Who Was Who in America

Biographical Titles Currently Published by Marquis Who's Who

Who's Who in America
  Who's Who in America supplements:
    Who's Who in America Birthdate Index
    Who's Who in America Classroom Project Book
    Who's Who in America College Alumni Directory
    Who's Who in America Index:
      Geographic Index, Professional Area Index
Who Was Who in America
  Historical Volume (1607-1896)
  Volume I (1897-1942)
  Volume II (1943-1950)
  Volume III (1951-1960)
  Volume IV (1961-1968)
  Volume V (1969-1973)
  Volume VI (1974-1976)
  Volume VII (1977-1981)
  Volume VIII (1982-1985)
  Index Volume (1607-1985)
Who Was Who in American History—Arts and Letters
Who Was Who in American History—The Military
Who Was Who in American History—Science and Technology
Who's Who in the World
Who's Who in the East
Who's Who in the Midwest
Who's Who in the South and Southwest
Who's Who in the West
Who's Who in American Law
Who's Who of American Women
Who's Who in Finance and Industry
Who's Who in Frontiers of Science and Technology
Who's Who in Religion
World Who's Who in Science
Directory of Women in Marquis Who's Who Publications
Index to Who's Who Books
Directory of Medical Specialists
Marquis Who's Who Directory of Online Professionals
Marquis Who's Who Directory of Computer Graphics
Marquis Who's Who in Cancer: Professionals and Facilities
Marquis Who's Who in Rehabilitation: Professionals and Facilities
Marquis International Who's Who in Optical Science and Engineering

Who Was Who in America®
with World Notables

Volume VIII
1982-1985

MARQUIS
Who's Who

Marquis Who's Who, Inc.
200 East Ohio Street
Chicago, Illinois 60611 U.S.A.

Library of Congress Catalog Card Number 43-3789
International Standard Book Number 0-8379-0214-2
Product Code Number 030301

Distributed in Europe by
Thompson, Henry Limited
London Road
Sunningdale, Berks
SL5 OEP, England

Distributed in Asia by
United Publishers Services Ltd.
Kenkyu-Sha Bldg.
9, Kanda Surugadai 2-Chome
Chiyoda-Ku, Tokyo, Japan

Manufactured in the United States of America

Table of Contents

Preface

The publication of Volume VIII of *Who Was Who in America* is an important step forward in the growth of a series of biographical reference books that seek to reflect both American history and the genealogical heritage of this country. The sketches are of deceased biographees in *Who's Who in America*.

The *Was* books (to use the shortened form by which they are better known) display the distinctive characteristics that have made *Who's Who in America* both an internationally respected reference work, and a household word in the country of its origin. Sketches not only were prepared by information supplied by the biographees themselves, but were approved and frequently revised by the subjects before being printed in a Marquis publication. As a result, many sketches contain personal data unavailable elsewhere. The preface to the first volume of *Who's Who in America* selected this fact as one of the volume's outstanding characteristics, and stated: "The book is autobiographical, the data having been obtained from first hands." Similarly, *Who Was Who in America* is largely autobiographical. Although condensed to the concise style that Marquis Who's Who, Inc. has made famous, the sketches contain essential facts. Inclusion of date of death and place of interment completes the sketches.

In continuing improvements introduced in previous volumes of *Who Was Who in America,* this volume includes sketches of some Marquis biographees known to be 95 years of age or older. Lacking current information regarding these individuals, we make such inclusions in the hope that our apologies will be accepted should errors occur. Sketches of recently deceased world notables also are included, particularly of those international figures whose careers had a direct bearing on the course of recent American history.

The result is far more than a biographical directory of some 112,000 deceased American notables within the covers of eight volumes. *Who Was Who in America* contains a vital portion of American history from the early days of the colonies to mid-1985. It is the autobiography of America.

Table of Abbreviations

The following abbreviations and symbols are frequently used in this book.

*Following a sketch indicates that the published biography could not be verified.

† Non-current sketches of *Who Was Who in America* biographees who were born 95 or more years ago (see Preface for explanation).

A.A. Associate in Arts
AAAL American Academy of Arts and Letters
AAAS American Association for the Advancement of Science
AAHPER Alliance for Health, Physical Education and Recreation
AAU Amateur Athletic Union
AAUP American Association of University Professors
AAUW American Association of University Women
A.B. Arts, Bachelor of
AB Alberta
ABA American Bar Association
ABC American Broadcasting Company
AC Air Corps
acad. academy, academic
acct. accountant
accg. accounting
ACDA Arms Control and Disarmament Agency
ACLU American Civil Liberties Union
ACP American College of Physicians
ACS American College of Surgeons
ADA American Dental Association
a.d.c. aide-de-camp
adj. adjunct, adjutant
adj. gen. adjutant general
adm. admiral
adminstr. administrator
adminstrn. administration
adminstrv. administrative
ADP Automatic Data Processing
adv. advocate, advisory
advt. advertising
A.E. Agricultural Engineer (for degrees only)
A.E. and P. Ambassador Extraordinary and Plenipotentiary
AEC Atomic Energy Commission
aero. aeronautical, aeronautic
aerodyn. aerodynamic
AFB Air Force Base
AFL-CIO American Federation of Labor and Congress of Industrial Organizations
AFTRA American Federation TV and Radio Artists
agr. agriculture
agrl. agricultural
agt. agent
AGVA American Guild of Variety Artists
agy. agency
A&I Agricultural and Industrial
AIA American Institute of Architects
AIAA American Institute of Aeronautics and Astronautics
AID Agency for International Development
AIEE American Institute of Electrical Engineers
AIM American Institute of Management

AIME American Institute of Mining, Metallurgy, and Petroleum Engineers
AK Alaska
AL Alabama
ALA American Library Association
Ala. Alabama
alt. alternate
Alta. Alberta
A&M Agricultural and Mechanical
A.M. Arts, Master of
Am. American, America
AMA American Medical Association
A.M.E. African Methodist Episcopal
Amtrak National Railroad Passenger Corporation
AMVETS American Veterans of World War II, Korea, Vietnam
anat. anatomical
ann. annual
ANTA American National Theatre and Academy
anthrop. anthropological
AP Associated Press
APO Army Post Office
Apr. April
apptd. appointed
apt. apartment
AR Arkansas
ARC American Red Cross
archeol. archeological
archtl. architectural
Ariz. Arizona
Ark. Arkansas
ArtsD. Arts, Doctor of
arty. artillery
ASCAP American Society of Composers, Authors and Publishers
ASCE American Society of Civil Engineers
ASHRAE American Society of Heating, Refrigeration, and Air Conditioning Engineers
ASME American Society of Mechanical Engineers
assn. association
assoc. associate
asst. assistant
ASTM American Society for Testing and Materials
astron. astronomical
astrophys. astrophysical
ATSC Air Technical Service Command
AT&T American Telephone & Telegraph Company
atty. attorney
AUS Army of the United States
Aug. August
aux. auxiliary
Ave. Avenue
AVMA American Veterinary Medical Association
AZ Arizona

B. Bachelor
b. born
B.A. Bachelor of Arts
B.Agr. Bachelor of Agriculture
Balt. Baltimore

Bapt. Baptist
B. Arch. Bachelor of Architecture
B.A.S. Bachelor of Agricultural Science
B.B.A. Bachelor of Business Administration
BBC British Broadcasting Corporation
B.C., BC British Columbia
B.C.E. Bachelor of Civil Engineering
B. Chir. Bachelor of Surgery
B.C.L. Bachelor of Civil Law
B.C.S. Bachelor of Commercial Science
B.D. Bachelor of Divinity
bd. board
B.E. Bachelor of Education
B.E.E. Bachelor of Electrical Engineering
B.F.A. Bachelor of Fine Arts
bibl. biblical
bibliog. bibliographical
biog. biographical
biol. biological
B.J. Bachelor of Journalism
Bklyn. Brooklyn
B.L. Bachelor of Letters
bldg. building
B.L.S. Bachelor of Library Science
Blvd. Boulevard
bn. battalion
B.&O.R.R. Baltimore & Ohio Railroad
bot. botanical
B.P.E. Bachelor of Physical Education
br. branch
B.R.E. Bachelor of Religious Education
brig. gen. brigadier general
Brit. British. Britannica
Bros. Brothers
B.S. Bachelor of Science
B.S.A. Bachelor of Agricultural Science
B.S.D. Bachelor of Didactic Science
B.S.T. Bachelor of Sacred Theology
B.Th. Bachelor of Theology
bull. bulletin
bur. bureau
bus. business
B.W.I. British West Indies

CA California
CAA Civil Aeronautics Administration
CAB Civil Aeronautics Board
Calif. California
C.Am. Central America
Can. Canada, Canadian
CAP Civil Air Patrol
capt. captain
CARE Cooperative American Relief Everywhere
Cath. Catholic
cav. cavalry
CBC Canadian Broadcasting Company
CBI China, Burma, India Theatre of Operations
CBS Columbia Broadcasting System
CCC Commodity Credit Corporation
CCNY City College of New York
CCU Cardiac Care Unit
CD Civil Defense

C.E. Corps of Engineers, Civil Engineers (in firm's name only or for degree)
cen. central (To be used for court system only)
CENTO Central Treaty Organization
CERN European Organization of Nuclear Research
cert. certificate, certification, certified
CETA Comprehensive Employment Training Act
CFL Canadian Football League
ch. church
Ch.D. Doctor of Chemistry
chem. chemical
Chem.E. Chemical Engineer
Chgo. Chicago
chirurg. chirurgical
chmn. chairman
chpt. chapter
CIA Central Intelligence Agency
CIC Counter Intelligence Corps
Cin. Cincinnati
cir. circuit
Cleve. Cleveland
climatol. climatological
clin. clinical
clk. clerk
C.L.U. Chartered Life Underwriter
C.M. Master in Surgery
C.&N.W.Ry. Chicago & Northwestern Railway
CO Colorado
Co. Company
COF Catholic Order of Foresters
C. of C. Chamber of Commerce
col. colonel
coll. college
Colo. Colorado
com. committee
comd. commanded
comdg. commanding
comdr. commander
comdt. commandant
commd. commissioned
comml. commercial
commn. commission
commr. commissioner
condr. conductor
Conf. Conference
Congl. Congregational, Congressional
Conglist. Congregationalist
Conn. Connecticut
cons. consultant, consulting
consol. consolidated
constl. constitutional
constn. constitution
constrn. construction
contbd. contributed
contbg. contributing
contbn. contribution
contbr. contributor
Conv. Convention
coop. cooperative
CORDS Civil Operations and Revolutionary Development Support
CORE Congress of Racial Equality
corp. corporation, corporate
corr. correspondent, corresponding, correspondence

C.&O.Ry. Chesapeake & Ohio Railway
C.P.A. Certified Public Accountant
C.P.C.U. Chartered Property and Casualty Underwriter
C.P.H. Certificate of Public Health
cpl. corporal
CPR Cardio-Pulmonary Resuscitation
C.P.Ry. Canadian Pacific Railway
C.S. Christian Science
C.S.B. Bachelor of Christian Science
CSC Civil Service Commission
C.S.D. Doctor of Christian Science
CT Connecticut
ct. court
crt. center
CWS Chemical Warfare Service
C.Z. Canal Zone

d. daughter
D. Doctor
D.Agr. Doctor of Agriculture
DAR Daughters of the American Revolution
dau. daughter
DAV Disabled American Veterans
D.C., DC District of Columbia
D.C.L. Doctor of Civil Law
D.C.S. Doctor of Commercial Science
D.D. Doctor of Divinity
D.D.S. Doctor of Dental Surgery
DE Delaware
dec. deceased
Dec. December
def. defense
Del. Delaware
del. delegate, delegation
Dem. Democrat, Democratic
D.Eng. Doctor of Engineering
denom. denomination, denominational
dep. deputy
dept. department
dermatol. dermatological
desc. descendant
devel. development, developmental
D.F.A. Doctor of Fine Arts
D.F.C. Distinguished Flying Cross
D.H.L. Doctor of Hebrew Literature
dir. director
dist. district
distbg. distributing
distbn. distribution
distbr. distributor
disting. distinguished
div. division, divinity, divorce
D.Litt. Doctor of Literature
D.M.D. Doctor of Medical Dentistry
D.M.S. Doctor of Medical Science
D.O. Doctor of Osteopathy
D.P.H. Diploma in Public Health
D.R. Daughters of the Revolution
Dr. Drive, Doctor
D.R.E. Doctor of Religious Education
Dr.P.H. Doctor of Public Health, Doctor of Public Hygiene
D.S.C. Distinguished Service Cross
D.Sc. Doctor of Science
D.S.M. Distinguished Service Medal
D.S.T. Doctor of Sacred Theology

D.T.M. Doctor of Tropical Medicine
D.V.M. Doctor of Veterinary Medicine
D.V.S. Doctor of Veterinary Surgery

E. East
ea. eastern (use for court system only)
E. and P. Extraordinary and Plenipotentiary
Eccles. Ecclesiastical
ecol. ecological
econ. economic
ECOSOC Economic and Social Council (of the UN)
E.D. Doctor of Engineering
ed. educated
Ed.B. Bachelor of Education
Ed.D. Doctor of Education
edit. edition
Ed.M. Master of Education
edn. education
ednl. educational
EDP electronic data processing
Ed.S. Specialist in Education
E.E. Electrical Engineer (degree only)
E.E. and M.P. Envoy Extraordinary and Minister Plenipotentiary
EEC European Economic Community
EEG Electroencephalogram
EEO Equal Employment Opportunity
EEOC Equal Employment Opportunity Commission
EKG Electrocardiogram
E.Ger. German Democratic Republic
elec. electrical
electrochem. electrochemical
electrophys. electrophysical
elem. elementary
E.M. Engineer of Mines
ency. encyclopedia
Eng. England
engr. engineer
engring. engineering
entomol. entomological
environ. environmental
EPA Environmental Protection Agency
epidemiol. epidemiological
Episc. Episcopalian
ERA Equal Rights Amendment
ERDA Energy Research and Development Administration
ESEA Elementary and Secondary Education Act
ESL English as Second Language
ESSA Environmental Science Services Administration
ethnol. ethnological
ETO European Theatre of Operations
Evang. Evangelical
exam. examination, examining
exec. executive
exhbn. exhibition
expdn. expedition
expn. exposition
expt. experiment
exptl. experimental

F.A. Field Artillery
FAA Federal Aviation Administration

FAO Food and Agriculture Organization (of the UN)
FBI Federal Bureau of Investigation
FCA Farm Credit Administration
FCC Federal Communication Commission
FCDA Federal Civil Defense Administration
FDA Food and Drug Administration
FDIA Federal Deposit Insurance Administration
FDIC Federal Deposit Insurance Corporation
F.E. Forest Engineer
FEA Federal Energy Administration
Feb. February
fed. federal
fedn. federation
FERC Federal Energy Regulatory Commission
fgn. foreign
FHA Federal Housing Administration
fin. financial, finance
FL Florida
Fla. Florida
FMC Federal Maritime Commission
FOA Foreign Operations Administration
found. foundation
FPC Federal Power Commission
FPO Fleet Post Office
frat. fraternity
FRS Federal Reserve System
FSA Federal Security Agency
Ft. Fort
FTC Federal Trade Commission

G-1 (or other number) Division of General Staff
Ga., GA Georgia
GAO General Accounting Office
gastroent. gastroenterological
GATT General Agreement of Tariff and Trades
gen. general
geneal. genealogical
geod. geodetic
geog. geographic, geographical
geol. geological
geophys. geophysical
gerontol. gerontological
G.H.Q. General Headquarters
G.N. Ry. Great Northern Railway
gov. governor
govt. government
govtl. governmental
GPO Governmental Printing Office
grad. graduate, graduated
GSA General Services Administration
Gt. Great
GU Guam
gynecol. gynecological

hdqrs. headquarters
HEW Department of Health, Education and Welfare
H.H.D. Doctor of Humanities
HHFA Housing and Home Finance Agency
HHS Department of Health and Human Services
HI Hawaii
hist. historical, historic

H.M. Master of Humanics
homeo. homeopathic
hon. honorary, honorable
Ho. of Dels. House of Delegates
Ho. of Reps. House of Representatives
hort. horticultural
hosp. hospital
HUD Department of Housing and Urban Development
Hwy. Highway
hydrog. hydrographic

IA Iowa
IAEA International Atomic Energy Agency
IBM International Business Machines Corporation
IBRD International Bank for Reconstruction and Development
ICA International Cooperation Administration
ICC Interstate Commerce Commission
ICU Intensive Care Unit
ID Idaho
IEEE Institute of Electrical and Electronics Engineers
IFC International Finance Corporation
IGY International Geophysical Year
IL Illinois
Ill. Illinois
illus. illustrated
ILO International Labor Organization
IMF International Monetary Fund
IN Indiana
Inc. Incorporated
ind. independent
Ind. Indiana
Indpls. Indianapolis
indsl. industrial
inf. infantry
info. information
ins. insurance
insp. inspector
insp.gen. inspector general
inst. institute
instl. institutional
instn. institution
instr. instructor
instrn. instruction
intern. international
intro. introduction
IRE Institute of Radio Engineers
IRS Internal Revenue Service
ITT International Telephone & Telegraph Corporation

JAG Judge Advocate General
JAGC Judge Advocate General Corps
Jan. January
Jaycees Junior Chamber of Commerce
J.B. Jurum Baccolaureus
J.C.B. Juris Canoni Baccalaureus
J.C.D. Juris Canonici Doctor, Juris Civilis Doctor
J.C.L. Juris Canonici Licentiatus
J.D. Juris Doctor
j.g. junior grade
jour. journal
jr. junior
J.S.D. Juris Scientiae Doctor

J.U.D. Juris Utriusque Doctor
jud. judicial

Kans. Kansas
K.C. Knights of Columbus
K.P. Knights of Pythias
KS Kansas
K.T. Knight Templar
Ky., KY Kentucky

La., LA Louisiana
lab. laboratory
lang. language
laryngol. laryngological
LB Labrador
lectr. lecturer
legis. legislation, legislative
L.H.D. Doctor of Humane Letters
L.I. Long Island
lic. licensed, license
L.I.R.R. Long Island Railroad
lit. literary, literature
Litt.B. Bachelor of Letters
Litt.D. Doctor of Letters
LL.B. Bachelor of Laws
LL.D. Doctor of Laws
LL.M. Master of Laws
Ln. Lane
L.& N.R.R. Louisville & Nashville Railroad
L.S. Library Science (in degree)
lt. lieutenant
Ltd. Limited
Luth. Lutheran
LWV League of Women Voters

m. married
M. Master
M.A. Master of Arts
MA Massachusetts
mag. magazine
M.Agr. Master of Agriculture
maj. major
Man. Manitoba
Mar. March
M.Arch. Master in Architecture
Mass. Massachusetts
math. mathematics, mathematical
MATS Military Air Transport Service
M.B. Bachelor of Medicine
MB Manitoba
M.B.A. Master of Business Administration
MBS Mutual Broadcasting System
M.C. Medical Corps
M.C.E. Master of Civil Engineering
mcht. merchant
mcpl. municipal
M.C.S. Master of Commercial Science
M.D. Doctor of Medicine
Md, MD Maryland
M.Dip. Master in Diplomacy
mdse. merchandise
M.D.V. Doctor of Veterinary Medicine
M.E. Mechanical Engineer (degree only)
ME Maine
M.E.Ch. Methodist Episcopal Church
mech. mechanical
M.Ed. Master of Education
med. medical
M.E.E. Master of Electrical Engineering
mem. member

meml. memorial
merc. mercantile
met. metropolitan
metall. metallurgical
Met.E. Metallurgical Engineer
meteorol. meteorological
Meth. Methodist
Mex. Mexico
M.F. Master of Forestry
M.F.A. Master of Fine Arts
mfg. manufacturing
mfr. manufacturer
mgmt. management
mgr. manager
M.H.A. Master of Hospital Administration
M.I. Military Intelligence
MI Michigan
Mich. Michigan
micros. microscopic, microscopical
mid. middle (use for Court System only)
mil. military
Milw. Milwaukee
mineral. mineralogical
Minn. Minnesota
Miss. Mississippi
MIT Massachusetts Institute of Technology
mktg. marketing
M.L. Master of Laws
MLA Modern Language Association
M.L.D. Magister Legnum Diplomatic
M.Litt. Master of Literature
M.L.S. Master of Library Science
M.M.E. Master of Mechanical Engineering
MN Minnesota
mng. managing
Mo., MO Missouri
moblzn. mobilization
Mont. Montana
M.P. Member of Parliament
M.P.E. Master of Physical Education
M.P.H. Master of Public Health
M.P.L. Master of Patent Law
Mpls. Minneapolis
M.R.E. Master of Religious Education
M.S. Master of Science
MS, Ms. Mississippi
M.Sc. Master of Science
M.S.F. Master of Science of Forestry
M.S.T. Master of Sacred Theology
M.S.W. Master of Social Work
MT Montana
Mt. Mount
MTO Mediterranean Theatre of Operations
mus. museum, musical
Mus.B. Bachelor of Music
Mus.D. Doctor of Music
Mus.M. Master of Music
mut. mutual
mycol. mycological

N. North
NAACP National Association for the
    Advancement of Colored People
NACA National Advisory Committee for
    Aeronautics
NAD National Academy of Design
N.Am. North America
NAM National Association of Manufacturers

NAPA National Association of Performing
    Artists
NAREB National Association of Real
    Estate Boards
NARS National Archives and Record
    Service
NASA National Aeronautics and Space
    Administration
nat. national
NATO North Atlantic Treaty Organization
NATOUSA North African Theatre of
    Operations
nav. navigation
N.B., NB New Brunswick
NBC National Broadcasting Company
N.C., NC North Carolina
NCCJ National Conference of Christians
    and Jews
N.D., ND North Dakota
NDEA National Defense Education Act
NE Nebraska
NE Northeast
NEA National Education Association
Nebr. Nebraska
NEH National Endowment for Humanities
neurol. neurological
Nev. Nevada
NF Newfoundland
NFL National Football League
Nfld. Newfoundland
N.G. National Guard
N.H., NH New Hampshire
NHL National Hockey League
NIH National Institutes of Health
NIMH National Institute of Mental Health
N.J., NJ New Jersey
NLRB National Labor Relations Board
NM New Mexico
N.Mex. New Mexico
No. Northern
NOAA National Oceanographic and
    Atmospheric Administration
NORAD North America Air Defense
NOW National Organization for Women
Nov. November
N.P.Ry. Northern Pacific Railway
nr. near
NRC National Research Council
N.S., NS Nova Scotia
NSC National Security Council
NSF National Science Foundation
N.T. New Testament
NT Northwest Territories
numis. numismatic
NV Nevada
NW Northwest
N.W.T. Northwest Territories
N.Y., NY New York
N.Y.C. New York City
NYU New York University
N.Z. New Zealand

OAS Organization of American States
ob-gyn obstetrics-gynecology
obs. observatory
obstet. obstetrical
O.D. Doctor of Optometry
OECD Organization of European
    Cooperation and Development

OEEC Organization of European
    Economic Cooperation
OEO Office of Economic Opportunity
ofcl. official
OH Ohio
OK Oklahoma
Okla. Oklahoma
ON Ontario
Ont. Ontario
ophthal. ophthalmological
ops. operations
OR Oregon
orch. orchestra
Oreg. Oregon
orgn. organization
ornithol. ornithological
OSHA Occupational Safety and Health
    Administration
OSRD Office of Scientific Research and
    Development
OSS Office of Strategic Services
osteo. osteopathic
otol. otological
otolaryn. otolaryngological

Pa., PA Pennsylvania
P.A. Professional Association
paleontol. paleontological
path. pathological
P.C. Professional Corporation
PE Prince Edward Island
P.E.I. Prince Edward Island (text only)
PEN Poets, Playwrights, Editors, Essayists
    and Novelists (international association)
penol. penological
P.E.O. women's organization (full name not
    disclosed)
pfc. private first class
PHA Public Housing Administration
pharm. pharmaceutical
Pharm.D. Doctor of Pharmacy
Pharm. M. Master of Pharmacy
Ph.B. Bachelor of Philosophy
Ph.D. Doctor of Philosophy
Phila. Philadelphia
philharm. philharmonic
philol. philological
philos. philosophical
photog. photographic
phys. physical
physiol. physiological
Pitts. Pittsburgh
Pkwy. Parkway
Pl. Place
P.&L.E.R.R. Pittsburgh & Lake Erie
    Railroad
P. O. Post Office
PO Box Post Office Box
polit. political
poly. polytechnic, polytechnical
PQ Province of Quebec
P.R., PR Puerto Rico
prep. preparatory
pres. president
Presbyn. Presbyterian
presdl. presidential
prin. principal
proc. proceedings
prod. produced (play production)

prodn. production
prof. professor
profl. professional
prog. progressive
propr. proprietor
pros. atty. prosecuting attorney
pro tem pro tempore
PSRO Professional Services Review Organization
psychiat. psychiatric
psychol. psychological
PTA Parent-Teachers Association
ptnr. partner
PTO Pacific Theatre of Operations, Parent Teacher Organization
pub. publisher, publishing, published
pub. public
publ. publication
pvt. private

quar. quarterly
q.m. quartermaster
Q.M.C. Quartermaster Corps.
Que. Quebec

radiol. radiological
RAF Royal Air Force
RCA Radio Corporation of America
RCAF Royal Canadian Air Force
RD Rural Delivery
Rd. Road
REA Rural Electrification Administration
rec. recording
ref. reformed
regt. regiment
regtl. regimental
rehab. rehabilitation
rep. representative
Rep. Republican
Res. Reserve
ret. retired
rev. review, revised
RFC Reconstruction Finance Corporation
RFD Rural Free Delivery
rhinol. rhinological
R.I., RI Rhode Island
R.N. Registered Nurse
roentgenol. roentgenological
ROTC Reserve Officers Training Corps
R.R. Railroad
Ry. Railway

s. son
S. South
SAC Strategic Air Command
SALT Strategic Arms Limitation Talks
S.Am. South America
san. sanitary
SAR Sons of the American Revolution
Sask. Saskatchewan
savs. savings
S.B. Bachelor of Science
SBA Small Business Administration
S.C., SC South Carolina
SCAP Supreme Command Allies Pacific
Sc.B. Bachelor of Science
S.C.D. Doctor of Commercial Science
Sc.D. Doctor of Science
sch. school

sci. science, scientific
SCLC Southern Christian Leadership Conference
SCV Sons of Confederate Veterans
S.D., SD South Dakota
SE Southeast
SEATO Southeast Asia Treaty Organization
sec. secretary
SEC Securities and Exchange Commission
sect. section
seismol. seismological
sem. seminary
s.g. senior grade
sgt. sergeant
SHAEF Supreme Headquarters Allied Expeditionary Forces
SHAPE Supreme Headquarters Allied Powers in Europe
S.I. Staten Island
S.J. Society of Jesus (Jesuit)
S.J.D. Scientiae Juridicae Doctor
SK Saskatchewan
S.M. Master of Science
So. Southern
soc. society
sociol. sociological
S.P. Co. Southern Pacific Company
spl. special
splty. specialty
Sq. Square
sr. senior
S.R. Sons of the Revolution
SS Steamship
SSS Selective Service System
St. Saint, Street
sta. station
stats. statistics
statis. statistical
S.T.B. Bachelor of Sacred Theology
stblzn. stabilization
S.T.D. Doctor of Sacred Theology
subs. subsidiary
SUNY State University of New York
supr. supervisor
supt. superintendent
surg. surgical
SW Southwest

TAPPI Technical Association of Pulp and Paper Industry
Tb Tuberculosis
tchr. teacher
tech. technical, technology
technol. technological
Tel.&Tel. Telephone & Telegraph
temp. temporary
Tenn. Tennessee
Ter. Territory
Terr. Terrace
Tex. Texas
Th.D. Doctor of Theology
theol. theological
Th.M. Master of Theology
TN Tennessee
tng. training
topog. topographical
trans. transaction, transferred
transl. translation, translated

transp. transportation
treas. treasurer
TV television
TVA Tennessee Valley Authority
twp. township
TX Texas
typog. typographical

U. University
UAW United Auto Workers
UCLA University of California at Los Angeles
UDC United Daughters of the Confederacy
U.K. United Kingdom
UN United Nations
UNESCO United Nations Educational, Scientific and Cultural Organization
UNICEF United Nations International Children's Emergency Fund
univ. university
UNRRA United Nations Relief and Rehabilitation Administration
UPI United Press International
U.P.R.R. United Pacific Railroad
urol. urological
U.S. United States
U.S.A. United States of America
USAAF United States Army Air Force
USAF United States Air Force
USAFR United States Air Force Reserve
USAR United States Army Reserve
USCG United States Coast Guard
USCGR United States Coast Guard Reserve
USES United States Employment Service
USIA United States Information Agency
USMC United States Marine Corps
USMCR United States Marine Corps Reserve
USN United States Navy
USNG United States National Guard
USNR United States Naval Reserve
USO United Service Organizations
USPHS United States Public Health Service
USS United States Ship
USSR Union of the Soviet Socialist Republics
USV United States Volunteers
UT Utah

VA Veterans' Administration
Va., VA Virginia
vet. veteran, veterinary
VFW Veterans of Foreign Wars
V.I., VI Virgin Islands
vice pres. vice president
vis. visiting
VISTA Volunteers in Service to America
VITA Volunteers in Technical Service
vocat. vocational
vol. volunteer, volume
v.p. vice president
vs. versus
Vt., VT Vermont

W. West
WA Washington (state)
WAC Women's Army Corps

Wash. Washington (state)
WAVES Women's Reserve. U.S. Naval Reserve
WCTU Women's Christian Temperance Union
we. western (use for court system only)
W. Ger. Germany, Federal Republic of
WHO World Health Organization
WI, Wis. Wisconsin
W.I. West Indies
WSB Wage Stabilization Board
WV West Virginia
W.Va. West Virginia
WY Wyoming
Wyo. Wyoming

YK Yukon Territory (for address)
YMCA Young Men's Christian Association
YMHA Young Men's Hebrew Association
YM & YWHA Young Men's and Young
  Women's Hebrew Association
Y.T. Yukon Territory
YWCA Young Women's Christian Association
yr. year

zool. zoological

Alphabetical Practices

Names are arranged alphabetically according to the surnames, and under identical surnames according to the first given name. If both surname and first given name are identical, names are arranged alphabetically according to the second given name. Where full names are identical, they are arranged in order of age — with the elder listed first.

Surnames beginning with De, Des, Du, however capitalized or spaced, are recorded with the prefix preceding the surname and arranged alphabetically, under the letter D.

Surnames beginning with Mac and Mc are arranged alphabetically under M.

Surnames beginning with Saint or St. appear after names that would begin Sains, and are arranged according to the second part of the name, e.g., St. Clair before Saint Dennis.

Surnames beginning with prefix Van are arranged alphabetically under the letter V. Surnames containing the prefix Von or von are usually arranged alphabetically under letter V; any exceptions are noted by cross references.

Compound hyphenated surnames are arranged according to the first member of the compound. Compound unhyphenated surnames are treated as hyphenated names.

Parentheses used in connection with a name indicate which part of the full name is usually deleted in common usage. Hence Abbott, W(illiam) Lewis indicates that the usual form of the given name is W. Lewis. In such a case, the parentheses are ignored in alphabetizing. However if the name is recorded Abbott, (William) Lewis, signifying that the entire name William is not commonly used, the alphabetizing would be arranged as though the name were Abbott, Lewis.

Who Was Who in America

AARON, ABRAHAM HIGHAM, physician; b. Buffalo, May 23, 1889; s. Aaron and Elizabeth (Wark) A.; M.D., U. Buffalo, 1912. Intern Buffalo Gen. Hosp., 1912-14, preceptor Charles D. Aaron, Detroit, 1914-18; attending physician emeritus; practice of medicine, specializing gastroenterology, after 1918; prof. clin. medicine U. Buffalo, 1932-56; dir. postgrad. and continuation studies, 1934-52, emeritus prof. clin. medicine, 1956; cons. physician Buffalo Gen. Hosp. Pres. Buffalo and Erie County Tb and Health Assn. Recipient Julius Friedenwold medal for outstanding achievement in gastroenterology, 1958; citations U. Buffalo, Am. Gastroent. Assn., 1960. Diplomate Am. Bd. Internal Medicine. Fellow A.C.P.; mem. A.M.A., Am. Gastroent. Assn. (pres. 1944-45). Editor of Gastroenterology, now emeritus. Home: Buffalo, NY. †

ABBOTT, CHESTER G., banker; b. Lynn, Mass., June 1, 1890; s. Lewis H. A.; A.B., Bowdoin College, 1913; LL.D., University of Maine; married Olive Barnes on October 16, 1915; children—Nancy B. (Mrs. James R. Thompson), Mary L. (Mrs. Edward J. Samp, Jr.). Salesman Henley-Kimball Co., Portland, Me., 1914-16, state mgr., 1916-25, v.p., gen. mgr., 1924-29; gen. sales mgr. Hudson Motor Car Co., Detroit, 1929-31, asst. gen. mgr., 1931-34, dir., 1929-35; pres. Transport Co., 1935-42; v.p. First Portland (Me.) Nat. Bank, 1942-49, pres. from 1950, dir. from 1938, also chmn. exec. committee; dir. Haverford Bros. Co., Oxford Paper Company, Me. Bonding and Casualty Co., Portland Stove Foundry. President board of overseers Bowdoin Coll.; past pres. Portland Community Chest. Member Am. (exec. com. nat. bank div.), Me. (past pres.) banker assns., C. of C. (past pres.). Home: Falmouth, Me. †

ABBOTT, CORNELLUS JAMES, indsl. engr.; b. Cleve., May 16, 1889; s. Alfred and Margaretha (Scheuer) A.; B.S., Case Sch. Applied Sci., 1911; m. Marguerite Gorsline, July 26, 1919; 1 son, Robert Cornelius. Contrn. engr., supt., 1911-14; plant engr., sales engr., spl. European rep., mgr. engring. Hydraulic Pressed Steel Co., Cleve., 1914-22; engring. cons., 1922-26; resident engr., asst. plant mgr. Pontiac div., Oakland Motor Car Co., 1926-28; indsl. engr. Ford, Bacon & Davis, Inc., 1928-30, from 1934, dir. from 1945, v.p., 1946-53, sr. v.p. from 1953; mng. dir. A.J. Brandt, Ltd., 1930-34, dir., v.p., 1932-34; gen. mgr., pres. Jacobs Aircraft Engine Co., 1940-45, dir., 1941-45. Mem. Zeta Psi. Clubs: N.Y. Athletic; Talbot Country, Miles River Yacht. Address: St. Michaels, Md. †

ABBOTT, GEORGE LAMB, business exec.; b. Camden, N.Y., Oct. 31, 1887; s. Anthony Wayne and Irene Bertha (Lamb) A.; Ph.B., Hamilton Coll., 1910; m. Nina Peirson Ostrander, June 12, 1923; 1 dau., Irene Peirson (Mrs. Kenneth Paul MacPherson). With Garlock Inc., Palmyra, New York, from 1911; as general manager, 1927-55, v.p., 1924-28, pres. 1928-55, treas., 1929-57, chmn. bd., chief exec. officer, 1955-59, dir., chmn. exec. com., from 1958; pres. Garlock Packing Co. of Can., Ltd., 1931-58, Mechanical Leathers, Inc., 1936-58; chmn. of bd. and dir. 1st Nat. Bank of Palmyra, 1929-36. Mem. Palmyra Bd. Edn., 1925-46, pres., 1941-46. Pres. Newark-Payne Community Hosp., Inc., from 1959. Trustee Hamilton Coll. Mem. Mechanical Packing Assn., Inc. (hon. pres.), The Newcomen Soc. of England (Am. Branch), Hamilton Coll. Alumni Assn. (past pres.), S.A.R., Delta Upsilon. Republican. Episcopalian. Mason. Clubs: Genesee Valley (Rochester); Union League (N.Y.C.); Fort Schuyler (Utica, N.Y.). Home: Palmyra, N.Y. †

ABBOTT, HELEN RAYMOND, writer; b. Boston, Mass., July 7, 1888; d. Thomas Alfred and Helen (Mitchell) A.; A.B., Mt. Holyoke Coll., 1910; short story course under Prof. Dallas Lore Sharp, Boston U., 1916, 17. Mem. D.A.R. Conglist. Clubs: Boston Authors, Manuscript, Appalachian Mountain (Boston); College, Woman's (Reading, Mass.). Author: The Merry Heart, 1918. Contbr. to mags. Home: Reading, Mass. †

ABBOTT, LEROY C(HARLES), orthopedic surgeon; b. Madelia, Minn., June 12, 1890; s. LeRoy and Maryanna (Paynter) A.; student U. of Minn., 1907-09, Pomona Coll., Claremont, Calif., 1909-10; M.D., U. of Calif., 1914; m. Margaret Mathews, Dec. 28, 1922; children—Susan Ann (Mrs. David Cole Sherwin) Margaret Mitchell (Mrs. Ben Scott Foster), Asst. dept. orthopedic surgery, U. of Calif. Hosp., 1916-17; asst. prof. surgery U. of Mich., 1920-23; prof. clin. orthopedic surgery Washington U., St. Louis, 1923-30; chief surgeon Shriners' Hosp. for Crippled Children, St. Louis, 1923-30; clin. prof. orthopedic surgery in charge U. of Calif., 1930-36, prof. orthopedic surgery in charge from 1936; cons. orthopedic surgeon San Francisco City and County Hosp.; chief orthopedic surg. service Children's and Franklin hosps.; visiting orthopedic surgeon Lagunda Honda Home, San Francisco; mem. deans' com. Vets. Hosp., Ft. Miley, San Francisco, from 1946; consultant orthopedic surgery, to sec. of war, 1943-45. Served as maj., Med. Corps, U.S. Army, 1917-19; with British at Edinburgh War Hosp. under Sir Harold Stiles, adjutant to Sir Robert Jones of British War Office, surgeon to St. Catherine's Lodge Hosp. in London, also chief surgeon dept. for care of bone and joint injuries in U.S. Base Hosps. 8 and 69, house surgeon Chalmers Hosp. and Royal Infirmary, Edinburgh, under Sir Harold Stiles, prof. surgery at U. of Edinburgh. Fellow Am. Coll. Surgeons; mem. Am. Orthopedic Assn. (pres. 1946-47), Am. Acad. Orthopedic Surgeons, A.M.A., Calif. State Med. Soc., Western Orthopedic Assn., Robert Jones Orthopedic Club, Am., Pacific Coast Surg. assns. Author of numerous articles. Home: San Francisco Calif.†

ABBOTT, OSCAR BERGSTROM, army officer; b. San Antonio, Tex., Oct. 8, 1890; s. Thomas Henry and Johanna (Heilickman) A.; student, Tex. Agr. and Mech. College, 1910-11, LL.B., Washington College of Law, 1936; m. Sally Elizabeth Stephens, Jan. 17, 1918; children—Albert William, Leonard Johnstone. Enlisted in 2d Inf. Tex. Nat. Guard, 1916, commd. 2d lt. cav., 1917, advanced through the grades to brig. gen. (temp.), 1943. Legion of Merit (Legionnaire). Mason. Clubs: Army-Navy (Washington, D.C.), Country (Arlington, Va.). Home: San Antonio, Tex. †

ABELL, GEORGE OGDEN, educator, astronomer; b. Los Angeles, Mar. 1, 1927; s. Theodore Curtis and Annamarie (Ogden) A.; m. Lois Everson, June 16, 1951; children: Anthony Alan, Jonathan Edward; m. Phyllis Fox, Mar. 10, 1972. B.S., Calif. Inst. Tech., 1951, M.S., 1952, Ph.D., 1956. Observer Nat. Geog. Soc.-Palomar Obs. Sky Survey, 1953-56; lectr. Griffith Obs., 1953-60; mem. faculty UCLA, 1956—, prof. astronomy, 1967—, chmn. dept., 1968-75; Guest Max-Planck- Institut für Physik und Astrophysik, Munich, Germany, 1965-66; vis. prof. Royal Obs., Edinburgh, Scotland, 1976-77; guest investigator Hale Obs., 1958—; cons. Space Tech Labs., 1958-59, Jet Propulsion Lab., 1962-66, Douglas Aircraft, 1964-66; prin. investigator U. Calif./Brit. Open U./BBC, TV series Understanding Space and Time, 1977-79; mem. exec. com. Com. for Sci. Investigation of Claims of the Paranormal; vis. prof. Am. Astron. Soc., 1962—. Author: Exploration of the Universe, 4th edit., 1982, Realm of the Universe, 1976, 3d edit., 1984, Drama of the Universe, 1978; editor: Science and the Paranormal, 1981, Objects of High Redshift, 1980, Evolution of the Early Universe and its Present Structure, 1983; Contbr. numerous articles to profl. jours. Mem. Internat. Astron. Union (pres. cosmology commn. 1979-82), Am. Astron. Soc. (com. chmn., counselor 1969-72), Astron. Soc. Pacific (dir., pres. 1968-70), Royal Astron. Soc., AAAS (councilor 1979-83), Sigma Xi. Investigated distbn. and properties of rich clusters and superclusters of galaxies, properties of 86 old planetary nebulae, origin of planetary nebulae Investigated distbn. and properties of rich clusters and superclusters of galaxies, properties of 86 old planetary nebulae, origin of planetary nebulae. Died Oct. 7, 1983.

ABELL, ROBERT EPHRAIM, surgeon; b. Lowrys, S.C., Oct. 12, 1887; s. Joshua Leland and Sophie (Erwin) A.; prep. edn., high sch., Lowrys; student Presbyn. Coll. of S.C., Clinton, S.C., 1 yr. Davidson (N.C.) Coll., 2 yrs.; M.D., U. of Md., 1912; m. Alice Hall Glenn, Oct. 12, 1916; children—Robert Ephraim, Sophie Erwin, Thomas Glenn. Resident surgeon Univ. Hosp., Baltimore, Md., 1912-15; a founder, 1915, from surgeon in charge, treas. and mgr. Chester Sanatorium; visiting surgeon Memorial Hosp., Abbeville, S.C., 1921-24; surgeon in charge Pryor Memorial Hosp., Chester, 1926-39; 1939; pres. and treas. of Abell Motors, Inc.; dir. Commercial Bank; mem. City Council, Chester; mem. Chester County War Memorial Commn. from 1948. Commd. 1st lt. Med. Corps, U.S.A., June 1918; went to France with Evacuation Hosp. No. 26; promoted capt., Oct. 1918; hon. discharged, Feb. 1, 1919, Fellow Am. Coll. Surgeons; mem. S.C. State Bd. Med. Examiners, S.C. Med. Assn. (pres. 1933-34), Beta Theta Pi, Nu Sigma Nu, Theta Nu Epsilon. Democrat. Presbyterian. Clubs: Chester Golf, Rotary, Hilton Head Hunting; Rush Medical Club (U. of Md.). Home: Chester, S.C. †

ABELL, THORNTON MONTAIGNE, architect; b. South Haven, Mich., Sept. 4, 1906; s. Charles Emery and Cora Ida (Webb) A.; m. Alma Florence Hatch, Aug. 6, 1927 (dec. 1976); 1 son, Jared; 1 stepson, David. Student, U. Mich., 1924, U. Calif. at Berkeley, 1927; B.Arch., U. So. Calif., 1931. Interior design instr. Chouinard Art Inst., 1950-52; vis. critic U. So. Calif. Sch. Architecture, 1953-61, 63-65. Designer, Clare C. Hosmer, Sarasota, Fla., 1925-26, Joseph J. Kucera, Pasadena, Calif., 1926, Marsh, Smith & Powell, Los Angeles, 1930-42, asso., Sumner Spaulding, Los Angeles, 1942-43, Adrian Wilson, Los Angeles, 1943-44, pvt. archtl. practice, Los Angeles, 1944—. Charter mem. Archtl. Guild, U. So. Calif.; Fellow A.I.A. (treas. So. Calif. chpt. 1958, dir. 1963-65, sec. Calif. council 1959, dir. 1958-63, 77—, v.p. So. Calif. chpt. 1977, pres. So. Calif. chpt. 1978). Died Apr. 2, 1984.

ABERNATHY, WILLIAM JACKSON, educator; b. Columbia, Tenn., Nov. 21, 1933; s. Sidney Guy and Estha Jackson A.; m. Claire St. Arnaud, Mar. 9, 1961; children: Evelyn Claire, William Jackson, Jannine Suzan. B.S. in Elec. Engring., U. Tenn., 1955; M.B.A., Harvard U., 1964, D.B.A., 1967. Project engr. film div. E.I. duPont, Columbia, 1955-56; project engr., project mgr. Gen. Dynamics Electronics, Rochester, N.Y., 1959-62; asst. prof. Grad. Sch. Bus., UCLA, 1966-68, Grad. Sch. Bus., Stanford U., 1968-72; William B. Harding prof. mgmt. of tech. Harvard U. Grad. Sch. Bus., Cambridge, Mass., 1972-83. Author: The Productivity Dilemma: Road Block to Innovation in the Auto Industry, 1978, (with Ginsburg) Technology and the Future of the Auto Industry, 1980, (with Clark and Kantrow) Industrial Renaissance: Producing a Competitive Future for America; editor: (with Sheldon and Prahaled) The Management of Health Care: A Technology Perspective, 1974. Served to 1st lt. USAF, 1959. Recipient McKinzie award Harvard Bus. Rev., 1980, 81. Mem. Nat. Acad. Engring. (panel chmn. of studies), AAAS. Home: Lexington, Mass. Died Dec. 29, 1983.

ABERNETHY, THOMAS PERKINS, prof. history; b. Collirene, Ala., Aug. 25, 1890; s. William Hinds and Anne (Pierce) A.; A.B., Coll. of Charleston, 1912; A.M., Harvard, 1916, Ph.D., 1922; Litt.D., Washington and Lee University, 1947; married Ida E. Robertson, Dec. 6, 1917. Acting asst. prof. history, Vanderbilt U., 1921-22; prof. of history, U. of Chattanooga, 1922-28; asso. prof. history, U. of Ala., 1928-30; asso. prof. history, U. of Va., 1930-37, Richmond Alumni prof. of history 1937-61, prof. emeritus, from 1961; vis. prof. U. Tex., 1961-62, U. Ariz., 1962-63. Chmn. Corcoran Sch. History, 1946-55. Served as 2d lt. inf., U.S. Army, 1918. Mem. Am. Hist. Assn., Miss. Valley Hist. Assn. (exec. com.), So. Hist. Assn. (pres. 1937), Va. Hist. Soc. (mem. exec. com.). Soc. Am. Historians, Raven Soc., Va. History and Govt. Textbook Commn., Phi Beta Kappa, Pi Kappa Phi. Club: Colonnade (U. of Va.). Author: The Formative Period in Alabama, 1922; From Frontier to Plantation in Tennessee, 1932; Western Lands and the American Revolution, 1937; Three Virginia Frontiers, 1940; The Burr Conspiracy, 1954; (with others) The Frontier in Perspective; The South in the New Nation, Vol. IV, 1961; (with others) Jacksonian Democracy, Myth or Reality?, 1962. Contbr. articles profl. jours. Ency. Brit., Am. Oxford Ency., Collier's Ency. Member editorial bd. Va. Quarterly Rev. Home: Charlottesville, Va. †

ABERT, DONALD BYRON, newspaper executive; b. Milw., Apr. 14, 1907; s. Byron H. and Lorraine K. (Haas) A.; m. Barbara Anne Grant, Aug. 1, 1936; children: Judith Abert Meissner, Barbara Abert Tooman, Grant. B.S., U. Wis., 1928. With Journal Co., pubs. Milw. Jour. and Sentinel and operator broadcast stas. WTMJ, WTMJ-TV, WKTI, Milw., from 1928; v.p. WKTI, 1952-60, exec. v.p., gen. mgr., 1961-68, pres., pub., 1968-85, chmn. bd., 1977-85, also dir.; pres. Matex, Inc.; treas., dir. Audit Bur. Circulations, 1964-74. Bd. dirs. United Community Services Milw., 1966-70; pres. Milw. council Boy Scouts Am., 1954-55; bd. dirs. Greater Milw. Com., Hosp. Area Planning Com., 1964-70, Newspaper Advt. Bur., from 1979; mem. bd. corp. Boys Club; trustee Harry J. Grant Scholarship Found., Milw. Boy Scout Fund, 1968-78; trustee Milw.-Downer Sem., 1946-58, pres., 1948-52; bd. dirs. Milw. Symphony Orch., pres., 1968-70; trustee Milw. Art Center, 1955-80, Marquette U. Recipient Silver Beaver award Boy Scouts Am. Mem. Am. Newspaper Pubs. Assn. (trustee found. 1972-78), Milw. Assn. Commerce, Phi Gamma Delta. Clubs: Milwaukee Country (Milw.), University (Milw.), Town (Milw.), Rotary (Milw.), Press (Milw.), Milwaukee (Milw.). Home: Milwaukee, Wis. Died July 6, 1985.*

ABLEWHITE, HAYWOOD SELLER, bishop; b. Cleveland, O., Sept. 11, 1887; s. James B. and Annie (Seller) A.; Adelbert Coll., Western Reserve U., 1907-09; A.B., Kenyon Coll., Gambier, O., 1915, D.D., 1930; grad. Bexley Hall Div. Sch. (Kenyon Coll.), 1915; m. Inez Fillmore, June 17, 1915; 1 dau., Inez Fillmore. Deacon, 1915, priest, 1916, P.E. Ch.; rector Ch. of Good Shepherd, Columbus, O., 1917-19, St. James Ch., Piqua, O., 1919-26, Ch. of St. Philip the Apostle, St. Louis, Mo., 1926-28; dean of St. Paul's Cathedral, Marquette, Mich., 1928-30; consecrated bishop of Marquette, Mar. 25, 1930. Mem. Delta Upsilon. Mason (32 deg. Home: Marquette, MI. †

ABRAMS, ALLEN, consultant; b. Butler Pa., Jan 27, 1889; s. Edward Everett and Mary Genevieve (Allen) A.; A.B., Washington and Jefferson Coll., 1910, M.S., 1915, D.Sc., 1937; B.S., Mass. Inst. Tech., 1915; m. Juanita Spyker, Nov. 15, 1919; children—Mary Catherine (Mrs. Douglas F. McKey), Jean Chilton (Mrs. H. Langdon Smith). Instr. chemistry Mass. Inst. Tech., 1915-16, 20-21; chemist Bemis Bros. Bag Co., 1916-17; chief chemist Cornell Wood Products Co., 1921-26; joined Marathon Corp., Rothschild, Wis., as tech. dir., 1926, became v.p., dir research, 1940, dir., 1943; indsl. cons. Arthur D. Little, Inc.; dir. Wausau Paper Mills Co., Sulphite Products Corp., Marathon Battery Co. Chmn. Nat. Academy of Science advisory board Quarter Master Corps Research and Development. Past dist. pres. Boy Scouts Am.; vice pres., Wausau Bd. Edn. Trustee Washington and Jefferson Coll. Served as lt. C.W.S. 1917-19, maj. C.W.S.; dep. dir., research and development div. O.S.S., 1943-44. Recipient honorary citation U. Wis., Phi Beta Kappa. Mem. Am. Forestry Assn., A.A.A.S., Am. Chem. Swedish, The Law, Nordic Law (past pres.). Home: Chgo., Ill. †

ABRAMSON, ARTHUR SIMON, educator, physician; b. Montreal, Que., Can., June 4, 1912; came to U.S., 1937, naturalized, 1942; s. Jacob J. and Dora (Rosenthal) A.; m. Ruth Mary Rumsey, Aug. 1, 1956; 1 son, Daniel Rumsey. B.S., McGill U., 1933, M.D., 1937. Diplomate: Am. Bd. Phys. Medicine and Rehab. (vice chmn. 1966-68). Intern Newark Beth Israel Hosp., 1938-39; resident Royal Victoria Hosp., Montreal, 1939-40, Montefiore Hosp., N.Y.C., 1940-41, Hosp. Joint Diseases, N.Y.C., 1941-42, Bronx VA Hosp., 1946-48; practice medicine, specializing in phys. medicine and rehab., N.Y.C., 1948-82; chief phys. medicine and rehab. service Bronx VA Hosp., 1950-55; clin. prof. phys. medicine and rehab. N.Y. Med. Coll., 1950-55; prof., chmn. dept. rehab. medicine Albert Einstein Coll. Medicine, 1955-82, Samuel Belkin Univ. prof., 1977-82; vis. prof. Ithaca Coll., 1958-76; various vis. professorships and lectureships. Cons. Kingsbrook Med. Center, Misericordia, Beth Abraham, VA hosps., Montrose, Bronx, and East Orange, Castle Point; Albee lectr. Kessler Rehab. Instn., 1964. Co-author: Care of Patient with Neurogenic Bladder, 1979; Mem. editorial bd., asso. editor: Archives of Phys. Medicine and Rehab, 1973-78; Contbr. articles profl. jours. Mem. Gov. Rockefeller's Council Rehab., 1961-65; past mem. Nat. Commn. Edn. Phys. Medicine and Rehab.; past mem. med. expert com. Am. Rehab. Found. Served to maj. AUS, 1942-46. Named N.Y.C. Disabled Man of Year, 1948; recipient President's trophy Handicapped Man of Year, 1956; Hon. Alumnus award Albert Einstein Coll. Medicine, 1974. Fellow N.Y. Acad. Medicine, Am. Acad. Phys. Medicine and Rehab. (pres. 1971-72, Zeiter lectr. 1975, Krusen Gold medal 1980), A.C.P.; mem. N.Y. Acad. Scis., AMA, Am. Congress Rehab. Medicine (recipient Gold Key award 1966, Coulter lectr. 1967), Am. Rheumatism Assn., Peruvian Soc. Urology (hon.), Peruvian Soc. Phys. Medicine and Rehab. (hon.). Home: Hartsdale, N.Y. Died Nov. 2, 1982.

ACHE, ATTILA MONTEIRO, Brazilian naval officer; b. Rio de Janeiro, Brazil, July 11, 1889; s. Marechal Napoleao and Constanca (Monteiro) A.; ed. Colegio Militar, Escola Naval, Escola de Submarinos, Escola de Engenharia, Escola de Guerra Naval; m. Dagmar Lima Franco, Mar. 4, 1911; children—Attila Franco Ache, Sydney Franco, Yvonne Franco. Commd. ensign, Brazilian Navy, 1910, and advanced through grades to rear adm., 1945; served in destroyer, Piaui, in Meditarranean, World War I; comd. several submarines and destroyers; comdg. officer cruiser Rio Grande do Sul, Jan. 1939-May 1940; dep. chief of navy minister's staff, May 1940-Jan. 1941; comdr. submarine squadron, Jan. 1941-Aug. 1945; chief of naval personnel, Nov. 1945-May 1947; on special mission to U.S., May 1947-Jan. 1948; naval attaché Brazilian embassy, Washington, from Jan. 1948; also serving as Brazilian Navy del. Joint Brazil-U.S. Defense Commn., and mem. Brazilian delegation Inter-Am. Defense Bd. Mem. Brazilian delegation and minister plenipotentiary to inauguration of President of Chile, 1938. Vice pres. Coselho de Imigracao e Colonizaco (Immigration and Colonization Bd.), 1938-45. Recipent Victory Medal World War I. Naval Merit of War with 3 stars World War II, Comdr. Order of Naval Merit, Gold Medal of Mil. Service, Medal in Commemoration of 50th Anniversary of Proclamation of Republic (Brazil), Comdr. Order of Naval Merit (Chile), Comdr. Order of Naval Merit (Paraguay), Official of Order of White Rose (Finland). Mem. Instituto Tecnico de Marinha. Roman Catholic. Clubs: Naval, Conselho Superior de Esportes, Liga de Esportes da Marinha (pres. 10 yrs.); Army-Navy, Army and Navy Country (Washington). Home: Washington, D.C. †

ACHI, WILLIAM CHARLES, judge; b. at Honolulu, H.T., July 1, 1889; s. William Charles and Maria (Alapai) A.; grad. St. Louis Coll., Honolulu, 1904, Oahu Coll., Honolulu, 1908; student Stanford, 1909-11, Yale, 1911-12, U. of Chicago, 1912-13; A.B., U. of Mich., 1914, LL.B., 1917; m. Rebecca K. Robinson, of Kainaliu, North Kona, H.T., June 7, 1910; children William Charles III, Richard Kelii, Mary Ann Arbor, Stanley Alpai, Rebecca K., Stanford H. Admitted to practice, U.S. Supreme Court, 1924, H.T. bar, 1917, and practiced at Honolulu, mem. Achi & Achi, until 1919; judge, Circuit Ct., 5th circuit, T.H., 1919-34; resumed practice at Lihue, Kauai, T.H. Mem. Calif. N.G., 1909. Assoc. mem. legal advisory bd., Selective Service Draft Bd., 1919; mem. Honolulu Civ. Service Commn., 1919. Mem. Am. Bar Assn., Bar Assn. Hawaii, Am. Soc. Internat. Law, Am. Geog. Soc., Hawaiian Hist. Soc., Native Sons and Daughters of Hawaii, Hale o na Alii, Kalanianaole Soc., Order of Kamehameha, Kauai Chamber Commerce, Pi Gamma Mu. Conglist. Mason (32 deg., Shriner), Zal Graz Grotto, Ann Arbor, Mich.; K.P., Ann Arbor. Clubs: Kauai Athletic, Kauai Boat, Kauai Fish and Game. Mem. Stanford U. Symphony Orchestra, 1910, Stanford U. baseball team, 1911, U. of Mich. Glee Club, 1916. Composer of college songs for Stanford, Yale, Mich., also of comic opera, "Pranks of Paprika" Democrat. Home: Hokulani, Kauai, T.H. †

ACKERMAN, DANIEL R., insurance exec.; b. Ridgewood, N.J., June 12, 1889. Asso. with Great American Ins. Co. since 1907, asst. sec., 1926, sec., 1929, v.p., 1931, chmn. bd. from 1947, dir. from 1946, chmn. exec. com. from 1952; chmn. bd., dir., chmn. exec. com. Am. Nat. Fire Ins. Co., Detroit Fire & Marine Ins. Co., Mass. Fire & Marine Ins. Co., Rochester Am. Ins. Co., Gt. Am. Indemnity Co.; pres., dir. One Liberty St. Realty & Securities Corp., Afia Finance Corp.; dir. Sanborn Map Co., Nat. Bd. of Fire Underwriters Building Corp., Sun Ins. Co., N.Y. Treas. Nat. Bd. Fire Underwriters. Mem. Am. Fgn. Ins. Assn. (trustee). Home: Spring Lake, N.J. †

ACKERMAN, JAMES WALDO, judge; b. Jacksonville, Fla., Jan. 1, 1926; s. James Waldo and Mary (Mundee) A.; m. Doris Ann Bivin, July 3, 1952; children: James Waldo III, Anne Francis, Philip William. B.S., Marquette U., 1947, J.D., 1949. Bar: Ill. 1949. Practiced, in Springfield, Ill., 1949-71, state's atty., Sangamon County, Ill., 1956-60; corp. counsel City of Springfield, 1960-62; asst. state treas. State of Ill., 1962-64, chief dep. atty. gen., 1970-71; atty. Springfield Election Commn., 1964-68; asso. gen. counsel Ill. Municipal League, 1966-68; formerly judge Ill. Circuit Ct., 7th circuit, Springfield; now judge U.S. Dist. Ct. Central Dist. Ill., Springfield, chief judge, 1982-84; adj. prof. dept. med. humanities So. Ill. U.; apptd. mem. Jud. Conf. Com. on Operation of Jury System, 1981. Contbr.: article Jour. Legal Medicine. Served with USNR, 1944-46, 52-54. Home: Springfield, Ill. Died Nov. 23, 1984.

ADAIR, EDWIN ROSS, diplomat; b. Albion, Ind., Dec. 14, 1907; s. Edwin L. and Alice (Prickett) A.; A.B., Hillsdale (Mich.) Coll., 1928; LL.B., George Washington U., 1933; LL.D., Ind. Inst. Tech.; m. Marian E. Wood, July 21, 1934; children—Caroline Ann (Mrs. David A. Dimmers), Stephen Wood. Admitted to Ind. bar, 1933, practiced law, Ft. Wayne; mem. 82d to 91st U.S. Congresses 4th Ind. Dist.; U.S. ambassador to Ethiopia, 1971-74. Mem. Gov.'s Commn. on Rights of Privacy, 1975-76. Past bd. dirs. Parkview Meml. Hosp.; bd. dirs. Eisenhower Scholarship Fund, Allen County Legal Aid, Religious Heritage Am., Youth for Christ; trustee Hillsdale Coll.; U.S. del. 18th Gen. Conf. UNESCO, Paris, 1974. Served in AUS, 1941-45. Mem. Ind. State, Ft. Wayne bar assns., VFW, Am. Legion, Interparliamentary Union (past del.), Delta Sigma Phi (past nat. pres.), Phi Alpha Delta. Mason (33 deg., Shriner). Home: Fort Wayne, Ind. Died May 1, 1983.

ADAM, CLAUS, educator, cellist, composer; b. Sumatra, Indonesia, Nov. 5, 1917; came to U.S., 1931, naturalized, 1935; s. Tassilo M. and Johanna (Musch) A.; m. Eleanor Randolph Bentz, Sept. 28, 1940; 1 dau., Elizabeth Johanna. Ed., Austria, Germany, Holland and U.S.; Philharmonic scholarship with, Joseph Emonts, 1935-38; scholar with, Emanuel Feuermann, 1938-43; orch. tng. with, Nat. Orch. Assn., 1935-40. Mem. faculty Juilliard Sch., 1955-83, Mannes Coll. Music, Phila. Coll. for Performing Arts. Asst. 1st cellist, Mpls. Symphony, 1940-43, 1st cellist, sta. WOR, N.Y.C., 1946-48, cellist, organizer, New Music String Quartet, 1948-54, mem., Juilliard String Quartet, 1955-74; Composer: Piano Sonata, 1950, String Trio, 1968, Song Cycle, Herbstgesängë , 1969, Concerto for Piano and Orch, 1973, String Quartet, 1975, Concerto Variations for Orch, 1976; numerous tours, U.S. and abroad, 1950-83; composer in residence, Am. Acad., Rome, 1976. Recipient grants and awards Ford Found., grants and awards Nat. Found. Arts, grants and awards Paderewski Found., grants and awards Naumberg Founds.; Guggenheim fellow, 1975-76. Died July 4, 1983.*

ADAMS, ALEXANDER PRATT, JR., banker; b. Savannah, Ga., May 24, 1914; s. Alexander Pratt and Mary Hamilton (Thomas) A.; m. Elizabeth Jamieson, July 19, 1941; children—Samuel Barnard, Mary Elizabeth Adams Odom. A.B., U. Ga., 1936; postgrad., Harvard U. Law Sch., 1936-39. Bar: Ga. bar 1938. Asso. firm Adams, Adams, Brennan & Gardner, Savannah, 1939-81; dir. Citizens & So. Nat. Bank, Atlanta, 1964-81, chmn. bd., 1978-79, also mem. credit com. and exec. com.; dir. Citizens & So. Holding Co., Carson Products Co., Savannah; mem. adv. bd. Citizens & So. Savannah. Mem. Bd. Aldermen, Savannah, 1946; asst. solicitor gen. Chatham County, 1947-48. Served with inf. AUS, 1941-45. Decorated Bronze Star medal. Mem. Am. Bar Assn., Ga. Bar Assn., Savannah Bar Assn. (pres. 1953), Assn. Ins. Attys., Chi Phi. Episcopalian. Clubs: Oglethorpe, Savannah Golf, Cotillion, Chatham, Century, Capital City.

ADAMS, ANSEL, photographer; b. San Francisco, Feb. 20, 1902; s. Charles Hitchcock and Olive (Bray) A.; m. Virginia Best, Jan. 2, 1928; children: Michael, Anne Adams Helms. Student piano, also spl. studies lit. and scis.; D.F.A. (hon.), U. Calif.-Berkeley, 1961, Yale U., 1973, U. Mass.-Amherst, 1974, U. Ariz., 1975, Harvard U., 1981. Piano performer and tchr., 1920-30, profl. photographer, 1932-84; dir. photography dept. Art Center Sch., Los Angeles, 1939-42, Golden Gate Internat. Exposition, San Francisco, 1940; vice chmn. dept. photography Mus. Modern Art, 1940-42; dir. photography dept. Calif. Sch. Fine Arts, San Francisco, 1946-49; dir. Ansel Adams Workshop, 1955-84. Author portfolios of original prints; over 30 books including Images, 1923-74; (with Nancy Newhall) monograph The Eloquent Light, 1963, 80, Death Valley, Yosemite Valley, 1960, (with Nancy Newhall) These We Inherit, America's Parklands; New Ansel Adams Photography Series, 3 vols.; monograph Polaroid Land Professional Photography Manual, Photographs of the Southwest, The Portfolios of Ansel Adams, Ansel Adams: Yosemite and the Range of Light, 1979, (with Nancy Newhall) The Camera, 1980, The Negative, 1982; The Print, 1983, Examples, The Making of 40 Photographs, 1983; Exhbns. include one man show An America Place, N.Y.C., 1936; also exhibits prin. cities of world, retrospective exhibit, Met. Mus. Art, N.Y.C., 1974, Mus. Modern Art, N.Y.C., 1979. Recipient Muir award Sierra Club, 1963; Conservation Service award U.S. Dept. Interior, 1968; Progress medal Photog. Soc. Am., 1969; Ansel Adams Conservation award Wilderness Soc., 1980; Presdl. medal of Freedom, 1980; named Hon. Photographer of 1981, Soc. Photog. Edn.; Guggenheim fellow, 1946, 48, 58; Chubb fellow Yale U., 1970. Fellow Royal Photo Soc. (London), Photographers Soc. Am., Am. Acad. Arts and Scis.; mem. Trustees for Conservation (pres. 1956-57), Sierra Club Calif. (dir. 1934-71), Friends of Photography (founder, chmn. bd. 1967. Club: Old Capitol (Monterey, Calif.). Calif.). Home: Carmel, Calif. Died Apr. 22, 1984.

ADAMS, CYRUS HALL, III, former retail store exec.; b. Chgo., Oct. 24, 1909; s. Cyrus Hall and Mary (Shumway) A.; student The Hill Sch., Pottstown, Pa., 1925-27; A.B., Princeton, 1931; m. Harriet Haynes, Aug. 14, 1936; children—Cyrus Hall IV, Mary Frances (Mrs. Eberhart). With Carson Pirie Scott & Co., Chgo., 1932-68, controller, 1954-63, asst. sec., 1961-63, asst. to pres., 1963-64, v.p. civic affairs, 1965-68. Mem. Chgo. Bd. Edn. Treas. Chgo. Hist. Soc.; bd. dirs. Better Govt. Assn.; trustee Hill sch. Mem. Chgo. Assn. Commerce and Industry. Home: Chicago, Ill. Died Jan. 29, 1985.

ADAMS, ELLIOT QUINCY, chemist; b. Medford, Mass., Sept. 13, 1888; s. Edward Perkins and Etta Medora (Elliot) A.; grad. high sch., Medford, Mass., 1904; B.S., Mass. Inst. Tech., 1909; Ph.D., U. of Calif., 1914; m. Jane J. Pidgeon, June 28, 1922 (died May, 1947); 1 dau., Dora C. (Mrs. Frank R. Arnold). Civil engring. asst. to E. P. Adams, Boston, 1904-05; research asst., General Electric Co., 1909-13; asst. in chemistry, University of Calif., 1914-15, instructor, 1915-17; organic and physical chemist, U.S. Bureau of Chemistry, 1917-21; physical chemist, research lab., incandescent lamp dept., Gen. Electric Co., 1921-28, lamp development lab. from 1929. Scoutmaster, 1910, neighborhood commr. from 1927, Boy Scouts America. Received Silver Beaver Award from Boy Scouts, 1941. Fellow A.A.A.S., Am. Phys. Soc., Mineral. Soc. America; mem. Am. Chem. Soc. Optical Soc. Am., Washington Acad. Scis., Universala Esperanto Asocio, Esperanto Assn. of N. Am., Illuminating Engring. Soc., Sigma Xi, Phi Lambda Upsilon. Unitarian. Author: (with W.E. Forsythe) Fluorescent and Other Gaseous Discharge Lamps, 1948. Contributor to Journal American Chemistry, Society, etc. Inventor (with Herbert L. Haller) of Kryptocyanine and other phtotgraphic sensitizing dyes. Home: Cleveland Heights, Ohio. †

ADAMS, GEORGE WORTHINGTON, educator; b. Jacksonville, Ill., Nov. 22, 1905; s. Albyn Lincoln and Minna (Worthington) A.; A.B., Ill. Coll., Jacksonville, 1927; A.M., Harvard, 1928, Ph.D., 1946; m. Mabel Rogers, Dec. 29, 1927; 1 dau., Pamela (Mrs. Charles Javis Meyers). Instr. English and history, Mass. Inst. Tech., 1928-30; asst. in history Harvard U. and Radcliffe Coll., 1930-33; asso. prof. history and social scis. MacMurray Coll. for Women, Jacksonville, 1933-37, and dir. summer session, 1937; assoc. prof., head dept. history Lake Forest (Ill.) Coll., 1937-42; dir. tng. div. 8, Met. Chgo. Office Civilian Def., 1942; asst. counsellor for vets. Harvard, 1945-46, sec. Grad. Sch. Arts and Scis., also mem. faculty, 1946-49, dean of spl. students and dean Univ. Extension, 1946-49; dir. Summer Sch. of Arts and Scis. and of Edn., 1947-49; dean of the coll. and prof. history Colo. Coll., 1949, dir. summer session, 1950; European dir. Salzburg Seminar in Am. Studies, 1954-58; prof. history So. Ill. U., 1958-61, 62-73, prof. emeritus, 1973-81, chmn. dept., 1958-61, 62-68; acad. v.p., prof. history U. Alaska, 1961-62. Mem. adv. council to the U.S. Civil War Centennial Commn., from 1958; editorial bd. Ulysses S. Grant Assn. Served as naval communications officer, USNR, overseas, Hawaii and Okinawa; disch. rank of lt. comdr., 1945. Recipient distinguished pub. service award Ill. Coll., 1959; Huntington Library Research award, 1967. Hon life mem. Austro-Am. Soc. Mem. Am., Miss. Valley hist. assns., Am. Assn. U. Profs., Nat. Assn. Deans and Dir. of Summer Session (sec. 1948-49). Author: Doctors in Blue: The Medical History of the Union Army in the Civil War, 1953. Editor: Mary Logan's Reminiscences of the Civil War and Reconstruction, 1970. Home: Carbondale, Ill. Died Nov. 5, 1981.

ADAMS, HARRIET STRATEMEYER (CAROLYN KEENE), author; b. N.J., circa 1893; d. Edward L. and Magdalene Stratemeyer; m. Russell Vroom Adams, 1916 (div. dec. 1966); children—Russell Vroom (dec.), Patricia, (Mrs. Harr), Camilla (Mrs. McClave), Edward. Grad., Wellesley Coll., 1915. Partner Stratemeyer Syndicate, 1930-82. Author, 1930-82, Dana Girls series, 1934-82, Nancy Drew series, 1930-82; also Nancy Drew Cookbook Clues to Good Cooking, 1973. Active ARC, Girl Scouts U.S., past Republican County committeewoman. Mem. League Am. Pen Women, Bus. and Profl. Women's Club. Clubs: N.J. Women's Press, Zonta, N.J. Wellesley, N.Y. Wellesley. Home: Maplewood, N.J. Died Mar. 27, 1982.*

ADAMS, J. STACY, psychologist; b. Brussels, Belgium, Mar. 16, 1925; s. Charles Stacy and Simonne (Herrman) A.; m. Antoinette Hamilton, Feb. 14, 1952 (div.); children: Michele, Erica. B.A., U. Miss., 1948; M.A., U. N.C., 1955, Ph.D., 1957. Dep. chief Attitude Research br. U.S. Army, Europe, 1948-53; asst. prof. Stanford U., Palo Alto, Calif., 1957-60; cons. Gen. Electric Co., N.Y.C., 1960-67; adj. asso. prof. Columbia U., 1962-67; R.J. Reynolds prof. U. N.C., Chapel Hill, 1967—; advisor behavioral research panel Gen. Electric Co., 1967-70; Mem. research com. NSF, 1968-69; mem. adv. com. Center for Creative Leadership, 1968-71. Author: (with D. Katz and R.L. Kahn) The Study of Organizations, 1980; others; contbr. articles to profl. jours. Served with U.S. Navy, 1942-46. Recipient Carolina Psychology Disting. Alumnus award U. N.C., 1977, Rendleman Doctoral Teaching award, 1980; Gen. Electric Co. grantee, 1967-69; NSF grantee, 1972-76. Mem. Am. Psychol. Assn., Acad. Mgmt. Office: Chapel Hill NC

ADAMS, LUCY LOCKWOOD, prof. English; b. New Haven, Conn., Dec. 9, 1890; d. William Ellison and Sara Elizabeth (Husted) Lockwood; A.B., U. of Redlands (Calif.), 1916; A.M., U. of Calif. 1917, Ph.D., 1925; m. George Irving Hazard, Sept. 16, 1909; children—Ellison Lockwood, Lucy Elizabeth Adelheid, Jacqueline Cecile Noel; m. 2d, Bertram Martin Adams, June 11, 1936. Began as a high sch. teacher, 1917; successively teacher English and history, Hilo, Hawaii, English and dramatics, Redlands High Sch., actg. asso. prof. English, U. of Redlands; with Mills Coll., Oakland, Calif., from 1920, successively as instr., asst. prof., asso. prof., English; extension lecturer U. of Utah, 1929-30; has taught summer sessions, U. of Calif., U. of Colo., U. of Calif. at Los Angeles. Author: The Frontier in American Literature, 1927. Compiler: In Search of America, 1930; Plays from the Drama Workshop, 1937. Home: Walnut Creek, Calif.†

ADAMS, NORMAN ILSLEY, JR., physicist; b. Winthrop, Mass., Sept. 20, 1895; s. Norman Ilsley and Mabel Estelle (George) A.; B.A., Yale, 1917, Ph.D., 1923; m. Genevieve A. Sloan, July 28, 1926; children—Norman Ilsley III, Harry Bell. Engr. dept. devel. and research AT&T, N.Y.C., 1923-24; mem. faculty Yale U., New Haven, 1925-85, prof. physics, 1944-64, prof. emeritus, 1964-85; vis. prof. U. Idaho, 1964, U. Del., 1965, Central Wash. State Coll., 1967; cons. engr. in radio broadcasting, 1927-85. Served as 2d lt., 301st Heavy Tank Bn., A.E.F., France, 1918; dir. Eatontown Signal Lab., Fort Monmouth, N.J., 1941-43; ret. rank lt. col. Registered profl. engr. (communications), Conn. Awarded Legion of Merit, World War II. Fellow Am. Phys. Soc.; mem. Res. Officers Assn., Ret. Officers Assn., Mil. Order World Wars, Order Lafayette, Gamma Alpha, Phi Beta Kappa, Sigma Xi. Republican. Episcopalian. Clubs: Appalachian Mountain; New Haven Lawn. Author: Principles of Electricity (with L. Page), 1931; Electrodynamics (with L. Page), 1940. Address: Gainesville, Fla. Died Mar. 19, 1985; interred Randolph Cemetery, Randolph, N.H.

ADAMS, SCOTT, librarian; b. Agawam, Mass., Nov. 20, 1909; s. Scott and Edith and Fisher (Ferre) A.; m. Barbara Winn, June 29, 1935; 1 dau., Susanna; m. Joan Titley, Jan. 19, 1974. A.B., Yale, 1930; M.L.S., Columbia, 1940. Dept. head Tchrs. Coll. Library, Columbia, 1940-42, Providence Pub. Library, 1943-45; acting librarian Armed Forces Med. Library, 1946-50; librarian U.S. NIH, Bethesda, Md., 1950-59; program dir., fgn. sci. information Office of Sci. Information Service, NSF, 1959-60; dep. dir. Nat. Library of Medicine, 1960-69; spl. asst. to the fgn. sec. Nat. Acad. Scis., 1970-71; sr. staff scientist sci. biol. communications div. George Washington U., 1972-73; prof. Sch. Edn., U. Louisville, 1973-75; asso. Urban Studies Center, 1975-78; sec. U.S. Book Exchange, Inc., 1952-53; Mem. internat. adv. com. documentation, libraries and archives to UNESCO, 1967-70, cons., 1971-82. Fellow AAAS (sec. information and communications sect. 1969-74), Med. Library Assn. (dir. 1952-55, pres. 1967-68); mem. D.C. Library Assn. (pres. 1948), Council Nat. Library Assns. (sec. 1954-55), Am. Soc. Information Sci. (pres. 1954-55), Spl. Libraries Assn., Nat. Acad. Scis. (chmn. com. on internat. sci. and tech. information programs 1974-75). Clubs: Mayflower Soc. (Louisville), Filson (Louisville); Yale (Washington), Cosmos (Washington). Home: Louisville, Ky. Died Oct. 3, 1982.

ADAMS, TRACY A., company exec.; b. Jaffrey, N.H., Apr. 3, 1889; s. Elmer J. and Alice (Bemis) A.; graduate Lowell Textile Inst., 1911; m. Louise Burleigh, June 28, 1916; children—Ann Hunt, Lucy A. Hunter. With Pacific Mills, 1911-17; v.p. Arnold Print Works, North Adams, Mass., 1917; gen. mgr., cons. engr. Barnes Textile Assos., Boston, 1943; exec. v.p., gen. mgr. U.S. Finishing Co., Norwich, Conn., 1949, pres. from 1949; cons. engr. Republican. Mason. Home: Peterborough, N.H. †

ADAMS, WALTER ALEXANDER, foreign service; b. Greenville, S.C., Dec. 16, 1887; s. William Alexander and Sarah Elvirah A.; student Clemson (S.C.) College; LL.B., Georgetown Univ., 1913; m. Betty Christine Eastman, Aug. 28, 1933. Began as clerk, U.S. Civ. Service, Washington, D.C., 1911; clk. Philippine Civ. Service to 1914; admitted to bar, U.S. Court for China, Shanghai, 1916; vice consul, Shanghai, 1916-18, Batavia, Java, 1918-20, Canton, China, and Swatow, China, 1920, Changsha, China, 1921; consul, Tsingtao, China, 1922-25, Chungking, China, 1925-27, Hankow, China, 1927, Nanking, China, 1929-31; consul gen., Hankow, 1931-34; consul gen., Harbin, Manchuria, 1934-37; assigned Div. of Far Eastern Affairs, Dept. of State, Oct. 1937, asst. chief, Jan. 1941. Clubs: Columbia Country (Washington, D.C.); Tsingtao International. Home: Greenville, S.C. †

ADELMAN, R. J., real estate executive; b. Chgo., June 21, 1915; s. Samuel and Rose (Colitz) A.; m. Betty Friend, Feb. 4, 1941; children: Jean Ruth, Betty Sue. A.B., U. Mich., 1936. With Arthur Rubloff & Co., Chgo., 1936-82, pres., 1952-70, chmn., chief exec. officer, 1970-80, chmn., 1980-82; dir. Chgo. Title & Trust Co., Avico Ltd. Mem. Ill. Aeros. Bd.; mem. Chgo. Airport Commn., 1980-82; bd. dirs., v.p. Greater N. Michigan Ave. Assn., Chgo. Served as 1st lt. USAAF, World War II. Mem. Am. Soc. Real Estate Counselors, Northwestern U. Assos., Soc. Indsl. Realtors, Farm and Land Inst. (real estate aviation chpt.). Clubs: Standard (Chgo.), Tavern (Chgo.); Lake Shore Country (Glencoe, Ill.); Ocean Reef (Key Largo, (Fla.). Home: Highland Park, Ill. Died Dec. 1, 1982.

ADLER, LUTHER, actor; b. N.Y.C., May 4, 1903; s. Jacob P. and Sarah (Lewis) A.; ed. Lewis Inst., Chgo.; studied for stage with parents; m. Sylvia Sidney (div. 1947); 1 son, Jacob Luther; m. 2d, Julie Hadley Roche, Apr. 1959. Stage appearance as child actor, Thalia Theatre, Bowery, N.Y.C., 1908; stage debut Provincetown Theatre, N.Y.C., 1921; appeared in numerous plays, including We Americans, 1927, Success Story, 1933, Awake and Sing, 1935, Paradise Lost, 1936, Golden Boy (N.Y.C. and London), 1938, Rocket to the Moon, 1939, Beggars are Coming to Town, 1945, A Flag is Born, 1946, Tovarich, 1952, A Month in the Country, 1956, A View From the Bridge (toured as Eddie Carbone), 1957-59; Mr. Rochester in Jane Eyre, 1943-44, also The Play's the Thing, N.Y.C., part of Shylock in Merchant of Venice, appearance St. James Theatre, London, part of Chebutykin in the Three Sisters, Lenin in The Passion of Josef D., Tevye in Fiddler on the Roof, 1965, (tour) 1966-67; Gen. Shi Pe' in Waltz of the Toreadors, 1969; Gregory Soloman in The Price, 1970; TV appearances include Playhouse 90, Mission: Impossible, Hawaii Five-O, Search, Streets of San Francisco; films include House of Strangers, D.O.A., South Sea Sinner, Under My Skin, Kiss Tomorrow Goodby, M. Magic Face, Desert Fox, Hoodlum Empire, Tall Texan, Miami Story, Girl in the Red Velvet Swing, Hot Blood, Crazy Joe. Office: Los Angeles, Calif. *

ADOLFSON, LORENTZ HENNING, univ. adminstr.; b. Chgo., Oct. 14, 1909; s. August H. and Eva (Bergstrom) A.; student Crane Jr. Coll., Chgo., 1929-30; B.A., Wabash Coll., 1933; Ph.D., U. Wis., 1942; m. Mildred Marie Jensen, Apr. 20, 1940; 1 dau., Carol Ann Rittle. Engaged in ins. bus., Chgo., 1926-29, mfg. and wholesale bus., Chgo., 1933-36; instr. polit. sci. univ. extension div. U. Wis.-Madison, 1938-42, asst. prof., 1942-44, dir., 1944-59, dean, 1959-64, dir. univ. summer sessions, 1954-64, chancellor Univ. center system, 1964-72, chancellor emeritus, 1972-85; state-wide lectr. on nat. and internat. affairs, 1938-44; head ICA Ankara (Turkey) project in pub. adminstrn. N.Y.U., 1957-58, head Wis. ednl. survey team, Uganda, also Kenya, 1966. edn. in Armed Forces, Dept. Def., 1961-63. Mem. Joint Interim Legislative Com. to Study County Govt. in Wis., 1945-46; mem. Wis. Radio Council, 1945-65, Youth Service Commn., 1947-49, Gov. Wis. Commn. Human Rights, 1947-57, Gov.'s Com. on UN Day (chmn. 1950-56); chmn. Wis. State Brotherhood, 1960; mem. Wis. Free Library Commn., 1951-57. Mem. Nat. U. Extension Assn. (pres. 1951-52), Assn. State U. and Land Grant Colls., Am. Assn. Jr. Colls. (commn. instrn.), Phi Beta Kappa, Tau Kappa Alpha, Phi Kappa Phi, Kappa Sigma, Blue Key. Club: Blackhawk (Madison). Home: Madison, Wis. Died July 3, 1985.

AGEE, CARL, educator; born Owen Co., Ky., Feb. 13, 1889; s. Alvies and Ollie (Nix) A.; student Eastern Ky. State Teachers Coll., Richmond, 1910-12; A.B., Transylvania Coll., Lexington, 1919; B.Th., Coll. of the Bible, Lexington, 1919; B.D., Yale, 1922; D.D., Culver-Stockton Coll., Canton, Mo., 1930; m. Ora Breeden, June 14, 1907; 1 dau., Wilma Louise. Taught in rural schs., Grant County, Ky., 1906-10; prin. high sch., Boonville, Ky., 1910-11, Holbrook, Ky., 1911-12; ordained ministry Christian (Disciples) Ch., 1912; pastor Flat Rock, Ky., 1912-15, Ewing, 1915-18, Lawrenceburg, 1918-22, 1st Ch., Phila., 1922-27, 1st Ch., Columbia, Mo., 1928-30; asso. dean, Bible Coll. of Mo., Columbia, 1930-34, dean, 1934-49, prof. N.T. lit. from 1949. Mem. Disciples of Christ. Home: Columbia, Mo. †

AGHNIDES, THANASSIS, Greek diplomat; b. Nigde, Province of Konia (Iconium) in Asia Minor, Turkey, Jan. 31, 1889; s. Prodromos and Anastasia (Aghnidou) A.; student Nat. Superior Coll., Phanar, Constantinople (Greek), and Coll. of St. Joseph, Cadi-Keuy, Constantinople (French); A.B., Anatolia Co., (an Am. Coll.), Marsivan, Asia Minor, 1908, LL.D., 1933; Barrister-at-Law, diploma, U. of Constantinople, 1908; LL.B., Paris U. Dir. press sect. Greek legation, London, 1918-19; mem. minorities sect. secretariat, League of Nations, 1919-20, disarmament sect., 1920-21, polit. sect., 1922-30 dir. disarmament sect., 1930-38, sec. gen. Disarmament Conf., 1932-34; under-sec. gen. League of Nations, 1939-42; sec.-gen. Montreux Conf. on Dardanelles, Montreux Conv., 1936; sec. gen. Capitulations Conf., Montreux, 1937, Nyon Conf., 1937; permanent under-sec. for fgn. affairs of Greece, 1942; Greek del. San Francisco Conf., Apr.-July 1945; pres. 6th com. in prep. commn., United Nations Orgn., Dec. 1945; Greek del. to Gen. Assembly, U.N., 1946; chief of Greek delegation, Gen. Assembly, Oct.-Dec. 1946; rapporteur of 5th com., Gen. Assembly, Jan. and Oct. Dec., 1946; chmn. advisory com. on administrative and budgetary questions UN, 1946-63; chmn. of International Civil Service Adv. Bd., 1948-58. Greek A. E. and P. to Ct. of St. James, London, 1942-47. Mem. Curatorium Acad. of International Law, The Hague, Netherlands. Club: St. James (London). Author (with Lord Perth and others) of a book on the International Secretariat of the Future, 1944. Contbr. articles on international orgn.; also lectures delivered in univs. of Oxford, London, Manchester, Bristol. Home: Geneva, Switzerland. †

AHERN, JOHN IRENAEUS, utility exec.; b. Weymouth, Mass., June 28, 1907; s. John W. and Catherine (Leary) A.; m. Marion Whitney Brown, Apr. 22, 1936. B.B.A., Boston U., 1930. Trainee Weymouth Light & Power Co., 1929-30, sales and advt., 1930-34; asst. mdse. mgr. New Eng. Power Service & Engring. Corp., 1934-36, editor, 1936-37, publicity dir., 1937-47; asst. v.p., dir. pub. relations New Eng. Electric System, Boston, 1947-50, v.p., from 1950; chmn., dir. Mass. Electric & Gas Assn.; chmn. bd. Mass. Electric Co., from 1968; dir. Fieldcrest Mills; mem. investment com. Union Warren Savs. Bank; finance com. dir. Boston Mut. Life Ins. Co.; dir. exec. com. Westville Homes Corp.; trustee exec. com. Amoskeag Co., Union Warren Savs. Bank; treas., dir. Issues Mgmt. Inc.; trustee Flatley REIT; dir. Fed. St. Capital Corp. Mem. exec. com. Mass. Com. Caths., Protestants and Jews; bd. govs. Boston U. Human Relations Center.; Bd. dirs., exec. com. Boston chpt. A.R.C.; bd. dirs. Family Counseling and Guidance Centers, Boston, Eunice K. Shriver Center for Mental Retardation; trustee Regis Coll., Walter E. Fernald State Sch.; chmn. bd. advisers Stonehill Coll; mem. pres. council Boston Coll. Served to lt. comdr. USNR, 1942-46. Clubs: Algonquin (Boston), Clover (Boston). Home: Newton, Mass.

AHLQUIST, RAYMOND PERRY, pharmacologist; b. Missoula, Mont., July 26, 1914; s. Perry Karl and Elsa Victoria (Ekroth) A.; m. Dorotha Mae Duff, Sept. 9, 1939. B.S., U. Wash., Seattle, 1935, M.S., 1937, Ph.D., 1940. Asst. prof. S.D. State U., 1940-44; mem. faculty Med. Coll. Ga., Augusta, from 1944, prof. pharmacology, from 1948, chmn. dept., 1948-63, 70-77; asso. dean Sch. Medicine, 1963-70, Charbonnier prof., from 1977. Author papers autonomic pharmacology. Recipient Oscar B. Hunter award clin. pharmacology Am. Soc. Clin. Pharmacology and Therapeutics, 1974; Albert and Mary Lasker Clin. Research award, 1976; Ciba award research hypertension, 1976; named Distinguished Alumnus U. Wash. Sch. Pharmacy, 1977. Fellow Am. Coll. Clin. Pharmacology, Acad. Pharm. Scis.; mem. Am. Soc. Pharmacology and Exptl. Therapeutics, Brazilian Pharmacology Soc., N.Y. Acad. Scis. Home: Augusta, GA.

AHRENS, DON E., motor exec.; b. Lodgepole, Neb., Dec. 31, 1890; s. George and Julia (Prosser) A.; B.S. in elec. engring., U. Neb., 1914; m. Lucile Sanders, Sept. 8, 1923; children—Gay, Peter, Jeffrey, Luise, Sara Jane. Gen. mgr. Cadillac div. Gen. Motors Corp., Chicago, Phila. and N.Y. City brs., gen. sales mgr., 1935, gen. mgr. from 1950, v.p. Gen. Motors Corp., 1950-56. Home: Bloomfield Hills, Mich. †

AIKEN, EARL FREDERICK, construction company executive; b. Portage, Wis., Mar. 15, 1921; s. Charles Walter and Emma Augusta (Schultz) A.; Ph.B., U. Wis., 1942; m. Mildred Patterson Cecil, May 30, 1951. With Morrison-Knudsen Co., Inc., from 1951, v.p., treas. Morrison-Knudson Internat. Co., and fgn. operating subsidiaries, from 1972, treas. parent co., Boise, Idaho, from 1976. Served with AUS, 1942-45. Mem. Am. Soc. Mil. Engrs., Beta Gamma Sigma. Republican. Lutheran. Club: World Trade (San Francisco). Home: Boise, Idaho. Deceased.

AIKEN, GEORGE DAVID, U.S. senator; b. Dummerston, Vt., Aug. 20, 1892; s. Edward W. and Myra A. (Cook) A.; grad. Brattleboro (Vt.) High Sch., 1909; m. Beatrice M. Howard, 1914 (dec.); children—Dorothy Howard (Mrs. Harry Morse), Marjorie Evelyn (Mrs. Harry L. Cleverly), Howard George (dec.), Barbara Marion (Mrs. Malcolm Jones); m. Lola Pierotti, June 30, 1967. With small fruit farm, 1912; started comml. cultivation of wildflowers, 1926. Sch. dir., Putney, Vt., 1920-37; mem. State Ho. of Reps., 1930-33, speaker 1933-34; lt. gov. Vt., 1935-37, elected Gov., 1937-41; elected to U.S. Senate, 1940, to fill vacancy for term ending Jan. 3, 1945; served, 1944-75. Mem. Windham County Farm Bur., Vt.

Hort. Soc. (pres. 1917-18), Putney Grange. Republican. Odd Fellow. Author: Pioneering with Wildflowers, 1933; Pioneering with Fruits and Berries, 1936; Speaking From Vermont, 1938. Home: Putney, Vt. Died Nov. 19, 1984.

AIKEN, HENRY DAVID, educator; b. Portland, Oreg., July 3, 1912; s. Frank Bethel and Miriam (Boskowitz) A.; m. Jean Flagler Scott; children—Katharine, Perry; m. Lillian Woodworth, Feb. 17, 1951; 1 son, David; m. Helen Rowland Geer, Nov. 17, 1958; children—Paula Hume, Henry David. A.B., Reed Coll., 1935; M.A., Stanford, 1937; M.A., Ph.D., Harvard; L.H.D., Ripon Coll., 1969. Asso. Columbia, 1944-45; asst. prof. U. Wash., 1945-46; asso. prof. Harvard, 1946-54, prof. philosophy, 1954-65; prof. philosophy and history of ideas Brandeis U., 1965-67, Charles Goldman prof. philosophy, 1967-80, emeritus, from 1980; vis. prof. U. Mich., Ann Arbor, 1953, 67. Author: The Age of Ideology, 1955, Reason and Conduct, 1962, The Predicament of the University, 1971; contbg. author: Value: A Cooperative Inquiry, 1950; Co-editor: Philosophy in the Twentieth Century, 1962; book editor: Jour. Philosophy, 1945-52; cons. editor: Philos. Review, 1950-54, Philosophy and Phenomenological Research, from 1974; Contbr. articles to profl., lit. jours. Guggenheim fellow, 1960-61; Alfred North Whitehead fellow Harvard, 1968-69. Mem. Am. Soc. Polit. and Legal Philosophy, Am. Philos. Assn., Am. Psychol. Assn., Am. Soc. Aesthetics, Hume Assn. Democrat. Home: Cambridge, Mass.

AINSWORTH, ROBERT ANDREW, JR., U.S. judge; b. Gulfport, Miss., May 10, 1910; s. Robert Andrew and Catherine (Wursch) A.; LL.B., Loyola U., New Orleans, 1932, LL.D. (hon.), 1967; LL.D. (hon.), Xavier U., New Orleans, 1953; m. Elizabeth Hiern, Oct. 14, 1933; children—Elisabeth (Mrs. Clarence Rareshide), Robert Andrew III, Leslie (Mrs. Vincent Maggio). Admitted to La. bar, 1932; practice in New Orleans, 1932-61; U.S. judge Eastern Dist. La., 1961-66, U.S. Ct. Appeals, 5th Circuit, New Orleans, 1966-81. Chmn. bd. mgrs. Council State Govts., 1955-56; mem. Charter Com. City New Orleans, 1951-52; founder La. Legislative Council, 1952; pres. Nat. Legislative Conf., 1955-56; mem. Presdl. Commn. on Intergovtl. Relations, 1961; chmn. com. on ct. adminstrn. Jud. Conf. U.S., 1969-78, chmn. adv. com. on appellate rules, 1978-81. Mem. La. Senate from Orleans Parish, 1950-61, pres. pro tem, 1952-56, 60-61. Mem. adv. council Loyola U. Law Sch. Recipient Weiss award NCCJ, 1966; Order of St. Louis medallion, 1976; St. Mary's Dominican Coll. medal, 1971; Herbert Harley award Am. Judicature Soc., 1976; Adjutor Hominum award Loyola U., 1977. Fellow Am. Bar Found.; mem. Blue Key, Order of Coif. Democrat. Roman Catholic. Author La. Civil Service Act. Adv. editors Tulane Law Rev. Home: New Orleans, La. Died Dec. 22, 1981.

AITKEN, WEBSTER, pianist; b. Los Angeles, June 17, 1908. Student, Emil Sauer and Artur Schnabel. Debut, Vienna, Austria, 1929, recitals in, Berlin, Rome, Salzburg, London; soloist with, Vienna Philharmonic Orch., Am. debut, Town Hall, N.Y.C., 1935; soloist with orchs. and chamber music ensembles throughout U.S.; performed: complete Franz Schubert piano sonatas, London and N.Y.C., 1938; rec. artist, EMS, Delos records. Mem. Am. Fedn. Musicians. Home: New York, N.Y.

AKIN, CHARLES VIVIAN, physician, pub. ofcl.; b. Meridian, Miss., May 23, 1890; s. Charles Vance and Jennie (MacCormack) A.; grad. Dallas Acad., Selma, Ala., 1903; B.S., Meridian Mil. Acad., 1907; M.D., Tulane U., Med. Sch., New Orleans, 1911; m. Arline Hardin, Aug. 16, 1911; children—Charles Armstrong, Elizabeth Allen (wife of David Heiman, U.S.A.). With U.S. Pub. Health Service, 1914-43, commd. asst. surgeon, 1914, passed asst. surgeon, 1918, surgeon, 1922, sr. surgeon, 1934; chief quarantine officer Port of N.Y., U.S. Quarantine Sta., Rosebank, S. I., N.Y., 1936-39; became asst. surgeon gen. U.S.P.H.S. and chief of Div. of Sanitary Reports and Statistics, Office of Surgeon Gen., Washington, D.C., 1939; commd. med. dir. Pub. Health Service, Mar. 1940; during service has had experience in control of bubonic plague, venereal and other communicable diseases and research in epidemiology; also as quarantine officer Mobile, Ala., and Panama Canal; in charge of N.Y. Quarantine Station, 1936-39; has improved methods of cyanide fumigation and rat-infestation inspection of vessels and developed Pub. Health Service system of radio pratique to eliminate quarantine inspection of qualified vessels; from U.S.P.H.S., as asst. surg. gen. 1942; asso. Brit. Ministry War Transport, 1943-45; dir. Clarke-Wayne Health Dept. 1946-60, med. cons. from 1960. Fellow Am. Pub. Health Assn.; mem. A.M.A., Miss. Pub. Health Assn., Commd. Officers Assn., Officers Assn., Delta Kappa Epsilon, Phi Beta Pi. Episcopalian. Home: Shubuta, Miss. †

ALBERT, JOHN, fgn. service officer, foreign correspondent; b. Vienna, Austria, Jan. 28, 1912; s. Louis and Mary (Glaser) A.; LL.B., Vienna U., 1936; student Vienna Sch. Journalism; m. Hildegard Janauschek, Oct. 29, 1934; children—Larry J., Carol A. Came to U.S., 1940, naturalized, 1945. Editor, later asst. mng. editor Telegrafen-Compagnie, Vienna, 1932-38; asst. fgn. news editor CBS, 1940-42; propaganda analyst, chief intelligence div. OWI, 1942-45; chief ct. interpreter Internat. Mil. Tribunal, Nuremberg, 1945-46; with USIA, from 1947, chief German service, 1948-53, West Europe br., 1953-57, European div., 1957-58, dir. Munich Program Center, 1958-62, chief central program services div. Voice of Am., Washington, 1962-66, chief news and current affairs, 1966-67, sr. news analyst, 1967-74, ret.; fgn. corr. Swiss and Austrian newspapers, from 1974. Recipient Superior Service awards, USIA, 1955, 74. Home: Silver Spring, Md. Died July 29, 1981.

ALBERTO, ALVARO, physico-chemistry educator; b. Rio de Janeiro, Brazil, Apr. 22, 1889; s. Prof. Alvaro Alberto da Silva and Maria (Teixeira da Motta) da S.; grad. Brazilian Naval Acad., 1910; student Brazilian Polytech. Sch., 1914-15; m. Tereza Otero, May 8, 1919; children—Alvaro, Tereza (Mrs. Humberto Freire de Carvalho), Leonardo. Officer in Brazilian Navy, 1910; instr. chemistry and explosives, Naval Acad., 1916-23, asst. prof., 1923-31, prof., 1931-42, became head of physics dept., 1942, chief prof. since 1931; also prof. of physico-chemistry; pres. and tech. adviser Rupturita (Explosives factory) since 1917. Served as navigator and gunner on Brazilian ships, World War I; patrol duty Amazon River Fleet, 1914-15. Brazilian rep. Atomic Energy Commn. of U.N., 1946; vice pres. League of Nat. Defense. Recipient Victory medal, 2 World Wars, 2 sea rescue medals: Amazon River, 1914; Atlantic, 1916; Navy gold medal for 40 yrs. service; Einstein prize (gold medal) from Brazilian Acad. of Science, 1936; Commend Cross of Naval Merit (Brazilian); Revista Maritima prize (gold medal), 1943-46. Chairman Third South American Congress of Chemistry, Rio de Janeiro, 1937; hon. mem. Brazilian Hist. and Geog. Inst., 1942; mem. Brazilian Soc. Chemistry (past pres. 1926-28), Brazilian Acad. Science (past pres. 1935-37). Clubs: Rotary (pres. 1935-36), Navy, Engineers. Author of over 200 memoirs, some published in book form. Home: Rio de Janeiro, Brazil. †

ALBERTSON, JACK, actor; b. Malden, Mass.; s. Leo and Flora (Craft) A.; m. Wallace Thomson, Oct. 31, 1952; 1 dau., Maura Dhu. Ed. pub. schs. Engaged in theatrical work, 1930—, including vaudeville, burlesque, radio and theatre; theatre prodns. include Meet the People, 1940, Strip for Action, 1942, Allah Be Praised, 1944, The Lady Says Yes, 1945, The Red Mill, 1946, The Cradle Will Rock, 1947, Make Mine Manhattan, 1948, High Button Shoes, 1948, Tickets, Please!, 1950, Top Banana, 1951, The Subject Was Roses, 1964 (Tony award best supporting actor), The Sunshine Boys, 1973; others; also numerous films including The Subject Was Roses (Oscar award best supporting actor), Justine, Roustabout, How to Murder Your Wife; Engaged in: also numerous films including Willie Wonka and the Chocolate Factory, 1972, Rabbit Run, The Poseidon Adventure, 1972; star: TV series Chico and the Man, from 1974; TV film Valentine, 1979, Marriage is Alive and Well (Recipient Emmy award outstanding lead actor comedy series 1976). Mem. Screen Actors Guild, Actors Equity, A.F.T.R.A. Beverly Hills CA Died Nov. 25, 1981.*

ALBIG, REED HARRISON, banker; b. McKeesport, Pa., Jan. 19, 1906; s. John William and Lenora (Reed) A.; m. Helen Spaide, May 11, 1940. Student, Gettysburg Coll., 1923; A.B., Amherst Coll., 1926; grad. study, Harvard. With McKeesport Nat. Bank, from 1924, v.p., 1929-32, exec. v.p., 1932-37, pres., 1937-76, chmn., from 1976; dir. Spaide Shirt Co., Butler, Pa., 1940-47, v.p., 1941-45, pres., 1945-47; dir. G.C. Murphy Co.; Mem. adv. com. Office Comptroller Currency, 1962. First pres. Mon Yough Conf. on Community Devel.; Bd. dirs. various community orgns. Passavant Hosp., Pitts. Served with USNR, 1943-45. Mem. Independent Bankers Assn. (pres. 1961-62, chmn. various coms.). Home: Allison Park, PA.

ALBIN, HAROLD CORNELIUS, govt. official; b. Stamford, Conn., July 13, 1888; s. Eugene and Rena Samantha (Waterbury) A.; B.S., U. of Ill., 1915; student Pa. State U., 1913; m. Christine May Cameron, Nov. 30, 1918; children—Marjorie (Mrs. Markham Van Fossen Lewis), Cameron Waterbury, Eloise Ann, Frances May, Harold Cornelius. Began as clerk, Chemical Nat. Bank and Plaza Bank, New York City, 1904-10; field investigator, Bur. Chemistry, U.S. Dept. Agr., 1915-19; sec.-treas., Southern States Produce Distributors, Valdosta, Ga., 1919-23; sales mgr. Fed. Fruit and Vegetable Growers, 1923-24; sec.-treas. Edgerton & Beers, Washington, D.C., 1924-35; dir. of procurement, Fed. Surplus Commodities Corp., 1935-39; U.S. Dept. Agr., from 1939. Am. mem. Internat. Emergency Food Com., 1943-46. Mem. Am. Rose Soc., Harrisburg, Pa.; Alpha Zeta. Independent. Mem. Soc. of Friends. Club: Cosmopolitan (Champaign, Ill.). Home: Arlington, Va. Deceased.

ALBION, ROBERT GREENHALGH, educator, author; b. Malden, Mass., Aug. 15, 1896; s. James Francis and Alice Marion (Lamb) A.; A.B., Bowdoin Coll., 1918, Litt.D., 1948; A.M., Harvard, 1920, Ph.D., 1924; Litt. D., Southampton Coll., 1970; L.H.D., U. Maine, 1971; m. Jennie Barnes Pope, Aug. 16, 1923 (dec. Sept. 30, 1976). Teaching fellow, Harvard, 1920-22; instr. history Princeton, 1922-24, asst. prof., 1924-28, assoc. prof., 1928-39, prof. history, 1939-49, dir. summer session, 1929-42; asst. dean faculty, 1929-43; vis. lectr. in oceanic history and affairs Harvard U., 1948-49, Gardiner prof. oceanic history and affairs, 1949-63, prof. emeritus, 1963-83; vis. prof. U. Conn., 1964-65, Emory U., Carleton Coll., 1966, U. Maine, 1966-72, Bowdoin Coll., from 1971; cons. U.S. Naval War Coll., 1965, NRC, 1968; pres. Am. Mil. Inst., 1941-45; trustee Naval Hist. Found., 1946-50; cons. Maritime Adminstrn., 1952-53; coordinator Munson Inst. Maritime History, 1955-66, dir., 1966-75; with Harvard-Navy Polaris Program, 1964-72; lectr. U.S. Mil. Acad., Nat. War Coll., U.S. Naval Acad., U.S. Coast Guard Acad. Served as 2d lt. Inf., 1918. Historian of Naval Adminstrn., asst. dir. naval history, Office Sec. of Navy, 1943-50; expert cons. War Dept., 1943. Awarded Presdl. Certificate of Merit, 1948. Trustee Penobscot Marine Mus., from 1960; overseer Bath (Maine) Marine Mus., from 1973; adv. bd. South St. Marine Mus., from 1969. Mem. Maine Hist. Sites Com., 1960-71; mem. Archives Adv. Bd., 1965-73, vice chmn., 1968-73. Hon. life mem. Soc. Nautical Research (Eng.), N.J. Hist. Soc. Mem. Maine Hist. Soc. (exec. com. 1958-76, pres. 1963-70), Theta Delta Chi, Phi Beta Kappa. Republican. Clubs: Cumberland (Portland, Maine); Faculty (Cambridge, Mass.). Author: Forests and Sea Power: The Timber Problem of the Royal Navy, 1926; Introduction to Military History, 1929; History of England and the British Empire (with W. P. Hall and J. B. Pope), 1937; Square Riggers on Schedule, 1938; The Rise of New York Port, 1815-60, 1939; Sea Lanes in Wartime (with J. B. Pope), 1942; The Navy at Sea and Ashore (with S.H.P. Read), 1947; Seaports South of Sahara, 1959; Forrestal and the Navy (with R. H. Connery), 1961; New England and the Sea (with W.A. Baker, B.W. Labaree), 1972; Five Centuries of Famous Ships, 1978. Editor: Philip Vickers Fithian; Journ. 1775-1776 (with L. Dodson), 1934; Exploration and Discovery, 1965; American Maritime Reprints, 1970. Editorial bd. Jour. Econ. History Am. Neptune, Essex Inst. Hist. Coll. Publs., Business Historical Review; also Naval and Maritime History: an Annotated Bibliography, 4th edit., 1972. Pioneered TV course for acad. credit, Harvard, 1959-60. Home: Groton, Conn. Died Aug. 9, 1983.

ALBRAND, MARTHA (MRS. SYDNEY J. LAMON), author; b. Rostock, Germany, Sept. 8, 1914; came to U.S., 1937, naturalized, 1947; d. Paul and Paula Freybe; m. Joseph M. Loewengard, 1932; m. Sydney J. Lamon., 1932. Student, U. Zurich. Author: No Surrender, 1942, Without Orders, 1943, Endure No Longer, 1945, Remember Anger, 1946, None Shall Know, 1947, Whispering Hill, 1948, After Midnight, 1949, Wait For the Dawn, 1950, Desperate Moment, 1951, Challenge, 1952, The Mask of Alexander, 1955, The Linden Affair, 1956, The Obsession of Emmet Booth, 1957, A Day in Monte Carlo, 1959, Meet Me Tonight, 1960, A Call from Austria, 1963, A Door Fell Shut, 1966, Rhine Replica, 1969, Manhattan North, 1971, Zurich/AZ 900, 1974, A Taste of Terror, 1976, Final Encore, 1978; also short stories in Ladies Home Jour. Recipient Le Grand Prix de Literature Policiere France, 1950. Home: New York, N.Y. Died June 17, 1981.

ALBRECHT, WILLIAM A(LBERT), soil scientist; b. Flanagan, Ill., Sept. 12, 1888; s. John and Barbara (Nafziger) A.; A.B., U. of Ill., 1911, B.S., 1914, M.S., 1915, Ph.D., 1919; m. Gertrude Lehman, June 8, 1920; 1 dau., Barbara (Mrs. J. Cortland G. Perct). Instr. soils, U. of Mo., 1916-19, asst. prof., 1919-20, asso. prof., 1920-30, prof., from 1930, chairman department of soils, from 1938; instr. soils, Biarritz (Fr.) Am. Univ., 1945-46; cons. Phillips Chem. Co. Fellow Am., Geog. Soc., Am. Acad. Applied Nutrition, A.A.A.S., Am. Soc. Agronomy; mem. Soc. Am. Bacteriologists, Soil Science Soc. of Am., Internat. Soc. of Soil Science, Am. Naturalists, Sigma Xi, Phi Kappa Phi, Gamma Sigma Delta, Omicron Delta Kappa, Gamma Alpha. Presbyterian. Cons. editor: Soil Science, Scientific Monthly, Plant and Soil (Holland). †

ALBRIGHT, E(DWIN) ROY, business exec.; b. Lee County, Ala., Dec. 25, 1887; s. John Oswell and Jessie (Middleton) A.; grad. pharmacy, Ala. Pharm. Sch., Mobile, Ala., 1909; m. Eleanor Druhan, Jan. 15, 1913; children—James Roy, John Oswell. Formed partnership with I. V. Wood as Albright & Wood Drug Store, Mobile, Ala., Nov. 1911, firm owns and operates 16 drug stores in Mobile and 1 in Meridian, Miss.; pres. of firm from 1926; treas. Ala. Bridge Commn. from 1936; dir. Home Savings & Loan Assn., Mobile, Ala. Mem. Ala. Nat. Guard, 1907; called to active service as 1st lt., Mexican Border, June, 1916; served as capt., 123d U.S. Inf., 5 mos. overseas, 1917-19. Trustee Ernest F. Ladd Memorial Stadium. Chmn. Am. Red Cross War Fund, Mobile County, 1945 (bd. dirs.); chmn. Ala. Beverage Control Bd., 1937-43. Mem. Nat. Assn. Chain Drug Stores (vice pres.), Mobile Retail Druggists Council (pres.), Mobile County Welfare Bd. (chmn.), Ala. Pharm. Assn. (v.p.), Mobile Chamber of Commerce (pres. from 1946). Democrat. Methodist. Am. Legion (comdr. 1935). Club: Rotary. Home: Mobile, Ala. †

ALBRIGHT, IVAN, artist; b. North Harvey, Ill., Feb. 20, 1897; s. Adam Emory and Clara Amelia (Wilson) A.; m. Josephine Medill Patterson; children—Joseph Medill Patterson, Alice Patterson, Adam Medill, Blandina Van Etten. Student, Northwestern U., 1915-16, U. Ill., Chgo., 1916-17; art studies, Ecole Regionale Beaux-Arts, Nantes, 1919, Art Inst. Chgo., 1920-23, Pa. Acad. Fine Arts, Phila., 1923, N.A.D., N.Y.C., 1924; L.H.D., Mundelein Coll., 1969; Ph.D. in Fine Arts, Lake Forest (Ill.) Coll., 1972; Ph.D. in Arts, Columbia Coll., Chgo., 1974, Art Inst. Chgo., 1977, Dartmouth Coll., 1978, Norwich (Vt.) U., 1980. Represented in permanent collections, Uffizi Gallery, Florence, Italy, Tate Gallery, London, Pompidou Center, Paris, Nat. Gallery, Washington, Met. Mus. Art, Mus. Modern Art, N.Y.C., Middlebury Coll., Bklyn. Mus., Guggenheim Mus., N.Y.C., Whitney Mus. Am. Art, N.Y.C., Carnegie Inst., Pitts., Art Inst. Chgo., Phila.

Mus. Art., Library of Congress, Washington, Wadsworth Athenaeum, Hartford, Conn., Nat. Mus., Jerusalem, Israel, Detroit Inst. Arts, Phoenix Mus. Art, Finch Gallery Art, N.Y.C., Pushkin Mus., Moscow, Russia, Ark. Arts Center, Dallas Mus. Fine Arts, Tex., Hirshhorn Collection, Washington, also in pvt. collections.; Exhibited group shows, Internationals Carnegie Inst., Pitts., Pan-Am. Internat., Balt., Century of Progress, Chgo., Golden Gate Internat., San Francisco, N.Y. World's Fair, Brussels World's Fair, Half Century Am. Art, retrospective, Chgo. Art Inst., 1964, Twentieth Century Portraits, Mus. Modern Art, N.Y.C., 50 Prints of the Year, One Hundred Am. Prints, The Artist Looks at People, Art Inst. Chgo., Realists and Magic Realists, Mus. Modern Art, N.Y., Masterpiece of the Month, Chgo. Art Inst., Corcoran Gallery Art, Washington, N.A.D., N.Y.; shown internat. in, London, Paris, Stockholm, Oslo, Rome, Venice, Berlin, Dusseldorf, Constantinople, Zurich, Tel Aviv, Arras, Milan, Toronto, Sao Paolo. Recipient John C. Shaffer prize Art Inst. Chgo., 1928, Silver medal, 1930, Brower prize, 1941, Harris bronze medal and award, 1943, print prize, 1945, Watson F. Blair prize, 1949, Cahn prize, 1950; silver medal Chgo. Soc. Artists, 1930; gold medal, 1931; Phila. Water Color Club prize Pa. Acad. Fine Arts, 1940; Temple gold medal, 1942; Fellowship prize, 1942; J. Henry Schiedt Meml. prize, 1956; 1st medal for best painting Met. Mus. Victory for Artists Exhbn., N.Y.C., 1942; Met. Mus. prize, 1952; Benjamin Altman prize N.A.D., 1944, 61; 1st prize 3d Nat. Print Exhbn., 1946; silver medal and award Corcoran Gallery of Art, Washington, 1955; H.M. 24th Carnegie Internat. Exhbn., Pitts., 1950; Northwestern U. Centennial degree Northwestern Ty., 1951; 5000 prize Dunn Internat.; 5000 prize Lord Beaverbrook Gallery, Frederickton, N.B.; 5000 prize N.S. Tate Gallery, London, Eng., 1962; Laureate State Ill. Lincoln Acad., 1968; Vt. Gov.'s award, 1975; Illustrious Moderns award, 1978; recipient Keys to City Warrenville, Ill., 1978; hon. fellow Ont. Coll. of Art, Toronto, 1980. Mem. Nat. Inst. Arts and Letters, Nat. Acad. Arts and Scis., Am. Watercolor Soc., Pa. Acad. Fine Arts Fellowship, Am. Acad. Arts and Letters, Chgo. Soc. Artists (past pres.), Phila. Water Color Club. Clubs: Casino (Chgo.), Saddle and Cycle (Chgo.), Tavern (Chgo.), Arts (Chgo.), Wayfarers (Chgo.); Lotos (N.Y.C.), Century (N.Y.C.); Round Table (Woodstock, Vt.). Home: Woodstock, Vt. Died Nov. 18, 1983.*

ALBRIGHT, MALVIN MARR, painter, sculptor, painter, under nom de plume Zsissly; b. Chgo., Feb. 20, 1897; s. Adam Emory and Clara Amelia (Wilson) A.; m. Cornelia Warren Fairbanks, Dec. 18, 1954. Ed., Art Inst. Chgo., Pa. Acad. Fine Arts, Beaux Arts Inst. Design. Has exhibited paintings and sculpture, 1927-83, including, NAD, Whitney Mus., Mus. Modern Art, all N.Y.C., Carnegie Inst., Pitts., Pa. Acad. Fine Art, Phila., Mus. Art Phila., Corcoran Gallery Art, Washington, Art Inst. Chgo., also in many important U.S. cities, Internat. fairs, spl. exhbns.; represented in permanent collections, Corcoran Gallery, Pa. Acad. Fine Arts, Toledo Art Mus., San Diego Art Mus., Butler Art Mus., Youngstown, Ohio, Library of Congress, others. Recipient numerous awards and prizes, 1922—, including; NAD; Corcoran Gallery Art; Art Inst. Chgo.; Dana Water Color medal Pa. Acad. of Fine Arts, others. Fellow Royal Soc. Arts (London), Internat. Inst. Arts and Letters, Pa. Acad. Fine Arts, Phila. Water Color Club; mem. NAD (academician), Nat. Sculpture Soc. Clubs: Tavern, Art, Saddle and Cycle; Peale (Phila.). Home: Fort Lauderdale, Fla. Died Sept. 15, 1983.

ALBRIGHT, PENROSE STRONG, educator; b. Winfield, Kans., Dec. 14, 1896; s. P. H. and Emma (Strong) A.; m. Mary Lucas, Apr. 27, 1924; children—Penrose Lucas, James Curtice, John Grover. B.S., Rensselaer Poly. Inst., 1922; M.S., U. Wis., 1929, Ph.D., 1936. With Southwestern Coll., Winfield, 18 years; instr. to prof., chmn. div. natural sci. and coordinator of war tng. service, faculty rep. armed services; head physics dept. Wichita State U., 1943-61, prof. emeritus, 1961-82; v.p., dir. Kansas-Okla. Oil & Gas Co. Author sci. articles. Bd. dirs. Congregational Found. Theol. Studies, 1969-75; mem. sci. adv. council Southwestern Coll. Honoree Penrose Albright chair of physics Southwestern Coll. Mem. Am. Chem. Soc., Am. Phys. Soc., AAAS, Kans. Acad. Sci. (pres. 1949-50), Am. Inst. Chemists, Am. Assn. Physics Tchrs., Am. Soc. Engring. Edn., Am. Legion. Republican. Clubs: Rotary (Wichita), Farm and Ranch (Wichita) (pres. 1954). Home: Wichita, Kans. Died Jan. 11, 1982.

ALDEN, HAROLD L., astronomer; b. Chicago, Ill., Jan. 10, 1890; s. David Adonijah and Emily Elizabeth (Worcester) A.; A.B., Wheaton (Ill.) Coll., 1912; M.S., U. of Chicago, 1913; Ph.D., U. of Va., 1917; married to Mildred Viola Davidson, December 25, 1917; children—Mary Louise (Mrs. Louis DillFranzen), Ruth (Mrs. James H. Wilson, Jr.), Harold Lee. Asst., Yerkes Observatory, Williams Bay, Wis., 1912-14; asst. and astronomer, Leander McCormick Observatory, U. of Va., 1914-25; asst. and asso. prof. astronomy, U. of Va., 1917-25; asst. and asso. prof. astronomy, Yale, and astronomer in charge, Southern Station, Yale U. Observatory, Johannesburg, South Africa, 1925-45; prof. astronomy and dir. Leander McCormick Observatory, U. of Va., from 1945. Instr. and later dir., U.S. Shipping Bd. Sch. of Navigation, Jersey City, N.J., 1918-19. Fellow Royal Astron. Soc., A.A.A.S.; mem. Am. Astron. Soc., Am. Assn. Variable Star Observers, International Astron. Union, Société Astronomique de France, Astron. Soc. South Africa (pres. 1932), South African Assn. for Advancement of Science, Phi Beta Kappa, Sigma Xi, Raven (U. of Va.) Club: Colonnade University of Va. Contbr. articles professional jours. Address: Charlottesville, Va. †

ALDERMAN, WILLIAM ELIJAH, educator; b. Glouster, O., Oct. 13, 1888; s. Nelson Kemper and Sarah Elma (Peugh) A.; Ph.B., Ohio University, 1909, LL.D. (honorary), 1954; A.M., Hiram Coll., 1910; grad. study Harvard University, 1912-14; Ph.D., Univ. of Wis., 1920; LL.D., Beloit Coll., 1958, Miami U., 1959; m. Wilhelmina R. Boelzner, June 15, 1912; children—Barbara Christine, Jane Elizabeth, Eleanor Margaret, William Elijah. Instr. in English, U. of Wis., 1914-20; asso. prof. English, Beloit (Wis.) Coll., 1920-21, prof., 1921-35, dean of men, dean of Coll., 1925-35; dean arts and sciences, prof. English Miami U., Oxford, O., from 1935, chmn. dept. English, 1935-47. V.p. in letters Wis. Acad. of Sciences, Arts, and Letters, 1930-33; mem. exec. com. Nat. Assn. of Deans and Advisers of Men, 1933-35, pres., 1935-36. Pres. Assn. of Presidents and Deans Wis. Colls., 1933-34. Mem. Am. Conf. Acad. Deans (vice pres. 1953, pres. 1954), Modern Lang. Assn., Phi Eta Sigma, Phi Beta Kappa, Phi Kappa Tau, Phi Mu Alpha, Omicron Delta Kappa. Club: Kiwanis. Republican. Presbyn. Contbr. articles to lit. jours. Home: Oxford, Ohio†

ALDRICH, CLYDE FRANK, reins. co. exec.; b. Pulaski County, Ark., Aug. 28, 1925; s. Frank and Mary (Haynes) A.; m. Gloria Lee Notwell, Dec. 30, 1972; children—Christopher F., Stephen L., Gary L., Laurie A., Robin L., Barry L. J.D., St. Louis U., 1950. Bar: Mo. bar 1950. Pvt. practice, St. Louis, 1950-58, city atty., St. Ann, Mo., 1950-52; asst. gen. counsel Kemper Group, Long Grove, Ill., 1958-69; pres., chief exec. officer, dir. Kemper Reins. Co., Long Grove, 1969-82; chmn. bd., chief exec. officer, dir. Kemper Reins. (Bermuda) Ltd., Kemper Europe Reassurances, S.A., Belgium; dir. Kemper Internat. Co., also subs. Served with AUS, 1943-46. Mem. Nat. Assn. Ins. Commrs. (reins. adv. com. chmn. 1976-82), Internat. C. of C. (trustee U.S. council 1975-82, vice chmn, reins. ins. com. 1979-82). Home: Barrington, Ill. Died 1982.

ALDRICH, JAMES THOMAS, physician; b. Dudley, N.C., May 14, 1890; s. John W. and Vicy (Artis) A.; B.S., Shaw U., Raleigh, N.C., 1916; M.D., Maharry Med. Coll., 1920; m. Athalia Freeman, Oct. 8, 1918. Gen. practice medicine, St. Louis, from 1924; mem. staffs Homer Phillips, Peoples, St. Mary's Infirmary hosps. Mem. A.M.AM., St. Louis Med. Soc., Nat. (pres. 1960-61), Mo. med. assns., Chi Delta Mu, Phi Beta Sigma. Republican. Baptist. Home: St. Louis, Mo. †

ALDRICH, ROBERT, motion picture dir., producer; b. Cranston, R.I., 1918; (m); children—Adell Aldrich, William, Alida Aldrich Shaffer, Kelly. Ed., U. Va. Pres. Assos. & Aldrich Co. Inc., Aldrich Studios. TV shows include China Smith, The Doctor; dir.: films Big Leaguer, Apache, Vera Cruz, Autumn Leaves, Ten Seconds to Hell, Angry Hills, No-Knife, Last Sunset, What Ever Happened to Baby Jane? , 4 for Texas, Hush, Hush Sweet Charlotte, Flight of the Phoenix, Dirty Dozen, Hustle, Emperor of the North, The Longest Yard, Twilight's Last Gleaming, Choirboys; producer, dir.: films World for Ransom, Kiss Me Deadly, The Big Knife, Attack!,, The Legend of Lylah Clare, The Killing of Sister George, Too Late the Hero, The Grissom Gang, The Frisco Kid, 1979. Mem. Dirs. Guild Am. (pres.). Home: Los Angeles, Calif. Died Dec. 5 1983.*

ALESSANDRONI, EUGENE VICTOR, jurist, civic leader; b. Capestrano, Italy, Jan. 24, 1887; s. Pierluigi and Carmela (Jafolla) A.; brought to U.S., 1891, naturalized, 1896; A.B., Central High Sch., Phila., 1903; LL.B., University of Pennsylvania, 1906; m. Ethel Hope Tumbelston, Jan. 6, 1909; 1 daughter, Hope. Admitted to the Pennsylvania bar, 1907, and began practice in Phila.; asst. dist. atty., 1919-27; elected judge Court of Common Pleas, 1st Dist. of Pa., for term, 1928-38, re-elected for terms, 1938-58. Dir. Phila. Symphony Orchestra Assn.; dir. Internat. Inst.; mem. bd. mgrs. U. of Pa.; pres. bd. Union Home; dir. Eagleville Sanatorium. Presidential elector, 1932. Mem. Law Acad. Phila. (vice-provost), Phila., Pa. and Am. bar assns., Am. Judicature Soc., Phila. U.N. Council, Foreign Policy Association, American Academy of Political and Social Sciences, Alpha Phi Delta; hon. mem. 1st Div. A.E.F. Mem. Order Sons of Italy (grand venerable, Dept. of Pa.). Clubs: Contemporary, Locust, Penn. Athletic, Lawyers, Socialegal. Awarded D.S.M. by U.S. Regular Vets Assn.; Humanitarian award by Order of B'nai B'rith. Home: Philadelpha, Pa. †

ALEXANDER, ARVIN J., lawyer; b. Lethbridge, Alta., Can., May 10, 1909; s. John M. and Lona (Ledford) A.; m. Anne Lawrie Valentine, Aug. 4, 1934; 1 son, Donald V. LL.B., Ohio State U., 1936, J.D., 1970. Bar: Ohio bar 1966. Partner firm Alexander, Ebinger, Fisher, McAlister & Lawrence, Columbus, 1946-84. Mem. Columbus City Council, 1939-43, pres., 1943; mem. Met. Airport Com., 1956-63; chmn. bd. trustees Columbus Better Bus. Bur. Central Ohio, 1958-61; pres. Citizens Research, Inc., 1962-64, chmn. bd., 1964-66; mem. Downtown Area Commn. Bd., 1965-75, life trustee, 1976-84; trustee, vice chmn. bd. trustees, chmn. exec. com. Mut. Investing Found., Columbus; trustee Columbus Sinking Fund, 1953-64, pres., 1957-58. Mem. Am., Ohio State, Columbus bar assns., Navy League (judge advocate 1963). Home: Columbus, Ohio. Died July 27, 1984.

ALEXANDER, GEORGE MILTON, pub. utility executive; b. near Morgantown, W. Va., November 10, 1867; s. John and Caroline (Conn) A.; LL.B. and B.S., W.Va. U., 1892; m. Gertrude Jamison, of Monongalia Co., W.Va., June 22, 1892; children—Virginia (Mrs. Robert E. Barnes), Edward Eugene. Admitted to W.Va. bar and began practice at Fairmont; prosecuting atty. Marion Co., W.Va., 1895-1900; pres. Bd. of Edn., Fairmont Independent Sch. Dist., 1911-1919. Served as capt., Ordinance Dept., U.S.A., World War. Mem. W.Va. State Bar Assn., U.S. Chamber Commerce, Phi Beta Kappa, Phi Sigma Kappa. Christian Scientist. Mason. Odd Fellow, Elk. Clubs: Maryland (Baltimore); Pittsburgh Athletic. Home: Fairmont, W.Va. †

ALEXANDER, GEORGE MURRELL, army officer; b. Va., Aug. 1, 1889; grad. Va. Mil. Inst., 1909; commd. capt. Inf., Va. Nat. Guard, July 1909; capt. Inf., Fed. Service, July 1917, advanced to maj., Sept. 1918; maj. Inf., Va. Nat. Guard, Nov. 1920, advanced to brig. gen., Oct. 1940; became comdg. officer Fed. Service, 91st Inf. Brigade, 29th Div., Ft. George G. Meade, Md.; overseas assignment, Sept. 1942.†

ALEXANDER, JAMES WENDELL, mathematics educator; b. Sea Bright, N.J., Sept. 19, 1888, s. John White and Elizabeth A.; B.S., Princeton, 1910, M.A., 1911, Ph.D., 1915; studied univs. of Paris and Bologna; m. Natalia Levitzkaja, Jan. 15, 1917; children—Irina, John. Began as instr. math. Princeton, 1911, asst. prof., 1920-25, assoc. prof., 1926-28, prof., 1928-33, prof. Inst. for Advanced Study, from 1933. Served as capt. tech. staff, Ordnance Dept., U.S. Army, 1917-18. Mem. Nat. Acad. Sciences, Am. Philos. Soc., Am. Math. Soc., Math. Assn. America, A.A.A.S., Phi Beta Kappa. Awarded Bôcher prize, Am. Math. Soc., 1929. Clubs: Am. Alpine, Quadrangle, Nassau. Contbr. to math. publs. Home: Princeton, N.J. †

ALEXANDER, LYLE THOMAS, soil scientist; b. Athens, Tex., Dec. 3, 1903; s. James C. and Maude (Dalton) A.; B.S. U. Ark., 1928. LL.D., 1958; Ph.D., U. Md., 1935; m. Helen Goodwin, June 7, 1927; children—Thomas Goodwin, Jennie Lyle (Mrs. Joseph F. Hodgson), Alice Maude (Mrs. John w. Huffman), Martha Sue (Mrs. David H. Bowman). Soil scientist Dept. Agr., 1928-83; chief soil survey labs., Soil Conservation Service, 1954-83; lectr. tropical soils Cornell U. 1957. Recipient Distinguished Service award Dept. Agr., 1956; Career Service award Nat. Civil Service League, 1959. Fellow A.A.A.S., Am. Soc. Agronomy; mem. Am. Chem. Soc., Soil Sci. Soc. Am., Sigma Xi. Presbyn. Home: Hyattsville, Md. Died Jan. 17, 1983.

ALEXANDER, SUMMERFIELD S., lawyer; b. Maryville, Mo., Aug. 15, 1887; s. Henry C. and Mary Elizabeth (Ammons) A.; LL.B., U. of Kan.; m. Anna Belle Horner, Sept. 1, 1910. Admitted to Kans. bar, 1907; co. atty. Kingman Co., Kans., 1910-12; U.S. atty. Dist. of Kans. from May 4, 1934. Mem. Phi Delta Phi. Democrat. Mason. Home: Kingman, Kan. †

ALFOLDI, ANDREW, educator, historian; b. Pomáz, Hungary, Aug. 27, 1895; came to U.S., 1955, naturalized, 1963; s. Antal and Charlotte (Klein) A.; m. Emma Seidl, Aug. 28, 1917; children—Emma, Andrew; m. Elisabeth Rosenbaum, Mar. 17, 1967. D.Phil., U. Budapest, 1919; D.Phil. (hon.), U. Utrecht, 1936, U. Ghent, 1949, U. Bonn, 1967, U. Paris, 1967. Mem. staff Hungarian Nat. Museum, 1919-23; prof. U. Debreczen, Hungary, 1923-29, Budapest, 1930-47, U. Berne, Switzerland, 1948-52, Basle, 1952-56, Inst. for Advanced Study, Princeton, N.J., 1955-81. Author numerous papers and books on Roman history. Recipient Gold Medal of the City of Rome, 1960; decorated Order Pour le mérite Fed. Republic of Germany; Order of Merit for Scis. and Arts Austria; Les Palmes Academiques France; Golden Cross of King George II Greece). Mem. Inst. of France, Royal Swedish Acad., Acad. Lincei Rome, Hungarian Acad.; corr. mem. British, Danish, Bavarian, Austrian, Bulgarian acads., Acad. Göttingen, Mainz, Lund; hon. mem. Pontificia Accdiarch Rome, Archaeol. Inst. Am., Soc. Antiquaries (London), Soc. for Promotion Roman Studies (London), Soc. Antiquaries of Scotland, German Archaeol. Inst., Finnish, Spanish archaeol. socs., Royal Numis. Soc. (London), Turkish Hist. Soc., others. Home: Princeton, N.J. Died 1981.

ALFREY, TURNER, JR., chemist; b. Siloam Springs, Ark., May 7, 1918; s. Turner and Cleo Ellen (Hogan) A.; B.S.Ch.E., Washington U., St. Louis, 1938, M.S. in Chemistry, 1940; Ph.D., Poly. Inst. Bklyn., 1943; m. Nancy Jeannette Farrington, Dec. 30, 1941; children—Robert Joseph, Nancy. Chemist, Monsanto Co., 1943-45; asso. prof. chemistry Poly. Inst. Bklyn., 1945-50; research scientist Dow Chem. Co., Midland, Mich., from 1950; vis. prof. M.I.T., 1974; Battelle vis. prof. Ohio State U., 1969. Recipient Bingham medal Soc. Rheology, 1960. Mem. Am. Chem. Soc. (Witco award 1973), Soc. Plastics Engrs. (Internat. award 1965), Am. Phys. Soc., Nat. Acad. Engring., Am. Acad. Mechanics, N.Y. Acad. Scis. Author: Mechanical Behavior of High Polymers, 1948; Copolymerization, 1952; Organic Polymers, 1967. Home: Midland, Mich. Died Aug. 10, 1981.

ALI, ASAF, governor Orissa, India; b. Delhi, India, May 1888; ed. St. Stephens Coll., Delhi, India; m. Aruna

Gangula, 1928. Called to bar, Lincoln Inn., London, Eng., 1912. Active in Indian public life from 1917; mem. Delhi Municipality (representing exclusively Muslim electorate), 23 yrs.; mem. Central Legislature (representing joint Hindu-Muslim-Sikh-Christian electorate), 1934-36; gen. sec. and dep. leader of Congress Party in Central Legislature when Pandit Jawaharlal Nehru assumed office; held portfolio of transport in Nehru cabinet in Interim Govt.; became first ambassador from India to United States America, 1946; gov. of Orissa, India since 1948. As lawyer has organized and conducted defence in celebrated trials, recent ones including that of officers of Indian Nat. Army, and that of leader of revolt in Kashmir. Author of numerous political and literary books in Urdu. Contbr. in Urdu and English to newspapers and literary magazines. Address: Cuttack, Orissa, India. †

ALIG, CORNELIUS O., JR., banker; b. Indpls., May 24, 1921; s. Cornelius O. and Cecilia (Wulsin) A.; m. Emily Norris, July 22, 1954; children—Cornelius, Marion, Frances, Alfred. A.B., Princeton, 1943. With Ind. Nat. Bank, Indpls., 1946-76, vice chmn., 1971-76; also dir.; v.p., dir. Ind. Nat. Corp., 1971-76; chmn. bd. First Nat. Bank & Trust Co., Plainfield, Ind., from 1965, Guarantee Auto Stores, Inc., Indpls. Water Co., Kalvar Corp.; trustee Century Realty Trust. Bd. dirs., treas. Park-Tudor Found.; clk.-treas. Town of Crows Nest; bd. dirs. Hundred Club, Ind. Dist. Export Council, Indpls Zool. Soc., Crown Hill Cemetery, Near North Devel., Ind. Central Univ. Found.; trustee Community Hosp. Found.; pres. Flanner House. Served with AUS, World War II. Decorated Bronze Star medal. Episcopalian. Clubs: Columbia (Indpls.), Woodstock (Indpls.), U.S. Auto (Indpls.) (treas.). Home: Indianapolis, Ind. Died July 26, 1981.

ALKEN, GEORGE DAVID, U.S. senator; b. Dummerston, Vt., Aug. 20, 1892; s. Edward W. and Myra A. (Cook) A.; grad. Brattleboro (Vt.) High School, 1909; m. Beatrice M. Howard, 1914; children—Dorothy Howard (Mrs. Harry Morse), Marjorie Evelyn (Mrs. Harry Leighton Cleverly), Howard, George, Barbara Marion (Mrs. Malcolm Jones). Began with small fruit farm, 1912; started comml. cultivation of wildflowers, 1926. School dir., Town of Putney, Vt., 1920-37; mem. State Ho. of Reps., 1930-33, speaker of the House, 1933-34; lt. gov., Vt., 1935-37, elected gov., 1937-41; elected to U.S. Senate, 1940, to fill vacancy for term ending Jan. 3, 1945; re-elected, 1944-50, 56-75. Mem. Windham Co. Farm Bur., Vt. Hort. Sec. (pres. 1917-18), Putney Grange. Republican. Odd Fellow. Author: Pioneering with Wildflowers, 1933; Pioneering with Fruits and Berries, 1936; Speaking From Vermont, 1938. Home: Putney, Vt. Died Nov. 19, 1984.

ALLABEN, FRED ROLAND, lawyer; b. Rockford, Ill., Sept. 19, 1901; s. John Elmer and Harriet (Strickland) A.; A.B., U. Mich., 1923, J.D., 1925; m. Apr. 17, 1925 (div.); children—Robert, Dorothy (Mrs. Dale L. Talbert), Lawrence; m. 2d, Leona M. Heise, Oct. 15, 1954; 1 son, John Randolph. Admitted to Mich. bar, 1925, U.S. Supreme Ct. bar, 1945, other fed. cts.; of counsel firm Allaben, Massie, Vander Weyden & Timmer, Grand Rapids, Mich., now ret.; city atty., Grand Rapids, 1946-48. Chmn. Kent County A.R.C., 1946-47, now hon. life mem. bd. dir. Recipient Distinguished Alumni Service award U. Mich. Alumni Assn., 1953, U. Mich. Alumni accolade, 1954. Fellow Am. Coll. Probate Counsel (past mem. bd regents, treas. 1965-66), Am. Bar Found. (life), Am. Coll. Trial Lawyers; mem. Grand Rapids (pres. 1952-53), Mich. (commr. 1947-50), Am. (ho. of dels. 1950-58; Mich. chmn. Am. Bar Center Project, 1953-54; ins. sect. council, 1949-54) bar assns., Internat. Assn. Ins. Counsel, Assn. Ins. Attys. (gov. 1950-58), Fedn. Ins. Counsel, Judicial Conf. Mich. (dir. 1955-68), Mich. Bar Found. (pres. 1954-68, life mem.), C. of C. (past chmn. better bus. bur. and state affairs com.), U. Mich Alumni Assn. (mem. exec. com., nat. dir. 1940-43, nat. com. law sch. fund), Phi Alpha Delta. Republican. Unitarian. Mason (32 deg., Shriner). Clubs: Barristers, Lawyers (U. Mich.); Mich. Union (life; U. Mich.); University (Ann Arbor). Author articles in legal and med. jours. Lectr. law insts. Home: Grand Rapids, Mich. Died June 16, 1985.

ALLCUT, EDGAR ALFRED, educator, mech. engr.; b. Birmingham, Eng., June 30, 1888; s. Thomas and Mary Jane (Jones) A.; B.Sc. with honors (Bowen research scholar), U.Birmingham, 1908, M.Sc., 1909; M.E., U. Toronto, 1931; m. Annie Josephine Walker, June 7, 1919; children—Monica Mary (Mrs. Philip Fitz-James), Stella Margaret (Mrs. Robert Muir). Asst. engr. Humphrey Pump Co., London, Eng., 1910-13; mgr. engring. and testing machine depts. W. & T. Avery, Ltd., 1913-17; chief insp. materials Austin Motor Co., 1917-20; asso. prof., later prof. and head dept. mech. engring. U. Toronto, 1921-56. Chmn. air pollution bd. City of Toronto, 1949-55; commissioner Ont. Energy Board, 1960; mem. Province of Ont. Labour Safety Council, from 1962; mem. com. substitute fuels NRC. Recipient Heslop gold medal, 1909; Herbert Akroyd Stuart prize Inst. Mech. Engrs., 1930; Plummer medal Engring. Inst. Can., 1943, Gzowski medal, 1947, Duggan medal, 1953. Fellow Am. Soc. M.E., Royal Aero. Soc.; mem. Nat. Indsl. Design Council Can., Engring. Inst. Can., Instn. Mech. Engrs. Assn. Profl. Engrs. Ont. Author: Materials and their Application to Engineering Design, 1922; An Introduction to Heat Engines, rev. edit. 1943; Principles of Industrial Management, rev. edit. 1950. Author tech. articles and papers. Home: Toronto, Can. †

ALLEBAUGH, FRANK IRVING, advt. and public relations consultant; b. Denver, Jan. 17, 1915; s. Charles Arthur and Margaret (Diegel) A.; student Denver U., 1934, Alexander Hamilton Inst., 1935, Colo. U. Extension, 1944; m. Pearl Elizabeth Murray, June 6, 1936; children—Judith Marie (Mrs. E.C. Viner, III), Kathleen D. (Mrs. Jack A. McCulley). Pub. relations U.S. Govt., Denver, 1935-43; engring. writer E.I. DuPont, 1943-44; indsl. advt. mgr. Gates Rubber Co., Denver, 1944-54; became account exec. Galen E. Broyles Co., Denver, 1954, v.p. Galen E. Broyles Co., Inc., 1957-60, exec. v.p., 1960-61; pres. Broyles, Allebaugh & Davis, Inc. 1961-69, chmn. bd., 1969-77; advt. and pub. relations cons., from 1977. Past chmn. Rocky Mountain council Am. Assn. Advt. Agys.; lectr. advt. U. Denver, Dever Pub. Schs. nat. convs. Past trustee Mktg. Communications Center, Princeton, N.J.; bd. dirs. Rocky Mountain Hosp., Denver. Recipient Silver medal award Am. Fedn. Advt., 1977. Mem. Bus. and Profl. Advt. Assn. (past nat. v.p., past Colo. pres.), Internat. Platform Assn. Club: Denver Press. Home: Denver, Colo.

ALLEMAN, G(ELLERT) S(PENCER), educator; b. Swarthmore, Pa., June 24, 1913; s. Gellert and Katharine Constable (Spencer) A.; m. Anita Lucille Lange, Dec. 19, 1953; 1 dau., Anne Katharine. B.A., Lehigh U., 1934; M.A., U. Pa., 1937, Ph.D., 1942. Instr. English Lehigh U., 1938-40, 42-47; asst. prof. English Newark Coll. Arts and Scis., Rutgers U., 1947-56, asso. prof. English, 1956-61, prof., from 1961, chmn. dept., 1962-66. Matrimonial Law and the Materials of Restoration Comedy, 1942; Co-editor: English Literature, 1660-1800: A Current Bibliography, 1954-64, also articles. Served with AUS, USAAF, 1942-46. Mem. Bibliog. Soc. U. Va., MLA, Modern Humanities Research Assn., Nat. Council Tchrs. English, Coll. English Assn., Nat. Rifle Assn., Phi Beta Kappa, Phi Eta Sigma. Home: Nutley, N.J.

ALLEN, ARTHUR EDGAR, osteopathic physician; b. Minneapolis, Minn., Dec. 13, 1888; s. Arthur Edgar and Agnes Amelia (Campbell) A.; student U. of Minn., 1907-10; D.O., Kirksville Coll. of Osteopathy, 1913; D.Sc., Kansas City Coll. of Osteopathy and Surgery; m. Edith McLaurin Mayers, Apr. 25, 1914; children—Arthur Edgar, Henry McLaurin. Practice of osteopathy since Aug. 1913. Sec. Minn. State Bd. Osteopathic Examiners and Registration, 1924-27; osteopathic mem. Minn. State Bd. Examiners Basic Scis., 1927-35. Mem. Am. Osteopathic Assn. (trustee 1928-38; pres. 1938-39; dir. research 1940-43), Minn. State Osteopathic Assn. (bd. of trustees; pres. 1923-24), Academy Applied Osteopathy (former trustee), Minneapolis Osteopathic Clinic, Zeta Psi, Mu Phi Delta, Iota Tau Sigma, Sigma Sigma Phi (hon.). Mason. Rotarian. Served as 1st lt., later capt., 4th Minn. Inf., 1917-19. Author, lecturer. Home: Wayzata, Minn. †

ALLEN, EDWARD SWITZER, educator; b. Kansas City, Mo., Dec. 12, 1887; s. Kenneth and Rose (Switzer) A.; A.B., Harvard, 1909, A.M., 1910, Ph.D., 1914; postgrad. U. Rome, 1911-13; m. Minne Elisabeth Muller-Liebenwalde, Aug. 9, 1915; children—Julius W., Rosemarie C. (Mrs. Hans Lechner), Hermann A. Master math. and physics Berkshire Sch., 1909-10; instr. math. Dartmouth, 1913-14, Brown U., 1914-15, U. Mich., 1915-19; asst. prof. W.Va. U., 1919-21; asso. prof. math. Ia. State U., 1921-43, prof., 1943-85; vis. prof. Grinnell Coll., 1960-62, Cottey Coll., 1964-65, Wartburg Coll., 1967-69. Charter chmn. Ia. Civil Liberties Union, 1935, also dir. Recipient annual award, Ia. Civil Liberties Union, 1961, Founder's award, 1973. Mem. Am. Assn. U. Profs. (chpt. pres.), Am. Math. Soc., Math. Assn. Am., Deutsche Mathematiker-Vereinigung, Circolo Matematico di Palermo, Fellowship of Reconciliation, Phi Beta Kappa, Sigma Xi. Socialist. Mem. Soc. of Friends. Author: Plane Trigonometry, 1936. Editor: McGraw-Hill Six-Place Tables, 6 edits., 1925-47. Translator: (with Mrs. Allen) Atom and Cosmos (Reichenbach), 1932; Lectures on Modern Geometry (Segre), 1961. Home: Ames, Iowa. Died May 8, 1985.

ALLEN, FREDERICK H., psychiatrist; b. San Jose, Cal., Dec. 6, 1890; s. James Monroe and Emma Sarah (Gage) A.; A.B., U. Cal., 1913, M.A., 1916, LL.D., 1953; M.D., Johns Hopkins, 1921; m. Nadell Gille, July 27, 1922. Resident psychiatrist Johns Hopkins Hosp., Balt. 1921-25; dir. Phila. Child Guidance Clinic, from 1925; clin. prof. psychiatry U. Pa. Med. Sch. and Grad. Sch. Recipient Phila. (Bok) award, 1950. Mem. Am. Psychiat. Assn., Am. Orthopsychiat. Assn. (pres. 1934-35), Internat. Assn. Child Psychiatry (pres. 1948-54), N.Y. Psychiat. Soc., Acad. Pediatrics, Am. Assn. Psychiat. Clinics for Chidren (pres. 1942-44), Acad. Child Psychiatrists (pres. 1955). Author: Psychotherapy with Children, 1941. Home: Phila., Pa. †

ALLEN, HARLAND HILL, economist; b. Loyalton, S.D., Dec. 9, 1887; s. Albert Barnes and Harriet Mabel (Hill) A.; m. Florence Brooks, May 28, 1927 (dec. Dec. 1964); children—Franklin (dec.), Rolaine Kay Allen Groves; m. Alma Louise Petersen, Aug. 8, 1965. Student, Dakota Wesleyan U.; LL.D. (hon.), Dakota Wesleyan U., 1958; A.B., Colo. Tchrs. Coll., 1916, A.M., 1917; postgrad., U. Chgo., 1920-21, Columbia U., 1924, univs. Paris, London, Berlin, Leipzig, summers 1926, 29. Editor, pub. Roscoe (S.D.) Reveille, 1911-12; supt. pub. schs., Kersey, Colo., 1915-16; prof. econs. North Tex. State Tchrs. Coll., Denton, 1917-19; fellow, teaching asst. U. Chgo., 1919-21; instr. econs. U. Ill., 1921-22; prof. econs., dean Sch. Commerce, Okla. Agrl. and Mech Coll., 1923-24; economist Halsey, Stuart & Co., Chgo., 1927-29, Foreman State Nat. Bank, 1929-31; pres. Growth Research, Inc. (successors to Harland Allen Assos., investment mgrs.), 1931-61, chmn. bd., 1961-68; founder, chief exec. Growth Industry Shares, Inc., 1946-64; dean Roosevelt Coll. Sch. Commerce, Chgo., 1947-49, exec. com., chmn. bd., 1959-63; charter mem. bd. La Salle Fund, Chgo.; fin. and indsl. research, S.Am., 1972; vis. lectr. Dakota Wesleyan U., 1973. Lectr., writer.; Author: Whither Interest Rates, 1939, The Businessman's Stake in American-Soviet Friendship, 1943, Investing for Growth-Why and How, 1957, How the Science Revolution is Changing the Social Order, 1964; series World Economic Perspectives for the 1970's, 1970-71, Portentous Credit Inflation, 1979; syndicated newspaper column Your Money Problems, 1924-29, Harland Allen Economic Letter, 1932-44; contbr.: articles to Business and Society; others. Bd. dirs. Dakota Wesleyan U., Mitchell, S.D., Edward A. Filene Good Will Fund; chmn. Chgo. chpt. Com. to Defend Am., 1941. Recipient Man of Year citation Dakota Weslyan U., 1961. Mem. Am. Econs. Assn., Am. Statis. Assn. (past pres. Chgo.). Unitarian. Clubs: City (dir.), Mid-Am, Investment Analysts (pres. 1932-33). Home: Tucson, Ariz. Died June 15, 1985.

ALLEN, HENRY ELLSHA, educator; b. Orange, N.J., June 13, 1902; s. E. Hubert and Jane Elizabeth (Durand) A.; A.B., Yale, 1924; A.M., Ph.D., U. Chgo., 1930; m. Helen Elizabeth Davis, June 18, 1927; children—Lenore Elizabeth (Mrs. Richard A. Robertson), Carolyn Ruth (Mrs. Craig M. Wiester). Tchr., Hill Sch., Pottstown, Pa., 1924-26; mem. faculty dept. religion, dir. Christian assn. Lafayette Coll., Easton, Pa., 1930-41; exchange prof. Occidental Coll., Los Angeles, 1939-40; pres. Keuka Coll., Keuka Park, N.Y., 1941-46; asso. dir. program Planned Parenthood Fedn. Am., 1946-47; coordinator students' religious activities U. Minn., 1947-70, prof., 1951-70; lectr. Haskell Inst., U. Chgo., 1933. Fellow Soc. Religion in Higher Edn., Harris Inst. Round Table, summer 1942; mem. Assn. for Coordination Univ. Religious Affairs, from 1960, v.p., 1960-61, pres. 1962. Chmn. intergroup relations com. Greater Mpls. Council of Chs., 1951-53; mem. Gov. Adv. Council on Children and Youth (chmn. com. on religious values 1953-61), Mpls. Round Table Nat. Conf. Christians and Jews (dir. from 1948); mem. Gov. Minn. Human Rights Com., 1950-67, vice chmn., 1956-61; chmn. com. religious observance Minn. Statehood Centennial Commn., 1958; del. White House Conf. Children and Youth, 1960; mem. Mpls. Mayor's Commn. on Human Relations, 1960-64; mem. nat. adv. com. Indian affairs Am. Civil Liberties Union, 1959-62, from 1973, chmn. internat. affairs com. Minn. Council Chs., from 1971. Bd. dirs. Minn. Fgn. Policy Assn., 1959-68, Internat. Center Students and Visitors, 1962-65, from 1970, Civic Orch. Mpls., 1959-62, from 1971, Community Services for Internat. Visitors, from 1971, Minn. br. Am. Civil Liberties Union, 1952-76, Greater Mpls. Council of Chs., 1948-53, from 1973. Recipient Order North Star, 1958; WTCN citation for Outstanding Community Service, 1962. Mem. Minn. Soc. Mayflower Descs., (jr. dep. gov. 1960-61), Religious Pub. Relations Council (life), Psi Upsilon. Conglist. Clubs: Skull and Bones, Professional Men's, Elizabethan (Yale); Campus (U. Minn.). Editor: Religion in the State University, 1950; Minnesota's Indian Citizens, 1965. Author: The Turkish Transformation, 1935. Home: Minneapolis, Minn. Died June 27, 1985.†

ALLEN, IRVING ROSS, advt. and sales counsel; born Chicago, Mar. 14, 1887; s. Marshall and Anna (Ross) A.; student pub. schs., Chicago; m. Olive Frederick, Dec. 22, 1918 (died 1938). Various sales and advertising activities including operation of own business, Chicago, 1908-19; v.p. and gen. mgr. H.W. Kastor & Sons Advt. Co., 1919-28; v.p. Critchfield Corp., 1928-37, and 1943-49; research and editorial dir. La Salle Sales Training Program, 1949; advt. and sales counsel with Brown Advt. Co., 1937-43; dir. Zenith Radio Corp. Served with U.S. Navy during World War I; lt. comdr., U.S.N.R., until 1938. Civilian aide to secretary of war for State of Ill. V.P. and trustee Henrotin Hosp., Chicago. Nat. sec. Mil. Training Camps Assn.; Civilian Army Council Fifth Army. Mem. board directors La Salle Extension U. Awarded certificate of appreciation War Department Distinguished Service Citation, 6th Service Command. Mem. S.A.R. Republican. Methodist. Clubs: Racquet, Augusta National Golf; Chicago, Chicago Athletic; Chicago Golf (Wheaton, Ill.). Author: The Ten Laws, 1916; The Money Maker,1919; You,1924.Home: Wheaton, Ill. †

ALLEN, JAMES SIRCOM, physicist, ret. educator; b. Halifax, N.S., Can., Aug. 11, 1911; came to U.S., 1911, naturalized, 1965; s. Samuel James M. and Eva (Sircom) A.; m. Mary E. Griswold, Nov. 28, 1936; 1 son, Richard C. B.A., U. Cin., 1933; Ph.D., U. Chgo., 1937. Asso. prof. Kan. State U., 1937-42; physicist Radiation Lab., Mass.

Inst. Tech., 1942-43; physicist Los Alamos Sci. Lab., 1943-46, cons., 1948-68; asst. prof. U. Chgo., 1946-48; prof. U. Ill., Urbana, 1948-73, ret., 1973. Author: The Neutrino, 1958. Fellow Am. Phys. Soc. Episcopalian. Club: Rotarian. Home: Taos, N.Mex. Died Sept. 15, 1983.

ALLEN, JOHN STUART, ret. ednl. adminstr.; b. Pendleton, Ind., May 13, 1907; s. Elwood D. and Stella (Anderson) A.; student George Sch., Newtown, Pa., 1921-24; A.B., Earlham Coll., 1928, LL.D., 1958; M.A., U. Minn., 1929; student Columbia, summer 1931; Ph.D., N.Y. U., 1936; Sc.D. (hon.), U. Tampa, 1958; L.H.D., U. South Fla., 1970; LL.D., U. West Fla., 1973; m. Grace H. Carlton, Aug. 23, 1933. Asst. in astronomy U. Minn., 1928-29; instr. Colgate U., 1930-36; asst. prof. astronomy, 1936-42, chmn. comprehensive phys. sci. course, 1931-42, dean of freshman, 1942; dir. div. higher edn. N.Y. State Edn. Dept., 1942-48; v.p. U. Fla., 1948-53, acting pres., 1953-55, exec. v.p., 1955-57; founding pres. U. South Fla., Tampa, 1957-70, pres. emeritus, 1970-82; spl. adviser to U. North Fla., from 1970; cons curricular, adminstrv. reorgn. U. Costa Rica, 1955. Dir. Univ. State Bank, Tampa. Bd. dirs. Tampa; exec. com. So. Regional Edn. Bd., 1960-64; bd. dirs. Princeton Ednl. Testing Service, 1961-65; mem. Nat. Commn. on Coop. Edn., 1968-71; exec. com. Nat. Commn. on Accreditation, 1968; mem. edn. com. on new instns. Am. Council Edn., 1968. Mem. Franklin Inst. Solar Eclipse Expdn., 1932; guest lectr. Hayden Planetarium, 1935; sci. cons., faculty workshop Assn. of Colls. and Univs. of N.Y. State, June 1941; trustee Dudley Obs., 1944-48; chmn. Com. on Approved Schs. for Vets. for N.Y. State, 1945-48; mem. N.Y. State Com. on Tech. Inst. Curriculums; state coordinator Vets. Edn. Council of N.E.A., 1947-1948; chmn. Fla. Certification Com. for Regional Edn., 1949-57; chmn. Fla. State Fulbright Com. 1950-57; mem. gov. adv. Council on Aging, 1960; mem. White House Conf. Aging, 1971; mem. Fla. council 100; mem. several other profl., ednl., community commns. Recipient Distinguished Alumnus citation U. Minn., 1962; Distinguished Alumni citation N.Y. U., 1971. Fellow A.A.A.S.; mem. Fla. Assn. Colls. and Univs. (pres. 1949-50, Distinguished Service citation 1971), Am. Astron. Soc., Royal Astron. Soc. of Can., Astron. Soc. of France, Fla. Acad. Scis., Newcomen Soc. of Eng., Nat. Collegiate Players, N.E.A., Albany Adult Edn. Council (pres. 1944-45), Fgn. Policy Assn., Greater Tampa C. of C. (gov.), Sigma Pi Sigma, Lambda Chi Alpha, Phi Delta Kappa, Sigma Xi, Omicron Delta Kappa, Alpha Kappa Psi, Pi Epsilon Delta, Pi Sigma Epsilon, Sinfonia. Mem. Soc. of Friends. Kiwanian (past pres.). Author or co-author several books, bulls. and articles. Home: Tampa, Fla. Died Dec. 26, 1982.

ALLEN, LINTON E., banker; b. Chipley, Ga., Mar. 22, 1889; s. John L. and Emma V. (Dickinson) A.; student Univ. Sch. for Boys, Stone Mountain, Ga., 1904-06; B.S., U. of Ga., 1909; student Eastman Bus. Coll., Poughkeepsie, N.Y.; m. Helen Ives Allen, Apr. 12, 1928; 1 dau., Helen Elizabeth. Began with Glynn County Bank, Brunswick, Ga., and became cashier, 1917; with Irving Nat. Bank, N.Y. City, 1919-23; v.p. Nat. Bank of Republic, Chicago, 1923-27; established Sanford (Fla.) Atlantic Nat. Bank, 1927, and served as pres., 1927-34; organized First Nat. Bank, Orlando, Fla., 1934, exec. v.p., 1934-36, pres., 1936-52, chmn. bd. from 1952; director Altantic Coast Line Railroad Co. Served as 2d lt., Inf., U.S. Army, World War I, major World War II. President Children's Home Society of Fla. (Central Fla. div.), 1947-50; Orlando Community Chest, 1945-46. Mem. Am. Bankers Assn. (mem. exec. council credity policy com.), Fla. Bankers Assn (past pres.), Phi Delta Theta. Presbyn. (elder, 1940-51, past pres. ch. sch. class; active in promotion and support of religious and humanitarian projects). Mason. Club: Rotary (past pres.). Home: Orlando, Fla. †

ALLEN, MORSE SHEPARD, educator; b. Brooklyn, Oct. 13, 1890; s. Charles M. and Carol (Shepard) A.; B.A., Wesleyan U., 1912, M.A., 1913; M.A., Columbia, 1913; student Oxford U., 1913-14; Ph.D., Princeton, 1920; m. Marjorie C. Hills, Aug. 20, 1918. Instr. English, Ohio Wesleyan U., 1914-16, asst. prof., 1916-20; asst. prof. Trinity Col., 1920-23, asso. prof., 1923-46, J. J. Goodwin prof. English, from 1946, head dept. 1946-58; sec. faculty, 1934-46. Mem. Am. Assn. U. Profs., Modern Lang. Assn., New England College English Association (pres. 1949-50), Conn. Hist. Soc., Phi Beta Kappa, Phi Nu Theta. Episcopalian. Author: Satire of John Marston. †

ALLEN, ROBERT CHESTER, mech. engr.; b. Hartford, Conn., July 16, 1889; s. Alden Josiah and Julia Frances (Allen); ed. pub. schs., Hartford; D.Sc. (hon.), Marquette U., 1960; m. Helen R. Kelley, July 2, 1932; children—Julia Rita, Eileen Rose, Robert Chester. With Terry Steam Turbine Co., Hartford, 1910-15, asst. engr., 1913-15; with Westinghouse Electric Corp., 1915-31, mgr. large turbine engring., 1926-31; mgr. engring. A.O. Smith Corp., 1931-34; chief engr. Murray Iron Works, Burlington, Ia., 1934-36; with Allis-Chalmers Mfg. Co., from 1936, sr. engring. cons. advanced power concepts, nuclear power systems, from 1960. Mem. spl. com. aircraft jet propulsion NACA, 1941; mission to U.K. for U.S. Navy aircraft jet propulsion devel., 1943; engring. large def. programs, steam turbines, aircraft superchargers, jet propulsion engines, World War II; rep. Am. Soc. M.E. at Verein Deutscher Ingenieure Centennial, W. Berlin, Germany, 1956. Recipient citation tech. advancements power engring. U. Wis., 1960. Fellow Am. Soc. M.E. Home: Wauwatosa, Wis. †

ALLEN, ROBERT L., med. dir. U.S.P.H.S.; b. New Castle, Pa., Nov. 4, 1888; s. John Calvin and Mary Newell (Wallace) A.; M.D., Jefferson Med. Coll., 1913; m. Jane Whitten, Dec. 1921; children—Jane (wife of Homer R. Allen, M.D.), Mary (Mrs. Richard Bischoff). Apptd. asst. surgeon U.S.P.H.S., Sept. 1914, med. dir., supervisor of all quarantine stations on U.S.-Mexican border, from 1937. Home: El Paso, Tex. †

ALLEN, RUTH ALICE, economist, teacher; b. Cameron, Tex., July 28, 1889; d. Thomas Franklin and Jennie (Adams) Allen; A.B., U. of Tex., 1921, M.A., 1923; Ph.D., U. of Chicago, 1933; unmarried. Teacher in pub. schs. of Texas, 1908-17; instr. dept. of economics, U. of Tex., 1923-28, prof. from 1940; supervisor southeastern region U.S. Bureau of Labor Statistics study of money disbursements of employed wage earners and clerical workers, 1934-35. Member women's advisory committee to War Manpower Board, 1942; pub. pannel mem. Nat. War Labor Bd., Region VIII, 1942-45. Mem. Am. Econ. Assn., Am. Assn. Univ. Profs., Southwestern Social Sci. Assn. (editor Quarterly 1941-47). Author: The Labor of Women in the Production of Cotton, 1930; The Great Southwest Strike, 1942; Chapters in "History of Organized Labor in Texas," 1941. Home: Austin, Tex. †

ALLER, CURTIS COSMOS, JR, educator, govt. ofcl.; b. Seattle, Sept. 22, 1918; s. Curtis Cosmos and Inga Pauline (Olsen) A.; B.A. in Econs. and Bus. magna cum laude, U. Wash., 1942; Ph.D., Harvard, 1958; B.Litt., Oxford (Eng.) U., 1950; m. Mary Aldridge, Feb. 21, 1954; children—Roger Curtis, John Cosmos, Thomas Arthur, Inga Maria. Prof. econs. San Francisco State Coll., 1959-85, dean Sch. Behavioral and Social Scis., 1982-85; staff dir. select subcom. labor U.S. Ho. of Reps., 1963-64; dir. Office Manpower Policy, Evaluation and Research, Manpower Adminstrn., Dept. Labor, 1965-85; arbitrator labor-manpower disputes, 1953-85. Mem. adv. council Bay View Fed. Savs. & Loan Assn., 1960-63; dir. Twin Pines Fed. Savs. & Loan Assn., 1963-85. Mem. Cal. Social Welfare Bd., 1962-85, also chmn. Campaign mgr. 7th Congl. Dist. Cal., 1956; co-chmn. Byron Rumford campaign for 17th Assembly Dist. Cal., 1962-64. Served with AUS, 1946-47. Rhodes scholar from Wash. State, 1948-50. Mem. Am., Western econs. assns., Indsl. Relations Research Assn., Nat. Planning Assn. Editor; (with Clark Kerr) West Coast Collective Bargaining Systems, 1955. Home: Washington, D.C. Died May 1, 1985.

ALLEY, JAMES BURKE, lawyer; b. Bedford County, Tenn., Sept. 13, 1894; s. Albert Rayford and Maud (Wardlaw) A.; prep. edn. Webb Sch., Bell Buckle, Tenn.; student Washington and Lee U., 1909-10; Okla. U., 1910-11; A.B., Columbia, 1914; LL.B., Harvard Law School, 1925; m. Esther Hall Lowe; children—Jane (Mrs. Anthony Jackson), James, Harrison, Cynthia (Mrs. Woodbury H. Andrews). With 1st Nat. Bank, Muskogee, Okla. 1914-16. J.P. Morgan & Co., N.Y. 1916-17; asst. sec. to v.p. and gen. counsel Indsl. Finance Corp., 1919-22; mem. Council Fgn. Policy Assn., Boston, 1923-25; practiced law in N.Y.C., 1925-32; partner, Glenn, Alley, Geer & Roberts, 1929-32; counsel Reconstrn. Finance Corp., in charge of bank reorgn. and recapitalization work, 1932-35, gen. counsel, March 1935-June 1937; dir. Commodity Credit Corp., Washington, First and Second Export-Import Banks of Washington, 1935-37; mem. law firm Auchincloss, Alley & Ducan, 1937-83; firm name changed to Hooker, Alley & Duncan, May, 1944. Rep. banking group in Havana and Washington, defaulted Cuban public works obligations, 1937; dir. African Metals Corp., Universitas, Ltd. Specializes in adminstrv. and anti-trust law and in law relating to orgn. and reorgn. of banking, business and railroad corps.; writer and speaker on subjects in field. Pres. bd. trustees, trustee Green Vale School, Glenhead, L.I. 1951-54; pres. Bd. Edn., Jericho, N.Y., 1945-46. Served with U.S. Navy, 1917-19. Mem. Am. Bar Assn., Assn. Bar City N.Y., Am. Judicature Soc., Council on Fgn. Relations. Beta Theta Pi. Democrat. Presbyn. Clubs: University, Pilgrims (N.Y.C.); Metropolitan. 1925 F Street (Washington); Ausable (St. Huberts, N.Y.); Millbrook Golf and Tennis. Millbrook Hunt (Millbrook, N.Y.). Home: New York, N.Y. Died Nov. 29, 1983.

ALLISON, JAMES RICHARD, physician; b. Brevard, N.C., Feb. 9, 1889; s. Elisha Montgomery and Roxie (Lanier) A.; A.B., U. of N.C., 1911; M.D., U. of Pa., 1914; post-grad. work N.Y. Skin and Cancer Hosp., Vanderbilt Clinic, London Post-Grad. Sch.; m. Susy FitzSimons, May 14, 1922; children—Frances Huger, James Richard, Christopher FitzSimons. Interne Presbyn. Hosp., Phila., 1914-15; dermatologist and allergist, Columbia, S.C., from 1920; consultant U.S. Vets. Hosp., Columbia Hosp. Served as surgeon, U.S. Navy, on U.S.S. President Grant, transport, World War I. Mem. A.M.A., Am. Acad. of Dermatology and Syphilology, Soc. for Investigative Dermatol., Southeastern Dermatol. Assn., Columbia Med. Soc. (past pres.), S.C. Med. Assn., Southern Med. Assn. (past pres. of sect.), Am. Legion. Democrat. Episcopalian. Contbr. articles to med. jours. Home: Columbia, S.C. †

ALLMAN, HEYMAN B., educator; b. Metz, Ind., July 12, 1890; s. John B. and Evelyn (Barron) A.; B.S., Tri-State College, 1910, also LL.D. (honorary), 1959; student Purdue University, 1918; A.M., Indiana U., 1931; m. Ethel Chard, June 8, 1916; children—Martha, John, Alice, William. Prin., supt. high schs., Ind., 1910-30; dir. supervised teaching Ind. U., 1930-36; dir. summer sessions, prof. sch. adminstrn. from 1946, prof. dept. edn. from 1946, dir. coll. and univ. placement service, from 1959; supt. schs., Muncie, Ind., 1936-46. Mem. state bd. edn., 1945-49; edn. adviser Pakistan Ministry of Edn. and ICA, 1954-56; dir. title III Edn. for Nat. Def., State Department of Edn., from 1959. Member National Edn. Assn., Ind. State Tchrs. Assn. (past pres.), C. of C., Phi Delta Kappa. Mem. Christian Ch. Mason. Clubs: Rotary, Ind. Sch. Men's. Co-author: Series of Spelling Books; Safety Education Contbr. profl. jours. Home: Bloomington, Ind. †

ALLOWAY, R(UPERT) BROOKE, lawyer; b. Columbus, Ohio, July 2, 1916; s. James William and Ninnette (McKinley) A.; B.A., Ohio State U., 1936; J.D., Harvard, 1939; m. Jane Denman Reason, Sept. 3, 1938; children—Jeremy Reason, Andrea Jane. Admitted to Ohio bar, 1939, also U.S. Supreme Ct.; law clk. to Judge Edward C. Turner, 1939-40; practice in Columbus, 1941-42, 49-76; mem. firm Topper, Alloway, Goodman, DeLeone & Duffey, and predecessors, 1949-76, sr. ptnr., 1969-76; spl. agt. FBI, Oklahoma City, Tulsa, Chgo., Indpls. and South Bend, Ind., 1942-44; contract termination atty. Studebaker Corp., 1944-46; asst. atty. gen. Ohio, Columbus, 1946-49; spl. counsel to atty. gen. Ohio, 1949-69. Mem. Jud. Council of Ohio, 1957-60. Mem. Centennial Commn., Ohio State U., from 1971. Vice chmn. Franklin County (Ohio) Republican Finance Com., 1963-65; counsel Ohio Rep. Finance Com., from 1966. Mem. adv. bd. Ohio State U., 1964-72, bd. overseers, 1950-51. Mem. Am., Ohio bar assns., Ohio State U. Assn. (1st v.p. 1961-62), Harvard Law Sch. Ohio Assn. (nat. v.p. 1964-65, pres. Ohio 1972-73), Ohio Hist. Soc., Soc. for Performing Arts, Columbus Gallery Fine Arts, Internat. Soc. Gen. Semantics. Clubs: Ohio State U. Faculty, Columbus, University, Scioto Country. Home: Columbus, Ohio. Office: Columbus OH. Died June 15, 1976.

ALLPORT, FLOYD HENRY, psychologist; b. Milw., Aug. 22, 1890; s. John Edward and Nellie Edith (Wise) A.; A.B., Harvard, 1913, Ph.D., 1919; m. Ethel Margaret Hudson, Oct. 5, 1917; children—Edward Herbert, Dorothy Fay, Floyd Henry; m. 2d, Helene Willey Hartley, Sept. 5, 1938. Instr. psychology Harvard and Radcliffe Coll., 1919-22; asso. prof. psychology U. N.C., 1922-24; prof. social and polit. psychology Syracuse U., from 1924, mem. Rumor Clinic, dir. Morale Seminar, World War II, dir. research on conformity behavior and theory of event-structure, from 1940; acting editor Jour. Abnormal and Social Psychology, 1921-24; dir. research on learning Washington office Maxwell Sch. Citizenship, under contract Office Naval Research, 1953-54; vis. prof. phychology U. of California, 1957-58, Mem. Social Science Research Council, 1925-27, 29-31; mem. research sub-com. Pres. Hoover's Conf. on Home Bldg. and Home Ownership, 1931; bd. dirs. Council for Democracy. Served from 2d lt. to 1st lt. F.A., U.S. Army, 1917-19, with AEF, 1918, Fellow A.A.A.S.; mem. Am. (council dirs. 1928-30), Eastern psychol. assns., Am. Sociol. Soc., Upper N.Y. Psychologists, Nat., Inst. Psychology, Soc. for Psychol. Study of Social Issues (council dirs. 1938-40; chmn. program com. 1938, chmn. 1940-41), Asso. Artists of Syracuse (pres. 1944-45), Sigma Xi, Phi Beta Kappa (hon.). Club: Harvard. Author: (with H.S. Langfeld) An Elementary Laboratory Course in Psychology, 1916, Social Psychology, 1924; (with D. Katz) Students' Attitudes, 1930; Institutional Behavior, 1933; Theories of Perception and the Concept of Structure, 1955; also articles in psychol. and social science jours. Home: Syracuse, N.Y. †

ALLPORT, HAMILTON, engineer, banker; b. Chicago, Ill., Nov. 13, 1890; s. Walter H. and Harriet (Hamilton) A.; M.E., Cornell U., 1914; m. Gile Davies, Nov. 29, 1919; children—Marian, Hamilton, J. Davies, Harriet H., Priscilla, Walter Frank. With bur. engring. statistics, N.Y.C. R.R., 1910; with James Hunter Machine Co., N. Adams, Mass., 1913; asst. engr., Underwriters' Labs., Inc., 1914-17; instr., asst. prof. Armour Inst. Tech. (Ill. Inst. Tech.), 1915-17, in charge hydraulic lab. and sr. thesis work; chief engr. Carson, Pirie, Scott & Co., Chicago, 1919; mech. engr. Plymouth Creamery System, Boston, 1920; mech. engr. E. B. Badger & Sons Co., gen. engring. service, Boston, Pittsburgh, New York, 1920-23; asst. to pres. and chief engr. The Glidden Co., Cleveland, 1923-25; v.p. A. B. Leach & Co., Chicago, 1925-33; partner James O. McKinsey & Co., McKinsey, Wellington & Co., engrs.; cons. engr.; pres., dir. Standard Silica Corp., Mid Continent Laundries, Chgo., Texas Hydro Electric Corp. (Seguin, Tex.); pres. Ind. Utilities Corp. (Corydon, Ind.), Cadillac (Michigan) Gas Company, Dakota Public Service Company (Woonsocket, S.D.); president, dir. Ry. Warehouses, Inc. (Cleveland); v.p. Midland Realization Co. (Chgo.), City Ice Co. (K.C.); Midland Utilities Co. (Chicago); dir. Moore Corp. (Joliet, Ill.), Grand Rapids (Mich.) Brass Co., Central West Pub. Service Co.

(Omaha), Henney Motor Co.; Consolidated Cement Corp. (Chicago); dir., chmn. exec. com. Central Scientific Company (Chicago). Mem. 1st O.T.C Fort Sheridan, Illinois, 1917; in France, 1917-19; served as lt. and capt. arty., regular army; participated in actions at British front, Verdun, St. Mihiel, Argonne-Meuse; lt. col. Reserve. Chmn. research com. Nat. Industrial Sand Assn. Mem. Am. Society M.E., Am. Institute Mining and Metall. Engrs., Soc. Mayflower Descendants, Soc. Col. Wars (gov.), Soc. Am. Mil. Engrs., Am. Chem. Soc., Chgo. Hist. Soc. (life), Mil. Order World War (life), Am. Legion, Art Inst. Chicago (life), Sigma Phi. Republican. Presbyn. Clubs: Chicago, Chicago Athletic Assn., University, Electric, Skokie Country; Chems. (N.Y.); Economic, Caxton, (Chgo.); Adventurers. Author: Photocharts, also portion of U.S. Artillery manual; contribution to various engring. and mil. pub. Inventor of power plant equipment widely used. Home: Glencoe, Ill. †

ALLYN, ARTHUR CECIL, museum director, lepidopterist; b. Chgo., Dec. 24, 1913; s. Arthur Cecil and Nelle (Musick) A.; m. Dorothy DeWitt, Mar. 21, 1938 (dec.); children: Dorothy Ann (Mrs. Christopher J. Lavick, Jr.), David D., William N. (adopted); m. Dorothy Dunklau, Apr. 22, 1972. Student, Dartmouth Coll., 1931-35, Beloit Coll., 1935; D.Sc. (hon.), U. Fla., 1981. Chmn. bd. A.C. Allyn & Co., Chgo., from 1969; pres., dir. Chgo. White Sox, 1961-69; mng. dir. Allyn Mus. Entomology of Fla. State Mus.; pres. Sarasota Jungle Garden, 1970-85; dir. Allyn Precision Tools (PTY) LTD, Mono Container (PTY) Ltd. Fellow Royal Entomol. Soc.; mem. Lepidopterists Soc., Sigma Chi. Presbyn. Club: University (Sarasota). Home: Sarasota, Fla. Died Mar. 22, 1985.

ALLYN, RICHARD, internist, cardiologist; b. Waverly, Ill., Oct. 16, 1913; s. Paul Richard and Lena (Turner) A.; m. Ruth Lefferts, Sept. 20, 1941; children—Thomas Richard, Barbara Loraine, Paul Lefferts, David Edwin. A.B. with high honors, U. Ill., 1935; M.D., Columbia U., 1939. Diplomate: Am. Bd. Internal Medicine (gov. 1981). Intern St. Luke's Hosp., N.Y.C., 1939-40, resident in internal medicine, 1940-41; spl. fellow in internal medicine Mayo Found., Rochester, Minn., 1941-42; practice medicine specializing in internal medicine and cardiology, Springfield, Ill., 1946-81; attending staff Meml. Hosp., Springfield, Ill., 1946-81, pres. med. staff, 1950, sr. attending staff, 1966-81, chmn. dept. medicine, 1951, 53; active staff St. John's Hosp., Springfield, 1946-81, pres. med. staff, 1969, chmn. dept. medicine, 1957-58, 65-66, 70-75; clin. asso. So. Ill. U. Sch. Medicine, 1971-73, clin. prof. medicine, 1973-81; Advisor planning com. So. Ill. U. Sch. Medicine, 1969-72; med. adviser local bd. SSS, 1950-81; mem. local med. group Ill. Adv. Com. for Med., Dental, Vet. and Allied Specialists, 1950-81; adv. com. on terminology Commn. Profl. and Hosp. Activities, Ann Arbor, Mich., 1971; med. adv. com. BiState Regional Med. Program, St. Louis, 1970-73; task force cardiovascular rehab. Nat. Heart and Lung Inst., 1973-75; proficiency evaluation program com. Coll. Am. Pathologists, 1973; mem. bd. commrs. Joint Commn. Accreditation of Hosps., 1978—, chmn. accreditation com., 1981—. Author: Library for Internists, 1973, Library for Internists II, 1976, Library for Internists III, 1979, Library for Internists IV, 1982. Ofcl. bd. 1st United Methodist Ch., Springfield, 1950-81, bldg. planning com., 1961-81, bd. trustees, 1962-81; mem. bishop's lay adv. com. Ill. Area Meth. Ch., 1965; active Boy Scouts Am., 1958-59; Bd. trustees MacMurray Coll., Jacksonville, Ill., 1962-81, treas., bd. trustees, exec. com., 1971; mem. Found. Med. Care Central Ill. Served to capt. M.C. AUS, 1942-46, ETO. Decorated Bronze Star; recipient Bronze tablet U. Ill., 1935, Distinguished Eagle Scout award Boy Scouts Am., 1971; Alexander Cochran Bowen scholar N.Y. Acad. Medicine, 1941-42. Fellow Am. Coll. Cardiology, A.C.P. (regent 1977-81, exec. com. bd. regents 1981, gov. Downstate Ill. 1970-76, exec. com. bd. govs. 1972-76, vice chmn. bd. govs. 1975-76, del. to AMA Ho. of Dels. 1978-81), Am. Coll. Chest Physicians, mem. AMA (intersplty. advisory bd. 1977-80, mem. exec. com. 1978-80, mem. task force on med. edn. 1980-81), Ill. Med. Soc. (chmn. sect. internal medicine 1960-61), Sangamon County Med. Soc, chmn. peer rev. com. 1981), Am. Soc. Internal Medicine, Ill. Soc. Internal Medicine (pres. 1960-62, mem. council), Am. Cancer Soc. (past chmn. Sangamon County chpt.), Springfield Med. Club (past pres.), Ill. Heart Assn. (pres. 1969-70, bd. dirs.), Am. Heart Assn. (fellow Council Clin. Cardiology), Sangamon County Heart Assn., Linnean Soc. N.Y., AAAS, Am. Ornithologists Union, Wilson Ornithol. Club, Nat. Audubon Soc., Springfield Audubon Soc., Soc. Mayflower Descs. in State of Ill. (life), Mayo Alumni Assn., Am. Birding Assn., Phi Beta Kappa, Sigma Xi, Phi Kappa Phi, Phi Eta Sigma, Alpha Kappa Lambda. Clubs: Illini Country (Springfield), Sangamo (Springfield); Masons, Rotary. Home: Springfield, Ill. Died Nov. 25, 1981.

AL-SAID, NURI, premier of Iraq; b. Baghdad, 1888; ed. Mil. Coll. and Mil. Staff Coll., Istanbul, Turkey. Participated in Arab revolt against Turkey prior to World War I; became comdr. in chief Iraq Army, 1921; several times minister of defense, also fgn. minister; first served as premier, 1930, also several times from, last appointment being Sept. 1950. Address: Baghdad, Iraq. †

ALSTON, WALTER EMMONS, former major league baseball mgr.; b. Butler County, Ohio, Dec. 1, 1911; s. William Emmons and Lenora (Neanover) A.; m. Lela Vaughn Alexander, May 10, 1930; 1 dau., Doria La Verne (Mrs. Harry Ogle). B.S. in Phys. Edn, Miami U., Oxford, Ohio, 1935. Mgr. Los Angeles Dodgers (and predecessor Bklyn. Dodgers), 1954-76, spl. cons., 1976-84; comml. sports announcer, Chgo., 1945. Author: (with Si Burick) Alston and the Dodgers, 1966, (with Don Weiskopf) The Complete Baseball Handbook: Strategies and Techniques for Winning, 1972, A Year At a Time, 1976. Named Major League Mgr. of Year Sporting News, 1955, 59, 63. Nat. League championship team 1955, 56, 59, 63, 65, 66, 74, World's Championship team 1955, 59, 63, 65; mgr. Nat. League All Star Team, 1954, 56, 57, 60, 64, 66, 67, 75. Home: Oxford, Ohio. Died Oct. 1, 1984.

ALTEMEIER, WILLIAM ARTHUR, surgeon; b. Cin., July 6, 1910; s. William A. and Carrie (Moore) A.; B.S., U. Cin., 1930, M.D., 1933; M.S. in Surgery, U. Mich., 1938; D.Sc. (hon.), Xavier U., 1973; m. Edna Wyss, June 16, 1934; children—William Arthur, Ann, George. Intern, Cin. Gen. Hosp., 1933-34; surg. resident Henry Ford Hosp., 1934-39, asst. resident, 1937-38, resident surgeon, 1938-39, asso. surgeon, 1939-40; instr. surgery U. Cin., 1940-43, asst. prof., 1943-52, Christian R. Holmes prof., chmn. dept., 1952-78, dir. research surg. bacteriology lab., 1940-83; dir. surg. services Cin. Gen. Hosp., 1952-78, clinician out-patient dept., 1943-83; surgeon-in-chief Holmes and Children's Hosps., 1952-78, prof. surgery, 1978-83; cons. surgeon Drake Meml., Cin. VA hosps.; limited pvt. practice, Cin., 1940-83. Responsible investigator contract subcoms. Surgeon Gen.'s Office, U.S. Army, numerous phys. conditions related to armed services, 1942-83, surg. cons., Japan and Korea, 1953; mem. div. med. scis. NRC, 1950-53, mem. subcom., burns, 1948-53, shock, 1950-53, trauma, 1953-67; chmn. surgery B study sect. NIH, 1972-74; cons. faculty medicine MEDCOM, 1972-83. Recipient Theodore Andrews McGraw award, David W. Yandell medal, Roswell Park Scroll and medal, citation award NCCJ, 1975; Harvey S. Allen Distinguished Service award Am. Bar Assn., 1978, fellow Grad. Sch. U. Cin., 1975. Diplomate Am. Bd. Surgery (bd. 1953-59, vice chmn. 1958-59). Fellow A.C.S. (mem. exec. com. bd. govs. 1972-75, chmn. subcom. surg. infections 1967-83, Distinguished Service award 1975, pres. 1978-79), mem. Central Surg. Assn. (treas. 1953-56, pres. 1958), Soc. Clin. Surgery (pres. 1962-64), Soc. Univ. Surgeons, So. Surg. Soc., Am. Surg. Assn. (pres. 1969-70), Am. Protologic Soc., Roy D. McClure Surg. Soc. (pres. 1966-70), AAAS, Am. Assn. Surgery of Trauma, Am. Cancer Soc., AMA, Am. Soc. Clin. Investigation, Assn. Am. Med. Colls., Cin. Acad. Medicine, Cin. Surg. Soc. (pres. 1956-57), Henry Ford Hosp. Med. Assn. (v.p. 1952-54, pres. 1954-56), Halsted Soc., Hist. and Philos. Soc., Internat. Soc. Surgery, Mont Reid Surg. Soc. (pres. 1971), Soc. Surg. Chmn., N.Y. Acad. Sci., Ohio State Med. Assn., Okla. Clin. Soc., Omaha Mid-West Clin. Soc., Western (council 1954-55, 1st v.p. 1957), Pan Pacific (v.p. 1969-72), Ohio surg. assns., Surg. Biology Club, Soc. for Surgery Alimentary Tract (pres. 1973-74), Allen O. Whipple Surg. Soc., Fred Coller Surg. Soc., Alpha Omega Alpha. Clubs: Rotary, Masons (33 deg.). Clubs: Commonwealth, Cincinnati, Queen City, Western Hills Country, Commercial, Queen City Optimist (pres. 1960-61). Author articles in field. Contbr.: Christipher's Textbook of Surgery, 1947, 56, 68; Nelson's Looseleaf of Surgery, 1948; Advances in Military Medicine, 1948; Surgery of Trauma, 1953; The Thyroid Gland, 1956; Surgery: Principles and Practice, 1957, 61, 66; Textbook of General Surgery, 1958; Complications in Surgery and Their Management, 1960; Cole and Elman's Textbook of Surgery, 1959, 1964, The Thyroid Gland, 1964; Surgical Bleeding, 1966; Lewis-Walters Practice of Surgery, 1974. Mem. editorial bd. Am. Surgeon, 1953-83, Annals of Surgery, 1955-83, Surgery, 1952, Current Therapy, 1958; Jour. Surg. Research, 1961-83. Home: Cincinnati, Ohio. Died Nov. 23, 1983.

ALTON, ROBERT M(INTIE), banker; b. Livingston, Mont., Apr. 1, 1889; s. Robert Davis and Anna (Mintie) A.; grad. Portland Acad., 1908; student U. Ore., 1908-09; LL.B., U. Mich., 1915; m. Frances Fowler, Mar. 14, 1922; chidren—Anne, Susan. Admitted to Ore. bar, 1916; law practice, Portland, 1915-17; asst. trust officer U.S. Nat. Bank, Portland, 1925, trust officer, head trust dept., 1933-37, v.p. from 1937, dir. from 1950. Gen. chmn. Community Chest campaign, Portland, 1948. Trustee Waverly Baby Home, Hallady Park Hosp., Friendly Rosenthal Found.; chmn. finance com. Pacific U. Served as 2d lt. to maj. 362d Inf., 91st Div., U.S. Army, 1917-19; chief contract retraining and settlement div., as lt. col., U.S.A.C., 1942-45. Mem. Am. Bankers Assn. (mem. exec. com.; pres. trust div. 1948). †

ALTSCHUL, HELEN G. (MRS. FRANK ALTSCHUL), civic worker; b. N.Y.C., May 9, 1887; d. Philip J. and Hattie (Lehman) Goodhart; A.B., Barnard Coll., 1907; m. Frank Altschul, Jan. 9, 1913; children—Charles, II (dec.), Margaret A. Lang, Edith A. Graham, Arthur Goodhart. Mem. bd. N.Y. Infirmary, from 1935, hon. v.p. Girls' and Boys' Service League N.Y.; trustee Barnard Coll. Mem. Am. Assn. U. Women. Clubs: Women's University (pres. 1947-49), Barnard College (pres. 1932-35), Cosmopolitan, Women's City. Address: Stamford, CT. †

ALVAREZ, VIDAURRE ANTONIO, diplomat of El Salvador; b. 1889; ed. Nat. U., San Salvador. With El Salvadorian Diplomatic Service missions in Nicaragua, Costa Rica, Mexico, Honduras, Spain, Portugal, The Vatican and Italy, 1927-50; chief protocol Ministry Fgn. Affairs, 1951-55; ambassador to Guatemala, 1955-60, to Spain, The Vatican and Switzerland, 1960-62; permanent rep. El Salvador to UN, from 1962. Address: New York, N.Y. †

ALVES, CHARLES STEBBINS, banker; b. Henderson, Ky., Mar. 28, 1887; s. Joseph Barnard and Annie (Henderson) A.; student high sch., Henderson, to sophomore grade; m. Catherine Triplett Kitchell, Sept. 20, 1907; children—Margaret Henderson, Elizabeth Merritt. Cashier Farmers Bank, Strausburg, Mo., at 19; organizer, 1910, Southwest Blvd. State Bank of Kansas City, Mo., disposed of interest in this bank, 1917, and organized the Peoples Trust Co. of which was pres. until Trust Co. was sold, 1927; dir., treas. Building Owners and Managers Assn.; vice-pres. Walnut Realty Co.; dir. Business Men's Assurance Co.; dir. Nat. Security Life Ins. Co. Bd. dirs. St. Luke's Hosp., Sunset Hill Sch. Assn. Democrat. Episcopalian. Clubs: Kansas City, Bankers', Mission Hills Country. Home: Kansas City, Mo. †

ALYEA, EDWIN PASCAL, surgeon; b. Clifton, N.J., Feb. 4, 1898; s. Joseph P.S. and Sarah Mae (Dinsmore) A.; B.S., Princeton U., 1919; M.D., Johns Hopkins U., 1923, postgrad., 1923-29; m. Nancy B. Anderson, June 9, 1926; children—Edwin Pascal, Nancy. Resident in medicine and instr. in surgery Johns Hopkins U. Sch. Medicine, 1923-26; resident, instr. in urology Brady Urol. Inst., Johns Hopkins Hosp., 1926-29; successively instr., asst. prof., asso. prof. surgery in charge urologic div. Duke U. Med. Sch., 1942, prof. urology, 1947-65, prof. emeritus, 1968-82; chief urology Duke U. Med. Center; cons. Watts, Lincoln, VA hosps., Durham, N.C., 1953. Mem. venereal disease com. NRC, Washington, 1940-42; mem. Nat. Med. Com. on Birth Control, 1933. Served with A.R.C., 1917; with heavy arty., O.T.C., U.S. Army, 1918. Diplomate Nat. Bd. Med. Examiners, Am. Bd. Urology. Fellow A.C.S. (gov. 1954); mem. Clin. Soc. Genito-Urinary Surgeons (pres. 1972), Am. Assn. Genito-Urinary Surgeons, Am. Urol. Assn., Urosurg. Soc., Johns Hopkins Surg. Soc., Am. Neisserian Med. Soc., Am., N.C. med. socs., So. Med. Assn., Southeastern (hon.), N.C., Fla. (hon.) urol. socs., Phi Beta Kappa, Alpha Omega Alpha. Contbr. numerous articles to profl. jours. Home: Durham, N.C. Died Feb. 1, 1982.

AMADO, GILBERTO, Brazilian diplomat; b. State of Sergipe, Brazil, May 7, 1887; s. Melchisedeck de Souza Amado and Ana de Lima Souza (Ferreira) Amado; LL.B., Law Sch. of Recife, Pernambuco, 1911; m. Alice de Barros Gibson, Nov. 9, 1911 (divorced 1931); children—Ana, Vera, Frederico. Prof. of law, Law Sch. of Recife, 1911-30; Fed. Congressman rep. State of Sergipe, 1914-24, mem. com. of finance and diplomacy of Chamber of Deputies, 1922-24; Brazilian del. to the Interparliamentary Confs. in Rome, London, Paris, Berlin, and Belgium, 1925-29; Fed. Senator, 1925-30; chmn. diplomatic and treaty coms. and mem. of finance com. of Senate, 1925-30; law prof., Univ. of Rio de Janeiro, 1931-32; prof. Inst. Franco-Brazilian of High Culture and lecturer Law Sch. of Paris, 1933; Brazilian del. to 7th Pan-Am. Conf., Montevideo, 1933; to Pan Am. Conf. of Commerce in Buenos Aires, 1935; law counselor to Ministry of Fgn. Affairs for Brazil, 1935-36; Brazilian ambassador to Chile, 1936; rep. Brazil, Internat. Labor Office, Geneva, Switzerland, 1947; Brazilian del. to Assembly of U.N., 1947. Journalist and writer since 1911, writer of fiction from 1940. Author: Chave de Salomão, 1914; Suave Ascencão (poetry), 1916; Grão de Areia (polit. and social essays), 1917; Aparencias e Realidades, 1922; Dansa sobre o Abismo, 1923; Dias e Horas de Vilbracão, 1933; Espirito do nosso Tempo, 1932; Tratado de Direito Publico, 1931, Tobias Barreto, 1935, Densidade e Tenuidade, 1935, O Meio Social e as Instituicões Politicas no Brasil, 1916 (latter books contain essays and studies in regard to historic development of politic and literary life in Brazil). Fiction (written while detained by the war in Switzerland, 5 yrs.): Inocentes e Culpados, 1940; Interesses da Companhia, 1942; Mariquinhas Camacho, 1947. Contbr. numerous articles and studies to newspapers and mags. of Brazil. Address: Hackensack, N.J. †

AMATEIS, EDMOND ROMULUS, sculptor; b. Rome, Italy, Feb. 7, 1897; s. Louis and Dora (Ballin) A.; m. Mildred Denison, Aug. 10, 1942 (dec. 1966); m. Dorothy Fisher Willis, May 24, 1968. Art edn., Beaux Arts Inst. Design, N.Y. City, 1916-17, 1920-21, Academie Julienne, Paris, 1919, Am. Acad. in Rome, 1921-24. Asso. of Nat. Acad., 1936, Nat. Academician, 1943. Instr. sculpture Columbia, 1928-32, Bennett Sch., 1938-40. Contbr. articles to profl. jours.; Exhibited, Met. Mus. Art, Phila. Acad. Fine Nat Acad. Design, others., Prin. works include busts, garden figures, folklore groups, Kansas City Liberty Meml., Balt. War Meml., U.S. Govt. Meml., Draguignan, France, also reliefs and portrait studies, Polio Wall of Fame, Georgia., Warm Springs Found. Served in F.A. U.S. Army, Apr. 1917-Aug. 1919; participating in battles of Chateau-Thierry, St. Mihiel, Meuse Argonne. Fellowship Am. Acad. in Rome, 1921-24; Henry O. Avery prize Archtl. League of N.Y., 1929; James E. McClese prize Pa. Acad. Fine Arts, 1933; Lindsey Sterling Morris

Medal Nat. Sculptor Soc. Designer of medal of Soc. of Medalists, 1940; U.S. Govt. medals for Typhus Commn. and Pacific Theatre of Operations; Liberty Hyde Bailey medal, 1958. Mem. Nat. Sculpture Soc. (pres. 1942-44, recipient Herbert Adams Meml. award for advancement of sculpture 1980), Alumni Assn. Am. Acad. in Rome, Nat. Inst. Arts and Letters. Address: Clermont, Fla. Died May 3, 1981.

AMES, HAROLD TAYLOR, industrial engineer; b. Antioch, Ill., Feb. 16, 1894; s. Chester C. and Mary Josephine (Taylor) A.; ed. pub. schs.; m. Katharine Fetrow, Mar. 21, 1925; children—Harold Fetrow, Janet Virginia. Identified with mfg. of automobiles. 1926-37; at various times pres. Duesenberg, Inc. of Ind., exec. v.p. Auburn Automobile Co. of Auburn, Ind., v.p. Cord Corp.; dir. King-Seeley Thermos Co.; pres., dir. The La Porte Corp. 1940-83, Chgo. Electric Mfg. Co., 1945-83, Nat. Stamping & Electric Works, 1948-83. Served as 1st lt. U.S. Air Service. 1917-19. Republican. Mason. Clubs: Chicago Athletic, Bob O'Link Golf: Thunderbird Country; Indian Hill. Home: Wilmette, Ill. Died June 3, 1983.

AMES, HARRY CLIFTON, lawyer; b. Williamsport, Pa., July 14, 1890; s. Alonzo Lighthall and Olive Ruth (Davis) A.; LL.B., Washington Coll. Law, 1923; m. Hilda Hinkel, Feb. 2, 1911; children—Jacquelin (Mrs. James M. Heilman), Harry Clifton. Admitted to D.C. bar, 1923; examiner, spl. agt. Bur. Pensions, Dept. Interior, 1912-20; atty.-examiner Interstate Commerce Commn., 1920-29; pvt. law practice, Washington, from 1929. Mem. Assn. Practitioners (pres. 1947-48), Assn. Motor Carrier Counsel, Am. Bar Assn., Asso. Traffic Clubs, Gamma Eta Gamma (hon.). Clubs: Traffic (N.Y. City); Cosmos, Columbia Country (Washington). Author interstate commerce law treatises. Home: Washington, D.C. †

ANDERSON, CHARLES S., mfg. exec.; b. Racine, Wis., Jan. 3, 1890; s. Soren C. and Jensine (Peterson) A.; student pub. schs., Racine; m. Sigma W. Amundsen, Sept. 25, 1912 (dec.); m. 2d, Elsie Ewens, June 14, 1938. Cost clk. J. I. Case Co., Racine, 1907-09, Mitchell Wagon Co., 1909-13; cost dept. mgr. Mitchell Auto Co., 1913; sec.-treas. Belle City Malleable Iron Co., 1913-23, sec., gen. mgr., 1923-26, v.p., sec., gen. mgr., 1926-35, pres., sec., 1935-58, chmn. bd., pres., 1958-59, chmn. board, chief exec. officer, 1959-61; chmn. bd., dir. Fabricast Mfg. Co., Woodstock, Ill.; dir. First Nat. Bank & Trust Co., Racine. Bd. dirs. Kendall Coll., Evanston, Ill.; pres. Curtis P. Kendall Found. Methodist (chmn. bd. trustees). Home: Racine, Wis. †

ANDERSON, EUGENE NEWTON, educator; b. Tehuacana, Tex., July 24, 1900; s. Jesse and Luda Lee (Newton) A.; m. Pauline Relyea, June 25, 1932; 1 son, Eugene Newton. A.B., U. Colo., 1921; Ph.D., U. Chgo., 1928; postgrad., U. Berlin, 1924-25. Instr. U. Chgo., 1925-32, asst. prof. European history, 1932-36; prof. European history Am. U., Washington, 1936-41; coordinator info., 1941-42; with Office Strategic Services, 1942-45; asst. chief div. cultural cooperation Dept. State, Washington, 1945, assoc. chief German-Austrian activities div., occupied areas, 1946-47; expert on humanities in German and Austrian univs. War Dept. and Am. Council Learned Socs., summer 1949; prof. European history U. Nebr., 1947-55; prof. European history UCLA, 1955-68, emeritus prof., 1968-84; vis. prof. U. Calif.-Santa Barbara, 1968-70; faculty Peshawar U., West Pakistan, summer 1961. Author: The First Moroccan Crisis: 1904-06, 1930, Nationalism and the Cultural Crisis in Prussia: 1806-15, 1939, The Humanities in the German and Austrian Universities, 1950, Process versus Power, 1952, The Prussian Elections of 1862 and 1863, 1954, The Social and Political Conflict in Prussia, 1858-64, 1954; Modern Europe in World Perspective, 1958; European Issues in the 20th Century, 1958; co-author: Political Institutions and Social Change in Continental Europe in the 19th Century, 1968; co-editor: Medieval and Historiographical Essays in Honor of J.W. Thompson, 1940; co-author: Europe in the 19th Century: A Documentary Analysis, 2 vols., 1961; co-editor, co-translator: Eckart Kehr, Battleship Building and Party Politics in Germany, 1894-1901, 1975; bd. editors: Jour. Modern History, 1952-55. Served with U.S. Army, 1918. Social Sci. Research fellow, 1930-31, 37. Mem. AAUP, Am. Hist. Assn. (chmn. program com. 1939), Phi. Beta Kappa, Phi Delta Theta. Presbyterian. Home: Santa Barbara, Calif. Died Nov. 18, 1984.

ANDERSON, FREDERICK, educator; b. Grosse Ile, Mich., Jan. 10, 1889; s. Frederick P. and Mary Campbell (Douglass) A.; A.B., Stanford, 1911; A.M., Harvard, 1912; Ph.D., Yale, 1915; m. Rebecca Motte Hart, June 19, 1919. Mem. faculty dept. of Romanic langs. Stanford from 1920. Mem. Am. Philos. Assn. Home: Stanford University, Calif. †

ANDERSON, FREDERICK WILLIAM, hematologist; b. Utica, N.Y., Apr. 20, 1921; s. Frederick Leslie and Claire Elma (Langworthy) A.; m. Betty Louise Brown, June 23, 1945; children: David O'Neil, Karen Dale Anderson Wood. A.B., Colgate U., 1941; M.D., U. Rochester, 1945. Intern Strong Meml. Hosp., Rochester, N.Y., 1945-46; resident in medicine Genesee Hosp., Rochester, 1949-51; instr. medicine U. Rochester, 1951-56, clin. asst. prof., 1956-69, clin. asso. prof., 1969-81; dir. clin. labs. Genesee Hosp., Rochester, 1951-67, assoc. dir., 1967-81, head hematology unit, 1962-81; cons. in medicine Monroe Community, Lakeside Meml. hosps. Chmn. med. adv. com. Rochester Regional ARC Blood Program, 1964-72; chmn. med. bd. St. John's Home, Rochester, 1972-81; USPHS clin. trainee in hematology U. Rochester, 1961-62. Served with M.C. AUS, 1946-48. Mem. Monroe County Med. Soc., Rochester Acad. Medicine, AMA, Am. Soc. Internal Medicine, Phi Beta Kappa, Alpha Omega Alpha. Presbyterian. Home: Rochester, N.Y. Died Oct. 30, 1981.

ANDERSON, HAROLD V(ICTOR), prof. chemistry; b. Manistique, Mich., Apr. 4. 1890; s. Johannes and Anna Christine (Nelson) A.; B.Chem. E., U. of Mich., 1912; M.S., Lehigh U., 1925; grad. student U. of Ill., 1928-29; m. Judity Botvidson, Aug. 1915 (dec. Jan. 1944); 1 son, Frank John; m. 2d. Eleanor Blanche Aldridge, June 28, 1947. Chemist Dixie Portland Cement Co., Richard City, Tenn., 1914-18, Air Nitrates Corp., Muscle Shoals; Ala., 1918; instr. chemistry Lehigh U., Bethlehem, Pa., 1918-21, asst. prof., 1921-30, asso. prof., 1930-41, prof. chemistry from 1941; tech. rep. and dir. research on project sponsored by Office Sci. Research and Development through Nat. Defense Research Com. at Lehigh U., 1941-46. Mem. bd. sch. dirs. and sec., Salisbury Township, Lehigh Co., Pa., 1937-49. Mem. Am. Chemical Society. American Crystallographic Association, Alpha Chi Sigma, Phi Eta Sigma, Kappa Sigma, Sigma Xi. Republican. Lutheran. Author: Qualitative Analysis (with T. H. Hazlehurst), 1941; Chemical Calculations (with J. S. Long), 1924, 5th revised edit., 1948. Home: Allentown, Pa. †

ANDERSON, HARRY PIERCE, ins. exec.; b. nr. Dunbarton, S.C., Aug. 7, 1890; s. Henry P. and Emma (Weatherbee) A.; student Orangeburg (S.C.) Coll., 1909-10; m. Julia Zeigler, Nov. 10, 1915; children—Harry Pierce, Norman Calhoun. With The Life Ins. Co. of Va. from 1913; agt., Columbia, S.C., 1913-15, asst. dist. mgr., 1915-16, asst. dist. mgr., Birmingham, 1916-19, mgr. Shreveport (La.) dist. office, 1919-23, mgr., Detroit, 1923-38, gen. mgr. four Mich. dist. offices, 1928-29, field supervisor, Western territory, home office, Richmond, Va., 1929-37, gen. supervisor all weekly premium dists., 1937-42, asst. v.p., 1942-48, v.p. charge weekly premium field offices and training, Richmond, from 1948. Officer on staff Gov. of S.C., 1947. Mem. Life Ins. Agency Management Assn. (board dirs.), Virginia State, Richmond Cs. of C., Democrat. Baptist (com. of finance; bd. endowment corp.). Mason (32 deg., Shriner). Home: Richmond, Va. †

ANDERSON, HUGO A., banker; b. Helsingborg, Sweden, May 20, 1887; s. Carl A. and Augusta C. (Mard) A.; m. Hilda A. Nelson, Sept. 5, 1914; children—Hugo August, Robert Orville, Donald Bernhard, Helen Catherine, Marie (Mrs. James Evans Cooney). Began as page First Nat. Bank of Chgo., 1901, became asst. cashier, 1919, asst. v.p., 1920, v.p., 1926-59, retired; dir. Gen. Dynamics Co., Champlin Oil & Refining Co., Union Asbestos & Rubber Co., City Products Co., Mem. Northwestern University Associates, Evanston, Ill. Presbyn. Clubs: Glenview, Chicago, Mid-day, Bankers (Chgo.). Home: Northbrook, Ill. Died June 10, 1983.

ANDERSON, JEREMY R., artist; b. Palo Alto, Calif., Oct. 28, 1921; m. Frances W. Whitney, 1947; children—Timothy and Bruce (twins), Jennifer. Student, San Francisco Art Inst., 1946-50. Lectr. U. Calif., Davis, 1974. One-man exhbns. at, Metart Gallery, San Francisco, 1949, Allan Frumkin Gallery, Chgo., 1954, Stable Gallery, 1954, Dilexi Gallery, San Francisco, 1960, 61, 62, 64, Los Angeles, 1962, Quay Gallery, San Francisco, 1970, 75, 78, Mus. Contemporary Art, Chgo., 1975, one-man retrospective show, San Francisco Mus. Art, 1966, annuals, 1948, 49, 51, 52, 53, 58, 59, 63, Whitney Mus. Am. Art Ann., 1956, 64, also 50 Calif. Artists exhbn., 1962-63, U. Ill., 1955, 57, Stanford U., 1962, Kaiser Center, Oakland, Calif., 1963, 2ieme Salon Internat de Galeries Pilotes, Lausanne, Switzerland, 1966, Portland Mus., 1968, Funk Show, U. Calif. at Berkeley, 1967, Los Angeles Mus., 1967, Expo '70, Osaka, Japan, San Francisco Mus. Art, 1972-73, Oakland Mus., 1973, 1970, J.P.L. Fine Arts, London, 1975, Calif. Painting and Sculpture, San Francisco Mus. Art, 1976, others; represented in perm. coll., Pasadena Art Mus., San Francisco Mus. Art, U. Calif., Berkeley, Mus. Modern Art, N.Y.C., Oakland Mus., Dallas Mus. Served with USNR, 1941-45. Recipient I.N. Walter Sculpture prize San Francisco Mus. Art, 1948; Abraham Rosenberg Found. Traveling Fellowship, 1950; Sculpture prize San Francisco Art Assn., 1959. Address: Mill Valley, Calif. Died June 18, 1982.

ANDERSON, NELS EHLERT, newspaper editor; b. Omaha, Neb., June 5, 1890; s. Hans Nissen and Anna Margaretha Louisa (Ehlert) A.; B., Pe., Southwest Missouri State Teachers College, 1911; A.B., Drury Coll., Springfield, Missouri, 1912, graduate study same college, 1913; m. Lucile Adams, July 10, 1919; children—Nels Adams, Anne, (Mrs. Sam Appleby). Managing editor Springfield Republican, 1914-19; vice consul at Saloniki, Greece, 1919-21; in charge editorial page St. Louis Times, 1921-32, also asst. gen. mgr., bd. dir.; treas. Alltype Printing Corp.; research work, Washington, 1938-39. Mem. Mo. Editorial Assn., Rep. Editors Assn., St. Louis Chamber of Commerce (air bd.). Episcopalian. Mason (K.T., Shriner). Club: North Hills Country. Author: Our States and Their State Flowers (with sister Chrissie J. Anderson); Our Social Status, The State Programme Idea; The National Flowers of the Pan American Union. Address: Springfield, Mo. †

ANDERSON, PAUL B., nat. ch. cons.; b. Madrid, Iowa, December 27, 1894; son B. Frank and Emma (Seashore) A.; A.B., U. of Iowa, 1920; grad. work Oxford U.; Th.D. (hon.), St. Sergius Theol. Inst., Paris; m. Margaret Holmes, July 8, 1925; children—Mary Roberta, John Peter. Entered fgn. service Y.M.C.A., Shanghai, China, 1913-17; dir. war prisoners' aid, Russia and Siberia, 1917-18; sr. sec. of N.A. Y.M.C.A. in Europe; dir., editor Russian YMCA press; cons. Nat. Council Chs. Decorated officer French Acad., Knight French Legion of Honor, Cross of Confraternity, St. Khetevan (Ga.), Hon. Officer Order of Brit. Empire (Gt. Britain). Author: Russia's Religious Future, 1935; People, Church and State in Modern Russia (Macmillan), 1944. Associate editor: The Living Church. Contbr. Fgn. Affairs Quar. Home: White Plains, N.Y. Died June 26, 1985.

ANDERSON, THEODORE W(ILBUR), religious exec.; b. Salina, Kan., July 4, 1889; s. Olof and Wilhelmina (Lundberg) A.; grad., North Park Coll., 1909; A.B., U. of Chicago, 1913, A.M., 1914; L.H.D., Augustana Coll., Rock Island, Ill., 1947; m. Evelynn Johnson, Aug. 30, 1916; children—Theodore Wilbur, Jane Evelyn (Mrs. Ernest G. Lindgren), Daniel Olof. Pres. Minnehaha Acad. (organized, 1913), Minneapolis, 1913-33; pres. Evang. Covenant Ch. of Am., 1933-59, pres. emeritus, from 1959; ordained, 1933. Decorated Royal Order North Star (Sweden), 1952. Mem. Phi Beta Kappa. Home: Evanston, Ill. †

ANDERSON, WILLIAM EVAN, internist; b. Mankato, Minn., Sept. 7, 1927; s. Evan Ernest and Naomi (Ahiskog) A.; m. Ramona Marie Baker, Mar. 26, 1951; 1 son, Evan William. A.B., Gustavus Adolphus Coll., 1950; M.D., U. Minn., 1954. Diplomate: Am. Bd. Internal Medicine, also subsplty. in gastroenterology. Intern St. Luke's Hosp., Duluth, Minn., 1954-55; resident in internal medicine VA Hosp., Mpls., 1955-58; instr. medicine U. Minn., 1958-60; asst. prof. medicine W.Va. U., Morgantown, 1960-67, asso. prof., 1967-74, prof., 1974-83, chmn. div. gastroenterology, 1967-80; cons. gastroenterologist VA Hosp., Clarksburg, W.Va., 1962-80; internist, gastroenterologist Braddock Med. Group, 1980-83. Served with USNR, 1945-46. Mem. AMA, Alpha Omega Alpha. Lutheran. Home: Cumberland, Md. Died Apr. 4, 1983.

ANDRAS, ROBERT KNIGHT, mining company executive; b. Lachine, Que., Can., Feb. 20, 1921; s. John Donald and Angela Eva (Knight) A.; m. Frances Hunt, Oct. 20, 1945; children: Robert Hunt, Angela Knight. Grad., Wesley Coll., Winnipeg, 1938; D. Pub. Service, Northland Coll., Ashland, Wis., 1970; LL.D., Lakehead U., 1978. Exec. Ford Motor Co., 1946-55; pres. 4 automotive equipment and leasing firms, Thunder Bay, Ont., Can., 1955-68; Liberal mem. Fed. Parliament, from 1965; apptd. mem. Queen's Privy Council for Can., cabinet minister without portfolio with responsibility for Indian policy, 1968, minister responsible for housing, 1969, minister of state for urban affairs, from 1971, minister consumer and corporate affairs and registrar gen. Can., 1972, minister manpower and immigration, 1972; pres. Treasury Bd., 1976, Bd. Econ. Devel. Ministers, 1978; sr. v.p., dir. Teck Corp., Vancouver, B.C.; dir. Lornex Mining Corp.; Nat. co-chmn. Liberal campaign, 1972; bd. dirs. Vancouver Bd. Trade. Served to maj. Canadian Army, 1942-46. Decorated Voluntary medal, France and Germany medal, Def. medal, War medal, 39-45; recipient Centennial medal, Jubilee medal. Mem. Elec. Vehicle Assn. Can. (dir.), Inter-Parliamentary Union, NATO, Commonwealth parliamentary assns., Alta. Indian Assn. (hon. pres. 1969). Clubs: Vancouver (Vancouver), Shaughnessy Golf and Country (Vancouver), Canadian (Vancouver); Le Cercle Universitaire (Ottawa). Home: Vancouver, B.C., Can. Deceased.

ANDREW, SEYMOUR LANSING, statistician; b. Boston, Mass., May 23, 1887; s. Samuel Worcester and Helen (Seymour) A.; student Roxbury Latin Sch., 1898-1904; A.B., Harvard, 1910; m. Katherine Murphy, May 11, 1910; children—Helen Edith, Seymour Lansing. Clerk Am. Telephone and Telegraph Co., 1910-14, foreign statistician, 1914-19, asst. chief statistician, 1919-21, chief statistician from 1921. Fellow Am. Statis. Assn., A.A.A.S.; mem. Am. Econ. Assn., Econometric Soc., Am. Polit. Science Assn., Acad. Polit. and Social Science, Economic Club of N.Y., Controllers Inst. of America, Am. Anthropol. Soc., Kappa Sigma. Episcopalian. Clubs: Harvard, Downtown Athletic, Railroad-Machinery. Home: Orange, N.J.†

ANDREW, WARREN, physician, biologist, author; b. Portland, Oreg., July 19, 1910; s. John and Alice (Lucke) A.; m. Nancy Valerie Miellmier, Aug. 18, 1936; 1 dau., Linda Nancy. B.A. summa cum laude, Carleton Coll.,

1932; M.S. (fellow), Brown U., 1933; Ph.D., Yale U., 1936, U. Ill., 1936; M.D., Baylor U., 1943; M.A. in Ch. History, Christian Theol. Sem., Butler U., 1974, M.A. in Religion, 1976; M.Th., Harvard U., 1979. Asst. instr. zoology Yale U., 1933-34, U. Ill., 1934-36; teaching fellow U. Ga., 1936-37, instr., fellow anatomy, 1937-39; instr. anatomy, sch. medicine Baylor U., 1939-41, asst. prof. anatomy, 1941-43; asso. prof. histology Southwestern Med. Coll., Dallas, 1943-45, prof., 1946-47; vis. prof. U. Montevideo, Uruguay, 1945-46; prof. anatomy, chmn. dept. sch. medicine George Washington U., 1947-48, 49-52; cons. anatomy George Washington U. Hosp., 1947-52; vis. prof. Washington U., St. Louis, 1948-49; cons. cytology VA Hosp., Martinsburg, W.Va., 1950- 52; Am. Mus. Natural History vis. investigator Lerner Marine Biol. Lab., Bimini, Bahamas, B.W.I., 1951; vis. scientist, Barro Colorado Island, C.Z., 1952; adviser anatomy, mem. exhibits com. Second Internat. Gerontol. Congress, 1951; prof. anatomy dir. dept. Bowman Gray Sch. Medicine, 1952-57; prof. Ind. U., Indpls., 1958-82; chmn. dept. anatomy Ind. U. (Sch. Medicine), 1958-71; lectr. Tokyo and Kyoto med. schs., Japan, summer 1960, Karachi, Pakistan, also Bombay and Jamnagar, India, summer 1962; vis. scientist U. Coll. Hosp. Med. Sch., London, 1970, U. Capetown, 1970, Bernice P. Bishop Mus., Honolulu, 1971; vis. prof. anatomy U. Hawaii, 1968; research fellow Yale Div. Sch., 1974-75, fellow in sci. and humanities, 1974-75; ofcl. del. Pan-Am. Congress Gerontology; editorial bd. Gerontologia, Basel, 1957—; rep. biology Internat. Research Com. Gerontology; participant IX Internat. Congress Cell Biology; IV Internat. Congress Gerontology, 1957; conf. aging of nervous system Nat. Neurol. Diseases and Blindness, 1957; conf. Aging Process, 1957; mem. Ind. Commn. on Aging, 1958-82; Ind. del. White House Conf. on Aging, 1961, 71. Author: Comparative Histology, 1959, Comparative Hematology, 1965, Microfabric of Man; One World of Science, 1966, The Anatomy of Aging in Animals and Man, 1971, (with Cleveland P. Hickman) Histology of the Vertebrates, 1974, The Lymphocyte in Evolution, 1977; contbg. author: (with Cleveland P. Hickman) Ency. Britannica; mem. editorial bd.: (with Cleveland P. Hickman) Gerontol. Newsletter, 1959-82, Quar. Bull. Ind. U. Med. Center, 1959; Columnist: (with Cleveland P. Hickman) Internat. Poetry Soc; Contbr. (with Cleveland P. Hickman) sci. articles to profl. publs. Mem. adminstrv. bd. Meridian St. Meth. Ch., Indpls. Recipient Distinguished Service Award U.S. Jr. C. of C., 1946; research award Gerontol. Found., 1959. Mem. Gerontol. Soc. (council and corp. 1950-53, 57-82), Internat. Assn. Gerontology (vice chmn. for biology, research com.), Am. Assn. Anatomists, Am. Soc. Zoologists, AAAS, Soc. Exptl. Biology and Medicine, Philos. Soc. Washington, Tex. Med. Assn., Tissue Culture Assn., Washington Soc. Pathologists, Washington Acad. Medicine, N.Y. Acad. Sci., Internat. Com. Standardization in Hematology, Biol. Soc. Montevideo, Amigos de la Naturaleza de Montevideo, Am. Soc. Electron Microscopists, Internat. Soc. Cell Biology, History of Sci. Soc., Am. Med. Soc. Vienna (life), Internat. Poetry Soc., Sigma Xi, Phi Beta Kappa, Phi Chi, Theta Phi. Clubs: Cosmos, Explorers (fellow). Research Bermuda Biol. Sta., 1959; mem. corp. Home: Indianapolis, Ind. Died Sept. 9, 1982.

ANDREWS, EMMET CHARLES, labor union executive; b. San Francisco, Aug. 3, 1916; s. Lincoln and Ada (Tiernan) A.; student public schs., San Francisco; m. Elizabeth Lucille Byrne, Apr. 8, 1938; 1 dau., Catherine Maurer. Postal clk., San Francisco, 1936-55; sec., pres. San Francisco local Nat. Fedn. Post Office Clks., 1938-55, nat. v.p., 1955-66; exec. aide United Fedn. Postal Clks., 1966-69; adminstrv. aide Am. Postal Workers Union, Washington, 1969-72, dir. indsl. relations, 1972-77, gen. pres., 1977-81; v.p. AFL-CIO Exec. Council. Mem. Am. Arbitration Assn. (dir.). Democrat. Home: Silver Spring, Md. Died Nov. 8, 1981.

ANDREWS, T. COLEMAN, accountant; b. Richmond, Va., Feb. 19, 1899; s. Cheatham William and Dora Lee (Pittman) A.; m. Rae Wilson Reams, Oct. 18, 1919; children: Thomas Coleman, Wilson Pittman. Ed. pub. schs., Richmond; D.C.S. (hon.), Pace Coll., 1954; LL.D. (hon.), U. Mich., 1955, Grove City Coll., 1963; Sc.D. (hon.), U. Richmond, 1955. Entered pub. acctg. profession, 1918; founder T. Coleman Andrews & Co. (C.P.A.s), Richmond, 1922; co-founder Bowles, Andrews & Towne (actuaries), Richmond, 1948; chmn. bd., pres. Am. Fidelity & Casualty Co., Inc., 1955-63; chmn. bd., pres. Fidelity Bankers Life Ins. Co., 1955-63, chmn. bd., 1963-65, Nat Liberty Life Ins. Co., Valley Forge, Pa., 1965-67; auditor pub. accounts Commonwealth of Va., 1931-33; comptroller, dir. finance, dir. utilities bus. office, exec. sec. sinking fund commn. City of Richmond, 1938-40; mem. staff dir. fiscal div. War Dept., 1941; contract renegotiation office Dept. Navy, 1942; officer USMC, 1943-45; on loan to Dept. State as chief acct., dir. transp. North African Econ. Bd., Algiers, 1943; mem. G-2) Gen. Staff, 4th Marine Aircraft Wing, Central Pacific, 1944-45; organizer, dir., corp. audits div. GAO, 1945-47; commr. internal revenue Dept. Treasury, 1953-55; chmn. acctg. and auditing study group 1st Hoover Commn., 1948. Ind. Democratic candidate for Pres., 1956. Decorated Bronze Star; named to Acctg. Hall of Fame Ohio State U.; recipient Alexander Hamilton Gold Medal award Dept. Treasury, 1955, 1st award Tax Execs. Inst., 1955, award for pub. service Virginians of Md. Mem. Richmond C. of C. (pres. 1958), Am. Inst. C.P.A.s (gold medal award for outstanding service 1947, pres. 1950-51), Va. Soc. C.P.A.s, Am. Acctg. Assn., Fed. Govt. Accts. Assn. Ind. Democrat. Episcopalian. Clubs: Commonwealth (Richmond), Country of Virginia (Richmond); Bohemian (San Francisco). Masons. Home: Richmond, Va. Died Oct. 15, 1983.

ANDRUS, CARLTON LEVERETT, naval officer; b. Feb. 10, 1888; m. Alda A. Andrus; 1 son Don L. (lt. M.C. U.S.N.). Entered U.S. Navy, 1917, and advanced through the grades to rear adm., 1946; dist. med. officer, 3d Naval Dist. Awarded Legion of Merit Medal, World War II. Fellow Am. Coll. of Surgeons, from 1950. Home: Los Gatos, Calif. †

ANDRUS, ELWIN A., lawyer; b. Troy Center, Wis., Mar. 28, 1904; s. Francis Leroy and Mary V. (Watrous) A.; m. Florence R. Stetson, June 15, 1925 (dec.); 1 son, Frank Stetson; m. Marion R. Olson, Aug. 9, 1952. LL.B., U. Wis., 1927. Bar: Wis. bar 1927, also U.S. Patent Office and U.S. Supreme Ct 1927. Practice with Edwin B.H. Tower, Jr., Milw., 1927-28; with patent dept. A.O. Smith Corp., 1928-29, charge patent dept., 1929-39, pvt. practice patent, trade-mark and copyright law, from 1939; asso. Andrus, Sceales, Starke, Sawall, Milw.; lectr. U. Wis. Law Sch., 1947-49; dir. Newport Corp., 1969-78, pres., 1973-78. Fellow Am. Coll. Trial Lawyers (pres. Wis. fellows 1974-79), Am., Wis. bar founds.; mem. Inter-Am. Bar Assn., Am. Bar Assn. (chmn. sect. patent, trademark and copyright law 1958-59), Milw. County Bar Assn., 7th Fed. Circuit Bar Assn. (pres. 1961-62), Wis. State Bar (chmn. sect. patent trademark, copyright law 1960- 62), Am. Patent Law Assn., Chgo. Patent Law Assn., Milw. Patent Law Assn. (pres. 1938-39), Internat. Patent and Trade Mark Assn. (exec. bd. 1955-57), Canadian Patent Inst., Milw. Engrs. Soc., Am. Judicature Soc., Am. Interprofl. Inst. (pres. Milw. chpt. 1973, nat. dir. 1974-77). Christian Scientist (ch. pres. 1960-63, 70-73). Clubs: Masons (32 deg.), Shriners, Lakes. Home: Sun City, Ariz.

ANDRUS, VALLE STEELE, railroad exec.; b. Turfants, Mich., Aug. 19, 1888; s. Sterling Glen and Catherine (Steele) A.; student pub. schs. Chgo.; extension courses law and econs.; m. Edna Brady, June 14, 1914; children—Elizabeth (Mrs. James Cummins), Robert, Margaret (wife of W.S. Busik, U.S.N.), With C.&N.-W. Ry., 1906-07; joined S.P. Co., 1908, r.r. operation, brakeman, trainmaster, asst. to supt. transportation, asst. to gen. mgr., asst. to v.p., 1909-32, mgr. bur. transportation research, 1932-42, asst. to pres. from 1942; pres. So. Pacific Equipment Co.; v.p. Sunset Ry. Republican. Episcopalian. Mason. Clubs: Pacific Railway, Olympic (San Francisco), Los Altos Country. Home: Menlo Park, Calif. †

ANDRY, E. ROBERT, emeritus educator; b. nr. Huntingburg, Ind., Sept. 24, 1907; s. George and (Mason) A.; m. Oma Belle Alvey, Aug. 30, 1931; children—Robert Bruce, Oma Kathryn. A.B., Butler U., 1930, A.M., 1934, B.D., 1934; Ph.D., Southern Baptist Theol. Sem., 1942. Ordained to ministry of the Christian Ch., 1934, and served rural chs. in, Ind., 1930-34, minister, Madison, Ind., 1934-38, Downey Ave. Ch., Indpls., 1938-44; head dept. religion Coll. Liberal Arts and Scis., Butler U., also prof. Bibl. history and lit., 1944-73, prof. emeritus, 1973-80, youth leader and counselor. Ford Found. fellow Jerusalem, 1952-53. Mem. Soc. Bibl. Lit. and Exegesis, Am. Acad. Religion, Am. Schs. Oriental Research, Kappa Delta Rho, Tau Kappa Alpha, Phi Kappa Phi, Theta Phi. Club: Lions (Westfield). Home: Westfield, IN.

ANGELL, ROBERT COOLEY, sociologist; b. Detroit, Apr. 29, 1899; s. Alexis Caswell and Fanny Carey (Cooley) A.; A.B., U. Mich., 1921, A.M., 1922, Ph.D., 1924; Hum.D., Western Mich. U., 1967; m. Esther Robbins Kennedy, Dec. 23, 1922; children—James Kennedy, Sarah Caswell. Instr. sociology U. Mich., Ann Arbor, 1922-26, asst. prof., 1926-30, asso. prof., 1930-35, prof., 1935-69, prof. emeritus, 1969-84, chmn. dept. sociology, 1940-52, dir. Coll. Honors Program, 1957-61; co-dir. Center for Research on Conflict Resolution, 1961-65; exec. dir. Sociol. Resources for Secondary Schs., 1966-71; dir. Tensions Project, UNESCO, Paris, 1949-50; mem. U.S. Nat. Commn. for UNESCO, 1950-56, vice chmn. commn., 1953; Deiches lectr. Johns Hopkins U., 1957. Mem. Charter Study Commn., Ann Arbor, 1953-55. Aviation cadet, 1918-19; capt., lt. col., A.C., 1942-45. Decorated Bronze Star. Mem. Internat. (pres. 1953-56), Am. (pres. 1951), Mich. sociol assns., ACLU, AAUP, Sociol. Research Assn., Mich. Acad. Scis., Arts and Letters, Internat. Studies Assn., Research Club (U. Mich.), Phi Beta Kappa, Delta Kappa Epsilon. Democrat. Author: The Campus, 1928; A Study in Undergraduate Adjustment, 1930; The Family Encounters the Depression, 1936; The Integration of American Society, 1941; The Moral Integration of American Cities. 1951; Free Society and Moral Crisis, 1958; Peace on the March, 1969; The Quest for World Order, 1979; also articles in sociol. jours. Editor: Am. Sociol. Rev., 1946-48. Home: Ann Arbor, Mich. Died May 12, 1984; interred Ann Arbor, Mich.

ANGEVINE, DANIEL MURRAY, physician; b. Saint John, N.B., Can., Oct. 8, 1903; s. James Edwin and Mary Edna (Irvine) A.; B.A., Mt. Allison U., 1924; M.D., C.M., McGill U., 1929; m. Dorothy Edna Shepherd, July 8, 1933; children—James Murray, Charles Douglas, Judith Melanie. Came to U.S., 1932, naturalized, 1942. Resident pathologist Montreal Gen. Hosp., 1929-30; intern U. Pa. Hosp., 1930-32; asst. pathologist N.Y. Hosp., also instr. and asst. prof. pathology, med. coll. Cornell U., 1932-40; pathologist A.I. duPont Inst., Wilmington, Del., 1940-45; vis. asst. prof. pathology U. Pa., 1940-45; dept. chmn. med. sch. U. Wis., Madison, 1945-68, prof. pathology, 1945-74, emeritus, 1974-83; pathologist U. Hosps., 1945-68; assoc. dir. research Armed Forces Inst. Pathology, 1968-74; area cons. pathology VA, 1946-68; cons. pathologist Surgeon Gen. U.S. Army, 1948-68, NRC, 1949-52, USPHS, 1947-52; mem. com. on skeletal system NRS, 1959-66; mem. study group in host factors in lung cancer Am. Cancer Soc., 1959; chief research pathologist Atomic Bomb Casualty Commn., Hiroshima, Japan, 1962-63, 74—, Nat. Adv. Cancer Council Bd., 1970-74; cons. in pathology VA Hosp., Madison, 1978-83, Wis. Alumni Research Found., 1975-83. Served from maj. to col. AUS, 1942-45; ETO. Mem. Am. Assn. Path. and Bact. (pres. 1961-62), Soc. Med. Consultants to Armed Forces, Am. Soc. Exptl. Path. (council, pres. 1953), Soc. Exptl. Biol. and Medicine (council 1950-52), Am. Soc. Clin. Investigation, Harvey Soc., A.M.A., Am. Rheumatism Assn. (exec. council), Am. Socs. for Exptl. Biology (chmn. fed. bd. 1954), Assn. Mil. Surgeons, Washington Acad. Medicine. Author: Atlas of Orthopedic Pathology, 1943. Contbr. to Confs. on Connective Tissue Macy Found., 1950-54; Mechanism of Inflammation (Jasmin and Robert), 1954; Diseases of Connective Tissue (Asboe-Hansen), 1954; Recent Trends in Pathology (Collins), 1959. Chief editor Archives of Pathology, 1963-73. Home: Madison, Wis. Died Feb. 8, 1983.

ANGRIST, ALFRED ALVIN, pathologist; b. Bklyn., Mar. 25, 1902; s. Isaac and Fannie (Levine) A.; m. Sylvia Maude Kasdan, June 9, 1932; 1 son, Burton M. B.S., Coll. City N.Y., 1922; also postgrad., Coll. City N.Y.; M.D., L.I. Coll. Medicine, 1926; postgrad., Columbia, Rutgers U., N.Y. Eye and Ear Infirmary, McGill U., Poly. Inst., Oak Ridge Inst. Nuclear Studies, Cornell U.; D.Sc. (hon.), Yeshiva U., 1970. Intern, resident Bronx, City, Met. hosps.; instr., asst. prof. pathology N.Y. Med. Coll., 1929-34, asso. prof. pathology, 1934-54; prof., chmn. emeritus dept. pathology Albert Einstein Coll. Medicine, 1954-69; dir. lab. services Bronx Municipal Hosp. Center, 1954-69; cons. Dist. Atty. of Queens County; cons. pathologist Queens Hosp. Center (other hosps.); Past bd. dirs. Health Ins. Plan Greater N.Y.; bd. govs. Isaac Alpert Research Inst. Editor: N.Y. State Jour. Medicine. Recipient Townsend Harris medal Coll. City N.Y., 1972; Alumni medal for distinguished service Downstate U. State N.Y. Fellow Coll. Am. Pathologists (founder); mem. Am. Assn. Pathology and Bacteriology, Am. Soc. Exptl. Pathology, Am. Soc. Clin. Pathology, N.Y. Acad. Medicine, N.Y. Pathol. Soc. (past pres.), Queens County Med. Soc. (past pres.), Queensboro Council Social Welfare (past pres.), Queensboro Tb and Health Assn. (dir.), Internat. Acad. Pathology, N.Y. State Med. Soc. (v.p. 1971), N.J. Soc. Pathology, AAAS, Am. Acad. Forensic Sci., Harvey Soc., Am. Fedn. Clin. Research, N.Y. Acad. Scis., N.Y. State Assn. Approved Pub. Health Labs., AMA. Home: Whitestone, N.Y. Died Mar. 19, 1984.

ANGSTMAN, ALBERT HENRY, judge; b. Farmington, Minn., Mar. 23, 1888; s. Jacob H. and Emma (Trout) A.; LL.B., St. Paul Coll. of Law, 1912; m. Mary Frances Chirgwin, Sept. 16, 1919; children—Albert C., Virginia Dawn (dec.), Dorothy May, Joan Frances. Admitted to bar, Minn. and Mont., 1912, and began practice at Helena, Mont.; asst. atty. gen. of Mont., 1921-28; asso. justice Supreme Court of Mont. for term, 1929-35; counsel Pub. Service Commn. of Mont., 1935-37; asso. justice Supreme Court of Mont., term 1937-43, 1945-46, from, 1956. Mem. Naval Reserve Force, World War I. Trustee Mont. Deaconess Sch., Mont. Children's Home and Hosp. Mem. Am. Legion. Methodist. Mason (past master); Elk, Eagle. Club: Kiwanis (pres. 1932). Home: Helena, Mont. †

ANTEVS, ERNST VALDEMAR, research geologist; b. Vartofta, Sweden, Nov. 20, 1888; s. Clas F. Ericsson and Ada S. Johansson; student Skara LÄroverk, 1901-09; Ph. Mag., 1912, Ph. Lic., 1916, Ph.D., 1917, U. of Stockholm; m. Ada E. Bradford, Oct. 8, 1929. Docent, U. of Stockholm, Sweden, 1917-35; research asso., Am. Geog. Soc., 1921-22, Carnegie Instn. of Washington, 1922-23, 1928-29, 1934-40, Geol. Survey, Canada, 1923-24, 1929-30, Harvard U., 1924-26; pvt. research from 1940; specialized in study of last glacial and post-glacial ages, especially problems of time, climatic variations, correlation, age of early man in America, changes of level of land and sea and tree growth as climatic indicator. Mem. Geol. Soc. America, Am. Meteor. Soc., Ecol. Soc., Phila. Acad. Natural Sciences, Am. Geog. Soc., A.A.A.S., Am. Geophys. Union, Assoc. Am. Geog., Soc. Am. Archaeol, Am. Anthropol. Assn. Received awards from Research Corporation New York, 1930. Author of many scientific articles and books on research pertaining mostly to the geologic and climatic history of the past 40,000 years. Address: Globe, Ariz. †

ANTHONY, CARL, lawyer; b. Linden, N.J., Oct. 30, 1929; s. Stanley Carl and Mary (Sheremeta) A. B.A.,

Cornell U., 1950, J.D., 1953. Bar: Calif. 1958, U.S. Ct. Mil. Appeals 1962, U.S. Supreme Ct 1968. Field claim rep. State Farm Mutual Automobile Ins. Co., San Francisco, 1956-58; assoc. William M. Pinney, Jr., San Francisco, 1958, John G. Evans, San Francisco, 1959-67; sole practice law, from 1967; Treas. Flournoy for Gov., San Francisco, 1974; mem. civic com. for Law Day USA, San Francisco, 1961-64, vice chmn. steering com., 1962; lectr. advanced legal edn. program Golden Gate U. Sch. Law, 1978; Chairperson for No. Calif. and Nev., Cornell Fund, 1966-67, 78-80. Served with USAF, 1953-55. Decorated Nat. Defense Service Medal. Mem. State Bar Calif., Bar Assn. San Francisco, Lawyers Club San Francisco (bd. govs. 1969-72), Am. Bar Assn., Am. Arbitration Assn. (lectr., panelist constrn. industry arbitration seminar 1978, mem. No. Calif. adv. council 1978-79, constrn. industry adv. com. 1976—, Whitney North Seymour Sr. arbitration medal 1980), Cornell Club No. Calif. (pres. 1964-65), Phi Alpha Delta. Club: Olympic. Home: San Francisco, Calif. Died Dec. 30, 1980.

ANTHONY, ERNEST LEE, educator; born Wescott, Neb., Sept. 6, 1888; s. Homer Gideon and Anne Elizabeth (Shoush) A.; B.S.A., University of Missouri, 1912, D.Sc., 1952; M.S., Pa. State Coll., 1914; student U. Copenhagen, Denmark, 1923; D.Agr., Mich. State Coll., 1954; m. Goldie Relura Swift, August 7, 1914; children—Helen Louise (Mrs. Paul E. Kindig), Betty Jane (Mrs. John Pearse). Instructor dairy husbandry, Pennsylvania State College, 1912-14, assistant professor, 1914-16, associate professor, 1916-19; prof. of dairy husbandry, W.Va. U., 1919-28; prof. dairy husbandry, Mich. State Coll., 1928-32, dean of agr., 1932-54. Awarded Am. Scandinavian fellowship, Denmark, 1923-24. Mem. Am. Dairy Science Assn. (pres. 1932), Am. Soc. Animal Production, Alpha Zeta, Alpha Gamma Rho. Mem. People Ch. (non-denominational). Club: Rotary, Author: Dairy Laboratory Manual, 1914; Dairy Cattle and Milk Production (with Eckles), 1955; also expt. station and coll. bulletins. Home: East Lansing, Mich. †

ANTHONY, HAROLD ELMER, zoologist; b. Beaverton, Ore., Apr. 5, 1890; s. Alfred Webster and Anabel (Klink) A.; student Pacific U., Forest Grove, Ore., 1910-11; B.S., Columbia, 1915, M.A., 1920; D.Sc., Pacific Univ., Forest Grove, Ore., 1934; m. Edith Irwin Demerel, Apr. 5, 1916 (died 1918); 1 son, Alfred Webster; m. 2d, Margaret Feldt, Feb. 22, 1922; children—Gilbert Chase, Margery Stuart. Field agent U.S. Biol. Survey, 1910-11; staff Am. Museum Natural History 1911-58; asso. curator of mammals, 1919-26, curator, 1926-58, chmn. 1942-58, honorary curator department conservation and general ecology, 1953-56, dean Council Sci. Staff, 1942-47, 51-52, 55-56, dep. dir. of mus., 1952-58; curator Frick Laboratory, from 1958. Member advisory bd. Nat. Parks Historic Sites, Buildings and Monuments of Nat. Park Service, U.S. Dept. Interior, 1946-54; mem. com. for preservation of natural conditions Ecol. Union, 1946-49; mem. Commn. Inst. of Belgian Congo, 1948-54. Engaged in exploration and research in N.Am., Panama, Ecuador, W. Indies, Chile, Africa, Burma, and other countries. Commd. 1st lt. F.A., Nov. 1917; capt., Sept. 1918; served in France, June-Sept. 1918. Member of the Com. Foundation for Study of Cycles, 1948. Fellow N.Y., Cal. acads. science, N.Y. Zoöl. Soc, mem. Am. Orchid Soc., Inc. (treas. from 1955), Am. Soc. Mammalogists (president 1935-37; trustee, 1928-53), Zoological Society London (corresponding member), Nat. Parks Association (trustee 1942-48, and from 1952), Arctic Institute of North America, Ecol. Soc. of Am., Society of Vertebrate Paleontology (charter member). Honorary member Sociedad Colombiana de Ciencias Naturales. Clubs: Men's Garden of N.Y. (pres. 1956-57), Boone and Crockett. Home: Englewood, N.J. †

ANTHONY, JOSEPH GARNER, lawyer; b. Phila., Dec. 19, 1899; s. Charles Howard and Rachel Edith (Humphreys) A.; m. Dorothy McClaren, June 29, 1926; children—Patricia A., Garner A. A.B., Swarthmore Coll., 1923; LL.B., Harvard, 1926. Bar: Hawaii bar 1926, Supreme Ct. of U.S 1936. Atty. gen. of, Hawaii, 1942-43, in pvt. practice, Honolulu, from 1943; Pres. Queen's Med. Center, Honolulu, 1945-49, v.p., 1949-75, bd. dirs., from 1976; regent U. Hawaii, 1951-58; del., chmn. judiciary com. Hawaii Constl. Conv., 1950. Author: Hawaii Under Army Rule; Contbr. 3articles to legal jours. Served with F.A. U.S. Army, World War I. Fellow Am. Bar Found.; mem. Am. Coll. Trial Lawyers, Am. Bar Assn. (state del. 1944-47, 53-62, bd. govs. 1961-64), Hawaii Bar Assn. (pres. 1937-39). Episcopalian. Clubs: Pacific, Oahu Country. Home: Honolulu, HI.

ANTON, JOHN J., banker; b. Chgo., May 20, 1889; s. John and Margaret (Heintz) A.; grad. St. Michael's High Sch., Chicago, 1904; student Am. Inst. Banking, 1906-12, Northwestern Sch. of Commerce, 1914-15; m. Isabel M. Hewson, June 9, 1915; children—John Francis, Richard Joseph, William Roy, James Henry. Became asso. with Union Trust Co., Chicago, 1906, asst. vice pres., 1929; v.p. First Nat. Bank of Chicago, 1929-54, ret. Mem. Ill. Bankers Assn. (pres. 1939-40). Clubs: South Shore Country, Chicago Athletic, Bankers. Address: Ft. Lauderdale, Fla. †

ANZALONE, JOSEPH JAMES, business exec.; b. Chicago, Nov. 20, 1889; s. Anthony and Anna (Congulosa) A.; student DePaul U., 2 yrs.; m. Frances Mary Burnam; 1 son, Edward Harry. Exec. The Van Sweringen Co., Cleveland, since 1922. pres., dir., from 1939; exec. Allegheny Corp., from 1929, v.p., sec. and dir., 1940-54; executive C&O. Ry., 1943-54, treas., 1951-54. Mem. Controllers Inst. Am. (pres. Cleveland control 1936, 1937), Cleveland Real Estate Bd. Home: Shaker Heights, Ohio†

APPEL, JAMES ZIEGLER, physician; b. Lancaster, Pa., May 15, 1907; s. Theodore Burton and Mary Hurford (Calder) A.; B.S., Franklin and Marshall Coll., 1928, Sc.D., 1952; M.D., U. Pa., 1932; m. Florence Burch, Aug. 4, 1933; children—Florence (Mrs. Joseph A. Pontius), Mary (Mrs. Crosby Smith), Nancy (Mrs. William Hess), Charlotte (Mrs. E. Hollihan), James. Intern, Robert Packer Hosp., Sayre, Pa., 1932-33; gen. practice medicine, Lancaster, 1933-35, surgery, from 1935; tng. surgery Lancaster Gen. Hosp., 1935-72; organizer, dir. health dept. Franklin and Marshall Coll., from 1943. Cons. Nat. Center Health Services Research and Devel., U.S. Dept. HEW, from 1968; mem. Pres.' Commn. Nursing Manpower, 1967, Pres.' Commn. Health Facilities, 1968. Adv. bd. Sears-Roebuck Found., 1955-61; sec. Am. Med. Research Found. of A.M.A., 1961-67, pres., 1964-79; trustee Sci. and Ednl. Trust, Med. Soc. Pa., pres., from 1960, pres. Pa. Area IX, PSRO, 1973-79. Served as lt. col. Pa. N.G., 1946. Fellow A.C.S.; mem Med. Soc. Pa. (trustee 1948-58), Med. Service Assn. Pa. (dir. 1945-57), AMA (trustee 1957-67, mem. commn. hosp. accreditation; pres. 1965-66), Lancaster City and County Med. Soc., Phi Beta Kappa, Chi Phi, Phi Alpha Sigma. Mem. United Church of Christ. Home: Lancaster, Pa. Died Aug. 31, 1981.

APPEL, MONTE, lawyer; b. Huron, S.D., Mar. 15, 1887; s. Samuel and Rose (Lyons) A.; A.B., U. of Wis., 1910; LL.B., Harvard, 1913; m. Gladys McGrew, June 16, 1926; children—Patricia, Jacquelin; m. 2d, Raimonda Bartol, January 16, 1965. Admitted to Minn. bar, 1913, D.C. bar, 1918; mem. firm Sanborn, Graves & Appel, St. Paul, 1917-18; practiced in Washington, 1920-33; later mem. Appel & Morton. Asst. counsel U.S. Shipping Board, 1917-18; spl. rep. of U.S. sec. of war, 1918-19; asst. atty. gen. of U.S., 1932-33; mem. Blair, Korner, Doyle & Appel, Washington, 1945-56, Cheavlier French Legion of Honor, 1918. Mem. Am., and District of Columbia bar assns., Delta Kappa Epsilon. Republican. Episcopalian. Club: Metropolitan (Washington, D.C.). Home: Washington, D.C. †

APPERLY, FRANK LONGSTAFF, prof. pathology; b. Victoria, Australia, July 26, 1888; s. William Berman and Pauline (Longstaff) A.; ed. Wesley Coll., Melbourne, Australia, 1903-06, Dublin-U., Ireland, 1913-15; M.A., Oxford U., Eng., 1916, M.D., 1920; M.D., Melbourne U., Australia, 1923, D.Sc., 1924; F.R.C.P., London; m. Elizabeth Mary Foley, June 26, 1915; children—Margaret Ann, Felicity Jean. Came to U.S., 1932. Sr. resident med. officer, Royal Northern Hosp., London, 1918-20; asso. prof. pathology, U. of Melbourne, 1920-32; physician to out-patients, St. Vincent Hosp., Melbourne, 1926-32; prof. pathology, Med. Coll. of Va., from 1932. Served as capt. Royal, Army Med. Corps. in Gallipoli, and Egypt, 1915-18. Awarded fellowship of Queen's Coll., Melbourne U.; Armytage and Syme Research prizes, Melbourne, 1922, 1923; Rhodes Scholar from Melbourne, 1910-13. Mem. Rhodes Scholarship com. of Va., 1937-38. Fellow of American College of Pathologists, 1947. Mem. Am. Assn. Exptl. Pathology, Am. Assn. Pathologists and Bacteriologists, A.A.A.S.; diplomat Am. Bd. Pathology, 1937. Episcopalian. Mason, Clubs: Current Events, Rotary (Richmond, Va.). Author: Patterns of Disease, 1951. Contbr. many research articles to med. jours. of U.S. Australia, England. Home: Richmond, Va. †

APPLE, WILLIAM SHOULDEN, assn. exec.; b. Spokane, Wash., July 28, 1918; s. Harry and Ann (Chon) A.; m. Lucille Harriet Josephs, May 3, 1942; children—Chandra Eden, Hugh Charles. Student, Wayne State U., 1945-46; B.S. in Pharmacy, U. Wis., 1949, M.B.A., 1951, Ph.D., 1954; D.Sc. (hon.), U. L.I., 1966, Union U., 1969. Instr. pharmacy U. Wis., 1951-53, asst. prof., 1953-56, asso. prof., chmn. dept. pharmacy adminstrn., 1956-58; asst. sec. Am. Pharm. Assn., Washington, 1958-59, sec., gen. mgr., 1959, exec. dir., 1959-80, pres., chief exec. officer, from 1980; del. U.S. Pharmacopeial Conv., Washington, 1960; mem. Com. 100 for Nat. Health Ins. Charter bd. dirs. Community Health Inc.; bd. dirs. Am. Assn. World Health Inc.; U.S. com. for WHO. Served to maj. AUS, 1941-46; lt. col. Res. Named Am. Druggist of Yr., 1961, 67, Rho Pi Phi Man of Yr., 1961; recipient J. Leon Lascoff Meml. award, 1961, Wayne State U. Distinguished Service award, 1962, Hugo H. Schaefer medal, 1966, Remington Honor medal, 1967; Colegio de Quimico Farmaceuticos de Chili, 1961; U. Wis. citation, 1965. Fellow AAAS; mem. National Drug Trade Conference (secretary-treas., pres. 1970), Am., Wis. (pres. 1956-57, chmn. bd. 1957-58) pharm. assns), Am. Council Pharm. Edn. (past pres.), Internat. Pharm. Fedn. (U.S. rep. 1959-74, v.p. from 1974), N.Y. Acad. Scis., Can. Pharm. Assn. (hon.), Japan Pharm. Assn. (hon.), Pharm. Soc. Gt. Britain (hon.), Rho Chi, Phi Lambda Upsilon, Phi Kappa Phi. Home: Falls Church, VA.

APPLEBY, STEWART, congressman; b. Asbury Park, N.J., May 17, 1890; s. Hon. T. Frank and Alice (Hoffman) A.; ed. Mercersburg Acad. and Rutgers U., class of 1913; married; children—Kathryn Alice, James Stewart. Licensed real estate and insurance broker; pres. Mattison Realty Co.; v.p. T. Frank Appleby Co., Reliance Realty Co.; developer of Wanamassa Park, and originator of Morgan Grade Crossing Elimination; elected member 69th Congress (1925-26), 3d Dist., N.J.; not a candidate for re-election or renomination. Enlisted U.S. Marine Corps, May 17, 1917; commd. capt. Marine Corps Reserve, 1925; flight duty on U.S.S. Los Angeles and J-3. Mem. Chi Phi, Kiwanis Internat., Newark Athletic Club. Member of Rutgers Alumni Council of Rutgers University. Home: Deal, N.J. †

APPLEGATE, ALBERT ANGELO, coll. adminstr.; b. Atlanta, Ill., Sept. 9, 1889; s. Albert Augustus and Clara, Angeline (Miller) A.; A.B., U. of Ill., 1914; M.A., U. of Mont., 1923; m. Grace Robinson, July 11, 1916; children—Roberta Grace, Albert Augustus. High sch. teacher, Butte, Mont., 1914-19; reporter, copyreader, Butte Standard, 1919-21; instr. U. of Mont., 1921-25; asso. editor, editorial writer, Boise (Ida.) Statesman, 1925-27; spl. writer Portland (Ore.) Oregonian, 1927; prof. journalism Baker Univ. Baldwin, Kan., 1927-29; polit. editor, editorial writer, Butte Post, 1928; mng. editor Bismarck (N.D.) Tribune, 1929; prof. journalism and printing S.D. State Coll., 1929-35; prof. of journalism, head dept., Mich. State University, 1936-55, director of speakers bureau, from 1956. Member of NRA committee for newspaper publishing industry, 1933. Mem. Sigma Delta Chi, Sigma Phi Epsilon. Republican. Presbyterian. Club: Rotary. Asso. editor: Headlining America, 1937, rev. edit, 1940; various monographs. contbr. tech. articles to Editor and Publisher. Home: East Lansing, Mich. †

APPLEGATE, KENNETH POMEROY, utilities executive; b. Englishtown, N.J., Dec. 27, 1890; s. Asher Tunis and Jennie Carson (Wilson) A.; student Troy (N.Y.) Acad., 1906-08; E.E., Rensselaer Poly. Inst., 1912; m. Marion Mount, Apr. 15, 1919; children—Kenneth Pomeroy, Asher Tunis. With Hartford (Conn.) Elec. Light Co. since 1912, president and dir. President Governmental Research Institute; secretary and life trustee Rensselaer Poly. Inst.; dir. Riverside Trust Co., Phoenix Ins. Co., Conn. Fire Ins. Co., Millstone Point Co., Nutmeg Power Co., Hartford Y.M.C.A. Served as lt. (j.g.), U.S. Navy, 1917-19. Mem. Am. Inst. E.E., C. of C. Conglist. Mason (32 deg.). Clubs: Rotary (pres. and dir.), University, Farmington Country, Hartford; Engineers (N.Y.). Home: West Hartford, Conn. †

APPLEMAN, JOHN ALAN, lawyer; b. Webster Groves, Mo., May 14, 1912; s. Milo Donaldson and Emma Catherine (Faust) A.; m. Jean Gerber, Jan. 9, 1935; 1 dau., Jean, 1 son (dec.). A.B., U. Ill., 1932, D.Law, 1935, M.A., 1950. Bar: Ill., Ky., Mass., D.C., U.S. Supreme Ct., other bars. Speaker, lectr. at univs., bar convs.; past pres. various corps.; legal adv. bd. Traumatic Medicine and Surgery for Atty. Condr. Prof. Trial Lawyers Seminar, 1963-72. Author: Automobile Liability Insurance, 1938, Insurance Law and Practice, 25 vols, 1940-46, 36 rev. vols., 1962-81, Preparing and Trying Cases in Illinois (2 vols.), 1950, Illinois Dramshop Briefs, 1951, rev. edit., 1960, Successful Jury Trials, 1952, Successful Appellate Techniques, 1953, Military Tribunals and International Crimes, 1954, 71, How To Use Life Insurance in Estate Analysis, 1954, Basic Estate Planning, 2 vols, 1957, Approved Appellate Briefs, 1958, How To Increase Your Money Making Power, 1959, rev. edit., 1964, 81, Cross-Examination, 1963, Preparation and Trial, 1967, Your Psychic Powers and Immortality, 1968, The Elusive Song, 1969, also fiction and poetry pub., under pseudonyms.; Long playing records and tapes entitled Examples of Cross Examination, 1960, 69; Contbr.: to numerous law jours. and revs. World Book Ency; popular periodicals, poetry jours. Fellow Internat. Acad. Trial Lawyers (gov. 1958-64, dean 1959-60), Internat. Soc. Barristers; mem. ABA, Ill. Bar Assn., Ky. Bar Assn., Champaign County Bar Assn. (gov. 1958-61, pres. 1959-60), Chgo. Bar Assn., Fedn. Ins. Counsel (pres. 1950-52, chmn. bd. govs. 1952-53), Phi Beta Kappa, Phi Eta Sigma. Presbyn. Address: Lake San Marcos, Calif.

APPLETON, HAROLD DONALD, biochemist, educator; b. N.Y.C., July 17, 1918; s. Frank and Jeanette (Goldenberg) A.; m. Gladys Frances Tordik, May 25, 1944. B.A., Bklyn. Coll., 1939; M.S., Purdue U., 1943. Diplomate: Am. Bd. Clin. Chemistry. Lab. asst. Otisville (N.Y.) Hosp., 1939-42; jr. chemist Bellevue Hosp., N.Y.C., 1946-48; chemist N.Y. U. Research Service and; Goldwater Meml. Hosp., 1948-54; sr. chemist Met. Hosp., N.Y.C., 1954-67, dir. dept. clin. chemistry, 1967-73, cons. clin. biochemist, 1972-81; asst. prof. biochemistry and pathology N.Y. Med. Coll., 1960-72, asso. prof. clin. biochemistry, 1972-76, prof., 1976-81, Grad. Sch. Med. Scis., 1972-81; cons. clin. biochemist Flower and Fifth Ave. Hosp., 1972-81. Contbr. articles to profl. jours.; chmn. bd. editors: Clin. Chemistry, 1957-62; mng. editor: 1962-70; editor: Clinica Chimica Acta, 1957-70. Co-chmn. United Jewish Appeal of Greater N.Y., 1959-81; bd. dirs., v.p. research Willcox Research Found. Served with inf. U.S. Army, 1942-46, ETO. Fellow Am. Assn. Clin. Chemistry (Fisher award 1968), Am. Inst. Chemists, N.Y. Acad. Scis.; mem. Am. Chem. Soc., AAAS. Home: Sherman, Conn. Died 1981.*

ARCHER, FRANKLIN MORSE, JR., lawyer; b. Camden, N.J., Sept. 17, 1902; s. Franklin Morse and Bessie (Chandlee) A.; m. Mary Joy Reeve, Sept. 22, 1928; children: Franklin Morse III, Mary Joy, Elizabeth A. (Mrs. Dow Drukker), William Reeve. Grad., Phillips

Exeter Acad., 1919; A.B., Princeton U., 1923; LL.B., Harvard U., 1926. Bar: N.J. 1928. Practiced in, Camden and, Haddonfield; partner firm Archer & Greiner, P.C., from 1928, counsel; asso. prof. U. Pa. Law Sch., 1933-49; Dir. Twitchco Inc.; ret. dir. Heritage Bancorp., Provident Mut. Life Ins. Co.; dir., chmn. exec. com. Heritage Bank, N.A.; Pres. N.J. Bd. Child Welfare, 1957-63; mem. regional adv. com. NLRB, 1960-61. Former mem. N.J. Supreme Ct. Com. on Appellate and Civil Rules.; Pres. Phila. Skating Club, Humane Soc., Ardmore, Pa., 1951-53; bd. mgrs. Cooper Hosp., Camden, pres., 1958-66, chmn. bd. mgrs., 1966; former trustee United Fund Camden County; trustee Community House, Moorestown, N.J.; past bd. dirs. World Wildlife Fund, Inc. Fellow Am. Coll. Probate Counsel (property, probate-trust law), N.J. (com. removal judges); mem. Am., N.J., Camden County bar assns. World Affairs Council Phila. (past dir.), N.J. Audubon Soc. (adv. com.), Phi Beta Kappa. Clubs: Rotarian (Camden) (past pres.); Princeton (Phila.), Philadelphia (Phila.), Sunday Breakfast (Phila.); Moorestown Field, Tavistock Country, Barnegat Light Yacht; Nassau (Princeton, N.J.). Home: Moorestown, NJ.

ARCHER, JEROME WALTER, educator; b. Milw., May 23, 1907; s. James A. and Anne (Herkens) A.; m. Anne Stanish, Aug. 19, 1933; 1 son, Robert Hugh. A.B. cum laude, Marquette U., 1930, M.A., 1932; postgrad., U. Chgo., 1936; Ph.D. (Univ. fellow 1939-40), Northwestern U., 1942. Chmn. dept. English West Milwaukee High Sch., 1930-36; mem. faculty Marquette U., 1936-63, prof. English, 1952-63, chmn. dept., 1948-63; chmn. dept. English Ariz. State U., Tempe, 1963-71, prof., 1963-77, prof. emeritus, 1977-82; cons. U.S. Office Edn., 1966-71. Co-author: A Reader for Writers, 3d edit, 1971, Exposition, 2d edit, 1971; Editor: Research and Development of English Programs in the Junior College, 1965; Author articles; contbr. to profl. jours. Mem. Nat. Council Tchrs. English (2d v.p., program chmn. 1956, dir. 1953-62, 69-72, chmn. nominating com. coll. sect. 1973, dir. European study tour 1960, adv. bd. Coll. English 1963-65), Modern Lang. Assn., Conf. Coll. Composition and Communication (chief exec. officer 1955), Medieval Acad. Am., Am. Dialect Soc., AAUP, English Club Greater Milw. (pres. 1949-51), Ariz. English Tchrs. Assn., English-Speaking Union (pres. Phoenix 1966-69, 74-76, dir. 1969-82), Phi Kappa Phi. Roman Catholic. Club: Mountain Shadows. Home: Scottsdale, Ariz. Died Aug. 19, 1982.

ARCHER, RAYMOND LEROY, clergyman; b. Adonis, W.Va., Oct. 31, 1887; s. William Jackson and Sarah V. (Twyford) A.; student Washington and Jefferson Coll., 1907-08; A.B., U. of Pittsburgh, 1911; A.M., Drew Univ., Madison, N.J., 1923; Ph.D., Hartford Sem. Foundation, 1935; student U. of Frankfurt, Germany, 1929; m. Edna Priscilla Caye, Apr. 27, 1916. Admitted to Pittsburgh Annual Conf. Methodist Episcopal Ch., 1909, ordained to ministry, 1911, commd. missionary to Buitenzorg, Java, Oct. 1911; served as missionary, 1911-20, supt. Java Dist., 1921-22; supt. Sumatra Mission (Medan), 1924-29; treas. Meth. Mission and mission supt. Annual Conf. (Singapore), 1933-42; asst. treas. Meth. Bd. Missions N.Y. City, 1942-44, asso. sec. Meth. Bd. Missions N.Y. City, 1945-50, bishop Singapore Area from 1950. Author: Mohammedan Mysticism in Sumatra, 1935. Home: New York, NY. †

ARDERY, JULIA HOGE SPENCER, civic worker, ex-Dem. nat. committeewoman; b. Richmond, Va., Sept. 16, 1889; d. Issac J. and Sally L. (Pendleton) Spencer; grad. Hamilton Coll., 1908; student Transylvania Coll., 1908-09; m. William B. Ardery, Apr. 14, 1910; children—William B., Winston B., Philip p. Vice chmn. Paris (Ky.) Sesquicentennial, 1939, Sesquicentennial Commn., Commonwealth of Ky., 1940-42; curator, chmn. restoration Duncan Tavern Historic Center, D.A.R., from 1940; mem. Ky. Historic Markers Com., 1949-64; mem. Ky. Commn. Preservation Historic and Archtl. Assets, from 1951; mem. exec. com. Ky. Civil War Centennial Com., 1958-65; Gov's Adv. Com. Ky. Hwys. Program, 1957-60. County chmn. fund drives A.R.C., World War II. Nat. elector sec. Electoral Coll., from 1944; del. Dem. Nat. Conv., mem. platform and resolutions com., 1956; Dem. nat. committeewoman for Ky., 1956-60. Trustee Kate McClintock Home for Aged Women, 1930-47. Mem. Bourban County (Ky.) Health and Welfare League (past pres.), Ky. Hist. Soc. (hon. v.p., mem. exec. com. 1932-61; distinguished service award Ky. 1968), Nat. Soc. Daus. of Founders and Patriots of Am., Order First Families Va. (burgess Ky. 1935-71), Soc. Descs. King William I the Conqueror (life founder), Brit.-Am. Soc. (life), Nat. Soc. Colonial Dames Am. in Commonwealth Ky., Internat. Soc. Daughters Barons Runnemede, D.A.R., Delta Delta Delta (outstanding alumnae award Ky. 1957). Mem. Disciples of Christ Ch. Club: Filson (Louisville). Author hist., general books, records. Address: Paris, KY. †

ARENDS, LESLIE CORNELIUS, congressman; b. Melvin, Ill., Sept. 27, 1895; s. George Teis and Talea (Weiss) A.; grad. high sch., Melvin, 1912; student Oberlin College, 1912-13; Doctor of Laws, Illinois Wesleyan University; m. Betty Tychon; 1 dau., Letty. Engaged in farming, from 1920; pres. Commercial State Bank, Melvin; mem. 74th to 91st Congresses 17th Ill. Dist., Rep. whip, ranking minority member Armed Services Committee and Committee on Standards of Official Conduct. Served USN, 1918; honorably discharged, 1919. Trustee of Ill. Wesleyan U., Mem. Am. Legion, Republican. Methodist. Mason (33 deg.). Home: Melvin, Ill. Died July 16, 1985.

ARIES, LEON JUDAH, surgeon; b. Chgo., Feb. 25, 1909; s. Frank and Lizzie (Narensky) A.; B.S., U. Ill., 1927, M.D., 1931, M.S., 1931; Ph.D., Northwestern U., 1940; m. Marie Dorothy Lhevine, Sept. 23, 1945; children—Jane Aries Levin, Elizabeth Aries Berman, Nancy. Intern, Cook County Hosp., Chgo., 1931-33, resident, 1933-35; practice medicine, specializing in surgery, Chgo., from 1935; asst. prof. surgery Northwestern U. Med. Sch., 1940-55; prof. surgery Cook County Grad. Sch., 1940-65, Chgo. Med. Sch., from 1957; attending surgeon Cook County Hosp., St. Joseph Hosp., Edgewater Hosp., Mt. Sinai Hosp.; pres. staff Edgewater Hosp., Chgo. Sec. br. Jewish Children's Bur.; trustee Francis Parker Sch. Served to maj. AUS, 1943-45. Recipient Chgo. Surg. Soc. award, 1940. Mem. A.C.S., Internat. Coll. Surgeons, Sigma Xi, Alpha Omega Alpha. Contbr. articles to profl. jours. Home: Chicago, Ill. Died Dec. 18, 1981.

ARLING, LEONARD SWENSON, physician, surgeon; b. Chicago City, Minn., Nov. 25, 1910; s. Charles Emil Swenson and Emily Charlotte (Carlson); B.S., U. Minn., 1933, M.B., 1934, M.D., 1936; m. Marion Arline Schroeder, June 24, 1938; children—Heather Marion (Mrs. Frank Louis Greenagel), Pamela Jill (Mrs. Walter A. Simmons), Bryan Jeremy. Intern, Receiving Hosp., Detroit, 1935-36; gen. practice medicine, Mpls., 1936-44, practice limited to indsl. medicine and surgery, from 1944; physician Twin Cities assembly plant Ford Motor Co. 1936-73; founder, dir. Medical, Inc., Mpls.; founder, co-owner and pres. N.W. Indsl. Clinic P.A., from 1944; mem. staff, chief of staff Met. Med. Center, Mpls., 1954. Mem. Gov.'s Adv. Com. on Employment of Physically Handicapped in Minn., 1948-55; regional cons. R.R. Retirement Bd. for Minn., N.D., S.D., Mont., Wis. Bd. dirs. United Hosp. Fund of Mpls. and Hennepin County, 1956-73, Jr. Achievement Mpls. and Hennepin County; bd. dirs., mem. investment com. Minn. Med. Found.; mem. Pres.'s Club, U. Minn. Found., E.T. Bell Assos., U. Minn. Diplomate Am. Bd. Preventive Medicine in occupational medicine. Fellow Indsl. Med. Assn. (chmn. small plants services com., sec. 1957-60); mem. AMA (chmn. joint conf. council indsl. health, chmn. state com. 1954, 55), Central States Soc. Indsl. Medicine and Surgery (gov., pres. 1956- 57), Minn. Med. Assn. (chmn. com. indsl. health 1948-55), Minn. Acad. Occupational Medicine and Surgery (pres. 1964), Medical Alumni Assn. of U. Minn. (pres. 1969), Am. Cancer Soc. (unit dir.; pres. Hennepin County unit 1964-65), C. of C. Greater Mpls., AAAS, Citizens League Greater Mpls., Isaac Walton League, Swedish-Am. Inst. Mpls., Photog. Soc. Am., Phi Rho Sigma. Lutheran. Mason (32 deg., K.T. Shriner). Clubs: Minneapolis; Midway (St. Paul). Home: Minneapolis, Minn. Died Jan. 9, 1979.

ARMBRUSTER, CHRISTIAN HERMAN, lawyer; b. Yonkers, N.Y., Mar. 14, 1921; s. Christian and Helen (Sergel) A.; B.A., Columbia U., 1944, LL.B., 1947. Admitted to N.Y. bar, 1948; assoc. firm Spence, Hotchkiss, Parker & Duryea, N.Y.C., 1947-48; partner firm Armbruster & Armbruster, N.Y.C., from 1948. Supr., Westchester County, 1949-59; mem. N.Y. State Assembly, 1959-66, N.Y. State Senate, 1967-68; trustee Yonkers Gen. Hosp.; adv. com. Pace Coll., Westchester. Served to maj. USAAF, 1943-46. Mem. Am. Legion. Mem. Reformed Ch. Club: Masons. Home: Bronxville, N.Y.

ARMBRUSTER, JOHN PHILIP, trust co. exec.; b. Bklyn., Aug. 1, 1919; s. Philip and Helen (Perdue) A.; student N.Y. State Bankers Sch. Agriculture, 1955-56, Stonier Grad. Sch. Banking, 1965-67; m. Evelyn Helen Worster, Dec. 28, 1941; children—J. Mitchell, Allan P., Dean F., Susan L. With Fed. Res. Bank N.Y., N.Y.C., 1937-57; with Long Island Trust Co., Garden City, N.Y., 1957-82, regional v.p., 1965-68, v.p., 1965-82, sec., 1972-82. Served with AUS, 1941-46, 51-52. Mem. Great Neck Businessmen's Assn. (pres. 1969-65, dir. 1963-66), Great Neck C. of C. (treas., dir. 1965-68). Club: Great Neck Lions. Home: Elmont, N.Y. Died 1982.

ARMENTROUT, JAMES SYLVESTER, clergyman, educator; b. Matuta, Tenn., July 14, 1887; s. Cyrus Bruce and Loutetia (Moore) A.; A.B., Washington Coll., 1905; B.D., Princeton Theol. Sem. (Old Testament fellowship), 1909; M.A., U. Pa., 1930; Ph.D., Yale, 1933; LL.D. (hon.), Waynesburg Coll., 1942; m. Jane Churchill Gulick, Aug. 23, 1909; 1 son, James Sylvester. Ordained to ministry Presbyn. Ch., 1908; pastor New Hope (Pa.) Ch., 1909-11; asst. pastor First Ch., Lancaster, 1911-14, Pine St. Ch., Harrisburg, 1914-17; dir. leadership edn. Bd. Christian Edn. Presbyn. Ch. U.S.A., 1917-44; prof. Christian edn. McCormick Theol. Sem., Chicago, from 1944. Mem. Nat. Council Chs. (div. Christian edn.), Am. Assn. Sch. Religious Edn., Phi Delta Kappa. Author: Administering the Vacation Church School, 1928. Home: Chicago, Ill. †

ARMENTROUT, WINFIELD DOCKERY, educator; b. Marshall, Mo., Nov. 2, 1889; s. Silas Winfield and Cora (Osborn) A.; A.B., Mo. Valley Coll., 1910; A.M., Columbia, 1914; grad. study, Ohio State Univ., 1922; Ed.D., Harvard Univ., 1926; LL.D., Missouri Valley College, 1936; m. Dora Sauer, Dec. 28, 1916; children—William Winfield, Jeanette, Instr., high sch., Chanute, Kan., 1910-11, Fort Scott, Kan., 1911-13; head of normal training dept., high sch., Topeka, Kan., 1914-15; asso. prof. edn. and psychology, Kan. State Teachers Coll., 1915-19; prin. jr. high sch., Lawrence, Kan., 1919-20; dir. instrn. and head of dept. training schs., Colo. State Coll. of Edn., 1920-31; v.p. Colo. State Coll. Edn., 1931-55, v.p. emeritus, 1955, acting pres., 1940-41; prof. education, cons. to faculty Colorado Woman's College, 1955-57; specialist in curriculum and textbook production George Peabody College, Seoul, Korea, from 1957; president Rocky Mountain Radio council, 1946-50; curriculum specialist, Denver pub. schs., half-time, 1922-23; extension lecturer in edn., Boston U., 1925-26; visiting prof. edn., Columbia U., summer 1927, U. of Hawaii, summer 1931. Mem. N.E.A., Phi Delta Kappa, Kappa Delta Pi, Pi Kappa Delta, Acacia. Conglist. Mason. Rotarian. Author: Introduction to Philosophy of Education (with H. S. Ganders and L.G.Thomas), 1947 Home: Greeley, Colo. †

ARMS, JOHN HEYL RASER, b. Williamsport, Pa., Feb. 28, 1888; s. Augustus Nice and Celeste Stoughton (Raser) A.; ed. Pingry Sch., Elizabeth, N.J., 1905; mech. engring., Cornell U., 1909; m. Dec. 1913, Edith Lucia Wilkinson (dec.); children—Robert (dec.), Richard Philip; m. Dec. 1929, Mary Darley Tucker (dec.); 1 son, Leonard Theodore; Instr. Rochester (N.Y.) schs., 1909-10; coordinating engr. Am. Wood Working Machinery Co., 1907-13; production control for Warner Bros. Co., Bridgeport, Conn., 1914-15; consultant in production control, 1915-17; asst. to exec. v.p. and in charge of personnel and plant operation Mfg. Co. of America, Phila., 1919-24; dealer service organization, Miller Rubber Company, Akron, Ohio, 1924-25; management consultant for various corporations, 1925-33; partner Arms & Madeheim, engineers, 1930-34; special agent U.S. and New Jersey Dept. of Labor, Employment Service, 1931-33; sec., gen. mgr. United Engring. Trustees, Inc., since 1933; sec. The Engring. Foundation from 1937; asst. sec. John Fritz Medal Fund Corp., 1935-39; sec. John Fritz Medal Board of Award from 1939; treas. Daniel Guggenheim Medal Fund, Inc., 1935-39, dir., 1937-39, and from 1940, sec. from 1944. In selective service div. U.S. War Dept., Phila., 1918, World War. Instr. and special examiner first aid and life saving, Am. Red Cross, 1927-35; director Oranges and Maplewood chapter; instructor in first aid N.Y. chapter, 1940-45; director Employment Conference Oranges & Maplewood Welfare Federation, 1930-33. Mem. A.S.M.E., Inst. Aeronautical Scis., Automobile Old Timers, Soc. Colonial Wars, Pa. Soc. S.R., Music Educators Assn. of N.J., Zeta Psi. Republican. Episcopalian. Mason (Shriner). Clubs: Engineers, Scarsdale (N.Y.) Golf. Home: Bronxville, N.Y. †

ARMSTRONG, DONALD, army officer, bus. exec., editor; b. Stapleton, N.Y., Apr. 15, 1889; s. Samuel Treat and Alice (Cobin) A.; A.B., A.M., Columbia, 1909; grad. Cours Superieur Technique de l'Artillerie, French Army, Paris, 1924; grad. Army Industrial Coll., 1927; LL.D. (hon.), Mt. Mary Coll., Milw.; m. Frances Richards Newcomb, Aug. 22, 1912 (dec. Dec. 1955); 1 son, Warren Putnam; m. 2d, Irene Troukatchoff de Fonton, Dec. 22, 1956. Commd. 2d lt. CAC, U.S. Army, 1910; served Ft. Monroe, Va., Fort William, Me., Fort Barrancas, Fla., Fort Monroe (coast defense adjutant); assigned to 35th Arty. Brigade, June 1918, as major, brigade adjutant; staff chief of artillery, A.E.F., Oct. 1918; attached to Direction de l'Artillerie, French Army, Paris, Jan. 1919; asst. mil. attaché, Am. Embassy, Paris, 1919-24; student officer, Centre d'Etudes Tactiques d'Artillerie, Metz, June 1920, French Coast Arty. Sch. Toulon, May 1921; transferred to Ordnance Dept., 1923; assigned to Watertown Arsenal, 1924, Planning Branch, Office Asst. Sec. of War, 1927; mem. F.A. Bd., Fort Bragg, 1931; Office Chief of Ordnance, as chief Maintenance Div., 1935; became exec. officer, Chicago Ordnance Dist., July 1939; promoted to brig. gen., May 22, 1942; chief Tank Automotive Center, Detroit, 1942; comdg. gen. Ordnance Replacement Training Center, Aberdeen, Md., 1943; comdt. Army Indsl. College, Washington, 1944; comdt. Industrial College of Armed Forces, 1945-46; asst. to chmn. exec. com. American Standards Association, 1946-47; v.p. U.S. Pipe & Fdry. Co., pres. and mem. bd. dirs., 1947-51; dir. Sloss-Sheffield Steel & Iron Co., United Concrete Pipe Corp., 1948-51. With Mut. Security Agency, Am. Embassy, Paris, 1952; dir. Editorial Adv. Services, Washington, 1953-56; comdt. national strategy seminars for reserve officers National War College, Washington, 1959, 60. Decorated Distinguished Service Medal, Legion of Merit (U.S. Army, United States Navy), Chevalier Legion of Honor; Order of Solidaridad (Panama); Victory medal with 2 clasps; Medal for Excellence, Columbia, 1945. Prof. lecturer, classics dept., George Washington U., 1937-39. Pres. Am. Mil. Inst., 1945-53, Nat. Acad. Econs. and Polit. Scis., 1953-54. Fellow A.A.A.S.; mem. N.Y. Hist. Soc., Newcomen Soc., Am. Sociol. Soc., Phi Delta Theta; fellow Royal Soc. Arts, Mason. Clubs: Army and Navy, Cosmos (Washington); University (N.Y.C.); Racquet, (Phila.). Contbr. to mags. Home: Washington, DC. †

ARMSTRONG, FREDERIC PALMER, banker; b. Keyport, N.J., Nov. 29, 1887; s. Frederic Francis and Mary Emma (Sellick) A.; student pub. schs., Keyport; m. Mable Jan Schenck, Oct. 18, 1910; children—Dorothy (Mrs. James F. Humphreys), Doris (Mrs. James G. Patton). Clk., various other positions Keyport Banking Co., 1903-29, pres., 1929-56; chmn. bd. Monmouth County Nat. Bank (merger Keyport Banking Company with other banks), from 1956, treasurer and director Surf Theater Company, Keyport Theater Co.; dir. Fed. Res.

Bank of N.Y. Commr. Port of N.Y. Authority, 1945-52. Mem. Monmouth Co. Bankers and Clearing House Assn. (past pres.), N.J. Bankers Assn. (pres. 1942-43). Republican. Mem. Reformed Ch. Club: Keyport Yacht. †

ARMSTRONG, GEORGE ALEXANDER, foreign service officer; b. Nyack, N.Y., Sept. 15, 1887; s. James Sinclair and Lizzie Howard (Welsh) A.; A.B., Princeton U., 1909; m. Elizabeth Inglis, Dec. 17, 1919 (died June 17, 1933); children—Mary Howard, George Alexander. Engaged in various business enterprises, 1909-24; vice consul at Zürich, Switzerland, 1924-28; consul at Nice, France, 1928-30; 2d sec. Am. Embassy, Warsaw, Poland, 1930-33, Berlin, Germany, 1933-35; Am. consul at Kingston, Jamaica, 1935-36; 2d sec. Am. Legation, Dublin, Irish Free State, 1936-37; consul at Colombo, Ceylon, 1937-39; 2nd sec. Am. Legation, Lisbon, Portugal, 1939; consul, Malaga, Spain, 1940-41, Manchester, Eng., from 1941. Served as 2d lt., U.S. Army, World War. Episcopalian. Club: University (New York). Home: New York, N.Y.†

ARMSTRONG, GEORGE THOMSON, phys. chemist; b. Castor, Alta., Can., Dec. 8, 1916; s. George Alexander and Margaret (Faris) A. (parents Am. citizens); m. Patricia Eliza Cadigan, June 16, 1945; children—Margaret Lucille Armstrong Chapman, Michael Faris Armstrong. B.S., U. Fla., 1939, M.S., 1943; Ph.D., Johns Hopkins U., 1948. Grad. asst. U. Fla., Gainesville, 1940-42; scientist Radiation Lab. Mass. Inst. Tech., Cambridge, 1942-45; jr. instr. Johns Hopkins U., 1945-48; instr. chemistry Yale U., 1948-51; lectr. Boston U., 1950-51; phys. chemist Nat. Bur. Standards, Washington, from 1951, chief thermochemistry sect., 1968-74, chief thermochem. measurements and standards, 1974-78, dep. chief chem. thermodynamics div., 1978; on detail to Office Toxic Substances EPA, 1978, 80; cons. in thermochemistry, calorimetry, energy-info. services; mem. Interunion Commn. on Biothermodynamics, from 1975, mem. IUPAC Commn. on Thermodynamics, 1977—. Contbr. articles to profl. jours.; Editor: Jour. Chem. Thermodynamics, from 1977. Mem. Woodside Park Civic Assn., from 1960; bd. dirs. Steamboat Run Community Assn., from 1978; treas., from 1980. Recipient Silver Medal award Dept. Commerce, 1967. Fellow Am. Phys. Soc., Washington Acad. Scis., AAAS (life); mem. Am. Chem. Soc., N.Y. Acad. Scis. (life), U.S. Calorimetry Conf. (dir. 1961-66, chmn. 1964, counsellor 1970-74, 77-80), Philos. Soc. Washington (council 1973-80, pres. 1978), ASTM (chmn. gaseous fuels com. 1974-79), Phi Beta Kappa, Sigma Xi, Phi Kappa Phi. Mem. United Ch. of Christ. Clubs: Cosmos (Washington), Potomac Appalachian Trail (Washington), St. Andrew's Society (Washington). Home: Silver Spring, MD.

ARMSTRONG, ROLF, artist; b. Bay City, Mich., April 21, 1889; s. Richard and Elizabeth (Scott) A.; student Chicago Art Inst., 1909-11, Julian Acad., Paris, 1920; unmarried. Address: New York, N.Y. †

ARMSTRONG, W(ALLACE) D(AVID), biochemist; b. Hunt County, Tex., July 8, 1905; s. Charles Alexander and Eva (Hulsey) A.; A.B., U. Tex., 1926, NRC fellow, 1926-27; M.S., NYU, 1928; Ph.D., U. Minn., 1933, M.D., 1937; Commonwealth Fund fellow, Copenhagen and London, 1938-39; Dr. Odontology, Stockholm, Sweden, 1955; m. Mary Elizabeth Garland, Aug. 19, 1929; children—Margaret Ann, John Wallace. Asst. in organic chemistry U. Tex., 1925-26; chemist Tex. Co., 1928-29; asst. dept. physiol. chemistry Med. Sch., U. Minn., 1929-33, instr., 1933-37, asst. prof., 1937-40, assoc. prof., 1940-43, prof., 1943-46, prof., head dept., 1946-74, Regents' prof. biochemistry, from 1973; dir. intramural research Nat. Inst. Dental Research, Bethesda, Md., 1974-76. Rockfeller fellowship, Stockholm, Sweden, 1950. Mem. Josiah Macy, Jr., Conf. on Metabolic Interrelations; cons. USPHS, Mpls. VA Hosp. Recipient Minn. Med. Soc. prize and award 1937; Pierre Fauchard Acad. medal, 1976. Fellow AAAS, Am. Coll. Dentistry (hon.; W.J. Gies award 1966); mem. Am. Soc. Biol. Chemists, Soc. Exptl. Biology and Medicine, Am. Chem. Soc., Minn. Path. Soc., Internat. Assn. Dental Research (pres. 1945-46; Biol. Mineralization award 1966, H.T. Dean award 1967), Biochem. Soc., Am. Physiol. Soc., Phi Chi, Alpha Omega Alpha, Phi Lambda Upsilon. Contbr. tech. jours. Home: Minneapolis, Minn. Died June 7, 1984.

ARNAUD, LEOPOLD, architect, educator; b. N.Y.C., Mar. 2, 1895; s. Leopold and Fortunée (Zarcharie) A.; grad. Lycée Janson de Sailly (U. Paris), 1914; B.Arch., Columbia, 1918, M.S. in Architecture, 1933; student École des Beaux Arts, Paris, 1919-24 (Architecte Diplômé par le Governement Francais); m. Blanchette Stearns, Nov. 5, 1927; children—Blanche Fortunée, Anthony Leopold. Archtl. designer Warren & Wetmore, architects, N.Y., 1924-29; designer Voorhees, Gmelin & Walker, N.Y., 1929-32; lectr. history of architecture Columbia, 1929-32, instr. architecture, 1933-35, asst. prof., acting dean Sch. Architecture, 1935-37, prof. history of architecture, 1937-42, Ware prof. architecture, 1942, dean architecture, 1937-60; dean emeritus and Ware prof. emeritus, 1960-84, dir. Sch. Painting and Sculpture, 1948-56, Sch. Dramatic Arts, 1948-53; dir. Casa Italiana, Columbia, 1950-55; vis. Carnegie prof. to S.A., 1943; Dept. State lectr. S.Am., 1954; with USIA, 1959-64; cultural attache Am. embassy, Brazil, 1960-62, Am. embassy, Spain, 1962-64. Served with F.A., U.S. Army U.S. Army, 1917-19, A.E.F., 13 months; wounded at Pexonne, 1918. Decorated Silver Star citation; recipient Silver medal Soc. des Architectes Diplômés par le Govt. Francais; Medaille du Profésseurat, Soc. des Architectes Provinciaux, France; chevalier Legion of Honor (France), 1949, officier, 1959; cav. officer Merito della Repubblica (Italy), 1955; knight Order Corpus Christi, Toledo (Spain), 1966; grand officier Order Isabela Catolica (Spain), 1976. Fellow AIA; mem. Assn. Collegiate Schs. Architecture (pres. 1940-42), Sch. Art League of N.Y. (pres. 1941-45), Theta Delta Chi; hon. mem. Instituto de Cultura Hispánica Madrid, socs. architects of Peru, Mexico, Buenos Aires, Ecuador and Colombia; corr. mem. Nat. Acad. Fine Arts, Argentina, Academie d'Archtecture de Paris. Clubs: Century, Columbia U., Ex-mems. of Squadron A. Contbr. to archtl. jours. Home: Fontainebleau, France. Died Dec. 9, 1984.

ARNDT, JOSEPH M, corp. ofcl.; b. Walnut Ridge, Ark., Feb. 25, 1887; s. Herman Arndt; m. Bertha Freund, Jan. 11, 1919; 1 son, Joseph M. Exec. v.p., dir., mem. exec. com. Gaylord Container Corp.; dir. Crown Zellerbach Corp. Mem.Fibre Box Assn. (dir.). Home: St. Louis, Mo.†

ARNOLD, AEROL, educator; b. Chgo., May 30, 1911; m. Anna Bing, Nov. 18, 1960. Ph.B., U. Chgo., 1931, M.A., 1933, Ph.D., 1937. Faculty U. Tex., 1936, U. Minn., 1937, Northwestern U., 1938; prof. English U. So. Calif., Los Angeles, from 1946. Author: Thomas Nashe's Criticism of the State of Education in England, 1947; Contbr. articles on Shakespeare and 20th Century poetry and fiction to profl. jours. Served with USAAF, 1943-46. Named All Univ. Prof. U. So. Calif., 1976. Mem. AAUP, MLA, Renaissance Assn. Am. Address: Los Angeles, Calif.

ARNOLD, ARCHIBALD VINCENT, army officer; b. Collinsville, Conn., Feb. 24, 1889; s. Theobald and Josephine Arnold; B.S., U.S. Mil. Acad., 1912; grad. Field Arty. Sch., Advanced Course, 1928. Command and Gen. Staff Sch., 1930, Army War Coll., 1935; m. Margaret Treat, Apr. 11, 1917; children—Margaret Cornell, Archibald Vincent, Joan Whitney, Charles Treat. Commd. 2d lt. Inf., U.S. Army, 1912, and advanced through the grades to general, 1941; participated in campaigns in the Aleutians, 1943, The Marshalls, 1944, liberation of the Philippines, Leyte, 1944-45, Okinawa, 1945; first Mil. Gov. of Korea, 1945; chief U.S. Del. on US-USSR Commn. for Korea, 1946; apptd. permanent maj. gen., 1947; retired for physical disability, 1948. Decorations; D.S.M. with Oak Leaf Cluster, Silver Star, Legion of Merit, Air Medal. Home: Cranberry Lake, N.Y.†

ARNOLD, CHARLES HARRISON, physician and surgeon; b. near Dorchester, Neb., Oct. 18, 1888; s. Henry and Ann Elizabeth (Gifford) A.; student Cotner U., Lincoln, and Valparaiso (Ind.) U.; M.D., Chicago Coll. Medicine and Surgery, 1913; studied at U. of Vienna, 1930 and 1933; m. Irma Sears, Jan. 20, 1912 (died 1926); children—Hubert Andrew, Faith Elizabeth; m. 2d, Winifred Owen McCoy, June 11, 1928. Began practice at Lincoln, 1913; chief surgeon and lecturer on surgery, Dr. Benjamin F. Bailey Sanatorium; mem. attending surg. staff and lecturer on surgery, St. Elizabeth's Hospital; mem. surg. staff Bryan Memorial Hosp.; surgeon for Travelers' Ins. Co.; spl. lecturer surg. dept. Creighton U. Sch. of Medicine, 1941-46; surg. consultant, Provincial Hosp.; hon. prof. of surgery West China Union Univ., Chengtu, Szechwan, China, Chinese Army Med Center, Shanghai; bd. dirs. Am. S.S. Union. Mem. adv. bd. Neb. State Hosp., Neb. Labor Commn. Trustee Wesleyan University; director, past v.p YMCA; member United Board for Christian Colls. in China. Delegate of A.M.A. to Internat. Goiter Conf., Berne, Switzerland, 1933. Served as officer U.S. Army, World Wars I and II, ret. lt. col.; mem. Lost Legion, 1917-18. Fellow Internat. Bd. Surgery (founder), Internat. Coll. Surgeons (trustee), Royal Society Medicine; hon. mem. Sao Paulo Surg. Soc.; mem. Am. and Neb. medical associations, Lancaster County Med. Soc., Am. Med. Assn. of Vienna, Nat. Mil. Surgeons Soc., Am. Assn. for Study of Goiter, mem. World Medical Assn., Order of the Purple Heart Nat. Aeronautic Assn., Am. Legion, 40 and 8, Vets. Fgn. Wars (past comdr.), Neb. Hist. Soc., Assn. Consultants World War II, Chinese Med. Soc. Am. Inter. Profl. Inst. (past pres.), Beta Theta Pi, Democrat. Member Christian (Disciples) Church (past elder). Mason (past master, past high priest, 32 degrees, past commander K.T., Shriner); Knight Red Cross of Constantine. Clubs: University, Polemic, Cosmopolitan, Hiram, Sojourners. Contbr. articles. Mem. editorial bd. Jour. Internat. Coll. Surgeons. Home: Lincoln, Neb. †

ARNOLD, DUANE, utility exec.; b. Sanborn, Iowa, Nov. 12, 1917; s. Grant D. and Beatrice (Short) A.; m. Henrietta Dows, Apr. 27, 1946; children—Margaret Helen, Duane, Elizabeth, Mary. B.A., Grinnell Coll., 1942. Dist. mgr. Iowa Electric Light & Power Co., Cedar Rapids, 1948-49, ops. supt., 1949-50, v.p. ops., 1950-54, v.p., gen. mgr., 1954-61, pres., 1961-69, 69, chmn., pres., 1969-83; chmn., dir. Perpetual Savs. & Loan Assn.; dir. Mchts. Nat. Bank, Cedar Rapids, Banks of Iowa; pres., dir. Cedar Rapids & Iowa City R.R., Iowa Land & Bldg. Co. Chmn. Community Chest, 1953; Trustee Iowa Center for Regional Progress; bd. dirs. Cedar Rapids YMCA, pres., 1959-60, Pub. Welfare Bur.; trustee NCCJ, Midwest Research Inst., Mercy Hosp., Cedar Rapids, Cedar Rapids Art Assn., Nature Center, Cedar Rapids; trustee, chancellor Herbert Hoover Presdl. Library Assn. Served with USMCR, 1942-45; lt. col. Res. Decorated Purple Heart, Bronze Star. Mem. Mo. Valley Elec. Assn. (pres. 1958), U.S. C. of C., Cedar Rapids C. of C. (pres., dir. 1969), Assn. for Bus. Edn. (dir.). Presbyterian (trustee, deacon. elder). Clubs: Masons, Shriners, Cedar Rapids Country; City (N.Y.C.), Midday (N.Y.C.). Home: Cedar Rapids, Iowa. Died Apr. 1983.

ARNOLD, RALPH JUDD, naval officer; b. Garden Grove, Ia., July 6, 1902; s. Harry Guy and Mabel (Judd) A.; B.S., U.S. Naval Acad., 1923; m. Mable Hutchinson, Nov. 25, 1925; m. 2d, Alica Crapo Jenkins, Jan. 17, 1936; children—Arnold, Marilyn Alyee. Commd. ensign, 1923, advanced through grades to rear adm.; served as line officer, 1923-35, trans. to supply corps, 1935; served U.S.S. Yorktown, 1942, at Naval Air Station, Seattle, 1942-43, on staff comdr. Fleat Air, S. Pacific, 1943-44; at Naval Air Station, Pensacola, Fla., 1944-45; in Navy Dept. and Munitions Bd., 1945-46; officer-in-charge Ordnance Stock office, Washington, 1947; asst. chief for supply Bur. Supplies and Accounts, Navy Dept., 1948-51; aviation supply officer, Phila., also district supply officer 4th Naval District, 1951-54; vice chief Naval Material, 1954; chief Bur. Supplies & Accounts, Dept. of Navy, 1954-60. Decorated: Navy cross, Bronze star, Commendation ribbon. Clubs: Army-Navy (Washington); Army-Navy Country (Arlington, Va.). Home: Arlington, Va. Died July 5, 1985.

ARNOLD, RICHARD MONROE, architect; b. Rome, Ga., Dec. 24, 1927; s. Ernest Monroe and Lena Cardwell (Waters) A.; m. Edwina Ruth Barnhill, Apr. 12, 1952 (dec. July 1980); children: Stephen Lang, Laura Lesley; m. Edeltraud Maria von Wittgenstein, Jan. 24, 1981. B.F.A., Tex. Christian U., 1950; postgrad., N.C. State Coll., Sch. Design, 1952-53. Registered architect, N.C., Ariz. Estimator Robert E. McKee, Inc., Santa Fe, 1951-52; draftsman, designer, architect Edwards, McKimmon & Etheredge (Architects), Raleigh, N.C., 1952-59; project architect Fred M. Guirey, Architect, Phoenix, 1959-60; v.p. Guirey, Srnka, Arnold & Sprinkle (Architects and Planners), Phoenix, 1961-75, pres., 1976-82, Archtl. Interiors, Inc., 1971-82; founder, pres. Ariz. Council of Professions, 1970-71; lectr. Ariz. State U. Coll. Architecture, 1970, 73, 75. Important works include Lowell Obs, Flagstaff, Ariz., Colonia Miramonte, Scottsdale, Ariz., Arts and Architecture Complex, Ariz. State U, Packard Stadium, Ariz. State U, Master Plan, Am. Grad. Sch. for Internat. Mgmt, Glendale, Ariz., 1st Nat. Bank Ariz. parking structure, Phoenix, Long Term Nursing Care unit VA Hosp, Phoenix, Cities Service Co. Office Bldg, Miami, Ariz. Fellow AIA (pres. Central Ariz. chpt. 1968); mem. Ariz. Soc. Architects (pres. 1969). Clubs: Phoenix Execs, University, Phoenix 100 Rotary. Office: Phoenix, Ariz.

ARNOLD, WILLIAM PERRY, retail department stores executive; b. Omaha, Mar. 21, 1925; s. John Chappel and Rachel Harriet (Heiss) A.; m. Barbara Lee Powell, Feb. 16, 1949; children: Stephen P., Alice Lee. B.S., U. Mo., 1947. With L.S. Ayres, Indpls., 1947-58; pres., gen. mdse. mgr. subsidiary John Bressmer Co., Springfield, Ill., 1958-64; v.p. mdse. and publicity, dir., mem. exec. com. L.S. Ayres & Co., 1964-68; exec. v.p., then pres., chmn. bd. J.W. Robinson Co., Los Angeles, 1968-74; vice chmn., exec. officer merchandising Asso. Dry Goods Co., N.Y.C., 1974-76, pres., exec. officer merchandising, 1976-79, pres., chief exec. officer, 1979-81, chmn., chief exec. officer, 1981-84, chmn. exec. com., 1984, also dir.; dir. Associated Dry Goods (U.K.) Ltd., Central Hudson Gas and Electric Corp., Poughkeepsie, Black & Decker Mfg. Co.; trustee, exec. com. Am. Savs. Bank, N.Y.C. Mem. adv. bd. Salvation Army, N.Y.C.; trustee Nat. Jewish Hosp. and Research Center, Denver. Clubs: N.Y. Athletic (N.Y.C.), Union League (N.Y.C.), Turf and Field (N.Y.C.). Home: Greenwich, Conn. Died Sept. 4, 1984.

ARNY, CLARA BROWN, home econ.; b. Grand Isl., Neb., June 19, 1888; d. Alfred F. and Mary A. (Richardson) B.; A.B., U. of Minn., 1913; A.M., Columbia U., 1922; student grad. schs., Stanford U. and Ohio State University; married Albert C. Arny, Oct. 12, 1946. Instructor rural schools, Minn., 1906-09, high sch., Red Oak, Ia., 1913-14, State Teachers Coll., Mankato, Minn., 1914-15; instr. home economics edn., U. of Minn., 1915-18, asst. prof., 1918-26, asso. prof., 1926-38, prof. 1938-53; lecturer Columbia U., 1924, 25, U. of Puerto Rico, 1940, U. of Conn., 1949, W.Va. U., 1951, U. of Ill., 1952; consultant, President Roosevelt's Advisory Com. on Edn., 1937. Pa. State Coll., Drexel Inst., Federal Office of Edn., 1940; Northwestern U. and Cornell U., 1944; U. of Toronto, 1947; consultant, Workshop of Am. Home Econ. Assn. and General Edn. Bd., 1946; also director of survey of home economics in liberal arts colls. for Am. Home Economics Assn. and North Central Assn. of Colls. and Secondary Schs., 1942-43. Recipient outstanding achievement award U. Minn. Fellow A.A.A.S.; member Nat. Society for Study of Education. Nat. Edn. Assn., League Women Voters, World Federalists, Mental Health Assn., American Ednl. Research Assn., Am. Assn. University Women, Am. Home Economics Assn. (chmn. evaluation com. (1946-52), Minn. Home Economics Assn. (past pres.), Minn. Acad. Sci., Omicron Nu, Pi Lambda Theta, Phi Upsilon Omicron. Republican. Unitarian. Clubs: College Women's (Minneapolis); Campus (U. of Minn.). Frequent contbr. to ednl. publs. Reviewer for Ency. of Ednl. Research, 1941. Co-author: The Teaching of Home Economics, 1928; Clothing Construction, 1934; Employment Opportunties for Women with Limited Home Economics Training, 1941; Minnesota Tests for

Household Skills, 1952. Author: A Study of Perequisite Sciences and Certain Sequent Courses at the University of Minnesota, 1941; Evaluation and Investigation in Home Economics, 1941; Home Economics in Liberal Arts Colleges, 1945; The Effectiveness of the High School Program in Home Economics, 1952; Evaluation in Home Economics, 1953. Editor: Marriage and Family Living (issue Health and Family Welfare), 1957. Home: St. Paul, Minn. †

ARON, RAYMOND CLAUDE FERDINAND, educator, author; b. Paris, France, Mar. 14, 1905; s. Gustave and Suzanne (Levy) A.; Agregation de Philosophie, Ecole Normale, Superieure and Faculty of Letters, Paris U., 1928, Doctorat es Lettres, 1938; LL.D., Harvard, 1958, U. Bale, 1960, U. Bruxelles, 1963; Doctor of Laws (hon.), Columbia Univ., 1966; m. Suzanne Gauchon, Sept. 5, 1933; children—Dominique (Mrs. Antoine Schnapper), Laurence. Sec., Center Social Studies, Ecole Normale Superieure, 1934-39; lectr. faculty letters U. Toulouse (France), 1939; editor Le France Libre, London, Eng., 1940-44; columnist Figuro, 1947-83; prof. faculty letters Paris U., 1955-83; Andrew D. White prof.-at-large Cornell U., 1965. Author: Introduction to the Philosophy of History, 1938; Century of Total War, 1951; Opium of the Intellectuals, 1955; Peace and War Among Nations, 1962. Home: Paris, France. Died Oct. 17, 1983.

ARONOWITZ, SAMUEL ETTELSON, lawyer; b. Albany, N.Y., 1890; s. Max and Dora (Ettelson) A.; A.B., Dartmouth, 1911; LL.B., Albany Law Sch., 1914, St. Rose Coll., 1971. Admitted to N.Y. bar, 1914; partner O'Connell & Aronowitz, Albany, from 1924; counsel, hon. dir. Nat. Comml. Bank & Trust Co. of Albany, from 1939; gen. counsel, trustee City & County Savs. Bank, from 1924; pres. Better Albany Living, Inc., from 1966. Mem. bd. fellows Brandeis U., 1952—; bd. Albany Med. Center Hosp., nat. exec. com. Am. Jewish Com., Jewish Welfare Bd., Joint Distbn. Com. Served as sgt. 309th Mach. Gun bn. 78th Div., World War I; col. judge adv. N.Y. Guard, 1940-48. Mem. Am., N.Y. State, Albany County bar assns., Federated Bar Assns. 3d Jud. Dist. (past pres.), Am. Legion (past comdr. dept. N.Y.). Republican. Jewish religion. Mason (Shriner). Clubs: Albany, Coloine Country (Albany); Dartmouth (N.Y.C.). Home: Albany, N.Y. †

ARONSON, IRENE H., artist; b. Dresden, Ger., Mar. 8, 1918; student Eastbourne (Eng.) Sch. Arts and Crafts, 1935-37, Slade Sch. Fine Arts, London, 1937-41, Ruskin Sch. Drawing, Oxford U., 1937-40, Atelier 17, 1945-55, Parsons Sch. Design, 1948; B.F.A., Columbia U., 1960; M.A. in Fine Arts and Fine Art Edn., 1962; certificates in drawing and design, U. London. One-woman exhbns. include Weyhe Gallery, N.Y.C., 1962, Smithsonian Instn., Washington, 1954, Brooks Meml. Art Gallery, Memphis, 1956, Towner Art Gallery, Eastbourne, 1961; group exhbns. include Am. Brit. Art Center, Bonestell Gallery, Mus. Modern Art, N.Y.C., 1942-45, Print Ann. at Bklyn. Mus., Art Gallery, Rome, Contemporarary Arts, 1950-51, Soc. Etchers, Chgo., U. So. Calif., Print Club of Phila., Creative Gallery, Nat. Acad., Pa. Acad., Boston Mus., Nat. Collection Fine Arts at Smithsonian Instn., 1951-53, Nat. Assn. Women Artists, N.Y.C., 1972; rep. permanent collections Mus. City N.Y., Ringling Bros., N.Y. Pub. Library, R.I. Mus. Art, Mus. Modern Art, N.Y.C., Met. Mus., Bezalel (Israel) Mus., Boston Mus. Fine Arts, Bibliotheque Nat., Paris, Royal Library, Brussels, Victoria and Albert Mus., London, also Rosenwald collections; works include illustrations, theatrical designs; asst. tchr. Walden Sch., N.Y.C., 1942-43, evening div. Coll. City N.Y., 1947-51; art instr. Bryant Youth and Adult Center, L.I., from 1954; tchr. jr. high sch. art, N.Y.C. Recipient Gold medal Eastbourne Sch. Arts and Crafts, 1936; 2d prize design Slade Sch., 1938, Eve Clendenin prize, 1954; medal of honor Nat. Assn. Women Artists, 1957; 1st graphic prize Knickerbocker Artists, 1958. Mem. AAUW. Comdr. art, travel publs. Address: Rego Park, NY.

ARTHUR, JOHN BURWELL, refractories co. exec.; b. Poplar Bluff, Mo., Jan. 29, 1889; s. Hiram David and Sophronia Carruthers (Jackson) A.; student pub. schs., Poplar Bluff, Mo., also Birmingham, Ala.; D.Engring., honoris causa, U. Mo. Sch. Mines and Metallurgy, 1958; m. Greeta B. Lawson, May 10, 1913; children—Dorothy E. (Mrs. Carl Bachmann), Betty Jane (Mrs. Robert G. Hook, Jr.). Office mgr. Sandoval Zinc Co., East St. Louis, Ill., 1910-11; office mgr. Cypress Lumber Co., Apalachicola, Fla., 1911-13; office mgr. Leach Lumber Co., Poplar Bluff, Mo., 1913-14; v.p., gen. mgr. A.P. Green Fire Brick Co. Mexico, Mo., 1914-29; pres., chmn. Mexico Refractories Co. (Mo.), from 1929; chmn. Nat. Refractories Co., Phila., from 1935; pres. Big Savage Refractories Co., Frostburg, Md., from 1938, Fire Brick Engrs., Inc. Cleve., from 1936, Niles Fire Brick Co. (Ohio), from 1954, Mexico Refractories Co. of Cuba, Havana, 1955—; dir. Refractories Engring. & Supplies, Ltd., Hamilton, Ont., Can., First Nat. Bank, Mexico, Mo., New Orleans Ct. Northern Ry. Co., St. Louis. Pres. KXEO Radio Sta., Mexico, Mo., 1959. Dir. Refractories Institute, Pitts., pres., 1959. Mem. Christian Ch. Clubs: Duquesene (Pitts.); Mexico City Country; Jefferson City Country; Merion Golf (Ardmore, Pa.). Home: Mexico, Mo. †

ASENSIO, MANUEL JOSÉ, air force officer; b. Highland Falls, N.Y., Apr. 10, 1906; s. José Manuel and Clara Marshal (Root) A.; B.S., U.S. Mil. Acad., 1927; B.S. in civil engring., U. Calif., 1931; student officers course Engr. Sch., 1931-32, Staff and Faculty Engr. Sch., 1940-42. Nat. War Coll., 1948-49; m. Ruth Margaret Sullivan, June 29, 1929; children—Manuel José, Joan Jay. Commd. 2d lt., 10th Cavalry, U.S. Army, 1927; promoted through grades to maj. gen.; trans. to Corps. Engrs., 1931; 3d Engrs., Schofield Barracks, T.H., 1932-35; 1st Engrs., Ft. DuPont, Dal., 1935-36; asst. to dist. mgr. Galveston, Texas, 1936-40; resident mgr. Home: Springfield, Va. Died Nov. 22, 1983.

ASH, FRANK CLARK, paper mfr.; b. Skaneateles, N.Y., Mar. 5, 1888; s. John and Nellie (Clark) A.; M.E., Syracuse U., 1909; m. Imogene Paddock, Oct. 12, 1915; children—Janet (Mrs. Henry C. Estabrook), Beatrice (Mrs. William S. Clark), Mary Ellen. In engring. dept. Syracuse Lighting Co., Syracuse, N.Y., 1909-10; engr. Crucible Steel Co., Syracuse, 1910-15; with Oswego Falls Corp., Fulton, N.Y., from 1915, pres. and dir. 1915-57; chmn. bd. Sealright-Oswego Falls Corp., 1957-64; member board of directors Niagara Mohawk Power Corp., Syracuse, New York, also First Trust & Deposit Company, Oswego County, Independent Telephone Company, Fulton, New York. Republican. Clubs: Fulton (Fulton); Century (Syracuse). Home: Fulton, N.Y. †

ASH, ROBERT, lawyer; b. Buffalo, Oct. 1, 1894; s. John Robert and Lucretia Elizabeth (Kingston) A.; m. Frances Halliburton Luna, Oct. 5, 1926; 1 dau., Fanchon. LL.B., George Washington U., 1918. Bar: D.C. bar 1918, Ct. Appeals bar 1918, U.S. Supreme Ct. bar 1918. Practiced in Washington; sr. partner Ash, Bauersfeld & Burton (and predecessor firms); specializing taxation; formerly Washington counsel Prentice-Hall, Inc.; dir. emeritus Potomac Nat. Bank, Md.; mem. adv. com. on fed. appellate rules Com. on Rules of Practice and Procedure, Jud. Conf. U.S., 1960-68. Author: How to Write a Tax Brief, 24th edit, 1980, Preparation and Trial of Tax Cases, 1957, Tax Problems Encountered in the General Practice of Law, 1960. Recipient Alumni Achievement award George Washington U., 1965, 77. Fellow Am. Bar Found.; mem. Am. Bar Assn. (tax counsel 1961-70, standing com. on fed. judiciary 1962-68, past chmn. com. appellate procedure, com. bureau practice and procedure), D.C. Bar Assn. (former vice chmn. council sect. administrv. law), Am. Law Inst., Am. Judicature Soc. Episcopalian. Clubs: Metropolitan (Washington); Chevy Chase (Md.); Burning Tree (Bethesda). Home: Bethesda, Md. Died Aug. 10, 1981.

ASHBRIDGE, SIR NOEL, ret. broadcasting corp. ofcl.; b. Wanstead, Essex, Eng., Dec. 10, 1889; s. John and Sylvia (Moore) A.; ed. Forest Sch., Snaresbrook, Essex, 1898-1907; B.Sc. in Engring., King's Coll., London U., 1911; m. Olive Maude Strickland, 1926, (dec. 1948), children—Wendy, Helen. With Yarrow & Co., British Thomson Houston Co., & The Lancashire Dynamo & Motor Co., 1911-14, Marconi's Wireless Telegraph Co. (Writtle Exptl. Sta.), 1920-26; asst. chief engr. British Broadcasting Co. (later named British Broadcasting Corp.), 1926-29, chief engr. and controller (engring.), 1929-43, dept. dir.-gen. of the corp. and tech. adviser to bd. of govs. 1943-47, was director of technical services, retired; dir. Marconi's Wireless Telegraph Company. Chmn. Radio Research Board; member Television Com.; mem. Nat. Physical Lab. (gen. bd., exec. com.; finance and promotions com.). Served with British Army, 1914-19; pvt., inf., 1914-16; drafted to Royal Engrs., Signals, 1916; lt., assigned as instr. on Signal Service work, 1917-18. President The Junior Institution of Engineers, 1949. Fellow King's Coll., London. Knight Bachelor (Great Britain), Knight Royal Order of Dannebrog (Denmark). Fellow Inst. Radio Engrs. (v. pres. since Jan. 1947); mem. Instn. elec. Engrs. (pres. 1941-42), Instn. Civil Engrs. Club: Athenaeum (London). Home: Sidcup, Kent, England. †

ASHBROOK, JOSEPH, editor; b. Phila., Apr. 4, 1918; s. William Sinclair and Mildred (Janney) A.; B.Sc., Johns Hopkins, 1939; M.Sc. in Astronomy, Case-Western Res. U., 1941; Ph.D. in Astronomy, Harvard, 1947; m. Martha Elizabeth Dowse, July 5, 1942; children—Catherine (Mrs. Michael S. Winer), Elizabeth (Mrs. Gerald D. Bowes), Jane, Susan (Mrs. Michael R. Humphrey). Physicist USN, Washington, 1942-45; instr. astronomy Yale, 1946-50, asst. prof., 1950-53; editor Sky Pub. Corp., Cambridge, Mass., 1953-80. Mem. Democratic Town Com., Weston, Mass., 1960-80. Mem. Am. Astron. Assn., Internat. Astron. Union (commn. on variable stars 1947-80, planets 1958-80, history of astronomy 1958-80), Am. Assn. Variable Star Observers (v.p. 1952-53), Medieval Acad. Am. Editor Sky and Telescope Mag., 1970-80. Home: Weston, Mass. Died Aug. 4, 1980.

ASHKIN, JULIUS, educator, physicist; b. Bklyn., Aug. 23, 1920; s. Isadore and Anna (Fishman) A.; m. Claire Ruderman, Sept. 1, 1946; children—Beth, Laura. A.B., Columbia, 1940, A.M., 1941, Ph.D. in Physics, 1943. Mem. staff Los Alamos Sci. Lab., 1943-46; asst. prof. U. Rochester, 1946-50; faculty Carnegie-Mellon Univ., from 1950, prof. physics, from 1958, chmn. dept., 1961-73. Fellow Am. Phys. Soc.; mem. Am. Assn. Physics Tchrs., AAAS. Home: Pittsburgh, Pa. Died June 4, 1982.

ASHLEY, RICHARD CHACE, chem. co. exec.; b. Providence, Mar. 26, 1927; s. Earl Hutchinson and Rachael Chace (Eddy) A.; m. Janet Eldridge Hills, Oct. 6, 1951; children—Richard Chace, Robin Whitney, Rachael Dicks, Randall Hills. B.S. in Chemistry, Brown U., 1950; postgrad., Harvard U., 1973. Chemist, prodn. supr. Uniroyal Corp., 1950-51; indsl. salesman Allied Chem. Corp., Morristown, N.J., 1951-60, regional sales mgr. Midwest, 1960-63, product mgr., mktg. mgr., dir. sales, 1963-69, div. officer, div. pres., 1970-77, group v.p., 1977-82; pres. Allied Chem. Corp. (Chems. Co. div.), 1979-82; chmn. bd. Allied Chem. Can. Ltd., 1979-82; dir. ENS Biols. Inc., 1980-82. Pres. Tokeneke Assn., 1974-75; v.p. Darien Land Trust, 1977; bd. dirs. Low Heywood Sch., 1974-75, Chem. Industry Council N.J. Served with USCG, 1945-46. Mem. Soc. Chem. Industry, Chem. Mfrs. Assn. (dir.). Clubs: Wee Burn Country, Ocean Reef, Norwalk Yacht. Home: Darien, Conn. Died Oct. 17, 1982.

ASHTON, LEONARD C., ins. exec.; b. Germantown, Pa., Apr. 23, 1887; s. Taber and Margaret Shotwell (Laing) A.; student Swarthmore Coll.; A.B., Harvard; LL.B., U. of Pa.; m. Ruth N. Potter, Jan. 27, 1917. With Provident Mut. Life Ins. Co. of Phila. from 1913, sec., 1918-29; v.p. and sec. from 1929. Home: Swarthmore, Pa.†

ASHTON, LINWOOD E., pres. First Portland Nat. Bank; b. Wilton, Me., Feb. 27, 1889; s. John Oliver and Nellie (Ellis) A.; m. Iva E. Libby, Dec. 29, 1910; children—Linwood E., Natalie Jean (Mrs. Jackson E. Blake), Iva Claire. Clerk, First Nat. Bank, Auburn, Me., 1905-06, Portland Nat. Bank, Portland, Me., 1907-10; bank examiner with auditing firm of Kansas City, 1910-13; with First Portland Nat. Bank from 1914, advancing from auditor, became pres. 1939, dir. 1925. Republican. Mason. Clubs: Cumberland, Woodfords. Home: Portland, Maine. †

ASKWITH, HERBERT, publishing company executive, public relations counselor; b. Boston, May 6, 1889; s. Barry and Gertrude (Aron) A.; m. Margaret A. Long, June 30, 1910; children: Bertram, Edna Abbey, Jean, Marjorie Louise. A.B. magna cum laude, Harvard U., 1907. Asst. English, comparative lit. Harvard U., 1907; mem. editorial staff Good Health Pub. Co., Battle Creek, Mich., 1908-12; publ. mgr. The Independent, N.Y.C., 1916-21; editor, pub. World Rev., 1922-26; v.p. Horace Liveright, Inc. (book pubs.), 1927-29, pub. relations counselor, N.Y.C., from 1935; cons. to pres. New Haven R.R., 1954-56. Author: A Common-Sense Guide to Children's Reading; editor: (with Arnold Herrick) This Way to Unity; author mag. and newspaper articles.; lectr.; frequent radio-TV guest speaker. Mem. N.Y. Gov.'s Panel Commuting Problems, 1959; initiator plan r.r. terminal and shopping center, New Rochelle, N.Y.; chmn. Westchester Commuters Group; mem. Larchmont Park Commn.; promotion Garden of a Million Tulips, N.Y. World's Fair, 1939. Twice recipient Bowdoin Lit. prize Harvard U.; endowed ann. Herbert Askwith Symposium on Higher Edn. Harvard U. Mem. Phi Beta Kappa. Clubs: Harvard (Westchester); Publicity (N.Y.C.) (v.p.). Home: Larchmont, N.Y. Died July 25, 1985.

ASPINALL, WAYNE NORVIEL, ret. congressman, cons.; b. Middleburg, Ohio, Apr. 3, 1896; s. Mack and Jessie Edna (Norviel) A.; A.B., U. of Denver, 1919; LL.B., Denver Law Sch., 1925; LL.D., U. Alaska, U. Denver; D.C.L., Colo. State U.; Dr.M.Eng., Colo. Sch. Mines; D.Pub. Service, Mesa Coll.; m. Julia E. Kuns, (dec. July 1969); children—Wayne Norviel, Owen Stewart, Richard Daniel, Ruth JoAnne (Mrs. John W. Flora); m. 2d, Essie Jeffers Best. Admitted to Colo. bar, 1925; practice law, also engaged in peach orchard industry; mem. Colo. Ho. of Reps., 1931-38, speaker, 1937, 38; state senator, 1939-49; mem. 81st to 92d congresses from 4th Colo. Dist.; chmn. Interior and Insular Affairs Com., Pub. Land Law Rev. Commn.; mem. Joint Com. Atomic Energy; cons. natural resources, Denver and Palisade, Colo. Apptd. mem. Mo. Basin Survey Commn. by Pres. Truman. Served with Signal Corps. U.S. Army, World War I; capt., assigned to mil. govt. service, World War II; legal expert with U.S. and English forces; participated in Normandy drive as Am. officer with Brit. 2d Army. Mem. Colo., Mesa County bar assns., Am. Legion, 40 and 8. Democrat. Methodist. Mason (33 deg., K.T., Shriner), Odd Fellow, Elk, Lion. Home: Palisade, Colo. Died Oct. 9, 1983.

ASTIN, ALLEN VARLEY, physicist; b. Salt Lake City, June 12, 1904; s. John Andrew and Catherine (Varley) A.; m. Margaret L. Mackenzie, Aug. 31, 1927; children—John Allen, Alexander William. A.B., U. Utah, 1925; M.S., N.Y. U., 1926, Ph.D., 1928; D.Sc., Lehigh U., 1953, George Washington U., 1958, N.Y. U., 1960. NRC fellow Johns Hopkins U., 1928-30; research asso. utilities research com. Nat. Bur. Standards, 1930-32, physicist, 1932-69, asst. chief ordnance devel. div., 1944-48, chief electronics and ordnance div., 1948-50, asso. dir., 1951-52, dir., 1952-69, dir. emeritus, from 1969; cons., chmn. inter-deptl. com. sci. research and devel., 1954-55; mem. NACA, 1952-58, Internat. Com. Weights and Measures, 1954-69, Naval Research Adv. Com., 1953-59, Def. Sci. Bd., 1956-69; chmn. com. on fed. labs. Fed. Council Sci. and Tech., 1962-69. Mem. Nat. Motor Vehicle Safety Adv. Council, 1968-72; U.S. coordinator U.S.-France Sci. Cooperation Program, 1969-75. Decorated Pres.'s Certificate of Merit U.S.; King's Medal United Kingdom; officer Legion of Honor France; recipient Rockefeller Pub. Service award; Distinguished Alumni award U. Utah, 1968; Standards medal Am. Nat. Standards Inst., 1969; Astin Polk Internat. Standards medal, 1974; Harry Diamond award IEEE, 1970. Fellow Am. Phys. Soc.,

AAAS, IRE; mem. ASTM, Am. Acad. Arts Scis., Instrument Soc. Am., Nat. Acad. Scis. (home sec. 1971-75), Am. Philos. Soc. (v.p. 1977-80), Washington Philos. Soc., Washington Acad. Scis., Am. Def. Preparedness Assn., Am. Inst. Aeros. and Astronautics (hon.), Standards Engr. Soc. (hon.), ADA (hon.), Am. Soc. Heating, Ventilating and Air Conditioning Engrs. (hon.), Sigma Xi, Phi Kappa Phi. Club: Cosmos. Home: Bethesda, MD.

ATCHLEY, DANA WINSLOW, physician, educator; b. Chester, Conn., July 8, 1892; s. William Abner and Florence Albertine (Ames) A.; B.S., U. Chgo., 1911; M.D., Johns Hopkins, 1915; D.Sc., Columbia, 1959; Docteur honoris causa U. Strasbourg (France), 1972; m. Mary Cornelia Phister, Sept. 21, 1916; children—Dana Winslow, John Adams, William Ames. Intern Johns Hopkins Hosp., Balt., 1915-16; asst. physician Presbyn. Hosp., N.Y.C., 1916-17, asst. vis. physician, 1917-19, 21-23, asso. attending physician, 1923-45, attending physician, 1945-58, cons., from 1958; practice medicine, specializing in internal medicine, N.Y.C., 1921-76; assoc. medicine Coll. Phys. and Surg., Columbia, 1921-25, asst. prof., 1925-30, asso. prof., 1930-41, asso. prof. clin. medicine, 1941-42, prof., 1942-58, prof. emeritus, 1958-82; cons. internal medicine Tuxedo (N.Y.) Hosp., Englewood (N.J.) Hosp., Nyack (N.Y.) Hosp., Rockefeller Found., Commonwealth Fund. Charter trustee Rutgers U. Pavilion named for him Columbia-Presbyn. Hosp. Mem. A.C.P. (master), Harvey Soc., Assn. Am. Physicians (Kober medal 1969), N.Y. Acad. Medicine, Am. Soc. Clin. Investigation, Johns Hopkins Soc. Scholars; hon. life mem. Am. Mus. Natural History. Episcopalian. Clubs: Knickerbocker Country, Century Assn. (N.Y.C.). Author: Physician: Healer and Scientist, 1961. Editor: Psychosomatic Medicine. Contbr. to Nelson's Loose Leaf System of Medicine and Cecil's Textbook of Medicine, articles to profl. jours. Home: Englewood, N.J. Died June 27, 1982.

ATKINS, FRANK DOUGLAS, JR., restaurant exec.; b. Seattle, May 12, 1931; s. Frank Douglas and Evelyn Anne (Ferm) A.; B.S., UCLA, 1957; m. Victoria Mayo Graham, Aug. 24, 1968. Audit supr. Ernst & Ernst, Los Angeles, 1957-64; asst. comptroller Technicolor, Inc., Hollywood, 1964-67; controller Revenue Control Systems div. Litton Industries, Inc., Beverly Hills, Calif., 1967-69; controller Host Internat., Inc., Santa Monica, Calif., 1969-84; treas., dir. Transp. Scis. Corp., Los Angeles, 1967-84. Trustee, West Coast U., 1979-84. Served with USN, 1950-54. C.P.A., Calif. Mem. Am. Inst. C.P.A.'s, Calif. Soc. C.P.A.'s, Phi Kappa Psi. Home: Marine Del Rey, Calif. Died Feb. 10, 1984.

ATKINSON, JUSTIN BROOKS, journalist; b. Melrose, Mass., Nov. 28, 1894; s. Jonathan H. and Garafelia (Taylor) A.; m. Oriana MacIlveen, Aug. 18, 1926; 1 step-son, Bruce T. MacIlveen. A.B., Harvard, 1917; L.H.D., Williams Coll., 1941; D.H.L., Adelphi Coll., 1960; LL.D., Pace Coll., Franklin and Marshall Coll., Brandeis U., 1965, Clark U., 1965, Washington Coll., 1966, L.I. U., 1967, Dartmouth, 1975. Reporter Springfield Daily News, 1917; instr. in English Dartmouth Coll., 1917-18; reporter and asst. to drama critic Boston Evening Transcript, 1919-22; asso. editor Harvard Alumni Bull., 1920-22; editor Book Rev., N.Y. Times, 1922-25, drama critic, 1925-42, 46-60, war corr., Chungking, China, 1942-44, news corr., Moscow, 1945-46, critic at large, 1960-65. Author: Skyline Promenades, 1925, Henry Thoreau, Cosmic Yankee, 1927, East of the Hudson, 1931, The Cingalese Prince, 1934, Broadway Scrapbook, 1947, Once Around the Sun, 1951, Tuesdays and Fridays, 1963, Brief Chronicles, 1966, Broadway, 1970, This Bright Land, 1972, (with Al Hirschfeld) The Lively Years, 1973; Editor: (with Al Hirschfeld) Walden and other writings of Henry David Thoreau, 1937, Complete Essays and other writings of Ralph Waldo Emerson, 1940, College in a Yard, 1957, The Pace Report, 1966, Sean O'Casey Reader, 1968. Served with U.S. Army, World War I. Recipient Pulitzer prize for journalism, 1947; mem. Theater Hall of Fame. Fellow Am. Acad. Arts and Scis. Democrat. Club: The Players (N.Y.C.). Home: Durham, NY.

AUERBACH, BEATRICE FOX, pres. G. Fox & Co., dept. store; b. Hartford, Conn., July 7, 1887; d. Moses and Theresa (Stern) Fox; ed. private schs. in Hartford, and travel abroad; m. George S. Auerbach, Apr. 5, 1911 (died Nov. 13, 1927) children—Georgette A. Koopman, Dorothy A. Schiro. After marriage lived in Salt Lake City until 1919. Asso. with father in management of G. Fox & Co., Hartford, 1928-38, pres. and mgr. from 1938. Established Auerbach Major at Conn. Coll. of New London, Conn.; also created and is head of Beatrice Fox Auerbach Foundation and Service Bur. for Women's Orgns. of Conn. Home: Hartford, Conn. †

AUGUSTINE, W(ALTER) O(RR), business exec.; b. Salem, O., 1890; s. David and Euphemia (Mackall) Lyman; B.S. Ohio State U.; m. Leah M. Weirich, Dec. 15, 1917; children—Ruth Jane (Mrs. Robert Battis), Joan Marie. With The Diamond Match Co., N.Y. City, from 1912, beginning as chem. engr., vice pres. in charge prodn.; pres. Uniform Chem. Products, Inc. Served with U.S. Army, World War I. Baptist. Home: Rahway, N.J.†

AUSTIN, ALLAN STEWART, engineer, construction executive; b. Cleve., Apr. 1, 1905; s. Wilbert J. and Ida M. (Stewart) A.; B.S., Yale, 1927; m. Margaret Stroup, July 29, 1929; 1 son, Richard C.; m. 2d, Winifred Nienhouse, Mar. 14, 1947; 1 son, James W. With Austin Co., Cleve., from 1928, successively foreman, Los Angeles, field engr., supt. and sales engr., London, Eng., sec., v.p., gen. sales mgr., 1953-58, pres., 1958-63, chmn. bd., from 1963, chief exec. officer, 1963-69; dir. Austin Co. Found. Trustee Lake Erie Coll., Hiram Coll., Ohio. Served from capt. to maj. AUS, 1943-46, Presbyn. Clubs: Kirtland (Ohio) Country; Gulfstream (Fla.) Golf; Redo; Union (Cleve.); Little (Delray Beach, Fla.); Club de Golf (Sotogrande, Spain). Home: Shaker Heights, Ohio. Died Apr. 3, 1981.

AUSTIN, EDWIN CHARLES, lawyer; b. Barrington, Ill., Mar. 28, 1892; s. Charles Henry and Luella (Hawley) A.; m. Marion Roberts, June 9, 1917; children—Barbara Austin Foote, Patricia Austin Sherer, Elizabeth Austin Lindsay. B.A., U. Wis., 1912; LL.B., Northwestern U., 1915, M.A., 1917. Bar: Ill. bar 1915. Since practiced in, Chgo.; mem. firm Sidley & Austin; counsel Chgo. Community Trust, 1944-64; mem. Ill. State Bd. Bar Examiners, 1925-27, Ill. State Bd. Examiners in Accountancy, 1934-37; mem. spl. commn. Ill. Supreme Ct., 1969; past dir. several corps. Mem. New Trier High Sch. Bd., 1919-20; mem. Glencoe Sch. Bd., 1927-31, pres., 1929-31; pres. Roycemore Sch., 1934-40, Cook County Sch. Nursing, 1943-44; trustee Am. Library Assn., Old Peoples Home, Evanston Hosp.; past chmn., past trustee Vassar Coll.; life trustee Northwestern U.; bd. dirs. Lyric Opera Chgo.; governing mem. Chgo. Orchestral Assn., Art Inst. Chgo. Served as lt. U.S. Navy, 1917-19. Recipient Alumni medal Northwestern U. Fellow Am., Chgo. bar founds.; mem. Am., Ill., Chgo. bar assns., Law Club (pres. 1966-67), Legal Club (pres. 1944-45), Order of Coif, Delta Sigma Rho, Sigma Phi, Phi Delta Phi. Republican. Congregationalist. Clubs: Chgo. (Chgo.), Comml. (Chgo.), Commonwealth (Chgo.), Mid-Day (Chgo.), Union League (Chgo.) (pres. 1935), Univ. (Chgo.), Execs. (Chgo.); Old Elm (Lake Forest, Ill.); Indian Hill (Winnetka, Ill.); Wausaukee (Wis.); Army and Navy (Washington). Home: Winnetka, Ill. Died Feb. 10, 1983.

AUSTIN, T. LOUIS, JR., utility exec.; b. 1919; (married). B.S. in Mining Engring, U. Ala., 1942. With Indsl. Generating Co., 1953-59; with Tex. Power & Light Co., from 1959, pres., chief exec. officer, 1967-72, chmn., from 1972; also dir; pres. Tex. Utilities Co., from 1972, chief exec. officer, from 1973, vice chmn. bd., 1974, chmn. bd., 1975, chmn. exec. com., chief exec., also dir.; dir. Dallas Power & Light Co. Served with USNR, 1942-45. Address: Dallas, Tex. *

AVERETT, ELLIOTT, banker; b. Chatham, N.J., Jan. 6, 1918; s. Elliott and Martha (Snead) A.; m. Julia Bancroft Fletcher, Dec. 12, 1947; children—Elliott III, Thomas Hamlett, Julia Hall. Student, Harvard Bus. Sch., 1958. With Bank of N.Y., 1940-82, asst. treas., 1949-52, asst. v.p., 1952-56, v.p., 1956-63, head nat. dept., 1958-63, exec. v.p., 1963-66, chmn. credit com., 1963-66, sr. exec. v.p., 1966-68, chief comml. banking officer, 1966-67, chief adminstrv. officer, 1967-73, pres., 1968-74, chief exec. officer, 1973-81, chmn. bd., 1974-82, also dir.; chmn. bd., chief exec. officer, dir. Bank of N.Y. Co., Inc.; chmn., dir. Bank of N.Y. Internat. Inc.; Centennial Ins. Co., La. Land & Exploration Co.; trustee Atlantic Mut. Ins. Co.; mem. N.Y. State Adv. Com. on Comml. Bank Supervision, 1965-67. Mem. Life Saving Benevolent Assn. N.Y., Council on Fgn. Relations, Inc.; trustee, treas. Seeing Eye, Inc., Morristown, N.J., 1958-70, pres., chmn., 1970-80, trustee, 1981-82; treas., v.p., bd. dirs. Greater N.Y. Fund, 1968-83, chmn., 1977; bd. dirs. Downtown Lower Manhattan Assn., UN Assn. U.S.A.; trustee Josiah Macy, Jr. Found.; mem. trustees com. N.Y. Community Trust, 1969-74; bd. govs. Hundred Year Assn. N.Y., Inc. Served to capt. AUS, 1941-46, ETO. Decorated Purple Heart, Silver Star medal. Mem. Assn. Res. City Bankers, Robert Morris Assos., N.Y., Clearing House Assn., Econ. Club N.Y., Am. Inst. Banking (chmn. adv. council N.Y. chpt. 1976-83), Am. Bur. Shipping, Internat. C. of C. (U.S. council). Clubs: Chicago; Down Town Assn. (N.Y.C.), Amateur Ski (N.Y.C.), Anglers (N.Y.C.); Somerset Hills Country, Pilgrims U.S, Union, Sky. Office: New York, N.Y. Died Jan. 12, 1982.

AVERY, WILLIAM TURNER, educator; b. East Cleveland, Ohio, Sept. 9, 1912; s. Leland Charles and Lela Grace (Gott) A.; B.A., Western Res. U., 1934, M.A., 1935, Ph.D., 1937; m. Frances Elizabeth Jordan, Mar. 28, 1948; 1 child, Frances Elizabeth Avery Haroy. Teaching fellow classics Case-Western Res. U., 1939-40; instr. Romance langs. and German, Fenn Coll., Cleve., 1940-42; instr. to assoc. prof. classics Dickinson Coll., 1946-48; assoc. prof. to prof. La. State U., 1948-55; prof., chmn. dept. classical langs. and lits. U. Md., 1955-78, prof. classical langs., 1978-82. Served as sgt. USAAF, 1942-45. Fellow Am. Acad. in Rome; mem. Dante Soc. Am., Nat. Assn. on Standard Med. Vocabulary, Classical Assn. Atlantic States, Am. Philol. Assn., Sigma Chi, Eta Sigma Phi, Phi Sigma Iota, Phi Eta Sigma. Contbr. to scholarly jours. in U.S., Europe. Home: Hyattsville, Md. Dec. Mar. 20, 1985. Interred Nat. Meml. Park, Falls Church, Va.

AVRUTICK, ABRAHAM NOAH, rabbi; b. Russia, Nov. 19, 1909; s. Fishel and Sosel (Shimshilevitch) AvR.; B.A., Yeshiva Coll., 1934; grad. Rabbi Isaac Elchanan Theol. Sem., Yeshiva U., 1929-36; D.H.L., Yeshiva U., 1966; m. Frances Ruth Feldman, Nov. 8, 1938; children—Rena AvRutick Barth, Judith AvRutick Berkowitz, Naomi AvRutick Simon. Came to Can., 1921, naturalized Am. citizen, 1943. Rabbi, 1936; pulpits held, Fitchburg, Mass., 1936-38, Newburgh, N.Y., 1938-46; rabbi Agudas Achim Synagogue, Hartford, Conn., from 1946; successively sec., treas., v.p. Rabbinical Council Am., pres., 1962-64, hon. pres., 1965; v.p. Yeshiva of Hartford; dir. Union of Orthodox Jewish Congregations Am. Active Community Chest, North End Citizens Com.; mem. Conn. Safety Commn.; mayor's mem. Com. on Hartford; bd. dirs. Hartford Jewish Fedn., Jewish Centre, Hebrew Home for Aged, Jewish Social Service. Recipient Mr. Success award Radio Sta. WCCC, Rabbinic Leadership award Union Orthodox Jewish Congregations Am., 1964. Editor: RCA Sermon Manual, 1960; contbr. articles to religious periodicals. Home: West Hartford, Conn. Died Nov. 13, 1982.

AXEEN, MARINA ESTHER, educator; b. St. Cloud, Minn., Nov. 29, 1921; d. Walter A. and Esther T. (Benson) A.; B.S., St. Cloud State Coll., 1945; B.S. in Library Sci., U. Minn., 1949, M.S. in Library Sci., 1953; Advanced Certification in Edn., U. Ill., 1965, Ph.D., 1967. Tchr. pub. schs., Duluth, Minn., 1946-47; head librarian Bethel Coll. and Sem., St. Paul, 1947-58; reference librarian St. Cloud State Coll., 1958-65; prof., chmn. dept. library sci. Ball State U., Muncie, Ind., 1967-81. Mem. ALA, Am. Assn. Library Schs., Assn. Coll. and Research Libraries, Assn. Ind. Media Educators, Ind. Library Assn. (chmn. Ind. educators reoundtable), Delta Kappa Gamma. Baptist (bd. Christian edn.). Contbr. articles to profl. jours. Home: Muncie, Ind. Died Nov. 10, 1981.

AXEL, PETER, physicist, educator; b. Bklyn., May 12, 1923; m. Shirley Thomas, 1954; 1 dau., Sarah. A.B., Bklyn. Coll., 1943; M.S., U. Ill., 1947, Ph.D. in Physics, 1949. Mem. staff elec. devel., radiation lab. Mass. Inst. Tech., 1943-46; asst. prof. physics U. Ill., 1949-55, asso. prof. physics, 1955-59, prof. physics, 1959-83. Guggenheim fellow; NSF sr. postdoctoral fellow. Fellow Am. Phys. Soc. (chmn. nuclear physics div. 1978-79). Spl. research nuclear physics, radioactivity, photon-induced reactions, electronics, nuclear instrumentation, nuclear accelerators. Home: Urbana, Ill. Died Feb. 3, 1983.

AXELRAD, JACOB, lawyer, educator, writer; born Philadelphia, May 25, 1889; s. Abraham and Celia (Zion) A.; LL.B., New York U., 1912, LL.M., 1913; m. Pauline Morse, Feb. 13, 1915; 1 dau., Muriel. Admitted to bar, 1913; practiced in state and federal courts, New York and Mass., 1913-46; lecturer from 1915; lecturer, Rand Sch. for Social Science, N.Y. City, 1944-45; asst. prof. of English, Sampson Coll., New York, 1946-47. Mem. Am. Assn. Univ. Profs. Author: Anatole France: a life without illusions, 1844-1924, 1944, translation rights French, Swedish, Spanish, Portuguese and Czechoslovakian; Patrick Henry—The Voice of Freedom, 1947. Contbr. articles to newspapers and mags. †

AXELROD, JAMES J., textile mill exec.; b. Boston, April 25, 1890; s. Max Axelrod and Dora Rutstein; married Miss Etta R. Abramson, Dec. 10, 1914; children—Gladys, Joseph, Allan. Treas., dir., Airedale Worsted Mills, Inc., Woonsocket, R.I., from 1937; with Lippitt Worsted Mills, Inc., Woonsocket, from 1944; treas. Crown Mfg. Co., Pawtucket, R.I., from 1945; dir. Wamsutta Mills. Trustee, Brandeis Univ. Home: Boston, Mass. †

AXELSON, JOHN S., electrical engineer; b. Toledo, Ia., July 20, 1890; s. Samuel E. and Dorothy (Walker) A.; B.S., in E.E., Ia. State Coll., 1913, E.E., 1923; m. Selma White, June 24, 1942; children—Paul, Rosalind, Ann. With Western Electric Co., Chicago, 1913-17; with Internat. Western Electric Co., 1918-19; mng. dir. Nat. Electric Light Assn., 1926-32; cons. engr., Chicago, from 1932. Mem. Am. Inst. Elec. Engrs., Edison Electric Inst. Club: University (Chicago). Home: Chicago, Ill. †

AXFORD, HIRAM WILLIAM, librarian, educator; b. Butte, Mont., Apr. 7, 1925; s. Harold Frederick and Della (Albert) A.; A.B., Reed Coll., 1950; M.A., U. Denver, 1958, Ph.D., 1968; m. Lavonne Brady, Nov. 11, 1956. Head librarian Denver Post, Inc., 1958-60; adj. prof. Grad. Sch. Librarianship, U. Denver, 1959-67, asst. dir. libraries, 1960-65, dir. libraries, 1965-67; dir. libraries, prof. history Fla. Atlantic U., Boca Raton, 1967-70; univ. librarian, prof. library sci. Ariz. State U., 1970-73; univ. librarian U. Oreg., Eugene, 1973-79; library cons. Bd. dirs. Center for Research Libraries, Chgo., 1975-80, chmn. bd., 1978-79. Fulbright lectr. U. Punjab, Lahore, West Pakistan, 1963-64. Served with AUS, 1943-46. Mem. A.L.A. (mem. com. on program evaluation and support 1976-77, mem. council 1975-79, chmn.), Assn. Coll. and Research Libraries (pres. 1974-75, mem. acad. status com. 1977-80), Library Automation, Research and Cons. Assn. (pres. 1970). Author: Gilpin County Gold, 1976. Mem. editorial bd. Library Acquisitions: Practice and Theory. Home: Eugene, Oreg. Died Aug. 12, 1980.

AYCOCK, WILLIAM LLOYD, M.D.; b. in Carroll Co., Ga., Feb. 25, 1889; s. Joseph Amis and Mary Elizabeth (Thomas) A.; Emory Univ., 1910-12; M.D., U. of Louisville, 1914; m. Eleanor Hickok Fuller, of Burlington, Vt., May 20, 1920; children—Harriet Fuller, Eleanor Fuller, Mary Elizabeth. Instr. bacteriology, N.Y. Post-Grad. Med. Sch., 1915-19; diagnostician N.Y. State Dept. of Health, 1916; dir. Poliomyelitis Research Lab., Vt. State Dept. of Health, 1919 to 1931; asst. prof. preventive medicine and hygiene, Harvard Med. Sch., from 1923; dir. research Harvard Infantile Paralysis Commn. from 1923. Served as 1st lt. U.S. Army, in charge of lab. Base Hosp. No. 8, A.E.F., Savenay, France, later on staff Central Labs., A.E.F., at Dijon, 1917-19. Mem. A.M.A., Am. Pub. Health Assn., Am. Epidemiol. Assn. Congregationalist. Contbr. numerous scientific articles in med. jours. Home: Canton, MA. †

AYRES, MARTHA OATHOUT, sculptor; b. Elkader, Ia., Apr. 1, 1890; d. Orlando De Shay and Mary (Ruegnitz) Oathout; A.B., Carleton Coll., Minn., 1911; student Art Inst. of Chicago, 1911-14; m. James Albert Ayres, of Deadwood, S.D., 1915; children—Carleton, Orlando, Catherine, Marx, Annabel, Dan. Teacher high sch., Sacred Heart, Minn., 1908-09; teacher of sculpture, Pomona, Calif., 1915; on homestead, Colo., 1918-23; sculpture work for Warner Bros. and Paramount Pictures, 1926. Awarded 1st prize Art Students League Exhbn., 1914. Prin. works: bas-relief of Ralph Waldo Emerson, Emerson High Sch., Pomona, Calif.; Fred B. Hill Memorial, Carleton Coll.; portrait bust of mother, State Bldg., Los Angeles; also "Bashful Baby," "Calling the Birds," portrait bust of Alfred Wallenstein (cellist), Wm. Greene, Adolph Lenzinger, Tom Mooney; Sundial "Purity," 87th St. Sch., Los Angeles, etc. Specializes on portraits and statues of children. Member Calif. Art Club, Am. League Against War and Fascism. Presbyterian. Home: North Redondo, CA. †

BABB, JERVIS JEFFERIS, business consultant; b. State College, Pa., April 28, 1902; s. Maurice Jefferis and Blanche Elsiegood (Vincent) B.; A.B., Haverford Coll., 1921; grad. work U. of Pa., 1921-22; M.B.A., Harvard, 1924; m. Ruth Hutchinson, June 5, 1926; 1 dau., Phyllis Elizabeth (Mrs. Donald Sheldon Perkins). Exec. v.p. and dir. S.C. Johnson & Son, Inc., Racine, Wis., 1944-50; pres. Lever Bros. Co., N.Y.C., 1950-55, chmn. bd., 1955-58; dir. Sucrest Corporation, Universal Foods Corporation, Gruen Industries, Inc., Lever Bros. Co., Guardian Life Insurance Company, Neptune Meter Co., American Can. Co.; trustee Dry Dock Savs. Bank; director Bank of N.Y., Bank of New York, Company, Incorporated. Mem. board of trustees Com. for Econ. Devel. Clubs: University, Economic of N.Y.; Duxbury (Mass.); Yacht; Kittansett. Home: New York, N.Y.

BABBIDGE, HOMER DANIELS, JR., educator; b. West Newton, Mass., May 18, 1925; s. Homer Daniels and Allalee Lavinia (Adams) B.; m. Marcia Joan Adkisson, Dec. 22, 1956; children: Aimee Allison, Sandra Allalee, Alexander Adams. B.A., Yale U., 1945, M.A., 1948, Ph.D., 1953, LL.D., 1969; LL.D., Ithaca Coll., 1960, Trinity Coll., 1969, Am. Internat. Coll., 1970; L.H.D., U. Hartford, 1963, Fairfield U., 1968, Rosary Hill Coll., 1969, U. New Haven, 1973; D.Pub. Adminstrn., Rollins Coll., 1971; D.Ped., R.I. Coll., 1972; Litt.D., Susquehanna U., 1977. Dir. financial aids, lectr. edn. Yale U., mem. bd. admissions, 1954-57; exec. fellow Pierson Coll., 1949-57, head resident counselor of freshmen, 1948-49, co-founder Am. studies at Yale for fgn. students, 1948; spl. asst. U.S. Commr. Edn., 1955-56; asst. to sec. HEW, 1957-58, dir. program fin. assistance to higher edn., 1958-59, asst. commr., dir. div. higher edn., 1959-61; v.p. Am. Council on Edn., 1961-62; pres. U. Conn., Storrs, 1962-72; master Timothy Dwight Coll., Yale U.; fellow Instn. for Social and Policy Studies, 1972-76; pres. Hartford Grad. Center, 1976-84; dir. Hartford Nat. Corp., Ency. Brit. Ednl. Corp., Security-Conn. Life Ins. Co. Author: Student Financial Aid: A Manual for Colleges and Universities, 1960, Noah Webster: On Being American, 1967, (with W.R. Rosenzweig) The Federal Interest in Higher Education, 1962; author, narrator: film series The Connecticut Heritage, 1976. Trustee Gannett Found., Wadsworth Atheneum, Conn. Pub. TV Corp., Mt. Sinai Hosp.; trustee Nat. Assn. Public TV Stas.; commr. Hartford Civic Center and Coliseum Authority. Named One of 10 Outstanding Young Men of Nation U.S. Jr. C. of C., 1959; recipient Distinguished Service medal HEW, 1961, Human relations award NCCJ, 1970; Outstanding Civilian Service medal Dept. Army, 1972; Gold award N.Y. Film Festival, 1977; award Corp. for Pub. Broadcasting, 1977. Clubs: Scroll and Key; Elizabethan (Yale), Fence (Yale); Hartford Twentieth Century, Monday Evening, Acorn; Century (N.Y.C.). Home: Hartford, Conn. Died Mar. 27, 1984.

BABCOCK, BRUCE L(ANDERS), lawyer, exec.; b. Willet, N.Y., Nov. 25, 1890; s. Adelbert S. and Minnie (Landers) B.; A.B., Colgate U., 1913; LL.B., Harvard, 1916; m. Julia Kingman Kingley, 1922; children—Kingman Kingsley, Bruce L. Admitted to N.Y. bar 1916; atty. legal dept. Endicott Johnson Corp., 1920-27, treas., dir. from 1927; dir. Marine Midland Trust Co. of So. N.Y., Endicott Trust Co.; trustee Binghamton Savs. Bank; mem. adv. com. Asso. Reciprocal Exchanges, N.Y. Trustee Colgate U. Pres. Susquenango Council Boy Scouts, 1945-46 (Silver Beaver). Campaign chmn. Broome County United Fund, 1954, pres. 1955. Rep. Conglist. †

BABCOCK, JOHN BRAZER, III, educator; b. Boston, Apr. 29, 1889; s. John B. and Harriet A. (Burditt) B.; S.B. in civil engring., Mass. Inst. Tech., 1910; m. Mildred Willard, Mar. 15, 1913; 1 son, Willard F. Asst. engr. Grand Trunk Ry., 1910; instrument man Canadian Pacific Ry., 1911; resident engr., Southern N.E. R.R., 1912; designing engr., Ambursen Hydraulic Constrn. Co. of Can., Ltd., 1913-15; instr. in ry. engring., Mass. Inst. Tech., 1916-19, asst. prof., 1919-25, asso. prof., 1925-28, prof. from 1928. Mem. Boston Soc. Civil Engrs. (pres., 1935), Am. Soc. C.E., Am. Ry. Engring. Assn., Am. Soc. for Engring. Edn., Am. Road Builders Assn. Republican. Club: New England Railroad. Author publs. on railway, highway and airport engring. Home: Newton Centre, Mass. †

BABCOCK, RODNEY WHITTEMORE, educator; b. Milton, Vt., July 22, 1890; s. Henry and Adele Calista (Stiles) B.; A.B., U. of Mo., 1912; M.A., U. of Wis., 1915, Ph.D., 1924; grad. study, U. of Pa., 1915-16; m. Josephine Luella Claus, July 22, 1915; children—John Henry, Jean Adele, Elliot Rodney. Instr. in mathematics Evansville (Wis.) Jr. Coll., 1912-14, U. of Pa., 1915-16, U. of Wis., 1916-25; asst. prof. mathematics, U. of Wis., 1925-29; prof. mathematics; DePauw U., 1929-30; dean Sch. of Arts and Sciences, Kan. State Coll. Agr. and Applied Science, 1930-55; dean emeritus, 1955; prof. mathematics, from 1955. Mem. Am. Math. Soc., Math. Assn. Am., Phi Delta Kappa, Gamma Alpha, Phi Kappa Phi, Pi Kappa Delta, Lambda Chi-Alpha, Sigma Xi, Pi Mu Epsilon. Republican. Methodist. Kiwanian. Home: Manhattan, Kan. †

BABER, ALICE, artist; b. Charleston, Ill., Aug. 22, 1928; d. Adin and Lois M. (Shoot) B. Student, Lindenwood Coll., 1946-47; B.A., Ind. U., 1950; postgrad., Fontainbleau (France) Sch. of Art, 1951. Lectr. in painting, design and lithography U. Calif., Santa Barbara, 1971, SUNY, Purchase, 1972-73, Post Coll., L.I., N.Y., 1973, Sch. of Visual Arts, N.Y.C., 1973-76; artist-in-residence Tamarind Inst., U. N.Mex., 1979. Numerous one-woman shows of paintings and/or lithographs, from 1958, latest being, Kunst-Galerie 63, Switzerland, 1978, Niagara U., Niagara Falls, N.Y., 1979, The Art Package, Chgo., 1979, Gallery West, Los Angeles, 1980, Galerie de'l Arte Nueva, Lima, Peru, 1980, Amerika Haus, Frankfurt, Germany, 1980, Lillian Heidenberg Gallery, N.Y.C., 1981, group shows, from 1957, latest being, Guggenheim Mus., N.Y.C., 1980, Orgn. Ind. Artists travelling exhbn., 1980-81; represented in permanent collections, Whitney Mus. Am. Art, N.Y.C., Mus. Modern Art, Bogota, Columbia, Met. Mus. Art, N.Y.C., Mus. Modern Art, N.Y.C., Guggenheim Mus., N.Y.C., Corcoran Gallery, Washington, Ga. Mus. Art, Atlanta, Nat. Art Gallery, San Salvador, Newark (N.J.) Mus., Nat. Mus. of Israel, Nat. Collection of Fine Arts, Washington and others, also numerous pvt. collections. Mem. Coll. Art Assn., Washington Women in Arts. Address: New York, NY.

BABSON, ARTHUR CLIFFORD, fin. exec.; b. Portland, Oreg., July 19, 1909; s. Sydney Gorham and Grace Bowditch (Campbell) B.; B.S., U. Oreg., 1931; m. Margery Tindle Grey, Aug. 3, 1946; children—John Pell, Robert Grey. With Union Terminal Coldstorage Co., Jersey City, 1932-36, asst. supt., 1935-36; with Babson's Reports, Inc., Wellesley Hills, Mass., from 1936, v.p., 1940-78, cons., from 1978; dir., mem. fiduciary com. Cape Ann Nat. Bank & Trust Co. of Gloucester (Mass.); dir. Sierra Pacific Power Co., Reno, Home Group Inc., N.Y.C., Gen. Devel. Corp., Miami, Fla., GDV Corp., N.Y.C.; dir., mem. exec. com. City Investing Co., Beverly Hills, Calif.; dir., mem. investment adv. com. Home Ins. Co., N.Y.C. Chmn. Sherborn (Mass.) Bd. Selectmen, 1964-70; trustee Sawin Acad. U.S. Naval rep. lt. comdr., Ceylon and So. India, 1942-45. Mem. Pilgrims of U.S., Chi Psi. Episcopalian. Home: Sherborn, Mass. Deceased.

BACHMAN, GEORGE WILLIAM, med. economist; b. Germantown, Ohio, May 12, 1890; s. George William and Katherine (Miller) B.; B.S., Heidelberg Coll., Tiffin, O., 1917; A.M., Columbia, 1923; Ph.D., U. of Chicago, 1927; D.Sc. Heidelberg College, 1944; unmarried. Professor of biology, Huping College, China, 1918-23, acting president, 1923-25; instr. in parasitology, Univ. of Chicago, 1927-28; assistant in parasitology, Johns Hopkins, 1928-29; asso. prof. of parasitology, Sch. of Tropical Medicine (auspices of Columbia U.), San Juan, Puerto Rico, 1930-31, acting dir., 1930-31, dir., 1931-41; prof. of parasitology, Columbia, 1931-41; field dir., Am. Bur. for Med. Aid to China, 1942-44; now member research staff, Brookings Institution. Awarded Rickets Memorial prize for research, U. of Chicago, 1928. Mem. Am. Soc. Parasitologists, N.Y. Acad. Science, American Society of Tropical Medicine, Washington Academy of Medicine, American Acad. of Tropical Medicine, Royal Soc. Tropical Medicine and Hygiene, Sigma Xi, Gamma Alpha. Mem. Reformed Church. Author: Health Resources in the United States; also reports, contbns. profl. publs. Home: Washington, D.C.†

BACKMAN, JULES, economist, educator, author; b. N.Y.C., May 3, 1910; s. Nathan and Gertrude (Schall) B.; m. Grace Straim, Oct. 18 1935; children—Mrs. Susan Patricia Frank, John Randolph. B.C.S., N.Y. U., 1931, A.M., 1932, M. B.A., 1933, D.C.S., 1935. Statistician Sydeman Bros., stock brokers, 1932-33; v.p., editor Econ. Statistics, Inc., 1933-35; with SEC, 1935; pub. utility research Madden & Dorau, 1936-37; instr. econs. Sch. Commerce, N.Y.U., N.Y.C., 1938-44, asst. prof., 1944-46, asso. prof., 1946-50, prof., 1950-60, research prof., 1960-75, prof. emeritus, 1975-82; dir. Scarsdale Nat. Bank; head econ. cons OPA, 1942, Brookings Instn., 1943; econ. advisor Steel Wage Cases, 1944, 49, 52; tech. adv. to industry mems. President's Cost of Living Com., 1944; econ. adv. to r.r. in wage and rate cases, 1946-60, N.Y. Joint Legis. Com. on Rents, 1953; mem. N.Y. Milk Shed Price Com., 1947-49, Gov's. Com. on Milk Mktg., 1961-65, Nat. Mktg. Adv. Com., 1967-69. Author: Government Price Fixing, 1938, Investment Dynamics, 1939, Rationing and Price Control in Great Britain, 1943, Economics of the Potash Industry, 1946, Surety Rate Making, 1949, (ed. and co-author) War and Defense Economics, 1952, Price Practices and Price Policies, 1953, Rate Policies and Rate Practices of the Post Office, 1954, Administered Prices, 1957, Wage Determination, 1959, Pricing: Policies and Practices, 1961, The Economics of the Electrical Machinery Industry, 1962, Advertising and Competition, 1967, Economics of the Chemical Industry, 1970, (with M.R. Gainsbrugh) Economics of the Cotton Textile Industry, 1946, Inflation and the Price Indexes, 1966; Editor, co-author: (with M.R. Gainsbrugh) Business Problems of the Seventies, 1973, Labor, Technology, and Productivity, 1974, Social Responsibility and Accountability, 1975, Multinational Corporations, Trade and the Dollar, 1974, Bus. and the Am. Economy, 1976-2001, 1976, Economic Growth or Stagnation, 1978, Business Problems of the Eighties, 1979, Regulation and Deregulation, 1980; econ. editor: (with M.R. Gainsbrugh) Trust & Estates mag, 1938-46; editorial writer: (with M.R. Gainsbrugh) N.Y. Times, 1943-48. Gen. chmn. Reform Jewish Appeal, 1966-69; cons. GAO, 1971-72; econ. adviser N.J. rate counsel, 1970-75; Mem. N.Y.U. Senate, 1962-65; trustee Union Am. Hebrew Congregations, 1976-82; chmn. bd. govs. Hebrew Union Coll., 1976-82. Recipient N.Y. Univ. Meritorious Service award, 1943, Madden award, 1960, Man of Year 1961 award G.B.A. Alumni N.Y.U.; Presidential citation N.Y. U., 1964; Am. Judaism award, 1970; Gt. Tchr. award N.Y. U., 1976; Founders medal Hebrew Union Coll., 1979. Hon. fellow Am. Statis. Assn.; mem. Am. Econ. Assn., Soc. Bus. Adv. Profs. (pres. 1955), N.Y. U. Alumni Fedn (pres. 1954-56), Beta Gamma Sigma, Phi Lambda Delta, Lambda Gamma Phi, Sigma Eta Phi (hon.), Alpha Phi Sigma (hon.). Clubs: N.Y.U. (chmn. bd. 1961-65, hon. life chmn. 1972-82), Metropolis Country (past dir.). Home: Scarsdale, N.Y. Died Mar. 25, 1982.

BACON, CLARENCE EVERETT, investment banking; b. Westbrook, Conn., Aug. 18, 1890; s. Clarence Everett and Katharine Sedgewick (Whiting) B.; B.S., Conn. Wesleyan Univ., 1913; m. Eva Peabody, Nov. 6, 1915 (divorced 1947); 1 dau., Anne Peabody. m. 2d Ramona Dillier, 1947. Salesman with Lee Higginson & Co., N.Y., 1914-16, Spencer Trask & Co., 1916-23, became partner, 1923, senior partner; president, treasurer and member board of directors Broadway Realty Co.; former v.p., dir. Mexican No. R.R.; vp., treas. Colo. Fluorspar Corp.; dir. Fresnillo Co.; dir., treas. Corp. of Yaddo; v.p., treas., dir. 880 Fifth Ave. Corp. (N.Y.C.). Trustee, chmn. investment com. Bennett Coll.; trustee, Wesleyan U., 1934-60, trustee emeritus; trustee So. Edn. Found., Inc., Spelman Coll. (Atlanta); trustee and chmn. finance coms. of Atlanta U. and Morehouse Coll., Atlanta, Ga. Served with 312th Inf., later lt. 48th Field Arty., 1917-19. Pres. bd. dirs. Montclair YMCA, 1925-36; exec. com. N.Y. State C. of C., 1933-36, 43-45, 49-52, 54-57; ex-gov. Assn. Stock Exchange Firms; trustee Community Chest, Montclair, 1937-45, pres. bd. 1939. Mem. S.A.R., New Eng. Soc. of New York (trustee 1939-42). Republican. Episcopalian (former vestryman). Clubs: Down Town, Down Town Athletic, Anglers (N.Y.C.); Maidstone, Devon Yacht (E. Hampton, L.I.); National Golf Links Am. (Southampton). Home: New York, NY†

BAER, REXFORD LEVERING, city official; b. Los Angeles, Nov. 25, 1931; s. Joseph Levering and Eunice Marguerite (Richardson) B.; B.A., Los Angeles State Coll., 1954; M.A. in Internat. Relations (Herman fellow 1957-59), U. So. Calif., 1959; postgrad. in law Southwestern U., from 1975; m. Cornelia Van Natta Goodwin, Aug. 21, 1959 (div.); children—Marianne Benora, Kathleen Goodwin. Asst. to dir. Sch. Internat. Relations, U. So. Calif., 1957-59; with USIA, 1959-68, dep. policy dir. Latin Am. and Cuban affairs, 1967-68; dir. So. Calif. region Inst. Internat. Relations, 1968-71, dir. West coast region 11E, 1971-74; freeway cons. and negotiator City of South Pasadena (Calif.), 1974-75. Mem. World Affairs Council, Town Hall, Com. Fgn. Relations, Los Angeles County Mus. Art. Served with AUS, 1954-57. Recipient Meritorious Service award USIA, 1961, 66. Mem. Delta Upsilon. Republican. Conglist. Home: San Gabriel, Calif. Died Jan. 11, 1985.

BAERG, GERHARD, educator; b. Hillsboro, Kan., Oct. 28, 1887; s. John and Margaret (Hildebrand) B.; A.B., U. Kan., 1916; A.M., Cornell U., 1918; Ph.D., 1920; m. Annette Dacier, June 30, 1930 (died Oct. 9, 1941); m. 2d, Marjorie Kendrick Lane, July 3, 1952. Instr. German, Wesleyan U., Conn., 1920-23; lecteur américain, Sorbonne, U. of Paris, 1923-24; lectr. on French culture Internationale Höjskole, Helsingör, Denmark, summer 1924; asst. to asso. prof. German, Wesleyan U., 1924-31; prof. German and head of German dept. DePauw U., 1931-54, prof. emeritus from 1954; guest prof. Gottingen U., Germany, summer 1949. Served as interpreter, 89th Div., U.S. Army, 1918-19. Mem. Modern Lang. Assn., Am. Assn. Tchrs. German (pres. 1943-44), Sigma Nu, Phi Delta Kappa, Phi Beta Kappa. Republican. Conglist. Author: The Supernatural in Modern German Drama, 1920; German Grammar Review with Composition, 1930: Alternate German Grammar Review, 1933; Deutschland, ein Kulturlesebuch, 1938. Home: Greencastle, Ind. †

BAETJER, ANNA MEDORA, scientist, educator; b. Balt., July 7, 1899; d. J. Frank and Katherine (Cook) B. B.A., Wellesley Coll., 1920; D.Sc., Johns Hopkins U., 1924, D.H.L. (hon.), 1979; D.P.H. (hon.), Woman's Med. Coll. Pa., 1953; D.Sc. (hon.), Wheaton Coll., 1966. Mem. faculty Johns Hopkins Sch. Hygiene and Public Health, Balt., 1923—, prof. environ. medicine, 1961-70, prof. emeritus, from 1970; cons. preventive medicine div. Office Surgeon Gen. U.S. Army, from 1943; mem. commn. environ. health Armed Forces Epidemiol. Bd., 1954-73; mem. com. on biol. effects of atmospheric pollutants NRC, 1970-73; cons. toxicology research div. Koppers Co., 1957-58; mem. Permanent Commn. and Internat. Assn. Occupational Health, from 1960; mem. adv. com. on safety pesticide residues in foods FDA, 1966-70; mem. occupational safety and health study sect. Nat. Inst. Occupational Safety and Health, HEW, 1968-70, 72-74; mem. nat. air quality criteria adv. com. EPA, 1972-76; mem. standards adv. com. on heat stress U.S. Dept. Labor, 1973-74; mem. noise control adv. bd. Balt. Health Dept., 1973-76; mem. com. on public info. in prevention occupational cancer NRC, 1975-77; mem. Armed Forces Epidemiology Bd., 1977-82; temporary adviser WHO, from 1978. Author: Women in Industry-Their Health and Efficiency, 1946; also articles research papers, chpts, in books.; Mem. editorial bd.: Archives Environmental Health, 1960-70, Excerpta Medica, 1976-77. Trustee Indsl. Health Found., from 1958, vice chmn., 1964-68. Recipient Disting. Civilian Services award U.S. Army, 1981, Outstanding Med. Educator award Am. Occupational Medicine Assn., 1983. Mem. Am. Physiol. Soc., Am. Public Health Assn., Am. Indsl. Hygiene Assn. (pres. 1951, Cummings Meml. award 1964), Am. Conf. Govt. Indsl. Hygienists (Herbert Stokinger award 1980), Am. Acad. Occupational Medicine (hon., Robert Kehoe award 1976), Am. Acad. Indsl. Hygiene (bd. 1968-72), Md. Acad. Scis. (trustee 1965-67), Phi Beta Kappa, Sigma Xi. Home: Baltimore, Md. Deceased.

BAGGARLY, FRANKLIN CLYDE, lawyer; b. Washington, Va., Apr. 14, 1890; s. Baldwin Bradford and Emma Jane (Moore) B.; B.S., Rappahannock Mil. Acad.; studied Randolph-Macon Coll., Ashland, Va.; spl. work U. of Va.; grad. Columbian George Washington) U.; grad. study Georgetown U.; studied law under Justices John M. Harlan and David J. Brewer of Supreme Court of U.S.; LL.B., Nat. U. Law Sch., 1908; m. Frances Willard Trott, of Anne Arundel Co., Md., Sept. 25, 1929. Editor Southern Mag., 1909-10; admitted to Va. bar, 1910; practiced at Richmond, Washington, Va., and Washington, D.C.; mem. common council and town atty., Washington, Va., 1914-18; chmn. legal advisory bd. and atty. for Govt. appeals, Rappahannock Co., Va., World War; atty. U.S. Dept. Justice, 1918, Bd. Contract Adjustment, War Dept. (asso. mem.), 1919; served as atty. select com. U.S. Senate in coal industry investigation, also asst. chief trial atty., Federal Trade Commn. Mem. Federal Bar Assn. (nat. pres., 1926-28), Soc. of Va. (pres. 1925-26), Pan State Soc. (v.p. 1927), Southern Soc. of Washington, Sigma Nu Phi. Mason (K.T., Shriner); mem. O.E.S. Club: Harper Country. Author: The History of Washington, Virginia—The First Washington of All, 1931. Home: Washington, D.C. †

BAGHDIGIAN, BAGDASAR KRIKOR, author; b. Armenia, Feb. 21, 1888; s. Krikor and Bezig (Kefeian) B.; came to U.S., 1904; B.S., Kan. State Agrl. Coll., 1916; grad. Mo. Sch. Social Economy, 1918; Mem. Mo. Writers' Guild, Kansas Authors' Club, Am. Quill Club, Sigma Delta Chi. Christian. Mason (32 deg.). Author: Essentials of Americanization, 1919; The Psalms of a Naturalized American, 1921; Americanism in Americanization, 1921; Americanism at Work, 1923; The Flag of Humanity (an interpretation of the American flag), 1923; In Defense of America, 1924; Tuning in with Life Forces for Health, Happiness, Power, Success, 1927. Lecturer. Founder and teacher of "The Four-Fold Secret of Mental, Physical, Spiritual, Dynamic Life"; also founder and dir. Better Citizenship Bur. of America, Commonwealth of Leaders. Home: Kansas City, Mo. †

BAILEY, CARLOS A(UGUSTUS), retired naval officer; b. Somerville, Mass., May 3, 1887; s. John Tewksbury and Alice Elizabeth (Bacon) B.; student Tufts Coll., Medford, Mass., 1906-07; B.S., U.S. Naval Acad., 1911; student Naval War Coll., Newport, R.I., 1936-37; m. Claire Lyons Millett, June 19, 1914; children—Carlos Augustus, Alice (wife of Lt. Comdr. F.A. Hooper), Ruth (wife of Lt. Comdr. Eugene H. Farrell), Tom Carroll, David Millett. Commd. ensign U.S. Navy, 1911, and advanced through grades to Commodore, 1945; sea service, various parts of the world; served various ships (U.S.S. Nebraska, Des Moines, Utah, McKee, Hopkins, Sturtevant, Mississippi, Medusa, Houston, Neville, Barnett), 1911-43; deputy comdt. and chief of staff, 9th Naval Dist., 1944-46; retired Nov. 1946. Served at sea, World Wars I and II; participated in 1st Pacific landing, Solomon Islands, World War II. Awarded Legion of Merit; received letters of commendation from Sec. of Navy and Pres. of U.S. Mem. Naval Acad. Alumni Assn., U.S. Naval Inst., SAR. Protestant. Home: Cuttingsville, Vermont.†

BAILEY, CLYDE H., biochemist; b. Minneapolis, Apr. 15, 1887; s. George W. and Sophie A. (McKenney) B.; student Sch. of Agr., U. of Minn., 1905; B.S., N.Dak. Coll. of Agr., 1913; M.S., U. of Minn., 1916; Ph.D., U. of Md., 1921; D.Sc. hon. causa, N.D. Agricultural Coll., 1951; m. Anne L. Wilkins, June 20, 1910; 1 dau., Barbara A. Analyst, Howard Lab., Minneapolis, 1905-07; scientific asst., Bureau Plant Industry, U.S. Dept. Agr., 1907-11; asst. later biochemist, Minn. Agrl. Expt. Sta., from 1911; asst. prof. biochemistry, U. of Minn., 1914-16, asso. prof., 1917-20, prof. from 1920; vice dir. Minn. Agrl. Expt. Station 1938-41, dean dept. agr., 1942-52, dean emeritus. Chemist Minn. Grain Inspection Dept., 1916-17; dir. Minn. State Exptl. Flour Mill, Minneapolis, 1921-24; dir. of research, Biscuit and Cracker Mfrs. Assn. of America, 1924-26; editor in chief Cereal Chemistry (jour. of Am. Assn. Cereal Chemists), 1924-31; adminstrator bakery div., Minn. Food Adminstrn., 1918. Fellow A.A.A.S., Konig, Deutsche Akad. Naturforscher; mem. Am. Chem. Soc. (chmn. agr. and food div., 1923-25), Am. Soc. Plant Physiology (chmn. Minn. sect., 1929-30), Sigma Xi (pres. Minn. Chapter, 1927-28), Gamma Sigma Delta (nat. sec. 1921-23, 1940-42; pres. Minn. Chap., 1922-23), Am. Assn. Cereal Chemists (pres. 1937-38), Phi Lambda Upsilon, Alpha Chi Sigma, Alpha Zeta. Mason. Clubs: Campus, Cosmopolitan, Rotary Internat. Author: Chemistry of Wheat Flour, 1925; Physical Tests of Flour Quality, 1940; Constituents of Wheat and Wheat Flour, 1944; also numerous bulletins and scientific papers covering results of original research. Thomas Burr Osborne medalist, 1932; Nicolas Appert medalist, 1946. Home: St. Pual, Minn. †

BAILEY, ROGER, architect, artist educator; b. Bradford, Pa., Oct. 3, 1897; s. Benjamin Milton and May (Andrews) B.; B.Arch., Cornell U., 1920; student L'Ecole des Beaux Arts, Paris, France, 1922-25; m. Elisabeth Lorch, Dec. 21, 1935. Engaged as practising and cons. architect, N.Y., 1929-32, Mich., 1932-49, Utah, from 1949; prof. architecture U. Mich., 1932-35, 38-49; vis. prof. Cornell U., 1936-38; head critic architecture Yale, 1936-38; prof. architecture U. Utah, 1949-66, emeritus prof., 1966-85, head dept., 1949-64, mem. univ. campus design com., 1958-64; exec. dir. Salt Lake Art Center, 1971-74, trustee, 1962-71. Mem. Citizens Adv. Com. Capital Improvements Salt Lake City, 1958; founder, co-dir. program archtl. psychology NIMH, 1961-68, prin. investigator research projects, 1964, 65, 69; project dir. State Rehab. Center, 1969-70; mem. State Adv. Com. on Rehab. Facilities, 1967; chmn. Com. on Archtl. Barriers, 1967; mem. tech. rev. com. Utah Div. on Aging, 1969-71; mem. adv. bd. YWCA, 1963-69. Bd. dirs. Utah Mental Health Assn., 1965-71; mem. bldg. com. Monterey Peninsula Mus. Art, from 1979, watercolor paintings in permanent collections: Monterey Peninsula Mus. Art, Monterey, Calif., Utah Mus. Fine Arts, Salt Lake City, Legion of Honor Mus. Art, San Francisco. Served to 2d lt., inf., U.S. Army, 1918. Recipient Paris prize, 1922; co-recipient Chgo. War Meml. Competition, 1930; recipient 1st Scarab Club water-color prize, Detroit, 1945; Architect of Year, Utah Producers Council, 1966. Fellow A.I.A. (bd. dirs. Detroit 1948, pres. Utah chpt. 1963, Cert. of Appreciation, Utah Soc. 1984), Assn. Collegiate Schs. Architecture (dir.), AAUP, U.S. Bldg. Research Inst., Nat. Soc. Applied Solar Energy. Episcopalian. Home: Pebble Beach, Calif. Died Apr. 20, 1985.

BAILEY, STEPHEN KEMP, educator; b. Newton, Mass., May 14, 1916; s. Albert E. and Marion B. (Hall) B.; m. Cornelia Wootton Brown, Aug. 31, 1940; children—Morris Edward, Lois Emerson. A.B., Hiram Coll., 1937; B.A. (Rhodes scholar), Oxford U., 1939; M.A., Harvard, 1943, Ph.D., 1948; LL.D. (hon.), Reed Coll., 1963, Union Coll., 1974, St. Mary's Coll., 1974; L.H.D. (hon.), Rosary Hill Coll., 1974; Litt.D. (hon.), Curry Coll., 1976. Research asso. Transcontinental Research, Inc., N.Y.C., 1939-40; dir. admissions Hiram Coll., 1941-42; asst. chief Am. Hemisphere div. Bd. Econ. Warfare, Washington, 1942; research fellow Social Sci. Research Council, Washington, 1946; asst. prof. govt. Wesleyan U., 1946-49, asso. prof., 1949-54; adminstrv. asst. Senator William Benton, 1951; William Church Osborn prof. pub. affairs Princeton U., 1954-59; dir. grad. program Woodrow Wilson Sch. Public and Internat. Affairs, Princeton, 1954-58; prof. polit. sci. Maxwell Grad. Sch. Citizenship and Public Affairs, Syracuse (N.Y.) U., 1959-74; dean Maxwell Grad. Sch., 1961-69; chmn. policy inst. Syracuse U. Research Corp., 1969-73; v.p. Am. Council on Edn., 1973-77; Francis Keppel prof. edn. policy and adminstrn. Harvard U., Cambridge, Mass., from 1977; sr. Fulbright lectr. Oxford U., 1957-58; staff asso. Public Adminstrn. Clearing House, Hoover Commn. on Orgn. Exec. Branch, Washington, 1948. Author: Roosevelt and His New Deal, 1938, Congress Makes a Law, 1950, (with Howard Samuel) Congress at Work, 1951, (with H. Samuel and S. Baldwin) Government in America, 1957, (with Robert Wood, Richard Frost, Paul Marsh) Schoolmen and Politics, 1962, The New Congress, 1966, (with Edith Mosher) ESEA: The Office of Education Administraters at Law, 1968, Congress in the Seventies, 1970, Education Interest Groups in the Nation's Capital, 1975, The Purposes of Education, 1976. Mayor, Middletown, Conn., 1952-54; Bd. dirs. Woodrow Wilson Found., 1958-63; bd. regents SUNY, 1967-73; trustee Hiram Coll., 1968—. Served as lt., OSS USNR, 1942-45. Recipient Disting. Service to Edn. plaque Council Chief State Sch. Officers, 1974, Disting. Service award Columbia, 1976. Mem. Am. Polit. Sci. Assn. (v.p. 1968-69), Nat. Acad. Edn., Am. Acad. Arts and Scis., Am. Soc. Pub. Adminstrn. (pres. 1967-68), AAUP, Assn. Am. Rhodes Scholars, Phi Delta Kappa. Conglist. Deceased.*

BAILEY, THOMAS ANDREW, historian, educator; b. San Jose, Calif., Dec. 14, 1902; s. James Andrew and Annie (Nelson) B.; m. Sylvia Dean, Aug. 28, 1928; 1 son, Arthur Dean. A.B. with great distinction, Stanford, 1924, A.M., 1925, Ph.D., 1927. Teaching fellow in history U. Calif., 1925-26; acting instr. in citizenship Stanford, 1926-27, asst. prof. history, 1930-35, asso. prof., 1935-40, prof., 1940, Margaret Byrne prof. Am. history, 1952-68, prof. emeritus, 1968-83; exec. head history dept., 1952-55, 57-59; instr. history and polit. sci. U. Hawaii, 1927-28, asst. prof., 1928-30; asst. prof. history U. Wash., summer 1931; vis. prof. diplomatic history George Washington U., 1936-37; vis. lectr. history Harvard, 1943-44, Cornell, 1950; Fellow Rockefeller Found. Internat. Relations and; mem. Inst. for Advanced Study, Princeton, N.J., 1939-40; Albert Shaw lectr. in diplomatic history Johns Hopkins, 1941; observer in, Europe; and civilian mem. staff Nat. War Coll., 1947. Mem. bd. editors: Pacific Hist. Rev, 1937-40; Author: Theodore Roosevelt and the Japanese-American Crises, 1934, A Diplomatic History of the American People, 1940, 10th edit., 1980, The Policy of the United States Toward the Neutrals, 1917-18, 1942, America's Foreign Policies; Past and Present, 1943, rev. edit., 1945, Woodrow Wilson and the Lost Peace, 1944 (awarded Commonwealth Club gold medal), Woodrow Wilson and the Great Betrayal, 1945, Wilson and the Peacemakers, 1947, The Man in the Street, 1948, America Faces Russia, 1950 (Gold medal Commonwealth Club), The American Pageant, 1956, 6th edit., 1979, Presidential Greatness, 1966, The Art of Diplomacy, 1968, Democrats vs. Republicans, 1968, Essays Diplomatic and Undiplomatic, 1969, Probing America's Past, 1973, (with Paul B. Ryan) The Lusitania Disaster, 1975, Voices of America, 1976, The Marshall Plan Summer, 1977, Hitler vs. Roosevelt, 1979, The Pugnacious Presidents, 1980, Presidential Saints and Sinners, 1981; Editor: (with F.A. Golder and J.L. Smith) The March of the Mormon Battalion, 1928, The American Spirit, 1963, 4th edit., 1978; Contbr. (with F.A. Golder and J.L. Smith) articles to profl. jours. Mem. Am. Hist. Assn. (pres. Pacific Coast br. 1959-60), Orgn. Am. Historians (pres. 1968), Stanford Inst. Am. History (dir. 1952-53), Soc. for Historians of Am. Fgn. Relations (pres. 1968), Phi Beta Kappa., Delta Sigma Rho. Home: Stanford, Calif. Died July 26, 1983.

BAILIE, ALEXANDER JOSEPH, ins. co. exec.; b. N.Y.C., Aug. 29, 1932; s. Alexander Harrigan and Agnes W. (Darragh) B.; m. Margaret E. Guilday, June 25, 1955; children—Maureen Antoinette, Joseph Alexander, Margaret Ellen, Michael Edward. A.B., Fordham U., 1954. With Met. Life Ins. Co., from 1954, apptd. officer, 1962; head Met. Life Ins. Co. (W. Coast office), 1965-67, actuary, N.Y.C., 1972-74, v.p. and actuary, 1974-76, sr. v.p. and actuary, 1976-77, sr. v.p. and chief actuary, 1977-80, sr. v.p., from 1980; dir. Met. Ins. & Annuity Co., Transatlantic Reins. Co. Fellow Soc. Actuaries; mem. Am. Acad. Actuaries. Home: Stamford, Conn.

BAILIET, JOHN MASON, gen. ins. broker; b. Appleton, Wis., July 29, 1890; s. David Henry and Ellen (Cannon) B.; ed. pub. schs. of Appleton; m. Vivian Irene Brega, February 14, 1912; children—Richard S., Ellen, David (dec.), Bette (Mrs. Donald C. Grefe). Teacher Freedom, Wisconsin, 1907-08, Cedar Point, Illinois, 1908-09; staff engineering department, U.P. R.R., Omaha, 1909-14; gen. ins., surety bond agt. and broker Balliet Agy., Inc., from 1914, chmn.; dir. Mich. Central R.R., Lake Erie and Eastern R.R., Pitts. & Lake Erie R.R.; mem. exec. com., dir. Detroit River Tunnel Co. Mem. Am. Arbitration Assn., Newcomen Soc. in N. Am. Elk, K.C. (4). Club: Butte des Morts Golf. Home: Appleton, WI. †

BAINBRIDGE, CHARLES NEWTON, engineer; b. Phila., Pa., Mar. 29, 1887; s. George M. and Mary Malinda (Coulston) B.; B.S. in C.E., Pa. State Coll., 1907, C.E., 1910; m. Lillian Schwab, of Chicago, Ill., Dec. 1910; children—Mary Katherine, Charles Newton. Began in employ Am. Bridge Co., 1907; instr. in civil engring. Pa. State Coll., 1908-09; with C.,M.,St.P.&P.R.R. Co. from 1909 (except 6 mos. with B.&O.R.R.), engr. of design; dir. Lombard (Ill.) Real Estate Improvement Co., First Trust Bank (Lombard). Mem. bd. trustees village of Lombard 10 years. Asso. mem. Am. Soc. C.E.; mem. Am. Ry. Engring. Assn., Phi Sigma Kappa. Republican. Methodist. Mason. Club: Collegiate (Chicago). Home: Lombard, Ill. †

BAINTON, ROLAND HERBERT, educator; b. Ikeston, Derbyshire, Eng., Mar. 30, 1894; came to U.S., 1902; s. James Herbert and Charlotte Eliza (Blackham) B.; m. Ruth Woodruff, June 8, 1921 (dec. 1966); children—Olive Mae (Mrs. Roger Robison), Herbert Woodruff, Joyce (Mrs. William Peck), Cedric, Ruth Mildred (Mrs. Richard Lunt). A.B., Whitman Coll., 1914; B.D., Yale, 1917, Ph.D., 1921. Instr. ch. history Yale, 1920-23, asst. prof., 1923-32, asso. prof., 1932-36, Titus St. prof. ecclesiastical history, 1936-62, prof. emeritus, 1962-84. Author: Castellio Concerning Heretics, 1935, David Joris, 1937, Bernardino Ochino, 1940, The Church of our Fathers, 1941, George Lincoln Burr, 1943, Here I Stand, A Life of Martin Luther, 1950, The Travail of Religious Liberty, 1951, The Reformation of the Sixteenth Century, 1952, Hunted Heretic: A Study of Michael Servetus, 1953, The Age of Reformation, 1956, What Christianity Says About Sex, Love and Marriage, 1957, Yale and the Ministry, 1957, Pilgrim Parson, The Life of James Herbert Bainton, 1958, Early Christianity, 1960, Christian Attitudes to War and Peace, 1960, El Alma Hispana, 1961, Medieval

Church, 1962, The Horizon History of Christianity, 1964, Erasmus of Christendom, 1968, Women of the Reformation, 3 vols, 1971, 73, 77, Behold the Christ, 1974, Yesterday, Today and What Next? Reflections on History and Hope, 1978, works transl. into 13 langs.; Contbr. articles to jours. Served with Quaker unit ARC, World War I. Conglist. Home: New Haven, Conn. Died Jan. 12, 1984.

BAIRD, ALEXANDER KENNEDY, educator; b. Pasadena, Calif., Nov. 22, 1932; s. A. Kennedy and Phyllis May (Stimpson) B.; m. Kathleen White, Oct. 1, 1965. B.A., Pomona Coll., 1954; M.A., Claremont Grad. Sch., 1957; Ph.D., U. Calif. at Berkeley, 1960. Instr. geology Pomona Coll., Claremont, Calif., 1955-56, 58-60, asst. prof. geology, 1960-64, assoc. prof. geology, 1964-70, prof. geology, 1970-85. NSF predoctoral fellow, 1957-58; NSF research grantee, 1963-68; NASA Viking scientist, 1972-79; prin. investigator NASA Mars Data Analysis Program, 1979-82; research assoc. NRC Jet Propulsion Lab., 1983. Fellow Geol. Soc. Am.; mem. Nat. Assn. Geology Tchrs., Am. Geophys. Union, Planetary Soc., Phi Beta Kappa, Sigma Xi. Home: Claremont, Calif. Died July 6, 1985.

BAIRD, FLAVE SAUNDERS, ry. exec.; b. Carbon Hill, O., Jan. 10, 1890; s. David Del and Ruth (Walters) R.; ed. pub. schs.; m. Edith Baer, Dec. 4, 1915 (died 1942); children—Miriam (Mrs. G. G. Simpson), Sarah Ruth (Mrs. George H. Hoover, Jr.); married second, Era Palmer Ryan on August 10, 1946. Began as stenographer, Norfolk and Western Ry. Co., Columbus, O., 1910-11, clerk, 1911-17, asst. chief clerk, 1917-20, chief clerk to asst. gen. freight agt., 1920-25, coal freight agt., Roanoke, 1925-27, asst. gen. freight agent, 1927-39, asst. freight traffic mgr., 1939, gen. coal freight agt., 1939-40, asst. vice pres. traffic, 1940-48, v.p. in charge of traffic from Jan. 1, 1949; dir. First Fed. Savings and Loan Assn. of Roanoke, Chesapeake Western Ry. Republican. Baptist. Mason, Kiwanian (pres. 1949). Home: Roanoke, Va.†

BAIRD, H.B., business exec.; b. Philadelphia, Nov. 23, 1888; s. Thomas Evans and Fanny (Brown) B.; student Haverford Sch., 1902-06, Hanover Inst. Tech., 1904-06; m. Ruth H. Cyphers, Sept. 3, 1938. Vice president Eastern Gas & Fuels Associates; pres. and dir. Castner, Curran & Bullitt, Inc., New England Coal & Coke Co.; dir. The Virginian Corp., Wyatt, Inc. Cambria Coal Mining & Mfg. Co., Wyatt Terminal Corp. Dir. Bituminous Coal Inst. Member Am. Soc. M.E. Clubs: Racquet and Tennis (New York); Racquet, University Barge (Phila.). Home: West Chester, Pa. †

BAIRD, SPENCER LAWRENCE, govt. ofcl.; b. Dodge City, Kan., Sept. 4, 1888; s. Joseph Charles and Josephine (Annison) B.; LL.B., U. Kan., 1911; m. Neva Rosalie Swartwout, Feb. 26, 1916; children—Dorothy Ann, Josephine (Mrs. Robert Smith Pine), Spencer Lawrence. Admitted to Kan. bar, 1911, Ida., 1914, Ore., 1927, Colo., 1936; practice of law, American Falls, Ida., 1913-26; atty. Power Co., 1914-18; asso. dist. counsel U.S. Bur. Reclamation, Portland, Ore., 1926-35, dist. counsel, Denver, 1935-41, Amarillo, Tex., 1941-51; chief counsel U.S. sect. Internat. Boundary and Water Commn., El Paso, from 1951; dir. Greensburg (Kan.) State Bank from 1940. Council commr. Boy Scouts Am., Denver, Amarillo, El Paso. Served with inf. U.S. Army, 1918. Mem. Am. Legion (post comdr.), Phi Delta Phi, Delta Tau Delta. Mason. Club: Rotary (dir., del. internat. conv., Rio de Janeiro). †

BAIRD, WALTER SCOTT, business exec.; b. Long Green, Md., Oct. 2, 1908; s. George William Curtis and Beulah (Dance) B.; m. Mary Davis, Sept. 28, 1937; children—Brinna, Nancy, Douglas Scott, Davis. A.B., St. John's Coll., 1930; Ph.D., Johns Hopkins, 1934. Instr. Harvard, 1934-35; physicist Watertown (Mass.) Arsenal, 1935-36; pres. Baird Assos., Inc., 1936-56; merged with Atomic Instrument Co., 1956; pres. merged corp. Baird Corp., Bedford, Mass., 1936-57, chmn., 1959-64, 67-82, pres., 1964-67; dir. Burr-Brown Research Corp., Tucson. Fellow Am. Acad. Arts and Scis.; mem. AAAS, Am. Inst. Mining, Metall. and Petroleum Engrs., Optical Soc. Am., Am. Inst. Physics, Sigma Xi. Clubs: Royal N.S. Yacht Squadron, Cruising of Am, St. Botolph. Home: Lexington, Mass. Died May 4, 1982.

BAKER, ALBERT ZACHARY, lawyer, former stock yards exec.; b. Whitesboro, Tex., Nov. 17, 1890; s. James Albert and Addie Isabella (Gilliland) B.; student U. Tenn., 1909-10; LL.B., Ohio No. U., 1924, John Marshall Law Sch., 1924; LL.D., Culver-Stockton Coll., 1956; L.H.D., California College Medicine, 1955; m. Grace D. Anderson, Feb. 21, 1914; children—Jane (Mrs. James J. Larson), Jean (Mrs. Hamilton W. Watt), Robert Gibson; m. 2d, Cornelia Anderson Thompson, Apr. 26, 1950; 1 stepson, Robert S. Thompson. With traffic dept. Morris & Co., Oklahoma City and Chgo., 1912-16; traffic mgr. Cleve. Provision Co., 1916-24; sec.-treas., commerce counsel Cleve. Union Stock Yards Co., 1924-25, pres., gen. mgr., 1925-46, 63-67, chmn. bd., 1925-68; dir., dep. chmn. Fed. Res. Bank Cleve., 1942-50, Nat. City Bank of Cleve., 1925-40. Pres. emeritus Am. Stock Yards Assn. Trustee emeritus Baldwin-Wallace Coll., from 1947. Mem. Cleve. C. of C. (past dir.), Cleve. Bar Assn., Delta Theta Phi. Mason (Shriner, 33), Rotarian (past pres. Cleve.; pres. Internat. 1955-56). Home: Kinsman, OH. †

BAKER, BENTON, lawyer; b. Bismarck, N.D., Dec. 31, 1889; s. Isaac P. and Julia Franklin (Barnes) B.; grad. Smith Acad., St. Louis, 1906; Ph.B., Yale, 1910; LL.B., 1915; m. Cornelia Francis Pickett, Aug. 9, 1919; children—Jessica Pickett (Mrs. Robert Frederic Barnard) and Benton. Admitted to N.D. bar, 1915, and practiced at Bismarck, 1915-26; held various civic, state and federal offices, 1917-26; spl. atty. U.S. Govt., Washington, D.C., 1926-28; specialized in practice of law of patents, trade marks and unfair competition from 1928, in N.Y.C., 1928-29, in Chgo., 1929-68; mem. Zabel, Baker, York, Jones & Dithmar, 1953-69; of counsel Zabel, Baker, York & Jones, Chgo., from 1969; spl. lectr. on patent law John Marshall Law Sch., 1944-56. Recipient 50 Year award N.D. Bar Assn., 1965. Mem. Am., 7th Fed. Circuit, Chgo. bar assns., Yale Law Sch. Assn. (grad. bd. 1957-60), Patent Law Assn. Chgo., Chgo. Civic Study Forum. University (Chgo.); Filson (Louisville). Author various papers and publs. Home: Santa Barbara, CA. †

BAKER, BURKE, ins. exec.; b. Waco, Tex., Aug. 9, 1887; s. Robert Holmes and Nellie (Faulkner) B.; B.A., U. Tex., 1909; grad. study Harvard, 1909-10; m. Bennie Brown, Oct. 11, 1911. Asst. cashier Tex. Trust Co., 1911-13; bond officer Bankers Trust Co., 1913-15; pres. Am. Briquet Co., Phila., 1915-19; pres. small oil prodn. cos., 1919-25; pres. Seaboard Life Ins. Co., Houston; president and chairman of the American General Life Insurance Company; formerly v.p. Houston Terminal Warehouse & Cold Storage Co.; dir. Manchester Terminal Corp., Houston, United Gas Corp., Shreveport, La. Mem. Texas Life Convention (former pres.), American Life Convention (dir.), Am. Bible Soc., Philos. Soc. Tex. (pres.). Presbyn. (Elder). †

BAKER, CROWDUS, cons.; b. Dallas, Feb. 27, 1906; s. Raymond Andrew and Alice Estella (Crowdus) B.; student Austin Coll., 1924-27; also LL.D.; LL.D., Villanova U.; Dr. Comml. Science (hon.), Suffolk University; m. Lorena Ann Proctor, July 5, 1928; 1 dau., Julie Ann. With Sears, Roebuck & Co., Dallas, Boston, Phila. Seattle, from 1929, gen. mgr. Boston mail order store, 1945-51, treas. co., 1951-63, v.p., comptroller, 1954-60, pres., 1960-68, vice chmn. bd., 1968-72, later dir.; dir. Archer-Daniels Midland Co., Simpsons-Sears, Ltd., Clark Equipment Co., Thomson Newspapers Inc. Bd. dirs. Sears-Roebuck Found.; trustee, Museum of Sci. and Industry, Chgo.; Jr. Achievement Chgo. Found.; v.p., dir. Jr. Achievement Chgo.; pres., dir. McGraw Wildlife Found. Mem. Northwestern U. Assos., Newcomen Soc. Clubs: Algonquin (Boston); Executives, Commercial, Chicago (Chgo.); Mid-Am. Home: Northfield, Ill. Died June 6, 1981.

BAKER, HAROLD WALLACE, civil engineer; b. Oneida, N.Y., Feb. 14, 1889; s. William M. and Fannie (Wallace) B.; B.E. in C.E., Union Coll., 1911, hon. D.Sc., 1936; m. Ethel M. Froass, Apr. 14, 1913; children—Wallace Froass, Jean Pauline. Engring. work on Coleman DuPont Road, Del. then asst. engr. for State of New York on barge, canal and highway constrn., later with Ludlum Steel Co., Watervliet, N.Y.; civil engr. Rochester (N.Y.) Bur. Municipal Research, 1921-24; commr. Pub. Works, City of Rochester, 1924-32; dir. constrn. Dist. of Columbia, 1932-34; city mgr. Rochester, Jan. 1934-June 1940; supervisor safety and fire protection Eastman Kodak Co. from 1940. Comdr. C.E. Corps, U.S. Naval Res. on active duty Navy Dept., Washington, D.C., from 1941. Mem. Am. Soc. C.E., Am. Water Works Assn., Internat. City Mgrs. Assn., Psi Upsilon, Sigma Xi. Unitarian. Mason (Shriner). Club: University. Home: Arlington, Va. †

BAKER, HERBERT HOWARD, business exec.; b. Toledo, O., Sept. 24, 1888; s. Rufus H. and Mary (Howard) Baker; ed. The Hotchkiss School, 1906; A.B., Yale Coll., 1910; m. Katharine M. Kinsey, Oct. 1, 1913. With Libbey Glass Co., Toledo, O., 1910-16; with Owens Bottle Co., Toledo, 1916-26; treas., 1920-26; with Libbey-Owens-Ford Glass Co., Toledo, from 1926, asst. to pres., 1926-28, v.p. and sec. from 1928. Dir. of Libbey-Owens-Ford Glass Co. Home: Toledo, Ohio. †

BAKER, HORACE BURRINGTON, educator, editor; b. Sioux City, Ia., Jan. 25, 1889; s. Robert Folen and Sophia Jane (Burrington) B.; B.S., U. Mich., 1910, Ph.D., 1920; m. Bernadine Barker, Dec. 21, 1941; children—Elizabeth C., Abigail B. Instr. to asst. prof. biology Colo. Coll., 1913-17; instr. zoology U. Mich., 1919; instr. zoology U. Pa., 1920-26, asst. prof., 1926-28, asso. prof., 1928-39, prof., from 1939, acting chmn. dept., from 1955; research fellow Phila. Acad. Nat. Sci., from 1925; research asso. Bishop Museum, Honolulu, from 1937. Served as 2d lt. F.A., U.S. Army, 1917-19. Mem. Am. Soc. Naturalists, Am. Soc. Zoologists, Am. Ecol. Soc., Am. Limnological Soc., Am. Malacological Union (pres. 1939), Am. Soc. Evolution, Am. Soc. Systematics, London Malacological Soc., Deutsche Malacozoologische Gesellschaft Soc., Sociedad Malacologica Cuba (hon.), Sigma Xi, Kappa Sigma. Unitarian. Editor for mollusks Biol. Abstracts, from 1925; editor, mgr. of The Nautilus, from 1932. Contbr. sci. periodicals. Home: Havertown, Pa. †

BAKER, JOANNA, prof. Greek, Simpson Coll. since 1889; d. Orlando Harrison and Mary C. (Ridley) B.; was taught Greek, Latin and French in childhood, by her parents, beginning the three languages at 4; read Homer in coll. at 8; moved to Algona, Ia., and entered coll.; apptd. tutor in Greek, Simpson Coll., when 16 yrs. old; grad. Cornell Coll., Ia., 1882 (A. M., 1985); tutor in Greek and sp'l student, Greek, German, French and music, De Pauw Univ., 1886-8 (A. M.), and admitted as an alumna ad eundem gradum; instr. Latin, De Pauw, 1888-9; student 1 term, 1895, in the Sauveur School of Languages, Amherst Coll., Mass.; post-graduate work Univ. of Chicago, 1896-1900 and 1902-3 (in residence 1898-9—other yrs. summers); A. M., Univ. of Chicago, 1903; asst. editor Indianola Herald, 1882-6; unmarried. Address: Indianola, Ia. †

BAKER, JOHN AUSTIN, exec., cons.; b. Paris, Ark., Feb. 22, 1914; s. John I. and Eloise Austin (Weems) B.; m. Susan Reed Toepfer, July 4, 1939; children—Roger William, James Karl, Robert Charles, David Allan, Judith Ann, Gordon Reed. B.S.A. (Danforth fellow), U. Ark., 1935; M.S., U. Wis., 1937; postgrad., Princeton, Harvard, U.S. Dept. Agr. Grad. Sch. Staff instr. U. Wis., 1935-36, 36-38, grad. fellow, 1938-39; economist, exec. officer Dept. Agr., 1937-51; program analyst, regional dir. FSA, Ark., La., Miss., 1939-43, FSA (Bur. Agrl. Econs.), 1937-39, 46-47; dir. land reform U.S. Mil. Govt., Korea, 1947-48, asst. to sec. agr., 1948-51; dir. legislative services Nat. Farmers Union, 1951-61; dir. agrl. credit Dept. Agr., 1961-62; asst. sec. of agr., mem. bd. CCC, 1962-69; pres. Community Devel. Services, 1969-81; assoc. James G. Patton Assocs., from 1970; exec. v.p. Green Thumb, Inc., 1974-80; Cons. U.S. Senate Com. Agr. and Forestry, 1971-73, U. Mass., S.D. Devel. Group, GAO, Four Winds Indsl. Found., Congl. Rural Caucus, U.S. Dept. State, 1958-60, CIA.; Mem. exec. com. Arlington Com. of 100, Coalition for Rural Devel.; Bd. dirs. Nat. Capital Democratic Club; adviser Dem. Nat. Com., 1948-76, 1981; White House Conf. on Aging; bd. dirs. Rural Am., Inc. Author: Guide to Federal Programs for Rural Development, 1975, Principles and Standards for Federal Program Evaluation and Analysis, 1975; Contbr. articles to profl. jours. Served from ensign to lt. USNR, 1943-46. Mem. Am. Agrl. Econ. Assn., Am. Econ. Assn., Nat. Planning Assn. (agrl. policy com.), Blue Key, Alpha Zeta, Alpha Gamma Rho, Phi Eta Sigma. Democrat. Home: Arlington, Va. Died Mar. 2, 1982.

BAKER, LEONARD JOEL, actor; b. Boston, Jan. 17, 1945; s. William Louis and Bertha (August) B. B.F.A., Boston U., 1967. Actor, various regional theatres, Balt., Louisville, Phila., Chgo., St. Louis; played various summer stock musicals in, Corpus Christi, Tex., Galveston, Tex., Saratoga Springs; off-Broadway debut in: musical Paradise Gardens East, 1969; appeared in: (Golden Globe nomination) films including Greenwich Village, 1976, The Hospital, 1972, The Paper Chase, 1974; Broadway debut in: films including Freedom of the City, 1974; other Broadway appearances: films including Secret Service, 1976, Boy Meets Girl, 1976; featured in: films including Life Class, Manhattan Theatre Club, 1976, Lesson of the Master at, Circle Repertory, 1976; performed: a one-man show at Spared, Brandeis U., 1975; TV appearances include On Our Own (Recipient Antoinette Perry (Tony) award for disting. achievement in theatre 1977, Drama Desk award for Broadway musical I Love My Wife 1976-77). Home: North Miami Beach, Fla. Died Apr. 12, 1982.

BAKER, LEONARD STANLEY, author; b. Pitts., Jan. 24, 1931; s. Charles and Bess (Schwartz) B.; m. Florence (Liva) Weil, Aug. 1, 1958; children: David, Sara. B.A., U. Pitts., 1952; M.S., Columbia U. Grad. Sch. Journalism, 1955. Reporter St. Louis Globe-Democrat, 1955-56; Washington reporter Newsday, 1956-65, author, editor, lectr., 1965—; vis. prof. U. Louisville, Boston U., George Washington U. Author: The Johnson Eclipse, 1966, Back to Back, 1967, The Guaranteed Society, 1968, Roosevelt and Pearl Harbor, 1970, Brahmin in Revolt, 1972, John Marshall—A Life in Law, 1974, Days of Sorrow and Pain—Leo Baeck and the Berlin Jews, 1978, Brandeis and Frankfurter—A Dual Biography, 1984. Served with U.S. Army, 1952-54. Recipient Pulitzer Prize for Biography, 1979; Gold medal Leo Baeck Inst., 1979. Jewish. Home and Office: Washington, D.C. Died Nov. 23, 1984.

BAKER, RICHARD TERRILL, educator; b. Coggon, Iowa, Mar. 27, 1913; s. Earle Alonzo and Grace Eloise (Terrill) B.; m. Marjorie Wilcox Coleman, Sept. 4, 1937; 1 son, Coleman E. A.B., Cornell Coll., Mt. Vernon, Iowa, 1934, D.D., 1946; M.S., Columbia, 1937; M. Div., Union Theol. Sem., N.Y.C., 1941. Mem. editorial staff Christian Adv. and Epworth Herald, 1934-36; asso. editor World Outlook, 1939-47; ordained to ministry Methodist Ch., 1941; asso. prof., acting dean Postgrad. Sch. Journalism, Chungking, China, 1943-45; corr. in Orient, 1945-46; asso. prof. journalism Columbia Grad. Sch. Journalism, 1947-52, prof., 1952-81, asso. dean sch., 1961-68, acting dean, 1968-70, 73; staff N.Y. Times, 1953-54; vis. prof. Nat. Chengchi U., Taipei, Taiwan, 1968, U. Sains Malaysia, Penang, 1975; adminstr. Pulitzer Prizes, 1976-81; Cons. religious affairs br. Office High Commnr. for, Germany, 1950. Author: The Seed and the Soil, 1941, Trumpet of a Prophecy, 1943, Ten Thousand Years, 1947, Darkness of the Sun, 1947, The Graduate School of Journalism, 1954, The Christian as a Journalist, 1961; Editorial bd.: Columbia Journalism Rev. Pulitzer traveling fellow, 1937-38; Decorated Victory medal Republic of China, 1947; recipient Columbia Journalism Alumni award, 1967. Mem. Assn. Edn. Journalism, Phi Beta Kappa. Home: New York, N.Y. Died Sept. 3, 1981.

BAKER, ROLLO C., university prof.; b. Middlebourne O., Oct. 2, 1888; s. Jacob W. and Alverda S. (Osburn) B.;

B.A., Ohio State U., 1915, M.A., 1917; Ph.D. in Anatomy, Univ. of Chicago, 1927; m. Iva Rovena Haas, Oct. 16, 1915; 1 son, Rollo Clyde. Grad. asst. in anatomy. Ohio State U., 1915-17, asst. 1917-18, instr., 1918-21, asst. prof., 1921-28, asso. prof. 1928-32; prof. from 1932; chmn. dept. of anatomy, 1933-43; sec. Coll. of Medicine, 1934-43; acting dean, 1943-44, sec. Coll. of Medicine and prof. anatomy, from 1944, asst. dean, from 1954; vis. prof. anatomy Univ. Tenn. Coll. of Medicine, summers of 1937-39. Mem. Am. Assn. of Anatomists, Ohio Acad. of Science, Sigma Xi, Alpha Omega Alpha, Phi Rho Sigma. Mason (Scottish Rite, Consistory). Clubs: Faculty, Crichton. Contbr. to scientific publs. on anatomy and the embrology of the nervous system; also embryology and anatomy of endocrine glands-phyaryngeal hypnosis. †

BAKER, STANNARD LUTHER, ins. co. exec.; b. Lansing, Mich., Mar. 2, 1900; s. Arthur Davis and Edith (Cooley) B.; m. Gladys Kinney, July 26, 1924. Student, Mich. State U., 1918-19, Northwestern U., 1919-21; B.A., U. Mich., 1922. With Mich. Millers Mut. Ins. Co., Lansing, 1922-83, successively file clk., asst. sec., v.p., 1922-44, pres. dir., 1944-65, chmn. bd., 1965-83. Mem. Sigma Nu. Clubs: Mason, Country of Lansing. Home: East Lansing, Mich. Died 1983.

BAKER, WAKEFIELD, JR., wholesale hardware co. exec.; b. San Francisco, July 2, 1922; s. Wakefield and Margaret (Madison) B.; student U. Calif. at Berkeley, 1942-43. Pres., Baker & Hamilton Co., San Francisco, from 1964, Bollibokka Land Co., from 1965. Club: Pacific Union (San Francisco). Home: San Francisco, Calif. Deceased.

BAKER, WALTER DAVID, govt. ofcl. Can.; b. Ottawa, Ont., Can., Aug. 22, 1930; s. David Edward and Olive Delphine (Laberge) B.; m. Lois Patricia Welch, June 2, 1956; children—David Richard, Jeffrey Andrew, Nancy Patricia. B.A., Carleton U., Ottawa, 1953; grad., Osgoode Hall Law Sch., Toronto, Ont., 1957. Bar: Called to Ont. bar 1957, created queen's counsel 1969. Asso. firm Bell, Baker, Thompson, Oyen & Webber, 1957-79; mem. Can. House of Commons, Ottawa, 1972-79, apptd. dep. opposition house leader, 1973-76, opposition house leader, 1976-79; mem. Queen's Privy Council for Can., 1979-83, pres., 1979-80; minister nat. revenue Can. Ministry Revenue, Ottawa, 1979-80; mem. Ottawa Bd. Trade.; Mem. Commonwealth Parliamentary Assn., Can. NATO Parliamentary Assn., Can.-U.S. Interparliamentary Group, Can. Group-Interparliamentary Union, Community Planning Assn. Can., Carleton County Law Assn., Ont. Mcpl. Assn., Ont. Fedn. Agr. Mem. Progressive Conservative Party. Mem. United Ch. of Canada. Clubs: Kiwanis, Richmond Curling (hon.), Carleton Heights Curling (hon.), Prescott Fish and Game. Home: Nepean, Ont., Can. Died Nov. 13, 1983.*

BAKER, WILLIAM AVERY, naval architect; b. New Britain, Conn., Oct. 21, 1911; s. William Elisha and Margaret MacDonald (Sanderson) B.; m. Ruth Stuart, May 2, 1936. S.B., Mass. Inst. Tech., 1934. Registered profl. engr., Calif., Mass. With shipbldg. div. Bethlehem Steel Co., 1934-64; curator Francis Russell Hart Nautical Mus., Mass. Inst. Tech., 1963-81; Trustee Plimoth Plantation, Inc. Compiler plans, specifications for hist. ships: Gjoa, 1948, Mayflower II, 1957, Adventure, 1970, Maryland Dove, 1978, constrn. com. revision, 1948, Safety of Life at Sea Conv, 1957-60, USCG working com. on stability and subdiv., 1961-81, com. on revision, 1930, load line conv.; Author: The New Mayflower, Her Design and Construction, 1958, Colonial Vessels, 1962, The Engine Powered Vessel, 1965, Sloops and Shallops, 1966, A History of the Boston Marine Society, 1968, C.J.A. Wilson's Ships, 1971; collaborator: New England and the Sea, 1972, A Maritime History of Bath, Maine, 1973, also numerous articles, chpts. in books.; Mem. editorial adv. bd.: Am. Neptune, 1952-81, Mystic Seaport, 1973-81. Fellow Pilgrim Soc. (trustee); mem. Soc. Naval Architects and Marine Engrs. (co-founder New Eng. sect. 1943, sec.-treas. 1943-44, chmn. 1957-58, sec.-treas. No. Calif. sect. 1949, hon. mem. 1980), Soc. Nautical Research, Hakluyt Soc., Boston Marine Soc., Harvard Musical Assn., Delta Upsilon. Home: Hingham, Mass. Died Sept. 9, 1981.

BAKER, WILLIAM EMERY, business exec.; b. Bushton, Ill., Dec. 11, 1887; s. William A. and Lillie (Frazier) B.; B.S., Rose Poly. Inst.; m. Rachel Thomas, May 14, 1913; children—Mrs. C. C. Young, Jr., William Robert. Engring. apprentice Westinghouse Elec. & Mfg. Co., 1911-12; prodn. engr. The Selby Shoe Co., 1912-14, Barney & Smith, 1914-16; supt. Delco Products Corp., 1916-24; vice pres. The Day Fan Electric Co., 1924-29; supt. motor div. Delco Products Corp., 1929-34; vice pres. in charge mfg. Servel, Inc., from 1934. Mem. Evansville Mfrs. Assn. (dir. and vice pres.), C. of C. Republican. Methodist. Mason (Shriner). Clubs: Elks, Evansville Country, Evansville Kennel. Home: Evansville, Ind. †

BAKKE, OSCAR, government official; b. Bergen, Norway, June 8, 1919 (parents U.S. citizens); s. Olaf E. and Karen N. (Knutsen) B.; B.A., Wagner Coll., 1941; student Bklyn. Law Sch., 1941, Agrl. and Tech. Coll. Tex., 1944, Columbia Law Sch., 1946; m. Astrid J. Josephensen, Oct. 2, 1943; children—Stephen H., Kenneth A., Robert O., Daniel B. With Civil Aero. Bd., 1946-74; reports editor accident investigation div., 1946-47, flight operations specialist internat. standards div., Bur. Safety Regulation, 1947-50, chief air carrier div. Bur. Safety Regulation, 1950-54, dep. dir. Bur. Safety Regulation, 1954-56, dir., 1956-57, dir. Bur. Safety, 1957-60; director Bur. Flight Standards, Fed. Aviation Agy., 1960-61, asst. adminstr. Eastern region, 1961-67, asso. adminstr. plans, 1967-68, acting dep. adminstr., 1968-74. Pres. Gateway Park Corp., Prince Georges Co., Md. Served as officer (pilot), USAAF, 1941-46; maj. Res. Asso. fellow Am. Inst. Aeros. and Astronautics; mem. Air Force Assn. Lutheran. Home: Camp Springs, Md. Died May 20, 1984.

BAKULEV, ALEKSANDER NIKOLAEVITCH, surgeon, educator; b. 1890. Sci. leader Inst. Cardio-Vascular Surgery of Acad. Med. Scis. in USSR; chief Faculty Medicine of 2d Med. Inst. of N. I. Pirogou; chief editor Big Med. Ency. Dep. of Supreme Ct. Academician. Pres. Acad. Medicine. Recipient prizes for organ sci. research into acquired and inherent diseases of heart, lungs and main blood vessels, for devel. methods of surg. treatment and introduction to routine of med. insts.; also Lenin prize. Address: Moscow, USSR. †

BALAMUTH, WILLIAM, educator; b. N.Y.C., Jan. 16, 1914; s. Maurice and Elizabeth (George) B.; B.S., Coll. City N.Y., 1935; Ph.D. (Univ. fellow), U. Calif. at Berkeley, 1939; m. Mollie Elizabeth Anderton, June 15, 1938; children—William Barry, Barbara Louise. Instr. zoology U. Mo., 1939-40; from instr. to assoc. prof. zoology Northwestern U., 1940-53; mem. faculty U. Calif. at Berkeley, from 1953, prof. zoology, from 1955, assoc. dean Coll. Letters and Sci., 1968-71, spl. faculty asst. to chancellor, from 1974; cons. commn. enteric infections Armed Forces Epidemiol. Bd., 1956-72. Bonnie Wallace LeClair fellow U. Freiburg (Germany), 1933-34. Fellow AAAS; mem. Am. Soc. Zoologists, Soc. Protozoologists, Am. Soc. Parasitologists, Am. Soc. Tropical Medicine and Hygiene, Phi Beta Kappa, Sigma Xi. Mem. editorial bds. jours. in field. Spl. research nutrition and differentiation free-living protozoa, parasitic amoebae. Home: Berkeley, Calif. Died June 10, 1981.

BALANCHINE, GEORGE, choreographer; b. Petrograd, Russia, Jan. 9, 1904; s. Meliton and Marie Balinchinvadze; grad. Imperial Sch. of Ballet, 1921, student Conservatory of Music, Petrograd; L.H.D., Brandeis U., 1965; m. Tanaguil LeClerq, Dec. 31, 1952 (div. 1969). Came to the U.S., 1933. Danced in state theatres of opera and ballet, Russia, 1915-24; toured Europe, then joined Ballets Russes de Serge Diaghilev; became dir. Royal Theater of Copenhagen, 1929; helped organize Ballets Russes de Monte Carlo, 1932; with Met. Opera House, N.Y.C., 1934-37; helped organize Sch. of Am. Ballet, 1934, now dir.; founded (with Lincoln Kirstein) Ballet Soc., 1946, now N.Y. City Ballet (toured U.S. and abroad, from 1950), artistic dir., ballet master N.Y. City Ballet; choreographer for motion pictures, plays, On Your Toes, Goldwyn Follies, Boys from Syracuse, Cabin in the Sky, I Married an Angel, ballets: The Nightingale, 1925; Barabau, 1925; Pastorale, 1927; Triumph of Neptune, 1927; Jack-in-the-Box, 1927; Apollon, 1928; Le Bal, 1929; Prodigal Son, 1929; Cotillion, 1932; Mozartiana, Errante, Seven Deadly Sins, 1933; The Nutcracker, 1954; Liebeslieder Waltzer, Ivesiana, Agon, Bugaku; Don Quixote, 1965, Sonatine, 1974. numerous others; collaborated on many ballets with Igor Stravinsky. Decorated Order Legion Honor (France). Mem. Greek Orthdox Ch. Author: Balanchine's Book of Ballet. Home: New York, N.Y. Died Apr. 30, 1983.*

BALCH, RICHARD HERROCKS, mfg. exec.; b. Bklyn., Mar. 2, 1901; s. Burton M. and Mary J. (Horrocks) B.; A.B., Williams Coll., 1921; LL.D., Hartwick Coll., 1955; m. Elizabeth S. Prescott. Sept. 15, 1928; children—Cynthia, James P., Barbara, Richard H. Vice pres. Horrocks Ibbotson Co., Utica, 1927-42, pres., 1942-67, chmn. bd., 1967-68; dir. Gladding Corp., S. Otselic, Divine Bros. Mfg. Co., Utica Fire Ins. Co. Pub. Service Commr., N.Y. State, 1955-60. Pres. Community Chest, Utica, 1949, mem. bd. edn. Democrat (del. nat. conv. 1944, 48; Dem. candidate lt. gov. N.Y., 1950; chmn. N.Y. state com. 1952-55). Presbyn. Mason. Clubs: Ft. Schuyler (Utica); Williams, Manhattan (N.Y.C.). Contbr. articles sporting goods publs. Home: Utica, N.Y. Died Mar. 15, 1984.

BALDERSTON, WILLIAM, retired corp. exec.; b. Boise, Idaho, Dec. 13, 1896; s. William and Stella B. (Sain) B.; C. E., U. of Wis., 1918; m. Susan Bowen Ramsay, Sept. 4, 1918; children—Eleanor (Mrs. J. M. Hoeffel. Jr.), Susan Ramsay (Mrs. T. W. Sears, Jr.), William James Claypoole. Lab. asst., chief inspr., factory mgr. v.p., dir. Ray-O-Vac, 1919-29; treasurer, Pioneer auto radio firm, Auto Radio Corp., Long Island, N.Y., 1929-30; mgr. car mfrs. div. Philco Corp., Detroit, Mich., 1930-41; vice pres. in charge of commercial div. and prod. of radar and radio equipment for Army and Navy, 1941-44; vice pres. in charge of operations and mem. exec. com. in charge of all mfg., engring. and purchasing activities of corp., exec. v.p. 1946-48, president, 1948-54, chairman of board of directors, 1954-58; Pioneer in commercialization of auto-radio. Dir. Greater Phila. Movement. Dir. Eisenhower Exchange Fellowship, Inc. Served as 1st lt., 33d F.A., U.S. Army, 1918-19. Awarded Presdl. Certificate of Merit, World War II. Mem. Iron Cross, Scabbard and Blade. Republican. Episcopalian. Clubs; Huntington Valley Country (Abington, Pa.); Union League (Phila.). Home: Meadowbrook, Pa. Died July 25, 1983.

BALDOCK, ROBERT HUGH, civil engr.; b. Trinidad, Colo., July 6, 1889; s. Rueben J. and Alice (Perry) B.; B.S., U. of Colo., 1938; C.E., 1939; D.Sc., U. of Ore., 1946; m. Austa Marchant, Mar. 15, 1913; children—Robert, Bonnie, Dorothy; m. 2d, Verona Watson Lehmer, Sept. 6, 1947. Engaged in ry., mining, hydroelectric and logging engring., 1908-15; successively transitman, resident engr., div. engr., maintenance engr., asst. chief engr., Ore. State Highway Dept., 1915-32, chief engineer, 1932-56; chief engineer Highway Mission to Iraq, from 1956; represents firm Edwards, Kelcgy and Beck, cons. engrs., Newark. Recipient George S. Bartlett award, 1950; named Engr. of Year by Profl. Engrs. Ore., 1954. Mem. Newcomen Soc. of Eng., Am. Assn. State Hwy. Ofcls. (pres.), Hwy. Research Bd. (mem. exec. com.), Am. Soc. C.E., Tau Beta Pi. Republican. Episcopalian. Mason. Club: University (Portland, Oregon). Contributor many technical bulletins on highway design. Home: Salem, Ore. †

BALDWIN, BILLY, interior designer; b. Roland Park, Md., May 30, 1903; student Princeton, Interior designer, N.Y.C. Author: Billy Baldwin Decorates, 1972; Billy Baldwin Remembers, 1974. Address: New York, N.Y. Died Nov. 25, 1983.*

BALDWIN, ERNEST J., coll. dean; b. Hewins, Kan., Dec. 24, 1890; s. William Worth and Winifred (Crawford) B.; B.S., U. Kan., 1915; M.S., 1916; Ph.D., Stanford, 1931; m. Madge Naomi Kring, Sept. 4, 1915; children—Donald, Barbara, JoAnn. Instr. chemistry U. S.D., 1916-17; state food and drug chemist, S.D., 1917-18; asst. prof. chemistry U. Ida, 1918-27; prof. chemistry, dean coll. liberal arts Ida. State Coll. from 1927. Mem. Am. Chem. Soc., A.A.A.S., Sigma Xi. Author: Inorganic and Analytical Chemistry, 1940. Contbr. articles profl. jours. Home: Pocatello, Ida. †

BALDWIN, HORACE STROW, physician; b. Englewood, N.J., Oct. 14, 1895; s. John Hall and Annie (Strow) B.; B.S., Wesleyan U., 1917; M.D., Cornell, 1921; m. Florence V. Reed, Sept. 3, 1924; children—Judith Ann Hutcheson, Horace (dec.). Intern N.Y. Hosp., 1921-23, dir. allergy clinic, 1935-61, asso. attending physician, 1947-61, consultant in med., 1961-83; pneumonia research Bellevue Hosp., 1923-27; practice medicine, specializing in allergy diseases, N.Y.C., 1927-68; asso. prof. clin. medicine Cornell, 1947-61. Cons. in medicine Nassau Hosp., Mineola, N.Y., North Country Community Hosp., Glen Cove, N.Y., Dobbs Ferry (N.Y.) Hosp., until 1968. Bd. dirs., v.p. Sunden Forest Preserve, Inc., 1955-65; v.p. Point O'Woods Assn., 1953-55. Trustee Wesleyan U., 1952-60; pres. Allergy Found. Am., 1953-57, chmn., 1957-66, v.p., 1966. Served as hosp. apprentice U.S. Navy, World War I, Diplomate in allergy Am. Bd. Internal Medicine. Fellow N.Y. Acad. Medicine (chmn. sect. internal medicine 1943), Am. Acad. Allergy (treas., pres. 1951-52); Sociedade Brasileria de Alergia (hon.), mem. Harvey Soc., N.Y. Acad. Scis., Delta Tau Delta. Episcopalian. Club: Field. Author sci. papers. Address: Sarasota, Fla. Died Nov. 3, 1983.

BALDWIN, ROGER NASH, public law consultant; b. Wellesley, Mass., Jan 21, 1884; s. Frank Fenno and Lucy Cushing (Nash) B.; A.B., Harvard U., 1904, A.M., 1905; LL.D., Washington U., 1968; Yale U., 1969, Brandeis U., 1969, Northwestern U., 1974, Haverford Coll., 1976; m. Madeleine Zabriskie Doty, Aug. 9, 1919 (div.); m. Evelyn Preston, Mar. 7, 1936 (dec. June 1962); 1 dau., Helen T. (dec.). Instr. sociology Washington U., St. Louis 1906-09; chief probation officer Juvenile Court, St. Louis, 1907-10; sec. Nat. Probation Assn., 1908-10; sec. St. Louis Civic League, 1910-17, St. Louis Children's Commn., 1913-14; dir. ACLU, N.Y.C., 1917-50, nat. chmn., 1950-55, adviser internat. work, from 1950, law faculty U. P.R., 1966-74. Cons. civil liberties U.S. occupation of Japan and Korea, 1947, Germany and Austria, 1948, 50, Govt. P.R., V.I., 1954-64; former chmn., hon. pres. Internat. League Human Rights, from 1946; bd. dirs. Nat. Audubon Soc., 1934-46; faculty New Sch. for Social Research, 1938-42; mem. Harvard Overseers' Com. on Econs. Dept., 1938-50. Recipient Am. Vets. Com. award, 1950; Florina Lasker civil liberties award, 1957; Order of Rising Sun (2d class), Emperor Japan; medal City of N.Y., 1966. Fellow Am. Acad. Arts and Scis. Author: (with Bernard Flexner) Juvenile Courts and Probation, 1912; Liberty under the Soviets, 1928. Editor: Kropotkin's Freedom Pamphlets, 1928; Civil Liberties and Industrial Conflict (Harvard Godkin lectures), 1938; A New Slavery, Forced Labor, 1953. Home: Oakland, N.J. Died Aug. 26, 1981.

BALDWIN, THOMAS WHITFIELD, prof. of English; b. Laurens County, S.C., Jan. 28, 1890; s. James Whitfield and Annie Jane (Anderson) B.; A.B., Erskine College, 1909; A.M., Princeton University, 1914, Ph.D., 1916; D.Litt., University of Illinois, 1959; married Elisabeth Regina Petrich, December 21, 1917; children—Ruth Marie, Elisabeth Grace, Cynthia Anne (adopted). Prin. and supt. of schs. in S.C., 1909-12; asst. Erskine Coll., 1912-13; prof. English and head of dept., Muskingum Coll., 1915-18, S.D. State Coll., 1918-20, Reed Coll., 1920-23; asst. prof. of English, Goucher Coll., 1923-25; with U. of Ill., from 1925, asst. prof. English, 1925-27, asso. prof., 1927-28, prof. English from 1928; visiting prof. English, U. Ia., summer 1927; visiting professor Southern Illinois U., 1958-59. Guggenheim fellow, 1931-32; Fulbright research scholar, United Kingdom, 1953-54. Mem. Modern Lang. Assn. Am., American Assn. University Professors, Shakespeare Association of America, Shakespeare Association (England), Phi Beta Kappa, Phi Kappa Phi. Southern Democrat. Methodist. Mason. Author: On The Literary Genetics of Shakespeare's Poems and Sonnets, 1950; William Shakespeare's Love's Labor's Won, 1957. Editor: Massinger's Duke of Milan, 1918; The Comedy of Errors, 1928; Earlier English Drama (Am. reviser), 1929; Trolius and Cressida, 1952; On the Literary Genetics of Shakespeare's Plays, 1592-94, 1959. Contbr. to profl., lit. jours. Home: Urbana, Ill.†

BALE, WILLIAM FREER, biophysicist, educator; b. Augusta, N.J., Jan. 2, 1911; s. Robert Osborne and Cora (Bales) B.; B.A., Cornell U., 1932; Ph.D., U. Rochester, 1936; m. Mary Ella Cardew, Apr. 28, 1939; children—Emily Catherine, Karen (Mrs. John A. Lauder II), Mary Elizabeth. Asso. in radiology U. Rochester (N.Y.), 1936-46, asso. prof. radiology, 1946-49, prof. radiation biology and biophysics, after 1949, then prof. emeritus. Staff mem. biophysic br. Div. Biology and Medicine, AEC, 1949-51, mem. adv. com. biology and medicine, 1963-70; mem. bd. sci. cons. Sloan-Keetering Inst. Cancer Research, 1962-72. Mem. Am. Phys. Soc., Am. Physiol. Soc. Radiation Research Soc., Soc. Exptl. Biology and Medicine, A.A.A.S., N.Y. Acad. Sci. Pioneer in uses of radioactive isotopes as tracers in biology; research, publs. on radiation biology and cancer immunology. Home: Rochester, N.Y. Died June 28, 1982.

BALFOUR, LLOYD G., mfr.; b. Wauseon, O., Jan. 6, 1887; s. Claude and Elizabeth (Lloyd) B.; LL.B., University of Indiana, 1907; A.B., University of Louisville; married Mildred McCann, Feb. 5, 1923. Admitted to bar, 1907; pres. and treas. L. G. Balfour Co., mfrs. of jewelry and kindred articles, from 1913. Mem. Sigma Chi (past grand consul), Phi Delta Phi. Formerly chairman Nat. Interfraternity Conf. Republican. Mason (32 deg., Shriner), Elk. Home: Norton, Mass. †

BALK, EUGENE NORMAN, lawyer; b. Toledo, Oct. 11, 1929; s. Harold H. and Mamie (Glow) B.; children—Angela J., Mark D., Lance C., Adele M. B.S. cum laude, Ohio State U., 1950; J.D. magna cum laude, Toledo, 1959; Advanced Mgmt. Program, Harvard U., 1979. Bar: Ohio bar 1959. Since practiced in, Lucas County; gen. counsel, mem. mng. partner com. The Andersons, 1967-83; partner firm Balk and Hess. Served to 1st lt., inf. U.S. Army, 1950-53. Fellow Ohio Bar Found.; mem. ABA, Ohio Bar Assn., Toledo Bar Assn., (com. chmn.), Toledo Legal Aid Soc. (trustee), Am. Judicature Soc., NAACP, U. Toledo Law Alumni Assn. (exec. com.), Gamma Sigma Delta, Phi Kappa Phi. Lutheran. Club: Rotary. Rotary. Home: Toledo, Ohio. Died Apr. 12, 1983.

BALL, FRED LINCOLN, drop forge co. exec.; b. Leskard, Ont., Can., Sept. 9, 1888; s. William J. and Sarah (Griffin) B.; LL.B., Cleve. Law Sch., 1911; m. Lulu Maud Bateman, Feb. 12, 1912; children—Robert L., Margaret Adele (Mrs. G. A. Craig), Frederick James, Gordon Bateman, Lewis Clark. Came to U.S., 1904, naturalized, 1911. With Park Drop Forge Co., Cleve., from 1907, sec., treas., 1907-54, pres., dir., from 1954; dir. Ohio Crankshaft Co., Cleve. Mem. sch. bd., Bratenahl, Ohio. Home: Cleveland, Oh. †

BALLANTINE, JOSEPH WILLIAM, polit. scientist; b. of Am. parents, Ahmednagar, India, July 30, 1888; s. William Osborn and Josephine Louise (Perkins) B.; A.B., Amherst, 1909; LL.D., Roanoke, 1947; m. Emilia A. Christy, Oct. 30, 1917 (dec. 1952); children—Elizabeth Copley, Alice Field, Louise Adele; married 2d Lealey Frost, Aug. 23, 1952. With Am. Fgn. Service, 1909-47; sec. Am. del. London Naval Conf., 1930; consul gen., Canton, China, 1930-34, Mukden, 1934-37; assigned to Dept. of State, 1937-41; consul gen., Ottawa, Can., 1941; assigned Dept. State, 1942; dir. office Far Eastern Affairs, Dept. State, 1944; special assistant to the sec. of State, 1945-Feb. 1947; advisor Internat. Prosecution Sect., Allied Mil. Tribunal for the East, 1946; staff Brookings Instn., 1947. Mem. Phi Gamma Delta. Conglist. Club: University (Washington). Author: Japanese as It Is Spoken, 1945; Formosa, 1952. Home: Silver Spring, Md. †

BALLARD, LLOYD VERNOR, sociologist; b. Magnolia, Wis., Aug. 22, 1887; s. George Albert and Augusta (Rosa) B.; A.B., Beloit (Wis.) Coll., 1912; A.M., Harvard, 1913; grad. student U. of Chicago, 1917-18, 1926; m. Eleanor Charlotte Brannon, June 14, 1922; 1 son, Lloyd Brannon (dec.). Instr. economics, Beloit Coll., 1913-15; asst. prof., 1915-18, assoc. prof., 1918-19, prof., from 1920, head dept. economics and sociology since 1921. Labor investigator Labor Relations Div., Emergency Fleet Corp., 1917-18; chmn. Council of Social Agencies, Beloit, 1932-34; pres. Community Welfare Assn., 1934-36; chmn. NRA Compliance Bd., Beloit, 1933-34; mem. bd. of State Dept. of Pub. Welfare, 1939-41, asst. dir. Div. of Child Welfare, 1941-42; dir. Wis. Welfare Council, 1942-43, president, 1943-46; member of advisory committee, School of Social Work, U. of Wis.; mem. Am. Public Welfare Assn., since 1945; mem. adv. council, Nat. Conf. on Family Relations; mem. Nat. Conf. Social Work; member com. on cooperation between nat. and state Confs. of Social Work; mem. state adv. com., div. of child welfare, State Dept. of Public Welfare, since 1943; chmn. state advisory bd. women's field army, American Association Control of cancer since 1943; consultant on delinquency, N.M. State Dept. of Public Welfare, 1943-45; sec. Beloit Coll. Faculty since 1947. Member Wisconsin State Committee on Russian War Relief; mem. bd. Wis. Assn. for Prevention of Alcoholism; v.p. Wisconsin Council on Alcoholism from 1950. Fellow Royal Econ. Soc. (England); mem. Am. Sociol. Soc., Mid-West Sociol. Soc. (sec. treas.; pres. 1947-48), Am. Acad. Polit. and Social Sci., Phi Beta Kappa. Tau Kappa Epsilon. Congregationalist. Mason. Club: Faculty and Alumni (Beloit). Author: Social Institutions, 1936. Contbr. articles to jours. Home: Beloit, Wis. †

BALLOTTI, GENO ARTHUR, found. exec.; b. Walsenberg, Colo., Dec. 28, 1930; s. Ernest James and Beatrice Mary (Pini) B.; m. Geraldine A. McCarty, Nov. 21, 1959; children—Geoffrey, Anne, Kathryn, Susan. B.A., Adams State Coll., 1953; M.A., U. Wyo., 1955; postgrad., Johns Hopkins U., 1958-60. Sr. English tchr. Florence (Colo.) High Sch., 1953-54; instr. Dept. English, U. Wyo., Laramie, 1954-55; spl. agt. Counter-Intelligence Corps, U.S. Army, 1956-57; asso. dir. John Hopkins U. Press, Balt., 1957-61; sec. Assembly on Univ. Goals and Governance, Harvard U., 1969-75; mgmt. bd. overseeing editorial/fin. ops. The Chronicle of Higher Edn., 1975-84; pub. Oceanus, Woods Hole (Mass.) Oceanographic Inst., 1974—; advisor Pres. of Stonehill Coll., N. Easton, Mass., 1972-84; asso. exec. officer Am. Acad. Arts & Scis., Harvard U., 1961-77. Author: Southwest Indian in Literature, 1955, The Embattled University, 1970; editor: Center Pieces, 1973-74. Asso. dir. Permanent Charity Fund of Boston, 1977-78, dir., 1978-84; Pres. Beaver brook Mental Health Assn., McLean Hosp., 1968-73; bd. dirs. Nat. Braille Press, 1961-78; trustee Fernald State Sch., Cambridge Center for Adult Edn.; ednl. cons. Boston Sch. Com., 1968-81, Change Mag., 1964-70; town meeting mem. Town of Belmont, 1968-81. Named Outstanding Alumnus Adams State Coll., 1968; Coe fellow U. Wyo., 1954-55. Roman Catholic. Clubs: Tavern, B & M Tennis, Cotuit Yacht Assn, Moose. Home: Belmont, Mass. Died Nov. 15, 1984.

BALMAIN, PIERRE, dress designer; b. St. Jean de Maurienne, Savoie, France, May 18, 1914; s. Maurice and Francoise (Ballinari) B.; student Lycee de Chambery, 1926-32; B.S. and B.L., U. Grenoble, 1932; studied architecture Ecole des Beaux Arts, Paris, 1932-34. Dress designer with Paris couturiers, 12 yrs.; continued designing while in service at front with the army, 1939-40; established in 1945 and operated own business, Paris. Conseiller du Commerce Exterieur, from 1953. Served with French Army, 1939-40. Decorated cross Legion of Honor (France); knight Order of Danebrog (Denmark); cavaliere Ufficiale dell'Ordine Al Merito della Repubblica Italiana. Home: Paris, France. Died June 29, 1982.

BALYEAT, RAY MORTON, physician; b. Arkansas City, Kan., Feb. 20, 1889; s. Reuben L. and Melissa Ellen (Hoffman) B.; A.B., U. of Okla., 1912, B.S. and A.M., 1916, M.D., 1918; m. Ann Bright, Feb. 12, 1920; children—Ray Milton, Rebecca Ann. Began practice at Oklahoma City, Okla., 1919; associate in medicine and lecturer on allergic diseases, U. of Okla., Med. Sch., from 1924; cons. physician, St. Anthony's Hosp., State Univ. Hosp.; dir. Balyeat Hay Fever and Asthma Clinic. Mem. AMA, ACP, Assn. for Study of Allergy (pres.), Okla. Acad. Science (v.p.), Phi Beta Pi, Phi Beta Kappa. Republican. Methodist. Club: Oklahoma. Author: Hay Fever and Asthma, 1926. Contbr. to Am. Jour. Med. Sciences. Southern Med. Jour., Jour. AMA, The Jour. of Allergy, Okla. State Med. Jour. Home: Oklahoma City, Okla. †

BAMBERGER, BERNARD JACOB, rabbi; b. Balt., May 30, 1904; s. William Burk and Gussie (Erlanger) B.; A.B., Johns Hopkins, 1923; Rabbi, Hebrew Union Coll., Cin., 1926, D.D., 1929, D.H.L., 1950; m. Ethel Ruth Kraus, June 14, 1932; children—Henry, David. Rabbi, Temple Israel, Lafayette, Ind., 1926-29, Congregation Beth Emeth, Albany, N.Y., 1929-44, Temple Shaaray Tefila, N.Y.C., 1944-70, rabbi emeritus, 1970-80. Mem. com. preparing new translation of Bible, Jewish Publ. Soc. Am.; pres. Central Conf. Am. Rabbis, 1959-61; pres. Synogogue Council Am., 1950-51; pres. World Union for Progressive Judaism, 1970-72. Mem. Soc. Bibl. Lit. and Exegesis, Am. Acad. Jewish Research. Author: Proselytism in the Talmudic Period, 1939; Fallen Angels, 1952; The Bible: A Modern Jewish Approach, 1955; The Story of Judaism, 1957; The Search for Jewish Theology, 1978; The Torah-A Modern Commentary: Leviticus, 1979; editor: Reform Judaism: Essays by Hebrew Union College Alumni, 1949; Studies in Jewish Law, Custom and Folklore (Jacob Z. Lauterbach), 1970-72. Contbr. essays learned and popular jours. Contbg edg. editor The Universal Jewish Ency. Home: New York, N.Y. Died June 14, 1980.

BANE, FRANK, government official, educator; b. Smithfield, Va., Apr. 7, 1893; s. Charles Lee and Carrie Howard (Buckner) B.; A.B., Randolph-Macon Coll., 1914, also LL.D.; student Columbia U., 1914-15; m. Lillian Greyson Hoofnagle, Aug. 14, 1918; children—Mary Clark, Frank. Prin. high sch., Nansemond County, Va., 1914, supt. schs., 1916-17; sec. Va. Bd. Charities and Corrections, 1920-23; dir. pub. welfare, Knoxville, 1923-26; assoc. prof. sociology U. Va., 1926-28; commr. pub. welfare Va., 1926-32; mem. President's Emergency Employment Com., 1930-31; dir. Am. Pub. Welfare Assn., 1932-35; lectr. pub. welfare adminstrn. U. Chgo., from 1932. Cons., Fed. Emergency Relief Adminstrn., 1933, pub. welfare adminstrn. Nat. Inst. Pub. Adminstrn., 1930, Brookings Instn., 1931-35; exec. dir. Fed. Social Security Bd., 1935-38; dir. div. state and local coop., adv. commn. Council Nat. Def., 1940-41; mem. civilian protection bd. Office Civilian Def., 1941; dir. field ops. OPA, 1941-42; mem. homes utilization div. Nat. Housing Authority, 1942; sec. Gov.'s Conf., 1938-59; exec. dir. Council State Govts., 1938-59; mem. adv. council Social Security, U.S. Senate Com. on Finance, 1947; dir. research fed.-state relations Com. on Orgn. exec. br. govt., 1948; chmn. cons. group med. edn. office Surg. Gen. USPHS, 1959; chmn. Adv. Commn. Intergovtl. Relations, from 1959; Regent's prof. govt. U. Calif., Berkeley, 1944-45. Served with A.C., U.S. Army, World War I. Mem. Am. Polit. Sci. Assn., Phi Kappa Sigma. Democrat. Club: Quadrangle. Contbr. to mags. Home: Alexandria, Va. Died Jan. 23, 1983.

BANFIELD, ARMINE FREDERICK, cons. geologist; b. Winnipeg, Man., Can., Jan. 27, 1909; s. Armine Frederick and Sarah (Boyd) B.; m. Cordelia May Dunkin, Nov. 1, 1941; children—Armine Frederick, Susan Del, James Andrew, Robert Hugh. Grad., St. John's Coll., Can.; B.S., McGill U., 1930; M.S., Northwestern U., 1933, Ph.D. in Geology, 1940. Instr. geology U. Man., 1930-31, Northwestern U., 1931-33; with Geol. Survey Can., summers 1930-32; geologist Island Lake Gold Mines, Man., 1933-35; chief geologist Beattie Gold Mines, Que., 1935-41; geologist Ventures, Ltd. (and subsidiaries), 1935-41, 45; cons. geologist, Noranda, Que., 1945-46; mgr. Aruba Gold Mines, Netherlands W.I., 1947, Equatorial Mining Corp., French Guiana, 1948; cons. geologist, 1948-78; partner Behre Dolbear & Co., Inc., N.Y.C., pres., 1972-76, chmn., 1976-78; head geol. expdn. to, Galapagos Islands and Ecuador, 1953; head field group for mineral reconnaissance for Iran Govt., 1958; tech. adviser OK Tedi Copper Project, Govt. Papua New Guinea, 1975-76, 78-79; Mem. library bd. Engrng. Socs. Library, N.Y.C., 1956-60, 60-64. Served as lt. RCAF, 1941-45. Mem. AIME (exec. com. N.Y. sect. 1959-61), Can. Inst. Mining and Metallurgy (life), Soc. Econ. Geologists (investment com. 1974-77), Mining and Metall. Soc. Am. (treas. 1967-77), Am. Inst. Profl. Geologists (pres. N.Y. sect. 1972, nat. exec. com. 1972). Clubs: Nutmeg Curling (Darien, Conn.) (sec., gov. 1966-70); Mining of Southwest (Tucson), Tucson Nat. Golf (Tucson). Home: Tucson, Ariz. Died Oct. 31, 1981.

BANG, FREDERIK BARRY, educator, physician; b. Phila., Nov. 5, 1916; s. A.F. and Carol (Klee) B.; A.B., Johns Hopkins, 1935, M.D., 1939; m. Betsy Garrett, June 1, 1940; children—Caroline Moyer, Molly Campbell, Axel Frederik. Intern U.S. Marine Hosp., Balt., 1939-40; fellow NRC, 1940-41; asst. Rockefeller Inst., Princeton, 1941-46; asst. prof. medicine Johns Hopkins, 1946-49, assoc. prof., 1949-53, prof., chmn. dept. pathobiology, from 1953; dir. Johns Hopkins Internat. Center Med Research and Tng., Calcutta, 1962-76. Fulbright fellow Nat. Inst. for Med. Research, London, Eng., 1955-56; Guggenheim fellow, 1961, 64. Served with M.C., AUS, 1943-46. Mem. Am. Soc. Tropical Medicine and Hygiene, Tissue Culture Assn., Interurban Clin. Club, Am. Soc. Immunologists, Am. Soc. Clin. Investigation, Am. Soc. Exptl. Pathology, Soc. Exptl. Biology and Medicine, Internat. Epidemiol. Assn., Am. Soc. Microbiology, Am. Soc. Cancer Research, Am. Soc. Parasitologists, Phi Beta Kappa, Sigma Xi. Editor: Adv. in Virus Research. Home: Baltimore, Md. Died Oct. 3, 1981.

BANGS, CLARE WILLIAM HOBART, college pres.; b. Auburn, Ind., May 5, 1890; s. Charles Henry and Virginia (Jennie) H. (Reynolds) B.; B.Pd. and A.B., Tri-State Coll., Angola, Ind., 1912; student Ind. U., U. of Chicago, King's Sch. of Oratory, Pittsburgh, Pa.; corr. course in civ. engrng.; A.M., Huntington (Ind.) Coll., 1913; m. Nellie A. Binning, July 18, 1917. Supt. of high schs. in Ind., 1909-12; prof. sociology and philosophy, 1912-14, pres. from 1914, Huntington (Ind.) Coll. Mem. Gen. Bd. of Edn. and Bd. of Trustees U.B. Ch., also gen. sec. edn. same. Mayor of College Park, Ind. Mem. Am. Acad. Polit. and Social Science, Assn. Am. Colls., Assn. Ind. Colls. (treas.), Am. Asiatic Assn.; charter mem. Edwardes Bangs Descendants. Republican. Investigator social problems, Chicago and St. Louis, various times; Chautauqua and commencement lecturer. Address: Huntington, Ind. †

BANGS, JOHN R., management educator; b. Balt., Sept. 13, 1892; s. John Robert and Maria (Rippel) B.; grad. Balt. Poly. Inst., 1914; M.E., Cornell U., 1921; postgrad. Columbia U. and NYU, 1929-30; m. Clara Margaretta Zeigler, Dec. 22, 1925; 1 dau., Mary Emilie Bangs Richler. Asst. dept. shop practice Balt. Poly. Inst., 1914-15, instr. elec. engrng., 1916-17; draftsman, designer, engr. Henry Smith & Son, Balt., 1918; instr. machine design Cornell U., 1919-20, instr. indsl. engrng, 1921-26, asst. prof., 1926-29, prof., head dept. adminstrv. engrng., 1930-43; dir. indsl., personnel relations Budd Co., Phila., 1943-57; prof. mgmt. U. Fla., 1958-63, prof. indsl. and personnel relations, from 1946, vis. prof. Div. Continuing Edn., asst. coach track team; arbitrator Fed. Mediation and Conciliation Service; cons. labor relations and edn. Detroit Edison Co.; mem. editorial and cons. staff Alexander Hamilton Inst.; tech. cons. War Manpower Commn. Named to Hall of Fame, Track and Field Fla., 1978. Mem. ASME, So. Econ. Assn., Am. Mgmt. Assn., Am. Arbitration Assn. (nat. panel), Atmos, Sphinx Head, Spike Shoe, Tau Beta Pi, Phi Kappa Phi, Kappa Tau Chi. Club: Gainsville Golf and and Country. Author: Factory Management, 1929; Industrial Accounting for Executives, 1930; Business and Industrial Management, 1934, rev. edit., 1941; (with G.R.

Hanselman) Accounting for Engineers, 1941; (with James W. Townsend) The Implications for Executives in the 1947 Labor-Management Relations Act, 1947; Plant Management, 1955; (with William V. Wilmot) Plant Management, 1963, Collective Bargaining, 1964; The Future of Collective Bargaining in the U.S., 1963; Labor's Goal for 64-more money, 1963; Teaching High School and College Track and Field Athletics, 1976; also author of booklets, privately printed; editor: (with L.P. Alford): Production Handbook, 1944; cons. and contbg. editor Personnel Handbook 1955, 58, Production Handbook, 1972; contbr. articles to profl. jours. Home: Gainesville, Fla. Died Dec. 31, 1980.

BANK, CARL C., army officer; b. Donnellson, Ia., Oct. 13, 1889; s. August Henry and Wilhelmina Lydia (Wendt) B.; student Highland Park Coll., Des Moines, Ia., 1907-08, Iowa State Teachers Coll., Cedar Falls, Ia., 1910-11; B.S., U.S. Mil. Acad., 1915; grad. F.A. Sch., battery officers course, 1921, advanced course, 1929, Chem. Warfare Sch., 1931, Command and Gen. Staff Sch., 1931; m. Hazel Edna Malone (died 1949); m. Edith May Hall, 1950. Commd. 2d lt., U.S. Army, 1915, and advanced through the grades to brig. gen.; retired 1947. Decorated Officer Legion of Honor (France), Legion of Merit with Oak Leaf cluster (U.S.). Home: Yucalpa, Cal. †

BANKS, TALCOTT MINER, lawyer; b. Englewood, N.J., June 23, 1905; s. Talcott M. and Olive H.S. (Dawes) B.; m. Kathleen Macy Hall, July 23, 1935 (dec. 1966); children—Ridgway, Oliver, Helen M.; m. Ann Smith Monks, June 23, 1967 (dec. 1970); m. Elisa C. Brooks, Aug. 8, 1973; dec. 1979. Grad., Hotchkiss Sch., Lakeville, Conn., 1924; A.B., Williams Coll., 1928, LL.D., 1975; LL.B., Harvard, 1931; LL.D., Northeastern U., 1971. Bar: Mass. bar 1931. Pres. Nat. Intercollegiate Lawn Tennis Assn., 1927-28; editorial staff Time mag., 1930; asso. firm Palmer & Dodge (and predecessors), Boston, 1931-41, mem. firm, 1944-80; gen. counsel Bd. Investigation and Research, Washington, 1941-44; dir. Comstock & Wescott, Inc. Contbr. articles to legal periodicals, mags. Hon. trustee Sterling and Francine Clark Art Inst., 1976-83; trustee emeritus Fessenden Sch., Williams Coll.; trustee New Eng. Conservatory Music; hon. pres. Boston Opera Assn., Inc.; chmn. bd. Boston Symphony Orch. Mem. ABA (chmn. spl. com. on securities laws and regulations 1940-42), Mass. Bar Assn., Boston Bar Assn., Am. Law Inst., Phi Beta Kappa, Kappa Alpha. Unitarian. Clubs: University (N.Y.C.); St. Botolph (Boston) (pres. 1949-53); Cruising of Am, Am. Alpine, Somerset; Hope (Providence); Dunes (Narragansett). Home: Lincoln, Mass. Died Aug. 2, 1983.

BANKSON, RUSSELL ARDEN, author; b. Mt. Hope, Wash., Feb. 21, 1889; s. Williamson B. and Celia B. (Fisher) B.; student State Coll. of Wash., Pullman, 1910-12; m. Ella Henneck, July 6, 1913; children —Rodger Russell, Norman Budd, Douglas Alan. City Editor Spokane (Wash.) Daily Chronicle, 1925-29; radio commentator; editorial staff. Spokane (Wash.) Spokesman-Review, 1938-42; chief, Project Reports Division, Central Utah Project, War Relocation Authority, 1943-44; chief publ. sect., War Relocation Authority, 1944-45; liaison. Information specialist, War Assets Adminstrn. (both Washington, D.C.), 1946; editorial dir. Asso. Country Newspapers, Spokane, Wash., 1947. Mem. Inland Empire Writers' Conf. (pres., 1934-35), Inland Empire Council Boy Scouts of America, Sigma Delta Chi; hon. mem. Colville Indian Tribe. Republican. Congregationalist. Mason. Sr. editor: Naval Reserve Training Publications. Author: Riders of the Breaks, 1931; Bitter Grass, 1933; Riders of the Badlands, 1934; Disaster Island, 1935; The Klondike Nugget, 1935. Contbr. fiction serials, short stories from 1920. Home: Spokane, Wash. †

BANNEROT, FREDERICK GEORGE, JR., refinery executive; b. Pitts., May 29, 1908; s. Frederick G. and Margaret R. (Long) B.; B.S., Yale, 1929; m. Mary Frances Palmer, Feb. 17, 1931; children—Frederick George III, Oroon Palmer. With Elk Refining Co., Charleston, W.Va., 1930—, successively refinery chemist, sec., v.p., exec. v.p., 1930-51, pres., 1951-69, chmn. bd., from 1969; dir. Kanawha Valley Bank, Chesapeake & Potomac Telephone Co. W.Va. Bd. dirs. Meml. Hosp.; trustee Morris Harvey Coll. Mem. C. of C. Episcopalian. Clubs: Edgewood Country, Berry Hills Country (Charleston); Duquesne (Pitts.). Amateur golf champion, W.Va., 1932, 33, 41. Home: Charleston, W.Va. Died June 27, 1980.

BANNING, MARGARET CULKIN, author; b. Buffalo, Minn., Mar. 18, 1891; d. William Edgar and Hannah Alice (Young) Culkin; m. Archibald Tanner Banning, Oct. 13, 1914; children—Mary Margaret, Archibald Tanner, William Culkin (dec.), Margaret Brigid (dec.); m. LeRoy Salsich, Nov. 15, 1944. A.B., Vassar Coll., 1912; cert., Chgo. Sch. Civics and Philanthropy, 1913. Russell Sage Found. fellow for research, 1913. Author: This Marrying, 1920, Half Loaves, 1921, Spellbinders, 1922, Country Club People, 1923, A Handmaid of the Lord, 1924, The Women of the Family, 1926, Pressure, 1927, Money of Her Own, 1928, Prelude to Love, 1929, Mixed Marriage, 1930, The Town's Too Small, 1931, Path of True Love, 1932, The Third Son, 1933, The First Woman, 1934, The Iron Will, 1935, Letters to Susan, 1936, The Case for Chastity, 1937, Too Young to Marry, 1938, Enough to Live On, 1939, Out in Society, 1940, Salud: A South American Journal, 1941, Letters from England, 1942, Conduct Yourself Accordingly, 1944, The Clever Sister, 1947, Give Us Our Years, 1949, Fallen Away, 1951, The Dowry, 1955, The Convert, 1957, Echo Answers, 1960, The Quality of Mercy, 1963, The Vine and the Olive, 1964, I Took My Love to the Country, 1966, Mesabi, 1969, Lifeboat Number Two, 1971, The Will of Magda Townsend, 1973, The Splendid Torments, 1976, A Place in the Country, 1979, Such Interesting People, 1979; Contbr. short stories to mags.; writer essays on phases Am. life and activities. Trustee Duluth (Minn.) Public Library, Nat. Fund Med. Edn., Nat. Health and Welfare Retirement Fund. Hon. mem. Jr. League (Duluth); mem. AAUW (ex-pres. Duluth), LWV, Authors League Am. (council 1948-50), League Am. Penwomen, P.E.N., Phi Beta Kappa. Republican. Roman Catholic. Clubs: Cordon (Chgo.); Northland Country, Tryon Country, Tryon Riding and Hunt, Bus. and Profl. Women's; Pen and Brush (N.Y.C.), Cosmopolitan (N.Y.C.). Home: Tryon, N.C. Died Jan. 4. 1982.

BANSER, HENRY P., machine manufacturing executive; b. Chgo., Oct. 5, 1914; s. Henry P. and Mary (DeBore) B.; m. Alma Watkins, Oct. 20, 1940 (dec. Oct. 1951); 1 son, Henry P. III (dec. July 1967); m. 2d, Tracie Falduto, Mar. 7, 1969; children—Valerie, Joanne, Dennise. Factory foreman Ross Mfg. Co., 1940; purchasing agt. E. I. Guthman & Co., 1940-44; sec.-treas. Electronic Comptometer Corp., Chgo., 1944-46, pres., chmn. from 1946; gen. mgr. Henald Mfg. Co., 1952; pres. Electronics Components Corp., 1947-80; chmn. bd. Atlas Cable Corp., Chgo., 1970-74. Home: Addison, Ill. Died Nov. 20, 1980.

BARBER, JOSEPH, editor, b. Lowell, Mass., June 20, 1909; assoc. Joseph and Grace Greenleaf (Harris) B.; student Phillips Acad., Andover, Mass., 1925-27; A.B., Harvard, 1931; student U. Munich (Germany), 1931-32; B.S. in Journalism, Columbia, 1933; m. Eileen Paradis, Feb. 15, 1936. Berlin corr. Hearst Newspapers, 1933-34; dir. publs. Am. Council, Inst. Pacific Relations, 1934-35; mng. editor Atlantic Monthly, 1935-38; pub. relations counsel, Honolulu, 1938-40; assoc. editor Washington Post, 1941-43; dir. Com. on Fgn. Relations in 33 cities, affiliate Council on Fgn. Relations, Inc., N.Y.C., 1946-63. Served from lt. (j.g.) to lt. comdr. USNR, 1943-46. Awarded Pulitzer traveling scholarship, 1933. Mem. Council Fgn. Relations. Clubs: Century, Harvard (N.Y.C.); St. Botolph (Boston). Author: Hawaii: Restless Rampart, 1941: Good Fences Make Good Neighbors, 1958; These Are The Committees, 1964; co-author: Political Handbook of the World, 1953. Editor: American Policy Toward Germany, 1947; The Marshall Plan as American Policy, 1948; Military Cooperation with Western Europe, 1949; American Policy Toward China, 1950; The Containment of Soviet Expansion, 1951; Foreign Aid and the National Interest, 1952; Foreign Trade and U.S. Tariff Policy, 1953; Diplomacy and the Communist Challenge, 1954; Alliances and American Security, 1960; Red China and Our U.N. Policy, 1961; Atlantic Unity and the American Interest, 1963. Home: Biddeford, Maine. Died Aug. 16, 1982.

BARBOUR, GEORGE B(ROWN), educator, geologist; b. Edinburgh, Scotland, Aug. 22, 1890; s. Alexander Hugh Freeland and Margaret Nelson (Brown) B.; prep. edn. Merchiston Castle, Edinburgh, 1898-1904; student Marburg Univ., Germany, 1904-05; M.A., (Hons.), U. of Edinburgh, 1911; M.A., Cambridge Univ., Eng., 1914; Ph.D., Columbia, 1929; m. Dorothy Dickinson, May 15, 1920; children—Hugh Stewart, John (Ian) Graeme, Freeland (dec.). Came to U.S. to reside, 1932. Prof. of geology, Peking Univ., China, 1920-22; prof. of applied geology, Peiyang Univ., Tientsin, 1922-23; prof. of geology, Yenching Univ., Peking, 1923-32; lecturer, Columbia, 1928-29; visiting lecturer, U. of Cincinnati, 1932-33; hon. lecturer Univ. of London, 1934-37; acting prof., Stanford U., 1935; visiting physiographer, Rockefeller Foundation, Peiping, 1934; asso. prof. of geology, U. of Cincinnati, 1937-38, prof. from 1938, dean coll. of liberal arts 1938-58; geomorphologist S. African Expdn., U. of Calif., 1947. Served with the Brit. Army overseas, 1914-19. Decorated Mons Star. Fellow Royal Soc. of Edinburgh; Geol. Soc. Am., Geol. Soc. Finland, Geol. Soc. London, Royal Geog. Soc., Geological Society Edinburgh, Ohio Academy Science (pres. 1948-49); member Association American Geographers, Geological Society France, Geol. Soc. China, Sigma Xi, Phi Beta Kappa (hon.), Omicron Delta Kappa; hon. mem. Chinese Geol. Survey, Soc. Belge de Geologie et d' Hydrologie. Presbyterian. Clubs: University (Cincinnati), Athenaeum (London). Author: Geology of Kalgan Area, 1929; Physiographic History of Yangtze River, 1934. Contbr. articles to scientific jours. Home: Cincinnati, OH. †

BARBOUR, WALWORTH, former U.S. ambassador; b. Cambridge, Mass., June 4, 1908; s. Samuel Lewis and Clara (Hammond) B.; grad. Phillips Exeter Acad., 1926; A.B., Harvard, 1930. Foreign service officer, 1931—; vice consul, Naples, Italy, 1932, Athens, Greece, 1933-36; vice consul, 3d sec., Baghdad, Iraq, 1936-39; vice consul, 3d sec., Sofia, Bulgaria, 1939-41, 2d sec., vice consul, Dec. 1941; 2d sec., vice consul, Cairo, Egypt, 1942-44; 2d sec., vice consul, Athens, Greece, Nov.-Dec. 1944, consul, Dec. 1944; assigned Dept. of State 1945-49; assigned minister-counselor, Moscow, U.S.S.R., 1949; dir. office Eastern European affairs State Dept., 1951-54; dep. asst. sec. of state for European affairs, 1954-55; U.S. minister London, Eng., 1955-61; ambassador to Israel, 1961-73. Clubs: University (Washington); Chevy Chase (Md). Died July 21, 1982.

BARDEN, HORACE GEORGE, accountant; b. Kenosha, Wis., Jan. 30, 1906; s. John T. and Eva (Holcomb) B.; B.S. in Accounting and Bus. Adminstrn., U. Wis., 1931; m. Laura Stauffacher, Sept. 21, 1929; children—Thomas P., Martha J. With Ernst & Ernst, C.P.A.s, 1931-68, various exec. capacities, Indpls. and Chgo., partner, 1951-68, mem. mng. com., 1956-68; speaker, writer profl. accounting and mgmt. cons. Mem. Am. Inst. Accountants (council, v.p.), Ill. Soc. C.P.A.s, Ind. Assn. C.P.A.s (past pres.), Nat. Assn. Cost Accountants (past pres. Indpls.), Phi Kappa Sigma, Beta Gamma Sigma, Beta Alpha Psi (hon.). Clubs: Chicago, University, Chicago (Chgo.); Bob-O'Link Country (Highland Park, Ill.); Westmoreland Country. Home: Kenilworth, Ill. Died Sept. 23, 1984.

BARDES, PAUL METZNER, insurance company executive; b. Wilkinsburg, Pa., July 21, 1929; s. Paul Metzner and Lillian (Schreiber) B.; m. Evelyn Kay Record, Nov. 1, 1976. Student, U. Pitts., 1947-48; B.B.A., Tulane U., 1957, J.D., 1959. Bar: La. bar 1959; C.L.U. C.P.C.U. Chpt. counselor Sigma Pi Fraternity, Elizabeth, N.J., 1948-51, 53; dist. claims mgr. Allstate Ins. Co., Northbrook, Ill., 1959-67; atty. Erie Ins. Exchange, Erie, Pa., 1967-72; v.p., gen. counsel, sec. Am. States Ins. Cos., Indpls., 1972—; underwriter Am. States Lloyds Ins. Co., Dallas, 1972—; sec.-treas. Ind. Ins. Guaranty Assn.; dir. City Ins. Agy., Inc. Bd. dirs. Young Reps., Allegheny County, Pa., 1950-51. Served with USMC, 1951-53. Mem. Sigma Pi. Club: Rotary. Home: Plainfield, Ind. Died July 3, 1984.

BARDIN, JAMES C(OOK), prof. Romance langs.; b. Augusta, Ga., Sept. 25, 1887; s. Henry Clay and Mary Ellen (Cook) B.; student, Newberry (S.C.) Coll., 1902-03; M.D., U. of Va., 1909; m. Sally Norvell Nelson, June 19, 1915; 1 son, James Nelson. Pathologist, Central State Hosp., Petersburg, Va., 1909-10; instr., Romance langs., U. of Va., 1910-26, prof. from 1926. Served as 1st lt., Med. Corps U.S. Army, 1919; from 1st lt. to lt. col., M.I. Res., 1921-42; lt. col., Air Corps., 1942; lt. col. hon. res. Mem. Am. Assn. Teachers Spanish, A.A.A.S., Am. Geog. Soc. Raven Soc., Mexico Pilgrims, Phi Beta Kappa, Theta Delta Chi. Club: Colonnade. Author: articles, Maya civilization, Latin-Am.; editor: Leyendas Historicas Mejicanas, 1917; El reino de los Incas, 1918. Home: Charlottesville, Va. †

BARDWELL, RICHARD W(OLEBEN), supt. schools; b. Tipton, Ia., May 14, 1889; s. Conrad Morton and Anna Louise (Woleben) B.; A.B., U. of Ill., 1910; A.M., U. of Chicago, 1922; grad. study, U. of Wis.; m. Gertrude Smith, July 10, 1912; children—Elizabeth, Richard, Roger W. Teacher and prin. pub. schs., Hebron, Ill., 1910-11; prin. pub. schs., Delavan, Ill., 1911-14; supt. pub. schs., Woodstock, Ill., 1914-23, Rock Island, 1923-28, Madison, Wis.. from 1928. Mem. Dept. of Superintendence of N.E.A., Psi Upsilon, Phi Delta Phi, and Phi Delta Kappa. Mason. Author: (with Ethel Mabie and J. C. Tressler) Elementary English in Action (series of textbooks), 1935. Home: Madison, WI. †

BARGHOORN, ELSO STERRENBERG, botany educator; b. N.Y.C., June 30, 1915; s. Elso S. and Elizabeth (Brust) B.; m. Margaret Alden MacLeod, Aug. 16, 1941 (div. 1951); children: Jonathan (dec.), Steven Frederick; m. Teresa Joan La Croix, July 21, 1953 (div. 1963); m. Dorothy Dellmer Osgood, Oct. 31, 1964. A.B., Miami U., Oxford, Ohio, 1937, D.Sc. (hon.), 1980; M.A., Harvard, 1938, Ph.D., 1941. Instr. biology Amherst (Mass.) Coll., 1941-43, asst. prof., 1944-46; asst. prof. botany Harvard, 1946-49, asso. prof., 1949-55, prof., from 1955; curator paleobot. collections, from 1949; Field service cons. to War Dept. OSRD, 1944-46. Contbr. articles to sci. jours. and books. Recipient Hayden Meml. award Phila. Acad. Natural Scis. Fellow Linnaean Soc. London; mem. Nat. Acad. Scis. (C.D. Walcott medal 1972), Geol. Soc. Am., Am. Acad. Arts and Scis., Bot. Soc. Am., Geochem. Soc., Phi Beta Kappa, Sigma Xi. Home: Carlisle, Mass.

BARIT, A. EDWARD, motor car mfg. exec.; b. Aug. 30, 1890. Associated with Hudson Motor Car Co., 1910-57, pres., 1936-54, also gen. mgr. and director; cons. Am. Motors Corp. 1954-57; dir. materiel Mitchell-Bentley Corp., from 1957.†

BARKALOW, FREDERICK SCHENCK, JR., educator, zoologist; b. Marietta, Ga., Feb. 23, 1914; s. Frederick Schenck and Katherine Aurelia (White) B.; B.S. in Chemistry, Ga. Inst. Tech., 1936; student Auburn U., 1936-38; M.S. in Zoology, U. Mich., 1939, Ph.D. (Rosenwald fellow 1946-47), 1948; m. Joan Metzger, Nov. 23, 1937; 1 dau., Joanna. Instr. zoology Auburn U., 1936-39, instr. botany and plant pathology, 1946; chief biologist Ala. Dept. Conservation, 1939-41; mem. faculty N.C. State U. of N.C., Raleigh, from 1947, prof. zoology, 1947-67, prof. zoology and forestry, 1968-79, prof. emeritus, 1979-82, head dept., 1950-63; cons. wildlife, 1939-82. Mem. Sec. Agr. Adv. Com. Multiple Use Nat. Forests, 1963-68; del. White House Conf. Conservation, 1962; panelist NSF, from 1959; mem. tropical biology panel U. Costa Rica, 1962; sr. vis. fellow to Great Britain for OEEC, 1960; cons. disease vector study in Alaska for Dept. Def., 1951. Chmn. edn. div. United Fund Raleigh, 1954, bd. dirs., 1955-58. Served to lt. col. AUS, 1941-46. Recipient Am. Motors Conservation award, 1967; Gov.'s award for Conservationist of Year, 1968; named to N.C. Conservation Hall of Fame, 1979. Fellow AAAS; mem. Archaeol. Soc. N.C. (pres. 1959-60), N.C. Acad. Sci. (v.p. 1962, pres. 1971), N.C. Wildlife Fedn. (sec. 1948, trustee from 1960, pres. 1965-66, 74-75, Am. Soc. Mammalogists (dir. 1961-71; chmn. land mammals com. 1961-66), Nat. Wildlife Fedn. (dir. region 3, 1978-82), Am. Ornithol. Union, Assn. Tropical Biology, Am. Soc. Systematic Zoology, Wildlife Soc., Phi Beta Kappa (pres. Wake County assn. 1954-55), Sigma Xi, Alpha Zeta, Xi Sigma Pi, Phi Kappa Phi (pres. N.C. State chpt. 1960-61), Phi Sigma. Contbr. numerous articles in field. Home: Raleigh, N.C. Died June 22, 1982.

BARKER, GEORGE JOHN, univ. prof.; b. Sparta, Wis., Oct. 5, 1889; s. George and Mary (Pasbrig) B.; B.S., U. of Wis., 1920, E.M., 1923; m. Cleophus Desmond, Sept. 10, 1913; children—Mary Helen, George Peter. Engr. Vinegar Hill Zinc Co., Galena, Ill., 1912-13; supt. Nat. Zinc Separating Co., Cuba City, Wis., 1913-17; research engr. Phosphate Mining & Fertilizer Div., Armour & Co., Nashville, Tenn. 1918-19; metallurgist Anaconda Copper Mining Co., Great Falls, Mont., 1920-21; prof. mining and metallurgy, U. of Wis., Madison, from 1922, chmn. dept. from 1948; pres. Vesper (Wis.) Tile & Brick Co.; sec.-treas. Coughlin Mining Co., Inc., Shullsburg, Wis.; cons. engr., Madison Wis. from 1936. Professional engr., Wis. Mem. Am. Soc. Engring. Edn. (mem. council), Am. Inst. Mining and Metall. Engrs. (bd. dirs. Chgo. sect.), Am. Foundrymen's Assn. (com. chmn.), Am. Soc. Metals (bd. dirs. Milw. chpt.), Soc. for Non-Destructive Testing, Gamma Alpha Sigma Xi. Roman Catholic. Clubs: Serra, Blackhawk Country, Madison Curling. Inventor Barker-Truog process of treatment of clays by pH control of base exchange properties, and holder 2 patents on the process. Home: Madison, Wis. †

BARKER, RAY W., army officer; born N.Y., Dec. 10, 1889; grad. Cav. Sch., 1920, F.A. Sch., Advanced Course, 1927, Command and Gen. Staff Sch., 1928. Army War Coll., 1940. Began as private, Cav., Sept. 1910; commd. 2d lt. Cav., Aug. 1913; transferred to F.A. as 1st lt., 1917, and advanced through the grades to brig. gen., Aug. 1942; maj. gen. (temp.) 1943; served major and lt. col. of field arty., World War I; Gen. Staff Corps, 1930-32; apptd. dir. of army div. to supervise demilitarization of Germany, July 1945; comdr. Am. occupation garrison, Berlin, and rep. on allied command, Oct. 1945; retired Mar. 1947. Supt. Manlius (N.Y.) Sch. from 1947. Address: Washington, D.C. †

BARLEY, FRANK JAY, mortgage co. exec.; b. LeRoy, Ill., Mar. 12, 1905; s. Frank Calfax and Florence (Martin) B.; student Ill. Wesleyan U., 1923-25; J.D., George Washington U., 1930; m. Evelyn Mildred Esch, Sept. 4, 1930; children—Martin A., Warren E. With D.C. govt., 1926-29; asst. treas. Commonwealth Investment Co., 1929-33; admitted to D.C. bar, 1930; assoc. Marsh & Rogers, Washington, 1930-33; asst. mgr. ins. dept. HOLC, 1933-41; adminstrv. officer WPB, 1941-44; chief personnel utilization project, Civil Service Commn., 1944-46, inspection div., 1946-48, asst. chief inspection div., 1948-49; chief, 1949-53, dir. bur. inspections, contact officer CSC and all fed. agys. on employee-mgmt. relations, 1953-61; asso. Waring and Son, Leonardtown, Md., from 1961; chmn. bd. Barley Mortgage Co. Inc., Waldorf and California, Md. Trustee St. Mary's County Home for Elderly. Mem. Phi Gamma Delta, Phi Delta Phi. Episcopalian. Home: California, Md. Died Oct. 1980.

BARLOW, MYRON C., prof. psychology; b. Chesterfield, Ida., Sept. 18, 1887; s. Truman H. and Fanny (Call) B.; A.B., U. of Utah, 1913; M.A., George Peabody Coll. for Teachers, 1924; Ph.D., U. of Chicago, 1926; m. Viola Ford, June 15, 1911; children—Thelma (Mrs. Thomas Freeman), Ford, Alice (Mrs. John I. Bradley), Dale. Teacher in public schools, 1908-17; agriculture, 1917-23; prof. psychology and head department of psychology University of Utah, 1926-48, retired real estate broker. Member Am. Assn. Univ. Profs., Phi Delta Kappa. Mem. Church of Jesus Christ of the Latter-Day Saints. Author: (pamphlet) Psychology of Building Good Study Habits. Contbr. articles to mags. Address: Los Angeles, Calif. †

BARLOW, SAMUEL LATHAM MITCHILL, composer; b. N.Y.C., June 1, 1892; s. Peter Townsend and Louise (Matthews) B.; student Groton Sch., 1904-10. Harvard, 1910-14; studied piano with Philipp, Paris, orchestration with Respighi, Rome; m. Ernesta Drinker, Mar. 10, 1928; 1 dau., Audrey Townsend (Mrs. W.R. Orndorff). Composer, lectr., writer. Composer: Mon Ami Peirrot (1st performance, Opera Comique Paris), 1934; Ballo Sardo (ballet), symphonic works played by Stokowsky, Goossens, Reiner, Paray, others; lectr. U. P.R., 1944. Pres., Citizens Com. for Govt. Art Projects; sec. and trustee Asia. Inst.; gov. Am. Composers Alliance; moderator of Forum for Democracy. Fellow Carnegie Found., 1943, mission to S.A. Trustee F.H. Beebe Fund, Boston; dir. Composers Forum, Hour of Music Concerts, Castle Hill Found.; pres. Am. Opera Soc. Served as 1st lt. A.E.F., 1917. Decorated Legion of Honor; Bundesverdienst-Kreuze 1st class (Bonn Govt.). Fellow Internat. Acad. Arts and Letters. Democrat. Club: Union (N.Y.C.). Author: The Astonished Muse, 1961. Contbr. various publs. Address: New York, N.Y. Died Sept. 19, 1982.

BARNARD, HARRY, biographer, journalist; b. Pueblo, Colo., Sept. 5, 1906; s. David and Paula (Halpern) Kletzky; m. Miriam Helstein, June 20, 1929; 1 dau., Karen; m. Ruth Eisenstat, Oct. 23, 1943; children—Judith, Ronald L., (Harry) David. Student, U. Denver, 1923-25; Ph.B. cum laude, U. Chgo., 1928; postgrad., John Marshall Law Sch., Chgo., 1937-38. Mem. editorial staff Chgo. Herald-Examiner, 1928-34; research staff Ill. Tax Commn., 1934-35; dir. research Chgo. Law Dept., 1935-42; dir. press relations U. Chgo., 1943; staff Detroit Times, 1943; chief editorial writer Chgo. Times, 1944; mem. staff Chgo. Sun, 1945-47, engaged in pub. relations and advt., 1948-58, biog. writer, lectr., tchr., writer other works, 1958-82; writer editorial page column Liberal at Large, Chgo. Daily News and Des Moines Register Syndicate, 1958-60; mem. faculty Am. politics Columbia Coll., Chgo., 1964-66; mem. dept. pub. relations Northwestern U., 1966-68; writer-in-residence, instr. biography and journalism Roosevelt U., Chgo., 1968-69; lectr. U. Chgo., 1958. Author: Eagle Forgotten, the Life of John Peter Altgeld, 1938, Rutherford B. Hayes and His America, 1954, Independent Man, the Life of Senator James Couzens, 1958; editor: (Pope John) Mater et Magistra, 1962, (with Preston Bradley) Along the Way, 1962, This Great Triumvirate of Patriots—The Story Behind Lorado Taft's Chicago Monument to George Washington, Robert Morris and Haym Salomon, 1971, The Forging of an American Jew, The Life and Times of Judge Julian W. Mack, 1974; contbr. to: other encys., mags. New Standard and; author privately distributed studies. Chmn. Altgeld Centennial Com., 1947; v.p. Nat. Com. to Abolish House Un-Am. Activities Com., 1962-64; publicist Henry Horner for Gov. Ill., 1932, E.J. Kelly for Mayor Chgo., 1935, 39; chmn. W. O. Douglas for Democratic presdl. nomination, 1952; bd. dirs. Chgo. Civil Liberties Com., 1940-42, Onward Neighborhood House Settlement, Chgo., 1962-69. Recipient Cooper Ohioana Library award, 1955; two selections in White House Library Am. Lit., 1962; Pontifical medal Pope John XXIII, 1963; Friends of Lit. award, 1975; Nat. Endowment Humanities fellow, 1974. Mem. Soc. Midwest Authors, Chgo. Press Vets, Phi Sigma Delta. Democrat. Jewish. Died Aug. 26, 1982.

BARNES, ALLAN CAMPBELL, foundation executive, obstetrician and gynecologist; b. Coldwater, Mich., Dec. 18, 1911; s. George Emerson and Myrtle Kendall (Montague) B.; A.B., Princeton U., 1933; M.D., U. Pa., 1937; M.S. in Obstetrics and Gynecology, U. Mich., 1941; m. Louise Young Kimball, June 5, 1937 (dec. May 1976); children—Katherine M. (Mrs. Robert Apter), Kimball M., Allan C., Miles T. Intern, U. Mich., Ann Arbor, 1937-39, resident, 1939-42, instr. obstetrics and gynecology, 1942-45; assoc. prof. obstetrics and gynecology Ohio State U., Columbus, 1945-47, prof., chmn. dept., 1947-53; prof., chmn. dept. obstetrics and gynecology Case-Western Res. U., Cleve., 1953-60; prof., dir. dept. obstetrics and gynecology Johns Hopkins, Balt., 1960-69; v.p. Rockefeller Found., N.Y.C., 1970-77; sr. fellow The Population Council, 1978-79; lectr. dept. Ob-Gyn, Bowman Gray Med. Sch., Winston Salem, N.C., 1979-82. Served to maj. AUS, 1942-45. Diplomate Am. Bd. Obstetrics and Gynecology. Fellow Am. Coll. Obstetrics and Gynecology; mem. Am. Assn. Obstetricians and Gynecologists, Am. Gynecol. Soc., Sigma Xi, Alpha Omega Alpha. Contbr. articles to profl. jours. Home: Winston Salem, N.C. Died June 13, 1982.

BARNES, DJUNA, author, poet, artist; b. Cornwall-on-Hudson, N.Y., June 12, 1892; d. Henry Wald and Elizabeth (Chappell) Barnes; student art Pratt Inst., Art Students League. Reporter, illustrator, spl. feature writer for newspapers, mags., 1913-31; short stories appeared in All-story mag., Smart Set, Morning Telegraph, Little Rev., Dial, Vanity Fair, Transatlantic Rev., others (pseud. Lydia Steptoe); one act plays produced by Provincetown Players, 1919-20, Studio Theatre of Smith Coll., 1926. Past trustee Dag Hammerskjöld Found. Mem. Nat. Inst. Arts and Letters, Authors Guild. Illustrator: A Book, 1923; (novel) Ryder, 1928; The Ladies Almanack, 1928, 2d edit., 1972; author Night Among the Horses, 1929; (novel) Nightwood, 1936; (play in verse) The Antiphon, 1958 (transl. into Swedish 1961); Spillway (short stories), 1962, 2d edit., 1972; The Selected Works of Djuna Barnes, 1962; represented in The Present Age (Edwin Muir), Vol. 5, England, The Widening Gyre, 1963, The Personal Voice, 1964, The World of Love, 1964, Modern Poetry, Little Treasury of American Prose, Modern Women in Love (transl. 6 langs.), Dial Anthology. Large oil painting, Alice, exhibited Art of this Century Gallery, N.Y.C., 1946 (McKeldin Library of U. Md. purchaser estate). Died June 19, 1982.

BARNES, HARRY C., corp. exec.; b. Bristol, Conn., 1889; 1st v.p. and dir. Associated Spring Corp., Bristol; dir. Washburn Wire Co., Phillipsdale, R.I. Pres. West Cemetery Assn., Bristol. Home: Bristol, Conn. †

BARNES, HORACE RICHARDS, educator; b. Haddonfield, N.J., May 8, 1887; s. Frederick Rigby and Louisa (Frank) B.; A.B., U. of Pa., 1911, A.M., 1913; LL.D., Washington Coll., 1928; m. Laura May Hibberd, June 13, 1916; children—Elizabeth Jean, Richard. Scholar in psychology and fellow in econs., U. of Pa., 1912-15; asst. prof., Drexel Inst., 1916-18; prof. Pa. Mil. Coll., 1918-19; bursar U. of Pa., 1919-21; prof. and head dept. econs., Franklin and Marshall Coll., Lancaster, Pa., from 1921, sec. bd. trustees, 1928-44. Pres. Civil Service Bd., Bur. of Police, Lancaster, 1930-34; dir. Nat. Indsl. Recovery Adminstrn., Lancaster, Co., 1933; asst. food adminstr. Del. County, 1917-18; chmn. Local Bd. No. 2, Lancaster Selective Service, 1940-44; mem. War Garden Com., Del. County. Mem. Am. Econs. Soc., Am. Acad. Polit. and Social Science, Lancaster Co. Hist. Soc. (exec. com.), Cliosophi Soc., Phi Sigma Kappa (nat. pres., 1930-32; mem. court of honor), Pi Gamma Mu (organized Franklin and Marshall chapter). Presbyn. (trustee). Republican. Mason. Author numerous articles of coll. frat. interest, and econ. history. Home: Lancaster, Pa. †

BARNES, JULIAN F., army officer; b. Washington, D.C., Oct. 14, 1889; grad. F.A. Sch., Advanced Course, 1923; honor grad. Command and Gen. Staff Sch., 1925; grad. Army War Coll., 1930. Commd. 2d lt., F.A., 1912, advanced through the grades to brig. gen., Sept. 1941. Address: Washington, D.C.*

BARNES, RALPH M., educator, indsl. engr.; b. Clifton Mills, W.Va., Oct. 17, 1900; s. John J. and Martha (Mosser) B.; B.S. in Mech. Engring., U. of W.Va., 1923, M.E., 1928; M.S., Cornell U., 1924, Ph.D., 1933; m. Mary Goodykoontz, June 13, 1931; children—Elizabeth, Carolyn Martha. Asst. to chief engr., U.S. Window Glass Co., Morgantown, W.Va., June-Sept., 1923; asst. engr. on product devel. Bausch & Lomb Optical Co., Rochester, N.Y., 1924-25; indsl. engr. The Gleason Works, Rochester, N.Y., 1925-26; instr. in indsl. mgmt. dept. of bus. orgn. and operation Coll. of Commerce, U. Ill., 1926-28; indsl. engr. Eastman Kodak Co., Kodak Park Works and Camera Works, Rochester, N.Y., summers, 1927-28-29, 30, 34, 35; cons. indsl. engr. Kodak Ltd., London, Eng., summer 1936, Dow Chem. Co., summer 1942; asst. prof. indsl. engring. mech. engring. dept. Coll. of Engring. U. Iowa, 1928-30, assoc. prof., 1930-34, prof., 1934-49, dir. of personnel, 1936-49, also dir. summer mgmt. course, 1939-48; now emeritus prof. engring. and prodn. mgmt. U. Calif. at Los Angeles. Served as cons. engr. during World War II. Cons. Fedn. Norwegian Industries, Swedish Industries, 1950; cons. to F.U.N.S.A., Montevideo, Uruguay, 1958, Spain, Mexico, Costa Rica, Japan, Peru, 1958-63. Recipient U. Mo. Honor award for distinguished service in engring., 1967. Fellow Internat. Acad. Mgmt., Soc. Advancement Mgmt. (Gilbreth Medal, 1941; Indsl. Incentive Award, 1951), ASME, Am. Inst. Indsl. Engrs. (Frank & Lillian Gilbretis Indsl. Engring. award 1969), AAAS; mem. Indsl. Mgmt. Soc., Am. Mgmt. Assn., Am. Soc. Engring. Edn., Tau Beta Pi, Sigma Xi, Sigma Iota Epsilon, Pi Tau Sigma, Alpha Pi Mu, Beta Gamma Sigma. Author: Work Measurement Manual, 1951; Motion and Time Study; Design and Measurement of Work, 6th edit., 1968; Work Sampling, 2d edit., 1957. Home: Los Angeles, Calif. Died Nov. 5, 1984.

BARNES, ROGER WILLIAM, physician; b. Littleton, Colo., Sept. 22, 1897; s. William Jull and Ada (Jull) B.; m. Oca Davis, Mar. 23, 1923; children—Bonnie Rae (Mrs. H. Hadley), Joanne (Mrs. C. Fisher), Joelle (Mrs. D. Emery), Richard (dec.), Duane, Dwight (dec.). A.B., Pacific Union Coll., 1922; M.D., Coll. Med., 1922; M.S., U. So. Calif., 1939; D.Sc., U. Okayama, Japan, 1954. Diplomate: Am. Bd. Urology. Intern Los Angeles County Hosp., 1922-23, resident in urology, 1923-25, pvt. practice medicine specializing in urology, Los Angeles, 1925-72, Loma Linda (Calif.) U. Med. Center, 1972-82; instr. urology Loma Linda U. Sch. Medicine, 1925-30, asst. prof., 1930-36, asso. prof., 1936-44, prof. surgery, 1944-65, distinguished service prof. urology, 1965-82, chmn. sect. surgery, 1948-63; chief dept. urology White Meml. Hosp., 1928-65; sr. attending surgeon, urology Los Angeles County Hosp., 1935-64, chmn. urology staff, 1957-60; sr. surgeon (resident) USPHS, 1942-61 Author: Endoscopic Prostatic Surgery, 1943, Urological Practice, 1954, Endoscopy, 1958, Urology Review, 1967, also articles med. jours. Fellow A.C.S., Internat. Coll. Surgeons, Societe Internat. d' Urologie; mem. AMA (chmn. urology sect. 1958), Am. Urol. Assn. (Ramon Guiteras award 1979), Calif. Med. Assn., Los Angeles County Med. Assn. (v.p. 1961, sec.-treas. 1963). Republican. Seventh-day Adventist. Home: Loma Linda, Calif. Died Jan. 19, 1982.

BARNES, WENDELL BURTON, banker; b. Ponca City, Okla., Aug. 23, 1909; s. Louis Seymour and Mary Elizabeth (Davis) B.; grad. Culver (Ind.) Mil. Acad., 1928; Ph.B., Brown U., 1932; LL.B., U. Mich., 1935; m. Lucile Wright, June 15, 1936; children—Wendell Burton, Nancy Louise, Shirley Lynne, William Graham Wright. Admitted to Okla. bar, 1935; asst. atty., Okla. Tax Commn., Okla. City, 1935-39; gen. counsel for Tulsa plant Douglas Aircraft Co., 1941-46; pvt. practice, 1946-53; gen. counsel Small Bus. Adminstrn., Washington, 1953-54, adminstr., 1954-59; sr. asso. Shearson, Hammill & Co., 1959-61, partner, 1961-62; with N.Y. Hanseatic Corp., N.Y.C., 1962-85; member board of directors Servo Corp. Am. Mem. Pres. Cabinet Com. Small Bus., 1956-59; mem. bd. dirs. Virgin Island Corp., 1958-59. Mem. Okla. Ho. Reps., 1950-52. Trustee Brown U. Recipient citation Brown U., 1959. Mem. Am., Fed. (nat. treas., nat. council), N.Y. bar assns., Izaak Walton League (pres. Okla., 1945), S.A.R., Soc. Cin., Psi Upsilon, Phi Delta Phi. Republican. Episcopalian. Home: Walnut Creek, Calif. Died June 11, 1985.

BARNET, ROBERT AYRES, JR., banker; b. Boston, Dec. 23, 1889; s. Robert A. and Sarah J. (Swasey) B.; m. Dorothy E. MacNab, Sept. 22, 1917 (dec. June 1957); children—Robert Ayres 3d, Virginia A. (Mrs. Ronald M. Killie); m. 2d, Dorothy deWitt Martin, June 6, 1959. With Am. Irving Savs. Bank, N.Y.C., from 1936, hon. chmn., from 1958, also trustee; dir. N. River Ins. Co. Home: Fairfield, Conn. †

BARNETT, FRANK EUGENE, lawyer, former corporation executive; b. Fairport Harbor, Ohio, July 14, 1912; s. George Forrest and Hazel (Roberts) B.; m. Virginia Severens Russ, Sept. 24, 1936 (div. 1953); 1 son, John Severns; m. Wana Allison, Dec. 31, 1954; 1 stepdau., Pamela Allison. A.B., Duke U., 1933; LL.B., Western Res. U., 1936. Bar: Ohio bar 1936, N.Y. bar 1943. Tax lawyer Lybrand, Ross Bros. & Montgomery, 1936-41; asso. Clark, Carr & Ellis, 1942-44, partner, 1945-68; Eastern gen. counsel U.P. R.R., 1951-60, v.p., 1955-60, v.p., gen. counsel, 1961-66, chmn. exec. com., 1967-69; chmn. bd., chief exec. officer Union Pacific Corp., U.P. R.R., 1969-77, O.S.L. R.R. Co., O. W. R.R. & N. Co., L.A. & S.L. R. R. Co., 1969-77, Spokane Internat. R.R. Co., 1971-77, Union Pacific Land Resources Corp., 1971-77, Union Pacific Mining Corp., 1971-77, Upland Industries Corp., 1971-77; chmn. bd. Champlin Petroleum Co., 1970-77; v.p., dir. St. Joseph & Grand Island Ry. Co., Utah Parks Co., 1969-77; of counsel firm Shea & Gould, 1977-80; trustee Seamen's Bank Savs.; Trustee, mem. exec. com. Union Pacific Found. Named R.R. Man of Yr. Modern R.R., 1975; recipient Seley award Seley Found., 1977. Mem. Am. Bar Assn., Assn. Bar City N.Y., Phi Delta Phi. Clubs: Econ. of N.Y. (N.Y.C.), Univ. (N.Y.C.), River (N.Y.C.); Preston Mountain (Kent, Conn.). Home: New York, N.Y. Died Apr. 4, 1985.

BARNETT, HENRY GREEN, English language educator; b. Leesburg, Fla., Dec. 13, 1890; s. Robert Howren and Sarah Elizabeth (Epperson) B.; A.B., Emory Coll. (now Emory U.), 1910; A.M., Columbia Univ., 1926; m. Bess Wood Sargent, Aug. 1, 1935. Teacher Soochow (China) Univ., 1920-21, Kwansei Gakuin, Kobe, Japan, 1921-22, Ewing Christian Coll., Allahabad, India, 1922-23, Lebanon Boys' Sch., Suq el Gharb, Syria, 1923-24, Sch. of Theology of Southern Meth. U., 1924-25; prof. English, Florida Southern Coll., Lakeland, Fla., from 1927. Methodist. Author: The Roof of the World (poems), 1916; Laical Letters, 1940; The Blanket on the Ground, 1944. Home: Lakeland, Fla. †

BARNETT, HERMAN L., lawyer; b. San Antonio, Dec. 12, 1893; s. Walter Michael and Fannie Edith (Lyon) B.; m. Irma Samson, Sept. 30, 1920; children—Marilyn, William Michael. A.B. summa cum laude, Tulane U., 1914, LL.B., 1916. Bar: La. bar 1916. Practiced in, New Orleans; sr. partner Guste, Barnett & Shushan, from 1957; dir. Continental Savs. & Loan Assn., 1922-70, dir. emeritus, from 1970; instr. pub. speaking Am. Inst. Banking, 1921, lectr. comml. law, 1930-43; spl. lectr. comml. law Tulane U. Sch. Commerce, 1922-29. Former mem. bd. editors: So. Law Quar. (Tulane Law Rev.). Chmn. New Orleans CSC, 1942-51; mem. exec. com. La. Civil Service League, from 1950, chmn. legal com., 1963-66; bd. dirs. Lighthouse for Blind, New Orleans, 1935-76, hon. life bd. dirs., 1976—. Served from 2d lt. to capt. U.S. Army, 1917-19, AEF. Recipient certificate of merit and key City of New Orleans, 1951, 66, Lemann Civil Service award, 1964; Distinguished Community Service award La. Civil Service League, 1977. Mem. Confrerie des Chevaliers du Tastevin (France), La. Law Inst., La. Civil Service League (gov. from 1954), ABA, La. Bar Assn., New Orleans Bar Assn. (1st v.p. 1936), Mil. Order World Wars (comdr. 1942-43), Res. Officers Assn., Am. Legion, La Coalition Patriotic Socs. (past pres.), New Orleans C. of C. (past chmn. nat. legis. com.), Order of Lafayette (charter), Phi Beta Kappa. Club: Kiwanis. Home: New Orleans, LA.

BARNETT, HOMER GARNER, educator emeritus; b. Bisbee, Ariz., Apr. 25, 1906; s. Lee and Lottie L. (McEuen) B.; A.B., Stanford, 1927; Ph.D., U. Calif., 1938; m. Judith H. Skaggs, Apr. 12, 1941; children—Linda Ann, Susan Marie. Research asso. anthropology U. Calif., 1937-38; instr. anthropology U. N.Mex., 1938-39; anthropologist bur. Am. ethnology Smithsonian Inst., 1944-46; asst. prof. anthropology U. Oreg., 1939-44, asso. prof., 1946-50, prof., 1950-71, prof. emeritus, 1971-85; staff anthropologist Trust Ter. Pacific Islands, 1951-53; mem. Research Council South Pacific Commn., 1952-53; cons. Netherlands New Guinea Govt., 1955. Sr. fellow NSF, 1956-57; fellow Center for Advanced Study in Behavorial Scis., 1964-65. Mem. Pacific sci. bd. Coast Adv. Com. Mem. AAAS, Am. Ethnol. Soc., Soc. Applied Anthropology (pres.), Phi Beta Kappa, Sigma Xi. Author: Innovation: The Basis of Cultural Change, 1953; Palauan Society, 1949; Anthropology in Administration, 1956; Coast Salish of British Columbia, 1955; Indian Shakers, 1957; Being a Palauan, 1959; The Nature and Function of the Potlatch, 1968; Being a Palauan, Fieldwork Edit., 1979; also articles on anthropology. Home: Eugene, Oreg. Died May 9, 1985; interred Rest House, Eugene.

BARNEY, WILLIAM POPE, architect; b. Columbus, Ga., Oct. 15, 1890; s. Charles Gorham and Francis (Pope) B.; B.S., Ga. Tech., 1911; M.S., U. Pa., 1913; Woodman-Gilette fellow, study Europe, 1921; m. Marian Greene, Aug. 8, 1915. Trainee offices Paul P. Cret, Charles Z. Klauder, 1915-22; with Davis Dunlap & Barney, 1923-29, W. Pope Barney & Asso., 1929-45; cons. firm Barney, Banwell, Armentrout & Divvens; principle works colls., schs., chs.; visiting critic Pa. State Coll. Adv. bd. Princeton. Lt. colonel Air Force Res. Awarded Gold Medal of Honor in Architecture, Archtl. League N.Y., 1929; winner competition for Phila. Housing; medal Paris Expn.; 1st mention Pan-Am. Exhbn., Monteivideo, Uruguay. Fellow A.I.A. (past chmn. nat. com. edn.), Internat. Inst. Arts and Letters; mem. Sandwich Hist. Soc. (past pres.), Sigma Xi, Scarab. Republican. Christian Scientist. Clubs: T Square (past pres., past design patron), Lions. Author: Architectural Highlights of Sandwich, New Hampshire, 1962. Contbr. articles profl. publs. Home: Center Harbor, N.H. †

BARNHILL, MAURICE VICTOR, judge; b. Halifax County, N.C., Dec. 5, 1887; s. Martin Van Buren and Mary (Dawes) B.; ed. priv. schs., Enfield (N.C.) graded schs.; Elm City (N.C.) Acad., U. of N.C. Law Sch.; LL.D., U. of N.C., 1946; m. Nannie Rebecca Cooper, June 5, 1912; children—Maurice Victor, Rebecca Arrington. Admitted to N.C. bar, 1909, and began practice in Raleigh, N.C., moving to Rocky Mount, N.C., 1910; pros. atty. Nash County, 1914-21; mem. State Legislature (House), 1921-23; judge Nash County Recorder's Court, 1923-24; judge N.C. Superior Court, 1924-37; assoc. justice N.C. Supreme Court, 1937-54; chief justice North Carolina Supreme Court, from 1954. Ex-chairman, board trustees Rocky Mount Graded Schs. and Nash County Highway Commn.; chairman N.C. Judicial Counsel from 1951. Member North Carolina Bar Assn., N.C. Bar, Inc., Sigma Chi; hon. mem. Phi Delta Phi, Law Sch. Democrat. Methodist. Mason (Shriner). Clubs: Benvenue (Rocky Mount, N.C.); Carolina Country (Raleigh, N.C.). Home: Raleigh, N.C. †

BARNITZ, WIRT WHITCOMB, editor lecturer; b. Hanover, Pa., June 13, 1887; s. Jacob Percy and Mary (Barnitz) B.; grad. high sch., Hanover, 1905; spl. study Harvard; unmarried. Lecturer on travel, etc., since 1912; spl. corr. New York World, Central Empires, Europe, 1915-16; founder of The Nomad (formerly Journeys Beautiful), editor, 1924-30. Assisted in orgn. War Camp Community Service, World War. Founder Nomad Orgn. for world peace through human contacts in travel. Traveled twice to Lapland for survey purposes preparatory to exploration of the outer reaches of Lapp tundra. Organizer, dir., plan for Home for Literary Workers. Club: The Explorers. Contbr. to Lippincott's, Harper's Weekly, Theatre Mag., Travel Mag., World Traveler, Spur, Country Life, Liberty, St. Nicholas, The Forum, etc. Author: Outline Course in Jounalism. Pioneer in radiolog broadcasting; —Castles and Their Ghosts,— most popular of his radio subjects; pioneer radio commentator. Lecturer on various topics. Home: New York, N.Y. †

BARNUM, WALTER, pres. Motorstokor Corpn.; b. N.Y. City, Feb. 3, 1887; s. William Milo and Annie Theresa (Phelps) B.; prep. edn., Westminster Sch., Simsbury, Conn.; B.A., Yale, 1910; m. Evelyn Humphrey, of N.Y. City, July 7, 1922; children—Burrall, Humphrey. Engaged in oil production, contracting and in real estate business, 1910-16; treas. Pacific Coast Co., operating coal mines, railroads and steamship cos. on Pacific Coast, 1916-25, pres., 1925-33, now dir.; pres. Motorstokor Corpn. since 1933; dir. The Pacific Coast Co., Richardson, Barnum & Co. Mem. Nat. Coal Assn. (dir.; pres. 1926-27), Delta Kappa Epsilon, Senior Soc. (Yale). Republican. Episcopalian. Clubs: Yale, Larchmont Yacht, New York Yacht, Cruising Club of America. Frequent speaker before representative bodies on production and distribution of coal. Home: New York, N.Y. †

BARNWELL, DAVID KITZMILLER, clergyman; b. Los Angeles, Oct. 7, 1900; s. Allen Yost and Julia (Kitzmiller) B.; A.B., U. Calif. at Berkeley, 1923; B.D., Union Theol. Sem., N.Y.C., 1928; student U. Edinburgh, 1928-29; D.D., Hillsdale Coll., 1946; m. Madeline Buzzell, July 1960. Ordained to ministry Baptist Ch., 1928; asso. sec. YMCA, U. Cal., 1923-24; pastor First Bapt. Ch., successor Christ Ch., Summit, N.J., 1929-68, minister emeritus, 1969-82; summer chaplain Hamilton Coll., Clinton, N.Y., summers, 1943-45; Nat. Council Chs. interchange preacher to Britain, 1959, chmn. interchange com.; lectr. Bapt. polity Union Theol. Sem., 1959-70. Bd. dirs. Union Theol. Sem., 1953-57, 58-70, dir. emeritus, 1970—. Mem. Union Theol. Sem. Alumni Assn. (pres. 1953-55), Athenaeum of Summit (pres. 1939-68), English-Speaking Union Kappa Chi. Home: Medford, N.J. Died Nov. 3, 1982.

BARR, ALFRED HAMILTON, JR., art historian; b. Detroit, Jan. 28, 1902; s. Alfred Hamilton and Annie Elizabeth (Wilson) B.; student Boys Latin Sch., Balt., 1911-18; A.B., Princeton, 1922, A.M., 1923, Litt.D., 1949; Ph.D., Harvard, 1946; Ph.D. (hon.), U. Bonn (Germany), 1958; Dr. Fine Arts, U. Buffalo, 1962, Yale, 1967; L.H.D., Columbia, 1969; m. Margaret Scolari-Fitzmaurice, May 27, 1930; 1 dau., Victoria Fitzmaurice. Instr. history of art Vassar Coll., 1923-24; asst. in fine arts Harvard, 1924-25; instr. art and archeol. Princeton, 1925-26; asso. prof. art, Wellesley Coll., 1926-29; dir. Mus. Modern Art, N.Y.C., 1929-43, dir. research in painting and sculpture, 1944-46, dir. collections, 1947-67, counselor to bd. of trustees, from 1967, v.p. bd., 1939-43, trustee, 1939-67. Mem. adv. com. on art Office of Coordinator of Inter-Am. Affairs, 1940-43; mem. adv. coms. Inst. of Modern Art, Boston, Cin. Modern Art Soc.; adv. council dept. art and archaeol. Princeton, 1946; vis. com. fine arts Fogg Art Mus., Harvard, 1958-60, chmn. from 1965, bd. overseers Harvard, 1964-70. Decorated cross, chevalier Legion of Honor, 1959; grand cross Order of Merit, West Germany, 1959; spl. merit award for notable creative achievement Brandeis U., 1964; N.Y. State award, 1968; award for distinguished service to arts Nat. Inst. Arts and Letters, 1968; award Art Dealers Assn. Am.; Skowhegan Gertrude Vanderbilt Whitney award 1974; award Internat. Art Dealers Assn., Cologne, Germany, 1975. Trustee Am. Fedn. Arts, 1948-55; pres. Found. for Arts, Religion and Culture, 1962-65. Mem. Assn. of Art Museum Dirs. (v.p. 1940-41), College Art Assn. (dir. 1943-48), Am. Assn. of Museums (councilor). Presbyn. Editor (with Holger Cahill): Art in America, 1936; American Painters Series, Penguin Books (London), 1944-45. Author: Cubism and Abstract Art, 1936; What is Modern Painting?, 1943; Picasso; Fifty Years of His Art, 1946; 20th Century Italian Art (with J.T. Soby), 1949; Matisse: His Art and His Public, 1951. Editor of 31 museum exhibition catalogs; Masters of Modern Art, 1954. Mem. editorial bd. Art Bulletin, 1939, Gazette des Beaux-Arts, 1940, Mag. of Art, 1942-52, Art Quar., 1953, Art in Am., 1957. Mary Flexner lectures, Bryn Mawr Coll., 1946. Home: New York, N.Y. Died Aug. 15, 1981.

BARR, DAVID PRESWICK, physician and educator; b. Ithaca, N.Y., Aug. 23, 1889; s. Fred C. and Priscilla (Preswick) B.; A.B., Cornell University, 1911, M.D., 1914; LL.D., Central Coll., 1929; Sc.D., Washington University (St. Louis), 1946; m. Mary Washington Walker, Nov. 26, 1919; children—Mary Sydney, Elizabeth; m. 2d Jean Fredrica Steadman, July 20, 1956. House officer Bellevue Hosp., N.Y. City, 1914-16; asst. physician, Russell Sage Inst., 1916-17, research fellow, 1919-22; instr. in medicine, Cornell U. Med. Coll., 1916-22, asst. prof. medicine, 1922-24; adj. asst. visiting physician, Bellevue Hosp., 1919-22, asst. physician, 1922-24; prof. medicine, Washington U., and physician in chief, Barnes Hosp., St. Louis, Mo., 1924-41; prof. medicine, Cornell U., physician in chief New York Hosp., 1941-57; pres., med. dir. Health Ins. Plan Greater N.Y., 1957-62; vis. prof. med. Nat. Def. Med. Center & Sch., China. Fellow A.C.P.; mem. A.M.A., Assn. Am. Physicians (pres. 1947), Soc. Clin. Investigation, N.Y. Acad. Medicine, Nu Sigma Nu. Home: New York, N.Y. †

BARR, ERIC L(LOYD), educator, retired naval officer; b. nr. Huron, S.D., Sept. 4, 1887; s. Andrew L. and Mary Ellen (Dale) B.; B.S., U.S. Naval Acad., 1911; grad. Naval War Coll., 1934; Ph.D., U. Wash., 1938; m. Ellen Culver, Aug. 19, 1911; children—Eric, Lloyd, Ellen Culver, Christopher Culver, Franklin Dale. Commd. ensign, U.S. Navy, 1912, advanced through grades to capt., 1939; comdg. officer submarines, 1915-20; assigned to 1st Naval Res. O.T. C. unit, U. Wash., 1926, asst. prof. naval sci., 1926-28, asso. prof., later prof. naval sci., 1936-45; sea duty, 1928-36; ret. from Navy, Sept. 1940; prof. naval sci. and tactics U. Wash., 1938-45; released from active duty U.S. Navy, as P.N.S. & T. and C.O. V-12, U. Wash., Oct. 31, 1945, dir. summer sessions from Nov. 1945. Decorated, Navy Cross, (Navy and Marine Corps medal. Mem. Am. Soc. Mil. Engrs., Am. Legion, Ret. Officers Assn., Municipal League Seattle, Episcopalian. Mason. Clubs: Faculty, Catalyst, Monday (Seattle). †

BARR, HARRY GORDON, business exec.; b. Liverpool, Eng. Oct. 20, 1889; s. James Clayton and Margaret (McLean) B.; student Liverpool Inst.; Ellesmere Coll., Shropshire, Eng.; m. Constance Baumann, June 18, 1919; 1 son James Clayton. Came to U.S., 1910, naturalized Am. citizen. Apprentice, J. I. Case Co., mfrs. farm machinery, 1910-12, clerk in purchasing dept., 1915, asst. purchasing agent, 1918, purchasing agent, 1923 general purchasing agt., 1938, v.p., from 1943, dir. from 1952. Life mem. Salvation Army Adv. Bd. Clubs: Racine Country, Somerset, (Racine); Chicago Athletic Assn. Republican. Episcopalian. †

BARR, JOSEPH MORAN, mayor; b. Pitts., May 28, 1906; s. James P. and Blanche (Moran) B.; grad. U. Pitts. Sch. Bus. Adminstrn., 1982; m. Alice White, June 4, 1949; children—Alice Elizabeth, Joseph Moran. Salesman. United Motors Service div. Gen. Motors, Pitts., 1924-29, George S. Dougherty Co., Pitts., 1929-36; mem. Pa. Senate, 1940-60; mayor, Pitts., 1959-70. Sec., Allegheny County Democratic Com., 1936; Bd. dirs. Pitts. chpt. A.R.C., Roselia Founding Home; trustee U. Pitts., Mercy Hosp., Carnegie-Mellon U., Carnegie Mus. Mem. Young Democrats of Pa. (pres. 1939), Young Democratic Clubs Am. (v.p. conv. assn.). Home: Pittsburgh, Pa. Died Aug. 26, 1982.

BARRACLOUGH, GEOFFREY, historian; b. May 10, 1908; s. Walter and Edith B.; student Bootham Sch., Oriel Coll., U. Munich, Merton Coll., Brit. Sch. at Rome. Fellow, lectr. St. John's Coll., 1936; lectr. U. Cambridge, 1937; prof. mediaeval history U. Liverpool, 1945-56; research prof. internat. history U. London, 1956-62; prof. history U. Calif., 1965-68, Brandeis U., 1968-84. Pres., Hist. Assn. (Gt. Britain), 1964-67. Author: Public Notaries and the Papal Curia, 1934; Papal Provisions, 1935; Mediaeval Germany, 1938; The Origins of Modern Germany, 1946; Factors in German History, 1946; The Mediaeval Empire, 1950; The Earldom and County Palatine of Chester, 1953; History in a Changing World, 1955; Early Cheshire Charters, 1957; editor Social Life in Early England, 1960; European Unity in Thought and Action, 1963; An Introduction to Contemporary History, 1964; The Crucible of Europe, 1976; (with R.F. Wall) Survey of International Affairs, 1955-56, 1956-58, 1958-60. Died Dec. 26, 1984.

BARRETT, GILBERT C., banker; b. Brooklyn, Apr. 26, 1889; s. Harry Freeman and Helen H. (Conklin) B.; student Charles Acad., Brooklyn; Am. Inst. Banking, N.Y. City; m. Marguerite Simmons, Oct. 18, 1916; children—Gilbert C., Jean (Mrs. Maurice J. Fitzgerald). With The Brooklyn Savings Bank from 1911, trustee from 1941, president, 1947-57, chairman of board of directors, from 1957. Served with U.S.N., 1918-19. Director American Red Cross (Brooklyn chpt.); trustee, asst. treas., Brooklyn Hosp., St. Christophers Hosp. for Babies; trustee, asst. treas., Brooklyn Inst. of Arts and Sci.; vice chmn. governing com. Bklyn. Children's Mus.; adv. bd. Salvation Army; dir. Savs. Banks Retirement System; dir., mem. exec. com. Institutional Securities Corp. Trustee Bklyn. War Meml.; mem. Nat. Inst. of Social Sciences; trustee, Polytech. Inst. of Brooklyn; mem. N.Y. City Anti-Crime Com., Inc.; adv. com. Civil Def. Mem. Downtown Bklyn. Assn. (dir.), C. of C., Am. Legion. Republican. Presbyn. Clubs: Skytop (Pa.), Lake Placid (N.Y.); Rembrandt, Rotary, Bankers (Bklyn.); Union League (N.Y.C.). †

BARRETT, JOE CLIFFORD, lawyer; b. Jonesboro, Ark., Mar. 29, 1897; s. William F. and Catherine (Siniard) B.; A.B., U. Ark., 1920; LL.B., George Washington U., 1924; LL.D., U. Ark., 1953; m. Bertha Campbell, Dec. 30, 1923; 1 dau., Dorine (Mrs. J.C. Deacon). Admitted to Ark. bar, 1922, practiced law, Jonesboro; sr. partner Barrett, Wheatley, Smith & Deacon, from 1943; city atty., 1926-30; dist. atty. St. Louis S.W. Ry. Lines, 1935-62. Mem. Nat. Conf. Commrs. on Uniform State Laws, 1943-63, life mem., 1963—, v.p., 1948-51, chmn. exec. com., 1951, pres., 1953-54; 59; mem. U.S. observer delegation 8th, 9th sessions Hague Conf. Pvt. Internat. Law, 1956, 60, U.S. delegation 10th session, 1964; U.S. delegation Diplomatic Conf. Uniform Law on Internat. Sale of Goods, 1964. Bd. mgrs. Council State Govs., 1959, Adv. Com. on Water Conservation and Use; adv. com. Commn. on Internat. Rules Jud. Procedure, 1959; mem. adv. panel U.S. Dept. State. Chmn. trustee Jonesboro Pub. Library, 1948-59. Recipient Outstanding Lawyer award Ark. Bar Assn. and Ark. Bar Found., 1960; Fellows Fifty-Yr. award Fellows Am. Bar Found., 1979. Mem. Am. Bar Assn. (ho. of dels. 1947-55, chmn. scope and correlation 1958, spl. com. on internat. unification of pvt. law 1957-61, chmn. sect. internat. and comparative law 1967-68, council), Am. Judicature Soc., Internat. Law Assn. (Am. br.), Am. Law Inst., Bar Assn. Ark. (past pres.). Democrat. Baptist. Lodges: Rotary, Masons. Clubs: Jonesboro Country, Little Rock. Home: Jonesboro, Ark. Died Oct. 7, 1980.

BARRIOS-SOLIS, OCTAVIO, consul gen. of Guatemala; b. Guatemala, Jan. 2, 1888; s. Mariano Barrios Auyon and Adelaide Solis Saens; B.Sc., Instituto Nacional de Varones, Guatemala, 1911; student Y.M.C.A. School Chicago, 1923-24, Chicago Dental Coll. and Loyola U., 1924-26; m. Jeannette Askren, Nov. 16, 1924. Consul gen. of Guatemala, at Chicago, from 1928. Mason. Deceased.

BARRON, TILTON MARSHALL, librarian; b. Phillipsburg, Kans., Jan. 19, 1916; s. James Walter and Minnie (Livermore) B.; A.B., Colo. Coll., 1937; B.L.S., Columbia, 1940; m. Betty Suzanne Clark, Dec. 28, 1946; children—James Tilton, William Clark, John Marshall. Library asst. N.Y.U. Libraries, 1937-40; evening supr. Bklyn. Coll. Library, 1940-41; circulation librarian Pa. State Coll., 1945-46; reference asst. Coll. City N.Y., 1947-48; librarian Ursinus Coll., 1948-54; librarian Clark U., 1954-78, librarian emeritus, 1978-84. Served as tech. sgt. USAAF, 1942-45. Mem. Am., Mass., New Eng. library assns., Bibliog. Soc. Am., Worcester Com. Fgn. Relations. Club: Bohemians. Home: Worcester, Mass. Died Aug. 24, 1984; buried Prospect Harbor, Maine.

BARROWS, MARJORIE, author; b. Chgo.; d. Ransom Moore and Caroline (Dixon) B. Student, Northwestern U., U. Chgo. Asso. editor Child Life, 1922-31, editor, 1931-38; co-editor Consol. Books, 1943-48; editor-in-chief Children's Hour, 1952-62; editor Treasure Trails, 1954-56, Jr. Treasure Chest, Family Weekly, 1954-62; Hon. mem. bd. govs. Heckscher Found., Nat. Council Radio Listeners. Author: About Ella Phant (juvenile), 1923, Muggins, 1931, Fraidy Cat, 1941, Four Little Kittens, Pirate of Pooh, 1936, Muggins Takes Off, 1964, Muggins' Big Balloon, 1965, Muggins Becomes a Hero, 1965, Favorite Stories of Muggins Mouse, 1966, That Parade, 1967, Little Red Boot, 1968, others; compiler: 100 Best Poems, 1931, 200 Best Poems, 1939, Organ Grinder's Garden, 1939, Box Office, 1943, The Children's Treasury, 1947, These Wonderful People, 1947, 1000 Beautiful Things, 1947, 56, 1000 American Things, 1948, 56, Read Aloud Poems, 1957-60, 5th edit., 1970, Treasure Trail Parade, 1957, (with Bennett Cerf) A Treasury of Humor, 1955, A Treasury of Beauty and Romance, 1959, The Family Reader, 1946, 61. Recipient scroll for contbn. lit. heritage of Chgo. Chgo. Found. for Lit.; hon. scroll Rand McNally. Mem. Inst. Am. Geneology, Soc. Midland Authors (dir.), Theta Sigma Phi (hon.), Zeta Phi Eta. Republican. Presbyterian. Club: Cordon (hon. mem., past v.p., sec.). Home: Evanston, Ill. Died Mar. 29, 1983.

BARRY, DAVID C., banker; b. Rochester, N.Y., Apr. 7, 1889; s. David and Elizabeth (Burrell) B.; A.M., Rutgers, 1941; m. Elizabeth D. Farber, Oct. 10, 1911; 1 dau., Ruth Elizabeth. Sr. v.p. Lincoln Rochester Trust Co., now ret., mem. adv. com. to dirs.; bus. cons.; dir. Bausch & Lomb Optical Co., Jas. Cunningham Son & Co., Inc., Mixing Equipment Co., Taylor Instrument Cos. Conglist. Clubs: Genesee Valley: Rochester (N.Y.) Country. Home: East Bloomfield, N.Y. †

BARRY, DAVID W., clergyman, association executive; b. Minneapolis, Kan., Nov. 7, 1917; s. Frank Touzlan and Sarah (McArthur) B.; m. Marion Virginia McAlister, July 5, 1942; children: Mary Katharine, David McAlister, Philip Monte, Samuel McArthur. B.A., Oberlin Coll., 1938; B.D., Chgo. Theol. Sem., 1941, D.D., 1955; postgrad., U. Chgo., 1941-44. Ordained to ministry Presbyn. Ch.; dir. urban research (Presbyn Bd. Nat. Missions), 1944-47; dir. Pathfinding Service, N.Y.C. Mission Soc., 1947-50, exec. dir., 1955-78; dir. research Nat. Council Chs., 1950-54. Pres. Fellowship Center, N.Y.C.; bd. dirs. North Side Center For Child Devel., N.Y. Theol. Sem., Opportunities Industrialization Center N.Y.C., Interfaith City-Wide Co-ordinating Com. Against Poverty, United Charities. Home: Armonk, N.Y. Died Apr. 5, 1984.

BARRY, JACK, TV host, producer; m. Patte Preble; children: Jeffrey, Jonathan, Barbara, Douglas Curtis. Formerly staff announcer Sta. WTTM, Trenton; owner, operator Sta. WGMA, late 1950s; in 1962 began packaging shows for Paramount's TV sta., Hollywood, Calif.; owned and operated Los Angeles music sta. KKOP-FM (changed to KFOX-FM), 10 yrs.; partner Barry & Enright Films, Inc., Colbert TV Sales, now constructing cable-TV system, Los Angeles area. Creator, host: Juvenile Jury, Mut. Radio Network, 1946, later on NBC-TV; later produced and hosted: shows including The Jack Barry Show; returned to network TV in mid-sixties, creating: Everybody's Talking for ABC; later becoming host of: ABC's summer series Generation Gap; produced and hosted: ABC's summer series The Reel Game, ABC, 1970; revived and syndicated: ABC's summer series Juvenile Jury through Four Star Prodns., 1970; packaged and hosted: ABC's summer series The Joker's Wild, CBS-TV, beginning 1972; began: ABC's summer series Hollywood's Talking, CBS-TV, 1973; now partner ABC's summer series, Barry & Enright Prodns., producers of Joker's Wild, Tic Tac Dough, Joker! Joker! Joker!!!,; hosted by Barry and: ABC's summer series Way Out Games; producer motion pictures. Died May 7, 1984.

BARRY, JAMES MILNE, utility exec.; b. San Francisco, Mar. 29, 1888; s. James Henry and Nellie Venetia (Barnum) B.; B.S., U. Cal., 1910; m. Sophie H. Lentz, Apr. 28, 1914. Elec. engr. Pacific Gas & Electric Co., Sacramento, 1910-12, Northwestern Electric Co., Portland, Ore., 1913-14; chief dept. of electricity, City of San Francisco, 1914-17; elec. engr. Gt. Western Power Co., San Francisco, 1917-18; various supervisory positions Ala. Power Co., 1918-25, v.p., 1925-27, v.p. in charge operations, 1927-32, v.p., gen. mgr., 1932-49, pres., 1949-52; chmn. exec. com. The Southern Co., from 1952, dir. Birmingham Fire & Casualty Co., Southern Company, Alabama Power Company, Central Ga. Ry. Company. Mem. Southeastern Electric Exchange (past pres.), Asso. Industries of Ala. (past dir.), Newcomen Soc. of Eng., A.S.M.E., Sigma Xi, Theta Xi, Tau Beta Pi. Presbyn. Kiwanian. Clubs: Mountain Brook, Vestavia Country. †

BARSKY, ARTHUR JOSEPH, educator, plastic surgeon; b. N.Y.C., Dec. 7, 1899; s. Joseph and Rebecca (Koengisen) B.; D.D.S., U. Pa., 1922; M.D., N.Y. Med. Coll., 1926; tng. plastic surgery N.Y. Postgrad. Med. Sch. and Hosp., 1927-34; postgrad. Sir Harold Gillies, London, Eng., 1934; m. Hannah Kahn, June 12, 1941; 1 son, Arthur Joseph III. Prof. emeritus surgery Albert Einstein Coll. Medicine 1955-82; cons. plastic surgeon Bronx (N.Y.) Municipal Hosp. Center, from 1955; cons. surgeon Beth Israel, Mt. Sinai, Bronx-Lebanon. Mem. tech. adv. com. cleft palate N.Y.C. Dept. Health, from 1960; sec.-gen. Internat. Fedn. Socs. Surgery Hand, from 1965. Pres. bd. Children's Med. Relief Internat. Served to lt. col., M.C., AUS, 1943-46. Recipient Health medal Govt. South Vietnam, 1969. Diplomate Am. Bd. Plastic Surgery, chmn. residency rev. com., 1964-66, Fellow N.Y. Acad. Medicine; mem. Am. Soc. Surgery Hand (founding mem., pres. 1965), Am. Assn. Plastic Surgeons, Am. Soc. Plastic and Reconstructive Surgeons (Hon. citation 1973), N.Y. Regional Soc. Plastic and Reconstructive Surgery (pres. 1963-64), Assn. Mil. Surgeons U.S., Am. Soc. Maxillofacial Surgeons, Am. Cleft Palate Assn., German Assn. Plastic Surgeons, Brazilian Coll. Surgeons, Hiroshima Soc. Medicine (advisor), AMA, N.Y.C., N.Y. State med. socs.; corr. mem. Brit. Assn. Plastic Surgeons; hon. mem. Peruvian Soc. Pediatric Surgery, Israel, Argentine, Japan socs. plastics surgeons, Plastic Surgery Soc. Colombia (S.Am.), Miss. Valley Med. Soc., Peruvian-N.Am. Med. Assn. Author: Plastic Surgery, 1938; Principles and Practice of Plastic Surgery, 1950; Congenital Anomalies of the Hand and Their Surgical Treatment. 1958; (in Spanish) Anomalias Congenitas de la Mano, 1962; Principles and Practice of Plastic Surgery (with Drs. S. Kahn and B.E. Simon), 1964; also numerous articles, chpts. in books. Home: New York, N.Y. Died Feb. 9, 1982.

BARTHOLOMEW, FRANK H., press assn. exec., b. San Francisco, Oct. 5, 1898; s. John William and Kate Leigh (Schuck) B.; LL.D., Oreg. State U.; m. Antonia Luise Patzelt, May 18, 1922. Joined U.P., Portland, 1921, v.p., 1930, later 1st v.p., dir. U.P. Assns., pres., gen. mgr., 1955-62, chmn. bd., 1962, emeritus, 1972, (became U.P.I. 1958) war corr. covering New Guinea, Aleutian campaign, 1943, Okinawa (10th Army), Luzon (38th Div.), 1945, Japanese surrender aboard U.S.S. Missouri, Tokyo Bay, 1945; atomic bomb tests, Bikini, 1946; war in China, Fall of Shanghai, 1949, Korean War, 1950, Indo China, 1954. Owner, Buena Vista Vineyards, Sonoma, Calif.; dir., mem. exec. com. San Francisco Fed. Savs. & Loan Assn., San Francisco. Served as 1st lt. Inf., U.S. Army, 1918. Recipient citations V.F.W., Gen. MacArthur, 1945, Gen. Omar N. Bradley award. Fellow Sigma Delta Chi; mem. Am. Legion. Mason (Shriner). Clubs: Bohemian, Press, World Trade (San Francisco); Foreign Correspondents (Tokyo); Balboa (gov.) (Mazatlan, Mexico). Home: Glenbrook, Nev. Died Mar. 26, 1985.

BARTLETT, CLAUDE JACKSON, psychologist, educator; b. Columbus, Ohio, Oct. 1, 1931; s. Claude Jay and Cecil (Richmond) B.; m. Gloria Kuechenberg, Aug. 29, 1953; children-Andrew William, Scott Jackson. B.S., Denison U., 1954; M.A., Ohio State U., 1956, Ph.D., 1958. Diplomate: Am. Bd. Examiners in Profl. Psychology. Asst. prof. psychology George Peabody Coll. for Tchrs., 1958-61; asst. prof. psychology U. Md., College Park, 1961-64, asso. prof., 1964-68, prof., from 1968, chmn. dept. psychology, 1968-78; cons. indsl. psychologist, pres. Tng. & Ednl. Research Programs, Inc. Recipient James McKeen Cattell awards, 1966, 68. Mem. Am. Psychol. Assn., Md. Psychol. Assn. (past treas.). Home: College Park, MD.

BARTLEY, NALBRO, writer; b. Buffalo, N.Y., Nov. 10, 1888; d. William Hamilton and Zayda Angie (Brandt) Bartley; ed. Buffalo High Sch., leaving high school in senior year; m. Martin Lee Clark, Apr. 25, 1933; 1 son, John (by previous marriage). Was reporter for Buffalo Morning Express, 1907-09; went to N.Y. City, 1909, as free lance writer; contbr. short stories to Munsey, and Street & Smith publs.; began writing for the Saturday Evening Post, 1917. Author: Paradise Auction, 1917; Bargain True, 1918; Woman's Woman, 1918; Gorgeous Girl, 1919; Careless Daughters, 1919; Gray Angels, 1920; Fair to Middling, 1921; Up and Coming, 1922; Judd and Judd, 1923; Bread and Jam, 1924; Pattycake Princess, 1925; Morning Thunder, 1926; The Mediocrat, 1927; The Fox Woman, 1928; Queen Dick, 1929; The Godfather, 1929; The Premeditated Virgin, 1930; Devil's Lottery, 1931; Second Flight, 1932; Breathless, 1933; Pease Porridge Hot, 1935. Home: San Francisco, Calif. †

BARTON, HENRY ASKEW, physicist; b. Pittsburgh, Pa., June 27, 1898; s. Henry L. and Caroline (Askew) B.; B.S., Princeton, 1919, E.E., 1921, A.M., 1924, Ph.D., 1925; m. May Vreeland, May 25, 1933; children—Joan, Jenneke. Telephone engr., Am. Telephone & Telegraph Co., New York, N.Y., 1921-23; prof. physics Cornell U., 1929-31; dir. Am. Inst. Physics, N.Y.C., 1931-57, adminstrn. cons. from 1957; pres. Sci. Manpower Commn., 1958; dir. Princeton Bank & Trust Co. Nat. Research fellow Harvard U., 1925-27; fellow Bartol Research Lab., 1927-29. Mem. Am. Phys. Soc., Optical Soc. America, Acoustical Soc. America, Am. Assn. Physics Teachers, Soc. of Rheology, A.A.A.S., Phi Beta Kappa, Sigma Xi. Clubs: Cosmos (Washington); University (New York); Nassau (Princeton). Home: Princeton, N.J. Died Oct. 11, 1983.

BARTON, JAMES RICHARD, real estate corporation executive; b. Pleasant Hill, Ill., Dec. 24, 1888; s. Dr. Perry Franklin and Elizabeth (Wells) B.; B.A., Hendrix Coll., Conway, Ark., 1913, LL.D., 1929; M.A., Teachers Coll., Columbia, 1921, grad. study, 1926; grad. study, U. of California, 1923; m. H. Neill Noe, June 10, 1914; children—Alice Elizabeth (Mrs. O. H. Miller), Paula Neill (Mrs. Earl Schenck, Jr.), Mary Carolyn (Mrs. Thos. Talbot), James Richard Jr. (U.S.A.A.F.), John William. Teacher rural schools, Ark. 1907-08; principal high schools, Kingsland and Melbourne, Ark., 1908-10; superintendent schs., Wainright, Okla., 1913-15; instr. edn. and modern langs. State Teachers Coll., Tahlequah, Okla., 1915-17; prin. high sch., Sapulpa, Okla., 1917-19; supt. city schs., Sapulpa, 1919-24, Okmulgee, Okla., 1924-25, Oklahoma City, 1925-31; pres. Great Northwest Finance Co., 1933-37, Pacific Realty Corp. from 1938; pres. Light Service Corp. (Newark); Coos Bay Assn., Asso. Coos Bay Land Owners; Major, Ore. State Guard, comdg. 2d Squadron, 1st Oregon Cavalry. Mem. Gov.'s Oklahoma Ednl. Survey Commn., Okla. Children's Code Commn. Dir. Oklahoma City Welfare Bd., Oklahoma City Y.M.-C.A., Oklahoma City C. of C.; mem. Oklahoma City Council Boy Scouts of Am.; mem. N.E.A. (life), Phi Delta Kappa. Methodist. Mason (K.T., Shriner). Clubs: Rotary (ex-pres.; dir.), Men's Dinner, Hillcrest, Twin Hills Golf and Country, Oklahoma City Golf and Country (Oklahoma City); Washington Athletic, Broadmoor Golf (Seattle); University (Portland). Lecturer on ednl. adminstrn. Home: Portland, Ore. †

BARTON, LEROY, consulting architect; born N.Y. City, Dec. 14, 1887; s. of Thomas Rowland and Elizabeth (Snow) B.; student public schools, N.Y. City, 1894-1905; Beaux Arts Soc., N.Y. City, 1906-10; grad. Command and Gen. Staff School, U.S. Army; m. Ann Parfitt, Jan. 29, 1913; Architect, N.Y. City, 1910-34, asso. with Aymar Embury II, 1912-34; asst. to sec. of the treasury, 1934-39, also acting supervising architect, Treas. Dept., 1939; archtl. advisor, Pub. Bldgs. Adminstrn., 1939-40. Served as capt., U.S. Army, 1917-20; col., U.S. Army, Insp. General's Dept., 1941-46; col. commanding, 177th Composite Group, 1947, retired 1948. Practicing as consulting architect. Awarded Legion of Merit, Army Commendation Ribbon; New York State Conspicuous Service Cross. Mem. Am. Inst. Architects, Archtl. League of N.Y., Am. Legion. Mason. Nat. Sojourner. Club: Cosmos. Home: Post Washington, N.Y. †

BARTTER, FREDERIC CROSBY, physician, med. research adminstr.; b. Philippine Islands, Sept. 10, 1914; came to U.S., 1927, naturalized, 1935; s. George Charles and Frances Crosby (Buffington) B.; m. Jane H. Lillard, May 25, 1946; children—Frederic Crosby, Thaddeus, Pamela Anne. A.B., Harvard Coll., 1935, M.D., 1940. Diplomate: Am. Bd. Internal Medicine. Intern Roosevelt Hosp., N.Y.C., 1941-42; research and clin. fellow in medicine Harvard Med. Sch. and Mass. Gen. Hosp., Boston, 1946-48; clin. investigator, specializing in endocrinology, 1946-83; commd. med. officer USPHS, HEW, 1942; dir. labs. USPHS Hosp., Sheepshead Bay, N.Y., 1942-44; med. officer in charge onchocerciasis investigation Pan Am. San. Bur., 1944-45; mem. staff Lab. Tropical Diseases, NIH, 1945-46; tutor biochem. scis. Harvard U., 1946-51; chief endocrinology br. Nat. Heart, Lung and Blood Inst., NIH, Bethesda, Md., 1951-73, clin. dir., 1970-76, chief hypertension-endocrine br., 1973-78; asso. prof. pediatrics Howard U., Washington, 1958-64, prof. pediatrics, 1965-78; clin. prof. medicine Georgetown U., Washington, 1965-78; asso. chief of staff for research Audie L. Murphy Vets. Hosp., 1978-83; prof. medicine U. Tex. Health Sci. Center, San Antonio, 1978-83. Contbr. over 300 articles on endocrinology and physiology to sci. jours. Recipient Meritorious Service medal NIH, 1970, Modern Medicine's Disting. Achievement award, 1977; Churchill fellow Cambridge, Eng., 1968-69. Fellow (hon.) Am. Coll. Cardiology, Royal Coll. Physicians; mem. Endocrine Soc. (Fred C. Koch award 1978), Am. Physiol. Soc., Assn. Am. Physicians, Am. Soc. Clin. Investigation, Salt and Water Club, Royal Soc. Medicine, Nat. Acad. Sci., Peripatetic Club, N. Am. Mycological Assn. Anglican. Home: San Antonio, Tex. Died May 5, 1983.

BARUS, MAXWELL, lawyer; b. Boston, Sept. 14, 1889; s. Carl and Anna Gertrude (Howes) B.; A.B., A.M., Brown U., 1910, LL.B. cum laude, Harvard, 1913; m. Jane Garey, Sept. 4, 1915; children—Carl, Anne (Mrs. David H. Seeley), Jane Ellen (Mrs. John Wehncke), David Nickerson. Admitted to Mass. bar, 1913, N.Y. State bar, 1915, also U.S. Supreme and other cts.; with firm Brandeis, Dunbar & Nutter, Boston, 1913-14; with firm Fish, Richardson & Neave, and predecessors, N.Y.C., from 1914, sr. partner, 1936-66, of counsel; from 1966. Alumni trustee Brown University, 1949-52; pres. bd. trustees Brookside Sch., Montclair, N.J., 1938-40. Served with USNRF, 1918-19. Mem. Am., N.Y. State bar assns., Bar Assn. City N.Y., N.Y. County Lawyers Assn., New York Patent Law Assn., Harvard Law Sch. Assn., Phi Beta Kappa, Sigma Xi, Alpha Delta Phi. Clubs: Brown University (past member board govs.) (N.Y.C.); Upper Montclair (N.J.) Country. Bd. editors Harvard Law Rev., 1911-13. Home: Upper Montclair, N.J. †

BARZINI, LUIGI, author, journalist; b. Milan, Italy, Dec. 21, 1908; s. Luigi and Mantica (Pesavento) B.; B.Lit., Columbia, 1930; m. Giannalisa Gianzana, Apr. 12, 1940; m. 2d, Paola Gadola, Sept. 12, 1949; children—Glovanna Ludovica, Benedetta, Luigi, Andrea, Franceseca. Travelling corr. for Corriere della Sera, Milan, 1931-40; editor Il Globo, Rome, 1944-47; contbr. Italian and fgn. magazines, 1954-65; mem. Italian Parliament for Liberal Party from Milan-Pavia, 1958-63. Author: Americans are Alone in the World, 1953; Mosca Mosca, 1961; L'Europa Domani Mattina, 1964; The Italians, 1964; (play) I Disarmati, 1957. Address: Rome, Italy. Died Mar. 30, 1984.

BASIE, WILLIAM (COUNT BASIE), composer, band leader; b. Red Bank, N.J., Aug. 21, 1904; s. Harvey Lee and Lillian (Child) B.; m. Catherine Morgan, July 12, 1942 (dec. 1983); 1 dau., Diane. Student pub. schs., Red Bank. Musician theatres, hotels, night clubs; pianist Benny Moten Band, Kansas City, 1929-36, band leader, 1936—. Broadway debut, Roseland Ballroom, 671938, jazz concert, Carnegie Hall, 1939; participated in jam session, Apollo Theatre, N.Y.C., 1940; motion picture debut: Reveille with Beverly, 1942; later roles in: Crazy House, 1943, theatre tours, various cities U.S.; guest star appearances radio show, TV spls.; toured with, Frank Sinatra, 1965, with, Tony Bennett, in Europe, performed at, Kennedy Inaugural Ball, command performance, Queen of Eng.; Numerous recs. Named most popular band Musicians Am., 1933; named Top Band Pitts. Courier ann. popularity poll, 1941; recipient All-Am. Band award Esquire, 1945, Jazz Merit award The Lamplighter, 1945, Down Beat internat. critics' poll winner, 1952-56, Kennedy Center Honors medal, 1981, Down Beat Readers Poll, 1983, Grammy award, 1983, numerous other awards U.S. and Europe. Mem. ASCAP, Dance Orch. Leaders Assn. (exec. bd. dirs.), NAACP. Died Apr. 26, 1984.*

BASS, STIRLING WESLEY, univ. prof.; b. Pittsburg, Tex., April 28, 1890; s. David Richard and Mary Elizabeth (Hart) B.; grad. S.W. Tex. Normal Sch., 1911; A.B., U. of Tex., 1927, A.M., 1932; grad. student U. of Colo., summers 1936, 40; m. Mary Hartson Boyd, Dec. 26, 1912 (dec. July 16 1921); children—Stirling Wesley, Mary (Mrs. Henry Hayne Crum); m. 2d, Mary Agnes Kirkbride, June 6, 1922; 1 dau., Helen (Mrs. Clarence Arthur Davis, Jr.) Supervisor elementary schs., 1919, prin., Provincial High Sch., Philippine Islands, 1920; instr., E. Tex. State Teachers Coll., 1921-22; prin. High Sch., Sulphur Springs, Tex., 1922-26; supt. city schs., Laredo, Tex., 1926-27; prof., head of dept. physics, Tex. Coll. of Arts and Industries, since 1927. Dir. Interscholastic League, 1935-45. Democrat. Mem. Christian ch. Mem. Am. Assn. Univ. Prof., Tex. Acad. of Sci. (pres. S. Tex. br., 1944-45), Am. Assn. of Physics Teachers. Mason. Home: Kingsville, Tex. †

BASSETT, CAROLYN FASSETT, publisher; b. Los Angeles; d. Ernest and Sarah Pierce (Miller) B.; student pub. schs., Glendale, Calif.; m. May 26, 1934; 1 son. With Security Pacific, Los Angeles; pres. Oxford Industries, Inc., Los Angeles, pub. Let's Live mag. Mem. Nat. Nutritional Foods Assn., Nat. Health Fedn. Home: Glendale, Calif. Died Apr. 28, 1985; interred Forest Lawn Cemetery, Los Angeles.

BASTIEN, RALPH HENRY, business exec.; b. Walkerville, Ont., Can., Nov. 2, 1893; s. Dennis Joseph and Eudora (Mickle) B.; ed. public schs., m. Blanche Roach, June 14, 1916; children—Betty (Mrs. Arthur M. Atterbury), Ralph Henry. Came to U.S., 1921 naturalized, 1928. Stenographer and state circulation mgr. The Detroit News, 1912-16; circulation mgr. London (Ont.) Free Press, 1916-18; sec. Booth Newspapers, Inc., Detroit, 1919-36, vice pres., 1936, gen. mgr. 1950, pres., 1952-59, also cons. and dir. Trustee of Cranbrook Academy Art. Presbyterian. Clubs: Lochmoor Golf, Grosse Pointe Yacht. Home: Grosse Pointe, Mich. Died July 2, 1984.

BATCH, JOHN MARTIN, research inst. exec.; b. Helena, Mont., Nov. 16, 1925; s. Otto Carl and Leah (Hartman) B.; m. Donna Rae Ogden, Jan. 11, 1973; children—Laura, James, Dana, Michelle. B.S., Mont. State U., 1949, M.S., 1950; Ph.D., Purdue U., 1955. Registered profl. engr., Wash. Research mgr. Gen. Electric Co., Richland, Wash., 1958-65; mem. staff Battelle-N.W., Richland, 1965-73; lab. dir. Battelle Columbus (Ohio) div., 1973-78; gen. mgr. project mgmt. div., gen. mgr. Office of Nuclear Waste Isolation, 1978-80, mem. corp. staff, from 1980, v.p., from 1976; dir. advanced com. dept. mech. engring. Ohio State U., from 1974. Author articles. Trustee Columbus Mus. Art; trustee chmn. fin. com. Columbus Coll. Art and Design. Served with U.S. Navy, 1943-46. Shell Oil Co. fellow, 1953. Mem. Am. Nuclear Soc., ASME, Sigma Xi, Sigma Alpha Epsilon. Episcopalian. Clubs: Scarlet and Gray Golf (Columbus); Elks. Home: Columbus, OH.

BATCHELDER, HOWARD TIMOTHY, educator; b. Greensboro Bend, Vt., Nov. 24, 1909; s. Charleton Harvey and Marcia Abigail (Fayer) B.; B.S., West Tex. State Coll., 1936; A.M., U. Mich., 1938, Ph.D., 1942; m. Mary Lockwood Sternenberg. Aug. 27, 1931; children—William Howard, Robert Wesley. Prin. Wildorado (Tex.) Pub. Sch., 1931-34, Lakeview Sch., Claude, Tex., 1934-35; high sch. prin., Dimmitt, Tex., 1935-37; prof. social sci. and edn. Miss. State Coll. for Women, 1939-41, prof. edn., head dept., 1942-43; asso. dean Sch. Edn., Ind. U., 1954-68, prof. edn., 1947-75; ednl. cons., editor films in tchr. edn. McGraw-Hill Book Co., Inc., 1947-57; adviser AID with U.S. Mission to Pakistan, 1960-67. Served from lt. (j.g.) to lt. comdr., USNR, 1943-46. Mem. NEA, Ind. Tchrs. Assn., Am. Assn. U. Profs., Phi Delta Kappa, Phi Kappa Phi, Pi Gamma Mu. Methodist. Author: (with McGlasson and Schorling) Student Teaching in Secondary Schools, 1965. Contbr. articles profl. jours. Home: Sun City, Ariz. Died Apr. 26, 1984.

BATES, FLOYD ELTON, railroad exec.; b. Allison, Ia., Jan. 3, 1889; s. Benjamin A. and Esther M. (Norris) B.; B.S. in Civil Engring., U. of Wisconsin, 1909, C.E., 1910; m. Elsie M. Dake, June 13, 1914 (dec.); children—John Harris, Robert Edward; m. 2d, Alice B. Cronin, Aug. 6, 1938. Draftsman, engring. dept., Chicago, Milwaukee, St. Paul and Pacific R.R., 1910-13 (except six mos. with Kansas City Terminal); asst. engr., Missouri Pacific R.R., 1913-19, asst. bridge engr., 1919-23, bridge engr., 1923-38, chief engr., 1938-45; exec. asst. to chief exec. officer and senior v.p., 1945-46, sr. exec. asst., 1946-56, v.p., from 1956; pres., v.p., dir. other railroads from 1945; dir. Nat. Bank of Commerce, Houston; mem. adv. com. Am. Nat. Bank Houston. Chmn. bd. Jr. Achievement, Inc., Houston. Mem. Am. Ry. Engineers Association. Clubs: Union League Chicago); Houston, River Oaks (Houston). †

BATES, STUART JEFFERY, prof. phys. chemistry; b. Toronto, Can., May 9, 1887; s. Stuart Samuel and Josephine Alice (Jeffery) B.; A.B., McMaster U., Toronto, 1907, A.M., 1909; Ph.D., U. of Ill., 1912; m. Hazel Constance Hooper, Aug. 9, 1917; children—Ruth Gwendolyn, Stuart Randolph. McMaster U. research asst., 1909-10; U. of Ill. fellow in chemistry, research asso. phys. chemistry, 1910-14; research asst. chemistry, Bur. of Standards; prof. phys. chemistry, Calif. Inst. Tech., from 1914. Mem. Am. Chem. Soc., Faraday Soc., Electrochemical Soc., A.A.A.S., Am. Assn. Univ. Profs., Sigma Xi, Phi Lambda Upsilon, Gamma Alpha, Baptist. Clubs: New Century, Athenaeum,(Pasadena). Home:Pasadena, Calif.†

BATES, WILLIAM BARTHOLEMEW, lawyer; b. Nacogdoches County, Tex., Aug. 16, 1890; s. James Madison and Mary Frances (Cook) B.; grad. Sam Houston State Teachers Coll., 1911; LL.B., Univ. of Texas, 1915; LL.D., conferred by the 7 state teachers colleges of Tex., 1944; LL.D., Baylor U., 1950; D.H.L., Trinity U., 1952; m. Mary Estill Dorsey, February 21, 1921; children—Juan (Mrs. Reagan Cartwright), Mary Dorsey. Practiced law, Bay City, Texas, 1915-17, Nacogdoches, Texas, 1919-21; district attorney, 2d Judicial District of Texas, 1921-22; partner Fullbright & Crooker, and successor firm, Fullbright, Crooker, Freeman, Bates & Jaworski, Houston, from 1923; dir. Gulf Atlantic Warehouse Co.,; chmn. bd. Bank of the Southwest (formerly Second Nat. Bank) of Houston. Commd. 2d lt., U.S. Army; served with 358th Inf., 90th Div., overseas; in Army of Occupation, Germany, 1918-19; twice wounded and promoted for gallantry in action. Mem. bd. edn. Houston Pub. Schs., 1927-35 (pres., 1932-35). Mem. bd. regents Tex. State Teachers Colls., 1937-43; pres., trustee M. D. Anderson Foundation (charitable orgn.); vice pres. Clayton Foundation for Research; trustee San Jacinto Mus. of History Assn.; gov., trustee S.W. Research Inst., San Antonio, Texas; chmn. bd. of regents U. of Houston; dir. Tex. Med. Center. Presbyterian. Mason (32, Scottish Rite). Clubs: Houston, River Oaks Country (Houston), Piney Woods Country (Nacogdoches, Tex.) Home: Houston, TX. †

BATSCHELET, CLARENCE EDMUND, geographer; b. Lock Haven, Pa., July 30, 1889; s. Jacob Ferdinand and Ida E. (Fisher) B.; A.B., Franklin and Marshall Coll., 1912; A.M., George Washington U., 1926; m. Nellie Abigail Welsh, Sept. 25, 1913; children—Helen Ruth, Dorothy Elizabeth, Eleanor Louise, Thelma Welsh, Melissa Ida, Clarence Edmund. Instr. mathematics, Franklin and Marshall Acad., 1912-13; with Census Bureau from 1914, geographer, from 1924. Fellow Am. Geog. Soc.; mem. Am. Statis. Assn., Assn. of Am. Geographers, U.S. Board on Geog. Names, Population Assn. of America. Republican. Methodist. Mason. Club: Cosmos. Home: Arlington, Va. Deceased.

BATTCOCK, GREGORY E., art critic, educator; b. N.Y.C., July 2, 1941; s. Gregory J. and Elizabeth B. B.A., Mich. State U., 1963; cert., Accademia di Belle Art, Rome, 1964; M.A., Hunter Coll., 1965; Ph.D., N.Y. U., 1979. Adj. asso. prof. art N.Y. U., from 1975; prof. art history William Paterson Coll., Wayne, N.J., from 1970; Am. corr. Art and Artists, from 1968; N.Y. corr. Domus, from 1967. Author: The New Art, 1964, New American Cinema, 1967, Minimal Art, 1968, Idea Art, 1973, Why Art, 1976, Beyond Appearance, 1980, The New Music, 1980; editor: Super Realism, 1975, New Ideas in Art Education, 1970; editor, pub.: Trylon and Perisphere. Address: Wayne, NJ.

BATTEY, GEORGE MAGRUDER, JR., journalist; b. Rome, Ga., Feb. 11, 1887; s. George Magruder and Mary Hamilton (Van Dyke) B.; student U. of Ga. and Princeton; unmarried. Enlisted in U.S.N., Apr. 16, 1917; 16 mos. with destroyer Reid in anti-submarine service. Mem. Chi Psi, Ga. Hist. Soc. Presbyn. Club: Princeton Terrace. Author: Humpty-Dumpty William and Co., 1916; Chart House Poems, 1918; 70,000 miles on a Submarine Destroyer, 1919; A History of Rome and Floyd County, Ga., 1922. Address: Washington, D.C. †

BA U, (AGGA MAHA THIRI THUDHAMMA), pres. of Burma; b. May, 1887; s. U Pho Hla and Daw Daw Nyun; B.A., Trinity Hall, Cambridge U., Eng., 1912, M.A., 1922; LL.D., Rangoon University, 1952; married Daw, Nyein, 1913 (dec.); married second, Daw Aye, 1923 (dec.); 3 sons, 1 dau. Called to bar, Eng., 1913; advocate Chief Ct. of Lower Burma, 1913-21; dist. judge, 1921-23; dist. and sessions judge, 1923-30; judge High Ct. Rangoon (under Brit. rule), 1930-47, chief justice, 1947-48; chief justice Union of Burma, 1948-52; elected first constl. pres. of Burma, Mar. 1952. Pres. Election Tribunal, 1937; remained during Japanese occupation, 1942-45; assisted drawing new constitution after Japanese surrender. Former chief commnr. Burma Ambulance Brigade, also chmn. Burma Red Cross; now patron of both. Home: Rangoon, Burma. †

BAUER, EDMOND S., chem. and equipment mfg. co. exec.; b. Astoria, N.Y., May 12, 1918; s. Edmond S. and Alice Gertrude (Cavanaugh) B.; m. Jean L. Benney, May 22, 1943; children—Carl Thomas, Jay Scott. B.S.Ch.E., Newark Coll. Engring., 1939. With Monsanto Co., 1942-79, group v.p., 1974-75, mng. dir., 1975, exec. v.p., 1975-79, dir., 1975-82; chmn., pres., chief exec. officer Fisher Controls Corp. Delaware, Clayton, Mo., 1979-82. Contbr. numerous articles on resins to profl. jours. Mem. Soc. Chem. Industry, Groupement International des Associations Nationales de Fabricants de Pesticides (dir. 1973-75), Nat. Agrl. Chems. Assn. (dir. 1970-76, chmn. 1974-75, exec. com. 1972-76). Clubs: Old Warson Country (St. Louis), St. Louis (St. Louis); Ponte Vedra (Fla.). Home: Saint Louis, Mo. Died June 8, 1982.

BAUER, FRANK STANLEY, educator; b. Blue Mound, Ill., Nov. 27, 1888; s. Charles and Alice (Wall) B.; B.S., U. of Ill., 1911; M.E., U. of Colo. 1915; m. Jessie McGinnies, Dec. 23, 1914; children—Frances Evelyn, William Charles. Instr. mech. engring. U. of Colo., 1911-14, asst. prof., 1914-19, asso. prof., 1919-22, prof. from 1922, head dept., prof. engring. drawing and machine design from 1936. Mem. Am. Soc. M.E., Am. Soc. E.E., Sigma Xi, Tau Beta Pi, Sigma Tau, Pi Tau Sigma. Registered mech. engr. Colo. Presbyn. Author: Engine, Boiler and Power Plant Design, 1929; Dynamics of Engines, 1944. Extensive travel in U.S., Can. Home: Boulder, Colo. †

BAUER, ROYAL D(ANIEL) M(ICHAEL), educator; b. Union, Mo., Oct. 25, 1889; s. Michael William and Rebecca Hannah (Witthaus) B.; B.S., U. of Mo., 1923; M.B.A., Northwestern, 1935; m. Helen Elizabeth Clark, June 30, 1921; children—Elizabeth Acheson (Mrs. Edward W. Kaminski, Jr.), Edward Clark, Mary Jocelyn (Mrs. James M. Kyle, III), Employed as clerk for the Bank of Union, Missouri, 1906-10.†

BAUER, WALTER HERMAN, academic dean; b. Red Oak, Iowa, Sept. 9, 1907; s. Philip J. and Emma M. (Herold) B.; B.S. in Chem. Engring., Ore. State Coll., 1929; Ph.D. in Phys. Chem., U. Wis., 1933; m. Ingeborg Marie Midelfart, Dec. 26, 1933 (dec. June 1, 1963); children—Karen Ingeborg (Mrs. Barry A. Taylor), Hans Philip, Dagny Marie (Mrs. Richard Wilcox). Asst. instr. U. Wis., 1929-33, research asst., 1933-34; faculty Rensselaer Polytech. Poly. Inst., 1934-72, prof. phys. chem., 1948-60, dean Sch. Sci., 1960-72, dean emeritus, 1972-80. Cons. industrials; spl. research fuels rocket launching, chem. and structure aluminum soap-hydrocarbon systems, explosive oxidation boranes and borane derivatives, rheology non-Newtonian systems. Served to capt. AUS, 1942-45. Fellow Am. Inst. Chemists, Am. Soc. Testing and Materials; mem. Am. Chem. Soc., Soc. Rheology, AAAS, Sigma Xi, Phi Lambda Upsilon, Alpha Chi Rho, Alpha Chi Sigma. Home: Troy, N.Y. Died Mar. 30, 1980.

BAUKE, JOSEPH PADUR, educator; b. Briesen, Germany, May 18, 1932; came to U.S., 1950, naturalized, 1957; s. Joseph and Maria (Padur) B. B.A., U. Cin., 1956, M.A., 1957; Ph.D., Columbia, 1963. Instr. German Columbia, N.Y.C., 1960-63, asst. prof., 1963-65, asso. prof., 1965-69, prof., 1969-83, chmn. dept. Germanic langs., 1967-79. Editor: Germanic Rev, 1966-83; Contbr. articles profl. jours. Mem. Germanistic Soc. Am. (pres. 1970), Phi Beta Kappa, Delta Phi Alpha. Home: New York, N.Y. Died Dec. 6, 1983.

BAUM, HARRY A., stock broker; b. Chgo., Oct. 4, 1902; s. Joseph and Mary (Silhovy) B.; m. Bessie Flagg, 1923 (dec. 1952); children—Jeane Baum Aiston, Harry Flagg; m. Odella Labounty, Mar. 7, 1954; children—Barbara Tera, Ralph Lemley. Student, Northwestern U., 1918-22, LaSalle Extension U., 1923-26. Floor mgr. Charles Sincere & Co., 1919-22; securities salesman Paul H. Davis & Co., Chgo., 1922-28; partner Benjamin E. Minturn & Co. (stock brokers), Chgo., 1929-31, Wayne Hummer & Co., 1932—; mem. Midwest Stock Exchange, 1932—, gov., 1954-57, 58-61, 63-66, chmn. fin. com., 1958-61, chmn. exec. com., 1963-66; allied mem. N.Y. Stock Exchange, gov., 1959—; chmn. Chgo. Assn. Stock Exchange Firms, 1952-54. Bd. dirs. LaSalle Extension U., 1947-62; chmn. bd. trustees Marmion Mil. Acad., 1960-63, chmn. exec. com., 1964—; affiliated mem. Monastic Community of Marmion Abbey, Cath. Order of St. Benedict, 1980—. Mem. Chgo. Assn. Commerce and Industry. Clubs: Execs, Chgo. Athletic Assn, Marmion Mil. Acad. Dads (pres. 1959-60). Home: Chicago, Ill. Died Jan. 7, 1984.

BAUM, HARVEY A., company exec.; b. Fentress, Va., June 13, 1889; s. Luther Paul and Penelope (Jackson) B.; student pvt. sch., Columbia; m. Lucille Kennedy, May 18, 1948; children—John, Harvey, Phyllis, Penelope (by former marriage). Pres. Atlantic Commn. Co., Inc. Home: Englewood, N.J. †

BAUM, JOHN HARRY, publisher; b. Lemoyne, Pa., Sept. 21, 1917; s. Harvey Emanuel and Cora Anna (Donkel) B.; A.B., Gettysburg Coll., 1939; m. Virginia Marie Hale, Mar. 23, 1940; children—J. Robert, Diane Marie, Deborah Mae, James A. With the Patriot-News Co., Harrisburg, Pa., from 1939, retail advt. mgr., 1953-59, advt. dir., 1959-63, gen. mgr., 1963-67, v.p., 1967, pub., 1968-81; v.p. Harrisburg Area Indsl. Corp., from 1956; dir. Dauphin Deposit Trust Co., Lemoyne Trust Div., Harris Savings Assn., Community Consumer Discount Co. Bd. fellows, Gettysburg Coll. Served with USNR, 1944-47. Mem. Newspaper Advt. Execs. Assn., Harrisburg Area C. of C. (pres. 1959), Sigma Alpha Epsilon. Lutheran. Kiwanian, Mason (Shriner, K.T., Jester). Club: Executives (Harrisburg). Home: Lemoyne, Pa. Died Sept. 16, 1981.

BAUM, MAURICE, educator; b. Ft. Wayne, Ind., May 9, 1901; s. James and Pearl (Pritzsky) B.; B.A. summa cum laude, Princeton, 1923; M.A., U. Chgo., 1926, Ph.D., 1928; m. Cecil Heilweil, June 10, 1923 (dec. 1965); 1 son, James Robert. Instr. philosophy Univ. Coll., U. Chgo., 1928-30; instr. U. Cin., 1931-32; prof., chmn. dept. philosophy Kent State U., 1932-69, ret., 1969. Mem. Am., Ohio (pres. 1968-69) philosophy assns. Home: Pacific Palisades, Calif. Died May 19, 1985.

BAUMANN, FREDERICK L(LEWELLYN), coll. prof.; b. Elgin, Ill., Aug. 28, 1889; s. Frank and Bertha May (Tuck) B.; Ph.B., U. of Chicago, 1917, A.M., 1925; Ph.D., Cornell U., 1928; m. Mabell Whalen Dixon, Apr. 26, 1911 (div. 1917) 1 son, Victor Hugh; m. 2d, Faye Bennett, Aug. 23, 1919. Officer, New Mexico Mil. Inst., 1919-23; instr. Carleton Coll., Northfield, Minn., 1925-27; prof. history Grinnell (Ia.) Coll. from 1927; also chmn. dept. history and social studies div. Served with U.S. Army Ambulance Corps, 1917-19. Awarded Cross of Merit (Italian Army), Mar. 19, 1919. Mem. Am. Hist. Assn., Am. Acad. Polit. and Social Science, Ia. Hist. Soc., Phi Beta Kappa. Author: Ancient and Modern Utopias; Sixteenth Century Renaissance England. Contbr. review articles to hist. revs. Conglist. Home: Grinnell, Ia. †

BAUSCH, CARL LOUIS, optical co. exec.; b. Syracuse, N.Y., June 20, 1887; s. George and Mary (Bloecker) B.; M.E., Syracuse U., LL.D. (hon.), 1956; m. Marian Milliman, Sept. 17, 1914; children—Carl Louis, William George. Began as machinist Bausch & Lomb Optical Company, 1909; toolmaker, 1910-12, assistant foreman, 1912-14, foreman, 1914-16, assistant superintendent, 1917-21, mechanical engr., 1921-28, v.p. in charge research and engring., 1935-56, hon. chmn. bd., from 1956; Bausch & Lomb Found., Smith Corona Typewriter Co., Trustee Syracuse U. Mem. Troop H, 1st Cav., N.Y. N.G., 1910-13; asst. chief Ordnance Dept., Rochester, N.Y., 1937-40. Director Convalescent Hosp., General Hosp. Life mem. Optical Soc. America, A.A.A.S.; mgr. Am. Soc. Mech. Engrs.; mem. Tau Beta Pi, Sigma Chi. Clubs: Rochester Country, Genesee Valley (Rochester). †

BAXTER, BATSELL BARRETT, educator, minister; b. Cordell, Okla., Sept. 23, 1916; s. Batsell and Frances Fay (Scott) B.; m. Mavis Wanda Roberts, Dec. 22, 1938; children—Barrett Scott, Richard Alan, John Douglas. B.A., Abilene Christian Coll., 1937, L.H.D. (hon.), 1979; M.A., U. So. Calif., 1938, Ph.D., 1944; B.D., Vanderbilt U., 1957. Prof. speech George Pepperdine Coll., 1938-45; prof. speech, chmn. dept. David Lipscomb Coll., 1945-54, chmn. Bible dept., from 1957; minister Hillsboro Ch., Nashville, 1951-80; speaker on nat. Herald of Truth (radio and TV religious programs), from 1960. Author: Heart of the Yale Lectures, 1947, Speaking for the Master, 1954, If I Be Lifted Up, 1956, Great Preachers of Today, Vol. I, 1960, Making God's Way Our Way, 1964, I Believe Because, 1971, America, It's Not Too Late, 1974, When Life Tumbles In, 1974, A Devotional Guide to Bible Lands, 1979, Family of God, 1980; editor: Upreach mag. Named Alumnus of Year Abilene Christian Coll., 1962. Mem. So. Speech Assn. (pres. 1951), Soc. Bibl. Lit. and Exegesis. Home: Nashville, Tenn.

BAXTER, FRANK CONDIE, educator; b. Newbold, N.J., May 4, 1896; s. Frank C. and Lilliam Douglas (Murdoch) B.; A.B.; U. Pa., 1923, A.M., 1925; Ph.D., U. Cambridge, 1932; postgrad. U. Calif., 1929-30; Litt.D. (hon.), U. So. Calif., 1955, Ripon Coll., 1957, Elmira Coll., 1959, La Salle Coll., Phila., 1963; D.F.A., Calif. Coll. Medicine, 1956; m. Lydia Spencer Morris, May 28, 1927; children—Lydia Morris, Francis Condie. With (Phila.) Pa. Salt Mfg. Co., 1912-17; mus. asst. U. Pa., 1921, asst. instr. zoology, 1922-23, instr. English, 1923-27; part time instr. English, Swarthmore Coll., 1925-27, U. Calif., 1929-30; asst. prof. U. So. Calif., 1930-33, asso. prof., 1934-36, prof. English, 1937-61, prof. English emeritus, 1961-82, chmn. univ. senate, 1947; pres. Oak Knoll Broadcasting Corp., Pasadena, from 1972; asst. to Dr. Harold S. Colton, sci. work in Painted Desert area, summers 1920, 21, 24. Recipient Peabody award, Sylvania, Ohio State U. awards; 7 Emmys from Acad. TV Arts and Sciences. Member AAUP, Phi Beta Kappa, Phi Kappa Phi, Beta Sigma Tau. Baptist. Maker original charts, models illustrating history printing, paper, history of alphabet, etc.; lectr. Pioneer Ednl. TV Programs; Shakespeare on TV; Now and Then; Harvest; The Written Word; The Bell System Science Series: Fair Adventure Series. Home: San Marino, Calif. Died Jan. 18, 1982.

BAXTER, HUBERT EUGENE, univ. prof.; b. Tonawanda, N.Y., Sept. 21, 1887; s. Eugene Charles and Margaret Ann (Gillie) B.; B.Arch., Cornell U., 1910, grad. study, 1911-14; m. Phebe Poole, June 22, 1927; children—Louise, Daniel Paine. With Lansing, Bley & Lyman, architects, Buffalo; 1910-12; instr., coll. of architecture, Cornell U., 1911-21, asst. prof., 1921-36, prof. from 1936. Mem. village bd., Cayuga Heights, N.Y., 1933-40, mayor, 1936-40. 1st lt., Res. mil. aviator, U.S. Air Service, 1917-19. Mem. Gamma Alpha, Tau Beta Pi. Author: Descriptive Geometry (with George Young, Jr.), 1921; Mechanics of Materials (with George Young, Jr.), 1927. Home: Ithaca, N.Y. †

BAXTER, JOHN LINCOLN, food processing executive; b. Brunswick, Maine, May 28, 1896; s. Hartley Cone and Mary (Lincoln) B.; A.B. cum laude, Bowdoin Coll., 1916, M.A. (hon.), 1961, LL.D. (hon.), 1970; m. Constance French, June 10, 1919 (dec. 1945); children—John L., Hartley Cone II; m. Beatrice Hennessey, Dec. 1952 (dec. July 1968). Tchr., Bowdoin Coll., 1916; mem. firm H.C. Baxter & Brother, food processors, Brunswick, 1917-65; pres. Snow Flake Canning Co., Brunswick, 1955-75, Puritan Sales Corp, 1935-65; v.p. Maine Canned Foods, Inc., Portland, Maine, 1930-65; dir. First Nat. Bank of Portland, Union Mut. Life Ins. Co., Rockland Rockport Lime Corp.; adv. council Liberty Mut. Life Ins. Co. Dir. New Eng. Council, 1924-25, sec., 1934-36, state chmn., 1936-40; chmn. Maine Joint Tax Conf., 1937; regional chmn. Com. Econ. Devel., 1943; mem. Maine Devel. Commn., 1943-53; cons. canned foods USDA, 1944. Trustee Bowdoin Coll. Served as 2d lt. U.S. Army, 1918; mem. Nat. Def. Adv. Council, 1940-41; chief processed foods sect., govt. presiding officer canned foods adv. com. OPM, WPB, 1941-43. Mem. Nat. Assn. Frozen Food Packers (v.p. 1953, pres. 1954), Maine Canners Assn. (pres. 1924-25), Phi Beta Kappa, Delta Kappa Epsilon. Contbr. mag. articles. Home: Topsham, Maine.

BAXTER, SAMUEL NEWMAN, JR., clergyman; b. Phila., Aug. 14, 1913; s. Samuel Newman and Lucy A. (Bolton) B.; B.A., Pa. State U., 1935; S.T.B., Gen. Theol. Sem., 1939, S.T.D., 1970; m. Catharine D. Fagan, June 8, 1940; children—C. Dallas Dixon, Lucy A. Bolton. Ordained deacon Episcopal Ch., 1939, priest, 1940; pastor in N.C., 1939-41, Pa., 1941-48; archdeacon Diocese of Western N.Y., 1948-54; rector Ch. of Good Shepherd, Austin, Tex., from 1954. Former sec. Ho. of Deputies and Gen. Conv. Episc. Church; sec. Diocese of Tex. 1965—. Mem. Theta Chi. Rotarian. Home: Austin, Tex.

BAXTER, SAMUEL SERSON, cons. engr.; b. Phila., Feb. 6, 1905; s. Matthew and Elizabeth (Serson) B.; m. Norma Ruth Winter, Oct. 8, 1932; children—Richard A., Linda C. Student, Drexel Inst. Tech. Evening Coll., 1921-25; D.Eng. (hon.), Drexel Inst. Tech., 1966. Registered profl. engr. Various engring. positions Bur. Engring., Phila., 1923-39, asst. chief engr., chief engr., 1946-52; asst. dir. Pub. Works, Phila., 1939-42; commr., chief engr. Water Dept., from 1972; cons. engr., from 1972; chmn. bd. East Girard Savs. Assn., Phila., from 1962. Vice pres. Phila. council Boy Scouts Am., 1963-68, pres., 1968-69; trustee Drexel U., from 1971. Served to maj. C.E. AUS, 1942-46. Named Engr. of Year Phila. chpt. Pa. Soc. Profl. Engrs., 1959; recipient nat. award Nat. Soc. Profl. Engrs., 1976. Pa. Fellow ASCE (dir. 1959-62, pres. 1971); mem. Am. Pub. Works Assn. (pres. 1947, chmn. research found. 1965-77), Am. Water Works Assn. (dir. 1959-62, pres. 1965-66), Engrs. Club Phila. (pres. 1963), Nat. Acad. Engring., Drexel U. Alumni Assn. (pres. 1969-73). Methodist. Club: Union League (Phila.). Home: Philadelphia, PA.

BAYLESS, JAMES LEAVELL, investment banking co. exec.; b. Houston, Feb. 10, 1925; s. Alec Clevel and Grace Norrell (Leavell) B.; m. Elizabeth Louise Langston, Dec. 15, 1950; children—James Leavell, Louise. B.B.A. in Fin, U. Tex., Austin, 1948. Salesman Rauscher Pierce Co., Houston, 1948-53, v.p., 1953-68, sr. v.p., 1968-70, exec. v.p., 1970-73, pres., 1973—, also dir.; dir. Alaska Interstate Co. Active United Fund; bd. dirs. Museum of Fine Arts, Houston, 1965-70, Holly Hall, 1949-60, Child Guidance Center, 1960-65, Goodwill Industries, 1972-78; chmn. adv. council Coll. Bus. Adminstrn. U. Tex., Austin, 1967-72; pres. Bus. Sch. Found.; Chmn. fin. George Bush campaigns for Ho. of Reps., 1968; for Senate, 1972. Served with USAAF, 1943-45. Decorated Purple Heart; named Outstanding Grad. Bus. Sch. U. Tex., 1967. Mem. Securities Industry Assn. (vice chmn. 1978-79), Kappa Sigma. Presbyterian (deacon, elder). Clubs: Houston Country, Bayou, Ramada, Dallas. Home: Houston, Tex. Died 1983.

BEACH, JOSEPH WATSON, ins. exec.; b. Hartford, Conn., Mar. 26, 1888; s. Charles Coffin and Mary Elizabeth (Batterson) B.; student U. Va., 1910, Williams Coll., 1911; m. Jessie Anderson, Apr. 25, 1912; m. 2d, Caroline Zezzette, Apr. 26, 1964. With Travelers Ins. Co. 1910-12; with Hartford Accident & Indemnity Co., 1914-17; with J. Watson Beach, Inc., from 1917, chmn. dir., from 1925; dir. Riverside Trust Co., United Bank & Trust Co. Pres. Bd. Edn. City Hartford, 1929-31; mayor, Hartford, 1933-35. Bd. dirs. St. Anthony Ednl. Found., Hartford Art Sch. Served as gunner's mate USN, World War I; lt. col. AUS, World War II. Mason. Clubs: St. Anthony (N.Y.C.); Hartford, Hartford Golf. Home: Farmington, CT. †

BEACH, P. GOFF, food co. exec.; b. Chgo., Dec. 25, 1914; s. Pierre Goff and Barbara S. (Young) B.; m. Mary Ellen Thompson, Sept. 12, 1942; children—Robert T., Thomas G., Nancy L., Sally A. Student, U. Ill., 1933-36; B.A. in Bus. Adminstrn, Northwestern U., 1940. With Oscar Mayer & Co., Chgo., 1936-82, plant mgr., Madison, 1952-53, v.p. operations, 1953-60, exec. v.p., 1960-66, pres., 1966-73, chief exec. officer, 1972-82, chmn. bd., 1973-82; dir. First Wis. Nat. Bank, Madison, First Wis. Corp., A.O. Smith Corp.; past dir. Western Pub. Co., Inc.; Mem. Adv. Council on Japan-U.S. Econ. Relations; past dir. Nat. Livestock and Meat Bd., Livestock Conservation, Inc.; dir. Grocery Mfrs. Am. Past pres. Madison Community Chest; past trustee Nutrition Found., Inc.; past bd. dirs. Big Bros. Dane County; trustee Northwestern U.; mem. adv. bd. Bus. Sch., U. Wis. Served to lt. (s.g.) USNR, 1943-46. Mem. Am. Meat Inst. (past chmn. bd.), Madison C. of C. (past v.p.), Wis. C. of C. (past dir.), Constrn. Users Round Table (past dir.). Clubs: Chicago; Madison (Madison), Maple Bluff Country (Madison) (past pres.); John Evans (Northwestern U.); Bascom Hill Soc. (U. Wis.). Home: Madison, Wis. Died Aug. 14, 1982.*

BEAL, RICHARD SIDNEY, clergyman; b. Denver, Colo., Dec. 10, 1887; s. Sidney and Henrietta Elizabeth (Arscott) B.; student William Jewell Coll., Liberty, Mo., 1908-11; D.D., Northern Bapt. Theol. Sem., 1935; m. Mona Lelia Ballfinch, Mar. 20, 1914; children—Richard Sidney, Elizabeth Rose, Charles Beckman, David Paul, Margaret Ruth. Began as railroad clk., 1903; ordained Bapt. ministry, 1910; pastor Forest City and Hume, Mo., 1909-11, Rich Hill, Mo., 1911-14. Victor, Colo., 1914-18, First Ch., Tucson, Ariz., from 1918. Mem. bd. mgrs. Ariz. Bapt. Conv. (mem. exec. com.); former mem. Gen. Council Northern Baptist Conv.; former mem. of bd. Am. Baptist Home Mission Soc.; dir. Rockmont Coll., Calif. Bapt. Theol. Sem., Los Angeles; former leader, Conservative Baptist Fellowship of Northern Baptists. Author of Lectures on The Book Revelation, 1932; Rivers in the

Desert, 10 volumes. Contbr. religious articles to mags. Home: Tucson Ariz. †

BEALE, GUY OTIS, railway exec.; b. Ettricks, Va., Sept. 24, 1888; s. John Thomas and Mary E. (Cousins) B.; ed. in pub. schs., bus. coll., U. Richmond; m. Hilda Booth, June 20, 1931; children—Mary Elizabeth, Guy Otis. With C. & O. Ry. Co. from 1908, v.p. for purchases from 1949. Served with A.E.F., France, 1918-19.†

BEAM, LURA, b. Marshfield, Me., Apr. 1, 1887; d. George Ellery and Nellie Hannah (Berry) B.; student U. of Calif., 1904-06; A.B., Columbia, 1908, A.M., 1917. Instr. in psychology, Gregory Normal Sch., Wilmington, N.C., 1908-10; instr. in edn., Le Moyne Normal Sch., Memphis, Tenn., 1910-11; asst. supt. edn., Am. Missionary Assn., 1911-19; with dept. of edn., Interchurch World Movement, 1919; asso. sec., research in edn., Council of Ch. Bds. of Edn., with intermittent studies for Assn. Am. Colleges, 1919-26; research in edn., Nat. Com. on Maternal Health, Inc., 1927-33, Gen. Education Bd., summer 1934. Chmn. com. on fine arts, Am. Assn. Univ. Women, from 1926. Republican. Congregationalist. Author: A Thousand Marriages (with Robert L. Dickinson), 1931; The Single Woman, 1933; also numerous pamphlets and articles in mags., giving results of educational surveys. Home: Bronxville, N.Y. †

BEAN, MONTE LAFAYETTE, drug chain exec.; b. Richfield, Utah, Jan. 23, 1899; s. Marquis L. and Annie Maria (Horne) B.; m. Birdie Sander, May 24, 1922; children—Beverly, Lamont, Audrey. Student, Latter-day Saints U., 1918-21. Mgr. Skaggs, Salt Lake City, 1913-29; div. mgr. Safeway Stores, Portland, Oreg., 1930-39; originator Tradewell Stores, Seattle, 1939-47; founder, dir. Payn Save, Inc., Seattle, from 1947. Author: These Mortal Years, 1977. Bd. dirs. Kidney Center. Served with USMC, World War I. Mem. Ch. of Jesus Christ of Latter-day Saints. Club: Rainer. Home: Seattle, Wash.

BEARD, BELLE BOONE, sociologist; b. Boone Mill, Va., Feb. 18, 1898; d. James William and Mary (Kleindienst) Beard; student Averett Coll., Danville, Va., 1913-15; A.B., Lynchburg (Va.) Coll., 1923; A.M., Ph.D., Bryn Mawr Coll., 1932; unmarried. Teacher of public schools, Franklin County, Va., 1915-18; asso. prof. of sociology and acting head dept. of economics and sociology, Sweet Briar (Va.) Coll., 1931-34, prof. of sociology and head of the department of sociology, 1934-63; chmn. division of social studies, 1946-49, head department of sociology, 1946-63; director of county and city organization State Dept. of Public Welfare (on leave from Sweet Briar Coll.), Richmond, Va. 1938-40; visiting prof. sociology, Vanderbilt U., Nashville, 1945-46; research professor New Mexico Highlands University, 1952-53. Fulbright lecturer to Korea, Seoul, 1961. Chairman, Merit System Council, State Dept. of Public Welfare, 1940-43; chmn. Va. Joint Merit System Council, 1943-53; pres. Va. Conf. of Social Work, 1936-37; mem. exec. com. Va. Welfare Council, 1935-41; v.p. Va. Interracial Commn., 1938-41; dir. Va. Council of Administrative Women in Edn., 1938-40, pres. 1940-42. Trustee Lynchburg Coll. from 1933, v.p., 1941. Fellow Gerontological Society, Am. Sociol. Soc.; mem. Internat. Assn. Gerontology, Societe Geriatric de Chile, Am. Probation Assn., Am. Assn. Sociol. Workers, Nat. Conf. Social Work, Am. Assn. of Univ. Women, Southern Sociol. Soc. (exec. com. 1936-40); Virginia Social Science Assn. (pres. 1942-44, v. pres., 1945-46). Julius Rosenwald Foundation Fellow, 1945-46; May K. Houck Foundation Fellow, 1959-60. Democrat. Member Disciples of Christ Church. Author: Juvenile Probation; also articles on juvenile delinquency and gerontology. Address: Sweet Briar, Va. Died Oct. 12, 1984.

BEARD, CHARLES EDMUND, transportation exec.; b. Toledo, O., Nov. 23, 1900; s. Hiram Ed. and Mamie (Reiser) B.; student Lake Forest Acad., Lake Forest Coll., Toledo U.; m. Rose Esther Wheaton, Feb. 3, 1923; children—Robert Don, Barbara Rose. Gen. traffic mgr. Braniff Airways, Inc., Oklahoma City, 1935-37, v.p. in charge traffic and sales, 1937, exec. v.p., 1947, pres. 1954-65. Home: Dallas, Tex. Died July 18, 1982.

BEARD, JAMES ANDREWS, author, food cons.; b. Portland, Oreg., May 5, 1903; s. Jonathan A. and Mary Elizabeth (Jones) B. Student, Reed Coll., 1920-21, D.H.L., 1976; student, U. Wash., 1931, Carnegie Inst. Tech., 1931-32. Pvt. tchr. cooking, Portland, 1932-37, tchr. country day sch., N.J., 1938; co-propr. Hors d'Oeuvre, Inc., N.Y.C., 1938-44; asso. dairy and vegetable farm, Reading, Pa., 1943; established clubs for United Seamen's Service throughout world, 1943-46, lectr., cooking demonstrator before groups, 1949—, food cons., 1956; propr. James Beard Cooking Classes., N.Y.C., 1955—. Active amateur theatrical group, Portland; appeared: on stage with Walter Hampden in revivals of Cyrano de Bergerac, 1924, 25, Othelo, 1925; radio, San Francisco and Portland, 1927-32; then as announcer for food commls.; featured on: TV food program Elsie Presents, 1946-47; guest on TV shows in, U.S., France and Eng., 1947-55; Author: Hors d'Oeuvre Canapes, 1940, Cook it Outdoors, 1941, Fowl and Game Cookery, 1944, Fireside Cookbook, 1949, James Beard's Fish Cookery, 1954, The Complete Book of Barbecue and Rotisserie Cooking, 1954, The Complete Cookbook for Entertaining, 1954, Jim Beard's New Barbecue Cookbook, 1958, James Beard's Treasury of Outdoor Cooking, 1960, The James Beard Cookbook, 1961; autobiography Delights and Prejudices, 1964, (with Alexander Watt) Paris Cuisine, 1952, (with Helen E. Brown) The Complete Book of Outdoor Cookery, 1955, (with Sam Aaron) How to Eat Better for Less Money, 1956, rev. edit., 1971, James Beard Cook Book, 1959, rev. edit., 1971, James Beard's Menus for Entertaining, 1965, How To Eat (and Drink) Your Way Through A French (or Italian) Menu, 1971, James Beard's American Cooking, 1972, Beard on Bread, 1973, Beard on Food, 1974, The Cooks Catalogue, 1975, New Fish Cookery, 1976, Theory and Practice of Good Cooking, 1977; weekly food column syndicated by, Universal Press Syndicate. Served with AUS, 1942-43. Decorated chevalier du Merite Agricole France). Address: New York, N.Y. Died Jan. 23, 1985.

BEARDSLEE, CLAUDE GILLETTE, philosophy educator; b. West Springfield, Mass., June 25, 1888; s. Clark Smith and Emma Gillette (Alvord) B.; A.B., Yale, 1909; B.D., Hartford (Conn.) Theol. Sem., 1912, S.T.M., 1913; M.A., U. of Southern Calif., 1922; Ph.D., Brown U., 1931; m. Pauline Dustin Johnson, Aug. 26, 1914 (died 1918); 1 dau., Caroline; m. 2d Louise Meech Miner, Sept. 23, 1920; children—Ruth, Betsy Remembrance, Claudia Gillette, Alvord Miner. Ordained to ministry Congl. Ch., 1914; pastor Southington, Conn., 1914-20; supt. of employment, Peck, Stow & Wilcox Co., Southington, 1920-21; grad. asst., later instr. and asst. prof. philosophy, U. of Southern Calif., 1921-24; pastor Kingston, R.I., 1924-29; grad. student asst. in philosophy, Brown U., 1929-31; prof. moral and religious philosophy, also chaplain, Lehigh Univ. from 1931. Served as pvt., advancing to 2d lt. arty., U.S. Army 1917-19. Mem. Am. Philos. Assn., Am. Assn. Univ. Profs., Phi Kappa Epsilon, Omicron Delta Kappa (nat. v.p.). Author: Analysis of Moral Problems, 1942. Republican. Mason. Home: Bethlehem, Pa. †

BECK, AUDREY PHILLIPS, state legislator; b. Bklyn., Aug. 6, 1931; d. Gilbert Wesley and Mary (Reilly) Phillips; B.A. with high honors and distinction in Econs., U. Conn., 1953, M.A., 1955; m. Curt Frederick Beck, Aug. 4, 1951 (div.); children—Ronald Pierson, Meredith Wayne. Instr. econs. U. Conn., Storrs, 1960-68; planning economist Windham Regional Planning Agy., 1968; mem. Conn. Ho. of Reps., 1969-75, asst. minority leader, 1973-75; mem. Conn. Senate, 1975-83, asst. majority leader, 1977-83; vis. prof. practical politics Center Am. Women and Politics, Eagleton Inst. Politics Rutgers U., 1973; spl. advisor U.S. del. UN Habitat, Vancouver, 1976. Mem. Mansfield Bd. Fin., 1965-71, mem. town govt. study com., 1967-68; pres. Tolland County Democratic Assn.; del. Dem. Nat. Conv., 1972; mem. com. legis. ethics and campaign financing Nat. Legis. Conf., 1973-75, com. sci. and tech., from 1975; mem. tax com. Council State Govts. Recipient Outstanding State Ofcl. award, 1973; Outstanding Woman Legislator award Bus. and Profl. Women's Clubs, 1976. Mem. League Women Voters, NOW, Am. Soc. Planning Ofcls. (pres.), Women's Polit. Caucus, AAUW, Conn. Fedn. Dem. Women's Clubs, Phi Beta Kappa, Phi Kappa Phi, Gamma Chi Epsilon, Delta Sigma Rho. Home: Storrs, Conn. Died Mar. 11, 1983.

BECK, AXEL JOHN, judge, lawyer; b. Sweden, May 6, 1894; came to U.S., 1906, naturalized, 1916; s. C. M. and Anna (Jonson) B.; m. Georgia C. Clark, Sept. 10, 1930; children—Byron John, Craig Allen. A.B., Morningside Coll., 1920; J.D., U. Chgo., 1922. Bar: Ill. bar 1923, S.D. bar 1924. Practiced in, Chgo., 1923-24, Union County, S.D., 1924—; organizer Bank of Union County, Elk Point, 1943, pres., chmn. bd., 1947-58, U.S. dist. ct. judge, 1958—; pres. Thermoflector Corp., North Sioux City, S.D. Republican nat. committeeman of S.D., 1948-57; also mem. exec. com. Mem. and officer Commn. on Uniform Laws for S.D.; mem. Nat. Conf. on Uniform Legislation, 1938-57; Mem. Elk Point Bd. of Edn., 1945-50, pres., 1949. Served as 2d lt. U.S. Army, World War I. Recipient Distinguished Service award Morningside Coll., 1966. Mem. Am. Legion (judge adv. Dept. of S.D.), State Bar of S.D., Am. Bar Assn., Pi Kappa Delta, Gamma Eta Gamma. Republican. Conglist. Club: Mason (32 deg., Shriner). Home: Aberdeen, S.D. Died Sept. 2, 1981.*

BECKENBACH, EDWIN FORD, mathematician, educator; b. Dallas, July 18, 1906; s. Charlie Geiger and Lucy Emma (Richardson) B.; m. Madelene Shelby Simons, Aug. 30, 1933 (div. June 1960); children—Edwin Simons, Madelene Lenann (Mrs. John Nye), Sonya Suzann (Mrs. Michael Morse); m. Alice Curtiss Tucker, June 24, 1960. B.A., Rice U., 1928, M.A., 1929, Ph.D., 1931. Nat. research fellow Princeton, Ohio State U., U. Chgo., 1931-33; instr. Rice U., 1933-40; asst. prof. U. Mich., 1940-42; asso. prof. U. Tex., Austin, 1942-45; prof. math. U. Calif. at Los Angeles, 1945-74, prof. emeritus, 1974-82; vis. prof. U. Sask., Can., summer 1940, U. Del., 1975-76; Cons. Rand Corp., Santa Monica, Calif., 1949-63; mem. Inst. for Numerical Analysis, Nat. Bur. Standards, 1948-50, Inst. for Advanced Study, Princeton, 1951-52; vis. scholar Swiss Fed. Inst. Tech., Zurich, 1958-59; mem. NSF Sch. Math. Study Group, 1958-60; writer African Edn. Program, Mombasa, Kenya, 1965; co-dir. 1st Internat. Conf. on Gen. Inequalities, Oberwolfach, W.Ger., 1976; co-dir. 2d conf., 1978, 3d conf., 1981. Author, editor: Construction and Applications of Conformal Maps, 1952, Modern Math. for the Engineer, 1st series, 1956, 2d series, 1961; Author: (with Richard Bellman) An Introduction to Inequalities, 1961, Inequalities, 1961, (with others) College Algebra, 1964, Modern Intro. Analysis, 1964, Applied Combinatorial Analysis, 1964, Essentials of College Algebra, 1965, Integrated College Algebra and Trigonometry, 1966, Modern School Mathematics, Course 1, 1967, Course 2, 1967, Algebra I, 1965, Algebra 2 and Trigonometry, 1968, Pre-Algebra, 1970, (with Robert C. James) Mathematics Dictionary, 3d edit, 1968, 4th edit., 1976, Modern College Algebra and Trigonometry, 1969, (with Robert Sorgenfrey) Analysis of Elementary Functions, 1970, Intermediate Algebra for College Students, 1971, Modern Analytic Geometry, 1972, (with C.B. Thompkins) Concepts of Communications: Interpersonal, Intrapersonal and Mathematical, 1972, (with others) College Mathematics for Students of Business and the Social Sciences, 1977, Procs. First Internat. Conf. Gen. Inequalities, 1978, Second, 1980, Third, 1982; Founding editor: (with others) Pacific Jour. Math, 1950-54; asso. editor (with others), 1955-82; Contbr. (with others) articles to profl. jours. Guggenheim fellow, 1958-59. Fellow AAAS; mem. Am. Math. Soc. (mem. council, mem. and chmn. com. printing and pub. 1956-61, chmn. com. to study fin. problems of math. revs. 1963-64), Math. Assn. Am. (chmn. com. publs. 1971-82), Soc. for Indsl. and Applied Math. (membership com. 1968-72), Nat. Council Tchrs. Math. (writer, coordinator summers 1964, 66), Indian Math. Soc., Societe Mathematique de France, Circolo Mathematico di Palermo, Assn. of Mems. of Inst. Advanced Study (chmn. Western com. 1980-82, trustee 1981-82), Sigma Xi, Phi Beta Kappa, Pi Mu Epsilon. Club: Riviera Tennis. Home: Los Angeles, Calif. Died Sept. 5, 1982.

BECKER, CARL R(AYMOND), business exec.; b. Ottumwa, Ia., Nov. 26, 1889; s. Frederick W. and Anna (Chapman) B.; student Yale, 1911-15; m. Ellen Dunn, Nov. 29, 1917. Pres. Thomas Young Orchids, Inc., Bound Brook, N.J., from 1932. Republican. Episcopalian. †

BECKER, FRANK J(OHN), congressman; b. Bklyn., Aug. 27, 1899; s. Maximilian and Eva (Sperling) B.; student Lynbrook pub. schs.; m. Anne Claire Ferris, June 30, 1923; children—Francis, Betty Ann (Mrs. Jack C. Myers), Robert. Ins. broker, Lynbrook, since 1945 dir. Lynbrook Fed. Savs. & Loan Assn., mem. 83d-87th Congress, 3d Congl. Dist. N.Y. Mem. Assembly, N.Y. Lesiglature, 1945-53, mem. ways and means com., chmn. charitable and religious societies com., chmn. joint legislative com. for study mil. law, 1948-53, bd. vis. U.S. Military Acad., West Point, 1954. Dir. Nassau Co. TB and Pub. Health Assn. Served with U.S. Army, 1918. Mem. Am. Legion (nat. vice chmn. pub. relations commn., past post and co. comdr.), Vets. Fgn. Wars, Holy Name Soc. Republican. Elk, K.C. Home: Lynbrook, N.Y. Died Sept. 4, 1981.

BECKER, MAURICE, artist; b. Nizhni Novgorod, now Gorki, Russia, Jan. 4, 1889; s. Isor and Rose (Simonoff) B.; brought to U.S. at age of 3; student Comml. High Sch., N.Y.C., 1 year; studied art with Robt. Henri and Homer Boss, N.Y.C.; m. Dorothy Baldwin, Sept. 28, 1918. Exhibited at Armory Show, 1913; contbg. art editor Masses (mag.), 1913-17; mem. art staff N.Y. Call and N.Y. Tribune, 1915; artist corr., West Indies, for Scripps N.E.A. Syndicate, 1917; painted in Mexico, 1921-23; exhibited with Orozco and Rivera in Mexico, 1922. Exhibited 1-man shows Whitney Studio, 1924, J.B. Neumann Gallery, Delphic Studio, 1930, Dorothy Paris Gallery, 1935, Artists Gallery, 1940, Macbeth Gallery, 1942, 45, A.F.I. Gallery, 1952, Hartert Galleries, 1954, 55, 57, Art of Today Gallery, 1955, Mansfield 1st Nat. Bank (Pa.). Exhibited maj. galleries, museums, U.S., Europe. Retrospective exhbn. oils, water colors and black and white, Berkshire Mus., Pittsfield, Mass., 1948, C.C.C. Gallery, Brighton Beach, N.Y.C.; included Met. Mus. Water Color Show, 1952-53, also in the 53 Contemporaries show Greenwich Gallery, N.Y.C., 1957, Armory Show's 50th Ann., N.Y.C., 1963, art exhbn. commemorating Warsaw Ghetto Uprising and founding State of Israel, N.Y.C., 1963. Represented in N.Y. Hist. Soc., Phila. Hist. Soc., Nicholas Gallery, N.Y.C., Chrysler Mus., Provincetown, Mass., Ringling Mus., Sarasota, Fla., U. Mich., Norfolk Mus. Arts and Scis., Local 65, AFL-CIO (mural), Chapellier Gallery, Bernhardt Crystal Gallery. Recipient Am. Fedn. Arts award, 1950. Mem. Fedn. Modern Painters and Sculptors, An American Group, Artists Equity Assn., Audubon Artists, N.C. Acad. of Arts and Scis. and Professions, N.Y. Hist. Soc. Address: Tioga, Pa. †

BECKER, ROBERT, sport writer; b. Terryville, S.D., Oct. 27, 1890; s. Henry E. and Stella (White) B.; A.B., Beloit (Wis.) Coll., 1912; m. Suzanne Dabney, June 16, 1917. Field naturalist with Field Museum of Natural History, Chicago, 1912-15; field work with U.S. Biol. Survey, 1916; again with Field Museum, 1917; outdoor editor Chicago Tribune since 1921; mng. editor Outdoorsman, Jan. 1945-50; editorial dir. Hunting and Fishing (combined with Outdoorsman), from 1951. Mem. Outdoor Writers Assn. of Am. (pres. 1930-31; pres. Ill. div., 1944-48), Sigma Chi. Republican. Conglist. Mason. Clubs: University, Campfire, Adventurers. Home: Lake Bluff, Ill. †

BECKETT, ERNEST J(OHN), business exec.; b. Wilton, Eng., Feb. 6, 1887; s. Richard and Emily J. (Titt) B.; ed. pvt. schs. in Eng.; m. Hilda Hansen, July 4, 1912; children—Richard Wilton, John Raymond. Came to U.S., 1907, naturalized, 1918. Filled various accounting and secretarial positions, 1907-20; asst. treas. Pacific Gas and Electric Co., San Francisco, 1920, financial asst. to pres.,

1927-43, treas. since 1943; vice pres., treas. and dir. Valley Elec. Supply Co., Fresno, Calif.; dir. Vallejo Elec. Light & Power Co. Mem. Am. Newcomen Soc., Pacific Coast Elec. Assn., Am. and Pacific Coast gas assns. Republican. Episcopalian. Clubs: Commonwealth (San Francisco); Golf and Country (Los Altos). Home: Palo Alto, Calif. Deceased.

BECKLEY, CHESTER ARTHUR, corp. exec.; b. York Co., Pa., Jan. 5, 1890; s. John and Mary (Ross) B.; B.S., Lycoming Coll., 1909; grad. study Syracuse U., 1909-12; student U.S. Coast Guard Acad., 1913-14; m. Maybelle H. Scott, June 6, 1916; children—Dorothy (Mrs. Maino desGranges), Jayne (Mrs. Peer deSilva). Joined T. A. Scott Co., Inc., New London Conn., 1919, with Merritt-Chapman & Scott Co., from 1923, v.p. in charge salvage facilities, operations and settlements, dir. 1948-56, also v.p., dir. four subsidiary corps.; pres., dir. Merritt-Chapman & Scott (West Indies) Inc. Commissioned officer, U.S. Coast Guard and U.S. Navy, 1914-19. Member Am. Soc. Naval Engrs., Am. Arbitration Assn., Phi Kappa Psi. Mason. Clubs: Propeller, India House. Home: Bellerose, NY. †

BECKSTEDT, MAX VICTOR, railroad exec.; b. Aultsville, Ont., Can., Sept. 11, 1888; s. Norris Levi and Isabelle (Shaver) B.; student pub. schs. Prescott, Ont., also bus. coll.; m. Emily Beale, Sept. 1, 1915; children—Ann, Emily. Came to U.S., 1905, naturalized, 1934. Joined D. & H. R.R., 1905, became gen. freight agt., 1936, gen. traffic mgr., v.p. traffic since 1946. Mem. Nat. Freight Traffic Assn. Episcopalian. Mason. Clubs: Albany (N.Y.) Country; Fort Orange; Traffic (N.Y.C., Boston and Montreal, Que.). †

BECKWITH, ALBERT EDWIN, telephone co. exec.; b. Albion, N.Y., Aug. 14, 1921; s. George D. and Elizabeth C. (Mauterstock) B.; m. Barbara J. Kessler, Apr. 26, 1980; children by previous marriage—David G., Nancy E. Various engring. positions Gen. Telephone Co. of Upstate N.Y., 1940-60, chief engr., Johnstown, N.Y., 1960-64, v.p. ops., 1964-71, Gen. Telephone Co. of Ind., Ft. Wayne, 1971-72, pres., from 1972, Gen. Telephone Co. of Mich., from 1981. Served in USAAF, 1942-46.

BECKWITH, EDSON EMERSON, airline exec.; b. Frankfort, N.Y., Oct. 28, 1930; s. H. Elting and Laura May (Spence) B.; m. Beatrice Jane Houseman, Aug. 12, 1961; children—John E., Amy S., Andrew McL. B.A., Hamilton Coll., Clinton, N.Y., 1953. With Chase Manhattan Bank, N.Y.C., 1957-66; asst. treas. Pepsico Inc., N.Y.C., 1966-70; v.p. fin. King Resources Co., Denver, 1971; v.p., treas. Braniff Internat. Corp., Dallas, 1972-80, sr. v.p. fin. services, 1980, exec. v.p.-fin., from 1981. Trustee Hamilton Coll., from 1979. Served with AUS, 1953-56. Mem. Fin. Execs. Inst. (chpt. dir. from 1974, pres 1979-80), Treas.'s Group N.Y.C. Club: Union League (N.Y.C.). Home: Dallas, Tex.

BEDFORD, EDWARD THOMAS, II, pres. Bush Terminal Bldgs. Co.; b. Brooklyn, N.Y., Aug. 1, 1888; s. Frederick Henry and Jennie V. (Dingee) B.; B.S., Amherst, 1910; m. Jessie Cook, Apr. 22, 1932; children—Edward Thomas, III, Barbara, Frederick Thomas, III. Pres. Candy Brands, Inc., Brooklyn, N.Y., 1931-34; pres. Columbia Refining Co., Long Island City, N.Y., since 1932; pres. Bush Terminal Bldgs. Co. from 1934; dir. Abercrombie & Fitch Co. Republican. Club: Union League. Home: Greenwich, Conn. †

BEDINGER, HENRY GRAYBILL, college pres.; b. Richwood, Boone Co., Ky., June 1, 1889; s. Henry Clay and Alice (Graybill) B.; A.B., Davidson (N.C.) Coll, 1911; B.D., Union Theol. Seminary, Richmond, Va., 1916; D.D., Davidson College, 1932; m. Alice Sturdivant Graham, Sept. 10, 1918; children—Henry Graybill, Tucker Graham, Alice Gordon, Lilian Baskerville. Teacher high sch., Decatur, Ga., 1911-13; supt.-evangelist home missions, Asheville (N.C.) Presbytery, 1916-18; chaplain C.A.C., A.E.F., 1918-19; pastor Presbyn. Ch., Hartsville, S.C., 1919-30; pres. Flora Macdonald Coll., Red Springs, N.C., from 1930. Democrat. Mason, K.P. Rotarian. Home: Red Springs, N.C. †

BEEBE, HAMILTON KELLER, lawyer; b. Chgo., Sept. 1, 1902; s. Walter Eugene and Katherine (Krausgrill) B.; A.B., U. Ill., 1923; J.D., Northwestern U., 1926; m. Helen McCullough, Oct. 9, 1926; children—Barbara Anne (Mrs. John G. Parrish, Jr.), James, Jane (Mrs. A. Richard Turner). Admitted to Ill. bar, 1926; partner firm Lord, Bissell & Brook, Chgo. Mem. Hinsdale Grade and Twp. High sch. bds., 6 yrs. Mem. Am., Ill., Chgo. bar assns., Lambda Chi Alpha, Delta Theta Phi. Republican. Episcopalian. Clubs: Law, Union League (Chgo.); Naples (Fla.) Country. Home: Fort Myers, Fla. Died Nov. 12, 1984; buried Naples, Fla.

BEEBE, WILLIAM BOVELL, lawyer; b. Wever, Iowa, May 1, 1919; s. Charles Howard and Ruth (Bovell) B.; m. Frances Jakobek, Aug. 5, 1950; children—Gerald Ross (by previous marriage), Beverly Ann, William Raymond, Thomas Bovell. Grad., Burlington Jr. Coll., 1938; A.B., George Washington U., 1946, LL.B., 1950. Legal adviser Office of Quartermaster Gen., Washington, 1950-51; practiced in, Washington, 1951—; mem. firm Glassie, Pewett, Dudley, Beebe & Shanks (and predecessor firms), 1955-84. Served to 2d lt. USAAF, 1941-45. Mem. Kappa Sigma, Phi Delta Phi. Clubs: Nat. Lawyers, Kenwood Golf and Country. Home: Bethesda, Md. Died June 9, 1984.

BEEBE, WILLIAM THOMAS, airline executive; b. Los Angeles, Jan. 26, 1915; s. Dewey Sheldon and Elsie (Thomas) B.; m. Nancy Lee Gragg, Feb. 3, 1951; children: Marshall J., Linda Lee, Deborah Susan. B.B.A., U. Minn., 1937. Coll. trainee Gen. Electric Co., 1938-40; personnel mgr. United Aircraft Corp., Hartford, Conn., 1940-46; v.p. Delta Air Lines, Inc., Atlanta, 1947-67, sr. v.p. adminstrn., 1967-70, pres., 1970-71, chmn. bd., chief exec. officer, 1971-80, chmn. bd., 1980-83, also dir.; dir. Am. Bus. Products, Inc., Provident Life & Accident Ins. Co. Former mem. Atlanta Bd. Edn.; mem. nat. adv. council Nat. Multiple Sclerosis Soc.; chmn. Ga. Soc. Prevention of Blindness. Episcopalian. Died June 9, 1984.

BEELKE, RALPH GILBERT, educator; b. Buffalo, Dec. 16, 1917; s. William and Elizabeth (Toy) B.; m. Hazel Hart, May 20, 1944; children—Christine, John, Ralph Alan. Diploma, Buffalo Sch. Fine Arts, 1939; Ed.B., U. Buffalo, 1939; M.A., Columbia Tchrs. Coll., 1947, Ed.D., 1952. Fabric designer, 1939-41, supr. art, Frankfort, N.Y., 1940-42, instr. art, Washingtonville, N.Y., 1947-49; deptl. asst. Columbia Tchrs. Coll., 1949-50; instr. art Md. State Coll., 1950-51; prof. art, chmn. dept. State U. N.Y. Coll., Fredonia, 1951-56; specialist edn. in arts U.S. Office Edn., 1956-58; exec. sec. Nat. Art Edn. Assn., 1958-62; head dept. of creative arts Purdue U., 1962-69, prof. art and design, 1969-77, head dept. creative arts, from 1977. Author: Curriculum Materials in Art Education, 1962; co-author: The Spectrum of Music, 1974; Editor: Art Edn. Bull, 1952-56, Art Edn, 1958-62; mem. good practices bd.: Arts and Activities mag, 1956-66; adv. editorial bd.: Sch. Arts mag, 1957-69; author: monthly column New Teaching Aids, 1954-62; paintings and prints in pvt. collections; exhibited regional and internat. shows. Mem. arts edn. delegation to, Soviet Union, 1960. Named Nat. Art Edn. Assn. Art Educator of Year, 1963. Mem. N.E.A., Coll. Art Assn., Am. Soc. Aesthetics, Am. Assn. U. Profs., Kappa Delta Pi, Phi Delta Kappa. Home: Lafayette, Ind.

BEERS, ROLAND FRANK, geologist, geophysicist; b. Owego, N.Y., June 6, 1899; s. Archibald Stephen and Jessie Bevans (Creveling) B.; m. Helen Elizabeth Clark, Oct. 29, 1921; children—Roland F., Barbara Helen. E.E., Rensselaer Poly. Inst., 1921; S.M., MIT,, 1928, Ph.D., 1943; postgrad., Harvard U. Grad. Sch. Arts and Scis., 1940-41. Instr. physics and elec. engring. Rensselaer Poly. Inst., Troy, N.Y., 1921-22; devel. engr. Western Electric Co., N.Y.C., 1922-23; mgr. A.S. Beers, Binghamton, N.Y., 1925; devel. engr. Raytheon Mfg. Co., Cambridge, Mass., 1925-26; physicist Submarine Signal Corp., Boston, 1927-28; party chief Geophys. Research Corp., Houston, 1928-31; party chief Geophys. Service, Inc., Dallas, 1931-34, v.p., 1934-36; pres., dir. The Geotechnical Corp., Dallas, 1936—; chmn. bd. and dir., 1947-56; pres., dir. Geotech. Corp. of Can., Ltd., Montreal, 1944-56; partner Beers and Heroy, Dallas, 1946-56; pres., dir. Roland F. Beers, Inc., 1955—; acad. dean Ethan Allen Community Coll., Manchester, Vt., 1973-75, then trustee; cons. AEC, 1957-85; pres. Geodynamics, Inc., Alexandria, Va., 1963-85; chmn. bd. Beers & Rodemann, Inc., Alexandria, 1957-85; pres. Knox Mining Corp., 1964-85; research asso., dept. geol. MIT, Cambridge, 1943-46; geophys. cons. U.S. Geol. Survey, Washington, 1943-46; mem. com. on measurement of geologic time NRC, 1945—, com. on seismic effects of detonations, 1945-46, com. on sedimentation, 1947—; head dept. fuel resources, prof. geophysics Rensselaer Poly. Inst., Troy, N.Y., 1948-52; permanent adv. com. geol. dept. So. Meth. U., 1947; mem. adv. com. on geophysics Office Naval Research; mem. com. on rock mechanics Nat. Acad. Scis.; mem. Vt. Higher Edn. Council. Contbr. to tech. publs. Trustee Russell Sage Coll., Albany Med. Coll., Vt. Acad.; Mem. nat. com. on seismology and gravity IGY. Fellow Geol. Soc. Am., AAAS, Am. Acad. Arts and Scis.; mem. Am. Assn. Petroleum Geologists, Soc. Exploration Geophysicists (chmn. best paper award com. 1946-47), AIME, IEEE Am. Geophys. Union, Seismol. Soc. Am., Photog. Soc. Am., Royal Photog. Soc. (London), ASTM, Sigma Xi, Eta Kappa Nu, Tau Beta Pi, Alpha Tau Omega. Presbyn. Clubs: Cosmos (Washington); Harvard (Boston); MIT (N.Y.C.); Petroleum (Dallas), Brook Hollow (Dallas). Home: Dorset, Vt. Died July 9, 1985; buried Oakwood Cemetary, Troy, N.Y.

BEESLEY, JOSEPH L., ins. exec.; b. Alert, Ind., Aug. 24, 1904; s. John W. and Mary (Stephenson) B.; m. Alta M. Biddinger, June 27, 1924; children—Lester, John E. A.B., DePauw U., 1926. C.L.U. With Equitable Life Assurance Soc. U.S., from 1926, beginning as trainee, successively cashier, Denver, Phoenix, Syracuse, asst. cashier, N.Y.C., cashier, Chgo., agy. mgr., Syracuse, field v.p. charge N.Y. area agys., 1953, sr. v.p. charge sales, 1955-61, sr. v.p., asst. to chmn., 1961-69, spl. rep., from 1969. Commr., treas. Nat. Commn. Community Health Services, 1962-66; mem. regional health adv. com. USPHS, 1968-71; trustee Am. Fund Dental Edn., 1961-69, DePauw U. Mem. Equitable Group Millionaires, Equitable Order of Excalibur, Nat. Assn. Life Underwriters (chmn. edn. com. Chgo.; dist. dir. Syracuse 1947-48), Life Agy. Mgrs. Assn., Syracuse Life Trust Council, Life Ins. Agy. Mgmt. Assn. (dir. 1961-63), Am. Coll. Life Underwriters (pub. relations com.), Am. Life Conv. (chmn. agy. sect. 1960), Agy. Officers Round Table (chmn. 1959-60), Phi Beta Kappa, Delta Chi. Methodist. Clubs: Masons, Rotary, Garden City Country, Union League. Home: Garden City, N.Y.

BEHRMAN, ROLAND AUGUSTUS, physician; b. Waltham, Mass., May 25, 1889; s. Augustus Henry and Emily Augusta (Wiesner) B.; M.D. cum laude, Tufts Coll., 1911; m. Edna I. Wheeler, May 26, 1917; children—Theodore M., John W., Robert J. Intern, Boston City Hosp., 1912-13; resident physician Boston Consumptive Hosp., 1914-15; practiced internal medicine Nantucket, Mass., 1915, Boston, 1916-17; mem. faculty Tufts Coll. Med. Sch., 1916-17, asst. medicine, 1917; with med. dept. John Hancock Ins. Co. from 1919, v.p., med. dir. from 1951. Served as capt. M.C., U.S. Army, France, Germany, 1917-19. Mem. A.M.A., Mass., Boston med. socs. Conglist. Contbr. articles med., ins. jours. Home: Marshfield, Mass. †

BEINECKE, EDWIN JOHN, trading stamp co. exec.; b. N.Y.C., July 1, 1913; s. Edwin John and Linda Louise (Maurer) B.; m. Helen Bryce Schiffer, Apr. 20, 1968; children—Sandra, Gretchen, Edwin. Student, Brown U., 1938. Various positions Mfrs. Trust Co., N.Y.C., 1935-37; v.p. Patent Scaffolding Co., L.I., 1948-58; with Sperry and Hutchinson Co., N.Y.C., from 1958, dir., from 1950, chmn. exec. com., from 1976; dir. Am. Mfrs. Mut. Ins. Co.; Mem. adv. bd. Yale Library Assos., 1971. Trustee Human Resources Sch., Alberton, N.Y., 1952; trustee Middlesex Sch., Concord, Mass., from 1977; chmn. Harry S. Truman Good Neighbor Award Found.; hon. chmn. U.S. Ski Team Fund, 1965. Served with U.S. Army, World War II. Recipient award Roth Sch. Bus. L.I. U., 1974; Distinguished leadership award L.I. Comml. Rev., 1971. Mem. Nat. Cowboy Hall of Fame, Norwich Area C. of C. Clubs: Union League, N.Y. Yacht, Ocean Reef, Westhampton Yacht Squadron, Westhampton Country, Creek, Indpls, Marco Polo. Home: Remsenburg, N.Y.

BEKINS, MILO W., business executive; b. Sioux City, Ia., Dec. 21, 1891; s. Martin and Katherine (Cole) B.; ed. pub. schs.; m. Dorothy E. Watson, Feb. 24, 1917; children—Barbara, Virginia, June, Milo. With automobile agy. Berkins Speers Motor Co., Los Angeles, 1909-16; successively chmn., vice chmn. dir. Bekins Van & Storage Co. of Cal., Los Angeles, Bekins Van & Storage Co. of Ariz., Phoenix, Bekins Van and Storage Co. of N.M., after 1948; officer Bekins Van Lines Co., Omaha, after 1939; dir., mem. finance com. Douglas Aviation Co.; dir. Citizens Nat. Bank. Mem. adv. bd., nat. council Boy Scouts Am., after 1948. Mem. Nat. Furniture Warehouse Assn. (past pres.), Cal. Van and Storage Assn. (past pres.), Beverly Hills C. of C. (past pres.). Mason (Shriner). Clubs: California, Los Angeles Country, Bel Air Bay (Los Angeles). Home: Los Angeles, Calif. Died Mar. 24, 1982.

BEKKER, KONRAD, economist; b. Berlin, Germany, May 24, 1911; s. Paul and Dorothea M. (Zelle) B.; Dr. fur., U. Basie (Switzerland), 1935, Ph.D., 1936; postgrad. fellow, Brookings Instn., 1938-39; m. Sarah McInteer, Mar. 15, 1944. Instr. econs. U. Ky., 1939-43; economist OSS, 1944-45, State Dept., 1945-81; adviser Joint Philippine-Am. Finance Commn., 1947. ECAFE working group on econ. development and placing. 1952, 56, ECLA meeting. La Paz, 1957; attache Am. embassy, New Delhi, India, 1951-53; 1st sec. Am. embassy, Rangoon, Burma, 1958-62; counselor for economic affairs Am. Embassy, Bern, Switzerland, 1962-64; 1st sec. Am. embassy, Bangkok, Thailand, 1964-81. Served to 2d lt. AUS, 1943-46. Mem. Am. Econ. Assn., Assn. Far Eastern Studies. Author articles. Home: New York, N.Y. Died June 26, 1981.

BELFIELD, JOHN COTTON, advertising executive; b. Phila., Apr. 2, 1906; s. Percy C. and Harriet (Coffin) B.; B.A., Pa. State U., 1928; m. Lillian F. Baker, Dec. 27, 1930; 1 dau., Nancy C. (Mrs. James Robert Bower). Account exec. N. W. Ayer & Son, advt., 1928-40; advt. mgr. Gelatin Products Corp., 1941-44; Detroit mgr. Good Housekeeping mag., 1944-45; joined Lewis & Gilman, Inc., advt., Phila., 1945, pres., chmn. bd. Mem. Delta Upsilon. Clubs: Merion Golf (Ardmore, Pa.); Racquet (Phila.). Home: Bryn Mawr, Pa. Died Mar. 13, 1982.

BELIVEAU, ALBERT, judge; b. Lewiston, Me., Mar. 27, 1887; s. Severin and Cedulie (Roberge) B.; LL.B., U. Me., 1911; LL.D., Assumption Coll., 1956; m. Margaret A. McCarthy, Aug. 6, 1935; children—Albert J., Severin M., Judith E. Admitted to Me. bar, 1911; practiced in Rumford, 1911-35; judge Superior Ct. Me., 1935-54; asso. justice Supreme Ct. of Me. from 1954. Address: Rumford, Me. †

BELKIN, JOHN NICHOLAS, zoologist, educator; b. Petrograd, Russia, Oct. 24, 1913; s. Nicholas Paul and Ina (Tardent) B.; came to U.S., 1928, naturalized, 1938; student Harvard U., 1931-33; B.S., Cornell U., 1938, Ph.D., 1946; m. Natalie Yantsin (div.); children—Nicholas J., Tanya, Natasha J.; m. Lorraine Lyla Marvin (dec. 1967); children—Laura T., Michael J., Elisabeth J.; m. Sharon Lee Shannon; 1 son, Karl E. Asst. then instr. entomology Cornell U., 1938-42, 46; asst. research specialist entomology Rutgers U., 1946; assoc. prof. biology Associated Colls. Upper N.Y., 1946-49; resident head biology dept. Mohawk Coll., Utica, N.Y., 1946-48, Sampson Coll., also Champlain Coll., 1948-49; mem. faculty UCLA, from 1949, prof. zoology, 1958-79, prof. emeritus, 1979-80. Served to capt. AUS, 1942-46; PTO. NSF grantee, 1955-66, USPHS grantee, 1962—, Med.

Research and Devel. Command, U.S. Army, 1963-76. Fellow AAAS, Entomol. Soc. Am.; mem. Soc. Systematic Zoology (council), Sigma Xi, Phi Kappa Phi. Author: The Mosquitoes of the South Pacific, 2 vols., 1962; Fundamentals of Entomology, 1972; also numerous research papers. Home: Los Angeles, Calif. Died Apr. 25, 1980.

BELKNAP, CHAUNCEY, lawyer; b. Roselle, N.J., Jan. 26, 1891; s. Chauncey and Emma Louise (McClave) B.; m. Dorothy Lamont, June 26, 1926; children—Louise (Mrs. David G. Carter), Robert Lamont, Barbara. Litt.B., Princeton, 1912; LL.B., Harvard, 1915. Bar: N.Y. bar 1916, D.C. bar 1966. Legal sec. to Justice Oliver Wendell Holmes, U.S. Supreme Ct., 1915-16; mem. firm Patterson, Belknap Webb & Tyler (and predecessor firms), N.Y.C., 1920-80, counsel, 1981-84; past dir. Am. Steel Foundries, Lehn & Fink Products Corp. Author: chpt. The Modern Princeton. Past mem. visitors com. Harvard Law Sch.; Trustee emeritus Princeton U., Internat. House, N.Y.C.; Pres. Nat. Alumni Assn. Princeton U., 1938-41. Commd. 2d lt., inf. U.S. Army, 1917; overseas with A.E.F., 1st Div. and G.H.Q., 1917-19; promoted capt. demobilized with rank maj. O.R.C. Decorated Legion of Honor France; cited by G.H.Q. U.S.). Fellow Am. Bar Found.; mem. Am. Law Inst., Am., N.Y. State (pres. 1960) bar assns), Bar Assn. City N.Y. (v.p. 1966), Harvard Law Sch. Assn. N.Y.C. (pres. 1957), N.Y. County Lawyers Assn., Phi Beta Kappa Assos., Phi Beta Kappa. Clubs: University (N.Y.C.), Century (N.Y.C.), Princeton (N.Y.C.). Home: New York, N.Y. Dec. Jan. 24, 1984.

BELL, ARTHUR DONALD, author, psychologist, university administrator; b. Vancouver, Wash., July 17, 1920; s. Arthur and Lois Myrtle (Cox) B.; m. Evelyn Brantley, June 2, 1944; 1 dau., Judy. B.A., William Jewell Coll., 1942; M.A., Southwestern Sch. Religious Edn., 1945, D.R.E., 1949; Ed.D. with honors, 1960; Ph.D., U. London; postgrad., Menninger Found. Clinic, Central Bapt. Theol. Sem., Asia Grad. Sch. State sec., coll. work Mo. Baptists, 1944-46; psychol. intern Miss. State Hosp.; dean, prof. religious edn. and psychology So. Ill. U., 1946-48; asst. to pres. chmn. dept. psychology Miss. Coll., 1948-51; dir. grad. studies, prof. psychology Sch. Religious Edn., Southwestern Bapt. Theol. Sem., 1951-60, prof. psychology and human relations, from 1963; exec. v.p.-pres. Howard Payne U., 1960-63; adj. prof. psychology Tex. Christian U., 1968-72; cons. in mental health U. Tex.; Vis. prof., lectr. Baylor U., U. Tex., Golden Gate Bapt. Theol. Sem., Philippine Bapt. Theol. Sem., Hong Kong Coll.; chmn. arts bd. St. John's Coll. Southwestern writing grantee, 1967, 70; adviser Baguio com. for AID grant to pres. Philippines, 1968. Author: Creative Arts, 1939, The Arts in Our Churches, 1948, How to Get Along with People, 1960, Spanish edit., 1972, Korean edit., 1975, The Changing Family and the Unchanging Word, 1967, In Christian Love, 1968, The Family in Dialogue, 1968, Chinese edit., 1978, The Family Together, 1968; co-author: Dimensions of Christian Writing, 1970, The Marriage Affair, 1972, (4 nat. book-of-month club selections), also articles in nat. publs.; Area editor: Ency. of So. Bapts; Papers and memoirs deposited in, Southwest Collection Tex. Tech. Biog. Hall, U. Manchester, Eng. Past pres. Tarrant County Mental Health Assn.; mem. Miss., Tex. mental health bds., chmn. archtl. awards, Santa Fe. Named Achiever, Alumnus of Year William Jewell Coll., 1971; recipient Wisdom award, 1971; Distinguished Alumni award Southwestern, 1977. Mem. Santa Fe Opera (patron), Old Santa Fe Assn. (v.p., trustee), Sigma Nu. Home: Santa Fe, NM.

BELL, CLARENCE EDWIN, railroad exec.; b. Lydia, S.C., Nov. 25, 1888; s. Thomas Edwin and Clara (McMeekin) B.; student pub. schs. Columbia, S.C.; m. Mabel Woolston Haines, Sept. 20, 1915; children—Clarence Edwin, Olin Lee, William (dec.). Locomotive fireman So. Ry., 1905; brakeman S.A.L. Ry., 1906-11, dining car steward, clk., 1911-16, chief clk. dining car dept., 1916-17, asst. supt. dining cars, 1917-23, supt. dining cars, 1923-35, passenger traffic mgr., 1935-48, gen. passenger traffic mgr., 1948-51, v.p. in charge passenger traffic and pub. relations, 1951-53, v.p. charge pub. relations, 1953-58; pres. Railway Advisory Services, Inc., from 1959, dir. Nat. Ry. Publ. Co. Mem. Newcomen Soc., United States Chamber of Commerce, American Association Dining Car Officers (past pres.), Am. Assn. Passenger Traffic Officers (past pres.), Am. Assn. R.R. Ticket Agts. Clubs: Princess Anne Country (Virginia Beach, Va.); Virginia, Norfolk Yacht and Country (Norfolk), Commonwealth (Richmond). Home: Richmond, Va. †

BELL, JOHN JAMES, banker; b. Chgo., Jan. 3, 1936; s. John J. and Antonia Marie (Czerwinski) Belohlavek. B.S. in Social Scis, U. Detroit, 1959. With Gen. Motors Corp., Detroit, 1960-73, sr. research analyst, community affairs, 1967-69; asst. nat. dir. pub. relations Chevrolet Motor div., 1969-73; exec. dir. corp. communications B.F. Goodrich Co., Akron, Ohio, 1973-75; dir. corp. communications Bendix Corp., Southfield, Mich., 1975-77; sr. v.p. Bank of Am. NT&SA, San Francisco, 1977-82, radio and TV news writer, 1956-59; bd. dirs. Washington Campus Program, Inc., San Francisco Archdiocese Communications Center; trustee U. Detroit; mem. public info. com. Bus. Roundtable. Named 1 of 10 Top Names in Corp. Public Relations Bus. Week mag., 1979. Home: Danville, Calif. Dec. Oct. 9, 1982.

BELL, ROBERT M., educator; b. Thomas County, Ga., June 15, 1889; s. William H. and Gertrude (Mims) B.; student Johnson Acad., 1910-13, Johnson Bible Coll., Kimberlin Hts., Tenn., 1913-16, B.A., 1918; student Manitoba U., Winnepeg, 1916-17; M.A., University of Tenn., Knoxville, 1924; Doctor of Laws, Milligan College, 1950; m. Myrtle Dekle, June 15, 1920; children—Robert Dekle, Betty Jane. Ordained to Christian ministry, June 1915, student minister, 1915-18; pastor, St. James Christian Ch., Winnipeg, Manitoba, 1918-19; provincial sec. Canadian Brotherhood Fedn., 1919-20; instr. economics and sociology, Johnson Bible Coll., 1920-23; instr. economics, U. of Tenn., 1923-41; pres. Johnson Bible Coll. from 1941; pastor, First Christian Church, Harriman, Tenn., 1923-44. Served as chaplain, World War I. Mem. Am. Econ. Assn., Am. Acad. Polit. and Social Science. Editor: Blue & White, from 1949. Home: Kimberlin Heights, Tenn. †

BELL, ROBERT SAMUEL, electronics company executive; b. Milw., May 29, 1915; s. Arthur Zwebell and Nina Louise (Jacobsen) B.; A.B., U. Calif., 1936; J.D., Harvard, 1940; D.Sc., Heald Engring. Coll., 1957; m. Carolyn Crowell, Jan. 2, 1943; 1 son, Robert McKim. Bar: Calif. 1940. Atty., Dept. of Justice, 1941-43; pvt. practice, 1946-48; owner, mgr. Burnham Mfg. Co., 1947-48, now merged into Packard-Bell; asst. to pres. Packard-Bell Electronics Corp., 1948, v.p., 1949-51, exec. v.p., 1951-56, pres. 1956-61, pres., chmn. bd. 1961-64, chmn. bd., from 1964; from 1968; dir. Gen. Telephone Co. of Calif. Vice pres., finance chmn., mem. exec. bd. Great Western area council Boy Scouts; bd. regents St. John's Hosp., Santa Monica; vis. com. Grad. Sch. Mgmt., U. Calif. Los Angeles; bd. dirs. Mchts. and Mfrs. Assn., Calif. Museum Found.; trustee Orthopaedic Hosp., Los Angeles. Served from pvt. to maj. USAAF, World War II; judge adv. 20th Air Force. Recipient Silver Beaver award Boy Scouts, 1958. Mem. Fed., Calif. bar assns., Los Angeles C. of C. (dir.), Navy League, Def. Orientation Conf. Assn., Town Hall, Radio Pioneers, Beverly Hills Wine and Food Soc., Judge Advs. Assn., Confrerie des Chevaliers du Tastevin (grand officer), Commanderie de Bordeaux, Chaine des Rotisseurs, Phi Kappa Sigma (dir.). Clubs: Harvard, Army-Navy, Jonathan, Bel Air Bay, Los Angeles Country (Los Angeles). Home: Los Angeles, Calif. Deceased.

BELUSHI, JOHN, actor, writer; b. Chgo.; m. Judy Jacklin, 1976. Former mem. Second City improvisation group, Chgo.; appeared in: Nat. Lampoon's rock/comedy revue Lemmings; writer, actor, then dir.: Nat. Lampoon's rock/comedy revue The Nat. Lampoon Radio Hour; actor, writer, dir.: Nat. Lampoon's rock/comedy revue The Nat. Lampoon Show; actor, writer: TV series Saturday Night Live, NBC-TV, 1975-79; TV appearances include spl. Richard Pryor Show; films include Go'in South, 1978, National Lampoon's Animal House, 1978, Old Boyfriends, 1979, 1941, 1979, The Blues Brothers, Continental Divide, 1981, Neighbors, 1981; rec. artist: films include Blues Brothers. Mem. AFTRA. Address: New York, N.Y.

BEMENT, DOROTHY MONTGOMERY, prin. girls' sch.; b. Lansing, Mich., June 14, 1890; d. Arthur Orrin and Vina Lou (Mosher) B.; A.B., Smith Coll., 1912, A.M., 1920. Teacher Miss Glendinning's Sch., New Haven, 1912-15, Miss Capen's Sch. for Girls, Northampton, 1915-21, Walnut Hill Sch., Natick, Mass., 1921-24; prin. Northampton Sch. for Girls from 1924. Mem. Headmistresses Assn. of the East, Nat. Assn. of Prins. of Schs. for Girls, N.E. Assn. of Schs. and Colls., Am. Assn. of Univ. Women. Conglist. Editor of Les Malheurs de Sophie, 1915. Home: Northampton, MA. †

BENCHLEY, NATHANIEL GODDARD, writer; b. Newton, Mass., Nov. 13, 1915; s. Robert and Gertrude (Darling) B.; B.S., Harvard U., 1938; m. Marjorie Bradford, May 19, 1939; children—Peter Bradford, Nathaniel Robert. Reporter, N.Y. Herald Tribune, 1939-41; asst. editor drama dept. Newsweek, 1946-47. Author: Side Street (novel), 1950; The Frogs of Spring (play), 1953; Robert Benchley (biography), 1955; The Great American Pastime (movie), 1956; One to Grow On (novel), 1958; Sail a Crooked Ship, 1960; The Off Islanders, 1961 (filmed as The Russians are Coming The Russians are Coming, 1965); Catch a Falling Spy, 1963; A Winter's Tale, 1964; The Visitors, 1965; A Firm Word or Two, 1965; The Monument, 1966; Welcome to Xanadu, 1968 (filmed as TV play Sweet Hostage), 1975; The Wake of the Icarus, 1969; Lassiter's Folly, 1971; The Hunter's Moon, 1972; Humphrey Bogart (biography), 1975; (novel) Portrait of a Scoundrel, 1979; Sweet Anarchy, 1979; also articles and fiction stories pub. various nat. mags., and several books for younger readers, including Gone and Back, 1971, Only Earth and Sky Last Forever, 1972, Bright Candles, 1974; Beyond the Mists, 1975; A Necessary End, 1976; Kilroy and the Gull, 1977; editor: The Benchley Roundup, 1954. Clubs: Pacific (Nantucket, Mass.); Coffee House; Century Assn. (N.Y.C.). Home: Siasconset, Mass. Died Dec. 14, 1981.

BENDER, MORRIS B., educator, neurologist; b. Russia, June 8, 1905; s. Boris and Anne (Nemirowsky) B.; came to U.S., 1914, naturalized, 1924; B.S., U. Pa., 1927, M.D., 1931; fellow Yale, 1936-37; m. Sara Spirtes, June 28, 1936; children—Barbara (Mrs. Martin Steiner), Adam, Barnaby, Victor, Leila. Intern Temple U. Hosp., 1931-32; resident neurology Montefiore Hosp., 1932-33, Mt. Sinai Hosp., 1933-35; head lab. exptl. neurology N.Y.U., 1938-43, mem. faculty, 1946-66, prof. clin. neurology, 1951-66; clin. prof. neurology Columbia Coll. Phys. and Surg., 1953, Goldschmidt prof. neurology, 1968-83; dir. neurology Mt. Sinai Hosp., N.Y.C., 1951-83, prof., chmn. dept. neurology Sch. Medicine, 1966-83, Henry P. Georgette Goldschmidt prof., chmn. emeritus, 1973-83; dir. neurol. service Bellevue Hosp., N.Y.C., 1951-61; adj. prof., neuropsychology program City U. N.Y., 1974; cons. visual scis. study sect. USPHS, 1962-64; mem. nat. research council VA, 1948. Served to comdr. USNR, 1943-46. Recipient Jacobi medal Mt. Sinai Hosp., 1957; So. Cross for sci. achievement (Brazil). Mem. Am. Neurol. Assn. (v.p. 1963 pres. 1972-73), Internat. Congress Neurology (treas. 1965-77, hon. treas., 1977), Am. Physiol. Soc., Alpha Omega Alpha; hon. mem. French, Israeli, Can., Brit. neurol. socs. Contbr. numerous articles in field. Spl. research vision perception. oculomotor system, neurophysiology. Home: Great Neck, N.Y. Died Jan. 23, 1983.

BENEDETTO, FRANCIS ARISTIDE, physicist, educator; b. Macon, Ga., Mar. 30, 1914; s. Aristide A. and Gertrude (Kennington) B.; A.B., St. Louis U., 1936; M.S., Fordham U., 1940, Ph.D., 1946; H.H.D. (hon.), Loyola U., New Orleans, 1978. Joined Soc. of Jesus, 1931, ordained priest Roman Catholic Ch., 1944; mem. faculty Loyola U., New Orleans, from 1947, prof. physics, from 1957, chmn. dept. physics and math., 1955-57, chmn. dept. physics, 1957-67, chmn. research grants com., 1958-63, chmn. sci. facilities com., 1961-65, exec. asst. to pres., from 1966, dir. creative improvement, from 1978, also mem., sec. bd. dirs., from 1965. Vice pres. communications WWL-AM-FM-TV, 1966-78. Chief radiol. sect. New Orleans CD, 1951-57, dep. chief, from 1957; regional counselor in physics for La., Am. Inst. Physics-Am. Assn. Physics Tchrs., 1961-63, 65-70. Trustee Spring Hill Coll., from 1973. Recipient spl. citation and award outstanding record tng. young scientists, Research Corp., 1957. Mem. Am. Phys. Soc., Am. Assn. Physics Tchrs., Am. Geophys. Union, La. Acad. Sci., New Orleans Acad. Sci., Sigma Xi, Sigma Pi Sigma, Blue Key. Spl. research cosmic rays. Contbr. articles. Address: New Orleans, La. Died Dec. 2, 1979; buried Mobile, Ala.

BENEDICT, HARRY E., corp. exec.; b. Neillsville, Wis., May 20, 1890; s. J. Sidney and Celia Ruth (Reed) B.; B.A., U. Wis.; m. Frances Holmburg, Apr. 16, 1921; children—Russell Reed, Stephen Gordon. Officer, Nat. City Bank, N.Y.C., 1918-19; asso. Frank A. Vanderlip, from 1919; pres. Elcamp Corp.; v.p. Barker Bros., Inc.; chmn. and dir. Palos Verdes Corp.; dir. Am. Airlines, Bill Bros. Pub. Co. Sec. Wis. Highway Commn., 1912-16. Exec. sec. War Savings Commn., Treasury Dept., Washington, 1917-18, War Loan Bd., 1918. Mason (32). Clubs: University India House, Downtown Athletic (N.Y.C.); Sleepy Hollow Country.†

BENITEZ, FRANCISCO, educator; b. Pagsangan, Laguna, P.I., June 4, 1887; s. Higinio and Soledad (Francia) B.; grad. Philippine Normal Sch., 1904; grad. Western Ill. Teachers Coll., 1908; B.S. in Edn., Columbia, 1910, M.A., 1914; m. Paz Marquez, of Lucena, P.I., Dec. 20, 1914; children—Francisco, Virginia, Roberto, Vicente. Supervisor Bur. of Edn., P.I., 1910-13; dir. Sch. of Edn., U. of Philippines, 1914-18; dean Coll. of Edn., same, since 1918. Editor Philippine Jour. of Edn. Pres. Philippine Normal Sch. Alumni Assn.; mem. bd. dirs. World Fed. of Edn. Assns. Recipient distinguished service medal, Columbia U., 1929. Mem. Nat. Federation of Teachers (pres. 1929-35), Inst. of Pacific Relations. Author: What is an Educated Filipino?, 1923; Story of Great Filipinos, 1924. Address: Manila, Philippines. Deceased.

BENJAMIN, ADAM, JR., congressman; b. Gary, Ind., Aug. 6, 1935; s. Adam and Margaret (Marjanian) B.; m. Patricia Ann Sullivan, July 31, 1966; children—Adam III, Alison Louise, Arianne. B.S., U.S. Mil. Acad., 1958; J.D., Valparaiso U., 1966. Bar: Ind. bar 1966, U.S. Supreme Ct. bar 1966. Zoning adminstr., City of Gary, 1963-65; exec. sec. to mayor Gary, 1965-66; atty. firm Benjamin, Greco & Gouveia, Gary, 1973-76; mem. Ind. Ho. of Reps. from Lake County, 1966-70, Ind. Senate from 4th Dist., 1970-76, 95th-97th Congresses from 1st Ind. Dist. Served with USMCR, 1952-54; from 2d lt. to 1st lt. U.S. Army, 1958-61. Mem. Am., Ind. bar assns. Office: Gary, Ind. Dec. Sept. 1, 1982.

BENJAMIN, RALPH JAMES, newspaper editor; b. Lafayette, Ind., Sept. 22, 1890; s. Rial and Evangeline (Conkling) B.; A.B., U. of Wash., 1914; m. Mabel M. Merrifield, May 14, 1916; children—Jackson Ralph, Jeanne Evelyn. Editor U. of Wash. Daily, 1914; reporter with Seattle Sun, 1914-15, Seattle Times, 1915; mng. editor Morning Olympian, Olympia, Wash., 1916-17; editor Evening Recorder and Morning Olympia, 1918-19; asst. city editor Seattle Star, 1919; editor Tacoma Times, 1921-28; editor Portland (Ore.) News, 1929-30; editor Seattle (Wash.) Star, 1930-31; editorial dir. Portland (Ore.) News-Telegram, Tacoma (Wash.) Times and Seattle (Wash.) Star, 1931-33; state supervisor of public utilities, 1934-38; supervisor of transportation, state Dept. Pub. Service, 1941; now pub. relations officer Joint Council of Teamsters, No. 28; editor The Washington Teamster. Mem. Sigma Delta Chi. Mason (32 deg., Shriner). Home: Seattle, Wash. †

BENN, BEN, artist; b. Russia, 1884; student Nat. Acad. Design (N.Y.C.), 1904-08. One man shows The Artists' Gallery, 1938, 41, 49; Egan Gallery, 1947, Hackner Gallery, 1950, 52, 53; Walker Art Center, 1953; Butler

Inst. Am. Art, 1954, Salpeter Gallery, 1956, 57, 59, Babcock Gallery, 1963, 65, 67, 70; exhibited group shows Pa. Acad. Fine Arts, Phila., 1942, 52, Met. Mus. Art, 1952, Whitney Mus. Am. Art, N.Y.C., 1932-34, 35, 49, 62-63, U. Neb., 1951, 52, 57, Riverside Mus., N.Y.C., 1954, 55, Musee Cantini, Marseille, France, 1956, Madison Sq. Garden, N.Y.C., 1958, Coliseum, N.Y.C., 1959. Providence Art Club, 1965, and numerous others; represented in permanent collections Albany (N.Y.) Inst. Art, Balt. Mus. Art, Butler Art Inst., Youngstown, O., Knoxville (Tenn.) Art Center, Kroller-Mueller Found., The Hague, The Netherlands, Met. Mus. Art, Mus. City N.Y., Newark Mus., Wlaker Found., Mpls., Watkins Meml. Gallery of Am. Univ., Washington, Whitney Mus. Am. Art, U. Minn., Mpls. Recipient Henry Scheidt meml. award, 1952, Carol Beck Gold medal; Marjory Waite award Am. Acad. Arts and Letters, 1971. Home: New York City, NY. †

BENNETT, ALONZO, business exec.; b. Graves County, Ky., Jan. 31, 1890; s. John B. and Mary Emma (Cox) B.; ed. pub. schs.; m. Florine Janice Dumbauld, Mar. 10, 1914. Employed in local freight office C.,R.I.&P. Ry., Memphis, 1906-08; loading clk., advancing to asst. sec. Memphis Terminal Corp., 1909-19; office and traffic mgr. Jerome Fentress & Co., cotton merchants, 1920-21; partner Finley & Bennett, 1922-25; traffic mgr. Federal Compress & Warehouse Co., 1925-40, v.p. since 1940, dir. and mem. exec. com. Mem. shippers' adv. com. Defense Transport Administration, National Cotton Council (vice chairman Tennessee-Kentucky State unit; delegate from Tennessee); mem. exec. and cotton coms. S.E. and S.W. Shippers Adv. Boards; mem. exec. com. and dir. Memphis Freight Bur.; past pres. Southwestern Indsl. Traffic League; mem. exec. com. Agrl. Council of Ark. (chmn. com. traffic and transportation); dir. Nat. Indsl. Traffic League (past pres., mem. exec. com.); sec.-treas. bd. dirs. Tenn. Compress and Cotton Warehouse Assn.; founder mem. Am. Soc. of Traffic and Transportation; mem. bd. dirs. Asso. Traffic Clubs of Am.; chmn. traffic and transportation com., Memphis C. of C., mem. Assn. I.C.C. Practitioners (com. on budget I.C.C.). Ark.-Mo. Ginners Assn., (mem. adv. exec. com.), Nat. Freight Traffic Assn. (mem. exec. com.), So. Traffic League, Asso. Traffic Clubs of Am. (dir.), Delta Council, Trans-Mo.-Kan. Shippers Board (cotton committee). Licensed to practice before Interstate Commerce Commission. Episcopalian. Mason. Clubs: Memphis Country, Memphis Traffic, Chicago Traffic, Railroad Passenger Traffic.†

BENNETT, EDWARD L., pres. Nat. Service Co.; b. Cambridge, Mass., 1888; grad. Harvard College, 1908. Pres. Nat. Service Companies. Trustee Cambridgeport (Mass.) Savings Bank; pres. and dir. Metropolitan Ice Co., Springfield Ice and Fuel Co.; v.p. and dir. Albany Castings Co., Walker Coal and Ice Co.; dir. Hoosac Storage and Warehouse Co., Nat. Assn. of Ice Industries, Nat. Service Ice Mfg. Co., New England Cities Ice Co., Cape Cod Laundry Co.; treas., dir., Murray Y-D Garage, Worcester. Home: Cambridge, Mass. †

BENNETT, HARRY JACKSON, educator; b. Bernice, La., Aug. 1, 1904; s. Ernest Jerome and Alice Gertrude (Jones) B.; m. Jane Tobie, Dec. 29, 1931; children—Carolyn (Mrs. Charles Donald Brown), Sarah Jane (Mrs. Edward Brash), Katherine Ann (Mrs. James Gregory May). B.S., La. State U., 1926; M.S., U. Ill., 1928, Ph.D., 1935. From instr. to prof. zoology La. State U., Baton Rouge, 1929-74, prof. emeritus, from 1975; asst. to dean Coll. Arts and Scis., 1938-42; dir. Marine Lab., 1946-56; dir. Sci. Tng. Programs Office, 1969-74, asso. dean Grad. Sch., coordinator research, 1973-74; fellow in zoology U. Ill., 1932-33; scientist, sr. scientist USPHS, 1947-49; prof. marine zoology Gulf Coast Research Lab., summers 1956-68; Mem. U.S. Schistosomiasis Commn., 1945-46, So. Regional Edn. Bd. Marine Scis. Com., 1953-54; dir. Vis. Scientist Program in La., 1958-65; cons. Mid-Continent Oil and Gas Assn., 1955-57, Outdoor Ednl. Center, St. Martin Parish Sch. Bd., Lafayette Natural History and Planetarium, from 1969. Contbr. articles to profl. jours. Served with San. Corps AUS, 1942-46. Decorated Bronze Star medal.; Distinguished Faculty fellow La. State U., 1968. Fellow AAAS (mem. council 1960-70); mem. Am. Soc. Parasitology, Am. Inst. Biol. Scis., Assn. Southeastern Biologists (pres. 1965-66), Am. Micros. Soc., Am. Soc. Zoologists, Am. Soc. Limnologists and Oceanographers, Soc. Systematic Zoology, La. Acad. Sci. (pres. 1969, Distinguished Service award 1973), Miss., Tenn. acads. sci., Assn. Acads. of Sci. (sec.-treas. 1962-65, pres. 1968-69, Distinguished Service award 1969), La. Sci. Tchrs. Assn. (pres. 1961-62, certificate of merit 1962), La. Jr. Acad. Sci. (chmn. 1957-65), Sci. Club, Sigma Xi, Phi Kappa Phi, Omicron Delta Kappa. Club: Kiwanian. Home: Baton Rouge, LA.

BENNETT, HOWARD CLIFTON, ret. coll. pres.; b. Cleburne, Tex., June 13, 1910; s. Howard C. and Lillie (Freeman) B.; student U. Tenn., 1928-29; B.A., Union U., Jackson, Tenn., 1936; Th.M., So. Bapt. Theol. Sem., Louisville, 1939; D.D., East Tex. Bapt. Coll., Marshall, 1948; m. Mary Lee Hurt, May 6, 1935; children—Marilyn (Mrs. George W. Hillyer III), Kate (Mrs. John E. Fite), Susan (Mrs. Kenneth B. Livingston). Ordained to ministry Bapt. Ch., 1935; pastor in Carthage, Tenn., 1939-41, Vivian, La., 1941-43, Kilgore, Tex., 1943-60; pres. East Tex. Bapt. Coll., 1960-76, trustee coll., 1944-53. Mem. exec. bd. Bapt. Gen. Conv. Tex., 1943-52; mem. Tex. Bapt. Edn. Commn., 1953-60, chmn., 1959-60. Chmn. Gregg County chpt. A.R.C., 1945. Trustee So. Bapt. Theol. Sem., 1958-68; chmn. bd. Roy H. Laird Meml. Hosp., Kilgore, 1952-58. Mem. Marshall C. of C., Sigma Alpha Epsilon. Rotarian. Home: Marshall, Tex. Died Apr. 15, 1985.

BENNETT, ORVAL, economist; b. Chrisney, Ind., Aug. 4, 1887; s. John Stephen and Matilda (Baker) B.; B.S., Central Normal Coll., Danville, 1910, A.B., 1911, LL.B., 1911; A.B., Ind. State Univ., 1915, Am., 1917; grad. study, U. of Ill., 1920, Harvard, 1921; LL.M., St. Louis Univ., 1922, J.D., 1923; Ph.D., Brookings Instn., 1924; m. Mae Estella Tate, Aug. 13, 1916. Admitted to Ind. bar. 1911, and practiced in Danville, 1910-11; instr. in economics U. of Ill., 1920; prof. of economics, Washington Univ., St. Louis, since 1947. Research economist with Federal Trade Commn., Washington, 1923-24. Served as economist and price specialist St. Louis-Dallas Dist., O.P.A., 1945; spl. rep. U.S. Employment Service and N.Y.A., St. Louis Dist., 1933-35. Fellow Royal Econ. Soc. of London, Brookings Instn., Washington. Non-Partisan in politics. Methodist. Author: Student Manual in Business Law, 1940; Public Finance (with Lippincott), 1949; Dumping et Concurrence Deloyal, Revenue Economique Internat., for Aug., 1938. Contbr. to Dictionary of Am. Biography. Home: St. Louis, Mo. †

BENNETT, ROY COLEMAN, newspaper editor; b. Centertown, Ky., July 2, 1889; s. James Coleman and Semarimus (Barnard) B.; student U. of Ky.; B.J., U. of Mo., 1914; m. Margaret Curtiss Wilson, June 14, 1931; children—Joan Elizabeth, Helen Louise. Was reporter Carthage (Mo.) Press, 1914-16; then reporter on St. Petersburg (Fla.) Times, 1916; city editor Gadsden (Ala.) Journal, 1917; state editor New Orleans (La.) States, 1917-18; mng. editor Lexington (Ky.) Herald, 1918; city editor Manila (P.I.) Cablenews-American, 1918-19; asso. editor Manila (P.I.) Bulletin, 1919-22; traveling corr. and polit. writer, China, 1922-23; copy reader and foreign editor Phila. Bulletin, 1923-26; editor and gen. mgr. Manila Daily Bulletin since 1926. Baptist. Republican. Mason (32 deg., Shriner), Elk. Clubs: Rotary, Army and Navy, Manila Polo (Manila); Baguio (P.I.) Country; American (Shanghai, China). Home: Quezon City, Philippines. †

BENNETT, RUSSELL HOADLEY, mining engr.; b. Mpls., Nov. 30, 1896; s. Russell Meridan and Helen (Harrison) B.; m. Miriam Fletcher, May 31, 1924; children—Winslow W., Helen H. (Mrs. W.J. Beus), Miriam (Mrs. D.S. Leslie, Jr.), Fletcher, Meridan, David T., Noel F. Grad., Phillips Acad., Andover, Mass., 1915; A.B., Yale, 1920; postgrad., Columbia, 1920-21. Registered profl. engr., Minn. Chmn. Electro Manganese Corp., Knoxville, Tenn., 1941-56; chmn. Placer Devel., Ltd.; dir. Meriden Iron Co., Mpls., Sargent Land Co.; owner, operator Shoderee Ranch, Pincher Creek, Alta., Can., 1932-72; Chmn. bd. trustees Dunwoody Indsl. Inst. Mpls., 1937-61. Author: also articles in profl. jours. Quest for Ore. Commr. representing City Mpls. in Met. Drainage Commn., 1927-31. Mem. Am. Inst. Mining and Metall. Engrs. (William Lawrence Saunders gold medal 1978). Republican. Methodist. Clubs: Minneapolis (N.Y.C.), Explorers. (N.Y.C.), Century Assn. (N.Y.C.). Home: Minneapolis, Minn. Deceased.

BENNETT, THOMAS F., banking; b. Brooklyn, N.Y., Aug. 5, 1887; s. James Joseph and Mary A. (FitzHarris) B.; m. Ethel K. Shean, Nov. 25, 1919. With Am. Exchange Nat. Bank, New York, 1905-18; asst. treas., U.S. Mortgage & Trust Co., New York, 1918-28; vice pres. and dir., Colonial Trust Co., New York, 1928-33; vice pres. Continental Bank & Trust Co. of N.Y., 1933-48; v.p. Chem. Corn Exchange Bank, 1948-52, ret., mem. 30 Broad St. adv. bd.; dir. D. Kaltman & Co., Noma Lights, Inc., Brewster, Badeau & Co. Inc. Home: Freeport, N.Y.†

BENNETT, WELLS IRA, dean; b. Red Creek, N.Y., Aug. 1, 1888; s. Hulbert James and Myrtie May (Wells) B.; B.A., Syracuse U., 1911, D.F.A., 1947; M.S., U. of Mich., 1916; m. Sybil C. Kennedy, Dec. 20, 1913; children—Phyllis Kennedy (wife of Dr. C. R. Lowe), Edward Wells. Architectural draftsman, 1911-12; instr. in drawing U. of Mich., 1912-18, asst. prof. drawing and architecture, 1919-27, asso. prof. architecture, 1927-36, prof. from 1936, dir. Coll. of Architecture, 1937-38, dean Coll. of Architecture and Design from 1938. Pres. Assn. Collegiate Schools Architecture, 1942-44. Served as designer, Construction Div., U.S. Army, 1918-19. Mem. Mich. State Bd. of Registration, Architects, Engineers and Surveyors, from 1939 (pres. 1945, 53). Fellow Am. Institute Architects (director Detroit chapter 1936-37; vice president 1944-45; pres. 1946-47; member nat. com. on honor awards 1953-57; chmn. honor awards com. Detroit chpt. 1954); mem. Bldg. Research Inst., Michigan Society Architects (director 1935-37, 1943-44), Michigan Housing Association (director 1926-37), National Association Housing Officials, National Society Planning Officials, Alpha Rho Chi, Phi Kappa Phi, Tau Sigma Delta. Club: University (Ann Arbor). Writer of many articles on architecture and housing. †

BENNETT, WILLIAM HUNTER, church official; b. Taber, Alta., Can., Nov. 5, 1910; s. William Alvin and Mary (Walker) B.; came to U.S., 1933, naturalized, 1942; B.S., Utah State U., 1936, M.S., 1948; Ph.D., U. Wis., 1957; m. Patricia June Christensen, Apr. 12, 1950; children—Camille Kay, William Bradford, Mary Ann, Julee Hazel, Deborah Pat, Jacqueline. Asst. county agr. agt. Salt Lake County, 1937; county agr. agt. Carbon County, Utah, 1937-42; mem. faculty Utah State U., 1937-70, prof. agronomy, 1956-70, asst. dir. extension 1956-58, dir., 1962-70, acting dean Coll. Agr., 1958-60, dean, 1960-62; counselor state presidency Ch. of Jesus Christ of Latter Day Saints, 1952-60, regional rep. council of twelve, 1967-70, asst. to council of twelve, 1970-77, mem. 1st Quorum of Seventy, 1977-80. Sec.-treas. Utah Edn. TV Found., 1958-59, v.p., 1959-80. Served to capt., inf. AUS, 1942-46. Mem. Crop Sci. Soc. Am., Sigma Xi, Phi Kappa Phi, Alpha Zeta, Alpha Gamma Rho, Phi Sigma, Alpha Tau Alpha, Epsilon Sigma Phi. Rotarian. Author, co-author sci. papers. Home: Bountiful, Utah. Died July 23, 1980.

BENNION, HOWARD SHARP, trade assn. exec.; b. Vernon, Utah, Sept. 7, 1889; s. Israel and Jeannette (Sharp) B.; B.S., U.S. Mil. Acad., 1912; grad. U.S. Army Engrs. Sch., Washington, 1915; m. Marian Morris Cannon, Sept. 16, 1920. Commd. 2d lt. Corps Engrs., U.S. Army, 1912, served in France as chief of camouflage service, later as exec. officer for chief engr. of A.E.F., World War I; asst. chief engr. Fed. Power Commn., 1920-24; dist. engr. charge flood control work on lower Mississippi, New Orleans; dir. engring. Nat. Electric Light Assn., 1926-33; asst. mng. dir. Edison Electric Inst., 1933-39, mng. dir., 1939—. Decorated D.S.M. (Army); French Legion of Honor; Cross of Valor (Poland). Fellow Am. Inst. E.E., mem. Am. Soc. Mil. Engrs. Mem. Ch. of Jesus Christ of Latter Day Saints. Home: New York, N.Y.†

BENNION, HUGH CLARK, college dean; b. Logan, Utah, Sept. 14, 1906; s. Edwin T. and Mary (Clark) B.; B.S. (Danforth Found. fellow 1930), Utah State U., 1931; M.S., Iowa State U., 1939; postgrad. U. Oreg., 1945-46; Ed.D., Oreg. State U., 1950; postgrad. UCLA and Berkeley, 1965; m. Rachel Parrish, Sept. 5, 1930 (dec. 1954); 1 dau., Jean (Mrs. Merle W. Johnson); m. 2d, Marjorie Owens, June 10, 1955; children—David, Craig. Mem. faculty Ricks Coll., Rexburg, Idaho, 1931-42, 45-65, head dept. psychology, 1945-65, dean faculty, 1952-72, dean faculty emeritus, 1972-82; dir. employee counseling Hill AFB, 1942-45; mem. subcom. asso. degree programs Nat. League Nursing, 1960-66, steering com. dept. asso. degree programs, 1966-69. Chmn. Madison County Community Chest, 1955. Mem. Am. Coll. Personnel Assn., Soc. Advancement Edn., Idaho Psychol. Assn., Nat., Idaho edn. assns., N.W. Jr. Coll. Assn. (chmn. instl., research com.), Phi Delta Kappa, Psi Chi, Gamma Sigma Delta. Republican. Mem. Ch. of Jesus Christ of Latter Day Saints. Rotarian (past pres. Rexburg). Home: Rexburg, Idaho. Died Dec. 8, 1982.

BENNS, F(RANK) LEE, prof. history; b. Barre, N.Y., Mar. 7, 1889; s. George Williams and Kate Lydia (Lee) B.; A.B., magna cum laude, Syracuse U., 1914, A.M., 1916, Litt.D., same, 1939; Am. Antiquarian Soc. fellow in history, Clark U., 1919-20, Ph.D., 1920; research in League of Nations Library, 1928-29; m. Jessie Angeline Coon, Apr. 5, 1915; 1 dau., Kate Lee (Mrs. Keith B. Robinson). Teaching fellow in history, Syracuse U., 1916-18; instr. in history, Ind. U., 1920, asst. prof., 1921, asso. prof., 1924, prof., 1930-54; visiting professor, summers, Syracuse U., 1920, U. of Wash., 1926, U. of Chicago, 1930 and 1935, U. of British Columbia, 1936 and 1941. Sec. gen. conf. Inst. of Politics, Williamstown, Mass., 1925. Fellow Royal Historical Society; member of American and Indiana State Hist. Socs., Indiana Academy of Social Sci., Phi Beta Kappa, Phi Gamma Delta. Awarded Justin Winsor prize, Am. Hist. Assn., 1920. Presbyterian. Author: Europe's Return to War, 1940; Europäische Geschichte Seit 1870, 1952; Europe From 1914, 8th edit., 1954; European History from 1870, 4th edit., 1955. Home: Rensselaer, Ind. †

BENOIT, RICHARD CHARLES, JR., electronic engr.; b. East Orange, N.J., May 16, 1917; s. Richard Charles and Mary F. (Tierney) B.; m. Josephine M. Rasulo, June 5, 1943 (dec. June 1971); children—Richard Joseph, Joseph Edward; m. Marilyn Heit Chazan, Apr. 28, 1973. Student, RCA Inst., 1936-37; cert., Air U. Command and Staff Coll., 1958; grad., Syracuse U. Modern Engring. Program, 1969; D.Eng., Clayton U., 1976, D.Internat. Affairs (hon.), 1976. Radio theatre sound serviceman, Highlands, N.J., 1934-40; electronic technician U.S. Army Signal Corps Labs., Ft. Monmouth, N.J., 1940-42; project engr. USAF Watson Labs., Red Bank, N.J., 1945-50; with USAF Rome Air Devel. Center, Griffis AFB, N.Y., from 1950, unit chief to sect. chief in areas of radio navigation and telecommunications, chief communications processing and distbn. sect., from 1968; tech. adviser Hdqrs. USAF, Europe, 1953, 55; mem. U.S. del. NATO Telecommunications Conf., 1959-67; USAF tech. adv. telecommunications Spanish Air Force, 1961-64; spl. communications cons. Albany (N.Y.) Med. Coll., Union U., 1959-64; U.S. project officer for telecommunications, tech. data exchange program U.S. and NATO nations, also Republic of Korea, from 1959; gen. chmn. ann. Mohawk Valley mgmt. seminars, 1960, 61; public relations dir. IEEE Nat. Communications Symposium, 1955-58, exec. vice chmn., 1959, gen. chmn., 1960, bd. govs., 1961-66. Contbr. articles to profl. jours. Chmn. non-partisan tech. adv. com. to Congressman Mitchell, N.Y.; past mem. citizens adv. council Marcy (N.Y.) Psychiat. Center. Served with USCGR, 1942-43; to ensign

U.S. Maritime Service, 1944-45. Recipient Key to City of Utica Utica C. of C., 1959, Key to City of Utica Mayor of Utica, 1960; four cash awards and certs. for invention contbns. Dept. Air Force, 1959-69; Superior Performance award, 1963; AF Systems Command cert. of merit, 1973. Fellow IEEE (internal dir. 1974-75, dir. Region I 1974-75, chmn. Mohawk Valley sect. 1969-70, sec. 1967-68, mem. del. to USSR), AAAS; mem. N.Y. Acad. Scis. Roman Catholic. Home: Utica, N.Y. Deceased.*

BENSON, HERBERT ALLEN, architect; b. New Orleans, Sept. 1, 1888; s. John Batiste and Rosalie Olivia (Leininger) B.; student pub. schs.; m. Lena Cohen, June 12, 1913; 1 dau., Jesselyn Rose (Mrs. Samuel Zurik). With Emile Weil, 1902-33, v.p., 1920-33; pvt. archtl. practice, New Orleans, 1933—; v.p. Central Savs. & Homestead Assn. Comdr. Office Civilian Def., World War II; chmn. bd. New Orleans Mid-Winter Sports Assn., The Sugar Bowl, 1940—; mem. Vieux Carre Commn., 1928-52. Vice pres. bd. Upper Pontalba Commn., 1939-49; mem. Nat. Housing Adv. Com. 1946-49; Dir. Magnolia Sch., 1940-55. Mason (Shriner). Club: Colonial Country of New Orleans. Home: New Orleans, La.†

BENSON, HOWARD HARTWELL JAMES, naval officer (ret.); b. Baltimore, Md., Oct. 8, 1888; s. Adm. William Shepherd and Mary Augusta (Wyse) B.; B.S., U.S. Naval Acad., 1909; grad., Naval War Coll., 1930, Army War Coll., 1935; m. Elizabeth Rea Thompson, May 12, 1917; children—Mary Rea (wife of Lt. Allan M. Hudson), Howard Hartwell James. Commd. ensign U.S. Navy, June 1911, advanced through grades to commodore, 1944; served in battleships, submarines, destroyers, capt. U.S.S. H-2, 1913-15; capt. patrol vessels and destroyer, Bay of Biscay, World War I; assignment at U.S. Naval Acad., 1930-32; exec. officer U.S.S. Tenn., 1932-34; shore assignment U.S. Navy Dept., 1935-36; capt. U.S.S. Reina Mercedes, 1938-41, U.S.S. Washington 1941-42; chief of staff, 7th Naval Dist. and Gulf Sea Frontier, 1942-46; retired from active service, 1946. Awarded Navy Cross, Legion of Merit, Victory medal, 2d Nicaraguan campaign, Am. Defense service, Am. Theatre and European Theatre medals; decorated with Order of So. Cross (Brazil), Oak Leaf emblem (Britain). Mem. Am. Soc. for Professional Geographers. Roman Catholic. K.C. Clubs: Army Navy, Army Navy Country (Washington), Yacht (N.Y. and Annapolis). Home: Annapolis, Md. †

BENSON, JOHN CABOT, lawyer; b. Heron Lake, Minn., Feb. 27, 1890; s. John Wesley and Mary Harriet (Cabot) B.; student Hamline U., U. Wis., also U. Minn.; m. Edna Frances Server, June 10, 1914; children—Margaret Eleanor (Mrs. Clark R. Fletcher, Jr.), Mary Lois (Mrs. Fenton M. Davison); m. 2d, Sara Wingate Jordan, Dec. 29, 1951. Admitted to Minn. bar, 1912; practiced in that state; mem. Faegre & Benson, Mpls. Pres. Asso. Finance Co.; dir., mem. exec. committee Mpls. Gas Co.; dir. Fed. Cartridge Corp. Counsel, dir., exec. com. Mpls. War Chest, 1941-45; organizer, 1st atty. Mpls. Legal Aid. Mem. Am., Minn., Hennepin County (pres. 1938-39) bar assns., S.A.R., Mayflower Society, Phi Delta Phi, Sigma Alpha Epsilon. Home: Minneapolis, MN. †

BENSON, JOHN EDWARD, chemist; b. Merchantville, N.J., Oct. 21, 1924; s. Victor and Mary Scott (Yeamans) B.; m. Jane Lindahl, Dec. 23, 1973. B.S., Pa. State U., 1950; M.A., Princeton U., 1953, Ph.D., 1956. Asst. prof. chemistry Pa. State U., 1956-61, Gettysburg Coll., 1961-64; assoc. prof. chemistry Dickinson Coll., 1964-67, prof., 1967-69, Dana prof., 1969-81, chmn. dept., 1965-71; cons. dept. chem. engring. Stanford U.; sci. cons. Served with USAAF, 1943-46. NSF sci. faculty fellow, 1964-65; recipient research grants NSF, 1969, research grants Research Corp., 1962. Mem. Am. Chem. Soc., AAAS, Catalysis Soc. Am., Sigma Xi. Research surface chemistry, adsorption and catalysis. Home: Menlo Park, Calif. Oct. 22, 1983.

BENSON, LAWRENCE KERN, lawyer; b. Lake Charles, La., Jan. 19, 1906; s. George William and Lotta Emma (Tannehill) B.; m. Adele Foster, Aug. 24, 1933; children—Lawrence Kern, Robert George. LL.B., Tulane U., 1927. Bar: La. bar 1927, Tex. bar 1929, U.S. Supreme Court bar 1964. Pvt. practice law, Hammond, La., 1927-29; asso. firm Baker, Botts, Parker & Garwood, Houston, 1929; asso. firm Milling, Benson, Woodward, Hillyer, Pierson & Miller (and predecessors), New Orleans, 1929-35, partner, from 1936; prof. law Tulane U., 1962-64.; Sec.-treas., past pres. Atchafalaya Land Corp.; adv. dir. La. Land and Exploration Co.; mem. civil law sect., adv. com. mineral law project La. Law Inst., 1963-74; vice chmn. La. Adv. Commn. on Coastal and Marine Resources, 1971-73; mem. La. Sea Grant Adv. Council, 1974-77; chmn. Continuous Revision Com. Mineral Code La. Law Inst., 1977-81. Bd. visitors St. Martin's Protestant Episcopal Sch.; Mem. Pub. Affairs Research Council, Council for Better La., Met. Area Com., New Orleans. Fellow Am. Bar Found.; mem. Am., La., New Orleans bar assns., Assn. Bar City N.Y., Am. Law Inst., Order Coif, Mid-Continent Oil and Gas Assn., Am. Judicature Soc., Ind. Petroleum Assn. Am., Bartolus Soc., Assn. Henri Capitant, Sigma Phi Epsilon, Phi Delta Phi. Republican. Presbyterian (trustee, elder). Clubs: Boston (New Orleans), Petroleum (New Orleans), Plimsoll (New Orleans), New Orleans Country (New Orleans); City (Baton Rouge). Home: New Orleans, LA.

BENSON, LUCILLE, actress; b. Richard City, Tenn., July 17, 1914; d. John B. and Elma Lee (Kirby) B. B.A. Huntington Coll. Appeared in: Broadway plays Hotel Paradiso; TV appearances include Bosom Buddies; appeared in: films Little Fauss and Big Halsy. Mem. Screen Actors Guild, Actors Equity, AFTRA. Democrat. Home: Scottsboro, Ala. Dec. Feb. 17, 1984.

BENSON, ROBERT GREEN, publisher; b. Nashville, Mar. 19, 1889; s. John T. and Eva (Green) B.; student Wallace U. Sch. 1902-05; grad. Vanderbilt U., 1909; m. Maggie Mai Phillips, Mar. 29, 1916. Partner Benson Printing Co., Nashville, 1909-68, John T. Benson Pub. Co., 1937-68; dir. Garden Publs. Inc., 1941-60. Mem. U.S., Nashville chambers commerce. Mason. Clubs: Rotary, Bell Meade Country, Cumberland (Nashville). Home: Nashville, TN. †

BENSON, WILLIAM AUGUST, v.p. Railway Express Agency, Inc.; b. Highwood, Ill., July 3, 1887; s. Charles J. and Mary (Melbourn) B.; ed. pub. and high schs., 1895-1905; m. Katherine K. Pratt, of Waukegan, Ill., Sept. 17, 1910; children—William F., Sherwood M., Frank E. M., Katherine E.M. Began work as telegraph operator and agt. C. & N.W. R.R., 1905; accountant various r.rs. etc., 1905-12; chief clk., Wells Fargo & Co., 1912-18; asst. to v.p. and pres., Am. Ry. Express Co., 1918-29; exec. v.p. Ry. Express Agency, Inc., 1929-34, v.p. in charge of operations from 1934; v.p. and dir. Ry. Express Agency of Calif. Republican. Baptist. Mason.†

BENT, BRUCE ROGER, investment co. exec.; b. Great Neck, N.Y., May 25, 1937; s. Arthur Thomas and Grace Regina (Melia) B.; B.B.A., St. Johns U., 1961; M.B.A., N.Y. U., 1965; m. Nancy Ann DiGiovanna, Nov. 9, 1963; children—Bruce Roger, Arthur. Research asst. L.F. Rothschild & Co., N.Y.C., 1961-63; portfolio mgr. Tchrs. Ins. & Annuity Assn., N.Y.C., 1963-67; dir. corporate fin. Stone & Webster Securities Corp., N.Y.C., 1967-68; partner Brown & Bent, N.Y.C., 1968-73; v.p., treas., dir. Res. Fund, N.Y.C., pres.; dir. Res. Mgmt. Corp., Hyperion Fund. Co-founder, trustee Leeway Sch. for Handicapped Children, Stony Brook, N.Y.; bd. dirs. United Community Fund, N.Y.C., Bishops Com. for Cath. Charities. Served with USMC, 1957-58. Roman Catholic. Home: Great Neck, N.Y. Deceased.

BENT, WILLARD OSBORN, retail company executive; b. Chgo., Dec. 22, 1912; s. Charles H. and Imo (Baker) B.; student Purdue U., 1931-32; m. Ruth Ward, July 15, 1939; children—Christopher, Dennis. Buyer, Montgomery Ward & Co., N.Y.C. 1933-42; mdse. mgr. Lord & Taylor, N.Y.C., 1946-48, Stewart's, Louisville, 1948-56, Famous-Barr, St. Louis, 1956-60; v.p. J. W. Robinson Co., Los Angeles, 1960-65; pres., chmn. bd., Garfinkel, Brooks Bros., Miller & Rhodes Inc., Washington, 1965-78, vice chmn., 1978-80. Served to lt. (s.g.) USNR, 1943-45. Clubs: Union League (N.Y.C.); University, Burning Tree Country (Washington); Talbot Country (Easton, Pa.); George Town. Office: Washington, D.C. Died Oct. 9, 1984.

BENTER, CHARLES, band leader; b. N.Y. City, Apr. 29, 1887; s. Sigmund and Sarah (Hirsch) B.; ed. pub. schs., N.Y. City; hon. Dr. of Music from Columbus Univ., 1929; m. Anna Matilda Benter, June 16, 1916; 1 dau., Anna Martha. Enlisted as apprentice boy musician in U.S. Navy, Mar. 20, 1905; made bandmaster at 19; organized Navy Band, 1919, and since its leader; went to Alaska with President Harding, 1923; promoted to lt. U.S. Navy, Mar. 1925, commd. lt. U.S. Navy by Act of Congress, 1935 (1st musician to attain officer's rank in music branch of the Navy); founder, officer in charge U.S. Navy School of Music; retired Jan. 1, 1942, after 37 years service; apptd. dir. Metropolitan Police Dept. Band, 1943. Various decoration for services in Cuba, Vera Cruz, World War, and for "good conduct." Mem. Am. Bandmasters' Assn., Am. Society of Composers, Authors and Publishers. Clubs: National Press Club, Army-Navy Country. Composer: (fantasia) A Day Aboard an American Man of War, Nov. 11, 1918, U.S. Navy Patrol; (marches) Irresistible, Lure of Alaska, Major Denby, Washington Times, Light Cruisers, Our Navy, Class of 91, U.S.N.A., Shenandoah National Park, All Hands, A Great American, The Submarine Force, Comairons, Navy Blue, Chief of Naval Operations, Amarillo, Commander Battle Force; (potpourri) Bits of Hits of Other Days; (humoresque) Strike up the Band, Here Comes a Sailor; (Habanera) Querida Mia, etc. Compiled, Lt. Charles Benter's Book of National Airs. Decorated Order of St. Sava, 4th class (Jugo-Slavia). Address: Washington, D.C. †

BENTLEY, F(RANKLIN) L(EE), coll. prof.; b. Albany, Mo., Oct. 23, 1887; s. William Newton and Mary M. (Dills) B.; B.S., Univ. Mo., 1913; M.S., Pa. State Coll., 1918; m. Nell M. Roberts, June 30, 1917. Asst. farm crops, Univ. Mo., 1913-14; asst. animal husbandry, 1914-16; instr., Pa. State Coll., 1916-18, asst. prof. animal husbandry, 1918-21, asso. prof., 1921-22, prof. animal husbandry since 1922, head dept. from 1927. Mem. Am. Soc. Animal Prodn., Am. Assn. Univ. Profs., Alpha Zeta, Gamma Sigma Delta, Farm House Frat. Democrat. Baptist. Clubs: State Coll. Rotary (past pres.), Centre Hills Country (past pres.). Contbr. numerous articles, circulars and bulletins on beef cattle and swine. Livestock editor, Pennsylvania Farmer from 1925. Judge of beef cattle at local, state, regional and nat. shows. Home: State Coll., Pa. †

BENTLEY, MAX, publicist; b. at Abilene, Tex., Nov. 18, 1888; s. Henry L. and Alice (Green) B.; ed. high sch., Abilene; m. Dimple F. McLemore, June 1, 1911; children—Alice (Mrs. Francis Cox), Josephine (Mrs. W. K. Kerfoot), Barbara. Reporter for the Abilene Reporter, 1906-11; reporter Corpus Christi (Tex.) Democrat, 1911-12, mng. editor, 1912-13; successively reporter, telegraph editor, city editor, news editor Houston (Tex.) Chronicle, 1914-20, mng. editor, 1920-23; free lance writer, on staff McClure's mag. and various other publs. 1923-26; one of founders of Abilene News (morning), 1926; managing editor, Abilene Reporter-News (morning-afternoon), 1926-36; editor and chmn. editorial bd. West Texas Today (monthly mag.); one of organizers and owners of Texas Publishers Assn., pub. a group of daily newspapers; radio news commentator, Texas State Network, 1938-39; activities and public relations dir. West Texas Chamber of Commerce since June 1, 1939. Past pres. West Tex. Press Assn.; ex-pres. Mng. Editors Assn. of Tex. Episcopalian. Has contributed articles to Dearborn Independent, McClure's Collier's, Harper's Scribner's Holland's Am. Forests and Forest Life, etc. Home; Abilene, Tex. †

BENTON, GEORGE YOUNG, clergyman; b. Livingston Manor, N.Y., May 11, 1890; s. Charles and Emogene (Stoutenburgh) B.; B.A., Syracuse U., 1913, hon. D.D., 1940; m. Ivanna Mae McConnell, Oct. 15, 1913; children—Martha Emogene, Charles Raymond. Ordained to ministry of Meth. Ch., 1919; pastor Meth. Ch., Freeville, N.Y., 1913-14, Westside Meth. Ch., Elmira, N.Y., 1916-22, First Meth. Ch., Oneida, N.Y., 1922-28, First Meth. Ch., Cortland, N.Y., 1928-38, Erwin Meth. Ch., Syracuse, N.Y., 1938-41; supt. Syracuse East Dist., 1941-47; Conference financial secretary, 1947-48, Conference financial secretary and treasurer since 1948. President Central New York Annual Conf. of Meth. Ch., Inc. Mem. bd. dirs. N.Y. State Council Chs.; mem. 1944-52 Northeastern Jurisdictional Conf. Meth. Ch.; mem. Com. of Two Hundred, Meth. Ch. Crusade for Christ; pres. Council of Chs., Syracuse Onondaga Co., 1948-49. Mem. Phi Beta Kappa, Delta Sigma Rho, Theta Beta Phi, Theta Chi Beta. Republican. Home: Syracuse, N.Y. †

BENTON, GLENN HARRISON, educator, clergyman; b. Savannah, O., Nov. 19, 1888; s. Harvey and Mary Ella (Cubbison) B.; student Coll. of Wooster, summer sessions, 1914-17; A.B., Oberlin Coll., 1921, A.M., 1923; student U. Chicago, summers 1925-28; Ph.D., U. Ia., 1932; m. Nellie Thomson, Aug. 29, 1914; children—Vivian LaVerne (wife of Dr. Stanley Wallace Terrill), Idella Maurine (Mrs. Henry Charles Hucker). Prof. history Drury Coll., Springfield, Mo., from 1921, dean, 1941-54; commr. General Assembly, Presbyn. Ch. U.S.A. 1928, moderator Synod Mo., 1947-48; lectr. on ednl., religious, diplomatic and internat. affairs. Mem. Carnegie Pub. Library Bd., Springfield, from 1941. Mem. Am. Assn. U. Profs., Pi Gamma Mu, Phi Eta Sigma, Delta Sigma Rho, Phi Alpha Theta. Mason. Presbyn. Contbr. articles in the Dictionary of Am. History; researcher. Home: Springfield, Mo. †

BENTZ, CHARLES WILLIAM, artist; b. Phila., June 8, 1888; s. Charles and Amelia (Suelke) B.; student Temple U., 1908-13, Indsl. Art Sch., 1904-06, 11-13, Pa. Acad. Fine Arts, 1943-46; m. Marjorie E. Mack, Aug. 31, 1917; children—Charles William, Philip H. Began career as profl. violinist 12 yrs.; then in real estate business; last 14 yrs. engaged exclusively in painting, and teaching painting to pvt. classes. Exhibited Phila. Sketch Club, Phila. Art Alliance, Pa. Acad. Fine Arts. Mem. Fellowship Pa. Acad. Fine Arts (pres. 1948-52), Phila. Art Alliance. Club: Phila. Sketch. Home: Berwyn, Pa. †

BENY, WILFRED ROY (ROLOFF BENY), artist, photographer, writer, book designer; b. Medicine Hat, Alta., Jan. 7, 1924; s. Charles John Francis and Rosalie M. (Roloff) B. B.A., B.F.A., U. Toronto, 1945; M.A., M.F.A. (Fellow), U. Iowa, 1947; postgrad., Columbia U., Inst. Fine Art, N.Y. U., 1947-48. One-man shows of paintings and graphic arts include, Paul Morihien Gallery, Palais Royal, Paris, 1952, Galleria del Milione, Milan, Italy, 1952, Art Gallery, Ont., 1954, Robertson Gallery, Ottawa, Ont., Can., 1954, Waldorf Galleries, Montreal, Que., Can., 1954, Western Can. Art Circuit Tour, 1955, Inst. Contemporary Art, London, 1955, Contemporaries Gallery, N.Y.C., 1956, Sagittarius, Rome, 1956, Paullo Barozzi Galleries, Venice, 1967, group shows throughout U.S. and Can. including, Nat. Acad., N.Y.C., Library of Congress, Washington, Bklyn. Mus., Carnegie Inst., Walker Art Center, Mpls., Cin. Art Center, Dallas Mus. Fine Art, Art Inst. Chgo., Art Assn. Montreal, Art Gallery Ont., Nat. Gallery Can., Ottawa, Canadian Nat. Exhbn., Toronto; represented in permanent collections, Nat. Gallery Can., Fogg Mus., Boston, Yale U. Mus., New Haven, Bklyn. Mus., Mus. Modern Art, N.Y.C., Redfern Gallery, London, Besalel Mus., Jerusalem, Milione Gallery, Milan and, numerous other pub. and pvt. collections, over 20 one-man photographic exhibits in museums, pvt. galleries, N.Y.C., Houston, Toronto, Montreal, Vancouver, London, Paris, Rome, Venice, Florence, Teheran, New Delhi; books of photographs include An Aegean Notebook, 1950, The Thrones of Earth and Heaven (Design prize Leipzig Book Fair 1958), A Time of Gods, 1962, Pleasure of Ruins, 1964, To Everything There Is a Season, 1967, Japan in Colour, 1967, India, 1969, Island-Ceylong, 1971, Roloff Beny in Italy, 1974, Persia: Bridge of Turquois, 1975, Iran: Elements of Destiny, 1978. Decorated knight Order of Mark Twain, officer

Order of Can.; recipient Centennial medal Govt. Can., 1967; Visual Arts award Canadian Council, 1968; John Simon Guggenheim fellow, 1952. Mem. Royal Canadian Acad. (life). Address: Lethbridge, Alta., Canada also Rome, Italy. Dec. Mar. 16, 1984.*

BERBERIAN, CATHY (MRS. LUCIANO BERIO), singer; b. Attleboro, Mass.; d. Ervant and Louise (Sudbeaz) B.; m. Luciano Berio, Oct. 1, 1950; 1 dau., Christina Luisa. Student, Columbia, Conservatorio G. Verdi, Milan, Italy; Fulbright scholar, with Giorgina Del Vigo, Milan, Italy, 1950-51. tchr. U. Vancouver, 1964, Rheiniscle Musikschule, 1965-66, Royal Conservatory, Toronto, 1971, Milan Conservatory, 1974, Liege Conservatory, 1977. Formerly engaged in theatre, also ethnic dancing, appearances European radio, also concerts, Europe, U.S., Can., Iran, Japan, 1958-83; performer vocal works avant-garde composers; music written for her by Bussotti, Cage, Milhaud, Pousseus, Stravinsky, Berio, including Sequenza III, Circles, Epifanie, Folk Songs; recs. for, Time, Boston, Wergo, Columbia, Philips, Angelicum, RCA, Telefunken records; Composer: Stripsody, 1966, Morsicathy, 1969, Anathema con Varie Azioni, 1970, Awake and Read Joyce, 1970-71. Recipient Grand Prix du Dique Academie Charles Cros, 1973. Address: Milan, Italy. Dec. Mar. 6, 1983.

BERCHTOLD, WILLIAM EDWARD, business counselor, writer, aerospace pioneer; b. Chgo., Apr. 9, 1905; s. John Andrew and Mary Ann (Lee) B.; A.B. cum laude, U. Ill., 1927; m. Paula Kathryn Cosby, July 28, 1939. Editor, writer AP, Champaign, Ill., Cleve., Columbus, Ohio and Washington, 1927-29, first aviation editor, 1928-29; dir. air transport sect. Aero. C. of C. Am., 1929-34, sec. 1st air traffic conf., 1930; v.p., dir. J. Stirling Getchell, Inc., N.Y.C., 1934-42, J. Walter Thompson, 1942-45; exec. v.p., dir. Foote, Cone & 1945-51; with McCann-Erickson, Inc., 1951-61, v.p., gen. mgr. midwest region, 1953-56; chmn. bd. Marschalk & Pratt, Communications Counselors, Inc., Market Planning Corp., Sales Communications, Inc., 1956-58; sr. v.p., chmn. plans rev. bd. McCann-Erickson Interpub., 1959-61; dir. Simmonds Precision Products, Inc., 1936-77, chmn. bd., 1939-74, vice chmn. bd., 1974-77, chmn. emeritus, 1977-81; pres. Pinnacle Products Corp., 1960-72; chmn. ICAI, 1968-70; pres. Growth Services for Bus., Inc., 1962-68, chmn. bd., from 1968; chmn. bd. Central Westchester Pub. Co., 1961-66. Life trustee Boy Scouts Am. Recipient Silver Beaver award Greater N.Y. council Boy Scouts Am. Mem. Am. Inst. Aeros. and Astronautics, Delta Chi, Sigma Delta Chi, Kappa Tau Alpha, Pi Alpha Mu. Episcopalian (vestryman). Clubs: Univ., Circumnavigators (pres. 1976-78), St. Hubert's Atrium (N.Y.C.); Tavern (Chgo.); Grosse Pointe Yacht, Old (Detroit). Editor: The Aircraft Year Book, 1929-34; contbr. articles to mags. Home: New York, N.Y. Died Sept. 14, 1981.

BERCKEMEYER, FERNANDO, Peruvian diplomat; b. Lima, Peru, July 24, 1904; s. Gustavo and Maria (Pazos-Varela) B.; student Inst. Lima, 1919, U. Notre Dame, 1917-1922; B.E., Rider Coll., Trenton, N.J., 1923; m. Claribel Rapp, Sept. 29, 1939. Vice consul for Peru, New Orleans, 1921-29, San Francisco, 1929-31, N.Y.C., 1931; counsul, Seattle, 1932-34; counsul gen., San Francisco, 1934-39, N.Y.C., 1939; charge d'affaires Peruvain embassy, London, Eng., 1943-44; E.E. and M.P., London, 1944-45, Stockholm, 1945-46; ambassador, London, 1946-49, Washington, 1949-63, 68-75. Del. to UN Assembly, London, Paris, N.Y.C. Bd. dirs. G. Berckemeyer & Co., Lima. Clubs: St. James's Travelers (London). Roman Catholic. Home: Lima, Peru. Died July 17, 1981.

BEREDAY, GEORGE ZYGMUNT FIJALKOWSKI, lawyer, sociologist; b. Warsaw, Poland, July 15, 1920; came to U.S., 1950, naturalized, 1955; s. Zygmunt B. and Halina (Piwko-Barylska) B.; m. Mary Hale Gillam, Dec. 21, 1954; children: Cornelia Krystyna, Mariko, Thaddeus Matthew Sigmund. B.Sc., U. London, 1944; B.A., U. Oxford, 1950, M.A., 1953; Ph.D., Harvard U., 1953; J.D., Columbia U., 1976; L.H.D., Susquehanna U., 1978; LL.D., Fla. Atlantic U., 1983. Mem. faculty Columbia U., 1955-76, prof. juvenile law, sociology, edn., 1977-83; exchange prof. U. Moscow, 1961; Fulbright prof. U. Tokyo, 1962; vis. prof. U. Hawaii, 1969-70, 79; Carnegie fellow in law and polit. sci. Harvard U., 1963-65, Burton lectr., 1972; dir. Japanese-Am. tchr. program Ford Found., 1964-68; dir. comparative juvenile law research Lounsbery Found., 1981-83; Convocation lectr. U. Wis., 1958; Phi Delta Kappa lectr. U. Ohio, 1964; Wolfson lectr. U. Oxford, 1971; Rosner lectr. City U. N.Y., 1975; mem. U.S. cultural mission to USSR, 1958, U.S. mission to Finland, 1966; U.S. del. 4th U.S.-Japan Cultural Conf., 1969; cons. U.S. Office Edn., 1966-70, OECD, 1970-71, UNESCO, 1971, Edn. Law Center, Rutgers Law Sch., 1974-75, Child Welfare League, 1974-75. Author; editor: Public Education in America, 1958, Liberal Traditions in Education, 1958, Politics of Soviet Education, 1960, Changing Soviet School, 1960, Comparative Method in Education, 1964, The Making of Citizen, 1966, Essays on World Education, 1969, Modernization and Diversity in Soviet Education, 1971, American Education through Japanese Eyes, 1973, Universities for All, 1973; founder, editor: Comparative Edn. Rev, 1957-67; joint editor: World Year Book Edn, 1957-67; gen. editor: Columbia Comparative Edn. Studies, 1964-83. Served with Polish Cavalry, 1938-42; Served with Brit. Parachute Regiment, 1942-45. Decorated Virtuti Militari of Poland, 1944. Mem. AAUP, Am. Bar Assn., N.Y. Bar Assn., Hawaii Bar Assn., Am. Hist. Assn., Am. Sociol. Assn., Comparative Edn. Soc., Harvard, Columbia law sch. assns. Clubs: Royal Automobile (London); Harvard (N.Y.C.). Home: New York, N.Y. also Honolulu, Hawaii. Dec. Oct. 22, 1983.

BERENDSEN, CARL AUGUST, New Zealand ambassador to U.S.; b. Sydney, Australia, Aug. 16, 1890; s. Ferdinand and Fannie (Asher) B.; LL.M., Victoria U. Coll.; m. Nellie Ellis Brown, Dec. 15, 1917; children—Ian Ellis, Keith Ellis. Sec. of external affairs, New Zealand Govt., 1928-43, permanent head Prime Ministers Dept., 1932-43, high commr. to Australia, 1943-44, minister to U.S., Washington, D.C., from 1944; del. U.N. Conf., San Francisco, 1945 and subsequent sessions of U.N. Gen. Assembly. Mem. Far Eastern Commn. to Tokyo, 1946; now New Zealand Ambassador to the United States. Decorated Knight Comdr. of St. Michael and St. George. Mem. Church of England. Home: Washington, D.C. †

BERESFORD, HOBART, educator; b. Vinton, Iowa, Dec. 6, 1896; s. Howard L. and Leah M. (Williams) B.; m. Lorene M. Kling, Aug. 20, 1925. B.S., Iowa State Coll., 1924, A.E., 1941. Registered profl. engr., Iowa, Idaho. Agrl. engr. Idaho Power Co., Boise, 1927-28; instr. U. Idaho, 1924-26, mem. faculty, 1928-46, Iowa State U., from 1946, prof. agrl. engring., now prof. emeritus. Contbr. numerous articles on agrl. enging. subjects in profl. jours. Named Engr. of Distinction Engrs. Joint Council. Fellow Am. Soc. Agrl. Engrs. (life); mem. Sigma Xi, Gamma Sigma Delta, Alpha Epsilon. Club: Rotarian (hon.). Home: Ames, Iowa.

BERG, DAVID ERIC, b. at Minneapolis, Minn., Jan. 13, 1890; s. Lars Pederson and Elizabeth (Skrefsrud) B.; B.A., U. of Minn., 1912; m. Alberta Elizabeth Lauer. Superintendent schools of Bruno, Minnesota, 1912-18, Grand Marais, Minn., 1913-14; with the University of Wisconsin survey, 1914, Madison Chamber of Commerce, 1915; asst. dir. Bur. Municipal Research, Akron, O., 1915-16; asst. sec. com. on criminal courts of Charity Orgn. Soc., N.Y. City, 1917; sec. charities and welfare com. of Phila. Chamber Commerce, 1917-21, also sec. of Phila. Welfare Federation; pres. Caxton Inst. of Extension Edn.; mng. editor Fundamentals of Musical Art. Lecturer on social statistics, Fordham U. Examiner Municipal Civil Service Commn., New York from 1936. Mem. 51st Pioneer Inf., 42d Div., A.E.F., 1918. Mem. Phi Delta Kappa. Author: Personality Culture by College Faculties, 1920; Introduction to Music, 1927; Art of Listening to Music, 1927; Beethoven and the Romantic Symphony, 1928; Choral Music and the Oratorio, 1928; The Modern Student, 1935. Home: Forest Hills, L.I., N.Y. †

BERGER, MORROE, educator, author; b. N.Y.C., June 25 1917; s. Morris and Frieda (Trotiner) B.; B.S.S., Coll. City N.Y., 1940; M.A., Columbia U., 1947, Ph.D., 1950; m. Paula Wainer, Mar. 7, 1943; children—Edward Morris, Keneth Harry, Laurence Philip. Mem. faculty Princeton U., from 1952, prof. sociology, from 1962, chmn. dept. sociology, 1971-74, dir. program Near Eastern Studies, 1962-68, 73-77, chmn. Council on Internat. and Regional Studies, 1968-77; chmn. joint com. Near and Middle East, Social Sci. Research Council and Am. Council Learned Socs., 1963-68; cons. 20th Century Fund, 1957, Congress Cultural Freedom, 1958-61, Ford Found., 1960-63, 67-68; adv. panel on Middle East, Dept. State; pres. Am. Research Center in Egypt., 1974-78. Mem. Middle East Studies Assn. (pres. 1967). Served with AUS, 1940-45. Author: Equality by Statute, rev. edit., 1967; Bureaucracy and Society in Modern Egypt, 1957; The Arab World Today, 1962; Islam in Egypt Today, 1970; Real and Imagined Worlds: The Novel and Social Science, 1977; also articles. Editor, translator: Madame de Stael on Politics, Literature and National Character, 1964. Home: Princeton, N.J. Died Apr. 7, 1981.

BERGER, NATHAN HALE, lawyer, banker; b. Brooklyn, N.Y., July 14, 1889; s. Harry Henry and Claire Paula (Firstman) B.; prep. edn. Erasmus Hall Acad. (Brooklyn); A.B., New York U., 1908, LL.B., 1909; m. Alice E. Zeisler, June 20, 1915; 1 dau., Claire Paula. Began practice of law, 1910; entered banking business, 1924; pres. Peoples Title & Mortgage Guaranty Co., 1926-28; v.p. Hayes Circle Nat. Bank (Newark, N.J.), 1928-30; pres. Peoples Nat. Bank & Trust Company (Belleville, N.J.), 1931-38; counsel Investment Building & Loan Assn., Barton Savings & Loan Assn.; pres. Wilson Construction Company, Reporting Corp., M.P. Hotel Co., Cosmo Hotels Corp., People's Mortgage Co.; chmn. Investment Foundation. Mason, Elk. Club: Kiwanis, Home: East Orange, N.J. †

BERGERON, VICTOR J., restaurateur; b. Calif., 1902; s. Victor and Marie (Camount) B. Ed. pub. schs., Calif. Opened restaurant Hinky Dink's, Oakland, Calif., 1934, Hinky Dink's (name changed to Trader Vic's), 1938; founder, chmn. other Trader Vic's in cities including, N.Y.C., Chgo., Beverly Hills, Portland, Oreg., Seattle, Denver, Washington, Scottsdale, Ariz., Kansas City, Emeryville, Calif., San Francisco, Tokyo, Japan, Dallas, Houston, St. Louis, Atlanta, Toronto, Ont., Can., Vancouver, B.C., Can. and, London, Eng., Munich, Germany, Singapore. Address: San Francisco, Calif. Died Oct. 11, 1984.

BERGERON, WILBUR LEE, educator, psychologist; b. Jefferson Parish, La., Aug. 29, 1925; s. V.S. and Sadie (Purifoy) B.; B.A., La. Coll., 1946; M.A., George Peabody Coll., 1947; Ed.D., U. Ark., 1953; m. Ann Hearn, May 14, 1949; 1 dau., Nancy Ann. Asst. prof. psychology La. Coll., 1947-51; psychologist La. State Colony and Tng. Sch., 1949, student counseling service U. Ark., 1951-53; psychology adviser La. Tech. U., Ruston, 1953-63, dir. psychol. services South, Monroe, La., 1963-65, prof., head dept. psychology, 1964-70, dir. div. ednl. research, 1966-72, assoc. dean research, from 1972; vocat. cons. Bur. Hearings and Appeals, Social Security Adminstrn., 1962-65; chmn. bd. Ruston Area Guidance Center, 1965; mem. regional mental health com. La. Council Handicapped Children, N. Central La. chpt. Council Exceptional Children; exec. dir. S. Central Region Research Lab., Little Rock, 1966. Mem. Am. Psychol. Assn., Am. Personnel and Guidance Assn., Nat. Vocat. Guidance Assn., Nat. Employment Counselors Assn., La. Guidance Assn. (pres. 1965), Ruston C. of C. Research in psychology of adolescence. Home: Ruston, La. Deceased.

BERGMAN, BERNARD AARON, editor; b. Chillicothe, Ohio, July 8, 1894; s. Eleazer and Carrie (Weiler) B.; B.A., Ohio State U., 1916; spl. student Universite de Poitiers, 1919; m. Sue Wells, 1922 (div. 1933); m. Frances Dellar, Mar. 17, 1933 (dec. Oct. 1965). Reporter, Chillicothe News Advertiser, 1915-16, Columbus (Ohio) Dispatch, 1917; public relations work, N.Y.C., 1919-31; mng. editor New Yorker mag., 1931-33; editor March of Events Page, Hearst Newspapers, 1933-35; successively Sunday editor, feature editor, exec. editor Phila. Record, 1935-42, also feature editor N.Y. Post, 1938; feature editor Pageant mag., 1946; dir. pub. relations Publicker Industries, Inc., 1947-55; editor, dir. Phila. Daily News, 1955-58; editor Jewish Exponent, Phila., 1958-61; editor Sunday mag. Phila. Bull., 1961-66, editor book div., 1966-69, book editor, from 1970, book columnist, from 1977; spl. instr. journalism U. Pa., 1951-52, lectr., 1960. Served as sgt. maj. U.S. Army, World War I; lt. col. USAAF, World War II. Recipient journalism award Temple U., 1956. Mem. Phi Beta Kappa, Zeta Beta Tau, Sigma Delta Chi. Democrat. Jewish. Clubs: Peale, Franklin Inn (Phila.). Author: The Smiling Corpse (with Philip Wylie), 1935. Phila. Bull. established B.A. Bergman award for outstanding lit. achievement in Greater Phila., 1974. Home: Philadelphia, Pa. Deceased.

BERGMAN, INGRID, actress; b. Stockholm, Sweden, Aug. 29, 1915; came to U.S., 1939; d. Justus and Friedel (Adler) B.; m. Peter Lindstrom, July 10, 1937 (div.); 1 dau., Pia; m. Roberto Rossellini; children—Roberto, Isabella and Ingrid (twins); m. Lars Schmidt, Dec. 21, 1958. Ed., Lyceum for Flickor and Sch. Royal Dramatic Theatre, Stockholm. Began acting in motion pictures and, stage plays in, Sweden; has played in motion pictures in, U.S., Intermezzo, 1939, Adam Had Four Sons, 1940, Rage in Heaven, 1940, Dr. Jekyll and Mr. Hyde, 1941, Casablanca, 1942, For Whom the Bell Tolls, 1943, Gaslight, 1944, Saratoga Trunk, 1945, Bells of St. Mary's, 1945, Notorious, 1946, Joan of Arc, Under Capricorn, Stromboli, The Greatest Love, Trip to Italy, Strangers, Fear, Anastasia, 1956, Paris Does Strange Things, 1957, Indiscreet, 1958, Inn of the 6th Happiness, 1958, Goodby Again, 1961, The Visit, 1963, The Yellow Rolls-Royce, 1964, Cactus Flower, 1969, Walk in the Spring Rain, 1969, Mixed Up Files of Mrs. Frankweiler, 1973, Murder on the Orient Express, 1974, A Matter of Time, 1976, Autumn Sonata, 1978; stage plays U.S.: Lilliom, 1940, Anna Christie, 1941, Joan of Lorraine, 1946, Tea and Sympathy, Paris, 1956-57, Hedda Gabler, 1963, Month in The Country, 1966, More Stately Mansions, 1968, Captain Brassbound's Conversion, 1970, The Constant Wife, 1975, Waters of the Moon, London, 1977 (Recipient Acad. award Acad. Motion Picture Arts and Scis. 1944, 56, N.Y. Film Critics Award 1956, TV Acad. award for The Turn of the Screw 1960); Author: stage plays Ingrid Bergman: My Story, 1980.*

BERKEY, BENJAMIN, photographic company executive; b. Podolsk, Russia, Jan. 1, 1911; came to U.S., naturalized, 1921; s. Isidore and Lena (Pisner) Berkowitz; m. Frances Picon, May 15, 1958; children: Dorothy, Harvey, Joseph, Robert, Gilbert, Belinda, Peter, Nina, David. B.B.A., CCNY, 1932. Chmn. bd. Berkey Photo, White Plains, N.Y., including; Willoughby Camera Stores, Berkeey Mktg. Corp., Berkey Tech. Co., 1933-82; chmn. bd. Wall Trading Corp., from 1980; chmn. bd., pres. Bentrose Corp., N.Y.C., 1958—. Chmn. City Coll. Fund, 1979-81, Baruch Coll. Fund, 1975-81, Cancer Dr. of Photo Industry, 1960-81. Named Man of Yr. City Coll., Man of Yr. Baruch Coll., Man of Yr. James Monroe High Sch., Man of Yr. Photog. Industry. Mem. Pioneer Club Camera Industry Japan (charter). Home: Scarsdale, N.Y. Died Dec. 16, 1984.*

BERKEY, RUSSELL STANLEY, naval officer; b. Goshen, Ind., Aug. 4, 1893; s. Albert and Lenora (Murray) B.; B.S., U.S. Naval Acad., 1916; student U.S. Naval War Coll., Newport, R.I., 1938-39; m. Eleanore Dickey Campbell, Jan. 15, 1919. Commd. ensign, U.S. Navy, 1916, advancing through the grades to rear adm., 1943; served on U.S.S. New York with Grand Fleet, North Sea, 1917-18; aide and sec. to Adm. W. V. Pratt, comdr. in chief U.S. Fleet, 1929-30; aide to Adm. Pratt, chief of naval operations, 1931-32; comd. gunboat Panay, Yangtze River, China, 1933-34, destroyer Smith-Thompson, Asiatic Station, 1934-36; asst. comdt., U.S. Naval Base, Iceland, 1941-42; comd. light cruiser U.S.S. Santa Fe (engaging in action in North, Central and South Pacific areas), 1942-43; rear adm. apptd. comdr. Cruiser Div. 15, assigned to duty in Southwest Pacific, from Dec. 1943; comd. Cruisers 7th Fleet and Task Forces 74 and 75, Dec. 1943-July 1945; participated in reoccupation of New Britain, New Guinea, the Admiralties, Morotai, all phases of the Philippine campaign and Tarakan, Brunei Bay and Balikpapan, Borneo; comdr. U.S. right flank forces, Battle of Suriago Strait in defense Leyte Beachhead; assigned duty in Office of Public Relations, Navy Dept., Washington, D.C., Sept. 1945. Awarded Legion of Merit with gold stars in lieu of 2d and 3d medals, Distinguished Service Medal, Navy Cross. Home: Lyme, Conn. Died June 17, 1985.

BERKOWITZ, DAVID SANDLER, history educator; b. Pitts., Aug. 20 1913; s. Abraham Jacob and Nellie (Sandler) B.; A.B., Harvard, 1938, A.M., 1940, Ph.D., 1946; m. Jessie Cohen, Sept. 8, 1940; children—Carl Sandler, Naomi Judith. Teaching fellow Harvard, 1939-41, Rogers travelling fellow, 1941-42; assoc. prof. history, chmn. dept. social sci. Emerson Coll., Boston, 1946-47; exec. officer Assn. Colls. and Univs. State N.Y., also cons. and liaison officer Commn. Need for State Univ. N.Y., 1946-48; mem. faculty Brandeis U., Waltham, Mass., 1948-83, prof. history, 1949-83, asst. to pres., dir. univ. planning, 1948-52. Vis. lectr. history Harvard, 1957-58; dir. New Eng. Transp. Co., 1956-62; dir., treas. Berkshire Assocs., Inc., 1959—; incorporator Waltham (Mass.) Savs. Bank, 1952-83. Bd. dirs. Waltham Family Service Assn., 1949-83, pres., 1959-61; incorporator Waltham Hosp., 1952—; bd. dirs. Region West Family Counseling Service, 1963—, mem. exec. com., 1963—, chmn. personnel com., 1963-66, chmn. community relations com., 1966-83; bd. dirs. Waltham Community Found., 1971-83, pres., 1971-73, treas., 1973-83. Recipient Washburn prize history Harvard, 1938; Folger Shakespeare Library fellow, 1965-66, sr. fellow, 1971-72; Am. Bar Found. legal history research fellow, 1972-73; Nat. Endowment for Humanities fellow, 1978-79. Mem. AAUP, Am. Hist. Assn., Renaissance Soc. Am., Conf. Brit. Studies, New Eng. Renaissance Conf. (permanent chmn. 1965—), Soc. History of Discoveries, Oxford Bibilog. Soc., Am. Printing Hist. Assn., Phi Beta Kappa. Author: Inequality of Opportunity in Higher Education, 1948; Bibliotheca Bibliographica Britannica, 1963; Catalogue of the Incunabula of Brandeis University Library, 1963; Aldine Dynasty of Humanistic Printers, 1963; Ancient Civilizations and the Founding of Libraries, 1964; From Ptolemy to the Moon; Progress in the Art of Exploration and Navigation, 1965; In Remembrance of Creation 1968. Home: Newtonville, Mass. Died Mar. 7, 1983.

BERNARD, DALLAS GERALD MERCER, banker; b. Fair Oak, Hampshire, Eng., Mar. 22, 1888; s. Edmund Bowen and Arabella Margaret (Piercy) B.; m. Elizabeth Addis, Nov. 16, 1922; children—Elizabeth Piercy (Mrs. G. W. Strang), Dallas Edmund, Margaret Anne (Mrs. W. G. Cleverly). With Jardine Matheson Co., Ltd., Hong Kong, 1911-28 Matheson & Co. Ltd., London, 1928-42; dir. Bank of Eng., 1936-49, dep. gov., 1949-54; chmn. Courtaulds, Ltd., 1962-64; dir. Proprietors of Hays Wharf, Ltd. Served with Royal Navy, 1903-06. Created Baronet, 1954. Home: Surrey, Eng. †

BERNARD, FLORENCE SCOTT (MRS. EBBERT LOUIS BERNARD), author; b. Clyde, O., July 19, 1889; d. Frank C. and Dora M. (Sloat) Scott; ed. pub. schs., Tiffin, Ohio; student short story writing and drama with Prof. Holliday, of Toledo U.; m. Ebbert Louis Bernard, Sept. 11, 1906; children—Dora Genevieve, Errol Hugh. Wrote first story at age of 14, and has since contributed many short stories to mags. Mem. Ch. of Chirst. Clubs: Toledo Writers'; Women's Educational. Author: Through the Cloud Mountain, 1922; Diana of Briarcliffe, 1923. Home: Toledo, Oh. †

BERNARD, HUGH JOHN, banker; b. Mt. Ayr, Ia., Oct. 26, 1889; s. George W. and Mary (Richardson) B.; student pub. schs. Traverse City, Mich.; m. Effie Clare Smith, Jan. 18, 1912; died Feb. 1920; 1 son, Dr. Lynn Allan; m. 2d, Hazel Silliman, June 18, 1921. Formerly vice president Bank of the Southwest, Houston, member of faculty, former chairman board of managers School Financial Public Relations, Chgo.; sect. leader Sch. Banking of the South, La. State U., Baton Rouge. Mem. Financial Pub. Relations Assn. (past pres.). Methodist (steward). Clubs: Houston, Pine Forest Country. †

BERNBACH, WILLIAM, advertising executive; b. N.Y.C., Aug. 13, 1911; s. Jacob and Rebecca (Reiter) B.; m. Evelyn Carbone, June 5, 1938; children—John Lincoln, Paul. B.C.S., N.Y. U., 1933. Dir. research N.Y. World's Fair, 1939-40; dir. postwar planning Coty, Inc., 1943-44; v.p. Grey Advt. Agy., 1945-49; pres. Doyle Dane Bernbach Inc., 1949-67, chmn., chief exec. officer, 1968-74, chmn. exec. com., chief exec. officer, 1974-76, chmn. exec. com., 1976-82; Disting. adj. prof. N.Y.U.; Vice chmn. Lincoln Center Film Com.; Bd. dirs., mem. exec. com. Legal Aid Soc., Salk Inst. Biol. Studies, Harper's Mag. Found. Bd. dirs. Internat. Eye Found.; bd. dirs. Mary Manning Walsh Home, Menninger Found., Friends of Am. Art in Religion, Inc.; chmn. bd., mem. exec. com. Municipal Arts Soc.; bd. dirs., vice chmn. Citizens Com. for N.Y.C.; mem. Urban Design Council of N.Y.C.; mem. bd. overseers Grad. Sch. Bus., N.Y. U.; mem. adv. bd. Library of Congress Center for the Book. Named Man of Year Pulse, Inc., 1966; mem. Copywriters Hall of Fame; recipient Madden Meml. award, 1968; Am. Acad. Achievement award, 1976; named Top Advt. Agy. Exec., 1969, One Person Who Did Most for Progress of Advt. Industry, 1963, 65, 66; elected to Advt. Hall of Fame, 1976. Mem. Am. Assn. Advt. Agys. (v.p., dir.; v.p., dir. Ednl. Found.). Clubs: N.Y. U. Alumni, City Athletic. Home: New York, N.Y. Dec. Oct. 2, 1982.

BERNDT, ALVIN HAROLD, investment company executive; b. Chgo., Nov. 19, 1913; s. Edward A. and Olga M. (Lehmann) B.; m. Marion C. Rising, Aug. 12, 1948; 1 child, Susan Berndt Mahoney. B.A., U. Ill., 1935; J.D., John Marshall Law Sch., 1938. Bar: Ill. bar 1939. Partner Lord Abbett & Co., N.Y.C., 1955-80, mng. ptnr., 1980-83; v.p., dir. Affiliated Fund, Inc., chmn., 1980-83; pres., chief exec. officer Lord Abbett Income Fund, Inc., 1980-83; chmn. Lord Abbett Bond-Debenture Fund, Inc.; pres., chief exec. officer, dir. Lord Abbett Developing Growth Fund, Inc., 1980-83; v.p. Lord Abbett Cash Res. Fund, Inc., 1979-80, pres., chief exec. officer, dir., 1980-83; mem. Investment Co. Inst.; rules com. SEC. Served to comdr. USN, 1941-46, PTO. Mem. Ill. Bar Assn., Sigma Nu. Presbyterian. Clubs: Wall St. (N.Y.C.); Apawamis (Rye, N.Y.). Home: Rye, N.Y. Dec. 1983.

BERRIGAN, EDMUND JOSEPH MICHAEL, JR. (TED BERRIGAN), poet; b. Providence, Nov. 15, 1934; m. Sandra Alper (div.); m. Alice Notley; children—Kate, David, Anselm. B.A., U. Tulsa, 1959, M.A., 1962. Tchr. Poetry Workshop, St. Marks Art Project, N.Y.C., 1966-67; vis. lectr. U. Iowa, 1968-69; poet-in-residence Northeastern Ill. U., 1969-76; editor, pub. C mag. and C Press, N.Y.C. Author: The Sonnets, 1964, Bean Spasms, 1967, Many Happy Returns, 1969, In the Early Morning Rain, 1971, Back in Boston Again, 1972, A Feeling for Leaving, 1974, Red Wagon, 1977, Nothing for You, 1978; Work appears in anthologies, Young American Poets, 1968, American Literary Anthology, 1968, All Stars, 1972. Served with U.S. Army, 1954-57. Recipient Poetry Found. award, 1964.*

BERRY, FRANK JOHN, railway exec.; born Orlew, N.D., Oct. 19, 1887; s. William and Ann Amelis (O'Hern) B.; student pub. schs. Lisbon, N.D.; m. Ellen Bates, Oct. 1936. Telegraph operator, relief agt. N.P. Ry., 1905-10, chief clk. to gen. agt., Winnipeg, Can., 1910-11, traveling freight agt., 1912, asst. gen. agt., 1913, gen. agt., 1920, Spokane, 1923, asst. gen. freight agt., Seattle, 1929, western traffic mgr., 1947, asst. gen. freight and passenger agt., Portland, Ore., 1932, asst. v.p. traffic, St. Paul, 1948, v.p. traffic since 1949. Served as 1st lt., U.S. Army, 1918-19. Mem. Am. Soc. Traffic and Transportation, Inc. (founder mem. 1949). Republican. Roman Catholic. Clubs: Town and Country, Minnesota (St. Paul); Union League (Chgo.); Tacoma; Rainier (Seattle); Arlington (Portland, Ore.). Home: St. Paul, Minn.†

BERRY, JACK, educator; b. Leeds, Eng., Dec. 13, 1918; came to U.S., 1963; s. Harry and Nellie (Butterfield) B.; m. Winifred Mary Ingle, Feb. 14, 1942; 1 son, Mark Adrian. B.A., Leeds U., 1939; Ph.D., London U., 1952. Lectr. London U., 1946-55, reader, 1955-60, prof., 1960-63; prof. Mich. State U., 1963-64; prof. linguistics Northwestern U., 1964-80. Home: Evanston, Ill. Died Dec. 1980.

BERRY, KEEHN W., banker; b. Glen Allen, Mo., Dec. 12, 1894; s. Pinkney Jasper and Ida (Keehn) B.; m. Mary Lois Brown, June 5, 1920; children—Keehn W., Mary Ellen. A.B., U. Mo., 1913, LL.B., 1915. Pres. Whitney Nat. Bank of New Orleans, 1937-69, chmn. bd., dir., 1969-81. Presbyn. Clubs: New Orleans Boston (New Orleans), New Orleans Country (New Orleans). Home: New Orleans, La. Dec. Sept. 7, 1981.

BERTHIAUME, PAUL WILFRED, computer info. co. exec.; b. Spokane, Wash., Feb. 16, 1935; s. Bernard Jesse and Regina (Paquette) B.; m. Adelaida Florez, Sept. 29, 1962; children—David Alan, John Robert. B.S. in Chem. Engring. magna cum laude, Gonzaga U., 1957; M.S. in Chem. Engring, Columbia U., 1959. With Electronic Assos., Inc., 1959-76, div. mktg. mgr., West Long Branch, N.J., 1968-69, v.p. mktg., 1970-76; also dir.; sr. v.p. mktg. New York Times Info. Bank, Parsippany, N.J., 1977-78, pres., from 1979. Trustee Charles Babbage Inst.; indsl. rep., computer systems tech. adv. com. Dept. Commerce, 1975-76. Mem. Soc. Computer Simulation (pres. 1975-76), Am. Fedn. Info. Processing Socs. (v.p. 1973-75), Nat. Computer Conf. (dir. 1971-75), IEEE Computer Soc., Sigma Xi. Roman Catholic. Died Oct. 16, 1981.

BERTKE, ELDRIDGE MELVIN, cell biologist; b. South Milwaukee, Wis.; s. Clinton Charles and Elsie (Wendt) B.; m. Emily Latchel, Apr. 23, 1950; children—Charles, Brian, William. B.S., U. Wis., 1950, M.S., 1951, Ph.D., 1955. Asst. prof., head dept. U. Dubuque, 1956-58; with Ariz. State U., Tempe, from 1958, prof. histology, cytology, dept. zoology, from 1967; cons. toxicology, pvt. industry, surgeon gen. U.S. Army, 1973-78; molecular biologist Inst. Research Walter Reed Army Med. Center, Washington, from 1970. Author: Cytology, 1968, 2d edit., 1974. Served with USAAF, 1943-46. Decorated DFC, Air medal with six oak leaf clusters.; Recipient Wis. Alumni Research Found. fellowship, 1952-55. Mem. N.Y. Acad. Sci., Am. Soc. Cell Biology, Electron Microscopy Soc. Am., Sigma Xi, Tri Beta, Phi Sigma. Methodist. Club: Masons. Home: Tempe, Ariz.

BESANT, ALVIN WILLIAM KENWAY, retail trade exec.; b. Winnipeg, Man., Can., June 20, 1933; s. William Joseph and Lillian Ruth (Kenway) B.; m. Jean Mary Nicol, Oct. 1, 1956; children—Christopher, Paul, Laura. B.A., United Coll., Winnipeg, 1954; postgrad., McGill U., 1965. Trainee Hudson's Bay Co., 1955-56, asst. dept. mgr., 1956-57; dept. mgr. Victoria, B.C., 1957-60; dept. mgr. Vancouver, 1960, mdse. mgr., 1960-61, Henry Morgan & Co., Ltd, Montreal 1961-66, store mgr., 1966-67; v.p. mktg. Singer Co. of Can., 1967-68; v.p. mdsg. Oshawa Wholesale Dept. Store div. Towers Dept. Stores, Toronto, 1968-69; exec. v.p., chief operating officer Gambles Can., Ltd., Winnipeg, 1969-73; v.p. drug and dept. stores Loblaw Cos. Ltd., Toronto, 1973-81; chmn. bd., pres. Boehmer Box Corp., Kitchener, Ont., 1974-81, Chant Paper Box Ltd., London, Ont., 1974-81, Wymark Printers & Lithographers, Ltd., Brantford, Ont. Bd. dirs. Man. Sports Fedn., 1970, Man. Theatre Centre, 1972-73. Mem. Metric Commn. of Can.; Mem. Am., Canadian mgmt. assns., Montreal, Toronto bds. trade, Canadian Paper Box Mfrs. Assn. (bd. dirs.), Winnipeg C. of C., Retail Council of Can., Mdse. Research Inst. N.Y., Internat. Council Shopping Centres. Home: Mississauga, Ont., Can. Died Aug. 8, 1981.

BESSEY, ROY FREDERIC, govt. ofcl.; b. Bklyn., Sept. 30, 1889; s. Samuel Emery and Caroline (Cahoone) B.; student evenings Northeastern U., 1909-11, Columbia, 1927-28, N.Y.U., 1928-29; m. Louise Dorothea Barnes, May 14, 1914; children—Carolyn (Mrs. West), Janet (wife Dr. Monroe Epstein), William Cahoone; m. 2d Mary Glenna Fisher, Oct. 20, 1945. Engring. dept. N.Y.C. R.R. B.&A. R.R., 1906-11; engring, designer Isthmian Canal Commn., Panama Canal, 1911-15; jr. engr. U.S. Reclamation Service, 1915; design, constrn. Nichols Copper Co., 1916; asst. mgr. a program div., bur. yards and docks Navy Dept., 1916-25, designing engr., 1932-33; cons. engr. port. waterway, terminal constrn. with George W. Goethals, Inc., Moores & Dunford, Inc., John Stewart, also v.p. Frederic R. Harris, Inc., 1925-32; engr. Nat. Park Service, 1933; regional insp. Fed. Emergency Adminstrn. Pub. Works, 1933; exec. officer Pacific N.W. Regional Planning Commn., also regional officer Nat. Resources Planning Bd., 1934-43; spl. advisor to adminstr. Bonneville Power Adminstrn., 1943-46; acting dep. dir. China office U.N. R.R.A., 1945; dir., chmn. Pacific N.W. field com., office of sec. Dept. Interior, 1946-53; consultant U.N. Tech. Assistance Adminstrn., part-time 1952-54. Resources for Future, Inc., Nat. Hells Canyon Assn., U.S.H.R. Govt. Operations Com.; vis. prof. polit. sci. U. Ore., 1960; cons. Dept. Interior, Dept. Health, Edn. and Welfare, Commerce. Mem. adv. com. on econ. policy Dem. Adv. Coun. Served with C.E., AEF, U.S. Army, 1918-19. Trustee Portland Art Assn., 1944-52, from 1960. Mem. Am. Soc. C.E., Nat. Planning Assn., Am. Polit. Sci. Assn. Unitarian. Club: Portland City. Home: Portland, Ore. †

BEST, ALLEN CHARLES, educator; b. Cleveland, N.Y., Apr. 22, 1911; s. Harry Eugene and Alta May B.; m. Elizabeth Papp, Sept. 16, 1938; children—Stephen Herbert, Janet Elizabeth. A.B., Syracuse U., 1935; S.T.B., Boston U., 1938, Ph.D., 1950; postgrad., Northwestern U., Cornell U. Psychologist, tchr. Rome State Sch. for Mentally Retarded, part-time, 1931-35; pastor North Falmouth and South Easton Congl. Chs., 1936-42; univ. chaplain, dir. N.Y. State Methodist Student Movement, Cornell U., 1942-58; prof., univ. chaplain SUNY, Alfred and Alfred U., 1958-60; v.p., dir. fin. devel. Greensboro Coll., 1960-62; dir. found. support parents programs, ch. relations, spl. prospects Syracuse (N.Y.) U., 1962-76; nat. dir. community relations and devel. literacy Vols. of Am., 1976-78, fund raising and public relations cons., from 1979. Author: Pastoral Work with Adjustment Problems, 1950; also numerous articles in psychology, edn., religion, marriage and the family. Exec. dir. Elmcrest Children's Center, 1977; Mem. commn. on religion and mental health Nat. Council Chs.; v.p. No. Syracuse Bd. Edn.; active United Fund Central N.Y., Onodaga County Mental Health Assn.; dir. Gladding Co. State chmn. Friends for Rockefeller; trustee St. Mary's Hosp., Am. Youth Hostel, Villa Gerard for Unmarried Mothers, Operation Crossroads Africa, Methodist Hosps. and Homes, Rescue Mission Bd. Syracuse; mem. council of elders Gerontology Center, Syracuse U.; mem. Meth. Found. Christian Higher Edn. Recipient Rockefeller award for disting. service to state. Mem. Am. Alumni Council, Am. Public Relations Assn., Am. Soc. Public Adminstrn., Am. Assn. Univ. Chaplains, Am. Assn. Pastoral Counselors, Syracuse U. Alumni Assn., Nat. Football Found. Rotarian. Home: North Syracuse, NY.

BEST, JOHN CARTER, cons., lectr., arbitrator; b. Shipley, Eng., Jan. 8, 1887; s. William Carter and Charlotte (Stainsby) B.; ed. Saltaire High Sch. and Ackworth Sch., Eng.; m. Helen Meincke, July 23, 1918; children—Patricia, Carter. Came to U.S., 1909, naturalized, 1918. Held various positions, 1909-17; vice pres. and gen. mgr. A.M. Meincke & Son, Inc., 1920-25; pres. Best Bros. Keene's Cement Co., 1926-37; vice pres. National Gypsum Co. 1938-56; v.p. Nat. Gypsum Co. (Canada), Ltd., A.A. Meincke & Son, Inc. Apptd. mem. gypsum industry adv. com., W.P.B., 1942. Nat. pres. Gypsum Association; dir. American Arbitration Association; also officer or director other trade assns. Served as 1st lt., U.S. Army, 1917-18. Republican. Episcopalian. Mason. Club: Buffalo. Contbr. to tech. publs. Address: Chatham, Cape Cod, Mass. †

BEST, MARSHALL AYRES, publisher; b. N.Y.C., Nov. 26, 1901; s. Albert Starr and Marjorie (Ayres) B.; m. Elizabeth Hoyt Worthington, 1939 (div.); children—Mary (Mrs. Mary Alcantara), John Ayres. A.B. summa cum laude, Harvard, 1923; postgrad., U. Grenoble Grenoble, France, 1923-24. With Viking Press (now Viking Penguin, Inc.), N.Y.C., 1925-82, dir., sec., 1927, gen. mgr., 1935, v.p., 1956-68, sr. editorial cons., 1969-82; gen. editor Viking Portable Library, from 1943. Dir., mem. exec. com. Am. Book Pubs. Council, 1962-65. Author poems, articles, translations; recorded Columbia Oral History, 1976. Mem. Phi Beta Kappa. Clubs: Century Assn. (N.Y.C.), Harvard (N.Y.C.); P.E.N. (v.p. 1967-70). Home: Sharon, Conn. Dec. 1982.

BEST, WILLIAM NEWTON, marine corps officer; b. Los Angeles, Calif., July 14, 1887; s. William Newton and Mary Elizabeth (Hayward) B.; student, Columbia, 1911; m. Lillian Nickerson, Aug. 30, 1919; children—William Newton, Lillian Nickerson. With engring. firms, So. Calif., 1911-16; commd. 2d lt. U.S.M.C., 1917, advanced through grades to brig. gen., 1946; served in U.S., Haiti, Hawaii, Santo Domingo, China, Nicaragua, Philippines, Cuba and at sea with the Fleet, Iceland, Pacific Ocean Area, Okinawa; retired Dec. 1, 1946. Mem. Phi Kappa Sigma. Republican. Protestant Episcopal. Mason. Clubs: Army Navy Country (Washington, Peking, China). †

BETHEA, JAMES ALBERTUS, physician, surgeon; b. Marion County, S.C., Oct. 30, 1887; s. William Walter and Sallie (Morrison) B.; student Clemson Coll., 1904-06, M.D., Tulane U., 1913; grad. Army Med. Sch., 1917; m. Margaret Hazel Bostrum, June 2, 1920; children—Margaret, Dorothy, Thomas Morrison, Commd. 1st lt. Med. Res. Corps. 1916, 1st lt. Regular Army, 1917, and advanced through the grades to major gen., Apr. 1948; intern in Touro Infirmary, New Orleans, 1913-15; med. practice, 1915-16; dir. Field Hosp., 4th Div., World War I; was chief surg., Far East Command, Tokyo, Japan; retired from Army; now exec. dir. Tex. State Hosps. and Spl. Schs. Diplomate Am. Bd. Surg. Fellow A.C.S.; mem. A.M.A., Assn. of Mil. Surgeons. Club: Army, Mason. Address: Austin, Tex. †

BETJEMAN, JOHN, poet, author; b. London, Eng., Aug. 28, 1906; s. Ernest Edward and Mabel Bessie (Dawson) B.; student Marlborough Coll., 1925-27, Magdalen Coll., Oxford, 1925-28; m. Penelope Chetwode, June 23, 1932; children—Paul, Candida. Book critic Daily Telegraph, from 1952; weekly column The Spectator, from 1954. Mem. Athenaeum. Mem. Ch. of Eng. Clubs: Beefsteak (London); Kildare Street (Dublin). Author: (poems) Mount Zion, 1931, Continual Dew, 1937, Old Lights for New Chancels, 1940, New Bats in Old Belfries, 1945, Selected Poems, 1950, A Few Late Chrysanthemums, 1954, Collected Poems, 1958 (Duff Cooper award; Foyle poetry prize); (prose) Ghastly Good Taste, 1933, First and Last Loves, 1953, (with John Piper) Murray's Guides to Books and Bucks and Berks; (anthologies) (with Geoffrey Taylor) English Landscape Poetry, English Love Poetry. Home: England. Died May 19, 1984.

BETTIS, VALERIE, dancer, choreographer; b. Houston; d. Royal Holt and Valerie Elizabeth (McCarthy) B.; m. Bernardo Segall, Sept. 20, 1943 (div. 1955); m. Arthur A. Schmidt, Sept. 26, 1959. Student, U. Tex. First profl. appearance, 1937, first solo performance, 1941, choreographer, 1942-82; made (with husband (pianist-composer) piano-dance recital tour, Central and South America, 1946; appeared in connection with work at, YMHA Dance Center, N.Y.C., 1947; dancer five solo modern dances, Jacob's Pillow Festival, Lee, Mass., 1947; dancer: legitimate stage prodns. on Broadway Haunted Heart, 1948, Inside U.S.A., Tiger Lily, As I Lay Dying, 1949; N.Y. State Theatre, Lincoln Center, N.Y.C., 1965; choreographer: Paul Whiteman's TV show, 1949; dancer and choreographer: TV shows Studio One, Omnibus, Kraft TV Theatre, Producers Showcase, Colgate Comedy Hour, Philco Playhouse, Your Show of Shows, Chevrolet Hour; dir.: TV shows If Five Years Pass, N.Y.C., 1962; dancer, actress, singer: TV shows Great to be Alive, 1949, Bless You All, 1950; ballet Street Car Named Desire, 1954; choreographer: ballet Peer Gynt, 1951, Slavenska-Franklin Ballet Co., N.Y.C., 1952, Our Town (NBC Spectacular), 1955; choreographer for: films Affair in Trinidad; Salome, 1952, Athena, 1954; actress The Women (NBC); guest artist: actress Three Penny Opera; actress: actress Back to Methuselah, 1957-58; stage dir.: London prodn. Ulysses in Nighttown, 1958; revival Virginia Sampler for 1960, Dallas Civic Ballet Co.; choreographer and performer: revival Golden Round and Early Voyagers; founder: revival Dancers Studio Found., Inc, 1964-73; co-dir.: ballet Improvisations Plus, 1968; re-staged: ballet A Streetcar Named Desire for, Nat. Ballet Co., 1974; dir., choreographer opera: ballet Adam and Eve, Joseph Jefferson Theatre Co., 1974; dir., choreographer: ballet Eden's Expressway, N.Y.C., 1975, The Corner and Poems, Echoes of Spoon River, N.Y.C., 1976, Randall Jarrell's Next Day, Public/Newman Theatre, 1978; revived, staged, directed: ballet The Desperate Heart, 1979; presented: ballet Leo Smit, Goodman Concert Hall, 1981 (Recipient Donaldson award, Mademoiselle award 1948). Home: New York, N.Y. Dec. Sept. 26, 1982.

BETTLE, GRISCOM, business exec. (ret.); b. Haverford, Pa., Feb. 19, 1890; s. Samuel and Helen Biddle (Griscom) B.; grad. St. Mark's Sch., 1910; A.B., Harvard, 1914; m. Dorothy Ball, Oct. 2, 1915 (died April 22, 1949); children—Griscom, Frances (Mrs. David A. Howard), Dorothy (Mrs. John R.S.S. Greenwood), Daniel Offley, Edith (Mrs. Frederick R. Drayton, Jr.), Helen Griscom (Mrs. William G. Baer). Vice pres. Central Elec. Co., Chicago, 1925-26; sales promotion mgr. Edward G. Budd Mfg. Co., Phila., 1927-36; pres. Fort Washington, Chemical Co., Pa., 1936-43; dir. The Budd Co., Globe Dye Works Co., Phila. Trustee Chatham Hall Sch., dir. Bryn Mawr (Pa.) Hosp. Served as capt. F.A., U.S. Army 1917-18. Republican. Mem. Society of Friends. Clubs: Philadelphia, Harvard (Phila.); Merion Cricket (Haverford, Pa.); Gulph Mills Golf (Conshohocken, Pa.); Jupiter Island (Hobe Sound, Fla.); Sakonnet Yacht, Sakonnet Golf (Little Compton, R.I.). Home: Hobe Sound, Fla.†

BETTONEY, WILFRED ESTEY, mech. engr.; b. Boston, Apr. 17, 1918; s. George V. and Helen A. (Estey) B.; m. Nellie Valkenburg, Sept. 27, 1942. B.S. in Mech. Engring. with distinction, U. Maine, 1939. With E.I. duPont de Nemours & Co., Inc., Wilmington, Del., from 1946, dir. petroleum lab., from 1962. Mem. Soc. Automotive Engrs. (dir.). Unitarian. Home: Wilmington, Del.

BETTS, CHARLES JULIUS, former state govt. ofcl.; b. Danbury, Wis., July 6, 1914; s. Thomas Britton and Ruby (Slack) B.; student Antioch Coll., 1934-35, Internat. Corr. Schs., 1937-40, U. Colo., 1939-41, Alexander Hamilton Inst., 1961; LL.B., Blackstone Sch. Law, 1960; m. Virginia Dare, Oct. 6, 1935; children—Earl Palmer, Mary Anna (Mrs. Jack A. Wilkerson), Burr Joseph. Architect with Roland L. Linder, Architect, 1937-47; cons. architect bd. church extension Disciples of Christ, Indpls., 1947-69; state bldg. commr. State of Ind., Indpls., 1969-76. Fellow AIA; mem. Ind. Soc. Architects (pres. 1958-59). Republican. Mem. Disciples of Christ. Contbr. articles to profl. jours. Home: La Grande, Oreg. Died May 4, 1984.

BETZNER, JEAN, educator; b. Montrose, Can., Mar. 22, 1888; d. David T. and Elsie Ann (Davidson) Betzner; B.S., Columbia Tchrs. Coll.; A.M., Columbia, Ph.D. Public sch. teacher, 1909-21, pvt. sch. teacher, 1921-30; mem. faculty Tchrs. Coll., Columbia, from 1930, prof. edn. Author: Everychild and Books, Exploring Literature (with Annie E. Moore). Home: Bronxville, N.Y. †

BEUTEL, FREDERICK KEATING, jurist, educator; b. Montgomery, Ala., Oct. 23, 1897; s. Conrad Frederick and Annie Margaret (Keating) B.; m. Nellie Irene McKinney, June 22, 1924; children: Fiora Ann, Beatrice Thorndyke. Student, U. Wash., 1917-19; A.B., Cornell U., 1921; LL.B., Harvard U., 1925, S.J.D., 1928. Began as clk. Puget Sound Bank, Tacoma, 1916; mgr. and propr. Beutel Bus. Coll., Tacoma, 1921-22; critic on editorial staff Ginn & Co., Boston, 1922-25, practiced law, Pitts., 1925-27, atty. to county controller, 1927; vis. prof. law U. Pa., 1931-32; dean La. State U. Law Sch., 1935-37; vis. prof. law Northwestern U., 1938-39; prof. law Coll. William and Mary, 1939-42; head cons. Coordinator Inter-Am. Affairs, 1941-42; mediator War Labor Bd., 1942; atty. to Alien Property Custodian, 1942-43; asst. solicitor Dept. Interior, 1944-45; dean U. Neb. Coll. Law, 1945-48, prof., 1949-63, U. Puerto Rico, 1963-65; vis. prof. law U. Ill., 1965-68, State U. N.Y., Buffalo, 1968-69, Ariz. State U., Tempe, 1969, Washington U., St. Louis, 1970-72. Author: Beutel's Brannon on Negotiable Instruments, 1948, Uniform Commercial Laws, 1950, Experimental Jurisprudence, 1957, German edit., 1970, Bank Officers Handbook, Banking Law, 1939, 1965, 70, 74, (with Milton Schroeder), 1982, Democracy or the Scientific Method, 1965, Experimental Jurisprudence and the Scienstate, 1975; Organizer, editor: Tulane Law Rev, 1929-31; editor: Fed. Bar Jour, 1944; Contbr. articles to law revs. Mem. AAUP, Fed. Bar Assn., Am. Law Inst. (life), Scabbard and Blade. Home: Scottsdale, Ariz. Dec. Nov. 22, 1983.

BEVAN, ARTHUR CHARLES, geologist; b. Delaware. O., Aug. 8, 1888; s. David Willard and Mary Leonora (Evans) B.; B.S., Ohio Wesleyan University, 1912, Sc.D., 1942; Ph.D., University of Chicago, 1921; student University of Missouri, summer, 1911; m. Mary Edna Arthur, June 17, 1914; 1 son, Robert (dec.). Asst. in geology, Ohio Wesleyan U., 1912-13, acting head dept., geology, 1913-14; instr. geology, Ohio State U., 1917-19; asst. prof. State U. of Mont., 1919-21; asst. geologist Mont. Bureau of Mines, 1919-22; asst. prof. geology, U. of Ill., 1921-29; geologist Ill. State Geol. Survey, 1923-29; asst. prof. of geology, U. of Chicago, summer 1924; state geologist of Va., 1929-47; prin. geologist Ill. Geol. Survey, 1947-55, emeritus. Sec. Assn. of Am. State Geologists, 1934-36, pres., 1937; v.p. Am. Assn. Advance Sci., 1945, editorial board; chmn., sec. Geology and Geography, 1945; president Va. Academy Sci., 1946; chmn. Nat. Research Council Division Geology and Geography, 1946-49. Fellow Geol. Soc. of America, A.A.A.S., Ohio Acad. Science; mem. Am. Assn. Petroleum Geologists, Soc. Econ. Geologists, Ill., Va. acads. sci., Geol. Soc. Washington, Alpha Sigma Phi, Sigma Xi. Writer on geology of Mont. Rockies, Ill. and Va. Home: Churchville, Va. †

BEVAN, GUY THEODORE MOLESWORTH, mfg. exec.; b. London, Eng., Mar. 17, 1890; s. Henry E. J. and Charlotte (Molesworth) B.; B.A.; M.A., St. Johns Coll. Cambridge U., Eng., 1912; m. Jean Munro, Aug. 11, 1920. Apprentice Metro-Vickers Electric & Mfg. Co.; Trafford Park, Eng. 1912-14; tech. dir. Willys-Overland Crossley, Ltd., Stockport, Eng., 1920-31; chief engr. Massey-Harris Co., Ltd., Toronto, 1931-44, v.p. engring. and research, 1944-50, v.p. coordinator, from 1950, v.p. dir. engring., Eastern Hemisphere, from 1953. Mem. Bd. Trade City of Toronto. Served as maj. Royal Engrs., Gt. Britain, 1914-20. Home: Leamington Spa, Eng.†

BHARUCHA-REID, ALBERT TURNER, mathematician, educator; b. Hampton, Va., Nov. 13, 1927; s. William Thaddeus and Mae Elaine (Beamon) Reid; m. Rodabé Phiroze Bharucha, June 5, 1954; children: Kurush Feroze, Rustam William. B.S., Iowa State U., 1949; postgrad., U. Chgo., 1950-53; D.Sci. (hon.),, Syracuse U.,, 1984. Research asst. math. biology U. Chgo., 1950-53; research asso. math. stats. Columbia U., 1953-55; asst. research statistician U. Calif., Berkeley, 1955-56; instr., asst. prof. math. U. Oreg., 1956-61; fellow Polish Acad. Scis., 1958-59; from asso prof. math. to prof. Wayne State U., 1961-81, asso. provost, dean grad. studies, 1976-81; prof. math. Ga. Inst. Tech., Atlanta, 1981-83; Disting. prof. math. Atlanta U., 1983-85; prof. applied math. Inst. Math. Scis., Madras, India, 1963-64; prof. Math. Research Center, U. Wis., Madison, 1966-67, Ga. Inst. Tech., 1973-74; mem. Grad. Record Exam. Bd., Princeton, N.J., 1978-82; bd. govs. Cranbrook Inst. Sci., Bloomfield Hills, Mich., 1977-80. Author or editor: Markov Processes and Their Applications, 1960 (Russian transl. 1969), Random Integral Equations, 1972, Approximate Solution of Random Equations, 1979, Probabilistic Methods in Applied Mathematics, 3 vols., 1968, 70, 73, Probabilistic Analysis and Related Topics, 3 vols., 1978, 79, 83; editor: Jour. Integral Equations; asso. editor: Stochastic Analysis and Applications. USAF research grantee, 1954-55; U.S. Army Research Office grantee, 1956-62, 77-81, 81—; NIH research grantee, 1966-69; NSF research grantee, 1969-71. Mem. Am. Math. Soc., AAAS, Inst. Math. Stats., Soc. Indsl. and Applied Math., N.Y. Acad. Scis., Polish Math, Soc., Bernoulli Soc., Soc. Math. Biology, Engring. Soc. Detroit, Nat. Assn. Mathematicians, Assn. Women in Math., London Math. Soc., Sigma Xi. Democrat. Episcopalian. Died Feb. 26, 1985.

BHATIA, AVADH BEHARI, physicist; b. India, Aug. 16, 1921; emigrated to Can., 1953, naturalized, 1965. B.Sc., U. Allahabad, 1940, M.Sc., 1942, D.Phil., 1946; Ph.D., U. Liverpool, Eng., 1951. Exhbn. scholar univs. Bristol and Liverpool, 1947-49; prof. theoretical physics Phys. Research Lab., Ahmedabad, 1950-52; Imperial Chem. Industries fellow U. Edinburgh, Scotland, 1952-53; fellow Nat. Research Council Can., Ottawa, 1953-55; mem. faculty U. Alta., Edmonton, 1955—, prof. physics, 1960—; dir. Theoretical Physics Inst., 1964-69; hon. prof. U. Liverpool, 1963-64; U.K. Sci. Research Council sr. vis. fellow Oxford (Eng.) U., 1978-79. Author: Ultrasonic Absorption, 1967, also research papers. Fellow Royal Soc. Can., Am. Phys. Soc.; mem. Can. Assn. Physicists; asso. mem. Acoustical Am. Address: Edmonton, AB, Canada. Died Sept. 27, 1984.

BIBLER, LESTER DAVID, physician; b. Findlay, Ohio, Jan. 13, 1902; s. Anson A. and Rosa A. (Friend) B.; m. Vera K. Moomaw, June 26, 1922; 1 son, David Anson. B.S., Ind. U., 1923, M.D., 1925. Diplomate: Am. Bd. Family Practice, also bd. dirs. Intern Methodist Hosp., Indpls., 1925-26, former mem. active staff; practicing physician, 1926-80; staff Winona Hosp., Methodist Hosp.; v.p. Muncie Oil & Coal Co., Capitol Med. Bldg., Indpls. Contbr. articles to med. jours. Bd. dirs. Ind. div. Am. Cancer Soc. Served to capt. M.C. USNR, 1940-46; comdg. officer Vol. Med. Unit 9-3 USNR. Recipient Maynard K. Hine medal Ind. U. Alumni Assn.; Lester D. Bibler chair formed Ind. U. Sch. Medicine. Mem. Am. Acad. Family Practice (past v.p.), AMA (chmn. com. med. practice, past chmn. sect. gen. practice; past trustee; past del. sect. gen. practice; 50 year mem., pres. elect 50 Yr. Club), Ind. Med. Assn. (past dist. councilor, past chmn. sect. gen. practice; 50 year mem.), Ind. Acad. Gen. Practice (past pres.), Indpls. Med. Soc., Am. Assn. Sr. Physicians (dir.), Indpls. C. of C., Am. Legion (past post comdr.), 40 and 8, Ind. U. Sch. Medicine Alumni Assn. (treas. from 1969, Alumnus of Yr. award 1981), 50 Yr. Club Am. Medicine (pres.), Phi Beta Pi (past pres. Ind.). Mem. Christian Ch. Clubs: Masons, Shriners, Jesters, Torch (past pres. Indpls.), Mercator (past nat. pres.). Home: Indianapolis, Ind. Died May 29, 1984.

BICKEL, WILLIAM FORMAN, business exec.; b. Pittsburgh, Mar. 12, 1890; s. Henry Wright and Lydia Forman (Paulson) B.; student Shady Side Acad., 1904-09; A.B., Princeton, 1913; m. Florence Croft, Apr. 26, 1917; children—William C., Harry C., Mary (Mrs. Robert W. Off). Pres. Woodland Stores, Inc., Pittsburgh, 1930-52; dir. Harbison-Walker Refractories Company, from 1932; treasurer executive committee Carnegie Hero Fund Commn.; vice pres., dir. Pitcairn-Crabbe Found. from 1928. Dir. Shady Side Acad. Presbyn. (trustee). Clubs: Fox Chapel Golf (dir.), Duquesne. Home: Aspinwall, Pa.†

BICKEL, WILLIAM HAROLD, educator, surgeon; b. Shamokin, Pa., July 4, 1909; s. Edwin Forrest and Florence (Simon) B.; B.A., Lawrence Coll., 1931; M.S., Northwestern U., 1935, M.D., 1936; M.S., Mayo Found., U. Minn., 1941; m. Annette Ray, Jan. 1, 1937; children—Barbara Carnell, Ruth Ann, Patricia, Priscilla. Intern, St. Luke's Hosp., Chgo., 1935-37; resident Hosp. Milw. Sanatorium, 1936-38; pvt. practice, asst. surgeon Internat. Harvester Co., Milw., 1936-38; fellow orthopedic surgery Mayo Med. Sch., U. Minn., Rochester, 1938-42, instr. to assoc. prof., 1942-59, prof. orthopedic surgery, 1959-74;

1st asst. orthopedic surgery Mayo Clinic, 1940-42, mem. staff, 1942-74; practice medicine, specializing in orthopedic surgery, Sun City, Ariz., 1974-77; cons., 1977-82. Civilian cons. orthopedic surgery Surg. Gen., ETO, 1958; mem. spl. med. adv. group, orthopedic cons. VA; adv. bd. Med. Specialties. Diplomate Am. Bd. Orthopedic Surgery, pres., 1959. Fellow A.C.S.; mem. Am.-Brit.-Canadian Travelling Fellowship Club, Am. Acad. Orthopedic Surgeons (pres. 1964), Minn. Med. Assn., Am., Tex. orthopedic assns., Interurban Orthopedic Soc., A.M.A., Am. Assn. Surgery Trauma, Clin. Orthopedic Soc., Internat. Soc. Surgery and Trauma, Sigma Xi. Home: Sun City, Ariz. Dec. Apr. 10, 1982.

BICKERMAN, ELIAS JOSEPH, historian; b. Russia, July 1, 1897; came to U.S., 1942, naturalized, 1948; s. Joseph and Sarah (Marguelies) B. A.B., U. Petrograd, 1915, Ph.D., 1918; Ph.D., U. Berlin, 1926; éleve diplome, École Pratique des Hautes Études, Paris, France, 1938. Privat-dozent U. Berlin, 1929-33; chargé de cours École Pratique des Hautes Études, Paris, 1933-40; chargé de recherches Centre National de la Recherche, 1937-42; prof. New Sch. for Social Research and École Libre, N.Y.C., 1942-46; research fellow Jewish Theol. Sem., N.Y.C., 1946-50; vis. prof. Columbia, 1948-49, prof. ancient history, 1952-67; with Inst. Advanced Study, Princeton, 1967-68; vis. prof. U. Judaism, Los Angeles, 1950-52, U. Cal. at Los Angeles, 1957, Jewish Theol. Sem., from 1968. Author: Der Gott der Makabaer, 1937, English transl., 1979, Institutions des Seleucides, 1938, From Ezra to the Last of the Maccabees, 1962, Chronology of Jewish. Address: New York, NY. Ancient World, 2d edit, 1967, Four Strange Books of the Bible, 1967, Studies in Jewish and Christian History, Vol. I, 1976, Vol. II, 1980, (with Morton Smith) The Ancient History of Western Civilization, 1976; Co-editor: (with Morton Smith) Revue Internationale des droits de l'Antiquité . Served with Russian Army, 1916-18. Recipient R. Kreglinger Triennal award U. Bruxelles, 1935, Asso. Études grecques, 1938, Lucas prize U. Tuebingen, 1976; Guggenheim fellow, 1949, 59. Fellow Am. Acad. Jewish Research, Brit. Acad. (corr.), Am. Acad. Arts and Scis. Jewish. Address: New York, NY.

BIDWELL, SETH ROLAND, lawyer, business exec.; b. Girard, Mich., May 6, 1900; s. Myron Elezer and Elizabeth Young (Ackerman) B.; J.D., U. Mich., 1924; m. Dorothy E. DeKleine, June 16, 1924; 1 son, Seth Macey. Admitted to Mich. bar, 1924; partner firm Bidwell, Schmidt & Martin, Grand Rapids, Mich., 1924-51; dir. Hasselbring Co., Niles Chem. Paint Co., Bijou Theatrical Enterprise Co., Butterfield Mich. Theatres Co., Blodgett Uncrated Furniture Co., Bradfield & Bidwell, Inc.; mem. Lansing bd. Mich. Nat. Bank; dir. Gross Telecasting Inc., Lansing. Trustee W.S. Butterfield Estate, Grand Rapids Youth Commonwealth; pres. Ingham County unit Am. Cancer Soc.; chmn. Ingham County chpt. ARC, 1952-53. Mem. Am. Bar Assn., State Bar Mich., Nat. Stationers Assn., SAR (past pres. Kent County), Phi Alpha Delta. Clubs: Masons (32 deg.), K.T., Shriners, Rotary (dir., v.p.), Peninsular (pres.), Kent Country (Grand Rapids); Paradise Valley Country, Scottsdale (Ariz.) Country; Lansing Country (past pres.), Automobile (Lansing); Circumnavigators (N.Y.C.). Home: Scottsdale, Ariz. Died May 27, 1981.

BIEBER, RALPH PAUL, univ. prof.; b. Hellertown, Pa., May 9, 1894; s. Rev. William John and Lillie Barbara (Sander) B.; A.B., Muhlenberg College, 1914. Litt.D., honorary, 1951; A.M., University of Pennsylvania, 1915, Ph.D., (Harrison scholar, 1915-16; Harrison fellow, 1916-18), 1918; m. Ida Louise Parker, Sept. 1, 1925; children—Dorothy (Mrs. Farley), William Instr. history Muhlenberg Coll., Allentown, Pa., 1918-19; asst. prof. history, Washington Univ., 1919-25, asso. prof. history, 1925-40, prof. from 1940, William Eliot Smith Prof. of History from 1950; chairman of the department of history, 1950-53; in Am. history summer sessions; Rutgers U., 1921, Univ. of Tex., 1924, 25, 27, U. Kan., 1928, U. Mo., 1937-40, U. N.M., 1954. Regional dir. Survey of Fed. Archives in Mo., 1936-37; mem. adv. com. Hist. Documents Survey in Mo., 1940-41. Awarded Social Sci. Research Council grant, 1940; Rockefeller Found. grant for research on Calif. Gold Rush of 1848-49, 1944-48. Fellow Huntington Library, Royal Historical Society, London, Am. Philos. Soc.; mem. Am. (contbr. local arrangements com. conv. St. Louis 1956), Miss. Valley (pres. 1947-48) hist. assns., nat. sectional and local hist. socs., Phi Beta Kappa, Sigma Phi Epsilon (hon). Club: Univ. of Pa. (St. Louis). Author or editor numerous hist. works, primarily on frontier U.S.; editor hist. jours. Contbr. to Dictionary of Am. Biography, 1928-36, Dictionary of Am. History, 1940, Britannica Book of Year (Ency. Brit.), 1940-56, 57; 10 Eventful Years, 1937-46 (Ency. Brit.), 1947. Specialist in The Frontier in the Trans-Miss. West, 1803-1808; British Colonial Adminstrn., 1675-1696. Home: University City, Mo. Died July 23, 1981.

BIEMILLER, ANDREW JOHN, labor union ofcl., congressman; b. Sandusky, Ohio, July 23, 1906; s. Andrew Frederick and Pearl (Weber) B.; m. Hannah Perot Morris, Dec. 20, 1929; children—Andrew John, Nancy Barbara. A.B., Cornell U., 1926; postgrad., U. Pa., 1928-31. Tchr. history Syracuse U., U. Pa., 1926-32; newspaper and labor relations positions, 1932-42; mem. Wis. legislature, 1936-42; with WPB, 1942-44; mem. 79th, 81st U.S. congresses, 5th Wis. Dist.; pub. relations counsellor, lectr., writer; spl. asst. to sec. interior, 1951-52; dir. dept. legislation AFL-CIO, 1956-82, chmn. staff com. on atomic energy.; Mem. labor-mgmt. adv. com. AEC; mem. mgmt.-labor textile adv. com. Dept. Commerce, 1961-82; mem. Presdl. Task Force on Career Advancement, 1966-67; mem. consumer com. on automobile ins. and compensation Dept. Transp.; mem. nat. petroleum adv. com. Dept. Interior; labor adviser Am. delegation GATT Conf., 1957, 61. Mem. Am. Fedn. Tchrs., Former Mems. of Congress (exec. bd.), Delta Kappa Epsilon. Democrat. Quaker. Clubs: Kenwood Golf and Country, Nat. Press. Home: Bethesda, Md. Died 1982.

BIENSTOCK, ABRAHAM LAWRENCE, lawyer; b. N.Y.C., Dec. 30, 1904; s. Alexander Myer and Matilda (Touster) B.; student Coll. City N.Y., 1922-24; LL.B., N.Y. U., 1927; m. Majorie Cahne, July 12, 1939; children—Patricia Grace Murdock Bienstock Williams, John James Murdock. Admitted to N.Y. bar, 1928, practiced N.Y.C.; sr. mem. firm Abraham L. Bienstock, N.Y.C., 1940-80; ltd. partner Hurt Oil Co., Ltd., Houston; chmn. bd. Intsel Corp.; dir., mem. exec. com., dir. R.H. Macy & Co., Inc., dir. Pechiney Ugine Kuhlmann Copr., chmn. exec. com., dir. Intsel Corp. Bd. mgrs. Hosp. for Spl. Surgery, N.Y.C.; bd. dirs. Univ. Settlement Soc.; trustee Bethsabee de Rothschild Found. for Arts and Scis. Mem. Council Fgn. Relations, Assn. Bar City N.Y., Am., N.Y. bar assns., N.Y. County Lawyers Assn. Clubs: Wall St. (N.Y.C.); Piping Rock, Locust Valley, L.I. Home: Syosset, N.Y. Died Nov. 14, 1980.

BIENVENU, RENE JOSEPH, university president; b. Colfax, La., Mar. 19, 1923; s. Rene J. and Corinne (Wells) B.; m. Catherine Nelken, Jan. 28, 1948; children—Steven, Elizabeth Ann, Patricia Renee. B.S., La. State U., 1944, M.S., 1949; Ph.D., U. Tex., 1957. Microbiologist Confederate Meml. Hosp., La., 1949-50; asst. prof. Northwestern State U., Natchitoches, La., 1950-58; dean Northwestern State U. (Coll. Sci. and Tech.), 1968-77, pres., from 1978; dean allied health La. State U., 1977. Contbr. articles to sci. jours. Served in USN, 1944-46. Mem. Natchitoches C. of C. (dir. from 1978), Am. Soc. Microbiology, La. Acad. Scis., La. Council of Deans, Nat. Brucellosis Research Council, Assn. Practitioners in Infection Control, La. Outdoor Drama Assn., Northwestern-Natchitoches Symphony Assn., Sigma Xi, Phi Kappa Phi, Beta Beta Beta, Phi Eta Sigma, Blue Key. Democrat. Roman Catholic. Club: Rotary. Address: Natchitoches, La. Dec. Jan. 27, 1983.

BIERER, JOHN M(ICHAEL), rubber goods mfr.; b. Cedarville, Va., Mar. 3, 1888; s. John M. and Susan (Painter) B.; B.S., Washington and Lee U., 1908, Mass. Inst. Tech., 1910; m. Ruth Coulter, June 14, 1913; children—John Coulter, Ruth Elizabeth (Mrs. John B. Ward), James Huntoon. With Boston Woven Hose & Rubber Co., Boston, from 1911, chemist, 1911-29, factory mgr., 1929-44, v.p., 1944-50, exec. v.p., 1950, pres. and gen. mgr., 1951-58, dir., from 1932; v.p. dir. Am. Biltrite Rubber Co., 1956-57; incorporator and trustee Newton Savings Bank. Member of Mass. Home Guard, 1917-19; spl. work in Q.M. Dept., U.S. Army, World War I. Vice pres., Newtom Com. on Pub. Safety, 1940, chmn., 1941-45. Mem. nat. exec. bd. Boy Scouts Am., 1940-58, life mem. nat. exec. bd., from 1958, nat. chmn. cub scouting, 1942-53, nat. chmn. explorer scouting, 1953-57; awarded Silver Beaver, Silver Antelope and Silver Buffalo. Fellow Instn. of the Rubber Industry (Eng.); mem. Am. Chem. Soc. (past chmn. rubber div.), Am. Soc. Testing Materials. Clubs: Union (Boston); Union Leagur (N.Y.C.); Brae Burn Country (Newton, Mass.). Home: Waban, Mass. †

BIERWIRTH, F(REDERICK) W(ILLIAM), utilities exec.; b. Elmwood, Ont., Aug. 29, 1889; s. John and Annie (Trent) B.; ed. pub. schs.; m. Ruth Granger, 1914; children—Jane (Mrs. Kenneth Simpson), Barbara (Mrs. Carl Giles Crowder), Granger. Prodn. and service br. Western Electric Co. Hawthorne Works, Chicago, 1912, head installation service, 1922, comml. contract mgr., 1926, gen. accounting supt. installation dept., N.Y. City office, 1924, gen. price mgr., 1927, asst. comptroller mfg., 1928, operating supt., Kearny (N.J.) Works, 1929, asst. works mgr., 1931, works mgr., 1935, head telephone sales dept., N.Y. City office, 1939, v.p. telephone div., 1942, v.p. telephone and installation div., 1951, v.p. finance from 1952; dir., mem. exec. com. Western Electric Co., Inc., pres., dir. Westrex Corp., 395 Hudson St. Corp.; dir. Bell Telephone Labs., Inc., Teletype Corp., No. Elec. Co., Ltd. Mem. N.Y. Elec. Soc. Clubs: Railroad-Machinery (N.Y.C.); Country (Upper Montclair, N.J.). Home: Upper Montclair, N.J. †

BIERY, JOHN CARLTON, chemical engineering educator; b. Jackson, Mich., Oct. 8, 1927; s. John Mahlon and Dorothy Christine (Schaibly) B.; B.S. Engring. in Chem. Engring., U. Mich., 1951; Ph.D. (Alumni Achievement Fund fellow, NSF fellow), Iowa State U., 1961; m. Glee Dudgeon, Dec. 23, 1950; children—Gay Maurene, John Dudgeon. With Dow Chem. Co., Rocky Flats Plant, Denver, 1951-58, research devel. engr., 1956-58; postdoctoral U. Wis., 1961-62; with Los Alamos Sci. Lab., 1962-70, asso. group leader, 1965-68, alt. group leader, 1968-70; assoc. prof. chem. engring. U. Ariz., 1970-71; chmn., prof. dept. chem. engring. U. Fla., Gainesville, 1971-81. Mgr., Unitarian Camp, Laforet, Colo., 1970. Served with AUS, 1946-47. Mem. Am. Inst. Chem. Engrs., N.Y. Acad. Scis., Sigma Xi, Tau Beta Pi, Phi Kappa Phi. Contbr. articles to tech. jours. Research in solvent extraction, manometers, tantalum corrosion by plutonium, surface tension, sodium tech., thermochem. hydrogen, coal gasification, heat transfer. Home: Gainesville, Fla. Died Jan. 9, 1981.

BIGGE, GEORGE EDMUND, govt. official; born Kalkaska, Michigan, October 24, 1887; son of Louis and Clara (Dietrich) B.; A.B., U. of Mich., 1922, A.M., 1923, Ph.D., 1931; LL.D. (honorary), Ferris Institute, 1958; married Ercell Venus Graham, July 26, 1917; children—Francis Elizabeth (dec.), George Edmund (dec.), Ercell Venus, Louis Graham, Joanna Mary, William Russell. Teacher rural schs., 1909, 1912, high sch., Big Rapids, Mich., 1913; ednl. dir. Mich. State Penitentiary, 1913-19; instr. U. of Mich., 1923-27; asst. prof. economics, Brown U., 1927-32, asso. prof., 1932-40, prof., 1940, chmn. of dept., 1936-40; mem. Social Security Bd., 1937-46; dir. Office Federal-State Relations, Fed. Security Agy., 1946-53; spl. asst. fed. state problems Dept. Health, Edn. and Welfare, from 1953. Chmn. R.I. Unemployment Compensation Bd., 1936. Mem. Am. Economic Association, American Academy Political and Social Science, American Association for Labor Legislation, Phi Beta Kappa, Delta Sigma Rho. Republican. Lutheran. Club: Exchange (Providence, R.I.). †

BIGGS, J. WILLIAM mfg.co. exec.; b. Detroit, May 22, 1932; s. Arthur Edward and Pauline Catherine (Maier) B.; m. Barbara Kliesrath, June 1, 1963. B.S. in Acctg. and Econs. cum laude, U. Md., 1954; M.B.A., Harvard U., 1962. C.P.A., Md. Dir. profit planning Cin. Milacron Co., 1963-68; staff asst. aquisitions Anaconda Co., 1968-69; mgr. budgets Singer Co., 1969-70; sr. cons. Xerox Corp., 1970-72; controller B-D div. Becton Dickinson & Co., 1972-76; v.p. fin., chief fin. officer Clarkson Industries, 1976-78, Ethan Allen Inc., Danbury, Conn., from 1978. Served to 1st lt. USAF, 1954-57. Mem. Fin. Execs. Inst., Am. Inst. C.P.A.'s, Harvard U. Bus. Sch. Alumni Assn., Harvard U. Bus. Sch. Club, Omicron Delta Kappa, Phi Kappa Phi. Home: Ridgefield, Conn.

BIGGS, JOHN, JR., judge, author; b. Wilmington, Del., Oct. 6, 1895; s. John and Rachel Valentine (Massey) B.; Litt.B., Princeton U., 1918, LL.D., 1956; LL.B., Harvard U., 1922, LL.D., 1969; LL.D., Lafayette Coll., 1948, Temple U., 1958, U. Del., 1960, Dickinson Sch. Law, 1962, Washington and Jefferson Coll., 1963; m. Anna Swift Rupert, Apr. 16, 1925; children—John III, Charles Rupert, Anna Swift Rupert. Admitted to Del. bar, 1922, since practiced in Wilmington; U.S. referee in bankruptcy Dist. of Del.; apptd. judge U.S. Circuit Ct. Appeals for 3d Circuit, 1937; chief judge 3d Jud. Circuit of U.S., 1939-65, circuit judge, 1965-79. Served in Ordnance and Tank Corps, U.S. Army, World War; civilian aide to sec. of war for Del., 1923-37. Recipient Isaac Ray award Am. Psychiat. Assn., 1955. Fellow Am. Psychiat. Assn., Am. Orthopsychiat. Assn.; mem. Wistar Assn., Am., Del., Fed. bar assns., Assn. Bar City N.Y., Am. Philos. Soc., Soc. Colonial Wars (past gov. Del.), SAR, Am. Legion, Century Assn., Order of Coif, Phi Alpha Delta. Mem. Soc. of Friends. Clubs: Metropolitan (Washington); Campus, Nassau (Princeton); Greenville Country; Philadelphia, Rittenhouse, Franklin Inn (Phila.); Wilmington Country; Harvard (N.Y.C.); Grolier. Author: Demigods, 1926; Seven Days' Whipping, 1928; Delaware Laws Affecting Business Corporations (with Stewart Lynch), 1935; The Guilty Mind, Psychiatry and the Law of Homicide, 1955. Contbr. mags., legal periodicals. Home: Wilmington, Del. Died Apr. 15, 1979.

BIGGS, ROBERT WILDER, mfg. co. exec.; b. Elyria, Ohio, Aug. 16, 1907; s. Hardy D. and Bessie (Wilder) B.; m. Eleanor Hughes, Jan. 30, 1932; 1 son, Robert Wilder. B.S. in Mech. Engring, Ohio No. U., 1930, Ph.D. (hon.), 1970. With Nat. Tube Co., 1930-38, Jones & Laughlin Steel Co., 1938-45; gen. mgr. operations Nat. Electric Products Co., Ambridge, Pa., 1945-51; v.p. mfg. Ball Bros. Co., Muncie, Ind., 1951-54; pres., dir. S. K. Wellman Co., Bedford, Ohio, 1954-65; pres., dir. Brush Wellman Inc., Cleve., 1965-69, chmn. bd., after 1969, now cons.; dir. Abex Corp., N.Y.C. Mem. Soc. Automotive Engrs., Newcomen Soc., Tau Beta Pi. Clubs: Country of Cleve, Union. Home: Chagrin Falls, Ohio. Died Nov. 1, 1984.

BILBY, RALPH MANSFIELD, business executive; b. Tucson, June 18, 1917; s. Ralph Willard and Marguerite (Mansfield) B.; student U. Ariz., 1935-40; m. Mary Eleanore Babbitt, Dec. 28, 1941; children—Meg, Diane Claire. Ralph Babbitt, Patricia Louise, Barbara Sue, Richard Joseph. Mgr. wholesale grocery dept. Babbitt Bros. Trading Co., Flagstaff, Ariz., 1946-56, v.p., 1956-69, supr. wholesale div. and trading posts, 1954-74, exec. v.p., 1969-75, pres., 1975-78; v.p., dir. Quality Industries, Phoenix, 1978-81; chmn. bd. Ariz. Pub. Service Co.; dir. 1st Nat. Bank of Ariz., 1976-81. Chmn. Ariz. Planning and Bldg. Commn., 1960-67; pres. Ariz. Acad., 1974-75; sec. Ariz. Bd. Regents, 1974-79, pres., 1979-81; 1st vice chmn. Ariz. Republican Central Com., 1956-58, 2d vice chmn., 1962-64; mem. Flagstaff City Council, 1954-58; trustee Am. Grad. Sch. Internat. Mgmt. Served to capt. U.S. Army, 1940-43; to maj. USAAF, 1943-45. Mem. United Indian Traders Assn. (past pres.), Flagstaff C. of C. (past pres.), Beta Gamma Sigma, Phi Delta Theta. Clubs: Phoenix Country, Elks. Home: Phoenix, Ariz. Died Apr. 1, 1981.

BILDERSEE, BARNETT, former public relations executive; b. N.Y.C., Apr. 6, 1911; s. Isaac and Selena (Ullman) B.; B.Litt., Columbia U., 1932; m. Ada Kogan, June 30, 1934 (dec. Jan. 1973); 1 child, Adele Bildersee Feldman. Reporter, N.Y. Evening World, 1928-31; corr. N.Y. Post-Phila. Pub. Ledger Syndicate, London, 1932-33; reporter Providence Jour., 1933-34; cable editor AP, N.Y.C., 1934-40; fgn. news editor, day city editor PM and N.Y. Star newspapers, 1940-49; with Allied Indsl. Research Consultants, Inc., 1949-56, v.p., 1953-54, exec. v.p., 1954-56, also dir.; v.p., chmn. plans bd. Tex McCrary, Inc., N.Y.C., 1957-58, exec. v.p., 1958-61, pres., 1961; pres. Martial & Co., Inc., 1961-63, Bildersee Pub. Relations, N.Y.C., 1963-76; vice chmn. Wallach/Reynolds/Bildersee, Inc.; dir. N.Y. Dental Service Corp.; lectr. N.Y. U. Sr. field rep. OWI, 1943. Bd. dirs. Brotherhood-in-Action, Inc. Mem. Soc. Silurians (pres.), U.S. Power Squadron, Sigma Delta Chi. Home: Port Saint Lucie, Fla. Died Sept. 2, 1984.

BILLINGSLEY, PAUL RAYMOND, surgeon; b. Lowellville, O., Oct. 25, 1887; s. Albert Magee and Eliza Vail (Boyd) B.; B.S., Cornell Coll., Mt. Vernon, Ia., 1910; M.D. (with distinction), Northwestern U., 1918; m. Frances Adelaide Bulot, Apr. 13, 1917; children—Ruth, Mary Frances, Paul. Instr. anatomy, Northwestern U. Med. Sch., 1913-19; interne Cook County Hosp., 1918-19; practiced at Sioux Falls, S.D., from 1920. Fellow A.M.A.; mem. S.D. State Med. Assn., Sioux Falls Acad., S.D. Soc. S.A.R., Sigma Xi, Alpha Omega Alpha, Nu Sigma Nu, Sigma Nu. Republican. Methodist. Mason. Home: Sioux Falls, S.D. †

BINDRA, DALBIR, educator; b. Rawalpindi, Pakistan, June 11, 1922; s. Jaswant S. and Lajiavati (Dhody) B.; B.A., Punjab U., 1941; M.A., Harvard, 1946, Ph.D., 1948; m. Jane Stewart, Aug. 5, 1959. Came to U.S., 1944. Teaching fellow psychology Harvard, 1946-47; asst. prof., dir. psychology lab. Am. U., Washington, 1947-49; asst. prof. McGill U., Montreal, Can., 1949-52, assoc. prof., 1953-61, prof., 1962-80, chmn. dept. psychology, 1975-80. Decorated Canadian Centennial medal. Fellow Am. Psychol. Assn. (div. physiol. and comparative psychology), Royal Soc. Can.; mem. AAAS, Canadian Psychol. Assn. (pres. 1958-59). Author: Motivation, a systematic reinterpretation, 1959; A theory of Intelligent Behavior, 1976. Editor: (with Jane Stewart) Motivation, 1966, 2d edit., 1971. Home: Montreal, Que., Can. Died Dec. 31, 1980.

BINGER, WALTER D(AVID), civil engr.; b. N.Y. City, Jan. 16, 1888; s. Gustav and Frances (Newgass) B.; student Phila. Textile Sch., 1908-09; S.B. in C.E., Mass. Inst. Tech., 1916; also studied abroad and at Harvard Engring. Sch.; m. Beatrice Bronson Sorchan, June 1, 1922; children—Charlotte (Mrs. Geo. Hasen), Frances, Bronson. Began in textile business, 1904; v.p. Thompson & Binger, Inc., engrs. and contractors, 1916-19; served as 2d lt. Signal Corps Constrn. Div., Jan.-Mar. 1918; with Air Service Constrn. Div.; A.E.F., Mar. 1918-Jan. 1919; pres. Thompson & Binger, Inc., 1920-28; v.p. R. H. Howes Construction Co., 1928-29; 1st v.p. Adelson Constructing & Engring. Corp., 1930-31; in private practice as cons. engr. since 1931; deputy commr. of sanitation in charge of engring. div., N.Y. City, 1934-38; (built Wards Island Sewage Treatment Works); commr. of Borough Works, Manhattan, charge of design and constrn. East River Drive and Harlem Drive, 1938-45; partner Binger-O'Connor-Orrok, Architect-Engineer, 1941-44, specializing work for Engineer Corps, U.S. Army; mem. Binger & Hammond, Associates, Consulting Engrs., 1944-45; vice-pres. City Investing Company, 1945-50; cons. engineer since 1950. Chmn. Nat. Tech. Adv. com., by appt. Sec. of War, 1941. Member visiting committee dept. civil and sanitary engring., Mass. Inst. Tech., 1944-46; chmn. Citizens Traffic Action Com., 1948. Mem. Am. Soc. Civil Engrs. (past dir. Met. Sect.; past nat. chmn. Nat. Com. on Civilian Protection in War Time; chmn. com. on program, 1944-45; nat. chmn. 1952), Instn. Civil Engrs. (London, Eng.); Citizens Union (former mem. legislative and exec. coms.). Newcomen Soc. of Eng., Am. Legion (past comdr. Willard Straight Post); mem. Amer. Inst. of Cons. Engrs., (mem. council, 1945). Clubs: Engineers, Technology, City, Midday (N.Y. City); Fairfield County Hunt (former gov.); Fairfield Beach (Conn.). Home: New York, NY. †

BINGHAM, ROBERT, magazine editor; b. Lima. O., Apr. 10, 1925; s. Rankin and Miriam (Kamerer) B.; grad. Phillips Exeter Acad., 1943. A.B. cum laude, Harvard, 1948; m. Janet McPhedran, May 13, 1950; children—Thomas, Anne, Peter. With Time mag., 1948; with The Reporter mag., 1948-64, mng. editor, 1957-64; mem. editorial staff New Yorker mag., 1965-82. Served with AUS, 1943-46. Home: Dobbs Ferry, N.Y. Died July 18, 1982.

BINKLEY, JAMES SAMUEL, surgeon, oncologist, radiologist; b. Guymon, Okla., July 31, 1908; s. James Garfield and Nellie Irene (Keller) B.; m. Kathrine Bretch, Mar. 8, 1941; children—Donald James, Keith Bretch. B.S., U. Okla., 1929, A.B., 1930; M.D., Harvard, 1932. Chief resident surgeon, also Rockefeller Clin.; fellow Meml. Hosp., N.Y.C., 1939, research fellow, 1936-40; med. dir. Am. Soc. for Control Cancer, Inc., Am. Cancer Soc., 1940-46; mem. surg. staff chest dept. Meml. Cancer Center; practice medicine, N.Y.C., 1940-42; organizer Cancer Center, Bethesda Naval Hosp., also; Long Beach Naval Hosp., 1942-46; sr. surgeon Los Angeles Tumor Inst., 1946-50; asso. prof. surgery U. Okla. Med. Sch., Oklahoma City, from 1950; mem. staff Bapt. Meml., Mercy, Presbyn. and Univ. hosps.; Med. dir. Standard Life & Accident Ins. Co.; cons. to ins. industry. Contbr. articles to profl. jours. Served to lt. comdr., M.C. USNR, 1942-46. Mem. A.C.S., A.M.A., Okla., Cal., N.Y., Los Angeles, N.Y.C., Oklahoma City, County med. socs., Oklahoma City Surg. Soc., Soc. Head and Neck Surgeons, Am. Radium Soc., James Ewing Soc., Phi Beta Kappa, Phi Beta Pi, Phi Delta Theta. Presbyn. Clubs: Kiwanian, Lake Aluma. Home: Oklahoma City, Okla.

BINZEN, FREDERICK WILLIAM, business exec.; born Brooklyn, Apr. 26, 1890; s. Frederick W. and Ella May (Albro) B.; student Lehigh U., 1910-11; m. Lucy Husted, Nov. 3, 1917; children—Frederick W., Peter H., David A. Dry Goods merchant, N.Y. City, 1911-25; asst. merchandise mgr. J. C. Penney Co., N.Y. City, 1926-29, merchandise mgr., 1929-49, 3d vice pres., 1945-46, 2d vice pres., 1946-47, exec. vice president, from 1947, dir. from 1935. Mem. Chi Phi. Republican. Clubs: Union League, Merchants (New York); Upper Montclair (N.J.) Country. Home: Montclair, N.J. †

BIRD, ANGUS EUGENE, banker; b. Guyton, Ga., July 16, 1888; s. Angus E. and Kitty (Stewart) B.; student Emory Coll., Oxford, Ga.; m. Cora Mary Jamar, Aug. 30, 1913; children—Mary Jamar, Kitty Stewart, Angus Eugene, Jr. With The Citizens & Southern Bank, Savannah, Ga., as utility clerk, Jan. 1910, bookkeeper, 1913, asst. cashier, 1917, transfered to Macon, Ga., as asst. cashier, 1918, became cashier, 1919, transferred to Athens, Ga., as exec. v.p., 1926; pres. Atlantic Savings and The Atlantic Nat. Banks of Charleston, S.C., Mar. 19, 1928; name of Atlantic Savings Bank changed to The Citizens & Southern Bank of S.C., transferred to Columbia, S.C.; hon. chmn. Citizens & Southern Nat. Bank of S.C.; dir. State Co., Record Publishing Co., State Commercial Printing Co. Trustee Emory U. Mem. C. of C., St. Andrews Soc., St. Cecilia Soc., Chi Phi. Club: Forest Lake Country (Columbia). †

BIRD, WILLIAM ERNEST, coll. pres. emeritus; b. Jackson County, N.C., July 21, 1890; s. Charles Asbury and Sarah Ermina (Terrell) B.; diploma Cullowhee Normal and Indsl. Sch., 1915; student Mars Hill Coll., 1912; A.B., U. N.C., 1917, postgrad., 1924-25; M.A., George Peabody Coll. for Tchrs., 1920; Doctor of Literature, Western Cal. Coll., 1960; m. Myrtle Wells, Aug. 16, 1916; children—Sarah Anne (Mrs. Engman), Charles Wells, Helen Gertrude (Mrs. Foreman). Tchr. pub. schs., Jackson County, 1909, 11; prin. Wilkesboro (N.C.) High Sch., 1917-19, Sylva High Sch., 1919-20; v.p., dean Western Carolina Coll., 1920-47, acting pres., 1947-49, dean, 1949-56, pres., 1956-57, pres. emeritus, from 1957; also part-time tchr. Pres. N.C. Coll. Conf., 1949-50. Mem. N.C. Council Poetry (chmn.), Modern Lang. Assn., Western N.C. Hist. Assn. (past pres.), N.E.A., N.C. Edn. Assn. Methodist. Mason, Rotarian (past pres.) Author: Lyrics of a Layman; History Western Carolina College, 1963; Level Paths: More Songs of the Layman; also research articles. Address: Cullowhee, N.C. †

BIRDSONG, H(ENRY) E(LLIS), prof. of journalism; b. Cooper Co., Mo., Apr. 17, 1887; s. John James and Jeston (Vaughan) B.; A.B., Univ. of Mo., 1912, B.J., 1913; master of philosophy, U. of Wis., 1924; m. Mabel Marquis, June 18, 1913; 1 dau., Virginia Jean (Mrs. David Scott Potts). Reporter, Kansas City (Mo.) Star, 1913-14; teacher and high sch. prin., Cooper Co. pub. schs., 1914-17; instr. in English and journalism, also dir. of publicity, Kansas State Teachers Coll., 1917-22; editor of Teaching (mag.), 1917-22, also newspaper corr.; instr. journalism, U. of Wis., 1922-24; prof. journalism and head of dept., Butler U., Indianapolis, 1924-27, Temple U., Phila., 1927-49, prof. from 1949; lectr. U. of Minn. Journalism Tour of Europe, summer, 1927. Mem. Association for Education in Journalism, American Assn. Univ. Professors, Sigma Delta Chi, Kappa Tau Alpha. Democrat. Protestant. Home: Glenside, Pa. †

BIRKENHAUER, FREDERICK WALLER, bakery exec.; b. Newark, Aug. 16, 1888; s. John and Lillian Pauline (Ziehr) B.; Litt.B. Princeton, 1910; m. Grace Marion Bittles, Apr. 12, 1916. Treas. N.Y. & Pacific Hop Co., 1910-17; pres. Butte County Hop Co., 1912-16; treas. Wagner Pastry Co., 1918-23. Wagner Pastries, Inc., 1923-25, Jochum Bros., Inc., 1923-25, Consumers Pie & Baking Corp., 1923-25; v.p. Pie Bakeries of Am., Inc., 1925-27, pres., 1927-31; chmn. bd., pres. Pie Bakeries, Inc., 1931-36; pres. Pie Bakeries of Mich., Inc., Pie Bakeries of N.Y., Inc., 1931-36; pres. Wagner Baking Corp., from 1936; also chmn.; bd. mgrs. Howard Savs. Inst., dir. Nat. Newark & Essex Banking Co., Williams Baking Co., Scranton, Pa. Trustee United Hospital of Newark, New Jersey. Honorary director YMCA; dir. Junior Achievement of Hosp. Crippled Children, Babies Hosp., Newark; trustee Newark Coll. Engring. Mem. Am. Inst. Baking (vice chmn., dir.), Am. Bakers Assn. (dir.). Clubs: Bakers of N.Y.; Bakers (Chgo.); Downtown (Newark); Morris County Country (Morristown, N.J.). Home: Madison, N.J. †

BIRMINGHAM, FREDERIC ALEXANDER, editor; b. N.Y.C., Nov. 13, 1915; s. John Francis and Louise (Westher) B.; B.A., Dartmouth, 1933; m. Ruth Frances Atherton, Nov. 8, 1941. Eastern editor Apparel Arts mag., 1935-36; mem. editorial staff Time mag., 1936-37; editor Ogden-Watney Pubs., 1938-39; sales promotion mgr. Esquire mag., 1941-45, mng. editor, 1952, editor-in-chief, 1952-56; exec. editor Gentleman's Quar., 1950-52; fashion editor Playboy mag., 1957-58; editorial dir. Gen. Pub. Co., 1959-62; editor Cavalier mag., 1963-66; spl. project editor Reader's Digest Assn., 1966-67; editorial dir. Status-Diplomat mags., 1967-68; sr. editor Status mag., N.Y.C., 1968-82; pres., exec. editor Third World News, Inc., 1968-82; lectr. Radcliffe Coll., U. Mo., Northwestern U., N.Y. U., Coll. City N.Y., C.W. Post Coll., New Sch. Social Research. Sr. editor OWI 1942-43. Served to lt. comdr. USNR, 1943-46. Mem. Overseas Press Club, Alpha Iota Epsilon, Sigma Phi Epsilon. Clubs: Tabard Inn, U. Mo. (Columbia, Mo.); Sanborn House, Dartmouth (Hanover, N.H.). Author: The Writer's Craft, 1957; It Was Fun While It Lasted, 1960; The Cookbook for Men, 1961; The Ivy League Today, 1962; How To Succeed At Touch Football, 1963; The Wedding Book, 1964. Author-editor: Girls From Esquire, 1953; The Esquire Book of Etiquette, 1954; The Esquire Drink Book, 1956; The Esquire Fashion Guide, 1958. Contbr. articles mags. and newspapers. Home: Scranton, Pa. Died Sept. 2, 1982.

BIRNKRANT, NORMAN HOWARD, lawyer; b. N.Y.C., Aug. 22, 1908; s. Maurice H. and Tillie (Schellberg) B.; m. Phyllis Zelens, Apr. 30, 1956; children—Terry Joy (Mrs. Gordon R. Miller), Madge Sue (Mrs. Thomas Grossman). J.D., Detroit Coll. Law, 1928; postgrad., U. Mich., 1928-32, U. Detroit, 1938. Bar: Mich. bar 1929. Since practiced in, Detroit; mem. firm Birnkrant, Birnkrant & Birnkrant, from 1928, sr. mem., from 1946; Mich. consul for Republic of Austria, from 1954, Austrian consul gen., from 1965; sec. Detroit Consular Corps, 1966—; dean Consular Corps Coll. and Internat. Consular Acad., 1971; Mem. world affairs com., internat. adviser world trade Greater Detroit Bd. Commerce, from 1954; sec. Inter-Am. Affairs Center, State Dept., 1942; guest lectr. internat. affairs Wayne State U., from 1955. Recipient Gold medal of honor for services behalf Republic Austria, 1959; Max-Reinhardt medal from mayor of Salzburg Austria, 1961. Mem. State Bar Mich., Am., Internat., Fed. (2d v.p.), Detroit bar assns.), Am. Soc. Internat. Law, Am. Trial Lawyers Assn., Am. Arbitration Assn., World Trade Club Detroit, Detroit Jr. C. of C., Detroit Alumni Assn. (pres. Detroit and Windsor 1952), Detroit Econ. Club (v.p., chmn. reception com.). Club: Cirumnavigators (N.Y.C. and); Cirumnavigators (Detroit). Address: Scottsdale, Ariz. Died June 17, 1983.

BIRTHRIGHT, WILLIAM C., labor union ofcl.; b. Helena, Ark., May 27, 1887; s. William Connell and Margaret Ellen (Linebaugh) B.; student pub. schs.; m. Birdie Lee Huss, June 29, 1910; 1 son, William. Joined Barbers Union, 1908; del. to Brit. Trade Union from AFL, 1937; pres. Barbers, Hairdressers Internat. Union from 1937; president-secretary Journeymen Barbers, Hairdressers, Cosmetologists and Proprietors' International Union; became vice president, AFL, 1940: vice president AFL-CIO. Chairman Selective Service Board 14 Indpls., 1940; mem. WSB, 1951-53. Chmn. bd. trustees Internat. Barber Schs. Ind. Democrat. Presbyn. Mason. Home: Indianapolis, Ind. †

BISHOP, CECIL WILLIAM (RUNT), ex-congressman; b. Johnson Co., Ill., June 29, 1890; s. William C. and Belle Z. (Ragsdale) B.; student Union Acad., Anna, Ill., 1907-08; m. Elizabeth Hutton, Dec. 25, 1913; 1 son, Jack Hutton. Learned tailoring trade while attending school; later became successively coal miner, telephone lineman, professional football and baseball player; 10 years in cleaning and tailoring business, Carterville, Ill.; city clerk, Carterville, 1915-17, postmaster, 1922-33; mem. 77th to 84th U.S. Congresses from 25th Ill. Dist.; exec. asst. to postmaster, P.O. Dept., Washington, 1955-56, ret., 1956; supt. div. indsl. plan and development Ill., 1957-58; counciliator Ill. Dept. Labor, from 1958. Member Ill. Postmasters Assn. (past sec.). Republican. Mem. Christian Ch. Woodman, K.P., Elk, Eagle, Oddfellow. Club: Lions (dist. gov. 1932-33; sec. Ill. 5 yrs; spl. internat. rep. U.S., Can., Mexico and Cuba 1934-40). Home: Carterville, Ill. †

BISHOP, HEWLETT RYDER, association executive, author, maritime consultant; b. Patchogue, N.Y., Feb. 12, 1909; s. Henry J. and Ethelinda (Ryder) B.; m. Ruth H. Truex, July 17, 1938; children: Hewlett Ryder, Marcia Louise. Ed., Mcht. Marine Tng. Center, Bklyn. With Roosevelt S.S. Co.; also U.S. Lines, 1927-41; designated master, 1938; port capt. U.S. Maritime Commn., 1941-42; mgr. cargo ops. Atlantic Coast dist. War Shipping Administrn., 1942-45; Atlantic Coast dir. Maritime Adminstrn., Dept. Commerce, 1945-64; pres. Nat. Cargo Bur., N.Y.C., 1964-74; U.S. rep. to Intergovt. Maritime Consultative Orgn., London, from 1964, chmn. internat. sub-com. on bulk cargoes, 1964-68, chmn. internat. sub-com. on containers and cargoes, 1969-74, chmn. container safety com., Geneva, Switzerland, 1972; adviser municipal state and fed. groups; devel. mecanno deck on tankers enabling additional cargo, World War II; Vice Chmn. Fed. Exec. Bd., 1962-63; gen. chmn. marine sect. Nat. Safety Council; mem. select com. Am. Mcht. Marine Seamanship Trophy. Author articles. Exec. com. Am. Mcht. Marine Library Assn. Recipient Meritorious Service medal Dept. Commerce, 1956, Career Service award Nat. Civil Service League, 1963, Distinguished Service medal for Americanism Am. Legion, 1952, Distinguished Pub. Service award USCG, 1973, sec.'s award Dept.

Transp., 1973. Mem. Am. Nat. Standards Inst., Maritime Assn. Port N.Y., Fed. Bus. Assn. (pres.), Propeller Club U.S. (gov.), Nat. Cargo Bur., Nat. Fire Protection Assn., Water Island Assn. (pres.), Life Saving Benevolent Assn. N.Y. Methodist (parish relations com.). Clubs: Mason, India House, Whitehall. Home: Oakdale, N.Y. Died Sept. 2, 1984; buried at sea.

BISHOP, JOHN MICHAEL, microbiology educator; b. York, Pa., Feb. 22, 1936; s. John Schwartz and Carrie Rutledge (Grey) B.; A.B., Gettysburg Coll., 1957; M.D., Harvard U., 1962; m. Kathryn Ione Putman, June 18, 1959; children—Dylan Michael Dwight, Eliot John Putman. Intern, Mass. Gen. Hosp., Boston, 1962-63, resident in internal medicine, 1963-64; fellow NIH, 1964-66; vis. scientist Heinrich Pette Inst., Hamburg, Germany, 1967-68; asst. prof. microbiology U. Calif., San Francisco, 1968-70, assoc. prof., 1970-72, prof., from 1972. Served with USPHS, 1964-66. Recipient Kaiser award in teaching U. Calif., 1969. Mem. Am. Soc. Biol. Chemists, AAAS, Am. Soc. Microbiology, Phi Beta Kappa, Alpha Omega Alpha. Assoc. editor: Jour. of Molecular Biology, 1973-77. Mem. editorial bd. Virology, 1970—, Jour. Biol. Chemistry, 1978—. Contbr. articles in field to profl. jours. Home: Belvedere, Calif.

BISHOP, JOSEPH WARREN, JR., lawyer, educator; b. N.Y.C., Apr. 15, 1915; s. Joseph Warren and Edna Priscilla (Dashiell) B.; m. Susan Carroll Oulahan, May 6, 1950; 1 son, Joseph Warren III. Grad. Deerfield Acad., 1932; A.B., Dartmouth Coll., 1936; LL.B., Harvard U., 1940. Bar: D.C. 1941, N.Y. 1954, Conn. 1963. Spl. asst. to undersec. war, 1940-42; with Office Solicitor Gen., Dept. Justice, 1947-50; asst. to gen. counsel U.S. High Commn. Occupied Germany, 1950-52; dep. gen. counsel, acting gen. counsel Dept. Army, 1952-53; pvt. practice law, N.Y.C., 1953-57; prof. law Yale Law Sch., 1957—, Richard Ely prof. law, 1968—; vis. prof. law U. Muenster, West Germany, 1965; faculty Salzburg Seminar Am. Studies, 1967; vis. fellow Clare Hall Cambridge (Eng.) U., 1974; vis. prof. U. Munich, W. Ger., 1980; asst. counsel trustees New Haven R.R., 1961-74; Expert cons. SEC, 1958. Author: Indemnifying and Insuring the Corporate Executive, 2d edit., 1980, Obiter Dicta, 1971, Justice Under Fire: A Study of Military Law, 1974; also articles, book revs. Served with AUS, 1943-46. Recipient Exceptional Civilian Service citation Dept. Army, 1953; Guggenheim fellow, 1974. Club: Century. Home: New Haven CT Office: New Haven CT

BISPLINGHOFF, RAYMOND LEWIS, business executive; b. Hamilton, Ohio, Feb. 7, 1917; s. Roscoe Earl and Isabelle (Lewis) B.; m. Ruth Doherty, June 20, 1944 (div.); children: Ross Lee, Ron Sprague. A.E., U. Cin., 1940, M.Sc., 1942; Sc.D., 1963, Swiss Fed. Inst. Tech., 1957; D.Eng. (hon.), Case Inst. Tech., 1965. Registered profl. engr., Mass., Mo. Engr. Aeronca Aircraft Corp., 1937-40, Wright Field, 1940-41; instr. U. Cin., 1941-43; engr. Bur. Aero., Navy Dept., Washington, 1943-46; asst. prof. Mass. Inst. Tech., 1946-48, asso. prof., 1948-53, prof., 1953-62; dir. Office Advanced Research and Tech., NASA, Washington, 1962-63, asso. adminstr., 1963-65, spl. asst. to adminstr., 1965-66; prof., head dept. aeros. and astronautics Mass. Inst. Tech., Cambridge, 1966-68; dean Coll. Engring., 1968-70; dep. dir. NSF, 1970-74; chancellor U. Mo-Rolla, 1974-77; sci. adviser to Mo. Gov., 1975-77; sr. v.p. for research and devel. Tyco Labs., Exeter, N.H., 1977-85, also dir., 1977-85; trustee MITRE Corp.; cons. Dept. Def.; adminstr. NASA, FAA; Wright Brothers lectr. Inst. Aero. Scis., 1955; Samuel P. Langley lectr. U. Pitts., 1962; 3d Ann. von Karman lectr. AIAA, 1965; vis. prof. U. Fla.; sr. lectr. M.I.T.; chmn. bd. No. Energy Corp.; dir. Allied Research Assos., Allied Systems Ltd., Gen. Aircraft Corp., Mobil-Tyco Corp., Grinnell Corp., Simplex Wire & Cable Corp.; mem. corp. adv. council Eastern Air Lines; chmn. sci. adv. bd. USAF; mem. Nat. Sci. Bd., Def. Sci. Bd.; pres. Internat. Council Aero. Scis.; chmn. investigative bds. for C-5A and B-1 aircraft USAF. Author: (with others) Aeroelasticity, 1955, Principles of Aeroelasticity, (with H. Ashley), 1962, Solid Mechanics, (with J.W. Mar and T.H.H. Pian), 1966, also numerous profl. papers.; Assos. editor: Jour. of Franklin Inst; cons. editor: McGraw Hill Ency. Technology. Mem. vis. com. Carnegie-Mellon U.; mem. vis. com. Princeton U.; trustee Nathaniel Hawthorne Coll. Recipient certificate of merit USAF; Sylvanus Reed award Inst. Aero. Scis., 1958; Distinguished Service medal NASA, 1967; Extraordinary Service medal FAA, 1968; Carl F. Kayan medal, 1971; Godfrey L. Cabot award, 1972; Distinguished Service award NSF, 1973; Exceptional Civilian Service medal USAF; hon. fellow Truman Library Inst. Fellow Am. Acad. Arts and Scis., AAAS, Inst. Aero. Scis., Am. Astronautical Soc., Am. Inst. Aeros. and Astronautics (pres. 1966), Royal Aero. Soc.; mem. Nat. Acad. Engring. (chmn. aeros. space engring. bd., chmn. com. on transp.), Nat. Acad. Sci., Internat. Acad. Astronautics, Engrs. Council for Profl. Devel. (dir.), Engrs. Joint Council (dir.), Sigma Xi, Phi Kappa Phi, Tau Beta Pi. Clubs: Mason. (Washington), Cosmos (Washington); Engineers (St. Louis); Explorers (N.Y.C.). Died Mar. 5, 1985.

BISSELL, PELHAM ST. GEORGE, III, judge, orgn. ofcl.; b. N.Y.C., Oct. 20, 1912; s. Pelham St. George and Mary Valentine Yale (Bissell) B.; m. Mary Alascia, Dec. 24, 1934. Grad., St. George's Sch., Newport, R.I., 1931; student, Columbia, 1931-34; A.B., Rutgers U., 1936; LL.B., N.Y.U., 1939. Bar: N.Y. State bar 1941. Asso. firm Barnes, Richardson & Colburn, N.Y.C., 1939-41, 45-51; law sec. to judge Ct. Gen. Sessions, N.Y. County, 1945-51; judge Civil Ct. City N.Y., 1952-81; Mem. S.R., 1933-81, gen. pres., 1961-64. Author: Descendents of Captain John Bissell, 1966. Asst. gov. gen. Soc. Mayflower Descs., 1960-63; comdr.-in-chief Soc. Am. Wars in U.S.A., 1961-64; Mem. Grand St. Boys Assn. Served to Lt. col. inf. AUS, World War II; col. Res. ret. Decorated Bronze Star medal; French Croix de Guerre; Belgian Croix de Guerre. Mem. Bar Assn. City N.Y., N.Y. County Lawyers Assn., Am., N.Y. State bar assns., Mil. Order Fgn. Wars (past comdr. N.Y. State), Am. Legion (past post comdr.), Soc. Colonial Wars, St. Nicholas Soc., Vets. Corps Arty. Soc. 1st Div., St. George's Soc., St. David's Soc., New Eng. Soc., Colonial Order Acorn, V.F.W., 40 and 8, Order of Founders and Patriots. Republican. Episcopalian. Clubs: Mason (33 deg.) (N.Y.C.), Elk. (N.Y.C.), Union League (N.Y.C.), N.Y. Rifle (N.Y.C.), N.Y. Athletic (N.Y.C.), Church (N.Y.C.); Army and Navy (Washington); St. Anthony. Home: New York, N.Y. Died July 11, 1981.

BITKER, BRUNO VOLTAIRE, lawyer; b. Milw., Feb. 5, 1898; m. Marjorie M. Mayer, 1957. LL.B., Cornell U., 1921. Bar: Wis. 1921. Gen. practice law, Milw., from 1921. Mem. Sewerage Commn. Milw., 1931-53; fed. ct. trustee Milw. Rapid Transit Line, 1950-52; spl. counsel to Gov. Wis., 1937; counsel State Banking Commn., 1938; cons. OPM, Washington, 1941; Wis. state counsel, dist. dir. OPA, 1942-44; spl. pros. atty. Milw., 1948; chmn. State Pub. Utility Arbitration Bd., 1947; mem., officer Gov.'s Commn. on Human Rights, 1947-56; chmn. Milw. Com. on Living Cost and Food Conservation, 1947, Commn. on Econ. Study Milw., 1948; mem. Mayor's Commn. on Human Relations, 1948-52; U.S. del. Internat. Conf. Local Govts., Geneva, 1949; U.S. rep. 1st World Conf. Lawyers, Athens, Greece, 1963, Geneva, 1967, Belgrade, Yugoslavia, 1971, Abidjan, Ivory Coast, 1973, Washington, 1975; chmn. Municipal Commn. on Mass Transp., 1954; lectr. div. continuing edn. Marquette U., 1961-62; chmn. Gov.'s Com. UN, 1959-76, hon. chmn., 1976-84; mem. Wis. adv. com. U.S. Commn. Civil Rights, chmn., 1960-71; mem. Nat. Citizens' Commn. Internat. Coop., 1965, U.S. Nat. Commn. for UNESCO, 1965-71, Pres.'s Commn. for Observance Human Rights Year, 1968-69, Wis. Bicentennial Commn., 1975-78; U.S. civic leadership del. to, Germany, 1964; U.S. rep. UN Internat. Conf. on Human Rights, Teheran, Iran, l41968; cons. Dept. State, 1968-73; del. Human Rights Conf., Uppsala (Sweden) U., 1972; U.S. rep. to UN Seminar on Human Rights, Geneva, 1978. Contbr. articles to legal jours, treatises on UN affairs. Trustee, adv. council Milw. Art Inst., from 1957. Served as lt. inf. U.S. Army, World War I. Recipient City of Milw. citation for distinguished pub. service, 1944; Amity award, 1950; Jr. Achievement award, 1959; citation Supreme Ct. Wis., 1978. Mem. ABA (mem. com. on world order under law 1978-80, internat. law sect. com. on genocide), Wis. Bar Assn. (hon. chmn. com. on world peace through law), Milw. Bar Assn., Fed. Bar Assn. Wis. (pres. 1945), Am. Soc. Internat. Law (human rights panel), World Peace through Law Center (charter, Geneva, mem. U.S. Helsinki Watch com. 1979—). Clubs: University (Milw.), Cornell Alumni of Wis. (Milw.). Home: Milwaukee, Wis. Dec. Apr. 12, 1984.

BIXBY, HAROLD MCMILLAN, banker; b. St. Louis, Mo., June 16, 1890; s. William Keeney and Lillian (Tuttle) B.; grad. Smith Acad., St. Louis, 1909; B.S., Amherst, 1913; m. Elizabeth Case, of St. Louis, Nov. 2, 1914; children—Frances Cushing, Elizabeth McMillan, Catherine Whittemore, Hebe Wise. Clk. Nat. Bank of Commerce, St. Louis, 1913-15; asst. to pres. Mo. Portland Cement Co., 1915-17; pres. Automatic Appliance Co., 1919-20; v.p. State Nat. Bank, 1920-29; pres. St. Louis Aviation Corpn. from 1929; dir. Mississippi Valley Trust Co., Lambert Pharmacal Co., Central States Life Insurance Co., Transcontinental Air Transport Co., Detroit Aircraft Corpn., Missouri Portland Cement Co., Emerson Electric Manufacturing Company, Corneli Seed Company. Enlisted U.S. Navy Aviation Ground Sch., Boston, Apr. 1918; flying service at Akron, O. One of Charles A. Lindbergh's principal backers for flight across Atlantic, 1927, and responsible for naming his plane the "Spirit of St. Louis." Pres. St. Louis Chamber Commerce, 1927-28. Mem. Psi Upsilon. Republican. Conglist. Clubs: Mo. Athletic, Noonday, St. Louis Country. Home: Clayton, Mo. †

BIXLER, JULIUS SEELYE, educator; b. New London, Conn., Apr. 4, 1894; s. James Wilson and Elizabeth James (Seelye) B.; A.B., Amherst Coll., 1916, A.M., 1920; Ph.D., Yale, 1924; student Union Theol. Sem., 1917-18, Harvard, 1923-24, U. of Freiburg, Germany, 1928-29; D.D., Amherst Coll., 1939; hon. M.A., Harvard, 1942, L.H.D., 1960; L.H.D., Union Coll., 1947, Wesleyan University, 1954, Carleton College, 1964, LL.D., University of Maine, 1948, Brown U., 1948, Bowdoin, 1952, Colby College, 1960; D.C.L., Acadia U., N.S., 1949; L.H.D., Bates Coll., 1958; Litt.D., Am. Internat. Coll., Springfield, Mass., 1961; Sc.D., Worcester Poly. Inst., 1962; m. Mary Harrison Thayer, September 21, 1918; children—Mary Harriet (Mrs. Thomas J. Naughton), Elizabeth Seelye (Mrs. Fred C. Bonner); Martha Harrison, Nancy Emerson (Mrs. Sanford M. Isaacs). Instr. Latin and English, American Coll., Madura, India, 1916-17; dir. religious activities, Amherst Coll., 1919-20; lecturer philosophy, American U., Beirut, Syria, 1920-22; asst. prof. religion and Biblical lit., Smith Coll., 1924-25, asso. prof., 1925-29, prof., 1929-33; lecturer on theology, Harvard, 1932-33, Bussey prof. of theology, 1933-42; president, Colby Coll., Waterville, Me., 1942-60, pres. emeritus, 1960—, Ingraham lecturer, 1967; educational consultant Thammasat University, Bangkok, 1962-63; lectr. U. Hawaii; fellow Center Advanced Studies, Wesleyan U., Middletown, Conn., 1961-62; Donald J. Cowling vis. prof. philosophy Carleton Coll., 1964; vis. prof. philosophy Bowdoin College, 1965; Distinguished vis. professor Univ. Me., 1969; acting dean Harvard Div. Sch., 1937, 40; Phi Beta Kappa vis. scholar, 1961-62; lectr. Salzburg Seminar in Am. Studies, 1951, 59, and 61; vis. prof. philosophy Bowdoin Coll., 1965; lectr. Am. U. Beirut, 1966; distinguished vis. prof. of philosophy University of Maine, 1969. Trustee of Smith Coll., Amherst Coll., Colby Coll.; president of the board directors, Nat. Council on Religion in Higher Edn., 1934-39. Mem. Am. Theol. Soc. (sec. 1930-35; pres. 1935-36), Am. Philos. Assn., Am. Acad. of Arts and Sciences, Alpha Delta Phi, Phi Beta Kappa, Delta Sigma Rho. Conglist. Author: Religion in the Philosophy of William James, 1926; Immortality and the Present Mood (Ingersoll lecture), 1931; Religion for Free Minds (Lowell Lectures), 1939; Resources of Religion and Aims of Higher Education (Hazen Lectures), 1942; Conversations with an Unrepentant Liberal (Terry Lecture), 1946; A Faith that Fulfills (Ayer Lectures), 1951; Education for Adversity (Inglis Lecture), 1952. Editor: (with R.L. Calhoun and H.R. Niebuhr) and contributor to The Nature of Religious Experience, 1937; contbr. to other symposia and theol. jours. Home: Jaffrey, N.H. Died Mar. 29, 1985.

BJORGE, GUY NORMAN, mining exec.; b. Underwood, Minn., July 13, 1887; s. Hans P. and Jonette (Sjordal) B.; Mining Engr., U. of Minn., 1912; hon. Dr.Eng., S.D. Sch. of Mines, 1939; m. Mabel Lee Turpin, Dec. 19, 1917; 1 dau., Rosemary Annette. Engr. Pickands Mather & Co., Gilbert, Minn., 1912; reconnaissance work in Venezuela for Barber Asphalt Paving Co., working as geologist, 1912-13; asst. chief engr. Pickands Mather & Co., 1913; chief geologist Old Dominion Co., Globe, Ariz., 1913-17; cons. mining geologist and engr., San Francisco, 1917-32; asst. gen. mgr. Homestake Mining Co., 1932-36, gen. manager, 1936-53, v.p., 1940-62, dir., 1940-64, consultant, from 1964; mem. of bd. of directors First Nat. Bank Black Hills, Black Hills Power and Light Company. Served as private in company three, O.T.S., 1918. Mem. Am. Inst. Mining and Metall. Engrs., Mining and Metall. Soc. Am., Soc. Econ. Geologists, Am. Mining Congress, Tau Beta Pi, Delta Upsilon, Sigma Rho. Republican. Clubs: Bohemian (San Francisco); Mining (N.Y.). Home: Berkeley, Cal. †

BJORK, RICHARD EMIL, college chancellor; b. Astoria, Oreg., Aug. 18, 1930; s. Carl E. and Mildred H. (McHugh) B.; m. Joan I. Pineda, June 13, 1953; children: Alison, Tracy. B.A., Yale U., 1952; M.A., Vanderbilt U., 1953; postgrad., U. Wash., 1954-55; Ph.D., Mich. State U., 1961. Dean of students Austin (Tex.) Coll., 1961-63; dean liberal arts SUNY, Plattsburgh, 1963-66; asst. to pres. Rochester (N.Y.) Inst. Tech., 1966-68; acting pres. Glassboro (N.J.) State Coll., 1968-69; vice chancellor higher edn. State of N.J., Trenton, 1968-70; pres. Stockton State Coll., Pomona, N.J., 1969-78; chancellor Vt. State Colls., Waterbury, 1978-85; mem. Nat. Adv. Com. Accreditation and Instl. Eligibility. Mem. corp. Cardigan Mountain Sch., N.H.; mem. nat. adv. council U.S. Army Command and Gen. Staff Coll. Served with USCG, 1953-56. Mem. Am. Polit. Sci. Assn., Am. Soc. Pub. Adminstrn., Am. Assn. Higher Edn., AAAS. Home: Montpelier, Vt. Deceased.

BLACK, ARCHIBALD, engineer; b. Inverness, Scotland, Oct. 2, 1888; s. John (author) and Marjorie (Robb) B.; came to U.S., 1906; Cooper Inst., New York; Cass Tech. Inst., Detroit; student Columbia U., extension and miscellaneous courses; m. Dorothy E. Stricker, Apr. 2, 1929; 1 dau., Dorothy Susan. Elec. work, Scotland and U.S.; with N.Y. Edison Co., Union Metallic Cartridge Co. (Bridgeport, Conn.), Detroit Edison Co., 1902-15; with Curtiss Aeroplane Co., Buffalo, N.Y., 1916; chief engr. L.W.F. Engring. Co., College Point, L.I., N.Y., 1917-18; aero engr. in charge aero specifications for Bur. Constrn. and Repair, Navy Dept., Washington, 1919-20; mem. firm A. & D. R. Black, cons. aero engrs., 1920-22; cons. air transport and industrial engr. from 1922; pres. Black & Bigelow, Inc., 1928-30; free lance writer, 1931-32; engr. and special writer The Port of New York Authority, 1933-39; engr. Republic Aviation Corp., Farmingdale, N.Y., 1940-41; Snead & Co., aeronautics div., 1942; Simmonds Aerocessories, Inc., 1943-45, cons. engineer from 1946. Designed airplane in which 1st Liberty engine was installed, Aug. 1917. Cons. engr. U.S. Air Mail Service, 1921. Mem. Inst. Aeronaut. Sci., Am. Soc. Mech. Engrs.; Am. Soc. for Metals. Author: Transport Aviation, 1926; Civil Airports and Airways, 1929; The Story of Bridges, 1936; The Story of Tunnels, 1937; The Story of Flying, 1st ed., 1940, 2d edition, 1943.†

BLACK, EDGAR B., transportation officer; b. Minneapolis, Minn., Oct. 16, 1888; s. Abraham B. and Clara (Francis) B.; ed. Renssalaer Poly. Inst., Troy, N.Y., 1907-10; m. Eileen L. Power, Dec. 20, 1904; children—Edgar B., Peter F., Charles T., John A. Salesman Republic Iron and Steel Co., Buffalo, N.Y., 1911-14; W. G. Heathfield and Co., 1914-16; Charles Kennedy and Co., 1916-17; Food Adminstrn. Grain Corp., 1917-20;

Charles Kennedy and Co., 1920-44 (all of Buffalo, N.Y.). War Food Adminstr., Washington, D.C., 1944-45; transportation officer, Prodn. and Marketing Adminstrn., Washington, D.C., 1945-47; ret. 1947. Clubs: Congressional Country (Washington); Buffalo Country, Gyro (Buffalo, N.Y.). Mason. Home: Eggertsville, N.Y. †

BLACK, FLOYD HENSON, educator; b. Bridgeport, Ill., Feb. 2, 1888; s. John Edwin and Ellen Jane (Finlay) B.; A.B., Carson and Newman Coll., Tenn., 1911, LL.D., 1932; studied in Paris, 1913, Southern Bapt. Theol. Sem., Louisville, Ky., 1915-16, U. of Chicago, summer, 1916; S.T.B., Andover Theol. Sem., 1917; S.T.M., Harvard, 1919; m. Zasafinka Kirova, 1914; 1 son, Cyril Edwin. Instr. in English and Latin, Robert Coll., Constantinople, Turkey, 1911-14, prof. Latin, 1919-26; pres. American Coll., Sofia, Bulgaria, from 1926. Pres. Instanbul Am. Coll. (comprising Robert College and Am. Coll. for Girls), 1944-55; mem. bd. mgrs. Admiral Bristol Hospital, Istanbul. Spl. asst. in Fgn. Service Auxiliary of State Dept., Oct. 1942-June 1944; mem. United States Educational Commission in Turkey. Former v.p. Bulgarian-Am. Soc.; pres. English Speaking League, Sofia. Mem. Turkish-Am. U. Assn., The Twentieth Assn. Boston (pres.), Inst. World Affairs (Warner, N.H.) (pres.). Conglist. Clubs: Congregational, Winthrop (Boston); Instanbul Propellor. Lectr. Bulgarian and Turkish affairs before clubs, schs. and colls. in U.S. Address: Arlington, Mass. Died Dec. 28, 1983.

BLACK, HAROLD STEPHEN, research engineer; b. Leominster, Mass., Apr. 14, 1898; s. Stephen A. and Julia S. (Bushnell) B.; B.S., Worcester (Mass.) Poly. Inst., 1921, D.Eng., 1955; m. Meta C. Spreen, July 1, 1934. With engring. dept. Western Electric Co., 1921-25; mem. tech. staff Bell Telephone Labs., Inc., Murray Hill, N.J., 1925-63; prin. research scientist Gen. Precision, Inc., Little Falls, N.J., 1963-66; communications cons., Summit, N.J., from 1966. Tchr., lectr., lit. critic. Mem. biomechanics com. Inst. Rehab. Medicine, N.Y. U. Med. Center, 1970-75, com. bioengring., from 1975, nat. bd. sponsors Inst. Am. Strategy, 1972; a founder Center for Internat. Security Studies, Am. Security Council Edn. Found. Recipient Nat. best Paper prize AIEE, 1934, Lamme gold medal, 1958; Modern Pioneer award NAM, 1940; John Price Wetherill medal Franklin Inst., 1941; certificate appreciation U.S. War Dept., 1946; Research Corp. sci. award, 1952, John H. Potts Meml. Award, 1959; medal Engrs. Club Phila., 1961; Honor award Wisdom Soc., 1969, named to Wisdom Hall of Fame, 1970. Registered profl. engr., N.Y. Fellow IEEE, AAAS, Franklin Inst., N.J. Acad. Sci., Intercontinental Biog. Assn., N.Y. Acad. Scis., Internat. Inst. Community Service, World-Wide Acad. Scholars, IRE, AIEE, Am. Biog. Inst.; mem. Audio Engring. Soc. (hon.), Am. Inst. Aeros. and Astronautics, Am. Def. Preparedness Assn., Nat. Geog. Soc., Internat. Platform Assn., Smithsonian Instn., UN Assn. U.S., Air Force Assn., Am. Security Council, Telephone Pioneers Am., Sigma Xi, Tau Beta Pi. Author: Feedback Amplifiers, 1936; Modulation Theory, 1953; also tech. and ency. articles. Research and devel. amplifiers, multichannel carrier telephone and telegraph systems, pulse position modulation, microwave radio relay systems, pulse code modulation microwave radio relay systems, laminated condrs., advanced communication and guidance feedback techniques pertaining to aerospace interests, telecommunications, advanced circuit techniques, new types feedback, feedforward, feedback-feedforward systems. Patentee in field. Address: Summit, N.J. Died Dec. 11, 1983.

BLACK, ROBERT DUNCAN, manufacturing company executive; b. White Hall, Md., Dec. 5, 1896; s. Samuel W. and Alice (Duncan) B.; student Northeastern U., 1915-17, L.H.D., 1963; m. Eleanor Watts, June 15, 1921; children—Brice (Mrs. Walter H. Bramman), Jean (Mrs. Thomas G. McCausland), Joyce (Mrs. Robert J. Franke). With Black & Decker Mfg. Co., Towson, Md., 1917-81, factory worker, staff sales office, mgr. Phila. br., advt. mgr., sales mgr., v.p. and sales mgr., v.p. in charge sales, v.p., 1917-54, exec. v.p., 1954-56, chmn. bd., pres., 1956-60, chmn. bd., 1960-68, hon. chmn. bd., chmn. exec. com., 1968-78, hon. chmn. bd., 1978-81, also dir.; dir. Conchemco Inc. Trustee emeritus, fellow Johns Hopkins; mem. corp. Northeastern U. Home: Timonium, Md. Died Mar. 21, 1981.

BLACK, ROBERT FOSTER, geology educator; b. Dayton, Ohio, Feb. 1, 1918; s. Stanley C. and Margaret (Martin) B.; m. Hernelda R. Lone, Feb. 12, 1944; children: John R., Dean S. B.A., Coll. of Wooster, 1940; M.A., Syracuse U., 1942; student, Calif. Inst. Tech., 1942-43; Ph.D., Johns Hopkins U., 1953. Geologist Roosevelt Wildlife Conservation Dept., N.Y. State, 1941-42, U.S. Geol. Survey, 1943-59; asso. prof. geology U. Wis., 1956-59, prof. geology, 1959-70, U. Conn., Storrs, 1970-83; cons. in field, 1942-83. Author papers in field. Recipient Alexander Winchell Disting. Alumni award Syracuse U. Fellow Geol. Soc. Am., Arctic Inst. N.Am.; mem. Soc. Econ. Geologists, AAAS, Am. Geophys. Union, Am. Soc. Photogrammetry, Assn. Engring. Geologists, Assn. Profl. Geol. Scientists, Soc. Econ. Paleontologists and Mineralogists, Internat. Glaciol. Soc., Am. Quaternary Assn. Home: Willimantic, Conn.

BLACK, WILLIAM, philanthropist, restaurant executive; b. Bklyn.; m. Jean Martin, 1951 (div. 1962); 1 child, Melinda; m. Page Morton, Mar. 27, 1962. Grad., Columbia, 1926, L.H.D. (hon.), 1967. Checker Washington Market; retail mcht. shelled nuts, N.Y.C.; organizer chain of stores Chock Full O' Nuts, N.Y.C., converted to restaurants, pres., chmn. bd., chief exec. officer; also owner coffee producing firm. Founder Parkinson's Disease Found., 1957; founder Page and William Black Postgrad. Sch. Medicine of Mt. Sinai Sch. Medicine, William Black Sch. Nursing, Lenox Hill Hosp., William Black Med. Research Bldg., Columbia U. Med. Center; bd. dirs. New Rochelle Hosp. Home: New Rochelle, N.Y. Dec. Mar. 7, 1983.

BLACKBURN, WALTER JUXON, publisher, broadcasting executive; b. London, Ont., Can., Mar. 18, 1914; s. Arthur Stephen and Etta Irene (Henderson) B.; m. Marjorie Ludwell Dampier, Nov. 9, 1938; children: Susan Blackburn Toledo, Martha Blackburn White. B.A. with honors in Bus. Adminstrn, London Central Collegiate Inst., U. Western Ont., 1936, LL.D. (hon.), 1977. Pres., mng. dir. London Free Press Printing Co. Ltd., from 1936, chmn. bd., pub.; chmn. bd. CFPL Broadcasting Ltd., CKNX Broadcasting Ltd.; pres. Wingham Investments Ltd.; dir. Can. Trust Co. Mem. adv. bd. YMCA-YWCA, London; mem. adv. council Orch. London. Served to 2d lt. Can. First Hussars, 1938-39. Mem. Can. Assn. Broadcasters, Can. Press, Newspaper Advt. Bur., Am. Newspaper Pubs. Assn. (sec. 1954-59). Anglican. Clubs: London, London Hunt and Country, Masons. Home: London ON Canada.

BLACKMAN, CHARLES FRANKLIN, fgn. service officer; b. Kansas City, Mo., May 20, 1911; s. Charles Franklin Sr. and Rae (Wood) B.; grad. Nat. War Coll., 1958; m. Martha Kearney, Nov. 15, 1946; children—Barbara, Charles III, Susan, Rebecca, Nan. Editorial staff Springfield (Mo.) Leader, 1934-36, Kansas City Star, 1936-42; U.S. resident officer, Heppenheim and Frankfurt, Germany, 1947-49; govt. ofcl. U.S. High Commn. to Germany, 1949-52; dir. Office German Programs, Dept. State, 1953; dep. pub. affairs officer Am. embassy, Rome, 1955-57; pub. affairs dir. U.S. Mission to Berlin, 1958-62; dir. Berlin task force USIA, Washington, 1962-64, pub. affairs adviser U.S. Maritime Adminstrn., 1964-66; counselor of embassy, Canberra, Australia, 1967-70; chief edn.-communication div. AID Office Population, 1970-75, population resources cons., 1975-76; staff mem. Hobcaw Barony, Baruch Found., Clemson U., Georgetown, S.C., 1976-78. Served to capt. USAAF, 1942-46. Mem. Am. Fgn. Service Assn. Clubs: Nat. Press (Washington); Refugee (Canberra); Journalists (Sydney, Australia). Home: Chevy Chase, Md. Died Feb. 12, 1980.

BLACKMER, LEONARD, pub. relations counsel, author; b. Flint, Mich., Aug. 18, 1889; s. Walter Merritt and Jennie Marie (Bogue) B.; student Lombard College, Galesburg, Ill.; married Lola Marie Young, Oct. 27, 1912. Faculty staff mem. U. of Wis., 3 yrs.; pub. relations surveys, financial campaigns for Near East Relief, Nat. Rep. Com., Calif. and Wis. community chests and numerous other instns. Mem. Am. Council on Pub. Relations, Nat. Assn. Pub. Relations Counsels, Am. Coll. Pub. Relations Assn. (formerly Am. Coll. Publicity Assn.). Nat. Publicity Council, Nat. Information Bur. Mason. Elk. Clubs: Publicity (New York); Publicity (Chicago); University (Madison, Wis.); Athletic, City (Milwaukee); Commonwealth (San Francisco). Author: The Campaign Set-Up, 1945; The Wisconsin War Fund, 1946. Contbr. articles on pub. relations, institutional financing and publicity to mags., periodicals, trade papers. Home: Westport, Conn.†

BLACKWELL, BETSY TALBOT, ret. editor; b. N.Y.C.; d. Hayden and Benedict (Bristow) Talbot; grad. Acad. St. Elizabeth, N.J., 1923; Litt.D., Dickinson Coll.; m. Bowden Washington, Dec. 11, 1925; m. 2d, James Madison Blackwell, Apr. 10, 1930; 1 son, James Madison IV. Fashion reporter for The Breath of the Avenue, New York 1923, successively asst. to fashion editor, beauty editor and fashion editor of Charm, 1923-31; advt. mgr. Sisholz Bros. dept. stores, 1931; with Tobe, fashion service, 1931-33; asso. Women's Orgn. for Nat. Prohibition Repeal, 1933; with Tobe 1933-35; fashion editor Mademoiselle 1935-37, editor in chief 1937-71; dir. Hanes Corp., Winston-Salem, N.C. Del. Am. Assembly; mem. Columbia U. Sch. of Gen. Studies Council; v.p. Fashion Group Inc., 1959-60, chmn. bd. govs., 1961-62; mem., past chmn. Coty Am. Fashion Critics' Awards; mem. adv. council Tobe-Coburn Sch. for Fashion Careers; mem. hon. adv. bd. N.Y. Fashion Designers, Inc. Mem. lay council Internat. Cardiology Found; mem. N.Y. council Hofstra U.; mem. pub. relations com. Girls Club Am. Recipient Pres.'s citation Lake Erie Coll. Mem. Fashion Group, Am. Soc. Mag. Editors (charter, exec. com.). Republican. Presbyn. Clubs: Nat. Press Club; Home: Ridgefield, Conn. Died Feb. 4, 1985.

BLACKWELL, HOYT, coll. pres.; b. Lancaster Co., S.C., Sept. 20, 1890; s. R. Lemuel and Mary (Hilton) B.; diploma, Mars Hill Coll., 1922; A.B., Wake Forest Coll., 1925, D.D., 1939; Th.M., Bapt. Theol. Sem., 1928; m. Olive English Brown, Sept. 12, 1934; children—Hannah Brown, Albert Lemuel, David Eric. Mem. of faculty Mars Hill (N.C.) College, 1928-38, pres. from 1938. Mem. N.E.A. Democrat. Baptist. Club: Civitan (Mars Hill). Address: Mars Hill, N.C. †

BLAI, BORIS, sculptor, educator; b. Russia, July 24, 1890; s. Michael and Esther (Anatopol) B.; ed. Kiev Imperial Acad. Fine Arts. Imperial Acad. Fine Arts, Leningrad, Ecole des Beaux Arts, 1912-13. Rodin apprentice, 1913; D.F.A., Florida Southern College, Lakeland, 1950; m. Manya Gourenko, Mar. 29, 1921; 1 son, Boris. Came to U.S., 1917, naturalized, 1931. Began as sculptor at age of 12; exhbns. in every country of Europe and in America, Annual Show Acad. Fine Arts, Pa., 1924-25, invted to Chicago Art Inst.; one-man show Grand Central Galleries, N.Y. City, 1934; asso. with R. Tait McKenzie in work, Canadian Memorial, Edinburgh, Scotland, statue of Gen. Wolfe, London; interested in progressive edn.; dir. of art. Oak Lane Country Day Sch., 1927-34; founder and dean Stella Elkins Tyler Sch. Fine Arts of Temple U., Elkins Park, Pa., 1934-59; consultant art department So. College. Founder, v.p. Long Beach. Island Found. Arts and Scis. Mem. Grand Central Galleries (New York), Art Alliance (Philadelphia), and Phila. Museum of Fine Arts. Home: Melrose Park, Pa. †

BLAIR, LORRAINE LOUISE, financial consultant; b. Milw.; d. Robert and Mina (Hesse) Schiller; student Mil. Downer Sem. and Coll.; children—Louise (Mrs. Richard Drury), Betty (Mrs. Carl Vaughn). Mgr. woman's dept. Mut. Life of N.Y., Milw., gen. agt. Continental Assurance Co.; mgr. woman's dept. Conn. Mut. Life Ins. Co., Chgo.; ins. broker, Chgo.; v.p. The Marshall Co., investments, Milw.; pres. treas. Lorraine L. Blair, Inc., investments and mut. funds, Chgo.; owner Baylor Ins. Agy. Founder, exec. dir. Finance Forum of Am. Mem. Nat. League Am. Pen Women, Midland Authors, Japan Soc. Chgo., Ill. Opera Guild, English-Speaking Union. Member of the Episcopalian Church. Clubs: Chicago Press (Chgo.); Reand Security: Answers to Your Everyday Money Questions. Organized, directed educational and pub. relations meetings Chgo. Stock Exchange, 1949; TV show Finance Forum of the Air. Lectr. before clubs and orgns. on finance, related subjects. Author: Answers to Your Everyday Money Questions, 1968. Home: Chicago, Ill. Died Nov. 17, 1984

BLAIR, WILLIAM MCCORMICK, investment banker; b. Chgo., May 2, 1884; s. Edward Tyler and Ruby (McCormick) B.; m. Helen Bowen, Feb. 10, 1912 (dec. 1972). B.A., Yale U., 1907; LL.D., Northwestern U., 1964; Litt.D., Lake Forest Coll., 1963. Partner William Blair & Co. Pres., life trustee Art Inst. Chgo.; life trustee U. Chgo., Field Mus. Natural History. Decorated chevalier French Legion of Honor; comdr. Royal Order of Vasa. Presbyterian (trustee, pres. congregation). Clubs: Chgo., Shoreacres, Comml., Old Elm (Chgo.); Racquet and Tennis (N.Y.C.). Home: Chicago, Ill. Died Mar. 29, 1982; buried Lake Forest Cemetery, Ill.

BLAKE, BERKELEY BARRINGTON, ch. official; b. of Am. parents at New Westminster, B.C., Can., Apr. 17, 1888; s. Jed Gilman and Isabel (Zealand) B.; Litt.B., U. of Calif., 1911; student Law Sch., Harvard, 1911-12; J.D., U. of Calif., 1913; student Pacific Unitarian Sch. for Ministry, 1922-23; S.T.D., Starr King School for the Ministry, 1950; m. Grace-Adele Parmele Smythe, Oct. 13, 1915; children—Jed Smythe, Charlotte, Frances. Admitted to Calif. bar, 1913, and practiced at San Francisco and Sacramento until 1922; ordained ministry Unitarian Ch., 1922; minister 1st Unitarian Ch., Sacramento, 1922-27; field sec. Am. Unitarian Assn., 1927-28, administrative v.p., 1928-33; minister Unitarian Ch., Santa Barbara, from 1933. Assistant professor Santa Barbara College, University of California, 1944, lecturer, 1945-46. Republican. Mason. Home: Santa Barbara, Calif. †

BLAKE, IRVING H(ILL), zoologist; b. Augusta, Me., Feb. 15, 1888; s. Fred S(umner) and F(lora) Etta (Chase) B.; A.B., Bates Coll., Lewiston, Me., 1911; A.M., Brown U., 1912; Ph.D., U. of Ill., 1925; m. Abigail M(argaret) Kincaid, Aug. 8, 1917. Instr. in zoology Ore. Agrl. Coll., 1912-15; instr. physiology Syracuse U., 1915-17; asso. prof. biology U. of Me., 1917-23; instr. zoology U. of Ida., 1925-26; prof. of zoology and anatomy U. of Neb. since 1926, chmn. dept. zoology from 1946; in charge zoology U. of Wyo. Sci. Camp, summers, 1933, 35-36; research work Marine Biol. Lab., Woods Hole, Mass., 1916, Cold Spring Harbor Biol. Lab., 1912; travel and field work in animal ecology in Ore., 1914, Me., (Northern Appalachians), 1923, Neb., 1928-29, Wyo. (Rocky Mountain forest studies), 1926; animal community reconnaissances, 1933, 35, 36, Colo. (slope exposure and high altitude studies) from 1937. Mem. Am. Asso. Univ. Profs., A.A.A.S., Ecol. Soc. of Am., Limnol. Soc. of Am., Wildlife Soc., Sigma Xi. Contbr. articles to sci. jours. Home: Lincoln, Nebr. †

BLAKE, JAMES HUBERT (EUBIE BLAKE), musician; b. Balt., Feb. 7, 1883; s. John Sumner and Emma (Johnstone) B.; m. Marion Gant Tyler, Dec. 27, 1945. Student Schillinger System of Composition, N.Y. U., 1949; D.H.L., Bklyn. Coll., 1973, Dartmouth, 1974; D.F.A., Rutgers U., 1974; Mus. D., New Eng. Conservatory Music, 1974. Began profl. piano career, 1901; became ptnr. vaudeville team Sissle and Blake, 1915; founder, Eubie Blake Music, (rec. co.), 1972. Collaborator: Broadway shows Shuffle Along, 1921, Blackbirds, 1930, Bubbling Brown Sugar, Eubie, 1979; mus. condr. Broadway shows, U.S.O. Hosp. Unit, 1941-46; now active pub. appearances, recording; appearances jazz festivals, Europe, mus. autobiography French TV.; Composer: songs including Baby Mine. Recipient numerous honors and awards. Mem. A.F.T.R.A., A.S.C.A.P., Negro Actors

Guild, Actors Equity. Club: Mason. Home: Brooklyn, N.Y. Dec. Feb. 12, 1983.*

BLAKE, JOHN BAPST, surgeon; b. Boston, Apr. 4, 1866; s. Dr. John George and Mary Elizabeth (McGrath) B.; A.B., Harvard, 1887, A.M., M.D., 1891; m. Anne Hastings, of Boston, Oct. 25, 1899. Asst. in anatomy, 1895-99, clin. surgery, 1899-1903, operative surgery, 1900-03; instr. surgery, 1908-10, asst. prof., 1910-19, Harvard Med. Sch. Visiting surgeon, Boston City Hospital, 1895-1911, surgeon-in-chief, 1911-19, consulting surgeon from 1919; visiting surgeon, Long Island Hospital, 1905-19; consulting surgeon, Boston Insane Hosp. Fellow Am. Surg. Assn., A.A.A.S.; mem. Boston Soc. Med. Improvement, Boston Med. Library Assn., Surg. Club (Boston), Boston Obstet. Soc., Mass. Med. Soc. Clubs: Harvard (Boston and New York); Union, Tavern, The Country. Author: Case Teaching in Surgery (with Herbert L. Burrell), 1904. Home: Boston, MA. †

BLAKENEY, JACK BYRD, publisher; b. Alvord, Tex., Mar. 30, 1913; s. James Benjamin and Neda (Ingram) B.; m. Pauline Lambert, Mar. 7, 1942; 1 dau., Melvetta. Student, John Tarleton Agrl. Coll., 1933-34; B.S., N. Tex. Tchrs. Coll., 1937. Nan. Asst. circulation mgr. Farm and Ranch, Holland's mags., 1941-42; asst. circulation mgr. Farmer-Stockman mag., 1942-71; v.p., chmn. bd. Farmer-Stockman Pub.Co., 1971-78; pub., gen. mgr. Farmer-Stockman mag., 1978-82. Chmn. N. Tex. Leukemia Assn.; ofcl. host Big D Charity Horse Show, 1971-77. Served to capt. USAAF, 1942-46. Mem. Agrl. Pubs. Assn. (dir.), Agrl. Circulation Mgrs. Assn., Southwest Hardware and Implement Assn. Mem. Ch. of Christ. Clubs: Dallas Press, Dallas Agr. Home: Dallas, Tex. Died Feb. 25, 1982; buried Restland, Dallas.

BLANCHARD, CLYDE INSLEY, management consultant and educator; born at Hutchinson, Kansas on October 6, 1888; s. of Ben and Avis (Insley) B.; student Swarthmore Coll., 1907-08; A.B., Baker U., Baldwin City, Kan., 1911; grad. courses in business, U. of Chicago, 1913; m. Garnet Benham, June 6, 1912; children—Lee Benham, Robert Mark, Howard Insley. Asst. prof. in bus., Ore. State Coll., 1913-15; prin., Standard Comml. Sch., Panama Pacific Internat. Exposition, San Francisco, Calif., 1915; head dept. bus. teacher training, U. of Calif., Berkeley, summers 1918-20; dir. bus. edn., pub. schs., Berkeley, 1922-25; with Gregg Pub. Co., N.Y. City, from 1927, dir. of research, 1927-37, general editor from 1938, mng. editor The Bus. Edn. World, monthly publ. for teachers, 1933-47; instr. court reporting, evening sessions, Hunter Coll., N.Y. City, 1935-41; prof. bus. edn., head grad. dept. bus. tchr. tng. U. of Tulsa, 1949-54, prof. management, 1954-56; vis. lectr. U. Colo., summer 1956-65; mgmt. cons. Consultant In-service Civilian Training, Fed. Govt., Washington, D.C., 1942-45. Mem. bd. directors Community Chest, Yonkers, N.Y., 1936-42. Mem. United Business Education Assn. (mem. exec. board), Nat. Shorthand Reporters Assn., Adminstrv. Mgmt. Soc., Systems and Procedures Assn. Am., S.A.R., Kappa Sigma, Delta Pi Epsilon. Author: Progressive Speed Building Tests, 1938; 20 Short Cuts to Shorthand Speed, 1939. Co-author: The English of Business, 1934; Gregg Typing, 1941; Ten Popular Bookkeeping Projects, 1941; Typing for Business, 1945; Gregg Speed Building for Colleges, 1951; Expert Shorthand Speed Course, 1951. Address: Tulsa, Okla. †

BLANCHETTE, ROMEO ROY, bishop; b. St. George, Ill., Jan. 6, 1913; s. Oscar and Josephine (Langlois) B.; B.A., St. Mary of Lake Sem., Mundelein, Ill., 1934, M.A., 1936, S.T.B., 1935, S.T.L., 1937; J.C.B., Pontifical Gregorian U., Rome, Italy, 1938, J.C.L., 1939. Ordained priest Roman Cath. Ch. 1937; notary Met. Tribunal Archdiocese Chgo., 1939-49, also asst. pastor Holy Name Cathedral; chancellor Diocese Joliet (Ill.), 1949-65, officialis, 1949-59, vicar gen., 1958-66, aux. bishop, 1965-66, bishop Diocese of Joliet, 1966-82. Chaplain Young Christian Students and Young Christian Workers, 1939-49; treas. Joliet Cathedral Bldg. Fund, 1950, Joliet High Sch. Bldg. Fund, 1953; bd. dirs. Joliet Sem. Bldg. Fund, 1960. Bd. dirs. Lewis Coll., Joliet Cath. Charities. Named domestic prelate, 1950, protonotary apostolic, 1959. Mem. Canon Law Soc. Am. (bd. dirs.). Died Jan. 11, 1982.

BLANDIN, AMOS NOYES, JR., judge; b. Bath, N.H., Dec. 20, 1896; s. Amos N. and Katherine (Woods) B.; m. Alberta Bell, July 15, 1937; children—Dale M., Joanna Bell, Jane Noyes. A.B., Dartmouth Coll., 1918, LL.D., 1951; LL.B., Harvard U., 1921; J.S.D., Suffolk U., 1948; LL.D., U. N.H., 1968. With Streeter, Demond, Woodworth & Sulloway, Concord, N.H., 1921; mem. firm Remick & Blandin, 1922-23; asso. Murchie & Murchie, 1923-29; mem. firm Murchie, Murchie & Blandin, 1929-41; mem. corp. Loan & Trust Savs. Bank, Concord, N.H., 1938-41; justice Superior Ct., 1941-1945, chief justice, 1945-47; asso. justice Supreme Ct. of N.H., 1947-66, jud. referee, 1966-78; mem. N.H. Jud. Council, 1945-47, N.H. Bd. Probation, 1947-63, chmn., 1961-63; mem. Bd. Rev. State Prison Sentences, 1975-77; lectr. law schs., colls. Author short stories, poems and legal articles. Chmn. N.H. Pub. Library Commn., 1943-50, N.H. Gov.'s Commn. on Pub. Disturbances, 1965-69; Trustee N.H. State Library, 1938-43, Coll. Advanced Sci., Canaan, N.H., 1961-63, Mary Hitchcock Meml. Hosp., Hanover, 1960-63. Served as 2d lt. F.A. U.S. Army, World War I. Recipient Robert Frost Contemporary Am. award, 1971. Mem. ABA, N.H. Bar Assn. (sec., treas. 1924-29), Am. Judicature Soc., Nat. Probation and Parole Assn. (adv. council judges), Am. Law Inst. (adv. group subject of agy.), Am. Acad. Polit. and Social Sci., Kappa Kappa Kappa, Dragon Sr. Soc. Democrat. Roman Catholic. Home: Hanover, NH.

BLANDING, SARAH GIBSON, educator; born Lexington, Ky., Nov. 22, 1898; d. William and Sarah Gibson (Anderson) Blanding; certificate from New Haven Normal Sch. of Gymnastics, 1919; A.B., U. of Ky., 1923; M.A., Columbia U., 1926; student London Sch. of Economics, London, 1928-29, Columbia U., summers, 1933, 34; LL.D., Syracuse U., U. of Ky., U. of Pa., Skidmore Coll., Russell Sage Coll., Rollins Coll., U. of Louisville, Mills Coll., Smith Coll., Brown U., N.Y.U., The Woman's College, U.N.C., Mt. Holyoke Coll., Knox Coll., U. Mich., Bennett College, Williams College, Chatham College; L.H.D., Keuka College Instructor Phys. Edn. University of Ky., 1919-23; acting dean of women, same, 1923-24, dean of women and asst. prof. polit. sci., 1926-37, dean of women and asso. prof. polit. science, 1937-41; dir. New York State Coll. of Home Economics, Cornell U., 1941-42, dean, 1942-46; pres. Vassar Coll., 1946-64, pres. emeritus, 1964-85. Nat. adv. com. UN Assn. U.S.A.; trustee Bennett Coll.; charter trustee Eisenhower Coll.; nat. adv. council Girl Scout U.S.A.; sponsor women's planning com. Japan Internat. Christian U. Found.; mem. nat. com. and adv. council, acad. freedom com. Am. Civil Liberties Union. Trustee, Chatham Coll., Wykeham Rise Sch., Scoville Library, Salisbury, Conn. Mem. Nat. Assn. Deans Women, Am. Assn. U. Women. Kappa Kappa Gamma. Democrat. Episcopalian (vestry). Club: Cosmopolitan (N.Y.C.). Home: Lakeville, Conn. Died Mar. 3, 1985

BLANNING, WENDALL YEAGER, lawyer; b. Williamstown, Pa., Nov. 13, 1888; s. William and Belle Jane (Yeager) B.; Ph.B., Dickinson Coll., Carlisle, Pa., 1912; m. Christine Anne Hoffman, Sept. 26, 1935; children—Robert Wendell, Bruce Jerome. Began as newspaper reporter, 1912; law librarian, 1913-14; admitted to Pa. bar, 1917, and practiced in Pa.; dir. Bureau of Pub. Convenience, Pub. Service Commn. of Pa., 1931-35; asst. dir. Bureau Motor Carriers, Interstate Commerce Commn., 1935-37, dir., 1937-58; practicing lawyer, Washington, from 1959. Served in inf. U.S. Army, 1917-19. Mem. Alpha Chi Rho. Republican. Methodist. Mason. Author: Public Utility Regulation in Pennsylvania, 1924. Home: Washington, D.C. †

BLATMAN, SAUL, medical educator; b. N.Y.C., Dec. 6, 1918; s. George Joseph and Bessie (Presel) B.; m. Ceevah Rosenthal, Apr. 10, 1954; children—Bettye Ann, Ceevah M., Robert N. B.A., Brown U., 1940; M.D., Duke, 1950. Intern, asst. resident N.Y. Hosp., 1950-52; resident, chief resident pediatrics Babies Hosp., N.Y.C., 1952-54; pvt. practice medicine, specializing in pediatrics, Manhasset, N.Y.; also Babies Hosp., N.Y.C., 1954-59; instr. pediatrics Columbia Coll. Physicians and Surgeons; also asst. attending physician Babies Hosp., N.Y.C., 1954-57; chief pediatrics Nat. Jewish Hosp., Denver, 1959-61; asst. clin. prof. pediatrics U. Colo. Med. Sch., 1959-61; asso. clin. prof. pediatrics N.Y. U. Sch. Medicine, 1961-67; asso. vis. pediatrician Bellevue Hosp., N.Y.C., 1961-67; prof. pediatrics Mt. Sinai Sch. Medicine, 1966-72; dir. pediatrics Beth Israel Med. Center, N.Y.C., 1961-72; prof. maternal and child health Dartmouth Med. Sch., from 1972, chmn. dept., 1972-78; dir. maternal and child health Dartmouth-Hitchcock Affiliated Hosps., N.H., 1972-78. Served to capt. AUS, 1943-46. Mem. Soc. Pediatric Research, Am. Pediatric Soc., Am. Acad. Pediatrics, Assn. Pediatric Edn. in Europe, Grafton County (N.H.) Med. Soc., N.E. Pediatric Soc. Home: Hanover, NH.

BLATT, BURTON, university dean, teacher educator; b. Bronx, N.Y., May 23, 1927; s. Abraham and Jennie (Starr) B.; m. Ethel Draizen, Dec. 24, 1951; children: Edward Richard, Steven David, Michael Lawrence. B.S., NYU, 1949; M.A., Columbia Tchrs. Coll., 1950; Ed.D., Pa. State U., 1956; L.H.D., Ithaca Coll., 1974. Tchr. mentally retarded children, N.Y.C., 1949-55; grad. scholar, grad. asst. Pa. State U., 1955-56; assoc. prof., coordinator spl. edn. So. Conn. State Coll., 1956-59, prof., chmn. spl. edn. dept., 1959-61; prof., chmn. spl. edn. dept. Sch. Edn. Boston U., 1961-69; Centennial prof., dir. div. spl. edn. and rehab., dir. Center on Human Policy, Syracuse U., 1969-76, dean Sch. Edn., 1976-85; former asst. commr. and dir. mental retardation Mass. Dept. Mental Health; former prin. cons. R.I. Commn. to Study Edn. of Handicapped Children; cons. U.S. Dept. Edn.; former mem. adv. bd. Joseph P. Kennedy Jr. Found. Author: (with S. Sarason, K. Davidson) The Preparation of Teachers, 1962, The Intellectually Disfranchised: Impoverished Learners and Their Teachers, 1967, (with F. Kaplan) Christmas in Purgatory, 1966, (with Frank Garfunkel) The Educability of Intelligence, 1969, Exodus from Pandemonium, 1970, Souls in Extremis, 1973, Revolt of the Idiots, 1976, (with D. Biklen and R. Bogdan) An Alternative Textbook in Special Education: People, Schools and Institutions, 1977, (with A. Ozolins and J. McNally) The Family Papers, 1979, In and Out of Mental Retardation, 1981, In and Out of the University, 1982, In and Out of Books, 1984, (with R. Morris) Perspectives in Special Education, 1984; also articles and monographs on mental retardation, spl. edn. and higher edn. Past bd. dirs. Epilepsy League Mass.; former chmn. Mass. Task Force on Edn. Mentally Handicapped; past mem. nat. adv. bd. Nat. Soc. Prevention Blindness; past mem. Mass. and N.Y. Govs.' coms. on Services to Children, Conn. Gov.'s Adv. Council Mental Retardation; past pres. and current mem. bd. visitors Syracuse Devel. Center; mem. N.Y. State Doctoral Council. Recipient ann. award Mass. Psychol. Assn., 1967, ann. award Mass. Assn. Retarded Citizens, 1968; Newell Kephart Meml. award Purdue U., 1974; award N.Y. State Assn. Tchrs. Mentally Handicapped, 1976; award Coll. of New Rochelle, 1980; ann. award Pioneer Devel. Ctr., 1983; Profl. Leadership award Young Adult Inst., 1983. Fellow Am. Assn. Mental Deficiency (past nat. v.p. edn., past editorial staff Am. Jour. Mental Deficiency, Mental Retardation, nat. pres. 1976-77, regional award 1973, nat. award 1974); mem. Council Exceptional Children (past mem. found. bd., past state pres., state dir., div. pres., chpt. award 1980), Assn. for Severely Handicapped, Phi Delta Kappa. Jewish. Home: Jamesville, N.Y. Died Jan. 20, 1985.

BLEE, HARRY HARMON, engineer; b. Santa Ana, Calif., May 13, 1887; s. Robert James and Amanda Jane (Harmon) B.; A.B., Stanford U., 1910, M.E., 1911; B.S., Occidental, 1911; grad. U.S. Army Sch. of Mil. Aeronautics, 1925; m. Gladys Howard. Instr. mech. engring., Stanford, 1911-12; successively asst. state mech. engr., state road engr. and state water supply engr., Calif., 1913-17 and 1920; private engring. practice, 1921-24 and 1926. Became connected with Aeronautics Br., U.S. Dept. Commerce, Feb. 1927, as sr. business specialist; made lecture tour of U.S.; was engineer-executive of Fact-Finding Com. on Airport Facilities for New York Met. Dist. and organized airport advisory service of the dept.; apptd. chief Div. of Airports and Aeronautic Information, 1928; dir. Aeronautic Development, U.S. Dept. Commerce, 1929-33; directed program of research on aids to air navigation; tech. advisor to U.S. delegation to 4th Pan-Am. Comml. Conf.; chmn. Nat. Coop. Research coms. on aero. Mem. interdepartmental Com. on Civil Airways, and Fed. Bd. of Surveys and Maps. Capt., A.C., U.S. Army (airplane engring. div.), 1917-19; mem. Air Corps Res. from 1919; col. A.A.F., 1941-48; in charge Civil Air Patrol anti-submarine and missing aircraft search and rescue operations and later in commd. of all C.A.P. activities; holds ratings of airplane pilot, airship pilot and spherical balloon pilot. Mem. Am. Soc. of Photogrammetry (pres. 1936). Mem. N.A.A. Contest Bd., 1932-38; mem. Commn. on Air Law, Fed. Aeronautique Internationale, 1935-38; chmn. Com. on Aerial Photography, Internat. Soc. of Photogrammetry, 1936-38; mem. Advisory Council of Fed. Bd. of Surveys and Maps, 1936-42. Presbyn. Address: Ashburn, Va. †

BLEICH, HANS HEINRICH, civil engineer; b. Vienna, Austria, Mar. 24, 1909; s. Friedrich and Antonie (Stern) B.; C.E., Tech. U., Vienna, 1933, D.Sc., 1934. Came to U.S. 1945, naturalized, 1950. Designing engr. bridges and indsl. plants, Austria, 1934-39; sr. engr. Braithwaite & Co., Ltd., London, Eng., 1940-44; research engr. Chance Vaught Aircraft div. United Aircraft, 1945; asso. engr. Hardesty & Hanover, N.Y.C., 1945-50; lectr. civil engring. Columbia, 1946-50, asso. prof., 1950-52, prof., 1953-77, prof. emeritus, 1977-85, dir. Inst. Air Flight Structures, 1954-77. Mem. ASCE, ASME, Am. Inst. Aeros. and Astronautics, Internat. Assn. Bridge and Structural Engring., Nat. Acad. Engring., Sigma Xi. Author: Design of Suspension Bridges, 1935. Editor: Buckling Strength of Metal Structures, 1952. Address: New York, N.Y. Died Feb. 9, 1985.

BLEICKEN, GERHARD DAVID, ins. exec.; b. Newton, Mass., Aug. 29, 1913; s. Gerhard and Beatrice (Douglas) B.; m. Ellene T. Mailhot (div.); children—Kurt Douglas, Eric, Carl Weeman; m. Ann M. Meacham; children—David H., Neil G. Student, Gettysburg Coll., 1931-32; J.D. cum laude, Boston U., 1938; D.C.S. (hon.), Suffolk U., 1973; LL.D. (hon.), Boston Coll., 1977, Emanuel Coll., 1978; L.H.D. (hon.), Northeastern U., 1977; student, Aspen Inst. Humanistic Studies, 1957, Sch. Indsl. Mgmt., M.I.T., 1958; grad., Naval Air Tng. Sch., R.I., Nat. Def. U. Bar: Mass. bar 1938, U.S. Supreme Ct. bar 1943. With John Hancock Mut. Life Ins. Co., Boston, 1939-79, chmn. bd., chief exec. officer, 1970-79, also dir.; dir. Arthur D. Little, Inc.; hon. dir. 1st Nat. Boston Corp., 1; st Nat. Bank of Boston; chmn. bd. Life Ins. Assn. Mass., 1976-77; mem. industries adv. com. Advt. Council, 1972-78; dir. Am. Research and Devel., Boston, 1970-72. Mem. program adv. com. Office Emergency Preparedness, 1958-73; mem. Am. Battle Monument Commn., 1969-78; mem. adv. com. on CD Nat. Acad. Scis., 1954-69; trustee Boston U., Boston Urban Found.; chmn. trustee council Boston U. Med. Center; bd. visitors UCLA Grad. Sch. Mgmt., 1967-78; bd. dirs. World Affairs Council, 1971-81; bd. overseers Boston Mus. Fine Arts, Boston Symphony Orch.; mem. Pres.'s Commn. on Personnel Interchange, 1974-77; trustee Boston Mus. Sci., 1973-81; exec. com. Mass. Com. Catholics, Protestants and Jews. Served at lt. USNR, 1943-46. Decorated comdr.'s cross Order Merit Fed. Republic Germany, 1976; recipient Presdl. Disting. Service award, 1968; Disting. Service citation Dept. Def., 1969; Disting. Community Service award Brandeis U., 1973; Disting. Citizen award Boy Scouts Am., 1977; Christian Herter award World Affairs Council, 1978; Benjamin Franklin fellow Royal Soc. Arts; Andrew Wellington Cordier fellow Sch. Internat. Affairs, Columbia U. Mem. UN Assn. U.S.A. (dir. 1973-79), Am. Law Inst. (life), Bostonian Soc. Episcopalian. Clubs: St. Botolph (Boston); Wianno Yacht. Home: Sherborn, Mass. Died Dec. 4, 1981.

BLESSING, RICHARD ALLEN, educator; b. Bradford, Pa., Sept. 11, 1939; s. Edward John and Eva Lou Ellen (Morrison) B.; m. Lisa Baepple, July 4, 1964; 1 son, Craig Edward. A.B., Hamilton Coll., 1961; M.A., Tulane U., 1963, Ph.D., 1967. Instr. English, football coach La. State U., New Orleans, 1964-68; asst. prof. Heidelberg Coll., Tiffin, Ohio, 1968-70; asst. prof. English U. Wash., Seattle, 1970-73, asso. prof., 1973-78, prof., from 1978. Author: Wallace Stevens' Whole Harmonium, 1970, Theodore Roethke's Dynamic Vision, 1974; poems Winter Constellations, 1977, A Closed Book,; Contbr. articles to profl. jours.; contbr. poetry to mags. Mem. Seattle Arts Commn., 1978. Guggenheim fellow, 1972-73; Am. Philos. Soc. grantee, 1970. Address: Seattle, Wash.

BLEWITT, THOMAS HUGH, physicist; b. Cleve., Feb. 8, 1921; s. Reginald T. and Ethyl (Arstall) B.; m. Agnes Winifred Herr, Sept. 4, 1943; children—Kenneth Thomas, Carol Alice. B.S. in Physics, Case Inst. Tech., 1942; B.S. in Meteorology, N.Y. U., 1943; D.Sc. in Physics, Carnegie Inst. Tech., 1950. AEC fellow Carnegie Inst. Tech., 1948-50; physicist Oak Ridge Nat. Lab., 1950-61; exchange scientiest Atomic Energy Establishment, Harwell, Eng., 1957-58; prof. Enrico Fermi Summer Sch., Ispra, Italy, 1960; sr. physicist Argonne (Ill.) Nat. Lab., from 1961; prof. materials engring. U. Ill. Chgo. Circle Campus, from 1965; cons. IAEA; vis. scientist Argentine Atomic Energy Com., 1969-70; vis. prof. U. Mo., 1977-78. Contbr. articles to profl. jours. Served to capt. USAAF, 1942-46. Fellow Am. Phys. Soc. Home: Wheaton, Ill.

BLISH, MORRIS JOSLIN, cons. chemist; b. Lincoln, Neb., Apr. 21, 1889; s. Frank May and Louise (Joslin) B.; B.Sc., U. of Neb., 1912, M.A., 1913; Ph.D., U. of Minn., 1915; m. Vera Buell, Apr. 21, 1921; 1 dau., Mary Louise. With Food Research Dept. Bur. of Chemistry, U.S. Dept. Agr., 1915-16; asst. chemist Mont. Agrl. Expt. Sta., 1916-22; chemist Neb. Agrl. Expt. Sta. and prof. agrl. Chemistry, U. of Neb., 1922-30; prin. chemist protein div., Western Regional Research Lab., U.S. Dept. Agr., Albany, Calif., from 1939; director research, Amino Products Co., Rossford, O., 1943; supvr. organic and biochemical research Internat. Minerals and Chem. Corp. until 1954, asso. Ariz. Research Labs., from 1954. Served as lt. Sanitary Corps, A.E.F., World War; major C.W.S., O.R.C. Fellow A.A.A.S., Am. Inst. Chemists; mem. N.Y. Acad. Sci., Am. Soc. Biol. Chemists, Am. Chem. Soc., Am. Assn. Cereal Chemists (pres. 1923-25), Indsl. Research Inst., Am. Inst. of Chemists, Sigma Xi, Phi Kappa Phi, Phi Gamma Delta, Alpha Chi Sigma. Thomas Burr Osborne medalist, 1936. Republican. Spl. work in wheat and flour chemistry, with emphasis on the proteins, enzymes, and the measurement and identification of factors governing wheat and flour quality. Home: Phoenix, Ariz. †

BLISS, FRANCIS WALTER, lawyer; b. Gilboa, N.Y., Apr. 27, 1892; s. Franklin W. and Alberta (Becker) B.; m. Margaret E. Schaeffer, June 22, 1918 (dec. June 24, 1956); children: Janet Schaeffer (Mrs. Snyder), Margaret Ellen (Mrs. Berdan), Martha Ann (Mrs. Grogan); m. Margaret A. Nethaway, Oct. 31, 1957. A.B., Cornell U., 1913; LL.B., Albany Law Sch., 1915, J.D., 1968; LL.D., Central Coll., Pella, Iowa, 1939. Bar: N.Y. bar 1915. Practiced in, Middleburgh, 1916-30, 77-82; county atty. Schoharie County, N.Y., 1922-26; justice Supreme Ct. N.Y., 1930-44, Supreme Ct. N.Y. (Appellate Div.), 1933-44; mem. firm Bliss & Bouck, Schoharie and Albany, N.Y., 1945-62; practice law, Schoharie, 1963-77; Pres. Howe Caverns, Inc., N.Y. Served as 1st lt. Signal Corps U.S. Army, 1917-18. Mem. Am., N.Y. State, Schoharie County bar assns. Mem. Reformed Ch. (bd. edn.). Clubs: Mason. Club (Albany), Fort Orange (Albany). Home: Middleburgh, N.Y. Dec. Sept. 8, 1982.

BLISS, LESLIE EDGAR, librarian; b. Poland, Herkimer County, N.Y., March 26, 1889; s. Jacob Henry and Alice Johnson (Stillman) B.; A.B., Colgate U., 1911; B.L.S., N.Y. State Library Sch., Albany, N.Y., 1913; m. Alice Marion Burnett, Feb. 26, 1914; children—Carey Stillman, Virginia Leland, Thayer Arnold. Asst. in legislative reference, N.Y. State Library, 1913-15; asst. Henry E. Huntington Library, San Marino, Calif., 1915-20, curator, 1920-25, acting librarian, 1925-26, librarian, from 1926. Member New York Historical Society, Phi Beta Kappa, and Phi Delta Theta. Republican. Clubs: Grolier (N.Y.C.); Roxburghe (San Francisco); Zamorano (Los Angeles). Home: Altadena, Cal. †

BLISS, RAY CHARLES, political party official; b. Akron, Ohio, Dec. 16, 1907; s. Emil and Emilie (Wieland) B.; m. Ellen F. Palmer., Nov. 26, 1959. A.B., U. Akron, 1935, L.H.D., 1968. Sec., treas. Wells & Bliss, Inc., 1933-37; pres. Tower Agys., Inc. (gen. ins.), Akron, 1947-81; Mem. Summit County Bd. Elections, 1936-78, chmn. bd., 1945-46, 49-50; chmn. Summit County Republican Central Com., 1942-64; mem. Ohio Rep. State Central and Exec. Com., 1944-74, chmn., 1949-65, mem. finance com., 1949-81; mem. Rep. Nat. Com., 1952-80, mem. exec. com., 1952-80, vice chmn., 1960-65, 70-80, chmn., 1965-69; del.-at-large Rep. Nat. Conv., 1952, 56, 60, 64, 68, 72, 76, mem. rules com., 1952, chmn. delegation, 1956, chmn. subcom. to select 1960 conv. site, chmn. 1968 site com., adviser site com., 1972, 76, vice chmn. Ohio delegation, 1960; chmn. Midwest Rep. State Chmns. Assn., 1953-65; chmn. Rep. com. on big city politics, 1961; chmn. Rep. State Chairmen's Adv. Com., 1962-65; adviser exec. com. on Nat. Conv. Arrangements Com., 1964, 72, 76, 80, chmn. conv. arrangements com., 1968; presiding officer Rep. Joint Leadership of Congress, 1965-69, Rep. Coordinating Com., 1965-69; mem. Rep. Nat. Rule 29 Com., 1973-74, chmn. subcom. 4, 1973-74; mem. Rep. Nat. Com. Bipartisan Com. to Study Methods of Financing Quadrennial Nat. Nominating Convs., 1973-81; mem. outreach adv. com. Rep. Nat. Com., 1977-80; Mem. Akron Regional Devel. Bd., U. Akron Devel. Found., 1970; trustee Akron U., 1970-74, 75-81, vice chmn., 1977-81, chmn. subcom. on devel., 1970-74, 75-81, mem. subcom. on fin., 1970-74, 75-80, chmn., 1980. Recipient U. Akron Alumni Honor award, 1965, Taylor A. Borradaile award Phi Kappa Tau, 1977. Mem. Blue Coats, Omicron Delta Kappa, Phi Kappa Tau, Phi Sigma Alpha. Episcopalian. Clubs: Mason (Akron) (32 deg.), Shriner (Akron), Kiwanian. (Akron), City (Akron), Portage Country (Akron), Fairlawn Country (Akron); Columbus (Ohio); Union (Cleve.); 1925 F Street (Washington). Home: Akron, Ohio. Died Aug. 6, 1981.

BLOCH, FELIX, physicist, educator; b. Zurich, Switzerland, Oct. 23, 1905; s. Gustav and Agnes (Mayer) B.; m. Lore C. Misch, Mar. 14, 1940; children—George J., Daniel A., Frank S., Ruth. Student, Fed. Inst. Tech., Zurich, Switzerland, 1924-27; Ph.D., Leipzig, Germany, 1928. Lectr. theoret. physics., Leipzig, 1932; assoc. prof. physics Stanford, 1934-36, prof., 1936-71, prof. emeritus, 1971-83; war research Stanford, Los Alamos, Harvard, 1942-45. Contbr. about 80 articles on atomic physics to sci. publs., since 1927. Recipient Nobel Prize in Physics, 1952; Lorentz Found. fellow Holland, 1930; Oersted Found. fellow, 1931; Rockefeller Found. fellow, 1933. Fellow Am. Phys. Soc. (pres. 1965-66), Am. Acad. Arts and Scis., Royal Soc. Edinburgh; mem. Nat. Acad. Scis., Royal Dutch Acad. Scis. Home: Zurich, Switzerland. Dec. Sept. 10, 1983.

BLOOD, ROBERT OSCAR, M.D., ex-gov.; b. Enfield, N.H., Nov. 10, 1887; s. William E. and Lorinda (Colby) B.; M.D., Dartmouth Coll., 1913, A.M., 1941; LL.D., Univ. of New Hampshire, 1941; m. Pauline Shepard, June 3, 1916; children—Robert O., Jr., Horace S., Emily. Interne Mary Hitchcock Memorial Hosp., Hanover, N.H., 1913-14; post grad. work in Boston and New York, N.Y.; mem. surg. and obstet. staff Margaret Pillsbury Gen. Hosp., Concord, N.H., since 1916; owner-mgr. Crystal Spring Farm, East Concord, N.H.; president City Realty Co. Governor of State of New Hampshire for term 1941-43, re-elected Governor for the term 1943-45. Served as lieut., later advanced through grades to maj., Med. Corps, U.S.A., 1917-19, with A.E.F. in France; lieut. col. M.O.R.C. since 1927. Decorated with Croix de Guerre (France); 26th Div. Distinguished Service Cross (U.S.). Fellow Am. Coll. Surgeons; mem. Am. Med. Assn., N.E. Obstet. and Gynecol. Soc., N.H. Surg. Soc., N.H. Med. Soc., Am. Legion. Republican. Congregationalist. I.O.O.F. Home: Concord, N.H. †

BLOODWORTH, JAMES NELSON, state justice; b. Decatur, Ala., Jan. 21, 1921; s. Benjamin M. and Marguerite (Nelson) B.; student Athens Coll., 1938-39; B.S., U. Ala., 1942, LL.B., 1947; m. Mary Jean Gregg, Sept. 27, 1963; children—Catherine, Sandra, Jean Marguerite. Admitted to Ala. bar, 1947; mem. firm Calvin and Bloodworth, Decatur, 1947-58; judge Recorder's Ct., Decatur, 1948-51; solicitor Morgan County, Decatur, 1951; judge 8th jud. Circuit Ct. Ala., 1959-68; assoc. justice Ala. Supreme Ct. 1968-80, ret., 1980; lectr. in law, from 1963. Co-chmn. Circuit Judges Seminars Ala., 1960-66; chmn. Ala. Pattern Jury Instrn. Com., 1966-68; pres. Morgan County Jury Com., 1966-68; faculty adviser Nat. Coll. State Trial Judges, 1967, Nat. Coll. State Judiciary Grad. Course, 1971; faculty Am. Acad. Jud. Edn., 1970-78. Pres. Decatur Boys Club, 1951; moderator N. Ala. Presbytery, 1965; mem. Ala. Bd. Pardons and Paroles, 1951-52. Chmn. Ala. Democratic Campaign Steering Com., 1961-63. Bd. dirs. Morgan County chpt. A.R.C., 1959-60. Served to capt. AUS, World War II. Decorated Bronze Star, Combat Inf. badge; named Outstanding Alumnus, U. Ala. Law Sch., 1980. Mem. Ala. Res. Officers Assn. (chpt. pres. 1959), Ala., Morgan County (pres. 1955) bar assns, Farrah Order of Jurisprudence, Phi Delta Phi, Kappa Alpha, Omicron Delta Kappa. Presbyn. (elder). Mason (K.T., Shriner), Rotarian (pres. Decatur 1953-54). Co-author: Index to Alabama Constitutional Convention of 1901, 1948. Home: Montgomery, Ala. Died 1981.

BLOOM, JULIUS, performing arts administrator, consultant; b. Bklyn., Sept. 23, 1912; s. Samuel Wolf and Sarah Yochebed (Ferman) B.; m. Emily Leah Spicer, Feb. 16, 1935; children: David Shepherd, Joseph Frederick. B.A., Rutgers U., 1933; postgrad., N.Y. U., 1934-36; L.H.D. (hon.), Buena Vista Coll., 1975. Assoc. editor The Literary World, 1934-35; instr. philosophy Rutgers U., Newark, 1935-36; editor Bklyn. Inst. Arts and Scis., Bklyn., 1936-37, asst. to dir., 1937-39, acting dir., 1939-41, dir., 1941-57; exec. dir. Nat. Inst. Music, N.Y.C., 1957-59; dir. concerts and lectures Rutgers U., 1959-72; exec. dir. Carnegie Hall Corp., N.Y.C., 1960-77, vice chmn. bd., dir. corp. planning, 1977-79, cons., 1979-84; Founder, gen. mgr. Bklyn. Symphony Orchestra, 1939-41; pres. Bklyn. Mus. Sch., 1956-62; cons. Cultural Devel. Greater Newark Devel. Council, 1959-66, Bucknell U., 1979—; music cons. Norwegian govt., 1957-61, Office Cultural Affairs, N.Y.C., 1962-65, Mexican govt., 1972—, Fundacão Orchestra Sinfônica Brasileira, 1978—, Columbia Pictures, 1980-82; adminstrv. cons. Center for Public Cinema, Inc., 1979-81, Internat. Fellowship for Arts, Culture and Edn., 1979—, Fundación Teresa Carreño, 1981-82, Beethoven Found., Inc., 1980-82; mktg. cons. Lodiar S.A., Geneva, 1980-82; advisor on community devel. Nat. Assn. Music Mchts., 1982—; cons. on theater design U. Judaism, Los Angeles, 1982—; dir., moderator Northwood Conf. on Creativity, Midland, Mich., 1982—; bd. dirs. Ferruccio Busoni Archives, 1983—. Author: The Year in American Music, 1946-47, 1947; contbg. editor: Metropolis mag., 1979—; Contbr. articles to profl. jours. Decorated officer Ordre des Arts et Lettres France). Mem. Am. Platform Guild (1st v.p. 1943-46, acting pres. 1946-47), Chamber Music Assos. (founder), Nat. Assn. Concert Mgrs. (exec. sec. 1953-57), Assn. Coll. and Univ. Concert Mgrs. (pres. 1962-64), Phi Beta Kappa. Home and Office: Brooklyn, N.Y. Died July 5, 1984.

BLOOM, MAX SAMUEL, wholesale distributor; b. Chgo., Aug. 2, 1907; s. Samuel and Mary (Becker) B.; m. Carolyn Gumbiner, June 11, 1930 (dec. 1966); children: Donald G., Stephen J., Barbara Kreml; m. Mary Frank Bernstein, Apr. 11, 1967 (dec. 1980). B.A., U. Chgo., 1927. With S. Bloom Inc., Chgo., 1927-83, chmn. bd. Chmn. Tobacco div. Combined Jewish Appeal, Chgo. Recipient Am. Jewish Com. Chgo. Human Relations award; recipient Alex Schwartz Meml. award, Chgo. Tobacco Table Stanley Loesser award, Merchandising award Cigarette Merchandise Assn. Mem. Ill. Assn. Tobacco Distributors (founder, past pres., dir.), Nat. Assn. Tobacco Distributors (Tobacco Hall of Fame 1967), Nat. Candy Wholesalers Assn. Club: Cliff Dwellers (Chgo.). Lodge: Rotary. Home: Chicago, Ill. Died Dec. 29, 1983.

BLOOMFIELD, ARTHUR L., prof. medicine; b. Baltimore, Md., May 30, 1888; s. Maurice and Rose (Zeisler) B.; A.B., Johns Hopkins, 1907, M.D., 1911; m. Julia Mayer, Oct. 16, 1920; children—Julia, Anne Elinor, Arthur John. With Johns Hopkins Sch. of Medicine as asst., instr., asso. and asso. prof. medicine, 1912-26; prof. medicine, Stanford, since 1926. Mem. A.M.A., Assn. Am. Physicians, Am. Soc. for Clin. Investigation. Home: San Francisco, Calif. †

BLOOMHARDT, PAUL FREDERICK, prof. of biography; b. Altoona, Pa., Jan. 28, 1888; s. John Daniel and Clara May (Isett) B.; A.B., Gettysburg (Pa.) Coll., 1909; student Gettysburg Theol. Sem., 1909-12; Ph.D., Johns Hopkins, 1918; m. Marjorie Blackburn, Mar. 23, 1918; children—Frederick Blackburn, Mrs. Dorothy Ruth Gaines. Began as teacher of Latin at Altoona (Pa.) High School, 1913; pastor at Lutherville, Maryland, 1915-17, at Buffalo, N.Y., 1920-23; prof. history, Newberry (S.C.) Coll., 1923-25; asso. professor biography, Wittenberg College, Springfield, Ohio, 1925-27, prof. from 1927; instr. history, Shrivenham (England) American Univ., 1945; lecturer on historical, political and sociological subjects to U.S. Armed Forces in Europe, 1946. Chaplain, lt. (j.g.), United States Navy, World War; attached to U.S.S. George Washington, 1918-19. Decorated Chevalier Order of Crown (Belgium), 1919. Mem. Am. Assn. Univ. Profs., Am. Oriental Soc., Am. Schs. of Oriental Research, Am. Hist. Assn., Phi Beta Kappa, Alpha Tau Omega, Lambda Mu. Lutheran. Clubs: Lowell, Men's Literary (Springfield). Contbr. to history and religious jours. Home: Springfield, Ohio. †

BLOOMINGDALE, ALFRED S., corporate executive; b. N.Y.C., Apr. 15, 1916; s. Hiram C. and Rosalind (Schiffer) B.; m. Betty Lee Newling, Sept. 14, 1946; children—Lee Geoffrey, Elisabeth Lee, Robert Russell. Grad., Brown U., 1938. Asst. mdse. mgr. Bloomingdale Bros., N.Y.C., 1938; Broadway and Hollywood producer, 1939-49; v.p. Diners' Club, Los Angeles, 1950-55, pres., 1955-70, chmn. bd., dir., 1964-70, cons., 1970-82; chmn. bd. Surfside 6 Floating Homes, Inc., Fort Lauderdale, Fla., 1970-82, Marina Bay Operating Co., Fort Lauderdale, 1973-82, Quadrox Corp., Los Angeles, 1974-82; chmn. bd., dir. Journey's End, Marietta, Ga.; dir. Lyman G. Realty Co., B. Bros., Realty Co., Beneficial Standard Corp., Marina Bay Hotel, Ft. Lauderdale. Bd. dirs. Internat. Rescue Com.; trustee emeritus Brown U.; bd. regents Loyola/Marymount Coll., St. John's Hosp. Decorated knight comdr. of St. Gregory. Mem. Acad. Motion Picture Arts and Scis., Westminster Alumni Assn., Delta Kappa Epsilon. Club: Brown University (Los Angeles). Home: Los Angeles, Calif. Dec. Aug. 23, 1982.

BLOOMQUIST, HOWARD RICHARD, corporate executive; b. Mpls., Sept. 16, 1918; s. Richard P. and Ruth M. (Holmgren) B.; m. Ingrid M. Brostrom, Feb. 14, 1941; children—Dennis, Diane (Mrs. W. Mowry Connelly), Laurel (Mrs. Paul Shields). Student, U. Minn., 1937-40; grad., Advanced Mgmt. Program, Harvard, 1958. Asst. advt. mgr. Pillsbury Mills, Inc., 1941-46; advt. mgr. Toni div. Gillette Co., 1946-49; gen. mgr. Lever Bros. Co., 1949- 53; with Gen. Foods Corp., 1953-68, gen mgr., 1962-63, v.p., 1963-67, group v.p., 1967-68; dir., sr. ptnr. McKinsey & Co., 1969-71; corp. v.p., pres. grocery products group (world-wide) W.R. Grace & Co., 1971-73; sr. v.p., pres. consumer products group Warner-Lambert Co., Morris Plains, N.J., 1973-77, sr. v.p. corp. mktg.-worldwide, 1977-80, also dir. Past trustee Greenwich (Conn.) Acad.; past vice chmn. United Way, Morris County, N.J. Mem. Am. Mgmt. Assn., Assn. Nat. Advertisers, Grocery Mfrs. Assn. Mem. Community Ch. (past chmn. ofcl. bd.). Clubs: Field (Greenwich); Harvard

Bus. Sch. (N.Y.C.). Home: Greenwich, Conn. Dec. Nov. 18, 1982.

BLOUNT, ROY EUGENE, army officer; b. Crawford, Tex., June 13, 1889; s. Ben F. and Ida (Bewley) B.; grad. Cav. Sch. Troops Officers course, 1926, Comd. and Gen. Staff Sch., 1932. Army Indsl. Sch., 1933; m. Lodie Drinkle, 1916. Commd. 2d lt. Texas Nat. Guard, 1912, capt., 1915; on active duty in federal service, Troop A, 1st Squadron Cav., Tex., N.G., 1916-17; promoted major, 1918; disch., 1920; commd. capt., cav., U.S. Army, 1920, and advanced through the grades to brig. gen., 1944; asst. chief of staff, G-3, 3d Div., 1932-37; exec. and comdr. 5th cav., 1938-39; faculty Cav. Sch., 1940; asst. chief of staff G-4, 1st Cav. Div., Fort Bliss, Tex., 1940-41; asst. chief, later chief of staff, Hdqrs. VII Corps, San Jose, Calif.; became asst. chief of staff, Hawaiian Dept. (Central Pacific Theater of Operations), May-Aug. 1943; assumed command Army Port and Service command. Central Pacific Theater of Operations, Aug. 1943. Decorated Distinguished Service Medal, Legion of Merit, Bronze Star Medal, Army Commendation Ribbon. Address: San Antonio, Tex. †

BLUHDORN, CHARLES G., corporate executive; b. Vienna, Austria, Sept. 20, 1926; came to U.S., 1942. Student, Coll. City N.Y., Columbia. Self-employed, 1946-56; chmn. bd., dir., mem. exec. com. Gulf & Western Industries, Inc., N.Y.C., 1958-83; dir. Paramount Pictures Corp., N.Y.C. Trustee Trinity Sch., N.Y.C.; co-chmn. N.Y. chpt. Am. Cancer Soc., U.S. Savs. Bond Drive. Served with USAAF, 1945. Recipient Disting. New Yorker award City Club N.Y. Address: New York, N.Y. Dec. Feb. 19, 1983.*

BLUM, ALEX ALADAR, artist; b. Budapest, Hungary, Feb. 7, 1889; s. Alexander and Rose (Sternberg) B.; student Cincinnati Art Acad., 1905-06; Nat. Acad. of Design, 1907-11; m. Helen Abrahams, 1917; children—Audrey Anthony, Robert Alex. Represented in Met. Mus. of Art, Boston Mus., Congl. Library of Washington, Wesleyan U., Yale U., Iowa State Coll., La. State U., N.Y. State Coll., Fordson Board of Education. Awarded Nat. Acad. of Design bronze medal, 1908; 1st prize for etching, 1909. Mem. Asso. Am. Artists. Home: Rye, N.Y. †

BLUM, ANNA OTTILLIA, lawyer; b. Monroe, Wis., Apr. 6, 1908; d. Samuel and Ottillia (Marty) B. B.A., U. Wis., 1929, LL.B., 1943. Bar: Wis. 1943. Practiced in Monroe, from 1943. Mem. Wis. Devel. Authority.; Pres. Green County Womens Republican Club, 1951-54. Mem. ABA, Wis. Bar Assn. (rep. to gov. body 1947-54), Green County Bar Assn. (pres. 1955, 71), Nat. Assn. Women Lawyers (pres. 1961-62, Wis. del. 1969-70), Green County Hist. Soc. (pres. 1951-54, treas 1958-69), Am. Legion Aux., Bus. and Profl. Women's Clubs (pres. Monroe 1976-79), Order of Coif, Phi Beta Kappa, Kappa Beta Pi. Club: Order Eastern Star. Home: Monroe, Wis. Died Apr. 20, 1985; buried Greenwood Cemetery, Monroe.

BLUM, STELLA, curator, educator; b. Schenectady, Oct. 19, 1916; d. Joseph and Mary (Kiskiel) Biercuk; m. George A. Blum, Oct. 5, 1939; children: Walter B., Eric George. B.F.A., Syracuse U., 1938. With Met. Mus. Art, N.Y.C., 1953—, assoc. curator, 1969-72, curator, 1972-85; adj. prof. NYU, 1979-85; guest curator Kyoto Costume Inst., Japan, 1975, 79, Kunsthaus Mus., Zurich, Switzerland, 1979, St. Louis Mus. Art, 1979, Victoria Gallery, Melbourne, Australia, 1981. Author: Victorian Fashions and Costumes from Harper's Bazar 1867-1898, 1974, Designs by Erte, 1976, Ackermann's Costume Plates, 1978, Everyday Fashions of the 20s, 1981, 18th Century French Fashion Plates, 1982. Recipient Arents Pioneer award Syracuse U., 1983; recipient citation Pratt Inst., 1983. Mem. Fashion Group (v.p.), Costume Soc. Am. (v.p.), Fashion's Inner Circle (pres.), Internat. Council Mus. (titular head costume com.). Home: Whitestone, N.Y. Died July 31, 1985.

BLYTHE, STUART OAKES, editor, writer; b. Rochester, N.Y., Mar. 5, 1890; s. Samuel George and Carolyn Hamilton (Oakes) B.; student Dartmouth, 1911, Ia. State Coll., 1912-13; A.B., U. of Wis., 1912; m. Gertrude Tunstall Edwards, Oct. 9, 1920; children—Kathleen Hamilton and Isabel Wilson (twins), Samuel George, 2d. Reporter, Oregon Jour., Portland, 1913-17; news staff U.S. Com. on Pub. Information, 1917-18; with Emergency Fleet Corp., 1918-19; asso. editor Country Gentleman, 1919-28, Washington rep., 1924-28; asso. editor Ladies' Home Jour., 1928-35; with Farm Jour., Inc. 1935-36; asso. editor Cal. Mag. of Pacific, 1936-39; asst. dir Am.-Cavalcade of a Nation, Golden Gate Internat. Expn., 1940; with Office Censorship, San Francisco, 1942-45, Cal. Dept. Employment, 1945-52. Mem. Theta Delta Chi, Sigma Delta Chi. Episcopalian. Club: Family (San Francisco). Home: Carmel, CA. †

BOAK, THOMAS ISAAC SLACK, mfg. exec.; b. Ellery, N.Y., Jan. 23, 1890; s. John William and Ida Helen (Ayers) B.; M.E., Cornell U., 1914; m. Anna Delora Sampson, July 5, 1915 (div.); children—Thomas Isaac Slack, Charles Edward, John; m. 2d. Josephine Anne Russell, Nov. 2d., 1956. Engr. N.Y.C. R.R., 1914-15, Art & Buttons, 1915-16. Duratex Co., 1916-17, Western Electric Co., 1917-19; works mgr. Internat. Oxygen Co., 1919-20; cons. engr., 1920-22; works mgr. Rumsey Pump Co., 1922-27, Goulds Pumps, Inc., 1927-32, Winchester Repeating Arms Co., 1932-50; pres., treas. Plume & Altwood Mfg. Co., from 1950. Trustee Cornell U., 1938-48. Mem. N.A.M. (dir. 1945-46). Home: Bristol, Conn. †

BOARDMAN, W. WADE, lawyer; b. New Richmond, Wis., Jan. 25, 1905; s. Stephen Charles and Adelia (Clapp) B.; m. Elizabeth Tucker, Sept. 11, 1929; 1 dau., Elizabeth (Mrs. John W. Prussing). Student, N.D. State U., 1923-26; LL.B., U. Wis., 1930. Bar: Wis. 1930. Practiced in Madison; partner firm Boardman, Suhr, Curry & Field; lectr. law U. Wis. Law Sch., 1934-46; Mem. bd. State Bar Commrs., 1946-73, pres., 1953-73; mem. Wis. State Jud. Council, 1950-53. Recipient Distinguished Alumnus award U. Wis. Law Alumni Assn., 1973. Mem. ABA, 7th Fed. Circuit Bar Assn., Dane County Bar Assn. (past pres.), State Bar Wis. (recipient award spl. merit 1972), Am. Bar Found., Am. Coll. Probate Counsel (regent 1966-72), Order of Coif, Phi Kappa Phi, Phi Kappa Psi, Phi Delta Phi. Club: Madison. Home: Madison, Wis. Died Mar. 18, 1983; buried Graceland Cemetery, Minerals Point, Wis.

BOATMAN, CONWAY, educator, clergyman; b. Stewart, Miss., July 30, 1889; s. William Henry and Mary Ann (Morehead) B.; A.B., Asbury Coll., Wilmore, Ky., 1915; A.M., Columbia, 1926; B.D., Drew Theol. Seminary, 1927; studied U. Chgo., summer 1929; D.D., Fletcher Coll., 1930; L.H.D., Union Coll., 1959; m. E(lmina) Carolina Brasher, June 23, 1915; children—John Paul, Joseph Brasher, Wilson Morehead. Teacher Asbury Coll., 1915-16; pastor M.E. Ch., Clear Lake and Burke, S.D., 1916-19; ednl. missionary in India, 1919-25; prof. and head dept. edn., Sterling (Kan.) Coll., 1927-28; pres. Ia. Nat. Training Sch. (for Christian leadership), Des Moines, 1928-31; pres. Snead Junior Coll., Boaz, Ala., 1931-39, Union College at Barbourville, Ky., 1938-59, president emeritus, from 1959. Member of the N.E.A., M.E. Church Ednl. Assn.; hon. member. International Longfellow Soc.; dir. Nat. Council of Clergymen and Laymen. Club: Kiwanian Internat., Rotary Internat. (hon. mem.). †

BOATNER, CHARLES KNOX, govt. ofcl.; b. Lawrence, Mass., Oct. 29, 1913; s. James William and Mary (Barfield) B.; student Tex. Christian U.; m. Alice Beatrice McCulloch, July 24, 1937; children—James Knox, Charles Knox, Arvel Davis. With Carter Publs., Inc., Ft. Worth, 1935-61, war corr., Pacific Theater, 1945, city editor, 1947-61; spl. asst. to Vice Pres. Johnson, 1961-63; asst. to sec., dir. information dept. Interior, 1964-70; asst. dir. S.W. region Nat. Park Service, Santa Fe, 1970-72, area asst. dir., Ft. Worth, 1972-82. Methodist. Home: Fort Worth, Tex. Died Mar. 2, 1982.

BOBBITT, ROBERT LEE, lawyer; b. Hillsboro, Tex., Jan. 24, 1888; s. Joseph A. and Laura (Duff) B.; student Carlisle Mil. Acad., 1907; N. Tex. Normal Coll., 1908-11; LL.B., U. Tex., 1915; m. Mary B. Westbrook, Apr. 20, 1918; 1 son, Robert Lee Jr. Admitted to Tex. bar, 1915; jr. partner firm Hicks, Hicks, Dickson & Bobbitt, Laredo and San Antonio, 1916-28; dist. atty. 49th Judicial Dist. Tex., 1928; atty. gen. Tex., 1929-30; asso. justice San Antonio Ct. Civil Appeals, 1935-37; chmn. Tex. Hwy. Commn., 1937-43; sr. partner Bobbitt, Brite, Bobbitt & Allen, from 1944. Pres. Central Securities Co., San Antonio, chmn. bd. S. Tex. Nat. Bank, San Antonio. Active local Boy Scouts Am., Salvation Army, YMCA. Mem. Tex. Ho. Reps., 1923-28, speaker, 1927-28; chmn., keynote speaker Tex. Democratic Conv., 1934. Mem. Tex. Dem. Exec. Com., from 1923. Presdl. Elector from Texas, 1944. Chmn. bd. trustees Tex. A. and I. College, 1932-35; regent N. Tex. State Coll., Denton. Served to capt., 90th Div., U.S. Army, 1917-19. Mem. Am., Tex., San Antonio bar assns., Am. Judicature Soc., Philos. Soc. Tex., Tex. Hist. Assn., Newcomen Soc., S. Tex. C. of C., Am. Legion, Chancellors (U. Tex.), Phi Delta Phi. Presbyn. (elder), Rotarian (pres., dist. gov.), Elk (Laredo). Home: San Antonio, Tex. †

BOCHNER, SALOMON, educator; b. Cracow, Poland, Aug. 20, 1899; came to U.S., 1933, naturalized, 1938; s. Joseph and Rude (Haber) B.; m. Naomi Weinberg, Nov. 1, 1937; 1 dau., Deborah. Ph.D., U. Berlin, 1921. Internat. Edn. Bd. fellow, 1925-27; lectr. Munich U., 1927-32; faculty Princeton, N.J., 1933-82, prof. math., 1946-82, Henry Burchard Fine prof. math., 1959-68; Edgar Odell Lovett prof. math. Rice U., Houston, 1968-82; Vis. prof. U. Calif. at Berkeley, 1953; cons. Los Alamos project, Princeton, 1951, NSF, 1952. Author: Fouriersche Integrale, 1932, Several Complex Variables, 1948, Fourier Transforms, 1949, Curvature and Betti Numbers, 1953, Harmonic Analysis and The Theory of Probability, 1955, Fourier Integrels, 1959, The Role of Mathematics in the Rise of Science, 1966, Eclosion and Synthesis: Perspectives on the History of Knowledge, 1969, Einstein Between Centuries, 1979; editor: Dictionary History of Ideas; cons. editor: McGraw-Hill Ency. of Sci. and Tech; Contbr. math. publs. Mem. Nat. Acad. Scis., Am. Math Soc. (Steele prize 1979). Home: Houston, Tex. Died May 2, 1982.

BOCK, ARLIE VERNON, prof. hygiene; b. New Albin, Ia., Dec. 30, 1888; s. John Julius and Hannah (Petersen) B.; A.B., Upper Ia. U., Fayette, 1910; M.D., Harvard University, 1915, D.Sc. (honorary), 1954; graduate study as Mosely traveling fellow from Harvard at Cambridge (Eng.) Univ., 1920-21, Ph.D., 1929; m. Sophia B. Eastman, June 5, 1926; 1 son, John Eastman. Resident physician Mass. Gen. Hosp., Boston, 1919-24, physician from 1928; assistant professor medicine. Harvard, 1924-30, associate professor, 1930-35. Henry K. Oliver professor of hygiene, 1935-54, emeritus, from 1954. Trustee Proctor Academy, Andover, New Hampshire. Served with U.S. Army Base Hosp. No. 5, attached to British E.F. in France, 1917-18; maj. M.C., U.S. Army. Fellow American Medical Assn., Am. Academy of Arts and Sciences; mem. Am. Soc. Clin. Investigation, Assn. Am. Physicians, Mass. Med. Soc., Sigma Xi. Republican. Clubs: Harvard (Boston and New York). Rewrote (with D. P. Dill) F. A. Bainbridge's Physiology of Muscular Exercise, 1931. Author numerous papers on the blood, surgical shock, etc. Home: Harvard, Mass. †

BOCKUS, HENRY L., physician; b. Newark, Del., Apr. 18, 1894; s. William Jones and Luella (Whiteman) B.; m. Rosalynd Foss, Jan. 13, 1935; 1 dau., Barbara Ann Aponte. M.D., Jefferson Med. Coll., 1917, D.Sc., 1958; D.Sc., Dickinson Coll., 1946, U. Pa., 1961; Dr. Honoris Causa, U. Central Venezuela, 1965, U. Cordoba, Argentina, 1967. Diplomate: Am. Bd. Internal Medicine (founder mem. subsplty. bd. gastroenterology). Resident physician Lenox Hill Hosp., N.Y.C., 1920-21; began practice as physician, Phila., 1921; now internist specializing in gastro-intestinal disorders and as gastroenterologist; organizer stomach clinic Grad. Hosp., U. Pa., 1921, asso. clinic, from 1921; prof. gastroenterology Grad. Sch. Medicine, U. Pa., from 1931; prof., chmn. dept. medicine, 1949-60, prof. medicine emeritus, from 1960; cons. physician Grad. Hosp.; chmn. bd. dirs. MEDICO, 1960-69; v.p. bd. dirs. CARE; cons. gastroenterologist Bryn Mawr Hosp., Abington Meml. Hosp., Phila. Naval Hosp.; hon prof. medicine U. Antioquia, Colombia, 1964; chmn. World Congress in Gastroenterology, Washington, 1958; hon. prof. U. Nacional de Cordoba, 1967. Author: Gastroenterology, 3 vols, 1943-46, rev., 1963-65 (transl. Portuguese, Spanish, Italian), 3d edit., 4 vols., 1974, Postgraduate Gastroenterology, 1950; contbr. sci. articles to med. jours. Trustee Jefferson Med. Coll., 1965-68. Served as lt., M.C. USN, 1917-19. Decorated comdr. Order Hipolito Unanue Peru; Order al Merito de Chile; El Sol de Peru Peru; comdr. Order Rio Branco Brazil; Order de Andres Bello Venezuela; Order of Merit Duarte Dominican Republic; recipient Caldwell medal Am. Roentgen Ray Soc., 1950; Strittmater award Phila. County Med. Soc., 1951; Modern Med. award for achievement, 1962; Disting. Service award MEDICO, 1975; Disting. Service award Pa. Med. Soc., 1978. Fellow A.C.P. (master), Royal Soc. Medicine (London) (hon.), Royal Soc. Arts (London), Nat. Acad. Medicine Mex. (hon.), Am. Coll. Gastroenterology (hon.); hon. mem. Gastroenterol. Assn. C.Am., Gastroenterol. Assn. Chile, Gastroenterol. Assn. Cuba, Gastroenterol. Assn. Switzerland, Gastroenterol. Assn. Venezuela, Gastroenterol. Assn. Peru, Gastroenterol. Assn. Brazil, Gastroenterol. Assn. Argentina, Gastroenterol. Assn. Uruguay, Gastroenterol. Assn. Can., Gastroenterol. Assn. Ecuador, Gastroenterol. Assn. Panama, Gastroenterol. Assn. Dominican Republic, Gastroenterol. Assn. Spain, Gastroenterol. Assn. India, Gastroenterol. Assn. Belgium, Gastroenterol. Assn. Germany, Gastroenterol. Assn. Colombia, Bockus Research Inst. of U. Pa., Bockus Internat. Soc. Gastroenterology, Orgn. Mundiale Gastroenterologia (pres. 1958-62, hon. pres. 1962—), Am. Gastroenterol. Assn. (past pres., recipient Friedenwald medal 1962), AMA (former chmn. sect. gastroenterology and proctology, distinguished service award 1970), Phila. Coll. Physicians, Phila. Pathologic Soc.; hon. asso. Am. Proctologic Assn., Phila. Art Alliance, Alpha Omega Alpha. Presbyterian. Clubs: Penn (Phila.), Phila. Country (Phila.); Peale. Home: Philadelphia, PA.

BODE, ALBERT WILLIAM, architect; b. Cin., Oct. 11, 1932; s. Albert Hagenbeck and Dorothy (Mercer) B.; student Carnegie Inst. Tech., 1952-53; B.S., U. Cin., 1957; m. Anna Jeanette Ainsworth, Apr. 16, 1955; children—Pamela, Mark, Grace, Elaine, Albert. Architect, prin. Glover-Smith-Nixon-Bode, Oklahoma City, and predecessors, from 1960. Mem. region 7 adv. panel on architecture Gen. Services Adminstrn., 1971-73. Mem. sr. exam. com. Nat. Council Archtl. Registration Bds., 1973-74. Mem. Oklahoma County Republican Exec. Com., 1967-69. Mem. bd. Village Library, 1967-69; bd. govs. Licensed Architects of Okla., sec.-treas., 1970-73, v.p., 1969-70, pres., 1973-74; life mem. Oklahoma City Arts Center. Recipient Ohio Soc. of AIA award of merit, 1957. Mem. AIA, Oklahoma City C. of C., Beta Theta Pi. Mem. Christian Ch. Important works include Dermatology Clinic Okla. U. Med. Center (Okla. AIA award of excellence), Okla. Bur. Investigation Bldg., Okla. Sci. and Arts Found. and Planetarium Bldg., Okla. Art Center Sculpture Ct., Oklahoma City U. Fine Arts Bldg., Oklahoma City Zoo Service Center Bldgs., Okla. Dept. Agr. Lab., Okla. Corp. Commn. Fuels Lab.; supervisory architect Mummers Theatre, Oklahoma City, 1970; food distbn. centers Nobel, Inc., Colo. and N.Mex., Griffin Grocery Co., Ark., Giant Wholesale Grocery, Tenn., SYSCO Food Systems, Tex., Grocers Supply, Ind.; also numerous Oklahoma City banks. Home: Oklahoma City, Okla. Deceased.

BODE, DIETRICH ADAM, clergyman; b. Youngstown, O., Sept. 16, 1888; s. George and Anna (Fiehler) B.; D.D. (hon.), Mission House Coll. and Sem., 1933; m. Clara M. Bixler, Sept. 16, 1913; children—Margaret C. (Mrs. L.M. Becker), Lorna M. (Mrs. R. Guthmuller), Paul, Nelda M. (Mrs. R. Topp), Arden, Carol A. (Mrs. J. Marty).

Ordained to ministry Ref. Ch. in U.S.A., 1912; pastor, Indianapolis, 1912-15, Erie, Pa., 1915-16, Rochester, N.Y., 1916-25, Phila., 1936-41, 1st Evang. and Ref. Ch., New Knoxville, O. from 1941; supt. Ottilie Orphan Home, Jamaica, N.Y. City, 1925-36. Home: New Knoxville, Ohio. †

BODENHAFER, WALTER BLAINE, sociologist; b. Kendallville, Ind., Feb. 26, 1887; s. Lee and Eva (Morgan) B.; student Transylvania U., Lexington, Ky., 1906-09; A.B., Ind. U., 1911, LL.B., 1912; A.M., U. of Kan., 1915; Ph.D., U. of Chicago, 1920; m. M. Edith Walker, Sept. 1, 1914. Instr. in sociology, U. of Kan., 1915-18, asst. prof., 1919-20; asso. prof. sociology, Washington U., 1920-23, prof. of sociology from 1923; prof. sociology, U. of Chicago, summer 1921. Chmn. family and old age div., Social Planning Council of St. Louis; mem. bd. of dirs. St. Louis Provident Assn. Mem. Am. Sociol. Soc., Soc. for Social Research, Am. Assn. Univ. Profs., A.A.A.S., Mid-west Sociol. Soc., Phi Delta Phi. Republican. Mason (32 deg., K.T., Shriner). Author: Social Organization and Disorganization (with S. A. Queen, and E. B. Harper), 1935. Contbr. Am. Jour. Sociology, Publs. Am. Sociol. Soc., etc. Home: St. Louis, Mo. †

BODENSTEIN, DIETRICH H. F. A., biologist, educator; b. Corwingen, East Prussia, Germany, Feb. 1, 1908; s. Hans and Charlotte (Lilienthal) B.; student U. Königsberg, (Germany), 1926-28, U. Berlin, 1928-33; Ph.D., U. Freiburg (Germany), 1953; m. Jean Coon, July 22, 1947; 1 dau. by previous marriage, Evelina (Mrs. William C. Suhler). Came to U.S., 1934, naturalized, 1940. Research asst. Kaiser Wilhelm Inst. Biology, Berlin, 1928-33; research asso. German-Italian Inst. Marine Biology, Rovigno d'Istria, Italy, 1933-34, Stanford Sch. Biology, 1934-41; John Simon Guggenheim Meml. Found. fellow dept. zoology Columbia, 1941-43; asst. entomologist Conn. Agrl. Expt. Sta., New Haven, 1944; insect physiologist, med. div. Army Chem. Center, Md., 1945-57; embryologist gerontology br. Nat. Heart Inst., Balt. City Hosps., 1958-60; Lewis and Clark prof. biology U. Va., Charlottesville, 1960-78, prof. emeritus, 1978-84, chmn. dept., 1960-73. Recipient Sr. U.S. Scientist award Alex von Humboldt Found., 1977. Mem. Am. Acad. Arts and Scis., Am. Soc. Zoologists, Am. Soc. Naturalists, Nat. Acad. Sci., Soc. Biology Brazil (hon.), Sigma Xi. Contbr. articles to profl. and sci. publs. Home: Charlottesville, Va. Died Jan. 5, 1984; buried Corwingen, Charlottesville.

BODINE, WILLIAM WARDEN, JR., organization executive; b. Villanova, Pa., May 29, 1918; s. William Warden and Angela Richardson (Forney) B.; m. Louise Richardson Dilworth, May 26, 1946; children—William Warden III, Lawrence D., Anne D., Barbara W. Grad., St. Paul's Sch., Concord, N.H., 1938; student, Harvard U., 1942. With Penn Mut. Life Ins. Co., Phila., 1951-83, asst. sec., 1952, financial sec., 1954-59; pres. Jefferson Med. Coll. and Med. Center, 1959-66; life trustee; pres. Arthur C. Kaufmann & Assocs., Inc. (mgmt. cons.), Phila., 1967-69; pres. World Affairs Council, Phila., 1969-83, chmn., 1983; dir. Sta. WHYY-TV. Bd. dirs., mem. exec. com. United Way Southeastern Pa.; v.p., mem. exec. com. YMCA, Phila.; bd. dirs., chmn. fund campaign Mental Health Assn. Southwestern Pa.; trustee Temple U., Episcopal Acad.; chmn. bd. Thomas Jefferson U., 1970-79; bd. dirs. Elwyn Inst., Crime Commn. of Phila.; bd. dirs. University City Sci. Center, chmn., 1980-83; bd. dirs. Art Alliance; 1st v.p. Free Library of Phila.; chmn. citizens adv. com. Center for Blind.; nat. bd. dirs. Smithsonian Instn.; bd. dirs. U. Pa. Press; Mem. Pa. Republican Finance Com. Served as lt. col. AUS, World War II. Decorated Legion of Merit, Purple Heart; Croix de Guerre with palm France; selected Young Man of Year Phila., 1950. Mem. Mil. Order World Wars, UN Assn. of U.S. (dir.), NCCJ (dir. Phila. region), Harvard Alumni Assn. (nat. dir.). Home: Villanova, Pa. Dec. Aug. 11, 1983.

BOEHM, KARL, opera conductor; b. Graz, Austria, Aug. 28, 1894; s. Leopold and Franz Boehm; student Gymnasium Graz, Vienna, Austria; m. Thea Linhard, May 2, 1927; 1 son, Karlheinz. Dir. Staatsoper, Hamburg, Dresden, Wien, Buenos Aires; condr. opera numerous countries. Home: Vienna, Austria. Died Aug. 10, 1981.

BOEHMER, FLORENCE ELISE, coll. dean; b. Springfield, Mo., Apr. 15, 1890; d. Charles Deterich and Katherine Dorothea (Wolf) B.; Teacher's Certificate, Southwest Mo. State Teachers Coll., 1911; A.B., Drury Coll., Springfield, Mo., 1912; A.M., U. of Illinois, 1918; Ph.D., Columbia Univ., 1932. Elementary sch. teacher, 1907-10; high sch. teacher, 1912-25; dir. of recreation, Nat. Coll. of Edn., Evanston, Ill., 1926-28; acting dean of women, Heidelberg Coll., Tiffin, O., 1928-29; dean of women, and asso. prof. edn., State Teachers Coll., Harrisonburg, Va., 1930-33; pres. Cottey Coll., Nevada, Mo., 1933-37; dean of women and coördinator of guidance activities, Drury Coll., from 1937. Mem. N.E.A., Nat. Assn. Deans of Women, Am. Assn. Univ. Women, Nat. Vocational Guidance Assn., Am. Personnel Assn., Business and Professional Women's Club, Mo. State Teachers Assn., Kappa Delta Pi, Pi Gamma Mu. Conglist. Home: Springfield, Mo. †

BOER, BENJAMIN C., lawyer; b. Apr. 25, 1889; s. John and Grace (Kuiper) B.; m. Helen Strathman, Oct. 16, 1971; 1 dau. (by previous marriage), Barbara Louise (Mrs. L. M. Irwin). B. Engring., U. Ia., 1913; LL.B., Case Western Res. U., 1917. Bar: Ohio bar 1917. Faculty Coll. Engring. U. Iowa, 1913-14, Case Sch. Applied Sci., 1914-17; practiced in, Cleve.; mem. firm Boer, Mierke, McClelland & Caldwell (and predecessors), after 1946; Mem. exec. com. Nat. Bar Presidents Assn., 1953-55. Fellow Am. Bar Assn. (spl. com. on disciplinary procedures 1953-55, Ho. Dels. 1955-56); mem. Ohio Bar Assn. (exec. com. 1945-50, v.p. 1950-51, pres. 1951-52), Cleve. Bar Assn. (exec. com. 1939-41), Order of Coif, Sigma Xi, Tau Beta Pi. Home: Lakewood, OH.

BOER, GERMAIN BONIFACE, accountant, educator; b. Rockne, Tex., Nov. 19, 1937; s. August H. and Lena M. (Bartsch) B.; m. Elinor Charles O'Brien, Jan. 25, 1964; children: Kathleen Marie, Robert James. B.S. in Commerce, St. Edward's U., 1960; M.B.A. in Acctg, Tex. Tech. U., 1961; Ph.D. in Bus. Adminstrn, La. State U., 1964. C.P.A., Tex. Various clerical and mgmt. positions Constant Service Co., Austin, Tex., 1955-56; asso. prof. acctg. Tex. Tech. U., Lubbock, 1964-66; asst. dean Tex. Tech. U. (Coll. Bus. Adminstrn.), 1964-66, asso. prof., 1967-68; faculty resident Arthur Andersen & Co., Chgo., 1966-67; project mgr. Nat. Assn. Accts., N.Y.C., 1968-70; asso. prof. acctg. Okla. State U., Stillwater, 1970-74, prof., 1974-77; prof. mgmt. Owen Grad. Sch. Mgmt., Vanderbilt U., Nashville, from 1977; spl. lectr. U. South Africa, summer 1971; cons. South Africa Iron and Steel, Inc., 1971, Minn. Dept. Public Welfare, 1974, Nat. Heart and Lung Inst., 1975, Okla. State Health Planning Commn., 1975-76, Coll. Am. Pathologists, 1979-81; founder Eight by Ten, Ltd., 1974, dir., Stillwater, Okla., 1974-77; dir. Mgmt. Tech. Group, Nashville. Contbg. author: Automation and Management in the Clinical Laboratory, 1972; author: Direct Cost and Contribution Analysis: An Integrated Management Accounting System, 1974, (with J.L. Bennington, G.E. Louvau, G.E. Westlake) Cost Effectiveness in the Clinical Laboratory, 1978; contbg. author: (with J.L. Bennington, G.E. Louvau, G.E. Westlake) Financial Management of the Clinical Laboratory, 1975; contbr. (with J.L. Bennington, G.E. Louvau, G.E. Westlake) articles on mgmt. acctg. to profl. jours. Bd. dirs. Ambiance Fine Arts, Inc., Nashville, Tenn., from 1981. Mem. Nat. Assn. Accts. (nat. dir. 1973-75, mem. research com. 1979-81, manuscripts dir. music city chpt. 1981-82, ednl. cons. and lectr. 1971-80), Am. Inst. C.P.A.'s, Am. Acctg. Assn. Roman Catholic. Home: Nashville, Tenn.

BOERKER, RICHARD HANS DOUAI, forest biologist; b. Brooklyn, N.Y., Oct. 19, 1887; s. John and Bertha (Douai) B.; A.B., Dartmouth, 1910; M.S. in Forestry, U. of Mich., 1911; Ph.D., U. of Neb., 1915; grad. student, New York U., 1918-19, Columbia, 1924; m. Irene Frances Bostwick, 1913; children—Allan Edwin, Huldah Irene, Janet Bertha, Ruth Elizabeth. Fellow in botany and investigator forest problems under Dr. C. E. Bessey, U. of Neb., 1914-15; with U.S. Dept. Agr., Forest Service, 1910-17; operating in Calif., Colo. and Wyo.; arboriculturist, Dept. of Parks, City of New York, 1917-18; consulting practice, specializing in street and highway planting, forest plantations, landscape and aesthetic forestry, 1917-18, 1919-21; dept. biology, Boys' High Sch., Brooklyn, 1918-19, Kingston (N.Y.) High Sch., from 1921; forestry expert timber cases, U.S. Dept. Justice, Court of Claims, 1920. Fellow A.A.A.S.; mem. Sigma Xi. Republican. Episcopalian. Author: A History of Forest Ecology, 1915; Ecological Investigation Upon Forest Trees, 1916; Our National Forests, 1918; also numerous articles in tech. jours. Address: Kingston, N.Y. †

BOGART, NEIL, record co. exec., film producer; b. Bklyn., Feb. 3, 1943; s. Al M. and Ruth M. (Markoff) Bogatz; married; 4 children. Student, Bklyn. Coll. Past account exec. Cash Box Mag.; past asst. to nat. promotion dir. MGM Records; past nat. promotion dir., v.p., gen. mgr. Cameo/Parkway Records; gen. mgr. Buddah Group, 1967-73; pres. Casablanca Records (now called Casablanca Records and Film Works), Los Angeles, 1974-80, Boardwalk Entertainment Co., Beverly Hills, Calif., 1980-82. Producer: films The Deep, 1976, Thank God It's Friday, 1978. Active Cedar-Sinai Med. Center, Betty Ford Cancer Center, Jewish Foster Child Care N.Y. Recipient Presidential award Nat. Assn. Record Merchandisers, 1977; named Man of the Year United Jewish Appeal-Fedn. Jewish Philanthropies, 1978. Died May 8, 1982.*

BOGERT, JOHN LYMAN, business executive; b. Flushing, L.I., N.Y., March 2, 1890; s. John Lawrence and Helen Lyman (Boardman) B.; student Flushing Institute, 1900-03; m. Katharine Plympton Curley, June 29, 1915; children—Peter Lawrence, Joan, Ann Thomas, Bruce Plympton. Clerk Nat. Bank of Commerce, New York, 1912-14; with Waltham Watch Co., 1914-20, dir. of sales and advertising, 1920-24; one of organizers Day-Bogert Advertising Agency, Boston, 1924, remaining until 1931; dir. of market research Lever Bros. Co., Inc., Cambridge, Mass., 1932-37; research dir. Lambert Co., New York, 1937; v.p. and dir. Benton & Bowles, Inc., 1937-42; vice-pres. in charge of research and development and director Standard Brands, Inc., since 1942. Enlisted for pilot training, U.S. Air Corps, 1917; completed ground sch. Mass. Inst. Tech. and Cornell U. Mem. Market Research Council of N.Y., Holland Soc. of New York. Home: New York, N.Y. †

BOGGS, A. MARIS (ANITA UARDA MARIS BOGGS), economist, educator, philanthropist; b. Philadelphia, Pa., Nov. 14, 1888; d. Benjamin Randolph and Mary Emma (Maris) B.; A.B., Bryn Mawr Coll., 1910; A.M., U. of Pa., 1911; A founder, 1913, and dean Bur. Commercial Economics and dir. same from 1922 (this is a philanthropic and ednl. instn. for promotion of internat. comity and understanding); spl. collaborator U.S. Bur. Edn. in visual instrn., 1915-25. Mem. Authors' League of America; hon. life mem. Md. Acad. of Science, Cleveland Photographic Soc.; fellow Royal Geog. Soc. Contbr. to various periodicals on internat. finance, economics, tariff, internat. relations, etc. Received thanks of U.S. Govt. and of various other nations, for constructive work in behalf of humanity. Decorated Order of the White Lion (Czechoslovakia) in recognition of eminent and distinguished services.†

BOHM, KARL, orch. condr.; b. Graz, Austria, Aug. 28, 1894; m. Thea Linhard, 1927; 1 son, Karlheinz. J.D., Karl-Franzens U., Graz; studied under, Eusebius Mandyczewski, Vienna, Austria. pres. London Symphony Orch., 1977. Condr., Graz City Theater, 1917-21, Munich (Germany) State Opera, 1921-27, gen. music dir., Darmstadt, Germany, 1927-31, condr., Vienna Philharmonic Orch., from 1933, Dresden (Germany) State Opera, 1934-42, Vienna State Opera, 1943-45, 54-56, Am. debut with, Chgo. Symphony Orch., 1956, condr., Berlin (Germany) Philharmonic Orch., N.Y. Philharmonic Orch., guest condr., Teatro San-Carlo, Naples, Italy, Teatro alla Scala, Milan, Italy, Teatro Colon, Buenos Aires, Argentina, Met. Opera, N.Y.C., condr., Salzburg (Austria) Festival, Bayreuth (Germany) Festival. Recipient numerous awards including; Schalk medal Vienna Philharmonic Orch.; Mozart medal Mozarteum, Salzburg and Mozart Soc.; Brahams medal Hamburg Germany; Music prize of Steiermark Austria; Berlin (Germany) prize of Art; named hon. gen. music dir. of Austria, 1964. Mem. German Performing Arts Acad. Home: Vienna, Austria. Died Aug. 14, 1981.*

BOHN, JOHN J., army officer; b. St. Paul, Minn., April 3, 1889; s. George W. and Cora Frances (Thompson) B.; student forestry Y. of Minn., 1908-09; grad. Troop Officers Course, Cav. Sch., 1921, Advanced Course, 1928. Command and Gen. Staff Sch., 1929, Army War Coll., 1932; m. Erma Valencia Yates, Aug. 24, 1921; children—John Yates, Joanne, Mary Lucile. Compass man, timber cruiser, topographer, Ariz., N.M., Ore., Wash., B.C., 1909-14; with mil. survey Northern Luzon, P.I., 1914-15; private 7th Cav., Feb. 24, 1914; commd. 2d lt., 1916, and advanced through the grades to brig. gen., July 25, 1942; with army, England and France, 1943-44; retired for disability in service, Feb. 1945. Mexican Expedition, 1916; with A.E.F., France, 1917-18. Decorated Silver Star, Bronze Star. Pres. Lenoir C. of C., 1949. Mem. Theta Delta Chi. Home: Lenoir, N.C. †

BOHSTEDT, GUSTAV, educator; b. Gnissau, Holstein, Germany, June 22, 1887; s. Asmus Heinrich and Anna (Rotermund) B.; brought to U.S., 1902, naturalized, 1913; B.S., U. Wis., 1915, M.S., 1916, Ph.D., 1925; m. Ruth Conway, July 3, 1918; children—Carl Conway, James Hunt, Engaged in farming and ranching, 1902-08; chief dept. animal industry Ohio Agrl. Experiment Sta. 1921-28; faculty mem. U. Wis., 1915-21, prof. animal husbandry from 1928, chmn. dept., 1945-53, Mem. com. of cons. on agr. The Rockefeller Found., 1952-55. Mem. Am. Soc. Animal Prodn. (sec.-treas. 1921-22, v.p. 1923-24, pres. 1925), Am. Dairy Sci. Assn., A.A.A.S., Am. Assn. U. Profs., Sigma Xi, Alpha Zeta, Theta Chi. Author publs. on livestock, nutrition, Made livestock surveys in Mexico, Colombia, Brazil. Home: Madison, Wis. †

BOJANOWSKI, JERZY, symphony condr.; b. Poland, June 18, 1895; s. Kamil Adam Wincenty and Wladyslawa Teresa (Bujalska) B.; m. Frances Krenz Welzant, 1937. Student, Mus. Coll., Warsaw, 1907-12, Mus. Acad., Vienna, Austria, 1913-14, Vienna U., 1913-14; student law, Kharkoff U., 1915-16. Condr., Warsaw Grand Opera, 1918-19, Opera of Pozman, 1919-25, mus. dir., Torun Opera, 1925-27, Lwow Opera, 1927-28, condr., Warsaw Grand Opera and Warsaw Philharmonic, also tour of European cities, 1928-32, Chgo. Symphony Orch., World's Fair, Chgo., Tulsa, Milw., Mpls., 1936-37, other cities in Middle West, 1932-38, Polish Ballet on European tour, N.Y. World's Fair, 1939, Chgo. Opera, 1941-42, Woman's Symphony Orch., Chgo., 1944-45, Milw. Stars Symphony Orch., 1941-51, mus. dir., Polonaise Found., Chgo., guest condr., Warsaw Philharmonic, 1973; mus. dir.: opera Halka, in English; Milw. premiere, 1977; artistic dir., Carillon Festival, Milw., 1979, 81; condr.: WTMJ-TV Peabody award concert, 1966; (Carillon Composition internat. prize Mechelen, Belgium 1971, 75, 79). Recipient Honor awards Am. Council Polish Cultural Clubs, 1966; Milw. Soc. PNA, 1968; award Merit minister of culture and art Poland, 1971. Fellow Internat. Inst. Arts and Letters. Address: Milwaukee, Wis.

BOK, BART JAN, astronomy educator; b. Hoorn, Holland, Apr. 28, 1906; came to U.S., 1929, naturalized, 1938; s. Jan and Gesina Annetta (Van Der Lee) B.; m. Priscilla Fairfield, Sept. 9, 1929 (dec. Nov. 1975); children: John Fairfield, Joyce Annetta. Student, U. Leiden, Holland, 1924-27, U. Groningen, 1927-29; Ph.D., 1932; D.Sc. (hon.), Ariz. State U., 1978, U. Nev., Las Vegas, 1979. Asst. in astronomy U. Groningen, 1927-29; R.W. Willson fellow in astronomy Harvard U., 1929-33, asst. prof., 1933-39, assoc. prof., 1939-46, Robert Wheeler Willson prof. astronomy, 1947-57; prof., head dept. astronomy

Australian Nat. U., 1957-66; dir. Mt. Stromlo Obs., nr. Canberra, 1957-66; prof. astronomy U. Ariz., Tucson, 1966-74, emeritus, 1974-83; head dept. and dir. Steward Obs., 1966-70; Past pres. commn. 33 Internat. Astron. Union. Author: The Distribution of Stars in Space, 1937, (with Priscilla F. Bok) The Milky Way, 1941, 5th edit., rev., 1981, (with F.W. Wright) Basic Marine Navigation, 1944, The Astronomer's Universe, 1958. Decorated Oranje-Nassau medal Netherlands; recipient Adion medal French Astronomers, 1971; Catherine De Wolf Bruce gold medal Astron. Soc. of Pacific, 1977. Fellow Australian Inst. Physics, Australian Coll. Edn., Royal Astron. Soc. (London) (asso.); mem. Internat. Astron. Union (v.p. 1970-73), Am. Astron. Soc. (pres. 1972-74, Henry Norris Russell prize lectr. 1982), AAAS, Nat. Acad. Scis., Am. Acad. Arts and Scis., Royal Soc. Scis., Uppsala, Sigma Xi; hon. mem. Royal Astron. Soc. Can., Royal Astron. Soc. N.Z., Astron. Soc. Australia; corr. mem. Royal Netherlands Acad. Arts and Scis., Royal Australian Acad. Sci. Home: Tucson, Ariz. Dec. Aug. 5, 1983.

BOLDT, GEORGE HUGO, U.S. dist. judge; b. Chgo., Dec. 28, 1903; s. George F. and Christine (Carstensen) B.; m. Eloise Baird, Nov. 17, 1928; children—Joan (Mrs. Hugh C. Sobottka), Virginia (Mrs. T. R. Riedinger), George B. A.B., U. Mont., 1925, LL.B., 1926; LL.D., Coll. Puget Sound, 1954; grad., Command and Gen. Staff Sch., Ft. Leavenworth, 1943; LL.D., U. Mont., 1961. Bar: Mont. bar 1926, Wash. bar 1928. Asso. W.D. Rankin, Helena, Mont., 1926-27; partner firm Ballinger, Hutson & Boldt, Seattle, 1928-45, Metzger, Blair, Gardner & Boldt, Tacoma, 1945-53; U.S. dist. judge (West dist. Wash.), 1953-71, chief judge, 1971, sr. judge, 1971-84; spl. asst. atty. gen. State of Wash., 1940, 50; U.S. del. 1st UN Congress on prevention of crime and treatment of offenders, Geneva, 1955; mem. com. on jud. facilities Am. Bar Assn.-A.I.A.; chmn. bd. visitors U. Puget Sound Law Sch.; mem. com. on operations and appraisals Fed. Jud. Center; Jud. Conf. rep. Sec. State Adv. Com. Internat. Law; chmn. Pay Bd., Econ. Stablzn. Program, Office of Pres., 1971-73. Trustee, pres. U. Mont. Found., 1975-76; trustee U. Puget Sound; also chmn. bd. visitors Law Sch. Served as lt. col. AUS, World War II. Mem. Am., Fed., Washington State, Pierce County bar assns., Am. Judicature Soc., Inst. Jud. Adminstrn., Am. Law Inst., Internat. Inst. Juridical Studies (gen. sci. com.), U.S. Jud. Studies (gen. sci. com.), U.S. Jud. Conf. (various coms.), Am. Legion, Phi Delta Phi, Sigma Chi. Republican. Presbyterian. Club: Mason (32 deg., Shriner). Home: Tacoma, Wash. Died Mar. 18, 1984.

BOLES, C. E., lawyer; b. Barren County, Ky., July 3, 1887; s. Charles E. and Eliza Jewell B.; A.B., Bethel Coll., 1906; LL.B., Columbia, 1915; m. Charlotte Bohannan, June 28, 1916 (dec. Oct. 1961); m. Margaret Pedigo Richey, July 30, 1969. Tchr., Marlin Tex., 1907-09, 1910-12, Terrell, 1909-10; legal practice, Glasgow, Ky., 1915-17, legal work, espionage, trading with enemy acts Solicitors Office, Post Office Dept., 1917-19; atty., examiner Internal Revenue, 1919-21, I.C.C., 1921-52; asst. dir. bur. finances, I.C.C., 1936-48, dir. bur. finance, 1948-54; legal practice, Washington, 1954-59, Glasgow, Ky., 1962-82; admitted to practice Supreme Ct. Dist. dir. Ky. Hist. Hwy. Marker Program. Candidate for Democratic nomination U.S. Senate, 1968. Mem. Ky. Bar Assn., Glasgow C. of C., Phi Gamma Delta, Democrat. Baptist. Mason. Clubs: The Filson (Louisville), Nat. Press; Rotary. Home: Glasgow, Ky. Died Jan. 14, 1982.

BOLL, CHARLES LOUIS, telephone co. exec.; b. St. Louis, June 13, 1931; s. Charles Mathias and Emma (Kohler) B.; A.B., Wash. U., 1956; m. Virginia Agnes Pogorzelski, May 28, 1955; children—Judith Catherine, Charles John, Carol Lynn. Outstate comml. mgr. Southwestern Bell Tel. Co., Poplar Bluff, Mo., 1957-59, information asst., pub. relations dept., St. Louis, 1959-61, unit mgr., Ferguson, Mo., 1961-62, supr. cash records treasury dept., St. Louis, 1962-65; cash mgr., stockholder relations Continental Tel. Corp., St. Louis, 1965-72, treas., 1972-82. Served with AUS, 1953-55. Mem. Fin. Mgmt. Assn., Nat. Health Welfare and Pension Plan Found. Roman Catholic. Home: Atlanta, Ga. Died Nov. 18, 1982.

BÖLL, HEINRICH, author; b. Cologne, Germany, Dec. 21, 1917; s. Viktor and Maria (Hermanns) B.; m. Annemarie Cech, 1942; children: Christoph (dec.), Raimund, René, Vincent. Student state schs., Cologne, 1924-37. Books include Der Zug war pünktlich, 1949, Wanderer, kommst du nach Spy, 1950, Die schwarzen Schafe, 1951, Wo warst du, Adam?, 1951, Und sagte kein einziges Wort, 1953, Nicht nur zur Weihnachtszeit, 1952, Haus ohne Hüter, 1954, Das Brot der frühen Jahre, 1955, So ward Abend und Morgen, 1955, Unberechenbare Gäste, 1956, Im Tal der donnerden Hufe, 1957, Irisches Tagebuch, 1957, Die Spurlosen, 1957, Dr. Murkes gesammeltes Schweigen, 1958, Billard um halb zehn, 1959, Erzählungen, Hörspiele, Aufsätze, 1961, Ein Schluck Erde, 1962, Ansichten eines Clowns, 1963, Entfernung von der Truppe, 1964, Als der Krieg ausbrach, 1962, Frankfurter Vorlesungen, 1966, Ende einer Dienstfahrt, 1966, Aufsatze, Kritiken, Reden, 1967, Hausfriedensbruch. Aussatz, 1969, Gruppenbild mit Dame, 1971, Gedichte, 1972, Neve politische und Literarische Schriften, 1973, Die verlorene Ehre der Katharina Blum, 1974, Drei Tage im März, 1975, Berichte zur Gesinnungslage der Nation, 1975, Einmischung erwünscht, 1977, Querschnitte, 1977, Werke I-V, 1977, Werke VI-X, 1978, Mein Lesebuch, 1978, Du fährst zu oft nach Heidelberg, 1979, Eine deutsche Erinnerung, 1979, Fürsorgliche Belagerung, 1979, Was soll aus dem Jungen bloss werden? Ode: Irgendwar mit Büchern, 1981, Vermintes Gelände, 1982, Das Vermaechtnis, 1982, Die Verwundung, 1983, Mein Trauriges Gesicht, 1984, Ein-Und Zusprueche, 1984, Bild-Bonn-Boenisch, 1984. Recipient numerous lit. prizes including; Group 47 prize, 1951; Rene Schickele prize, 1952; Kritikerpreis, 1952/53; So. German Narrator prize, 1953; Eduard Van der Heydt prize, 1957; Charles Veillon prize, 1960; Lit. prize Cologne, 1961; Nobel prize for lit., 1972; Carl von Ossietzky Medal, 1974; Premio Latina, 1980; hon. prof. numerous univs. Mem. Am. Acad. Arts and Letters (hon.), German Acad. for Lang. and Poetry, PEN (past pres.), Am. Acad. Arts and Scis. (hon.). Address: Hürtgenwald-Grosshau, Federal Republic Germany. Died July 16, 1985.

BOLLAY, WILLIAM, cons. engr.; b. Stuttgart, Germany, Jan. 14, 1911; came to U.S., 1924, naturalized, 1929; s. Frederick J. and Dorothea Frieda (Kramer) B.; m. Jeanne Marie Brinsley, Aug. 30, 1934; 1 dau., Melody Jeanne (Mrs. Bollay Kladnik). B.S., Northwestern U., 1933, Sc.D. (hon.), 1959; Ph.D., Calif. Inst. Tech., 1936. Instr. Calif. Inst. Tech., 1936-37, Harvard, 1937-41; with aerophys. lab. N. Am. Aviation, 1945-51; tech. dir. Aerophys. Devel. Corp., 1951-58; cons. engr., 1958-62; vis. prof. Stanford U., 1963-68, Mass. Inst. Tech., 1962-63, U. Calif. at Los Angeles, 1948-54, cons. engr., Santa Barbara, Calif., from 1968; Mem. sci. adv. bd. USAF, 1949-54, U.S. Army Aviation, from 1961; mem. NACA and NASA subcoms., from 1941; dir. Commn. Engring. Edn., 1962-65. Served with USNR, 1941-45. Decorated Legion of Merit; recipient Wright Bros. lecture award, 1951. Fellow AAAS, AIAA (dir. 1968-70). With Werner von Braun developed concept of first U.S. satellite.

BOLLENBACHER, PAUL E(DWARD), educator; b. Celina, O., Nov. 6, 1889; s. Charles Louis and Mary Elizabeth (Bauer) B.; student Wooster (O.) Coll., 1910-11, Ohio State U., 1911; A.B., U. of Mich., 1914, A.M., 1918; student Strasburg, 1920 Leipzig, Germany, 1921; m. Larve Shean, Aug. 25, 1921; children—Mary (Mrs. Hugo Hartig), Paul John, Charles. Instr. German, St. Olaf Coll., Northfield, Minn., 1914-18, prof. German, chmn. German dept. from 1924. Served with U.S. Army World War I. Mem. Am. Assn. Teachers of German. Democrat. Home: Northfield, Minn. †

BOLLENS, JOHN CONSTANTINUS, political science educator, publisher; b. Pitts., Dec. 27, 1920; s. Constantinus John and Annie (Free) B.; m. Virgene Ruth Anderson, Sept. 21, 1945; children: Ross John, Scott Alan. A.B., Coll. of Wooster, 1942; A.M., Duke, 1948; Ph.D., U. Wis., 1948. Research dir. Municipal League, Seattle, 1945-47; adminstrv. analyst U. Calif. at Berkeley, 1947-50, lectr. polit. sci., 1949-50; asst. prof. polit. sci. U. Calif. at Los Angeles, 1950-55; acting dir. Bur. Govtl. Research, 1954-55, asso. prof., 1955-60, dir. urban studies, 1958-62, prof., from 1960; pres. Palisades Publishers, from 1972; Cons. govt., pvt. orgns.; exec. sec. Western Govtl. Research Assn., 1947-50; spl. asst. to dir. Internat. City Mgrs. Assn., 1950; dir. met. areas study Council State Govts., 1955-56; exec. officer, research dir. Met. St. Louis Survey, 1956-57; exec. dir. Met. Community Studies, Dayton, Ohio, 1957-59; dir. study city charter, govtl. orgn., Los Angeles, 1962-63; mem. Los Angeles County Citizens Economy and Efficiency Com., 1964-73, Los Angeles Citizens Com. Zoning Practices and Procs., 1967-69, Los Angeles County Pub. Adminstr.-Pub. Guardian Adv. Commn., 1973-75; cons. to Adv. Commn. on Intergovtl. Relations, from 1967. Author: The Problem of Government in the San Francisco Bay Region, 1948, Appointed Executive Local Government, 1952, California Government and Politics, 7th edit, 1981, The States and the Metropolitan Problem, 1956, Special District Governments in the United States, 1957, Exploring the Metropolitan Community, 1961, A Study of the Los Angeles City Charter, 1963, The Metropolis: Its People, Politics and Economic Life, 4th edit, 1982, Communities and Government in a Changing World, 1966, A Program to Improve Planning and Zoning in Los Angeles, 1968, Governing a Metropolitan Region: The San Francisco Bay Area, 1968, American County Government, 1969, The City Manager Profession: Myths and Realities, 1969, A Study of the Los Angeles County Charter, 1970, Yorty: Politics of a Constant Candidate, 1973, A Guide to Participation, 1973, Jerry Brown: In a Plain Brown Wrapper, 1978, Political Corruption: Power, Money, and Sex, 1979, How To Be a Successful Student, 1982. Mem. Los Angeles Am. Revolution Bicentennial Com., 1974-76, v.p., 1974-76; mem. Los Angeles Bd. Civil Service Commrs., 1973-77, pres., 1974; mem. Los Angeles County CSC, from 1979. pres., 1982. Mem. Am. Polit. Sci. Assn., Am. Soc. Pub. Adminstrn. (pres. Los Angeles area chpt. 1962-63), Phi Beta Kappa. Home: Pacific Palisades, Calif.

BOLOTOWSKY, ILYA, artist, educator; b. St. Petersburg, Russia, July 1, 1907; s. Jules J. and Anastasia (Shapiro) B.; student Gymnasia, Baku, Caucasus, 1915-19, Coll. St. Joseph, Constantinople, Turkey, 1920-23, French Coll., 1920-23, N.A.D., N.Y. Sch. Art, 1924-30; postgrad. research art U. Wyo., 1949-51; m. Meta Cohen, Sept. 17, 1947; 1 son, Andrew. Came to U.S., 1923, naturalized, 1929. Head dept. art Black Mountain Coll., 1946-48; asso. prof. art U. Wyo., 1948-57; prof. art Coll. Edn., New Paltz, N.Y., 1957-65; adj. prof. Hunter Coll., 1963-64; chmn. dept. fine arts Southampton Coll. (L.I.), from 1965; vis. prof. Bklyn. Coll., 1954-56. One-man shows G.R.D. Studios, 1930, N.Y.C. New Art Circle, 1946-52, Pinacotheca, 1947, 50, Borgenicht Gallery, 1954, 56, 58, 59, 61, 63, 65, 68, 70, 72, 74, 76, 78, retrospective one-man show, 1969-70, London (Eng.) Arts Gallery, 1971, London Arts Gallery, Detroit, 1971, Solomon R. Guggenheim Mus., 1974, Nat. Collection Fine Arts, Smithsonian Instn., 1975, Schloss-Remseck Galerie, Stuttgart, Germany, 1975, Basel (Switzerland) Art Fair, 1975; exhibited in shows U.S. Western Europe, Japan, Argentina, traveling show U. Colo., U. Art Mus., Albuquerque, Iowa Mus. Art, Newport Harbor Art Mus., Balboa, Cal.; rep. permanent collections Whitney Mus., Phillips Gallery, Washington, Yale U. collection, Phila. Mus., Munson-Williams-Proctor Inst., Utica, N.Y., Guggenheim Mus., Brandeis U., Frederick Olsen Found., Guilford, Conn., Mus. Modern Art, N.Y.C., Lyman Allyn Mus., New London, Conn., R.I. Sch. Design, Chase Manhattan Bank, Walter Chrysler Mus., Provincetown, Mass., Mus. Fine Art, Birla Inst., Calcutta, India, South Mall, Albany, N.Y.; represented in permanent collections Musée d'Art Moderne, Ceret, France, Götheborg, Sweden, Walker Art Center, Mpls., Larry Aldrich Mus., Ridgefield, Conn., Met. Mus. Art, N.Y.C., also pvt. collections; executed murals Cinema I, N.Y.C., North Central Bronx Hosp., 1973, four murals New Social Security Bldg., Chgo., 1976; developed painting style on 3 dimensional constrns., 1961; creative writer, playwright. Served with AUS, 1942-43, USAAF, 1943-45. Recipient 1st prize for painting N.A.D., 1929, 30; for editorial work and translation Mil. Dictionary, 1942; grant for exptl. film work, State U. N.Y. Research Found., 1959-60; 1st prize Midwest Film Festival for film Metanoia, 1963; prize Nat. Inst. Arts and Letters, 1971. John Simon Guggenheim Found. fellow, 1973. Fellow Internat. Inst. Arts and Letters (life, prize); mem. Am. Abstract Artists (pres. 1957-58), Nat. Soc. Mural Painters, Fedn. Modern Painters and Sculptors. Home: Sag Harbor, N.Y. Died Nov. 22, 1981.

BOLTEN, JOSEPH STIRLING, U.S. Pub. Health Service; b. Maspeth, L.I., N.Y., Aug. 15, 1889; s. Lewis and Rae (Chapin) B.; M.D., U. of Pa. Grad. Sch., 1911; m. Rae W. Johnstone, 1913; children—Richard Stirling, Ruth Josephine. Commd. asst. surgeon U.S. P.H.S., 1913, passed asst. surgeon, 1917, surgeon, 1921, sr. surgeon, 1933, med. dir., 1939; medical officer in charge U.S. Quarantine Station, Brownsville, Tex. Mem. Am. Med. Assn. Presbyn. Mason (K.T., 32 deg., Shriner). Home: Brownsville, Tex. †

BOLTON, GUY, playwright; b. England, Nov. 23, 1887; s. Reginald Pelham and Alice (Behenna) B.; ed. in England, also studied architecture in France; m. 2d, Virginia de Lanty, 1933; children (by 1st marriage)—Richard, Joan, Peggy, Guy. Playwright since 1914; author or co-author of about 80 plays produced in N.Y. City and London, including The Dark Angel, Polly-with-a-Past, Sally, Lady Be Good, Girl Crazy, Grounds for Divorce, Anything Goes, O, Boy!, Rio Rita, Theatre, Follow the Girls, Theirs is Tomorrow; also motion pictures The Love Parade, Weekend at the Waldorf, Till the Clouds Roll By. Mem. S.A.R. Home: Rensenburg, L.I., N.Y.†

BOLTON, T. COULSTON, educator; b. Phila., Dec. 17, 1887; s. George Gregson and Jane Emma (Holt) B.; B.S., Univ. Pa., 1913, A.M., 1917; m. Phyllis Price, Mar. 12, 1921; children—Hilda (Mrs. Robert J. Roman), Phyllis Vivian (Mrs. Neil Thomas Letham), Bruce. Clerk, Phila. Nat. Bank, 1906-10; salesman, Union Central Life Ins. Co., N.Y. City, 1913-15; instr., Wharton Sch., Univ. Pa., 1915-18; asso. editor, Alexander Hamilton Inst., N.Y. City, 1919-21; lecturer in ins., Wall St. div., N.Y. Univ., 1920-21; prof. of ins., head dept., Syracuse Univ., from 1921; lecturer for retail inst. of Nat. Retail Lumberman's Dealers Assn. since 1946, Am. Inst. Banking, Syracuse, 1921-35; instr. for life ins. salesmen preparing for Chartered Life Underwriter's exam. since 1930. Served as chief yeoman, U.S. Navy, overseas, 1918-19. Served as teacher Army Specialized Training Program, 1943-44. Chartered Life Underwriter, 1930. Mem. Am. Assn. Univ. Teachers of Ins., Am. Assn. Univ. Profs., Am. Soc. Chartered Life Underwriters, Beta Gamma Sigma (past pres. and sec.), Alpha Sigma Phi. Republican. Baptist Club: Faculty Men's. Author books and contbr. articles to bus. publs. Spl. fields: ins. and finance. Home: Syracuse, N.Y. †

BOLTON, THEODORE, librarian, author; b. Columbia, S.C., Jan. 12, 1889; s. Benjamin Meade and Henrietta Louise (Liebau) B.; student Corcoran Sch. of Art, Washington, D.C., 1908-12; diploma Pratt Inst., 1915; Library Science diploma, 1924; B.L.S., 1942; B.S., in Education, New York University, 1937, M.A., 1940; Harvard, summers, 1937, 39; M.F.A., Columbia U., 1955; m. Helen Stevens, 1930. Library asst. Pub. Library, Washington, 1911-13; instr. in drawing, high schs., Brooklyn, 1915-17; with Library of Congress, 1918-21, Brooklyn Pub. Library, 1924-26; librarian Century Club since 1926. Mem. Am. Library Association, New York Library Club; American Antiquarian Society. Author: (books) Early American Portrait Painters in Miniature, 1921; Early American Portrait Draughtsmen in Crayons, 1923; American Book Illustrators, 1938; (with H. B. Wehle) American Miniatures, 1927; (with I. F. Cortelyou) Ezra Ames of Albany, 1955. Translator and illustrator of The Wonderful History of Peter Schlemihl (by A. von Chamisso),

1923; Diane de Turgis (by Prosper Mérimée), 1925. Home: New York. †

BOMAR, WILLIAM PURINTON, corporate executive; b. Lookout Mountain, Tenn., Aug. 9, 1886; s. David Terry and Anna E. (Purinton) B.; m. Jewel Nail, Nov. 2, 1915 (dec. Oct. 1965); 1 child, William Purinton; m. Portia Goulder Hamilton, July 1, 1966. B.S., Yale, 1908. With Bewley Mills, Fort Worth, 1909-57, pres., gen. mgr., 1943-57; past pres. Inland Investment Co.; chmn. bd. Chicasha Cotton Oil Co., 1961-82; past chmn. bd. Houston Gen. Ins. Group; dir. Tex. Utilities Co., Tex. Electric Service Co., State Res. Life Ins. Co., Southwestern Expn. and Fat Stock Show, Flour Mills Am., Inc., Mo.-Kans.-Tex. R.R. Co.; Pres. Ft. Worth Grain and Cotton Exchange, 1925. Chmn. bd. W. I. Cook Childrens Hosp., Ft. Worth, from 1928; bd. dirs. Tex. Research Found., Retina Found., Boston. Mem. Millers Nat. Fedn. (past pres.), Am. Mixed Feed Mfrs. Assn. (past pres.), Ft. Worth C. of C. Presbyterian (chmn. bd. trustees). Clubs: Ft. Worth (Ft. Worth) (past pres.), Rivercrest Country (Ft. Worth); Masons. Home: Forth Worth, Tex. Dec. Mar. 8, 1982.

BONAFEDE, VINCENT IGNATIUS, physician; b. Buffalo, Mar. 5, 1906; s. Joseph and Providence (Anselmo) B.; m. Carolyn Constantine, Sept. 18, 1943; children—Virginia Isabel, Mary Lee. M.D., U. Buffalo, 1930. Diplomate: Am. Bd. Psychiatry and Neurology (psychiatry). Intern Allied Sisters Hosps., Buffalo, 1930-31; resident Meyer Meml. Hosp., Buffalo, 1931; asst. physician St. Lawrence Psychiat. Center, Ogdensburg, N.Y., 1931-32; asst. physician, sr. psychiatrist, supervising psychiatrist Craig Developmental Center, Sonyea, N.Y., 1933-52, asst. dir., 1952-60, dir., 1960-76; cons. psychiatrist Mt. Morris Tb Hosp., 1935-71, Craig Developmental Center, from 1976, Nicholas H. Noyes Meml. Hosp., from 1977. Mem. Livingston County Bd. Health, from 1976; med. cons. Livingston County Tb Clinic, from 1976; chief psychiatrist Elmira Reformatory, 1959-63; med. examiner S.S.S., 1943-73; chpt. chmn. blood bank ARC, 1976-79; examiner Am. Cancer Soc., 1978-79; cons. Livingston County Family Planning Clinic, 1978-79; Chmn. Sonyea Community Chest, 1941-50; exec. bd. Genesee council Boy Scouts Am., from 1967, v.p., 1976-77; mem. adv. council Charles G. May Occupational Center, 1970-76. Fellow Am. Psychiat. Assn. (cert. mental hosp. adminstr.), Am. Assn. on Mental Deficiency; mem. A.M.A., N.Y. State Med. Soc. (pres. 7th dist. br. 1965-67), Livingston County Med. Soc. (pres. 1954, 73-74, trustee 1975-79), Am. Epilepsy Soc., Genessee Valley Psychiat. Soc., Neuron Club (sec. 1959-75, pres. 1975-76), Am. Assn. Psychiat. Adminstrs. (pres. N.Y. State chpt. 1969-70), Assn. Med. Rehab. Dirs. and Coordinators (med. rehab. dir.), Buffalo Acad. Medicine, Rochester Acad. Medicine, Nat. Guild Cath. Psychiatrists, N.Y. Trudeau Soc., Livingston County Hist. Soc., Mt. Morris Hist. Soc. Republican. Roman Catholic. Clubs: K.C, Elk, Rotarian (pres. Mt. Morris 1960-61, 69-70, gov.'s aide Dist. 712 1961-62). Address: Mount Morris, NY.

BOND, JAMES CLARENCE, assn. ofcl.; b. Grant City, Mo., Aug. 2, 1889; s. William R. and Mary Josephine (Martin) B.; A.B., Westminster Coll., Fulton, Mo., 1912; B.S., Northeast Mo. State Teachers Coll., Kirksville, Mo., 1915; A.M., Columbia, 1925; student U. of Colo., 1928, U. of Chicago, 1934-38; m. Alma R. Magee, Aug. 30, 1916; children—Betty Jean, James Clarence. Teacher of social studies, Macon (Mo.) High Sch., 1914-16; supt. of schs., Keytesville, Mo., 1916-19, Memphis, Mo., 1918-19, Macon, Mo., 1920-25; prin. Franklin Sch., Kansas City, Mo., 1925-28, Henry C. Kumpf Sch., 1928-37; pres. Teachers Coll., Kansas City, Mo., 1937-42, dean Teachers Coll. Div., Junior and Teachers Coll., 1942-44, when discontinued; prin. Paseo High Sch., Kansas City, Mo. from 1945. Silver Beaver Award for Distinguished Service to Youth by Boy Scouts of Am.; Kansas City Cath. Community Council citation for distinguished community service, 1952; Alumni Achievement in Edn. Award, Westminster Coll., 1950. Mem. bd. dirs. Kans. City Area Council, Boy Scouts Am.; chmn. Leadership Training and Advancement Com., mem. bd. dirs. Nat. Council. Mem. N.E.A., Am. Assn. Sch. Adminstrs., Mo. State Tchrs. Assn., Phi Delta Kappa, Kappa Alpha, Nat. Soc. for the Study of Edn. Presbyn. Clubs: Schoolmasters, Elementary Principals, South Kansas City Business, Rotary, Professional Men's. Home: Kansas City, Mo. †

BOND, RAYMOND T., publisher. With Dodd, Mead & Co., N.Y.C., 1920-81; beginning as salesman, successively advt., publicity and promotion mgr., 1925-57, sec., 1935-81, pres., 1957-64, also editor, chmn. Editor mystery bologies, nature books. Died July 16, 1981.

BOND, THOMAS JACKSON, educator, chemist; b. Ennis, Tex., Aug. 16, 1912; s. John Henry and Frances (Puckett) B.; B.S., North Tex. State U., 1938, M.S., 1939; Ph.D., U. Tex., 1950; m. Edith Lyle Gorman, June 3, 1939; children—Anedith (Mrs. Jeffrey E. Nash), Thomas Jackson, Robert Gorman. Instr. chemistry Tex. Coll. Arts and Industries, Kingsville, 1941-43; faculty Baylor U., Waco, Tex., from 1943, prof. chemistry, chmn. dept., from 1965. Mem. Am. Chem. Soc., Am. Soc. Biol. Chemists, Sigma Xi. Mason. Spl. research growth factors, intermediate metabolism, comparative studies effects chem. carcinogens and non-carcinogens on essential cell constituents. Home: Waco, Tex. Died Dec. 16, 1981.

BONESTEEL, VERNE CLINTON, banker; b. Huron, S.D., Apr. 23, 1890; s. Charles Henry and Mary Perry (Davies) B.; grad. high sch., Huron; A.B., class orator, U. of Wis., 1912; m. Laura Louise Schoenert, Nov. 18, 1915; 1 son, John Martin. With James Valley Bank, Huron, advancing to cashier, 1912-18; nat. bank examiner, State of S.D., 1918-19; v.p. Security Nat. Bank, Sioux City, Ia., 1919-28; pres. Am. Nat. Bank, Aurora, Ill., 1928 to consolidation, Jan. 1, 1930, with First Nat. Bank of Aurora, of which has since been pres.; also pres. First Am. Corpn. Trustee Jennings Sem., Aurora, Buena Vista Coll., Storm Lake, Ia. Treas. Ia. Bankers Assn., 1927-28; mem. Kappa Sigma. Republican. Presbyn. Mason (32 deg., Shriner). Clubs: Union League, Kiwanis. Contbr. articles to banking and financial journals. Home: Aurora, Ill. †

BONI, ALBERT, publisher; b. N.Y.C., Oct. 21, 1892; s. Charles and Bertha (Seltzer) B.; ed. Cornell U., 1909-10; Harvard U., 1910-12; m. Nell van Leeuwen, Sept. 14, 1917; 1 son, William F. Founded Washington Square Players, 1915, later the Theatre Guild; established the Little Leather Library, 1915-17, Boni and Liveright, 1917; founder, pres. Albert and Charles Boni, Inc., from 1923. Invented Microprint and Readex reading projector; pres. Readex Microprint Corp., 1940-74, chmn. bd., 1974-78; chmn. bd. Readex Microprint Corp. (U.K.), Ltd. Founder Modern Library. Recipient citation Rochester Mus. Arts and Scis., 1944; Pioneer medal Nat. Microfilm Assn., 1961. Fellow Nat. Microfilm Assn., F.R.M.; mem. Am. Documentation Inst., A.L.A., Optical Soc. Am., Royal Soc. Photography, Soc. Motion Picture and TV Engrs., Soc. Photog. Scientists and Engrs. Editor: Modern Book of French Verse, 1920; A Guide to the Literature of Photography and Related Subjects, 1943; Photographic Literature-A Subject Catalogue and Index to two million books and articles, 1962; Photographic Literature 1960-70, 1972. Co-inventor silver haloid film eliminating gelatin and capable of 200x reduction. Office: New York, N.Y. Died July 30, 1981.

BONINE, CHESLEIGH ARTHUR, geologist; b. Sorrento, Fla., Mar. 25, 1888; s. Joel Carter and Lola (Hemery) B.; ed. Central High Sch., Washington, 1904-08; E.M., Lehigh U., 1912; grad. study Johns Hopkins; m. Beulah Whiteman, Nov. 22, 1913; 1 dau., Ann. Field work, U.S. Geol. Survey, until 1917; cons. oil and gas work since 1917, in N.M., N.D., Mont., Okla., Ky., Pa., Wyo., etc.; instr. geology, Lehigh U., 1917-18; with Pa. State Coll. since 1918; prof. geol. emeritus; co-operating geol. State Geol. Survey of Pa. Member Society of Economic Geologists, Phi Delta Theta, Tau Beta Pi, Sigma Xi, Sigma Gamma Epsilon. Republican. Lutheran. Author bulletins of U.S. Geol. Survey and numerous repts. Home: State College, Pa. †

BONISTEEL, ROSCOE OSMOND, lawyer; b. Sidney Crossing, Ont., Can., Dec. 23, 1888; s. Milton Fremont and Frances Anna (Whyte) B.; brought to U.S., 1891; student Dickinson Coll., 1908, LL.D., 1952; LL.B., U. Mich., 1912, LL.D., 1964; D.Sc., Cleary Coll., 1953; m. Lillian Coleman Rudolph, Sept. 12, 1914; children—Jean Ellen (Mrs. William C. Knecht), Betty Dame (Mrs. Wm. Judson Johnson), Frances Coleman (Mrs. Willis Allan Fisher), Roscoe Osmond, Nancy Ann (Mrs. Harry Calcutt). Admitted to Mich. bar., from 1912, since practiced law; dir. Mich. Life Ins. Co., R & B Machine Tool Co., State Bank of Frankfort, Ann Arbor Bank, Northwestern Savs. & Loan Assn. (Traverse City). County, city atty. Ann Arbor, 1921-28; del. Republican State Convs.; del. Rep. Nat. Conv., Kansas City, 1928, Chgo., 1944, presdl. elector, 2d Mich. Congl. Dist., 1932; mem. Mich. Constl. Conv., 1961-62. Served as capt. U.S. Air Service, 1918-19; mem. Mich. War Preparedness Commn., Washtenaw County, 1918. Chmn. bd. appeals Mich. Selective Service. Dir. U. Mus. Soc. U. Mich.; dir. Mich. Soc. for Crippled Children, 1934, 35; regent U. Mich., 1946-60; bd. govs. Wayne State U., 1956-59, William L. Clements Library, U. Mich.; trustee Rackham Fund, U. Mich.; trustee Rackham Fund, U. Mich.; trustee Dickinson Coll., Cleary Coll.; chmn. bd. trustees Nat. Music Camp, Interlochen, Interlochen Arts Acad. Mem. State Bd. Law Examiners Mich., 1945-52. Mem. Am. Bar Assn. (mem. resolutions com. 1937-39; ho. of dels. 1936-41, mem. (Mich.) on com. uniformity of legislation in U.S. 1943-61), State Bar Mich. (pres. 1936-37), Hist. Soc. Mich. (pres. 1961-62), Am. Law Inst., Am. Legion (judge adv. Mich. 1934-35), Huquenot Soc. Can., Huquenot Soc. Mich., Phi Kappa Sigma. Republican. Presbyn. Mason (33 deg.), Rotarian (dist. gov. 1934-35), Kiwanian (hon.). Clubs: University, Dickinson College Alumni of Mich. (pres.), Ann Arbor, Ann Arbor Golf and Outing, Detroit, Detroit Athletic. Home: Ann Arbor, MI. †

BONNER, EUGENE (MACDONALD), composer, writer; b. Washington, N.C., July 24, 1889; s. William Tripp and Eugenie (Huggins) B.; grad. Peabody Inst. Conservatory Music, 1911; grad. study mus. composition, London, Eng. and Paris, France, 1911-15, instrumentation and conducting with Rubin Goldmark and Walter Rothwell, 1915-17. Music critic London (Eng.) Telegraph and London Musical Standard, 1914-16; asst. editor, music critic Outlook mag., N.Y.C., 1927-29, Bklyn. Eagle, 1928-29; music critic New York Daily Mirror, Cue mag.; guest critic New York Herald Tribune, 1943-45; mng. editor Musical Record, N.Y.C., 1940-41; program dir. orchestra, librarian radio sta. WQXR, N.Y.C., 1943-47; free lance articles music and related subjects. Mus. compositions include: La Femme Muette (opera) in collaboration with Anatole France, excerpts played by Balt. Symphony Orchestra, 1927; The Venetian Glass Nephew (opera), Vanderbilt Theatre, N.Y.C., 1931; The Gods of the Mountain (opera) with Lord Dunsany, Nat. Orchestral Assn. under Leon Barzin, Carnegie Hall, 1937; White Nights (symphonic poem), N.Y. Philharmonic Symphony Soc., condr. John Barbirolli, 1939. Phila. Orchestra, condr. Eugene Ormandy, 1941; Whispers of Heavenly Death (suite voice and orchestra), Phila. Orchestra, condr. Ormandy, soloist Marjorie Lawrence, Acad. Music, Phila., 1941, also Nat. Orchestral Assn., Leon Barzin and Marjorie Lawrence, 1941; Concertino for Piano and String Orchestra, Wallenstein's Symphonic Strings broadcast, 1941, WQXR String Orchestra, 1945-46, concert performances, London, Brussels, Geneva, 1925-37; Taormina (orchestral suite) broadcast WOR and WNYC, 1936, 41. Served as top-sgt. heavy art., U.S. Army, 1917-19; 2 diplomatic missions to Eng. and France, 1915, 16. Recipient Munich Fellowship, MacDowell Club, 1937. Mem. Nat. Assn. American Composers and Conductors Music Critic's Circle (charter). Author: The Club in the Opera House, 1949; Sicilian Roundabout, 1952. Dir., editor-in-chief: A Bibliography of the Anthropological, Ethnological and Religious Origins of the Dance, 1934-39. †

BONNET, HENRI, diplomat; b. Chateauponsac, France, May, 1888; s. J. Th. and Marie Thérèse (Lascoux) B.; ed. Lycées de Tours et Paris, Université de Paris, Ecole Normale Supérieure de Paris; m. Helle Zervoudaki, Aug. 29, 1932. Prof. history, U. of Paris, 1912; foreign editor, Ere Nouvelle, 1919; mem. secretariat. League of Nations, 1920-31; dir. Internat. Inst. of Intellectual Cooperation, also sec. gen. Permanent Conf. Hautes Etudes Internationales, also vice pres. Center of Studies of Foreign Policy in Paris, and mem. Superior Council of Scientific Research, 1931-40; prof. polit. science, Ecole Libre des Hautes Etudes, New York, N.Y.; mem. exec. com. 'France Forever'in U.S., 1941, vice chmn. Chicago chapter, 1942, exec. v.p. nat. organization, 1943; commr. for information Com. Nat. Liberation, Algiers, 1943; minister for information Provisional Govt. of French Republic, 1944; ambassador of France to U.S., 1944-55. Decorated Croix de Guerre. Grand Officer Legion of Honor. Vice pres. Internat. League of Rights of Man, 1942. Mem. editorial board of Free World, 1941. Special adviser World Citizens Assn., Chicago, Ill., 1941. Author of several books, also articles and studies on cultural subjects and foreign politics. Home: Paris, France. †

BONNETT, LELAND BREWER, elec. exec.; b. Geneva, N.Y., Nov. 11, 1889; s. William I. and Emma H. (Brewer) B.; E.E., Syracuse U., 1910; m. Irene E. White, Feb. 28, 1912. Engring. and sales Gen. Electric Co., Schenectady, N.Y. and N.Y.C., 1910-23; engring. Bklyn. Edison Co., 1923-26, in charge purchasing, 1926-38; with Consol. Edison Co. of N.Y., Inc., From 1938, v.p. from 1940; dir. N.Y. Steam Corp. Pres. Bklyn. Bureau of Social Service, Licensed engr., N.Y. Fellow Am. Inst. E.E.; mem. Am. Soc. M.E., Am. Gas Assn. (dir.). Club: Engineers (N.Y.C.). Home: Brooklyn, N.Y. †

BONNEY, HERBERT STAATS, JR., lawyer; b. Culpeper, Va., Jun 6, 1907; s. Herbert Staats and Barnett (McGaughey) B.; m. Ann Margaret Hudnall, July 19, 1941; children—Samuel Robert, Joseph James, Frances Ann, Susan Dove. B.A. Austin Coll, Sherman, Tex., 1931; B.S., U. Okla., 1932; LL.B., So. Methodist U., 1936. Bar: Tex. bar 1936, U.S. Supreme Ct. bar 1959. Practiced in, Dallas; partner firm Bonney, Wade & Stripling, 1969-77; gen. counsel Monkey Grip Rubber Co. Bd. dirs. Dallas Jr. C. of C., 1935-36; pres. Park Cities Dad's Club, 1963-64; Mem. Austin Coll. Devel. Commn., 1975-81. Served with USNR, 1943-46. Recipient Meritorious Service award Austin Coll. Alumni, 1972. Mem. Am. Bar Assn. (taxation com.), Am. Judicature Soc., Tex. State Bar., Austin Coll. Alumni Assn. (pres. 1970-71). Republican. Methodist. Club: Dallas Country. Home: Dallas, Tex. Died Apr. 4, 1982.

BONNIE, ROBERT PALEN, chem. mfr.; b. Nashville, Dec. 2, 1889; s. Robert P. and Maude (Williams) B.; grad. Andover Acad., 1907; Ph.B. Yale, 1911. Engaged in mining and engring., 1911-13; wholesale mcht., 1914-16; chem. mfr., from 1920; sec. treas. Ky. Color & Chem. Co., from 1920, pres. from 1957; pres. Inland Waterways Co., from 1930; pres. Louisville Central area, dir. Harshaw Chem. Co.; dir. Am. Barge Line Co., Mem. Ky. Bd. Flood Control and Water Usage. Treas. Rep. City and County Exec. Com. Pres. bd. overseers U. Louisville; v.p. Norton Meml. Infirmary; treas. Children's Hosp., Louisville. Served as capt. U.S. Army, 1917-19. Mem. Louisville Bd. Trade (past pres.), Asso. Industries Ky. (past pres.), N.A.M. (past dir.). Clubs: Pendennis, River Valley, Louisville Country, (Louisville). Home: Louisville, Ky. †

BOOMER, GEORGE O(WENS), business exec.; b. Plano, Ill., June 11, 1888; s. Martin and Annie (Kangley) B.; m. Rosella Thatcher, Nov. 26, 1914; children—John Thatcher, Barbara Owens, Marian Sarah. Dir., chmn. exec. com. Chemetron Corp.; dir., chmn. Premier Thermo-Plastics Co.; dir. Louisville Trust Co. Mem. Ky. C. of C. Republican. Clubs: Pendennis, Country (Louisville). Home: Louisville, Ky. †

BOONE, JAMES BUFORD, SR., newspaper pub.; b. Newnan, Ga., Jan. 8, 1909; s. James Edwin and Maude (McKoy) B.; m. Frances Herin, Sept. 15, 1929; children—Janette (Mrs. Younkin), James B. A.B., Mercer U., 1929; LL.D. (hon.), Colby Coll., 1957; D.H.L. (hon.), U. Ala., 1979. Reporter Macon (Ga.) Telegraph and News, 1929-38, city editor, 1938-40, mng. editor, 1940-42; spl. agt. FBI, 1942-46; editor Macon Telegraph, 1946-47; pub. Tuscaloosa News, 1947-68; pres. Tuscaloosa Newspapers, Inc., 1954-68, chmn. bd., 1968-74, ret., 1974; pres. Tuscaloosa Hotel Co., 1963-65. Pres. Black Warrior council Boy Scouts Am., 1949; chmn. YMCA bldg. fund campaign, 1954; mem. Pulitzer awards jury, 1958. Recipient Pulitzer prize for editorial writing, 1957; George Washington medal for editorial writing Freedoms Found., 1957; Lovejoy award Colby Coll., 1957; Algernon Sydney Sullivan award U. Ala., 1968; Outstanding Alumnus of Year award Mercer U., 1979. Baptist. Club: Country. Home: Tuscaloosa, Ala.

BOORKMAN, CHARLES JOHN, librarian; b. Aurora, Ill., Mar. 31, 1909; s. Charles John and Clara (Frey) B.; A.B., U. Ill., 1933, B.L.S., 1938; M.A., U. So. Calif., 1954; m. Ruth Ellen Reuss, Sept. 19, 1939; children—Jo Anne, Mary Elizabeth Harrelson. Librarian regional project Nat. Youth Adminstrn., Quoddy Village, Maine, 1938-42, Fifth Service Command, War Dept., Columbus, Ohio, 1942-43; sci. librarian San Jose State Coll., 1945-48; librarian Los Angeles State Coll., 1948-49; dir. univ. library Calif. State U., Long Beach, 1949-76, dir. emeritus, 1976-83. Served with USNR, 1943-45. Mem. A.L.A., Kappa Delta Rho, Phi Kappa Phi. Rotarian. Author bibliographies for Nat. Youth Adminstrn. Home: Long Beach, Calif. Died Aug. 1, 1983; buried Spring Lake Cemetery, Aurora, Ill.

BOOTH, JOHN EDWARD, lawyer; b. N.Y.C., Nov. 7, 1897; s. John T. and Mary (Larkin) B.; m. Katherine Keeler, June 30, 1928; children—John T., Grace-Mary G. A.B., Amherst Coll., 1923; LL.B., Fordham U., 1927. Bar: N.Y. bar 1927. Practiced law, N.Y.C.; dir. Iroquois Brands Ltd., J. W. Wilson Glass Co. Chmn. North Suffolk County chpt. A.R.C.; Bd. dirs. Huntington (N.Y.) Hosp., 1940-47, pres. bd., 1943-47; trustee North Country Sch., Lake Placid; trustee, treas. Nightingale-Bamford Sch., N.Y.C. Served as lt. (j.g.) USNR, 1917-21. Mem. St. George Soc. N.Y.C., Delta Kappa Epsilon. Club: National Arts (bd. govs., pres.). Home: Bridgeport, Conn. Died Nov. 9, 1984.

BOOTHBY, RALPH EDWIN, educator; b. Medford, Mass., June 2, 1890; s. Charles Herbert and Edith Mabel (Weeks) B.; grad. high sch., Medford, 1907; A.B., cum laude, Harvard, 1912; m. Marion Louise Brooks, of West Medford, Mass., July 12, 1917; children—Lawrence Warren, Norman Bostwick, Theodora. Master, St. Stephen's Sch., Colorado Springs, Colo., 1912-15, headmaster, 1915-22; prof. edn. and dir. Antioch Sch., Yellow Springs, Ohio, 1922-23; dir. Park Sch., Cleveland, Ohio, 1923-24; headmaster Western Reserve Acad., Hudson, Ohio from 1924. Mem. Progressive Edn. Assn. (advisory bd.), Sigma Alpha Epsilon. Episcopalian. Clubs: University (Cleveland); Harvard (Boston); Wantastiquet Trout Club (Weston, Vt.). Home: Hudson, OH. †

BOOZ, DONALD ROBERT, mgmt. cons.; b. Evanston, Ill., Oct. 10, 1920; s. Edwin G. and Helen (Hootman) B.; A.B., Williams Coll., 1942; Indsl. Adminstr., Harvard, 1943, M.B.A., 1947; m. Jean Hennesy O'Connor; children—Michelle Storrs, Edwin George, John Storrs. Faculty Harvard Bus. Sch., 1946-50; with Jewel Tea Co., Inc., 1951-58: engaged as mgmt. cons., from 1958; chmn. Donald R. Booz and Assos., Inc., Chgo., from 1961. Served as officer USAAF, World War II. Mem. Inst. Mgmt. Cons. (founding), Harvard Bus. Sch. Assn. (exec. council). Clubs: Chicago Economic, Harvard Business School (past pres.) (Chgo.). Author: (with Learned and Ulrich) Executive Action, 1951; (with Ulrich and Lawrence) Management Behavior and Foreman Attitude, 1949. Home: Chicago, Ill. Died Aug. 16, 1982.

BORDEN, WILLIAM A., army officer, engr., cons.; b. Ft. Sam Houston, San Antonio, Tex., Mar. 20, 1890; s. William Cline and Jennie Ella (Adams) B.; M.E., Cornell U., 1912; grad. Ordnance Sch. of Application, 1917, Army Industrial Coll., 1925, Army War Coll., 1933; M.B.A., Harvard U., 1928; m. Dorothy Adams, Oct. 6, 1917; children—Dorothy Adams, (Mrs. Hugh B. Vickery), Ann Carlin (Mrs. Ramon de'Murias), Cynthia Ayres (Mrs. Theodore A. Ayers). Commd. 2d lt., CAC, 1912, advanced through grades to brig. gen., 1944; served as dir. new developments div. War Dept., 1944-46; mem. joint com. on new weapons and equipment Joint Chiefs of Staff, 1944-46; mem. Research Bd. for Nat. Security, 1945-46, Nat. Inventors Council, 1945-46, adv. com. Office-Science Research and Development, 1945-46, military advisory board to officer in charge Atomic Bomb Project, 1945-46, operating com. on release of sci. information, 1945-46; liaison officer to pres. Publ. Board, 1945-46, 1946; chief engineer with Dewey & Almy Chemical Co., Cambridge, Mass., 1946-48, vice president, engineering, 1948-55, mgmt. and engrng. cons., from 1955; dir. Farrington Mfg. Co. Decorated D.S.M., Legion of Merit (U.S.); Hon. Comdr. .Order Brit. Empire. Registered profl. engr. Mass., D.C. Mem. Officers Assn., Nat. Geog. Soc., Am. Ordnance Assn. (charter, hon. life mem.), Delta Kappa Epsilon, Scabbard and Blade. Club: Army and Navy (Washington). Author tech. articles in various publs. Address: Washington, D.C. †

BORDENAVE, ENRIQUE, diplomat; b. Barrero Grande, Paraguay, Oct. 30, 1889; s. Abdon and Dolores (Franco) B.; Doctor in Law, U. of Asuncion, Paraguay; student U. of Buenos Aires, Argentine, and U. of Paris; m. Margot Legeren, June 10, 1932; children—Henry, Margarita. E.E. and M.P. from Paraguay to U.S. from 1933. Vice pres. Corporation Paraguaya; pres. Industria Paraguaya de Carnes. Decorated Legion of Honor (France); Great Cross of Carlos de Cespedes (Cuba); Order of Merit (Chile); Order of Isabel la Catolica (Spain). Catholic. Address: Washington, D.C. †

BOREMAN, HERBERT STEPHENSON, judge; b. Middlebourne, W.Va., Sept. 21, 1897; s. Kenner S. and Eva (Wells) B.; m. Cornelia K. Campbell, July 23, 1924; children—Evelyn (Mrs. C. A. Parks), Cornelia (Mrs. McVey Graham), Herbert Stephenson. LL.B., W.Va. U., 1920. Bar: W.Va. bar 1920. Practice of law, Parkersburg, W.Va., 1920-54; asst. U.S. Dist. Atty., 1923-27; pros. atty. Wood County, W.Va., 1929-33; mem. W.Va. Senate, 1942-50; judge No. Dist. of W.Va., U.S. Dist. Ct., Parkersburg, 1954-59; judge U.S. Court of Appeals, 4th Circuit, 1959-71, sr. judge, from 1971. Mem. W.Va. Commn. Uniform State Laws, 1950-54; nominee for gov. W.Va., 1948; Bd. govs. W.Va. U., 1932-36, vis. com. coll. law, 1950-54. Mem. ABA, W.Va. Bar Assn. (v.p.), Wood County Bar Assn. (pres. 1934), W.Va. U. Alumni Assn. (past pres.). Republican. Presbyterian. Home: Parkersburg, W.Va. Died Mar. 26, 1982.

BORNEMEIER, WALTER CARL, surgeon; b. Cass County, Nebr., Apr. 22, 1901; s. Charles and Lena (Schlueter) B.; B.A., North Central Coll., 1923, L.H.D., 1970; M.D., Northwestern U., 1929; m. Mabel Kemp, May 29, 1926; children—Lois Mary (Mrs. Louis John Kettle), Beatrice Ann (Mrs. Ralph Fiedler), Walter Carl II. Practice in Chgo., 1929-73; mem. staff Ill. Masonic Hosp., 1934-73, sr. attending surgeon, 1938-73; hon. cons. surgeon Resurrection Hosp.; instr. surgery Northwestern U. Med. Sch., 1934-52; prof. surgery U. Ill. Sch. Medicine, 1972. Pres. Tb Inst. Chgo. and Cook County, 1962-64. Pres. Niles Township High Sch. Bd. Edn., 1952. Hon. trustee North Central Coll. Served to maj., M.C., AUS, World War II; MTO. Recipient Distinguished Alumnus award North Central Coll., 1962; Merit award Northwestern U., 1971. Diplomate Am. Bd. of Surgery. Fellow A.C.S.; mem. A.M.A. (pres. 1970-71), Chgo. (past pres.), Ill. med. socs., Chgo. Surg. Soc. Rome (hon.), World Med. Assn., Phi Chi, Scabbard and Blade. Lutheran. Mason (33 deg.). Contbr. med. jours. Died Nov. 4, 1983.

BORSODI, RALPH, economist and author; b. N.Y. City, Dec. 20, 1888; s. William and Bertha (Wang) B.; privately educated; M.A., Saint John's Coll., Annapolis, 1941; m. Myrtle Mae Simpson, Aug. 14, 1911 (died Dec. 24, 1948); children—Ralph William, Edward M.; married 2d Mrs. Claire B. Kittredge, Sept. 6, 1950. Founder Sch. of Living, Suffern, N.Y.; mem. editorial bd. of Free America. Chancellor University of Melbourne, Fla., 1954. Author numerous books, latest publs., Edn. and Living, 2 vols., 1948; Social Pluralism, 1952; Challenge of Asia, 1957. Home: Melbourne, Fla. †

BORTIN, DAVID, lawyer; b. Pa., Sept. 23, 1886; s. Samuel Bortin and Jenny B.; ed. Central high sch.; Gratz Coll.; LL.B., Univ. of Pa.; m. Edna Nathan of Chicago, Dec. 11, 1916; 1 son, George. With Furth & Singer, later, Furth, Singer & Bortin, member of firm Bortin and Frater; director of Loft Candy Co., City Stores, Bond & Mortgage Co., Girard Life Ins. Co., Bankers Securities Corp., Factors Corp., of America. Mem. bd. of law examiners; former school dir.; dir. Phila. Gas Commn.; vice pres. Commercial Museum and Convention Hall; gov., Glens Mills Schs., gov. Mt. Sinai Hosp. Chmn. legal advisory bd. Div. Robin Hood Dell Orchestra, Inc. during World War I. Trustee (life) Free Libraries of Phila.; dir. Bd. City Trusts, Phila. Member Am., Pa., Phila. bar associations. Mason. Clubs: Lawyers, Brandeis, Pa. Athletic, Philmont Country, Pen and Pencil, Bankers (N.Y.). Author: Jews of Spain and Portugal during the Inquisition. Home: Philadelphia, Pa. †

BOSHES, BENJAMIN, physician, educator; b. Chgo., Feb. 15, 1907; s. Jacob and Ethel (Laffer) B.; grad. Crane Jr. Coll., Chgo., 1926; M.B., Northwestern U., 1929, B.S., 1930. M.D., 1931, M.S., 1934, Ph.D., 1938; m. Virginia Tarlow, June 14, 1931; children—Janet (Mrs. Charles A. Stern) Roger Arnold. Intern Cook County Hosp., Chgo., 1930-31; faculty Northwestern U. Med. Sch. 1932—, chmn. dept. neurology and psychiatry, 1952—; psychiatrist Inst. Juvenile Research, 1936-41; practice of medicine, specializing neurology and psychiatry, Chgo., 1931—; sr. cons. neurology VA Hosp., Hines, Ill.; cons. neuropsychiatry VA Hosp., Downey, Ill.; sr. cons. neuropsychiatry VA Research Hospital, Chicago; cons. neurology Fifth Army; consultant Federal Aviation Agency, 1968—. Served from capt. to lt. col. AUS, 1941-46; chief neuropsychiatry service 12th Gen. Hosp. Mem. Am. Acad. Neurology, A.M.A., Am. Neur. Assn., Am. Psychiat. Assn., Chgo. Neur. Soc. (pres. 1954-55), Ill. Psychiat. Soc. (pres. 1948), Central Neuropsychiat. Assn. (pres. 1955), Assn. Research Nervous and Mental Diseases, Am. Epilepsy Society, Sigma Xi, Alpha Omega Alpha. Author articles on neurology, psychiatry. Chief editor Frontiers in Neurology. Home: Winnetka, Ill. Died Apr. 13, 1984.

BOSS, CHARLES FREDERICK, JR., clergyman, church sec.; b. Washington, D.C., July 22, 1888; s. Charles Frederick and Katie V. (Doyle) B.; Bachelor Religions Edn., Boston U., 1922; grad. work Am., Harvard and Northwestern Univs.; LL.D., Adrian Coll., 1946; m. Hazel Stuart Price, June 8, 1910; children—Hazel Anna (wife of Capt. Leo W. Padden), Ruth Charlotte (Mrs. James H. Morito). Began as transit man with civil engr., 1906; successively mem. engring. dept., Chesapeake and Potomac Telephone Co.; topographic draftsman, U.S. Post Office Dept.; with div. topography, U.S. Geol. Survey; ordained to ministry of Methodist Ch.; served as pastor of churches in Washington Dist. of Baltimore (Md.) Conf. of Methodist Ch.; teacher Biblical subjects, church history and psychology in community schs. of Religious edn., Wellesley (Mass.), Hyde Park (Mass.), Fall River (Mass.); dir. religious work, community ch. sch., Readville, Mass.; dir. religious edn. Baltimore Conf. of Meth. Ch., 1922-26; mem. bd. edn. Meth. Ch. supt. church sch. div. and dir. bur. ednl. research, 1926-33; exec. sec. Commn. on World Peace of Meth. Ch. Chicago, from 1936. Accredited official observer, press rep. and consultant to United Nations Conf. by Dept. of State, 1945; mem. dept. internat. justice and good will Fed. Council of Churches of Christ in Am.; mem. exec. com. Internat. Council of Religious Edn.; mem. nat. council Fellowship of Reconcilliation; mem. Phila. Conf., 1941, Del. Conf., 1942, Round Table Conf. of Internat. Leaders, Princeton, N.J., 1943, Cleveland Conf., 1945; mem. Sherwood Eddy Seminar in Europe to study conditions in various countries, 1937; conducted seminar in six European countries for young Methodist delegates to Amsterdam Conf., 1939. Mission of Peace for Meth. Commn. on World Peace to Europe 1947, 48. Editor: World Peace Newsletter. Home: Evanston, Ill. †

BOSS, WALLACE LAMONT, banker; b. St. Paul, Oct. 31, 1905; s. Andrew and Evalena (LaMont) B.; m. Charlotte Bullen Wells, July 20, 1929; children—Wallace Andrew, Garrett Wells, Janet Charlotte Boss Hearon. B.S., U. Minn., 1928. Clk. Mchts. Nat. Bank, St. Paul, 1923-24, 28-29; rep. First Nat. Bank, St. Paul, 1929-38, asst. cashier, 1938-46, v.p., 1946-68, sr. v.p., exec. officer, 1968-70; ret. chmn. bd. St. Anthony Park State Bank. Past chmn. St. Paul Open Golf Tournament; past regional dir. Minn. War Finance Com.; past state campaign chmn. Minn. div. Am. Cancer Soc. King Boreas XX of St. Paul Winter Carnival. Mem. St. Paul Jr. C. of C. (past treas.), U.S. Jr. C. of C. (past treas.), St. Paul Area C. of C. (past treas., past dir.), Minn. Bankers Assn. (past pres.), U. Minn. Alumni Assn. (past treas., past dir.), Ramsey County Hist. Soc. (past dir.). Presbyterian (elder). Home: St Paul, Minn. Died Jan. 16, 1981.

BOSUSTOW, STEPHEN, movie producer-distbr.; b. Victoria, C., Can., Nov. 6, 1911; s. Stephen and Irene (Ure) B.; m. Audrey M. Stevenson, Nov. 16, 1935 (dec. Nov. 1975); children—Stephen H., Nicky O. Student pub. schs. Founder, pres. UPA Pictures, Burbank, Calif., 1941-61; founder, chmn. bd. Stephen Bosustow Prodns., Santa Monica, Calif., from 1961. Animation artist with, U.B. Iwerks, Los Angeles, 1931-32, artist with, Walter Lantz, Universal Pictures, 1932-34, artist, writer, Walt Disney Studios, Burbank, Calif., 1934-41, on Mickey Mouse cartoons, Snow White and 7 Dwarfs, Bambi, Fantasia; (Recipient Oscar award for best produced animated cartoons Acad. Motion Pictures Arts and Scis. for Gerald McBoing Boing 1952, When Magoo Flew 1954, Magoo's Puddle Jumper 1956). Address: Santa Monica, Calif.

BOSWORTH, FREDERIC MANNING, lawyer; b. Lakewood, Ohio, Sept. 2, 1900; s. Frederick C. and Sarah (Manning) B.; student Case Inst. Tech., 1917-20; E.E., Ohio State U., 1921; LL.B., Case-Western Res. U., 1925; m. Lucy Sawyer, July 1, 1931; 1 dau., Constance (Mrs. Paul Eric Kriikku). Admitted to Ohio bar, 1925, U.S. and Can. patent offices, 1928; assoc. firm Maky, Renner, Otto & Boiselle, Cleve. Registered mech. engr., Ohio. Mem. Cleve. Bar Assn. (hon.), Am., Cleve. patent law assns., Tau Beta Pi, Phi Delta Phi, Phi Delta Theta. Clubs: Clifton, University, Rowfant, Avon Oaks. Home: Rocky River, Ohio. Died Nov. 10, 1983.

BOTKIN, HENRY, artist; b. Boston, Apr. 5, 1896; s. Albert and Anna (Dachinick) B.; m. Rhoada Lehman, Sept. 16, 1930; children—Toinette, Glenn. Student, Mass. Sch. Art, 1915-19; student Art Students League, Paris. Illustrator, Sat. Eve. Post, Harpers Bazaar, Vogue, others, 1919-28, painter, 1929-83; represented in permanent collection, numerous museums, including, Met. Mus. Art, Library of Congress, Mus. Modern Art, Boston, Mus. Fine Arts, Whitney Mus., others throughout U.S., pvt. collections throughout, U.S., 91 one-man exhbns., Paris, Boston, Washington, Kansas City, Denver, Los Angeles, San Francisco, N.Y.C., Chgo., other cities, group shows including, Whitney, Carnegie Internat., Corcoran, Art Inst. Chgo.; art adv. leading Am. collectors.; Contbr. to: George Gershwin, 1938, Esquire, 1943; Co-editor: Abstract Art, 1957. Recipient numerous awards including purchase awards Acad. Arts and Letters, 1967, 74, 75. Fellow Internat. Inst. Arts and Letters; mem. Am. Abstract Artists (pres. 1954-55), Fedn. Modern Painters and Sculptors (pres. 1958-59, 60-61), Artists Equity (pres. 1952-53). Rep. by 16 paintings Walter P. Chrysler, Jr. collection. Home: New York, N.Y. Dec. Mar. 4, 1983.

BOTTA, RICO, naval officer; b. Nov. 2, 1890. Entered U.S. Naval Reserve, Nov. 30, 1921, and advanced through the grades to rear admiral; transferred to U.S. Navy, Nov. 30, 1921; apptd. comdr. U.S. Naval Air Material Center, Phila. Address: Washington, D.C. †

BOTTORFF, CHARLES RUSSELL, hardware mfg. co. exec.; b. Goshen, Ky., Mar. 1, 1889; s. Robert and Mattie (Moore) B.; ed. pub. schs.; m. Norma Herzer, Oct. 8, 1913 (dec. 1955); 1 dau., Anne (Mrs. William H. Fields); m. 2d, Mildred G. Miller, Mar. 2, 1957. With Belknap Hardware & Mfg. Co. (now Belknap Inc.), Louisville, from 1907, specialty sporting goods and cutlery salesman, buyer, dir., asst. treas., dir. sales, pres., 1930-55, chmn. bd., 1955-69, dir., cons., 1969 from 1969; dir. First Nat. Bank, Ky. Trust Co., First Ky. Co. Bd. dirs. Louisville Community Chest, Louisville Found. Named Hardware Man of Year, Phila. Assn. Mfrs., 1953. Presbyn. Mason. Clubs: Louisville Country, Pendennis (Louisville). Home: Louisville, KY. †

BOUCHER, PAUL ROBERT, government official; b. Cambridge, Mass., Apr. 13, 1942; s. Paul Andrew and Jeannette Ellen (LaPointe) B.; m. Ginette Louise Beaudoin, July 29, 1967; children—Eric Paul, Nicole Marie. B.S., Merrimack Coll., Andover, Mass., 1963; J.D., Suffolk U., 1969. Bar: Mass. bar 1970. Spl. agt. U.S. Naval Intelligence, Boston and Alexandria, Va., 1964-72; atty. U.S. Dept. Justice, Washington, 1972-79; insp. gen. SBA, Washington, 1979-82. Home: Vienna, Va. Dec. July 4, 1982.

BOULT, SIR ADRIAN CEDRIC, symphony conductor; b. Chester, Eng., Apr. 8, 1889; s. Cedric Randal and Katharine Florence (Barman) B.; Mus.D., Christ Church, Oxford, 1912; M.A. Royal Conservatory, Leipzig, 1913; LL.D., Birmingham U., 1930; hon. Mus.D., University Edinburgh, 1922. Cambridge University, 1953; married Ann Mary Grace Bowles, July 1, 1933. Mem. musical staff Royal Opera, Covent Garden, London, 1914; mem. teaching staff, Royal Coll. Music, 1919-30, 62-83; dir. music Brit. Broadcasting Corp., 1930-42; chief conductor BBC Symphony Orchestra till 1950. London Philharmonic Orchestra, 1950-57; conductor City of Birmingham Orchestra, 1924-30, 59-60; guest condr. Royal Philharmonic Orchestra, Liverpool Philharmonic Soc., London Symphony, also symphonies in Vienna, Prague, Barcelona, Zurich, Budapest, Paris, New York, Boston, Sweden; president London Philharmonic Orchestra. Served War Office and Commission Internat. de Ravitaillement, 4 years. World War. Recipient Gold Medal, Harvard Glee Club, 1956. Fellow Royal Coll. of Music; hon. mem. Royal Acad. Music; hon. fellow Christ Church, Oxford U. Clubs: Athenaeum, (London). Contbr. to musical jours. London, Eng. Died Feb. 23, 1983.

BOURNE, FRANK CARD, classics educator; b. Wells, Maine, July 17, 1914; s. Moses Avander and Grace (Card) B.; A.B., Princeton, 1936, M.A., 1940, Ph.D., 1941. Mem. faculty Princeton, 1946-76, prof. Classics, 1966-76, Kennedy prof. Latin emeritus, 1976-83; master Grad. Coll., 1954-58. Served with USAAF, 1941-45. Mem. Vergilian Soc. Am. (sec.-treas. 1951-54), Classical Assn. Atlantic States (pres. 1957), Am. Philol. Assn., Assn. Internat. d'Epigraphie Latine, Assn. Internat. de Papyrologues. Author: Public Works of Julio-Claudians and Flavians, 1946; A History of the Romans, 1966; (with Johnson and Norton) Ancient Roman Statutes, 1961. Editor: Decline and Fall (Gibbon), 1963. Home: Wells, Maine. Died Nov. 19, 1983.

BOURNE, GRANVILLE HARMAN, pub. utility co. exec.; b. Bklyn., Aug. 6, 1889; s. William G. and Margaret P. (Tonge) B.; grad. high sch.; m. Violet A. Kelly, Apr. 22, 1924; children—Granville Harman, Donald Winthrop. With Hodenpyl, Walbridge & Co., pub. utility banking and operating, N.Y.C., 1906-12; accountant Hodenpyl, Hardy & Co., N.Y.C., 1912-25, partner, 1925-28; asst. sec., asst. treas. Commonwealth & So. Corp., and predecessors, N.Y.C., 1916-34, comptroller, 1934-45, v.p., comptroller, 1945-47, pres., 1947-49, also dir., officer operating utility companies in system, 1916-49; pres. Commonwealth Services, Inc., N.Y.C., 1947-55, chmn. bd. from 1955. Served with U.S. Army, 1918-19. Mem. Controllers Inst. Am., Edison Electric Inst., Am. Gas Assn., Am. Mgmt. Assn., N.Y. State C. of C. Clubs: Downtown Athletic (N.Y.C.); Upper Montclair Country (Montclair, N.J.). Home: Glen Ridge, N.J. †

BOUSLOG, JOHN SAMUEL, physician; b. Logan, Ill., Oct. 13, 1890; s. George Sylvester and Mary Elizabeth (Wasson) B.; A.B., U. of Colo., 1914, M.D., 1916; m. Nina Audrey Brown, May 23, 1915; 1 son, John William (dec.). Intern, U. Hosp., Boulder, Colo., 1916-17; pvt. practice Boulder, 1916-18; radiologist, Denver, from 1918; instr. physiol. chemistry, summer sch. U. of Colo., 1914; asst. prof. radiology, med. sch., 1940-43, asso. clin. prof. radiology, 1943-52, clinical professor of radiology since 1952; associate roentgenologist Selmene Winter Found., 1922-27; roentgenologist gastro-enterology Child Research Council, 1922-27; radiologist St. Lukes Hosp., 1934-45, St. Anthony Hosp., 1918-56 (pres. staff, 1937-38), Children's Hosp. (staff sec., 1930-34), Am. Med. Center, Beth Israel Hosp., 1922-56 (pres. staff 1934-35), Jewish Nat. Home for Asthmatic Children; cons. staff Presbyn., St. Luke's hosps., Childrens Hosp.; cons. radiologist Colo. Gen. Hosp.; civilian cons. Fitzsimmons Gen. Hosp. Denver; surgeon in res. U.S.P.H.S. Sec. National Conference Med. Service, 1948-49, pres., 1949-50; mem. adv. com. Coop. Med. Advt. Bur., A.M.A., 1944-46, chmn. Ann. Conf. Constituent State Med. Assns., 1943. Served with Med. Adv. Bd., World War I; radiologist, World War II; sec. Med. Adv. Board; capt. Med. Res. Corps, U.S. Army, 1925-35. Recipient of Selective Service medal; gold medal Radiol. Society N.A., 1955; medal Colorado division American Cancer Society, 1955. Diplomate Am. Bd. Radiology. Fellow Am. Coll. Radiology (state councilor 1944-47, bd. chancellors 1948-52, chmn. 1950-51, pres. 1952-53), A.A.A.S., Am. Coll. Chest Physicians; mem. Radiol. Soc. N.A. (bd. dirs. 1945-49, pres. 1950-51), Am. Roentgen Ray Soc., Am. Radium Soc., Inter-American Coll. Radiology, Society of Nuclear Medicine, American Cancer Society (dir. 1953-59; president of Colorado section 1952-54), Assn. Study Neoplastic Diseases, Colorado, Rocky Mountain (president 1956-57) radiological societies, American Numismatic Association, Rocky Mountain Cancer Found., Am. Trudeau Soc., Denver Clin. and Path. Soc., C. of C., Phi Beta Pi, Alpha Chi Sigma, Acacia. Mason (Shriner, 32 deg., K.T.). Clubs: Athletic, City (Denver). Author articles in profl. jours. Home: Denver, Colo. †

BOUTELL, HUGH G., mechanical engineer; b. Chicago, Ill., Mar. 9, 1890; s. Henry Sherman and Euphemia (Gates) B.; B.S., George Washington U., 1912; m. Mary Maling Bourne, Sept. 14, 1915; 1 dau., Suzette (Mrs. Alfred Francis Hopkins, Jr.). Dynamometer car engr. Southern Ry., 1914-16; draftsman Baldwin Locomotive Works, 1916-18; asst. engr. physicist Nat. Bur. Standards, 1918, chief information sect., 1919-46, asso. engr., mech. engr., editor Tech. News Bulletin, 1919-46. Life mem. Mil. Order Loyal Legion; mem. Ry. and Locomotive Hist. Soc., Railroadians of Am., Brotherhood of Live Steamers. Republican. Episcopalian. Author: National Advisory Committee for Aeronautics Report Number 44 (with H. C. Dickinson), 1920; War Work of the Bureau of Standards, 1921; Visitors' Manual of the Bureau of Standards, 1937. Contbr. numerous articles to tech. publs. Address: Santa Barbara, Calif. †

BOVARD, JAMES MOORHEAD, coll. trustee; b. Greensburg, Pa., Apr. 14, 1901; s. Harry Foster and Mary (Moorhead) B.; A.B., Yale, 1924; LL.B., U. Pitts., 1927, LL.D., 1950; m. Carroll E. Donner, Jan. 30, 1942; stepchildren—Joseph William, Carroll Donner. Asso. or partner law firm Moorhead & Knox, 1927-48; pres. Forbes Nat. Bank Pitts., 1939-48; pres. bds. of trustees of Carnegie Inst. and Carnegie Library of Pitts., 1948-67, pres. emeritus, 1967-82; trustee emeritus Carnegie-Mellon U., 1948-82, chmn., 1948-66; dir. Equitable Gas Co.; trustee Dollar Savs. Bank. Dir. Pitts. Regional Planning Assn., Eye and Ear Hosp. Pitts. Trustee Sarah Mellon Scaife Found. Served as lt. col. USAAF, 1942-45. Home: Pittsburgh, Pa. Died Mar. 26, 1982.

BOVE, CHARLES FREDERICK, surgeon; b. Brooklyn, N.Y., Dec. 15, 1890; s. Mark M. and Ida A. (Serrill) B.; M.D., U. of Md., 1913; A.B., Sorbonne, Paris, 1921; M.D., Faculté de Paris, 1923; m. Suzel de Cambefort, Dec., 1920 (divorced Jan., 1939); 1 son, Clifford Hilton; m. 2d, Edith M. Lahellec, Aug. 7, 1940. Began practice of medicine, 1915; Intern St. Joseph Hosp., 1913-15; post grad. student John Hopkins Univ., surgeon American Hospital of Paris, 1923-40; asso. attending, Beth-David Hosp., N.Y. City. Served as maj. (mil. surgeon) with A.E.F. during World War I. Mem. A.M.A., N.Y. County Med. Soc., French Assn. Surgeons (Paris, France). Knight of Legion of Honor (France). Anglican. Clubs: Polo, T.N.T., American (Paris). Address: New York, N.Y. †

BOWDEN, A. BRUCE, banker; b. New Martinsville, W.Va., Aug. 17, 1908; s. Dr. George S. and Ora (Zimmerman) B.; B.A., Washington and Jefferson Coll., 1929; grad. Rutgers U. Grad. Sch. Banking, 1952; m. Mildred Bastian, June 26, 1937; 1 son, Alan Bruce. With Mellon Securities, 1937-42, Gulf Oil Corp., 1942-44; with buying dept. Mellon Securities Corp., 1946-47; asst. v.p. First Boston Corp., 1947-48; with Mellon Nat. Bank & Trust Co., 1948-73, v.p., 1951-63, senior vice president, 1963-65, executive vice pres., 1965-66, president, 1967-73; director of Allegheny Ludium Steel Corp., Dresser Industries, Incorporated, Dravo Corporation, Vice president of board of directors Western Pa. Hosp.; trustee Tb League of Pittsburgh. Served as lt. USNR, World War II. Home: Pittsburgh, Pa. Died Mar. 18, 1983.

BOWDEN, NICHOLLS WHITE, civil engr.; b. Tangipahoa, La., Mar. 23, 1888; s. Lemuel H. and Mary L. (Draughon) B.; B.S., La. State U., Baton Rouge, 1908, C.E., 1928; m. Willie F. Bates, Nov. 20, 1912; children—Elizabeth Bowden Millice, 1st Lt. Nicholls White (killed in action, Italy, Oct. 27, 1943). Surveyman, surveyor, junior engineer, United States Engineers Department, Nashville and Chattanooga, Tennessee, 1908-22; assistant, principal assistant, state highway (chief) engineer, La. Highway Commn., Baton Rouge, 1922-28; engr., later senior engr., U.S. Engr. Dept., Pittsburgh, Pa., 1928-35; sr. engr. on temp. duty, office chief of engrs. U.S. Army, Washington, D.C., 1933-35, in connection with engring. investigation pub. works projects for Mississippi Valley Com.; prin. and head hydraulic engineer, chief of river control branch Tennessee Valley Authority from Jan. 1936; regional water consultant Tenn. and Cumberland River basins for Water Resources Com. of Nat. Resources Planning Bd., 1936-42; alternate mem. Water Resources Committee 1938 until disbanded in 1943; mem. com. on evaluating constructed projects Pres.' Water Resources Commn., Washington, 1950. Mem. Am. Soc. C.E., Tau Beta Pi, Sigma Tau Sigma, Phi Kappa Phi. Methodist. Mason. Author articles on operation of multiple-purpose reservoir systems; also 1st and 2d prize winning articles on open channel river improvement. †

BOWDEN, RAY B., trade assn. exec.; b. Eskridge, Kan., Aug. 5, 1890; s. John and Lemmie (Campbell) B.; student Montana State Coll., 1925-27, U. of Mont., 1927-28; m. Grace Child, Aug. 20, 1916; children—Gladys Rae (Mrs. Martin Maracek) John Child and Mary Joan (Mrs. Kingsley Suits) (twins). Began as a County sch. tchr., 1907; supt. schs., Alta Vista, Kan., 1913-15; copy editor, Kansas City (Mo.) Journal, 1915; city editor, Pocatello (Ida.) Daily Chronicle, 1915-16; city editor, Boise (Ida.) Daily Statesman, 1916; newspaper reporter, Butte (Mont.) Daily Post and Anaconda Standard, 1916-17; publicity dir., Mont. Food Adminstrn., 1918; advt. mgr., Sawyer (chain) stores, 1919; editor of pubns. Mont. State Coll., 1920-30; engaged in trade assn. work (grain and feed), from 1930; sec. Texas Grain and Feed Assn., Ft. Worth; former assistant to pres. Grain and Feed Dealers Nat. Assn. Mem. Am. Trade Assn. Execs., Epsilon Sigma Phi, Sigma Delta Chi, Pi Kappa Alpha. Mason. Clubs: University (Washington). Home: Ft. Worth, Tex. †

BOWEN, CHARLES FRANCIS, novelist; b. Manchester, N.H., Jan. 13, 1889; s. Charles Henry and Josephine Bernardine (Daley) B.; student Valparaiso (Ind.) Univ., 1908-09; Boston U. Law Sch., Mass., 1914-15; m. Helen Elizabeth Rawlins, Sept. 2, 1921. Enlisted as pvt. Nat. Guard of N.H., Dec. 1915; provisional 2d lt., R.A., C.A.C., 1915-16; regimental adjt., 1st Army Hdqrs. Regt., A.E.F., 1917; sec. Gen Staff, 32d Div., France and Germany, 1918-19; dir. State Planning and Development Commn., N.H., 1934-36; sec. to gov. N.H., 1937-39; brig. gen., U.S. Army, 1940-47; maj. gen. N.G., N.H., from 1951; State dir. Selective Service, New Hampshire, 1940-47; adjutant gen. New Hampshire, 1939-54. Vice pres. Mt. Washington Observatory from 1942. Member State Commn. for Promotion of the Wealth and Income of the People of N.H.; Nat. com. on Civilian Defense; Am. Legion, 1941-42; Vets. Fgn. Wars. Awards: Silver Star Medal; Legion of Merit; Army Commendation Medal; Croix de Guerre with palm; Bene Merentibus Decoration (Poland); Chevalier, Royal Order of the White Eagle (Jugoslavia). Republican. Roman Catholic. Club: Rotary (Manchester, N.H.). Author: Lost Virgin (hist. novel), 1958. Home: Manchester, N.H. †

BOWEN, CHARLES PARNELL, JR., mgmt. cons.; b. West Collingswood, N.J., Feb. 20, 1914; s. Charles P. and Helen (Sheets) B.; B.S., Mass. Inst. Tech., 1935; m. Hope Ludlow, Dec. 24, 1937; children—Geoffrey, Carla, Deborah, Eve. Time study engr. Gen. Electric Co., 1935-40; indsl. engr. Carnegie Ill. Steel Co., 1940- 41, Ingersoll Steel & Disc div. Borg-Warner, 1941-43, Bell Aircraft, 1943-44; with Booz, Allen & Hamilton, N.Y.C., 1944—, partner, 1948-62, coordinating partner Eastern region, mem. exec. com., 1957-61, pres., dir., 1962-70, chmn., dir., 1970-76, hon. chmn., 1976-81; dir. Money Market Assets, Inc. Clubs: Chicago, Attic (Chgo.); University, Sky, N.Y. Yacht (N.Y.C.); Indian Harbor Yacht. Home: Greenwich, Conn. Died Sept. 27, 1981.

BOWEN, KENNETH BLOUNT, clergyman; b. near Plymouth, N.C., Dec. 25, 1889; s. William Horace Della Estelle (Harrison) B.; A.B., Atlantic Christian Coll., Wilson, N.C., 1912; B.D., The Coll. of the Bible (fellow in religious edn.), Lexington, Ky., 1917; A.M., Transylvania Coll., Lexington, Ky., 1918, D.D., 1946; merit scholarship Union Theol. Sem., 1918-20; A.M., Columbia, 1919; m. Onnolee Avery, Sept. 4, 1923; children—Avery, Betsy, Brenda. Practice teaching Horace Mann Sch., 1919-20; pastor Central Ch. Disciples, Auburn, N.Y., 1920-25, The Memorial Ch. Disciples, Ann Arbor, Mich., 1925-27, The Madison Av. Ch. Disciples, Covington, Ky., 1927-45; pres. The Coll. of the Bible, Lexington, Ky., 1945-48; now pastor Morgan Park Christian Ch., Disciples, Chicago, Del. Oxford and Edinburgh, 1937, Conf. 1937. Mem. War Service com. Disciples of Christ; exec. com. Red Cross and U.S.O. Mem. exec. com. Fed. Council of Chs., New York; mem. Pi Kappa Alpha, Theta Phi. Independent. Mason, Club: Informal (Lexington). Contbr. to Disciple publs. Traveled abroad 4 times to study econ., social and religious conditions. Home: Chicago, Ill. †

BOWEN, RAYMOND BROWER, indsl. developer; b. Mpls., Aug. 16, 1888; s. Millard Fillmore and Gertrude (Morgan) B.; grad. Hotchkiss Sch., 1908; B.S., Sheffield Sci. Sch., Yale, 1912; m. Virginia van Santvoord, Sept. 25, 1915; children—Van Santvoord, John G., Barbara (Mrs. Harry M. Scoble, Jr.). Advt. staff Review of Reviews, 1913, Nation's Bus., 1919-23, The Outlook, 1914-17, 23-25; advt. dir. New Yorker mag., 1925-53, dir. from 1926; exec. v.p. Bennington County Indsl. Corp., from 1958. Served with AS, U.S. Army, World War I. Clubs: Yale (N.Y.C.); Ekwanok Country (Manchester, Vt.). Home: Bennington, Vt. †

BOWER, ADELAIDE HOWELL, writer; b. Atlanta, Ga., May 21, 1889; d. Evan Park and Julia Adelaide (Erwin) Howell; ed. pub. and pvt. schs., Lucy Cobb Inst., (Athens, Ga.) and Peeples-Thompson Sch., New York; m. Byron Bower, 1914 (divorced). Engaged in newspaper work from 1923; editor Short Story Dept., Sunday American, Atlanta, from 1923. Mem. League of Am. Penwomen, Atlanta Writers' Club. Known as "The friend of the beginner-writer." Author, lecturer, teacher, short story technique. Home: Atlanta, Ga. †

BOWERS, HAROLD C., banker; b. Wykoff, Minn., Aug. 13, 1889; s. Robert and Carrie (Farrington) B.; student pub. schs., Minn.; Claribel Westaby, June 23, 1915; children—Mildred (Mrs. Smith), Wanda (Mrs. Joe Ward). With banks in Hettinger, New Leipzig, Regent, N.D., 1911-12; bookkeeper, asst. mgr., v.p. Regent Grain Co., Regent, also New England, N.D., 1912-24; cashier First State Bank, Regent, 1924-45; mgr. Bank of N.D., Bismarck, since 1945. Mem. N.D. State Banking Bd., 1940-45. Presbyn. Mason (Scottish Rite, Shriner), Royal Order Jesters, Elk. Home: Bismarck, N.D. †

BOWLER, HENRY REGINALD, denominational sec.; b. Milford, Neb., Feb. 14, 1889; s. Edwin Parker and Caroline (Holden) B.; A.B., Linfield Coll., 1909, D.D., 1938; Rhodes Scholar, St. John's Coll., Oxford, Eng., B.A., 1916, M.A., 1920; m. Helen Grace McCron, Oct. 4, 1922; children—David Livingstone, Elizabeth Ann (Mrs. R. M. Appelbaum). Teacher in pub. high schools of Salt Lake City, Utah, 1916-17; secretary to Doctor John R. Mott, 1917-19; research and writing, Hist. Bur. Nat. War World Council, Y.M.C.A., 1920-21; asst. exec. sec., Gen. Bd. Promotion, Northern Bapt. Conv., 1921-24, sec. lit. and asst. treas., Council Finance and Promotion, 1924-48; recording sec., Northern Baptist Conv., 1946-49, budget adviser from 1948; secretary Commn. of Appraisal, Laymen's Fgn. Missions Inquiry, 1931-32; mem. Bapt. Joint Com. on Pub. Affairs; mem. bd. mgrs. Central Dept. Ch. World Service, mem. bd. mgrs. Am. Bible Soc., commn. on missionary edn. Nat. Council Chs. of Christ in U.S.A. Democrat. Baptist. Collaborated in writing book, Service with Fighting Men, 1922. Home: Hollis, N.Y. †

BOWLES, AUBREY RUSSELL, JR., lawyer; b. Richmond, Va., May 31, 1896; s. Aubrey Russell and Ida Gertrude (Hockaday) B.; A.B., Richmond Coll., 1915; A.M., Harvard, 1920; LL.B., U. Va., 1923; m. Martha Mary Hoadly, Jan. 15, 1927; children—Mary Hoadly (dec.), Aubrey Russell III. Admitted to Va. bar, 1922, since practiced in Richmond; asso. firm McGuire, Riely & Eggleston, 1923-32, Bowles, Anderson and Boyd, 1942-57, firm now Bowles and Bowles; pres. Va. Bonded Warehouse Corp., 1942-57; former sec., gen. counsel Nolde Bros., Inc. Pres. Family Service Soc., 1940-43. Former mem. exec. com., bd. dirs. Richmond area Community Chest; past bd. mgrs. Silver Hill Found; exec. officer Brit. mission of War Damages Commn. of the Gen. Peace Commn., 1919. Served as 1st lt., 3d Cav., U.S. Army, AEF, 1917-19; Hdqrs. comdt. advanced G.H.Q.; comdg. officer Hdqrs. Troop 3d Army, AEF. Fellow Am. Bar Found.; mem. Am. Coll. Trial Lawyers, Jud. Council Va., Am. Law Inst., Am. Judicature Soc., Internat. Assn. Ins. Counsel, Fedn. Ins. Counsel, Va. Trial Lawyers Assn., Am. (ho. of dels. 1957-58), Va. (exec. com. 1949-52), W.Va. (hon.), Richmond bar assns., Va. State Bar (exec. com. and council 1948-57, pres. 1955-56), Inst. Jud. Adminstrn., Inc., Nat. Assn. R.R. Trial Counsel, Raven Soc. (U. Va.), Va. Hist. Soc., Am. Legion, Soc. 40 and 8, Am., Va. power boat assns., Soc. Cin., Meml. Guidance Clinic (past dir.), Assn. Bar City N.Y. (asso.), U. Va. Law Sch. Assn., Judicial Conf. Va., Jud. Conf. U.S. 4th Circuit, Jamestowne Soc., Phi Beta Kappa, Kappa Sigma, Phi Delta Phi. Episcopalian. Clubs: Country of Virginia, Farmington Country. Contbr. articles to profl. publs. Home: Richmond, Va. Died Apr. 20, 1984.

BOWMAN, JAMES SCHENCK, civil, hydraulic engr.; b. West Liberty, Ia., Apr. 29, 1889; s. Joseph Stanley and Phebe Wheeler (Schenck) Bowman; B.C.E., State University of Iowa, 1913; m. Sadie Richmond, Apr. 6, 1914; children—Joseph Richmond, James William; married 2d, Opal Morgan, May 23, 1938. Began as rodman, Northern Pacific Railroad, 1907; drainage and highway engineer, Algona, Ia., 1913-14; asst. engr., Miami Conservancy Dist., Dayton, O., 1915-18; irrigation engr., Estate of L. Z. Leiter, Clearmont, Wyo., 1919; hydraulic engr., Fargo Engring. Co., Jackson, Mich., 1920-27, with L. F. Harza Chicago, 1928-32; instr. hydraulic engring., U. of Wisconsin, 1933, with engring. dept., Tenn. Valley Authority, Knoxville, Tenn., since 1933, head of project planning div., 1934-43, head of water control planning dept., 1943-55, on special assignments TVA, 1955-59, cons. engr., from 1955. Mem. Am. Soc. C.E. Ky. Civil War Round Table, Tenn. Hist. Soc., Son of the Revolution (Tennessee Chapter), Tau Beta Pi. Mem. bd. of stewards Church Street Methodist Ch. Mason. Club: Smoky Mountains Hiking (Knoxville). Contbr. chapter on Spillway Crest Gates in Handbook of Applied Hydraulics, 1942. Co-author; The Holston-French Broad Country, A History of Knox County, Tennessee, 1946. Home: Knoxville, Tenn. †

BOWMAN, LE ROY EDWARD, author; b. Elgin, Ill., Nov. 21, 1887; s. Frank Edward and Bertha May (Tuck) B.; A.B. with honors, U. Chgo., 1911, postgrad., 1911-12; Ph.D., Columbia, 1954; m. Garda Brown Wise, Sept. 23, 1942; children (by former marriage)—Bruce, Mary Ellen. Dir. receiving and shipping dept. Elgin Butter Co. (Ill.), 1905-07; dir. Greenpoint Neighborhood Assn., Bklyn., 1913-17; dir. nat. personnel dept. War Camp Community Service, 1917-18; mem. dept. social sci., Columbia, 1917-31, dir. tng. sch. for community workers, 1920-23, organizer, dir. N.Y.C. Recreation Com., 1919-27; organizer summer exptl. schs. in various cities on Rosenwald Fund grant under Child Study Assn. Am., 1931-35; organizer discussion project U.S. Dept. Agr., 1935; dir. United Parents Assn. Greater N.Y. (200 parent orgns.), 1935-38; forum leader and dir. S.C. and Vt. state forum demonstrations, U.S. Office Edn., 1938-39; free-lance lectr., 1940-41; supr. bur. adult edn., tng. forum leaders, organizing intercultural community leagues, N.Y. State Edn. Dept., 1942-46, Bklyn. Coll., 1946, advanced steadily, asso. prof., 1954-58. Chmn. Ch. World Service Study Com. to Korea and Hong Kong, 1960. Bd. dirs. Consumer's Coop. Services, N.Y.C., 1925-28; trustee and lectr. Rochdale Inst., 1936-44; bd. dirs. Eastern Coop., Inc., 1948-49. Sec. and editor Nat. Community Center Assn., 1922-30; sec. sect. on community Am. Sociol. Soc., 1924-29; mem. central com. Am. Assn. for Study Group Study Group Work, 1941-43. Mem. Liberal Party, vice chmn. N.Y., from 1960. Recipient honor award N.Y.C. League for Indsl. Democracy, 1962. Author: Wilderness of American Prosperity (Benn), 1929; (with Margaret Lighty) Parenthood in a Democracy (Parents Inst.), 1935; Community Programs for Summer Play Schools (Child Study), 1936; How to Lead Discussion (Woman's Press), 1939; Organization and Leadership of Group Discussions and Forums (N.Y. State Edn. Dept.), 1943; The American Funeral, 1959; Youth and Delinquency, 1960; Reactions to N.Y. City Fair Housing Practices Law, 1960. Home: Brooklyn, N.Y. †

BOWMAN, PAUL HAYNES, coll. pres., clergyman; b. nr. Johnson City, Tenn., July 5, 1887; s. Samuel J. and Sue V. (Bowman) B.; A.B., Bridgewater Coll., 1910, LL.D., 1944; B.D., Crozer Theol. Sem., Chester, Pa., 1913; A.M., U. Pa., 1913; D.D., Blue Ridge Coll., 1918, Juanita Coll., 1925; LL.D., Roanoke Coll., 1944; m. Flora Hoover, Aug. 12, 1913; children—Paul Hoover, Grace (Mrs. Robert Koons), John Evans, Gene. Ordained to ministry Ch. of the Brethren, 1907; minister Bethany Ch. Brethren, Phila., 1913-15; pres. Blue Ridge (Md.) Coll., 1915-17; prof. philosophy Bridgewater Coll., 1918-19, pres., 1919-45, pres. emeritus, from 1950; ednl. specialist U.S. Office Edn., 1945-46; gen. rep. Ch. World Service, N.Y. City, 1948-51; livestock farmer nr. Timberville, Va., from 1946; dir. Farmers & Mchts. Bank. Pres. Rockingham Pub. Library, from 1948. Moderator, Ch. of Brethren, 1937, 1942, 1949, mem. Gen. Brotherhood Bd., 1929-47, also from 1951. Mem. Nat. Council Chs. Christ in Am. (commn. mem.), Tau Kappa Alpha. Republican. Home: Timberville, Va. Deceased.

BOWMAN, WILLARD EUGENE, publisher; b. Hartford City, Ind., Sept. 5, 1889; s. Aurelius A. and Mary C. (Russell) B.; grad. Hartford City High Sch., 1907; m. Mary Pauline Smith, July 30, 1912; children—Mrs. Gerald T. O'Donoghue, Mrs. Basil T. Moore, Richard Eugene. Reporter for Hartford City Times Gazette, 1907; publicity work for Indiana State Rep. Com., etc., 1914-16; news editor and editorial writer Detroit Journal, 1916-20; Washington corr. for Toledo Blade, Detroit Journal and Newark (N.J.) Star-Eagle, 1920-22; mng. editor and editor, Newark Star-Eagle, 1922-35; executive v.p. and publicity dir. L. Bamberger & Co., 1935-37; editor Newark (N.J.) Star-Eagle, 1937-40 (Star-Eagle was consolidated with Newark Morning Ledger); asso. pub. Newark (N.J.) Star-Ledger since 1941; past pres. Broad St. and Mchts. Assn. (Newark). Clubs: Newark Advertising (past pres.), Downtown, Kiwanis (Newark); National Press (Washington, D.C.); N.J. State Press Assn. (past pres.). Home: East Orange, N.J. †

BOWRING, EVA, former govt. ofcl., rancher; b. Nevada, Mo., Jan. 9, 1892; d. John F. and M. Belle (Hinkes) Kelly; m. T. F. Forester, 1911; children—Frank H., James Harold, Jo Donald; m. 2d, Arthur Bowring, Apr. 13, 1928 (dec. 1944). Cattle rancher, operator Bar 99 Ranch, Merriman, Neb., 1928-85; Hereford breeder; U.S. senator, Neb., 1954; mem. Fed. Bd. Parole, 1956-64. Mem. adv. com. Neb.-S.D. Regional Med. Program, from 1965. Trustee Neb. Children's Home Soc. Died Jan. 8, 1985.

BOYCE, JOHN SHAW, forest pathologist; b. Belfast, Ireland, Nov. 9, 1889; s. Robert Robinson and Sarah Jane (Waring) B.; brought to U.S., 1891, naturalized, 1911; B.S., U. of Neb., 1911, M.F., 1912; Ph.D., Stanford, 1917; hon. M.A., Yale, 1929; m. Lillian Marion Jameson, May 16, 1917; 1 son, John Shaw. Forest guard U.S. Forest Service, 1910, forest asst., 1911-12; scientific asst., and asst. pathologist Div. Forest Pathology, U.S. Dept. Agr., 1919-20, pathologist in charge of Portland (Ore.) br., 1920-28; prin. silviculturist and dir. Northeastern Forest Expt. Sta., U.S. Forest Service, 1928-29; prof. forest pathology, Yale U. and principal pathologist U.S. Dept. of Agriculture from 1929. U.S. del. Internat. Congress of Forestry and Touring, Grenoble, France, 1925. Served as 2d lt. Air Service, U.S. Army, 1918. Chmn. com. forestry NRC, 1940-42. Fellow Soc. Am. Foresters, A.A.A.S.; mem. of Am. Forestry Assn., Am. Phytopathol. Soc., Bot. Soc. of America, Conn. Acad. Science, Mycol. Soc. of America, N.E. Botanical Club, Soc. Am. Foresters, Sigma Xi. Author books and papers on tree diseases and decay of wood. Home: New Haven, Conn. †

BOYD, CHARLES ALEXANDER, educator, scientist; b. Snohomish, Wash., Mar. 4, 1917; s. Charles Alexander and Hazel (Gainer) B.; student Mt. Vernon Jr. Coll., 1935-37; B.S., U. Wash., 1939; M.S., Oreg. State Coll., 1941; Ph.D., U. Wis., 1948; m. Isabel Withycombe, June 20, 1942; children—Susan, Charles, Elizabeth. Research asso. Allegheny Ballistic Lab., 1942-45; chemist Argonne Nat. Lab., 1946-47; project asso. U. Wis., 1948-50, asst. prof. phys. chemistry, 1950-51; phys. chemist Camp Detrich, 1951-53; sci. warfare adviser weapons systems evaluation group Dept. Def., 1953-56, asst. dir. research, 1956-58, dir. research, dir. weapons systems evaluation div. Inst. Def. Analyses, 1958-62; chief scientist Aeroprojects, Inc., 1962-65; sr. research asso. Ordnance Research Lab., Pa. State U., 1965-70; tchr. sci. dept. State College (Pa.) Area High Sch., 1970-74; dir. alternative program State College Area Sch. Dist., 1974-79. Mem. Fellow A.A.A.S.; mem. Faraday Soc., Sigma Xi, Phi Lambda Upsilon, Sigma Pi Sigma, Alpha Chi Sigma, Phi Delta Kappa. Club: Cosmos (Washington). Home: Port Matilda, Pa. Died Nov. 1, 1980.

BOYD, CHARLES PARKER, textile mfr.; b. Boston, Aug. 24, 1887; s. Charles Marshall and Jennie Eliza (Parker) B.; student Volkman Sch., Boston, 1906, Phila. Textile Sch., 1907-08; m. Marion Leslie Knott, Sept. 28, 1909; children—Leslie (Mrs. Harold Davis), Charles Marshall II, Marion (Mrs. W. Guthrie, Jr.), Jennie E. (Mrs. V. Murray Smith), Charles Parker, Natalie (Mrs. J. Cann). Apprentice Am. Woolen Co., Boston, 1908-10; with Nat. Shawmut Bank, Boston, 1910-12; with Jeremiah William & Co., 1912-31, partner, 1917-31; dir. Beacon Mfg. Co., Swannanoa, N.C., from 1912, pres., from 1934, chmn.; founder Boyd & Sons Mfg. Co., Phila., 1931, pres., from 1931; dir. Sacheme Mills, Winder, Ga., Oconec Mills, Westminster, S.C. Served with U.S. Army, 1917-18. Republican. Episcopalian. Clubs: Racquet, British Officers (Phila.); New York Yacht. Home: Rosemont, Pa. †

BOYD, HAROLD BUHALTS, orthopaedic surgeon, ret. educator; b. Chattanooga, Dec. 2, 1904; s. Clarence J. and Marie Frances (Buhalts) B.; M.D., Loma Linda (Calif.) U., 1932; m. Jean Frances Stewart, Feb. 23, 1933; children—Heather (Mrs. Charles Lindsay), Julia (Mrs. Orville W. Swarner, Jr.), Jean Frances (Mrs. H. Maynard Lowry). Intern, Los Angeles County Hosp., 1931-32; resident Kern County Hosp., Bakersfield, Calif., 1932-34; fellow in orthopaedic surgery Campbell Clinic, Memphis, 1934-36, partner, 1937-74, chief of staff, 1962-70; mem. staff Baptist Meml. Hosp., pres., 1952, Crippled Children's Hosp. Sch.; mem. staff LeBonheur Childrens Hosp.; cons. orthopaedic surgeon John Gaston Hosp. Civilian orthopedic cons. for Surg. Gen. U.S. Army to Japan and Korea, 1951; instr. U. of Tenn., 1940-41, asst. prof., 1941, asso. prof. orthopaedic surgery, 1944-59, prof. orthopaedic surgery, head orthopaedic dept., 1959-72, emeritus, 1972-81; vis. orthopedic prof. Ohio State U., 1961, N.Y. Orthopaedic Hosp., 1973; Camp vis. prof. U. Calif., 1962; F.W. Horner vis. prof. McGill U., 1969; vis. prof. Hosp. for Spl. Surg., N.Y.C., 1972, Shafa Hosp., Tehran, Iran, 1976, U. South Ala., 1978; Baer vis. prof. Johns Hopkins U., 1978; trustee Jour. Bone and Joint Surg., 1966-71. Pres. trustees Campbell Found.; trustee Orthopaedic and Research Edn. Found. 1960-65, pres., 1964-65. Decorated Nat. Order So. Cross, Brazil, 1953; named Alumnus of Year Loma Linda U., 1954, Tenn. Physician of Year, 1973. Diplomate Am. Bd. Orthopedic Surgery (mem. bd. 1964-69). Fellow Am. Acad. Orthopaedic Surgeons (pres. 1953), A.C.S. (gov. 1958-61, Tenn. pres. 1965-66), NIH (surg. study sect. 1957-61); mem. AMA, Am. Orthopaedic Assn., Westen Surg. Assn., Am. Soc. Surgery of the Hand, Société Internationale de Chirugie Orthopédique et de Traumatologie, Med. and Surg. Assn. of Quito, Bolivian Surg. Soc., Memphis and Shelby County Med. Soc. (pres. 1957); hon. mem. Chilean soc. Orthopaedics and Traumatic Surg. Soc., Brit., South African orthopaedic assns., la Sociedad Latino Americana de Orthopedia y Traumatologia, Venezuelean Soc. Orthopaedic and Traumatic Surgery, Iranian Orthopedic Soc. (hon.), Sigma Xi, Alpha Omega Alpha. Contbr. articles to profl. jours. Contbg. author Campbell's Operative Orthopaedics, 1939-71. Home: Carlsbad, Calif. Died May 29, 1981.

BOYD, LINN JOHN, physician, educator; b. Detroit, Sept. 30, 1895; s. David Armitage and Laura M. (Staffin) B.; M.D., U. Mich., 1918; m. Madeline H. Young, June 8, 1918. In gen. practice, Addison, Mich., 1919-20; asso. prof. medicine Med. Sch. U. Mich., 1920-22, asso. prof. medicine, dir. research labs., 1922-25; in practice, Lansing, Mich., 1925-26; prof. medicine, head dept. pharmacology, N.Y. Med. Coll., 1926-58, clin. prof. medicine, dir. Div. Grad. Studies, 1958-63, cons. Grad. Sch., 1963-70; dir. of medicine, Met. Hosp., 1937-50, also pres. med. board, 1940-50; cons. medicine, U.S. Marine, Sea View Hosp. (S.I.), Otisville Sanatorium (N.Y.), Monmouth Meml. Hosp.; pres. med. bd. Bird S. Coler Meml. Hospital; chmn. med. bd. N.Y. Med. Coll.-Met. Hosp. Center, 1955-58; med. examiner N.Y., 1947-58; dep. chief examiner Nat. Bd. Med. Examiners, 1948-58. Served in U.S. Navy, League Island and Grey's Ferry naval hosps., 1918-19; lt. USNRF. Fellow Am. Coll. Gastroenterology (hon.), Am. Coll. Cardiology, A.C.P.; mem. N.Y. Heart Assn., Harvey Soc., Sigma Xi, Alpha Omega Alpha, Alpha Sigma, Alpha Kappa Kappa. Episcopalian. Mason, K.P. Research in lesser known drugs. Author of textbooks on roentgenology of heart and great vessels, also on pharmacology, cardiology and electrocardiography. Home: Stamford, Conn. Died Oct. 4, 1981.

BOYD, P. M., editor, clergyman; b. Fairburn, Ga., June 29, 1889; s. James La Fayette and Frances (Harper) B.;

student Reinhardt Coll., Waleska, Ga.; B.A. and D.D., Fla. So. Coll., Lakeland, Fla.; m. Mary Emma Baggett, June 9, 1914 (died July 25, 1925); children—William Baggett, Thomas Stewart; m. 2d, Mary Frances Sharp, Aug. 19, 1927. Began as evangelist; ordained ministry M.E. Ch., S., 1928; asso. pastor First Ch., Orlando, Fla., 1928-32; pastor College Heights Ch., Lakeland, 1932-36; chaplain Fla. So. Coll., Lakeland, 1932-36; pastor First Ch., Jacksonville, 1936-41; dist. supt. Methodist Ch., Tampa, 1941-March. 1945; Pastor Christ Methodist Church, St. Petersburg, 1945-46; second Pastorate First Ch., Jacksonville, 1946-55; supt. Miami dist. Fla. Conf., Meth. Ch., 1955-61; editor Fla. Christian Advocate, 1933-36, bus. mgr., 1934-36. Del. Gen. Conf. M.E. Ch. S., 1938; del. Gen. Conf., Meth. Ch., 1944, Jurisdictional Conf., 1956, Southeastern Jurisdictional Conf., 1940, 44-52; mem. exec. com. Bd. Publs. Chmn. trustees Meth. Children's Home, Enterprise, Fla.; chmn. Wesley Found. Commn. U. Fla., 1940-41; vice chmn. bd. trustees Fla. So. Coll., 1953-61, chmn. endowment commn. Mem. Internat. Soc., Pi Gamma Mu, Theta Phi. Mason. Home: Jacksonville, Fla. †

BOYD, RICHARD MOODY, transp. cons.; b. Louisville, Jan. 16, 1915; s. Moody and Nellie Field (Dickinson) B.; A.B., U. Ky., 1936; m. Dale Crowe, May 24, 1941; children—Richard Hart, David Parker. Gen. agt. I.C. R.R., 1936-48; with PPG Industries, Inc., 1949-70, v.p. traffic, transp., 1966-70; dir. N. Am. Car Corp., Chgo., 1969-72, pres., 1970-72; regional mgr. Nat. R.R. Passenger Corp., 1972-76; transp. cons., 1976-82. Served to col. Transp. Corps. AUS, 1941-46. Mem. nat. Freight Traffic Assn. (pres. 1967), Nat. Indsl. Traffic League (pres. 1960-62), Am. Soc. Traffic and Transp., Nat. Def. Transp. Assn. (v.p. 1965-66), Traffic Club Pitts. (pres. 1965-66), N.Y.C., Am. Legion, Sigma Phi Epsilon. Home: Kenilworth, Ill. Died June 15, 1982; buried Odd Fellows Cemetery, Madisonville, Ky.

BOYD, ROBERT STEWART, pub. co. exec.; b. N.Y.C., May 17, 1908; s. Robert J. and Esobel (Bole) B.; m. Evelyn Allan Power, June 25, 1936; 1 dau., Lee Allan. Student bus. adminstrn., Columbia, 1932; student, Wesleyan U., Middletown, Conn., 1933. Traffic rep. Eastern Air Lines, 1933-35; dist. sales mgr. Gen. Foods, Inc., 1935-41; dir. war workers recruiting Mfrs. Assn. Syracuse, N.Y., 1942-44; account exec. Young & Rubicam, 1945-46; advt. mgr. Nat. Biscuit Co., 1947-55; v.p., pub. Curtis Pub. Co., from 1956; formerly with marketing and sales Good Housekeeping, N.Y.C.; now pres. S. Boyd & Assos., Mendham, N.J.; publishers cons. Wonderful World of Ohio; dir. Nat. Analysts, Inc.; Pres. Grocery Mfrs. Assn. Syracuse, 1940-41, Advt. Club Syracuse, 1942; chmn. communications Ret. Sr. Vol. Program; mem. exec. com. Dept. Aging; host, dir. weekly program RSVP Srs. Speak Out, Sta. WRAN. Pres. N.Y.C. Youth Devel. Com.; Republican campaign mgr. 7th Congl. Dist., N.J., 1951-52; treas. N.J. for Eisenhower, 1951-52; pres. Ridgewood (N.J.) Rep. Club, 951-52.; Trustee, exec. com. Am. Freedom from Hunger Found.; trustee Prospect Hill Sch., Newark.; Mem. N.Y. N.G., from 1938. Named hon. chief 3 tribes Can. Indians; recipient award Voluntary Action Center, 1978; also citations advt. clubs St. Louis, citations advt. clubs Mpls., citations advt. clubs Miami, Fla., also; Reading, Pa. Mem. Morristown Beard Sch. Alumni Assn. (trustee 1976), Delta Kappa Epsilon. Clubs: Syracuse Univ, Mendham Golf. Address: Chester, NJ.

BOYD, THOMAS ALVIN, research adminstr.; b. Fairview O., Oct. 10, 1888; s. William Charles and Amanda (Bell) B.; student Muskingum Coll., 1908-09, Franklin Coll., 1913-14; B. Chem. Engring., Ohio State U., 1918, Chem. Engr., 1938, D.Sc., 1953; D. Engring., U. Detroit, 1952; D.Sc., Wayne State U., 1955; m. Grace Jean Bethel, June 25, 1919; 1 dau., Elinor Jean. Research chemist, research div. Dayton Metal Products Co. (O.), 1918-19; research chemist, asst. head fuel dept. Gen. Motors Research Div. (merger Dayton Metal Products Co. with Gen. Motors Corp.), Dayton, 1919-25, Detroit, 1925-47; research cons., lectr. in field. Recipient Lamme medal for meritorious achievement in engring. Ohio State U., 1939, Thomas Midgley award Detroit sect. Am. Chem. Soc., 1966. Fellow A.A.A.S.; mem. Am. Soc. Testing Materials (dir. 1943-45, v.p. 1945-47, pres. 1947-48), Am. Inst. Chemists (hon.), Am. Chem. Soc., Soc. Automotive Engrs. (Horning Meml. medal 1948), Engrs. Soc. Detroit (dir. 1941-47, pres. 1943-44), Soc. for History Tech., Am. Soc. Engring. Edn., Sigma Xi, Phi Lambda Upsilon, Tau Beta Pi. Presbyn. Clubs: Boat, Torch, Economic (Detroit); Chemists (N.Y.C.). Author: Gasoline—What Everyone Should Know About It, 1925; Research—The Pathfinder of Science and Industry, 1935; Professional Amateur, A Biography of Charles Franklin Kettering, 1957. Editor: Prophet of Progress Selections from the Speeches of Charles F. Kettering, 1961. Contbr. articles to profl. jours. Home: Grosse Pointe Park, MI. †

BOYD, THOMAS HENRY, investment banker; born Clarksville, Tenn., Aug. 12, 1890; s. John Hardgrove (D.D.) and Ellen Morris (Henry) B.; A.B., Princeton, 1913; LL.B., Northwestern U., 1916; m. Katharine Winslow Kingsley, June 18, 1918; 1 son, Kingsley. Admitted to Ore. State bar, 1916; atty. Geary & Boyd, Portland, 1916-17, Clark, Kendal & Co., 1919-21; with Blyth & Co., Inc., from 1921, Portland, Ore. office, 1921-35, Chgo., 1935-42, N.Y. from 1942, v.p. from 1938, dir. from 1952; dir. Iron Fireman Mfg. Co., Cleve. Served to 1st lt. inf., 91st div. A.E.F., U.S. Army, 1917-19. Mem. Ore. State Bar, Delta Tau Delta, Phi Delta Phi. Clubs: Bond, Municipal Bond (pres. 1939; Chgo.); Municipal Bond, Downtown Athletic (N.Y.C.); Shelter Island Yacht, Gardiners Bay Golf. †

BOYD, WILLIAM CLOUSER, educator, researcher; b. Dearborn, Mo., Mar. 4, 1903; s. William Oliver and Wilmuth (Clouser) B.; m. Lyle A. Gifford, June 9, 1931 (div. 1966); 1 child, Sylvia Lyle; m. Cassandra Girard Crosby, 1967. A.B., Harvard U., 1925, M.A., 1926; Ph.D., Boston U., 1930; student, Sch. Oriental Studies, Cairo, Egypt, 1949-50. Teaching fellow Boston U. Sch. Medicine, 1926, mem. faculty, from 1930, prof. immunochemistry, research, 1948-69, prof. emeritus, 1969-83; head dept. biochemistry (U.S. Naval Med. Research Unit No. 3), Cairo, 1949-50; research collaborator (Brookhaven Nat. Lab.), 1956-57; vis. prof. biochemistry and nutrition U. P.R. Med Sch., San Juan, 1970-71; research assoc. U. Calif.-San Diego, 1974-83. Author: (with Fritz Schiff) Blood Grouping Technic, 1942, Fundamentals of Immunology, 1943, 4th edit., 1966, Genetics and the Races of Man, 1950, (with B.S. Walker and I. Asimov) Biochemistry and Human Metabolism, 1952, (with I. Asimov) Races and People, 1955, Introduction to Immunochemical Specificity, 1962, also 300 articles in tech. jours. Guggenheim fellow, 1935; Fulbright fellow, 1952. Fellow Am. Acad. Arts and Scis., N.Y. Acad. Sci.; mem. Am. Assn. Immunologists (pres. 1959-60), Am. Assn. Human Genetics (pres. 1957), Am. Rocket Soc., Am. Assn. Phys. Anthropologists, Brit. Assn. Immunologists (hon.), Sigma Xi. Club: Boston Mycological (pres. 1960). Home: Falmouth, Mass. Dec. Feb. 19, 1983.

BOYDEN, ROGER TALBOT, govt. ofcl.; b. Phila., Oct. 1, 1887; s. Amos J. and Annie Lucinda (Sherman) B.; student Mass. Inst. Tech., 1906-09; B.S. in C.E., George Washington U., 1921, LL.B., 1925; m. Florence Mae Jones, Oct. 1928 (dec. June 1942). Surveyor, draftsman, rodman, instrumentman, 1908-15; admitted to D.C. bar, Supreme Ct., Ct. of Appeals, 1925; with ICC, from 1915, beginning as engr. bur. valuation, successively examiner bur. valuation, examiner bur. finance, chief sect. loans and reorgns., asst. dir. bur. finance, 1915-54, dir. bur. finance, from 1954. Mem. Phi Sigma Kappa, Phi Alpha Delta. Home: Washington, D.C. †

BOYER, BENJAMIN FRANKLIN, legal educator; b. St. Joseph, Mo., Sept. 17, 1904; s. John Sidney and Ruby (Hale) B.; m. Marion L. Lehr, Oct. 20, 1928; 1 dau., Judith Ann (dec.). Student, U. Va., 1922-24; A.B., U. Mo., 1926, J.D., 1928; LL.M., Columbia U., 1941; LL.D., Waynesburg Coll., 1952, Dickinson Sch. Law, Carlisle, Pa., 1959. Bar: Mo. 1928, Pa. 1950. Asst. atty. Mo. State Hwy. Commn., 1928-33; mem. firm Otto & Boyer, Washington, Mo., 1933-37; faculty Sch. Law, U. Kansas City (now U. Mo. at Kansas City), 1937-47, assoc. prof. law, 1937-42, prof. law, 1942-47; asst. to dean Sch. Law, U. Kansas City (Sch. Law), 1938-39, chmn. law faculty, 1939-40, dean, 1940-47; dean, prof. law Temple U. Sch. Law, Phila., 1947-65, prof., 1965-69; prof. law U. Calif. at Hastings Coll. Law, 1969-79; Alternate mem. regional enforcement commn. WSB, 1952; Bd. curators Lincoln U. of Mo., Jefferson City, 1939-44; bd. advisers Pa. Tax Inst., 1948-61; Mem. Mo. Supreme Ct. Com. on Civil Procedure, sub-com. on suggestion and plan, 1939-41; chmn. Personnel (Civil Service) Bd. of Kansas City, 1946-47. Editor: (with others) Selected Readings on the Legal Profession, 1962, Materials on Professional Responsibilities of the Legal Profession, 1967. Mem. Health and Welfare Council Phila., 1964-69; mem. Commn. on Standards and Accreditation of Services for the Blind, Nat. Accreditation Council of Agys. Serving the Blind and Visually Handicapped, Pa. Gov.'s Commn. on Labor Legislation, 1953-54; bd. dirs. Legal Aid Soc. Phila., 1954-69, pres., 1960-69; council mem. Phila. Medico-Legal Inst., 1955-69. Commd. 2d lt. Inf. Res. U.S. Army, Feb. 1927; apptd. lt. col., Inf. May 1943; col. 1945; active duty under Res. Commn. 1941-46; instr. Commd. and Gen. Staff Sch. at Ft. Leavenworth Nov. 1942-Dec. 1945, Kans.; comdt. Phila. O.R.C. Sch. 1950-51. Recipient Arthur von Briesen medal Nat. Legal Aid and Defender Assn., 1968. Mem. Am., Mo., Pa., Kansas City, Phila., San Francisco bar assns., Mo. Bar (sr. counsellor 1978), Nat. Acad. Arbitrators, Am. Arbitration Assn. (vol. panel), Lawyers Assn. Kansas City, Am. Law Inst. (life mem.), Am. Judicature Soc., Phi Beta Kappa Associates, Order of Coif, Phi Delta Phi, Alpha Pi Zeta, Sigma Nu, Phi Beta Kappa. Clubs: Mason (San Francisco) Shriner; Rockhill Tennis. Home: Kansas City, Mo. Died Aug. 1, 1985.

BOYER, J. U., banker; b. St. André-Avellin, July 30, 1899; s. Onésime and Enelie (Beaudry) B.; m. Laurette Hetu, July 3, 1948; 1 dau., Michèle. With Provincial Bank of Can., from 1918, beginning with managerial positions, Montreal, Ottawa, and Windsor, Ont., successively mgr. Main Office, Montreal, gen. mgr., v.p., exec. v.p., 1918-57, pres., from 1957, also dir.; pres. Les Immeubles Pro-Can Limitée; dir. Crown Life Ins. Co., Gatineau Lumber & Builders Supply, Ltd., Le Pavillon du Meuble Ltée, Les Libraries Pilon, Inc. Mem. Montreal Bd. Trade. Pres. l'Institut Bruchesi de Montreal, Inc., Les Camps de Santé Bruchesi; life gov. l'Ecole de Commerce De Quebec, Inc., Hosp. Notre-Dame, l'Hopital St. Justine; chmn. bd. Hôpital St.-Jean-de-Dieu; hon. mem. Montreal Symphony Orch.; dir. La Colonie Notre Dame, Inc., mem. Canadian Welfare Council. Decorated Medal Pro Ecclesia et Pontifice, 1949. Mem. Canadian Bankers' Assn. (pres. 1949, hon. pres. 1951-58), Nat. Athletic Assn. (gov.), Am. Bankers Assn. (v.p. for Can. 1949-51), Internat. C. of C. (dir. Canadian council), Montreal, Montreal Jr. (gov.) chambers commerce. Clubs: St. Laurent Kiwanis; Cercle de la Place d'Armes; Seigniory; Laval Sur de Lac; Saint Denis; Outre-mont. Home: Laval, Que., Can.

BOYLE, JOHN S., county judge; b. Chgo., July 17, 1901; s. Michael and Maria (O'Malley) B.; m. Mary Sullivan, June 9, 1945. LL.B., DePaul U., 1926. Bar: Ill. bar 1926. Practiced in, Chgo., asst. corp. counsel, 1931-33, asst. states atty., Cook County, 1933-39, states atty., 1948-52; judge Superior Ct. Cook County, 1960-63; chief justice criminal ct., 1963; chief judge Circuit Ct. Cook County (constl. consolidation of all Cook County cts.), 1964-78, ret., 1978; chief judge of chief judges State of Ill., 1974-77. Alderman, Chgo., 1939-43; Pres. Nat. Conf. Met. Cts., 1966; Del. Democratic Nat. Conv., 1952, 56, 60. Recipient Chgo. Crime Commn. Spl. Commendation award, 1963, 1st Law award Lincoln Acad. Ill., 1965, Award Merit Celtic Legal Soc., 1965, Distinguished Service award Tau Epsilon Rho, 1966, VIP citation in jurisprudence Catholic Women's Club Ill., 1966, Distinguished Achievement award DePaul U., 1968, Man of Year award Cath. Lawyers Guild Chgo., 1970, Lex Legio award De Paul U., 1973; Tom C. Clark Distinguished Service award, 1974. Mem. Fed. Bar Assn., ABA, Ill. Bar Assn., Chgo. Bar Assn. (Disting. Service award 1979), West Suburban Bar Assn. (pres. 1957), Phi Alpha Delta (Chgo. Alumni award 1949). Democrat. Clubs: Executive (dir.), Law, Butterfield Country. Home: Oak Park, Ill.

BOYLE, WILLIAM ANTHONY, labor union exec.; b. Bald Butte, Mont., Dec. 1, 1904; s. James P. and Catherine (Mallin) B.; m. Ethel V. Williams, June 3, 1928; 1 dau., Antoinette. Asst. to internat. pres. United Mine Workers Am., 1948-60, internat. v.p., 1960-63, internat. pres., 1963-72. Vice chmn. Nat. Coal Policy Conf.; mem. President's Adv. Com. Labor-Mgmt. Policy. Dir., mem. exec. com. National Bank, Washington. Home: Washington, D.C. Died May 31, 1985.

BOYLES, GEORGE ROBERT, banker; b. Chgo., Aug. 26, 1890. Examiner Chgo. Clearing House Assn., 1920-28; v.p., dir. Lake View State Bank, 1928-30; pres., chmn. Madison & Kedzie Trust & Savs. Bank, 1930-33, Merchants National Bank in Chgo., 1934-62; vice chmn. Central Nat. Bank (merger Merchants National Bank of Chicago, 1962-66, adviser, from 1966. President of Palisades Park Properties Incorporated, 1952-64; pres. Bahia Vista, Inc. Mem. Am. (treas. 1955-57), Ill. (pres. 1943-44) bankers assn. Clubs: Chgo. Athletic Assn., Bankers, Executives (Chgo., Ill.); Palisades Park Country (pres. 1951-53); Oak Park Country. Home: Oak Park, Ill. †

BOZA, HECTOR, mining engr.; b. Lima, Peru, Dec. 12, 1888; s. Benjamin Boza; ed. Lima (Peru) schs., student U. of Mo., U. of Wisconsin, U. of Illinois. Minister public works, Peru; delegate to Pan-Am. Conf., Lima, 1938; pres. Inter-Am. Com. of public works, New York, 1944; Peruvian del. to U.N. Gen. Assembly, London, New York; senator, mem. Fgn. Affairs, Com. of Peruvian Senate. Dir. several mining and indsl. orgns. Deceased.

BOZORTH, RICHARD MILTON, research physicist; b. Salem, Ore., Apr. 10, 1896; s. Scott and Elizabeth Flint (Dearborn) B.; A.B., Reed Coll., 1917; Ph.D., Cal. Inst. Tech., 1922; m. Louise Huntley, Aug. 3, 1921; children—Katherine (Mrs. E. Bruce Whitesell), Alison (Mrs. J. W. Fowle). Teaching fellow Cal. Inst. Tech., 1919-21; du Pont fellow, 1921-22; research fellow 1922-23; research physicist, Bell Telephone Labs. and Western Electric Co., N.Y.C. and Murray Hill, N.J., 1923-61; U.S. del. Internat. Union Pure and Applied Physics, London, 1934, Amsterdam, 1948; mem. Naval Tech. Mission, Japan, 1945-46, Amsterdam, 1948; with IBM Watson Research, 1961-66, Naval Ordnance Lab., 1961-70; lectr. in field. Chmn. NRC-Nat. Acad. Sci. panel; founder Ann. Conf. Magnetism and Magnetic Materials, 1955. Served with United States Army, 1917-19. Fulbright research prof. U. Tokyo, 1961-62; U. K. sr. vis. fellow Oxford U., vis. fellow Brasenose Coll., 1968. Fellow Am. Phys. Soc.; mem. Phys. Soc. of Japan, Am. Inst. Elec. Engrs. (ofcl. rep. to Japan 1953) A.A.A.S., Am. Soc. Metals, Crystallographic Assn. Author: Ferromagnetism, 1951; also sci. papers. Asso. editor Jour. Applied Physics, 1937-39. Editorial bd. Jour. Applied Physics, I.E.E.E. Magnetics (hon. life mem.); contbr. Ency. Brit., 1947, 56, 71, chpts. to various books. Patentee magnetic materials. Home: Short Hills, N.J. Deceased.

BRACKEN, AARON FRANCIS, agronomist; b. Freedom, Wyo., Oct. 11, 1890; s. Aaron Franklin and Amelia (Hanson) B.; B.S., Utah State Agrl. Coll., 1914, M.S., 1923; student Univ. of Minn., 1926-27, State Coll. of Ia. summer 1936; m. LaVern Miller, Oct. 30, 1917; children—Thora Mae, (Mrs. Wm. B. Ward), Barbara Donnell (Mrs. Dale Balls), Alice (Mrs. Burdette Peterson). Asst. agronomist, Utah State Agrl. Coll., 1914-16, 1920-24, asso. agronomist, 1924-46, agronomist since 1946; county agrl. agt., Morgan and Summit Counties, Utah, hdqrs. Coalville, 1917-18; scientific asst., U.S.D.A., Bureau Plant Industry, hdqrs. Nephi, Utah, 1918-20; state planning cons., Nat. Resources Bd., 1934-35; agronomist for Syrian Govt., Damascus, Syria, 1947-48; owner and operator farm near Nephi, Utah, since 1919. Fellow Am. A.A.S.; mem. Am. Soc. Agronomy (sec., Western br., 1930, pres., 1931). Am. Assn. Univ. Profs., Utah Acad. Sciences, Arts, and Letters, Phi Kappa Phi, Sigma Xi. Republican. Mem. Ch. of Jesus Christ of Latter Day Saints. Contbr. articles on various problems of crops and soils largely dealing with dryland agriculture in Utah publs. Home: Logan, Utah. †

BRACKEN, JAMES LUCAS, editor, writer; b. Greensburg, Kan., Nov. 20, 1913; s. John N. and Grace (Lucas) B.; m. Frances Cadzow, Mar. 24, 1943; children—Thomas R. J., Dorothy C., Frances Margaret Bracken Huessy. Corr. Brit. newspaper syndicates, writer agrl. publs., 1933-37; field editor, later exec. editor Pacific N.W. Farm Trio, Spokane, 1937-42; mng. editor Western Metals mag., Los Angeles, 1946; editorial writer, asst. to mng. editor The Spokesman Rev., Spokane, 1947-48, mng. editor, 1949-78, editor, 1978. Served to capt. AUS, 1942-46. Contbr. to World Book Ency., also other publs. Home: Spokane, Wash. Died May 19, 1984; interred Spokane, Wash.

BRADDY, HALDEEN, English language educator; b. Fairlie, Tex., Jan. 22, 1908; s. John Winfield and Lena Moss (Rountree) B.; B.A., E. Tex. State U., 1928; M.A., U. Tex., 1929; Ph.D., N.Y. U., 1934; m. Virginia Bell, June 19, 1927. Instr. English, N.Y. U., 1929-38; prof. Tex. Christian U., 1938-42; supr. Tex. Tech U., 1943-44; assoc. prof. U. Kans., 1944-45; lectr. Tulane U., 1946, U. So. Calif., 1946; prof. English U. Tex. at El Paso 1946-78, prof. emeritus, 1978-80; research prof., 1963-64. Served as 1st lt. USAAF, 1942-43. Grantee Am. Council Learned Socs., 1937; named East Tex. State U. Distinguished Alumnus, 1972; recipient U. Tex. at El Paso Faculty Research award, 1972. Mem. Tex. Folklore Soc. (pres. 1951-52, program chmn. 1952), Rocky Mountain MLA (pres. 1972-73), Kappa Sigma. Mem. Christian Ch. Author: Chaucer's Parlement of Foules, 2d edit., 1969; Chaucer and the French Poet Graunson,, 2d edit., 1968; Glorious Incense, The Fullfillment of Edgar Allan Poe, 2d edit., 1968; Cock of the Walk, Legend of Pancho Villa, 1955, 2d edit., 1970; Hamlet's Wounded Name, 1964, 2d edit., 1974; Pershing's Mission to Mexico, 1966, 2d edit., i973; Pancho Villa Rides Again, 1967; Mexico and the Old Southwest, 1971; Geoffrey Chaucer, 1971; Three Dimensional Poe, 1973; The Paradox of Pancho Villa, 1978; rev. editor Jour. Am. Folklore, 1945. Home: El Paso, Tex. Died Aug. 16, 1980; buried Ft. Bliss Nat. Cemetery, Tex.

BRADEN, SAMUEL RAY, clergyman, educator; b. Derby, Kan., June 18, 1888; s. Ed(ward) and Jennie (Wardell) B.; A.B., Coll. of Emporia, Kan., 1910; B.D., McCormick Theol. Sem., 1919; grad. work Princeton, 1912, U. of Chicago, 1919; Ph.D., U. of Mo., 1924; m. Mary E. Altman, of Emporia, Kan., May 26, 1913; children—Samuel Edward, John Altman, Mary Elizabeth. Supt. schs., Derby, Kan., 1910; teacher Paxton Training Sch., Kiungchow, Island of Hainan, China, 1913-15; ordained Presbyn. ministry, 1913; pastor Cottonwood Falls, Kan., 1915-17, Logan Sq. Ch., Chicago, 1917-19; prof. religious edn., Bible Coll. of Mo., 1919-24; dean and acting president Blackburn Coll., Carlinville, Ill., 1924-25; head of psychology and edn. dept., Tusculum Coll., Greeneville, Tenn., 1925-26; acting pres. Mo. Valley Coll., Marshall, Mo., 1926-27; pastor First Presbyn. Ch., McAlester, Okla., from 1929. T.B. Blackstone fellow in N.T., McCormick Theol. Sem., 1919. Mem. Am. Sociol. Soc., Phi Delta Kappa. Republican. Contbr. to religious jours. Home: McAlester, Okla. †

BRADFORD, EUGENE FRANCIS, univ. adminstr.; b. Bangor, Me., Mar. 5, 1889; s. William Henry and Mary Ellen (Wilson) B.; A.B., Bowdoin Coll., 1912; A.M., Harvard, 1913, Ph.D., 1927; m. Marjorie Campbell, Dec. 26, 1919; 1 son, Edwin Campbell. Instr. English, Syracuse U., 1913-17, asst. prof., 1919-23, asso. prof., 1923-25, prof., 1927-28, dir. admissions, 1919-28; dir. admissions Cornell U., 1928-46, registrar, from 1930, exec. com., vice chmn. Coll. Entrance Exam. Bd. Mem. commn. on higher instns. Middle States Assn. Served as 1st lt. 308th Inf., 77th Div. U.S. Army, 1917-19, Oise-Aisne, Mense-Argonne Offensives. Mem. Modern Lang. Assn. Am., Am. Assn. U. Profs., Phi Beta Kappa, Phi Kappa Phi, Delta Kappa Epsilon. Republican. Unitarian. †

BRADFORD, JAMES COWDON, investment banker; b. Nashville, Nov. 24, 1892; s. Alexander and Leonora (Bisland) B.; student Vanderbilt U., 1909-12; m. Eleanor Avent, May 11, 1926; children—Eleanor, James C. Partner Davis Bradford & Co., 1912-52; pres. Piggly Wiggly Stores Inc., 1923-25; ptnr. J. C. Bradford & Co. Served as 1st lt. F.A., U.S. Army, 1917-19. Episcopalian. Mason (32 deg., Shriner). Clubs: Belle Meade, Cumberland. Home: Nashville, Tenn. Dec. Dec. 1981.

BRADFORD, KARL SLAUGHTER, army officer; b. Washington, D.C., June 28, 1889; s. Ben Boyland and Nellie Irene (Harvey) B.; student U. of Va., 1906-07; B.S., U.S. Mil. Acad., 1911; grad. Machine Gun Officers Sch., Ecole Speciale Militaire, St. Cyr, France, Cavalry Sch., Command and Gen. Staff Sch. and Army War Coll.; m. Loraine Allen Sickel, Dec. 27, 1917; 1 daughter, Sally Harvey (Mrs. Richard Peck, Jr.). Commissioned 2d lt., U.S. Army, 1911; promoted through grades to brig. gen., 1941; served at various times in 2d, 3d, 4th, 15th and 26th Cavalry Regts.; comdr. 1st Cavalry Brigade, Fort Bliss, Tex.; 1941-43; instr. U.S. Mil. Acad., 1914-18, and Cavalry School, 1934-36. Member Cavalry Board, 1921-25. Dep. pres. War Dept. Manpower Bd., 1943-46; Retired from Dec. 1946. Awarded Legion of Merit. Mem. Soc. of the Cincinnati, Beta Theta Pi, Clubs: Army and Navy, Army and Navy Country (Washington). Editor of Cavalry Jour., 1926-27. Home: Washington, D.C. †

BRADFORD, ROBERT FISKE, former governor of Massachusetts, lawyer; b. Boston, 1902; A.B., Harvard, 1923, LL.B., 1926, LL.D., 1948. Admitted to Mass. bar 1927; partner Palmer & Dodge; dir. Cambridge Trust Co.; honorary dir. Olivetti Underwood Corp.; trustee Boston Five Cents Savs. Bank, Investment Trust of Boston. Gov. Mass., 1947-49. Trustee Simmons College; senior warden King's Chapel. Home: Cambridge, Mass.

BRADFORD, WILLIAM LESLIE, pediatrician, educator; b. Sedalia, Mo., June 8, 1898; s. John Asbury and Minnie Jane (Price) B.; m. Lenora Dee Dalton, Oct. 27, 1928; 1 child, William D. A.B., U. Mo., 1921; M.D., Washington U., St. Louis, 1923. Intern St. Louis City Hosp., 1923-24; asst. health officer for, Mo., 1924-26; resident pediatrics Strong Meml. Hosp., Rochester, N.Y., 1926-27; AAAS, bacteriology and pathology U. Rochester Sch. Medicine and Dentistry, 1927-28, instr. pediatrics, 1928-30, asst. prof., 1930-34, assoc. prof., 1934-49, asst. dean, 1947-54, prof., from 1950, head dept., 1952-64; Disting. vis. prof., pediatrics U. Mo., 1965; cons. AEC. Contbg. editor various pediatric books, encys.; Contbr. articles to profl. jours.; Editor jour.: Pediatrics. Served with U.S. Army, 1918. Recipient gold medal U. Rochester Med. Alumni, 1960; Alumni award U. Mo, 1965; Alumni award Washington U., 1970. Mem. Am. Pediatric Soc. (chmn. council), Soc. Pediatric Research (v.p.), Soc. Exptl. Biology and Medicine, Soc. Am. Bacteriologists, Am. Acad. Pediatrics, Am. Pub. Health Assn., AAAS, Alpha Omega Alpha, Sigma Xi, Sigma Nu, Tri Chi, Nu Sigma Nu. Clubs: Mason. (Rochester), Genesee Valley (Rochester). Home: Rochester, N.Y. Dec. Nov. 11, 1983.

BRADLEE, STANWOOD GORDON, investment broker; b. Newton, Mass., Aug. 7, 1889; s. Harry Homer and Florence (Blaikie) B.; student Boston Latin Sch.; m. Clara Mae Fraser, Oct. 11, 1915; children—Charlotte (Mrs. Wilbur G. Burbridge), Merrill Gordon. Entered bus. with Codman, Grew & Co., 1905, firm changed name to Weld, Grew & Co., 1908, partner 1919, partner Jackson & Curtis, 1930; consol. with Weld, Grew & Co., 1930; partner Paine, Webber, Jackson & Curtis, later consol. from 1942; dir. Gen. Acceptance Corp. Home: Centerville, Mass. †

BRADLEY, ALBERT, foundation executive; born at Blackburn, Eng., May 29, 1891; s. Walter and Maria (Winward) B.; B.S., Dartmouth, 1915, LL.D., 1954; A.M., U. Mich., 1916, Ph.D., 1917, univ. fellow in econs., 1915-17; m. Helen Worcester, June 12, 1920; children—Charles W., Jeanne (Ingels). Assistant to comptroller Gen. Motors Corp., 1919; successively asst. comptroller asst. treas. and gen. asst. treas., v.p., 1929-42, exec. v.p. 1942-56, chmn. bd., 1956-58, now men. bd. dirs. Chmn. bd. trustees Alfred P. Sloan Found., until 1962, trustee, hon. chmn.; trustee Dartmouth Coll., 1953-61, then trustee emeritus; trustee Sloan-Kettering Institute, 1953-61. Served as 1st lt. U.S. Army, World War I. Mem. Phi Beta Kappa. Conglist. Clubs: University, Blind Brook, Round Hill, Country of Detroit; N.Y. Athletic, (N.Y.C.); Augusta National Golf; Gulf Stream Golf. Home: Greenwich, Conn. Died Sept. 11, 1983.

BRADLEY, BRUCE EMANUEL, naval officer; b. Raleigh, N.C.; s. William Harrison and Bessie Myrtle (Hickock) B.; grad. U. Va., 1926; m. Gertrude Elizabeth Mueller, Sept. 19, 1931; children—Gertrude Elizabeth (Mrs. Urschel), Bruce Emanuel. Commd. lt. (j.g.) M.C. USN, 1926, advanced through grades to rear adm., 1954; assigned Naval Hosp., Chelsea, Mass., 1926-27, then 7th Div., USMC, Nicaragua; stationed P.I., China, U.S., 1933-36; staff Naval Advanced Base Hosp., Bougainville and Finchaven, New Guinea, 1942-44, Naval Hosp., Long Beach, Cal., Bethesda, Md., Key West, Fla., then Oakland, Cal., 1948-54; joined staff med. bur. U.S. Navy, Washington, and became its dep. chief, 1955. Mem. A.M.A., Nu Sigma Nu. Home: Arlington, Va. Died Sept. 5, 1984.

BRADLEY, FREDERICK GORDON, Canadian govt. ofcl.; b. St. John's Newfoundland, Mar. 21, 1888; s. Norman N. and Evangeline M. (Trimm) B.; student Methodist Coll.; LL.B., Dalhousie U., 1914; read law with Justice Kent; m. Ethel Louis Roper, June 22, 1923; 2 sons, John Roper, Frederick Gordon. Admitted to bar as solicitor, 1914, created Kings Counsel, 1928; practiced as partner Sir A. B. Morine, 1918-22, under own name, 1922-24, 1933-39; chief magistracy, 1933-39. Elected to House of Assembly for District of Fort de Grave, 1924; Minister without portfolio in Munroe cabinet, 1924-26; resigned to take seat as Independent in House of Assembly, 1926; elected and apptd. mem. cabinet without portfolio, 1928; apptd. solicitor general, 1929; leader Liberal opposition in House Assembly, 1932-33; chief magistracy 1933-39; elected to Nat. Conv. as chmn. and served as leader 1st del. to Ottawa, 1946; apptd. Sec. State Can., 1949; mem. parliament Bonavista-Twillingate, 1949. Mem. treasury bd., Dept. Finance; pub. health and charities commn.; vice chmn. Statutes Consolidation Commn. Liberal. Mem. United Church of Can. Mason. Odd Fellow. Home: East Ottawa, Ont., Canada. †

BRADLEY, PRESTON, clergyman; b. Linden, Mich., Aug. 18, 1888; s. Robert McFarlan and Anna Elizabeth (Warren) B.; student Alma (Mich.) Coll., 1905-06; studied law, Flint, Mich., 1906-09; spl. work U. Mich., 1909-10; D.C.L., Hamilton Coll. Law, Chgo.; LL.D., Lake Forest Coll., 1938; D.D., Meadville Theol. Sch., 1939, Yankton Coll., 1966; m. Grace Wilkins Thayer, Nov. 25, 1915 (dec. 1950); one son, James (dec.); m. June Haslet, June 30, 1952. Student pastor, Grand Blanc, Mich., 1907-09, Ch. of Providence (Presbyn.), Chgo., 1911-12; withdrew from Presbyn. Ch., July 1, 1912, began preaching independently; founded Peoples Ch., Chgo., July 5, 1912; services at Wilson Ave. Theatre, 1913-19, Pantheon Theatre, Sheridan Rd., 1919-26; ch. built own bldg., costing furnished $750,000, dedicated, Oct. 10, 1926; united with Unitarian Conf., Feb. 9, 1922, accepting full fellowship with Unitarian Ch., Feb. 9, 1923; continued as pastor Peoples Ch., sr. pastor, until 1968. Bd. dirs. Chgo. Pub. Library, 1925-77; mem. Ill. State Tchrs. Coll. and Normal Sch. Bds. Recipient Merit award Ill. Dept. Conservation, 1952; Good Human Relations award Dale Carnegie Club Internat., 1955. Mem. Art Inst. Chgo., Izaak Walton League Am. (pres. 1930), Drama League Am., Phi Phi Alpha (Alma), Pi Gamma Mu. Clubs: Chgo. Press, City, Adventurers (Chgo.); Nat. Arts (N.Y.C.); Authors (London, Eng.). Author: Courage for Today, 1934; Mastering Fear, 1935; Power from Right Thinking, 1936; Life and You, 1940; New Wealth for You, 1941; Meditations, 1941; My Daily Strength, 1943; Happiness Through Creative Living, 1955; Along the Way, 1962; Between You and Me, 1967. Address: Chicago, Ill. Died June 1, 1983.

BRADLEY, R. FOSTER, univ. prof.; b. Troy, S.C., Nov. 30, 1889; s. Robert Foster (D.D.) and Martha (Wideman) B.; A.B., Univ. S.C., 1911, A.M., 1914; Ph.D., Univ. Wis., 1933; m. Rhoda Vandiver, June 21, 1917; children—Louise Ayer (Mrs. Frank R. Adams), James Vandiver. Assistant, University of South Carolina, 1911-12; instr. Georgia Tech., 1912-13; teacher of English, Columbia (S.C.) High Sch., 1913-14; teaching fellow, Univ. Wis., 1914-15, asst., 1915-17, instr. 1919-21, asst. prof. Romance langs., 1921-36; prof. and chmn. dept. Romance langs., Washington and Lee Univ. from 1936, Ball professor 1947. Served as 1st lt., U.S. Army, 1917-19; overseas March 1918-April 19. Mem. Am. Assn. Teachers of French, Am. Assn. Teachers of Spanish, Am. Assn. of Univ. Profs., Phi Beta Kappa. Presbyterian. Editor: French Literature before 1800 (with R. B. Michell), 1935; French Literature of the Nineteenth Century (with R. B. Michell), 1935; Eight Centuries of French Literature (with R. B. Michell), 1951. Home: Lexington, Va. †

BRADLEY, WILLIAM T., clergyman; b. Derry, Ireland, Oct. 3, 1911; s. William J. and Veronica (Cowley) B. Student, Mt. St. Mary Coll., Emmitsburg, Md., 1929-31; A.B., St. Charles Coll. Sem., Columbus, Ohio, 1933; postgrad., Mt. St. Mary Sem., Norwood, Ohio, 1933-37. Ordained priest (Roman Catholic Ch.), 1937, archdiocesan supt. schs., Santa Fe, 1944-64, archdiocesan dir. hosps., 1945-64, also archdiocesan dir. charities, from 1944; named Domestic Prelate by Pope Pius XII, 1950; apptd. diocesan consultor, 1951-64; resident chaplain St. Catherine Indian Sch., from 1950. Author articles. Chaplain N.M. Legislature Senate and House alternately, 1945-64; del., mem. state com. Mid-Century White House Conf. on Children and Youth; 1st v.p. Catholic Hosp. Assn., U.S. and, Can., 1956-57; mem. N.Mex. Fair Employment Practices Com., 1954-69, chmn., 1959-69; chmn. N.Mex. Health Com. Sch. Health, 1958, N.Mex. Bd. Edn. High Sch. Com., 1958. Mem. Nat. Catholic Edn. Assn. (exec. com., supt. dept. 1953-58). Club: K.C. (4 deg.). Home: Santa Fe, NM.

BRADWAY, JOHN SAEGER, educator; b. Swarthmore, Pa., Feb. 17, 1890; s. William and Jennie (Saeger) B.; A.B., Haverford Coll., 1911, A.M., 1915, LL.D., 1957; LL.B., U. Pa., 1914; m. Mary Henderson, June 11, 1921. Admitted to Pa. bar, 1914 practiced in Phila.; asst. atty. Phila. Legal Aid Soc., 1914-20; chief counsel Phila. Municipal Legal Aid Bur., 1920-22; pvt. practice, 1920-29; sec. Nat. Assn. Legal Aid Orgns., 1922-40 inclusive, pres., 1940-42; visiting prof. law and dir. legal aid clinic, U. of Southern Calif., summer, 1928, prof. and dir. same, 1929-31; prof. law and dir. legal aid clinic Duke U., Durham, N.C., 1931-59 vis. prof. U. of N.C. sch., social work, 1950-59; prof. law Hastings Coll. Law, 1960-65; law faculty Calif. Western U., San Diego, from 1965. Mem. Am. (chmn. legal aid com. 1938-39, sec. section family law 1958-62), Cal., Pa. (chmn. legal aid com. 1923-56), N.C. (chmn. legal aid com. 1933-51, 53-59), Phila., San Francisco bar assns., Order of Coif, Phi Beta Kappa, Phi Alpha Delta, Pi Gamma Mu, Tau Kappa Alpha. Republican. Rotarian (pres. Durham, N.C. 1936-37). Author. Contbr. law revs. Address: San Diego, Calif. †

BRADY, HUGH PICKEN, lumber co. exec.; b. Sitka, Alaska, Feb. 19, 1891; s. John Green and Elizabeth (Patton) B.; m. Mary Somerville Schieffelin, June 22, 1921; 1 dau., Cornelia Schieffelin (Mrs. H.G.A. Meili). Grad., Phillips Andover Acad., 1910; B.A., Yale, 1914; postgrad., U. Wash., 1959. Asst. mgr. A.C. Dutton Lumber Co., 1915-22, sec., 1920-22; owner, mgr. Colby Lumber Co., 1924-32; partner Brady & Ketcham Lumber Co., 1924-32; pres. Brady Internat. Lumber, Inc., Seattle, 1933—; now chmn. bd. Exec. com. Yale Alumni Bd., 1952-57, nat. com. chmn., 1955-57. Del.-at-large, 1961-66, del., 1967-72; chmn. council com. Yale Forestry Sch., 1961-66, mem. com., 1966-69; mem. exec. com. Snoqualmie Nat. Forestry Adv. Council, Sitka Hist. Restoration

Assn.; alumni rep. Phillips Andover Acad., 1940-62; Trustee Wash. Forestry Conf., Keep Wash. Green Assn. Recipient Yale medal, 1952; Outstanding Service award Wash. State Forestry Conf., 1973; named Distinguished Zete, 1960; fellow Davenport Coll. Yale, 1961-82. Fellow Forest History Assn.; mem. Wash. Conservation Soc. (past pres.), Yale Assn. Western Wash. (pres., chmn.), Zeta Psi (past nat. pres.), Alpha Delta Tau. Republican. Episcopalian. Clubs: University, Tennis, Washington Athletic, Seattle Yacht, Corinthian Yacht; Yale (N.Y.C.). Home: Seattle, Wash. Died Apr. 13, 1982.

BRADY, SCOTT (GERARD KENNETH TIERNEY), actor; b. Bklyn., Sept. 13, 1924; s. Lawrence Hugh and Mary Alice (Crowley) T.; m. Lisa Tirony, Dec. 24, 1967; children—Timothy Eamon Charles Francis, Terence Michael Anthony Vincent. Ed., Roosevelt High Sch., Yonkers, N.Y., 1939-42, Bliss-Hayden Drama Sch., Beverly Hills. Films include In This Corner, 1947, Born to Fight, Canon City, He Walked by Night, Port of New York, Undertow, Kansas Raider, Undercover, Girl, Model and the Marriage, Broker, Bronco Buster, Montana Belle, Untamed Frontier, Yankee Buccaneer, Bloodhounds of Broadway, Perilous Journey, El Alamein, White Fire, Johnny Guitar, Law vs. Billy the Kid, Gentlemen Marry Brunettes, Vanishing American, They Were So Young, Terror at Midnight, Mohawk, Maverick Queen, Fort Utah, Arizona Bushwackers, Dollars, The Loners, Wicked, Wicked, The China Syndrome, 1979, Gremlins, 1983. Served with USNR, 1942-45. Mem. Acad. Motion Picture Arts and Scis. Roman Catholic. Club: N.Y. Athletic. Address: Los Angeles, Calif. Died Apr. 16, 1985.

BRAGARNICK, ROBERT, marketing executive; b. Milw., June 22, 1919; s. Harry and Elizabeth (Maltz) B.; B.S., U. Pa.; m. Ruth Welander, Sept. 22, 1949; children—Peter Harry, Ellen Lisa. Successively with Ted Bates, Inc., Dancer-Fitzgerald-Sample, Blow-Beirn-Toiga, Inc., Revlon, Inc.; v.p., dir. Joseph E. Seagram & Sons, Inc., 1957-61; pres. Robert Bragarnick, Inc., marketing counsellors, 1961-85. Mem. exec. com. People to People Internat.; bd. dirs. St. John's U. Club: Westhampton Country. Home: New York, N.Y. Died May 14, 1985.

BRAISTED, FRANK A., naval officer; b. Detroit, Mich., Feb. 12, 1889; s. William C. and Lillian M. (Phipps) B.; B.S.M.S., U.S. Naval Academy, 1909; M.S., Columbia, 1916; sr. course, Naval War Coll., 1930; m. Margaret K. Buzard, Oct. 19, 1916; children—William R., Frank A., Jr. Commissioned ensign, U.S. Navy, 1911, and advanced through grades to rear admiral, 1942; served as midshipman, U.S.S. Connecticut and Delaware; served aboard U.S.S. New York and U.S.A.T., Dakotan; in command U.S.S. Beale, 1918 (spl. commendation); commanded destroyers Breckeridge, Fairfax and Hurlbert; Navy Yard Development Board, 1924-27; U.S.S. Tennessee, 1927-29; prodn. supt. Norfolk Navy Yard, 1930-32; command U.S.S. Sacramento, 1932-34; Army Indsl. Coll. and Personnel War Plans, 1935-37; command U.S.S. Trenton, 1937-39; dir. Naval Reserves, 9th Naval Dist., 1939-40; commander Transports Service Force, Pacific Fleet, 1940-42; commander Operational Training Command, Pacific Fleet, 1943-44; comdt. Naval Operating Bases, Guantanamo Bay, Cuba and Bermuda, B.W.I., 1944-46; pres. Board of Inspection and Survey from 1946. Awarded Legion of Merit, 1944. Address: Washington, D.C. Died Dec. 24, 1981.†

BRAMAN, JAMES D'ORMA, savs. and loan exec., former mayor of Seattle; b. Lorimor, Iowa, Dec. 23, 1901; s. Jacob Wesley and Susie Mae (Huntzinger) B.; student pub. schs., Bremerton, Wash.; m. Margaret V. Young, Nov. 27, 1920; children—James D'Orma, Robert C. Pres. Braman Millwork Supply Co., 1920-29, Braman Mill & Mfg. Co., Inc., Bremerton, 1929-43, Braman Lumber & Hardware Co., Inc., Seattle, 1946-56; chmn. bd. Shoreline Savs. & Loan Assn., Seattle, from 1952; mem. Seattle City Council, 1954-64; mayor of Seattle, 1964-69; asst. sec. U.S. Dept. of Transp., 1969-70. Rep. Seattle to Wash. State World's Fair Commn., 1957-62; mem. Seattle Center Adv. Commn.; mem. adv. council U.S. Conf. Mayors; chmn. Puget Sound Governmental Com.; mem. nat. council, pres. Chief Seattle council Boy Scouts Am. Trustee Pacific Sci. Center Found.; trustee, mem. steering com. Century 21 Corp., 1959-62. Served to comdr. USNR, 1942-46. Recipient Silver Beaver award Boy Scouts Am., 1949. Mem. Nat. League Cities (chmn. com. transp. and communications, mem. exec. bd.), Japan-Am. Conf. of Mayors and C. of C. Presidents (exec. com.), Seattle C. of C. Republican. Mason, Kiwanian. Home: Seattle, Wash. Deceased.

BRAMMER, KURT WILLIAM, elec. constrn. co. exec.; b. Copenhagen, Denmark, Apr. 25, 1905; s. William Heinrich and Asta (Larsen) B.; came to U.S., 1923, naturalized, 1929; grad. high sch.; m. Mary Elizabeth Bagnall, Nov. 4, 1939; children—Mary Olive and Elizabeth Ann (twins). With L.E. Myers Co., Chgo., 1925-79, dir., 1946-79, v.p., 1950-55, exec. v.p., 1955-63, pres., 1963-76, chmn. 1946-79, 1970-79, cons., 1979-82. Mem. Nat., Cook County, Chgo. elec. contractors assns. Republican. Congregationalist. Clubs: Masons, Shriner, Union League (Chgo.); Country of N.C. (Pinehurst). Home: Pinehurst, N.C. Died July 15, 1982.

BRANCH, RUSSELL T., engring. exec.; b. Port Jervis, N.Y., June 5, 1889; s. George E. and Almeda L. (Van Noy) B.; M.E., Stevens Inst. Tech., 1912, E.D., 1952; m. Lelia G. McGaw, Sept. 1, 1914; children—Russell T., F. Elizabeth, George E., Kathryn. With Stone & Webster Engring. Corp., N.Y.C., from 1912, in direct supervision of elec. and mech. installations, and resident engr. on constrn. projects, 1912-22, supt. of constrn. in direct responsible charge of constrn. of various projects, 1922-30, constrn. mgr. in supervisory charge constrn. projects, 1930-33, vice pres. and sr. constrn. mgr. in exec. charge constrn. activities, 1933-43, exec. vice pres. in exec. charge constrn. electromagnetic plant and related works, War Dept. atomic bomb plant at Clinton Engr. Works, Oak Ridge, Tenn., also gen. direction all constrn. operations of corp., 1943-44, pres., 1944-55, chmn., 1955 from, also dir. Mem. Army Ordnance Assn., Newcomen Society (N.Y. com.), Sigma Nu. Republican. Clubs: Manhasset Bay (L. I.) Yacht; Stevens Metropolitan, India House (New York). Home: Manhassett, L.I., N.Y. †

BRAND, GEORGE E., lawyer; b. Houghton, Mich., June 11, 1888; s. George and Isabella (Monville) B.; LL.B., University of Michigan (Ann Arbor), 1912, LL.M. (honorary), 1949; associate editor Mich. Law Review; m. Elsie B. Jones, June 25, 1914; children—George E. (lt. U.S. Navy), Marjorie A. (wife of Charles R. Turner), Barbara E. (wife of Lt. G. Neilan Smith). Admitted to bar, 1912; associated with Bernard B. Selling, Detroit, Mich., 1912-13; partner in firm Selling & Brand, 1913-18; individual practice from 1918. Chmn. Wayne County (Mich.) Selective Service Appeal Bd., 1940-44. Mem. Mich. Bd. of Law Examiners, 1933-38. Mem. Am. Judicature Soc. (chmn. bd. dirs., 1942-45, pres. from 1945), Am. Bar Assn. (govt. from 1947; del. from 1936; com. on unauthorized practice of law, 1936-37; spl. com. on law lists, 1939-40; com. on professional ethics and grievances, 1940-45 and 1946-49), State Bar of Mich. (commr. at large 1935-38, pres. 1937-38), Detroit Bar Assn. (bd. dirs. 1928-37, pres. 1934-35), Gamma Eta Gamma, Woolsack Soc. Clubs: Lawyers (New York); Detroit, Detroit Athletic. Author: Unauthorized Practice Decisions, 1937. Home: Detroit, Mich. †

BRANSON, KATHARINE FLEMING, educator; b. Coatesville, Pa., Feb. 7, 1887; d. Henry James and Mary Francis (Parke) B.; grad. high sch., Coatesville, 1903, The Misses Shipley Sch., Bryn Mawr, Pa., 1905; A.B., Byrn Mawr Coll., 1909. Teacher, St. Mary's Sch., Mount St. Gabriel, Peekskill, N.Y., 1910-12, Girton Sch., Winnetka, Ill., 1912-14, Miss Beard's Sch., Orange, N.J., 1914-17, also dir. studies, 1919-20; sec. Miss Madeira's Sch., Washington, D.C., 1917-19; headmistress The Katharine Branson Sch., Ross, Calif., from 1920. Presbyn. Club: Women's City (San Francisco).†

BRAUCHER, ROBERT, judge; b. N.Y.C., Feb. 23, 1916; s. Howard S. and Edna Vaughan (Fisher) B.; m. Mary Elizabeth King, Jan. 15, 1942; children—Roberta, William King, Jean, Karen. A.B. with high honors, Haverford Coll., 1936; LL.B. magna cum laude, Harvard, 1939. Bar: N.Y. bar 1939, Mass. bar 1950. Asso. firm Hughes, Richards, Hubbard & Ewing, N.Y.C., 1939-41; vis. prof. law Harvard Law Sch., Cambridge, Mass., 1946-49, prof. law, 1949-71; asso. justice Supreme Jud. Ct. Mass., 1971-81; Fulbright lectr. Chuo and Tokyo univs., Japan, 1959; vis. prof. law U. Minn., 1968-69; cons. N.Y. Law Revision Commn.; v.p. Nat. Commn. on Uniform State Laws, 1967-70; Mass. commr. Uniform State Laws, 1954-71; reporter Restatement of Contracts 2d, 1960-71; mem. Mass. Statutory Spl. Com. on Code of Ethics, 1961-62, Mass. Atty. Gen. Adv. Council on Conflict of Interest; chmn. Nat. Commn. on Consumer Finance, 1969-71, Nat. Inst. for Consumer Justice, 1971-73. Author: (with Riegert) Documents of Title, 3d edit, 1978, (with Fuller) Basic Contract Law, 1964, (with Riegert) Introduction to Commercial Transactions, 1977; Editor: (with Riegert) Harvard Law Rev, 1937-39. Vice-pres. Unitarian- Universalist Laymen's League, 1965-66; mem. Belmont Sch. Com., 1961-68, chmn., 1966-68. Served to maj. USAAF, 1941-45, CBI; Served to maj. USAAF, PTO; to lt. col. USAF Res., 1946-55. Decorated Legion of Merit, D.F.C., Air medal. Mem. Atlantic Union Com., Am. Vets. Com., ABA (mem. council sect. corp. law 1973-77, bd. of editors 1975-81), Mass. Bar Assn., Am. Legion, Am. Law Inst. (mem. council 1972-81), Phi Beta Kappa. Republican. Unitarian. Home: Arlington, Mass. Died Aug. 26, 1981.

BRAULICK, EDWARD JOSEPH, clergyman; b. Albany, Minn., Mar. 8, 1887; s. Frank Paul and Henrietta (Radtke) B.; B.A., Wartburg Coll., Clinton, Ia., 1907; student Wartburg Theol. Sem., 1907-10, U. of S.D., 1912-13; M.A., Capitol U., Columbus, O., 1916; student U. of Minn., summers 1914, 15, U. of Tex., 1930-33; D.S.T., Am. Theol. Sem., 1941; B.L.D., Temple Hall, 1946; m. Ida Penzer, Aug. 19, 1911; children—Roald Edward, Hiltrude Irene, Paulus Henry, Ruth Arlene, Edith Mae, Wilfred James. Prof. of English, Eureka (S.D.) Luth. Coll., 1910-13. Wartburg Normal Coll., Waverly, Ia., 1913-17; pastor Luth. Ch., Oelwein, Ia., 1917-29; prof. of Bible, Tex. Luth. Coll. at Seguin, Tex., 1929-35; pres. Wartburg Coll., Waverly, Ia., 1935-45; pastor Lutheran Ch., Seguin, Texas from 1945. President Texas Lutheran Chautauqua, 1929-32. Vice pres. Am. Luth. Ch., 1950-52; treas. Bd. of Mexican Missions, Luth. Ch., 1929-35; ex-pres. Oelwein Sch. Bd., Iowa Dist., Luth. Ch.; mem. Four-Minute Men, Luth. Orphans' Home Soc. Mem. Assn. Collegiate Registrars, Am. Lutheran Ednl. Conf.; ex.pres. Nat. Luth. Ednl. Conf. Republican. Lion. Author of books, latest being: Lutheran Church Polity. Home: Seguin, Tex. †

BRAUN, THEODORE WILLIAM, public relations executive; b. Newark, Dec. 26, 1901; s. Adam and Elizabeth (Bayles) B.; m. Beatrice Banning, July 3, 1920. Spl. student, Harvard Sch. Bus. Chmn. bd. Braun & Co., Los Angeles, from 1936; past dir. Corp. for Pub. Broadcasting.; Cons. comdg. gen. Fourth Army, Western Def. Command, 1941-43; dir. tech. info. div. A.S.F., 1944; staff mem. Gordon Gray Report to Pres., U.S. fgn. and econ. policy, 1950; mem. spl. com. on reorgn. NSC, 1953, asst. to sec. treas., 1953-54, cons., 1955, mem. adv. com. to sec. def. on gen. mil. tng., 1962; gov. U.S. Postal Service, 1971, 72. Past pres. Hollywood Bowl Assn.; trustee Harvey Mudd Coll., Good Samaritan Hosp., Los Angeles. Mem. C. of C., Town Hall (past gov., past pres.). Clubs: Metropolitan (Washington, N.Y.C.); Men's Garden of Los Angeles (Los Angeles) (past pres.), Bel Air Country (Los Angeles), California (Los Angeles) (past pres.); Eldorado Country (Indian Wells, Calif.). Home: Los Angeles, Calif. Dec. Mar. 26, 1983.

BRAUTIGAN, RICHARD, author; b. 1935. Author: A Confederate General from Big Sur, 1965, Trout Fishing in America, 1967, The Pill Versus the Springhill Mine Disaster, 1968, In Watermelon Sugar, 1969, Rommel Drives on Deep into Egypt, 1970, The Abortion: An Historical Romance, 1971, Revenge of the Lawn, 1971, The Hawkline Monster-A Gothic Western, 1974, Willard and His Bowling Trophies: A Perverse Mystery, 1975, Sombrero Fallout: A Japanese Novel, 1976, Dreaming of Babylon: A Private Eye Novel 1942, 1977, June 30th, June 30th, 1978, The Tokyo-Montana Express, 1980. Address: New York, N.Y. Died Oct. 25, 1984. *

BRAWNER, JAMES PAUL, educator; b. Magazine, Ark., Aug. 10, 1902; s. Robert L. and Eva Mae (Thomason) B.; A.B., Washington and Lee U., 1924, A.M., 1925; Ph.D., U. Ill., 1935; m. Kirby Lee Smith, June 21, 1925. Faculty Ark. State Tchrs. Coll., 1925-29; asst., instr. U. Ill., 1929-35; faculty W.Va. U., from 1935, asst. prof. English, 1936-45, asso. prof., 1945-52, chmn. dept., 1949-67, prof., 1952-72, prof. emeritus, 1972-84. Vis. prof. U. Ark., Eastern Mich. State U., Ypsilanti, faculty U. Tng. Center, Florence, Italy, 1945. U.S. cons. Office Edn., Dept. Health, Edn. and Welfare, 1966. Mem. Internat. Assn. U. Profs. English, Modern Lang. Assn., Am. Assn. U. Profs. Nat. Council Tchrs. English, Phi Beta Kappa (nat. council, pres. South Atlantic dist. 1967-70), Phi Kappa Phi, Sigma Upsilon. Author: The Wars of Cyrus, 1942. Author articles on English drama, Am. writers. Home: Morgantown, W.Va. Died Aug. 7, 1984.

BRCIN, JOHN DAVID, sculptor; b. Gracac, Yugoslavia, Aug. 15, 1899; s. David and Milica (Kesich) B.; pres. edn., gymnasium, Gracac; came to U.S., 1913; student Valparaiso U., 1961-17; B.F.A., Art Inst., Chgo., 1946; M.A., Ohio State U., 1930; m. Blanche Elizabeth Moore, June 14, 1923. Instr. modeling and drawing Mpls. Sch. Art, 1922-23; head of sculpture dept. Layton Sch. Art, Milw., 1923-24; instr. modeling Rockford (Ill.) Coll., 1934-36. Prin. works: Mark Twain (owned by City of Chgo.); Caroline (owned by Witte Meml. Mus., San Antonio); portrait bust of Judge Elbert H. Gary for Gary Commerical Club; meml. tablet to Newton, Mann, 1st Unitarian Ch. of Omaha; Rudulph Hering Medal for Am. Soc. C.E.; meml. tablet to Benjamin Franklin Lounsbury, Washington Blvd. Hosp., Chgo.; sculpture for Joslyn Meml. Art Mus., Omaha, (home of Symphony Orch. of Omaha); monument to Cyrus Hall McCormick, campus of Washington and Lee U.; monument to Gov. Henry Horner, Grant Park, Chgo.; Stephen Decatur Monument for Decatur, Ill., heroic portrait bust of Stepehn Decatur for U.S. Naval Acad., Annapolis; bust of Mark Twain for North Central Coll., Naperville, Ill.; exhibited at N.A.D., Pa. Acad. Fine Arts, Art Inst. Chgo., Detroit Inst. Arts, Mus. Fine Arts, Houston, Cal. Palace of Legion of Honor, Bklyn. Mus., Albright Art Gallery, Buffalo, Dayton Art Inst., White Meml. Mus., San Antonio, John Herron Art Inst., Indpls., Milw. Art Inst.; represented in permanent collections U. Ill., Roosevelt U., Pioneer Mus. Art, Stockton, Cal., Evansville (Ind.) Mus. Arts, various pub. schs. Bryan Lathrop European traveling fellow Art Inst., Chgo., 1920, certificate of merit, 1922, Mrs. John C. Shaffer prize, 1923, William M.R. French meml. gold medal, 1926 Municipal Art League portrait prize, 1945; Catherine Barker Spaulding prize, Hoosier Salon, Hickox prize, 1936; Mem. Nat. Sculpture Soc. Club: Cliff Dwellers. Author: The Sculpture of John David Brcin, 1967. Died Oct. 31, 1983.

BRECHER, SAMUEL, artist; b. Boryslaw, Austria; came to U.S., 1910, naturalized, 1922; s. Louis and Pauline (Furchtsam) B.; m. Florence Kaplan, June 18, 1933. Grad., Soc. Home: New York, NY. N.Y.C., 1921; student, Nat. Acad. Design, N.Y.C., 1921-25, N.Y. U., 1934-35; studied with, Charles W. Hawthorne, Provincetown, Mass. faculty Newark Sch. Fine and Indsl. Arts, 1946-74. Exhibited one man shows, A.C.A. Gallery, N.Y.C., 1935, Hudson D. Walker Gallery, N.Y.C., 1938, 40, Kraushaar Galleries, N.Y.C., 1942, 44, 92d St. YMHA, N.Y.C., 1946, Babcock Galleries, N.Y.C., 1949, 51, Merrill Gallery, N.Y.C., 1962, YMHA Bergen County, N.J., 1966, Winston Gallery, Ft. Lee, N.J., 1970-77, Cottage Gallery, Provincetown, Mass., 1979, 82, St. Peter's Coll. Art Gallery, Jersey City, N.J., 1983, others; exhibited group shows in museums, throughout

U.S.; represented in permanent collections, Met. Mus. of Art, N.Y.C., Walker Art Center, Mpls., Newark Mus. of Art, Fla. So. Coll., Lakeland, Fla., Smithsonian Instn., Tel Aviv and Ein Harod Mus., Israel, Jewish Mus., N.Y.C. Recipient First Salmagundi Club Prize in Oil Painting, 1950, prize in oil painting N.Y. State Fair, 1951, Audubon prize in casein, 1953, second prize Art League of L.I., 1954, Audubon prize oil painting, 1956, 83, Talens prize for oil painting Allied Artists Exhbn., 1960, first prize Nat. Soc. Casein Painters, 1962, prize for oil painting Painters and Sculptors Soc. N.J., 1982. Mem. Audubon Artists, Allied Artists, Nat. Soc. Casein Painters, N.J. Painters and Sculptors Soc. Home: New York, NY.

BRECKENRIDGE, JAMES DOUGLAS, educator; b. N.Y.C., Aug. 8, 1926; s. Clarence E. and Erna (Gritschke) B.; m. Dorte Ulrich, Jan. 8, 1964; children—Alexander D., Susanne U. A.B., Cornell U., 1945; M.F.A., Princeton, 1949, Ph.D., 1957. Curator Corcoran Gallery Art, Washington, 1952-55, Balt. Mus. Art, 1955-60; research fellow Am. Council Learned Socs., 1959-60; vis. assoc. prof. U. Pitts., 1960-61; assoc. prof. dept. art Northwestern U., 1961-66, prof., 1966-83, chmn. dept., 1964-72, chmn. dept. art history, 1972-74; art critic Chicago's Am., 1962-64; Mem. Inst. Advanced Study, Princeton, N.J., 1974-75; Bd. dirs. Internat. Center of Medieval Art. Author: Numismatic Iconography of Justinian 11, 1959, Likeness, 1969. Sr. fellow Nat. Endowment for Humanities, 1970-71; Fulbright research fellow Bulgaria, 1982. Fellow Am. Numis. Soc., Royal Numis. Soc., Royal Soc. Arts; mem. Coll. Art Assn. Am. (dir.), Am. Inst. Archeology, Soc. Archtl. Historians, Mediaeval Acad. Am. (councillor), Municipal Art Commn. Evanston (pres. 1972-75), Midwest Art History Soc. (pres.). Home: Evanston, Ill. Dec. Dec. 18, 1982.

BRECKNER, ELMER LEANDER, educator; b. Chapin, Ill., Sept. 13, 1888; s. Augustus and Laura Belle (Hamilton) B.; A.B., B.S., U. of Mo., 1913; A.M., U. of Wash., 1939; student U. of Mont., summers 1914, 15, Wash. State Coll., summer 1917, U. of Wash., summers 1916, 24, 26, 29; m. Eugenia Vaughan, June 14, 1916; 1 son, Norman Vaughan. Teacher and prin. pub. schs., Mo., Okla., Mont., Wash. and Ida., 1906-18; prin. high sch., Olympia, Wash., 1919-20, supt. pub. schs., 1920-31; supt. pub. schools, Tacoma, Wash., 1931-37; asst. supt. in charge of administration and finance. Member of N.E.A., Washington Education Assn., Nat. Soc. for Study of Edn., Progressive Edn. Assn., Phi Delta Kappa, Phi Alpha Delta. Democrat. Methodist. Mason. Kiwanian. Home: Tacoma, Wash. †

BREDELL, HAROLD HOLMES, lawyer; b. Indpls., June 18, 1907; s. Jesse Bailey and Flora E. (Glasscock) B.; m. Victoria Schreiber, Apr. 20, 1939 (dec. Dec. 1975); children—Harold H., Philip K. A.B., Butler U., 1929; LL.B., Harvard, 1932. Bar: Ind. bar 1932. Practiced in, Indpls.; mem. firm Bredell Martin McTurnan & Meyer, 1947-80; chmn. Vernon Fire & Casualty Ins. Co., Vernon Gen. Ins. Co.; pres., dir. Vernon Financial Corp., Ins. Investment Corp.; lectr. Ind. Law Sch., 1938-40. Contbr. legal jours. Bd. dirs. Festival Music Soc., 1978-82. Served as lt. USNR, 1944-46. Mem. ABA (treas., mem. bd. govs. 1949-59, bd. dirs. endowment 1959-75, treas. 1959-65, v.p. 1969-71, pres. endowment 1971-73), Ind. Bar Assn., Indpls. Bar Assn., C. of C., Ind. Soc. Chgo., Ind. Harvard Law Assn. Republican. Episcopalian. Clubs: Lawyers (Indpls.), Harvard (Indpls.), Columbia (Indpls.); Highland Country, Traders Point Hunt. Home: Indianapolis, Ind. Died Feb. 23, 1982.

BREDER, CHARLES MARCUS, JR., biologist; b. Jersey City, June 25, 1897; s. Charles Marcus and Albertine Louise (Agthe) B.; D.Sc. (hon.), Newark U.; m. Ruth B. Demarest, Nov. 18, 1918; children—Charles Marcus III, Richard Frederick; m. 2d, Ethel Lear Snyder, Apr. 17, 1933; m. 3d, Priscilla Rasquin, Jan. 3, 1967. With U.S. Bur. Fisheries, 1919-21; aquarist N.Y. Aquarium, 1921-25, research asso., 1925-33, asst. dir., 1933-37, acting dir., 1937-40, dir., 1940-43, research asso., 1944-83; curator, chmn. dept. fishes and aquatic biology Am. Mus. Natural History, 1944-60, dept. ichthyology, 1960-65, curator emeritus, 1965-83. Participant numerous sci. expdns. including Marsh Darien (Panama), 1924, Mexican Cave expdn., 1940, Fla. tarpon lab., 1938-42, Ecuador for OSRD, 1942, NRC Commn. utilization marine shore resources, 1943; Lerner Marine Lab., Bimini, Bahamas, 1947-57; research asso. Am. Mus. Nat. History, 1926-43, Bingham Oceanographic Found., Yale, 1933-57; vis. prof. N.Y. U., 1941-52. Mem. adv. bd. Mote Marine Lab., 1958-66, bd. dirs., research asso., 1967-75. Fellow N.Y. Zool. Soc., AAAS, N.Y. Acad. Sci. (A. Cressy Morrison prize 1925); mem. Am. Fisheries Soc., Am. Soc. Ichthyologists and Herpetologists (pres. 1932, gov. 1932—), Am. Soc. Zoologists, Chgo. Acad. Scis. (hon. life). Author: Fishes of the Atlantic Const., 1929. Contbr. to numerous tech. jours. Home: Englewood, Fla. Died Sept. 28, 1983.

BREDVOLD, LOUIS IGNATIUS, prof. English; b. Springfield, Minn., July 20, 1888; s. Ludvig L. and Nila (Nillson) B.; student Luther Coll., Decorah, Ia., 1903-07; A.B., U. of Minn., 1909, A.M., 1910; Ph.D., U. of Ill., 1921; grad. study, U. of Chicago, 1913-14; m. Emilie Ray Bowman, Sept. 17, 1923. Teacher in high schs., 1910-13; instr. English, Ia. State Coll., 1914-16; fellow in English, U. of Chicago, 1913-14; instr. English, U. of Ill., 1916-17 and 1919-20, fellow in English, 1920-21; instr. in English, U. of Mich., 1921-23, asst. professor, 1923-27, associate professor, 1927-30; professor, 1930 from, Henry Russell lecturer, 1957, chmn. of dept. of English, 1936-47; visiting prof., U. of Chicago, summers, 1926, 31, Johns Hopkins, 1933, U. of Minn., summer, 1935, Northwestern U., summer, 1938; visiting prof., Univ. of Calif. (Berkeley), 1947. Served as 1st lt. Co. I, 343d Inf., and Co. M, 39th Inf., U.S. Army, 1917-19, World War. Mem. Modern Lang. Assn. Am. (editorial bd. 1938-48). Mich. Acad., Am. Assn. Univ. Profs., Phi Kappa Phi. Awarded John Simon Guggenheim Foundation fellowship, 1929-30. Republican. Clubs: University, Research, Tudor and Stuart (Baltimore). Author: The Intellectual Milieu of John Dryden, 1934. Editor: Contbr. to mags. Home: Ann Arbor, Mich. †

BREEDING, EARLE GRIFFITH, M.D.; b. Denton, Md., Feb. 14, 1888; s. William R. and Cora G. B.; M.D., U. of Md. Sch. of Medicine and Coll. Phys. and Surg., 1913; m. Mary Brining, Sept. 10, 1919; one dau. Practiced at Washington, D.C., from 1917; specializes in treatment of nose, throat and ears; prof. oto-laryngology, George Washington Med. Sch. Fellow Am. Coll. Surgeons; mem. Am. Med. Assn., Med. Soc. of D.C. Democrat. Episcopalian. Clubs: Rotary, Congressional Country. Home: Washington, D.C. †

BREEN, JOHN WILLIAM, athletics mgr.; b. Milw., May 9, 1907; s. Charles Archibald and Kate (Walker) B.; m. Elizabeth Grey, Aug. 20, 1938; children—John William, Anne Breen, Andy. Ph.B., Carroll Coll., 1935; M.S., U. Wis., 1942. Asso. prof., head coach and athletic dir. Carroll Coll., Waukesha, Wis., 1938-49; asso. prof., head coach, athletic dir. Lake Forest (Ill.) Coll., 1949-57; dir. player personnel Chgo. Cardinals football team, 1957-59; v.p., dir. pub. relations Houston Oilers football team, 1959-72, gen. mgr., from 1971. Served to lt. comdr. USNR, 1942-45. Recipient U.S. Football Writers honesty award, 1973; named to Hall of Fame Carroll Coll., 1973, Hall of Fame Lake Forest Coll., 1974. Mem. Tau Kappa Epsilon. Presbyn. (elder). Clubs: Mason, Champion Golf. Home: Houston, Tex. Died Feb. 9, 1984.

BREIT, GREGORY, physicist, educator; b. Russia, July 14, 1899; s. Alfred and Alexandra (Smirnova) B.; came to U.S., 1915, naturalized, 1918; A.B., Johns Hopkins, 1918, A.M., 1920, PH.D., 1921, LL.D. (hon.), 1976; D.Sc. (hon.), U. Wis., 1954; m. Marjorie MacDill, Dec. 30, 1927. Nat. Research fellow U. Lelden, Holland, 1921-22, Harvard, 1922-23; asst. prof. physics Minn. U., 1923-24; math. physicist dept. terrestrial magnetism Carnegie Inst., Washington, 1924-29; prof. physics, N.Y. U., 1929-34, U. Wis., 1934-47; prof. physics Yale, 1947-58, Donner prof. 1958-68; Distinguished prof. physics SUNY, Buffalo, 1968-73, Distinguished prof. emeritus, 1973-81; research assoc. Carnegie Inst., Washington, 1929-44; vis. mem. Inst. for Advanced Study, Princeton, N.J., 1935-36; resident Technische Hochschule, Zurich, Switzerland, 1928. War work; degaussing Naval Ordnance Lab., Washington Navy Yard, 1940- 41; sect. mem. OSRD, NDRC 1940-42; coordinator fast neutron project Met. Lab., U. Chgo., 1942; Radiation Lab. Johns Hopkins, 1942-43; Aberdeen Proving Ground, Md., 1943-45. Recipient Franklin medal Franklin Inst. Phila., 1964; Nat. Medal of Sci., 1967. Fellow Am. Phys. Soc. (T.I. Bonner prize 1969), IEEE, Phys. Soc. (London), AAAS, Am. Acad. Arts and Scis., Washington Acad. Sci., Geophys. Union; mem. Nat. Acad. Sci., Phi Beta Kappa, Sigma Xi. Contbr. articles to profl. jours. Address: Buffalo, N.Y. Died Sept. 13, 1981.

BREMER, EDITH TERRY, social service administrator; born at Hamilton, N.Y., Oct. 9, 1889; d. Benjamin Stites and Mary Colfax (Baldwin) Terry; A.B., U. Chgo., 1907; grad. study Chgo. Sch. Social Work, 1907-08, N.Y. Sch. Social Work, 1911. Univ. Geneva, 1925, N.Y. Univ., 1955 from; married Harry M. Bremer, Sept. 4, 1912. Survey women in trade unions, Chgo., 1907-08; field study Chgo. Juvenile Ct., 1908; spl. agt. U.S. Immigration Commn., 1909-10; worker fgn. born U. Chgo. Settlement, 1909-10; nat. organizer work for immigrant girls, nat. bd. YMCA, 1910-18; exec. div. fgn. born women Nat. War Work Council, 1918-22; exec. dept. Immigration and Fgn. Communities, pioneer Internat. Inst. Movement, 1922-36; co-founder Internat. Social Service (formerly Internat. Migration Service), 1926; founder Am. Fedn. Internat. Institutes, Inc., N.Y.C. (formerly Nat. Inst. Immigrant Welfare), exec. dir. 1936-54, dir. emeritus, 1954 from; acting dir. Internat. Inst. N.Y., Inc., 1955-58, executive vice pres., 1958 from; leader of development U.S. Displaced Persons Program, 1948-52; mem. adv. com. Refugee Relief Program, 1954. Dir. Maniu Roumanian American Relief Foundation; mem. bd. Polish Am. Social Service Bureau. Decorated by Pres. Masaryk, Order of White Lion, Czechoslovakia, 1927; awarded citation as useful citizen U. Chgo. Alumni Assn., 1951; Nat. Fellowship award for activities Internat. Inst. Movement, Phila. Fellowship Commn., 1953; mem. N.Y. com. on immigration and naturalization. Mem. Am. Acad. Polit. and Social Sci., Am. Assn. Social Workers, Internat. Conf. Social Work. Methodist. Club: Chicago (New York City). Sponsor Folk Songs of Many Nations, compiled by Florence Botsford. Contbr. frequent articles Social Work Year Book, Annals, U.S. Immigration Review, Survey, Rural Life, others. Home: Port Washington, N.Y. †

BRENNAN, EDWARD THOMAS, fgn. service officer; b. Toorak, Australia, Feb. 28, 1921; s. William Rowley and Katherine Angela (Donovan) B.; came to U.S., 1922, naturalized, 1924; B.S. in Fgn. Service, Georgetown U., 1949; m. Denise Helen Meier, Dec. 31, 1945; children—Kevin, Denise, Edward Thomas, Peter. Joined U.S. Fgn. Service, 1941; assigned Dept. State, 1941-42, charge diplomatic courier ops. for Latin Am., South Pacific and No. Europe, 1947-50, chief couriers, 1952-53, officer charge European region, Paris, 1953-54, Frankfurt am Main, Germany, 1954-56; assigned Am. embassy, Manila, 1957-59, Tunis, Tunisia, 1959-63; dep. chief mission, counselor Am. embassy, Bangui, Central African Republic, 1963-66; assigned Nat. War Coll., Washington, 1966-67; spl. asst. internat. affairs div. plans and ops. USAF, 1967-68, asst. dep. dir. plans for policy, 1968-69, dir. Office Multilateral Policy and Programs, Dept. State, 1969-71, U.S. consul gen., Thessaloniki, Greece, 1971-75; counselor of embassy for refugee and migration affairs U.S. Mission to UN, Geneva, 1975-; alt. del. U.S. del. to 16th Gen. Conf., UNESCO, Paris, 1970; del. exec. bd. Intergovtl. Com. on European Migration, also exec. coms. UN High Commn. for Refugees, Geneva, 1976-77. Served as aviator USNR, 1942-47, 50-52. Recipient Exceptional Civilian Service commendation Dept. Air Force, 1970; Superior Service award Dept. State, 1971, 79. Mem. Am. Fgn. Service Assn., U.S. Naval Inst., Georgetown U. Alumni Assn. Clubs: Army and Navy, Am. Internat. (Geneva). Home: Bethesda, Md. Died Sept. 25, 1979

BRENNAN, VINCENT M., judge; b. Mt. Clemens, Mich., Apr. 22, 1890; s. Charles T. and Mary Agnes (Morrison) B.; A.B., Detroit Coll., 1909; LL.B., Harvard Univ., 1912; M.A., Univ. of Detroit, 1914; LL.D., from same university, 1927; m. Ruth Hurley July 17, 1915; children—Ann (Mrs. Richard Moore), Vincent M., John Hurley. Legal adviser to Mich. State Labor Dept., 1912-13; asst. corp. counsel, Detroit, 1915-20; mem. Mich. Senate, 1919-20, mem. 67th Congress (1921-23), 13th Mich. Dist. Judge Circuit Court, Wayne County, Mich., 5 terms, 1924-54; author Brennan Act, passed by Mich. legislature, 1919, in behalf of World War Vets. Past pres. Cardinal Newman Foundation of Detroit, Mem. Michigan State Bar, Detroit Bar Assn., Delta Theta Phi. K.C. (4 deg.), Clubs: Harvard (Mich.), Detroit Golf. Home: Detroit, Mich. †

BRENNER, JAMES EMMET, law educator; b. Rensselaer, Ind., Nov. 10, 1889; s. John J. and Carrie (Mantor) B.; B.S. U.S. Naval Acad., 1913, grad. study, 1919-20; J.D., Stanford, 1927; m. Florence M. Marshall, Sept. 12, 1914; children—James Emmet, John Marshall. Admitted to Calif. bar, 1927; exec. sec. State Bar of Calif., 1929-30, research dir., 1930-51; law librarian, Stanford, 1927-32, associate prof. law, 1928-36, professor of law, 1936-55, emeritus professor of law, from 1955. Director of Western area, Am. Law Inst. and Am. Bar Assn. for continuing legal edn.; mem. Council for Survey of Legal Profession. Recalled to active duty as lt. comdr. United States Navy, May 1941, promoted to rank of captain, 1944. Member American, California, San Francisco bar associations, Delta Theta Phi, Order of the Coif. Mem. Presbyn. Ch. Clubs: Bohemian, Commonwealth (San Francisco); Army and Navy (Washington, D.C.); St. Francis Yacht Club (San Francisco); Officers Club (Annapolis). Mem. adv. bd. Am. Bar Assn. Jour. Home: Palo Alto, Calif. †

BRERETON, WILLIAM DENNY, JR., naval officer; b. Globe, Ariz., Dec. 15, 1887; s. William Denny and Helen (Hyde) B.; ed. pub. and private grade schs., Pittsburgh; m. Nancy Harrison Collins, May 1, 1912; children—Helen Hyde (Mrs. Robert Dwight Swezey), Nancy Marshall, Sara Burton. Became midshipman, U.S. Navy, 1904; promoted through grades to capt.; comdr. U.S. transport and U.S.S. Elcano in Far East, World War; later comdr. U.S.S. Brooklyn; now naval attaché, Argentine. Decorated Comdr. Order of Leopold, II; Victory medal. Clubs: Army and Navy, Chevy Chase, Washington. Home: Pittsburgh, Pa.†

BRESLER, EMANUEL HAROLD, med. educator; b. Pensacola, Fla., Mar. 2, 1919; s. Joseph and Rae (Berson) B.; B.S., U. Fla., 1941; M.D., Tulane, 1947; m. Jean Barnett, Sept. 3, 1950; children—Harvey Joel, Eve Michele, Jonathan Daniel. NIH cardiovascular research fellow Tulane, New Orleans, 1948-50; instr. physiology N.Y. U. Bellevue Sch. Medicine, 1950-51; pvt. practice medicine Miami, Fla., 1953-55; mem. faculty Tulane U., 1955-81, asso. prof. medicine, 1959-63, prof., 1963-81; dir. research VA Hosp., New Orleans, 1957-76, med. investigator, 1976-81. Served to capt. AUS, 1943-46, USAF, 1951-53. Diplomate Am. Bd. Internal Medicine. Mem. Am. Physiologic Soc., Biophysical Soc., Am. Soc. Nephrology, A.M.A., Am. Fedn. Clin. Research, A.A.A.S., Am. Heart Assn., Phi Beta Kappa (recipient Querens Rives Shore award). Devel. of theory of peritubular physicochemical determinats of fluid absorption across kidney tubules with particular reference to regulation of volume of body fluid. Home: New Orleans, La. Died June 21, 1981.

BREUER, MARCEL LAJOS, architect; b. Pecs, Hungary, May 22, 1902; s. Jacques and Franciska (Kan) B.; grad. Magyar Kir, Forealiskola, Pecs, Hungary, 1920; M.A., Bauhaus, Weimer, Germany, 1924; Dr. Govt. Hungary (hon.), 1968; D.Arts, Harvard U., 1970; D.F.A. (hon.), Pratt Inst., 1969; D.Arts (hon.), U. Notre Dame; m. Martha Erps, Aug. 14, 1926; m. Constance Leighton, Mar. 30, 1940. Master of Bauhaus, Dessau, Germany, 1925-28; architect Berlin, 1928-31; archtl. commns. and travel in Spain, Morocco, Switzerland, Germany, Hungary, Greece and Eng., 1931-35; architect, London, 1935-37; assoc. prof. archtl. dept. Harvard U., 1937-46; partner Walter Gropius & Marcel Breuer, Cambridge, Mass., 1937-42. Recipient Washington award Am. Hungarian Studies Found., 1967, Thomas Jefferson Found. medal U. Va., 1968, 1st Internat. prize La Rinascente's Compasso d'Oro for indsl. 1957, Bard award City Club N.Y., 1964, 68; award for Whitney Mus., N.Y. State Council on Arts, 1967, Fifth Ave. Assn., 1967, Met. Washington Bd. of Trade award, 1969, Concrete Industry Bd. award, 1969, 70. Fellow AIA (awards include N.Y. chpt. medal of Honor 1965, Gold medal 1968, award for excellence 1970, Honor award 1970, 72, 73), Am. Acad. Arts and Scis.; mem. Nat. Inst. Arts and Letters (v.p. 1968); hon. mem. Archtl. Soc. Colombia, Archtl. Soc. Peru, Archtl. Soc. Argentina. Clubs: Harvard, Century (N.Y.C.). Author: Sun and Shadow, Marcel Breuer, 1921-61; Marcel Breuer: New Buildings and Projects; contbr. articles to jours. Home: New York, N.Y. Died July 1, 1981.*

BREWER, JOHN WITHROW, educator; b. Boston, Mar. 26, 1904; s. Daniel Chauncey and Genevieve (Withrow) B.; A.B. maxima cum laude, Princeton, 1926, M.A., 1930, Ph.D., 1932; student Harvard Law Sch., 1926-28; m. Thelma Lillian Martin, Aug. 22, 1943. Instr. polit. sci. George Washington U., 1933-34, asso. prof. internat. law, 1939-46, prof., 1946-73, prof. emeritus internat. law and polit. sci., 1973-82, head dept. polit. sci., 1946-63; instr. Dartmouth, 1934-35; asst. prof. polit. sci. Conn. State Coll., 1935-38, asso. prof., 1938-39; vis. prof. U. So. Calif., 1950-82. Served with U.S. Army, 1942-46. Decorated Legion of Merit. Mem. Phi Beta Kappa. Home: Harvard, Mass. Died Dec. 27, 1982.

BREWSTER, STANLEY FARRAR, lawyer; b. Cincinnati, Oh., Aug. 22, 1889; s. Joseph William and Margaret King (MacFadden) B.; A.B., U. of Cincinnati, 1910; Harvard Law Sch., 1910-13; J.D., New York U., 1922, S.J.D., 1923; m. Dorothy Livingston Williams, July 8, 1930; children—Dorothy Edwards, William. Admitted to N.Y. bar, 1922, D.C. bar, 1930; lectr. on finance N.Y.U., prof. law Washington Coll. of Law, 1933-40. Served as lt., inf., with AEF in France and Eng.; capt. Judge Adv. Gen. (Res.), 1933, maj., 1936, lt. col., 1942; judge adv. gen. Greenland Base Command, 1941-42, Judge Adv. Nat. Res. Officers Assn., 1936-38. Mem. Am., D.C., Fed. bar assns., Soc. Mayflower Descendants, S.A.R., Mil. Order World War, Am. Legion. Clubs: Army and Navy, Harvard (Washington); Harvard (N.Y.C.); Army and Navy Country (Arlington, Va.); Merion Cricket. Author: Legal Aspects of Credit, 1923; Analysis of Credit Risks, 1924; Bankruptcy, 1925; Twelve Men in a Box, 1935; Analysis of Federal Securities Act, 1935; Federal Procedure, 1940.†

BRICKER, GEORGE W(ALTER), mgmt. counsellor, lawyer; b. N.Y.C., Oct. 13, 1902; s. George Walter and Frances Eugenie (Cossart) B.; m. Elizabeth Cooper Jack, June 28, 1930; children—Jacqueline (Mrs. Russell J. Lewicki), Elizabeth (Mrs. W. Bruce Johnson). B.S., Mass. Inst. Tech., 1923; M.B.A., Harvard, 1925; J.D., Northeastern U., 1933. Bar: Mass. bar 1933. Pub. accountant H.C. Hopson & Co., Inc., N.Y.C., 1925-29; pub. utility cons. O'Hare-Lewis, Boston, 1929-36; practice law, Boston, 1933-36; mgmt. cons. Robert Heller & Assos., Inc., Cleve., 1936-52; v.p. Celanese Corp. Am., 1952-58, cons., 1958-63; lectr. So. Meth. U., 1958, Okla. State U., 1959, profl. mgmt. counselor, 1958-81, practice law, Chatham and Dennisport, Mass., 1972-81; cons. N.H. Pub. Service Commn., 1933, 34, UN, 1971; marketing adviser Investment Adv. Centre Pakistan, Karachi, 1965-66, chief tech. adviser, 1966-67; UN tech. assistance expert for Govt. Yugoslavia, 1973; IESC vol. cons. for Govt. Brazil, 1974; Mem. task force on Post Office Dept. project Commn. Orgn. Exec. Br. Govt., 1948. Author, pub.: Bricker's Internat. Directory of University Sponsored Executive Development Programs, annually 1970-80; asso. editor, 1981—. Trustee, treas. Child Edn. Found., 1956-57. Recipient Medalha Pro Mundi Beneficio Brazilian Acad. Humanities, 1975. Mem. Am. Bar Assn., Mass. Bar Assn., Am. Soc. Tng. and Devel., N. Am. Soc. Corp. Planning, Newcomen Soc. Club: Harvard (N.Y.C.); Harvard (Boston). Home: South Chatham, Mass. Died June, 1981.

BRIDGES, WILLIAM ANDREW, author; b. Franklin, Ind., Jan. 27, 1901; s. Harry and Katherine (Vaught) B.; m. Lynn Vandivier, July 31, 1924 (dec. 1949); m. Lucille Hedges, 1962 (dec. 1968); m. Nana Hedges Marts, 1969 (dec. 1977). A.B., Franklin Coll., 1923, Litt.D., 1952. Reporter European edit. Chgo. Tribune, Paris, 1923-25, European edit. Chgo. Tribune (Riviera edit.), Nice, 1924; reporter Franklin Star, 1925; reporter rewriter desk N.Y. Times, Paris, France, 1926-28; reporter N.Y. Sun, 1929-34; editor, curator of publs. N.Y. Zool. Soc., 1935-66. Author: Wild Animals of the World, 1948, Zoo Babies, 1953, Zoo Expeditions, 1953, Zoo Pets, 1955, Zoo Doctor, 1957, Zoo Celebrities, 1959, (with Lee S. Crandall) A Zoo Man's Notebook, 1966, The Bronx Zoo Book of Wild Animals, 1968, The New York Aquarium Book of the Water World, 1970, Zoo Careers, 1971, Gathering of Animals, 1974; Contbr. publs. Mem. Phi Delta Theta. Democrat. Baptist. Home: Pleasantville, N.Y. Dec. Mar. 28, 1984.

BRIDGHAM, FRANK NELSON, business exec.; b. Melrose, Mass., June 18, 1890; s. Edgar Cary and Charlotte Abbe (Stratton) B.; A.B., Boston U., 1910; LL.D. (honorary), Western N.E. College; married Marie Rice, June 7, 1919; children—Harriette Anne (Mrs. Vernon G. Beatty), Charlotte Marie (Mrs. Hubert C. H. Woodard). Dir. Strathmore Paper Co., 1926 from, vice president, 1942-51, treasurer, 1946-51, president, 1951-60, chairman of the board, 1957 from; dir., chmn. bd. Premoid Corp.; dir., asst. treas. Rising Paper Co.; dir. Third Nat. Bank & Trust Company, Springfield, Massachusetts. Board directors Springfield Goodwill Industries; treasurer Horace A. Moses Found., Inc., West Springfield, 1924-47, pres., 1947 from; trustee Springfield Coll., Boston U., Wilbraham Acad., Western N.E. Coll., N.E. Deaconess Hosp., Boston, Moses-Ludington Hosp., Ticonderoga, N.Y. Served as 2d lt. U.S. Army, World War I. Mem. Writing Paper Mfrs. Assn. (past pres.). Methodist. Clubs: Colony, Civitan (Springfield); Longmeadow (Mass.) Country, Metropolitan (N.Y.C.). Home: Springfield, Mass. †

BRIER, JOHN CROWE, educator; b. nr. Huddersfield, Eng., Feb. 27, 1889; s. Ward and Mary Jane (Crowe) B.; came to U.S., 1897, naturalized, 1918; B.S., U. of Mich., 1912, M.S., 1913; m. Grace Streibert, Sept. 12, 1913. Mem. faculty U. of Mich. since 1917, prof. chem. engring. from 1918; cons. chem. engr. since 1917. Major, U.S. Army Res., 1930-41; lt. col., active service, Ordnance Div., 1942; chief proof officer, 1942-43. commdg. officer, 1943-46, both at Southwestern Proving Ground Hope, Ark.; col., 1946. Home: Gregory, Mich. †

BRIGGS, CHARLES WILLIAM, lawyer; b. Cairo, Ia., July 30, 1887; s. Edward Samuel and Lucy Maria (Weaver) B.; A.B., U. Ia., 1909; LL.B., Harvard, 1913; m. Lois Ione Johnson, June 3, 1922; children—Warren Marshall, Edward Samuel, Charles William. Admitted to Ia. bar, 1912, Minn. bar, 1919; practicing lawyer, Wapello, Ia., 1913-17, pros. atty., 1914-17; mem. Briggs and Morgan, and predecessor firms, St. Paul, from 1919; counsel Weyerhaeuser Company, from 1940; member board of directors, mem. exec. com. First Trust Co. of St. Paul. Served as capt. Inf., U.S. Army, World War I, France, 1918; lt. col. Inf. Res., 1932-46. Mem. Minn. State and Am. bar assns., Am. Judicature Soc., Am. Interprofl. Inst., Am. Polit. Sci. Assn., Am. Soc. Internat. Law, Fgn. Policy Assn., Delta Sigma Rho. Republican. Conglist. Mason. Clubs: Minnesota, Athletic, Informal (St. Paul). Home: St. Paul, Minn. †

BRIGGS, ERNEST, artist; b. San Diego, Dec. 24, 1923; s. Ernest and Emma (Docili) B.; student Cal. Sch. Fine Art, San Francisco, 1947-50; m. Anne Arnold, Aug. 7, 1961. Exhibited one man shows at Metart Gallery, San Francisco, 1949, Stable Gallery, N.Y.C., 1954, 55, San Francisco Art Assn. Gallery, 1956, Howard Wise Gallery, N.Y.C., 1960, 62, 63; exhibited group shows at Jewish Mus., N.Y.C., 1967, Yale Art Gallery, 1968; rep. permanent collections at Carnegie Inst., Pitts., Mich. State U., Rockefeller Inst., N.Y.C., Whitney Mus. Am. Art, N.Y.C., San Francisco Mus. Art; faculty U. Fla., 1958. Pratt Inst., 1961-84, Yale, 1968. Served with USAAF, 1943-46; CBI. Home: New York, NY. Died June 12, 1984.

BRIGGS, EUGENE STEPHEN, ins. exec.; b. Howard County, Mo., Feb. 1, 1890; s. Thomas Hale and Susan Almyra (Pyle) B.; B.S., Central Coll., Fayette, Mo., 1912; B.S. in Edn., U. of Mo., 1917, M.A., 1921; Ph.D., Tchrs. Coll. (Columbia), 1934; grad. study U. Ia., summer 1932; m. Mary Gentry, Aug. 19, 1914; children—Stephen Gentry (dec.), Eleanor Sue, William B. Sci. tchr. Moberly, Mo., 1912-13; high sch. prin. at Carrollton, Slater and Trenton, Mo., 1913-19; prin. high sch., Okmulgee, Okla., 1919-23, scupt. schs., 1925-28; pres. State Tchrs. Coll., Durant, Okla., 1928-33; dir. adult edn. Mo. State Dept. of Edn., 1934-35; pres. Christian Coll., Columbia, Mo., 1935-38; pres. Phillips U., Enid, Okla., 1938-61; professor edn., Univ. of Ark, summer 1926, Wash. State Coll., summer 1927; asst. in teacher-training dept. Teachers Coll. (Columbia), 1934; pres. Okla. Motor Club, 1960-62, Nat. Investors Life Ins. Co., Okla., from 1959; pres. Investors Equity Corp., Oklahoma. Vice president, Okla. Adv. Com. to Commn. on Civil Rights, 1958-61. Founder Okla. Vocational Guidance Conf., 1929; state chmn. YMCA 1931-33; hon. chmn. Oklahoma Cancer Fund Drive, 1960-61; mem. State Correlation Commn. (Disciples of Christ) (exec. com. 1940-61); v.p. Internat. Conv., Disciples of Christ, 1942-44; chmn. Salt Plains Council Boy Scouts Am., 1940-43 (mem. Nat. Council); mem. Am. Seminar, 1938, 39, 41; mem. Com. on Effective Ministry, Disciples of Christ, 1940-47; mem. Okla. Coordinating Bd., 1940-42. Mem. bd. dirs. Conference of Christians and Jews, 1947-49; chmn. Brotherhood Week (Okla.), 1948 state chmn. Crusade for Freedom, 1952, March of Dimes, 1954; sec. Okla. Higher Edn. Found., 1955-61, mem. bd., from 1951, pres., 1954-55; adv. com. Nat. Citizens Commn. on Education, from 1950; dir. Christian Bd. Publs.; mem. Oklahoma Coll. Pres'. Council, sec., 1928-33; hon. state chmn. Okla. Cancer Crusade, 1960-61 Recipient service plaque Okla. State University; service awards Salvation Army, Lions Internat. Inducted Oklahoma Hall of Fame, 1951. Life mem. N.E.A. (exec. com. of dept. higher edn. 1943-46). Oklahoma Edn. Assn.; mem. Nat. Soc. for Study of Edn., S.A.R. (v.p.), Blue Key, Phi Delta Kappa, Kappa Delta Pi, Pi Gamma Mu. Democrat. Mem. Disciples of Christ. Mason (K.T., Shriner). Clubs: Lions (dir. 1943-50, internat. pres. 1948-49), Hi-Twelve. Author: (with V.M. Pratt) A Finding and Broadening Course in Public Speaking, 1933; Preparation of Secondary Teachers in Teachers Colleges for Guiding and Directing Extra-Class Activities, 1935. Author, editorial page, Lions Magazine, 1948-49. Editor Phillips U. Bull., 1938-61. Contbr. to ednl. and religious mags. Home: Oklahoma City, Okla. †

BRIGGS, LLOYD ARNOLD, investment co. exec.; b. Ortonville, Minn., Apr. 15, 1916; s. Leslie Arnold and Cynthia Estelle (Brown) B.; m. Ruth Helyn Zotter, Dec. 11, 1943. B.B.A., U. Minn., 1939. With Procter & Gamble Co., 1939, Hardware Mut. Casualty Co., 1939-40; spl. agt. FBI, 1940-45; with Addressograph-Multigraph Co., 1946-48; with Am. Photocopy Equipment Co., Evanston, Ill., 1948-63, exec. v.p., 1956-63; also dir.; v.p. Bell & Howell Co.; pres. Bus. Equipment Group, 1964-67, Dempster Investment Co., from 1967; pres. Ditto, Inc.; chmn. bd. Océ Industries Inc., Chgo.; dir. Stover Water Softener Co., Nat. Bank North Evanston, Pulaski Road Corp., Chgo., B.K. Elliott Corp., Pitts., Computer Copies Corp., N.Y.C.; U.S. cons. to Van Der Grinten N.S., Venlo, Holland. Mem. Chgo. Crime Commn.; Bd. dirs. St. Francis Hosp., Evanston, Ill. Mem. Soc. Former Spl. Agts. FBI, Delta Upsilon. Clubs: Royal Palm Yacht and Country (Boca Raton, Fla.), Bankers (Boca Raton, Fla.); Pine Tree Golf (Boynton Beach, Fla.); Execs. (Chgo.), Mid-Am. (Chgo.); North Shore Country (Glenview, Ill.); Bob O'Link Golf (Highland Park, Ill.). Home: Boca Raton, Fla. Died Sept. 28, 1981.

BRIGGS, ROBERT WILLIAM, biologist, educator; b. Watertown, Mass., Dec. 10, 1911; s. Robin John and Bridget (McGonigle) B.; m. Janet Elizabeth Bloch, Sept. 27, 1940 (div. 1980); children—Evan William, Alexander Bloch, Meredith; m. Françoise Bacher Teviotdale, 1980. B.S., Boston U., 1934; Ph.D., Harvard U., 1938. Research fellow McGill U., Montreal, Que., Can., 1938-42; mem. Inst. Cancer Research, Phila., 1942-56; prof. biology Ind. U., Bloomington, 1956-63, research prof., from 1963, chmn. dept., from 1969, then prof. emeritus. Mem. Am. Soc. Naturalists, Genetics Soc. Am., Am. Soc. Zoologists, Nat. Acad. Scis., Am. Acad. Arts and Scis., Soc. Study Devel. and Growth. Home: Bloomington, Ind. Dec. Mar. 4, 1983.

BRIGHTMAN, HAROLD WAN, dept. store pres.; b. Fall River, Mass., Nov. 5, 1889; s. Charles and Abbie J. (Albert) B.; A.B., Harvard, 1911; m. Florence Pennington, Jan. 28, 1914; children—Emerson Eliot, Robert Lloyd. Stockboy Wm. Filenes Sons Co., Boston, 1911-12, various positions merchandising div., 1912-18, asst. to gen. mdse. mgr., 1918-21, div. mdse. mgr., 1921-24; div. mdse. mgr. Abraham F. Strauss, Brooklyn, 1924-27, Gimbel Bros., New York, N.Y., 1927-30; dir. mdse. mgr., L. Bamberger & Co., Newark, N.J., 1930-35, vice pres. and general mdse. mgr., 1935-44; exec. mdse. dir. Meir & Frank, Portland, Ore., 1944-45; sr. vice pres. Lit Bros., Phila., 1945-47, pres., 1947-54; chmn. bd. Swern & Co., Trenton, N.J., 1947-54; v.p., dir., mem. exec. com. City Stores Co., N.Y.C.; mem. adv. com. Tradesmen's Land Title Bank & Trust Co., Phila.; dir. Bonwit Teller, (Phila.), Bankers Securities Corp., Phila. Transportation Co. Hon. chmn. bd. Nat. Consumer-Retailer Council, N.Y.C.; v.p., dir. Phila. Better Bus. Bur.; mem. retail adv. bd. Drexel Inst. Tech., Phila.; trustee, mem. exec. com. Am. Heritage Found., N.Y.C.; mem. adv. bd., Phila. Council Chs.; mem. finance adv. com. Phila. YWCA; chmn. Phila. div. Nat. Conf. Christians and Jews. Recipient civilian certificate of award for distinguished pub. service to USN from sec. of navy, Mem. C. of C. (past chmn., dir., mem. exec. com.), Clubs: Harvard, (N.Y.C.); Union League (Phila.); Smoke Rise (Butler, N.J.). Contbr. articles in field. Home: Butler, N.J. †

BRILLANT, JULES ANDRE, public utility exec.; b. St. Octave de Metis, Que., Can., June 30, 1888; s. Joseph and Rose (Raiche) B.; B.Sc., St. Joseph U., N.B., 1939, LL.D., 1942; Dr. Comml. Sci. (hon.), Montreal U., 1943; Dr. in Social Scis., St. Louis U., 1955; Dr. of the University, Montreal U., 1959; m. Rose Coulombe, Dec. 27, 1923 (dec. 1933); children—Jacques, Aubert, Carol, Madeleine, Suzanne; m. 2d. Agnes Villeneuve, Feb. 1, 1940. Asst. mgr. Canadian Nat. Bank, Amqui, 1911; mgr. Banque Hochelaga Rimouski, 1918; pres. Canada & Gulf Terminal Ry. Co., Ltd. 1947, Bonaventure & Gaspe Telephone Co., Ltd., 1953; chmn. bd. Quebec Telephone, 1961, Les Prévoyants du Can.; director Dominion Steel & Coal Corp., Dominion Coal Co., Ltd., Can. Wire & Cable Co., Limited, also Hawker Siddeley Canada, Limited hon. president Administration & Trust Co., from 1966. Vice president, Rimouski Technical and Marine Sch., from 1936. Mem. Legislative Council of Que., 1942. Decorated comdr. Order Brit. Empire; comdr. Order St. Gregoire le Grand; knight devotion grace Sovereign Mil. Order Malta in Can. Mem. Red Cross Soc. (hon. mem. Que. Provincial div.), Newcomen Soc. Eng., Canadian Legion (hon. sect. pres.), Société d'Administrn. et de Fiducie (dir.). Liberal. Roman Catholic. Clubs: Garrison (Que.); Montreal. Home: Rimouski, Que., Can. †

BRILLOUIN, LEON N(ICHOLAS), scientist, educator; b. Sevres, France, Aug. 7, 1889; s. Marcel and Charlotte (Mascart) B.; student U. Munich, 1913; Ph.D., U. Paris, 1920; m. Stephanie Prussak, Dec. 5, 1912; 1 dau., Bella (Mrs. Gilbert Boris). Came to U.S., 1941, naturalized, 1949. Prof. U. Paris (Institut H. Poincare, chair theoretical physics), 1928-32; prof. College de France, Paris, 1932-48; gen. dir. French Nat. Broadcasting System, July 1939-Jan. 1941; visiting prof., U. Wis., 1928; U. Mich., summer 1929; prof., U. Wis., 1941-42, Brown U., 1942-43; defense research work, Columbia (applied mathematics group), 1943-45; research lectr. Cruft Lab., Harvard U., 1946, Gordon McKay prof. applied mathematics, 1947-49; dir. electronics edn., Internat. Bus. Machines Corp., N.Y. City, 1949. Radio engr. rank of lieut., French Army, 1914-49. Hon. fellow Indian Acad. of Scis., India, 1938; mem. N.Y. Acad. Sci. Author; La theorie des quanta et l'atome de Bohr, 1923, Les Mesures en haute frequence, 1923; Selected papers on Wave-mechanics, 1928; L'atome de Bohr, 1930; les statisiques quantiques, 1939; Quantenstatistik, 1931; (also a Russian translation); Notion elementaires de Mathematiques, 1935; Les Tenseurs en Mecanique, 1938, 1946; Wave propagation, 1946. Collector modern French paintings. Home: New York, N.Y. †

BRINK, CAROL RYRIE, author; b. Moscow, Idaho, Dec. 28, 1895; d. Alexander Ryrie and Henrietta (Watkins) Ryrie; student Portland Acad. 1912-14, U. Idaho, 1914-17, D.Litt., 1965; B.A., U. Calif., 1918; m. Raymond W. Brink, July 12, 1918; children—David Ryrie, Nora Caroline. Began writing stories for children about 1925. Awarded Newbery medal for year's most distinguished contbn. to juvenile lit., 1935; ann. award So. Calif. Council Lit. Children, 1966. Mem. Nat. League Am. Pen Women, Calif. PEN, Authors' League Am., Women in Communications, Phi Beta Kappa, Gamma Phi Beta. Presbyn. Club: Faculty Women's. Author: Caddie Woodlawn, 1935 (Newbery medal 1935); Harps in the Wind (adult biography), 1947; Stopover (novel), 1951; Family Grandstand (Jr. Lit. Guild selection), 1952; The Highly Trained Dogs of Prof. Petit (Children's Book Club selection), 1953; The Headland (award Friends Am. Writers), 1955; Family Sabbatical (Jr. Lit. Guild selection), 1956; Strangers in the Forest, The Pink Motel, 1959; The Twin Cities, 1961; Château Saint Barnabé, 1962; Snow in the River (McKnight Family Lit. Fund award 1966; prize Nat. League Am. Pen Women), 1964; Andy Buckram's Tin Men (Jr. Lit. Guild selection), 1966; Winter Cottage, 1968; Two Are Better Than One, 1968; The Bad Times of Irma Baumlein, 1972; Louly, 1974; The Bellini Look, 1976; Four Girls on a Homestead, 1977. Editor: Best Short Stories for Children, 1935; Best Short Stories for Boys and Girls, 1936, 37, 38, 39. Contbr. stories and verse for children to popular mags. Home: San Diego, Calif. Died Aug. 15, 1981.

BRINK, RAYMOND WOODARD, coll. prof.; b. Newark, N.J., Jan. 4, 1890; s. Clark Mills and Helen (Bacon) B.; B.S., Kan. State Coll., 1908, B.S., in E.E., 1909; A.M., Harvard, 1915, Ph.D., 1916; grad. work U. of Grenoble and U. of Paris, 1916 and 1924, Collège de France, 1917 and 1925; m. Carol Ryrie, July 12, 1918; children—David Ryrie, Nora Caroline. Instr. in math., U. of Ida., 1909-12, U. of Minn., 1912-13; Harvard traveling fellow at Paris, 1916-17; lecturer in mathematics, U. of Edinburgh, 1919-20; asso. prof. of mathematics, U. of Minn., 1920-28, prof. from 1928; chmn. dept. of mathematics, 1928-32, and from 1939. Served in S.R.C., 1917-18. Fellow A.A-.A.S. (sec. sect. A 1944-51); mem. Math. Assn. Am. (pres. 1941-42, gov., 1943-48), Am. Math. Soc., Edinburgh Math. Soc., Sigma Xi. Baptist. Club: Campus. Asso. editor Transactions of Am. Mathematical Society, 1927-31. Author numerous books on mathematics. Editor: Appleton-Century Mathematics Series. Contbr. articles in analysis to math. jours. †

BRINK, RODNEY LIDDELL, editor, pub.; b. Saginaw, Mich., Nov. 9, 1889; s. Guy Kimball and Annabel (Liddell) B.; student high schs., Minneapolis, Minn., 1903-07; m. Veda Wiebens, of San Diego, Calif., Jan. 14, 1922; 1 son, MacDonald. Reporter San Diego (Calif.) Sun, 1913-15, city editor, 1919-21; reporter San Diego Union, 1916-17; editor Sacramento Star, 1922-23; mng. editor Los Angeles Record, 1924-31; editor and pub. Boisé (Ida.) Capital News, 1932-35; editor Seattle Star since 1935; editor in chief Scripps League of Newspapers, hdqrs. Seattle, Wash., since 1937. Served as 2d lt. Air Corps, U.S.A., World War. Christian Scientist. Home: Bellevue, Wash.†

BRINKLEY, HOMER LEE, coops. exec.; b. Linneus, Mo., Mar. 26, 1898; s. Floyd O. and Maude Emily (Howe) B.; B.S., La. State U., 1919, postgrad., 1922; m. Alice May Brogan, Sept. 5, 1925 (dec.); 1 son, Homer (dec.); m. Dorothy Fowler Munster, Nov. 27, 1965. Mgr. cotton livestock farms, La., 1919-21; instr. agr. La. State U., 1922; state supr. La. State U., farm trainees war VA, 1923; county agt. Calcasieu Parish, La., 1924-28; gen. mgr. Am. Rice Growers Coop. Assn. and Exchange (covering rice belt La., Tex., Ark.), Lake Charles, La., 1928-50; exec. v.p. Nat. Council Farmer Coops., from 1950; dir. Dominion Nat. Bank, Falls Church, Va., chmn. audit com.; former dir. Central Bank for Co-ops., FCA, Washington; past trustee, mem. exec. com. Am. Inst. Cooperation, Washington; cons. Am. del. Conf. on Internat. Orgn., San Francisco; mem. U.S. del. 3d Inter-Am. Conf. on Agr., Caracas, Venezuela, 1945; del. White House Conf. on Conservation, 1962; chmn. Agrl. Internat. People-to-People Program, 1962; mem. U.S. Food for Peace Council, 1962; adv. com. World Food Congress, 1963; past mem. govtl. adv. coms. Dir. Found. for Am. Agr.; pres. Nat. Council Farmer Co-ops., exec. com., chmn. labor-mgmt. com., 1944-45; past pres. La. Council Farmer Coops.; past mem. fgn. agrl. trade policy com. USDA; bd. suprs. La. State U., 1940-54, Citzens League S.W. La. (former pres.); mem. U.S. del. FAO, Geneva, 1957, Rome, 1953; del. Internat. Fedn. Agr. Producers, Rome, 1953, chmn. N.Am. regional conf., 1962; chief Presdl. Fgn. Agrl. Trade Mission Asia, 1954; mem. Dept. Agr. nat. com. on agrl. research, policy, 1952-57, Pres.'s Spl. Com. on Civilian Nat. Honors, 1956; adviser U.S. del. to Gen. Agreement on Trade and Tariffs, Geneva, 1956, 61-62; adv. com. on rural rehab. Dept. Agr., 1961-64; exec. com. U.S. Freedom from Hunger Found., 1961-65; mem. com. on co-ops. AID. Mem. nat. com. Boy Scouts Am. Served 2d lt. U.S. Army, 1918; capt. La. N.G., ORC, 1925-35. Mem. Am. Legion, Lambda Chi Alpha, Alpha Zeta. Methodist. Club: Metropolitan (Washington). Home: Falls Church, Va. Died Sept. 6, 1983.

BRINKWORTH, JOHN J., v.p. N.Y. Central R.R.; b. Buffalo, July 3, 1887; ed. St. Joseph's Collegiate Inst. Buffalo. Vice pres. N.Y. Central R.R. from 1947. Address: Chicago, Ill. †

BRINTON, ANNA, educationalist; b. San Jose, Cal., Oct. 17, 1887; d. Charles E. and Lydia Shipley (Bean) Cox; A.B., Stanford, 1909, M.A., 1913, Ph.D., 1917; LL.D., Mills Coll., 1937, Swarthmore Coll., 1950, Earlham Coll., 1961; m. Howard H. Brinton, July 23, 1921; children—Lydia (Mrs. John Van G. Forbes), Edward, Catharine (Mrs. John R. Cary), Joan (Mrs. Kent Erickson). Instr. Latin, Coll. of Pacific, 1909-12, Stanford, 1912-13; student Am. Acad. in Rome, 1913-14; instr., later prof. Latin, Mills Coll., 1916-22; mem. student relief group Am. Friends Service Com., Germany, 1920; prof. Latin, Earlham Coll., 1922-28; acting prof. classics Stanford, summers 1927, 28; prof. archaeology Mills Coll., 1928-36, dean faculty, 1933-36; research fellow Woodbrooke Selly Oak Colls., Eng., 1931-32, asso. dir. Pendle Hill Sch., Wallingford, Pa., 1936-49; bd. dirs. Am. Friends Service Commn., 1936-52, commnr. in India and China, 1946, rep. in Japan, 1952-55, vice chmn., 1958 from. Exec. bd. Nat. Council Chs., 1950-52, 56-60. Mem. Am. Assn. U. Women, Phi Beta Kappa, Mem. Society of Friends. Author: Maphaeus Vegius, 1940; Fourteen Woodcuts, 1930; A Pre-Raphaelite Aeneid, 1934; also Pendle Hill pamphlets, 7, 38, 62. Editor: Then and Now: Quaker Essays, Historical and Contemporary, 1960. Home: Wallingford, Pa. †

BRISSON, FREDERICK, theatrical producer; b. Copenhagen, Mar. 17, 1913; s. Carl Brisson; m. Rosalind Russell (dec. Nov. 1976); m. Arlette Janssen, May 1978. Student, Rossall Coll., Fleetwood, Eng. Assoc. producer Gaumont-British, Eng.; talent agy. rep. Brit. and Am. talent, Eng.; jr. ptnr. Vincent Agy., Hollywood. Producer motion pictures in, Eng.; Two Hearts in Three-Quarter Time, Prince of Arcadia, Moonlight Sonata; motion pictures in Hollywood; producer: 22 Broadway plays including Mixed Couples, Coco, Pajama Game, Under the Yum Yum Tree; films including Mrs. Pollifax-Spy. Trustee Los Angeles Internat. Film Expn. (FILMEX); founder, co-chmn. Rosalind Russell Med. Research Center for Arthritis, U. Calif., San Francisco. Spl. cons. to sec. of war World War II; also lt. col. AAF; chief office radio propaganda. Decorated U.S. Legion of Merit; King Christian X medal Denmark; recipient N.Y. Drama Critics award for Five Finger Exercise. Clubs: St. James's (London); Eldorado Country (Indian Wells, Calif.); Racquet and Tennis (N.Y.C.). Died Oct. 8, 1984.

BROCK, POPE FURMAN, lawyer; b. Avalon, Ga., Oct. 13, 1888; s. William Thomas and Eliza Jane (Keeling) B.; A.B., U. Ga., 1911, LL.B., 1913; LL.D., Piedmont Coll., Oglethorpe U., 1956; m. Alice Matthews, Mar. 30, 1921; children—Pope F., Mary Jane. Instr. history dept. U. Ga., 1911-14; admitted to Ga. bar, 1913, practiced in Macon, 1914-32; mem. firm Brock, Sparks & Russell, 1920-32, mem. Spalding, MacDougald, Sibley & Brock, Atlanta, 1935, Spalding, Sibley, Troutman & Brock, 1936-42; gen. counsel Coca-Cola Co., Atlanta, 1942-54, ret., continues in adv. capacity; chmn. bd. dirs. Fulton Nat. Bank of Atlanta, Fulton Nat. Corp., 1958-77, adv. dir., 1977-83; dir. Piedmont Securities Co., Acmaro Securities Co., Guaranty Investment Co., Dupre Mfg. Co.; arbitrator N.Y. Stock Exchange. Chmn., Local Govt. Commn. Atlanta and Fulton County, Ga., 1966. Trustee, a founder U. Ga. Found., 1937-57; bd. regents U. System Ga., 1943-49, chmn. bd., 1947-49; trustee Oglethorpe U., 1944-59, chmn. bd. trustees, 1956-59; trustee Univ. Center in Ga., 1954-77. Mem. task force on water resources and power devel. 2d Hoover Commn. on Govt. Reorgn. Mem. Inter-Am., Internat. Am., Ga., Atlanta bar assns., Am. Judicature Soc., U. Ga. Alumni Soc. (pres. 1931-32), Nat. Council Juvenile Ct. Judges and Nat. Juvenile Ct. Found. (asso.), World Assn. Lawyers for Peace (founding), Phi Beta Kappa Assos., Phi Beta Kappa. Club: Piedmont Driving. Home: Atlanta, Ga. Died July 19, 1983.

BROCKEL, HARRY CHARLES, educator; b. Chgo., Sept. 18, 1908; s. Thomas J. and Margaret (Strachan) B.; m. Ella M. Searth, Nov. 4, 1936; 1 dau., Leslie Jeanne. Student, U. Wis., Marquette U., 1926-31. Various positions City Milw. Bd. Harbor Commrs., 1926-36, sec., 1936-42, municipal port dir., 1942-68; faculty U. Wis., Milw., 1969-79; Vice chmn. Wis. Deep Waterways Commn., 1945-69, Gt. Lakes Commn.; chmn. Wis. Gov.'s Com. St. Lawrence Seaway Project, from 1952; adv. bd. St. Lawrence Seaway Devel. Corp., 1954-69; U.S. adv. bd. Coastal Zone Adminstrn., 1973-75; port adviser to Nat. Govt. Venezuela, 1975-76; chmn. Gt. Lakes Compact Commn. Wis.; adv. bd. Gt. Lakes Pilotage Adminstrn.; fed. port controller Gt. Lakes-St. Lawrence Seaway Ports; mem. export expansion council Dept. Commerce; cons. on port and shipping matters to U.S. Sec. Transp., 1973-74. Author: The Milwaukee River, 1968; co-author: The Great Lakes Transportation System, 1976; Contbr. articles to jours. Mem. adv. council on naval affairs World Affairs Council.; Trustee Gt. Lakes Found. Recipient good govt. award Milw. Jr. C. of C., 1951, Distinguished Pub. Service award Milw. Assn. Commerce, 1954, Nat. Pub. Service award Fraternal Order Eagles, 1954, Pere Marquette award Marquette U., 1956; Distinguished Engring. Service award U. Wis., 1958; award Cosmopolitan Club, 1959; award Milw. Found., 1960; Gold medal S.A.R., 1973. Mem. Am. Assn. Port Authorities (pres. 1949, dir.), Gt. Lakes Harbors Assn., Nat. Rivers and Harbor Congress (dir.), Am. Soc. Mil. Engrs., USCG League, USCG Aux., Am. Soc. for Pub. Adminstrn. (pres. Milw. chpt.), Navy League U.S., Gt. Lakes Model Shipbuilders Guild, Internat. Assn. Shipmasters, Civil War Round Table, Assn. Municipal Engrs., Alpha Kappa Psi (hon.). Clubs: Mason. (Milw.), Milwaukee Athletic (Milw.), Executives (Milw.), Milwaukee Traffic (Milw.), Milwaukee Transportation (Milw.), Milwaukee Yacht (Milw.), Port of Milwaukee Propeller (Milw.), World Trade (Milw.); Propeller U.S. (nat. v.p. 1951), Chicago Traffic. Home: Milwaukee, Wis. Died Oct. 28, 1981.

BRODBECK, MAY, university administrator; b. Newark, July 26, 1917; d. Louis and Etta (Bragar). B.A., N.Y. U., 1941; M.A., U. Iowa, 1945, Ph.D., 1947. Mem. faculty U. Minn., 1947-74, prof. philosophy, 1959-74, chmn. dept., 1967-70, dean grad. sch., 1972-74; v.p. for acad. affairs, dean faculties U. Iowa, Iowa City, 1974-81, 83, Carver prof. philosophy, 1974-83, Carver prof. philosophy emerita, 1983; fellow Center for Advanced Study in Behavioral Scis., Stanford, Calif., 1981-82; vis. lectr. Cambridge (Eng.) U., 1970; vis. prof. U. Md., 1964; dir. Grad. Record Exam. Bd., 1972-76, Nat. Center Higher Edn. Mgmt. Systems, 1977-83. Author: American Non-Fiction, 1900-1950, 1952; author, editor: Readings in the Philosophy of the Social Sciences, 1968; Co-editor: Readings in the Philosophy of Science, 1953; editorial bd.: Philos. Studies, 1950, Philosophy of Sci, 1959—, also numerous articles. NSF research grantee, 1966-68; Fulbright research scholar Italy, 1962-63; Social Sci. Research Council faculty fellow, 1955-58. Mem. Am. Philos. Assn. (sec.-treas. 1955-57, v.p. 1970-71, pres. 1971-72), Nat. Assn. State Univs. and Land Grant Colls. (chmn. council acad. affairs 1980-81), Philosophy Sci. Assn., AAUP. Home: Menlo Park, Calif. Dec. Aug. 2, 1983.

BRODERICK, JAMES JOSEPH, actor; b. Charlestown, N.H., Mar. 7, 1927; s. James Joseph and Mary Elizabeth (Martindale) B.; m. Patricia Biow, May 29, 1949; children—Martha, Janet, Matthew. Student, U. N.H., 1944-45; grad., Neighborhood Playhouse Sch. of the Theatre, N.Y.C. Appeared in: Broadway plays Johnny No Trump, 1964, Let Me Hear You Smile, 1973; films include Alice's Restaurant, 1968, Dog Day Afternoon, 1975; appearing in: films include Family, ABC-TV, 1976-81; toured fifteen countries with Helen Hayes in The Glass Menagerie, 1961; (also Emmy award nominee as best actor.). Served with USN, 1945-46. Named TV Father of Yr., 1977; Critics Circle award nominee, 1977. Mem. Actors Equity Assn., Screen Actors Guild, AFTRA. Home: New York, N.Y. Dec. Nov. 1, 1982.

BRODEUR, ARTHUR GILCHRIST, prof. English, writer; b. Franklin, Mass., Sept. 18, 1888; s. Clarence Arthur and Mary Cornelia (Latta) B.; A.B., Harvard, 1909, A.M., 1911, Ph.D., 1916; m. Maude Noland, Aug. 31, 1912; married 2d, Florence Weyant, November, 25, 1945; married 3d Josephine Thompson, May 29, 1950. Instr. in English, U. Cal. 1916-18, asst. prof., 1918-22, asso. prof., 1922-30, prof., 1930-55, emeritus, 1955 from. Mem. Philol. Assn. of Pacific Coast, Modern Language Assn. of Am., Am.-Scandinavian Found. Knight 1st class Royal Order of Vasa (Sweden), 1944. Democrat. Club: Adventure Campfire. Author: The Altar of the Legion (with Farnham Bishop), 1926; The Pageant of Civilization, 1931. Translator: The Prose Edda (Vol. V., Scandinavian Classics), 1916. Home: Sebastopol, Cal. †

BRODIE, ARNOLD FRANK, educator, biochemist; b. Boston, Dec. 31, 1923; s. Harry E. and Tessie (Getman) B.; B.A., Northeastern U., 1946; M.S., Boston U., 1947; postgrad. Mass. Inst. Tech., 1949; Ph.D., U. Pa., 1952; m. June Wiskind, Nov. 24, 1948; children—Todd D., Leslie S. Research asst., biochem. lab. Mass. Gen. Hosp., Boston, 1952-54; research biochemist Leonard Wood Meml. Lab., Harvard Med. Sch., 1954-56, asso. microbiology, 1956-60, asst. prof. microbiology, 1960-63; prof. microbiology U. So. Calif. Med. Sch., 1963-81, chmn. dept. biochemistry, 1970-81. Recipient Creative scholarship and research award, 1969. Fellow Royal Soc. Health, Am. Acad. Microbiology; mem. Am. Soc. Microbiology (chmn. div. physiology), Acad. Northeastern U., Am. Soc. Biol. Chemistry, A.A.A.S., Am. Chem. Soc. Home: Pasadena, Calif. Died Jan. 24, 1981.

BRODIE, RENTON KIRKWOOD, soaps and detergent manufacturing executive; b. Portland, Ore., Sept. 12, 1887; s. George A. and Georgiana Sargent (Carpenter) B.; B.S., Ore. State Coll., 1908, D.Sc., 1936; M.S., U. of Chicago, 1911; m. Caroline Buchanan, Sept. 13, 1911. Asst. in chemistry, Ore. State Coll., 1908-09, instr., 1909-13, asst. prof., 1913-15, asso. prof., 1915-18; fellow Mellon Inst., U. of Pittsburgh, 1918-19; chemist The Procter and Gamble Co., Cincinnati, 1919-23, chemical supt., 1923-26, dir. of manufacture and tech. research, 1927-31, v.p. manufacturing, 1931-42, v.p. 1942-54, adminstrv.

v.p., 1954-55, Member of the American Chemical Society, Am. Oil Chemists' Soc., Am. Inst. Chem. Engrs., A.A-.A.S. Clubs: Cincinnati Country, Queen City, Commercial. Home: Cincinnati, OH. †

BROEMAN, CHARLES WILLIAM, lawyer; b. Cin., Jan. 16, 1890; s. Frank and Mary (Meyers) B.; m. Ina Warner, June 15, 1915; children—Dwight Warner, Betty (Mrs. Thomas Jos. Klinedinst). A.B., U. Cin., 1911; LL.B., Cin. Law Sch., 1913. Bar: Ohio bar 1913. Practiced in, Cin.; pres. Charles W. Broeman Co., Cin., 1930-81; dir. Hennegan Co., Tresler Oil Co., Leyman Corp.; dir. emeritus 1st Nat. Bank of Cin. Mem. Cin. Bar Assn. Clubs: Queen City (Cin.), Optomist (Cin.). Home: Cincinnati, Ohio. Died Jan. 19, 1981; buried Spring Grove, Cincinnati.†

BROGAN, ALBERT PERLEY, prof. philosophy; b. Omaha, Neb., July 22, 1889; s. Francis Albert and Maude Haskell (Perley) B.; student U. of Neb., 1907-09; A.B., Harvard, 1911, A.M., 1912, Ph.D., 1914; m. Mary Cleo Rice, Sept. 26, 1916; children—Mary Rice, Francis Albert. With U. of Tex. since 1914, instr. philosophy until 1917, adjunct prof., 1917-23, asso. prof., 1923-25, prof., 1925-65, asst. dean Grad. Sch., 1932-36, dean, 1936-58, prof. emeritus. Mem. Am. Philos. Asso. (pres. western div. 1932), A.A.A.S., Conf. Deans of Southern Grad. Schs. (pres. 1948). Contbr. Philos. Rev., Jour. of Philosophy and Internat. Jour. Ethics. Home: Austin, Tex. †

BROGGINI, ADRIAN JOSEPH, engring. and constrn. co. exec.; b. Lakewood, Ohio, Oct. 16, 1912; s. Andrew and Letitia (Sinton) B.; m. Virginia Reutter, Aug. 15, 1934; children—Carol Ann (Mrs. Anson W. Krickl), Judith Elin (Mrs. D.L. Gunner), Adrienne Joan (Mrs. Paul Lindquist). B.S. in Chem. Engring, U. Mich., 1934. Registered profl. engr., Mass. With E.B. Badger & Sons Co., Boston, 1936-50, v.p., 1948-50; with Stone & Webster Engring. Co., Boston, 1950-53; with Badger Co., Inc., 1953-77, pres., chief exec. officer, treas., dir., 1957-68, chmn., chief exec. officer, dir., 1968-71, chmn., 1971-77, dir., 1971-85, cons., 1977-85; dir. Badger Morrocco, Badger Ltd., London, Eng., Badger N.V., The Hague. Mem. Corp. Wentworth Inst., Boston. Mem. Nat., Fla. engring. socs., Am. Inst. Chem. Engrs., Trigon, Tau Beta Pi. Clubs: University Mich, President's; Country (Brookline, Mass.); Brae Burn Country (Newton, Mass.); Algonquin (Boston); Beach (Palm Beach, Fla.); Lost Tree Country (North Palm Beach, Fla.); Bald Peak Country (Melvin Village N.H.). Home: Wellesley Hills, Mass. Died Feb. 3, 1985; buried Newton Cemetery, Mass.

BROIDA, DAN, chemical company executive; b. Springfield, Ill., Aug. 24, 1913; s. Joseph and Mary B.; m. Roma Rosalyn Milder, Oct. 30, 1949; children—Joel Gary, Richard Allan, Melanie Susan, Marna Jeanne. B.S.Ch.E., Washington U., St. Louis, 1936. Vice pres. Midwest Cons. Inc., St. Louis, 1936-48; founder, chmn. bd. Sigma Chem. Co., St. Louis, from 1948; chmn. bd., dir. Sigma-Aldrich Corp., St. Louis, 1972-82; dir. Sigma-London Chem. Co. Served to maj. AUS, 1941-45. Home: Saint Louis, Mo. Dec. 1982.

BROMBERG, BEN GEORGE, aero. engr.; b. N.Y.C., Feb. 14, 1915; s. Louis and Anne (Steinhouse) B.; m. Pauline Riggs, May 10, 1941 (dec.); 1 son, Jeffrey; m. Margaret Ann Warnier, Aug. 31, 1981. B.S. (Sylvanus Reed fellow), N.Y. U., 1936, M.S., 1937; Sc.D. (Consol. Vultee fellow), M.I.T., 1947. Chief tech. engr. research Consol. Vultee Aircraft Corp., 1939-45; research asso., instr. lab. Mass. Inst. Tech., 1945-47; chief engr. missile div. McDonnell Aircraft Corp., St. Louis, 1947-59, v.p., 1959-68; v.p., gen. mgr. McDonnell-Douglas Astronautics Co., Eastern div.; McDonnell Douglas Corp., 1968-73; also dir.; exec. v.p. McDonnell Douglas Astronautics Co., Huntington Beach, Calif., also corp. v.p. parent co., 1973-80, cons., from 1980; instr. servomechanisms Washington U., 1951; space sci. research and devel. com. St. Louis U., from 1962; vis. com. dept. aeros. and astronautics Mass. Inst. Tech., 1962-66. Contbr. papers to profl. lit. Mem. Berg Sci. Found., St. Charles High Sch.; Bd. dirs. McDonnell Scholarship Found. Recipient Alumni Achievement award N.Y. U., 1970-71; Distinguished Pub. Service medal NASA, 1974. Fellow Brit. Interplanetary Soc., Am. Inst. Aeros. and Astronautics; mem. Aerospace Industries Assn. (missile and space council), Navy League U.S., IEEE (sr.), Am. Phys. Soc., Engring. Council Profl. Devel. (coll. accreditation bd.), Sigma Xi. Club: Nat. Space. Home: Huntington Beach, Calif.

BROMLEY, CHARLES VINSON, JR., stockbroker; b. Wayne, W.Va., Mar. 2, 1902; s. Charles Vinson and Pauline Napfer (Fry) B.; student Va. Mil. Inst., 1918-19; B.S., U.S. Mil. Acad., 1923; m. Elizabeth Patton Walker, June 12, 1929; 1 son, Charles Vinson III. Commd. 2d lt., Cav., U.S. Army, 1923, advanced through grades to maj. gen., 1951; assigned 7th Cav., Ft. Bliss, Tex., 1928-32, 26th Cav., P.I., 1932-35, with 1st Cav., Ft. Knox, Ky., 1935-37, Inf. Sch., Ft. Benning, Ga., 1937; staff Armored Force Hdqrs., Ft. Knox, 1940-43; regt. comd. 6th Armored Div., then 12th Armored Div., 1943-46, chief staff 12th Armored Div., 1st Armored Div., occupation duties, 1946-47; exec., G.3 Div. EUCOM Hdqrs. Died May 23, 1984.

BROOKFIELD, DUTTON, clothing mfg. co. exec.; rancher; b. Kansas City, Mo., Dec. 31, 1917; s. Arthur D. and Elizabeth (Blish) B.; B.S., U. Mo., 1939; m. Betty Bell, Nov. 16, 1940; children—Karen Ann, Arthur Dutton II, Charles R., Betty Bell. Pres. Unitog Co., Kansas City, 1953-79; dir. Northwestern Mutual Life Ins. Co., Milw., mem. exec. com., 1971-79; dir. First Nat. Bank, First Nat. Charter Corp. (both Kansas City, Mo.), Southwestern Bell Telephone Co., St. Louis, Am. Can Co., Greenwich, Conn., Kansas City Power & Light Co.; rancher Lee's Summit, Mo. Mem. Bd. Police Commrs., Kansas City, 1957-61; dir., v.p. Kansas City (Mo.) Crime Commn., 1964; bd. dirs. United Funds, Inc., Kansas City, 1964; bd. dirs. Civic Council Greater Kansas City, pres., 1973-74; bd. dirs. Am. Royal Assn., Starlight Theatre; chmn. Jackson County Sports Complex Authority. Nat. chmn. U. Mo. Devel. Fund, 1968-71; chmn. athletic council U. Mo., 1952-55; vice chmn. trustees U. Mo. at Kansas City, 1962; trustee Midwest Research Inst., 1955—; trustee Barstow Sch., pres. bd., 1958. Mem. NAM (dir.), Nat. Assn. Uniform Mfrs. (dir. 1965), U. Mo. Gen. Alumni Assn. (pres. 1955-56), C. of C. Greater Kansas City (pres. 1973). Republican. Presbyn. Clubs: Kansas City, Kansas City Country, Rotary (pres. 1954-55) (Kansas City); River, Carriage. Home: Kansas City, Mo. Died July 23, 1979.

BROOKS, DOUGLAS WALWORTH, cotton mfr., planter, investments; b. Deeson, Miss., Apr. 24, 1890; s. Josiah C. and Annie D. (Walworth) B.; ed. Vanderbilt U.; unmarried. Pres. Aileen Mills Co., Biscoe, N.C., Union Compress & Warehouse Co., Memphis; operator cotton plantations, Mississippi; dir. Bank of Lake Village, Ark. Formerly; pres. Newburger Cotton Co., Memphis; dep. chmn. bd. Fed. Res. Bank of St. Louis; pres. and treas. Am. Cotton Shippers Assn. Clubs: Memphis Country, Memphis Hunt and Polo, Tennessee (Memphis). Home: Memphis, Tenn. †

BROOKS, FORREST EDMUND, cons. engr.; b. Kansas City, 1890; John Bryns and Jennie Priday (Cadle) B.; B.S. in Elec. Engring, Case Inst. Tech., 1912; m. Ruth Hetzel, Apr. 30, 1923; children—Mary Jane, Forrest Edmund, Ruth Lee. With N.Y. Telephone Co., N.Y.C., 1912-55, successively engr., engr. plant extension, chief engr., 1912-50, v.p., 1950-55; cons. engr., from 1955; directed survey of transit facilities N.Y. Met. area conducted by Met. Rapid Transit Commn. and Port N.Y. Authority. With Office Civilian Def., World War II; mem. group under Fed. contract (project East River) to study Civil Def., 1951, 52. Served to maj. Signal Corps, U.S. Army, 1917-19; col. N.Y. N.G., 1941-54. Recipient citation in communications mgmt. Case Inst. Tech., 1953. Licensed profl. engr., N.Y. Fellow I.E.E.E.; mem. Am. Inst. Cons. Engrs., N.Y. C. of C., Commerce and Industry Assn. N.Y., Ohio Soc. N.Y., Eta Kappa Nu (past nat. pres.), Sigma Nu. Episcopalian. Clubs: Engineers (trustee mem. bd. mgmt.), N.Y. Railroad, Railroad-Machinery (N.Y.C.); Scarsdale (N.Y.), Golf; Skytop (Pa.). Home: Scarsdale, NY. †

BROOKS, GEORGE WILLIAM, coll. dean; b. Macon, Ga., June 7, 1918; s. John William and Lois (Henderson) B.; B.S., Ind. U., 1941, M.S., 1942, Ed.D., 1955; LL.B., LaSalle Extension U., 1947; m. Fannie E. Crafton, May 25, 1945; 1 son, George W. (dec.). Instr., Voorhees Jr. Coll., 1942-43; asst. prof. social studies Prairie View A. and M. Coll. of Tex., 1943-53; prof. social studies and edn. S.C. State Coll., Orangeburg, 1955-59, chmn. dept. social studies, 1959-60, dean Sch. Grad. Studies, 1960-80. Mem. council on coop. coll. projects TVA, 1963-80. Mem. Am. Assn. Sch. Adminstrs., N.E.A., Nat. Council for Social Studies, S.C. Psychol. Assn., Palmetto Edn. Assn. (parliamentarian ho. of dels. 1959-80), Kappa Alpha Psi, Phi Delta Kappa, Phi Alpha Theta, Pi Gamma Mu. Mason (Shriner). Home: Orangeburg, S.C. Died Apr. 13, 1980.

BROOME, JOHN PARRAN, govt. ofcl.; b. Broome's Island, Md., Sept. 4, 1888; s. John and Nannie (Peterson) B.; student U. of Md., 1904-06, Columbia Night Sch., 1920-21, 1926-27; m. Elsa Deming, Apr. 14, 1928. With engring. corps., B. & O. R.R., Baltimore, 1910-13; gen. supervisor, DuPont Co., Parlin, N.J., 1915-21; city mgr., Salem, Va., 1922-26, Summit, N.J., 1926-31, Petersburg, Va., 1935-39; regional dir. Public Housing Adminstrn., Atlanta, 1939-48; asst. commr. for Public Housing Adminstrn., Washington, from 1948. Operator 2 farms in Southern Maryland from 1950. Home: Arlington, Va. †

BROSNAN, DENNIS WILLIAM, ry. ofcl.; b. Albany, Ga., Apr. 14, 1903; s. D. William and Sarah Elizabeth (Wimbish) B.; B.S., Ga. Inst. Tech., 1923; m. Louise Geeslin, Nov. 24, 1927; 1 son, Dennis William, III. Resident engr. Ga. State Highway Dept., 1923; with So. Ry. System, from 1926, v.p., 1952-60, exec. v.p., 1960-62, pres., from 1926, dir.; pres., dir. So. Ry. Co., Ala. Great So. R.R. Co., La. So. Ry. Co., Cin., New Orleans & Tex. Pacific Ry. Co., New Orleans & Northeastern R.R. Co., New Orleans Terminal Co., Ga. So. & Fla. Ry. Co., Carolina & Northwestern Ry. Co., Live Oak, Perry & Gulf R.R. Co., So. Ga. Ry. Co., Atlantic & East Carolina Ry. Co., Interstate R.R. Co., Ala. Indsl. Realty Co., Johns River Terminal Co., Ga. Indsl. Realty Co., dir. Richmond, Fredricksburg and Potomac R.R. Company, Richmond-Washington Co., Am. Security & Trust Co. (Washington), Citizens & So. Nat. Bank Atlanta; chmn. bd., chief exec. officer Central Ga. Ry. Co., Ga. and Fla. Ry. Co.; chmn., exec. com. Savannah & Atlanta Ry. Co., South Western Rd. Co.; chairman Wrightsville and Tennessee Railroad Company. Board directors Nat. Coal Policy Conf., Boys Clubs Am., So. States Indsl. Council; bus. adv. bd. Sch. Bus. Adminstrn. Am. U. Trustee Nat. Safety Council. Mem. Am. Soc. Sales Execs., Assn. Am. Railroads (pres.), Phi Sigma Kappa. Baptist. Mason. Clubs: River; Chevy Chase, 1925 F Street, Metropolitan (Washington); River (Jacksonville, Fla.); The Club (Birmingham, Ala.); Pendennis (Louisville). Home: Washington, D.C. Died June 14, 1985.†

BROSNAN, JOHN F(RANCIS), lawyer; b. N.Y.C., May 23, 1890; s. Michael L. and Nora B. (Cotter) B.; student De LaSalle Inst., 1904-09; B.C.E., Manhattan Coll., 1911, M.A., 1913, hon. LL.D., 1935; LL.D. (hon.), Fordham U., 1949; LL.B., N.Y. U., 1914, J.D., 1914, LL.D., 1958; D.C.L., St. Johns U., 1952; LL.D., Cath. U. Am., 1955, Iona Coll., 1958, Union Coll., 1959, LeMoyne Coll., 1959, Canisius Coll., 1959, Nat. U. Ireland, 1960; D.C.S., Pace Coll., 1957; Pd.D., St. Bonaventure U., 1957; m. Irene V. Bannin, June 30, 1923; children—John Patrick, Mary Ellen (Rev. Sister Mary Ellen), Vincent Michael. Admitted to N.Y. bar, 1915, D.C. bar, 1966; legal sec. to Hon. John P. Cohalan, 1915-21, law asst. to surrogates Cohalan and Foley, 1922-23; mem. firm Rushmore, Bisbee & Stern, and successors, N.Y.C., 1928-69; counsel firm Cusack & Stiles, N.Y.C., from 1970; mem. N.Y. State Temporary Commn. Against Discrimination, 1944, adv. bd. Prevailing Rate Wages on Pub. Works, 1946. Trustee State U., 1948, Moreland commr. investigating harness racing, 1953; elected regent Univ. State of N.Y., 1949, vice chancellor of regents, 1957, chancellor, 1957-61, regent emeritus, 1974; trustee Roger Williams Straus Meml. Found., Catholic Charities, Archdiocese of N.Y.; mem. Cardinal's Com. Laity for Cath. Charities; mem. bds. Servants of Relief for Incurable Cancer, Marquette League for Cath. Indian Missions, Health and Hosp. Council N.Y., St. Vincent's Hosp., N.Y.C., N.Y. Foundling Hosp., William Nelson Cromwell Found.; sr. trustee Manhattan Coll., chmn., 1967-70, trustee emeritus, 1973; chmn. N.Y. Brotherhood Week of NCCJ, 1958. Served as pvt. U.S. Army, World War I. Decorated Bros. Christian Schs. (affiliated mem.), Knight of Malta (bd. founders), knight Grand Cross Holy Sepulchre; recipient medal Manhattan Coll., 1938, medal St. De LaSalle, 1951, medal Am. Irish Hist. Soc., 1958; medal N.Y. Acad. Pub. Edn., 1958, George Washington Honor medal Freedoms Found. at Valley Forge, 1961, LaSallian medal of Bros. of Christian Schs., Manhattan Coll., 1967, Papal medal Pro Ecclesia at Pontifica, 1971, Elizabeth Seton Coll. Gold Medal award, 1972. Fellow Am. Bar Found., N.Y. Bar Found.; mem. Am. Judicature Soc., N.Y. County Lawyers Assn. (past pres.), Am., N.Y. Cath. Hist. Soc., Cath. Med. Jurisprudence, Assn. Bar City N.Y., U.S. Cath. Hist. Soc., Cath. Lawyers Guild, Am. Irish Hist. Soc. (council), Manhattan Coll. Alumni Soc. (past pres., medal of Honor 1960), Blessed Sacrament Conf. of St. Vincent de Paul Soc. (past pres.), Xavier Alumni Sodality (past pres.), Soc. Friendly Sons of St. Patrick (past pres.), Delta Chi. Clubs: K.C. (hon. life; Charles Carroll Gen. Assembly award 1960); City Midday (N.Y.C.). Home: New York, N.Y. Died Apr. 12, 1982.†

BROSNAN, THOMAS JOSEPH, power co. exec.; b. Washington, Apr. 7, 1905; s. John D. and Margaret (Hanlon) B.; m. Jean Swindeman, Nov. 3, 1931; children—Thomas Joseph, Jean A. (Mrs. George F. Leger), John Houston. B.S. in Elec. Engring, Catholic U. Am., 1925. With Westinghouse Electric Co., 1925-30, gen. engr., 1926-30; distbn. engr. Buffalo Niagra Electric Power Corp., 1930-50; chief engr. Western div. Niagara Mohawk Power Corp., Syracuse, N.Y., 1950-63, v.p., asst. chief engr., 1963-66, v.p., chief engr., 1966-73, v.p. research and devel., environmental matters, 1973-75, cons., from 1975, also dir.; v.p., chief engr., dir. Canadian Niagara Power Co., Ltd., from 1966; v.p., dir. St. Lawrence Power Co., 1966-75; v.p. Empire State Power Resources, Inc., from 1974. Former pres., dir. Cerebral Palsy Assn. Western N.Y.; past trustee United Fund Erie County. Fellow I.E.E.E. (past chmn. Niagara Frontier sect., past chmn. transmission and distbn. com.), Edison Electric Inst. (past. chmn. transmission and distbn. com.; exec. com. engring. and operating div.), Conf. Internationale des Grands Reseaux Electriques, Am. Assn. Engring. Edn., N.E. Power Coordination Council (chmn. council 1973-77, past chmn. system design coordinating com.), Nat. Electric Reliability Council (exec. bd.), Atomic Indsl. Forum, Am. Standards Assn. Clubs: Century, Buffalo Yacht. Home: Fayetteville, NY.

BROUGHER, WILLIAM E., army officer; born in Miss., Feb. 17, 1889; B.S., Miss. Agr. and Mech. Coll., 1910; grad. Command and Gen. Staff Sch., 1923, Army Indsl. Coll., 1933, Army War Coll., 1938, Inf. Sch. Tank Course, 1939; m. Frances Kelly, 1914; children—Doris, Betty, Frances. Commd. 2d lt., Inf., U.S. Army, Oct. 7, 1911, and advanced through the grades to brig. gen., Dec. 1941 (advanced by Gen. MacArthur for leadership in the Philippine Islands); served as major of Inf., World War I; served through the Bataan campaign, Philippines; taken prisoner in Japanese occupation of Philippine Islands; liberated Mukden, Manchuria, Aug. 1945. Became comdg. gen., Ft. McClellan, Ala., 1946; comdg. gen. Camp Gordon, Augusta, Ga., 1949; lectr. Decorated D.S.M. Mem. Am. Legion, Rotary. Mason (32 deg.). Author (poems) The Long Dark Road (8th edit.), 1947. Home: Atlanta, Ga. †

BROUGHTON, DONALD BEDDOES, chemical engineer; b. Rugby, Eng., Apr. 20, 1917; came to U.S., 1924, naturalized, 1934; s. Walter and Emily (Beddoes) B.; m. Natalie Waitt, Feb. 20, 1943. Asst. prof. chem. engring. M.I.T., 1943-49; with process div. UOP, Inc., Des Plaines, Ill., 1949-84, assoc. tech. dir., 1979. Recipient Alpha Chi Sigma award for chem. engring. research Am. Inst. Chem. Engrs., 1967. Fellow Nat. Acad. Engring., Am. Inst. Chem. Engrs.; mem. Am. Chem. Soc. (Rohm & Haas award in Separation Sci. and Tech. 1983), Am. Petroleum Inst. Home: Evanston, Ill. Died Dec. 2, 1984.

BROWER, CHARLES HENDRICKSON, business exec.; b. Asbury Park, N.J., Nov. 13, 1901; s. Charles Hendrick and Mary Amelia (Henderickson) B.; B.Sc., Rutgers, 1925; m. Mary Elizabeth Nelson, July 8, 1930; children—Brock Hendrickson, Charles Nelson, Anne Clayton, Teacher Bound Brook (N.J.) High Sch., 1925-26; joined Batten, Barton, Durstine, Osborn, New York, N.Y. as writer, 1928, vice pres. and dir., 1940-46, exec. v.p. charge creative services, 1946, mem. exec. com., 1951, gen. mgr., vice chairman executive committee, 1957, president chairman executive committee, 1957-64, chmn. bd., 1964-70. Life trustee of Rutgers U. Mem. Westfield (N.J.) Bd. Edn. 1945-48. Mem. Alpha Chi Rho. Republican. Episcopalian. Clubs: University (N.Y.); Echo Lake (Westfield). Home: Westfield, N.J. Died July 23, 1984.

BROWN, ABNER WOLCOTT, business exec.; b. Antioch, Cal., Jan. 1, 1889; s. Collins Munroe and Elizabeth (Wolcott) B.; B.S., U. Cal., 1910; m. Lavinia Bouche, Sept. 18, 1920. Joined Pabco Products, Inc. (formerly Paraffine Cos., Inc.), 1919, traffic mgr. from 1926, sec. from 1943. Served as 2d lt., U.S. Army, World War I. Mason.†

BROWN, CHARLES C., army officer; b. Houston, Tex., Jan. 3, 1890; s. Orville LeRoy and Sue Dee (Grainger) B.; B.S., Va. Mil. Inst., Lexington, Va., 1910; m. Anna Marie Sahm, June 24, 1916. Graduate, First Officers Training Camp, Fort Riley, Kan., commd. capt., inf., O.R.C., 1917; served with 92d (colored) Div., A.E.F., through World War I; promoted major, battalion comdr. 317th Ammunition Train, 1918; appt. capt., Q.M.C., U.S. Army, 1920, transferred to Field Arty., 1924, and advanced through the grades to brig. gen., 1944. Address: Washington, D.C.†

BROWN, CHESTER MELVILLE, chem. co. exec.; b. Cape Girardeau, Mo., Nov. 24, 1907; s. Edward Eugene and Emma I. (Caudle) B.; student Southeast Mo. State Coll., 1925-27, U. Mo., 1927-29; m. Nelda Juanita Prather, June 11, 1937; children—Stewart Dean, Stephen Mel, Phyllis Irene. With Allied Chem. Corp., 1929-69, trainee, successively supt., prodn. mgr., dir. sales, v.p., 1929-57, pres. Gen. Chem. div., 1957, pres. Nat. Aniline div., 1958-59, pres. co., 1959-69, also chief exec. officer, 1962-69, chmn. bd. dirs., 1962-69, dir., 1959-74; dir. Nat. State Bank, Elizabeth, N.J. Trustee Wells Coll., Aurora, N.Y., Vail-Deane Sch., Elizabeth. Mem. Am. Ordnance Assn., Synthetic Organic Chem. Mfrs. Assn., Mfg. Chemists Assn. Presbyterian. Home: Cape Girardeau, Mo. Died Aug. 12, 1981.

BROWN, DAVID E., state health officer; b. Ruston, La., Nov. 5, 1888; s. David E. and Elnora (Still) B.; M.D., Univ. of Tenn., 1910; m. Mae Jordan, Apr. 4, 1912; 1 son, David E. Gen. practice of medicine La., since 1910; state health officer, from 1943. Has served as mem. House of Rep. of La., and mem. La. State Senate. Mem. A.M.A., La. State Med. Soc., Am. Pub. Health Assn. Democrat. Methodist. Home: Baton Rouge, La. Deceased.

BROWN, EDMUND, JR., corp. exec., economist; b. Norfolk, Conn., Apr. 27, 1890; s. Edmund and Mabel S. (Shaw) B.; B.A., Amherst Coll., 1912; Ph.D., Columbia, 1924; m. Margaret A. Johnson, Mar. 17, 1936; children—Deborah Glassbrook, Geoffrey Norton. Faculty mem. U. Mo., 1916, U. Richmond, 1922, sch. commerce U. N.C., 1923-25; v.p. Brookmire Econ. Service, 1925-29; head research Lehman Corp., N.Y. City, 1929-45; v.p., 1941-45; head research Clark Dodge & Co., N.Y. City, 1946; v.p., dir. Investors Management Corp., Fundamental Investors, Investors Management Fund, N.Y. City, 1947, pres., dir., from 1948. Served as sgt., M.I., World War I. Author: Control of the Port, 1924; Marketing, 1925; Determinants of Investment Practice, 1934, numerous spl. reports. Home: Greenwich, Conn. †

BROWN, EDMUND RANDOLPH, publishing co. exec.; b. Everett, Mass., Sept. 2, 1888; s. Joseph and Mary Somers (Hosmer) B.; m. Alice Needham Very, June 22, 1916; children—Rosalys, Edmund Hosmer, Charlotte Brown Jackson, Cynthia, Martha Brown Bragg. A.B., Harvard, 1909. Pres. Four Seas Co., Boston, 1909-30, Bruce, Humphries, Inc., Boston, 1930-64, The Branden Press, Inc., Boston, from 1964; treas. Lit. Publs. Found, Inc. Editor: Internat. Pocket Library, from 1930, Poetry Jour, 1910-30, Poet Lore, from 1930, The World in Books, from 1960, Mem. Harvard Music Assn. Club: Sharon Chess. Home: Boulder, Colo.†

BROWN, EVERETT ERNEST, army officer; b. Vinton County, O., Dec. 15, 1889; ed. Marietta (O.) Coll., grad. Inf. Sch. company officers course, 1926, command and Gen. Staff Sch., 1938. In federal service on border duty, 4th Inf., Ohio Nat. Guard, 1916-17; with 166th Inf., France, 1917-18; participated Champagne-Marne, Aisne-Marne and Chateau Thierry engagements; disch., 1919; commd. 1st lt., U.S. Army, 1920, and advanced through the grades to brig. gen., 1944; asst. chief of staff, G-4, Hdqrs. VII Corps Area, Dec. 1941-May 1942, G-2, Hdqrs. VIII Corps, Brownwood, Tex., 1942; later assigned duty in Southwest Pacific Area. Decorated Legion of Merit with 2 Oak Leaf Clusters, Silver Star. Address: Washington, D.C.†

BROWN, FOSTER SARGENT, former univ. pres.; b. Leyden, N.Y., Sept. 18, 1908; s. Wallace Duane and Ruth Belle (Jackson) B.; B.S., St. Lawrence U., 1930, M.A., 1933, LL.D., 1961; Ed.D., Columbia U., 1950; L.H.D., Clarkson Coll. Tech., 1965; m. Catherine Pickard, June 27, 1936; children—Ruth Jackson (dec.), Susan Houghton, Wallace David, Celia Elizabeth, Irving Foster. Teaching prin. Coeymans (N.Y.) Union Sch., 1930-33; supervising prin. Roeliff Jansen Central Sch., Hillsdale, N.Y., 1935-43; supt. schs. Suffern (N.Y.), 1943-51; dean State U. Coll., Cortland, N.Y., 1951-52; pres. State U. Coll., Oswego, N.Y., 1952-63; pres. St. Lawrence U., 1963-69, now emeritus; hon. life mem. N.Y. State Congress Parents and Tchrs.; dir. St. Lawrence Nat. Bank. Mem. adv. bd. St. Lawrence Seaway Devel. Corp.; bd. dirs. St. Andrews Sch., Boca Raton, Fla.; mem. Morristown (N.Y.) Found. Pres., trustee emeritus St. Lawrence U.; bd. advisers Pine Crest Sch., Ft. Lauderdale, Fla. Mem. St. Lawrence County Hist. Assn., Phi Delta Kappa, Sigma Alpha Epsilon. Presbyterian. Rotarian. Contbr. to ednl. jours. Home: Morristown, N.Y. Died Feb. 14, 1985.

BROWN, FRANK ARTHUR, JR., biologist, educator; b. Beverly, Mass., Aug. 30, 1908; s. Frank Arthur and Arletta Esten (Robinson) B.; m. Jennie Wentworth Pettegrove, June 24, 1934; children: Charlotte, Frank Arthur, Marilyn Diane. A.B., Bowdoin Coll., 1929, Sc.D. (hon.), 1983; M.A., Harvard U.; Ph.D., Harvard U., 1934. Austin Teaching fellow Harvard, 1929-32, teaching asst. in zoology, 1932-34; instr. U. Ill., 1934-37; asst. prof. zoology Northwestern U., Evanston, Ill., 1937-40, assoc. prof., 1940-46, prof., from 1946, chmn. dept. biol. scis., 1949-56, Morrison prof. biology, 1956-76, emeritus, 1976-83; instr. Mt. Desert Biology Lab., summer 1940; vis. prof. U. Chgo., summer 1941; nat. lectr. Sigma Xi, 1968; assoc. and book rev. editor Physiol. Zoology, 1942-76; in charge dept. invertebrate zoology Marine Biol. Lab., Woods Hole, Mass., 1945-49. Author: Selected Invertebrate Types, 1950, Comparative Animal Physiology, 1950, 61, Biological Clocks, 1962, The Biological Clock: Two Views, 1970, An Introduction to Biological Rhythms, 1976; contbr. articles to profl. jours. Trustee Marine Biol. Lab., 1946-71, emeritus, 1976-83; trustee John G. Shedd Aquarium, 1969-77, hon., 1977-83. Recipient award of merit Found. for Study of Cycles, 1966; Disting. Educator award Bowdoin Coll., 1979. Fellow AAAS, Animal Behavior Soc.; mem. AAUP, Am. Soc. Zoologists (v.p. 1954), Am. Soc. Limnology and Oceanography, Am. Physiol. Soc., Soc. Study Growth and Devel., Ill. Acad. Sci., Soc. Extpl. Biology and Medicine, Am. Inst. Biol. Scis., Am. Soc. Naturalists (v.p. 1956), Soc. Gen. Physiologists (pres. 1955), Ecol. Soc. Am., Am. Soc. Plant Physiologists, Am. Geophys. Union, Soc. Chronobiology, Internat. Soc. Biometeorology, N.Y. Acad. Scis., Explorers Club, Sigma Xi, Gamma Alpha, Phi Sigma, Delta Upsilon. Conglist. Club: Harvard (Chgo.). Home: Woods Hole, Mass. Dec. May 19, 1983.

BROWN, GEORGE (ALFRED), British govt. ofcl.; b. London, Eng., Sept. 2, 1914; s. George Brown; m. Sophie Levine; 2 daus. Jr. clk. London's financial dist.; fur salesman John Lewis Partnership Ltd., 1931-36; organizer Transport and Gen. Workers' Union, 1936-44; mem. parliament for Belper, 1945-70; joint Parliamentary sec. to Ministry Agr. and Fisheries, 1947; vice chmn. def. com., 1960-70, mem. exec. com. Western European Union, 1960-70, minister of works, 1951; mem. Privy Council, Labour Party, 1951, mem. parliamentary com., 1955-85, also opposition spokesman on def., on home affairs, dep. leader, v. chmn., chmn. orgn. subcom., 1960-63, chmn. home policy subcommittee, 1963-70; foreign secretary, 1966-68. Member of the Nat. Youth Adv. Council; Brit. rep. Council of Europe's Consultative Assembly, 1951-53, 60; indsl. adviser Daily Mirror, London, from 1953. Bd. govs. Repton Sch. Home: London, Eng. Died June 3, 1985.

BROWN, GEORGE RUFUS, engineer, corporate executive; b. Belton, Tex., May 12, 1898; s. Riney Louis and Lucy Wilson (King) B.; m. Alice Pratt, Nov. 25, 1925; children—Nancy Nelson Brown Negley, Alice Maconda Brown O'Connor, Isabel Anne King Brown Wilson. Student, Rice U.; C.E., Colo. Sch. Mines. Chmn. fin. com., founding dir. Tex. Eastern Transmission Corp., ret., 1974; chmn. bd. Brown & Root, Inc.; dir. Halliburton Co., First City Bancorp.; dir. emeritus ITT, Southland Paper Mills, Inc., La. Land & Exploration Co., Texasgulf, Inc., Trans World Airlines. Former chmn. bd. trustees William M. Rice U.; trustee, pres. Brown Found. Episcopalian. Home: Houston, Tex. Dec. Jan. 22, 1983.

BROWN, H. TEMPLETON, lawyer; b. St. Joseph, Mo., Feb. 5, 1902; s. Robert A. and Mary (Guitar) B.; m. Jessie McLaren Hosmer, Oct. 17, 1928; children—H. Templeton, Jessie Grace (dec.). Grad., Phillips Andover Acad., 1919; A.B., Yale U., 1923; LL.B., Harvard U., 1926. Bar: Mo. bar 1926, Ill. bar 1943, U.S. Supreme Ct. bar 1943. Partner firm Brown, Douglas & Brown, St. Joseph, 1926-42, Mayer, Brown & Platt (and predecessors), Chgo., 1942-83; dir. emeritus UAL, Inc., United Air Lines, Inc.; dir. Scott, Foresman & Co., A.M. Castle & Co. Chmn. pres.'s council Nat. Coll. Edn.; mem. Northwestern U. Assos., Chgo. Zool. Soc.; dir. emeritus Northwestern Meml. Hosp., Chgo. Mem. Am. Bar Assn., Ill. Bar Assn., Chgo. Bar Assn., D.C. Bar, Am. Bar Found., Am. Judicature Soc., Am. Soc. Internat. Law, Am. Coll. Trial Lawyers, Bar Assn. 7th Fed. Circuit, Beta Theta Pi. Republican. Episcopalian. Clubs: Indian Hill Country (Chgo.), Onwentsia Country (Chgo.), Old Elm Country (Chgo.), Chgo. (Chgo.), Commonwealth (Chgo.), Comml. (Chgo.). Home: Winnetka, Ill. Dec. Sept. 26, 1983.

BROWN, HARLAN CRAIG, librarian; b. Cleve., Jan. 26, 1906; s. Edgar Dwight and Harriet J. (Weakley) B.; A.B., U. Minn., 1930, B.S., 1931; A.M., U. Mich., 1935; m. Helen Abel, June 16, 1936. Asst. librarian S.D. State Coll., 1931-34; gen. service asst. U. Mich. Library, 1935-36; circulation librarian N.C. State Coll., 1936-39, librarian State Coll. Agr. and Engring., 1939-64; asso. dir. D.H. Hill Library, N.C. State U. at Raleigh, 1964-71, dir. emeritus, 1971-82. Served to capt. AUS, 1942-46; maj. Res. ret. Mem. S.D. Library Assn. (v.p. 1933-34), N.C. Library Assn. (v.p. 1946-48, pres. 1949-51, life), Phi Kappa Phi. Democrat. Unitarian. Home: Raleigh, N.C. Died Oct. 10, 1982.

BROWN, HARRY LOWRANCE, state senator; born Forsyth County, Ga., Sept. 23, 1888; s. Berrien Holcombe and Sallie (Scruggs) B.; grad. A. and M. Sch., Clarkesville, Ga., 1911; B.S., in Agr., U. of Ga., 1916; Sc.D., Clemson (S.C.) Coll., 1937; m. Effie Garrett, Sept. 13, 1916 (died Nov. 22, 1925); 1 dau., Carroll Marie (Mrs. Garner T. Haupert); m. 2d, Lucie Mae Neville, Sept. 7, 1927. Scientific asst. in animal husbandry U.S. Dept. Agr., Jan.-Sept. 1917; state agt. in marketing Ga. Agrl. Extension Service, 1919; county agt. Fulton County, Ga., 1920-32; asst. dir. Agrl. extension, Athens, Ga., 1932-34, dir. agrl. extension, Athens, Ga., 1934-37; asst. sec. U.S. Dept. Agr., Washington, D.C., Jan. 1937-Dec. 1939; asst. dir. Agrl. Relations Dept., Tenn. Valley Authority, Knoxville, Tenn., 1939-41; gen. agent Farm Credit Adminstrn. of Columbia, S.C., 1941-47; vice chancellor U. System of Ga., 1947-49; dean, dir. agr. U. Ga., 1949-50, farm operator from 1950. Pub. mem. Selection Bd., U.S. Dept. of State, Washington, 1951; state senator, 40th Ga. Dist., 1953-54. Served as chief storekeeper with A.S., U.S.N., 1917-19. Mem. joint Brazil-U.S. Tech. Commn., Clayton C. of C. (pres. Rabun Co.), Alpha Zeta. Democrat. Baptist. Mason. Club: Rotary (Clayton, Ga.). Contbr. agrl. articles to newspapers and agrl. jours. Home; Mountain City, Ga. †

BROWN, IRVING H(ENRY), author, educator; b. Madison, Wis., Oct. 29, 1888; s. Charles N. and Nellie M. (Williams) B.; A.B., U. of Wis., 1911, A.M., 1912; Ph.D., Columbia, 1921; m. Mary Sullivan, of Chicago, June 24, 1916; children—William Woodberry, Elizabeth Marya. Began as instr. U. of Wis., 1912; later at U. of Cincinnati; asst. prof. Romance langs., Grad. Sch., Columbia, since 1924. American corr. Gypsy Lore Soc. (Eng.); mem. Am. Assn. Univ. Profs., Delta Tau Delta. Author: Nights and Days on the Gypsy Trail, 1922; Leconte de Lisle, 1924; Gypsy Fires in America, 1924; Deep Song, 1929; Romany Road, 1932. Translator: Enemies of Women, by Blasco Ibáñez, 1918. Contbr. to Forum, Travel, Survey Graphic, Romanic Review, Bookman, Jour. of Philosophy, Jour. Gypsy Lore Soc., The Britannica. Known as an authority on the Am. Gypsy. Address: New York, N.Y.

BROWN, JAMES GRADY, educator; b. Winona, Miss., Feb. 27, 1920; s. John James and Lovenia (Bridges) B.; m. Vivian Harris, Jan. 21, 1966. A.B., George Washington U., 1948, M.A., 1949; Ed.D., U. Md., 1961. Bus. edn. tchr., also prin. Balt. city schs., 1948-57; instr. bus. adminstrn. U. Md., 1957-61; asst. dean adminstrn., asso. prof. bus. adminstrn. George Washington U., 1961-66; prof., chmn. dept. bus. edn. Central Mich. U., 1966-77; prof. bus., head dept. Miss. State Coll. for Women, 1967-69; prof. bus. edn. Ga. State U., Atlanta, 1969-71; prof., head dept. bus. Miss. U. for Women, Columbus, from 1971; vis. prof. bus. edn. U. N.D., summer 1972, Memphis State U., 1969. Pres. Eastern Bus. Assn., 1963. Served with USAAF, 1941-45. Mem. Nat. Bus. Edn. Assn. (exec. bd. 1960- 63), Adminstrv. Mgmt. Assn. (v.p., exec. bd. Washington chpt. 1961- 63), N.E.A., Am. Bus. Communication Assn., Phi Delta Kappa, Delta Phi Epsilon. Home: Columbus, Miss.

BROWN, JAMES RAPHAEL, JR., manufacturing company executive; b. Phila., July 8, 1924; s. James Raphael and Jo Anna (Williams) B.; m. Jeanne Amy Maroney, Nov. 5, 1965; children—Constance Brown Black, Carolyn Brown Sander, James Randall, Cynthia, James Roland, Jeanne Ralphael. B.S. in Mech. Engring, U. Pa., 1943, M.S., 1948; M.B.A., Harvard U., 1959. With Baldwin-Lima-Hamilton Co., Eddystone, Pa., 1949-59, div. mgr., until 1959; dir. mfg. Dresser Industries, Inc., Dallas, 1959-60; adminstrv. exec. v.p. Clark Bros., Olean, N.Y., 1961-62; pres., chief exec. officer UMC Industries, St. Louis, 1962-70; with Dresser Industries, Inc., 1970-82, sr. v.p. ops., 1974-75, exec. v.p., 1976-81, pres., 1981-82, also dir. Served with USAAF, 1943-46. Decorated D.F.C., Purple Heart, Air medal; recipient Outstanding Leadership award ASME, 1977. Clubs: Bent Tree Country (Dallas), Brook Hallow (Dallas), Petroleum (Dallas); River Oaks (Houston), Petroleum (Houston); Old Warson Country (St. Louis). Home: Dallas, Tex. Dec. July 19, 1982.

BROWN, JOSEPH, sculptor, lectr.; b. Phila., Mar. 20, 1909; s. Max and Lena (Novak) B.; m. Gwyneth Noreen King, Aug. 19, 1939. Student, Temple U., 1927-31; B.S. (hon.), Temple U.; D.F.A., Temple U., 1980; D.F.A. (hon.), Western Md. Coll., 1978. Profl. boxer, 1929-30; sculpture studio asst. to Dr. R. Tait McKenzie, 1931-38; boxing coach Princeton U., 1937-62, instr., resident sculptor, 1939-45, asst. prof., resident sculptor, 1945-48, asso. prof., 1948-62, prof., 1962-77, prof. emeritus, 1977-85; Mem. Phila. Art Commn. Exhibited in one-man shows at, Nat. Acad. Arts and Letters, 1948, Yale U., 1952, 56, 60, Johns Hopkins U., 1965, U. Va., 1957, Bucknell U., 1958, Colgate U., 1958, Princeton U., 1938-66, Springfield Coll., 1964, U. Bridgeport, 1957, NEA, Washington, 1964, Sessler Gallery, Phila., 1963, Braverman Gallery, N.Y.C., 1969, Lehigh U., 1950, Olympic Games, Mexico City, 1968, Mangel Gallery, Phila., 1975, group shows at, Nat. Acad. Design, 1933-78, Pa. Acad. Fine Arts, 1932-42, Chgo. Art Inst., 1940, Archtl. League of New York, 1933, 35, Phila. Art Alliance, Phila. Mus., 1949, N.J. Art Mus., N.J. Pavilion, Worlds Fair, N.Y.C., 1965, Can. Olympic House, Expo '67; represented in permanent collections at, N.J. Art Mus., Pa. Acad. Fine Arts, Kennedy Meml. Library, Madison Sq. Garden, Nat. Acad. Design, also numerous univs., important works include two heroic bronze statues, White Athletic Center, Johns Hopkins U., heroic stone carving, St. Barnabus Ch., Phila., AAU swimming monument, Yale U., heroic bronze, McGonigle Hall, Temple U., four 16 foot bronze statues, Vets. Stadium, Phila.; Contbr. articles to profl. jours. Trustee Pop Warner Little Scholars, Service to Youth award, 1973. Recipient Barnett prize Nat. Acad. Design, 1944, 1st medals for sculpture Montclair Art Mus., 1940, 1st medals for sculpture DeVinci Soc., Phila., 1951, Creative award Am. Acad. Phys. Edn., 1968; assoc. academician Nat. Acad. Design; elected to Cultural Hall of Fame South Phila. High Sch., 1957; Athletic Hall of Fame Temple U., 1975. Fellow Nat. Sculpture Soc.; mem. Nat. Assn. for Sport and Phys. Edn., Nat. Sport Hall of Fame, Order of Owl, Temple U. Club: Franklin Inn. Home: Princeton, N.J. Died Mar. 12, 1985.

BROWN, KENNETH HAROLD, lawyer; b. Montreal, Que., Can., Apr. 12, 1908; s. Ernest and Ruby (Kirkus) B.; B.A., McGill U., 1929; B.A., B.C.L., Oxford U., 1932; m. Agnes Morton, Aug. 8, 1934; children—Micaela Margaret (Mrs. William S. Wilson), Alan Geoffrey Lloyd. Called to bar, Eng., 1932, Que., 1933, created Queen's counsel, 1947; practiced in Montreal, 1933-80; mem. firm, now counsel Lafleur, Brown, de Grandpré, and predecessor firms, 1933-80. Dir. Dubonnet, Inc., Can. Stebbins Engring. & Mfg. Co., Ltd. Emeritus mem. bd. govs. McGill U. Served to lt. col. Canadian Army, 1941-45. Decorated Order Brit. Empire. Mem. Canadian Bar Assn., Psi Upsilon. Home: Montreal Que., Canada. Died Nov. 11, 1980.

BROWN, LEE HENRY, c. of c. exec.; b. Saranac Lake, N.Y., Mar. 22, 1890; s. Henry W. and Carrie (Wilkins) B.; student pub. schs., Saranac Lake; m. Grace Evelyn Nugent, July 23, 1921 (div.); 1 dau., Elizabeth (Mrs. John P. Pappas). Asst. gen. sec. Holyoke (Mass.) YMCA, 1912-20; mng. sec. Westfield C. of C., 1920-24; mng. sec. Portsmouth (N.H.) C. of C., 1924-28; personal counsellor Wm. L. Fletcher, Inc., 1928-42; pvt. practice personal counsellor, 1942-49; personnel mgr. R.H. Hinkley Co., Boston, 1949-59; mem. staff Boston YMCA, 1959-64; exec. v.p., dir. Mass. C. of C., Boston, from 1964. Justice of Peace, 1967-68. Mem. Gov.'s Com. on Tourism, 1968-69, Gov.'s Com. on World Trade, 1969-70, Gov.'s Com. on Port of Boston, 1968-69. Kiwanian (pres.). Club: Adirondack Shillelagh (founder). Home: Boston, MA. †

BROWN, LINDSEY, librarian; b. Fall River, Mass., Oct. 27, 1888; s. George Pitman and Edna (Lindsey) B.; A.B. cum laude, from Harvard University, 1910, A.M., from same university, 1911; certificate, Library Sch., N.Y. Pub. Library, 1920; m. Dorothy K. Puddington, Dec. 28, 1920. Teacher history pub. and pvt. schs., 1911-18; asst. to dir. War Service Exchange, 1918; asst. reference librarian, Princeton U., 1920-21; asst. librarian, New Haven Pub. Library, 1921-25; librarian Waterbury Pub. Library, 1925-29; librarian New Haven Pub. Library from 1929. Mem. Conn. Library Assn., Mass. Library Assn., New Haven Colony Hist. Soc. Unitarian. Clubs: Graduate, Yale Faculty (New Haven). †

BROWN, LYLE, justice Arkansas Supreme Court; b. 1908; A.B., Henderson State U.; M.A., So. Meth. U. Admitted to Ark. bar, 1935; then assoc., justice Ark. Supreme Ct., Little Rock. Died May 1, 1984.

BROWN, MARK, radiologist, educator; b. Miami, Fla., Dec. 31, 1925; s. Leo and May (Marmur) B.; B.S., U. Miami, 1946; M.D., Vanderbilt U., 1950; m. Julia Dudley Hudson, Jan. 24, 1953; children—Karen Lynn, Lisa Ann, Leslie Carol. Intern, Vanderbilt U. Hosp., 1950-51; asst. resident surgeon U. Miami Sch. Medicine, 1955-56; resident radiologist Mallinckrodt Inst. Radiology, Barnes Hosp.-Washington U. Med. Center, St. Louis, 1956-59; research asso. anatomy Sch. Medicine Vanderbilt U., Nashville, 1951-52; instr. radiology Washington U. Sch. Medicine, St. Louis, 1959-60; mem. faculty Med. Coll. Ga., Augusta, 1963-83, prof. radiology, 1963—, chmn. dept. radiology, 1963-74, chief sect. nuclear medicine, 1971-83; cons. radiology VA Hosp., Augusta, Ga., 1963-83, Eisenhower Med. Center, Ft. Gordon, Ga., 1964-83, Gracewood (Ga.) State Hosp., 1964-83; aj. prof. Ga. Inst. Tech., Atlanta, 1968-73. Trustee Am. Registry Radiol. Technologists, 1969-73. Served to capt. USAF, 1953-55. Diplomate Am. Bd. Radiology, Am. Bd. Nuclear Medicine. Fellow Am. Coll. Radiology. Home: Augusta, Ga. Died Nov. 19, 1983; buried Augusta, Ga.

BROWN, MATTHEW L., orgn. adminstr.; b. Springfield, OH., Feb. 24, 1889; s. John E. and Emma (Boland) B.; student pub. schs. Springfield; m. Winifred M. Bosler, Apr. 17, 1912; 1 son, Matthew M. Sec. Ohio State Aerie, tri-state dir. for Ohio, Ky., W.Va. Frat. Order Eagles, 1931-44, mng. organizer, 1944, adminstrv. dir. since 1949, active in establishing Meml. Found., Jr. Order of Eagles, Eagles Nat. Life Ins. Co., Eagles' employee pensions, Pres. Clark Co. (OH.) Health League; mem. bd. Community Fund of Springfield, A.R.C.; chmn. bd. Hosp. Bldg. Com.; mem. bldg. com. Clark Co. Children's Home; gen. mgrs. Clark Co. Indsl. Exhibit; mgr., condr. bond issue for hosps., parks, schs., sewer systems; organizer Aid to Aged Adminstrn. (OH.), apptd. adminstr. by Gov. George White, 1934; mem. various hosp. bds. Mem. Springfield C. of C., A.F. of L. Democrat. Roman Catholic. Elk, K.C. Home: Springfield, Ohio. †

BROWN, MELFORD LOSEE, clergyman; b. Canton, N.Y., Aug. 21, 1887; s. Melford G. and Fannie Margaret (Losee) B.; B.S., St. Lawrence U., 1908; grad. Gen. Theol. Sem., 1911; studied Columbia; m. Edith Livingston, of N.Y. City, Sept. 21, 1914 (died 1919). Deacon, 1911, priest, 1912. P.E. Ch.; jr. curate, All Angels Ch., N.Y. City, 1911-12, sr. curate, 1912-14; rector Ch. of Ascension, Mt. Vernon, N.Y., since 1914. Home: Mt. Vernon, N.Y. †

BROWN, NESTOR MELLOY, ret. foods co. exec.; b. Akron, Ohio, Nov. 15, 1914; s. Ellsworth Grant and Emma Elizabeth (Rector) B.; m. Virginia Wallace Zinkhann, Dec. 23, 1939; children—Jane (Mrs. Edward Benedick), Victoria Ann (Mrs. Douglas Cushman), Rebecca Ellen (Mrs. Mark Ewing). B.S. in Mech. Engring, U. Akron, 1939. Indsl. engr. Am. Hard Rubber, Akron, 1939-40; indsl. engr. Nat. Screw & Mfg. Co., Cleve., 1940-42; asst. supt. Defiance Pressed Steel Co., Marion, Ohio, 1942-44, Omar Mills, Inc., Omaha, 1944-45; v.p. prodn. Taylor Reed Corp., Glenbrook, Conn., 1945-50; sr. v.p. Welch Foods Inc., Westfield, N.Y., 1964-67, exec. v.p., 1967-77, pres., 1977-80, ret., 1980, also dir. Mem. Concord Grape Assn. (pres. 1966), N.Y. State Canners and Freezers Assn. (pres. 1968), Am. Mgmt. Assn., Grocery Mfrs. Presbyn. Club: Tequesta (Fla.) Country. Home: Tequesta, Fla.

BROWN, PAUL MARVIN, JR., oil refining company executive; b. Amite, La., Nov. 5, 1893; s. Paul Marvin and Mary Alice (Perry) B.; A.B., Centenary Coll., 1916, LL.D., 1966; A.M., So. Meth. U., 1917; m. Willie Eleanor Cavett, July 30, 1918; children—Eleanor (Mrs. Greve), Charles Ellis. Instr. classical langs. Centenary Coll., 1917-18; asst. cashier Am. Nat. Bank, Shreveport, La., 1919-25, cashier, 1925-30; cashier Continental Am. Bank and Trust Co., Shreveport, 1930-35; pres., gen. mgr. Bayon State Oil Corp., Shreveport, from 1935; became receiver Comml. Nat. Bank Shreveport, 1936, resigned; pres. Ida Gasoline Co., Inc., 1957-81, Uni Prodn. Co., Inc., 1966-81, chmn. bd. La. Bank and Trust Co., 1956-75, chmn. emeritus, 1975-81, pres. Caddo Light Aggregate Co., Inc., 1959-81. Pres. Better Bus. Bur., Shreveport, 1963-64; treas., dir. Gulf South Research Inst., 1965-74; mem. La. Commn. Higher Edn. Facilities, 1965-73; pres. Pub. Affairs Research Council of La., 1962-63. Mem. La. Civil Service Commn., 1941-48, 52-56, (chmn. 1947-48, 52-56). Trustee Centenary Coll., treas. 1933-41, chmn., 1941-65, now chmn. emeritus, hon. life trustee. Served with U.S. Army, 1918-19; AEF. Mem. Kappa Alpha, Omicron Delta Kappa. Democrat. Methodist. Mason (K.T.). Clubs: Rotary (dist. gov. 1964-65), Shreveport. Home: Shreveport, La. Dec. Sept. 7, 1981. Interned Shreveport, La.

BROWN, PHILIP BRANSFIELD, lawyer; b. Middletown, Conn., Mar. 30, 1924; s. Philip Joseph and Elizabeth Pauline (Bransfield) B.; B.A. (Olin scholar), Wesleyan U., Middletown, 1944; LL.B. (bd. editors Law Jour.), Yale, 1946; m. Elinor Merrill Kenney, Feb. 7, 1959; children—Elizabeth, Sarah, Marcia. Admitted to Conn. bar, 1946, D.C. bar, 1947, U.S. Supreme Ct., 1950; asso., then partner firm Cox, Langford, Stoddard & Cutler, Washington, 1946-62; partner firm Cox, Langford & Brown, 1962-78, Squire, Sanders & Dempsey, 1978-80; sec., dir. Stanwick Corp., Ordibel, Inc.; sec. Italian Econ. Corp. Chmn. bd. trustees Wesleyan U., 1969-80; pres. bd. dirs. Madeira Sch., Greenway, Va., 1971-75. Trustee Lake Placid Edn. Found. Decorated officier l'Ordre de la Couronne, commandeur l'Ordre de Leopold II (Belgium). Mem. Am., D.C. bar assns., Belgian Am. C. of C. (dir.), Yale Law Sch. Assn. (pres. Washington 1956-57, mem. nat. exec. com. 1957-58), Phi Beta Kappa. Clubs: Metropolitan, Nat. Capital Democratic (Washington); Union (Cleve.). Home: Washington, D.C. Died Jan. 2, 1980.

BROWN, REED MCCLELLAN, educator; b. Germantown, O., Jan. 28, 1888; s. Orvon Graff and Lulu (Reed) B.; A.B., Twin Valley Coll., Germantown, 1906; Ph.B., Yale, 1910; m. Julia Wilson, June 12, 1912; children—Reed McClellan, Celeste Foster. Instr. Miami Mil. Inst., 1910-13, comdt. of cadets, 1930-32, pres. from 1932. Methodist. Mason (32 deg., Shriner). Clubs: Rotary, University. Home: Germantown, Ohio.

BROWN, ROBERT ALFRED, editor; b. Detroit, Feb. 1, 1918; s. Joseph Smith and Pearl (Moore) B.; m. Sarah Gene Warner, Aug. 26, 1941; children—Nikolyn Brown McDonald, Kathleen Brown Polage, Susan Brown Haywood, Scott, Mary Beth Brown McGonagle. Student, Flat River Jr. Coll., 1936-38; B.J., U. Mo., 1940. Editor Dexter (Mo.) Messenger, 1940-41; reporter Kennett (Mo.) Dunklin County Democrat, 1941-43, Daily Capital News, Jefferson City, Mo., 1945-46; statehouse reporter U.P. Assns., Little Rock, 1946-49, bur. mgr., Santa Fe, N.Mex., 1950-52, Albuquerque Jour., 1952-53, mng. editor, 1953-64, exec. editor, 1964-67, editor, 1967-76, sr. editor, from 1976. Commr., 181st gen. assembly United Presbyn. Ch. U.S.A., 1969. Served with AUS, 1943-45, ETO. Recipient Jud. Media award State Bar N.Mex., 1974. Mem. N.Mex. Press Assn. (pres. 1970), Sigma Delta Chi (Dan Burrows Meml. award N.Mex. chpt. 1974). Presbyn. Home: Albuquerque, NM.

BROWN, ROBERT CLARENCE, JR., patent lawyer; b. Evanston, Ill., Sept. 7, 1906; s. R. Clarence and Ella (Pierce) B.; B.S., Northwestern U., 1926, J.D., 1928, M.S., 1929; m. Alice Haas, June 15, 1931; children—Lawrence Haas, Warren Pierce, Ronald Owen. Admitted to Ill. bar, 1929, pvt. practice patent law, Chgo., 1929-81; partner firm Mann, Brown, McWilliams and Bradway, 1950-76; of counsel firm Mason, Kolehmainen, Rathburn & Wyssig, 1976-81; v.p. Internat. Research and Devel. Co., 1949-66. Cons. dir. tech. devel. div. WPB, 1942-43; chmn. Assn. Def. Com. of Chicago Tech. Socs.; pres. North Shore Area council Boy Scouts Am., 1949-51, exec. com. region 7, 1953-81, hon. life mem. exec. com., 1968—, vice chmn., 1962-64; past chmn. adv. council Northwestern U. Technol. Inst.; trustee Northwestern U., 1965-69. Mem. Am., Chgo. bar assns., Chgo Patent Law Assn. (pres. 1961), Northwestern U. Alumni Assn. (pres. 1963-64), Tau Beta Pi, Delta Tau Delta, Phi Alpha Delta. Republican. Presbyterian. Clubs: Northwestern U., Physics, Union League (Chgo.); Exmoor Country (Highland Park, Ill.); Three Lakes Rod and Gun (pres. 1973-75). Home: Highwood, Ill. Died May 21, 1981.

BROWN, RONALD FREDERICK, chemist, educator; b. Washington, Apr. 14, 1910; s. Virgil Lee and Laura Lee (Hoover) B.; B.S., U. Md., 1932; A.M., Harvard, 1937, Ph.D., 1939; m. Allie M. Sandridge, Mar. 24, 1935; children—Karen A., Stephen M. Instr. Harvard, 1939-40, Purdue U., 1940-42; asst. prof. U. So. Calif., Los Angeles, 1942-48, asso. prof., 1948-55, prof., 1955-75, prof. emeritus, 1975-84, head dept. chemistry, 1953-56, 1958- 63. Vis. research asso. Cal. Inst. Tech., 1963-64; responsible investigator OSRDCMR, 1943-45. Sr. Fulbright research fellow Imperial Coll., U. London, 1956-57. Fellow AAAS; mem. Am. Chem. Soc., AAUP, Sigma Xi, Phi Kappa Phi, Phi Lambda Upsilon, Alpha Chi Sigma. Author: Organic Chemistry, 1975; also tech. articles. Home: Laguna Hills, Calif. Died Mar. 3, 1984; buried Pacific Ocean.

BROWN, SANBORN C(ONNER), physicist; b. Beirut, Lebanon, Jan. 19, 1913; s. Julius Arthur and Helen Elizabeth (Conner) B.; parents U.S. citizens; A.B., Dartmouth, 1935, A.M., 1937; Ph.D. (Kramer fellow 1937-38), Mass. Inst. Tech., 1944; m. Lois L. Wright, June 21, 1940; children—Peter M., Stanley W., Prudence E. Asst. physics Dartmouth, 1935-37; teaching fellow Mass. Inst. Tech., 1938-41, instr. physics, 1941-45, asst. prof., 1945-49, asso. prof., 1949-62, professor, 1962-75; associate dean of the Graduate School, 1963-75. Mem. board dirs. Metcom, Inc. (Salem, Mass.). Mem. Sch. Com., Lexington, Mass., chmn., 1961-75. Tech. adviser U.S. del. 2d UN Internat. Conf. on Peaceful Uses Atomic Energy, Geneva, 1958; chmn. planning com. Internat. Conf. on Physics Edn., Paris, 1960; U.S. del. Internat. Atomic Energy Agy. Conf. on Plasma Physics and Controlled Thermonuclear Fusion, Salzburg, Austria, 1961; mem. U.S. nat. com., pres. on physics edn. Internat. Union of Pure and Applied Physics. Recipient Distinguished Service citation Am. Assn. Physics Tchrs., 1962. Fellow Am. Acad. Arts and Scis. (chmn. Rumford com. 1955-58, chmn. com. on ednl. activities 1957-61), Am. Phys. Soc. (chmn. div. electron physics 1951-52); mem. Am. Assn. Physics Tchrs. (chmn. com. sci. apparatus for ednl. instns. 1955-60, treas. 1955-62, mem. commn. on coll. physics). Sigma Xi (nat. lectr. 1961). Author: Base Data of Plasma Physics, 1959; Count Rumford, Physicist Extraordinary, 1962. Co-editor: International Education in Physics, 1960. Contbr. profl. jours. Home: Lexington, Mass. Died Nov. 28, 1981.

BROWN, SEVELLON, newspaper editor; born Washington, Apr. 23, 1913; s. Sevellon and Elizabeth Bonney (Barry) B.; student Amherst Coll., 1931-34; M.S., Columbia, 1936; m. Margaret Durkee, July 11, 1936 (div. 1958); children—Deborah Ann, Bonney Baxter; m. Janice Oakley Van De Water, Dec. 27, 1958. Assoc. editor Pathfinder Mag., 1937-39; Washington corr. Providence Evening Bull., 1939-42; chief Washington bur. Providence Journal-Bulletin, 1942-44, assistant to editor, 1946-49, assoc. editor, 1949-53, editor, 1953-68. Trustee Providence Public Library. Served as 2d lt. OSS, AUS, 1944-46. Pulitzer traveling scholar in Europe, 1936-37. Internat. (chmn. Am. com.), Am. press insts., New Eng. Soc. Newspaper editors (pres. 1960-61). Home: Providence, R.I. Died July 20, 1983.

BROWN, THEODORE DANA, banker; b. Denver, Jan. 8, 1922; s. Dana W. and Lillian (Bullis) B.; m. Barbara Towne, Oct. 3, 1943; children—Pamela (Mrs. Eric Sankey), Carolyn (Mrs. Gray Hawken). A.B., U. Denver, 1943; LL.B., Harvard, 1948. Asst. trust officer Internat. Trust Co., Denver, 1948-51; v.p., trust officer Security State Bank of Sterling, Colo., 1952-54, exec. v.p., 1954-62, pres., 1962-70, chmn. bd., 1970-73; also dir., chmn. bd., dir. Farmers State Bank, Yuma, Colo., 1963-76, vice-chmn., 1976-85; exec. v.p., dir. First Nat. Bank of Denver, 1970-73, pres., 1973-76, chmn. bd., 1976-85; chmn. bd., chief exec. officer 1st Nat. Bancorp., 1978-85; dir. Routt County Nat. Bank (div. CF and I Steel Corp.). Trustee Colo. Coll., Nat. Jewish Hosp. Research Center. Served with Supply Corps. USNR, 1943-45. Home: Englewood, Colo. Died Apr. 4, 1985.

BROWN, THOBURN KAYE, army officer; b. Clyde, N.C., Oct. 26, 1888; s. Thomas Wilson and Eliza Matilda (Haun) B.; student U. of Tenn., 1906-08; B.S., U.S. Mil. Acad., 1913; grad. Cav. Sch., 1923; distinguished grad. Command and Gen. Staff Sch., 1924; grad. Army War Coll., 1933; m. Frances Scratchley, Oct. 27, 1917; children—George Scratchley (U.S. Army), Thomas Wilson (U.S. Army). Commd. 2d lt., Cav. U.S. Army, 1913, and advanced through grades and ret. brig. gen., Oct. 31, 1948; instr. U.S. Army Schs., 1924-38. Decorated Legion of Merit, Bronze Star, Mexican Campaign World War I, European Theatre Medal with 1 battle star, Am. Theatre and Defense Medals, Commdr. British Empire, Legion of Honor. Croix de Guerre with palm (France), Order of Southern Cross (Brazil), Grand Cross Order of the Crown (Italy). Mem. Phi Gamma Delta. Clubs: Army and Navy Country (Washington D.C.), El Rio Golf and Country (Tucson, Airz.). Home: Tucson, Ariz. †

BROWN, TIMOTHY, judge; b. Madison, Wis., Feb. 24, 1889; s. Frederic M. and Annie H. (Storer) B.; A.B., U. Wis., 1911; LL.B., Harvard, 1914; m. Margaret S. Titchener, 1921 (dec. 1936); 1 son, Timothy; m. 2d, Louise Coxon, July 16, 1936. Admitted to Wis. bar, 1914, practiced in Madison, 1914-49; ct. commr. Dane County, 1926-49; exec. counsel to Govs. Goodland and Rennebohm of Wis., 1945, 1947-49; commr. Pub. Service Commn. of Wis., 1939; justice Wis. Supreme Ct. 1949-64, chief justice, 1962-64, resident judge, from 1964. Served to lt. (j.g.) USN, 1917-19. Mem. Am., Wis. bar assns., Am. Legion, V.F.W., Order of Coif, Beta Theta Pi. Club: Mendota Yacht. Home: Madison, WI. †

BROWN, WILLIAM FULLER, JR., electrical engineering educator; b. Lyon Mountain, N.Y., Sept. 21, 1904; s. William Fuller and Mary Emily (Williams) B.; A.B., Cornell, 1925; Ph.D., Columbia, 1937; m. Nancy Shannon Johnson, Aug. 17, 1936; 1 son, Eric Ramsay. Tchr. Carolina Acad., Raleigh, N.C., 1925-27; lectr. Columbia, 1928-38; asst. prof. Princeton, 1938-43; contract employee Naval Ordnance Lab., Washington, 1941-43, sr. physicist, 1943-45; research physicist Sun Oil Co., Newtown Square, Pa., 1946-55; sr. research physicist Minn. Mining & Mfg. Co., 1955-57; prof. elec. engring. U. Minn., Mpls., 1957-73, prof. emeritus, 1973-83; presenter tutorial Internat. Magnetics Conf., 1983. Research on magnetism, electricity, elasticity, applied theoretical physics, numerical calculation and statistics; guest prof. Max-Plank-Institut fûr Metallforschung, Stuttgart, 1963-64. Mem. adv. com. on ferromagnetism Office Naval Research, 1949-55. Recipient Meritorious Civilian Service award Dept. of Navy. Fulbright scholar Weizmann Inst. Sci., Rehovot, Israel, 1962. Fellow AAAS, Am. Phys. Soc., N.Y. Acad. Scis. (A. Cressy Morrison award, 1967), IEEE (Centennial medal 1983); mem. Magnetics Soc. (hon. life), Am. Soc. Info. Sci., Am. Assn. Physics Tchrs. (Coulomb's law com. 1944-50), Philos. Soc. Washington, Internat. Soc. Gen. Semantics, Operations Research Soc. Am., Inst. Math. Statistics, Soc. Natural Philosophy, Phi Beta Kappa, Sigma Xi, Tau Beta Pi, Phi Kappa Phi. Author: Magnetostatic Principles in Ferromagnetism, 1962; Micromagnetics, 1963, 78; Magnetoelastic Interactions, 1966. Mem. editorial bd. IEEE Transactions on Magnetics. Contbr. Handbook of Physics (E.U. Condon, editor); Ency. of Physics (S. Fluegge, editor). Translator Soviet Physics JETP. Contbr. articles to sci. jours. Home: Saint Paul, Minn. Died Dec. 12, 1983; buried Powhatan, Ohio.

BROWN, WILLIAM RUSSELL, lawyer; b. Holly Springs, Miss., July 5, 1914; s. Horace Brightberry and Aileen (Blackburn) B.; B.B.A., U. Tex., 1937, LL.B., 1937; m. Ruth Cunningham, Apr. 19, 1941; children—Betsy (Mrs. Thomas M. Smith III, Virginia, Russell. Admitted to Tex. bar, 1937, since practiced in Houston; with firm Baker & Botts, and predecessors, partner, 1948-83; gen. counsel, dir Houston Lighting & Power Co.; dir. Houston Industries, Inc., Primary Fuels, Inc., Utility Fuels, Inc. Served to lt. USNR, 1943-45. Decorated Bronze Star. Fellow Tex. Bar Found.; mem. Am. (council pub. utility sect. 1974-77), Tex. (council pub. utility law sect. 1976-77), Houston bar assns., Newcomen Soc., Chancellors, Friar Soc., Order of Coif, Delta Tau Delta, Beta Gamma Sigma. Clubs: Houston, Houston Country. Democrat. Episcopalian. Home: Houston, Tex. Died Apr. 8, 1983.

BROWN, WOOD, lawyer; b. Ruston, La., Oct. 26, 1905; s. Samuel Wood and Mary Gertrude (Mayfield) B.; A.B., Davidson Coll., 1926; LL.B., Tulane U., 1930; J.S.D., Yale, 1931; m. Martha Hyland, Feb. 14, 1933; children—Wood, Claiborne Hyland (dec.), Peter Howard. Admitted to La. bar, 1930; asso. firm Spencer, Phelps, Dunbar & Marks, New Orleans, 1931-41; partner firm Montgomery, Barnett, Brown & Read, and predecessor, from 1942; lectr. law sch. Tulane U., from 1934, prof., 1941-65, prof. emeritus, 1965-82; mem. bd. adv. editors Tulane Law Rev. Chmn. bd. Supervisors Elections for New Orleans, 1940-48; pres. Bur. Govtl. Research of New Orleans, 1950-52, mem. Civil Service Commn., 1953-58. Past Pres. So. area YMCA, past pres., dir. New Orleans; dir. Protestant Home for Aged; pres. New Orleans Community Chest, 1962-65, bd. dirs., 1965-69; trustee Pub. Affairs Research Council La.; trustee So. Eye Bank, Gulf States Eye Surgery Found.; mem. exec. bd. New Orleans council Boy Scouts Am. Research fellow Southwestern Legal Found. Mem. Am. Law Inst., Am., La., New Orleans (past v.p.) bar assns., Am. Assn. Ins. Counsel, New Orleans C. of C., Order of Coif, Sigma Chi, Phi Delta Phi. Presbyn. Club: Boston. Home: New Orleans, La. Died Oct. 29, 1982; buried Slidell, La.

BROWNE, JOHN BARTON, b. Plymouth, Eng., Apr. 23, 1887; s. John and Florence Emily (Andrews) B.; ed. Queens Coll., Taunton, Eng. and Bowden Coll., Manchester, Eng.; m. Eva Eckhardt, May 1, 1904; 1 son, John Boynton. Editor Saturday Review, Denver, Colo., 1907-08; feature writer, Los Angeles (Calif.) Examiner, 1910-15; served with French Army, 1915-17 (invalided home 1917); field dir. Am. Red Cross, San Francisco Area, 1919-20; editor California Outdoors and In from 1921; official rep. of Nat. Museums of France in U.S., Can. and Mexico since 1928. Mem. Dramatists Guild of Authors' League of America. Mem. A.A.A.S., Seismol. Soc. America. Awarded Palmes Academiques and Officier de I'Instruction Publique (France), Officer d'Academie. Democrat. Episcopalian. Clubs: Los Angeles Athletic. Authors, Surf and Sand, Hollywood Athletic, Riviera Golf. Contbr. to Saturday Evening Post, Los Angeles Examiner, California Outdoors and In. Co-author: Tell Us of the Night, 1941. Home: Los Angeles, Calif. †

BROWNELL, AMANDA BENJAMIN HALL (MRS. JOHN ANGELL BROWNELL), author; b. Hallville, Conn., July 12, 1899; d. Joseph and Caroline (Lucas) Hall; ed. pvt. schs.; courses in short story writing and English versification, New York U. and Columbia U.; m. John Angell Brownell (U.S. Navy), Aug. 28, 1923; 1 son, John Angell. Contbr. many short stories to women's mags., and poems in Harper's, Century, N. Am. Rev., etc.; awarded yearly prize by Poetry Soc. America for poems entitled The Dancer in the Shrine, and I'll Build My House, also Poetry Magazine (Chicago, Ill.) prize for The Ballad of the Three Sons, 1924. Episcopalian. Author: The Little Red House in the Hollow, 1918; Blind Wisdom, 1920; The Heart's Justice, 1922—all fiction; The Dancer in the Shrine (verse), 1923; (verse) Afternoons in Eden, 1932; Cinnamon Saint (poem), 1937; Honey Out of Heaven (collection of lyrics), 1938; Unweave a Rainbow (lyrics), 1942. Home: New London, Conn. Died Sept. 10, 1981.

BROWNELL, GEORGE ABBOTT, lawyer; b. N.Y.C., May 13, 1898; s. George Francis and Anne (Abbott) B.; m. Katharine Gray Dodge, June 8, 1946. A.B., Harvard, 1919, A.M., 1920, LL.B., 1922. Bar: N.Y. 1922. Practiced in, N.Y.; mem. firm Davis, Polk & Wardwell (and predecessors), 1922-30, partner firm, from 1930, of counsel, 1972-79; Personal rep. Pres. U.S., rank of Minister to, India. Middle East, 1946, Mexico 1948, spl. asst. to sec. air force, 1950; Trustee Bklyn. Savs. Bank, 1965-73; cons. to State Dept., 1946-57. Trustee Leake and Watts Childrens Home, 1932-76, N.Y. U. Med. Center, 1948-76, Lenox Hill Hosp., 1945-76, Seeing Eye Inc., 1939-74; bd. overseers Harvard, 1960-66. Served from pvt. to 2d lt. F.A. U.S. Army, 1918; from lt. col. to brig. gen. USAAF, 1942-45; brig. gen. O.R.C., 1947. Decorated Order of So. Cross Brazil).; D.S.M. U.S.; Selective Service medal; recipient William Nelson Cromwell medal N.Y. County Lawyers Assn., 1968. Fellow Am. Bar Found.; mem. Am. N.Y. State bar assns., N.Y. County Lawyers Assn., Bar Assn. N.Y.C. (v.p. 1968-70), Am. Law Inst. Club: Century (N.Y.C.). Home: New York, NY.

BROWNING, NOLAN, banker; b. Missouri, Oct. 27, 1899; s. William E. and Ada (Adair) B.; A.B., U. Okla., 1922; M.B.A., Harvard, 1925; m. Dorothy Wetherby, Sept. 3, 1932. With Bank of Am. Trust & Nat. Savs. Assn., from 1926, sr. v.p., 1959-64, Clubs: Stock Exchange, California (Los Angeles). Home: Los Angeles, Calif.

BRUCE, ALEXANDER DOUGLAS, car heating co. exec.; b. Guelph. Ont., Can., July 1887; s. George R. and Francas (Burgess) B.; grad. Guelph Collegiate Inst., 1902; m. Herby Johnson. Oct. 24, 1914; m. 2d. Elizabeth Reid, Nov. 10, 1939. Came to U.S., 1910, naturalized, 1925. Clk., J. B. Armstrong Carriage Co., 1902; sec. Standard Fitting & Valve Co., Guelph, 1907-10; purchasing agt. Chicago Car Heating Co., Chgo., 1910-14, Canadian rep., Montreal, 1914-17; sec. Vapor Corp. (formerly Vapor Heating Corp.), 1917-26, v.p., 1926-40, exec. v.p., 1940-45, pres., 1945-63, chmn. bd., from 1963; chmn. bd. Amercon Corp., Phila., from 1966. Republican. Methodist. Mason. Clubs: Union League, Rotary. Chicago, Executives (Chgo.); Skokie (Glencoe, Ill.). Home: Winnetka, Ill. †

BRUCE, E(DWIN) L(AWSON), JR., manufacturer; born Kansas City, Missouri, July 31, 1892; son of Edwin Lawson and Eva (Glenn) B.; student U. of Wis., 1911-13; m. Betty Cunningham, Mar. 18, 1914; children—Eva Gene (Mrs. Carey G. Bringle), Betty (Mrs. Sydney R. Miller, Jr.), Irene (Mrs. Irene Bruce Mitchell). With E. L. Bruce Co., from 1913, dir., from 1922, v.p., 1925-45, pres., 1945-62, later chairman board, director E. L. Bruce Co., Inc., became honorary chairman board, 1965; pres., dir. Miss. & Skuna Valley R.R. Co.; dir., St.L-S.F. R.R.; dir., exec. com. (Union Planters Nat. Bank. Mem. So. Hardwood Traffic Assn. (dir.), Newcomen Soc. (Eng.). Episcopalian. Clubs: Memphis Country, University, Lumbermen's, Internat. Concatenated Order of Hoo Hoo, Rivermont (Memphis). Home: Memphis, Tenn.

BRUCE, HOMER LINDSEY, ret. lawyer; b. Blanco, Tex., Aug. 24, 1892; s. William Herschel and Lillie Ora (Hart) B.; B.A., U. Tex., 1913; B.A. (Rhodes scholar), Oxford U., Eng., 1915, M.A., 1919; LL.B., Harvard, 1920; m. Anna Clara Chrisman, Aug. 18, 1917 (dec. 1959); children—Homer Lindsey, Robert Chrisman (dec.), Caroline (Mrs. Peter B. Vanderhoef); m. 2d, Dorothy Murie Blue, Mar. 24, 1964. Admitted to Tex. bar, 1920, practiced in Houston; sr. partner firm Baker and Botts, from 1920. Dir. Imperial Sugar Co. Served as capt. U.S. Army, World War I, AEF in France; lt. col. Res. Mem. Am., Houston bar assns., State Bar Tex., Beta Theta Pi. Clubs: Friars; Houston Country, Houston, Plaza Houston, Panorama Country, Conroe. Home: Houston, Tex. Died 1979.

BRUCE, JAMES WILLIAM, fuel co. exec.; b. Dorchester, Mass., Feb. 21, 1921; s. William B. and Isabella (McMillan) B.; certificate Bentley Coll. Accounting and Finance, 1946; B.A., Northeastern U., 1951; grad. Advanced Mgmt. Program, Harvard U., 1963; m. Margaret C. Hoffman, July 20, 1945; children—William B., Robert E., Laurie C. With Eastern Gas & Fuel Asso., Boston, 1940-84, treas., 1966-76, v.p., 1970-84, asst. to pres., 1976-77, v.p. corp. relations, 1977-84; treas. Boston Gas Co., 1964-66; dir. U.S. Mut. Liability Ins. Co. Mem. adv. com. Boston council Boy Scouts Am. Mem. New Eng. Gas Assn., Financial Execs. Inst., Mass. Soc. C.P.A.'s. Club: Treasurers (Boston). Home: Yarmouth Port, Mass. Died May 22, 1984.

BRUCE, ROBERT WATSON, telephone co. exec.; b. Stuttgart, Ark., May 5, 1903; s. George C. and Edna L. (Watson) B.; student Franklin (Ind.) Coll., 1921-23; B.S., U. Cal. at Berkeley, 1926; m. Ruth W. Anshutz, June 22, 1929; 1 son, Richard Chandler. With Pacific Tel. & Tel. Co., from 1926, successively residential salesman, mgr. offices in San Francisco, San Rafael, Bakersfield and Reno, div. comml. mgr., Sacramento, asst. v.p. Cal. operations, 1926-58, vice president, 1958-59, asst. v.p. of co., from 1959. Chmn. communications service Nev. Civil Def., 1946-52; communications adv. bd. Cal. Disaster Orgn., 1954-60; adv. com. Cal. Taxpayers Assn., 1955-60. Past bd. dirs. Bakersfield and Reno YMCA's; pres. Reno YMCA, 1951; v.p. S.W. area council YMCA, 1952; bd. dirs. Nev. region Boy Scouts Am., 1948-52. Mem. Kappa Delta Rho. Clubs: Press and Union League, Commonwealth. Home: Kentfield, Cal.

BRUCH, HILDE, psychiatrist, psychoanalyst, author, educator; b. Germany; came to U.S., 1934, naturalized, 1940; d. Hirsch and Adele (Rath) B.; 1 adopted nephew, Herbert. M.D., U. Freiburg, 1929. Diplomate: Am. Bd. Pediatrics, Am. Bd. Child Psychiatry. Pediatric tng. Leipzig U. Clinic; pediatrician Babies Hosp., N.Y.C., 1934-53; psychiat. tng. Johns Hopkins, 1941-43; psychoanalytic tng. Washington Balt. Inst., 1941-45; asso. psychoanalyst Psychoanalytic Clinic for Tng. and Research, Columbia, 1947-64; clin. prof. psychiatry Coll. Physians and Surgeons, 1953-58, clin. prof., 1958-64; attending psychiatrist N.Y. State Psychiat. Inst., 1954-64, dir. children's psychiat. service, 1953-55, psychotherapeutic supr., 1955-64, pvt. practice psychoanalysis and child psychiatry, N.Y.C., until 1964; prof. psychiatry Baylor Coll. Medicine, 1964-78, prof. emeritus, 1978-84. Author: Don't Be Afraid of Your Child, 1952, The Importance of Overweight, 1957, Studies in Schizophrenia, 1959, Eating Disorders: Obesity, Anorexia Nervosa and the Person Within, 1973, Learning Psychotherapy: Rationale and Ground Rules, 1974, The Golden Cage: The Enigma of Anorexia Nervosa, 1978; Contbr. articles to profl. jours. Wartime work on food habits for NRC. Recipient numerous awards in field. Life fellow Am. Psychiat. Assn.; mem. Internat. Psychoanalytic Assn., Am. Psychoanalytic Assn. Home: Houston, Tex. Died Dec. 15, 1984.

BRUECKNER, LEO JOHN, educator; b. Streator, Ill., Apr. 21, 1890; s. Herman and Leonore (Schneider) B.; student U. of Mich., 1909-11; A.B., U. of Ia., 1913, A.M., 1915, Ph.D., 1919; m. Agnes Holland, December 24, 1917; children—Richard, Keith, John, Patricia. Supt. of schs., Lowden, Ia., 1913-14; fellow U. of Ia., 1915-16; research dept. Detroit Pub. Schs., 1916; mem. faculty, Detroit Teachers Coll., 1916-17 and 1919-20, asst. dean, 1921-22; prof. elementary edn., U. of Minn., from 1922; dir. instructional research Minneapolis Pub. Schs., 1922-28; mem. Gary Sch. Survey, 1916-17; mem. Sch. Bldg. Survey, Cleveland Heights, OH., 1920; dir. study of elementary edn. for Regents Inquiry into Character and Cost of Public Education in New York, 1936-38. Chief, sect. on elementary edn., Office Military Govt., American Zone, Germany, 1947-48. Served as capt. Sanitary Corps. U.S. Army, in Intelligence Service, 1917-19; chief psychol. examiner, Camp Lewis, 1918; charge of rehabilitation Letterman Hosp., 1918-19. Mem. N.E.A., Nat. Society for Study of Edn., American Research Assn., Nat. Soc. Coll. Teachers Edn., Nat. Council Teachers of Mathematics. Sigma Nu, Phi Delta Kappa. Lutheran. Clubs: Campus,

Scholia. Author: How to Make Arithmetic Meaningful (with F. E. Grossnickle), 1947. Author and co-author many diagnostic and remedial tests in arithmetic and reading; contbr. many articles in year books, jours. and bulls. Home: Minneapolis, Minn. †

BRUENNER, ADOLPH F., lawyer; b. N.Y.C., June 12, 1889; s. Adolph and Frederica (Grabow) B.; ed. Brown U.; LL.B., LL.M., New York University; m. Marie A. Wolf, June 30, 1914; 1 son, Frederick H. Admitted to N.Y. bar, N.J. bar; practice in Hollis, New York. Director Factory Mutual Liability Ins. Co., Automobile Mut. Ins. Co., Amica Credit Corp., Amica Underwriting Corp. (all Providence). Mason. Address: Hollis, N.Y. †

BRUMBAUGH, AARON JOHN, college pres.; b. Hartville, Stark Co., O., Feb. 14, 1890; s. Francis and Frances (Gehman) B.; student Mt. Union Coll., Alliance, O., summers 1908, 09; B.A., Mt. Morris (Ill.) Coll., 1914; M.A., U. of Chicago, 1918; m. Marjorie Ruth Sherrick, May 31, 1914. Teacher rural schs., 1908-9; supt. Mecca Twp. Consolidated Sch., Trumbull Co., O., 1908-9; supt. schs., Mt. Morris, 1914-15; head English dept. Mt. Morris Coll., 1915-17, dean and prof. edn., 1918-21, pres. from 1921, same coll. Mem. N.E.A. Mem. ch. of Brethren (Dunkers). Clubs: Ben Ezra. Lecturer teachers' institutes, also lyceum lecturer. Home: Mt. Morris, Ill. †

BRUMBAUGH, G. EDWIN, architect; b. Huntingdon, Pa., Aug. 27, 1890; s. Martin Grove and Anna (Konigmacher) B.; B.S. Arch., Univ. of Pa., 1913; m. Frances Hover Anderson, Feb. 11, 1914. Started independent practice of architecture, Phila., Pa., 1916; Gwynedd Valley, Pa. Bldgs. include residences, schs., chs., etc.; specialist in residential work, particularly early Am. style and restoration of historic bldgs. which include; Ephrata Cloisters, Ephrata, Pa., Daniel Boone Homestead near Reading, Pa., Pottsgrove, Pottstown, Pa., for Commonwealth of Pa., Germantown Acad., David James Dove House (occupied by Pres. George Washington), Grumblethorpe, (John Wister House), and Gloria Dei (Old Swedes' Ch., Phila.; recent commns. include restorations of bldgs. at Washington Crossing, Pa. and Valley Forge, Pa. for Commonwealth of Pa. Fellow A.I.A., Pa. German Soc. (dir.), Montgomery County Hist. Soc., Pa. Hist. Assn., Swedish Colonial Soc., Sigma Xi. Dir. Pa. Sch. of Horticulture for Women, Ambler, Pa. Republican. Mem. Christian Science Ch. Author: Colonial Architecture of the Pennsylvania Germans, 1931. Contbr. articles on archtl. and hist. subjects to various mags. Home: Gwynedd Valley, Pa. †

BRUMLEY, ALBERT EDWARD, music pub., composer; b. Spiro, Okla., Oct. 29, 1905; s. William Sherman and Sarah Isabelle (Williams) B.; m. Goldie Edith Schell, Aug. 30, 1931; children—Bill, Albert Edward, Tom, Bob, Jack, Betty (Mrs. Billy John Pockrus). Student, Hartford (Ark.) Mus. Inst., 1926-30. Pres. Brumley/Hartford Interprises, Powell, Mo., 1948-75, Circuit clk., recorder of deeds, McDonald County, Mo., 1942-44. Composer over 600 gospel and religious songs. Mem. Nashville Songwriters Assn.'s Hall of Fame, Gospel Music Assn. Hall of Fame, Nashville. Mem. Ch. of Christ. Home: Powell, Mo. Died Nov. 15, 1977.

BRUNIE, HENRY C., banker; b. N.Y. City, Nov. 16, 1900; s. Henry and Josephine (Rinckhoff) B.; student Cornell U., 1919-21; m. Anna H. Fuller, Sept. 26, 1931; children—Ann H., Susan W. With Bankers Trust Company (N.Y. City), 1921-24, Brown Bros. Harriman & Co., 1924-31; v.p. Standard Investing Corp., 1929-31; sales and syndicate mgr., Kidder, Peabody & Co., 1931-33; partner L. A. Mathey & Co., 1933-39; pres. and dir. Empire Trust Co. from May 16, 1939; pres. and dir. Empire Safe Deposit Co. from June 13, 1939; dir. Dome Mines, Ltd., Gen. Reinsurance Corp., Home Ins. Co., N.Y. Capital Mgmt. Co. of Can., Ltd., Guaranty Reins. Co. Ltd., Gen. Reins. Life Corp., Southwestern Research & Gen. Investment Co., Narragansett Capital Corp. Dome Petroleum Ltd. Hon. chmn. United Hosp. Fund. Trustee v.p. Roosevelt Hosp. Clubs: Bankers, Bond, Links Cornell, River, Economic, Round Hill (Conn.); Recess; Clove Valley Rod and Gun; Cotton Bay (Eleuthera, Nassau). Home: Stamford, Conn. Died Apr. 11, 1985.

BRUNSTETTER, ROSCOE, lawyer; b. Westmoreland County, Pa., Nov. 12, 1890; s. Lester and Elizabeth (Hough) B.; Ph.B., Grove City Coll., 1915; LL.B., U. Pitts., 1918; m. Mary Gertrude McCune, Aug. 17, 1920. Admitted to Pa. bar, 1918. Fla. bar, 1925, U.S. Supreme Ct., 1926; practice of law, Miami, Fla., from 1926. Commissioner of City of Coral Gables, 1933-37, mayor, 1935-37. Dir., past pres. Fla. Soc. Crippled Children; dir. Children's Home Soc. Fla., Fla. region Nat. Conf. Christians and Jews, Dade County Society for Crippled Children; chairman Dade County chpt. National Found. Infantile Paralysis; chmn., dir. Variety Children's Hosp. of Miami; trustee U. Miami. Mem. Am., Fla., Dade County bar assns., Greater Miami Airport Assn. (past pres.), So. Fla. Hist. Soc., Fairchild Tropical Garden. Am. Legion, Julian Eaton Ednl. Found., Newcomen Soc. in N.A. Clubs: Coral Reef Yacht, Variety Lions (past pres., past dist. gov.) (Miami); Coral Gables Country, Riviera Country, Century (Coral Gables, Fla.); Committee of One Hundred (Miami Beach, Fla.). Home: Coral Gables, Fla. †

BRUSH, RAPP, army officer; b. Fort D. A. Russell, Wyo., Nov. 7, 1889; s. Daniel Harmon and Harriett (Rapp) B.; student Phillips Exeter Acad., 1904-08, U. of Ill., 1909-11; distinguished grad. Command and Gen. Staff Sch., 1923, Army War Coll., 1926; m. Alice Hall, Feb. 24, 1915; 1 son, Rapp. Commd. 2d lt., U.S. Army, 1911; promoted through grades to col., Jan. 1, 1940, brig. gen., Apr. 7, 1941, major gen., May 1942; mem. War Dept. Gen. Staff Corps, 1927-31; retired with rank of major general, 1945, Comd. 40th Inf. Div., World War II; combat operations incl. invasion of Luzon and capture of Clark Field; invasion and liberation Islands of Panay and Negros Occidental, P.I., Jan.-July 1948. Decorated D.S.M., Silver Star, Legion of Merit, Bronze Star and Air Medals; Comdr. Royal Order St. Olav (Norway). Home: Menlo Park, Calif. †

BRUSH, ROBERT MURRAY, hotel executive; b. Denver, July 1, 1913; s. Roy Arthur and Adele (Twitchell) B.; m. Marjorie C. Culver, Oct. 12, 1945; children: Richard L., John T., Robert Murray (dec.), Frederick Culver. B.S., Cornell U., 1934. From steward to mgr. Basin Harbor Club, Vt., 1934-39; asst. to pres. Hosts, Inc., Springfield, Mass., 1940-42; gen. mgr. Wayland Manor, Providence, 1946-47, Sheraton-Biltmore, 1947-48; asst. to gen. mgr. Sheraton Corp. Am., Boston, 1948-50, v.p., 1950-59, sr. v.p., 1959-69; v.p. TraveLodge Internat., Inc., El Cajon, Calif., 1969-71, sr. v.p., 1971-76, also dir.; v.p. Cox Hotel Corp. Vice pres. Cultural Fund Boston.; bd. dirs., mem. exec. com. San Diego Conv. and Visitors Bur., 1973-76, mem. adv. com., 1976-80; bd. dirs. Travelers Aid Soc., 1976-83, treas., 1979-81, pres., 1981-84. Served from lt. to maj. USAAF, 1942-46. Mem. Northeast Hotel Assn., Cornell Soc. Hotelmen (pres. 1951), Boston C. of C., New Eng. Council (past dir.), Am. Hotel and Motel Assn. (industry adv. com.), Calif. Hotel and Motel Assn. (dir. 1973—), Sigma Nu. Clubs: Rancho Santa Fe Country (Rancho Santa Fe), Rancho Santa Fe Men's Golf (Rancho Santa Fe) (gov. 1978-81, v.p. 1979, 80), Rotary (Rancho Santa Fe); Los Ancianos. Home: Rancho Santa Fe, Calif. Dec. June 17, 1984.

BRYAN, ALBERT V(ICKERS), judge; b. Alexandria, Va., July 23, 1899; s. Albert and Marion (Beach) B.; m. Marie Gasson, Dec. 1, 1923; children: Albert Vickers, Henry Gasson. LL.B., U. Va., 1921. Bar: Va. bar 1920. Practiced in, Alexandria, 1921-47; judge U.S. Dist. Ct. for Eastern Dist. Va., 1947-61, from 1961, U.S. Circuit Ct. Appeals, 4th Circuit, 1961-72; mem. Va. Bd. Corrections, 1943-45, Va. Bd. Law Examiners, 1944-47. Bd. visitors U. Va., 1956-64, rector, 1960-64. Mem. Am., Va. bar assns., Am. Law Inst., Raven Soc., Phi Beta Kappa, Phi Kappa Sigma, Phi Delta Phi, Omicron Delta Kappa. Home: Alexandria, Va. Dec. Mar. 13, 1984.*

BRYAN, JACOB FRANKLIN, III, ins. co. exec.; b. Jacksonville, Fla., Feb. 26, 1908; s. Jacob Franklin and Olive (Gibson) B.; m. Josephine Hendley, May 25, 1935; children—Jacob F., IV, Carter Byrd, Kendall Gibson. Student, Fla. Bus. U., 1927-28; LL.D. (hon.), Bethune-Cookman Coll., 1965. With Ind. Life and Accident Ins. Co., Jacksonville, from 1927, v.p., dir., 1948-57, chmn. bd., pres., 1957-79, chmn. bd., chief exec. officer, from 1979; chmn. bd., pres. Herald Life Ins. Co., Jacksonville, 1960-79, chmn. bd., chief exec. officer, from 1979; dir., mem. trust com. Fla. Nat. Bank; dir. Fla. Fed. Savs. and Loan Assn., from 1955, v.p., from 1974, dir. Indsl. Am. Corp. Mem. U.S. Indsl. Council, from 1967, mem. exec. com., v.p. for Fla., from 1970; mem. com. Bold New Jacksonville Program, 1968; chmn. Community Planning Council Jacksonville Area, from 1968; mem. Fla. Pub. Sch. Bd., 1968-69, Fla. State Ins. Advisory Com., Fla. Council of 100, from 1967; chmn. Health Systems Agy. of N.E. Fla. Area 3, 1964-70; mem. state advisory group Fla. Regional Med. Programs, from 1967; mem. contract com. HUD, from 1970; chmn. Fla. Gov.'s Art Commn.; mem. Downtown Devel. Authority, Fla. Gov.'s St. Augustine Hist. Restoration and Preservation Commn., 1969-74, Commn. on Quality in Edn., from 1967; exec. adviser N. Fla. council Boy Scouts Am., 1961-71; lay adv. bd. St. Vincent's Hosp.; chmn. adv. com. Eartha White Nursing Home, Jacksonville, 1965-66; bd. dirs. United Negro Coll. Fund, March of Dimes, Child Guidance Clinic, Jacksonville Art Mus., United Fund for Jacksonville, Girls Club Jacksonville; bd. dirs. Fla. Heart Assn., 1968-70, chmn. fund drive, 1969-70; Bd. dirs. N.E. Fla., 1964-75, pres., 1968-69; bd. dirs., mem. Pres.'s Club, Meth. Hosp. Found., from 1981; past nat. bd. dirs. Am. Cancer Soc., past pres., hon. life bd. dirs. county unit, bd. dirs., Fla., 1964-71, hon. life mem.; bd. dirs. Life Underwriting Tng. Council, Jacksonville Symphony Assn., Jacksonville Cathedral Found., 1963-72; mem. devel. com. Salvation Army, from 1980; mem. nominating com., mem. nat. chmn.'s centennial club ARC, from 1981; trustee Bethune-Cookman Coll., Jacksonville U., Bapt. Meml. Hosp., Episcopal High Sch., Jacksonville; bd. fellows U. Tampa. Recipient Spl. Service award Fla. Cancer Soc., 1959, Ted Arnold award Jacksonville Jaycees, CHIEF award Ind. Colls. and Univs., 1971; Order of Dolphin-Bronze Patron award U. Jacksonville, 1981; named Boss of Year Arlington Jaycees, 1960, Boss of Year Am. Bus. Women's Assn., 1965, Man of Year Fla. Assn. Life Underwriters, 1960, and other awards. Fellow Royal Hort. Soc. (Eng.); mem. Jacksonville C. of C. (past bd. govs.), Fla., Jacksonville hist. socs., Life Insurers Conf. (past bd. dirs.), Nat. Assn. Over the Counter Cos. (advisory council from 1973), Jacksonville Geneal. Soc., NAM, Newcomen Soc., SAR (past pres.), SCV, Alpha Kappa Psi (hon. life). Episcopalian. Clubs: Seminole, Fla. Yacht, River, Timuquana Country, Ye Mystic Revellers, Meninak. Home: Jacksonville, Fla.

BRYAN, JOHN EDWARD, editor; b. Cleve., Nov. 24, 1913; s. Charles F. and Rose (Matt) B.; student Adelbert Coll., 1931-34, Western Res. U.; m. Allane Hoyt Horner, Nov. 25, 1933; children—John C., Nancy; m. 2d, Helen Urban, Jan. 6, 1944. Promotion and pub. relations dir. Gen. Outdoor Advt. Co., 1934-40; estate analyst Conn. Gen. Life Ins. Co., 1940-41; asst. promotion dir. Cleve. Press, 1942; editor lamp publ. Gen. Electric Co., 1943-45; reporter Cleve. Plain Dealer, 1945-48, financial editor, 1948-72, bus. columnist, 1972-79; fin. relations cons. Mem. Cleve. Soc. Sec. Analysts, Nat. Security Traders Assn., Soc. Am. Bus. Writers, Alpha Delta Phi, Sigma Delta Chi. Club: Mid-Day. Contbr. articles mags. Home: Palm Harbor, Fla. Died Aug. 17, 1984.

BRYAN, LESLIE AULLS, transportation economist; b. Bath, N.Y., Feb. 23, 1900; s. Daniel Beach and Anna (Aulls) B.; m. Gertrude Catherine Gelder, Aug. 22, 1931; children: Leslie A., George G. B.S., Syracuse U., 1923, M.S., 1924, J.D., 1939; Ph.D., Am. U., 1930; Sc.D. (hon.), Southwestern, 1972. Prof. bus. adminstrn. Southwestern Coll., Winfield, Kans., 1924-25; asst. coach of track Syracuse U., 1925-42, dir. athletics, 1934-37, also instr., 1925-28, asst. prof. transp., 1928-31, assoc. prof., 1931-39, prof., 1939-45, Franklin prof. transp., 1945-46; also pres. Seneca Flying Sch., Syracuse, N.Y., 1943-46; dir. Inst. Aviation; prof. mgmt. U. Ill., 1946-68, emeritus, 1968-85; aviation advisory bd. Norwich U., 1954-59; mem. Pres. Kennedy's Task Force on Aviation Goals, 1961; U. Ill. faculty rep. Intercollegiate Conf. (Big Ten), 1959-68, acting dir. athletics, 1965-66; Dir. aviation State of N.Y., 1945; Pres. Eastern Intercoll. Boxing Assn., 1936-38, N.Y. State Aviation Council, 1944-46, Traffic Club of Syracuse., 1942; Transp. cons. Nat. Resources Planning Bd., 1942-44; aviation cons. New Standard Ency., from 1947; mem. nat. aerospace ednl. adv. com. Civil Air Patrol, 1948-68, chmn., 1965-66; mem. bd. aero. advisers, State of Ill., 1949-69; tech. assistance bd. Link Found., 1953-71; adv. com. FCDA, 1957-60; chmn. Pres. Eisenhower's Gen. Aviation Facilities Planning Group, 1957-58; adv. com. Washington Internat. Airport, 1958-62; cons. FAA, 1959-62; mem. adv. bd. Air Tng. Command, 1964, cons., 1965-69; mem. adv. bd. Ill. State Archives, from 1980. Author: Aerial Transportation, 1925, Industrial Traffic Management, 1929, Principles of Water Transportation, 1939, (with others) Aviation Study Manual, 1949, (with Wilson) Air Transportation, 1949; (with others) rev. Fundamentals of Aviation and Space Technology, 1968; Traffic Management in Industry, 1953, Aulls-Bryan and Allied Families, 1966, Aulls Genealogy, 1974, Thomas Bryan and Some of His Descendants, 1979, Immigrant Ancestors, 1981; also monographs and articles.; Adv. editor: Nat. Air Rev, 1948-50; editorial adviser (aeros.), Holt, Rinehart & Winston, Inc., 1960-64, bd. editors, Air Affairs, 1949-51; cons.: Our Wonderful World, 1954-55; contbr.: World Book Ency, 1952-68, Funk and Wagnalls New Ency, 1947—, Compton's Pictured Ency, 1959-85, McGraw Hill Ency. of Sci. and Tech, 1959; cons. editor: Above and Beyond Ency, 1967-85, Illustrated Ency. of Aviation and Space, 1970. Bd. dirs. Nat. Found. for Asthmatic Children, 1956-65; Pres. Arrowhead council Boy Scouts Am., 1954-60, mem. at large nat. council, 1960-70, regional exec. bd., 1959-70. Served as lt., inf. and Air Corps U.S. Army, 1917-19, overseas; col. USAF Res.; Res. ret. Awarded Sec. War Commendation, 1946; Arents medal, 1955; Brewer Trophy, 1953; Sigma Delta Chi award, 1955; Air Power award, 1956; Silver Beaver award Boy Scouts Am., 1957; Silver Antelope, 1959; Tissandier diploma Fedn. Aeronautique Internat., 1958; distinguished service award Am. Assn. Airport Execs., 1959; Continental Air Command certificate of recognition, 1960; Nat. Aero. Assn. certificate of recognition, 1966; FAA distinguished pub. service award, 1965; Elder Statesman of Aviation, 1966; Distinguished Alumni award Am. U., 1969; Letterman of Distinction award Syracuse U., 1969; Patriots medal, 1968; Minuteman award S.A.R., 1976; others. Fellow U. Aviation Assn. (pres. 1948-49, Wheatley award 1955); mem. Am. Soc. Traffic and Transp. (bd. examiners 1948-60), Nat. Aerospace Edn. Council (pres. 1952-53, 64-66, dir. 1953-54, 59-64, 66-67), Nat. Aero Assn. (v.p. 1953-56, 60-61, 65-66, dir. 1950- 52, 54-55, 57-59, 62-64), Civil Air Patrol (Distinguished Service medal 1954), Am. Assn. Airport Execs. (v.p. 1953-55, pres. 1955-56, dir. edn. 1952-68, hon. life mem.), Am. Inst. Aeros. and Astronautics, Acad. Mgmt., ICC Practitioners Assn., Aerospace Writers Assn., Soc. of Cincinnati, Nat. Air and Space Mus. (Hall of Honor), Nat. Huguenot Soc. (pres. Ill. 1971-73, Disting. Service medal 1976, pres. gen. 1977-78, hon. pres. gen. 1979—), Newcomen Soc. N.Am., Scabbard and Blade, Am. U. Alumni Assn. (chmn. bd. govs. 1970-71), S.A.R. (genealogist gen. 1973-75, trustee 1975-76, 77—, v.p. gen. 1976-77, pres. Ill. 1974-76), Ill. Geneal. Soc. (pres. 1972-73, Distinguished Leadership award 1974), Soc. War 1812 (asst. adj. gen. 1975-85, pres. Ill. 1976-81), Arnold Air Soc., Pershing Rifles, Sigma Alpha Tau, Alpha Eta Rho, Phi Gamma Mu, Zeta Psi, Phi Delta Phi, Phi Kappa Alpha, Alpha Kappa Psi, Phi Kappa Phi, Alpha Phi Omega, Kappa Phi Kappa, Alpha Delta Sigma, Delta Nu Alpha, Tau Omega, Beta Gamma Sigma. Home: Champaign, Ill. Died June 24, 1985.

BRYAN, WRIGHT, ret. univ. adminstr., former editor; b. Atlanta, Aug. 6, 1905; s. Arthur Buist and Inez (Sledge)

B.; m. Ellen Hillyer Newell, Oct. 12, 1932; children—Ellen Newell (Mrs. N. Bryan Tozzer), Mary Lane (Mrs. John K. Sullivan), William Wright. B.S., Clemson Coll., 1926, Litt.D., 1956; postgrad., U. Mo. Sch. Journalism, 1926-27; LL.D., Coll. of Wooster, 1958. Reporter, 1924, sports editor, 1926, Greenville (S.C.) Piedmont; with Atlanta Jour., 1927-53, successively reporter, city editor, mng. editor, asso. editor and mng. editor, editor, 1945-53; editor Cleve. Plain Dealer, 1954-63; v.p. devel. Clemson (S.C.) U., 1964-70; war corr. for Atlanta Jour. and NBC, 1943-45. Author: Clemson: An Informal History of the University, 1889-1979. Chmn. Ga., Press. Inst., 1942, Atlanta chpt. A.R.C., 1950-51; pres. Atlanta Rotary Club, 1953; first v.p. Welfare Fedn. of Cleveland, 1960-61; Bd. overseers, bd. dirs. Sweet Briar Coll. Recipient Medal of Freedom for services as war corr. Mem. Am. Soc. Newspaper Editors (pres. 1953), Clemson Alumni Assn. (pres. 1958, Distinguished Alumnus award), Sigma Delta Chi, Phi Kappa Psi. Methodist. Clubs: Capital City (Atlanta), Piedmont Driving (Atlanta), Nine O'Clocks (Atlanta); Overseas Press (N.Y.C.); Poinsett (Greenville, S.C.). Captured by German army, Sept. 12, 1944, liberated Jan. 22, 1945. Home: Clemson SC

BRYANT, HAROLD W., lawyer; b. Mayville, Mich., Feb. 1, 1888; s. Allison L. and Marian W. (Phillips) B.; A.B., DePauw U., 1910; LL.B., Harvard, 1913; m. Mary V. Harrison, June 20, 1912; children—John H., Richard W., Stephen A., Harold W. Admitted to Mich. bar, 1913; city atty. East Grand Rapids, Mich., 1928-53; sec.-treas. Waters Bldg. Co.; dir. Union Bank of Mich., Ton Tex Corp., Colonial Banking Co. Trustee, sec. M.J. Clark Meml. Home. Mem. Am. Bar Assn., Phi Beta Kappa, Delta Kappa Epsilon. Methodist. Home: Grand Rapids, Mich. †

BRYANT, PAUL WILLIAM, university football coach, athletic director; b. Kingsland, Ark., Sept. 11, 1913; s. Wilson Monroe and Ida (Kilgore) B.; m. Mary Harmon Black, Aug. 3, 1934; children—Mae Martin (Mrs. John Tyson), Paul William. B.S., U. Ala., 1939. Asst. football coach U. Ala., 1936-40, Vanderbilt U., 1940-41; head football coach U. Md., 1945, U. Ky., 1946-53, Tex. A&M Coll., 1954-57, U. Ala., 1958-82; head coach Sugar Bowl games, 1951, 62, 64, 67, 73, Orange Bowl, 1950, 63, 65, 66, 75, Cotton Bowl, 1952, 1967, 72, Blue Bonnet Game, 1960, 70, Gator Bowl, 1957, 1968, Liberty Bowl Game, 1959, 69, 76, Great Lakes Bowl Game, 1947; Dir. First Nat. Bank, Federated Guaranty, R.L., Zeigler Co., Inc., all Tuscaloosa. Author: Building a Championship Football Team, 1960. Active local YMCA, United Fund, Heart Fund, Tb Seal drive.; Trustee Am. Football Coaches Assn., Pop Warner Hall of Fame. Served to lt. comdr. USNR, 1941-45. Recipient Legion of Honor award Tex. Upsilon chpt. Sigma Nu, 1956, Ann. award Louisville Optimist Club, 1950, Meritorious Service plaque Ky. Press Assn., 1951, plaque D.C. chpt. U. Ala. Alumni Assn., 1962, Outstanding Citizen Ky. award Ky. Press Assn., 1950, Silver Anniversary award Sports Illustrated mag., 1960, Outstanding Achievement in Coll. Football award Dapper Dan Club, Pitts., 1962, Worlds No. 1 Coach award Birmingham (Ala.) Downtown Action Com., 1965; named to Ark. Hall of Fame, 1965, hon. col. Ala. Militia, 1963, Ark. traveler, 1959; hon. Texan, 1954, adm. Tex. Navy, 1954, adm. of Lake Martin Ky., 1962, Ky. Col., 1950, Coach of Yr. in SW, 1956, in SE Conf., 1961, 64, 72, 74, Coach of Yr. Coach and Athletic mag., 1955, 56, 60, 61, 64; Coach of Yr. Am. Football Coaches Assn., 1961, 72, 73; Dist. III Coach of Yr. medallion, 1964; Citizen of Yr., Teleprompter Cable TV, 1975; U. Ala. athletic dormitory named Paul Bryant Hall, 1965; stadium named Bryant-Denny Stadium, 1976. Mem. Am. Football Coaches Assn. (pres. 1972), Jasons, Sigma Nu, Omicron Delta Kappa. Methodist (steward). Clubs: A (U. Ala.), Athletic Letterman's. Home: Tuscaloosa, Ala. Dec. Jan. 26, 1983.*

BUCHANAN, DOUGLAS N., educator, neurologist; b. Scotland, Jan. 14, 1901; s. Andrew Dick and Mary (Nisbet) B.; M.A., B.Sc., M.B., Ch.B., U. Glasgow (Scotland), 1925; postgrad. Trinity Coll., Cambridge (Eng.) U., 1925-30, U. Paris, 1924, 31; M.D. (hon.), U. San Carlos de Guatemala, 1956; m. Marian Anderson, 1930. Formerly mem. faculty staff Nat. Hosp. Nervous Diseases, London, Eng; mem. faculty Med. Sch., U. Chgo., from 1932, prof. neurology 1940-83; neurologist U. Chgo. Hosps., from 1932; attending and cons. neurologist Children's Meml. Hosp., Chgo., from 1935. Cons. neurologist D.R.G., NIH, Washington, 1964-68, chmn., 1968-71. Mem. Am. Neurol. Assn., Am. Pediatric Soc., Chgo. Neurol. Soc. (pres. 1956). Home: Chicago, Ill. Died May 11, 1983.

BUCHANAN, EDWIN, banker; b. Ripley, O., Oct. 28, 1890; s. Thomas and Katherine Elizabeth (Bell) B.; A.B., Ohio State U., 1911; m. Marietta McClure, Apr. 9, 1914; 1 son, Thomas Edwin. Began with Union Nat. Bank, Columbus, 1911; asst. mgr. and examiner, Columbus Clearing House, 1912-16, mgr. and examiner, 1917-18; cashier The Ohio Nat. Bank, Columbus, 1919-20, vice pres., 1921-29, pres., 1928-35; vice-pres. First Wis. Nat. Bank, Milwaukee, Wis., since 1935. Treas. Liberty Loan Com., Franklin Co., Ohio, World War I. Treas. Milwaukee chapter Am. Red Cross, 1936-38, chmn., 1940-43, treas. from 1947. Chmn. finance com., Milwaukee Co. Council Boy Scouts, 1938-39; treas. Wis. chpt. Arthritis and Rheumatism Found., from 1960. Pres. Better Bus. Bur. Milwaukee, 1940-42; mem. bd. govs. Nat. Assn. Better Bus. Burs., Inc., 1941-43. Mem. Assn. Reserve City Bankers, 1920-56. Mem. Wis. Bankers Assn. (mem. ednl. com. 1940-42), Wisconsin Council on Alcoholism (treas. 1951-57), Ohio Bankers Assn. (treas. 1927-29); mem. Milwaukee Co. Council Am. Cancer Soc. (campaign chairman, 1947, 56), Sigma Phi Epsilon (national chairman board trustees, 1926-32, grand treas., from 1932; grand president, 1955-56). Republican. Presbyterian. Clubs: University, Blue Mound Country; Bankers (Chicago). Home: Milwaukee, Wis. †

BUCHANAN, JOSEPH BOYD, shoe mfr.; b. Fulton, Mo., Dec. 13, 1888; s. John Harvey and Sallie Merriwether (Wren) B.; ed. pub. schs. of Fulton; m. Irene Kestley, Nov. 27, 1915; children—Jane Anne, Elizabeth Marie, William John, Thomas Boyd. With Roberts, Johnson & Rand Shoe Co. (now Internat. Shoe Co.), St. Louis, 1908-12; a founder, officer Nunn-Bush Shoe Co., Milw., from 1912, pres., 1947-60, chmn. bd., from 1960. Clubs: Wisconsin, West more Country. Home: Wauwatosa, Wis. †

BUCHER, GEORGE HEISLER, mfg. exec.; b. Sunbury, Pa., July 24, 1888; s. John Beard and Hannah (Heisler) B.; grad. Pratt Inst., Brooklyn, N.Y., 1909; E.E., Stevens Institute of Technology, 1943; D.Eng. (hon.), Pratt Institute Brooklyn, 1956; married Bertha I. Rhoads, Dec. 26, 1911; children—Martha Elizabeth (Mrs. Jules W. Beuret, Jr.), Ruth Rhoads (Mrs. Paul L. Rude), Alma Rhoads (Mrs. Paul Bartel), Irene Rhoads (Mrs. Wm. R. Worthy, Jr.), George David. Graduate engineering student Westinghouse Company, East Pittsburgh, Pa. 1909-11; export department of Westinghouse Company (from 1915 Westinghouse Electric Internat. Co.), New York, 1911-20, assistant to gen. mgr., 1920-21, asst. gen. mgr., 1921-32, v.p. and gen. mgr., 1932-34, pres. and general manager, 1934-36, president, 1936-44, chairman board since 1944; vice president and Eastern District mgr. Westinghouse Electric & Mfg. Co., N.Y., 1935-36, exec. v.p., Pittsburgh, 1936-38, dir. from 1937, president, 1938-46 (name changed to Westinghouse Electric Corp., 1945), vice chairman bd., 1946-51, member executive com. from 1946. Director of Canadian Westinghouse Company, Ltd., Peoples 1st Nat. Bank and Trust Co. Mem. Am. Inst. Elec. Engrs., Am. Soc. Mech. Engrs., Tau Beta Pi. Clubs: University, Duquesne (Pitts.), Wall Street (N.Y.).†

BUCHER, OLIVER BOONE, army officer; b. Bridgewater, Va., Dec. 5, 1890; s. Dr. David Andrew and Annie (Lindsay) B.; student Portsmouth (Va.) High Sch., 1907-09; B.S. in C.E., Va. Mil. Inst., 1917; m. Evelyn Bayly Hoge, Dec. 26, 1917; children—Evelyn Bayly (wife of Lt. Col. F. T. Unger), Oliver B. (1st lt. Army Air Corps). Civil engr., S.A.L. Ry., 1909-13; commd. 2d lt., Coast Arty. Corps, 1917; promoted through grades to brig. gen., 1943. Awarded Liberty Medal, 1918, Defense medal, 1941, American Theatre Campaign medal, 1944. Mem. Kappa Alpha, Scabbard and Blade. Mason. Home: Frankfort, Ky.†

BUCK, ARTHUR EUGENE, public finance; born Carter County, Tenn., Mar. 6, 1888; s. John Bell and Sarah Eliza (Range) B.; Ph.B., Milligan (Tenn.) Coll., 1910; B.Sc., U. of Tenn., 1913; M.A., Columbia, 1916; student at Training Sch. for Pub. Service, N.Y. City, 1916-17; m. Frances Hyder, Sept. 19, 1913 (died 1930); son, Arthur Eugene; m. 2d, Beatrice L. Stone, April 30, 1931; children—Keith Taylor, John Milward. Staff mem. N.Y. Bur. Municipal Research, 1917-53; dir. New York City budget study for Mayor's Committee on Management Survey, 1951-52; technical adviser to U.S. Bureau of the Budget, 1934-35 and 1939-40; adviser to Ill. state director of finance, 1941-42; project dir. of budgeting study, Commn. on Orgn., Executive Branch of Govt. (Hoover Commn.), 1948-49; consultant President's Committee on Administrative Management on fiscal organization, procedure, the nat. govt., 1936-37; project dir. fiscal matters, Conn. and Mich. reorgn. studies, 1949-50; hon. life mem. Municipal Finance Officers' Assn. of U.S. and Can., Governmental Research Association; consultant for New York State Commn. on Fiscal Affairs, 1953-54. Author several books on govtl. budgeting and finance; contbr. govt. jours., monographs, pamphlets. Home: Norwalk, Conn. †

BUCK, CLAYTON DOUGLASS, senator, gov.; b. in Del., Mar. 21, 1890; s. Francis N. and Margaret (Douglass) B.; prep. edn., Friends' Sch., Wilmington, Del.; student U. of Pa.; m. Alice duPont Wilson; children—Clayton Douglass, Dorcas Van Dyke. Was engaged in road-bldg. engring. work, Del.; chief engr., Del. State Highway Dept., 1920-29; gov. of Del. 1929-37; U.S. senator from Del. for term beginning Jan. 1943; pres. Equitable Trust Co., Wilmington. Republican. Episcopalian. Clubs: Union League, Wilmington, Wilmington Country. Home: Wilmington, Del. Deceased.

BUCK, FRANK E(UGENE), business exec.; b. Mayfield, Calif., Dec. 6, 1889; son Frank Eugene and Alice Belle (Allen) B.; ed. pub. schs.; m. Alice Meyer, Sept. 17, 1923. Entire career with Golden State Company, Limited, San Francisco; director of the Bank of Cal., Pacific Gas & Electric Co. Home: Menlo Park, Calif. †

BUCKINGHAM, EARLE, mechanical engr.; b. Bridgeport, Conn., Sept. 4, 1887; s. Francis Smith and Mary Hills (Kingman) B.; student U.S. Naval Acad., 1904-06; m. Nina Walmsley Morgan, Aug. 5, 1911; children—Emily Fisher, Janet Olive, Forrest Morgan, Eliot Kingman. With Graphophone Co., Bridgeport, Conn., 1906-08, Winchester Repeating Arms Co., New Haven, 1908-09, Veeder Mfg. Co., Hartford, 1909-11, Royal Typewriter Co., Hartford, 1911-14, Canadian Car & Foundry Co., New York, 1915, Winchester Repeating Arms Co., 1916-17, Pratt & Whitney Co., Hartford, 1919-24; prof. emeritus mech. engring., Mass. Inst. Tech.; now tech. dir. Gear Systems, Inc., West Concord. Capt and maj. Ordnance Dept. U.S. Army, 1917-19; maj. O.R.C. Worcester Reed Warner medal Am. Soc. M.E., 1945, Edward P. Connell Award by American Gear Mfrs. Assn., 1950; Gold Medal, Am. Soc. of Tool Engrs., 1957. Mem. Nat. Screw Thread Commn. since 1920; mem. Soc. Automotive Engrs.; asso. mem. Am. Soc. Mech. Engrs. Episcopalian. Mason. Author: Principles of Interchangeable Manufacturing, 1921; Involute Spur Gears, 1922; Spur Gears, 1928; Dynamic Loads on Gear Teeth, 1931; Manual of Gear Design, 1937; Production Engineering, 1942; Analytical Mechanics on Gears, 1949; Dimensions and Tolerances for Mass Production, 1954. Home: Belmont, Mass. †

BUCKISCH, WALTER G. M., educator; b. Burlington, Ia., Dec. 20, 1888; s. Christian and Valeska (Schreiber) B.; grad. Morris High Sch., N.Y. City, 1906; A.B., Columbia, 1910, A.M., 1913; Ed. D., Stanford, 1935; D.Sc. in Edn. honoris causa, Univ. of Manila, 1934; m. Laura Esther Storts, May 30, 1918; children—Robert Livingston, Herbert William. Teacher, Philippine Islands, 1912-16; prin. high sch., 1916-18; div. supt. schs., Surigao, Camarines, La. Union and Bulacan, P.I., 1918-25; chief of academic div., gen. office, Bur. Edn., P.I., 1925; commr. pvt. edn., P.I., 1926-32, technical adviser to the governor-general, 1933; professorial lecturer, U. of Philippines, 1928-33, U. of Santo Tomas, 1930-33; Indian Field Service, Ariz. and N.M., 1936-38; Republican. Mem. Pi Gamma Mu, Phi Delta Kappa. Author: The Relation Between Private Education and the State in the Philippines; also articles in mags. Home: Van Nuys, Calif. †

BUCKLER, LESLIE HEPBURN, law educator; b. London, Eng., July 4, 1890; s. Thomas and Leslie Hepburn (Buckler) Pollard, of Baltimore; came to U.S., 1896, naturalized and assumed mother's family name, 1914; student Boys Latin Sch., Baltimore, 1901-08; A.B., Johns Hopkins, 1912, A.M., 1914; m. Eise Miles, Aug. 18, 1935. Admitted to Md. bar, 1915, N.Y. State bar, 1920; asso. with firm of Glenn and Ganter, N.Y. City, 1919-29; mem. law faculty, U. of Va. from 1929, James Monroe prof. of law and chmn. com. on grad. studies, dept. of law, from 1949. Mem. Am. Law Inst., Am. and Va. bar assns. Home: Charlottesville, Va. †

BUCKLEY, ALFRED, fuel oil, heating equipment and dental supplies exec.; b. Providence, Dec. 24, 1890; s. Alfred and Margaret (Gray) B.; student pub. schs.; m. Helen Agnes Searles, Apr. 2, 1934; children—Cyril H., Alfred David L., Carter Y., Richard B. Pres., treas. Buckley & Scott, Inc., Providence; pres. Smith-Holden, Inc.; dir. Indsl. Nat. Bank. Bd. dirs. Home for Aged. Episcopalian. Home: Providence, RI. †

BUCKLEY, FRANK MICHAEL, psychologist, educator; b. Boston, Apr. 9, 1918; s. Frank Michael and Anna Teresa (Kelly) B.; m. Ruth V. Healy, May 25, 1957; children—Teresa, Jacqueline, Jane, Marlene, Monica, Kara. A.B., Coll. Holy Cross, Worcester, Mass., 1941; M.A., Boston Coll., 1946; Ed.D., Harvard U., 1954. Instr. psychology Ariz. State U., Tempe, 1946-49; asst. prof., then asso. prof. Boston Coll., 1949-60; prof. psychology Grad. Sch., Assumption Coll., Worcester, 1960-71, chmn. dept., dir. grad. program psychology and edn., 1962-67, dir. counseling and psychol. services, 1960-65; vis. prof. Duquesne U., Pitts., 1969-70, prof. psychology, from 1971; lectr. Harvard U., 1960-62; vis. lectr. Clark U., Worcester, 1966-68; cons. Mass. Gen. Hosp., Boston, 1959-66, Worcester Youth Center, 1963-66, Western Psychiat. Inst. and Clinic, Pitts., from 1976; bd. dirs. Worcester Mental Health Assn., 1962-71, Pastoral Counseling Inst., Worcester, 1963-70; speaker internat. psychology confs., Paris, 1961, Amsterdam, 1963, London, 1964, Tilburg, 1976, Phila., 1977, Copenhagen, 1980. Contbr. articles to prof. publns., chpts. to books. Mem. Am. Psychol. Assn., Mass. Psychol. Assn., Pa. Psychol. Assn., Am. Group Therapy Assn., AAUP. Club: Harvard (Pitts.). Home: Pittsburgh, PA.

BUCKLEY, JOHN WILLIAM, petroleum company executive; b. N.Y.C., June 22, 1920; s. William F. and Aloise (Steiner) B.; m. Ann B. Harding, Nov. 1949 (div. dec); children: Mary, Aloise, John M. B.A., Yale U., 1942. Engaged in exploratory and producing aspects of oil, various fgn. countries; pres., dir. Pantepec Internat., Inc.; dir. Can. So. Petroleum, Ltd. Served from pvt. to 1st. lt. AUS, 1942-46, N. Africa, France. Mem. Nat. Rifle Assn. Roman Catholic. Clubs: Camp Fire of America; Racquet and Tennis (N.Y.C.), Union League (N.Y.C.). Home: Lakeville, Conn. Died Dec. 1, 1984. *

BUCKLEY, JOSEPH, clergyman; b. St. Paul, Sept. 3, 1905; s. James Augustine and Mary (Magner) B. Student, Marist Coll., Washington, 1925-27; S.T.D., Angelico U., Rome, Italy, 1931; M.A. in Philosophy, U. Notre Dame, 1947. Joined Soc. of Mary, 1925; ordained priest Roman Catholic Ch., 1931; prof. theology and philosophy Marist Coll., 1931-34, Notre Dame Sem., New Orleans, 1934-41,

46-52, 58-59, 72—; lectr. U. Notre Dame, 1946, summers 1949, 50-51; founding pastor St. Pius X Parish, Bedford, O., 1952-58; provincial Washington Province, Soc. of Mary, 1959-61, 70-72, superior gen., 1961-69; Voting mem. Vatican Ecumenical Council II and First Synod Bishops, 1967; mem. New Orleans Archdiocesan Clergy Senate, 1975—. Author: Man's Last End, 1949, Christian Design for Sex, 1952, Purity, Modesty, Marriage, 1960; Translator: from French to English The Three Stages of Spiritual Life, 3 vols, 1956. Served to maj. Chaplain Corps AUS, 1942-46. Decorated Bronze Star medal. Mem. Am. Philos. Assn., Am. Cath. Theol. Soc., Am. Legion (chaplain La. 1950-51, Ohio 1953-54, Italy-Greece 1969-70). Home and office: New Orleans LA

BUCKNER, GEORGE WALKER, JR., ch. ofcl.; b. Pike County, Mo., Oct. 1, 1893; s. George Walker and Anna (Griffth) B.; student Culver-Stockton Coll., 1911, Southport (Eng.) Univ. Sch., 1912-13, Langenburg (Germany) Gymnasium Schule, 1913; A.B., Culver-Stockton Coll., 1914, A.M., 1915, L.L.D., 1940; A.M., Central Wesleyan Coll., 1916; D.D., Hastings Coll., 1925; D.Litt., Atlantic Christian Coll., 1953; m. Winifred Magee, Aug. 24, 1915; children—Susan (Mrs. Philip Jackson), Julia Anna (Mrs. Raymond Wheeler), Georgia Winifred (Mrs. Roland Pierre). Ordained minister Disciples of Christ, 1915; pastor chs. at Mokane, La Monte and Lee's Summit, Mo., 1916-21; pastor First Christian Ch., Hastings, Nebr., 1921-27; also prof. Bibl. lit. Hastings Coll., 1922-24, prof. sociology, 1926-27; pastor Central Ch. of Christ, Grand Rapids, Mich., 1927-35; editor World Call, internat. mag. of Disciples of Christ, 1935-61; internat. commr. Council of Christian Unity (Disciples of Christ), from 1961; interim minister St. Paul's Christian Ch., Raleigh, 1964-65, 67; grad. lectr. Phillips U., 1940; lectr. Union Sem., P.R., 1947. Exec. sec. Council on Christian Unity, 1941-61; mem. exec. com. Fed. Council Chs. of Christ in Am., 1940-50; mem. Am. Com. World Council of Chs., 1944-48; mem. dept. internat. affairs of Nat. Council Chs.; mem. exec. bd. N.C. Council Chs., from 1975; mem. bd. Ecumenical Inst., Switzerland, from 1948; del. to World Conf. on Faith and Order Edinburgh, and to World Conf. on Church, Community and State, Oxford, 1937; del. to World Missionary Conf., Madras, India, 1938; fraternal del. Conf. of Chs. of Christ in Gt. Britain and Ireland, 1945; del. Assembly World Council of Chs., 1948, 1954, adviser, 1961; mem. Central Com., World Council Chs., 1948-61, founding; on ecumenical, editoral mission to the Middle East and Asia, 1961-62; com. Christian U. in Japan; delivered Earl lecture Pacific Sch. of Religion, 1949, Cuthrell lectures Atlantic Christian Coll., 1952; mem. commn. on social action N.C. Council Chs., ofcl. rep., from 1966; mem. Protestant Catholic Editorial Study Mission to Israel, 1970; planner, leader Interfaith Study Tour to Israel, 1973; mem. nat. adv. com. Am.-Israel Cultural Found.; spl. rep. Lexington Theol. Sem., from 1968. Recipient citation Nat. and World Council Chs., 1960. Clubs: Indianapolis Athletic, Wranglers, Asso. Ch. Press (past pres.); overseas mem. Authors Club of London, Eng. Author: Concerns of a World Church, 1943; The Winds of God, 1947. Contbr. articles to religious and sociol. publs.; lectr. Staff corr. The Christian Century, 1939-61. Address: Charlotte, N.C. Died Mar. 23, 1981.

BUDD, THOMAS ALLIBONE, educator; b. Phila., June 16, 1890; s. James Marshall and Alice (Zehnder) B.; B.S., U. Pa., 1912, A.M., 1923; m. Kathryn M. Smith, Apr. 18, 1927; 1 dau., Susan (Mrs. Wm. D. Johnson). Instr. accounting U. Pa., 1912-17; 19-22, asst. prof., 1923-28, asso. prof. finance, 1929-36, prof. finance, 1937-52, prof. accounting and finance from 1952, chmn. finance dept., 1928-45, chairman of the accounting dept., 1945-53. From 1955, director of student personnel Wharton School Finance and Commerce, 1921-35, vice dean, 1936-54, acting dean, 1954-55, vice dean, from 1955. Served as ensign United States Naval Reserve Forces, 1917-19; edn. dir. A.S.T.P., 1943-46. Mem. Am. Acad. Polit. and Social Sci., Am. Econ. Assn., Am. Assn. U. Profs., Nat. Tennis Umpires Assn., Beta Gamma Sigma, Pi Gamma Mu, Beta Alpha Psi, Phi Kappa Psi. Republican. Episcopalian. Clubs: Merion Cricket, Phi Kappa Psi. Author: The Interpretation of Accounts (with E. N. Wright), 1927; Financial and Business Statements, 1947; Accounting Principles (with Dean Russell Stevenson), 1953; Financial Statements. 1959. Home: Merion Station, Pa. †

BUDRYS, JONAS, consul gen. of Lithuania; b. Kaunas, Lithuania, May 10, 1889; s. Jonas and Anna (Wizer) B.; grad. Gymnasium in Kaunas, 1898-1907; m. Regina Kashuba, Oct. 21, 1926; 1 child, Algirdas. Govt. employee at Ministry of Communication, Russia, 1907-09; with Russian Army in Caucasus, 1909-10; Ministry of Communications, 1911-12; county deputy chief, Ministry of Interior, 1912-14; military intelligence service of Army, 1914-17, staff military comd. at Viadivostok (Siberia) as capt., 1917; head of Lithuanian Intelligence Service in Lithuania, 1921; lt. gov. province of Klaipéda, Feb. 1923, gov., Apr.-Nov. 8, 1925; head of Dept. in Interior Affairs, 1927-28; consul gen. in Koenigsberg, Germany, 1928-36, New York from 1936. Officer of Military Cross in Lithuania; Comdr. of Order Grand Duke of Gediminas; Honorary Citizen of New York City, 1940. Home: New York, N.Y. †

BUECHE, ARTHUR MAYNARD, manufacturing company research executive; b. Flushing, Mich., Nov. 14, 1920; s. Bernard Paul and Margaret (Rekart) B.; children—Kristine L., Arthur J., Margaret K., Elizabeth M. A.S., Flint (Mich.) Jr. Coll., 1941; B.S. in Chemistry, U. Mich., 1943; postgrad., Ohio State U., 1943; Ph.D., Cornell U., 1947; D.Sc., St. Lawrence U., 1971, Union Coll., 1973, Poly. Inst. N.Y., 1979, SUNY, 1980; LL.D., Knox Coll., 1973; D.Eng., Rensselaer Poly. Inst., 1975; Sc.D., Clarkson Coll., 1975, U. Akron, 1975. Registered profl. engr., N.Y. Research asso. Cornell U., 1947-50; with Gen. Electric Co., 1950-81, mgr. chemistry research dept., 1961-65, v.p. research and devel., Schenectady, 1965-78, sr. v.p. tech., 1978-81; dir. Bus. Devel. Services, Inc.; trustee Schenectady Savs. Bank, 1966-78; mem.-at-large NRC, 1966, bd. human resources, 1973-74, commn. on human resources, 1979-81; mem. chemistry vis. com. Harvard U., 1970-76; mem. Dept. Commerce statutory vis. com. Nat. Bur. Standards, 1972-75, chmn., 1974-75; cons. NASA Research and Tech. adv. council, 1968-74; mem. sci. and tech. policy panel Pres.'s Office Sci. and Tech., 1970-71; mem. adv. council Nat. Govs.' Council on Sci. and Tech., 1973-81; mem. Pres.'s Adv. Group on Sci-Tech.-Econ. Policy, 1975-76; mem. roster of cons. to adminstr. ERDA, 1976-77; mem. various coms. NSF; mem. corp. vis. com. for sponsored research MIT, 1971-81, mem. corp. vis. com. for dept. elec. engring. and computer scis., 1979-81; past mem. adv. com. Sch. Metallurgy and Materials Sci., U. Pa.; bd. overseers Sch. Metallurgy and Materials Sci., U. Pa. (Sch. Engring. and Applied Scis.), 1979-81; mem. IMS adv. bd. U. Conn., 1979-81; bd. visitors Sch. Engring., Duke U., 1980-81; mem. N.Y. adv. com. for Atmospheric Scis. Research Center, 1972-78; Councilor exec. com. Gordon Research Confs., 1960, chmn. bd. trustees, 1966; trustee Albany Med. Coll., Hudson-Mohawk Assn. Colls. and Univs., 1969-78, Com. for Econ. Devel., 1980-81; council Coll. Engring., Cornell U., chmn., 1974—; mem. Rensselaer Council, 1972-81; trustee Rensselaer Poly. Inst., 1975-81. Bd. mgrs. Ellis Hosp., 1970-78; bd. dirs. Sunnyview Hosp. and Rehab. Center, 1969-78; mem. metal properties council Engring. Found., 1966-81, vice chmn., 1972-74, chmn., 1974-76. Recipient Am. Soc. for Metals medal, 1978; Indsl. Research Inst. medal, 1979; award for disting. contbn. Soc. for Research Adminstrs., 1979; Gold medal Am. Inst. Chemists, 1980; Centennial medal ASME, 1980. Fellow Am. Phys. Soc. (chmn. exec. com. div. high polymer physics 1953), AAAS; mem. Am. Chem. Soc. (chmn. div. polymer chemistry 1963, bd. dirs. 1966), Am. Inst. Physics (council), Indsl. Research Inst. (dir., v.p. 1973, pres. 1975-76), Dirs. Indsl. Research, Am. Mgmt. Assn. (v.p. research and devel. div. 1972-73), Empire State C. of C. (past v.p.), Nat. Acad. Scis. (Forum com., co-chmn. forum on energy 1974, fin. com. 1980—), Nat. Acad. Engring. (council), Conn. Acad. Sci. and Engring., Sigma Xi, Tau Beta Pi, Alpha Chi Sigma, Gamma Alpha, Phi Kappa Phi, Phi Lambda Upsilon. Clubs: Mohawk Golf (Schenectady), Mohawk (Schenectady); Brooklawn Country (Fairfield, Conn.); Cornell of N.Y. Patentee polymer field. Home: Albany, N.Y. Dec. Oct. 22, 1981.

BUELL, ELLEN LOUISE, dir. nursing; b. Earlville, N.Y., May 11, 1889; d. Floyd Clark and Nellie (Douglass) Buell; grad. Sch. of Nursing, Faxton Hosp., Utica, N.Y., 1911; certificate in pub. health nursing, Simmons Coll., Boston, 1918; B.S., in Edn., Columbia U. Teachers Coll., 1928; unmarried. Engaged in nursing, 1911-17; supervisor visiting nurse service. Henry St. Settlement, N.Y. City, 1918-20; tuberculosis nursing, Utica (N.Y.) Dept. of Health, 1920-22; successively supervisor visiting nurse service, field dir. and edn. dir. Henry St. Settlement, 1922-30; organizer, 1930, and dir. Dept. Pub. Health Nursing, Syracuse U. Coll. of Medicine, until 1943; dir. programs in pub. health nursing, Frances Payne Bolton School of Nursing, Western Reserve University, Cleveland, 1943-52, Mem. Am. Pub. Health Assn., Nat. Orgn. for Pub. Health Nursing, National League Nursing Edn., Am. Nurses Assn., Am. Assn. Univ. Women, Pi Lambda Theta. Contbr. to professional mags. Home: Earlville, N.Y. †

BUELL, WAYNE HERBERT, coll. chmn.; b. Lewis, Ind., July 2, 1913; s. Clifford and Grace Edith (Miller) B.; m. Vita Schaefer, Oct. 21, 1939. B.Chem. Engring., Lawrence Inst. Tech., 1936, D.Engring. (hon.), 1958; M.S., Wayne State U., 1951. Instr. math. and chemistry Lawrence Inst. Tech., Southfield, Mich., 1936-44, prof. chemistry, 1946-48; dir. research Aristo Corp., Detroit, 1944-46, v.p., dir. research, 1948-51, exec. v.p., dir., 1951-64; pres. Lawrence Inst. Tech., 1964-77, chmn., chief exec. officer, 1977—. Author papers in field. Pres. Russell Lawrence Found., 1960-62. Recipient award sci. merit Am. Foundrymen's Soc., 1970. Mem. Am. Chem. Soc., Am. Foundrymen's Assn. Home: Southfield, Mich. Deceased.

BUFF, MARY MARSH, writer, artist; b. Cincinnati, O., Apr. 10, 1890; d. Andrew Jackson and Elizabeth (Wade) Marsh; student Cincinnati Art Academy, 1910; student of painting, Bethany College, Lindsborg, Kansas, 1911-13 (Bachelor of Painting); student U. of Okla., 1909-11, Acad. of Fine Arts, Chicago, 1916; m. Conrad Buff, July 6, 1922; children—Conrad, David Marsh. Art supervisor, Lewiston, Mont., 1914-17; head art dept., State Teachers Coll., Albion, Ida., 1917-21; asst. art curator, Los Angeles Museum, 1921-22; art critic of Saturday Night, 1925-26. Author several books, latest being: The Apple and The Arrow, 1951; Magic Maize, 1953: Hurry Skurry and Flurry, 1955; Hah-Nee, 1956; Elf Owl, 1958. Mem. Writer's Guild, P.E.N. Contbr. Child Life. Home: Pasadena, Cal. †

BUFFINGTON, ALBERT FRANKLIN, educator; b. Pillow, Pa., July 11, 1905; s. John N. and Lizzie (Hepler) B.; A.B., Bucknell U., 1928; student U. Berlin (Germany), 1926; A.M., Harvard, 1932, Ph.D., 1937; m. Dorothy Lorine Harris, June 20, 1932; children—Albert Franklin, Lorine Harris. Head German dept. Central High Sch., Scranton, Pa., 1928-30; instr. German, Harvard, 1930-37; from instr. to asso. prof. langs. U. N.H., 1937-45; mem. faculty Pa. State U., 1945-80, prof. German, 1948-65, emeritus, 1965-80, acting head dept., 1964-65; prof. German, Ariz. State U., 1965-75, prof. emeritus, 1975-80; weekly broadcasts in Pennsylvania German radio sta. WKOK, 1946-59; lectr. for USIS in Rheinpfalz, Germany, 1961. Mem. Modern Lang. Assn. (chmn. comparative lit. group 1951-52), Pa. German Soc. (bd. dirs., publs. com. 1948-65), Pa. German Folklore Soc. (bd. dirs., publs. com. 1948-65), Am. Assn. Tchrs. German. Author: (with W.E. Boyer and D. Yoder) Songs Along the Mahantongo; Pennsylvania Dutch Folksongs, rev. edit., 1964; (with P.A. Barba) A Pennsylvania German Grammar, rev. edit., 1965; The Reichard Collection of Early Pennsylvania German Plays, 1962; Dutchified German Spirituals, 1965; Pennsylvania German Secular Folksongs, 1974. Home: Scottsdale, Ariz. Dec. June 18, 1980.

BUGAS, JOHN STEPHEN, business exec.; b. Rock Springs, Wyo., Apr. 26, 1908; s. Andrew P. and P. and Nell (Ladamus) B.; J.D., U. Wyo., 1934, LL.D., 1946; m. Margaret Stowe McCarty, Aug. 13, 1938; children —Helen Patricia, Margaret Jane, Elizabeth Diane John Kerr, Cheyenne, 1934-35; spl. agt. FBI, Washington, 1935, Los Angeles, 1935-36, Omaha, 1936, spl. agt. in charge, Juneau, Alaska, 1936-37, Birmingham, Ala., 1937-38, Detroit, 1937-38, Detroit, 1938-43; indsl. relations exec. Ford Motor Co., 1944-59, v.p. indsl. relations 1946-59, v.p. internat. group, 1957-65, v.p., cons., dir., 1965-68, also mem. exec. and operating coms.; dir. One William Street Fund, Inc., Standard Oil Co. (Ind.), Kelsey-Hayes Co. Bd. dirs. dirs. Boy's Clubs Detroit, Boys' Clubs Am. Clubs: Detroit, Yondotega Detroit Athletic; Bloomfield Hills (Mich.) Country; Country of Fla. (Par, Fla.). Home: Bloomfield Hills, Mich. Died Dec. 2, 1982.

BUHLER, CURT FERDINAND, historian, librarian; b. N.Y.C., July 11, 1905; s. Conrad and Martha (Warburg) B.; m. Alexandra M. London, Nov. 19, 1927 (div. Mar. 1939); 1 son, Conrad Alexander (dec.); m. Frances Lynham, Apr. 28, 1939 (dec. Nov. 1966); m. Lucy Jane Ford, July 10, 1971; 1 step-dau., Lucile Ford Schoettle. A.B., Yale, 1927; Ph.D., Trinity Coll., U. Dublin, 1930, Litt.D., 1947; postgrad., U. Munich, 1931-33; Litt.D. honoris causa, Columbia U., 1980. Staff printed books Pierpont Morgan Library, 1934-48, keeper printed books, 1948-66, research fellow for texts, 1967-73, emeritus, 1973-85., hon. fellow, 1974-85.; Del. Union Académique Internationale, Brussels, 1957-85; vis. fellow All Souls Coll., Oxford, 1969; Mem. adv. council U. Notre Dame, 1972-85. Author: The Sources of the Court of Sapience, 1932, The Dicts and Sayings of the Philosophers, 1941, The Bible, Manuscripts and Printed Bibles from the Fourth to the Nineteenth Century, 1947, (with Selmer) The Melk Salbenkrämerspiel, 1948, Fifteenth Century Books and the Twentieth Century, 1952, The University and the Press in Fifteenth Century Bologna, 1958, William Caxton and His Critics, 1960, The Fifteenth Century Book, 1960, Neue Kunst und neue Welt, der Buchdruck und Amerika, 1963, The History of Tom Thumbe, 1964, The Epistle of Othea, 1970, Early Books and Manuscripts, Forty Years of Research, 1973, also articles, essays to learned publs. Rosenbach fellow U. Pa., 1947, 58-59; Guggenheim fellow, 1965, 77, 78. Fellow Medieval Acad., Am. Acad. Arts and Scis., Gutenberg Gesellschaft, Brit. Acad. (corr.); mem. Am. Philos. Soc. (com. on library), Bibliog. Soc. Am. (pres. 1952-54), Am. Council Learned Socs. (sec. 1960-74, chmn. 1974-85), Early English Text Soc. (council 1971-85), Modern Lang. Assn. (exec. council 1956-60), Bibliog. Soc. Eng. (treas. U.S. 1949-64), Renaissance Soc. Am. (pres. 1961-63), Ligue Internationale de la Librarie Ancienne (hon.), Union Academique Internat. (dir. 1968-71), Dante Soc. Am. (com. on hon. mems.), Phi Beta Kappa. Clubs: Century Assn. (N.Y.C.), Grolier (N.Y.C.); Cosmos (Washington); East India (London); Royal Dublin (Dublin), University (Dublin); Gutenberg Gesellschaft (Mainz). Home: New York, N.Y. Died Aug. 2, 1985.

BULL, HENRY BOLIVAR, educator, biochemist; b. Stateburg, S.C., June 16, 1905; s. DeSaussure and Caroline (Reese) B.; B.S., U. S.C., 1927; M.S., U. Minn., 1928, Ph.D., 1930; postgrad. U. Rochester, 1928-29; m. Fredrica Alway, Feb. 13, 1935; 1 dau., Jean. Instr. U. Minn., 1929-31; NRC fellow U. Berlin (Germany), 1931-32; asst. prof. U. Minn., St. Paul, 1932-36; postdoctoral fellow U. Vienna (Austria), 1934; faculty Northwestern U. Med. Sch., Chgo., 1936-52, prof., 1945-52; vis. prof. Calif. Inst. Tech., Pasadena, 1943; prof., head dept. biochemistry U. Iowa, Iowa City, 1952-63, research prof. biochemistry, 1963-73, prof. emeritus, research scientist, 1973-82. Mem. Am. Chem. Soc., Am. Soc. Biol. Chemists, Soc. Gen. Physiologists, Biophys. Soc. Author: Biochemistry of the Lipids, 1937; Physical Biochemistry, 1943; Introduction to Physical Biochemistry, 1964; also numerous articles. Research on phys. chemistry of proteins, surface chemistry of proteins, titration of proteins. Home: Iowa City, Iowa. Died Apr. 2, 1982; interred Oakland Cemetery, Iowa City, Iowa.

BULL, MASON, lawyer; b. Redfield, S.D., Mar. 7, 1903; s. Roy Taylor and Ida (Mason) B.; m. Kathryn M. Doyle, June 3, 1933 (dec. Dec. 20, 1975); children—Mason (dec.), Jane Ann (Mrs. Weihaupt), David, Nicholas. A.B., Harvard, 1924; J.D., Northwestern U., 1929. Bar: Ill. bar 1929. Mem. firm Bull, Ludens, Potter & Burch, Morrison, 1935-83; mem. law dept. C.M., St.P. & P. R.R. Co., 1929-35; master-in-chancery Whiteside County Circuit Ct., 1940-65. Fellow Am. Coll. Trial Lawyers, Am. Bar Found.; mem. ABA, Ill. Bar Assn. (gov. 1957-64, 1st v.p. 1961-62, pres. 1962-63), Whiteside County Bar Assn., Am. Judicature Soc., Am. Law Inst. Republican. Conglist. Clubs: Mason. (Chgo.), University (Chgo.), Harvard (Chgo.). Home: Morrison, Ill. Died Feb. 24, 1983.

BULLARD, WILLIS CLARE, lawyer, corp. exec.; b. Toledo, June 15, 1916; s. Clare N. and Anna (Davidson) B.; A.B., Western Mich. U., 1939; J.D., U. Mich., 1942; m. Virginia Gilmore, June 29, 1941 (div. Oct. 1970); children—Willis Clare, David G., Jonathan K.; m. 2d, Leota Carroll, Nov. 28, 1970. Admitted to Mich. bar, 1942; asso. Dyer, Meek, Ruegsegger & Bullard and predecessor firms, Detroit, 1942-53, sr. partner, 1953-79. Dir., Kelly Services, Inc.; chmn. bd. Down River Casting Co., from 1956; pres. Mill Supply & Machine Co., from 1960; sec., dir. Dawson Carbide Industries, Inc., Gorham Tool Co.; dir. Inst. Temporary Services. Mem. Nat. Def. Exec. Res., Dept. Commerce, from 1962, chmn. Mich. Nat. Def. Exec. Res., from 1973. Mem. exec. com. United Rep. Fund Mich. Mem. Am., Mich., Detroit bar assns., Nat. Assn. R.R. Trial Counsel, Assn. ICC Practitioners, Nat. Tech. Services Assn. (dir.), Pine Lake C. of C., Delta Theta Phi. Clubs: Copper (N.Y.C.); Detroit, Propeller, Recess (Detroit); U. Mich. (pres. 1958-59) (Grosse Pointe, Mich.); Bloomfield Open Hunt (Bloomfield Hills, Mich.). Author: Equal Employment Opportunity Laws and The Temporary Contract Service, 1968. Home: Bloomfield Hills, Mich. Died 1979.

BULLIS, HAROLD EDMUND, assn. consultant; b. Manlius, N.Y., July 24, 1888; s. George E. and Ida H. (Wood) B.; M.E., Cornell U., 1909; LL.D., Philippine Women's University, 1960; m. Miriam Payne, July 14, 1923; children—Edmund Payne, Carolyn. Engaged in C. of C. organization and publicity work, 1910-17; editor Am. Chamber Commerce Journal, Manila, P.I., and pres. Philippine Publicity Service, 1920-22; sent by Gov. Gen. Leonard Wood on spl. mission to rulers of Indo-China, Siam, Federated Malay States, Straits Settlements, Dutch Indies, Borneo, 1922-23; in charge mission to U.S. of Premier Herriot of France, Chinese High. Commn., 1923-24, and Pulaski mission from Poland, 1929; chief of Organized Reserve Sect., Gen. Staff, U.S. Army, 1924-27; exec. officer Nat. Com. for Mental Hygiene, 1930-42; cons. Del. Soc. Mental Hygiene; spl. cons. USPHS; cons. Philippine Govt., Philippine Womens U., 1954; round-the-world lectr. tour as cons. on mental health education World Fedn. Mental Health, 1960. Nat. vice pres. Americans for the Competitive Enterprise System. Secretary of Committee for Research in Dementia Praecox. Served from capt. to lt. col., arty., U.S. Army, World War I, as col., claims div., AUS, World War II. Decorated Legion of Merit, Bronze Star Medal, Commendation Ribbon with two oak-leaf clusters, also eight fgn. decorations; named Man of Yr., Del. C. of C., 1963. Fellow Royal Geog. Soc.; mem. Founders and Patriots Am., S.A.R., A.A.A.S., Am. Legion, and several fgn. socs. Republican. Mason (33). Rotarian. Clubs: Explorers, Circumnavigators, Army and Navy, Nat. Press (Washington); Manila (P.I.) Polo. Author several books, including: Human Relations in Action. Home: Wilmington, DE. †

BULLOCK, HENRY MORTON, clergyman; b. Chgo., Dec. 6, 1902; s. Hugh Morton and Alma Pauline (Smith) B.; Ph.B., Emory U., 1924, B.D., 1925; B.D., Yale, 1927, Ph.D., 1932; m. Julia Sargent, Aug. 16, 1937; 1 child, David Morton. Ordained to ministry Methodist Ch., 1927; pastor Union City, Ga., 1924-25, Concord Park Ch., Orlando, Fla., 1925-26, Cheshire, Conn., 1927-28, Bayshore Ch., Tampa, Fla., 1928-29; prof. of English Bible, Blackburn Coll., Carlinville, Ill., 1929-35; prof., head dept. religion Millsaps Coll., Jackson, Miss., 1935-42; vis. prof. Scarritt Coll., Nashville, 1939; pastor Jefferson St. Meth. Ch., Natchez, Miss., 1942-45, First Meth. Ch., Gulfport, Miss., 1945-49, Capitol Street Meth. Ch., Jackson, 1949-52; editor of church sch. publs. Meth. Ch., Nashville, 1953-72; minister edn. Brentwood (Tenn.) United Meth. Ch., 1972-84. Chmn. bd. ministerial tng. Miss. Meth Conf., 1940-44, 48-52; mem. gen. bd. Nat. Council Chs. of Christ, 1954-66, mem. exec. bd. dept. ednl. devel., 1964-72. Trustee Scarritt Coll., 1964—. Mem. Phi Beta Kappa, Omicron Delta Kappa, Tau Kappa Alpha. Author: A History of Emory University, 1936, The Divine Fatherhood, 1945. Editor: (with Edward C. Peterson) Young Readers Bible, 1965. Contbr. to ednl. and religious publs. Home: Nashville, Tenn. Dec. Oct. 29, 1984.

BULTMAN, FRITZ, painter, sculptor; b. New Orleans, Apr. 4, 1919; s. Anthony F. and Pauline (Angele) B.; student New Orleans Arts and Crafts Sch., Munich (Germany) Prep. Sch., New Bauhaus, Chgo., Hans Hofmann Sch. Fin Arts, N.Y.C.; m. Jeanne Lawson, Dec. 24, 1943; children—Anthony Frederick IV, Johann. Tchr., Grad. Art Sch., Hunter Coll., 1959-63, Sch. Edn., Pratt Inst., 1958-59, 62-63; cons., artist-in-residence in fine arts Provincetown Fine Arts Workshop, Provincetown, Mass., 1968-69; exhbns. include Hugo Gallery, N.Y.C., 1947-50, Kootz Gallery, N.Y.C., 1951-53; one man shows include Stable Gallery, N.Y.C., 1958, Martha Jackson Gallery, N.Y.C., 1959, Delgado Mus., New Orleans, 1959, Mayer Gallery, N.Y.C., 1960, Stadler Gallery, Paris, France, 1960-63, Tibor de Nagy Gallery, N.Y.C., 1963-65, Arts Club, Chgo., 1965. Vice pres. Bultman Mortuary Co., New Orleans, from 1954. Mem. Tougaloo (Miss.) Coll. Art Com. Italian Govt. scholar, 1950-51; Fulbright fellow in France, 1964-65; recipient Sculpture award Am. Show, Art Inst. Chgo., 1964. Home: Provincetown, Mass. Died July 20, 1985.

BUMBY, HORACE ABRUM, mfg. exec.; b. Burnett, Wis., Aug. 22, 1890; s. John Colley and Olive (Wells) B.; A.B., Ripon Coll., 1912; m. Merle Elizabeth Hockenbury, Aug. 14, 1915; children—John Edgar, Ann (Mrs. Arthur Fallon). Mem. sales dept., Swift & Co., Chicago, 1912-14; sec.-treas. Ripon (Wis.) Milk Co., 1914-19, pres., 1920-29; president Marshfield (Wis.) Milk Co., 1927-29; treas. Speed Queen Corp., Ripon, 1939, pres., gen. mgr. and dir. since 1910; pres. and dir. Ripon Foods, Inc. from 1930; v.p. and dir., Advertiser's Mfg. Co. from 1921; pres. Speed Queen div. McGraw-Edison Co., Elgin, Montello (Wis.) Products Co., from 1944; dir. McGraw Edison Co., Ripon (Wis.) State Bank, Jefferson (Wis.) Co. Bank. Trustee Ripon Coll. Pres. Republican Ednl. Found. Mem. Wis. Mfrs. Assn. (dir.). Pi Kappa Delta. Mason. Clubs: Rotary, Chicago Athletic Assn.; Wisconsin, University (Milw.); South Hills (Fond du Lac); Koshkonong Mound Golf (Ft. Atkinson); Meadow Spring Golf (Jefferson, Wis.); Madison (Madison, Wis.). Home: Jefferson, Wis. †

BUNDY, WALTER ERNEST, educator, author; b. Spiceland, Ind., Jan. 22, 1889; s. Frank and Cora Anna (Pickett) B.; prep. edn., Spiceland Acad.; A.B., De Pauw U., 1912; S.T.B., Boston U. Sch. of Theology, 1915, Jacob Sleeper fellow, 1916, Ph.D., 1921; grad. study Basel (Switzerland) U., 1916-17; m. Claire Anna Gass-Maritz, June 16, 1919; children—George Richard, Virginia Claire, Frank Raymond. Prof. English Bible, De Pauw U., from 1919. In Mil. Intelligence Service, stationed at Basel as vice consul, 1917-19; mem. Am. Peace Mission to Vienna, Austria, 1919. Mem. Soc. Bibl. Lit. and Exegesis, Soc. of Midland Authors, Phi Beta Kappa, Beta Theta Pi. Republican. Methodist. Co-editor and contbr.: The Spirit of Scholarship (Phi Beta Kappa Anniversary vol.), 1940. Home: Greencastle, Ind. †

BUNKER, ELLSWORTH, ambassador; b. Yonkers, N.Y., May 11, 1894; s. George R. and Jean Polhemus (Cobb) B.; A.B., Yale U., 1916, LL.D., 1959; LL.D., Mt. Holyoke Coll., 1962, Windham Coll., 1963, Georgetown U., 1976, St. Michael's Coll., 1978, U. Vt., 1979; m. Harriet Allen Butler, Apr. 24, 1920 (dec.); children—Ellen (Mrs. Fernando Gentil), John Birkbeck, Samuel Emmet; m. Carol C. Laise, Jan. 3, 1967. Dir. Nat. Sugar Refining Co., 1927-66, pres., 1940, chmn. bd., 1948-51; dir. Centennial Ins. Co.; trustee Atlantic Mut. Ins. Co.; U.S. ambassador to Argentina, 1951, Italy, 1952-53, India, 1956-61, also Nepal, 1956-59; mediator Dutch-Indonesian dispute over West New Guinea, 1962; cons. to sec. of state, 1963; U.S. rep. on council OAS, 1964-66; ambassador-at-large, 1966-67; ambassador to Vietnam, 1967-73; ambassador-at-large, 1973-78; pres. Am. Nat. Red Cross, 1953-56. Trustee Hampton Inst. (hon.), Asia Found., Expt. in Internat. Living (hon.), Vt. Council on World Affairs (hon. pres.), Fgn. Policy Assn. (hon.), New Sch. for Social Research (hon.), Bur. Social Sci. Research, Population Crisis Com.; trustee George C. Marshall Found.; assoc. fellow Calhoun Coll., Yale U. Decorated grand cross knight Republic of Italy; recipient Presdl. Medal of Freedom with Spl. Distinction, 1963, 68, Am. Statesman award Freedoms Found., 1970, Sylvanus Thayer medal, 1970, Gen. George Catlett Marshall award, 1974, Presdl. award for disting. civilian service, 1979. Mem. Council on Fgn. Relations, Am. Acad. Arts and Scis. Home: Putney, Vt. Died Sept 27, 1984.

BUNN, GEORGE WALLACE, JR., banker; b. Springfield, Ill., Jan. 28, 1890; s. George Wallace and Ada (Richardson) B.; Litt. B., Princeton, 1912; L.H.D., Blackburn Coll., 1956; m. Melinda Jones, Oct. 9, 1920; children—Sally, George Wallace, Linda. Reporter N.Y. Sun, 1912-14; with John W. Bunn and Co., wholesale grocers, 1919-28; with Springfield Marine Bank, from 1928, pres. now chmn. bd.; dir. Capitol Grocery Co., Ill. Nat. Ins. Co. Served as 1st lt., 333 Machine Gun Bn., 1917-19. Pres. Springfield War Fund Council, 1942-46, Springfield Park Bd., 1932-33, Springfield Pub. Library Bd., 1939-42; trustee Lawrenceville (N.J.) Sch., Blackburn Coll., Carlinville, Ill. Mem. Abraham Lincoln Hist. Assn. (pres.). Republican. Presbyn. Clubs: Sangamo, Ill. Country (Springfield); University (Chicago); Princeton (N.Y.). Home: Springfield, IL. †

BURBANK, REGINALD, physician; b. Pittsfield, Mass., July 26, 1888; s. Charles Henry and Jennie Halford (Brooks) B.; grad. Phillips Acad., Andover, Mass., 1908; A.M., Trinity Coll., Hartford, 1911; M.D., Cornell, 1915; m. Marion B. Powers, Dec. 2, 1916; children—Marion (Mrs. John Walker McNeely), Jeanne, Margaret (Mrs. Arthur Curtis Welch), Reginald, Jr., m. 2d, Kathryn Poole Muse, July 26, 1943. Asst. surgeon New York Orthopedic Hosp., 1916-26; chief arthritis clinic Cornell Med. Coll., 1917-19; instr. arthritis, chief arthritis clinic, Bellevue Med. Coll., 1919-26; cons. on arthritis Brooklyn Hosp., from 1926; dir. arthritis clinic St. Clare's Hosp., from 1940; practice of med. limited to gout, arthritis, allied rheumatoid diseases. Fellow New York Acad. Medicine; mem. Am. Soc. for Study of Arthritis (chmn.), Physicians Scientific Soc., Am. Soc. Bacteriol., N.Y. County Med. Soc., N.Y. State Med. Soc. Republican. Mem. Dutch Reformed Ch. Mason. Clubs: Union, Grolier. Contbr. numerous monographs to scientific jours. Home: New York, N.Y. †

BURCHAM, PAUL BAKER, educator; b. Fayette, Mo., Feb. 22, 1916; s. Frank E. and Bula (Richardson) B.; B.A., Central Coll., 1935; M.A., Northwestern U., 1938, Ph.D., 1941; postgrad. U. Chgo., 1942; m. Helen Kennard Spencer, Dec. 27, 1941; children—Jane, Ann. Instr., asst. prof., asso. prof. U. Mo., Columbia, 1946-54, prof., 1954-85, chmn. dept. math., 1948-66. Served to capt. USAAF, 1942-46. Mem. Am. Math. Soc., Math. Assn. Am. Author: (with Ewing and Betz) Differential Equations with Applications, 1954. Home: Columbia, Mo. Died Mar. 13, 1985.

BURCHILL, GEORGE PERCIVAL, business exec.; b. S. Nelson, N.B., Can., Nov. 3, 1889; s. John Percival and Eliza Bacon (Wilkinson) B.; B.S., U. N.B., 1910, LL.D. (hon.), 1940; D.C.L. (hon.), Kings Coll., Halifax, N.S., 1954; m. Jean Gordon Garden, Feb. 26, 1916; 1 son, John Garden. Pres. George Burchill & Sons, Ltd.; chmn. N.B. Telephone Co.; dir. Montreal Trust Co., Bathurst Power & Paper Co., Ltd. Apptd. senator of Can. 1945 Mason (grand master). Home: N.B., Can. †

BURCK, JACOB, editorial cartoonist, painter; b. Poland, Jan. 10, 1904; s. Abraham and Rebecca (Lev) B.; m. Esther Kriger, Jan. 12, 1933; children—Joseph, Conrad. Student, Cleve. Sch. Art, Art Students League of N.Y.; studied portrait painting with, Albert Sterner, N.Y.C., 1924-26; pupil, Boardman Robinson. Exhibited, Cleve. Mus. Art, 1924, Whitney Mus. Am. Art, Mus. Modern Art; exhbn. murals, Fine Arts Bldg., N.Y.C., Archtl. League, Chgo. Art Inst.; creator: daily editorial cartoon Chgo. Sun-Times (Recipient Pulitzer prize 1941, profl. journalistic frat. award Sigma Delta Chi 1942, Birmingham Mus. Art 1st prize editorial cartooning 1958). Mem. Sigma Delta Chi. Home: Chicago, Ill. Died May 11, 1982.*

BURDEN, WILLIAM ARMISTEAD MOALE, financier; b. N.Y.C., Apr. 8, 1906; s. William A. M. and Florence Vanderbilt (Twombly) B.; m. Margaret Livingston Partridge, Feb. 16, 1931; children: William A. M. (dec.), Robert Livingston (dec.), Hamilton Twombly, Ordway Partridge. A.B. cum laude, Harvard U., 1927; D.Sc., Clarkson Coll. Tech., 1953; LL.D., Fairleigh Dickinson U., 1965, Johns Hopkins U., 1970. Analyst aviation securities Brown Bros., Harriman & Co., N.Y.C., 1928-32; charge of aviation research Scudder, Stevens & Clark, N.Y.C., 1932-39; v.p., dir. Nat. Aviation Corp. (aviation investment trust), N.Y.C., 1939-41; v.p. Def. Supplies Corp. subs. RFC, 1941-42; spl. aviation asst. Sec. of Commerce, 1942-43; mem. NACA, 1942-47; asst. sec. Commerce for Air, 1943-47; U.S. del. Civil Aviation Conf., 1944; chmn. U.S. del. interim assembly Provisional Internat. Civil Aviation Orgn., 1946; aviation cons. Smith Barney & Co., Inc., 1947-49; partner William A.M. Burden & Co., 1949—; spl. asst. for R & D to Sec. of Air Force, 1950-52; mem. Nat. Aeros. and Space Council, 1958-59; U.S. ambassador to Belgium, 1959-61; mem. U.S. Citizens Commn. for NATO, 1961-62; dir. emeritus Am. Metal Climax, CBS, Inc.; cons. Aerospace Corp. Author: The Struggle for Airways in Latin America, 1943, Peggy and I, 1982. Trustee, past chmn. Inst. for Def. Analyses; trustee, past pres., chmn. Mus. Modern Art; hon. life gov. Soc. of N.Y. Hosp., 1950—; trustee emeritus Columbia U.; trustee Fgn. Service Edn. Found., French Inst. in U.S.; regent Smithsonian Instn., 1962—; bd. dirs. Atlantic Council U.S., 1961—; bd. govs. Atlantic Inst., 1964—. Decorated comdr. Cruzeiro do Sul Brazil; comdr.'s cross Order of Merit Fed. Republic Germany; grand official El Sol del Peru Peru; grand officer French Legion of Honor; comdr.'s cross Order of Merit Italy; grand cordon Order of Leopold Belgium; asso. comdr. (Bro.) Order of St. John. Mem. Council Fgn. Relations (hon. dir.), AIAA, France-Am. Soc. (pres.), Council French-Am. Socs. in N.Y. (chmn.). Clubs: Somerset (Boston); The Brook (N.Y.C.), Racquet and Tennis (N.Y.C.), River (N.Y.C.), Links (N.Y.C.), Century (N.Y.C.); Metropolitan (Washington); Buck's and White's (London); Jockey (Paris). Home: New York, N.Y. Died Oct. 11, 1984.

BURDICK, DEAN LANPHERE, pharmaceutical consultant; b. Little Genesee, N.Y., June 12, 1920; s. Herman R. and Mary A. (Lanphere) B.; A.B., U. Mich., 1943; m. Onilee L. Shaner, Aug 28, 1942; children—Dean Lanphere, Kathryn L. Mng. editor publs. Corning Glass Works, 1945-48; copy head advt. dept. Abbott Labs., 1948-52; exec. v.p. creative head William Douglas McAdams, Inc., 1952-56; pres. Burdick & Becker, Inc., pharm. advt., N.Y.C., 1956-61; pres. Dean L. Burdick Assocs., Inc., 1961-75; creative cons. pharm. industry, 1975-84. Congregationalist. Clubs: Ponte Vedra (Fla.) Country; Clinton (Conn.) Country. Home: Madison, Conn. Died Apr. 3, 1984.

BURDICK, RAYMOND T(ERRY), economist; b. Lima, N.Y., May 5, 1889; s. John Alfred and Emma C. (Terry) B.; B.S., Cornell, 1912; M.S., Colo. State Agrl. Coll., 1922; Ph.D., U. of Chicago, 1940; m. Lina M. Odell, Aug. 14, 1913 (died Apr. 22, 1931); m. 2d. Ethel M. Barnhart, June 18, 1932; 1 stepdau. Louise Barnhart, Instr. and asst. prof. agronomy, U. of Vt., 1912-18; accountant Holt Mfg. Co., Stockton, Calif., 1918-19; asso. prof. agronomy, Colo. State Agrl. Coll., 1919-21, asso. prof. economics, 1921-43, head dept. economics, sociology and history from 1943; in charge farm management research, Colo. Agr. Expt. Sta. from 1921, chmn. Western Regional Livestock Marketing Com. since 1947. Mem. Fort Collins (Colo.) Bd. Edn., 1938-43. Chmn. Colo. Wartime Prodn. Capacity Com., (agr.), 1943-47. Fellow A.A.A.S.; mem. Am. and Am. Farm economic assns., Western Farm Economic Assn. (pres., 1950-51). Methodist (chmn. bd. trustees, 1949-51). Old Fellow. Club: Kiwanis (pres., 1931). Home: Fort Collins, Colo. †

BURDINE, WILLIAM M., business exec.; b. Verona, Miss., May 11, 1889; s. William M. and Mary B.; student pub. schs. Chmn. bd., dir. Burdines, Inc., Miami, Fla., pres. †

BURGERS, J. M., Avco Victor Emanuel distinguished prof. Grad. Sch. Aero., Cornell U. prof. emeritus Inst. Phy. Sci. and Tech., U. Md. Died 1981.

BURGESS, EDWIN HAINES, railroad ofcl.; born Columbus, Kan., Sept. 1, 1888; s. Francis F. and Sarah (Kelsey) B.; A.B., Pacific Coll., Newberg, Ore., 1909; B.S., State Coll. Wash., 1910, LL.D., 1951; LL.B., U. Pa., 1914; m. Ruth Wayland, June 1915; 1 son, dec. Admitted to New York bar, 1915. Md. bar, 1947; practiced in N.Y.C. as asst. gen. solicitor and gen. solicitor Lehigh Valley R.R. Co., 1914-42; prin. high sch., Sprague, Wash., 1910-11; lecturer on New York Practice, Law Sch., U. of Pa., 1924-48; chmn. Trunk Line Assn., and chmn. Traffic Exec. Assn., Eastern Railroads, 1942-46; v.p. and gen. counsel Baltimore and Ohio R.R. Co., Balt., 1946 from; dir. Buffalo, Rochester and Pitts. Ry. Co., Dayton & Union R.R. Co. Chief counsel U.S. R.R.'s Wage Case, 1947, U.S. R.R. Rate Case, 1952. Trustee Oscar G. Murray Railroad Employes Benefit Fund. Chmn., Civilian Components Policy Bd., U.S. Dept. Def., 1950-51. Mem. Am., N.Y. State, N.Y. Co., Md., and Baltimore City bar assns., Am. Law Inst., Am. Classical League, Assn. Am. Univ. Professors, Assn. I.C.C. Practitioners (pres. 1941-42), Newcomen Soc. England, Pilgrims of U.S., Phi Beta Kappa. Congregationalist. Mason. Clubs: Railroad (New York). Maryland, Baltimore Country, Merchants (Baltimore); Traffic (Chicago).†

BURGESS, ROBERT WILBUR, statistician; b. Newport, R.I., July 25, 1887; s. Isaac Bronson and Ellen (Wilbur) B.; grad. Morgan Pk. Acad., 1905; A.B., Brown U., 1908, hon. Sc.D., 1948; Rhodes scholar, 1908-11; B.A., Oxford U., 1910; Ph.D., Cornell 1914; m. Dorothy Cross, Jan. 1, 1925; children—Mary Ellen, Dorothy Cleveland, Margaret Cross. Instr. in mathematics, Purdue, 1911-12; asst. in mathematics, Cornell, 1912-14, instr., 1914-16; instr. mathematics, Brown University, 1916-17, assistant professor, 1919-25; statistician and economist, Western Electric Co., 1924-52; cons. statistics from 1952; dir. Bur. of Census, Dept. Commerce, from 1953. Served as first lieutenant, O.R.C., duty at Washington, D.C., Oct. 1917-May 1918; 1st lt., capt., maj. N.A., duty with statistics br. Gen. Staff. Washington, May 1918-Sept. 1919; maj. O.R.C., 1919-29. Fellow Am. Statis. Association (v.p. 1939); member Conference of Business Economists, American Math. Assn., Am. Economic Association,. Econometric Society, Institute of Mathematical Statistics. Brown Engineering Association (president 1942). Economic Principles Commission Nat. Assoc., of Mfrs., 1944. Delta Upsilon, Phi Beta Kappa and Sigma Xi fraternities. Baptist. Clubs: Downtown Athletic, Brown University (New York); Huguenot Yacht. Author: Introduction to the Mathematics of Statistics; chapter on research for gen. administration in "Scientific Management in Am. Industry." Contbr. math. or statis. articles in Am. Jour. Mathematics, Physical Rev., Am. Oxonian, Encyclopedia Britannica, etc. Home: Pelham, N.Y. †

BURKE, HAROLD P., judge; b. Rochester, N.Y., June 6, 1895; s. Peter and Jennie (Noonan) B.; LL.B., U. Notre Dame, 1916; m. Margaret M. McKay, June 30, 1927; 3 children. Admitted to N.Y. bar, 1920, practiced in Rochester; 2d dep. gen. State of N.Y., 1934-37; judge U.S. Dist. Ct., Rochester, 1937-81. Democrat. Club: K.C. Home: Rochester, N.Y. Died July 17, 1981.

BURKE, JAMES A., congressman; b. Boston, Mar. 30, 1910; student Lincoln Prep. Sch., Suffolk U.; m. Aileen McDonald. Former registrar vital statistics, Boston. Served as spl. agt. in Counter Intelligence, World War II. Mem. Mass. Gen. Ct., 10 years; asst. majority leader Mass. Ho. of Reps., 4 years; mem. 86th-87th Congresses, 13th Mass. Dist., 88th-95th Congresses, 11th Dist. Mass. Home: Milton, Mass. Died Oct. 13, 1983.

BURKE, JAMES VINCENT, JR., lawyer; b. Pitts., Dec. 28, 1911; s. James Vincent and Alice (Hesson) B.; m. Mary E. Brown, Jan. 26, 1952. B.A. cum laude, Notre Dame U., 1933; LL.B., U. Pitts., 1936. Bar: Pa. bar 1937. Assoc. with firm Campbell, Thomas & Burke (and predecessors), Pitts., 1937-42, 46-59, 61-81, ptnr., 1946-59, 61-81; gen.

counsel Dept. of Def., 1959-61; Dir. Tyson Metal Products, Inc., Allegheny Installations, Inc.; dir. Ziegler Meat Co. Bd. dirs. St. Francis Gen. Hosp. Served as lt. USNR, 1942-46, ETO. Mem. ABA (ho. of dels. 1952- 60, 62-71), Pa. Bar Assn., Fed. Bar Assn., Allegheny County Bar Assn. (pres. 1958), Am. Law Inst.; Fellows Am. Bar Found. Clubs: Duquesne (Pitts.), Notre Dame (Pitts.) (Man of Year award 1960). Home: Pittsburgh, Pa. Dec. Oct. 26, 1981.

BURKE, VINCENT C., postmaster; b. Louisville, Ky., Jan. 27, 1887; s. Michal J. and Mary (Doyle) B.; ed. high sch. and Spencerian Bus. Coll., Louisville; m. Julia Burns, Oct. 6, 1915; children—Mary Virginia, William V., Vincent C. Clerk Louisville post office, 1906; apptd. post office insp., Jan. 1914, dep. 1st asst. postmaster gen., May 1933; postmaster, Washington, D.C., Mar. 6, 1936. Democrat. Catholic. K.C. Home: Washington, D.C. Deceased.

BURLEY, WILLIAM V., corp. exec.; b. Albemarle Co., Va., Sept. 29, 1890; s. William R. and Ella V. (Craddock) B.; grad. Washington (D.C.) Inst. Accountancy; m. Selena Gist Browning, Aug. 19, 1915; children—William V., Jr., Doris Burley (Mrs. Maxwell). With Statistical Service Co., Washington, 1911-12; Pierce Butler & Pierce Mfg. Co., Syracuse, N.Y., 1912-13; So. Ry. Co., Washington, 1913-16; S. H. Kress & Co., N.Y. City, 1916-17, Price, Waterhouse & Co., 1917-22; with Nat. Lead Co. and affiliated interests since 1922, mem. comptroller's dept. Nat. Lead Co., 1922-25, mgr. St. Louis br., 1939-48, dir. 1940, v.p 1943, mem. exec. com. 1948; sec., treas. and dir. Mueler Brass Foundry Co., St. Louis, 1925-34 (also sec., treas. and dir., Carran Bearing Metal Co., Ludlow, Ky., 1925-34); asst. gen. mgr. and comptroller, dir. Magnus Co., Inc., N.Y. City, 1935-39; pres., dir. Magnus Metal Corp., Magnus Brass Mfg. Co. (Cincinnati); also gen. mgr., Magnus Metal and Magnus Brass Divs. of Nat. Lead Co. also v.p., dir., mem. exec. com. Nat. Lead Co. since 1948; dir. Baker Castor Oil Co., American Bearing Corp. Mem. Railway Business Association (mem. governing bd.), Am. Ordnance Assn., The Newcomen Soc. Clubs: The Lawyer's, Economic, Winged Foot Golf, N.Y. Railroad (New York); Larchmont (N.Y.) Yacht; Boothbay Harbor Yacht; Chgo. Home: New York, NY. †

BURMAN, BEN LUCIEN, writer; b. Covington, Ky., Dec. 12, 1895. s. Sam and Minna B.; A.B., Harvard, 1920; m. Alice Caddy, Sept. 19, 1927. Began as reporter Boston Herald, 1920; asst. city editor Cin. Times Star, 1921; spl. writer N.Y. Sunday World, 1922; staff contbr. N.E.A. (Scripps Howard Newspapers), 1927; wrote literary revs. for The Nation and other publs.; regular contbr. Readers Digest; contbr. Saturday Rev. Served as mem. 2d Div., A.E.F., severely wounded at Soissons, France, July 1918. Bd. dirs. Authors' League Am., P.E.N. Author: Steamboat Round the Bend, 1933 (filmed starring Will Rogers); Blow for a Landing, 1938 (awarded Southern Authors prize for most distinguished book); Rooster Crows for Day, 1945 (Thomas Jefferson Meml. prize); Everywhere I Roam, 1949; Children of Noah, 1951; High Water at Catfish Bend, 1952; The Four Lives of Mundy Tolliver, 1953; Seven Stars for Catfish Bend, 1956; It's a Big Country, 1956; The Street of The Laughing Camel, 1959; The Owl Hoots Twice at Catfish Bend; It's a Big Continent, 1962; The Generals Wear Cork Hats, 1963, The Sign of the Praying Tiger, 1966; Blow A Wild Bugle for Catfish Bend, 1967; Look Down That Winding River, 1973; High Treason at Catfish Bend, 1977. Was the first writer to reach Free French in Africa ater French collapse; war corr. attached Free French and Brit. 8th Army, 1941. Decorated French Legion of Honor, 1946; recipient So. Ill. U. Capt. Donald T. Wright Marine award Congress Water Resources—U. So. Ill.; Gold medal for distinguished services to Am. lit. Dutch Treat Club. Died Nov. 12, 1984.

BURNET, DANA, author; b. Cincinnati, O., July 3, 1888; s. Edward Warren and Alice Ann (Dana) B.; grad. Woodward High Sch., Cincinnati, 1907; LL.B., Cornell, 1911; m. Marguerite Elsie Dumary, of Brooklyn, N.Y., Nov. 26, 1913. With Evening Sun, New York, 1911-18. Mem. Chi Phi. Author: Poems, 1915; The Shining Adventure, 1916; The Lark; It is a Strange House, 1925; Angel Food (3 act comedy), 1927; Four Walls (3 act play, with George Abbott), 1928; The Boundary Line (3 act drama), 1931. Contbr. to mags.†

BURNETT, WILLIAM RILEY, Author; b. Springfield, Ohio, Nov. 25, 1899; s. Theodore Addison and Emily Updike Colwell (Morgan) B.; m. Whitney Forbes Johnstone; children: William Riley III, James Addison. Student, Ohio State U., 1919-20. Statistician, State of Ohio, 1921-27, writer, 1928—. Author: Little Caesar, 1929, Iron Man, 1930, Saint Johnson, 1930, The Silver Eagle, 1931, The Giant Swing, 1932, Dark Hazard, 1933, Goodbye to the Past, 1934, The Goodhues of Sinking Creek, 1934, King Cole, 1936, The Dark Command, 1938, High Sierra, 1940, The Quick Brown Fox, 1942, Nobody Lives Forever, 1944, Tomorrow's Another Day, 1945, Romelle, 1946, The Asphalt Jungle, 1949, Little Men, Big World, 1951, Vanity Row, 1952, Adobe Walls, 1953, Captain Lightfoot, 1954, Pale Moon, 1956, Underdog, 1957, Bitter Ground, 1958, Mi Amigo, 1959, The Goldseekers, 1962, The Widow Barony, 1963; also fiction others; story The Ivory Tower, in The Best Short Stories of 1946; has received 3 book club selections: story Little Caesar (Lit. Guild); Iron Man, Dark Hazard, (Book of the Month),

Little Caesar, and The Asphalt Jungle translated into 12 languages, The Great Escape (Screen Writers award for best drama 1963), The Roar of the Crowd, 1964, Cool Man, 1968; Author: many screen plays, including Wake Island, 1942. Recipient O. Henry Meml. award for best short story, 1930. Mem. Acad. Motion Picture Arts and Scis. Democrat. Episcopalian. Club: Players (N.Y.). Address: Los Angeles, Calif. *

BURNHAM, ALAN, architect; b. Englewood, N.J., Feb. 10, 1913; s. Enoch Lewis and Cora (Sellers) B.; m. Frances Hotchkiss Berking, Mar. 22, 1947; children—Roderick Hotchkiss, Cora Lewis. Student, Avon (Conn.) Old Farms, 1929-30, Fountain Valley Sch. of Colo., Colorado Springs, 1930-32; B.S., Harvard, 1936; B.Arch., Columbia, 1940. With Bur. Yards and Docks USN (camouflage), Washington, 1941-43; overseas duty USN, Trinidad, B.W.I., 1944-46; with Alex D. Crosett & Assos. (architects), N.Y.C., 1946, Walter Dorwin Teague, indsl. designer, 1946-47, Frederick L. Ackerman and Harold R. Sleeper (architects), N.Y.C., 1947-48, Trio Industries, Inc., N.Y.C., 1948-49, Lorimer Rich & Robbins Conn (architects), N.Y.C., 1949-50; office of Henry S. Churchill, N.Y.C., 1950-52; indsl. div. Ebasco Service, Inc., 1952-60, Burns & Roe, Inc., 1960-62, Shanley & Sturges, 1962-65; exec. dir. Landmarks Preservation Commn., 1965-72, dir. research, 1972-78; cons. to, Biltmore, Asheville, N.C.; lectr. New Sch., 1964-81. Contbr. to jours. and mags.; Edited: Richard Morris Hunt Family Papers, 1939, New York Landmarks, 1963. Fellow AIA; mem. Soc. Archtl. Historians, Nat. Trust, L.I., N.Y. hist. socs., Municipal Art Soc. (past dir.). Clubs: Harvard (N.Y.C.); Century Assn. Home: Greenwich, Conn. Dec. Mar. 3, 1984.

BURNHAM, WILBUR HERBERT, artist, designer stained glass murals; b. Boston, Feb. 4, 1887; s. Wilbur Leroy and Mary (Oxley) B.; student Mass. Sch. Art, 1904-08; also France, Eng., Italy and Spain; m. Etta Mae Miller, June 22, 1912; 1 son, Wilbur Herbert. Began as designer stained glass, 1906; designer Harry E. Goodhue, Boston, 1906-16, Horace J. Phipps Co., Boston, 1916-18; mem. firm Ball & Burnham, 1918-20, Phipps, Ball & Burnham, 1920-22; in bus. alone, 1922 from. Stained glass represented in Cathedral of St. John the Divine, Washington Cathedral, Ch. St. Vincent DePaul, Los Angeles, many others. Fellow Royal Soc. Arts; mem. Mediaeval Acad. Am. Am. Fedn. Arts. Stained Glass Assn. Am. (pres. 1939-41), Boston Soc. Arts and Crafts (master craftsman), Mass. Sch. Art Alumni, Copley Soc. (pres. 1951-53). Recipient Gold medal Boston Tercentenary Art Exhbn., 1930; diplome de Medaille d'Argent, Paris Expn., 1937; Craftsmanship medal A.I.A., 1947. Republican. Episcopalian. Writer, lectr. on stained glass. Home: Wakefield, MA. †

BURNS, BERYL ILES, hosp. adminstr.; b. Unionville, Mo., Apr. 22, 1889; s. William Arthur and Mary Ethalinda (Jones) B.; A.B., U. of Missouri, 1916; A.M., U. of Mich., 1918; M.D., U. of Iowa, 1924; Ph.D., Northwestern U., 1933; m. Hallie, Almeda Hendrick, Apr. 5, 1915; children—Mary Evelyn (Mrs. Morgan Blum), Betty June (Mrs. Frederick Albert Hook). Asst. in anatomy, U. of Mich. Sch. of Medicine, 1916-17, instr. anatomy, 1917-18; instr. anatomy, U. of Iowa, Sch. of Medicine, 1918-24, asst. prof. anatomy, 1924-25; prof. anatomy U. of Utah, Med. Sch., 1925-32, dean, 1929-32; fellow, Neurol. Inst., Northwestern U., 1931-32; prof. anatomy La. State U. Med. Sch., 1932-45, dean, 1939-45; administrator of hosps., U. of Texas Med. Branch, Galveston, Tex., 1945-49, commr. of hosps., Kansas City, Mo., from 1949. Mem. Am. Assn. Anatomists, A.A.A.S., Tex. Acad. Science, A.M.A., Amer. Hospital Assn., Phi Kappa Phi. Sigma Xi. Phi Beta Pi. Author: various articles on anatomy and med. edn. Home: Kansas City, Mo. †

BURNS, DANIEL MATTHEW, advertising agency executive; b. Bklyn., Aug. 1, 1918; s. Isaac Matthew and Mary Cecilia (Hodell) B.; m. Adele Valerie Casey, July 28, 1945; children: Daniel Matthew, Eugene, Clare, Margaret, Christopher, Adele, Theresa, Stephen, Barbara. B.A., St. Francis Coll., Bklyn., 1940; postgrad., Fordham U. Vice pres., editor Bottling Industry, Gussow Publs., 1946-53; with William Esty Co., Inc., N.Y.C., 1953-83, sr. v.p., 1968-83, dir. sales promotion services, 1967-83; pres. Daniel M. Burns Communications, from 1984. Chmn. council regents St. Francis Coll., 1976-78. Served to 1st lt. AUS, 1942-46. Mem. Mktg. Communications Execs. Internat. (pres. 1979-81), St. Francis Coll. Alumni Assn. (pres. 1958). Republican. Roman Catholic. Home: Garden City, NY.

BURNS, MATTHEW JAMES, union official (ret.); b. Appleton, Wis., Nov. 6, 1887; s. Andrew and Mary (Davey) B.; ed. pub. schs.; m. Sarah Elvira Hendricksen, Oct. 22, 1912; children—Vera Marie (Mrs. Harold Hinman), Russel Matthew, Bernard, Jerome Dallem. Engaged in paper making trade 1902-20; apptd. gen. organizer, Internat. Brotherhood of Paper Makers, 1920, internat. sec., 1922-28, internat. pres., 1929-40, and 1943-47; labor economist, W.P.B., 1941-42, alternate mem. over-all appeals bd., asst. dir., pulp and paper div., W.P.B., 1943. Retired Dec. 1947; mem. govt. staff working on Defense Mobilization from 1951. Roman Catholic. Home: Albany, N.Y. †

BURNS, ROBERT M(ARTIN), chemist; b. Longmont, Colo., Jan. 9, 1890; S. Thomas and Mattie (Ash) B.; A.B., Univ. of Colo., 1915, A.M., 1916, D.Sc., (hon.), 1945;

Ph.D., Princeton, 1921; m. Ada Kneal, September 11, 1924; 1 dau., Nadia (Mrs. John Gould). Instructor University of Colorado, 1915-17; research chemist, Barrett Company, Edgewater, N.J., 1921-22, Western Elec. Co., New York, 1922-25; mem. technical staff Bell Telephone Labs., Murray Hill, N.J., 1925-55, chem. dir., 1945-55; sci. adviser Stanford Research Inst., from 1955, dir. European office, 1957-59, 60-61, dir. phys. and biol. research, 1959-60. Served as second lieutenant, United States Army, 1918-19; chmn. of OSRD Naval Com. on Corrosion, 1944-45. Soc. of Chem. Industry, Perkin Medal, 1952. Mem. Am. Chem. Soc., (chmn. N.Y. Section, 1949-50; recipient of the Acheson medal 1956), Electrochemical Soc. (president 1943, secretary, 1947-49), A.A.A.S., also Tau Beta Pi, Kappa Delta Pi, Sigma Xi, Phi Beta Kappa, Delta Tau Delta, Alpha Chi Sigma (nat. pres. 1924-28). Clubs: N.Y. Chemists, (honorary member), Green Mountain (president N.Y. section 1937), Appalachian Mountain (chairman N.Y. chapter 1946). Author: Protective Coatings for Metals (with W. W. Bradley), 1955. Contbr. to chem. jours. Home: Woodside, Cal. †

BURNS, SIR ALAN, govt. ofcl.; b. St. Kitts, B.W I., Nov. 9, 1887; s. James and Agnes (Delisle) B.; student St. Edmund's Coll., Ware, Eng.; m. Kathleen Hardtman, May 10, 1914; children—Benedicta, Barbara. Apptd. Colonial Civil Service, 1905, served in Leeward Islands, 1905-12, Nigeria, 1912-24, Bahama, 1924-28, Nigeria, 1929-34; apptd. Gov. of British Honduras, 1934; asst. under sec. of state for the Colonies, 1950; gov. of the Gold Coast, 1941; permanent U.K. rep. on trusteeship council of UN, 1947-56. Decorated Knight Grand Cross Order St. Michael and St. George, Knight of Order of St. John. Club: Athenaeum (London). Author: History of Nigeria, 1929; Colour Prejudice, 1948; Colonial Civil Servant, 1949; History of the British West Indies, 1954; In Defence of Colonies, 1957. Home: Putney Heath, London, Eng. †

BURNTVEDT, THORVALD OLSEN, clergyman; b, Kragerö, Norway, May 29, 1888; s. Andreas Olsen and Pauline Ingeborg (Hansen) B.; came to U.S., 1903; naturalized, 1917; A.B., Augsburg Acad. and Coll., Minneapolis, Minn., 1912; C.T., Augsburg Theol. Sem., 1915; student Bibl. Sem., New York, 1919-20, U. of Minn., summer, 1929, Northwestern Conservatory of Music, Minneapolis, 1908-09; LL.D., St. Olaf Coll., 1934; D.D., Luther Theol. Seminary, St. Paul, 1954; m. Anna Constance Tollefson, Aug. 24, 1921; children—Gloria Anne, Gratia Muriel, Thorvald Robert. Ordained to ministry of Luth. Ch., June, 1915; pastor Olivet Luth. Ch., Tacoma, Wash., 1915-18, Trinity Luth. Ch., Brooklyn, N.Y., 1919-20, Trinity Luth. Ch., Minneapolis, 1920-30; lecturer Luth. Bible Inst., 1922-29, Augsburg Theol. Sem., 1926-29; pres. The Luth. Free Ch. (of America) since June, 1930; pres. Luth. Deaconess Home and Hosp., Mpls.; dir. Nat. Luth. Council. Decorated by King of Norway. Comdr. Cross of Royal Order of St. Olaf, 1946. Mem. Advisory Council American Bible Society. Compiled (with sec.) Annual Reports Luth. Free Ch. since 1931. Author of several religious booklets; contbr. to religious jours. Co-editor The Concordia Hymnal and a book of Family Devotions, Life and Light. Home: Minneapolis, Minn. †

BURPEE, DAVID, seedsman; b. Phila., Apr. 5, 1893; s. Washington Atlee and Blanche (Simons) B.; student Cornell U., 1913; D.Sc. (hon.), Bucknell U., 1959, Del. Valley Coll. Sci. and Agr., 1972; m. Lois Torrance, July 18, 1938; children—Jonathan, Blanche Elizabeth (Mrs. Michael R. Dohan). Asst. to father in seed bus., Phila., 1914; chief exec. officer W. Atlee Burpee Co., 1915-70, dir., until 1977. Hon. dir. Del. Valley Coll. Sci. and Agr., Doylestown, Pa., Bucknell U.; bd. dirs. Welcome House, Doylestown, Pa.; former dir. emeritus Abington Meml. Hosp. Recipient Gold seal Nat. Council State Garden Clubs, 1964; Am. Home Achievement medal, 1964; Gold medal for outstanding contbn. to horticulture Men's Garden Club Los Angeles, 1974; certificate of appreciation Men's Garden Club of Delaware Valley, 1975; Liberty Hyde Bailey medal Am. Hort. Soc., 1978; cert. of appreciation All-Am. Selections. Mem. Am. Seed Trade Assn. (dir., past pres.), Soc. War 1812, Canadian Soc. Phila. (hon. life pres.), English-Speaking Union, Pa. Soc. N.Y. (v.p.), Pa. S.R., Am. Hort. Council (citation 1958), Royal Hort. Soc., Nat. Sweet Pea Soc. Gt. Britain (Henry Eckford Meml. medal 1963), Scottish Nat. Sweet Pea Soc., Société Nationale d'Horticulture de France, Newcomen Soc. N.A., Phila. Soc. Promoting Agr. (Agrl. award 1950), Men's Garden Clubs Am., Quaker City Farmers Club, Delta Mu Delta (hon.), Alpha Zeta (hon.), Delta Upsilon. Republican. Clubs: Union League (v.p. 1933-35), Racquet (Phila.); Hillsboro (Fla.). Plant breeder; created, introduced new hybrid flowers, vegetables. Home: Doylestown, Pa. Died June 24, 1980.

BURR, HUGH CHAMBERLIN, clergyman; b. Gloversville, N.Y., Aug. 27, 1890; s. Geroge C. and Katherine Little (Chamberlin) B.; A.B., Princeton, 1911; grad. Union Theol. Sem., 1915; grad. work, 1915-16; A.M., Columbia U., 1916; D.D., Kalamazoo (Mich.) Coll., 1933; m. Frances Rousseau Williams, Jan. 16, 1917; children—Jonathan Williams, Theodore Sumner, Sec. Philadelphian Soc. (Y.M.C.A.), Princeton, 1911-12; student minister Madison Av. Presbyn. Ch., N.Y. City, 1912-15, asst. minister, 1915-16; ordained ministry Bapt. Ch., 1915; minister Portland Street Ch., Haverhill, Mass., 1916-21, First Ch., Elmira, N.Y., 1921-30, First Ch. Detroit, Mich., 1930-38; sec. Fed. Chs. of Rochester and vicinity, Inc. from Feb. 1, 1938. Mem. Princeton Charter Club, Am. Hymn Soc., Theta Phi; mem. bd. of mgrs., N.Y. Bapt. Missionary Conv., 1926-29, 1938-40; pres. Detroit Council Religious Edn., 1931; v.p. Detroit Council of Chs., 1931, pres., 1933, 1934; v.p. Detroit Bapt. Missionary Soc., 1932, 1935, 1936, 1937; mem. program com. Northern Baptist Conv., 1931, chmn. nominating com., 1934, resolutions com. 1938; chmn. com. on relations with other religious bodies, 1940-47; mem. exec. com. Fed. Council of Churches, 1933-37 and 1940, adv. com. 1946-48; chairman central department of field administration National Council of Churches; treasurer Association Council Sec., 1940, president, 1942, 50; mem. Coordinating Conf. of 140 of Nat. Interdenominational Bodies, 1941, Constutition com. 1940; exec. com. of planning com. National Council, Chs. of Christ, 1948, secretary of Baptist Commission on relations with the Disciples of Christ, 1944-47. Mem. bd. trustees, Internat. Council of Religious Edn., 1946. Home: Rochester, N.Y. †

BURROUGHS, EDMUND, lawyer; b. Amherst, Mass., Feb. 16, 1890; s. George Stockton and Emma (Plumley) B.; A.B., Oberlin Coll., 1911; LL.B., Harvard, 1914; m. Esther Ann Swinehart, Sept. 24, 1921; children—Anne Caroline (Mrs. Halbert Frank), Elizabeth Frances (Mrs. Paul Addison Frank, Jr.). Admitted to Ohio bar, 1914; asso. firm M.B. & H.H. Johnson, Cleve., 1914-16; mem. firm Buckingham, Doolittle & Burroughs, Akron, O., from 1943. Instr., Akron Night Law Sch., evening session Akron U.; dir. Burkhardt Consol. Co., Gilbert Lumber Co., Inc., Met. Investment Co., Skillwood Products, Inc., Spiral Brushes, Inc. Served as 2d lt. U.S. Army, 1918-19; AEF in France. Mem. Am., Ohio, Akron (pres. 1933-34) bar assns., Am. Judicature Soc., Akron C. of C. (1st v.p. 1950-51). Conglist. (chmn. trustees 1938). Rotarian. Club: City (pres. 1956 Akron). Home: Akron, OH. †

BURROWES, HILLIER M(CCLURE), prof.; b. Wallkill, N.Y., Aug. 6, 1887; s. Charles Wesley and Jennie Roberta (McClure) B.; A.B., Yale, 1908, student, 1910-11; M.A., U. of Mo., 1916; summer student U. of Pittsburgh, Pa.; m. Augusta Berlin Williams, June 22, 1912; 1 dau., Helen McClure (Mrs. Joseph Willis Crowell). Instr. English, Lafayette Coll., 1908-10, U. of Mo., 1911-19; prof. and head depts. of English and pub. speaking, Park Coll., Parkville, Mo., 1919-21, coach of debate; substitute prof. of English, Northwest Mo. State Teachers Coll., Maryville, summer of 1920; prof. of English, Grove City (Pa.) Coll., since 1921, coach of debate. Served as 1st lt. Ordnance U.S. Army, 1917-19; Capt. Ordnance with Pittsburgh Ordnance Dist., 1942-46; as major ret. Awarded Army Commendation for work as historian. Mem. Pa. Speech Assn., Debating Assn. Pa. Colleges (past pres.), Nat. Council Teachers of English, Am. Legion (past county and dep. dist. comdr.), Am. Ordnance Assn., Pi Kappa Delta. Republican. Presbyterian. Home: Grove City, Pa. †

BURROWS, ABE, playwright, dir.; b. N.Y.C., Dec. 18, 1910; s. Louis and Julia (Salzberg) B.; m. Carin Smith Kinzel, Oct. 2, 1950; children: James Edward, Laurie Ellen (Mrs. Peter Grad). Student, Coll. City N.Y., 1928-29, Sch. of Finance, N.Y. U., 1929, 30, 31. Writer of: This is New York, for CBS, 1938-39, Texaco Star Theatre, CBS, 1939, Rudy Vallee-John Barrymore program, NBC, 1940, Duffy's Tavern, CBS and NBC, 1941-45, writer-producer, Paramount Pictures, 1946; writer: Joan Davis program, CBS, and, Ford Program, 1946; writer and star: Abe Burrows Show, CBS, 1946-47; made personal appearances in theatres and night clubs, 1947-48, writer-performer-producer, CBS, 1949; writer and star of: Breakfast with Burrows, CBS, 1949, Abe Burrows Almanac, CBS-TV, 1950; also in: This is Show Business, CBS-TV and, We Take Your Word, CBS Radio, and TV, 1950; co-author: musical comedy Guys and Dolls, 1950 (Tony award); dir.: musical Two on the Aisle, 1951; co-author, dir.: musical Three Wishes for Jamie, 1952; author, dir.: musical Can-Can, 1953, First Impressions, 1959; dir.: play Reclining Figure, 1954, Golden Fleecing, 1959; author, dir.: play Say, Darling, 1958; co-author, dir.: play How To Succeed in Business without Really Trying, 1961; dir.: musical What Makes Sammy Run? , 1964; author, dir.: Am. version Cactus Flower, 1965; dir.: Broadway play Forty Carats, 1968; Broadway musical Happy Hunting; adapter, dir.: play Four on a Garden, 1972; dir.: Broadway play No Hard Feelings (Recipient Radio Critics award for best comedy show 1947, N.Y. Drama Critics Award as co-author Guys & Dolls 1951, as co-author How To Succeed in Business without Really Trying 1961, Pulitzer prize as co-author How To Succeed in Business without Really Trying 1961, Tony award as co-author and dir. 1961); Composer lyricist and performer, Decca Record Album, Columbia Record album, Abe Burrows Sings? , 1950; Author: song The Girl with the Three Blue Eyes, 1944, Abe Burrow's Song Book, 1955, Solid Gold Cadillac; screenplay, 1956; co-author: Broadway musical comedy Silk Stockings; autobiography Honest, Abe, 1979. Mem. Dramatists Guild (v.p. 1964), ASCAP, AFTRA, Writers Guild Am. West, Dirs. Guild Am., Soc. Stage Dirs. and Choreographers, Explorers Club. Died Dec. 17, 1985.

BURT, ALFRED LEROY, prof. history; b. Listowel, Ont., Can., Nov. 28, 1888; s. Christian Kimbal and Sarah Jane (Large) B.; B.A., U. of Toronto, 1910; B.A., Corpus Christi Coll., Oxford, Eng. (Rhodes scholar from Ont. 1910), 1912, M.A., 1916; married Dorothy Duff, August 18, 1915; children—Dorothy Forrest (Mrs. J. S. Johnson), Mary Duff (Mrs. A. L. Leinback), John Arthur, Joan Elizabeth (Mrs. S. E. Jenness). Came to U.S., 1930. Lecturer in history, University of Alberta, Canada, 1913-16, asst. prof., 1916-20, asso. prof., 1920-21, prof. and head dept. of history, 1921-30; prof. of history, U. Minn., 1930-57, prof. emeritus, 1957 from; prof. Carleton Coll., Ottawa, Can., 1957-58. Served as lt. Canadian O.T.C., 1916-18; with Canadian Tank Batn., 1918-19. Co-winner Belt prize and Robert Herbert Memorial prize, Oxford, 1913; Tyrell Medal, Royal Soc. Can., 1946. Fellow Royal Historical Soc.; mem. Can.-U.S. Com. on Edn., Am., Canadian (pres. 1949-50) hist. assns., Acad. Polit. Science. Canadian Polit. Science Assn. Author several books, including: The Old Province of Quebec, 1933; The United States, Great Britain and British North America, 1940; A Short History of Canada for Americans, 1942; The Evolution of the British Empire and Commonwealth from the American Revolution, 1956. Edited Makers of Canada, Vol. III., 1926. Contbr. to Cambridge History of British Empire; The United States and Its Place in World Affairs, 1918-43; also to jours. Home: Minneapolis, Minn. †

BURT, WILBUR F., business exec.; b. Ocean Grove, N.J., 1890; grad. Amherst College, 1912. Vice pres. and dir. Socony-Vacuum Oil Co., Inc. Dir. Houdry Process Corp. Home: New York, N.Y. Deceased.

BURTNESS, THORSTEIN WARREN, retired ry. exec.; b. Chgo., Aug. 11, 1887; s. Theodore and Marie (Holth) Bjertnes; student sch. commerce, Northwestern, 1914-16; m. Ruth Ericksen, Sept. 10, 1924; children—Thorstein Warren, Jr., Ruth Elizabeth. With C., M., St.P.&P. R.R., 1902-52, clk. accounting dept., 1902-15, chief clk. to gen. auditor, 1915-16, chief clk. to pres., 1916-20, office asst. to pres., 1920-24, corp. sec., 1924-52. Trustee Wheaton Coll., 1939 from. Protestant. Home: Wheaton, Ill. †

BURTON, CLARENCE G(ODBER), congressman; born Providence, R.I., Dec. 14, 1886; s. Joseph G. and Annie (Severn) B. Became treas. Lynchburg Hosiery Mills, Inc., 1907, pres. from 1921; pres. Lynchburg Fed. Savings & Loan Assn.; dir. Comml. Trust & Savings Bank. Mem. Lynchburg City Council, 1942-48; mayor of Lynchburg, 1946-48. Elected mem. 80th Congress (1947-49), 6th. Va. Dist. (by spl. election Nov. 1948); mem. 81st-82d Congresses (1949-53). Dist. Pres. Memorial Hosp., Lynchburg. Mem. Commn. on World Service and Finance, Va. Meth. Conf. Democrat. Elk. Clubs: Lynchburg Rotary (past pres.), Natural Bridge Appalachian Trail (past pres.). Home: Lynchburg, Va. Died Jan. 18, 1982.*

BURTON, HARRY B., former mayor; b. Climax, Greenwood Co., Kan., Oct. 22, 1887; s. Charles Lane and Mary Elizabeth (Bennett) B.; self-ed.; m. Rose Elizabeth Stenger, Dec. 23, 1909. V.p. Mid-Continent Fuel Co.; mayor of Kansas City, Kan., 1921-3. Mem. Switchmen's Union of N.A. Democrat. Methodist. Mason (32 deg., Shriner). Club: Optimist. Home: Kansas City, Kan. †

BURTON, LAURENCE V(REELAND), consultant; b. Aurora, Ill., Apr. 15, 1889; s. Charles Pierce and Cora Lena (Vreeland) B.; B.S., U. Ill., 1911, M.S., 1914; Ph.D., Yale University, 1917; m. Isabel Clegg, Aug. 17, 1921 (deceased on August 12, 1965). With Libby, McNeill & Libby, 1915-17, 22-24, Nat. Canners Assn., 1919-21, Ill. Canners Assn., 1921-22, Foulds Milling Co., 1924-28, McGraw-Hill Pub. Co., 1928-47; exec. dir. Packaging Inst., N.Y.C., 1947-55, cons. food processing and packaging, from 1955; contbg. editor Package Engrng. Leader 2-man Reverse Flow team under ECA invited by Anglo-Am. Council on Prodn. to visit Eng., 1951. Served as pvt. to 1st lt. San Corps, World War I; corr. SWPA, 1944, Combined Intelligence Objectives Survey, 1945. Recipient Internat. award Inst. Food Technologists, 1957. Mem. Am. Soc. Testing Materials, Tech. Assn. Pulp and Paper Industry, Inst. Food Technologists (pres. 1941-42), Am. Chem. Soc., Soc. Am. Microbiologists, Am. Assn. Cereal Chemists, Packing Inst., Met. Bakery Prodn. Men's Assn., N.Y. Acad. Scis., Soc. for Investigation of Recurring Events, Phi Kappa Sigma. Phi Tau Sigma. Club: Yale (N.Y.C.). Author: Week-End Painter, 1948. Contbr. profl. jours. Home: Scarsdale, N.Y. †

BURTON, PHILLIP, congressman; b. Cin., June 1, 1926; 1 dau., Joy. A.B. in Polit. Sci, U. So. Calif., 1947; LL.B., Golden Gate Law Sch., 1952. Bar: Calif. bar 1952, U.S. Supreme Ct. bar 1956. Practice law, San Francisco; mem. Calif. Assembly, 1956-64; chmn. com. social welfare; mem. 88th-97th congresses 6th dist. Calif.; mem. interior and insular affairs coms., edn. and labor com., chmn. nat. parks and insular affairs subcom.; chmn. House Democratic Caucus, 1975-76; U.S. del., chmn. North Atlantic Treaty Assn. Conf. Past nat. officer Young Democrats; a founder Calif. Dem. Council; sec.-treas. 88th Congress Dem. Club; chmn. Dem. Study Group, 1971-72. Served with USN, World War II, Korea. Mem. Blue Key (dist. officer). Home: San Francisco, Calif. Dec. Apr. 10, 1983.*

BURTON, RICHARD (RICHARD JENKINS), actor; b. Pontrhydfen, South Wales, Nov. 10, 1925; m. Sybil Williams (div. 1963); 2 children; m. Elizabeth Taylor, Mar. 15, 1964 (div.); m. Susan Hunt, 1976 (div. 1983); m. Sally Anne Hay, July 3, 1984. Ed., Exeter and Oxford. Lst stage appearance in: Druid's Rest, Royal Court Theatre,

Liverpool, Eng., 1943; later on London stage; Brit. debut in film Last Days of Dolwyn, 1948; on London stage in A Phoenix Too Frequent; N.Y. stage debut Phoenix Too Frequent, 1950; later appeared: N.Y. stage debut Legend for Lovers, 1951; on Broadway in Time Remembered; then musical Camelot, also Equus, 1976; U.S. tour of Camelot, 1980-81; Broadway and U.S. tour of Private Lives, 1983; title role in: Broadway prodn. Hamlet, Old Vic Company, Edinburgh Festival, 1953; continued 1953-54 season with, Old Vic Company; later appeared in: Hollywood film debut in My Cousin Rachel, 1954; other films include Circle of Two; TV roles in Wuthering Heights, 1958, Divorce His, Divorce Hers, Brief Encounter; title role in: TV miniseries Life of Richard Wagner, 1982; appeared as White Knight: TV prodn. Alice in Wonderland, 1983; later appeared in: recs. include A Personal Anthology; (Recipient Golden Globe award 1954, 78; also, 7 acad. awards nominations.); Author: A Christmas Story, 1964, Meeting Mrs. Jenkins, 1965. Served with RAF, 1944-47.

BURTT, HAROLD ERNEST, prof. psychology; b. Haverhill, Mass., Apr. 26, 1890; s. Winslow Jordan and Annie Belle (Boyer) B.; A.B., summa cum laude, Dartmouth, 1911; A.M., Harvard, 1913, Ph.D., 1915; m. Ruth M. Macintosh, June 7, 1916; 1 son, Benjamin Pickering. Instr. psychology, Simmons Coll., Boston, 1915-18, Harvard, 1916-18; consulting psychologist, Canadian Consol. Rubber Co., 1919; instr. psychology, 1919-20, asst. prof., 1920-21, prof. 1922, chmn. psychology dept. from 1939 Ohio State University. Served as chmn. sub-com. on aviation of Psychol. Com. Nat. Research Council, World War I, and aided in developing psychol. methods for selecting aviators; capt. A.S. Aeronautics, Oct. 22-Dec. 24, 1918, at Princeton, N.J. Expert consulant to War Dept. in connection with planning Separation Centers, World War II. Member A.A.A.S. (vice president Psychology Sect., 1949), American Psychological Assn. (council of dirs., 1933-36), American Assn. Applied Psychology (council of dirs., 1938-40), Am. Statis. Assn., Am. Marketing Assn., Phi Beta Kappa. Sigma Xi. Baptist. Author: Applied Psychology, 1948, abridged edit. 1952; rev. edit. 1957; and others. Contbr. research articles to psychol. jours. Address: Columbus, OH. †

BURWELL, HARVEY S., army officer; b. Winsted, Conn., Apr. 20, 1890; s. Dr. Robert Merritt and Harriet Ilizabeth Burwell; B.S., Norwich U., Northfield, Vt., 1913; grad. Am. Service Flying Sch., 1917; grad. Air Corps Tactical Sch., 1932, Command and Gen. Staff Sch., 1934; rated command pilot, combat observer; m. Alice Colladay, July 21, 1915; 1 son, Dane. Commd. 2d lt., Cavalry, U.S. Army, Nov. 3, 1913, and advanced through the grades to brig. gen., Sept. 23, 1942; transferred to Aviation Sect., Signal Corps, 1917, Field Arty., 1916, Air Service, 1920; comdg. gen. Lowry Field, Colo., and Amarillo Air Base, Texas, since 1942. Retired, 1944, with Legion of Merit. Home: Denver, Colo. †

BURWELL, LINA, mem. Dem. Nat. Com.; b. Birmingham, Ala., Aug. 31, 1890; d. Eugene and Emma (Rehwaldt) Weinberg; student pub. schs.; m. Earle G. Burwell, Dec. 3, 1912; children—Eleanor Borden (Mrs. Maurice L. Snider), Orrin Earle. Jerome Ellis, Robert Randolph. Active Democratic Party 30 yrs., formerly precinct com. woman, Casper, state vice chmn. del. nat. conv., mem. nat. com., presdl. elector, 1948. Com. Nat. Found. Infantile Paralysis. Mem. Wesleyan Service Guild (co-ordinator). Methodist. Home: Casper, Wyo. †

BUSCH, ALFRED H., corporate executive; b. Chgo., 1919; ed. U. Wis., 1942; LL.B., De Paul U., 1947. Sec. Stewart-Warner Corp., 1953-59, sec.-treas., 1959-64, v.p., sec.-treas., 1964-77, sr. v.p., sec.-treas., 1977-79, sr. v.p., treas., from 1979, also dir. Office: Chicago, Ill. Dec.

BUSH, LUCIUS MASON, osteopath; b. Pompey, N.Y., Sept. 5, 1887; s. Allen Edgar and Florence Adelaide (Crandall) B.; student Syracuse U., 1907-09; D.O., Am. Sch. of Osteopathy, Kirksville, Mo., 1912, Phila. College of Osteopathy, 1920; married Ethel Waldron, December 13, 1911; children—William Mason, M.D., Florence Marguerite (Mrs. Gerard Langoler), James Allen, M.D., Practiced osteopathy, Hartford, Connecticut, 1912; Jersey City, N.J., 1912-21, New York City from 1921; specializing in ear, nose and throat. Mem. Am. Osteopathic Assn. (chmn. ear, nose and throat sect, 1921-22), N.Y. State and N.Y. City osteopathic assns., Am. Osteopathic Soc. of Ophthalmology, Rhinology and Otolaryngology, Sigma Nu, Theta Nu Epsilon, Theta Psi, Monks Head. Republican. Presbyterian. Mason. Clubs: Winged Foot Golf (Mamaroneck, N.Y.); Hermitage Country (Magog); Skytop. Author: Common Sense Health, 1935; The Secret of Sinusitis and Headaches, 1938. Contbg. author to Clinical Osteopathy, 1917. Contbr. articles to professional and health jours. Speaker before osteopathic socs. Pioneer in osteopathic methods of treating sinusitis, adenoids, mastoiditis, deafness. Home: Pelham, N.Y. †

BUSH-BROWN, HAROLD, architect; b. Paris, France, of Am. parents, Nov. 3, 1888; s. Henry Kirke and Margaret (Lesley) B.; grad. Newburgh (N.Y.) Acad., 1907; A.B., Harvard, 1911; M.Arch., 1915; m. Marjorie Conant, Aug. 16, 1924, 1 son, Richard Lyman. Began as archtl. draftsman, 1910; prof., head dept. architecture Georgia Institute of Technology (formerly Ga. Sch. Tech.), 1925-56, formerly dir. sch. architecture, prof. emeritus, from 1956; sr. partner Bush-Brown, Gailey & Heffernan, architects. Designed 7 dormitories, dining-hall, 6 classroom bldgs., lab. bldgs., auditorium, library, gynmasium at Georgia Sch. Tech. and Guggenheim Sch. Aeros. Chmn. Joint committee on teaching architecture for A.I.A.-Assn. Collegiate School Architecture. District officer for Ga. of Historic Am. Bldg. Survey, 1936-37. Served as ensign, lt. jr. grade, U.S.N.R.F., 1917-20. Fellow, Am. Inst. Architects; mem. Am. Planning and Civic Assn. Democrat. Unitarian. Club: Harvard of New York and Atlanta. Home: Duxbury, Mass. †

BUSHMILLER, ERNIE, cartoonist; b. N.Y.C., Aug. 23, 1905; s. Ernest George and Elizabeth (Hall) B.; m. Abby Bohnet, July 9, 1930. Student, N.A.D. With United Features Syndicate, from 1931. Former comedy writer for, Harold Lloyd, comedian, Hollywood, Calif., former cartoonist, N.Y. World, N.Y. Graphic; creator: cartoon Fritzi Ritz; also comedy strip Fritzi Ritz and Nancy; comic books pub. monthly. Mem. adv. bd. Salvation Army. Mem. Soc. Illustrators, Nat. Cartoonists Soc. Clubs: Dutch Treat, Artists and Writers, Banshees. Home: Stamford, Conn. Dec. Aug. 15, 1982.*

BUSIGNIES, HENRI GASTON, electronic-communications engr.; b. Sceaux, France, Dec. 29, 1905; s. Henri and Juliette (Benoit) B.; degree in elec. engring., Paris, 1926; D.Sc., Newark Coll. Engring., 1958; D.Engring., Poly. Inst. Bklyn., 1970; m. Cecile Phaeton, July 15, 1931; 1 dau., Monique (Mrs. Francis Roland Stolz). Came to U.S., 1940, naturalized, 1953. Research, devel. engr. Les Laboratoires, Le Materiel Telephonique, Paris labs. Internat. Tel.& Tel. Corp., 1928-35, dept. head, 1935-38, head project on direction finders, radar, instrument landing, receivers, antennas, 1938-41; lab. head Fed. Telecommunication Labs. Internat. Tel. & Tel. Corp., Nutley, N.J., 1941-46, dir., 1946-48, tech. dir., 1948-54, exec. v.p., 1954-56, pres. 1956-75, pres. ITT labs. div., 1958-75, v.p., 1960-65, gen. tech. dir. corp., 1960-75, sr. v.p., chief scientist, ret., 1975, chief scientist emeritus, 1975-81; dir. Am. Optical Corp. Recipient Lakhovsky award Radio Club of France, 1926; certificate commendation for outstanding service USN, 1947; Presdl. certificate of Merit, 1948; Pioneer award air nav. I.R.E., 1959; Indsl. Research Inst. medal, 1971. Fellow IEEE (David Sarnoff award 1964, Internat. Communications award 1970, Edison medal 1977), Nat. Acad. Engring., Radio Club Am. (Armstrong medal 1975, dir. 1977); mem. French Engrs. in U.S., Soc. French Civil Engrs., French Soc. Advancement Scis. Roman Catholic. Club: Alliance Francaise. Contbr. articles to profl. publs. Patentee in field; inventor MTI Radar. Home: Montclair, N.J. Died June 19, 1981.

BUSSING, WILFRID CHARLES, pub. co. exec.; b. Evansville, Ind., Nov. 8, 1889; s. Bernard J. and Alice (Doyle) B.; grad. high sch., Evansville, Ind.; m. Katherine Kittinger, Jan. 25, 1915 (dec. 1927); children—Marilyn, Wilfrid, Charles; m. 2d, Lois MacCammon, Mar. 26, 1929. Advt. mgr. Terre Haute (Ind.) Post, 1909; pub. Evansville (Ind.) Rev. 1912; bus. mgr. Evansville Press Co., 1916-26, became pres., 1936; advt. dir. Rocky Mountain News, Denver, 1926-29; gen. mgr. Indpls. Radio Sta. WKBF, 1929-31; advt. dir. Balt. Post, 1931-34; bus. mgr. Evansville Press, 1934-39; pres. Evansville Printing Corp., 1939-65, pubs. Evansville Courier, Evansville Press, Sunday Courier and Press, Bussing Investment Corp., 6th and Lincoln Corp., Mich. and Main Corp.; v.p., sec. Lois Anne Investments Inc. Trustee, exec. com. U. Evansville; past pres. bd. overseers St. Meinrad Coll.; bd. dirs. Evansville Indsl. Found. Chmn. adv. bd. Little Sisters of the Poor. Mem. C. of C. Roman Catholic. Knight of Malta. Clubs: Evansville Country, Evansville Petroleum; University of Notre Dame. Home: Evansville, IN. †

BUSSMANN, HARRY T., mfg. exec.; b. St. Louis, 1889; s. Bernard and Regina (Kroeger) B.; m. Catherine Anna Bussmann, Jan. 26, 1910; children—Kathryn Bruening, Harry T., Dr. D. W. Vice pres. Bussmann Mfg. Co., St. Louis, from 1914; dir. McGraw Electric Co. Roman Catholic. Home: St. Louis, MO. †

BUTCHER, HARRY C., radio-TV consultant; born Springville, Ia., Nov. 15, 1901; s. Harry C. and Myrtle Abbie (Kimball) B.; A.B., in Journalism, Iowa State Coll. (Coll. of Agrl. and Mech. Arts), 1924; m. Ruth Barton, June 8, 1924 (divorced, Apr. 1946); 1 dau. Beverly; m. 2d, Mary Margaret Ford, May 7, 1946. Dir. of information and editor Ill. Agrl. Assn. Record, Chicago, 1924-26; mng. editor Fertilizer Review and asst. to exec. nat. Fertilizer Assn., Washington, D.C., 1926-29; opened Washington Office, Columbia Broadcasting System in 1929, dir. Washington office, 1929-32 and Mgr. WJSV (now WTOP), Washington, D.C., 1932-34, v.p. in charge, Washington, 1934-42; pres. Cable TV of Santa Barbara, Inc. Commissioned lt. commander, U.S. Naval Reserve, Sept. 16, 1939, advancing to capt., Nov. 1944; assumed active duty, Communications Div., Navy Dept., Mar. 1, 1942; assigned as aide to Gen. Eisenhower, June 1942. Mem. So. Cal. Broadcasters Assn., Radio Pioneers, Naval Order of the U.S. (commandery), Sigma Phi Epsilon and Sigma Delta Chi. Mem. Church of God. Mason, Elk. Clubs: Nat. Press; University, Channel City (Santa Barbara); Author: My Three Years With Eisenhower, 1946. Home: Santa Barbara, Calif. Died Apr. 22, 1985.

BUTLER, FRANCIS PEABODY, stock broker; b. Chgo., Apr. 12, 1887; s. Hermon Beardsley and Jessie (Peabody) B.; grad. Hill Sch., 1905; B.A., Yale, 1909; m. Deborah Hunter, Aug. 31, 1912; children—Deborah (Mrs. C. Wanton Balis), Jessica (Mrs. Alfred C. Sheffield), Hermon B. (dec.). Partner Peabody, Houghteling & Co., Chgo., 1910-27, Butler, Sr. & Co., Chgo., 1927-29, E. H. Rollins, Chgo., 1929-32; salesman, partner Alfred L. Baker & Co., 1932-39; partner Betts, Borland & Co., Chgo., from 1939; dir. Gen. Portland Cement Co. Trustee Church Home for Aged Persons, Chgo.; bd. mgrs. Chgo. YMCA. Clubs: Attic (Chgo.); Onwentsia (Lake Forest, Ill.); Elihu (Yale). Home: Lake Forest, Ill. †

BUTLER, LEE DAVID, business executive; b. Dunmore, Pa., Feb. 6, 1897; s. James Samuel and Ethel Blanch (Frey) B.; m. Margaret Burchard Fine, June 23, 1930; children: Lee David, Margo Butler Lorig, Adele Butler McLennan. A.B., Princeton U., 1922, M.A., 1924. Pres., treas. Lee D. Butler, Inc., Washington, 1930-79; owner-mgr. Kinloch Farm, 1941-81; dir. Potomac Electric Power Co., 1948-79, mem. exec. com., 1952-79; chmn. exec. com. Woodward & Lathrop, 1967-77, dir., 1950-77. Vice-pres., dir. Nat. Symphony Orch.; pres. United Community Services, Washington, 1950-52; chmn. blood donor service D.C. chpt. A.R.C., World War II, chmn. war fund campaign, Washington area, 1945; bd. dirs. Emergency Hosp., Washington; bd. dirs., exec. com. Atlantic Rural Expn., 1951-82, v.p., 1981; alumni trustee Princeton U., 1952-56. Mem. Va. Angus Assn. (pres. 1962), Phi Beta Kappa. Episcopalian. Clubs: Princeton (Washington) (pres. 1942-45), Met. (Washington); Chevy Chase (Md.). Home: Supply, Va. Died Dec. 31, 1981.

BUTLER, PAUL, bus. exec.; b. Chgo., June 23, 1892; s. Frank O. and Fannie (Bremaker) B.; grad. U. Ill., 1916. Pres., Butler Co., Chgo.; chmn. bd. J.W. Butler Paper Co.; pres., gen. mgr. Butler Paper Cos., Kansas City, Detroit, Los Angeles, New Orleans, Mpls., Phoenix, Denver, Southwestern Paper Cos., Dallas, Ft. Worth, Houston, Pacific Coast Paper Co., San Francisco, Standard Paper Co., Milw., Butler Paper Co., Inc., Ft. Wayne, Ind.; chmn. bd. Butler Aviation Co. bases at Midway, O'Hare, Meigs (Chgo.), Alexander Field (Wisconsin Rapids), Logan Internat. (Boston), Palm Beach (Fla.) Internat., Washington Nat., LaGuardia (N.Y.C.); Helicopter Air Lift (Chgo.), San Francisco Internat. Airport, Palm Springs (Cal.) Airport; pres., gen. mgr. Mid-States Paper Co., Terre Haute, Ind., Sun Ranch, Cameron, Mont. Served as lt. AS, U.S. Army. Mem. Soc. Colonial Wars, Chgo. Hist. Soc., Art Inst., Chgo. Natural History Mus. Clubs: Oak Brook (Ill.) Polo (pres. 1924-30); Army and Navy (v.p., acting pres. 1924-26); York Golf (pres. 1926-35); Racquet Attic, Union League, Chicago Golf; India House, Meadow Brook (N.Y.C.); Everglades, Seminole (Palm Beach, Fla.). Home: Oak Brook, Ill. Died June 24, 1981.

BUTLER, RICHARD AUSTEN (LORD BUTLER), ednl. adminstr; b. Attock Seral, India (now Pakistan), Dec. 9, 1902; s. Montagu Sherard Dawes and Ann Gertrude (Smith) B.; student Marlborough; M.A., Pembroke Coll., Cambridge; LL.D., Cambridge, 1952, Nottingham, 1953, Bristol, 1954. Sheffield, 1955, St. Andrews U., Glasgow, Reading, 1959; D.H.L., Oxford, 1952; married Sydney Elizabeth Courtauld, Apr. 20, 1926 (dec.); children—Richard Clive, Adam Courtauld, Samuel James, Sarah Teresa Mary; married 2d, Mollie Montgomerie Courtauld, 1959. Fellow Corpus Christi Coll., Cambridge, 1925-29; mem. Parliament, Saffron-Walden, 1929-65; parliamentary under-sec. state for India, 1932-37; sec. Ministry of Labour, 1937-38; under-sec. of state for Fgn. Affairs, 1938-41; pres. bd. edn., 1941-45, minister of labor, 1945; chmn. Nat. Union of Conservative and Unionist Assns., 1945-51; chancellor of the Exchequer, 1951-55; Lord Privy Seal, 1956-59; also leader House of Commons, 1956-62, home secretary, 1957-62, chairman of Conservative party, 1959-62; first secretary of state, 1962-63, secretary of state for foreign affairs, 1963-65. High steward Cambridge Univ., chancellor Sheffield U., after 1959; now master of Trinity College, Cambridge University. Mem. Indian Franchise Com., 1931; mem. Privy Council com. for Reform of Channel Islands Govt.; 1946. Privy councillor, 1945. Decorated Companion of Honour, 1954; honorary fellow Corpus Christi College of Cambridge, 1952. President of Union Society, 1924. Modern Language Association, 1940, Nat. Assn. for Mental Health, 1946, Royal Soc. Lit., 1951, Brit. and Fgn. Schs. Socs., 1945; chmn. council Royal India Soc., Anglo Netherlands Soc., 1946. Clubs: Athenaeum, Carlton, Farmers, Beefsteak. Grillions (London). Address: Cambridge, Eng. Died Mar. 8, 1982.

BUTLER, WILLIAM PITT, vice-pres. Kellogg Co.; b. Battle Creek, Mich., Nov. 22, 1888; s. Hiland George and Clara B. (Kellogg) B.; ed. high sch.; m., 1909; children—William P. (dec.), Charlotte (Mrs. Howard S. Welch), Robert. Plant mgr. Armour Grain Co., 1918-27; asst. supt. Kellogg Co., 1927-32; plant mgr. Kellogg Co. of Can., London, Ont., 1932-39; v.p. and plant mgr. Kellogg Co. from 1939. Consultant, War Manpower Commn. Republican. Mason. Clubs: Battle Creek Saddle and Hunt. Home: Battle Creek, Mich. †

BUTTERFIELD, LYMAN HENRY, historian; b. Lyndonville, N.Y., Aug. 8, 1909; s. Roy Lyman and Ethel (Place) B.; A.B., Harvard, 1930, A.M., 1934; Litt.D., Franklin and Marshall Coll., 1952, Bucknell U., 1953; D.Hum., Washington Coll., 1963; LL.D., Monmouth

Coll., 1975; L.H.D., U. Southeastern Mass., 1976; m. Elizabeth Anne Eaton, June 15, 1935; children—Fox, Hester. Instr., tutor English, Harvard, 1930-37; asst., asso. prof. English, Franklin and Marshall Coll., 1937-46; asst., asso. editor Papers of Thomas Jefferson, Princeton, 1946-51; dir. Inst. Early Am. History and Culture, Williamsburg, Va., 1951-54; editor-in-chief Adams Papers, Mass. Hist. Soc. (20 vols. pub. by Harvard U. Press 1961-75), 1954-75, emeritus, 1975-82. Bd. editors Quar., lectr. history Coll. William and Mary, 1951-54; lectr. history Harvard, 1955-64; cons. editor history Harvard U. Press, 1965-75, hon. cons. editor, from 1975. Died Apr. 24, 1982.

BUTTS, ALLISON, metallurgist; b. Poughkeepsie, N.Y., Apr. 26, 1890; s. Allison and Arrie Elizabeth (Mosher) B.; student Riverview Mil. Acad., 1901-07; A.B., Princeton, 1911; S.B., Mass. Inst. of Tech., 1913; m. Charlotte Beatrice Rogers, July 31, 1918 (died Oct. 4, 1920); 1 son Philip Guernsey; m. 2d, Eva Lillian Rogers, June 17, 1924; 1 dau., Virginia Jane. Smelter foreman U.S. Metals Refining Co., 1913-14, research chemist, 1914-16; asst. in metallurgy, Lehigh U., 1916-17, instr., 1917-20, asst. prof., 1920-28, asso. prof., 1928-38, prof. from 1938, dept. head, 1952-56. Dir. Baby Health Station 1923-27. Mem. jury of award, Lincoln Welding Found., 1942, 47. Investigator and Tech. representative, National Defense Research Committee, 1944-46. Mem. American Institute Mining and Metall. Engineers (chmn. edn. div., dir. 1950-52), Electrochemical Soc., Am. Soc. for Metals, Inst. of Metals of Great Britain, American Soc. for Engineering. Edn. (sec. div. of Mineral Technology, 1937-40), Sigma Xi. Presbyterian (pres. bd. of trustees So. Ch., Bethlehem, Pa., 1930-32). Editor: Methods of Nonferrous Metallurgical Analysis, 1928; Copper, the Metal, Its Alloys and Compounds, 1954. Recipient Stoughton Award for contbns. to metallurgy, 1955. Home: Bethlehem, Pa. †

BUTTS, HALLECK ALLISON, commercial attaché; b. Valley Falls, Kan., Aug. 12, 1888; s. Halleck David and Emma Julia (Ladd) B.; prep. edn., Ball High Sch., Galveston, Tex.; grad. Riverview Mil. Acad., Poughkeepsie, N.Y., 1907; grad. Georgetown University School of Foreign Service, 1920; m. Marie Edith Gluek, Dec. 20, 1930. With Leyland S.S. Lines, Galveston, 1909-11; claims adjuster legal dept., A., T. & S.F. Ry., Galveston, 1912-19 (except 1 yr.); sergt. Aero Squadron, later sergt. and lt. Field Arty. Res., U.S.A., 1917-18; apptd. trade commr. U.S. Dept. of Commerce, and assigned to Tokyo, Japan, June 1920; commercial attaché from Apr. 7, 1927. Mem. Delta Phi Epsilon. Episcopalian. Mason (Shriner). Home: Galveston, Tex. †

BYRNES, JOHN W., lawyer; b. Green Bay, Wis., June 12, 1913; s. Charles W. and Harriet (Schumacher) B.; m. Barbara Preston, 1947; children—John, Michael, Bonnie, Charles, Barbara, Elizabeth. A.B., U. Wis., 1936; LL.B., 1938. Bar: Wis. bar 1939, D.C. bar 1972. Mem. Wis. Senate, 1941-45, 79th-92d Congresses from 8th Wis. Dist.; with firm Foley, Lardner, Hollabaugh & Jacobs, Washington. Mem. Wis., D.C. bar assns. Republican. Home: Arlington, Va. Died Jan. 12, 1985.

CABANISS, JELKS HENRY, lawyer; b. Union Springs, Ala., Mar. 7, 1887; s. Edward H. and Martha F. (Jelks) C.; A.B., U. Ala., 1906, A.M., 1907, LL.B., 1908; m. Elizabeth Morris, Apr. 17, 1912; children—Elizabeth Morris (wife of Henry Chesley Daniel, U.S.N.), Jelks Henry (U.S. Army). Admitted to Ala. bar, 1908, since practiced in Birmingham; mem. firm Cabaniss & Johnson since 1908, partner since 1912, dir., finance com. Protective Life Ins. Co., 1917-53; dir. McWane Cast Iron Pipe Co., Birmingham, 1922-53, Moore-Handley Hardware Co., Birmingham, 1948-58, So. Cement Co., 1940-53, Allison Lumber Co., Bellamy, Ala., 1951-53. Pres. community chest, Birmingham and Jefferson Co., 1942-44. Served with U.S. Army, 1917-19. Mem. Ala., Am., Birmingham bar assns., Phi Beta Kappa, Sigma Alpha Epsilon, Phi Delta Phi. Presbyn. Clubs: Birmingham Country (past pres.), Mountain Brook. Home: Birmingham, Ala. †

CAFFERY, EDWARD, consular service; b. St. Mary Parish, La., Feb. 14, 1889; s. Donelson and Bethia Celestine (Richardson) C.; student Princeton, 1908-10, in Europe, 1910-12, University of Virginia Law Sch., 1912-13; m. Daphne Winchester Gillis, of New Orleans, La., Apr. 21, 1920; children—Susan Winchester, Marie Nanette, Chloe Felicia, Lila Marguerite De Lesseline. Apptd. vice consul and assigned to Bucharest, Rumania, 1921, consul, 1924; consul, Habana, Cuba, 1925-28, in charge consulate-gen., Jan.-Sept. 1927; consul, San Jose, Costa Rica, 1928-31, Niagara Falls, Can., from May 1931. Served as 1st lt., inf., U.S.A., 1917-19. Democrat. Presbyn. Clubs: Chevy Chase, Army and Navy, Rotary. Address: Niagara Falls, Canada. †

CAHILL, FRED VIRGIL, educator; b. Davton, Wash., Feb. 13, 1916; s. Fred Virgil and Grace Violet (Crossler) C.; B.A., U. Nebr., 1937, M.A., 1938; Ph.D., Yale, 1941; m. Nan Walker Hardin, Mar. 25, 1952. Instr. govt. U. Ore., 1941-42, asst. prof., 1946-47; asst. prof. govt. Yale, 1947-51, prof. govt. U. Mass., 1953-55, dean arts and scis., 1955-60; dean gen. studies N.C. State Coll., 1960-63, dean of liberal arts, 1963-71, prof. politics, 1971-84. Served to lt. col. AUS, 1942-46, 51-53. Mem. Phi Beta Kappa, Phi Kappa Phi. Democrat. Conglist. Author: Judicial Legislation, 1952; (with R.J. Steamer) The Constitution, Cases and Comment, 1960. Home: Raleigh, N.C. Died May 23, 1984; buried Arlington Nat. Cemetery.

CAINE, WALTER EUGENE, utility executive; b. Buffalo, Apr. 4, 1908; s. Howard Ellsworth and Dora (Squier) C.; B.B.A., U. Buffalo, 1930; M.B.A., Northwestern U., 1931; m. Jeanette Wenborne, Dec. 22, 1932; children—Stephen Howard, Edward Arthur, Martin Squier. Sr. rate analyst Pub. Service Commn. of Wis., Madison, 1932-38; asst. chief rate div. Rural Electrification Adminstrn., Washington, 1936; asst. chief div. rates and research Fed. Power Commn., Washington, 1938-44; assoc. dir. Survey Electric Industry, Twentieth Century Fund, N.Y.C., 1940; dir. bur. stats., sec. accounting sect. Am. Gas. Assn., N.Y.C., 1944-48; dir. gas planning div. Petroleum Adminstrn. for Def., Dept. Interior, Washington, 1951-52; sec., treas. Tex. Eastern Transmission Corp., Shreveport, La., 1948-50, v.p., treas., 1950-53, v.p. gas sales and mktg., Houston, N.Y.C., 1953-67, v.p. corporate services div., Houston, 1967-72, instr. U.S. Dept. Agr. Grad. Sch., Washington, 1943-44. Mem. gas industry adv. council Dept. Interior, 1954-57, mil. petroleum adv. bd., 1957-62. Mem. future requirements com. Denver Research Inst., U. Denver, 1961-73, vice chmn., 1970-72, chmn., 1972-73; bd. dirs. Houston Council on Human Relations, 1973-76, exec. com., treas., 1973-74; regional exec. Nat. Alliance Businessmen, 1972-74. Mem. Am. Gas Assn., Am. Def. Preparedness Assn. (mem. nat. council 1960-61), U.S. C. of C. (com. on econ. policy 1963-66, task force on financing state, local govt. 1966-67), N.Y. Soc. Security Analysts, Fin. Analysts Fedn., N.Y. Soc. Gas Lighting, Newcomen Soc. N.Am., Am. Econ. Assn., Nat. Planning Assn. (nat. council 1969-74), N.Am. Manx Assn., Soc. Friends Nat. Army Mus., Buffalo Cavalry Assn., Confederate Air Force, Internat. Commn. Jurists., Co. Mil. Historians, Confederate Air Force, U.S. Armor Assn. Clubs: Cosmos (Washington); Sky (N.Y.C.); Shreveport; Houston, Lakeside Country (Houston). Author: (with A.R. Burns) Electric Power and Government Policy, 1948; Gas Facts, 1948. Home: Houston, Tex. Dec. Oct. 3, 1979.

CALDER, ROBERT (GEORGE), business exec.; born Glen Ridge, N.J., Aug. 31, 1888; s. James and Mary (Von Helwig) C.; B.S., St. Lawrence U., 1910; student Philippine Constabulary Officers Training Sch., Aug.-Nov. 1911; m. Maude Ethel Martin, June 8, 1915; 1 son, Robert George, Jr. In wholesale and retail oil business, 1921-46; with Standard Oil Co. of N.J., 1931-46; real estate investment and development from 1946; v.p. and dir. Kesbec, Inc., subsidiary Standard Oil Co. of N.J., successor to Kesbec Sales Co., 1921-46; v.p. and director Edlar Realty Corp., Real Estate Holding Co.; dir. Union Bag & Paper Corp. Served as lt., Philippine Constabulory, 1911-12, major, United States Army, 1912-20. Mem. Camp Fire Club of Am., Briarcliff, N.Y., Alpha Tau Omega (St. Lawrence U.). Republican. Club: Quaker Hill Country (Pawling, N.Y.). Home: Pawling, N.Y †

CALDWELL, MILLARD F, JR., judge; born in Knoxville, Tennessee, Feb. 6, 1897; s. Millard Fillmore and Martha Jane (Clapp) C.; student Carson and Newman Coll., 1913-14, U. of Miss., 1917-18, U. Va., 1919-22; LL.D., LL.D., Rollins Coll., U. Fla., Florida Southern University, Florida State University; married Mary Rebecca Harwood, Feb. 14, 1925; children—Millard Fillmore III (dec.), Sally, Purkins McCord, Susan B. Dodd. Admitted to Tenn. bar 1922, Fla. bar, 1925; served as prosecuting atty. and county atty., Santa Rosa County, Fla., and city atty., Milton; elected to Fla. State Legislature, 1928 and 1930; mem. 73d to 76th congresses (1933-41), 3d Fla. Dist.; voluntarily retired from Congress to resume practice of law at Milton and Tallahassee, Fla.; elected governor of Florida for term 1945-49; Fed. Civil Defense administrator 1950-52; justice Florida Supreme Court 1962-69, chief justice, 1967-69. Del. Interparliamentary Union, The Hague, 1938, Oslo, 1939; mem. Exec. Council American Group Interparliamentary Union. Chairman National Governors Conference, 1946-47; pres. Council of State Governments, 1946-48; chmn. bd. of control So. Regional Edn., 1947-50; chmn. Fla. Commn. Constl. Government, 1957-66. Served as pvt. and 2d lt., F.A., U.S. Army, World War I. Mem. Am. Judicature Soc., Newcomen Soc., Huguenot Soc., S.A.R., Alpha Kappa Psi, Blue Key, Kappa Sigma, Phi Alpha Delta. Democrat. Home: Tallahassee, Fla. Died Oct. 23, 1984.

CALDWELL, WALLACE EVERETT, prof. ancient history; b. Brooklyn, N.Y., Apr. 26, 1890; s. Frank Eddy and Anna Frances (Horton) C.; A.B., Cornell Univ., 1910; Ph.D., Columbia, 1919; student U. of Ghent, 1921-22; m. Harriet Elvira Wilmot, June 8, 1915; children—Edward Everett, Robert Wallace, Martha Belle Wilmot. Asst. master, Bethlehem (Pa.) Prep. Sch., 1910-12; master, Allen-Stevenson Sch., N.Y. City, 1912-14; fellow, Columbia, 1914-15; instr., Ind. U., 1915-16; teacher, High Sch. of Commerce, N.Y. City, 1916-17; instr., Columbia, 1917-21; fellow Commn. for Relief in Belgium Edn. Foundation, 1921-22; asso. prof. of ancient history, U. of N.C., 1922-28, prof. from 1928, chmn. dept. of history, 1951-53. Mem. King's County com. of Prog. Party, 1912-14. Mem. Am. Hist. Assn., Classical Assn., Am. Philological Assn., Am. Archaeol. Inst. (past v.p.), Archeol. Soc. N.C. (pres. 1933-36), Soc. Mayflower Descs. (gov. N.C. Soc. 1942-45), Colonial Wars (asst. general N.C. 1958), S.A.R., Acadia, Phi Beta Kappa, Mason (32 deg. K.T., past grand master, past grand high priest; past sovereign grand master grand council). Author: Hellenic Conceptions of Peace, 1919; The Ancient World, 1937; World History (with E. H. Merrill), 1949; Popular History of the World (with E.H. Merrill), 1950; Readings in Ancient History (with W.C. McDermott), 1952. Translator: Thebes (by Jean Capart), 1926. Home: Chapel Hill, N.C. †

CALDWELL, WALTER BRUCE, steel exec.; b. Boston, May 15, 1890; s. Edward and Lucy (Morse) C.; M.E., Cornell, 1912; m. Catherine Stackpole, Oct. 21, 1913. Pres. Calumet Steel div., Chicago, and Franklin (Pa.) Steel div. of Borg-Warner Corp. Home: Chicago, Ill. †

CALE, EDGAR BARCLAY, univ. adminstr.; b. Uniontown, Pa., Aug. 31, 1910; s. Charles H. and Myrtle (Barclay) C.; m. Lynetta Gerhardt, June 20, 1932; children—Audrey Arlene (Mrs. Frank Bedford), Barbara Jeanne (Mrs. Jack S. Overton), Edgar Barclay, Patricia Anne (Mrs. Gerald Beaver); m. Pearl Allen, Mar. 21, 1971 (dec. died June 1977)); m. Margery Frye Davidson, July 8, 1978. Student, U. Pitts., 1928-30; B.A., U. Pa., 1932, M.A., 1934, Ph.D., 1940. Mem. faculty polit. sci. U. Pa., 1937-53; exec. sec. Phila. Charter Commn., 1949-51; chief edn. div. U.S. mission to Thailand, 1953-56; prof. polit. sci. U. Buffalo, 1956-61, dir. devel., 1956-58, vice chancellor planning and devel., 1958-61; vice chancellor devel., also prof. higher edn. U. Pitts., 1961-66; pres. Univ. and Coll. Assos., Washington, 1966-68; dean Motorola Exec. Inst., Vail, Ariz., 1968-74; asst. to pres. Biscayne Coll., Miami, Fla., 1974-75; dir. continuing services, prof. Center for Higher Edn., Nova U., Ft. Lauderdale, Fla., 1975-82; cons., lectr. Berlin (Germany) Inst. Mgmt., 1972; ednl. cons. Motorola, Inc.; Asst. dir. U. Pa. Bi-Centennial, 1939-40; acad. dir. U.S. Naval Flight Prep. Sch., 1943-44, Refresher Sch. V-7 Officers Candidates, 1944-45; moderator, dir. U. Pa. Forum of Air, 1944-53; dir. Motorola Inst. Mgmt., Geneva, Switzerland and Bangkok, Thailand, 1972-73. Mem. sch. bd., Upper Darby, Pa., 1948-53; Bd. dirs. Pitts. History and Landmarks Found., Consultants Overseas Relations, Park Sch., Buffalo. Rockefeller social sci. fellow, 1941-42; Penfield traveling scholar diplomacy, 1942-43. Mem. Am. Coll. Public Relations Assn., Am. Polit. Sci. Assn. Presbyterian. Clubs: Univ. (Pitts.); Tower (Ft. Lauderdale). Home: Fort Lauderdale, Fla. Died Feb. 26, 1982.

CALEB, FRANK, arts adminstr.; b. Ft. Smith, Ark., Sept. 13, 1937; s. Phillip Ivor and Frances Irene (Johnston) C.; m. Victoria Russell, Sept. 5, 1970; children—Vanessa, Phillip. M.M., Yale U., 1962. Gen. mgr. Duluth (Minn.) Symphony Orch., 1972-73; asst. mgr., dir. devel. Lyric Opera of Chgo., 1973-78; pres. Milw. Symphony Orch., from 1978; trustee Evanston (Ill.) Art Center, 1973-78, v.p., 1975-78. Weekly columnist, Duluth Herald, 1972-73; contbr. numerous articles on music and the arts to profl. jours. Trustee St. Paul Opera Co.; bd. dirs. Chgo. Theatre of the Deaf.; Mem. bd. deacons First Presbyterian Ch. of Evanston, Ill., 1974-77. Mem. Am. Symphony Orch. League, Opera Am., Old English Sheepdog Club Am. Clubs: Univ, Tower. Home: Milwaukee, Wis.

CALEY, EARLE RADCLIFFE, chemist, educator; b. Cleve., May 14, 1900; s. John Radcliffe and Minnie (Mitchell) C.; m. Grace Fowles Cochran, Dec. 24, 1925; children: Grace Virginia (Mrs. Walter F. Feist), Robert Cochran, Paul Cochran. Student, Case Inst. Applied Sci., 1918-20; B.Sc., Baldwin-Wallace Coll., 1923, D.Sc. (hon.), 1967; M.S., Ohio State U., 1925, Ph.D., 1928. Instr., then asst. prof. Princeton, 1928-42; chemist Agora Excavation staff, Athens, Greece, 1937; chief chemist Wallace Labs., New Brunswick, N.J., 1942-46; mem. faculty Ohio State U., from 1946, prof. chemistry, from 1957, vice chmn. dept., 1949-60. Author: Analytical Factors and Their Logarithms, 1932, The Composition of Ancient Greek Bronze Coins, 1939, Composition of Parthian Coins, 1954, (with J.F.C. Richards) Theophrastus on Stones, 1956, Analysis of Ancient Glasses, 1962, Orichaleum and Related Ancient Alloys, 1964, Analysis of Ancient Metals, 1964, Metrological Tables, 1965, (with J.S. Belkin) Eucharius Roslin the Younger on Minerals and Mineral Products, 1978; also articles and chpts. to books. Recipient Lewis prize Am. Philos. Soc., 1940, Research prize Ohio Jour. Sci., 1952, citation Am. Classical League, 1954. Fellow AAAS, Internat. Inst. Conservation Historic and Artistic Works, Ohio Acad. Sci., Am., Royal numismatic socs.; mem. Am. Chem. Soc. (Dexter award 1966), Archeol. Inst. Am. (pres. Columbus 1959), History Sci. Soc. Presbyn. (elder). Home: Columbus, OH.

CALEY, GLENN HINTON, ry. official; b. Middletown, N.Y., Oct. 25, 1888; s. George James and Katharine (Jakley) C.; ed. high sch.; studied elec. and mech. engring., Internat. Corr. Sch.; m. Anna DeWitt, Apr. 11, 1917; children—Mary Katharine, Ruth Barbara (Mrs. Howard Schwiebert). Began as clk. in elec. and signal dept. New York, Ontario & Western R.R., Middletown, Jan. 1905, advanced through various positions, gen. mgr., Apr. 1937-June 1938; v.p. and gen. mgr., dir., D.&H. R.R. Co., Albany, N.Y., from June 1938; v.p., gen. mgr., dir. Greenwich & Johnsonville Ry. Co., Wilkesbarre Connecting R.R. Co., Cooperstown & Susquehanna Valley R.R., Cooperstown & Charlotte Valley R.R. Co., Chateaugay & Lake Placid Ry. Co., Ticonderoga R.R. Co. (all subsidiaries of D.&H. R.R.), Northern Coal & Iron Co., Hudson River Estates, Inc.; member board mgrs. Delaware & Hudson Co.; dir. National Commercial Bank and Trust Company, Albany, Licensed professional engr. Mem. N.Y. State Soc. Professional Engrs., Newcomen Soc.,

Assn. Am. Railroads. Republican. Congregationalist. Mason (K.T.). Clubs: Canadian, Railroad (New York); Fort Orange, Schuyler Meadows (Albany). Home: Middletown, N.Y. †

CALHOON, RICHARD PERCIVAL, educator; b. Sewickley, Pa., Feb. 3, 1909; s. George Percival and Elizabeth Cavett (Sigman) C.; m. Frances Clark Abercrombie, July 2, 1940; children—Kathryn, Susan, Carol, Bruce. A.B., U. Pitts., 1930, A.M., 1932. Instr. U. Pitts., 1930-34; labor adminstr. NRA, 1934-35; referee under Davis-Bacon Act, 1936; asst. to factory mgr. Ansco Corp., Binghamton, N.Y., 1936-37; pub. relations and tng. dir. U.S. Rubber Co., Naugatuck, Conn., 1937-41; personnel dir. Kendall Mills, Charlotte, N.C., 1941-46; prof. personnel adminstrn. U. N.C., 1946-79; cons. in personnel adminstrn. Arbiter Am. Arbitration Assn., Fed. Conciliation and Mediation Service, N.C. Dept. Labor. Author: Moving Ahead on Your Job, 1946, Problems in Personal Administration, 1949, (with C.A. Kirkpatrick) Influencing Employee Behavior, 1956, (with E.W. Noland and A.M. Whitehill) Cases on Human Relations in Management, 1958, Managing Personnel, 1963, Cases in Personnel Management and Supervision, 1966, 2d edit., 1971, Personnel Management and Supervision, 1967, Coaching in Supervision, 1974, (2d edit. (with Thomas H. Jerdee), 1981, also research publs., articles. Mem. Acad. Mgmt., AAUP, Nat. Acad. Arbitrators, Eugene Field Soc. (hon.), Delta Sigma Pi (hon.), Beta Gamma Sigma (hon.). Democrat. Home: Chapel Hill, NC.

CALHOUN, PATRICK, JR., transportation exec.; b. Atlanta, Ga., Apr. 30, 1891; s. Patrick and Sally Porter (Williams) C.; student Taft Sch., 1907-12; Ph.B., Yale, 1915; m. Lucy Botts, May 30, 1924 (dec. 1936); m. 2d Mrs. Lucy Gayle Kelly, Nov. 15, 1937 (dec. 1940); step-children—William C. Kelly, Gayle Kelly (Mrs. Edw. A. Schaefer, Jr.); m. 3d Louise Campbell Foster, Feb. 28, 1944; 1 stepson, James Campbell Foster. Coal and oil operator, 1913-17; coal and river transportation, Frankfort, Ky., 1919-22, Louisville, from 1922; v.p. Am. Commercial Barge Line Company, 1927, pres., 1935-57; chairman, 1957-60, also president of subsidiaries including Jeffersonville Boat & Machine Company; director Inland Waterways from 1929. Served as aviation cadet to 2d lt. U.S. Army, air service, 1917-19. A.E.F. Home: Prospect, Ky. Died Oct. 14, 1983.

CALHOUN, WILBUR PERE, univ. prof., consulting economist; b. Wadsworth, O., Mar. 22, 1889; s. Charles Alexander and Alice Cary (Dempster) C.; A.B., Hiram Coll., 1913; A.M., U. of Mich., 1914; m. Zella Irene Kreider, Sept. 16, 1916; 1 son, William Kreider. Instr. economics, Dartmouth Coll., 1914-15; instr. economics, U. of Mich., 1915-19, asst. prof. 1919-23; asst. prof. finance, U. of Cincinnati, 1923-24, prof. finance from 1924. Mem. Am. Econ. Assn., Economists' Nat. Com. on Monetary Policy, Am. Finance Assn. Beta Gamma Sigma, Pi Rho Phi. Presbyn. Club: Bankers. Home: Cincinnati, Ohio. †

CALLAHAN, FRANK HOWARD, clergyman; b. Pittsburgh, Pa., July 21, 1889; s. Rev. Frank Howard and Agnes Lena (Beatty) C.; A.B., Allegheny Coll., Meadville, Pa., 1912, D.D., 1932; S.T.B., Boston U., 1915; m. Mary Sowash Maxwell, July 24, 1922; children—Elizabeth Maxwell, Frank Howard III, Mary Constance. Ordained ministry Meth. Ch., 1919; asso. minister 1st Ch., Pittsfield, Mass., 1919-21, Centre Church, Malden, 1921-23; mem. president's staff, Boston U., 1922-23; minister, Needham, 1923-25, St. James Ch., Springfield, 1925-26. William Street Ch., Delaware, O., 1926-29, Broad St. Ch., Columbus, O., 1929-33, Windermere Ch., Cleveland, 1933-38, First Ch., Akron, 1938-42, Church of St. Paul and St. Andrew, New York, 1942-51; field sec. Meth. Hospital of Brooklyn, 1951-59; exchange-preacher to England and Scotland, 1936. With Norton-Harjes Ambulance, French Army, 1917; with Y.M.C.A., A.E.F., 1918. Recipient Freedoms Found. sermon award, 1950, 57. Mem. Bklyn. Clerical Union, Phi Delta Theta, Chi Alpha, N.Y. Quill Club, Mason. Home: Meredith, N.H. †

CAMALIER, RENAH F., lawyer; b. Washington, Oct. 8, 1890; s. George A. and Rena Irene (Fearing) C.; LL.B., Nat. U., 1924; m. Helen F. Edwards. Admitted to D.C. bar, 1926, U.S. Supreme Ct., 1938, Colo. Supreme Ct., 1940, also fed. cts.; clk. Water Dept., Washington, 1908-14, 15-17; clk.-reporter Pub. Utilities Commn., Washington, 1914-15; sec. Asst. Sec. Navy, 1917-20, Sen. Alva B. Adams, 1923-24, 33-40; examiner Fed. Trade Commn., 1925-27; asst. U.S. atty. Dept. Justice, Washington, 1927-30; pvt. practice law, Washington, 1930-33, 42-51; counsel Senate Com. on D.C. Affairs, 1940-41; mem. nat. appeals bd. U.S. Coast Guard from 1951; commr. D.C. from 1952. Fuel oil coordinator O.P.A., 1942-43. Bd. dirs. Y.M.C.A.; dir. Met. Police Boys Club. Mem. D.C., Am., Fed. bar assns., Friendship Citizens Assn., Washington Bd. Trade, Am. Bus. Assn., D.C. Soc. Natives, Interfaith Com. Catholics Protestants Jews. Methodist (chmn. bd. trustees). Mason (Shriner, K.T., 33 deg.). Home: Washington, D.C. †

CAMERON, BARNEY GEORGE, newspaper exec.; b. Spokane, Wash., Jan. 3, 1911; s. Gilbert L. and Minnie (Bond) C.; student Willamette U., 1929-30, U. Oreg. extension, 1934; m. Betty Hayford Fosdick, July 24, 1932; children—Ann, Joan. Circulation exec., Salem, Oreg., also Los Angeles Examiner, 1930-34; circulation mgr. Portland (Oreg.) News-Telegram, 1934-39; circulation dir. Scripps League Newspapers, 1939-42; with Seattle Star, 1942-46, Pitts. Post-Gazette, 1946-51; circulation dir. N.Y. Herald Tribune, 1951-56, v.p., bus. mgr., dir. 1956-61; v.p., bus. mgr. Pitts. Press, 1961-65, v.p. bus mgr., 1965-75, pres., 1975-76, ret., 1976; dir. Gateway Farms. First v.p. St. Francis Hosp.; bd. dirs. Pitts. Opera, Inc. Named to Newspaperboy Hall of Fame, 1979. Mem. Amen Corner (bd. govs.), Pa. Soc. Mason (Shriner), Rotarian (dir. 1967-69); mem. Soc. of Silurians. Clubs: Pittsburgh Press, Duquesne (dir. 1969-72), Allegheny (dir.), Variety (former asst. chief barker) (Pitts.); Overseas Press of Am. Home: Pittsburgh, Pa. Died Aug. 16, 1984.

CAMP, ERNEST W., commr. of customs; b. Saginaw, Mich., June 30, 1887; ed. pub. schs., 1 yr. U. of Mich.; LL.B., Georgetown U., 1912. Sec. to Congressman Joseph W. Fordney, becoming actively interested in tariff subjects; clk. Com. on Ways and Means of Ho. of Rep., 1919-22; apptd. chief Div. of Customs, Dept. of Treasury, Jan. 18, 1922, dir. Mar. 4, 1923; commr. of customs from 1927. Attended Internat. Economic Conf. at Geneva as Adviser from Treasury Dept., May 1927. Address: Washington, D.C. †

CAMP, JAMES LEONIDAS, JR., business executive; b. Franklin, Va., June 7, 1895; s. James Leonidas and Carrie Fountain (Savage) C.; m. Mary Clav, May 21, 1918; 1 child, James Leonidas, III. A.B., Wake Forest Coll., 1914; student, Columbia., 1914-15; D.Sc. (hon.), U. Richmond, 1958. Began as lumber plant worker, 1915-19; with Camp Mfg. Co., Franklin, 1919-56, successively salesman, v.p., head sales, 1919-26, pres., dir., 1926-56, chmn. bd., dir., 1956; chmn. exec. com. Union Camp Corp., 1956-69; dir. Va. Nat. Bank; trustee Am. Forest Products Industries, Inc. Chmn. bd. dirs. J.L. Camp Found., Inc.; trustee U. Va. Grad. Sch. Bus. Adminstrn., Va. Found. Ind. Colls., Nat. Fund for Med. Edn., Bapt. Orphanage, Salem, Va., U. Richmond. Served with USN, 1918. Mem. Am. Paper and Pulp Assn. (exec. com.), NAM (past bd. dirs.), Nat. Lumber Mfrs. Assn. (bd. dirs.), Va. Mus. Fine Arts, Newcomen Soc. N.A., English-Speaking Union, Phi Kappa Sigma. Democrat. Baptist. Clubs: Princess Anne Country (Virginia Beach); Country (Richmond), Commonwealth (Richmond), Virginia (Richmond); Farmington Country (Charlottesville, Va.). Home: Franklin, Va. Dec. Feb. 27, 1983.

CAMP, LAWRENCE HICKS, paper mfg. co. exec.; b. Brunswick, Va., Oct. 30, 1915; s. David O. and Eva (Bennett) C.; grad. Ferrum Jr. Coll., 1935; student Va. Mech. Inst., nights, 1936-44. With Carter Bros., Inc., 1936-44; staff accountant Leach, Calkins & Scott, 1944-49, partner, 1949-61; with Chesapeake Corp. Va., West Point, 1961-82, treas., 1963-69, v.p. finance, 1966-68, sr. v.p., 1968, exec. v.p., 1968-69, chief exec. officer, 1968-82, pres., 1969-82, also dir.; treas., dir. Balt. Box Co., Binghamton Container Co., Greenlife Products Co., Miller Container Corp., Scranton Corrugated Box Co., So. Corrugated Box Corp., David Weber Co. Home: West Point, Va. Died June 2, 1982.*

CAMPAIGNE, JAMESON GILBERT, editorial cons., author; b. Bklyn., Jan. 16, 1914; s. Curtis and Edna Amory (Foote) C.; A.B., Williams Coll., 1936; m. Edith Louise Baker, Jan. 15, 1938; children—Jameson, Markham Baker, Jeffrey, Catherine. Sales work Yardley & Co., Ltd., 1936-40; radio writer Compton Advt., Inc., N.Y.C., 1940-43; chief editorial writer Indpls. Star, 1946-51, editor editorial page, 1952-60, editor, 1960-69, editorial writer, columnist, 1969-73; editorial writer N.Y. Daily News, N.Y.C., 1973-76; editorial cons., author, 1976-85. Served with USMCR, 1943-46. Recipient Lincoln Nat. Life Found. award for best editorial on Lincoln (2); Freedoms Found. medal, 1951, 53, award, 1952, 57; Ind. U. Writers Conf. award, 1960. Mem. Mont Pelerin Soc. Author: American Might and Soviet Myth, 1960; Check-off, 1961. Contbr. to Sat. Eve. Post, Internat. Background. Home: Encinitas, Calif.

CAMPBELL, ANNE (MRS. GEORGE W. STARK), writer; b. Lynn, St. Clair Co., Mich., June 19, 1888; d. H. J. and Mina (Atkinson) C.; ed. high sch.; m. George W. Stark, feature writer, of Detroit News, August 28, 1915; children—George Winter, Alison Jean, Richard Campbell. Began writing verse for the Detroit News, 1922; work syndicated by Asso. Newspapers, N.Y. City.†

CAMPBELL, CLARENCE SUTHERLAND, sports association executive; b. Fleming, Sask., Can., July 9, 1905; s. George A. and Annie M. (Haw) C.; m. Phyllis L. King, Nov. 17, 1955. B.A., LL.B. (Rhodes scholar), U. Alberta, 1926; M.A., Oxford U., 1928, B.C.L., 1929. Bar: Queen's Counsel, Alta. Barrister, Edmonton, Alta., 1929-40; pres. Nat. Hockey League, Montreal, Can., 1946-77, hon. chmn. bd. govs., 1977-84. Pres. Lakeshore Gen. Hosp. Found. Served to lt. col. Canadian Army, 1940-46. Decorated Order Brit. Empire. Mem. Law Soc. Alberta. Home: Montreal, Que., Can. Died June 24, 1984.

CAMPBELL, HOWARD E., congressman; b. Pittsburgh, Pa., Jan. 4, 1890; s. Charles A. and Ada Louise (Wensel) C.; attended U. of Pittsburgh; unmarried. Mem. 79th Congress (1945-47), 29th Pa. Dist. Pres. Pittsburgh (Pa.) Real Estate Bd. from 1943. Trustee Shadyside (Pa.) United Presbyn. Ch. Republican. Mason. Club: Civic of Allegheny County (Pa.). Home: Pittsburgh, Pa. Deceased.

CAMPBELL, JAMES ALLAN, physician; b. Moweaqua, Ill., Nov. 29, 1917; s. Frank Arthur and Gertrude Mary (Dowling) C.; m. Elda Schaffer Crichton, Sept. 23, 1944; children: James Allan, Bruce Crichton, Douglas Karr. A.B., Knox Coll., Galesburg, Ill., 1939, D.Sc. (hon.), 1965; M.D., Harvard U., 1943; L.H.D. (hon.), Lake Forest (Ill.) Coll., 1968. Diplomate: Am. Bd. Internal Medicine. Asst. resident in pathology Billings Hosp., Chgo., 1941-42; asst. pathology U. Chgo. Med. Sch., 1941-42; intern, then asst. resident in medicine Boston City Hosp., 1943-45, resident, 1945-46; teaching fellow medicine Harvard U. Med. Sch., 1944-45; asst. medicine Thorndike Meml. Lab., 1945-46; Harvey Cushing fellow Johns Hopkins Hosp. and Med. Sch., 1947-48; prof. medicine U. Ill. Med. Sch., 1951-71; attending physician Albany (N.Y.) Hosp., 1951-53; also dean, prof. medicine Albany Med. Coll., 1951-53; asst. attending physician Presbyn. Hosp., Chgo., 1948-51, asso. attending, 1951, chmn. dept. medicine, 1953; pres., trustee successor Rush-Presbyn.-St. Luke's Med. Center, 1964; prof. medicine Rush Med. Coll., 1971-83; dir. Morton-Thiokol,Inc.; bd. dirs. Hosp. Research and Ednl. Trust; past planning dir. edn. in health fields Ill. Bd. Higher Edn., 1964-68; Balfour vis. prof. medicine Mayo Found., 1975; Trustee Knox Coll., Sprague Meml. Inst., 1973-83. Author articles in field. Served as capt. M.C. AUS, 1946-47. Fellow A.C.P.; mem. Am. Clin. and Climatol. Assn., Central Soc. Clin. Research, Central Soc. Clin. Investigation, N.Y. Acad. Scis., Alpha Omega Alpha (past pres., dir.). Home: Chicago, Ill. Died Nov. 19, 1983.

CAMPBELL, MURDOCH A., lawyer; b. Graniteville, Vt., 1889; student U. Mo. and Nat. U., Washington. Admitted to Vt. bar, 1917, practiced in Northfield, Vt.; asst. sec. Vt. senate, 1927-31, sec., 1931-33; commr. motor vehicles, 1933-41. Served with 172d Inf., U.S. Army, 1917-19; in Fed. service, Feb.-Dec. 1941. Home: Northfield, Vt. †

CAMPBELL, RONALD IAN, diplomat; b. June 7, 1890; s. Sir Guy Campbell; ed. Eton Coll., Magdalen College, Oxford. Entered diplomatic service, 1914; apptd. minister to U.S. from Great Britian, 1941.†

CAMPBELL, ROY STUART, shipbuilding exec.; b. Detroit, Mich., Apr. 9, 1889; s. Dr. James J. and Agnes Ada (Fair) C.; B.S. in Marine and Naval Architecture, U. of Mich., 1912; m. Constance Stephenson, Sept. 13, 1919. With N.Y. Shipbuilding Corp., Camden, N.J., from 1934, pres. and gen. mgr. from 1942. Home: Woodbury, N.J. Deceased.

CAMPBELL, RUTH RAMSDELL (MRS. JAMES FRANCIS CAMPBELL), author; b. Manistee, Mich., Feb. 11, 1888; d. Thomas Jefferson and Nettie (Stanton) Ramsdell; ed. in Paris, France, until twelve; grad. Detroit Sem., 1902; m. James Francis Campbell, Sept. 23, 1908 1 son, Colin. Editor The Hudsonian and Children's Mag., since 1929. Author: The All Alone House, 1923; The Runaway Smalls, 1923; That Pink and Blue Affair, 1923; Kiddies and Grown-ups Too, 1924; The Cat Whose Whiskers Slipped, 1925; The Turtle Whose Snap Unfastened, 1927; Small Fry and the Winged Horse, 1927. Contbr. Munsey's, Child Life, etc. Home: Detroit, Mich.†

CAMPBELL, WILLIAM A., army officer; b. Salt Lake City, Dec. 27, 1887; s. John and Lena (Bronnolson) C.; Command and Gen. Staff Sch., 1932-34, Army War Coll., 1936-37; m. Thirza Hansen, Aug. 25, 1912; children—Cora (Mrs. Howard E. Allen), Elizabeth, William Ardery, Robert Hansen. Commd. 2d lt. 1st Utah Cavalry, 1916; 1st lt. 146th F.A. (France); capt. 33d F.A., Camp Meade, Md.; instr. R.O.T.C. U. of Utah, 1919-23; Hawaiian Dept., 1923-27; Field Artillery Sch., Ft. Sill, Okla., 1927-32; instr. Nat. Guard of Utah, 1934-36; instr. Command and Gen. Staff Sch., 1937-41; comdg. officer 49th F.A. 1941; Gen. Staff, G.H.Q. until Apr. 18, 1942. Commanded Field Artillery of 3rd Inf. Div. Apr.-June 1944, in U.S., N. Africa, Sicily, Italy. Asst. comdt. Command and Gen. Staff Sch., Ft. Leavenworth, Kan., since Aug. 1944; temp. rank of brig. gen. Address: Fort Leavenworth, Kan.†

CAMPBELL, WILLIAM WILSON, banker; b. Forrest City, Ark., Feb. 9, 1889; s. Silas Calvin and Jessie (Griggs) C.; student Eastman Coll., Poughkeepsie, N.Y., 1908-09; LL.D. (hon.), U. Ark., 1949; m. Victoria Mann, Dec. 14, 1916; children—William Mann Ann. President of the First National Bank of Eastern Arkansas, Forrest City, Arkansas, from 1923-54, chmn. bd., chief exec. officer, from 1954; dir. Arkansas Power and Light Corporation, Federal Reserve Bank, Memphis, First Arkansas Development Finance Corporation; mem. fed. adv. council, Eighth Fed. Res. Dist., St. Louis Fed. Res. Bank chairman of regional adv. committee to comptroller of currency Eighth National Bank Region. State chairman Ark. War Finance Com.; mem. cotton adv. com. Commodity Credit Corp., Washington; adv. com. R.F.C., Little Rock, Ark.; chmn. state highway finance adv. com.; mem. Memphis and Ark. Bridge Commn., 1945, Hoover panel on loan agencies, 1954; vice chmn. Ark. Indsl. Development Commn.; mem. White House Conf. on Edn. Trustee Arkansas Coll., Forrest City Library; dir. Ark. Crippled Children's Hosp.; dir., trustee Ark. Tb Sanatorium; mem. So. Presbyn. Gen. Assembly's Bequest Com.; chmn. Presbyn. Found. Investment Com. Synod Arkansas; mem.

Ark. Com. for Salk Inst.; state chmn. Ark. Farmers Home Adminstrn. U.S. Dept. Agr. Recipient Hon. Life Membership award 4-H Clubs; Man of Year in Service to Ark. Agr., Progressive Farmer, 1951. Mem. Soil Conservation Society of America (hon.), Ark. C. of C. (dir.), Mid-South Fair Assn. Memphis (dir.), Am. Bankers Assn. (mem. exec. council; chmn. agrl. commn., pres. nat bank div., chmn. state adv. com. U.S. Savs. Bank div.), Ark. Bankers Assn. Presbyn. Mason (33 deg.). Clubs: Rotary, Young Bus. Men's (Forrest City).†

CANADAY, JOHN EDWIN, writer, art critic; b. Ft. Scott, Kans., Feb. 1, 1907; s. Franklin and Agnes F. (Musson) C.; m. Katherine S. Hoover, Sept. 19, 1935; children: Rudd Hoover, John Harrington. B.A., U. Tex., 1929; M.A., Yale U., 1933. Tchr. art history, dept. architecture U. Va., 1938-50; head sch. art Newcomb Coll. Tulane U., New Orleans, 1950-52; chief div. edn. Phila. Mus. art, 1953-59; art critic N.Y Times, 1959-77; vis. prof. U. Tex.-Austin, 1977. Author: (24 portfolios) The Metropolitan Seminars in Art, Mainstreams of Modern art, 1959, Embattled Critic, 1962, Culture Gulch: Notes on Art and Its Public in the 1960's, 1969, (with katherine H Canaday) Keys to Art: Lives of the Painters, 4 vols., Baroque Painters, 1972, Late Gothic to Renaissance Painters, 1972, Neo-Classic to Post-Impressionist Painters, 1972, Artful Avocado, 1973, What is Art, 1981; 7 mystery novels under pseudonym Matthew Head. Served with USMCR, 1944-45. Home: New York, N.Y. Died July 19, 1985.

CANHAM, ERWIN DAIN, newspaper editor, radio and TV commentator; b. Auburn, Maine, Feb. 13, 1904; s. Vincent Walter and Elizabeth May (Gowell) C.; B.A., Bates Coll., 1925, Litt.D., 1946; B.A., M.A. (Rhodes scholar), Oxford U. (Eng.); numerous hon. degrees, including L.H.D., Boston U., 1948, Yale U., 1949; LL.D., Principia Coll., 1951, Tufts U., 1958, Temple U. 1959; Litt.D., Brigham Young U., 1962; LL.D., Lafayette Coll., Bowdoin Coll., 1967; m. Thelma Whitman Hart, May 10, 1930 (dec.); children—Carolyn (Mrs. R. Shale Paul), Elizabeth (Mrs. Lyle Davis); m. Patience M. Daltry. Reporter, Christian Sci. Monitor, 1925, covered ann. sessions of League of Nations Assn., 1926, 27, 28; chief corr. Christian Sci. Monitor at League of Nations Naval Conf., 1930, corr. Geneva, Switzerland, 1930-32, head of Washington Bur., 1932-39, gen. news editor, 1939-41, mng. editor, 1941-44, editor, 1945-64, editor-in-chief, 1964-74, editor emeritus, 1974-82; nation-wide polit. surveys and covered trips of Am. Presidents; attended inauguration Philippine Commonwealth Govt. and wrote on Far East, 1935; dep. chmn. U.S. delegation UN Conf. on Freedom of Information, 1948; U.S. alt. del. UN Gen. Assembly, 1949; mem. U.S. Commn. for Info., U.S. Nat. Commn. for UNESCO, 1948-51; mem. Pres.'s Commn. on Campus Unrest, 1970; plebiscite commr. North Marianas Islands, 1975, resident commr., 1976-82. Chmn. Fed. Res. Bank of Boston, 1962-67. Bd. dirs. Nat. Safety Council, v.p. religious leaders, 1964-68; bd. dirs. Resources for Future; trustee Boston Pub. Library, pres., from 1968; trustee Robert A. Taft Inst. of Govt., 20th Century Fund, Bates Coll., Simmons Coll., Wellesley Coll.; mem. corp. Northeastern U. Radio commentator, 1938-39, from 45. Decorated hon. comdr. Order Brit. Empire; officer French Legion Honor; Order of George I (Greece); grand distinguished service cross Order of Merit (German Federal Republic); Grand Silver Badge of Honor (Austria); recipient John Peter Zenger award U. Ariz., 1970. Fellow Am. Acad. Arts and Scis.; mem. U.S. C. of C. (chmn. bd. 1960, dir.), Am. Soc. Newspaper Editors (pres. 1948-49), Assn. Am. Rhodes Scholars, Phi Beta Kappa, Delta Sigma Rho. Christian Scientist. Mason (33 deg.). Clubs: Gridiron, Nat. Press, Overseas Writers (Washington pres. 1938-40); Tavern; Harvard (Boston); Saturday. Author: (with others) Awakening: The World at Mid-Century, 1951; New Frontiers for Freedom, 1954; Committment to Freedom, 1958; (with DeWitt John) The Christian Science Way of Life, with A Christian Scientist's Life, 1962. Editor: Man's Great Future, 1959. Home: Saipan, North Mariana Islands. Died Jan. 3, 1982.

CANNON, CARL LESLIE, librarian; b. Smith Center, Kan., Dec. 16, 1888; s. Willis and Emma Belle (Pollock) C.; A.B., U. of Kan., 1912; B.L.S., N.Y. State Library Sch., 1917; m. Lillian C. Gruskin, June 3, 1926; 1 dau., Cynthia Anne. Began at newspaper work and later in the offices of the A.T.&S.F. Ry., Topeka, Kan.; asst. Newark (N.J.) Free Pub. Library, summer 1916; with New York Pub. Library, 1917-32, asst. in information div. until 1918, chief of acquisition div., 1919-32, supt. book order office, 1926-32; chief of accessions div., Yale Univ. Library, 1932-39; became asso. in Bibliography, Brown U. Library, 1939. With U.S. Army, 1918. Mem. A.L.A. (exec. bd.), Conn. Library Assn. (pres. 1939-40), Am. Library Inst., Pi Upsilon (U. of Kan.). Author: Publicity for Small Libraries, 1929; American Book Collectors and Collecting from Colonial Times to the Present, 1941. Compiler: Journalism (bibliography), 1924; Order and Accession Department (based on earlier edits. by F. F. Hopper), 3d edit., 1930. Editor: Narratives of the Trans-Mississippi Frontier (8 vols.), 1932; Guide to Library Facilities for National Defense, 1940. Mem. advisory council Dictionary of Am. History, 1937-40.†

CANNY, FRANCIS CHARLES, lawyer; b. Dayton, O., Aug. 26, 1889; s. Anthony and Elizabeth (Hughes) C.; A.B., U. of Dayton, 1909; LL.B., Georgetown U., 1913; m. Helen Esther Rowling, Apr. 18, 1917; children—Mary Frances, Helen Louise, Suzanne. Admitted to Ohio bar, 1913; mem. Ohio Ho. of Rep., 1917-18; asst. pros. atty., Montgomery County, 1931-33; served as U.S. dist. atty. for Southern Dist. of Ohio; now in practice at Dayton. Democrat. Home: Dayton, Ohio. †

CANOLES, M. ALICE, Dem. nat. committeewoman; b. Baltimore County, Md., Jan. 10, 1890; d. Charles E. and Mary Ann (Kimble) Chester; ed. pub. sch. of Orangeville; student Md. State Tchrs. Coll., 2 yrs.; m. Edward A. Canoles, Apr. 21, 1907; children—Zedith A. (Mrs. Dominic Sartori), Florence S. (Mrs. Alfred Speca). Active in social work, 30 yrs., also in work of A.R.C.; Dem. nat. committeewoman for Md., 1944-48 and Jan. 1951-July 1952. Organizer Women's 26th Ward Original Orgn. Dem. Club (pres. 29 yrs.); mem. O'Conor Dem. Club, City wide Dem. Club, United Dem. Women's Club of Md., Civic League. Mem. Nat. Woman's Party. Lutheran. Mem. Order Eastern Star. Home: Baltimore, Md. †

CANOVA, JUDY, comedienne, singer, actress; b. Starke, Fla., Nov. 20, 1916; d. Joseph Francis and Henrietta (Perry) C.; children by previous marriage—Julieta England, Diana Canova Rivero. Student pub. schs., Starke, and private tutors. Performed on radio, in Fla., 1928; appeared with: Paul Whiteman Show, N.Y.C.; starred in: radio shows Judy Canova Show (NBC), 12 yrs; appeared in: Broadway shows Yokel Boy; toured with: Broadway shows No No Nanette; appeared in: numerous films including Cannonball; others; rec. artist, RCA, Tops; appeared as guest: on TV shows Dinah Shore Show; others; headliner for state fairs. Home: Los Angeles, Calif. Died Aug. 5, 1983; interred Forest Lawn Meml. Park, Glendale, Calif.

CANT, GILBERT, writer; b. London, Eng., Sept. 16, 1909; ed. Leeds (Eng.) Boys Modern Sch.; m. Barbara Nickelhoff, Sept. 20, 1930 (div.); children—Geoffrey David, John Gilbert Hubbard; m. 2d, Ruth Abramson, Dec. 18, 1966. Came to U.S., 1930, naturalized, 1940. Reporter, Yorkshire Post, Leeds, 1927-28, No. Whig, Belfast, No. Ireland, 1929; asst. editor Royal Gazette and Colonist Daily, Bermuda, 1929-30; N.Y. corr. for Brit. newspapers, 1930-37; feature writer N.Y. Post, 1937-42, war editor, 1942- 44; contbg. editor Time mag., 1944-52, asso. editor, 1952-78; cons. editor Look mag., 1979. Recipient Russell L. Cecil award Arthritis and Rheumatism Found., 1957, 66; Albert Lasker Med. Journalism award, 1961, 65. Mem. Am. Ornithologists Union, Brit. Trust for Ornithology. Clubs: Explorers, Collectors (N.Y.C.); Orienta Yacht (Mamaroneck). Author: The War at Sea, 1942; America's Navy in World War II, 1943; The Great Pacific Victory, 1946; Male Trouble: A New Focus on the Prostate, 1976; also articles, pamphlets. Editor: This Is the Navy, 1944. Died Aug. 1982.

CANTRELL, JAMES RANDALL, surgeon; b. Norman, Okla., Aug. 8, 1922; s. Roy F. and Bernice H. (Nisbett) C.; m. Elizabeth Stehly, June 27, 1953; children—Randall, Beth, Martha, Jane, Roy. A.B., Johns Hopkins U., 1944, M.D., 1946. Diplomate: Am. Bd. Surgery, Am. Bd. Thoracic Surgery. Intern Johns Hopkins U. Hosp., 1946-47, asst. resident in surgery, 1947-48, 50-52, resident in surgery, 1952-53, practice medicine specializing in thoracic surgery, Balt., 1953-60, Seattle, 1960-83; instr. in surgery Johns Hopkins U. Sch. Medicine, 1952-55, asst. prof. surgery, 1955-58, asso. prof., 1958-60, Seattle area rep. admissions com., 1962-83; attending surgeon U. Wash. Hosp., Seattle, 1960-83; mem. staff Harborview Med. Center, Seattle, 1960-83; Swedish Hosp. Med. Center, Seattle, 1975; cons. VA Hosp., Seattle, 1960-83, Children's Orthopedic Hosp., Seattle, 1972-83; sec. Wash. Bd. Med. Examiners, 1966-68, chmn., 1973-76. Contbr. numerous articles on pathology and thoracic surgery to med. jours. Mem. Mayor's Traffic Safety Task Force, Seattle, 1972-74. Served to capt. M.C. AUS, 1948-50. Mem. ACS (chmn. operating room asst. com. 1964-66, bd. govs. 1973—, exec. com. 1976-83), AMA (com. on drugs 1963—), Wash. Med. Assn. (del. 1962-72, health manpower council 1974-83), Seattle, Samson Thoracic surg. socs., King County (Wash.), Balt. City med. socs., Soc. Univ. Surgeons, Am., North Pacific, Pacific Coast surg. assns., Am. Cancer Soc., Am. Assn. Thoracic Surgery, Phi Beta Kappa, Sigma Xi, Omicron Delta Kappa, Alpha Omega Alpha. Home: Mercer Island, Wash. Died Nov. 11, 1983; buried Sunset Hills, Bellevue, Wash.

CAPONIGRI, ALOYSIUS ROBERT, educator; b. Chgo., Nov. 16, 1915; s. Nicholas and Lucia (Sorrocco) C.; m. Winifred Phyllis Franco, Oct. 6, 1946; children—Victoria Marie, Robert John, Lisa Marie. A.B., Loyola U., Chgo., 1935, M.A., 1936; student, Harvard U. Grad. Sch., 1937-39; Ph.D., U. Chgo., 1942. Instr. State U. Ia., 1943-46; mem. faculty U. Notre Dame, 1946-83, prof. philosophy, 1956-83; lectr. Inst. Luigi Sturzo, Rome, 1961; distinguished vis. prof. Loyola U., Chgo., 1963; vis. lectr. U. Padova, Bologna, spring 1964, 68, 71, Genoa, Milan, also Luigi Sturzo Inst., Rome, 1964, 65, 71; vis. prof. philosophy U. Madrid, Spain, 1964-66; mem. editorial bd. U. Notre Dame Press; also mem. U. Notre Dame Press (univ. Grad. Council.); Sec.-treas. Assos. Philos. Inquiry; mem. nat, selection bd. Fulbright Program, 1958-60; fellow Folger Shakespeare Library, 1975; vis. scholar Harvard Center for Italian Renaissance Studies, summer 1975; lectr. U. Okla., 1976, Symposium on Religion Art in Am., Vatican City, 1976, Fordham U., 1976. Author: Time and Idea, 1953, History and liberty, 1955, History of Western Philosophy, 5 vols, 1964-70, The New Art of Criticism of Giambattista Vico, The Historical Theory of Natural Law in Giambattista Vico; Editor: Modern Catholic Thinkers, 1960, Masterpieces of Catholic Literature, 2 vols, 1964, Contemporary Spanish Philosophy, 1967; Translator: Major Trends in Mexican Philosophy, 1966, On Essence (Xavier Zubiri), 1973. Fulbright fellow, 1950-51, 71; Rockefeller fellow, 1953, 74-75; grantee Am. Philos. Soc., 1960; grantee Am. Council Learned Socs., 1963; grantee Comité Conjunto Hispano-Norte-Americano para Asuntos Educativos y Culturales, 1979. Mem. Am., Am. Cath. philos. assns., Metaphysics. Soc. Am., Cath. Commn. Cultural and Intellectual Affairs, Instituto Luigi Sturzo Roma (corr.). Home: South Bend, Ind. Died March 2, 1983.

CAPOZZOLI, LOUIS JOSEPH, congressman; b. Cosenza, Italy, Mar. 6, 1901; s. Gabriele and Cristina (Ciongola) C.; brought to U.S., 1906; LL.B., Fordham U., 1922; m. Adele Valli, Sept. 25, 1927; children—Louis Joseph, Christine Annette, Gloria Adele. Admitted to N.Y. Bar, 1923, asst. dist. atty., N.Y. County, 1930-37; mem. N.Y. State Assembly, 1939-40; mem. 77th and 78th Congresses (1941-45), 13th N.Y. Dist. Mem. Grand St. Boys' Assn., John De Salvio Dem. Assn. Mem. Rapallo Lawyers Assn. Catholic. Democrat. Elk. Greenwich Village Assn. (N.Y. City). Home: New York, N.Y. Died Oct. 8, 1982.

CAPPON, LESTER JESSE, historian; b. Milw., Sept. 18, 1900; s. Jesse and Mary Elizabeth (Geisinger) C.; m. Dorothy Elizabeth Bernet, June 25, 1932; children—Mary Elizabeth (Mrs. William B. Yarbrough) (dec.). Student, State Tchrs. Coll., Milw., 1918-20; diploma, Wis. Conservatory Music, 1920; A.B., U. Wis., 1922, M.A., 1923; M.A., Harvard, 1925, Ph.D., 1928. Stanley Bernet. Tchr. English Boy's Tech. High Sch., Milw., 1923-24; research asso. history, inst. for research social sci. U. Va., 1926-27, 1928-30, archivist library, 1930-40, asst. prof. history, 1930-45, cons. archives, 1940-45, hon., 1945-81, asso. prof. history, 1945; dir. Va. Hist. Records Survey, 1936-37, Va. World War II History Commn., 1944-45; editor publs. Inst. Early Am. History and Culture, Williamsburg, Va., 1945-55, dir., 1955-69; archivist Colonial Williamsburg, Inc., 1945-52, archival cons., 1952-69; sr. fellow Newberry Library, Chgo., 1969-70, Distinguished research fellow, 1975-76, emeritus, 1976-81; editor-in-chief Atlas of Early American History, Newberry Library, 1970-75; lectr. history Coll. William and Mary, 1946-69, emeritus, 1969-81; lectr. history U. Calif. at Riverside, winter 1976; lectr. archives Am. U., 1947-53; dir. Inst. on Hist. and Archival Mgmt., Radcliffe Coll., 1956-60. Author: Bibliography of Virginia History Since 1865, 1930, Virginia Newspapers, 1921-1935, A Bibliography, 1936, A Plan for the Collection and Preservation of World War II Records, 1942, Virginia Gazette Index, 1736-80, 1950, others.; Editor: William and Mary Quar, 1955-56, 62-63, The Adams-Jefferson Letters, 1959, Atlas of Early American History: The Revolutionary Era, 1760-1790, 1976, Travel Journals of Jared Sparks, 1826-30; Contbr. articles to profl. jours. Mem. community council, Williamsburg, 1951-53; bd. dirs. Univ. Press Va., 1962-66; mem. adv. bd. Ill. State Archives, 1973-77, No. Ill. Regional History Center, No. Ill. U., DeKalb, 1977-80. Fellow Soc. Am. Archivists (sec. 1942-50, v.p. 1955, pres. 1957); mem. Am. Antiquarian Soc., Am. Hist. Assn., So. Hist. Assn. (pres. 1949), Am. Assn. State and Local History, Orgn. Am. Historians, Mass. Hist. Soc., Va. Hist Soc., Wis. Hist. Soc., Albemarle County (Va.) Hist. Soc. (editor 1940-45), Colonial Soc. Mass., Nat. Parks Assn., Am. Forestry Assn., Wilderness Soc., Phi Beta Kappa (hon.), Sigma Pi, Phi Mu Alpha-Sinfonia, Sigma Delta Chi. Democratic. Episcopalian. Clubs: Sierra, Caxton. Home: Williamsburg, Va. Died Sept. 1981.

CAPRON, LAWRENCE ROLLIN, ry. official; b. Litchfield, Ill., June 27, 1888; s. Charles Rollin and Lylete Ann (Lawrence) C.; ed. elementary schs., St. Paul, Minn.; m. Eva Belle McCurdy, May 27, 1912. Office boy C., B.&Q. R.R., 1902-03; office boy Frank B. Kellogg (later sec. of state), 1903; with N.P. Ry., 1903-37, beginning as office boy and later clerical positions in freight traffic dept., then asst. gen. freight agent, in St. Paul, 1915-20, in Seattle, 1920-21, asst. freight traffic mgr., St. Paul, 1921-24, freight traffic mgr., 1924-37; asst. v.p. C.B.&Q. R.R., Chicago, 1937-38, vice pres., 1938 from, dir.; v.p. Colo. & Southern Ry. Co., Ft. Worth & Denver Railway Company; member board directors Belt Ry. Co. of Chicago, Paducah & Ill. R.R. Co., Ill. No. Ry. Rep. Clubs: Union League (Chicago); Minnesota, St. Paul (St. Paul). Home: Evanston, Ill. †

CAREWE, SYLVIA, painter, tapestry artist; b. N.Y.C.; d. Lewis and Esther (Oghstal) C.; 1 son. John. Student, Columbia. One-man shows (tapestries), French & Co., 1960, 62, tapestries and banners, Community Ch., N.Y.C., 1964-69, Fordham U., (1970), paintings, A C A Gallery, 1948, 53, 54, 56, 58, 61, Riley Gallery, both N.Y.C., 1959, Three Arts, Poughkeepsie, N.Y., 1947, 52, 54, 58, 60, Barnett Aden Gallery, Washington, 1950, Tersa Karlis Gallery, Westport. Conn., 1955, Decatur (Ill.) Art Center, Ball State Tchrs. Coll., Art Assn., Richmond (Ind.), Butler Inst. Am. Art. U. Ind., 1955, 68, Wittenborn's One-Wall Gallery, N.Y.C., 1957, Galerie Katie Granoff, Paris, France, 1957, Butler Inst. Am. Art. tapestries, 1960, U. N.C., 1962, also various colls., univs.; headdresses for Aristophanes The Birds, Cooper Union, 1960; exhbn. pastel paintings for tapestry, Donnell Art Library, N.Y.C., 1968; exhibited works in many group shows including, Mus. Modern Art, Whitney Mus., Mus. Bruge, Belgium, Standliche Mus., Rotterdam, Boston Mus. Fine Arts, Bklyn.Mus., Phila. Print Club, Smith Mus., Springfield, Mass., Columbia (S.C.) Mus. Art, Ga. Mus. Arte; represented in permanent collections, Met. Mus. Art, N.Y.C., Whitney Mus. Am. Art, Musee de l'Arte Moderne, Paris, Finch Coll. Art Mus., Paris, Nat. Mus., Djakarta, Indonesia, Brandeis U., Butler Art Inst., Howard U., Tel Aviv Mus., Joseph H. Hirshhorn Mus., Washington, also pvt. collections, works used for mag. covers; appeared in: film Liberated Laundromat, 1971. Recipient ann. award A C A Gallery competition for 1st one-man show, 1947. Mem. Artists Equity, Am. Soc. Contemporary Artists, Archtl. Guild, Am. Watercolor Soc., Phila. Print Club, N.Y. Soc. Women Artists, Nat. Soc. Women Artists, Atelier 17, Friends of Whitney Mus., Mus. Modern Art, Guggenheim Mus., Municipal Art Soc., Women in Arts. Club: Women's City. Address: New York NY

CAREY, JANE PERRY CLARK, polit. scientist; b. Washington; d. John C. and Addie (Burr) Clark; m. Andrew Galbraith Carey, Jan. 10, 1942. A.B., Vassar Coll.; A.M., Columbia; Ph.D., Columbia, 1931. Research sec. Internat. Migration Service, 1922-28; instr. econs. Mt. Holyoke Coll., 1928-29; cons. Com. on Ellis Island, U.S. Sec. Labor, 1933; mem. staff Pres.'s Com. on Econ. Security, 1934-35; cons. U.S. Social Security Bd., 1935-43; prin. tng. specialist U.S. Civil Service Commn., 1943; mem. various fed., state wage bds., 1934-40; asst. adviser on displaced persons U.S. Dept. State, 1944-46, cons., 1946-47; expert cons. Germany U.S. Mil. Govt., 1948; cons. Dept. State, 1951, 64-67; chief investigator U.S.A. and Can. refugee survey UN High Commr. for Refugees, 1952; asst. prof. govt. Barnard Coll., Columbia, 1938-53; Research guest Greek Govt., 1965, Sweden, 1968, 70, Turkey, 1969, Iran, 1965, 70, 75, 78; guest King's Coll., Cambridge (Eng.) U., 1979; mem. U.S. Fulbright Commn. for Italy, 1953-54, Aspen Persepolis Conf., Iran, 1975. Author: Deportation of Aliens from United States to Europe, 1931, The Rise of a New Federalism, 1938, The Uprooted People of Europe and European Recovery, 1948, Italy: Change and Progress, 1963, (with A.G. Carey) The Web of Modern Greek Politics, 1968; Contbr. (with A.G. Carey) articles and book revs. to profl. publs. Pres. Consumers League N.Y., 1941-42; Trustee Vassar Coll., 1943-51, Mt. Vernon Jr. Coll. and Sem. for Girls, 1942-50; bd. dirs. Robert Coll., Istanbul, Salzburg Seminar in Am. Studies; past bd. dirs. Anatolia Coll., Thessaloniki, Greece, Am. Women's Vol. Service, Consumers' League N.Y.; past dir., mem. exec. com. Fgn. Policy Assn. Recipient Robert Noxon Toppan prize in constl. law Columbia, 1928 (1st time to a woman), research awards Council for Research Social Sci., 1935, 38, 48; Decorated Order Italian Solidarity. Mem. Council on Fgn. Relations, Am. Polit. Sci. Assn., Am. Italy Soc. (dir.), Soc. for Italian Hist. Studies, Am. Acad. Polit. Sci., Middle East Studies Assn., Am. Inst. Iranian Studies, Conf. Group on Italian Politics. Methodist. Clubs: Cosmopolitan (N.Y.C.), Colony (N.Y.C.), Contemporary (N.Y.C.). Home: New York, N.Y. Died Oct. 24, 1981.

CARGILL, IAN PETER M., internat. bank ofcl.; ed. Oxford U. With Indian Civil Service, 1938-47, British Treasury, London and Washington 1948-52; with IBRD, 1952-80, asst. dir. dept. operations Far East, 1957-61, dir. operations dept. Far East, 1961-66, dir. Asia dept., 1966-68, dir. South Asia dept., 1968-72, regional v.p. Asia, 1972, v.p. finance, from 1973. Died July 10, 1981.

CARLILE, WILLIAM ALONZO, lawyer, former judge; b. Webber's Falls, Okla., Oct. 30, 1887; s. William and Flora (Hamilton) C.; student U. Ark., also Bacone Coll., Muskogee, Okla.; read law under Walter Scott Moore; m. Ethel Hefton, Dec. 16, 1908; children—William G., Robert Kenneth; m. 2d, Edna Ohm, Aug. 22, 1944. Admitted to Okla. bar, 1913, practiced in Sallisaw, Vian, Chandler and Oklahoma City; judge, Sequoyah County, 1918, atty. for county, 1920; 1st asst. county atty., Oklahoma County, 1945-48; dist. judge Oklahoma and Canadian counties, 1949-56; justice Okla. Supreme Ct., 1956-59. Mem. Okla. Ho. of Reps., 1925-27, Okla. Senate, 1932-36. Democrat. Baptist. Mason (32 deg., Shriner), Elk, K.P. †

CARLISLE, SAMUEL, motion picture exec.; b. Glasgow, Scotland, Jan. 21, 1887; s. Samuel and Mary (Black) C.; student pub. schs. Glasgow; m. Marie T. Faribault, Jan. 21, 1930; children—Edith Adele, Lucille Marie. Came to U.S., 1906, naturalized, 1920. Employee Title Guaranty & Trust Co., Brooklyn, 1907-09, Bank of British N.A., N.Y. & Can., 1909-15, Price, Waterhouse & Co., N.Y. City, 1915-26; joined Warner Bros. Pictures, Inc., N.Y. City, 1926, as controller, asst. treas., dir., from 1934; treas. dir. Stanley Co. of Am. Served as corpl., 107th Inf., U.S. Army, 1917-19. Clubs: Advertising (N.Y. City), Country (Rockville Centre, N.Y.). Home: Rockville Centre, N.Y. †

CARLOUGH, EDWARD F., labor union ofcl.; b. Bronx, N.Y., Aug. 31, 1903; ed. pub. schs.; m. Florence Sweeney. Journeyman sheet metal worker, N.Y.C., 1924-40; pres., bus. mgr. local 28, Sheet Metal Workers Internat. Assn., N.Y.C., 1940-51, gen. sec.-treas., Washington, 1951-59, gen. pres., 1959-70, pres. emeritus, 1970-85. Died July 9, 1985.

CARLSON, ALBIN EDMUND, business exec.; b. Chgo., Nov. 16, 1905; s. Victor and Sophie (Mattson) C.; m. Esther Virginia Stevens, June 20, 1931; children—Stephen Edmund (dec.), Candace (Mrs. Harry G. Beatty, Jr.). B.S., Northwestern U., 1928; L.H.D., Nat. Coll. Edn., 1976. C.P.A., 1941. Former vice chmn., dir. Hartford Plaza bank, Chgo.; former pres., dir. Comptometer Corp (now Walter Kidde Co.); former exec. v.p., dir. Continental Telephone Co., Wilmington, Del., Theodore Gary & Co., Gary Service & Investment Co.; pres., dir. Asso. Tel. & Tel. Co.; v.p., dir. Inland Telephone Co., Middle States Utilities, Inc., Automatic Electric (Can.), Ltd., Community Telephone Co., Automatic Electric Sales (Can.), Ltd., Automatic Electric Co., Chgo., Anglo-Canadian Telephone Co., Montreal; incorporator, former dir. Citizens Nat. Bank, Boca Raton; past dir. Ill. Mid-Continent Life Ins. Co., Penn Controls Inc. Life trustee Nat. Coll. Edn., Evanston, Ill.; past trustee Asso. Colls. Ill., Garrett Theol. Sem., Evanston; bd. regents Marymount Coll., Boca Raton, Fla.; bd. dirs. Caldwell Theatre Co., Inc., Boca Raton. Recipient Wisdom award of Honor. Mem. Am. Inst. Accountants, Fla. Atlantic Music Guild, Beta Alpha Psi. Republican. Methodist. Clubs: Boca Raton Hotel (Boca Raton), Royal Palm Yacht and Country (Boca Raton). Address: Boca Raton Fla.

CARMICHAEL, HOWARD HOAGLAND (HOAGY CARMICHAEL), composer, actor; b. Bloomington, Ind., Nov. 22, 1899; s. Howard Clyde and Lida Mary (Robison) C.; LL.B., Ind. U., 1926, D.Mus., 1972; m. Ruth Mary Meinardi, Mar. 14, 1936; children—Hoagy Bix, Randy Bob; m. 2d, Dorothy Wanda McKay, June 20, 1977. Composer, radio artist, rec. artist; writer for Broadway shows and moving pictures, TV shows; star of own radio program CBS; also TV show Saturday Night Rev., and Laramie; played feature roles in films To Have and Have Not, Johnny Angel, Canyon Passage, Best Years of Our Lives, Night Song, Young Man with a Horn, 1950, Belles on Their Toes, 1952, Las Vegas Story, Timberjack. Mem. A.S.C.A.P., Kappa Sigma, Theta Tau Alpha, Theta Nu Epsilon. Republican. Mem. Christian Ch. Clubs: Thunderbird Country, La Costa Country. Compositions include: Stardust, Rockin' Chair, Lazybones, Little Old Lady, Washboard Blues, Skylark, Two Sleepy People, Blue Orchids, Georgia on My Mind (state song of Ga.), Ole Buttermilk Sky, Lazy River, Hongkong Blues, In the Cool, Cool, Cool of the Evening (Oscar award 1951), The Memories of You, I Get Along Without You Very Well, Small Fry. Author: The Stardust Road, 1946; (autobiography) (with Stephen Longstreet) Sometimes I Wonder, 1965. Home: Rancho Mirage, Calif. Died Dec. 27, 1981.

CARMICHAEL, JAMES H, business exec.; b. Newark, Apr. 2, 1907; s. James H. and Margaret (Miner) C.; ed. Suffield Mil. Acad., Conn.; student Univ. So. Calif.; m. Jessie Northrup, July 4, 1930; children—Joan, Judith. Chief pilot Pa.-Central Airlines, 1936, v.p. charge operations, 1940, exec. v.p., 1945; dir. Capital Airlines-P.C.A., 1941-58, pres., 1947-57, chmn. bd. dirs., 1957-58; corporate v.p. Fairchild Engine & Aircraft Corp., 1958-59, pres., 1959-60; pres. J.H. Carmichael & Assos., Washington; former chmn. bd. Airlift Internat., Inc. Head Tech. Indsl. Intelligence Com. to study German comml. and mil. transp. aviation; mem. industry adv. com. NACA. Mem. Fed. City Council, Washington, Nat. Capital Planning Com. Mem. bus. adv. com. Am. U. Recipient Airmail Flyer's Congl. Medal of Honor, 1935, Horatio Alger award, 1958. Mem. Transp. Assn. Am. Clubs: Nat. Press, University. Home: Sumner, Md. Died Dec. 1, 1983.

CARMICHAEL, KATHERINE KENNEDY, univ. ofcl.; b. Birmingham, Ala., Oct. 1, 1912; d. Daniel Malcolm and Ruby (Kennedy) Carmichael; A.B., Birmingham-So. Coll., 1932; M.A., Vanderbilt U., 1939, Ph.D., 1943. Tchr. high sch. nr. Birmingham, 1932-36; tchr. elementary sch., Birmingham 1936-38; instr. English, mem. staff dean of women Tex. State Coll. Women, 1939-40; asst. prof. English, dean of women Western Md. Coll., 1942-44; instr., later chmn. dept. English, Hockaday Sch., Dallas, 1944-46; vis. lectr. English, U. Wis., summer 1946; dean of women, instr. English, U. N.C., 1946-72, asso. dean students for supportive services, 1972-75, asso. dean student affairs, 1976-77; Istanbul lang. and cultural asso., 1977-78; Fulbright lectr. English, Philippine Normal Coll., Manila, 1951-52; vis. Smith-Mundt prof. U. Saigon (Viet Nam), 1961-62. Bd. visitors Peace Coll., 1968-71, 75-76. Fellow Vanderbilt U., 1940-41; Delta Kappa Gamma scholar, 1955-56. Recipient Distinguished Alumni award Birmingham-So. Coll., 1970. Mem. AAUW (Md. dir. 1941-42, N.C. dir. 1952-54), D.A.R., Assn. Women Deans, Adminstrs. and Counselors (pres. N.C. 1963-65), N.C. Lit. and Hist. Soc. (bd. awards 1952-54), Modern Lang. Assn., English Speaking Union (local bd. 1970), Delta Kappa Gamma (N.C. scholarship chmn. 1952-54, chpt. pres. 1965-67), Chi Delta Phi, Alpha Chi Omega, Mortar Board. Democrat. Presbyn. Club: Faculty (U.N.C.) (sec. 1954-55), Author: A Critical Edition of the Early Poems of John Keats, with a Philosophical Supplement, 1943. Home: Istanbul, Turkey. Died June 26, 1982.

CARNEIRO LEAO, ANTOÑIO, Brazilian educator; b. Recife, Pernambuco, July 2, 1887; s. Antonio Carlos and Elvira de Arruda Carneiro Leao; ed. Faculty of Law of Recife (degree in Law, 1911). Journalist and lawyer, 1910-18, 1927-29; founder of mag. "O Economiste", 1919, and dir., 1920-27; dir. gen. of edn., Fed. Dist., 1922-26; sec. of justice and edn., 1929-30; prof. Brazil Summer Sch., Rio de Janeiro, 1928, 29; rep. to 2d Nat. Edn. Conf., São Paulo, 1929, v.p. 3d Conf., Rio de Janeiro, 1931; dir. indsl. normal school, 1931-33; prof. of French, Colegio Pedro II, Rio de Janeiro, 1932-37; became prof. of edn. Inst. of Edn., Rio de Janeiro, and prof, school adminstrn., U. of Rio de Janeiro, 1933; dir. Dept. of Edn., Rio de Janeiro, 1935; studied ednl. trends in U.S., 1934-35. Author of numerous ednl. books. Home: Rio de Janeiro, Brazil. †

CARNEY, CHESNEY M., lawyer, banker; b. Silver Hill, W.Va., Apr. 16, 1901; s. Ellis B. and Julia (Jones) C.; m. Elise Gibson, Sept. 23, 1933. A.B., W.Va. U., 1924, LL.B., 1926. Bar: W.Va. bar 1926. Since practiced in, Clarksburg; partner firm Steptoe & Johnson, Clarksburg, Charleston, W.Va. and, Washington, 1930-69, of counsel, 1969-82, dir., Clarksburg Community Bank. Mem. Order of Coif, Theta Chi, Phi Delta Phi. Republican. Episcopalian. Club: Rotarian. Home: Clarksburg, W.Va. Died Aug. 20, 1982.

CARPENTER, ARTHUR WHITING, chem. engr.; b. Wellsville, N.Y., Mar. 30, 1890; s. Samuel and Clara (Whiting) C.; S.B., Mass. Inst. Tech., 1913, M.S. in Chem. Engring.; m. Irma Coon, May 8, 1948. City chemist, Alliance, O., 1914; chemist water purification plant. Akron, O., 1915-17; tech. service engr. Goodyear Tire & Rubber Co., Akron, 1919-21, devel. engr., 1923-26; supt. Holtite Mfg. Co., Balt., 1922; devel. engr. B. F. Goodrich Co., Akron, 1927, mgr. testing labs., 1928-55; cons. chem. engr., rubber technologist, from 1955. Loaned by B. F. Goodrich Co. to Nat. Resources Security Bd., Sept. 1948; asst. dir. raw materials OPM, to 1949; prin. indsl. specialist and cons. rubber conservation div. WPB, 1941-42. Served from 1st lt. to capt., San. Corps, U.S. Army, 1918-19. Recipient Charles Goodyear medal Am. Chem. Soc., 1957. Fellow Am. Inst. Chemists; mem. Am. Soc. Testing Materials (pres. 1946-47; hon. mem. 1955), Am. Inst. Chem. Engring., Nat. Soc. Profl. Engrs., Am. Chem. Soc., Lambda Chi Alpha, Alpha Chi Sigma. Republican. Conglist. Mason. Clubs: Torch, University, Fairlawn Country (Akron). Contbr. chpt. on Physical Testing and Specifications in Am. Chem. Soc. Monograph No. 74, The Chemistry and Technology of Rubber, 1937. Obtained authors and edited books pub. by Am. Soc. for Testing Materials; Symposium on Rubber, 1932; Symposium on the Applications of Synthetic Rubbers, 1944. Contbr. numerous tech. papers on testing and instruments to sci. and trade jours. Home: Akron, OH. †

CARPENTER, CLARK BAILEY, metallurgist; b. Girard, Kan., May 21, 1888; s. Jesse Ryan and Jane (McMurray) C.; B.S. in Mining, U. Kans., 1915, M.S. in Mining, Mass. Inst. Tech., 1922; m. Mabe I. Ashby, Aug. 25, 1917; 1 dau., Barbara Ann. Mining engr., Anaconda Copper Mining Co., 1916-17; asst. prof. of metallurgy, Colo. Sch. of Mines, 1920-21, asso. prof., 1922-36, prof. since 1936; cons. metallurgist for Gen. Iron Works, and C.S. Card Iron Works, Denver. Served as 1st lt. Engring. Corps U.S. Army, 1917-20. Mem. Am. Soc. Metals, Am. Foundrymens Assn., Am. Inst. Mech. Engrs., Sigma Xi, Tau Beta Pi, Sigma Gamma Epsilon. Republican. Mason (K.T.). Club: University (Denver). Home: Golden, Colo. †

CARPENTER, CLIFFORD EARL, newspaperman; b. East Syracuse, N.Y., Mar. 15, 1909; s. Edmund B. and Helen (Pehl) C.; student U. Rochester; m. Ethel LeFevre, Oct. 20, 1933; 1 son, Scott E. With Democrat & Chronicle, Rochester, 1933-73, police reporter, gen. assignments reporter, yachting columnist, asst. city editor, Sunday editor, copy reader, copy desk chief, acting mng. editor, editorial writer, 1953-57, editor editorial page, 1957-60, editor, 1960-67, editorial columnist, 1967-73; reporter Canandaigua Daily Messenger, 1931-33. Pres. Nat. Conf. Editorial Writers, 1963-64, now life mem.; editorial bd. Rochester Gannett Newspapers, 1970-73. Named goodwill ambassador to S.A., Rochester, 1958; recipient Community Social Service award 1972, Citizen of Year award Kiwanis, 1973. Fellow Rochester Mus. Arts and Scis.; mem. U.S. Power Squadron (sr.), U.S. Coast Guard Aux. Home: Sun City Center, Fla. Died July 22, 1981.

CARPENTER, DEAN, hotel exec.; b. Port Chester, N.Y., Aug. 4, 1902; s. Harry S. and Mary Newton (Dean) C.; student Haverford (Pa.) Coll., 1921-22; married Rosemary Hilton, Dec. 7, 1925; children—Connie Ann, Anthony Dean. Asso. with N.Y. City dealers in old prints, paintings and antique furniture, 1923-31; with Hilton Hotels since 1931, v.p., dir. and gen. mgr. Roosevelt Hotel, N.Y. City, 1945-51; v.p. spl. European rep. Hilton Internat. Corp., 1952-56; gen. mgr. Savoy-Hilton Hotel, N.Y.C.; v.p., director Hilton Hotels Internat.; promoted, designed, built and operated El Ranchotel, El Paso, Tex., 1939-42. Mem. Am., N.Y. hotel assns., Am. Arbitration Assn. (nat. panel), Nat. Hotel Expo. N.Y.C. Better Bus. Bur., Greater N.Y. Safety Council. Clubs: N.Y. Athletic (N.Y.C.); Sakonnet G.C. (R.I.); Tavern. Home: Little Compton, R.I. Died Nov. 9, 1981.

CARPENTER, ESTHER, educator; b. Meriden, Conn., June 4, 1903; d. Ernest Charles and Nettie Jane (Hale) Carpenter; B.A., Ohio Wesleyan U., 1925, D.Sc. (hon.), 1956; M.S., U. Wis., 1927; fellow biology, Bryn Mawr Coll., 1927-28; Ph.D., Yale, 1932. Research asst. embryology Carnegie Inst. Tech., 1932-33; part-time instr. Albertus Magnus Coll., 1933-34; mem. faculty Smith Coll., 1933-68, prof. zoology, 1953-68, chmn. dept., 1955-60, Myra M. Sampson prof. zoology, 1963-68. Research

Strangeways Research Lab., Cambridge, Eng., 1953-54, 61. Howald scholar Ohio State U., 1942-43. Mem. Tissue Culture Assn., Growth Soc., Am. Soc. Cell Biology, Am. Soc. Zoologists, Am. Assn. Anatomists, Sigma Xi. Conglist. Author articles thyroid, pituitary, vitamin A. Home: Northampton, Mass.

CARPENTER, HARRY GORDON, univ. trustee; b. Starkville, Miss., Feb. 9, 1890; s. Vivian Murrey and Eudora (Hagin) C.; B.S., Miss. State U., 1910; grad. study Ont. A. and M. Coll., also U. Wis.; m. Annie Watson Barnard, July 19, 1919; children—Ladye Barnard (Mrs. W. E. Freitag), Vivian Margaret (Mrs. W. R. Rodgers). Faculty, Tex. A. and M. Coll., 1911-13; county agt., 1914-20; dir. First Nat. Bank, Vicksburg, Miss., Baird & Có., wholesale hdwe., Greenville, Miss., Hollendale Livestock Sales Co. County chmn., past pres. A.R.C.; v.p. Andrew Jackson council Boy Scouts Am., also dist. chmn.; state dir. YMCA. Trustee Miss. State Coll., Blue Mountain Coll.; trustee, past president board trustees of state-owned colleges. Recipient Silver Beaver award Boy Scouts Am. Member Newcomen Soc. Am. Farm Bur. (pres., dir.), Miss. Econ. Council, Delta Council (dir.). Democrat. Club: Rotary (past pres.). Address: Rolling Fork, Miss. †

CARPENTER, KAREN ANNE, singer; b. New Haven, Mar. 2, 1950; d. Harold Bertram and Agnes Reuwer (Tatum) C.; (married). Student, Long Beach (Calif.) State Coll., 1967-69. Vice pres. Ars Nova Inc.; co-producer Richard Carpenter Prodns. Jr. Singer: The Carpenters; rec. artist, A&M Records, Hollywood, Calif., 1969-83, semi-finalist (ll Am. Coll. Show 1968, 69), recipient (18 gold records in U.S., 49 worldwiae, also, 7 platinum records and, 2 silver records, 3 Grammy awards, 1 AMA award.). Chmn. Am. Cancer Soc. Sweepstakes winner Battle of the Bands, Hollywood Bowl, 1966. Home: Downey, Calif. Died Feb. 4, 1983.

CARPENTER, RUSSELL PHELPS, office supply and, art products co. exec.; b. Chgo., Sept. 6, 1900; s. William W. Seymour and Viola (Phelps) C.; m. Mary Howe, Dec. 28, 1927; children—William, Carlisle C. Jones, Virginia. B.A., Dartmouth Coll., 1923. With Sanford Corp., Bellwood, Ill., 1923-83, chmn. bd., 1950-83. Pres. YMCA, Oak Park, Ill., 1956, bd. dirs., 1935-83; pres. Chgo. Council on Alcoholism, 1972-73, bd. dirs., 1967-83. Clubs: Masons, Rotary. Home: Oak Park, Ill. Died Feb. 20, 1983.

CARPENTER, WILLIAM WESTON, sch. adminstrn.; b. Lawrence, Kan., Mar. 2, 1889; s. William Thomas and Helen Eva (Weston) C.; A.B., U. of Kan., 1912, A.M., 1917; studied U. of Ariz.; Ph.D., Columbia, 1926; m. Doris Melvina Cotey, Dec. 27, 1914; children—Barbara Cotey, William Weston, Edward Thomas. Teacher of science high schs. of Ariz., and head of Science dept., Phoenix Union High Sch., until 1920; dean Phoenix Jr. Coll., 1920-23; prof. of teaching physical science, George Peabody Coll. for Teachers, Nashville, Tenn., 1925-27, prof. sch. administration, 1927-28; prof. edn., U. of Mo. since 1928 Educational Reorganization advisor, Japan, 1948-50. Served as 2d lt. inf., U.S. Army, World War; 1st lt. Ariz. National Guard. Received Silver Beaver award, Boy Scouts America. Past chmn. research com. Am. Assn. of Jr. Colleges. Mem. N.E.A. (life mem.), Am. Assn. Univ. Profs., Assn. for Higher Edn., Am. Ednl. Research Assn., Nat. Soc. for Study of Edn., Nat. Council Schoolhouse Constrn., Phi Delta Kappa, (past nat. secretary), Kappa Delta Pi. Democrat. Presbyn. Author: Certain Phases of the Administration of High School Chemistry, 1925; (with John Rufi) The Teacher and the School; (with John Rufi) The Teacher and Secondary School Administration, 1931; (with Ralph Yakel) State and National School Administration, 1931, revised, 1934, 37, 39, revised by William Weston Carpenter, 1951, 54; (with L. G. Townsend) Community School Administration, 1936, revised 1948, 1951; (with W. E. Rosentengel) Community School Finance Problems, 1936, revised 1939; (with N.E. Viles) Community School Building Problems, 1934, revised 1940; The Organization and Administration of The Junior College, 1939; (with G.H. Marshall and Clara W. Marshall) The Administrator's Wife, 1941; Schoolhouse Planning and Construction 1946; Suggestions for Procedure for Missouri Boards of Education (with A. G. Capps and L. G. Townsend), 1950, rev., 1956; (with A. G. Capps) selected Readings, State and National School Administration, 1951, rev., 1954; Evaluating The Educational Services in the Local School District (with A. G. Capps and L. G. Townsend), 1955; Local School Administration in Action (with L. G. Townsend), 1956; Titles of Dissertations in Edn. Accepted by U. of Mo. 1916-58 (with A. G. Capps), 1958. Home: Columbia, Mo. †

CARR, CHALMERS RANKIN, orthopedic surgeon; b. Asheville, N.C., Oct. 27, 1907; s. Claude and Annie (Rankin) C.; A.B., Davidson Coll., 1928; postgrad. U. N.C. Med. Sch., 1931-33; M.D., Jefferson Med. Coll., Phila., 1936; m. Willie Alexander, May 8, 1933; children—Chalmers Rankin, William A., Alice C. Singer. Intern, Jefferson Med. Coll. Hosp., 1936-38; commd. lt. (j.g.) M.C., USN, 1938, advanced through grades to capt., 1951, ret., 1954; fellow orthopedic surgery Lahey Clinic, Boston, 1943, N.C. Orthopedic Hosp., Gastonia, 1947; chief orthopedic surgery U.S. Naval Hosp., Oakland, Calif., 1948-51, U.S. Naval Hosp., Bethesda, Md., 1951-54; practice in Charlotte, N.C., from 1954; chmn. bd. Miller Clinic, Inc., Charlotte, 1954-77, emeritus, 1977-84; chief orthopedic surgery Charlotte Meml. Hosp., 1958-60, 66-69; chief med. staff emeritus Orthopaedic Hosp., Charlotte; hon. staff orthopaedic surgeon Hunters-ville (N.C.) Hosp., Southeastern Gen. Hosp., Lumberton, N.C.; mem. cons. staffs Presbyn., Meml., Mercy hosps.; hon. cons. emeritus Charlotte Rehab. Hosp., from 1977. Fellow Soc. Internat. de Chirurgeric Orthopedia et Traumautologic; mem. A.C.S. (gov. 1966-75), Am. Orthopedic Assn., Am. Acad. Orthopedic Surgeons, A.M.A., Mecklenberg County Med. Soc. (past pres.), Med. Soc. State N.C. (speaker ho. of dels. 1969-76), Assn. Surgeons So. R.R.'s (pres. 1966), Charlotte C. of C., N.C. Orthopaedic Soc. (past pres.), Pi Kappa Phi, Phi Chi. Republican. Presbyn. Clubs: Linville (N.C.) Country; Quail Hollow. Contbr. articles to med. jours. Home: Charlotte, N.C. Died Jan. 31, 1984.

CARR, EDWARD HALLETT, historian, author; b. June 28, 1892; ed. Trinity Coll., Cambridge (Eng.) U. Temporary clk. British Fgn. Office, 1916; with British Delegation to Peace Conf., 1919; temporary sec. British embassy, Paris, France, 1920-21; assigned Fgn. Office: 1922-25; 2d sec. legation, Riga, 1925-29; assigned Fgn. Office, 1929-30; asst. adviser League of Nations affairs, 1930-33; 1st sec., 1933; resigned from Fgn. Service, 1936; Wilson prof. Internat. politics Univ. Coll., Wales, Aberystwyth, 1936-47; dir. fgn. publicity Ministry Information, 1939-40; asst. editor The Times, 1941-46; tutor politics Balliol Coll., Oxford U., 1935-55; fellow Trinity Coll., Cambridge U., 1955-82. Decorated comdr. Order British Empire, 1920. Author: Dosotevsky, 1931; The Romantic Exiles, 1933; Karl Marx: A Study in Fanaticism, 1934; International Relations Since the Peace Treaty, 1937; Michael Bakunin, 1937; The Twenty Years Crisis, 1919-1939, 1939; Britain: A Study in Foreign Policy from Versailles to the Outbreak of the War, 1939; Conditions of Peace, 1942; Nationalism and After, 1945; The Soviet Impact on the Western World, 1946; Studies in Revolution, 1950; A History of Soviet Russia, vol. I, 1950, vol. II, 1952, vol. III, 1953 (all under title The Bolshevik Revolution, 1917-1923), vol. IV, 1954 (The Interregnum, 1923-24), vol. V, 1958, vol. VI, 1959 (Socialism in One Century, 1924-1926), vol. VII (2 parts), 1964; German-Soviet-Relations Between the Two World Wars, 1919-1939, 1951; The New Society, 1951; What is History?, 1961. Club: Oxford and Cambridge. Address: Cambridge, Eng. Died Nov. 7, 1982.

CARR, JOE CORDELL, sec. state Tenn.; b. Cookeville, Tenn., June 20, 1907; s. Sidney Forrest and Laura (Burton) C.; student pub. schs., Nashville; m. Mary Oliver Hart, Sept. 12, 1934; children—Carolyn (Mrs. George N. Welch III), Joe Cordell. Bill clk. Tenn. Ho. of Reps., 1929-33, asst. chief clk., 1933-37, reading clk., 1937-39, chief clk., 1939-41, 53-55; State of Tenn., Nashville, 1941-45, 47-49, 57-76. Pres. Tenn. Bapt. Brotherhood. Organizer, sec. Young Democratic Clubs Tenn., 1933, pres., 1934; sec. Young Dem. Clubs Am., 1937, pres., 1941. Served with AUS, 1944-45. Mem. Am. Legion, 40 and 8, Soc. Amateur Chefs. Baptist (deacon). Mason (33, Shriner, Jester). Clubs: Exchange (pres. 1954), Elks. Home: Nashville, Tenn. Died Oct. 12, 1981.

CARR, OPHELIA SMITH TODD, educator; b. "Chilesburg", nr. Lexington, Ky., Oct. 27, 1887; d. Dabney and Mary Clifton (Smith) Carr; A.B., U. of Ky., 1925, grad. sch., 1925-26, law sch., 1927-28; student U. of Chicago Law Sch., summer, 1927. Teacher high sch., Lawrenceburg, Ky., 1909-10; elementary and high schs. Lexington, 1910-18; finance and statis. work, Office Chief of Ordnance, Washington, D.C., 1918-22; teacher Hamilton Coll., Lexington, Ky., 1922-28; dean and academic head, Chatham Hall, Chatham, Va., 1928-33; prin. Stuart Hall, Staunton, Va., 1933-43; head, St. Katharine's School, Davenport, Ia., 1943-47; admitted to Ky. bar, 1928. Mem. Am. Genetic Assn., AAAS. Democrat. Episcopalian. Address: Lexington, Ky. †

CARR, RAYMOND NORMAN, musician; b. Franklin, Ind., Nov. 20, 1890; s. Norman and Eliza Esther (Wood) C.; A.B., Shurtleff Coll., Alton, Ill., 1911; student U. of Chicago, summer 1911; diploma Northwestern Sch. of Music, 1915; Mus.B., Am. Conservatory of Music, Chicago, 1924; studied pvtly. under masters; m. Alta May Foreman, Jan. 18, 1913; children—Malcolm Judson Foreman, Raymond Norman Wood, Margaret Esther May. Teacher, Chicago and suburbs, 1911-15; asso. supervisor of music, pub. schs. Minneapolis, Minn., 1915-19; dir. dept. of music State Teachers Coll., Kirksville, Mo., 1919-21; dean Sch. of Fine Arts and prof. singing and choral music, Des Moines U., 1921-26; dean, Coll. of Music, Kan. Wesleyan U., Salina, Kan., 1926-28; founder, 1928, and dir. Salina Conservatory of Music. Tenor soloist, choral dir. and lecturer. Mem. Music Supervisors Nat. Conf., Ia. State Teachers' Assn. (pres. music sect., 1923-24). Republican. Methodist. Mason (32 deg., Shriner). Author: Building the School Orchestra, 1923. Home: Salina, Kan. †

CARROLL, JAMES ALBERT, JR., oil exec.; b. Brunswick, Ga., Mar. 27, 1890; s. J. A. and Eloise (Allen) C.; student N.M. Mil. Inst., 1903-06; m. Gladys Freeman, Sept. 15, 1915; 1 dau., Patricia E. (wife of capt. D. J. McCaughey, U.S.A.A.F.). With Prairie Oil & Gas Co., Kan., 1916, Standard Oil Co. (Ind.), 1919-27, gen. auditor, 1927, Pan Am. Petroleum Transport Co., N.Y.C., from 1927, comptroller, 1928-31, v.p., treas., 1932-51, later financial v.p., mem. bd., exec. com. (also officer subsidiaries); financial vice-pres. member board of directors, executive committee, American Oil Company, from 1954. Served in Okla. N.G., Mexican border campaign, 1916-17, U.S. Army, 1918. C.P.A., Colo. Mem. S.A.R. Conglist. Home: Scarsdale, N.Y. †

CARROLL, JOHN ALBERT, U.S. senator; b. Denver, July 30, 1901; LL.B.; Westminster Law Coll.; m. Dorothy R. Doyle; 1 dau., Diane Ruth. Asst. U.S. district atty., 1933-34; dist. atty of Denver, 1937-41; regional atty. Rocky Mountain area, OPA, 1942-43; mem. 80th-81st Congresses, 1st Colo. Dist. U.S. senator from Colo., 1957-62; member of senate judiciary interior coms. Served at Corregidor, P.I., World War I; Africa, Italy, Corsica, France, World War II. Died Aug. 31, 1983.

CARROLL, WILLIAM JOSEPH, fire control manufacturer; b. Boston, Nov. 9, 1890; s. Samuel J. and Ellen (Mahoney) C.; student pub. schs., Boston; m. Helen J. Kennedy, Apr. 5, 1918; children—William Joseph, Helen (Mrs. Laurence McCloud), Jean, Nancy (Mrs. David Birmingham). Sales mgr. The Gamewell Co., Newton Upper Falls, Mass., 1920-32, chmn. 1956-58, president and chief executive officer, from 1958; gen. mgr. Rockwood Sprinkler Co., from 1932; pres., dir. Worcester-Rockwood, Ltd., Montreal, Can., from 1932; trustee Bay State Savs. Bank. Mem. Worcester County Metal Trade (pres. 1957-59), Nat. Automatic Sprinkler and Fire Control Assn. (pres. 1941-44). Home: Worcester, Mass. †

CARSON, BRUCE LYNN, publisher; b. Grand Junction, Colo., Aug. 6, 1934; s. Porter and Martha (McBain) C.; m. Susanne Strohmeier, Feb. 15, 1958; children—Deborah Lynn, Scott Paterick, Matthew James. B.S. in Bus. Adminstrn, U. Denver, 1959; postgrad., U. Calif., Los Angeles. Accountant Atlantic Mut. Ins. Co., 1958-60; financial analyst, corp. tax accountant United Calif. Bank, Los Angeles, 1960-64; exec. v.p., gen. mgr. Lab. World mag., Los Angeles, 1964-77, pub., 1974-77; asso. pub. Clin. Lab. Products mag., Crystal Lake, Ill., from 1977; pres. Internat. Med. Mktg. Services, Inc., from 1974; cons. in field. Active local YMCA. Served with USAF, 1952-56. Mem. Med. Mktg. Assn., Midwest Pharm. Advt. Club. Republican. Episcopalian. Home: Crystal Lake, Ill.

CARSON, DAVID BYERS, cons.; b. Pitts., Sept. 1, 1890; s. Theodore Freulingheusyen and Louise (Ochsenhirt) C.; C.E., Ohio State U., 1913; m. Rose Steinfeld, Nov. 29, 1917; children—Susan Marion, David Byers III, Robert Sterling; m. 2d, Helen Foster, Oct. 20, 1945. Rodman, later draftsman, asst. tc. valuation engr. Toledo & Ohio Central Ry., Columbus, O., 1913-15; insp., later clk., sales agt. Carbon Steel Co., Pitts., 1915-17, dist. sales mgr., 1919-20; dist. sales mgr. Tacony Steel Co., Cleve., 1921-23; asst. sales mgr., later sales mgr., mgr. research and devel. dept. Central Alloy Steel Corp., Massillon, O., 1923-29; v.p., treas. Asso. Alloy Steel Corp., Cleve., 1930-32; v.p. Pitts. Steel Co., 1935-44; v.p. sales, exec. v.p., dir. Sharon steel Corp., 1932-59, cons. Dir. iron and steel div. NPA, Washington, 1950, mem. Moblzn. Controls Task Force. Served as 1st lt. AUS, 1917-19. Mem. Army Ordnance Assn., Nat. Sales Execs., A.I.M., Am. Iron and Steel Inst., (dir.), Am. Soc. Metals, Delta Upsilon. Republican. Presbyn. Clubs: Duquesne (Pitts.); Cleveland Athletic; Youngstown, Youngstown Country (Youngstown, O.); Coral Ridge Country (Ft. Lauderdale, Fla.); Sharon Country (Pa.). Home: Delray Beach, FL. †

CARSON, GEORGE BARR, JR., historian, educator; b. Ancon, C.Z., Oct. 16, 1915; s. George Barr and Edna (Hess) C.; m. Dorothy Alberta Klemer, Sept. 5, 1936; children: Michael Frederic, Donald Richard, Jane Isabelle. B.A., Coll. Wooster, 1935; M.A., U. Chgo., 1940, Ph.D., 1942. Instr. Monticello Coll., 1942- 45; asst. prof. U. Ky., 1945-47; prof. history, chmn. div. social sci. N.Y. State Tchrs. Coll., New Paltz, 1947-49; asst. prof. U. Chgo., 1949-56; also editor Jour. Modern History; sr. fellow Russian Inst., Columbia, 1951-52; dir. service center for tchrs. history Am. Hist. Assn., also editor publ. series, 1956-61; prof. history, chmn. dept. Oreg. State U., 1961-80; vis. prof. U. Colo., summer 1955, George Washington U., spring 1958, 61, N.W. Interinstl. Council for Study Abroad, Avignon, 1978. Author: (with Louise F. Brown) Men and Centuries of European Civilization, 1948, Electoral Practices in the USSR, 1955, (with T. Walter Wallbank and Alastair M. Taylor) Civilization Past and Present. Vol. II, 1969, Russia Since 1917: The Once and Future Utopia, 1972; Editor: Latvia: An Area Study, 2 vols, 1956; adv. bd.: Hist. Abstracts, 1953-60; exec. bd.: Social Edn, 1960-61; mem. adv. com.: Soviet Studies in History, from 1975; adv. bd.: Gov.'s State Hist. Records, from 1977. Recipient Webb-Smith essay prize on modern European revolutionary history, 1976. Mem. Am. Hist. Assn., Am. Assn. Advancement Slavic Studies (chmn. Far Western Slavic cong. 1966-67), AAUP. Home: Corvallis, Ore.

CARSON, HIRAM JOHN, utilities cons.; b. Council Bluffs, Ia., Nov. 26, 1887; s. George and Rachel Leslie (Boyce) C.; B.S. in mech. engring., Ia. State Coll., 1910; m. Marguerite Sinclair, Mar. 9, 1918; children—Gweneth Leslie, David Sinclair, Mary Susanne (Mrs. Howard E. Jessen), Frances Edith Alden (Mrs. James I. McNelis). Engaged as cadet engineer with The Peoples Light Co., Davenport, Ia., 1911-13; gen. supt. Muscatine (Ia.) Lighting Co., 1913-15, since 1915; gen. mgr. Cedar Rapids (Ia.) Gas Co., 1915-30, from 1930; successively asst. v.p., chief engr., supt. operations, v.p. in charge operations No.

Natural Gas Co., 1930-49, 1st v.p., 1950-52, dir., 1942-52; cons. utility natural gas pipe line adminstrn. dir. Peoples Natural Gas Co. Served as capt. Engrs. and C.W.S., 1917-18. Chmn. midwest natural gas com. W.P.B. Recipient Am. Gas Assn. Distinguished Service award, 1951. Mem. Am. (chmn. transmission com. 1946-49, chmn. nitrogen removal com.), Midwest (pres.) gas assns., Fgn. Relations Com., Soc. Mayflower Descendants, Alden Kindred Soc., Phi Kappa Psi. Presbyn. Mason. Home: Berkeley, Cal. †

CARSON, JOHN (JOSEPH), writer; born at Johnson County, Ind., Nov. 16, 1889; s. William and Mary (Gleason) C.; student pub. and parochial schs., Indianapolis, Ind., 1895-1902, Manual Training High Sch., 1903-05; m. Ardelia Elizabeth Carson, May 3, 1916; children—Mary Katherine, Elizabeth Jane, Joan. Clk. Van Camp Packing Co., 1905-10; reporter and city editor Indianapolis Sun and Ind. Daily Times, 1911-18; Washington corr. for St. Louis Globe Democrat, St. Louis Republic, Baltimore Sun, Baltimore Evening Sun, Scripps-Howard Alliance, 1918-24; sec. Senator James Couzens, 1924-36; was consumers' counsel Nat. Bituminous Coal Commn.; director research and information Cooperative League of U.S.A., Washington; commr. Fed. Trade Commn. 1949-53; writer, Washington Corr. from 1953. Catholic. Clubs: National Press, Columbia Country (Washington). Address: Washington, D.C. †

CARSON, ROBERT, author; b. Clayton, Wash., Oct. 6, 1909; s. Franklin Pierce and Blanche Ethel (McClaren) C.; m. Mary Jane Irving, Feb. 11, 1938. Student, Am. Inst. Banking. Various positions, 1928-35, scenarist, novelist, mag. writer, 1935-42, writer, 1945-83. Producer, CBS-TV, 1954-55; motion pictures written include Action of the Tiger, Man With Wings, Light That Failed, Bundle of Joy; sound version Desperados, Beau Geste, Western Union; movies from serials, short stories include Reformer and the Redhead, Across the Pacific, Perilous Holiday, You Gotta Stay Happy; (Received Acad. award for motion picture A Star is Born 1937); Author: The Revels are Ended, 1936, Stranger in our Midst, 1947, Magic Lantern, 1952 (Book-of-the-Month Club selection), Quality of Mercy, 1954, Love Affair, 1958, My Hero, 1961, An End to Comedy, 1963, The Outsiders, 1966, The December Syndrome, 1969, The Golden Years Caper, 1970, Jellybean, A Tale of the Old West, 1974; contbr. fiction and travel articles to nat. mags., Works transl. Danish, Italian, German, Dutch, Norwegian, Swedish, Turkish. Served as lt. col. USAAF, 1942-45. Mem. Writers Guild Am., Screen Writers' Guild (exec. bd. 1951-53). Home: Los Angeles, Calif. Died Jan. 19, 1983.

CARTER, AMON, JR., publisher; b. Ft. Worth, Dec. 23, 1919; s. Amon G. and Nenetta (Burton) C.; B.B.A., U. Tex., 1941. With Carter Publishers 1936-82, pres. 1952-74; director American Airlines, Incorporated, 1957-82. Served as captain, U.S. Army, 1941-45; prisoner of war, Germany, 1943-45. Decorated Purple Heart, Bronze Star. Member Kappa Sigma. Club: Exchange. Home: Fort Worth, Tex. Died July 24, 1982.

CARTER, ELMER ANDERSON, editor; b. Rochester, New York, July 19, 1890; s. George Cook and Florence Lucretia (Young) C.; student Harvard, 1908-12; m. Edna Felicia Billups, Apr. 1922; 1 dau., Sarah Elizabeth; m. 2d, Thelma Charles Johnson, June 1927. Teacher mathematics and dir. athletics, Prairie View, (Tex.) State Coll., 1914-18; exec. sec. Urban League, Columbus, 1920-21, Louisville, 1921-23, St. Paul and Minneapolis, 1923-28; editor Opportunity, Journal of Negro Life, 1928-42; mem. Unemployment Ins. Appeal Bd., 1937-45. Served in 92d Div., U.S. Army, with A.E.F., 1918-19. Mem. Unemployment Ins. State Advisory Council, 1935-37. Mem. N.Y. State Commn. Against Discrimination. Mem. exec. com. Boy Scouts (N.Y. City). Mem. exec. bd. Negro Actors Guild of America, Am. Legion, Alpha Phi Alpha. Member board of trustees, Town Hall, New York City. Independent Democrat. Club: Reveille (N.Y. City). Contbr. articles and revs. to jours. Home: New York, N.Y. †

CARTER, JERRY WILLIAMS, mem. Dem. Nat. Com.; b. Barbar Co., Ala., Aug. 11, 1887; s. Dr. Wilbur Wesley and Mary Blanche (Williams) C.; student pub. schs. Tenn. and N.C.; m. Mary Frances Holifield, Oct. 27, 1907; children—Jerry, Burnette Dansby, Robert Gordon, Francis Hunter, Sidney Cates, William Holifield, David Hinton. Salesman and city mgr. Singer Sewing Machine Co., Tenn. and North Fla., 1907, mgr., 1912; Fla. State hotel commr., 1917-29. Elected Fla. ry. and pub. utilities commr., 1934-55. Mem. Dem. Nat. Com., Fla. from 1948. Baptist. Democrat. Mason (Shriner), Eastern Star, Odd Fellow. Elk, Moose, Modern Woodmen, Praetorium, Royal Sons of Rest. Clubs: Hopping Fleas, Bearcat. Home: Tallahassee, Fla. †

CARTER, LOUIS HAYWARD, exec.; born Somerville, Mass., Oct. 14, 1890; M.S., Tufts Coll. Dir. Am. Agrl. Chem. Co. Trustee Tufts Coll. Mem. Delta Upsilon. Club: University (N.Y.C.).†

CARTER, MILTON ELI, lawyer, accountant; b. South Bend, Ind., Oct. 13, 1890; s. Eli Wiley and Mary Susan (Eagy) C.; student Nat. U. Law Sch., Washington, D.C., 1924-26; m. Hazel Mary Reed, May 3, 1917; children—David Reed (dec.), John Wiley, Marion Emilye, Mary Marjorie. Began as newsboy, 1901; successively clerk, store accountant, salesman, cost accountant and public accountant; advisory auditor Bur. of Internal Revenue, 1919-20; certified pub. accountant; admitted to Mo. bar, 1926, and tax atty.; sr. tech. advisor Dept. Internal Revenue, 1933-36; apptd. asst. to commr. internal revenue, 1936, head Chicago div.-tech. staff from 1939. Enlisted 1st O.T.C., Ft. Sheridan, Ill., May 13, 1917; commd. 1st lt., U.S. Inf., Aug. 15, 1917, capt. 344th Inf., 86th Div., July 1918. Mem. Bar of U.S. Supreme Court, Bar of Mo., Am. Legion, Vets. Foreign Wars, Sigma Nu Phi. Democrat. Catholic. Club: Manor Country (Washington, D.C.). Home: Evanston, Ill. †

CARTER, SOLON JEHU, lawyer; b. Bloomingdale, Ind., Sept. 1, 1888; s. Daniel G. and Cora (Ferguson) C.; prep. edn., DePauw Prep. Sch., Greencastle, Ind.; A.B., Miami U., Oxford, O., 1909, LL.D., 1919; m. Augusta Mitch, Nov. 22, 1912; children—John Solon, Eleanor Hadley, Jane Blair. Admitted to Ind. bar, 1910, practice law, Indianapolis; mem. Matson, Carter, Ross & McCord, 1923-30, counsel for Nat. Paper Board Assn. Advanced from private to Lt., Ind. N.G., 1910-15; capt., later maj., lt. col. and col., F.A., U.S. Army, World War. Judge, Marion Superior Ct., Indianapolis, 1919-23; special master in chancery, U.S. Dist. Ct., Southern Dist. Ind.; candidate for the nomination for U.S. Senate, Republican ticket, Ind., 1928. Mem. Am. and Ind. State bar assns., Phi Delta Theta. Decorated Croix de Guerre (France). Quaker. Mason. Clubs: Columbia, Players, Indianapolis Country. Home: Indianapolis, Ind. †

CARTER, THOMAS MILTON, educator; b. Chaplin, Ky., Feb. 29, 1888; s. Ambrose B. and Susan M. (Burns) C.; A.B., Ill. Wesleyan U., 1914; S.T.B., Garret Bibl. Inst., 1917; M.A., Northwestern U., 1921; Ph.D., U. Chgo., 1923; m. Frances H. Berry, Aug. 25, 1922; children—Virginia (Mrs. J. D. Norton), Geraldine (Mrs. Thomas F. Donaldson), Suzanne (Mrs. John E. Walker). Chautauqua lectr. summer 1919; asst. to pres. Hamline U., 1919-20; head dept. edn. Albion Coll., 1923 from; vis. prof. summer schs. U. Neb., U. Pa., Northwestern U., U. Ohio, U. Louisville. Served from 1st lt. to col. Chaplains Corps. AUS, World War I and II. Decorated Oak-Leaf-Cluster. Mem. Am. Psychol. Assn., Am. Ednl. Research Assn., Am. Acad. Polit. and Social Scis., N.Y. Acad. Scis., Michigan Schoolmasters Club (pres.), Mich. Coll. and U. Placement Assn. (pres.). Contbr. articles prof. jours. Home: Albion, Mich. †

CARTER, WILLIAM BEVERLY, JR., ambassador; b. Coatesville, Pa., Feb. 1, 1921; s. William Beverly and Maria (Green) C.; m. Carlyn Brown Pogue, Nov. 27, 1971; 1 son, William Beverly III; stepchildren—Dion Pogue, Ann V. Pogue. A.B., Lincoln U., 1944; student, Temple U. Sch. Law, 1946-47, New Sch. Social Research, 1950-51. Reporter Phila. Tribune, 1943-45; city editor Phila. Afro-Am. Newspaper, 1945-48; dir., partner Journalists Assos., Phila., 1948-55; pub. Pitts. Courier, 1955-64; press attache Am. embassy, Nairobi, Kenya, 1965-66; counselor embassy, Lagos, Nigeria, 1966-69; dep. asst. sec. state African affairs Dept. State, Washington, 1969-72, U.S. ambassador to United Republic of Tanzania, Dar Es Salaam, 1972-75, spl. asst. to asst. sec. state for African affairs, 1975-76, U.S. ambassador to Republic of Liberia, 1976-79, ambassador-at-large, 1979-81. Mem. subcommn. prevention discrimination and protection minorities UN, 1972-82; Mem., acting chmn. D.C. Bd. Higher Edn., 1972; sec. Pa. Commn. Civil Rights, 1957-60; Candidate U.S. House of Reps. 4th Congl. Dist., 1954. Mem. Nat. Newspaper Publishers Assn. (pres. 1958), Lincoln U. Alumni Assn. (exec. sec. 1952-55), Am. Fgn. Service Assn., Alpha Boule, Sigma Pi Phi, Kappa Alpha Psi. Home: Washington, D.C. Died May 9, 1982.

CARTWRIGHT, GEORGE EASTMAN, physician, educator; b. Lancaster, Wis., Dec. 1, 1917; s. Walter Clark and Vera (Eastman) C.; B.A., U. Wis., 1939; M.D., Johns Hopkins, 1943; m. Helene Cleare, Sept. 1, 1948; children—Jane Ann, Margaret Ann, Christine Ann, Candace Helene, Peter Edmund. Intern, Johns Hopkins, 1943-44, resident, 1944-45; research on internal medicine, Salt Lake City, 1947-80; prof., chmn. dept. medicine U. Utah Coll. Medicine, 1967-80. Served to capt., M.C., AUS, 1945-47. Author: Diagnostic Laboratory Hematology, 1968. Contbr. over 250 articles on hematology to med. jours. Home: Salt Lake City, Utah. Died Apr. 8, 1980.

CARUS, CLAYTON DOUGLAS, educator; b. Mich., Oct. 10, 1889; s. Charles Stuart and Harriet Elvira (Hunt) C.; A.B., Stanford, 1913, M.A., 1917; Ph.D., U. Va., 1930; m. Vallance Arnott, May 14, 1913. Instr. Wash. State Coll., 1919-21; asso. prof. U. So. Cal., 1921-29, prof. from 1930, chmn. dept. marketing, trade, transportation from 1930. Publ mem. 10th region War Labor Bd., 1942-45; chief fgn. country analyst Bur. Econ. Warfare, 1943. Mem. Pacific Coast Econs. Assn., Am. Assn. U. Profs., Delta Sigma Pi, Delta Phi Epsilon (nat. bd. govs.), Phi Kappa Phi, Beta Gamma Sigma. Author: Japan—Its Resources and Industries (with McNichols), 1944. Home: Los Angeles, Calif. †

CARVER, HARRY CLYDE, educator; b. Waterbury, Conn., Dec. 4, 1890; s. Harry Darwin and Anna Jane (Lewis) C.; B.S., U. Mich., 1915; m. Louise Baltzer, Sept. 2, 1929; children—Barbara Anne (dec.), Anne Louise. Instr. U. Mich., 1916-18, asst. prof., 1918-25, asso. prof., 1925-36, prof. math. from 1936. Served as operations analyst, U.S. 8th Air Force, Eng., 1944-45. Fellow Am. Statis. Assn., Inst. Math. Statistics and Czechoslovakian Statistical Soc. Author: Introduction to Mathematical Statistics, 1949; Air Navigation, 1943; Mathematical Statistical Tables, 1950. Founder and editor, 1930-1938, of Annals of Mathematical Statistics. Home: Ann Arbor, Mich. †

CARVER, KAUFFMAN LOWELL, banker; b. Los Angeles, May 10, 1888; s. Samuel Ashmead Wood and Stella (Winans) C.; A.B. Pomona Coll., 1912; m. Rosamond Reimers, May 1915; children—Muriel R. (Mrs. Jerome D. Barnum, Jr.), Jean M. (Mrs. Robert E. Bennett), Carleton Samuel. Joined Crescent Creamery Co., 1912, salesmgr., 1915-26, v.p., gen. mgr., 1922-26; dir. Seaboard Nat. Bank, 1922-36, pres., 1933-36; dir. Carver Investment Co., 1922-48, chmn. bd., treas., 1946-48; v.p., dir. Arden Farms Co. since 1926; v.p. Bank of Am. Nat. Trust & Savs. Assn., 1936-53, v.p., mgr. 7th and Olive St., office, Los Angeles, 1944-53, member adv. council bd. dirs., 1953 from; dir., v.p. Old Colony Paint & Chem. Co., 1951 from; dir. Pendleton Tool Industries, Inc., counselors Investment Fund, Inc., California Metal Enameling Company. Dir. Great Western Livestock Exhibit Assn., 1936-48; mem. bd. trustees San Marino City Sch. Dist., 1930-48, pres. bd., 1933-48; trustee K. L. Carver Educational Foundation. Member Los Angeles C. of C. (chmn. farm-city relations sub-committee 1955-57), Southern Cal. Cattlemen's Assn. (dir., treas., 1950-53), So. Cal. Hist. Soc. Clubs: California, Valley Hunt, Newport Harbor Yacht, Stock Exchange, Cinema (Los Angeles); San Marino (Cal.) City. Home: San Marino, Cal. †

CARVER, ROY JAMES, bus. exec., inventor; b. Preemption, Ill., Dec. 15, 1909; s. James and Laura (Risley) C.; B.S., U. Ill., 1934; m. Lucille Avis Young, Aug. 22, 1942; children—Charlotte, Roy James, Clayton Charles, John Alexander, Martin Gregory. With Ill. Dept. Pub. Rds., 1934-38; founder Carver Pump Co., 1938, Carver Foundry Products, 1954; founder, chmn. Bandag, Inc., Muscatine, Iowa, 1957-81; founder, pres. Carver Tropical Products, 1968-81; dir. First Nat. Bank of Rock Island. Bd. dirs. U. Iowa Found., Augustana Coll., Rock Island; mem. Muscatine Art Center; leadership mem. Boy Scouts Am. Recipient Horatio Alger award. Mem. Aircraft Owners and Pilots Assn., Nat. Aeros. Assn., Muscatine C. of C. Elk. Clubs: President's (U. Ia.); President's (U. Ill.); Geneva Golf and Country (Muscatine). Home: Muscatine, Iowa. Died June 16, 1981.

CARY, CHARLES A(USTIN), business exec.; b. Machias, Me., Mar. 14, 1890; s. George F. and Charlotte (Coleman) C.; student Washington Acad., 1902-06; A.B. magna cum laude, Bowdoin Coll., 1910, M.A. (hon.), 1950; S.B., Mass. Inst. Tech., 1912; m. Frances D. Campbell, Aug. 26, 1913; children—George F., Mary C. (Mrs. James C. Rea Jr.), Campbell. Mem. engring. dept. Electric Bond & Share Co., N.Y. City, 1912-17, asst. to chief engr., 1917-18; with E. I. du Pont de Nemours & Co., 1918-55, asst. mgr. nylon div., 1940-44, mgr., 1944-45, asst. gen. mgr. rayon dept., 1945-46, v.p., mem. exec. com., 1947-55, ret., 1955, dir., 1947 from; chmn. bd. Internat. Freighting Corp., 1948-55; dir. Del. Power & Light Co. Trustee Bowdoin Coll.; mem. bd., v.p. Wilmington YMCA; mem. internat. com. YMCA's U.S. and Can.; pres. United Community Fund No. Del., 1953-55; v.p., mem. bd. Welfare Council Del. Mem. United Community Funds and Councils Am. (bd. mem. 1957-60), Greater Wilmington Development Council (bd.), Internat. Missionary Council (chmn. N. Am. adv. com.), C. of C., Delta Kappa Epsilon. Republican. Presbyn. Clubs: Wilmington Country, Du Pont Country, University & Whist of Wilmington; Northeast Harbor (Me.) Fleet. Home: Wilmington, Del. †

CARY, JOSEPH BRACKENRIDGE, exec.; born Ft. Wayne, Ind., May 23, 1890; s. Harry Ellsworth and Edith Hannah (Brackenridge) C.; student St. Paul's Sch., Garden City, L.I., 1903-05, Pawling (N.Y.) Sch., 1907-09; Ph.B., Sheffield Sci. Sch., Yale, 1912; m. Margaret Ransom Porter Jan. 1, 1926; children—Joseph Brackenridge, Virginia Ransom (Mrs. Forrest A. Read, III). Apprentice Am. Steel Foundries, Chester, Pa., 1911-12; engr. and supt. Am. Malleables Co., Lancaster, N.Y., 1912-17; mgr. operations Air Reduction Co., N.Y. City, 1919-21; vice-pres. Am. Malleables Co., 1921-25; operating mgr. Beaver Products Co., Buffalo, N.Y., 1925-27; v.p. and gen. mgr. Niagara Sprayer & Chem. Co., Inc., mfr. insecticides, Middleport, N.Y., 1928-41, pres. from 1942; mem. bd. directors Food Machinery Corp., San Jose. Served as pvt. Signal Corps and 2d lt. A.S., U.S. Army, 1917-18. Republican. Presbyterian. Clubs: Saturn (Buffalo); San Jose Country, St. Claire. Home: San Jose, Calif. †

CARY, WILLIAM LUCIUS, lawyer, educator; b. Columbus, Ohio, Nov. 27, 1910; s. William Lincoln and Ellen (Taugher) C.; m. Katherine L.F. Cooper, 1954; children—Linn F.C., Katherine F.C. A.B., Yale, 1931, LL.B., 1934; M.B.A., Harvard, 1938; LL.D., Amherst, 1965. Bar: Ohio bar 1934, also Mass., D.C., N.Y., Ill. bars 1934. Atty. Squire, Sanders & Dempsey, Cleve., 1934-36, SEC, Washington, 1938-40; spl. asst. to atty. gen. tax div. Dept. Justice, Washington, 1940-42; counsel Office Coordinator of Inter-Am. Affairs, Brazil, 1942; lectr. finance, law Harvard Grad. Sch. Bus. Adminstrn., 1946-47; prof. law Northwestern U. Sch. Law, 1947-55; prof. law Columbia, 1955-83, Dwight prof. law, 1964-83; Vis. prof. U. Calif. at Berkeley, summer 1950, Stanford, summer

1954, Yale, 1957-58, 72, U. Paris I, 1976; dir. Newark Telephone Co., Ohio; counsel Patterson, Belknap, Webb & Tyler; chmn. SEC, 1961-64; mem. public oversight bd. Am. Inst. C.P.A.'s. Co-author: Effects of Taxation on Corporate Mergers, 1951, The Law and the Lore of Endowment Funds, 1969; Author: Politics and the Regulatory Agencies, 1967, Cases and Materials on Corporations, 1958, 69, 80. Served as maj. USMCR; with OSS, 1944-45, Rumania and Yugoslavia; dep. dept. counsellor Dept. Army, 1951-52. Mem. Am., N.Y. bar assns., Am. Law Inst., Am. Acad. Arts and Scis., Phi Beta Kappa. Presbyn. Clubs: Century (N.Y.); Met. (Washington). Died Feb. 7, 1983.

CASAGRANDE, ARTHUR, civil engr., educator; b. Haidenschaft, Austria, Aug. 28, 1902; came to U.S., 1926, naturalized, 1931; s. Angelo and Anna (Nussbaum) C.; m. Erna M. Maas, Nov. 9, 1940; children—Vivien Alice, Sandra Maas. Ing. (civil engr.), Tech. Univ. Vienna, 1924, Dr. techn., 1933, Dr.h.c., 1965; S.M. (hon.), Harvard, 1942; Dr. (hon.), Nat. U. Mexico, 1952; Dr. L.C., U. Liège, Belgium, 1975. Asst. hydraulics Tech. U., Vienna, 1924-26; research asst. U.S. Bur. Pub. Rds., Mass. Inst. Tech., 1926-32, lectr., Harvard, 1932-34, asst. prof., 1934-40, asso. prof., 1940-46, prof. soil mechanics and found. engring., 1946-73, Gordon McKay prof. emeritus, from 1973; cons. numerous fed., state, municipal and pvt. engring. orgns. on found. and earth dams in, U.S., Can., Latin Am., Europe, Near and Far Eastern Countries, Africa; cons. U.S. C.E., Panama Canal, Organizer 1st Internat. Conf. Soil Mechanics and Found. Engring., Cambridge, June 1936. Decorated Order Rio Branco Brazil; recipient Desmond Fitzgerald medal Boston Soc. Civil Engrs., 1936, Clemens Herschel prize, 1932, 51, structural sect. prize, 1947; Arthur M. Wellington prize ASCE, 1950; research prize, 1959; Karl Terzaghi award, 1963; Distinguished Civilian Service medal from sec. army, 1967; award merit Am. Inst. Cons. Engrs., 1973; Goethals medal Soc. Mil. Engrs., 1979; Casagrande Geotech. Bldg., CE Waterways Expt. Sta., Vicksburg, Miss., named in his honor, 1978; Rankine lectr. Instn. Civil Engrs., London, 1960. Fellow Geol. Soc. Am., AAAS; mem. Am. Acad. Arts and Scis., ASCE (hon., Terzaghi lectr. 1964, Edmund Friedman Profl. Recognition award 1968), Boston Soc. Civil Engrs. (hon. pres. 1957-58), Am. Soc. Engring. Edn., Transp. Research Bd., Am. Geophys. Union, Mexican Soil Mechanics Soc. (hon.), Soil Mechanics Soc. Venezuela (hon.), Japanese Soil Mechanics Soc. (hon.), Brazilian Assn. Soil Mechanics (hon.), Soc. Harvard Engrs. and Scientists, Internat. Soc. Soil Mechanics and Found. Engring. (pres. 1961-65), Nat. Acad. Engring., Nat. Acad. Exact, Physical and Natural Scis. Argentina (hon.), Sigma Xi. Home: Belmont, Mass. Died Sept. 6, 1981.

CASAGRANDE, JOSEPH BARTHOLOMEW, educator; b. Cin., Feb. 14, 1915; s. Louis Bartholomew and Alma (Hausske) C.; m. Mary Deveney, Aug. 15, 1945 (dec. July 1967); children—Louis Bartholomew, Mary Leonora, Laurie Jean, Katherine Alma; m. Mabel Stevenson Navarro, Sept. 23, 1969. B.A., U. Wis., 1938; B.A. Wis. scholar, 1938-39; Ph.D. (Univ. fellow 1940-41), Columbia, 1951. Instr. anthropology Queens Coll., summer 1949, U. Rochester, 1949-50; adj. asso. prof. Am. U., 1953-56; lectr. Fgn. Service Inst., 1956; prof. anthropology U. Ill., Urbana, 1960—, head dept. anthropology, 1960-67; dir. Center Internat. Comparative Studies, 1968-82; Exec. sec. 29th Internat. Congress Americanists, N.Y.C., 1949; field trips to, Comanche, Okla., 1940, Ojibwa, Wis., 1941, Navaho, Ariz., 1956, Ecuador, 1962, 63, 64, 65, 66-67, 68, 69, 70, 72; staff mem. Social Sci. Research Council, 1950-60, dir., 1961-63; mem. adv. panel in anthropology NSF, 1962-64, adv. com. for social scis., 1966; mem. behavioral scis. study section NIH, 1965-69; mem.-at-large div. behavioral scis. Nat. Acad. Scis.-NRC, 1969-71. Author: Comanche Linguistic Acculturation, 1955, also numerous articles.; Editor: In the Company of Man; Twenty Portraits by Anthropologists, 1960. Served to 1st lt. AUS, 1942-46. Recipient Demblzn. award Social Sci. Research Council, 1946-47, 48-49; Guggenheim fellow, 1966-67; NSF research grantee, 1966-67, 70-71. Fellow Am. Anthrop. Assn. (exec. bd. 1961-63, pres. 1972-73), AAAS, Royal Anthrop. Soc. Gt. Britain and Ireland; mem. Am. Ethnol. Soc. (past pres.), Soc. Applied Anthropology (regional v.p. 1960-61), Anthrop. Soc. Wash. (sec. 1953-56), Linguistic Soc. Am., Phi Beta Kappa. Home: Urbana, Ill. Died June 29, 1982.

CASE, ADELAIDE TEAGUE, religious education; b. St. Louis, Mo., Jan. 10, 1887; d. Charles Lyman and Lois Adelaide (Teague) C.; grad. Brearley Sch., N.Y. City, 1904; B.A., Bryn Mawr, 1908; M.A., Columbia, 1919, Ph.D., 1924. Teacher, St. Faith's Sch., Poughkeepsie, N.Y., 1908-09; librarian Ch. Missions House, New York, 1914-16; instr. religious edn., New York Training Sch. for Deaconesses, 1917-19; with Teachers Coll. (Columbia) as asst. in religious edn., 1919-20, instr. in edn., 1920-24, asst. prof., 1924-28, asso. prof. from 1928. Episcopalian. Clubs: Women's City, Bryn Mawr, Town Hall. Author: Liberal Christianity and Religious Education, 1924; As Modern Writers See Jesus, 1927. Home: New York, N.Y.†

CASE, ANNA, soprano singer; b. Clinton, N.J., Oct. 29, 1889; d. Peter Van Nuyse C.; ed. pub. schs., South Branch, N.J.; vocal training under Mme. Augusta O. Renard, N.Y. City; m. Clarence H. Mackay, July 18, 1931. Began as church singer at Plainfield, N.J.; debut as a Dutch boy in "Werther," with Met. Opera Co., New York, 1909, and mem. of Co., until 1917; roles include Sophia, in "Der Rosenkavalier," Olympia, in "Tales of Hoffman," Micaela, in "Carmen," etc.; has appeared on the concert stage in U.S., Europe and Can. Home: Roslyn, N.Y. †

CASE, CLIFFORD PHILIP, lawyer, former U.S. senator; b. Franklin Park, N.J., Apr. 16, 1904; s. Clifford Philip and Jeannette (Benedict) C.; m. Ruth M. Smith, July 13, 1928; children: Mary Jane (Mrs. William M. Weaver), Ann (Mrs. John C. Holt), Clifford Philip III. A.B., Rutgers U., 1925, LL.D., 1955; LL.B., Columbia U., 1928; LL.D., Middlebury Coll., 1956, Rollins Coll., 1957, Rider Coll., 1959, Bloomfield (N.J.) Coll., 1962, Columbia, 1967, Princeton, 1967, Upsala Coll., 1969, Yeshiva U., 1976, Fairleigh Dickinson U., 1979, Kean Coll., N.J., 1979, Ramapo Coll., 1979; D. Pub. Service, Seton Hall U., 1971. Asso. Simpson Thacher & Bartlett, N.Y.C., 1928-39, mem. firm, 1939-53; of counsel Curtis Mallet Prevost Colt & Mosle, N.Y.C. and Washington, from 1979; Washington counsel firm Shanley & Fisher, Newark, from 1981; Mem. Rahway (N.J.) Common Council, 1938-42; mem. N.J. House of Assembly, 1943, 44; mem. 79th-83d U.S. congresses from 6th N.J. Dist., resigned, 1953, U.S. Senator from, N.J., 1955-79; mem. coms. Fgn. Relations, Appropriations, select com. on Intelligence; mem. Tech. Assessment Bd.; U.S. del. UN Gen. Assembly, 1966; del. Republican Nat. Conv., 1956, 60, 68, leader N.J. del., 1976; vis. prof. polit. sci. Rutgers U., 1979. Chmn. bd. Freedom House, from 1979; Pres. Fund for the Republic, 1953-54; trustee Rutgers U., 1945-59; bd. dirs. Columbia Jour. Law and Social Problems. Recipient medal for excellence Columbia Law Sch. Alumni Assn., 1974. Mem. Assn. Bar City N.Y., Am., N.Y. State, N.Y. County, D.C. bar assns., Council Fgn. Relations, Phi Beta Kappa, Delta Upsilon, Phi Delta Phi. Republican. Presbyn. Clubs: Century Assn. (N.Y.C.); Essex (Newark); Federal City (Washington). Home: Washington, DC.

CASE, JOHN CROWTHER, former oil co. exec.; b. Rochester, N.Y., Jan. 29, 1892; s. Howard Brown and Elizabeth (Crowther) C.; m. Anne Taylor, Nov. 28, 1916; children—John H., Honor E. (Mrs. John P. Runyon). Student, Marlborough Coll., Eng., 1906-10, Institut Minerva, Zurich, Switzerland, 1911-12. Joined Vacuum Oil Co., 1912, asst. to mgr. producing dept., N.Y., 1920-25, mgr. producing operations, Europe, 1925-37; mgr. producing dept. Socony-Vacuum Oil Co., Inc., 1937, dir., 1943, v.p. dir. charge producing, 1946-57, ret., 1957; dir. Columbian Petroleum Co., Arabian Am. Oil Co. Chmn. bd. trustees Am. U. Beirut, 1955-64; bd. dirs. Near East Coll. Assn.; Mem. Morris Twp. Sch. Bd., 1928-50. Served as 1st lt., inf. 78th Div. U.S. Army, World War I, 1918-19. Mem. Am. Geog. Soc., Pilgrims, Council Fgn. Relations, Arctic Inst. N.Am. (chmn. bd. govs. 1955). Clubs: Alpine (London); Am. Alpine (N.Y.C.) (past pres.), Adirondack Mountain Reserve-Ausable (N.Y.C.), Century Assn. (N.Y.C.); Alpine of Canada (Benff); Morristown; Akademischer Alpen (Zû rich). Home: Keene Valley, NY.

CASE, RICHARD WERBER, lawyer; b. Washington, Mar. 21, 1918; s. Ralph Hoyt and Erwin (Werber) C.; m. Elizabeth J. Carson, Sept. 30, 1943. A.B., U. Md., 1939, LL.B., 1942. Bar: Md. bar 1942. Practiced in, Balt.; ptnr. firm Smith, Somerville & Case (and predecessors), from 1958; dir. T. Rowe Price Prime Res. Fund, Inc., T. Rowe Price New Income Fund, Inc., T. Rowe Price Tax-Free Income Fund Inc., T. Rowe Price Tax-Exempt Money Fund, Inc., T. Rowe Price U.S. Treasury Money Fund, Inc.; Spl. tax counsel County Commrs. of Baltimore County, 1951; chmn. Baltimore County Tax Survey Commn., 1958-59. Contbr. articles to profl. jours. Mem. Md. Bd. Edn., 1949-52; chmn. Md. Tax Survey Commn., 1949-51; asst. atty. gen., Md., 1947-49; chmn. com. rev. financing Md. Health Activities, 1954-55; mem. com. med. care Md. Planning Commn., 1956-63; chmn. Md. Savs. and Loan Study Commn., 1960-61; mem. Constl. Conv. Commn., chmn. com. state finance and taxation, 1965-67, conv. del., 1967; Trustee Peabody Inst. Balt., from 1953, chmn., from 1977; trustee Balt. Mus. Art, 1971-77; bd. dirs. Md. Sch. Blind, from 1956; bd. regents U. Md., 1960-75, vice chmn., 1970-75; trustee Johns Hopkins U., from 1975. Fellow Am., Md. bar founds.; mem. Am., Md., Balt. bar assns., Am. Law Inst., Order of Coif. Presbyn. Clubs: Maryland (Balt.), Hamilton Street (Balt.), Center (Balt.). Home: Sparks, MD.

CASEY, HUGH JOHN, army officer; Bklyn,. N.Y., July 24, 1898; s. John J. and Margaret (Miles) C.; student of civil engring., Brooklyn Polytech. Inst., 1914-15; B.S. (Distinguished Grad.), U.S. Mil. Acad., 1918; grad. Engrs. Sch., Civil Engring. Course, 1920, Company Officers Course, 1927; Dr. Engring., Technische Hochschule, Berlin, Germany (Freeman fellowship on hydraulic research), 1935; Dr. Engring. (honorary), New York University, 1955; m. Dorothy Ruth Miller, May 13, 1922; children—Patricia Adams, Hugh Boyd, Keith Miles. Commd. 2d lt., U.S. Army, 1918, advanced through grades to maj. gen., 1944; instr. Engineering School and company commander of the 219th Engineers, 1918-19; various engring. and instrnl. assignments, 1919-40; Chief Design and Engineering Section; Office Q.M. Gen., Washington, D.C., 1940-41; chief engr. U.S. Army Forces in Far East, Philippine Islands, Oct. 1941-Mar. 1942; chief engr. G.H.Q., S.W. Pacific Area, Australia, G.H.Q., 1942-44; comdg. Gen. Army Service Comd., 1944-45; chief engr. G.H.Q. Armed Forces in Pacific Area (Philippines and Tokyo), 1945-46; Far East Comd. (Tokyo), 1946-49, ret. 1949; exec. v.p. Pa. Hosp., Phila., 1950; 1st v.p. Melrose Distillers, Inc.; corporate sec., asst. to chmn. Schenley Industries, N.Y.C., from 1951; chmn. New York City Transit Authority, 1953-55; director Radiation Applications, Incorporated. Chairman lay advisory board Met. Hospital; member consultors group Manhattan College. Decorated D.S.C., D.S.M. with cluster, Silver Star, Legion of Merit, Bronze Star Medal, Distinguished Service Star with cluster, Presidential Unit Citations (4), Distinguished Marksman, Distinguished Pistol Shot (U.S.); Grand Officer Order of Orange and Nassau (Netherlands); Comdr. Order of British Empire. Officer, Legion of Honor (France). Fellow Am. Soc. C.E.; mem. Soc. Am. Mil. Engrs.; hon. mem. Instn. of Engrs., Australia, Philippine Assn. Civil Engrs., Philippine Assn. Elec. and Mech. Engrs., Permanent Internat. Assn. Navigation Congress. Clubs: Army and Navy, Army, Navy and Marine Corps Country (Washington); University (N.Y.). Contbr. Tech. jours. Home: New York, N.Y. Died Aug. 30, 1981.

CASEY, RALPH DROZ, prof. journalism; b. Aspen, Colo., May 8, 1890; s. James and Linda (Droz) C.; A.B.; U. of Wash., 1913, also A.M.; Ph.D., U. of Wis., 1929; m. Lois Elda Osborne, May 26, 1921. Began as reporter Seattle Post-Intelligencer, 1913, later political reporter and then asst. city editor; asst. prof. of journalism, State U. of Mont., 1916-19, U. of Wash., 1919-20; gen. assignment reporter New York Herald, 1920-21; rewrite desk, Seattle Post-Intelligencer, 1922, then publicity department of Seattle Chamber Commerce; asso. prof. journalism, University of Oregon, 1922-27, prof., 1929-30; asst. in journalism, University of Wisconsin, 1927-28; fellow in political science, same univ., 1928-29; prof. journalism and dir. School of Journalism, University of Minnesota, 1930-58, dir. emeritus, from 1958; vis. prof. in Journalism, Stanford, 1958, U. Cal. at Berkeley, 1959. Cons. O.W.I., 1942, and Bureau of the Budget, 1942-43. Mem. Heywood Brown Award Committee, 1957; member of the committee on pressure groups and propaganda, Social Science Research Council, 1930-34. Member board of judges, N. W. Ayer Newspaper Typography Contest, 1933. Awarded Guggenheim fellowship, 1937-38. Received 1946 nat. awards of Sigma Delta Chi and Kappa Tau Alpha for research in journalism; Distinguished Service Citation in Journalism, U. Wis., 1958; Eric W. Allen Meml. Lectr., U. Ore., 1958. Mem. Commn. on Tech. Needs of Press, Radio and Film, UNESCO, 1948. Mem. Am. Assn. Schs. and Depts. of Journalism (pres. 1957), Assn. Tchrs. Journalism, Am. Polit. Sci. Assn. (dir. seminar on pub. affairs reporting 1957), Am. Soc. Newspaper Editors (distinguished service mem.), Nat. Conf. Editorial Writers, Internat. Press Inst. (asso.), Beta Theta Pi, Alpha Delta Sigma, Sigma Delta Chi, Phi Beta Kappa. Author: (with Glenn C. Quiett) Principles of Publicity, 1926. Editor: Propaganda and Promotional Activities—An Annotated Bibliography (with H.D. Lasswell and B. L. Smith), 1935; revised edition, same editors, Propaganda, Communication and Public Opinion, 1946; (with others) Essays, Verse and Letters of J. M. Johanson, 1920; (with Frank Luther Mott) Interpretations of Journalism, 1937. Asso. editor Pacific Review, 1920-22; on staff American Boy mag., summer 1926; editor Journalism Quarterly, 1935-45, editorial bd. since 1945. Home: Minneapolis MN.†

CASEY, RALPH EDWARD, lawyer; b. Boston, May 25, 1911. A.B., Harvard U. 1932, LL.B., 1935; LL.M., Georgetown U., 1941. Bar: Mass. bar 1935. Pvt. practice law, Boston, 1935-39; with GAO, Washington, 1939-55, assoc. gen. counsel charge contracts, litigation and maritime activities, 1948-55; counsel Hardy Com. on U.S. Govt. Ops., 1950-52; chief counsel Mcht. Marine and Fisheries Com., 1955-56; pres. Am. Mcht. Marine Inst., Inc., 1956-68; exec. v.p. Am. Inst. Mcht. Shipping, 1969-70; spl. counsel Mcht. Marine and Fisheries Com., 1970-71, chief counsel, 1971-72; mem. firm Haight, Gardner, Poor & Havens, Washington.; Vice pres. Internat. Shipping Fedn., London, Eng., 1965-68; vice chmn. bd., chmn. exec. com. Nat. Com. Internat. Trade Documentation, 1967-70. Address: Washington, D.C. Dec. Feb. 23, 1982.

CASEY, RICHARD GARDINER, Australian diplomat; b. Brisbane, Queensland, Australia, Aug. 29, 1890; s. Richard Gardiner and Evelyn Jane (Harris) C.; B.A., Trinity Coll., Cambridge, 1913; m. Ethel Marian Sumner Ryan, June 24, 1926; children—Jane Alice Camilla, Richard Charles Donn. Began as engr., 1913; liaison officer between Australian Govt. and foreign office, 1924-31; mem. Ho. of Rep. for Corio, 1931-40; asst. Federal treas., 1933-35; treas., 1935-39, minister in charge of development, 1937-39, minister for supply and development, 1939-40; Australian minister to U.S. from 1940; appointed Privy Councillor, 1939. Served in World War, 1914-18 (metioned in despatches). Decorated Distinguished Service Order, Military Cross. Mem. Australian del. to Coronation and Imperial Conf., 1937; rep. Australia at London Conf. on Conduct of War, Nov. 1939. Clubs: Oxford, Cambridge (London); Melbourne (Melbourne). Home: Berwick, Victoria, Australia.†

CASPER, HENRY WEBER, educator; b. Milwaukee, Aug. 3, 1900; s. John Bernard and Eleanor (Weber) C.; student St. Stanislaus Sem., 1927-31; A.B., St. Louis U., 1932, A.M., 1935; S.T.L., St. Marys Coll., 1941; Ph.D., Catholic U. of Am., 1947. Entered Soc. of Jesus, 1927;

ordained priest, 1940. Instr. Regis Coll., Denver, 1935-37; with Creighton U., Omaha, Neb., from 1946, research prof. of history, dean grad. sch., 1947-58, asso. prof. history, 1958-62, professor of history, 1962-72; prof. history Marquette U., Milw., from 1972. Member Nebraska advisory committee to Federal Commn. on Civil Rights, 1958. Historian of Catholic Archdiocese of Omaha, 1954. Mem. Am. Hist. Soc., Catholic Hist. Soc., Omaha Com. Fgn. Relations, Jesuit Ednl. Soc., Neb. Greater Omaha hist. socs. Conf. Christians and Jews, Pi Gamma Mu, Alpha Sigma Nu (national faculty rep. 1954—). Republican. Author: American Attitudes toward Rise of Napoleon III, 1947; The Church on the Northern Plains, 1838-1874, 1960. Home: Saint Paul, Minn.

CASSARD, PAUL, naval officer; b. Prince Frederick, Md., July 30, 1890; s. William Gilbert and Edith (Dowell) C.; graduate, U.S. Naval Acad., 1913; m. Minna Dessez, Aug. 15, 1925, 1 dau., Karen. Commd. ensign, 1913, advanced through grades to capt., 1941; served on U.S.S. Wyo. in occupation of Vera Cruz, Mexico, 1914, on destroyer operating out of Queenstown, Ireland, World War I; became naval aviator, 1920; mem. U.S. Naval Mission, Brazil, 1926-29; Office of Naval Intelligence, Eastern Sea Frontier, Hdqrs., N.Y., World War II; mem. Navy's Bd. of Review, Discharges and Dismissals, from 1945, pres., from 1947. Episcopalian. Clubs: New York Yacht; Army and Navy Army Navy Country (Washington, D.C.). Home: Washington, D.C. †

CASSAT, DAVID BERRYHILL, corp. exec., religious assn. ofcl.; b. Vail, Iowa, Jan. 25, 1894; s. David Williams and Lillian (Berryhill) C.; A.B., Parsons Coll., 1916, LL.D., 1955; m. Ruth Boleyn Lyon, Apr. 20, 1922; children—George Lyon, Jean Boleyn (Mrs. Earl S. Christman, Jr.). With Interstate Finance Corp., Dubuque, Iowa, 1925-67, pres., 1935-61, chmn., 1961-67; chmn. bd., dir. Sunrise Golf Devel. Corp., Ft. Lauderdale, Fla., Pub. Utilities Corp., Uniflow Gas Corp. (both Sunrise Golf Village, Fla.); past pres., dir. Presbyn. Life, Inc., Phila.; dir. Am. Trust & Savs. Bank, Dubuque; hon. dir. Am. Finance System, Inc., Wilmington, Del. Mem. City Council Sunrise Golf Village, 1961-67. Voting del. World Council Chs., Evanston Assembly, 1954; treas., mem. exec. com., mem. gen. bd., 1957-69, mem. finance and bus. com., investment com., donor support com. Nat. Council Chs. U.S.A.; mem. planning and function com. Iowa Council Chs., 1968-82. Past pres. Dubuque Community Chest; chmn. Ia. Study Com. on Higher Edn., 1957-61; mem. Iowa Coordinating Council on Edn. Beyond High Sch., 1967-82. Life bd. dirs. U. Dubuque. Served as 2d lt., inf. U.S. Army, World War I. Mem. Am. Finance Conf. (pres. 1936-37, past chmn. exec., pub relations cons.), Am. Indsl. Bankers Assn. (life hon. dir., life hon. mem. exec. com), Nat. Council Presbyn. Men (pres. 1954-55). Presbyn. (mem. bd. missions 1947-53). Rotarian (past pres. Dubuque). Home: Fort Lauderdale, Fla. Died Apr. 3, 1982; buried Linwood Cemetery, Dubuque, Iowa.

CASSIDY, JOHN EDWARD A., lawyer; b. Ottawa, Ill., Jan. 31, 1896; s. Andrew Douglas and Margaret Lucile (Fox) C.; LL.B., U. of Notre Dame, 1917; m. Susan Marie Casey, Aug. 11, 1923 (dec.); children—John Edward, James A. (dec.), Susanne Isabella, Colleen Margaret, Marilyn Frances, Thomas Vincent, Owen David, Douglas Joseph and Diane Marie (twins). Admitted to Ill. bar, 1917; gen. practice after 1921; mem. Cassidy, Cassidy, Quinn & Lindholm; atty. gen. Ill., 1938-41; dir. Peoria-Jour. Star, Inc., Sheridan Bank: Commissioner of the Illinois State Welfare Dept. Del. Dem. nat. convs., 1932-36, 40, 56. Mem. Ill. Conf. repealing 18th Amendment, 1933. Lt. inf., 101st Machine Gun Batt., A.E.F., World War. Decorated Order Purple Heart (U.S. Army). Illinois gov., Notre Dame Foundation; mem. Citizens Com., U. of Ill.; mem. advisory com., Labor and Indsl. Relations, U. Ill., mem. law council U. Notre Dame, Mem. Am. Bar Assn. (com. on coordination of law enforcement agencies; Criminal Law Sect.), Ill. State Bar Assn. (bd. of govs.), Peoria Bar Association (president), Am. Coll. Trial Lawyers, Peoria Assn. of Commerce (dir. and pres.), U. of Notre Dame Alumni Assn., Am. Legion; national councillor; dir. Ill. Chamber of Commerce. Democrat. Catholic. K.C. Clubs: Creve Coeur, Peoria Country; Union League (Chicago). Home: Peoria, Ill. Died Mar. 25, 1984.

CASSINGHAM, ROY B., business exec.; b. Gilman, Ill., Sept. 4, 1889; s. Ora W. and Elmira (Burns) C.; student Univ. of Ill.; m. Ada M. McKinney, Nov. 19, 1927 (dec.). President and director Internat. Cellucotton Products Co., Chicago; dir. Upper Avenue Bank, Chicago, Berkeley Mills, Inc., Balfour, N.C. Mem. Delta Tau Delta. Home: Chicago, Ill. †

CASTAÑEDA CASTRO, SALVADOR, pres. El Salvador; b. Cojutepeque, El Salvador, Aug. 6, 1888; grad. Escuela Politecnica Militar; m. Josefa Castro; several children. Entered Army of El Salvador, 1905, advancing the rank of brig. gen., 1929; dir. Escuela Politecnica Militar, 1931; minister of interior, 1931-34; Partido Unificacion candidate for president, 1944, elected pres., 1945. Mason. Address: San Salvador, El Salvador, Central America. Deceased.

CASTELHUN, DOROTHEA (MRS. W. K. BASSETT), author; b. Newburyport, Mass., Dec. 30, 1889; d. Karl and Elise (Brednich) C.; grad. high sch., Newburyport, 1907; student Radcliffe Coll., 1909-12; student Temple Business Sch., Washington, D.C., 1912; m. W. K. Bassett; 1 son, Oliver Castelhun Bassett. Was reading editor for Encyclopedia Britannica, New York, 1914-17; copy writer N. W. Ayer Adv. Agency, Phila., 1918-24; asso. editor Carmel Cymbal, Pacific Weekly. Author: Penelope's Problems, 1928; Penelope and the Golden Orchard, 1924; (with Daisy Bostick) Carmel at Work and Play, 1924; The House in the Golden Orchard, 1925; Penelope in California, 1926; Dene Avery's Legacy, 1930; Frills, 1931; also short stories in mags. Address: Carmel, Calif.†

CASTLE, GORDON BENJAMIN, educator; b. Portland, Ind., Aug. 10, 1906; s. Arthur D. and May (Brake) C.; A.B., Wabash Coll., 1928; A.M., U. Calif., 1930, Ph.D., 1934; m. Berta Boyd, May 17, 1931; children—Lynn, Margit. Biologist termite investigations com. U. Calif., 1928-31, teaching fellow, 1931-34; instr. U. Mont., 1934-36, asst. prof., 1936-38, asso. prof., 1938-39, prof., 1939-62, chmn. dept. zoology, 1938-48, dir. biol. sta., 1938-62, sr. acad. dean, dean Coll. Arts and Scis., 1949-52, dean Grad. Sch., 1952-57, acting pres., 1958-59; prof. zoology Ariz. State U., Tempe, 1962-76, prof. emeritus, 1976-83, chmn. dept., 1962-64, v.p., 1964-67. Mem. exec. bd. Campfire Girls, 1945-49. Mem. A.A.A.S., Am. Ecol. Soc., Am. Soc. Zoologists, Ariz. Acad. Scis. Democrat. Died Feb. 17, 1983.

CATE, BERT CLARENCE, educator; b. Wyoming, Wyo. Co., N.Y., Feb. 8, 1887; s. Clarence Thomas and Nora Marcia (Butler) C.; grad. Middlebury Acad., Wyoming, 1905; A.B., Williams Coll., 1909; m. Ruth Eliza Spencer, of Pennellville, N.Y., Aug. 15, 1912; children—Dorothy Jane, Margaret Butler, Louis Clarence, Barbara Ruth, William Ward. Teacher Cook Acad., Montour Falls, N.Y., since 1909, headmaster since 1918. Republican. Mason. Rotarian. Home: Montour Falls, N.Y.†

CATHARINE, ROBERT MACFARLAND, banking; b. Jersey City, N.J., Dec. 9, 1888; s. Theodore and Mary Anne (MacFarland) C.; ed. pub. schools of N.Y. City; m. Mildred Holliday, Nov. 6, 1913; children—Virginia (Mrs. John J. Mueller), Robert M. Bank clerk, Title Guarantee & Trust Co., 1905-22; asst. cashier, Bank of the Manhattan Co., Jamaica, 1923-28, vice pres. in charge uptown divs. (Bronx and Washington Heights), 1928-30; v.p. N.Y. Title & Mortgage, 1930-33; deputy administrator Fed. Housing Administration, Washington, D.C., 1934-36; comptroller and trustee of Dollar Savings Bank, N.Y.C., 1936-38, exec. v.p., 1938-41, pres., 1941-62, chmn. bd. trustees, 1957-62, chmn. exec. com., from 1962; trust adv. bd. Chase Manhattan Bank, N.Y.; dir. Md. Casualty Co., Balt. Mem. banking bd. State N.Y., 1947-56. Mem. Savs. Bank Assn. State N.Y. (p.p.) Nat. Assn. Mutual Savs. Banks (pres. 1952-53). Republican. Presbyn. Clubs: Union League (pres. 1954-55), The Links (N.Y.C.). Home: New York, N.Y. †

CATLEDGE, TURNER, newspaper man, author; born Ackerman, Mississippi, March 17, 1901; son Lee Johnson and Willie Anna (Turner) C.; grad. Phila. (Miss.) High Sch.; B.Sc., Miss. State Coll., 1922; Litt. D., Washington and Lee University; Doctor of Humane Letters, Southwestern at Memphis; LL.D. University of Kentucky; m. 2d Abby Izard, 1958; children (by previous marriage)—Mildred Lee, Ellen Douglas. Began as all-around man on Neshoba (Miss. Democrat. 1921; resident editor Tunica (Miss.) Times, 1922-23; mng. editor Tupelo (Miss.) Journal, 1923; reporter Memphis (Tenn.) Commercial Appeal, 1923-27, Baltimore (Maryland) Sun, 1927-29; city staff New York Times, N.Y. City, 1929, corr. Washington bur. 1930-36, chief Washington news corr., New York Times, 1936-41; chief corr. Chicago Sun, 1941-42, editor in chief, 1942-43; nat. correspondent New York Times, 1943-44, mng. editor, 1951-64, executive editor, 1964-70. Mem. Pulitzer Prizes Adv. Com. Mem. A.P. Mng. Editors Assn., Am. Press Inst. (adv. bd.), Am. Soc. Newspaper Editors (dir., pres. 1961), Sigma Delta Chi. Clubs: Nat. Press, Gridiron, Overseas Writers, Metropolitan (Washington); Dutch Treat, Overseas Press, Century, Players, Silurians, Creek (N.Y.); Boston (New Orleans). Author: (with Joseph W. Alsop, Jr.) The 168 Days, 1937. Contbr. articles to mag. Home: New York, N.Y. Died Apr. 27, 1983.

CAUDILL, WILLIAM WAYNE, architect, educator; b. Hobart, Okla., May 25, 1914; s. Walter H. and Josephine (Moores) C.; m. Edith Roselle Woodman, Feb. 5, 1940; children—Susan Kent, William Wayne. B.A., Okla. State U., 1937; M.Arch., Mass. Inst. Tech., 1939; LL.D., Eastern Mich. U., 1957. Founder firm Caudill Rowlett Scott (Architects), Houston, 1946; founder architecture div. Tex. Engring. Expt. Sta. Tex. A. and M. Coll., 1948, prof., 1950-61; Wm. Watkin prof. architecture, dir. Rice U. Sch. Architecture, 1961-71; vis. lectr. Princeton, Harvard, Cornell U., N.C. State Coll., Washington U. Author: Architecture By Team, Space for Teaching, Building for Learning, So You Want to Build a School. Served with C.E. AUS, also; Served with C.E. USNR, 1942-46. Fellow A.I.A. (chmn. nat. sch. com.). Methodist. Home: Houston, Tex. Died 1983.*

CAUGHRAN, B. HOWARD, lawyer; b. near Fayetteville, Tenn., Nov. 6, 1890; s. William Hamilton and Hazeltine (Ashby) C.; graduate student Morgan School, Fayetteville, Tennessee, 1909; Trinity Coll. (now Duke U.), 1911-12; LL.B., Cumberland U., 1916-17; m. Effie East, June 5, 1918; children—Joan (Mrs. Ray E. Miller), John Hamilton. School teacher, Kelso and Huntland, Tenn., 1909-10; Foreman Ark., 1912-15; ins. business, Fayetteville, Tenn., 1915-16; admitted to Tenn. bar, 1917, Ind., from 1920, practiced at Indpls.; asst. U.S. Attorney, So. Dist. Ind., 1933-40, U.S. Attorney, 1940-50; mem. Dowden, Denny, Caughran & Lowe. Pvt., U.S. Army, Fort Logan, Colo., 1917; hon. disch. as 2d lt., 1919. Mem. Am., Ind. State, and Indianapolis (pres. 1942) bar assns., Delta Sigma Phi, Sigma Delta Kappa (hon.). Democrat. Presbyn. Home: Indianapolis, Ind. †

CAULEY, FRANK WILLIAM, architect, lawyer; b. Chgo., Aug. 25, 1898; s. Frank F. and Margaret E. (Byrnes) C.; m. Rosalie Hill, Aug. 26, 1925 (dec. 1966); 1 son, Francis Hill; m. Sarah Smith, Aug. 2, 1966. B.S., Armour Inst. Tech., 1922; LL.B., Chgo. Kent Coll. Law, 1938; J.D. (hon.), Ill. Inst. Tech., 1970. Bar: Ill. bar 1956. Architect Victor C. Carlson Orgn. (hotels, stores and apts.), 1932-34, archtl. office, Evanston, Ill., 1924-41, from 46, practice in, Ill., N.C. and Wis.; pres., dir. Frank W. Cauley, Inc. (architects), from 1940, Waterford Corp. (real estate), from 1940, Delaware Investment Corp. (securities), Evanston, from 1946; asst. works mgr., also mdse. mgr. Victor Mfg. and Gasket Co., Chgo., 1941-45; pres. Ercom Corp. (contracts with Naval Research Lab.), Washington, 1945; Lectr. Northwestern U., 1962; Mem. Nat. Trust for Historic Preservation; chmn. Com. for Restoration Old Market House of Galena, Ill.; chmn. adv. com. on market house restoration State architect of Ill.; preservation officer historic bldgs., State of Ill. Works include numerous residences in classical revival style, Ill., Wis., Va., 1940-50; 1926 apt. bldg. designated Evanston Hist. Landmark. Mem. A.I.A. (preservation officer hist. bldgs. No. Ill. and Chgo.; del.), Nat. Soc. Archtl. Historians, Evanston, Chgo. hist. socs., Scarab (hon.). Republican. Club: University (Chgo.).

CAUTHEN, BAKER JAMES, clergyman; b. Huntsville, Tex., Dec. 20, 1909; s. James S. and Maude (Baker) C.; A.B., Stephen F. Austin Coll., Nacogdoches, Tex., 1929; M.A., Baylor U., 1930, D.D., 1945; Th.M., Southwestern Bapt. Theol. Sem., 1933, Th.D., 1936; m. Eloise Glass, May 20, 1934; children—Carolyn, Cauthen Mathews, Ralph. Ordained to ministry Bapt. Ch., 1927; pastor Poly. Bapt. Ch., Fort Worth, 1933-39; prof. missions Southwestern Bapt. Theol. Sem., Fort Worth, 1935-39; missionary Fgn. Mission Bd., So. Bapt. Conv., 1939-45, sec. for the Orient, 1945-53, exec. sec., 1954-79, exec. dir., to 1979; ret., 1979; tchr. missions Golden Gate Bapt. Theol. Sem., 1980-84. Home: Richmond, Va. Dec. Apr. 15, 1985. Interned Hollywood Cemetary, Richmond.

CAVERLY, RAYMOND N., ins. exec.; b. Minneapolis, Mar. 13, 1890; s. Amos and Ellen (Sexton) C.; A.B., Catholic U. of Am., 1910; LL.B., U. Minn., 1913; m. Rene Stacey, Sept. 5, 1916; 1 son, Robert J. Admitted to bar, 1913; mem. firm Caverly Diamond, Dwyer and Lawler, N.Y. City, from 1932; atty., Globe Indemnity Co., 1913-31; v.p., Fidelity and Casualty Co. from 1931, v.p., Continental Ins. Co., Fidelity Phoenix Fire Ins. Co., Niagara Fire Ins. Co., Am. Eagle Fire Ins. Co., from 1949; dir. Am. Eagle Fire Ins. Co. Mem. Internat. Assn. Ins. Counsel, Am., N.Y. State and N.Y. City bar assns. Mem. Friendly Sons of St. Patrick. Clubs: Baltusrol Golf (Springfield, N.J.); University, Lawyers, Casualty and Surety (N.Y. City). Home: South Orange, N.J. †

CAWLEY, FRANCIS RIGGS, association executive; b. Ottumwa, Iowa, May 13, 1911; s. Lawrence Edmund and Mabel Lee (Riggs) C.; m. Ruth Katheryn Nelson, Oct. 12, 1940; children—Mary Helen, Thomas Michael, Marjorie Anne. Ph.B. in B.A. magna cum laude, U. Notre Dame, 1933; J.D., Georgetown U., 1937; postgrad. in budget adminstrn, Am. U., 1936. Bar: D.C., Supreme Ct. bars. Clk. NRA, 1933-36; chief budget, purchase and travel sect. REA, 1936-37, budget officer, 1938-39, U.S. Housing Authority, 1939-40; chief budget and planning br. OPM, 1941; budget officer, chief mgmt. services br. WPB, 1942, budget officer, dir. div. budget adminstrn., 1943-45; budget officer, dir. office of budget and mgmt. Dept. Commerce, 1945-52; v.p. Mag. Pubs. Assn., 1952-63; exec. dir. Lithographers and Printers Nat. Assn., 1963-64, Label Mfrs. Assn., Inc., 1964-76; Washington rep. Agrl. Pubs. Assn. Acting budget officer ECA, 1948; former mem. faculty Syracuse, Georgetown, Fla. State univs. Recipient Outstanding Service award Fed. Govt.; Am. Assn. for Pub. Info. Edn. Research award. Fellow Soc. for Advancement Mgmt.; mem. Graphic Arts Assn. Execs. (life), Phi Alpha Delta. Democrat. Roman Catholic. Home: Falls Church, Va. Dec. Nov. 17, 1980.

CEFOLA, MICHAEL, educator, chemist; b. Barile, Italy, Oct. 22, 1908; came to U.S., 1919, naturalized, 1924; s. Arcangelo and Vincenza (Labella) C.; m. Alice Elizabeth Robertiello, Aug. 14, 1948; 1 child, Michael A. B.S., Coll. City N.Y., 1933; Ph.D., N.Y.U., 1941. Research asso. U. Chgo. Manhattan Project, 1942-44, Mass. Inst. Tech. Radiation Lab., 1944-45; microchemist Socony Vacuum Oil Co., N.Y.C., 1945-47; nuclear chemist G.E. Knolls Atomic Power Lab., Schenectady, N.Y., 1947-50; prof. chemistry Fordham U., 1950-83. Contbr. articles to profl. jours. Fellow N.Y. Acad. Scis.; mem. Am. Chem. Soc., Am. Microchem. Soc. (hon. past chmn.), New Eng. Assn. Chemistry Tchrs., Sigma Xi, Phi Lambda Upsilon. With Dr. G.T. Seaborg first isolated plutonium at U. Chgo.; patentee on purification of plutonium. Home: Scarsdale, N.Y. Died Feb. 12, 1983.

CELIO, ENRICO, Swiss diplomate; b. Ambri, Tessin, Switzerland, June 19, 1889; s. Emilio and Maria (Danzi) C.; ed. colls. at Balerna, Milan, Einsiedeln, and univs. of Florence and Milan; Docteur es Lettres and Licencié en Droit, U. of Fribourg; m. Elsy Grolimund, July 1920. Lawyer from 1931; editor Popolo e Liberté, 1915-19; mem. Grand Council, Tessin, Switzerland, 1917-32, presided 1932; Nat. Council, Berne, Switzerland, 1923-32; elected Fed. Councilor, 1941; pres. Swiss Confederation, 1942, 48; Swiss minister of transport (chief of dept. mails and rys.) 1941-50, minister of Switzerland in Italy since 1950. Mem. Société des Etudiantes Suisses. Mem. Swiss Conservative Party. Roman Catholic. Address: Rome, Italy. †

CERNY, ROBERT GEORGE, architect, educator; b. LaCrosse, Wis., June 11, 1908; s. George J. and Helen P. (Salverson) C.; B. Arch., U. Minn., 1932; M.Arch., Harvard, 1933; m. Vivian M. Boucher, Aug. 21, 1934; children—Robert Leon, Susan Mari. Asso. architect TVA, 1934-36; faculty architecture U. Minn.; partner Jones & Cerny, 1937-42, Thorshov & Cerny, architects, Mpls., 1942-60; pres. Cerny Assos., Inc., architects, engrs., planners, Mpls., 1960-85. Mem. Mpls. Inst. Arts, Walker Art Center, Downtown Council Mpls. (pres. 1966-67, dir.), NCCJ. Nelson Robinson, Jr. travelling fellow (Harvard) 1934. Fellow A.I.A. (pres. Mpls. chpt. 1964-65, mem. bldg. industry nat. com.); mem. C. of C., Minn. Soc. Architects, A.A.U.P., Am. Hosp. Assn., Soc. Am. Mil. Engrs., U. Minn. Alumni Assn. (dir.). Clubs: Harvard (Mpls.); Campus, Faculty and Alumni (U. Minn.); Minneapolis; Wayzata Country; Town and Country. Contbr. designs, bldgs. to archtl. mags. Home: Excelsior, Minn. Died Jan. 31, 1985.

CERVANTES, ALFONSE J., mayor; b. St. Louis, Aug. 27, 1920; ed. St. Louis U. Pres. Cervantes and Asos., gen. ins., St. Louis; mem. St. Louis City Council, 15th ward, 1949-63, pres. bd. aldermen, 1959-63; mayor St. Louis, 1965-73. Founder St. Louis Ambassadors domestic and fgn. trade promotion orgn. and sponsor cultural activities St. Louis; founder St. Louis Bus. Devel. Commn. Named Outstanding Man of Year, St. Louis Jr. C. of C., 1955, also Met. St. Louis C. of C.; recipient numerous citations human rights orgns. local, nat. Mem. Young Pres. Orgn. (past. nat. treas., nat. bd. dirs.). Democrat. Home: St. Louis, Mo. Died June 22, 1983.

CHAGALL, MARC, artist; born Vitebsk, Russia, July 7, 1887; student l'Académie de St. Petersburg. Ceramist, painter, illustrator, engraver, watercolorist; went to Paris, 1910; painter numerous pictures, including, Moi et le Village, 1910-14; exhibited in Berlin, 1914; designer costumes and decorations, also executed murals for Theatre Julif, Moscow, 1919; returned to Paris, 1929, and made engravings for Ames Mortes (Gogol), 1929; Fables de la Fontaine, 1930; also for the Bible (to be issued in 1956); visited U.S., 1941; designer costumes for ballets: Aleko (Tchaikovsky), The Firebird (Stravinsky); had retrospective exhbns. Mus. Modern Art (N.Y.C.), Art Inst. Chgo. (all 1946); retrospective exhbn. Musée d'Art Moderne, Paris, 1947; also exhbns. Tate Gallery (London), museums of Amsterdam, Israel, Turin, Zurich, Berne, Basle. Recipient Carnegie prize, 1939; Internat. prize for engraving Blennial at Venice, 1948. Member American Academy Arts and Letters (hon.). Author and illustrator: Ma Vie, 1931. Illustrator: Mille de une nuits; Contes de Bocace. Home: Vence, Alpes Maritimes, France. Died Mar. 28, 1985.

CHALON, JACK, anesthesiologist, educator; b. Cairo, July 7, 1920; came to U.S., 1965, naturalized, 1972; s. William and Helen (Hirsch) C.; m. Barbara Elizabeth Coombs, Oct. 22, 1948; children: Mary Coombs, Jonathan William. M.B., B.S., univs. London and Edinburgh, 1946. Diplomate: Am. Bd. Anesthesiology, Soc. Apothecaries of London. Intern Eastern Gen. Hosp., Edinburgh, 1946-47; resident surgery and anesthesiology Sinai Hosp., N.Y.C., 1965-67; instr. to asst. prof. Albert Einstein Coll. Medicine, Bronx, N.Y., 1968-74; assoc. prof. anesthesiology NYU Med. Ctr., 1974-78, prof., 1978-84, pvt. practice medicine, Aldershot, Eng., 1949-64; assoc. dir. anesthesiology, dir. lab. pulmonary cytology, chief of labs. NYU Med. Ctr.; cons. anesthesiologist Manhattan VA Hosp.; cons. to chief med. examiner N.Y.C. Assoc. editor: Survey of Anesthesiology; assoc. editor: Sphere; author: Humidification of Anesthetic Gases, 1981; contbr. articles to profl. jours. Served with M.C. Royal Army, 1947-49; Served with M.C. Territorial Army, 1950-58. Fellow Am. Coll. Anesthesiologists, Royal Soc. Medicine, N.Y. Acad. Medicine (chmn. anesthesiology and resuscitation sect. 1978-79), Am. Coll. Chest Physicians; mem. AMA, N.Y. Soc. Anesthesiologists, Am. Soc. Anesthesiologists, AAAS, Brit. Med. Assn., Pan Am. Med. Assn., Internat. Anesthesia Research Soc., Assn. Police Surgeons Gt. Britain, Internat. Acad. Cytology, N.Y. Acad. Scis. Home: Tarrytown, N.Y. Died June 19, 1984.

CHAMBERS, MELBER, lawyer; b. N.Y.C., July 20, 1901; s. Walter Albert and Evangeline (Bowers) C.; m. Katherine Audley Heigho, Aug. 4, 1933; children: Ann Audley Chambers Holloway, Robert Alan. A.B., Cornell U.; LL.B., Harvard U. Bar: N.Y. Formerly partner, now of counsel firm Sage, Gray, Todd & Sims, N.Y.C., 1926—; spl. master N.Y. Supreme Ct., 1978—; Dir. Jersey Central Power & Light Co., 1940-44, Am. Radio Co., 1948-71, Concel, Inc., 1965-72. Pres. Correctional Assn. N.Y., 1958-70; Trustee Goddard Coll., 1962-72. Home: New York NY Office: New York NY

CHAMBERS, RALPH HAMILTON, engineer; b. St. Joseph, Mo., Apr. 17, 1871; s. Robert Hamilton and Alice Cornell (Wheelock) C.; C.E., Rensselaer Polytechnic Inst., 1893; Dr. Engring., 1937; m. Corinne Martin Darling, May 27, 1896; children—Corinne Martin, Robert Hamilton. Asst. engr., Troy Water Commn., 1893-94; asst. engr., King Bridge Co., Cleveland, O., 1894-96, engr. and mgr. Boston office, 1896-99; mem. firm Chambers & Hone, cons. engrs., N.Y. City, 1900-10; asst. chief engr., The Foundation Co., constrn. engrs., N.Y. City, 1911, chief engr., 1911-14; also gen. mgr., 1914; v.p. and chief engr. Jarrett Chambers Co., engring. contractors, N.Y. City, 1915-26; cons. engr., 1926-29; v.p. The Foundation Co., 1929-38; cons. engr. 1938-40; v.p. and dir. The Foundation Co., 1940-43, cons. engr. since 1943. Mem. ASCE, Renssaelaer Soc. Engrs., Sigma Xi. Republican. Conglist. Clubs: Engineers, Century. Designer of plans or construction or both, of the difficult foundations for high buildings in N.Y. Home: New York, N.Y. †

CHANDLER, ALFRED WHITE, naval officer; b. Newport, R.I., June 17, 1890; s. John Whitehead and Mary (White) C.; student Wenonah (N.J.) Mil. Acad., 1911-12; D.D.S., Univ. of Pa., 1915; m. Ruth Hathaway Jenkins, Apr. 17, 1922; children—Ruth, Alfred, Janie. Commnd. lt. (j.g.), U.S. Navy, 1917, capt., 1940, rear adm., 1946. Sr. dental officer, naval sta., Virgin Islands, W.I., 1917-19, various shore stas., U.S., 1919-27, U.S.S. Saratoga, 1927-29; instr. U.S. naval dental sch., Washington, D.C., 1930-34; sr. dental officer, U.S.S. Relief, 1934-36, naval air sta., Pensacola, Fla., 1936-40, U.S. N.A., 1940-43, U.S. naval training sta. San Diego, Calif., 1943-44; dist. dental officer, 11th naval dist., 1944-45; inspector and chief dental div., Bureau of Medicine, U.S. Navy Dept., Washington, D.C., 1945-47. Mem. Sigma Nu. Protestant. Home: Chevy Chase, Md. †

CHANDLER, GEORGE, actor; b. Waukegan, Ill., June 30, 1898; s. George William and Abigail Mary (Beck) C.; B.S., U. Ill., 1922; m. Catherine Marie Ward, Jan. 15, 1936; children—George Gary, Ward Leslie, Michael Charles. Actor, Chatauqua, vaudeville, stock cos.; appeared numerous motion pictures, 1927-85, including The Virginian, Jessie James, Across the Wide Missouri, Island in the Sky, High and Mighty; performed as Uncle Petrie in Lassie TV series; TV role Ichabod and Me, CBS, guest star numerous TV shows. Pres. bd. trustees Screen Actors Guild Producers Pension and Welfare Plan, 1962; pres. permanent charities com. Motion Picture Industry, 1963; adv. bd. Motion Picture Museum. Served as 2d lt., F.A., 1918-19. Recipient Achievement award U. Ill., 1962. Mem. Screen Actors Guild (president 1960-63, first vice president from 1964-65), Delta Upsilon, Beta Gamma Sigma, Alpha Kappa Psi, Pierrots. Home: Studio City, Calif. Died June 12, 1985.

CHANDLER, LOREN ROSCOE, surgeon; b. Selma, Calif., Apr. 22, 1895; s. Wilbur Fiske and Edna Marie (Goble) C.; A.B., Stanford U., 1920, M.D., 1923; Sc.D. (hon.), Univ. Southern California, 1952; m. Elva Beal, Nov. 16, 1921; children—Craig Clayton, Loran. Surg. training Stanford U. Hosp., 1923-25; mem. dept. of surgery, Stanford U., from 1923; professor of surgery, 1938-60, professor emeritus, 1960-82; dean School of Medicine, 1933-53. Fellow A.C.S.; mem. Cal. Acad. Medicine (v.p. 1941, pres. 1942), Assn. Med. Colls. (v.p. 1937-38; pres. 1941-42), A.M.A., Pacific Coast Surg. Assn., (pres. 1954), Am. Surg. Association. Nu Sigma Nu, Zeta Psi. Dir. and v.p. Coll. of Physicians and Surgeons Sch. of Dentistry, San Francisco, 1937-54. Republican. Protestant. Club: Bohemian (San Francisco). Author articles profl. jours. Home: San Francisco, Calif. Died Oct. 16, 1982.

CHANDLER, PAUL GLADSTONE, coll. pres.; b. Princeton, Ky., Nov. 7, 1889; s. Joseph Stroud and Elizabeth Ann (Pillow) C.; A.B., Ky. Wesleyan Coll., Winchester, 1914; A.M., Columbia, 1920, Ph.D., 1930; m. Kathleen Hicks, Sept. 6, 1927; children—Elizabeth Ann (deceased), John Paul, Barbara Lee. Engaged as teacher in rural school and high school in Kentucky, 1908-11; principal Lindsay Wilson Training Sch., Columbia, Ky., 1914-17; head dept. edn., State Normal Coll., Kent, O., 1920-27, Teachers Coll., Millersville, Pa., 1927-37; pres. Clarion (Pa.) State Teachers Coll. from 1937. Mem. N.E.A., Kappa Delta Pi, Phi Delta Kappa, Phi Sigma Pi. Methodist. Mason (K.T., Shriner), Elk, Kiwanian. †

CHANDLER, THOMAS, utility exec.; b. Sault Ste. Marie, Mich., Aug. 31, 1887; s. William and Cata (Oren) C.; B.C.E., University of Mich., 1910; m. Ethol Anderson, June 22, 1915; children—William, Mary Ruth. Supt. Edison Sault Electric Co., 1910-17, v.p., 1917-21, pres., 1921-44. Served as capt. of engrs., U.S. Army, 1917-19. Republican. Episcopalian. Home: Sault Ste. Marie, Mich. †

CHAO, YUEN REN, educator; b. Tientsin, China, Nov. 3, 1892; s. Heng Nien and Lai Sun (Feng) C.; brought to U.S., 1910; A.B., Cornell, 1914; Ph. D., Harvard, 1918; Litt. D. (hon.), Princeton, 1946; LL.D., University of California at Berkeley, 1962; m. Buwei Yang, June 1, 1921; children—Rulan, Nova, Lensey, Bella. Instr. physics Cornell, 1919-20; instr. philosophy and Chinese Harvard, 1921-24, lectr., 1941-46; prof. Chinese Nat. Tsing Hua U., 1925-29; chief sect. linguistic Academia Sinica since 1929; vis. prof. U. Hawaii, 1938-39, Yale, 1939-41; prof. oriental langs. and linguistics U. Cal., 1947-52, Agassiz prof. Oriental langs. and lit., 1952-60, professor emeritus, 1960-82. Faculty Research lectr., 1967. Linguistics Soc. Am. chair Linguistic Inst., Univ. of Mich., 1967; China Foundation chair on linguistics Nat. Taiwan U., 1959; Fulbright research scholar Kyote U., 1959. Mem. com. on unification nat. lang., com. music edn. Chinese Ministry Edn.; cons. Bell Telephone Labs.; del. to UNESCO confs. Fellow Am. Acad. Arts and Scis.; mem. Academia Sinica. Sci. Soc. of China. Am. Anthrop. Assn., Am. Oriental Society (president 1960), Philosophy Science Soc., History Sci. Soc., Linguistic Soc. Am. (pres. 1945), Comité International Permanent de Linguistics, Acoustical Soc. Am., A.A.A.S. Author: New Book of Rhymes, 1923; Studies in the Modern Wu Dialects, 1928; Phonetics of Yao Folksongs, 1929; Love Songs of the Sixth Dalai Lama (with Yu Dawchyuan), 1929; The Chunghsiang Dialect, 1939; Cantonese Primer, 1947; Concise Dictionary of Spoken Chinese (with L.S. Yang), 1947; Mandarin Primer, published 1948; Problems in Linguistics, published 1960; Language and Symbolic Systems, 1968; Grammar of Spoken Chinese, 1968; Readings in Sayable Chinese, 3 volumes, 1969. Composer: Songs of Contemporary Poems, 1928; Children's Festival Songs, 1934. Translations in Chinese and English. Contbr. to bulls., jours. and encys. Home: Berkeley, Calif. Died Feb. 24, 1982.

CHAPIN, F(RANCIS) STUART, sociologist; b. Brooklyn, N.Y., Feb. 3, 1888; s. Charles Brookes and Florence Adelaide (Johnson) C.; U. of Rochester, N.Y., 1905-08; B.S., Columbia, 1909, A.M. 1910, Ph.D., 1911; univ. fellow in sociology, 1910-11; m. Nellie Estelle Peck, Sept. 7, 1911 (died Nov. 29, 1925); children—Edward Barton, Francis Stuart, Florence Estelle; m. 2d, Eula Elizabeth Pickard, Feb. 19, 1927. Mem. faculties Wellesley Coll., Smith Coll., Univ. Minn., 1911-53; mem. editorial staffs various publs., from 1923; editor Harper's Social Science Series 1926-63; mem. adv. board Sociological Abstracts of N.Y., 1957-64. Cons. to Community Research Assos., from 1953, North Carolina Board of Higher Edn., from 1963; mem. com. hygiene of housing, Am. Pub. Health Assn., 1936-57; chmn. bd. commrs. Asheville Housing Authority, 1962-64. Recipient Alumni Medal, Columbia U., 1940. Pres. Consumer Behavior, Inc., 1952-62. Chrmn. seminar on exptl. methods 4th World Congress Sociology, Stresa, Italy, 1959. Fellow Am. Statis. Assn., A.A.A.S. (v.p. sect. K 1943), Am. Sociol. Soc. (pres. 1935), Royal Soc. Health (London), Sociol. Research Assn. (pres. 1936); mem. Acad. Certified Social Workers, Am. Assn. U. Profs. (chpt. pres. 1942-43), Nat. Assn. Social Workers (chpt. pres. 1932-33), American Council of Learned Societies (delegate 1939-42), Social Science Research Council. Clubs: Automobile, Campus, Asheville Civitan, Mountain City of Asheville (N.C.). Author books including: Experimental Designs in Sociological Research, 1947, rev. edit., 1955. Editor-in-chief Social Sci. Abstracts, 1928-32. Home: Asheville, N.C. †

CHAPIN, HARRY FORSTER, singer, songwriter; b. N.Y.C., Dec. 7, 1942; s. James Forbes and Elspeth (Burke) C.; attended U.S. Air Force Acad.; student Cornell U., Ithaca, N.Y., 1960-64; Litt.D. (hon.), Adelphi U., 1978, Dowling Coll., 1979; m. Sandra Campbell Gaston, Nov. 28, 1968; children—Jaime, Jono, Jason, Jenny, Josh. Filmmaker, 1965-71; singer, songwriter, 1971-81; albums recorded include: Heads & Tails, 1972, Sniper & Other Love Songs, 1972, Short Stories, 1973, Verities & Balderdash, 1974, Portrait Gallery, 1975, Greatest Stories Live, 1976, Road to Kingdom Come, 1976, Dance Band on the Titanic, 1977; Living Room Suite, 1978, Legends of the Lost and Found, 1979, Sequel, 1980; composer book and lyrics for plays Night That Made America Famous, Zinger. Pres. Story Songs Inc. Hon. chmn. Suffolk County Hunger Hearings; trustee Performing Arts Found. of L.I., (N.Y.); founding trustee World Hunger Year; mem. President's Commn. on Internat., Domestic and World Hunger; bd. dirs. Eglevsky Ballet, 1979—, L.I. Bus. Assn., 1979—. Acad. award nominee for best feature documentary, Legendary Champions (1st prizes N.Y. and Atlanta film festivals), 1969; Grammy nominee for best new artist, 1972, for best male vocal performance, for Cats in the Cradle, 1975; recipient Rock Music award for pub. service, 1976, 77, Humanitarian award B'nai B'rith, 1977, L.I. Advertisers Man of Year award, 1977, Lone Eagle award L.I. Pub. Relations Soc.,

1978; named One of 10 Outstanding Young Men, U.S. Jaycees, 1977. Mem. Screen Guild, AFTRA, ASCAP, Nat. Assn. Rec. Arts, Sci., Am. Fedn. Musicians, Actors Equity. Author: Looking...Seeing, 1975. Composer for Make a Wish, Emmy award winning TV series for children, 1974. Address: Huntington, N.Y. Died July 16, 1981.

CHAPIN, JOHN REVERE, investment broker; b. Milton, Mass., July 8, 1888; s. Henry Bainbridge and Susan Torrey (Revere) C.; A.B. Harvard, 1910; m. Margaret DeFord, June 20, 1911; children—John Revere, Joan, Alice Anne, Susan R., Margaret DeFord, Henry DeFord. Sec., dir. United Mchts. & Mfrs., N.Y.C., from 1928; partner Kidder, Peabody Co., from 1941. Club: Somerset (Boston). Home: Brookline, Mass. †

CHAPIN, KATHERINE GARRISON, author; b. Waterford, Conn., Sept. 4, 1890; d. Lindley H. and Cornelia Garrison (Van Auken) Chapin; ed. private schs., N.Y. City; m. Francis Biddle, Apr. 27, 1918; 1 son, Edmund Randolph. Speaker on contemporary poetry, analysis of Am. poetry and on craft of poetry writing to schs. and colls.; fellow in Am. Letters of the Library of Congress from 1944. Democrat. Clubs: Cosmopolitan (N.Y.); Cosmopolitan, Art Alliance (Phila.). Wrote poems and ballads for choruses. Author books including: Plain Chant for America, 1942; Sojourner Truth (3 act play), 1948. Home: Washington, D.C. †

CHAPIN, VINTON, ambassador, service officer; b. Paris, France, Apr. 17, 1900 (parents U.S. citizens); s. Amory and Anna Marie (Dickinson) C.; grad. St. Marks' School, 1919; A.B., Harvard, 1923; m. Lilian Aldrich Winchester, Jan. 25, 1938; children by previous marriage—Richard, Charles Winchester, Gordon Winchester, Aldus. With Lee Higginson Co., investment bankers, Boston, 1923-26; fgn. service officer, 1927-61; vice consul. Prague, 1929, consul, 1930; London Naval Conference, 1930; sec. delegation to Internat. Tech. Cons. Com. on Radio Communication, Copenhagen, 1931; asst. to under-sec. state, 1931-35; divisional asst., 1935; 2d sec., Prague, 1936-38. London, 1938-40, Dublin, 1940. Am. Legation (later Embassy), Port-au-Prince, Haiti, 1941; 1st sec. Am. Embassy, Rio de Janeiro, Brazil, 1944, The Hague, Netherlands, 1946; counselor Am. Legation, Dublin, Ireland; 1947-49. Manila, Philippines, 1949-51; faculty Nat. War Coll., Washington, 1951-52; fgn. service insp., 1953; dep. assistant sec. gen. for polit. affairs NATO, Paris, 1952-55; counselor of embassy and minister Am. Embassy, Havana, 1955-57; ambassador to Luxembourg, 1957-60; with U.S. delegation UN Conf. for Internat. Orgn., San Francisco, Cal., 1945. Served with USMC, 1918-19. Clubs: Chevy Chase (Md.); Metropolitan (Washington). Home: Dublin, N.II. Died Sept. 15, 1982.

CHAPMAN, ALBERT K(INKADE), mfg. exec.; born Marysville, O., May 31, 1890; s. Charles S. and Anna T. (Kinkade) C.; A.B., Ohio State, 1912, A.M., 1913, LL.D., 1956; Ph.D., Princeton, 1916; Doctor Science, Clarkson Coll. Tech., 1965; m. Ercil Howard, Aug. 14, 1916; children—Ercil (Mrs. George Haywood Hawks, Jr.), Elizabeth (Mrs. Hiram G. Hanson). Engaged in physiol. optics research, Clark U., Worcester, Mass., 1916-17; with Eastman Kodak Co., Rochester, N.Y., 1919-66, v.p., asst. gen. mgr., 1941-43, v.p., gen. mgr., 1943-52, pres., 1952-60, vice chairman board of directors, 1960-62, chairman bd., 1962-66, chmn. exec. com., 1961-66, dir., 1943-66; v.p., dir. Eastman Gelatine Corp.; dir. Kodak Ltd., Canadian Kodak Co., Ltd.; adv. com. to bd. Lincoln-Rochester Trust Co. Member corp. Rochester Community Chest, Inc. Honorary hon. chmn. bd. trustees, hon. chmn. exec. com. bd. trustees, hon. vice chairman of the advisory council committee of Rochester Institute. Tech.; hon. trustee U. Rochester; trustee and member of the executive com. Geo. Eastman House, Inc.; bd. mgrs. Rochester Meml. Art Gallery, Eastman School of Music. Served as 1st lt., in sci. and research div., U.S. Signal Corps, later 1st lt. and capt. (development work on aerial photography), U.S. Army Air Service World War I; maj. in Army Ordnance Reserve 1924-27. Decorated Knight French Legion of Honor, 1955. Mem. Rochester Mus. Assn., Royal Society Arts, Ohio State U. Assn., Soc. Photog. Scientists and Engrs., Photographic Society of America, Princeton Graduate Alumni Assn., YMCA, Phi Beta Kappa, Sigma Xi. Republican. Presbyn. Mason. Clubs: Genesee Valley, Country, University, Rochester. Home: Rochester, N.Y. †

CHAPMAN, ALGER BALDWIN, lawyer; b. Hempstead, L.I., N.Y., Nov. 2, 1904; s. Hannibal Hamlin and Lotta Lulia (Proctor) C.; m. Elizabeth Ives, Aug. 20, 1929 (dec.); children—Alger, Carol, William (dec.), Hilda; m. Catherine C. Hubbard. A.B., Williams Coll., Williamstown, Mass., 1926; LL.B., Columbia, 1930; LL.D., Adelphi College, 1957, St. Lawrence U., 1964; D.Pub. Service, Brigham Young U., 1968. Bar: D.C. bar 1932, N.Y. bar 1940. Atty. legislative counsels' office U.S. Senate, 1930-32; mem. firm Donovan Bond & Alvord, Washington, 1932-34; partner firm Alvord & Alvord, 1934, partner in charge N.Y.C. office, 1939-45; commr. taxation and finance, pres. State Tax Commn., N.Y., 1945-48 (except 6 mos. in 1946); with Chapman & Bryson (and successor firm Chapman, Walsh and O'Connell), N.Y.C., 1948-59; partner successor firm Hawkins, Delafield & Wood, 1959-64; chmn. bd., chief exec. officer, pres. Beech-Nut Life Savers, Inc. (name changed to Squibb Corp. 1971), 1958-68, chmn. bd., 1968-75, also dir. dir. Adams Express Co. Life mem. bd. trustees Adelphi Coll., 1949-83, chmn. bd., 1949-57; trustee Edward John Noble Foundation, YMCA Greater N.Y.; trustee, past chmn. Tax Found.; past pres. Nat. Assn. Tax Adminstrn.; past trustee N.Y. State U., 1946, 50; Campaign mgr. Republican candidate for gov., N.Y., 1946, 50; state campaign mgr. Rep. candidate for pres., 1948, 52, 56; treas. N.Y. Rep. State Com., 1950-58. Mem. Am., N.Y. State bar assns. (Sigma Phi.). Clubs: Metropolitan (N.Y.C.); Ft. Orange (Albany, N.Y.); Nat. Press (Washington); Siwanoy Country (Bronxville, N.Y.); Nat. Golf Links Am. (Southampton, N.Y.). Home: Anagansett, N.Y. Died Nov. 3, 1983.

CHAPMAN, CLYDE RAYMOND, lawyer; b. Fairfield, Me., July 23, 1889; s. George Mansur and Laura Evelyn (Keene) C.; A.B., Bowdoin Coll., 1912; LL.B., Me. Law Sch., Bangor, 1917; m. Eva May Humphrey, Feb. 14, 1919; 1 son, Gordon. Admitted to Me. bar, 1918; clk. Me. Ho. of Rep., 1919-33; judge Belfast Municipal Ct., 1920-24, city solicitor, 1923-24; co. atty. Waldo County, 1925-33; atty. gen. of Me., 1933-37; in private practice. Mem. Am. Bar Assn., Me. Bar Assn., Nat. Assn. of Attorneys General (president, 1936-37), Zeta Psi, Phi Alpha Delta, Republican. Unitarian. Mason (32 deg., K.T., Shriner). Club: Lions. Home: Belfast, Maine. †

CHAPMAN, SYDNEY, mathematician, geophysicist; b. Eccles, Lancashire, Eng., Jan. 29, 1888; s. Joseph and Sarah Louisa (Gray) C.; B.Sc. in Engring., Manchester U., 1907, M.Sc., 1908, D.Sc., 1912; B.A. in Math., Cambridge U., 1911, M.A., 1914, Sc.D., 1958; M.A., Oxford U., 1946; Sc.D., U. Alaska, 1958, U. Mich., 1960, U. Colo., 1962, U. Paris, 1962, University of Exeter, 1963, U. Newcastle, 1965, U. Sheffield, 1967; Dr. Technology (honorary), Brunel Univ., 1968; m. Katharine Steinthal, Mar. 23, 1922; children—Cecil Hall, Robert Gray, Mary Milnes (Mrs. Ian McAlley), Richard Joseph Ernest. Chief asst. Royal Obs., Greenwich, 1910-14, 1916-18; lectr. math. Trinity Coll., Cambridge, Eng., 1914-19; prof. Manchester U., 1919-24, Imperial Coll. Sci. and Tech., London, 1924-46; prof. natural philosophy Oxford U. 1946-53; research asso. Cal. Inst. Tech., 1950-51; prof. geophysics U. Alaska, from 1951; research staff High Altitude Obs., Boulder, Colo., from 1955; sr. research scientist Inst. Sci., Tech., U. Mich., 1959-65. Pres. Spl. Commn. Internat. Geophys. Yr., 1953-59. Hon. fellow Trinity Coll., Cambridge, 1957, Queen's Coll., Oxford, Imperial Coll., London; recipient Antonio Feltrinelli internat. prize Academie Nazionale dei Lincei, Rome, 1956, Bowie medal Am. Geophys. Union, 1962, Symons Meml. Gold Medal Royal Meteorol. Soc., 1965, Hodgkins medal Smithsonian Instn., 1965. Fellow Royal Soc. London (Copley medal 1964); mem., past pres. London Math. Soc., Royal Meteorol. Soc., Royal Astron. Soc., London Phys. Soc., Internat. Union Geodesy and Geophysics, Internat. Assn. Meteorology, Internat. Assn. Terrestrial Magnetism and Electricity, fellow Am. Phys. Soc.; hon. mem. many learned socs. Author: Earth's Magnetism, 1936; (with T. G. Cowling) Mathematical Theory of Non-Uniform Gases, 1939; (with J. Bartels) Geomagnetism, 1940; IGY: Year of Discovery (Edison prize as best 1959 sci. book for youth), 1959; Solar Plasma, Geomagnetism and Aurora, 1964. Address: Boulder, Colo. †

CHAPPELL, ELLWOOD BLAKE, judge; b. Osmond, Neb., May 4, 1889; s. Will Henry and Pleasant May (Turner) C.; Ph.G., U. of Neb., 1912, LL.B., 1916, A.B., 1923; m. Myra May Stenner, April 10, 1918; children—True Louise, James Williams, Mary Jean. Admitted to Neb. bar, 1916, and since practiced in Lincoln; municipal judge, 1925-29; dist. judge, 3rd Judicial Dist. of Neb., 1929-43; asso. justice Supreme Court of Neb. since Jan. 7, 1943; lecturer, U. of Neb., 1925-45. Member Lincoln (past pres.), Neb. State (past pres.), and Am. bar associations, American Legion (past commander), 40 and 8, C. of C., Delta Chi, Delta Theta Phi. Republican. Protestant. Mason (32 deg., Scottish Rite, K.C.C.H.), Elk. Club: Zodiac. †

CHARANIS, PETER, educator; b. Lemnos, Greece, Aug. 15, 1908; s. George and Chresanthy (Stroumtsos) C.; m. Madeleine Schiltz, Aug. 5, 1939; children—Alexandra, Anthony. B.A., Rutgers U., 1931, LL.D. (hon.), 1980; Ph.D., U. Wis., 1935; postgrad., U. Brussels, Belgium, 1936-38; postgrad. hon, U. Thessalonica, 1972. Faculty Rutgers U., 1938-85, prof., 1949-63, Voorhees prof. history, 1963-76, emeritus, 1976-85, chmn. dept., 1964-66; Vis. prof. U. Wis., 1950-51; vis. scholar Harvard at Dumbarton Oaks, 1956-57, 78-79; former mem. bd. scholars Harvard at Dumbarton Oaks (Dumbarton Oaks Research Library); mem. Am. Nat. Com. Byzantine Studies, 1963-85; editorial staff Byzantinoslavica; former mem. com. Gennadeion, Am. Sch. Classical Studies, Athens. Author: monographs on history Byzantine Empire and medieval Near East; Editorial adv. bd.: monographs on history Greek-Roman and Byzantine Studies, 1956-68, The Greek Orthodox Theological Rev, Neo-Hellenika; cons. editor: monographs on history Comparative Studies in Society and History, 1958-73; gen. editor: monographs on history Rutgers Byzantine series. Trustee Holy Cross Greek Orthodox Theol. Sch. Guggenheim fellow, 1956-57; Decorated comdr. Royal Order of Phoenix Greece).; Recipient Distinguished Research award Adv. Bd. Research and Grad. Edn.; Lindback Found award for distinguished teaching. Mem. Soc. Macedonian Studies (hon.), Am. Hist. Assn., Acad. Athens (corr.), Medieval Acad. Am., Soc. Ch. History. Home: Highland Park, N.J. Died Mar. 23, 1985.

CHARLES, ERNEST, composer, tenor; b. Mpls., Nov. 21, 1895; s. William Bruno and Louise Augusta (Baker) Grosskopf; m. Mrs. Maurice Willard Ames, Sept. 1, 1940; 1 son (by 1st marriage), William Kenniston. Ed. pub. schs., Mpls.; studied harmony, U. So. Calif., summer, 1922. Pres. Ecco Music, Inc.; formerly asst. exec. sec. Am. Guild Musical Artists. Has appeared as tenor, Pro Musica Soc., San Francisco, recitals in, N.Y.C., Pitts., Los Angeles, Wichita, San Diego; Composer: choral God is Our Strength, Spring in Vienna; solo Nay, Do Not Weep; My Lady Walks in Loveliness. Nat. patron Delta Omicron Sorority, 1941; hon. mem. Phi Mu Alpha Sinfonia, nat. mus. frat., U. Nebr., 1941. Served with 1st Minn. F.A., 1916. Fellow Am. Inst. Fine Arts; mem. ASCAP. Republican. Episcopalian. Clubs: Los Angeles Country; Apollo (Mpls.) (hon.); Bohemians (New York). Home: Beverly Hills, Calif.

CHARNEY, JULE GREGORY, meteorologist, oceanographer; b. San Francisco, Jan. 1, 1917; s. Ely and Stella (Litman) C.; A.B., U. Calif. at Los Angeles, 1938, M.A., 1940, Ph.D., 1946; postgrad. (NRC fellow), U. Oslo, Norway, 1947-48; D.Sc. (hon.), U. Chgo., 1970; children—Nicolas, Nora, Peter. Instr., lectr. physics-meteorology U. Calif. at Los Angeles, 1942-46; research asso. U. Chgo., 1946-47; mem., dir. meteorology project Inst. Advanced Study, Princeton, N.J., 1948-56, long term mem., 1952-56; prof. meteorology Mass. Inst. Tech., 1956-81, Alfred P. Sloan prof., 1966-81, chmn. dept., 1974-77. Chmn. U.S. com. for Global Atmospheric Research Program, Nat. Acad. Sci., 1968-71. Recipient Robert M. Losey award Inst. Aero. Scis., 1957, Symons Meml. gold medal Royal Meteorol. Soc., 1961, Hodgkins medal Smithsonian Instn., 1968, Internat. Meteorol. Orgn. prize, 1971. Guggenheim fellow Cambridge (Eng.) U., also Weizmann Inst. Sci., Israel, 1972-73; Overseas fellow Churchill Coll., Cambridge U., 1972-81. Fellow Am. Geophys. Union (pres. meteorol. sect. 1970-81, Bowie medal 1976), Am. Meteorol. Soc. (Meisinger award 1949, Carl-Gustav Rossby medal 1964), World Meteorol. Orgn., Nat. Acad. Scis., Am. Acad. Arts and Scis., Royal Swedish (fgn. mem.), Norwegian acads. scis., Phi Beta Kappa. Author articles dynamic meteorology, oceanography. Died June 16, 1981.

CHASE, CHARLES HENRY, educator; b. Portland, Maine, Aug. 14, 1910; s. Frank Cushing and Lena Ernestine (Crocker) C.; m. Elizabeth Elois Cummings, Aug. 23, 1936; children—Astrid, Frank Charles. B.S., U.S. Mil. Acad., 1933; M.S., George Washington U., 1969; grad., Armed Forces Staff Coll., 1947, Army War Coll., 1951, Naval War Coll., 1953. Commd. 2d lt. U.S. Army, 1933, advanced through grades to maj. gen., 1961; served with (101st Airborne Div.), ETO, World War II, asst. div. comdr., 1956-57; chief staff (XVIII Airborne Corps), 1957-59; chief (Mil. Assistance Adv. Group), Cambodia, 1959-61; comdg. gen. (2d Inf. Div.), 1961-62; chief staff (U.S. Strike Command), 1962-64; dep. chief staff (Allied Forces Central Europe), 1964-66; chief staff U.S. Army, Europe, 1967-68; lectr. mgmt. sci. Fla. Inst. Tech., Melbourne. Decorated D.S.M., Silver Star, Legion Merit with oak leaf cluster, Bronze Star with 2 oak leaf clusters; decorated by France; decorated by Belgium; decorated by Holland; decorated by Republic of Korea. Mem. Assn. U.S. Army, 101st Airborne, 2d Inf., 25th Inf. div. assns. Home: Satellite Beach, Fla. Dec. Mar. 12, 1981.

CHASE, DANIEL, author; b. Newark, N.J., Jan. 31, 1890; s. Everett Almont and Lydia Lieta (Simpson) C.; B.S., Dartmouth, 1914; unmarried. Served as lt. Ordnance Dept., U.S.A, World War; attached to Air Service and R.A.F. Trustee Holliston Pub. Library. Mem. Sigma Nu. Mason. Author: Flood Tide, 1918; The Middle Passage, 1923; Hardy Rye, 1926; Pines of Jaalam, 1929; Backfire, 1931. Home: Holliston, Mass.†

CHASE, HAROLD WILLIAM, educator; b. Worcester, Mass., Feb. 6, 1922; s. Louis and Bessie (Lubin) C.; m. Bernice M. Fadden, July 3, 1944; children—Bryce Stephen, Eric Lewis. A.B., Princeton U., 1943, M.A., 1948, Ph.D., 1954. Asst. prof. polit. sci. U. Del., 1948-50; asst. prof. politics Princeton U., 1952-57; prof. polit. sci. U. Minn., 1957-77, 81-82, dep. asst. sec. def. for res. affairs, Washington, 1977-80; adv. editor Scribner's Pub. Co., 1960-73; vis. prof. Columbia U., 1963-64, Nat. War Coll., 1965-66, U. Chgo., 1966-67, U. Calif., San Diego, 1981. Author: (with Paul Dolan) The Case for Democratic Capitalism, 1964, Federal Judges: The Appointing Process of Federal Judges, 1972, (with Craig Ducat) Corwin's Constitution and What It Means Today, 1973, Constitutional Interpretation: Casebook in Constitutional Law, 1974. Chmn. Minn. Ethical Practices Bd., 1976-77. Served to maj. gen. USMC Res., 1942-46, 50-52, 68-69. Decorated Legion of Merit with oak leaf cluster, Purple Heart with oak leaf cluster; recipient Disting. Teaching award U. Minn., 1961. Mem. Am. Polit. Sci. Assn. Home: Minneapolis, Minn. Died Jan. 13, 1982.

CHASE, HARRIE BRIGHAM, judge; b. Whitingham, Vt., Aug. 9, 1889; s. Charles Sumner and Carrie Emily (Brigham) C.; prep. edn., high sch., Wilmington, Vt. and Phillips Exeter (N.H.) Acad.; student Dartmouth College, 1908-09, Boston University School Law, 1910-12; LL.D., Dartmouth College, 1939; m. Mina Annis Gilman, Mar. 7, 1912; children—Madeline Harriet, Alice Natalie, Dana

Charles. Admitted to Vt. bar, 1912, and began practice at Brattleboro; mem. firm Chase & Chase, 1912-19; state's atty., Windham County, Vt., Feb.-May 1919; judge, Superior Court, Vt., 1919-27, chief judge, 1926-27; asso. justice, Supreme Court, Vt., 1927-29; judge, United States Court of Appeals, 2nd Judicial Circuit, from Feb. 1, 1929. Trustee Brattleboro Retreat. Mem. Am. and Vt. State bar assns., Chi Phi, Phi Delta Phi. Republican. Universalist. Mason, Odd Fellow. Club: Dartmouth (New York). Home: Brattleboro, Vt. †

CHASE, JACKSON B(URTON), congressman; b. Seward, Neb., Aug. 19, 1890; s. Edward and Nellie (Ford) C.; student U. Neb., 1910-12; LL.B., U. Mich., 1913; m. Loretta Slater, Aug. 24, 1915. Admitted to Neb. bar, 1921, asst. atty. gen. Neb., 1921-22; practice of law, Omaha, 1923-42; chmn. Neb. Liquor Control Commn., 1945-46; judge 4th Jud. Dist. Neb., 1946-54; mem. 84th Congress, 2d Neb. Dist. Mem. Neb. State Legislature, 1933-44. Served with F.A., U.S. Army, 1919; maj. Judge Adv. Gen. Dept., AUS, 1942-45. Mem. Am. Bar. Assn., Omaha C. of C., Com. Fgn. Relations, Mich Alumni Assn., Phi Delta Phi, Chi Phi. Elk, Eagle, Mason (Shriner). Club: Kiwanis (dir. Omaha). Home: Omaha, Neb. †

CHASE, MARY COYLE, dramatist; b. Denver, Feb. 25, 1907; d. Frank Bernard and Mary (McDonough) Coyle; ed. pub. schs., Denver; student U. Denver, 1921-23, U. Colo., 1923-24; Litt.D., U. Denver, 1947; m. Robert Lamont Chase, June 7, 1928; children—Michael Lamont, Colin Robert, Barry Jerome. Began as newspaper reporter, 1924; reporter, Rocky Mountain News, Denver, 1928-31; free-lance corr. Internat. News Service and United Press, 1932-36; publicity dir., N.Y.A., Denver, 1941-42, Teamsters Union, 1942-44. Recipient William MacLeod Raine award Colo. Authors League, 1944. Pulitzer Drama Award for Play Harvey, 1944-45. Mem. Dramatist Guild. Author: (plays) Now You've Done It, 1937; Sorority House (produced as motion picture 1938); Too Much Business, 1938; Harvey, 1944; Next Half Hour; Mrs. McThing, 1952; Bernardine, 1952; Loretta Mason Potts, 1958; The Prize Play, 1961; Midgie Purvis, 1963; The Dog Sitters, 1963; Mickey, 1969; Cocktails with Mimi, 1973. Died Oct. 1981.*

CHASE, W(ILLARD) LINWOOD, educator; b. Island Falls, Me., May 14, 1897; s. Willard Orin and Ina Lizzie (Penney) C.; student Aroostook (Me.) State Normal Sch., 1914-16; A.B., U.Me., 1920, LL.D., 1955; A.M., Techers Coll., Columbia, 1927, Ph.D., 1935; married Ruth Hazel Spinney, Nov. 6, 1918; children—Ruth (Mrs. William L. Schubert), Robert, Priscilla (Mrs. Dennis L. Heindel), Elizabeth (now Mrs. William F. Read). Public school teacher Orono, Me., 1916-17, Old Town Me., 1917-18, Waltham, Mass., 1920-22; supt. of schs., Canton, Me., 1922-24, Boothbay Harbor, Me., 1924-25; teacher Horace Mann Sch., Teachers Coll., Columbia, 1925-28; asst. prof. of edn., Boston Univ., 1928-35; headmaster, Country Day Sch. for Boys, Newton, Mass., 1935-40; professor of education Boston University, 1940-53, 57-61, dean School of Education, 1953-57. Served as 2d lieutenant Q.M.C., 1918-19; organizer and moderator N.E. Jr. Town Meeting of the Air, 1943-45. Mem. N.E.A., Assn. for Supervision and Curriculum Development Nat. Soc. Study of Edn., Am. Ednl. Research Assn., Am. Unitarian Assn. (mem. bd. dirs., 1943-46), Nat. Council for Social Studies (pres. 1947), Jr. Town Meeting League (pres. 1946-47), Phi Delta Kappa, Phi Beta Kappa. Republican. Unitarian. Author books including: America in The World (with Marion Lansing and Allan Nevins), 1949; Leaders in Other Lands (with Jeanette Eaton and Allan Nevins), 1950; Pioneer children of America (with Caroline D. Emerson and Allan Nevins), 1950; Makers of the Americas (with Marion Lansing and Allan Nevins), 1951. Home: Hingham, Mass. Died July 18, 1983.

CHAUNCEY, CHARLES C., army officer; born Tex., Oct. 31, 1889; grad. Air Corps Tactical Sch., 1931, Command and Gen. Staff Sch., 1936; rated command pilot, combat observer, tech. observer. Began as private Aviation Sect., Oct. 1917; commd. 2d lt., May 1918, and advanced through the grades to brig. gen., Aug. 1942; became chief of staff, 3d Air Force, E.T.O., May 1942; chief of staff, Mediterranean Allied Air Forces, North Africa, Jan. 1944; apptd. dep. chief of air staff, Army Air Forces, Washington, D.C., June 1945. Address: Fort Myer, Va. †

CHAVANNES, ALBERT LYLE, electric utility exec.; b. Knoxville, Tenn., Dec. 19, 1897; s. Adrian Leon and May (Sharp) C.; m. Margaret Florence McCown, June 19, 1923; children—Adrian E., Dorothy W. (Mrs. John A. Flynn), Theodore E. B.S. in Elec. Engring, U. Tenn., 1918, grad. student, 1919-22; grad. student, U. Chgo., 1920; extension student bus. adminstrn., U. Calif., 1943. Prodn. engr. Westinghouse Electric Corp., 1919; instr. math. U. Tenn., 1919-22; instr. elec. engring. U. Ill., 1922-23; with So. Calif. Edison Co., Los Angeles, after 1923, gen. auditor, 1947-49, asst. treas., mgr. ins., 1949-59, sec., after 1959, Rea Investment Co., Los Angeles. Mem. Pacific Coast Electric Assn., Electric Club Los Angeles, Phi Gamma Delta, Phi Kappa Phi, Tau Beta Pi. Republican. Presbyn. Clubs: Mason (Los Angeles) (Shriner, K.T.), Breakfast (Los Angeles). Home: Glendale, Calif. Died Nov. 12, 1984.

CHAYEFSKY, PADDY, writer; b. N.Y.C., Jan. 29, 1923; s. Harry and Gussie (Stuchevsky) C.; B.S., Coll. City N.Y., 1943; m. Susan Sackler, Feb. 24, 1949; 1 son, Dan. Writer TV dramas, 1952-82; writer, asso. producer films Marty, 1955, Bachelor Party, 1957, The Goddess, 1958, Middle of the Night, 1959, The Americanization of Emily, 1964; writer-producer The Hospital, 1971, Network, 1975; Altered States, 1979; Broadway dramas, including: Middle of the Night, 1956, The Tenth Man, 1959, The Passion of Josef D., 1964, The Latent Heterosexual, 1968; writer, co-producer Broadway play Gideon, 1961-82; pres. Carnegie Prodns., 1957, S.P.D. Corp., 1959, Sudan Corp., 1956-82, Sidney Prodns., Inc., 1967-82, Simcha Prodns., 1971-82. Served in AUS, World War II. Decorated Purple Heart. Mem. Dramatists Guild, Screenwriters Guild Am., Writers Guild Am., Screen Actors Guild, AGVA. Author: (anthology) Television Plays by Paddy Chayefsky, 1955; The Goddess, 1958; Middle of the Night, 1958; The Tenth Man, 1960; Gideon, 1961; The Passion of Josef D., 1964; (play and book) The Latent Heterosexual, 1968: Altered States (novel), 1978. Address: New York, N.Y. Died Aug. 1, 1982.

CHEDSEY, WILLIAM REUEL, mining engr.; b. Boulder, Colo., Feb. 11, 1887; s. Nathan L. and Florence (Earhart) C.; grad. Manual Training Sch., Denver, Colo., 1904; E.M., Colo. Sch. of Mines, 1908; D.Eng. 1938; grad. courses in elec. and mech. engring., U. of Ida., 1908-10; m. Cora Belle Sapp, 1915 (dec.); children—William J. (dec.) George L., Frank E., Charles B.; m. 2d, Elizabeth Slattery Granger, May 9, 1949. Instr. surveying Colo. Sch. of Mines, 1906-08; director of Missouri School of Mines and Metallurgy, and director of Mo. State Mining Expt. Station, 1937-41; consulting mining engr., Golden, Colo., 1941-43; consultant, U.S. Navy, Washington, D.C., from 1943; state chief of training, Ohio War Manpower Commission, and research consultant on fuels, Ohio State Univ., Engring. Expt. Sta., 1944-46; prof. of mining engineering, U. Ill., from 1946; U.S. Govt. Engring. Education Mission to Japan, 1951; consulting practice and mine examinations in many states. Mem. Am. Inst. Mining and Metall. Engrs. (chmn. Edn. Div., 1940, 41); Mining and Metall. Society of Am.; Coal Mining Inst. America (pres. 1937), Engineers Council for Professional Development, American Mining Congress, Am. Soc. for Engring. Education (chmn., Mo. Sect. 1938), Tau Beta Pi, Phi Kappa Phi, Sigma Gamma Epsilon, Triangle, Alpha Phi Omega, Kappa Sigma, Protestant. Home: Champaign, Ill. †

CHEEVER, JOHN, writer; b. Quincy, Mass., May 27, 1912; s. Frederick L. and Mary D. (Liley) C.; m. Mary M. Winternitz, Mar. 22, 1941; children—Susan, Benjamin Hale, Federico. Student, Thayer Acad.; Litt.D. (hon.), Harvard U., 1978. Author: The Way Some People Live, 1942, The Enormous Radio, 1954, The Wapshot Chronicle, 1957 (Nat. Book award 1958), The Housebreaker of Shady Hill, 1959, Some People Places and Things That Will Not Appear in My Next Novel, 1961, The Wapshot Scandal, 1964, The Brigadier and the Golf Widow, 1964, Bullet Park, 1969, The World of Apples, 1973, Falconer, 1977, Collected Stories (Critics Circle award, McDowell medal 1979, Recipient Pulitzer prize 1979). Mem. Am. Acad. Arts and Letters (Howells medal for fiction 1965), Nat. Inst. Arts and Letters., Nat. Inst. Arts. Address: Ossining, N.Y. Died June 18, 1982; buried First Parish Cemetary, Norwell, Mass.*

CHENERY, CHARLES MORRIS, pres. N.Y. Water Service Corp.; b. Richmond, Va., Dec. 13, 1888; s. James Hollis and Ida Burnley (Taylor) C.; student pub. schools, Ashland, Va.; m. Marguerite Anchambault, June 29, 1918. Pres. and dir. N.Y. Water Service Corp. since April 1, 1937; pres., dir. Western N.Y. Water Co., Buffalo, N.Y. (Suburban), from 1937; pres. and dir. South Bay Consol. Water Co., Long Island, N.Y., from 1937; pres. and dir. Rochester (N.Y.) and Lake Ontario Water Service Corp. from 1937. Republican. Episcopalian (vestryman Christ's Ch., Pelham). Clubs: Pelham Country (Pelham Manor, N.Y.); Southern Soc. of New York. Home: Pelham Manor, N.Y. †

CHENEY, HOWARD L., architect; b. Chicago, Ill., Aug. 12, 1889; s. of Elmer Sprague and Ellen (Hayward) C.; B.S. U. of Ill., 1912; married. Cons. architect Pub Bldgs., Adminstrn. and Civil Aeronautics Authority. Served with 31st Div. U.S.A., 106th Engrs., World War Major U.S. Army Air Force, 1942-44; served overseas. Fellow AIA (pres. Chicago chapter, 1929-31); mem. Soc. Am. Mil. Engineers, Tau Beta Pi, Delta Kappa Epsilon. Mason (32 deg.). Clubs: University (Chicago), Cosmos (Washington). Home: Chicago, Ill.†

CHERNEV, IRVING, author; b. Priluki, Russia, Jan. 29, 1900; came to U.S., 1904; s. William and Molly (Budnitzky) C.; m. Selma Kulik, Mar. 13, 1927; 1 child, Mel. Ed., N.Y.C. Formerly with fine papers industry, the most recent co. being Marquardt & Co. Inc., N.Y.C., 1957-68, Tchr., lectr. on chess. Author: Curious Chess Facts, 1937, Chessboard Magic!, 1943, Winning Chess Traps, 1946, The Russians Play Chess, 1947, The Bright Side of Chess, 1948, The 1000 Best Short Games of Chess, 1955, Logical Chess Move by Move, 1957, Combinations: The Heart of Chess, 1960, Practical Chess Endings, 1961, The Most Instructive Games of Chess Ever Played, 1965, The Chess Companion, 1968, Wonders and Curiosities of Chess, 1974, The Golden Dozen: The Twelve Greatest Chess Players of All Time, 1976, Capablanca's Best Chess Endings, 1978, The Compleat Draughts Player, 1981; co-author: Chess Strategy and Tactics, 1933, An Invitation to Chess, 1945, Winning Chess, 1948, The Fireside Book of Chess, 1949. Clubs: Marshall Chess (N.Y.C.); Mechanics Chess (San Francisco). Chess Master. Address: San Francisco, Calif. Dec. Sept. 29, 1981.

CHERRINGTON, HOMER VIRGIL, educator; b. nr. Gallipolis, Ohio, Jan. 21, 1891; s. Lozier L. and Susan (Drummond) C.; A.B., Ohio U., 1914; A.M., U. Mich., 1921; A.M., Harvard, 1922, Ph.D., 1940; m. Maria Grover, Sept. 1, 1926 (dec. Jan. 1978). Tchr., Athens (Ohio) High Sch., 1914-16; asst. prof. English, Ohio U., 1917-18, asst. prof. English, econs., 1919-21, prof. econs., 1925-29, prof. fin., 1956-61, emeritus prof., 1961-82; prof. econs. Cornell Coll., Mt. Vernon, Iowa, 1922-25; prof. commerce State U. Iowa, 1929-47; vis. prof. Northwestern U., summer 1945, prof. fin., 1947-56, prof. emeritus, 1956-82; Cameron distinguished prof. bus. Trinity U., San Antonio, 1961-62; vis. prof. fin. Stanford, summers 1956-58, 60; lectr. mortgage banking seminars, Chgo.; ednl. cons. Mortgage Bankers Assn. Am., 1954-56, faculty Sch. Mortgage Banking, jointly with Northwestern U., 1954-59. Served as 2d lt. AUS, 1918. Recipient certificate of merit Ohio U. Alumni Assn., 1957. Mem. Am. Econ. Assn., Phi Beta Kappa, Delta Sigma Pi, Tau Kappa Alpha, Beta Gamma Sigma. Methodist. Author: The Investor and the Securities Act, 1942; Business Organization and Finance, 1948. Co-editor: Mortgage Banking, 1953. Home: Cleveland, Ohio. Died May 18, 1982.

CHESKIN, LOUIS, marketing and motivational research specialist; b. Kiev, Russia, Feb. 19, 1909; s. Joseph and Mary (Bugendler) C.; came to U.S., 1921, naturalized, 1921; M.A., Lewis Inst.-Ill. Inst. Tech., 1932; m. Vivian Martin, Aug. 14, 1948; 1 dau., Bonnie Lynn. Instr., Lewis Inst.; dir. arts div., exptl. projects on psychol. effect design and color Chgo. Bd. Edn., 1935-40; dir. Color Research Inst., Chgo., 1945-81; pres. Louis Cheskin Assos., Chgo., 1950-81. Pres., Greater Chgo. Adult Edn. Council, 1962-65. Mem. Midland Authors, Chgo. Assn. Commerce and Industry, Ill. C. of C., Am. Inst. Mgmt., Internat. Platform Assn., Am. Acad. Polit. and Social Sci. Unitarian. Clubs: Cliff Dwellers, Executives (Chgo.); Directors (London). Author 15 books, 1940-81, latest being The Cheskin System for Business Success, 1973. Contbr. articles to profl. publs. Home: Chicago, Ill. Died Oct. 10, 1981.

CHESLOCK, LOUIS, composer; b. London, Eng., Sept. 25, 1898; s. Jacob and Rebecca (Neumark) C.; to U.S., 1901, naturalized, 1913; certificate violin Peabody Conservatory Music, 1917, certificate harmony, 1919, Artist diploma, 1921; D. Musical Arts, Peabody Inst., 1964; m. Elise Brown Hanline, May 31, 1926; 1 son, Barry. Violinist, Balt. Symphony Orch., 1916-37, guest condr., 1928, 1944, 1950, asst. concert master, 1932-37; instr. violin Peabody Conservatory Music, 1916-70, instr. composition, counterpoint and orchestration, 1922-76, chmn. dept. theory, 1950-68. Premiere of opera The Jewel Merchants (play by James Branch Cabell) Balt., Feb. 26, 1940. Premier ballet Cinderella, Balt., 1946, enlarged version, 1958; premiere of string quartet Pan Am. Union, Washington, 1957; performances of orchestral prize works, Washington, 1935, San Diego, Cal., Rochester N.Y., 1936, Akron, O., 1942, Guatemala, 1950, Israel, 1955, P.I., 1955, Belgium, 1956, Puerto Rico, 1956, Chile, Argentina and Panama, 1961, Singapore and Bombay, 1967, Boston, 1970, Washington, 1971, Portugal, 1971, 73. Recipient Peabody alumni prize 1921, Chgo. Daily News prizes for compositions for piano, violin, violoncello and orchestra, 1923, 24; prize Nat. Composers' Clinic Contest for choral composition, 1942; hon. mention Chicago Theatre symphonic contest, 1923; hon. mention N.Y. Women's Symphony Orch. contest, 1938; elected to Balt. City Coll. Hall of Fame, 1960, numerous other awards. Wrote: Introductory Study on Violin Vibrato, 1931; Graded List of Violin Music, 1948; H.L. Mencken on Music, 1961. Composer of symphonic, operatic and ensemble works; also compositions for violin, piano, voice, etc. Home: Baltimore, Md. Died July 19, 1981.

CHEVALIER, ELIZABETH PICKETT, author; b. Chgo., Mar. 25, 1896; d. Montgomery and Alma (Osborne) Pickett; A.B., Wellesley Coll., 1918; Litt.D., Transylvania Coll., 1943, Occidental Coll., 1966; m. Stuart Chevalier, Oct. 17, 1936. Publicity dir. ARC Nursing Service, Washington, 1918-19; hist. research, writing, 1919-23; author, dir. scenics and short subjects Fox Studios, N.Y.C., 1923-24, Hollywood, Calif., 1925-28; scenarist, writer original stories Fox West Coast Studios, 1926-28; author, scenarist, asso. producer first Am. full length color motion picture Redskin, starring Richard Dix, released by Paramount, 1928. Mem. bd. incorporators Am. Nat. Red Cross, 1944-47 (dissolution), mem. nominating com. for 1947 Red Cross Nat. Conv., mem. adv. com. on orgn., 1946; mem.-at-large bd. govs., 1947-52, woman mem. bd. govs. com. nat. blood program, 1947-51; pub. adviser U.S. del. 15th World Health Assembly, UN; mem. Calif. Welfare Study Commn., 1961-63. Trustee Occidental Coll. and SW Mus.; Calif. dir. Robert E. Lee Meml. Found., 1954-65. Mem. Nat. Soc. Colonial Dames Am. (nat. chmn. patriotic services Com. 1954-56), P.E.N. Democrat. Presbyn. Clubs: Sulgrave (Washington); Cosmopolitan, Pen and Brush (N.Y.C.); Town (Pasadena, Calif.). Author: Official History of American Red Cross Nursing Service World War I; The American National Red Cross: Its Origin, Purposes and

Service, 1922; Redskin, 1928; (novel) Drivin' Woman, 1942. Home: Los Angeles, Calif. Died Jan. 3, 1984.

CHEVALIER, HAAKON MAURICE, author; b. Lakewood, N.J., Sept. 10, 1901; s. Emile and Therese (Roggen) C.; m. Ruth Bosley, 1922 (div. 1931); 1 son, Jacques Anatole; m. Barbara Lansburgh, 1931 (div. 1950); children—Suzanne Andrée, Haakon Lazarus; m. Carol Lansburgh, 1952; 1 dau., Karen Anne. Student, Stanford, 1918-20; A.B., U. Calif., 1923, A.M., 1925, Ph.D., 1929. Prof. French U. Calif., 1929-46. Author: Anatole France and His Time, 1932, For Us the Living, 1949, The Man Who Would be God, 1959, Oppenheimer: The Story of a Friendship, 1965, The Last Voyage of the Schooner Rosamond, 1970; Translator: Andre Malraux's Man's Fate, 1934, Days of Wrath, 1936, Louis Aragon's Bells of Basel, 1936, Louis Aragon's Residential Quarter, 1938, The Secret Life of Salvador Dali, 1942, Vladimir Pozner's The Edge of the Sword, 1942, First Harvest, 1943, Gontran de Poncins' Home is the Hunter, 1943; André Maurois' Seven Faces of Love, 1943, Salvador Dali's Hidden Faces, 1944, Joseph Kessel's Army of Shadows, 1944, Denis de Rougemont's Devil's Share, 1944, Vercors' Three Short Novels, 1947, Simon Gantillon's Vessel of Wrath, 1947, Salvador Dali's 50 Secrets of Magic Craftmanship, 1948, Salvador Dali: On Modern Art, 1957, Stendhal's A Roman Journey, 1957, René Grousset's Chinese Art and Culture, 1959, Michel Seuphor's The Sculpture of This Century, 1960, Aragon's Holy Week, 1961, Michel Seuphor's Abstract Painting, 1962, Henri Michaux's Light Through Darkness, 1962, Michel Seuphor's Abstract Painting in Flanders, 1963, Bob Claessen's and Jeanne Rousseau's Our Bruegel, 1969, Pierre Galante's André Malraux, 1971, Jerzy Szablowski's Flemish Tapestries, 1972; others.; Contbr. to various mags. Mem. P.E.N., Authors League Am., Assn. Internationale des Interprètes de Conférence, Assn. des Traducteurs Littéraires de France. French interpreter U.N. Conf., San Francisco, 1945, War Criminals Trials, Nurnberg, 1945-46, UN, Lake Success, N.Y., 1946 Home: Paris, France. Died July 11, 1985.

CHEW, NORMAN BRADFORD, truck mfg. co. exec.; b. San Francisco, Feb. 21, 1924; s. Walter Marcus and Gladys Eleanor (Pye) C.; B.M.E., Bradley U., 1949; postgrad. Advanced Mgmt. Program, Harvard U., 1966, Northwestern U. Inst. Internat. Mgmt., Burgenstock, Switzerland, 1978; m. Mary-Alice Rondthaler, Mar. 1946 (dec. June 1972); children—Bradford (dec.), Sherry, Mike, Geoffrey; m. Bettina Mae Gedrose, June 11, 1976; stepchildren—Steven Gedrose, Kenneth Gedrose, Christopher Gedrose, Andrew Gedrose. With Stone & Webster Engring. Co., 1949; engr. Freightliner Corp., Portland, Oreg., 1950-58, chief engr., 1958-66, v.p. and sr. v.p. engring., 1966-74, exec. v.p. ops., 1975-80, also dir.; pres. Consol. Metco, Portland, 1974-76, gen. mgr., 1974-75, also dir. Trustee, treas., chmn. fin. com. Oreg. Episcopal Schs.; bd. dirs. Portland Chamber Orch.; com. mem. Portland council Boy Scouts Am. Served with USN, 1942-46. Registered profl. engr., Oreg. Mem. Soc. Automotive Engrs. (dir.), Am. Mgmt. Assn., World Affairs Council. Republican. Clubs: Portland Rotary, Lake Oswego Sailing, Willamette Sailing, Multnomah Athletic. Contbr. articles to profl. jours. Patentee in truck and truck parts field. Home: Oswego, Oreg. Died Sept. 25, 1980.

CHEWNING, LEWIS GARLAND, ret. box co. exec.; b. Spotsylvania County, Va., Feb. 14, 1905; s. Lynn P. and Kate (Waller) C.; student Hampden-Sydney Coll., 1923-24, U. Richmond, 1924-25; LL.D., Hampden-Sydney Coll., 1968; m. Mary Beverly Chenery, June 14, 1928; 1 dau., Mary Beverly (Mrs. Frank Talbott III). Propr. Lewis G. Chewning, Inc., realtor, Richmond, 1934- 50; pres. Va. Folding Box Co., Inc., subsidiary W.Va. Pulp and Paper Co., 1950-70, ret., 1970, also dir.; hon. dir., exec. com. Life Ins. Co. Va.; dir., mem. exec. and trust coms. Va. Trust Co. Mem. Richmond Planning Commn., 1942-49, Va. Hosp. Bd., 1955-56; campaign gen. Richmond Area Community Chest, 1944; campaign chmn. Richmond chpt. A.R.C., 1945. Bd. trustees Hampden-Sydney Coll., 1947-84, chmn., 1958-69, chmn. finance com., 1969-84; finance com. Union Theol. Sem., Richmond, 1948-84; bd. trustees Richmond Meml. Hosp., 1950-84, Richmond chpt. A.R.C., 1960-84. Va. Found Ind. Colls., 1960-84; mem. bd. trustees, mem. exec. com. Richmond Corp; bd. dirs. Richmond Found., 1943-84. Mem. Va. (past dir.), Richmond (past pres.) chambers commerce, Soc. Colonial Wars Va., Omicron Delta 1946. Presbyn. (elder, trustee). Clubs: Commonwealth (past gov.), Country of Virginia (past gov.) (Richmond). Home: Richmond, Va. Died May 5, 1984.

CHICHESTER, HARVEY NELSON, ins. assn. exec.; b. Bklyn., Jan. 28, 1917; s. Harvey Nelson and Helen Frances (Wilshusen) C.; m. Mazie Louise Locke, Dec. 18, 1944; children—David N., A. Lance, Todd H., Glen C. Student, Bklyn. Coll., evenings 1937-42; LL.B., St. John's U., 1950. Bar: N.Y. bar 1951. With Chubb & Son, N.Y.C., 1934-42, 46; ins. coordinator War Assets Adminstrn., 1946-50; with AFIA Worldwide Ins., Wayne, N.J., 1950-81, gen. counsel, 1967-81, sec. bd., 1971-81; sec., dir. AFIA Worldwide Life Ins. Co., Del. Reins. Co. Chmn. cub scouts and instl. rep. Nassau County council Boy Scouts Am., 1954-60; Bd. dirs. Babe Ruth League Baldwin, Inc., 1959-67, Bapt. Children's Home L.I., Bklyn., from 1971; bd. mgrs. Bapt. Home Bklyn., from 1969. Served to 1st lt. inf. AUS, 1942-46, PTO. Decorated Purple Heart. Mem. Am. Fgn. Law Assn. (sec. 1971-72, dir. from 1973), Am. Bar Assn., N.Y. County Lawyers Assn., Am. Soc. Internat. Law. Home: Oak Ridge, NJ.

CHICKERING, ARTHUR MERTON, educator; b. North Danville, Vt., Mar. 23, 1887; s. Orville Elmore and Alice Elizabeth (Finley) C.; Ph.B., Yale, 1913; M.S., U. of Wis., 1916; Ph.D., U. of Mich., 1927; m. Mabel Adele Kehler, Feb. 13, 1909; children—Alice Pope (Mrs. Orville Crays), Orville Merton, Donald Hugh. Asst. and instr. biology, Beloit (Wis.) Coll., 1913-18; prof. biology, Albion (Mich.) Coll. since 1918, chmn. div. science and math., chmn. divisional council, 1932-56; asso. in arachnology, Mus. Comparative Zoology, Harvard, 1952 from. Mem. Mich. Bd. Examiners in Basic Sci., 1941-55. Researcher on gen. biol. of spiders; 7 seasons of field work on spiders, Central America, from 1928; research associate Museum of Comparative Zoology, Harvard, summers, 1934 from. John Simon Guggenheim Memorial fellow, 1957. Fellow A.A.A.S. (mem. council from 1936), Entomol. Society of America; mem. Am. Micros. Soc. (treas. 1925-52, pres. 1952-53), Mich. Acad. Science, Arts and Letters (pres. 1936; council from 1935), Soc. for Study of Evolution, Am. Soc. Zoologists, Soc. Systematic Zoologists, Chicago Acad. Sci. (hon. life mem.), Sigma Xi, Phi Beta Kappa, Am. Soc. for the Study of Human Genetics, Entomol. Soc. of Am., Am. Assn. of Univ. Profs. Independent Republican. Methodist. Author tech. papers pub. in profl. jours. Home: Albion, Mich. †

CHILDS, JOHN LAWRENCE, educator; b. Eau Claire, Wis., Jan. 11, 1889; s. John Nelson and Helen Janette (Smith) C.; A.B., U. of Wis., 1911; A.M., Columbia, 1924, Ph.D., 1931; m. Grace Mary Fowler, July 22, 1915. Graduate sec., U. of Wis., 1911-12, Intercollegiate Dept., Y.M.C.A., 1912-16; foreign sec. Internat. Com. Y.M.C.A., Pekin, China, 1916-27; with Teachers Coll., Columbia U., from 1928, prof. philosophy of edn. 1937-54, prof. edn. emeritus, from 1954; vis. prof. U. Mich., 1957-58, U. Ill., 1958-59, So. Ill. U., 1960-61; vis. prof. philosophy S. Ill. U., Carbondale, 1962-63, adj. prof., from 1964; lectr. U. of Wis., 1965. Vice chmn. Liberal Party, mem. Nat. Com. on Acad. Freedom, Am. Civil Liberties Union; mem., National Commission Am. Federation of Teachers on Educational Reconstruction; mem. A.F. of L. Postwar Com. Awarded Order of Abundant Harvest by Chinese Nat. govt. for famine relief work, 1921; Nicholas Murray Butler silver medal, 1951; Wm. H. Kilpatrick award, philosophy of education, 1956; Educational award Wayne State Univ., 1958; League for Indsl. Democracy award, 1959; award from the John Dewey Society, in 1965. Fellow A.A.A.S., Nat. Council Religion in Higher Education; mem. National Academy of Education; member of Am. Philos. Assn., Am. Polit. Sci. Assn., N.E.A., Am. Edn. Fellowship, Sigma Delta Chi, Phi Alpha Tau, Kappa Delta Pi, Delta Sigma Rho. Club: Nassau (Princeton, N.J.). Author books including: Education and the Philosophy of Experimentalism, 1931; The Educational Frontier with others), 1933; America, Russia and the Communist Party with George Counts), 1943; Education and Morals, 1950; American Pragmatism and Education, 1956; (with others) Education in the Age of Science, 1959. Home: Carbondale, Ill. †

CHILLSON, CHARLES WHITE, aerospace engineer; b. Los Angeles, Mar. 12, 1910; s. Charles Foster and Mary Boone (White) C.; m. Rosa Grey deWaard, Oct. 23, 1944. B.S., Stanford, 1931; postgrad., Cal. Inst. Tech., 1931-35. Design, test, controllable pitch propellers Green Assocs., Los Angeles, 1931-36; with propeller div. Curtiss Wright Corp., 1936-71, chief engr. in rocket dept., 1945-50; tech. dir. Curtiss Wright Corp. (Curtiss div. (formerly propeller div.)), 1963-71; on leave to assist tech. monitoring mil. satellite program U.S. Dept. Def., Inst. Def. Analysis, Advanced Research Projects Agy., Washington, 1959-60, aerospace cons. engr., 1971-84. Served as col. a/s Tech. Intelligence Corps USAAF, 1945. Fellow Am. Inst. Aeros. and Astronautics (nat. dir. Am. Rocket Soc. 1950-52, pres. 1952, dir. N.Y. sect. 1953-56, pres. 1955). Patentee propellers, multi-engine synchronizers, rocket engines, other aircraft components Home: Santa Barbara, Calif. Died Aug. 20, 1984.

CHISOLM, JAMES JULIAN, b. Winchester, Ky., Dec. 24, 1889; s. James Julius (D.D.) and Mary Virginia (Tweed) C.; A.B., Princeton, 1911; M.D., Johns Hopkins, 1915; m. Eva A. Frierson, Oct. 14, 1920; children—James Julian, Mary Frierson. Resident house officer, Johns Hopkins Hosp., 1915-16, asst. in laryngology, 1916-17, asst. resident surgeon, 1917-18, instr. in clin. laryngology, 1918-20, asso. in same from 1920. Commd. 1st lt., Med. R.C., 1918; mem. Md. Med. Advisory Bd., 1917-18; overseas duty, Med. Corps, U.S.A., 1918-19. Mem. A.M.A., Baltimore Med. Soc., Johns Hopkins Surg. Soc., Phi Beta Kappa. Democrat. Presbyn. Club: Clinical. Home: Baltimore, Md. †

CHOLLAR, ROBERT GANUN, found. exec.; b. Syracuse, N.Y., Feb. 10, 1914; s. Walter Edward and Estelle Augusta (GaNun) C.; m. Thelma Lucille Holt, Sept. 22, 1934; children—Charles Edward, Brian Holt, Richard Robert. Student, Dartmouth, 1931-32; B.A., Antioch Coll., 1933-34; D.Sc. (hon.), Ind. Inst. Tech., 1972. Joined Nat. Cash Register Co., Dayton, Ohio, 1933, analytical chemist, research chemist, head chem. research dept., dir. research, v.p. research, 1954-59, v.p. research and devel., 1959-64, v.p., group exec. research and devel., mfg., 1964-71; pres., chmn. bd. C.F. Kettering Found., Dayton, 1971-81, chmn., 1981-82; dir. Dayton Power & Light Co.; Past mem. tech. adv. com. Cox Coronary Heart Inst.; mem. exec. com. Dayton-Miami Valley Consortium, Engring. and Sci. Inst. Dayton. Nat. commn. coop. edn. Thomas Edison Found.; mem. tech. adv. bd. U.S. Dept. Commerce; mem. sci. adv. council Ohio Bd. Regents; council mem. Nat. Affairs Center for Television.; Bd. overseers Sloan-Kettering Inst. for Cancer Research; past trustee Greater Washington Edn. Communications Assn. Mem. Am. Chem. Soc., Indsl. Research Inst. (pres. 1960-61), Tau Beta Pi, Chi Phi. Clubs: Engineers' Dayton (past pres.), Moraine Country, Ohio Commodore; University (N.Y.C.). Patentee fields synthetic rubber, plastics, printing. Home: Dayton, Ohio. Died 1982.

CHOW, VEN TE, educator, engring. cons.; b. Hangchow, China, Aug. 14, 1919; s. Chung Tan and Chin Yu (Young) C.; came to U.S., 1947, naturalized, 1962; B.S., Nat. Chiao Tung U., 1940; M.S., Pa. State U., 1948; Ph.D., U. Ill., 1950; Sc.D., Andhra U. (India), 1975; D.Eng., Yuengnam U. (Korea), 1976; D. honoris causa, Université Louis Pasteur de Strasbourg, France, 1976; m. Lora Y. Shu, June 3, 1961; children—Margot, Marana. Teaching positions Gt. China Sch., Shanghai, 1940-41, U. Utopia, Shanghai, 1941-43, China Agrl. and Textile Engring. Coll., Shanghai, 1943-45, Nat. Chiao Tung U., Shanghai, 1946-47; civil engr. Bur. Pub. Works, Taiwan, 1945-46; research asst. Pa. State U., 1947-48; research asst. U. Ill., Urbana, 1948-51, asst. prof. civil engring., 1951-55, asso. prof. hydraulic engring., 1955-58, prof., 1958-81, asso. mem. Center for Advanced Study, 1962-63. Dir. NSF Watershed Experimentation System, 1963-77; mem. adv. panel Water Resources Center, from 1964; cons. City and County Honolulu, 1959, 65-66, 68-69, Harza Engring. Co., Chgo., 1968, 73, Oahu Environ. Consultants, Honolulu, 1969, Union Carbide Corp., 1970, Hanson-Rodriques & Assos., Santo Domingo, Dominican Republic, 1971-73, Sinotech Engring. Consultants, from 1972, Tri-County Engring. Inc., 1973, from 77, Alfred Benesch & Co., Chgo., 1974, Murphy L. Clark, Anchorage, 1975, McMillan & Binch, Toronto, Ont., Can., 1975, Papillion Valley (Nebr.) Preservation Assn., 1975-76, TAMS, N.Y.C., 1977-78, others; mem. U.S. nat. com. irrigation, drainage and flood control Internat. Commn. on Irrigation and Drainage, from 1961; Nat. Acad. Scis.-NRC U.S. nat. com. for Internat. Hydrological Decade, 1965-75, mem. steering com., 1966-73; mem. various adv. groups Nat. Acad. Sci., 1967-77; mem. U.S. adv. com. Internat. Inst. Applied Systems Analysis subcom. on water resources, 1974-81; disting. cons. on water resources problems developing nations and world water conderence UN Secretariat, 1968-74; mem. adv. panel to U.S. Dept. Interior Water Resources Sci. Info. Center, 1968-72; UNESCO cons. to establish Centre Applied Hydrology Brazil, 1967, Internat. Hydrological program, 1974, U. Costa Rica, also in Lima, Peru, 1969; AID expert to India, 1970; chmn. internat. adv. panel on Morava River water resources systems devel., Yugoslavia, 1971-81; cons P.R. Dept. Pub. Works, 1969, TVA, 1972, Côrporación Dominicana de Electricidad, Dominican Republic, 1972-81, Departamento de Aquas e Energia Electrica, Sao Paulo, Brazil, 1973, water mgmt. Dept. State, 1973-75; distinguished vis. prof. Nihon U. (Japan), 1977; pres. World Congress on Water Resources, 1973, 75, 78. Recipient A. Epstein Meml. award, 1955; Chinese Inst. Engrs. N.Y. Achievement award, 1965; John R. Freeman Meml. Lectr. award Boston Soc. Civil Engrs., 1972; TRW lectr. award, 1974; Profl. Achievement award Chinese Engrs. and Scientists Assn. So. Claif., 1975; Silver Jubilee Commerative medal Internat. Commn. Irrigation and Drainage, 1975; Louis Pasteur medal, 1976; registered profl. engr., Va. Sr. mem., Hwakang China Acad., 1969; Fulbright-Hays sr. scholar, 1974; academian Academia Sinica, 1974; NSF distinguished scholar, 1974. Fellow Am. Acad. Mechanics (founding mem.), Internat. Water Resources Assn. (founding mem.; pres., chmn. exec. bd. 1972-77), Am. Geophys. Union (vis. scientist 1965-72, chmn. Robert E. Horton Fund 1972-74, v.p. hydrology sect. 1972, pres. 1974-76), Am. Acad. Arts and Scis.; mem. N.Y. Acad. Scis., Korean Assn. Hydrological Sci. (hon.), Am. Soc. Engring. Edn. (Western Electric Fund award 1974, Vincent Bendix award, 1977), ASCE (Research prize 1962), Internat. Assn. Hydraulic Research, Internat. Assn. for Hydrological Scis. (U.S. com. Internat. Union Geodesy and Geophysics subcom. 1973-81), Nat. Acad. Engring. (mem. panel natural hazards and disasters, 1972, com. on remote sensing for devel. 1975-77), Academia Sinica (academician), Sigma Xi, Phi TAu Phi (pres. Mid-Am. chpt.), Phi Kappa Phi, Phi Kappa Epsilon, Chi Epsilon (hon. faculty mem.). Author: Open-Channel Hydraulics, 1959. Editor-in-chief: Handbook of Applied Hydrology; editor Advances in Hydrosci., 1964—, Jour. Hydrology, 1969-81; cons. editor McGraw-Hill Book Co., N.Y.C., 1962-81; adv. editor Devels. in Water Scis., 1974-81; mem. editorial bd. Remote Sensing of Environment-An Interdisciplinary Jour., 1967-71, Geophys. Surveys-An Internat. Jour. Geophysics 1971-81; Water Supply and Management, 1977-81; mem. adv. bd. Fluid Mechanics-Soviet Research, 1972-81; editor-in-chief Water Internat., 1975-81. Contbr. articles to profl. jours. Home: Urbana, Ill. Died July 30, 1981.

CHRISTENSEN, BERNHARD MARINUS, educator; b. Porterfield, Wis., Oct. 21, 1901; s. Nels and Inger (Kristensen) C.; A.B., Augsburg Coll., Minneapolis, Minn., 1922; student Augsburg Sem., 1922-25; Th.B., Princeton Theol. Sem., 1927, Th.M., 1927; student Univs. of Berlin and Göttingen, 1927-28; Ph.D., Hartford Sem. Found., 1929; special study University of Oslo (Norway), 1959; Litt.D., Luther Coll., 1962, Coll. of St. Thomas, 1965; m. Lily Gracia Gundersen, Aug. 6, 1935; children—Nadia Margaret, Naomi Grace, Mary Thorynne, Marina Kirsten, Sonya Ruth. Teacher of Bible and history, Oak Grove Sem., 1925-26; assistant pastor Trinity Lutheran Church, Brooklyn, New York, 1928-30; professor philosophy and theology, Augsburg College and Seminary, 1930-38, pres., 1938-62; prof. theology Luther Theol. Sem., 1963-84. President National Lutheran Educational Conf., 1944; mem. exec. com. Am. Lutheran Conference, 1934-54; chairman mayor's council on Human Relations, Minneapolis 1948-50; member Minnesota UNESCO Committee; member Citizen's Club (dir.); bd. dirs. Mpls. Community Chest and Council, 1953-59; bd. dirs. Mpls. YMCA, Mpls. Bd. Pub. Welfare. Decorated Knight 1st class Royal Order of St. Olav, Norway, 1954. Mem. Am. Assn. for UN (dir. Minn. div.). Lutheran. Club: Skylight. Author: Fire Upon the Earth, 1941; He Who Has No Sword, 1964; also religious booklets. Editor: The Presence, 1929. Asso. editor Jour. Am. Luth. Conf., 1938-43; editor The Luth. Messenger, 1931-34. Home: Minneapolis, Minn. Died July 11, 1984.

CHRISTENSEN, EARL PERRY, accountant; b. Detroit, July 19, 1921; s. Hans and Sarah Ann (Perry) C.; m. Virginia Quinn Miller, May 6, 1944; children—John, David, Philip, Paul, Jeffry. B.S.C., Detroit Inst. Tech., 1943. Accountant Price Waterhouse & Co. (C.P.A.'s), 1941-80, partner, Stamford, Conn., 1961-80. Served to 1st lt. USAAF, 1943-46; to capt. USAF, 1951-53. Mem. Am. Inst. C.P.A.s, Stamford Assn. C.P.A.s. Clubs: Hemisphere (N.Y.C.); Woodway Country (Darien, Conn.). Home: New Canaan, Conn. Died Aug. 30, 1980.

CHRISTENSEN, LEW FARR, choreographer, ballet director; b. Brigham City, Utah, May 6, 1909; s. Chris and Mary Isabelle (Farr) C.; m. Giselle Caccialanza, May 10, 1941; 1 son, Chris. Soloist, ballet master Ballet Caravan, N.Y.C., 1936-41, Am. Ballet, N.Y.C., 1941, Ballet Soc., N.Y.C. Ballet, 1946-52; dir. San Francisco Ballet, 1952-84; Mem. Adv. Com. on Arts, Washington, 1963-69, Cal. Arts Commn., 1963-66. Served with AUS, 1942-46. Recipient Capezio Dance award, 1984. Home: San Bruno, Calif. Died Oct. 9, 1984. *

CHRISTIANSON, ROBERT JAMES, lawyer; b. Robbinsdale, Minn., Nov. 22, 1908; s. Theodore and Ruth (Donaldson) C.; B.A., LL.B., U. Minn., 1934; m. Louise Brown, Aug. 8, 1936; children—Robert James, Jean Louise Christianson Grussing. Admitted to Minn. bar, 1934, since practiced in Mpls.; mem. firm Faegre & Benson, and predecessors, 1944-81; dir. Red Wing Shoe Co., Inc., Durand Canning Co., Buhler-Miag Inc., Faribault Canning Co., Butter-Kernel Products, Inc., Minnetonka Boat Works, Inc. Mem. Order of Coif, Psi Upsilon, Phi Delta Phi. Republican. Congregationalist. Clubs: Mpls., Minikahda (Mpls.). Pres., recent case editor U. Minn. Law Rev., 1933-34. Home: Edina, Minn. Died Nov. 4, 1981.

CHRISTIE, ALDEN BRADFORD, architect; b. Montclair, N.J., Apr. 3, 1935; s. John Alden and Elizabeth (Hubbell) C.; m. Jane Elsie Tyler, June 21, 1958. A.B., Harvard, 1957, M.Arch., 1961. Prin. Cambridge Seven Assos., Inc. (architects), Mass., 1962-67; asso. RTKL Assos., Inc. (architects and planners), Balt., 1968-70, 72—; sr. architect Balt. City Dept. Planning, 1977, prin. city planner, 1978; prin. Alden B. Christie (cons. architect), Balt., 1971-72; asst. in graphics Harvard Grad. Sch. Design, 1963-65, asst. prof. architecture, 1965-67. Exhibit architect, U.S. Pavilion, Expo 67, Montreal.; Important works include Vocat.-Tech. Center (award of Excellence Am. Inst. Steel Constrn. 1972), Calvert County, Md. Recipient Alpha Rho Chi medal in architecture, 1961, Progressive Architecture Ann. Design awards, 1964, 65. Mem. AIA. Address: Baltimore MD

CHUBB, JOHN EVERSON, former railroad official; b. Edgewood, Pa., July 12, 1912; s. Lewis Warrington and Mary Porter (Everson) C.; student Carnegie Inst. Tech., 1931-32; B.C.E., Ohio State U., 1935; m. Ida Anita Straube, July 20, 1936; children—John Everson, William St. John II. With Pa. R.R. (name changed to Penn Central), 1935-71, v.p. 1967-71; pres., chmn. bd. Detroit, Toledo & Ironton R.R., Ann Arbor R.R., Manistique & Lake Superior R.R., 1963-67; v.p., chief engr., dir. Strasburg R.R. Co., 1957-71; pres., chmn. bd. No. Central Rwy. Co., 1970-71. Chmn. bd. trustees Detroit Inst. Tech., 1966-70. Mem. Am. Ry. Engring. Assn., Soc. Cin., Sigma Xi, Tau Beta Pi. Episcopalian. Clubs: Rotary, Out-of-Town (Cape Charles). Home: Eastville, Va. Died Sept. 2, 1983.

CHUBB, PERCY, II, insurance executive; b. East Orange, N.J., Apr. 1, 1909; s. Hendon and Alice (Lee) C.; m. Corinne Roosevelt Alsop, May 28, 1932; children: Hendon II, Percy III, Corinne R.R. (Mrs. Zimmermann), Joseph A., James P., L. Caldecot. Student, St. Paul's Sch., 1922-27; Ph.B. (Timothy Dwight fellow), Yale, 1931. Asso. Chubb & Son, Inc. (formerly Chubb & Son), ins. underwriters), N.Y.C., 1931, partner, 1935-41, 45-59, pres. dir., 1959-65, chmn., 1965-70, dir., 1959-74, dir. emeritus, 1974-77; chmn., dir. Chubb Corp., 1968-70, chmn. exec. com., 1970-74, dir, 1968-78; dir. Fed. Ins. Co., 1945-78, pres., from 1948, chmn. bd., 1964-70, chmn. exec. com., 1970-74, Vigilant Ins. Co., 1970-74, dir., 1945-78; Joined U.S. Maritime Commn. in Wash. to establish war risk ins. orgn., 1941; dir. Wartime Ins. War Shipping Adminstrn., 1942-43, asst. dep. administr. for fiscal affairs, 1943-45, asst. dep. administr., fiscal and shipping relations, 1945; Headed U.S. delegation to Planning Com. of United Maritime Authority, London, Eng., 1944. Author: From 60 North to 60 North, 1951, Cruising Guide for the Windward and Leeward Islands of the Eastern Caribbean, 1961, Who Hath Desired the Sea, 1980. Trustee, pres. Victoria Found., Inc.; trustee Mystic Seaport, Inc., chmn. bd., from 1980; trustee St. Paul's Sch., 1956-75. Awarded Presdl. Certificate of Merit, 1947; decorated hon. officer Order Brit. Empire. Mem. U.S. Yacht Racing Union. Clubs: River (N.Y.C.), Downtown Assn. (N.Y.C.), N.Y. Yacht (N.Y.C.) (commodore 1967-68). Home: Chester, NJ.

CHUNN, CALVIN ELLSWORTH, former state ofcl.; b. Jonesboro, Ark.; s. John Calvin and Sally Gelena (Kirby) C.; m. Florence Jenkins, Oct. 19, 1945; children—Adele Gelena, Lawrence Jenkins. B.A., U. Ark., 1937; M.S., Northwestern U.; Ph.D., U. Mo. With Jonesboro Daily Tribune, AP, head dept. journalism U. Tulsa, 1946-48; prof. U. Mo., 1949-50; dir. pub. relations Tex. Christian U., 1950-53; edn. dir. So. div. NAM, 1953-58; dir. Okla. State U. Sch. Communications, 1958-59; dir. health edn. Am. Acad. Pediatrics, 1959-62; editor research publs. Calif. Dept. Mental Hygiene, Sacramento, 1962-65; chief bur. textbooks Calif. Dept. Edn., 1965-78. Author: Of Rice and Men, 1946, Oklahoma Publications Law, 1948, The Publication Laws of Oklahoma, A Digest, 1950, Not to the Strong Alone, 1963, The Man Who Invented Baseball, 1967, Blood Under the Sun, 1967, Not By Bread Alone, The Saga of Valley Forge, 1981; also short stories, mag. articles. Served as maj., inf. AUS, 1941-46. Decorated Silver Star, Purple Heart with two oak leaf clusters, Bronze Star with one cluster, Combat Inf. badge. Mem. SAR (pres. Calif. 1974-75, pres. gen. 1978-80), Mil. Order World Wars (comdr. Calif. 1977-78), Descs. of Washington's Army at Valley Forge (comdr.-in-chief 1980-82), Descs. of Colonial Govs., Ams. of Royal Descent, Order of Three Crusades, Soc. of Cin., Order Founders and Patriots, Sons and Daus. of Pilgrims (Calif. gov. from 1980), Order of Magna Charta, Crown of Charlemagne, Kappa Sigma. Methodist. Clubs: Masons, Shriners. Home: Fair Oaks, Calif.

CHURCH, EARL FRANK, photogrammetrist, civ. eng.; b. Parish, N.Y., Aug. 11, 1890; s. Fred A. and Emma (Redington) C.; grad. high sch., Parish, also 2 yrs. additional course; C.E., Syracuse University, 1911, Dr. Engring. honoris causa, 1951, also 5 yrs. work in music. With U.S. Coast and Geodetic Survey 1911-24, in charge at U.S. Coast and Geodetic Survey of the least squares adjustment and math. computation of geod. survey of Hawaiian Island, 1923-24; asst. prof. applied mathematics Syracuse U., 1927-31, asso. prof. aerial photogrammetry, 1931-39, prof., 1939-50, ret. Commd. 1st lt. engrs., President's executive order, Sept. 1917; duty with A.E.F. in France, Oct. 1917-Apr. 1919; in charge, at hdqrs. 2d Army, geodetic computations in topog. div. of intelligence sect., and trained all officers and enlisted men for this work. Commended by Gen. Bullard; citation by Gen. Pershing, "for meritious work in geodetic work in France"; citation by French Govt., also Order of Silver Palm, Officer d'Académie. Official del. for U.S. at Congress of Internat. Fed. of Surveyors, London, 1934. Recipient of Photogrammetry Award, 1947. Mem. Soc. Am. Military Engrs., Am. Soc. of Photogrammetry, Am. Geophysical Union, Theta Tau, Tau Beta Pi, Sigma Xi, Pi Mu Epsilon; asso. mem. Am. Soc. Civil Engrs. Mason (K.T., Shriner). Author books including: Elements of Photogrammetry, 1944. Home: Parish, N.Y. †

CHURCH, FRANK, lawyer, former U.S. senator; b. Boise, Idaho, July 25, 1924; s. Frank Forrester and Laura (Bilderback) C.; m. Bethine Clark, June 21, 1947; children: Frank Forrester, Chase. B.A., Stanford U., 1947, LL.B., 1950; student, Harvard U., 1948. Bar: Idaho 1950, D.C. 1981. Practiced in, Boise, until 1956, U.S. senator from, Idaho, 1957-81, chmn. fgn. relations com., 1979-81; chmn. Spl. Com. on Aging, 1971-78; Select Com. Study Govtl. Ops. in Intelligence Activities, 1975-76; co-chmn. Spl. Com. on Nat. Emergencies and Delegated Emergency Powers, 1973-76; partner firm Whitman & Ransom, Washington, 1981-84; mem. U.S. Mission to UN, 1966. State chmn. Idaho Young Democrats, 1952, 54, nat. conv., 1960, Presdl. candidate, 1976. Served as 1st lt. M.I. AUS, World War II. Recipient nat. award Am. Legion Oratorical Contest, 1941, Joffre Debate medal Stanford, 1947; One of Ten Outstanding Young Men award Nat. Jr. C. of C., 1957. Home: Bethesda, Md. Died Apr. 7, 1984.

CHYNOWETH, BRADFORD G., army officer; b. Ft. Warren, Cheyenne, Wyo., July 20, 1890; s. Edward and Emilie (Grethen) C.; B.S., U.S. Mil. Acad., 1912; grad U.S. Engr. Sch., 1915, Tank Sch., 1921, Command and Gen. Staff Sch., 1928, Army War College, 1932; married Grace Woodruff, 1920; children—Frances Emilie (Mrs. Jean M. Sauvageot), William Edward, Ellen Mary (Mrs. R. R. Soule). Commd. 2d lt. Corps Engrs., U.S. Army, 1912, and advanced through the grades to brig. gen., 1941. Decorated Distinguished Service Medal. Clubs: Army and Navy, Chevy Chase (Washington); Berkeley Tennis., Commonwealth. Home: Berkeley, Cal. †

CLABAUGH, SAMUEL FRANCIS, bus. exec.; b. Birmingham, Ala., Mar. 6, 1890; s. John Henry and Martha Hinton (Graves) C.; A.B., U. Ala., 1909, A.M., 1910, LL.B., 1919; m. Mary Bacon Duncan, Oct. 30, 1913; children—Samuel F. (dec.), Mary (Mrs. Arthur F. Wright) (dec.), Elizabeth (Mrs. John G. Johnson), Jean (Mrs. Henry C. Hiles), Doris (Mrs. Ivan Jadan); m. 2d, Maitland Thompson Linney, Mar. 17, 1948. Pub., Tuscaloosa (Ala.) News, 1910-14; v.p., cashier City Nat. Bank, 1919-26; pres. Ala. Nat. Life Ins. Co., 1926-27; pres. Protective Life Ins. Co., 1927-37, chmn. bd., 1937-39; chmn. bd. Fed. Home Loan Bank of Winston-Salem, 1939; pres. Atlantic Life Ins. Co., 1939-41; govt. ofcl., 1949-53; bus. cons. indsl. moblzn. and indsl. def.; research cons. Center for Strategic Studies, Georgetown U.; pres. Westchester Corp., Washington, 1959. Exec. com. Life Ins. Sales Research Bur. (vice chmn.), 1931-32. Served to col. U.S. Army, 1940-49, faculty Indsl. Coll. of Armed Forces, 1947-49. Awarded Legion of Merit. Mem. Alumni Soc. U. Ala. (past pres.), Tuscaloosa C. of C. (past pres.), Druid City Hosp. (past pres.), Birmingham C. of C. (past pres.), Phi Beta Kappa, Beta Gamma Sigma, Sigma Alpha Epsilon. Methodist. Kiwanian (past internat. treas.). Clubs: Army and Navy, Cosmos (Washington). Co-author: East-West Trade: Its Strategic Implications, 1964; Trading with the Communists: A Research Manual, 1968. Contbr. on econ. warfare to Ency. Brit. Address: Washington, DC. †

CLAGETT, ROBERT HORATIO, editor; b. at Centerville, Tenn., May 31, 1888; s. Robert Montgomery and Tommie (Easley) C.; student Columbia (Tenn.) Mil. Acad., 1905-08; m. Elenora White, of Jackson, Tenn., Nov. 2, 1915; children—Robert, Nelle White. Instr. mil. science and history, Meth. Coll., Terrell, Tex., 1908-11; established The Citizen, weekly newspaper, Centerville, 1911; state editor Jackson (Tenn.) Sun, 1912; on staff Hattiesburg (Miss.) News, 1912-13; mng. editor Jackson (Tenn.) Sun, 1913-18; asso. editor Columbia (Tenn.) Herald, 1918-19; mng. editor Rome (Ga.) News Tribune, 1919-26; asso. editor Memphis (Tenn.) Evening Appeal, 1926-28; pub. Knoxville (Tenn.) Journal, 1928-37, editor since 1937. Republican. Episcopalian. Mason. Clubs: Cherokee Country, Irving, Rotary. Home: Knoxville, Tenn. †

CLAIR, MATTHEW W., JR., bishop; b. Harpers Ferry, W.Va., Aug. 12, 1890; s. Matthew Wesley and Fannie Meade (Walker) C.; student Syracuse U., 1909; B.A., Howard U., 1915; S.T.B., Boston U., 1918; S.T.M., Iliff Sch. Theol., 1927; D.D., Morgan U., 1934, Gammon Theol. Sem., 1936; m. Ethel C. Smith, Nov. 25, 1920; children—Phyllis Ann, Ethel Maxine (Mrs. Jasper Wilson). Ordained to ministry Meth. Ch., 1917; prof. practical theology Gammon Theol. Sem., 1936-40; pastor St. Mark Meth. Ch., Chgo.; bishop Meth. Ch. Council Bishops, N.Y.C. Mem. bd. dirs. E. Stanley Jones Union. Served as chaplain, 320th Labor Bn., U.S. Army, World War I. Mem. Ch. Fedn. of Greater Chgo., Gen. Conf. Commn. Ministerial Tng. of Meth. Ch., Pi Gamma Mu, Alpha Phi Alpha. †

CLAIR, MILES NELSON, cons. civil engr.; b. Lickdale, Pa., Sept. 7, 1900; s. Harry Monroe and Victoria (Sussana) C.; B.S. in Engring., Drexel Inst. Tech., 1921, D.Eng. (hon.), 1960; S.M. in Civil Engring., Mass. Inst. Tech., 1923; m. Carolyn Florence Green, June 16, 1928; children—Cynthia Yorke (Mrs. Stan Norkin), Valerie de Luce (Mrs. John D. Stelling), Ardith Monroe. Positions with constrn. orgn. in field and office, 1919-22; asst. instr. Mass. Inst. Tech., 1923-24; instr. civil engring. Drexel Inst. Tech., 1924-25; with Thompson & Lichtner Co., Inc., Brookline, Mass., 1925-82, pres., 1949-82; projects include civilian and mil. airports; spl. lectr. Mass. Inst. Tech., Northeastern U., Harvard. Mem. Am. Com. on Large Dams; mem. bldg. code com. City of Boston, 1936-65; air transp. com. New Eng. Council, 1958-62; adv. com. bldg. U.S. C. of C., 1960-82; mem. mayor's adv. com. on pub. bldgs., Newton, Mass., 1960-64; mem. U.S. State Dept. People to People Commn. to S. Am., 1973. Adv. bd. South End Boys Club, Boston 1940-82; nat. councillor U.S.O., 1957-82; pres. Salvation Army Assn. Greater Boston, 1958-61; mem. Mass. Com. on Children and Youth, 1964-82. Recipient Bronze Keystone medal Boys Club Am., 1958; citation of achievement City of Phila., 1961; Man and Boy award Boys Club Am. and Salvation Army, 1963; Howard Coonley medal U.S.A. Standards Inst., 1968; Others award Salvation Army, 1973; named hon. col. Salvation Army Assn., 1967. Fellow Am. Soc. C.E. (pres. New Eng. sect. 1948; chmn. standards com.), SAR (life); mem. Am. Soc. for Testing Materials (pres. 1961-62), Am. Concrete Inst. (dir. 1940, hon. mem.), Am. Standards Assn. (v.p. 1961-62, dir.), Boston Soc. Civil Engrs. (Herschel prize 1950, Ralph W. Horne Fund award 1966, pres. 1954-55, constrn. standards bd. 1950-82), Boston Aero. Club, Nat. Aero. Assn., Phi Kappa Phi, Tau Beta Pi. Mason. Author numerous tech. papers, contbr. articles to tech. publs. Pioneered devel. ready-mixed concrete, light-weight aggregates, precast concrete, constrn. quality control use of compacted fills for bldg. founds. Home: Waban, Mass. Died 1982.

CLAMPETT, BOB, filmmaker, cartoonist; b. San Diego, May 8, 1914; s. Robert C. and Joan (Merrifield) C.; m. Sody Stone, June 25, 1955; children: Robert, Ruth Ann, Cheri. Student, Otis Art Inst. Cartoonist King Features Syndicate, 1926-31; designer 1st Mickey Mouse dolls for Walt Disney, 1929-30; animator, writer, dir. Looney Tunes & Merrie Melodie cartoons (Bugs Bunny, Tweety, Daffy Duck, Porky Pig), Warner Bros., 1931-46; owner, operator Bob Clampett Studio, Hollywood, Calif.; filmed Charlie McCarthy, 1938; created prodns. for Columbia Pictures, Republic Studio, MCA, 1946-48; appeared on CBS-TV, 1948; lectr. at univs. and film festivals worldwide. Created: Cecil hand puppet and Time for Beany; TV series for, Paramount, Sta. KTTV and CBS, 1949-59; TV series on Beany and Cecil; color cartoon series for, United Artists, 1959-61, for, ABC-TV, 1962-67; distributed by, ABC Films, 1968-76, ICI, 1977-84; host: (with Orson Welles) Bugs Bunny Superstar; theatrical feature, 1975-78; writer-dir.: film Snafu for Signal Corps (Govt. citation); Created: Tweetie Pie, Porky (Pig) and Beans cartoon characters for, Warner Bros.; and one of the creators of: Bugs Bunny, 1934-41; author: book series Beany and Cecil; author and composer songs for TV puppet shows, 1948-58 and, Cartoons with Sody Clampett, 1959-62. Mem. Pres.'s People to People Com., 1956. Recipient 3 Emmy awards, Grand Shorts award, Billboard award, Ink Pot award for achievement in comic art medium, PTA award; honored by Cinematheque Francaise, Paris. Mem. ASCAP., Dirs. Guild Am., Acad. TV Arts and Scis. Patentee dimensional animation process; collector Warner Bros. original animation art work. Died May 2, 1984.

CLANCY, JOHN THOMAS, surrogate; b. Long Island City, N.Y., Apr. 11, 1903; s. Patrick J. and Mary Ann (Ryan) C.; LL.B., Fordham U., 1925; m. Patricia O'-Rourke, Mar. 17, 1936. Admitted to N.Y. bar, 1931; practice in Long Island City, 1931-59; asst. atty. gen. N.Y. State, 1939-42; spl. asst. U.S. atty. gen. OPS, 1951-53; pres. Borough of Queens, N.Y., 1959-63; mem. N.Y.C. Bd. Estimate, 1959-63; surrogate Queens County, N.Y., 1963-71. Chairman for Queens, United Hospital Fund, 1957; mem. St. John's Univ. Council, 1959-85, Queens Cancer Com., 1957-85; grand marshal St. Patrick's Day Parade, 1961; adv. com. 1964-65 N.Y. World's Fair. Bd. dirs. Boys Club Queens. Recipient Silver Medallion, Nat. Conf. Christians and Jews, 1956, Annual award, 1958; Man of Year award Queens Boys Club, 1961, S. Queens Boys Club, 1960. Div. 10 Ancient Order Hibernians, 1938, Temple Menorah, Great Neck, N.Y., 1960; awards Queensboro Council Social Welfare, 1960, Urban League Greater N.Y., 1960; Americanism award Am. Legion, 1961, Interfaith award Vets. Fgn. Wars, 1961; Youth Service award Queens YMCA, 1961, Woodhaven Community Service award, 1961. Mem. Am., N.Y. State, Queens County (past pres.) bar assns., Queens C. of C. (pres. 1952-59, dir. 1949-85), Ancient Order Hibernians, Holy Name Soc. Democrat. Roman Cath. Elk, Rotarian (past pres. Queens). Club: North Hills Golf (pres. 1952-56) (Douglaston, N.Y.). Home: Jackson Heights, N.Y. Died May 14, 1985.

CLAPP, ALFRED LESTER, coll. prof.; b. Fort Scott, Kan., Sept. 16, 1889; s. Charles Lucius and Ida Maria (Baker) C.; B.S., Kan. State Coll., 1914. M.S., 1934; student U. of Minn., 1937-38; m. Stella Opal Cady, June 7, 1918; children—Betty Jean (Mrs. Blaine Brandenburg), Bonnie Lou (Mrs. Phil McIntyre), Aleta Faye (Mrs. Everett R. Meyer). Superintendent agronomy farm, Kansas State College, 1914-15; dist. leader county agents and extension agronomist, Extension Div., Kan. State Coll., 1920-31, asst. agronomist, asso. agronomist, and agronomist Dept. of Agronomy from 1931, prof. of agronomy from 1939. Dir. of agr., Kan. State Fair, 1938-40; farm crops judge, Okla. State Fair, 1937-46; judge at Internat. Hay and Grain Show from 1935. Mem. Kansas Crop Improvement Assn. (sec. 1935-46), Internat. Crop Improvement Assn. (sec. 1936-39, pres. 1940-41, hon. mem. 1949), Am. Society Agronomy, Phi Kappa Phi, Alpha Zeta, Gamma Sigma Delta, Epsilon Sigma Phi, Sigma Xi. Republican. Methodist. Author articles in farm jours. Home: Manhattan, Kans. †

CLAPP, WILLIAM JACOB, former utility cons.; b. Greenville, S.C., Sept. 27, 1903; s. Crawford and Caroline (West) C.; m. Hazel Quigg, Sept. 30, 1926; 1 son, Jack C. B.S., Clemson U., 1923. With Fla. Pub. Service Co., 1925-45, gen. supt., 1938-43; merger with Fla. Power Corp., 1946, prodn. engr., 1946-47, prodn. supt., 1947-50, v.p., 1950-51, exec. v.p., 1952-67, pres., chmn. bd., 1967-68, cons. engr., 1968-80. Former chmn. Fla. Devel. Commn.; mem. Fla. Worlds Fair Authority.; Chmn. bd. overseers Stetson Coll. Law, St. Petersburg, Fla.; trustee Stetson U., DeLand, Fla. Served from capt. to maj. C.E. AUS, World War II. Recipient Outstanding Citizen award St. Petersburg Jr. C. of C., 1954, Fla. Econ. Devel. award First Research Corp., 1958, Mgmt. Achievement award Soc. Advancement Mgmt. of U. Fla., 1958. Mem. Am. Inst. E.E., ASME, Southeastern Electric Exchange (dir., past pres.), Edison Electric Inst. (past pres., past chmn. policy com. on atomic power), So. Mil. Engrs., Am. Legion, Res. Officers Assn., Com. of 100 St. Petersburg, Sigma Tau, Beta Gamma Sigma. Methodist. Home: St Petersburg, Fla.

CLARK, BERTON S., food technology consultant; born in North Russell, New Yor, September 26, 1888; son Leland Dewitt and Flora (Clark) C.; B.S., St. Lawrence U., 1911, Sc.D., 1927; m. Alice Morrell, Oct. 11, 1916. Asst. chemist research dept. Gen. Chem. Co., L.I. and N.Y.C., 1911-12, works chemist, Camden, N.J., 1912-15; research chemist food and container research Am. Can Co., N.Y.C., 1915-26; mgr. research Pacific dist., San Francisco, 1926-42, asso. dir. research, 1942-44, dir. research, Maywood, Ill., 1944-51, sci. dir., 1951-53; mem. adv. bd. q.m. research and development, chmn. container packing, packaging and preservation, Nat. Research Council, 1949-53, mem. food and nutrition bd. from 1953, sec. Agrl. Research Inst., 1952; cons. U.S.D.A., mem. food and nutrition bd., 1953-57, chairman conf. com. on food standards, from 1954; research director for Maine Sardine Industry, 1954-60. Mem. U.S. operations mission to Israel, 1961. Recipient Nicholas Appert award for Distinguished Service in Food Tech., 1959. Member National Canners Association. (research dir. west br. lab., San Francisco, 1926-27), Q.M. Food and Container Inst. (pres. 1948-49, chmn. bd. 1950), Can. Mfrs. Inst. (chmn. tech. com. World War II, chjmn. research com. 1952-53), Inst. Food Tech. (chmn. Chgo. sect. 1951, pres. 1953), Q.M. Assn., Am. Chem. Soc., Sigma Alpha Epsilon. Author numerous articles. Home: Oak Park, Ill. †

CLARK, CHARLES SPENCER, utility exec.; b. Seattle, June 8, 1912; s. Elmer Baily and Adah (Spencer) C.; S.B., U. Wash., 1933, Ph.D., 1975; M.B.A., Harvard U., 1935; m. Myra Snowdon, Apr. 19, 1939; children—Linda Clark Helsell, Snowdon B.J., Margaret Adah, Charles Spencer. Engr., Allied Chem. & Dye Corp., 1935-37; oil operator, 1937-42; operating mgr. Van Waters & Rogers, Inc., Seattle, 1942-46; pres. Chemi-Serve, Inc., Seattle, 1946-52; chmn. emeritus Cascade Natural Gas Corp., Seattle, from 1977; dir. Norcen Energy Resources Ltd., Toronto, Gaz Met., Montreal, No. and Central Gas Corp. Ltd., Greater Winnipeg Gas Co., Gaz du Que., Coleman Collieries Ltd. Bd. dirs. Fred Hutchinson Cancer Center, Pacific N.W. Research Found., A Contemporary Theatre, U. Wash. Arboretum Soc.; mem. men's adv. bd. Children's Orthopedic Hosp., Seattle. Mem. Pacific Coast Gas Assn., Acad. Mgmt., Zeta Psi. Republican. Episcopalian. Clubs: Golf, Univ., Rainier, Yacht, Tennis (Seattle); Vancouver (B.C., Can.); Rosedale (Toronto). Home: Seattle, Wash. Deceased.

CLARK, CLARE CLYDE, lawyer; b. Conway, La., Mar. 13, 1888; s. Edward Levin and Susan Hibernia (Mayo) C.; A.B., La. State U., 1911, LL.B., 1913, J.D., 1968; m. Mary Collins Thatcher, Jan. 14, 1922. Admitted to La. bar, 1913, since practiced in Shreveport; pvt. practice, 1914-15; partner firm Cook, Clark, Egan, Yancey & King, and predecessors, from 1957. Mem. exec. bd. La. Bapt. Conv., 1935-41; exec. com. So. Bapt. Conv., 1956-61; mem. Shreveport Municipal Fire and Police Civil Service Bd., 1944-47. Trustee M.E. Dodd Found., 1930-41. Served as 2d lt. F.A., U.S. Army, 1918. Mem. Am., La., Shreveport bar assns., Am. Legion, Phi Delta Phi. Democrat. Baptist (deacon from 1927, chmn. bd. 1930-64). Mason (Shriner). Clubs: Shreveport, Shreveport Country. Home: Shreveport, LA. †

CLARK, DEAN ALEXANDER, physician; b. St. Paul, Feb. 7, 1905; s. Charles Alexander and Georgia (Dean) C.; A.B., Princeton U., 1927; B.A. (Rhodes scholar), Oxford U. 1929, B.S., 1930; M.D., Johns Hopkins U., 1932; m. Katherine Goldthwaite Dorr, July 12, 1937 (div. 1962); children—Anna Jane, Stephen Higginson, Rosalind Carden, William Dean; m. Harriet Fidler Jones, 1962. Intern medicine Johns Hopkins Hosp., 1932-33; asst. resident medicine and neurology N.Y. Hosp., N.Y.C., 1933-34; NRC fellow medicine and neurophysiology Cornell, 1934-35; intern, asst. resident Henry Phipps Psychiat. Clinic, Johns Hopkins Hosp., 1935-37; intern Trudeau (N.Y.) Sanatorium, 1938; study med. care in Appalachian bituminous coal fields, 1939; passed asst. surgeon (res.) USPHS, 1939-41, surgeon (res.), 1941-44, sr. surgeon (res.), 1944-45, sr. surgeon (regular) 1945, med. dir. (res.), from 1945, surveys med. care; former assoc. prof. pub. health practice Columbia; med. dir. Health Ins. Plan Greater N.Y., 1945-49; gen. dir. Mass. Gen. Hosp., Boston, 1949-62; clin. prof. preventive medicine Harvard Med. Sch., 1953-62; research prof. med. and hosp. adminstrn. Grad. Sch. Pub. Health, U. Pitts., 1962-70; mem. staff John J. Kane Hosp., 1970-76. Fellow Am. Pub. Health Assn., N.Y. Acad. Med.; mem. Am. Coll. Hosp. Adminstrs., Am. Acad. Arts and Scis. Contbr. to sci. jours. Home: Pittsburgh, Pa. Died Mar. 30, 1982.

CLARK, EMORY T., manufacturing company executive; b. 1905; married. Gen. contractor, Chgo.; contractor, 1929-33; with Clark Oil and Refining Corp., 1933—, chief exec. officer, dir., 1934-50, sec., treas., now pres., chief exec. officer, also dir. Address: Milwaukee, Wis. Died 1984.*

CLARK, EUGENE EDWIN, mfg. exec.; b. N.Y. City, Sept. 27, 1888; s. William George and Mary (Cook) C.; student pub. schs.; m. Jane E. Shea, Jan. 3, 1917 (died Sept. 1947); children—William George, John Edwin; m. 2d Sally E. Powers, Dec. 21, 1948. Mgr. Constant Angle Arch Dam Co., 1918-23; pres. Masterench Corp., 1923-26; treas. Heller Bros. Co., Newark, 1926-28, v.p. and mgr. Ohio br., 1928-33; pres., dir. and gen. mgr. Am. Screw Co. from 1933; pres. Am. Guaranty Corp., United Guarantee Corp.; dir. Industrial Nat. Bank of Providence. Home: Foster Center, R.I. †

CLARK, EVANS, editor; born in Orange, N.J., Aug. 9, 1888; s. William Brewster (M.D.) and Fanny H. (Cox) C.; prep. edn. pvt. schs., N.Y.C., and Hill Sch., Pottstown, Pa.; B.A., Amherst Coll., 1910; grad. study Harvard, 1910-11; law study Columbia, 1911-14, M.A., 1913; m. Freda Kirchwey. Nov. 9, 1915; children—Brewster (dec.), Michael, Jeffrey (dec.). Instr. govt. Princeton, 1914-17; asso. editor The Utilities Mag., 1917-19; co-organizer, 1920, mng. dir. The Labor Bur., Inc., 1920-24; bus. mgr. N.Y. Call, 1924; asso. editor Advertisers Weekly, 1924-25; spl. editorial, book review and feature writer on econ. subjects, also asst. to Sunday editor N.Y. Times, 1925-28, mem. editorial bd., 1954-62, editorial contributor, 1962-64; executive director 20th Century Fund, Inc., 1928-53, member bd. trustees, 1953 from. Chmn. bd. dirs. Nat. Pub. Housing Conf., 1935-37; co-founder and mem. Pub. Affairs Com., 1935-37; co-organizer, sec. Council for Democracy, 1940-49; mem. music com. U.S. Coordinator Inter-Am. Affairs, 1940-42. Dir. Hillside Housing Corp., 1941-42, Group Health Coop., Med. Adminstrn. Service, 1942-45; trustee Spring Hill Sch., 1933-38; trustee Film Council of Am., 1948-52, chmn. bd., 1949-50; dir. N.Y. State Citizens Council, 1944-50; chmn. bd. Alumnae Adv. Center, 1952-54, vice chmn., 1954-56; chmn. pub. policy com. The Advt. Council, 1946-50, vice chmn., 1950 from, director, 1945-60; member board of trustees Joint Council on Economic Education, 1952-53; incorporating mem. Health Ins. Plan of N.Y.C., from 1945; mem. bd. dirs. Group Health Dental Ins., from 1965. Fellow Am. Geog. Soc.; mem. American Council on NATO, Alpha Delta Phi. Clubs: Century, Harvard, Town Hall, Fire Bell (N.Y.C.); Cosmos (Washington). Author: Financing the Consumer, 1930; How to Buget Health, 1933. Co-author: Boycotts and Peace, 1932; The Internal Debts of the United States, 1933; Stock Market Control, 1934. Fire alarm dispatcher N.Y. Fire Dept. Emergency Auxiliary Corps, 1942-45. Home: N.Y.C.; also East Hampton, N.Y. †

CLARK, GILBERT EDWARD, diplomat; b. Thompson Ridge, N.Y., Jan 15, 1917; s. Theodore Gilbert and Kathryn Cornelius Morgan (Jones) C.; m. Lyla Elaine Sween, Apr. 7, 1943; children: Bonnie Lee, Theodore Edward, George Kirsten. B.A., Syracuse U., 1938, M.A., 1940. Reporter Middletown (N.Y.) Times Herald, 1937; grad. asst. instr. Syracuse U., 1938-39; prodn. mgr. Whitney Graham Pub. Co., Buffalo, 1940-41; asst. prof. Syracuse U., 1946; with Dept. State, 1946—, info. officer, vice consul Am. consulate gen., Bombay, India, 1946-49, consul, 1949-51; pub. affairs staff Bur. Near Eastern, South Asia and African Affairs, 1951-53; 2d sec., consul, 1st sec. Am. legation, Tangier, Morocco, 1953-56; detailed to Bur. Budget, Exec. Office of Pres., 1956-57, Dept. State, 1957-58; assigned to Nat. War Coll., 1958-59; Am. consul gen., Amsterdam, Netherlands, 1959-61; counselor of embassy, dep. chief of mission Am. embassy, Pretoria, Transvaal, Republic South Africa, 1961-65; dir. Office West Africa Affairs, Dept. State, 1965-66; country dir. So. Africa Affairs, 1966-68, ambassador to, Mali, 1968-70, to, Senegal and The Gambia with residence in Dakar 1970-73, fgn. service insp., 1974, sr. insp., 1975-81; fgn. affairs cons. Congl. Research Service, 1975-84. Bd. dirs. Washington Internat. Coll., Leopold Senghor Found.; mem. adv. com. Sister Cities Internat.; mem. vestry St. Patrick's Episcopal Ch. Served as lt. col. Signal Corps AUS, 1941-45, CBI. Decorated Bronze Star; grand officer Nat. Order Lion, Senegal). Mem. Am. Fgn. Service Assn., Nat. War Coll. Alumni Assn., Assn. Diplomatic and Consular Officers Ret., Sigma Delta Chi, Alpha Phi Omega. Home: Washington, D.C. Died May 9, 1984.

CLARK, HERBERT ALLEN, ins. exec.; b. Chelsea, Mich., Sept. 10, 1889; s. John and Mary (Cunningham) C.; m. Florence Mahoney, June 24, 1911. With Firemen's Ins. Co. of Newark, from 1925, v.p., dir., from 1930; with Underwriters Salvage Co. of Chgo., from 1921, v.p., dir., 1935, now pres.; chmn. Underwriters Adjusting Co., Chgo.; dir. Oil Ins. Assn. Home: River Forest, Ill. †

CLARK, JAMES RICHARD, lawyer; b. Cincinnati, O., Jan. 6, 1889; s. John and Dora (Conley) C.; A.B., St. Xavier Coll., Cincinnati, 1907, A.M., 1909; LL.B., Y.M.C.A. Night Law Sch., Cincinnati, 1910; m. Helen Herschede, Sept. 11, 1916; children—Mary Helen, John Francis, James Richard, William Donald, Dorothy Mae, Thomas Henry, Nancy Lee, Suzanne. Began practice at Cincinnati, 1910; mem. Ohio Ho. of Reps., 1913-15; asst. U.S. atty. Southern Dist. of Ohio, 1916-20, U.S. atty., 1920-22; special asst. atty. U.S. atty gen., 1922-23; mem. Council City of Cincinnati, 1936-37; mem. State Banking Advisory Bd., 1937. Mem. American, Cincinnati and Ohio State bar assns. Democrat. K.C., Elk. Club: Hyde Park Golf. Author of Ohio Blue Sky Law and Bipartisan Jury System of Ohio; successfully prosecuted 13 socialists evading draft, and other notable cases. Home: Cincinnati, Ohio. †

CLARK, JOHN BALFOUR, textile mfr.; b. Newark, Mar. 23, 1898; s. J. William and Margaretta (Cameron) C.; student St. Mark's Sch.; m. Marjorie Ward, Aug. 3, 1935; children—Rosalie (Mrs. Richard Farnsworth Hunnewell), Robert John B. With Clark Thread Co., Newark, 1920-54, pres., dir., 1928-54, co. now Coats & Clark, Inc., of which pres., 1954-64; pres., dir. J. & P. Coats (R.I.) Inc. (now part of Coats & Clark, Inc.), Pawtucket, R.I., Jonas Brook Bros., Inc., Newark; dir., trustee Mfrs. Hanover Trust Co.; dir; Am. Ins. Co., Newark, Centennial Ins. Co., Standard Brands, Atlantic Mutual Insurance Company, American Chicle Company (N.Y.C.), Bigelow-Sanford Carpet Company, Incorporated. Treasurer of Grand Jury Association of N.Y. Co.; mem. United Rep. Finance Com., N.Y. Mem. St. Andrews Soc. of N.A. Burns Soc. of N.Y. Mason. Clubs: Racquet and Tennis, Links, Piping Rock, Recess, Okeetee, Brook, Links Golf. Home: Long Island, N.Y. Died July 21, 1982.

CLARK, LORD KENNETH MCKENZIE, writer; b. London, Eng., July 13, 1903; s. Kenneth McKenzie and Margaret Alice (McArthur) C.; student Winchester Coll., 1917-22; M.A., Trinity Coll., Oxford U., 1925, D.Litt.; LL.D., Glasgow U.; D.Litt., Columbia; m. Elizabeth Winifred Martin, Jan. 10, 1927; children—Alan, Colin, Colette. With Bernard Berenson, Florence, Italy, 1926-27; keeper dept. fine art Ashmolean Museum, Oxford, 1931-33; dir. Nat. Gallery, 1934-45; surveyor King's Pictures, 1934-44; dir. film div., then controller home publicity Ministery Information, 1939-41; Slade prof. fine art Oxford, 1946-50, 61-62; chmn. Arts Council Gt. Britain, 1953-60. Chmn. Ind. TV Authority, 1954-57 adv. council Victoria and Albert Mus., Conseil des Musics Nationaux; bd. Nat. Art Collections Fund, 1961-62; trustee British Mus., Nat. Galleries Scotland. Decorated Companion of Honour, Knight Commander of the Bath; comdr. Legion of Honor (France); comdr. Lion of Finland; Order of Merit, Grand Cross, 2d Class (Austria). Fellow Brit. Acad., Royal Soc. Lt.; mem. Swedish Acad., Spanish Acad. Clubs: The Travellers, The Saint James (London, Eng.). Author: The Gothic Revival, 1929; Landscape into Art, 1949; Piero della Francesca, 1951; Leonardo da Vinci (rev. edit.), 1952; Moments of Vision, 1954; The Nude, 1956; Looking at Pictures, 1960; Rembrandt and the Italian Renaissance; Ruskin Today, 1964; others. Home: Kent, England. Died May 20, 1983.

CLARK, MARGUERITE SHERIDAN, writer, editor; b. Madison, Wis.; d. Andrew Jackson and Louise (Davis) Sheridan; m. William Alexander Clark, Nov. 23, 1926. Ed., Columbia U.; postgrad., Sch. Journalism, 1924-26. Med. editor Newsweek mag., N.Y.C., 1941-61; writer-editor Cornell U. Med. Coll., 1961-65; sci. writer Cybertek, Inc., N.Y.C., 1965. Author: Medicine on the March, 1949, After the Doctor Leaves, 1954, Medicine Today, A Decade of Progress, 1960, Why So Tired? The Whys of Fatigue and the Ways of Energy, 1962; Contbr. articles to nat. publs. Recipient Nat. Headliner's award for consistently accurate and informative reporting in field of medicine, 1947. Mem. Nat. Assn. Sci. Writers (pres.), Theta Sigma Phi. Episcopalian. Clubs: Cosmopolitan (N.Y.C.), Pen and Brush (N.Y.C.). Home: New York NY

CLARK, MARK WAYNE, retired army officer, former military college president; born Madison Barracks, New York, May 1, 1896; son of Col. Charles Carr and Rebecca C.; ed. Highland Park (Ill.), High Sch.; B.S., U.S. Mil. Acad., 1917; grad. Inf. Sch., 1925; command and Gen. Staff Sch., 1935; Army War Coll., 1937; LL.D., Pa. Mil. Coll., Loyola Univ., Clemson Coll., U. of So. Cal., Oberlin Coll., U. of San Francisco, U. of S.C., U. Akron, Belmont Abbey Coll., Butler U.; D.P.S., University of Vienna, University of Naples, also, The Citadel; D.C.L., Oxford University; D.Sc., U. of Florence; L.H.D., Newberry College; m. Maurine Doran, May 17, 1924 (dec.); children—Patricia (Mrs. Gordon H. Oosting) (dec.), William Doran (maj., U.S. Army nat.); m. 2d, Mrs. Mary Millard Applegate, Oct. 17, 1967. Commd. 2d lt., Infantry, 1917, advanced through the grades to gen., 1945, ret. 1953; commander-in-chief of U.S. Occupation Forces in Austria and U.S. High Commr., 1945; U.S. mem. Allied Commn. for Austria; dep. U.S. Sec. of State, 1947, with Council of Fgn. Ministers negotiating a treaty for Austria; head of 6th Army, 1947-49; Western Area rep. of Sec. of Defense for Unification of Facilities and Services, 1948-49; chief of Army Field Forces, Ft. Monroe, Va., 1949-52; comdr. in chief, U.N. Command in Korea; comdg. gen. U.S. Army Forces in Far East; gov. Ryukyu Islands 1952; pres. The Citadel Mil. Coll. of S.C., 1954-66, pres. emeritus, 1966-84. Recipient many mil. decorations. Episcopalian. Author: Calculated Risk, 1950; From the Danube to the Yalu, 1954. Address: Charleston, S.C. Died Apr. 17, 1984.

CLARK, NELSON RAYMOND, packer; b. La Grange, Ill., Aug. 4, 1887; s. Nelson Charles and Alice (Gibbs) C.; A.B., Harvard, 1908; m. Madalene Tillson, Jan. 25, 1913; children—Nelson Raymond, Peggy. Started with Swift & Co., 1908, mgr. wool dept., 1913, transferred to dairy and poultry div. 1927, v.p. from 1928, dir. from 1944. Club: University. Home: La Grange, Ill. †

CLARK, RALPH B., tannery ofcl.; b. Plymouth, Mass., Apr. 15, 1889; s. William H. and Lucy Jane (Collingswood) C.; student Lowell Textile Inst.; m. Agnes Murray, Dec. 2, 1914. Gen. mgr. tanneries and dir., Endicott Johnson Corp. Home: Endicott, N.Y. †

CLARK, ROSCOE W., mfg. exec.; b. Russell, Pa., Mar. 21, 1887; s. DeForest and Mary (Lauffenberg) C.; student pub. schs., N.Y.; m. Myra DeVoe, Apr. 5, 1914; children—Hugh DeVoe, Robert Wesley. Vice pres., gen. mgr. G. M. Crown Metal Constrn. Co., 1910-16; chief engr., mgr. contract div. Art Metal Constrn., Jamestown, 1916-58, president of Jamestown division, 1958-60, director, 1926-60, vice chairman, 1958-60, vice president of Art Metal, Incorporated, from 1960. Mason (32 deg.). Clubs: Jamestown Trap and Skeet, Moon Brook Country (Jamestown, N.Y.); Chaut Lake Yacht (Lakewood, N.Y.). Home: Lakewood, N.Y. †

CLARK, SAMUEL ORMAN, JR., lawyer; b. Woodbridge, Conn., July 9, 1900; s. Samuel Orman and Pauline C. (Marquard) C.; Ph.B., Sheffield Sci. Sch., Yale, 1921; student Yale Grad. Sch., 1921-22; LL.B., magna cum laude, Yale Law Sch., 1928; m. Charlotte I. Northrop, Jan. 3, 1931. Civil engr. Stone & Webster, Boston, 1922-26; admitted to N.Y. bar, 1929, Conn. bar, Dist. of Columbia bar, bar U.S. Supreme Court; practice with Milbank, Tweed & Hope, and its predecessor, Masten & Nichols, New York, 1928-31; with Chambers & Hesselmeyer, New Haven, Conn., 1932-34; chief atty., protective com. study, Securities and Exchange Commn., Washington, D.C., 1934-38, dir. of reorganization div., 1938-39; asst. atty. gen., Dept. of Justice, in charge of tax div., July 1939-Dec. 1945; partner Hewes & Awalt, Washington, D.C., and Hartford, Conn., 1946-49; partner Awalt, Clark & Sparks, Washington. Mem. Am. Bar Assn., Dist. of Columbia Assn., Alpha Chi Rho, Phi Delta Phi, Order of Coif. Democrat. Clubs: Graduate (New Haven, Conn.); Metropolitan, Yale (Washington, D.C.). Contbr. to legal jours. Home: Bradenton, Fla. Died Jan. 21, 1975.

CLARK, SHERMAN ROCKWELL, naval officer, stockbroker; b. Balt., Nov. 16, 1899; s. James Francis and Edna Sherman (Rockwell) S.; B.S., U.S. Naval Acad., 1922; grad. Naval War Coll., 1935, Nat. War Coll., 1948; m. Eliza Lane Dugan, Dec. 19, 1929; 1 son, David Sherman Rockwell. Commd. ensign, U.S. Navy, 1922 and advanced through grades to rear adm., 1951; comdr. Hilary Pollard Jones, Destroyer Div. 14 and Desrons 7 and 14, Atlantic, Desron 50, Pacific, World War II; head dept. English, history and govt. U.S. Naval Acad., 1944-46; chief staff, comdr. 2d Fleet, 1948-50; with Office Chief Naval Ops., 1950-53; comdr. Destroyer Flotilla 4, Atlantic Fleet, 1953; with Office Chief of Naval Operations, 1954-55; comdr. Tng. Command Atlantic Fleet, 1955-57, dep. comdt. Indsl. Coll. Armed Forces, 1957-59, chief mil. assistance adv. group, Italy, 1959-61; ret., 1961; head investment trust dept. Clark, Melvin & Co., Annapolis, Md., 1961-80. Decorated Legion of Merit, Gold Star, Bronze Star; recipient Gold medal Olympic Games, 1920. Mem. Naval Inst. Clubs: Army and Navy (Washington); Annapolis Yacht. Home: Annapolis, Md Died Nov. 8, 1980.

CLARK, SYDNEY AYLMER, author; b. Auburndale, Mass., Aug. 18, 1890; s. Francis Edward and Harriet Elizabeth (Abbot) C.; grad. Newton (Mass.) High Sch., 1908; A.B., Dartmouth Coll., Hanover, N.H., 1912; m. Margaret Elliott, June 24, 1916; children—Margery Jacqueline, Donald Elliott. Began as teacher of English and history, Hill Sch., Pottstown, Pa., 1914; teacher Country Day Sch., Kansas City, Mo., 1915-17; with C. W. Whittier & Bro., real estate, Boston, 1917-28; in Rio de Janeiro, Brazil, 1924-25; began writing short stories, 1924. Decorated First class Order of Stella della Solidarieta Italiana; knight Royal Order of the North Star (Sweden); Medalla de Bronce al Mérito Turistico (Spain); chevalier l'Ordre du Merite Touristique (France). Member of Psi Upsilon. Congregationalist. Author travel books called All the Best In covering Hawaii, Caribbean, Europe, Mexico, Japan, Italy, Mediterranean, South America, and ten other areas; All the Best in the South Pacific, 1961. Editor with Signal Corps, War Dept., 1944-45; ind. writing and lecturing, from 1945. Home: Sagamore Beach, Mass. †

CLARK, WARREN WILLIAM HERMAN, univ. prof.; born Union County, Ore., June 22, 1887; s. John Marion and Sarah Elizabeth (Horner) C.; A.B., Willamette U., Salem, Ore., 1914, A.M., 1922; student U. of Wash., 1916, 1936, U. of Calif., 1922, 1926; m. Gertrude Jane Luthy, Dec. 31, 1914; children—Corliss Ailene (Mrs. John W. Cotton), Carol Gertrude (Mrs. John H. Bowers, Jr.). Head of science dept. Astoria (Ore.) High Sch., 1914-15. Salem Sch. System, 1915-23; asst. prin. of high sch., Salem, Ore., 1918-23; asst. prof. chemistry Willamette U., 1923-35, prof. physical sciences from 1936. Mem. A.A.A.S., Ore. Acad. Science (chmn. geology div. 1948-49), Am. Assn. Coll. Profs., Seismol. Soc. of Am., Salem Geol. Soc. (hon. life mem.). Democrat. Methodist. Home: Salem, Ore. †

CLARK, WILLIAM BELL, author, advertising; b. Mechanicsburg, Pa., Sept. 26, 1889; s. William Patterson and Kate Stees (Bell) C.; grad. Harrisburg (Pa.) Tech. Sch., 1907; m. Grace Mildred Wrigley, Nov. 5, 1915; children—William Bell, Donald Wrigley. In newspaper work, Harrisburg and Phila., 1907-19; asst. sec. Pa. War History Commn., 1919-21; rep. of N. W. Ayer & Son, advertising, 1921-39, v.p., 1939-47. Mem. Naval History Foundation, Pa. Hist. Soc., Pa. Geneal. Soc., Soc. S. of R. (1st v.p.). Republican. Presbyterian. Author: The History of the 79th Division, A.E.F., 1922; When the U-Boats Came to America, 1929; Lambert Wickes, Sea Raider and Diplomat, 1932; Gallant John Barry, Naval Hero, 1938; Captain Dauntless, The Story of Nicholas Biddle of the Continental Navy. Has specialized in research on naval history from 1919. Home: Evanston, Ill. †

CLARK, WILSON D., JR., bank exec.; b. Lee, Mass., July 6, 1887; s. Wilson D. and Jessie (Pultz) C.; m. Sue E. MacWilliams, Oct. 29, 1910; children—Edward P., Alexander M., Jessie Clark Merrell. In banking business 42 yrs.; pres. Day Trust Co., Boston; chmn. bd. Arlington Five Cents Savings Bank, Arlington, Mass.; trustee and chmn. on finance com. Mt. Holyoke Coll., South Hadley, Mass.; trustee and chmn. Robbins Library, Arlington; vice. pres., trustee Symmes-Arlington Hosp., Arlington. Club: Union (Boston). Home: Arlington, Mass. †

CLARKE, CHARLES GALLOWAY, lectr., author, cinematographer; b. Potter Valley, Cal., Mar. 19, 1899; s. Charles Edwin and Anna Electa (Millington) C.; ed. pub. schs., Los Angeles; m. Marian Nora Bowden, Apr. 25, 1931; 1 dau., Mary Clarke Fleming. Dir. photography Hollywood studios, 1920-61; lectr. advanced cinematography U. Calif. at Los Angeles, 1961-65; motion pictures filmed include Viva Villa, 1934, Miracle on 34th Street, 1947, Carousel, 1956, The Barbarian and the Geisha, 1958. Served with F.A., U.S. Army, World War I. Mem. Am. Soc. Cinematographers (pres. 1950-54, treas. 1966-83), Acad. Motion Picture Arts and Scis. Clubs: Westerners, Los Angeles Corral, Zamorano, Adventurer's (Los Angeles). Author: Professional Cinematography, 1964; The Men of the Lewis and Clark Expedition, 1970; co-author: American Cinematographer Manual, 1973. Died July 1, 1983.

CLARKE, GILMORE DAVID, cons. engr., landscape architect; b. N.Y.C., July 12, 1892; s. Gilmore and Johanna F. (Knubel) C.; m. Emma Elizabeth Vought, Aug. 16, 1917; children—Elizabeth Nelson (Mrs. Peter Tower), Edward Perry, Doris Jean (Mrs. Maurice C. Bond); m. Mary Elizabeth Sprout, July 11, 1941 (dec. Sept. 1962); m. Dolores Nancy Bedford, Apr. 5, 1968. Student, Dwight Sch., N.Y., 1907-09; B.S., Cornell U., 1913; L.H.D., Yale, 1940. Practiced as landscape architect, 1913-82; landscape architect Westchester County Park Commn., 1923-35; cons. engr., landscape architect numerous local, state, fed. commns., spl. constrn. authorities; mem. bd. archtl.-engring. consultants UN Hdqrs., N.Y.C.; mem. bd. design Met. Life Ins. Co. Housing Projects, 1938-49, chmn., 1945-49; prof. Coll. Architecture, Coll. Engring. Cornell U., 1935-50; dean Coll. Architecture, Coll. Engring. Cornell U. (Coll. Architecture), 1938-50, prof. landscape architecture emeritus, 1963-82; practice landscape architecture, also civil engring. firm Clarke & Rapuano, 1935-62; pres. Clarke & Rapuano, Inc., 1962-72; Cons. landscape architect N.Y. World's Fair, 1964-65; Mem. Nat. Commn. Fine Arts, 1932-50, chmn., 1937-50; mem. Art Commn. City N.Y., 1950-53, N.Y. State Planning Council, 1935-41, Bd. Design N.Y. World's Fair, 1949; landscape architect mem. Adv. Bd. Architects, U.S. Capitol, 1956-82; cons. N.Y. State Power Authority; mem. adv. com. on Arts, Dept. State; mem. Smithsonian Art Commn., 1940-67. Author: Sonnets-, 1949-1962, 1963-1966, A Septet of Sonnets, 1968-81. First scout commr. Borough of Bronx, N.Y.C., Boy Scouts Am., 1916-17; Trustee Am. Acad., in Rome, 1931-71, trustee emeritus, 1971—; chmn. bd. trustees Bayard Cutting Arboretum, now emeritus; trustee Am. Mus. Natural History.; Adv. com. Grad. Sch. Design Harvard, 1932-44. Served from lt. to capt. 6th Engrs., 3d Div. U.S. Army, World War, 1917-19. Decorated Silver Star, Order of Purple Heart.; Recipient Medals of Honor Archtl. League N.Y., 1931, Medals of Honor Nat. Sculpture Soc., 1970; Frank P. Brown medal Franklin Inst., 1945. Fellow Am. Soc. Landscape Architects (pres. 1949-50), Royal Soc. Arts, Franklin Inst. (life); mem. AAAL, Nat. Inst. Arts and Letters, Am. Inst. Cons. Engrs., ASCE (life); hon. mem. AIA, NAD, Société Francaise D'Architecture de Jardins, Tau Beta Pi. Republican. Presbyn. Clubs: Metropolitan (N.Y.C.), Century (N.Y.C.); Cosmos (Washington). Home: New York, NY. Died Aug. 6, 1982.

CLARKE, MARY EVELYN, philosophy educator; b. Weymouth, Eng., July 26, 1890; d. Albert Augustus and Florence Emily (Portbury) Clarke; ed. in pvt. schs., Weymouth, Eng., and Stuttgart, Germany; B.A., King's Coll., U. of London, 1918, M.A., 1920, Ph.D., 1926. Lecturer in philosophy, King's Coll., London, 1920-21, U. of South Wales, Cardiff, 1921-22; instr. philosophy Smith Coll., 1923-27, asst. prof., 1927-30, associate professor, 1930-37, professor, from 1937. Member American Philos. Assn., Aristotelian Society (British), American Association University Profs. Mem. British Labor Party. Episcopalian. Author: A Study in the Logic of Value, 1928. Contbr. articles in professional jours. Home: Northampton, Mass. †

CLARKSON, ROSS, trust co. exec.; b. Port Hope, Ont., Can., May 9, 1888; s. John B. and Louisa (Scarff) C.; student Montreal schools; Doctor Civil Laws, Bishop's University; Doctor of Laws, McGill University; married to Elsie Florence Trenholme, September 12, 1916; children—Joan D. (Mrs. B. G. Miller), Ross T., Sheila E. (Mrs. Alan A. Sharp). Clk. Alliance Assurance Co., Montreal, 1904-08; with Royal Trust Co., from 1908, mgr., 1922-43, general manager, 1943, vice pres., dir., from 1945, president, 1950-55, chairman of the bd., 1955-62, hon. pres., from 1963; dir. Brit. Am. Bank Note Co., Ltd., Great Lakes Paper, Ltd., Can. Iron Foundries, Limited; also Imperial Chemical Industries of Canada, Limited. President of Montreal Bd. Trade, 1939. Served as capt. and adj. Grenadier Guards, 1916, with Canadian Forestry Corps in France, 1917-19. Anglican. Clubs: Canadian of Montreal (pres.), Mount Royal, St. James' (Montreal). Home: Westmount, Can. †

CLASON, CHARLES RUSSELL, congressman; b. Gardiner, Me., Sept. 3, 1890; s. Oliver Barrett and Lizzie Julia (Trott) C.; A.B., Bates Coll., Lewiston, Me., 1911; LL.B., Georgetown U., 1914; B.A. in jurisprudence, Oxford U., England, 1917; m. Emma M. Pattillo, of Truro, Nova Scotia, Aug. 4, 1928. Admitted to Mass. Bar, 1917, and practiced in Boston, asso. with Gaston, Snow, Saltonstall & Hunt, 1917-19; mem. firm Simpson, Clason & Callahan, Springfield, Mass., from 1919; asst. dist. atty., Western Dist. Mass., 1922-26, dist. atty., 1927-30; mem. 75th Congress (1937-39), 2d Mass. Dist. Served in Coast Arty.,

U.S.A., 1918. Rhodes scholar from Me. to Oxford U. Decorated with Medaille du Roi Albert for services on Commn. for Relief in Belgium, 1914-15. Trustee Bates Coll. Mem. Hampden Co. Bar Assn., Phi Beta Kappa. Republican. Methodist. Mason. Clubs: Rotary, University (Springfield, Mass.); Congressional Country (Washington, D.C.). Home: Springfield, Mass. Died July 7, 1985.

CLAUDE, ALBERT, cell biolchemist; b. Longlier, Belgium, Aug. 24, 1898; (parents Am. citizens). Doctorate in medicine and surgery, Liège U., 1928, doctor honoris causa, 1975; doctor honoris causa, U. Modena, 1963, U. J. Purkinje, Brno, 1971, Rockefeller U., 1971, Université Catholique de Louvain, Belgium, 1975, Rijksuniversiteit te gent, Belgium, 1975. Cell biochemist; with Institut für Krebsforschung Berlin U. and Kaiser Wilhelm Institut, Berlin-Dahlem, 1928-29; faculty Rockefeller Inst. (now Rockefeller U.), from 1929, prof. emeritus, 1972-83; dir. Jules Bordet Inst., Brussels, 1948-72, prof. emeritus, 1971-83; prof. Université Libre de Bruxelles, from 1948, prof. emeritus, 1969—; vis. research prof. Johnson Research Found., 1967; Vol. Brit. Intelligence Service, World War I. Decorated Brit. War medal, 1918; Interallied medal, 1918; grand cordon de l'Ordre de Leopold II Belgium; comdr. Order of Palmes académiques, France; recipient prize Fonds National de la Récherche Scientifique, 1965; medal Belgian Acad. Medicine; Louisa G. Horwitz prize Columbia U., 1970; Paul Ehrlich and Ludwig Darmstaedter prize, 1971; Nobel prize in medicine and physiology for work done 30 years ago at Rockefeller Inst. Med. Research (now Rockefeller U.), 1974. Mem. Belgian Académie Royale de Médecine, French Académie Nationale de Médecine, Am. Acad. Arts and Scis. (hon.), Koninklijke Academie voor Geneeskunde (Belgium, hon.), Belgium Academie Royale des Sciences, Lettres et Beaux Arts (asso.), Institut de France (asso.), Internat. Soc. Cell Biology, Société française de Microscopie Electronique (hon.), Am. Assn. Cancer Research (hon.), Société belge de Biologie Cellulaire (hon.), Société française de Biologie (hon.). Founder modern cell biology; first to isolate a cancer virus by chem. analysis and characterize it as a RNA virus; first to use electron microscope to study normal and tumor cells; author technique to separate cells constituents quantitatively by differential centrifugation and carry out the inventory of their biochem. functions. Died May 23, 1983.

CLAUSE, ROBERT LEWIS, glass manufacturer; b. Kokomo, Ind., Feb. 23, 1890; s. W. L. and Elizabeth Ann (Fish) C.; student Sewickley (Pa.) Acad., 1902-07; M.E., Cornell U., 1914; m. Mary Agnes Grove, Apr. 14, 1915; children—Nancy Elizabeth (Mrs. John M. Trainer), Barbara Ann, (Mrs. Henry F. Devens II) Mary Grove (Mrs. George Heard). Draftsman Pittsbg. Plate Glass Co., 1914-15, asst. supt., 1917-19, gen. supt., 1921-27, director from 1922, v.p., 1926-40, exec. v.p., 1940-41, pres. 1941-44, vice chmn. bd. of dirs. from Jan. 1, 1944; director Peoples First National Bank & Trust Company. Dir. Tuberculosis League of Pittsburgh. Republican. Presbyterian. Clubs: Duquesne, Allegheny Country, Sewickley Hunt, Rolling Rock, Edgeworth. Home: Sewickley, Pa.†

CLAUSEN, ROBERT THEODORE, biologist, educator; b. N.Y.C., Dec. 26, 1911; s. Adam Peter and Mary (Blum) C.; m. Edna Wadleigh Rublee, Jan. 31, 1942; children—Eric Neil, Joanna Margaret, Thomas Paul, Heidi Elizabeth. A.B., Cornell U., 1933, A.M., 1934, Ph.D., 1937. Mem. faculty Cornell U., 1933—, prof. biology, 1949-77; collaborator Dept. Agr., 1943. Author: Sedum of the Trans-Mexican Volcanic Belt, 1959, Sedum of North America North of the Mexican Plateau, 1975. Mem. Am. Inst. Biol. Sci., Ecol. Soc. Am., Bot. Soc. Am., Am. Soc. Plant Taxonomists, Torrey Bot. Club, Am. Fern Soc. (past pres.), N.E. Bot. Soc. Home: Ithaca NY

CLAVAN, IRWIN, architect; b. Newport News, Va., Feb. 1, 1900; s. Harry E. and Rachel (Holzweig) C.; m. Virginia Moschak, Jan. 18, 1952; 1 son, Peter. B.Arch., U. Pa., 1921, M.Arch., 1922. Registered profl. architect, N.Y. Projects- mgr. Shreve, Lamb & Harmon, architects, 1926-33, Shreve, Lamb & Harmon, architects (including Empire State Bldg.), 1930-31, pvt. practice, from 1934. Asso. architect: Parkchester, N.Y.C., 1937-39; architect: Stuyvesant Town, Riverton and Peter Cooper Village, N.Y.C., 1946-48; architect devel. and 1st sect.: Gateway Center, Pitts., 1950-52; cons. architect: Equitable Life Bldg, San Francisco, Met. Life Ins. Co. Recipient medal Société des Architectes Diplomes Governement Francais, 1922. Mem. A.I.A. Home: New York, NY.

CLAYTON, JEAN PAUL, equipment mfg. co. exec.; b. Sterling, Ill., Oct. 3, 1888; s. Gilbert Oliver and Mary Adeline (Robinson) C.; B.Engring., Tulane, 1909, D.Engring., 1942; M.E.E. (research fellow), U. Ill., 1911; m. Helen Electa Burbank, June 2, 1915; children—Jean Paul, Hugh Burbank, Helen Ruth. With Central Ill. Pub. Service Co., Mattoon, Ill., 1912-32, v.p., 1919-32, pres., 1932; asst. to pres. Super-Power Co. Ill., 1928-32; v.p. in charge operations Middle West Utilities Co., 1932; chief system officer Commonwealth Edison Co., Pub. Service Co. of No. Ill., Western United Gas & Electric Co., No. Ill. Utilities Co., Chgo. Dist. Electric Generating Corp., 1932-49; v.p. Power Dispatchers Equipment Co., from 1952. mem. Ill. Legislature Commn. on Future Rd. Program, 1931-33; chmn. Com. on Elimination of Grade Crossings, Springfield, Regional Hwy. Com. for Springfield and Sangamon County, 1930-32. Organizer charity fund drive Catholic Charities Springfield-Springfield Council Charities, 1931. Fellow Am. Inst. E.E.; mem. Am. Soc. M.E., Western Soc. Engrs. (chmn. awards com. 1941-45, Octave Chanute medal 1938). Ill. State Electric Assn. (past pres.), Springfield (pres. 1926-27), Ill. (pres. 1930-32, chmn. bd., 1932-35) chambers commerce; Sigma Xi. Club: Union League (Chgo.). Discoverer, developer new analysis of cylinder performances of reciprocating engines, used in Am. engring. colls.; compiler Illinois-Its Resources-Development and Possibilities. Home: Winnetka, IL. †

CLEARY, EDWARD JOHN, cons. engr.; b. Newark, June 16, 1906; s. Daniel A. and Bertha (Geiges) C.; B.S., Rutgers U., 1929, M.S., 1933, C.E., 1935, Sc.D., 1959; D.Eng., Rose-Hulman Inst. Tech., 1972; m. Adelaide Rogers, June 16, 1934; children—Edward R., Kathleen S., Daniel H., Adelaide Ellen. Field engr. Utilities Power & Light Corp., Chgo., 1929-31; mem. editorial staff Engr. News Record (pub. McGraw Hill Co.), 1935-49, exec. editor, 1945-49; exec. dir., chief engr. Ohio River Valley Water Sanitation Commn., Cin., 1949-67, cons., 1967-84; prof. emeritus environ. health U. Cin., 1976-84; cons. emeritus U.S. Army Med. Research and Devel. Command, 1978. Bd. dirs. Resources for Future, Washington. Registered profl. engr., N.Y., Ohio, N.J. Diplomate Am. Acad. Environ. Engrs. Mem. ASCE (hon.), Water Pollution Control Fedn. (hon.), Engring. Soc. Cin., Am. Pub. Works Assn. (pres. 1952), Pub. Works Hist. Soc. (pres. 1977), Am. Water Works Assn. (hon.), Acad. Aquatic Ecosystems (dir.), Inter Am. Assn. San. Engring., Nat. Acad. Engring., Sigma Xi, Tau Beta Pi, Delta Upsilon. Roman Catholic. Clubs: Cosmos, Westlake Yacht. Co-author: Bulldozers Come First, 1944; author: The Orsanco Story, 1967. Home: Westlake Village, Calif. Died Apr. 1, 1984.

CLEARY, WALTER HENRY, justice state supreme ct.; b. Lyndonville, Vt., Nov. 17, 1887; s. John and Louise (McArthur) C.; grad. Lyndon Inst., 1906; A.B., Middlebury Coll., 1911; LL.B., Boston U., 1915; LL.D. (honorary), Holy Cross Coll., 1943, Saint Michael's College, 1958; J.S.D., Suffolk U., 1949; m. Arlene Mary Decoteau, Nov. 28, 1917; children—John McArthur, Louise Ellen (Mrs. Charles D. Horvath). Admitted to Vt. bar, 1916 and practiced at Newport, 1916-34; also U.S. commr.; city atty., Newport, Vt., 1922-34; pres. Nat. Bank Newport, 1933-34; superior ct. judge, 1934-38, chief superior ct., 1938-48, justice Vt. Supreme Ct. from 1948, now chief justice. Trustee Middlebury Coll., from 1941, St. Michaels Coll., from 1947, Lyndon Inst., Vt. State Library, from 1949. Mem. American Bar Association, Vermont Bar Assn. (president 1932-33), Phi Beta Kappa, Phi Delta Phi, Delta Upsilon. Home: Newport, Vt. †

CLEAVER, WILLIAM JOSEPH, author; b. Hugo, Okla., Mar. 24, 1920; s. William Edward and Delpha Marie (Richardson) C.; m. Vera Fern Allen, Oct. 4, 1945. Commd. U.S. Army Air Corps; advanced through grades with U.S. Air Force. Author: (with Vera Cleaver) Ellen Grae, 1967, Lady Ellen Grae, 1968, Where the Lilies Bloom, 1969 (Nat. Book award nominee), Grover, 1970 (Nat. Book award nominee), The Mimosa Tree, 1970, I Would Rather Be a Turnip, 1971, The Mock Revolt, 1971, Delpha Green & Company, 1972, Me Too, 1973, The Whys and Wherefores of Littabelle Lee (Nat. Book award nominee), 1973, Dust of the Earth, 1975 (Spur award, Lewis Carroll Bookshelf award), Trial Valley, 1977, Queen of Hearts, 1978 (Nat. Book award nominee), A Little Destiny, 1979, The Kissimmee Kid, 1981. Recipient Air Medal with 2 clusters. Home: Winter Haven, Fla.

CLEBSCH, WILLIAM ANTHONY, religious studies educator; b. Clarksville, Tenn., July 27, 1923; s. Alfred and Julia (Wilee) C.; m. Betsy Berkeley Birchfield, June 10, 1944; children: William Ernst, Sarah Elizabeth Clebsch Veblen. B.A., U. Tenn., 1946; B.D., Theol. Sem. Va., 1946, S.T.M., 1951; Th.D., Union Theol. Sem., N.Y.C., 1957; M.A. status, Clare Coll., Cambridge U., 1959-60. Lectr. religion, Episcopal chaplain Mich. State U., 1946-49; instr., asst. prof. ch. history Theol. Sem. Va., 1949-56; assoc. prof., prof. history Theol. Sem. of S.W., 1956-64; assoc. prof. religion Stanford U., 1964-67, prof. religious studies and humanities, 1967-84, George Edwin Burnell prof. religious studies, 1980-84, chmn. humanities spl. programs, 1967-73, chmn. religious studies, 1973-80, chmn. Am. studies, 1975-80, vice chmn. faculty senate, 1968-69, chmn., 1969-70, vice chmn. adv. bd., 1977-80, chmn., 1980-81; cons. on religion World Book Ency.; sr. fellow NEH, 1971-72, 76-77, 80-81; vis. fellow in religious studies, asso. fellow Silliman Coll., Yale U., 1971-72; vis. prof. religion U. N.C., also Duke U., 1976-77; fellow Center for Advanced Study in Behavioral Scis., 1980-81; trustee Scholars Press, 1979—. Author: (with C.R. Jaekle) Pastoral Care in Historical Perspective, 1964, England's Earliest Protestants, 1964, From Sacred to Profane America, 1968, Christian Interpretations of the Civil War, 1969, American Religious Thought, 1973, Christianity in European History, 1979. Mem. Am. Soc. Ch. History (pres. 1972), Council Study of Religion (chmn. 1974-76), Am. Acad. Religion (pres. 1979-80), Nat. Humanities Faculty (dir. 1968-73). Home: Stanford, Calif. Died June 12, 1984.

CLEE, LESTER HARRISON, clergyman; b. Thompsonville, Conn., July 1, 1888; s. Frederick and Margaret (Kelley) C.; ed. Worcester (Mass.) High Sch., 1900-05; D.D., Cumberland U., 1934, Washington and Jefferson U., 1940; LL.D., Bloomfield Coll., 1951; married Katherine Steele, Aug. 9, 1911; 1 son, Gilbert Harrison. Boys' sec. Y.M.C.A., Quincy, Mass., 1908-11; sec. boys' work Y.M.C.A., Providence, R.I., 1911-15; dir. boys' work N.Y. City Sunday Sch. Assn., 1915-18; asst. minister West End Presbyn. Ch., N.Y. City, 1918-22; minister Baptist Ch., Rutherford, N.J., 1922-26, 2d Presbyn. Ch., Newark, 1926-50; president N.J. Civil Service Commn. from 1951; speaker House of Assembly, State of N.J., 1935; elected to N.J. Senate, 1936. Rep. candidate for gov. of N.J., 1937; mayor Chester, N.J., from 1953. Chmn. Ch. Extension Com., Newark Presbytery, 1941-52; dir. Bloomfield Coll. and Sem. Trustee Presbyn. Hosp., 1942-50, Blair Acad. from 1951; synod chmn. Restoration Commn., 1947-48. Chmn. State Labor Mediation Bd., 1950-51. Dist. Gov. N.J. Lions' Clubs, 1923, 24, 25. Home: Chester, N.J. †

CLELAND, HENRY LLOYD, sch. principal; b. Monmouth, Ill., Apr. 14, 1890; s. David Martin and Anna (Pollock) C.; A.B., Westminster Coll., New Wilmington, Pa., 1913; Officers' Training Sch. Saumur, France, 1918; A.M., Columbia, 1928; grad. student Univ. of London (spring), 1919; Univ. of Pittsburgh (summer) 1923; Ped.D., Westminster College, 1942; married Eugenia Margaret Jones, June 25, 1921; 1 dau., Jane Morrow. Teacher, New Castle, Uniontown, Bellevue, Pittsburgh, Pa., 1913-32; with Pittsburgh sch. system as vice prin., prin., dir. of guidance, dir. of personnel, 1932-46; pres. Westminster Coll., from 1946; principal, Pittsburgh (Pa.) Secondary Schools. Served with U.S. Army, 1917-19. Dir. Pittsburgh Teachers' Assn., Girls' Service Club of Pittsburgh, Westminster Coll. Mem. Pa. State Edn. Assn., N.E.A., Am. Assn. Sch. Adminstrs., Am. Council of Teacher Examiners, Phi Delta Kappa. United Presbyterian Ch. Club: Rotary. Home: Pittsburgh, Pa. †

CLEMENCE, RICHARD VERNON, economist; b. Greenville, R.I., Oct. 13, 1910; s. Richard R. and Lora Eliza (Oatley) C.; Ph.B., Brown U., 1934, A.M., 1936; M.A., Harvard, 1940, Ph.D., 1948; m. Eleanor Prescott, Dec. 5, 1942; 1 dau., Melissa. Instr. econs. Boston U., 1937-38; asst. econs. Mass. Inst. Tech., 1939-42; research asso. Nat. Bur. Econ. Research, 1942-43; head dept. econs. Pine Manor Jr. Coll., 1945-47; faculty Wellesley Coll., 1947-82, prof. econs., 1958-82, chmn. dept., 1956-82, A. Barton Hepburn prof. econs., 1966—, also dir. program econ. edn. Cons. economist New Eng. Econ. Edn. Council, Kingston Ins. Agy. Dir. Benjamin Chase Co.; dir. fgn. operations div. Paine Brook Assos. Served with AUS, 1942-44. Life fellow Royal Econ. Soc., Nat. Assn. Bus. Economists (dir. internship program in econs.); mem. Am. Econ. Assn., Am. Finance Assn., Econ. History Assn., Am. Statis. Assn., Econometric Soc., Paine Brook Assos. (dir.), Internat. Mark Twain Soc. (hon.), Phi Beta Kappa. Author: The Schumpeterian System, 1950; Income Analysis, 1951; The Economics of Defense, 1953; also numerous articles. Filler editor The Enterprise. Home: Wellesley, Mass. Died Nov. 8, 1982.

CLEMENTS, CHARLES L., banker; b. Berrien County, Ga.; s. David C. and Martha (Baskin) C.; m. Lena Pafford, 1915; children—Bertha Virginia, Frances Marian, Charles L. Student, Ga. A. and M. Coll. Sec. Valdosta Drug Co., Ga., 1923-26; cashier, v.p. Miami Beach Bank & Trust Co. (now Merc. Nat. Bank), Fla., 1926-33; pres. Chase Fed. Savs. & Loan Assn., 1933-64, chmn. bd., from 1964; chmn. Community Nat. Bank of Bal Harbour, Miami Beach; propr. C.L. Clements Ins. Agy., Inc., from 1943. Former pres. Community Chest, Dade County, Fla. Mem. U.S. Savs. and Loan League (past pres.), Miami Beach C. of C. (past pres.), Com. of One Hundred (dir.). Clubs: Rotarian. (Miami Beach), Bath (Miami Beach), Surf (Miami Beach) (bd. govs.), LaGorce Country (Miami Beach), Biscayne Bay Yacht (Miami Beach), Indian Creek Country (Miami Beach). Home: Miami Beach, Fla.

CLEMENTS, EARLE C., senator; born Morganfield, Ky., Oct. 22, 1896; student U. of Ky.; m. Sara Blue; 1 dau. Elizabeth Hughes. Served as official in Ky. 28 yrs., successively in offices of sheriff, county clerk, judge, and state senator; majority floor leader, Ky. State Senate, 1944; mem. 79th and 80th Congresses (1945-49), 2d Ky. Dist.; gov. of Ky., 1947-50; U.S. senator from Ky., 1950-56; asst. Dem. leader 83d Congress; farmer. Home: Morganfield, Ky. Died Mar. 12, 1985.

CLEMENTS, GEORGE L., chain store executive; b. Chgo., Feb. 24, 1909; s. Fred and Ina (Small) C.; student U. Ill., 1926; hon. doctorate Loyola U.; m. Ruth Howell, Sept. 1, 1933; children—Lynne, John. Assoc. with Jewel Cos., Inc., Chgo., 1929-78, dir., 1948-78, pres., 1951-65, chmn. bd., 1965-70, chmn. exec. com., 1970-73. Past chmn. Nat. Assn. Foods Chains. Active Chgo. council Boy Scouts Am., United Settlement Appeal, Nat. Fund for Med. Edn., Chgo. Crusade of Mercy, Hinsdale Caucus. Chmn. Ill. State Bd. Higher Edn., 1969-72. Clubs: Hinsdale Golf (gov.); Desert Forest Golf. Home: Carefree, Ariz. Dec. June 13, 1985.

CLEMMER, HENRY AUSTIN, bakery exec.; b. Hatfield, Pa., Mar. 3, 1888; s. J. K. and Emma (Landis) C.; student bus. coll., Norristown, Pa., 1906-07; m. Lucia Speaker, April, 1924; 1 son, Calvin L.; m. 2d, Ethel A. Butterfield, 1945. With Sunshine Biscuits, Inc., from 1910, sec., asst. treas. from 1932, dir. from 1936. Dir. Queens Co. Boy Scouts. Mem. Queensboro C. of C. (dir.). Club: Queensboro Rotary. Home: Hollis, N.Y. †

81 WHO WAS WHO

CLENDENIN, WILLIAM RITCHIE, musicologist, educator; b. Sparta, Ill., July 23, 1917; s. Harry Orrin and Sarah Mabel (Ritchie) C.; m. Virginia June Van Zandt, June 14, 1941; 1 son, William Ritchie. B.Mus., U. Ill., 1940; S.M.M., Union Theol. Sem., 1942; Ph.D., U. Iowa, 1952. Organist, choirmaster Trinity Ch., Columbia, S.C., 1942-44; asst. prof. music Queens Coll., 1944-46, Iowa State U., 1946-49; asst. prof. music U. Colo., 1952-59, asso. prof., 1959-68, coordinator grad. studies music, from 1961, prof., from 1968; organist, choirmaster St. John's Episcopal Ch., Boulder, Colo., 1953-62; music reviewer Boulder Daily Camera, 1953-67. Author: Music: History and Theory, 1965, (with Louis Trzcinski) Visual Aids in Western Music, 3d edit, 1967, History of Music, 1974, (with Ritchie Clendenin) A Modern Edition of Girolamo Fantini's Trumpet Method (1638), 1977. Chmn. Univ. United Fund Drive, 1956. U. Colo. Faculty fellow, 1965-66; research grantee, 1965, 75. Mem. Am. Musicol. Soc. (chmn. Rocky Mountain chpt. 1956-58, 1968-69), Pi Kappa Lambda (pres. Alpha Tau chpt. 1973-75), Phi Mu Alpha, Alpha Kappa Lambda. Club: University. Home: Boulder, Colo.

CLEVELAND, FORREST FENTON, educator, physicist; b. Pendleton County, Ky., Jan. 10, 1906; s. George Edwin and Flora (Wyatt) C.; m. Marguerite Ewalt, Aug. 17, 1929. A.B., Transylvania Coll., 1927; M.S., U. Ky., 1931, Ph.D., 1934; postgrad. summers, U. Chgo., 1932, 33, 39, U. Mich., 1939. Sci. tchr. Middlesboro (Ky.) High Sch., 1927-28; physics tchr. Henry Clay High Sch., Lexington, Ky., 1928-30; instr. physics U. Ky., 1930-34; sci. tchr. Highland Jr. High Sch., Louisville, 1934-35; prof. physics and math., chmn. dept. Lynchburg (Va.) Coll., 1935-39; faculty Ill. Inst. Tech., Chgo., 1939-71, prof. physics, 1943-71; adj. prof. elec. engring. U. Ky., 1972-85; vis. prof. physics Ohio State U., summer 1947; Transylvania Coll., summer 1929. Editor, pub.: Spectroscopia Molecular, 1952-81; asso. editor: Jour. Chem. Physics, 1950-53; Author physics manuals, numerous articles. Co-recipient Research prize Va. Acad. Sci., 1939. Fellow Am. Phys. Soc., AAAS; mem. AAUP, Am. Assn. Physics Tchrs., Soc. Applied Spectroscopy (hon.), Coblentz Soc., Sigma Xi, Sigma Pi Sigma. Home: Lexington, Ky. Died Feb. 5, 1985; buried Lexington Cemetery.

CLEVELAND, JOHN LUTHER, chmn. Guaranty Trust Co. of New York; b. Cleburne, Tex., Mar. 11, 1891; s. John L. and Annie (Upshaw) C.; ed. public schools, Cleburne, and Eastman's Sch., Poughkeepsie, N.Y., m. Elizabeth Ames, Nov. 29, 1921; children—Charles Ames, John L., Jr., Elizabeth. Asst. cashier Am. Nat. Bank of Muskogee, Okla., 1910-16; v.p. and dir. Am. Nat. Bank of Oklahoma City, Okla., 1916-23; v.p. and dir. Guaranty Trust Co. of New York, N.Y. 1923-44, pres., 1944-47, chmn. bd. dirs., 1947-59; chmn., exec. com. Morgan Trust Co., N.Y., 1959-61; dir. Anaconda Co. Clubs: Links (N.Y. City); Blind Brook (Port Chester, N.Y.); Bankers Club of Am. (L.I.); Nat. Golf Links (Southhampton, New York). Home: Pelham Manor, N.Y. Died July 1, 1984.

CLEVERDON, ERNEST GROVE, banker; b. Marlow, Ala., Sept. 28, 1900; s. Walter I. and Millicent (Grove) C.; B.A., U. Ala., 1924; m. Marian Hauser, Oct. 8, 1927; children—John Hauser, Walter Irving. With Mchts. Nat. Bank Mobile, 1929-68, cashier, 1938-65, exec. v.p., 1963-68, ret., 1968, dir. until 1968, hon. dir., 1968-85. Pres., America's Jr. Miss. Scholarship Found., 1963—; dir., past pres. Mobile Symphony and Civic Music Assn.; pres. Mobile County Found. Pub. Higher Edn., 1961—. Bd. dirs., past pres. Mobile chpt. ARC; past pres. Jr. Achievement Mobile; past bd. dirs., past 1st v.p. Mobile Better Bus. Bur.; bd. dirs. Group Aid for Retarded Children; past dir. Ala. Motorist Assn., Birmingham; v.p., trustee, chmn. exec. com. U. of S. Ala.; past bd. dirs., past treas., now hon. bd. dirs. Am.'s Jr. Miss Pageant, 1970-85; past v.p., bd. dirs. Ala. Council on Econ. Edn., U. Ala.; trustee Tb and Health Assn. Mobile County, 1960-85; pres., bd. dirs. Mobile Area Pub. Higher Edn. Found., from 1961; mem. Ala. Council on Arts and Humanities, 1979-85. Named Educator of Year, Phi Delta Kappa, 1965, Mobilian of Year, 1962; recipient Civic award Alpha Kappa Psi, 1969; First Alumni Assn. Service award U. South Ala., 1970, First Distinguished Service award, 1976. Mem. English Speaking Union (past pres. Mobile br.), Mobile C. of C. (chmn. edn. com. 1957-70), Beta Gamma Sigma, Beta Alpha Psi (hon. mem. Mobile chpt.). Methodist (trustee, treas.). Clubs: Lions (past pres. Mobile), Masons (32 deg., knight comdr. ct. of honor), Shriners. Home: Mobile, Ala. Dec. July 24, 1985. Interned Mobile, Ala.

CLEW, WILLIAM JOSEPH, newspaper editor; b. Middletown, Conn., June 28, 1904; s. Timothy J. and Anne (Taylor) C.; m. Mona Gallivan, Oct. 12, 1928; children—William Taylor, Harvey Taylor and Carole Clew Hoey (twins), Elizabeth Barrow Clew Kampmeinert. Student, Wesleyan U., Middletown, 1926-27. Reporter Middletown Press, 1923-25; mem. staff Hartford (Conn.) Courant, 1925—, asst. mng. editor, 1949-66, mng. editor, 1966-74, Middle East corr., 1974—; mem. expdn. Operation Deep Freeze to South Pole, 1964; search expdn. for lost bomber Lady Be Good, 1960; mem. Conn. Freedom of Info. Commn., 1977—. Author articles. Mem. Middletown Bd. Edn., 1945-49, Haddam (Conn.) AP Edn., 1956-60. Served as capt. AUS, 1942-43. Recipient Yankee Quinn award Acad. New Eng. Journalists, Sigma Delta Chi, 1980. Mem. New Eng. AP News Execs. Assn. (pres. 1965-66), Res. Officers Assn., AP Mng. Editors Assn., Am. Soc. Newspaper Editors, Ret. Officers Assn., Sigma Delta Chi. Roman Catholic. Clubs: Explorers (N.Y.C.), Overseas Press (N.Y.C.); Nat. Press (Washington). Home: Haddam CT

CLIFFORD, RALPH KIBBE, steel corp. exec.; b. Anderson, Ind., Jan. 13, 1890; s. F. L. and Sallie E. (Kibbe) C.; B.S., U. of Mich., 1914; m. Isabel Hamilton, Oct. 18, 1925; children—Constance Anne, Clara Emily. With Continental Steel Corp. since 1916, beginning as chief chemist, v.p. in charge operations, 1939-43, dir. from 1941, vice pres. and gen. mgr., 1943-46, pres., 1947-55; chmn. bd., director, mem. exec. com., 1955 from; dir. Pub. Service Co. of Ind. Mem. Am. Iron and Steel Inst. (dir.). Presbyn. Home: Kokomo, Ind. †

CLINTON, LAWRENCE MARTIN, justice Nebr. Supreme Ct.; b. Sidney, Neb., Mar. 21, 1915; s. Frank and Mary (Mikkelsen) C.; m. Virginia Martin, Nov. 27, 1948; children—Lawrence M., Kathryne A., Marie, Mark. A.B., Creighton U., 1940, LL.B., 1940. Bar: Nebr. bar 1940. Practiced in, Sidney, 1946-71, county atty., Cheyenne County, Nebr., 1947-51, city atty., Sidney, 1953-71; justice Nebr. Supreme Ct., from 1971. Co-author: Practitioners' Handbook for Appeals in the Courts of Nebraska. Served with AUS, 1941-46. Decorated Bronze Star; recipient Alumni Achievement citation Creighton U., 1980. Mem. Nebr. Bar Assn., Am. Judicature Soc., Am. Legion. Roman Catholic. Clubs: Rotary, K.C. Home: Lincoln, Nebr.

CLITHEROE, LORD (SIR RALPH ASSHETON), banker, industrialist; b. nr. Clitheroe, Eng., Feb. 24, 1901; s. Sir Ralph and Mildred (Master) Assheton; M.A. with honours in history, Christ Church, Oxford U., 1923; m. Sylvia Hotham, Jan. 24, 1924; children—Bridget (Mrs. Marcus Worsley), Ralph John, Nicholas. Called to bar Inner Temple, 1925; M.P. for Rushcliffe, City of London, Blackburn, 1934-55; mem. House of Lords, 1955-84; privy counsellor, 1944-84; financial sec. Treasury Dept., 1942-44; chmn. Borax Holdings, 1958-84, Mercantile Investment Trust, 1956-84; vice chmn. John Brown & Company, 1959-84, Tube Investments; deputy chairman Nat. Westminster Bank; director of U.S. Borax and Chemical Corporation, also Coutts & Co., Nat. Mut. Life Assn. Australia, English & Calddonian Investment Trust, Union Miniere, Nat. Westminster Bank, Ltd., Rio Tinto Zinc Corp., Ltd., Nat. Provincial & Rothschild (Internat.) Ltd., others. Vice-lt. County Lancashire, 1956-84; justice of peace, 1934-84; Created Lord Clitheroe, 1955; High Steward of Westminster, 1962. Fellow Soc. of Antiquaries. Home: Clitheroe, England Died Sept. 18, 1984.

CLOSE, HUGH WILLIAM, textile manufacturing executive; b. Phila., Nov. 18, 1919; s. Hugh William and Marian Lucy (Crandall) C.; m. Anne Kingsley Springs, Nov. 23, 1946; children—Lillian Crandall (Mrs. Erskine B. Bowles), Frances Allison Hart, Leroy Springs, Patricia (Mrs. Thomas G. Hastings), Elliott Springs, Hugh William, Derick Springsteen, Katherine Anne. B.S., U. Pa., 1942; grad., Exec. Program, U. N.C., 1959; LL.D. (hon.), U. S.C., 1967. With Springs Mills, Inc., N.Y.C., from 1946, beginning as mem. sales staff, Fort Mill, S.C.; succesively apprentice Springs Mills, Inc. (Springs Cotton Mills); asst. supt., asst. mgr. Springs Mills, Inc. (Fort Mill plant), gen. supt. card and spinning, asst. gen. mgr., asst. to pres., v.p., 1946-59; pres., dir. Springs Mills, Inc., 1966-69, chmn., from 1969; dir., chmn. Kanawha Ins. Co., L&C Devel. Corp., Lancaster & Chester Ry., Leroy Springs & Co., The Springs Co., Carolina Loan & Realty Co., Am. Ins. Agy., Inc., Carolina's Northwestern Ry; dir. Charter Properties, Inc. Commr. 5th dist. S.C. Dept. Parks, Recreation and Tourism, 1967-78; chmn. bd. dirs. Elliott White Springs Found., Frances Ley Springs Found.; bd. dirs. U. S.C. Devel. Adv. Council, J.E. Sirrine Textile Found., Bus. Partnership Found. Coll. Bus. Adminstrn. U.S.C.; trustee S.C. Coll. Council, Inc. Served as pvt. AUS, 1942; ensign to lt. (s.g.) USNR, 1942-46. Named Textile Man of Year N.Y. Bd. Trade, 1963. Mem. Am. Textile Mfrs. Inst., Inc. (pres. 1972-73, dir.), S.C. Textile Mfrs. Assn. (dir., v.p. 1977-78), Newcomen Soc. N. Am., Phi Gamma Delta, Beta Gamma Sigma. Episcopalian. Club: Lions (Fort Mill). Home: Fort Mill, SC.

CLOUSE, JOHN HENRY, prof. engring.; b. Somerset, O., April 22, 1887; s. William Henry and Bertha (Green) C.; diploma, elec. engring., Ohio U., 1911; S.B. (indsl. arts), Armour Inst., 1920, S.B. (mech. engring.), 1921, M.E., 1925; student, U. of Chicago, 1920-30, 1931-32; m. Ruth Mary Cowan, June 5, 1930. Apprentice instr., I.C.R.R., 1913-16; instr., mech. engring., U. of Ark., 1916-19; head, dept., physics, Sioux Falls (S.D.) high sch., 1921-29; instr., mech. engring., U. of Notre Dame, 1929-30; asst. prof. mech. engring., Ore. State Coll., 1930-31; asso. prof. of physics, U. of Miami, 1932-41, prof., physics, 1941-42, coordinator, civilian pilot training, 1939-41, area supr., engring. sci. management, War Training Program, 1940-42, prof. from 1945, head dept. physics, 1945-52, dean engring. from 1947; specialist in engring. edn., U.S. Office of Edn., 1942-43; test engr., Lion Mfg. Co., 1944-45. Named Engr. of the Year, So. Fla., 1954. Served as mech. engr., USN, 1943-44. Mem. Sioux Falls Engring. Soc. (life mem.; sec.), Am. Soc. Mech. Engrs. (chmn. Fla. sect., 1940-41), Am. Soc. Engring. Edn., Fla. Acad. Scis., Sigma Xi (local pres., 1954-56), Phi Kappa Phi, Omnicron Delta Kappa. Democrat. Catholic. Author papers before socs. Home: Coral Gables, Fla. †

CLYDE, WILFORD WOODRUFF, gen. contractor; b. Springville, Utah, Oct. 27, 1889; s. Hyrum Smith and Elanora (Johnson) C.; B.S. in Elec. Engring., U. Utah, 1913; m. Henrietta Palfreyman, Oct. 1, 1913 (dec. Sept. 1922); children—Wilford Cornell, Blaine Palfreyman, William Russell, Ila Mae (Mrs. Vernon O. Cook); m. 2d, Jennie Ailene Palfreyman, Sept. 21, 1923; children—Louise (Mrs. Blake H. Gammell), Carol (Mrs. David E. Salisbury). Chmn. bd. W. W. Clyde & Co., gen. contractors, Springville, from 1927; pres. Knight Ideal Coal Co., Carbon County, Utah, from 1948, Utah Service, Inc., Springville, from 1940, Utah Valley Indsl. Supply Co., Springville, from 1961, Ideal Nat. Ins. Co., Salt Lake City, from 1958; v.p. Geneva Rocks Products Co., Owen, Utah, from 1954; adv. com. Farmers and Merchants br. Walker Bank & Trust Co., Provo, Utah. Pres. Utah Nat. Parks council Boy Scouts Am., 1952-64. Mayor of Springville, 1942-44. Bd. regents U. Utah, from 1963. Mem. Asso. Gen. Contractors Am. (pres. intermountain br. 1939), Springville C. of C. (pres. 1943). Mem. Ch. of Jesus Christ of Latter Day Saints (bishop, mem. high council Springville Stake). Kiwanian (pres. Springville 1939). Home: Springville, UT. †

CLYNE, CHARLES TERENCE, advt. exec.; b. Phila.; s. Charles T. and Mary (Reall) C.; A.B., Amherst (Mass.) Coll.; m. Frances Donelon, Oct. 6, 1946; children—Terence Donelon, Michael John. Vice pres. Free & Peters, Inc., 1937-46; exec. v.p. The Biow Co., Inc., N.Y.C., 1946-54; vice chmn. bd. McCann-Erickson, Inc., 1954-61; chmn. bd. M.E. Prodns., 1954-61; exec. v.p. Maxon, Inc., 1962-64, pres., 1964; pres. Clyne Co., Inc., 1965-81, also chmn. bd.; chmn. bd. Coral TV Corp., 1965-70. Served as col. with Eighth Air Force, World War II. Decorated Bronze Star with oak leaf cluster, Legion of Merit, Croix de Guerre. Clubs: Maidstone, Devon Yacht (East Hampton, N.Y.); N.Y. Athletic, Met. (N.Y.C.); Bridgehampton, Greenwich Country; Palm Bay, Bath and Tennis, Jockey (Miami, Fla.); Racquet, Tennis (Palm Springs, Calif.). Home: Greenwich, Conn. Died Nov. 30, 1981.

COAN, FRANK SPEER, specialist, Office of War Information; b. Urumia, Persia (now Rezaieh, Iran), Mar. 26, 1889; s. Frederick Gaylord and Ida Jane (Speer) C.; (parents U.S. citizens); A.B., Williams Coll., 1911; B.D., Hartford Theol. Sem., 1917; student New Coll., Edinburgh and Mansfield Coll., Oxford, 1914-15; m. Janet Tryon Stone, Sept. 21, 1918; children—Mary Frances, Ellen Stone, Stuart Frederick Gaylord, Nancie Somerville, Janet Speer. With E. S. Woodworth & Co., grain commn. mchts., Minneapolis, 1911-13; Y.M.C.A. sec. with B.E.F. in Mesopotamia and India, 1915-16; Y.M.C.A. sec. with A.E.F., France, 1917-18; Y.M.C.A. sec., Lahore and Hyderabad (Deccan), India, 1919-31; free lance lecturer on internat. affairs, 1931-34; gen. sec. English-Speaking Union of U.S., 1935-42; Near and Middle East expert, Office of War Information, from 1942. Awarded Brit. Gen. Service Medal, 1918. Mem. Phi Gamma Delta. Presbyterian. Home: Princeton, N.J. Deceased.

COBB, WILLIAM BALLINGER, lawyer; b. Kansas City, Kans., Dec. 3, 1894; s. Alfred H. and Carrie Lee Place; m. Olivine Steffens, Aug. 19, 1939; children: Stephen Henry, Stephanie Marguerite; m. Lee Ann Koth, Sept. 12, 1959. A.B., U. Wyo., 1916; LL.B., Kans. U., 1920, J.D., 1968. Bar: Wyo. 1920, Hawaii 1948. Practice law, Casper, Wyo., 1920-41; surplus property officer Dept. Interior for Hawaii, 1945-47, practice law, Hawaii, from 1948, Honolulu; bankruptcy judge U.S. Dist. Ct., Hawaii, 1962-76; Mem. Wyo. State Legislature, 1925-29; arbitrator industries and Internat. Longshoreman's and Warehousemen's Union AFL-CIO, Sugar, Pineapple and Longshore Unions; dir. CD Agy., Hawaii, 1950-53; pub. mem., chmn. Hawaii Employment Relations Bd.; chmn. Territorial Traffic Safety Com., 1958-64. Candidate for del. to Congress, 1950. Served with U.S. Army, 1917-19, 41-46; col. Judge Adv. Gen. Corps 1954. Decorated Legion of Merit. Mem. Am. Legion, VFW, Res. Officers Assn., Am. Bar Assn., Bar Assn. Hawaii, Ret. Officers Assn., Assn. U.S. Army. Clubs: Mason (Shriner), Elk, Kiwanian. Home: Honolulu, HI.

COBB, WILLIAM J., business exec.; b. Atlanta, Ga., Aug. 31, 1888; s. Eldorado H. and Elisia (Kinney) C.; grad. student in economics; married, Sept. 25, 1919; children—William J., Nell. Vice pres. Melville Shoe Corp., New York, N.Y. Mem. Y.M.C.A., Boy Scouts of Am., Mem. Economic Soc. of New York, Am. Marketing Assn., Nat. Retail Shoe Assn. (dir.), New York County Republican Club. Club: New York Salesmanager. Contbr. articles on shoes and leather to mags. and jours. Home: New Rochelle, N.Y. Deceased.

COBLENTZ, STANTON ARTHUR, author; b. San Francisco, Aug. 24, 1896; s. Mayer and Mattie (Arndt) C.; m. Flora Bachrach, 1922. A.B., U. Calif., 1917, A.M., 1919. Mem. staff San Francisco Examiner, 1919-20; book reviewer N.Y. Times, N.Y. Sun, N.Y. Herald, Internat. Book Rev., 1920—. Author: books including An Editor Looks at Poetry, 1947, The Sunken World, 1948, Unseen Wings; anthology, 1949, Garnered Sheaves; verse, 1949, New Poetic Lamps and Old, 1950, Into Plutonian Depths, 1950, After 12,000 Years, 1950, Time's Travelers, 1952, From Arrow to Atom Bomb, 1953, From a Western Hilltop, 1954, Under the Triple Suns, 1954, The Rise of the Anti-Poets, 1955, The Pageant of Man, 3d edit, 1957,

Villains and Vigilantes, 1957, Magic Casements, 1957, The Blue Barbarians, Out of Many Songs, The Long Road to Humanity, 1959, My Life in Poetry, 1960, Next Door to the Sun, 1960, Atlantis and Other Poems, 1960, The Runaway World, 1961, The Swallowing Wilderness, 1961, Redwood Poems, 1961, The Generation That Forgot to Sing, 1962, The Moon People, 1964, The Last of the Great Race, 1964, The Lizard Lords, 1964, Avarice: A History, 1965, Ten Crises in Civilization, 1965, Demons, Witch Doctors and Modern Man, 1965, The Paradox of Man's Greatness, 1966, Lord of Tranerica, 1966, The Poetry Circus, 1967, The Crimson Capsule, 1967, The Pageant of the New World, 1968, Aesop's Fables; rhymed versions, 1968, The Day the World Stopped, 1968, The Power Trap, 1970, The Militant Dissenters, 1970, The Challenge to Man's Survival, 1972, Selected Short Poems, 1974, The Lone Adventurer, 1975, Strange Universes: New Selected Poems, 1977, Sea Cliffs and Green Ridges: Poems of the West, 1979; compiler: Modern American Lyrics, 1924, Modern British Lyrics, 1925, The Music Makers, 1945, Unseen Wings, 1949, Poems to Change Lives, 1960, Sea Cliffs and Green Ridges: Poems of the West, 1979; editor: Wings A Quarterly of Verse, 1933-60; contbr. to newspapers and mags.; book reviewer: Los Angeles Times. Winner Peace Poetry Contest San Francisco Chronicle, 1918, Star Poem Contest The Poetry Rev., London, 1924; 1952 award Lyric Found. for Traditional Poetry, N.Y. Mem. Authors League Am., Poetry Soc. Am. Address: Monterey, Calif. Died Sept. 6, 1982.

COCHRAN, DWIGHT M., corp. dir.; b. Lexington, Ill., Aug. 16, 1904; s. William and Elizabeth Ann (Jones) C.; B.S., U. Chgo., 1927; m. Stella Catherine Adams, Feb. 22, 1936; children—Dwight M., Stella Ann. With I.C. R.R., Chgo., 1922-23, White Weld & Co., 1927-30; asst. sales mgr. Kroger Co., Cin., 1931-38; dir. Eastern sales Joseph Schlitz Brewing Co., 1938-43; with Safeway Stores, Inc., 1943-56, v.p., 1951-56, dir., 1952-56; dir. Kern County Land Co., 1956-68, exec. v.p., 1957-59, pres., 1959-68, chief exec. officer, 1960-68; dir. Watkins-Johnson Co.; hon. dir. United Calif. Bank. Life trustee U. Chgo. Mem. Delta Upsilon. Republican. Presbyn. Clubs: Pacific-Union, Bohemian (San Francisco); Burlingame (Calif.) Country; Marrakesh Golf (Palm Desert, Calif.); Eldorado Country (Indian Wells, Calif.). Home: Palm Springs, Calif. Died Jan. 2, 1983.

COCHRAN, HARRY ALVAN, educator; b. Elk County, Pa., June 25, 1890; s. Robert Francis and Elizabeth Ann (Berkey) C.; B.S., Univ. Pitts., 1916; M.S., Temple Univ., 1924; Ed.D., 1930; LL.D., LaSalle Coll., 1936, Ursinus Coll., 1951; m. Molly Anderson, July 16, 1919; children—Bryce Clark, Robert Anderson, William Cody. Teacher pub. and high schs., Pa., 1909-14, high sch., St. Louis Mo., 1916-20; asst. prof. commercial edn., U. of Pittsburgh, 1920-21; prof. finance, Temple U., from 1921, dir. sch. of bus., 1925-34, dean, sch. bus. from 1934, dir. summer schs., 1925-46. Treas. Temple U., 1945-55, v.p.; from 1955; sec. Phila. County Bd. Pub. Asst., 1939-41. Served in O.T.C., Ft. Riley, Kan., 1917. Mem. Am. Economic Assn., N.E.A., Phi Delta Kappa, Delta Sigma Pi, Beta Gamma Sigma. Republican. Episcopalian. Mason. (Shriner). Home: Glenside, Pa. †

COCHRAN, JACQUELINE (MRS. FLOYD B. ODLUM), aviatrix; b. Pensacola, Fla.; D.Sc. (hon.), Northland Coll., 1960; LL.D. (hon.), Elmira Coll., 1955; Litt.D. (hon.), Russell Sage Coll., 1955, D.Mil.Sci. (hon.), Northeastern U., 1977; m. Floyd B. Odlum, May 11, 1936. With cosmetics industry from age 14; owner of cosmetic mfg. co., 1935-63; received pilot's license after 3 weeks tng., Roosevelt Field, L.I., 1932; additional tng. in Calif. for 1 yr., equal to U.S. Navy course in groundwork and flight; flew comml., transport and army pursuit planes and bombers; only Am. woman entrant in McRobertson London-Melbourne race, 1934; 1st woman to fly in Bendix transcontinental race, 1934; winner 1st place in women's div. and 3d place against field of men in Bendix race, 1937; winner of Bendix race, 1938, 2d place, 1946, and 3d place, 1948; 1st woman to pass sonic barrier and exceed speed of sound in Sabre jet F-86, 1953; holder internat., U.S. 2,000 Kilometer records and numerous other speed, distance and altitude records including flights in 1964 at more than twice the speed of sound, world speed records Lockheed F-104-G Starfighter, 1963, 64; piloted bombing plane across the North Atlantic, June 1941; took group of Am. women pilots to Eng., Mar. 1942, for service with Brit. Air Transport Aux., in which she held rank of flight capt.; apptd. dir. Women Pilots, U.S. Air Force, July 1943, after having headed Woman Pilot Tng. program of Army Air Force for several months; commd. lt. col. in USAF Res., 1948, col., 1969. Cons. NASA; dir. Storer Broadcasting Co. Mem. Calif. State and Riverside County Republican Central Com. Trustee George Washington U., from 1962; bd. dirs. Air Force Acad. Found.; trustee Air Force Mus. Found.; v.p. Air Force Hist. Found.; trustee Donald Douglas Mus. and Library; hon. bd. dirs. Am. Hall Aviation History; permanent trustee Internat. Women's Air and Space Mus. Decorated D.F.C. with two oak leaf clusters, Legion of Merit; Order Legion Honor (France); Pionierkette Winderose (W. Germany); recipient Clifford Burke Harman trophy Internat. League of Aviators, 1937, 38, 39, 46, 50 (for years 1940-49), 53; Distinguished Civilian Service award Air Force Assn., 1948; Mitchell award for gen. serial achievements, 1937; McGough Meml., 1940; D.S.M. (only civilian woman to receive this award); Gold medal Fedn. Aeronautique Internationale, 1953; Zonta Achievement award, 1957; elected to Aviation Hall of Fame, 1971; memorabilia dedicated as permanent display Air Force Acad., Colorado Springs, Colo., 1975; pvt. papers donated to Dwight D. Eisenhower Library, Abilene, Kans., 1975. Fellow Soc. Exptl. Test Pilots (hon.); mem. Ninety-Nines (internat. orgn. of women pilots) (pres. 1942-43), Fedn. Aeronautique Internationale (sr. v.p. 1956-57, pres. 1959), Internat. Acad. Astronautics (hon. life), Bus. and Profl. Womens' Clubs Calif., Nat. Aero. Assn. (hon. pres.). Club: Zonta. Author: The Stars at Noon, 1954. Address: Indio, Calif. Died Aug. 9, 1980.

COCHRAN, THOMAS EVERETTE, clinical psychologist, minister, writer, lecturer; born Shepherdsville, Kentucky, 1889; son of James Nathan and Margaret Elizabeth (Howlett) C.; A.B., U. of Richmond (Va.), 1911; A.M., U. of Chicago, 1914. B.D. in Practical Sociology, 1915; Th.D. in Relig. Edn., Crozer Theol. Sem., 1916; Ph.D., U. of Pa., 1921; m. Irma Elizabeth Holding, June 6, 1921; children—Thomas Everette, William Malcolm. Professor math., sociology, Columbia Coll., Lake City, Fla., 1911-13, prof. edn. and psychology, 1916-17; prof. edn. and psychology and dir. sch. of edn., Wake Forest (N.C.) Coll., 1917-21; prof. secondary edn. and sch. administration and dir. summer sch., Flora Macdonald Coll., Red Springs, N.C., 1919; prof. ednl. psychology and ednl. tests and measurements, Western State Teachers Coll., Cullowhee, N.C., summers 1920-25; dean and prof. edn. and psychology, Judson Coll., Marion, Ala., 1921-26; prof. of edn. and psychology, dir. summer sch. and junior dean, Georgetown Coll., 1926-30; prof. psychology and edn., Centre Coll., 1930-53; prof. emeritus 1953; prof. psychology and edn., Transylvania Coll., summer 1930; prof. psychology, Berea Coll., summer 1931 Center Coll., Summers 1932-53; licensed to preach 1908, Baptist minister in connection with college teaching for 20 years in various churches; was certified as a clinical psychologist by the Kentucky State Board of Psychology, 1950; director Orlando Guidance and Counseling Center. Member of the Florida Psychological Assn., So. Assn. Psychology and Philosophy, Nat. Religious Edn. Assn., Kappa Phi Kappa, Lambda Chi Alpha. Baptist. Mason (past master Franklin Lodge, Danville, Ky.); Order of Eastern Star (worthy grand patron of Ky., 1934-35), Order White Shrine of Jerusalem, Daughters America, Kiwanian. Author: History of Pub. Sch. Edn. in Fla.; Elements of Gen. Psychology—An Outline; A Guide to the Study of Ednl. Psychology; Eastern Star Addresses; Manual for the Study of Adolescent Psychology; Workbook in Adolescent Psychology; Laboratory Studies in General Psychology; Cochran Group Test of Mental Ability, Advanced Examination, Forms A & B; Syllogistic Reasoning Test; Introversion-Extroversion Test; Dominance-Submission Test; Emotional Stability Test, and articles in ednl. and psychol. journals. Home: Orlando, Fla. †

CODY, JOHN CARDINAL, cardinal, archbishop of Chgo.; b. St. Louis, Dec. 24, 1907; s. Thomas Joseph and Mary (Begley) C. Grad., St. Louis Prep. Sem., 1926; Ph.D., N.Am. Coll., Rome, 1928, S.T.D., 1932, D.Canon Law, 1936. Ordained priest Roman Catholic Ch., 1931; aux. bishop Diocese St. Louis, 1947-54, co-adjutor with right of succession to bishop of, St. Joseph, Mo., 1954, bishop of, 1955; coadjutor to Archbishop-Bishop of, Kansas City-St. Joseph, Aug., 1956; bishop of, Kansas City-St. Joseph, Oct. 1956; coadjutor with right of succession to Archdiocese New Orleans, 1961, apostolic adminstr., 1962-64, archbishop, New Orleans, 1964, Chgo., from 1965; elevated to Sacred Coll. of Cardinals, 1967; Mem. Sacred Congregation Clergy; chancellor Cath. Ch. Extension Soc.; nat. chaplain Nat. Cath. Soc. Foresters; high spiritual dir. Cath. Order Foresters. Mem. N.Am. Coll. Alumni Assn., Nat. Conf. Cath. Bishops. Address: Chicago, Ill.

COE, FRED(ERICK) A(TKINS), paper manufacturer; b. Harrison, N.J., Feb. 3, 1889; s. Harry Barwood and Rosetta Wilhelmina Frederica (Horstmann) C.; student Woods Bus. Coll., Newark, 1904, Newark Tech. Sch., night, 1905-07, 1908-09, Mechanics' Inst., N.Y. City, nights, 1910-11, Columbia, nights, 1914-18; B.S., Cooper Union, 1918, C.E., 1921; m. Ella Louise Mullen, Mar. 10, 1911; children—Beatrice E. (Mrs. Ben F. Ingraham), Fred A. Jr. Plant engr., W.Va. Pulp & Paper Co., Mechanicsville, N.Y., 1922-42, asst. mill mgr., 1942-47, mill mgr. from 1947, dir. since 1948; dir. and mem. exec. bd., Indian River Co., Albany, N.Y., from 1947. Licensed profl. engr., N.Y. State Dir. Associated Industries of N.Y. State; mem. Tech. Assn. of the Pulp and Paper Industry, Omega Delta Phi. Episcopalian (vestryman). Mason. Club: Masonic. Home: Mechanicsville, N.Y. †

COE, SAMUEL GWYNN, college prof.; b. Blacksburg, Va., Dec. 28, 1888; s. Henry Slicer and Cornelia (Pettigrew) C.; student Randolph-Macon Acad., Front Royal, Va., 1904-06; A.B., Washington and Lee U., 1909, M.A., 1916; Ph.D., Johns Hopkins, 1926; m. Anna Ford, of Front Royal, Sept. 10, 1921; children—Ann Louise, Ruth Beverly. Instr. Randolph-Macon Acad., 1909-11; prin. Va. high schs., 1911-15 and 1919-23; prof. history, Southern Coll., Lakeland, Fla., from 1926. Commd. 2d lt. U.S.A., 1917; instr. in history, A.E.F.U. of Beaune, Cote d'Or, France, 1919. Mem. Phi Beta Kappa, Pi Gamma Mu. Wrote "The Mission of William Carmichael to Spain," in Johns Hopkins Studies, 1926, William Carmichael in Dictionary of Am. Biography. Home: Lakeland, Fla. †

COEN, HARRY B., motors corp. exec.; b. Columbus, O., Jan. 27, 1888. Locomotive fireman C. & O. R.R., 1906, locomotive engr., 1910; prodn. supt. Ford Motor Co., Columbus, 1914; automobile dealer, 1916-29; with prodn. div. of motor transport, Detroit Region, Gen. Motors Corp., during World War I, gen. mgr. of parts mfg. plant, Columbus, 1923-33, supt. sheet metal div. Chevrolet Div., Flint, Mich., 1933, gen. supt. mfg., 1935, mgr. Chevrolet operations, Flint, 1937, mem. personnel staff, central office, Detroit, 1939, dir. labor relations to 1946, now v.p. in charge of employe relations staff. Address: Detroit, Mich. †

COFFMAN, HAROLD COE, govt. ofcl.; b. Moran, Kan., Sept. 13, 1889; s. Jesse Hughes and Laura (Coe) C.; grad. Kan. State Teachers Coll., Emporia, 1910; A.B., U. of Kan., Lawrence, 1915; grad. student George Williams Coll., Chicago, 1916-17, U. of Chicago (fellow), 1916-17; A.M., U. of Mich., 1922; Ph.D., Columbia, 1936; m. Aletha Morrow, June 19, 1917; children—Ray Harold, Kenneth Morrow, Nita Lee. Tchr., prin. pub. schs., YMCA worker, 1907-26; prof., chmn. department philosophy and psychology, Mich. State Coll., 1927-28; prof. psychology and education Northwestern U., 1928-30, 1935-36, prof. lectr. 1936 from; cons. psychologist, Riverside Church, N.Y.C., 1930-35; pres. and trustee George Williams Coll., Chgo., 1936-53; pres. Asso. Colls. Ill., Inc., Chgo., 1953-54; chief edn. div. U.S. Operation Mission, Egypt, 1955 from. Mem. S.E. Chgo. Commn. Del. World's Com. Y.M.C.A.'s Plenary Meeting and Consultation on Leadership Training, Denmark, 1950. Mem. adv. selection com. Fulbright Act, Internat. Exchange of Persons. Chmn. 8th Annual Chicago Recreation Conf.; collaborator, Div. of Program Surveys of the U.S. Govt. Served as 1st lt. U.S. Army, World War I. Recipient Danish Medal, King Christian den Tiendes Frihedsmedaille. Fellow Nat. Council on Religion in Higher Edn., chmn. 1931-33; mem. Am. Assn. Univ. Profs., Am. Psychol. Assn., National Com. for Mental Hygiene, N.E.A., Association of Consulting Psychologists, Adult Education Council of Chicago, Am. Assn. for Study of Group Work, Phi Delta Kappa, Beta Epsilon, Pi Gamma Mu. Baptist. Clubs: University (Evanston); Union League, Colony, Rotary (Chgo.); Torch (Lansing). Author: American Foundations—A Study of Their Role in the Child Welfare Movement, 1936. Contbr. to jour. Mem. reviewing com. for Dictionary of Education.†

COGAN, DAVID HAROLD, corporate executive; b. nr. Barton, Vt., Jan. 10, 1909; s. Bened and Annie (Grant) C.; m. Martha Sharp, 1957; 1 son, Bruce M. Student, Northeastern U., 1926-30. Sales engr. Hytron Corp., Salem, Mass., 1930, sales mgr., 1931; pres., dir. Air King Products Co., Inc., Bklyn., 1946-54, Royal Wood Products Co., Inc., 1946-54, King Assocs., Inc., 1946-54, CBS-Columbia, Inc., 1951-54, Seymour Chevrolet Sales, Inc., 1954-67, Continental Discount Fund, Inc., 1955-64, Tri-Continental Realty Corp., 1960-67, Victoreen Instrument Co., 1957-74; pres. treas., dir. D.H. Cogan, Inc., 1952-65, Pathe Radio Corp., 1942-54, Ravac Electronics Corp., 1942-57, Continental Holding Corp., 1954-61; v.p. dir. Hytron Radio & Electronics Corp., 1931-54, CBS, Inc., 1951-54, CBS-Hytron, 1951-54; treas., dir. Atlantic Realty, Inc., 1952-57, Continental Holding Corp., 1954-61; dir. Premier Microwave, 1963-83; chmn. bd. Mirawal Corp., 1955-56, VLN Corp., 1955-74, Phaostron Instrument & Electronic Co., 1966-69, Bohn Bus. Machines, Inc., 1964-68, Colonial Press, Inc., 1967-74, Dreyfus Consumer Bank, 1982-85, Dreyfus Life Ins. Co., 1982-85; chmn. bd., pres. Nuclear Electronics Ohio, Inc., 1955-59; vice chmn. bd., dir. Sheller-Globe Corp., 1974-85; pres., treas., dir. D.H.C. Inc., 1967-79, Natick Corp., 1973-85; dir., chmn. exec. com. Estey Organ Co., 1956-64; dir. Dreyfus Tax Exempt Bond Fund, Inc., Dreyfus Tax Exempt Money Market Fund, Inc., The Dreyfus Corp. Vice pres., sec., dir. L. Peter Cogan Found.; pres., treas., dir. David H. Cogan Found.; bd. dirs., trustee Northeastern U.; bd. dirs. Nat. Energy Found.; trustee Nat. Commn. for Coop. Edn.; chmn. bd. Am. Council for Nationalities Service. Mem. N.A.M., Radio Electronic TV Mfrs. Assn. Clubs: Stamford Yacht; Princeton (N.Y.C.). Home: Stamford, Conn. Died Jan. 26, 1985.

COGSWELL, FRANKLIN DEWEY, religious educator; b. Beatrice, Neb., June 13, 1889; s. Ben Reuben and Harriet Franklin (Hill) C.; A.B., U. of Denver, 1912; student Union Theol. Sem., New York, 1915-17; A.M., Teachers Coll., Columbia, 1917; Dr. Christian Service, Hillsdale College, 1944; Doctor of Letters, Univ. of Denver (Colo.), 1947; m. Elizabeth Stocker Fraser, Sept. 3, 1919. Professor of English Ewing Christian Coll., Allahabad, India, 1912-15; ednl. sec. Missionary Edn. Movement of U.S. and Can., 1917-46, general sec., 1946-50; gen. director Commn. on Missionary Edn., Nat. Council Churches of Christ in the U.S.A. from 1950. Member Phi Beta Kappa, Sigma Delta Chi. Presbyterian. Editor: interdenom. books for study of home and foreign missions. Home: Caldwell, N.J. †

COHAGEN, CHANDLER CARROLL, architect, Masonic officer; b. near Pierson, Ia., Apr. 24, 1889; s. John R. and Mary Francis (Turner) C.; B.S., U. of Mich., 1915; m. Flora John Brown, Sept. 18, 1917. Pres. McIver, Cohagen & Marshall (architects), Billings and Great Falls, Mont., 1915-20, McIver & Cohagen, 1920-36; independent practice as Chandler C. Cohagen, Billings, Montana, from 1936; chief architect on Eau Claire Ordnance Plant for Smith, Hinchman and Grylls, 1942;

83 WHO WAS WHO

secretary and director Treasure State Development Company. International trustee DeMolay Foundation, Inc.; mem. executive board of Grand Council of Order of DeMolay, from 1929, grand master, 1938-39, grand treasurer, from 1953; inspector general honorary 33 deg. Scottish Rite, Southern Jurisdiction, from 1937. Mem. Billings City Council, 1925-26; pres. State Bd. Archtl. Examiners, 1922-24, 36-61; pres. Nat. Council Archtl. Registration Bds., 1962-63; gov. 11th Dist. Mont. State Advisory Planning Bd.; pres. Billings Commercial Club, 1937; pres. Billings Y.M.C.A., 1925-45, Montana Y.M.-C.A., from 1956, board of directors of North Central Region; formerly vice president and trustee Billings Polytechnic Inst.; formerly sec., trustee Inter-mountain Coll., Billings; pres. International DeMolay Foundation, Inc. Awarded Academic medal by American Inst. Architects, 1915. Fellow A.I.A. (pres. Mont. Chpt. 1928-36), Internat. Inst. Arts and Letters; mem. Royal Order Scotland, Am. Soc. Heating and Ventilating Engrs. (life mem.), Alpha Rho Chi (founder, nat. archon), Delta Phi, Tau Sigma Delta. Republican. Mem. Disciples of Christ Ch. Mason (33 deg., K.T., Shriner); grand master Mont. Grand Lodge, A.F. & A.M. 1951-52. Club: Kiwanis (pres. 1949). Home: Billings, Mont. †

COHEN, BENJAMIN VICTOR, lawyer; b. Muncie, Ind., Sept. 23, 1894; s. Moses and Sarah (Ringold) C.; Ph.B., U. Chgo., 1914, J.D., 1915; S.J.D., Harvard, 1916; LL.D., Dropsie Coll., 1952, Ball State U., 1969, Brandeis U., 1975; D.H.L., Hebrew Union Coll.-Jewish Inst. Religion, 1979; Admitted to Ill. bar, 1916, N.Y. State bar, 1924; sec. to U.S. circuit judge, 1916-17; atty. U.S. Shipping Bd., 1917-19; counsel Am. Zionists, Peace Confs., London, Paris, 1919-21; pvt. practice N.Y.C., 1922-33; asso. gen. counsel PWA, 1933-34; gen. counsel Nat. Power Policy Com., 1934-1941; spl. asst. to U.S. atty. gen., concerned with pub. utility holding co. litigation, 1936-38; adviser Am. ambassador to Gt. Britain, 1941; asst. to dir., Office Econ. Stblzn., 1942-43; gen. counsel Office of War Moblzn., 1943-45; counselor Dept. State, 1945-47; assisted Congl. coms. in drafting Securities Act 1933, Securities and Exchange Act 1934, Utility Holding Co. Act 1935, Fair Labor Standards Act 1937; legal adviser Internat. Monetary Conf., Breton Woods, N.H., 1944; mem. Am. del. Dumbarton Oaks Conf., 1944, Berlin Conf., 1945, Council Fgn. Ministers, London, 1945, Moscow, 1945, 47, Paris, 1946, N.Y.C., 1946, Paris Peace Conf., 1946; sr. adviser Am. del. UN Gen. Assembly, London, N.Y., 1946, mem. del., Paris, 1948, 51, N.Y.C., 1949, 50, 52; U.S. rep. before Internat. Ct. Justice, The Hague, 1950; U.S. rep. on UN Disarmament Commn., 1952; Oliver Wendell Holmes lectr. Harvard Law Sch., 1961; David Miles Meml. lectr. Hebrew U. Jerusalem, 1965; mem. adv. panel internat. law Dept. State, 1968; Royer lectr. U. Calif. at Berkeley, 1974. Recipient Isaiah award, Washington chpt. Am. Jewish Com., 1969. Mem. Phi Beta Kappa. Author: The United Nations Constitutional Development, Growth and Possibilities, 1961; also articles. Home: Washington, D.C. Died Aug. 16, 1983.

COHEN, CHARLES L., mfg. co. exec.; b. Chgo., July 8, 1895; s. Charles and Lena (Broslov) C.; student U. Chgo. 1912-13; LL.B., Webster Coll. Law, 1917; m. Thelma Panama, June 15, 1921; children—Donald, Joann. Admitted to Ill. bar 1917; jr. partner M. Snower & Co., 1913-17, sec., 1917-24, pres., treas., 1924-54; chmn. bd. Opelika Mfg. Corp., from 1954. Republican. Jewish religion. Mason; mem. B'nai B'rith. Clubs: Standard, Bryn Mawr Country (past pres.); Tamarisk Country (Palm Springs, Calif.). Home: Palm Springs, Calif. Deceased.

COHEN, HERBERT ERWIN, lawyer, supermarket exec.; b. Utica, N.Y., Nov. 3, 1932; s. Moe and Mae (Greenbaum) C.; m. Phyllis Simonovitz, July 14, 1957; children—Linda Jean, Michael Howard, David Jonathan. A.B., U. Mich., 1953; J.D., Union U., 1957; LL.M. in Taxation, N.Y. U., 1958. Bar: N.Y. bar 1958, also U.S. Supreme Ct 1958. With firm Strang, Wright, Combs, Wiser & Shaw, Rochester, N.Y., 1958-59, Marine Midland Corp., Buffalo, 1959-61; individual practice law, Albany, N.Y., 1961-64; with Newkirk Assos., Inc., 1964-65; sr. v.p., gen. counsel, sec. Price Chopper Markets, Inc. (Golub Corp.), Schenectady, 1965-83; dir. Community State Bank; lectr. N.Y. State Bar Assn., Practising Law Inst., Albany Law Sch., Am. Mgmt. Assn., Food Mktg. Inst. Vice pres. Albany Jewish Family Services, 1971-73, pres., 1973-75, also trustee, 1967-77; trustee Daus. of Sarah Home for the Aged, Troy, N.Y., 1969-77, treas., 1974-76, v.p., 1976-77; bd. dirs. Albany Jewish Community Council. Mem. N.Y. State Bar Assn., Food Mktg. Inst. (lawyers and economists com.). Jewish (trustee congregation). Home: Albany, NY. Died Apr. 9, 1983.

COHEN, IRA, neurological surgeon; b. Long Branch, N.J., Aug. 4, 1887; s. Maurice Samuel and Rosalie (Meyer) C.; B.S., Columbia, 1909, M.D., 1911; m. Dorothy Dreyfuss, Mar. 31, 1927. Interne, Mount Sinai Hosp., N.Y. City, 1911-14, adjunct surgeon, 1920-32, attending neurol. surgeon, 1932-50, cons. Served in Med. R.C. World War I; discharged as maj.; commd. colonel Med. Res. Corps, 1939; disqualified for active service in World War II. Diplomate Am. Bd. of Surgery and Neurological Surgery. Fellow Am. Coll. Surgeons, A.M.A., N.Y. Acad. Medicine; mem. Am. and N.Y. neurol. socs., N.Y. Surg. Soc., Mil. Order World Wars. Author numerous sci. papers. Home: Stratford, Conn. †

COHEN, JOSEPH GEORGE, educator; b. Berezino, Russia, Dec. 5, 1888; s. Matthew and Ida (Lasciak) C.; came to U.S., 1891, naturalized, 1897; A.B., Coll. of City of N.Y., 1908; A.M., N.Y. Univ., 1912, Pd.M., 1913, Ph.D., 1914; L.H.D. (honorary) Yeshiva University, 1961; married Emma Naomi Mabel, Nov. 22, 1925; children—Vera, Michael. Teacher and supervisor, pub. schs. of N.Y. City, 1908-25; instr. edn., Coll. of City of N.Y., 1921-25, asst. prof. edn., 1925-27, asso. professor, 1927-32; prof. edn., Brooklyn Coll., 1932-49; chmn. dept. edn., 1932-46; dir. extension div., 1932-34, dir. div. grad. studies, Bklyn. Coll., 1935-49; asso. dean tchr. edn., pub. colls. N.Y.C., 1949-51, dean, 1951-58; vis. prof. Am. Studies U. Bar Ilan, Israel, 1958-59; ednl. adviser Police Dept., N.Y.C., 1925-26; ednl. cons. Paramount Famous Players Corp., 1926-28; ednl. consultant N.Y. State Dept. of Edn., 1945-46. Served as pvt., U.S. Army, 1917-18; 1st lt., Res. Corps, 1918-21. Recipient Townsend Harris Medal, 1954. Member American Assn. Univ. Profs., Am. Academy Polit. and Social Science, Nat. Soc. of Coll. Teachers of Edn., N.E.A. (member dept. of superintendence), Phi Beta Kappa, Kappa Delta Pi. Co-author (with William Scarlet): Modern Pioneers, 1931; editor: Robinson Crusoe; author numerous articles on ednl. subjects. Home: Hampton Bays, N.Y. †

COHEN, NEHEMIAH MYER, merchant; b. Palestine, Jerusalem, Sept. 10, 1890; s. Jehuda and Leah (Dennenberg) C.; ed. Jerusalem; m. Naomi Halperin, Sept. 10, 1908; children—Emanuel, Israel, Lillian (Mrs. Lawrence P. Solomon). Came to U.S., 1915, naturalized, 1921. Ordained Orthodox rabbi, 1914; mem. clergy in U.S., 1915-21; with Giant Food Inc., 1936-84, pres., 1949-64, chmn. bd., 1964-84, gen. mgr., 1964; pres. Giant Foods Properties, 1957-84. Cabinet mem. United Jewish Appeal; mem. bd. United Givers Fund. Home: Washington, D.C. Died June 5, 1984.

COIT, DOROTHY, dramatic coach, author; b. Salem, Mass., Sept. 25, 1889; d. Robert and Eliza (Atwood) Coit; A.B., Radcliffe Coll., 1911; unmarried. Teacher of history, English and dramatics, Buckingham Sch., Cambridge, Mass., 1911-22; joint dir. Children's Theatre, from 1922; teacher of drama in Trent School, N.Y. Director reportory prodns.; Aucassin and Nicolete, The Tempest, The Rose and the Ring, etc. Episcopalian. Club: Cosmopolitan (N.Y.). Author: books: Ivory Throne of Persia; Kai Khosru and other plays for children. Address: New York, N.Y. †

COKE, ROSSER J., lawyer; b. Dallas, Tex., Aug. 3, 1888; grad. West Tex. Military Acad.; LL.B., Washington & Lee Univ., 1911. Admitted to Tex. bar, 1911; sr. mem. firm Coke & Coke. Vice pres. and dir. Universal Mills, Fort Worth, Tex. (atty.), Lone Star Cement Corp. (atty. Tex. div.); treas, atty. and dir. Dallas Hudson Co.; atty., mem. trust com. and dir. First Nat. Bank in Dallas; dir. Dallas Railway & Terminal Co., Gulf, Colorado & Santa Fe Railway. Vice pres. Navy League of the U.S. Mem. Bar Assn. Dallas, State Bar Texas, Am. Bar Assn., Phi Delta Phi. Home: Dallas, Tex. †

COLBURN, FRANCIS PEABODY, artist, educator; b. Fairfax, Vt., Oct. 20, 1909; s. John Edward and Florence (Read) C.; m. Gladys LaFlamme, Dec. 23, 1934; 1 son, David. Ph.B., U. Vt., 1934, Litt.D., 1974; spl. student painting, Bennington Coll.; scholar, Art Students League, N.Y.C.; L.H.D., U. Vt. Resident artist U. Vt., Burlington, 1942-84, chmn. art. dept., 1946-84; dir. Craftsbury Chamber Players, Inc. Exhibited one-man shows, Knoedler, McBeth galleries, Green Mountain Gallery, N.Y.C., Wood Gallery, Montpelier, Vt., also coll. and univs., group shows, Carnegie Inst., Corcoran Gallery, Whitney Mus. Am. Art, N.A.D., Audubon Artists Assn., Boston Inst. Contemporary Art, Chgo. Art Inst., Pasadena Art Inst., Cordova Mus., Boston, Conn. Acad. Art.; (Recipient awards for paintings Springfield (Mass.) Mus. Fine Arts, Boston Inst. Contemporary Art, San Francisco Palace Legion of Honor, Fleming Mus.); Author: Letters Home and Further Indiscretions, 1978, recs. of New Eng. humor. Trustee Vt. Symphony Orch. Mem. Vt. Art Tchrs. Assn. (pres.), So., No. Vt. art assns., Vt. Council on Arts (Distinguished Service award 1968), Artists Equity, Delta Psi. Episcopalian. Francis Peabody Colburn Gallery named in honor, U. Vt., 1974. Home: Burlington, Vt. Died Mar. 16, 1984.

COLDWELL, MAJOR JAMES WILLIAM, member of Parliament, Can.; b. Seaton, Devon, Eng., Dec. 2, 1888; s. James Henry and Elizabeth (Farrant) C.; ed. Heles Sch. Exeter, Eng., 1902-04, Royal Albert Memorial, University Coll., Exeter, 1905-09; m. Norah Gertrude Dunsford, July 22, 1912 (dec. June 26, 1953); children—John Maj. R.C.A.F.), Margaret Norah. Came to Canada, 1910; teacher, Dowling, Alberta, 1910-11; principal of school, Sedley, Saskatchewan, 1911-14, Regina, 1914-34; nat. sec. Co-op. Commonwealth Fedn., 1934-37, nat. chmn., 1938-42. Mem. House of Commons, Can., since 1935; House leader of Co-op. Commonwealth Fedn. from 1940. Nat. pres., 1942, re-elected 1944, served 1945-49. Del. Commonwealth Parliamentary Conf., London, 1941, 48, Ottawa, 1952; 8th Internat. Conf. Inst. Pacific Relations, 1942; leader Canadian del. Conf. of Labour, Socialist & Co-operative Political Parties of British Comonwealth of Nations, London, 1944, Toronto, 1947; visited Canadian battle line Northwest Europe, 1944. Mem. official Can. del. San Francisco Conf., 1945. Member Canadian Delegation, U. N. Assembly, N.Y., 1946, 50; mem. League for Indsl. Democracy U.S. (v.p.), Canadian Red Cross, Can. Inst. Internat. Affairs, United Nations Soc. of Can. (hon. v.p.), Univ. Club (Ottawa). Anglican. Author: Left Turn, Canada, etc. Home: Ottawa, Ont., Can. †

COLE, EDWARD CYRUS, educator; b. Pawtucket, R.I., Mar 26, 1904; s. Washington Leverett and Fanny Ethel (Nicholson) C.; m. Alice Sylvia Crawford, Sept. 6, 1930; children—Ann Frances Cole Berquist, James Washington Leverett. A.B., Dartmouth, 1926; M.F.A., Yale, 1942. Mem. faculty Yale, 1930—, asso. prof., 1946-71, emeritus, 1971—; prodn. mgr. Yale (Sch. Drama), 1946-66, exec. officer, 1959-64, acting dean, 1965-66, sr. faculty fellow, 1966-67; fellow Timothy Dwight Coll., 1959-71, asso. fellow, 1973—, Yale Alumni Bd., 1962-71, Assembly of Assn. Yale Alumni, 1972-77; practice as theatre planning cons., 1937—; central com. Am. Coll. Theater Festival, 1962-71, dept. nat. coordinator, 1969-71 (Gold medal 1972, Silver medal 1973); Bd. dirs. Yale Alumni Fund, 1962-71, Theatre Haven, Inc., 1970-78. Author: (with Harold Burris-Meyer) Scenery for the Theatre, 1938, 2d edit., 1972, Japanese edit., 1975, Theatres and Auditoriums, 1949, 2d edit., 1964, with supplement, 1975. Bd. govs. Am. Playwrights Theatre, 1963-72. Recipient Treasury citation for war bond sales, 1944; award Theta Alpha Phi, 1958; Founders award U.S. Inst. Theatre Tech., 1971. Fellow Am. Ednl. Theatre Assn. (pres. 1958, Merit award 1964), Am. Council for Arts in Edn. (dir. 1972, founding fellow 1973); mem. ANTA (dir., exec. com. 1953-69, 2d v.p. 1962, sec. 1967-68), Nat. Council Arts in Edn. (dir. 1962-72, exec. sec. 1962-66), U.S. Power Squadrons (life), AAUP, Mystic Seaport Branford hist. socs., Branford Land Trust, Conn. Conservation Assn., Hutmens Assn., New Eng. Theatre Conf. (regional citation 1967), New Haven Power Squadron, Zeta Psi. Episcopalian. Clubs: Yale (New Haven), Dartmouth (New Haven); Appalachian Mountain (life). Home: Branford CT Office: New Haven CT

COLE, FRANK L., physician, army officer; b. Paris, Ida., June 11, 1890; s. Walter C. and Louisa (Birdneau) C.; grad. So. branch U. of Ida., 1909; M.D., U. of Ill., 1914; m. Orba Ellsworth, June 2, 1917; children—Frank E., Josephine. Interne, City and County Hosp., St. Paul, 1914-16; in pvt. practice of medicine, Rigby, Ida., 1916-17; commd. 1st lt., M.C., U.S. Army 1917, and advanced through grades to brig. gen., 1948; assigned asst. and chief of surgery Trinler Gen. Hosp., Honolulu, 1928-31; chief gen. surgery Letterman Gen. Hosp., San Francisco, 1931-36; asst. chief surgeon Walter Reed Gen. Hosp., Washington, 1936-40; chief of surgery Army and Navy Gen. Hosp., Hot Springs, Ark., 1940-42; comdg. officer in various army hosps., 1942-46; chief cons. in surgery to The Surgeon Gen., 1946-48; comdg. gen. Letterman Gen. Hosp., 1948; now chief Med. and Health Services. Cal. Civil Def. Office. Decorated Legion of Merit, Army Commendation ribbon. Diplomate Internat. Bd. Surgery. Fellow A.C.S. (gov.). Internat. Coll. Surgeons; mem. A.M.A., Phi Beta Pi. Republican. Mason. Home: Daly City, Cal. †

COLE, JAMES P., prof. Math.; b. Galveston, Tex., Nov. 10, 1889; s. Robert E. L. and May (Perry C.; B.S., in C.E., La. State U., 1912, M.S., 1925; m. Una Currie, Jan. 26, 1913; children—Jim, Genevieve (Mrs. Paul Leslie), Bobby, Tommy, Coleen. Inst. mathematics La. State U., 1919-26; head mathematics dept., Louisiana Polytechnic Inst. 1926-32; dean student affairs La. State U., 1932-41, dir. high sch. relations, 1941-46, dir. student life and prof. math., since 1946. Served with inf., U.S. Army, 1913-19, retired as major; col. La. State Guard and exec. officer, 1943-46. Mem. La. Golf Assn. (pres. 1944-47), Am. Legion (dept. comdr. of La., 1942-43, nat. exec. com., 1943-45), Am. Math. Soc., Am. Math. Assn., Omicron Delta Kappa, Phi Kappa Phi, Kappa Sigma. Democrat. Catholic. Clubs: Baton Rouge Rotary, Baton Rouge Golf and country. Author: Plane and Spherical; Trigonometry Business Mathematics; Military Instructors Manual (Albany, N.Y.), 1917. Home: Baton Rouge, La.†

COLE, KENNETH S(TEWART), biophysicist, educator; b. Ithaca, N.Y., July 10, 1900; s. Charles Nelson and Mabel (Stewart) C.; m. Elizabeth Evans Roberts, June 29, 1932 (dec. 1966); children: Roger Braley, Sarah Roberts. A.B., Oberlin Coll., 1922; Sc.D. (hon.), 1954; Ph.D., Cornell U., 1926; Sc.D. (hon.), U. Chgo., 1967; M.D. (hon.), U. Uppsala, 1967. Fellow NRC, Harvard U., 1926-28; research fellow Gen. Edn. Bd., Leipzig, 1928-29, asst. prof. physiology Columbia, 1929-37, asso. prof., 1937-46; Cons. physicist Presbyn. Hosp., N.Y.C., 1929-46; fellow Guggenheim Found., Inst. Advanced Study, Princeton, 1941-42; prin. biophysicist, metall. lab. U. Chgo., 1942-46, prof. biophysics and physiology, 1946-49; tech. dir. Naval Med. Research Inst., Bethesda, 1949-54; chief lab of biophysics Nat. Inst. Neurol. Diseases and Blindness, NIH, Bethesda, Md., 1954-66, sr. research biophysicist, 1966-77, scientist emeritus, 1978-84; regents prof. U. Calif., Berkeley, 1963-64, prof. biophysics, 1965-77, adj. prof. neuroscis., San Diego, 1980-84; vis. prof. physiology and biophysics U. Tex. Med. Br., Galveston, 1972-84; Priestley lectr. Pa. State Coll., 1939; Tennent lectr. Bryn Mawr Coll., 1941. Mem. bd. Biol. Lab., Cold Spring Harbor, 1940-45; Trustee Marine Biol. Lab., Woods Hole, Mass., 1947-55, 56-64, emeritus, 1966—. Decorated Order of So. Cross Brazil; recipient Nat. Medal of Sci., 1967. Fellow Am. Acad. Arts and Scis., Am. Phys. Soc., AAAS, N.Y. Acad. Sci.; mem.

Nat. Acad. Scis., Am. Physiol. Soc. (council 1963- 65), Société philomatique Paris, Soc. Gen. Physiologists, Biophys. Soc. (council 1957-62, pres. 1963), Royal Soc. London (fgn.), Sociedade de Bologia de Chile (hon.), Sociedade Brasileira de Biologia (hon.), Sigma Xi, Alpha Epsilon Delta (hon.), Epsilon Chi (hon.). Club: Cosmos (Washington). Died Apr. 18, 1984.

COLE, LOUIS WILLIAM, former mfg. exec.; b. N.Y.C., July 1, 1890; s. Michael and Esther Gertrude (Manne) C.; B.S., Cooper Union, 1912, E.E., 1916; m. Estelle Melnick, June 8, 1920; children—Thomas M., Carol (Mrs. Millard Rothenberg). Draftsman Met. Switchboard Co., N.Y.C., 1905-09; constrn. engr. Tucker Electric Constrn. Co., N.Y.C., 1910-11; comml. mgr. Columbia Metal Box Co., 1911-14, chief emgr., 1914-18; pres. gen. mgr. Fed. Pacific Electric Co., Newark, 1918-50, chmn. bd. 1950-69. Mem. Am. Inst. E.E., Nat. Elec. Mfrs. Assn., Tau Beta Pi. Home: Harrison, NY. †

COLE, SYLVAN, chain store exec.; b. Los Angeles, Sept 2, 1889; s. Nathan Cohn and Fannie (Prager) C.; student pub. schs. of Los Angeles; m. Dorothy B. Stein, Mar. 5, 1917; children—Sylvan, Charles Norman, Richard. With Walter E. Deutsch. founded the Dollar Shirt Shops, Los Angeles, 1911, name changed to Nat. Shirt Shops, 1917, and to Nat. Shirt Shops of Del., Inc., 1934, pres. many years, chmn. bd., treas. and dir. co. and all its subsidiary corps. from 1942. Dir. and mem. exec. com. Inst. of Distbn.; mem. exec., adminstrv. coms. Am. Jewish Com. Gov. Joint Defense Appeal. Mem. Met. Mus. Art, Mus. Natural History, Mus. Modern Art. Club: Harmonie.†

COLIN, RALPH FREDERICK, lawyer; b. N.Y.C., Nov. 18, 1900; s. William and Elizabeth (Benjamin) C.; m. Georgia Talmey, June 2, 1931; children: Ralph Frederick, Pamela Talmey (Lady Harlech). A.B., CCNY, 1918; LL.B., Columbia U., 1921. Bar: N.Y. 1922. Assoc. Rosenberg & Ball, N.Y.C., 1921, mem., 1926, later Rosenberg, Goldmark & Colin; of counsel Rosenman Colin Freund Lewis & Cohen; dir., gen. counsel CBS, 1927-69, Columbia Artists Mgmt., Inc.; adminstrv. v.p., gen. counsel Art Dealers Assn. Am. Cons. editor: Air Law Rev.; contbr. to law reviews and art periodicals. Active early devel. art theatres, N.Y.C.; past dir. Provincetown, Greenwich Village, Actors theatres.; bd. dirs., trustee, v.p. Philharm. Symphony Soc. N.Y., 1942-56; trustee, hon. sec. Baron de Hirsch Fund, 1935-56; trustee, v.p. Mus. Modern Art, N.Y.C., 1954-69, vice chmn. internat. council; trustee Hosp. Joint Diseases, 1932-52, chmn. bd., 1949-51, pres., 1951-52; mem. vis. com. dept. fine arts and Fogg Mus., Harvard U., 1951-73, 75—; bd. visitors Columbia Law Sch., 1961—; bd. dirs. Richard and Dorothy Rodgers Found., Bernheim Found., Woodheath Found.; bd. dirs. CBS Found., 1953-69, pres., 1956-69; bd. dirs. Am. Fedn. Arts, 1946-56; chmn. radio broadcasting div. Nat. War Fund, 1943-44. Mem. Assn. Bar City N.Y. (exec. com. 1942-46, mem. com. on judiciary 1948-51, com. on grievances 1956-61, chmn. spl. com. on pub. and bar relations 1956-59, v.p. 1960-61, chmn. com. profl. ethics 1961-62), N.Y. County Lawyers Assn., ABA, Fed. Communications, N.Y. State bar assns. Home: New York NY Office: New York NY

COLLES, ALVIN ROBERT, co. exec.; b. Downs, Iowa, Oct. 6, 1922; s. Joseph Hubert and Ellen Victoria (Jacobson) C.; m. Mona Jacqueline Everetts, May 3, 1952; children—Timothy, Mark. B.S., U. Ill., 1948. With Ernst & Ernst, Los Angeles and Honolulu, 1948-52, 61-65; with Lear Siegler Corp., Los Angeles, 1952-61, Transam. Corp., San Francisco, 1965-69; with Occidental Life Ins. Co. Calif., Los Angeles, 1969-83, chief fin. officer, 1980-83. Served with USN, 1943-46, PTO; Served with USN, ATO. Mem. Am. Inst. C.P.A.'s, Am. Council Life Ins., Office Mgmt. Assn. Home: Brea, Calif. Died 1983.

COLLETT, C(HARLES T(AGGART), transportation exec.; b. Pine Bluff, Ark., Aug. 8, 1888; s. Charles A. and Sarah M. (Bedford) C.; student pub. schs.; m. Lucille Virginia Eddy, Oct. 14, 1909 (div.); children—Shirley (Mrs. J. E. Knox), Ruth (Mrs. George M. Lillig). Claim clk. St.L.-S.F. R.R., St.L., 1907-10, rate clk. St.L., also Oklahoma City, 1910-11, chief clk. to asst. gen. freight agt., Oklahoma City, 1911-12; gen. agt. S.P. Co., 1912-16, K.C., 1916-18, St.L., 1920-23, Chgo., 1923-26, asst. to traffic mgr., 1926-29, asst. freight traffic mgr., 1929-38, freight traffic mgr., 1938-51, gen. traffic mgr. from 1951. Mem. Nat. Freight Traffic Assn. Clubs: Chicago, Union League, Traffic. Home: Chicago, Ill. †

COLLIER, CHARLES ALLEN, business exec.; b. Atlanta, Ga., Sept. 5, 1888; s. Charles and Susan (Rawson) C.; student Ga. Tech., 1905-09; m. Elizabeth Sturgeon, Nov. 30, 1910; children—Elizabeth, Mary, Henrietta. Wiring and motor insp., power sales engr. Ga. Ry & Power Co., Atlanta, 1909-22; gen. sales mgr. Ga. Power Co., 1922-27, v.p., 1927-53, dir., 1938 from; cons. So. Services, Inc., Birmingham, Ala. Trustee Atlanta YMCA. Maj., Specialist Res., ret.; maj. Ga. Wing Civil Air Patrol, exec. officer, World War II. Mem. Am. Inst. E.E. Assn. Edison Illuminating Cos., Edison Elec. Inst., Southeastern Electric Exchange, So. Hist. Soc., Ga. Soc. Profl. Engrs., Soc. Am. Archaeology, Soc. Am. Mil. Engrs., Newcomen Soc. Eng. (Am. br.), Chi Phi. Democrat. Mason. Clubs: Army and Navy (Washington); Capital City, Inquiry, Piedmont Driving (Atlanta). Author articles on elec. subjects, advt. and community development. Originated Ga. Better Home Towns Program, 1944. Home: Atlanta, Ga. †

COLLINGS, ELLSWORTH, educator; b. McDonald County, Mo., Oct. 23, 1887; s. Thomas Jefferson and Sallie Betheny (McBee) C.; B.S., U. of Mo., 1917; M.A., Columbia, 1922, Ph.D., 1924; m. Lessie Lee Garren, Dec. 25, 1907; 1 dau., Jewell Opal. With U. of Oklahoma from 1922, dean School of Education, 1926-45, professor secondary education, from 1945. Mem. N.E.A., Okla. Edn. Assn., Progressive Edn. Assn., A.A.A.S., Okla. Acad. Science, Phi Delta Kappa, Kappa Delta Pi, Phi Beta Sigma. Democrat. Baptist. Author books on schs. and sch. supervision. Co-Author: Psychology for Teachers (with M. O. Wilson), 1933; The 101 Ranch, 1937; Adventures in the Dude Ranch Country, 1942. Home: Norman, Okla. †

COLLINGS, JOHN KEMPTHORNE, JR., beverage co. exec.; b. Bayonne, N.J., Jan. 30, 1928; s. John Kempthorne and Victoria (Middleton) C.; student Maritime U., State N.Y., 1947; B.A., Columbia U., 1952; m. Barbara Wheeler Brinkman, Nov. 10, 1951; children—Jeffrey Kempthorne, Deborah Wheeler, John Kempthorne III, Mark Kempthorne. Exec. v.p. Henze Instrument & Valve Inc., Hoboken, N.J., 1956-65; gen. mgr. ITT Nesbitt, Phila., 1965-66, exec. v.p. Environ. Products div. ITT, Phila., 1967-68, pres. Wire and Cable div., 1969; pres., chief exec. officer Aqua-Chem. Inc., Milw., 1969-71, chmn., chief exec. officer, 1972-76, chmn. bd., pres., 1976-78, dir., 1969-81; v.p. The Coca-Cola Co., Atlanta, 1978-79, exec. v.p., 1979-81, vice chmn., 1981, also dir.; dir. Marine Corp., Milw., Parker Pen Co., Janesville, U.S. Trustee Peddie Sch., Hightstown, N.J., 1971—. Served to lt. USNR, 1952-54. Home: Atlanta, Ga. Died June 25, 1981.

COLLINS, ARTHUR SYLVESTER, JR., army officer; b. Boston, Aug. 6, 1915; s. Arthur Sylvester and Anne T. (Farrell) C.; B.S., U.S. Mil. Acad., 1938; grad. Command and Gen. Staff Coll., Armed Forces Staff Coll., Army War Coll., 1953; M.A. in Internat. Relations, George Washington U., 1964; m. Naomi Cashmore Wulfsberg, Nov. 20, 1948; children—Dennis Charles, Kevin Arthur, Maureen Ray Collins Saunders. Commd. 2d lt. U.S. Army, 1938, advanced through grades to lt. gen., 1967; assigned 13th and 14th inf. regiments, Panama, 1938-41; battalion comdr. 130th Inf., Hawaii, 1942-43; regtl. comdr., New Guinea, Morotai and Luzon, 1944-46; with tactical dept. U.S. Mil Acad., 1948-52; comdr. 1st regt., U.S. Mil. Acad., 1950-52; regtl. comdr. 10th Inf., Germany, 1955-56; mem. faculty Army War Coll., 1956-59; spl. asst. tng. to chief U.S. Army Adv. Group, also G-3 adviser to 1st Republic Korea Army, 1959-60; J- 5 plans div. Joint Chief Staff, 1960-61; J-1, J-3, chief Staff USSTRICOM, 1961-63; dir. office personnel, Dept. Army, 1963-64, asst. dep. chief staff mil. operations, 1964-65; comdr. 4th Inf. div., Fort Lewis, Wash., and Vietnam, 1965-67; asst. chief staff force devel. Dept. Army, 1967-70; comdr. 1st Field Force, Vietnam, 1970-71; dep. comdr.-in-chief U.S. Army Europe, 1971-74. Mem. adv. bd. S.W. Wash. State Coll.; pres. Transatlantic council Boy Scouts Am. Decorated Silver Star, Legion of Merit with oak clusters, D.S.M. with 3 oak leaf clusters. Bronze Star with 2 oak leaf clusters, Air medal, Combat Inf. badge; recipient Terence Cardinal Cooke award, 1974. Mem. Tacoma C. of C. (bd. dirs.). Kiwanian, Rotarian (hon.). Author: Common Sense Training, 1978. Contbr. articles to various publs. Home: Alexandria, Va. Dec. Jan. 7, 1984. Interned West Point, N.Y.

COLLINS, CARL INGERSOLL, mfg. exec.; b. Asheville, N.C., June 29, 1890; s. Willis E. and Mary (Ingersoll) C.; B.S., Ga. Tech., 1912; m. Dorothy Crump, Oct. 18, 1921; children—Thomas C., John I. Engr. Atlantic Steel Co., 1912-15; supt. U.S. Cartridge Co., 1915-17; sales engr. Hyatt Roller Bearing Co., 1919-23; supt., gen. mgr. Morris & Bailey Steel Co., 1923-33; gen. supt. Cuyahoga Works Am. Steel & Wire Co., 1933-35, mgr. Worcester (Mass.) dist., 1935-42; exec. v.p. Wickwire Spencer Steel Co., 1942-44; pres. Superior Steel Corp., 1944-57; president, director Copperweld Steel Company; mem. board of directors of Commonwealth Trust Co. Served with U.S. Army, World War I. Mem. Am. Iron and Steel Inst. (dir.), Chi Phi. Presbyn. Clubs: Worcester, Tatnuck Country, Duquesne, Univ., Rolling Rock, Oakmont Country, Fox Chapel Golf. †

COLLINS, FORRES MCGRAW, investment banking exec.; b. Tupelo, Miss., Feb. 27, 1926; s. Frederick Hunter and Lucy (McGraw) C.; m. Emilie Marie Lapeyre, Jan. 7, 1954; children—Forres McGraw, Emilie Marie Lapeyre. Student, Southwestern La. Inst., 1943-44; B.A., Tulane U., 1948. Salesman Henri Duizend Co., New Orleans, 1948-49, George Tessier Co., New Orleans, 1949-51, Am. Viscose Corp., New Orleans, 1951-52; v.p., dir. Longino & Collins, Inc., New Orleans, 1952-54; partner Howard, Weil, Labouisse, Friedrichs & Co. (investment bankers), New Orleans, 1954-71, sr. v.p., dir., 1971-83; pres., dir. Bayou Johnson Oyster Co., New Orleans, 1969-83. Served to lt. USNR, 1944-46. Mem. Tulane U. Alumni Assn., Phi Lambda Epsilon, Phi Delta Theta, Kappa Delta Phi. Clubs: Bond (pres. 1962), New Orleans Country, Boston, Stratford, Lake Shore, Recess. Home: New Orleans, La. Died Sept. 7, 1983; interred New Orleans, La.

COLLINS, MAURICE, government official; b. Waterford, Ireland, Nov. 29, 1888; s. John and Bridget (Quinlan) C.; student Mt. Sion and Waterpark Co., Ireland; LL.B., Nat. Univ. Law Sch., 1928; m. Elizabeth White King, Feb. 20, 1915. Clerk and bookkeeper, U.S. Treasury Dept., 1913-18; head bookkeeper Bureau of War Risk Ins. and Vets. Bur., 1919-22; chief accounting div., Vets. Bureau, 1922-30; dir. of finance Vets. Adminstrn. since 1943; asst. commr. accounts and deposits U.S. Treasury, 1934-38; asst. to Dir. of Budget, 1938-39; exec. asst. to Fed. Security Administrator, also asst. to dir. of defense, health and welfare service, 1939-43; asst. Fed. Security administrator since 1945. Served in U.S. Army, 1918-19. Mem. Am. Inst. of Accountants. Mem. Am. Legion. Roman Catholic. Home: Washington, D.C. †

COLLINS, ORELL TEX, chem. co. exec.; b. Letcher County, Ky. June 19, 1923; M.E., Purdue U., 1948; grad. Advanced Mgmt. Program, Harvard U., 1976; m. Barbara Blatchford, Sept. 18, 1948; children—Peggy, Paul, Jeffrey. Salesman, Barber Coleman Co., to 1956; with Nalco Chem. Co., 1956-85, sr. v.p., Oak Brook, Ill., 1968-72, exec. v.p., 1972-77, pres., chief operating officer, 1977-79, pres., chief exec. officer, 1979-82, chmn. bd., 1982-84, chmn. exec. com., 1984-85. Mem. pres.'s council Purdue U. Served with USAAF, World War II. Registered profl. engr., Ill. Mem. ASME, Am. Petroleum Inst., Mfg. Chemists Assn. Republican. Presbyterian. Clubs: Butler Nat. Golf, Butterfield Country, Country of N.C.; Chgo. Athletic Assn. MidAm. (Chgo.). Died Mar. 15, 1985.

COLLINS, RICHARD EDWARD, architect; b. Staunton, Va., Oct. 13, 1910; s. William Meem and Margaret (McLaughlin) C.; B.S., Catholic U. Am., 1932; m. Cecilia Ann Tomulty, Dec. 29, 1934; children—Richard Edward, Kathleen (Mrs. Philip A. Stevens), Margaret (Mrs. Richard O. Ives), Mary (Mrs. Blair Lee IV). With Bur. Yards and Docks, Navy Dept., 1938-46, chief designer, 1942-46; pvt. practice architecture, Washington and Silver Spring, Md., 1946-56; mem. faculty Catholic U. Am., 1946-66, prof., 1960-66; partner firm Collins & Kronstadt (now Collins & Kronstadt, Leahy, Hogan, Collins, Architects, Planners, Engineers), Silver Spring, from 1956. Recipient Gen. Excellence in Architecture award A.I.A.; Soc. Beaux Arts Architects medal; Assn. Fed. Architects First award, numerous other awards. Fellow A.I.A. Home: Silver Spring, Md. Died Sept. 25, 1981.

COLLINS, ROWLAND LEE, English language educator; b. Bristow, Okla., Sept. 17, 1934; s. John Leland and Velma Grace (Jones) C.; m. Sarah Jo Huff, Apr. 10, 1965; children: Robin Elizabeth, Michael John, Catherine Grace. A.B. in English and Humanities cum laude, Princeton, 1956; M.A. (Woodrow Wilson Found. fellow), Stanford, 1959, Ph.D., 1961. Teaching assoc. Stanford, 1958-59; lectr. English Ind. U., 1959-61, instr., 1961-62, asst. prof. English, 1962-65, assoc. prof., 1965-67; prof. U. Rochester, 1967-85, acting chmn. dept. English, 1970-71, chmn., 1972-81; Council of Humanities fellow Princeton, 1965-66; Woodrow Wilson Found. campus rep. Ind. U., 1963-67, U. Rochester, 1982-85. Author: Anglo-Saxon Vernacular Manuscripts In America, 1976; Editor: Fourteen British and American Poets, 1964, Beowulf, 1965; Contbr.: bibliographies to New Cambridge Bibliography of English Lit., vol. III, 1969, vol. I, 1974; Editorial cons.: bibliographies to Victorian Studies, 1963-66; editorial bd.: bibliographies to Your Musical Cue, 1964-69, U. Rochester Library Bull, 1969—; founding editor: bibliographies to Year's Work in Old English Studies, 1968—; asso. editor: bibliographies to Old English Newsletter, 1968—; Author numerous articles, revs. on Old English manuscripts lit. and wills, lexicography, linguistic history, Tennyson, Shakespeare, opera, electronic music, archtl. history, poetry, and lit. history to profl. jours. Trustee Keuka Coll., 1976-85; Acad. advisor Montfort Jones and Allie Brown Jones Found., 1961-73, trustee, 1973—, vice chmn., 1974—; mem. Landmark Soc. of Western N.Y., 1968—, trustee, 1970—, sec., 1974-78, pres., 1978-80; mem. Rochester Preservation Bd., 1969-75, vice chmn., 1969-71, chmn., 1971-74; bd. dirs. Hillside Children's Center, 1977-85. John Simon Guggenheim Found. fellow, 1965-66. Fellow Rochester Mus. and Sci. Center; mem. Internat. Assn. Univ. Profs. English, Guild of Scholars (sec.-treas. 1975-78), Modern Lang. Assn. Am. (sec. Old English group 1964, chmn. 1964, del. assembly 1977-79), Assn. Depts. English (dir. 1980—), Medieval Acad. Am., Early English Text Soc., Bibliog. Soc. Am., Cambridge (Eng.) Bibliog. Soc., Bibliog. Soc. (London), English Inst., Tennyson Soc. (Am. rep. 1967-85), Citizens' Assn. East Ave., Park-Meigs Neighborhood Assn. (pres. 1975-76), Rochester Hist. Soc., Meml. Art Gallery, Rochester Area Ednl. TV Assn., Friends of Rochester Public Library (dir. 1976-85), English-Speaking Union (chmn. br. com. scholarship 1969-72). Democrat. Episcopalian (commn. to evaluate seminarians 1974-75). Clubs: Grolier, The Club, Faculty. Home: Rochester, N.Y. Died May 17, 1985.

COLLINS, SAMUEL CORNETTE, mech. engr.; b. Democrat, Ky., Sept. 28, 1898; s. John Wesley and Rachel Ellen (Caudill) C.; m. Lena Arbragine Masterson, Sept. 4, 1929. B.S., U. Tenn., 1920, M.S., 1924; Ph.D., U. N.C., 1927, D.Sc. (hon.), 1957; LL.D. (hon.), St. Andrews U., Scotland, 1967. Prof. chemistry Carson-Newman Coll., 1925-26, E.Tenn. State Tchrs. Coll., 1928-30; research assoc. Mass. Inst. Tech., 1930-35, asst. prof. chemistry, 1935-42, assoc. prof., 1942-46, assoc. prof. mech. engring., 1946-49, prof. mech. engring., 1949-64; v.p. Arthur D. Little, Inc. and Cryogenic Tech., Inc., Cambridge, Mass., 1964-71; research chemist Naval Research Lab., Washington, 1971—. Contbr. articles on cryogenic apparatus to profl. jours. Recipient Wetherill medal Franklin Inst., 1951, Kamerlingh Onnes Gold medal Netherlands Refrigeration Soc., 1958, first Samuel C. Collins award Cryogenic Engring. Conf., 1965. Fellow Am. Acad. Arts and Scis. (Rumford medal 1965), ASME (Gold medal 1968); mem. Nat. Acad. Scis. Baptist. Home: Fort Washington, Md. Died June 19, 1984.

COLLINS, WALTER LANSING, educator; b. New Madison, O., Dec. 16, 1889; s. Charles Wesley and Alice (Addleman) C.; Ph.B., Lebanon U., 1917; B.A., Wilmington (O.) Coll., 1921; M.A., U. of Cincinnati, 1926, Ph.D., 1928; m. Mabel Reynolds, Sept. 1912; children—Paul, Walter, Mary Louise. Teacher and supt. schs., Warren County, O., 1914-17; dir. tech. edn., Y.M.C.A. Schs., Columbus, O., 1918-20; supt. schs., West Alexandria, O., 1921-26; instr. summer sessions, Lebanon U. and Wilmington Coll., 1915-21; held Baldwin and Taft fellowships, U. of Cincinnati, 1926-28; instr. and dir. extension teaching, same univ., 1928-29; asst. prof. edn. and dir. grad. work, Teachers Coll., U. of Cincinnati, 1929-32; pres. Wilmington Coll., 1932-40; dir. Div. of Instrn., State Dept. of Edn., Ohio, 1940-44; supt. schs., Kenton, Ohio, from 1945. Commd. major, U.S. Army, May 1943, serving overseas. Member Nat. Edn. Assn., Am. Assn. Univ. Profs., Phi Delta Kappa, Zeta Sigma Pi. Republican. Mason. Mem. Soc. of Friends. Clubs: Commercial, Rotary. Author: Citizens in the Making, 1928; also series of work books on citizenship training. Compiler and editor (with others) of Abstracts of Masters and Doctors Dissertations (U. of Cincinnati), 1931. Home: Kenton, O. Deceased.

COLMAN, GEORGE TILDEN, fgn. service officer; b. Elmira, N.Y., Jan. 3, 1888; s. Harry John and Caroline (Tilden) C.; A.B., Williams Coll., 1908, A.M., 1909; student Cornell U., 1909-10; Ph.D., University of Chicago, 1914; m. Myrth King, Oct. 12, 1928; 1 son, George Tilden; children by previous marriage—Ruth Elizabeth (Mrs. Victor Peterson), Catherine Tilden (wife of Capt. Robert Spika, U.S.A.A.F.), Sager Tilden. Began as teacher, Phillippine Islands, 1911-13; professor Hiran (Ohio) College, 1914-15, Mackenzie College, São Paulo, Brazil, 1915-17; entered U.S. Foreign Service, 1918; vice consul, São Paulo, Brazil, 1918-19; vice consul de carriere assigned to Rio de Janeiro, 1920, Punta Arenas, Chile, 1923-25; asst. to pres., Horlick's Malted Milk Corp., Racine, Wis., 1925-41; sr. econ. analyst, U.S. Dept. of State, assigned to São Paulo, Brazil, 1941-46, vice consul in charge, Natal, Brazil, 1947. Consul in charge, Belem, Para, Brazil, 1948, retired, 1958. Organizer Greeley (Colo.) br. Boys Club Am. Mem. Am. Assn. for U.N. (pres Weld County chpt.). Home: Greeley, Colo. †

COLOWICK, SIDNEY PAUL, biochemist, educator, editor; b. St. Louis, Jan. 12, 1916; s. Michael and Frieda (Singer) C.; m. Grace Shaffel, 1943; 1 son, Frank Shaffel; m. Maryda Swanstrom, 1951; children: Ann Maryda, Susan, Nancy. B.S., Washington U., 1936, M.S., 1939, Ph.D., 1942. Instr. pharmacology Washington U., 1943-44, asst. prof., 1945-46; asso. Pub. Health Research Inst., N.Y.C., 1946-48; asso. prof. biochemistry U. Ill. Coll. Medicine, Chgo., 1948-49; asso. prof. biology Johns Hopkins U., 1950-54, prof., 1954-59; Am. Cancer Soc. prof. microbiology Vanderbilt U., 1959-85, Harvie Branscomb Disting. prof., 1978. Editor: (with Nathan O. Kaplan) Methods in Enzymology, 1955-85; exec. editor: Archives Biochemistry and Biophysics, 1970-74. Recipient Eli Lilly award Am. Chem. Soc., 1947. Mem. Am. Soc. Biol. Chemists, Am. Chem. Soc., Internat. Union Biochemistry (enzyme commn.), Nat. Acad. Sci., Am. Acad. Arts and Scis. Home: Nashville, Tenn. Died Jan. 9, 1985.

COLPITTS, HERBERT GRANGER, corp. exec.; b. Warren, Pa., May 23, 1889; s. Kenneth Thompson and Dorothy (Granger) C.; student high sch., Warren, O.; m. Margaret Jeannette Webb, Feb. 1, 1914; children—Nancy, Herbert, Edwin. Began as file clerk, Inland Steel Co., 1907; clerk, later office mgr. Chief Printing Co., Hammond, Ind., 1909-15; joined Colpitts Mfg. Co., Chicago, 1916, as v.p., later pres.; dir. National Printing Co. Address: River Forest, Ill. Deceased.

COLSTON, JAMES ALLEN, educator; b. Quincy, Fla., July 27, 1909; s. Meadie and Anica (Jordan) C.; B.S., Morehouse Coll., 1932, LL.D., 1959; M.A., Atlanta U., 1933; postgrad. Columbia, summers 1938, 39, 40, U. Chgo., 1945-46; Ph.D., N.Y. U., 1950; LL.D., Monmouth Coll., 1954, Bethune Cookman Coll., 1977; L.H.D., Westminster Coll., 1966, Gettysburg Coll., 1969; Litt.D., Knoxville Coll., 1968, Lafayette Coll., 1976; m. Wilhelmina Thelma White, Dec. 22, 1935; children—Jean, Alliece. Instr., E. P. Johnson Sch., Atlanta, 1932-33; prin. Rigby Jr. High Sch., Ormond, Fla., 1933-38; dir. Ballard Sch., Macon, Ga., 1938-43; instr. Atlanta U., summer 1941; workshop dir. Hampton Inst., Grad. Study Center, Jacksonville, Fla., summer 1942; pres. Bethune-Cookman Coll., Daytona Beach, 1942-46; dir. pub. relations Hampton Inst., 1946-47; pres. Ga. State Coll., Savannah, 1947-49; lectr. in edn. N.Y.U., 1949-50; chmn. dept. edn. A. and T. Coll., Greensboro, N.C., 1950-51; pres. Knoxville Coll., 1951-66, Bronx Community Coll. of City U. N.Y., 1966-76; prof. A. & T. State U., Greensboro, 1976-82; trustee Dollar Savs. Bank. Exec. v.p. Hall of Fame for Great Ams. Mem. commn. on curriculum Am. Assn. Jr. Colls.; mem. com. on disadvantages State U. N.Y.; mem. Bronx adv. council State Commn. for Human Rights; mem. exec. bd., chmn. advancement com. Bronx Boy Scouts; mem. N.Y. State Health Planning Adv. Council; mem. council on admissions City U. N.Y.; mem. adv. council to Joint Legislative Com. on Higher Edn.; chmn. Commn. on Theol. Edn. in Southeastern States, U.P. Ch. in U.S.A.; mem. Fordham Rd. Devel. Corp.; mem. adv. com. Bronx Service Center, A.R.C. Greater N.Y. Bd. dirs. A.R.C., Internat. Visitors Center, So. Regional Council, YMCA Greater N.Y., Council of Higher Ednl. Instns., N.Y.C., Gallaudet Coll., Robert R. Moton Meml. Inst., Sickle Cell Found.; Found.; bd. dirs., vice pres. vice chmn. pub. edn. com. Am. Cancer Soc.; chmn. com. ednl. service, bd. dirs. United Negro Coll. Fund; trustee U.P. Found., Princeton Theol. Sem., Bronx Lebanon Hosp., Bennett Coll.; chmn. bd. trustees Johnson C. Smith Theol. Sem., Wilmington, Del.; state exams. bd. regents U. State N.Y.; adv. com. Eastern Music Festival. Mem. N.C. (life), Am. tchrs. assns., Am. Assn. Sch. Adminstrs., Am. Council on Edn., NEA (dept. higher edn.), Boy Scouts Am., Bronx C. of C. (dir.), NAACP, New Homemakers of Am. (hon., adv. com.), Traid-Bus. and Profl. Men, Nat. Geog. Soc., Assn. for Higher Edn., Nat. Council United Presbyn. Men (exec. com., v.p.), Phi Beta Kappa, Phi Delta Kappa, Alpha Kappa Mu, Sigma Pi Phi, Beta Epsilon. Presbyn. Mason (scholarship com. State Ga.), Rotarian. Club: Greensboro Men's. Home: Greensboro, N.C. Died Jan. 21, 1982.

COLT, THOMAS CLYDE, JR., retired museum administrator; b. Orange, N.J., Feb. 20, 1905; s. Thomas Clyde and Florence (Clery) C.; student Blair Acad., Blairstown, N.J., 1920-22; B.S., Dartmouth Coll., 1926; m. Martha Belle Patterson Willingham, June 17, 1933 (div. 1950); children—Thomas Clyde III, Jon Landstreet, Corinne Patterson; m. Priscilla Crum, Apr. 4, 1950; children—Christopher, Penelope, Susannah. Writer, critic, N.Y., 1926-27; assoc. Rehn Galleries, N.Y., 1927-29; trustee Richmond Acad. Arts, 1933-35; sec. Va. Art Alliance, 1934-35; curator (title later changed to dir.) Va. Mus. Fine Arts, 1935-42, 45-48; dir. Portland (Oreg.) Art Mus., 1948-56; dir. Art Inst., Dayton, Ohio, 1957-75; past pres. Colt Bros. Inc.; exec. com. Ohio Art Council, 1965-70; pres. Intermus. Conservation Assn., 1968-70. Served with USMCR, 1929-31, 42-45; naval aviator, 1930, lt. col. Res. ret. Decorated Star Solidarity 2d class (Italy). Mem. Assn. Art Museum Dirs. (hon.). Compiler art catalogues, booklets. Home: Dayton, Ohio. Dec. Mar. 6, 1985.

COLTON, ROGER B., army officer; born N.C., Dec. 15, 1887; Ph.B., Yale, 1908; M.S., Mass. Inst. Tech., 1920; grad. Coast Arty. Sch., Engring. Course, 1922, Advanced Course, 1927, Command and Gen. Staff Sch., 1928, Army War Coll., 1938; m. Ora Carter, 1917; one daughter, Shirley (Lotz). Commd. 2d lt., C.A.C., Nov. 1910; transferred to Signal Corps as major, 1930, and advanced through the grades to brig. gen., Jan. 1942, major gen., Aug. 1942; served as lt. col., C.A.C., World War I; chief Signal procurement, supply and engring., later in charge Air Force electronic equipment, World War II; retired as maj. gen., Feb. 1, 1946. Awarded Legion of Merit and Distinguished Service Medal. Mem. U.S. delegation, Internat. Radio Consulting com. (C.C.I.R.) Sept.-Nov., 1934. Vice president, Fed. Telephone & Radio Corporation; dep. tech. dir. International Tel. & Tel. from 1952. Fellow Am. Inst. Elec. Engrs., senior mem. Inst. Rad. Engrs. Mem. Sigma Xi, Theta Xi. Author: Army Ground Communications, Radar in the United States Army. Home: New York, N.Y. †

COLWELL, ALEXANDER HUNTER, physician; b. Pittsburgh, Pa., Oct. 16, 1887; s. William Wilson and Sarah Ellen (Hunter) C.; M.D., University of Pittsburgh, 1914; m. Nancy Ann Martin, October 10, 1916; children—Alexander Hunter, Nancy Ann. Interne Western Pa. Hospital, 1914-15; Mellon fellow in med. research, 1915-16; asso. prof. medicine, U. of Pittsburgh since 1934; mem. staff St. Francis, Magee and Presbyn. hosps. Chmn. Mayor's Advisory Com. on Municipal Hosps., 1934. Served with A.E.F. in France, World War; hon. discharged with rank of capt., 1919. Mem. Am. Med. Assn., Med. Soc. State of Pa. (pres. 1935-36), Allegheny County Med. Soc. (pres. 1930-31), Soc. Biol. Research, Pittsburgh Acad. Medicine, Alpha Omega Alpha. Ind. Republican. Mem. United Presbyn. Ch. Mason. Club: University. Contbr. to professional jours. Home: Pittsburgh, Pa. Deceased.

COLWELL, LULA PULLIAM (MRS. HOWARD G. COLWELL), church official; b. LaBelle, Mo., Apr. 6, 1890; d. David T. and Lillian Belle (Rice) Pulliam; student Colo. Women's Coll., 1909-10; A.B., University Colo., 1921; M.A. (hon.), Brown U., 1950; L.H.D. honora causae, Berkeley Bapt. Div. School, 1954; married Howard G. Colwell, June 26, 1913; children—Robert P., Lillian M. (Mrs. Ray Patterson), David G. Sec., D. T. Pulliam Co., Worland Wyo., and Loveland, Colo., from 1939; mem. bd. dir. First Nat. Bank of Loveland. Consol. Home Supply Ditch & Reservoir Co. Pres. No. Baptist Convention, 1949-50, mem. finance com. and rep. at World Council of Churches, Amsterdam, 1948. Mem. Phi Beta Kappa. Trustee Colo. Women's Coll., Denver, Bacone Coll., Okla. Baptist. Home: Loveland, Colo. †

COMBS, HUGH D(UNLAP), ins. co. exec.; b. Yonkers, N.Y., Dec. 30, 1889; s. Franklin Pierce and Rosetta (Dunlap) C.; student Mt. Hermon Sch., 1913; LL.B., St. Lawrence U., 1921; m. Edith Eskesen, Oct. 24, 1922; 1 dau., Edith (Mrs. Carl W. Schmidt). Admitted to N.Y. bar, 1921, Md., 1935; exec. v.p., director U.S. Fidelity & Guaranty Company, Baltimore, 1948, senior executive vice president; dir. Fed. Seaboard Terra Cotta Corp., Fidelity Ins. Co. of Can., Del Mar Corp. Mem. Internat. Assn. Ins. Counsel, Am. Bar Assn., Am. Legion. Clubs: Baltimore Country, Merchants. Author articles on ins. Home: Baltimore, Md. †

COMISH, NEWEL HOWLAND, economist; b. Mountain Home, Utah, Jan. 30, 1888; s. Robert N. and Emma J. (Howland) C.; B.S., Utah Agrl. Coll., 1911; student U. of Chicago, 1913-14; M.S., U. of Wisconsin, 1915, Ph.D., 1929; m. Louise Larson, May 8, 1913; children—Dr. Alison Thorne, Mrs. Elaine Strawn, Newel William, Conrad Howland. Farm owner and mgr. from 1913; instr. in English and history, high sch., Snowflake, Ariz., 1911-13; instr. in economics and sociology, Ore. State Agrl. Coll., 1915-17, asst. prof., 1917-18, asso. prof., 1918-20, prof., 1920-32; prof. business administration, U. of Ore. from 1932; prof., U. of Calif., summer 1924; visiting prof. 1940 summer session U. of Utah, and 1941 summer session U. of Pittsburgh. Chmn. Third and Fourth War Loan Campaign of Lane County, 1943, 1944. Mem. of the Nat. Tariff Research Com., 1931-33, Nat. Social Science Research Com. on Agrl. Coöperation; sales training dir. Lipman, Wolfe & Company, 1945. Fellow A.A.A.S.; mem. Am con. Assn., Am. Farm Economic Assn., American Marketing Association, Coöperative League of America, Am. Assn. of Univ. Profs., League of Western Writers, Royal Econ. Soc., Phi Kappa Phi, Alpha Kappa Psi, Alpha Kappa Delta, Pi Kappa Phi, Order of the Spoon; mem. Oregon Trail Council of Boy Scouts of Am. since 1938. Club: Eugene Lions. Author books including: Small Scale Retailing, 1946, 48. Collaborator of Engle's Marketing in the West, 1946. Contbr. to A Century of Progress, 1929. Mem. adv. council Living Age. Contbr. to sci. and bus. mags. Home: Eugene, Oreg. †

COMMAGER, HENRY STEELE, historian, educator; b. Pitts., Oct. 25, 1902; s. James Williams and Anna Elisabeth (Dan) C.; m. Evan Carroll, July 3, 1928; children: Henry Steele, Nellie Thomas McColl, Elisabeth Carroll; m. Mary E. Powlesland, July 14, 1979. Ph.B., U. Chgo., 1923, M.A., 1924, Ph.D., 1928; postgrad. (Am.-Scandinavian Found. scholar), U. Copenhagen, 1924-25; hon. fellow, Peterhouse Cambridge (Eng.) U.; Litt.D., Washington Coll., Chestertown, Md., Ohio Wesleyan U., 1958, Monmouth Coll., 1959, U. Pitts., Marietta Coll., Hampshire Coll., 1970; Ed.D., R.I. Coll. Edn.; LL.D., Merrimack U., Carleton Coll., 1966, Dickinson Coll., 1967, Columbia U., 1969, Ohio State U., 1970, Gonzaga U., Mich. State U., U. Pa.; L.H.D., Brandeis U., 1960, Alfred U., U. Hartford, 1962, U. Puget Sound, 1963, Wilson Coll., 1970, U. Mass., 1972; D.Litt., Mich. State U., 1960, Franklin and Marshall Coll., 1962, Cambridge U., 1962, W. Va. U.; D.H.L., Maryville Coll., 1970, numerous others. Mem. faculty NYU, 1929-38, prof. history, 1931-38, Columbia U., 1938-56, Sperenza lectr., 1960; lectr. Am. history Cambridge U., 1942-43; Pitt prof. Am. history, 1947-48; Harold Vyvyan Harmsworth prof. Am. history Oxford (Eng.) U., 1952; Zuskind prof. Brandeis U., 1954-55; prof. U. Copenhagen, 1956; prof. Am. history Amherst (Mass.) Coll., 1956-72, Simpson lectr., 1972-84; hon. prof. U. Santiago, Chile; Bacon lectr. Boston U., 1943; Richards lectr. U. Va., 1944; lectr. Salzburg Seminar in Am. Studies, 1951; Gotesman lectr. Uppsala U., 1953; spl. lectr. for Dept. State, German univs., 1954; vis. prof. U. Aix-en-Provence, Nice, France, summer 1957; lectr. U. Jerusalem, summer 1958; Commonwealth lectr. U. London, Eng., 1964; Harris lectr. Northwestern U., 1964; lectr. U. Mexico, 1965; Patton lectr. Ind. U., 1977; vis. prof. Harvard U., U. Chgo., U. Calif., others; cons. OWI, Eng. and; U.S.; mem. U.S. Army War Hist. Commn., Historians Commn. Air Power; cons. U.S. Army, SHAEF, 1945. Author: (with S.E. Morison) The Growth of the American Republic, 1930, 2d vol., 1939, Theodore Parker, 1936, (with A. Nevins) The Heritage of America, 1939, (with E.C. Barker) Our Nation, 1941, (with A. Nevins) America: the Story of a Free People, 1943, rev. edit., 1966, Majority Rule and Minority Rights, 1944, The Story of the Second World War, 1945, The Blue and the Gray, 2 vols, 1950, The American Mind, 1950, Living Ideas in America, 1951, Robert E. Lee, 1951, Freedom, Loyalty, Dissent, 1954 (spl. award Hillman Found.), Joseph Story, 1956, (with G. Brunn) Europe and America since 1942, 1954, (with R.B. Morris) The Spirit of Seventy-Six, 2 vols, 1958, Great Declaration, 1958, Great Proclamation, 1960, Crusaders for Freedom, 1962, History: Nature and Purpose, 1965, Freedom and Order, 1966, Search for Usable Past, 1967, Was America a Mistake? , 1968, The Commonwealth of Learning, 1968, The American Character, 1970, The Discipline of History, 1972, The Empire of Reason: How Europe Imagined and America Realized the Enlightenment, 1978; editor: Documents of American History, 1934, 9th edit., 1973, Tocqueville, Democracy in America, 1947, The St. Nicholas Anthology, 1947, America in Perspective, 1947, Second St. Nicholas Anthology, 1948, Living Ideas in America, 1951, 64, Atlas of American Civil War, 1958, Immigration in American History, 1961, Why the Confederacy Lost the Civil War, History of the English Speaking Peoples (Churchill), Major Documents of the Civil War, Theodore Parker, an Anthology, Lester Ward and the Welfare State, The Struggle for Racial Equality, 1967, 72, Winston Churchill, Marlborough, 1968, Baedeker's United States, Britain Through American Eyes, 1973, Jefferson, Nationalism and the Enlightenment, 1975, (with others) The Spirit of Seventy-Six, 1975, This Day and Generation (Edward Kennedy), 1979, The

Rise of the American Nation, 50 vols. (in process). Trustee Am.-Scandinavian Found., Am. Friends Cambridge U. Decorated knight 1st class Order Dannebrog; recipient Herbert B. Adams award Am. Hist. Assn., 1929; Guggenheim fellow, 1960-61. Fellow Am. Scandinavian Soc.; mem. Am. Acad. Arts and Letters (Gold medal for history 1972), Mass. Hist. Soc., Am. Antiquarian Soc., Phi Beta Kappa. Democrat. Clubs: St. Botolph's (Boston); Century (N.Y.C.); Lansdowne (London). Died Apr. 2, 1984.*

CONANT, W(ILLIS) GARRETT, educator; b. Passaic, N.J., May 7, 1888; grad. Morris Acad., Morristown, N.J., 1906; A.B., Brown U., 1910; grad. study Harvard, 1920. Headmaster and propr. Blake Tutoring School, Tarrytown-on-Hudson, 1911-1920; dir. Cambridge Tutoring Sch., N.Y. City, from 1920; established summer sch. for boys at Williamstown, Mass., 1926. Served as instr. F.A., Officers' Training Sch., Camp Tyler, 1918-19; founder, 1927, pres., Cambridge Junior Coll., Williamstown, Mass., and Pinehurst, N.C. Del. Ford Permanent Peace Conf. at The Hague, 1915-16. Clubs: Brown Univ., Graduates' (New York); Philips Manor Yacht. Home: New York, N.Y. †

CONARRO, HARRY WIBORG, steel mfr.; b. Warren, Pa., Nov. 22, 1890; s. Charles Twining and Clara (Trushel) C.; student Wharton Sch., U. Pa., 1909. LL.B., U. Pa., 1913; m. Eleanor W. Russell, Jan. 10, 1924; children—Eleanor W. (Mrs. Robert R. Voigt), Harry Wiborg; m. 2d, Anne L. Kandelaft, Nov. 23, 1951. Asst. treas. Struthers Wells Co., Warren, 1916-18, treas., 1918-20, gen. mgr., 1920; v.p. Struthers Wells Corp., 1932-55, exec. v.p., 1955-56, pres., chief exec. officer, 1956-61, became chairman of the executive committee, 1961, also director, consultant; general manager, treas. Warren Axe & Tool Co., 1920-49; sec.-treas. DeLuxe Metal Furniture Co., 1926-49; dir. Warren Nat. Bank; cons. Struthers Sci. & Internat. Corp., N.Y.C. Mem. Newcomen Soc., Pa. Soc. Republican. Presbyn. Club: N.Y. Athletic. Home: Warren, Pa. †

CONDLIFFE, JOHN B., economist; b. Melbourne, Australia, Dec. 23, 1891; s. Alfred Bell and Margaret (Marley) C.; ed. Canterbury Univ. Coll., Gonville and Caius Coll., Cambridge; D.Sc., New Zealand, D. Letters (hon.), 1957; LL.D., Occidental Coll., 1942; m. Olive G. Mills, June 20, 1916; children—John Charles (dec.), Peter George, Margaret Mary. Prof. econs. Canterbury Coll., Christchurch, New Zealand, 1920-26; research sec. Inst. Pacific Relations, 1927-30; prof. econs. U. Mich., 1930-31; mem. League of Nations Secretariat, 1931-37; prof. commerce U. London, 1937-39; prof. econs. U. Calif., 1940-58, also dir. teaching Inst. of Econs., 1947-52; cons. Res. Bank of New Zealand, 1957; asso. dir., Div. of History and Econs., Carnegie Endowment, 1943-48; sr. economist Stanford Research Inst., 1961-67. Rapporteur-general Internat. Studies Conf., 1937-39; chmn. Geneva Research Center, 1937-39; chmn. internat. research com. Inst. of Pacific Relations, 1942-45. Adviser Indian Nat. Council Applied Econ. Research, 1959-60. Decorated hon. knight comdr. Order St. Michael and St. George; recipient Henry E. Howland Meml. prize, Yale U., 1939; Wendell Willkie prize, 1950; Sir James Wattie prize, 1972. Decorated Gold Cross Order of Phoenix (Greece). Mem. Royal Econ. Soc., Am. Econ. Assn., Econ. Soc. Australia and N.Z. Author books including: The Commerce of Nations, 1949; The Welfare State in New Zealand, 1959; The Development of Australia, 1964; Te Rangi Hiroa: The Life of Sir Peter Buck, 1972; Defunct Economists, 1973. Home: Walnut Creek, Calif. Died Dec. 23, 1981.

CONDON, HARRY RUTH, cons. forest engr.; b. Conshohocken, Pa., Nov. 19, 1887; s. Patrick and Anne Elizabeth (Ruth) C.; student U. Pa., 1907; B.S. (forestry), Pa. State Coll., 1913; m. Nell Elizabeth Warren, June 3, 1920; 1 son, Richard Warren (dec.). Asst. forester Pa. R.R., 1913-27, forester, 1927; v.p., gen. mgr. Am. Mond Nickel Co., 1927-29; v.p. Century Wood Preserving Co., 1929-35, Wood Preserving Corp., Pitts., 1935-39, Koppers Co., 1939-53, 1953; cons. forest engr. Served as capt. C.E., U.S. Army, World War I; mem. commn. to negotiate peace, 1918-19. Mem. Soc. Am. Foresters Am. Wood Preservers Assn. (past pres.), Am. Ry. Engrs. Assn., Alpha Gamma Rho. Republican. Presbyn. Club: Duquesne (Pitts).†

CONGER, ALLEN C(LIFTON), zoology educator; b. Zanesville, O., Nov. 23, 1887; s. Charles Levi and Eva Myrtilla (Peairs) C.; B.S., Ohio Wesleyan U., 1908; A.M., Ohio State U., 1912; grad. study, U. Mich., 1916-17; m. M. Vesper Bright, Sept. 10, 1912; children—Charles William (deceased), Martha Elizabeth, John Allen. Prof. of biology, Wilmington (Ohio) Coll., 1909-12; instr., zoology, Mich. Agrl. Coll., 1912-16; asst. prof., 1916-19, assoc. prof., 1919-23; assoc. prof. zoology Ohio Wesleyan U., 1923-35, prof., 1935-53, registrar, 1933-53, professor and registrar emeritus, from 1953; consultant Michigan Fish Commn., 1921-23. Mem. AAAS, Phi Beta Kappa, Sigma Xi, Omicron Delta Kappa, Phi Kappa Psi. Republican. Methodist. Author bulletins and numerous articles on economic zoology, birds and natural history. Home: Mountain View, Calif. †

CONKLIN, FREDRIC L., naval officer; b. Manchester, Mich., Apr. 12, 1888; s. Abraham Benjamin and Elizabeth (Mills) C.; M.D., U. of Mich., 1913; m. Delphine Tyler Sellers, Mar. 9, 1921. Surgical interne, U. of Mich. Hosp., 1913; practiced medicine, Grand Ledge, Mich., 1914; entered Naval Med. Sch., Washington, 1914; commd. lt. (j.g.), U.S. Navy, 1915, and advanced through grades to rear adm., 1946; assigned in charge of orthopedics, later chief of surg. service, U.S. Naval Hosp., Chelsea, Mass., 1924-28; with U.S. Marines, Managua, Nicaragua, 1928-30 (assisted in organizing med. depts. of Nicaraguan Army, established their first hosp. and served as med. dir. of all med. activities); chief of surg. service U.S. Naval Hosp., New York City, 1930-32, Philadelphia, Pa., 1932-33 and 1936-39; exec. officer U.S. Naval Hosp., Canacao, P.I., 1934; regtl. surgeon 4th Marines, Marine Expeditionary Force, Shanghai, China, 1935; chief of surg. service, later exec. officer, U.S. Naval Hosp., San Diego, Calif., 1939-42; organized U.S. Naval Mobile Hosp. No. 5, Naval Med. Supply Depot, Brooklyn, N.Y., 1942, established and comd. the hospital, which was set up in New Caledonia, having additional duty as mem. Hosp. Standardization Bd., which visited all naval hosp. activities in South Pacific Area; med. officer in command U.S. Naval Hosp., Palm Beach, Fla., 1945-46; dist. med. officer Ninth Naval Dist., Great Lakes, Ill. from 1946. Decorated Legion of Merit, Victory (World War I and World War II), Nicaraguan Campaign, Defense, Pacific Area, Phillippine Liberation ribbons. Mem. founders group Am. Bd. of Surgery. Fellow Am. Coll. Surgeons; mem. Am. Med. Assn. Address: Great Lakes, Ill. †

CONLEY, EUGENE, tenor; b. Lynn, Mass., Mar. 12, 1908; s. Reuben Anthony and Josephin (Farnsworth) C.; student pub. schs. Lynn; studied with Ettore Verna; m. Winifred Heidt, Mar. 9, 1948; m. Alvah Lea, July 9, 1960. Began as ch. soloist; singer local radio stas.; toured with Boston Male Choir; 1st profl. appearance in Robin Hood, Boston Light Opera Co.; sang with Handel-Haydn Soc. in Messiah; soloist Commonwealth Symphony; appeared in radio program NBC Presents Eugene Conley; guest engagements NBC Symphony under Arturo Toscanini and Frank Black; N.Y. operatic debut in Rigoletto, as the Duke, Bklyn. Acad. Music, 1940; toured transcontinentally with San Carlo Opera Co., also with New Opera Co. under Fritz Busch; featured lyric tenor Cin. Summer Opera Co., summers; appeared with Mexico Nat. Opera Co., N.Y.C. Center Opera Co., New Orleans Opera Assn.; toured Europe, singing in numerous opera houses, 1947-48; various concerts, U.S. and Can., 1949-50; also appeared City Center Opera, Covent Garden Opera, London, Teatro Colon, Buenos Aires; also soloist with Stokowski and New York Philharmonic in 5 concerts Carnegie Hall; also sang at LaScala Opera House, Milan, Italy. 1949, 50, 51; debut in title role of Faust, Met. Opera; guest artist Stadium Concerts, N.Y.C., summer 1950; appeared in La Boheme, Arena, Verona, Italy, 1950; sang with Netherlands Opera and Holland Festival, 1957; frequent appearances leading network radio and TV programs including Voice of Firestone; soloist Presidential Inauguration, 1953; appeared in 20th Century-Fox short Of Men and Music: recordings for London FFRR; Am. premiere Stravinskys Rakes Progress, Met. Opera, 1953: artist tenor in residence with rank prof. Sch. Music, North Tex. State U., 1960-78, ret., 1978; pvt. voice tutor, Dallas, 1978-81; mem. faculty, soloist Summer Vocal Inst., Am. Inst. Mus. Studies, Graz, Austria, 1971, 1973, 76, 77. Mem. Met. Opera Assn., LaScala Opera Co. in Milan, San Francisco Opera Co., New Orleans Opera, N.Y.C. Center Opera Co., Cin. Zoo Opera Co., Chgo. Opera Co., Royal Opera House in Stockholm, Opera Comique in Paris, Nat. Opera of Mexico City, Am. Assn. U. Profs., Nat. Assn. Tchrs Singing, Ft. Worth Opera Co. (bd.), Am. Guild Mus. Artists (life mem. bd.). Home: Denton, Tex. Died Dec. 18, 1981.

CONNERAT, WILLIAM SPENCER, lawyer; b. Savannah, Ga., May 7, 1889; s. Clarence S. and Laura (Spencer) C.; student Univ. Virginia Law Sch., 1910-11; LL.B., U. Ga., 1912; m. Josephine N. Crisfield, Dec. 17, 1927; children—Josephine (Mrs. Fred M. Blanton), William Spencer, Pearce Crisfield, Laura Spencer (Mrs. Freeman N. Jelks, Jr.). Admitted to Ga. bar, 1912, practiced in Savannah; sr. mem. Connerat, Dunn, Hunter, Houlihan, Maclean & Exley and predecessors, 1946 from; secretary Savannah Dist. Authority, 1951-61. Mem. Ga. Legislature, 1945-46. Mem. bd. officer Protestant Episcopal Ch. in Diocese of Ga., treas. Diocese of Ga., 1950 from. Served as capt. 320th F.A. 82d Div., U.S. Army, World War I. Cited for exceptional service Meuse-Argonne offensives. Mem. Chi Phi. Clubs: Oglethorpe, Century, Cotillion (Savannah). Home: Savannah, GA. †

CONNORS, JOHN STANLEY, publishing company executive; b. Worcester, Mass., July 26, 1925; s. Frank J. and Lucy A. (Kennedy) C.; m. Catherine Lightbourne; children: Susan, Patricia, Kathleen, Richard, Jane, John, Allison White. Student, Mich. State Coll., 1943, 46-49, U.S. Mil. Acad., 1945-46. With advt. dept. N.Y. Daily News, 1949-53; merchandising dir. R.W. Orr Assocs., Inc., 1953-56; with N.Y. World Telegram & Sun, 1956, Am. Weekly, 1956-59; with Sat. Evening Post, N.Y.C., 1960-65, N.Y. sales mgr., 1963, nat. sales mgr., 1963-65, advt. dir., 1965; pub. Holiday, 1967-68; v.p. Curtis Pub. Co., 1964-71; v.p., pub. Psychology Today mag., 1968-71; pres., pub. Travel and Leisure mag.; exec. v.p. Am. Express Pub. Corp. (wholly owned subs. Am. Express Co.), dir., mem. exec. com., 1979-84; pres., pub. Internat. Rev. of Food and Wine mag. (Am. Express pub. affiliate.); Chmn. adv. bd. masters degree program New Sch. for Social Research. Served with AUS, 1943-45. Mem. Mag. Pubs. Assn. (dir.), Pacific Area Travel Assn., Caribbean Travel Assn., Am. Soc. Travel Agts., World Travel Orgn., Travel Industry Assn. Am., African Travel Assn. (v.p. bd. dirs. 1976—, pres. N.Y. chpt. 1976-79, 1st African individual achievement award), Delta Sigma Phi, Alpha Phi. Roman Catholic. Clubs: N.Y. Atrium, Sky, Netherlands. Home: New York, N.Y. Died Apr. 5, 1984. *

CONQUEST, VICTOR, chemist; b. Kan., Feb. 7, 1896; s. Harrison and Amanda (Huffman) C.; student U. Kan., 1916, U. Dijon (France), 1919; m. Ella W. Bensing, May 19, 1920; children—Dorothy Lee (Mrs. Campbell), Victor B., Robert D. Research chemist Armour & Co., Chgo., 1926-31, dir. research, 1931-49, gen. mgr. research div., 1949-51, v.p. research div., 1951, v.p., European rep., 1960-62; dir. Armour-Bezons, Bezons (S. & O.) France, Armour-Hess Chesm., Ltd., Leeds, Eng.; dir. Armour-Erba Pharm. Co., Milan, Italy, 1961, adviser in research mgmt., 1962-84. Mem. chem. meats sub-com. Nat. Acad. Scis. Joint Argentine-U.S. Commn. for Study of Foot and Mouth Disease. Recipient Nicholas Appert medal, 1953; Indsl. Research Inst. medal, 1956. Mem. Am. Chem. Soc., Am. Oil Chemists Soc., Inst. Food Technologists, Phi Tau Sigma. Contbr. articles profl. publs. Home: Chicago, Ill. Died June 24, 1984.

CONRIED, HANS (FRANK FOSTER), actor; b. Balt., Apr. 1, 1915. Began career in Shakespearian radio prodn., other radio prodns. included The Great Gildersleeve, My Friend Irma, Life With Luigi; appeared summer stock in Too Young to Kiss, Texas Carnival, Behave Yourself, Rich, Young and Pretty, World in His Arms, Jet Pilot, Three for Bedroom C.; on Broadway in Can-Can; stage prodns. include Generation, Take Her, She's Mine, Tall Story, Don't Drink the Water, Spofford, Girls, Irene; motion pictures include It's A Wonderful World, Duley, The Wife Takes a Flyer, The Falcon Takes Over, Blondie's Blessed Event, Nightmare, Journey into Fear, His Butler's Sister, Senator was Indiscreet, Nancy Goes to Rio, My Friend Irma, Big Jim McClain, Walt Disney prodn. Peter Pan, The 5000 Fingers of Dr. T., Bus Stop, Affairs of Dobie Gills, You're Never Too Young, Davy Crockett King of the Wild Frontier, Birds and the Bees, Cat from Outer Space, Dramatic School, The Birds and the Bees, The Shaggy D.A.; appeared on TV in Danny Thomas Show, Fractured Flickers, Stump the Stars, Great Voices from Great Books, The Tony Randall Show, Died Jan. 5, 1982.

CONSIDINE, JOHN JOSEPH, advt. exec.; b. Jersey City, Sept. 6, 1941; s. Joseph Patrick and Helen (Hrezak) C.; m. Catherine Christine Noone, Nov. 26, 1966; children—Elizabeth Mairead, Laura Bridget, Adam Christopher, Kate Ann. B.S. in Psychology, St. Peter's Coll., 1963. Research analyst Prudential Ins. Co., 1964-66; research mgr. The Mennen Co., 1966-68; research adminstr. Gillette Corp., 1968-69; sr. v.p. account service, corp. dir. research W.B. Doner & Co., Detroit, 1969-82; dir. W.B. Doner. Mem. Am. Marketing Assn. (dir. Detroit chpt. 1972-82), Am. Mgmt. Assn., Adcraft Club Detroit. Home: West Bloomfield, Mich. Died May 4, 1982.

CONVERSE, PAUL D., economist, prof.; b. Morristown, Tenn., Mar. 8, 1889; s. Rev. James B. and Almeda (Dulaney) C.; B.A., Washington and Lee U., Lexington, Va., 1913, M.A., 1914; LL.D., 1944; m. Gertrude Graver, July 3, 1918; children—Paul Lee, Louise Dulaney. Former mem. faculty Washington and Lee U., U. Pitts.; mem. faculty U. of Ill. 1924 from, prof. marketing, dept. head. Mem. Am. Marketing Assn. (past pres.). Paul D. Converse Award established in his name, Am. Marketing Assn., 1946. Author: Marketing Methods and Policies, 1921; Selling Policies, 1927; Elements of Marketing 1930; Essentials of Distribution, 1936; Introduction to Marketing (with F. M. Jones), 1948; and others, also monographs. Contbr. various publs. Home: Urbana, Ill. †

CONWAY, MARINUS WILLETT, hospital supt.; b. Cincinnati, O., June 22, 1888; s. Marinus Willett and Mary E. (Corbly) C.; grad. Woodward High Sch., Cincinnati, 1906; M.D., Ohio-Miami Coll. of Medicine (U. of Cincinnati), 1910; m. Maude E. Bryan, of Elwood, Ind., Oct. 18, 1912; 1 son, Marinus Willett. Asst. supt. Eastern State Hosp. (mental), Medical Lake, Wash., 1912-21; engaged in gen. practice of medicine in Cheney, Wash., 1921-33; supt. Eastern State Hosp. from 1933. Mem. Wash. State and Spokane County med. socs., Omega Epsilon Phi. Democrat. Home: Medical Lake, Wash. †

CONWAY, WILLIAM IGNATIUS, lawyer; b. Aledo, Ill., Feb. 10, 1900; s. Patrick J. and Julia A. (Kennedy) C.; m. Jane S. Steele, Jan. 12, 1952; children—Jane, Mary. A.B., Loras Coll., 1924; LL.B., Georgetown U., 1928. Bar: D.C. bar 1927, Ill. bar 1928. Spl. agt. F.B.I., 1928-33, chief investigator assigned inquiry involving ofcl. corruption in, Bklyn., 1938-42, law practice, Chgo., 1933-38, 45-82. Served from capt. to lt. col. USAAF, 1942-45. Mem. Chgo. Bar Assn. Roman Catholic. Club: Union League (Chgo.). Home: Oak Park, Ill. Died Nov. 11, 1982.

COOGAN, JOHN LESLIE (JACKIE COOGAN), actor; b. Los Angeles, Oct. 26, 1914; s. John Henry and Lillian Rita (Dolliver) C.; m. Dorothea Odetta Hanson, May 27, 1950; children—John Anthony, Joann Dolliver, Leslie Diane (Mrs. Mitchell), Christopher Fenton. Student, Santa Clara U., 1931-32, U. So. Calif., 1933-34. Appeared in numerous motion pictures, 1916-84, including, Skinner's Baby, 1916, The Kid, 1919, The Actress, 1953, Fine Madness, 1965, Shakiest Gun In The West, 1967, Rogues Gallery, 1967, Little Sister, 1968, Marlo, 1968, Durango, 1975; appeared on numerous TV shows, 1947—; including Playhouse 90, 1955, Studio One, 1956, Johnny Carson, 1965, Mike Douglas, 1965, Regis Philbin, 1966, Les Crane, 1966, Joey Bishop Show, 1967, U Don't Say, 1967, Truth or Consequences, 1967, Woody Woodbury, 1967, Name of the Game, 1968, 69, 70, Red Skelton, 1970, Jeanie, 1970, Julia, 1970, The Interns, 1970, Partridge Family, 1970, Stump the Stars, 1970, Barefoot in the Park, 1970, Matt Lincoln, 1970, This Is Your Life, 1977, Adams Family, 1977; television series Cowboy G-Men, 1951-53, McKeever and Colonel, 1960s, Addams Family, 1963-65; appeared in: stage plays Blue Denim, 1967, Make a Million, 1968, Sweet Bird of Youth, 1968, Odd Couple, 1969, Come Blow Your Horn, 1969; toured, U.S. and Europe, (with Donald O'Connor), 1950, U.S., (with Ted Cassidy), summer stock, 1963-65; Author: Jackie Coogan Child Labor Law, 1937. Served with USAAF, 1941-45, CBI. Decorated D.F.C., Air medal; recipient Papal medal Pope Pius 10th, 1924, Order of King George Greek Govt., 1924, Justinian Cross Greek Orthodox Ch., 1924. Mem. Screen Actors Guild, A.F.T.R.A., Am. Guild Variety Artists, Equity, Acad. Motion Picture and Television Arts and Scis. Home: Palm Springs, Calif. Died March 1, 1984.

COOK, DONALD C., business cons.; b. Escanaba, Mich., Apr. 14, 1909; s. Nelson and Edith (Bryant) C.; m. Winnifred V. Carlsen, Dec. 4, 1943; 1 son, Nicholas Bryant. A.B., U. Mich., 1932, M.B.A., 1935; J.D., George Washington U., 1939, LL.M., 1940; 4 hon. degrees. C.P.A., Md. Financial examiner registration div. SEC, 1935-36, utilities analyst, pub. utilities div., 1937-42, asst. dir., 1943-45; spl. counsel U.S. Ho. of Reps. Com. Naval Affairs, 1943-45; exec. asst. to atty. gen. of U.S., 1945-46; dir. Office Alien Property, U.S. Dept. Justice, 1946-47; partner Cook and Berger, law offices, 1947-49; commr. SEC, 1949-53, vice chmn., 1950-52, chmn., 1952-53; chief counsel preparedness investigating subcom. Senate Armed Services Com., 1950-52; with Am. Electric Power Service Corp., from 1953, exec. v.p., 1954-61, pres., 1961-72, chmn. bd., 1972-76; dir., mem. exec. com. Am. Electric Power Co., 1960-76, pres., 1961-72, chmn. bd., chief exec. officer, 1971-76, cons., 1976-81; dir., chief exec., pres. subsidiaries Appalachian Power Co., Ind. & Mich. Electric Co., Ky. Power Co., Kingsport Power Co., Ohio Power Co., Wheeling Electric Co., Central Appalachian Coal Co., Franklin Real Estate Co., Ind. Franklin Realty, Inc., Cardinal (Operating Co., South Bend Mfg. Co., Twin Branch R.R. Co., W.Va. Power Co., Am. Electric Power Service Corp., Beech Bottom Power Co., Inc., Central Coal Co., Central Ohio Coal Co., Central Operating Co., Kanawha Valley Po r Co.), *1961-76; pres. Ohio Valley Electric Corp. (and subs.), until 1976; cons. Am. Electric Power System; gen. partner Lazard Freres and Co.; dir. Am. Broadcasting Cos., Inc., Amerada Hess Corp., Gen. Dynamics Corp., Pacesetter Systems. Contbr. articles on legal, financial and accounting subjects to profl. jours. Trustee George Washington U. Mem. Am., Mich. bar assns., Am. Accounting Assn., Am. Inst. C.P.A.'s, Am. Judicature Soc., Theta Xi, Phi Delta Phi, Beta Gamma Sigma. Democrat. Episcopalian. Clubs: Univ. (N.Y.C.), U. Mich. (N.Y.C.); Nat. Capital Democratic (Washington), Metropolitan (Washington), George Washington U. (Washington); U. of Mich. Presidents. Home: New York, N.Y. Died Dec. 16, 1981.

COOK, EARL FERGUSON, geology educator; b. Bellingham, Wash., May 24, 1920; s. Earl Ferguson and Helen (Royer) C.; m. Jean E. Wiltse, June 21, 1947 (div. 1964); children: Jeanette, Randall, Cynthia. B.S. in Mining Engring., U. Wash., 1943, M.S. in Geology, 1947, Ph.D. in Geology, 1954; student, U. Paris, 1945-46, U. Geneva, 1948-49. Instr. geology U. Wash., 1947-48, Stanford U., 1948; geologist Geophoto Services, Denver, 1949-51; mem. faculty U. Idaho, 1951-64, dean Coll. Mines, prof. geology, 1957-64; dir. Idaho Bur. Mines, 1957-64; prof. geology, asso. dean coll. geoscis. Tex. A & M U., College Station, 1965-71, prof. geography and geology, dean, 1971-81, Disting. prof., Harris prof. geoscis., 1981-83; exec. sec. div. earth scis. Nat. Acad. Scis.-NRC, Washington, 1963-66; geologist Gulf Oil Corp., summers 1955, 56. Served with AUS, 1943-46, ETO. Decorated Purple Heart. Mem. Geol. Soc. Am., AIME, Assn. Am. Geographers, Soc. Econ. Geologists, Am. Inst. Profl. Geologists. Address: College Station, Tex. Died Oct. 11, 1983.

COOK, GEORGE ANDRUS, mem. Nat. Mediation Bd.; b. Bloomington, Ill., May 5, 1889; s. Charles Albert and Vie (Andrus) C.; ed. public schs. and business coll. of Bloomington; m. Bertha Sparks, Sept. 14, 1918; children (by former marriage)—Edith Cook Gonoude, Vie Cook Arres. Began as ry. clerk Chicago and Alton, Bloomington, Ill., 1905; timekeeper Chicago and Alton, Kansas City, Mo., 1912-16; traveling auditor Chicago & Great Western, Chicago, 1917-19; wage schedule expert and examiner U.S.R.R. Labor Bd., Chicago, 1920-26; mediator and sec. U.S. Bd. of Mediation, 1926-34; sec. Nat. Mediation Bd., Washington, D.C., 1934-37, mem. of bd. from Jan. 1938, chmn., 1940-41, 1942-43. Republican. Mem. Christian Ch. Mason (32 deg., Shriner). Clubs: National Capital Skeet, National Capital Casting, Washington Gun (Washington, D.C.); Illinois Bait and Fly Casting (Chicago); San Francisco Tyee Club. Contbr. to outdoor mags. articles on angling. Home: Washington, D.C. †

COOK, HAROLD HUNTTING, investment banker; b. N.Y., 1903; s. Ferdinand H. and Mary W. (Aldrich) C.; A.B., Williams Coll., 1926; m. Alice Doyle, Oct. 2, 1928 (div.); children—Joan M., Anne H. (Mrs. Forbes Durey); m. 2d, Mrs. Catherine Johnson Baehr, Dec. 15, 1961; stepchildren—John J. Baehr, Jr., Carla Baehr. With Spencer Trask & Co., N.Y.C., 1926-33, 41-68, gen. partner, 1944-68, sr. v.p., dir. Spencer Trask & Co., Inc., 1968-69, cons., 1969-72; utility specialist C.W. Young & Co., 1933-35; mgr. bond dept. Reynolds & Co., 1935-37; sec. Reynolds Metals Co., 1937-41. Gov. of N.Y. Stock Exchange, 1962-68. Chmn. alumni fund Williams Coll., 1945-47, mem. alumni exec. com., 1945-47; pres. bd. trustees Collegiate Sch., N.Y.C., 1949-52, Kimberley Sch., Montclair, N.J., 1949-52. Mem. Nat. Assn. Securities Dealers (gov. 1956-59), Investment Bankers Assn. (gov. 1955-58), Pilgrims Soc., Soc. Colonial Wars, S.R., Alpha Delta Phi. Clubs: Bond of N.Y. (pres. 1958-59); Downtown Assn.; U.S. Seniors Golf Assn.; Paradise Valley Country (pres. 1976-77, dir.). Home: Scottsdale, Ariz. Died Sept. 23, 1981; interred Quogue, L.I.

COOK, HOWARD, trust co. exec.; b. Mexico, Mo., Nov. 30, 1889; s. Sam B. and Olivia (Hord) C.; student pub. schs.; m. Gertrude Shuman, June 4, 1921; children—Sam B., Howard W. With Central Mo. Trust Co., Jefferson City, from 1906, 2d asst. treas., 1916, 1st asst. treas., 1919, dir., 1919, v.p., 1921, pres., 1931-55, chmn. bd., 1955-71, chmn. exec. com., 1968-71, chmn. emeritus, from 1971. Served to capt. inf. U.S. Army, 1917-18. Home: Jefferson City, MO. †

COOK, HOWARD WILLARD, author, pub.; b. Syracuse, N.Y., Dec. 12, 1890; s. Edward Allen and Albertina Lee (Case) C.; grad. Sewanee (Tenn.) Mil. Acad., 1908 (valedictorian); unmarried. Formerly with editorial dept. Doubleday, Page & Co.; sec. Moffat, Yard & Co. from 1919. Episcopalian. Club: Players. Author: Our Poets of Today, 4th edit. 1922. Contbr. to The Mentor Assn., New York Sun, Chicago Evening Post, etc. Home: Norwalk, Conn. †

COOK, JOHN RICHARD, chmn. Arrow-Hart & Hegeman Electric Co.; b. Centerville, Md., July 9, 1887; s. John R. and Emma (Perry) C.; B.D., Trinity Coll.; 1910; m. Mildred C. Corson, 1916 (dec.). Cashier Travelers Ins. Co., 1911-12; sales Levering & Carrigues, 1912-14; underwriter London & Lancashire Fire Ins. Co., 1914-18; with Arrow-Hart & Hegeman Electric Co., Hartford, Conn., as service mgr., 1918, and later sales mgr., gen. mgr. and v.p. until 1932, when elected pres.; dir. Hartford Steam Boiler Inspection & Ins. Co., Soc. for Savings Bank, National Fire Insurance Company, Phoenix Mutual Life Insurance Company. Member board of trustees Trinity Coll.; mem. bd. dirs. American School for the Deaf. Mem. Delta Psi. Clubs: Electrical Mfrs., Hartford, Hartford Golf. Home: Hartford, Conn. †

COOKE, C(HARLES) WYTHE, geologist; b. Baltimore, Md., July 20, 1887; s. Henry Lane and Alice Wilson (Slemmer) C.; A.B., Johns Hopkins, 1908, fellow, 1911-12, Ph.D., 1912; Field asst., Md. Geol. Survey, 1908-12; geologist U.S. Geol. Survey 1910-56; research associate Smithsonian Institution, 1956 from; also geologist Geol. Survey of Dominican Republic, 1919; geologist Tropical Oil Co., Colombia, S.A., 1920. Fellow A.A.A.S., Geologic Society America, Paleontological Society (editor, 1937-46, vice president, 1948), member Washington Academy Sciences (editor, 1930-31; member of board managers 1932-35), Geol. Soc. Washington (sec. 1923-24; treas. 1930-35; vice-president, 1940), Phi Beta Kappa, Gamma Alpha, Delta Upsilon. Clubs: Cosmos, Washington Canoe (mem. board mgrs., 1940-47), Midriver Geology of Florida, 1945. Contbr. chapters in books and articles on geol. subjects. Editor Jour. Paleontology, 1937-46. Home: Washington, D.C. †

COOKE, ROY FRANCIS, real estate cons.; b. Athol, Mass., June 6, 1904; s. Charles Henry and Lillian (Smith) C.; m. Miriam Reed, Oct. 8, 1927; children—Roy Francis, Joanne (Mrs. Dwight Eames), Mary Lou (Mrs. Arlan MacKnight). Student, Boston U., 1923-24, Harvard Grad. Bus. Sch., 1939-40, Mass. Mil. Acad., 1943-44. Teller, bookkeeper Athol (Mass.) Savs. Bank, 1924-30; with R.F. Cooke Industries, Orange, Mass., 1930-55; asst. commr. FHA, Washington, 1957-61, real estate cons., from 1961; cons. SBA of N.H. Mem. mil. staff Gov. Christian A. Herter, 1952-56; concert master Greenfield Symphony Orch.; chmn. Fin. Com. Town of Athol, 1940-41; pres., adminstr. Athol Meml. Hosp., 1949-56; Bd. dirs. Franklin County Pub. Hosp., Greenfield, Mass., North Quabbin Health Service, YMCA, N.H. Kidney Assn.; commr. Boy Scouts Am.; trustee Wesley Theol. Sem., Washington, Nat. Kidney Found. Served to col. Mass. N.G. Mem. Nat. Wood Workers Mfrs. Assn. (pres. 1935-40), U.S. C. of C. (mem. policy com. 1943-47), Internat. Christian Leadership (treas. 1960-65), Res. Officers Assn. U.S. (pres. nat. orgn., pres. Mass chpt.), N.H. Res. Officers Assn. (pres.), Ancient and Honorable Arty. Co. Mass., Nat. Soc. 1st Inf. Div., Concord (N.H.) Bd. Realtors. Methodist (mem. finance com. 1966-73, asst. treas. 1972-73, lay del. 1967-73). Clubs: Masons, Shriners, Kiwanis (life fellow found.; dist. gov.), Skytop, Men's (v.p.), Ellinwood. Home: Concord, NH.

COOKE, STRATHMORE RIDLEY BARNOTT, metallurgist, educator; b. Wanganui, New Zealand, Jan. 4, 1907; s. Charles Ridley and Lilian Dawn Auckland (Barnott) C.; B.S., U. New Zealand, 1928, B.E., 1929; Assoc., Otago Sch. of Mines, U. Otago, 1929; M.S., Mo. Sch. Mines, 1930; Ph.D., U. Mo., 1933; m. Helen Ruth Cahill, Oct. 14, 1933; 1 son, S.R. Bruce. Came to U.S., 1929, naturalized, 1941. Research metallurgist Mo. Expt. Sta., 1933-36; asst. prof. Mo. Sch. Mines and Metallurgy, 1936-39; research prof. Mont. Sch. Mines, 1939-46; prof. metallurgy, mineral dressing U. Minn. Sch. Mines, 1946—, head sch. mines and metallurgy, 1957-60, chief dir. metall. engring., 1960-63, prof. metall. engring., 1963-70, prof. Sch. Earth Scis., 1970-74, prof. emeritus, 1974-85. Mem. AIME (Legion of Honor); Am. Inst. Mining, Mettalurgical and Petroleum Engrs. (Disting. Mem. award 1978), Mineral. Soc. Am., Brit. Astron. Assn., Sigma Xi, Phi Kappa Phi, Theta Tau, Kappa Sigma, Tau Beta Pi. Contbr. articles in field. Home: Robbinsdale, Minn. Dec. June 13, 1985. Interned Minneapolis, Minn.

COOKE, TERENCE JAMES, Cardinal, bishop; b. N.Y.C., Mar. 1, 1921; s. Michael and Margaret (Gannon) C. Student, Cathedral Coll., N.Y.C.; B.A., St. Joseph's Sem., Yonkers, N.Y., 1945; M.S. in Social Work, Catholic U., 1949. Ordained priest Roman Catholic Ch., 1945; asst. pastor St. Athanasius Ch., Bronx, N.Y.; also chaplain St. Agatha Home, Nanuet, N.Y., 1946-47; asst. dir. Cath. Youth Orgn., also dir. youth activities, N.Y.C., 1949-54; procurator St. Joseph's Sem., Yonkers, N.Y., 1954-57; sec. to Cardinal Spellman, 1957-58; named papal chamberlain, vice chancellor Archdiocese N.Y., 1958, domestic prelate, chancellor, 1961-65, vicar gen., 1965-68, titular bishop of Summa and aux. bishop, N.Y., 1965-68, archbishop of N.Y., 1968—, created cardinal, 1969. Home: New York, N.Y. Died Oct. 6, 1983.

COOKE, WILLARD RICHARDSON, univ. prof.; b. Galveston, Tex., Sept. 6, 1888; s. Henry Pendleton and Caroline Louisa (Richardson) C.; B.A., U. of Tex., 1908, M.D., 1912; m. Aline Ruth Austin, Apr. 25, 1914; children—Henry Austin, Willard Richardson, John Rogers. Rotating internship, John Sealy Hosp., Galveston, Tex., 1912-13; instr., obstetrics and gynecology, U. of Tex., 1913-21; asso. prof., 1921-24; professor U. of Tex.; obstetrician and gynecologist in chief, John Sealy Hospital, from 1924. Captain, U.S. Army, 1917-19, (inactive status). Member Galveston County Med. Soc. (ex.-pres.), South Tex. Dist. Med. Soc. (ex.-pres.), Tex. Med. Assn. (ex-chmn., section on obstetrics and gynecology), Southern Med. Assn. (ex-chmn., section on obstetrics and gynecology), Pan-Am. Med. Assn. (ex-v.p.), Tex. Surgical Society (ex-vice pres.) A.C.S., Houston Gynecological and Obstet. Soc., Central Assn. Obstetricians and Gynecologists (ex- pres.), Am. Assn. Obstetricians, Gynecologists, and Abdominal Surgeons (pres., Am. Gynecol. Soc. (v.p.), Am. Bd. of Obstetrics and Gynecology (dir.), Alpheus Freedman Africanus King Soc. (hon.), A.M.A., Tex. Assn. Obstetricians Gynecologists. Episcopalian. Clubs: Boat, Country (Galveston). Author, textbook Essentials of Gynecology; co-author, Curtis' Obstetrics of Gynecology and American Encyclopedia of Medicine, also many articles appearing in professional jours. †

COOLEDGE, HELEN MCGREGOR, univ. prof.; b. Panora, Ia., July 23, 1889; d. James Wilson and Lucena (Booton) McGregor; B.S., U. of Mo., 1914, A.B., 1917; A.M., Teachers Coll. Columbia U., 1921; m. Nelson F. Cooledge, July 27, 1924. High sch. teacher household arts, Nevada, Mo., 1914-17; head home econ. dept. Ark. State Coll., 1917-20; instr. foods and nutrition Cornell Univ., 1922-24; homemaker and part-time teacher home econ. Ark. Poly. Coll., 1929-38; head home economist and homemaker, U. of S.D., from 1938. Mem. Am. Assn. Univ. Profs., Am. Assn. Univ. Women, Business and Professional Women, S.D. Edn. Assn., C. of C., Am. Home Econ. Assn., S.D. Home econ. Assn., Woman's soc. Christian Service, Delta Kappa Gamma. Methodist. Clubs: Federated Garden, Dames, Faculty Woman's. Author of articles in mags., radio talks. Won $75 prize for definition of Home Economics, 1948. Home: Vermillion, S.D. †

COOLEY, VICTOR E., business exec.; b. Cloverdale, Calif., July 31, 1890; student University of California, 1908-11; married Helen F. Pierce, Feb. 18, 1922; children—Richard P., Ann Frances, Mary Katherine, Helen Victoria. Became president and director Southwestern Bell Telephone Company, 1947, chmn. from 1950; dir. First National Bank, St. Louis, Missouri, Scruggs-Vandervoort-Barney, Inc., Southeast Mo. Telephone Co., Am. Central Ins. Co. Home: Clayton, Mo. †

COOLIDGE, HAROLD JEFFERSON, international conservationist; b. Boston, Jan. 15, 1904; s. Harold and Edith (Lawrence) C.; m. Helen Carpenter Isaacs, Apr. 25, 1931 (div. 1972); children: Nicholas, Thomas, Isabella; m. Martha Thayer Henderson, May 26, 1972. Grad., Milton Acad., 1922; student, U. Ariz., 1922-23; B.S., Harvard, 1927, Cambridge (Eng.) U., 1927-28; D.Sc., George Washington U., 1959, Seoul Nat. U., 1965, Brandeis U., 1970. Asst. mammalogist Harvard African Expdn. to Liberia, Belgian Congo, 1926-27; leader Indo-China div. Kelley-Roosevelt's Field Mus. Expdn., 1928-29; asst. curator mammals Mus. Comparative Zoology, Harvard, 1929-46, asso. mammalogy, 1946-70; leader Asiatic Primate Expedition, 1937; exec. dir. Coolidge Found.,

1946-51; exec. dir. Pacific sci. bd. Nat. Acad. Scis.-NRC, 1946-70; collaborator U.S. Nat. Park Service, 1948-85; Sec. Am. Com. Internat. Wild Life Protection (now Am. Com. Internat. Conservation), 1930-51, chmn., 1951-71, hon. chmn., 1971—; hon. cons. Bernice P. Bishop Mus., 1953-85; cons. OBOR, U.S. and Indonesia; adviser Pacific Studies Peabody Mus. Salem, 1974—; pres. Internat. Union for Conservation Nature and Natural Resources, 1966-72, hon. pres., 1972-85, v.p. internat. commn. nat. parks, 1948-54, 63-66, chmn., 1958-63, mem., 1963-76, hon. mem., 1976—, chmn. species survival service commn., 1949-58, mem., 1958-76, hon. mem., 1976-85; sec. gen. 10th Pacific Sci. Congress, Honolulu, 1961; chmn. 1st World Conf. on Nat. Parks, Seattle, 1962; Bd. dirs. L.S.B. Leakey Found., U.S. World Wildlife Fund, 1962—; bd. dirs. Internat. World Wildlife Fund, 1966-78, mem. of honor, 1979-85; bd. dirs. Inst. Nat. Pour la conservation de la Nature de Zaire (hon.), Charles Darwin Found. for Galapagos Islands, Research Ranch, Inc.; hon. mem. bd. dirs. Island Resources Found.; v.p. Fauna Preservation Soc., U.K.; bd. dirs. emeritus Hawaii Pacific Tropical Botanic Gardens, African Wildlife Leadership Found.; trustee William P. Wharton Conservation Trust, Sci. and Aeros. Adv. Com., Lindbergh Fund; chmn. Lindbergh Fund; corp. Boston Mus. Sci.; adv. bd. Cultural Survival Inc., 1975—; mem. adv. council Internat. Crane Found., 1977—; hon. pres. H. J. Coolidge Ctr. for Environ. Leadership; hon. mem. NRC, Philippines.; hon. dir. Bat Conservation Soc. Author: (with Theodore Roosevelt) Three Kingdoms of Indo-China, 1933; sci. publs. on primates, internat. conservation. Served to maj. AUS, 1943-45. Decorated Mil. Legion of Merit U.S.; decorations from Ecuadorian, French, Laotian, Annamite, Cambodian, Belgian govts., Prince of Netherlands; recipient 75th Anniversary medal of merit U. Ariz., 1960; Hutchinson medal Garden Club Am., 1963; Albright medal Am. Scenic and Historic Preservation Soc., 1969; Silver medal Internat. Achievement award U.S. Nat. Parks Centennial Commn., 1972; Browning award Smithsonian Instn., 1978; Phillips medal Internat. Union Conservation of Nature and Natural Resources, 1978; J. Paul Getty Wildlife Conservation prize, 1979. Fellow N.Y. Zool. Soc. (gold medal 1969), Pacific Sci. Assn. (hon. life); mem. Am. Soc. Mammalogists (life), Common Cause, Caribbean Cons. Assn., Inst. Nat. Parks Belgian Congo (dir. 1955-60), Nat. Parks and Conservation Assn. (sec. 1946-59, dir. 1959-74), Pacific Sci. Assn. (U.S. mem. Pacific sci. council 1962-72), Monticello Assn., Chgo. Mus. Natural History (life), Internat. Inst. Differing Civilizations (Brussels), Cercle Zoologique Congolaise (hon., Belgium), Zool. Soc. London (corr.), Sigma Xi. Episcopalian. Clubs: Harvard Travellers (Boston), Tavern (Boston); Cosmos (Washington); Harvard (N.Y.C.), Boone and Crockett (N.Y.C.), Explorers (N.Y.C.) (chmn. edn. com. 1976). Home: Beverly, Mass. Died Feb. 14, 1985.

COOLIDGE, JOHN TEMPLEMAN, JR., artist; b. Boston, Mass., Dec. 28, 1888; s. John Templeman and Katharine Scollay (Parkman) C.; A.B., Harvard, 1911; grad. Sch. of Mus. of Fine Arts, Boston, 1917; m. Susannah Cunningham, Apr. 25, 1916; children—Francis Parkman (dec.), John Templeman, III, Paul Constant, Gloria, Susannah Harriet. Painter of landscapes and magazine illustrator; traveled 1 yr. in British E. Africa taking photographs and moving pictures of wild animals. Contbr. nature articles to Scribner's Mag. Served as 2d lt. S.R.C., Air Service, in U.S., World War. Mem. Am. Mus. Natural History, Boston Soc. Natural History. Republican. Unitarian. Club: Tavern (Boston). Home: Readville, Mass. †

COOLING, WILLIAM PETER, insurance company executive; b. Los Angeles, Nov. 5, 1915; s. Parke A. and Zuleika (Henderson) C.; A.B., DePauw U., 1936; m. Barbara Butler Fox, May 11, 1979; children—Virginia (Mrs. John E. Hollett III), Susan (Mrs. David D. Babcock), Mary (Mrs. Wayne L. Ritter Jr.). With Indiana Group, Inc. and subsidiary cos., Indpls., from 1936, exec. v.p., 1956-58, pres., from 1958, also chmn. bd.; chmn., dir. Cooling-Grumme-Mumford Co., Inco Finance, Inc., Central Adjusting Co., Inc., Consol. Information Service Corp. dir. Mayflower Corp., Aero Mayflower Transit Co., Inc., Am. Fletcher Nat. Bank & Trust Co., Am. Fletcher Corp., Citizens Gas and Coke Utility. Pres., Goodwill Industries Am., Washington 1970-73, bd. dirs., 1971-74; bd. dirs. United Fund Greater Indpls., Central Ind. council Boy Scouts Am., Indpls. Goodwill Industries; bd. dirs., past pres. Hoosierland Rating Bur., Ind. Traffic Safety Council. trustee Christian Theol. Sem., 1967-73, DePauw U. Mem. Ind. Insurors Assn. (dir.), Ins. Inst. Ind. (pres., dir.), Indpls. C. of C. (dir.) Methodist. Mason, Kiwanian. Clubs: Meridian Hills Country, Columbia, Indpls. Athletic. Home: Indianapolis, Ind. Deceased

COOMBS, CHARLES ANTHONY, banker; b. Newton, Mass., Apr. 9, 1918; s. Charles Harold and Florence (Campbell) C.; A.B., Harvard, 1940, M.P.A., M.A., 1942, Ph.D., 1953; m. Ilona Harman, Apr. 5, 1945; 1 dau., Claire. With Fed. Res. Bank N.Y., 1946-75, sr. v.p. charge fgn. function, 1959-75; fin. cons., dir. Discount Corp. N.Y., Am. Internat. Group, Am. Express Internat. Banking Corp., First Chgo. Internat. Banking Corp. Fed. Res. rep. meetings Bank Internat. Settlements, Basle, Switzerland; fin. adviser Am. Mission to Greece, 1947; mem. Presdl. Task Force Promoting Fgn. Investment in U.S., 1963. Served with AUS, 1942-44. Recipient Distinguished Service award Treasury Dept., 1968; commendatore award Italian govt., 1975. Mem. Council Fgn. Relations. Club: Morris County Golf. Author: The Arena of International Finance, 1976; also articles in field. Home: Green Village, N.J. Died Sept. 20, 1981.

COOMBS, RALPH ROLAND, ins. exec.; b. Orange, Mass., July 22, 1888; s. Roland Morton and Emma Jane (Cook) C.; student pub. schs., Boston; univ. extension courses, comml. coll.; m. Irene Berry, Apr. 18, 1918; children—Lucille Dorothy (Mrs. Ray A. Johnson), Joanne (Mrs. William R. Richard, Jr.), Ralph Roland. With Mass. Mut. Life Ins. Co., Springfield, from 1907, dept. mgr., 1931, asst. sec., 1932-39, asst. to pres., 1939-44, 2d v.p., 1944-48, v.p., 1948-50, adminstrv. v.p. from 1950. Pres., dir. Vis. Nurse Assn., 1936-50; trustee Better Business Bur., 1942-50, United Fund, 1941-53. Served with U.S. Army, World War I. Mem. Life Office Management Assn. (past bd. dirs.), Springfield C. of C. (past v.p., dir.). Conglist. Mason. Contbr. articles profl. management jours. Home: Springfield, Mass. †

COON, ERNEST D., univ. prof.; b. Pierre, S.D., Nov. 17, 1889; s. Hiram Southwick and Myra (Robarts) C.; B.S., U. of N.D., 1920, M.S., 1922; Ph.D., U. of Wis., 1932; m. Janet Rae Duncan, June 7, 1923. Instr. chemistry U. of N.D., 1922-27, asst. prof. 1927-34, asso. prof., 1934-41, prof. chemistry from 1941 and head of the chemistry department, 1950-51, from 1957, member adminstrv. com., 1940-52. Member bd. trustees Wesley Coll., sec. to bd., from 1937. Served with U.S. Navy, 1917-19; in radio and submarine service; instr. Harvard U.S. Naval Radio Sch., 1918. Mem. Am. Chem. Soc. (mem. div. exec. committee, chairman of the Red River Valley section 1952-53, national councilor from 1957, North Dakota Academy Sci. (pres. 1937-38, 1938-39), Am. Assn. Univ. Profs., Sigma Xi, Methodist. Club: Fortnightly (Grand Forks). Home: Grand Forks, N.D. †

COOPER, CHAUNCEY IRA, college dean; b. St. Louis, May 31, 1906; s. Ira Luther and Mattie Salina (Horton) C.; B.S. in Pharmacy, U. Minn., 1934, M.S., 1935; m. Marie Taylor, June 7, 1937; 1 son, Chauncey M.; foster children—William R. Hyde (M.D.), Jeanne H. Lofton. Instr. pharmacy Meharry Med. Coll., Nashville, 1927-32; instr. pharmacy Howard U., 1935-38, assoc. prof., acting dean Coll. Pharmacy, 1938-41, prof., dean after 1941. Founder, organizer Nat. Pharm. Assn., pres., 1947, exec. sec., after 1950; editor Jour. Nat. Pharm. Assn., after 1955. Recipient award for leadership Washington Pharm. Assn., 1957; Chauncey I. Cooper award established by Nat. Pharm. Assn. Mem. Am. Pharm. Assn., Am. Assn. Colls. Pharmacy, Washington Pharm. Assn., Beta Kappa Chi, Alpha Phi Alpha. Club: Pigskin (Washington). Home: North Chevy Chase, Md. Died Sept. 30, 1983.

COOPER, G. WILHELMINA, modeling agy. exec.; b. Cullemborg, Holland, May 11, 1939; d. Willy Robert and Klasina (Van Straten) Behmenburg; m. V. Bruce Cooper, Feb. 15, 1965; children—Melissa, Jason. Fashion model, Chgo., 1959, Paris, 1960, N.Y.C., 1961-67; appeared on over 280 mag. covers including numerous Vogue mag. covers; founder Wilhelmina Model Agy., N.Y.C., 1967, pres., until 1980; dir. Wilhelmina Models, Inc., N.Y.C., Wilhelmina West, Inc., Wilhelmina Artists Reps., Los Angeles. Mem. Internat. Model Mgrs. Assn., Screen Actors Guild, AFTRA, Fashion Group (officer). Author: The New You, 1978. Home: Cos Cob, Conn. Died Mar. 1, 1980.

COOPER, JOHN CROSSAN, JR., lawyer; b. Balt., Oct. 16, 1901; s. John Crossan and Louisa Carrel (Jenkins) C.; A.B., Princeton, 1923; LL.B., Yale, 1927; m. Eleanor Chalfant, Jan. 28, 1930; children—John C. III, Louisa J., Harriet W. Partner, Venable, Baetjer & Howard, 1937; dir. Balt. Savs. Bank, Baltimore, Canton R.R. Co., Canton Co. of Balt., Cottman Co. Trustee Johns Hopkins U., Gilman Sch.; trustee Johns Hopkins Hosp., chmn., 1965-71. Mem. Am., Md., Balt. (pres. 1954-55) bar assns. Democrat. Roman Catholic. Clubs: Maryland, Elkridge (Balt.); Brook (N.Y.C.). Home: Baltimore, Md. Died Nov. 19, 1980.

COOPER, LESTER IRVING, TV producer; b. N.Y.C., Jan. 20, 1919; s. Samuel and Clara (Levine) C.; m. Audrey Rosemary Levey, July 1, 1949; children: Kim, Elizabeth, Matthew. Student, NYU, 1936, Columbia U. extension, 1936. Writer, Warner Bros., Hollywood, Calif., 1937-41, screenwriter, J. Arthur Rank-Brit. Nat. Pictures, London, 1945-49, chief copy editor, Esquire mag., 1949-50, with Lester Cooper Prodns., films, 1953-55, CBS, 1953-55, NBC, 1955-58; supervising producer, head writer: PM, Westinghouse Broadcasting Co., 1959-61; producer: Exploring the Universe, 1962-64; with: ABC News, 1965—; creator, writer, dir., exec. producer: Animals Animals Animals (Emmy award, Peabody award, Action for Children's TV award), 1976-81 (Ohio State U. award); (Recipient Journalism TV award AMA 1967, Albert Lasker Med. Journalism award 1970); Writer-producer: Hemingway's Spain, 1968 (Peabody award), Can You Hear Me?, 1967, Heart Attack, 1969, This Land is Mine, 1970; creator: Make a Wish (Peabody award 1971), 1971 (Emmy award 1974). Served with AUS, 1941-45. Mem. Dirs. Guild Am., Writers Guild Am. Home: Westport, Conn. Died June 6, 1985. *

COOPER, STUART, corp. official; b. Clayville, N.Y., July 31, 1887; s. Charles Frank and Emily Cornelia (Avery) C.; E.E., Syracuse U., 1914; m. Mary Green Bailey, May 22, 1920. Asst. constrn. engr., later statistician and distribution engr., New York & Queens Electric Light & Power Co., 1914-17; distribution engr. Counties Gas & Electric Co., 1917-18; asst. to elec. engr. United Gas Improvement Co., 1918-19; v.p. and mgr. Charleston Consol. Ry. & Light Co., 1919-27; v.p. and mgr., later pres., S.C. Power Co., 1927-28; v.p. Phila. Suburban Counties Gas & Electric Co., 1928-29; v.p. United Gas Improvement Co., 1929-43; pres. and dir. Delaware Power & Light Co., 1943-56, chmn. bd. dirs. and exec. com., 1956-59, chmn. exec. com., 1959 from, dir. subsidiary cos.; dir. Farmers Bank State of Del., Phila., Balt. & Washington R.R. Mem. Edison Electric Inst., Am. Gas Assn. (dir.), Am. Inst. E.E., Tau Beta Pi, Delta Upsilon. Presbyterian. Clubs: Wilmington, Wilmington Country. Rotary. Home: Wilmington, Del. †

COOPERMAN, PHILIP, educator; b. N.Y.C., Dec. 3, 1918; s. Meyer and Bessie (Wolocizer) C.; m. Elsie B. Rosenson, Oct. 8, 1950; children—Gene D., Lawrence J. B.S., Coll. City N.Y., 1938; M.S., N.Y.U., 1948, Ph.D., 1951. Physicist USN Dept., Balt., 1941-43; physicist Los Alamos Sci. Labs., 1944-46, Research Corp., Bound Brook, N.J., 1951-56; sr. mathematician Gulf Oil Corp., Hamarville, Pa., 1956-58; asst. prof. U. Pitts., 1958-60; dir. research and devel. Research-Cottrell, Bound Brook, 1960, cons., 1959-60, 61-62; prof. math. Fairleigh-Dickinson U., Teaneck, N.J., from 1961; cons. U.S. Steel Corp., 1959; Precipitair Pollution Control, Inc., 1967-72, Mikropul Corp., 1977-79; tech. editor All Clear Mag., 1969-71; reviewer Math. Revs., 1963-69; hon. vis. prof. U. Wollongong, Australia, 1975. Contbr. articles to profl. jours.; reviewer: Jour. Electrostatics, U.K. Served with C.E. AUS, 1943-46. Fgn. fellow Inst. of Electrostatics (Japan); mem. Air Pollution Control Assn., IEEE, Am. Math. Soc., Math. Assn. Am., Electrostatic Soc. Am. Patentee in field. Home: Teaneck, NJ.

COOVER, MERVIN SYLVESTER, engring. edn.; b. Shippensburg, Pa., Dec. 9, 1890; s. George Benjamin and Mary Alice (Lutz) C.; E.E., Rensselaer Poly. Institute, 1914; m. Frances Amy Potter, June 6, 1917; children—Mervin Potter, George Bertrand, Martha Claire. Student engr., N.Y. Central Railroad, 1914-15; prof. and head of department of electrical engring., Ia. State Coll., Ames, Ia., from 1935; dir. naval training sch. (elec.), Ia. State Coll., 1942-44. Served with 37th Engrs., A.E.F., during World War I. Asst. regional coordinator, radio technician training, engring., science, management defense training, 1942-43. Mem. Am. Inst. E.E. (rep. Engrs. Council Profl. Development, 1948-51, exec. com. 1945; Edison Medal com., 1941-43, 1944-46; Washington Award Commn., 1946-48; rep. Hertz Award Com., 1944-53; engrs. joint council; chmn. region VI, engring. Manpower commn., 1951-53), Soc. Promotion Engring. Edn. (chmn. 1942), Ia. Engring. Soc. (recipient John Dunlap Meml. Award, 1938; rep. 5th Dist., 1939; dir. 1939; v.p. profl. div., 1940; chmn. com. on special awards, 1941-46; chmn. publs., 1943; chmn. membership com., 1942; pres. 1944); honorary mem. Phi Kappa Phi, Tau Beta Pi, Eta Kappa Nu, Sigma Tau, Alpha Sigma Phi. Registered professional engr., State of Iowa. Author many papers in tech. and professional publs., also Notes on Electric Railway Engineering, 1930-31, Principles of Electric Traction, 1931-32 and 1933. Home: Ames, Iowa. †

COPELAND, JO, fashion designer; b. N.Y.C.; d. Samuel and Minna (Emelin) C.; m. Edward Joseph Regensburg, 1923 (div. 1944); children—Anthony S., Lois Adele (Mrs. Robert Gould); m. Mitchell Benson, May 8, 1953. Student, Parson's Sch. Design, Art Students League, N.Y.C. Comml. artist, 1918-21; sketcher, designer Pattulo, 1921-29; dress mfr. Jo Copeland, Inc., 1931-37; with Pattullo-Jo Copeland, Inc., 1938-70, v.p. charge designing, 1938-70; now free lance cons.; writer series on fashion for Phila. Enquirer; cons., lectr. Fashion Inst. Tech., also adviser community resources to students design and merchandising. Adv. bd. Steven's Coll.; pres. Manhattan League of Indsl. Home for Blind; mem. adv. bd. Girls Club N.Y. Recipient Nieman Marcus award; Am. Silk Assn. award; citation Phila. Mus. Art; medal Ordre de la Courtoisie de France, 1961; award Girls Club of N.Y., 1961. Mem. Fashion Group, Council Fashion Designers Am. (founder mem.). Home: New York, NY.

COPELAND, LAMMOT DU PONT, financial executive; b. Wilmington, Del., May 19, 1905; s. Charles and Louisa d'Andelot (du Pont) C.; m. Pamela Cunningham, Feb. 1, 1930; children: Lammot du Pont, Louisa Copeland Duemling, Gerret van S. B.S. in Indsl. Chemistry, Harvard, 1928; LL.D., U. Del., 1962, U. Pa., 1963, Am. U., 1964; D.Sc., Jefferson Med. Coll., 1963; H.H.D., Washington Coll., 1965; D.Sc. in Commerce, Drexel Inst.; D.Engring., PMC Colls., 1971. With E.I. du Pont de Nemours & Co., Inc., 1929-83, dir., 1942-83, mem. finance com., 1943-59, sec., 1947-54, v.p., 1954-62, chmn. finance com., 1954-59, mem. exec. com., 1959-67, pres., chmn. exec. com., 1962-67, chmn. bd., 1967-71, mem. fin. com., 1962-83; dir. Dupont Co. Can., Montreal, 1949-63. Trustee Longwood Found.; trustee, treas. Eleutherian Mills-Hagley Found.; bd. overseers Harvard Coll., 1964-70; trustee, past pres. Henry Francis duPont Winterthur Mus.; hon. dir., past pres. Wilmington Soc. Fine Arts; vice chmn. bd. Del. Safety Council; trustee U. Pa., 1951-66. Decorated officer Legion of Honour France; officer Order of Leopold Belgium; comdr. Order Couronne de Chene Luxembourg). Mem. Pilgrims U.S., Am. Chem. Soc., Harvard Alumni Soc. (dir. 1953-56), Mil.

Order Loyal Legion, Nat. Rifle Assn., Soc. Colonial Wars Del. (gov.), Walpole Soc., Huguenot Soc. Am., Soc. Mayflower Descs., Am. Antiquarian Soc., Am. Philos. Soc. Clubs: Wilmington (Wilmington), Wilmington Country (Wilmington), Vicmead Hunt (Wilmington), Greenville Country (Wilmington); Harvard (N.Y.C.), University Links (N.Y.C.); Capitol Hill (Washington). Home: Greenville, Del. Died July 1, 1983.

COPPEDGE, ROY FLEMISTER, store corporation executive; born Pike Co., Ga., July 20, 1889; son of Zachary Taylor and Dora Virginia (Wood) C.; student pub. schs. of Atlanta, Ga.; m. Norma Jones, Oct. 19, 1911; children—Louise (Mrs. Bernarde Edward Anderson), Roy Flemister. Store mgr. S. H. Kress & Co., N.Y. City, 1909-25, dist. mgr., 1915-25, buyer 1925-31, supervisor of buying, 1929-31; exec. v.p. McCrory Stores Corp., N.Y. City, 1931-39, pres., 1939-45, chmn. bd. 1945 from, chief executive officer, 1945-59; chmn. exec. bd. McCrory-McLellan Stores; dir., mem. exec. com. McCrory Corp.†

CORBETT, ROGER BAILEY, college president; b. Morgantown, W.Va., Feb. 11, 1900; s. Lee Cleveland and Evelyn N. (Northrup) C.; B.S., Cornell U., 1922, M.S., 1923, Ph.D., 1925; Litt. D. (hon.), College of Artesia, N.M.; m. Faith L. Rogers, Nov. 25, 1927 (died 1939); children—Roger Lee, Ann Francis; m. 2d, Elizabeth Burn Rutter, July 22, 1963. Instr. Cornell U., 1924-25; economist, instr., extension service, 1925-40; dir. Agrl. Expt. Sta., U. Md., 1940-43; exec. sec.-treas. Am. Farm Bur. Fedn., 1943-47; asso. dean and dir. Coll. of Agr., U. Md., 1947-49; agrl. counsel Nat. Assn. Food Chains, 1949-55; pres. New Mexico State University, 1955-70. Past mem. El Paso br. Federal Reserve Board; director of Shop Rite, Inc., Farah Manufacturing Co., Inc. Member national council Boy Scouts Am. Past pres. Am. Country Life Association, Northeastern Dairy Conference; president of Farm Film Foundation. Served as acting sgt. World War I. Mem. N.E.A.., Am. Acad. Polit. and Social Scis., Newcomen Soc. N.Am., Phi Kappa Phi, Alpha Zeta, Kappa Delta Rho, Epsilon Sigma Phi, AGFU, Scabbard and Blade (hon.). Episcopalian. Rotarian (past. pres.). Author numerous expt. sta. and extension service bulls., also articles. Address: Las Cruces, N.M. Died Jan. 25, 1984.

CORCORAN, THOMAS GARDINER, lawyer; b. Pawtucket, R.I., Dec. 29, 1900; s. Thomas Patrick and Mary Josephine (O'Keefe) C.; A.B. and A.M., Brown U., 1922; LL.B., Harvard, 1925, S.J.D., 1926; m. Margaret J. Dowd; 6 children. Sec. to Oliver Wendell Holmes, asso. justice Supreme Court of U.S., 1926-27; asso. Cotton & Franklin, lawyers, N.Y.C., 1927-32; counsel R.F.C., Washington, 1932, 34-41; asst. to sec. of Treasury, 1933; spl. asst. to atty. gen. of U.S., 1932-35; assisted congl. coms. in drafting Securities Act of 1933, Fed. Housing Act, 1933, Securities Exchange Act of 1934, Pub. Utility Holding Company Act of 1935, Fair Labor Standards Act of 1938; now in pvt. practice with Corcoran, Youngman and Rowe, Washington. Trustee Brown U., 1964-69. Democrat. Roman Catholic. Home: Washington, D.C. Died Dec. 6, 1981.

CORCORAN, WILLIAM HARRISON, chem. engr.; b. Los Angeles, Mar. 11, 1920; s. William H. and Enid (Winchester) C.; m. Martha Nell Rogers, Nov. 7, 1942; children—Sally Kay (Mrs. Raymond K. Fisher), William Owen. B.S., Calif. Inst. Tech., 1941, M.S., 1942, Ph.D., 1948. Chem. engr. Cutter Lab., 1941-42; devel. engr., research supr. Calif. Inst. Tech., 1942-46, NRC predoctoral fellow, 1946-48; dir. tech. devel. Cutter Lab., 1948-52; asso. prof. chem. engring. Calif. Inst. Tech., 1952-57, prof., from 1957, exec. officer chem. engring., 1967-69, v.p. inst. relations, 1969-79, Inst. prof., from 1979; sci. dir., v.p. Don Baxter, Inc., 1957-59, sci. cons., from 1959; dir. Superior Farming Co., KTI, Inc.; Dir. Industry Edn. Council San Gabriel Valley, from 1965; chmn. council, dir. Engrs. Council for Profl. Devel., 1975-78; v.p. Accreditation Bd. for Engring. and Tech., 1980; trustee, mem. exec. com. Assn. Independent Calif. Colls. and Univs., 1972-79; bd. dirs. Huntington Inst. Applied Med. Research, from 1973, sec., 1974-77, v.p., from 1977; bd. dirs. Villa Esperanza, Pasadena, Calif., from 1976; chmn. Air Force Inst. Tech. subcom. of bd. visitors Air U., 1975-78. Author: (with J.B. Opfell and B.H. Sage) Momentum Transfer in Fluids, 1956, (with W.N. Lacey) Introduction to Chemical Engineering Problems, 1960; Asso. editor: (with W.N. Lacey) Jour. Quantitative Spectroscopy and Radiative Heat Transfer, 1971; editorial adv. bd.: (with W.N. Lacey) Internat. Chem. Engring; mem. publs. bd.: (with W.N. Lacey) Chem. Engring. Edn, from 1967; chmn. (with W.N. Lacey), 1967-68, 75-77; Contbr. (with W.N. Lacey) articles to profl. jours. Recipient Educator of Yr. award chpt. 99 Am. Soc. Tool and Mfg. Engrs., 1968; Civic Achievement award So. Calif. sect. Am. Inst. Chem. Engrs., 1970; Westinghouse Engring. Teaching Excellence award, 1970; Phillips Petroleum Co. lectr. in chem. engring., 1971; Distinguished Alumnus Los Angeles Sch. Dist. Bicentennial, 1976; Ednl. Achievement award Calif. Soc. Profl. Engrs., 1976; Teaching Excellence award Associated Students Calif. Inst. Tech., 1977; scroll of appreciation USAF, 1979. Fellow Am. Inst. Chem. Engrs. (Founders award 1974, pres. 1978), Inst. for Advancement Engring. (Engr. of Yr. 1980), AAAS; mem. Am. Soc. Engring. Edn. (chmn. ad hoc rev. com. on engring. and engring. tech. studies 1975-77, Lamme award 1979), Am. Chem. Soc., ASME, Am. Def. Preparedness Assn., Am. Inst. Chemists, Am. Inst. Aeros. and Astronautics, Nat. Acad. Engring., Nat. Acad. Engring. of Mex. (corr.), Sigma Xi, Tau Beta Pi. Home: San Gabriel, Calif.

CORDELL, OSCAR L., business exec.; b. Helenwood, Tenn., May 26, 1887; s. John and Emma (Ryan) C.; ed. at pub. schs.; m. Eda Turley, Nov. 17, 1909; children—John Turley, David Oscar, Emily May (Mrs. John Thomas Scott). Petroleum refining and marketing from 1907; dir. and pres. Bareco Oil Co. from 1939. Republican. Presbyterian. Mason. Clubs: Tulsa, Southern Hills Country. Home: Tulsa, Okla. †

CORENA, FERNANDO, bass; b. Geneva, Switzerland, Dec. 22, 1916; emigrated to U.S., 1954; s. Dimitri and Ugolina (Albertini) C. Bacalaurea, U. Frybourg, Switzerland. Operatic debut in Arena of Verona, La Scala, Milan; leading bass with, Metropolitan Opera, at Theatro Colon, Buenos Aires, Stattsoper, Berlin, Covent Garden, London, Lyric Opera, Chgo., San Francisco Opera, Vienna Staatsoper, Grand Theatre, Geneva, Rome Opera, Vienna Staatsoper, Florence Maggio Musicale et Comunale; also appeared in, Brussels, Nice, Paris, Lisbon, Barcelona, Hartford, Houston, Miami, New Orleans, Phila., Washington., festival appearances include, Salzburg, Edinburgh, Holland, Athens. Home: Castagnola, Switzerland. Died Nov. 26, 1984.

COREY, GEORGE RAYMOND, utilities exec.; b. Jewett, O., Jan. 17, 1887; s. Thomas and Henrietta (Jolley) C.; LL.B., Univ. Utah, 1921; m. Mathilda Frazee, Oct. 21, 1913 (dec. Jan. 24, 1935); 1 son, George Raymond; m. 2d, Anne L. Harris, Aug. 9, 1938. With Utah Power & Light Co., from 1913, gen. counsel 1937-44, v.p., dir., gen. counsel and sec. 1944-51, exec. v.p., dir., sec. from 1951. Admitted to Utah bar 1921. Mem. C. of C. Protestant Episcopal. Mason. Clubs: Alta. Country.†

COREY, MARIAN EDITH, editor; b. Saranac Lake, N.Y., 1888; d. Alembert L. and Jane Elizabeth (Lynch) C.; A.B., Syracuse (N.Y.) U., 1912. With U.S. Shipping Bd., London, Eng., 1922-24; asso. editor Brit. Delineator Mag., 1924-26, asso. fashion editor Am. edit., 1926-30, fashion editor, 1930-34; editor Butterick Fashion Book, 1930-34, McCall's Pattern Book from 1934; writer monthly series, Adventures in Sewing, McCall Corp. from 1946. Mem. Fashion Group, Alpha Gamma Delta. Author: McCall's Complete book of Dressmaking, 1951. Contbr. articles Canadian Home Jour., 1931-34, fashion articles McCall's Mag., 1934-49. Home: Pelham, N.Y. †

COREY, STEPHEN MAXWELL, univ. prof.; b. July 21, 1904, Rochester, N.Y.; s. Stephen Jared and Edith (Webster) C.; B.S., Eureka (Ill.) Coll., 1926, LL.D. (honorary), 1960; M.A., University of Illinois, 1927, Ph.D., 1930; student University of Chicago, 1935; married Martha Robb, 1929; (deceased 1952); 1 son, John Douglas; married 2d, Elinor Karp Levie, 1953; step-children—Barbara, Tim, James. Fellow University Illinois, 1926-28; various assignments U. Ill., De Pauw U., U. Neb., U. Wis., 1928-40; prof. ednl. psychology U. Chgo., 1940-48, supt. lab. schs., 1940-44, dean of students, social sci. div., dir. Audio-visual Materials Center, 1944-48; prof., exec. officer Horace Mann-Lincoln Inst. for Sch. Exptmtn., from 1948, head dept. msychol. Found. and Services, 1955-57, dean, 1955-59, Tchrs. Coll., Columbia; I.C.A. technician assigned to Ministry of Edn., India, 1959-62. Trustee Eureka Coll., 1940-45; Film Council, 1947-51, Teaching Films Custodians, 1949-60; dir. Lisle Fellowship Found., 1949-52; edn. adv. W. K. Kellogg Found., from 1957. Fellow Am. Psychol. Assn.; mem. Nat. Soc. Study Edn. (chmn. 1949-57, yearbook com.; dir.), A.A.A.S., Am. Assn. Sch. Adminstrs., American Education Research Assn. (member of executive com. 1958-60), N.E.A. (dir. Dept. Suprs. and Curriculum Dirs., 1944-47, exec. com. 1953-56, pres., dept. audio-visual instrn. 1947-48), Sigma Xi, Lambda Chi Alpha, Phi Delta Kappa. Club: Men's Faculty. Author: (with others) Schools for a New World, 1947; Audio-visual Instructional Materials, 1949; Action Research and Education, 1953; Instructional Leadership, 1954. Mem. bd. editors Jour. Ednl. Psychology, 1952-57, Sch. Rev., 1940-49, Contributing editor Jour. Exptl. Education, 1936-54; also Childhood Edn., 1943-46; Education Digest, 1954-57. Chmn. adv. com. Encyclopedia Britannica Films (formerly Erpi), 1943-48. Contbr. to Encyclopedia of Educational Research and various profl. pubs. Home: New Delhi, India. Died 1984.

CORI, CARL FERDINAND, educator, biochemist; b. Prague, Czechoslovakia, Dec. 5, 1896; came to U.S., 1922, naturalized, 1928; s. Carl I. and Maria (Lippich) C.; m. Gerty Theresa Radnitz, Aug. 5, 1920 (dec. 1957); 1 son, Carl Thomas; m. Anne FitzGerald Jones, Mar. 23, 1960. Student, Gymnasium, Austria, 1906-14; M.D., German U. Prague, 1920, U. Trieste, Italy, 1974; Sc.D., Yale, Western Res. U., 1947, Boston U., 1948, Cambridge U., Eng., 1949, U. Granada, Spain, 1966, Brandeis U., 1965; Sc.D. hon. degrees, Monash U., Melbourne, Australia, 1966, Washington U., St. Louis, 1967, St. Louis U., 1967, Gustavus Adolphus Coll., 1963. Asst. in pharmacology U. Graz, Austria, 1920-21; biochemist State Inst. for Study Malignant Disease, Buffalo, 1922-31; prof. pharmacology and biochemistry Washington U. Sch. Medicine, 1931-66; cons. biochemistry, vis. lectr. Mass. Gen. Hosp., Harvard U. Med. Sch., Boston, 1966-84, dir. Enzyme Research Lab., 1966-84; mem. faculty Harvard Med. Sch., 1966-84. Contbr. articles, chiefly on carbohydrate metabolism and enzymes of animal tissues to Am. sci. jours.; Mem. editorial bd.: Biochimica et Biophysica Acta. Recipient Nobel Prize in medicine and physiology, 1947; Willard Gibbs medal Am. Chem. Soc., 1948; Sugar Research Found. award, 1947, 50; Lasker award, 1946; Squibb award, 1947; St. Louis award. Mem. Nat. Acad. Scis.; hon. mem. Harvey Soc.; mem. Am. Soc. Biol. Chemists, Am. Chem. Soc. (Mid-West award 1946), A.A.A.S., Royal Soc. London, Am. Philos. Soc., Sigma Xi. Home: Cambridge, Mass. Died Oct. 20, 1984.

CORLETT, BEN CALLISTER, banker; b. Napa, Cal., Feb. 11, 1889; s. Robert and Elizabeth (Derry) C.; B.S., U. Cal. at Berkeley, 1912; m. Evangeline Gosling, June 11, 1921; children—Robert William, Benjamin Callister. From clk. to v.p. and cashier First Nat. Bank, Napa, 1914-38; v.p., mgr. in Napa, Bank of Am., 1938-43; supt. banks, Cal., 1943-46; v.p. Am. Trust Co., San Francisco, 1946-58; sr. v.p. Am. Bankers Assn., Washington, from 1958, pres. state bank div., 1958; pres. Cal. Bankers Assn., 1934-35. Served as capt. U.S. Army, World War I. Home: Washington, D.C. †

CORLETT, CHARLES HARRISON, army officer; b. Burchard, Neb., July 31, 1889; s. Charles Milton and Mary Eliza (Stafford) C.; ed. Monte Vista Grade and High schs., 1895-1907, Nat. Prep. Acad., 1908-09; A.B., U.S. Mil. Acad., 1913; m. Amy Mildred Bond, Mar. 14, 1916 (died Sept. 29, 1926); m. 2d, Pauline Wherry, Aug. 12, 1928. Worked on cattle ranches in Colo. until entering mil. acad.; commd. 2d lt. and assigned to 30th Inf., Fort St. Michael, Alaska, 1913; resigned from Army May 29, 1919, to become mgr. Quemado Sheep & Cattle Co. in N.M.; reentered Army as major, July 1, 1920; promoted through grades to major general, Sept. 23, 1942; apptd. commander U.S. Troops, Kiska, 1943; comd. 7th Infantry Div., Kwajalein campaign, Marshall Islands, 1943; Comd. 19th Corps of 1st Army in invasion of Europe, June-October 1944; comdg. 36th Corps, Camp Gruber, Okla., until retirement, May 31, 1946. Now engaged in fruit and stock raising, Las Huertas, Espanola, N.M. Chmn. board trustees of Santa Fe Clinic, Inc.; member managing board, School of American Research. Decorated D.S.M. (Army), D.S.M. (Navy), Silver Star (2), Legion of Merit, Mexican and Victory medals (U.S.), Chevalier Legion of Honor (France), Estrella de Abdon Calderon (Ecuador), Comdr. Order of Leopold with palm, Croix de Guerre with palm (Belgium); Grand Officer Order Orange and Nassau (Holland). Mem. Christian Ch. Mason. Club: Army-Navy Country (Washington). Address: Espanola, N.Mex. †

CORLETTE, LYLE H., business exec.; b. Ossian, Ia., Oct. 7, 1888; s. Horace B. and L'Belle (Hall) C.; B.S. in Elec. Engring., and B.S. in Mech. Engring., Ia. State Coll., 1910, E.E., 1915; m. Edith M. MacCulley, May 22, 1919; children—Douglas L., Sally L., Suzanne. Elec. engr., 1910-28; dist. sales mgr. in N.Y. for A.C.F. Motors Co., 1928-32; dist. sales mgr. J. G. Brill Co., N.Y. City, 1932-44; vice pres. A.C.F.-Brill Motors Co., Phila., 1945-50; pres. Faber Engineering Co., Inc., from 1950. Served as 2d lt. (pilot), U.S. Army Air Force, 1917-19, Mem. Phila. C. of C. Republican. Presbyterian. Mason (Shriner, K.T.). Clubs: Engineers (New York); Racquet Club, Phila. Country. Home: Bala-Cynwyd, Pa. †

CORN, IRA GEORGE, JR., business exec.; b. Little Rock, Aug. 22, 1921; s. Ira George and Martha (Vickers) C.; m. Louise Touchstone, Feb. 8, 1947 (div. Mar., 1961); children—Jay, John, Laura. Student, Little Rock Jr. Coll., 1941; A.B., U. Chgo., 1947, M.B.A., 1948. Trainee marketing Gen. Electric Co., N.Y.C., 1947-48; asst. prof. So. Meth. U., 1948-54; corporate, financial cons., Dallas, 1954-66; pres. Community Water Service, Dallas, from 1960; co-founder Tyler Corp., Dallas, 1966, dir., from 1966; chmn. C & H Transp. Co., Dallas, from 1966; co-founder Mich. Gen. Corp., Dallas, 1968, chmn. bd., chief exec. officer, from 1968; chmn. bd. dirs. Aces Internat., Inc., Dallas; chmn. Pinnacle Books, Inc., N.Y.C.; TV economist Channel 33, Dallas; speaker profl. orgns., Dallas, N.Y.C., Washington; exec. com. Commn. for Publicly Held Cos., N.Y.C. Author: Play Bridge With The Aces, 1972, The Story of the Declaration of Independence, 1977, Businessman Answers Questions Asked by College Students, 1980; author monographs; also syndicated column Aces on Bridge. Trustee Aberrant Behavior Center, Dallas, Dallas Acad.; mem. council on Grad. Sch. Bus., U. Chgo. Served from pvt. to sgt. AUS, 1942-46. Mem. Nat. Assn. Bus. Economists, U. Chgo. Alumni Assn. (chmn. Dallas chpt. from 1955, nat. com. corporate support from 1969), Am. Contract Bridge League (pres. 1979-80, chmn. 1980-81, dir.), The Aces (capt., founder), S.A.R., Sigma Chi (Significant Sig award 1979). Presbyterian. Club: Economist's (Washington). Mem. world champion bridge team, 1970, 71, 77. Home: Dallas, Tex.

CORNER, GEORGE WASHINGTON, anatomist, medical historian; b. Balt., Dec. 12, 1889; s. George Washington and Florence (Evans) C.; A.B., Johns Hopkins, 1909, M.D., 1913; Dr. honoris causa, Cath. U. Chile, 1942; D.Sc., U. Rochester, 1944, Boston U., 1948, Chgo., 1958, Jefferson, 1971, Rockefeller U., 1975; LL.D., Tulane U., 1955, Temple U., 1956, Johns Hopkins, 1975; M.D.S. (hon.), Women's Med. Coll., Phila., 1958; D.Sc., Oxford U., 1950, M.A., 1952; D.Litt., U. Pa., 1965; m. Betsy Lyon Copping, Dec. 28, 1915 (dec. 1976); children—George Washington, Hester Ann (dec.). Med. asst. Grenfell Labrador Mission, summers, 1912-13; asst. anatomy

Johns Hopkins, 1913-14; resident house officer Johns Hopkins Hosp., 1914-15; asst. prof. anatomy, U. Calif., 1915-19; assoc. prof. anatomy Johns Hopkins, 1919-23, prof. emeritus of embryology; prof. anatomy U. Rochester, 1923-40, also curator Med. Library, 1938-40; dir. dept. of embryology Carnegie Inst. Washington, 1940-56; historian Rockefeller Inst., 1956-60; exec. officer Am. Philos. Soc., 1960-77, editor, from 1977; George Eastman vis. prof. Oxford U., 1952-53; Vicary lectr. Royal Coll. Surgeons, London, 1936; Vanuxem lectr. Princeton, 1942; Terry lectr. Yale, 1944; research prof. Commonwealth Fund, U. Louisville Med. School, 1946; U.S. del. Internat. Congress of Endocrinology, 1941, pres. congress, 1964; pres. Internat. Congress of Anatomists, 1960. Mng. editor, Am. Jour. Anatomy, 1939-41. Trustee emeritus Samuel Ready Sch. Recipient Squibb award Soc. Study of Internal Secretions, 1940, Presdl. Certificate of Merit, 1948; Passano Found. award, 1958; Dale medal Brit. Soc. of Endocrinology, 1964; Marshall medal Brit. Soc. Study Fertility, 1973; Welch medal Am. Assn. History Medicine, 1975; Franklin medal Am. Philos. Soc., 1979; fellow Balliol Coll., Oxford, 1952-53, Rochester Mus. Arts and Scis., 1943. Hon. fellow Royal Soc. Edinburgh, Royal Coll. Obstetrics and Gynecology London; mem. Royal Soc. London (fgn.), Am. Assn. Anatomists (sec. 1930-38, pres. 1946-48, Henry Gray award 1979), Soc. Exptl. Biology and Medicine, Am. Philos. Soc. (v.p. 1953-56), Nat. Acad. Scis. (v.p. 1953-57), Anat. Soc. Gt. Britain (hon.), Am. Assn. History Medicine (pres. 1954-55), Phi Beta Kappa, Sigma Xi, fgn. corr. mem. numerous socs.; hon. mem. and fellow Am. and fgn. socs. Clubs: Century (N.Y.C.); Franklin Inn (Phila.). Author books, 1927—; also numerous papers in field. Address: Philadelphia, Pa. Died Sept. 28, 1981.

CORNING, ERASTUS, II, mayor; b. Albany, N.Y., Oct. 7, 1909; s. Edwin and Louise (Maxwell) C.; m. Elizabeth N. Platt, June 23, 1932; children—Erastus III, Elizabeth (Mrs. Dudley). A.B., Yale, 1932. Pres. Albany Assos., Inc., 1932—, mayor, Albany, 1942—; Mem. N.Y. State Assembly, 1936, N.Y. State Senate, 1937-41; del. N.Y. State Constl. Conv., 1967, Democratic Nat. Conv., 1944, 48, 52, 56, 60, 64, 68, 72, 76, 80. Served with AUS, 1944-45, ETO. Mem. Am. Legion, VFW, Phi Beta Kappa, Chi Psi. Home: Albany, N.Y. Died May 28, 1983.

CORNWALL, JOSEPH SPENCER, choir conductor; b. Mill Creek, Utah, Feb. 23, 1888; s. Joseph Alexander and Mary Ellen (Spencer) C.; student Latter Day Saints U., 1904-08, U. of Utah, 1910-13, Northwestern U. (summers), 1914-16, Columbia U. Sch. of Music, 1916; m. Mary A. Haigh, June 11, 1913; children—Marian, Joseph Haigh, Bonnie, Margaret, Allen S., John Shirley, Carol. Teacher of piano 1908-33; teacher Manassa (Colo.) Sch., 1909-10; music supervisor at Granite Dist., 1913-29; Granite Dist. music supervisor, Salt Lake City, 1929-36; choir dir. Salt Lake City Tabernacle from 1936; guest choral condr. Music Educators Conf., Long Beach, Calif., 1939. Guest dir. United Protestant Church choirs, 1952. Mem. Church of Latter Day Saints (Mormon). Home: Salt Lake City, Utah. †

CORREIA, OSCAR, diplomat of Brazil; b. Curityba, Parana, Brazil, Aug. 1, 1887; m. Antonietta, June 16, 1917; 1 dau., Sonia Maria. Began as consular attaché, 1912; consul gen. at N.Y. City, to July 1945; with Foreign Office, Rio de Janeiro. Roman Catholic. Mem. Soc. of Foreign Consuls of New York (pres. 1943).†

CORSON, FRED PIERCE, bishop; b. Millville, N.J., Apr. 11, 1896; s. Jeremiah and Mary E. (Payne) C.; m. Frances Beaman, Mar. 22, 1922; 1 son, Hampton Payne. A.B., Dickinson Coll., Carlisle, Pa., 1917, A.M., 1920, D.D., 1931, L.H.D., 1944; B.D., Drew U., 1920; also; L.H.D. numerous hon. degrees including, St. Charles Borromeo Cath. Sem., 1981. Ordained to ministry Methodist Episcopal Ch., 1920, consecrated bishop, 1944, pastor, Jackson Heights, N.Y., New Haven, Port Washington, N.Y., Simpson Ch., Bklyn., until 1929; supt. Bklyn. So. Dist., N.Y. East Conf., 1930-34; pres. Dickinson Coll., 1934-44, also trustee; permanent chaplain Faith of Our Fathers Chapel, Freedoms Found., 1968-85; titular pastor Old St. George's Ch., 1968-85; bishop-in-residence Christ United Meth. Ch., St. Petersburg, Fla.; mem. ecumenical theol. symposium 41st Eucharistic Congress.; trustee Wyoming Sem., Pennington Sch. for Boys, Drew U., Westminster Theol. Sem., Lycoming Coll.; hon. pres. trustee Temple U.; pres. Council Bishops, 1952-53; fraternal messenger to Gen. Conf. Brazil, 1950; v.p. Meth. World Council, 1956-61, pres., 1961-66, now sr. presiding bishop; ofcl. Meth. rep. Kirchentag Assembly, Stuttgart, Ger., 1952; mem. Bishops Commn. for Meth.-Catholic Conversations, 1968-85; sr. cons. to schs. and colls. United Meth. Ch., 1968—; civilian dir. 32d Coll. Tng.; spl. lectr. various colls. and univs., 1945—, del. to gen. conf., 1932, 40, 44; mem. univ. senate, mem. book com., world peace commn. Detachment (air crew), 1943-44; mem. Nat. Council Chs. of Christ, Com. on Internat. Goodwill, Pa. Gov.'s Com. for Revision State Constn.; chmn. Sec. of War's Clergy Commn. To Inspect Occupied Countries of Europe, 1948; ofcl. rep. Meth. Ch. to Centennial Celebration of Methodism in China, 1948; ofcl. Meth. rep. to Army and Navy Chaplains, Japan, 1948; del. World Council Chs., 1954; religious cons. Armed Forces in Far East Command, 1954; chaplain Republican and Democratic nat. convs., 1948, 52; del., observer 2d Vatican Council, Rome, 1962, 63, 64, 65; pres. Gen. Bd. Edn., Meth. Ch., 1948-60. Author: (with others) Augustin Cardinal Bea; editor: Bridges To Unity; contbr.: Documents of Vatican II. Bd. dirs. Freedoms Found., Valley Forge, Pa. Recipient Yorktown medal Soc. of Cin.; Kappa Sigma Man of Year, 1950; St. Olav medal Norway, 1964; Gourgas medal (Masonic decoration), 1964; Royal Order of Scotland; Phila. Pub. Relations award, 1965; decorated knight Royal Order Scotland, 1977; Meritorious Leadership award World Meth. Ch., 1979; named to Football Found. Hall of Fame; named Ark. Traveler, 1983. Mem. Newcomen Soc., Phi Beta Kappa (Bicentennial fellow 1976), Phi Beta Kappa Assos., Kappa Sigma, Omicron Delta Kappa, Tau Kappa Alpha. Clubs: Masons (N.Y.C., Phila.) (33 deg.); KT; Kiwanis (N.Y.C., Phila.), Union League (N.Y.C., Phila.). Home: Cornwall, Pa. Died Feb. 16, 1985.

CORSON, ROBERT WILLIAM, mfg. co. exec.; b. Chgo., Feb. 1, 1922; s. Ralph Maurice and Cora (Kohlsaat) C.; grad. Phillips Exeter Acad., 1938; A.B., Harvard, 1942, M.B.A., 1943; m. Constance Elaine Barrett, June 26, 1943; children—Marshall Ayer, Dara Barrett. With Textron, Inc., 1946-50; asst. controller Saco-Lowell Shops, 1950-58; v.p., controller Howe Scale Co., 1958-61; with Foxboro Co. (Mass.), 1961-80, sec., 1964-68, treas., 1967-80, v.p., 1980, also dir.; dir. Morton Shoe Cos., Inc., South Shore Nat. Bank. Bd. dirs., v.p. Internat. Bus. Center New Eng.; trustee, pres. Milton (Mass.) Hosp. Served to lt. USNR, 1943-46. Mem. Hosps. Laundry Assn. Mass. (trustee), Machinery and Allied Products Inst. (financial council), U.S. C. of C. Home: Milton, Mass. Died Nov. 24, 1980.

CORTÉS PÉREZ, FIDEL, bishop; b. Tumbisca, Mex., Apr. 21, 1912 Ordained priest Roman Cath. Ch., 1939, elevated to bishop of, Chilapa, Mex., 1958, consecrated, 1959. Address: Chilapa, Mexico.

CORWIN, MARGARET TRUMBULL, college dean; b. Phila., Pa., Nov. 29, 1889; d. Robert Nelson and Margaret Wardell (Bacon) Corwin; A.B., Bryn Mawr College, 1912; hon. M.A., Yale Univ., 1934; Litt.D., Rutgers U., 1943, Beaver College, 1947; unmarried. Sec. Yale Press, 1912-17; exec. sec. woman's com. of Conn. Div. of Council of Nat. Defense, 1917-18; canteen worker Y.M.C.A., A.E.F., France, 1918; exec. sec. Grad. Sch., Yale U., 1918-34; dean N.J. Coll. Women, Rutgers U., from 1934. Dir. N. Atlantic sect., Am. Assn. U. Women, 1924-28, Convenor exchange Com. Internat. Fedn. U. Women, 1937-47, asst. treas., 1947-50. Pres. Middle States Assn. Colls. and Secondary Schs., 1946-47; mem. commn. Insts. of Higher Edn. from 1948; mem. exec. com. Coll. Entrance Exam. Bd., 1950-52. Mem. Phi Beta Kappa. Club: Cosmopolitan (New York). Home: New Brunswick, N.J. †

COTTAM, HOWARD REX, former ambassador, educator, ofcl.; b. St. George, Utah, July 27, 1910; s. Heber and Edith (Brooks) C.; m. Katherine Stokes, Aug. 30, 1934; 1 dau., Lillian Meredith. A.B., Brigham Young U., 1932; Ph.B., U. Wis., 1938, Ph.D., 1941; student, Nat. War Coll., 1952. Asst. prof. Pa. State Coll., 1940-42; chief rent examiner OPA, Pitts., 1942; prin. agrl. economist U.S. Dept. Agr. and chief program appraisal War Food Adminstrn., N.E. region, N.Y.C., 1942-44, agrl. economist U.S. embassy, Paris, France, 1944-46, agrl. attache U.S. embassy, Rome, 1946-47, 1st sec. and consul, 1947-50, counselor embassy and chief food and agrl. div. E.C.A. spl. mission to Italy, 1950-52; U.S. resident liaison officer to FAO of U.N., 1951-52; also U.S. mem. on commodity problems, com. on relations with internat. orgns., del. 6th conf.; chmn. appeals com. UN FAO; assigned to Nat. War Coll., Washington, 1952-53, counselor of embassy for econ. affairs, The Hague, dep. dir. of U.S. operation missions to Netherlands, 1953-55, counselor of embassy and ICA rep., The Netherlands, 1955-56, counselor of embassy, dir. U.S. operations mission to Brazil, 1956-57, minister for econ. affairs, dir. mission, 1957-60; dep. asst. sec. Bur. Nr. Eastern and South Asian Affairs, U.S. Dept. State, 1960-63; Am. ambassador, Kuwait, 1963-69; N. Am. rep. of FAO/UN, 1969-74, cons., 1974; chmn. adv. com. Am.-Arab Assn. for Commerce and Industry, 1978-79; vis. prof. Am. U., Washington, 1974-84; adviser to U.S. delegate FAO Council, Rome, 1950, 51, 52, Internat. Cotton Adv. Council, 1952; U.S. observer Internat. Fedn. Agrl. Technicians, Geneva, 1947, at Internat. Conf. Proposed David Lubin Acad., Rome, 1949; Alternate U.S. mem. permanent com. Internat. Inst. Agrl., Rome, 1947; alternate agrl. mem. U.S. Trade Agreements Com., Annecy, France, 1949; treas., bd. mem. Netherlands-U.S. Ednl. Found., 1953-56; alternate U.S. mem. Internat. Tin Study Group, The Hague, 1955-56; Hon. pres. Internat. Sch. of Kuwait, 1963-69; trustee Near East Found., 1969-78; bd. advisers Airline Passengers Assn., 1969-76; ex officio trustee Am. Freedom from Hunger Found., 1969-72; mem. adv. panel World Population Soc., 1973—; bd. dirs. Am. Near East Relief Agy., 1972-75; mem. external adv. com. World Food Inst., Ames, Iowa, 1973-74. Mem. Soc. Internat. Devel. (dir. Washington chpt. 1972-73), Washington Fgn. Affairs Inst., UN Assn. (mem. bd., v.p. Capitol Area div. 1973—, 3d v.p. 1976-78), Am. Agrl. Econs. Assn., AAAS. Clubs: Cosmos (Washington), DACOR House (Washington). Home: Washington, D.C. Died Apr. 2, 1984.

COTTER, WILLIAM ROSS, congressman; b. Hartford, Conn., July 18, 1926; s. William W. and Mary E. (O'Loughlin) C. B.A., Trinity Coll., 1949. Aide to Gov. Abraham Ribicoff, 1955-58, dep. ins. commr. Conn., 1958-64, ins. commr., 1964-70; mem. 92d-97th Congresses. Active Greater Hartford Community Chest.; Treas. Conn. Democratic Central Com., 1961-73. Roman Catholic. Clubs: K.C, Elk, Wethersfield (Conn.) Country, Hartford. Home: Hartford, Conn.

COTTERMAN, HAROLD F., univ. dean; b. Farmersville, O., Oct. 22, 1887; s. Marcus Ward and Martha (Brubaker) C.; student prep. dept. Miami U.; B.S., Ohio State U., 1916; student U. Wis., summer 1916; A.M., Columbia 1917; Ph.D., American U., 1930; m. Mae Yingling, June 13, 1914; children—Harold F., Martha Ann (Mrs. William Randolph Talbott), Jean (deceased). Elementary sch. prin., Montgomery County, O., 1906-09; dean and prof. of agrl., Ohio Northern U., Ada, 1913-15; instr., agrl. edn., Ohio State U., 1916; prof. agrl. edn., Md. State Coll. (U. of Md.), 1917-46, dean of edn., 1917-23; state supervisor of vocational agriculture Md. State Dept. of Edn., 1917-23, 1935-46; instr., Johns Hopkins, summer 1918; dir. summer session, U. of Md., 1919-23, asso. dean, Coll. of Edn., 1923-37, asst. dean (charge instruction), Coll. of Agr., 1937-46, dean of Univ. faculty, 1946- 57, dean emeritus, from 1957. Mem. Am. Assn. for Advancement of Science, Am. Assn. Univ. Profs., N.E.A., Am. Vocational Assn., Middle States Assn. of Colls. and Secondary Schs. (exec. com.), Md. State Teachers Assn., Md. Vocation Assn. (pres., 1928), Kappa Alpha, Phi Kappa Phi, Alpha Zeta, Phi Delta Kappa, Kappa Phi Kappa, Omicron Delta Kappa. Democrat. Episcopalian. Grange (state lecturer, Md., 1936-48). Clubs: Cosmos (Washington); Federal School Men's (pres. 1940-41). Kiwanis (pres., 1939, Prince George Co., Md.). Home: College Park, Md. †

COTTING, CHARLES EDWARD, banker; b. Boston, Mass., May 15, 1889; s. Charles Edward and Ruth Stetson (Thompson) C.; prep. edn., Noble and Greenough Sch., Dedham, Mass.; A.B. Harvard U., 1911; m. Sarah H. Winslow, July 26, 1939. Began with Lee, Higginson & Co., investment bankers, Boston, 1911, partner, from 1922; chairman bd., Lee Higginson Corp.; v.p. and dir. Lee Higginson Safe Deposit Co.; dir. Fifty Associates. Jones & Lamson Machine Co., Blackstone Mutual Fire Insurance Company, Me. Central R.R., Portland Terminal Company; vice chairman of the board of trustees Provident Inst. for Savings, Boston. Served as 1st lt., later capt., Air Service, U.S. Army, 1917-19. Dir. Travelers Aid Soc. Boston. Trustee, treas. Mass. Found.; treas. Franklin Found., Mass. Heart Assn.; mem. visiting com., grad. sch. business adminstrn. Harvard; mem. corp. Mass. Gen. Hosp.; treas. Indsl. School for Crippled Children; trustee and president Boston Home for Incurables; trustee Boston Lying-in Hosp., Mt. Auburn Cemetery, The Seeing Eye. Mem. nat. exec. bd. Boy Scouts America; mem. exec. com. Mass. Soc. Prevention Cruelty to Children; mem. corp. Cardigan Mountain Sch., Canaan, N.H.; treas. Mass. Soc. of Cincinnati. Unitarian. Clubs: Harvard, Union, Somerset, Odd Volumes, Bond (mem. bd. govs.) (Boston): Harvard, Knickerbocker (New York). Home: Boston, Mass. †

COTTINGHAM, HAROLD FRED, educator; b. Charleston, Ill., Dec. 11, 1913; s. Fred Hervey and Frances (Coon) C.; B.Ed., Eastern Ill. State U., 1935, Pd.D. (hon.), 1956; M.A., U. Iowa, 1940; Ed.D., Ind. U., 1947; m. Violet Costello, June 4, 1941; children—Rebecca, Sarah. Tchr., Ill. high schs., 1936-42; instr. U.S. Navy, Ind. U., 1942-44; instr. psychology, guidance dir. William Woods Coll., Fulton, Mo., 1944-45; dir. guidance and research Moline (Ill.) schs., 1945-48; assoc. prof. psychology Fla. State U., Tallahassee, 1948-53, prof. edn., from 1953, head dept. guidance and counseling, 1958-68; John Mosler prof. Fordham U., N.Y.C., 1968-69; summer tchr. Ark. State Coll., N.Y.U., Colo. State Coll., U. Iowa, Boston U., Northwestern La. Coll., U. So. Calif., Brigham Young U., Eastern Wash. Coll.; lectr. U. Miss., Ohio U., Butler U., U. Rochester, Mankato State Coll., U. Ala., Mich. State U., Marshall U., Ohio State U., Ball State U.; speaker guidance assns. in Miss., Ala., Ky., Pa., Ohio, La., Tenn. Cons. mem. subcom. counseling and testing, nat. manpower adv. com. Dept. Labor, 1963-67, 69-70, regional counseling cons., 1969-70. Diplomate Am. Bd. Profl. Psychology. Mem. Nat. Vocat. Guidance Assn. (pres. 1962-63), Am. Personnel and Guidance Assn. (pres. 1964-65), Am. Psychol. Assn. (fellow div. counseling psychology), Fla. Psychol. Assn., Fla. Assn. Deans and Counselors (pres. 1954-56), Am. Coll. Personnel Assn., Assn. Counselor Edn. and Supervision, So. Assn. Counselor Edn. and Supervision (pres. 1971-72), Nat. Register Health Service Providers in Psychology, Kappa Delta Pi, Phi Delta Kappa. Author: Guidance in Elementary Schools, 1956; (with Hopke) Guidance in the Junior High School, 1961; Counseling Guidance and Personnel Services, 1971; (with Burck and Reardon) Counseling and Accountability; Methods and Critique, 1973. Editor: Guidance Bull., 1953-63. Contbr. to profl. jours., encys. Home: Tallahassee, Fla. Died Aug. 19, 1981.

COTTRELL, LEONARD S., JR., social psychologist; b. Hampton Roads, Va., Dec. 12, 1899; s. Leonard Slater and Ruth Ella (Roane) C.; B.S., Va. Poly. Inst., 1922; M.A., Vanderbilt U., 1926; Ph.D., U. Chgo., 1933; m. Anita Rucker, Aug. 27, 1927; children—Leonard Slater III, Susan Rucker. Instr. sociology U. Chgo., 1931-35; asst. prof. sociology Cornell U., 1935-38, prof., 1938-39, prof. sociology, chmn. dept. sociology and anthropology, 1939-48, dean, Coll. Arts and Scis., 1948-51, vis. prof.,

1951-53; adj. prof. sociology N.Y.U., 1952-68; vis. prof. sociology and psychology U. N.C., Chapel Hill, 1968-72; staff social psychologist Russell Sage Found., 1951-67, sec. found., 1959-67; on leave to serve as chief sociologist research br., information, edn. O.C.S., War Dept., 1942-45; chmn. adv. group on psychol. and unconventional warfare Research and Devel. Bd., Dept. Def., 1952-53, mem. adv. panel, 1954-59; mem. sci. adv. bd. USAF, 1955-58; mem. Army Sci. Adv. Council, 1956-58; nat. adv. council NIMH, 1955-59; adv. com. social scis. NSF, 1959-64. Mem. sci. research adv. bd. Nat. Assn. Retarded Children, 1959-65; chmn. adv. com. on behavioral research Office Emergency Planning, Nat. Acads. Sci.-NRC, 1960-63; mem. Pres.'s Panel on Mental Retardation, 1961-62; chmn. citizens adv. council to Pres.'s Com. on Juvenile Delinquency and Youth Crimes, 1961-65, also chmn. tech. review panel to com., 1961-65; chmn. bd. dirs. Telemann Soc. N.Y., 1959-64. Served with U.S. Army, 1918. Fellow AAAS, Am. Sociol. Assn. (pres. 1949-50); mem. Sociol. Research Assn. (pres. 1949-50), Am. Philos. Soc., Social Sci. Research Council, Am. Psychol. Assn., Law and Soc. Assn. (trustee), Phi Beta Kappa, Sigma Xi. Club: Cosmos (Washington). Co-author 4 books to 1941; (with Sylvia Eberhart) American Opinion on World Affairs in the Atomic Age, 1948; (with S.A. Stouffer) The American Soldier, 1949; (with Nelson Foote) Identity and Interpersonal Competence, 1955; (with Stanton Wheeler) Juvenile Delinquency: Its Prevention and Control, 1966. Editor: Sociometry, 1956-60; former assoc. editor Psychiatry, Social Forces; joint editor Sociology Today; Problems and Prospects, 1959. Home: Chapel Hill, N.C. Died Mar. 20, 1985.

COUCH, NATALIE FRANCES, lawyer; b. Nyack, N.Y., Nov. 24, 1887; dau. Louis Bradford and Natalie (Kreuder) C.; prep. edn., Dana Hall, Wellesley, Mass., 1905-07; LL.B., cum laude, Fordham U., 1924. Sec. to Judge Arthur S. Tompkins, justice Supreme Court of New York, 24 yrs.; police justice, village of Grand View-on-Hudson. Organizer and hon. pres. Women's Republican Club of Nyack; mem. bd. govs. Women's Nat. Rep. Club; sec. N.Y. State Rep. Exec. Com.; eastern dir. women's div. Rep. Nat. Com. 1936 campaign. Mem. Am. and N.Y. State bar assns., Nat. Assn. Women Lawyers, N.Y. Women's Bar Assn. (hon.), Rockland County (N.Y.) Bar Assn. (pres.), Rockland County Conservation Assn., Rockland County Soc. (pres.), Kappa Beta Pi. Presbyn. Club: Rockland Country. Home: Grand View-on-Hudson, N.Y.†

COUGHLIN, HOWARD, union exec.; b. N.Y.C., Apr. 5, 1913; s. John and Elizabeth (Walsh) C.; student parochial schs., spl. courses. Local union pres., bus. mgr., 1937-42; organizer AFL, 1942-46; v.p. Office and Profl. Employees Internat. Union, 1951-53, pres., 1953-79, ret., 1979; mem. gen. bd., mediation panel AFL-CIO. Mem. N.Y. State Temporary Commn. on Jud. Conduct; mem. N.Y. State Banking Bd. Mem. Pres.'s Com. Equal Employment Opportunity, N.Y. State ManpoWer Planning Council. Mem. Am. Arbitration Assn. (chmn. exec. com., chmn. bd. dirs.). Home: Bronxville, N.Y. Died Jan. 19, 1984.*

COULTER, ELLIS MERTON, educator; b. nr. Hickory, N.C., July 20, 1890; s. John Ellis and Lucy Ann (Propst) C.; student Rutherford (N.C.) Coll., 1905-09; Concordia Coll., Conover, N.C., 1909-10; A.B., U. N.C., 1913; A.M., U. Wis., 1915, Ph.D., 1917; Litt.D., Marietta Coll., 1948; LL.D. (hon.), U. N.C., 1952; Mem. history faculty Marietta Coll., 1917-19; asso. prof. history U. Ga., 1919-23, prof., 1923-58, Regents prof. emeritus, 1958-81. Vis. prof., lectr., numerous colls. and univs. Trustee, Wormsloe Found., Savannah, Ga. Lutheran. Author numerous books from 1922, those from 1950 include: Wormsloe, 1955; Lost Generation, 1956; Auraria, 1956; Confederate States of America, 1861-65; John Ellis Coulter, Small-Town Businessman of Tarheelia, 1962; Joseph Vallence Bevan, Georgia's First Official Historian, 1964; Georgia Waters, 1965; Old Petersburg and the Broad River Valley of Georgia, 1965; The Toombs Oak, The Tree that Owned Itself, and other Chapters of Georgia, 1966; William Montague Browne, Versatile Anglo-Irish American, 1823-1883, 1967; Daniel Lee, Agriculturist, His Life North and South, 1972; George Walton Williams, The Life of a Southern Merchant and Banker, 1820-1903, 1976; also hist. articles; editor several books including The Journal of Peter Gordon, 1732-1735, 1963. Mng. editor emeritus Ga. Hist. Quar. to 1981. 1st pres. So. Hist. Soc. Home: Athens, Ga. Died July 5, 1981.

COURTNEY, WIRT, congressman; b. Franklin, Tenn., Sept. 7, 1889; s. Wirt and Anne (Neely) C.; ed. Battleground Acad., Franklin, Tenn., 1903-07, Vanderbilt University, 1907-11, Sorbonne, Paris, 1918-19; m. Currey Taylor, 1919; children—Jane Anne (Mrs. Alexander Klieforth), Wirt, III, Richard Eastman, Robin Spencer. Admitted to Tennessee bar; practiced, 1911-17; lt. Inf., United States Army, with A.E.F. (wounded), 1917-19; law practice, 1919-32; adjutant gen. of Tenn., 1932; brig. gen. Tenn. Nat. Guard; circuit judge, 1933-39. Mem. 76th to 80th Congresses (1939-49), 7th Tenn. Dist. Mem. Sigma Chi. Democrat. Episcopalian. Mason (Shriner), Elk. Home: Franklin, Tenn.†

COUSINS, PAUL MERCER, educator; b. Luthersville, Ga., Dec. 1, 1889; s. Dr. Solon Bolivar (Bapt. minister) and Lou Ella (Fuller) C.; A.B., Mercer U., 1910, LL.D., 1936; A.M., Columbia, 1919; m. Marjorie Nowell, Aug. 30, 1923; 1 son, Paul Mercer. Began as tutor Greek, Mercer U., 1909-10; instr. Greek and English, Locust Grove Inst., 1910-15, v.p., 1912-15; prof. English, Shorter Coll., 1915-34, head of dept. from 1918, v.p., 1933, and pres. from 1933. Mem. Sigma Nu. Democrat. Baptist. Kiwanian. Home: Rome, Ga. †

COVELL, DAVID RANSOM, clergyman; b. Richfield Springs, N.Y., Mar. 14, 1887; s. Luther W. and Lefa Ann (Ransom) C.; A.B., George Washington U., 1910, A.M., 1914, L.H.D., 1936; B.D., Gen. Theol. Sem., New York, N.Y., 1915; grad. student Oxford (Eng.), 1914; m. Mary Scheurman, Mar. 7, 1916; children—Mary Ransom, David Ransom. Ordained to ministry of Protestant Episcopal Ch., deacon, 1913, priest, 1914; became exec. sec. Diocese of Southern Ohio, 1935-40; field sec. The Forward Movement of Episcopal Ch., 1940-42; supt. Episcopal City Mission and rector The Mariners Ch., Detroit, Mich., 1942-45; chaplain Hobart Coll., Geneva, N.Y., 1945-50; rector St. Luke's Parish, Hudson, Mass., since 1950. Chaplain, St. Elizabeth's Govt. Hosp. for Insane, Washington, D.C., 1916-24. Capt., chaplain organized reserves, U.S. Army, 1922-42. Mem. Am. Assn. Social Workers, Mental Hygiene Soc., Am. League for Abolition of Capital Punishment (mem. bd.), Soc. Mayflower Descendants, S.R., Pyramid. Mason (K.T.). Clubs: Detroit Boat, Mariners, Propeller (Detroit); University (Geneva); Rotary. Author: Discussion Outlines for Young Peoples Societies, 1934; Introduction to Practical Parish Procedure, 1944. Home: Hudson, Mass. †

COWAN, WOOD MESSICK, cartoonist, writer; b. Algona, Ia., Nov. 1, 1889; s. James McKelvey and Raechel Marion (Foster) C.; student Chgo. Art Inst., 1909-12; m. Frances Daines Metcalf, Dec. 15, 1929; children—Conrad Metcalf, Thaddeus McKelvey. Cartoonist, Chicago Inter Ocean, 1909, New Orleans Item, 1911-13, Washington Times, 1914-15; sports writer, cartoonist Adams Syndicate, N.Y.C., 1918-24, N.Y. World, 1925-28, N.E.A. Service, 1929-39; pres.-editor Artists & Writers Service, newspaper feature service, Westport, Conn., 1946. Comic panel cartoons contbns. to Judge, Life, Argosy, Colliers, from 1920; editorial cartoonist Bridgeport (Conn.) Post 1949-60, New Haven Register, from 1958. Mem. Conn. Ho. of Reps. for Weston, 1951-53, from 1955; first selectman Weston Connecticut, 1956-57; mem. of Fairfield County Court House Building Commission, 1956-57. Mem. Rep. Town Com. of Weston. Mem. Westport Artists (pres. 1949), Artists & Writers Assn. Author Flying Andy, Flying A News. Co-author, illustrator: Famous Figures of the Old West. Home: Weston, Conn.

COWART, RALPH W., prof. education; b. Luverne, Ala., Jan. 7, 1890; s. James Hansford and Mary Jane (Larkin) C.; B.Ped., Ala. State Normal Sch., 1910; B.S., U. of Ala., 1914; A.M., Columbia, 1921, grad. work, Columbia, 1923-24, U. of Michigan, 1928-29; m. Gladys Godbey, June 29, 1920. Teacher pub. schs. Ala., 1910-12; prin. high sch., 1914-15; supt. city schs., Albany, Ala., 1915-18, 1919-23, 1924-25; exec. sec. Ala. Edn. Assn., 1925-27; prof. edn., dir. supervised teaching, dir. teacher placement bur. U. of Ala., 1927-50; asst. dean Coll. Edn., 1948-59, now interim dean. Served in U.S. Army, 1918-19; with A.E.F. Mem. N.E.A., Ala. Edn. Assn., Am. Assn. U. Profs., Phi Beta Kappa, Phi Delta Kappa, Kappa Delta Pi. Democrat. Methodist. Author ednl. books. Contbr. to sch. jours. †

COWDEN, THOMAS KYLE, govt. ofcl.; b. Hickory, Pa., June 14, 1908; s. John M. and Nettie M. (Mitchel) C.; B.S., Ohio State U., 1930, M.S., 1931; Ph.D., Cornell U., 1937; LL.D., Purdue U., 1966; m. Clara Williams, Feb. 6, 1937; children—John W., Jean W. Research Pa. State Coll., 1931-36; teaching, research Purdue U., 1937-43; dir. research Am. Farm Bur. Fedn., 1943-49; head dept. agrl. econs. Mich. State U., 1949-54, dean Coll. Agr. and Natural Resources, 1954-69; asst. sec. agr. U.S. Dept. Agr., 1969-73, counselor to sec. agr., 1973-78; tchr. Mich. State U. Cons. various govtl. and bus. agys. Mem. Am. Farm Econs. Assn. (past pres.), Sigma Xi, Phi Kappa Phi, Alpha Zeta, Alpha Gamma Rho. Contbr. articles on mktg. and agrl. policy to periodicals. Home: Arlington, Va. Died Dec. 18, 1983.

COWIE, CHARLES DURNO, business exec.; b. Insch, Aberdeenshire, July 25, 1887; s. Peter and Margaret (Phillip) C.; ed. Insch pub. schs.; m. Carrie May Fairbairn, Apr. 11, 1914; 1 son, John P. Clerk, Town & County Bank, Aberdeen, Scotland, 1904-08; ledgerkeeper Home Bank, Toronto, Ont., Can., 1908-10; accountant Home Bank, Sandwich, Ont., 1910-11; cashier Can. Northern Railway, Toronto, 1911-16; special work in connection with Royal Commn. apptd. to make a valuation of and inquire into affairs of Can. Northern Ry. Co., 1916-17; spl. work in connection with Canadian Northern Ry. Arbitration, 1917-18; asst. to v.p. Canadian Nat. Rys., Toronto, 1918-23, asst. to v.p., Montreal, P.Q., 1923-32, treas., 1932-45, vice pres. and treas. from 1945, vice pres. and treas. Canadian Nat. Steamships, Ltd., from 1945; treas. Trans-Canada Air Lines from 1937. Clubs: St. James's, The Engineers, Kanawaki Golf, Prince Consort Lodge. Home: Montreal, Can. †

COWLES, ALFRED, economist; b. Chgo., Sept. 15, 1891; s. Alfred and Elizabeth (Cheney) C.; A.B., Yale, 1913; m. Elizabeth Livingston Strong, May 10, 1924 (div. 1939); children—Richard Livingston, Ann; m. 2d, Louise Lamb Phelps, Oct. 24, 1949. Journalist, Spokesman Rev., Spokane, Wash., 1913-15; pres. Cowles & Co., finance, Colorado Springs, 1925-38; economist, 1933-84, pres. Cowles Commn. for Research in Econs., Colorado Springs, 1933-39, Chgo., from 1939. Hon. bd. dirs. Passavant Meml. Hosp.; trustee Colorado Springs Fine Arts Center (hon.); colleague Colo. Coll. Fellow Econometric Soc., A.A.A.S.; mem. Internat. Statis. Inst. Club: Commercial (Chgo.). Author: Common Stock Indexes, 1938; The True Story of Aluminum, 1958. Contbr. to Econometrica, Jour. Am. Statis. Assn. Home: Lake Forest, Ill. Died Dec. 28, 1984.

COWLES, GARDNER, publisher; b. Algona, Iowa, Jan. 31, 1903; s. Gardner and Florence M. (Call) C.; m. Lois Thornburg, May 17, 1933 (div. 1946); children: Lois Cowles Harrison, Gardner, III, Kate Cowles Nichols; m. Jan Streate Cox, May 1, 1956; 1 dau., Virginia. Grad., Phillips Exeter Acad., 1921; A.B., Harvard U., 1925; LL.D. (hon.), Drake U., 1942, Coe Coll., 1948, L.I. U., 1955, Grinnell Coll., 1957, Colls. Hobart and William Smith, 1968; L.H.D., Bard Coll., 1950, Cornell Coll., 1951, Mundelein Coll., 1968; Sc.D., Simpson Coll., 1955; Litt.D., Iowa Wesleyan Coll., 1955, Morningside Coll., 1958. City editor Des Moines Register, 1925, news editor, 1926-27; asso. mng. editor Des Moines Register and Tribune, 1927, mng. editor, 1927-31, exec. editor, 1931-39, asso. pub., 1939-43, pres., 1943-71; chmn. bd., editor in chief Cowles Communications, Inc., N.Y.C., 1937-71, hon. chmn. bd., 1971-83, Cowles Broadcasting, Inc., 1983-85; dir. emeritus United Air Lines, UAL, Inc.; domestic dir. Office of War Information, Wash., 1942-43; resigned; with Wendell Willkie, round world flight, 1942. Trustee U. Miami, Drake U., Tchrs. Coll., Columbia U.; Trustee emeritus Mus. Modern Art. Mem. Am. Soc. Newspaper Editors (former mem. bd.), Des Moines C. of C. (dir. 1930-47), Greater Des Moines Com. Harvard Class of 1925 (treas.), Phi Beta Kappa (hon.), Delta Sigma Pi, Alpha Delta Sigma. Clubs: Des Moines; Blind Brook (Purchase, N.Y.); Harvard (N.Y.C.), Links (N.Y.C.), Economic (N.Y.C.), Knickerbocker (N.Y.C.); Indian Creek Country (Miami Beach, Fla.), The Bath (Miami Beach, Fla.); Nat. Golf Links Am; Shinnecock Hills Golf (Southampton, N.Y.). Home: Surfside, Fla. Died July 8, 1985.

COWLES, JOHN, newspaper publisher, editor; b. Algona, Ia., Dec. 14, 1898; s. Gardner and Florence (Call) C.; grad. Phillips Exeter Acad., Exeter, N.H., 1917; A.B., Harvard, 1920 as of 1921; LL.D. (hon.), Boston U., 1941, Grinnell Coll., 1955, Harvard, 1956; Litt. D., Jamestown (N.D.) Coll., 1946; L.H.D., Coe Coll., 1956; Simpson Coll., 1957, Drake U., 1958; LL.D., Macalester Coll., 1958, University Rochester, 1959, Carleton College, 1961, Allegheny Coll., 1963; m. Elizabeth Morley Bates, July 1923; children—Elizabeth Morley (Mrs. Arthur A. Ballantine, Jr.), Sarah Richardson (Mrs. John M Bullitt), John, Russell. In newspaper work since 1920; 2nd v.p. Asso. Press, 1929, 1st v.p., 1930, bd. dirs., 1934-43; dir. of the Audit Bureau of Circulation, 1929-33; pres. The Mpls. Star & Tribune Co. (and predecessor corps.) since 1935; chmn. bd. The Des Moines Register and Tribune Co.; director First Nat. Bank of Minneapolis. Spl. asst. to lend-lease adminstr., E. R. Stettinius, Jr., Washington, D.C., 1943 (received Presidential Certificate of Merit for service; mem. gen. adv. com. U.S. Arms and Disarmament Agency; member of the Business Council. Served as pvt., U.S. Army, 1918. Member bd. of Trustees Am. Assembly. Columbia U., mem. bd. overseers Harvard, 1944-50, 60-66. Trustee Carnegie Endowment for Internat. Peace, Phillips Exeter Acad., 1936-54; trustee Gardner Cowles Foundation, Minneapolis Foundation, Ford Foundation, Minneapolis Society of Fine Arts. Mem. Hoover Commn. Com. on Nat. Defense, 1948; Nat. Citizen's Com. for Pub. Schs.; mem. com. for White House Conf. on Edn., 1954-55. Recipient Centennial award, Northwestern U., 1951; Journalism Award, U. Minn., 1956. Mem. Am. Legion, S.A.R., Sigma Delta Chi (past hon. pres.), Alpha Kappa Psi (hon.). Mason. Clubs: Minneapolis, Woodhill (Minneapolis); The Des Moines; The Metropolitan (Washington); Mill Reef (Antigua, West Indies). Author chapter on journalism in "American Now," 1938; also newspaper series, "Britain Under Fire," 1941; Report on Asia, 1956. Home: Minneapolis, Minn. Died Feb. 25, 1983.

COX, HERMAN GRAHME, JR., architect, engr.; b. Ft. Worth, Aug. 16, 1907; s. Herman Grahme and Agnes (Kerfoot) C.; m. Harriett Elizabeth Copeland, June 18, 1932; children—Mary Lynn Cox Grow, Carol Lee (Mrs. Glen Cope), Herman Grahme, III. B.S., Tex. A and M U., 1929. Registered profl. engr., Tex. Architect Am. Airway, Dallas, 1929-33, airport engr., State of Tex., 1934, pvt. practice architecture and engring., Ft. Worth, 1935-40, from 46. Author: Your Dachshund, 1966. Chmn. Zoning Bd. Adjustment, 1951-60, Animal Control Authority, 1953-61, City Planning Commn., 1961-67, Central Bus. Dist. Redevel. Com. Town Hall, 1964; all breed judge Am. Kennel Club. Served to lt. col., C.E. AUS, 1940-45. Decorated Legion of Merit. Fellow AIA; mem. Tex. Soc. Architects, Nat., Tex. socs. profl. engrs., Tau Beta Phi. Club: Ft. Worth. Home: Fort Worth, Tex.

COX, LEMUEL WILSON, railway exec.; b. Phila., Oct. 7, 1889; s. Joseph John and Theresa (Pierce) C.; student Phila. Sch. Pedagogy, 1908-10, U. Pa. Evening Sch., 1914-17; m. Florence Martha Brounley, Dec. 16, 1911. Clk. office of sec. N.&W. Ry. Co., Phila., 1910-20, asst.

sec., 1920-30, sec., 1939-53, v.p. charge finances, 1953 from, also dir.; dir. The Mut. Fire, Marine and Inland Ins. Co. Mem. Assn. Am. Railroads, Am. Soc. Corporate Secs., Financial Analysts of Phila., Republican. Mason. Clubs: Union League, also Right Angle (Phila.). Home: Radnor, Pa. †

COX, NORMAN WADE, clergyman; b. Climax, Ga., Oct. 28, 1888; s. Barclay Wade and Alice Louise (Brock) C.; B.A., Mercer, 1914. D.D., 1928; Th.M., Southern Bapt. Theol. Sem., Louisville, Ky., 1918; m. Osye Lee Matthews, Sept. 7, 1910; children—Graham Wade, Sara Margaret. Ordained to ministry Southern Bapt. Ch., 1910; pastor successively First Ch., Barnesville, Ga., Portsmouth, Va., Savannah, Ga., and Meridian, Miss., until 1931; pastor First Ch., Mobile, 1931-32, Fifth Av. Ch., Huntington, W.Va., 1932-39; again in Meridian, Miss., from June 1939. Received 6093 accessions to chs. in 23 yrs. Mem. bd. trustees Shorter Coll. (Rome, Ga.), Southern Bapt. Theol. Sem., Southwestern Bapt. Theol. Sem. Mason (Shriner), Rotarian. Author: Why the Skepticism of Christian Youth?; Youth's Return to Faith, 1938. Contbr. many papers and articles on religious subjects; author of "A Daily Tryst with God", a daily devotional used as a syndicated newspaper feature; author of "Tramping Trails of Faith", a weekly editorial published in newspaper since 1932. Editor The Baptist Messenger, 1936-39. Home: Meridian, Miss. †

COX, ROY, banker; b. Hartville, Mo., June 1888; s. Argus and Emma C.; A.B., Baker U., Baldwin, Kan., 1910; m. Juliet Williams, Jan. 28, 1914; 1 son, Roy. Manager for Freehold Investment Co., Springfield, 1910-15; cashier Am. Savings Bank, Springfield, 1915-18; with auditing dept., U.S.A., stationed at Paris, France, Sept. 1918-Apr. 1919; v.p. Trinidad (Colo.) Nat. Bank, 1919-21, pres. from Oct. 1921. Pres. Colorado Bankers Assn., 1924-25. Republican. Mason (K.T., 32 deg., Shriner), K.P. Club: Rotary (ex-pres.). Home: Trinidad, Colo. †

COXE, GEORGE HARMON, author; b. Olean, N.Y., Apr. 23, 1901; s. George H. and Harriet C. (Cowens) C.; m. Elizabeth Fowler, May 18, 1929; children: Janet, George III. Student, Elmira Free Acad., 1918-19, Purdue U., 1919-20, Cornell U., 1920-21. With Santa Monica (Calif.) Outlook, 1922; successively with Los Angeles Express, Utica (N.Y.) Observer Dispatch, N.Y. Comml. and Elmira Star-Gazette, to 1927; advt. work Barta Press, Cambridge, Mass., 1927-32; writer Metro-Goldwyn-Mayer, 1936-38, 44; dir. Mystery Writers Am., 1946-48, 69-70, pres., 1952. Author numerous mystery books, from 1935, Lady Killer, 1949, Inland Passage, 1949, Eye Witness, 1950, The Frightened Fiancee, 1950, The Widow Had a Gun, 1951, The Man Who Died Twice, 1951, Never Bet Your Life, 1952, The Crimson Clue, 1953, Uninvited Guest, 1953, Focus on Murder, 1954, Death at the Isthmus, 1954, Top Assignment, 1955, Suddenly a Widow, 1956, Man on a Rope, 1956, Crime Photographer; radio, 1943-52, Murder on Their Minds, 1957, One Minute Past Eight, 1957, The Impetuous Mistress, 1958, The Big Gamble, 1958, Triple Exposure, 1959, Slack Tide, 1959, One Way Out, 1960, The Last Commandment, 1960, Error of Judgement, 1961, Moment Author Violence, 1961, The Man Who Died Too Soon, 1962, Mission of Fear, 1962, The Hidden Key, 1963, One Hour To Kill, 1963, Deadly Image, 1964, With Intent To Kill, 1965, The Reluctant Heiress, 1965, The Ring of Truth, 1966, The Candid Imposter, 1968, An Easy Way To Go, 1969, Double Identity, 1970, Fenner, 1971, Woman With A Gun, 1972, The Silent Witness, 1973, The Inside Man, 1974, No Place for Murder, 1975, Masterpieces of Mystery, 1976; contbr. short stories, serials, novelettes to mags. and anthologies, 1932—; war corr., 1944. Recipient Grand Masters award, 1964. Mem. Authors Guild, Sigma Nu, Phi Zeta. Republican. Clubs: Old Lyme (Conn.) Country, Old Lyme Beach; Cornell (N.Y.C.); Spanish Wells Golf (Hilton Head, S.C.). Home: Old Lyme, Conn. Died Jan. 30, 1984.

COXE, JOHN E., supt. of edn.; b. Watson, Louisiana, July 14, 1887; s. William Potts and Margie Selina (Webb) C.; A.B., U. of La., 1909, A.M., 1928; student U. of Chicago, 1921, U. of Ohio, 1939; m. Hazel Grimm, March 29, 1929. Prin. of high schs., La., 1909-13; supt of edn., Livingston Parish, La., 1913-20; elementary and high sch. supervisor, State Dept. of Edn., 1920-39; state supt. of edn., 1940-48. Sec. La. State Bd. of Edn.; mem. bd. of managers, Delgado Trades Sch.; exofficio mem. Tulane Ednl. Fund. Mem. La. Teachers Assn., Nat. Edn. Assn. Nat. Assn. of Sch. Adminstrs., Prog. Edn. Assn., Kappa Phi Kappa. Home: Baton Rouge, La. †

CRABBE, BUSTER CLARENCE L., actor, bus. exec.; b. Oakland, Calif., Feb. 7, 1908; s. Edward C.S. and Agnes (McNamara) C.; m. Adah Virginia Held, Apr. 13, 1933; children—Susan Ann Crabbe Fletcher, Cullen Held. B.A., U. So. Calif., then; student Law Sch. Exec. dir. Cascade Industries. Appeared in Flash Gordon and Buck Rogers films for, Paramount Studios and Universal Studios, also as; Billy the Kid for, Producers Releasing Corp.; appeared in 170 films for, Paramount, Universal, Columbia and MGM studios; with, Billy Rose's Aquacade, N.Y. World's Fair, 1940, later formed, Buster Crabbe's Aquacade, TV appearances on TV as; Captain Gallant of the Foreign Legion, also: Buck Rogers; Author: Energistics. Mem. Hutchinson River council Boy Scouts Am. Mem. 1st group Swimming Hall of Fame; winner Gold medal for swimming 1932 Olympics. Mem. Sigma Chi. Republican. Home: Scottsdale, Ariz. Died Apr. 23, 1983.

CRABLE, ALVIN LAWRENCE, educator; b. Wolfe City, Tex., Nov. 27, 1889; s. James Marion and Martha Lawrence (Craig) C.; A.B., Austin Coll., Sherman, Tex., 1917; A.M., University of Oklahoma, 1927; Ph.D. (hon.), Austin Coll., 1937; m. Claudia Mae Church, May 8, 1918; children—Alvin Lawrence, Martha Jo, Henry Bennett. Teacher in Tex. schools, 1914-19; supt. of Collinsville, Tex. school, 1919-21; prin. high sch., Marietta, Okla., 1921-23, Durant, Okla., 1923-24; supt. Marietta schs., 1924; high sch. inspector, 1924-29; dir. of corr. study and extension classes Okla. A. and M. Coll., 1929-36; state supt. pub. instrn., Okla., 1936-47. Fed. employee; spl. asst. to nat. adminstr. War Assets Adminstrn.; spl. study in field operations of Agency in closing out surplus property, from April 1948. Served at Camp Travis and Camp McArthur, World War I. Mem. Am. Legion (past comdr. Marietta post, past comdr. Payne County post), Okla. Edn. Assn. Democrat. Baptist. Mason (32 deg.). Home: Oklahoma City, Okla. †

CRAIG, CECIL C(ALVERT), educator; b. Otwell, Ind., Apr. 14, 1898; s. Harley Eben and Lula (Abbott) C.; A.B., Ind. U., 1920, A.M., 1922; Ph.D., U. Mich., 1927; Am-Scandinavian Found. Fellow, Lund U., Sweden, 1924-25; m. Ruth Swan, Sept. 3, 1927; 1 dau., Mary Elizabeth. Instr. in mathematics, Ind. U., 1920-22; instr. mathematics, U. Mich., 1922-24, 1925-29, asst. prof., 1931-36, asso. prof., 1936-42, prof. mathematics, 1942-46, prof. mathematics and dir. statis. research lab. from 1946; Nat. Research Council fellow, 1929-31, fellow Rockefeller Found., 1937-38; instr. in intensive courses in statis. quality control in various univs. during World War II and from 1945. Recipient Shewhart medal, Am. Soc. Quality Control, 1957. Fellow Inst. Math. Statistics (pres., 1942, 43), Am. Statis. Assn., Am. Soc. Quality Control; mem. Am. Math. Soc., Math. Assn. of Am., The Biometrics Soc., Am. Assn. Univ. Profs., Mich. Soc. for Quality Control Assn. Computing Machinery, Phi Beta Kappa, Sigma Xi, Sigma Nu. Contbr. tech. articles on math. statistics to profl. jours.; mem. editorial bd. of Mathematical Tables and Other Aids to Computation and of Industrial Quality Control. Clubs: University, Golf and Outing (Ann Arbor). Home: Ann Arbor, Mich. Died June 16, 1985.

CRAIG, LESLIE WILSON, banker; b. Fidelity, Ill., Sept. 5, 1888; s. Tunis II, and Lucy Elizabeth (Wilson) C.; ed. pub. schs. of Jersey County; m. Nellie May Day, Oct. 9, 1915. Clerk, Central Savings Bank, Monroe, La., 1907-12; cashier, Farmers State Bank, Medora, Ill., 1912-19; asst. v.p. Nat. Stockyards Nat. Bank, East St. Louis, Ill., 1919-21; vice pres., Am. Trust Co., El Paso, Texas, 1921-22; asst. v.p., Security Trust & Savings Bank, Los Angeles, Calif., 1922-24, vice pres., 1924-29; vice pres. Security-First Nat. Bank, Los Angeles, Calif., since 1929, dir. from 1946; pres. Kings County Land and Cattle Co., Inc., Lemoore, Calif., from 1935. Democrat. Methodist. Clubs: Calif., Los Angeles Country. Home: Los Angeles, Calif. †

CRAIG, W(ILLIAM) MARSHALL, clergyman; b. Anderson, S.C., May 28, 1889; s. Sam M. and Mamie (Partlow) C.; student Demarest Coll.; D.D., Furman U., Baylor U.; m. Loulie Cullum, Oct. 21, 1915. Ordained to ministry, Baptist Ch.; pastor Gaston Av. Bapt. Ch., Dallas from 1927; broadcaster 1st Bapt. Radio Hour, Atlanta, Jan. 1946. Preacher annual Texas State Conv., Amarillo, 1930, So. Bapt. Conv., St. Petersburg, Fla., 1932. Vice pres. So. Bapt. Conv., 1951. Pres. Tng. Union in Va.; trustee Baylor U., Baylor U. Hosp.; bd. mem. Howard Payne Coll., Texas State Bd.; chmn. Relief and Annuity Bd. Club: Kiwanis. Home: Dallas, Tex. †

CRAIGHEAD, FRANK COOPER, entomologist; b. Craighead's, Pa., Oct. 7, 1890; s. Charles Cooper and Agnes (Miller) C.; B.A., Pa. State Coll., 1912; M.S., George Washington U., 1915; Ph.D., 1919; m. Caroline Johnson, of Alexandria, Va., Oct. 1915; children—John Johnson and Frank Cooper (twins), Jean Caroline. With U.S. Dept. Agr., Washington, 1912-20; in employ Dominion Agrl. Dept., Can., 1920-23; again with U.S. Dept. Agr. since 1923; in charge forest insect investigations of U.S. Bur. Entomology. Fellow A.A.A.S.; mem. Soc. Am. Foresters, Soc. Economic Entomologists, Washington Entomol. Soc., Washington Acad. Science, Alpha Zeta. Club: Cosmos. Home: Washington, D.C. †

CRAM, MILDRED, author; b. Washington, D.C., Oct. 17, 1889; d. Nathan Dow and Mary Olivia (Queen) Cram; student Barnard School for Girls, N.Y. City; also studied abroad; m. Clyde Stanley McDowell. Writer of books, motion picture plays, stories from 1918. Author: Stranger Things, 1923; The Tide, 1924; Scotch Valley, 1928; Madder Music, 1930; Forever, 1935; Kingdom of Innocents, 1940. Motion pictures: Forever and Mary Smith, U.S.A., 1943; Life and Love of Anna Pavlowa (Alex. Korda Prodn.). Contbr. fiction to mags.; articles to Ladies Home Journal, etc. Home: Montecito, Santa Barbara, Calif. Address: New York, N.Y. †

CRAMER, CLARENCE HENLEY, educator; b. Eureka, Kans., June 23, 1905; s. David H. and Irma M. (Henley) C.; m. Elizabeth A. Garman, Dec. 27, 1949. A.B., B.S. in Edn, Ohio State U., 1927, A.M., 1928, Ph.D., 1931. Asso. prof. history So. Ill. U., 1931-42; dir. personnel Nat. War Labor Bd., 1943-44, UNRRA Germany, 1944-47, Internat. Refugee Orgn., 1947-48; asso. and acting dean Case Western Res. U. Sch. Bus., 1949-54; dean Case Western Res. U. Sch. Bus. (Adelbert Coll.), 1954-69, prof. history, 1949—, chmn. dept., 1963-67. Author: Royal Bob—The Life of Robert G. Ingersoll, 1952, Newton D. Baker—A Biography, 1961, Open Shelves and Open Minds, 1972, American Enterprise: Free and Not So Free, 1972, Case Western Reserve: A History of the University, 1826-1976, 1976, and separate vols. on its law, library and engring. schs. Mem. Western Res. Hist. Soc. (trustee), Phi Beta Kappa, Delta Tau Delta, Elide (trustee). Club: Cleve. Skating. Home: Cleveland OH

CRANE, BARRY, director, producer; b. Detroit; m. Shirlee Roseberg; m. Arline Anderson; children: Ben, Shari. Student, U. Mich. Formerly with, Pasadena Playhouse, then prodn. asst., King Bros., then from 2d asst. dir. to prodn. mgr., 4 Star TV, then assoc. producer-dir., Paramount Co.; then producer: Mission Impossible, all from 1960-79; now dir.: TV shows Trapper John. Mem. Dirs. Guild Am., Producers Guild Am., Writers Guild, Am. Contract Bridge League (6-time winner McKenny trophy, World Mixed Pair champion). Home: Studio City, Calif. Died July 5, 1985.

CRANE, BRUCE, paper co. exec.; b. Dalton, Mass., July 27, 1909; s. W. Murray and Josephine Porter (Boardman) C.; A.B., Yale, 1931; m. Winnie Davis Long, May 14, 1932; children—Winnie and Davis (twins). With Crane & Co., Inc., Dalton, 1931-85, pres., gen. mgr., 1951-75, chmn. bd. dirs., 1975-85; dir. Agrl. Nat. Bank, Pittsfield, Mass., Berkshire Life Ins. Co., Pittsfield. Mem. Dalton Sch. Com., 1945-51; mem. Gov.'s Council Mass., 1953-56. Republican nat. committeeman for Mass., 1964-80. Mem. Writing Paper Mfrs. Assn. (pres. 1951-52). Home: Dalton, Mass. Died June 2, 1985.

CRATER, ROBERT WINFIELD, newspaperman; b. Newcomerstown, Ohio, Jan. 8, 1912; s. Edward Irving and Hazel M. (Bramhall) C; student pub. schs.; m. Lucille R. Salladay, Aug. 15, 1930; 1 dau., Carroll Crater Volchko. With J.G. Bair Co., Cambridge, Ohio, 1930-36; reporter Coshocton (Ohio) Tribune, 1936-42; reporter Columbus (Ohio) Citizen, 1942-45, city editor, 1945-50; Washington corr. Cleve. Press, Cin. Post and Times Star, Columbus Citizen-Jour., 1950-77, ret., 1977. Mem. Sigma Delta Chi, Alpha Phi Gamma. Home: University Park, Md. Dec. Jan. 26, 1985. Interned Adelphi, Md.

CRAWFORD, JOHN CALVIN, JR., lawyer; b. Maryville, Tenn., July 24, 1906; s. John Calvin and Mary Maud (Farnham) C.; m. America Arey Moore, Jan. 1, 1933; children—Carolyn (Mrs. J. Calvin Chesnutt). John Calvin, Duncan Venable. A.B., Maryville Coll., 1927; LL.B., Harvard, 1931. Bar: Tenn. bar 1931. Pvt. practice, Maryville, 1931-53, 61-82; U.S. dist. atty. Eastern Dist. Tenn., 1953-61; Dir. Bank of Maryville. Mem. adv. commn. rules practice and procs. Supreme Ct. Tenn., 1966-74; State senator, Tenn., 1941-45; mayor of Maryville, 1947-53, mem. utilities bd., from 1963, chmn., from 1969; chmn. City of Maryville Indsl. Devel. Bd., 1964-75, Presdl. elector, 1964. Mem. Am., Tenn., Maryville bar assns. Republican (del. nat. conv. 1952). Presbyterian (ruling elder from 1934). Clubs: Mason (33 deg.), Lions. Home: Maryville, Tenn. Dec. Dec. 24, 1982.

CRAWFORD, KENNETH GALE, journalist; b. Sparta, Wis., May 27, 1902; s. Robert Levy and Madge (Gale) C.; m. Elisabeth Bartholomew, July 21, 1928; children—William, Gale. B.A., Beloit Coll., 1924, Litt.D., 1954; LL.D., Olivet Coll. Reporter and bur. mgr. UPI, St. Paul, St. Louis, Cleve., Lansing and Indpls., 1924-27, Washington corr., 1927-29; columnist Buffalo (N.Y.) Times, 1929-32; Washington corr. N.Y. Post, 1932-40; Washington corr. and bur. mgr. PM (newspaper), 1940-43; war corr. Newsweek, N. Africa, Italy, Middle East, Eng., France, 1943-44, Washington corr., polit. columnist, 1944-70, formerly syndicated newspaper columnist; now free lance writer. Author: The Pressure Boys, 1939, Report on North Africa, 1943. Pres. Am. Newspaper Guild, 1939-40. Decorated Navy Commendation U.S.; French Liberation medal. Mem. Sigma Chi. Clubs: Nat. Press (Washington), Overseas Writers (Washington); Players (N.Y.C.). Home: Washington, DC.

CRAWFORD, WILLIAM DONHAM, b. Little Rock, June 22, 1923; s. Sidney Robert and Blanche (Donham) C.; m. Colene King, June 6, 1947; children: Carol, Bruce Donham, Philip King. Student, U. Ark., 1941-43; B.S., U.S. Naval Acad., 1947; M.S., Calif. Inst. Tech., 1948. Chief Office Sci. and Tech., Pan Am. Union, Washington, 1949-50; staff AEC, 1951-54; with Middle South Utilities, Inc., N.Y.C., 1955-63, asst. sec., asst. treas., 1956-59, v.p., 1959-63, Consol. Edison Co., N.Y., 1963-69, adminstrv. v.p., 1966-69; mng. dir. Edison Electric Inst., N.Y.C., 1969-70, pres., 1971-78; now dir.; chmn., chief exec. officer Gulf States Utilities Co., Beaumont, Tex., from 1978, now ret., hon. chmn. bd.; dir. First City Bank Beaumont; adv. dir. Comml. Nat. Bank, Little Rock. Trustee Thomas A. Edison Found.; bd. dirs. Am. Nuclear Energy Council. Served with USN, 1947-49. Club: Baltusrol Golf (Springfield, N.J.). Home: Beaumont, Tex. Died Sept. 1, 1984.

CRAWFORD, WILLIAM HULFISH, cartoonist; b. Hammond, Ind., Mar. 18, 1913; s. William Hulfish and Katharine (McCulland) C.; B.A., Ohio State U., 1935; m. Claire Olita Trillo, Feb. 11, 1950; children—Katharine,

Dale. Cartoonist, Washington Post and Washington Daily News, 1936-38; editorial page cartoonist Newark News, 1938-62; chief editorial page cartoonist Newspaper Enterprise Assn., N.Y.C., 1962-82; illustrator of 19 books; profl. sculptor and lectr. Mem. Nat. Cartoonists Soc. (pres. 1960-61, named Best Editorial Cartoonist in Country 1957, 58, 59, 66). Club: Dutch Treat (N.Y.C.). Home: New York, N.Y. Died Jan. 6, 1982.

CREEL, CECIL WILLIS, agrl. cons.; b. Angola, Ind., Oct. 22, 1889; s. Lorenzo Dow and Estella Frances (Willis) C.; student Mont. Agri. Coll., Bozeman, Mont., 1904-06; Tri-State Coll., Angola, Ind., 1906-07, Kan. State Agrl. Coll., 1907-09; B.S. in Agr., Univ. of Nevada, 1911; D. Agr., Univ. of Maryland, 1939; m. Laura Belle Stevens, June 5, 1915 (dec.); children—Marshall Stevens, William Lorenzo (dec.), Jane Estelle; m. 2d, Mille La Rayne Malley, July 17, 1945. Began career at Agricultural Experiment Station, Purdue University, 1911-12; special agent in charge agrl. education Indian Service, Dept. of Interior, 1912-13; in charge research and extension Pacific Northwest Field Sta., Bur. Entomology, U.S. Dept. Agr., Forest Grove, Ore., 1914-19, in charge Bur. campaign to stimulate food production in N.W. during World War; county agt., leader Agrl. Extension Service, U. of Nev., 1919-21, dir. agrl. extension, 1921-41, 43-52, dean of agr., 1945-49; agriculturist Fgn. Agr. Service, U.S. Dept. Agr., in Israel, 1953; consultant to Foreign Operations Administration, 1954-55; cons. Dept. State, 1956-62. Elector Hall of Fame for Great Ams., N.Y. U., from 1955. Rep. nominee for U.S. Sen. from Nev., 1942. Chmn. extension sect. Assn. State Univs. and Land-Grant Colls. 1933, chmn. Com. on Extension Orgn. and Policy, 1936-37; pres., 1938, Washington rep., 1940-41; exec. sec. Nev. State Bd. of Charities and Pub. Welfare, 1933-34; state civil works adminstr., 1933-34. Fellow A.A.A.S.; mem. Farm Bur., Grange, Phi Kappa Phi, Sigma Alpha Epsilon, Epsilon Sigma Phi. Mason (32 deg.), grand master R. & S.M., Nev., 1947, K.T., Knight Red Cross Constantine, Sovereign Joan of Arc Conclave 1957, Intendant Gen. Imperial Council, Div. Nev. 1960; Shriner Potentate Kerak Temple, 1951, mem. imperial council Masonic relations com., Jester, Reno Ct. 33, dir. 1924. Rotarian. Author: articles and bulls. Home: Reno, Nev. †

CREIGHTON, THOMAS HAWK, architect; b. Phila., May 19, 1904; s. Frank W. and Maude (Hawk) C.; m. Gwen Lux, 1959; children by previous marriage—Thomas Hawk, Anne Genung. A.B., Harvard, 1926; grad., Beaux Arts Inst. Design, 1929. Archtl. designer Shultze & Weaver, Charles B. Meyers, N.Y.C., Freeman, French, Freeman, Burlington, Vt., 1926-38; sr. architect, dept. hosps., N.Y.C., 1938-40; asso. Alfred Hopkins & Assos., 1940-46; editor Progressive Architecture, 1946-63, editorial dir., 1963-64; partner, v.p. John Carl Warnecke & Assos. (architects), San Francisco, 1963- 66, architect and planner, Honolulu, 1966; Adj. prof. architecture, Columbia; 962-63; vis. lectr. U. Hawaii, 1968-69, univ. architect, 1970; spl. columnist Honolulu Advertiser, 1968-84. Author: Planning To Build, 1945, Houses, 1947, Building for Modern Man, 1949, The American House Today, 1951, Quality Budget Houses, 1954, Designs for Living, 1955, (with Katherine Morrow Ford) Contemporary Houses, 1961, The Architecture of Monuments, 1962, American Architecture, 1964, The Lands of Hawaii: Their Use and Misuse, 1977. Mem. Honolulu Planning Commn., 1971-74. Fellow AIA; mem. Constrn. Specifications Inst. (hon.). Home and Office: Honolulu, Hawaii. Died Oct. 6, 1984.

CRENNEN, ROBERT EARL, world news service exec.; b. Mpls., June 13, 1929; s. Leo Patrick and Alice Signe (Dahlin) C.; B.A. in Journalism (Univ. scholar), U. Mont., 1951; postgrad. U. Minn., 1951; m. Beverly Mae Rich, Sept. 22, 1951; children—Kristi Roxanne, Thad Geoffrey. Reporter, Mpls. Tribune, 1951; with UPI, 1954-84, bus. mgr. Pacific div., San Francisco, 1963-68, mgr. S.W. div., Dallas, 1969-76, v.p. central zone, Chgo., 1977-84. Served with CIC, U.S. Army, 1952-54. Mem. Sigma Delta Chi, Sigma Nu, (life). Clubs: Dallas Press, North Dallas Racquet, Lake Bluff (Ill.) Racquet, Cross and Cockade. Home: Lake Bluff, Ill. Died May 19, 1984.

CRENSHAW, GEORGE WEBSTER, cartoonist; b. Los Angeles, Oct. 23, 1917; s. Charles Robert Lafayette and Alpha (Allen) C.; m. Betty Sedam, Mar., 1980; children by previous marriage—Kenneth, Joseph, Marilyn, Thomas. Student, U. Calif., Berkeley, 1938-40, Northwestern U., 1942, Harvard U., 1943. pres., owner Masters Agy., Capitola, Calif., from 1968. Animator, Disney Studios, 1938-39, Paramount Studios, 1940-42, M.G.M. Studios, 1946-48; cartoonist: syndicated features The Muffins, Columbia Features, 1957-59, Nubbin, King Features, 1958-71, Belvedere, Field Newspaper, from 1961, Simpkins, N.Y. News, 1971-75, Gumdrop, United Features, 1977-79; publisher: syndicated features Belvedere Books, 1964, 70, 82. Served with USNR, 1942-46. Home: Aptos, Calif. Deceased.

CRESTON, PAUL, composer; b. N.Y.C., Oct. 10, 1906; s. Gaspare and Carmela (Collura) Guttoveggio; m. Louise Gotto, July 1, 1927; children—Joel Anthony, Timothy William. Student pub. schs., N.Y.C. Organist St. Malachy's Ch., N.Y.C., 1934-67; faculty N.Y. Coll. Music, 1964-68; distinguished vis. prof. Central Wash. State Coll., Ellensburg, 1967, composer-in-residence, prof. music, 1968-75. Made concert tour as pianist and accompanist, 1936; mus. dir.: The Hour of Faith Program, ABC, 1944-50; Author: Rational Metric Notation. Guggenheim fellow in composition, 1938, 39; Recipient citation of merit Nat. Assn. Am. Composers and Condrs., 1941, 43; music award Nat. Inst. Arts and Letters, 1943; N.Y. Music Critics award for Symphony No. 1, 1943; Alice M. Ditson award for Poem for Harp and Orch., 1945; Fedn. Music Clubs award for Symphony No. 2, 1947; Music Library Assn. award for Two Choric Dances, 1948; 1st prize for Symphony No. 1 Paris Referendum Concert, 1952; State Dept. grant as Am. specialist for Israel and Turkey, 1960; gold medal Nat. Arts Club, 1963; Composer award Lancaster Symphony, 1970. Life fellow Internat. Inst. Arts and Letters; mem. Nat. Assn. Am. Composers and Condrs. (pres. 1956-60, life mem.), ASCAP (dir. 1960-68), Bohemians (gov. 1950-68), Nat. Music Council (exec. com. 1950-68), Kappa Kappa Psi, Phi Kappa Lambda, Pi Mu Alpha Sinfonia. Home: San Diego, Calif. Died Aug. 24, 1985.

CREVISTON, RUSSELL GOOD, pub. relations exec.; b. Grant Co., Ind., Oct. 24, 1889; s. Henry Clay and Josephine (Lobdell) C.; student Ind. State Normal Sch., Ind. U., 1909-13; m. Louise Wigger, Sept. 25, 1918. Gen. mgr. Wigger Co., Marion, Ind., 1914-16; a founder Am. Legion, asst. nat. adj., nat. adj., 1919-25; gen. mgr. Eastern States Indsl. League, Springfield, Mass., 1925-27, Plumbing and Heating Industries Bureau, Chgo., 1927-29; sales promotion mgr., dir. advt. and sales promotion Crane Co., Chicago, 1929-39, dir. pub. relations from 1939; industry cons. govt. dept. Bd. dirs. Chgo. Bldg. Congress, Ry. Bus. Assn.; mem. indsl. health and safety com. N.A.M.; mem. constrn. and civic development department. com. C. of C. U.S. Served as lt. to capt. Inf., U.S. Army, 1916-18, maj. gen. staff War Dept., 1919. Mem. Ind. Soc. Chgo. (v.p.), Phi Delta Kappa. Republican. Episcopalian. Mason. Club: Chgo. Press (charter mem.). Assisted development Am. Legion in 48 states, U.S. tys, 17 fgn. countries, Inter-Allied Vets. Fedn., Overseas Decoration Service, dir. Legion's campaign for $6,000,000 endowment for relief orphans of vets., donated Creviston Cup for winning Drum Corps. Home: Evanston, Ill. †

CRICKARD, MASON, banker; b. Huttonsville, W.Va., Dec. 28, 1887; s. Patrick and Amanda (Moyers) C.; student Davis and Elkins Coll.; A.B., W.Va. Wesleyan Coll.; m. Mabel Gates, Jan. 18, 1918. With Union Trust Co., Charleston, W.Va., 1914-29; pres., dir. Bank of Dunbar from 1918; dir. Charleston Nat. Bank, pres. 1952, chmn.; dir. Charleston Fed. Savs. & Loan Assn., 1934-52, v.p., 1934, pres., 1952. Mem. W.Va. Bd. Edn. Trustee Charleston Meml. Hosp. State treas. W.Va., U.S.O., World War II. Mem. W.Va. (pres. 1933-34, chmn. resolutions com., chmn. taxation and legislation com.) Am. (mem. exec. council, v.p. nat. bank div.) bankers assns., Charleston C. of C. Democrat. Presbyn. Mason (Shriner). Home: Charleston, W.Va. †

CRISPO, ANDREW J(OHN), art dealer; b. Phila., Apr. 21, 1945. Ed., St. Joseph's Coll. Pres. Andrew Crispo Gallery, Inc., N.Y.C., from 1973. Editor, contbg. author: Pioneers of American Abstraction, 1973, Ten Americans: Masters of Watercolor, 1974, Twelve Americans: Masters of Collage, 1977; specialist in Am. and European paintings of 18th, 19th and 20th centuries, antiquities of English and French origin of 17th, 18th, 19th and 20th centuries. Forbes fellow Fogg Art Mus. Home: New York, N.Y. Deceased.

CRIST, FREDERIC EUGENE, security co. exec.; b. Dayton, Ohio, Dec. 1, 1916; s. William H. and Devone (Double) C.; m. Leta Clark, Apr. 8, 1939; children—Barbara, Beverly. A.B., Miami Coll., Dayton, 1935; LL.B., N.Y. U., 1950. Bar: N.Y. bar 1951, U.S. Supreme Ct. bar 1951. Indsl. administr. Am. Machine & Foundry Co., 1950-53; sec., dir., mem. exec. com. Sun Chem. Corp., 1953-57; exec. v.p., mem. exec. com. Barnes Group, Inc., 1957-66, dir., 1958-80; pres., dir., mem. exec. com. Electronics Splty. Co., Los Angeles, 1966-68; exec. v.p., mem. exec. com., dir. Burns Internat. Security Services Inc., Briarcliff Manor, N.Y., 1968-70, pres., 1970-72, chmn. bd., chief exec. officer, 1972-78; mem. adv. com. Am. Stock Exchange, 1972-78. Bd. dirs. Conn. Mfg. Assn., 1964-66; Mem. bd. finance, Bristol, Conn., 1963-66; Bd. dirs. Bristol ARC, 1960-62, Bristol United Fund, 1960-63; corporator Bristol Hosp., 1957-66. Mem. N.Y. Bar Assn.; mem. Order Eastern Star. Clubs: Mason, Shriner, Hundred (dir.), Explorers, Union League, Whispering Pines Country, Mt. Kisco Country, Heritage Country. Home: Whispering Pines, NC.

CRITTENBERGER, WILLIS DALE, army officer; b. Anderson, Ind., Dec. 2, 1890; s. Dale Jackson and Effie Alice (Daniels) C.; grad. U.S. Military Acad., 1913, Cav. Sch., 1924, Command and Gen. Staff Sch., 1925, Army War Coll., 1930; m. Josephine Frost Woodhull, June 23, 1918; children—Willis Dale, Jr., Townsend Woodhull (killed in Rhine crossing, March 23, 1945), Dale Jackson. Commd. 2d lt., United States Army, 1913, and advanced through the grades to lt. general (temporary), June 3, 1946; military intelligence officer, Manila, P.I., 1932-34; assigned 1st Cav. (mechanized), 1934, and from that time associated with development of mechanization in army; on duty Office of Chief of Cavalry, Washington, D.C., 1938-40; chief of staff 1st Armored Div., Fort Knox, Ky., 1940-41; comdg. gen., 2d Armored Brigade, 2d Armored Div., 1941-42, 2d Armored Div., Feb.-July 1942, 2d Armored Corps, 1942-43; organizer and comdr. III Armored Corps (later redesignated XIX Corps), 1943; comdg. gen. XIX Corps, Eng., Jan.-Mar. 1944; comdg. gen. IV Corps, Italian Campaign, 1944-45, the corps fighting continuously for 401 days, northward from Rome and across Po River; received unconditional surrender of German Ligurian Army, Apr. 29, 1945; comdg. gen. Caribbean Defense Command and Panama Canal Dept., with hdqrs. Quarry Heights, C.Z., from Oct. 1945. Decorated Distinguished Service Medal with oak leaf cluster, Bronze Star Medal, Mexican Border Campaign, World War I, World War II, European Theater Campaign and Am. Theater Campaign medals (U.S.), Star of Abdon Calderon, 1st class (Ecuador), Legion of Honor, Croix de Guerre (France), Medalha de Guerra, Ordem do Merito Militar, Medalha de Pampanha, Cruzeiro do Sul, Grand Official (Brazil), Order of Ayacucho, Gran Official (Peru), Silver Star for Valor, Grand Officer, Order of St. Maurice and St. Lazzaro, Mil. Order of Malta (Italy), Order of Vasco Nunez de Balboa (Panama). Address: New York, N.Y. †

CRITZ, HARRY HERNDON, banker; b. Teague, Tex., Feb. 26, 1912; s. Ivan Chancelumm and Suzie (Herndon) C.; m. Sarah Alice Gregor, Feb. 26, 1938 (dec.); children—Terry (Mrs. Russell A. Mericle, Jr.), Harry Kimbrough, James Richard; m. Joy Bell, Dec. 20, 1974; 1 dau., Renee Denise. Student, Tex. A. and M. Coll., 1929-31; B.S., U.S. Mil. Acad., 1935. Commd. 2d lt., arty. U.S. Army, 1935; advanced through grades to lt. gen.; assigned 1st Inf. Div. Africa and Europe, 1941-46; sec. (Arty. Sch.), 1948-50; assigned (Army War Coll.), 1950-51; Hdqrs. (6th Army), San Francisco, 1951-52, (I Corps and 8th Army), Korea, 1953-54, Office Asst. Sec. Def. for Internat. Affairs, 1954-57; chief staff (101st Airborne Div.), Ft. Campbell, Ky., 1957-60; sec. staff (SHAPE), Paris, France, 1960- 63; comdg. gen. (101st Airborne Div.), Ft. Campbell, 1963-64, (U.S. Army Arty. and Missile Center); also comdt. (U.S. Army Arty. and Missile Sch.), Ft. Sill, Okla., 1964-67; comdg. gen. (I Corps Korea), 1967-68; comdg. gen. Fourth U.S. Army, Ft. Sam Houston, Tex., 1968-71, ret., 1971; pres. Ft. Sill Nat. Bank, Okla., from 1971. Decorated D.S.M., Silver Star, Legion of Merit with two oak leaf clusters, Bronze Star medal with oak leaf cluster; also fgn. decorations. Home: Fort Sill, Okla. Died May 2, 1982.

CROMWELL, RICHARD P., ret. ins. co. exec.; b. Medford, Mass., Dec. 12, 1903; s. Harry P. and Edith (Graves) C.; m. Margaret Elizabeth Miller, Oct. 12, 1933; children—Virginia, Robert, John. Student, Harvard, 1925. Pres. Cromwell & Co., 1931-50; former sr. v.p. Am. Mut. Liability Ins. Co., Boston; now ret.; v.p. Allied Am. Mut. Fire Ins. Co. and Am. Policyholders Ins. Co.; former pres. Lexington Savs. Bank, now ret. Mem. planning bd., sch. com., Lexington. Mem. Boston Security Analysts Soc. (past pres.). Home: Osterville, Mass.

CROSBY, ELIZABETH CAROLINE, anatomist, educator; b. Petersburg, Mich., Oct. 25, 1888; d. Lewis Frederick and Frances (Kreps) C.; 1 adopted dau., Kathleen Palmer. B.S., Adrian (Mich.) Coll., 1910; M.S., U. Chgo., 1912, Ph.D. (fellow in anatomy), 1914), 1915; Sc.D. (hon.), Adrian Coll., 1939; Sc.D., Marquette U., 1957, Denison U., 1959, Smith Coll., 1967, Women's Med. Coll., 1967, U. Mich., 1970; LL.D. (hon.), Wayne State U.; M.D. (hon.), U. Groningen, Netherlands, 1958; L.H.D. (hon.), Med. U. S.C., 1980. Prin. Petersburgh High Sch., 1915-18; supt. schs., Petersburgh, 1918-20; mem. faculty Mich. Med. Sch., 1920-59, prof. anatomy, from 1958, prof. emeritus, cons. neurosurgery, from 1959; prof. emeritus anatomy U. Ala. Med. Center, Birmingham, cons. anatomy, from 1964; lectr. Marischal Coll., U. Aberdeen, Scotland, 1939-40, sr. research fellow, 1960; vis. prof. U. P.R., 1949; Henry Russel lectr. U. Mich., 1946; Max Peet lectr. Univ. Hosp., U. Mich., 1949; Mellon lectr. U. Pitts. Med. Sch., 1951; Eben J. Carey Meml. lectr. Marquette U.Med. Sch., Milw., 1952; guest lectr. French Neurol. Conf., 1955; Henry Burr Ferris lectr. Yale U. Med. Sch., 1958; Mayo Clinic lectr., 1963; lectr. Ot. Lectr. series Tulane U., 1965; Ohio State U. lectr., 1966; Marion Hines lectr. Emory U., 1966; Neurosci. lectr. U. La., New Orleans. Co-author: Comparative Anatomy of the Nervous Systems of Vertebrated, including Man, 1936, Correlative Neurosurgery, 1955, 2d edit., 1969, 3d edit., 1980, Correlative Anatomy of the Nervous System, 1962, Comparative Correlative Neuroanatomy of the Vertebrate Telencephalon, 1980. Recipient Nat. Medal of Sci., 1979; award Nat. Med. Women's Assn., 1981. Mem. Ala. Acad. Sci., Am. Assn. Aanatomists, Harvey Cushing Assn. (hon.), Cajal Club, Internat. Brain Research Orgn., U. Mich. Alumni Assn., Research Commn. World Fedn. Neurology, Soc. Neurosci., So. Soc. Anatomists, Univ. Research Club, Washtenaw County Med. Soc., Women's Research Club, Sigma Xi, Phi Kappa Phi; asso. and/or hon. mem. other assns. Home: Dexter, Mich.

CROSBY, PAUL TRACY, physician; b. Seneca Falls, N.Y., Feb. 21, 1890; s. John Francis and May Estelle (Williams) C.; Syracuse Univ., 1913, M.D., 1915; m. Dorothy Frances Barnes, 1912; 1 son, John Barnes. Interne, St. Joseph's Hosp., Syracuse, 1915-17; in practice, specializing in psychiatry, from 1928; coordinator Vets. Med. Service Plan, Regional Office of Vets. Adminstrn., Syracuse, from 1947. Commd. lt. (j.g.), Med. Corps. U.S. Navy, 1917, and advanced through the grades to rear adm., 1947; Decorated Silver Star (Army), Navy Cross (U.S.), Croix de Guerre (France). Diplomate Am. Bd.

Psychiatry. Fellow Am. Psychiatric Assn.; mem. Mohawk Valley Neuropsychiatric Soc., Neuron Club, Onondaga Co. Med. Soc. Phi Delta Theta, Nu Sigma Nu. Republican. Episcopalian. Home: De Witt, N.Y. †

CROSBY, SUMNER MCKNIGHT, educator; b. Mpls., July 29, 1909; s. Franklin Muzzy and Harriet (McKnight) C.; m. Sarah Rathbone Townsend, Oct. 19, 1935; children—Sumner McKnight, William F., Frederick T., Gerrit L. Student, Blake Sch., Hopkins, Minn., 1916-26, Phillips Acad., Andover, Mass., 1926-28; A.B., Yale, 1932, Ph.D., 1937; student, Ecole des Chartes, Paris, France, 1934-35; A.F.D. (hon.), Mpls. Sch. Art, 1965. Instr. Yale, 1936-40, asst. prof. history of art, 1940-43, 1945-47, asso. prof., 1947-52, prof., 1952-78, prof. emeritus, 1978-82, chmn. dept. history art, 1947-53, 62-65; excavated in Abbey Ch. St. Denis, north of Paris, summers 1938, 39, 46, 47, 48, 67, 68, 69, 71; curator Art Gallery, 1946-78; fellow Berkeley Coll., Yale, 1939-82; chmn. Carolyn Found.; dir. The Crosby Co. Vis. com. fine arts Harvard, 1959-65; mem. vis. com. dept. art and archaeology Princeton, 1962-68; Dir. Internat. Center Medieval Art, 1956-82, pres., 1965-68; mem. internat. com. history art, 1950-75. Author: Abbey of St. Denis I, 1942, L'Abbaye Royale de Saint-Denis, 1952, The Apostle Bas-Relief at Saint-Denis, 1972; Mem. bd., Speculum, 1946-54; Editor: Art Through the Ages, 1959, Religious Art in France Thirteenth Century, Corpus Vitrearum Medii Aevi; Mem. editorial bd.: Art Bull. Trustee Am. Fedn. Arts, 1940-45, 49-50; Mem. Coll. Art Assn., dir., 1939-45 and 1947-52, pres., 1940-44; exec. sec. Am. Council of Learned Socs. Com. on Preservation of Cultural Materials in War Areas, 1943-44; spl. adviser Am. Commn. for the Protection and Salvage of Artistic and Historic Monuments in War Areas, 1944-46; spl. adv. on Restitution of Cultural Materials Dept. State, 1945. Recipient Guggenheim F.; festschrift in his honor, 1976; Decorated chevalier Legion d'Honor; officier Ordre des Arts et Lettres. Mem. Medieval Acad. Am., Archaeol. Inst. Am. (trustee 1966-69), Société d'Archéologie Francaise, Soc. Nat. des Antiquaires de France (hon.), Am. Philos. Soc., Am. Acad. Arts and Scis., Alpha Delta Phi. Republican. Presbyn. Clubs: Century Assn. (N.Y. City), Yale (N.Y. City); Walton Fishing (Cornwall Bridge, Conn.); Elizabethan, Wolf's Head of Yale. Home: Woodbridge, Conn. Died Nov. 16, 1982.

CROSS, MAURICE CONDIT, univ. prof.; b. Urbana, Ohio, Mar. 20, 1890; s. Henry Webster and Irene A. (Condit) C.; student Wooster (Ohio) Coll., 1913-14; A.B., Ohio State, 1916, A.M., 1920, Ph.D. 1926; m. Helen Moore, Aug. 31, 1926. Supt. of schools, Butler, O., 1916-18; instr. econs. and accounting, Ohio State U., 1918-19, 1920-21; instr. econs., Purdue, 1919-20; prof. prodn. mgt., Syracuse U., since 1922, chmn. dept. prodn. mgt., coll. bus. adminstrn., 1922-56; vis. prof. Coll. Bus. Adminstrn., U. Tex., 1956-59. Served as pvt. Co. B. 309 Engrs., 84 Div., U.S. Army, 1918. Mem. Sigma Iota Epsilon, national president, 1940-48), Phi Kappa Phi, Beta Gamma Sigma. Republican. Conglist. Author: Types of Business Enterprises, 1928. Home: Syracuse, N.Y. †

CROSS, RICHARD, insurance company executive, lawyer; b. Tulsa, Oct. 27, 1940; s. T.R. and Lucy (Smothers) C.; m. Nancy Ellen Ash, Nov. 11, 1967 (div.); 1 child, Alan Wade. B.S., Okla. State U., 1967; J.D., S.Tex. Coll. Law, 1970. Bar: Tex. bar 1970, U.S. Supreme Ct 1976. Asst. probate judge, Harris County, Houston, 1967-70; sr. partner Nations & Cross, Houston, 1971-73; pres. Ins. Corp. of Am., Property & Casualty Ins. Co., Houston, 1973-83; Instr. S.Tex. Coll. Law. Author: Opening and Administering the Texas Guardianship, 1970; Editor: S.Tex. Law Jour, 1969-70. Mem. ABA (past nat. chmn. law student div., Silver Key of Recognition), Tex. Bar Assn., Am. Judicature Soc., Tex. Trial Lawyers Assn., Order of Lytae (past pres.), Phi Alpha Delta. Home: Houston, Tex. Died June 21, 1983.

CROSS, WILLIAM THOMAS, social service; b. nr. Mexico, Mo., May 1, 1887; s. John Newton and Olivia McClure (Harris) C.; A.B., U. of Mo., 1908, A.M., 1909; studied U. of Chicago; m. Dorothy Embry, Aug. 21, 1919. Connected with St. Louis School of Philanthropy, also research work of Russell Sage Foundation, New York, 1908-9; sec. Mo. State Bd. Charities and Corrections, also instr. sociology, U. of Mo., 1909-13; gen. sec. Nat., Conf. Charities and Correction, now Nat. Conf. of Social Work, 1913-20; survey officer, Ill. State Dept. of Pub. Welfare, 1920-21; trust dept., Chicago Trust Co. from 1921; faculty, U. of Chicago, 1921-2. Mem. Nat. Conf. of Social Work, Am. Sociol. Soc. Methodist. Clubs: Quadrangle, City (treas.) Home: Chicago, Ill. †

CROUSE, CECIL IDELL, lawyer, milk co. exec.; b. Freehold, N.J., Mar. 13, 1898; s. William Henry and Matilda (Miller) C.; A.B., Princeton, 1921; LL.B., U. Pa., 1927; m. Elisabeth van de Velde Bunting, Oct. 20, 1934; children—Gerrit Van Asmus, Stephen Miller. Admitted to N.Y. bar, 1929, Chgo. bar, 1931; atty. Coudert Bros., N.Y.C., 1927-28; with Davis, Polk, Wardwell, Gardiner & Reed, N.Y.C., 1928-30, Cutting, Moore & Sidley, Chgo., 1930-32; with law dept. The Borden Co., 1932-67, asst. v.p. charge law dept., 1941-53, v.p. charge law dept., 1953-67, also director; director of The Borden Co., Ltd., Toronto, Member of Am., N.Y. State bar assns., Assn. Bar City of N.Y. Clubs: Union League (N.Y.C.); Wee Burn Country (Darien). Home: Darien, Conn. Died July 31, 1983.

CROW, ALLEN BENJAMIN, business exec.; b. St. Louis, June 4, 1887; s. Benjamin Franklin and Amanda S. (Allen) C.; student Colo. Coll., 1909-11; A.B., Columbia, 1913; student Detroit Inst. Tech., 1922, U.S. Forest Products Lab., 1925; LL.D., U. Detroit, 1941; m. Eleanor G. Thomas, July 24, 1913 (deceased November 14, 1961); children—Walter Allen, Agnes Louise (Mrs. Ray A. Coppenger). Office secretary Y.M.C.A., Keokuk, Iowa, 1906-07, membership sec., Colorado Springs, 1907-09, gen. sec., Prospect Park br., Bklyn., 1913-16, gen. sec., Evanston, Ill., 1916-18, asso. personnel sec. nat. war work council, Chgo., 1918-19, city indsl. sec., Detroit, 1919-21; Mich. dir. China Famine Fund, 1921; sales, advt. mgr. Strand Lumber Co., Detroit, 1921-25; asst. to pres. F.M. Sibley Lumber Co., and affiliates, 1925-44; founder, pres. Econ. Club of Detroit, 1934-62; dir. Wabeek State Bank, 1942-55; trustee First Liquidating Corp., 1942-49. Dir. Music Settlement Sch., Salvation Army; mem. adv. bd. United Found.; mem. Civic Searchlight. Recipient award Jr. Achievement of S.E. Mich., 1958. Mem. Detroit Bd. Commerce, Detroit Real Estate Bd., Am. Acad. Polit. Sci., Detroit Comml. Secs., Newcomen Soc. Eng., Detroit Com. Fgn. Relations, Columbia Club Mich. (pres.), Engring. Soc. Detroit, Phi Beta Kappa, Phi Gamma Delta, Alpha Kappa Psi. Republican. Bapt. Mason (K.T.) Clubs: Economic (dir.), Adcraft, Aero of Mich., Detroit Golf. Home: Detroit, Mich. †

CROW, LESTER DONALD, teacher educator, author; b. Dundee, Ohio, Mar. 31, 1897; s. William Caldwell and Mary (Olmstead) C.; m. Alice von Bauer, June 11, 1927 (dec. Jan. 1966); m. Rosamond M. Hardy, July 9, 1969. A.B., Ohio U., 1923, L.H.D. (hon.), 1972; M.A., N.Y. U., 1924, Ph.D., 1927; LL.D., St. Lawrence U., 1975; Litt.D., Mt. Union Coll., 1976; L.H.D., Bklyn. Coll., 1983. Tchr. high schs., Ohio, 1919-22, Pelham, N.Y., 1924-26; prof. edn. Mary Washington U., Fredericksburg, Va., 1926-27; asst. prof. edn. Leigh U., Bethlehem, Pa., 1927-28; prof. N.Y. U., 1929-30; dir. edn. Pelham Inst., N.Y.C., 1930-32; mem. faculty Bklyn. Coll., 1932-67, prof., 1958-67, emeritus prof. edn., 1967-83; mem. com. to evaluate secondary schs. Middle Atlantic States Colls. and Secondary Schs., 1947-49; mem. U.S. Commn. for Tchr. Edn. Program, Japan, 1950-51. Author: numerous books including An Introduction to Education, 3d edit, 1974, Educational Psychology, rev. edit, 1963, Introduction to Guidance, 2d edit, 1961, Child Psychology, 1953, Readings in General Psychology, 1954, Sex Education in a Growing Family, 1959, How to Study, 1963, Psychology and Human Adjustment, 1967, General Psychology, rev. edit, 1972, Human Development and Adjustment, 1973, Autobiography, As the Crow Flies, 1977, Personality, 1978, Self-Discipline, 1980, Psychology of Childhood, 1981; contbr. articles to profl. jours. Pres. Midwood Park Property Assn., Bklyn., 1955-65. Recipient Certificate of Merit Ohio U. Alumni Assn., 1970, Alumni award Mt. Union Coll., 1974; Lester D. Crow room named in his honor Bklyn. Coll., 1983. Mem. Am. Personnel and Guidance Assn. (life), N.Y. Acad. Sci. (life), Kappa Delta Pi (hon. life), Phi Delta Kappa (life). Club: N.Y. Schoolmaster's (past pres). Home: Hollywood, Fla. Died June 30, 1983.

CROWNS, GEORGE HENRY, fraternal ins. exec.; b. Kaukauna, Wis., May 9, 1888; s. Cornelius and Mary (Ryan) C.; LL.B., Marquette U., 1915; m. Henrietta Kizerow, Sept. 9, 1919 (dec. Dec. 1930). Admitted to Wis. bar, 1916, practiced in Kewaunee, 1916-17; county judge Kewaunee County, Wis., 1925-44; dir. Catholic Order of Foresters, Chgo., 1936-44, hig sec., 1944-56, high chief ranger, from 1956. Dir. Ins. Fedn. Ill., Chgo. Served as lt., U.S. Army, 1917-19. Mem. Wis. Bar Assn. (past pres. 14th Jud. Circuit), Am. Legion (past comdr. Kewaunee), Third Div. Soc. U.S. Army, Izaak Walton League, Nat., Ill. fraternal congresses Am., Nat. Council Cath. Men. K.C. Home: Nekoosa, Wis. †

CRUIKSHANK, BURLEIGH, clergyman; b. Montreal, Can., June 4, 1890; s. Peter and Elizabeth (Scott) C.; came to U.S., 1890, naturalized 1918; student, Blair Acad., Blairstown, N.J., 1910-12; A.B., Washington and Jefferson Coll., Washington, Pa., 1915, hon. D.D., 1927; student Princeton Theol. Seminary, 1915-18, Princeton Univ. Grad. Sch., 1916-17; hon. LL.D., Beaver Coll., Pa., 1935; m. Gladys Taylor, 1915; 1 dau., Priscilla (Mrs. Theodore W. Lacy); m. 2d, Barbara Book, Nov. 26, 1928; children—Martha Book, Burleigh. Minister, Presbyn. Ch., Chatham, N.J., 1918-21; asst. minister, First Presbyn. Ch., Pittsburgh, Pa., 1921-22; minister, Westminster Presbyn. Ch., Steubenville, O., 1922-28, St. Paul Presbyn. Ch., Phila., Pa., 1928-41, The Presbyn. Ch. of Chestnut Hill, Phila., Pa., from 1941. Selected All-Am. football center, 1915. Mem. Phi Kappa Psi. Republican. Presbyterian. Clubs: Union League (Philadelphia), Philadelphia Cricket. Home: Philadelphia, PA. †

CRUM, MASON, univ. prof.; b. Rowesville, S.C., Nov. 22, 1887; s. W. C. and Nonie (Neeley) C.; A.B., Wofford Coll., 1909; student Vanderbilt U., 1910, Harvard, 1912; Ph.D., University of South Carolina, 1925, Doctor of Letters, 1950; married Katherine Howell, April 20, 1914; children—Mason (dec.), Frances (Mrs. Colin Munroe), Kit (Mrs. Frank M. Irwin), Mary, Pat, Madison. Ordained to the ministry of the Methodist Church, 1923; prof. of religious education, Columbia College, 1920-30; asso. prof. Bibl. lit. Duke, 1930-50, prof., 1950-57, emeritus, 1957 from. Mem. N.C. Coll. Teachers of Religion (past pres.), Nat. Council Family Life, White House Conf. Children and Youth. Am. Assn. for Advancement of Sci., Am. Assn. Univ. Profs., N.C. Edn. Assn., Inst. Afro-Am. Studies, Methodist Hist. Soc. (v.p. Southeastern jurisdiction), Southeastern Council Family Relations (v.p.). Chi Phi, Omicron Delta Kappa, Pi Gamma Mu. Democrat. Club: Duke U. Faculty. Author, several books including Store of Lake Junaluska, 1950; The Negro in the Methodist Church, 1950.†

CUDDY, LUCY HON, banker; b. Waldron, Ark., Aug. 2, 1889; d. Daniel and Maggie (Gaines) Hon; m. Warren N. Cuddy, Aug. 15, 1917; children—David Warren, Daniel Hon. A.B., U. Ark., 1911. Tchr. high schs., Ark., Alaska, 1911-17; dir. 1st Nat. Bank, Anchorage, from 1942, chmn. bd., from 1958. Mem. Anchorage Women's Club (hon.), chmn. art show, 1952; chmn. bd. Anchorage council Girl Scouts, 1935-41; chmn. 1st drive Anchorage United Good Neighbors, 1956; bd. regents U. Alaska, 1957-63. Recipient Distinguished Alumna citation U. Ark., 1961. Mem. Cook Inlet Hist. Soc. Democrat. Home: Anchorage, AK.

CUDKOWICZ, GUSTAVO, exptl. pathologist; b. Zurich, Switzerland, July 27, 1927; came to U.S., 1959, naturalized, 1969; s. Isidoro and Adele (Weinstock) C.; m. Adriana Vitta, Oct. 6, 1957; children—Elena Mara, Ariel David, Merit Ester. B.A., Liceo Alessandro DaFano, Milan, Italy, 1946; M.D., U. Milan, 1952. Intern U. Hosps., Milan, Italy, 1952; resident radiology Nat. Cancer Inst., Milan, 1953-55; fellow biochemistry U. Uppsala, Sweden, 1953-54; fellow biology div. Oak Ridge Nat. Lab., Tenn., 1960, biologist, 1961-65; asst. prof. dept. gen. pathology U. Milano Sch. Medicine and Nat. Cancer Inst., 1955-59; asso. cancer research scientist Roswell Park Meml. Inst., Buffalo, 1965-67, prin. research scientist, 1967-69; asso. research prof. microbiology SUNY, Buffalo, 1967-69, prof. pathology and microbiology, 1969—; mem. tumor immunology sci. rev. group Nat. Cancer Inst., NIH, 1972-73; co-organizer theme 4th Internat. Congress of Immunology, Paris, France, 1980; ad hoc mem. sci. rev. com. NIH, 1972—, Am. Cancer Soc., 1978—. Editor: Tumors and Microbes, 1978, Natural and Induced Cell-Mediated Cytotoxicity, 1979; editorial bd.: Transplantation, 1972-75, Immunological Communications, 1972—, Jour. of Immunopharmacology, 1978—, Jour. of Reticuloendothelial Soc, 1979—, Cancer Immunology and Immunotherapy, 1981—. Served with M.C. Italian Army, 1956-57. Italian Nat. Research Council fellow, 1952; Internat. Atomic Energy Agy. fellow, 1960; Internat. Eleanor Roosevelt Cancer fellow, 1976; NIH grantee, 1969—; Am. Cancer Soc. grantee, 1968-72, 79—. Mem. Am. Assn. Pathologists, Am. Assn. for Cancer Research, Reticuloendothelial Soc., Internat. Soc. Exptl. Hematology, Soc. for Exptl. Biology and Medicine, Transplantation Soc., Am. Assn. Immunologists, AAAS. Discoverer of natural resistance to bone marrow transplants. Home: Amherst NY Office: Buffalo NY *

CUKOR, GEORGE DEWEY, motion picture director; b. N.Y.C., July 7, 1899; s. Victor F. and Helen (Gross) C. Began as asst. stage mgr. N.Y. prodns.; directed many N.Y. prodns. starring such players as Ethel Barrymore, Jeanne Eagels, Laurette Taylor, etc.; stage dir., Empire Theatre, N.Y.C., for Frohman Co., 1926-29, dir. and mgr., Lyceum Theatre, Rochester, N.Y., 1921-28; entered motion picture field, 1929; became dir. for, Metro-Goldwyn-Mayer Corp., 1933; dir.: Little Women, 1933, David Copperfield, 1934, Romeo and Juliet, Camille, 1936, Holiday, 1937, Zaza, 1938, The Women, 1939, Susan and God, 1939, Philadelphia Story, 1940, A Woman's Face, The Twins, Keeper of the Flame, 1942, Gaslight, 1943, Winged Victory, 1943, Double Life, 1947, Edward My Son, 1948, Adam's Rib, 1949, A Life of Her Own, Born Yesterday, 1950, Kitty and the Marriage Broker, 1951, The Marrying Kind, 1951, Pat and Mike, 1952, The Actress, 1953, It Should Happen To You, 1954, A Star is Born, 1954, Bhowani Junction, 1955, Les Girls, 1957, Wild is the Wind, 1957, Heller in Pink Tights, 1958, Let's Make Love, 1959, The Chapman Report, 1961, My Fair Lady, 1964 (Acad. award), Justine, 1968, Travels With My Aunt, 1972, Love Among the Ruins, 1974 (Emmy award), The Blue Bird, 1976, The Corn Is Green, 1979, Rich and Famous, 1981. Hon. discharge U.S. Army. Home: Los Angeles, Calif. Died Jan. 24, 1983.

CULBERTSON, WALTER LEROY, petroleum co. exec.; b. Dederick, Mo., July 29, 1918; s. Alfred and Ethel Ida (Belong) C.; B.S. in Mech. Engring., Kans. State U., 1939; m. Wanda Marian Atkins, Sept. 30, 1940; children—Philip, Robert. With Phillips Petroleum Co., Bartlesville, Okla., 1939-80, now sr. v.p. corp. planning and budgeting. Mem. ASME, Nat. Soc. Profl. Engrs., Am. Inst. Chem. Engrs. Republican. Mem. Christian Ch. (Disciples of Christ). Club: Bartlesville Hillcrest Country. Home: Bartlesville, Okla. Died July 12, 1980.

CULLER, ELMER AUGUSTIN KURTZ, prof. psychology; b. Louisville, O., Oct. 11, 1889; s. John and Amanda (Kurtz) C.; student Mt. Union Coll., Alliance, O., 1905-07; A.B., Juniata Coll., Huntingdon, Pa., 1910; B.D., Union Theol. Sem., New York, 1913; student U. of Berlin, 1913-14, U. of Leipzig, 1914-15; Ph.D., U. of Chicago, 1922; unmarried. Instr. in psychology, Ohio State U., 1916-20, U. of Wis., 1920-23; asso. in psychology, U. of Ill., 1923-27, asst. prof., 1927-28, asso. prof., 1928-36, prof., 1936-38; prof. psychology, U. Rochester,

1938-54, emeritus, dir. Psychology and Animal Hearing labs.; asso. professor U. of Chicago, summer, 1929. Awarded Howard Crosby Warren medal by Soc. of Exptl. Psychologists, 1938. Mem. council of dirs. and chmn., program com., Am. Psychol. Assn.; pres. Midwestern Psychol. Assn.; v. chmn., Div. anthropology and psychology, Nat. Research Council; mem., sect, com. for psychology, Am. Assn. for Advancement of Science; mem. of corp., Psychometric Soc.; mem. bd. dirs. Eastern Psychol. Assn. Fellow A.A.A.S., Acoustical Soc. America; member Rochester Acad. of Science; Am. Soc. for Research in Psychosomatic problems., Am. Physiol. Soc., Soc. of Exptl. Psychologists, Sigma Xi. Mem. Ch. of the Brethren. Clubs: Appalachian Mt.; Faculty, X Club (University of Rochester). Contbr. articles on hearing and conditioning to profl. jours. Asso. or cons. editor Jour. of Comparative Psychology, Jour. of Exptl. Psychology, Jour. of Psychology, Psychol. Record, Psychometrika. Home: Columbus, OH. †

CULLOM, NEIL P., lawyer; b. N.Y. City, Mar. 4, 1887; s. Cornelius P. and Rassalee (Gardenhire) C.; B.S., Vanderbilt U., 1908; LL.B., Yale, 1911; m. Janet DeLong, Jan. 12, 1922. Admitted to N.Y. State bar, 1912, and from practiced in N.Y. City; dir. R. Hoe & Co., Inc. (also chmn. bd. from 1950), 72d St. & Park Corp., Unity Fire Ins. Co. of New York. Mem. Am. Bar Assn., Assn. of the Bar of the City of New York, New York Law Institute. Clubs: The University, Down Town Association. Home: New York, N.Y. †

CULLUM, ROBERT BROOKS, retail company executive; b. Dallas, May 10, 1912; s. Ashley Wilson and Eloise (Brooks) C.; B.S., So. Methodist U., 1933; m. Dorothy Rogers, July 6, 1934; children—Betsy Cullum (Mrs. George Bolin), Sally (Mrs. Houston Holmes Jr.), Dan Rogers, Robert Brooks. Chmn. bd. dirs. Cullum Companies, Inc., Dallas; dir. Dallas Fed. Savs. & Loan Assn., Dallas Power & Light Co., Dr. Pepper Co., Republic Nat. Bank Dallas. Pres. State Fair of Tex., 1966, pres. Dallas Citizens Council, 1972; dir. Dallas Council World Affairs, dir. North Tex. Commn., 1972. Bd. dirs. Blue Cross Blue Shield Tex., Tex. Research Found.; trustee Callier Speech and Hearing Center, Southwestern Med. Found.; trustee, mem. bd. govs. So. Methodist U. Mem. Nat. Assn. Food Chains, Republic Assn. Food Chains, Super Market Inst. (pres. 1966-67), Dallas C. of C. Cotton Bowl Athletic Assn., So. Methodist U. Alumni Assn. Methodist. Clubs: Chaparral, City, Dallas, Dallas Country, Eldorado Country Imperial, Koon Kreek Klub. Home: Dallas, Tex. Died Dec. 12, 1981.

CUMMING, WILLIAM ALBON, Can. govt. research and devel. exec.; b. Detroit, July 16, 1926; s. Clyde and Minerva (Good) C.; m. Phyllis Jean Miller, Aug. 30, 1947; children—Brian C., Gordon B. B.Sc. in Engring. Physics, Queen's U., Kingston, Ont., Can., 1947. With Nat. Research Council of Can., Ottawa, Ont., 1947—, asso. v.p. labs., 1973-74, v.p. ops., 1974-76, v.p. labs., 1976-78, sr. v.p., 1978—. Recipient Pub. Service Outstanding Achievement award Can. Govt., 1985. Mem. IEEE (sr.), Assn. Profl. Engrs. Ont., Engring. Inst. Can., Can. Soc. Elec. Engring. Home: Ottawa, Ont., Can. Died May 8, 1985; buried Beechwood Cemetery, Ottawa.

CUMMINGS, L(ESLIE) O(LIN), univ. dean; b. Baltimore, Md., June 19, 1888; s. Olin Marshall and Hattie Eleanor (Dodge) C.; A.B., Harvard, 1910, A.M., 1911, grad. study, 1912-14, Ed.D., 1921; m. Grace A. Preble, June 10, 1914 (died May 11, 1939); children—Stearns Preble, Bruce (dec.), Leslie; m. 2d, Sara Louise Allen, Mar. 21, 1942; children—Allen, Sala, Eleanor, Lewis, Margaret. Principal Stone Grammar Sch., Walpole, Mass., 1910-12; dir. playgrounds, Walpole, summers 1911, 12, Somerville, Mass. summers 1912-13; supt. schs., Franklin and Wrentham, Mass., 1914-18; instr. in edn., Harvard, 1920-21, asst. prof. edn., 1921-27, asso. prof., 1927-30; prof. edn. and head of dept., U. of Buffalo, 1930-31, dean of Sch. of Edn. from 1931, and dir. of Summer Session from 1934. Dir., mem. exec. com. Memorial Center and Urban League of Nat. Urban League, Buffalo, pres. 1938; consultant Ednl. Policies Com. Mem. Am. Assn. of Sch. Administrators, Am. Assn. Univ. Profs., Phi Beta Kappa, Phi Delta Kappa, SigmaAlphaEpsilon. Mason. Home:Orchard Park, N.Y.†

CUMMINGS, NATHAN, industrialist; b. St. John, N.B., Can., Oct. 14, 1896; s. David and Esther (Saxe) C.; m. Ruth Lillian Kellert, Dec. 30, 1919 (dec. Mar. 1952); children: Beatrice Violet Mayer, Herbert Kellert, Alan Harris. Ed., Economist Tng. Sch., N.Y.C.; hon. degree, Catholic U. Am., Kenyon Coll., The Citadel, U.N.B. (Can.), Tel Aviv U., Israel. Shoe bus., 1914-17, wholesale shoe bus., 1917-24, shoe mfg., 1924-30, importing gen. mdse., 1930-34, mfg. buscuits and candy, all in Can., 1934-38; pres. C.D. Kenny Co., Balt., 1939-85; acquired Sprague Warner & Co., Chgo., 1942, Western Grocer Co. and; Marshall Canning Co. of, Marshalltown, Iowa, 1944; acquired Reid, Murdoch & Co., Chgo., 1945; chm. bd. Consol. Grocers Corp., Chgo., 1947-68; chm. bd. Consol. Grocers Corp. (name changed to Consol. Foods Corp.), 1954, since which time more than 50 cos. have been acquired, now hon. chmn.; mem. exec. com.; dir. Gen. Dynamics Corp. Governing life mem. Art Inst. Chgo.; hon. trustee Met. Mus. of Art; patron Montreal Mus. Fine Arts; patron, governing mem. Mpls. Soc. Fine Arts; mem. citizens bd. U. Chgo.; hon. trustee Mt. Sinai Sch. Medicine; life gov. Jewish Gen. Hosp., Montreal; patron Lincoln Center Performing Arts. Decorated officier French Legion of Honor; commendatore Order of Merit Italy; commandador Order of Merit Peru). Clubs: Chicago; Canadian (N.Y.C.), Board Room (N.Y.C.). Home: New York, N.Y. Died Feb. 19, 1985.

CUMMINS, JAMES DIRICKSON, clergyman; b. Smyrna, Del., Sept. 12, 1888; s. Alfred Lee and Elva Culbreth (Carrow) C.; St. Stephen's Coll., 1907; U. of Pa., 1910; Phila. Div. Sch., 1913; m. Katharine Whaley, Oct. 4, 1917; 1 son, James Dirickson. Deacon, 1913, priest, 1914, P.E. Ch.; missionary, Diocese of Ore., 1913-15; curate, St. Paul's Chapel, Trinity Parish, New York, 1915-16; rector St. Paul's Parish, Centerville, Md., 1916-19; elected headmaster St. Paul's Sch. for Boys, Baltimore (declined), 1919; dean and rector of Christ Ch. Cathedral, New Orleans, La., 1919-26; summer special preacher Trinity Church, Boston, Grace Church, N.Y., York Harbor, Maine, 1923-26; archdeacon of East La., 1920-26; asso. minister, Emanuel Ch., Boston, 1926-30; acting vicar Beaconsfield, England, summer 1930; rector Ch. of the Holy Name, Swampscott, 1930-50, rector emeritus from 1950; delegate to General Convention, 1919, 22; del. Provincial Synods, 5 times; high sch. teacher English and ancient history, 1918-19. V.p. Prison Reform Assn. of La., 1920-24; La. del. Am. Prison Congress, 1921, 22; mem. com. of visitors to Federal Leper Hosp., 1920-26; mem. Gen. Com. Am. Ch. Congress from 1923; mem. bd. dirs. New Orleans Charity Orgn. Soc., 1925-27; formerly pres. Church School Union (Boston); mem. exec. com. Episcopal City Mission, 1929-32; trustee Public Library 1939-48; also member many diocesan and civic cons. Fellow Am. Geog. Society; mem. Sons of the Revolution. Mason (K.T.). Clubs: University, Harvard Musical Assn., Appalachian Mountain. Lecturer; special teacher; writer of articles and criticisms; traveled widely; spent 4 months in Palestine and Egypt, 1921. Home: Ocean City, Md. †

CUNNINGHAM, ALAN GORDON, British fgn. service; b. England, May 1, 1887; s. Prof. D. J. Cunningham; student Royal Mil. Acad., Woolwich, Eng. Received 1st commn. 1906, served in World War I as brig. maj. and Gen. Staff Officer (2d grade); Gen. Staff officer, Straits Settlements, 1919-21; at Naval Staff Coll., 1925; commd. brevet lt. col., 1928; instr. Machine Gun Sch., 1928-31; commd. lt. col., 1935; at Imperial Defense Coll., 1937; comdr. 1st div. Royal Arty., 1937-38; commd. maj. gen., 1938; comdr. 5th Anti-Aircraft Div., 1938; comdr. 66th and 51st Highland Divs., 1940; lt. gen. in command British forces in victorious Ethiopian campaign; field comdr. 8th Army; high commr. Palestine and Transjordan until British withdrawal. Awarded Distinguished Service Order, Mil. Cross; Knight Grand Cross of the Order of St. Michael and St. George, Knight Comdr. of the Bath; Comdr. Legion of Merit (U.S.). Address: London, Eng. †

CUNNINGHAM, FLOYD FRANKLIN, geographer, educator; b. Flat Rock, Ill., Dec. 24, 1899; s. Carl Homer and Lillie Alberta (Seitzinger) C.; student Eastern Ill. U., Charleston, 1916-18; B.Ed., Ill. State U., Normal, 1926; postgrad. U. Chgo., 1926-27; A.M., Clark U., 1928, Ph.D., 1930. Tchr. rural schs., Crawford County, Ill., 1918-22; prin. Emerson Sch., Berwyn, Ill., 1925-27; instr. geography Ill. State U., 1925; prof., head dept. geography U. North Ala., Florence, 1929-47, dir. visual edn., 1938-47, instr. civil air regulations, air nav. and meteorology, 1939-42; vis. prof. geography George Peabody Coll. for Tchrs., Nashville, summer 1935; prof. geography Am. U., Biarritz, France, 1945-46; lectr. in geography, info. and edn. div. U.S. Army in Germany and Austria, 1946; Fulbright lectr. in geography Am. U. and Ain Shams U., Cairo, Egypt, 1953-54; prof., chmn. dept. geography So. Ill. U., Carbondale, 1955-58, prof. geography, dir. lab. climatology, 1958-66, prof. emeritus, 1966-84; distinguished vis. prof. geography Western Ky. U., 1966-70. Served with U.S. Shipping Bd. in Can., Eng. and Germany, 1919; del. from Ala. to Internat. Geog. Congress, Warsaw, Poland, 1934. Recipient Distinguished Service award Western Ky. U.; Disting. Alumni award Ill. State U., 1978; hon. Ky. col. Fellow Nat. Council for Geog. Edn. (pres. 1941-43), Am. Geog. Soc.; mem. Assn. Am. Geographers, AAUP (pres. So. Ill. chpt. 1959-60), Ill. Geog. Soc. (pres. 1948-49), Ill. Acad. Sci., Nat. Travelers Club, Am. Assn. for UN, Am. Soil Conservation Soc., Am. Forestry Assn., Am. Platform Assn., Ill., Crawford County hist. socs., Ill., So. Ill. geneal. socs., Kappa Delta Pi, Gamma Theta Upsilon. Democrat. Methodist (trustee). Kiwanian (life mem.). Author: Laboratory Manual in the Geography of North America, 1930; (with C.F. Jones) Laboratory Manual in the Geography of South America, 1931; (with Samford and McCall) You and Regions Near and Far, 1964, You and the United States, 1964, You and the Americas, 1965, You and the World, 1966; 1001 Questions Answered About Water Resources, 1967. Contbr. articles to profl. jours. Condr. travel study courses around world. Home: Carbondale, Ill. Died Apr. 22, 1984.

CUNNINGHAM, HARRY FRANCIS, ret. army officer; b. Washington, D.C., Apr. 15, 1888; s. Joseph Harry and Theodora (Bradley) C.; ed. Worcester Polytechnical Institute and various ateliers, Paris, France; Ecole Supérieure de Guerre, Paris; m. Adèle Ferrand; children—Harry Francis (U.S. fgn. Service), Joseph Harry II (Air Forces). Was archtl. draftsman in the Supervising Architect's office, U.S. Treasury Dept., 1905-09; later with Wood, Donn & Deming, Hornblower & Marshall, Clarke Waggaman; est. office on own account, 1911; architect in devastated regions, France, 1920-22; in Washington, D.C., 1922-24, Florida 1924-28; with Goodhue Associates, in charge continuation Neb. Capitol, 1928-30; prof. architecture, U. of Neb., 1930-34; practicing in Washington, 1934-40; re-entered Army, 1940. Works: Dennis Hotel and Shuffleboard Club and numerous residences, St. Petersburg, Fla.; Burning Tree Club Bldg., Washington; Tower of Neb. State Capitol, Lincoln, Neb.; plans for 17 villages Dept. of Aisne, France; Brazilian Embassy and Heatherington Apts., Washington, also numerous residences. Served as capt. and maj., inf., machine guns, in A.E.F.; lecturer on citizenship, Camp Dix, N.J., 1932-35; active Reserve officer (maj. and lt. col., inf.); recalled to active duty in Army on May 10, 1940, as lt. col., Gen. Staff, in Mil. Intelligence Service; promoted col., June 12, 1941; chief of first U.S. Mission to Free French Africa, Aug. 1941-Feb. 1942; military observer in Free French Africa and Belgian Congo, 1942-43; participated with Free French (Tchad troops) in Fezzan-Tripoli Campaign, Dec. 1942-Jan. 1943. Transferred to Air Corps, Oct. 1943. Asst. C. of S., A-2, Fifth Air Force, 1943-45; mem. Central Intelligence Group, Mar.-Sept., 1946; faculty of Armed Forces Staff College, Oct. 1946-July 1947; P & O Div., Army Gen. Staff July 1947-Dec. 1948, special consultant since January 1949. Hon. corporal, Tchad Regt. Senegalese Riflemen. Medals: Victory, Army of Occupation (Germany, World War I; Japan, World War II), National Defense, Europe-Africa Theatre, American Theatre, Pacific Theatre, Philippine (American); Legion of Honor, Croix de Guerre with Palm, Fighting French Forces, Colonial Wars, Verdun (French); Officer Oder of the Lion (Belgium). Member Am. Mil. Inst., Mil. Order Fgn. Wars, Mil. Order Carabao, Mil. Order World War, National Sojourners, Heroes of '76, American Institute Architects (emeritus). Fellow, American Geographical Soc. Republican. Mason. Clubs: Grolier, New York. Author various books on architecture and numerous articles on architectural and military subjects. Home: Lincoln, Neb. †

CUNNINGHAM, JAMES VINCENT, poet; b. Cumberland, Md., Aug. 23, 1911; s. James Joseph and Anna Mattingly (Finan) C.; m. Barbara Francesca Gibbs, June 18, 1937 (div. 1942); 1 dau., Marjorie Ann (Mrs. George Lupien); m. Dolora Gallagher, Mar. 26, 1945 (div. 1949); m. Jessie MacGregor Campbell, June 3, 1950. Student, St. Mary's (Kans.) Coll., 1928; A.B., Stanford, 1934, Ph.D., 1945. Instr. Stanford, 1937-45; asst. prof. U. Hawaii, 1945-46, U. Chgo., 1946-52, U. Va., 1952-53; asso. prof. then prof. English Brandeis U., Waltham, Mass., 1953-85, Univ. prof., 1976-80, emeritus, 1980-85, chmn. dept., 1953-59, 61-62, 68-69; chmn. Brandeis U. (Sch. Humanities), 1960-61, 70-71; Vis. prof. Harvard, 1952, U. Wash., 1956, Ind. U., 1961, U. Calif. at Santa Barbara, 1963, Washington U., St. Louis, 1976. Author: The Helmsman, 1942, The Judge is Fury, 1947, Doctor Drink, 1950, The Quest of the Opal, 1950, Woe or Wonder; The Emotional Effect of Shakespearean Tragedy, 1951, The Exclusions of a Rhyme: Poems and Epigrams, 1960, Tradition and Poetic Structure, 1960, The Journal of John Cardan, 1964, To What Strangers, What Welcome, 1964, The Renaissance in England, 1967, The Collected Poems and Epigrams, 1971, Collected Essays, 1977, Dickinson: Lyric and Legend, 1980. Guggenheim fellow, 1959-60, 67; Nat. Endowment for Arts grantee, 1966-67. Home: Sudbury, Mass. Died Mar. 30, 1985.

CUNNINGHAM, JOHN BISSELL, educator, mining engr.; b. Cass City, Mich., Dec. 31, 1887; s. John William and Margaret (Bissell) C.; student Albion (Mich.) Coll., 1907-10; E.M., Mich. Coll. of Mines, Houghton, 1913, M.S., 1931; student Columbia, 1916; m. Blanche Briggs, Dec. 17, 1926; 1 dau., Sally. Instr., Mich. Coll. of Mines, 1913-16, asst. prof., 1916-17, prof., 1917-25; prof. of metallurgy, Univ. of Ariz. from 1925; metallurgist, U.S. Bur. of Mines, summers, 1943, 44, 50. Mem. Am. Inst. of Mining and Metall. Engrs., A.A.A.S., Am. Soc. of Engring. Edn., Tau Beta Pi. Mason. Author Bur. of Mines publs. on Lithium, 1948. Holder patents on molybdenum. Address: Tucson, Ariz. †

CUNNINGHAM, JOHN PHILLIP, advt. exec.; born Lynn, Mass., Sept. 17, 1897; s. John F. and Mary E. (Ryan) C.; A.B., Harvard Coll., 1919; m. Patricia Fitzpatrick, Oct. 1, 1924. Artist, 1919-21; copywriter for Newell-Emmett Co., N.Y. City, 1921-30; partner Newell-Emmet Advt. Agency, N.Y. City, 1930-50; exec. v.p. Cunningham & Walsh, Inc., 1950-54, pres., 1954-85, also chmn. bd. Dir. N.Y. Heart Assn. Served as ensign, U.S. Navy, 1917-19. Mem. Am. Assn. Advt. Agencies (chmn. of the board, 1952). Roman Catholic. Clubs: University, Union League, Harvard, Lotos, Riverdale Yacht, Nipnichsen. Contbr. articles in advt. publs. Home: Riverdale-on-Hudson, N.Y. Died Feb. 23, 1985.

CUNNINGHAM, PAUL HARVEY, congressman; b. Indiana County, Pa., June 15, 1890; s. Robert Harvey and Sarah Jane (McQuaide) C.; grad. Pa. State Normal Sch., Indiana, Pa., 1911; A.B., U. of Mich., 1914, LL.B., 1915; LL.D., Sterling College, Kansas, 1954; married Harriett French Plummer, Dec. 1918; children—Paul Harvey, Edward Plummer (U.S. Marines; killed in action, Siapan, Nov. 15, 1944), Harriet Sarah; m. 2d Gail Fry, Dec. 26, 1926. Admitted to Mich. bar, 1915, Iowa bar, 1920; practiced at Grand Rapids and Grand Haven, Mich.,

1915-17, Des Moines, Ia., from 1920; mem. law firm Strock, Cunningham, Sloan & Herrick, 1922-29; sr. mem. firm Cunningham & Emery from 1929. Mem. Iowa State Legislature, 1933-36; mem. 77th Congress, 6th Iowa Dist., 78th to 85th, 5th Ia. Dist. Served 1st lt., World War I; former capt. 168th Inf., Ia. Nat. Guard. Dir. Ia. Children's Home Soc. Mem. Sigma Phi Epsilon. Republican. United Presbyn. Mason, Odd Fellow. Clubs: Frontier, Cosmopolitan, Spectator, Six-Foot (Des Moines). Home: Des Moines, Ia. †

CUNNINGHAM, PAUL MILLARD, writer-editor; b. Stigler, Okla., Oct. 25, 1915; s. Marcus and Nora (Modlin) C.; B.A., U. Ark., 1937; m. Marian Frances Wimmers, Feb. 11, 1961; children—Barry, Gary (dec.); stepchildren—John, Daniel, David Schardine. Reporter, Ft. Smith (Ark.) Times-Record and S.W. Am., 1937; reporter Cin. Post (now Post and Times-Star), 1937-68, editorial writer, editor editorial page, 1968-75, asst. editor editorial-op-ed pages, 1975-77. Instr. U. Cin. Eve. Coll., 1945-55. Home: Cincinnati, Ohio. Died June 17, 1984.

CUNNINGHAM, WILLIAM ALEXANDER, III, army officer; b. Athens, Ga., May 10, 1911; s. William Alexander II and Elizabeth (Ritter) C.; B.S., U.S. Mil. Acad., 1934; m. Madera Maddux, June 16, 1937; children—William Alexander IV, Susan Madera. Commd. 2d lt. U.S. Army, 1934, advanced through grades to maj. gen., 1961; bn. comdr. N. African invasion, 1943; prin. staff officer Okinawan invasion, 1945; assigned Army Gen. Staff, 1948-50, Army War Coll., 1952; plans and policy officer CINCPAC Joint Staff, 1952-55; regtl. comdr. 1st Inf. Div., 1955-57, chief staff, 1957-58; G-3, 8th U.S. Army, 1958-59; asst. div. comdr. 1st Cav. Div., 1959-60; asst. comdt. Command and Gen. Staff Coll., 1960-61; dep. chief staff personnel and adminstrn. Hdqrs. U.S. Army, Europe, 1961-63; comdg. gen. 24th Inf. Div., 1963-65; comdg. gen. Hdqrs. IV U.S. Army Corps., 1965-66; transp. programs coordinator, N.Y.C., 1966-68; asst. gen. mgr. Pacific Architects & Engrs., Saigon, Vietnam, 1968-69; exec. dir. Lake Lanier Devel. Authority, Atlanta, 1969-74. Chief U.S. delegation Council Internat. Mil. Sports, from 1962, hon. mem., from 1963. Decorated Silver Star, Legion of Merit, Bronze Star with 2 oak leaf clusters, Commendation ribbon with 1 oak leaf cluster, Purple Heart, Combat Inf. badge, Presdl. citation, D.S.M., Korean Order of Ulchi. Club: Army and Navy. Home: Mathews, Va. Died Sept. 25, 1983.

CURRY, ARTHUR RAY, librarian; b. Cleburne, Tex., Mar. 21, 1889; s. James Silas and Ella Annie (Ray) Elam C.; B.A., University of Texas, 1916; B.L.S., University of Illinois, 1921; m. Miriam Marguerite Lewis of Indianapolis, Ind., May 28, 1924; children—Jean Eloise, Landon. Teacher consecutively, Abilene (Tex.) Christian Coll., Greenville (Tex.) High Sch., Allen Mil. Acad., Bryan, Tex., until 1919; reference librarian U. of Okla., 1921-23; exec. sec. Pub. Library Commn. of Ind., June 1, 1923-June 1, 1925; librarian Mary Couts Burnett Library, Tex. Christian U., Fort Worth, 1925-33; librarian Rosenberg Library, Galveston, from 1934. Mem. A.L.A. (life), Tex. Library Assn. (treas. 1929-34, 1st v.p. from 1934), Southwestern Library Assn. (treas. from 1934), Galveston Rotary Club (editor "Port Wheel," since 1935). Unitarian. Address: Galveston, Tex. †

CURRY, HASKELL BROOKS, mathematician, educator; b. Millis, Mass., Sept. 12, 1900; s. Samuel S. and Anna (Baright) C.; A.B., Harvard, 1920, A.M., 1924; postgrad. Mass. Inst. Tech., 1920-22; Ph.D., U. Göttingen (Germany), 1930; NRC fellow U. Chgo., 1931-32; Sc.D. (hon.), Curry Coll., 1966; m. Mary Virginia Wheatley, July 3, 1928; children—Anne Wright (Mrs. Richard Shaner Piper), Robert Wheatley. Research asst. in physics Harvard, 1922-23, instr., 1926-27; instr. Princeton, 1928-29; asst. prof. Pa. State U., 1929-33, assoc. prof., 1933-41, prof., 1941-60, Evan Pugh research prof., 1960-66, emeritus, 1966-82; prof., dir. Inst. Foundational Research, U. Amsterdam, 1966-70, emeritus, 1970-82; vis. Andrew Mellon prof. U. Pitts., 1971-72. Mem. Inst. Advanced Study, Princeton, 1938-39; Fulbright research scholar, vis. prof. U. Louvain, Belgium, 1950-51, hon. vis. prof., from 1951; honors examiner Swarthmore Coll., 1936, 37. Mathematician Frankford Arsenal 1942-44, Johns Hopkins Applied Physics Lab., 1944-45, Aberdeen Proving Ground, 1945-46; mem. Conf. Bd. Math. Scis., 1958-63; U.S. nat. com. Internat. Union History and Philosophy of Sci., 1959-63. Trustee Curry Coll., 1940-51. Served as pvt. Harvard unit SATC, 1918. Recipient medal U. Louvain, 1951. Mem. Assn. Symbolic Logic (pres. 1938-40), AAAS (council 1937), Am. Math. Soc. (council 1945-47), Am. Philos. Assn., Math. Assn. Am., Am. Ornithologists Union, Nat. Geog. Soc., Academie Internationale de Philosophie des Sciences (assessaur 1961-65, v.p. 1965-69), Nederlandse Ornithologische Unie, Wiskundig Genootschap to Amsterdam, Sigma Xi, Pi Mu Epsilon, Sigma Pi Sigma. Author: Outlines of a Formalist Philosophy of Mathematics (Amsterdam), 1951; A Theory of Formal Deducibility, rev. edit., 1957; (with Robert Feys) Combinatory Logic, Vol. 1 (Amsterdam), 1958; Foundations of Mathematical Logic, 1963, reprinted, 1977; (with Hindley and Seldin) Combinatory Logic, vol. 2, 1972. Home: State College, Pa. Died Sept. 1, 1982.

CURTIS, CLAUDE DAVIS, college pres.; b. nr. Maryville, Tenn., Dec. 28, 1887; s. Moses Bryant and Eliza (Davis) C.; B.S., Hiwassee Coll., Madisonville, Tenn., 1907; post grad. work, U. of Tenn.; m. Edna Cochran of Maryville, July 30, 1908; children—Hubert Cochran, Charles Robert, Anna Louise. Prin. pub. schs., Friendsville, Tenn., 1907-08; head dept. science, Maryville Poly. Sch., 1908-14; supt. city schs., Maryville, 1914-23; pres. Martha Washington Coll., Abingdon, Va., 1923-31; asso. pres. Sullins Coll., Bristol, Va., from 1931. Mem. Pi Gamma Mu. Republican. Member M.E. Ch., S. Club: Civitan (pres.). Wrote Three Quarters of a Century at Martha Washington College. Home: Abingdon, Va. †

CURTIS, EDWARD ELY, prof. of history; b. Chicago, Ill., July 4, 1888; s. Edward Lewis and Laura Elizabeth (Ely) C.; A.B., Yale Univ., 1910; A.M., Yale Univ. Grad. Sch., 1911, Ph.D., 1916; m. Elizabeth Plant Anketell, June 24, 1914 (dec.); m. 2d, Muriel Anne Streibert, July 15, 1924. Instr. in history, Yale, 1911-15; asst. prof. history, Wellesley Coll., 1916-22, asso. prof. history, 1922-31, Ralph Emerson prof. N. Am. history, Wellesley Coll., from 1931, chmn. dept. of history and polit. science, 1936-42. Mem. Am. Hist. Assn., Am. Polit. Science Assn., Inter-Am. Bibliog. Assn., Am. Soc. Internat. Law. Episcopalian. Author: The British Army in the American Revolution, 1926. Contbr. to sketches in Dictionary of American Biography. Home: Wellesley, Mass. †

CURTIS, FRANCIS DAY, educator; b. Portland, Ore., Aug. 6, 1888; s. Edward David and Frances Gertrude (Case) C.; B.S., U. Ore., 1911, A.M., 1922; fellow, Columbia, 1924, Ph.D., 1924; m. Edith Clements, June 12, 1915; children—Dorothy (Mrs. Tom H. Kinkead), Allison (Mrs. Charles L. Burleigh). Tchr. high sch., Ore., 1911-23; with Sch. Edn., U. Mich., 1924-53, prof., 1933-53, emeritus, from 1953, sec., 1941-47. Chmn. com. on research in teaching sci. U.S. Office of Edn., 1947-52; vis. prof. U. Cal., summers 1931, 48. U. Hawaii, summer 1936. Univ. Texas, summer 1938. U. Ill., summer, 1941, Colorado State Coll. Edn., summer 1942, U. Cal. Los Angeles, 1954. Fellow A.A.A.S. (v.p., chmn. sect. Q, 1948-49); mem. N.E.A. (pres. sci. sect. 1929), Nat. Council Elementary Sci. (pres. 1941), Nat. Assn. Research in Sci. Teaching (pres. 1932), Phi Beta Kappa, Phi Delta Kappa, Delta Tau Delta, Acacia. Republican. Mason. Author: Some Values Derived from Extensive Reading of General Science, 1924; A Digest of Investigations in the Teaching of Science, Vol. I, 1926. Vol. II, 1931, Vol. III, 1939; A Synthesis and Evaluation of Subject Matter Topics in General Science, 1929; Investigations of Vocabulary in Textbooks of Science for Secondary Schs., 1938. Joint author textbooks of gen. sci., 1929. 36, 43, 49, 58; of biology for secondary schs. 1934, 40, 49, 58. Research editor Sci. Edn., 1935-46; contbr. Year Books of Nat. Edn. Assn. Dept. Superintendence, 1927, 28. High School Curriculum Reorganization, 1933. Year Books N.S. S.E., 1932, 35, 47, Research Bulletin. A.E.R.A., 1934, 37, 42, 45. Joint Year Book A.E.R.A. and D.C.I., 1938. Mental Measurements Year Books. 1938, 40; also to ednl. jours. Home: Ann Arbor, Mich. †

CURTIS, JAMES WASHINGTON, army officer; b. Jefferson City, Mo., Oct. 3, 1888; s. Richard Washington and Virginia Lee (Cooper) C.; ed. Ky. Mil. Inst. and U. of Pa.; grad U.S. Inf. Sch., 1923. Command and Gen. Staff Sch., 1928; m. Muriel Alberta Cothran, Feb. 7, 1924; children—Virginia Cothran, James Washington. Commd. lt., inf., U.S. Army, 1917, advanced through the grades to brig. gen., 1943; instr. Cornell U., 1928-32; mem. faculty, Inf. Sch., 1935-39; chief of staff Replacement and School Command, Army Ground Forces. Awarded Silver Star, French Fourragère. Mem. Phi Kappa Tau. Mason (K.T., Shriner). Home: El Paso, Tex. †

CURTIS, JOHN KIMBERLY, physician; b. Redlands, Calif., Mar. 14, 1905; s. Clinton James and Lucy (Kimberly) C.; B.A., Yale, 1928; M.D., Columbia, 1932; m. Margaret McAllister, Oct. 5, 1936; children—Kimberly J., James McAllister, Catherine. Intern, Presbyn. Hosp., N.Y.C., 1932-34, asst. attending physician, 1935-42; resident 1st div. Bellevue Hosp., N.Y.C., 1934-35; asso. prof. U. Wis., Madison, 1951-53, prof. internal medicine, 1953-76, emeritus prof., 1976-85; chief medicine VA Hosp., Madison, 1951-68. Served with M.C., USNR, 1942-46; ETO. Mem. Wis. Heart Assn. (pres. 1956-57), Dane County Med. Soc. (pres. 1952-53). Research pulmonary physiology. Home: Madison, Wis. Died July 5, 1985.

CURTIS, JOSIAH MONTGOMERY, publishing company executive; b. Elm Grove, W.Va., Nov. 11, 1905; s. Allen and Zelda (Epstein) C.; m. Alma Heidee, Oct. 13, 1945. A.B., W.Va. U., 1928, L.H.D., 1966; postgrad., U. Buffalo, 1931-32. Reporter, sub-editor Wheeling (W.Va.) News Register, 1928-29; city editor Morgantown (W.Va.) Dominion-News, 1930-31; reporter Buffalo Evening News, 1931-34, asst. city editor, 1934-37, city editor, 1937-42; asso. dir. Am. Press Inst., 1947-51, dir., 1951-65, exec. dir., 1965-67; v.p. Knight-Ridder Newspapers, Miami, Fla., 1967-79, cons., 1979-82; prof. Grad. Sch. Journalism, Columbia; lectr. journalism Columbia, other univs.; Mem. adv. bd. Am. Press Inst., 1968-82; mem. journalism com. DePauw U., 1968-82. Served to maj. AUS, 1942-45. Nat. fellow Sigma Delta Chi, 1958; cited by Philippine Govt., 1958. Mem. Sigma Delta Chi, Phi Delta Theta. Home: Miami, Fla. Died Nov. 25, 1982.

CURTIS, PAUL ALLAN, JR., shooting expert; b. New York, Mar. 28, 1889; s. Paul A. and Catherine Irving (Mackenzie) C.; ed. Trinity Sch. (New York), Friends Acad, (Locust Valley, L.I.), and at Glasgow, Scotland; m. Sarah Duval Floyd, of Upperville, Va., June 2, 1917 (died Apr. 13, 1924); 1 son, Paul A.; m. 2d, Alice Gaffney of Boston, July 30, 1924; m. 3d, Mabel Blackburn Smith, of Hamilton, Bermuda; 1 son, Colin Mackenzie. Asst. illuminating engr. New York Edison Co., 1911-12; with Macbeth-Evans Co., Pittsburg, Pa., 1914-18; sales mgr. Mitchell Vance Co., New York, 1920-27; shooting editor Field and Stream Publishing Co., New York, 1919-34; editor of Game, 1934-35, National Sportsman, 1937-38. Mem. 1st Cavalry, New York National Guard, Mexican border service, 1916; commd. 1st lt. U.S.A., Nov. 1917; instr. of equitation, Washington, D.C.; capt., July 1918; went to France, July 1918; a.d.c. to Gen. McRoberts; hon. discharged, Jan. 1919. Episcopalian. Clubs: Players, Camp Fire of America; joint master of Star Ridge Hunt. Author: Outdoorsman's Handbook, 1920; Sporting Firearms of Today in Use, 1922; American Game Shooting, 1927; Upland Game Bird Shooting in America, 1930; The Book of Guns and Gunning, 1934; The Highlander, 1937; Sportsmen All, 1938. Contbr. to The Sportsman, Polo, etc. Authority on mil. and sporting firearms and shooting. Home: Devonshire, Bermuda. †

CURTIS, WALTER LOUIS, JR., naval officer; b. Ahoskie, N.C., July 25, 1915; s. Walter Louis and Ruth (Dowell) c.; student U. N.C., 1932-33; B.S., Wake Forest Coll., 1935; postgrad. Gen. Line Sch., 1946-47, Indsl. Coll. Armed Forces, 1957-58; m. Janet Hartz Gallagher, Dec. 7, 1956; stepchildren—Janet Gallagher (Mrs. Charles Linran), Linda Gallagher. Commd. ensign USNR, 1937, trans. to U.S. Navy, 1946, advanced through grades to rear adm., 1965; pilot, landing signal officer U.S.S. Hornet, 1941-42, U.S.S. Princeton, 1942-44; air officer in new U.S.S. Princeton, 1945-47; chief staff officer to comdr. Atlantic Res. Fleet, 1948-50; comdg. officer Scouting Squadron 31, 1950-52; staff officer Office Chief Naval Operations, Navy Dept., Washington, 1952-54; exec. officer U.S.S. Randolph, 1954; asst. operations officer Staff Comdr. Sixth Fleet, Mediterranean, 1955-57; assigned European Command Div., 1958, Joint Staff Office, Joint Chiefs Staff, 1959, Office Chmn., Joint Chiefs Staff, 1960; comdr. U.S.S. Thetis Bay, 1961-62, U.S.S. Kitty Hawk, 1962-63; chief staff, aide to comdr. First Fleet, 1963-64; asst. chief naval personnel for personnel control Bur. Naval Personnel, Navy Dept., Washington, 1964-66; comdr. Carrier Div. Nine, 1967-84. Decorated Bronze Star. Home: San Diego, Calif. Died Apr. 11, 1984.

CURTISS, CHARLES DWIGHT, engr., assn. exec.; b. Camden, Mich., Dec. 23, 1887; s. Manly Jackson and Addie Elmira (Alward) C.; B.S., Mich. State Coll., 1911; M.A., Columbia, 1915; C.E., Ia. State Coll., 1916; m. Dorothea Davis, July 18, 1919; children—Charles Dwight, Martha. Instr. civil engring. Mich. State Coll., 1911-13; supt. asphalt plant Continental Pub. Works Co., 1914; bridge insp. Mich. State Highway Dept., 1915; asst. engr. Ia. State Highway Commn., 1915-17; testing and insp. engr. J.B. McCrary Co., Atlanta, 1917; asst. to chief U.S. Bureau of Public Roads, Department of Commerce, 1919-27, chief div. control, 1927-43, dep. comr. finance and management 1943-55, commr. 1955-57; spl. asst. to exec. v.p., Am. Road Builders Association, from 1958. 1st lt. to capt., A.E.F., 1917-19. Recipient Gold Medal, Dept. Commerce; Alumni award, 1953, Centennial award, 1955, Mich. State U.; George S. Bartlett award for contbn. to hwy. proggress, 1957. Mem. Am. Soc. C.E. (1st exec. com. hwy. Div. and sec. of div. 1923-47, chmn. exec. com. 1926; past pres. D.C. sect.), Am. Assn. State Highway Officials (exec. com.), Am. Rd. Builders Assn., Nat. Acad. Scis., Hwy. Research Bd. (chmn. exec. com. 1963); hon. mem. Inst. Traffic Engrs. Mason (32 deg.). Club: Cosmos (Washington). Home: Kensington, Md. †

CURTISS, URSULA REILLY (MRS. JOHN CURTISS, JR), author; b. Yonkers, N.Y., Apr. 8, 1923; d. Paul and Helen (Kieran) Reilly; m. John Curtiss, Jr., May 24, 1947; children: Katherine, John, Paul, Kieran, Mary. Student pub. schs. Fashion copywriter Gimbels, N.Y.C., 1944, Macy's, 1944-45, Bates Fabrics, Inc., 1945-47. Author: Voice Out of Darkness, 1948, The Second Sickle, 1950, The Noonday Devil, 1951, The Iron Cobweb, 1953, The Deadly Climate, 1954, The Stairway, 1955, Widow's Web, 1956, The Face of the Tiger, 1957, So Dies the Dreamer, 1960, Hours to Kill, 1961, The Forbidden Garden, 1962, The Wasp, 1963, Out of the Dark, 1964, Danger: Hospital Zone, 1966, Don't Open the Door!, 1968, Letter of Intent, 1971, The Birthday Gift, 1976, In Cold Pursuit, 1977, The Menace Within, 1979, The Poisoned Orchard, 1980, Dog in the Manger, 1982, Death of a Crow, 1983. Recipient Zia Award, 1963. Mem. Crime Writers' Assn. Home: Albuquerque, N.M. Died Oct. 10, 1984.

CURZON, CLIFFORD, concert pianist; b. London, England, May 18, 1907; s. Michael and Constance (Young) C.; student Royal Acad. of Music, London, 1920; studied later under Katharine Goodson; also studied under Schnabel, Berlin, 1923; under Landowska and Boulanger, Paris, 1930; m. Lucille Wallace, July 16, 1931. Toured Europe for British Council, 1936 and 1937; recent tours throughout world; coast to coast tours in U.S.A. Fellow Royal Acad. Music, London. Comdr. British Empire 1958. Home: London, England. Died Sept. 1, 1982.

CUSACK, JOHN FRANCIS, lawyer; b. Chgo., Dec. 13, 1904; s. James Joseph and Eileen Nellie (Fitzgerald) C.; Ph.B., U. Chgo., 1928, J.D., 1930; m. Magdalene M.

Hanousek, Dec. 29, 1937; children—John Francis, Judith (Mrs. John G. Ryan), James J., Raymond R., Richard W., Thomas E., Magdalene H., Ana C. Admitted to Ill. bar, 1931; partner Cusack & Cusack, 1931-82; dir. Hazeltine Research, Inc., Chgo. Chmn., Motion Picture Appeal Bd. Chgo., 1968-77; mem. Dept. Urban Renewal, 1969-82; chmn. Friends Chgo. Schs. Com., 1966-70. Bd. dirs. South Shore Commn. Home: Chicago, Ill. Died Sept. 24, 1982.

CUSHING, CHARLES COOK, educator, composer; b. Oakland, Calif., Dec. 8, 1905; s. Henry Dexter and Edna (Cook) C.; m. Charlotte Crosby Cerf, Aug. 11, 1935; children—Jennifer (Mrs. Jennifer Curtis), Elizabeth (Mrs. Richard John Lamb), Jonathan Caleb. A.B., U. Calif. at Berkeley, 1928, M.A., 1929; student of, Nadia Boulanger, Paris, France, Ecole Normale de Musique, 1929-31. Mem. faculty U. Calif. at Berkeley, from 1931, prof. music, 1949-68, conductor univ. Concert Band, 1934-52. Composer: 2d Sonata for Violin and Piano, 1932, Thesmaphoriazusae (incidental music), 1933, Carmen Saeculare, 1935, String Quartet No. 2 in A, 1936, Three Eclogues for 2 Clarinets and Bassoon, 1938, Psalm XCVII for Chorus and Band, 1939, Phrygian Toccata (piano), 1941, Wine from China (men's chorus and piano 4 hands), 1945, Lyric Set (flute, soprano, viola), 1946, Saint Ursula and The Radishes (men's chorus, contralto solo, 4 winds), 1946, Divertimento (4 movements for string orch.), 1947, Fantasy (flute, clarinet, bassoon), 1949, Angel Camp (variations for concert band), 1952, What are Years? (mixed chorus), 1954, Sonata for Clarinet and Piano, 1957, Poem for Baritone and Orch, 1958, Laudate Pueri (suite for 2 clarinets), 1959, Cereus (poem for orch.), 1960, Ondine (incidental music), 1961, The Tempest (incidental music), 1964, Intermezzo (incidental music), 1967; also many songs to texts Am. poets. Recipient George Ladd Prix de Paris, 1929-31; decorated chevalier Legion of Honor France, 1952; commn. Ford Found., 1959. Home: Berkeley, Calif. Dec. Apr. 13, 1982.

CUSHMAN, CLARISSA WHITE FAIRCHILD, author; b. Oberlin, O., Jan. 13, 1889; d. Charles Grandison and Adelaide Frances (Deane) Fairchild; A.B., Oberlin Coll., 1911; m. Robert Eugene Cushman, Dec. 25, 1916; children—Robert Fairchild, John Fairchild. Editorial asst. Charles E. Merrill Co., 1911-13; mem. editorial staff Vogue Magazine, 1913-16. Mem. Phi Beta Kappa. Democrat. Conglist. Author: The New Poor (pub. also in Eng.), 1927; But For Her Garden (pub. serially as "Judith", also pub. in Eng.), 1935; The Bright Hill, pub. serially, 1935, in book form, 1936, also pub. in Eng.; This Side of Regret (pub. serially as "Trial by Marriage", also pub. in Eng.), 1937; The Other Brother (pub. serially, 1939, in book form, 1939); I Wanted to Murder (Mary Roberts Rinehart prize novel, pub. serially and in book form, 1940); Young Widow (pub. serially, 1941, in book form, 1942). Contbr. serial novels to mags.†

CUSHMAN, ROBERT EVERTON, JR., marine corps officer; b. St. Paul, Dec. 24, 1914; s. Robert E. and Jennie Lind (Cumley) C.; B.S., U.S. Naval Acad., 1935; m. Audrey Boyce, Jan. 17, 1940; children—Roberta Lind, Robert Everton III. Commd. 2d lt. USMC, 1935, advanced through grades to gen. 1972; numerous U.S. and overseas command and staff assignments, 1935-57; asst. to v.p. for nat. security affairs, 1957-61; comdg. gen. 3d div., Okinawa, 1961-62; asst. chief staff G-2 and G-3, Hdqrs. USMC, Washington, 1962-64; comdg. gen. 4th and 5th Marine Div. and Marine Cor. Base, Camp Pendleton, Cal., 1964-67; comdg. gen. III Marine Amphibious Force and I Corps Tactical Zone Vietnam, 1967-69; dep. dir. CIA Washington, 1969-71; comdt. USMC, Washington, 1972-75. Mem. bd. control U.S. Naval Inst. Proc., 1957-61. Decorated Navy Cross, D.S.M. (2), Legion of Merit, Bronze Star; Order May (Argentina); Nat. Order 3d and 4th class, Army and Navy Distinguished Service Order 1st class, Cross Gallantry with 2 palms (Vietnam); Order Mil. Merit. Nat. Security Merit 2d class (Korea). Episcopalian. Died Jan. 2, 1985.

CUTLER, IVAN BURTON, educator; b. Salt Lake City, Jan. 11, 1924; s. Ralph and Virginia (Burton) C.; B.S., U. Utah, 1947, Ph.D., 1951; m. Beth Ashton, June 6, 1945; children—Coy Cutler Hogan, Claudia Cutler Van Orden, Christopher A., Raymond A., Bonita Cutler Hughes, Connie, Ralph A., Willard A., Louise, Paul A. Instr. ceramic engring. U. Utah, Salt Lake City, 1951-52, asst. prof., 1952-56, asso. prof., head dept. ceramic engring., from 1956, prof., 1959-67, prof. mech. engring., from 1965; vis. prof. ceramic engring. U. Ill., 1967-68. Chmn. Gordon Research Conf., 1965; liaison scientist Office Naval Research, London, Eng., 1972-73; mem. Internat. Inst. for Sci. of Sintering, Internat. Com. on Reactivity Solids. Served to ensign USNR, 1944-46. Fellow Am. Ceramic Soc., mem. Brit. Ceramic Soc., Sigma Xi, Phi Kappa Phi, Tau Beta Pi. Home: Centerville, Utah. Died July 26, 1979; buried Salt Lake City.

CUTLER, LAWRENCE MARK, physician, univ. trustee; b. Old Town, Maine, Oct. 22, 1906; s. Edwin and Rachel (Rawinski) C.; m. Catherine Epstein, Oct. 14, 1939; children—Eliot, Joshua, Joel. B.A., U. Maine, 1928; M.D., Tufts U., 1932; LL.D., Colby Coll., 1974. Intern Me. Gen. Hosp., Portland, 1932-33; house officer Boston City Hosp., 1933-34; pvt. practice, Bangor, Maine, 1934-41, from 46; chief med. service Eastern Maine Gen. Hosp., Bangor, 1950-68; cons. staff Eastern Maine Med. Centre, 1968—; Mem. arthritis and metabolic diseases adv. council NIH, 1951-55; Mem. Bangor Sch. Bd., 1945-55, chmn., 1948-52; del. White House Conf. Edn., 1955; chmn. Gov. Maine Adv. Com. Edn., 1957-58; mem. Com. Coordination High Edn. of Me.; adviser to the State Legislature, 1967-68; mem. Nat. Com. Support Pub. Schs., from 1963; Bd. trustees U. Maine, from 1956, v.p., 1962-63, pres., 1963-73; bd. dirs. Eastern Me. Guidance Center, Bangor, 1960-64. Served to lt. col., M.C. AUS, 1941-46, PTO. Decorated Bronze Star. Mem. Maine Penobscot med. assns., Am. Jewish Hist. Soc. (exec. council 1965-67), Bangor Mechanics Assn. Home: Bangor, ME.

CUTLER, SAMUEL, merchandising exec.; b. Russia, Sept. 15, 1890; s. William and Sophie (Sprints) C.; brought to U.S. 1910, naturalized 1914; ed. high sch.; m. Thelma Weingroff, Feb. 1, 1917; children—Elaine Doris (Mrs. Richard J. Yadwin). Stanley C. With Sears, Roebuck & Co., 1907-20; mfg. exec. Cutler & Roe, Newark, 1920-31; with Nat. Bellas Hess, Inc., Kansas City, Mo., from 1931, v.p., 1936-56, pres., from 1956. Home: East Orange, N.J.†

CUTSHALL, ELMER GUY, lecturer, educator; b. Independence, Ia., June 17, 1890; s. Eli Grant and Maria Cornelia (Blake) C.; A.B., Cornell College, Ia., 1913, D.D., 1928; A.M., State U. of Ia., 1914; student Northwestern U.; B.D., Garrett Bibl. Institute, 1918, graduate work, Th.M., D.D., 1931; Ph.D., cum laude, Univ. of Chicago, 1922; post-grad. work in psychology, U. of Pa., 1923; LL.D., Kan. Wesleyan U., 1931; m. Neva Irene Moss, June 24, 1914; children—Valdor Blake, Vivian Moss (Mrs. John Bartlett Edwards), Vernon Hayes, Vincent Keet; married 2d, Lucile Skutley, 1953. Ordained to ministry of Meth. Church, 1915; pastorates in Ia. and Ind. until 1918; pastor Palatine, Ill., 1919-20; Meth. chaplain, U. of Pa., 1920-23, also dir. religious edn., Christian Assn. of U. of Pa., part of the time; pres. W.Va. Wesleyan Coll., 1923-25; pres. and prof., philosophy of religion, Iliff Sch. Theology, Denver, 1925-32; chancellor Neb. Wesleyan U., 1932-37. Holder of Swift fellowship Univ. of Chicago, 1919-20. Organizer Wesley Foundation of City of Phila. and dir. 1920-23; an incorporator of Wesley Foundation of Colo.; sec. bd. control Wesley Foundation of Colo., 1925-31; del. Gen. Conf. of M.E. Ch., 1928, 32; del. to Meth. Ecumenical Conf., Altanta, 1931; mem. Univ. Senate M.E. Ch., 1928-32; mem. Bd. of Edn. of M.E. Church, 1932-36; chmn. Neb. Delegation to Gen. Conf., 1936. Inst. lecturer for Rotary Internat. Mem. Alpha Phi Omega, Delta Theta Chi, Phi Beta Kappa, Pi Gamma Mu, Pi Kappa Delta, Phi Kappa Phi. Republican. Mason. Clubs: Rotary, Denver Rifle. Author: Analysis and Comparison of the Elements involved in the Hearing and the Singing of the Pitch of a Tone; Philosophy of Methodism. Asso. editor Pi Gamma Mu, 1925-35. Has held forums in 1470 cities; given 7400 lectures including addresses to 1534 different high schools, and 98 colls. and univs. Traveled in Europe and Nr. East, 1937-38. Home: Manitou Springs, Colo. †

CUTTING, JOHN CLIFTON, newspaper man; b. Cambridge, Mass., Apr. 21, 1890; s. Edwin Ashley and Fanny (Ward) C.; ed. pub. schs., Rindge sch.; m. Kathryn Rose Coonan, Mar. 7, 1914. Reporter Cambridge Tribune, 1911, Nashua (N.H.) Telegraph, 1912, Boston Globe, 1913, Washington Star, 1914; asst. Sunday editor New York Herald, 1917; reporter New York Evening World, 1919; magazine editor Evening World, 1920; editor Selznick News Reel, 1921, Kinogram News Reel, 1922, Inst. Am. Meat Packers, 1923. Clubs: Adventurers', Dutch Treat (New York). Home: Chicago, Ill. †

DADY, SISTER MARY RACHAEL, educator; b. Kellogg, Minn., July 17, 1888; dau. John and Mary Ann (Dwyer) Dady; A.B., Coll. of Saint Teresa, Winona, Minn., 1914; A.M., Columbia, 1916; Ph.D., Catholic Univ. of Am., 1939. Mem. Sisters of Third Order Regular of St. Francis of Congregation of Our Lady of Lourdes, Rochester, Minnesota. Registrar College of Saint Teresa, Winona, Minn., 1918-26, sec., 1926-28, teacher dept. of philosophy, 1930-37, 39-46, pres. from 1946. Mem. Am. Cath. Philos. Assn. Author: The Theory of Knowledge of Saint Bonaventure, 1939. Home: Winona, Minn. †

DAHLGREN, LAWRENCE JUNGBLOM, lawyer; Chgo., Aug. 21, 1906; s. A. Godfrey and Amanda W. (Jungblom) D.; J.D., John Marshall Law Sch., Chgo., 1926; m. Lorna Rasmussen, Jan. 1, 1945 (dec. Aug. 1976); children—Beverly Freytag Durham, Phyllis Freytag Funovits. With Chgo. Title & Trust Co., Chgo., 1922-28; admitted to Ill. bar, 1928, practiced in Chgo.; practice law, 1928-80; partner firm Bergstrom, Rohde, Dahlgren & Olson, 1968-73; of counsel Ruff & Grotefeld, Ltd., 1973-80; asst. to pres. Telephone and Data Systems, Inc., 1973-78; v.p., sec., dir. Melin Tool Co., Inc., Cleve.; dir. Zelzer Mgmt., Inc., Chgo. Pres., dir. Layman Tithing Found., Chgo.; past pres., trustee Arlington Heights Park Dist.; trustee Luth. Inst. Human Ecology, Luth. Gen. Hosp., Inc., Park Ridge, Ill., 1952-73. Served to lt. comdr. USNR, 1942-45. Mem. Am., Chgo. bar assns., Nordic Law Club, Am. Srs. Golf Assn., Am. Legion, VFW, Delta Theta Phi. Lutheran. Clubs: Swedish (Chgo.), Oak Park (Ill.) Country. Home: Chicago, Ill.

DAKAN, EVERETT LEROY, educator; b. Savannah, Mo., June 29, 1889; s. Spencer Brown and Elsie Jane (Watts) D.; B.S., U. Mo., 1918; student U. Wis., 1931, U. Mich. 1932; m. Gladys Ayers, Sept. 14, 1916; children—Elsie Jane, Everett Ayers. Instr. U. Mo., 1917-18; prof. S.D. State Coll., 1918-19; extension specialist Ohio State U., 1919-23, prof., from 1924, chmn. dept. poultry sci., 1924-55, tchr. ornithology, 1933-40. Relocation officer War Relocation Authority, 1943-45. Mem. Audubon Soc. (pres. Columbus chpt. 1935-36), Am. Assn. U. Profs., Poultry Sci. Assn., Gamma Sigma Delta, Author: The Effect of Artificial Light on Growth and Reproduction of Fowls, 1936; Ohio and the Poultry Industry, 1939; Hatchery Sanitation, 1939; Goose Raising, 1951; Poultry editor of The Ohio Farmer, 1924-55. Home: Columbus, OH. †

DALE, JAMES G., lawyer; b. N.Y.C., Jan. 7, 1888; A.B., N.Y.U., 1909, J.D., 1913. Admitted to N.Y. bar, 1912; practice in Rochester; mem. firm Harris, Beach, Keating, Wilcox, Dale & Linowitz. Mem. Am., N.Y. State, Monroe County bar assns., Phi Beta Kappa.†

DALEY, JOSEPH T., bishop; b. Connerton, Pa., Dec. 21, 1915. Ed., Charles Borromeo Sem., Phila.; D.D. Ordained priest Roman Cath. Ch., June 4, 1941, titular bishop Barca and aux. bishop, Harrisburg, 1963-67, coadjutor bishop with right of succession, 1967-71, bishop of, Harrisburg, Pa., 1971-85. Address: Harrisburg, Pa. Deceased. *

DALI, SALVADOR, artist; b. Figueras, nr. Barcelona, Spain, May 11, 1904; s. Salvador and Felipa (Domeneck) D.; m. Gala Dali, Sept. 1935. Student pub. sch. and pvt. acad. conducted by, Bros. of the Marist Order, Figueras, Sch. of Fine Arts, Madrid, 1921-26. Designed jewelry, furniture, and art nouveau decorations, 1929-31; symbolic interpretations of legend of William Tell and Millet's The Angelus, 1934; made first visit to, U.S., 1934, series of beach scenes at, Rosas, Spain, literal pictures of his dreams, 1934-36; decorated residence of, Edward James, London, 1936; made 3 visits in, Italy, 1937-39; designed: Dali's Dream House, N.Y. World's Fair, 1939; made 2d visit to, U.S., 1940; Ballets Bacchanale, Met. Opera House, 1939; music, Richard Wagner; scenery and costumes by Dali Labyrinth book; costumes, scenery by Dali; music Schubert), 1941, Cafe de Chiuita, Spanish Festival, Met. Opera, 1942, Exhbns. include one-man shows, Julien Levy Gallery, N.Y., 1933, Arts Club, Chgo., 1941, Dalzell Hatfield Galleries, Los Angeles, Calif., Mus. Modern Art, N.Y. (exhibit loaned to many cities U.S.), Knoedler Gallery, N.Y., many in, Paris, London, Barcelona, and N.Y.C., retrospective exhbn., Rotterdam, 1970-71; Author: autobiography Secret Life of Salvador Dali, 1942, Diary of a Genius, 1965, The Unspeakable Confessions of Salvador Dali, 1976. Recipient 5000 Huntington Hartford Found. award, 1957. Completed two paintings, portrait of Helen of Troy, Joseph Greeting His Brethren, before he was 10; influenced by Italian Futurists, 1923-25; became a Surrealist, Paris, France, 1929. Home: Cadaquès, Spain.

DALRYMPLE, SHERMAN HARRISON, union official; b. Walton, W.Va., Apr. 4, 1889; s. Herbert Clarence and Eliza Eleanor (Atkinson) D.; ed. pub. sch., Mt. Lebanon, W.Va.; m. Esta Robinson, Jan. 3, 1914 (dec.); 1 dau., Juanita Faye (dec.); m. 2d, Grace Moomaw, Oct. 2, 1928. Worked in rubber industry, 1909-10, oil fields, 1911-14; again in rubber industry, 1914-17 and 1919-35; pres. Goodrich Local Union, Am. Fed. of Labor, 1934-35; pres. United Rubber Workers of Am., Internat. Union (C.I.O.) from Sept. 1935. Served successively as private, corporal, sergt., gunnery sergt. and 2d lt., U.S. Marine Corps, Apr. 1917-Aug. 1919. Decorated with Fourragere and Croix d'Guerre. Editor United Rubber Worker (monthly publn.). Home: Akron, Ohio †

DALTON, DOROTHY UPJOHN, univ. trustee; b. Kalamazoo, Oct. 28, 1890; d. William Erastus and Rachel (Babcock) Upjohn; student Western Mich. Normal Sch. (now U.), 1908-09, Kalamazoo Coll., 1909-10; A.B., Smith Coll., 1914; grad. Washington Sq. Players (later Theater Guild) Sch. Theater, 1915; m. Allan DeLano, Feb. 5, 1919 (div. May 1926); children—Barbara (Mrs. Gauntlett), Suzanne (Mrs. Preston Parish); m. 2d Howard Dalton, Mar. 21, 1945 (dec. Apr. 1949). Mem. Provincetown Players, N.Y.C., 1916-18; charter mem. Kalamazoo Civic Players, from 1930, hon. pres. bd. dirs., from 1963; bd. dirs. Upjohn Co., Kalamazoo, 1916-25, 29-64; mem. bd. W. E. Upjohn Unemployment Trustee Corp., 1934-63. Mem. adv. bd. Borgess Hosp., Kalamazoo; mem. governing bd. World Fedn. Mental Health; bd. dirs. Kalamazoo Symphony Orch., Kalamazoo Outpatient Psychiat. Clinic, Kalamazoo br. Mich. Mental Health Assn.; trustee Western Mich. U.; hon. trustee Kalamazoo Coll.†

DALY, EDWARD JOSEPH, airline exec.; b. Chgo., Nov. 20, 1922; s. Edward Michael and Charlotte Grace D.; m. Violet June Chandler; 1 child, Charlotte. Student, U. Ill., U. Santa Clara, 1967; grad. in applied human relations, Dale Carnegie Inst., 1975. Vice pres. S. O'Carrol Midway Aviation, Chgo., 1947-48; pres., chmn. bd. World Airways, Inc., Oakland, Calif., 1950-84; pres. Skycoach Aircraft Corp.; v.p., gen. mgr. Monarch Air Service; pres. Nationwide Freight Forwarders, Inc.; owner, dir. First Western Bank, 1968-73. Regent U. Santa Clara. Served to sgt. U.S. Army, 1942-45. Decorated Purple Heart; recipient numerous awards, including: NAACP award, 1969; cert. of honor State Calif., 1975; U.S. award of Merit USO, 1975; U.S. award of honor U.S. Army, 1975; Easter Seal award Greater San Francisco/Oakland Crusade, 1976-81; Internat. Fellowship medal King Jordan, 1977; United Way award, 1978; Research Philanthropic award Nat. Jewish Hosp., 1978;

Achievement award State Md., 1981; Dept. Def. award, 1966; Achievement medal Republic Mali, 1977; named Man of Yr. USO, 1974; Disting. Citizen State Nev., 1977. Mem. USAF Assn., Internat. Air Carrier Assn., Nat. Air Carrier Assn. (dir.), Flying Samaritans, Nat. Council YMCA's, Nat. Alliance Businessmen, SAR. Roman Catholic. Clubs: Wings, U.S. Aero, Commonwealth Calif, Orinda Country, St. Francis Yacht, Silverado Country, Royal Aero. Died Jan. 21, 1984.

DALY, LEO ANTHONY, architect; b. Omaha, July 29, 1917; s. Leo Anthony and Madeline D. (Peterson) D.; m. Rosemary Gaughan, May 31, 1941; children—Leo Anthony III, John Gaughan. Student, Creighton U., 1935-36, LL.D. (hon.), 1971; B.S., Cath. U. Am., 1939; LL.D. (hon.), U. Nebr., 1976. Architect Leo A. Daly Co., Omaha, 1939-41, partner, 1941-48, v.p., 1948-52, pres., treas., 1952-81; dir. InterNorth, Inc., Omaha, Northwestern Bell Telephone Co., Omaha, U.S. Nat. Bank, Omaha; mem. profl. adv. council Coll. Architecture U. Nebr., Lincoln. Trustee Nebr. Ind. Coll. Found.; bd. dirs. Jr. Achievement; bd. dirs. Boy Scouts Am., Mid-Am. Council; dir. Boys Clubs Omaha; chmn. Nebr. Arts Council, 1973-76; bd. dirs. Mid-Am. Arts Alliance, 1973-76; chmn. capital fund dr. United Way Midlands, Omaha, 1978-79, gen. chmn., 1959; pres. bd. govs. Ak-Sar-Ben; dir. Omaha Devel. Council; trustee Omaha Indsl. Found.; mem. Citizens Consultation Com., SAC; cons. to bd. Creighton U.; trustee Creighton/Nebr. Health Found.; mem. chancellor's adv. council U. Nebr., Omaha. Recipient Exceptional Service medal USAF, Builder of Year award U. Nebr., Lincoln, 1980, Citizen of Year award United Way Midlands, 1978, Man of Year award Notre Dame Club Omaha and Council Bluffs, 1977, Medal of Independence His Majesty King Hussein Jordan, 1975, Creighton-Manresa medal Creighton U. and Jesuit Community, 1974, Alumni award Cath. U. Am., 1962. Fellow AIA (Edward C. Kemper award), Soc. Am. Mil. Engrs.; mem. Nat. Council Archtl. Registration Bds., Royal Inst. Brit. Architects, Architects Registration Council U.K., Royal Australian Inst. Architects (asso.), Soc. Archtl. Historians, Assn. Collegiate Schs. Architecture, Cons. Engrs. Council, Nebr. Soc. Architects, Profl. Engrs. Nebr., Fedn. Internationale des Ingenieurs-Consuls, Practising Designers Ltd. London (hon.), Omaha C. of C., Tau Sigma Delta. Roman Catholic. Clubs: Country (Omaha), Plaze (Omaha), Omaha (Omaha), Press (Omaha); Marco Polo (N.Y.C.); Nebraska (Lincoln). Home: Omaha, Nebr. Died June 16, 1981.

DAME, LAWRENCE, author, planter, art critic; b. Portland, Maine, July 2, 1898; s. Edward Lawrence and Katherine (Gunn) D.; ed. Harvard U., Ecole des Hautes Etudes Sociales (Paris), Univ. of Grenoble, Univ. of Toulouse (France), Instituto de Burgos (Spain), Boston U.; m. Rachel Wells, Sept. 25, 1958. Editorial staffs, 1919-39; explored Yucatan and Quintana Roo, 1940-41; relief worker Unitarian Service Com., Portugal, 1941; art editor and special writer Boston Herald-Traveler, 1940-48; staff critic Art Rev., (London), 1950-53; with Turkish Times, Istanbul, il Mattino d'Italia Centrale, Florence, and Rome Daily Am., 1952-53; assoc. editor Nantucket (Mass.) Inquirer and Mirror, 1953-54; art, books and theatre editor Sarasota (Fla.) Herald-Tribune, 1954-61; with Social Pictorial, Palm Beach, Fla., from 1961; dir. art. Palm Beach Post, 1959-74; dir. Harvard U. News Office, 1943-45, 46-47; radio commentator sta. WJNO, Palm Beach. Pres. Palm Beach Art Council, from 1974; civil def. organizer Jamaica, 1974-75. Served arty., France, 1917-18. Decorated by French and Portuguese govts. for war work, 1941, officer Order of Merit (France). Mem. SAR, Soc. Colonial Wars, Wine and Food Soc. of Boston (gov.), Wine and Food Soc. of Palm Beach (pres.), Harvard Musical Assn., Sarasota Literary Forum (pres.). Clubs: Vet. Motor Car of Am., Rolls-Royce Owners, Overseas Press (New York), Harvard (Palm Beach); Jamaica Press Assn.; Pacific, Wharf Rat (Nantucket Island, Mass.). Author: New England Comes Back, 1940, Yucatan, 1941; Maya Mission, 1967; Backabush Jamaica; co-author: Boston Murders, 1948. Contbr. articles to mags. Cycling and Wine authority. Home: Jamaica, West Indies. Died May 27, 1981.

DAMON, MASON ORNE, lawyer; b. Ft. Dodge, Iowa, Sept. 7, 1905; s. Edward Orne and Georgia Anna (Mason) D.; m. Harriet Louise Provost, June 16, 1930; children—Mason Orne (dec.), Laura Provost (Mrs. G. Thomas Martin). A.B., Amherst Coll., 1926; J.D., Harvard, 1929. Bar: N.Y. bar 1930. Practiced in, Buffalo; partner firm Damon, Morey, Sawyer & Moot (predecessors), 1940-79, of counsel, from 1979; with procurement legal div. Dept. Navy, 1943-46; gen. counsel Bur. Ships, 1945-46; part-time prof. U. Buffalo Law Sch., 1942-43; sec. Bell Aircraft Corp., 1957-60, Bell Aerospace Corp., 1960-70; mem. adv. bd. Western region Bank of N.Y., from 1976; dir. Bank of N.Y. Co., Inc., 1969-76, Niagara Frontier Bank of N.Y., 1969-75. Pres. bd. dirs. Buffalo Pub. Library, 1949-54; trustee Buffalo and Erie County Pub. Library, 1954-80, trustee emeritus, from 1980, vice chmn., 1954-55, chmn., 1956-57, 66-67; trustee Park Sch., Buffalo, 1947-71, v.p., 1948-55, pres., 1955-57; bd. dirs. Internat. Inst. Buffalo, 1962-76, pres., 1969-75. Served to lt. comdr. USNR, 1943-45. Fellow Am. Bar Found.; mem. Phi Beta Kappa, Delta Sigma Rho, Beta Theta Phi. Clubs: Buffalo, Midday (pres. 1954), Saturn. Home: Buffalo, NY.

DANA, RICHARD HENRY, univ. ofcl.; b. N.Y.C., Mar. 5, 1912; s. Richard Henry and Ethel Nathalie (Smith) D.; grad. cum laude, Phillips Exeter Acad., 1930; A.B. cum laude, Harvard, 1934; m. Nina Katharine Montgomery, Nov. 20, 1948; children—Richard Henry, Cornelia Marshall, Nathalie Pepperrell. Engaged in promotion, also as acting sales mgr. Alfred A. Knopf, 1935-39; founder, pres. Music Press, Inc., 1939-49; promotion mgr. J.B. Lippincott Co., Phila., 1950-52, Ballantine Books, 1952-54; asst. to David Rockefeller in personal and philanthropic activities, 1955-69; bus. mgr. publs. Asso. Council of the Arts, N.Y.C., 1970; asst. sec. Rockefeller U., N.Y.C., 1970-84. Pres. Diller Quaile Sch. Music, N.Y.C., 1966-73. Bd. mgrs. Seamen's Ch. Inst., 1961-72; bd. dirs. Contemporary Music Soc., 1960-84. Served to 1st lt. AUS, 1942-45; ETO. Club: Century (N.Y.C.). Home: New York, N.Y.

DANBY, JOHN BLENCH, editor; b. North Riding, Yorkshire, Eng., June 3, 1905; s. John and Edith A. (Smith) D.; student pub. schs., Eng., also Del., Pa.; m. Helen Agnes Boyce, June 14, 1941; children—David Boyce, Deborah Boyce. News editor Wilmington (Del.) Jour. Every Evening, 1934-42; asst. telegraph news editor N.Y. Herald Tribune, 1942-45; successively asst. articles editor, asso. editor, editor Liberty mag., N.Y.C., 1945-50; exec. editor Redbook mag., N.Y.C., 1950-60; managing editor Good Housekeeping magazine, N.Y.C., from 1960, now executive editor. Member President's Committee on Employment of the Handicapped. Member of the American Civil Liberties Union. Clubs: National Press (Washington); Overseas Press (N.Y.C.). Home: Fair Lawn, N.J. Died Apr. 23, 1983.

DANENBERG, EMIL CHARLES, college president, pianist; b. Hong Kong, July 30, 1917; came to U.S., 1926, naturalized, 1941; s. Emil F.X. and Elsie (Gardner) D.; m. Mary Ann Brezsny, June 23, 1951. A.B., UCLA, 1942, A.M., 1944; D.Mus., Marietta (Ohio) Coll., 1980; H.H.D., Franklin Coll., Ind., 1980. Faculty Oberlin (Ohio) Coll., 1944-82, prof. pianoforte, acting dean, 1970-71; dean Conservatory Music, 1971-75, pres. Oberlin Coll., 1975-82. Concert debut, 1922, New York debut, 1950, concert tours, throughout U.S. and Europe. Mem. Am. Fedn. Musicians (life), AAUP, Music Tchrs. Nat. Assn., Phi Beta Kappa, Phi Mu Alpha, Pi Kappa Lambda. Home: Oberlin, Ohio. Died Jan. 16, 1982.

DANFORTH, JOSEPH D., chemist, educator; b. Danville, Ill., Mar. 7, 1912; s. James and Bertha Ann (Garrard) D.; m. Geraldine Hoffman, July 6, 1940; children—James Davis, Cheryl, David Edward, Patricia Ann. B.A., Wabash Coll., 1934; Ph.D., Purdue U., 1938. Research chemist Universal Oil Products Co., 1938-47; mem. faculty Grinnell Coll., from 1947, prof. chemistry, from 1953, Roberts Honor prof., 1962-63, chmn. dept. chemistry, 1961-64, Dack prof. chemistry, from 1964; vis. scientist chemistry for colls. Am. Chem. Soc., from 1959, mem. vis. scientist com., dir. high sch. program chemistry, 1961-64; cons. in field. Hon. cons. sci. teaching sect. UNESCO, 1964. Author. Recipient Coll. Chemistry Tchr. award Mfg. Chemists Assn., 1963. Mem. Midwest Assn. Chemistry Tchrs. (pres. 1962), Am. Chem. Soc. (treas. div. chem. edn. 1967), A.A.A.S., Ia. Acad. Sci., Phi Beta Kappa. Clubs: Mason, Elk. Pantentee in field. Home: Grinnell, Iowa.

D'ANGELO, LOUIS, singer with Metropolitan Opera Assn.; b. Naples, Italy, May 6, 1888 (now Am. citizen); s. Ernest and Russo D'A.; m. Ruocco D'Angelo, July 7, 1912; children—Caroline Antoinette (Mrs. Philip A. Ardisonne), Elvira Lorraine (Mrs. Dominic P. Ardisonne), Louise Anna (Mrs. Jerry Lombardo). With Aborn Opera Co., 1914-15, Ravinia Opera (Chicago), 1916-30, San Francisco Opera Assn., 1928-40, Metropolitan Opera Assn., N.Y.C., from 1918; played over 350 parts in opera; played the part of Kegal in the English production of The Bartered Bride, presented by Metropolitan Opera Assn., 1940. Roman Catholic. Sang with Caruso during his last three years, with Scotti and Hempel in the first production of The Daughter of the Regiment. Address: Jersey City, N.J. †

DANIEL, HAWTHORNE, author; b. Norfolk, Nebr., Jan. 20, 1890; s. Dr. David Rush and Nancy Ann (Kyner) D.; m. Nelle M. Ryan, 1922; 1 child, Nancy Nelle. Student, U.S. Naval Acad., 1908, Iowa State Coll., 1909-10, N.Y. U., 1914-15, Columbia U., 1914-15. Reporter Omaha Bee, 1915; editorial staff World's Work, 1916-23; mng. editor Boys' Life, 1923-25; editor Natural History, Mag., 1927-35; curator, printing and pub. Am. Mus. Natural History, 1927-35; mng. editor The Commentator, 1936-39, Visited the Arctic Coast of Can. on mag. assignment, 1921, Navy war Corr., World War II; with Army and Navy, in Pacific, Asiatic, Mediterranean and European areas, visited islands of, Pacific and, E. Indies, Australia, India, China, etc.; lectr. Author: (introduction by Franklin D. Roosevelt) numerous books including Ships of the Seven Seas, 1925, End of Track, 1936 (medal of Oreg. Trail Meml. Assn.), For Want of a Nail (The Influence of Logistics on War), 1948, Judge Medina: A Biography, 1952, The Inexhaustible Sea, (with Frances Minot), 1954, The Captain Leaves His Ship, (with Jan Cwiklinski), 1955, The Happy Warrior; (with Emily Smith Warner) a biography of Alfred E. Smith, 1956, The Ordeal of the Captive Nations, 1958 (citation from Assembly of Captive European Nations 1960), The Hartford of Hartford, 1960, Public Libraries for Everyone, 1961, Ferdinand Magellan; biography, 1964, A Different Kind of War, (with Vice Adm. Milton E. Miles), 1967, also articles and short stories in mags. Ensign USNR, 1917; officer U.S.S. Harvard; duty in Bay of Biscay and English Channel; lt. U.S. Tank Corps, 1918-19; 303d and 306th Bn. in U.S., Eng. and France; as reconnaissance officer. Awarded U.S. Navy commendation. Clubs: Explorers (N.Y.C.); Boonsboro Country (Lynchburg, Va.). Home: Lynchburg, Va. Dec.

DANIELS, DRAPER, advertising consultant, author; b. Morris, N.Y., Aug. 12, 1913; s. John Albert and Fanny Martha (Draper) D.; m. Louise Parker Lux Cort, Oct. 9, 1937 (div. 1967); children—John, Bruce, Marie, Curtis; m. Myra Janco, Aug. 18, 1967. B.S., Syracuse U., 1934. Sales, advt. depts. Vick Chem. Co., N.Y.C., 1935-40; copywriter Young & Rubicam, N.Y.C., 1940-44, 46-47, copy chief, Chgo., 1947, v.p., 1948, chmn. plans bd., 1949-54; copy supr. McCann-Erickson, Kenyon & Eckhardt, N.Y.C., 1944-46; copy supr. Leo Burnett Co., Inc., Chgo., 1954, v.p., 1954-56, v.p. in charge copy, mem. plans bd., 1956-57, dir., v.p. charge creative depts., 1957-58, exec. v.p. creative services, exec. com., 1958-61, chmn. exec. com., dir., 1961-62; nat. export expansion coordinator U.S. Govt., 1962-63; exec. v.p. McCann-Erickson, Inc., 1963-64, Compton Advt. Inc., 1964-65; chmn. bd., chief exec. officer Draper Daniels, Inc., Chgo., 1965-77; Mem. adv. bd. Sch. Journalism, Syracuse U.; adv. bd. Coll. Bus. Adminstrn. Roosevelt U., also fellow. Author: Giants, Pigmies, and Other Advertising People, 1974. Mem. Mfg. Export Adv. Com., Ill., 1967, 70; Chmn. Democratic Central Com., Lake County, Ill., 1954-56; del. Dem. Nat. Conv., 1956. Address: Marco Island, Fla. Died May 7, 1983.

DANIELS, FRED HAROLD, business exec.; b. Worcester, Mass., 1887; s. Fred Harris and Sarah L. (White) D.; student Yale, 1909, Mass. Inst. Tech., 1911; m. Eleanor G. Goddard, June 2, 1915; children—Eleanor (Mrs. Samuel C. Bronson), Bruce. With B.F. Sturtevant Co., Boston, 1911-13; with Riley Stoker Corp. from 1913, pres., gen. mgr., dir., 1926-50; now chmn. bd.; dir. Badenhausen Corp.; trustee Peoples Savs. Bank, Worcester; dir. A. W. Cash Co., Mechanics Nat. Bank, State Mut. Life Assurance Co. Fellow American Society of Mechanical Engineers. Mason. Clubs: Engineers (N.Y.C.); Worcester, Tatnuck Country (Worcester). †

DANIELS, JONATHAN WORTH, editor, author; b. Raleigh, N.C., Apr. 26, 1902; s. Josephus and Addie Worth (Bagley) D.; A.B., U. N.C., 1921, M.A., 1922; postgrad. Columbia U. Law Sch., 1922-23; m. Elizabeth Bridgers, Sept. 5, 1923 (dec. Dec. 1929); 1 dau., Elizabeth Bridgers (Mrs. C. B. Squire); m. Lucy Billing Cathcart, Apr. 30, 1932; children—Lucy Daniels Inman, Adelaide (Mrs. B. J. Key), Cleves (Mrs. Steven Weber). Reporter Louisville Times; then reporter Raleigh (N.C.) News and Observer, Washington corr., 1925-28, assoc. editor, 1932-33, editor, 1933-42, exec. editor, 1947, editor, 1948-70, editor emeritus, 1970-81; founder, contbr. Island Packet, Hilton Head Island, S.C., from 1970; asst. dir. Office Civilian Def., 1942; adminstrv. asst. to Pres., 1943-45; press sec. to Pres., 1945; U.S. mem. UN subcom. on Prevention of Discrimination and Protection of Minorities, 1947- 53; mem. pub. adminstrv. bd. ECA and Mut. Security Agy., 1948-53; mem. Dem. Nat. Com. from N.C., 1949-52; mem. Fed. Hosp. Council, 1949-53; on editorial staff, Fortune mag., N.Y.C., 1930, 31-32; contbr. weekly page, A Native at Large, to Nation, 1941-42. Trustee Vassar Coll., 1942-48; Guggenheim fellow, 1930-31. Mem. Delta Kappa Epsilon. Democrat. Episcopalian. Club: Nat. Press (Washington). Author: Clash of Angels (novel), 1930; A Southerner Discovers the South, 1938; A Southerner Discovers New England, 1940; Tar Heels: A Portrait of North Carolina, 1941; Frontier on the Potomac, 1946; The Man of Independence, 1950; The End of Innocence, 1954; The Forest is the Future, 1957; Prince of Carpetbeggars, 1958; Mosby, Gray Ghost of the Confederacy, 1959; Stonewall Jackson, 1959; Robert E. Lee, 1960; The Devil's Backbone; The Story of the Natchez Trace, 1962; They Will Be Heard, 1965; The Time Between The Wars, 1966; Washington Quadrille, 1968; Ordeal of Ambition-Jefferson, Hamilton, Burr, 1970; The Randolphs of Virginia, 1972; The Gentlemanly Serpent, 1974; White House Witness 1942-45, 1975. Contbr. articles and revs. to mags. Home: Hilton Head Island, S.C. Died Nov. 6, 1981.

DANIELSON, GORDON CHARLES, educator, physicist; b. Dover, Idaho, Oct. 28, 1912; s. Gust and Olga (Olson) D.; m. Dorothy Edna Thompson, June 24, 1939; children—Ellen Kathleen (Mrs. Karl Richard Fox), Lee Robert, Keith Gordon, Neil David. B.A., U. B.C., 1933, M.A., 1935; Ph.D., Purdue U., 1940. Research physicist U.S. Rubber Co., Detroit, 1940-41; asst. prof. physics U. Idaho, 1941-42; asso. group leader Beacons Radiation Lab., Mass. Inst. Tech., 1942-46; mem tech. staff Bell Telephone Labs., Murray Hill, N.J., 1946-48; asso. prof. physics Iowa State U., Ames, 1948-53; prof. physics, sr. physicist Inst. for Atomic Research, 1953-83, chmn. physics grad. adv. com., 1951-53, mem. metallurgy curriculum com., 1949-54, chmn. physics colloquium com., 1959-60, distinguished prof. scis. and humanities, 1964-83; Mem. metallurgy and solid state rev. com. Argonne Nat. Lab., 1960-63, chmn., 1962-63; mem. solid state panel Nat. Acad. Scis.-NRC, 1962-72; cons. NSF, 1963-66; civilian cons. USAF, Eng., 1944-45; chmn. com. on thermoelectric conversion Office Naval Research, 1958. Contbr. articles prof. jours., books. Recipient Army-Navy certificate appreciation, 1948; Guggenheim fellow U. Cambridge, Eng., 1958-59. Fellow Am. Phys. Soc. (exec. com. div. solid state physics 1963-66), Iowa Acad. Sci.; mem. Am. Inst. Physics (vis. scientist 1960-72), UN Assn. (pres. Ames chpt. 1964-66), Sigma Xi (pres. Iowa State U. chpt. 1967-68). Unitarian (past pres., treas. Ames fellowship). Research on practical Fourier analysis, domain orientation in barium titanate, surface physics, thermal diffusivity, tungsten bronzes, semi-conducting compounds. Home: Ames, Iowa. Died Sept. 30, 1983.

DANIELSON, JOHN OSWALD, university official; b. Park Rapids, Minn., July 2, 1913; s. John Otto and Mary (Quinlivan) D.; B.S., Wis. State Coll., Superior, 1940; M.A., U. Wis., 1942, postgrad., 1947, 50-51, 52; m. Phyllis G. Strong, Sept. 19, 1942; 1 child, Rosannah Mary. Grad. asst. U. Wis., 1940-42; civil service USN, 1942-43; prof. math. U. Wis., Superior, 1946-55, chmn. dept. math., 1955-57, dean instrn. 1957-62, exec. v.p., 1962-72, vice chancellor, 1972-78, vice chancellor emeritus, 1978-85. Chmn. Wis. Engring. Edn. Improvement Com., 1967; past pres. Wis. Adv. Com. Extension Programs; past vice chmn. Wis. Planning Com. Edn. Beyond High Sch.; past mem. Wis. Higher Edn. Com. on Inter-instnl. Cooperation. Pres. Superior Assn. Commerce, 1963-64. Pres. Holy Family Hosp., Superior, 1969-71; past bd. dirs. N. Wis. Areawide Comprehensive Health Planning Orgn.; bd. dirs., v.p. U. Wis.-Superior Found.; bd. dirs., mem. exec. com. Health Service Agy. of Western Lake Superior. Served from ensign to lt. (s.g.), USNR, 1943-46. Mem. Soc. Instrnl. and Applied Math., Wis. Acad. Arts and Scis., Math. Assn. Am., A.A.A.S., Wis. Edn. Assn., Lake Superior Ednl. Assn., Superior Hist. Soc. (past v.p.), Pi Mu Epsilon, Phi Delta Kappa, Fex Frat., Sigma Pi Sigma. Club: Optimists (dir. Superior 1957-59, past pres.; dist. lt. gov., 1961-85). Home: Superior, Wis. Died June 23, 1985.

DANILEVICIUS, ZENONAS, physician, author, editor; b. Petrograd, Russia, May 13, 1915; came to U.S., 1947, naturalized, 1953; s. Boleslovas and Martha (Paliunas) D.; m. Joana Sakevicius, Oct. 3, 1937; children—Rita Marija Danilevicius Fernandez, Daina Marija Danilevicius Dumbrys, Linas Zenonas. M.D., Vyt.D., U. Kaunas, Lithuania, 1938. Intern U. Hosp., Kaunas, 1937-38; resident internal medicine Mil. Hosp., Kaunas, 1938-41; dir. Second City Policlinic, Kaunas, 1941-44, Nursing Sch., UNRRA, Schwaebisch Gmuende, Bavaria, 1946-47; intern St. Anthony Hosp., Chgo., 1947-48; pvt. practice medicine, Chgo., 1949-63; sr. editor A.M.A. Jour., Chgo., from 1963; Expert witness at hearings U.S. Congl. Ways and Means Com., 1961; Chmn. sci. program com. Hosp. St. Anthony, Chgo., 1960-63. Author: Zmogus, Physiology, 1943; Contbr. articles, transls. to profl. jours. Mem. Am. Med. Writers Assn., Cath. Lithuanian Acad. Sci., Chgo. Med. Soc., AMA, Internat. Soc. History Medicine, Am. Soc. History Medicine, Am. Soc. Internal Medicine. Home: Chicago, Ill. Died Apr. 15, 1981.

DANNAY, FREDERIC, writer; m. Rose Koppel; children—Douglas, Richard. Vis. prof. U. Tex., Austin, 1958-59. Co-writer with late Manfred B. Lee under pseudonym Ellery Queen; Co-author: Roman Hat Mystery, 1929, French Powder Mystery, 1930, Dutch Shoe Mystery, 1931, Tragedy of X, 1932, Greek Coffin Mystery, 1932, Tragedy of Y, 1932, Egyptian Cross Mystery, 1932, American Gun Mystery, 1933, Tragedy of Z, 1933, Siamese Twin Mystery, 1933, Drury Lane's Last Case, 1933, Chinese Orange Mystery, 1934, Adventures of Ellery Queen, 1934, Spanish Cape Mystery, 1935, Halfway House, 1936, Door Between, 1937, Challenge to the Reader, 1938, Devil To Pay, 1938, Four of Hearts, 1938, Dragon's Teeth, 1939, New Adventures of Ellery Queen, 1940, 101 Years' Entertainment, 1941, Calamity Town, 1942, Detective Short Story; bibliography, 1942, Sporting Blood, 1942, There Was an Old Woman, 1943, Female of the Species, 1943, Misadventures of Sherlock Holmes, 1944, Best Short Stories from Ellery Queen's Mystery Magazine, 1944, Casebook of Ellery Queen, 1945, Murderer Is A Fox, 1945, Roques' Gallery, 1945, To the Queen's Taste, 1946, The Queen's Awards, 1946-53, Murder by Experts, 1947, 20th Century Detective Stories, 1948, Ten Days' Wonder, 1948, Cat of Many Tails, 1949, Double Double, 1950, Literature of Crime, 1950, Origin of Evil, 1951, Queen's Quorum, 1951, Calendar of Crime, 1952, King Is Dead, 1952, Scarlet Letters, 1953, The Golden Summer, 1953 (under pseudonym Daniel Nathan), Glass Village, 1954, Ellery Queen's Awards, 1954-57, Q.B.I, 1955, Inspector Queen's Own Case, 1956, In the Queens' Parlor, 1957, Finishing Stroke, 1958, Ellery Queen's Mystery Anns, 1958-61, Ellery Queen's Anthologies, 1960—, Quintessence of Queen, 1962, To Be Read Before Midnight, 1962, Mystery Mix, 1963, Player on the Other Side, 1963, And On the Eighth Day, 1964, Double Dozen, 1964, Queens Full, 1965, Fourth Side of the Triangle, 1965, 20th Anniversary Annual, 1965, Study in Terror, 1966, Crime Carousel, 1966, Face to Face, 1967, All-Star Lineup, 1967, Poetic Justice, 1967, House of Brass, 1968, Mystery Parade, 1968, Q.E.D, 1968, Cop Out, 1969, Murder Menu, 1969, Minimysteries, 1969, Last Woman in His Life, 1970, Grand Slam, 1970, Golden 13, 1971, Fine and Private Place, 1971, Headliners, 1971, Mystery Bag, 1972, Crookbook, 1974, Murdercade, 1975, Aces of Mystery, 1975, Masters of Mystery, 1975, Giants of Mystery, 1976, Crime Wave, 1976, Magicians of Mystery, 1976, Masterpieces of Mystery, 20 vols, 1976-82, Searches and Seizures, 1977, Champions of Mystery, 1977, Cops and Capers, 1977, X Marks the Plot, 1977, Crimes and Consequences, 1977,

Faces of Mystery, 1977, Masks of Mystery, 1978, A Multitude of Sins, 1978, Napoleons of Mystery, 1978, Wings of Mystery, 1979, Scenes of the Crime, 1979, Secrets of Mystery, 1979, Ellery Queen's Mystery Mag, 1941-82; (Co- recipient Edgar Allan Poe awards (Edgars) 1945, 47, 49, 51, 60, Grand Master). Address: Larchmont, N.Y. Died Sept. 3, 1982.*

DANNELLY, CLARENCE MOORE, supt. schs.; b. Wetumpka, Ala., July 23, 1889; s. John Milton and Lena Augusta (Stephens) D.; B.Pd., State Normal Sch., Troy, Ala., 1907; A.B., Birmingham-Southern Coll., 1912, L.H.D.; A.M., George Peabody Coll. for Teachers, 1926; Ph.D., Yale, 1933; Litt.D., Southwestern U. (Tex.); LL.D., Centenary Coll.; m. Mary Newton Farnham, June 28, 1910; children—Clarence Moore (dec.), Hermione, Mary Farnham, (dec.), Frank Perry. Supt. city schs., Evergreen, 1908-10; prin. Etowah Co. High Sch., Attalla, Ala., 1912; in ednl. dept. Rand McNally & Co., Chicago, Ill., 1913-15, 1917-19; dept. edn., state of Ala., 1915-17; supt. Sunday sch. work, Ala. Conf., M.E. Ch., S., 1919-28; also supt. dept. of adminstration, Gen. S.S. Bd., M.E. Ch., S., 1926; pres. Ky. Wesleyan Coll., 1928-32; professor education, University of Alabama, 1934-36; superintendent of city and county schools, Montgomery, Alabama, from July 1, 1936. Ex-pres. Gen S.S. Council, M.E. Ch., S.; Lay Leader, Ala. Conf. Meth. Ch. 1941-52; mem. jud. council Meth. Ch., 1952-56. Vice pres. N.E.A., 1946-47. Mem. Am. Assn. Sch. Adminstrs. (adv. council, 1947-49), N.E.A., Ala. Edn. Assn., Alpha Tau Omega, Phi Delta Kappa, Omicron Delta Kappa, Kappa Delta Pi, Kappa Phi Kappa. Democrat. Mason (K.T., Shriner), K.P., Rotarian. Former mem. editorial bd. The Sch. Exec. Contbr. ednl. jours. Home: Montgomery, Ala. †

DARGUSCH, CARLTON SPENCER, lawyer; b. Batavia, N.Y., Aug. 19, 1900; s. Julius Herman and Etta (Burnham) D.; m. Genevieve Johnston, Nov. 6, 1923; children—Carlton Spencer (dec.), Evelyn Byrd (Mrs. Charles A. Lanphere). Student, Ind. U., 1921-22, Ohio State U., 1922- 25. Legislative draftsman Ohio Gen. Assembly, 1925; atty. Tax Commn. of Ohio, 1925-33, tax commr. of, Ohio, 1933-37, resigned, Jan. 1937, engaged in pvt. practice of law, specializing in taxation, Columbus, Ohio, 1937-84; dir. Clark Grave Vault Co.; cons. Engring. Manpower Commn.; Mem. com. specialized personnel, asst. dir. manpower ODM, 1955-57; mem. U.S. del. Conf. Applied Research in Europe, Vienna, Austria, 1956, India, 1958, USSR, 1960. Author: (with John R. Cassidy) Estate and Inheritance Taxation, 1930, rev. 1956, (with Jack H. Bertsch) The Operation of Selective Service in World War II, 1956. Trustee Ohio State U., 1938-59, 63-65, chmn. bd. trustees, 1944-45, 51-52, 58-59; dir. Ohio State U. Research Found., 1951-62. Active duty lt. col., Judge Adv. General's Dept. U.S. Army, 1940-47; dep. dir. nat. hdqrs. SSS promoted colonel 1942; brig. gen. 1946. Awarded D.S.M., 1946. Mem. Omicron Kappa Upsilon (hon.), Kappa Sigma, Phi Delta Phi, Mil. Order World Wars. Clubs: Mason. (Md.), Chevy Chase (Md.); Army and Navy (Washington); Columbus Country (Columbus), Columbus (Columbus), Ohio State Faculty (Columbus), Ohio State U. Sphinx (Columbus); Engineers (N.Y.C.), Chemists (N.Y.C.), The Players (N.Y.C.); Union (Cleve.); Queen City (Cin.). Helped draft plans for SSS, World War II and present; also plans for Universal Mil. Tng Home: Columbus, Ohio. Died Aug. 21, 1984.

DARLING, C(HESTER) COBURN, business exec.; born Pawtucket, R.I., Nov. 13, 1887; s. Lyman Morse and Abby (Rockwood) D.; student St. George's Sch., Newport, R.I., 1902-06; Class of 1910, Princeton; m. Marian Preston, Nov. 6, 1912; children—C. Coburn (officer, R.C.A.F., missing in action Aug. 1943), Eleanore (Mrs. William Everdell, 3d). Clerk, Rhode Island Ins. Co., Providence, 1910-12; local mgr. Jackson & Curtis Investment Securities, Boston, 1912-14, br. E. C. Randolph, mem. N.Y. Stock Exchange, Providence, 1914-18; mem. Miller & George, investment securities, Providence, 1920-38; member of the board directors The Avco Mfg. Corp. N.Y. Trustee Memorial Hosp., Pawtucket, R.I. Served as 1st lt., A.E.F., U.S. Army, 1918-19. Mem. Soc. Colonial Wars. Republican. Conglist. Mason. Clubs: Hope, Agawam Hunt (Providence); Colonial (Princeton); Racquet and Tennis, Links (N.Y. City); Reading Room, Yacht (Edgartown, Mass.). Home: Providence, RI. †

DARROW, GEORGE MCMILLAN, scientist; b. Springfield, Vt., Feb. 2, 1889; s. Guy Calvin and Maria (Barnet) McM.; A.B., Middlebury Coll., 1910; A.M., Cornell, 1911; Ph.D., Johns Hopkins, 1927; m. Grace Elizabeth Chapman, Aug. 19, 1919; children—Leslie, Edith, Carol, Wilson, George, Dan. With U.S. Bur. Plant Industry since 1911, prin. horticulturist in charge deciduous fruit prodn., Beltsville, Md., 1946-54; charge small fruit prodn. U.S. Department Agr. from 1954. Member A.A.A.S., Am. Genetic Assn. (mem. council from 1943, v.p., 1950-51), Am. Soc. Hort. Sci. (v.p., 1947-48, pres., 1948-49), Am. Phytopath. Soc., Washington Bot. Soc., Kappa Delta Rho. Mem. editorial bd., Jour. Heredity, 1922-44. Specialties: Research in small fruits, breeding of berries, polyploidy in fruit improvement. Home: Bowie, Md. †

DART, JUSTIN, business executive; b. Evanston, Ill., Aug. 17, 1907; s. Guy Justin and Laura (Whitlock) D.; m. Ruth Walgreen, Oct. 9, 1929 (div. 1939); children: Justin Whitlock, Peter Walgreen; m. Jane O'Brien, Dec. 31, 1939; children: Guy Michael, Jane Campbell, Stephen.

A.B., Northwestern U., 1929. With Walgreen Co. (drug store chain), Chgo., 1929-41, gen. mgr., 1939-41, dir., 1934-41; joined Rexall Drug Co. (became Dart Industries, Inc.), 1941, v.p., dir., 1942; pres. Dart Industries Inc., 1946-75, chmn., chief exec. officer, 1966-80; chmn. exec. com., dir. Dart & Kraft, Inc., 1980-84; dir. emeritus United Air Lines and; UAL, Inc. Chmn. bd. trustees U. So. Calif., 1967-71, trustee, 1972-84; trustee Los Angeles County Mus. Art, Hosp. Good Samaritan, Los Angeles; bd. dirs. Eisenhower Med. Center, Palm Desert, Calif. Republican. Clubs: Bohemian (San Francisco); Los Angeles Country, California; Cypress Point (Pebble Beach, Calif.); Eldorado Country (Palm Desert). Died Jan. 26, 1984.

DAUB, GUIDO HERMAN, chemist, educator; b. Milw., Dec. 16, 1920; s. Guido Ernst and Pauline Louise (Frentzel) D.; m. Katharine Powell, June 26, 1948; children—Guido William, Elisabeth, John Powell. B.S. in Chemistry, U. Wis., 1944, M.S., 1947, Ph.D. in Organic Chemistry, 1949. Chemist Rohm and Haas Co., Phila., 1944-45; faculty U. N.Mex., Albuquerque, 1949—, asst. prof. chemistry, 1949-54, assoc. prof., 1954-61, prof. chemistry, 1961-84, dept. chmn., 1970-81; dir. U. N.Mex. (Los Alamos Grad. Center), 1958-63. Co-author: Basic Chemistry, 1972, 77, 81; contbr. articles to publs. Recipient honor scroll N.Mex. Inst. of Chemists, 1975; recipient various research grants NIH, various research grants U.S. AEC, various research grants Dept. Energy. Mem. Am. Chem. Soc., Blue Key, Sigma Xi, Alpha Chi Sigma, Phi Lambda Upsilon, Phi Kappa Phi. Presbyterian. Club: University Golf Assn. Home: Albuquerque, N.Mex. Died June 4, 1984.

DAUERTY, JAMES SHACKELFORD, clergyman; b. Pittsburgh, Pa., Feb. 12, 1887; s. William MacConnell and Rida Allen (Mullen) D.; A.B., Lafayette Coll., 1910; A.M., Princeton, 1912; grad., Princeton Theol. Sem., 1913; Th.B., Th.M., Philadelphia Div. Sch., 1930, Th.D., 1932; m. Cora Leland Roberts, June 20, 1917; children—Barbara Anne (Mrs. John Charles Rhoades), James Shackelford, Charles Vernou Roberts. Ordained to Presbyn. ministry, 1913; pastor Columbus, N.J., 1913-18, Moorestown, N.J., 1918-45; adviser to General Assembly's com. on the Book of Common Worship, 1931; special lecturer on Presbyn. worship, Phila. Divinity Sch., 1931, Western Theol. Sem., Pittsburgh, 1939, Faculty Club of the Gen. Theol. Sem., N.Y., 1942; moderator of the Synod of N.J., 1941-42. Mem. Worship Commn. Fed. Council, Worship Commn. Western Sect. World Alliance of Ref. Chs., General Assembly's Com. on Revision of The Book of Common Worship (sec.), Soc. Bibl. Lit., Am. Soc. Ch. Hist. Del. Western Sect. to United Ch. of Can., 1942. Clubs: Presbyterian Ministers' Social Union, Canterbury, Twentieth Century, Wranglers (Philadelphia), Symposium (Princeton). Author: Index and List of Sources of Prayers in "The Book of Common Worship" of the Presbyterian Church, U.S.A., 1932; Ancient Hymns and Canticles in "The Handbook to The Hymnal," 1935; "Worship of the Reformed Churches" in Christendom, 1939. Contbr. articles to religious jours. Home: Clearwater, Fla. †

DAVENPORT, FRED MARSHALL, physician, educator; b. Scranton, Pa., Nov. 30, 1914; s. Fred Marshall and Laura May (Church) D.; m. Clara J. Dommerich, June 14, 1941; children—Laura May, Steven Marshall, Clara Josephine. B.A., Columbia, 1936, M.D., 1940, Sc. Med.D., 1945. Asst. prof. dept. epidemiology U. Mich. Sch. Pub. Health, Ann Arbor, 1951-52, assoc. prof., 1953-58, prof., 1958-77, prof. emeritus epidemiology and internal medicine, 1977-82; chmn., 1969-82; asst. prof. internal medicine Univ. Hosp., Ann Arbor, 1951-52, assoc. prof., 1953-58, prof., 1958-77; Dir. Commn. on influenza Armed Forces Epidemiological Bd., Office of Surgeon Gen., 1955-71; chmn. U.S. Viral Disease Panel, U.S. Japan Coop. Med. Sci. Program, NIAID, 1969-73; adv. panel on virus diseases WHO, from 1958. Bd. dirs., chmn. bd. sci. dirs. Center for Research in Diseases of Heart and Circulation and Related Disorders, from 1973. Served to capt., M.C. AUS, 1942-46. Mem. Am. Epidemiological Soc., Fedn. Socs. Exptl. Biology, Am. Soc. Bacteriologists, Am. Acad. Microbiology, Assn. Epidemiology Program Dirs. Sch. Pub. Health, Central Soc. for Clin. Research, Am. Assn. Immunologist, Harvey Soc., Robert Koch Inst. (hon.), Assn. Am. Physicians, Am. Soc. Clin. Investigation, Soc. Exptl. Biology and Medicine, Am. Pub. Health Assn., Assn. Tchrs. Preventive Medicine, Am. Soc. for Microbiology, Mich. Health Officers Assn., Internat. Epidemiol. Assn., Pan Am. Med. Assn., Research Club of U. Mich., Alpha Omega Alpha, Delta Omega. Home: Ann Arbor, Mich. Dec. Mar. 2, 1982.

DAVENPORT, JOHN SIDNEY, III, lawyer; b. Richmond, Va., Mar. 14, 1905; s. John Sidney and Marguerite (Warwick) D.; m. Edna Wylie McAdams, June 23, 1932 (dec. Nov. 1966); 1 dau. Marguerite Warwick (Mrs. J. Stephen Lord); m. Eliza Tabb Mason, May 4, 1968 (dec. Aug. 1976). B.A., Yale, 1927, LL.B., 1930. Bar: Va. bar 1930. Practiced in, Richmond; sr. partner Denny, Valentine & Davenport, 1939-66, Mays, Valentine Davenport & Moore, from 1967; with Office Gen Counsel WPB, 1942-44, OSS, 1944-45; dir. Little Oil Co. Inc., Richmond Fed. Savs. & Loan Assn. Mem. Richmond City Council, 1948-52; vice mayor, Richmond, 1948-50; Bd. dirs., past pres. Sheltering Arms Hosp.; former trustee Funds of Diocese Episcopal Ch. Recipient Good Govt. award

Richmond First Club, 1962, Spl. award for outstanding community service Jr. C. of C., 1962. Fellow Am. Coll. Trial Lawyers, Am. Bar Found.; mem. ABA, Va. Bar Assn. (past pres.), Richmond Bar Assn. (past pres.), Richmond C. of C. (past pres.), Corbey Ct., Alpha Delta Phi, Phi Delta Phi. Episcopalian. Clubs: Country of Va. (Richmond); Alfalfa (Washington); Shenandoah (Roanoke, Va.). Home: Richmond, VA.

DAVID, HENRY, consultant; b. N.Y.C., Dec. 5, 1907; s. George and Esther (Silver) D.; m. Bryna Ball, Nov. 20, 1959; 1 child (by previous marriage), Paul Allen. B.A., CCNY, 1929; M.A., Columbia, 1930, Ph.D., 1936; M.A., Cambridge, 1969. Instr. history dept. CCNY, 1930-38; lectr. New Sch. for Social Research, 1936-37; prof. history dept. Queens Coll., 1938-54; prof. grad. sch. bus. Columbia U., 1954-59; prof. econs., dean grad. faculty polit. and social sci. New Sch. for Social Research, 1959-61, pres. sch., 1961-63; dir. research BBC, 1942-45, adviser on Am. affairs, 1945-47; cons. Rand Corp., 1948-55, 63-64; exec. dir. Nat. Manpower Council, 1951-61, mem., 1961-66; head office sci. resources planning NSF, 1964-66; exec. sec. div. behavioral scis. Nat. Acad. Scis.-NRC, 1966-73; exec. dir. Assembly Behavioral and Social Scis., 1973-74; prof. pub. affairs Lyndon B. Johnson Sch. Pub. Affairs, U. Tex., Austin, 1974-78; dir. vocat. edn. study Nat. Inst. Edn., Dept. Edn., 1977-82; Pitt prof. U. Cambridge, Eng., 1969-70; cons. editor labor Random House; U.S. alternate del. UNESCO Gen. Conf., 1972; cons. Internat. Inst. for Applied Systems Analysis, Laxenburg, Austria, 1974-76, U.S. Congress Office of Tech. Assessment, 1976. Author: History of the Haymarket Affair, 1936, 58, Manpower Policies for a Democratic Society, 1963, (with others) History of Western Civilization, 1935, Labor Problems in America, 1940, House of Labor, 1951, America in Crisis, 1952; 11 publs. Nat. Manpower Council, 1952-65, Common Frontiers of the Social Sciences, 1957, Public Education in America, 1958; contbr. (with others) articles and reviews to periodicals.; Co-editor: (with others) The Economic History of the United States Series, 1945-84; Contbg. editor: (with others) Labor and Nation, 1946-52, Am. editor Futures, 1972-80; contbg. editor: (with others) Interim and Final Reports on the Vocational Education Study and related publs., 1977-81. Chmn. bd. trustees Inst. for Future. Benjamin Franklin fellow Royal Soc. of Arts; mem. Am. Hist. Assn., Indls. Relations Research Assn., Acad. Polit. Sci., AAAS, Phi Beta Kappa. Home: Washington, D.C. Died Jan. 21, 1984.

DAVIDS, MARK, investment banker; b. Los Angeles, Apr. 4, 1896; s. Mark A. and Elizabeth (Pickering) D.; A.B., Stanford, 1917; m. Helen L. Mosher, Sept. 15, 1923 (dec. 1946); children—Mark M., Suzanne; m. 2d, Ann Robinson, Oct. 29, 1949. Pacific coast dist. mgr. Reading Iron Co., 1923-25; sales mgr. Banks Huntley & Co., Los Angeles, 1925-30; Chgo. resident partner B.B. Robinson & Co., 1930-39; exec. v.p. Lester & Co., investment bankers, Los Angeles, 1940-51; gen. partner successor co. Lester, Ryons & Co., 1951-69; ltd. partner Hornblower, Weeks, Hemphill Noyes, 1969-78; Trustee Boys Republic, 1959-79. Served as 1st lt. U.S. Army, World War I; AEF in France. Mem. Investment Bankers Assn. (gov. 1959-61, v.p. 1964). Mason. Clubs: Bond (pres. 1959), California (Los Angeles); El Dorado Country. Home: Los Angeles, Calif. Died Dec. 25, 1979; interred Inglewood Cemetery, Calif.

DAVIDS, RICHARD CARLYLE, writer; b. Bagley, Minn., May 15, 1913; s. Ole and Annie Marie (Sunderland) D. B.A. magna cum laude, U. Minn., 1937. Tchr. pub. sch., Shevlin, Minn., 1931-33; field editor The Farmer, St. Paul, Minn., 1937-39; assoc. editor Better Homes & Gardens Mag., Des Moines, 1940-42, Farm Jour., Phila., 1948-66; producer 1st issue Ranger Rick Mag., Nat. Wildlife Fedn., Washington, 1966; editor Dynamic Maturity, Washington, 1975-77, free lance writer, 1966-75, from 77; Mem. Minn. Gov.'s Adv. Bd. on Natural Resources, 1972-75. Author: This Is Our Land, 1940, The Man Who Moved a Mountain, 1970, How to Talk to Birds, 1972, Garden Wizardry, 1976, Lords of the Arctic, 1982. Served with USAAF, 1942-46. Decorated Legion of Merit.; Winner of Howard W. Blakeslee award for med. writing Am. Heart Assn., 1961. Mem. Phi Beta Kappa, Sigma Delta Chi. Democrat. Lutheran. Originator concept human resource. Home: Bagley, Minn.

DAVIDSON, HOWARD CALHOUN, army officer; b. Wharton, Tex., Sept. 15, 1890; s. Dr. John Calhoun and Lily (Carleton) D.; student Tex. A. & M. Coll., College Station, Tex., 1907-09; LL.D. (honorary) Texas A. and M., College, 1946; B.S., U.S. Mil. Acad., 1913; grad. Air Corps Tactical Sch., 1933. Army War Coll., 1940; m. Mary Perrine Patterson, Oct. 8, 1921 (died 1950); children—Stuart Carleton, Mary Howard, Julia Shaw and Frances Patterson (twins); m. Eva Rucker Finn, 1958. Commd. 2d Lt., U.S. Army, 1913; advanced through grades, becoming brig. gen., Apr. 7, 1941; apptd. comdr. 10th Air Force, India, Aug. 1943. Promoted to rank of major general, 1944; director First National Bank of Arlington, Va. Decorated Distinguished Flying Cross, D.S.M., Air Medal, Order of Leopold (Belgium), Order Abdon Calderon, 2d Class (Ecuador). Comdr. British Empire, Order Cloud and Banner (China). Purple Heart. Trustee Charlotte Hall (Md.) Mil. Acad.; dir. Air Force Aid Soc. Mem. Aero. Assn. Methodist, Mason (Shriner). Clubs: Chevy Chase, Army and Navy (Washington). Home: Washington, D.C. †

DAVIDSON, J(OSEPH) LEROY, educator; b. Cambridge, Mass., Mar. 16, 1908; s. Edward A. and Mary (Susser) D.; A.B., Harvard, 1930; M.A., Inst. Fine Arts, N.Y.U., 1936; Ph.D., Yale, 1951; m. Martha Aginsky, Aug. 38, 1932; 1 son, Gergory Edward. Asst. dir., curator Walker Art Center, Mpls., 1939-43; research analyst War Dept., Washington, 1943-45; visual art specialist Dept. of State, Washington, 1945-47; asst. prof. Yale, 1947-55; prof. U. Ga., 1955-56; prof. art history Claremont Grad. Sch., 1956-61; prof. art history U. Calif. at Los Angeles, 1961-76, chmn. dept. art, 1970-72; Maude I. Kerns vis. distinguished prof. Oriental art U. Oreg., Eugene, 1976; participant archeol. expdn. India, 1963-64. Fulbright fellow, 1952-53. Author: Lotus Sutra in Chinese Art, 1954. Contbr. articles to profl. jours. Home: Pacific Palisades, Calif. Died Mar. 18, 1980.

DAVIDSON, RITA CHARMATZ, judge; b. Bklyn., Sept. 1, 1928; d. Michael and Eiga (Rokeach) Charmatz; m. David Sternheimer Davidson, Aug. 27, 1950; children: Minna Kohn, Leo Charmatz. B.A. with honors, Goucher Coll., 1948, LL.D., 1979; LL.B., Yale U., 1951. Bar: D.C. 1952, Md. 1963. Individual practice law, Washington and Montgomery County, Md., 1951-67; chairperson Montgomery County Bd. Appeals, 1960-64; commr. Md. Nat. Park and Planning Commn., 1967; zoning hearing examiner Montgomery County, 1967-70; sec. Md. Dept. Human Resources, 1970-72; asso. judge Ct. Spl. Appeals Md., 1972-79, Ct. Appeals Md., Annapolis, 1979-85; chairperson Gov.'s Commn. on Jobs for Vets. and; Gov.'s Interagy. Com. on Childhood Devel., 1970-72. Recipient Woman of Year award Balt. Bus. and Profl. Women, 1971; Disting. Citizen's award State of Md., 1973; Leadership award Silver Spring C. of C., 1973; Focus Women's award Montgomery County, 1980; Humanitarian award Citizens Awards Com. Balt., 1980; others. Mem. Am. Bar Assn., Md. Bar Assn., Montgomery County Bar Assn., D.C. Bar Assn., Women's Bar Assn., Nat. Assn. Women Judges, Nat. Assn. Women Lawyers, Am. Judicature Soc., Md. Jud. Conf., Yale Law Sch. Assn., Am. Law Inst. Home: Chevy Chase, Md. Died 1985.

DAVIES, DAVID WILLIAM, writer; b. Winnipeg, Man., Can., May 23, 1908; s. Owen H. and Catherine C. (McCaffrey) D.; m. Thelma E. Stengel, Nov. 10, 1936. A.B., U. Calif. at Los Angeles, 1932, A.M., 1940; Ph.D., U. Chgo., 1947. Mem. staff Henry E. Huntington Library, San Marino, Calif., 1927-28, asst. dept. rare books, 1936-38; research asst. to Herbert I. Priestley, Bancroft Library, U. Calif., 1933-36, in charge rare books and manuscripts, 1938-41; asst. prof. edn., librarian Utah State Coll., 1941-43; dir. libraries U. Vt., 1946-47; librarian Pomona, Claremont and Claremont Men's colls., 1947-52, Honnold Library for the Claremont Colls., 1952-67; staff writer Lloyd Corp. Ltd., 1973-74; writer Elsevier Pub. Co., Amsterdam, 1974-78; lectr. Calif. State U., Fullerton; prof. library sci. Immaculate Heart Coll.; lectr. history books and printing; vis. sr. lectr. Coll. Librarianship, Wales, 1967-68; Lectr. on Am. libraries in Netherlands under auspices Internat. Univ. Found., 1950. Author: The World of The Elseviers, 1580-1712, 1954, A Primer of Dutch 17th Century Overseas Trade, 1961, Dutch Influence on Elizabethan Culture, 1963, Elizabethans Errant, the Strange Fortunes of Sir Thomas Sherley and His Three Sons, 1967, An Enquiry into the Reading of the Lower Classes, 1970, The Evergreen Tree, 1971, Public Libraries as Culture and Social Centers, 1974, The Last Compaign of Sir John Moore, 1974, Grant Dahlstrom and the Castle Press, 1981, Clyde Brown, His Abbey and His Press, 1982; Editor: Sir Roger Williams' The Actions of the Low Countries, 1963, E.A. Abbott, Flatland, 1978; asso. editor: A Concordance to the Essays of Sir Francis Bacon, 1973. Served as 1st sgt. AUS, 1943-46. Guggenheim fellow, 1963-64. Home: Claremont, Calif.

DAVIES, HESTER ROGERS, school prin.; b. Avoco, Pa., Dec. 26, 1887; d. Rev. John Rumsey and Isabel (Moffat) D.; A.B., Wellesley, 1910; A.M., U. of Chicago, 1925; unmarried. Teacher history, Stevens Sch., Germantown, Pa., 1912-19; teacher history, Walnut Hill Sch. for Girls, Natick, Mass., 1919-29, prin. from 1932; teacher history, Spence Sch., New York, 1929-32. Mem. Am. Assn. Univ. Women, Headmistress Assn. of East, Wellesley Coll. Teachers Assn., Zeta Alpha. Presbyterian. Clubs: Wellesley(New York); Middlesex. Home: Natick, Mass.†

DAVIES, ISAIAH, army officer; b. near Columbus, Kan., July 12, 1890; s. William Benjamin and Mollie (Calvert) D.; ed. pub. and high schs. in Kan.; m. Beatrice Whitaker, June 2, 1915; children—Zela Louise (wife of Lt. Col. Robert C. McBride), Virginia Lee (wife of C. W. Corbett). Pvt. Inf., May 1912-Feb. 1914; transferred to Aviation Sec., Signal Corps, Air Corps and Army Air Forces, Feb. 1914, advanced through the grades to brig. gen., April 21, 1942; rated command pilot and combat observer; chief of staff, Eleventh Air Force; comd. squadron under Gen. Wm. Mitchel during bombing demonstrations off Va. Capes in 1921, when the German battleships were sunk, the first to be sunk by bombs. Mason. Club: Army and Navy (Washington). Home: Baxter Springs, Kans. †

DAVIES, ROBERT HOLBORN, container company executive; b. Galesburg, Ill., Sept. 19, 1919; s. Gomer and Ethel Mae (Holborn) D.; m. Eleanor Belle Cogan, May 12, 1940; children: Michael Joseph, Stephen Dewi. Student, U. Minn., 1936-39, Santa Ana Coll., 1939. Cons. engr. Lincoln Electric Co., Cleve., 1943-49; v.p. Baker Raulang Co., Cleve., 1949-51, Clark Equipment Co., Buchanan, Mich., 1951-59; pres. Electric Autolite Co., Toledo, 1959-63; chmn. bd. Eltra Corp., Toledo, 1963-64; pres. Sangamo Electric Co., 1964-76, Holborn Co., Toledo, 1976-80; sr. v.p., dir. corp. devel. Owens-Illinois Inc., Toledo, from 1980; dir. Toledo Edison Co., Dana Corp., Itel Corp. Pub.; mem. Hudson Inst. Mem. Soc. Automotive Engrs., Aircraft Owners and Pilots Assn., Nat. Aero. Assn., Material Handling Inst. (past pres.). Clubs: Toledo (Toledo), Belmont Country (Toledo), Toledo Country (Toledo), Toledo Tennis (Toledo), Shadow Valley (Toledo); N.Y. Yacht (N.Y.C.), Sky (N.Y.C.); Union League (Chgo.), Chicago (Chgo.). Address: Toledo, OH.

DAVIES, WALTER L. J., banker; b. Portland, Ore., Oct. 17, 1889; s. Rees D. and Elizabeth (Jones) D.; ed. pub. schs.; m. Marion Peacock, July 23, 1938. Began as messenger U.S. Nat. Bank, Portland, Ore., 1908. successively asst. cashier, asst. v.p., 1908-34. v.p. from 1934, now also dir. Served at lt., U.S. Army; with A.E.F., World War I. Republican. Mason (32 deg., Shriner). Clubs: Arlington, University (Portland, Ore.). Home: Portland, Ore. †

DAVIS, ALLISON, social anthropologist, psychologist, educator; b. Washington, Oct. 14, 1902; s. John Abraham and Gabrielle Dorothy (Beale) D.; m. Alice Elizabeth Stubbs, June 23, 1929 (dec. 1966); children: Allison Stubbs, Gordon Jamison; m. Lois L. Mason, Jan. 7, 1969. A.B., Williams Coll., 1924; M.A. in English, Harvard U., 1925; M.A. in Anthropology, 1932; postgrad. in anthropology, London Sch. Econs., 1932-33; Ph.D., U. Chgo., 1942. Co-dir. field research in social anthropology Harvard U., Cambridge, Mass., 1933-35; prof. anthropology Dillard U., New Orleans, 1935-38; research asso. in psychology Inst. Human Relations, Yale U., New Haven, 1938-39; research asso., asst. prof. human devel. U. Chgo. Center on Child Devel., 1939-42; asst. prof. edn. U. Chgo., 1942-47, asso. prof., 1947-48, prof., 1948-70, John Dewey Distinguished Service prof., 1970-83; vice chmn. com. on manpower retraining Dept. Labor, 1968-72; mem. Pres.'s Com. on Civil Rights, 1966-67; dir. Great Books Found., 1970-83; lectr. Harvard U., Smith Coll., U. Pitts., U. Wis., U. Rochester; George E. Miller Distinguished prof. U. Ill., 1965; Prentiss M. Brown Distinguished Service prof. Albion Coll., 1970. Author and co-author: eight books in field, including Children of Bondage, 1940, Deep South, 1941, Father of the Man, 1947, Social-Class Influences upon Learning, 1948, Manual, Davis-Ells Test of Problem Solving Ability, 1953, Psychology of the Child in the Middle Class, 1960, Cultural Deprivation, 1964, Leadership, Love and Aggression, 1983; contbr. numerous book chpts. Center for Advanced Studies in Behavioral Scis. fellow, 1959-60; named Educator of Year Edn. jour., 1971; recipient Distinguished Service medal Tchrs. Coll., Columbia U., 1977; Spencer Found. grantee, 1978-80, 81-82. Fellow Am. Acad. Arts and Scis.; mem. Am. Psychiat. Assn. (Solomon Carter Fuller award 1977), Phi Beta Kappa, Sigma Xi, Phi Delta Kappa. Home: Chicago, Ill. Died Nov. 21, 1983.

DAVIS, CURTIS WOODWARD, glass mfr.; b. Charleston, W.Va., Jan. 4, 1901; s. Henry and Lizzie (Brazeal) D.; student pub. schs., Charleston; m. Mary Emory Londeree, Jan. 8, 1922; children—Curtis Woodward, David E. With Libbey-Owens-Ford Co., Toledo, 1923-81, successively clk. stores dept., Charleston, supr. stores, established new stores system, Rossford, O., office mgr. Charleston plant, in charge control dept., indsl. engring. div. at Toledo, asst. mgr. Rossford plant, mgr., gen. factories mgr., Toledo, v.p., 1949-55, exec. v.p. prodn., 1955-59, exec. v.p., 1959-63, pres., 1963-64, pres., chief exec. officer, 1964-67; dir. Colonial Mdse. Co., Toledo, Harrison Marina, Toledo, Ohio Citizens Trust Co. Trustee Toledo YMCA, Toledo Hosp., Toledo Mus. Art. Baptist. Mason. Clubs: Sylvania Country, Toledo, Belmont Country (Toledo). Home: Toledo, Ohio. Died July 16, 1981; buried Ottawa Hills Meml. Park.

DAVIS, EDWARD WILSON, consultant; b. Cambridge City, Ind., May 8, 1888; s. Walter Clarance and Della Mendenhall (Wilson) D.; B.S., Purdue U., 1911, E.E., 1918; m. Jessie Mary Campbell, June 4, 1914; children—Jane, Martha, Ruth. Elec. engr. Westinghouse Electric & Mfg. Co., 1911, Gen. Electric Co., 1912; instr. mathematics, U. of Minn., 1913-15; engr. Mesaba Iron Co., 1915-18; with U. Minn., 1918-55, prof. and supt. Mines Expt. Sta., 1925-55; dir., 1938-55; metall. consultant to Reserve Mining Co., from 1955. Member Am. Mining Congress, Am. Inst. Mining and Metall. Engrs., A.A.A.S., Eastern States Blast Furnace and Coke Oven Assn., Phi Kappa Sigma. Republican. Mason. Clubs: Minneapolis Engineers, Campus. Author Mines Expt. Sta. bulls. on taconite. Home: Silver Bay, Minn. †

DAVIS, EUGENE W., lawyer; b. 1889; LL.B., U. Kan. Admitted to Kan. bar, 1915; practiced in Topeka; apptd. U.S. dist. atty., 1953. Address: Topeka, Kans. †

DAVIS, FLOYD ARNOLD, clergyman; b. McDonald, Ohio, Oct. 14, 1926; s. Ivan C. and Marguerite D.; m. Gayle Kuhn Rose, Jan. 24, 1947; children—James B., Christopher I., Paul D., Donald F., Wayne A., Harold L. D.D., Denver Baptist Bible Coll., 1974, B.A., 1975. Ordained to ministry Bapt. Ch., 1953; pastor chs. in, Ohio,

Okla., Colo., 1947-70; pastor Olivet Bapt. Ch., Kansas City, Kans., 1970-76; exec. dir. Assn. Baptists for World Evangelism, Cherry Hill, N.J., from 1976; chmn. bd. dirs. Faith Bapt. Bible Coll., Amkeny, Iowa, 1965-75; founder, 1st pres. Regular Bapt. Ch. Builders, Inc., Colo., 1963; mem. council Gen. Assn. Regular Bapt. Chs., 1973-77, chmn., 1976; bd. dirs. Assn. Baptist World Evangelism, from 1962. Served with USNR, 1944-45. Fellowship Baptists for Home Missions, 1960-76. Home: Marlton, NJ.

DAVIS, GENE BERNARD, artist; b. Washington, Aug. 22, 1920; s. Arthur G. and Edna Mae (Stout) D.; m. Florence Elizabeth Coulson, Nov. 24, 1960. Student, U. Md., 1938-39, Wilson Tchrs. Coll., Washington, 1939-41. Asst. prof. Corcoran Gallery Art Sch. Painting, Washington; instr. painting and drawing Am. U., 1968-69; artist-in-residence Skidmore Coll., N.Y., summer 1969, U. Va., 1972. One man shows, Corcoran Gallery Art, 1964, 68, 70, 78, MIT, 1966, Hofstra U., 1966, San Franciso Mus. Art, 1968, Washington Gallery Modern Art, 1968, Jewish Mus., 1968, Walker Art Center, 1978, Bklyn. Mus., 1982, Carnegie-Mellon Mus., Pitts., 1983; group shows, Chgo. Art Inst., Los Angeles County Mus., Detroit Mus. Fine Arts, Brandeis U. Mus., Mus. Modern Art, Buenos Aires, Rio de Janeiro, Art Gallery of Toronto, Can., Munson-William-Proctor Inst., Utica, N.Y., Corcoran Gallery of Art, Washington, Walker Art Center, Mpls., Isaac Delgado Mus., New Orleans, Atlanta Art Assn., Mus. Modern Art, 1966, San Francisco Mus. Art, U.S. Embassies Art Program, White House Art Program, Los Angeles Country Mus., 1964, Whitney Mus., 1967, 69, 71. Recipient Bronze medal Corcoran Gallery Biennial Am. Painting, 1965; grant for contbn. to Am. art Nat. Council on Arts, 1967; Guggenheim fellow, 1974-75. Address: Washington, D.C. Died Mar. 30, 1985.

DAVIS, GIFFORD, educator; b. Portland, Maine, June 11, 1906; s. Marshall and Marguerite (Gifford) D.; A.B., Bowdoin Coll., 1927; A.M., Harvard, 1928, Ph.D., 1933; m. Helen Adams Peabody, Aug. 9, 1930; children —Elizabeth Hale (Mrs. Charles Usher, Jr.), Anne Webster. Instr., Romance langs., tutor Harvard, 1929-30; faculty Duke, 1930-, prof. Romance langs., 1953-76, prof. emeritus, 1976-84, chmn. dept., 1957-64, dir. summer sch. Spanish studies, 1950-56, dir. undergrad. studies in Spanish, 1964-73. Mem. Am. Assn. Tchrs. Spanish and Portuguese (past pres. N.C.), S. Atlantic Modern Lang. Assn., AAUP. Presbyterian (elder). Contbr. articles on 19th century novel and medieval period in Spanish lit. to profl. lit. Home: Durham, N.C. Died July 18, 1984.

DAVIS, GLENN B., naval officer; b. Norwalk, O., Jan. 2, 1892; s. Albert William and Emma Laura (Benson) D.; B.S., U.S. Naval Acad., 1909-13; m. Ruth Pinkney Manahan, May 15, 1915; 1 son, Glenn Benson. Commd. ensign, 1913, promoted through grades to rear adm. Club: Army and Navy (Washington D.C.). Home: Norwalk, Conn. Died Sept. 9, 1984.

DAVIS, H(ARRY) NORMAN, flour mill executive; b. Birmingham, Eng., Nov. 18, 1888; s. Harry Osmond and Alice (Bill) D.; student pvt. schs., Cheltenham, Eng.; m. Lillian Harriet Taylor, Sept. 3, 1919; children—Alice Jane (Mrs. G. F. Perman), Norman Robert. With Ogilvie Flour Mills Co., Ltd., Montreal, Can., from 1905, beginning with various sales positions, successively sales mgmt. staff, asst. gen. mgr., v.p., 1905-52, pres., from 1952; pres. Canada Grain Export Co., Vancouver; v.p. Gerber-Ogilvie Baby Foods, Ltd., Niagara Falls; dir. Consol. Bakeries, Toronto, Indsl. Grain Products, Ft. William, McGavin Bakeries, Ltd., McGavin, Ltd., Vancouver; dir. Canadian com. Northern Assurance Co. Gov. Dominion Drama Festival. Episcopalian. Mason (33 deg.). Home: Westmount, Que., Can. †

DAVIS, HERBERT PERRY, prof. dairy husbandry; b. Montagu, Mich., Aug. 22, 1889; s. Smith Cornell and Meta Caroline (Perry) D.; B.S., U. of Mo., 1911; M.S., Pa. State Coll., 1914; m. Esther Gertrude Greiner, July 20, 1915; children—Carolyn Lenne (Mrs. William Wood McKittrick), Herbert Perry (dec.), Frederic (dec.). Asst. in dairy husbandry, U. of Ill., 1911; asst. in dairy husbandry, later instr., Pa. State Coll., 1911-14; asst. dairy husbandman, later dairy husbandman and editor dairy div. bur. animal industry, U.S. Dept. Agr., 1914-19; prof. dairy husbandry and vice dir., Idaho Agrl. Expt. Sta., U. of Idaho, 1919-21; prof. dairy husbandry, U. of Neb. from 1921. Official delegate U.S. World's Dairy Congress, Berlin, 1937. Socio Corr. Soc. Italiana Per Il Progresso Della Zootechnica, Milano, Italy, 1948. Fellow A.A.A.S.; member American Dairy Sci. Assn. (hon.) (past pres.), Am. Soc. Animal Prodn. (chmn. dairy production sect., 1944), Am. Genetics Assn., Neb. Acad. Sci., Am. Assn. U. Profs. (past pres. local chapter), Nat. Edn. Assn., Am. Inter-profl. Inst., Gamma Sigma Delta, Alpha Zeta. Conglist. Mason. Clubs: Rotary (past pres.), Eckles. Author: Livestock Enterprise (with others) (Lippincott) Contbr. to tech. jours. Home: Lincoln, Neb. †

DAVIS, JAMES BURNAM, development, investment and management consultant; b. Lilly, Ill., July 22, 1909; s. Charles William and Etta Eliza (Rutherford) D.; Conservation fellow Harvard, 1950-51, M.A., 1966; m. Delpha Lee Payne, Mar. 24, 1931; children—Carol Anne, Patricia Louise; m. 2d, Mary Martha Banks, Jan. 28, 1949. High sch. tchr., Maysville, Ky., 1929; tchr., basketball coach, Washington, Ky., 1929-30; economist Brookings Instn., 1934; economist, adminstrv. officer, agriculturist Dept. Agr., 1935-43; prin. agriculturist, chief program operations E. Central region A.A.A., 1943; chief marketing div. E. Central region Prodn. and Marketing Adminstrn., 1946-47, agriculturist Prodn. and Marketing Adminstrn., 1947-51, chief program devel. and operating methods, 1951, acting chief Pakistan br. TCA, 1951-52; sr. fgn. affairs officer specializing S. Asia, TCA, ICA, 1952-56, dep. chief agriculturist U.S. Tech. Coop. Mission to India, 1956-58, staff ICA, Washington, 1958-60; chief food and agr. officer AID, Lagos, Nigeria, 1961, Iran, 1965, Afghanistan, 1966, dep. assoc. dir., Vietnam, 1968, assoc. dir., 1969-73; mgmt. and evaluation cons., Europe, Asia, Africa, Latin Am.; now devel., investment and mgmt. cons. Served from lt. (j.g.) to lt. USNR, 1943-46. Methodist. Home: Falls Church, Va. Died July 3, 1979.

DAVIS, JAMES CURRAN, lawyer, also ex-congressman; b. Franklin, Ga., May 17, 1895; s. Thomas Benjamin and Lura Viola (Mooty) D.; student Reinhardt Coll., 1909-10, Emory Coll., 1910-12; m. Mary Lou Martin, Dec. 26, 1932; 1 dau., Mary Martin (Mrs. Edward G. Bowen). Admitted to Ga. bar, 1919; gen. law practice, Atlanta, 1919-34; DeKalb Co. rep. Ga. State Gen. Assembly, 1924-28; atty. Ga. Dept. Indsl. Relations, Atlanta, 1928-31; atty., DeKalb Co., 1931-34; judge superior cts., Stone Mountain Jud. Circuit, 1934-47; mem. 80th-87th U.s. Congresses, 5th Dist. of Ga.; dir. DeKalb County Fed. Savs. & Loan Assn. Del. Dem. Nat. Conv., 1952; mem. Ga. Dem. Exec. Com. Served in USMC, 1917-19. Mem. Sigma Alpha Epsilon. Methodist. Mason. Clubs: Atlanta Lions, Lawyers of Atlanta (past pres.), Ga. Motor (dir.). Home: Stone Mountain, Ga. Died Dec. 28, 1981.

DAVIS, JAMES ELMER, educator; b. Barneveld, Wis., Apr. 22, 1887; s. David J. and Sarah (Williams) Davies; student (Platteville) Wis. State Normal Sch., 1901-05; A.B., U. of Wis., 1912, A.M., 1913; m. Frances A. Walker, Aug. 25, 1920; children—David James, Francis Llewellyn, John Henry. Teacher, public schs. in Wis. and S.D., 1905-10; instr., and asst. prof. mathematics, Pa. State Coll., 1913-17; instr., mathematics, U. of Wis., 1919-22; asst. prof. and chmn. dept. of mathematics, U. of Ark., 1922-23; asst. prof. mathematics, Drexel Inst. of Tech., 1923-25; asso. prof. and chmn. dept. engring. extension, Pa. State Coll., 1925-26; asso. prof., Drexel Inst. of Tech., 1926-42, prof. and chmn. dept. of mathematics from 1942. Served as lt., capt., 313th Inf., A.E.F., 1917-19; commandant, Univ. Detachment, Univ. of Toulouse, France, 1919; capt. to colonel, inf., O.R.C., from 1920. Univ. scholar, U. of Wis., 1912-13. Mem. Am. Math. Soc., Math. Assn. of Am., Phi Beta Kappa, Gamma Alpha, Acacia, Scabbard and Blade. Mason. Presbyn. (mem. bd. trustees and treas.). Club: The Players (mem. bd. govs. and treas.). Home: Swarthmore, Pa. †

DAVIS, JAMES PORTER, b. Tennille, Ga., Aug. 31, 1889; s. Thomas Joel and Kate (Skipper) D.; A.B., Mercer U., 1908; studied U. of Chicago, summer 1911, Columbia, 1916-17; m. Mabel G. Scott, June 16, 1917 (dec. June 1950); children—James Porter (killed in action, 1944), Edwin Lanier, Theodore, Jean Katherine; m. 2d, Helen Louise Van Tuyl, Mar. 25, 1951. Began as teacher in secondary schs., 1908-16; Am. consul at Marseilles, France, 1917-21, Bangkok, Siam, 1921-22, Shanghai, China, 1922-25; engaged in pvt. business, 1925-33; successively economic advisor to NRA, exec. sec. Ulman Com. on Prison Labor Problems; mem. Prison Industries Reorganization Bd. and exec. sec. same, 1935-40; later consultant Price Stabilization Div., Nat. Defense Advisory Commn.; asso. price exec., liaison officer with Canadian Wartime Prices and Trade Bd.; adviser on price control to Cuban and Bolivian govts.; acting territorial dir., Puerto Rico; adviser on Latin-Am. Relations. Regional administrator, Territories and Possessions, Office of Price Adminstrn.; dir. Div. Office of Territories, Dept. of Interior, from Sept. 1947. Democrat. Episcopalian. Home: Falls Church, Md. †

DAVIS, JAMES ROBERT, civil engr.; b. St. Louis, June 24, 1924; s. Paul Lee and Alma Nora (Schlottach) D.; m. Lou Ann Walter, July 2, 1948; children—Kenneth Lee, Claire Luann, Bruce Robert. B.S., Calif. Inst. Tech., 1948, M.S., 1949. Registered profl. engr., Calif., Nev. Staff engr. Frederick J. Converse Co., 1949-50, 52-56; partner, chief engr. Converse Found. Engring. Co., Pasadena, Calif., 1956-63; v.p. Converse Found. Engrs., Pasadena, 1963-69; pres. Converse Davis Dixon Assos., Pasadena, 1969-78; chmn. bd. chief exec. officer Converse Ward Davis Dixon, Pasadena, from 1978; Planning commr., City of W. Covina, Calif., 1968-70. Served with USNR, 1943-46, 50-52. Fellow Am. Cons. Engrs. Council (dir. 1971), Inst. Advancement Engring. (Outstanding Engr. Merit award 1977); mem. ASCE, Cons. Engrs. Assn. Calif. (pres. 1970), Calif. Inst. Tech. Alumni Assn. (dir. 1976-79), Structural Engrs. Assn. Calif. Club: Rotary. Home: West Covina, Calif.

DAVIS, JOHN MORGAN, judge; b. Shenandoah, Pa., Aug. 9, 1906; s. William J. and Sarah R. (Jones) D.; m. Eva B. Pierson, June 18, 1932; children: Patricia Anne, Carole Joan, John Morgan. B.S., U. Pa., 1929, LL.B., 1932; postgrad., Sch. Banking, Rutgers U., 1942. Bar: Pa. 1933, U.S. Supreme Ct. bar 1933. Practiced in, Phila., 1933-52; v.p. Seaboard Radio Broadcasting Corp., 1937-51; gen. counsel Nat. Assn. Broadcasters, 1944-46; chmn. Community Broadcasting Corp., 1951-64; judge Ct. Common Pleas, 1952-58; lt. gov. Pa., 1959-63; judge Fed. Dist Ct. for Eastern dist. Pa., 1964—, now. sr. judge.; Chmn. Gov.'s Com. on Edn.; former sec. Pa. Labor Relations Bd. Recipient numerous awards. Mem. Am. Judicature Soc., Lawyers Club Phila., Socialegal Club Phila., Welsh Soc., Phi Alpha Delta (hon.), Lambda Sigma Kappa. Baptist (trustee). Lodge: Masons. Office: Philadelphia PA

DAVIS, JULIUS E., lawyer; b. Mpls., Apr. 21, 1912; s. Isadore and Molly (Edelman) D.; student Lawrence U., 1929-30; B.S., U. Minn., 1933, J.D., 1936; m. Lillian Stacia Kropman, May 26, 1940; children—Stephen J., Lawrence A. Admitted to Minn. bar, 1936, since practiced in Mpls.; pvt. practice, 1936-38; mem. firm Robins & Davis, 1938-43; sr. partner Robins, Davis & Lyons, Mpls., 1946-79; pres., dir. Ro-Vis, Inc., Daviland Corp.; chmn. bd., dir. Edina-France, Inc.; dir. Kodicor, Inc., Equity Capital Co., EQC Co., Inc., Jennie-O Foods, Inc., Willmar, Minn., Big Bear Stores, Columbus, Ohio, Lakeside Village Apts., Inc., Culver City, Calif., Oprel Holding Co., Inc., Balt. Pres., U. Minn. Found.; trustee Friends African Art. Served with AUS, 1943-45. Mem. Am., Minn., Hennepin County bar assns., Nat. Lawyers Club, U. Minn. Law Sch. Alumni Assn. Clubs: Mpls.; Drug and Chem. (N.Y.C.); Jockey (Miami). Home: Minneapolis, Minn. Died Mar. 16, 1979.

DAVIS, LOYAL, neurol. surgeon; b. Galesburg, Ill., Jan. 17, 1896; s. Albert and Laura (Hensler) D.; student Knox Coll., 1912-14, D. Sc. (hon.), 1933; M.D., Northwestern U., 1918, M.S., 1921, Ph.D., 1923; D.Sc. (hon.), Temple U., 1961; m. Edith Luckett, May 21, 1929; children—Richard, Nancy. Intern Cook County Hosp., 1918-19; surg. asst. to Dr. A.B. Kanavel, Chgo., 1920-23; fellow NRC, 1922-24; vol. asst. to Dr. Harvey Cushing, 1923-24; asso. prof. surgery Northwestern U., 1925-32, prof., chmn. dept. surgery, 1932-63, emeritus prof., 1964-82; cons. neurol. surgery VA, 1927-63; attending surgeon Passavant Meml. Hosp., 1929-63. Served as lt. M.C., World War I; col. AUS, 1942-43; ETO. Hon. fellow Royal Coll. Surgeons Eng., Royal Coll. Surgeons Edinburgh; fellow A.C.S. (chmn. bd. regents 1960-62; pres. 1963); mem. AMA, Am. Neurol. Soc., Soc. Neurol. Surgeons (pres.), Am. (pres. 1957), So., Western surg. assns., Soc. Clin. Surgery, James IV Assn. Surgery (pres. 1970-73), Halsted Soc., Beta Theta Pi. Club: Casino. Editor Surgery, Gynecology and Obstetrics 1938-63. Died Aug. 19, 1982.

DAVIS, MERRILL S., surgeon, univ. trustee; b. Miami, Ind., Mar. 11, 1890; s. George Washington and Sadie (Perry) D.; A.B., Ind. U., 1912, M.D., 1914; orthopedic resident Harvard Med. Sch., 1918-19; m. Mary Josephine DeMarcus, Sept. 6, 1913; children—Joseph, Richard. Pvt. practice specializing in orthopedic, gen. surgery, Marion, Ind.; founder, dir. Davis Clinic. Pres. Davis Med. Found.; trustee, v.p. James Whitcomb Riley Meml. Assn.; trustee Ind. U., 1950-52, 59-62. Chmn. bd. Riverside Meml. Hosp. Served with M.C., U.S. Army, 1917-19. Recipient Ind. U. Distinguished Alumni Service award, 1963. Fellow Am., Internat. colls. surgeons; mem. A.M.A., Grant County Med. Soc., Ind. Bone and Joint Club (founder, past pres.), Ind. U. Med. Sch. Alumni Assn. (a founder, 1st pres.), Ind. U. Alumni Assn. (pres. 1945-47; recipient Ind. U. plaque). Home: Marion, Ind. †

DAVIS, MORGAN JONES, geologist; b. Anson, Tex., Nov. 19, 1898; s. John Wesley and Gabrella (Jones) D.; student Tex. Christian U., 1916-18; B.A. in Geology, U. Tex., 1925; student Harvard Grad. Sch. of Bus. Adminstrn., 1947; D.Eng. (hon.), Colo. Sch. Mines, 1964; m. Veta Clare Moore, Aug. 8, 1926; children—Morgan J., Jr., James H. Worked on Tex. cattle ranch, 1915-16; engr., later asst. supt., Tulsa Spavinaw Water Project, 1921-24; became geologist Humble Oil & Refining Co., 1925; with Nederlandsche Kolonidale Petroleum Maatschappij, geologist in Java, resident geologist producing fields, Sumatra, Indonesia, 1929-34; with Humble Oil & Refining Co. (name now Exxon U.S.A.), 1934, chief geologist, 1941, mgr. exploration dept., 1946, dir. in charge exploration, 1948, v.p., 1951-56, exec. v.p., 1956-57, pres., 1957-61, chmn. board, chief exec. officer, 1961-63; dep. chmn. bd. dirs. Fed. Res. Bank of Dallas, 1961-63; cons., dir. First City Nat. Bank, Houston. Bd. trustees Kinkaid Sch., Houston; mem. vis. com. Grad. Sch. Bus. Adminstrn., Harvard, 1963-68; adv. council Geology Found., U. Tex. Bd. dirs., past pres. Nat. Space Hall of Fame. Recipient Distinguished Service award, Tex. Mid-Continent Oil and Gas Assn., 1960. Mem. Philos. Soc. Tex., Houston Geol. Soc. (life), Tex. Hist. Assn., Am. Assn. Petroleum Geologists (pres. 1952-53; Sidney Powers award distinguished achievement 1972), Assn. Profl. Geol. Scientists, Am. Petroleum Inst. (dir.), Mid-Continent Oil and Gas Assn., Am. Geog. Soc., Am. Inst. Mining, Metall. and Petroleum Engrs. Tex. Acad. Sci., Am. Geophys. Union, Geol. Soc. Am. (pres. 1968-69), Sigma Iota Epsilon, Delta Kappa Epsilon, Sigma Gamma Epsilon. Mason. Clubs: Harvard Business School, Houston Country, Ramada, River Oaks, Petroleum, Bayou (Houston); Boston (New Orleans); Mill Reef (Antigua, W.I.); St. Charles Bay Hunting (Rockport, Tex.); Twenty-Five Years of Petroleum Industry (pres. 1963). Home: Houston, Tex. Died Dec. 31, 1979.

DAVIS, NORRIS GARLAND, educator; b. Bartlett, Tex., Feb. 15, 1916; s. Emet Graves and Jennie (Shults) D.; student John Tarleton Coll., 1933-35; B.J., U. Tex., 1937, M.J., 1938; postgrad. U. Wis., 1941-43; Ph.D., U. Minn., 1954; m. Edith Bess Pennington, June 3, 1939;

children—Dan Garland, Dana Bess. Reporter Corpus Christi (Tex.) Caller-Times, 1938-40; instr. Tex. A.&M. Coll., College Station, 1940-41; asst. prof. journalism U. Tex., Austin, 1946-55, asso. prof., 1955-62, prof., 1962-81, chmn. journalism dept., 1965-76, asso. dean Sch. Communication, 1976-79. Bd. dirs. Tex. Student Publs. Mem. pub. relations com. Tex. div. Am. Cancer Soc., 1963-65. Served with AUS, 1943-46. Recipient Teaching Excellence award U. Tex. Students Assn., 1961, Teaching Excellence award, Piper Found., 1963, Friend of Tex. Press award, 1976, Tex. Daily Newspaper Assn. award, 1977. Mem. Internat. Council Indsl. Editors (pres. Austin chpt. 1966-67), Assn. Edn. Journalism, Southwestern Journalism Congress (pres. 1970-71), Tex. Journalism Edn. Council (pres. 1977-78), Sigma Delta Chi, Kappa Tau Alpha (nat. pres. 1977-78). Author: The Press and the Law in Texas, 1956; (with others) Modern Journalism, 1962. Contbr. articles to profl. jours. Home: Austin, Tex. Died Apr. 15, 1981.

DAVIS, POSEY OLIVER, educator, exec., writer; b. Athens, Ala., Aug. 15, 1890; s. Richard Scoggins and Malinda Elizabeth (Barker) D.; B.S., Ala. Polytechnic Inst., 1916; m. Mildred Kilburn, June 19, 1918. Teacher pub. schs., 1909-12; horticulturist Ala. Expt. Sta., 1916-17; argiculturist Southern Ry., 1917-18; connected with boys' 4-H Club work, Ala. Poly. Inst., 1918-20; with Progressive Farmer, 1920; dir. publicity, Ala. Poly. Inst., 1920-37, exec. sec. and registrar, 1932-37; dir Extension Service, 1937-59, Chmn. Ala. Cotton Textile Indsl. Relations Bd., 1933; gen. mgr. radio station WAPI, Birmingham, 1928-32; chmn. Ala. Soil Conserv. Com. since 1939, Ala. PMA Committee since 1937; mem. Industry Com. No. 1 under Fair Labor Standards Act of 1938; chmn. extension service section Assn. Land Grant Colls. and Univs., 1946 (elected 4-yr. member com. on organization and policy, 1942); dir. First National Bank, Auburn, Ala. Pres. Southeastern Resources Development Association, 1950-51, Assn. So. Agr. Workers, 1951-52; chmn. Ala. Rural Development Com., from 1956; mem. Ala. State Bd. Agr., from 1937, mem. adv. bd., State Dept. Conservation. Mem. state bd. Ala. Cancer Soc. Declared by the Progressive Farmer. "The Man of the Year" in Alabama Agriculture, 1939; awarded medal and certificate by American Farm Bureau Federation for distinguished service to American agriculture; lecturer; regular writer for newspapers and farm journals. Mem. Phi Kappa Phi, Gamma Sigma Delta, Alpha Zeta, Alpha Gamma Rho, Omicron Delta Kappa, Epsilon Sigma Phi. Democrat. Mem. Christian Ch. Mason (Shriner), Kiwanian; mem. Kiwanis Internat. Com. on Publicity, 1930-31, chmn. Com. on Agr., 1942; pres. Auburn Kiwanis Club, 1932. Author: One Man; A Century of Science on Alabama Farms. Home: Auburn, Ala. †

DAVIS, RALPH WILLIS, lawyer; b. Derry, N.H., June 28, 1890; s. Albert Augustus and Ella (Fellows) D.; Dartmouth, 1908-13; Columbia Law Sch., summer, 1914; Yale Law Sch., 1915-17; m. Marion Sullivan, Nov. 18, 1922; children—Marion Virginia, Barbara Arline. Admitted to N.H. bar, 1920, and began practice at Manchester; mem. McLane, Davis & Carleton; dir. First Nat. Bank, Derry. Mem. N.H. Ho. of Rep., 1921-23; atty. gen. of N.H., term 1929-34. Served as seaman, advancing to ensign, U.S. Navy, 1917-20. Trustee Trust Funds, Derry, 1920. Chmn. N.H. Racing Commn., 1933-35. Republican. Conglist. Home: Manchester, N.H. †

DAVIS, RAYMOND W(EBBER), banker; b. Hillsboro, N.D., Oct. 15, 1887; s. Harry W. and Clara E. (Webber) D.; B.A., University of Maine, 1911, LL.D. (honorary), 1957; married Hazel S. Small, February 2, 1918; children—Donald E., Dorothy A. With Guilford Trust Co. (Me.), from 1911, successively clk., sec., sec. and treas., 1911-28, pres., from 1928; dir. Eastern Trust & Banking Co. (Bangor). Adminstr. Piscataquis County OPA, 1942-44. Trustee U. Me., 1936-56, pres. bd., 1952-54; pres., director Guilford Meml. Library, from 1928. mem. Me. Bankers Assn. (pres. 1936-37; pres. group 4, 1933-34), Phi Gamma Delta. Mason. Club: Executives (Bangor). Home: Guilford, Me. †

DAVIS, RICHARD BEALE, educator; b. Accomack, Va., June 3, 1907; s. Henry Woodhouse and Margaret Josephine (Wills) D.; m. Lois Camp Bullard, Aug. 25, 1936. A.B., Randolph-Macon Coll., 1927, Litt.D. (hon.), 1955; A.M., U. Va., 1933, Ph.D., 1936; Litt.D. (hon.), Coll. William and Mary, 1979; L.H.D. (hon.), Eastern Ky. U., 1980. Instr. English McGuire U. Sch., Richmond, Va., 1927-30, Randolph-Macon Acad., 1930-32; instr., teaching fellow U. Va., 1933-36; asso. prof. Mary Washington Coll. U. Va., 1936-40; asso. prof. U. S.C., 1940-46, prof. English, 1946-47; prof. English, in charge Am. lit. U. Tenn., 1947-62, Alumni Distinguished Service prof. Am. lit., 1962-77, prof. emeritus, from 1977; vis. prof. Am. lit. U. Va., summers, 1938-42, U. Tex., 1949; research grantee Huntington Library, 1947, 50, Am. Philos. Soc., 1951-52, 58, 62, Folger Library, 1955, Am. Council Learned Socs., 1966, Colonial Williamsburg, 1964; Fulbright vis. prof. U. Oslo, 1953-54; U.S. State Dept. lectr. to Indian univs., 1957; vis. prof. Claremont Grad. Sch., 1957, Duke, 1965; chmn. So. Humanities Conf., 1960—. Author: Francis Walker Gilmer-Life and Learning in Jefferson's Virginia, 1939, (with Fredson Bowers) George Sandys-A Bibliographical Catalogue of Printed Editions in England to 1700, 1950, George Sandys, Poet-Adventurer, 1955, The Abbé Corréa in American, 1955, William Fitzhugh and His Chesapeake World, 1676-1701, 1963, Intellectual Life in Jefferson's Virginia, 1790-1830, 1964 (Am. Assn. State and Local History award 1963), American Literature through Bryant, 1969, Literature and Society in Early Virginia 1608-1840, 1973, Intellectual Life in the Colonial South, vols. 1-3, 1978 (Nat. Book award for history 1979), A Colonial Southern Bookshelf, 1979; contbr. (with Fredson Bowers) articles to profl. jours.; Editor: (with Fredson Bowers) Tenn. Studies in Lit, 1956-72, Correspondence of Thomas Jefferson and Francis Walker Gilmer, Chivers' Life of Poe, 1952, The Colonial Virginia Satirist, 1967, Collected Poems of Samuel Davies, 1723-1761, 1968, The Wept of Wish-ton-Wish (Cooper), 1970, The Letters of the British Spy (William Wirt), 1970, (with C.H. Holman, L. Rubin, Jr.) Southern Writing, 1970; Co-editor: (with C.H. Holman, L. Rubin, Jr.) American Cultural History, 1607-1829, 1961. Served with USNR, 1943-46. Guggenheim fellow, 1947, 60-61; Nat. Endowment for Humanities fellow, 1974; Chancellor's research scholar, 1976-77; Nat. Humanities Center fellow, 1979-80. Mem. S. Atlantic MLA (pres. 1964-65), MLA (chmn. Am. lit. sect. 1975), Bibliog. Soc. Am., AAUP, Raven Soc., Internat. Assn. Profs. English, Va. Hist. Soc. (hon.), Am. Antiquarian Soc., Blue Key, Phi Beta Kappa, Phi Kappa Phi, Lambda Chi Alpha, Sigma Upsilon. Episcopalian. Clubs: Colonnade (U. Va.); Arlington (Ky.); Cosmos (Washington). Address: Knoxville, Tenn. Dec. Mar. 30, 1981.

DAVIS, RICHARD FRANCIS, educator, university official; b. Keene, N.H., Aug. 30, 1924; s. Leston Francis and Bessie Viana (Barrett) D.; m. Carolyn Bernice Turner, June 18, 1950; children: Richard F., Rebecca L. B.S., U. N.H., 1950; M.S., Cornell U., 1952, Ph.D., 1953. Asst. prof. animal nutrition Cornell U., 1953-54; asst. prof. dairy sci. U. Md., College Park, 1954-56, asso. prof., 1956-58, prof., 1958-85, head dept. dairy sci., 1956-81, acting chmn. div. agrl. and life scis., 1973-74, asso. provost agrl. and life scis., 1981-85. Author: Modern Dairy Cattle Management, 1962; contbr. articles on animal nutrition to profl. jours. Served with U.S. Army, 1944-46. Mem. AAAS, Am. Inst. Nutrition, Am. Dairy Sci. Assn., Am. Soc. Animal Sci., N.Y. Acad. Sci., Washington Acad. Sci., Sigma Xi, Phi Kappa Phi, Alpha Zeta. Methodist. Club: Rotary (College Park) (pres. 1973-74). Home: Adelphi, Md. Died Jan. 3, 1985.

DAVIS, T(HOMAS) COLBURN, business exec.; b. Kanawa County, W.Va., Jan. 17, 1887; s. T.O.M. and Elizabeth (Dickinson) D.; student West Virginia public schools; married Sara Swisher, August 10, 1917; children—Thomas Colburn (deceased), Helen (Mrs. Herbert C. Wohlers). With Kanawha Nat. Bank, Charlestown, W.Va. to 1916; located in New York, 1927; dir. Mo. Pacific R.R., from 1941, Mich. Chemical Corporation, from 1941; pres., director Centennial Development Co., from 1944; dir. Am. Chain & Cable Co., Detroiter Mobile Homes, Mobile Homes Finance Co., Brightwater Paper Co., W. T. Morris Foundation, John J. Nesbitt, Inc., Sormir Petroleum Corp.; exec., trustee, Wm. T. Morris estate from 1946. Border service with W.Va. N.G.; overseas, World War I; student War Coll., 1923; mem. War Dept. Gen. Staff 1924-27. Clubs: Army and Navy (Washington); Racquet (St. Louis); Detroit; Saginaw (Mich.); Pine River Country (Alma, Mich.). Home: Saint Louis, Mich. †

DAVIS, WALLACE, lawyer; b. Russellville, Ark., July 12, 1888; s. Jeff and Ina (McKenzie) D.; student U. of Ark. and Vanderbilt U.; m. Ethel Riley, Dec. 26, 1929. Admitted to Ark. bar, 1910, practiced in Little Rock; mem. Pace Davis & Pace; atty. gen. Ark., 1915-17; mem. Dem. Nat. Com., 1916-20. Presbyterian. Home: Little Rock, Ark. †

DAVIS, WILLIAM VIRGINIUS, naval consultant; b. Savannah, Ga., Jan. 28, 1902; s. William Virginius and Winifred (Bonney) D.; B.S., U.S. Naval Acad., 1924; m. Margaret Cary, Oct. 1, 1927; children—Judith Cary, Mary Winifred, William Virginius, Margaret Wright. Commd. ensigh USN, 1924, advanced through grades to vice adm., 1956; comdg. officer Torpedo Squadron 5, USS Yorktown, 1940-41; officer in charge aircraft armament unit Air Sta., Norfolk, Va., 1941-43; staff, comdr. aircraft Central Pacific Force, Pacific Fleet, 1943-44, dep. chief staff for operations, 1944, comdr. shore-based air force forward area Central Pacific, 1944, 1944, chief staff hdqrs. strategic air force Pacific Ocean Areas, 1944-45; comdr. USS Tulagi, 1945-46; project coordinator operational devel. force Atlantic Fleet, Norfolk, 1946-47; dir. flight tests Air Test Center, Patuxent River, Md., 1947-50, comdg. officer, 1951; comdg. officer USS Franklin D. Roosevelt, 1950-51; dep. comdr. field command Armed Forces Spl. Weapons Project, Sandia Base, 1952-55; comdr. carrier div. 5, Pacific Fleet, 1955-56; dep. chief Naval Operations (Air), 1956-58; dep. comdr.-in-chief U.S. Atlantic Fleet, 1958-60; sr. mil. adviser Lockheed Aircraft Corp., 1960-64; exec. dir. USS Alabama Battleship Commn., 1964-72, navy and mil. cons., 1972-74. Mem. NACA 1956-58. Decorated D.F.C., Legion of Merit; Most Noble Order Crown Thailand 1st class. Recipient Nat. Air Council ann. award for helicopter devels., high altitude jet flight, 1949. Home: Fairhope, Ala. Died July 25, 1981.

DAVISON, DENVER N., former chief justice Okla. Supreme Ct.; b. Rich Hill, Mo., Oct. 9, 1891; s. Benjamin P. and Lottie (Jones) D.; J.D., U. Okla., 1915; m. Barbara Wilhelm, July 29, 1917 (dec.); 1 son, Denver B. (dec.); m. Lillian Richardson Wright, Sept. 5, 1976. Practiced law, Coalgate, Okla., 1915-27, Ada, Okla., 1927-37; mem. Supreme Ct. Okla., Oklahoma City, 1937-78, chief justice on three occasions. Mem. original Will Rogers Commn. Served with U.S. Army, World War I. Mem. Alpha Tau Omega, Phi Delta Phi. Clubs: Elks, Masons, K.P., Rotary (charter mem., past pres.). Home: Oklahoma City, Okla. Died Apr. 28, 1983.

DAVISON, RUSSELL LEE, educator; b. Southampton, Cumberland Co., N.S., Aug. 15, 1887; s. Arthur John and Olive Adelia (Phinney) D.; brought to U.S., 1892; grad. Dean Acad., Franklin, Mass., 1910; A.B., Tufts Coll., 1914; m. Ency Harrington Case, June 13, 1916. Teacher Dean Acad. until 1919; employment mgr., Walpole, Mass., 1919-20; prin. Goddard Sem., from 1921. Mem. Theta Delta Chi. Universalist. Home: North Billerica, Mass. †

DAVY, CHARLES EARL, corp. exec.; b. Dowagiac, Mich., Feb. 27, 1890; s. Charles Humphry and Emma (Moore) D.; student pub. schs., Pitts.; m. Ethyl J. Thatcher, Nov. 7, 1935. Dir. engring. operations and mem. engring. bd. Chrysler Corp.; asso. with advanced engring. designs and procurement of vital material. Active in aircraft and tank engine programs, World War II. Mem. Detroit Bd. of Commerce, Franklin Inst. Club: Detroit Athletic. Home: Detroit, Mich. †

DAWLEY, POWEL MILLS, educator, clergyman; b. Newport, R.I., Mar. 1, 1907; s. William James and Mabel Cleveland (Wilson) D.; Ph. B., Brown U., 1929, A.M., 1931, D.D., 1965; B.D. (Phillips Brook fellow), Episcopal Theol. Sch., 1936, D.D., 1961; Ph.D., U. Cambridge (Eng.) Corpus Christi Coll., 1938; S.T.D., Gen. Theol. Sem. 1955; m. Dorothy Wainwright Knapp, Dec. 1, 1941; children—Victoria Wainwright, Pamela Wilson, Dorothy Maris. Ordained dean P.E. Ch., 1935, priest, 1936; asso. rector St. David's Ch., Balt., 1938-42; dean St. Luke's Cathedral, Portland, Me., 1942-45; prof eccles. history Gen. Theol. Sem., N.Y.C., 1945-71, sub-dean, prof. emeritus, 1971—. Mem. Am. Soc. Ch. History, Lambda Sigma Nu. Mason (32 deg.). Author: The Religion of The Prayer Book, 1943; Chapters in Church History, 1950; The Words of Life, 1950; John Whitgift and the English Reformation, 1954; The Episcopal Church and its Work, 1955; Our Christian Heritage, 1959; The Story of the General Theological Seminary, 1969; The Story of the General Theological Seminary, 1969. Home: Brunswick, Maine. Died July 10, 1985.

DAWSON, FRANCIS MURRAY, hydraulic and sanitary engring.; b. Truro, N.S., Canada, Sept. 3, 1889; s. Charles Murray and Ellen (Dickie) D.; B.S. in C.E., N.S. Tech. Coll., Halifax, N.S., 1910; M.C.E., Cornell U., 1913; E.D. (honoris causis), Syracuse U., N.S. Tech. Coll.; m. Lettie Palmer Heaton, January 11, 1919; children—John Howard, Murray Heaton, Susan Alice (dec.), Ursula Jean (adopted), Letitia Alice. Came to U.S., 1922. Began as engr. constrn. and survey work. Transcontinental and Grand Trunk Pacific Ry., 1906; instr. civil engring. and engr. Dock constrn., Halifax, 1910-12; asst. prof. hydraulics, Cornell U., 1921-22; asso. prof. hydraulics, U. of Kan., 1922-24, prof., 1924-28, actg. dean of men, 1926-28; prof. hydraulics and sanitary engring., U. of Wis., 1928-36; dean Coll. of Engring., U. of Ia., from 1936, has been cons. engr. on many projects. Chmn. com. for nat. plumbing code; men. Ia. Natural Resources Council, Iowa Hwy. Research Board. Served as capt. Canadian Engrs. in France, 1915-19. Awarded Mil. Cross (Can.). Mem. Am. Soc. C.E. (dir.), Engr. Coll. Research Council (chmn. 1946-50), Am. Soc. Engring. Edn. (v.p. 1946-50, pres. 1950-51), Nat. Research Council (exec. com.), Am. Geophysics Union, Am. Water Works Assn., Am. Sewage Works Assn., Sigma Xi, Tau Beta Pi, Sigma Tau. Triangle. Conglist. Club: University. Author profl. books and articles. Home: Iowa City, Ia. †

DAWSON, JOHN ALBERT, investment dealer, religious ofcl.; b. Chgo., Sept. 3, 1904; s. John Henry and Ida Louise (Hellman) D.; student Northwestern U., 1925-27; LL.D. (hon.), Alderson-Broaddus Coll.; m. Annie Joe Howel, Mar. 24, 1934; children—Ann (Mrs. Myron Stanton), Mary (Mrs. William R. Dunar), John H. Gen. partner John A. Dawson & Co., Chgo., 1931-71; mem. Midwest Stock Exchange, Chgo., 1950-71. Past world chmn. men's dept., mem. exec. com. Bapt. World Alliance; past pres. Chgo. Bapt. Assn., Am. Bapt. Conv., Am. Bapt. Assembly, Green Lake, Wis. Mem. Chgo. Crime Commn.; mem. at large Nat. council Boy Scouts Am. Trustee Central Bapt. Children's Home, Bapt. Home and Hosp., Maywood, Ill., Bapt. Theol. Union (U. Chgo.), No. Bapt. Theol. Sem., Oakbrook, Ill; chmn. trustees Judson Coll., Elgin, Ill. Mem. Nat. (trustee), Ill. (past pres.) socs. S.A.R., Soc. Mayflower Descs. in Ill. (gov. 1960-63), Navy League U.S., Soc. Colonial Wars, Phi Kappa Sigma. Republican. Club: N Men's (Northwestern U.). Home: Wilmette, Ill. Died Oct. 20, 1979; buried Rosehill Cemetery, Chgo.

DAWSON, MITCHELL, lawyer, writer; b. at Chicago, Ill., May 13, 1890; s. George Ellis and Eva (Manierre) D.; Ph.B., U. of Chicago, 1911, J.D., 1913; m. Rose Hahn, Mar. 8, 1921; children—Hilary, Jill, Gregory. Admitted to Ill. bar, 1913, and practiced since at Chicago; mem. Dawson & Dawson, 1917-26 and 1933-35, Dawson, Dawson & Schneberger, 1926-33; in pvt. practice. Served with Ambulance Service, U.S. Army, July 1917-Mar.

1918; sergt. Intelligence Corps, U.S. Army, Mar. 1918-Jan. 1919. Dir. and sec.-treas. Chicago Civic Broadcast Bur., 1934-35; mem. exec. com. Cook County Consumers Council, 1933-35; mem. Adult Edn. Council of Chicago (dir.). Mem. Chicago Bar Assn. (pub. relations counsel, chmn. pub. relations com. 1934-37), Ill. State Bar Assn., Am. Bar Assn. (chmn. public relations com. of sect. on bar orgn. activities 1936-38; mem. com. on econ. condition of the bar 1937-39), Internat. Bar Assn., Chicago Law Inst., Authors League America, Delta Chi. Club: City (dir.; v.p. 1943-44). Author: The Magic Firecrackers, 1949. Editor of the Chicago Bar Record, 1934-35, 1939-42. Contributed column of legal comment to Chicago Daily News and other papers, 1926-31; contributor to Harper's, Atlantic, New Yorker, Saturday Evening Post, Reader's Digest, etc. Lecturer on newspaper law, Medill Sch. of Journalism, Northwestern U., 1943-44. Chmn. Winnetka Caucus Com., 1945. Home: Winnetka, IL. *

DAY, JAMES OZRO, govt. official; born Decatur, Miss., Nov. 30, 1888; s. Samuel Marion and Eliza P. (Clark) D.; student Droughons Sch. of Commerce, 1907, Miss. Heights Acad., 1908-10; LL.B., Washington and Lee U., Lexington, Va., 1912; m. Maude Barbara Reeves, Oct. 1, 1918; 1 dau., Daysidel (Mrs. Thomas James Bruister). Admitted to Miss. bar, June 1912; in gen. practice of law, 1920-28; state senator, 27th Dist., Miss., 1928-32; Circuit Court judge, 1933; asst. U.S. dist. atty., 1938-42; U.S. dist. atty., 1942-48; atty., penal div. Internal Revenue Service, U.S. Treasury Dept., from 1948; apptd. counsel for U.S. Senate Com. governing District of Columbia, Wash., D.C., for term beginning Jan. 1, 1945. Served in U.S. Army, World War I, 1917-19. Trustee Tutwiler High Sch., Delta State Teachers Coll. Mem. Am. Legion. Mason (Scottish Rite). Clubs: Lions; Chamber of Commerce. Address: Atlanta, Ga. †

DAY, JAMES WARREN, accountant; b. Brownwood, Tex., Dec. 10, 1903; s. William Riley and Martha Jane (Warren) D.; m. Tommie Hazel Diestelhorst, Mar. 22, 1934; 1 dau., Diane Shepherd. A.B., Tex. Christian U., 1928, M.A., 1929. C.P.A., Tex. Sr. partner Day, Benton & Covey, 1949; partner Day, Benton & Frazier (C.P.A.'s), 1949-69; now asso. Brantley, Spillar & Frazier (C.P.A.'s); prof. evening coll. Tex. Christian U., 1936-62; sec., dir. William N. Edwards & Co. (investment bankers), 1944-66, Hopkins County Broadcasting Co., Sulphur Springs, Tex., 1948—; dir. Tex. Commerce Bank of Fort Worth. Former mem. citizens council Scott and White Meml. Hosp., Scott, Sherwood and Brindley Found.; past v.p., dir. Met. Dinner Club Greater Ft. Worth; past mem. lay adv. bd. St. Joseph Hosp.; adv. council S.W. Bapt. Theol. Sem. Recipient Distinguished Service award U.S. Jr. C. of C., Ft. Worth, 1933; Distinguished Alumnus award Tex. Christian U., 1966. Mem Am. Accounting Assn., Municipal Fin. Officers Assn. of U.S. and Can., Nat. Assn. Cost Accountants (pres. Ft. Worth chpt. 1950-51), Am. Inst. Accountants, Tex. Soc. C.P.A.'s, Joint Civilian Orientation Conf. No. 19, Def. Orientation Conf. Assn. Ind. Democrat. Baptist. Clubs: Mason (Ft. Worth), Elk (Ft. Worth) (past exalted ruler), Optimist (Ft. Worth) (pres. Ft. Worth 1939-40, dist. gov. 1945-46, internat. pres. 1952-53, chmn. boys work council 1959-60), Knife and Fork (Ft. Worth), Fort Worth (Ft. Worth). Home: Fort Worth TX

DAY, ROBERT JAMES, magazine cartoonist; b. San Bernardino, Calif., Sept. 25, 1900; s. James Anderson and Estelle Strowbridge (Brooks) D.; m. Ethel H. Fabian, Aug. 29, 1904; children: Estelle E., James Anderson II. Student, Otis Art Inst., 1919-27. Mem. art dept. Los Angeles Times, 1919-27, Los Angeles Examiner, 1927-29, N.Y. Herald Tribune, 1930. Contbr.: other nat. mags. Punch, advt. campaigns nat. corps., cartoons exhibited throughout, U.S., Europe.; Author: All Out for the Sack Race, 1945; Illustrator: We Shook the Family Tree, 1946, Fun Fare, 1949, Lower Prices Are Coming, 1950, (Arthur Godfrey) Stories I Like to Tell, 1952, (Dorothy Rickard) Little Willie, 1953, (William Zunsser) Any Old Place With You, 1957, Seen Any Good Movies Lately, 1958, (Jack Olsen) The Mad World of Bridge, 1960, (Jonathan Rhodes) Over the Fence is Out, 1961, (Cory Ford) What Every Bachelor Knows, 1961, (Jane Goodsell) I've Only Got Two Hands and I'm Busy Wringing Them, 1966, (Leo Rosten) Rome Wasn't Burned in a Day, 1972. Address: Gravette, Ark. Died Feb. 7, 1985.

DAY, WILLIAM EDWIN, former judge; b. Washington, July 17, 1912; s. Ralph Edwin and Mary Agnes (Smith) D.; LL.B., Nat. U., 1935, LL.M., M.P.L., 1937; m. Mary Redmond, May 28, 1938. Admitted to D.C. bar, 1936; with GPO, 1931-37; instr. printing Coll. Engring., Carnegie Inst. Tech., 1937-40; pvt. practice law, Washington, 1940-41; spl. atty. antitrust div. Dept. Justice, 1941-42, spl. asst. to atty. gen. antitrust div., 1945-49; commr. U.S. Ct. Claims, 1949-73, sr. trial judge, 1973-74. Served to lt. comdr. USCGR, 1942-45. Mem. Am., D.C. bar assns. Club: Army-Navy Country (Arlington). Home: New Smyrna Beach, Fla. Died Sept. 9, 1981.

DAYHOFF, MARGARET OAKLEY, biochemist; b. Phila., Mar. 11, 1925; d. Kenneth Wilson and Ruth Prettyman (Clark) Oakley; m. Edward S. Dayhoff, May 29, 1948; children—Ruth Elizabeth, Judith Elaine. B.A., N.Y. U., 1945; M.A., Columbia U., 1946, Ph.D., 1948. Postdoctoral research asst. Rockefeller Inst. for Medical Research, N.Y.C., 1948-51; postdoctoral research fellow U. Md., College Park, 1957-59; head dept. chem. biology Nat. Biomed. Research Found., Washington, 1960—, asso. dir. research, 1962-83; asso. prof. physiology and biophysics Georgetown U. Med. Sch., 1970-77, prof., 1977-83; bd. dirs. Nat. Biomed. Research Found., 1978-83; mem. adv. com. NIH, 1972-75. Editor: Atlas of Protein Sequence and Structure, 1965-83. NIH grantee, 1963-83; NASA grantee, 1964-83. Fellow AAAS; mem. Am. Soc. Biol. Chemists, Am. Chem. Soc., Biophys. Soc. (sec. 1971-79, pres. 1980-83), Internat. Soc. Study Origins of Life (mem. council), Council of Biology Editors, N.Y. Acad. Scis., Am. Soc. Cell Biology. Head Protein Sequence Reference Data Collection, Nucleic Acid Sequence Data Base. Home: Silver Spring, Md. Died Feb. 5, 1983.

DEACON, EUGENE L., banker, engr.; b. Everly, Ia., Aug. 9, 1888; s. Eugene H. and Helen (Lippincott) D.; B.S. in C.E., Ia. State Coll. Agr. and Mech. Arts, 1911; m. Henrietta A. Wiese, Dec. 25, 1911 (died Jan. 31, 1917); 1 dau., Thais Dorothy; m. 2d, Hazel E. Kator, May 1, 1919; 1 son, John E. Constrn. engr., George A. Fuller Co., Chicago and Detroit, 1911-16; gen. supt. A. J. Smith Constrn. Co., June 1919-Feb. 1921; in pvt. real estate business and bldg. constrn., Detroit, 1921-26; mem. staff Union Trust Co., Detroit, in charge erection 40-story Union Trust Bldg., 1926-29, v.p., in charge operation, maintenance and rentals same and other office bldgs., and miscellaneous property from 1929; pres. and treas. Taber-Deacon Co., office and home furnishings; prin. organizer and pres. Brightmoore State Savings Bank, 1924. Served as 1st lt., later capt. Signal Corps, U.S.A., June 1917-Aug. 1918; maj. Air Service, Aug. 1918-Jan. 1919; engr. in charge constrn. aviation camps at Rantoul, Ill., Kelly Field No. 2, San Antonio, Tex., Houston, Tex., Lake Charles, La.; later in gen. charge all aviation camp constrn., and in charge Aviation Repair Depot Sect. Mem. Acacia fraternity. Republican, Conglist. Mason (K.T., Shriner). Club: Detroit Athletic. Home: Detroit, Mich. †

DEALEY, JAMES QUAYLE, JR., ret. educator; b. Providence, Sept. 21, 1899; s. James Quayle and Clara (Learned D.; A.B., Brown U., 1920; B.A. (Rhodes Scholar 1921-23), Oxford (Eng.), U., 1923, M.A., 1928; Ph.D., Harvard, 1928; m. Esther Poole Reed, June 24, 1932; 1 son, William Reed. With personnel dept. Lycoming Rubber Co., 1920; trust dept. R.I. Hosp. Trust Co., 1924-25; instr. govt. Harvard, 1925-28; asst. prof. polit. sci. Western Res. U., 1928-31; asst., then asso. prof. Hamilton Coll., 1931-46; with hist. sect. War Dept., 1946-47; prof. polit. sci. U. Toledo, 1947-70, prof. emeritus, 1970-85, chmn. dept., 1954-65. Pres. Toledo Council World Affairs, 1961-63. Mem. Oneida County (N.H.) Pub. Welfare Com., 1937-43. Served with inf., U.S. Army, 1918, from capt. to lt. col. AUS, 1943-46. Mem. Am., Canadian Polit. sci. assns., Phi Beta Kappa, Phi Kappa Phi, Delta Upsilon. Home: Toledo, Ohio. Died Apr. 25, 1985.

DEAN, ABNER, artist; b. N.Y.C., Mar. 18, 1910; s. Louis and Deana (Grozcky) Epstein. A.B., Dartmouth, 1931; student, N.A.D., 1927. Free lance artist drawings for advt., illustrations and cartoons for mags., 1931-82. Author: satirical drawings It's a Long Way to Heaven, 1945, What Am I Doing Here? , 1947, And on the Eighth Day, 1949, Come As You Are, 1952, Cave Drawings for the Future, 1954, Wake Me when Its Over; verse and cartoons, 1955, Not Far From the Jungle, 1956, Abner Dean's Naked People, 1963. Mem. Soc. Illustrators. Patentee multilevel folding table, indsl. bldg. system assembly. Address: New York, N.Y. Dec. June 30, 1982.

DEAN, HAROLD CHURCHILL, utilities exec.; born Canton, S.D., Mar. 25, 1888; s. Frank M. and Charlotte (Paxton) D.; E.E., U. of Ill., 1909; m. Katherine E. French, June 7, 1913; children—Charlotte (Mrs. Frank W. Appleton, Jr.), John, Anne (Mrs. Albert R. Dow). Served as elec. engr. in charge dept. gas and electricity City of Chicago, 1914-16; asst. to pres. N.Y. and Queens Electric Light & Power Co., 1916-17, gen. supt., 1917-34, v.p. and dir., 1934-45; v.p. Consol. Edison Co., 1945-53, ret.; mem. Queens adv. bd. Mfrs. Trust Co.; vice pres., trustee College Point Savs. Bank. Trustee Mt. Olivet Cemetery. Former mem. War Labor Bd.; cons. from World Power Conf. to ECOSOC. Mem. N.Y.C. Bd. Edn., 1946-50. Fellow Am. Inst. E.E.; mem. Community Service Soc. (trustee, mem. adminstrv. com.), Tau Beta Pi, Eta Kappa Nu. Clubs: Rotary (N.Y.); Douglaston. Home: Douglaston, N.Y. †

DEAN, L(INDLEY) RICHARD, univ. prof.; b. Charlotte, Vt., Dec. 28, 1887; s. James Richard and Alma (Collins) D.; A.B., Dartmouth Coll., 1909; A.M., Princeton, 1910, Ph.D., 1914; student, Am. Sch. Classical Studies, Athens, Greece, 1914-15; m. Belle Wierman Bream, July 21, 1920; 1 son, Richard Albert. Instr. in classics, Princeton, 1912-13, 15-16; asst. prof., Dartmouth Coll., 1916-18; prof., Earlham Coll., 1918-21; prof., Denison Univ., Granville, Ohio, from 1921. Mem. Am. Philol. Assn., Phi Beta Kappa, Sigma Phi Epsilon. Mem. Friends Ch. Home: Granville, Ohio. †

DEANE, ALBERT LYTLE, corporation official; b. Chicago, Ill., Mar. 31, 1888; s. Albert Lytle and Lillie (Willard) D.; ed. pub. schs. and Culver Mil. Acad.; m. Claire Courteol, of Granby, Mo., Mar. 18, 1911; 1 son, Lyttleton. Draftsman, 1906-07; with Hall's Safe and Lock Co., 1907-09; draftsman and mining supt. in Mexico, 1909-13; mgr. in Mexico for Nat. Corr. Sch., 1913-15; with Guarantee Securities Co., New York and San Francisco, 1915-17; asst. to pres. Anglo-Calif. Trust Co., 1917-18; with Gen. Motors Acceptance Corpn., 1919-29; gen. mgr. Motors Holding Div. of Gen. Motors Corpn., 1929-34 and from 1935; dir. Gen. Motors Acceptance Corpn., Gen. Exchange Ins. Corpn. Dep. Adminstr. Federal Housing Adminstrn., 1934-35. Dir. Children's Village, Dobbs Ferry, N.Y. Democrat. Conglist. Clubs: Economic, Town Hall (New York). Author: Investing in Wages, 1932; The Deane Plan. Home: White Plains, N.Y.†

DEANE, PHILIP B., banker; b. Middleboro, Mass., Aug. 16, 1889; s. Leonidas and Anna Davis (Pratt) D.; B.S., Haverford Coll., 1911; m. Louise Spahr, Apr. 10, 1920. Various sales and exec. positions, U.S. and abroad, Sharp & Dohme, Phila., York Safe & Lock Co. (Pa.), Read Standard Corp., York, Pa.; pres., dir. Central Market Corp.; dir. York Nat. Bank & Trust Co., S. S. White Dental Mfg. Co., Phila., Central Market Corp., York, Pa. Staff Lend Lease Adminstrn., Washington, 1942-44. Pres. of bd. trustees YWCA, Blind Center. Member of the Newcomen Soc. N.Y. Mason. Clubs: Circumnavigators of New York; Rotary (past gov.). Home: York, Pa. †

DE ANGELI, MARGUERITE, writer; b. Lapeer, Mich., Mar. 14, 1889; d. Shadrach G. and Ruby A. (Tuttle) Lofft; student pub. schs.; m. John de Angeli, Apr. 2, 1910; children—John, Arthur, Ted, Maurice, Nina (Mrs. Alfred Kuhn). Author, illus. children's books: The Door in the Wall, 1949; Just Like David; Marguerite de Angeli's Book of Nursery and Mother Goose Rhymes; Black Fox of Lorne, 1956; The Old Testament Selected and Illustrated, 1960; Marguerite de Angeli's Favorite Hymns, 1963; The Goose Girl, 1964; Turkey for Christmas, 1965; (autobiography) Butter at the Old Price, 1971. Home: Philadelphia, PA. †

DEAR, CLEVELAND, ex-congressman; b. Sugartown, La., Aug. 22, 1888; s. James M. and Sarah Jane (Harper) D.; A.B., La. State U., 1910, B.L., 1914; m. Marion Anderson, of Milwaukee, Wis., Apr. 19, 1922; children—Marion, Cleveland. Admitted to La. bar, 1914; dist. atty. 9th Judicial Dist. of La., 1920-33; mem. 73d and 74th Congresses (1933-37), 8th La. Dist. Mem. La. Bar Assn., Dist. Attys.' Assn. of La., Am. Legion, 40 Hommes et 8 Chevaux, Sigma Alpha Epsilon. Democrat. Baptist. Mason (32 deg.), Elk. Home: Alexandria, La.†

DEARING, GEORGE BRUCE, educator; b. Erie County, Pa., Jan. 11, 1918; s. James Roscoe and Clara (Patterson) D.; A.B., Allegheny Coll., 1939, LL.D. (hon.), 1965; M.A. in English, State U. Ia., 1940, Ph.D., 1942; M.A. in Psychology, Swarthmore Coll., 1954; student Inst. Coll. and U. Adminstrs., Harvard Bus. Sch., 1958; m. Betty Boltz, June 29, 1940; children—Mary Susan, James Bruce. Instr. English, U. Minn., 1942-43, Cornell U., 1946-47; asst. prof. English, Swarthmore Coll., 1947-50, from asst. to asso. prof., 1952-57, dir. Bell Program in Liberal Arts for Execs., 1956-57; vis. prof. English, U. Mass., summer 1956; prof. English, dean Sch. Arts and Sci., U. Del., 1957-65; pres. State U. N.Y. at Binghamton, 1965-71; vice chancellor acad. programs State U. N.Y., Albany, 1971-76; Univ. prof. humanities Upstate Med. Center, State U. N.Y., Syracuse, 1976-85. Active Boy Scouts Am.; bd. dirs. Am. Humanities Center 1958-85. Served with USNR, 1943-46, 50-52; capt. Res. Am. Council Learned Soc. faculty study fellow, 1952-53. Mem. Coll. English Assn. (dir. 1951-52, 60-63, pres. 1953), Assn. Land Grant Colls. and State Univs. (chmn. div. arts and scis. 1963), Modern Lang. Assn., Nat. Council Tchrs. English, Am. Assn. U. Profs., Eastern Assn. Coll. Deans, Am. Conf. Acad. Deans, Soc. Advancement Edn. (trustee 1966), Phi Beta Kappa, Psi Chi. Episcopalian. Contbr. articles profl. jours. Home: Skaneateles, N.Y. Died July 14, 1985.

DE ARRUDA PEREIRA, ARMANDO, Brazilian ceramic engineer, organization executive; b. São Paulo, Brazil, 1889; early edn. in Italy; student Escola Politecnica (São Paulo), Seafield Park Engring. Coll. and U. of Birmingham (England); C.E., New York U. Practiced as civil engr., Brazil, formerly for Sorocabana Ry.; vice pres. Ceramica São Caetano, São Paulo, from 1923. Mem. 1st Rotary Regional Ibero-Am. Conf., Valparaiso (sponsored adoption of internat. medium of exchange). Became sec. Rotary Club of São Paulo, 1932; became gov. 72d Rotary Internat. (Brazil), 1934; mem. Comité Internacional de Revistas and 2d vice-pres. Rotary Internat., 1937-38; elected pres. Rotary Internat., 1940. President Fedn. Industries of São Paulo; mem. Conselbo Técnico Economia e Finançes; mem. Comissões de Planejamento para o Brasil; delegate Brazil Inter-Am. Conf., Mexico City, Mar. 1945. Mem. ASCE, Royal Soc. Arts. Sponsor Pan-Am. Clubs (for school children). Contbr. to mags. and author of book describing his trip down the Araguaya and Tocantins rivers (tributaries of the Amazon); other books and also translations from English to Portuguese. Address: São Paulo, Brazil. †

DEBO, ANGIE, author; b. Beattie, Kan., Jan. 30, 1890; d. Edward P. and Lina E. (Cooper) D.; A.B., U. of Okla., 1918; A.M., U. of Chicago, 1924; Ph.D., U. of Okla., 1933. Rural school teacher, Okla., 1913-15; prin. North Enid village school, 1918-19, teacher of history, senior high sch., Enid, 1919-23; teacher of history, West Texas State

College, Canyon, Texas, 1924-33; curator Panhandle-Plains Historical Museum, Canyon, Tex., 1933-34; free lance writing, 1934-47; teacher Stephen F. Austin State Coll., Nacogdoches, Tex., 1 summer; editor W.P.A. Indian-Pioneer History Project, 6 months; state supervisor W.P.A. Writers Project, Okla., 1940-41; curator of maps, library Okla. A. & M. Coll., Stillwater, from 1947. Conducted survey of Indian settlements in Eastern Oklahoma for Indian Rights Assn., summer 1949. Recipient of Alfred A. Knopf history fellowship ($1200), May 1942. Member Phi Beta Kappa, Pi Gamma Mu. Democrat. Methodist. Author: several books latest of which are: Oklahoma: Foot-loose and Fancy-free, 1949; The Five Tribes of Oklahoma, 1950; The Five Civilized Tribes of Oklahoma, 1951. Editor: (John M. Oskison, assistant) Oklahoma: A Guide to the Sooner State, 1941; The Cowman's Southwest, 1953.†

DEBOW, RUSSELL ROBINSON, judge; b. Lovejoy, Ill., Aug. 5, 1913; s. John W. and Bettie E. (Robinson) DeB.; m. Ruth Willa Duncan, Dec. 28, 1937; 1 dau., Dolores Diana. B.Ed., Ill. State Normal U., 1935; postgrad., Georgetown U. Law Sch., 1951-53; J.D., DePaul U., 1954. Bar: Ill. bar 1955. Dir. recreation, Lovejoy, 1935; asst. area dir. WPA, East St. Louis, Ill., 35-37; asst. area dir. Nat. Youth Adminstrn., East St. Louis, 1937-41, state officer for Negro affairs, 1941-42, asst. to regional dir., Chgo., 1942-43; with Doehler-Jarvis Corp., Chgo., 1943-46; nat. field rep. Robert S. Abbot Pub. Co. (pubs. Chgo. Defender), 1946-49; sales mgr. Robert S. Abbot Pub. Co. (Chgo. Defender), 1949-51; asst. to dir. OPS, Washington, 1951-53; asst. to U.S. congressman, Chgo., 1954-61, practiced in, 1955-62, dep. commr. dept. investigation, City Chgo., 1962-65, adminstrv. asst. to mayor, 1965-67; magistrate Circuit Ct. Cook County, 1967-71, assoc. judge, 1971, judge, 1971—; Cons. spl. mission to Africa ICA, 1961; labor cons. USOM to Liberia, ICA, 1961. Mem. Cook County Bar Assn. (past v.p., gen. sec., dir.), Chgo. Bar Assn., ABA, Nat. Bar Assn. (past chmn. jud. council), World Assn. Judges, Am. Arbitration Assn. (nat. panel arbitrators). Home: Chicago IL Office: Chicago IL

DEBUS, KURT HEINRICH, government official; b. Frankfort/Main, Germany, Nov. 29, 1908; s. Heinrich P.J. and Melly (Graulich) D.; M.S. in Elec. Engring., Darmstadt (Germany) Tech. U., 1936, Ph.D. in Elec. Engring., 1939; LL.D., Rollins Coll., 1967; hon. doctorate Fla. Tech. U., 1969, Fla. Inst. Tech., 1970; m. Irmgard Helene Brueckmann, June 30, 1937; children—Ute, Sigrid (Mrs. William R. Northcutt). Came to U.S., 1945, naturalized, 1959. Asst. prof. elec. engring. Darmstadt Tech. U., 1939-42; test engr., later flight test dir. Peenemuende Rocket Center, 1942-45; dep. dir. guidance and control div., later staff asst. to Wernher von Braun rocket research and devel. div., U.S. Army Ordnance, 1945-52; dir. missile firing lab. Army Ballistic Missile Agy., 1952-60; dir. Launch Operations Center, NASA, 1960-63, John F. Kennedy Space Center, NASA, 1963-74, mem. mgmt. council Office Manned Space Flight, 1962-74, mem. sr. council Office Space Sci., 1962. Chmn. Brevard County (Fla.) U.S. Savs. Bond Dr., 1962-74; chmn. Brevard-Indian River campaign Muscular Dystrophy Assn. Am., after 1969. Trustee Fla. Inst. Tech. Scholarship Fund. Recipient Exceptional Civilian Service award, 1959; Frank A. Scott Gold Medal award, Am. Ordnance Assn., 1964; NASA Outstanding Leadership award, 1964; Pioneer Windrose award, Order Diamond, 1965; AAS Space Flight award, 1968; Career Service award Nat. Civil Service League, 1969; Distinguished Service Medal NASA, 1969, Apollo Achievement award, 1969; Americanism medal D.A.R., 1969; Nat. Space Hall of Fame, 1969; decorated Comdr's Cross Order Merit (Fed. Republic Germany). Fellow Am. Inst. Aeros. and Astronautics (Lewis Hill award 1974); mem. Am. Ordnance Assn. (life), Nat. Geog. Soc., Brit. Interplanetary Soc. (adv. bd. 1968), German Soc. Rocket Tech. and Space Flight (hon.), Nat. Acad. Engring., Hermann Oberth Gesellschaft (Honor ring 1971, hon. mem.). Deutsche Gesellschaft fur Raketentechnikûnd Raumfahrt (hon.), Instrument Soc. Am. (hon.), M.B.L.S. (adv.). Home: Cocoa Beach, Fla. Died Oct. 10, 1983.

DECK, ARTHUR CLARENCE, editor; b. Salt Lake City, Feb. 20, 1908; s. Jacob Conrad and Dorothea (Hegemeier) D.; student U. Utah, 1924-28; m. Winnifred Willey, Dec. 28, 1936; children—Stephanie Ann Churchill John Willey. Exec. editor Salt Lake Tribune, Salt Lake City, 1950-81; bd. dirs. Newspaper Agy. Corp. Mem. C. of C., Am. Soc. Newspaper Editors (pres. 1973-74), Beta Theta Pi, Theta Tau, Sigma Delta Chi. Club: Alta (Salt Lake City). Home: Salt Lake City, Utah. Died Mar. 12, 1981.

DECKER, DONALD GILMORE, univ. adminstr.; b. Elizabeth, Colo., Jan. 7, 1914; s. Sidney and Nellie (Gilmore) D.; m. Doris Ritter, Dec. 23, 1937 (dec. 1953); 1 dau., Judith C. (Mrs. John Gilbert); m. Doris Stricklan, Mar. 14, 1955. B.S., Eastern Mich. U., Ypsilanti, 1935; M.A., Colo. State Coll., 1937; Ph.D., Columbia, 1943; Sc.D. (hon.), Mich. State Normal U., 1951. Faculty U. No. Colo., from 1937, prof. sci. edn., from 1948, chmn. div. sci., 1948-54, dean of coll., 1955-70, provost, from 1970; dean U. No. Colo. (Sch. Ednl. Change and Devel.), from 1971; research asso. bur. ednl. research and sci. teaching Columbia Tchrs. Coll., 1940-43; research asso. Manhattan project, Oak Ridge, 1943-45; Mem. council instrn. Colo. Dept. Edn., from 1958; adv. com. Colo. Com. Study Edn. Beyond High Sch.; adv. bd. Colo. Senate Com. on Edn., from 1959; mem. Sci. Materials Center, from 1959; Ednl. Policies Commn., from 1960; adv. bd. Products Design Co., from 1959. Mem. bd. editors: L.W. Singer Science Series, Grades 1-9, 1957-59; Ednl. collaborator, Coronet Films, from 1958; Contbr. articles to ednl. jours. Mem. Colo. Sci. Assn. (pres. sci. sect. 1944), Nat. Sci. Tchrs. Assn. (pres. 1959-60), Nat. Assn. Research Sci. Teaching, Internat. Council Elementary Sci., Colo. Schoolmasters Club, Lambda Sigma Tau, Sigma Phi Epsilon. Club: Rotarian. Home: Greeley, Colo.

DECKER, GEORGE NIXON, corporate exec.; b. Springfield, Mass., Sept. 27, 1914; s. George Henry and Mary (Nixon) D.; student Rochester (N.Y.) Sch. Commerce, 1932-33, Ohio U., 1934-35, Niagara U., 1935-37; m. Rosemary Agnes Charlotte Morgan, Apr. 8, 1939; children—Sharon Lee (Mrs. James Williams), Robert Charles. Accountant, Van Vechten Milling Co., Rochester, N.Y., 1937-38; self employed grain broker Decker Grain Co., Rochester, 1938-40; supr. gen accounting IBM Corp., Rochester, 1940-43; successively asst. comptroller, comptroller, v.p., first v.p. Kellogg div. Am. Brake Shoe Co., Rochester, 1943-59, pres. Kellogg div., Oxnard, Cal., 1959-62, pres. Abex Corp. Group Aerospace Cos., Oxnard, 1962-70; pres., chief exec. officer Ventura Internat., Inc., Oxnard, from 1971, also dir.; dir. Travel City, Inc., Sherman Oaks, Calif.; v.p., dir. Coastal Pipco Co., Oxnard, from 1973, Athletic Supply Co. Hawaii, Ltd., Honolulu, B. F. Schoen, Inc., Honolulu, from 1976. Active in County Republcan Club. Mem. Fin. Execs. Inst. Club: Las Posas Country. Home: Camarillo, Calif. Died Oct. 18, 1980.

DECKER, JOHN PETER, educator; b. Ione, Wash., Dec. 27, 1915; s. Peter G. and Clara (Ness) D.; m. Roxielee Farmer, Sept. 2, 1940; children—Peter Gary, Roxanne, Sharon Lee. B.S., U. Idaho, 1938; A.M., Duke U., 1940, Ph.D., 1942; cert., U.S. Army Air Force Sch. Aviation Medicine, 1942. Asst. prof. botany dept. U. Nebr., Lincoln, 1946-47, SUNY, Syracuse, 1947-54; dir. audio-visual prodns. Bklyn. Botanic Garden, 1954-55; research physiologist U.S. Forest Service, Tempe, Ariz., 1955-63; prof. Sch. Engring., Ariz. State U., Tempe, 1963-81, prof. emeritus, 1981-82. Author: Handbook of Time-Zero, 1972, Solving Personality Clashes with Time-Zero, 1978. Served with USAAF, 1942-46. Fellow AAAS; mem. Am. Soc. Plant Physiologists (patron). Republican. Mem. Congregational Ch. Major discoveries include five methods for showing photorespiration, common diagnostic for personality clashes, technique for removing semantic barrier that prevents improvement of edn. Home: Tempe, Ariz. Died Oct. 2, 1982.

DE CREEFT, JÒSE, sculptor; b. Guadalajara, Spain, Nov. 27, 1884; s. Mariano and Rosa (Champane) de C.; student sculpture Augustine Querol Studio, Madrid, 1900-04, Academie Julien, Paris, France, 1905-07, Maisons Greber, Paris, 1911-14; m. Alice Carr, May 15, 1928; children—William, Nina; m. 2d, Lorraine Helen Goulet, Nov. 12, 1944; 1 dau., Dona Maria. Came to U.S. 1929, naturalized, 1940. First exhibited Seattle Art Museum, 1929; exhbns. also include annually at Georgetta Passedolt Gallery, N.Y.C., 1936-49, also Fine Arts Pavilion N.Y. World's Fair, 1964, White House Festival of Arts, Washington, 1965, Kennedy Galleries, N.Y.C. 1969, 70, 72, 73, 74; one-man retrospective New Sch. for Social Research, Art Center, 1974, New Sch. and Hirschhorn Mus. and Sculpture Garden, 1975; tchr. sculpture Art Students League, 1944-48, 57-82; tchr. New Sch. Social Research, N.Y.C., 1932-48, 57-60, Norton Sch. of Art, West Palm Beach, Fla., winters 1948-49, 50-51, Skowhegan (Maine) Sch. Painting and Sculpture, summers 1948-49. Commd. Alice in Wonderland 16 foot Bronze group, N.Y., 1957, mosaic Bronx Municipal New Nurses Residence and Sch., 1961, bronze relief Pub. Health Lab., Bellevue Hosp., N.Y.C., 1966; represented in permanent collections Met. Art. Mus., Whitney Mus. Am. Art, Mus. Modern Art, Phila. Mus. Art, Bklyn. Mus., Pa. Acad., Seattle Art Mus., Smithsonian Instn., Vatican. Recipient 1st prize for sculpture (Torso) Acad. Julien, 1906, Met. Mus. Art (Maternity, granite), 1942, Gold Medal Pa. Acad. (head of Rachmaninoff, beaten lead), 1945; anonymous prize (figure, Maturity), Audubon Artists, 1956, gold medal, 1954, first prize, 1957; award Nat. Sculpture Soc., 1969; commd. Poet by Fairmont Park Art Assn., 1950; Ford Found. award, retrospective exhibit, 1961; decorated commendador Orden de la Isabella Católica (Spain); recipient Florence Brevoort Eichemeyer prize Columbia U., 1975; Gold medal of honor Nat. Arts Club, N.Y.C., 1975; Homage to Jose deCreeft, Spanish Inst. and Consulate Spain, 1976. N.A. Fellow Nat. Sculpture Soc., Sculptor's Guild, Fedn. Modern Painters and Sculptors; mem. Acad. Arts and Letters Artists' Equity (dir.), Audubon Artists (dir.), Nat. Soc. Lit. and Arts, Hispanic Soc. Am. (corr.). Books about: Jose de Creeft, by Jules Campos, 1949; The Sculpture Jose de Creeft, 1972. Home: New York, N.Y. Died 1982.

DEDMON, EMMETT, author, editor; b. Auburn, Nebr., Apr. 16, 1918; s. Roy Emmett and Cora Christine (Frank) Deadman; m. Claire Catherine Lyons, June 19, 1945; 1 child, Jonathan. A.B., U. Chgo., 1939; L.H.D., George Williams Coll., 1965, Roosevelt U., 1973; LL.D., Nebr. Wesleyan U., 1967. Asst. fgn. editor Chgo. Times, 1940; columnist, critic Book Week, lit. supplement Chgo. Sun, 1946-47; lit. editor Chgo. Sun-Times, 1947, drama critic, 1950, asst. Sunday editor, 1953, asst. mng. editor, 1955-58, mng. editor, 1958-62, exec. editor, 1962-65, editor, 1965-68; v.p., editorial dir. Chgo. Sun-Times and Chgo. Daily News, 1968-78; sr. cons. corporate and pub. affairs Hill & Knowlton, Chgo., 1978-83; Mem. nat. acad. council Valparaiso U. Author: Duty to Live, 1946, Fabulous Chicago, 1953, rev. edit., 1981, Great Enterprises, 1957, A History of The Chicago Club, 1960, China Journal, 1973. Pres. YMCA Met., Chgo., 1965-68; trustee U. Chgo., Chgo. Hist. Soc., United Way of Chgo., Newberry Library, Pullman Ednl. Found. Served with USAAF, 1940-45; P.O.W. 1943-45. Decorated Air medal. Mem. Am. Soc. Newspaper Editors, Soc. Am. Historians, Air Force Assn., Sigma Delta Chi, Phi Kappa Psi. Lutheran. Clubs: Casino, Carlton, Tavern, Chicago, Commercial, Economic, Glen View. Home: Chicago, Ill. Dec. Sept. 18, 1983.

DEEN, BRASWELL DRUE, congressman; b. Appling County, Ga., June 28, 1893; s. Samuel Lee and Mary Victoria (Altman) D.; Ph.B., Emory U., 1922; m. Corinne Smith, of Lawrenceville, Ga., July 1, 1918; children—Mildred Louise, Braswell Drue, Walter George. Pres. South Ga. Junior Coll., McRae, Ga., 1924-27; supt. of schs., Tennille, Ga., 1922-24; owner Alma (Ga.) Times since 1928. Mem. 73d and 75th Congresses (1933-39), 8th Ga. Dist. Democrat. Methodist. Clubs: Kiwanis (Waycross, Ga.); Bacon County Recreational (Alma). Home: Alma, Ga. Died Nov. 28, 1981.

DEERING, ARTHUR LOWELL, dean coll. of agr. and dir. extension service; b. Denmark, Me., Jan. 13, 1888; s. Arthur Myron and Mary (Lowell) D.; student Bridgton Acad., North Bridgton, Me.; B.S., U. of Me., 1912; (hon.) D.Sc., U. of Me., 1934; m. Freda Bowman, June 30, 1915 (dec.); children—Mary L., Marjorie B., Robert B., Helen M.; m. 2d Crystal Bowman, June 15, 1926. Engaged as teacher agr., high sch., 1912; Kennebec County Agt., Extension Service, Coll. of Agr., 1912-20; county agt. leader for the Extension Service, 1920-30; asst. dir. for the Extension Service, 1927-30; dir. of the Extension Service for Me., 1930-33; dean Coll. of Agr. and dir. Extension Service from 1933; dir. Farm Credit Bd. (First Dist.). Served as Field Sec. Kennebec County Food Production Com. during the World War. Mem. Epsilon Sigma Phi, Alpha Zeta, Phi Kappa Sigma. Mason. Home: Orono, Maine. †

DEEVER, ROY MERWIN, univ. adminstr.; b. Frankfort, Kans., Sept. 13, 1915; s. O.H. and Dora Christine (Van Dyke) D.; m. Virginia Maxine Casad, May 24, 1942; children—Douglas Roy, Virginia Diane. B.A., Southwestern Coll., 1937; M.Ed., U. Okla., 1941, Ed.D., 1959; Litt.D., Huron Coll., 1974. Supt. schs., Woodward, Okla., 1955-58; prof. ednl. adminstrn. Ariz. State U., Tempe, from 1959; dir. Ariz. State U. (Bur. Ednl. Research ano Services), 1962-*7, acting dean, 1977-78, asso. dean, from 1978; pres. Instroteach, Inc., Tempe, from 1968, Saguaro Dancorp., Tempe, from 1965; v.p. Tempe Mcpl. Facilities Corp., from 1970; dir. United Bank Ariz., Phoenix; vis. prof. U. Alaska, 1966, Calif. State U., San Jose, 1965, U. Hawaii, 1971, 73, 74-76, Southeastern Mass. U., 1973, Western Mich. U., 1976, 77; pres. nat. council Instrument for Observation of Teaching Activities, from 1972. Author: Evaluation of Teaching Effectiveness in the Church, 1968, Five Areas of Church Teacher Competence, 1968, Education 1980 A.D, 1968, Design for a Lifetime: Learning in a Dynamic Social Structure, 1970, The Role of the Teacher in Society, 1970, Arizona State University in the Years Ahead, 1971, Development of a Model Pre-Service Training Program for Beginning Church Teachers, 1972, Instructional Modules, Teacher Preparation for Class Session, 1973, Classroom Control, 1974, Instrument for Observation of Teaching Activities in Higher Education, 1975, The Role of the Teacher in Higher Education, 1975, Yhe Role of the Instructor in Health Care, 1975, The Role of the Church Teacher, 1979. Bd. dirs. United Fund; bd. dirs. Tempe United Way, pres., 1976-*8. Served with USAF, 1942-46. So. Assn. fellow, 1958-59. Mem. Assn. Sch. Adminstrs., Ariz. Assn. Sch. Adminstrs., Tempe C. of C., Phi Delta Kappa. Methodist (lay leader, chmn. bd. stewards, mem. ednl. and mission commns.). Home: Tempe, Ariz.

DE FORD, EARL H., army officer; b. Stuart, Ia., Sept. 1, 1890; s. Franklin and Jane Isabelle (Clark) DeF.; LL.B., Drake U., Des Moines, Ia., 1911; grad. Air Corps Tactical Sch., Langley Field, 1929, Command and General Staff Sch., Ft. Leavenworth, Kan., 1935; m. Zoe Kester, Dec. 25, 1913; 1 dau., Jane Isabelle. Practiced law, 1911-17; commd. capt. Inf. Res., 1917, capt. Regular Army, Inf., 1920; major, Air Corps, 1935, and advanced to brig. gen., 1943; comdg. gen. XI Bomber Command. Decorated Distinguished Flying Cross, Air medal, for action against Japanese, World War II. Clubs: Alta, Rotary (Salt Lake City), Kiwanis (Okla. City). Mason (Shriner). Home: Des Moines, Iowa. †

DEFRANCE, SMITH J., aero research engr.; b. Battle Creek, Mich., Jan. 19, 1896; s. John B. and Lena A. (Smith) DeF.; B.S., University of Michigan, 1922, Dr. Engring., 1953; LL.D., U. Cal., 1952; m. Ruth Patterson, July 20, 1922. Research engr. NACA (now NASA), 1922-47, director Ames Aero. Lab., 1947-58, director of Ames Research Center, 1958-67. Served as airplane pilot Army of U.S., 1917-19. Decorated Silver Star medal and Medal for Merit; recipient Nat. Civil Service League Career award, 1964. Fellow Inst. Aero. Scis. (v.p.); mem.

A.A.A.S., Am. Legion, Sigma Xi, Tau Beta Pi. Episcopalian. Mason. Clubs: Rotary, Quiet Birdmen; Fremont Hills Country. Author tech. reports. U.S. Govt. Home: Los Altos, Calif. Died May 6, 1985.

DE GRAFF, ARTHUR CHRISTIAN, med. educator; b. Paterson, N.J., Dec. 3, 1899; s. Christian and Trina (Cooper) D.; B.S., N.Y.U., 1920, M.D., 1921; m. Dorothy Dodd, June 30, 1926; children—Arthur Christian, Elliott Dodd, Eric William. Intern, resident physician Bellevue Hosp., N.Y.C., 1921-24; instr. medicine Univ. and Bellevue Med. Coll., 1923-24; Crile research fellow physiology Western Res. U. (now Case Western Res. U.), 1924-25; instr. physiology N.Y.U. Med. Coll., 1925-27, Samuel A. Brown prof. therapeutics, 1932-83; specialist heart disease; vis. physician Bellevue Hosp., 1936-83; cons. medicine Nassau Hosp., Mineola, N.Y., St. Agnes Hosp., White Plains, N.Y.; cons. cardiologist Mount Vernon (N.Y.) Hosp., Manhattan VA Hosp., United Hosp., Port Chester, N.Y., Yonkers (N.Y.) Gen. Hosp., Peninsula Gen. Hosp., Rockaway Beach, N.Y., Lawrence Hosp., Bronxville, N.Y.; mem. cons. staff N.Y. Infirmary, Phelps Meml. Hosp., Ossining, N.Y.; chmn. med. bd. Irvington House; attending physician Univ. Hosp., N.Y.U. Med. Center. Past pres. U.S. Pharmacopoeia. Fellow A.C.P., Am. Coll. Cardiology; mem. Am. Soc. for Pharmacology and Exptl. Therapeutics, A.M.A., Soc. Exptl. Biology and Medicine, Am. Fedn. Clin. Research, Am. Physiol. Soc., Am. Soc. Clin. Investigation, N.Y. Acad. Med., N.Y. Heart Assn. Am. Soc. for Clin Pharmacology and Therapeutics (past pres.), New York County Med. Soc., Am. Heart Assn. (council basic sci.), Harvey Soc., Soc. Alumni Bellevue Hosp., Sigma Xi, Alpha Omega Alpha, Editorial bd. Am. Heart Jour., Clin. Pharmacology and Therapeutics. Home: Warm Mineral Springs, Fla. Died May 25, 1983.

DEGRAFF, JOHN TELLER, lawyer; b. Amsterdam, N.Y., May 25, 1902; s. Edward T. and Anna V. (Taylor) DeG.; B.S. magna cum laude, St. Lawrence U., 1922, LL.D. (hon.), 1972; LL.B., Albany Law Sch., 1925; m. Audrey B. Brown, Aug. 18, 1923; children—John T., Richard, David A.; m. 2d, Pauline R. Gibson, Apr. 15, 1970. Admitted to N.Y. State bar, 1925; mem. firm DeGraff, Foy, Conway and Holt-Harris, Albany; counsel N.Y. State Legislative Commn. Extension Civil Service, 1939-41. Mem. N.Y. State Bd. Law Examiners, 1940-49, pres., 1949-69; chmn. Nat. Conf. Bar Examiners, 1951-52; chmn. N.Y. State Tenure Commn., 1944-61. Trustee St. Lawrence U., from 1959. Mem. Am. (ho. dels.), N.Y. State (v.p. 1955-61) bar assns., Am. Law Inst., Phi Beta Kappa, Tau Kappa Alpha, Alpha Tau Omega. Justinian. Clubs: Albany Country; Ft. Orange; Mill Reef (Antigua). Contbr. articles to mags., profl. jours. Home: Albany, N.Y. Died Sept. 19, 1983.

DE GRAFF, ROBERT FAIR, publisher; b. Plainfield, N.J., June 9, 1895; s. James W. and Carrie (Milliken) de G.; student The Hotchkiss Sch., 1911, 12; m. Doreas Marie Bomann, June 14, 1920. Began with Doubleday Page & Co., 1922; dir. Doubleday Doran & Co., 1930-36; v.p., dir. Garden City Pub. Co., Inc., 1930-36; pres. Blue Ribbon Books, Inc., 1936-38; pres. Pocket Books, Incorporated, 1939-50, chairman of the board of dirs. from 1950. Served as 2d lt. Ordnance Reserve Corps, 86th Div., U.S. Army, 1918. Trustee, Village of Upper Brookville, N.Y.; dir. Council of Books in Wartime, Armed Forces Editions, Inc. Republican. Presbyterian. Clubs: Racquet and Tennis, Dutch Treat, Cove Neck Tennis, Piping Rock, Coffee House. Home: New York, N.Y. Died Nov. 2, 1981.

DE GRAZIA, ETTORE TED, artist; b. Morenci, Ariz., June 14, 1909; s. Domenico and Lucia (Gagliardi) DeG.; B.A., U. Ariz., 1944 B.S., M.A., 1945; m. Marion Sheret, June 14, 1946. Exhibited in numerous one man shows, 1932-82; works appeared in Ariz. Hwys. and other mags.; important collections include Kino Collection, scenes from life of Jesuit priest Father Eusebio Kino, Way of the Cross; paintings depicting 15 Stas. of the Cross presented to Newman Catholic Student Center, U. Ariz., 1964; painting Los Ninos reproduced as UNICEF greeting card, 1960. Recipient Achievement award U. Ariz., 1968. Mem. Sinfonia. Author: Ah-Ha-Toro, 1967; Yaqui Easter, 1968; The Rose and the Robe, 1968. Built Gallery in the Sun, 1965; M-Collection, 1971; De Grazia and His Mountain, The Superstition, 1972; DeGrazia Paints Cabeza de Vaca: The First Non-Indian in Texas, New Mexico and Arizona, 1973; De Grazia Moods, 1974; De Grazia Paints the Legends of the Papago Indians, 1975; De Grazia Paiants the Apache Indians, 1976; Christmas Fantasies, 1977. Died Sept. 17, 1982.

DEHNKE, HERMAN, lawyer; b. nr. Napoleon, O., Nov. 26, 1887; s. Hermann and Katherine (Sattler) D.; student Ferris Inst., 1907-08; LL.B., Valparaiso U., 1912; m. Maude F. Dodge, Sept. 1, 1913; children—Spray (Mrs. Gordon Clack), Helen (Mrs. Dane M. Smith), Theodore, Grace (Mrs. William Ogden), Carl. Admitted to Mich. bar, 1911, practiced in Harrisville; pros. atty. Alcona County, Mich., 1915-27; judge 23d Jud. Circuit, Alcona, Oscoda and Iosco counties, 1928-59. Del. Mich. Constl. Conv., 1961-62. Mem. Am., Mich., 23d Circuit bar assns., Mich. Judges Assn. (past pres.), Mich. (pres. 1949-51, trustee), Nat. (dir.-at-large, sec.) Tb assns. Presbyn. Mason, Odd Fellow (grand master 1934-35). Club: Lions. Home: Harrisville, Mich. †

DE JONG, MEINDERT, author; b. Wierum, The Netherlands, 1906; m. Beatrice McElwee. A.B., Calvin Coll. Author: The Wheel on the School (Newbery award 1954), The Little Cow and the Turtle, The House of Sixty Fathers, Along Came a Dog, The Mighty Ones, The Last Little Cat, Nobody Plays with a Cabbage, The Singing Hill, Journey From Peppermint Street, (Nat. Book award 1968), Far Out the Long Canal, Puppy Summer, A Horse Came Running, The Easter Cat, The Almost All-White Rabbity Cat. Recipient Internat. Hans Christian Andersen Award for children's lit., 1962, Nat. Cath. Regina award, 1972; Distinguished Alumni award Calvin Coll., 1975. Address: Allegan, Mich.

DE KAUFFMANN, HENRIK LOUIS HANS, Danish ambassador to U.S.; b. Frankfurt am Main, Germany, Aug. 26, 1888; s. Chamberlain Aage and Mathilde (von Bernus) de K.; LL.M., 1911; hon. LL.D., Bates Coll., Lewiston, Me., 1941; m. Charlotte MacDougall, Nov. 18, 1926. Sec. to Ministry of Foreign Affairs, Copenhagen, 1912-13; sec. of consulate gen., N.Y., 1913-15; sec. to Ministry of Foreign Affairs, Copenhagen, 1915-16; sec. of legation, Berlin, 1916; chief of div. Ministry Fgn. Affairs, Copenhagen, 1921; E.E. and M.P. to Rome, 1921-31, to Peiping and Tokyo, 1924-31, to Bangkok, 1928-31; dep. del. to Assembly of League of Nations, 1931; E.E. and M.P. to Oslo, 1932-39; E.E. and M.P. to U.S., 1939-47; ambassador from 1947; signed agreement granting U.S. bases in Greenland, 1941; joined U.N. declaration, on behalf of "Free Danes," 1942. Member international confs. at Hot Springs, 1943, Atlantic City, 1943, Bretton Woods, 1944. Mem. Denmark's first free cabinet after the liberation while still holding post as E.E. and M.P. to U.S.; head of Danish delegation at founding of the U.N., San Francisco, 1945, Food and Agr., Quebec, U.N.R.R.A. Conf., Atlantic City, 1946. Pres. Food and Agr. Orgn. Conf., Copenhagen, 1946, chmn. Danish delegation, U.N. Conf., N.Y., 1946-49. Decorated Grand Cross and Silver Cross of Order of Dannebrog. Home: Washington, D.C. †

DE KRUIF, PAUL, writer; b. Zeeland, Mich., Mar. 2, 1890; s. Hendrik and Hendrika J. (Kremer) de K.; B.S., U. of Mich., 1912, Ph.D., 1916; m. Rhea Barbarin, Dec. 11, 1922. Bacteriologist, U. of Mich., 1912-17, Rockefeller Inst., 1920-22; reporter for Curtis Publishing Company from 1925; consultant Chicago Board of Health, Michigan State Health Department Laboratories. Served as lieut. Sanitary Corps, U.S. Army, 1917, capt., 1917-19. Collaborator with Sinclair Lewis, on Arrowsmith, 1925. Author: Our Medicine Men, 1922; Microbe Hunters, 1926; Hunger Fighters, 1928; Seven Iron Men, 1929; Men Against Death, 1932; Why Keep Them Alive?, 1936; The Fight for Life, 1938; Health Is Wealth, 1940; Kaiser Wakes the Doctors, 1943; The Male Hormone, 1945; Life Among the Doctors, 1949. Contbr. to Reader's Digest. Home: Holland, Mich.

DELAND, THORNDIKE, mgmt. cons.; b. Cleve., Aug. 16, 1888; s. Rawle and Ella (Wheelwright) D.; ed. pub. schs.; m. Janet Dunbar, Oct. 12, 1917; children—Thorndike, Rawle. With Detroit Bd. Commerce, 1903-06; asst. sec. Chgo. Assn. Commerce, 1906-09, Boston C. of C., 1909-11, sec. Denver C. of C., 1911-16; supr. U.S. Navy Shipyard, Phila., 1919; labor mgr. Henry Sonneborn Clothing Factory, Balt., 1919-20; with Asso. Mdsg. Corp., N.Y.C., 1920-26; organizer Thorndike Deland Assos., mgmt. cons.-exec. personnel recruitment, N.Y.C., 1926, sr. partner, from 1926. Chmn. legislative com. N.Y. Bd. Trade, from 1961. Mem. Scarsdale (N.Y.). Library Bd. Served to 1st lt. U.S. Army, 1916-19; AEF in France and Germany. Decorated D.S.C.; Croix de Guerre with palm and star, Legion of Honor (France). Mem. U.S., N.Y. chambers commerce, Sales Execs. Club N.Y., Advt. Club N.Y., Am. Legion (past post comdr.). Am. Ordnance Assn., I.R.E., Am. Air Force Assn., Nat Retails Merchants Assn. Clubs: Union League, Rotary (N.Y.C.); Am. Yacht (Rye, N.Y.); Town (Scarsdale). Home: Scarsdale, N.Y. †

DELANO, FRANK ELMER, advt. exec.; b. East Orange, N.J., May 23, 1911; s. Frank Elmer and Lyda May (Cahill) D.; B.S., Lehigh U., 1933; student Duke U., 1932, N.J. Law Sch., 1933-34; m. Rosalie Jean Leistikow, Aug. 31, 1939 (dec. Apr. 1972); 1 son, Frederick Cahill; m. 2d Frances Senie Klein, May 29, 1973. Radio mgr., exec. Young & Rubicam, advt., 1933-40, 1941-42, 1945-47; account exec. Warwick & Legler, advt., 1940-41; vice chmn. bd., dir. Foote, Cone, Belding, advt., N.Y.C., until 1972. Served as lt. aviation U.S. Navy, 1942-45; lt. Res. Fellow Royal Geog. Soc., Royal Acad. Arts and Scis.; mem. S.A.R., E. Africa Profl. Hunters Assn., Am. Wildlife Soc., Conseil Internat. de la Chasse, Smithsonian Instn. Assos., Assn. des Chasseurs et Pecheurs Gabonais, Assn. Former Intelligence Officers, Republican. Home: Rye, N.Y. Died Mar. 3, 1985; buried Greenwood Union Cemetery.

DE LAPP, GEORGE LESLIE, bishop; b. East Delavan, Wis., Nov. 4, 1895; s. Lawson LeGr and Carrie Elizabeth (West) DeL.; m. Ardyce Lucile Case, July 25, 1926; children—Cicely Anne, Patricia Lucile, George Leslie. Ed. high sch., Mpls.; extension courses, U. Minn., YMCA, Am. Inst. Bankers, Graceland Coll. Clk. First Nat. Bank, Mpls., 1913-17; connected with F.A. Bean Properties, Inc. (farming ops.), 1918-28; bishop Minn. dist. Reorganized Ch. Jesus Christ of Latter Day Saints, 1926-28; bishop of Lamoni (Iowa) Stake, 1928-31, counselor to presiding bishop, hdqrs., Independence, Mo., 1931-40, presiding bishop and trustee in trust, 1940-66, then bishop.; cons. Zionic Research Inst., Inc., Independence. Author: Quarterly Materials (Herald Pub. House), 1941-42, book, 1973. Former trustee Kansas City Gen. Hosp. and Med. Center; mem. Harry S. Truman-Jackson County Sports Complex Authority, 1966-75, treas., 1966-73, chmn., 1974-75. Served with AUS, 1917-18. Home: Independence, Mo. Died Dec. 1, 1981; buried Mound Grove, Independence.

DE LA RUE, SIDNEY, govt. ofcl.; b. Haddonfield, N.J., Aug. 22, 1888; s. William Henry and Katherine (Brandriff) de la Rue; spl. work U. of Pa., 1907-09; m. Mary Sasse, 1928. With Bur. of Insular Affairs, War Dept., U.S. Mil. Govt. of Dominican Republic, as spl. agt., accountant, supply and purchasing officer, supervising accountant and acting dir. Dominican Dept. of Posts, Telegraph, etc., hdqrs., Trujillo, 1918-20; auditor of Liberia, hdqrs., Monrovia, 1921-22, gen. receiver and financial adviser of Liberia, 1922-24, 1924-28; counsellor to Minister of Finance, Turkey, hdqrs., Istanbul, 1924; financial adviser and gen. receiver of Haiti, 1929-41; pres. Haitian Nat. Bank of Issue, 1935-41; consultant on Caribbean, War Shipping Adminstrn., Washington, D.C., Mar.-Aug., 1942; consultant to U.S. sect., Anglo-Am. Caribbean Commn., Aug.-Sept. 1942; chief, Caribbean Office, 1942-44; spl. asst., Office of Lend-Lease Adminstrn., 1943-44, mission to London U.S.-British Caribbean policy, 1942; consultant and special asst. U.S. sect., Caribbean Commn., Dept. of State, Washington, 1944-46, adviser, Office of Near Eastern and African Affairs, 1948, cons. T.C.A. Near East and African Development Programs, 1951-53; chmn. adv. com. U.S. Civil Service Commn., 1953-54, consultant on territorial allowances, 1954-57; dep. director Econ. and Financial Mission Republic of Peru, 1949-50. Former sr. v.p. Stettinius, Assocs., Inc., Liberia Co., Washington. Fellow Geographic Socity of New York. Club: Metropolitan of Washington, D.C. Author: Land of the Pepper Bird, 1931; also economic and financial treatises on the Rep. of Liberia, Rep. of Haiti and the West Indies. Sepcialist in financial and econ. adminstrn. of African and West Indies terrs. Home: Easton, Md. †

DELL, DONALD LUNDY, lawyer; b. Savannah, Ga., June 17, 1938; s. Julian Peter and Margaret Jullien (Lundy) D.; B.A., Yale, 1960; LL.B. (Noble Found. fellow), U. Va., 1964; m. Carole Marie Osche, Mar. 21, 1971; children—Alexandra Lundy and Kristina Osche (twins). Admitted to D.C. bar, 1964, Va. bar; with firm Hogan & Hartson, Washington, 1965-67; spl. asst. to dir. OEO, Washington, 1967-68; sr. partner firm Dell, Craighill, Fentress & Benton and predecessor, Washington, 1969-80. Bd. dirs. Washington Area Tennis Patrons Found., 1970-80, Am. Council on Internat. Sports, 1975-80; trustee Robert F. Kennedy Meml. Found. Named Washingtonian of the Yr., 1975. Mem. D.C., Va. bar assns., Yale Scroll and Key Honor Soc. Democrat. Roman Catholic. Clubs: Columbia Country; University, Met., Les Ambassadeurs. Columnist, Washington Star newspaper, summer 1973. Mem. U.S. Davis Cup Tennis Team, 1961, 62, 63, capt., 1968-69; TV tennis sportscaster, 1974-79. Home: Potomac, Md. Died Oct. 21, 1980.

DEL MANZO, MILTON CARL EDWARD, educator; b. Milwaukee, Wis., Dec. 29, 1889; s. Ernest and Bertha (Bachmann) Del M.; student U. of Dubuque (Ia.), 1909-13; B.A., State U. of Ia., 1915, M.A., 1921, Ph.D., 1924; m. Mildred R. Dewees, Aug. 28, 1916; children—Donald Dewees, Jessie Elizabeth. Teacher, high sch., Dallas Center, Ia., 1916-18, supt. schs., 1918-20; same, West Branch, Ia., 1920-21; prin. University Schs., State U. of Ia., 1922-24; prof. edn. U. of Kan., and supt. schs., Lawrence, 1924-25; asso. Internat. Inst., 1925-32, asso. dir. from 1932; asst. prof. edn., Teachers Coll., Columbia, 1927, prof. from 1928, provost from 1929. Dir. Manhattanville Neighborhood Center, New York; mem. bd. Uptown Y.M.C.A., N.Y. City. Mem. N.E.A., Am. Assn. School Adminstrators, Coll. Teachers of Edn., Phi Delta Kappa, Kappa Delta Pi. Author: The Financing of Education in Iowa (with others), 1924; Public School Bonding in Iowa, 1926. Contbr. on edn. Home: New York, N.Y. †

DEL MAR, ROLAND HADDAWAY, army officer; b. Attica, Ind., Feb. 11, 1908; s. Carlos Florio and Mabelle Antoinette (Leonard) del M.; m. Elizabeth Kathryn Adams, Oct. 11, 1930; 1 dau., Mareen Duvall del Mar Braddock. Student, Coll. of Wooster, 1930; grad., Cavalry Sch., 1942, Command and Gen. Staff Coll., 1945, Armed Forces Staff Coll., 1950, Army War Coll., 1954, Command Mgmt. Sch., 1956. With Internat. Harvester Co., 1928-41; commd. capt. U.S. Army, 1941, advanced through grades to maj. gen., 1962; asst. div. comdr. (4th Armored Div.), 1956; readiness officer AFSE (NATO), Naples, 1958-59, ops. officer, 1959-60; comdg. gen. Combat Command A, 1st Armored Div., 1960-61, Antilles Command, P.R., 1961-63; dir. Inter. Am. Def. Coll., 1963-66; Chmn. Md. Commn. Latin Am. Affairs; vice chmn. Balt. Dist. Export Council. Pres. Charles Delmar Found.; pres. Americas Found.; trustee Coll. of Wooster; bd. dirs. Pan-Am. Devel. Found.; v.p. Internat. Student House. Decorated Disting. Service medal, Legion of Merit, Bronze Star medal, D.S.M., UN medal. Mem. U.S. C. of C., Am. Legion, Md., Frederick County hist. socs., SAR, Chevalier du Tastevin, Latin Am. Studies Assn., Southeastern Conf. Latin-Am. Studies, Mil. Order

World Wars, Pan-Am. Soc. (v.p.), Center for Inter-Am. Relations, Spanish Inst., Washington Inst. Fgn. Affairs, English-Speaking Union, Nat. Steeplechase and Hunt Assn., Sigma Delta Pi. Episcopalian. Clubs: Masons (Washington), Shriners (Washington), Nat. Sojourneur (Washington), Internat. (Washington), Capitol Hill (Washington), City Tavern (Washington), Army-Navy (Washington), Univ. (Washington), Explorers (Washington). Home: Knoxville, MD.

DELONG, JAMES EDWIN, engine manufacturer; born Zionsville, Ind., May 31, 1889; s. James and Frances (Havens) D.; ed. M.E., Purdue Univ.; m. Esther M. Rogers, Nov. 6, 1912; 1 son, Roger Garfield. Asst. engr. Rutenber Motor Co., 1912-14; sec.-treas. Rutenber Electric Co., 1914-17; factory mgr. Indiana Truck Corp., 1919-23; with Waukesha Motor Co., Waukesha, Wis., since 1923, successively as mgr. of oil field sales, 1923-28, asst. gen. mgr., 1929-33, v.p., 1933-36, elected pres. and gen. mgr., 1936. During World War, served as capt., 1st Div., Ammunition Train, A.E.F., U.S. Army. Home: Waukesha, Wis. †

DEL RIO, DOLORES, actress; b. Durango, Mex., Aug. 3, 1908; d. Jesus and Antonia (Lopez Negrete) Asunsolo; educated Convent of San Jose, Mex.; m. Lewis A. Riley, Nov. 24, 1960. Appeared numerous films, including Johanna, 1925; Pals First, 1925; High Steppers, 1925; The Whole Town is Talking, 1925; What Price Glory, 1926; Gateway to the Moon, 1926; The Loves of Carmen, 1927; Resurrection, 1927; Ramona, 1928; Revenge, 1928; Evangeline, 1929; The Bad One, 1930; The Dove, 1931; Bird of Paradise, 1932; Flying Down to Rio, 1933; Wonder Bar, 1934; The Widow from Montecarlo, 1935; Madame Dubarry, 1935; I Live for Love, 1935; Accused, 1936; Lancer Spy, 1937; International Settlement, 1938; The Man from Dakota, 1939; Journey into Fear, 1941; Flor Silvestre (Mexico), 1942; Maria Candelaria (Mexico), 1943; Las Abandonadas (Mexico), 1944; Bugambilia (Mexico), 1945; La Otra (Mexico), 1945; La Selva De Fuego (Mexico), 1946; The Fugitive, 1947; Historia De Una Mala Mujer (Argentina), 1948; La Malquerida, 1949, La Casa Chica, 1949, Deseada, 1950, Dona Perfecta, 1951 (all Mexico); Senora Ama (Spain); star play Anastasia, U.S., 1956; Medio Tono (Mexico), 1957; star TV program Public Prosecutor, 1958; star Mexican theatre Lady Windermere's Fan, 1958, then theatre tour in Mexico, 1959; actress films De Mujer a Mujer, 1960; Flaming Star, U.S., 1961; Ghosts (Mexico), 1962; El Pecado De Una Madre, 1962; star film, Cheyenne Autumn, 1963; actress TV, Return to Glory, Murietta, both Hollywood, 1964; actress film Once Upon A Time, Italy, with Sofia Loren, Omar Shariff, 1966; Mexican film Casa De Mujeres, 1968; appeared Mexican TV dedicated to her biography entitled Biography, 1969; appeared Marcus Welby TV program, The Legacy, 1972; play Camille in Mexico City, 1970-71, film The Sons of Sanchez, 1977. Pres. bd. dirs. Nursery of Actors Union of Mex.; pres. Festival Internacional Cervantino. Roman Catholic. Club: Acapulco Yacht. Home: Mexico. Died Apr. 11, 1983.

DEMARAY, ARTHUR E., former dir. National Park Service; b. Washington, D.C., Feb. 16, 1887; s. Edward A. and Emma (Register) D.; ed. pub. sch. and high sch., Washington, D.C.; m. Alfrida Briggs, Nov. 10, 1913; 1 dau., Elise Anderson. With Nat. Park Service, Dept. of Interior, Washington, D.C., from 1917, becoming successively topographic draftsman, 1917, editor, 1919, administrative officer, 1926, sr. administrative officer, 1929, exec. officer, 1930, asso. dir., 1933-51, ret. Mem. (formerly pres.) Government Services, Inc., dir., treas. Nat. Park Concessions, Inc. Decorated by King of Sweden with order of Knight of Vasa, 1927; Cornelius Amory Pugsley silver medal, Am. Scenic and Historic Preservation Soc., 1942, gold medal, 1951. Mem. Nat. Council for State Parks, Am. Planning and Civic Assn., Biological Society Washington, Demarest Family Assn., Am. Inst. Landscape Artists (corr. mem.). Home: Chevy Chase, Md. †

DEMENT, ROBERT LEE, dentist; b. Meridian, Miss., Nov. 24, 1887; s. Charles Pinckney and Mary (McInnis) D.; student Marion (Ala.) Mil. Inst., 1903-05, Meridian Male Coll., 1905-07; D.D.S., Atlanta Dental Coll. (Emory Univ. Sch. Dentistry), 1916; m. Emile Walker, Oct. 9, 1912. In pvt. practice dentistry, Atlanta, since 1916; prof. periodontology Atlanta-Southern Dental Coll. (now Emory Univ. Sch. of Dentistry), 25 yrs. Fellow Internat. Coll. Dentists; mem. Am. Dental Assn. (past chmn. periodontia sect.). Am. Acad. Periodontology (past pres.), Southern Acad. Periodontology (past pres.), Pierre Fauchard Acad., Ga. Dental Assn. (past pres.), Fifth Dist. Dental Soc. of Atlanta (past pres.), Northern Dist. Dental Soc., Omicron Kappa Upsilon, Psi Omega. Democrat. Presbyterian. Home: Atlanta, Ga. †

DEMERIT, MERRILL, chief power engr., Tenn. Valley Authority; b. Lake Mills, Wis., Oct. 13, 1890; s. Milan White and Nellie Hatley (Wilson) D.; B.S. in E.E., U. of Wis., 1914; m. Grace A. Neupert, Sept. 14, 1914 (dec.); children—Robert Neupert, Gordon Merrill (dec.), Paul Merrill, Merrill. Testman Gen. Elec. Co., 1914; inspection and tests Wagner Elec. & Mfg. Co., 1915-16; distbn. engr. Detroit Edison Co., 1918-21; asst. comml. mgr. West Penn Power Co., 1922, distbn. engr., 1923-25, distbn. mgr., 1926-27, asst. to pres., 1927-29, asst. chief engr., 1929-34, gen. engr., 1935-40; power consultant O.P.A., 1941-42; chief power engr., W.P.B., 1943-44; chief power engr. Tennessee Valley Authority, from 1941; member Defense Electric Power Unit, Dept. of Interior. Fellow Am. Inst. of Elec. Engrs.; mem. Soc. of Am. Military Engineers. Club: Chattanooga Golf and Country. Pub. complete set Electrical Distribution Standards and Construction Standards; numerous tech. articles on elec. distrbn., transmission and generation. Home: Signal Mountain, Tenn. †

DE MICHEAL, DONALD ANTHONY, mag. editor; b. Louisville, May 12, 1928; s. Joseph and Ernestine Elizabeth (Lefler) DeM.; student Ind. U., 1957-59, U. Louisville, 1960; m. Anna Elizabeth Murphy, June 5, 1948; children—David Sidney, Deborah Ann. Profl. musician on drums and vibraharp, 1944-82; leader band, 1951-60; author jazz criticism, 1959—; mem. staff Down Beat mag., 1960-67, editor-in-chief, 1961-67; editor Actual Specifying Engr. mag., 1967-78, editor, asso. pub., 1971-78; editor-pub. Plate World mag., Niles, Ill., 1979-82; music editor Scholastic Roto, 1968-69; music columnist Youth Enterprises Syndicate, 1969-71; pres. Jazz Inst. Chgo., 1976-78. Author: (with Alan Dawson) A Manual for the Modern Drummer, 1962. Editor, compiler: Jazz Record Review, Vols. 5-8, 1961-64; INBEX Digest, 1971. Home: Chicago, Ill. Died Feb. 4, 1982.

DEMOTTE, RALPH J., business exec.; b. Chicago, Ill., Jan. 18, 1890; s. Fletcher and Josephine (Portman) DeM.; ed. pub. schs. of Eureka, Ill., and extension courses; m. Meda Engle, Oct. 2, 1912; 1 dau., Mary Ellen (Mrs. Howard T. Robertson). Supt. Dickinson and Co., canning factory, Eureka, Ill., 1908-17; joined Sears, Roebuck & Co., Chicago, 1917; gen. mgr. Kansas City, Mo., operations, 1929-40, became treas. Sears, Roebuck & Co., 1940, director, 1942; dir. All State Ins. Co., Sears-Community State Bank. Clubs: Chicago, Bob-O-Link, Executives. Home: Chicago, IL. †

DEMPSEY, JACK, owner Jack Dempsey Restaurant, N.Y.C.; former world's heavyweight boxing champion. Address: New York, N.Y. Died May 31, 1983.

DENBY, EDWIN ORR, writer; b. Tientsin, China, Feb. 4, 1903 (parents U.S. citizens); s. Charles and Martha (Orr) D.; grad. Hotchkiss Sch., 1918; student Harvard, 1919-22, Schule Hellerau-Laxenburg (Austria), 1925-27. Dancer, State Theatre, Darmstadt, Germany, 1928-29, with Claire Eckstein, Berlin and Munich, Germany, 1930-33, with Marietta von Meyenburg, Switzerland, 1935; dancer, collaborator text N.Y. musical Horse Eats Hat, 1936; choreographer Negro ballet Knickerbocker Holiday, 1938; dance critic Modern Music, 1936-42, N.Y. Herald Tribune, 1942-45; contbr. magazines in field. Guggenheim fellow, 1948; recipient award Poets' Found., 1965, Dance mag., 1966. Mem. P.E.N. Author: (dance criticism) Looking at the Dance, 1949; (poems) In Public, In Private, 1948, Mediterranean Cities, 1956; (dance and art) Dancers, Buildings and People in the Streets, 1965; (librettos) Die Neue Galathee, 1928; The Second Hurricane, 1937. Died July 1983.

DENEMARK, GEORGE WILLIAM, education accreditation agency administrator; b. Chgo., Nov. 13, 1921; s. August Frederick and Harriet (Holly) D.; m. June Elaine Breidigam, Feb. 13, 1945; children: Eric, David, Gail. A.B., U. Chgo., 1943, M.A., 1948; Ed.D., U. Ill., 1956. Instr. U. Ill., Urbana, 1949-50; asst. prof. edn. Boston U., 1950-52; exec. sec. Assn. for Supervision and Curriculum Devel., Washington, 1952-56; asst. dean, prof. Coll. Edn. U. Md., 1956-58; dean, prof. Sch. Edn. U. Wis., Milw., 1958-67; dean, prof. Coll. Edn., U. Ky., Lexington, 1967-82, prof., 1982-83; dir. Nat. Council for Accreditation of Tchr. Edn., Washington, 1983—; cons. tchr. edn. and curriculum, Brazil, Colombia, P.R., V.I., Venezuela.; Chmn. adv. bd. ERIC Clearinghouse on Tchr. Edn. Editor: Ednl. Leadership, 1952-54; Chmn. editorial adv. bd.: Jour. Tchr. Edn, 1962-63. Trustee Joint Council on Econ. Edn.; bd. dirs. Escola Johnson, Fortaleza, Brazil; adv. bd. World Book, 1965-69. Served to lt. (j.g.) USNR, 1943-46. Mem. N.E.A. (life, chmn. nat. commn. on tchr. edn. and profl. standards 1967-68), Nat. Assn. State U. and Land Grant Colls. (chmn. com. on edn. for teaching profession 1968-69), Am. Assn. Colls. for Tchr. Edn. (pres. 1972-73), Assn. Supervision and Curriculum Devel., Nat. Soc. for Study Edn., Phi Delta Kappa. Home: Washington, D.C. Died May 26, 1985.

DENHOFF, ERIC, pediatric neurologist; b. Bklyn., June 5, 1913; s. Joseph Ira and Lillian (Linsky) D.; m. Sylvia Brooklyn, July 8, 1945; children—Donald G., Joseph I., Barbara L. B.S., U. Vt., 1934; M.D., 1938; ScD. (hon.), Brown U., 1980. Diplomate: Am. Bd. Pediatrics. Intern St. Luke's Hosp., New Bedford, Mass., 1938-39; resident Boston City Hosp., 1939-41, Bradley Hosp., East Providence, R.I., 1941-42; practice medicine specializing in pediatric neurology, Providence, from 1946; mem. staffs R.I. Hosp., Bradley Hosp.; med. dir. Meeting Street Sch. Children's Rehab. Center, from 1947; Gov. Center Sch., from 1962; clin. prof. pediatrics Brown U., from 1972. Contbr. articles to profl. jours.; Mem. editorial bd.: Clin. Pediatrics, from 1970, Jour. Learning Disabilities, from 1970. Served with M.C. U.S. Army, 1941-45. Mem. Am. Acad. Pediatrics, Am. Acad. Cerebral Palsy, Am. Acad. Neurology, Am. Psychiat. Inst., R.I. Med. Soc., Mass. Med. Soc., Sigma Xi, Alpha Omega Alpha. Democrat. Jewish. Home: Providence, RI. Office: Providence RI

DENMARK, ANNIE DOVE, college president; b. Goldsboro, N.C., Sept. 29, 1887; d. Willis Arthur and Sara Emma (Boyette) Denmark; prep edn., high sch., Goldsboro; diploma in piano, Meredith Coll., Raleigh, N.C.; studied piano under Raphael Joseffy, N.Y.C., 1909. Virgil Piano Sch., 1917, Alberta Jonas, 1916-17; student Chautauqua Instn., dept. religion, summers 1921-27; A.B., Anderson (S.C.) Coll., 1925. Instr. piano, Buies Creek (N.C.) Acad., 1908-09, Tenn. Coll., Murfreesboro, 1910, Shorter Coll., Rome, Ga., 1910-16; instr. piano Anderson Coll., 1917-25, dean of women, 1925-26, pres., from 1928. Mem. So. Assn. Colls. for Women (pres., 1934-35). Trustee of W.M.U. Training School, Louisville, Ky. Democrat. Baptist. Hon. Litt.D. conferred by Furman U., 1941. Author: White Echoes, 1932. Home: Goldsboro, N.C.†

DENNES, WILLIAM RAY, educator; b. Healdsburg, Sonoma County, Calif., Apr. 10, 1898; s. Edward Frederick and Harriet (Ray) D.; A.B., U. Cal. at Berkeley, 1919, M.A., 1920, LL.D., 1966; D.Phil., Oxford U., Eng., 1923; LL.D., N.Y. U., 1951; m. Margaret Munroe Stevenson June 22, 1923; children—Richard, Margaret (Mrs. Edwin Honig). Mills fellow in philosophy, U. Calif., 1920, instr. philosophy, 1923-24, asst. prof., 1924-27, asso. prof., 1927-32, 33-36, prof., 1936-82, chmn. dept., 1941-43, 44-48, Mills prof. intellectual and moral philosophy, civil polity U. Calif. at Berkeley, 1958-65, emeritus, 1965-82, dean grad. div., 1948-55; asso. prof. philosophy Yale, 1932-33; vis. prof. philosophy, Harvard, 1935, Stanford, 1941, 43; Woodbridge Meml. lectr. in philosophy Columbia, 1958; vis. prof. philosophy So. Ill. U., 1966; vis. prof. philosophy U. Va., 1967, U. Calif., Santa Cruz, 1970-71. Served with USN, 1918-19; asst. dir. Manhattan Dist. Los Alamos Project, 1943. Awarded Univ. medal U. Cal., 1919; Rhodes Scholarship, Corpus Christi Coll., Oxford, 1920-23; Guggenheim fellowship in Germany and Eng., 1929-30. Pres. assn. grad. schs. Assn. Am. Univs., 1952; chmn. grad. council Assn. Land-Grant Colls. and Univs., 1952; mem. Conf. on Sci., Philosophy and Religion, 1952. Fellow Royal Soc. Arts, AAAS; mem. Am. Philos. Assn. (pres. Pacific div. 1945), Mind Soc. Gt. Britain, Phi Beta Kappa (pres. Alpha chpt. Calif., 1941-42), Alpha Kappa Lambda. Democrat. Club: Faculty (Berkeley). Author books in field; (latest) Naturalism and the Human Spirit (with John Dewey and others), 1944; Civilization and Values, 1945; East-West Philosophy (with others), 1951; Symbols and Values (with others), 1954; Some Dilemmas of Naturalism, 1960; C.I. Lewis on the Morally Imperative, 1969; co-author 18 vols. in philosophy, U. Calif. Publs., co-editor, 1941-60. Home: Berkeley, Calif. Died May 2, 1982.

DENNEY, ROBERT VERNON, judge; b. Council Bluffs, Iowa, Apr. 11, 1916; s. Arthur J. and Helen (Weaver) D.; student Peru State Tchrs. Coll., 1933-34, U. Nebr., 1934-36; LL.B. cum laude, Creighton U., 1939; m. Ruth Conklin, Dec. 21, 1940; children—Vernon, David, Michael, Deborah Admitted to Nebr. bar, 1939; practice in Nebr., 1939-40, 45-81; spl. agt. FBI, 1940-41; atty. Jefferson County, Nebr., 1947, Fairbury, 1951; mem. 90th-91st Congresses 1st Dist. Nebr.; U.S. dist. judge, Nebr., 1971-81. Pres. Fairbury Indsl. Devel. Corp., 1960; mem. Fairbury Sch. Bd., 1956. Chmn. Jefferson County Republican Com., 1960, Nebr. Rep. Party, 1960-64. Served to lt. col. USMCR, 1942-45; PTO. Decorated Bronze Star; recipient Alumni Merit award Creighton U., 1976. Mem. Fairbury C. of C. (past pres.), Am. Legion (past post comdr.), V.F.W. Mason (K.T., Shriner), Lion. Clubs: Fairbury Executives (pres.), Fairbury Country (pres.). Presbyn. (elder). Home: Omaha, Nebr. Died June 26, 1981.

DENNING, RICHARD (LOUIS ALBERT DENNINGER), actor; b. Poughkeepsie, N.Y., Mar. 27, 1914; s. Louis Andrew and Anna Marie (Bohrmann) Denninger; m. Evelyn F. Ankers, Sept. 6, 1942; 1 dau., Diana Dee. M.A. in Bus. Adminstrn. magna cum laude, Woodbury Coll., 1934. Actor, Paramount Pictures, Hollywood, Calif., 1936-45; free-lance actor stage, screen, radio and TV, from 1945; motion pictures include Adam Had Four Sons, 1941, Beyond the Blue Horizon, 1942, An Affair to Remember, Day The World Ended, 1956, Black Scorpion, 1957, Gun That Won the West, 1955, Seven Were Saved, 1946, Crooked Web, 1955, Lady Takes a Flyer, 1958, Desert Hell, 1958, Emergency Squad, Golden Gloves, 1940, Black Beauty, 1946, Twice Told Tales, 1963; others; star: TV series Mr. and Mrs. North, 1952-54, The Flying Doctor, 1959, Michael Shayne, 1960-61, Karen, 1965; featured actor as the governor in: TV series Hawaii Five-O, from 1968. Mem. exec. bd. Maui council Boy Scouts Am., from 1970; Adv. bd. Woodbury Coll. Served with USNR, 1942-45. Mem. Gamma Sigma Pi, Phi Gamma Kappa. Mem. Christian Ch. (deacon, moderator, lay reader). Clubs: Maui Country, Newport Sailing, Kamaole Skin Divers. Address: Beverly Hills, Calif.

DENNY, GEORGE PARKMAN, physician; b. Brookline, Mass., June 2, 1887; s. Arthur Briggs and Francis (Gilbert) D.; A.B., Harvard, 1909; M.D., 1913; m. Charlotte Hemenway, July 2, 1914; chidldren—Charlotte (Mrs. J.J. Knox), George Parkman, Nancy A. (Mr. C.H. Weed). Intern Peter Bent Brigham Hosp., Boston, 1913-14, asso. vis. physician, 1925-35; asso. med. sch. Harvard, 1919-21; vis. physician Beverly Hosp., 1925-41; practice, specializing in internal medicine, Boston, 1920-41; mgr. V.A. Hosp., West Roxbury, Mass., 1949-52, Boston, from 1952. Mem. bd. overseers Harvard,

1947-53; trustee Home for Aged Men, Farm and Trade Sch., Boston. Served as 1st lt. to capt. M.C., U.S. Army, 1917-19, maj. to col., 1942-46. Decorated Legion of Merit. Fellow A.C.P.; mem. A.M.A., Mass. Med. Soc. Clubs: Somerset, Tavern (Boston). Home: Milton, MA. †

DENSFORD, KATHARINE JANE (MRS. CARL A. DREVES), nursing; born in Crothersville, Indiana, December 7, 1880; the daughter of Loving Garriott and Mary Belle (Carr) Densford; preparatory dept., Oxford Coll. for Women, Oxford, O.; A.B., Miami U., 1914, LL.D., 1950; M.A., U. of Chicago, 1915; D.Sc., Baylor U., 1945; Vassar Training Camp for Nurses, Poughkeepsie, N.Y., 1918; R.N., U. of Cincinnati Coll. of Nursing and Health, 1920; student Teachers Coll., Columbia U., 1937; m. Carl Arminius Dreves, August 8, 1959. Began as grade and high sch. teacher, 1915-18; later served as head nurse, supvr. of nurses, dir nursing service and instr. various places, 1920-30; prof. nursing and dir. Sch. of Nursing, U. of Minn., 1930-59, professor and director emeritus from 1959; guest instr. various schs., 1926-60, mem. nat. nursing advisory committee A.R.C., 1944-46, 56-62; cons. various organizations on nursing, including U.S. Army Nurse Corps, 1948-52, VA Nursing Service. Nat. co-chmn. Am. Nurses' Found. Campaign, 1960-63, nat. co-chmn. adv. council of found., from 1963. Mem. Governor's Commission on Status of Women, from 1963; mem. Minn. State Bd. of Health, from 1961. Member of various local, state and nat. assns. coms. and leagues in nursing edn. and hosps.; mem. Am. Assn. U. Women, Am. Association University Professors, Am. Nurses Association (president 1944-48), International Council Nurses (second vice president 1947-57), Nat. Assn. Parliamentarians, Nat. Health Assembly, Sigma Theta Tau (nat. pres., 1941-45), Am. Fgn. Policy Assn., Alpha Tau Delta (nat. pres. 1936-38), Phi Beta Kappa. Author chptrs. in profl. books; co-author: (Densford and Everett) Ethics for the Modern Nurse, 1946; co-author: (Densford, Gordon and Williamson) Counselling Program in Schools of Nursing, 1946; many articles on nursing edn. profl. Home: St. Paul, Minn. †

DENT, ALBERT WALTER, health education consultant; b. Atlanta, Sept. 25, 1904; s. Albert and Daisey (Thomas) D.; A.B., Morehouse Coll., 1926, LL.D., 1947; LL.D., Bishop Coll., 1969, Tulane U., 1969; m. Ernestine J. Covington, June 23, 1931; children—Thomas Covington, Benjamin Albert, Walter Jesse. Auditor, Atlanta Life Ins. Co., 1926; v.p. Safety Constrn. Co., Houston, 1927-28; alumni sec. Morehouse Coll., 1928-31; supt., Flint-Goodridge Hosp. of Dillard U., 1932-41; bus. mgr. Dillard U., 1935-41, pres., 1941-69; cons. Health Edn. Authority of La., from 1969. U.S. del. World Health Assembly, 1948, 55, 58; cons. health adv. com. fgn. Operations Adminstrn., 1954. Bd. dirs. So. Regional Council, from 1944, v.p., 1952-65; bd. dirs. Nat. Orgn. Pub. Health Nursing, 1944-50, Com. for Nation's Health 1946-52; bd. dirs. Nat. Health Council, from 1949, pres., 1953-55; bd. dirs. United Negro Coll. Fund. Mem. Commn. on Health Careers, from 1958; mem. La. adv. com. Civil Rights Commn., from 1959; bd. dirs. Nat. Med. Fellowship, Inc., from 1959; bd. assocs. Chgo. Theol. Sem., from 1962; mem. Nat. Commn. Community Health Services, from 1962, Fed. Hosp. Council 1946-50, 61. Trustee Meharry Med. Coll., 1951-54; mem. com. on fellowships Ford Found., 1951-54. Fellow Am. Coll. Hosp. Adminstr.; mem. Assn. Colls. and Secondary Schs. for Negroes (pres. 1948-49), Am. Hosp. Assn. (commn. hosp. care), U.S. Children's Bur. (commn. on children and youth), Nat. Planning Assn. (com. on South, exec. com. from 1952), Nat. Tb Assn. (pres. 1965-66), Nat. Student Health Assn. (pres. 1942-48), Nat. Conf. Hosp. Adminstrs. (chmn. 1936-42), Morehouse Coll. Alumni Assn. (pres. 1936-39), Omega Psi Phi (past grand basileus). Home: New Orleans, La. Died Feb. 12, 1984.

DENT, JOHN K., railroad exec.; b. Litchfield, Ky., June 6, 1888; s. Samuel R. and Georgeia (Bassett) D. Engaged in r.r. work from 1905; now v.p. L. & N. R.R. Mem. Ky. bar. Clubs: Pendennis, Big Spring Country. Home: Bashford Manor Lane, Ky. †

DENTLER, CLARA LOUISE (MRS. WILLIAM J. DENTLER), writer and historian; b. Pawtucket, R.I., July 17, 1887; d. Franklin Howes and Emeline Elizabeth (Grant) Snow; A.B., Wittenberg Coll., Springfield, O., 1911; B.D., Hamma Divinity Sch., 1914; grad. student U. of Glasgow, research student Nat. Scottish Museum, Edinburgh, and British Museum, London, 1922-24; m. William Jacob Dentler, June 8, 1911. Prof. English, lecturer on Am. Life and Instns., in Facultá di Magistero, Royal Univ., Florence, Italy, 1946-47. Mem. Am. Assn. Univ. Women, British Poetry Soc. (London). Author: Katherine Luther of the Wittenberg Parsonage, 1925; Contemporary World, Vol. I, 1934, Vol. II, 1937; Wittenberg, the Cradle of the Reformation, 1942. Contbr. of large number of articles to various publs. in U.S. and Europe. Address: Florence, Italy. Deceased.

DENTON, JAMES G., justice Tex. Supreme Ct.; b. 1917. B.A., Tex. Tech. U.; student, U. Tex. at Austin Law Sch. Bar: bar 1941. Asso. justice Tex. Supreme Ct., 1971—. Address: Austin, Tex.

DENTON, WILLARD KIRKPATRICK, banker; b. N.Y. City, Mar. 9, 1899; s. Charles Allen and Mabel (Kirkpatrick) D.; grad. Washington Irving High Sch., Tarrytown, N.Y., 1917; student various courses in banking and economics, Columbia U. and Am. Savings and Loan Inst.; m. Faith de Baubigny, Feb. 15, 1947; 1 son, Willard K. Denton. Clerk, R.R. Co-op. Bldg. and Loan Assn., N.Y. City, 1921-23, asst. treas., 1923, treas. and dir., 1924, vice pres.-treas. and dir., 1924-30; special deputy supt. of banks for State of N.Y., 1930-38; exec. vice pres. and trustee Metropolitan Savings Bank, N.Y. City, 1938-42, became pres. and trustee Mar. 1942; became pres. and trustee Manhattan Savings Instn., May 1942; pres. and trustee Manhattan Savings Bank since July 1942, chmn. of the bd. trustees, since March 1967. (this bank formed by successive combination of Metropolitan Savings Bank, Manhattan Savings Instn. and Citizens Savings Bank); chmn., chief exec. officer East N.Y. Savs. Bank, 1966-70; mem. adv. bd. Chemical Bank & Trust Co. dir. U.S. Fire Ins. Co., Savings Bank Trust Co.; chmn. Fed. Deposit Ins. Corp. Com. of Assn. of Mutual Savings Banks; mem. Fed. Deposit Ins. Corps Savings Banks Council; mem. council of adminstrn. N.Y. Savings Assn. Trustee Nat. Fund Med. Edn.; mem. bd. dirs. YMCA; mem. N.Y. Cancer Com., N.Y. Bus. Development Corp. Served as seaman 2d class, U.S. Navy, 1918-19; lt. (j.g.), U.S. Coast Guard, 1941-42. Chmn. exec. com. Group IV, Savings Banks Assn., State of N.Y. Mem. N.Y. War Finance Com. (mem. exec. com.; exec. mgr.; chmn. N.Y. Co.), 1944-45. Mem. East Side Chamber of Commerce (dir.), Fifth Avenue Association (dir. 1958), Am. Legion. Mason. Clubs: Union League (N.Y.C.); Bedford Golf and Tennis. Home: Mt. Kisco, N.Y. Died Aug. 20, 1984.

DERBY, WILFRID NEVILLE, coast guard officer; born Newark, N.J., Dec. 4, 1889; s. Henry and Ellen (Auster) D.; ed. Stevens Sch., and Webb Acad.; B.S., Coast Guard Acad., 1911; m. Ruth McChesney, Mar. 23, 1921; children—Wilfrid Neville, Ruth Alice. Cadet, U.S. Coast Guard, 1908, advancing through grades to rear adm., 1947; supt. U.S. Coast Guard Acad. from 1947. Mem. Newcomen Soc. Address: New London, Conn. †

DE RIVERA, JOSE, sculptor; b. West Baton Rouge, La., Sept. 18, 1904; s. Joseph and Honorine (Montamat) Ruiz; m. Rose Covelli, 1926; 1 son, Joseph; m. Lita Jeronimo, 1955. Student drawing with, John W. Norton, Chgo.; student drawing with sculpture in, Spain, Italy, France, Greece, Egypt; D.F.A. (hon.), Washington U., St. Louis. Sculpture critic Yale, 1953-55; mem. faculty N.C. State Coll. Sch. Design, 1957-60. Exhibited numerous galleries, museums, univs., 1930-85, including, De Cordova Mus., Whitney Mus. Am. Art, Ind. U., Smith, Mt. Holyoke colls., Galerie Claude Bernard, Paris, Zurich Art Mus., Stockholm Mus. Modern Art, Stedelijk Mus., Amsterdam, Seattle World Fair, Washington Gallery Modern Art, Battersea Park, London, Pub. Edn. Assn. N.Y., Arts Club Chgo., White House, Washington, U. N.M., Los Angeles County Mus., Phila. Mus. Art, La Jolla (Calif.) Mus. Contemporary Art; represented in numerous permanent collections. Served with USAAF. Recipient Watson F. Blair prize Art Inst. Chgo., 1957; Creative Awards medal Brandeis U., 1969; others.; Nat. Inst. Arts and Letters grantee, 1959. Mem. Nat. Inst. Arts and Letters.; mem. Midwestern Psychol. Assn. Home: New York, N.Y. Died Mar. 19, 1985.

DERNER, GORDON FREDERICK, psychologist, educator, university official; b. Buffalo, Apr. 9, 1915; s. Henry F. and Nettie Ellen (Hamilton) D.; B.S., SUNY, Buffalo, 1942; M.A., Columbia U., 1943, Ph.D., 1950; postgrad. William Alanson White Inst. Psychoanalysis, Psychiatry and Psychology, 1946-50; m. Margaret F. Rafter, Sept. 17, 1942; children—Jonathan F. (dec.), Kurt F. Research asso. Boy Scouts Am., 1942-43; cons. psychologist Columbia Grammar Sch., N.Y.C., 1943-44; psychologist Grasslands Hosp., Valhalla, N.Y., 1944-46; instr. Columbia U., N.Y.C., 1945-51, lectr. psychology, 1951-68; supervising psychologist Psychol. Services Center, Adelphi U., Garden City, L.I., 1951-83, from asso. prof. to prof. psychology Adelphi U., 1951-83, dir. clin. psychology program, 1951-83, dir. postdoctoral program in psychotherapy, 1961-83, dean Inst. Advanced Psychol. Studies, 1962-83; dir. Biofeedback Research Center, Franklin Gen. Hosp.-Adelphi Inst. Advanced Psychol. Studies, 1976-83; vis. prof. Syracuse U., 1953, U. Iowa, 1962, Calif. Sch. Profl. Psychology, San Diego, 1976, U.S. Internat. U., 1976-83; pvt. practice, 1943-83; cons. psychologist Siani Temple, Mt. Vernon, N.Y., 1950-52; cons. Lawrence (N.Y.) Public Schs., 1955-57, North Shore Neuropsychiat. Center, Roslyn, N.Y., 1958-64, VA, 1957-83, Oakland County (Mich.) Juvenile Ct., 1960-83; spl. examiner N.Y.C. CSC, 1954-83; adv. council N.Y. State Bd. Examiners in Psychology, 1956-67; field selection officer Peace Corps., 1963-70, trainee devel. officer, 1970-72, Chmn. bd. N.Y. Cystic Fibrosis Research Assn., 1953-56; bd. dirs. Nassau Council Churches Counseling Service, 1965-70, Nassau Tb and Public Health Assn., 1958-73, chmn. nominating com., 1965-67. Paul Dawson Eddy award for disting. service Adelphi U., 1978; diplomate Am. Bd. Profl. Psychology, Am. Bd. Psychol. Hypnosis. Fellow N.Y. Acad. Scis., Soc. Personality Assessment, Royal Soc. Health (London), Soc. Psychol. Study Social Issues; mem. Am. Acad. Psychotherapists (charter mem., dir. 1956-60), Am. Psychol. Assn. (fellow divs. cons. psychology, clin. psychology and psychotherapy; mem. test standards com. 1954-55, pres. div. cons. psychology 1972-73, div. psychotherapy 1974-75, div. clin. psychology 1975-76; exec. bd. 1967-70, 73-76; council of reps. 1966-83; Disting. Psychologist award div. psychotherapy 1977), Eastern Psychol. Assn. (dir. 1977-83), N.Y. State Psychol. Assn. (dir. 1955-66, chmn. clin. div. 1957-58, pres. 1959-60), Nassau County Psychol. Assn. (founder, dir. 1951-83, pres. 1951-53), Indian Psychol. Assn. (life), N.Y. Soc. Clin. Psychology (Disting. Psychologist award 1979), N.Y. Soc. Clin. Psychologists, Biofeedback Soc. Am., AAUP. Author: (with M. Aborn) Clinical Diagnosis of Intelligence, 1950; Certain Aspects of the Psychology of the Tuberculous, 1952; contbr. articles to profl. jours.; asso. editor: Handbook of Clinical Psychology, 1965; Encyclopedia of Psychiatry, Psychology, Neurology and Psychoanalysis, 1977; mem. editorial bd. The Clinical Psychologist, 1965-83, Psychotherapy: Theory, Research and Practice, 1964-83, Profl. Psychology, 1969-83; instrumental in establishing first univ.-based profl. sch. psychology. Home: Garden City Long Island, N.Y. Died Sept. 11, 1983.

DE ROCHEMONT, RICHARD GUERTIS, motion picture, TV producer; b. Chelsea, Mass., Dec. 13, 1903; s. Louis L. G. and Sarah Wilson (Miller) de R.; m. Helen Bentley Bogart, Apr. 11, 1924 (dec. Aug. 15, 1975); m. Jane Louise Meyerhoff, Feb. 25, 1976. A.B., Harvard U., 1928. Reporter N.Y. Am., 1928, N.Y. Sun, 1929; fgn. editor Movietone Newsreel, 1930-31; dir. for France Fox Movietone, 1931-34; gen. fgn. mgr. The March of Time, 1934-40; mng. editor The March of Time div. Time, Inc., 1940-43; producer March of Time, 1943-52; ind. producer for Dept. State, Ford Found., NBC, etc., 1952-53; v.p. J. Walter Thompson Co., N.Y.C., 1953-55; pres. Vavin, Inc., 1955-82; war corr. Life; accredited to French Army, 1939-40; war corr. March of Time; accredited U.S. Forces, 1944-45. (Recipient Motion Picture Acad. award for prodn. of A Chance to Live 1949). chevalier du Merite Agricole, 1938; promoted to officier, 1959; decorated officier Legion d'Honneur, 1945; France; officier Ordre du Merite Touristique, 1959; comdr. Ordre du Mérite Nat., 1979; France). Mem. France Forever (nat. pres. 1943-46). Episcopalian. Clubs: Paris-American (N.Y.C.) (pres. 1962-64), Harvard (N.Y.C.), Williams (N.Y.C.), Coffee House (N.Y.C.); Cercle Interallié 0 (Paris); Overseas Press of America (gov. 1940-43, 48, 57-63, trustee corrs. fund 1945-82). Home: Flemington, N.J. Dec. Aug. 4, 1982.

DE ROTHSCHILD, ALAIN JAMES GUSTAVE JULES, banker; b. France, Jan. 7, 1910; ed. U. Paris. Vice pres. Banque Rothschild; pres. Compagnie du Nord, 1968-82. Mayor, Chamant, France. Decorated officer Legion of Honor, Croix de Guerre. Address: Paris, France. Died Oct. 18, 1982.

DESBOROUGH, ALMA HINCHMAN, orgn. ofcl.; born Camden, N.J., Sept. 3, 1890; d. Howard and Josephine (Dithmar) Hinchman; ed. pub. schs. of Camden; extension courses Columbia and Hamilton univs.; m. Edmonds A. Desborough, June 28, 1917 (died 1918); 1 son, Paul Hinchman. Asst. exec. sec., The Needlework Guild of America, Inc., Phila., 1934-41, nat. exec. sec. from 1941; sec. Labrador br. of the Needlework Guild (aids work started by Sir Wilfred Greenfell) from 1947. Good Will Ambassadress of the City of Phila. Mem. Nat. Assn. Women Broadcasters, C. of C. (nat. rep.). Club: Business and Profl. Womans (internat., nat. and local brs.), N.J. Republican Womens. Appears in radio programs. Home: Haddonfield, N.J. †

DESIMONE, SALVATORE VINCENT, consulting engineer; b. N.Y.C., Jan. 25, 1924; s. Gabriel and Gemma (Amato) DeS.; m. Damaris Hamilton Smith, May 8, 1948; children: Ursula, Dorothy, Tiffany. B.C.E., Coll. City N.Y., 1948; postgrad., Columbia, 1948-49, 50-53. Registered profl. engr., N.Y., N.J., Conn., Mass., Fla., La., Ohio, Ky., D.C., Ga. Structural engr. Moran, Proctor, Freeman & Mueser, N.Y.C., 1948-51; chief structural dept. Brown Guenther, Booss, N.Y.C., 1952-53, structural engr., 1951-52; with Mueser, Rutledge, Johnston & DeSimone, N.Y.C., 1953—, asso., 1960-65, partner, 1966—; Vice pres. N.Y. Bldg. Congress, 1976—. Tech. adv. com. Village of N. Tarrytown, N.Y., 1976—; tech. adv. com. Ardsley, 1956-59; mem. Ardsley Zoning Com., 1956-59; bd. dirs. Phelps Meml. Hosp., 1977-80. Served as 1st lt. inf. AUS, 1943-46. Decorated Purple Heart. Mem. N.Y. Assn. Cons. Engrs. (dir. 1976-80), ASCE, Am. Concrete Inst., Am. Cons. Engrs. Council, N.Y. Assn. Cons. Engrs., The Moles, Prestressed Concrete Inst., Concrete Industry Bd., Delta Kappa Epsilon. Club: Univ. Home: Tarrytown NY Office: New York NY

DESMOND, JOHN J(OSEPH), JR., investment counselor; b. Boston, May 31, 1887; s. John Joseph and Anne Louise (Guider). A.B. cum laude, Harvard, 1909, A.M. final honors, 1910, Ed.D., 1949; LL.D., Stonehill Coll.; Ph.D. (hon.), New Bedford Institute of Technology; M.S. (honorary), Bradford College of Technology; married to Mary Wight Murphy, Oct. 18, 1930; children—Mary Louise, John Joseph, Richard Lewis. Submaster Saugus (Mass.) High Sch., 1909-11, Roberts Sch., Cambridge, Mass., 1911-13; headmaster Chicopee (Mass.) High Sch., 1913-21; supt. schs., Chicopee, 1921-46; became the commr. edn. Commonwealth of Mass., 1946; investment counselor Draper, Sears & Co., Boston; dir. College Courses, Incorporated. Director Chicopee Coop. Bank; corporator Chicopee Savs. Bank. Chmn. Bd. Collegiate Authority, Mass., from 1946; mem. adv. council U.S. Commr. Edn. from 1949; mem. corp. Mass. Inst. Tech.; vis. com. Harvard Coll., Hayden Meml. Library; chmn. Oct. Conf. Exchange Edn. Opinion, 1936, 52; approving authority for med. schs., nursing schs., pharmacy schs. Chmn. adv. com. Mass. Commn. Against Discrimination.

Trustee Mus. Fine Arts, Mus. Sci., Commn. on Rehabilitation, U. Mass., Lowell Textile Inst., Bradford-Durfee Tech. Inst., New Bedford (Mass.) Textile Inst. Served as lt., Motor Transport Div., A.U.S., World War I, res. officer, 1918-29. Mem. N.E. Supts. Assn. (pres.), Mass. Sch. Supts. Assn. (pres.), Am. Assn. Sch. Adminstrs., Chief State Sch. Officers Council. Kiwanis Internat. (lt. gov. N.E. dist., 1930). Clubs: Milton (Mass.) Town; Harvard, Ninety-Six (Boston); Massachusetts Schoolmasters (pres. 1930). Home: Milton, Mass. †

DESRUISSEAUX, PAUL, lawyer, bus. exec., former Canadian senator; b. Sherbrooke, Que., Can., May 1, 1905; s. Geoffroy Francois and Sarah (Gauthier) D.; m. Celine Duchesne, June 16, 1945; children—Louis (dec.), Francois, Helene, Pierre. Grad., St. Charles Coll., 1928, Montreal Coll., 1931; grad. law, U. Montreal, 1934; postgrad., Babson Inst., 1935, Harvard, 1935-36; LL.D. (hon.), U. Sherbrooke, 1964; Ph.D. in Bus. Adminstrn, Hamilton State U. Bar: Que. bar 1934, created King's counsel 1948, Queen's counsel 1953. Practiced in, Sherbrooke; sr. mem. Desruisseaux, Fortin, Rouillard, until 1960, senator div., Wellington, 1966-80; past chmn. La. Tribune, Inc., CHLT, CHLT-FM and CHLT-TV, 1955-67; chmn. Melchers Distilleries Ltd., 1967-75; pres. St. Regis Investment Co., 1948-67, Sherbrooke Hotel & Motel Co., 1948-59, Que. Telemedia, Inc., 1967-70, Telegram Printing & Pub. Co., Ltd., 1955-70, Delta Services, Inc., 1963-67, Radio and TV Sherbrooke, Inc., 1955-67, Desmont Research and Devel. Inc., 1967-80, Cablevision, 1965-80, Desruisseaux Corp., 1961-74; Société Tele-Cinema, Inc., 1954-73, Cinema Plaza, Inc., 1965-73; v.p. Cinema Premier, Inc., 1953-73; dir. Westmount Life Assurance Co., Ltd., 1964-76, Canadian Gen. Electric Co., Ltd., 1964-76, Royal Bank of Can., Que., 1962-77, Provigo, 1969-74, PPG Industries, 1970-77, Monde Internat. Corp., 1971-77. Asst. Asst. commr. Cath. Scouts of Sherbrooke, 1937-39; Mem. Canadian br. Commonwealth Parliamentary Assn., Canadian group Interparliamentary Union, NATO Parliamentary Assn.; Bd. govs. Sherbrooke Hosp.; pres. Sherbrooke Red Cross Soc., 1954-57; bd. govs. U. Sherbrooke, 1957-74, v.p. bd. trustees, 1961-71; bd. regents U. Ottawa, 1960-66; chmn. hon. bd. govs. Que. Assn. Retarded Children, from 1961; bd. dirs. PPG Found., 1970-77. Served with Royal Canadian Arty., 1942-45. Recipient medals Latin union l'Alliance Francaise; Bene Merenti medal; decorated comdr. Royal Order St. Gregoire Gt.; knight Magistral Order Malta; Human Relations award Canadian Council Christians and Jews; named hon. chief Abenakis Indians. Mem. A.I.M. (fellow pres.'s council), Sherbrooke C. of C., Sherbrooke Fusiliers (hon. mem. Officers Club), P.Q. C. of C. (past gov.), Canadian Research Assn., Canadian Assn. for Advancement Sci., Canadian Bar, St. Francis Bar (past counsellor, past treas.), Canadian Daily Newspaper Pubs. Assn., Canadian Press (dir.), Canadian French Daily Assn. (past pres.). Roman Catholic. Clubs: Hillcrest Ski (North Hatley) (co-founder, life, North); Sherbrooke Social. Home: Sherbrooke, Que. Deceased.

DESSUREAULT, JEAN MARIE, senator, lumber dealer; b. Ste. Genevieve de Batiscan, Que., Dec. 30, 1888; s. Aime and Marie-Anne (Rousseau) D.; ed. Sacred Heart Coll., St. Anne de la Perade and Victoriaville, Que.; m. Aurore Vallee, June 30, 1913 (dec. 1954); children—Louise (Mrs. Will C. Kelliher), Marthe (Mrs. Kenneth F. Brown), Suzanne (Mrs. Robert M. Ross), Claire (Mrs. Martin Garneau); m. 2d, Elise Dion, Sept. 21, 1957. Pres., J.M. Dessureault, Inc.; propr. J.M. Dessureault Lumber Co.; v.p. La Banque Canadienne Nationale, 1944-64, Quebec Land & Realty Co., La Compagnie de Courtage Immobilier de Quebec Ltee; dir. Trust Gen. du Can., Hotel Windsor, Mortreal, mem. Senate of Can., from 1945. Alderman, Quebec City, 1922-26. Bd. govs. Sch. Commerce, Laval U. Decorated chevalier l'Ordre Equestre du St. Sepulcre de Jerusalem. Apptd. hon. lt. col. Que. Regt., 1937. Liberal. Roman Catholic. Clubs: Quebec Garrison; Reform; University. Home: Sillery, Quebec, Canada. †

DESTLER, CHESTER MCARTHUR, history educator; b. Wyncote, Pa., July 27, 1904; s. Lewis Wesley and M. Louise (Griesemer) D.; A.B. cum laude, Coll. Wooster, 1925; A.M., U. Chgo., 1928, Ph.D. (Henry Milton Wolf fellow), 1932; m. Katharine Hardesty, Sept. 9, 1936; children—Paul Lewis, Irving McArthur, Anne Louise, William Wallace. Instr. history Coll. of Ozarks, 1925-28; research asst. U. Chgo., 1930-31; asst. prof. history Albion Coll., 1931-34; prof. history Ga. Tchrs. Coll., 1934-41, dir. jr. div., 1935-41; prof. U. System of Ga., 1937-41; prof., chmn. dept. history Conn. Coll., 1942-54, Charles J. MacCurdy prof. Am. history, 1949-54. Faculty summers Tulane U., 1940, U. N.C., 1941, Elmira Coll., 1941-42, Cornell, 1942, 52; vis. prof. Yale, 1945, 50-51, Cornell U., 1953, U. Bridgeport, 1973. Mem. editorial bd. Miss. Valley Hist. Rev., 1946-49, Soc. Edn., 1946-51; pres. Ga. Council Social Studies, 1939-41; mem. ednl. adv. bd. Am. Heritage, 1946-49; mem. Mystic (Conn.) Seaport, 1947-52; mem. adv. council Conn. Bicentennial Commn. on Am. Revolution; chmn. Conn. Minimum Wage Bd. Laundry Industry, 1950-51. Fellow Berkeley Coll., Yale, 1945-46, 66-70, assoc. fellow, 1946-66, 71-84; Library of Congress fellow in Am. civilization, 1945-46; recipient Everett Edwards award in agrl. history, 1957. Mem. Assn. for Study Conn. History (pres. 1970-71), Agrl., Conn. hist. socs., Orgn. Am. Historians, Am., New Eng. hist. assns., N.E. Assn. Social Sci. Tchrs. (pres., 1950-51), Aux. Inst. Living (dir.). Phi Beta Kappa. Democrat. Conglist. (mem. N.E. Bd. Pastoral Supply 1947-50, moderator Hartford Assn. 1977-79). Author: American Radicalism, 1865-1901: Essays and Documents, 1946; Joshua Coit, American Federalist, 1962; Henry Demarest Lloyd and the Empire of Reform, 1963; Roger Sherman and Independent Oil Men, 1967; Connecticut: The Provision State, 1973. Sr. editor Studies in Social Progress, 1938. Editor: The Democratic Process, 1948; Liberalism As A Force in History, 1953. Contbr. articles to hist., econ. jours. Home: West Hartford, Conn. Died Sept. 30, 1984.

DEUEL, THORNE, anthropologist; b. Millbrook, N.Y., Dec. 15, 1890; s. Thorne and Laura Howard (Haight) D.; B.S., U.S. Mil. Acad., 1912; student Columbia, 1924-28; Ph.D., U. Chgo., 1935; m. Nora Wing Quain, Aug. 29, 1924; children—Thorne, William Townsley. Instr., later asst. prof. sociology Syracuse (N.Y.) U., 1928-33; asst. anthropology U. Chgo., 1931-34, research asso., 1934-38, dir. archaeol. expdns., central and so. Ill., 1932-37; dir. archaeol. survey Miss. Valley, 1931-38; dir. Ill. State Museum of Natural History and Art, 1937-63, senior scientist, 1963-65, director emeritus and research associate, from 1965. Served from second lieutenant to maj., U.S. Army, 1912-19, jr. mil. aviator, aviation sect. Signal Corps, 1917-19, active duty, 1942-45, lt. col., 1943; fgn. service in China and India, 1943-44. Fellow Am. Anthropol. Assn., Soc. for Am. Archaeol. (sec.-treas. 1940-42), A.A.A.S.; mem. Ill. Acad. Sci. (librarian, pres. 1949-50), Am Assn. Museums, Midwest Mus. Conf. (pres. 1950-51), Mo. Archaeol. Soc. (life), New York Academy of Sciences (life), Sigma Xi. Author: Rediscovering Illinois (with F.C. Cole), 1937; Illinois Records of 1000 A.D., 1948; Men's Venture in Culture, 1950; Hopewellian Dress in Illinois, 1952; The Modoc Shelter, 1957; American Indian Ways of Life, 1958. Editor: Hopewellian Communities in Illinois, 1952. Contbr. profl. jours. Home: Springfield, Ill. †

DEUSING, MURL, producer; b. Milw., Sept. 5, 1908; s. Henry and Olga (Henning) D.; m. Mildred Nickels, May 25, 1928. B.E., U. Wis., 1933. Asst. curator edn. Milw. Pub. Mus., 1932-45, curator edn., 1945-59; during this period adminstr. audiovisual library serving Milw. schs., also pioneered mus. TV Programs; photographer wild life Walt Disney's True Life Adventures, Zoo Parade, Warner Bros., also lectr. wild life and travel, 1939-84; owner Murl Deusing Film Prodns., classroom teaching films, from 1946; dir. Mus. Sci. and Natural History, St. Louis, 1959-61; producer TV programs Nat. Ednl. TV and Radio Center, N.Y.C., 1961-77, producer Murl Dausing Safari TV series, 1964-77. Author: Soil, Water and Man, 1936. Recipient Distinguished Alumnus award U. Wis.-Milw. Alumni Assn., 1971. Mem. AAAS, Wis. Soc. Ornithology (past pres.), Am. Assn. Museums (counselor 1959), Izaak Walton League (past nat. dir., past sec. Wis.), Midwest Mus. Conf. (past pres.), Acad. Sci. St. Louis, Wis Acad. Sci., Nat. Conservancy, Wilderness Soc., Nat. Parks Assn. Home: Clermont, Fla. Died Dec. 18, 1984.

DEUTSCH, BABETTE, writer; b. N.Y.C., 1895; A.B., Barnard Coll. (Columbia), 1917; Litt.D. (hon., Columbia, 1946. Lectr. poetry Columbia U., 1944-71, sr. lectr., 1960-71; hon. cons. Library of Congress, 1961-66; chancellor Acad. Am. Poets. Recipient Disting. Alumna award Barnard Coll., 1977. Mem. P.E.N., Nat. Inst. Arts and Letters (sec.), Am. Acad. Arts and Letters. Author: Banners (verse), 1919; Honey Out of the Rock (verse), 1925; A Brittle Heaven (novel), 1926; In Such a Night (novel), 1927; Potable Gold (criticism), 1929; Fire For the Night (verse), 1930; Epistle to Prometheus (verse), 1930; Mask of Silenus (novel), 1933; This Modern Poetry (criticism), 1935; One Part Love (verse), 1939; Heroes of the Kalevala (juvenile), 1940; It's a Secret (juvenile), 1941; Walt Whitman, Builder for America (juvenile), 1941; The Welcome (juvenile), 1942; Rogue's Legacy (novel), 1942; Take Them, Stranger (verse), 1944; The Reader's Shakespeare (criticism), 1946; Poetry in Our Time (criticism), 1952, 56, 58, 63, rev. edit., 1963; Animal, Vegetable, Mineral (verse), 1954; Poetry Handbook, 1957, 58, 62, 69, 74; Coming of Age: New and Selected Poems, 1959, 64; Collected Poems, 1919-1962, 63; I Often Wish (juvenile), 1966; The Collected Poems of Babette Deutsch, 1969. Co-translator: The Steel Flea (juvenile), 1943; Tales of Faraway Folk (juvenile), 1952; More Tales of Faraway Folk (juvenile), 1963. Editor: The Poems of Samuel Taylor Coleridge (criticism), 1967. Translator several vols. verse including The Twelve by Alexander Blok, Eugene Onegin by Pushkin, Poems from The Book of Hours by Rilke, 1941, 75; Two Centuries of Russian Verse, 1966; There Comes a Time (juvenile), 1969. Scholarship established in her name by classmates at Barnard Coll., 1977. Home: New York, N.Y. Died Nov. 13, 1982.

D'EVELYN, CHARLOTTE, coll. prof.; b. San Francisco, May 23, 1889; d. Frederick William and Susan (Taylor) D'Evelyn; B.L., Mills Coll., 1911; Ph.D., Bryn Mawr Coll., 1917. Instr. Mount Holyoke Coll., 1917-20, asst. prof., 1920-23, asso. prof. 1923-31, prof. English lit. from 1931, chmn. dept. English lang. and lit., 1939-47. Research work England and Ireland, 1915-16, 1929-30, and summers, 1931-39. Mem. Modern Lang. Assn., Modern Humanities Research Assn., Medieval Acad. of Am., Am. Assn. Univ. Profs. (mem. council 1941-43). Am. Assn. Univ. Women, Phi Beta Kappa. Editor: Meditations on The Life of Christ, 1921; Peter Idley's Instructions to his Son, 1935; The Latin Text of the Ancrene Riwle, 1944. Home: South Hadley Mass. †

DEWELL, WILBUR, cosmetic co. exec.; b. Cushing, Ia., Dec. 1, 1890; s. George Allen and Agnes Woodside (Moore) D.; student Morningside Coll., Sioux City, Ia.; m. Minna Ehlers, Nov. 24, 1909; 1 son, Lloyd (dec.). Sales mgr. Churchill Drug Co., Burlington, Ia., 1922-27; with McKesson & Robbins, Inc., 1927-56, v.p., 1934-56, dir., 1943-56; gen. mgr. McKesson Labs., Bridgeport, Conn., 1929-56; with Lanolin Plus, Inc., Newark (merged to form Bishop Industries, Inc. 1962), from 1958, chmn. bd., dir., until 1972; chmn. bd. Dewell & Edell, Inc., Newark; Frough Constrn. Co., N.Y.C. and Bridgeport, Savoy Industries, Inc., Long Island City, N.Y. Named Ky. col., 1941. Mason (Shriner), Rotarian. †

DEWEY, ERNEST WAYNE, educator; b. Hutchinson, Kans., May 20, 1925; s. Ernest A. and Violet (Hampton) D.; m. Helen Josephine Scamell, Apr. 11, 1949; children—Ernest Ralph, William Frederick, James Franklin. B.A., U. Kans., 1949, M.A., 1950; Ph.D., U. Tex., 1954. Vis. instr. U. Kans., 1953-54; asst. prof. Okla. State U., 1954-58, assoc. prof., 1958-60; prof., chmn. philosophy U. S.D., 1960-66; prof., chmn. philosophy U. Toledo, 1966-76, prof., 1976-82; symposia-rev. editor Philosophy Forum, 1970-74. Served with AUS, 1943-46. Mem. AAUP, Am. Philos. Soc., Ohio Philos. Soc., Southwestern Philos. Soc. (sec. treas. 1957-58, editor Newsletter 1957-59), Am. Soc. for 18th Century Studies, Phi Alpha Theta, Pi Gamma Mu. Democrat. Home: Toledo, Ohio. Dec. Mar. 21, 1982.

DEWEY, EVELYN, psychologist; b. Minneapolis, Minn., Mar. 5, 1889; d. John and Alice (Chipman) D.; B.A., Barnard Coll., New York, 1911. Dir. psychol. survey, N.Y. City, 1918-20. Author: Schools of Tomorrow, 1915; New Schools for Old, 1919; Methods and Results of Testing School Children, 1920; The Dalton Laboratory Plan, 1922. Home: New York, N.Y. †

DEWEY, GODFREY, author, educator, bus. exec.; b. N.Y.C., Sept 3, 1887; s. Melvil, Annie (Godfrey) D.; ed. Albany (N.Y.) Acad.; A.B., Harvard, 1909, Ed.M., 1921, Ed.D., 1926; m. Marjorie Kinne, May 28, 1914; children—Kinne (dec.), Katharin, Arthur Kinne (dec.), Margaret Ann, Stuart Kinne (dec.). Exec. officer, Lake Placid Co. and allied corporations. 1908-32, chairman of the executive committee, 1955-62; pres., treas. Dewey Shorthand Corp., from 1937; president, director Forest Press. Inc., 1951-61. President III Olympic Winter Games Committee, 1929-32; trustee Lake Placid Club Education Foundation, from 1924, vice president, from 1958; mem. board trustees Emerson College, 1940-51; pres. Emerson Coll., 1949-51. Trustee Northwood Sch., 1954-61, chmn., 1954-59. Recipient Freedoms Found. award, 2d place, 1950, 62. Sec. Simplified Spelling Board, 1921-46, Spelling Reform Association. 1932-46, Simpler Spelling Assn. from 1946; hon. mem. Nat. Shorthand Reporters Assn., N.Y. State Shorthand Reporters Assn.; pres. Essex Co. Tuberculosis and Pub. Health Assn., 1935-37. Mem. N.E.A., Am. Legion, Grange, Phi Delta Kappa. Mason. Republican. Episcopalian. Clubs: Lake Placid; Harvard (N.Y.C.). Author numerous books including Relative Frequency of English Speech Sounds and the Dewey Shorthand series of textbooks; also articles. Home: Lake Placid Club, N.Y. †

DEWITT, PAUL B(URTON), lawyer; b. Sheldon, Ia., Apr. 15, 1910; s. Jesse Arthur and Pearl (Monk) DeW.; A.B., A.M., Univ. of Ia., 1931; A.M., Harvard, 1934; LL.B., Univ. of Mich., 1937; m. Else Hvistendahl, May 31, 1943; 1 son, Jon Lance. Admitted to Ia. bar, 1937, practiced with Shull and Marshall, Sioux City, 1937-38; chief leg. drafting bur. and state law librarian, State of Ia., 1939-40; asst. sec. Am. Judicature Soc., Ann Arbor, Mich., 1941; reporter, rules com., Supreme Court of Ia., Des Moines, 1941-42; exec. sec. Assn. of the Bar of the City of New York from 1945; sec. Nat. Conf. of Judicial Councils from 1941. Served as lt. U.S. N.R., 1942-46, then lt. comdr. Mem. Am. Bar Assn. (alternate del. to U.N., 1946, sec. spl. com. on improving judicial adminstrn., chmn. sect., of bar activities, 1947-49; dir. state coms., sect., jud. adminstrn., 1948-51; mem. Ho. of Dels.), Ia. Bar Assn. (sec. 1941-42), Phi Beta Kappa, Phi Delta Theta. Episcopalian. Club: Century (N.Y.). Editor Annual Handbook Nat. Conf. of Jud. Councils. Home: New York, N.Y. Died May 14, 1985.

DEWITT, WILLIAM ORVILLE, baseball exec.; b. St. Louis, Aug. 3, 1902; s. William Joseph and Lulu May (Sowash) D.; student St. Louis U., 1925-27, Law Sch., 1928-31, Washington U., 1927-28; m. Margaret Holekamp, Mar. 21, 1936; children—Joan, Donna Dorothy, William O. Office boy for St. Louis Browns, 1916, v.p., gen. mgr., 1936-48, pres., 1949-51, v.p., 1952-53; stenographer St. Louis Cardinals, 1917-25, treas., 1926-35, v.p., 1936; asst. gen. mgr. N.Y. Yankees, 1954-56; baseball coordinator, 1957-59; pres. Detroit Baseball Co., 1959-60; v.p., gen. mgr. Cin. Baseball Club Co., 1960-61; pres., gen. mgr., owner Cin. Reds, 1961-66; baseball cons., 1967-72; pres. William O. DeWitt & Assos.; chmn. bd. Cin. Coliseum Corp., Chgo. White Sox, from 1975. Mem. Major League Exec. Council, 1948-50, and from 77; mem. Com. to Select Vet. Players to Baseball Hall of Fame, from 1972. Admitted to Mo. bar, 1931, Fed. bar, 1958, U.S. Supreme Ct., 1972. Named Maj. League Exec. Yr., 1944. Mem. Mo. Bar Assn., Bar Assn. St. Louis, Delta Theta Phi, Alpha Sigma Nu. Mason (33 deg., Shriner). Presbyn. Clubs: University (St. Louis); Queen City, Recess, Cincinnati Country, One Hundred, Commonwealth (Cin.); Little

(Gulfstream, Fla.); Ocean (Delray Beach). Home: Cincinnati, Ohio. Died Mar. 3, 1982.*

DE YOUNG, HENRY CHUNG, (surname changed from Chung to De Young by Supreme Court of D.C., 1923), author; b. Soor Chun, Pyeng Ahn Province, Korea, Feb. 28, 1890; s. Yong Poke and Si (Lee) Chung; came to U.S., 1905; grad. Teachers' Coll., Kearney, Neb., 1915; A.B., U. of Neb., 1917, A.M., 1918; fellow in economics, Northwestern U., 1918-19; Ph.D., American U., Washington, D.C., 1921; m. Lillie E. Lawson, of Muskogee, Okla., June 3, 1924. Elected peace envoy to Paris Conf. by the Koreans residing in America, Hawaii, Mexico, China and Russia, but departure from U.S. was blocked by cable from Sec. Lansing to State Dept. Korean del. to Press Congress of the World, at Honolulu, T.H., 1921; Korean commr. to America and Europe, from 1920; mem. Korean delegation to Conf. on Limitation of Armament, Washington, D.C., 1921-22; v.p. New Ilhan & Co. Mem. Korean Nat. Assn., Press Congress of the World (v.p.). Presbyn. Clubs: Authors, Civic (New York); Nat. Press (Washington, D.C.). Author: Korean Treaties, 1919; The Oriental Policy of the United States, 1919; The Case of Korea, 1921. Home: Kearney, Neb. †

DIAZ, RAFAELO, operatic tenor; b. San Antonio, Tex., May 16, 1888; s. Rafaelo and Rose (Umscheid) D.; ed. West Tex. Mil. Acad. and St. Mary's Coll., both of San Antonio; studied music at Stern Conservatory, Berlin; Début with Boston Opera Co., Nov. 1911; later with Hammerstein Opera Co.; joined Metropolitan Opera Co.; high lyric tenor; has appeared in concerts throughout U.S. Theosophist. Address: New York, N.Y. †

DICK, HASELL HUTCHISON, foreign service officer; born at Rock Hill, S.C., June 29, 1888; U.S. Naval Academy, 2 1/2 years; married. Apptd. consul bar asst., 1911; dep. consul gen., Yokohama, 1911, vice consul, 1912; Dept. of State, 1915; vice consul, Jerusalem, 1915, Basel, 1917, Geneva, 1919; Dept. of State, 1920; consul, Sydney, Nova Scotia, 1924, Rangoon, 1926, Port Elizabeth, 1929; consul, Amoy, 1933; sec. Diplomatic Service, 1937; consul, Strasbourg, 1937, Bordeaux, 1939, Nantes, 1940, Bordeaux, 1941; Dept. of State, 1941; consul gen., Dakar, Senegal, French West Africa, 1946. Address: Washington, D.C. Deceased.

DICK, PHILIP KINDRED, science fiction author; b. Chgo., Dec. 16, 1928; s. Joseph Edgar and Dorothy (Kindred) D.; m. Tessa Busby, Apr. 18, 1973; 1 child, Christopher; children by previous marriages—Laura, Isolde. Student, U. Calif., Berkeley, 1950. Books include Solar Lottery, 1955, Time Out of Joint, 1959, The Man in the High Castle, 1962, The Simulacra, 1964, Martian Time-Slip, 1964, Do Androids Dream of Electric Sheep? 1968, We Can Build You, 1972, The Golden Man, 1980, VALIS, 1981. Recipient Hugo award, 1962; John W. Campbell Meml. award, 1974. Mem. Sci. Fiction Writers Am. Episcopalian. Died March 2, 1982.

DICKEMAN, RAYMOND LOUIS, energy cons.; b. Lime Ridge, Wis., Aug. 9, 1922; s. Louis and Abigail (Foley) D.; m. Janice Leatherberry, Sept. 29, 1945; children—Kathleen, Marcia, Dianne, Nancy, Mary. B.S., U. Wis., 1947, M.S., 1948. Mgr. nuclear physics devel. Gen. Electric Co., Richland, Wash., 1948-56, mgr. reactor tech., 1956-59, mgr. mfg., 1959-60, gen. mgr. fuels preparation dept., 1960-62, gen. mgr. N-reactor dept., 1962-66, gen. mgr. Hanford atomic products dept., 1966-67, gen. mgr. domestic turnkey projects, 1967, gen. mgr. nuclear plant projects dept., 1967-69; pres., chmn. bd., chief exec. officer Exxon Nuclear Co., Inc., Exxon Nuclear Internat., Inc., Jersey Nuclear Avco Isotopes, Inc., Exxon Nuclear GMbH, 1969-78; chmn. bd., pres. Dickeman Assos., Bellevue, Wash., 1980-83, internat. energy cons. Served with AUS, 1943-45. Mem. Nat. Acad. Engring., Atomic Indsl. Forum (dir.), Nat. Nuclear Energy Council, other tech. and mgmt. socs. Home: Bellevue, Wash. Died Mar. 12, 1983.

DICKERMAN, MARION, educator; b. Westfield, N.Y., Apr. 11, 1890; d. Edwin and Emily (Willey) D. Student, Wellesley Coll., 1907-09; A.B., Syracuse U., 1911, Pd.B., 1912, A.M., 1912. Instr. Canisteo (N.Y.) High Sch., 1912-13, Fulton HIgh Sch., 1913-18; dean N.J. State Normal Sch., Trenton, 1920-21; instr. Bryn Mawr (Pa.) Coll. Summer Sch., 1922, 23; instr. Todhunter Sch., N.Y.C., 1922-27, prin., 1927-39; asso. princ. Dalton Schs., 1939-42; dir. pub. edn. Am. Arbitration Assn., 1942-44; instr. Hunter Coll., 1944-45; Panel mem. region 2 Nat. Labor Relations Bd.; ednl. dir. Mystic Seaport, Mystic, Conn., 1945-62. Co-author: Invincible Summer an Intimate Portrait of the Roosevelts; Lectr., writer on current ednl., polit. topics; appeared: Chronology show, NBC, 1972. Alt. Democratic Nat. Convs., 1928, 32, 36, 40; mem. Com. on Resolutions, 1940; Mem. Pres.'s Commn. to Study Indsl. Relations in Gt. Britain and Sweden, summer 1938, Conf. on Children in a Democracy, Apparel Industry Com., Bd. Edn., Columbia U. Oral History Project.; Bd. dirs. Nat. Sci. for Youth Found. Served in record dept. Endell St. Mil. Hosp. 1918-19, London, Eng. Mem. AAUW (pres. N.Y. br. 1938-39), New Canaan Hist. Soc., Nat. League Am. Pen Women. Democrat. Episcopalian. Club: Cosmopolitan. Home: Kennett Square, Penn. Died May 16, 1983.

DICKERSON, THOMAS MILTON, educator, accountant; b. Webster County, Ky., Feb. 2, 1898; s. Daniel Webster and Mina (Witherspoon) D.; student U. of Mich., 1919-21; B.A., Bowling Green (Ky.) Coll. of Commerce, 1924; A.B., Western Ky. State Teacher's Coll., 1926; M.B.A., Northwestern U., 1929; C.P.A., Ky., 1934, Ohio, 1937; m. Nell Caldwell Vaughn, Nov. 28, 1922; 1 dau., June Nelle (Mrs. John E. Sturgis). High school prin., Simpson County, Ky., 1921-23; asst. prof. accounting Bowling Green Coll. of Commerce, 1923-28, head dept., 1929-30; teaching fellow Northwestern U., 1928-29; asst. prof. econ. U. of Louisville (Ky.), 1930-31; asst. sec. Nat. Assn. Cost Accountants, 1931-34; chief staff accountant Nat. Com., Municipal Accounting, 1934-35; Western Res. U., 1935-63, asso. prof. accounting, 1935-42, prof., 1942-63; head accounting dept., 1936-62, dir. div. bus. adminstrn., 1943-48; lectr. in accounting Coll. of Bus. Adminstrn., U. South Fla., Tampa, 1963-70; vis prof. accounting Grad. Sch. Bus., Stanford, summer 1956. Mem. Am. Accounting Assn. (v.p. 1952), Am. Inst. C.P.A.'s, Ohio C.P.A. Soc., Nat. Assn. Accountants (mem. nat. bd., dir. 1939-46), Delta Sigma Pi, Beta Alpha Psi (past pres., grand council), Beta Gamma Sigma. Democrat. Presbyn. Author articles, pub. addresses. Home: Charlotte, N.C. Died July 29, 1982; interred Franklin, Ky.

DICKINSON, LESTER E., univ. prof.; b. St. Cloud, Minn., Mar. 27, 1890; s. George A. and Mary Ann (McComb); A.B., U. of Minn., 1914; m. Adelaide Thielman, June 17, 1916; 1 son, Thomas Allan. Began as teacher in pub. schs., Minn. and Mont., 1914-20; instr., asst. prof. and asso. prof. English, Wayne U., 1920-47, professor of English from 1947; trustee American Hosp.-Med. Benefit, Detroit. Member Modern Lang. Assn. of Am., Am. Assn. Univ. Profs., Coll. English Assn. Home: Ferndale, Mich. †

DICKINSON, PORTER, newspaper publisher; b. Glasgow, Ky., Mar. 10, 1906; s. Michael Hall and Emma Raus (Smith) D.; student U. Wash., 1925-26; m. Eleanor Roberts, July 26, 1930; 1 son, Robert Brewster. Pub. Honolulu Star-Bull., from 1927, now pub. emeritus, from 1972; pres. Hawaii Newspaper Agy., 1962-70; v.p., dir. Guam Publs., Inc., 1970-72, Mariana Publs., Inc., 1970-72; dir. C. Brewer & Co., Ltd., First Hawaiian Bank, Andrade & Co.; hon. consul of Finland for Hawaii, from 1961. Chmn. adv. bd. Hawaii Salvation Army, 1949-51, 67. Bd. dirs. Better Bus. Bur. Decorated Order Finnish Lion. Mem. Honolulu C. of C. (pres. 1952-53), Am. Newspaper Pub. Assn., Hawaii, Calif. newspaper pubs. assns. Republican. Rotarian (pres. Honolulu 1947-48, dist. gov. 1951-52), Mason (Jester). Home: Honolulu, Hawaii. Died July 9, 1984.

DICKINSON, WILLIAM HAROLD, former mfg. co. exec.; b. Ft. Worth, Nov. 16, 1910; s. John William and Harriet (Dickey) D.; B.S. in Elec. Engring., Tex. A. and M. U., 1930; m. Lathia Rosamond Benton, Aug. 17, 1934 (dec. 1952); m. 2d, Mary Kathryn Border, Aug. 19, 1953; children—Elaine (Mrs. Thomas Anthony Phillips), Thomas William, Robert William. With Westinghouse Electric Corp., 1930-56, dir. mfg. engring., Pitts., 1950-56; with A.O. Smith Corp., Tipp City, Ohio, 1956-60, 69-75, works mgr. Electric Motor div., 1956-57, gen. mgr., 1957-60; v.p. Midland-Ross Corp., gen. mgr. Power Controls div., Owosso, Mich., 1960-68; v.p., dir. Midland-Ross of Can. Ltd., 1965-68; dir. Dolly Toy Co., Tipp City, 1956—; v.p., dir. Tipp City Shopping Center, 1961-77; dir. Owosso Savs. Bank, 1960-68; dir. Greenville Center, 1972-77; adviser on electric mfg. industry to Govt. of India, 1949. Mem. adv. bd. Owosso Coll., 1966-68; chmn. Owosso drive United Fund, 1968-69; v.p., dir. Shiawassee County (Mich.) United Fund, 1968-69; trustee Owosso Meml. Hosp., 1960-69, pres., 1964-67. Methodist (former chmn. bd. trustees, adminstrv. bd., council on ministries). Club: Troy Country. Home: Troy, Ohio. Died Sept. 21, 1983.

DICKMANN, BERNARD FRANCIS, mayor; b. St. Louis, Sept. 7, 1888; s. Joseph Francis and Maria (Eilers) D.; unmarried. Clk. W. R. Chivvis Hardware Lumber Co., 1904-06; with Jos. F. Dickmann Real Estate Co. from 1906, pres.; mayor City of St. Louis, 2 terms 1933-41. Served as gunnery sergt. U.S.M.C., World War. Mem. advisory bd. Salvation Army of St. Louis; mem. St. Louis Real Estate Exchange (ex-sec. and ex-pres.), St. Louis Chamber of Commerce (bd. dirs.), Merchants Exchange. Mem. Am. Legion (past comdr. Clarence Sodeman Post), Forty and Eight. Exalted Ruler Elks, 1926-29. Club: Missouri Athletic. Home: St. Louis, Mo. †

DICKSON, JOHN DAWSON, lawyer, corp. official; b. Angelica, N.Y., Nov. 18, 1890; s. Dawson and Frances J. (Shaw) D.; student Wilsonian Acad., Angelica, N.Y., 1905-08, St. John's Mil. Acad., Manlius, N.Y., 1908-10, Amherst College, 1910-12; B.L., Albany Law Sch., Union Univ., 1916; m. Mary D. Sweet, Nov. 18, 1920; children—Fanny Jane, Marilyn Sweet. Admitted to N.Y. bar, 1917; mem. Dickson & Dickson; sec. Allegany County Fair Assn., 1919-21; apptd. receiver Pittsburgh, Shawmut and Northern R.R. Co., 1923, pres. from 1923; pres. Shawmut Mining Co., Shawmut Coal and Coke Co., Kersey Mining Co., Tyler Coal Co., Shawmut Commercial Co., Shawmut Realty Corp. of Pa., Shawmut Realty Corp. of N.Y. Dir. Eastern Bituminous Coal Assn., First Trust Co. of Wellsville, Bank of Angelica, N.Y. Served as capt. U.S. Army, World War. Republican. Methodist. Mason. Clubs: Olean City; Wellsville Country; National Republican. Home: Wellsville, N.Y. †

DIEFENDORF, CHARLES H., trust company exec.; b. Buffalo, Feb. 22, 1890; s. Warren J. and Caroline (Haas) D.; m. Charlotte Wilke, 1918; children—Charlotte, David. With Marine Trust Co. of Western New York, beginning as messenger, became exec. v.p. 1931, dir. 1934, pres. 1942-56, chmn. exec. com. and chief exec. officer, from 1956; pres. and dir. Marine Midland Corporation; dir. Marine Midland Trust Co. of N.Y., Peter Cooper Corp., Am. Steamship Co., Internat. Salt Co., Gen. Baking Co., Erie Railroad Co., Dunlop Tire & Rubber Corp., Buffalo Ins. Co., Carborundum Co., Niagara Share Corp. Mem. bd. dir. Hist. Soc., Kleinhans Music Hall, Millard Fillmore Hosp. (Buffalo). Mem. Council, U. of Buffalo. Clubs: Bankers of America; Buffalo, Saturn, Buffalo Country; The Links (New York). Home: Buffalo, N.Y. †

DIEHL, GEORGE WEST, minister; b. in Northumberland County, Pa., Dec. 7, 1887; s. Oliver Judson and Nellie Eliza (West) D.; student Hampden-Sidney Coll., 1907-10; A.B., Washington and Lee U., 1913; B.D., Union Theol. Sem., 1916; A.M., U. of Richmond, 1917; grad. study Columbia, 1923, U. of Chicago, 1930-31; LL.D. (honorary), Concord College, 1964; m. Iva Carruth Shafer, September 3, 1917. Prin. Brownsburg (Va.) High Sch., 1910-11, Grundy (Va.) Presbyn. Sch., 1917-20; personnel and ednl. dir., Carter Coal Co., 1920-24; pres. Concord State Normal Sch., Athens, W.Va., 1924-29; pres. Morris Harvey College, 1929-30; ad interim supply, 1st Presbyterian Ch., Houston, Tex., Jan.-Mar. 1932; pastor First Presbyterian Church, Corpus Christi, Tex., 1932-49, Oxford Presbyterian Church, Lexington, Va., from 1949-63; minister without charge, from 1963. Public member of panel 8th Regional War Labor Board; member bd. of adjustment, City Planning Board; founder, headmaster Presbyn. Day Sch. from 1945; commissioner Corpus Christi Council, Girl Scouts, 1935-39; member committee Gulf Coast Council, Boy Scouts of America; co-chmn., Nat. Conf. of Christians and Jews; pres., South Tex. Tree Assn.; mem. Rockbridge County Board of Education, from 1956; director Rockbridge County Farm Bureau, 1956-58; chmn. Rockbridge County Civil War Centennial Com., from 1959; pres. bd. dirs. Botetourt-Rockbridge Regional Library, 1957-63; moderator Western Tex. Presbytery, 1940-41, Lexington (Va.) Presbytery, 1957; historian Lexington Presbytery, from 1958. Commnr., gen. assembly, Presbyn. Ch. U.S., 1943. Former chaplain 150th Inf., W.Va. Nat. Guard; corporal, Co. A, 4th Va. Inf., 1912-15. Member N.E.A. (life), Sons of the American Revolution, Am. Legion (chaplain Post 248), Corpus Christi Ministerial Assn. (pres. 1935), Memorial Museum Association (president), The Rockefeller Family Association, Institute American Geneaology, Soc. Am. Archives, Nat., Va. genealogical societies, Pi Gamma Mu, Tau Kappa Alpha, Alpha Psi Omega, Phi Delta Kappa, Delta Theta Chi. Democrat. Presbyn. Mason (32 deg., K.T., Shriner, Past-Grand Eminent Prelate K.T. of Tex.; Elk. Club: Kiwanis (ex-pres.), Ruritan. Trustee Schriener Inst., Fred Roberts Meml. Hosp. Author: The Tringle of Life, 1926; Chapel Chimes (syndicate); Bugles on the Hills, 1941; We Presbyterians, 1948; Virginia Vignettes, 1952; The Flaming Frontier, 1955; Saga of Hamilton's School House, 1956; The Deacons of Virginia, 1958; The Family of Philip Long (1678-1755), 1963; others. Home: Lexington, Va. †

DIEHM, VICTOR CHRISTIAN, broadcasting executive; b. Sparrows Point, Md., Nov. 7, 1902; s. Christian O'Brien and Mary (Hackman) D.; student U. Md., 1925, Peabody Conservatory Music, 1925; Dr. Art of Oratory, Staley Coll., 1954; m. Hazel Virginia Loose, Dec. 19, 1936; children—Elizabeth Anne (Mrs. Richard I. Bernstein), Victor Christian. Entered radio broadcasting in Balt., 1926; with Steinman Group, Lancaster, Pa., 1931-46; owner WAZL and WVCD-FM, Hazleton, Pa., from 1946; formed Vic Diehm Radio Group, 1948, operated radio stas. in Biddeford, Me., Boston, Allentown, Pa., Meadville, Pa., Tallahassee, Fla., 1948-60; pres., chief exec. officer MBS, N.Y.C., 1969-72; v.p. Pocono Downs Raceways, Inc. Mem. Pa. Indsl. Devel. Authority, from 1955. Pa. lay del. Nat. Am. Cancer Soc. Bd., from 1971. Candidate Pa. Senate, 1966. Past trustee Bloomsburg (Pa.) State Coll. Recipient Coronet Mag. award for outstanding pub. service, 1950, VFW Nat. award for distinguished local service, 1962, Bronze medal ACS; named Pa. Broadcasters ambassador of good will; Vic Diehm Day in Pa. proclaimed by gov., Nov. 6, 1969, also day in his honor, June 10, 1972. Mem. Nat. (dir.), Pa. (past pres.) assns. broadcasters, Radio Advt. Bur. (chmn. 1963-64), Pa. C. of C. (past pres.). Methodist. Mason (Shriner, Jester), Elk, Kiwanian. Home: Conyngham, Pa. Died Aug. 17, 1980.

DIETRICH, NEIL KITTRELL, naval officer; b. Hopkinsville, Ky., Sept. 29, 1901; s. Charles Henry and Minnie (Lander) D.; B.S., U. S. Naval Acad., 1923; m. Janet Jenkins, Nov. 7, 1927; 1 dau., Diane (wife of Lemuel C. Shepherd, III, U.S.M.C.). Commd. ensign U.S.N., 1923, advanced through grades to rear admiral, 1951; U.S. Naval attache Am. Embassy, London. Decorated Legion of Merit, Navy Commendation Ribbon, Comdr. British Empire, French Croix de Guerre. Clubs: Army and Navy Country. Home: Washington, D.C. Died June 3, 1982.

DIETRICH, NOAH, business exec.; born Batavia, Wis., Feb. 28, 1889; s. John and Sarah (Peters) D.; grad. Janesville (Wis.) High Sch.; m. Carol Hoyt, May 23, 1936; children—John, Anthony Paul, Caroline, Susan (by previous marriage)—Mrs. John G. O'Hara, Mrs. Elizabeth Jewell. Bankteller, cashier, 1907-11; real estate and pub. utility auditor, 1911-17; petroleum development and distrbn. accounting, 1917-19; Haskins & Sells, 1919-20; comptroller automobile distbr., 1920-25; exec. Hughes Tool Co., 1925; dir. Loma Uranium Corp., Gulf Brewing Co., Nat. Bank of Commerce of Houston, Trans World Airlines, Inc. Mem. adv. bd. N A M. (past regional v.p. and dir.). Clubs: Ramada (Houston); Los Angeles Country, Balboa Bay, Beach, Walker Lake. Home: Beverly Hills, Calif. †

DIETRICH, ROY KAISER, lawyer; b. Kansas City, Mo., Sept. 19, 1889; s. David and Margaret (Kaiser) D.; A.B., U. Kan., 1910; LL.B., K.C. Sch. Law, 1912; m. Gale Galbaugh Gossett, May 5, 1915; children—Alfred G., John D., Sanford R., William G. Admitted to Mo. bar, 1912, practiced in Kansas City; sr. partner Dietrich, Tyler & Davis, and predecessors, from 1912. Chmn. local Selective Service Bd., 1940-45. Dir., gen. counsel William Volker, Charities Fund; counsel Roanridge Rural Trg. Found.; dir. Research Hosp. Mem. Am., Mo. State, Kansas City bar assns., Lawyers Assn. Kansas City, Phi Beta Kappa, Phi Alpha Delta, Delta Upsilon, Republican. Episcopalian. Club: U. (Kansas City). Home: Kansas City, Mo. †

DIETZ, ALBERT ARNOLD CLARENCE, biochemist, educator; b. Port Huron, Mich., Aug. 15, 1910; s. Frederick W. and Sophia (Klenk) D.; m. Lelah May Johnstone, Nov. 27, 1937; children—William A.J., Robert J.M. B.S., U. Toledo, 1932, M.S., 1933; postgrad., U. Heidelberg, Germany, summer 1934, U. Mich., summer 1935; Ph.D., Purdue U., 1941. Biochemist Enza-Vita Labs., Toledo, 1933-39, U.S. Rubber Co., Detroit, 1942-43, Inst. Med. Research, Toledo Hosp., 1943-59, Armour and Co., Chgo., 1959-60; NDRC fellow Purdue U., 1941-42; with VA Hosp., Hines, Ill., from 1960; research asst. prof. biochemistry Chgo. Med. Sch., 1962-69; asso. prof. Loyola U. Stritch Sch. Medicine, 1969-74, prof., from 1974. Contbr. articles to profl. jours. Pres. Toledo PTA, 1951-53. Recipient Chgo. Clin. Chemist award, 1977. Fellow AAAS; mem. Am. Chem. Soc. (past chmn. Toledo sect.), Am. Assn. Clin. Chemists (chmn. Chgo. sect. 1969-71, dir. 1975-77, pres. 1979), N.Y. Acad. Scis., Ill. Acad. Sci., Council Sci. Soc. Presidents (sec. from 1980), Sigma Xi. Club: Torch (pres. 1963-64). Home: LaGrange, Ill.

DIETZ, DAVID HENRY, editor, author; b. Cleve., Oct. 6, 1897; s. Henry William and Hannah (Levy) D.; A.B., Western Res. U., 1919, Litt.D., 1948; LL.D., Bowling Green State U., 1954; m. Dorothy B. Cohen, Sept. 26, 1918; children—Doris Jean, Patricia Ann, David Henry. Editorial staff Cleve. Press, 1915-77; sci. editor Scripps-Howard Newspapers, 1921-77; lectr. gen. sci. Western Res. U., 1927-50; mem. subcom. on publicity, div. med. sci. NRC, 1940-46; cons. Surg. Gen. U.S. Army, 1944-47; at Bikini with Army-Navy Task Force One for atomic bomb test, as news corr., radio commentator, summer 1946. Pres., Shaker Heights Library Bd., 1944-76; trustee Mt. Sinai Hosp., Cleve., 1961-70. Recipient numerous awards including Pulitzer prize for journalism, 1937, Albert Lasker Med. Journalism award, 1954, Ohioana Career medal, 1958, James T. Grady award, 1961. Fellow Am. Geog. Soc., Royal Astron. Soc., AAAS Ohio Acad. Sci.; nat. fellow Sigma Delta Chi; mem. Nat. Assn. Sci. Writers (charter, 1st pres.), Am. Astron. Soc., Astron. Soc. Pacific, Société Astronomique de France, Sigma Xi, Zeta Beta Tau, Omicron Delta Kappa (hon.). Clubs: Rowfant Oakwood, Mid-Day, City, (Cleve.); National Press (Washington). Author: The Story of Science, 1931; Medical Magic, 1937: Atomic Energy in the Coming Era, 1945 (transl. into 13 langs.); Atomic Science, Bombs and Power, 1954; All About Satellites and Space Ships, 1958; All About Great Medical Discoveries, 1960; All About the Universe, 1965; Stars and the Universe, 1968; The New Outline of Science, 1973. Contbr. atomic bomb article Ency. Brit., 1946 edit., also Brit. Book of Year, 1946. Home: Shaker Heights, Ohio. Died Dec. 9, 1984.

DIETZ, HOWARD, librettist; b. N.Y.C., Sept. 8, 1896; m. Tanis Montagu, 1937; 1 child, Liza Dietz Shaw; m. Lucinda Goldsborough Ballard, July 31, 1951; stepchildren—Robert F.R. Ballard, Jenifer Ballard (Mrs. Walter Romberg). Student, Townsend Harris Hall, Columbia, 1913-17. Began as newspaper reporter; dir. publicity and advt. Goldwyn Pictures Corp., N.Y.C., 1918-24; continuing since merger into Metro-Goldwyn-Mayer, 1924, apptd. v.p., 1940; Screen and radio Info. Please chmn. U.S. Treasury, 1941-58. Author: June Goes Downtown, 1923, Dear Sir, (with Jerome Kern), 1924, Merry-Go-Round, (with Morrie Ryskind), 1927, The Little Show, 1929, Second Little Show, 1930, Three's a Crowd, 1930, Bandwagon, (with George S. Kaufman), 1932, Flying Colors, 1932, Revenge With Music, 1934, At Home Abroad, 1935, Follow the Sun; prod. in, Eng., 1936, Between the Devil, 1937, (with Vernon Duke) Dancing in the Streets, 1943, Jackpot, 1944, Sadie Thompson, (with Reuben Mamoulian), 1944, Inside U.S.A, 1948, Fledermaus, for Met. Opera Co., 1950, The Bandwagon; motion picture, 1953, The Gay Life, 1961, Jennie, 1963; (with Arthur Schwartz) also English adaption of Bell for Adano; autobiography Dancing in the Dark, 1974; movie That's Entertainment, 1975, 76; composer: (with Arthur Schwartz) songs Something to Remember You By; numerous others.; Contbr. (with Arthur Schwartz) to periodicals. Served with U.S.N., 1917-19. Mem. ASCAP. Clubs: Regency, Sands Point Golf. Address: New York, N.Y. Died July 30, 1983.

DIGBY, BASSETT, writer; b. London, Eng., Jan. 25, 1888; s. late George Beverly Wyatt and Minnie (Keeling) D.; ed. privately and London Univ. College Sch.; m. Miss D. S. Johnson, of Warsaw, Poland, July 18, 1915. In London office Chicago Daily News, 1909-10; on staff of Knickerbocker Press, Albany, N.Y., 1910; traveling and studying in Siberia, 1911; on staff Phila. Public Ledger, 1912-13; in Siberia, Mongolia and Manchuria, making ethnol. studies and collections of fauna and flora, 1914; explored N.E. coast of Baikal and discovered in N.E. Siberia skull and horn of extinct woolly rhinoceros, first tusks of baby mammoth, and other mammoth remains; disguised as Siberian peasant, visited lamaseries along Mongolian border. War corr. of Chicago Daily News in Egypt, Scandinavia, Balkans, Poland and Russia, from 1914. Extensive contbr. to Am. and European publications. Author: (with Richardson Wright) Through Siberia. Fellow Royal Geog. Soc. Address: Chicago, Ill.†

DIGGES, J. DUDLEY, state justice; b. La Plata, Md., Jan. 8, 1912. A.B., St. John's Coll., 1933; LL.B., U. Md., 1936. Bar: Md. bar 1936. Judge 7th Jud. Circuit, 1949-69; asso. justice Md. Ct. Appeals, 1969—. Address: Annapolis, MD.

DIKE, KENNETH ONWUKA, educator; b. Nigeria, Dec. 17, 1917; s. Nzekwe and Felicia (Anere) D.; student Achimota Coll., Ghana, 1938-39, Fourah Bay Coll., Sierra Leone, 1939-43; B.A., U. Durham (Eng.), 1943; M.A., U. Aberdeen (Scotland), 1947, LL.D., 1961; Ph.D., London U., 1950, LL.D., 1963; LL.D., Northwestern U., 1962, Leeds (Eng.) U., 1963, Columbia U., 1965, Princeton, 1965; D.Litt., Boston U., 1962, Birmingham (Eng.) U., 1964, Ahmadu Bello U., Nigeria, 1965, Ibadan (Nigeria) U., 1975, U. Ghana, 1979; D.Sc., U. Moscow (USSR), 1963; m. Ona Patricia Olisa, Mar. 5, 1953; children—Chinwe Maureen, Chukwuemeka George, Nneka Helen, Ona Olive, Obiora Kenneth. Came to U.S., 1970. Lectr. history U. Coll., Ibadan, Nigeria, 1950-52, sr. lectr., 1954-56, prof. history, 1956-60, vice prin., 1958-60, vice chancellor, 1960-67; sr. research fellow West African Inst. Social and Econ. Research, Ibadan U., 1952-54; Andrew W. Mellon prof. African history Harvard U., 1970-83, chmn. com. on African studies, 1972-83. Chmn. Commn. Rev. Ednl. System Eastern Region, 1959; mem. Ashby Commn. Higher Edn. in Nigeria, 1957; chnn. organizing com. Internat. Congress Africanists, 1962; chmn. Nigerian Antiquities Commn., 1954-67. Fellow Am. Acad. Arts and Scis., Royal Hist. Soc., Kings Coll., Brit. Hist. Assn., mem. Nat. Archives Nigeria (founder, dir. 1951-64), Hist. Soc. Nigeria (pres. 1955-67), Assn. Commonwealth Univs. (chmn. 1965-66). Clubs: Commonwealth Soc. (London); Metropolitan (Lagos, Nigeria); Odd Volumes (Boston). Author: Trade and Politics in the Niger Delta, 1830-1885, 1956; Report on the Preservation and Administration of Historical Records in Nigeria, 1953; A Hundred Years of British Rule in Nigeria, 1957; The Origins of the Niger Mission, 1958. Home: Belmont, Mass. Died Oct. 26, 1983.

DILLARD, HARDY CROSS, former judge, legal educator; b. New Orleans, Oct. 23, 1902; s. James Hardy and Avarene Lippincott (Budd) D.; B.S., U.S. Mil. Acad., 1924; student U. Va., 1919-20, 24-27, LL.B., 1927; student U. Paris, 1930-31; LL.D. (hon.), Tulane U., 1971, Washington Coll., 1976; m. Janet Gray Schauffler, Nov. 16, 1934 (dec. July 1970); children—Joan Jarvis, Hardy Schauffler; m. Valgerdur Nielsen Dent, Dec. 9, 1972. Admitted to Va. bar, 1927; practiced in N.Y., 1929-30; Carnegie endowment fellow in internat. law U. Paris, 1930-31; mem. faculty law U. Va., 1927-29, 31-37, prof., 1938-58, James Monroe prof., 1958-70, asst. dean, 1937-40, dean Law Sch., 1963-68; judge Internat. Ct. Justice, The Hague, 1970-79; mem. arbitral tribunal Beagle Channel Case between Chile and Argentina, 1971-77; dir. Inst. Pub. Affairs, 1938-42; vis. prof. law Columbia U., 1962-63; cons., lectr., W. Ger., 1950; Fulbright lectr. Oxford U., summer 1953; Carnegie lectr. Hague Acad. Internat. Law, 1957; mem. com. to study non-tech. instrn. in armed forces Sec. of Def., 1961-62; Tucker lectr. Washington and Lee U.; Sibley lectr. U. Ga.; Irvine lectr. Cornell U.; Bailey lectr. La. State U.; Mooers lectr. Am. U.; others. Trustee Va. Episcopal Sch., 1952-61; mem. adv. council U.S. Air Force Acad. Mem. Commn. Constl. Revision for Va., 1968. Served as maj. AUS, 1942, lt. col., 1942, col., 1943; comd. and staff assignments, European and Far Eastern Theatres, 1943-45; cons. Brookings Instn., 1947-50; dir. studies Nat. War Coll., 1946, mem. bd. cons., 1951-54, cons., from 1956. Decorated Legion of Merit with oak leaf cluster, Bronze Star medal; recipient Raven award, 1957, Thomas Jefferson award, 1967; Distinguished Civilian award U.S. Air Force, 1970; Wolfgang Friedman Meml. award Columbia U., 1979. Fellow World Acad. Sci. and Letters; mem. Am., Va., W.Va. bar assns., Am. Soc. Internat. Law (pres. 1962-63), Am. Law Inst. (council, hon. v.p. 1963-79, hon. pres. 1979-82), Am. Soc. Polit. and Legal Philosophy, Soc. of Cincinnati (hon.), Order of Coif, Phi Beta Kappa, Beta Theta Pi, Phi Delta Phi, Omicron Delta Kappa. Democrat. Episcopalian. Author: Some Aspects of Law and Diplomacy, 1957; editor: Va. Bar News, 1956-62; Proceedings of Inst. of Pub. Affairs, 8 vols; adv. editor Va. Quarterly Rev., 1937-70; editorial bd. Am. Jour. Internat. Law; contbr. articles and reviews to numerous profl. and non-tech. jours. Home: Charlottesville, Va. Died May 12, 1982.

DILLENBACK, LEMUEL CROSS, educator; b. Cobleskill, N.Y., Apr. 7, 1890; s. Jonas and Helen (Spraker) D.; A.B., Carnegie Inst. Tech., 1913, A.M., 1914; m. Hazel McIntosh Soper, Nov. 29, 1919; children—Mary Louise (Mrs. James Pierce Butler Jr.), Lemuel Cross. Instr. architecture U. Ill., 1915-17, asst. prof., 1920-23, asso. prof., 1923-25, prof., 1925-30; prof. architecture Columbia, 1930-34; prof. architecture Syracuse U., 1934-58, acting dir. dept., 1936, dir., 1937-45, dean Coll. Fine Arts and dir. Sch. Architecture, 1945-58. Served to lt. comdg. officer USAAF, World War I. Recipient Merit award Carnegie Alumni Fedn., 1955. Registered Architect, N.Y. Fellow A.I.A. (pres. Central N.Y. chpt. 1946-47), Syracuse Soc. Architects (v.p. 1937-38, pres. 1942-43), Sigma Nu, Phi Kappa Phi, Sigma Upsilon Alpha, Alpha Chi Tau, Tau Sigma Delta. Republican. Lutheran. Rotarian. Home: Syracuse, NY. †

DILLING, MILDRED, harpist; b. Marion, Ind.; d. Frank M. and Rachel (Freel) Dilling; student harp, N.Y.C., with Henriette Renie, Pris; m. Clinton W. Parker, Oct. 9, 1943 (dec. 1948). European debut, Salle Erard, Paris; Am. debut, Aeolian Hall, N.Y.C.; concerts in Europe, N. and S. Am., Can., Middle and Far East and Near East; world tours for State Dept.; numerous recitals, symphony, radio and TV appearances; starred in film Adventures in Music, 1940; organized 1st harp sextet to play Radio City Music Hall; 1st harpist to play on radio in Ireland; 7 engagements at White House; tchr. harp Ind. U. Sch. of Music, 1957; in charge 14th annual master class and workshop U. Calif. at Los Angeles, summer 1977. Hon. mem. Sigma Alpha Iota. Editor, collector: Old Tunes for New Harpists, 10th edit., 1971; 30 Little Classics, 7th edit., 1971. Owner largest pvt. collection harps ever assembled. Home: New York, N.Y. Died Dec. 30, 1982.

DILLMAN, RAY EUGENE, lawyer; b. Vernal, Utah, Apr. 22, 1890; s. Simon Peter and Julia Ellen (Davis) D.; student Brigham Young U., 1909-10; LL.B., U. of Utah, 1913; grad. work, U. of Chicago, 1913-14; m. Mildred M. Miles, July 1, 1916; children—Ray Earl, Miles, Naomi, Mary Dorothy. Admitted to Utah bar, 1912; city atty. Roosevelt, Utah, 1920-34; county atty. Duchesne County, 1915-17; mem. state senate, 1928-32, pres. of senate, 1930; in pvt. practice from 1915; president Roosevelt State Bank. President of Western States Mission, Church of Jesus Christ of Latter-Day Saints, Denver, Colorado. Trustee Utah State Agricultural College; trustee Utah School for Deaf and Blind; trustee Duchesne County School District; mem. Utah State Board Education. Mem. State Water Storage Commn.; Colo. River Commn. Rep. candidate for gov., 1936. Mem. Beta Theta Pi. Republican. Mem. Ch. of Latter Day Saints (pres. Western States Mission). Clubs: Barristers (pres.), University. Home: Denver, Colo. †

DILLON, EDWARD SAUNDERS, physician; b. Woodbury, N.J., March 21, 1890; s. Rev. Edward and Mary (Saunders) D.; A.B., Princeton, 1911; M.D., Harvard, 1916; m. Eugenia Vansant, May 26, 1923; children—Edward Vansant, John Saunders, Eugenia Epting, Richard Snowdon, Charles William Larue. Interne, Penn. Hosp. 1917-18; practice of medicine in Phila. since 1923; chief, div. of metabolism, Phila. Gen. Hosp.; adjunct physician, Pa. Hosp.; asso. prof. diseases of metabolism, Grad. Sch. of Medicine, U. of Pa.; asst. med. dir. Pa. Mutual Life Ins. Co. Served as capt., Royal Army Med. Corps, 1916; U.S. Army Med. Corps, 1918-19. Fellow Am. Coll. of Physicians, Phila. Coll. of Physicians; mem. A.M.A., Phila. County Med. Soc. (chmn., com. on diabetes), Am. Diabetes Assn. (pres., 1947-48), Rittenhouse Astronom. Soc. Republican. Presbyterian (elder). Contr. articles to med. jours., chiefly on diabetes. Home: Narberth, Pa. Deceased.

DILLON, JOHN HENRY, physicist; b. Ripon, Wis., July 10, 1905; s. Frank George and Hattie (Barnes) D.; A.B., Ripon Coll., 1927, Sc.D. (hon.), 1950; Ph.D., U. Wis., 1931; M.S. (hon.), Lowell Textile Inst., 1951; m. Bernice Olmsted, June 18, 1935 (dec. Aug. 1960); m. 2d, Rena Quinn Perkson, Apr. 4, 1963; stepchildren—Howard N. Perkson, Pamela Perkson Brown. Physics research group Firestone Tire & Rubber Co., 1931-37, head physics div., 1937-45, asst. dir. research, 1945-46; dir. research Textile Found. and Textile Research Inst., 1946-51; dir. Textile Research Inst., Princeton, N.J. 1951-82, pres. 1959-82, vis. lectr. Princeton, 1947-82, prof. dept. chem., 1952-82. Chmn Gordon Research Conf. Textiles, 1949; chmn. physicists group Nat. Acad. Sci.-NRC adv. panels to Nat. Bur. Standards. 1961-82. Trustee Phila. Coll. Textiles and Sci.; member board of trustees Ripon College. Recipient Harold DeWitt Smith Memorial medal, 1955. Fellow Am. Phys. Soc. (chmn. div. high polymer physics 1944). The Textile Inst. (Eng.); mem. Am. Inst. Physics (gov. bd. 1957-59), Am. Assn. Textile Chemists and Colorists, Am. Assn. Textile Technologists. Am. Chem. Soc., Am. Soc. Testing Materials, Fiber Soc. (pres. 1961-62), Soc. Rheology (pres. 1957-59), Soc. Chem. Industry Gt. Britain. Phi Beta Kappa. Sigma Xi. Club: Nassau. Author numerous articles in sci. and trade jours. Mem. editorial bd. Jour. Applied Polymer Sci., 1960-82. Holder U.S. and fgn. patents. Home: Princton, N.J. Died June 28, 1982.

DILLON, JOHN JOSEPH, lawyer; b. Indpls., Aug. 1, 1926; s. John J. and Margaret (Sweeney) D.; student Xavier U., 1947-49; LL.B., Ind. U., 1952; LL.D., Marian Coll., 1972; m. Anna C. Dean, Jan. 19, 1957; children—Anne Margaret, John Joseph, Denise Marie. Admitted to Ind. bar, 1952; counsel Indpls. Legal Aid Soc., 1953-56; city atty. Indpls., 1956-64; atty. gen. Ind., 1965-69; mem. firm Dillon, Hardamon & Cohen, Indpls.; comdg. gen. 38th Inf. Div. Ind. N.G.; adj. prof. Ind. U. Sch. Law, Indpls. Pres., Marian Coll. Assocs., Indpls., 1963. Bd. dirs. Indpls. Legal Aid Soc., from 1963, also pres.; vice chmn. bd. trustees Marian Coll.; bd. dirs. Catholic Charities Indpls., Indpls. Civic Ballet Soc.; trustee Indpls. and English Found. Served with USAAF, World War II; maj. gen. USNG. Mem. Am., Ind. bar assns., Lawyers Assn. Indpls., 500 Festival Assocs., Ind. U. Law Sch., Indpls. Alumni Assn. (pres., dir.), Aircraft Owners and Pilots Assn., Sigma Delta Kappa. Democrat. Home: Indianapolis, Ind. Died June 21, 1983.

DILLON, PAUL WASHINGTON, mfg. exec.; b. Sterling, Ill., June 3, 1883; s. Washington Moorehead and Sarah Jane (Martin) D.; student Shattuck Mil. Acad., Faribault, Minn., 1901-03; m. Crete Blackman, Nov. 16, 1904 (dec.); children—Crete Blackman (Mrs. John W. Bowman) (dec.), Margaret (Mrs. Goddard), Washington Martin. With Northwestern Steel & Wire Co. (formerly Northwestern Barb Wire Co.), dir., 1908-80, pres., 1920-38, 40-51, treas. 1921-48, chmn. bd., 1938-80; dir. Northwestern Products Corp., Sterling, Ill. Served as capt. U.S. Army, World War I. Presbyn. Clubs: Rock River Country (Sterling); Union League (Chgo.). Home: Sterling, Ill. Died Feb. 25, 1980.

DILWORTH, JOHN RICHARD, educator; b. Dubuque, Iowa, May 21, 1914; s. Johnson and Edna (Ferris) D.; B.S., Iowa State U., 1937, M.S., 1938; Ph.D., U. Wash., 1956; m. Alice Beatrice Carey, Sept. 2, 1937 (dec. June 13, 1968); children—Anne Louise (Mrs. Daniel Morgan Ford), John Richard, Mary Alice (Mrs. Mark Stewart); m. Leona Fletcher, June 15, 1976. Instr. La. State U., Baton Rouge, 1938-41, asst. prof., 1946; mem. faculty Oreg. State U., Corvallis, from 1946, prof., head dept. forest mgmt., from 1955. Cons. Mason, Bruce & Girard, Portland, Oreg., summer, 1948, Bur. Land Mgmt., Portland, summer, 1956, Thompson Tree Farm, Corvallis, summer, 1954; pres. Green Peak Tree Farm, Corvallis, from 1965; research scientist Pacific NW Forest and Range Expt. Sta., Portland, summers 1947, 53; vis. scientist Swiss Forest Expt. Sta., Zurich, 1961; co-chmn. Swedish-Am. Forestry Conf., Stockholm, 1958. Served with AUS, 1941-46. Weyerhaeuser fellow, 1952-53. Mem. Oreg. State Employees Assn. (pres. 1964-65), Soc. Am. Foresters, Corvallis C. of C. (dir. 1963-64), Am. Soc. Photogrammetry, Am. Forestry Assn., Western Forestry and Conservation Assn., AAAS, Phi Kappa Phi, Alpha Zeta, Xi Sigma Pi, Phi Eta Sigma, Gamma Sigma Delta. Republican. Episcopalian. Clubs: Century, Triad, Elks, Kiwanis, Corvallis Country. Author: Variable Probability Sampling, 1976; Log Scaling and Timber Cruising, 1976. Home: Corvallis, Oreg. Died June 15, 1981.

DIMIT, CHARLES PARSON, vice pres. prodn. and dir. Phillips Petroleum Co.; b. Crawfords Corners, Pa., 1888. Mason. Home: Bartlesville, Okla. †

DINKELOO, JOHN GERARD, architect; b. Holland, Mich., Feb. 28, 1918; s. William and Bessie (Brouwer) D.; student Hope Coll., 1936-39; B.Arch. in Archtl. Engring., U. Mich., 1942; m. Thelma Ann Van Dyke, Jan. 30, 1943; children—Carter John, Janje, Dirk Van Dyke, Tessa, Christian Van Dyke, Hanni, Kaaren. Designer, Skidmore, Owings & Merrill, Chgo., 1942-43, chief prodn., 1946-50; partner Eero Saarinen & Assos., Birmingham, Mich. and Hamden, Conn., 1959-66, Kevin Roche-John Dinkeloo and Assos., Hamden, from 1966; prin. works include TWA Terminal at Kennedy Airport, 1961, Dulles Airport, 1962, CBS Hdqrs. Bldg., N.Y.C., 1965, Oakland (Calif.) Mus., 1967, Ford Found. Adminstrn. Bldg., N.Y.C., 1967, Gateway Arch, Jefferson Nat. Expansion Meml., St. Louis, 1965, Morse and Stiles colls., Yale, 1963. Trustee Hope Coll. Served as officer USNR, 1943-46. Recipient Bard award for Ford Found. Bldg., 1968. Mem. A.I.A. Devel. structural neoprene plazing gaskets, laminated metalized heat reflecting glass, exposed structural bldg. components of corrosion resistant steel. Home: Hamden, Conn. Died June 15, 1981.

DINNICK, JOHN SAVERY, investment banker; b. Toronto, Ont., Can., Oct. 29, 1911; s. Wilfrid and Alice Louise (Conlin) D.; children—Martha, Sarah, Victoria. Student, St. Andrew's Coll., 1924-26, Upper Can. Coll., 1926-30, Trinity Coll., U. Toronto, 1931-33. With McLeod Young Weir Ltd., Toronto, 1933—, pres., 1960—, chmn. bd., 1970-75, hon. chmn. bd., 1975-77, fin. cons., 1977—, also dir.; fin. cons. I.F.C., World Bank; dir. Canron Ltd., Photo Engravers & Electrotypers Ltd. Bd. dirs. Donwood Found. Served with RCAF, 1940-45. Mem. Investment Dealers Assn. Can. (pres. 1969-70). Club: Canadian (Toronto) (past pres.). Home: Toronto ON Canada Office: Toronto ON Canada

DI PRIMA, RICHARD CLYDE, educator, mathematician; b. Terre Haute, Ind., Aug. 9, 1927; s. Clyde and Ethel (Phillips) DiPrima; m. Maureen P. Clune, Nov. 27, 1954; children: Shivaun, Richard Clyde. B.S., Carnegie Inst. Tech., 1950, M.S., 1951, Ph.D., 1953. Research asso.

MIT, 1953-54; research fellow Harvard U., 1954-56; research physicist Hughes Aircraft Co., 1956-57; mem. faculty Rensselaer Poly. Inst., 1957-84, prof. math., 1962-84, assoc. dean Grad. Sch., 1968-72, chmn. Faculty Council, 1969-70, chmn. dept. math. scis., 1972-81, Eliza Ricketts Found. prof. math., 1979-84; cons. to industry, 1961—; Fulbright lectr. Weizmann Inst. Sci., Rehovoth, Israel, 1964-65; mem. com. recommendations U.S Army basic sci. research Nat. Acad. Sci.-NRC, 1976-84, chmn., 1981-84; mem. sci. council Inst. Computer Application, Sci. and Engring., NASA-Langley Research Center, 1977—, chmn., 1981-82; mem. adv. bd. Office Math. Scis. NRC, 1979—; mem. vis. com. Center for Application of Math.; also dept. math. Lehigh U. Author: Elementary Differential Equations and Boundary Value Problems, 1965, 3d edit., 1977, Elementary Differential Equations, 1965, 3d edit. 1977, Introduction to Differential Equations, 1970; editor: Physics of Fluids, 1973-76; mem. editorial bd.: Mechanics Research Communications, 1973-84. Mem. budget com. Troy United Fund, 1960-64; mem. adv. bd. Albany Diocesan Office Health and Social Services, 1966-70, v.p., 1969-70. Served with AUS, 1946-48. Guggenheim fellow, 1982-83; Fulbright research fellow Weizmann Inst., 1983. Fellow Am. Acad. Mechanics (pres. 1976-77), Am. Phys. Soc., ASME (exec. com. 1977-82, chmn. 1981-82, William H. Wiley Disting. Faculty award 1980); mem. Am. Math. Soc., Am. Math. Assn., Soc. Indsl. and Applied Math. (mem. council 1970—, v.p. for programs 1975-77, trustee 1977-80, pres. 1978-80), Soc. Natural Philosophy, Conf. Bd. Math. Scis. (exec. com. 1975-78), Sigma Xi. Home: Troy, N.Y. Died Sept. 10, 1984.

DIRAC, PAUL ADRIEN MAURICE, physicist, educator; b. Bristol, Eng., Aug. 8, 1902; s. Charles Adrien Ladislas and Florence Hannah (Holten) D. D.Sc., Bristol U., 1921; Ph.D., U. Cambridge, 1926. Vis. lectr. U. Wis., 1929, U. Mich., 1929, Princeton U., 1931; Lucasian prof. math. U. Cambridge, 1932-69; mem. Inst. Advanced Studies, Princeton, NJ, 1947-48, 58-59; prof. physics Fla. State U., Tallahassee, 1971-84. Author: Principles of Quantum Mechanics, 1930, 4th edit., 1958, Lectures on Quantum Mechanics, 1966, The Development of Quantum Theory, 1971, Spinors in Hilbert Space, 1974, General Theory of Relativity, 1975. Recipient Nobel prize in physics (with Erwin Schrodinger), 1933; recipient Royal Medal, 1939, Copley medal Royal Soc. London, 1952, Order of Merit, 1973. Fellow Royal Soc.; mem. Nat. Acad. Scis. (fgn. assoc.). Home: Tallahassee, Fla. Died Oct. 20, 1984.*

DISALLE, MICHAEL VINCENT, lawyer, governor Ohio; b. N.Y.C., Jan. 6, 1908; s. Anthony and Assunta (D'Arcangelo) DiS.; student Central Cath. High Sch., Toledo; J.D., Georgetown U., 1931; LL.D., Notre Dame U., 1949, Miami U., 1959, Bowling Green State U., U. Toledo, Kent State U., U. Akron, 1960; D.H.L., Ohio U., 1963; M.S. (hon.), U. Bridgeport, 1951; m. Myrtle Eugene England, Dec. 19, 1929 (separated); children—Antoinette, Barbara, Constance, Diana, Michael E. Admitted to Ohio bar, 1932, and began practice in Toledo; sr. mem. DiSalle, Green & Haddad; asst. dist. counsel Home Owners Loan Corp., 1933-35; mem. Ohio Ho. of Reps., 1937-38; asst. city law dir. City of Toledo, 1939-41, mem. city council, 1942-47, vice mayor, 1944-48, mayor (city mgr.), 1948-50; dir. price stblzn., Washington, 1950-52; apptd. dir. econ. stblzn., 1952; gov. Ohio, 1959-63; practice law, Columbus, Ohio, 1963-66, Washington, from 1966; counsel Chapman, Duff & Paul (formerly Chapman, Gadsby, Hannah & Duff), Washington, from 1971; Disting. prof. U. Mass. Originator, first chmn. Toledo Labor-Mgmt. Citizens Com. (Toledo Plan), 1945 (plan has been adopted by other cities for mediation labor disputes); an organizer and 1st pres. Ohio Assn. Municipalities, 1949; chmn. adv. bd. U.S. Conf. Mayors, 1949; del. Internat. Union Cities, Geneva, 1949. Mem. Pres.'s Adv. Com. on Intergovtl. Affairs, 1961-63; mem. panel of arbitrators Internat. Centre Settlement of Investment Disputes, 1967-74. Named outstanding man of year Jr. C. of C., 1944, outstanding alumnus Georgetown Student Bar Assn., 1962; recipient award Interfaith Movement, 1962. Mem. Am., Fed. Ohio, Columbus, Toledo bar assns., Bar Assn. D.C., Delta Theta Phi. Democrat. Roman Catholic. Home: Washington, D.C. Died Sept. 16, 1981.

DISCHER, CHARLES DALE, manufacturing and marketing company executive; b. Kalamazoo, July 22, 1924; s. Charles V. and Ethel (Bailor) D.; m. Patricia E. Krause, June 12, 1948; children: Brett, Christine. A.B., Kalamazoo Coll., 1949; M.A., Mich. State U., 1951. C.P.A., Mich. registered prin. Nat. Assn. Securities Dealers. Staff mem. firm Seidman & Seidman, Grand Rapids, Mich., 1951-54; servicing mgr. Albert Mortgages, Inc., Grand Rapids, 1954-56; sec. treas. Baxter Laundries Corp., Grand Rapids, 1956-63; v.p.; investment officer Amway Corp., Ada, Mich., 1963-84; pres., dir. Amway Mgmt. Co., Amway Mut. Fund, Amway Stock Transfer Co.; chmn. bd. Halcyon Petroleum, Inc.; dir. Preferred Properties Inc. Mem. exec. bd. Grand Valley Council Boy Scouts Am., 1968-84. Bd. assocs. Carthage Coll., Kenosha, Wis., 1971-84; bd. advisers Ferris State Coll., Big Rapids, Mich., YWCA, Grand Rapids. Served with AUS, 1943-46. Decorated Purple Heart. Mem. Am. Inst. C.P.A.s, Mich. Assn. C.P.A.s. Lutheran (treas.). Clubs: D.A.V, Peninsular. Home: Grand Rapids, Mich. Died Apr. 2, 1984.

DISESA, JOSEPH DANIEL, lawyer; b. Norwalk, Conn., May 17, 1916; s. Nicholas Joseph and Ida Romano (D'Elia) DiS.; m. Rose A. Pelliccia, June 11, 1949; children—Verdi J., Angela R., Victoria M., Ann L., Susan Nichola. B.S., Georgetown U., 1937, J.D., 1940. Bar: Conn. bar 1944, U.S. Dist. Ct. bars 1945. Mem. firm DiSesa, Hogan & Shure, New Haven, 1977-83, sr. partner, 1977-83; chmn. bd. Talley Industries, Mesa, Ariz.; dir. State Nat. Bank, Bridgeport, Conn., UMC Electronics Co., North Haven, Conn., Earmark, Inc., Hamden, Conn. Mem. New Haven Devel. Commn., 1974-83; pres. New Haven Devel. Corp., 1975-83; trustee Hosp. St. Raphael, 1973-83; bd. regents Georgetown U., 1980-83; pres. Legal Assistance Assn., New Haven, 1966-69. Served with USNR, 1941-43. Recipient Hall of Fame award Jr. Achievement, 1978. Mem. Georgetown U. Alumni Assn. (pres. 1980), Am. Bar Assn., Conn. Bar Assn., New Haven County Bar Assn. (past pres.), Am. Judicature Soc. Clubs: New Haven Country (N.Y.), New Haven Lawn (N.Y.), Quinnipiack (N.Y.), Turf and Field (N.Y.). Home: New Haven, Conn. Dec. 1983.

DISNEY, RICHARD LESTER, judge, Tax Court of the U.S.; born Richland, Kansas, June 6, 1887; s. Wesley and Elizabeth (Matney) D.; student U. of Kan., 1906-08, U. of Ariz., 1908-10; A.B. in jurisprudence, Oxford U., England (Rhodes Scholar), 1912; m. Harriet F. Mitchell, Sept. 6, 1914; children—Richard Lester Jr., Mitchell Keith, Iris Dawn, Gloria Elizabeth. Admitted to Okla. bar, 1913; practiced in Muskogee until 1917; mem. Oklahoma Ho. of Rep., 2 terms; practiced Ardmore, Okla., 1917-29, Oklahoma City, 1929-36; candidate for congressman, 5th Okla. Dist., withdrew when apptd. mem. U.S. Bd. of Tax Appeals, position held from 1936 (judge, The Tax Court of the United States). Mem. Oklahoma bar association. Democrat. Mason. Mem. Christian Ch. Club: National Press (Washington, D.C.). Home: Washington, D.C. †

DITZ, GEORGE ARMAND, lawyer; b. Stockton, Calif., June 5, 1889; s. George and Mary (Troescher) D.; A.B., Stanford U., 1911, Harvard Law Sch., 1911-12, J.D., Stanford U. Law School, 1912-13; m. Janet True Adams, June 3, 1914; children—Janet True (Mrs. Lawrence C. Ford), George Armand, John Adams. Admitted to bar, 1913; partner firm of Neumiller & Ditz, 1916-62, now counsel to Neumiller, Beardslee, Diehl & Siegert. Trustee Stanford U., from 1942; bd. govs. Stanford U. Hosps., 1955-58; mem. Am. Red Cross, (chmn. San Joaquin Co. chpt.; 1943; War Fund chmn., 1944-46; mem. Nat. Bd. Govs., 1947-50; mem. Pacific area adv. council, 1950-53, chmn. 1953); chmn. resolutions com., Nat. Conv., 1952; mem. bd. dirs. San Joaquin-Calaveras Council Boy Scouts of Am., 1936-53, mem. adv. bd. from 1953, mem. exec. com. Region XII, from 1953, mem. Nat. Council, 1954. Trustee Katharine Branson Sch., Ross, Cal., 1947-52. Mem. American Judicature Soc., San Joaquin Pioneer & Hist. Soc. (dir.); American Law Inst., San Joaquin County Bar Assn., State Bar of Calif., Am. Bar Assn., Calif. Hist. Soc., Phi Delta Phi, Phi Beta Kappa. Clubs: Yosemite (Stockton); Bohemian, Commonwealth (San Francisco). Home: Stockton, Calif. †

DIVERTY, MARSHALL HAND, lawyer; b. Woodbury, N.J., June 15, 1888; s. Henry B. and Ellie S. (Steelman) D.; B.S., U. Pa., 1910; M.A., 1912; LL.B., 1913; m. Mabel Greene, June 7, 1917; 1 dau., Jane (Mrs. Donald C. MacFarland); m. 2d, Louise Bancroft, Mar. 29, 1935. Admitted to N.J. bar, 1913, practiced in Camden, specializing trial and probate matters. Mem. Am., N.J., (pres.), Gloucester County, Camden bar assns., N.J. Soc. Pa., Trail Riders Canadian Rockies, Theta Delta Chi. Methodist. Mason (Shriner). Club: Union League (Phila.). Home: Woodbury, N.J. †

DIVINE, CHARLES, author; b. Binghamton, N.Y., Jan. 20, 1889; s. Charles S. and Emma (Harding) D.; A.B., Cornell U., 1912; m. Elizabeth Davies, of New York, Oct. 18, 1926. On staff New York Sun, 1912-16, the last year as spl. corr. attached to ex-President Roosevelt. Enlisted in 27th Div., U.S.A., and commd. 2d lt.; served with A.E.F.; demobilized in France, 1919; traveled in France, Spain and N. Africa; contbr. to The Sun, Century Mag., etc.; free lance writer and contbr. of short stories to various mags. Author: City Ways and Company Streets (poems), 1918; Gypsy Gold (poems), 1923; The Road to Town (poems), 1925; Cognac Hill (novel), 1927; also several one-act plays. Home: New York, N.Y. †

DIVINE, THOMAS FRANCIS, educator; b. Kansas City, Mo., Aug. 23, 1900; s. James Francis and Agnes (Herson) D.; A.B., St. Louis U., 1923, A.M., 1924; Ph.D., U. London, Sch. Econs. (Eng.), 1938; Geneva Inst. Internat. Relations, summers 1935-37. Entered Soc. of Jesus, 1917; ordained priest, 1930; instr., Loyola U., Chgo., 1924-26, Creighton U., Omaha, 1926-27; asst. prof. soc. scis. and asst. dean, Rockhurst Coll., Kansas City, 1931-32; instr. Marquette U., Milw., 1933-34, asst. prof. econs., 1938-42, dean Coll. Bus. Adminstrn., prof. econs., 1942-59, prof. econs., editor Marquette Bus. Rev., from 1963, dean emeritus; prof. econs. St. Louis U., 1960-63. Dir. Marquette Labor Coll., 1941-49, Marquette Inst. Indsl. Relations, 1941-49, head econs. dept., 1942-48; v.p. Council for a Lasting Peace, 1943, pres. 1945; part-time pub. mem. Nat. War Labor Bd., Region 6, 1943-44; pub. panel mem., 1944-45; mem. nat. panel arbitrators Am. Arbitration Assn.; dir. Citizens Conf. on Internat. Econ. Union, 1947-52. Mem. Cath. Econ. Assn. (pres. 1943, exec. council 1944-46), Am. Econ. Assn., Am. Assn.

Collegiate Schs. Bus. (exec. com. 1953-56), Beta Gamma Sigma (nat. exec. com. 1955-63). Author tariff pamphlet and mag. articles; also (book) Interest: An Historical and Analytical Study in Economics and Modern Ethics, 1959. Editor-in-chief Rev. Soc. Economy, 1947-59. Contbr. to book, encys. Home: Milwaukee, Wis. Died Mar. 31, 1979.

DIX, CHARLES HEWITT, geophysicist, educator; b. Los Angeles, Mar. 27, 1905; s. Charles Arthur and Florella (Hewitt) D.; B.S., Calif. Inst. Tech., 1927; M.A., Rice Inst., 1928, Ph.D., 1931; m. Josephine Bayley Weber, Nov. 5, 1970. Instr. math. Rice Inst., 1929-34; research geophysicist Humble Oil Co., 1934-37; geophysicist Socony-Vacuum Oil Co., 1939-41; chief geophysicist United Geophys. Co., 1941-48, v.p., 1942-48; mem. faculty Calif. Inst. Tech., 1948-73, prof. geophysics, 1953-73, emeritus, 1973-84; cons. in field. Fulbright fellow, 1963-64. Mem. Am. Phys. Soc., Am. Geophys. Union, Seismol. Soc. Am., Soc. Exploration Geophysicists (hon.), AAAS, Phi Beta Kappa. Author: Seismic Exploration for Oil, 1952. Home: Pasadena, Calif. Died Dec. 10, 1984.

DIXON, IRA ALLEN, bank ofcl.; b. Iroquois Co., Ill., Sept. 25, 1890; s. James W. and Annie (Huber) D.; student U. Ill., 1909-12; m. Cecil Thompson, Dec. 4, 1913; children—Dale, Greta, Gretchen (Mrs. Howard E. Wilson), Glen. Admitted Ind. bar, 1913; practiced law and engaged in gen. ins. bus., from 1913, Kentland, 1940-52; owner, pub. Newton County Enterprise, 1928-33; postmaster, Kentland, 1931-35; mem. staff U.S. senate banking and currency com., 1952-54; mem. Fed. Home Loan Bank Board, 1954-62. Pros. atty., Newton Co., 1944-47; atty., Kentland, 1948-52; mem. sch. bd., 1928-32. Mem. Ind. State Rep. Com., 1942-50. Mem. Ind. Bar Assn., C. of C., Ind. Soc. Chgo. and Washington, Theta Delta Chi. Methodist. K.P., Eagle. Rotarian. Home: Washington, D.C. †

DIXON, ROBERT ELLINGTON, naval officer; b. Richland, Ga., Apr. 22, 1906; s. Robert Joshia and Willie (Osburn) D.; student Marion (Ala.) Inst., 1922-23; B.S., U.S. Naval Acad., 1927; m. Mary Cornelia Baldwin, Aug. 28, 1930; 1 dau., Cornelia Baldwin (Mrs. Robert Xavier McKee). Commd. ensign USN, 1927, designated naval aviator, 1930, advanced through grades to rear adm., 1955; comdr. U.S.S. Avocet, 1940, U.S.S. Palau, 1948. U.S.S. Valley Forge, 1952, Scouting Squadron 2 U.S.S. Lexington in Battle of Coral Sea, action at Bougainville and Salamau-Lae, 1942; staff 3d Fleet Pacific campaigns, 1943-44; comdr. U.S. Taiwan Patrol Force, 1956; chief Bur. Aero., Navy Dept., after 1957. Mem. adv. com. Nat. Air Museum. Decorated Navy Cross, Legion of Merit, Presdl. Unit citation. Home: Virginia Beach, Va. Died Oct. 21, 1981.

DOBBINS, JAMES T(ALMAGE), chemist, univ. prof.; b. Boonville, N.C., Feb. 11, 1888; s. Nathan C. and Sophronia C. (Reece) D.; A.B., U. of N.C., 1911, A.M., 1912, Ph.D., 1914; m. Lila Shore, June 20, 1917; children—Christine (Mrs. Robert H. Taylor), James Talmage. Instr., N.C. State Coll., 1914-18; asso. prof. chemistry U. of N.C., 1918-30, prof. chemistry from 1930, Mem. Am. Chem. Soc., Soc. Pub. Analysts, Sigma Xi, Alpha Chi Sigma. Democrat. Baptist. Author: Semi Micro Qualitative Analysis, 1943. Home: Chapel Hill, N.C. †

DOBSON, WILLIAM ARTHUR CHARLES HARVEY, sinologist; b. London, Aug. 8, 1913; s. William Archibald Harvey and Daisy Harriet (Hamlyn) D.; children—Guy St. Clair, Iain St. Clair. B.A., Oxford U., 1945, M.A., 1947, D.Litt., 1960. Lectr. Chinese Oxford U., 1948-52; prof., head dept. East Asian studies U. Toronto, 1952-64, prof. Chinese, 1964-79, prof. emeritus, 1979—; Ashley fellow Trent U., Peterborough, Ont., Can., 1980—. Author: Late Archaic Chinese, 1959, Early Archaic Chinese, 1962, Mencius, 1963, Late Han Chinese, 1964, Language of the Book of Songs, 1968, A Dictionary of Chinese Particles, 1974. Served to lt. col. Brit. Army. Recipient Molson prize Can. Council, 1973; decorated Order of Can., 1975. Mem. Am. Oriental Soc., Assn. Asian Studies, Philol. Soc. London. Office: Peterborough ON Canada

DOCKERAY, JAMES CARLTON, economist; b. Grand Rapids, Mich., Aug. 16, 1907; s. Floyd Carlton and Katherine Caroline (Eddy) D.; m. Isabel Ruth McRoberts, Sept. 2, 1935; children: George Carlton, William Floyd, Susan Ruth. B.A., Ohio Wesleyan U., 1929; M.A., Ohio State U., 1931, Ph.D., 1936. Student acct. Chesapeake & Potomac Telephone Co., 1929-30; asst. econs. Ohio State U., 1931-35; instr. Iowa State Tchrs. Coll., 1935-36; asso. prof. econs. and bus. adminstrn. James Millikin U., 1936-42; prof. fin. U. Md., 1942-46; fiscal and fin. economist Dept. Commerce, 1946-61; professorial lectr. George Washington U., 1946-55, prof. fin., chmn. dept. govt. and bus., 1955-64, asst. dean Sch. Govt. Bus. and Internat. Affairs, 1964-66, dean, 1966-73, emeritus, 1973-84; cons.; lectr. Grad. Sch. Banking, Rutgers U., 1952-55; dep. mem. FHLB, 1938; cons. statis. control div. USAAF, 1943-45. Author: Public Utility Taxation in Ohio, 1938, (with W.H. Husband) Modern Corporation Finance, 7th edit, 1972. Mem. Am. Econ. Assn., Nat. Acad. Pub. Adminstrn. (study panel), Am. Finance Assn., Washington Soc. Investment Analysts. Club: Econs. (Orlando, Fla.). Home: Maitland, Fla. Died Sept. 30, 1984.

DOCKERY, HENRY CLAY, lawyer; b. Rockingham, N.C., July 27, 1887; s. Henry Clay and Minnie LeGrand (Everett) D.; A.B., Wake Forest Coll., 1909; studied law Wake Forest and U. N.C., 1909-11; m. Alice Lund Christensen, July 16, 1949. Admitted to N.C. bar, 1911; practiced in Rockingham, 1911-15. Charlotte from 1915; mem. Whitlock, Dockery, Ruff and Perry; co. atty., Macklenburg Co., 1931, 32. Served as mem. bd. dirs. Macklenburg Co. Community Chest from 1940, pres., 1944, 45, campaign chmn., 1946, 47, 49. Served with 81st Div., World War I; maj., N.C. Nat. Guard (Judge Advocate Gen.), 1921, 22, 23. Named Charlotte's Man of the Year, 1949. Mem. N.C. Bar Assn., Mecklenburg Bar Assn. (pres. 1942). Baptist. Mason (Shriner). Elk. Mem. Sigma Nu. Home: Charlotte, N.C. †

DOCKING, ROBERT BLACKWELL, former governor Kansas, banker; b. Kansas City, Mo., Oct. 9, 1925; s. George and Mary Virginia (Blackwell) D.; m. Meredith Martha Gear, 1950; children—William Russell, Thomas Robert. B.S. with honors, U. Kans., 1948; grad., Grad. Sch. Banking, U. Wis.; LL.D., Benedictine Coll., Washburn U. With Union State Bank, Arkansas City, Kans., 1956-59, pres., 1959-83; mayor, Arkansas City, 1963-66, gov., Kans., 1967-75; chmn. Kans. Venture Capital, Inc.; pres. City Nat. Bank & Trust Co., Guymon, Okla.; asst. treas., dir. Kans. Public Service Co.; owner Docking Ins. Agy., Arkansas City, Docking Devel. Co., Oxford, Kans.; pres., dir. Union State Bank, Arkansas City; dir. 4th Nat. Bank & Trust Co., Wichita, Kans., 1st Kans. Life Ins. Co., Newton, Cimarron, Kans.; Investment Co., Inc., Cimarron Ins. Co., Inc., Cimarron Life Ins. Co., Plains Ins. Co., Cimarron Fin. Co.; former chmn. Interstate Oil Compact Commn.; chmn. Midwest Gov.'s Conf., 1971-73; mem. Kans. Bank Mgt. Commn. Mem. City Commn. Arkansas City, Winfield, 1963-66; past pres. Community Chest; pres. United Fund; chpt. chmn. A.R.C., 1961; chmn. Kans. Cancer Crusade, 1975, Douglas County Democratic Com., 1954-56; v.p. Kans. Dem. Vets., 1957; trustee Wesley Hosp. Found., U. Kans. Endowment Assn., Menninger Found., Midwest Research Inst. Served from pvt. to 1st lt. USAAF, 1943-46. Named Young Man of Year Kans. Jr. C. of C., 1959; recipient Distinguished Service citation U. Kans., Ellsworth medallion, 1981; Disting. Kansan award, 1981. Mem. Arkansas City C. of C. (pres.), Am. Legion (comdr. Arkansas City, Kans.), Cowley County Bankers Assn., Am. Bankers Assn., Ind. Oil and Gas Assn., Kans. Livestock Assn., Internat. Platform Assn., Am. G.I. Forum, Am. Assn. for UN, U. Kans. Alumni Assn. (pres.), Am. Assn. Criminology, Beta Theta Pi, Beta Gamma Sigma, Delta Sigma Pi. Clubs: Mason (32 deg., Shriner), Elk, Eagle, Rotarian. Home: Arkansas City, Kans. Dec. Oct. 8, 1983.

DODD, HAROLD, naval officer; b. New York, N.Y., Nov. 10, 1890; s. Capt. Arthur Wright (U.S. Navy) and Margaret (Zochos) D.; ed. pub. schs., Newport, R.I., and Berkeley, Calif.; grad. U.S. Naval Acad., 1912; M.S., Columbia U., LL.B., George Washington U., 1930; grad. Naval War Coll., sr. course, 1929. Commd. ensign, U.S. Navy, 1912, and advanced through the grades to commodore, 1944; served in U.S. ships Michigan, Florida, Pennsylvania, Turner, Kennison, Medusa, Saratoga, Mississippi, Trenton and Honolulu; aide on staff of comdr. Div. Nine, Battleship Force Two, Atlantic Fleet (operating with British Grand Fleet), 1917; on duty in patent section Judge Advocate General's Office, Navy Dept., Washington, D.C., 1927-30, in administrative, admiralty, and international law div., 1932-39, asst. to Judge adv. gen., 1939; after comdg. U.S.S. Honolulu, 2 yrs., became chief of staff and aide to comdt. Naval Operating Base, Trinidad, B.W.I.; became comdt. Naval Operating Base, Rio de Janeiro, Brazil, 1943; chief of Naval Mission and sr. naval mem. Joint Defense Commn., Rio de Janeiro, 1944. Decorated Mexican Service, Asiatic-Pacific Area Campaign and Am. Area Campaign medals, Victory Medal with silver star and Grand Fleet clasp, Am. Defense Service Medal with Fleet clasp. Home: New York, N.Y. Deceased.

DODDRIDGE, PHILIP, retired army officer; born in Mattawan, N.J., April 13, 1887; son Charles Edward and Amelie Baird (Alcott) D.; student Cheltenham Mil. Acad., 1893-1905; m. Grace Winifred Woods, July 21, 1915; children—Winifred (Mrs. Paul H. DuPras), Phyllis (Mrs. William E. Braye). Served in Inf., U.S. Army, 1917-41; capt. to col. Adj. Gen. Dept., 1941-47; prof. mil. sci. and tactics Joliet (Ill.) High Sch. and Jr. Coll. R.O.T.C., 1919-20, Boise (Ida.) High Sch. R.O.T.C., 1939-41; adj. gen. A.A.C., 1942-47; served in P.T.O., World War II; ret. 1947; civil def. dir., State Ida., 1950-53. Decorated Legion of Merit, Bronze Star Medal, Commendation Medal with oak leaf cluster. Mem. Mil. Order World Wars. Kiwanian. Home: Boise, Ida. †

DODDS, HAROLD WILLIS, former univ. pres.; b. Utica, Pa., June 28, 1889; s. Samuel and Alice (Dunn) D.; A.B., Grove City (Pa.) Coll., 1909; LL.D., 1931; A.M., Princeton, 1914, LL.D., 1957; Ph.D., U. Pa., 1917; LL.D., Yale, 1933, Dickinson U., Am. U. Rutgers U., N.Y. U., Harvard, Williams Coll., 1934, U. Cin., 1935, U. Pa., 1936, Dartmouth, 1937, Purdue U., 1938, Tulane U., 1941, Tusculum, 1945, U. N.C., 1946, Oberlin Coll., 1947, Toronto U., 1947, Washington and Lee U., 1949, U. Glasgow, 1951, Brown U., 1954, U. Cal., U. Mich., McGill U., 1955, Dropsie Coll., Colgate U., 1957, U. B.C., 1958, U. Manchester, 1959, U. N.B., Centre Coll., 1963; D.C.L., U. Pitts., 1957; D. Social Sci., Laval U., 1952; Litt.D., Columbia, 1934, Hahnemann Med. Coll., 1937, U. Hawaii, 1949; L.H.D., Hobart Coll., 1936, Bucknell U., 1958; H.H.D., Coll. Wooster, 1938; m. Margaret Murray, Dec. 25, 1917. Instr. econs., Purdue U., 1914-16; exec. sec. U.S. Food Adminstrn., Pa., 1917-19; asst. prof. polit. sci. Western Res. U., 1919-20; sec. Nat. Municipal League, 1920-28, editor Nat. Municipal Rev., 1920-23; prof. politics Princeton, 1927-34, pres. univ., 1933-57. Electoral adviser Govt. Nicaragua, 1922-24; tech. adviser pres. Tacna-Arica Plebiscitary Commn., 1925-26; chief adviser pres. Nat. Bd. Elections Nicaragua, 1928; cons. Cuban Govt. in election law and procedure, 1935. Chmn., Pres.'s Com. on Integration Med. Services of Govt., 1946; mem. Pres.'s Adv. Commn. on Universal Tng., 1947; chmn. task force on personnel, 2d Hoover Commn., 1954-55; chmn. Am. delegation Anglo.-Am. Conf. on Refugee Problem, Bermuda 1943. Named comdr. Order of King Leopold, 1937. Mem. Am. Acad. Arts and Scis., Am. Philos. Soc., Phi Beta Kappa. Presbyn. Clubs: Athaeneum (London, Eng.): Century, Princeton (N.Y.C.); Nassau (Princeton). Author: Out of This Nettle...Danger, 1943; The Academic President—Educator or Caretaker?, 1962; also numerous articles, surveys and reports in polit. Home: Princeton, NJ. †

DODDS, NUGENT, lawyer; b. Mount Pleasant, Mich., June 17, 1887; s. Francis H. and Mollie (Nugent) D.; student Mich. State Normal Coll., Mount Pleasant, 1903-05; Olivet (Mich.) Coll., 1905-07, Georgetown Law Sch., 1909-10; LL.B., U. of Mich., 1913; m. Dorothy Vaughan Shaddick, June 6, 1907; 1 son, Edward Shaddick. In practice of law, Mount Pleasant, Marquette and other cities of Mich., 1913-24; spl. asst. to atty. gen. of U.S., 1924-30; acting head of criminal div., Dept. of Justice, Aug. 1930-Feb. 1931; asst. atty. gen. of U.S., in charge criminal prosecutions, 1931-33; gen. practice of law, Washington, D.C., 1933-43; legal cons. Div. Patent Adminstrn., Office Alien Property Custodian, 1943-44; mem. Vested Property Claims Com., Office Alien Property Custodian, 1945-48; spl. asst. to Atty. Gen. of U.S., 1948-52. Mem. Am. Patent Law Assn. Republican. Episcopalian. Club: Cosmos. Home: Washington, D.C. †

DODGE, CLEVELAND E., financier; b. N.Y.C., Feb. 5, 1888; s. Cleveland H. and Grace (Parish) D.; m. Pauline Morgan, 1919; children—Elizabeth (Mrs. Bolling W. Haxall), Cleveland E., Joan (Mrs. Frederic Rueckert, Jr.). A.B., Princeton U., 1909, Ph.D., 1959; LL.D., Presbyn. Coll., 1941, N.Y. U., 1952, Columbia U., 1954; L.H.D., Springfield Coll., 1951; Litt.D., U. Ariz., 1958. With Phelps Dodge Corp., N.Y.C., 1910-67, v.p., 1924-61, now hon. dir. Trustee Tchrs. Coll. Columbia, Princeton U., 1941-45; hon. trustee Grant Found., Am. Mus. Natural History; nat. bd. dirs.; mem. exec. com. internat. com. YMCA; bd. dirs. YMCA Greater N.Y., pres., 1925-35; bd. dirs. Near East Found., pres., 1930-53; bd. dirs. Council Chs. City N.Y.; trustee Woodrow Wilson Found., pres., 1950; emeritus dir. Internat. House.; Chmn. Bronx Adv. Planning Bd., 1938-44; v.p. U.S.O., N.Y. Com. Served with 304th F.A. U.S. Army, 1917-19. Decorated Cross of Grand Comdr. Royal Order George I, 1953; Greece; Order of Homayoun, 1955; Iran).; Recipient Russell Colgate citation as layman of year, 1954. Mem. AIME, Mining and Metall. Soc. Am. (pres. 1937). Presbyn. Clubs: University (N.Y.C.), Princeton (N.Y.C.). Home: Riverdale, N.Y. Dec. Nov. 24, 1982.

DODGE, HOMER LEVI, physicist, educator, lecturer; born in Ogdensburg, New York, October 21, 1887; son Orange Wood and Isabella (Donaghue) Dodge; A.B., Colgate U., 1910; M.S., State U. of Iowa, 1912, Ph.D., 1914; Sc.D., Colgate U., 1932, U. of Vt., 1945; LL.D., Middlebury Coll., 1945; student Columbia, summer, 1913; m. Margaret Mary Wing, Sept. 5, 1917; children—Alice Isabella (Mrs. Stewart R. Wallace), Norton Townshend. Asst. instr. physics State U. Ia., 1910-12, demonstrator, 1912-13; instr., 1913-15, asst. prof., 1915-19; prof. physics, Univ. of Okla., 1919-44, head of dept., 1919-42, dir. Sch. of Engring, Physics, 1924-42, dean of Grad. Sch., 1926-44; founder U. of Okla. Research Inst., dir., 1941-44, nat. counselor, 1953-63; director Okla. State Bureau of Standards, 1919-44. Dir. Office Sci. Personnel, Nat. Research Council, Washington, D.C., 1942-44; pres. Norwich U., 1944-50 president emeritus since 1950, director Cabot Fund Program in Aviation, 1950-53, chairman of Cabot Fund Administrative Committee, 1949-59; cons. to War Manpower Commn. and War and Navy Depts., 1942-44; mem. div. phys. scis., Nat. Resrch. Council, 1944-46. Topographic aid U.S. Geolog. Survey, 1906-11, junior topographer, 1911-14; editor research in physics dept. of "School Science and Mathematics," 1916-24. Course expert in physics, Com. on Edn. and Spl. Training War Dept., 1919; mem. nat. advisory com. for engring., science and management defense training 1941-45. Mem. governing bd. Am. Inst. of Physics, 1932-39; Policy Commn., 1942-47; pres. bd. trustees Okla. Sch. of Religion, 1927-44; mem. acad. adv. bd. U.S. Merchant Marine Acad., 1947-52. Fellow American Assn. Advancement Science, Am. Phys. Soc. (mem. council 1936); mem. Am. Assn. Physics Teachers (1st pres. 1930-32; Am. Assn. Univ. Profs. (member council, 1931-33; field director survey of college and univ. teaching, 1932-33), Newcomen Society of England, American Society for Engring. Education (mem. council, 1942-47; mem. engring. edn. mission to Japan, 1952), Wilderness Society, National Parks Association, Sigma Xi, Phi Beta Kappa, Phi Gamma Delta, Sigma Pi Sigma (national pres. 1947-50, nat. lectr. on Soviet education 1957-58). Orsted medalist —for notable contributions to teaching of physics,— 1944. Conglist. Clubs: Cosmos (Washington, D.C.); University Club (Boston, Massachusetts), Appalachian Mountain, Green Mountain, Rotary. Author: Problems in Physics Derived from Military Situations and Experience, War Dept., 1919; Laboratory Manual of Physics (with D. E. Roller), 1926. Contbr. research papers, articles on advances in physics and on ednl. subjects. Research on ednl. systems Europe, Soviet, Great Britain. Pioneer canoe trips Green-Colorado River System, St. Lawrence River. Many illustrated travel lectures. Home: Mechanicsville, Md. Died June 29, 1983.†

DODSON, EDWIN STANTON, teacher educator, consultant; b. Empire, Nev., Mar. 26, 1921; s. George J. and Mary (Larsen) D.; m. Rose Arenaz, Aug. 6, 1949. B.A., U. Nev., 1942; M.A., U. Oreg., 1948, U. Calif., 1966; Ed.D., U. Calif., 1967. Tchr. public schs., McGill, Yerington, Reno, all Nev., 1942-49, elementary sch. prin., Battle Mountain, Nev., 1949, Austin (Nev.) Public Sch., 1949-50, supt. schs., Lovelock, Nev., 1950-55, prin. elementary, jr. high, high schs., Reno, Nev., 1955-66, asst. supt. schs., 1966-67; assoc. prof. schs. adminstrn. U. Nev., Reno, 1967-71, prof., from 1971; cons. Washoe County Sch. Dist., from 1967, Washoe County Tchrs. Assn., 1967-68, Nev. PTA, 1978, Nye County Sch. Dist., 1978, Lander County Sch. Dist., 1978, Carson City Sch. Dist., 1981, Storey County Sch. Dist., 1981, Lyon County Sch. Dist., 1981, 82, Nev. Sch. Trustees Assn., 1968, Nev. Dept. Edn., 1968, 78. Author: Vocational Education and the Comprehensive High School: A Challenge to Administrators, 1968. Fulbright scholar in comparative edn. Finland, France, 1960. Mem. NEA, Nev. Edn. Assn. (dir. 1965-67), Washoe Prins. Assn. (pres. 1963-64), Nev. Assn. Sch. Adminstrs. (exec. sec. 1974-79), Am. Assn. Sch. Adminstrsn. (nat. adv. council 1966-69, 75-78), Phi Delta Kappa, Phi Alpha Theta, Phi Kappa Phi. Home: Reno, Nev.

DODSON, OWEN VINCENT, author; b. Bklyn., Nov. 28, 1914; s. Nathaniel and Sarah Elizabeth (Goode) D.; B.A., Bates Coll., 1936, D.Litt., 1977; M.F.A., Yale U., 1939. Instr. Atlanta U., 1938-42, also dir. drama; dir. drama Spelman Coll., 1938-41; instr. Hampton Inst., 1942-43, then dir. drama; prof. drama Howard U.; poet-in-residence Ruth Stephen Poetry Center U. Ariz., spring 1969; now cons. Harlem Sch. Arts, N.Y.C.; dir. summer theatre The Theater Lobby, Washington; condr. seminars in theatre and playwriting; lectr. in field. Exec. sec. Am. Film Center, N.Y.C.; mem. Com. Mass Edn. in Race Relations; bd. dirs. Am. Negro Theatre. Rosenwald fellow, 1945; Guggenheim fellow, 1953; Rockefeller Found. fellow, 1968. Recipient Paris Rev. prize for short story The Summer of Fire, 1956. Mem. Phi Beta Kappa. Author numerous books including (Poems) Powerful Long Ladder, 1946, The Confession Stone: A Song Cycle Sung by Mary about Jesus, 1970; (novels) Boy at the Window, 1951, Come Home Early, Child, 1977; (play) Divine Comedy, 1977; The Harlem Book of the Dead, 1978. works represented in numerous anthologies. Died June 21, 1983.

DOERING, GRACE BERNARDINA (MRS. JOHN W. MCCORD), lawyer; b. Cleve., June 16, 1890; d. Anton and Frances J. (Langer) D.; m. John W. McCord, July 25, 1957. A.B., Case Western Res. U., 1911; J.D. magna cum laude, Baldwin Wallace Coll., 1925; LL.M., Cleve. State U., Cleve.-Marshall Coll. Law, 1927. Bar: N.Mex. bar 1925, Ohio bar 1931, U.S. Supreme Ct. bar 1960. Instr. public high schs., Ohio, 1911-20; staff Albuquerque Morning Jour., 1920; asso. John F. Simms, N.Mex., 1925-26; law asst. Ct. Appeals, 8th Dist. Ohio, 1926-33; asso. Doering, Doering & Doering, from 1933; Prof. appellate practice and procedure Grad. Sch., Cleve.-Marshall Coll. Law, 1933-38; asst. dir. law, City of Cleve., 1935-42; regional atty. OPA, 1942; Public mem. 5th regional tripartite panel Nat. Labor Bd., 1943-45; v.p. Nat. Assn. Women Lawyers Found., 1956-57. Author: (with John Sherman Long) McCord of Alaska: Statesman for the Last Frontier, 1975; Contbr. (with John Sherman Long) articles to profl. publs. Trustee Legal Aid Soc. Recipient recognition awards for civic and profl. activities, including citation bd. govs. Case Western Res. U., 1963. Fellow Ohio State Bar Found.; mem. Nat. Assn. Women Lawyers (pres. 1957-58, del. ho. of dels. to Am. Bar Assn. 1958-59), ABA (1st woman assembly del. to ho. of dels. 1957), Fed. Bar Assn. (hon. mem.), Ohio Bar Assn. (hon. mem.), Cleve. Bar Assn. (hon. mem.), Cuyahoga Bar Assn. (trustee 1938-49, life), Internat. Assn. Women Lawyers, Am. Judicature Soc., Cleve. Law Library, Citizens League, LWV, Bus. and Profl. Women (hon.), AAUW, Alumnae Assn. Flora Stone Mather Coll. Case Western Res. U. (life), Nat. Woman's Party, Czechoslovak Soc. Am. (hon.), Nat. Conf. Bar Presidents, Cleve. Women Lawyers Assn. (pres. 1954-56), Phi Beta Kappa, Phi Alpha Delta (life). Clubs: Women's City (Cleve.) (sponsor), College (Cleve.) (hon.). Home: Cleveland, OH. †

DOERING, OTTO CHARLES, JR., lawyer; b. Wilmette, Ill., Oct. 29, 1904; s. Otto Charles and Mabelle Ione (Montgomery) D.; LL.B., Cornell U., 1927; m. Lucy S. Thomas, June 9, 1927; children—Rogers Montgomery, Paul Edward, Otto Charles III. Admitted to N.Y. bar, 1927, practiced in N.Y.C.; mem. firm Donovan Leisure Newton & Irvine, 1935-79. Pres., Field Photo Meml. Home, Reseda, Cal. Served to lt. col. AUS, 1942-45, exec. officer OSS. Decorated Legion of Merit (U.S.); Order Brit. Empire; Order White Elephant (Thailand). Mem. Am., N.Y. State bar assns., Assn. Bar City N.Y., Clubs: St. Andrew's Golf (Hastings-on-Hudson, N.Y.); Lake Placid (N.Y.). Home: Scarsdale, N.Y. Died July 12, 1979.

DOHENY, WILLIAM JOSEPH, clergyman, jurist, author, educator; b. Merrill, Wis., May 30, 1898; s. William R. and Bridget (O'Connor) D. J.U.D. (Dr. Roman and Canon Law), Cath. U. Am., 1927. Bar: Admitted as adv. and atty., Sacred Roman Rota and Apostolic Signatura 1932. Entered Congregatio a Sancta Cruce, 1919; ordained priest Roman Cath. Ch., 1924; title monsignor conferred, 1948; asst. superior Fgn. Mission Sem., Washington, 1925-28, acting superior, 1928-29; superior Holy Cross Internat. Coll., Rome, Italy, 1929-34; superior Sem. of Our Lady of Holy Cross, North Dartmouth, Mass., 1934-35, North Easton, Mass., 1935-37, Holy Cross Coll., Cath. U. Am., 1937-41; asst. superior gen. Congregation of Holy Cross, Washington and N.Y.C., 1941-45, gen. supr. studies, 1945—; prof., legal ethics U. Notre Dame, 1945-48; asso. justice Tribunal of Sacred Roman Rota, Vatican City, 1948—, presiding judge, 1960—; legal expert 2d Vatican Council, 1952—; judge Appellate Court of Vatican City. Consultor Sacred Congregation of the Sacraments, 1950—, Sacred Congregation of the Rites, 1950—; Charter mem. Riccobono Seminar of Roman Law, Washington. Author: Church Property: Modes of Acquisition, 1927, Canonical Procedure in Matrimonial Cases, 1937, Canonical Procedure in Matrimonial Cases, Vol. II, 1946, Practical Manual for Marriage Cases, 1938, Practical Problems in Church Finance, 1941, The Pater Noster of St. Teresa, 1942, Give Us This Day Our Daily Bread, 1944, Our Life in Christ, 1945, Papal Documents on Mary, 1954, We Priests Need Prayers, 1975, Holy Communion and the Most Blessed Trinity, 1976, Our Lady in Our Life, 1977, The Marvels of Divine Grace, 1977, The Selected Writings of Archbishop Martinez, 1977, St. Vincent de Paul and His World, 1978, St. Paul the Apostle: His Life and Times, 1978, The Best of Abbot Marmion, 1979, The Way that Leads to God, 1979, The Revelations of St. Gertrude, 1979, The Book of the Divine Consolations of Blessed Angela of Foligno, 1979, The Jewels of St. Jane Frances de Chantal, 1980, Boylan's Best, 1980, The Life of St. Birgitta of Sweden, 1980, Cardinal Newman: His Life and Spirituality, 1981, Prat, The Life of our Lord, Jesus Christ, 1981, Symposium on Mental Prayer, 1981, Bossuet—Meditations on the Gospels, 1981. Hon. life mem. Canon Law Soc. of Am. (1st pres. 1938), K.C. Home: Vatican City Vatican State

DOHERTY, RICHARD P., economist, mgmt. cons., indsl. relations and tv exec.; b. Wilton, N.H., May 5, 1905; s. Edward and Myra J. (Duval) D.; m. Dorothea M. Sullivan, May 30, 1933; 1 dau., Judith Dale. A.B. magna cum laude, Clark U., 1925; A.M., Brown U., 1926, grad. fellow, 1927-28. Prof. econs. Boston U., 1928-46, head econs. dept., 1940-45; v.p., dir. labor relations Nat. Assn. Radio and TV Broadcasters, 1946-54; pres. TV-Radio Mgmt. Corp., from 1954, TV-Radio Properties Corp., from 1964; U.S. mgmt. del. ILO, Geneva, Switzerland, 1949-67; mgmt. mem. Internat. Social Security Experts Com., 1962-70; industry mem. WSB, 1951-52; founder, exec. dir. Indsl. Relations Council Met. Boston, 1940-46; industry adviser Pres. Truman's Labor Mgmt. Conf., 1945. Author: Interpretation Business and Financial Conditions, 1934, Structure American Business, 1937, Economic Organization of Society, 1939, Essentials of Collective Bargaining, 1946, Broadcasting and Business Cycles, 1950, Taft Hartley Act and Broadcasting Industry, 1948, Wage Policy and Administration, 1954, Pitfalls in Collective Bargaining, 1955, TV: America's Growth Industry, 1964, Appraisal of the International Labor Organization, 1965; Contbr. articles to profl. jours. Dir. Mass State Civil Def., 1941-45; chmn. East Coast Civil Def. Council, 1942-45. Awarded Pres. Certificate of Merit for civil def., 1945. Mem. Am. Econs. Assn., Am. Assn. Bus. Economists, Broadcast Pioneers, Broadcasters Club Assn., Phi Beta Kappa. Clubs: Hyannis Yacht; Circumnavigators (Washington), Broadcasters (Washington). Home: Dennis, Mass. Died Jan. 21, 1982.

DOLE, WILLIAM, painter, educator; b. Angola, Ind., Sept. 2, 1917; s. W. Earl and Edna Helen (Cowan) D.; m. Kathryn Lee Holcomb, Feb. 14, 1941; children—William, Heidi, Hilary, Deirdre, Deborah, Jonathan, Kathryn. A.B., Olivet Coll., 1938; D.F.A., 1978; M.A., U. Calif.-Berkeley, 1947. Lectr. art U. Calif.-Berkeley, 1947-49, asst. prof. art, Santa Barbara, 1949-57, assoc. prof., 1957-61, prof., 1961-83, chmn. dept. art, 1958-63, 71-74. One-man shows, Galerie Springer, Berlin, 1956, 64, McRoberts and Tunnard Gallery, London, 1966, Staempfli Gallery, N.Y.C., 1974, 76, 78, 80, Phillips Collection, 1979, group shows include, Pa. Acad. Fine Arts, 1950, 60, 65, 67, Downtown Gallery, N.Y.C., 1963, 64, U. Ill., 1965, 67, Bklyn. Mus., 1972, 81, Andrew Crispo Gallery, N.Y.C., 1977; represented in permanent collections, including, Bklyn. Mus., Chase Manhattan Bank, Fogg Art Mus., Harvard U., Joseph H. Hirshhorn Mus. and Sculpture Garden, Washington, Honolulu, Pa. acads. fine arts, Santa Barbara, U. Iowa museums art, Walker Art Center, Mpls., Atlantic-Richfield Co. Sustaining trustee Santa Barbara Mus. Art. Served with AC U.S. Army, 1942-45. Recipient Art award Am. Acad. and Inst. Arts and Letters, 1978. Episcopalian. Home: Santa Barbara, Calif. Dec. Jan. 13, 1983.

DOLIN, ANTON, dancer, choreographer; b. Sussex, Eng., July 27, 1904; s. George H. and Helen Maude (Healey) Kay. Ed. pvt. tutors; dramatic tng. with, Italia Conti; ballet tng. with, Grace Cone, Princess Seraphine Astafieve and, Bronislava Nyinskao. Lectured at Oxford and Cambridge univs. and on radio in, England, Australia and U.S. Began as actor, 1915, with, Diaghileff Co., 1921-29, prin. dancer, Sadler's Wells, 1931-35; danced, acted: leading role in Ballerina, London, 1933, and in, Precipice, London, 1934, founder, dir., prin. dancer, Markova-Dolin Ballet, 1935-38, toured with, Original Ballet Russe, Australia, 1939, premier danseur or guest artist, Ballet Theatre, until 1946; dancer, choreographer: ballet in revue Seven Lively Arts, N.Y.C., 1944-45; organizer, dancer ballet in revue, new Markova-Dolin group, touring, U.S., C.Am., Mexico, 1935-38, 45, 47-48, guest artist, Original Ballet Russe, 1946-48, founded (with Markova), group that became, London's Festival Ballet, 1949; artistic dir., prin. dancer, 1949-61, formed and toured with, Stars of Ballet, 1961, dir., choreographer, Rome Opera Ballet, 1962, artistic adviser, Les Grand Ballets Canadiens.; Creator of: Diaghileff ballets Les Biches; Own: choreography Quintet, N.Y.C., 1940, Capriocioso and Pas de Quatre, Chgo., 1940; Has danced and acted in many motion pictures.; (Recipient Dance Mag. award 1981); Author: Divertissement, 1930, Ballet Go Round, 1938, Pas de Deux: the Art of Partnering, 1949, Alicia Markova, 1953, Autobiography, 1960. Home: New Bedford, Mass. Dec. Nov. 25, 1983.

DOLL, AUGUST PHILLIP, oil executive; b. Cincinnati, Jan. 17, 1887; s. August and Effie (Phillipp) D.; ed. Ohio Mechanics Inst.; m. Olga Moorhaus, Dec. 9, 1913. Started as salesman Edwards Mfg. Co. in 1907, later sales mgr.; in 1916 with Corcoran-Victor Co. as comptroller and dir.; sec.-treas. and sales mgr. Thomas J. Corcoran Lamp Co., Cincinnati, O., 1919, pres., 1925; named changed in 1931 to Corcoran-Brown Lamp Co., continued as pres. until Dec. 1937; became pres. The Valvoline Oil Co. (name changed to Freedom-Valvoline Oil Co.), 1938, vice chmn. bd.; dir. and mem. exec. com. Columbia Gas & Electric Corp.; dir. Am. Thermos Co., Globe Wernicke Co., Aluminum Industries, Cincinnati. Plastene Corp., Mem. Wyoming Civic Center Orgn. Mason (Grotto, Shriner), Elk. Clubs: Cincinnati, Queen City (hon. mem.), Wyoming Golf, Cincinnati Country. Home: Wyoming, Ohio. †

DOMENICALI, CHARLES ANGELO, educator, physicist; b. Albuquerque, Dec. 27, 1917; s. Pietro Luca and Angelina (Selva) D.; m. Maxine Elinor Lind, Mar. 11, 1944; children—Dena Ann, Peter Lind, Donna Lynne. B.S., U. N.Mex., 1939; Ph.D., Mass. Inst. Tech., 1949. Physicist U. N.M., 1942; research asso. magnetism Mass. Inst. Tech., 1947-49; asso. prof., chmn. physics dept. Alfred (N.Y.) U., 1949-52; research physicist, sect. head Franklin Inst. Labs., Phila., 1952-55, cons., 1965; research physicist, head solid state physics sect. Honeywell Research Center, Hopkins, Minn., 1955-57, sr. research physicist, 1957-61; vis. lectr. elec. engring. U. Minn., 1959; prof. physics Ariz. State U., Tempe, 1961-63; research physicist Union Carbide Research Inst., Tarrytown, N.Y., 1963-64; prof. physics Temple U., Phila., from 1965, chmn. physics dept., 1965-68. Contbr. articles profl. jours. Mem. Am. Phys. Soc., N.Y. Acad. Scis., Am. Assn. Physics Tchrs. Home: Philadelphia, PA.

DONAHUE, EDWARD JOSEPH, banker; b. Penn Yan, N.Y., Dec. 1, 1889; s. Edward and Mary Ellen (DeWan) D.; LL.B., Georgeton U.; m. Elizabeth V. Abbott, Oct. 17, 1925; 1 son, Edward Abbott. With 1st Nat. Bank of Geneva, N.Y., 1908-15; nat. bank examiner, 1915-20; asst. cashier Union Exchange Nat. Bank, N.Y., 1920-25; asst. v.p. Chatham-Phoenix Nat. Bank, N.Y., 1925-30; v.p. Chase Nat. Bank, N.Y. City, from 1930. Roman Catholic. Home: Forest Hills, N.Y. †

DONAHUE, RUSSELL B., finance company executive; b. Oak Park, Ill., Sept. 29, 1921; m. Carol Anderson; 6 children. B.S. in Fin, Northwestern U., 1951. Successively with Gen. Electric Co., McGraw Edison Co., Comml. Credit Co.; pres. bus. fin. div. James Talcott, Inc., Oak Brook, Ill.; also exec. v.p. parent co.; retired sr. exec. v.p., dir. Assos. Comml. Corp. Served with USAAF, 1943-45. Mem. Nat. Comml. Fin. Conf. (chmn. bd.), Northwestern U. Alumni Club of Chgo. (dir. 1975-77). Mem. Evang. Covenant Ch. of Am. Home: Hinsdale, Ill.

DONAHUE, STEPHEN J., ret. bishop; ordained priest Roman Cath. Church, May 25, 1918; apptd. aux. bishop of N.Y., 1934. Home: New York, N.Y. Died Aug. 17, 1982.

DONALD, GEORGE KENNETH, consul general; b. Mobile, Ala., Nov. 27, 1890; s. Harry Gordon and Kate Lea (Gazzam) D.; A.B., Yale, 1912; m. Cherry Hempstead, Sept. 1912; children—Robert Gordon, Katharine Lea, Richard Hempstead. Apptd. consul at Maracaibo, Venezuela, June 22, 1914; consul at Nuevo Laredo, Mexico, Mar.-Sept. 1917, Aguascalientes, 1917-18, Sydney, N.S., 1918-19, Tegucigalpa, Honduras, 1919-22, Johannesburg, S. Africa, 1922-28; consul gen. at Guatemala, 1928-32, chargé d'affaires and 1st sec., 1932-33; consul gen. at St. John's, Newfoundland, 1933-34; consul gen. at Milan, Italy, 1934-37, at Southampton, Eng., 1937-41, Windsor, Ont., Can., 1941-45, St. John's, Newfoundland, 1946-47, ret. 1947. Episcopalian. Address: Washington, D.C. †

DONNELLY, CHARLES EDWARD, lawyer; b. Oswego, N.Y., Aug. 1, 1890; s. Charles Edward and Elizabeth (Henrick) D.; LL.B., U. So. Cal., 1912; m. Dorcas Metcalf, Apr. 21, 1920; children—George Swanwick, Margaret E. (Mrs. Ellsworth H. Kendig), Charles Edward. Admitted to Cal. bar, 1912, since from practiced Los Angeles; with Donnelly, Clark, Chase & Haakh and predecessor firms, from 1914. Mason (32 deg.). Clubs: California, Athletic, Stock Exchange (Los Angeles); Newport Harbor Yacht (Newport Beach, Cal.). Home: Los Angeles, CA. †

DONOHUE, HAROLD DANIEL, congressman; b. Worcester, Mass., June 18, 1901; s. Cornelius and Margaret (Lyons) D.; student, Northeastern Univ., 1925; unmarried. admitted to Mass. Bar, 1925; practiced in Worcester; mem. 80th-91st Congresses, 4th Dist. Alderman, pres. bd. and acting mayor, Worcester. Entered United States Navy, Dec. 1942; disch. as lt. comdr. Dec. 1945. Mem. bd. trustees Worcester County bar assns., Am. Legion, World War II Vets. Assn. (Worcester). Democrat. Roman Catholic. Elk, K.C., Eagle. Home: Worcester, Mass. Died Nov. 4, 1984.

DONOHUE, MARK NEARY, lawyer; b. Wilmington, Del., Nov. 18, 1905; s. Michael and Mary Ellen (Neary) D.; m. Hazel W Wright, Nov. 24, 1934; children—Mark (dec.), Nancy, Mary Ellen (Mrs. Daniel L. Wulff). B.A., U. Del., 1927; LL.D., Harvard U., 1930. Bar: Del. bar 1930, N.Y. State bar 1931. Practice Law, N.Y.C., from 1930; assoc. firm Hoguet & Neary, N.Y.C., 1930-38; partner firm Brumbaugh, Graves, Donohue & Raymond (and predecessors), N.Y.C., from 1938. Fellow Am. Coll. Trial Lawyers; mem. Am., N.Y. State bar assns., Assn. Bar City N.Y. (chmn. exec. com. 1965, treas. 1967-70), N.Y. County Lawyers Assn., Am. Patent Law Assn., N.Y. Patent Law Assn. (pres. 1961). Home: Chatham, N.J. Died Nov. 1, 1983.

DONOVAN, DENNIS FRANCIS, judge; b. Champion, Mich., Apr. 9, 1889; s. Michael and Mary (Harrington) D.; LL.B., U. Mich., 1913; m. Alice Gertrude Flaherty, Dec. 2, 1916; children—Mary Gertrude (Mrs. A.C. Kelly), Dennis Francis. Admitted to Mich. bar, 1913, Minn. bar, 1914, since practiced in Minn.; U.S. dist. judge for Dist. of Minn., from 1945, sr. judge. Mem. Minn. 11th Jud. Dist., Am. bar assns. Democrat. Roman Catholic. Rotarian (past pres.) Clubs: Kitchi Gammi, Athletic, Minnesota (St. Paul); Minneapolis. Home: Rochester, MN. †

DONOVAN, HENRY A(UGUSTUS), ex. govt. ofcl.; b. Boston, July 18, 1889; s. Cornelius and Ellen Theresa (Haley) D.; grad. English High Sch., Boston, 1906; m. Sadie Elizabeth Hanley, Oct. 15, 1912; 1 dau., Dorothy Catherine (Mrs. William Phillips); m. 2d, Beatrice Downer Holland. Stenographer New Haven R.R., Boston, 1906-10; with U.S. Dept. Agr., from 1910, successively stenographer, chief clk. bur. soils, bus. mgr. bur. chemistry and soils, asst. to chief bur. chemistry and soils, asst. chief bur. for mgmt., bur. agrl. chemistry and engring., asst. chief bur. mgmt., bur. agrl. and indsl. chemistry, 1910-53, dep. asst. adminstr. memg. Agrl. Research Service, 1953-59 (retirement age), now mgmt. cons. with the dept.; mem. dept. office techniques and operations Dept. Agr. Grad. Sch., from 1940, chmn. dept., mem. grad. sch. council, 1948-64. Mem. Soc. Personnel Adminstrn., Am. Soc. Pub. Adminstrn. Home: Washington, D.C. †

DOOLE, GEORGE ARNTZEN, aviation company executive; b. Quincy, Ill., Aug. 12, 1909; s. George Andrew and Naomi (Arntzen) D.; B.S., U. Ill., 1931; M.B.A., Harvard, 1939; pilot, then chief pilot Pan Am. World Airways, N.Y.C., 1934-46, regional dir. Middle East and Asia, 1946-53; pres. The Pacific Corp., Washington, from 1953, then dir.; dir. Air Am., Inc., Air Asia Co., Ltd., Washington, 1953-85; pres., chmn., dir. Arntzen and Co. (name formerly DHM Co.), Quincy, 1949-85; dir. Civil Air Transport Co. Ltd., Taiwan, 1955-85, Air Am., Ltd., Hong Kong, Tai-Pacific Services Co. Ltd., Bangkok. Mem. U.S. presdl. team during negotiation 1st Air Transport Services agreement between U.S. and India, 1946. Gov. adm. Bristol Hosp., Istanbul, Turkey, 1946-51. Served from cadet to col. USAF, World War II, Korea. Decorated Order of Cedars (Lebanon). Mem. Clipper Pioneers, Am. Inst. Aero. and Astronautics, Nat. Aero. Assn., Order of Daedalions. Clubs: Wings, Harvard, Explorers (N.Y.C.); Army and Navy, Aero (Washington); Chevy Chase (Md.); St. George's (Beirut, Lebanon). Home: Washington, D.C. Dec. Mar. 8, 1985. Interred, Quincy, Ill.

DOOLEY, DENNIS A., lawyer, state librarian; b. Boston, Mass., Dec. 20, 1889; s. Dennis C. and Rose A. (Connolly) D.; A.B., Boston Coll., 1912; LL.B., Suffolk Univ. Law Sch., 1920; LL.D. (hon.) Boston Coll., 1932; m. Edith A. Doyle, June 16, 1915; 1 dau., Edith F. (Mrs. William A. Johnson). Dep. chief examiner, Mass. Civil Service Commn., 1913-19; asst. dir. div. univ. extension, Mass. Dept. of Edn., 1919-29; dean Boston Coll. Law Sch., 1929-36; State Librarian Commonwealth of Mass. from 1936. Mem. Bar Assn. City of Boston, Nat. Assn. of State Libraries (pres., 1941-48), Am. Library Assn., Mass. Library Assn., Spl. Libraries Assn., Am. Assn. Law Libraries. Democrat. Roman Catholic. Editor, Index, State Bar Assn. Proc., 1942. Home: Jamaica Plain, Mass. †

DOOLEY, EDWIN BENEDICT, former congressman; b. Bklyn., Apr. 13, 1905; s. Joseph Augustus and Isabelle (Delaney) D.; A.B., Dartmouth, 1927; LL.B., Fordham U., 1930; m. Harriette M. Feeley, Oct. 7, 1926 (dec. Jan. 1952); 1 son, Edwin Benedict; m. 2d, Anita M. Gillies, 1955 (dec. 1962); m. 3d, Margaret Sheefel Bailhe, Jan. 9, 1964. Feature writer N.Y. Sun, 1927-38; v.p. Don Spencer Co., advt. agy., 1938-40; dir. pub. relations Gen. Foods Corp., 1940-46; asso. Inst. Pub. Relations, 1946-48; exec. dir. N.Y. State div. Am. Cancer Soc., 1948-50; dir. pub. relations and advt. Health Ins. Plan Greater N.Y., 1950-55; mem. 85th to 87th Congresses, 26th Dist. N.Y. State, 1956-62; v.p. Jones, Brakeley & Rockwell. Chmn., N.Y. State Athletic Commn., 1966-75; mem. N.Y. State com. Nat. Capitol Sesquicentennial Commemoration, 1951; pub. relations com. Boy Scouts Am., 1948-50. Mayor, Mamaroneck, N.Y., 1950-56. Bd. dirs. Community Chest. Republican. Clubs: Dartmouth (pres. Westchester 1953-54); Touchdown (chmn. 1945-46), University (Mamaroneck); Capitol Hill (Washington); Boca Raton Hotel and Club; Bankers of Boca Raton, Knights of Malta; N.Y. Athletic. Home: Boca Raton, Fla. Died Jan. 25, 1982.

DOOLING, HENRY CHEESMAN, army officer; b. Clayton, N.J., June 23, 1887; s. John W. and Sylvia S. (Cheesman) D.; student Temple Coll., 1904; M.D., Medico-Chirurgical Coll., Philadelphia, Pa., 1908; m. Nellie May Essler, June 1, 1909; children—Frances Jean, George Halvor (dec.), Edith Sylvia (Mrs. M. L. Cooley, Jr.). Engaged in practice as physician, Norwood, Pa., 1909-17; entered Med. Corps, U.S. Army, 1917, and advanced through the grades to brig. gen.; serving as chief health officer, Panama Canal. Served in France during World War I; later assignments, Walter Reed Gen. Hosp. (Washington), Gorgas Hosp. (Ancon, C.Z.), William Beaumont Gen. Hosp. (El Paso), Station Hosp. (Fort Riley, Kan.); Army, 1947; med. dir., State Sanitorium, South Mountain, Pa. Fellow Am. Coll. Physicians; mem. Am. Med. Assn., Am. Bd. Internal Medicine, Isthmian Med. Assn., Assn. Mil. Surgeons, Am. Trudeau Soc. Mason. Address: South Mountain, Pa. †

DOOMAN, EUGENE HOFFMAN, diplomat; b. Osaka, Japan, Mar. 25, 1890; B.S., Trinity Coll., 1911; student Columbia U., 1 yr.; married. Apptd. student interpreter, Japan, 1912; vice counsul and interpreter, Kobe, 1915-20, Taihoku, 1920-21; asst. Japanese sec., Tokyo, 1921-26, asst. Japanese sec. and 2d sec., Apr.-May 1926, Japanese sec. and 2d sec., 1926-30; 1st sec., London, 1931; counselor of Embassy, Tokyo, since Jan. 5, 1937. Accompanied Ambassador Dawes to conf. with dels. attending session of Council of League of Nations concerning Manchuria, Paris, 1931; adviser Preliminary Naval Conversations, Oct.-Dec. 1934, London Naval Conf., 1935-36; to Dept. of State, June 1942. Address: Washington, D.C. Deceased.

DOREMUS, ROBERT BARNARD, university dean; b. Newton, Mass., May 19, 1915; s. Robert Proudfit and Eleanor (Barnard) D.; m. Betty Bartlett Holt, Apr. 26, 1941 (dec. May 1970); children—John Barnard, Andrew Bartlett. A.B., Harvard, 1935, A.M., 1936, Ph.D., 1940. Faculty U. Wis.-Madison, 1940-42, 46-82, prof. English, 1953-82, asst. dir. freshman English, 1946-47, asst. dean U Coll. Letters and Sci., 1947-50, assoc. dean, 1950-82. Author: Writing College Themes, 1960; Editor: (with Lacy and Rodman) Patterns in Writing, rev. edit, 1963. Served to capt. USAAF, 1942-46. Mem. MLA. Home: Madison, Wis. Dec. Aug. 1, 1982.

DORF, ERLING, geologist; b. Nysted, Nebr., July 19, 1905; s. Alfred T. and Thyra Axelsen (Dreier) D.; m. Ruth Kemmerer, Apr. 3, 1934; children—Thomas (dec.), Norman Kemmerer, Robert Erling, Martha Dreier. B.S., U. Chgo., 1925, Ph.D., 1930. Asst. instr. U. Chgo., 1926-27, fellow geology, 1928-30; instr. Princeton, 1926-3O, asst. prof., 1930-40, asso. prof., 1940-46, prof. geology, 1946-74, emeritus, 1974-84, curator paleobotany, 1930-74, emeritus, 1974-84; research asst. Carnegie Instn. of Washington, 1926-45; lectr. U. Pa., 1936-42, Princeton Adult Sch., 1964-84; research curator Phila. Acad. Sci., 1936-46; prof. geology Wagner Free Inst. Sci., 1948-81; vis. lectr. Villanova U., 1963-67; vis. prof. Rutgers U., 1968-70, Fairleigh-Dickinson U., 1975; dir. NSF summer geol. conf., Mont., 1964-73; paleobot. cons. U.S. Nat. Mus.; chmn. com. on paleobotany NRC, 1941-46. Author: Pliocene Floras of California, 1933, Upper Cretaceous Floras of Rocky Mountain Region, 1942; Editor: Guidebook for Field Trips, Geol. Soc. Am., 1957; Bd. editors: Rev. Palaeobotany and Palynology, also Palaeogeography, Palaeoclimatology, Palaeoecology, 1968-84; Contbr. articles to geol. and bot. jours. Bd. dirs. Princeton chpt. A.R.C., 1942-53, 60-66, vice chmn., 1964; nat. awards selection bd. Rec. for Blind, 1976-84; mem. Princeton Twp. Bd. Health, 1960-76, Flood Control Com., 1976-84, Environ. Com., 1977-84, Environ. Design Rev. Com., 1977-84; trustee Princeton Community Players, 1950-53, 56-58, Princeton Country Day Sch., 1946-56, Stony Brook-Millstone-Watersheds Assn., 1974-78; cons. Ednl. Testing Service, 1969-73; U.S. del. Indian Sci. Congress, 1953; sci. collaborator Nat. Park Service, 1954-58. Fellow AAAS (council 1947-57), Geol. Soc. Am., Paleontol. Soc. Am. (v.p. 1943), Bot. Soc. Am., N.J. Acad. Sci. (adv. council 1978-84); mem. Nat. Assn. Geology Tchrs. (v.p. east sect. 1956-57, pres. 1957-58, Neil Miner award 1963, Ralph Digman award 1967), A.A.U.P., N.J. Geol. Soc., Internat., Am. assns. plant taxonomists, Yellowstone-Bighorn Research Assn. (council 1961-84, pres. 1964-66, hon. life), Am. Inst. Biol. Scis., Am. Geol. Inst., Atlantic Coastal Plain Assn., Paleobot. Soc. India (hon.), Mont. Geol. Soc. (hon. life), Royal Danish Acad. Arts and Scis. (fgn.), Sigma Xi, Kappa Epsilon Pi, Alpha Tau Omega. Club: Nassau (pres. 1961). Home: Princeton, N.J. Died Apr. 16, 1984.

DORFMAN, ALBERT, physician; b. Chgo., July 6, 1916; s. Aron and Anna (Schwartzman) D.; m. Ethel Steinman, Sept. 1, 1940; children—Abby, Julie. S.B., U. Chgo., 1936, Ph.D., 1939, M.D., 1944. Instr. biochemistry U. Chgo., 1939-42, asst. prof. pediatrics, 1948-53, assoc. prof., 1953-57, prof., 1957-82, chmn. pediatrics dept., 1961-72; dir. LaRabida-U. Chgo. Inst., 1957-67, Richard T. Crane Disting. Service prof. pediatrics, 1965-82; chief biochemistry Army Med. Sch., Washington, 1946-48; dir. Joseph P. Kennedy, Jr., Mental Retardation Research Center, 1965-82. Contbr. articles to sci. jours. Recipient E. Mead Johnson award for research in pediatrics, 1957, Borden award for research in pediatrics, 1971, City of Hope Nat. Med. Center award for med. research, 1971. Mem. Am. Chem. Soc., Am. Soc. Biol. Chemists, Am. Acad. Arts and Scis., Am. Heart Assn., Am. Rheumatism Soc., Soc. Pediatric Research, Am. Pediatric Soc., Nat. Acad. Scis., Inst. Medicine, Am. Acad. Pediatrics, AAAS, Am. Soc. Cell Biology, Arthritis and Rheumatism Found., Biochem. Soc., Chgo. Pediatric Soc., Inst. Medicine Chgo., Inst. Soc., Ethics and Life Scis., Internat. Soc. Developmental Biology, Midwest Soc. Pediatric Research, Soc. for Complex Carbohydrates, Soc. Developmental Biology. Home: Chicago, Ill. Dec. July 27, 1982.

DORFMAN, SAUL, pianist, educator, musician; b. Chgo., May 18, 1912; s. Louis and Hilda (Goldenberg) D.; m. Helen Gordon, July 17, 1941; 1 child, Marc. Student, U. Chgo., 1940-42, Leipzig (Germany) State Conservatory of Music, 1930-32, State Coll. Music, Berlin, Germany, 1932-33. Prof., chmn. dept. piano Chgo. Musical Coll., Roosevelt U., 1945-74; music dir. Beth Emet Synagogue, Evanston, Ill., 1951-84. Piano soloist, Chgo. Symphony Orch., 1926, 34, concerts, Germany, 1930-33; appeared concerts also soloist various symphony orchs., U.S., numerous appearances pianist; lectr. radio and TV; Contbg. editor: Piano Quar. Recipient Gold medal Am. Conservatory of Music, 1925; Chicagoland Piano Playing Tournament Grand prize, 1927. Mem. Am. Assn. U. Profs., Music Tchrs. Nat. Assn., Soc. Am. Musicians (pres. 1971-73), Nat. Guild Piano Tchrs. Jewish. Home: Chicago, Ill. Dec. Feb. 2, 1984.

DORSON, RICHARD M., folklorist, historian, educator; b. N.Y.C., Mar. 12, 1916; s. Louis Jasper and Gertrude (Lester) D.; A.B., Harvard, 1937, M.A., 1940, Ph.D., 1943; m. Dorothy Diamond, 1940 (div. 1948); 1 son Ronald; m. 2d, Gloria Irene Gluski, Aug. 8, 1953; children—Roland Jeffrey, Linda. Instr. history Harvard, 1943-44; from instr. to prof. history Mich. State U., 1944-56; prof. history and folklore Ind. U., Bloomington, 1957-71, Distinguished prof., 1971-81, dir. Folklore Inst., 1963-81. Fulbright vis. prof. U. Tokyo, 1956-57; mem. ednl. adv. bd. John Simon Guggenheim Meml. Found., 1971-81; mem. council Smithsonian Instn., 1977-81; cons. Nat. Endowment for Humanities, 1972-75, Harvard Sheldon fellow, 1942, Library of Congress fellow, 1946, Guggenheim fellow, 1949, 64, 71; Am. Council Learned Socs. fellow, 1952, 61. Recipient Chgo. Folklore prize, 1947, 65, 69. Mem. Am. Folklore Soc. (pres. 1966-68), Am. Hist. Assn., Orgn. Am. Historians, Am. Studies Assn. Club: Cosmos. Author: Jonathan Draws the Long Bow, 1946; Bloodstoppers and Bearwalkers, 1952; Negro Folktales in Michigan, 1956; Negro Tales from Pine Bluff, Arkansas and Calvin, Michigan, 1958; American Folklore, 1959; Folk Legends of Japan, 1961; American Negro Folktales, 1967; The British Folklorists, A History, 1968; American Folklore and the Historian, 1971; Folklore, Selected Essays, 1972; America in Legend, 1973; Folklore and Fakelore, 1976. Editor: numerous vols. including African Folklore, 1972; Folklore and Traditional History, 1973; Folktales Told Around the World, 1975. Founder, editor Jour. Folklore Inst., 1963-81. Contbr. articles to jours. Home: Bloomington, Ind. Died Sept. 11, 1981.

DORTICOS, TORRADO OSVALDO, pres. of Cuba; b. 1919; student Havana U. Admitted to bar and practiced law; leader Castro revolutionary movement in Cienfuegos, 1957-58, imprisioned, Dec. 1958; escaped and fled to Mexico, returned upon success of revolution; minister revolutionary laws, 1959; pres. of Cuba, 1959-83. Mem. Cuban Nat. Bar Assn. (v.p.). Home: Havana, Cuba. Died June 23, 1983.

DOUB, GEORGE COCHRAN, govt. official; born Cumberland, Md., July 25, 1902; s. Albert A. and Anne Peyton (Cochran) D.; B.A., Johns Hopkins, 1923; LL.B., U. Md., 1926; m. Sophy Tayloe Snyder, Feb. 6, 1932; children—Anne Augustin, Sophy Tayloe, George Cochran. Admitted to Md. bar, 1926; asst. gen. solicitor Western Md. Ry. Co., 1928-30, gen. atty., 1930-34; partner Parker, Carey & Doub, 1934-40, Marshall, Carey & Doub,

1940-50, Marshall, Carey, Doub & Mundy, 1950-53. U.S. atty. Dist. of Md., 1953-56; asst. atty. gen. of U.S. charge civil div., 1956-61. Mem. for Balt. on character com., Ct. Appeals of Md., 1935-52; mem. Commn. to Revise Corporation Laws of Md., 1948-52. Rep. candidate atty. gen., Md., 1946. Dir. Mental Hygiene Soc. Md., 1947-52, Tb Assn. Md., 1947-51. Served as lt. comdr., USNR, World War II. Mem. Am., Fed. (nat. council), Md. (exec. council 1950-51), Baltimore City (chmn. com. civil procedure 1946-48) bar assns., Am. Judicature Soc., Am. Law Inst. Clubs: Green Spring Valley Hunt, Maryland, 14 West Hamilton Street, Bachelors Cotillion (Balt.); Centruy Assn. (N.Y.C.). Home: Owings Mills, Md. Died Oct. 30, 1981.

DOUB, HOWARD P., physician; b. Hagerstown, Md., Sept. 30, 1890; s. Louis P. and Ella (Newcomer) D.; A.B., Western Md. Coll., 1913; M.D., Johns Hopkins, 1917; m. Helen Ringrose, June 21, 1919; 1 son, Gerald P. Extern roentgenology Johns Hopkins Hosp., 1917-18; asso. roentgenologist Grace Hosp., Detroit, 1918-23; roentgenologist Detroit Receiving Hosp., 1921-23; radiologist-in-chief Henry Ford Hosp., Detroit, 1923-55, cons. radiology, from 1955. Cons. roentgenology Review Draft Bd., 1917-18, 42-45. Recipient gold medal Am. Coll. Radiology, 1962. Fellow Am. Coll. Radiology (president 1954-55); mem. Interamerican College of Radiology, A.M.A., American Radium Society, American Roentgen Ray Soc., Radiol. Soc. North America (president 1938; editor, Radiology, 1941-66, emeritus, from 1966; awarded Gold medal, 1950), Detroit X-ray and Radiol. Soc., Radiol. Soc., Columbia (corr. mem.), Tex. Radiol. Soc. (hon. mem.), Sociedad Radiologeia Panamena (hon.), Rocky Mountain Radiological Society (honorary member). Republican. Contbr. articles radiol. subjects. Home: Detroit, Mich. †

DOUDS, CHARLES TUCKER, government official; b. Plumville, Pa., Apr. 11, 1898; s. James Bothel and Margaret Jane (Morrow) D.; B.S., Pa. State U., 1922; M.A., Columbia, 1929; m. Ella Anna Fowler, June 11, 1926; 1 child, Charles Fowler. Sec., U. Rochester YMCA, 1922-28; staff, student div. Nat. Council YMCA, 1929-32; sec. Pa. Com. for Old Age Security, 1935-36; regional dir. Nat. Labor Relations Bd., 1937-42, asst. dir. field div., 1942, regional dir. N.Y., 1942-57, regional dir. Newark, N.J., 1957-58; chief labor manpower div. Fgn. Econ. Adminstrn., Washington, 1946-47; dir. bur. mediation State of Pa., 1958-69; labor arbitrator, 1969-82; chief of staff Gov.'s Commn. to Revise Pub. Employe Law, 1968. Alumni rep. on bd. trustees Pa. State U., 1956-76. Served with U.S. Army, 1918. Mem. Am. Soc. Pub. Adminstrn., Assn. Labor Relations Agys. (hon. life, pres. 1965-66), Nat. Acad. Arbitrators, Harrisburg Civil War Roundtable. Lutheran. Club: Penn State (pres. Harrisburg area 1967-68). Author: (verse) I Remember Another April, 1976. Contbr. articles to profl. jours. Home: Camp Hill, Pa. Dec. Jan. 10, 1982.

DOUGHERTY, CHARLES FREDERICK, railway exec.; b. Winfield, Kan., June 2, 1889; s. Lorenzo Dow and Corrie Ellis (Wilson) D.; student pub. schs.; m. Ita Boreal Upton, Aug. 11, 1917; children—Ann Withers (Mrs. E. J. Carlson, Jr.), Charles Frederick. With M.P. R.R., from 1905. Gen. manager of the Western dist., Kansas City, from 1951. Served as maj. U.S. Army, 1917-20, col., 1942-45. Decorated Bronze Star; Croix de Guerre with palms (France); Vittori Emanuel II (Italy). Mem. Am. Legion. Episcopalian. Mason (Shriner). †

DOUGLAS, ALEXANDER EDGAR, physicist; b. Melfort, Sask., Can., Apr. 12, 1916; s. Donald and Jessie Florence (Carwardine) D.; B.A., U. Sask., 1939, M.A., 1940; Ph.D., Pa. State U., 1948; m. Phyllis Helene Wright, July 26, 1945; children—Nancy Phyllis, Donald James, Andrew Alexander. Research scientist acoustics lab. Nat. Research Council Can., Ottawa, Ont., 1941-46, spectroscopy lab., 1948-68, dir. div. physics, 1968-73, prin. research officer Herzberg Inst. Astrophysics, 1973-80. Fellow Royal Soc. Can., Royal Soc. (London), Am. Phys. Soc.; mem. Can. Assn. Physicists (medal 1970, pres. 1975-76). Contbr. numerous articles on molecular structure and molecular spectra to profl. jours. Home: Ottawa, Ont., Can. Died July 26, 1981.

DOUGLAS, JOHN JEFFERSON, computer cons.; b. Cave-in-Rock, Ill., Oct. 14, 1935; s. Ulys J. and Rose Marie (Henry) D.; m. Monna Loy Nail, July 23, 1960; children—Kelley Jefferson, Kristen Neile. B.S. in Elec. Engring, Ariz. State U., 1965, M.S., 1969. Program dir. Series 6000, Honeywell/Gen. Electric Info. Systems Div., Phoenix, 1968-71; v.p., dir. mktg. services Courier Terminal Systems, Inc., Tempe, Ariz., 1971-74, v.p. ops., 1974-76, exec. v.p., 1976-78; v.p., gen. mgr. Computer Terminal Systems Ops., ITT Courier Terminal Systems, Inc., 1978-79, pres., 1979-80, computer cons., Paradise Valley, Ariz., 1980—; Mem. dean's adv. council Sch. Engring., Ariz. State U., Tempe, 1979; mem. Gov.'s Energy Conservation Com., 1979—. Served with USN, 1953-56. Home and Office: Paradise Valley AZ

DOUGLAS, MARJORY STONEMAN, author; b. Minneapolis, Minn., Apr. 7, 1890; d. Frank B. and Lillian (Trefethen) Stoneman; A.B., Wellesley Coll., 1912; Litt. D. (honorary), University of Miami, 1952; divorced. Reporter Miami (Florida) Herald, 1915-18; with overseas dept. publicity, Am. Red Cross in Europe, 1918-20; asst. editor and columnist, Miami Herald, 1920-23; free lance short story and article writer for Saturday Evening Post and other nat. mags., 1924-40; asso. prof. English, University of Miami, 1925-29; lecturer history of short story, Summer Inst. Lit., Pa. State Coll., 1929; book editor, Miami Herald, 1942-49; dir. Winter Inst. Lit., U. of Miami, 1944; dir. Mus. Sci. and Natural History, Miami, from 1954; pres. Hurricane House, Pubs., Inc., Coconut Grove, Fla.; lectr. Fla. history Miami-Dade Junior Coll. President Dade County Conf. on Civic Affairs, from 1964. Mem. Soc. Women Geographers Wash. Received 2d prize O. Henry Meml. Collection, 1928. Author: (play) The Gallows Gate, 1928; (book) The Everglades; River of Grass (Rivers of Am. series), 1947; Road to the Sun, 1951; (Junior novel) Freedom River, 1953; Hurricane, 1958; Alligator Crossing, (published) 1959; The Key to Paris (Junior book); Florida, The Long Frontier, pub. 1967; also writer editorial column in New York Times, 1950; book reviews for N.Y. Herald-Tribune, 1949; editor University of Miami Press, 1960-63, dir. emeritus, from 1963. Home: Coconut Grove, Fla. †

DOUGLAS, MELVYN, actor; b. Macon, Ga., Apr. 5, 1901; s. Edouard G. and Lena (Shackelford) Hesselberg; m. Helen Gahagan, Apr. 5, 1931; children—Gregory, Peter Gahagan, Mary Helen. Began as actor, 1919; appeared in stock with Jessie Bonstelle; played in Free Soul, Jealousy, Tonight or Never, N.Y.C.; motion pictures include: As You Desire Me, She Married Her Boss, others; appeared in Time Out for Ginger, Broadway, cross country tour and Australia, 1953-55. Co-producer ex-G.I. hit mus. rev. Call Me Mister; actor, producer, dir. (motion pictures) Blandings Builds His Dream House, 1947, The Great Sinner, 1948, Carriage Entrance, 1949, On the Loose, 1951, Billy Budd, 1962, Hud, 1963 (recipient Acad. award for best supporting actor 1963); The Americanization of Emily, 1964; appeared in Rapture, 1965, Hotel, 1967, I Never Sang For My Father (nominated for Acad. award), 1970, One Is A Lonely Number, The Candidate, 1972, The Tenant, 1976, That's Entertainment, Part 2, 1976, Twilight's Last Gleaming, 1977; also (stage shows) Two Blind Mice, 1949, Bird Cage, 1950, Let Me Hear the Melody, 1951; Little Blue Light, 1951; Glad Tidings, 1951-52; Inherit the Wind, 1955-56; Waltz of the Toreadors, N.Y.C. and on tour; The Gang's All Here, 1959-60; The Best Man, 1960-61; appeared in Do Not Go Gentle Into the Night, CBS-TV, 1967, Spofford, on Broadway, 1967-68. Mem. follow-up program White House Conf. on Children in a Democracy, mem. State Relief Commn., State Dept. Soc. Welfare. Del. Nat. Conv., 1940; mem. nat. com. La Guardia-Norris Independent Voters Comm.; state chmn. (Cal.) Apptd. head Arts div. Office Civilian Def. Served from pvt. to maj. AUS, 1942-46; CBI. Recipient Tony award for best actor on Broadway, 1960. Mem. Players, Screen Actors Guild (dir.), Res. Officers Assn. Died Aug. 4, 1981.

DOUGLAS, WALTER SPALDING, civil engineer; b. Cranford, N.J., Jan. 22, 1912; s. Walter Jules and Elizabeth Appleton (Spalding) D.; m. Jean Gairdner Moment, May 6, 1938; children—David, Joanne, Nancy. Grad., Phillips Exeter Acad., 1929; B.A., Dartmouth, 1933; M.S. in Civil Engring, Harvard, 1935. Structural steel detailer Nashville Bridge Co., 1935-37; asst. to chief engr. N.Y. World's Fair, Inc., 1937-39; assoc. engr. Parsons, Brinckerhoff, Hall & Macdonald, N.Y., 1939-42, 46-52; partner Parsons, Brinckerhoff, Quade & Douglas, 1952-75, sr. partner, chmn. bd., 1966-75. Prin. works include responsibility for design, constrn. mgmt. San Francisco Bay Area, Atlanta Rapid Transit System, Caracas, Venezuela; design Combat Operations Center, N.Am. Air Def., Colo., Toledo Port Authority Marine Terminal. Trustee Hillside Cemetery, Plainfield, N.J.; bd. govs. Muhlenberg Hosp., Plainfield, 1950—, pres., 1958-59; bd. dirs. Newport (R.I.) Hosp., 1977-85. Served to lt. comdr. USNR, 1942-45. Recipient citation Engring. News-Record, 1966, Moles Assn. award for Outstanding Achievement in Constrn., 1970, hon. citation Newcomen Soc., 1975; inducted into Hall of Fame, Am. Pub. Transp. Assn., 1984. Fellow ASCE (James Laurie prize 1969, named one of ten outstanding men in constrn. of last 50 years 1975); mem. Am. Inst. Cons. Engrs. (past v.p.), Soc. Am. Mil. Engrs., Nat. Acad. Engring. Clubs: Dartmouth (N.Y.C.); Conanicut Yacht (Jamestown, R.I.). Home: Jamestown, R.I. Died Mar. 1985.

DOUGLASS, ALFRED EUGENE, mfg. exec.; b. Allentown, Pa., Jan. 16, 1888; s. William Merton and Helen Louise (Billings) D.; student Mercersburg (Pa.) Acad., 1906; m. Jean Melicent Ellis, Dec. 7, 1907 (dec.); children—Alfred Eugene, Donald Stoughton, Elizabeth Laurene (Mrs. Max Hess). Supr. Allentown Portland Cement Co., 1912-18, pres., dir., 1939-51, chmn., 1951-57, chmn. exec. com., 1957-61; mgr. crushing dept. Fuller-Lehigh Co., Fullerton, Pa., 1918-25; v.p., gen. mgr. Fuller Co., machinery mfrs., Catasaugua, 1926-29, pres., 1929-39, dir., chmn. exec. com., 1939-54, pres., 1954-57, chmn. bd., from 1957; dir. emeriti First Nat. Bank Allentown. Mem. C. of C., Am. Soc. Mech. Engrs. Republican. Episcopalian, Elk. Clubs: Livingston, Lehigh Country (Allentown); Catasauqua, Lehigh Valley Engineers. Home: Allentown, PA. †

DOVENMUEHLE, GEORGE HENRY, mortgage banker; b. Chgo., Jan. 29, 1895; s. Henry C. and Louise K. (Hoffman) D.; A.B., Yale, 1916; m. Mary E. Dyer, June 8, 1922; children—George Henry, Elizabeth D. Asst. mgr. H.F.C. Dovenmuehle & Son, wholesale shoes, Chgo. 1916-24; hon. chmn. Dovenmuehle, Inc., 1924-84; bd. dirs. Metropolitan Housing Council, Goodwill Industries. Served as capt. 344th Inf., U.S. Army, 1917-19. Mem. Mortgage Bankers Assn. Am. (past bd. dirs.), Chgo. Assn. Commerce and Industry (bd. dirs.), Chgo. Real Estate Bd. (v.p. 1935), Chgo. Mortgage Bankers Assn. (past pres.), Alpha Delta Phi. Republican. Conglist. Clubs: Chicago Athletic Assn., Indian Hill; Commercial. Home: Winnetka, Ill. Died Oct. 3, 1984.

DOW, FRANK, commr. of customs; b. Sangerville, Me., Feb. 8, 1888; s. James and Effie (Davis) D.; student U. Me.; m. Alice Packard, Sept. 1, 1913; children—Packard, Mary Ferry. With U.S. Customs Service from 1910, now commr. of customs. Home: Silver Spring, Md. †

DOW, GROVE SAMUEL, prof. sociology; b. Bowling Green, Mo., Oct. 7, 1888; s. Ernest Wentworth and Blanche (Hinman) D.; A.B., William Jewell Coll., Liberty, Mo., 1909; A.M., Brown U., 1911; studied Harvard and University of Chicago; m. Olive Brashers, of Bolivar, Mo., Aug. 17, 1914; children—Grove Samuel, Evelyn Hinman, John Brashers. Prof. history, Me. Central Inst., 1912-13; prof. sociology, Olivet (Mich.) Coll., 1914-18; prof. economics and sociology, U. of N.M., 1918-19; prof. sociology, Baylor U., 1919-22; same, U. of Denver, 1923-26; acting professor of sociology, W. Va. Univ., Jan.-Aug., 1927, asso. prof. 1927-29; prof. sociology State Teachers Coll., Springfield, Mo., from 1929. Mem. exec. com. Colo. Conf. Social Work. Lecturer, U. of Kansas summer 1919, U. of Texas, summer 1921. Mem., Am. Sociol. Soc., Am. Assn. Univ. Profs., Child Welfare League of America, Nat. Child Labor Com., Alpha Kappa Delta, etc. Democrat. Baptist. Clubs: University, Kiwanis (Springfield); City (Denver). Author: Introduction to the Principles of Sociology, 1920; Society and Its Problems, 1922; Social Problems of To-Day, 1925; Crime and Its Prevention, 1927. Home: Springfield, Mo. †

DOW, JAMES WILSON, physician, educator; b. Worcester, Mass., Sept. 8, 1917; s. Edwin Arthur and Lily (Caton) D.; m. Helen Louise Pollard, Mar. 10, 1945; children—Duncan, Kate; m. Beverly Anne Brooks, May 26, 1967; children—James Buchanan, Christian Davidson. B.S., Harvard, 1941; M.D., Tufts U., 1944. Intern R.I. Hosp., Providence, 1944-45; resident Lahey Clinic, Boston, 1945-46, House Good Samaritan, Brookline, Mass., 1946-47, Peter Bent Brigham Hosp., Boston, 1947-49, practice medicine specializing in cardiology and biomed. engring., 1948-58, Phila., 1958-62, Chgo., 1966-73, specializing in internal medicine, prospective cardiology, indsl. medicine, 1973-85; instr. medicine, dir. Circulation Lab., Children's Med. Center, Boston, 1949-51; asst. prof. medicine Tufts Med. Sch.; also dir. Circulation Lab., Boston City Hosp., 1953-58; adj. prof. med. sci., dir. biomed. engring. tng. program Drexel Inst. Tech., 1960-62; head biophys. scis. sect. tng. br. Nat. Inst. Gen. Med. Scis., NIH, 1962-66; prof. medicine U. Ill. Med. Center, 1966-70; prof. bioengring., head bioengring. program U. Ill. at Chgo. Circle Coll. Engring., 1966-85; prof. and chmn. biomed. engring. Rush Presbyn. St. Luke's Med. Center, Chgo., 1970-75, prof. medicine, 1970-85; Pres. Dow Med. Care, Inc., 1973-75; med. dir. Northwest Center for Early Disease Detection, Inc., Hoffman Estates, Ill., 1975-85. Home: Hanover Park, Ill. Died June 4, 1985; buried Hanover Park.

DOW, PETER STAUB, graphics and engring.; b. Knoxville, Tenn., Feb. 11, 1887; s. Samuel Billings and Marie (Aebli) D.; student U. of Tennessee, 1906-08; C.E., Dartmouth Coll., 1911; unmarried. Asst. supt., Hastings Pavement Co., New York, N.Y., 1911; field instr. surveying, Thayer Sch. of Civil Engring., Dartmouth Coll., 1910; instr. graphics and engring., Dartmouth Coll., 1912-17, asst. prof., 1917-25, prof. and head of department, 22 years, professor emeritus from June 1952; instructor Stevens Inst. Tech. summers 1912-14; inspector concrete highways, Portland Cement Mfrs., 1914; instr. in railroad construction Thayer Sch. of Civil Engring., 1917. Instr. in concrete and drafting, Dartmouth Coll. Training, Nat. Army, 1917, instr. in charge surveying and map making, 1918; instr. Dartmouth College V-12 Unit, 1943-45. Fellow Am. Assn. for Advancement of Sci., Royal Soc. Health; mem. Soc. Am. Mil. Engrs., S.A.R. (N.H. soc.), Am. Soc. C.E. (life), Dartmouth Society of Engineers (life), Am. Public Health Assn., Am. Assn. Univ. Profs., N.H. Acad. Sci., Phi Gamma Delta, Gamma Alpha. Address: Knoxville, Tenn. †

DOW, ROBERT C., lawyer; b. Seven Rivers, N.M., July 10, 1888; s. James Leslie and Mary (Neatherlin) D.; father a sheriff in N.M., in pioneer times; grad. N.M. Mil. Inst., Roswell, N.M., 1909; LL.B., Washington and Lee U., Lexington, Va., 1912; m. Florence Jessamine Henderson, June 2, 1915; children—Mary Frances, James Leslie. Admitted to N.M. bar, 1912, and began practice at Carlsbad; mem. N.M. Ho. of Rep., 1915; dist. atty. Fifth Jud. Dist. of N.M., 1917-21; atty. gen., N.M., 1927, 28; prosecuted 19 murder cases and secured 14 convictions; judge advocate gen. of N.M. Mem. N.M. Bar Assn. Democrat. Methodist. Mason, Odd Fellow, Woodman, Elk. Brought up a cowboy and has not forgotten how to use the lariat; won first prize in calf-roping contest, at Carlsbad, 1925, defeating 3 men, including the world-champion roper; invited to rope the first calf leaving the chute, at Chicago yearly contest, on New Mexico Day, 1927. Home: Santa Fe, N.M. †

DOWDEN, RAYMOND BAXTER, artist; b. Coal Valley, Pa., Dec. 25, 1905; s. Samuel Louis and Catherine (Baxter) D.; m. Anne Ophelia Todd, Apr. 1, 1934. B.A., Carnegie Inst. Tech., 1930; fellow, Tiffany Found., Oyster Bay, N.Y., 1931-32. Tchr. Cherry Lawn Sch., Darien, Conn., 1934-35, Carnegie Inst. Tech., 1930-33; part-time tchr. Manchester Ednl. Center, Pitts., 1930-33; tchr., pub. relations dir., 1928; trustee Starr Commonwealth for Boys, Albion, Mich., 1945-55; prof. art Cooper Union Sch. Art and Architecture, N.Y.C., 1936-70, head dept., 1945-67, prof. emeritus, 1970—; dir. Yale-Norfolk (Conn.) Art Sch., 1952-59. Designer, Westinghouse Electric Co., 1930, part-time designer, Petgen Stained Glass Co., Pitts., 1928-30; free-lance advt., design, illustration, 1936—, works exhibited, Dartmouth Coll., Manhattanville Coll., Purchase, N.Y., Pratt Inst., Bklyn., Hunt Bot. Library, Pitts., Soc. Ind. Artists, N.Y.C., G.R.D. Gallery, N.Y.C., Whitney Mus. Biennial, Internat. Water Color shows, Chgo., Elliott Gallery, Pitts., Carnegie Inst., Gulf Gallery, Pitts.; designer Murals for Westinghouse at, Chgo. Worlds Fair, 1933, Murals for, West Side Center, N.Y.C., stained glass windows, St. Mary's Ch., Homestead, Pa. Mem. Tau Sigma Delta. Home: New York City N.Y.

DOWDEY, CLIFFORD SHIRLEY, JR., author; b. Richmond, Va., Jan. 23, 1904; s. Clifford Shirley and Bessie (Bowis) D.: grad. John Marshall High Sch., Richmond, Va., 1921; student Columbia, 1923-25; Litt.D., Ripon Coll.; m. Frances Wilson. July 13, 1944 (dec. July 1970); children—Frances, Sarah; m. 2d, Carolyn De Camps, Sept. 9, 1971. Reporter, book reviewer Richmond News Leader, 1925-26; editorial staff Munseys and Argosy (mags.), book reviewer for N.Y. Sun, 1926-28, editor pulp mags. Dell Pub. Co., 1928-29, 1933-35; free lance writer, 1929-33, 35-79; lect. in creative writing U. Richmond; has lived in Va., Fla., Conn., Ariz., Tex., Calif., N.C. and N.Y.C., doing research and writing. Guggenheim fellow, 1938. Mem. Soc. Am. Historians. Episcopalian. Author books including: Bugles Blow No More (novel), 1937; (history) Experiment in Rebellion, 1946; Weep for My Brother (novel), 1950; (novel) Jasmine Street 1952; The Proud Retreat, 1953; (history) The Land They Fought For; The Story of the South as the Confederacy, 1832-1865, 1955; The Great Plantation, 1957; History: Death of a Nation, 1958; Lee's Last Campaign (history), 1960; The Wartime Papers of R.E. Lee (editor, writer), 1961; The Seven Days (history), 1964; Lee (1 vol. biography), 1965; The Virginia Dynasties (history), 1969; The Golden Age (history), 1970; (with Louis Manarin) The History of Henrico County, 1984. Contbr. to Saturday Rev., McCall's, Ladies Home Jour., Holiday, American Heritage, Atlantic Monthly, Ency. Brit. Author originals to motion pictures. Home: Richmond, Va. Died May 30, 1979; buried Hollywood Cemetery, Richmond, Va.

DOWDLE, WALTER REID, microbiologist; b. Irvington, Ala., Dec. 11, 1930; s. Ruble Charles and Rebecca (Powell) D.; m. Mabel Irene Graham, Apr. 2, 1953; children—Greta Denise Dowdle Rackley, Robert Reid, Jennifer Leigh. B.S., U. Ala., 1955, M.S., 1957; Ph.D., U. Md., 1960. Tech. asst. U. Ala., 1953-55, research asst., 1955-57, U. Md., 1957-60; with respiratory virology unit Center for Disease Control, Atlanta, 1960-72, dir. virology div., from 1973; dir. WHO Collaborating Center for Influenza and Collaborating Center for Virus Reference and Research; mem. expert adv. panel on virus diseases WHO, from 1966; asso. prof. Sch. Pub. Health, U. N.C., from 1964; asso. mem. com. on influenza Armed Forces Epidemiology Bd., from 1969; chmn. orthomyxovirus study group Internat. Commn. for Nomenclature of Viruses, from 1971; mem. U.S. influenza del. to USSR, 1974, 76; coordinator U.S.-USSR Collaborative Agreement on Influenza and Acute Respiratory Diseases, from 1974; mem. virology task force NIAID, NIH, from 1976. Mem. editorial bd.: Jour. Clin. Microbiology, from 1974; mem. editorial com.: Ann. Rev. Microbiology, from 1976. Served with USAF, 1948-52. WHO hon. fellow, dept. microbiology John Curtin Sch. for Med. Research, Australian Nat. U., Canberra, 1972-73. Fellow Am. Acad. Microbiology; mem. Am. Soc. Microbiology, Infectious Disease Soc. Am., Soc. for Exptl. Biology and Medicine, AAAS, Sigma Xi. Home: Atlanta, GA.

DOWLER, FRANCIS WALTON, lawyer; b. London, Ont., Can., June 19, 1917; s. Robert Henry and Margaret Katherine (Peart) D.; m. Dorothy Louise Davis, July 7, 1951; children—Sandra Margaret Louise, Sheila Bernice, Daphne Louise. B.A. with honours in Bus, U. Western Ont., 1941; grad., Osgoode Hall Law Sch., 1944. Bar: called to bar Ont 1944, named Queen's counsel 1959. Read law with Fraser, Beatty, Tucker, McIntosh & Stewart, 1941-44; practice in, London, 1947-81; ptnr. Ivey & Dowler, 1951-81. Mem. Delta Upsilon. Mem. United Ch. of Can. Clubs: London, London Hunt and Country. Home: London, Ont., Canada. Dec. June 16, 1981.

DOWNS, CHARLES RAYMOND, consulting chem. engr.; b. New Haven, Conn., Mar. 17, 1888; s. Walter Root and Lillian Gay (Burwell) D.; Ph.B., Sheffield Scientific Sch., Yale University, 1909, Ph.D., 1912; children—Walter Burwell, Carolyn Clifford (Mrs. George Burnett). Lab. instr. chemistry, Sheffield Sci. Sch., 1909-12; research chemist Barrett Co., Edgewater, N.J., 1912-17, chief chemist research dept., 1917-22; chem. engr. charge spl. development Nat. Aniline & Chem. Co., Buffalo, 1922; v.p., sec. Weiss & Downs, Incorporated; N.Y. City, 1923-44; pres. Chemists Building Co. of New York, 1944-45; president and director The Calorider Corp., Stamford, Conn., 1937-64; consulting chem. engr. since 1943. Mem. Referee Bd. Office Prodn. Research and Devel. WPB, 1942-44; cons. Army Corps Engrs., 1948-51. Registered profl. engr., N.J. Awarded Howard N. Potts gold medal, Franklin Inst., Phila., 1922; Grasselli gold medal, Am. Sec. of Soc. Chem. Industry, London, 1926. Mem. Am. Inst. Chemical Engrs. (past dir., rep. on Com. for Econ. Development 1945-46), Am. Chem. Soc. (past councillor, chmn. N.Y. sect. 1928; chmn. Nichols Medal Jury of Award 1929; chmn. Western Conn. sect. 1936), Soc. Chem. Industry of London (exec. com. Am. sect. 1939-42), Am. Inst. City of N.Y. (bd. mgrs. 1932-35, 1945-49, council of awards, 1940-43), Am. Inst. Chemists, Am. Assn. Advancement Sci., National, Connecticut societies of professional engineers, Yale Engring. Association, Sigma Xi, Alpha Chi Sigma. Independent Republican. Conglist. Mason (32 deg., K.T.). Clubs: Yale, Chemists of N.Y. (pres. 1944-45, v.p. 1926-28, 1939-40, trustee 1926-32, 39-44, hon. trustee, chmn. symporiarchs 1936-38). Author: The Technical Organization—Its Development and Administration, 1924. Occasional contbr. to sci. publs. Patentee. Home: Verona, N.J. †

DOWNS, JAMES CHESTERFIELD, JR., property mgmt.; b. Des Moines, Oct. 18, 1905; s. James Chesterfield and Frieda (Braun) D.; student U. Ill., 1923-25; D.C.S., U. Fla., 1952; m. Florence Finn, June 20, 1929; children—James Anthony, Carolyn, Suzanna. Asso. Edward C. Waller, Chgo., 1926-28; mgr. property mgmt. Baird & Warner, 1929-31; with Foreman Nat. Bank, 1931; founder, former chmn., of counsel Real Estate Research Corp.; mgr. br. office Draper & Kramer, 1931-33; v.p. Dayton Keith & Co., Chgo., 1933-38; spl. lectr. univs. Fla., Leland Stanford, Notre Dame; dir. Chgo. Title & Trust Co. Housing and redevel. coordinator City of Chgo., 1954-57; chmn. lay bd. consultors Mercy Hosp. Trustee U. Chgo., 1957-81. Mem. Chgo. Assn. Commerce and Industry (dir.), Inst. Real Estate Mgmt. (pres. 1938-39), Theta Chi. Democrat. Roman Catholic. Clubs: Commerical (pres. 1960), Mid-America, Economic (pres. 1959), Chicago (Chgo.). Author: Principles of Real Estate Management, 1950. Home: Geneva, Ill. Died Oct. 26, 1981.

DOWNS, SYLVESTER DEWITT, army officer; b. Greenville, Pa., Feb. 28, 1889; s. Sylvester Day and Mary Hannah (Goldinger) D.; student, Thiel Coll., Greenville, Pa., 1909, B.S., U.S. Mil. Acad., 1914; grad. F.A. Sch., Ft. Sill, Okla., 1925; honor grad., Command and Gen. Staff Sch., 1927; m. Evelyn Murphy, Feb. 1, 1916; children—Katherine Evelyn (Mrs. Chester L. Johnson), Mary Elizabeth. Commd. 2d lt., Cav., 1914, and advanced thru the grades to brig. gen., 1943; cavalry officer, 1914-18, F.A., 1918-43; with Am. forces in Germany, 1921-22; instr. F.A. Sch., 1923-26; Gen. Staff Corps, 1929-32; instr. N.Y. Nat. Guard, 1932-35, Command and Gen. Staff Sch., 1935-39. Home: Greenville, Pa. †

DOWNS, THOMAS JOSEPH, lawyer; b. Terre Haute, Ind., Mar. 7, 1904; s. James Edward and Mary Gertrude (Cannon) D.; m. Frances M. Mayrose, June 2, 1931; children—Sara Ann (Mrs. Eugene P. O'Brien), Ellen (Mrs. Daniel de la Torre). Student, Ind. State U., 1922-23; J.D., Georgetown U., 1928. Bar: Ill., D.C. bars. Partner Downs & Scheib, 1942-50, Downs, Johnson & Zahler, Chgo. and Washington, 1950-53, Thomas J. Downs, Chgo. and Washington, 1953-70, Downs & Pierce, 1970-83; pub. adminstr., Cook County, 1957-62; mem., pres. Med. Center Commn., 1953-73. Asst. atty. gen. Ill., 1968—; Del. Republican Nat. Conv., 1940, 48, 56, 60, 68, 76; Rep. nominee 2d Ill. Dist. U.S. Congress, 1942, 44. Recipient 175th Anniversary medal of Honor Georgetown U. Sch. Law, 1964. Mem. Am., Ill., Chgo. bar assns., Bar Assn. 7th Fed. Circuit, Am. Judicature Soc., Delta Chi. Clubs: Union League (Chgo.), Executives (Chgo.), Press (Chgo.). Home: Chicago, Ill. Dec. Mar. 25, 1983.

DOYLE, ROBERT EMMETT, association executive; b. Washington, July 11, 1915. Student, George Washington U. With Nat. Geog. Soc., Washington, 1934-80, asst. sec., 1951-58, assoc. sec. for membership, 1958-61, v.p., 1961-67, v.p. and sec., 1967-76, trustee, 1975-84, pres., 1976-80, vice chmn. bd., 1980-84. Served in U.S. Army, World War II. Address: Washington, D.C. Dec. Mar. 20, 1984.

DRACH, EDMUND L., chem. exec.; b. Chgo., Jan. 5, 1887; s. Edmund A. and Emilie (Diecke) D.; LL.B., Chgo. Kent Coll. Law, 1912; m. Agnes Mabel Johnson, Jan. 29, 1919; children—Aurie Jane (Mrs. Lester Hornbrook), Lois Marjorie. Joined Purch, Abbott Labs., North Chicago, 1910, v.p. from 1947, dir. since 1930. Mem. Nat. Assn. Purchasing Agts., Chgo. Perfumery, Soap & Extract Assn., Inc., Chgo. Drug and Chem. Assn. (pres. 1933-34), Phi Delta Phi. Republican. Methodist. Mason. Clubs: Chicago Athletic; Evanston Golf. Home: Wilmette, Ill. †

DRAKE, GEORGE LINCOLN, forest cons.; b. Laconia, N.H., Apr. 7, 1889; s. Benjamin F. and Mary (Drowne) D.; student N.H.U., 1908-09; B.S., Penn State Coll., 1912; m. Dora A. Polley, Oct. 15, 1915; 1 dau., Barbara (Mrs. William H. Collins, Jr.). Employed U.S. Forest Service, Alaska, Ore. and Wash., 1912-30; joined Simpson Loggins Co., Shelton, Wash., 1930, v.p., 1946-53; forest consultant, Tacoma, Washington. President Pacific Logging Congress, 1937. Trustee Wash. Forest Fire Assn. Recipient Testimonial award, Wash. State Coll. Mem. Western Forestry and Conservation Assn. (pres. 1944), Soc. Am. Foresters (pres. 1952-53). Theta Chi, Alpha Zeta, Xi Sigma Pi. Mason. Home: Shelton, Wash. †

DRAKE, ROBERT TUCKER, lawyer; b. Wilmette, Ill., Feb. 16, 1907; S. Lyman and Jennie M. (Keith) D.; m. Martha B. Swan, Sept. 14, 1929; children—Janet D. (Mrs. Robert H. Morris), Helen (Mrs. John E. Sanford). A.B., Dartmouth, 1929; LL.B., Columbia, 1934. Bar: N.Y. bar 1934, D.C. bar 1935, Ill. bar 1937. Practiced in, Washington, 1934-36, Chgo., 1937-42, 49-82; assoc. firm Alden, Latham & Young, Chgo., 1937-42; atty. NLRB, Chgo., 1942-47; mem. firm Foss, Schuman & Drake, Chgo., 1960-82; assoc. prof. law U. Idaho, Moscow, 1947-49; labor arbitrator, from 1982. Bd. dirs. Sierra Club Legal Def. Fund, 1977-82. Mem. Ams. for Democratic Action (dir.), World Without War Council (dir. Chgo.), ACLU (chmn. div. 1954-57), Internat. Peace Acad. (U.S. com. 1973—), UN Assn. Chgo. (v.p. div. 1975-82). Clubs: University (Wis.), Wausaukee (Wis.); Skokie (Ill.); Country; Cliff Dwellers (Chgo.), Literary (Chgo.). Home: Winnetka IL Office: Chicago IL

DRESSER, LAURENCE L., engr.; b. Litchfield, Mich., Aug. 4, 1895; s. Niles E. and Lou G. (Sherk) D.; B.S., Tri-State Coll., 1923, LL.D., 1951; m. La Vera L. McAllister, Dec. 29, 1915 (dec. Jan. 1946); children—Robert Mac, Doris L. (Mrs. Roehm A. West, Jr.), James M.; m. 2d, Mrs. Georgina McClain, Sept. 28, 1954. Founder, former chmn. bd. Dresser Engring. Co., Tulsa. Registered profl. engr., Okla., Tex., Kans., La., Ark., N.M. Mem. Nat. (past pres.), Okla. (past pres.) socs. profl. engrs., Tulsa C. of C., Sigma Tau (hon.), Tau Beta Pi. Mason (Shriner, Jester), Rotarian. Clubs: Farm, Knife and Fork, Engineers. Headliners, Southern Hills Tulsa (Tulsa); Engineers of Dallas, Chapparal, Dallas. Home: Tulsa, Okla. Died Dec. 19, 1980.

DREVLOW, WILLIAM EDWARD, lt. gov. Ida.; b. Round Prairie, Minn., Jan. 23, 1890; s. Fred and Anna (Helmbrecht) D.; student pub. schs., Minn.; m. Adaphenia Heinrich, Jan. 17, 1913; children—Maurice W., Raymond D. Creamery operator, Eldred, Minn., 1908-09; with Bates & Rogers Constrn. Co., 1910-14; mech. engr. constrn. dams Mont. Power Co., 1914-17, Northwest Electric Co., Portland, 1917-19; farmer, Tekoa, Wash., 1919-24, Craigmont, Ida., from 1943; locomotive crane operator Potlach Forests, Lewiston, 1925-43; chmn. Union Warehouse & Mercantile Co. Mem. Ida. Ho. of Reps., 1947, 51, 53, Ida. Senate, 1955, 57; lt. gov. Ida., from 1959. Democrat. Lutheran (council 1932-38). Club: Idaho Flying Legislators (organizer, sec. 1947, pres. 1953). Home: Craigmont, Ida. †

DREW, THOMAS BRADFORD, educator, chem. engr.; b. Medford, Mass., Feb. 9, 1902; s. Henry Jay Washburn and Henrietta Cook (Cole) D.; S.B., Mass. Inst. Tech., 1923, S.M., 1924; m. Alice Wait, June 9, 1930; children—Mary, Emilie, Sarah. Instr. chem. engring. Drexel Inst., 1925-28, Mass. Inst. Tech., 1929-34; research and design chem. engr. E.I. du Pont de Nemours & Co., Wilmington, Del., 1934-40, cons., 1950-62; asso. prof. chem. engring. Columbia, 1940-45, prof., 1945-65, exec. officer, 1948-57; vis. prof. chem. engring. Mass. Inst. Tech., 1959-60, prof. chem. engring., 1965-67, prof. emeritus, 1967-85; cons. Ford Found., New Delhi, 1962, 63, 66; Ford Found. program specialist Birla Inst. Tech. and Sci., New Delhi, India, 1964-65; with Nat. Def. Research Com. (sect. XI), 1941-43, also Manhattan Dist. Projects, SAM Labs., 1943, TNX div. E.I. du Pont de Nemours & Co., 1943-44; cons. Brookhaven Nat. Labs., Upton, L.I., N.Y., 1947-72, mem. adv. com. on phys. sci., 1947-48, chmn. adv. com. on engring., 1947-55; mem. com. sr. reviewers AEC, 1952-57. Fellow N.Y. Acad. Sci., A.A.A.S., Am. Inst. Chem. Engrs. (William H. Walker award 1937, Max Jakob Meml. award 1967); mem. Mass. Soc. of Cin. (v.p. 1975-77, pres. 1977—), ASME (hon.; Max Jakob Meml. award 1967), Am. Chem. Soc., Sigma Xi, Phi Lambda Upsilon, Tau Beta Pi, Theta Tau. Democrat. Unitarian. Club: Chemists (N.Y.C.). Author: Vector and Polyadic Analysis; also author of papers on chem. engring. Editor: Advances in Chemical Engineering. Home: Peterborough, N.H. Died May 5, 1985.

DREWES, WERNER, painter, graphic artist; b. Canig, Germany, July 27, 1899; came to U.S., 1925, naturalized, 1936; s. Georg and Martha (Schaefer) D.; m. Margaret Schrobsdorff, 1924 (dec. 1959); children: Harold, Wolfram, Bernard; m. Mary Lischer, 1960. Student, Bauhaus, Dessau, Germany, 1927. Traveled in, Italy, Spain, S.Am., U.S., Japan, Korea, Russia, 1923-27; tchr. fine arts Columbia U., N.Y.C., 1937-40, Bklyn. Coll., 1945, Sch. of Design, Chgo., 1946, Washington U., St. Louis, 1947-65. Represented in collections in pub. libraries in, Newark, N.Y.C., Boston, Honolulu Acad., Yale and Washington U., art mus. in, St. Louis, Chgo., Bklyn., Phila., San Francisco, Fogg Mus., Boston, Mus. Modern Art, N.Y.C., Library of Congress, Washington, Victoria and Albert Mus., London, Nat. Gallery Am. Art, Nat. Gallery, Washington, Guggenheim Mus., Met. Mus., N.Y.C., and, others. Home: Reston, Va. Died June 21, 1985.

DREWRY, JOHN ELDRIDGE, educator; b. Griffin, Ga., June 4, 1902; s. Judson Ellis and Verdi May (Harrell) D.; m. Kathleen Merry, Dec. 24, 1925 (div. 1949); 1 child,

Milton Lee (dec.); m. Miriam Thurmond, Mar. 16, 1950. A.B., U. Ga., 1921, B.J., 1922, A.M., 1925; postgrad., Columbia U., summer 1924, 25. Reporter, news editor Athens (Ga.) Banner-Herald, 1921-23, book reviewer, from 1923; corr. book reviewer Atlanta Jour., 1921-39; book reviewer Atlanta Constn., from 1939; corr. Christian Sci. Monitor, 1927-40; instr. journalism Henry W. Grady Sch. Journalism, U. Ga., Athens, 1922-24, adj. prof., 1924-26, assoc. prof., 1926-30, prof., from 1930, dir., dean, 1940-69, dean emeritus, 1969-83, organizer press bur., 1921, publicity dir., 1921-28, 1930-32; asso. editor Henry W. Grady Sch. Journalism, U. Ga. (Alumni Record), 1925-39; lectr. journalism Lucy Cobb Inst., 1925-26; state mail editor A.P., Atlanta, summer 1926; editor Univ. Items, summers 1927-32; organizer, univ. dir. Ga. Scholastic Press Assn.; univ. adminstr. George Foster Peabody Radio and TV Awards, Ga. Radio and TV Inst., Ga. Press. Inst., So. Indsl. Editors Inst., Edn.-Industry Confs. Pub. Relations and Advt.; first sec., nat. joint com. profl. edn. for journalism; mem. exec. com., formerly mem. Council on Research in Jour., AASDJ. Author, co-author, editor books, 1924-83, including, Concerning the Fourth Estate, 1938, Post Biographies of Famous Journalists, 1942, Book Reviewing, 1946, More Post Biographies, 1947, Journalism at Mid-Century, 1950, Journalism Enters a New Half Century, 1951, New Horizons in Journalism, 1952, Advancing Journalism, 1953, Journalism Is Communications, 1954, Dimensional Journalism, 1955, Communications Problems and Progress, 1956, Communications: Key to So Much, 1957, The What, Why, and How of Communications, 1958, Are We Communicating? , 1959, Attaining Goals via Better Communications, 1960, Onward and Upward with Communications, 1961, Diagnosis and Prognosis in Journalism, 1962, Better Journalism for a Better Tomorrow, 1963, Communications Cartography, 1964, Higher Ground for Journalism, 1965, Writing Book Reviews, 1966, Greater Communications Effectiveness, 1966, A Forward Look for Communications, 1967, Journalistic Escalation, 1968, New Heights for Journalism, 1969; Contbr.: book column Publishers Auxiliary; syndicated book rev. column New Book News; articles to mags. Mem. Ga. Bicentennial Commn., 1933. Lt. col. staff Gov. Ellis Arnall. Named to Dixie Bus. Hall of Fame for Living; also recipient Distinguished Service award, 1954; recipient gold key award Columbia Sch. Press Assn., 1954; plaque Internat. Council Indsl. Editors, 1966; Distinguished Service awards U. Ga. Alumni Soc., 1969; Distinguished Service awards Ga. Press Assn., 1969; Distinguished Service awards Ga. Assn. Broadcasters, 1969. Mem. Am. Assn. Tchrs. Journalism (pres. 1930), Am. Council Edn. Journalism, Ga. Edn. Assn., Newcomen Soc., Phi Beta Kappa (pres. U. Ga. chpt. 1948-49), Phi Kappa Phi, Sigma Delta Chi, Kappa Tau Alpha (nat. pres. 1958-60), Omicron Delta Kappa, Digamma Kappa, Kappa Alpha (So.), Phi Eta Sigma, Blue Key Council. Democrat. Baptist (chmn. deacons 1946-47). Clubs: Rotarian (past pres.), Gridiron. Home: Athens, Ga. Dec. Feb. 11, 1983.

DREXEL, ROGER EDWARD, chem. co. exec.; b. Rochester, N.Y., Feb. 10, 1920; s. Edward Anthony and May Rose (Laemmel) D.; m. Rose A. Kracsun, Jan. 14, 1950; 1 dau., Suzanne Louise Drexel Sensing. B.S. in Chem. Engring, U. Rochester, 1941; Sc.D., M.I.T., 1944, Ch.E., 1946. With E.I. duPont de Nemours & Co., Wilmington, Del., from 1944, v.p. plastic products and resins, 1979-80, v.p. polymer products, from 1980. Mem. Am. Chem. Soc., Am. Inst. Chem. Engrs., Phi Beta Kappa, Sigma Xi.

DRICK, JOHN EDWARD, ret. bankers; b. Williamsport, Pa., Nov. 26, 1911; s. George R. and Charlotte (Quinn) D.; grad. Phillips Acad., Andover, Mass., 1930; B.S., Sheffield Sci. Sch., Yale, 1934; m. Caroline Whitehead, Mar. 14, 1936; children—Judith (Mrs. Toland), George Randall, Helen (Mrs. Peter Hayes). With First Nat. Bank, Chgo., 1935-77, v.p. petroleum and term loan div., 1951-64, sr. v.p. charge term loan div., 1964-65, exec. v.p., 1965-69, pres., 1969-74, chmn. exec. com., 1974-77, hon. dir. to 1982; dir. Stepan Chem. Co., MCA, Inc., Outdoor Sports Industries, Inc., Oak Industries, Central Ill. Pub. Service Co. Clubs: Chicago, Commercial Jupiter Hills; Exmoor. Died Feb. 16, 1982.

DRINKWATER, TERRELL CROFT, ret. air transportation exec.; b. Denver, July 15, 1908; s. Ray Lawrence and Geraldine (Croft) D.; A.B., Univ. of Colo., 1930; LL.B., 1932, LL.M., 1933; m. Helen Louise Kiddoo, Sept. 5, 1933; children—Terrell Thomas, Dorsey Ann. Practiced law in Denver, specializing aeronautical law, 1933-42; exec. vice pres., dir., gen. mgr. Continental Air Lines, Inc., 1942-44; vice pres., Am. Airlines, Inc., 1944-47; v.p., dir., Am. Overseas Airlines, Inc., 1945-47; pres., dir., Western Airlines, Inc., 1947-70; dir. Southern Cal. Edison Co., Union Bank, Los Angeles, Pacific Mut. Life Ins. Co., Los Angeles. Cons. to United States delegation in negotiation of internat. air pacts with United Kingdom at Bermuda, 1946. Mem. Colo. State Aeronautics com., 1938-42. Dir. Los Angeles chpt. A.R.C.; director YMCA. Mem. Air Transport Assn. Am. (mem. bd. dirs. 1942-44, 47-48, 53-54, 59-60, 67-68), Los Angeles C. of C. (pres. 1952), Am. Bar Assn., Chi Psi, Phi Delta Phi. Republican, Presbyterian. Clubs: University (Colo.); Burning Tree (Washington); California, Los Angeles Country. Died Jan. 5, 1985.

DRISCOLL, EDGAR J(OSEPH), govt. ofcl.; b. Chelsea, Mass., Jan. 2, 1890; s. John H. and Julia A. (Crowley) D.; student pub. schs. Boston; m. Katharine E. Rooney, July 21, 1917; children—John, Edgar, Philip, Katharine (Mrs. Richard C. Withington), Sheila (Mrs. Ingersol Cunningham), William, Robert. Entered investment bus., 1907; v.p. A.B. Conant Co., Inc., 1921-36; sole propr. Edgar J. Driscoll & Co., investments-analyses; pres., dir. Nat. Appraisal Co.; dir. Lessells Assos., Scully Signal Co. Dir. Boston Municipal Research Bureau. Chief consumers sect. Region 5 Civilian Def., Greater Boston, 1941; regional dir. rent control for N.E. states, 1942-54; mem. Unpaid Spl. Commn. to study paroles and pardons systems of Mass.; chmn. A.R.C. Served as lt., 99th Aero Squadron, A.S., Zone of Advance A.E.F., 1918-19. Mem. Am. Irish Hist. Soc. K.C. Clubs: Downtown, Clover (Boston). Home: West Roxbury, Mass. †

DRISCOLL, MARGARET WEYERHAEUSER (MRS. WALTER BRIDGES DRISCOLL), church and assn. exec.; b. Cloquet, Minn., Oct. 20, 1902; d. Rudolph M. and Louise B. (Lindeke) Weyerhaeuser; m. Walter Bridges Driscoll, Nov. 27, 1926 (dec. 1937); children—Walter John, Rudolph W. B.A., Vassar Coll., 1923; L.H.D., Macalester Coll., 1948, Westminster Coll., Pa., 1958, Coll. of Santa Fe, 1973, U. So. Calif., 1978. Past bd. mgrs., treas., fin. chmn. Ch. Women United; trustee emeritus Macalester Coll., St. Paul; former v.p. United Presbyn. Found.; bd. dirs., past pres. Child Welfare League Am.; chmn. Christian Ministry in Nat. Parks; trustee, v.p. Opera Assn. N.Mex., Nat. Ghost Ranch Found., Abiquiu, N.Mex. Pres., trustee Santa Fe Opera Found.; trustee Sch. of Am. Research, Santa Fe; trustee emeritus Presbyn. Hosp. Center, Albuquerque, Mus. of N.Mex. Found.; past chmn., trustee emeritus St. John's Coll., Santa Fe; past mem. bd. regents N.Mex. Highlands U., Las Home: Santa Fe, NM.

DROHAN, THOMAS EDWARD, food company executive; b. Newton, Mass., Dec. 1, 1927; s. Francis Edward and Marie R. (Scully) D.; m. Sabra Elizabeth Kent, Nov. 21, 1956; children: Thomas Edward, Sabra Elizabeth, Michele Marie, Daniel Kent. Student, Sorbonne, U. Paris, 1948; B.A. cum laude, Harvard U., 1949. Nat. advt. and promotion mgr. Best Foods, N.Y.C., 1950-55; product mgr. Lever Bros., N.Y.C., 1955-59; sales and mktg. mgr. Manteca Canning Co., San Francisco, 1959-61; with Foremost Dairies, Inc., San Francisco, 1961-70, gen. mgr. div. grocery products, mktg. v.p., to 1970; v.p., gen. mgr. food products div. Foremost Foods Co., 1970, pres., to 1976; with Foremost-McKesson, Inc. (now McKesson Corp.), San Francisco, 1967-84, exec. v.p., 1976-77; pres., chief exec. officer Foremost-McKesson, Inc.(now McKesson Corp.), 1978-84; also dir. Foremost-McKesson, Inc. (now McKesson Corp.); dir. Calif. Can. Bank, San Francisco. Mem. Rockefeller U. Council; mem. bd. overseers, com. on univ. resources Harvard U.; bd. dirs. Hospice of Marin, San Rafael, Calif., mem. fund-raising and long-range objectives coms.; bd. dirs. sec. Tiburon (Calif.) Found. Served to 1st lt. Signal Corps, U.S. Army. Recipient Martin Luther King Jr. Humanitarian award, 1979. Mem. Calif. State C. of C. (dir.), Advt. Council (dir.), Grocery Mfrs. Am. (dir.). Clubs: The Links (N.Y.C.); Olympic (San Francisco). Home: Greenbrae, Calif. Dec. May 4, 1984.*

DRUMMOND, ROSCOE, columnist; b. Theresa, N.Y., Jan. 13, 1902; s. John Henry and Georgia Estella (Peppers) D.; m. Charlotte Bruner, Sept. 11, 1926 (dec.); 1 child, Geoffrey (dec.); m. Carol Cramer, June 1, 1978. B.S.J., Syracuse U., 1924; Litt.D., Dartmouth Coll., 1947; D.H.L. (hon.), Principia Coll., Elsah, Ill.; LL.D., Syracuse U., 1955; postgrad., Ricker Coll., 1962. Reporter for Christian Sci. Monitor, Boston, 1924, continuing as asst. city editor, asst. to exec. editor, chief editorial writer, European editorial mgr., gen. news editor, mem. editorial bd., exec. editor, 1934-40; chief Washington News Bur., 1940-53; creator State of the Nation; on leave as dir. infor. ECA in Europe, Paris, 1949-51; chief Washington Bur. N.Y. Herald Tribune, 1953-55; and author syndicated column Washington; now Washington columnist for Los Angeles Times Syndicate and; Christian Sci. Monitor. Author: (with Gaston Coblentz) Duel at the Brink, 1960; Contbr. to (with Gaston Coblentz) Am. and Brit. mags.; lectr. (with Gaston Coblentz). Trustee Freedom House, 1962-67. Recipient prize for best editorial pub. in an Am. newspaper on significance of Internat. Press Exhbn. at Cologne, 1928; George Arents award for proficiency in journalism, 1946. Mem. Am. Soc. Newspaper Editors, Alpha Kappa Psi, Sigma Phi Epsilon, Beta Gamma Sigma, Sigma Delta Chi. Clubs: Gridiron (Washington), Overseas Writers (Washington), Nat. Press (Washington), Cosmos (Washington); Masons. Address: McLean, Va. Dec. Sept. 30, 1983.

DRUMMOND, W(ILLIAM) R(EXFORD), communications exec.; b. Sullivan, Ind., Nov. 6, 1890; s. Robert S. and Nannie (Hinckley) D.; student Internat. Corr. Schs., 1906-09; m. Roberta A. Jones, Jan. 1, 1913; 1 son, William Robert. With Western Union Telegraph Co., N.Y.C., from 1909, beginning as Morse operator and office mgr., successively chief bookkeeper and traveling auditor, div. auditor and asst. auditor, gen. supr. methods and asst. comptroller, 1909-52, became controller, 1952, retired as vice pres. and controller, 1957; pres., dir. Franklin Telegraph Co. (Mass.), The Gold & Stock Telegraph Co. (N.Y.), Internat. Ocean Telegraph Co. (N.Y.), Phila. Local Telegraph Co. (Pa.), Am. Union Telegraph Co. (N.J., Pa.), Empire & Bay States Telegraph Co. (N.Y.), Havana District Telegraph Co. of Cuba, Lynchburg & Abingdon Telegraph Co (Va.), N.Y. Mutual Telegraph Co. (N.Y.), Pacific & Atlantic Telegraph Co. of U.S. (Pa.), Southern & Atlantic Telegraph Co. (N.Y.), Washington & New Orleans Telegraph Co. (Va.) Ocean Telegraph Co. (Mass.), Western Union Distbn. Service, Inc. (N.Y.); v.p., dir. Western Union Services, Inc. (N.Y.) Internat. Telegraph Co. (Me.). Home: Hampton, N.J. †

DRUSHAL, JOHN GARBER, ret. coll. pres.; b. Lost Creek, Ky., July 16, 1912; s. George Emery and Ada (Garber) D.; A.B., Ashland Coll., 1935, LL.D., 1969; M.A., Ohio State U., 1938, Ph.D., 1951; L.H.D., Coll. of Wooster, 1977, Wittenberg U., 1977; m. Dorothy Loree Whitted, June 12, 1938; children—Michael, Jane (dec.), Richard, Douglas. Instr., Ashland Coll., 1936-37, U. Mo., 1938-39; asst. prof. Capital U., 1939-46; prof. Coll. of Wooster (Ohio), 1946-63, dean of coll., 1963-66, dean, v.p. acad. affairs, 1966-67, acting pres., 1967-68, pres., 1968-77. Instr. summers Bowling Green State U., 1941, U. Mo., 1942, Queens Coll., 1948; dir. Citizens Nat. Bank. Pres., Wooster City Council, 1960-70. Trustee Ashland Coll.; v.p. trustee Ohio Retirement Homes at Wooster. Mem. AAUP (past chpt. pres.), Speech Assn. Am., Acad. Polit. Sci., Central States Speech Assn. (past. sec.), Ohio Assn. Coll. Tchrs. Speech (past sec., pres.), Ohio Assn. Speech and Hearing Therapists (past pres.), Ohio Coll. Assn. (past exec. sec., past pres.), Wooster Auto Club (dir.), Delta Sigma Rho (past nat. v.p.; Distinguished Alumni award 1973). Presbyterian. Club: Rotary (past pres. Wooster). Author: (with Bonthius, Davis) The Independent Study Program in the United States, 1957. Home: Lakeville, Ohio. Died Dec. 3, 1982.

DUBIN, ISADORE NATHAN, pathologist; b. Montreal, Que., Can., July 13, 1913; s. Moses Labe and Sarah (Mettarlin) D.; m. Alberta Simkevitz, June 21, 1940 (div. May 1969); children: Mary Louise, Elizabeth Simone, William Lyle. B.Sc., McGill U., 1935; M.D., 1939. Diplomate: Am. Bd. Pathology. Intern medicine Royal Victoria Hosp., Montreal, 1939; asst. resident, resident pathology St. Luke's Hosp., Cleve., 1940-42; asst. resident pathology Duke Hosp., Durham, N.C., 1942-44, asst. pathologist, 1944-45; attendant pathologist John Gaston Hosp., Memphis, 1945-49; pathologist, prof. pathology Women's Med. Coll. Hosp., Phila., 1955-85; chief pathology service Phila. Gen. Hosp., 1955-66; cons. pathology VA Hosp., Phila., 1955-85; asst. pathology Duke U., Durham, 1942-43, instr., 1943-44, asso. pathology, 1944-45; asst. prof. pathology U. Tenn. Coll. Medicine, Memphis, 1945-48, asso. prof., 1948-49; spl. lectr. U. Miss., 1948-49; spl. research fellow Nat. Cancer Inst., Bethesda, Md., 1949-50, Nat. Heart Inst., U. Berne, Switzerland, 1970; chief hepatic pathology sect. Armed Forces Inst. Pathology, 1951-55; lectr. pathology U.S. Naval Hosp., Phila., 1961-85; mem. ad hoc com. isoniazid and liver disease Center for Disease Control, USPHS, 1971-72; cons. NRC, 1963-67, EPA, 1976-78. Contbr. articles to med. jours. Served to maj. M.C. U.S. Army, 1951-53. Fellow A.C.P., AAAS; mem. Am. Assn. Pathologists and Bacteriologists, Am. Soc. Exptl. Pathology, Am. Assn. Study Liver Diseases, Internat. Acad. Pathology, Am. Osler Soc., Path. Soc. Phila. Home: Wynnewood, Pa. Deceased.

DUBINSKY, DAVID, labor leader; b. Brest-Litovsk, Poland, Feb. 22, 1892; s. Zallel and Shaine (Wishingrad) D.; ed. Zionist and Knoshtat schs., Poland and evening schs., N.Y.C.; LL.D. (hon.), Columbia, 1968; m. Emmal Goldberg, 1915; 1 dau., Jeannette. Came to U.S., 1911, naturalized, 1916. Baker's apprentice, Poland; active bakery worker's union and because of activities banished to Siberia at age of 16; returned to European Russia, then came to U.S.; learned cloak cutting trade; joined Local 10, Internat. Ladies Garment Workers Union, 1911, mgr.-sec., 1921-29; v.p. Internat. Ladies Garment Workers Union, 1922-29, gen. sec., treas., 1929-32, pres., 1932-65; v.p. AFL-CIO; v.p. and mem. exec. council A.F. of L., 1934-36, resigned, 1936, because of views on inds. unionism; rep. A.F. of L. to Governing Body Internat. Labor Office, Geneva, Switzerland, 1935; mem. Conf. on Workers Edn. called by Internat. Fed. Trade Unions, London, Eng., 1936, and Conf. Internat. Clothing Workers Fedn., 1936. Co-founder Am. Labor Party in State of N.Y., 1936, also presdl. elector for Am. Labor Party and Democratic Party, 1936; apptd. mem. Wage and Hour ladies' apparel industry coms., 1938-41, also mem. Spl. Wage and Hour P.R. Com., 1940; vice chmn. Am. Labor Conf. on Internat. Affairs; labor rep., Nat. Coat and Suit Indsl. Recovery Bd., 1942; founder, vice-chmn. Liberal Party, N.Y. State, 1944; bd. dirs. Willkie Meml., 1945; A.F.L. rep. Mgmt. and Labor Conf., elected v.p. A.F.L. exec. council, 1945; A.F.L. cons., U.N. Econ. and Social Council, 1946; mem. Trade Union Adv. Com. on Internat. Labor Affairs of U.S. Dept. Labor; mem. bd. dirs. Am. Overseas Aid-U.N. Appeal for Children. Apptd. Apr. 1941, to War Dept. Bd. on claims for tax amortization of emergency defense facilities; bd. dirs. Nat. War Fund, Joint Distbn. Com., Greater N.Y. dirs. Willkie Meml., 1945; AFL rep. Mgmt. and Labor Conf., re-elected v.p. AFL exec. council, 1945; AFL cons., U.N. Econ. and Social Council, 1946; mem. Trade Union Adv. Com. on Internat. Labor Affairs of U.S. Dept. Labor; mem. bd. dirs. Am. Overseas Aid-U.N. Appeal for Children; mem. AFL com. Labor's Com. for the election of Truman, 1948; AFL del. Internat. Confedn. Free Trade Unions, London, 1949, Stockholm, 1953, mem. gen. council, 1949; apptd. mem. War Dept. Bd. on claims for tax amortization of emergency defense facilities, 1941. Pres.'s Adv. Com. on

Labor-Mgmt. Policy, 1961; bd. dirs. Nat. War Fund, Joint Distbn. Com., Greater N.Y. Fund, F. D. Roosevelt Meml. Found.; mem. spl. com. on labor standards and social security apptd. by sec. of state. Decorated King's medal (England); Medal of Grand Cavalier (Italy); recipient Humanitarian Service award Eleanor Roosevelt Cancer Found., 1961, Golden Door award Am. Council for Nationalities Service, 1965. Freedom award Internat. Rescue Com., 1966, Diamond Jubilee medal for service to labor Mayor J. Lindsay, 1973; named Senior Citizen of the Year, Gov. Rockefeller, 1970. Founder Ams. for Democratic Action, 1947; mem. exec. com. of Citizens' Com. to Support the Marshall Plan, Workers Edn. Bur.; mem. Greater N.Y. for United Negro Coll. Fund, 1948. Fellow Am. Acad. Arts and Scis.; mem. Nat. Sponsors Com. of Am. Heart Assn., 1948, Nat. Conf. Christians and Jews (nat. labor chmn. Brotherhood Week, 1964). Home: New York, N.Y. Died Sept. 17, 1982.

DUBOIS, JOSIAH ELLIS, JR., lawyer; b. Camden, N.J., Oct. 21, 1912; s. Josiah Ellis and Amelia (Ayles) DuB.; m. Dorothy Frances Clement, June 12, 1937; children—Robert Clement, Jeraldine Dale. A.B., U. Pa., 1931, LL.B., 1934. Bar: D.C. bar 1938, N.J. bar 1940. Law clk. gen. counsel's office U.S. Treasury Dept., Washington, 1936-38; gen. practice law, partner firm DuBois & DuBois, Camden, 1938-41; atty. gen. counsel's office Treasury Dept., 1940-43, chief counsel fgn. funds control div., 1943, asst. gen. counsel, 1944, asst. to sec. treasury, 1944-83; gen. counsel War Refugee Bd., 1944-83; pvt. practice, Camden, 1946-59; ptnr. firm DuBois, Maiale & Du Bois, 1959-83. Mem. spl. mission, C. Am., 1941, North Africa, 1942-43, accompanied sec. treasury to Eng., France on spl. mission for pres., 1944; mem. Allied Reparations Com., Moscow, 1945, U.S. delegation Berlin Conf., 1945; dep. chief counsel for War Crimes (charge I.G. Farben case), Nuremburg, Germany, 1947-48. Author: The Devil's Chemists, 1952. Mem. Am., N.J. bar assns., Order of Coif. Club: Franklin Chess (Phila.). Home: Pitman, N.J. Dec. Aug. 1, 1983.

DU BOIS, RAOUL PENE, costume and set designer; b. N.Y.C., Nov. 29, 1914; s. Raoul George-Gontran Pene and Bessie (Hetherington) Du B. Designer sets for several prodns., Paris; 1st designs in N.Y.C. were costumes for Life Begins at 8:40, Winter Garden, 1934; since designer: Jumbo, 1935; 1st London design: Home and Beauty, 1937; designer: Broadway shows The Two Bouquets, Leave It to Me, The Ziefeld Follies, 1938, Du Barry Was a Lady, Too Many Girls, One for the Money, Aquacade, 1939, Two for the Show, Panama Hattie, Hold on to Your Hats, 1940, Liberty Jones, 1941, Carmen Jones, 1943, The Firebrand of Florence, Are You With It? , 1945, Heaven on Earth, Lend an Ear, 1948, Alive and Kicking, Call Me Madam, 1950, Make a Wish, 1951, New Faces of 1952, In Any Language, 1952, Wonderful Town, Maggie, Charley's Aunt, John Murray Anderson's Almanac, 1953, Mrs. Patterson, 1954, Plain and Fancy, The Vamp, 1955, Ziegeld Follies (sets and costumes for 3 different prodns.), Carmen Jones (costumes only), 1957, Gypsy (costumes only), 1959, Maurice Chevalier (decor and lighting), The Student Gypsy, 1963, PS I Love You, Royal Flush, 1964, Darling of the Day, 1968, double-bill Peter and the Wolf and Here and Now, Rondelay, 1969, No, No, Nanette, 1971, Rain, 1972; costumes and decor for Irene, 1973, Gypsy, London, 1973, N.Y.C., 1974, Doctor Jazz, 1975, Sugar Babies, 1979; costumes for Colette, Denver, 1982; designer for: Ballet Russe de Monte Carlo, Denver, 1982; designer films, 1941-45; films including Louisiana Purchase, Layd in the Dark, Dixie, also others. Recipient Tony award for Wonderful Town and No, No, Nanette. Died Jan. 1, 1985.*

DUBOIS, THEODORA MCCORMICK (MRS. DELAFIELD DUBOIS), author; b. Brooklyn, N.Y., Sept. 14, 1890; d. Eliot and Laura Case (Brenton) McCormick; ed. Halsted Sch., Yonkers, N.Y., 1900-09; m. Delafield DuBois, on April 27, 1918 (deceased on January 6th, 1965); children—Theodora Delafield, Eliot. Republican. Episcopalian. Author books including: Rogues Coat, 1949; Its Raining Violence, 1949; High Tension, 1950; Wc Merrily Put to Sea, 1950; Solution T25, 1951; Fowl Play, 1951; The Cavalier's Corpse, 1952, Freedom's Way, 1953; The Listener, 1953; Seeing Red, 1954; The Emerald Crown, 1955; The Love of Fingin O'Lea, 1957; Rich Boy-Poor Boy, 1961; Captive of Rome, 1962; Tiger Burning Bright, Shannon Terror, Dangerous Rescue (under pen name Theodora McCormick), The Late Bride, all 1964; The High King's Daughter, 1965. Contbr. fiction to various mags. Home: S.I., N.Y. †

DUBOS, RENE JULES, bacteriologist; b. Saint Brice, France, Feb. 2O, 1901; came to U.S., 1924, naturalized, 1938; s. Georges Alexandre and Adeline Madeleine (De Bloedt) D.; m. Marie Louise Bonnet, Mar. 23, 1934 (dec. 1942); m. Letha Jean Porter, Oct. 16, 1946. Student, Coll. Chaptal, Paris, 1915-19, Institut Nat. Agronomique, Paris, 1919-21; Ph.D., Rutgers U., 1927, Sc.D. (hon.), 1949; Sc.D. (hon.), Rochester U., 1941, Harvard, 1942, Paris U., 1950, New Sch. for Social Research, N.Y.C., 1956, U. Rio de Janeiro, Dartmouth; M.D. (hon.), Liege U., 1947, Yeshiva U., 1961, U. Alta., 1963, U. Pa., 1965, U. Calif., 1965; hon. degree, Colby Coll., 1966, Carleton Coll., 1966, St. John's U., 1968, Queen's U., Can., 1969, U. Sherbrooke, Can., 1969, Loyola U., 1970, Clark U., 1970, Kalamazoo Coll., 1971, Bard Coll., 1971, Marquette U., 1971, Williams Coll., 1971, Cath. U., 1972, U. Calgary, 1972, Assumption Coll., 1974, Benedictine Coll., 1974, Jefferson U., 1974, Montclair State Coll., 1975, Rockefeller U., 1975, St. Peter's Coll., 1975, Kenyon Coll., 1976, Marietta Coll., 1978. Asst. editor staff Internat. Inst. Agr., Rome, 1922-24; research asst. soil microbiology, instr. bacteriology N.J. Exptl. Sta., Rutgers U., 1924-27; fellow Rockefeller Inst. Med. Research, 1927-28, asst., 1928-30, asso., 1930-38, asso. mem., 1938-41, mem., 1941-42, 44-56, mem., prof., Rockefeller U, 1957-71, prof. emeritus, from 1971; George Fabyan prof. comparative pathology, prof. tropical medicine Harvard Med. Sch., 1942-44. Author: books including The Bacterial Cell, 1945, Bacterial and Mycotic Infections of Man, 1948, Louis Pasteur-Free Lance of Science, 1950, The White Plague-Tuberculosis, Man-Society, 1952, The Dreams of Reason, 1961, Pasteur and Modern Medicine, 1960, The Unseen World, 1962, The Torch of Life, 1962, Health and Disease, 1965, Man Adapting, 1965, So Human an Animal, 1968, Man, Medicine and Environment, 1968, Reason Awake: Science for Man, 1970, (with Barbara Ward) Only One Earth, 1972, A God Within, 1972, Choisir d'etre humain, 1974, Beast or Angel: Choices That Make Us Human, 1974, The Professor, the Institute and DNA; Oswald T. Avery, 1976, The Wooing of Earth, 1980, Quest, Reflections on Medicine, Science, and Humanity, 1980, Celebrations of Life, 1981. Served in French Army, 1921-22. Recipient numerous awards including Howard Taylor Ricketts award U. Chgo., 1958; Passano award AMA, 1960; Robert Koch Centennial award R. K. Inst., Berlin, Germany; Sci. Achievement award AMA, 1964; gold medal and prize Pacific Sci. Center, 1966; Pulitzer prize, 1969; Prix Internat. de l'Institut de la Vie; Washburn award, 1974; Cullum Geog. medal, 1975; Tyler Ecology award, 1976. Mem. Nat. Acad. Scis., Am. Philos. Soc., NRC. Club: Century Assn. Home: New York, NY.

DUBUFFET, JEAN, French painter; b. LeHavre, France, July 31, 1901; s. George S. and Jeanne (Paillettle) D.; studied art Ecole des beaux-arts, Le Havre; m. Paulette Bret, Feb. 25, 1927; 1 dau.; m. 2d, Lili Dubuffet. Wholesale wine mcht., Paris, 1930-39, 40-46; painter, 1931-34, 1942-85; exhibited Galerie Rene Drouin, Paris, 1944, Pierre Matisse, Cordier-Warren galleries, Mus. Modern Art, N.Y.C.; executed murals Vue de Paris, Grand Paysage, 1945-46; exhibited statuettes Galerie Rive Gauche, 1954; retrospective exhbn. Mueée des arts decoratits, Paris, 1961. Prin. paintings include: Mirobolus, Macadam et Cie, Sols et terrains, Hautes Pâtes, Corps de dames, la Vie de famille, Paysages mentaux, Tables pay sagées, Pierres philosophiques, Texturologies. Address: Paris, France. Died May 12, 1985.*

DUCKWORTH, T.A., ins. co. exec.; b. Albany, Mo., Mar. 26, 1912; s. Thomas Alexander and Sally (Edwards) D.; student Central Coll., Fayette, Mo., 1930-33; LL.B., U. Mo., 1936; m. Edwina Nelson, July 12, 1941; children—Sally (Mrs. David P. Hansen), Celeste Nelson (Mrs. James Natwick), Jane Chilton. Admitted to Mo. bar, Wis. bar; with Employers Ins. of Wausau (Wis.), 1936—, sec., 1957-60, sr. v.p., sec., 1960-74, exec. v.p., 1974-75, pres., 1975-77, chmn., 1977—; dir. 1st Am. Nat. Bank, Wausau, Forward Communications Corp., Wausau. Mem. sr. council Wis. Lung Assn.; bd. dirs. The Leigh Yawkey Woodson Art Mus., Inc., Wausau, Wausau Hosps., Inc.; v.p. Daniel Storey Found., Wausau; bd. dirs. Wausau Story Drum and Bugle Corps; mem. area adv. group U. Wis. Center, Wausau; bd. curators Central Methodist Coll., Fayette, Mo. Mem. Wausau Area C. of C. (past pres.), Delta Theta Phi, Phi Kappa Delta. Presbyn. (elder). Mason (Shriner), Rotarian. Home: Wausau, Wis. Died Feb. 7, 1985; interred Wausau, Wis.

DUDGEON, FARNHAM FRANCIS, editor; b. St. James, Minn., Feb. 16, 1912; s. Hugh G. and Mary Josephine (Nugent) D.; student St. John's U., 1928-29; B.S., U. N.D., 1934; m. Gould Crook, July 6, 1937; children—Michael, Patrick, Timothy, Colleen. Labor relations, investigative work N.D. state, fed. agencies, 1934-39; mem. editorial staff Western Newspaper Union, 1939-42, editor-in-chief, 1942-52; editor and pub. Feature Publs., Inc., 1952-85. City commr., mayor pro tem, Frankfort, 1965-66, mayor, 1967. Mem. Sigma Delta Chi, Theta Chi, Phi Delta Kappa. Roman Catholic. K.C. Contbr. weekly news analysis to 2,500 community newspapers 1940-43. Home: Frankfort, Ky. Dec. Jan. 23, 1985.

DUDLEY, LAVINIA PRATT, editor; b. N.Y. City; d. Charles H. and Harriet (Hartman) Pratt; student N.Y.U.; Litt.D. (hon.), Mo. Valley Coll., 1947; m. Ivan Ross Dudley, Feb. 19, 1927 (dec. December 1961). Began career as assistant to dean sch. retailing N.Y.U., 1921-24; asst. to Am. editor, also mgr. editorial office Ency. Brit., 1925-29, mgr. book shops, 1930-33; ednl. dir. Brit. Jr., editor study units for rural schs., 1934-38; asst. editor Ency. Americana, 1939-47, exec. editor Americana publs., 1948-59, editor in chief, 1959-64; cons. editor Am. Peoples Encyclopedia, N.Y.C., 1964, consultant, since 1965-84. Named professional woman of year for State of N.Y., 1959. Fellow Am. Geog. Soc.; mem. Acad. Polit. Sci., Nat. Audubon Soc. Republican. Club: Women's U. (N.Y. City). Editor Americana Reading Guides in engring., chemistry, commerce, agr., Latin Am. Home: New York, N.Y. Died Sept. 30, 1984.

DUDLEY, WILLIAM EWART, clergyman; b. Leintwardine, Herefordshire, Eng., Oct. 4, 1887; s. Rev. William and Lucy Ann (Shingler) D.; student Bede Collegiate, Sunderland, Eng., 1900-03, Oswestry (Eng.) Prep. Collegiate, 1903-05, Univ. of N.D., 1912-16; B.A., Wesley Coll., Grand Forks, N.D., 1918, D.D., 1926; spl. study, Harvard University, 1919; LL.D., Defiance College, Defiance, Ohio; m. Estelle R. Leibeler, July 12, 1912; children—William Hugh, Robert Brisbourne. Came to U.S., 1910 naturalized citizen, 1916. Ordained ministry M.E. Ch., 1915; student pastor West Bronwich, Staffordshire, and Ludlow, Shropshire, Eng., 1907-10; home missionary, La Riviere, Man., Can., 1910-11; student pastor Lakota (N.D.) Union Ch., 1912-15, Forest River (N.D.) M.E. Ch., 1917-18; pastor Crookston (Minn.) Congl. Ch., 1917-18; First Congl. Ch., Winona, Minn., 1918-21, Park Av. Congl. Ch., Minneapolis, 1921-29, Flatbush Congl. Ch., Brooklyn, N.Y., 1929-42, First Congl. Ch., Toledo, O., 1942-48; interim ministry, St. James United Ch., Montreal; Trinity United Ch., Charlottetown; Prince Edward Isl., Can., 1949. British interchange preacher and speaker, alternate years, 1919-36. Scottish Rite Mason. Contbr. articles, verse and hymns. Home: 10 Grafton St., Charlottetown, P.E. Island, Can. Address: Toledo, Ohio. †

DUENSING, DAVID L., food processing company executive; b. 1922; married. Student, Wright Jr. Coll., 1940, U. Fla., 1942. With Armour & Co., Phoenix, 1946-77, 80-85, various advt. and mktg. positions, 1946-60; v.p., dir. mktg. Armour Grocery Products Co., 1960-68; pres. Armour-Dial Inc. subs. (name changed from Armour Grocery Products Co. 1968, 1964-68; exec. v.p. Armour & Co., 1977-85; pres. Armour-Dial Inc., 1977-85; dir. DeSoto Inc, Wayne-Gossard Corp. Served to 1st lt. USAF, 1942-46. Home: Phoenix, Ariz. Died Jan. 19, 1985.

DUFF, JOHN CARR, educator; b. Pitts., July 23, 1901; s. Alexander McGill and Edna (Carr) D.; Ph.B. cum laude, Kenyon Coll., 1923, A.M., 1924; Ph.D., N.Y. U., 1934; m. Gladys Hays, July 1, 1922; children—Robert Russell, John Hays, Thomas. Tchr. high sch., 1924-25; organizer LaFayette Jr. High Sch. and Benjamin Franklin Jr. High Sch., Uniontown, Pa., 1925; prin. Benjamin Franklin Jr. High Sch., 1925-30; supervising prin. Dist. 6, Scarsdale, N.Y., 1935-37; successively teaching fellow, instr., asst. prof. to prof. Sch. Edn. N.Y. U., asst. dean, 1946-48, chmn. dept. adult edn., 1948-59, prof. adminstrn. and supervision, 1959-67, mem. div. advanced studies, mem. staff Center for Field Services, co-ordinator Summer Sch., Chautauqua, 1950-52; cons. in field. With War Dept., 1943-45; mem. summer faculty U. P.R., 1958, 59, U. Fla., 1958, State U. N.Y. at Buffalo, 1963; mem. project on cost of edn. N.Y. State Dept. Edn., 1959-60; sr. cons. Bur. Ednl. Studies and Services, lectr. adminstrn. Sch. Edn., Hofstra U., 1967-82. Cons. on tng. Girl Scouts U.S. Served with U.S. Army, 1918; tng. specialist and civilian dir. civilian tng. Office Q.M. Gen., World War II. Recipient Study award Fund for Adult Edn., 1955-56. Mem. Adult Edn. Assn. U.S., AAUP, Am. Assn. Sch. Adminstrs., Collegiate Assn. Devel. Ednl. Adminstrn., St. Andrew's Soc. N.Y.C., Phi Delta Kappa, Kappa Delta Pi (hon.). Mason. Author books, including: (with Cox and McNamara) Basic Principles of Guidance, 1948. Editor The Clearing House, 1935-36. Home: Garden City, N.Y. Died June 1, 1982.

DUFFY, BRIAN FRANCIS, clergyman, educator; b. N.Y.C., Apr. 23, 1917; s. Thomas Charles and Ellen (Sullivan) D. B.A., St. Bonaventure U., 1942; M.A., 1947, Columbia, 1956; doctoral candidate, Columbia, 1958. Ordained priest Roman Catholic Ch., 1946; asst. prin. Bishop Timon High Sch., Buffalo, 1947-53; head dept. theology St. Bonaventure U., 1953-54, dean, 1954-55, Siena Coll., Loudonville, N.Y., 1958-64, pres., 1964-70, prof. English, 1970-83. Address: Loudonville, N.Y. Dec. May 18, 1983.

DUFFY, EDWARD C., utilities exc.; b. Cambridge, N.Y., Mar. 5, 1909; s. Edward D. and Helen A. (McClallen) D.; B.S. in Mech. Engring., U. Notre Dame, 1930; m. Helene M. Playford, Oct. 23, 1931; children—Maureen Helene (Mrs. R.L. Forrester), Robert Francis, Linda Mary. Engring. and constrn. depts. Consol. Edison Co. N.Y., Inc., 1930-42; engr. Long Island Lighting Co., Mineola, N.Y., 1942-45, supt. generating stas. and substas., 1945-48, mgr. elec. prodn., 1948-50, asst. v.p., 1950-53, v.p., 1953-58, sr. v.p., 1958-65, exec. v.p., 1965-68, pres., 1968-75, vice chmn., 1974-76, also dir.; dir. L.I. Trust Co., Litco Corp.; trustee Green Point Savs. Bank. Fellow ASME (Prime movers award 1955); mem. Am. Gas Assn. (dir. 1968-70), Soc. Gas Lighting, I.E.E.E., L.I. Assn. Commerce and Industry. Clubs: Garden City (N.Y.) Golf; North Fork Country; Notre Dame N.Y. Home: Floral Park, N.Y. Died Mar. 3, 1983.

DUFFY, EDWARD W., banker; b. 1926; (married). B.S., Utica (N.Y.) Coll., 1950. Asst. nat. bank examiner Treasury Dept., 1950-52; cashier, asst. trust officer Carthage Nat. Exchange Bank, 1952-56; with Marine Midland Bank, NA, Buffalo, from 1956, pres., chief exec. officer, Utica, 1969-71, Syracuse, N.Y., 1971-73, pres., chief exec. officer, then chmn. bd. main office, 1973-75, chmn. bd., pres., chief exec. officer, 1975-76, chmn. bd., chief exec. officer, from 1976, also dir.; chmn. bd., chief exec. officer Marine Midland Banks Inc.; dir. Hong Kong & Shanghai Banking Corp., Niagara Mohawk Power Corp., Utica Mut. Ins. Co., Buffalo Forge Co. Served with USNR, 1943-46. Address: Buffalo, NY.

DUGAN, GEORGE, newspaperman; b. Toledo, Feb. 9, 1909; s. George and Mary Eleanor (Blauvelt) D.; student Blair Acad., 1925-27, U. Mich., 1927-31; m. Josephine Rearick, Nov. 24, 1937; 1 son, Brian. Reporter Religious News Service, 1938-47; reporter N.Y. Times, 1947-49, religious news editor, 1949-65, reporter, 1965-78. Served as Spl. Agt. CIC, AUS 1945-47. Awarded Asso. Ch. Press award of merit, 1952, Nat. Religious Publicity Council award, 1950, James O. Supple Meml. award, 1955, Religious Heritage Am. award 1972. Mem. Religious Newswriters Assn. (pres. 1951-52), Alpha Delta Phi, Sigma Delta Chi. Home: Hillsdale, N.J. Died May 25, 1982.

DUKE, JOHN WOODS, composer, pianist; b. Cumberland, Md., July 30, 1899; s. Harry Kearney and Matilda Adina (Hoffman) D.; teacher's certificate, Peabody Cons. of Music, Baltimore, 1918; diploma Allegany County Acad., Cumberland, 1915; m. Dorothy E. Macon, Dec. 23, 1922; children—John Macon, Edith Karen. Began as teacher piano, Smith Coll., 1923, prof. music from 1938; spent sabbatical year in Europe, 1929-30; has appeared in many concerts and recitals, giving 1st performances of contemporary works; compositions have been performed in concerts in New York, Boston and various other cities in the East. Mem. S.A.T.C., Columbia U., 1918. Mem. A.S.C.A.P., American Association University Professors. Composer numerous songs, solo, chamber and orchestral works, also an operetta. Home: Northampton, Mass. Died Oct. 26, 1984.

DUNBAR, CHARLES ELMER, govt. securities dealer; b. Pitts., Dec. 24, 1912; s. William Kuhn and Elizabeth Atwood (Biggs) D.; B.S., Yale, 1935; m. Hester Ann Waring, Dec. 7, 1935; children—Beverly Value McNaull, Elizabeth Atwood (Mrs. Gustav Koven), Anne Waring (Mrs. Anthony W. Miller) With Discount Corp., N.Y.C., 1938-81, pres., 1965-67, chmn. bd. 1967-81; dir. Tri-Continental Corp., Grumman Corp.; trustee East River Savs. Bank. Trustee Franklin and Marshall Coll. Clubs: Crusing Club of Am.; N.Y, Yacht, Metropolitan (N.Y.C.); New Bedford (Mass.) Yacht. Home: New Vernon, N.J. Died Nov. 13, 1981.

DUNBAR, RALPH MCNEAL, librarian; b. Elkton Md., July 7, 1890; s. Boulden Biddle and May Belle (McNeal) D.; A.B., George Washington U., 1912; A.M., Columbia U., 1914; student U. Chicago, 1935-37; m. Grace J. Sleeper, July 6, 1918; 1 son, Ralph Biddle (dec.). Library asst. Pub. Library of D.C., 1907-12; instr. 23d St. Prep. Sch., N.Y. City, 1912-13; in charge traveling library dept. Brooklyn Pub. Library, 1913-17, supt. of supplies, 1917-18, asst. reference librarian, 1918-19; field librarian Morale Div., Bur. of Navigation, U.S. Navy Dept., 1919-24; asst. librarian and asso. prof., Ia. State Coll., 1924-37; chief Library Service Div., U.S. Office of Education, 1938-56, director Library Services Br., 1956-58; dir. A.L.A. library resources fact-finding project, from 1958. Officer candidate Field Atty. Officers Sch., Camp Zachary Taylor, 1918. Received A.L.A. fellowship award, 1935-36. Mem. A.L.A., (exec. bd.), A.A.A.S., D.C. Library Assn., N.E.A. Assn. Coll. and Reference Libraries, Special Libraries Assn. Club: Cosmos (Washington). Writer of bulls. for U.S. Office of Edn.; contbr. to profl. jours. †

DUNCAN, D(AVID) C(HRISTIE), physicist; born Churchville, N.Y., July 30, 1889; s. James and Margaret (Christie) D.; A.B., Univ. of Mich., 1911, MS., 1913, Ph.D., 1924; m. Mildred Webb, Aug. 28, 1913; children—Gordon Webb, Donald Christie. Instr. in physics, Purdue Univ., 1911-18; prof. of physics Pa. State U., from 1918; acting head physics dept., 1950-53, emeritus prof., from 1953; sr. engr. HRB-Singer, 1953-55, consultant to United States government, from 1955. Member A.A.A.S., American Assocation Physics Teachers, American Assn. Univ. Profs., Am. Inst. Physics, Am. Phys. Soc., Am. Soc. for Engr. Edn., Chi Phi, Phi Kappa Phi, Sigma Xi, Sigma Pi Sigma, Alpha Epsilon Delta. Republican. Presbyn. Home: State College, Pa. †

DUNCAN, FREDERICK GELLER, insurance executive; b. N.Y.C., Apr. 24, 1911; s. William A. and Grace W. (McWilliam) D.; B.A., Princeton, 1932; m. Janet St. Clair Mullan, Mar. 12, 1938 (div. 1963); 1 son, William Mullan; m. 2d, Grace Sager Rippin, Mar. 15, 1963. With Guaranty Trust Co., N.Y.C., 1933-50, asst. treas., 1947-50; with N.Y. Life Ins. Co., 1950-76, asst. treas., 1952-57, asst. v.p., 1957-61, 2d v.p., 1961-70, treas., 1970-76, ret., 1976; mem. Midtown adv. bd. Mfrs. Hanover Trust Co. Trustee Russell Sage Found., 1957-73; Served from lt. (j.g.) to lt. comdr., USNR, 1942-45; Africa and S. Pacific. Home: Lyme, Conn. Died Dec. 18, 1983.

DUNCAN, LAURENCE ILSLEY, judge; b. Concord, N.H., Oct. 5, 1906; s. Charles and Charlotte (Ilsley) D.; m. Doris M. Hackett, June 25, 1932; children—Stuart B., James H.S. A.B., Dartmouth Coll., 1927; LL.B., Harvard, 1930. Bar: N.H. bar 1930. Engaged in law practice, 1930-45; asso. justice N.H. Superior Ct., 1945-46, N.H. Supreme Ct., 1946-76. Del. N.H. Constl. Conv., 1938, 41; mem. N.H. Bd. Bar Examiners, 1941-44; Former mem. council League N.H. Craftsmen; trustee Concord Hospital, 1944-63, 67-78. Mem. Am., N.H. bar assns., Am. Judicature Soc., Phi Beta Kappa, Phi Alpha Delta (hon.), Sigma Nu. Republican. Conglist. Address: Concord, NH.

DUNCAN, LOUIS CHARLES, manufacturing company executive; b. Kokomo, Ind., Feb. 20, 1913; s. John P. and Nellie C. (Stevens) D.; m. Marguerite Dewees, Sept. 3, 1934 (dec. Aug. 1968); children: Carole (Mrs. William Kuehn), Craig; m. Eileen Hastings, Apr. 26, 1969. B.A., Ind. U., 1933; LL.D. (hon.), Buena Vista Coll. From br. mgr. to vice chmn. Household Internat., Chgo., 1939-78; chmn. bd. Sealy Inc., Chgo., 1978-85; chmn. East West Capital Corp.; dir. CAM-OR Corp., Indpls., East West Mut. Stock Corp., A.I. Corp., Lexicon Corp., Denver. Bd. dirs. Am. Heart Assn.; mem. adv. council U. Ill.; bd. dirs. Ill. Council Econ. Edn. Served as field dir. ARC, World War II. Recipient Disting. Service award Nat. Consumer Finance Assn., 1970. Mem. Chgo. Commerce and Industry Assn., Mid-Am. Com., English Speaking Union, Chgo. Council Fgn. Relations. Presbyterian (elder). Clubs: Union League (Chgo.), Mid-Am. (Chgo.), Executives (Chgo.), Economic (Chgo.); Hinsdale Golf (Ill.); Army Navy (Washington). Home: Oak Brook, Ill. Died July 8, 1985.

DUNCAN, THOMAS CLARK, utility exec.; b. Pitts., July 16, 1905; s. Thomas S. and Margaret N. (Clark) D.; E.E., Cornell U., 1927; m. Thelma M. Ashworth, Jan. 26, 1927; children—Thomas A., William C., Margaret E. (Mrs. Donald R. Woodley). With Consol. Edison Co. N.Y., Inc., and predecessors, 1927-70, asst. v.p., 1962-64, v.p., 1964-67, sr. v.p., 1968-69, exec. v.p., 1969-70; exec. dir. N.Y. Power Pool, 1971-73. Fellow I.E.E.E. Club: Cornell (N.Y.C.). Home: Port Washington, N.Y. Died Feb. 18, 1985; interred Nassau Knolls, Port Washington, N.Y.

DUNCAN, WALTER, oil company executive; b. La Salle, Ill., Jan 11, 1889; s. Nicholas W. and Mary Ann (Stuart) D.; m. Velma M. Twomey, Oct. 24, 1914; children—Edward J., J. Walter, Vincent J., Raymond T. Ph.B., U. Notre Dame, 1912, LL.D., 1956. Engaged in ins. bus., 1912-83, in oil bus., 1937-83; pres. Walter Duncan, Inc., La Salle, 1956-83. v.p., dir. La Salle State Bank. Mem. bd. lay trustees U. Notre Dame. Served to 2d lt., inf. U.S. Army, World War I. Decorated Knights of Malta. Roman Catholic. Club: K.C. Address: LaSalle, Ill. Dec. May 12, 1983.

DUNHAM, STUART A., editor; b. Binghamton, N.Y., Jan. 24, 1920; s. Fay B. and Helen (Clark) D.; student Oberlin Coll., 1938-40; m. Maureen McNamara; children—Caroline, Sara, Elisabeth. Reporter, Binghamton Press, city editor, until 1965; editor Camden (N.J.) Courier-Post, 1965-67, Hartford (Conn.) Times, 1967-71; exec. editor Rochester (N.Y.) Times-Union, Democrat and Chronicle, from 1971. Home: Pittsford, N.Y. Died.

DUNLAP, JAMES EUGENE, educator; born Ripon, Wis., Oct. 31, 1889; s. Augustus Eugene and Jessie C. Cooke (Frazer) D.; A.B., Ripon Coll., 1910, L.H.D., 1951; A.M., U. of Mich., 1914, Ph.D., 1920; m. Gertrude Florence Clark, June 8, 1917; children—James Edward, Robert Bruce. Instr. Latin Ohio State U., 1915-19; asst. prof. Latin Ind. U., 1920-23; acting asst. prof. Latin U. of Mich., 1919-20, asst. prof. Greek and Latin, 1923-28, asso. prof., 1928-40, prof. from 1940, chmn. dept. classical studies, 1946-57. Mem. Am. Philol. Assn., Classical Assn. Middle West and South, Phi Kappa Phi. Home: Ann Arbor, Mich. †

DUNLAP, S(AMUEL) BENJAMIN, judge; b. St. Charles County, Mo., Feb. 22, 1888; s. Robert Hamilton and Ada Caroline (Pearce) D.; LL.B., La Salle Extension Univ., Chicago, Ill., 1918; m. Elizabeth Jacoby Bedford, Oct. 12, 1910; children—Robert Benjamin, Dorothy Elizabeth (Mrs. David Brown). Bookkeeper, 1910-13; city clerk, Caldwell, Ida., 1913-18; probate judge, Canyon County, 1919-20; gen. law practice, 1919-42; justice Supreme Court of Idaho, 1943-44. Mayor of Caldwell, 1929-30, elected prosecuting attorney, Canyon County, 1932; elected Democratic presidential elector from Idaho, 1940. Member American Idaho, and 7th Judicial District of Idaho bar assns., Elk, Odd Fellow. Club: Caldwell Kiwanis, Am. Rose Soc. Home: Caldwell, Idaho. †

DUNLOP, EDWARD ARUNAH, pub. co. exec., assn. exec.; b. Pembroke, Ont., Can., June 27, 1919; s. Edward A. and Emily Mabel (Ferguson) D.; m. Dorothy Joyce Tupper, Aug. 12, 1944; children—Edward A., Charlotte Mary Ferguson. B.A., Trinity Coll., U. Toronto, 1945; LL.D. (hon.), Queen's U., 1975. Dir. casualty rehab. div. Dept. Vets. Affairs, Ottawa, Ont., 1945-49; mng. dir. Arthritis Soc., Toronto, 1949-81; pres. Toronto (Ont.) Sun Pub. Corp., 1971-81, also dir.; dir. Edmonton Sun Pub. Corp., United Press Can. Mem. Provincial Parliament for York-Forest Hill constituency, 1963-71, chmn. select com. on election law, 1968-71, minister without portfolio, 1971; trustee Toronto Gen. Hosp. Served to lt. col. Queen's Own Rifles of Can., 1937-44. Decorated George medal Order Brit. Empire. Hon. mem. Can. Rheumatism Assn., Can. Soc. for Clin. Investigation, Am. Rheumatism Assn. Conservative. Home: Toronto ON Canada.

DUNN, BURTON, banker; b. Corpus Christi, Tex., Apr. 4, 1889; s. Pat F. and Clara J. (Brown) D.; grad. Alamo City Bus. Coll., San Antonio, 1907; m. Buena V. Hill, June 30, 1917; children—Frances (Mrs. Samuel Seltzer), Lura (Mrs. Blake Sweat), Juliana (Mrs. Hart Smith), Patsy Ruth (Mrs. Edward Singer). Formerly with Corpus Christi State Nat. Bank, pres., 1950-56, chmn. exec. com.; rancher on Padre Island, Tex., from 1937; dir. First Savs. Assn., Corpus Christi. Trustee Ada Wilson Crippled Childrens Hosp., M.G. and Johnnye D. Perry Found. Rotarian (past pres. Corpus Christi). Home: Corpus Christi, Tex. †

DUNN, NEIL HARRISON, banker; b. Alexandria, Neb., Oct. 31, 1888; s. Lee J. and Maude (Enslow) D.; prep. edn., high sch., Lincoln, Neb., and Shattuck Sch., Faribault, Minn.; student U. of Neb., 1908-09; m. Gratia Green, Sept. 25, 1912; children—Neil H., William James, Derick Clive. Cashier State Bank of Elk Creek, Neb. 1912-15, State Bank of Superior, 1916; cashier First Nat. Bank, Hastings, 1917-19, pres. from 1919; pres. Farmers State Bank, Ayr, Neb.; dir. Clarke Hotel Co. Trustee Hastings Coll. Republican. Presbyn. Mason (32 deg., K.T., Shriner). Rotarian. Home: Hastings, Neb. †

DUNN, ROGER ELLIOTT, savs. and loan exec.; b. Long Beach, Calif., Nov. 11, 1925; s. Rex A. and Norma A. (Molley) D.; B.S. in Econs., U. Calif., Santa Barbara, 1950; m. Norma Josephine Johnson, Nov. 25, 1948; children—Susan Lynn, Allison Ann, Lon Edward. With Community Savs. & Loan Assn., Long Beach, 1950-79, chmn. bd., 1975-79; sec., dir. Financial Fedn., Inc., 1959-79. Served in USNR, 1944-46. Republican. Clubs: Rotary (Long Beach); Virginia Country. Home: Long Beach, Calif. Died 1979.

DUNN, WILLIAM CARLETON, mfg. exec.; b. Kansas City, Mo., Mar. 28, 1890; s. George and Mina M. (Foster) D.; M.E., Armour Inst. Tech., 1912; m. Agnes Walker, Apr. 27, 1915. Field engr. Internat. Harvester Co., 1912-13; development engr. Detroit Lubricator Co., 1913-14; gen. mgr. H. J. Walker Co., 1914-20; pres. Ohio Crankshaft Co., Cleve., 1920-55, chmn. bd., from 1955; v.p. Park Drop Forge Co., Cleve., 1928-55, dir., from 1928; dir. Union Commerce Bank, Harris-Seybold Co., Asso. Industries (all Cleve.), Hercules Motors Corp. (Canton, O.). Mem. Soc. Automotive Engrs., Newcomen Soc. N.A., Cleve. C. of C. (past dir.), Phi Kappa Sigma. Home: Cleveland, Ohio. †

DUNNE, ROBERT ELMER, lawyer; b. San Francisco, May 21, 1912; s. Frederick F. and Cecelia F. (Dunleavy) D.; LL.B., Southwestern U., Los Angeles, 1942; m. Jean Dwyer, Sept. 13, 1952; children—Robert Eugene, Patrick Dwyer, Maureen Leslie, Kevin Michael. Admitted to Calif. bar, 1942, practiced law, Los Angeles; partner firm Dunne, Shallcross & Kane, from 1970; dir. Angeles Winter Devel. Corp. Served with AUS, 1942-45. Decorated Purple Heart, Bronze Star. Mem. Am., Los Angeles County bar assns., Calif. State Bar, Am. Bd. Trial Advocates, Am. Judicature Soc., Stanford U., U. San Francisco alumni assns., Serra Club. Republican. Roman Cath. Home: Flintridge, Calif. Died Sept. 7, 1978; buried Los Angeles.

DUQUE, GABRIEL CARLOS, lawyer; born Los Angeles, Feb. 1, 1890; s. Tomás Lorenzo and Eleuteria (de Galdos y Belzaguy) D.; B.L., Univ. Calif., 1914; grad. law study Harvard, 1914-15; m. Mary Withers McAlister, Aug. 16, 1927; children—Gabriel Carlos, James McAlister. Admitted to Calif. bar, 1915, U.S. Supreme Ct., 1918; partner Duque & McKinley, Los Angeles, 1922-57; director, mem. executive trust, chmn. dirs. examining coms. Security-First Nat. Bank of Los Angeles. Trustee, pres. Barlow Sanatorium Assn., 1945-52; chmn. Cal. Community Found.; dir. Good Hope Med. Found., 1954-58. Served as ensign to lt. (j.g.) U.S. Navy, 1917-19. Mem. Am., Calif. State and Los Angeles bar assns., Psi Upsilon, Phi Delta Phi. Clubs: California, Bel-Air Bay, Country (Los Angeles). Home: Los Angeles, Calif. †

DURANT, ARIEL, writer; b. Russia, May 10, 1898; d. Joseph and Ethel (Appel) Kaufman; came to U.S., 1900, naturalized, 1913; student Columbia U.; LL.D., L.I. U., 1968, Litt.D., 1968; L.H.D., Akron U., 1969, Ripon Coll., 1970; m. Will Durant, Oct. 31, 1913; 1 dau., Ethel Benvenuta. Collaborator with husband on books, 1957-81; publs. include The Age of Reason Begins, 1961; The Age of Louis XIV, 1963; The Age of Voltaire, 1965; Rosseau and Revolution, 1967 (Pulitzer prize 1968); The Lessons of History, 1968; Interpretations of Life, 1970; The Age of Napoleon, 1975; A Dual Autobiography, 1977. Recipient Huntington Hartford Found. award creative writing, 1963, Presdl. medal of Freedom, 1977; named Woman of Year in Lit., Los Angeles Times, 1965. Address: Los Angeles, Calif. Died Oct. 25, 1981.

DURHAM, GEORGE HOMER, educator, church executive; b. Parowan, Utah, Feb. 4, 1911; s. George Henry and Mary Ellen (Marsden) D.; m. Eudora Widtsoe, June 20, 1936; children—Carolyn, Doralee (Mrs. R.H. Madsen), George. A.B., U. Utah, 1932; Ph.D., U. Calif. at Los Angeles, 1939; LL.D., Ariz. State U., 1971, Ind. State U., 1976, State Coll. So. Utah, U. Utah, 1977; D. Pub. Service, Brigham Young U., 1975. Finance div. mgr. Zion's Coop. Merc. Inst., Salt Lake City, 1935-36; fellow, asst. U. Calif., Los Angeles, 1937-39, vis. prof., summer 1950; polit. sci. dept. Utah State Coll., 1939-42, Swarthmore Coll., 1942-43, U. Utah, 1944-60; dir. Inst. Govt., U. Utah, 1946-53, head polit. sci. dept., 1948-53, v.p. univ., 1953-60; pres. Ariz. State U., 1960-69; Utah commr. higher edn., Salt Lake City, 1969-76; research prof. U. Utah, 1976-77; mng. dir. hist. dept. Ch. of Jesus Christ of Latter-day Saints, 1977-85; Mem. Western Interstate Commn. for Higher Edn., 1955-60, 69-76; mem. Ariz. State Bd. Edn., 1960-66; mem. U.S. nat. commn. for UNESCO, 1955-57,59; cons., current affairs analyst KTVT, Intermountain TV Corp., Salt Lake City, 1956-58;

mem. lang. adv. devel. bd. U.S. Office Edn., 1959-63; mem. Air Force ROTC adv. panel to sec. air force, 1961-64, Army ROTC Panel, 1968-70; adviser Army Command and Gen. Staff Coll., 1970-73; mem. Bd. Fgn. Scholarships, 1963-66; Bd. dirs. Am. Council on Edn., 1967-70, Ari. Acad., 1964-69, Phoenix Symphony, 1961-69; adv. bd. Utah Symphony, 1969-85, Am. Grad. Sch. Internat. Mgmt. Author: Joseph Smith: Prophet-Statesman, 1944, The Adminstration of Higher Education in Montana, 1958, other monographs.; Contbg. editor: The Improvement Era, 1946-70. Mem. world-wide exec. com. Sunday schs. Ch. of Jesus Christ of Latter-day Saints, 1971-73; pres. Salt Lake Central stake, 1973-76; regional rep. Council of 12, 1976-77; mem. First Quorum of the Seventy, 1977-85. Mem. Am. Polit. Sci. Assn. (exec. council 1949-51), Western Polit. Sci. Assn. (pres. 1948), Am. Soc. Pub. Adminstrn. (council 1949-51, v.p. 1952, pres. 1959-60), Nat. Acad. Pub. Adminstrn., Pi Gamma Mu, Pi Sigma Alpha, Phi Kappa Phi. Clubs: Timpanogos, Windsor. Home: Salt Lake City, Utah. Died Jan. 10, 1985.

DURKEE, RODNEY STUART, petroleum exec.; born Omaha, Neb., Sept. 4, 1887; s. William Porter and Anna Matilda (Jewell) D.; student U. Neb., 1904-05; m. Harriet Newell Close, Mar. 10, 1910; children—Stuart Hills, Margaret (Mrs. Sevellon Brown 3d). Comptroller, Panama-Pacific Internat. Exposition, San Francisco, 1912-16, Gen. Petroleum Corp. of Calif., Los Angeles, 1916-29, Standard Oil Co. of N.Y., 1929-33, Socony-Vacuum Co., Inc., N.Y. City, 1933-38; exec. v.p. and dir. Lane-Wells Co., Los Angeles, 1938-39, pres., 1939-54, chmn. bd., 1954. Mem. Am. Inst. Mining and Metall. Engrs., Controllers Inst. Am. (past director, past national pres.), Am. Petroleum Inst., Petroleum Equipment Suppliers Assn., Cal. Mfrs. Assn. (past pres., dir.), Western Personnel Inst. (treas., dir.), Los Angeles Area Bldg. Funds (dir.). Republican. Episcopalian. Clubs: California, San Gabriel (Calif.) Country. Home: San Marino, Calif. †

DURKEE, WILLIAM PORTER, lawyer, government official; b. Chgo., Apr. 27, 1919; s. William Porter and Helen Chapman (Stookey) D.; m. Dorcas Mary Dunklee, Nov. 12, 1946; children—William Porter, Mary Vaughan, Edward Chapman. A.B. cum laude, Dartmouth, 1941; LL.B., Yale, 1947. Bar: Cal. bar 1949, Colo. bar 1949. Staff Am. embassy, London, Eng., 1943-44; ptnr. Dunklee, Dunklee & Durkee, Denver, 1949-82; Assoc. dir., exec. dir. Am. Com. United Europe, 1950-52; cons. U.S. Govt., 1952; attaché Am. embassy, Paris, France, 1955-58, U.S. Dept. State, 1958-61; dir. fed. assistance Office Civil Def., Dept. Def., 1961-62, dep. asst. sec. def., 1962-64, dir. civil def., 1964-66; v.p. Europe, Free Europe, Inc.; with responsibility for Radio Free Europe, 1967-68, pres., 1968-75. Served with King's Royal Rifle Corps Brit. Army, 1941-44. Recipient Distinguished Civilian Service award Dept. Army, 1965, 66. Mem. State Bar Cal., Colo. Bar Assn., Council on Fgn. Relations, Celer et Audax (London, Eng.), Psi Upsilon, Phi Delta Phi. Episcopalian. Home: Washington, D.C. Dec. May 6, 1982.

DURLAND, LEWIS HUDSON, university administrator; b. Watkins Glen, N.Y., Jan. 5, 1908; s. Charles M. and Clara A. (Johnson) D.; m. Margaret J. Carry, Jan. 8, 1939; children—Anne, Katharine; m. Barbara Underhill, Jan. 1969. A.B., Cornell U., 1930. With adminstrv. offices Cornell U., Ithaca, N.Y., from 1936, treas., 1948-73, treas. emeritus, 1973-82; chmn. First Nat. Bank & Trust Co., Ithaca, 1958-78, chmn. emeritus, 1978-82; dir. Security N.Y. State Corp., SCM Corp., Raymond Corp., Park Broadcasting Inc. Trustee Duncan Hines Found., Ithaca Coll.; v.p., treas. Griffis Found. Mem. Am. Littoral Soc., Friends Ithaca Coll., Chi Phi. Clubs: Cornell of N.Y, Cornell U. Tower, Maganassippi Fish and Game, Beaverkill Trout, Union League. Home: Ithaca, N.Y. Dec. Sept. 2, 1982.

DURRELL, LAURENCE WOOD, botanist and plant pathologist; b. Lincoln, Neb., Feb. 16, 1888; son Willis Gorton and Bellita (von Stubenrauch) D.; B.S.A., O. State U., 1914; M.S., Ia. State Coll., 1917, Ph.D., 1923, D.Sc., 1959; m. Nana E. Kenoyer, Aug. 27, 1917; children—Dorothy, Mary. Instr. plant pathology Ia. State Coll., 1917-19; field asst. U.S.D.A., 1917-19; plant pathologist state fruit sta. Mo., 1919-21; asst. pathologist Ia. State Exp. Sta., 1921-24; prof. and head dept. botany and plant pathology Colorado State U., chief plant pathology sect. Colo. Agr. Expt. Sta., 1924-53, dean Coll. Sci. and Arts, emeritus dean and dept. head, from 1953. Work on corn diseases, smut of wheat, disease problems of Colo. on stock poisoning plants, soil fungi. Fellow A.A.A.S.; mem. Ecol. Soc. Am., Internat. Phycological Soc., Am. Microscopial Soc., Mycological Soc. Am., Am. Phytopathol. Soc., Colo.-Wyo. Acad. Sci. (chmn. orgn., 1927, sec.-treas., 1928-29; pres. 1930), Physchol. Soc. of Americas, Mountain States Society of Electron Microscopists, Sigma Xi, Phi Kappa Phi, Gamma Sigma Delta. Home: Ft. Collins, Colo. †

DURRETT, JAMES J(OHNSON), physician; b. Tuscaloosa Co., Ala., Mar. 2, 1889; s. Ebb Joseph and Sallie (Johnson) D.; B.S., U. of Ala., 1908, M.S., 1909, grad. in pharmacy, 1910; M.D., Harvard, 1914; m. Doris Irene Goodhope, June 24, 1944; 1 son, James Joseph. Instr. biology, U. of Ala., 1909-11; health officer, Tuscaloosa Co., Ala., 1915-17; asst. epidemiologist U.S.P.H.S., 1917-20; supt. Dept. of Health, prof. pub. health U. of Tenn., Memphis, 1920-28; chief drug div. Food and Drug Adminstrn., 1928-31; dir. professional relations, chmn. research com., E. R. Squibb & Sons, N.Y., 1931-36; chief drug div., prin. tech. advisor, Food and Drug Adminstrn., 1936-41; dir. Bur. of Med. Opinions, Fed. Trade Commn., 1941-51; dean Med. Coll. of Ala., U. Ala., 1951-55, cons. to pres. univ., from 1955. Mem. Sigma Xi. Home: Birmingham, Ala. †

DURRETT, WILLIAM YANCY, Boy Scout executive; b. Weatherford, Tex., Mar. 20, 1889; s. Geo. F. and Roma (Williams) D.; prep. edn., high sch., Weatherford; student Bethel Coll., McKenzie, Tenn.; Theol. Sem., McKenzie, Tenn.; m. Eunice Cooper Johnson, Nov. 24, 1910; 1 dau., Marguerite Pearl. Ordained ministry Cumberland Presbyn. Ch., 1910; pastor successively Olney, Tex., New Holland, Ill., Springfield, Mo., Knoxville, Tenn., Nashville, 1920-23, Chattanooga 1923-25; retired from pastorate of the largest ch. in the denomination on account of ill health; dist. mgr., E. Tenn. dist., Conn. Mutual Life Ins. Co. Chaplain U.S.N., Sept. 1917-Apr. 1920. Exec., Boy Scouts of America, 1926-27. Democrat. Mason. Club: Civitan (pres.). Home: Knoxville, Tenn. †

DUWEZ, POL EDGARD, materials science educator; b. Mons, Belgium, Dec. 11, 1907; s. Arthur and Jeanne (Delcourt) D.; Metall.E., Sch. Mines, Mons, 1932; D.Sc., U. Brussels, 1933; D.Sc. (research fellow), Calif. Inst. Tech., 1935; m. Nera Faisse, Sept. 4, 1935; 1 dau., Nadine, Instr., prof. Sch. Mines, Mons, 1935-40; research engr. Calif. Inst. Tech., Pasadena, 1941-45, chief materials sect. jet propulsion lab., 1945-54, assoc. prof. materials sci., 1947-52, prof., from 1952; Campbell Meml. lectr., 1967; mem. sci. adv. bd. to chief of staff USAF, 1945-55. Recipient Charles B. Dudley award ASTM, 1951; Francis J. Clamer medal Franklin Inst., 1968; Gov. Cornez prize (Belgium), 1973; Paul Lebeau medal French Soc. for High Temperature, 1974. Fellow AIME (C.H. Mathewson Gold medal 1964), Am. Soc. Metals (Albert Sauveur Achievement medal 1973); mem. Nat. Acad. Scis., Nat. Acad. Engring., Am. Ceramic Soc., Am. Acad. Arts and Scis., AAAS., Brit. Inst. Metals, Société Française des Ingenieurs Civils, Sigma Xi. Contbr. articles to profl. jours. Home: Pasadena, Calif. Died Dec. 31, 1984.

DUX, CLAIRE, singer; b. nr. Bydgoszcz, Poland, Aug. 2, 1890; ed. Bydgoszcz and Berlin; musical edn., Berlin and Milan; m. Charles H. Swift, Aug. 1926. Début at Cologne, 1909; sang with Caruso, at Royal Opera House, Berlin, and leading lyric soprano there, 1911-18; sang in opera at London, Stockholm, Copenhagen, etc., and with symphony orchestras in larger cities of Europe; came to America, 1921; joined Chicago Civic Opera Co., 1923; principal rôles in "Marriage of Figaro", "Boheme", "Lohengrin", "Pagliacci", "Magic Flute", "Rosenkavalier", "Meistersinger", "Rigoletto", "Faust", etc. Decorated by German, Swedish, Danish and Russian govts. Home: Chicago, Ill. †

DVORAK, RAYMOND FRANCIS, ret. educator; b. Algonquin, Ill., Mar. 31, 1900; s. Frank and Katharin (Prybl) D.; B.S., U. Ill., 1922, B.Mus., 1926; D.Mus. (hon.), Ill. Wesleyan U., 1950; m. Florence Marie Hunt, Feb. 1, 1936; children—Robert Regis, Katharine Louise, Theresa Anne, Anton Karel. Tchr., Urbana (Ill.) High Sch., 1922-25; faculty U. Ill., 1925-34; prof. music U. Wis., Madison, 1934-70, emeritus prof., 1970-82, dir. bands, 1934-68. Mem. summer sch. faculty Chgo. Mus. Coll., 1923, 28, Nat. Music Camp, Interlochen, Mich., 1930, 31, Juilliard Sch. Music, 1932, Emporia (Kans.) State Coll., 1937, U. Calif. at Los Angeles, 1947, Wash. State Coll., Ellensburg, 1954-55, pres. Wis. Rehab. Assn., 1956-58; mem. Wis. Gov.'s Com. of Employment Handicapped, 1959-69; chmn. for Wis., Christmas Seals campaign, 1964; mem. Mayor Madison Com. Employment Handicapped, 1961-69. Bd. dirs. Wis. Neurol. Found., 1959-62. Served with U.S. Army, world War I. Named Wis. Handicapped Man of Year, 1955; recipient citation of honor Nat. Cath. Music Educators Assn., 1963; named Wis. Catholic Layman of Year, 1963; recipient Honor award Duquesne U., 1965; Honors Service award Pacific U., 1965, also citations President's and Gov.'s coms. employment handicapped, 1952; plaque in recognition G. LeBlanc Corp., 1967, Service to Mankind Award Wis. dist. Sertoma Internat., 1970, Distinguished Service award Wis. Alumni Assn., 1972, Distinguished Service award Wis. Music Educators Conf., 1974; John Philip Sousa band award Instrumentalist mag., 1977. Mem. Am. (pres. 1960), Wis. (pres. 1950) bandmasters assns., A.S.C.A.P., Coll. Band Dirs. Nat. Assn. (pres. 1948), Midwest Nat. Band and Orch. Clinic dir. from 1947, medal of honor 1970, Am. Legion; hon. life mem. Am. Fedn. Musicians; hon. mem. Iowa, S.D. Bandmasters assns., Scabbard and Blade, Phi Beta Mu, Kappa Kappa Psi, Delta Sigma Omicron (hon life), Phi Kappa Phi, Phi Eta Sigma, Phi Mu Alpha, Roman Catholic. Rotarian. Author: The Band on Parade, 1936; The Art of Flag Swinging, 1938; (films) On Wisconsin, 1953, Marching Along with Sousa, 1956. Home: Madison, Wis. Died Nov. 15, 1982.

DWAN, ALLAN, motion picture director; b. Toronto, Ont., Can., Apr. 3, 1885; s. Michael Joseph and Mary Jane (Hunt) D.; E.E., U. Notre Dame, 1907. Began career as scenarist, scenario editor and dir. Am. Film Co., San Diego, 1909; producer, dir. Look Who's Laughing, RKO Pictures, 1941; dir. Rise and Shine, 20th Century Fox, 1942; producer, dir. Here We Go Again; dir. Friendly Enemies, Up In Mabel's Room, Around the World, Abroad with Two Yanks, Brewster's Millions, Northwest Outpost, Driftwood, Montana Belle, Calendar Girl, Inside Story, Sands of Iwo Jima, Surrender, Belle Le Grand, Wild Blue Yonder, I Dream of Heanie, Woman They Almost Lynched, Flight Nurse, Silver Lode, Passion, Cattle Queen of Montana, Escape to Burma, Pearl of the South Pacific, Tennessee's Partner, Slightly Scarlet, Hold Back the Night, Restless Breed, Rivers Edge; retired, 1965. Home: Van Nuys, Calif. Died Dec. 21, 1981.†

DWIGHT, EDWARD HAROLD, mus. dir.; b. Cin., Aug. 2, 1919; s. Harold S. and Rosalind (Vail) D.; m. Ruth Roudebush, Jan. 20, 1944; children—Timothy, Allen. Student, Yale, 1937-39, Art Acad. Cin., 1939-40, St. Louis Sch. Fine Arts, 1940-41, Cornell U., summer 1941. Art critic Cin. Post, 1945; asst. to dir. Cin. Art Mus., 1946-47; dir. Cin. Modern Art Soc., 1947-49, asst. curator painting and sculpture, 1949-54; curator Am. art, 1954-55, Layton Collection; dir. Milw. Art Center, 1955-62; dir. Mus. Art, Munson-Williams-Proctor Inst., Utica, N.Y., 1962-80, dir. emeritus, 1980—; guest instr. Xavier U., 1954-55; guest lectr. Am. art U. Wis., 1956-57. Contbr. articles to profl. publs. Ford Found. fellow, 1961; Mus. Profl. Fellowship grantee Nat. Endowment for Arts, 1973; Barra Found. grantee, 1978. Mem. Assn. Art Mus. Dirs. Club: Fort Schuyler (Utica). Home: Clinton, NY Office: Utica, NY

DWYER, JOHN PHILIP, columnist, music and drama critic; b. Rochester, N.Y., Nov. 4, 1913; s. Eugene J. and Clara C. (Connell) D. Student, U. Rochester, 1931-35; B.A. in Music, Eastman Sch. Music, 1937. Music, drama critic Rochester Evening News, 1937-39; reporter N.Y. Sun, 1939-40, U.P. Radio, 1940-42; news editor ABC Broadcasting Co., N.Y.C., Washington, 1945-49; music editor, lively arts critic Buffalo Evening News, 1956. Served with USAAF, 1942-45. Mem. Music Critics Assn. (past v.p.). Address: Buffalo, NY.

DYDE, WALTERS FARRELL, univ. adminstr.; b. Kingston, Can., Sept. 30, 1890; s. S.W. and Jenny (Farrell) D.; M.A., Queens U., 1911, U. Alberta, 1912; B.A., Oxford U. (Rhodes Scholar), 1919; Ph.D., Columbia, 1929; m. Marguerite Stuart, Aug. 20, 1918; children—James Farrell, Jane Christina (Mrs. Richard Miller). Came to U.S., 1922, naturalized, 1940. Instr. classics U. Alberta (Can.), 1912-13; territorial supt. edn., Yukon Ty., Can., 1919-22; asst. prof. edn. U. Colo., 1924-26, asso. prof., 1926-29, prof. edn., 1929-59, chmn. coordinating com. on nat. def., 1940-42, adminstrv. asst. to pres., 1942-43, dean univ., 1943-47, v.p., 1947-59, emeritus; summer lectr. Peabody Coll., 1924, U. Manitoba (Can.), 1932, 36. Harvard, 1937; cons. on higher edn. to Dept. Edn. of P.I., also Fulbright lectr. in edn. Centro Escolar U., 1954-55. Served as maj., Royal F.A., B.E.F., World War I. Awarded Mil. Cross (Brit.) 1918, Mem. Nat. Acad. Polit. Sci., John Dewey Soc., Nat. Soc. for Study Edn. Home: Boulder, Colo. †

DYER, ELIZABETH, univ. dean; b. Cincinnati, O., Dec. 21, 1890; d. Franklin Benjamin and May (Archibald) Dyer; student U. of Cincinnati, 1908-10; A.B., Vassar Coll., 1912; diploma Simmons Coll., Prince Sch. of Edn. for Store Service, 1914; unmarried. Teacher Waterbury High Sch., 1914-15; asst. dir. Prince Sch., Simmons Coll., 1915-17; personnel dir. Rike-Kumler Co., 1917-18; supervisor, Carnegie Inst. Tech. Research Bur. for Retail Training, 1918-22; coordinator prof. New York Sch. of Retailing, 1922-24; became dir. Univ. Cincinnati, Coll. home economics 1924, dean 1940-52. Mem. Am. Home Econ. Assn., N.E.A., Am. Assn. U. Women, League of Women Voters, Delta Kappa Gamma, Chi Omega (pres. from 1952), Omicron Nu. Club: Women's City. Author: Textile Fabrics, 1923; A Manual for Shoe Departments, 1920. Contbr. to mags. Home: Cincinnati, Ohio. †

DYER, THOMAS, clergyman; b. Pulaski, Tenn., Feb. 18, 1888; s. Zachary Taylor and Sarah Anna (Carden) D.; prep. edn., Massey Prep. Sch., Pulaski, Tenn.; student Bethel Coll., McKenzie, Tenn., and Vanderbilt U.; m. Alice Josephine Leslie, May 6, 1924. Ordained ministry Cumberland Presbyn. Ch., 1910; pastor successively Addison Av. Ch., Nashville, Odessa Ch., First Ch., Kansas City, Mo., until 1927, First Ch., Ellsworth, Kan., from Feb. 1, 1927. Served as pvt. 3d Antiaircraft Batt., July-Nov. 1918; 1st lt., chaplain, Nov. 11, 1918-Sept. 18, 1919; served overseas in Army of Occupation; now capt., chaplain O.S.A. Res. Mem. Nat. Bd. of Missions, Cumberland Presbyn. Ch., 4 yrs.; reorganized ch. at Odessa and organized ch. at Kansas City. Democrat. Mason (32 deg., Shriner); mem. O.E.S. Home: Ellsworth, Kan. †

DYKMAN, JACKSON ANNAN, lawyer; b. Brooklyn, N.Y., July 11, 1887; s. William Nelson and Isabel (Annan) D.; B.A., Yale, 1909; LL.B., Harvard Law School, 1912; D.C.L., Nashotah House, 1947; m. Susan Brewer Merrick, Feb. 3, 1915. Admitted to New York bar, 1913; clerk Dykman, Oeland & Kuhn, 1913-15; partner of the law firm Cullen & Dykman, Bklyn., from 1915. Trustee Estate Belonging to Diocese of L.I., 1922-62, chancellor, 1925-52, standing com. Diocese of L.I., 1922-62; trustee Gen. Theol. Sem., 1925-61. Mem. Nat. Council Protestant Episcopal Ch., 1943-49. Served as lt. col., judge adv., U.S. Army, 1917-19, special asst. to atty. gen. U.S., 1942-46, 1950-52. Fellow Am. Bar Found.; mem. Soc. Colonial Wars, Am., N.Y. State (pres. 1944), Nassau County, Bklyn. bar assns., Assn. of Bar of City of N.Y., Alpha Delta Phi. Republican. Clubs: The Links, Recess, Yale (N.Y.C.); Piping Rock (L.I.). Author: White and Dykman, Annotated Constitution and Canons of the Protestant Episcopal Church, 1953. Joint master Meadow Brook Hounds, 1931-33. Home: Glen Cove, NY. †

DYSINGER, WENDELL STUART, college dean; b. Freeport, Ill., Mar. 13, 1897; s. William S. and Laura (McColm) D.; A.B., Wittenberg Coll., 1918; B.D., 1921; M.A., State U. Iowa, 1929, Ph.D., 1933; m. A. Ruth Fraser, May 10, 1921; children—Robert Holmes, Dale Wendell. Ordained to ministry United Luth. ministry, 1921; pastor 1st Ch., Los Angeles, Oakland, Calif. and Iowa City; research asst. U. Iowa, 1933-37; dir. personnel Thiel Coll., Greenville, Pa., 1937-40; dean, dir. personnel MacMurray Coll., Jacksonville, Ill., 1940-61, v.p., dean coll., 1961-65, v.p., dean emeritus, 1965-83; acting acad. dean McKendree Coll., Lebanon, Ill., 1965-68; cons. psychologist Dept. Mental Health, State of Ill., 1968-74. Mem. motion picture research com. Payne Found.; mem. adv. council Inst. for Juvenile Research State of Ill.; personnel cons. Am. Council on Edn.; dir. tri-coll. study (Hanover, Wittenberg, MacMurray colls.) for U.S. Office Edn. Diplomate Am. Bd. Examiners in Profl. Psychology. Fellow Am. Psychology Assn.; mem. Ill. Psychol. Assn. (pres. bd. examiners), Ill. Guidance and Personnel Assn., Midwest Assn. Coll. Deans, Am. Bd. Psychol. Services (sec., treas.), Am. Coll. Personnel Assn., North Central Assn. Acad. Deans (pres.), Nat. Vocat. Guidance Assn., Sigma Xi, Phi Gamma Delta. Rotarian. Author: Emotional Response of Children to the Motion Picture Situation, 1933; Self-Measurement for College Students, 1935; College Know-How, 1957. Contbr. articles to jours. Home: Jacksonville, Ill. Died Feb. 7, 1983.

DZVONCHIK, JOSEPH, clergyman; b. Losia, Province of Galicia (formerly Austria, later Poland), Jan. 4, 1888; s. Onisim and Eva (Detch) D.; ed. public school and high school, Mayfield, Pa.; student Zitomir (Russia) Theol. Sem., 1903-05, Russian Orthodox Sem., Minneapolis, Minn., 1906-11; special law course, Youngstown (O.) Law Sch., 1 yr.; special social science course, Western Reserve U., 1 yr.; m. Ellen Ripich, July 20, 1911; children—Nicholas, Nadezda (Mrs. Linwood M. Winslow), Joseph, Anna (dec.). Ordained priest of Russian Orthodox Church of America, 1911; became dean of Midwestern Dist., 1919. Central Pa. Dist., 1921; elevated to rank of archpriest, 1925. Elected mem. Metropolitan Council at All American Conf., 1937; resigned as secretary, 1946, re-elected member (same) at Cleveland (O.) Sobor, 1946. nat. spiritual adviser Federated Russian Orthodox Clubs of America since 1941; national executive secretary Russian Orthodox Ch. of North America since 1939; del. from North America to All Russian Ch. Conf. (Sobor), Moscow, 1945. Pres. Racial Council, Stamford, Conn., 1935-37. Pres. Russian Orthodox Clergy Assn. to 1941, Russian Orthodox Clergy Alumni Assn., 1935-45. Mem. bd. St. Vladimir Theol. Sem., New York, N.Y. Awarded crucifix with decoration by Bishops' Council, 1941. Author: Russian Orthodox Prayer Book, 1942; My Trip to Moscow, 1945. Home: Whitestone, N.Y. †

EADY, SIR (CRAWFORD) WILFRID GRIFFIN, Brit. govt. ofcl., economist; b. Argentina, Sept. 1890; s. G. Griffin Eady; ed. Clifton, and Jesus Coll., Cambridge; m. Elizabeth M. Laistner, 1915; 2 sons. Entered Home Civil Service, 1913, and advanced through positions of responsibility, becoming undersec. of state in Home Office, in charge of air raid precautions (A.R.P.), 1938; additional dep. chmn. Bd. of Customs and Excise, 1940-41, chmn., 1941-42; joint 2d sec. of the treasury since 1942. Chmn. Brit. delegation Bretton Wood Monetary Conf., 1944. Mem. court of govs. London Sch. of Economics; prin. Working Men's Coll., London, since 1941. Companion St. Michael and St. George, 1932, Companion of Bath, 1934, Knight Comdr. Order Brit. Empire, 1939, Knight Comdr. of Bath, 1942. Home: London, Eng. †

EAKIN, ROBERT EDWARD, chemistry educator; b. LaGrande, Oreg., Jan. 23, 1916; s. Robert S. and Netta (Kiddle) E.; B.S., Oreg. State U., 1937, M.A. (Standard Brands fellow), 1939; Ph.D. (Standard Brands fellow), U. Tex., Austin, 1942; m. Esther Aline, Oct. 13, 1940; children—Timothy, Patrick, Michael, Kelly. Research biochemist Nutrition Clinic, Hillman Hosp., Birmingham, Ala., 1941-42; research assoc. U. Cin. Med. Sch., 1941-43; asst. to full prof. chemistry U. Tex., Austin, 1946-79; cons. Eli Lilly & Co., Clayton Biochemical Found. for Research. Served with USNR, 1943-46. Mem. Am. Assn. Biol. Chemists, Am. Chem. Soc., AAAS, Phi Lambda Upsilon, Sigma Xi, Phi Kappa Phi, Phi Delta Theta. Presbyn. Author: (with others) Biochemistry of the B Vitamins, 1951. Home: Austin, Tex. Died Oct. 19, 1979.

EAST, JOHN H., JR., govt. adminstr.; b. Rising City, Neb., Feb. 27, 1890; s. John H. and May (Emerson) E.; grad. Colo. Sch. Mines, 1910; m. Arlie Conaway, Dec. 8, 1918; 1 son, John H. Asso. with Chile Copper Co., Chuquicamata, Chile, 1916-22. Locust Mountain Coal Co., Shenandoah, Pa., 1923-28, U.S. Gypsum Co., Alabaster, Mich., 1928-33; J. R. Bazley, Inc., Pottsville, Pa., 1934-37; regional dir. Region IV, U.S. Bur. Mines, Denver, from 1949. Mem. Am. Inst. Mining Engrs., Am. Soc. Safety Engring., Colo. Sci. Soc. Mason. Author articles profl. publs. †

EATON, SARGENT FLINT, merchant; b. Boston, Mass., Oct. 23, 1888; s. Austin Hardy and Nellie (Choate) E.; A.B., Dartmouth, 1911; m. Esther Denholm Cooke, Oct. 2, 1915; children—Elizabeth Choate (Mrs. Cuyler H. Shaw), Sargent Sheffield. In mdse. div., Filene's, Boston,

Mass., 1911-16; owner, Eaton Co., Portland, Me., 1916-24; asst. to exec. v.p., Saks, N.Y. City, 1924-26; pres., dir., chmn. Howland's, Bridgeport, Connecticut, from 1926; member of the exec. com., dir., mem. trust investment com., 1st Nat. Bank & Trust Co., Bridgeport; dir. Bridgeport Peoples Savings Bank; vice pres., dir., mem. exec. com., finance com., Bridgeport Hosp.; v.p., dir., Bridgeport Chamber of Commerce; dir. Community Chest and War Council, Conn. Pub. Expenditure Council. Mem. Nat. Retail Dry Goods Assn. (mem. exec. com., dir.). Republican. Conglist. Clubs: Brooklawn, University, Rotary. Home: Fairfield, Conn. †

EBERHARD, RAY C(HARLES), lawyer; b. La Crescent, Minn., Aug. 12, 1890; s. Charles C. and May L. (Mason) E.; LL.B., University of Southern California, 1915; m. Lucy Dorival, September 30, 1915; children—Elisabeth E. Zeigler, Mildred E. Younger. Admitted to Calif. bar, 1914; deputy city attorney, Los Angeles, and assistant counsel to Municipal Dept. Water and Power, 1916-24, during litigation establishing right of city to distribute water from Los Angeles Aqueduct and to operate municipal power system; counsel to bondholders' com., reorganizing irrigation dists. and private corps., Ore., Ida., Utah, Ariz., Calif., 1923-31; mem. Eberhard & Zeigler, specializing in public law and water rights, Los Angeles from 1931; Mem. adv. com., Legislative Interim Com. on Revision Calif. Constrn. counsel Teacher Organizations, of Los Angeles, spl. asst. counsel Met. Water District of Southern California (Colorado River project), and consulting counsel California State Dept. of Public Works, 1939. Mem. Governor's Com. on Central Valley Project, 1939-42. Counsel, Calif. Municipal Utilities Assn., counsel Pacific Coast Building Officials' Conference. Has drafted many bills and constitutional amendments affecting municipally owned enterprises and education. Member U.S. Treasury Southern California Commission Salary Deductions (war bonds). Mem. Am., Los Angeles, Calif. State (mem. Ho. Dels., 1946-47-48), bar associations, Examiner, California State Bar, California Public Power League (former member executive committee). Republican. Methodist. Clubs: Trojans (dir.), Los Angeles Athletic, Pacific Coast, Hollywood Athletic, Deauville, Riviera Country, Peter Pan Woodland. Contbr. articles on legal and polit. subjects to mags. Home: Los Angeles, Calif. †

EBLEN, AMOS HALL, lawyer; b. Alton, Mo., Apr. 26, 1906; s. Joseph L. and Meekee (Gum) E.; LL.B., U. Mo., 1931, A.B., 1932; S.J.D., Harvard, 1934; m. Marguerite George, Aug. 11, 1932; children—Larry H., Gary T. Admitted to Mo. bar, 1930, Ky. bar, 1938; prof. law U. Mo., 1931-33, U. Ky., 1934-42; vis. prof. Emory U., 1935, Ohio State U., 1940-41; asso. Smith & Leary, attys., Frankfort, Ky., 1942-43, 46-50; reporter Ct. of Appeals of Ky., Frankfort, 1950-56, judge, 1958-59; mem. firm Eblen, Howard & Milner, Lexington, Ky., 1959-75, Eblen, Milner, Rosenbaum & Wilson, Lexington, 1975-79; individual practice law, Lexington, 1979-80; sec. Jud. Council of Ky., 1950-58, Ky. Bd. Bar Examiners, 1949-50; mem. Ky. Bd. Bar Commrs., 1963-69. Served to capt. AUS, 1943-46. Mem. Ky. Bar Assn. Baptist. Home: Frankfort, Ky. Died Dec. 5, 1980.

ECCLES, GEORGE STODDARD, banker; b. Baker, Oreg., Apr. 9, 1900; s. David and Ellen (Stoddard) E.; m. Dolores Doré, Mar. 4, 1925. B.S., Columbia Sch. Bus. 1922; LL.D., U. Utah, 1963, Utah State U., 1970, Westminster Coll., 1974; H.H.D., Brigham Young U., 1978. Asst. cashier First Security Bank Utah, Nat. Assn. (formerly 1st Nat. Bank of Ogden), 1922, v.p., 1923, pres., 1934-75, chmn. bd., from 1934; chmn. exec. com., dir. First Security Bank of Idaho Nat. Assn.; v.p., dir. First Security Corp., 1928-46, chmn. bd., chief exec. officer, dir., 1975-82; mem. exec. com. Aubrey G. Lanston & Co., Inc., N.Y.C.; dir. Utah Internat., Inc., San Francisco, U.P. Corp. N.Y., Farmers Group, Inc., Los Angeles, Amalgamated Sugar Co., Ogden, Am. Bankers Life Assurance Co. Fla., Am. Bankers Ins. Co. Fla., Anderson Lumber Co., Ogden Union Ry. & Depot Co.; advisor to Sec. of Treasury; hon. life dir. Texasgulf, Inc., N.Y.C.; Past pres., hon. life mem. dir., mem. exec. com. Assn. of Registered Bank Holding Cos. Trustee Los Angeles Found. Otology; past bd. dirs. Nat. Indsl. Conf. Bd.; treas. bd. trustees U. Utah. Served in inf. U.S. Army, World War I. Mem. Am. Bankers Assn., Assn. Res. City Bankers (past pres., hon. life), Internat. Monetary Conf. (past chmn., hon. life mem.), C. of C., Alpha Kappa Psi, Sigma Chi. Clubs: Ogden Golf and Country, Alta, Salt Lake Country; Eldorado Country (Palm Desert, Calif.). Home: Salt Lake City, Utah. Dec. 1982.

ECCLESTON, J(AMES) HOUSTON, clergyman; b. Chestertown, Md., May 10, s. John Bowers and Augusta (Chambe) A.B., Princeton, 1856; studied theology Div. Sch., W. Phila.; (S.T.D., Griswold, 1873; D.D., Princeton, 1904); m. Helen McLoud 1887. Deacon, 1865, priest, 1866, P.E. Ch.; rector St. Matthew's and later of Ch. of the Saviour, Phila.; elected bishop of Iowa, 1875, disputed and declined; elected bishop of W. Va., 1877, declined; later rector Emmanuel Ch., and Ch. of the Atonement, Baltimore; elected dean Theol. Sem. of Va., 1898, declined; pres. Standing Com. Diocese of Md. and rector Emmanuel Ch., from Jan., 1884; mem. Bd. Missions, P.E. Ch. Address: Baltimore, Md. Deceased.

ECHOLS, JOHN MINOR, linguist, educator; b. Portland, Oreg., Mar. 25, 1913; s. John Minor and

Florence Crawford (McGuffin) E.; B.A., U. Va., 1937, M.A., 1938, Ph.D., 1940; summer student U. Mich., 1938-40; m. Nancy Worthington Doner, June 7, 1941; children—Jane McGuffin, John Minor III, Florence Doner. Instr. German and Swedish, U. Chgo., 1947; asso. prof. linguistics, dep. dir. Fgn. Service Inst., Dept. State, 1947-52; asso. prof. linguistics Cornell U., 1952-57, prof. linguistics, 1957-78, emeritus, 1978-82, chmn. dept. Far Eastern studies, 1956-61. Dir., cons. Ford Found. and Inst. Internat. Edn. English Lang. Teaching Project, Indonesia, 1952-55. Served as lt. comdr. USNR, 1942-47; asst. naval attaché Am. legation, Stockholm, 1944-47. Recipient honor award Dept. State, 1951. Fellow Am. Anthrop. Assn.; mem. Linguistic Soc. Am. (life), Assn. Asian Studies (v.p. 1976-77, pres. 1977-78), Am. Oriental Soc., Phi Beta Kappa. Presbyn. Author: (with Hassan Shadily) An Indonesian-English Dictionary, 1963, An English-Indonesian Dictionary, 1975. Home: Ithaca, N.Y. Died June 23, 1982.

ECKENRODE, ROBERT THOMAS, railroad executive; b. Harrisburg, Pa., Nov. 12, 1927; s. Robert Thomas and Helen Gertrude (Oaster) E.; m. Isabel F. O'Leary, Sept. 29, 1951; children—Pamela Ellen Eckenrode Magyar, Robert Thomas, III, David M., Cynthia A. B.Chem-.Engring., Villanova (Pa.) U., 1951; M.A., Fordham U., 1964. Registered profl. engr., Mass. Dir. Frankford Arsenal, Phila., 1949-56; sr. v.p. Dunlap & Assocs., Inc., Darien, Conn., 1956-69; exec. v.p. Am. Stock Exchange Inc., N.Y.C., 1969-80; group v.p. Nat. Railroad Passenger Corp., 1980-82; adj. prof. Fairfield (Conn.) U., 1975-80; chmn. Amex Commodities Exchange, Inc., 1978-79. Served with USN, 1947-48. Mem. Fin. Execs. Inst., N.Am. Soc. Corp. Planners, Am. Mgmt. Assn., Ops. Research Soc. Am., Inst. Mgmt. Scis., Sigma Xi. Home: Alexandria, Va. Dec. Apr. 27, 1982.

ECKERMAN, WILLIAM CHARLES, social scientist; b. Saginaw, Mich., Oct. 29, 1934; s. Ernest Francis and Catherine Mary (Shea) E.; m. Margaret Ann Moore, June 25, 1960; children—William Moore, Thomas Patrick. B.A. in Econs, U. Mich., 1956, M.A. in Econs, 1957, Ph.D. in Social Psychology, 1963. Study dir., head field office Survey Research Center, U. Mich., 1960-66; sr. social psychologist Mich. Health and Social Security Research Inst., Detroit, 1966-67; group mgr., then center dir. Research Triangle Inst., Research Triangle Park, N.C., 1967-74, v.p. social sci., 1974-83. Author: Public Concepts of the Costs and Utility of Higher Education, 1964, Factors Affecting The Validity of Self-Reports of Drug Use, 1978. Mem. Am. Psychol. Assn., Am. Sociol. Assn., AAAS, Am. Assn. Public Opinion Research, Phi Kappa Phi. Roman Catholic. Club: North Ridge Country. Home: Raleigh, N.C. Died June 12, 1983.

ECKERT, OTTO E., engineer; b. Saginaw, Mich., Jan. 13, 1890; s. Fred Carl and Kunigunda (Popp) E.; B.C.E., U. of Mich., 1912; m. Clara Elizabeth Horning, Oct. 1, 1913; 1 dau., Barbara Ann (Mrs. Joseph Anton). Asst. city engr., Saginaw, Mich., 1912-17; asst. engr. with constructing Q.M., Camp Custer, 1917; asst., then acting state sanitary engr. for Mich., 1918; city engr., Lansing, Mich., 1919-21, 1923-27; contracting builder, 1922; gen. mgr. Bd. of Water and Electric Light Commrs., Lansing, since 1927. Mem. Lansing City Plan Commn., 1922-46. Regent, U. of Mich., from 1946. Mem. ASCE, ASME, Am. Inst. E.E., Am. Pub. Power Assn. (past pres.), Mich. Engring. Soc. (past pres.), Tau Beta Pi. Mason. Club: Rotary. Home: Lansing, Mich. †

ECKLEY, FREDERICK RALPH, JR., telephone co. exec.; b. Delaware, Ohio, Aug. 22, 1914; s. Frederick Ralph and Mary Taylor (May) E.; B.S.C., Ohio State U., 1936; m. Helen Warren, June 21, 1941; children—Marcia Eckley Yearout, Deborah Eckley Briggs. With N.J. Bell Telephone Co., 1936-47; with AT&T, 1947-52, 56-61, dir. personnel and pub. relations long lines, 1959-61; with Northwestern Bell Telephone Co., 1952-56, asst. v.p. sales and mdsg., 1955-56; with Mich. Bell Telephone Co., Detroit, 1961-62; v.p., gen. mgr., dir. mem. exec. com. Ohio Bell Telephone Co., Cleve. 1962-64, pres., dir., 1966-77; exec. v.p. AT&T, N.Y.C., 1964-66; dir. Republic Steel Corp., Eaton Corp., Nationwide Real Estate Investments, Addressograph Multigraph Corp. Mem. Navy League U.S., Ohio Soc. N.Y., Ohio (dir.), Cleve. (dir.) chambers commerce, Telephone Pioneers Am., Newcomen Soc., Phi Gamma Delta. Clubs: Gulfstream Golf; Pepper Pike, Union, Country (Cleve.); Delray Beach (Fla.), Delray Beach Yacht. Home: Delray Beach, Fla. Died Aug. 28, 1982; interred Knollwood Cemetery, Cleveland, Ohio.

ECKSTEIN, GUSTAV, physiologist, author; b. Cincinnati, O., Oct. 26, 1890; s. Gustav and Emma (Imig) E.; D.D.S., Cincinnati Coll. of Dental Surgery, 1911; M.D., U. of Cincinnati, 1924; studied Harvard Univ.; L.H.D., Hamilton College, 1939; m. Francesca Benedica, Apr. 19, 1919. Instructor in physiology. College of Medicine, Univ. of Cincinnati, 1922-33, asst. prof., 1933-35, asso. prof. from 1935. Author: Nogochi, 1931; Lives, 1932; Kettle, 1933; Hokusai, 1935; Canary, 1936; Christmas Eve, 1940; In Peace Japan Breeds War, 1943; The Pet Shop, 1945. Died Sept. 23, 1981.

ECKSTEIN, OTTO, economics educator; b. Ulm, Germany, Aug. 1, 1927; came to U.S., 1939, naturalized, 1945; s. Hugo and Hedwig (Pressburger) E.; m. Harriett Mirkin, June 27, 1954; children: Warren Matthew, Felicia, June.

A.B., Princeton U., 1951, LL.D. (hon.), 1966; A.M., Harvard U., 1952, Ph.D., 1955. Mem. faculty Harvard, 1955-84, prof. econs., 1963, Paul M. Warburg prof. econs., 1975-84; pres. Data Resources, Inc., 1969-81, chmn., 1981-84; dir. Paine Webber, Inc. Author: Water Resource Development, 1958, (with J.V. Krutilla) Multiple Purpose River Development, 1958, (with others) Economic Policy in Our Time, 1963, Public Finance, 1963, (with others) Econometrics of Prices, 1972, Parameters and Policies in the U.S. Economy, 1976, The Great Recession, 1978, Core Inflation, 1981, The DRI Model of the U.S. Economy, 1983; editor: Foundations of Modern Economics Series, 1962—, (with others) Rev. Economics and Statistics, 1962-71. Tech. dir. employment, growth and price levels study Joint Econ. Com., U.S. Congress, 1959-60; mem. President's Council of Econ. Advisers, 1964-66, Nat. Adv. Council on Econ. Opportunity, 1967-69, President's Commn. on Income Maintenance Programs, 1968-69; mem. research adv. bd. Com. for Econ. Devel., 1967-70, Belmont Hill Sch., 1975-84; trustee Radcliffe Coll., 1979-84. Served with AUS, 1946-48. Fellow Econometric Soc., Am. Statis. Assn., Nat. Assn. Bus. Economists; mem. Am. Econ. Assn. (exec. com. 1967-70, v.p. 1981), Eastern Econ. Assn. (pres. 1983-84). Home: Lexington, Mass. Dec. Mar. 22, 1984.

EDDINS, DANIEL STONEWALL, pres. Plymouth Motor Corp.; b. Waco, Tex., Apr. 13, 1887; s. Daniel Stonewall and Mamie (Harrison) E.; grad. high sch.; studied economics, commercial law and accounting, 1 1/2 yrs.; m. Ora May Rounsaville. Locomotive repairs for mechanical training, 3 1/2 yrs.; automobile dealer and distributor, 1911-18; branch mgr. Chevrolet Motor Co., 1918-22; regional mgr. Chevrolet Motor Co., 1922-24; asst. gen. sales mgr., Chevrolet Motor Co., 1924-25; vice-pres. and sales mgr. Olds Motor Works, 1925-29; pres. and gen. mgr. Olds Motor Works, 1929-32; with General Motors Corp., Detroit, 1932-34; v.p. and gen. mgr. Plymouth Motor Corp., Detroit, 1932-34; v.p. and gen. mgr., 1934. Clubs: Athletic (Detroit); Golf; Grosse Point Yacht. Home: Detroit, Mich. Deceased.

EDDY, CLYDE, lecturer, author; b. Round Mountain, Tex., Mar. 30, 1889; s. Daniel Leland and Mary (Skelton) E.; Ph.C., U. of Calif., 1912; grad. study Columbia, 1921-23, New Sch. of Social Research, N.Y. City, 1923-25; m. Kathleen Kirby, Mar. 15, 1912; 1 son, Richard Langston. Editor Pacific Pharmacist, San Francisco, 1915-16, The Druggists Circular, N.Y. City, 1916-27; dir. edn. and research, Bray Pictures Corp., 1927; mgr. merchandising dept. E. R. Squibb & Sons, N.Y. City, from 1928. Lecturer from 1927. Enlisted man, U.S. Navy, 1906-08; mem. photographic div., U.S. Signal Corps, France, 1918-19. Leader of Eddy Colo. River Expdn., 1927; mem. Pathe-Bray Colo. River Expdn., 1927; leader Eddy-Frazier Colo. River Expdn., 1934. Mem. Am. Pharm. Assn. (vice-pres.; ex-pres. N.Y. branch), Am. Med. Editors Assn. (v.p.); hon. mem. Am. Scenic and Historic Preservation Soc.; fellow Royal Geog. Soc. (London), American Geographical Soc. of N.Y. Clubs: Explorers, Adventurers (N.Y.C.). Author several books, adventure and travel articles, also business articles. Editor: Today in Pharmacy and Ideas. Home: Mathews County, Va. †

EDDY, WALTER LEWIS, ex-sec. Federal Reserve Bd.; b. Newport, R.I., Aug. 19, 1889; s. George Alfred and Fannie Stanton (Eldred) E.; ed. pub. schs.; m. Esther L. Swain, of Washington, D.C., Mar. 24, 1915; children—Walter Lewis, Esther L. Began as asst. to sec. of Federal Reserve Bank Organization Com., 1914; identified with Federal Reserve Bd. as sec. to gov. of Bd., then asst. sec. to Bd. and sec., 1923-31. Mason (32 deg., Shriner). Home: Washington, D.C. †

EDENS, JAMES DRAKE, JR., investment exec.; b. Blaney, S.C., May 13, 1925; s. J. Drake and May (Youmans) E.; m. Ferrell McCracken, May 28, 1946; children—Robert Manning, Jenny. B.S. in Bus. Adminstrn, U. S.C., 1949. Vice pres. Edens Food Stores, Inc. (merged with Winn-Dixie Stores, Inc. 1955), Columbia, S.C., 1946-55; founder, pres. Edens-Turbeville Gen. Ins. Agy., Columbia, 1956-64, engaged in mgmt. of personal investments in securities and real estate, farming and timber mgmt., from 1965. Mem. Nat. Adv. Bd. for Sports Fisheries and Wildlife, Dept. Interior, chmn., 1969-72; chmn. S.C. Wildlife and Marine Resources Commn.; mem. adv. bd. Voluntary Action Com. Lexington and Richland Counties; bd. dirs., past 1st v.p. Alston Wilkes Soc.; trustee S.C. Arthritis Found., Columbia (S.C.) Coll., from 1974, Alston Wilkes Found.; mem. U. S.C. Acad. and Athletic Scholarship Program, U. S.C. Ednl. Found.; mem. adminstrv. bd., chmn. pastoral counseling service com. Trenholm Rd. United Meth. Ch.; chmn. S.C. Republican Party, 1963-65; del. Rep. Nat. Conv., 1964, 68, 76; mem. Rep. Nat. Com. for S.C., 1965-72, vice chmn., 1965-72. Served with USMC, 1943-46, PTO. Mem. S.C., Greater Columbia chambers commerce, Nat. Wildlife Fedn., S.C. Farm Bur., Nat. Audubon Soc., Nat. Rifle Assn., Wilderness Soc., Ducks Unlimited, U. S.C. Alumni Assn. Methodist (lay preacher). Clubs: Mason. (Columbia), Palmetto (Columbia), Forest Lake Country (Columbia); Grand Nat. Quail of Okla, Camellia Ball. Home: Columbia, SC.

EDGAR, CAMPBELL DALLAS, naval officer; b. Washington, D.C., Aug. 23, 1889; s. Comdr. Webster Appleton and Matilda (Emory) E.; student Manlius Sch., 1907-08; B.S., U.S. Naval Acad., 1912; m. Ysabel Rising, Sept. 15, 1920; 1 son, Dallas Sargent. Commd. ensign U.S. Navy, 1912, advanced through grades to rear admiral, 1947; served in U.S.S. Sampson, based at Queenstown, Ireland, 1917-18; div. of squadron comdr. in amphibious operations, Algiers (North Africa), Sicily, Salerno (Italy), Normandy, So. France, 1942-44; comdr. transport squadron, Pacific, 1945; ret. from active service, Jan. 1, 1947. Awarded Legion of Merit, 3 gold stars; decorated officer, Legion of Honor, Croix de Guerre with palm (France). Home: Carmel, Calif. †

EDGERTON, ALANSON HARRISON, educator; b. Elba, N.Y., May 16, 1890; s. Freeman and Susan (Norton) E.; grad. Rochester (N.Y.) Inst. of Technology, 1909; B.S., Columbia, 1913, A.M., 1917, Ph.D., 1925; m. Nicholas Grierson Stewart, Mar. 24, 1914; 1 son, Stewart Edgerton. Teacher, Plattsburg (N.Y.) State Normal Sch., 1909-10; chmn. dept. indsl. edn. and applied arts, prof. edn. U. Wis., 1924-28, dir., prof. vocational guidance, 1928-44, prof. edn., charge counselor tng., 1944-60, prof. edn. emeritus, from 1960; summer guidance workshop dir. No. Mont. Coll., 1960-62; personnel consultant Bancroft Dairy Co., Wis., job family series cons. Science Research Associates, Chicago, Illinois Guidance con., Wis. Dept. Pub. Instruction. Chmn. Personnel Board (civil service), City of Madison, Wis. Mem. N.E.A. (high sch. curriculum chmn., 1927-28), Nat. Soc. for Study of Edn. (chmn. yearbook com., 1922-24), Nat. Vocational Guidance Assn. (v.p. 1926-27, pres. 1928, trustee 1929-30, 36-41, recipient Distinguished Service citation 1963), Wis. Guidance Association (hon. life), American Personnel and Guidance Assn. (hon. life), Alpha Sigma Phi, Phi Sigma Phi, Phi Delta Kappa. Conglist. Clubs: Taus (New York); University Faculty (Madison). Author books, the latest: Techniques of Guidance and Personnel Services, 1948; The Keys to Job Success, 1952; Opening the Doors to Successful Careers, 1952; Vocational Guidance Kit for U.S. Armed Forces, 1953; Career Information Kit for Civilians, 1954; Career Information Kit and Counselor Manual, 1958, revised edits. and new supplements for older kits, 1963; Career-Planning Guide Book for Parents, 1958, revised edits., 1961, 63; Dairy Personnel Placement Tests, 1962-63. Compiler and contributor professional publications. Editor of Make and Do sects. Book of Knowlege, 1924-25; director Nat. Occupational Trend and Guidance Evaluation studies, from 1926. Guidance cons. World Book Ency. Author syndicated column, It's Your Job. Home: Madison, Wis. †

EDMINSTER, TALCOTT W., agricultural engineer; b. East Freetown, Mass., Oct. 1, 1920; s. Albert and Elizabeth (Talcott) E.; B.S. in Agrl. Engring., U. Mass., 1942; M.S., U. Ga., 1943; m. Marian Jeanne Wilson, June 3, 1944; children—Linda Kay Edminster Gregory, Talcott Ross, Vicki Deen Edminster Schmeltz, Corinne Gail Edminster Vucci. With Soil Conservation Service, U.S. Dept. Agr., Va., 1944-52, subsequently work project leader fed. drainage research program, asst. chief and then chief Eastern soil and water mgmt. research br. Agrl. Research Service, Beltsville, Md., assoc. dir. soil and water conservation research div., dep. adminstr., assoc. adminstr., adminstr., 1971-78, dep. dir. Sci. and Edn. Adminstrn., 1978-80. Bd. dirs. U.S.-Israeli Binat. Sci. Found., 1976-79, U.S.-Israeli Binat. Agrl. Research and Devel. Fund, 1978-80. Decorated officier de l'Ordre Lu Mérite Agricole, French Ministry Agr., 1979; recipient William A. Jump Meml. award, 1951; Superior award Dept. Agr., 1951, Distinguished Service award, 1973; Career Service award Nat. Civil Service League, 1975. Fellow AAAS, Am. Soc. Agrl. Engring. (chmn. soil and water div. 1954, v.p. 1956-57, pres. 1968-69), Am. Soc. Agronomy, Soil Conservation Soc. Am., Internat. Commn. Agrl. Engring. (v.p. 1974-79, pres. 1979-80). Author coll. textbooks. Contbr. articles to profl. jours. Home: College Park, Md. Died Nov. 1980.

EDMUNDS, JOHN OLLIE, university chancellor; b. Higgston, Ga., Mar. 1, 1903; s. Plato D. and Lee S. (Ganey) E.; m. Emily Bryant, July 17, 1934 (dec. 1959); children—John, Jane; m. Martha Lee, 1978. A.B., John B. Stetson U., 1925, A.M., 1927, LL.B., 1928, LL.D., 1943; LL.D., U. Richmond, 1970; Litt.D. (hon.), U. Miami, 1951, Jacksonville U., 1964; D.Hum. (hon.), Rollins Coll., 1963. Bar: Fla. bar 1927. Practiced in, DeLand, Fla., 1927-30; judge Duval County, Jacksonville, Fla., 1931-44; pvt. practice, Jacksonville, 1944-48; pres. John B. Stetson U., DeLand, 1948-67, chancellor, 1967-84; partner Gualala Redwoods, 1949-84. Mem. Pres.'s Com. Devel. Scis. and Engrs., 1959-60; Duval County chmn. War Savs. Bond Com. U.S. Treas., 1942; mem. Fla. Land Use and Control Commn., 1957-58. Served as lt. (j.g.) USCGR; exec. officer Jacksonville Bn. Port Security Force, 1943-44. Recipient Freedom's Found. Award, 1952, 55, 68. Mem. Assn. Am. Colls. (pres. 1959), Omicron Delta Kappa, Phi Alpha Delta, Theta Alpha Phi, Delta Sigma Phi. Democrat. Baptist (pres. Conv. 1961). Clubs: Masons (33 deg.), Shriners, Rotary, Ponte Vedra; Timuquana Country (Jacksonville), River (Jacksonville); Lake Beresford Yacht (DeLand); University (N.Y.C.); Olympic (San Francisco). Candidate for U.S. Senate 1944. Home: DeLand, Fla. Dec. Apr. 2, 1984.

EDWARDS, BYRON MALET, banker; b. Bladenboro, N.C., June 1, 1888; s. Daniel Baxter and Mary Turner (Edwards) E.; attended Bladenboro elementary and high schs., 1894-1905; LL.D. (honorary), Univ. S.C., 1953; married Sadie Bridger Edwards, Aug. 23, 1907; children—Emma Marie (Mrs. James Wesley Hunt), Jettye Vivian (Mrs. Albert Edward Lee), Byron Marion, Robert Livingston, Sadie Bridger. Telegraph operator and station agent, Bladenboro, Southern Pines and Aberdeen, N.C., 1905-11; general mgr. Bennettsville & Cheraw R.R., Bennettsville, S.C., 1911-18; cashier Planters Nat. Bank, Bennettsville, 1918-23; vice pres., Columbia Nat. Bank, Columbia, 1923-25; vice pres., The South Carolina Nat. Bank of Charleston, Columbia, 1925-40, pres. and dir., 1940-51, chmn. bd. from 1952. Asst. sec. U.S. Treasury, 1941, consultant to the secretary, 1941-46. Dir. S.C. Ins. Co., Columbia, Liberty Life Insurance Co., Greenville, S.C., Standard Warehouse Co., Columbia; dir. Jefferson Hotel Co., Columbia, Bladenboro Cotton Mills, Marlboro Cotton Mills, Bridges Corp., Seaboard Airline Railroad Co., S.C. Electric & Gas Co.; mem. advisory bd. Hampton (S.C.) plant Westinghouse Electric Co. Director RFC, Charlotte, 1932-51, Nat. War Fund, Inc., N.Y. Trustee Furman U., Benedict Coll. S.C. Found. Ind. Colls., Nat. Endowment Fund, A.R.C. (mem. adv. com.); chmn. bd. trustees Bapt. Found. S.C.; chmn. adv. bd. Providence Hosp., Columbia. Democrat. Baptist. Clubs: Columbia, Forrest Lake Country (Columbia). Home: Columbia, S.C.†

EDWARDS, CHARLES REID, surgeon; b. Medley, W. Va., 1888; M.D., U. Md., 1913. Intern. University Hosp., 1913-15, now vis. surgeon; practice of medicine, specializing surgery, Balt., from 1937; vis. surg. staff Church Home and Infirmary, Union Meml. Hosp.; prof. surgery U. Md. Fellow A.C.S., Am. Surg. Assn.; mem. A.M.A., Soc. Clin. Surgeons, So. Surg. Assn., Am. Assn. Surgery Trauma.†

EDWARDS, DANIEL RICHMOND, soldier; b. Moorville, Tex., Apr. 9, 1888; s. Jefferson Dudley and Joan Richmond (Sutton) E.; B.A., Tex. Agrl. and Mech. Coll., 1910; M.Litt., Columbia Sch. of Journalism, New York, 1920; m. Frances Sullivan, June 21, 1921; 1 dau., Joan Frances. Enlisted in U.S. Army, June 1, 1912; served in Philippines, at Vera Cruz and with Tex. Rangers until 1917; went to France with First Div., U.S.A., Apr. 1917; participated in battles at Cantigny and Soissons; wounded and lost arm and leg. Awarded Congressional Medal of Honor for "intrepidity and bravery above and beyond the call of duty," at Soissons; D.S.C. for "extraordinary heroism" at Cantigny; Legion d'honneur, Medelle de guerre and Croix de guerre with 3 palms (France); Distinguished Conduct Medal (Eng.); Meddi de guerre, Black Star (Italy); King Albert's Cross, Croix de guerre (Belgium); War Cross (Poland); Medal for Valor (Montenegro). Served as press rep. of Warren G. Harding's presidential campaign, also under apptmt. of President Harding, as spl. expert in rehabilitation, etc., of U.S. Vets'. Bur., 1923-26; Govt. dir. in campaign for reinstation of war risk insurance, 1926. Dir. pub. relations Internat. Broadcasting Corpn. from 1926; v.p. Robb Chemical Co., Inc., Adv. Film Service Corpn. Mem. Soc. of Engrs. for Prevention of Crime, Am. Aviation Foundation. Republican. Clubs: Flyers, Commodore Athletic, Republican, Texas Agrl. and Mech. Club of New York. Lecturer on crime, athletics and aviation. Home: Baldwin, L.I., N.Y. †

EDWARDS, JAMES D., univ. dean; b. Eclectic, Ala., Nov. 5, 1914; s. James DeAra and Lula (Harris) E.; B.A., Bob Jones U., 1936; student Gregg Coll., summer 1937, La. State U., summers 1938-39; M.A., U. Mich., 1941; LL.D., Northwestern Schs., 1952; m. Carolyn Elizabeth Reynolds, May 31, 1939; children—James D., Carolyn DeAra. Dean of men Bob Jones U., Greenville, S.C., 1936-43, prof. Am. history 1943—, coll. dean, 1943-47, dean sch. commerce, 1947-48, dean students, 1947-53, dean of adminstrn., 1953-81. Mem. N.E.A., So. Hist. Assn., U. Mich., Bob Jones U. (pres. 1952-54) alumni assns. Home: Greenville, S.C. Died Aug. 20, 1981.

EDWARDS, LESTER RICHARD, business exec.; b. LaCrosse, Wis., Aug. 10, 1890; s. Julius Augustus and Olive (Spicer) E.; M.E., Ill. Inst. Tech., Chgo., 1912; m. Caroline K. Steckhahn, Sept. 1, 1915; children—Jean Olive (Mrs. Webster C. Ericson), Betty Lou (Mrs. Kenneth R. Hall), Charlotte Helen (Mrs. Harlan L.R. Anderson), Joyce Lillian (Mrs. Charles K. Test). Partner Edwards & Daley, Elkhorn, Wis., 1906-11; salesman, sales mgr. Aeroshade Co., Waukesha, 1912-17; mgr. P. Hohenadel Jr. Canning Co., Janesville, 1919-22; pres. Garden Canning Co., also Fairview Farms Co., Evansville, 1922-25; asst. to pres. Kieckhefer Container Co., Milw., 1925-29, sec.-treas., 1925-35 (also officer subsidiary, affiliated firms); sec.-treas., sales and prodn. mgr. Eddy Paper Corp., Chgo., 1930-35; pres., treas. dir. gen. mgr. Northeastern Container Corp., Bradford, Pa., 1935-56; v.p., dir. Nat. Container Corp., N.Y.C., 1943-56, president co., 1956-57 (also v.p., director six subsidiaries); vice president, director Marinette, Tomahawk & Western R.R. Co., 1946-56; pres., dir. Bradford Publs., Inc., from 1943, Hotel Emery Corporation, Bradford, 1944-64, Radio Sta. WESB, from 1946, Port Allegany Corp., 1947-62, Urell, Inc., Tioga, Pa., from 1953, Orchard Apts., Inc., Bradford, from 1952, Warren (Pa.) Apts., Inc., 1952-54, Travel Network, Inc., Susquehanna Chem. Co., from 1955, Penn Capital Corp., 1959-66; v.p. Owens-Ill. Glass Co., 1957-60, general manager paper products div., 1956-58; v.p. Condor Corp.; v.p., dir. Nat. Bottle Corp., from 1960, Star City Glass Company, from 1960; partner Smith Ins. Agy.; director Whitewater Canning Co. Humbird Canning Co. (Wis.). Pres., dir. McKean County chpt. Am. Cancer Soc., 1939-56, dir. Pa. div., from 1955, pres.,

1959-60, del.-dir. 1962-mem. bd. of dirs., mem. exec. committee, from 1963; v.p., dir. Bradford U.S.O.; trustee YMCA; dir. Nat. Edn. and Research Inst., Tb and Health Soc.; chmn. bd. dirs. Bradford Hosp., 1945-55. Served as ensign USNR, 1917-19. Mem. Pennsylvania, Bradford (U.S. councilor, past pres.) C.'s of C., Am. Legion, 40 et 8, Pa. Soc. (N.Y.C.), Newcomen Soc. N.Am. Presbyn. Mason (32 deg., Shriner), Elk. Clubs: Rotary (past pres.), Bradford, Pennhills. Home: Bradford, Pa. †

EDWARDS, LYFORD PATERSON, social scientist; b. London, Can., July 2, 1882; s. James Stevenson and Mary Elizabeth (Smyth) E.; student McGill U., 1901-03; B.A., University of Chicago, 1905; M.A., 1917, Ph.D., 1919; Western Theol. Seminary, Chicago, 1905-07, Columbia, summer, 1915; D.D. Bard College, 1947; married Helen Winthrop Gray, June 16, 1923. Deacon, 1907, priest, 1908, P.E. Ch.; rector St. Matthew's Ch., Evanston, Ill., 1907-13; Curate St. John's Ch., Staten Island, N.Y., 1913-14; instr. Nashotah (Wis.) Prep. Sch., 1914-16, Rice Inst., Houston, Tex., 1917-19; asso. prof., St. Stephen's (now Bard) College, 1919-24, professor of social science, 1924-47, professor emeritus since 1947, dean, 1927, provost, 1928. Asso. rector Trinity Ch., Bridgeport, Conn., 1947. Member American Sociol. Soc., Am. Acad. Polit. and Social Science, Kappa Sigma. Author: The Transformation of Early Christianity, 1919; The Natural History of Revolution, 1927. Address: Fairfield, Conn. Died July 24, 1984.

EDWARDS, MARCIA, educator; b. El Paso, Tex., Oct. 22, 1901; d. W. Lister and Ella (Pickett) Edwards; A.B., Coll. of Puget Sound, 1925, D.Sc. (hon.), 1953; A.M. (fellow Am. Assn. Collegiate Registrars), U. Minn., 1931. Ph.D., 1935. Instr. Coll. of Puget Sound, 1926-27, asst. registrar, 1927-30; research fellow U. Minn., 1931-33, instr. ednl. psychology, 1933-36, asst. prof., 1936-40, asso. prof., 1940-46, prof. 1946-70, asst. to dean coll. of edn., 1938-42, asst. dean., 1942-53, asso. dean from 1953. Mem. Mpls. Citizens' Com. of Pub. Edn., 1951-60. Mem. U. Minn. Alumni Association, Minn. Psychol. Assn., Am. Coll. Pessonnel Assn. (past treasurer), Am. Personnel and Guidance Assn., Am. Psychol. Assn., Nat. Vocational Guidance Assn., N.E.A., Nat. Soc. Study Edn., Am. Assn. U. Women, Pi Lambda Theta, Psi Chi. Home: Minneapolis, Minn. Died Oct. 28, 1984.

EFFINGER, ROBERT CRAIG, banker; b. Staunton, Va., May 24, 1890; s. John Frederick and Fannie Strother (Smith) E.; B.S., U. Va., 1914; m. Anne Turley, July 30, 1923; 1 son, Robert Craig. Cons. economist and statistician, 1919-26; with Irving Trust Co., N.Y.C., 1927-54, v.p., 1931-54, ret. Enlisted U.S. Army, 1917, served 1st lt. Gen. Staff and Am. Commn. to Negotiate Peace. A.E.F., 1918-19, disch. rank capt., 1919. Mem. Zeta Psi. Episcopalian. Author: ABC of Investing, 1947. Home: Staunton, VA. †

EGAN, WILLIAM ALLEN, governor of Alaska; b. Valdez, Alaska, Oct. 8, 1914; s. William Edward and Cora (Allen) E.; grad. high sch., Valdez; LL.D., Alaska Meth. U., U. Alaska; m. Neva McKittrick, Nov. 16, 1940; 1 son, Dennis William. Mem. Ho. of Reps., Alaska Ty., 1941, 43, 47, 49, 51, Senate, 1953, 55; del., pres. Alaska Constl. Conv., 1955-56; Tennessee Plan senator to Washington, to promote statehood for Alaska, 1956-58; gov. Alaska, 1959-66, 71-75; dist. mgr. Equitable Life Assurance, 1967-70. Councilman City of Valdez, 1937-38, mayor, 1946; chmn. Western Gov.'s Conf., 1961-62. Mem. Pioneers of Alaska, V.F.W., Am. Legion. Address: Anchorage, Alaska. Died May 6, 1984.

EGGERSS, H. A., b. Persia, Ia., 1890; ed. Univ. of Wis. Pres., Container Co., Van Wert, Ohio; president and dir., Continental Can Co., Inc.; pres. Gould Paper Co., Lyons Falls, N.Y., Continental Can Corp.; dir. Van Wert (Ohio) Nat. Bank, Cameron Can Machinery Co., Chicago, Continental Can Co. of Canada, Ltd., Montreal Que., Continental Can Corp., Havana, Cuba, Continental Overseas Corp., New York City. Home: New York, N.Y. †

EGGERT, HERBERT FLETCHER, ins. exec.; b. Bklyn., Apr. 2, 1887; s. John Fletcher and Marietta (deBaun) E.; student pub. schs., Bklyn.; m. Mary Parker Westvelt, Nov. 5, 1913 (dec. Dec. 19, 1947); children—Herbert Fletcher, Mary Westervelt (Mrs. Walter Buel Potts); m. 2d, Nancy Ann Dolf, June 9, 1951. Runner, clk. claims dept. Atlantic Mut. Ins. Co., 1902-07; adjusting, brokerage activities Mather & Co., N.Y.C., 1907-13; partner Parsons & Co., gen. ins. adjusters, 1913-16. Parsons & Eggert, 1916-19, merged Marsh & McLennan, 1919; v.p., dir. Marsh & McLennan, Inc., 1923-48, vice chmn. bd., 1948-58; pres., dir. Sandacres Assos., Inc., 1930-48, chmn. from 1948; chmn., exec. com., dir. Transatlantic Reins. Co.; chmn., dir. International Cessions Co.; Tech. sec. bd. survey and cons. engrs. U.S. Shipping Bd., 1917, mem. adv. ins. com., 1918, asst. dir. div. ins., 1918-19. Mem. Life Sav. Benevolent Assn. (trustee, mem. finance com.), Maritime Assn. Port of N.Y. (ins. com.), Assn. Average Adjusters (chmn. 1919-20), Insurance Society of New York. Episcopalian Church (trustee). Clubs: India House (bd. govs.); Metropolitan, Downtown Assn., Church (N.Y.C.); Everglades, Bath and Tennis (Palm Beach, Fla.); Quogue Field, Quogue Beach, Turf and Field. Home: New York, N.Y. †

EGGLESTON, ARTHUR FRANCOIS, business exec.; b. Meriden, Conn., Nov. 19, 1890; s. Jere Dewey and Elizabeth Christy (Duncan) E.; student Williston Sem. Prep. Sch., Easthampton, Mass.; B.A., Cornell U., 1913; m. Grace Louise Lane, Dec. 29, 1914 (dec. Aug. 1930); 1 dau., Gertrude Elaine (Mrs. Robert T. Turton); m. 2d, Frances Evelyn Nordaby, Jan. 25, 1933; 1 dau., Polly Jane (Mrs. Foster M. Johnson, Jr.). With The Lane Constrn. Corp., 1914-78, beginning as sales mgr. and paymaster, successively sec., v.p., pres. and gen. mgr., chmn. bd., chief exec. officer, mem. bd. dirs.; sec., pres. chmn. bd. John S. Lane & Son, Inc.; trustee City Savs. Bank, Meriden. Formerly pres., dir. Meriden Hosp., Meriden YMCA; former chmn. bd. mgrs. Bradley Home. Served as 2d lt., inf. U.S. Army, World War I. Conglist. Clubs: Home (Meriden); Pine Orchard (Conn.) Yacht; New Haven Country, Quinnipiack (New Haven); Vero Beach (Fla.) Golf, Riomar Yacht, Riomar Golf (Vero Beach). Home: Meriden, Conn. Died Oct. 29, 1978.

EGGLESTON, H. R., coll. prof.; born Walton, N.Y., Feb. 25, 1890; s. Judah and Maria A. (Bowen) E.; B.S., Hamilton Coll. (Root fellowship in science), 1912, D.Sc., 1950; A.M., Harvard, 1913; student Bermuda Sta. for Biol. Research, summer 1915, Univ. Chicago, summer 1916, Franz Stone Lake Lab., Ohio State Univ., summers 1925, 26, Univ. Mich. Biol. Sta., summer 1927; m. Mildred Claire Cunningham, Sept. 3, 1913; children—Arthur Gurdon, Tom. Prof. biology, Buena Vista Coll., Storm Lake, Ia., 1913-15; instr. biology, Marietta (Ohio) Coll., 1915-17, prof. biology, chmn. dept., from 1917; bacteriologist in charge water purification plant, Marietta, 1918-50; bacteriologist, board of health, 1922-50; splist. Ohio Biological Survey, Mollusca Survey, summers, 1929, 30, 31. Fellow A.A.A.S., Ohio Acad. Sci.; mem. Am. Soc. Biology Tchrs., Ecol. Soc. Am., Limnol. Soc. Am., Malacol. Union, Sigma Xi, Omicron Delta Kappa, Beta Beta Beta. Author bulls., spl. papers, Ohio Acad. Sci. Home: Marietta, OH. †

EGK, WERNER JOSEPH, composer; b. Auchsesheim, Bavaria, May 17, 1901; s. Joseph and Maria (Buck) E.; student Conservatory for Music, Augsburg, Germany, also U. Munich; m. Elisabeth Karl, Mar. 29, 1923; 1 son, Titus. Conductor, Staatsoper, Berlin, 1936-40; dir. High Sch. for Music, West Berlin, 1950-53; permanent guest condr. Staatsoper Munich, from 1950. Composer: (operas) Die Zaubergeige, 1935; Peer Gynt, 1938; Columbus, 1941; Irische Legende, 1955; Der Revisor, 1956; Die Verlobung in San Domingo, 1963; Siebzehn Tage und vier Minuten, 1966; (ballets) Joan von Zarissa, 1940; Abraxas, 1948; Ein Sommertag, 1950; Die Chinesische Nachtigall, 1953; Cassanova in London; also works for orch., solos for orch. Mem. League German Composers (pres.), Acad. der Künste Berlin West, Acad. der schönen Künste Munich, Deutsche Akademie der Künste Berlin. Rotarian. Home: Munich, Germany. Died July 10, 1983.

EHRICKE, KRAFFT ARNOLD, space engineer; b. Berlin, Germany, Mar. 24, 1917; came to U.S., 1947, naturalized, 1955; s. Arnold F. and Ruth (Konietzko) E.; m. Ingeborg Mattull, Jan. 16, 1945; children: Krista, Astrid, Doris. M.S. in Aero. Eng, Tech. U., Berlin, 1942, courses atomic physics and celestial mechanics, 1941-42; L.H.D., Nat. Tchrs. Coll., Evanston, Ill., 1961. Devel. engr. V-2 propulsion system, Peenemuende, Germany, 1942-45; jet propulsion engr. Dept. Army, Ft. Bliss, Tex., 1947-50; chief gasdynamics sect. Army Ballistic Missile Center, Redstone Arsenal, Ala., 1950-52; preliminary design engr. Bell Aircraft Corp., 1952-54; with Convair div. Gen. Dynamics Corp., 1954-65, design specialist, 1954-55, chief design and systems analysis, 1956-57; asst. to tech. dir. Convair-Astronautics, 1957-58, originator, also program dir. Centaur space vehicle, 1958-62, dir. advanced studies dept., 1962-65; asst. div. dir. astrionics div. N.Am. Aviation, Autonetics div., Anaheim, Calif., 1965-68; chief scientist space systems and applications space div. N.Am. Rockwell Corp., Downey, Calif., 1968-73; exec. adviser N.Am. space ops. Rockwell Internat. Corp., 1973-76; mgr. N.Am. space ops. Rockwell Internat. Corp. (NASA contract Space Industrialization Study Space div.), 1976-77; founder, pres. Space Global Co., 1977-84. Author: Space Flight, Vol. I, Environment and Celestial Mechanics, 1959, Vol. II, Dynamics, 1961, (with E.A. Miller) Exploring the Planets, 1969, Beyond Earth, 1971, Cosmic Engineering (in Russian); numerous articles. Recipient 1st Guenther Loeser medal for best paper (The Satelloid) presented during 6th Internat. Astronautical Congress Internat. Astronautical Fedn., 1956, G. Edward Pendray award Am. Rocket Soc., 1961, Astronautics award Am. Rocket Soc., 1957, I.B. Laskowitz award N.Y. Acad. Scis., 1972; named to Internat. Aerospace Hall of Fame, 1966. Fellow Am. Inst. Aeros. and Astronautics, Brit. Interplanetary Soc., Deutsche Ges. f. Weltraumforschg. (pres. 1942-43); mem. Internat. Acad. Astronautics. Introduced microwave reflector concept for long-distance power transmission, 1972, Lunar Slide Lander Concept, 1977 Home: La Jolla, Calif. Died Dec. 11, 1984.

EICHLER, RUDOLPH J., investment banker; b. San Diego, 1889. Vice chmn. bd. Bateman, Eichler & Bingham, Inc. Home: Santa Barbara, Calif. *

EIDE, RANDOLPH, telephone company executive; b. Lee, Ill., May 25, 1888; s. Tollef Torris and Christine (Greve) E.; A.B., University of Illinois, 1910; m. Edna Ruth Phillips, January 17, 1917; children—Catherine Christine (Mrs. John C. Grant, Jr.), Randolph, John Henry, Richard Phillips. Special insp. N.Y. Telephone Co., N.Y.C., 1911-13; supervisor traffic, Eastern Mo. and Ark., for Southwestern Bell Telephone Co., St. Louis, 1913-16; supervisor traffic Mich. Bell Telephone Co., Detroit, 1916-17; supt. traffic (Ohio) Central Union Telephone Co., Columbus, 1917-20; gen. supt. traffic Ohio Bell Telephone Co., 1921-23, gen. mgr., 1923-24, v.p., 1925-30; president, 1930-52, chairman of board from 1952, member executive com. from 1930, director from 1924; director Union Bank of Commerce, Cleveland; trustee, Society for Savings, Cleveland, O. Treasurer Cleveland Community Fund; president Cleveland C. of C., 1931-32. Trustee Univ. Sch. of Cleveland; trustee, Case Institute of Technology, Cleveland; member, St. Luke's Hosp. Assn., Cleveland, since 1935; Governor's Civil Defense Advisory Council for Ohio. Decorated St. Olav Medal, Order of St. Olav, Norway, Frihetsmedalje of King Haakon VII of Norway. Fellow Am. Inst. Elec. Engrs. Republican. Lutheran. Pres. Telephone Pioneers of America, 1946-47 (pres. N. C. Kingsbury chapter 1939-40). Clubs: Union, Mid-Day, Mayfield Country. Home: Cleveland Heights, Ohio. †

EIDSON, JOHN OLIN, educator; b. Johnston, S.C., Dec. 10, 1908; s. Olin Marvin and Margaret (Rushton) E.; m. Perrin Cudd, Aug. 7, 1952. A.B., Wofford Coll., 1929, Litt.D. (hon.), 1954; M.A., Vanderbilt U., 1930; Ph.D., Duke, 1941. Faculty U. Ga., Athens, 1936-68; beginning as instr. English, successively dean U. Ga. (Coordinate Coll.); dir. U. Ga. (U. Center in Ga.); dean U. Ga. (Coll. Arts and Scis.), 1957-68; pres. Ga. So. Coll., Statesboro, 1968-71; vice chancellor Univ. System of Ga., 1971-76; Fulbright prof. Am. studies U. Bonn, Germany, 1977-78; vis. prof. Am. lit. U. Freiberg, Germany, 1956. Author: Tennyson in America, 1943, Charles Stearns Wheeler; Friend of Emerson, 1951, (with W.W. Davidson) Reading for Pleasure, 1948; Editor: (with W.W. Davidson) Ga. Rev, 1950-57; mem. editorial bd. (with W.W. Davidson), 1957-74; Contbr. (with W.W. Davidson) articles and revs. to scholastic jours. Vice pres. Coastal Empire council Boy Scouts Am., 1970-71; exec. bd. Atlanta Area council, 1973-83; pres. Fifty Yr. Club of Wofford Coll., 1980-83, U. Ga. Bot. Garden, 1981-83. Served from lt. to maj., inf. AUS, 1942-46; lt. col. Res. Recipient M.G. Michael award for research, 1950. Mem. Am. Studies Assn., Modern Lang. Assn. Am., S. Atlantic Modern Lang. Assn., Assn. State Univs. and Land-Grant Colls. (mem. senate 1963-66), Southeastern Am. Studies Assn. (pres. 1966-68), Conf. Acad. Deans So. States (sec.-treas. 1965-66, v.p. 1966-67, pres. 1967-68), Nat. Council Coll. Arts and Sci., English Assn. London, Newcomen Soc. N.Am., Am. Assn. State Colls. and Univs., Statesboro C. of C., Tennyson Soc. Eng., Sphinx, Phi Beta Kappa (chmn. S. Atlantic dist. 1958-61, pres. Coastal Ga.-Carolina assn. 1970-72), Pi Kappa Delta, Phi Kappa Phi, Delta Phi Alpha (nat. sec. 1929-34, mem. nat. council 1969-83), Tau Kappa Alpha, Kappa Delta Pi, Phi Delta Kappa, Kappa Phi Kappa. Methodist (mem. ofcl. bd.). Club: Rotarian. Home: Atlanta, Ga. Died Jan. 27, 1983; buried Greenlawn Meml. Garden, Spartanburg, S.C.

EILERS, LOUIS KENNETH, chemical company exec.; b. Gillespie, Ill., Apr. 11, 1907; s. William H. and Minnie (Luken) E.; A.A., Blackburn Coll., 1927; B.S., U. Ill., 1929; M.S., U. Va., 1930; Ph.D., Northwestern U., 1932; D.Sc. (honorary), Blackburn College, 1957; married C. Frances Wampler, Oct. 18, 1930; children—Carol, Lois, Carl, Richard, William. With Eastman Kodak Co., Kodak Park, Rochester, N.Y., 1934-72, successively chemist, supt. roll coating dept., asst. mgr. film mfg., asst. to gen. mgr. Kodak Park, asst. gen. mgr. Kodak Park, 1934-56, v.p., asst. gen. mgr. Eastman Kodak Co., 1956-59; pres. Eastman Chem. Products, Inc., 1959-60, vice chmn. bd. dirs., from 1960, also chief exec. officer, chmn. bd.; president Tenn. Eastman Company, Texas Eastman Company, Carolina Eastman Corp. Mem. Am. Chem. Soc., Photog. Soc. Am., Sigma Xi, Phi Lambda Upsilon, Alpha Chi Sigma. Club: Oak Hill Country (Rochester). Address: Kingsport, Tenn. Died Aug. 20, 1984.

EISEMAN, PHILIP, banker; b. Boston, Mar. 11, 1904; s. Ludwig and Selma (Weil) E.; m. Marion B. Becker, June 14, 1930; 1 dau., Anne (Mrs. Thomas S. Walker). Grad., Phillips Andover, 1921; B.S., Harvard, 1925, M.B.A., 1927. With Old Colony Trust Co., Boston, 1927-30; asst. treas. Old Colony Trust Assos. (name later changed to Bay Banks, Inc.), Boston, 1931-40, treas., v.p., 1940-48, pres., 1948-66, dir., 1948-74, chmn. bd., 1966-69. Hon. trustee Combined Jewish Philanthropies; corporator Mt. Auburn Hosp. Served to lt. col. Signal Corps.; Served to lt. col. AUS, 1943-46. Hon. mem. Assn. Bank Holding Cos. Clubs: Harvard (Boston), Union (Boston); Cambridge, Belmont (Mass.) Country. Home: Swampscott, Mass.

EKLUND, NILS O., JR., ret. corp. exec.; b. Portland, Oreg., June 4, 1911; s. Nils O. and Signe (Anderson) E.; m. Elizabeth Loukes Fairchild, July 12, 1930; children—Karin Anna, Jay Dee (dec.). Student, U. Oreg., 1928-30, Behnke Walker Bus. Coll., Portland, 1930; LL.D., Golden Gate U. (1977). Salesman (Standard Oil Co. of Calif.), Portland, 1930-33, supr., 1933-38; sales mgr. Boyd Coffee Co., Portland, 1938-41; successively engr., asst. supt. and supt. assembly operations Portland and Vancouver shipyards Kaiser Co., Inc., 1942-45; successively supt., asst. gen. supt., gen. supt. Kaiser Frazer Corp., Willow Run, Mich., 1946-48; tech. cons. Motor House, Ltd., Bombay, India, 1948; successively asst. Midwest sales mgr., Midwest sales mgr., gen. sales mgr. Kaiser Motors Corp., 1949-52, asst. exec. v.p., 1952-54; gen. mgr. Detroit engine div. Willys Motors, Inc., 1954-56; asst. v.p. Henry J. Kaiser Co., Oakland, Calif., 1956-59; v.p. Kaiser Industries Co., Oakland, 1959-72, sr. v.p., 1972-76; mem. adv. bd. Douglas Mgmt. Corp., 1977-80; Pres., dir. District Adminstrn. Bldg. Corp., 1966-80. Mem. Calif. Citizens Legis. Adv. Commn., 1957-61; gen. campaign chmn., pres. Alameda County United Fund, 1959-61, mem. exec. com., bd. govs., 1959-61; v.p. United Way of Bay Area, 1959-61, mem. exec. com., bd. govs., 1959-65, pres., chief exec. officer, 1963-64, 66, trustee, 1966-76; mem. nat. adv. council United Community Funds and Councils of Am., 1963-66; mem. adv. bd. Calif. State U., Hayward, 1962-68, chmn. adv. bd., 1966-68, emeritus mem., 1968-80; mem. exec. com., panel chmn. Gov.'s Transp. Task Force, 1967-68; chmn. citizens adv. com. to rules com. Calif. Senate, 1967-68; bd. dirs. Internat. House U. Calif., 1966-74; mem. Bay Area Transp. Study Commn., 1963-69, chmn., 1965-69; chmn. Oakland Transp. Task Force, 1972-74, Alameda County Health Care Services Adv. Commn., 1970-72; gen. chmn. regional com. for better service Oakland Airport, 1971-76; Pres. Oakland Devel. Found., 1964-75; bd. dirs. San Francisco Bay Area Council, vice chmn. steering com., 1963-76; trustee Golden Gate U., from 1964, chmn. bd. trustees, 1974-77; chmn. bd. govs. Research Inst., 1974-76; bd. dirs., pres., chief exec. officer Dunsmuir House Research and Ednl. Corp., 1968-72; bd. dirs. Better Bus. Bur., 1974-76; pres., chief exec. officer Oakland Symphony Orch. Assn., 1973-76. Mem. Oakland C. of C. (dir., pres. 1962-63), Sigma Phi Epsilon. Clubs: Bohemian, 100 (dir. 1962-65, pres. 1964). Home: Mendocino, Calif. Died Oct. 31, 1980.

ELBIN, PAUL NOWELL, educator; b. Cameron, W.Va., Apr. 21, 1905; s. Harry and Nellie (Nowell) E.; student Fairmont (W.Va.) State Coll., 1923-25; A.B., Ohio State U., 1926; A.M., Tchrs. Coll., Columbia U., 1928, Ph.D., 1932; D.D., Davis and Elkins Coll., 1960; Litt.D., W.Va. U., 1965; m. Helen Elizabeth Pierce, Sept. 3, 1929. Tchr., Cameron High Sch., 1926-27; with West Liberty (W.Va.) State Coll., 1928-85, head dept. English and speech, also chaplain, 1928-35, pres., 1935-70, dean interfaith chapel, prof. speech, 1970-71; prof. speech Ohio U., 1971-73; exec. dir. Oglebay Inst., 1944-46; music editor Wheeling (W.Va.) News Register, 1947-61; staff writer Etude music mag., 1953-56. Pres., Wheeling Symphony Soc., 1973-75, Ohio Valley Arts Council, 1978-85. Mem. Am. Guild Organists (dean Wheeling chpt.). Admitted to Wheeling Presbytery, 1956; interim minister Westminster Presbyn. Ch., 1974, 78, Cove United Presbyn. Ch., Weirton, W.Va., 1979, 1st United Presbyn. Ch., Wheeling, 1979-85. Author: The Improvement of College Worship, 1932; The Bible Question Bee, 1943; Brotherhood Through Religion, 1944; The Enrichment of Life, 1945; Fifty Devotional Services, 1950; Worship for the Young in Spirit, 1956; The Paradox of Happiness, 1975. Home: West Liberty, W.Va. Died May 13, 1985.

ELBRICK, CHARLES BURKE, ambassador; b. Louisville, Ky., March 25, 1908; s. Charles J. and Lillian (Burke) E.; A.B., Williams Coll., 1929; m. Elvira Lindsay Johnson, July 27, 1932; children—Alfred Johnson, Valerie Burke. Vice consul, Panama, C.Z., 1931; student Fgn. Service Sch., 1932; vice consul Southampton, England, 1932-34; 3d sec. Port-au-Prince, 1934-37, Warsaw, Poland, 1937-38, Praha, 1938-39, Warsaw, Poland, 1939, Bucharest, 1939, Warsaw (Angers, France), 1939-40, Madrid, Spain, 1940; vice consul Lisbon, Portugal, 1940-41; 3d sec. Lisbon, Portugal, 1941, 2d sec., 1941-43, Tangier, 1934-44; Div. of African Affairs, Dept. of State, 1944-45; 1st sec., Warsaw, Poland, 1945; asst. chief, Div. Eastern European Affairs. Dept. State, 1946-48; student Nat. War Coll., 1948-49; counselor of embassy, Habana, 1949-51; counselor N. Atlantic Council Delegation London, 1951, Paris, 1952-53; dep. asst. sec. of state, Dept. of State, 1953-56, asst. sec. of state, 1957-58; Am. ambassador to Portugal, 1958-63; American ambassador to Yugoslavia, Belgrade, 1964-69, Brazil, 1969-83. Mem. Phi Delta Theta. Clubs: Metropolitan. Chevy Chase (Washington). Home: Gilbertsville, N.Y. Died Apr. 13, 1983.

ELDERDICE, J(AMES) RAYMOND, author; b. Baltimore, Apr. 2, 1889; s. Rev. James Luther and Letitia Cumae (Hayman) E.; grad. Western Md. Prep. Sch., Westminster, Md., 1906; student Western Maryland College, 1906-08; m. Florence Margaret Cahall, April 23, 1926. On staff of Baltimore Sun, May-Sept. 1908; asst. sec. Travelers and Mchts.' Assn., Baltimore, 1908-09; staff writer Standard Pub. Co., Cincinnati, Jan.-Sept. 1914. Asso. editor, 1921-23, editor, 1923-27, Federalsburg Courier; newspaper corr., 1924-31. Democrat. Author: The Last Ditch, 1915; T. Haviland Hicks, Freshman, 1915; T. Haviland Hicks, Sophomore, 1915; T. Haviland Hicks, Junior, 1916; T. Haviland Hicks, Senior, 1916. Writing photoplays for The Thomas A. Edison Co., 1917. Enlisted in Med. Corps, U.S.A., July 2, 1917. Literary critic, from 1933. Contbr. stories to American Boy, St. Nicholas, Sport Story, David C. Cook publs., and other juvenile publs. Home: Federalsburg, Md.†

ELDJARN, KRISTJAN, former pres. of Iceland; b. Iceland, Dec. 6, 1916; s. Thorarinn and Sigrun Eldjarn; student U. Copenhagen, 1936-39; M.A., U. Iceland, 1944, Ph.D., 1957; m. Halldora Kristin Ingolfsdottir, Feb. 6, 1947; children—Olof (Mrs. Stefan O. Stefansson), Thorarinn, Sigrun, Ingolfur. Asst. curator Nat. Mus. Iceland, 1945-47, dir., 1947-68; pres. of Iceland, 1968-80. Decorated grand master Order Falcon, also fgn. decorations. Mem. Icelandic Sci. Soc. Research archaelogy Iceland, Greenland and Newfoundland, 1937-67. Author archaeol. papers. Home: Bessastadir, Iceland. Died Sept. 15, 1982.

ELDREDGE, LAURENCE HOWARD, lawyer, educator, author; b. Cold Spring, N.J., Mar. 18, 1902; s. Irvin H. and Marie Louise (Benton) E.; m. Helen Biddle Gans, Sept. 30, 1926; children—Mary Harriet, Deborah (Mrs. duPont), Helen Louise (Mrs. James W. Bradley). B.S., Lafayette Coll., 1924, Litt. D., 1970; LL.B., U. Pa., 1927. Bar: Pa. bar 1927, Calif. bar 1972. Reporter Pub. Ledger, Phila., 1924-25; writer syndicated news articles, 1925-27; assoc. Montgomery & McCracken (formerly Roberts & Montgomery), 1927-38; mem. firm Norris, Lex, Hart & Eldredge, 1944-56; prof. law Temple U., 1928-33, adj. prof., 1947-52; assoc. in law U. Pa., 1933-34, 1937-38, prof. law, 1938-44; lectr. med. jurisprudence. U. Pa. (Grad. Sch. Medicine), 1958-59, U. Pa. (Med. Sch.), 1940-68; vis. prof. law Columbia, spring, 1941, summer, 1946; vis. prof. law Hastings Coll. Law, San Francisco, 1970-71, prof. law, 1971-79, prof. emeritus, 1979-82; spl. dep. atty. gen., Pa., 1948-49; Past chmn. bd. Pa. Alcoholic Beverage Study, Inc.; past pres. Better Bus. Bur. of Phila., Inc. (dir. 1940-71); Pres. Phila. Art Alliamce, 1949-66. Author: Eldredge on Modern Tort Problems, 1941, Pennsylvania Annotations to Restatement, Torts, Vols. I and II, 1938, 1938, Trials of a Philadelphia Lawyer, 1968, The Law of Defamation, 1978, Revising reporter, Restatement of the Law of Torts, 1946-47, Reporter decisions Supreme Ct. Pa, 1942-68; Editor, Pa. Bar Assn. Quar., 1938-42; Author articles and book revs. in law publs. Former chmn. bd. Mrs. John S. Sheppard Found.; sec.-treas. Magee Meml. Hosp., 1953-59, trustee, 1946-59; pres. Episcopal Hosp., 1946-53, Mus. Council, Phila., 1958-59; bd. dirs. Hosp. Council, 1952-60. Served from lt. to comdr. USCGR; supt. Coast Guard Vol. Port Security Force Tng. Sch., World War II, Phila. Recipient citation Lafayette Coll., 1960; Phila. Art Alliance medal achievement 1966. Fellow Royal Soc. Arts London; mem. Am. Law Inst. (life mem., adviser on torts and evidence), Phila. Medico-Legal Inst. (pres.), ABA, Pa. Bar Assn. (Phila Bar Assn., chmn. bd. govs. 1960-61), San Francisco Bar Assn., State Bar Calif., Soc. Mayflower Descs. (past gov.), Soc. Colonial Wars Commonwealth Pa. (past sec.), Colonial Soc. Pa. (gov. 1962-64), Lafayette Coll. Alumni Assn. (pres. 1961-62), S.R., Phi Beta Kappa, Phi Beta Kappa Assos. (past dir.), Delta Upsilon (meritorious service award 1961), Pi Delta Epsilon, Delta Theta Phi, Order of Coif (pres. U. Pa. chpt. 1959-61). Republican. Episcopalian. Clubs: Mason, Franklin Inn, Union League, Penn, Lawyers of Phila; Bohemian (San Francisco), University (San Francisco). Home: San Francisco, Calif. Dec. July 17, 1982.

ELIEL, HARRIET JUDD, ednl. adminstr., civic worker; b. Evanston, Ill., Dec. 29, 1890; d. George T. and Sarah B. (Blanchard) Judd; A.B., U. Cal. at Berkeley, 1913, M.A., 1923; student Columbia Tchrs. Coll., 1919-20; m. Paul Eliel, Aug. 2, 1913; children—Leonard P., Stewart J. (dec.), Eleanor R. (Mrs. John J. Breslin), Jean A. (Mrs. Roger McCoy). Founder, dir. John Dewey Sch., Berkeley, 1921-24; instr. parent edn. Berkeley pub. schs., 1921-24; instr. family life edn., 1930-33; dir. N. Cal. Great Books Found., 1948-50; regional dir. Inst. Internat. Edn., 1952-57; administrative associate to foreign student adviser Stanford University, from 1957. Member of Berkeley Board Education, 1931-35, pres., 1933-35; pres. Cal. League Women Voters, 1933-37, San Francisco League Women Voters, 1942-44; mem. adv. council Cal. Employment Service, 1935-39; sec. Nat. League Women Voters, 1936-42; mem. Com. of 25 to Study State Govt., 1941-42, Cal. Com. Children and Youth, 1945-52; chmn. Cal. Com. Study Transient Youth, 1950-52. Mem. adv. com. San Francisco State Coll.; trustee San Francisco Museum Art; dir. San Francisco Family and Children's Agy., San Francisco Social Hygiene and Health Assn., Bay Area Child Care Com. Mem. Kappa Alpha Theta, Prytanean Soc., Torch and Shield. Address: San Francisco. †

ELIOT, ETHEL COOK, author; b. North Gage, N.Y., Apr. 15, 1890; d. Cornelius C. and Carrie L. (Holton) Cook; m. Professor Samuel Atkins Eliot, Jr., July 10, 1915; children—Frances Torka, Alexander, Patience Ann. Roman Catholic. Author: The Little House in the Fairy Wood, 1918; The House Above the Trees, 1921; The Wind Boy, 1923; The House on the Edge of Things, 1923; Buttercup Days, 1924; The Vanishing Comrade, 1924; Fireweed, short stories in various mags., 1925; Waul and Dyke, Inc., 1926; Storey Manor, 1927; The Dryad and the Hired Boy, 1928; The Gay Mystery, 1931; Ariel Dances, 1931; Green Doors, 1933; Her Soul to Keep, 1935; Angels' Mirth, 1936; Roses for Mexico, 1946. Home: Northampton, Mass. †

ELKINS, JAMES ANDERSON, banker, lawyer; b. Huntsville, Tex., Sept. 25, 1879; LL.B., U. Tex., 1901; m. Isabel Mitchell (dec.); children—W.S., James Anderson. Partner firm Vinson, Elkins, Searls & Connally, Houston; sr. chmn. bd. First City Nat. Bank, Houston. Mem. Am. Tex., Houston bar assns. Home: Houston, TX. †

ELLERD, HARVEY G., vice-pres. Armour & Co.; b. Sioux City, Ia., May 1, 1888; s. George and Mary (Conkleman) E.; student Morningside Coll., Cornell Univ.; m. Mildred Minard, Jan. 23, 1913; children—Harvey G., Jane Ellerd Keers. With Armour & Co. from 1907, vice pres.; dir. Central Nat. Bank in Chicago. Pres. Chicago Assn. Commerce and Industry since 1949. Home: Chicago, Ill. †

ELLETT, ALEXANDER, physicist; b. Chillicothe, Mo., Sept. 5, 1894; s. Andrew Jackson and Bessie (Lane) E.; A.B., U. Colo., 1922; Ph.D., Johns Hopkins, 1923; m. Onabelle Townsend, Jan. 16, 1921; children—Elizabeth Onabelle, Charles Alexander. Norman Townsend. Wilma June. NRC fellow, 1923-25; asst. prof. physics U. Ia., 1925-28. asso. prof., 1928-29, prof., 1929-40; chmn. sect. E. div. A. Nat. Def. Research Com., 1939-41, chief div. 4, 1941-45; dir. research Zenith Radio Corp., Chgo., 1945-59, v.p. charge research, 1949-63, v.p. spl. sci. projects, 1963. Decorated Medal for Merit, 1948. Fellow Am. Phys., Soc.; mem. I.R.E. Club: Cosmos (Washington). Contbr. articles profl. jours. Home: Carmel, Calif. Died Nov. 26, 1981.

ELLINGSON, EMIL OSCAR, chemistry educator; b. Nicollet, Minn., Oct. 14, 1887; s. Andrew and Sigri (Lokensgaard) E.; student normal sch., Madison, Minn., 1895-99; B.S., St. Olaf Coll., Northfield, Minn., 1906; A.M., U. of Wis., 1910. Ph.D., 1912; m. Lena Boraas, June 27, 1903; children—Eveline Lenore (Mrs. Paul Cornelius Johnson), Joseph Edward Norris, Russell Orlando, Rudolph Conrad, Vivian Margaret. Arthur Gordon (dec.). Instr. U. of Wis., 1913-19; prof. of chemistry, St. Olaf Coll., from 1919, head of dept. from 1924. Mem. Am. Chem. Soc., Sigma Xi, Gamma Alpha. Lutheran. Wrote: Qualitative Analysis and articles on topics of scientific interest. Home: Northfield, Minn. †

ELLINGTON, ELMER VERNE, educator; b. Peru, Mo., Feb. 8, 1888; s. William P. and Mary V. (Steele) E.; B.S. in Agr., U. of Mo., 1910; m. Ruth W. Broman, Feb. 26, 1919; 1 d. (Mrs. John Pritchard). Extension splist. U. of Ida., 1910-11, asso. prof. dairying, 1912-13, prof. dairying and dairyman Experiment Sta., 1913-16; asst. in charge dairy extension, U.S. Dept. Agr., Washington, D.C., 1917-22; prof. dairy husbandry, head of dept., and dairy husbandman Experiment Sta., State Coll. of Wash., 1922-45, dir. Agr. Extension Service, 1945-54, emeritus; also vice dean Coll. Agr., asst. dir. of Expt. Sta.; chmn. extension service sects., Land Grant Colleges. Assn. Fellow A.A.A.S.; mem. Am. Dairy Science Assn. (pres. Western Div. 1927; dir. 1937-40), Wash. State Dairymen's Assn. (sec.), Northwest Science Assn., Pullman Chamber of Commerce (pres. 1928); also member of Alpha Zeta, Phi Kappa Phi, Gamma Sigma Delta and Beta Theta Pi fraternities. Democrat. Mem. Episcopalian Church. Mason (Shriner), Elk. Club: Pullman (pres. 1929), Kiwanis. Author of numerous scientific papers and pamphlets. Home: Pullman, Wash. †

ELLIOT, HENRY M., business exec., cons.; b. New Haven, Jan. 23, 1889; s. William H. and Helen (Chittenden) E.; student Yale univ.; m. Gladys D. Richter, 1918; children—Beatrice (Mrs. Charles C. Wooster), Henry M., Phebe, Pamela (Baronessa Pamela Abbruzzese), Jared, John, Hope (Mrs. John B. Carter). Associated with the Winchester Repeating Arms Company, New Haven, 1911-13; manufacturing, sales and sales administration, DeLong Hook & Eye Company, Phila., 1914-17; sales mgr., Manning Abrasive Co., Troy, New York, 1920-28; v.p. Behr-Manning Corp., 1928-50, 1st v.p., 1950-54; former pres. dir. Norton-Pike Co., ret., 1954; mng. dir. Coated Abrasives Mfrs. Inst.; pres. B-M Holding Corporation, 1950-62. Past president, director Albany County Tuberculosis Association. Served as capt. Ordnance Dept., U.S. Army, 1917-20. Mem. Am. Ordnance Assn., Newcomen Soc. Clubs: Yale (N.Y.C.); Schuyler Meadows (Loudonville). Home: Loudonville, N.Y. †

ELLIOTT, BEN G., mech. engr., educator; b. North Platte, Neb., Feb. 17, 1889; s. Frederick and Susan (Potts) E.; B.S., Rose Poly. Inst., 1910, M.S., 1911; M.E., U. Wis., 1913; m. Georgia Mae Buchanan, Dec. 22, 1915; children—Dorothy Mae (Mrs. Robert Sneed), Georgia Ann (Mrs. Paul Handt). Apprentice with Union Pacific Railroad, Allis-Chalmers Manufacturing Co., McKeen Motor Car Co., 1906-10; machinist, road engr. McKeen Motor Car Co., 1911-12; fellow mech. engring. U. Wis., 1912-13, instr. mech. engring. extension div., 1913-15, asso. prof. charge dept., 1917-19, prof. mech. engineering, 1919-59, professor mech. engring. emeritus, from 1959, chmn. dept. mech. engring., college engring., from 1947; asso. prof. mech. engring. U. Neb., 1915-17. Dist. rep., sect. on edn. and tng. U.S. Shipping Bd., World War I; advisor to dir. sci. adv. com. SSS, Wis.; sec. Wis. State Tchrs. Retirement Bd. Registered profl. engr., Wis. Fellow A.S.M.E. (v.p. 1953-56); mem. Nat. Soc. Profl. Engrs. (past nat. v.p. and dir.), Am. Soc. for Engring. Edn., National Assn. Power Engineers (university coordinator Am. Power Conference), Triangle (honorary), Pi Tau Sigma, Sigma Tau, Tau Beta Pi. Democrat. Presbyn. Mason (33 deg.). Club:

Technical, University (Madison); Kiwanis (past dist. gov.). Author: The Gasoline Automobile, 1915; The Automobile Chassis, 1923; Automobile Power Plants, 1923; Automobile Repairing, 1924; also articles on engring., ednl. subjects. Home: Madison, Wis. †

ELLIOTT, COLIN FRASER, government official; b. Winnipeg, Manitoba, Can., Oct. 7, 1888; s. William Moore and Maria (Smith) E.; B.A.Sc., Toronto Univ., 1912; C.E., Osgood Hall, Toronto, 1915; m. Marjorie Sypher, Sept. 8, 1920; children—Roy Fraser, Mary Marjorie. Enrolled as solicitor of Supreme Court, 1915; called to bar, 1915; solicitor, Income Tax Div., 1919, then counsel, asst. commr., 1929-32; commr., 1932-43; dep. minister Nat. Revenue (taxation), from 1943; A.E. and M.P. of Can. in Chile, from Oct. 1946. Dir. Ottawa Carleton Coll. Served with Can. Expeditionary Force in Can., Eng., France, 1915-19. Decorated Companion St. Michael and St. George, 1944. Mem. United Ch. of Can. Home: Ottawa, Ont., Can. †

ELLIOTT, IVAN A., lawyer; b. White Country, Ill., Nov. 18, 1889; s. B. F. and Nellie (Belle) Elliott; student U. of Ill., 1911-13; LL.B., Ill. Wesleyan U., 1916; m. Malen Stinson, Oct. 12, 1922; children—Ivan A., Norman J. Admitted to Ill. bar, 1917; in practice of law from 1919; atty. gen. of Ill. 1948-50; member Supreme Court, State of Illinois, 1949-53; mem. firm Conger & Elliott; director First Nat. Bank, Carmi, Ill., White County Abstract Co. Served as lt., later capt. arty., A.E.F., 1917-18; brig. gen. Ill. Res. Militia; lt. col., coast arty., in active service, 1942-44. Mem. Am. Leg. (past state comdr.), Phi Alpha Delta. Democrat. Presbyterian. Home: Carmi, Ill. †

ELLIOTT, LOUIS D., government exec.; b. Ithaca, N.Y., Apr. 4, 1889; s. O. L. and Ellen (Coit Brown) E.; B.A., Stanford, 1911, Ph.D., 1923; m. Helen Nagel, Dec. 22, 1913; children—Robert D., David G., Margaret Anne. Chemist U.S. Bureau of Chemistry, U.S. Dept. Agr., 1913-18; chemist Nat. Canners Assn., 1918-22; chem. and administrative officer U.S. Food and Drug Adminstrn., from 1923, asso. commr. foods and drugs. Home: Falls Church, Va. †

ELLIOTT, RICHARD MAURICE, prof. psychology; b. Lowell, Mass., Nov. 3, 1887; s. Thomas Henry and D. Lilla (Naylor) E.; A.B., Dartmouth, 1910; A.M., Harvard, 1911, Ph.D., 1913; U. of Berlin, 1913-14; m. Mathilde Rice, Dec. 5, 1929. Sheldon fellow, Harvard Univ., 1913-14; instr. psychology, Harvard, 1914-15, Yale, 1915-18; asso. prof. psychology U. of Minn., 1919-23, prof. from 1923, chmn. dept., 1919-51. Commd. 1st lt. S.C., U.S. Army, Feb. 3, 1918, and assigned as psychol. examiner; capt., Oct. 28, 1918; hon. discharged, Apr. 26, 1919. Fellow A.A.A.S., Am. Psychol. Assn. (council of dirs. 1931-33, council of representatives, 1946-48, board of directors, 1946-48); mem. Social Science Research Council (council of dirs. 1939-44). Mem. div. of anthropology and psychology Nat. Research Council, 1947-50. Dir. The Psychological Corp., 1931-47. Mem. Phi Beta Kappa, Kappa Kappa Kappa. Unitarian. Editor of The Century Psychology Series. Home: St. Paul, Minn. †

ELLIS, GILBERT R., finance company executive; b. Mo., 1915 With Household Internat. (formerly Household Finance Corp.), 1935-82, v.p., 1956-65, sr. v.p., 1965-66, exec. v.p., 1966-72, pres., 1972-76, chief exec. officer, 1973-82, chmn. bd., 1974-82, also chmn. exec. com. Home: Highland Park, Ill. Dec. Nov. 13, 1982.

ELLIS, HUBERT SUMMERS, congressman; b. Hurricane, Putnam County, W.Va., July 6, 1887; ed. public schools and Marshall Coll.; married. Engaged in insurance business, from 1920; mem. 78th to 80th Congresses (1943-49), 4th W.Va. Dist. Republican. Served in U.S. Army, World War I; 20 months with 150th F.A. 42d Div., in France. Mem. Am. Legion (dept. comdr. 1933-34). Home: Huntington, W.Va. Deceased.

ELLIS, ROBERT H., advertising agency executive; b. Evanston, Ill., May 21, 1929; s. Carl G. and Florence M. E. B.S., Northwestern U., 1951. Sales mgr. S.O.S. Co., Chgo., 1956-58; mktg. mgr. Econs. Labs., N.Y.C., from 1958; then exec. v.p., dir. Batten, Barton, Durstine & Osborne, Inc., N.Y.C.; pres. REL Corp. Served with USNR. Home: New York, N.Y. Dec. June 1, 1982.

ELLIS, ROY, coll. pres.; b. Seymour, Mo., Mar. 9, 1888; s. David Franklin and Cornelia (Pyatt) E.; student Southwest Missouri State College, 1909-11; A.B., B.S. in Edn., U. of Mo., 1914; A.M., Harvard, 1917; grad. study Columbia, 1921-23, Ph.D., 1930; m. Frances Myrtle Nations, March 8, 1923; 1 son, David Owen. Teacher, rural schs. Wright County, Mo., 1906-09; prin. Central Grammar Sch., Texarkana, Ark., 1911-12; supt. schs., Greenfield, Mo., 1914-16; prof. economics, Southwest Missouri Teachers Coll., 1918-26, pres. from 1926. Served as sergt., inf. and cav., U.S. Army, World War. Mem. N.E.A., Mo. State Teachers Assn., Phi Beta Kappa, Phi Delta Kappa, Phi Delta Phi. Republican. Baptist. Clubs: University, Kiwanis. Author: Manual for the Study of the Principles of Economics, 1924; Manual for the Study of Economic Problems, 1924; Civic History of Kansas City, Missouri, 1930. Home: Springfield, Mo. †

ELLIS, WILLIAM EDWARD, naval officer; b. Burlington, N.C. Nov. 7, 1908; s. Charles Britt and Margaret (Cannady) E.; B.S., U.S. Naval Acad., 1930; m. Barbara Elizabeth Decker, Dec. 24, 1934; 1 son, William Edward. Commd. ensign U.S. Navy, 1930, advanced through grades to vice adm., 1964; designated naval aviator, 1932; various assignments in ships and ashore, U.S. and C.Z., 1932-42; comdr. Escort Fighting Squadron 26, 1942-43; comdg. officer Air Group 18, 1943-44; air officer U.S.S. Intrepid, 1944-45, exec. officer, 1945; chief staff officer to comdr. Naval Air Bases, 12th Naval Dist., 1945-48 comdg. officer Fleet All Weather Tng. Unit, Atlantic, 1948-50; assigned Naval War Coll., 1950-51, Joint Staff Office, Joint Chiefs Staff, 1951-53; comdr. U.S.S. Badoeng Strait 1953-54; chief staff and aide to comdr. Operations Devel. Forces, 1954-56; comdr. aircraft carrier U.S.S. Forrestal, 1956-57; chief staff and aide to comdr. Carrier Div. 6, 1957-58; dir. air warfare div. Office Chief Naval Operations, 1958-59; asst. chief field support Bu. Naval Weapons, 1959-61; comdr. Carrier Div. 2, 1961-62; asst. chief naval operations air, Navy Dept., 1962-64; comdr. 6th Fleet, Mediterranean, 1964-66; chief staff to NATO's Supreme Allied Condr., Atlantic, Norfolk, Va., 1966-68. Decorated Navy Cross, D.F.C., Air medal, Navy Commendation medal, D.S.M., numerous unit and area ribbons. Home: Pensacola, Fla. Died Sept. 26, 1982.

ELLISON, JEROME, editor, author; b. Maywood, Ill., Oct. 28, 1907; s. Earl J. and Vera D. (Engmark) E.; children—Jerome III (dec.) and Judith Ann (twins), Julie. Student, U. Wis., 1925-26; A.B., U. Mich., Ann Arbor, 1930; M.S., So. Conn. State Coll., 1966. Editor Mich. Gargoyle, U. Mich., 1929, Circle of Zeta Psi, 1930-32; asst. editor Life mag., 1932-33; asso. editor Readers Digest, 1935-42; editor-in-chief Liberty mag., 1942-43; mng. editor Collier's mag., 1943-44; editorial dir., bur. overseas publs. OWI, 1944-45; instr. in mag. journalism N.Y. U., 1945; founder Asso. Mag. Contbr., Inc.; editor, pub. The Magazine of the Year, 1946-47; with journalism dept. Ind. U., 1955-60; founder, editor, pub. Best Articles & Stories mag., 1957-61; lectr. English and humanities New Haven Coll., 1964-66, prof. English and humanities, 1966-75; lectr. continuing edn. div. U. Conn., 1964-66. Free-lance cartoonist, also writer monthly column for, Life mag., 1933-34; Author: books including John Brown's Soul, 1951, Report to the Creator, 1955; pseudonym N. Emorey: books including A Serious Call to an American (R) Evolution, 1967, mass edit., 1971, God on Broadway, 1971, (with Arthur Ford) The Life Beyond Death, 1972, The Last-Third-of-Life Club, 1973, Life's Second Half, The Dynamics of Aging, 1978; Contbr.: (with Arthur Ford) essays to New Eng. Quar; articles and stories in numerous periodicals. Mem. Phenix Soc. (founder, pres. 1973—), Zeta Psi. Episcopalian. Home: Guilford, Conn. Died June 9, 1981.

ELLISON, J(OHN) MALCUS, chancellor; b. Burgess' Store, Va., Feb. 2, 1889; s. Robert J. and Maggie J. (Stepter) E.; A.B., Virginia Union University-College, 1917, LL.D., 1950; A.B. in Edn., 1925; A.M., Oberlin Grad. Sch. of Theology, 1927; student Columbia U. and Union Theol. Sem., 1931-32; Ph.D., Drew U., Madison, N.J., 1933; LL.D., Morhouse Coll., 1955, Va. State Coll., 1960; m. Mabel C. McWilliams, July 23, 1917 (died Jan. 25, 1919); children—Mabel Constance (Mrs. Hugh Merrill Scoggins, Jr.) and Geraldine McWilliams (Mrs. Francis A. Kornegay) (twins); m. 2d, Ophelia I. Gray, June 14, 1920 (died Sept. 25, 1925); 1 son, John Malcus; m. 3d, Elizabeth B. Balfour, June 18, 1933. Ordained to ministry of Baptist Church, pastor, Shiloh Bapt. Ch., 1913-26, also prin. Northern Neck Industrial Acad., 1917-18, Rosenwald High Sch., 1918-26; prof. sociology and college pastor, Virginia State Coll., 1927-34, also spl. research investigator Va. Poly. Inst., Blacksburg, Va., 1928-34, pastor, First Bapt. Ch., South Orange, N.J., 1931-34; pastor Zion Bapt. Ch., Washington, D.C., 1934-36; also prof. religious edn. Howard Univ., 1934-36; pres. Va. Union Univ., Richmond, Va., 1941-55, chancellor, from 1955, also professor. College Cons. Baptist Bd. Edn., Am. Baptist Ch. Vice chmn. Va. Commn. on Interracial Cooperation; mem. Negro Organization Soc. of Va., Richmond Council on Interracial Orgn., Nat. Assn. Advancement Colored People, Nat. Teachers Assn., Am. Assn. Private (or Church Related) Colls., Am. Sociol. Assn., Alpha Phi Alpha. Mason. Author: The Negro Church in Rural Virginia, 1930; Negro Organization and Leadership in Relation to Rural Life in Virginia, 1933; Negro Life in Rural Virginia, 1865-1934, 1934 (all pub. Va. Poly.); Art of Friendship, 1940; Tensions and Destiny, 1953; They Who Preach, 1956; They Sang Through the Crisis, 1961. Address: Richmond, Va. †

ELLSBERG, EDWARD, engineer, author, retired naval officer; b. New Haven, Nov. 21, 1891; s. Joseph and Edna (Lavine) E.; m. Lucy Knowlton Buck, June 1, 1918; 1 dau., Mary Phillips (Mrs. Goldwin Smith Pollard). Student, U. Colo., 1910, Eng.D., 1929; B.S., U.S. Naval Acad., 1914; postgrad., 1916; M.S., MIT, 1920; Sc.D., Bowdoin Coll., 1952; L.H.D., U. Maine, 1955. Served with USN, until 1926, advancing through grades to lt. comdr., promoted to comdr. by Spl. Act of Congress, 1929 for work as salvage officer raising U.S. Submarine S-51 from sea bottom, 1926, and initial operations on S-4, 1927, reappointed, World War II, advanced to rear adm., 1951, salvage officer, Red Sea, Western MTO; participated in (Normandy Invasion), 1944; in connection with installation of artificial harbors along Normandy coast; supr. shipbuilding USN, for, Cleve. area, 1945; Chief engr. Tide Water Oil Co., 1926-35, cons. engr., 1935-41. Author numerous books, fiction and non-fiction, 1927—; including On The Bottom, 1928, Under The Red Sea Sun, 1946, No Banners, No Bugles, 1949, The Far Shore, 1960; frequent mag. contbr. including. Decorated D.S.M., Legion Merit with oak leaf cluster; comdr. Order Brit. Empire. Mem. N.J. Soc. Profl. Engrs., Am. Petroleum Inst., Naval Inst., Am. Polar Soc., Soc. Am. Historians, Soc. Am. Mil. Engrs., Am. Acad. Polit. and Social Sci. Clubs: Army and Navy (Washington); Explorers; Causeway (Southwest Harbor, Maine); Northeast Harbor Fleet, Ends of the Earth; Pot and Kettle (Bar Harbor). Inventor under-water torch for cutting steel; designer system for salvaging submarines; inventor in field petroleum; designer low pressure desalinization systems in gen. use in naval vessels. Home: St Petersburg Beach, Fla. Dec. Jan. 24, 1983.

ELMLARK, HARRY EUGENE, newspaper feature syndicate exec.; b. Hudson, N.Y., July 25, 1909; s. David and Anna (Finkelstein) E.; B.S., U. Va., 1931; m. Lillian Rosenthal, Sept. 17, 1933; 1 dau., Walli (Mrs. Jerome Kellert). Reporter, Washington Post, 1931-33; free-lance mag. and newspaper writer, 1933-36; with Washington Star Syndicate, and predecessor, N.Y.C., 1936-79, gen. mgr., v.p., 1958-62, pres., 1962-79, also editor; sr. editor Universal Press Syndicate, N.Y.C., 1979-80. Died 1980.

ELSE, GERALD FRANK, educator; b. Redfield, S.D., July 1, 1908; s. Frank Marston and Minnie Marylouise (Beckman) E.; student U. Neb., 1924-27; A.B. summa cum laude, Harvard, 1929, M.A., 1932, Ph.D., 1934; L.H.D., U. S.D., 1975; LL.D., U. Nebr., 1976; m. Martha Post Wight, June 15, 1939, (dec. 1961); children—Susan Else Wyman, Stephen (dec. 1974); m. 2d, Gladys Hart Burian, Jan. 1, 1976. Instr. in Greek and Latin, Harvard, 1935-38, faculty instr., 1938-42; prof., head dept. classics U. Iowa, 1945-57; prof. Greek and Latin, U. Mich., 1957-76, chmn. dept. classical studies, 1957-68, founder, dir. Center for Coordination Ancient and Modern Studies, 1969-76, prof. emeritus, 1977-82; asso. Nat. Humanities Center, N.C., 1979. Mem. Nat. Council on Humanities, 1966-72, vice chmn., 1968-71. Served as capt. USMCR, 1943-45. Fellow Am. Acad. Arts and Scis.; mem. Am. Philol. Assn. (pres. 1964), Classical Assn. Middle W. and S. (pres. 1955-56), Archaeol. Inst. Am., Heidelberg Acad. Scis. (corr.), Phi Beta Kappa. Author: Aristotle's Poetics: The Argument; The Origin and Early Form of Greek Tragedy; The Structure and Date of Book 10 of Plato's Republic; The Madness of Antigone. Translator: Poetics (Aristotle). Contbr. articles, revs. on classical subjects to periodicals. Home: Ann Arbor, Mich. Died Sept. 6, 1982.

ELSING, WILLIAM TADDES, lawyer; b. Bisbee, Ariz., May 8, 1910; s. Morris J. and Celestine (Marks) E.; m. Ferol Cox, May 29, 1941. Student, Stanford, 1928, U. Calif. at Berkeley, 1929; J.D., U. Ariz., 1933. Bar: Ariz. bar 1933, Calif. bar 1946. Practiced in, Prescott, Ariz., 1933-38, Phoenix, 1938-84;. chmn. bd. govs. Ariz. Dept. Mineral Resources, 1969-76. Served with CIC AUS, 1942-45. Mem. Am., Calif., Ariz., Maricopa County bar assns., Soc. Mining Engrs., Am. Inst. Mining, Metall. and Petroleum Engrs., AAAS, Phi Delta Phi. Republican. Presbyn. Home: Phoenix, Ariz. Died July 1984.

ELSON, SAM, lawyer; b. N.Y.C., Dec. 25, 1908; s. Alex and Sarah (Reichick) E.; A.B., Washington U., St. Louis, 1927, LL.B., 1930; J.S.D., Yale, 1931; m. Gertrude Clemens Palmer, June 28, 1934; children—Edward C., David L., Dorothy M., (Mrs. Donald Rosenthal). Admitted to Mo. bar. 1930; mem. faculty Washington U. Sch. Law, 1931-35; asso. firm Husch, Eppenberger, Donohue, Elson & Cornfeld, and predecessor, St. Louis, 1932-80, partner, 1936-80. Mem. St. Louis Council Human Relations, 1949; pres. Jewish Community Relations Council St. Louis, 1947-51. Bd. dirs. Jewish Fedn. St. Louis, 1952-55. Sterling fellow Yale Law Sch., 1930; recipient alumni citation Washington U. Mem. Am., Mo. bar assns., Bar. Assn. St. Louis, Am. Law Inst., Am. Judicature Soc., Mo. Assn. Social Welfare, NCCJ, St. Louis Com. Fgn. Relations, Phi Beta Kappa, Order of Coif, Order of Artus. Contbr. articles legal jours. Mng. editor St. Louis Law Rev., 1930. Home: St. Louis, Mo. Died Sept. 4, 1980.

ELTON, REUEL WILLIAM, trade assn. exec.; born Pittsburgh, Pa., May 9, 1890; s. Reuel William and Blanche Belle (Aikins) E.; ed. pub. schs.; m. Mary Ellen Reid, Aug. 3, 1935. Exec. sec., 80th Div. Vets. Assn., 1920-21; adjutant gen., Vets. of Fgn. Wars, 1921-25; campaign management, Am. City Bur., 1926; asst. mgr., Pittsburgh C. of C., 1926-30; asst. mgr., Nat. Paint, Oil and Varnish Assn., N.Y. City, 1930-32; mgr. Pittsburgh

Better Bus. Bur., 1933; sec. and exec. v.p., Nat. Paint, Varnish & Lacquer Assn., Washington, 1934-47; gen. mgr., exec. v.p. Am. Trade Assn. Execs., 1947-56; sec. emeritus Am. Soc. Assn. Execs. Washington; exec. sec. Ft. Lauderdale (Fla.) Sales Execs. Club. Served to capt., Inf., U.S. Army, 1917-18. Decorated Legion Honor (France). Republican. Presbyn. Home: Ft. Lauderdale, Fla. †

ELVING, PHILIP JULIBER, chemistry educator; b. Bklyn., Mar. 14, 1913; s. Bernard David and Rose (Juliber) E.; m. Beulah Londow Round, June 20, 1937; children: Elizabeth Elving Bass, Louise Elving Carr. A.B., Princeton U., 1934, A.M., 1935, Ph.D., 1937. Instr. chemistry Pa. State U., 1937-39, prof., 1949-52; instr. chemistry Purdue U., 1939-41, asst. prof., 1941-43, asso. prof., 1947-49; head analytical, phys. chemistry div., research lab. Publicker Industries, Inc., 1943-45; asst. dir. chem. research, 1945-47; vis. prof. chemistry Harvard U., 1951-52, Hebrew U., 1966, 73, 81; prof. chemistry U. Mich., Ann Arbor, from 1952, Hobart H. Willard prof. chemistry, from 1981; mem. Internat. Com. for Electrochem. Thermodynamics and Kinetics, 1960-69, NRC Com. Analytical Chemistry, 1958-61. Editor: (with I.M. Kolthoff) Treatise on Analytical Chemistry, from 1959, (with J.D. Winefordner) Chemical Analysis Series, from 1957; contbr. articles to profl. jours. Recipient Anachem award Detroit sect. Am. Chem. Soc., 1958, Fisher award, 1960. Mem. Am. Chem. Soc. (div. chmn.), Electrochem. Soc. (dir.; div. chmn.), Polarographic Soc., Soc. Analytical Chemistry, Brit. Chem. Soc., Phi Beta Kappa, Sigma Xi, Phi Lambda Upsilon. Jewish. Home: Ann Arbor, Mich.

ELY, WALTER RALEIGH, JR., judge; b. Baird, Tex., June 24, 1913; s. Walter Raleigh and Lucy Ann (McCoy) E.; m. Billie Bernice Gambill, Oct. 27, 1937; 1 son, William Raleigh; m. m 2d, Ruby Ilene Walters, Sept. 18, 1945; 1945. A.B., U. Tex., 1935, LL.B., 1935; LL.M., U. So. Calif., 1949, LL.D., 1973. Bar: Tex. bar 1935, Calif. bar 1945. Gen. practice, Abilene, Tex., 1935-39, asst. atty. gen., Tex., 1939-40; judge U.S. Ct. Appeals, 9th Circuit, 1964-84; Mem. exec. com. Calif. Conf. State Bar Dels., 1957-60; spl. counsel U.S. Senate, 1955. Contbr. articles to profl. jours. Bd. dirs. Los Angeles County Bar Found., Travel Program for Fgn. Diplomats. Served with USMCR, 1941-44. Decorated Silver Star medal. Fellow Am. Coll. Trial Lawyers; mem. Am., Tex. bar founds., ABA (ho. of dels. 1961-64), Los Angeles County Bar Assn. (pres. 1962), Marine Corps Res. Officers Assn. (hon. life), VFW, Order of Coif, Phi Delta Phi, Delta Kappa Epsilon. Methodist. Clubs: Mason (Los Angeles) (Shriner, K.T.), Los Angeles (Los Angeles), Athletic (Los Angeles), Chancery (Los Angeles); Lakeside Golf of Hollywood; Navy Golf Course (Los Alamitos, Calif.). Home: Sunset Beach, Calif. Died Oct. 9, 1984.

EMBRY, NORRIS WULKOP, company exec.; b. Louisville, Aug. 18, 1890; s. Henry Foster and Laura (Baker) E.; student pub. schs.; m. Elizabeth Pickett Ball, May 17, 1916; children—Betty Ball (Mrs. Warren Williams), Norris. Factory employee Bell Coggeshall Box Co. (later known as Embry Box Co.), Lsvl., 1911, salesman, 1915, Embry Box Co. merged with 12 other box mfrs. to form Gen. Box Co., 1922, mgr., Lsvl., 1922-25, asst. to sales mgr. Chgo. office, 1925-30, dist. sales mgr., plant mgr., Bklyn., 1930-35, pres., dir., 1935-52, chmn. bd.; president and dir. Embry Lumber Co., from 1956. Mem. Wirebound Box Mfrs. Assn. Home: Ft. Lauderdale, Fla. †

EMBRY, THOMAS ERIC, judge; b. Pell City, Ala., June 14, 1921; s. Frank Bernard and Isabella (Mungall) E.; m. Bedford Stall, Jan. 6, 1945; children—Corinne Embry Vickers, Frances Alden Embry Burchfield. LL.B., U. Ala., 1947. Bar: Ala. bar 1947. Partner firm Embry & Embry, Pell City, Ala., 1947-48; individual practice law, Birmingham, Ala., 1949-55; partner firm Beddow, Embry & Beddow, Birmingham, 1956-74; justice Supreme Ct. Ala., Montgomery, from 1975; adj. mem. faculty dept. criminal justice U. Ala., Birmingham. Served to capt. U.S. Army, 1943-46. Mem. Ala., Birmingham bar assns., Am., Ala. trial lawyers assns., Am. Judicature Soc., Internat. Soc. Barristers. Democrat. Roman Catholic. Home: Birmingham, Ala.

EMERSON, FAYE MARGARET, actress; b. Elizabeth, La., July 8, 1917; student San Diego State Coll.; m. William Wallace Crawford, 1941 (div. 1942); 1 son, William Wallace Crawford III; m. 2d, Elliott Roosevelt, Dec. 3, 1944 (div. 1950); m. 3d Skitch Henderson, 1950. Joined summer stock group St. James Repertory Theater, Carmel, Cal.; appeared in comedy Here Today, San Diego Municipal Theater, 1941; motion picture actress Warner Brothers, 1941-46, films including Bad Men of Missouri, Juke Girl, Murder in the Big House, Blues in the Night, The Desert Song, Hollywood Canteen, The Very Thought of You, Hotel Berlin, Danger Signal, Her Kind of Man; Eastern stage debut, Cape Playhouse, Dennis, Mass., 1946; first appeared on Broadway, 1948; plays include Here Today, The Play's the Thing, Goodbye My Fancy, Parisienne; on radio in My Silent Partner, NBC, 1949; began TV career with CBS, 1949; TV show, NBC, 1950; star Faye Emerson's Wonderful Town, 1951; panel mem. I've Got a Secret. Recipient ann. TV award Look mag., 1951. Died Mar. 9, 1983.

EMERSON, GLADYS ANDERSON, biochemist, nutritionist; b. Caldwell, Kans., July 1, 1903; d. Otis Anderson and Louise (Williams) Anderson. A.B., B.S., U. Sci. and Arts Okla., 1925; M.A., Stanford, 1926; Ph.D., U. Calif. at Berkeley; Ph.D. (Univ. fellow), 1932; postgrad., U. Göttingen, 1932-33. Teaching asst. U. Sci. and Arts, Okla., 1923-25; asst. Stanford, 1925-26; research asso. Inst. Exptl. Biology, U. Calif. at Berkeley, 1933-42; vis. lectr. pharmacology med. sch. U. Calif. at San Francisco, 1945; research asso. Sloan-Kettering Inst. Cancer Research, 1950-53; head dept., animal nutrition Merck Inst. Therapeutic Research, Rahway, N.J., 1942-56; dir. nutrition Merck, Sharp & Dohme Research Labs., 1956-57; Marie Curie lectr. Pa. State U., 1951; research lectr. Iowa State U., 1952; prof., chmn. dept. home econs. U. Calif. at Los Angeles, 1957-61, prof. nutrition, 1961-70, prof. emeritus, from 1970,; head div. nutrition Sch. Pub. Health, 1961-69; vis. lectr. biochemistry and nutrition U. Nebr., 1958; lectr. univs., sci. and profl. socs., Japan, 1964, 65, 67, 70, 75; engaged in research OSRD, 1943-45; mem. liaison and sci. adv. bd. Q.M. Food and Container Inst., 1949-50; food and nutrition research com. NRC, 1952; mem. Food and Nutrition Bd., 1959-64, mem. com. dietary allowances, 1960-64; exec. council Am. Bd. Nutrition, 1959-68; panelist Rensselaer Poly. Inst. indsl. council, 1955; mem. U.S. nat. com. Internat. Union Nutrition Scientists, 1958-62; organizing com. 5th Internat. Congress Nutrition, 1961; vice chmn. panel on new foods White House Conf. on Food, Nutrition and Health, 1969; del. confs. in field; instr. trainees Peace Corps, 1962, 63, 64. Author articles to books and sci. jours.; Asso. editor: Jour. Nutrition, 1952-56. Mem. State Nutrition Com., 1966-69; mem. Calif. Nutrition Council, 1971—, So. Calif. Com. on Food and Nutrition, from 1973; sponsor Calif. Freedom from Hunger Com., 1966-70, sci. adviser, 1970-74; mem. sci. bd. Meals for Millions, 1970-79, hon. trustee, 1979—, mem. nominating com. nutrition program com., 1977; expert witness FDA, FTC, 1972-76; mem. So. Calif. com. ONA-U.S.A., 1974-76; chmn. So. Calif. com. WHO, 1973-75; Mem. bd. So. Calif. Friends Soochow U., 1970—; mem. Los Angeles Interagy. Disaster Com., 1976. Recipient Garvan medal Am. Chem. Soc., 1952; named to Okla. Hall Fame, 1943, to; Univ. Scis. and Arts Okla., 1972. Fellow Am. Inst. Chemists, A.A.A.S., N.Y. Acad. Scis., Am. Pub. Health Assn., Am. Inst. Nutrition (councillor 1952-55, chmn. membership com. 1964, fellows com. 1975-78, history of nutrition com. 1976-78); mem. Am. Chem. Soc. (chmn. women's service com. 1953-58), Am. Soc. Biol. Chemists, Soc. Exptl. Biology and Medicine, Gordon Research Conf. (chmn. vitamins and metabolism 1952, vice chmn. 1951), Pan Am. Med. Assn. (nutrition council 1959-60), UN Assn. So. Calif. (mem. council from 1974, v.p. community relations and edn. 1976-78), Los Angeles World Affairs Council, Town Hall of Calif., Sigma Xi, Delta Omega (nat. pres. 1951), Sigma Delta Epsilon, Iota Sigma Pi (nat. v.p. 1945, nat. pres. 1951-57, nat. hon. mem.). Co-isolator Vitamin E, 1936 Home: Santa Monica, Calif. Deceased.

EMERSON, GOUVERNEUR VINCENT, ret. army officer, physician; b. Milford, Pa., Mar. 8, 1889; s. Henry Everett and Helene (Burbage) E.; m. M.D., Medico Chirurgical Coll., Philadelphia, 1914; grad. Army Med. Sch., Washington, 1917; m. Marie V. McLaughlin, Nov. 2, 1919; children—Teresa Burbage (Mrs. William E. Wilkins), 1st Lt. Henry E. Emerson, U.S.A. Interne Phila. Gen. Hosp., 1914-16. Served as 1st lt., Med Corps, U.S. Army, 1917, promoted through grades to brigadier gen., 1948. Supervising physician Bur. Tuberculosis Control, Pa. Dept. of Health. Fellow Am. Coll. Surgeons; mem. American Med. Assn. Decorated Legion of Merit, Catholic. Home: Milford, Pa. †

EMERSON, JAMES GORDON, univ. prof.; b. Volney, Ia., Apr. 11, 1889; s. James Pembroke and Anna Margaret (Tangeman) E.; B.S., Ia. State Coll., 1912; student Harvard Law Sch., 1912-13, U. Calif. Law Sch., summer 1914; J.D., Stanford, 1915; m. Edith Willmann, Sept. 23, 1922; 1 son, James Gordon. Station agt., Chicago, Gt. Western Ry., 1903-06, telegrapher, chief div. telegrapher, summers 1907, 08; admitted to Calif. Bar, 1914; instr. and asst. prof. pub. speaking, Kan. State Coll., 1915-17, prof. and dept. head, 1917-21, vis. prof., 1925-26; mem. faculty Stanford from 1921, prof. speech and drama from 1950, dir. debate, 1921-32, 1943-45 and 1948-52. Mem. Kan. State Coll. panel of speakers, World War I. Dir. Western Region, Office of Coordinator of Inter-Am. Affairs Discussion Contest 1943-44. Served with U.S. Army, 1918-19, U.S., France and Germany, Mem. Am. and Western speech assns., Am. Assn. U. Profs., Order of Coif, Phi Alpha Delta, Delta Sigma Rho. Conglist. Contbr. articles on spl. subjects, also book revs. in speech and lang. publs. Home: Palo Alto, Calif. †

EMERSON, LYNN ARTHUR, educator; b. Twin Lakes, Minn., July 20, 1890; s. Robert and Mary (Wilson) E.; E.E., U. of Minn., 1911; Ph.D., N.Y.U., 1932; m. Lottie Campbell, June 22, 1915; children—Mary Elizabeth, Margaret Louise, Robert Campbell, Ruth Ann (Mrs. Keith A. Zilk), Helen Harriet (Mrs. Donald E. Smith). Teacher and principal of the Dunwoody Institute at Minneapolis, 1916-18 and 1921-22; asst. supt. schs., Yonkers, N.Y., 1936-38; prof. of indsl. edn., coll. of agr., Cornell, 1938-46, asst. dean, coll. of engring. (part time), 1944-46, prof. of indsl. and labor relations, sch. of indsl. and labor relations, 1946-55, acting dir. of extension, 1946-47; vocational edn. specialist with Research Found., State University of N.Y., Israel Project, 1955-57; consultant: Pres.'s Adv. Com. on Edn., 1937; Nat. Youth Adminstrn., 1938-40; Ill. Legislative Commn. on Higher Edn., 1944; N.Y. State Com. on Tech. Insts., 1945-46; New Haven Sch. Survey, 1946-47; Study of Vocational Schs. of N.Y.C., 1948-51; Ark. Legislative Commn. Higher Edn., 1950; United States Office of Education, Washington, 1957-60; ICA, Cambodia, 1961; pvt. cons. in vocational and tech. edn.; also cons. N.C. Edn. Dept. Mem. Am. Vocational Assn., Am. Tech. Edn. Assn., Nat. Assn. Indsl. Teacher Trainers, Am. Soc. of Training Dirs., Phi Kappa Phi, Tau Beta Pi, Phi Delta Kappa. Democrat. Methodist. Author publs. including: How to Prepare Training Manuals, 1952; Technical Training in the United States, 1962. Contbr. articles in periodicals. Home: Chevy Chase, Md. †

EMERY, EARNEST WESLEY, educator; b. Sedalia, Mo., Sept. 26, 1887; s. William Henry and Rebecca Ann (Treadway) E.; grad. high sch., Washington, Ind., 1909; student Central Normal Coll., Danville, Ind., summer 1909; A.B., Ind. Central Coll., Indianapolis, Ind., 1915; A.M., Ind. U., 1923; m. Lota Maude Snyder, Apr. 14, 1911; children—Richard Edwin, Donald Gale, Earnest Merle. Pastor U.B.Ch., Logansport, Ind., 1914-15; ednl. missionary U.B.Ch., in Sierra Leone, W. Africa, 1915-18; field rep. and treas., Ind. Central Coll., 1918-23; pres. York (Neb.). Home: York, Nebr. †

EMMET, HERMAN LEROY, business exec.; b. New Rochelle, N.Y., Sept. 26, 1889; s. Robert Temple and Helena Van Cortlandt (Phelps) E.; A.B., Yale, 1912; m. Helen Dunscomb Auerbach, June 22, 1912; children—Lydia Field (Mrs. Lewis Croxton Williams), Katherine Hone (Mrs. Gerald Ames Bramwell), Anna Paige (Mrs. Gloster Beveridge Aaron), Herman LeRoy, Helena Van Cortlandt (Mrs. John Buffington-Tredway). Prodn. clerk Gen. Elec. Co., Schenectady, N.Y., 1912-15; asst. to prodn. mgr., 1915-20, prodn. mgr., 1920-29, works mgr. Gen. Elec. Co., Erie, Pa., from 1929; dir. 1st Nat. Bank of Erie; mem. bd., Pa. Assn. for the Blind; past pres. Community Chest of Erie County; vice pres. and mem. bd. Community Chests and Councils, Inc., New York City; pres. Community and War Fund of Erie County; past pres. and mem. bd. trustees of Hamot Hosp., Erie, Pa. Mem. Acad. of Polit. Sci., Am. Soc. M.E., Newcomen Soc., Navy League of U.S., Am. Mus. of Natural History. Republican. Episcopalian. Clubs: Erie, Kahkwa (Erie); University, Yale, Racquet and Tennis (New York City); Chagrin Valley Hunt (Cleveland); Mohawk, Mohawk Golf (Schenectady); Tobique Salmon (Nictau, Can.); Rolling Rock (Pittsburgh). Home: Erie, Pa. †

EMMET, ROBERT R(UTHERFORD) M(ORRIS), naval officer; b. New Rochelle, N.Y., Jan. 27, 1888; s. Robert Temple and Helena Van Cortlandt (Phelps) E.; grad. U.S. Naval Acad., 1908; m. Beulah Eaton Hepburn, Oct. 17, 1914; children—Robert Temple, Beulah Eaton, Barton Hepburn, John Patten. Commd. ensign U.S. Navy, June 1910, and advanced through grades to rear adm., Aug. 1946; comd. U.S.S. Texas, 1938-40; transports amphibious force, Atlantic Fleet, 1941-43; U.S. Naval Training Center, Great Lakes, Ill., 1943-45; ret., 1946. Awarded Navy Cross for services on board U.S.S. Canonicus (mine layer), 1918; D.S.M. for services rendered during forced landing at Fédala, Morocco, 1942. Clubs: New York Yacht, University (N.Y. City); Chevy Chase (Md.); Indian Creek Country (Miami Beach, Fla.). Home: Miami Beach, Fla. †

EMMONS, RALPH LEWIS, lawyer; b. Borodino, Onondaga County, N.Y., Mar. 15, 1890; s. Milton and Laura (Stanton) E.; A.B., U. of Mich., 1915; LL.B., Cornell U., 1918; m. Ellen O'Brien. Nov. 25, 1915; children—Ralph Lewis, Jr., Mary Dorothy, William Gerard, Charles Milton, Ann Jeannette, Paul Myron, Maurice Frederick, Joseph Franklin, Laura Elizabeth (dec.), Roger Lee. Teacher in rural schools, 1909-11; assistant in economics, Cornell U., 1916-18; asso. editor Cornell Law Quar., 1917-18; admitted to N.Y. bar, 1919; began practice in Binghamton with Jenkins, Deyo & Hitchcook; own law office from 1926; atty. N.Y. State Tax Commn. for Broome County, 1929-36; U.S. atty., Northern Dist. of N.Y., 1936-43; govt. appeal agent, draft bd. No. 449, 1944-47; bd. govs. Am. Civic Assn. from 1948. Mem. Am., N.Y. State, Broome County bar assns. Democrat. Roman Catholic. Home: Binghamton, N.Y. †

EMPSON, WILLIAM, poet, critic; b. Yorkshire, Eng., Sept. 27, 1906; s. Arthur Reginald and Laura (Micklethwait) E.; B.A., Magdalene Coll., Cambridge (Eng.) U., 1929, M.A., 1935; m. Hester Henrietta Crouse, Dec. 1941; children—William Hendrick Magador, Jacobus Arthur Calais. Prof. English lit. Bunrika Daigaku, Tokyo, Japan, 1931-34, Peking (China) Nat. U., 1937-39, 46-52, Sheffield (Eng.) U., 1958-84, Chinese editor BBC, 1941-46. Fellow Royal Soc. Lit. Author: Seven Types of Ambiguity, 1930; Poems, 1935; Some Versions of Pastoral, 1935; (verse) The Gathering Storm, 1940; The Structure of Complex Words, 1951; Collected Poems, 1955; Milton's God, 1961. Home: London, England. Died Apr. 15, 1984.

ENDRESS, HENRY, soc. exec.; b. S.I., N.Y., Nov. 18, 1914; s. Karl Frederick and Mina (Graf) E.; m. Clare Marie LeBlanc, July 20, 1942; children—Lee Henry, Lori Clare. B.A., Wagner Coll., 1938; Litt. D. (hon.), 1956; postgrad. English, Columbia U., 1938-39; LL.D. (hon.), Gettysburg Coll., 1959. Feature writer, columnist S.I. Advance, 1936-39, 79-80; publicity dir., registrar Wagner Coll., 1938-39; publicity dir. S.I. C. of C., 1939-41; exec. dir. S.I. Community and War Chest, 1941-45, Conn. State War Fund, New Haven, 1945; asso. dir. stewardship and laymen's movement United Luth. Ch., N.Y.C., 1946-49, exec. dir., 1949-63; mem. exec. council Luth. Ch. in Am., 1968-69; mem. Luth. Commn. on Handicapped, 1980—; v.p. Wilfrid (Ont., Can.) Laurier U., 1963-69, acting pres., 1967-68; exec. dir. Luth. Resources Commn., Washington, 1969-79; mem. Religious Heritage of Am., 1978—; v.p. Vesper Soc., San Leandro, Calif., 1980—; lectr. George Washington U. Sch. Adult Edn., 1978. Asso. film producer, Cathedral Films, Hollywood, Calif., 1947-52, Louis DeRochemont Assos., N.Y.C., 1952-53; theatrical film Martin Luther, Halas & Bachelor Cartoon Films, London, 1956; exec. sec. theatrical film, Luth. Film Assos., N.Y.C., 1951-53, mem. com. prodn., 1953-80; TV spl. The Joy of Bach, 1978-79; Author: (with others) Doing God's Work, 1948, Franklin Clark Fry-A Palette for a Portrait, 1972, Writing for the Religious Market, 1956, Mr. Protestant, 1962, Stewardship Explorations, 1963; contbr. (with others) articles to profl. jours. Mem. nat. religious adv. council CBC, 1965-69, vice chmn., 1968-69. Named Luth. Layman of 1954 Fedn. Luth. Clubs, Luth. Layman of 1955 Luth. Soc. N.Y., Luth. Layman of Kitchener-Waterloo Luth. Brotherhood, 1967; Fund Raiser of Yr. Nat. Soc. Fund Raising Execs., 1980. Mem. Religious Pub. Relations Council, Luth. Laymen's Fellowship (pres. 1975-77), Luth. Laymen's Movement for Stewardship, Nat. Assn. Hosp. Devel., Nat. Soc. Fund Raising Execs. Clubs: Nat. Lawyers (Washington), Nat. Press. Canadian (Washington). Home: Hayward CA Office: San Leandro CA

ENGBERG, EDWARD JOHN, hosp. supt., physician; b. Mpls., Sept. 29, 1887; s. John and Hilda (Johnson) E.; M.D., U. Minn., 1913; postgrad. course neurology, Phila. Postgrad. Sch. Neurology, 1916; m. Dagmar Larson, Jan. 22, 1917; children—Robert W., Kathryn D. Intern Mounds Park Sanitarium, St. Paul, 1913-14; pvt. practice neuro-psychiatry, St. Paul, 1914-37; supt. Faribault (Minn.) State Sch. and Hosp., from 1937; teaching asst. neurology U. Minn. Med. Sch., 1915-19. Mem. Minn. Bd. Med. Examiners, 1929-35, sec., 1930-35; mem. Minn. Bd. Health and Vital Statistics, 1935-37. Served to capt., M.C., U.S. Army, 1917-19. Diplomate Am. Bd. Psychiatry and Neurology. Life fellow Am. Psychiat. Assn.; fellow A.M.A.; mem. Minn., Rice County med. socs., Minn. Psychiat. Soc., Minn. Soc. Neurol. Scis., Central Neuro-psychiat. Assn., Am. Assn. Mental Deficient, Am., Minn., Rice County assns. retarded children, Faribault C. of C., Am. Legion Phi Rho Sigma, Alpha Omega Alpha. Baptist. Elk, Rotarian, Mason. Club: St. Paul Athletic. Contbr. profl. jours. Address: Faribault, Minn. †

ENGEL, LEHMAN, composer, conductor, author; b. Jackson, Miss., Sept. 14, 1910; s. Ellis and Juliette (Lehman) E. Student, Cin. Conservatory, Cin. Coll. Music, Cin. U.; fellow, Juilliard Grad. Sch., 1930, grad., 1934; pvt. student with, Roger Sessions, 1935; Mus.D., Boguslawski Coll. Music, 1944; L.H.D., Millsaps Coll., 1971; Mus.D. (hon.), U. Cin., 1971. pres. Arrow Music Press, Inc.; dir. Mus. Theatre Workshop, Broadcast Music, Inc., N.Y.C., Los Angeles, Nashville, Toronto; exec. dir. mus. theatre devel. Columbia Pictures-Screen Gems; lectr. Cin. Coll. Conservatory Music, Wagner Coll., S.I., Smithsonian Instn.; adv. bd. Sch. Performing Arts, Music Sch. Henry St. Settlement, N.Y.C. Condr., Lewisohn Stadium, 1951, New Friends of Music, Town Hall, N.Y.C., 1952, mus. dir., State Fair Musicals, Dallas, 1949-52; condr.: lyric theatre others; composer incidental music for; composer, condr. incidental music; many documentary and instructional films for, U.S. Navy; composer: concert works for various solo instruments, orch., voices, also Pierrot of the Minute; opera, 1928, The Soldier, 1956; works for TV, films, radio, condr. Bajour; mus. theatre cons. to, Columbia Pictures, recs., RCA-Victor, Columbia, Decca, Brunswick, Atlantic; guest condr., St. Louis Municipal Opera, 1968, Porgy and Bess with Turkish State Opera, The Consul at Temple U. Festival; world premiere: Scarlett, Tokyo, 197O; guest condr., Boston Symphony Orch.; condr.: Lost in the Stars, Kennedy Theatre, 1972; artistic dir., Sigmund Romberg Festival, Acad. of Music, Phila., 1973, participant seminars, Yale U., 1975, N.Y. U., 1976, Banff Arts Centre., (Recipient Bellamann award 1964, scroll Consular Law Soc. 1968, Los Angeles Drama Critics Circle award 1980, Northwood Inst. award 1981, decoration Republic Austria, Nat. Endowment Humanities grantee.); Author: Planning and Producing a Musical Show, 1956, rev. edit., 1974, The American Musical Theatre, 1967, Words with Music, 1971, Getting Started in the Theatre, 1973, This Bright Day; autobiography, 1975, Their Words are Music, 1975, The Critics, 1976, The Making of the Musical, 1977, Renaissance to Baroque, 7 vols. Served to lt. USNR, 1942-45. Mem. League Composers (composers com.), Composers and Lyricists Guild Am. (v.p.). Home: New York, N.Y. Dec. Aug. 29, 1982.

ENGEL, MARIAN RUTH, novelist; b. Toronto, Ont., Can., May 24, 1933; d. Frederick Searle and Mary Elizabeth (Fletcher) Passmore; children—William and Charlotte (twins). B.A., McMaster U., 1955; M.A., McGill U., 1957. Tchr. Mont. State U., Missoula, 1957-58, The Study, Montreal, Que., Can., 1958-60, St. John's Sch., Nicosia, Cyprus, 1962-63; writer-in-residence U. Alta., Edmonton, Can., 1977-78, U. Toronto, 1980-81. Free-lance writer: novels include No Clouds of Glory, 1968, The Honeyman Festival, 1970, Monodromos, 1974, Joanne, 1975, Inside the Easter Egg, 1975, Bear, 1976, The Glassy Sea, 1978, The Year of the Child, 1981, Islands of Canada, 1981; books for children include Adventure at Moon Bay Towers, 1975, My Name Is Not Odessa Yar Rev, 1977; contbr.: short stories and articles to numerous mags. and newspapers including N.Y. Times Book Rev; (Recipient Gov. Gens. award for Best Novel in English in Can. for Bear 1976). Trustee Toronto Pub. Library Bd., 1974-77; mem. Toronto Book Prize com., 1974-77. Mem. Assn. Canadian TV Radio Artists, Writers Union Can. Mem. New Democratic Party. Home: Toronto, Ont., Can. Died Feb. 16, 1985.

ENGEL, SAMUEL GAMILEL, motion picture producer; b. Woodridge, N.Y., Dec. 29, 1904; s. Morris Hyman and Mary (Berman) E.; Ph.G., Union U., 1924; m. Ruth Franklin, Dec. 4, 1936; children—Charles Franklin, Mark Ethridge. Dir., Imperator Prodns., Inc. Vice chmn. of the board Brandeis Institute; mem. pres.'s council Loyola U., Los Angeles, California. Served as lieutenant, United State Navy, 1942-45; comdr., USNR. Mem. Screen Producers Guild, Acad. Arts and Scis. (v.p.), Screen Writers Guild, Rho Pi Phi. Mason. Home: Beverly Hills, Calif. Died Apr. 7, 1984.

ENGEL, WILLIAM, physician; b. Brooklyn, N.Y., Feb. 2, 1887; s. David and Rosa (Hess) E.; student Eckley Prep. Sch., 1904-05; M.D., Long Island Coll. and Hosp., 1909; m. Mildred Bristol Fuller, Nov. 11, 1962. Interne Long Island Coll. Hosp., Brooklyn, N.Y. 1909-11; physician, Brooklyn and N.Y. City, 1911-17; capt. Med. Corps, U.S. Army (with A.E.F.), 1917-20; physician N.Y., from 1920, ret. Decorated D.S.C. (U.S.). Fellow Am. Assn. Phys. Therapy, N.Y. Assn. Phys. Therapy); mem. N.Y. State, N.Y. County (honorary life member) med. socs., Internat. Papillon Soc. (v.p. Am. br.). Mason. Clubs: Boca Raton; La Coquille (Palm Beach, Fla.). Author: Sensible Dieting, 1939; This Naughty World; Aristocrats Anonymous. Contbr. to jours. and mags. Breeder of Papillon dogs. Home: Boca Raton, Fla. †

ENGELHARDT, NICKOLAUS LOUIS, JR., ednl. cons.; b. Auburn, N.Y., July 8, 1907; s. Nickolaus Louis and Bessie (Gardner) E.; B.S., Yale, 1929; A.M., Columbia, 1938, Ph.D., 1939; m. Florida Beatrice Kramer, Nov. 30, 1933; children—David, John (dec.). Asso. devel. air transp. in Pitts. Aviation Industries Corp. and as asst. to v.p. Transcontinental and Western Air, Inc., 1929-36; mem. staff Harrison & Fouilhoux, architects, N.Y.C., 1936-38; research asso. div. field studies Tchrs. Coll., Columbia, 1938-40; prof. edn. U. Fla., 1939-40; dir. research Newark Pub. Sch. System, 1940-43, vis. lectr. U. Wis., 1941; ednl. cons. CAA, 1942; dir. Air-Age edn. research Am. Airlines, N.Y.C., 1943-47; prof. N.Y. U., summer 1949; cons. to bds. edn. and architects in planning sch. bldgs. and orgn. sch. systems as mem. firm Engelhardt & Engelhardt, Inc., N.Y.C., 1947-83, now chmn. bd. Cons. to Fla. Work Conf. on Sch. Problems and So. States Work Conf., 1941. Mem. Newark Def. Council, 1942; mem. bd. edn. Edgemont Dist., Scarsdale, 1948-51; cons. N.Y. State Citizens Com. for Pub. Schs.; dir. Denver Congress on Air Edn., 1945, World Congress of Air Edn., 1946. Recipient Frank B. Brewer trophy for outstanding contbn. aviation edn. by Nat. Aeros. Assn., 1947. Fellow A.A.A.S.; mem. Am. Assn. Sch. Adminstrs., N.E.A., Am. Ednl. Research Assn., Phi Delta Kappa, Theta Xi. Author: School Building Costs, 1939; Planning Community Schools (with N.L. Engelhardt), 1940; Social Trends and the Schools, 1941; Education for the Air Age, 1942; New Frontiers of Our Global World, 1942; (with N.L. Engelhardt and S. Leggett) Planning Secondary School Buildings, 1950, Planning Elementary School Buildings, 1952; School Building and Planning Handbook, 1956; Complete Guide for Planning New Schools, 1970. Contbr. to profl. periodicals. Died Apr. 23, 1983.

ENGERT, CORNELIUS VAN H., former U.S. ambassador; b. Vienna, Austria, Dec. 31, 1887; s. John Cornelius and Mary (Babbitt) E.; brought to U.S. as child; B.Litt., U. Cal., 1909, M.Litt., 1910, student Law Sch., 1908-11; Le Conte Meml. fellow Harvard, 1911-12; m. Sara Cunningham, Dec. 16, 1922 (dec. 1972); children—Roderick, Sheila (Mrs. F. Gillen). Teaching fellow history U. Cal., 1909-11; attaché Am. embassy, Constantinople, Turkey, 1912-16, represented embassy at Chanak during Dardanelles campaign, 1914-15; spl. mission to Syria and Palestine, 1916-17, interned by Turks for several weeks upon rupture diplomatic relations with U.S., 1917; attached to Viscount Ishii's Japanese mission to U.S., 1917; 3d sec. Am. legation, The Hague, 1917-19; asst. to U.S. High Commr., Constantinople, 1919-20; 2d sec. legation, Tehran, Iran, 1920-22; first U.S. Diplomatic officer to visit Kabul, Afghanistan, 1922; Dept. State, 1922-23; 1st sec. Am. embassy, Havana, Cuba, 1923-25, San Salvador, C.Am., 1925-26, negotiated and signed Treaty Friendship between U.S. and Republic El Salvador, 1926; 1st sec. Santiago, Chile, 1926-27, Caracas, Venezuela, 1927-30, Peking, China, 1930-33, Cairo, Egypt, 1933-35; minister resident and consul gen., Addis Ababa, Ethiopia (during Italian War), 1935-37; chargé d'affaires, Tehran, 1937-40; consul gen. Beirut and Damascus, 1940-42; in charge Brit. interests, Syrian campaign, 1941; 1st U.S. minister plenipotentiary to reside in Kabul, Afghanistan, 1942-45; traveled overland, Kabul to Moscow, via Bokhara and Samarkand, 1945, visited Katmandu, Nepal, 1945; asst. and acting diplomatic adviser UNRRA, 1946-47; spl. mission to Middle East, 1946; rep. Internat. Bank for Reconstrn. and Devel., Middle East, India, Pakistan and Ceylon, 1948-51; founder (with others) Anglo-Am. Coll., Oxfordshire, Eng., 1966, lectr. at coll., 1968; founder (with others) Am. Friends of Middle East, Inc., 1951, mem. bd. dirs. 1951-70. Cons. Common Market, 1959-85. Awarded lectureship for 1954 in Turkey, Iran, Afghanistan, Pakistan and India; hon. comdr. Order Brit. Empire; asso. knight Order of Saint John of Jerusalem. Fellow Am. Geog. Soc., Royal Geo. Soc., Royal Central Asian Soc.; charter mem. English-Speaking Union (pres. Washington br. 1951-58, then v.p., mem. bd.) Presbyn. Clubs: Sierra (San Francisco); Royal Societies (London). Home: Washington, D.C. Died May 12, 1985.

ENGLEHART, FRANCIS AUGUSTUS, army officer; b. Laclede, Mo., Mar. 1, 1890; s. Henry Franklin and Mary Elizabeth (Johnson) E.; B.S., U.S. Mil. Acad., 1913; student special course, U. Of Minn., 1919-20; grad. Army Industrial Coll., Washington, D.C., 1933; M.B.A., Grad. Sch. Bus. Administrn., Harvard, 1935; m. Imogen Norton, Dec. 27, 1916; children—Imogen Elizabeth (wife of Maj. George Overton Riggs), Francis Augustus, Nancy Louise (wife of Capt. David Baldwin Conard), Norton Franklin. Commd. 2d lt., Coast Artillery Corps, U.S. Army, 1913, advancing through the grades to brig. gen., 1944; instr. mathematics, U.S. Mil. Acad., 1916-19, Coast Arty. Sch., Ft. Monroe, Va., 1920-21; transferred to Ordnance Dept., 1921; served successively at Frankford Arsenal, Philadelphia, Pa.; ordnance officer 6th Corps Area, Chicago, Ill.; Rock Island (Ill.) Arsenal; harbor defenses of Manila and Subic bays, P.I.; Office of Chief of Ordnance, Washington, D.C.; ordnance officer, 2d Div., Fort Sam Houston, Tex., ordnance officer 4th Corps Area, Atlanta, Ga., 2d Army, Memphis, Tenn., China-Burma-India Theatre; Office Chief of Ordnance, Washington, D.C.; ordnance officer Central Pacific Theatre; now ordnance officer Pacific Ocean Areas. Home: Bennington, Vt. †

ENGLISH, ADA JEANNETTE, librarian; b. Washington, N.J., June 11, 1889; d. Walter B. and Bertha Gertrude (Opdyke) Cox; ed. New York U.; B.A., Rutgers U., 1927, M.A., 1930; B.S., Columbia U. Library Sch., 1932; m. Philip M. English, 1907 (dec.); 1 son, Wilton Opdyke. Library asst., Bayonne, New Jersey Public Library, 1920-22; became librarian N.J. Coll. for Women (now Douglass Coll.), librarian emeritus, historian, 1942-54; organizer, N.J. Coll. for Women Library Sch., 1927, dir. 1927-28, acting dir. from 1951. Member of New Brunswick Finnish Relief Drive (chairman 1940). Mem. Am. Assn. Univ. Profs., Spl. Library Assn., Am. Library Assn., Assn. Coll. and Reference Libraries (chmn. finance comm. for coll. and research libraries, 1947-49), N.J. Library Assn. (chmn. scholarship com., 1930-33, chmn. membership and hosp. coms., 1938-39, pres. 1942-43 chmn. library action com. 1946-47). Columbia U. Library Sch. Alumni Assn. (reg. chmn. for N.J. and Pa., 1938-39), League of Women Voters (v.p. New Brunswick League, 1945-47) Zonta Internat. (pres. New Brunswick chap., 1935-38), mem. Urbana League New Brunswick Forum, Delta Kappa Gamma, Kappa Delta Pi. Author numerous magazine articles. Home: New Brunswick, N.J. †

ENGLISH, E(UGENE) SCHUYLER, editor, author; b. N.Y.C., Oct. 12, 1899; s. Eugene Montgomery and Clara (Stoiber) E.; m. Eva Linde Schultz, March 2, 1937 (dec. August 1956); m. Ruth Hill Kephart, July 4, 1959. Grad., Phillips Acad., Andover, Mass., 1918; student, Princeton, 1918-20; Litt.D. Wheaton (Ill.) Coll, 1939. Sec. Sterling Pure Food Co., Phila., 1920-21; asst. purchasing agt. Curtis Pub. Co., 1922-31; pres. Am. Bible Conf. Assn., Inc., 1930-47; mng. editor Revelation mag., 1931-39; mem. faculty Phila. Sch. Bible, 1935-47, pres., 1936-39; asso. editor Our Hope mag., 1939-45, editor, 1946-58, The Pilgrim (missionary publ.), 1944—; radio broadcaster Phila. Stas. on Bible Study themes, 1935-46. Author: Studies in the Gospel According to Matthew, 1935, By Life and By Death, 1938, The Life and Letters of St. Peter, 1941, Studies in the Gospel According to Mark, 1943, Studies in the Epistle to the Colossians, 1944, The Shifting of the Scenes, 1945, H.A. Ironside, Ordained of the Lord, 1946, Things Surely to Be Believed, 1946, Studies in I and II Thessalonians, 1947, Robert G. Lee, A Chosen Vessel, 1949, Re-Thinking the Rapture, 1951, Studies in the Epistle to the Hebrews, 1954; Editor-in-chief: Pilgrim Edition of The Holy Bible, 1948; Chmn. editorial com.: New Scofield Reference Bible, 1967; Editor: Revised N.T. Berkley Bible, 1969, A Companion to New Scofield Reference Bible, 1972. Served as pvt. U.S. Army, Sept.-Dec. 1918. Home: Merion PA

ENGLISH, MAURICE, author, publisher; b. Chgo., Oct. 21, 1909; s. Michael and Agnes (Sexton) E.; m. Fanita Blumberg, Apr. 25, 1945; children—Jonathan Brian, Deirdre Elena. A.B. magna cum laude, Harvard, 1933. Journalist, U.S. and Europe, 1933-53; editor, pub. Chicago mag., 1953- 57; freelance writer, 1957-61; mng. editor, sr. editor U. Chgo. Press, 1961-69; founding dir. Temple U. Press, Phila., 1969-76; founder Pulvinar Press, 1975; dir. U. Pa. Press, 1979-83. Author: (anthology writings Louis Sullivan) The Testament of Stone, 1963; poems Midnight in the Century, 1964, A Savaging of Roots, 1974; translations Selected Poems of Eugenio Montale, 1966; play The Saints in Illinois, 1969, Choosing the God, 1976. Fulbright fellow France, 1966-67. Mem. Phi Beta Kappa. Home: Philadelphia, Pa. Died Nov. 18, 1983.

ENGLISH, PAUL X., army officer; b. Richmond, Va., Sept. 29, 1889; s. Robert Emmett and Madeline Augustine English; grad. Va. Mil. Inst., 1911, Chem. Warfare Sch., 1924, Command and Gen. Staff Sch., 1928, Army War Coll., 1933; m. Edith Maloney, June 30, 1924; 1 son, Paul X., Jr. Commd. 2d lt., Inf., U.S. Army, 1912, capt., May 1917; transferred to Chem. Warfare Service as major, 1924, and advanced through the grades to brig. gen., Jan. 1942; exec. officer, Office Chief of Chem. Warfare Service, 1939-41, chief, indsl. service, 1941-44; chief of staff, Hdqrs. 7th Service Command since 1944. Decorated Legion of Merit. Mem. Sigma Phi Epsilon. Clubs: Army and Navy (Washington, D.C.); Omaha, Omaha Athletic.†

ENGLISH, SPOFFORD GRADY, consulting chemist; b. Mt. Pleasant, Tenn., Nov. 16, 1915; s. Spofford G. and Ruby May (Warnock) E.; student U. Chattanooga, 1933-34; B.S., U. Okla., 1938, M.S., 1940; Ph.D., U. Calif. at Berkeley, 1943; m. Muriel K. Frodin, Sept. 18, 1942; children—Susan P., Elizabeth H., Helen W. Chemist, Okla. Geol. Survey, 1936-40; teaching asst. chemistry U. Calif. at Berkeley, 1940-42; group leader Manhattan Project, U. Chgo., 1942-43; sect. chief chemistry div. Clinton Lab., Oak Ridge, 1943-46; asst. prof. chemistry U. Calif. at Berkeley, 1946-47; mem. staff AEC (became ERDA 1975), 1947-76, dep. dir. research, 1960-61, asst. gen. mgr. research and devel., 1961-73, assoc. dir. div. phys. research, 1973-76, chmn. plowshare adv. com., 1960-76; chemistry cons., 1977-81; tech. adviser U.S. del. UN Disarmament Conf., London, 1955, U.S. del. Conf. Cessation Nuclear Weapons Test, Geneva, 1959; mem. U.S. del. IAEA, 1956. Mem. Phi Beta Kappa, Sigma Xi. Home: Bethesda, Md. Died Apr. 6, 1981.

ENGRAM, WILLIAM CARL, psychologist, educator; b. Frankfort Heights, Ill., Aug. 12, 1921; s. William and Joyce B. (Horrell) E.; m. Barbara J. Knapp, Aug. 7, 1954; children: Pamela Sue, Melanie Jane, William Marc. A.B., Washington U., 1949; M.A., U. Mo., 1951; Ph.D., Cornell U., 1966. Instr. psychology U. Mo., 1951-52, counselor, 1952; counselor, instr. psychology Stephens Coll., 1953; asso. prof. to prof. psychology, chmn. dept. Lindenwood Coll., St. Charles, Mo., 1953-64; counselor Univ. Counseling Service, Cornell U., 1964-65; spl. instr. Elmira Coll., 1965-66; assoc. prof. psychology State U. N.Y. at Albany, 1966-67; dir. counseling services Alfred U., 1967-69, prof., 1967-81, chmn. dept. psychology, 1967-72, dir. grad. program in psychology; pvt. practice psychology, 1972-81; cons. N.Y. State Dept. Social Services, 1975-81. N.Y. state committeeman Liberal party, 1967-72; co-chmn. Steuben County com., 1968-70; Bd. dirs. Genesee Valley (N.Y.) Civil Liberties Union, chmn. local chpt.; bd. dirs. So. Tier Legal Services, 1974-79, pres., 1976, v.p., from 1977; v.p. Nat. Register of Health Services Providers. Served with AUS, 1942-46. Mem. Am., Eastern, N.Y. State psychol. assns., Am. Psychology-Law Soc., Am. Orthopsychiat. Assn., Fedn. Am. Scientists, AAAS, AAUP, N.Y. Acad. Scis., Psi Chi, Alpha Pi Zeta. Home: Hornell, NY.

ENGSTROM, ELMER WILLIAM, engr.; b. Minneapolis, Aug. 25, 1901; s. Emil and Anna (Nilssen) E.; B.S., U. of Minn., 1923; Sc.D., hon., New York U., 1949; LL.D., Findlay College, 1960, Rider College, 1962, West Virginia University, 1962; m. Phoebe Leander, July 28, 1926; one son William Leander. Began as development engr. and advanced to div. engr. Gen. Elec. Co., Schenectady, N.Y., 1923-30; div. engr. RCA Mfg. Co., 1930-31, dir. gen. research, 1932-39, dir. research, 1939-42, dir. gen. research RCA Labs Div. of Radio Corp. of America, 1942-43, research dir., 1944-45, vice pres. in charge research, 1945-51, v.p. charge RCA Labs. Division, 1951-54, exec. v.p. research and engring. RCA, 1954-55, sr. exec. v.p., 1955-61, pres., dir., 1961-65; dir. RCA Communications, Inc., NBC. Former chmn. research and engineering adv. panel on electronics Office Sec. of Def., Wash. also mem. Def. Sci. Bd. Mem. adv. com. research div. Coll. Engring., N.Y.U., from 1949; mem. exec. com., bd. govs. Am. Swedish Hist. Found. Chmn. Hoover Medal Bd. of Award, 1962. Recipient Outstanding Achievement award University Minnesota, 1950; Progress Medal award, Society Motion Picture and TV Engrs., 1955, John Ericsson Medal, Am. Soc. Swedish Engrs., 1956, Christopher Columbus Internat. Prize in Communications, 1959, Medal of Honor, Electronic Industries Assn., 1962; decorated Comdr. Order Merit Italian Republic. Fellow Am. Inst. E.E., I.R.E. (dir. 1949); mem. N.A.M., Indsl. Research Inst., Inc. (pres. 1948-49), Nat. Security Indsl. Assn., Sigma Xi (past pres. local chpt.) Presbyn. Clubs: Nassau. Rotary (past pres. local club). Author numerous tech. articles. Home: Princeton, N.J. Died Oct. 30, 1984.

ENNEN, ROBERT CAMPION, librarian; b. Detroit, Aug. 25, 1922; s. George L. and Oramel (Ballentine) E. A.B., John Carroll U., 1952; M.A. in L.S, U. Mich., 1958, M.A. in Classics, 1960, Ph.D. in Library Sci, 1962. Asst. dir. library Univ. Notre Dame, Ind., 1962-72; dir. libraries Loyola Univ., Chgo., 1972-83. Home: Chicago, Ill. Dec. Mar. 12, 1983.

ENTENZA, JOHN DYMOCK, educator, author, editor, publisher; b. Calumet, Mich., Dec. 4, 1905; s. Antonio P. and Ellen S. (Dymock) E.; student Stanford, Tulane U., U. Va.; LL.D., Ill. Inst. Tech., 1968; 1 son, Kenneth Keating. Editor-pub. Arts and Architecture mag., 1940-60; dir. Graham Found. Advanced Studies Fine Arts, Chgo., 1960-71; spl. adviser to chancellor, prof. architecture and art U. Ill., Chgo. Circle Campus, 1973-84. Cons. Bur. Reclamation, Dept. Interior. Mem. steering com. Master Plan for Humanities and Arts, Ill. Bd. Higher Edn.; v.p., dir. Internat. Design Conf., Aspen, Colo.; v.p., trustee Mus. Contemporary Art, Chgo., Tamarind Found., Los Angeles, Nat. Citizens Com. for Broadcasting; mem. Commn. on Chgo. Hist. and Archtl. Landmarks; mem. Yale council com. Sch. Architecture; bd. visitors Carnegie-Mellon U.; adviser Nat. Endowment for Arts; mem. task force for architecture, planning and design Ill. Inst. Tech., 1976; mem. Council for Arts, Mass. Inst. Tech., 1971-84; bd. dirs. emeritus, spl. adviser Graham Found. for Advanced Studies in Fine Arts, 1971-84. Hon. mem. AIA, also Los Angeles and Chgo. chpts. AIA, recipient Disting. Service citation AIA, Inspiration in Architecture medal, 1979, also spl. award Calif. Council; award Am. Soc. Interior Designers, 1976; medalist Yale Sch. Art and Architecture, 1966. Clubs: Tavern (Chgo.); Century (N.Y.C.). Home: Chicago, Ill. Died Apr. 27, 1984.

EPPINK, NORMAN ROLAND, artist; b. Cleve., July 29, 1906; s. Herman and Catherine (Koch) E.; m. Helen Louise Brenan, June 15, 1931; 1 dau., Karen Eppink Remington. B.E.A., Cleve. Art Inst., 1928; M.A., Western Res. U., 1936. Instr. art Lakewood (Ohio) public schs., 1928-30; med. illustrator Cleve. Clinic Found., 1930-33; lectr. Cleve. Mus. Art, 1935-36; tchr. art Cleve. public schs., 1936-37; instr. art Emporia (Kans.) State U., 1937-47, prof. art, head dept., 1947-75, prof. emeritus, 1975-85; Bd. dirs. Kans. Fed. Art, 1946-49, Kans. Cultural Arts Commn., 1965-67. Author: 101 Prints, 1971; one man shows include, Wichita Art Mus., 1944, Nat. Gallery of Art, 1968-70, Cleve. Public Library, 1967, Denver U. Library, 1968, Topeka Public Library, 1969, Paine Art Center, Oshkosh, Wis., 1969; represented in permanent collections at, Brit. Mus., Chgo. Art Inst., Cleve. Mus. Art, Los Angeles County Mus. Art, Met. Mus. Art.; (with wife) two-man show, Topeka Pub. Library Gallery, 1977. Club: Rotary. Home: Emporia, Kans. Died June 14, 1985.

EPPLER, WILLIAM BURGESS, investment banker; b. Scranton, Pa., July 13, 1921; s. H. Rufus and Phoebe (Burgess) E.; m. Jeannette Smith, June 17, 1950; children—Richard Beall, John Rufus, Jennifer, Margaret. Pres. Eppler, Guerin & Turner, Inc., Dallas, from 1951. Served to capt., F.A. AUS, 1942-46, N. Africa, Italy. Episcopalian. Clubs: Dallas, Dallas Country. Home: Dallas, Tex. Dec. 1982.

EPSTEIN, BENJAMIN ROBERT, association executive; b. N.Y.C., June 11, 1912; s. Hyman and Sadie (Ziess) E.; m. Ethel Schwartz, Oct. 21, 1935; children: Ellen, David. Ph.B. cum laude, Dickinson Coll., 1933, L.H.D., 1963; exchange fellow, Inst. Internat. Edn., U. Berlin, 1934-35; traveling fellow, U. Pa., 1934, 38, M.A., 1936; LL.D., Talladega Coll., 1957. Instr. German U. Pa., 1935-36; faculty Coatesville (Pa.) High Sch., 1936-38; staff N.Y. Fedn. Jewish Charities, 1938; staff Anti-Defamation League of B'nai B'rith, 1939-44, dir. Eastern region, 1944-47, nat. dir., 1947-79, nat. commr., from 1956; translator; mem. Pres.'s Commn. on Holocaust, 1978. Author: (with Arnold Forster) The Troublemakers, 1952, Germany-Nine Years Later, (with Jacob Alson and Nathan C. Belth) Crosscurrents, (with Arnold Forster), 1956, Some of My Best Friends, 1962, Danger on the Right, 1964, The Radical Right: Report on the John Birch Society and Its Allies, 1967, (with Arnold Foster) The New Anti Semitism, 1974. Exec. v.p. A.D.L. Found., 1979-83; chmn. bd. Fire Island Synagogue, 1979-83, Ocean Beach Community Fund, 1979-83; mem. U.S. del. Madrid Conf. on Security Corp. in Europe, 1980. Recipient Ellis Island award, 1978. Mem. Bur. Intercultural Edn. (dir.), Nat. Assn. Intergroup Relations Officers, Assn. Jewish Community Relations Workers, Phi Epsilon Pi., B'nai B'rith. Clubs: Harmonie, Friars. Home: New York, N.Y. Dec. May 2, 1983.

EPSTINE, HARRY M., business executive; b. Chillicothe, O., Apr. 2, 1899; s. Benjamin and Bella (Adolph) E.; m. Jane B. Metzger, Apr. 6, 1936; children: Beatrice, Marianna. Student engring., U. Mich.; LL.D. (hon.), St. Vincent Coll. Asst. gen. mgr. Summerfield & Hecht, Detroit, 1919-30; with May Stern & Co., Pitts., 1931-82, pres., 1948-82; pres. Epley Land Co., Millard Realty Co., Porter-Gratiot Realty Co.; v.p. Riverview Homes; dir. Comml. Bank & Trust Co. Trustee Falk Med. Fund, Allegheny Gen. Hosp.; bd. dirs. Am. Cancer Soc., Better Bus. Bur.; treas., trustee Montifiore Hosp.; bd. dirs. St. Vincent's Coll.; nat. exec. com. Conf. Fedns. and Welfare Funds, Am. Jewish Com.; hon. pres. United Vocational and Employment Service; bd. dirs. United Jewish Fund, Fedn. Philanthropies, YM and YWHA, Atlantic Union Com.; co-chmn. NCCJ. Served with U.S. Army, 1917-18. Clubs: Furniture (Chgo.), Standard (Chgo.); Westmoreland (Pitts.), One Hundred (Pitts.), Concordia (Pitts.). Home: Pittsburgh, Pa. Dec. Sept. 10, 1982.

ERB, ALLEN H., clergyman, hosp. supt.; b. Newton, Kan., Dec. 9, 1888; s. Tillman H. and Elizabeth Hess) E.; grad. acad., Hesston (Kan.) Coll., 1911; m. Ethel Estella Cooprider, June 20, 1912. Ordained to ministry of Mennonite Ch., Oct. 1912; pastor near McPherson, Kan., 1912-16; supt. Mennonite Sanitarium, La Junta, Colo., from 1916; administrator Lebanon (Ore.) Hospital from 1950; built The Mennonite Hosp. and Sanitarium, 1926-28; evangelist portions of each year; ordained bishop of Mennonite Ch., 1939. Moderator Gen. Conf., 1943-47; mem. missions com. Mennonite Bd. of Missions and Charities, 1941-47. Trustee Colo. Hosp. Assn., 1948-51. Home: Lebanon, Oreg. †

ERICKSON, ERNEST I., hosp. adminstr.; b. Aurora, Ill., Dec. 17, 1887; s. Eric Otto and Johanna Sofia (Nord) E.; ed. pub. schs. of Ill.; m. Anna Thelander, June 18, 1919 (dec. Apr. 26, 1941); children—Betty Louise (Mrs. Stanley Stake), Ruth Joan (Mrs. Byron Swedberg), John Rudolph; m. 2d, Blanche Lauger, Aug. 25, 1945. Asst. sec. Am. Well Works, Aurora, Ill., 1913-17, sec.-treas., Dallas, Tex., 1918-22; asst. supt. Augustana Hosp., Chicago, 1923-24, acting supt., 1924-25, supt. from 1925. Trustee Hosp. Service Corp. (Blue Cross), Chicago, Central Savs. and Loan Assn., Chicago, Am. Coll. Hosp. Adminstrs., Chicago Hosp. Council. Mem. Am. Hosp. Assn., (pres. 1951-52), Am. Protestant Hosp. Assn., Ill. Hosp. Assn., Chicago Hosp. Council. Republican. Luther. Club: Swedish. Home: Chicago, Ill. †

ERLANDER, TAGE, prime minister of Sweden; b. Ransäter, Värmland, Sweden, June 13, 1901; s. Erik and Alma (Nilsson) E.; M.A., U. of Lund, 1928; m. Aina Andersson, 1930; children—Sven, Bo. Began in journalism, then entered polit. career; became mem. city council, Lund, 1931-38; mem. second chamber Swedish Riksdag, 1933-44, from 1949, 1st chamber, 1945-48; apptd. sec. Ministry of Social Affairs, 1938-44; minister without portfolio in Coalition Cabinet, 1944-45; minister of edn. and church affairs in Social Dem. Cabinet, 1945-46; premier of Sweden 1946-49. Mem. Social Democratic Party (chmn. since 1946). Mem. Swedish Luth. Ch. Co-editor Svensk Uppslagsbok (ency.), 1932-38. Home: Stockholm, Sweden. Died June 21, 1985.

ERNST, JOHN LOUIS, advt. agy. exec.; b. Pine Bluff, Ark., Dec. 24, 1932; s. Albert C. and Christine (Vinent) E.; m. Lois R. Geraci, June 12, 1971; children—Ann Marie, Catherine Teresa, Laura Elizabeth, Christine Margaret. B.S., Spring Hill Coll., Mobile, Ala., 1954; student, Georgetown U. Law Sch., 1957. Stock broker Washington Planning Co., 1957-58; sales exec. Am. Airlines, Washington, Phila. and N.Y.C., 1958-62; account exec. Ted Bates Advt. Agy., N.Y.C., 1962-65; sr. v.p., mgmt. dir. Marschalk Advt. Agy., N.Y.C., 1965-68; dir. Interpub. Service Corp., 1967-69; sr. v.p., mng. dir. McCann-Erickson Advt. Agy., N.Y.C., 1969-70; pres. Ernst-Van Praag, N.Y.C., 1970-75; chmn. bd. A.V.E. Corp., N.Y.C., 1974-75; chmn. bd. Advt. to Women, Inc., N.Y.C., from 1975. Served to capt. USMC, 1954-57. Home: New York, NY.

ERVIN, JOHN WESLEY, lawyer, educator, minister; b. Los Angeles, June 22, 1917; s. Frank Earl and Lillian Pearl (Gray) E.; m. Patricia Connelly, May 24, 1958; children by previous marriage—Nancy Gray Ervin Kleeman, Shelley Hutchinson Ervin Fehring, John Chipman Gray. Student, UCLA, 1935-39; J.D., U. Calif.-San Francisco, 1944; LL.M. (research fellow 1945-47), Harvard, U., 1945, S.J.D., 1955. Bar: Calif. 1944. Research asst. to justice Calif. Supreme Ct., 1943-44; prof. law Northeastern U. Law Sch., 1945-46; prof. law, dir. and editor ann. Insts. on Fed. Taxation, U. So. Calif., 1947-70; sr. mem. firm Ervin, Cohen & Jessup, Beverly Hills, Calif., 1953-82; spl. adviser on fed. tax legislation to Sec. Treasury, 1955; ordained to ministry Ch. of People; local pastor United Methodist Ch.; Founding mem. Found. Establishment Internat. Criminal Ct.; Vice pres. bd. trustees, gen. counsel Philos. Research Soc., Internat. Communications Found.; sec., gen. counsel, trustee Internat. Found. for Integral Psychology; bd. dirs., founding mem., v.p. for legal affairs Assn. for Holistic Health, 1974-78; bd. dirs. UN Assn. Los Angeles, now pres. Author: Federal Taxation and the Family, 1955, Spiritual Healthline and Spirit of Holistic Health, 1978. Recipient Distinguished Internat. Lawyer certificate, 1972, UN Peace medal, 1978. Mem. ABA (chmn. publs. com. taxation sect. 1954-55), Calif. Bar Assn., Beverly Hills Bar

Assn., Am. Law Inst., Am. Judicature Soc., Order of Coif, Phi Delta Phi. Office: Beverly Hills, Calif. Dec. Apr. 16, 1982.

ERVIN, SAMUEL JAMES, JR., former U.S. senator; b. Morganton, N.C., Sept. 27, 1896; s. Samuel J. and Laura Theresa (Powe) E.; m. Margaret Bruce Bell, June 18, 1924; children—Samuel James III, Margaret Leslie (Mrs. Gerald Hansler), Laura Powe (Mrs. William E. Smith). A.B., U. N.C., 1917, LL.D., 1951; LL.B., Harvard, 1922; LL.D., Western Carolina Coll., 1955, Wake Forest U., 1971, George Washington U., Davidson Coll., St. Andrews Presbyn. Coll., 1972, Boston U., 1973, U. N.C. at Charlotte, 1974, Drexel U., 1974, Colgate U., 1974, U. Cin., 1974, Belmont Abbey Coll., 1975, Warner Pacific Coll., 1975, Anderson Coll., 1976, U. N.C.-Greensboro, 1983; Dr. Pub. Adminstrn., Suffolk U., Boston, 1957; L.H.D., Wilkes Coll., 1973, Chgo. State U., 1977; Litt.D., Catawba Coll., 1974; D.Con.L., Appalachian U., 1974; J.D., New Eng. Sch. Law, 1975; D. Pub. Service, U. West Fla., 1983. Bar: N.C. 1919. Engaged in gen. practice, Morganton, 1922-85; rep. from Burke County N.C. Gen. Assembly, 1923, 25, 31; judge Burke County Criminal Ct., 1935-37, N.C. Superior Ct., 1937-43; resigned to resume practice law; rep. in Congress from 10th N.C. Dist., 1946-47; asso. justice N.C. Supreme Ct., 1948-54; U.S. senator from N.C., 1954-74; mem. Senate armed services com., judiciary com., chmn. separation of powers subcom., govt. operations com., Presdl. campaign activities select com.; Mem. N.C. Bd. Law Examiners, 1944-46, N.C. Democratic Exec. Com., 1930-37. Author: The Watergate Conspiracy, Humor of a Country Lawyer. Trustee Morganton Graded Schs., 1927-30, U. N.C., 1932-35, 1945-46, Davidson Coll., 1948-85. Served with Co. I, 28th Inf., 1st div. U.S. Army, World War I; French front. Decorated French Fourragere, Purple Heart with oak leaf cluster, Silver Star, D.S.C.; U.D.C. cross mil. service. Mem. ABA, N.C. Bar Assn., N.C. State Bar, Jr. Am. Legion, V.F.W., D.A.V., Soc. 1st Div., Army and Navy Legion Valor, Morganton C. of C., Am. Judicature Soc., N.C. Lit. and Hist. Assn., So. Hist. Assn., Soc. Mayflower Descs. N.C. (gov. 1950-52), Gen. Alumni Assn. U.N.C. (pres. 1947-48), Soc. Cincinnati, S.A.R., Sigma Upsilon, Phi Delta Phi. Democrat. Presbyn. Clubs: Mason (33 deg., K.T.), Moose, Kiwanian, Kip. Home: Morganton, N.C. Died Apr. 23, 1985.

ESGATE, ARTHUR TREAT, Fed. official; b. Marion, Iowa, July 26, 1887; son of Edwin J. and May A. (Treat) E.; B.A., Cornell College, Mount Vernon, Iowa, 1909; married Helen W. Weaver, August 17, 1916. Clerk Cedar Rapids (Ia.) National Bank, 1909-12; successively auditor, cashier, vice president and director, Valley Bank and Trust Co., Phoenix, Ariz., 1913-32; examiner, R.F.C., Washington, D.C., 1932-33; dir. of Regional Agrl. Credit Div., Farm Credit Administration, 1933-35, dep. gov., 1935-38; exec. v.p. Federal Farm Mortgage Corp., 1936-40; dep. prodn. credit commissioner, 1940-52; prodn. credit commr., 1952-54; dep. dir. Short Term Credit Services, 1954-55; dep. gov., from 1955. Mem. Sigma Nu. Episcopalian. Home: Falls Church, Va. †

ESHLEMAN, EDWIN D., b. Lancaster County, Pa., Dec. 4, 1920; s. Reeder L. and Mary (Barbara) E.; m. Kathryn E. Dambach, Dec. 26, 1942; children: E. Bruce, R. Lee. B.S. in Polit. Sci., Franklin and Marshall Coll., 1942; postgrad., Temple U., 1948. Tchr. pub. schs., 1946-49; mem. Pa. Ho. of Reps. from Lancaster County, 1954-66; majority and minority whip; mem. 90th-94th congresses 16th Dist. Pa.; circuit prof. Franklin and Marshall Coll.; dir. Lancaster 1st Fed. Savs. & Loan Assn.; Vice chmn. Pa. Higher Assistance Agy., 1963-67. Author: Congress, The Pennyslvania Dutch Seat. Served with USCGR, 1942-45. Recipient Disting. Service award Pa. Jr. C. of C., 1956; Disting. Alumni award Franklin and Marshall Coll., 1974; Nat. Silver medal of Merit, VFW, 1975; named to Pa. Young Rep. Hall of Fame, 1966. Mem. Am. Legion (Outstanding Citizen award 1976), VFW, Amvets. Home: Lancaster, Pa. Died Jan. 10, 1985.

ESKELUND, KARL I., Danish diplomat; b. Steenstrup, Denmark, Jan. 15, 1890; s. Peder Nielsen and Elisa (Meisling) E.; Dr. of Law, U. Copenhagen, 1915; m. Lotte Pernat, July 5, 1945. Journalist, Politiken, Copenhagen, 1915, parliamentary corr., 1917-30; chmn. Journalists Union, 1930-38, chmn. Internat. Union Journalists, 1937-38; chief press dept. Fgn. Office, 1938-45; consul. gen., Wellington, New Zealand, 1945-49, chargé d'affaires, 1946-49; dep. chief Danish Embassy, Bonn. Germany, 1950-51; Danish minister, Prague, Czechoslovakia. 1951-55; dep. del. Denmark to UN, 1955-56; ambassador, Denmark to UN, 1956-58. Danish Ambassador to Yugoslavia, from 1958. Address: Belgrade, Yugoslavia. †

ESPOSITO, ANTHONY H., labor union exec.; b. Naples, Italy, Jan. 30, 1888; s. Frank and Maria (Matarese) E.; brought to U.S., 1899, naturalized, 1916; student pub. schs. Italy, parochial sch., N.Y.C.; m. Helen Blum, Jan 13, 1911; children—Arthur, Elsie. Mgr. Union Toy and Novelty Workers local 223 since 1933. Pers. Internat. Union Doll and Toy Workers of U.S. and Can., A.F.L. Roman Catholic Address: New York, N.Y. †

ETHRIDGE, WILLIE SNOW (MRS.), author; b. Savannah, Ga., Dec. 10, 1900; d. William Aaron and Georgia (Cubbedge) Snow; A.B., Wesleyan Coll., Macon, Ga., 1920; Litt.D., U. Kentucky, 1942, m. Mark Foster Ethridge, Oct. 12, 1921; children—Mary Snow, Mark, Georgia, David. Reporter, Macon (Ga.) Telegraph, 1920; writer newspaper and magazine articles since 1920, contbg. to well known publications. Awarded Carl Schurs Foundation-Fellowship, 1933. Trustee Wesleyan Coll. (Macon), Lincoln Inst. (Pleasant Ridge, Ky.). Democrat. Club: Womens,Country, Pendennis River Valley (Lousville): Kiwanis. Author books including: As I Live and Breathe, 1937; Mingled Yarn, 1939; I'll Sing One Song, 1941; This Little Pig Stayed Home, 1944; It's Greek To Me, 1948; Going to Jerusalem, 1950; Let's Talk Turkey, 1952; Nila. 1956; Summer Thunder, 1959; Russian Duet, 1959; There's Yeast in the Middle East, 1963; I Just Happen to Have Some Pictures, 1964; You Can't Hardly Get There from Here, 1965. Home: Moncure, N.C. Died Dec. 14, 1982.

ETS, MARIE HALL, (MRS. HAROLD ETS) author, illustrator; b. Milw.; d. Walter Augustus and Mathilda (Carhart) Hall; m. Milton T. Rodig, Nov. 30, 1917 (dec. Jan. 1918); m. Harold N. Ets, June 6, 1930 (dec. June 1943). Student, N.Y. Sch. Fine and Applied Art, 1916-17; Ph.B., U. Chgo., 1924; student art, Art Inst., Chgo.; student, Chgo. Sch. Civics and Philanthropy, U. Chgo., Columbia U. Author, illustrator: children's books Mister Penny, 1935, The Story of a Baby, 1939, In the Forest, 1944, (with Ellen Tarry, A.A. Alland) My Dog Rinty, 1946, Oley: The Sea Monster, 1947, Little Old Automobile, 1948, Mr. T.W. Anthony Woo, 1951, Beasts and Nonsense, 1952, Another Day, 1953, Play With Me, 1955, Mister Penny's Race Horse, 1956, Cow's Party, 1958, (with Aurora Labastida) Nine Days to Christmas: A Story of Mexico, 1959, Mister Penny's Circus, 1961, Gilberto and the Wind, 1963 (honor book N.Y. Herald Tribune Children's Spring Book Festival 1963), Automobiles for Mice, 1964, Just Me, 1965, Bad Boy, Good Boy, 1967, Talking Without Words, 1968; adult book Rosa: The Life of an Italian Immigrant, 1970, Elephant in a Well, 1972, Jay Bird, 1974. Vol. resident Chgo. Commons, 1919-29; orgn. for Child Health in Czechoslovakia, A.R.C., 1921-22; investigator U.S. Coal Commn., W.Va. and So. Ill. mining camps, 1923. Recipient prize N.Y. Herald Tribune Spring Book Festival, 1947; honor book Internat. Jury for H.C.; Andersen medal Stockholm, 1956; recipient Caldecott medal, 1960. Home: Inverness, Fla.

EVANS, CHARLES (CHICK EVANS), JR., golf and sporting writer; b. Indianapolis, Ind., July 18, 1890; s. Charles and Lena (Young) E.; student Northwestern U.; m. Esther Lael Underwood, Sept. 18, 1928. Special writer for Hearst's newspapers, 1912-21. Has been connected with investment banking business since 1911. Vice-pres. Beloit Dairy Co., Chicago. Mem. Phi Delta Theta. Author: Chick Evans' Golf Book, 1921; How to Play Golf, 1924; Ida Broke (with Barrie Payne), 1929. Western interscholastic golf champion 1906, 07, 08; western junior golf champion 4 times, 1907-10; Chicago City Champion 6 times, 1907-14; western amateur champion 8 times, 1909-23; western open champion, 1910; United North and South champion, 1911. French amateur champion, 1911; Am. amateur champion, 1916, 20; Am. open champion, 1916. Engaged in exhbns. under the Western Golf Assn., during World War, that netted over $300,000 for Am. Red Cross. He and Bobby Jones the only golfers to win the national open and national amateur golf championships the same year. Chmn. Nat. Collegiate Athletic Assn. Golf Com. from 1937; Ill. State Commr. Golden Gate Internat. Expn., 1939. Home: Chicago, Ill. †

EVANS, DAVID WOOLLEY, advertising and public relations executive; b. Salt Lake City, Mar. 5, 1894; s. John Alldridge and Florence (Neslen) E.; m. Beatrice Cannon, Sept. 9, 1920; children—David C., Robert C., Edmund C., Wayne C., Carleton C. A.B., U. Utah, 1915; Ph.D. (hon.), Utah State U., 1978, H.H.D. (hon.), 1979. Copywriter, account exec., v.p., adv. mgr. Stevens & Wallis, Inc., Salt Lake City, 1919-43; editor, gen. mgr. Utah Farmer, 1931-33; pres., gen. mgr. David W. Evans, Inc., Salt Lake City, 1943-65, chmn. bd., chief exec. officer, 1965-68, chmn. bd., 1968-72, founder, chmn., dir., 1972-82; dir. Utah Resources Internat., Inc., 1st Thrift & Loan, Utah Woolen Mills.; Vis. lectr. Brigham Young U., 1969-70. Contbr. articles to various publs. Coordinator Mormon exhibits N.Y. World's Fair Pavilion, 1962-65; mem. info. service com. Ch. of Jesus Christ of Latter-day Saints, 1957-72; mem. exec. com. western region Boy Scouts Am., 1968-73; exec. bd. Gt. Salt Lake council, mem.-at-large nat. council; mem. Republican pub. relations adv. panel 90th congress; active pub. relations, publicity for numerous candidates Rep. party, 1948-70; mem. adv. bd. Coll. Bus., U. Utah, 1976-82, mem. govt. transition com., City of Salt Lake City, 1979. Served with Signal Corps U.S. Army, 1918. Recipient spl. citations for information campaign and legislative liaison for Upper Colorado River Project, 1956; Silver medal Advt. Fedn. Am.-Printer's Ink mag., 1966; Distinguished Service award dept. communications Brigham Young U., 1966; Disting. Alumni award U. Utah, 1971; Disting. Achievement in Communications award, 1976. Mem. Advt. Fedn. Am. (hon. life), Counselors Pub. Relations Soc. Am., Newcomen Soc. N.Am., U.S. C. of C. (govt. ops. and expenditures com. 1964-69). Mem. Ch. Jesus Christ of Latter-day Saints. Clubs: Rotary, Timpanogos. Home: Salt Lake City, Utah. Dec. July 25, 1982.

EVANS, GORDON GOODWIN, educator; b. Bklyn., Feb. 13, 1921; s. William Fuller and Beatrice Annie (Briley) E.; A.B., Princeton, 1942; Ph.D., Harvard, 1950; m. Doletha Soorn Watt, Oct. 14, 1944; children—Doletha Marian, William Soorn, Jocelyn Briley, Lawrence Watt, Ruth Christina, Charlotte Deirdre, Chemist, E.I. du Pont de Nemours & Co., Inc., Buffalo, 1942-43; instr. chemistry Tufts U., 1949-52, asst. prof., 1952-65, asso. prof., 1965—, chmn. dept., 1966-68. Served with AUS, 1943-46. Mem. Am. Chem. Soc., AAAS, New Eng. Assn. Chemistry Tchrs. (pres. 1973-75), Am. Assn. U. Profs. Unitarian-Universalist. Home: Bedford, Mass. Dec. May 19, 1980. Interned Tewksbury, Mass.

EVANS, GREGG M(ILLER), coll. prof.; b. Emporia, Kan., June 14, 1890; s. Jeremiah Evan and Margaret Elizabeth (Miller) E.; A.B., Coll. of Emporia, 1912; M.S., U. of Chicago, 1922; Ph.D., Pa. State Coll., 1928; m. Ruth Elizabeth Swanson, Sept. 11, 1919; children—Irvin Miller, Elizabeth Ruth, Nancy Carolyn. Teacher high schs., 1915-17; prof. chemistry and physics, Yankton (S.D.) Coll., from 1922. Served as 1st lt. inf., U.S. Army, with A.E.F., 1917-19. Member Am. Chem. Soc., South Dakota Academy of Science. Republican. Conglist. Asst. editor: Outline of Organic Chemistry, 1937. Contbr. sci. articles to jours. Home: Yankton, S.D. †

EVANS, HAWTHORNE CLOUGH, JR., coll. pres.; b. Morristown, Tenn., Aug. 18, 1927; s. Hawthorne Clough and Lily (Myers) E.; m. Barbara Teagarden, Dec. 18, 1963; 1 son, Mark Richard. B.A., Carson-Newman Coll., 1950; M.A., Columbia U., 1951; Ed.D., U. Tenn., 1958; postgrad., U. Colo., 1956, Lafayette Coll., 1951. Band dir. Morristown (Tenn.) Jr. High Sch., 1951-54; guidance counselor Morristown City Schs., 1954-55; prin. Rose Elem. Sch., Morristown, 1955-56, Roberts Elem. Sch., Morristown, 1958-60; asso. prof. edn. and psychology Carson-Newman Coll., Jefferson City, Tenn., 1960-62, placement dir., 1962-63, dir. student teaching, 1963-67, chmn. dept. psychology and edn., dir. tchr. edn., 1966-67; pres. Lees-McRae Coll., Banner Elk, N.C., from 1967; dir. N.C. Nat. Bank, Banner Elk; adv. bd. Newland br. Watauga Savs. & Loan. Author: mus. comedy Tom; contbr. to mags and newspapers. Camp dir. Camp at Buck Hill Falls, Pa., 1962-67; former mem. exec. bd. and area chmn. Daniel Boone council Boy Scouts Am., now mem. adv. council, scoutmaster, 1945-80; former adminstr. Ky-Tenn. Circle K; dir. charge organizer, 1st exec. dir. Boy's Club Jefferson City, former mem. bd. dirs.; adviser Cherokee Tribe; former mem. bd. dirs. Blue Ridge Health Council, Urban and Rural Council, Avery County C. of C.; liaison officer Res. Officer Tng. Corps, Air Force Acad.; trustee, treas. N.C. Ind. Coll. Fund; bd. dirs. N.C. Student Theatre Guild Inc.; former mem. exec. council Blue Ridge Council for Arts; commr., chmn. Presbyterian survey com. Presbyn. Ch. U.S. Gen. Assembly; elder, past moderator local ch.; former mem. exec. bd. Upward Bound; former mem. bd. govs. Highland U. Served with USAAF, 1946-48; lt. col. USAF Res. Named Young Man of Year Morristown Jr. C. of C., 1955, Young Man of Year Morristown Jr. C. of C., Avery County (N.C.), 1974; Tenn. Tchr. of Year Tenn. Fedn. Women's Clubs, 1957; U.S. Airman of Year USAF Res.; recipient Silver Beaver award, Scoutmaster's award, Scouter's key Boy Scouts Am., 1958; Tenn. Col., Ky. Col. Mem. Nat. Edn. Assn., Tenn. Edn. Assn. (past chmn. guidance sect.), Morristown Edn. Assn. (past pres.), Nat., Tenn. assns. student teaching, Internat. Platform Assn., N.C. Assn. Jr. Colls. (v.p. 1975, pres. 1977-79), Tenn. PTA, Order of Arrow (vigil mem.), Phi Kappa Phi, Phi Delta Kappa, Phi Theta Kappa (hon.). Club: Kiwanism (lt. gov. Carolina dist. 1972-73); Kiwanism (Jefferson City and Banner Elk) (internat. com. youth services 1979-80, gov. 1977-78, dist. chmn. gov.'s flying squad, co-chmn. dist. med-winter conf., dist key club com., mem. Internat. Commn. on Youth Services 1979-80, Internat. Commn. on Kiwanis Edn. 1980-81). Home: Banner Elk, NC.

EVANS, JEAN CHARLES, univ. adminstr.; b. DeMotte, Ind., July 17, 1923; s. Paul French and Evangeline Mae (Ollman) E.; m. Helen Magda Kaldahl, Nov. 22, 1944; children—Jean, Sigrid Paula and Sandra Helena (twins), Kristie Suellen. B.S., Purdue U., 1950; M.S., Mich. State U., 1957; Ph.D. (Kellogg Found. fellow), U. Wis., 1959. Extension editor U. Md., 1950-52; spl. reports editor Mich. State U., 1955-57; research asso. U. Wis., Madison, 1959-60; asst. dean extension U. Mo., 1960-65; v.p. univ. extension Okla. State U., Stillwater, 1965-74;

chancellor U. Wis. Extension, Madison, from 1974. Served with USN, 1944-46. Recipient Appreciation cert. Nat. 4-H Found. Mem. Nat. Assn. State Univs. and Land Grants Colls. (chmn. extension council 1972), Nat. Univ. Continuing Edn. Assn. (pres. 1980-81), Wis. Adult Edn. Assn., Alpha Zeta, Phi Kappa Phi, Phi Delta Kappa, Gamma Sigma Delta. Methodist. Home: Madison, Wis.

EVANS, JOHN KRYDER, ret. mfr.; b. Elk Lick, Pa., July 9, 1890; s. John Miles and Ellelia (Bott) E.; Ph.B., Franklin and Marshall Coll., 1911; m. Marion Lloyd Hallowell, Oct. 21, 1916; 1 dau., Janet (Mrs. Alexander McBride 3d). Salesman, asst. sales mgr. Arbuckle Bros., N.Y.C., 1911-18; asst. to pres. Franklin Baker Co., Hoboken, N.J., 1918-27; v.p. Gen. Foods Corp., ret. 1955, gen. mgr. Maxwell House div., Hoboken, 1927-55; cons., exec. com. Pan-Am. Coffee Bur., 1956-65. Trustee, exec. com. Franklin and Marshall Coll., from 1940; adv. bd. Pace Coll., N.Y.C., 1935-56. Del. 1st World Coffee Conf., Rio de Janeiro, 1958. Recipient Order of So. Cross, Brazil, 1960. Mem. Nat. Coffee Assn. (hon. life; dir. 1939-51, 53-54, exec. com. of bd. 1945-50). Am. Brazilian Soc., Phi Kappa Sigma. Mem. Soc. of Friends. Clubs: Union League (Phila.); Bankers of Am. (N.Y.C.); Granite (Toronto, Ont., Can.). Home: South Orange, NJ. †

EVANS, LUTHER HARRIS, former univ. ofcl.; b. nr. Sayersville, Tex., Oct. 13, 1902; s. George Washington and Lillie (Johnson) E.; A.B., U. Tex., 1923, M.A., 1924; Ph.D., Stanford, 1927; D.H.L., Yale, 1946; D.Litt., Brown U., 1953; LL.D., Pa. Mil. Coll., U. B.C., 1948, Loyola Coll., 1950, Columbia, 1953, Dartmouth, 1956, Adelphi Coll., 1960, Denison U., 1961; H.H.D., Washington U., 1959, Marietta Coll., 1962; m. Helen Murphy, Sept. 12, 1925; 1 son, Gill Coter. Inst. freshman orientation course Stanford, 1924-27; instr. govt. N.Y.U., 1972-28; instr. polit. sci. Dartmouth, 1928-30; assst. prof. politics Princeton, 1930-35; dir. hist. records survey WPA, 1935-39; dir. legis. reference service Library of Congress, 1939-40, chief asst. librarian, acting librarian, 1940-45, librarian, 1945-53; mem. U.S. Nat. Commn. UNESCO, 1946-52, 59-63, chmn., 1952, mem. exec. bd. UNESCO, 1949-53, dir.-gen. 1953-58, U.S. del. or adviser Gen. Conf., 1947-53; cons. internat. studies programs U. Tex., 1959; dir. survey fed. deptl. libraries Brookings Instn., 1959-61; dir. project on ednl. implications of automation NEA, 1961-62; dir. internat. and legal collections Columbia, 1962-67, dir. internat. collections, 1967-71; dir. Popular Printing Inc. Mem. organizing com. World Conf. on Role of Univs. in Quest of Peace, 1963-69; chmn. exec. com. Commn. to Study Orgn. of Peace, 1964-76; chmn. U.S. del. Inter-Am. Copyright Conf., Washington, 1946, Universal Copyright Conv., Geneva, 1952; chmn. bd. dirs. Com. for the World Univ., 1974-81, People to People Communications; bd. dirs. Council on Internat. and Polit. Affairs; mem. U.S. Com. for Refugees, 1961-81, chmn., 1963-67; vice chmn. Nat. Book awards Adv. Com., 1964-71; mem. governing bd. New Directions; mem. bd. World Without War Council; mem. corp. Franklin Book Programs. Decorated by govts. Brazil, France, Japan. Lebanon, Peru, Mem. World Federalists U.S.A. (pres. 1971-75), U.S. People for UN (pres. 1966-76), ACLU, ALA (life), NEA (life), Am. Soc. Info. Sci., Am. Antiquarian Soc., World Acad. Art and Sci., Soc. Internat. Devel., Mexican Soc. Internat. Law, UN Assn. U.S.A. (vice chmn. bd. dirs. N.Y. 1972-76). Author: The Virgin Islands from Naval Base to New Deal, 1945. Editor: (with George E. Arnstein) Automation and the Challenge to Education, 1962; (with others) Federal Department Libraries, 1963, 66; The United States and UNESCO, 1971; editor Am. Documentation quar., 1961; chmn. adv. com. World Peace News, N.Y.C., 1969-81. Contbr. articles to profl. jours. Home: San Antonio, Tex. Died Dec. 23, 1981.

EVANS, MELVIN HERBERT, ambassador, physician; b. Christiansted, St. Croix, V.I., Aug. 7, 1917; s. Charles Herbert and Maude Eloise (Rogiers) E.; m. Mary Phyllis Anderson, Aug. 26, 1945; children: Melvin Herbert, Robert Rogiers, William Charles, Cornelius Duncan. S.B., Howard U., 1940, M.D., 1944, LL.D. hon., 1972; M.P.H., U. Calif.-Berkeley, 1967; L.H.D. hon., Morgan State U., Balt., 1971. Physician in charge Frederiksted Mcpl. Hosp., St. Croix, 1945-48; chief mcpl. physician V.I. Govt., St. Croix, 1951-56, 57-59, commr. of health, 1959-67; gov. U.S. V.I., 1969-75; mem. 96th Congress from V.I., 1979-80, ambassador to Trinidad and Tobago, 1981-84; fellow in cardiology Johns Hopkins Hosp., Balt., 1956-57; chmn. V.I. Bd. Med. Examiners, 1959-67. Chmn. bd. trustees Coll. of V.I., 1962-69; chmn. So. Govs. Assn., 1973-74; mem. Republican Nat. Com. from V.I., 1976-82. Sr. asst. surgeon USPHS, 1948-50. Recipient Disting. Alumni award Howard U., 1970; recipient Trustee Merit award Fairleigh Dickinson U., 1970. Fellow ACP; mem. Am. Assn. Pub. Health Physicians (charter), V.I. Med. Soc. (past pres.), Pan Am. Med. Assn., St. Croix C. of C. (pres. 1977-78). Mem. Wesleyan Ch. Lodges: St. Croix Rotary; Masons. Home: Christiansted, St. Croix, V.I. Died Nov. 27, 1984.

EVARTS, HARRY FRANKLIN, assn. exec.; b. Troy, N.Y., July 20, 1928; s. Leslie Herbert and Lenora Marie (Chapman) E.; student Sampson (N.Y.) Coll., 1948-49; B.S.C., Ohio U., 1951, M.S., 1952; D.B.A., Harvard, 1959; m. Drusilla Ann Riley, Sept. 9, 1951 (div. Aug. 1969); children—Dale Irene, Leslie Alan, Valerie Dru, Jill Ann. Work standards and methods engr. Gen. Motors Corp., 1952-55; indsl. engr. Gardner Bd. & Carton Co., 1955-57; asst. prof. prodn. mgmt. Northwestern U., 1958-63; asso. prof. Ohio U., 1963-65, prof. bus. adminstrn., dean Coll. Bus. Adminstrn., 1965-70; pres. Bryant Coll., Smithfield, R.I., 1970-76, also trustee; dir. ednl. services Am. Mgmt. Assns., 1976-85. Cons. ICA and Japan Productivity Center, 1960; dir. Internat. Data Sci., Inc. Trustee Nichols Coll., 1978; bd. dirs. Ohio Council Econ. Edn., 1966-70, R.I. Council Econ. Edn., 1971-76, Internat. Mgmt. Devel-Inst., Kenya, 1970, Zambia, 1971, 73. Served with AUS, 1946-48; PTO. Ford Found. fellow, 1956-58. Mem. Acad. Mgmt., Beta Gamma Sigma. Unitarian. Club: University. Author: (with others) Operations Management, 1961; Introduction to PERT, 1964; also articles, chpts. in books. Home: New York, N.Y. Died July 3, 1985.

EVERETT, CURTIS THOMAS, foreign service officer; b. Scottsville, Ky., Dec. 9, 1890; s. George Miller and Alice (Cage) E.; B.S., Vanderbilt, 1915, M.A., 1916; spl. course, Sorbonne, Paris, 1919; m. Agnes Madeleine Wyler, Apr. 15, 1931. Instr. Fla. Mil., Acad. (Green Cove Springs), 1911-13. Bowen Prep. Sch. (Nashville, Tenn.), 1916, North State School (Asheville, N.C.), 1916-17; U.S. vice consul, Liege, Belgium, 1920-22, Stuttgart, Germany, 1922-24, Bombay, India, 1924-26; consul, Bombay, 1926-27, Frankfort, Germany, 1928, Geneva, 1928-41; sec. at Paris for duty at Vichy, 1941-42; consul at Toronto, Aug. 1942, Apr. 1947; consul at Basel, Switzerland, from Apr. 1, 1947. Served at Ft. Oglethorpe T.C., Aug.-Nov. 1917; commd. 2d lt., F.A.; arrived in Fr., Aug. 1918; 1st lt., Oct. 1918; arty. information officer 156th F.A. Brig., 81st Div.; hon. disch., Aug. 1919. U.S. del. to Conf. to facilitate the Internat. Circulation of Films of an Ednl. Character, Geneva, 1933, 1938. Mem. Am. Acad. Polit. and Social Science, Alpha Tau Omega. Club: Bombay Gymkhana (Bombay).†

EVERETT, SALLIE BAKER, mem. Dem. Nat. Com.; b. Palmyra, N.C., Feb. 26, 1888; d. LaFayette John and Pattie Norman L. Baker; student Meredith Coll., 1905-09; m. Benjamin Bryan Everett, Feb. 25, 1914; children—3 daus., 2 sons. Partner with husband in extensive farming ginning and merc. bus., Palmyra. Vice chmn. N.C. Dem. Exec. Com., 1942-48, 50; mgr. women's campaign for Gov. W. B. Umstead, 1952; chmn. women's div. N.C. Farm Bur., 1942-52; mem. from N.C. Dem. Nat. Com., from 1952; mem. exec. com. representing women So. region, from 1956. Dir. Agrl. Found., N.C.; State Coll., N.C. Farm Bur. Recipient Distinguished Service award, N.C. Farm Bur., 1947; named Progressive Farmers Woman of the Year, N.C., 1946. Mem. N.C. State Fedn. Women's Clubs (pres. local club 1939-40, 14th N.C. dist. 1942-44; chmn. state dept. edn. 1939-41). Home: Palmyra, N.C. †

EVERS, ALBERT JOHN, architect; b. Westside, Ia., Aug. 17, 1888; s. Henry and Elisabeth (Heiner) E.; B.L., University of California, 1911; m. Sepha Pischel, Dec. 5, 1916; children—Henry Kaspar, Albert John (killed in action, Normandy, July 28, 1944), Elisabeth Marion, William Dohrmann. Licensed architect, 1912; with Rockefeller Foundation, Peking Union Med. Coll., Peking, China, 1916-20; private architectural practice, San Francisco, 1920-34; chief architectural supervisor Federal Housing Adminstrn. for Northern Calif., 1934-36; chief of specification Golden Gate Internat. Expn., 1936-38; executive director San Francisco Housing Authority, 1938-43; Assistant State director War Manpower Commn., 1943-45; priv. practice, Meyer & Evers, 1946-57; consulting architect, 1957-61, retired 1961. Director Dohrmann Comml. Co., Federal Home Loan Bank, Los Angeles, 1937-46. Mem. of the State Bd. of Architectural Examiners for 8 years, pres. 2 years. Fellow A.I.A. (past dir.), State Assn. Calif. Architects (ex-pres.), Chi Phi. Republican. Mason. Club: Bohemian (San Francisco). Home: Ross, Cal. †

EVERTS, ALBERT PAINE, finance; b. Philadelphia, Pa., Aug. 6, 1887; s. Rev. William Wallace and Dolly Elizabeth (Paine) E.; A.B., Harvard, 1909 (as of 1910); student Grad. Sch. Bus. Adminstrn., 1909-10; m. Fannie Foster Tower, Apr. 24, 1915 (deceased July 29th, 1961); m. second, to Mrs. Helen C. Ross, on September 26th, 1964; children—Carolyn (Mrs. James A. Stewart), Albert Paine, Nelson Tower. Associated with firm Paine, Webber & Co., Boston, Mass., 1910, partner, 1919; partner Paine, Webber, Jackson & Curtis, 1942-57, limited partner, from 1957. Vice pres. board aldermen, Newton, Mass., 1944-45. Gov. N.Y. Stock Exchange, 1950-54; chmn. spl. gifts Mass. Republican Finance Com., 1944; chmn. Mass. War Finance Com. for 3d War Loan. Dir. Boston Better Business Bureau; v.p. New Eng. Baptist Hosp., New Eng. Home for Little Wanderers; former trustee Boston Museum of Science, Mt. Holyoke Coll., Mass. Forest and Park Assn.; gov. Assn. Stock Exchange Firms, 1942-46; former gov. and v.p. Investment Bankers Assn. Am.; former gov. Nat. Assn. Security Dealers. Clubs: Harvard (Boston); Country (Brookline); Brae Burn Country. Home: Newtonville, Mass. †

EVES, WILLIAM, III, church exec.; b. Wilmington, Del., Oct. 11, 1889; s. Hiram Pyle and Mary Kirk (Horner) E.; grad. Friends Sch., Wilmington, 1906; B.S., Princeton, 1911, E.E., 1913, A.M. (hon.), 1954; grad. work edn., U. Pa., summers 1922, 25; m. Julia Downman Thom, Oct. 16, 1915; children—Benjamin Miller, Mary Elizabeth (Mrs. Dongkyu Bak), Rebecca Thomas (Mrs. Carl F. Ullrich). Works engr. Am. Vulcanized Fibre Co., Wilmington, 1913-19; vice chmn. child feeding mission in Germany, Am. Friends Service Com., 1919-21, chmn., 1924; faculty George Sch., Bucks County, Pa., 1921-55, dean, dir. admissions, 1926-36, vice prin., 1936-55; gen. sec. Phila. Yearly Meeting, Soc. of Friends from 1955; bd. dirs. Am. Friends Service Com., from 1925, chmn. fgn. service sect., 1925-48, vice chmn., 1947, 56-62; bd. dirs. Pendle Hill, Wallingford, Pa., Friends ednl. and religious center. Vice chmn., bd. dirs. National Carl Schurz Association: board directors Citizens Council of Delaware County, Pa. Mem. N.E.A., Am. Inst. E.E., Princeton Engrng. Assn., Phi Beta Kappa. Club: Princeton (Phila.). Home: Swarthmore, Pa. †

EVINS, JOSEPH LANDON, former congressman; b. DeKalb County, Tenn., Oct. 24, 1910; s. James Edgar and Myrtie (Goodson) E.; A.B., Vanderbilt U., 1933; LL.B., Cumberland U., 1934, Ll.D., 1958; postgrad. George Washington U., 1938-40; m. Ann Smartt, June 7, 1935; children—Joanna (Mrs. Malcolm Carnahan, Jane (Mrs. Robert J. Leonard), Mary-Adelaide. Admitted to Tenn. bar, 1934; gen. law practice, Smithville, Tenn., 1934-41; atty. FTC, Washington, 1935-38, asst. sec., 1938-40; v.p. First Nat. Bank, Smithville, Tenn. 1944-54, pres., 1954-63, hon. chmn. bd., 1963-84; mem. 80th-82d Congresses, 5th Tenn. Dist., 82d-94th Congresses, 4th Congl. Dist. mem. com. on appropriations, chmn. select com. small bus., chmn. subcom. on pub. works AEC appropriations, former chmn. ind. offices subcom. on appropriations; now spl. counsel and cons. to Gov. Tenn. Del., Democratic Nat. Convs., 1952-76; Tenn. campaign mgr. Johnson-Humphrey, 1964. Trustee David Lipscomb Coll., Nashville, Cumberland Coll., Lebanon, Tenn. Tech. and M.T.S.U. Founds. Served to maj. AUS, 1942-46; ETO. Received Dem. nomination as state senator, 12th Tenn. senatorial dist. (declined nomination for pub. office during war), 1944; recipient numerous state and nat. awards and citations for pub. service after serving 30 years in Congress. Mem. Am. Legion, VFW, Army Res. Corps. 40 and 8, Amvets, Phi Kappa Sigma, Phi Delta Phi. Clubs: Army-Navy, Commodore, Masons (33 deg.), Shriners, Elks, Lions. Author: Understanding Congress, 1963. Home: Smithville, Tenn. Died Mar. 31, 1984.

EWALD, JOHN A., cosmetic mfr.; b. Maspeth, L.I., N.Y., Dec. 22, 1901; s. Adolph R. and Catherine C. (Fitting) E.; student N.Y.U.; m. Olive Schumacher, Dec. 31, 1924 (dec. Jan. 1950); 1 son, John A.; m. 2d Emma Lepotsky, Mar. 10, 1954. With Avon Products, Inc., N.Y.C. 1920-84, chmn. bd., chief exec. officer, 1962-67, chmn. exec. com., dir., 1967-84; dir. Marine Midland Trust Co. of N.Y. Member of the Board of dirs. Nassau Hosp., Mineola, N.Y.; adv. bd. mem. fund raising com. Salvation Army. Mem. Toilet Goods Assn., Inc. (dir.). Presbyn. Mason. Clubs: Union League (N.Y.C.), Garden City (N.Y.) Golf, Thunderbird Country (Palm Springs, Cal.), U.S. Seniors Golf Assn. Home: Garden City, N.Y. Died Sept. 20, 1984.

EWALD, PAUL P., physicist; b. Berlin, Germany, 1888; Ph.D., U. Munich, 1912; M.A., U. Belfast, 1946; D.Sc., Stuttgart U., 1954; Dr.hic., U. Paris, 1958, U. Munich, 1968; D.Sc., Adelphi U., 1966, Poly. Inst. Bklyn., 1972; Prof. theoretical physics Poly. Sch., Stuttgart, 1921-37; prof. math. physics Queen's U., Belfast, North Ireland, 1939-49; head physics dept. Poly. Inst. Bklyn., 1949-57, prof. physics, 1949-59. Fellow Royal Soc. (Gt. Britain), Phys. Soc. Britain, Am. Phys. Soc. (chmn. solid state div. 1961-62), Am. Acad. Arts and Scis., Deutsche Akademie der Naturforscher (Leopoldina); hon. mem. Deutsche Mineralog. Ges., Société Francaise de Minéralogie et de Cristallographie, Cambridge Philos. Soc.; corr. mem. Acad. Scis. Göttingen and Munich; mem. Internat. Union Crystallography (pres. 1960-63, exec. com. 1948-66), Am. Crystallographic Assn. (pres. 1952). Author: Fifty Years of X-ray Diffraction, 1962; other books, articles. Address: Ithaca, NY. †

EWELL, LOIS, operatic soprano; b. Memphis, Tenn., Jan. 1887; d. James Levi E.; ed. Erasmus Hall, New York; studied voice with Frederick Haywood, later with Lombardi and Vannini, at Florence, Italy, and Guilliard, at Paris, France. Début with Fritzi Scheff, in "Babette"; sang in "Forty-Five Minutes from Broadway," "Merry Widow," etc. Address: New York, N.Y. †

EWING, DWIGHT TARBELL, coll. prof.; b. Winterset, Ia., 1888; s. Frederick Walter and Effe (Tarbell) E.; B.S., Parsons Coll., 1911; M.S., U. of Chicago, 1915, Ph.D.,

1920; m. Grace Sandiland, Aug. 1915; children—Betty, John, Jeanette, Richard, Robrt. Du Pont fellow, also Nat. Research Council work on mustard gas, World War I; prof. phys. chemistry Mich. State Coll. from 1930; worked on Manhattan project, 1943-44. Received award for meritorious research, Sigma Xi Sci. Soc., Mich. State Coll., 1948. Mem. Am. Chem. Soc., Phys. Soc., Electrochem. Soc., Optical Soc. of Am. Electrophys. Soc., Sigma Xi, Alpha Chi Sigma, Phi Kappa Phi, Sigma Pi Sigma. Contbr. numerous articles on phys. chemistry, electro-chemistry, spectroscopy and phys. properties of vitamins in chem. research publs. Holds 7 patents on electroplating of chromium and other electro-chemical processes. Home: East Lansing, Mich. †

EWING, ORMAN WILLIAM, mem. Dem. Nat. Committee; b. Rockport, Mo., Sept. 10, 1888; s. Abraham Lincoln and Ina Luella E.; ed. high sch.; m. Leola Howe, of Ogden, Utah, Apr. 27, 1909; children—Lowell Howe, Orma Alberta, Phyllis Leola, William Strevell, Bonnie Joyce. Began as railroad brakeman, 1906, later ins. solicitor; began land law practice, 1919; large land owner in Utah and Wyo.; pres. Westland Co. (Wyo. holding corpn.); v.p. Gebo Consolidated Co., Gem Oil Co., Black Mountain Petroleum Co.; sec.-treas. Utah Paraffine Co. Mem. Dem. Nat. Com., Utah, (from 1932). Presbyn. Elk. Student early western history and lecturer on same and pub. land questions. Home: Salt Lake City, Utah. †

EYRING, HENRY, educator; b. Colonia Juarez, Mexico, Feb. 20, 1901; came to U.S., 1912, naturalized, 1935; s. Edward Christian and Caroline (Romney) E.; m. Mildred Bennion, Aug. 25, 1928; children—Edward Marcus, Henry Bennion, Harden Romney; m. Winifred Brennan, Aug. 13, 1971; children—Eleanor Gwendoline, Patricia Margaret, Joan Morag, Bernice Heather. B.S., U. Ariz., 1923, M.S., 1924; Ph.D., U. Cal., 1927; postgrad., U. Berlin, 1929-30; D.Sc., U.. Utah, 1952, Northwestern U., 1953, Princeton, 1956, Seoul (Korea) Nat. U., 1963, Brigham Young U., 1965, Western Res. U., 1966, Denison U., 1967, Marquette U., Notre Dame U., 1969; LL.D., Ind. Central Coll., 1964. Instr. U. Ariz., 1924-25; teaching fellow U. Calif., 1925-27; instr. U. Wis., 1927-28, research asso., 1928-29; lectr. U. Calif., 1930-31; research asso. Princeton, 1931-36, asso. prof., 1935-38, prof., 1938-46; dean Grad. Sch., U. Utah, 1946-67, Disting. prof. chemistry, from 1967; dir. fundamental research Textile Found., Textile Research Inst., 1944-46. Author: (with Glasstone, K.J. Laidler) Theory of Rate Processes, 1941, Quantum Chemistry, (with J. Walter, G.E. Kimball), 1944, (with Frank H. Johnson, Milton J. Polissar) Kinetic Basis of Molecular Biology, 1954, (with Edward M. Eyring) Modern Chemical Kinetics, 1963, (with others) Statistical Mechanics and Dynamics, (with A.S. Krauz) Kinetics of Deformation, 1975, (with Dennis Caldwell) The Theory of Optical Activity, 1971, (with Mu Shik Jhon) Significant Liquid Structures), 1978, (with S.H. Lin and S.M. Liu) Basic Chemical Kinetics, 1980; also numerous articles.; Editor: (with S.H. Lin and S.M. Liu) Ann. Rev. Phys. Chemistry. NRC scholar, 1929-30; Recipient 9th ann. prize AAAS, 1932; plaque and honorarium Research Corp., 1949; Irving Langmuir award chem. physics Gen. Electric Found., 1968; Nat. Medal Sci., 1966; Madison Marshall award, 1968. Mem. Am. Acad. Arts and Scis., Nat. Acad. Scis., Am. Philos. Soc., Am. Chem. Soc. (Gibbs medal Chgo. sect. 1968, dir. 6th dist. 1949-51, pres. 1962, Peter Debye award 1964, Berzelius medal 1979, Wolf prize 1980, Joseph Priestley medal 1975, Bingham medal 1981), Nat. Sci. Bd., AAAS (dir., past pres.). Republican. Mem. Ch. of Jesus Christ of Latter-day Saints. Home: Salt Lake City, UT.

FABIAN, MICHAEL ROBERT, advertising executive; b. Budapest, Hungary, Dec. 7, 1932; came to U.S., 1941; s. Tibor and Elisabeth (Partos) F.; m. Betty B. Borjeson, July 28, 1956; children: David, John, Jennifer. B.A., Wesleyan U., 1954. Asst. account exec. Grey Advt., N.Y.C., 1956-58; asst. advt. mgr. Hudson Pulp & Paper, N.Y.C., 1958-60; mktg. dir. W.B. Doner Co., Phila., 1960-62; pres., chief exec. officer March Direct Mktg., N.Y.C., 1962-85; pres. Barry Blau & Ptnrs., Westport, Conn., 1984-85. Served with U.S. Army, 1954-56. Mem. Direct Mktg. Assn. (chmn. pres.'s club 1972-74 Silver Mailbox award), Direct mktg. Creative Guild (pres. 1976-78, 82-85), Direct Mktg. Idea Exchange. Clubs: Hundred Million, Weston Field. Home: Weston, Conn. Died July 10, 1985.

FABLE, ROBERT COOPER, JR., lawyer; b. Sellersville, Pa., Dec. 7, 1910; s. Robert C. and Janet E. (Grayson) F.; B.S., Temple U., 1931, LL.B., 1935; m. Ethel Smith Nock, Sept. 4, 1935 (dec. Oct. 1968); 1 child Janet Ann, (dec. Mar. 1968); m. Margaret Siebert Jansky, Feb. 28, 1969. Admitted to Pa. state bar, also U.S. cts., 1935; practiced in Phila., 1935-43; with VA, Washington, 1946-70, legislative atty., asst. dep. adminstr. vets. affairs, 1946-58, dep. gen. counsel, 1958-63, gen. counsel, 1963-70. Served to capt., AUS, 1943-46. Decorated Legion of Merit; recipient Meritorious Service award VA, 1957, Distinguished Career award VA, 1970. Mem. Am., Fed. bar assns., Sigma Phi Epsilon. Conglist. Mason (32). Club: Nat. Lawyers. Home: Sunapee, N.H. Died Jan. 2, 1982.

FAEGRE, JOHN BARTHELL, lawyer; b. Flandreau, S.C., Oct. 3, 1889; s. Albert and Sarah Jane (Barthell) F.; A.B., U. Minn., 1911, LL.B., 1913; m. Mary Bohn, Oct. 20, 1910; children—John Barthell, Robert. Admitted to Minn. bar, 1913, and since practiced in Minneapolis; mem. firm Faegre & Benson from 1923; dir. C., R.I. & P. Ry. Co. Mem. bd. dirs., mem. exec. com. Mpls. Found. Mem. Phi Delta Phi, Beta Theta Pi. Republican. Episcopalian. Clubs: Minneapolis, Minikahda (Mpls.); Woodhill Country (Wayzata, Minn.); Chgo. Home: Wayzata, MN. †

FAGAN, FRANK, retail co. exec.; b. N.Y.C., July 31, 1905; s. James and Antoinette (Holahan) F.; m. Valeska Hubbard, Dec. 29, 1934; children—Andrea, Peter, Dona Amy. Student pub. schs.; lit. and lang. studies, Columbia. Asst. advt. mgr. wholesale div. W. & J. Sloane, 1924-26, advt. mgr. retail stores, 1926-28; mdse. mgr. John Wanamaker, Phila., 1928-31; pres. mdsg. and promotion div. Felix Lillenthal, 1931-34; with Young & Rubicam, Inc., 1934-64, mdsg. exec., 1934-38, account exec., 1938-41, v.p., account supr., 1943, mem. exec. com. and plans bd., 1946, sr. v.p., 1953-58, exec. v.p., 1958-64; pres. S. T. Preston & Son, Inc., Greenport, N.Y., 1959-79, chmn., from 1979. Clubs: New York Yacht, Manhasset Bay Yacht. Home: Orient, NY.

FAGAN, JOHN JOSEPH, labor union exec.; b. Chgo., Oct. 15, 1927; s. Ralph T. and Mary A. (O'Brian) F.; m. Harriet Lerner, May 24, 1974; children—Patricia, John Jr., Daniel. Student, U. Chgo., 1962-63. Bus. rep. Local 46, Laundry, Dry Cleaning and Dye House Workers Internat. Union, Chgo., 1964-70; gen. sec., treas. Textile Processors, Service Trades, Health Care, Profl. and Tech. Employees affiliate Internat. Brotherhood Teamsters, Chgo., 1970-75, gen. pres., from 1975. Served with U.S. Navy, 1944. Roman Catholic. Clubs: Kiwanis, Moose. Address: Chicago, Ill.

FAGE, ARTHUR, scientist; b. Portsmouth, Eng., Mar. 4, 1890; s. William John and Annie (Crook) F.; Asso., Royal Coll. of Sci., 1912; Diploma, Imperial Coll. of Sci. and Tech., 1914; m. Winifred Eliza Donnelly, Sept. 1, 1920 (died 1951); children—John Donnelly, Christine Mary. Engaged in aerodynamic research from 1912; supt. aerodynamics div. Nat. Phys. Lab., Teddington, Eng., 1946-52, retired. Decorated Commander Order British Empire. Fellow Royal Soc. (London), Royal Aero. Soc., Inst. Aero. Scis. Author sci. papers. Home: Teddington, Middlesex, Eng. †

FAGG, FRED DOW, JR., former univ. president; b. Bklyn., July 30, 1896; s. Fred Dow and Ida Alzina (Chase) F.; A.B., U. of Redlands, 1920, LL.D., 1939; A.M., Harvard University, 1921; J.D., Northwestern University, 1927, LL.D. (honorary), 1950; married, Vera Wilkes, August 25, 1924; children—Barbara Louise and Fred Dow. Asst. in economics, Harvard, 1921-23; instr. in economics, Northwestern U., 1923-27; asst. and asso. prof. economics, U. Southern Calif., 1927-29, also asst. dean of Coll. of Commerce and lecturer Sch. of Law, 1927-29; exchange prof., Inst. für Luftrecht, Königsberg, Germany, 1928-29; prof. law, Northwestern U., 1929-47, dean School of Commerce, 1938-39, v.p. and dean of faculties 1939-47; mng. dir. Air Law Inst., Chicago, 1929-39; founder and editor-in-chief Jour. of Air Law, 1930-37; mng. editor Jour. of Radio Law, 1930-31; legal adviser Federal Aviation Commn., 1934-35; legal counsel U.S. Senate Sub-Com. on Aircraft Investigation, 1935-36; dir. air commerce, Dept. of Commerce, 1937-38; cons. expert, Civil Aeronautics Authority, 1938-39; dir. Northwestern U. Inst. Aeronautics, 1946-47; pres. U. So. Cal., 1947-57; dir. Southern California Edison Co., Union Oil Co. of Cal. Dir. Freedoms Found.; chmn. bd. Air Pollution Found., 1954-55, 57-58, 59-61; mem. Western Interstate Commn. on Higher Edn., 1955, chmn., 1958-59. Member of the Illinois Aeronautics Commission. 1931-37; sec. Nat. Assn. of State Aviation Officials, 1932-37; Am. mem. Comité Internat. Technique d'Experts Juridques Aériens, 1934-40; mem. National Advisory Com. for Aeronautics, 1937-38; chairman of Calif. Aeronautics Commission, 1947-49. Served as 2nd lt., pilot 92d Aero Squadron, A.E.F., 1917-18. Mem. Am., Ill. State, Chicago and Los Angeles bar assns., State Bar of Calif., Delta Theta Phi, Pi Kappa Delta, Delta Sigma Rho, Alpha Kappa Psi, Order of Coif, Alpha Eta Rho, Phi Beta Kappa, Phi Kappa Phi, Blue Key. Baptist. Clubs: Calif. and University (Los Angeles); Law, Legal (Chicago). Contbr. to law reviews. Home: Pasadena, Calif. Died Oct. 14, 1981.

FAHRENWALD, ARTHUR WILLIAM, metall. engr., educator; b. Yankton, S.D., May 22, 1890; s. Frank and Caroline (Nelson) F.; student prep. sch., Rapid City, S.D., 1906-10; B.S., S.D. State Sch. of Mines, Rapid City, 1914; m. Lola Grace Ellsworth, May 31, 1916; children—Arthur William, Mary Low, Richard Ellsworth. Research metallurgist Butte & Superior Mining Company, Butte, Montana, 1914-15; ore dressing research engineer for the United States Bureau of Mines, 1919-29, consultant engr. same, from 1930; dean Sch. of Mines, U. of Ida., 1929-30 and 1934-54, prof. and head depts. mining and metallurgy, 1930-55, emeritus dean of mines and research prof., from 1955; dir. Idaho Bur. Mines and Geology; cons. metallurgist Internat. Nickel Co. of Can. and Horne Copper Corp. (Noranda, Que.), 1927-29, Basic Magnesium, Inc., Las Vegas, Nev., and Northwest Magnesite Co., Chewelah, Wash., 1941 and 1942. Inventor of ore dressing processes and machines. Recipient Robert H. Richard award Am. Inst. Mining and Metall. Engrs., 1956; Inland Empire Engr. of the Yr., Nat. Soc. Profl. Engrs. Mem. Am. Inst. Mining Metall. and Petroleum Engrs., Nat. Soc. Profl. Engrs., Sigma Xi. Author books. Contbr. articles on engring. and mining. Home: Moscow, Ida. †

FAIN, SAMUEL S., educator; b. Chicago, Dec. 25, 1909; s. Morris and Ella (Magidson) F.; m. Elizabeth Romola Miller, Jan. 14, 1935; children—Joan Muriel Fain Gusinow, Marilyn Romola Fain Freed. B.Mus. Edn., Northwestern, 1940; M.A., U. Ariz., 1951; D.Mus. Arts, U. So. Cal., 1956; pvt. lessons on various musical instruments. Band and orch. dir. Chgo. Pub. Schs., 1930-40; instr. pub. sch. music Am. Conservatory Music, Chgo., 1936-40; prof. music U. Ariz., 1942-76, prof. emeritus, from 1976; vis. prof. music U. So. Cal., summer 1956; condr. Tucson Symphony Orch., 1945-50. Contbr. to profl. jours. Mem. Music Educators Nat. Conf., Kappa Kappa Psi, Phi Delta Kappa, Phi Mu Alpha. Home: Tucson, Ariz.

FAIRCHILD, LOUIS W., publisher; b. Glen Ridge, N.J., Mar. 3, 1901; s. Edmund W. and Catherine (Boyd) F.; grad. Princeton, 1924; m. Gertrude A. Helm; children—John B., Anne B. Chmn. bd. Fairchild Publications, Inc., N.Y.C. Home: New York, N.Y. Died Oct. 16, 1981.

FAIRLEY, FRANCIS HILLIARD, lawyer; b. Monroe, N.C., Oct. 3, 1915; s. Frank Hilliard and Janie (Phifer) F.; m. Ella Doris McGuinn, Aug. 24, 1951; children—Mary Jane, Ella Frances. B.A. with honors, U. N.C., 1935; student and teaching-fellow, Grad. Sch., 1935-36, LL.B., 1939; student, Columbia U. Sch. Law, 1936-38. Bar: N.C. bar 1939, also U.S. Supreme Ct., Ct. Claims, ICC, FCC, Tax Ct., Treasury Dept., U.S. Ct. Internat. Trade 1939. Law clk. to chief judge U.S. Ct. Appeals, 4th Circuit, 1939-40; sr. partner firm Fairley, Hamrick, Monteith & Cobb, Charlotte, N.C., 1939—; pros. atty. City of Charlotte, 1941; sr. asst. U.S. atty. Western Dist. N.C., 1948-53; Dir., vice chmn. So. Nat. Bank; dir., chmn. bd. Ruth's Salads Corps. of N.C. and S.C.; dir., sec. Catawba Loan & Finance Co.; dir. Daniels Constrn. Co., Lawyers Service Corp., Lenoir Finance Co., J.V. Griffith Co., Eastover Assn.; instr. negotiable instruments and comml. law Am. Inst. Banking, 1946-49, 51-52; Mem. Charlotte Estate Planning Council; chmn. Nat. Conf. Lawyers and Life Ins. Cos., 1976—, vice chmn., 1974-76. Contbr. articles to profl. jours. Mem. N.C. Democratic Exec. Com., 1960—; Bd. dirs. N.C. Law Found. Served to lt. comdr., naval aviator USNR, 1941-45, ETO, PTO. Fellow Am. Bar Found., Am. Coll. Probate Counsel, Comml. Law Found. (dir. 1968—); mem. Am. Acad. Polit. and Social Scis., Acad. Polit. Sci., Am. Law Inst. (life), Am. Judicature Soc., Assn. Bar City N.Y., Internat. Bar Assn., N.C. Bar Assn. (past v.p.), Inter-Am. Bar Assn., Fed. Bar Assn., ABA (life; ho. dels. 1962—, vice chmn. life ins. law com., banking law com.), Mecklenburg County Bar Assn. (exec. com. 1950-54, past chmn. programs com. 1949-55), N.C. State Bar (pres. 1962-63, past v.p., chmn. exec. com., mem. council), Am. Legion (life; post comdr.), 40 and 8, Comml. Law League Am. (bd. govs. 1963-69, v.p. 1966-67, pres. 1967-68), S.A.R. (life; v.p. 1979-80, pres. 1980-81), S.C.V., Fedn. Ins. Counsel, Nat. Assn. Probate and Bank Attys., Def. Research Inst., Nat. Conf. Bar Presidents, U. N.C. Law Alumni Assn. (dir. 1953-64, pres. 1959-60), V.F.W., N.C. Law Found., N.C. Ednl. Found., Robert Burns Soc., U. N.C. Gen. Alumni Assn. (life; dir. 1948-51, class agt. ann. alumni giving), Columbia U. Law Sch. Alumni Assn. (Harlan Fiske Stone fellow; ann. fund dir.), Charlotte Opera Assn., Mint Mus. Art, Charlotte Symphony Soc., Charlotte Regional Ballet, Order of Grail, Order of Golden Fleece, Charlotte C. of C., Scribes, Phi Beta Kappa Assos., Phi Beta Kappa, Phi Delta Phi (province pres. 1947-64, internat. pres. 1967-69, chief justice from 1969). Episcopalian (sr. warden, lay leader). Clubs: Carmel Country (pres. 1957), City, Execs, Cotillion; Charlotte Country (Charlotte), Univ. (Charlotte), Rams (Charlotte), Towne (Charlotte). Home: Charlotte, N.C. Deceased.

FALCONE, PETER, advt. agy. exec.; b. Schenectady, Mar. 15, 1936; s. O. Peter and Carmen C. (Farone) F.; m. Sally Rogers, Dec. 17, 1960; children—Lisa Pennell, Wendy Rogers. B.A., Union Coll., 1959. Sr. copywriter Gen. Electric Co., 1960-64; account exec. Benton & Bowles (Advt.), N.Y.C., 1964-68; pres., dir., founder Celebrity Systems, Inc., N.Y.C., 1968-70; exec. v.p., dir. Doyle Dane Bernbach, Inc., N.Y.C., from 1970. Served with USAF, 1960. Mem. Frozen Food Inst. (nat. com.), Sigma Phi. Club: Innis Arden Golf (Old Greenwich, Conn.). Home: Old Greenwich, Conn.

FALES, EUGENE W., army officer; b. LaSalle, Niagara County, N.Y., Sept. 16, 1887; s. Henry Marshall Warren and Sarah Christiana (Smith) F.; student Rutgers Coll., 1906-09; grad. Command and Gen. Staff Sch., 1926, Tank Sch., 1927, Army War Coll., 1928, French Tank Sch., Versailles, 1933; m. Hélène Margaret Baker. May 16, 1919; children—Warren, Philippe. Commd. 2d lt., 1st U.S. Inf., 1912, and advanced through the grades to maj. gen., 1944; with Mexican Punitive Expdn., 1916-17; with A.E.F., France and Germany, 1918-19; army liaison officer with Gen. Smedley D. Butler, U.S. Marine Corps, 1921-24; War Dept. Gen. Staff, 1928-32; with French Tank Regt., 1933; mem. Inf. Bd., 1934-36; comd. Tank and Motor Sch., 1936-38; exec. officer, Office Chief of Inf., 1939-41; comdg gen. Inf. Replacement Training Center. Camp Roberts. Calif., 1941-43; comdg. gen. Inf. Replacement Training Center, Camp Blanding, 1943-45; comdg. gen., Ft. Lewis, Wash., 1945-46. Mem. Delta Upsilon.

Clubs: Army and Navy, Army-Navy Country (Washington); Valley Club of Montecito (Santa Barbara); Monterey Peninsula Country. Home: Monterey, Calif. †

FALK, ISIDORE SYDNEY, bacteriologist, pub. health med. economist, social security expert; b. Bklyn., Sept. 30, 1899; s. Samsin and Rose (Stolzberg) F.; m. Ruth Hill, Mar. 18, 1925 (dec. July 17, 1982); children: Sydney Westervelt, Stephen Ackley. Spl. student, Sheffield Sci. Sch. Yale U., 1915-17, Ph.B., 1920, Ph.D., 1923. Asst. dept. pub. health Yale U., 1915-20, instr., 1920-23; prof. pub. health Yale U. (Sch. Medicine), 1961-68, prof. emeritus, adj. lectr., 1968-84; asst. prof. bacteriology U. Chgo., 1923-26, assoc. prof., 1926-29, prof., 1929; asst. dir. Bur. Child Welfare, Chgo. Dept. Health, 1926-27; assoc. dir. Com. on Costs of Med. Care, 1929-33; research assoc. Milbank Meml. Fund, 1933-36; staff mem. U.S. Com. on Econ. Security, 1934-35; with Div. Research and Statistics, Social Security Adminstrn., Washington, 1936-54, dir., 1940-54; cons. on health services United Steelworkers of Am., 1958-80; pvt. cons. on pub. health and social security. Author numerous books, since 1923, primarily in field med. care.; Conducted several health surveys and; compiled reports thereon.; Contbr. numerous tech. papers to jours.; mem. editorial bds. various profl. jours. Vice chmn. bd. dirs., exec. dir. Community Health Care Center Plan, New Haven, 1967-79. Served with AUS, 1918; Mem. govt. adv. coms. World War II. Decorated Congl. Selective Service medal; officer Ordre de Honneur et Merite, Haiti, 1953; cabalero Orden de Vasco Nunez de Balboa, Panama, 1956; recipient various profl. awards and hon. memberships. Fellow Am. Public Health Assn. (Sedgwick Meml. Gold medal 1973), AAAS; mem. and officer several profl. assns. Research in eugenics of infant welfare, theory of microbic virulence, microbic cause of influenza, econs. of med. care and pub. health, social ins., nat. health ins. group practice prepayment plans and health maintenance orgns., quality of med. care Home: New Haven, Conn. Died Oct. 4, 1984.

FALLS, LAURENCE EDWARD, ins. exec.; b. West Point, Miss., Mar. 1890; s. Walter L. and Hettie L. (Wise) F.; ed. pub. schs. Milwaukee and Cleveland; m. Amy C. Horr, Apr. 21, 1917; m. 2d, Edith F. Morgan, Nov. 16, 1942. With Western Reserve Ins. Co., Cleveland, 1907-12; employed by Ernst & Ernst, Cleveland, 1912; traveling auditor and in automobile dept., Aetna Affiliated Cos., Nov. 1912-Jan. 1915; local and gen. ins. agent, Cleveland, 1915-23; with The Am. Ins. Co. from May 1, 1923, successively as spl. agent in Ohio, supt. of agents, Newark, 1924-26, asst. sec., Newark, 1926-27, v.p. from 1927, dir. from 1930; v.p. and dir. Bankers Indemnity Ins. Co., Dixie Fire Ins. Co., Greensboro, N.C., The Columbia Fire Ins. Co., Dayton, O. Dir. U.S. P. & I. Agency, Inc.; dir. Insurance Inst. of Am., sec. treas., 1948; mem. Ins. Soc. of N.Y., Ins. Soc. N.J.; vice pres. and trustee, Community Hosp. Clubs: Essex County Country, Essex Skytop, Drug and Chemical, Dartmouth College (N.Y. City); Gyro. Author: Manual on Use and Occupancy, Leasehold, Rents and Profits Insurance. Home: Maplewood, N.J. †

FALSGRAF, WENDELL ALBERT, lawyer; b. Cleve., June 18, 1904; s. Albert E. and Daisy V. (McDonald) F.; m. S. Catherine Johnson, Sept. 22, 1928; children—William Wendell, Sherwood Nourse. A.B., Western Res. U., 1926, J.D., 1928. Bar: Ohio bar 1928. Partner Falsgraf, Reidy, Shoup and Ault, Cleve., 1931-69, counsel, 1970-71, Baker & Hostetler, Cleve., from 1971. Pres. Citizens League Cleve., 1946-47, Nationalities Service Center, 1965-67; Mem. U.S. 6th Region Loyalty Bd., 1949-52; Trustee Cleve. YMCA, 1954-57, Western Res. U., 1946-50; trustee Hiram (Ohio) Coll., 1965-75, hon. trustee, from 1975. Recipient of the Jr. C. of C. Award, 1938; Distinguished Alumnus award Case Western Res. U., 1968; Fletcher Reed Andrews Distinguished Alumnus award Law Sch., 1974; Univ. medal, 1976; Alumnus of Year award Adelbert Coll., 1976; Outstanding Service award Nationalities Services Center, Cleve., 1976. Fellow Am. Bar Found., Soc. Benchers (chmn. 1975-76), Garfield Soc. (chmn. 1972-75), Am. Coll. Probate Counsel (gov. Ohio 1965-72), Ohio State Bar Found. (trustee 1965-68); mem. ABA (ho. dels. 1960-64, chmn. citizenship com. 1962-68, mem. council section on individual rights and responsibilities 1965-68), Ohio Bar Assn. (chmn. client security fund com. 1973), Cleve. Bar Assn. (pres. 1957-58), Case Western Res. U. Law Sch. Alumni Assn. (pres. 1959-60), Delta Upsilon, Phi Delta Phi, Sigma Delta Chi (dir. No. Ohio chpt. 1960-62). Clubs: Union (Cleve.), City (Cleve.) (pres. 1946), Cheshire Cheese (Cleve.) (pres. 1955), Rotary (Cleve.) (pres. Cleve. East 1938-39), Canterbury Golf (Cleve.) (pres. 1958); Royal Poinciana Golf (Naples, Fla.). Home: Chagrin Falls, OH.

FANE, IRVIN, lawyer; b. Dallas, Nov. 17, 1904; s. Benjamin and Johanna (Weil) F.; m. Bernice L. Smith, May 7, 1929; children—Lawrence S., Bruce E. A.B., LL.B., U. Mo., 1928; L.H.D. (hon.), Hebrew Union Coll.-Jewish Inst. Religion, 1969. Bar: Mo. bar 1928. Practiced in, Kansas City; partner firm Spencer, Fane, Britt & Browne (and predecessors), from 1928; Mem. Kansas City Bd. Police Commrs., 1953-57; mem. Adminstrv. Conf. U.S., 1961-62; mem. legal adv. com. Nat. Power Survey, 1963-64. Chmn. bd. Union Am. Hebrew Congregations, 1963-67, hon. chmn., from 1971; mem. Am. bd. World Union Progressive Judaism, from 1958; pres. Congregation B'nai Jehudah, Kansas City, 1940-45, trustee, from 1937; a founder Jewish Welfare Fedn. Kansas City, 1933, mem. bd., 1933-38, 50-55; a founder Jewish Community Center Kansas City, 1935, v.p., 1943-45; Bd. dirs. Starlight Theatre Assn., Downtown, Inc.; bd. counsellors Menorah Med. Center, Kansas City; hon. dir. Rockhurst Coll.; bd. govs. Hebrew Union Coll.-Jewish Inst. Religion, Cin., 1963-67; mem. Greater Kansas City Sports Commn., from 1966; pres. U. Mo. Law Sch. Found., 1970-71; mem. nat. adv. council U. Mid-Am., 1974-77; bd. curators U. Mo., 1971-77, pres., 1973-74. Recipient Night of Sports award, 1960; Disting. Service medallion Am. Heart Assn., 1963; U. Mo. Alumni Assn. citation of merit, 1966; Brotherhood award NCCJ, 1967; Human Rights medallion Am. Jewish Com., 1978. Mem. Internat., Am., Fed. Energy, Kansas City bar assns., Mo. Bar, Lawyers Assn. Kansas City, Am. Judicature Soc., Kansas City C. of C., U. Mo. Alumni Assn., QEBH Hon. Soc., Zeta Beta Tau, Phi Delta Phi (hon.). Republican. Clubs: Oakwood Country (Kansas City, Mo.), Kansas City (Kansas City, Mo.). Home: Kansas City, MO.

FANKHAUSER, GERHARD, educator; b. Burgdorf, Switzerland, Mar. 11, 1901; s. Max and Anna (Hermann) F.; student U. Geneva, U. Zurich; Ph.D., U. Berne, 1924; m. Erna Koestler, Aug. 28, 1931; children—David Andreas, Anne and Marguerite (twins). Instr. zoology U. Berne, Switzerland, 1925-29; Rockefeller Found. fellow U. Chgo., Yale, 1929-31; asst. prof. biology Princeton, 1931-39, asso. prof., 1939-46, prof., 1946-81, Edwin Grant Conklin prof. biology, 1956-69, emeritus, 1969-81. Mem. A.A.A.S., Am. Soc. Zoologists, Am. Assn. Anatomists, Am. Genetics Soc., Am. Soc. Naturalists, Soc. Study Growth, Internat. Inst. Embryology, Internat. Soc. Cell Biology, Sigma Xi. Contbr. articles in field. Home: Princeton, N.J. Died Oct. 2, 1981.

FANTE, JOHN THOMAS, writer; b. Denver, Apr. 8, 1909; s. Nicholas Peter and Mary (Capolungo) F.; student U. Colo., Regis Coll., Denver; m. Joyce H. Smart, July 31, 1937; children—Nicholas, Daniel, Victoria, James. Writer numerous screenplays including Full of Life, 1957 (nominated Acad. award best screenplay 1957), Walk on the Wild Side, Reluctant Saint, My Six Loves, 1962. Author: Wait Until Spring Bandini, 1938; Ask The Dust, 1939, 67; Full of Life, 1952; (collection short stories) Dago Red, 1940; Bravo Burro, 1969; Brotherhood of the Grape, 1977. Recipient Nat. Cath. Theatre Drama award, 1964. Contbr. to nat. mags. Home: Malibu, Calif. Died May 8, 1983.

FARNSWORTH, JERRY, artist; b. Dalton, Ga., Dec. 31, 1895; s. Samuel and Lavinia (Pou) F.; m. Helen Alton Sawyer, Aug. 26, 1924. Student, Corcoran Sch., Washington; pupil, Charles W. Hawthorne, Provincetown, Mass. Carnegie vis. prof. art, artist in residence U. Ill., 1942-43; dir., instr. Farnsworth Sch. of Art, Sarasota, Fla. Exhibited in, N.Y.C., Chgo., Washington, Phila., Toledo, St. Louis, Cleve., others, represented in, Met. Mus., N.Y.C., by "Annabella", bought 1940, Whitney Mus. Am. Art, by "My Neighbor Miss Williams", bought 1942; permanent collection, Syracuse U.; Author: Portrait and Figure Painting. Awards include: honorable mention Chgo. Art Inst., 1940; Portrait prize Nat. Arts Club, N.Y.C., 1941; purchase prize Los Angeles Mus., 1945; First purchase prize High Mus., Atlanta, for Loraine of Truro, 1946; Maynard Portrait prize Nat. Acad., 1952; purchase prizes Chrysler Mus. Art, Norfolk, Va.; Asso. Nat. Academician, 1933; Nat. Academician, 1935. Mem. Provincetown Art Assn. Club: Nat. Arts (N.Y.C.). Home: Sarasota FL

FARRELL, FOSTER F., assn. exec.; b. Des Moines, Ia., Sept. 15, 1898; s. John Francis and Annie (Beck) F.; ed. public schs., Des Moines, Ia., student Kemper Mil. Sch., Boonville, Mo., 1917-19, U. of Nebraska, 1920-21; m. Josephine M. Wallace, Oct. 11, 1930. Began as municipal bond buyer, 1922; bond buyer, George M. Bechtel Co., 1922-33; representative Port of Astoria Bondholders Com. and City of Astoria Bondholders Com., 1933-35; sec.-treas. and mgr. Nat. Fraternal Congress of America from 1935. Mem. Delta Tau Delta. Mason (Shriner), Rotarian. Club: Illinois Athletic (Chicago). Home: Chicago, Ill. †

FARRELL, JOHN EDWARD, lawyer; b. South Orange, N.J., Apr. 29, 1907; s. John and Johanna (Hefferman) F.; m. Margaret Spellane, Jan. 31, 1942; children—Margot, Ellen, John, Paul, Jane. Student, Fordham U., 1927-28; J.D., Georgetown U., 1932. Bar: N.J. bar 1933. Pvt. practice, Newark, 1933-41; with P. Ballantine & Sons, Newark, 1941-67, sec.-counsel, 1951-54, v.p., 1954-64, pres., 1964-67, chmn. bd., 1967, then engaged in practice of law, Newark; of counsel Shanley & Fisher; trustee Howard Savs. Bank, Newark; dir. Yeast Products, Inc., Clifton, N.J. Trustee Essex County Blood Bank, Seton Hall U. Served to maj. USAAF, 1942-45. Fellow Am. Bar Found.; mem. ABA, N.J., Essex County bar assns. Roman Catholic. Home: South Orange, N.J. Dec. Dec. 3, 1983.

FARRINGTON, ELIZABETH PRUETT, ret. govt. ofcl.; b. Tokyo, Japan, May 30, 1898; d. Robert Lee and Josephine (Baugh) Pruett; A.B., U. Wis., 1918; m. Joseph Rider Farrington (dec. June 1954); children—Beverly (Mrs. Hugh F. Richardson), John. Pres. Dist. League Republican Women, Washington, 1947-49; nat. chmn. pub. relations Nat. Fedn. Women's Rep. Clubs, 1947-49, nat. pres., 1949-53; elected del. to Congress from Hawaii to succeed husband who died, 1954, reelected, 1954-57; pres., dir., Honolulu Star Bull., 1957-61, Hilo Tribune-Herald, 1957-61; pres. Hawaiian Broadcasting System, 1960-61; pres., dir. Star-Bull. Printing Co., 1957-61; chmn. bd. dirs. Honolulu Lithograph Co., 1958-61; dir. Office Territories, Dept. Interior, 1969-72. Mem. Am. Assn. U. Women, Nat. Council Chs., Theta Sigma Phi, Alpha Omicron Pi. Mem. Disciples of Christ. Clubs: Congressional, Capitol Hill (Washington). Home: Honolulu, Hawaii. Died July 21, 1984.

FARSON, JAMES NEGLEY, writer; b. Plainfield, N.J., May 14, 1890; s. Enoch and Grace (Negley) F.; B.S. in C.E., U. of Pa., 1914; m. Eve Stoker, Sept. 22, 1920; 1 son, Daniel Negley. Began as engr. in Manchester, Eng., 1914; sold army and navy supplies to Russian govt. for mfrs., 1914, for own company, 1915-17; sales mgr. Mack Internat. Motor Truck Co., Chicago, 1923-24; foreign corr. Chicago Daily News, 1924-35, serving in India, Egypt and throughout Europe, and stationed in London, 1931-35. Scout pilot with rank of lt., British Royal Flying Corps in Egypt, World War; spent two subsequent yrs. in woods of British Columbia for recuperation of wounded leg. Mem. London Assn. Am. Newspaper Correspondents, (pres. 1933-34), Phi Gamma Delta, Phi Kappa Beta. Club: Savage (London). Author: Sailing Across Europe, 1926; Daphnes in Love, 1927; There's No End to It, 1929; Seeing Red, 1930; Black Bread and Red Coffins, 1930; The Way of a Transgressor (Literary Guild book of the month for Feb. 1937), 1936; Transgressor in the Tropics, 1937; Story of a Lake, 1939; Behind God's Back, 1941; Going Fishing, 1942. Contbr. short stories. Home: London, England. †

FARWELL, ALBERT DAY, investment exec.; b. Chgo., May 28, 1888; s. Francis C. and Fannie N. (Day) F.; student Hill Sch., Pottstown, Pa.; B.A., Yale; m. Edith Hill Foster, Jan. 6, 1917. With John V. Farwell, Chgo., 1910-17, pres., N.Y.C. 1919-24; pres. Quaker Mfg. Co., Chgo., 1925-29; with Spencer Trask & Co., Chgo., 1929-34; sr. partner Farwell Chapman & Co., 1934-60; partner William Blair & Company, Chgo., mem. New York Stock Exchange; dir. Liquid Carbonic Co., 1957-58; dir. Mickleberry Food Products Co. Trustee J. G. Shedd Aquarium Mus.; pres., bd. trustees YMCA (Chgo.). Clubs: Onwentsia (Lake Forest); Shoreacres, Lake Bluff; The Attic (Chgo.). Home: Lake Forest, Ill. †

FARWELL, LORING CHAPMAN, educator; b. Chgo., June 29, 1915; s. Edward Parris and Elizabeth (Farwell) F.; B.S., Mass. Inst. Tech., 1937; M.B.A., Northwestern U., 1940, Ph.D., 1955; m. Martha Jane Campbell, Jan. 31, 1942; children—Edward Parris III, David Loring. With Sheridan, Farwell and Morrison, Chgo., 1937-39; mem. faculty Northwestern U., 1946-81, prof. econs., 1955-81. Served with AUS, 1941-46. Mem. Am. Econ. Assn., Am. Fin. Assn., Econometric Soc., Inst. Mgmt. Scis. Author: (with G. Leffler) The Stock Market, 3d edit., 1963; (with J.T. O'Neil and V. Boyd) Quantitative Controls for Business, 1965; (with others) Financial Institutions, 5th edit., 1971. Home: Northfield, Ill. Died Apr. 6, 1981.

FARY, JOHN G., congressman; b. Chgo., Apr. 11, 1911; m. Lillian Makowski, 1934; children—James, Marian. Student, Loyola U., Chgo., Real Estate Sch., Ill., Midwest Inst. Mem. Ill. Gen. Assembly, 1955-75; mem. 94th-97th congresses from 5th Ill. Dist. Mem. Polish Nat. Alliances, Polish Roman Catholic Union. Democrat. Roman Cath. Clubs: Moose, Eagles, Lions, K.C, Kiwanis. Home: Chicago, Ill. Died June 7, 1984.

FASICK, CLYDE AUGUSTUS, clergyman, educator; b. Mifflin, Pa., Aug. 13, 1887; s. William Sherman and Esther Star (Greenland) F.; student Dickinson Sem., Williamsport, Pa., 1907; A.B., Pa. Coll., Gettysburg, 1914, grad. study, 1914-15; grad. study Univ. of Pa., summer 1915; M.A. from University of the South, 1934; m. Esther Ruth Kennedy, of Mifflin, Pa., June 8, 1929. Instr., pub. schs., Pa., 1907-10; ordained ministry M.E. Ch., 1915; pastor Mercersburg, Pa., 1915-17; successively instr., comdt. and headmaster, with rank of capt., maj., and lt. col., Sewanee Mil. Acad., since 1919; dir. Camp Greenbrier for Boys, Alderson, W.Va. Served as 2d lt., later 1st lt., U.S.A., 1917-19, instr. officers training schs., Aug. 1917-Mar. 1919; capt., inf., R.C. Mem. Am. Legion, Phi Delta Theta. Republican. Mason. Address: Sewanee, Tenn.†

FASSBINDER, RAINER WERNER, director, producer, writer; b. Bad Worishofen, W. Ger., May 31, 1946; s. Helmut and Liselotte Pempeit (Eder) F. Ed. public schs., various drama schs. including, Fridl-Leonhard Studio, Munich. W. Ger. Actor: Munich Action Theater, 1967; founder: Munich Antiteater, 1968; author, producer avant-garde adaptations of classical plays, 1968-70; author: various plays including The Bitter Tears of Petra von Kant, 1971; dir.: numerous feature and TV films including Love is Colder than Death, 1969, Katzelmacher, 1969 (W. Ger. Film Critics prize and Fed. Film prize), Beware of a Holy Whore, 1970, Why Did Herr R. Run Amok?, 1970 (Fed. Film prize), The Bitter Tears of Petra von Kant, 1972, Fox and His Friends, 1974, Ali-Fear Eats the Soul, 1974 (Critics award at Cannes Film Festival), Theater am Turm, Frankfurt, W. Ger., 1974-75 (Recipient Patron award (Gerhard-Hauptmann prize), TV award German Acad. Producing Arts, various other internat. film festival prizes.). Mem. PEN. Home: Munich, Federal Republic of Germany. Dec. June 10, 1982.*

FAUL, HENRY, educator, nuclear geophysicist; b. Prague, Czechoslovakia, July 17, 1920; B.S., Mass. Inst. Tech., 1941, Ph.D., 1949; M.S., Mich. State U., 1942. Prof. geology U. Pa., Phila., 1966-81. Author: Ages of Rocks, Planets and Stars, 1966; Nuclear Clocks, 3d edit., 1976. Editor: Nuclear Geology, 1954. Research geochemistry and geophysics. Died Sept. 16, 1981.

FAVERTY, FREDERIC EVERETT, educator; b. Sparta, Ill., Sept. 29, 1902; s. Clarence Walter and Amelia (Riemer) F.; A.B., Washington U., 1924; M.A., Harvard, 1929, Ph.D., 1930; m. Margaret Ellen Beckett, June 20, 1934; children—Kathleen Margaret, Richard Beckett. Instr. English, Western Res. U., 1925-28; instr. English, Northwestern U., 1930-33, asst. prof., 1933-39, asso. prof., 1939-45, prof. and chmn. dept. of English, 1945-58, Morrison prof. English, 1958-71, Morrison prof. emeritus, 1971-81. Book reviewer Book World, Chgo. Tribune; cons. on Victorian lit. to publs. Modern Lang. Assn., 1960-81; cons. div. research and humanities Nat. Found. Arts and Humanities, 1966; Ph.D. examiner U. Toronto (Ont.), 1967. Mem. bd. overseers vis. com. to dept. English, Harvard, 1954-58, mem. ad hoc com. joint appointment in English and gen. edn., 1953. Recipient Friends of Lit. award, 1957. Mem. AAUP, MLA, Phi Beta Kappa (mem. Christian Gauss Award com. 1957-60, chmn. 1960). Presbyn. Editor: Northwestern Univ. Press, 1945-50. Author: Mathew Arnold the Ethnologist, 1951; Your Literary Heritage, 1958. Editor, contbr. The Victorian Poets: a Guide to Research, 1968; mem. editorial bd. jour. Victorian Studies, 1958-60; adv. bd.. Victorian Poetry, 1964-81. Contbr. to Harvard Studies in Philology and Literature; Modern Philology, Studies in Philology, others. Club: University (Evanston). Home: Evanston, Ill. Died Aug. 9, 1981.

FAYMONVILLE, PHILIP R., army officer; b. Calif., Apr. 30, 1888; B.S., U.S. Mil. Acad., 1912; grad. Chem. Warfare Sch., 1933, Army Indsl. Coll., 1933, Army War Coll., 1934. Commd. 2d lt., C.A.C., U.S. Army, 1912; transferred to Ordnance Dept. as capt., 1920, and advanced through the grades to brig. gen., Jan. 1942; served as major and lt. col., Ordnance Dept. World War I; in charge Lend-Lease in Russia, Aug. 1942; dir. Research and Development, Army Service Forces, 1945.†

FEDER, AARON, physician, educator; b. N.Y.C., May 1, 1915; s. Herman and Fannie (Trenner) F.; m. Beatrice Wallance, Dec. 25, 1941; children: Carol (Mrs. Philip Glatsein), Jane Louise (Mrs. Harlan M. Dellsy). Student, N.Y.U., 1931-34; Exchange scholar, Harvard Med. Sch., 1937; M.D. with honors, U. Md., 1938. Intern Hosp. Joint Diseases, N.Y.C., 1938-40, resident, 1940, practice medicine specializing in internal medicine, Jackson Heights, N.Y., 1940-83; mem. faculty Cornell U. Med. Sch., 1940—, clin. prof. medicine, 1965-85, 1st Irene and I. Roy Psaty Disting. prof. in clin. medicine, 1984-85; vis. prof. LaGuardia Hosp., 1974; attending physician N.Y. Hosp., L.I. Jewish Hillside Med. Center; vis. physician Bellevue Hosp., 1953-68; mem. med. malpractice panel N.Y. State Supreme Ct.; cons. physician Booth Meml. Hosp., North Shore U. Hosp., Long Beach Meml. Hosp.; cons. NIH, 1976-79; mem. med. adv. bd. Hebrew U.-Hadassah; del. internat. Congresses in field. Contbr. articles to profl. jours.; Assoc. editor: N.Y. State Jour. Medicine. Co-chmn. physicians div. United Jewish Appeal Greater N.Y., 1963-85, past chmn., Queens div.; mem. exec. com. Fedn. Jewish Philanthropies, 1950-85; gov. YMHA-YWHA of Central Queens. Served from 1st lt. to maj., M.C. AUS, 1942-45, PTO. Recipient Myrtle Wreath award for disting. service Hadassah; U. Md. Med. Alumni Assn. award for outstanding contbns. to medicine and disting. service to mankind, 1980. Fellow A.C.P. (founding pres. chpt., council), Am. Coll. Cardiology, N.Y. Acad. Medicine, N.Y. Acad. Scis., N.Y. Cardiol. Soc. (past dir.), Royal soc. Health Gt. Britain, Royal Soc. Medicine, Cornell U. Med. Coll. Alumni (hon.), U. Md. Med. Alumni (v.p. 1978-79, 82-84); mem. Med. Soc. State N.Y. (past del., past sect. chmn., com. on prizes and awards), Harvey Soc., Am. Fedn. Clin. Research, Am. Soc. Tropical Medicine, Am. Heart Assn., Assn. Am. Med. Colls., Assn. Mil. Surgeons, AAAS, Sigma Xi, Alpha Omega Alpha (hon.). Home: Great Neck, N.Y. Died Mar. 19, 1985.

FEIL, HAROLD, physician; b. Bay Shore, L.I., N.Y., June 26, 1889; s. George E. and Lillian (Stein) Cohen; M.D., Ohio Wesleyan U., 1911; A.B., U. Denver, 1914; m. Nellie Elgutter, July 29, 1915; children—George Herbert, Mary (Mrs. Herman Hellerstein), Edward Rosewater. Intern Michael Reese Hosp., Chgo., 1911-13; vol. asst. U. Coll. Hosp. Med. Sch., London, 1919-20, Western Res. U., 1921-22; pvt. practice internal medicine and cardiology, Cleve., from 1920; asso. physician Mt. Sinai Hosp., Cleve., 1916-33, physician in chief, 1948-50, cons. medicine, from 1951, physician Cleve. City Hosp., 1921-33; asso. physician U. Hosp., Cleve., 1933-55, hon. staff, from 1956; asst. clin. prof. medicine Western Res. U., 1933-38, asso. clin. prof., 1938-47, clin. prof., 1947-55, emeritus, from 1955; cons. Mt. Sinai Hosp.; med. adv. com. Maternal Health Clinic. Served as lieutenant, M.C., U.S. Army, 1918-19, captain, 1926-30. Alumni award Western Res. U. Med. Alumni, 1961. Diplomate Am. Bd. Internal Medicine. Fellow A.A.A.S., A.C.P.; mem. Central Soc. Clin. Research, Cleve. Acad. Medicine (v.p. 1931), Ohio Med. Assn., A.M.A., Am. Heart Assn., Am. Soc. Study Arteriosclerosis, Cleve. Area Heart Soc. (pres. 1951), Cleve. Med. Library Assn. (dir. from 1926, pres. 1948-49) Handerson Med. History Soc. (pres. 1959), Ohio Acad. History of Medicine (president 1961), Sigma Xi. Clubs: Medical Arts, Rowfant, Oakwood (Cleve.). Author: Coronary Heart Disease, A Personal, Clinical Study, 1964. Asso. editor Circulation Research, 1955-57. Contbr. to New Gould Med. Dictionary, 1946, 56, Current Therapy, 1956, 63. Research in cardiovascular diseases. Home: Cleveland, OH. †

FEINGOLD, BENJAMIN FRANKLIN, physician; b. Pitts., June 15, 1900; s. Mayer Jacob and Ray Libbie (Robins) F.; m. Helene Samuels, June 21, 1951. B.S., U. Pitts., 1921, M.D., 1924. Intern Passavant Hosp., Pitts., 1924-25; fellow in pathology U. Goettingen, Germany, 1927; house officer children's clinic U. Vienna, Austria, 1928-29; clin. instr. pediatrics Northwestern U., 1929-32; attending physician in pediatrics and infectious diseases Los Angeles County Gen. Hosp., 1932-38; attending physician in pediatrics Cedars of Lebanon Hosp., 1932-41, chief pediatrics, 1945-51; attending physician in pediatrics Los Angeles Children's Hosp., 1932-51, asso. in allergy, 1945-51; with Kaiser Found. Hosp. and Permanente Med. Group, from 1971; established all depts. allergy for No. Calif., chief allergy, 1951-69, chmn. central research com., 1952-70, dir. lab. med. entomology, 1957-70, chief emeritus dept. allergy, San Francisco, 1969-82. Author: Introduction to Clinical Allergy, 1973, Why Your Child is Hyperactive, 1975, The Feingold Cookbook for Hyperactive Children, 1979; contbr. numerous articles on allergy and basic immunology to profl. jours. Served to comdr. USNR, 1941-45, PTO. Mem. Am. Acad. Pediatrics, Am. Acad. Allergy. Home: San Francisco, Calif. Dec. Mar. 23, 1982.

FEINSINGER, NATHAN PAUL, educator; b. Bklyn., Sept. 20, 1902; s. Israel Bernard and Rebecca (Neighstock) F.; A.B., U. Mich. 1926, J.D., 1928, LL.D. (hon.), 1973; m. Bettie Whitney, Jan. 15, 1940; children—Greg, Ellen, Peter. Sociolegal research, Columbia Law Sch., 1928-29; asst., then asso., prof. law U. Wis., 1929-73, prof. emeritus, 1973-83, co-dir. Center for Teaching and Research in Disputes Settlements, Seminar in Methods of Disputes Settlement, Labor Relations Law; former vis. prof. law univs. of Chgo., Mich., Stanford, 1934, 36, 53, 58. Successively asso. gen. counsel, dir. nat. disputes and pub. mem. Nat. War Labor Bd., Washington, 1942-46; chmn. Wage Stabilization Bd., 1951-52. Spl. asst. to atty. gen. and gen. counsel, Wis. Labor Relations Bd., 1937-39; spl. rep. sec. of labor in labor disputes, 1946-49; chmn. presdl. fact finding bd. in steel, meat packing, airlines labor disputes, 1946, 48. Mem. Am. Bar Assn., Nat. Acad. Arbitrators, Order of Coif, Phi Beta Kappa, Phi Kappa Phi (hon.), Phi Delta Phi (hon.), Druids. Club: University. Author: Stearns on Suretyship, 1937; Cases and Materials on Partnerships, 1939; Cases and Materials on Labor Law, 1940. Home: Madison, Wis. Died Nov. 1, 1983.

FELDMAN, MARTY, writer, comedian, film director; b. London, 1933; m. Lauretta. Movie appearances include Every Home Should Have One, 1969, Young Frankenstein, 1974, The Adventures of Sherlock Holmes' Smarter Brother, 1976, Sex with a Smile, 1976, Silent Movie, 1976; star, co-writer, co-dir.: Movie appearances include The Last Remake of Beau Geste, 1977; TV comedy writer BBC Movie appearances include; appeared: TV series The Frost Report; star: summer replacement series Dean Martin Presents the Golddiggers; also the: summer replacement series Marty Feldman Comedy Machine, 1972, numerous guest appearances; writer-dir. film: In God We Trust, 1980. Mem. Dirs. Guild Am. Office: Beverly Hills, Calif. Dec. Dec. 2, 1982.

FELLNER, WILLIAM JOHN, economist, educator; b. Budapest, Hungary, May 31, 1905; s. Henry and Margaret (Leipziger) F.; m. Valerie Korek, Jan. 4, 1936; 1 dau., Anna Valerie Thomas. Student, U. Budapest, 1922-23; B.S., Fed. Inst. Tech., Zurich, 1927; Ph.D., U. Berlin, 1929. Ptnr. in mfg. firm, Budapest, 1929-38; lectr. econs. U. Calif.-Berkeley, 1939-40, asst. prof., 1941-42, assoc. prof., 1943-47, prof., 1947-52; prof. econs. Yale, 1952-73, Sterling prof. econs., 1959-73, Sterling prof. emeritus, 1973-83, chmn. dept. econs., 1962-64; resident scholar Am. Enterprise Inst., 1972-73, 75-83; cons. U.S. Treasury Dept., 1945, 49-52, 69-73; mem. Pres.'s Council Econ. Advisers, 1973-75; vis. lectr. Havard, 1950-51; Alfred Marshall lectr. U. Cambridge, 1957. Author: A Treatise on War Inflation, 1942, Monetary Policies and Full Employment, 1946, 2d edit., 1947, Competition Among the Few, 1949, Trends and Cycles in Economic Activity, 1956, Emergence and Content of Modern Economic Analysis, 1960, Probability and Profit, 1965, Towards a Reconstruction of Macroeconomics, 1976; joint author: Survey of Contemporary Economics, 1948, Money, Trade and Economic Growth, 1951, Studies in Income and Wealth, Vol. 16, 1954, Economic Policies and Inflation, 1972, A New Look at Inflation, 1973; project dir., contbr.: Contemporary Economic Problems, 1976—; Joint editor: Readings in the Theory of Income Distribution, 1946; mem. editorial bd.: Am. Econs. Review, 1950-52; Contbr. articles to various econs. jours. Decorated comdr., cross Order of Merit (W. Ger.); recipient Bernhard Harms prize Inst. World Economy, U. Kiel, 1982. Fellow Am. Acad. Arts and Scis., Econometric Soc.; mem. Am. Econ. Assn. (exec. com. 1955-58, pres. 1969), Bavarian Acad. Scis. (corr.), Phi Beta Kappa (hon.). Clubs: Mory's (New Haven); Yale (N.Y.C.); Cosmos (Washington). Home: Washington, D.C. Dec. Sept. 15, 1983.

FELTS, SAM LEE, state justice; b. Cheatham County, Tenn., Sept. 29, 1889; s. George W. and Sarah (Perry) F.; LL.B., Cumberland U., 1914; student U. Paris (France), 1918; m. Jane Jackson, Dec. 27, 1924; children—Samuel Lee, Philip Wyatt. Admitted to Tenn. bar, 1914; mem. firm Duke & Felts, Ashland City, 1915-17; asso. firm Jordan, Stokes, Jr., Nashville, 1919-21; mem. firm Chambers, Williams & Felts, 1922-24; asso. O. W. Hughes, 1926-28, Albert Williams, Nashville, 1929-37; presiding judge Ct. Appeals of Tenn., 1950-58; asso. justice Supreme Ct. of Tenn. Mem. Tenn., Nashville bar assns., Nashville Library Assn., Am. Legion, Order Coif. Democrat. Methodist. Home: Nashville, Tenn. †

FENTON, MARTIN, securities exec.; b. Washington, Jan. 7, 1908; s. Charles Wendell and Alice (Rochester) F.; m. Katharine Elinor Douglas, Oct. 9, 1931; children—Alice D. (Mrs. Alice F. Kuhns), Martin, Wendell, Edith Douglas (Mrs. Roger Tuckerman), Prudence. Grad., St. Mark's Sch., 1925; A.B., Yale, 1929. Trainee M.W. Kellogg Co., 1930-31; auditor Nat. City Bank, N.Y.C., 1931-33; mgr. Laird & Co., N.Y.C., 1933-41; partner Laird & Co. (then Laird, Inc.), Wilmington, Del., 1946-56, pres. corp., 1956-64, chmn., 1964-67; pres., investment mgr. Christiana Securities Calif., Inc., from 1978; cons. White Weld & Co., Inc., Wilmington; dir. Christiana Cos., Inc. Served to lt. col. USMCR, 1941-46. Decorated Bronze Star. Episcopalian. Clubs: Cypress Point (Pebble Beach, Calif.); Wilmington Country (pres. 1957-62), Wilmington. Home: Pebble Beach, Calif.

FENTRESS, CALVIN, JR., insurance; b. Hubbard Woods, Ill., Oct. 30, 1907; s. Calvin and Paulina Stearns (Lyon) F.; grad. Berkshire Sch., 1926, Princeton, 1931; m. Frances E. Wood, Oct. 1931; children—Audrey, Calvin III, Mary Hardwick, Robert Wood. In investment business, Lee, Higginson & Co., 1931-32; with Allstate Ins. Co. and Allstate Fire Ins. Co. since Apr. 1932, in investment dept., 1932-36, became treas., 1937, v.p. and treas., 1938, exec. vice pres. and sec., 1940, pres. and mem. finance com., 1941, pres. and treas., 1944-45, pres., 1945-57, chmn. 1957-66, chmn. finance com., 1966-83, also dir.; dir. Continental Illinois Nat. Bank and Trust Company of Chicago, Baker, Fentress & Co., Consol. Financial Corp., No. Ill. Gas Co., Sears Roebuck & Co. Clubs: Commonwealth, Chicago, Commercial (Chgo.); Onwentsia (Lake Forest, Ill.). Home: Lake Forest, Ill. Died July 16, 1983.

FERGUS, E(RNEST) N(EWTON), agronomist; b. Shelby County, O., Mar. 19, 1892; s. John Shannon and Jennie Alice (Stoner) F.; B.Sc. Ohio State U., 1916, M.S., 1918; Ph.D., U. Chgo., 1931; m. Audrey Smith, Mar. 11, 1916 (dec.); children—Janet Ann (Mrs. George Francis Spragens), Charles Shannon. married 2d, Katherine J. Bascom, Oct. 23, 1957. Asst. in soils and crops Purdue U. Agrl. Expt. Sta., 1918-20; instr. in farm crops U. Ky., 1920, asst. prof., 1923, asso. prof., 1928, prof., 1938, prof. agronomy, 1962-64, prof. emeritus, 1964-85; area dir. grad. study, 1952-62; agronomist in charge pasture and forage crops investigations, Ky. Agrl. Experimental Sta., 1936-54, agronomist charge crops sect., 1954-62; collaborator in forage crops research U.S. Dept. of Agr., 1936-61; dir. Ky. Research Found., 1945-64, v.p., 1959-64; dir. vis. scientists program Ky. Academy Science and National Sci. Found., from 1964. Sec. agronomy sect. Assn. So. Agrl. Workers, 1938-39, vice chmn., 1939-41, chmn., 1941-42; mem. planning conference of Nat. Found. Seed Project, 1951-56. Southern Seedsmen's Man of Year award, 1954. Fellow A.A.A.S., Am. Soc. Agronomy (chairman div. agronomic application 1951, div. agronomic edn. 1952, div. crop prodn., mgmt. 1953); mem. Am. Assn. U. Profs., Sigma Xi, Gamma Sigma Delta, Alpha Zeta. Presbyn. (commr. Gen. Assembly, 1937, 48). Co-author: Field Crops Management, 1942, rev. edit., 1949; Southern Field Crops Management, 1944, rev. edit., 1949; Field Crops, 1958; and others. Home: Lexington, Ky. Died Jan. 3, 1985; buried Lexington Cemetery, Lexington, Ky.†

FERGUSON, CHESTER HOWELL, lawyer, corporation executive; b. Americus, Ga., July 1, 1908; s. Sidney Hugh and Barbara (White) F.; m. Louise Lykes, Dec. 2, 1939; children—Stella Louise, Howell Lykes. Student, Mercer U., U. Ala.; J.D., U. Fla., 1930. Bar: Fla. bar 1930. With Macfarlane, Ferguson, Allison & Kelly (and predecessors), Tampa, 1930-83, mem. firm, 1935-83; chmn. MBS, Inc., 1959-60; vice chmn., dir. LTV Corp.; chmn. Lykes Bros., Inc., 1969-83, First Fla. Banks, Inc., 1st Nat. Bank in Palm Beach, 1970-79; dir. Am. Ship Bldg. Corp., Youngstown Sheet & Tube Co., Lykes Bros. S.S. Co., Inc., Lykes Pasco Packing Co., Knight & Wall Co., Bank of Clearwater, 1st Nat. Bank Fla., Lewis State Bank, Tampa Ship Repair & Dry Dock Co., Inc., Kennesaw Life & Accident Ins. Co. Dir. CD Hillsborough County, also Gulf Coast dist. Fla., 1947-63; trustee U. Tampa, 1950-83; bd. regents Fla. State U. System, 1969-83. chmn., 1965-69. Served from 1st lt. to col. USAAF, 1942-46; asst. chief staff CBI. Decorated Air medal, Legion of Merit, Bronze Star, also Chinese decoration. Mem. Fla. C. of C., Greater Tampa C. of C. (bd. govs.), Am. Legion, Air Force Assn., Mil. Order World Wars, Newcomen Soc., Am., Fla., Tampa bar assns., Am. Coll. Trial Lawyers, Maritime Law Assn., Am. Coll. Probate Counsel, Blue Key, Phi Delta Theta, Omicron Delta Kappa, Phi Delta Phi, Beta Gamma Sigma. Episcopalian (sr. warden). Clubs: Rotary (Tampa), Univ. (Tampa), Tampa Yacht and Country (Tampa), Palma Ceia Golf and Country (Tampa), Merrymakers (Tampa), Ye Mystic Krewe of Gasparilla (Tampa). Home: Tampa, Fla. Dec. Mar. 3, 1983.

FERGUSON, CLARENCE CLYDE, JR., diplomat, law educator; b. Wilmington, N.C., Nov. 4 1924; s. Clarence Clyde and Georgeva (Owens) F.; m. Dolores Zimmerman, Feb. 14, 1954; children: Claire Oberone, Hope Elizabeth, Eve Maria. A.B., Ohio State U., 1948; LL.B., Harvard U., 1951; LL.D., Rutgers U., 1966, Williams Coll., 1975. Bar: Mass. 1951, N.Y. 1953. Asst. dept. gen. edn. Harvard U., 1950-52, teaching fellow Law Sch., 1951-52; assoc. Baltimore, Paulson and Canudo, N.Y.C., 1952-54; asst. U.S. atty. So. Dist. N.Y., 1954-55; prof. law Rutgers U. Law Sch., 1955-63; gen. counsel U.S. Commn. Civil Rights, 1961-63; dean, prof. law Howard U. Law Sch., 1963-69, prof. law, 1975-83; Henry L. Stimson prof. law Harvard U.; spl. U.S. coordinator relief to civilian victims of Nigerian Civil War, 1969-70, ambassador to Uganda, 1970-72; dep. asst. sec. for African affairs Dept. State, Washington, 1972-73; U.S. rep. ECOSOC, N.Y.C., 1973-75. Author: (with A.P. Plaustein) Desegregation and the Law: The Meaning and Effect of the School Segregation Cases, 2d edit., 1960, Enforcement and Collection of Judgements and Liens, 1961, Secured Transactions, Article IX Uniform Commercial Code in New Jersey, 1961; also numerous articles, revs.; editor: Materials on Trial Presentation, 1958. Civil rights adviser to Gov. Rockefeller of N.Y., 1959-64, mem. several presdl. commns., cons. to govt., 1955-83, U.S. expert UN sub-commn. on discrimination, 1964-83; treas. East Orange (N.J.) Housing Authority, 1959-61; bd. dirs. legal def. and ednl. fund NAACP, 1962—; trustee Inst. Policy Studies, 1962—. Served with AUS, 1942-46, ETO, PTO. Decorated Bronze Star. Mem. ABA, Fed. Bar Assn. (nat. council 1963—), Assn. Am. Law Schs. (exec. com. 1965—), D.C. Circuit Jud. Conf., Phi Beta Kappa. Office: Cambridge, Mass. Dec. Dec. 21, 1983.

FERGUSON, HOMER, federal judge; b. Harrison City, Pa., Feb. 25, 1888; s. Samuel and Margarete (Bush) F.; m. Myrtle Jones, June 20, 1913; 1 dau., Amy Margaret (Mrs. Charles Robert Beltz). Student, U. Pitts., 1910-11; LL.B., U. Mich., 1913, LL.D., 1951; LL.D., Kalamazoo Coll., Detroit Coll. Law, Muhlenberg Coll. Bar: Mich. bar 1913. Practiced law, 1913-29, circuit judge, 1929-43, U.S. senator from, Mich., 1943-54, U.S. ambassador to, Philippines, 1955-56; assoc. judge U.S. Ct. Mil. Appeals, 1956-71, sr. judge; sat as one-man grand jury, Wayne County, Mich., 1939-42; Prof. law Detroit Coll. Law. Mem. Am., Mich., Detroit bar assns., Washington Inst. Fgn. Affairs, Interparliamentary Union, Am. Judicature Soc., Sigma Delta Kappa. Presbyn. Clubs: Sr. Men's (Grosse Pointe); Met. (Washington); K.T. Home: Grosse Pointe, Mich. Dec. Dec. 17, 1982.

FERGUSON, JAMES SHARBROUGH, history educator; b. Anguilla, Miss., Dec. 31, 1916; s. James Elbert Jenkins and Delle Prudence (Clark) F.; m. Frances Hardy Cottrell, June 3, 1939 (dec. Nov. 1978); children: Frances Cottrell, Elizabeth Lynn; m. Sarah Thompson Shepherd, Oct. 18, 1980. A.B., Millsaps Coll., 1937, LL.D., 1974; A.M., La. State U., 1940; Ford scholar, Yale U., 1952-53; Ph.D., U. N.C., 1953. Instr. math. Amory (Miss.) High Sch., 1937-39; teaching fellow La. State U., 1939-42; Gen. Edn. Bd. fellow U. N.C., 1942-43, instr. history, 1943-44; asst. prof. history Millsaps Coll., 1944-46, asso. prof., 1946, prof., 1947-62, acad. dean, 1954-62; prof. history U. N.C. at Greensboro, 1962-84, dean grad. sch., 1962-64, acting chancellor, 1964-65, 66-67, vice chancellor, 1966, chancellor, 1967-79, Univ. Disting. prof., 1979-84,; vis. assoc. prof. summer session Tulane U., 1947. Contbr. articles hist. jours. Dir. Christian Citizenship Seminar, Miss. Meth. Youth Fellowship, 1954; trustee St. Andrew's Presbyn. Coll. Mem. AAUP, Orgn. Am. Historians, So., Miss. hist. assns., N.C. Lit. and Hist. Assn., Phi Beta Kappa (hon.), Pi Kappa Alpha, Alpha Epsilon Delta, Eta Sigma Phi, Phi Kappa Phi, Pi Kappa Delta, Omicron Delta Kappa. Methodist. Club: Civitan (Greensboro). Home: Greensboro, N.C. Died Sept. 24, 1984.

FERGUSON, LUCIA (CAROLINE) LOOMIS (MRS WALTER FERGUSON), columnist; b. Boggy Depot, Indian Ty., Mar. 29, 1887; d. Enos Osborne (M.D.) and Lena (Arbogast) Loomis; ed. St. Xavier's Acad., Denison, Tex., 1902, Hardin Coll., Mexico, Mo., 1903-04; diploma Sch. of Fine Arts (U. of Okla.), 1907; m. Walter Ferguson, Nov. 7, 1908; children—Loomis Benton, Ruth Elva, Thomas Bruce. Associated with husband in publication of Cherokee Republican 10 yrs., becoming known through a column under her name devoted to the interests of women; returned to newspaper writing as columnist of Oklahoma News, 1923, and from 1925 has regularly syndicated "A Woman's Viewpoint" in the Scripps-Howard newspapers. Mem. Am. Assn. Univ. Women, Business and Professional Women's Club, Okla. Hall of Fame, Y.W.C.A., Phi Beta Kappa, Kappa Alpha Theta, Theta Sigma Phi; hon. mem. Am. Women's Assn. Home: Tulsa, Okla. †

FERGUSON, WHITWORTH, elec. constrn. co. exec.; b. Walcott, Iowa, Oct. 30, 1900; s. Charles Andrew and Edna (Whitworth) F.; m. Dorothy Anger, June 25, 1924; children—Barbara Jean (Mrs. Frederic H. Federlein), Whitworth, Donald Richard. B.S. in Elec. Engring, Iowa State U., 1921; postgrad., Mass. Inst. Tech., 1921-23; D.Sc. (hon.), Webber Coll., Babson Park, Fla., 1963. Vice pres. Robertson Electric Co., Buffalo, 1923-35; chmn. Ferguson Electric Constrn. Co. Inc., Buffalo, from 1935, Ferguson Electric Equipment Corp., Buffalo, from 1953; chmn. Buffalo br. Fed. Res. Bank N.Y., 1963-65; dir. Erie Lackawanna R.R. Co.; Vice chmn. N.Y. State Atomic and Space Devel. Authority, 1962-76; dep. dir. Erie County Civil Def., from 1953. Chmn. Creative Edn. Found.; pres. Ferguson Found.; past pres. United Fund Buffalo; trustee Hosp. Service Corp. Buffalo, Millard Fillmore Hosp.; bd. regents Canisius Coll.; trustee Buffalo YMCA; mem. Mass. Inst. Tech. Future Planning Com. Served to col. USAAF, World War II. Recipient Civic Affairs citation U. Buffalo, 1958; Engring. citation Iowa State U., 1963; Man of the Yr. award Buffalo C. of C., 1968; Disting. Achievement citation, 1971; Chancellor's medal SUNY, Buffalo, 1972; Walter P. Cooke award U. Buffalo Alumni Assn., 1972; Lobdell Disting. Service award M.I.T., 1981. Mem. Buffalo C. of C. (pres. 1959-60, chmn. nuclear com. from 1963), Newcomen Soc., Def. Orientation Conf. Assn. Presbyn. (elder). Home: Buffalo, NY.

FERGUSSON, ERNA, author; b. Albuquerque, N.M., Jan. 10, 1888; d. Harvey Butler and Clara Mary (Huning) Fergusson; grad. Girls Collegiate Sch., Los Angeles, 1907; B.Pd., U. of N.M., 1912; M.A., Columbia, 1913. Teacher Albuquerque Pub. Schs., 1914-17; Red Cross home service sec. State Supervisor of N.M., 1919; reporter Albuquerque Herald, 1920; dude wrangler Albuquerque and Santa Fe, N.M., 1920-27; writer and lecturer from 1925. With Division Education, Office Coordinator Inter-American Affairs, Washington, D.C., 1944. Mem. Phi Mu. Democrat. Author books including: Murder and Mystery in New Mexico, 1948; New Mexico: A Pageant of Three Peoples, 1951; also many articles. Address: Mexico City, Mexico. †

FERGUSSON, HARVEY, writer; b. Albuquerque, N.M.; Jan. 28, 1890; s. Harvey Butler and Clara Mary (Huning) F.; pres. edn. N.M. Mil. Inst., U. N.M.; A.B., Washington and Lee U., 1911; m. Rebecca McCann, 1927 (dec. 1927). Reporter Washington Herald, Savannah Morning News, Richmond Times-Dispatch, 1912-13; with Washington bur. Chgo. Record-Herald, 1913-14; editor F. J. Haskin Newspaper Syndicate, 1914-22; engaged lit., motion picture work, from 1922; Guggenheim fellow, 1935. Mem. Phi Kappa Psi. Author: The Blood of the Conquerors, 1921; Capitol Hill, 1923; Women and Wives, 1924; Hot Saturday, 1926; Wolf Song, 1927; In Those Days, 1929; Footloose McGarnigal, 1930; Rio Grande, 1933; Modern Man—His Belief and Behavior, 1936; The Life of Riley, 1937; Home in the West, 1945; People and Power, 1947; Grant of Kingdom, 1950; The Conquest of Don Pedro, 1954 (Lit. Guild Selection). Home: Berkeley, Cal. †

FERNSTROM, KARL D(ICKSON), business engineer; born St. Paul, Minn. Oct. 14, 1887; s. Henning and M. Louise (Dickson) F.; student, Carleton Acad., Northfield, Minn., 1899-1900; grad., Horace Mann Sch., N.Y. City, 1906; S.B., Mass. Inst. of Tech., 1910; m. Katherine VanDyke Bangs, Oct. 18, 1921 (divorced 1945); 1 son, Karl Dickson; m. 2d, Dorothy Weston Bond, July 7, 1945; children—Henning, John Dickson. Asst. instr. in physics, Mass. Inst. of Tech., 1910-12; student apprentice Fairbanks-Morse, Beloit, Wis., 1912-13; works mgr. and supt., Columbia Plate Glass Co., Blairsville, Pa., 1913-16; asst. plant engr. and supt. of transportation, Newport News Shipbuilding and Dry Dock Co., 1916-20; works mgr. Nat. Conduit and Cable Co., Hastings-on-Hudson, 1920; supervisor r.r. cars and locomotive bldg. operations, Newport News Shipbuilding and Dry Dock Co., 1920-25; successively instr., asst. prof., asso. prof. economics dept., Mass. Inst. of Tech., 1925-30; prof. bus. mathematics dept. of bus. and engring. adminstrn., 1930-46; (on leave, 1940-46); prof. bus. mgt., Lowell Inst. for Indsl. Foremen, 1932-37; vice pres. and gen. mgr., dir., mem. of exec. com. N.C. Shipbuilding Co., Wilmington, 1940-42; gen. mgr. Office Rubber Dir., Washington, D.C., 1942-43; chief operating officer Harrisburg (Pa.) Machine Co. and Springfield (Mass.) Foundry and Machine Co., 1943-44; vice pres. of prodn., Cramp Shipbuilding Co., Phila., 1944-46; vice pres. prodn. and gen. mgr. Am. Machine and Foundry Co., N.Y. City and Brooklyn, 1946-48, vice pres., 1948-50; indsl. management consultant with Foster Wheeler Manufacturing Corporation from November 1950. Member Society of Naval Architects and Marine Engrs., Theta Delta Chi. Republican. Episcopalian. Author with others: Organization and Management of a Business Enterprise, 1935. Home: New York, N.Y. †

FERREYROS, ALFREDO, Peruvian ambassador; born Lima, Peru, Sept. 17, 1887; s. Carlos and Rosa (Ayulo) F.; grad. Recoleta Coll., Sch. of Agr., Lima, 1907; postgrad. student in sugar tech., La. State Univ., 1908; m. Ana Gaffron, Aug. 13, 1911. Mgr. of sugar state, Peru, 1911-25; pvt. bus., Liverpool and London, Eng., 1925-38; dir. several banking, commercial and bus. instns., Peru, 1939-47; ambassador to U.S., since Jan. 1948. Peruvian del. to sugar confs., Europe from 1931. Internat. Sugar Conf., London, 1937; Peruvian rep., Internat. Sugar Council; pres., Camara Algondonera del Peru, 1941-42; pres., Council of Econ. Supt., Peru, 1942-43; mem. consultative com. for fgn. affairs, Peru, 1944-47. Awarded Gran Cruz de la Orden del Sol del Peru. Travel in U.S., Hawaii, Java in connection with sugar technological work, 1908-10.†

FERRIN, EVAN F(ISHER), univ. prof., investigator; b. Marcus, Ia., Feb. 9, 1888; s. Joseph and Elizabeth (Fisher) F.; B.S., Ia. State Coll., 1911; M. Agr., 1920; m. Stella Drennan, June 22, 1912; children—Harold Evan, Lora Jean. Instr. in animal husbandry Ia. State Coll., 1911. Tex. A. and M. Coll., 1912; asst. prof. animal husbandry Ia. State Coll., 1912, asso. prof., 1913-18; asso. prof. Kansas State Coll., 1918-20; prof. animal husbandry U. Minn. 1920-56, head of department, 1949-56, prof. emeritus, 1956; investigator swine nutrition and management; mem. bd. dirs. St. Paul Union Stockyards Co. Judge swine state and nat. shows from Pacific coast to Eastern corn belt, from 1920. Mem. Livestock Hall of Fame. U. Minn., 1956. Mem. Livestock Breeders Association (director). American Society for Animal Production. Alpha Zeta, Gamma Sigma Delta, Delta Sigma Rho, Theta Delta Chi, Block and Bridle. Methodist. Researcher in swine nutrition and management, Kan. and Minn. agrl. expt. stas. Contbr. articles to bulls. and jours. Home: St. Paul, Minn. †

FERRIS, JOHN ORLAND, newspaper editor; b. Winchester, Ind., Nov. 7, 1893; s. Charles Elliott and Ethel Mae (Chenoweth) F.; ed. pub. schs.; m. Veda Roller, May 1, 1923 (div. 1929); 1 son, Hugh R.; m. 2d, Esther May Wallace, June 18, 1931 (dec. 1969). Reporter, Winchester Daily News, 1910-11; staff Muncie (Ind.) Evening Press, 1911-18; city editor Muncie Star, 1919-24; mem. editorial dept. Miami (Fla.) Herald, 1924-26; news editor Muncie Star, 1926-35, mng. editor, 1935-60, editor, 1960-74, editor emeritus, 1974-81. Served with U.S. Army, 1918-19. Mem. Am. Legion. Mason (K.T., 32 deg., Shriner), Rotarian. Home: Muncie, Ind. Died June 17, 1981.

FERROGGIARO, F. A., banker; b. San Francisco, May 12, 1890; s. Natale and Anna (Guinasso) F.; m. Delphine Lerda, Aug. 1, 1916; children—Delphine (Mrs. E. Q. Reed), Fred L. (dec.); m. Kathleen del Piano Wolf, July 25, 1974. Ed. pub. schs., San Francisco. With Bank of Am. NT & SA, San Francisco, from 1906, v.p., mgr. Oakland main office, 1931-40, exec. v.p., 1940-49, dir., from 1940, hon. dir., chmn. gen. finance com., from 1944, sr. vice chmn. bd., 1949-54, chmn. bd., 1954-55; hon. dir. BankAm. Corp.; hon. chmn. bd. Lucky Stores, Inc., Dublin, Calif.; dir. C.P. Nat. Utilities Co. Regent St. Mary's Coll. of Calif. Republican. Roman Catholic. Clubs: Elk (San Francisco), Druid (San Francisco), K.C. (San Francisco), Olympic (San Francisco); Claremont Country (Oakland). Home: Oakland, Calif.

FESLER, PAUL HILL, hospital supt.; b. Stanberry, Mo., May 13, 1890; s. John Elmer and Agnes (Cunning) F.; student Epworth U., 1903-04, Marion (Ind.) Normal Sch., 1908-09; m. Alma Leah Watkins, June 10, 1916; children—Dorothy Lee, Jeanne Pauline. Stenographer and court reporter State Auditor's Office, Okla., 1911-14; chief clk. Med. Sch., U. of Okla., 1914-16; sec. Med. Sch. and supt. Univ. Hosp., Oklahoma City, 1916-27; supt. hosps., U. of Minn., 1927-32; supt. Wesley Memorial Hosp., Chicago, since 1932. Trustee Northwestern U., Wesley Memorial Hospital, Methodist Deaconess Pension Fund. Mem. American Hospital Assn. (pres. 1931-32; trustee 1932-33), Minn. Hosp. Assn. (pres. 1930-31), Western Hosp. Assn.; pres. Okla. Hosp. Assn., 1926-27, Chicago Hosp. Assn., 1933-35, Ill. Hosp. Assn. (trustee), Bd. of Hosps. and Homes for M.E. Ch., Am. Protestant Hosp. Assn. (trustee), Nat. Meth. Hosps. and Homes Assn.; dir. Cook County Sch. of Nursing; Pres. Ill. Assn. for the Crippled. Democrat. Methodist. Mason. Club: Union League. Contbr. to hosp. jours.†

FEUER, SAMUEL GUSTAVE, physician; b. N.Y.C., July 18, 1903; s. David and Eva (Sher) F.; student Columbia, 1922; M.D., N.Y.U., 1925; m. Ruth Nadelson, Sept. 6, 1926; children—Adele Glaubman (dec.), Barbara (Mrs. Donal Keller). Intern, Bellevue Hosp., N.Y.C., 1925-26; pvt. practice medicine, N.Y.C., 1926-81; former cons. Jewish Chronic Disease Hosp., St. Francis Hosp., Roslyn, L.I.; dir. emeritus phys. medicine and rehab. L.I. Coll. Hosp., Prospect Heights Hosp.; former cons. phys. medicine, rehab. VA Hosp., Miami, Fla.; former clin. asso. prof. phys. medicine and rehab. Downstate U. N.Y. Med. Center. Cons. Police Dept. N.Y.C., 1948-70. Mem. Human Rights Advocacy Commn. for Retarded and Handicapped, Miami; cons. rehab. Sunland Tng. Center for Retarded Children. Comdr. M.C., USNR, 1942-65, active service, 1942-45; ret. comdr. N.Y. Naval Militia. Diplomate Am. Bd. Phys. Medicine and Rehab. Fellow Am. Acad. and Congress Phys. Medicine, Internat. Coll. Angiology, Am. Acad. Compensation Medicine, Am. Geriatrics Soc., A.C.P., N.Y. Acad. Medicine; mem. Am. Soc. Phys. Medicine (life), AMA, N.Y. State, Kings County med. socs., Phi Delta Epsilon (life). Mason. Home: Hollywood, Fla. Died June 25, 1981.

FEUER, STANLEY BURTON, motion picture executive, lawyer; b. South Bend, Ind., Oct. 2, 1928; s. Samuel R. and Bess R. (Cohen) F.; m. Frances Schwolsky, Oct. 9, 1955; children: Pamela T., Wendy M., Thomas C. B.A., Yale U., 1950, LL.B., 1953. Bar: N.Y. 1955, Ind. 1957. With firm Breed, Abbott & Morgan, N.Y.C., 1955-57; asst. sec. Studebaker Corp., 1957-63, sec., corp. atty., 1963-67; v.p., gen. counsel Studebaker-Worthington, Inc., 1968-71; dir. STP Corp., 1968-71; v.p., gen. counsel GAF Corp., 1971-74, Metro-Goldwyn-Mayer Inc., Culver City, Calif., 1974-80; v.p., gen. counsel, corp. sec. Metro-Goldwyn-Mayer Film Co., Culver City, 1980-82; gen. counsel, corp. sec. MGM/UA Entertainment Co., Culver City, 1982-84. Served to lt. (s.g.) USCGR, 1953-55. Mem. ABA. Home: Los Angeles, Calif. Died Sept. 15, 1984.

FICKLEN, JACK HOWELLS, editorial cartoonist; b. Waco, Tex., Apr. 18, 1911; s. Fielding and Bessie (Howells) F.; student So. Methodist U., 1930-32, Dallas Creative Center, 1964; m. Mary Alice Brown, Oct. 21, 1950; children—Molly Bess, Jack Howells, Robert F. Copyboy, Dallas News, 1928-35, layout artist, photog. retoucher, 1935-37, sports cartoonist, 1937-40, editorial cartoonist, 1937-40, 46-77, ret., 1977; syndicated cartoonist Register & Tribune Syndicate, Des Moines, 1940-45. Book illustrator, free lance cartoonist, 1930-80, owner, mgr. Avalon Features Syndicate, editorial cartoon service, Dallas, 1960—; work exhibited Archives Am. Art, Detroit, U. Mo. Sch. Journalism, Wayne State U., Congl. Record, Presdl. Mus., Odessa, Tex.; permanent exhbn. Assn. Am. Editorial Cartoonists Assn., Dallas Hall of State. Dir. communications Dallas County Civil Def., 1958-60. Bd. dirs. Tex. Council Wildlife Fedn. Served with AUS, 1940-46; ETO; lt. col. Res. ret. Decorated Bronze Star medal, Croix de Guerre avec paisne (Belgium). Mem. Am. Editorial Cartoonists Assn., Res. Officers Assn., Artists and Craftsmen Assn. Dallas (pres. 1975-76). Democrat. Presbyn. Illustrator: Fundamental Principles of Driving, 1945; Self Government by Texans, 1950; represented in Best Editorial Cartoons of 1972, 74. Home: Dallas, Tex. Died Oct. 20, 1980.

FIEDELBAUM, HERMAN, hotel operator; b. Austria, Dec. 25, 1889; s. Moses and Elka Dora (Roth) F.; m. Helena Reitman, Nov. 21, 1915; children—Maurice, Leo A., Betram, Irwin. Came to U.S., 1905, naturalized, 1922. Mfr. ladies dresses, 1912-25; engaged in bldg. constrn., 1925-33, in ins. bus., 1926-40, as hotel operator, from 1938; chmn. bd. Fields Hotels, N.Y.C., from 1955. Bd. dirs. Jewish Meml. Hosp., N.Y.C., Infants Home of Bklyn.; pres. Stuyvesant Polyclinic, N.Y.C. Home: N.Y.C. 17. †

FIELDER, PARKER CLINTON, legal educator; b. Chgo., Oct. 20, 1918; s. Harold Clinton and Adrienne (Parker) F.; m. Marguerite Sparks, June 16, 1943 (dec. 1976); children—Sydney (Mrs. Terry Seaver), Pamela (Mrs. Robert Wyatt); m. Bonnie Cummins, Feb. 12, 1977. B.S. in Commerce, Northwestern U., 1941; LL.B., U. Tex., 1948. Bar: Tex bar 1948, also U.S. Supreme Ct., other fed. cts 1948. Accounting-auditor Sears, Roebuck & Co., Chgo., 1941-42; prof. law U. Tex., 1948-53, William H. Francis, Jr. prof. law, 1961-85; partner firm Turpin, Kerr, Smith & Dyer, Midland, Tex., 1953-61; vis. prof. U. Pa., 1964-65, So. Meth. U., summer 1968, U. Utah, 1976, Am. U., 1983; research assoc. charge tax project Tex. Legis. Council, 1950; gen. counsel, dir. Permian Corp., 1959-61; spl. cons. Tex. Legis. Property Tax Com., 1974-75. Author articles in field. Editor-in-chief: Tex. Law Rev, 1947-48. Served to capt. AUS, 1942-46; col. Res. Mem. Am. Bar Assn., State Bar Tex. (vice chmn. com. continuing legal edn. 1961-64), Am. Law Inst., Order of Coif, Phi Delta Phi, Chancellors. Mem. Christian Ch. (mem. bd., tchr.). Home: Austin, Tex. Died Jan. 9, 1985.

FIELDING, TEMPLE HORNADAY, author, foreign correspondent; b. N.Y.C., Oct. 8, 1913; s. George Thomas II and Helen Ross (Hornaday) F.; m. Nancy Parker, Oct. 17, 1942; 1 child, Dodge Temple. A.B. cum laude, Princeton, 1939. columnist Hall Syndicate, 1956-57; founder, 1958, Temple Fielding's Epicure Club of Europe; chmn., pres. Fielding Publs., Inc., 1966-83; columnist met. editor Ladies' Home Jour., 1968-83; travel contbg. editor Travel and Leisure, 1970-83; Profl. writer, 1939-83; contbr.: articles Travel and Leisure, Reader's Digest, Saturday Evening Post, Harper's, Life, Mademoiselle, Town and Country, Cosmopolitan, Nations Business; fgn. corr.: articles Town and Country, in Mexico, 1942, Harper's and Reader's Digest, in Yugoslavia, 1944, Reader's Digest, Sat. Eve. Post and Cosmopolitan, in Europe and Africa, 1946, in Ethiopia for, Internat. News Service, 1946; corr.: articles for Sat. Eve. Post, in Arctic, N.W. Territories, Can., 1948; fgn. corr. 13 S.Am. countries for same mags. articles, 1949; newspaper feature writer: articles Christian Sci. Monitor, 1940-49; TV film producer: series on The Fieldings in Europe, NBC, 1954; Author: A Guide to Fort Bragg, 1942-83, Fielding's Travel Guide to Europe, annually 1948-83, Fielding's World Currency Converter, annually 1974-83, Fieldings' World Time Converter, annually, 1967-83, (with Nancy Fielding) Fieldings Shopping Guide to Europe, annually 1957-83, Fielding's Low Cost Guide to Europe, annually 1967-83, Fielding's Living Guide Toll-free Information Service, 1977; Contbr. to: (with Nancy Fielding) Deadline Delayed, 1946. Served to maj. AUS., 1941-45. Recipient Info. Fund award; decorated knight's cross Haederstegn, knight Royal Order Dannebrog Denmark; knight's cross Order Queen Isabel La Catolica; comdr. Order Merito Civil; Gold and Silver medals Order Merito Turistico Spain; knight Royal Order Vasa Sweden; Gold Decoration of Honor Austria; Gold and Silver medals Paris; Silver medal Copenhagen; Hijo Adoptivo City of Pollensa; knight Tuborg League; officer Order des Coteaux Commanderie; Silver medal l'Hospitalite France; Gold Plaque of Merit Federazione Italiana Pubblici Esercize; Cross comdr. Order Merito della Repubblica Italiana Italy; recipient Princeton University Medal of Honor, Distinguished Achievement award Class of, 1939; Flor de Almendro award Spain; named hon. citizen of Amsterdam and Copenhagen; recipient Red Badge of Courage USMC, 1963; spl. citation Pres. Kennedy, 1963; Non Sibi Sed Patria award USMC Res. Officers Assn., 1964. Mem. Union Europeene des Clefs d'Or (hon.), Am. Soc. Journalists and Authors (past pres.), Soc. Am. Travel Writers, Asso. Corresponsales de Prensa Iberoamericana, Grand Order European Tour Operators (hon.), Arctic Inst. (Can.), Adventurers of Denmark (hon.). Clubs: Century (N.Y.C.), Overseas Press (N.Y.C.) (past gov.), Vets. of OSS (N.Y.C.); Saratoga Yacht (Fla.); Travelers Century (Los Angeles); Ski of Great Britain (London); Guild of King Christian IV (Denmark), Knights of Olefant (Denmark); Flying Dutchmen (Netherlands); Lion Watchers (Ethiopia). Address: New York, N.Y. Dec. May 18, 1983.

FIENUP, WILLIAM FRED JOHN, realty co. exec.; b. New Melle, Mo., Dec. 16, 1890; s. Henry Fred and Elise (Hetlage) F.; student City Coll. Law and Finance, St. Louis, also Alexander Hamilton corr. courses; m. Gertrude May Lehr, Oct. 12, 1918; children—Wilbur, Raymond. From office boy to office mgr. Am. Can Co., 1907-22; with R.C. Can Co., St. Louis, 1922-68, exec. v.p., 1961, pres., 1961-68; pres. Justine Realty Co. Bd. dirs. St. Louis YMCA; sec.-treas. Found. for Jr. Trapshooters. Mem. Nat. Fibre Can and Tube Assn. (pres. 1960-61; bd. dirs. from 1961), N.A.M., U.S., Mo., St. Louis chambers commerce. Lutheran. Mason (32). Inventor easy opening biscuit can, spl. telescope can. Home: Chesterfield, MO. †

FIGLEY, KARL D., physician; b. Toledo, O., Apr. 12, 1887; s. Melvin Morgan (D.D.) and Minnie Estelle (Walker) F.; B.S., Ohio Weseleyan Univ., 1908; M.D. Jefferson Med. Coll., 1913; m. Margaret Patterson Morgan, Apr. 23, 1919; children—Melvin Morgan, Harriet Jane (Mrs. George Curtis Urschel, Jr.). Interne King's County Hosp., Brooklyn, 1914-15; resident physician German Hosp., N.Y. City, 1916; pvt. practice medicine, Toledo, from 1920, splist. in allergies from 1928; attdg. phys. Toledo Hosp.; occaisonal lecturer, Univ. Mich. Med. Sch. from 1940. Capt. Med. corps, World War I, A.E.F., 1917-19. Fellow: A.C.P., Am. Acad. Allergy (pres. 1948), A.M.A. Diplomate Am. Bd. Internal Medicine, 1943. Mem. A.R.C. (mem. bd. trustees Toledo chpt.), Toledo Mental Hygiene Assn. (mem. bd. trustees); Alpha Omega Alpha. Republican. Protestant. Clubs: Rotary International Inverness, Toledo. Contbr. articles to med. publs. Home: Westmoreland, Toledo 7. †

FILAS, FRANCIS LAD, priest, theology educator; b. Cicero, Ill., June 4, 1915; s. Thomas Martin and Emily (Seery) F. A.B., Loyola U. Chgo., 1937, M.A., 1943; S.T.D., W. Baden (Ind.) Pontifical U., 1952. Joined Soc. of Jesus, 1932; ordained priest Roman Catholic Ch., 1945; tchr. theology U. Detroit, 1946-48; prof. theology Loyola U., Chgo., 1950-85, chmn. dept., 1959-67; writer, lectr. Cana Conf., also; family counselling; spl. research theology St. Joseph; lectr. radio, TV. Vice pres. Documentation and Research Center, North Am. Soc. of Josephology, St. Joseph's Oratory, Montreal, Can., 1952-62. Author: The Man Nearest to Christ, 1944, The Family for Families, 1947, Joseph and Jesus, 1952, His Heart in Our Work, 1952, Joseph Most Just, 1956, The Parables of Jesus, 1959, St. Joseph and Daily Christian Living, 1959, Joseph: The Man Closest to Jesus, 1962, Sex Education in the Family, 1966, St. Joseph After Vatican II, 1968, How to Read Your Bible, 1978; Recorded albums and tapes on family life, mental depression and philosophy of religion, 1964—; filmstrips on Bibl. history and geography of Israel Documentaries on Shroud of Turin. Mem. Am. Mariological Soc., Cath. Bibl. Assn., Holy Shroud Guild (v.p.). Spl. research on Pontius Pilate coins' imprints on Shroud of Turin. Address: Chicago, Ill. Died Feb. 15, 1985.

FINDEISEN, JOHN ORSON, business exec.; born Nashville, Tenn., May 21, 1889; s. John Edward and Lulu M. (Hill) F.; B.S., in Mech. Engring., U. Pa., 1912; m. Myrtle M. McKee, Oct. 4, 1916; 1 son, John Orson. Vice pres., merchandise dir. True Temper Corp. Served as 1st lt., Ordnance Corps, U.S. Army, World War I. Mem. Alpha Chi Rho. Republican. Episcopalian. Clubs: Country, Union, Hermit, Skating (Cleveland). Home: Chagrin Falls, Ohio. †

FINDLAY, ALLAN, lawyer; b. Watson, Sask., Can., Aug. 17, 1914; s. Roy Pattullo and Muriel (Stephens) F.; m. Dorothy Graham Smith, Aug. 9, 1947; children—Marion Morris, Carol Reid, Paul, Allan, Donald. B.A., King's U., 1934; postgrad., Dalhousie U. Law Sch., 1934-35; B.A., Oxford (Eng.) U., 1938, B.C.L., 1939. Bar: Called to N.S. bar 1946, Ont. bar 1946, created Queen's counsel 1954. With firm Tilley, Carson & Findlay (and predecessor), Toronto, from 1946, partner, from 1950; Dir. Canadian Pacific Ltd., Kerr Addison Mines Ltd. Served with RCAF, 1941-45. Rhodes scholar for N.S., 1936. Clubs: Toronto (Toronto), Rosedale Golf (Toronto). Home: Toronto ON, Canada.

FINN, SAMUEL LAWRENCE, lawyer, corp. exec.; b. N.Y.C., June 3, 1890; s. Samuel and Ida (Schwartz) F.; student U. Dayton, 1920-22. H.H.D., 1957; m. Lillian R. Evans, Sept. 15, 1917; children—Chester E., Celeste F. (wife of Dr. Robert Klein). Admitted to Ohio bar, 1914, practiced in Dayton; partner Estabrook, Finn & McKee, from 1920. Sec., dir. Hewitt Soap Co., Inc.; pres. Chester Investment Co.; pres., dir. Ludlow Realty Co., Dayton; v.p., dir. Nat. Foundry & Furnace Co., Mercer Foundry Co., Harkit Sales Co., Dayton, Victor Realty Co.; treas., dir. Stroop Agrl. Co., Troylon Farms, Inc.; sec., dir. T.K. Bar Cattle Co., Grays Realty Co., Burton Sanford Investment Co., dir., mem. exec. com. Dayton Power & Light Co., mem. bd. dirs. other corps. Past pres. Dayton Community Chest; secretary Metropolitan Community Studies, Inc.; mem. Selective Service Commn. Ohio, World War II. Pres. bd. trustees Dayton U.; trustee Dayton Found. Mem. Am., Ohio, Dayton bar assns. Clubs: Lawyers; Newcomen; Towne, Bicycle. Home: Dayton, OH. †

FINNEY, NAT(HANIEL) S(OLON), newspaper correspondent; b. Stewartville, Minn., Oct. 10, 1903; s. Ross Lee and Caroline (Mitchell) F.; A.B., U. of Minn., 1927; m. Flora Edwards, Apr. 5, 1930. Reporter, Minneapolis Star, 1925-26, 1927-29; with Harcourt, Brace & Co., pubs., 1929-30; editor, bldg. trade publ., 1930-33; reporter, Minneapolis Star, 1933-35; city editor, Mpls. Star Jour., 1935-39, feature editor, 1939-41; Washington correspondent, Minneapolis Star and Tribune, Look Mag., 1941-50; editorial page editor Minneapolis Star, 1950-53; chief Washington bur. Buffalo Evening News since 1953. Received Raymond Clapper Memorial Award, 1947; Pulitzer Prize for Nat. Affairs Reporting, 1948. Outstanding Achievement award U. Minn., 1952. Mem. Overseas Writers, White House Corrs. Assn., Chi Phi, Sigma Delta Chi. Club: National Press, The Gridiron (Washington); Chevy Chase. Home: Bethesda, Md. Died Dec. 18, 1982.

FIROR, J(OHN) WILLIAM, SR., agricultural economist; b. Thurmont, Md., Sept. 23, 1887; s. William Leonard and Anna Catharine (Wisotzkey) F.; B.S. (horticulture), Univ. of Md., 1908; student, Univ. of Chicago, summer, 1909. Cornell Univ., summer, 1910; grad., U.S. Sch. of Arty. Fire, 1918; M.S. (agr.). Univ. of Ga., 1931; m. Mary Valentine Moss, June 15, 1920; children—Anne Byrd (Mrs. Andrew M. Scott), David Leonhard, John William, Hugh Valentine. Teacher, prep. sch., Bethel Mil. Acad. Warrenton, Va., 1908-10; mem. faculty Univ. of West Va., 1911; mem. faculty, Univ. of Ga., 1912-51 (with leaves of absence for mil. service, pvt. bus., 1920-22, and various agrl. activities for State of Ga.); organized Dept. of Agrl. Econs., U. Ga., 1928, now prof. emeritus of agricultural econs., ret. Mem. of Ga. State Com. Agrl. Adjustment Research project, 1934; state leader, Agrl. Program Planning project, 1935-36; mem. staff Governor's Agrl. and Indsl. Development Bd., Ga., 1944-45; mem. City Council, Athens, Ga., 1947-48. Served as 1st lt., A.E.F., 1917-19; edn. officer and dir. of troop sch., U.S.A.A.F., Lowry Field, Colo., 1942-44. Mem. Am. Legion, Vets. of Fgn. Wars, Am. Farm Econs. Assn., Agrl. Econs. Assn. of Ga. (organizer, 1945), Beta Gamma Sigma. Phi Kappa Phi, Alpha Kappa Psi. Democrat. Author articles on agrl. subjects. Home: Athens, Ga. †

FISCHELIS, ROBERT PHILIPP, pharmacist, adminstr.; b. Phila., Pa., Aug. 16, 1891; s. Philipp and Ernestine (Kempt) F.; Ph.G., Medico-Chirurgical Coll. of Phila., 1911, Ph.C., 1912, Pharm.D., 1913; B.Sc. in chemistry, Temple U., 1913; Pharm.M., Phila. Coll. of Pharmacy, 1918; spl. courses U. of Pa., 1916-18; hon. Pharm.D., U. of Conn. Coll. of Pharmacy, 1934; hon. Sc.D., Rutgers Univ., 1942; Phila. Coll. Pharmacy and Sci., 1945; married Juanita Celestine Deer, February 24, 1919. Instr. in pharmacy and organic chemistry, Medico-Chirurgical Coll., Phila., 1912-14; chemist H. K. Mulford Co., 1916-19; spl. lectr. Phila. Coll. Pharmacy, 1917-45; cons. pharmacist and chemist since 1919; cons., adv., or mem. control bds. or commns. various govtl. agencies, state and federal; commissioned sr. pharmacist U.S.P.H.S. Res., 1945, pharmacist dir. (col.), 1950; cooperating state ofcl. Food and Drug Administration, Federal Security Agency 1926-44; mem. research staff Com. on Costs of Medical Care, 1929-33; founder Pa. Pharmacist, editor, 1916-19; founder N.J. Jour. of Pharmacy, editor, 1927-30 and 1935-46. Served as sergt. 1st class in Chem. Warfare Service, U.S. Army, 1918. Adviser Am. delegation Internat. Health Conf., 1946; member exec. com. Nat. Health Assembly, 1948-49; hon. cons. Bur. Medicine and Surgery, U.S. Navy; cons. to surgeon gen. U.S. Army; cons. to Office Civil Defense Planning and Nat. Security Resources Bd. professorial lecturer George Washington Univ. Mem. N.J. State Bd. of Health, 1939-47. Mem. revision com. U.S. Pharmacopoeia 1940-50; mem. Am. Council on Pharm. Edn.; mem. com. on drugs and medical supplies, division medical sciences, National Research Council. Fellow A.A.A.S.; Am. Pub. Health Assns.; mem. Am. Social Hygiene Assn. (sec. 1945-49). Am. Pharm. Assn., Am. Chem. Soc., A.M.A., Nat. Assn. Bds. of Pharmacy, and several other profl. and sci. socs., also Am. Legion. Episcopalian. Club: Chemists (N.Y.C.). Collaborator (with 38 others) Remington's Practice of Pharmacy, 7th edition, 1926. Co-author books; editor various publications. Contbr. to various pharm. and sci. jours.; editorial dir. Jour. Am. Pharm. Assn. Awarded Remington Medal by Am. Pharm. Assn., 1943; Lascoff Award, Am. Coll. Apothecaries, 1952. Home: Washington, D.C. Died Oct. 14, 1981.

FISCHER, HAROLD ROBERT, banker; b. Kewanee, Ill., Aug. 28, 1902; s. Emil and Sarah (Hodge) F.; student U. Chgo., 1920-21, Am. Inst. Banking, Grad. Sch. Banking, Rutgers U., 1945; m. Goldie Gamble, May 21, 1925; children—James Robert, Nancy Jean and Sally Ann (twins). Bookkeeper, asst. cashier and trust officer Union State Savs. Bank & Trust Co., Kewanee, Ill., 1922-31; asst. receiver Ill. State Bank Liquidation, 1931-42; asst. cashier First Granite City Nat. Bank, 1942-44, v.p., 1944-46, pres. 1946-68, chmn. bd., 1968-71, vice chmn., 1971-77. Past chmn., dir. Tri-Cities Port Authority. Bd. dirs. United Fund, YMCA; past chmn. Tri-Cities ARC, Tri-Cities Community Chest, Cahokia council Boy Scouts Am.; past chmn. bd. trustees So. Ill. U. Mem. Tri-Cities C. of C.

Methodist. Elk. Club: Granite City Optimist. Home: Granite City, Ill. Died July 10, 1985.

FISCHER, HUGO BREED, civil engineer, educator; b. Lakehurst, N.J., Mar. 16, 1937; s. Hugo Carl and Sara Breed (Lindsay) F.; B.S., Calif. Inst. Tech., 1958, M.S., 1963, Ph.D., 1966; m. Frances Jocyln Best, Feb. 10, 1962; children—Gavin, Mirren. Asst. prof. civil engring. U. Calif., Berkeley, 1966-70, assoc. prof., 1970-74, prof., 1974-83; pres. Hugo B. Fischer. Served with USAF, 1958-62. Recipient Straub award, 1966. Mem. ASCE (Croes medal 1969, Hilgard prize 1971, Huber prize 1974), Internat. Assn. Hydraulic Research, Am. Geophys. Union, Sigma Xi. Sr. author: Mixining in Inland and Coastal Waters, 1979. Home: Berkeley, Calif. Dec. May 22, 1983.

FISCHETTI, JOHN, cartoonist; b. Brooklyn, N.Y., Sept. 27, 1916; s. Pietro and Emanuela (Navarra) F.; student Pratt Inst., 1937-40; D.F.A. (hon.) Colby Coll., 1969; m. Karen Mortenson, Oct. 25, 1948; children—Peter, Michael. Worked on animated films for Walt Disney; drew his 1st editorial cartoons for Chgo. Sun (now Sun-Times); did illustrations for Coronet, Esquire, Sat. Eve. Post, Collier's N.Y. Times; became syndicated cartoonist Newspaper Enterprise Assn., 1950, staff cartoonist N.Y. Herald Tribune, 1962; later cartoonist Publishers' Newspaper Syndicate (now subsidiary Field Enterprises Inc.); chief editorial cartoonist Chgo. Daily News; with Field Newspaper syndicate. Served with Signal Corps, AUS. Recipient Pulitizer Prize, 1969; named Best Editorial Cartoonist, Nat. Cartoonist Soc., 4 times, Sigma Delta Chi award, 1954, 56, Am. Civil Liberties award, 1972, N.Y. Newspaper Guild Front-page award, 1962. Died Nov. 18, 1980.*

FISH, HAMILTON, congressman; b. Garrison, Putnam County, N.Y., Dec. 7, 1888; s. Hamilton F.; A.B., cum laude, Harvard, 1910; studied law same univ., 1910-11; m. Grace, dau. Alfred Chapin, former mayor of Brooklyn, N.Y., Sept. 24, 1921. Vice-president John C. Paige & Co., gen. ins.; mem. N.Y. Assembly, 1914-16; elected to 66th Congress (1919-21) to fill vacancy caused by resignation of Hon. Edmund Platt; reëlected 67th to 78th Congresses (1921-45), 26th N.Y. District. Commd. captain Colored Inf., 15th N.Y. Vols., later known as 369th Inf.; took part in Battle of Champagne, July 15, 1918, and Sept. following; maj. inf., 4th Div., Army of Occupation; grad. Army and Gen. Staff Coll., A.E.F.; col. of reserves. Republican. Home: Newburgh, N.Y.†

FISH, ROBERT L., author. Author numerous books including Incredible Schlock Holmes, 1966; The Bridge That Went Nowhere, 1968; Murder League, 1968; Xavier Affair, 1969; Rub-A-Dub-Dub, 1971; Green Hell, 1971; The Tricks of the Trade, 1972. Recipient Edgar novel awards Mystery Writers Am., 1962, short story awards, 1972, 73. Home: Trumbull, Conn. Died Feb. 23, 1981.

FISHEL, WAITE PHILIP, prof. metallurgy; b. Pleasant City, O., Dec. 9, 1890; s. John Benson and Anna May (Bugher) F.; B.S., Ohio University, 1918; M.S., Ia. State Coll., 1922, Ph.D., 1936; m. Ruth Spaid, Dec. 5, 1912; 1 son, Myron Philip. Instr. chemistry, Ohio Univ., 1917-19; grad. student and instr. Ia. State Coll., 1919-23; became instr. metallurgy Vanderbilt U., Nashville, Tenn., 1923, later asst. prof. and asso. prof., prof. metallurgy from 1941. Mem. Am. Chem. Soc., Am. Soc. for Metals, Am. Inst. Mining and Metall. Engrs., Am. Foundrymens Assn. Torch (Ohio U.), Sigma Xi, Delta Tau Delta. Member Christian Ch. Home: Nashville, Tenn. †

FISHER, ADRIAN SANFORD, lawyer, former univ. dean; b. Memphis, Jan. 21, 1914; s. Hubert Frederick and Louise (Sanford) F.; A.B., Princeton, 1934, LL.D., 1965; LL.B., Harvard, 1937, Georgetown U., 1977; m. Laura Graham, Jan. 12, 1945; children—Laura Donelson, Louise Sanford. Admitted to Tenn. bar, 1938; law clk. to Supreme Ct. Justice Brandeis, 1938, Justice Frankfurter, 1939; atty. various govt. agys., 1939-41; asst. chief. Fgn. Funds Control div. U.S. Dept. State, 1941-42; asst. to asst. sec. of war, 1944; solicitor U.S. Dept. Commerce, 1947-48; gen. counsel AEC, 1948-49; legal adviser Dept. State, 1949-53; dep. dir. U.S. Arms Control and Disarmament Agy., 1961-69, U.S. rep. ENDC, Geneva, 1964, 66-69, U.S. ambassador to Conf. of Com. on Disarmament Geneva, 1977-83; pvt. law practice, former asso. Covington & Burling; v.p. counsel Washington Post Co.; prof. internat. law and internat. trade, Georgetown U. Law Center, dean, 1969-75, Francis Cabell Brown prof. internat. law, 1975-77; legal adviser to U.S. Del. to Press, Paris, 1952; mem. Pres.'s Commmn. on Immigration and Naturalization; mem. U.S. Panel Permanent Ct. Arbitration. Tech. adviser to U.S. judges, Internat. Mil. Tribunal, Nuremberg, Germany, 1946. Served to capt. USAAF, 1942-43, 45. Awarded Legion of Merit. Mem. Am. Law Inst., Am. Bar Assn., Bar Assn. D.C., Phi Beta Kappa. Democrat. Presbyn. Club: Metropolitan (Washington). Home: Washington, D.C.. Died Mar. 18, 1983.

FISHER, ARTHUR NORMAN, dir., producer; b. Bklyn., Feb. 6, 1934; s. David and Ann (Landman) F.; student Hunter Coll., 1951-53, Syracuse U., 1955; children—Shari, Dani Yale. Producer-dir. numerous TV shows and series including: Andy Williams Series, 1969-71, Sonny & Cher, 1971-75, Cher Spls., Neil Diamond Spl., Donny and Marie series, 1975-78; producer, dir. NBC-Universal. Served with USNR, 1953-55. Recipient Emmy award, 1972. Mem. Dirs. Guild Am. (award 1978), Writers Guild Am., Producers Guild Am., Nat. Acad. TV Arts and Scis. Author: Garden of Innocence. Home: Los Angeles, Calif. Died Feb. 22, 1984.

FISHER, LOUIS JOSEPH, lawyer, organization executive; b. Waterbury, Conn., Mar. 13, 1901; s. Louis and Philomena (de Zinno) F.; m. Ethel McMullan, Dec. 29, 1931; children: Louis Joseph III, John Reed, David Kendall. Student, N.Y.U., 1921, U. N.C., 1925. Bar: N.C. bar 1925. Practiced in, High Point; asst. county atty. Guilford County, 1932-43; pros. atty. High Point Municipal Ct., 1946-51, 60-81. Mem. Amateur Athletic Union U.S., 1936-81; pres. Carolinas Assn., 1942-50, nat. publicity chmn., 1950, nat. chmn. law and legislation com., 1951-57, mem. exec. com. fgn. relations, 1948-81, trustee surplus funds, 1955-81, chmn. championships awards, 1959-60, 1st v.p., 1959-61, pres., 1961-81; chmn. Sullivan award com., 1973-81; charter Mercury Athletic Club, High Point, 1941, pres., 1941-43; chmn. High Point Boxing and Wrestling Commn., 1941-81; bd. dirs. U.S. Olympic Assn., 1952-56, 56-60, 60-81, mem. games coms., 1952-81, womens swimming com., 1952-81, U.S. rep., 1956-60; U.S. rep. Internat. Amateur Athletic Fedn., 1962-81; asso. counselor U.S. Olympic Com., 1973-81, mem. internat. relations com., 1977; hon. dir. French-Swiss Ski Coll., Boone, N.C.; Sec. Guilford County Rd. Elections, 1933-46; govt. appeal agt. local SSS, 1940-81; Vice chmn. Guilford County Dem. Exec. Com., 1931-33; chmn. High Point Twp. Dem. Exec. Com., 1931-33; mem. N.C. Dem. Com., 1940-46; del. Nat. Dem. Conv., 1944; mayor Pinehaven Village, N.C., 1954-56; Trustee Col. Harry B. Henshell Found. Recipient citations and certificates for SSS service; award for contbn. to amateur athletics Citizens Savs. Athletic Found., 1977; named High Pointer of Week High Point Enterprise, Dec. 1961; Tar Heel of Week Raleigh News and Observer, Apr. 1962; citation for sportsmanship from Mo. Legislature; Louis J. Fisher award established by Carolinas assn. U.S. Amateur Athletic Union, 1956. Fellow Internat. Soc. Barristers; mem. ABA, N.C. Bar Assn., 18th Jud. Bar Assn., High Point Bar Assn. (pres. 1951-52, award for distinguished service 1951), Fed. Bar Assn. (pres. chpt. 1975-81), N.C. Bar (mem. council), Amateur Athletic Union (chmn. nat. adv. com., counsellor N.C.), High Point C. of C., High Point Hist. Soc. (dir.), Comml. Law League Am., Am. Judicature Soc., Fed. Bar Assn., So. Furniture Club (dir.), Delta Theta Phi. Clubs: 1859, Elks. Home: High Point, NC.

FISHER, RONALD AYLMER, scientist; b. East Finchley, Eng., Feb. 17, 1890; s. George and Katie (Heath) F.; Sc.D., Gonville and Caius Coll., Cambridge U., 1913; D.Sc., Am. U., 1932, Harvard, 1936, U. London, 1946, U. Chgo., 1952; LL.D., Calcutta U. 1939, Glasgow U., 1947; m. Ruth Eileen Guinness, Apr. 26, 1918; 2 sons, 6 daus. With Rothamsted Expt. Sta., 1919-33; Galton prof. U. London, 1933-43; Balfour prof. U. Cambridge, from 1943. Created Knight, 1952. Fellow Royal Soc.; mem. Nat. Acad. Scis., Am. Acad. Arts and Scis., Am. Philos. Soc. Royal Swedish Acad. Scis., Royal Danish Acad. Scis., Specialty theoretical, applied statistics, theory of evolution, exptl. genetics.†

FISHER, RUSSELL SYLVESTER, pathologist, state ofcl.; b. Bernie, Mo., Nov. 15, 1916; s. Jacob R. and Russee (Solomon) F.; m. Marjorie Parker, Nov. 27, 1937; children—Patricia Fisher McHold, Martha Fisher Ryker. B.S., Ga. Sch. Tech., 1937; M.D., Med. Coll. Va., 1942. Diplomate: Am. Bd. Pathology (trustee from 1969, pres. 1979). Intern Henry Ford Hosp., Detroit, 1942-43, resident, 1943-44; research fellow Harvard U. Med. Sch., Boston, 1946-49; chief med. examiner State of Md., Balt., from 1949; prof. forensic pathology U. Md. Med. Sch., from 1949; lectr. forensic pathology Johns Hopkins U., from 1949; asso. in forensic pathology Johns Hopkins U. (Sch. Hygiene and Pub. Health), from 1955; mem. Md. Adv. Council on Comprehensive Planning, 1968-69; sec., treas. bd. dirs. Md. Med.-Legal Found., Inc. Contbr. articles to profl. jours. Served with USNR, 1944-46. Named Pathologist of Yr., awarded jointly by Am. Soc. Clin. Pathologists and Coll. Am. Pathologists, 1979. Fellow Am. Acad. Forensic Sci. (pres. 1960-61); mem. AMA (del. from 1966, council on med. edn. from 1973, chmn. 1978-79, liaison com. grad. med. edn. 1974-79, chmn. 1977), Med. and Chirurg. Faculty Md. (pres. 1969-70), Balt. City Med. Soc., Am. Soc. Clin. Pathologists, Coll. Am. Pathologists, Nat. Assn. Med. Examiners (chmn. exec. com. 1968-69), Am. Assn. Pathologists, Bacteriology, Internat. Acad. Pathologists, Am. Assn. Blood Banks (dir. from 1972). Home: Crownsville, MD.

FISHER, SHELTON, publisher; b. Memphis, May 7, 1911; s. Lester Alan and Edna (Shelton) F.; m. Louise Tait, June 27, 1936; children—Shelton Tait, Anthony Kent, Anne Louise (Mrs. Jonathan Colby), Christopher Alan. Student, Columbia, 1929-30; B.S., U.S. Naval Acad., 1934; D.Litt., Westminster Coll., 1968; LL.D., Susquehanna U., 1968. With Curtis Pub. Co., 1935-38, McCann-Erickson Advt., 1938-40; joined McGraw-Hill Pub. Co. (now McGraw-Hill, Inc.), 1940; promotion mgr. Business Week, 1940-42; sr. v.p. McGraw Hill Pubs., 1958-62, pres., 1963-65, McGraw-Hill, Inc., 1966-74, chief exec. officer, 1968-75, chmn. bd., 1974-76; cons. to bd., 1976-85; chmn. Am. Bus. Press, 1964-66; dir. Borden, Inc., 1969-76, Rockwell Mfg., Inc., 1970-73; dir. Sperry Rand Corp., NL Industries, Koger Properties, Inc., Salzburg Seminar Am. Studies. Asst. pub.: Science Illustrated, 1946-49; pub.: Power, 1949-57, Fleet Owner, 1954-58, Elec. Merchandising, 1957-59. Trustee U.S. Naval Acad. Found., Westminster Coll.; mem. Mgmt. Advisory Bd. Mayor N.Y.C. Served as lt. comdr. USNR, 1942-46. Mem. Delta Kappa Epsilon. Clubs: University (N.Y.C.); Wee Burn Country. Home: Darien, Conn. Died Mar. 15, 1985.

FISHER, WALTER H(ARRISON), lawyer; b. Roseboro, N.C., Oct. 22, 1889; s. Alex F. and Mary Louise (Owen) F.; grad. Buies Creek (N.C.) Acad., 1911, Wake Forest (N.C.) Coll., 1915; m. Lossie S. Herring, Mar. 27, 1917; children—Walter Clark, J. Franklin. Admitted to N.C. bar, 1915, and began practice at Clinton; U.S. dist. atty., Eastern N.C. Dist., 1929-34; in practice at Clinton. Mem. N.C. State Senate, 1915-17, 1919-21; Rep. nominee for state solicitor, 1922, 26, for mem. Congress, 1924, for lt. gov. of N.C., 1928, for justice Supreme Court, 1934; del. to Rep. Nat. Conv., 1928. Methodist. Home: Clinton, N.C. †

FISHER, YULE, former assn. exec.; b. Edwardsville, Ill., Jan. 15, 1912; s. Martin Hamilton and Marguerite Wheeler (Metcalfe) F.; A.B., Am. U., 1932; LL.B., J.D., George Washington U., 1935; m. Genevieve Wilder Marsh, June 3, 1949; children—David Yule, Genevieve Cutler, Charles Martin. With Nat. Hwy. Users Conf., Washington, 1934-69, dir., 1968-69; exec. v.p. Hwy. Users Fedn. for Safety and Mobility, Washington, 1970-71; adv. bd. Columbia Fed. Savs. & Loan. Bd. mgmt. Camp Letts, YMCA. Chmn., Nat. Com. on Uniform Traffic Laws, 1964-73. Served to lt. comdr. USNR, 1942-45. Recipient Alumni award Am. U., 1964; citation for Distinguished Service Nat. Com. Uniform Traffic Laws, 1971; Silver Beaver award Boy Scouts Am., 1939. Mem. Hwy. Research Bd., Alpha Tau Omega. Contbr. articles to profl. lit. Home: Chevy Chase, Md. Died Mar. 11, 1983.

FISHLEIGH, CLARENCE TURNER, automotive engineer; b. Chgo., July 31, 1895; s. John A. and Henrietta P. (Turner) F.; m. Thea Holste, May 16, 1923; children—Elayne Fishleigh Bramwell, Marilyn Fishleigh Pierce. B.S. in Elec. Engring, U. Mich., 1917; J.d., Detroit Coll. Law, 1939. Bar: Mich. bar 1939, Ill. bar 1952. Registered profl. engr., Ill., Mich., N.Y., Ohio, Fla., Tex. Mech. prodn. engr. Ford Motor Co., Highland Park, Mich., 1919-22; exptl. motor testing asst., prodn. mgr. Am. Car and Foundry Co., Chgo., 1922-23, Rich Tool Co., Detroit, 1923-24; mgr. Clarence T. Fishleigh Co., Wilmette, Ill., 1924-30; assoc. engr., cons. engr. Walter T. Fishleigh, Detroit, 1930-47, cons. automotive engring., patents, 1947-51, Chgo., 1951-73, Deerfield, Ill., 1973-82. Served as 2d lt. A.C. U.S. Army, 1917-19. Decorated Croix de Guerre France. Mem. Nat. Ohio socs. profl. engrs., Soc. Automotive Engrs., ASME, Western Soc. Engrs., Engring. Soc. Detroit, Am., Mich. patent law assns., Patent Law Assn. Chgo., Chgo. Bar Assn., Ill. Bar Assn., Mich. Bar Assn., Kappa Sigma, Sigma Nu Phi. Club: Union League (Chgo.). Home: Deerfield, Ill. Dec. Sept. 2, 1983.

FISK, JAMES BROWN, physical scis. research exec.; b. West Warwick, R.I., Aug. 30, 1910; s. Henry James and Bertha (Brown) F.; B.S., Mass. Inst. Tech., 1931, Ph.D., 1935; M.A. (hon.), Harvard U., 1947; D.Sc., Carnegie Inst. Tech., 1956, Williams Coll., 1958, Newark Coll. Engring., 1959, Columbia U., 1960, Colby Coll., 1962, N.Y.U., 1963, Rutgers U., 1967. Drew U., Harvard, 1969; D.Eng., U. Mich., 1963, U. Akron, 1963; LL.D., Lehigh U., 1967, Ill. Inst. Tech., 1967. Fairleigh Dickinson U., 1973; Litt.D., Newark State Coll., 1969; m. Cynthia Hoar, June 10, 1938; childlren—Samuel, Zachary, Charles. Research asst. aero. engring. Mass. Inst. Tech., 1931; Proctor traveling fellow Trinity Coll., Cambridge, Eng., 1932-34; teaching fellow physics Mass. Inst. Tech., 1934-36; mem. Soc. of Fellows, Harvard, 1936-38, sr. fellow, 1949; asso. prof. physics U. N.C., 1939; electronics research engy., asst. dir. phys. research Bell Telephone Labs., 1939-47, dir., 1949-51, dir. research phys. scis., 1952-54, v.p. research, 1954-55, exec. v.p., 1955-58, dir., 1955-74; pres. Bell Telephone Labs, 1959-73, chmn. bd., 1973-74; dir. Cummins Engine Co., Am. Cyanamid Co., Equitable Life Assurance Soc., Corning Glass Works, Cabot Corp., Neptune Internat. Co. Gordon McKay prof. applied physics, Harvard, 1947-49; dir. div. research AEC, 1947-48, mem. gen. adv. com., 1952-58; mem. President's Sci. Adv. Com., 1957-60, cons., 1960-73. Mem. corp. Mass. Inst. Tech.; trustee John Simon Guggenheim Meml. Found., Alfred P. Sloan Found.; bd. dirs. Sloan-Kettering Inst. for Cancer Research; bd. overseers Harvard, 1961-67. Recipient Indsl. Research Inst. medal, 1963; citation Midwest Research Inst., 1968; Washington award Western Soc. Engrs., 1968; Advancement Research medal Am. Soc. Metals, 1974, Hoover medal, 1975; Presdl. certificate of Merit, World War II. Fellow Am. Phys. Soc., Am. Acad. Arts and Scis., I.E.E.E.; mem. Nat. Acad. Engring. (Founders medal 1975), Nat. Acad. Sci., Am. Philos. Soc., Sigma Xi, Tau Beta Pi. Clubs: Harvard (N.Y.C.); Ausable (St. Huberts, N.Y.); Somerset Hills Asso. editor Phys. Rev., 1945-48. Contbr. articles to profl. periodicals. Home: Basking Ridge, N.J. Died Aug. 10, 1981.

FITCH, A(LBERT) L(EWIS), b. Byron Center, Mich., Oct, 3, 1887; s. Charles Lewis and Nancy (Rumbaugh) F.; A.B. Albion (Mich.) Coll., 1911, A.M., 1912; Ph.D., U. of Mich., 1916; m. Emma Elizabeth Leeson, Jan. 1, 1914. Teacher of science, Allegan (Mich.) High Sch., 1913-15; research physicist Western Electric Co., New York,

1916-19; asso. prof. of physics, Univ. of Me., 1919-21, prof., 1921-39, resigned 1939. Mem. A.A.A.S., Am. Physical Soc., Gamma Alpha, Sigma Xi, Phi Kappa Phi. Methodist. Address: New Sharon, Maine.†

FITT, FRANK, clergyman; b. Limerick, Ireland, Sept. 10, 1889; s. Francis Matthew and Harriette (Longbottom) F.; came to U.S., 1905, naturalized citizen; A.B., Williams Coll., 1911; B.D., Union Theol. Sem., 1914; A.M., Columbia, 1915; D.D., Alma (Mich.) Coll., 1931; m. Harriett Bradley, Aug. 15, 1918; children—Mary Bradley (Mrs. Gerald McCarthy), Alfred Bradley. Ordained to ministry of Presbyterian Church, 1915; pastor Highland Park (Ill.) Presbyn. Ch., 1918-30, Grosse Pointe Memorial Ch., Grosse Pointe Farms, Mich., from 1931. Mem. bd. trustees, Lake Forest (Ill.) Coll., 1919-30, Presbyn. Home: 1918-24, Presbyn. Ch. Extension, Chicago, 1924-30, Detroit, 1931-34 and 1936-39. Contbr. to religious publs. Home: Grosse Pointe Farms, Mich. †

FITZ, JOHN ALLEN, ednl. adminstr.; b. Hampton, Iowa, June 8, 1908; s. Stephen Roberts and Edna May (Watson) F.; m. Helen Ann Scott, June 15, 1933; children—Marilyn Ann (Mrs. Mark McClure), Jonelle (Mrs. Nathan L. Simmons), Stephen Scott. A.A., Santa Ana (Calif.) Jr. Coll., 1928; A.B., U. Calif. at Berkeley, 1930, M.A., 1937; student, U. So. Cal., 1945-50; Ed.D., U. Denver, 1955. Secondary sch. tchr., 1931-38, curriculum coordinator, 1938-39, supt. schs., 1939-50, univ. prof., 1952-58; joined U.S. Fgn. Service, 1955, inservice tchr. ednl. adviser, Ethiopia, 1955- 57, edn. adviser, Iran, 1958-60, chief edn. adviser, Salisbury, Rhodesia, 1961-62, Washington, 1963-66; program co-ordinator State Tech. Services Act Programs at U. Calif. at Los Angeles, from 1967; field worker Rocky Mountain Sch. Study Council, 1951-52. Mem. Assn. Supervision and Curriculum Devel., Nat. Soc. Study Edn., AAUP, African Studies Assn., Am. Fgn. Service Assn., Soc. Internat. Devel., Phi Delta Kappa. Home: Anaheim, Calif.

FITZGERALD, ALBERT JOSEPH, former union exec.; b. Sept. 21, 1906. With Gen. Electric Co., 1928-41; pres. local 201, United Elec., Radio and Machine Workers Am., Lynn, Mass., 1939-41, pres. Dist. 2, New Eng., 1940-41, gen. pres., N.Y.C., 1941-78, ret., 1978; sec.-treas. Mass. CIO, 1939-42, v.p. CIO, 1942-49, CIO rep. Selective Service Commn., World War II; asso. mem. War Labor Bd., World War II. Died Mar. 22, 1982.

FITZGERALD, HAROLD ALVIN, former newspaper publisher; b. St. Johns, Mich., Aug. 3, 1896; s. Howard Harold and Zylpha Irene (Shaver) F.; m. Elizabeth Millis, June 16, 1923; children—Howard Harold II, Nancy E. Connolly, Richard Millis. A.B., U. Mich., 1917; LL.D., Oakland U., Mich. State U. With Pontiac (Mich.) Daily Press, 1919-69, telegraph editor and bus. mgr., to 1930, editor and mgr., 1930-44, pub., 1944-66; ret. as chmn.; 1st v.p. A.P., 1951-54, dir., 1954-63; dir. Grand Trunk Ry., 1940-70, Fed. Home Loan Bank Ind.-Mich., 1950-59; v.p. Hillsdale (Mich.) News, 1940-72. Contbr. to: others. Look mag. Former trustee Kingswood, Cranbrook, Brookside schs., Bloomfield Hills, Mich.; former dir. Mich. Soc. for Crippled Children.; Mem. Mich. Constl. Commn., 1942; vice chmn. Cranbrook Found., Bloomfield Hills, 1945-65; Bd. dirs. Ams. Found.; chmn. Univ. Oakland Found. Served as 2d lt., Air Service U.S. Army, 1917-18. Hon. alumnus Mich. State U. Mem. Am. Soc. of Newspaper Editors, Inter-Am. Press Assn. (dir. 1957-68, hon. life dir.), Am. Legion, Alpha Delta Phi, Sigma Delta Chi. Episcopalian (former vestryman). Clubs: Rotarian, Bloomfield Hills Country (past pres.), Orchard Lake Country; Spring Lake Country (Grand Haven, Mich.); Univ. of Mich. (Ann Arbor); Marco Polo (N.Y.C.). Home: Pontiac, Mich. Died Dec. 10, 1984.

FITZGERALD, ROBERT, (STUART FITZGERALD) writer; b. Geneva, N.Y., Oct. 12, 1910; s. Robert Emmet and Anne Montague (Stuart) F.; m. Sarah Morgan, Apr. 19, 1947 (div. div. 1982); children—Hugh Linane, Benedict Robert Campion, Maria Juliana, Peter Michael Augustine, Barnaby John Francis, Caterina Maria Teresa.; m. Penelope Laurans, May 16, 1982. Grad., Choate Sch., Wallingford, Conn., 1929; A.B., Harvard U., 1933; student, Trinity Coll., Cambridge (Eng.) U., 1931-32. Reporter N.Y. Herald Tribune, 1933-35; writer Time mag., 1936-49; instr. lit. Sarah Lawrence Coll., 1946-53, Princeton, 1950-51; fellow Sch. Letters, Ind. U., 1952—; vis. prof. U. Notre Dame, 1957, U. Wash., 1961, Mt. Holyoke Coll., 1964, Harvard U., 1964-65, Nicholas Boylston prof., 1965—, prof. emeritus, 1981. Author: Poems, 1935, A Wreath for the Sea, 1943, In the Rose of Time, 1956, Spring Shade, 1971; Translator: Oedipus at Colonus (Sophocles), 1941, Odyssey (Homer), 1961, Chronique, Birds (St. John Perse), 1961-66, Iliad (Homer), 1974, Aeneid (Virgil), 1983, (with Dudley Fitts) Alcestis (Euripides), 1935, Antigone (Sophocles), 1939, Oedipus Rex (Sophocles), 1949. Guggenheim fellow, 1953, 71; recipient Shelley award Poetry Soc. Am., 1955; grantee creative writing Ford Found., 1959; recipient Bollingen prize for transl., 1961, Landon award for transl., 1976; Ingram Merrill Lit. award, 1978. Fellow Am. Inst. Arts and Letters (award 1957), Am. Acad. Arts and Scis., Acad. Am. Poets (chancellor 1968). Roman Catholic. Clubs: Harvard (N.Y.C.); Saturday (Boston). Address: Cambridge, Mass. Died Jan. 16, 1985.

FITZGIBBONS, GERALD ALOYSIUS, educator; b. Detroit, Mich., July 8, 1888; s. Patrick and Catherine (Barrett) F.; B.A., U. of Detroit, 1909; M.A., St. Louis U., 1918. Joined Soc. of Jesus (Jesuits), 1909; ordained priest R.C. Ch., 1923; instr. in history and English, Creighton U., Omaha, Neb., 1913-15, St. Mary's (Kan.) Coll., 1918-20, Loyola U., Chicago, 1926-27; dir. and asso. editor "The Queen's Work," St. Louis, 1927-31; pres. St. John's U., Toledo, 1931-36; became provincial Chicago Province of the Soc. of Jesus, Sept. 1936; dir. Jesuit Seminary Assn., 1937-39; pastor Bellarmine Chapel, Cincinnati, 1939-45; dir. Laymen's Retreat League of Mich., from 1945. Address: Bloomfield Hills, Mich. †

FITZ-HUGH, GLASSELL SLAUGHTER, otolarynogologist, educator; b. Charlottesville, Va., May 1, 1907; s. Glassell and Orie (Slaughter) Fitz-H.; m. Dorothea Minor Meredith, Sept. 9, 1937; children: Glassell Slaughter, George Meredith, Elizabeth Morrison. Student, Augusta Mil. Acad., 1925-27; M.D., U. Va., 1933. Diplomate: Am. Bd. Otolaryngology. Intern, resident Charity Hosp., New Orleans, 1933-35, U. Va. Hosp., Charlottesville, 1935-37; faculty sch. medicine U. Va., 1937—, prof. otolaryngology, 1951-77, prof. emeritus, 1977-84, chmn. dept., 1951-75, vice chmn. dept., 1975-77; Former mem. communicative disorder research tng. com. NIH. Served as capt. to lt. col. M.C. AUS, 1942-46. Fellow A.C.S. (past rep. to residency rev. com. for otolaryngology); mem. AMA, So. Med. Assn., Med. Soc. Va., Va. Soc. Ophthalmology and Otolaryngology, Am. Acad. Ophthalmology and Otolaryngology, Am. Laryngol. Rhinol. and Otological Soc. (pres. 1967), Am. Acad. Facial Plastic and Reconstructive Surgery, Am. Otological Soc., Am. Laryngol. Assn. (pres. 1974), AAUP, Thomas Jefferson Soc., U. Va. Gen. Alumni Assn. (bd. mgrs.), Am. Soc. Head and Neck Surgery, Soc. U. Otolaryngologists, Va. Acad. Scis., Va. Hearing Found., Am. Council Otolaryngology, Nat. Rehab. Assn., Alpha Omega Alpha. Presbyn. Home: Charlottesville, Va. Oct. 2, 1984.

FITZPATRICK, ALOYSIUS MARK, clergyman; b. Au Sable, Mich., Apr. 25, 1889; s. Edward and Catherine Amelia (Kennedy) F.; student Assumption Coll., Windsor, Ont., Can., 1905-07, St. Thomas Coll., Houston, Tex., 1907-09; S.T.D., Propaganda U., Rome, Italy, 1913, J.C.L., 1912. Ordained priest Roman Cath. Ch., Rome, 1913; asst. pastor St. James Ch., Grand Rapids, Mich., 1913-18, chancellor of Diocese of Grand Rapids, pastor St. Thomas parish and editor Catholic Vigil, 1919-26; editor. The Catholic Universe Bulletin, official newspaper of Diocese of Cleveland, O., 1929; diocesan dir. The Catholic Press from 1937; dir. Cath. Press Union. Served as 1st lt. (chaplain), U.S. Army, 1918-19. Mem. K.C. Home: Cleveland, Ohio. †

FITZ-PATRICK, FRANK GAMBLE, railroad exec.; b. Hamilton, Ont., Can., Aug. 28, 1889; s. Peter Edward John and Minnie Coleman (Wilson) Fitz-P.; brought to U.S., 1893, naturalized, 1903; ed. pub. schs. and bus. coll. in Chicago; m. Maude Miller, March 16, 1918. Clerk, Frank Parmelee Co., 1904-06; with C.&N.-W.Ry. from 1906, as car record and tracing clerk, ticket clerk, cashier and accountant, Chicago, traveling agt., Pittsburgh, New York City, gen. agt., Detroit, 1920, New York, 1920-37, gen. eastern agt., New York, 1937-38, chief traffic officer, Chicago, June 1938-44, vice pres. from June 1944; vice president C.,St.P.M.&O. Ry., since May 1942; vice president North Western Warehouse Co. Served as private to 1st lieutenant, U.S. Army, 1917-19. Mem. Chicago Assn. of Commerce. Mason. Clubs: Union League, Traffic, Chicago (Chicago); Traffic (New York); Minnesota (St. Paul); Minneapolis. Home: Richmond, Ill. †

FITZWATER, OTTIS TEASLEY, utilities exec.; b. Ky., Jan. 22, 1906; s. Henry Elliott and Amy (Bastin) F.; ed. pub. schs.; m. Paula Leigeber, Sept. 30, 1926; children—Donald E., Richard E. With Indpls. Power & Light Co. (and predecessor firm), 1923-79, beginning as timekeeper, successively mem. gen. accounting dept., asst. treas., treas., v.p., 1923-57, pres., 1957-66, chmn. bd., pres., 1966-67, chmn. bd., chief exec., officer, 1967-71, chmn. exec. com., 1971-76, also dir.; dir. Indpls. Life Ins. Co. Bd. dirs. Indpls. United Fund, Crossroads council Boy Scouts Am.; trustee Ind. Central U. Mem. Ind. (dir.), Indpls. (hon. v.p.) chambers commerce, Mem. Ch. of God. Mason (Shriner). Clubs: Columbia, Meridian Hills Country, Indianapolis Athletic (Indpls.). Home: Indianapolis, Ind. Died 1979.

FIXX, JAMES FULLER, editor, writer; b. N.Y.C., Apr. 23, 1932; s. Calvin Henry and Marlys (Fuller) F.; m. Mary J. Durling, June 11, 1957 (div. 1973); children: Paul, John, Elizabeth, Stephen. Student, Ind. U., 1950-52; B.A., Oberlin Coll., 1957. Reporter, Sarasota (Fla.) Jour., 1957-58; feature editor Saturday Rev., 1958-66; exec. editor McCall's, 1966-67, editor, 1967-69; sr. editor Life, 1969-71; articles editor Audience mag., 1971-72; mng. editor Horizon, 1974-76; cons. Pres.'s Council on Phys. Fitness and Sports, 1979-84. Author: Games for the Superintelligent, 1972, More Games for the Superintelligent, 1976, The Complete Book of Running, 1977, Solve It!, 1978, Jim Fixx's Second Book of Running, 1979, Jackpot!, 1982. Mem. Conn. Gov.'s Com. on Fitness, 1980-84. Home: Riverside, Conn. Died July 20, 1984.

FLANAGAN, WILLIAM FRANCIS, education association executive; b. Warwick, R.I., Apr. 10, 1911; s. William Francis and Sarah Frances (Tierney) F.; m. Helen C. Flynn, Aug. 4, 1952 (dec.); children—William Francis III, John J., Sarah A., James V., Ellen L. A.B., Providence Coll., 1936, Ed.D., 1973; M.Ed., R.I. Coll., 1947, Ped.D. (hon.), 1971; Ph.D., U. Conn., 1955; D.A., U. R.I., 1974; Sc.D., Bryant Coll. (hon.), 1979; D.H.L., Roger Wms Coll (Hon), 1978. Tchr. Lockwood High Sch., 1936-40; vice prin. Aldrich Hich Sch., Warwick, R.I., 1940-52, prin., 1952-56; coordinator Warwick Adult Edn. Program, 1949-56; vis. prof. U. Conn., summer 1956; prof. edn. R.I. Coll., 1956-64, dir. summer session, 1958-64, asst. dir. grad. and extension div., 1956-58, dir. grad. studies, 1958-64; pres. R.I. State Systems of Jr. Colls., 1964-78, R.I. Jr. Coll., 1964-78; exec. dir. R.I. Ind. Higher Edn. Assoc., Warwick, R.I., 1979-84. Mem. corp. Providence Coll; trustee Roger Williams Coll.; mem. corp. Kent County Meml. Hosp., Peoples Savs. Bank, R.I., R.I. Hosp.; pres. New Eng. Jr. Coll. Council; chmn. Comm. on Govtl. Affairs, Nat. Council State Dirs. Community Colls.; mem. U.S. Congl. Adv. Comm. on Community Colls.; mem. adv. bd. Tchrs. Coll., Columbia U Center for Community Colls.; chmn. R.I. Public Higher Edn. Council; mem. Govs. R.I. Council on Vocat. Edn. Served to lt. USN, 1942-45. Recipient listing Alumni award Prov. Coll., 1962; Charles Carrol award R.I. Ed. Assoc, 1959; Regents' award State Board of Regent for Ed, 1978; citation for disting. service to edn. R.I. Senate, 1970; citation for disting. service to edn. R.I. House, 1978; Regents' citation Pres. Emeritus R.I. Jr. Coll., 1978; Service Above Self award Providence Rotary, 1978; Man of Yr. award Warwick Rotary, 1979; named to R.I. Heritage Hall of Fame, 1981. Mem. Nat. Assoc. Ind. Colls. and Univs., Nat. Inst. Inc. Colls. and Univs., Assn. Higher Edn., R.I. Secondary Sch. Prins. Assn., R.I. Supts. Assn., Phi Delta Kappa. Roman Catholic. Home: Warwick, R.I. Dec. Jan. 9, 1984.

FLANDERS, HELEN HARTNESS, author, ballad collector, lectr.; b. Springfield, Vt., May 19, 1890; d. James and Lena (Pond) Hartness; grad. Dana Hall, Wellesley, Mass., 1909; M.A., Middlebury Coll., 1942; m. Ralph E. Flanders, Nov. 1, 1911 (dec. Feb. 1970); children—Helen Elizabeth (Mrs. William Whitney Ballard), Anna Hartness (Mrs. Henry P. Balivet, Jr., dec.), James Hartness. Fellow Internat. Inst. Arts and Letters; mem. Am. Northeast folklore socs., Soc. Ethnomusicology, Internat. Folk Music Council, Internat. Congress Ethnol. and Anthrop. Scis., A.A.A.S., poetry socs. Am. and Vt., Washington Lit. Soc., D.A.R., Nat. League Am. Pen Women. Conglist. Clubs: Altrurian, Sulgrave (Washington). Author books; also ballad collections (with others) Vermont Folk-Songs and Ballads, 1931; A Garland of Green Mountain Song, 1934; Country Songs of Vermont, 1937; New Green Mountain Songster, 1939; Vermont Chapbook, 1941; Ballads Migrant in New England, 1953; (poetry anthology) Green Mountain Verse, 1943; Ancient Ballads Traditionally Sung in New England, Vol. I, 1960, Vol. II, 1961, Vol. III, 1963, Vol. IV, 1965; Country News Items and other Poems, 1965. Home: Springfield, Vt. †

FLANIGAN, HORACE C., banker; b. New York, N.Y., July 26, 1890; s. John and Elizabeth (Adams) F.; C.E., Cornell U., 1912; post grad. student engring., U. of Munich, and Tech. Sch. of Munich, 1913-14; m. Aimee Magnus, Oct. 23, 1920; children—John, Peter Magnus, Marjorie Nell, Robert Michael. With Adams Flanigan Co., N.Y., 1914-31; became v.p., dir. Manufacturers Trust Co., 1931, pres., 1951-56, chairman bd., 1956-61; chmn., exec. com. Mfrs. Hanover Trust Co., 1961-62, dir., cons., from 1962; dir. Discount Corporation of New York, also Hilton Hotels Corp., Anchor Hocking Glass Corp.; trustee Dolar Savings Bank of N.Y. Bd. dirs. World's Fair, 1964; nat. bd. Muscular Dystrophy Assn.; bd. dirs. Inst. for Muscle Diseases. Served as ensign, USNR, 1918. Trustee emeritus Cornell U. Dir. Beekman Downtown Hosp., Boys Club. Mem. Bankers Club of Am. (gov.). Clubs: Manursing Island (Rye, N.Y.); The Links, Madison Sq. (N.Y.); Round Hill (Greenwich, Conn.); Clove Valley Rod and Gun (N.Y.); Blind Brook (Port Chester, N.Y.). Address: New York, N.Y. †

FLATHER, WILLIAM JAMES, JR., pres. Wm. J. Flather, Jr., Inc.; b. Washington, D.C., Mar. 1, 1890; s. William J. and Emma A. (Felt) F.; student Univ. Sch., Washington, D.C., Princeton U.; m. Helen R. Noyes, Apr. 12, 1916; children—William J., 3d, Georgianna Noyes, Agnes Haskell. Employed with The Riggs Nat. Bank of Washington, D.C., 1911-15, Glover & Flather, 1915-33; founded Wm. J. Flather, Jr., Inc., 1933, pres., from 1933; chmn. bd. G. Calvert Bowie, Inc.; director emeritus, cons. Am. Security & Trust Co.; dir. Security Storage Co., Washington, Eltra Corp., Security Assets Corp.; member board, mem. exec. com. Columbia Title Ins. Co., D.C. Served in U.S. Army Air Corps, 1917-19. Member of Phi Beta Kappa. Episcopal. Clubs: Metropolitan, Chevy Chase; India House (N.Y.). Home: Washington, D.C. †

FLEMING, FOY BURWELL, lawyer; b. Sparta, Ga., Oct. 13, 1921; s. Thomas Farrar and Ava Butler (West) F.; A.B., U. Tex., 1947; LL.B., U. Miami, 1949; m. Joanne Louise Tait, Apr. 15, 1948; children—Victoria Ann, Paula Joan, Roger Tait. Admitted to Fla. bar, 1949, since practiced in Ft. Lauderdale; partner firm Fleming, O'Bryan & Fleming, 1949-85; chmn. Am. Nat. Bank and Trust Co., Ft. Lauderdale, 1962-85, Sunrise Am. Nat. Bank, Ft. Lauderdale, 1963-74, Southport Am. Nat. Bank, Ft. Lauderdale, 1973-76, First Bancshares Fla., Inc., 76-85. Bd. dirs. United Fund Broward County, 1955; trustee Nova U. of Advanced Tech., 1966-70, Pine Crest Prep. Sch., 1967-69. Served to lt. (j.g.) USNR, 1943-46.

Mem. Am., Fla. bar assns., C. of C. Greater Ft. Lauderdale (dir. 1967-85). Home: Highlands, N.C. Died July 12, 1985; interred Meml. Gardens, Ft. Lauderdale, Fla.

FLEMING, ROBERT HENRY, government official; b. Madison, Wis., Jan. 30, 1912; s. Robert H. and Mabel Clair (Scanlan) F.; m. Jean Elizabeth Heitkamp, June 27, 1936; children—Robert Henry, Frederick Heitkamp. B.A., U. Wis., 1934; Nieman fellow, Harvard, 1950. Reporter Madison Capital Times, 1931-43, Milw. Jour., 1945-53; Midwest bur. chief Newsweek mag., 1953-57; corr. ABC, 1957-61, chief Washington bur., 1961-65; dep. press sec. to Pres. U.S., 1966-68; asst. dir. USIA, 1968-69; staff Ho. of Reps., 1969-81. Contbr. to: Nieman Reports. Served as officer, inf. AUS, 1943-45. Recipient Distinguished Service award U. Wis., 1959. Presbyterian (deacon). Home: Washington, D.C. Died Dec. 10, 1984.

FLETCHER, C. PAUL, foreign service officer; b. Ridgefarm, Ill., Apr. 1, 1890; s. Albert I. and Belle (Newlin) F.; student U.S. Mil. Acad., West Point, N.Y., 1911-12; B.S., U. of Ill., 1914; m. Esther Avent, Feb. 8, 1917; children—Nancy Elizabeth (Mrs. George Choremi), Patricia Avent. Plantation operator, Hickory Valley, Tenn., 1920-23; vice consul, Toronto, Can., 1924-29, consul, 1929-33; with Department of State, Washington, D.C., 1933-37; secretary in the diplomatic service, 1937; consul, Alexandria, Egypt, 1937-41; with Dept. of State, Washington, D.C., 1942; consul, Basra, Iraq, 1942-44, Gibraltar, 1944-47; consul general, Casablanca, 1947-49; with the Department of State from 1949. Served as 1st lieutenant, later capt., U.S. Army, 1917-19; A.E.F., 1918-19. Mem. Assn. Graduates U.S. Mil. Acad., Am. Fgn. Service Assn., Am. Legion, Psi Upsilon. Address: Washington, D.C. †

FLINN, JOHN CUNNINGHAM, motion pictures; b. Evanston, Ill., May 6, 1887; s. John J. and Mary Talbot (Cole) F.; ed. pub. and high schs.; m. Courtney Luella Ames, Feb. 9, 1911; children—Marjorie Thayer, John C. With New York Herald, 1907-15, play reviewer and asst. dramatic critic last 4 yrs.; connected with motion picture business from 1915, first as adv. and publicity mgr., Lasky Feature Co., later Famous Players-Lasky Corpn.; then pres. Metropolitan Pictures Corpn.; v.p. Pathe Exchange, Inc.; v.p., gen. mgr. Producing Distributing Corpn.; v.p. Producers Internat. Corpn., Cinema Corpn. America, Cecil B. De Mille Pictures Corpn. Exploited "The Covered Wagon" in U.S. London and Paris. Republican. Christian Scientist. Home: Yonkers, N.Y. †

FLINT, E(INAR) P(HILIP), chemist; born Wardner, Ida., Aug. 10, 1908; s. Oscar Frederick and Mathilda Charlotte (Peterson) F.; B.S., U. of Wash., 1930; A.M., George Washington U., 1932; Ph.D., U. of Md., 1936; m. Adele Cavanagh, Nov. 6, 1937; children—Robert Bryan, James Frederick. Research chemist clay and silicate products div. Nat. Bur. of Standards, Washington, 1930-44; supervisor of inorganic chem. sect. Armour Research Found., Chicago, 1944-46, became chmn. ceramics and minerals dept., 1946; dir. inorganic research Mallinckrodt Chemical Works, St. Louis, 1954-56; head inorganic research Arthur D. Little, Incorporated, Cambridge, Mass., from 1956. Mem. Institute of Ceramic Engineers, American Inst. Mining and Metall. Engrs., Am. Ceramic Soc., (chmn. Chgo. sect. 1948-49), Am. Chem. Soc., Sigma Xi. Clubs: Chicago Chemists (chmn. finance com. 1949-50). Contbr. articles to tech. jours. Home: Wellesley, Mass. Died Jan. 17, 1984.

FLOCKHART, ROBERT SEATON, clergyman; b. Plymouth, Eng., Jan. 15, 1889; s. John and Mary (Edwards) F.; ed. State Normal Sch., Springfield, S.D., also Sioux City Business Coll. until 1909; Friends U., Wichita, 1909-11, Gen. Theol. Sem., 1911-14; D.D., Tabor (Ia.) Coll., 1927; m. Marguerite Alice Meyer, Jan. 10, 1917; 1 dau., Mary Louise (Mrs. John Windsor Persse). Ordained deacon P.E. Ch., 1914, priest, 1915, rector Grace Ch., Chanute, Kan., 1914-15; asso. rector All Saints Ch., Omaha, 1915-17; successively rector Ch. Resurrection, Fernbank, Cin., Ch. Ascension, Cin., St. Thomas Ch., Sioux City, Ia., St. John's Ch., Western Run, Balt., 1929, St. Thomas's Ch. New Haven, 1934-50, Trinity Ch., Lime Rock, Conn., 1917-58; Nat. crusader, N.D., 1927; asso. sec. field dept. Nat. Council P.E. Ch., 1928-32, dep. Gen. Conv., Washington, Cleve., 1943; mem. Coll. Preachers, Washington, 1928-33; diocesan missioner, Washington, 1930, 32; dir. Diocesan Ch. Mission of Help, 1929-33; mem. City Mission Staff, Balt.; mem. faculty Racine Conf., 1931; leader clergy confs. Diocese Me., 1931; chaplain Hannah More Acad., Balt., 1933-34; instr. Md. Diocesan Normal Sch., 1933-34; pres. New Haven Clerical Assn., 1935-37; mem. faculty Pomfret Summer Conf., Diocese Conn., 1936-40, mem. com. old age benefits, 1937; pres. New Haven Missionary Assn., 1935-38; mem. Church Scholarship Soc.; chmn. New Haven Archdeaconry Div. Budget and Program, 1941-43; mem. Diocesan Dept. Budget and Program, 1941-43; mem. diocesan dept. missions and mem. standing com. Diocese Conn., 1943-50, mem. exec. council, 1948-50. Rotarian. Home: Baltimore, MD. †

FLOWERS, WALTER, lawyer, company executive, former congressman; b. Greenville, Ala., Apr. 12, 1933; s. Walter W. and Ruth (Swaim) F.; m. Beverly Burns; children: Vivian Victoria, Walter Winkler III, Victor Woodley. A.B., U. Ala., 1955; LL.B., 1957; Rotary Found. fellow, U. London, 1957-58; LL.D., St. Joseph's Coll. Bar: Ala. 1957, Miss. 1960, D.C. 1978. Sr. ptnr. firm Flowers and Shelby, Tuscaloosa, Ala., 1961-68; mem. 91st to 95th Congresses, 7th Dist. Ala.; mem. com. on judiciary, chmn. subcom. adminstrv. law and govtl. relations, mem. com. on sci. and tech., chmn. subcom. fossil and nuclear energy, select com. on aging, mem. Democratic steering and policy com.; mem. ethics com.; mem. commn. on revision Fed. Ct. Appellate System; ptnr. firm Collier, Shannon, Rill, Edwards & Scott, Washington, 1979; v.p. charge govt. relations Wheelabrator-Frye, Inc., 1979-83; group v.p. The Signal Cos., Inc., 1983-84; vis. disting. prof. polit. sci. U. Ala., 1979. Former mem., chmn. Tuscaloosa Civil Service Bd.; mem. platform com., drafting subcom. Dem. Nat. Conv., 1976. Served to 1st lt. U.S. Army Res., 1958-59. Mem. ABA, Miss. Bar Assn., Ala. Bar Assn., D.C. Bar Assn., Phi Beta Kappa, Omicron Delta Kappa, Jasons Soc., Phi Delta Phi, Sigma Alpha Epsilon. Democrat. Episcopalian. Lodge: Rotary. Home: McLean, Va. Dec. Apr. 13, 1984.

FLUKE, JOHN MAURICE, electronic test equipment manufacturing company executive; b. Tacoma, Dec. 14, 1911; s. Lee and Lynda Pearl (Epley) F.; m. Lyla Adair Schram, June 5, 1937; children: Virginia Lee Fluke Gabelein, John Maurice, David L. B.S. in Elec. Engring., U. Wash., Seattle, 1935; M.S. in Elec. Engring. (scholar), MIT, 1936; LL.D. (hon.), Gonzaya U., 1982. Registered profl. engr., Conn., Wash. Engr. Gen. Electric Co., 1936-40; founder John Fluke Mfg. Co. Inc., Stamford, Conn., 1948, pres., 1948-52, Seattle, 1952-71, chmn. bd., chief exec. officer, 1971-84; chmn. bd., chief exec. officer John Fluke Internat. Co., 1966—; dir. Peoples Nat. Bank Wash., Gen. Telephone Co., N.W.; leader Wash. Trade Mission to Orient, 1965; pres. Wash. Research Council, 1961-73; mem. exec. bd. Seattle King County Safety Council, 1962-63; chmn. bd., hon. life mem. Seattle Area Indsl. Com., 1962-66; mem. exec. com. Assn. Wash. Bus., 1966-78; mem. Pres.'s blue ribbon panel Dept. Def., 1969-70, chmn. electronic test equipment task force, 1974-78; mem. trade mission to, Eng. and Scotland, 1964; civilian aide to Sec. Army, 1974-78; mem. Snohomish County Econ. Devel. Council, 1972-73. Bd. dirs. Doctors Hosp., Seattle, 1969-73, Seattle Hist. Soc., 1974-84, Seattle Found., 1970-84; v.p. bd. dirs. Seattle Symphony, 1969-84, chmn. vis. com. U. Wash. Coll. Elec. Engring., 1976-84; trustee Pacific Sci. Center, Seattle, 1971-78, Gonzaga U., 1980-84, bd. dirs. Econ. Devel. Council Puget Sound, 1976-84; chmn. personnel; dir. selection com. City of Seattle, 1969; chmn. endowment fund Seattle Symphony, 1967, 77-79; mem. corp. vis. com., dept. elec. engring. and computer sci. MIT, 1976; pres. chmn. bd. Seattle Jr. Achievement, 1973-78, nat. dir., regional chmn., 1975-78, mem. field adv. commn., 1977, chmn. emeritus, 1976-78; mem. planning and devel. com. Salvation Army, 1976; mem. annual fund bd. U. Wash., 1975-78. Served with USNR, 1940-46. Recipient Corp. Leadership award, 1976; Decorated Legion of Merit; recipient Charles A. Coffin award Gen. Electric Co., 1940; Howard Vollum Sci. and Tech. award Reed Coll., 1976; Man of Yr. award Mountlake Terr. C. of C.-State Adv. Council, 1966; named Small Bus. Man of Year, 1966, Hon. Citizen NCCJ, 1983; First Citizen of Seattle, 1979; fellow Seattle Pacific U., 1970—; John M. Fluke Disting. Chair in Mfg. established in his honor at U. Wash., 1982; Cascade Symphony honoree, 1983; mem. Northwest Ornamental Horticulture Soc. Fellow IEEE (engring. edn. and accreditation com. 1971-72, Regional Pub. Service award 1967, Industralist of Year award 1966); mem. Am. Electronics Assn. (chmn. internat. trade task force 1979—), Am. Security Council, Instrument Soc. Am. (hon.), Seattle C. of C. (bd. dirs. 1960—, pres. 1965-66, life mem.), Tau Beta Pi (pres. 1934-35), English Speaking Union. Republican. Lutheran. Clubs: Rainier (Seattle); U. Wash. Pres.'s; Rotary (Vocat. Service award 1978) (Seattle); Seattle Golf. Patentee in field. Home: Seattle, Wash. Dec. Feb. 11, 1984.

FLYGARE, WILLIS H., educator; b. Jackson, Minn., July 24, 1936; B.A., St. Olaf Coll., 1958, D.Sc., 1976; Ph.D., U. Calif. at Berkeley, 1961; m. Ruth Swansson, Aug. 17, 1958; children—Karna Louise, John Alan, Amy Lynn, Sarah Ann. Mem. chemistry faculty U. Ill., Urbana, 1961-81, prof., 1966-81. Mem. Nat. Bur. Standards Office Standards Re Data Evaluation Panel, 1973-76, Solid State Scis. Panel, 1973-78, Naval Studies Bd., 1976-80; mem. rev. com. chem. div. Argonne U. Assn., 1972-78; mem. dirs. rev. com. Lawrence Livermore Lab., 1977-80. Recipient Fresenius award Phi Lambda Upsilon, 1971; Leo Hendrick Baekeland award, 1973; Irving Langmuir award, 1981; Centenary medal Chem. Soc. London. Alfred P. Sloan fellow, 1964-68, Guggenheim fellow, 1972, 78. Fellow Am. Phys. Soc.; mem. Nat. Acad. Scis., Am. Chem. Soc., Am. Acad. Arts and Scis. Asso. editor Jour. Chem. Physics, 1969-71, Rev. Sci. Instruments, 1972-74, Chem. Revs., 1976-81; mem. editorial adv. bd. Chem. Physics; mem. editorial rev. com. Ann. Rev. Phys. Chemistry, 1974-79, mem. materials research council, 1968-81; editorial bd. Nouvean Jour. de Chemie, 1976. Home: Urbana, Ill. Died May 18, 1981.

FLYNN, BERNARD JOSEPH, lawyer; born Baltimore, Feb. 10, 1888; s. Bernard and Mary (McGann) F.; student Calvert Hall Coll. (Baltimore), 1901-05, U. Md., 1908; LL.D. (hon.), La Salle Coll.; m. Teresa Margaret Berger, Aug. 31, 1937. Admitted to Md. bar, 1908, and since practiced in Baltimore; asso. justice Traffic Court, 1922-24; sec. Supervisors of Elections, 1925-34; U.S. atty. for Md. since 1934. Served as sec. K. of C. activities, Camp Meade, Md., 1917-20. Mem. Am., Federal, Md. State and Baltimore bar assns., Barristers Club, Am. Judicature Soc., Md. Historical Society, American-Irish Historical Society, Hibernian Society, Maritime Law Association. Democrat. Roman Catholic. Club: University, Knights of Columbus (Baltimore). Home: Baltimore, Md. †

FOERSTER, HARRY ROBERT, physician; b. Milwaukee, Wis., Sept. 1, 1889; s. Erwin and Sophia (Hottinger) F.; B.S., U. of Wisconsin, 1912; M.D., U. of Pennsylvania, 1914; post grad. student Vanderbilt Clinic, Columbia, 1916-17 and 1919; m. Katharine Flynn, Jan. 8, 1918; children—Harry Robert, Richard Deveraux. In practice of medicine, specializing in dermatology and syphilology, Milwaukee, Wis., from 1920; former asso. prof. dermatology Marquette U., later clin. prof. and head of dept.; asso. prof. dermatology U. of Wisconsin, 1924-56; sr. cons. in charge of post graduate dermatology training, U.S. Veteran's, Milwaukee County hosps.; member staff Milwaukee, Columbia, Milw. Children's hosps., 1st lt., later capt., M.C., U.S. Army, 1917-19; with A.E.F.; capt., later major, Med. Res. Corps, to 1936. Pres. bd. trustees Village of Chenequa, Wis. Mem. A.M.A. (sec. sect. dermatology and syphilology 1933-35, chmn. 1936), Am. Acad. Dermatology (president 1940), Milwaukee Acad. Medicine (pres. 1930, trustee 1930-31), Royal Soc. Medicine (hon. mem. dermotology sect.), Am. Dermatol. Assn. (sec. 1940-48, pres. 1948-49), Soc. Investigation Dermatology (past vice pres.), Med. Soc. Milwaukee County (pres.), Phi Gamma Delta, Alpha Mu Pi Omega. Clubs: University (director) (Milwaukee); Chenequa (Wis.) Country. Contbr. to several books and to med. jours. Home: Milwaukee. †

FOERSTER, NORMAN, univ. prof.; b. Pittsburgh, Pa., Apr. 14, 1887; s. Adolph Martin and Henrietta M. (Reineman) F.; A.B., Harvard, 1910; A.M., U. of Wis., 1912; Litt.D., U. of the South, 1931, U. of N.C., 1948; D.H.L., Grinnell Coll., 1946; England, 1920-21, France and Germany, 1927-28; married Dorothy Haskell, February 21, 1911; children—Donald Madison, David Bruce. Instr. in English, U. of Wis., 1911-14; asso. prof. English, U. of N.C., 1914-19, prof., 1919-30; dir. School of Letters and prof. English, U. of Ia., 1930-44; visiting professor English, Duke Univ., 1948-51; pres. Coll. English Assn., 1941; member Modern Lang. Assn. America (exec. council, 1939-42), Modern Humanities Research Association, Society of American Historians, Phi Beta Kappa (honorary mem. 1949). Author: Outlines and Summaries, 1915; Sentences and Thinking (with J. M. Steadman, Jr.), 1919, 23, enlarged edit., Writing and Thinking, 1931, 41, 52; Nature in Am. Literature, 1923; American Criticism, 1928; The American Scholar, 1929; Toward Standards, 1931; The American State University, 1937, The Future of The Liberal College, 1938, The Humanities and the Common Man, 1946. Co-Author: The Reinterpretation of American Literature, 1928; The Intent of the Critic, 1941; Literary Scholarship, 1941; the Humanities After The War, 1944. Editor: Essays for College Men (collaborators F. A. Manchester and Karl Young), 1913, second series, 1915; Selected Literary Essays from James Russell Lowell (with Will D. Howe), 1914; Chief American Prose Writers, 1916, 19, 31; American Ideals (with W. W. Pierson, Jr.), 1917; English Poetry of the 19th Century (with G. R. Elliott), 1923; American Poetry and Prose, 1925, 34, 47, 52, 57; Humanism and America, 1930; American Critical Essays, 1930. Contbr. to various jours. Home: Santa Barbara, Cal. †

FOGARTY, CHARLES FRANKLIN, mining co. exec; b. Denver, May 27, 1921; s. Charles Franklin and Mabel Still Fogarty; m. Wilma Marguerite Wells, Oct. 14, 1943; children—Charles M., Harry W., Patricia Ann F. Kappus, Mary E., Catherine Sue F. Peterson, Joan M., Paul T., Theresa E. E.M., Colo. Sch. Mines, 1942, D.Sc., 1952. Registered profl. engr., Tex. Exploration geologist Socony Vacuum Oil Co. of Colombia, S.A., 1946-50; geologist Texasgulf Inc., 1952-53, asst. mgr. exploration dept., 1953-54, mgr. exploration dept., 1954-57, v.p., mgr. exploration dept., 1957-61, sr. v.p., 1961-64, exec. v.p., 1964-68, pres., 1968-73, chmn. bd., chief exec. officer, 1973-81, also dir.; chmn., dir. Texasgulf Can. Ltd., 1966-81; dir. Compania Exploradora del Istmo. (S.A.), Mexico, Sulphur Export Corp., Lehman Corp., Armco Inc., Greyhound Corp. Trustee Colo. Sch. Mines, also Research Inst. Served to maj. C.E. AUS, 1942-46. Recipient Distinguished Achievement medal Colo. Sch. Mines, 1962; Hal W. Hardinge award, 1969. Mem. Mining and Metall. Soc. Am. (pres. 1967-68), Am. Inst. Mining and Metall. Engrs., Am. Assn. Petroleum Geologists, Canadian Inst. Mining and Metallurgy, Can.-Am. Com., Soc. Exploration Geophysicists, Houston Geol. Soc., Am. Petroleum Inst., Nat. Acad. Engring., Am. Mining Congress (vice chmn. from 1977, dir.), Sulphur Inst. (dir.), Chem. Mfrs. Assn. (dir.), Copper Devel. Assn. (dir.), Zinc Inst., Com. Econ. Devel. (dir.), Newcomen Soc. N.Am., Tau Beta Pi, Sigma Gamma Epsilon, Kappa Sigma, Scabbard and Blade. Roman Catholic. Clubs: Mining (N.Y.C.), Sky (N.Y.C.), Economic (N.Y.C.), University (N.Y.C.); Houston; Westchester Country (Rye, N.Y.); Blind Brook (Port Chester, N.Y.). Home: Darien, Conn. Died Feb. 11, 1981.

FOGEL, SEYMOUR, artist; b. N.Y.C., Aug. 25, 1911; s. Benjamin and Lillian (Jones) F.; m. Barbara Clark, Nov. 6, 1936; children: Gail, Jared Allen. Student, Art Students League, N.Y.C., 1929, NAD, 1929-32. asst. prof. art U. Tex., 1946-54; vis. prof. Mich. State U., 1960; lectr. colls., from 1948. Artist, mural painter, 1934—; Artist one-man shows include, McNey Inst.; San Antonio, Houston, Santa Barbara and Ft. Worth mus., M. Knoedler Gallery, Duveen Graham, 1955, 81-83, Allan Stone Gallery, N.Y.C., Stamford (Conn.) Art Mus., 1981, also Can., S.Am., Eng., group shows include, Met. Mus., Whitney Mus., Mus. Modern Art, Archtl. League N.Y., Berlin, Hamburg, 1980, 81, represented in permanent collections, Whitney Mus., Dallas and Houston mus., Hirshhorn Collection, Mich. State U., U. Mo., City St. Louis Art Mus., Ft. Worth Art Center, Nat. Archives Am. Art, executed numerous stained, glass, paintings and mosaics for sch., hosps., govt. bldgs., pvt. instns., including lobby for, Social Security Bldg., Washington, 1942, Hoffmann-LaRoche Research Tower, Nutley, N.J., 1964, U.S. Fed. Bldg., Ft. Worth, 1966, Bklyn. pub. schs., 1967, U.S. Customs Ct. Bldg., N.Y.C., 1968, Gouveneur Hosp., N.Y.C., 1971, Bellevue Hosp., 1973, Sch. 383, Bklyn., 1976, New Park West High Sch., N.Y.C., 1976-77. Recipient awards U.S. Govt. sponsored competitions for mural painting, 1940-41; Silver medal Archtl. League N.Y., 1958; 1st prize Gulf Caribbean Internat., Houston, 1956; 1st prize Tex. Gen. Exhbn., 1956. Mem. Archtl. League N.Y. (past v.p.). Home: Weston, Conn. Died Dec. 4, 1984.

FOGELQUIST, DONALD F., educator; b. Sioux City, Iowa, Aug. 23, 1906; s. Frederick C. and Anna (Lundgren) F.; B.A., Wash. State U., 1930, M.A., 1933; Ph.D., U. Wis., 1941; m. Helen Rasmussen, July 1, 1939; children—Alan Frederick, Mark Stephen, James Donald. Mem. faculties Wash. State U., U. Miami, U. Fla., 1938-42; prof. Spanish, UCLA, 1948-80; dir. Paraguayan-Am. Cultural Center, Asuncion, Paraguay, 1945-46; lectr. in Latin Am. under auspices State Dept., 1959. Served to lt. comdr. USNR, 1942-45. Fulbright fellow, 1962-63. Mem. Inst. Internat. de Lit. Iberio-americana, Am. Assn. Tchrs. Spanish and Portuguese. Author: Juan Ramón Jimenez, 1958; Españoles de Amèrica y Americanos de España, 1968; Juan Ramón Jiménez, 1976. Episcopalian. Home: Pacific Palisades, Calif. Dec. Dec. 10, 1980. Interred St. Mathews Ch., Pacific Palisades, Calif.

FOGG, PHILIP SHEARER, b. Battle Creek, Mich., July 28, 1903; s. Alvah Lemont and Delia (Shearer) F.; m. Jean Adix, July 30, 1935; children—Jonathan, James (dec.). A.B. cum laude, Stanford, 1925; M.B.A. magna cum laude, Harvard, 1929; D.Sc. (hon.), Harvard. Chief statistician Rand McNally & Co., San Francisco, 1925-27; investment analyst Tri-Continental Corp., N.Y.C., 1929-30; lectr. Am. Inst. Banking, Los Angeles, 1932-38, Inst. Govt., U. So. Calif., Los Angeles, 1937, Calif. Sch. Design, Pasadena, 1937-41; prof. bus. econs., registrar Calif. Inst. Tech., Pasadena, 1930-41; treas. Consol. Electrodynamics Corp., Pasadena, 1937-41, exec. v.p., 1941-45, chmn. bd., 1945-65, pres., 1945-61; vice chmn. Bell & Howell Co., 1961-66, dir., 1960-73, Royal Industries, Inc., 1965-77, Security Pacific Nat. Bank of Los Angeles, 1954-75; chmn. exec. com. Lear Siegler, Inc., 1965-73, dir., 1954-73; Spl. adviser AEC, 1947-49. Author articles on taxation, fed. finance. Mem. vis. com. for astronomy Harvard U., 1954-64; trustee Harvey Mudd Coll., Claremont, Calif., Art Center Coll. of Design, Pasadena; bd. dirs. Pasadena Found. Med. Research. Mem. C. of C. (pres. 1948-49), Calif. Inst. Tech. Assos., Phi Beta Kappa. Republican. Clubs: Rotary (Pasadena) (pres. 1950-51), Lincoln (Pasadena), Twilight (Pasadena) (pres. 1966-67), Valley Hunt Home: Pasadena, Calif. Annandale Golf (Pasadena).

FOILES, KEITH ANDREW, publisher; b. Genoa, Ill., Mar. 14, 1926; s. Harold Gustus and Harriet Cordelia (Robinson) F. B.A., Augustana Coll., Rock Island Ill., 1950; M.A., U. Denver, 1954. Tchr. English, Carlmont High Sch., Belmont, Calif., 1955-57; with Harcourt Brace Jovanovich, N.Y.C., 1957-83, v.p., dir. sch. dept., 1976-78, sr. v.p., head sch. materials and human assessment group, 1978-83. Served with USNR, 1943-46. Mem. Am. Numisatic Assn. Club: Vanderbilt Athletic. Home: New York, N.Y. Dec. 1983.

FOLEY, HENRY MICHAEL, educator; b. Palmer, Mass., June 1, 1917; s. Henry Michael and Rosemary (O'Neill) F.; B.S., U. Mich., 1938, M.S., 1939, Ph.D., 1942; m. Margaret Moore, Mar. 27, 1943 (div. 1959); children—David, Barbara; m. 2d. Barbara Mallard, Apr. 19, 1959. Teaching asst. U. Mich., 1939. Coffin fellow, 1940-42, research for OSRD, 1942-43; research on proximity fuse for OSRD, Washington, 1944-45; instr. physics advancing to prof. Columbia, 1946-82, chmn. dept. physics, 1957-60, 72-73; research atomic and nuclear physics; Guggenheim fellow, 1954-55; Fulbright lectr., Netherlands, 1955; U.S. Office Naval Research, London, 1968-69. Fellow Am. Phys. Soc. (chmn. div. electron and atomic physics 1972); mem. Am. Assn. Physics Tchrs. Home: New York, N.Y. Died Aug. 14, 1982.

FOLEY, PAUL, retired advertising executive; b. Pontiac, Mich., Mar. 12, 1914; s. Raymond M. and Mary (Hautekeur) F.; m. Sophye M. Balicki, Oct. 31, 1937 (div. 1979); children: Susan Mary, Peter Michael, Jane Celeste; m. Lydia E. Silvani, Dec. 5, 1980. B.A. magna cum laude, U. Notre Dame, 1937, LL.D. (hon.), 1976; L.H.D. (hon.), Art Ctr. Coll. Design, 1979. Reporter Chgo. Evening Am., 1937-38; editorial staff Detroit Free Press and Pontiac (Mich.) Press, 1938-39; copywriter Grace & Bement, Inc., advt. agy., 1940-43; exec. v.p., dir. MacManus, John & Adams, Inc., 1946-55; v.p., mgr. McCann-Erickson, Inc., Detroit, 1955-56, sr. v.p., dir., mgr. home office, N.Y.C., 1956-71, vice chmn. bd. dirs., 1963-64, chmn. bd. dirs., 1964-71; also chief exec. officer; pres., chief exec. officer Interpub. Group Cos., 1971-77, chmn. bd., chief exec. officer, 1977-79, chmn. fin. com., 1980-82, dir., 1980-83; With OWI, N.Y.C., 1943, bur. chief, Instanbul, Turkey, 1944-45. Trustee, U. Notre Dame, 1969-83. Recipient Human Relations award Am. Jewish Com., 1973; For N.Y. award City Club N.Y., 1973; Advt. Man of Yr. award Assn. for Help Retarded Children, 1976; Outstanding Exec. award Fin. World, 1977; Silver Apple award Boys Towns of Italy, 1977; Inducted into Advt. Hall of Fame, 1983. Home: New York, N.Y. Died Oct. 30, 1983.

FOLGER, JOHN CLIFFORD, b. Sheldon, Iowa, May 28, 1896; s. Homer and Emma (Funston) F.; m. Mary Kathrine Dulin, Nov. 2, 1929; children—John Dulin, Lee Merritt. B.S., State Coll. Washington, 1917; M.S., 1918. Chmn. bd. Folger Nolan Fleming Douglas Inc., Piedmont Mortgage Co., Washington; dir. Allbritton Communications, WJLA TV; mem. adv. bd. IBM, Hilton Hotels, Am. ambassador to, Belgium, 1957-59; Former mem. bd. govs. New York Stock Exchange. Chmn. Rep. Nat. Finance Com., 1955-57, 60-61; Gen. chmn. Washington Community Chest, 1940; chmn. D.C. chpt. ARC, 1942, now hon. chmn.; mem. Washington Cathedral.; Pres. Investment Bankers Assn. Am., 1943-45. Mem. Nat. Inst. Social Sci. Republican. Clubs: Alfalfa (Washington), The Brook (Washington), Chevy Chase (Washington), Metropolitan (Washington), 1925 F Street (Washington); Down Town Assn. (N.Y.C.); Everglades (Palm Beach), Bath and Tennis (Palm Beach). Home: Washington DC

FOLLEY, A.J., lawyer; b. Oletha, Tex., Nov. 28, 1896; s. George Washington and Rebecca Ann (Roberts) F.; m. Blance Bass, May 28, 1929 (dec. 1960); 1 child, Frances F. Notestine; m. Rowena Jones Cowan, July 28, 1962. A.B., Baylor U., 1921, LL.B., 1925. Tchr. English and math. Frederick (Okla.) High Sch., 1921-23; tchr. history Baylor U., 1922-24, admitted to, Tex. bar, 1925, gen. practice law, Floydada, Tex., 1925-35; dist. atty. 110th Jud. Dist., Tex., 1929-34; dist. judge, 1934-37; assoc. justice Ct. Civil Appeals, Amarillo, Tex., 1937-43; judge Commn. of Appeals Tex. Supreme Ct., 1943-45; asso. justice Supreme Ct. Tex., 1945-49; now mem. firm Folley, Snodgrass & Calhoun. Trustee Baylor U., 1948-62. Fellow Am. Coll. Trial Lawyers, Am. Bar Found.; mem. ABA (ho. of dels. 1962-66), State Bar Tex. (pres. 1959-60). Presbyn. Club: Rotarian. Home: Amarillo, Tex. Dec. May 1982.

FONDA, HENRY, actor; b. Grand Island, Nebr., May 16, 1905; s. William Brace and Herberta (Jaynes) F.; m. Shirlee Adams; children by previous marriage, Jane, Peter, Amy (adopted). Student, U. Minn., 1923-25. Began as actor, Community Playhouse, Omaha, 1925, appeared with other little-theater and touring companies; appeared in: The Farmer Takes a Wife, N.Y.C., 1934, Blow Ye Winds, N.Y.C., 1938, in motion pictures since, 1935; including The Farmer Takes a Wife, 1935, Trail of the Lonesome Pine, 1936, You Only Live Once, 1937, Wings of the Morning, 1937, Jezebel, 1938, Jesse James, 1939, Young Mr. Lincoln, 1939, Grapes of Wrath, 1940, Lady Eve, 1940, Male Animal, 1941, Ox Bow Incident, 1942, My Darling Clementine, 1946, The Long Night, The Fugitive, A Miracle Can Happen, 1947; on legitimate stage in Broadway prodn. Mr. Roberts (later in film of same name), 1949, Point of No Return, 1952, Caine Mutiny Court Martial, 1953, First Monday in October, 1979; films Tin Star, 1957, Stage Struck, 1958, Warlock, The Man Who Understood Women, 1959, Advise and Consent, 1961, The Longest Day, How the West was Won, 1963, Fail Safe, The Best Man, 1964, Sex and the Single Girl, In Harm's Way, Battle of the Bulge, The Rounders, 1965, The Dirty Game, A Big Hand for the Little Lady, 1966, Welcome to Hard Times, Firecreek, Yours, Mine and Ours, 1967, The Boston Strangler, Madigan, 1968, Once Upon a Time in the West, Too Late The Hero, 1969, Cheyenne Social Club, There Was a Crooked Man, The Red Pony, 1970, Sometimes a Great Notion, 1972, The Serpent, Ash Wednesday, 1973, Midway, 1976, Rollercoaster, 1977, The Swarm, 1978, My Name Is Nobody, 1974, Tentacles, 1977, The Great Smokey Roadblock, 1978, Fedora, 1979, Meteor, 1979, The Journey of Simon McKeever, 1979, Wanda Nevada, 1979; stage plays Two For the Seesaw, 1958, A Gift of Time, 1962, Generation; toured in Clarence Darrow, 1974, 75; TV appearances include The Alpha Caper, 1973, Collision Course, 1976; series Captains and the Kings, 1976; (Recipient Tony award 1979, Achievement award Kennedy Center 1979, Life Achievement award Am. Film Inst.). Served from seaman 1st class to lt. USN, 1942-45; attended q.m. sch. Naval Tng. Base, San Diego. Died Aug. 12, 1982.*

FONTANNE, LYNN, actress; b. London, Eng.; d. Jules Pierre Antoine and Frances Ellen (Thornley) F.; m. Alfred Lunt. L.H.D., Dartmouth, 1954; L.H.D. hon. degrees, Temple U., Brandeis U, N.Y.U., Beloit Coll., Art Inst. Chgo., Emerson Coll., Yale, Carroll Coll., St. Thomas Aquinas Coll., Russell Sage Coll. Made first stage appearance as a child at the, Drury Lane Pantomime; first London appearance, 1909; first New York appearance: as Harriett Bludgeon in Mr. Preedy and the Countess, Nov. 7, 1910; played Gertrude in Milestones on tour and later in the revival; small parts in My Lady's Dress; then followed Quadrille, 1954, The Great Sebastians, 1956, The Visit, 1958-60; Played: (with Alfred Lunt.) in motion picture The Guardsman. Recipient Presdl. Medal of Freedom, 1964; Antoinette Perry award; Emmy award. Address: Genesee Depot, WI. Died July 30, 1983.

FOOTE, MERRILL NEWTON, surgeon; b. Carolyn, N.Y. Oct. 21, 1888; s. Isaac N. and Augusta A. (Merrill) F.; grad. Cornell U.; M.D., Columbia; m. Ruth H. Sackman, June 1, 1922; children—Jane M. (Mrs. W. Nicholas Kruse), Carol P. (Mrs. Robert H. T. Davidson), Shirley R. (Mrs. Jerald Melum). Dir. surgery Carson C. Peck Meml. Hosp., Bklyn.; former mem. faculty dept. surgery L.I. Coll. Medicine; dir. emeritus dept. surgery St. John's Episcopal Hosp., Bklyn.; attending surgeon Bklyn. Cancer Inst., Kingston Av. Hosp., John E. Jennings Hosp.; cons. surgeon Lutheran Med. Center, Luth. Hosp., Cumberland Hosp., Brookhaven Meml. Hosp., Victory Meml. Hosp., Beth-El Hosp., Evang. Deaconess Hosp., Prospect Heights Hosp., Caledonian Hosp., Bklyn. Hebrew Home and Hosp. for Aged, Good Samaritan Hospital (West Islip, Long Island), Jamaica Hosp., Mather Meml. Hosp., Southside Hosp., Bklyn. Infants and Nursery. Trustee Packer Collegiate Inst. Served with Am. Ambulance Co., U.S. Army, World War I; AEF in France. Recipient Distinguished Cross, Diocese L.I. Diplomate Am. Bd. Surgery (a founder). Fellow A.C.S. (gov. 1941-57, regent from 1957; pres. Bklyn. and L.I. chpt. 1950), So. Surg. Assn., Royal Acad. Medicine (London), American Surgical Association; member of the American Goiter Association (past pres.), N.Y. Gastroenterological Soc. (past pres.), Royal Soc. Medicine London, Bklyn. (past pres.), Queensborough (hon.) surg. societies, International Society Surgery (titular mem.). A.M.A. Med. Society Kings County, N.Y. State Medical Society, Kongelig Norsk Seilforenine. Episcopalian (vestry). Clubs: Rembrandt (past pres.); University, Brooklyn Heights Casino (Bklyn.); Cornell, N.Y. Athletic (N.Y.C.); Sportsmen's; St. Regis Big Game Hunting; Wyandanch Sportsmens; Bellport Bay Yacht (ex-commodore), Great South Bay Yacht Racing Assn. (past pres.). Contbr. numerous articles med. jours. Home: Brooklyn, N.Y. †

FOOTE, WALTER AMBROSE, consular service; b. Greenville, Tex., June 25, 1887; s. James Edward and Bessie (Hodges) F.; A.B., E. Tex. Normal Coll., Commerce, 1906; student Ottoman U., Istanbul, Turkey, 1908-09; A.M., American U., Washington, D.C., 1932, Ph.D., 1935; m. Margaret E. B. Robinson, Sept. 25, 1919. Served in U.S. Navy, 1907-15 and 1917-20, resigning as lt., Sept., 1920, to enter consular service; consul at Port Said, 1920-22, Prague, 1922-24, Hamburg, 1924-27, Medan, Sumatra, 1927-31; asst. chief of press div., Dept. of State, Washington, D.C., 1931-34; consul in charge at Batavia, Java., 1934-38; consul, Melbourne, Australia, 1938-40; appointed consul gen., Batavia, Java, Aug. 1, 1940; 1st sec. Am. Legation, Canberra, Australia, and consul gen., Batavia. Java; temporarily assigned, Melbourne, 1942; became counselor of embassy, Colombo, Ceylon, 1948. Mem. Psi Chi Omega. Episcopalian. Address: Washington, D.C. †

FORD, O'NEIL, architect; b. Pink Hill, Tex., Dec. 3, 1905; s. Leonidas Bertram and Lula (Sinclair) F.; student N. Tex. State Coll., 1923-25; m. Wanda Graham, Aug. 29, 1941; children—Wandita, Michael O'Neil, Linda Elizabeth, John Douglas. With David R. Williams, architect, Dallas, 1926-30; pvt. practice, 1930-34; with U.S. Rural Indsl. Planning Agy., 1934-35; charge planning rural communities Fed. Emergency Relief Adminstrn., 1935-36; prvt. practice, Dallas, 1936-37; partner A. B. Swank, Dallas, 1937-39; partner Jerry Rogers, San Antonio, 1941-53; Rockefeller traveling fellow, 1953; engaged in private practice, 1953-54; mem. O'Neil Ford and Assos., from 1954; ptnr. Ford, Powell & Carson, San Antonio. Research on lift-slab system Southwest Research Inst., cons. Inst. Inventive Research, 1951-54; mem. architects adv. com. PHA, from 1950; cons. architect Southwest Found. Research and Edn., 1954; exec. architect San Antonio Housing Authority, 1950-53; vis. prof., lectr. univs. and colls. in U.S., Europe; work consists of instl. bldgs., schs., residences, labs., indsl. bldgs. Mem. vis. com. to sch. architecture Mass. Inst. Tech., from 1957. Mem. jury archtl. competitions. Served as flying instr., USAAF, World War II. Recipient honor award Tex. Soc. Architects competition, 1956. Certified Nat. Council Archtl. Registration Bds. Mem. A.I.A. (state capitol plan bd.), San Antonio Conservation Soc. (hon.), Hist. Survey Com. Address: Denver, Colo. Died July 21, 1982.

FOREMAN, CARL, film writer, director, producer; b. Chgo.; s. Isidore and Fanny (Rozin) F.; m. Estelle Barr; 1 dau., Carla; m. Evelyn Smith; children: Jonathan, Amanda. Student, U. Ill., Northwestern U., John Marshall Law Sch. Mng. dir. Open Road Films, Ltd., London, 1952-75; Bd. govs. Brit. Film Inst., 1965-71, Brit. Nat. Film Sch., 1971-75; mem. pub. media panel U.S. Endowment for Arts, 1976-77. Motion pictures include Young Winston, High Noon, The Guns of Navarone, The Bridge Over the River Kwai, Born Free, The Victors. Served with AUS, World War II. Decorated comdr. Royal Order Phoenix Greece, comdr. (hon.) Most Excellent Order Brit. Empire; recipient Writer of Year award Variety Club of London, 1972. Fellow Royal Soc. Arts; mem. Writers Guild Am. (Laurel award for distinguished screen writing 1969, Valentine Davies award for disting. service to film community 1977), Writers Guild Gt. Britain (pres.

1968-76, award for distinguished service to writers 1968, Best Brit. Screenplay award 1971), Israel Screen Writers Guild (founder, hon. pres.). Clubs: Savile (London), Garrick (London). Address: New York, NY. Died June 26, 1984.

FORESTER, MAX HENRY, mining exec.; b. N.Y.C., Nov. 23, 1889; s. John M. and Ottilie (Broesing) F.; A.B., Oberrealschule, Marburg-Hessen, Germany, 1908; M.F., Yale, 1910; m. Jean McGraw, Oct. 4, 1919; children—Nancy (Mrs. John A. Padden, Jr.), Barbara (Mrs. A.A. DeGregory), Miriam (Mrs. William F. Sours), Susan (Mrs. John C. Hagan, III). With U.S. Forest Service, Ariz., 1910-12; chief forestry dept. Consol. Coal Co., Ky., 1912-17, foreman, supt., gen. supt. mining operations, Ky., Pa., 1919-38, gen. mgr. W.Va. div., 1938-41, gen. mgr. all divs., 1941-43, v.p. in charge Westen div., Jenkins, Ky., 1943-46; v.p. Pitts.-Consol. Coal Co. from 1948. Served with U.S. Army, 1917-19; detached service U.S. Mil. Govt., Germany, 1946-48. Mem. Am. Inst. Mining Engrs., Engrs. Soc. Western Pa., Am. Legion, Am. Ordance Assn. Home: Pittsburgh, Pa. †

FORGAN, JAMES BERWICK, banker; b. Minneapolis, Minn., Jan. 12, 1890; s. James B. and Mary E. (Murray) F.; LL.D. Williams Coll., Williamstown, Mass.; m. Margaret Meeker, Jan. 24, 1914. With the First Nat. Bank of Chicago from 1909, as clerk, 1909-19, asst. cashier, 1919-22, asst. v.p., 1922-26, v.p., 1926-44, dir., 1929-67, vice chmn. bd., 1945-60, hon. chmn., 1960-67, hon. dir., from 1967. Trustee emeritus Williams Coll. Mem. Chgo. Assn. Commerce (v.p. 1931-32); hon. trustee Chgo. YMCA; hon. trustee Presbyn.-St. Lukes Hosp. Clubs: University, Casino, Chicago, Shoreacres (Lake Forest). Home: Lake Forest, Ill. †

FORNOFF, CHARLES WRIGHT, lawyer, educator; b. Pana, Ill., June 25, 1900; s. John Henry and Grace (Wright) F.; A.B., U. Ill., 1922, M.A., 1923, Ph.D., 1926, J.D., 1932; m. Inda Wilson, June 14, 1928; 1 dau., Jane. Admitted to Ill. bar, 1932; instr. history State U. Ia., 1924-25; asst. history, polit. sci. U. Ill., 1925-28; asst. prof. history, polit. sci. U. Ark., 1928-30, asst. prof. law, 1936-37; partner Fornoff & Fornoff, Pana, 1932-36; asst. prof. law U. Utah, 1937-38; asso. prof. law U. Idaho, 1938-39, U. Toledo Coll. Law, 1939-82, acting dean, 1942-46, dean, 1946-60. Mem. AAUP, Am., Ohio bar assns., Am. Judicature Soc., Assn. Am. Law Schs. (mem. numerous councils and coms.), League Ohio Law Schs. (sec.-treas. 1946-51, pres. 1951-52), Phi Beta Kappa, Order of Coif. Co-author: Anatomy of Modern Legal Education, 1961. Contbr. articles to law jours. Home: Toledo, Ohio. Died Feb. 5, 1982.

FORREST, MATTHEW GALBRAITH, naval architect; b. Johnstone, Scotland, July 8, 1906; s. John and Jean (Galbraith) F.; brought to U.S., 1906, naturalized, 1912; B.S., U. Mich., 1927; postgrad. Bklyn. Poly. Inst., 1935-36; certificate in Celestial Navigation, Weems Sch. Navigation, 1937; m. Elizabeth Dickinson, July 28, 1937; children—Matthew Dickinson, Jonathan Lee. With Fed. Shipbldg. & Dry Dock Co., Kearny, N.J., summers 125-26; jr. sci. dept. N.Y. Shipbuilding Co., Camden, N.J., 1927; marine technician marine dept. Gulf Refining Co., N.Y.C., 1928; designer, engr. Gibbs & Cox, Inc., N.Y.C., 1928-34, asst. naval architect, 1934-52, v.p. naval architecture, 1956-67, executive vice president, 1967-83. Member International Conference for Safety of Life at Sea, 1960. Mem. Bd. Edn., Chatham, N.J., 1947-54. Co-founder, past v.p., bd. dirs. Morris County (N.J.) Assn. Mental Health; trustee Chatham Pub. Library. Served with U.S. Navy, World War II; PTO. Decorated Naval Certificate Commendation; recipient Capt. Joseph H. Linnard prize Soc. Naval Architects and Marine Engrs., 1948, Distingished Alumnus citation U. Mich., 1953; David W. Taylor medal Soc. Naval Architects and Marine Engrs., 1968, chmn. publs. com. 1968-83, American Soc. Naval Engrs. Presbyn. Home: Chatham, N.J. Died Mar. 23, 1983.

FORREST, WILBUR STUDLEY, newspaperman; b. Annawan, Ill., Feb. 13, 1887; s. Benjamin Franklin and Marie (Studley) F.; grad. Bradley Poly. Inst., Peoria, Ill., 1909; m. Floss M. Springer, Oct. 23, 1914; children—Edgar Hull, Yvonne, Benjamin. Began as reporter Peoria Journal, 1909; with United Press Assn., Chicago, 1910, mgr. northwestern br., Milwaukee, Wis., 1910-12, reporter, Washington, D.C., 1912-14, mgr. Cleveland (O.) br., 1914-15; asst. gen. European mgr., 1915-16, mgr. in France, attached to French Gen. Hdqrs. as war corr. on the field, 1917-18; corr. New York Tribune, with Am. Gen. Staff, 1918, with U.S. Army on Rhine until July 1919, corr. in Mexico, 1919-20, Haiti, 1921, corr. for France, 1921-27, spl. writer, Washington, 1927-29, China and Japan, 1929, Washington, 1930, N.Y. City, 1931; apptd. exec. asst. to pres. and dir. New York Tribune, Inc., 1931, asst. editor, 1939-50. Trustee Union Dime Savings Bank, New York. Past pres. N. Y. State Soc. of Newspaper Editors; mem. White House Corrs. Assn., Overseas Writers. Past pres. Am. Soc. Newspaper Editors. Decorated Legion of Honor and Officer Pub. Instruction (France). Republican. Episcopalian. Clubs: Nat. Press; Long Island Country (Eastport, L.I.); Dutch Treat (New York). Home: Manhasset, L.I., N.Y. †

FORSBERG, ROBERT LEE, ret. utility exec., fin. cons.; b. Columbus, Ohio, May 20, 1916; s. Frederik and Martha (Vorpe) F.; B.S.C., Miami-Jacobs Bus. Coll., Dayton, O., 1939; m. Janet L. Blakley, Jan. 27, 1942; children—Terry Lee, James Lind. Successively budget dir., comptroller, dir. market research Airtemp div. Chrysler Corp., 1936-58; with G.E. Schumacher, Dayton, 1958-61; with Ariz. Pub. Service Co., Phoenix, 1961-76, treas., 1963-80, asst. sec., 1963-80, fin. v.p., 1967-71, exec. v.p. fin. and corporate affairs, 1971-75, v.p. corp. services, 1975-76, also dir.; fin. cons., 1976-80, Bd. dirs. United Fund, 1963-69, treas., 1966, pres., 1967, 68; treas. Phoenix operation Guide Dogs for Blind, 1964-68; mem. fin. com., adv. bd. Theodore Roosevelt council Boy Scouts Am., 1964-66; fin. com., adv. bd. ARC, 1972-80, chmn. centennial roll call com. Maricopa County chpt. Served with AUS, 1944-46. Mem. Am., Pacific Coast (chmn. exec. com., adminstrv. services sect. 1968) gas assns., Phoenix Soc. Fin. Analysts (pres. 1968-69), Fin. Execs. Inst. (pres. Ariz. chpt. 1975-76), Financial Analysts Fedn., Nat. Assn. Accountants, Pacific Coast Electric Assn., Edison Electric Inst., Newcomen Soc. N. Am., A.I.M. (pres.'s council), Phoenix C. of C., Ariz. Acad., Phi Theta Pi. Home: Phoenix, Ariz. Died Feb. 5, 1980.

FORSTER, DONALD FREDERICK, economist, university president; b. Toronto, Ont., Can., July 13, 1934; s. Frederick F. B.A., U. Toronto, 1956; A.M. (Woodrow Wilson fellow, Imperial Oil fellow), Harvard U., 1958. Research asst. on ofcl. biography of W.L.M. King, Ottawa, Ont., 1958-60; Lectr. in polit. economy U. Toronto, 1960-63, asst. prof. polit. economy, 1963-65, asso. prof. economics, 1965-70, prof. economics, 1970-73, vice provost and exec. asst. to pres., 1967-70, 70-71, acting exec. v.p. (acad.) and provost, 1971-72, v.p., provost, 1972-75, pres., from 1983, prof. dept. economics Coll. Social Sci.; pres. U. Guelph Ont., 1975-83; econ. adviser Tanzania Ministry of Econ. Affairs and Devel. Planning, 1970; bd. govs. U. Guyana, Georgetown, 1976-80; mem. exec. com. Council Ont. Univs., Toronto, 1976-80, chmn. exec. com., 1977-79; bd. dirs. Assn. Univs. and Colls. Can., Ottawa, 1977-80; econ. advisor Govt. of Papua New Guinea, 1974; cons. on ofcl. history of Dept. Trade and Commerce, Ottawa, 1963-65, cons. on ofcl. biography of C.D. Howe, 1964-65; mem. Econ. Council Can., Ottawa, 1981-84. Author: (with M.A. Bienefeld) Economics for Business, 1964, (with J. W. Pickersgill) The Mackenzie King Records, vol. II, 1968, vol. III, 1970, vol. IV, 1970; editor: (with M. H. Watkins) Economics: Canada, 1963; asst. editor: Can. Ann. Rev., 1964-70; rev. editor: Can. Jour. Econs. and Polit. Sci.; contbr.: articles to Can. Ann. Rev, 1961-70. Research on Canadian-Australian devel. and trade relations. Home: Guelph Ont., Canada. Died Aug., 1983.

FORSTER, HENRY, real estate exec.; b. N.Y. City, Mar. 21, 1889; s. Frederick P. and Edith (Allen) F.; A.B., Harvard, 1911; m. Helena Livingston Fish, Aug. 28, 1920; children—Henry Hamilton, Bayard Stuyvesant, Sheila Emily (Mrs. Anthony G. Morris), Christopher Allen, Hamilton Fish. President, dir., Brown, Harris, Stevens Inc., N.Y.C., 1951-59, vice chmn., 1959-60, dir. predecessor cos., 1926-59; vice chmn. Douglas Gibbons-Hollyday & Ives, Inc., 1960-62; trustee First Nat. Real Estate Trust, from 1962. Dir. Nat. Econ. Council, Inc., Fresh Air Association of St. John. Clubs: Harvard, Racquet and Tennis, Fifth Avenue (N.Y.C.). Home: Garrison-on-Hudson, N.Y. †

FORSTER, WALTER LESLIE, cons.; b. Leeds, Eng., June 30 1903; s. John Mark and Margaret (Forster) F.; m. Lorna Bonstow, Feb. 3, 1936; 1 son, John. B.Sc., Leeds U., 1924. Engr. Royal Dutch-Shell Group, Mexico, Venezuela, Rumania, Egypt, 1925-40, gen. mgr., Colombia, 1946-47, Venezuela 1947-50, cons., 1951-85; dir. various companies. Served as col. Brit. Army, 1940-46. Decorated comdr. Order Brit. Empire, Legion of Merit U.S.). Fellow Inst. Petroleum London. Home: Westmount, Ont., Can. Died Feb. 15, 1985.

FORSYTHE, EDWIN B., Congressman; b. Westtown, Pa., Jan. 17, 1916; s. Albert H. and Emily (Matlack) F.; m. Mary McKnight, Aug. 24, 1940; 1 dau., Susan. Grad. high sch. Gen. mgr. Locust Lane Farm Dairy, Moorestown, N.J., 1933-60, sec.-treas., 1960-78; mem. 91st-97th congresses from 6th N.J. Dist., 98th Congress from 13th N.J. Dist.; ranking minority mem. mcht. marine and fisheries com. 98th congress from 13th N.J. Dist., mem. Republican com. on coms., exec. com. Rep. personnel com., mem. com. on standards of ofcl. conduct; Sec. Bd. Adjustment, Moorestown, 1948-52; mem. Bd. Health, 1953-62; mayor City of Moorestown, 1957-62; chmn. Planning Bd., 1962-63; committeeman Moorestown Twp., 1953-62; mem. N.J. Senate, 1964-70. Mem. bd. N.J. Legaue Municipalities, 1958-62; del. Rep. Nat. Conv., 1968, 76; bd. dirs. Burlington YMCA. Recipient Citizen of Yr. award Combined Service Clubs Moorestown, 1962; named Legislator of Yr. N.J. Assn. Chosen Freeholders, 1968, Legislator of Yr. Nat. Wildlife Fedn., 1980. Mem. South Jersey Milk Dealers Assn. (pres. 1958-61), N.J. Milk Industry Assn. (pres. 1960-62). Quaker. Home: Moorestown, N.J. Died Mar. 29, 1984.*

FORT, JOHN PORTER, author; b. Mount Airy, Ga., Oct. 4, 1888; s. John Porter and Lula Hay (Ellis) F.; B.S., U. of Ga., 1909, LL.B., 1911; grad. study Harvard Law Sch., 1911-12; LL.M., Chattanooga (Tenn.) Law Sch., 1914; grad. study Sorbonne, Paris, 1919; m. Louise Douglas Frazier, of Chattanooga, Nov. 28, 1922; children—John Porter, James Frazier, Keith. Admitted Tenn. bar, 1912, practiced at Chattanooga until 1918; mem. editorial staff, sec. Chattanooga News, 1920-25; pres. Fort Coal & Land Co. Served as pvt., hdqrs. troop, 6th Div., U.S.A., World War. Mem. Phi Beta Kappa. Democrat. Episcopalian. Author: Light in the Window, 1928; Stone Daugherty, 1929; God in the Straw Pen, 1931. Contbr. of poems and articles to Forum, Esquire, Harper's, Saturday Evening Post, Scribner's, Vanity Fair. Home: Lookout Mountain, Tenn.†

FORTAS, ABE, lawyer, former asso. justice U.S. Supreme Ct.; b. Memphis, June 19, 1910; s. William and Ray (Berson) F.; m. Carolyn Eugenia Agger, July 9, 1935. A.B., Southwestern Coll., Memphis, 1930; LL.B., Yale, 1933. Asst. prof. law Yale, 1933-37; asst. dir. corporate reorgn. study SEC, 1934-37, cons., 1937-38; asst. dir. SEC (Pub. Utilites Div.), 1938-39; gen. counsel PWA, 1939-40, PWA (bituminous coal div.), 1939-41; dir. div. of power Dept. Interior, 1941-42, undersec. dept., 1942-46; past mem. firm Arnold, Fortas & Porter, Washington; asso. justice U.S. Supreme Ct., 1965-69; mem. firm Fortas & Koven, Washington, from 1970; Acting gen. counsel Nat. Power Policy Com., 1941; mem. Pres.'s Com. to Study Changes in Organic Law P.R., 1943; adviser U.S. delegation to UN, San Francisco, 1945, London, 1946; vis. prof. law Yale U., 1946-47. Contbr. to legal, other periodicals. Chmn. bd. dirs. Kennedy Center Prodns., Inc.; trustee Carnegie Hall Corp., John F. Kennedy Center for Performing Arts, Marlboro Sch. Music. Mem. Fed., Am., FCC bar assns., Order of Coif, Phi Beta Kappa, Omicron Delta Kappa. Address: Washington, DC.

FORTIN, JACQUES, law commission administrator; b. Matane, Que., Can., Mar. 10, 1937; s. Louis-De-Gonazague and Georgette (Gregoire) F.; m. Micheline McDuff, May 30, 1964; children: Jean-Francois, Isabelle. B.A., U. Montreal, 1957, LL.M., 1961, diplôme d'etudes superieures, 1963, LL.D., 1971. Bar: Que. 1962. Assoc. Cutler, Lachapelle & Lamer, Montreal, Que., Can., 1962-64; prof. law U. Montreal, 1964; project dir. Law Reform Commn. of Can., Ottawa, 1972-74, now v.p., cons., 1974-85. Author: La Preuve Penale, 1984; co-author: Traite De Droit Penal, 1982. Died Jan. 28, 1985.

FOSCUE, HENRY ARMFIELD, furniture mfr.; b. Jamestown, N.C., Mar. 9, 1904; s. John Edward and Vera (Armfield) F.; m. Valworth McMillan, Dec. 22, 1933; children—Ellen Valworth, Henry Armfield. B.B.A., U. N.C., 1926; D.Hum., U. N.C., Raleigh, 1964; D.H.L., U. N.C., Greensboro, 1966; LL.D., U. N.C., Chapel Hill, 1981; L.H.D., N.C. State U., 1964. Sales dept. Globe Furniture Co., High Point, N.C., 1926-35, sec., sales mgr., 1935-50, pres., from 1950; founder, pres. Colony Tables, Inc., Henry of High Point; pres., chmn. So. Furniture Expn. Bldg.; dir. Hatteras Yacht Co., High Point. Pres. N.C. Indsl. Council, 1951-52; mem. Exec. Mansion Fine Arts Commn. N.C.; exec. com. Assn. Governing Bds. Univs. and Colls.; Founder, pres. Furniture Found., Inc.; bd. dirs. Home Econs. Found., Bus. Found., N.C. Engring. Found., N.C. State U.; chmn. trustees U. N.C., Chapel Hill, from 1972; trustee, mem. exec. com. Consol. U. N.C., from 1953. Named Man of Year in Furniture Industry, 1948, High Point Man of Year, 1972; recipient Brotherhood citation Nat. Conf. Christians and Jews, 1965. Mem. So. Furniture Mfrs. Assn. (chmn. ednl. com., past. dir., mem. exec. com., pres. and chmn.), N.A.M. (dir. 1951-54). Club: Cofounders (Med. Sch. U. N.C.) (pres.). Home: High Point, N.C. Died Mar. 7, 1985; buried Oakwood Cemetery, High Point.

FOSTER, BLAIR, lawyer; b. Boston, Sept. 15, 1888; s. Frank Osborne and Mary Armstead (Blair) F.; student Worcester Poly. Sch., 1912; LL.B., Atlanta Law Sch., 1913; m. Carol Frances Spratt, Sept. 6, 1912. Admitted to Ga. bar, 1913; practiced in Atlanta; asst. U.S. dist. atty., Atlanta, 1917-18; asso. Robert C. & Philip H. Alston, 1918-21; mem. Foster & Stockbridge, 1913-17, Alston, Foster, Sibley & Miller, and predecessors, 1921-51; dir. Higgins-McArthur Co.; mem. adv. bd. Citizens & So. Nat. Bank, Atlanta; ret. 1951. Mem. Ga. State (bd. govs. 1935-38), Am. and Atlanta bar assns., Phi Gamma Delta. Clubs: Lawyers, Capital City, Piedmont Driving (Atlanta). Home: Clinton, Conn. †

FOSTER, EUGENE MARTIN, army officer; b. Springfield, Mass., May 28, 1889; s. David Martin and Florence Eugenia (Yates) F.; ed. pub. schs., bus. schs. and Emerson Inst., Washington; grad. Army Indsl. Coll., 1934, Army War Coll., 1939; m. Anita Helen Heitmuller, Nov. 15, 1916; 1 dau., Patricia Ann. Commd. capt. A.U.S., 1917, capt., finance dept. U.S. Army, 1920, advanced through grades to maj. gen. and chief of finance U.S. Army, 1949; overseas service, Pacific and Europe. Awarded Commendation Ribbon, Legion of Merit. Episcopalian. Mason. Clubs: Army and Navy (Washington). Home: Chevy Chase, Md. †

FOSTER, FRANCES ALLEN, educator; b. Providence, Mar. 13, 1887; d. Samuel James and Evelyn Leonard (Allen) Foster; A.B., Brown U., 1909; Ph.D., Bryn Mawr Coll., 1913. Instr., later asst. prof. Carleton Coll., Northfield, Minn., 1914-19; asso. prof. Lawrence Coll., Appleton, Wis., 1919-24; asso. prof., later prof. Wells Coll., Aurora, N.Y., 1924-27; asso. prof. Vassar Coll., Poughkeepsie, N.Y., 1927-40. prof. from 1940; head English dept. Am. Coll. for Girls, Istanbul, Turkey, 1920-30. Mem. Modern Lang. Assn. of Am., Mediaeval Acad. of Am., Linguistic Soc. of Am., Am. Assn. U. Profs., Am. Fedn. Tchrs., Phi Beta Kappa. Editor: Stanzaic Life of

Christ, 1924; Northern Passion, 1912-13, 31. Home: Poughkeepsie, N.Y. †

FOSTER, HAROLD RUDOLF, cartoonist, writer; b. Halifax, N.S., Can., Aug. 16, 1892; s. Edward Lusher and Janet Grace (Rudolf) F.; came to U.S., 1921, naturalized, 1934; student Chgo. Art Inst., 1922-24, Am. Acad., 1925-26, Chgo. Acad., 1926-27; m. Helen Lucille Wells, Aug. 28, 1915; children—Edward Lusher, Arthur James. Artist, Stovals Co., Winnipeg, Man., Can., 1911-13, T. Eaton Co., Winnipeg, 1913-15, Buckley Studios, Winnipeg, 1915-21, Jahn & Ollier Engraving Co., Chgo., 1921-27, Palenske-Yount Co., Chgo., 1921-36; writer cartoonist: Tarzan of the Apes, 1933-37, Prince Valiant, 1937-79. Recipient Banshees Silver Lady, King Features Syndicate, 1952, Sam statuette Swedish Acad. Cartoons, 1969. Fellow Royal Acad. Arts (London); mem. Nat. Cartoonists Soc. (Reuben 1957, plaque for Best Story Strip 1964, plaque for Best Spl. Feature 1966, 67). Home: Spring Hill, Fla. Died July 25, 1982.

FOSTER, J. J., coal corp. exec.; b. Lewiston, W.Va., Jan. 5, 1889; s. John Alexander and Alice (Peters) F.; grad. arts and sci. Marshall Coll., Huntington, W.Va.; m. Jenny Pryce Coffman; 1 dau., Jane B. (Mrs. Harry W. Adams, Jr.). Various positions Island Creek Coal Co., Huntington, W.Va., v.p., dir. Nat. Bank of Logan, W.Va. Mem. Logan Coal Operators Assn. (pres.), N.A.M., Nat. Coal Assn. †

FOSTER, JOHN STRICKLAND, lawyer; b. Birmingham, Ala., May 16, 1907; s. John Strickl and Aline (Bush) F.; m. Dorothy Jean McCrackin, June 30, 1961. B.A., Vanderbilt U., 1929; LL.B., U. Ala., 1931. Bar: Ala. bar 1930. Practiced in, Birmingham; formerly partner Graham, Bibb, Wingo & Foster; partner Foster & Conwell; mem. faculty Birmingham Sch. Law, 1933-50, asst. city atty., Birmingham, 1935-48, county atty., Jefferson County, 1948-75. Vice pres. Young Democrats Ala., 1935; pres. Jefferson County Anti-Tb Assn. Served from capt. to lt. col., JAGC AUS, 1942-46. Mem. Birmingham Bar Assn. (past sec.-treas., exec. com.), Am. Legion (past pres. Jefferson County council, state comdr.), Delta Kappa Epsilon, Omicron Delta Kappa, Phi Delta Phi. Clubs: Masons, Shriners, Elks. Home: Birmingham, Ala.

FOSTER, STANHOPE, lawyer; b. Riverhead, N.Y., Nov. 22, 1890; s. Sylvester M. and Alice M. (Swezey) F.; student Moravian Boys' Sch., Neuwied, Germany, 1904; A.B., Yale, 1911; LL.B., N.Y. Law Sch., 1913; m. Annette A. Hale, July 11, 1922; 1 dau., Clara Louise Jeppesen. Of counsel Brown, Wood, Fuller, Caldwell & Ivey, N.Y.C., from 1944; dir. American Natural Gas Company, Cities Service Co., Empire Gas & Fuel Co., Lawyers Co-Operative Publishing Company. Member American and N.Y. State bar assns., Assn. of Bar of City of N.Y., Phi Beta Kappa, Beta Theta Pi. Home: Great Neck, N.Y. †

FOSTER, WILLIAM CHAPMAN, business executive, government official; b. Westfield, N.J., Apr. 27, 1897; s. Jed S. and Anna Louise (Chapman) F.; m. Beulah Robinson, May 9, 1925; 1 son, Seymour Robinson. Student, Mass. Inst. Tech., 1918; LL.D., Syracuse U., 1957, Rutgers U., 1968, Bowdoin U., 1968, Yale, 1969; D.Pub. Service, George Washington U., 1963; H.L.D., Kenyon Coll., 1968. Officer, dir. Pressed and Welded Steel Products Co., Inc., 1922-46; under-sec. commerce, 1946-48; dep. U.S. spl. rep. ECA, 1948-49, dep. adminstr., 1949-50, adminstr., 1950-51, dep. sec. def., 1951-53; pres. Mfg. Chemists Assn., Inc., 1953-55; exec. v.p., dir. Olin Mathieson Chem. Corp., 1955-58, dir., v.p., sr. adviser, 1958-61; chmn. bd., pres. United Nuclear Corp., 1961; dir. U.S. ACDA, 1961-69; chmn. bd. Porter Internat. Co., 1970-84; Chief U.S. rep. 18th Nation Disarmament Conf., 1962-69; U.S. del. UN, 1964-66, 68; U.S. rep. UN Disarmament Commn., 1965. Served with U.S. Army, World War I; dir. purchases div. Army Services Forces and spl. rep. Under-sec. of War on procurement for USAAF, World War II. Decorated U.S. Medal for Merit; recipient commendations for civilian service from War Dept. Def., Disting. Honor award ACDA, 1969. Mem Arms Control Assn. (chmn. bd. until 1981), Bus. Council (hon.). Clubs: Metropolitan (Washington), Cosmos (Washington), Chevy Chase (Washington). Home: Washington, D.C. Died Oct. 14, 1984.

FOTH, JOSEPH H(ENRY), economist; b. near Whitewater, Kan., May 28, 1888; s. Henry and Mary (Graber) F.; A.B. Univ. Okla., 1913, A.M., 1914; Ph.D. Univ. Chicago, 1924; student Univ. Mich. summer 1938; LL.B., Washburn Municipal University, 1949; married Ethel Wilson, Sept. 13, 1916; children—Edith Elizabeth, Maxine Mae, Joseph Richard. Head, dept. econs. and sociology Kalamazoo (Mich.) Coll., 1915-22, Univ. Rochester (N.Y.), 1922-36; forum leader in forums sponsored by United States Commr. of Edn., serving in Wichita, Milwaukee, Portland (Ore.) and Seattle, 1936-37; head, dept. econs. and bus. adminstrn., Washburn Coll., Topeka, Kan., 1937-39; exec., dir. of Citizens League of Kansas City, 1939-41; O.P.A. information exec. for Kan., 1941-43; prof. of econs. and dir. student employment, Washburn Municipal Univ., 1943, and head dept. econs. and bus. adminstrn. from 1945. Mem. Topeka C. of C. Topeka Citizens Forum (mem. council); Phi Beta Kappa, Delta Sigma Rho, Pi Kappa Delta (nat. historian and mem. council, 1919-21), Pi Gamma Mu, Phi Alpha Delta. Mason. Baptist. Club: Kiwanis. Author: Trade Association, 1930. Contbr. to the Dictionary of American History 1938. Journal of the Bar Assn. of the State of Kansas, 1946. Specialist in corp. finance and investments. Home: Topeka, Kans. †

FOURNET, JOHN BAPTISTE, judge; b. St. Martinville, La., July 27, 1895; s. Louis Michel and Marcelite (Gauthier) F.; grad. La. State Normal, 1915; LL.B., Louisiana State University, 1920. LL.D., 1956; married Rose M. Dupuis, February 1, 1921 (divorced); children—Lela Mae Ann (Mrs. Roger Vincent), John Dupuis; married 2d Sylvia Ann Fournet. Admitted to Louisiana bar, 1920; practice law, St. Martinville, 1920, Baton Rouge, 1921-22, Jennings, 1922; served as mem. La. Ho. of Reps., and as speaker, 1928-32; lt. gov. of La., 1932-35; asso. justice Supreme Ct. of La., 1935-49, chief justice from Sept. 1949. Served as pvt., U.S. Army, 1918. Mem. Am. and La. bar assns., Am. Judicature Soc., Conf. of Chief Justices, Order of Coif, Gamma Eta Gamma, Phi Alpha Delta, Pi Lambda Beta, Pi Gamma Mu. Democrat. Mason (32 degree, Shriner). Clubs: New Orleans Country, New Orleans Athletic, Internat. House. Home: New Orleans, La. Died June 2, 1984.

FOWLER, GEORGE ALBERT, clergyman; b. Washington, D.C., Dec. 22, 1889; s. George Washington and Mary Elizabeth (Conway) F.; grad. Pennington (N.J.) Sem., 1913; student Wesleyan U., Middletown, Conn., 1913-14; grad. Drew Theol. Sem., Madison, N.J., 1917; D.D., McKendree Coll., Lebanon, Ill., 1934; m. Grace Catharine Milne, June 28, 1916; children—Grace Mary, Joyce Madison. Ordained M.E. ministry, 1917; pastor East Moriches, L.I., 1917; apptd. asso. supt. Metropolitan Dist. Anti-Saloon League of N.Y., 1917; supt. Anti-Saloon League, Western Dist. of N.Y., 1919-25; asso. pastor First Ch., Tulsa, Okla., 1925-27; pastor First Ch., Stillwater, Okla., 1927-28, Trinity Ch., Kansas City, Mo., 1928-33, First Ch., Oak Park, Ill., Apr. 1933-Oct. 1941; supt. Chgo. no. district Meth. Ch. 1941-45; pastor St. James Ch., Chgo., 1945-53, St. Johns, 1953-60, now asso. pastor Rader Meml. Meth. Ch., Miami, Fla. Del. Uniting Conf., 1939, Gen. confs., 1944, 52, Jurisdictional confs., 1944, 52, 8th Ecumenical Conf., Oxford, Eng., 1951. Trustee Wesley Foundation, Urbana, Ill., Wesley Hosp., Chgo.; dir. Christian Bus. Mens Found.; past pres. Ch. Fedn. Greater Chgo. Mem. Nat. (dir.), Ill. (p.p.) temperance leagues, South Shore Ministerial Assn. (v.p.), World Meth. Council (del.), Internat. Soc. Theta Phi, Beta Theta Pi. Mason (32 deg.). Clubs: Kiwanis, Lake Shore (Chgo.); Flamingo; Bookfellows; Miami Shores Country. Address: Miami Shores, Fla. †

FOX, CAROL, opera producer; b. Chgo., June 15, 1926; d. George Edward and Virginia (Scott) Fox; grad. Girls Latin Sch., Chgo.; pvt. voice studies with Giovanni Martinelli, Edith Mason, Vittorio Trevisan, Virgilio Lazzari, also studied in Italy; Mus.D. (hon.), Chgo. Conservatory, 1955; LL.D., Rosary Coll., 1958; L.H.D., Lake Forest Coll., 1961; m. C. Larkin Flanagan, June 22, 1957; 1 daughter, Victoria. Founder Lyric Theatre of Chgo. (became Lyric Opera of Chgo.), 1952, pres., gen. mgr., 1952-56, gen. mgr., 1956-81. Mem. women's bd. U. Chgo., Loyola U. Decorated Cavaliere al Merito della Republica Italiana; Commendatore nell' Ordine Al Merito della Republica Italiana; recipient Chgo. medal merit, 1958; Internat. Achievement award World Peace, Trade Fair and Chgo. Assn. Commerce and Industry, 1959; Chicagoan Yr. Arts, Jr. Assn. Commerce and Industry, 1961. Mem. Chgo. Jr. League. Died July 21, 1981.*

FOX, EDWARD LYELL, writer; b. New York, Sept. 29, 1887; s. Walter and Mary (Lyell) F.; New York High Sch. of Commerce and Rutgers Coll.; m. Eleanor R. Ward, June 6, 1912. Began as newspaper and mag. writer, New York, 1908; on staff New York Sun, until latter part of 1911; v.p., mng. editor, Wildman Magazine and News Service, from Jan. 1, 1912. War corr. for Forum Mag. and Illustrated Sunday Magazines, 1914-16. Commd. capt., 349th Field Arty. N.A., 1917. Club: Beta Theta Pi (New York). Author: Behind the Scenes in Warring Germany, 1915; Wilhelm Hohenzollern and Co., 1917; The New Gethsemane, 1917. Contbr. to mags. Home: New York, N.Y. †

FOX, EDWIN GORDON, elec. engr.; b. Milwaukee, Jan. 1, 1887; s. Edwin M. and Frances K. (Gordon) F.; B.S., U. of Wis., 1908; m. Erma Wohlenberg, Nov. 13, 1913. Service engr., later sales engr. Gen. Elec. Co., Ft. Wayne, Ind., 1908-14; engr. in charge elec. design Steel & Tube Co. of Am., Indiana Harbor, Ind., 1914-20; elec. engr. Freyn Engring. Co., cons. engrs., Chicago, 1920-34, v.p., 1934-51; v.p. Koppers Co., Inc. (which acquired former co.) and operating mgr. Freyn dept. from 1951. Engring. work (steel industry) in Soviet Union as mem. group of engrs. supplied by Freyn Engring. Co., 1928-33, in Holland, 1939, Colombia, S.A., 1948, 1950. Fellow Am. Inst. E.E.; mem. Assn. Iron and Steel Engrs., Western Soc. Engrs. (pres. 1940), Brit. Iron and Steel Inst., Phi Gamma Delta. Episcopalian. Clubs: Chicago Engineers, South Shore Country, University (Chicago). Author: Principles of Electric Motors and Control, 1924; Electric Drive Practice, 1928; Electric Drive for Blooming and Slabbing Mills (in Russian), 1933. Contbr. articles to tech. publs. Holder patents on steel industry equipment. Home: Chicago, Ill. †

FOX, FRANCES BARTON, writer; b. Bullitt Co., Ky., Jan. 19, 1887; d. Fontaine Talbot and Mary Pitkin (Barton) F.; ed. pub. and pvt. schs., Louisville. Presbyn. Author: The Heart of Arethusa, 1918; also contbr. stories to mags. Home: Louisville, Ky. †

FOX, IRVING, lawyer; b. N.Y.C., June 11, 1909; s. Herman and Sadie (Low) F.; m. Lenore Galowitz, Aug. 6, 1933; children—Eric Roger, Steven Andrew. B.S., N.Y. U., 1930, J.D., 1932. Bar: N.Y. bar 1933. Practiced in, N.Y.C.; mem. firm Netter, Lewy, Dowd, Fox, Ness & Alfieri, from 1962; counsel to Netter, Dowd & Alfieri, N.Y.C. Nat. treas. Thanks to Scandinavia, Inc., Phi Sigma Delta Found.; Trustee Charles Kriser Found., Beth Israel Hosp., N.Y.C., Kidney Found. N.Mex., Albuquerque. Served to lt. USNR, 1944-46. Mem. Am., N.Y. State bar assns., N.Y. Country Lawyers Assn. Home: Tarrytown, NY.

FOX, JACK VERNON, newspaperman; b. St. Joseph, Mo., Nov. 28, 1918; s. Forest R. and Josephine (Halley) F.; B.J., U. Mo., 1940; m. Feryle Dawson, Feb. 17, 1941; children—Stephen Patrick, Linda. With United Press, 1940-82, successively writer, Kansas City, Denver, staff war cable desk, N.Y.C., rewrite desk, N.Y.C., corr., London, 1949-51, bur. mgr., 1951-53, feature editor, N.Y.C., 1954-58, roving corr., 1958-63, 66-68, news feature editor, 1963-66, corr. Los Angeles, 1968-82. Mem. Sigma Delta Chi. Home: Los Angeles, Calif. Died Jan. 15, 1982.

FOX, JOHN GASTON, physicist, educator; b. Biggar, Saskatchewan, Can., Mar. 5, 1916; s. Jacques Gaston and Lulu Margaret (Connell) F.; B.Sc., U. Saskatchewan, 1935, M.Sc., 1937; Ph.D., Princeton, 1941; m. Constance Mary Sullivan, July 15, 1947; children—Wendy Elizabeth, Grant Sullivan, Paul John. Came to U.S., 1940, naturalized, 1955. Physicist Hercules Powder Co., 1941-45, Los Alamos Sci. Lab., U. Calif., 1945-46, asst. prof. physics Carnegie Inst. Tech., 1946-49, asso. prof., 1949-56, asst. head dept., 1950-56, prof., from 1956, head dept., 1956-61; vis. prof. Indian Inst. Tech., Kanpur, India, 1967-69, program leader, 1971-72. Physicist, Laboratoire Joliot-Curie de Physique Nucleaire, Orsay, France, 1962-63. Fellow Am. Phys. Soc.; mem. AAUP, Am. Assn. Physicists in Medicine, Am. Assn. Physics Tchrs., Soc. Nuclear Medicine, Sigma Xi, Phi Kappa Phi. Contbr. numerous articles. Home: Oakmont, Pa. Died July 24, 1980.

FOX, LAWRENCE MOYSES, merchandising exec.; b. Streator, Ill., Sept. 1, 1889; s. Herman and Tillie (Moyses) F.; student The Peacock Sch. Pres. Nat. Mfr. & Stores Corp., Atlanta; chmn. bd. Charles Kaufman Co., New Orleans, Fox Mfg. Co., Rome, Ga., Stanle Lachman & Co., Chattanooga, Lawson Investment Co., Atlanta. Mem. bd. Jewish Center, Jewish Old Age Home, Jewish Welfare Fund, Am. Jewish Com. Mason (32 deg., Shriner). Clubs: Standard U. Chgo., 1933-36; intern Evanston (Ill.) Hosp., 1937-38; staff internat. health div. Rockefeller Found., 1938-49; acting dir. Obion-Lake County (Tenn.) Health Dept., 1949; prof. epidemiology Sch. Medicine Tulane U., 1949-58, Wm. Hamilton Watkins prof. epidemiology, dir. div. grad. pub. health, 1958-60, vis. prof. epidemiology, from 1960; chief div. epidemiology, mem. Pub. Health Research Inst. City of N.Y., Inc., from 1960; adjunct prof. epidemiology Columbia Sch. Pub. Health, from 1960, N.Y.U. Sch. Medicine, from 1960. Cons. Communicable Disease Center, United States Public Health Service, member rickettsial disease commission, Armed Forces Epidemiological Board, from 1955; member virus and rickettsial study sect. Nat. Insts. Health, 1958-62, mem. bd. sci. counselors, div. biologic standards, 1959-62; med. com. Army Chem. Corps Adv. Council, from 1956; cons. epidemiology U. Ala. Sch.†

FOX, LOYD JOHN, dairy products processing co. exec.; b. Peola, Wash., Dec. 8, 1916; s. Paul Roy and Mayme Etta (Johnson) F.; m. Louise McElvain, Sept. 11, 1938; children—Vicki Lee, Barbara Jane. B.S. in Dairy Mktg, Wash. State U., 1940. With Dairy Coop. Assn., Portland, Oreg., 1940-46; with Safeway Stores Inc., from 1946, plant ops., 1959-62, mgr. milk dept., 1962-66, mgr. dairy div., Oakland, Calif., from 1966, v.p., from 1972. Mem. United Dairymen Assos. (dir. from 1979), Nat. Dairy Council (dir. from 1979), Calif. Dairy Council (dir. 1966-72). Clubs: Rotary, Diablo Water Ski, Am. Water Ski Assn. Home: Oakland, Calif.

FOX, ROBERT JOHN, clergyman; b. N.Y.C., Apr. 18, 1930; s. John Bernard and Margaret (Dunleavy) F.; B.A., St. Joseph's Sem. and Coll., 1953; M.S.W., Nat. Cath. Sch. Social Services, 1958; D.D. (hon.), Lafayette U., Easton, Pa., 1973. Ordained priest Roman Cath. Ch., 1955; parish asst. Holy Family Ch., Manhattan, 1955-56; student placement Monroe County Welfare, Rochester, N.Y., 1957, Family and Children's Soc., Balt., 1958; asso. dir. Family Service, Cath. Charities, N.Y.C., 1958-61; Fulbright lectr. social work, Montevideo, Uruguay, 1961-63;

coordinator Spanish community action Archdiocese of N.Y., 1963-70; dir. Full Circle Assos., N.Y.C., 1970-84; asso. prof. theology Marymount Coll., 1967-72; dir. Inst. Intercultural Communication, N.Y.C., 1959-61; vice chmn. Archdiocesan Social Justice Task Force, N.Y.C., 1970-74; founder, dir. Summer in the City, N.Y.C., 1964-84; initiator The Thing in the Spring, 1967, Mansight, 1971. Trustee CIDOC, Guernavaca, Mex., 1967-74. Home: New York, N.Y. Died Apr. 27, 1984.

FOX, WALTER C., JR., lawyer; b. Mpls., Nov. 21, 1890; student U. Cal.; LL.B., Golden Gate Coll., 1917. Admitted to Cal. bar, 1917; mem. firm Chickering & Gregory, San Francisco. Mem. Am. Bar Assn., Bar Assn. San Francisco, State Bar of Cal.†

FOY, NORMAN WARD, bus. exec.; b. Balt., July 25, 1895; s. Joseph Franklin and Winifred (Wroten) F.; m. Marie Elmont Browning, June 7, 1916; children—Norman Ward, Constance Browning; m. Madelyn Marie Burns, Oct. 16, 1930; children—Patricia (Mrs. Paul B. Allodi), Brian Burns (dec.). Ed. pub. schs. and high sch., Balt. and Cambridge, Md. With Carnegie Steel Co., 1912-17; salesman and dist. sales mgr. Republic Iron & Steel Co., Phila., Buffalo, Boston and Birmingham, 1919-30; with Republic Steel Corp., from 1930, gen. mgr. sales, 1937-53, v.p. charge sales, 1953-61, dir., 1956-62; With steel div. WPB, 1941-44; dir. steel div., active in initiating and developing controlled materials plan for budgeting and distbn. steel, copper and aluminum for war purposes; asst. adminstr. N.P.A., Washington, 1951, N.P.A. (charge metals and minerals bur.). Served as 1st lt. C.E. U.S. Army, World War I. Mem. Am. Iron and Steel Inst. Clubs: Union (Cleve.), Pepper Pike (Cleve.), Country (Cleve.). Home: Chagrin Falls, Ohio. Died Sept. 30, 1981.

FRAENKEL, OSMOND KESSLER, lawyer; b. N.Y.C., Oct. 17, 1888; s. Joseph E. and Emily (Kessler) F.; A.B., M.A., Harvard, 1908; LL.B., Columbia, 1911; m. Helene Esberg, Dec. 11, 1913; children—Carol Fraenkel Lipkin, Nancy Fraenkel Wechsler, George K. Admitted to N.Y. bar, 1910; mem. firm Goldsmith & Fraenkel, 1916-28, Goldsmith, Jackson & Brock, 1928-42, Fraenkel, Jackson & Levitt, 1942-45; counsel Hays, St. John, Abramson & Schulman, later Hays, St. John, Abramson & Heilbron, N.Y.C., 1945-83; counsel N.Y. Civil Liberties Union, 1934-55, A.C.L.U., 1955-77. Chmn. hearings bd. Dept. Welfare City of New York, 1935-51. Recipient Florina Lasker award N.Y. Civil Liberties Union, 1973. Mem. Assn. Bar City N.Y., New York County Lawyers Assn. (past dir.), Nat. Lawyers Guild (past v.p., exec. bd. pres. N.Y. chpt.), Am. Arbitration Assn. Author: The Sacco-Vanzetti Case, 1931; Our Civil Liberties, 1945; The Supreme Court and Civil Liberties, 1960; The Rights You Have, 1971. Editor: The Curse of Bigness, 1934. Contbr. articles to legal periodicals. Home: New York, N.Y. Died May 16, 1983.

FRAKER, CHARLES FREDERIC, educator; b. Alma, Colo., Nov. 15, 1888; s. Charles Fremont and Sarah Eleanor (Roberts) F.; A.B., Colorado Coll., 1919; A.M., Harvard, 1920, Ph.D., 1931; m. Selva Larramendi, July 16, 1921; 1 son, Charles Frederic. Teacher Laoag, P.I., 1913-15; supervisor of traveling teachers and curator of Industrial Museum, Manila, 1915-16; instr. Romance langs., Colorado College, 1920-21; instr., Harvard, 1922-24, 1931-32; asst. prof., Northwestern U., 1924-30; mem. faculty U. of Mass. from 1932, prof., head dept. Romance langs., 1947-55, emeritus, from 1955. Awarded Selective Service medal, 1947. Mem. Am. Assn. U. Profs. Rotarian. Home: Vero Beach, Fla. †

FRAME, FLOYD HILL, b. Salesville, O., Dec. 5, 1887; s. John Shannon and Alice Rebecca (Perry) F.; prep. edn., Carnegie Tech. Night Sch., Pittsburgh, Pa.; A.B., Clark Coll., Worcester, Mass., 1912; postgrad. work, Wesleyan U., Columbia and Mass. Inst. Tech.; E.E., Worcester Poly. Inst., 1924; m. Florence Hortense Isham, Aug. 10, 1915; children—John Warren, Russell Elliott. Asst. physics dept., Wesleyan U., Conn., 1912-13; lab. asst. Gen. Electric Co., Pittsfield, Mass., 1913-14; instr. physics and electricity, Mo. Sch. of Mines and Metallurgy, 1914-17, successively asst. prof. physics and electricity, asst. prof. elec. engring., asso. prof., until 1925, prof. elec. engineering and head of dept., 1925-48, electrical consultant from 1948. Entered United States Army at Ft. Riley, Kan., May 17, 1917; commd. 1st lt. ordnance, Aug. 1917; capt. Oct. 1918; comdg. officer 306 Mobile Ordnance Repair Shop, attached to 81st Div., overseas; hon. disch. June 1919. Mem. Phi Kappa Phi, Sigma Xi, Kappa Sigma. Conglist. Home: Rolla, Mo. †

FRAMPTON, HOLLIS, film-maker, educator; b. Wooster, Ohio, Mar. 11, 1936; s. Hollis William and Nellie Virginia (Cross) F.; student Western Res. U., 1954-57; m. Marcia Trimble Steinbrecher, Sept. 17, 1966 (div. Sept. 1974). Asst. prof. art Hunter Coll., 1969-73; vis. lectr. film history Sch. Visual Arts, N.Y.C., 1970-71; vis. lectr. art history Cooper Union, 1970-73; asso. prof. Center Media Study, State U. N.Y. at Buffalo, 1973-84. Mem. video selection com. Anthology Film Archives, N.Y.C., 1974-84; mem. film panel N.Y. State Council on Arts, 1976-84. Grantee Friends of New Cinema, 1970, Nat. Endowment Arts, 1975, Creative Artists Pub. Service Program, 1975, Am. Film Inst. Ind. Filmmaker Program, 1977. Reprospective exhbns. include Walker Art Center, 1972, Mus. Modern Art, 1973, Royal Film Archive Belgium, 1974, Anthology Film Archives, 1975. Film prodns. include: Surface Tension, 1968; Palindrome, 1969; Zorns Lemma, 1970; Hapax Legomena, 1972; Solariumagellani, 1974. Died Mar. 30, 1984.

FRANCIS, DOUGLASS, educator; b. Leicester, Eng., Sept. 29, 1889; s. Douglas and Louisa (Greasley) F.; grad. Marlboro and Sandhurst Mil. Coll., England; unmarried. Came to U.S., 1923. Adjutant Palo Alto (Calif.) Mil. Acad., 1923-25; supt. West Coast Mil. Acad., Palo Alto, from 1925. Served as 2d lt., lt., capt. and maj., British Royal Flying Corps, World War; retired from Army, 1922. Decorated Air Force Cross (Brit.); Croix de Guerre (French). Episcopalian. Address: Palo Alto, Calif. †

FRANCIS, JOHN JOSEPH, lawyer; b. Orange, N.J., June 19, 1903; s. Theodore Thomas and Mary (Moran) F.; LL.B., Rutgers U., 1925, LL.D., 1959; LL.M., N.Y. U., 1947; LL.D. (hon.), Seton Hall U., 1979; m. Penelope Connolly, Dec. 26, 1933; children—John J., Cynthia, Hugh. Admitted to N.J. bar, 1926; asso. law firms, Newark, 1926-37; mem. firm Foley & Francis, 1937-47; adv. master Ct. of Chancery, 1947-48; judge Essex County Ct., 1948-53, appellate div. Superior Ct., 1953-57; asso. justice Supreme Ct. of N.J., 1957-72; temporary spl. counsel State Commn. Investigation, 1972-73; lectr. Rutgers U. Law Sch., 1973-84. Chmn. adv. com. jud. conduct N.J. Supreme Ct., 1974-84; chmn. adv. com. on jud. selection Fed. Dist. Ct., 1979-84. Trustee Village South Orange, 1946-47. Recipient award meritorious services Rutgers Law Alumni Assn.; Disting. Jud. Service award N.J. Supreme Ct., 1978. Mem. Am., N.J., Essex County (pres. 1942-43) bar assns., Rutgers Law Alumni Assn. Club: Bay Head (N.J.) Yacht, Morristown. Asso. editor N.J. Law Jours., 1943-47, 72-84. Contbr. articles profl. jours. Home: South Orange, N.J. Died July 5, 1984.

FRANCISCO, CLYDE TAYLOR, educator; b. Virgilina, Va., June 2, 1916; s. Luther T. and Nancy (Firesheets) F.; A.B., U. Richmond, 1939, D.D., 1962; Th.M., So. Baptist Theol. Sem., 1942, Th.D., 1944; m. Nancy Lee Anderson, Dec. 26, 1940; children—Don Richard, Carol Lee. Ordained to ministry Bapt. Ch., 1940; pastor in Va. and Ky., 1936-44; interim pastor in Ky. and W.Va., 1953-61; mem. faculty So. Bapt. Theol. Sem., from 1944, John R. Sampey prof. O.T. interpretation, from 1951; vis. prof. Fitzwilliam Coll., Cambridge (Eng.) U., 1975-76, Bapt. Theol. Sem., Penang, Malaysia, 1979. Mem. Soc. Bibl. Lit. and Exegesis, Am. Acad. Religion, Internat. Platform Assn., Phi Beta Kappa. Author: Introducing the Old Testament, 1950, rev., 1977; Studies in Jeremiah, 1961; The Book of Deuteronomy, 1964; I and II Chronicles, Broadman Bible Commentary, 1970. Translator; Proverbs, New Berkeley Version of the Bible, 1970; Genesis (Revised) Broadman Bible Commentary, 1973. Home: Louisville, Ky. Died Aug. 21, 1981; buried Cave Hill Cemetery, Louisville.

FRANK, ELI, JR., lawyer; b. Balt., Aug. 29, 1902; s. Eli and Rena (Ambach) F.; m. Amy Heilbronner, May 7, 1928; children—Marcia Frank Allina, Victoria Frank Albert. B.A., Johns Hopkins U., 1922; LL.B., Harvard U., 1925. Bar: Md. bar 1925. Asso. firm Beeuwkes, Skeen & Oppenheimer, Balt., 1925-34; chief counsel U.S. Bur. Customs, 1934-36; asst. gen. counsel Treasury Dept., 1936; partner firm Laucheimer & Frank, Balt., 1936-55, Frank, Bernstein, Conaway & Kaufman, 1943-66, Frank, Bernstein, Conaway and Goldman, from 1966; mem. rules com. Md. Ct. Appeals, 1946-54; mem. Appellate Ct. Jud. Commn. Md., 1971-76. Mem. bd. sch. commrs. Balt. City, 1957-62, pres., 1962-68; commr. Edn. Commn. of States, 1966-68; trustee Johns Hopkins U., 1959-76; chmn. trustees Johns Hopkins Fund, 31961-66. Mem. ABA (ho. of dels. 1968-70), Md. Bar Assn. (pres. 1969-70), Am. Law Inst., Bar Assn. Balt. City, Harvard Law Sch. Assn. Md. (pres. 1967-68). Clubs: Johns Hopkins (Balt.), Center (Balt.), 14 West Hamilton St. (Balt.); Rule Day, Lawyers Round Table. Home: Baltimore, MD.

FRANK, MILTON HENRY, cons.; b. Niles, Mich., July 23, 1888; s. Bishop Quesnel and Nancy Jane (White) F.; B.S., Purdue U., 1912, E.E., 1915; m. Hazel Shadley, Aug. 29, 1917. Clk. N.Y.C. R.R., Elkhart, Ind., 1909-10; apprentice Ft. Wayne (Ind.) Electric Works, 1911; various engring. positions, Ind., Ill., Mich., 1912-18; local mgr. Eastern Wis. Electric Co., Fond du lac, 1918-22, div. mgr., 1922-30; asst. to v.p. Wis. Power & Light Co., Madison, 1930-33, So. div. mgr., 1933-34, asst. to pres., 1935-36, v.p., 1936-46, exec. v.p., 1946-53; v.p. Franklin Van Sant Assos., Inc., 1954-63; pres. M.H. Frank Co., 1964-70. Mem. Newcomen Soc., Nat. Assn. Life Underwriters (million dollar round table life mem.), Wis. Utilities Assn. (past pres.), Wis. Union (life), Pub. Relations Soc. Am. (pres. Wis.; nat. v.p. central dist. 1954), YMCA, Purdue Alumni Assn., Iron Key, Acadia, Tau Beta Pi, Republican. Conglist. Mason, Rotarian. Clubs: Madison, Technical (Madison); Union League (Chgo.). Home: Madison, WI. †

FRANK, NATHANIEL HERMAN, educator, physicist; b. Boston, Mar. 18, 1903; s. Abraham and Fannie Katherine (Goldberg) F.; S.B., Mass. Inst. Tech., 1923. Austin fellow, 1925, Sc.D., in Physics, 1926; m. Louise Elizabeth Temme, 1929; 1 son, Christopher Temme. With Mass. Inst. Tech., 1924-84, successively asst. elec. engring., instr. physics, asst. prof., asso. prof., 1924-44, prof., 1944-84, head dept., 1952-62; fellow, Munich, 1929, Inst. Advanced Study, 1936. With NDRC; expert cons. Office Sec. War. Fellow Am. Phys. Soc., Assn. Physics Tchrs., Am. Acad.; mem. Sigma Xi, Sigma Alpha Mu, Tau Beta Pi. Author: Introduction to Mechanics and Heat; Introduction to Electricity and Optics; Introduction to Theoretical Physics, Mechanics, Electromagnetism (with J. C. Slater). Research in electron theory of metals, theory of design of electronuclear accelerators. Died Feb. 19, 1984.

FRANKENSTEIN, ALFRED, art critic, curator; b. Chgo., Oct. 5, 1906; s. Victor Samuel and Irma (Rosenthal) F.; Ph.B., U. Chgo., 1932 (attended intervals between 1925-32); Yale, 1930; m. Sylvia Lent, Apr. 18, 1935; children—John, David. Music editor, Review of Reviews Corp., 1930-32; asst. to Herman Devries, music editor Chgo. American, 1930-34; instr. music U. Chgo., 1932-34; music critic San Francisco Chronicle, 1934-65, art critic, 1934-79; curator Am. art M.H. de Young Meml. Mus., 1979-80; program editor San Francisco Symphony Orch., 1935-63; lectr. Am. art U. Calif., 1950-74; instr. Harvard, summer 1951, 52, 67; tchr. Salzburg Seminar in Am. Studies, 1962, 64; lectr. in Am. studies Mills Coll., 1955-70; adj. prof. Am. art N.Y. U. 1969-70; lectr. Am. art Stanford, 1972-81; v.p. San Francisco Art Commn., 1976-81. Guggenheim fellow for research on William Michael Harnett, Am. still life painter, 1947. Mem. Newspaper Guild, Am. Studies Assn., Internat. Assn. Art Critics. Author: (with Arthur K.D. Healy) Two Journeyman Painters; After the Hunt, 1953, 69; Angels Over the Altar, 1961; The Royal Visitors, 1963; A Modern Guide to Symphonic Literature, 1967; The Reality of Appearnce, 1970; William Sidney Mount, a Documentary Biography, 1976; Karel Appel, 1980. Co-author: The World of Copley, 1970. Died June 22, 1981.

FRANKLIN, CHARLES BENJAMIN, organization executive; b. Jefferson County, Kans., Oct. 15, 1891; s. Joseph Manning and Lucy Virginia (Kunkel) F.; m. Elizabeth Turner, Aug. 20, 1929 (div.); 1 dau. Elizabeth Logan Burg; m. Margaret Lavona Barnum, Jan. 20, 1940; children: Margaret Lee, Benjamin Barnum. A.B., Washburn Coll., 1913; student, Columbia U., 1924; A.M., Harvard U., 1927; D.H.L., Washburn Coll., 1967. Pres. Associated Chautauquas, 1919-32; pub. Jayhawk Mag., 1922-23; state bus. mgr. of, Kans., 1933-36; pres. Knife and Fork Club Internat. and Associated Clubs, from 1938; dir. Am. Platform Guild, 1945-47. Editor: Famous After Dinner Speeches, 1949, The Dinner Club Movement, 1954. Pres. Native Sons of Kans., 1928-29, Rotary Club of Topeka, 1929-30. Served as 2d lt. Air Service, World War I. Mem. Internat. Platform Assn. (bd. govs., awards 1965, 67, 70), Am. Legion, 40 and 8. Republican. Congregationalist. Club: Saturday Night Lit. Lodges: Masons; Shriners. Home: Topeka, Kans. Died July 4, 1983.

FRANKLIN, EDWARD CLAUS, physician; b. Berlin, Ger., Apr. 14, 1928; came to U.S., 1939, naturalized, 1944; s. Ernest A. and Ilse (Joachim) F.; m. Dorothea Zucker, May 15, 1956; 1 dau., Deborah. B.S. magna cum laude, Harvard U., 1946; M.D., N.Y. U., 1950. Diplomate: Am. Bd. Internal Medicine. Intern Beth Israel Hosp., 1950-51; resident Montefiore Hosp., 1951-52, VA Hosp., Bronx, N.Y., 1954-55; research asso. Rockefeller U., 1955-58; asst. prof. medicine N.Y. U., 1958-63, asso. prof., 1964-68, prof., from 1968, chmn. rheumatic study group, 1968; dir. Irvington House Inst., 1973; adviser NIH, Am. Heart Assn. Contbr. 250 articles to profl. jours. Served as 1st lt. U.S. Army, 1952-54. Named Career Scientist N.Y.C. Health Research Council. Fellow Josiah Macy Found., Arthritis Found. (sr. investigator); mem. Nat. Acad. Scis., Soc. Clin. Investigation, Am. Soc. Biol. Chemistry, Am. Assn. Immunologists, Am. Rheumatism Assn., Harvey Soc., AAAS, Am. Assn. Physicians. Democrat. Jewish. Home: New York, NY.

FRANKLIN, HAROLD BROOKS, theatres; b. N.Y. City, Apr. 4, 1890; s. Samuel and Tillie (Taube) F.; LL.B., Coll. City New York, 1906; m. Anna May White, Dec. 12, 1913; 1 son, Elbert White. Vaudeville booking agt., N.Y. City, 1910-14; producer of dramatic and musical stock cos., 1914-18; mgr. Shea Theatres, Buffalo, N.Y., 1918-22; chief of theatre dept. Paramount-Publix Corpn., 1922-27; pres. Fox-West Coast Theatres, 1927-30; pres. Hughes-Franklin Theatres, nat. motion picture theatre chain, from 1931; pres. Brookin Corpn., Kenlin Corpn., Boulevard Corpn. Dir. Calif. State Chamber Commerce. Republican. Christian Scientist, Mason (Shriner). Clubs: Masquers, Calif. Yacht (Los Angeles); Lambs, Motion Picture (New York). Author: Motion Picture Theatre Management, 1926; Sound Motion Pictures, 1927. Contbr. to Motion Pictue Herald and bulls. of Soc. Motion Picture Engrs. Home: Beverly Hills, Calif. †

FRANTZ, GEORGE ARTHUR, clergyman; b. Kittanning, Pa., Oct. 23, 1888; s. George Elias and Margaret (Wardian) F.; B.A., Grove City (Pa.) Coll., 1910, D.D., 1926; S.T.M., Western Theol. Sem., Pittsburgh, 1913; graduate study Marburg University, Germany, 1914, Trinity College, Glasgow, Scotland, 1914-15; D.D., Wabash College, 1929; LL.D., Tusculum Coll., 1946; married Amy Constance Kellogg, May 9, 1913; children—Elinor Gertrud, Sara Margaret, Barbara Ann, John Arthur. Ordained ministry Presbyn. Ch., 1913; asst. pastor E. Liberty Presbyn. Ch., Pittsburgh, 1913-14; minister First

Presbyn. Ch., Oakdale, Pa., 1915-18, First Presbyn. Ch., Van Wert, O., 1918-26, First Presbyn. Ch., Indianapolis, Ind., 1926-53; interim pastor First Ch. Oak Park, Ill., 1954-55, East Liberty Ch., Pitts., 1955-57, First Plymouth Congl. Ch., Lincoln, Neb., from 1960; guest professor homiletics Western Theol. Sem., Pitts., 1955-58; Taylor lectr. McCormick Theol. Sem., Chgo., 1955. Trustee Louisville Theological Seminary. Mem. Bd. of Christian Edn., Presbyterian Church in U.S.A. Trustee Butler Univ. (Indianapolis), Western Theol. Sem. (Pittsburgh), Hanover (Ind.) Coll. Mason (32 deg.). Clubs: Indianapolis Literary, Curry and Saddle, Indianapolis Athletic. Wrote "Good Taste," "Immune"; Book of Mercies, 1952.†

FRANTZ, LEROY, bus. exec.; b. Wilmington, Del., Apr. 28, 1888; s. Jacob Frick and Gertrude Lavina (Osborne) F.; Litt.B., Princeton, 1910; m. Henrietta Beiler Glossbrenner, Apr. 21, 1914; children—Doris Osborne (Mrs. Robert Winslow Carrick), Jeanne (Mrs. Earl B. Douglass, Jr.), Leroy. Pres. Dentist's Supply Co., N.Y.C., 1944-49; pres. Leroy Frantz, Inc., from 1949; dir. emeritus 1st Westchester Nat. Bank, New Rochelle; hon. dir. Internat. Flavors & Fragrances, Inc., N.Y.C. Past dir. Huguenot YMCA. Mem. C. of C. Republican. Clubs: Princeton (N.Y.C.); Cap and Gown (Princeton, N.J.); Lauderdale Yacht (Ft. Lauderdale, Fla.); Larchmont Yacht, N.Y. Yacht. Home: Davenport Neck, NY. †

FRANZBLAU, ABRAHAM NORMAN, psychiatrist; b. N.Y.C., July 1, 1901; s. Manes and Esther Eva (Blau) F.; m. Rose Nadler, Dec. 21, 1923; children—Michael, Jane Franzblau Isay. B.S., Coll. City N.Y., 1921; Ph.D., Columbia, 1934; M.D., U. Cin., 1937; L.H.D. (hon.), Hebrew Union Coll.-Jewish Inst. Religion, N.Y., 1958, P.C., 1970. Psychometrist, ednl. clinic Coll. City N.Y., N.Y.C. Bd. Edn., also Vets. Bur., 1921-23; founder, prin. Hebrew Union Coll. Sch. Tchrs., N.Y.C., 1923-31; prof. edn. and psychology Hebrew Union Coll., Cin., 1931-37, pastoral psychiatry, 1937-43; also Hebrew Union Coll. (Grad. Sch. Applied Religion), Cin., 1938-43; intern Jewish Hosp., Cin., 1937-38; resident May Inst. Med. Research, Cin., 1938-40; asst. to surgeon gen. USPHS, Washington, 1943-46; prof. pastoral psychiatry and dean Hebrew Union Coll.-Jewish Inst. Religion, N.Y.C., 1946-57; practice psychiatry, N.Y.C., from 1949; attending psychiatrist Mt. Sinai Hosp., 1949—; founder dept. pastoral psychiatry Hebrew Union Coll., Cin., 1937; founder Sch. Edn., 1946, Sch. Sacred Music, N.Y.C., 1948, Sacred Music Press, N.Y.C., 1950, Am. Conf. Cantors, N.Y.C., 1951; dir. commn. research Union Am. Hebrew Congregations, 1928-31. Author: Religious Belief and Character, 1935, Road to Sexual Maturity, 1954, Primer of Statistics for Non-Statisticians, 1958, (with R.N. Franzblau) A Sane and Happy Life, 1962, Erotic Art of China, 1977; contbg. author: (with R.N. Franzblau) Comprehensive Textbook of Psychiatry, 1976, The Sexual Experience, 1977, also 75 articles. Bd. visitors N.Y. State Rehab. Hosp., from 1962; v.p. Arts of Theatre Found.; bd. dirs. Met. Synagogue, N.Y.C. Served as maj. USPHS, World War II. Recipient Maimonides award Milw. Med. Center, 1973. Fellow Am. Psychiat. Assn. (life, chmn. nat. task force religion and psychiatry 1971); mem. Am. Psychosomatic Assn., Am. Geriatric Soc., N.Y. State Soc. Clin. Psychiatry (pres. 1970-72), N.Y. Acad. Medicine, N.Y. State, N.Y. County med. socs., AMA, Soc. Sci. Study Religion, Alpha Omega Alpha, Kappa Delta Pi; hon. mem. Central Conf. Am. Rabbis, N.Y. Assn. Reform Rabbis, Am. Conf. Cantors, Nat. Council Jewish Edn., Nat. Conf. Jewish Communal Service, Commn. Jewish Edn. Address: New York, N.Y. Died Oct. 29, 1982.

FRATES, WILLIAM SNOW, lawyer; b. Edmonton, Alta., Can., May 16, 1917; s. John Enos and Susan Izora (Snow) F.; m. Sara Williamson Tennille, June 17, 1960; children—William Snow, John Michael, William G. Tennille, Barbara Elizabeth Frates Kelley, Judith Ann Frates Meyer, Stephen Howard, Frederick Snow. B.S. in Bus. Adminstrn; LL.B., U. Fla., 1941, J.D., 1967. Bar: Fla. bar 1941. Asso. Loftin, Calkins, Anderson & Scott, Miami, 1942-46; partner Loftin, Anderson, Scott, McCarthy & Preston, 1951-52, Nichols, Gaither, Green, Frates & Beckham, 1952-61, Frates, Floyd, Pearson, Stewart, Richman & Greer, Miami, 1961-80, Frates, Jacobs, Farrar, Novey & Blanton, Miami, 1980—; partner Miami Dolphins Ltd., 1969-76; pres. Snow Haven Farm, Inc.; lectr. U. Fla. Coll. Law; chmn. U.S. Dist. Ct. Grievance Com., from 1973. Chmn. Metro Study Commn. Dade County, Fla., 1970-71, Campaign Reform Spending Com. of Dade County, 1974; co-chmn. unit F, chmn. legal div. United Way of Dade County, 1974; pres. Mental Health Assn. for Southeastern Fla., 1955-56, Fla. Assn. Mental Health, 1955; mem. Orange Bowl Com.; chmn. bd. Third Century U.S.A., 1970-73; chmn. bd. Community TV Found. S. Fla., 1971-76, emeritus, from 1976; bd. govs. Pub. Broadcasting Service, 1976-80; bd. dirs. Vizcayans, 1969, Nat. Assn. Mental Health, 1956-57; trustee Pub. Health Trust Dade County (Jackson Meml. Hosp.), 1973-79, chmn. bd., 1976-77; trustee U. Fla. Law Center Assn., from 1970, chmn., 1975-78; bd. advs. Fla. Internat. U.; vis. com. Sch. Medicine, U. Miami, bd. govs. med. div., from 1978; exec. bd. dirs. S. Fla. council Boy Scouts Am., from 1977. Served to capt. AUS, 1942-46. Recipient Disting. Eagle award, 1978, Gold medal Law-Sci. Acad. Am., 1958; Distinguished Alumnus award U. Fla., 1976; Gov.'s award Fine Arts Concil Fla., 1976. Fellow Internat. Acad. Trial Lawyers (dir. 1968-73), Acad. Fla. Trial Lawyers, Law-Sci. Found. Am. (nat. pres. 1959), Internat. Soc. Barristers (dir. 1970-73, pres. 1973), Am. Bar Found.; mem. ABA, Fla. Bar Assn. (past com. chmn.), Dade County Bar Assn., Assn. Trial Lawyers Am. (asso. editor r.r. law jour. 1952-65, adv. com. student advocacy program 1966), Am. Judicature Soc., Nat. Audubon Soc., Bankers Club Miami, Greater Miami C. of C. (bd. govs. 1968-70, 74-79, v.p., exec. com. 1968-70), Nat. Eagle Scout Assn., Baden-Powell Guild, Order of Coif, Fla. Blue Key (hon.), Phi Delta Phi, Phi Kappa Tau. Democrat. Methodist. Clubs: Coral Reef Yacht (Miami), Biscayne Bay Yacht (Miami), Miami (Miami), Am. (Miami). Home: Coral Gables, Fla. Died Mar. 22, 1984.

FRAWLEY, ERNEST DAVID, publisher; b. Brockton, Mass., Apr. 17, 1920; s. Arthur Henry and Viola (Morse) F.; m. Natalie Pingree, Oct. 29, 1948 (dec. Dec. 30, 1962); children: Betsy, Cynthia, Susan; m. Elizabeth von Thurn, Nov. 19, 1965. A.B., Middlebury Coll., 1942; student, Bread Loaf Grad. Sch. English, summers 1940, 41. Staff mem. N.E. regional magazine Boston Transcript, 1946; with advt. dept. Dewey & Almy Chemical Co., Cambridge, Mass., 1947-48, Green Mountain Pubs. (baseball publs.), Boston, 1948-49; pub., treas., dir. Child Life mag., 1949-56; circulation dir., asst. bus. mgr. Harvard Bus. Review, Harvard Grad. Sch. Bus. Adminstrn., 1956-63, controller, 1963-71, gen. mgr., 1971-79, pub., 1979-84; trustee, adminstr. Internat. Marketing Inst., 1960-70, treas., 1961-70; dir. Comml. Bank & Trust Co., Wilmington, Mass., 1962-65, W. A. Wilde Co., Bus. Research Corp.; cons. U.S. Dept. State, 1960-70, Dept. Commerce, 1960-66; Sec. Boston Conf. on Distbn., 1961-64. Trustee Thayer Pub. Library, Braintree, 1964-79; trustee Mass. Hort. Soc., 1976-79. Served as lt. (s.g.) USNR, 1942-45. Mem. Am. Marketing Assn., Nat. Planning Assn. (nat. council 1970), Am. Arbitration Assn., Delta Kappa Epsilon. Club: Harvard. Home: Braintree, Mass. Died Dec. 9, 1984.

FRAWLEY, JAMES JEROME, railroad exec.; b. Buffalo, Sept. 28, 1888; s. Michael and Eliza (Hennessy) F.; student pub. and parochial schs., Buffalo. Joined N.Y.C. R.R. as messenger, Buffalo, 1902, asst. supt. Erie div., 1937-40, supt., 1940-45, asst. gen. mgr., Cleve., 1945-47, Syracuse, N.Y., 1947, gen. mgr. Lines East, 1947-49, asst. v.p. N.Y. Central System, N.Y.C., 1949-51, v.p. operations and maintenance from 1951; v.p. operations and maintenance P.&E.B. R.R., Chicago River & Ind. R.R. Co., Ind. Harbor Belt R.R. Co., Lake Erie & Eastern R.R. Co.; dir. N.J. Junction R.R. Co. Republican. Roman Catholic. Home: Riverdale, N.Y. †

FRAZIER, ADRIAN W., constrn. contractor; b. St. Louis, 1888; grad. Washington U., 1909. Chmn. dir. Frazier-Davis Constrn. Co., St. Louis; treas., dir. Bridges Asphalt Paving Co.; dir. First Nat. Bank, St. Louis, Scruggs-Vandervort & Barney Dry Goods Co. Dir. Washington U. Home: Richmond Heights, Mo. †

FREDA, WESTON HARRY, clergyman; b. Chester, N.S., Can., Dec. 8, 1888; s. Harding William and Frances (Morash) F.; ed. Acadia Acad., Wolfville, N.S., 1908-10. Newton Theol. Instn., 1911; completed studies privately; D.D., Franklin (Ind.) Coll., 1926; m. Nina Evelyn Embree, Dec. 25, 1912; children—Evelyn (Mrs. Mason Billard Wells), Thornton George. Came to U.S., 1917, naturalized, 1924. Ordained to ministry of Baptist ch., 1912; pastor, Nova Scotia, 1912-17; pastor Clarendon Street Baptist Church, Boston, 1917-24, Church of the Master, Cleveland, Ohio, 1924-28, exec. and lecturer, 1928-33; pastor First Baptist Church, Galesburg, Ill., 1933-39, Baptist Temple, Rochester, N.Y., Jan. 1939-Oct. 1944, pastor emeritus Bapt. Temple, Rochester. Trustee Colgate-Rochester Seminary since 1944. Formerly dir. Advertising Club, Cleveland, O. Mem. Tau Kappa Epsilon. Republican. Author: The Biggest Business of Life, 1925; Why Life Cracks Up, 1936. Contbr. to Galesburg (Ill.) Register-Mail from 1937. Home: Rochester, N.Y.†

FREDEN, GUSTAF, educator; b. Saronville, Neb., Jan. 29, 1889; s. Anders Gustaf and Anna Ulrika (Westling) F.; grad. Real Gymnasium, Stockholm, Sweden, 1910; B.A., Augustana Coll., Rock Island, Ill., 1924; M.A., U. of Ia., 1925, Ph.D., 1927; m. Hazel Mae Westerlund, Sept. 6, 1925; children—Martha Mae, Leona Anna. Physical dir. Bethany Coll., Lindsborg, Kan., 1912-13; supervisor physical education and hygiene, city schs., Nashville, Tenn., 1913-17; research asst. U. of Ia., 1925-27; apptd. head Dept. of Edn., La. Poly. Inst., 1928, dean Sch. of Edn., 1933-45; retired. Enlisted in U.S. Army, Sept. 1917; commd. 2d lt., 42d ("Rainbow") Div., 1918, 19; hon. disch., June 1919. Mem. Am. Legion, Phi Delta Kappa. Lutheran. Mason (Shriner). Contbr. on ednl. topics. Home: Rock Island, Ill. Deceased.

FREDRICKSON, JAY WARREN, educator; b. Salt Lake City, Dec. 21, 1917; s. Sherman and Lethea Rebecca (Rockwell) F.; m. Marie Cowsert Swift, May 6, 1974; children by previous marriage—Jon H., Teresa Kay (Mrs. Gary McCarbery), Sherman R. B.S., U. Utah, 1947, Ph.D., 1949. Prof., head dept. metallurgy Pa. State U., 1949-52; sect. head The Dow Chem. Co., Midland, Mich., 1952-62, research dir., mgr. new bus. and minerals exploration, metals dept., 1962-65, mgr. tech. service and devel. metals dept., 1965-69; prof., dir. Grad. Inst. Tech., U. Ark., 1969—; adj. lect. U. Mich., 1959; bd. dirs. Geo-Met Reactors Ltd., Ont., Can., 1964-67. Trustee Foundry Edn. Found. Served to lt. col. AUS, 1940-46. Decorated Bronze star with 2 clusters, Croix de Guirre with palm. Mem. Am. Soc. Metals (past chmn.), Am. Inst. Mining and Metall. Engrs., Soc. Automotive Engrs. (governing bd.), Sigma Xi, Theta Tau, Sigma Gamma Epsilon, Phi Kappa Phi, Phi Lambda Upsilon. Club: Rotarian. Home: North Little Rock AR

FREEDHEIM, EUGENE H., lawyer; b. Leadville, Colo., Mar. 16, 1900; s. Alfred A. and Carrie (Heitler) F.; A.B., U. Colo., 1921; J.D., Harvard, 1924; m. Mina Koperlik, Mar. 2, 1927; children—Joan F. Collins, Donald K., David E. Admitted to Ohio bar, 1925, since practiced in Cleve.; partner firm Hahn, Loeser, Freedheim, Dean & Wellman. Dir. Akro Corp., Wickman Corp. Hon. life trustee Mt. Sinai Hosp. (Cleve.); trustee Cleve. Community Chest, 1956-72, Welfare Fedn. Cleve., 1952-57 (chmn. case work council 1949-50), Family Service Assn., 1953-62, Youth Bur., 1952-58, Jewish Community Fedn. (life); life trustee Jewish Family Service Assn. Cleve., pres., 1945-49; pres. Family Service Assn. Am., 1957-59; dir. Nat. Council for Homemaker-Home Health Aide Services, 1965-78, treas., 1969-73, exec. com., 1967-84; mem. Lawyer's Com. for Civil Rights Under Law, 1966-84, trustee, 1967-84; mem. nat. bd. Nat. Conf. Social Welfare, 1966-68; trustee Cleve. Playhouse, 1966-72, 75-84, Cleve. Playhouse Found., 1972-84; vis. com. Sch. Law, Case-Western Res. U., 1958-68. Recipient distinguished service award Cleve. Community Chest, 1956; Eisenman award Jewish Community Fedn., 1970. Fellow Am. Bar Found. (life); mem. Cleve. (pres. 1955-56), Ohio, Am. (rep. to Nat. Conf. Lawyers and Social Workers 1961-70) bar assns., Am. Law Inst., Am. Arbitration Assn. (dir. 1965-69, life mem.) Phi Beta Kappa Assos. (life mem.). Jewish. Clubs: Oakwood, City, (Cleve.). Home: Shaker Heights, Ohio. Died Dec. 19, 1984; interred United Jewish Cemeteries, Cleveland, Ohio.

FREEDLANDER, A. L., rubber mfr.; b. Wooster, O., June 6, 1889; s. David Lewis and Anna F.; B.S. in chemistry, Case Sch. of Applied Science, Cleveland, O., 1911; D.Sc. (honorary) Ashland College, 1957; unmarried. Rubber chemist and compounder, development engr., B. F. Goodrich Co., Akron, O., 1911-19; factory mgr. and dir. development research, Dayton (O.) Rubber Mfg. Co., 1919-21, vice pres., asst. gen. mgr. and dir. development, 1921-36, became pres. and gen mgr., 1936; founder, past chmn. bd. and chief exec. officer, now chmn. exec. com. and dir. Dayco Corp., Dayton; 1st pres., founder Copolymer Corp., Baton Rouge; mem. rubber adv. com. RFC, from 1951. Mem. bd. directors of the Dayton Art Institute. Served with the 134th F.A., U.S. Army, 1916-17; rubber consultant to Air Force, 1917-18. Recipient John Pottinger World Trade Award, 1952. Deputy chief, rubber branch, W.P.B., 1941, rubber consultant, 1942-43; consultant and chmn. synthetic tire cord and yarn com. Office of Rubber Dir., W.P.B., from 1943; mem. Rubber Industry adv. com. NPA. Active Dayton Philharmonic Orch. Knighted by Norway, Denmark. Mem. Nat. Mgmt. Assn., Rubber Mfrs. Assn. (past dir.) Am. Chem. Soc., Newcomen Soc. Club: Dayton Foremen's (a founder, 1st pres.). Patentee in field. †

FREEMAN, JOHN GEORGE, physician; b. Willmar, Minn., Nov. 11, 1918; s. George Herman and Mata (O'Neill) F.; 1 son, Michael J. B.A. cum laude, Gustavus Adolphus Coll., 1940; M.B., U. Minn., 1943; M.D., 1944; fellow neurology and psychiatry, Mayo Found., 1944-45, 48-50. First asst. psychiatry Mayo Clinic, 1950-51; clin. dir. Fergus Falls (Minn.) State Hosp., 1951-54; clin. dir., asst. supt. Jamestown (N.D.) State Hosp., 1954-59; research psychiatrist U. Nebr. Med. Sch. and Nebr. Psychiat. Inst., 1959-61; supt. Mont. State Hosp., 1961-63; asst., then asso. supt. Stockton (Calif.) State Hosp., 1963-67, med. dir., 1972-75, DeWitt (Calif.) State Hosp., 1967-70; med. dir. local programs Dept. Mental Hygiene No. Calif. Region, 1970-72; psychiatrist Napa (Calif.) State Hosp., 1975-81; asst. clin. prof. div. mental health U. Calif., Davis, 1972-76. Contbr. articles to profl. jours. Served to capt., M.C. AUS, 1945-47. Fellow Am. Psychiat. Assn.; life mem. AAAS. Home: Nevada City, Calif.

FREEMAN, OTIS WILLARD, coll. pres. emeritus, educator; b. Otsego, Mich., Apr. 13, 1889; s. Franklin Allen and Laura (Gibson) F.; B.A., Albion (Michigan) College, 1910; M.S., Michigan University, 1913; student Northwestern Univ., 1923-24; Ph.D., Clark University, Worcester, Mass., 1929; m. Laura O. Cowell, Aug. 5, 1914; children—Annie Laura (dec.), Helen Margaret (Mrs. Paul G. Miller), Franklin (deceased), Ruth Alice (Mrs. Francis R. Coelho). Teacher in public high schools in Michigan, also Mont. and Calif., 1910-21; instr. summer normal schs., Mont. and San Francisco, 1915-23; instr. geology, Northwestern U., 1923-24; prof. geography, and head dept. phys. sci. Eastern Wash. Coll. Edn., 1924-50, pres. 1951-53; acting prof. geology U. Hawaii, 1927-28; acting prof. geography Indiana U., 1943-46; visiting prof. geography, summer session, Western Reserve U., 1929, Reed Coll., 1940, U. of Wash., 1941; prof. geography State Tchrs. Coll., Indiana, Pa., from 1954. Specialist in geog. higher edn., U.S. Office Edn., 1948; visiting prof. geog., U. of Hawaii, 1948-49; visiting lecturer Universtiy of Arizona, 1959-60. Nat. Council Geographers Teachers; acting state geologist, Indiana, 1945. Awarded Richard Elwood Dodge prize Nat. Council Geog. Tchrs., 1947; Distinguished Service award Nat. Council Geog. Edn., 1958. Member Assn. American Geographers Assn., Pacific Coast Geographers (president,

1935, editor, 1935-39, and secretary, 1946-48), American Meteorological Soc., Northwest Scientific Assn. (sec. 1933-38, editor 1939-43, pres. 1948), Pa. Ednl. Assn., Northwest Conservation League (pres. 1940), American Geophysical Union, A.A.A.S., Pa. Acad. Sci., Phi Beta Kappa (hon.), Sigma Xi, Sigma Nu. Conglist. (state moderator for Wash., 1939). Rotarian. Author books, latest: Essentials of Geography, 1949. Geog. editor Education, 1943-55. Contbr. and co-editor several geog. publs., latest: Essentials of Geography, 1949, rev. 1959; Geography of the Pacific, 1951; Conservation of Northwest Resources, 1951; Resources of Washington, 1954; World Geography, 1957. Contbr. ednl. and sci. mags. Address: Seattle, WA. †

FREEMAN, THOMAS BENNETT, indsl. cons.; b. Vineyard, Ark., Mar. 19, 1887; s. George Wellington and Zora (Bennett) F.; B.A., University of Arkansas, LL.D. (honorary), 1943; m. Margaret wilson, April 17, 1919; children—Leslie Jean (Mrs. Thomas E. Deacy, Jr.), Bennette (Mrs. William H. Hartz, Jr.). Pres. Freeman & Co. in Arkansas, 1910-29; vice-pres. and general manager Scott-Burr Stores Corp., a subsidiary of Butler Bros., Chicago, 1929-35, pres., 1936-39; pres. Butler Brothers, 1939-47, chmn. bd., 1947-48, ret.; dir. Wilson & Co., Inc., Chgo. Mem. 6th Regional War Labor Board, 1943-45. Pres. Chicago Assn. of Commerce and Industry, 1945-47. Dir. Cook Co. Sch. Nursing, 1946-49; trustee Inst. of Design, 1944-49, mem. adv. bd. to Chgo. Park District, 1945-50. Trustee U. Chgo. Cancer Research Found., 1947-53; mem. council med. and biol. research U. Chgo., 1949-53; dir. Tucson Festival of Arts, 1950-55, Tucson Med. Center, 1951-55, Tucson Symphony Soc., 1952-56. Mem. Newcomen Soc. Eng. Grand trustee, Sigma Chi, 1935-48. Clubs: Glen View Country (Golf, Ill.); Tucson (Ariz.) Country; University, Rotary, Chicago, Commercial (Chgo.). Address: Tucson, Ariz. †

FREIN, JOSEPH PETER, constrn. cons.; b. St. Louis, May 22, 1904; s. Jacob Peter and Mary Ellen (Sullivan) F.; engring. extension student, Washington U., St. Louis; m. Margaret Mary Peters, June 8, 1929; children—Michael James, Elizabeth Margaret. Office engr., chief survey party, also insp., div. sewers and paving, City St. Louis, 1925-30; engr. W.E. Callahan Constrn. Co., St. Louis, 1930-43; with Morrison-Knudsen Co., Inc., 1943-70, chief engr., Boise, Idaho, 1951-60, v.p. charge engring., 1960-68, v.p. fgn., 1968-69, dir., 1959-70; v.p. Morrison Knudsen Internat. Co., Inc., 1968-70; now ind. constrn. cons. Mem., chmn. constrn. subcom. U.S. Com. on Large Dams, Internat. Commn. on Large Dams, 1969-74; cons. Superior Ct. Calif. in litigation related to Oroville Underground Powerhouse, 1974-75. Mem. Am. Arbitration Assn. (nat. panel arbitrators 1968-83). Contbg. author, editor-in-chief: Handbook of Construction Management and Organization, 2d edit., 1979. Co-inventor, patentee deep bridge pier founds. Home: Boise, Idaho. Died Mar. 24, 1983.

FREITAG, OTTO FREDERICK, educator in dental science; b. St. Louis, Mar. 24, 1889; s. William C. and Katherine C. (Reisch) F.; D.D.S., St. Louis U., 1915; m. Edna Evelyn Schulte, Oct. 4, 1916; 1 dau., Juanita Constance (Mrs. Samuel Hudson Bowring). Pvt. practice dentistry, St. Louis, 1915-17, and from 1919; mem. faculty St. Louis U. Sch. Dentistry from 1919, prof. of operative dentistry, 1926-37, vice dean from 1926, supt. clinic, 1923-43, dir. dept. oral diagnosis and treatment planning from 1943. Served with Dental Corps, U.S. Army, 1917-19; overseas 10 mos.; disch. rank of major. Mem. Federation Dentaire Internationale, Internat. Assn. Dental Research, Am. Coll. Dentists, Am. Dental Assn., Mo. State Dental Assn., St. Louis Dental Soc., St. Louis Soc. Dental Sci., A.A.A.S., Omicron Kappa Upsilon (charter mem., 1934, v.p., 1948, pres., 1950). Home: University City, Mo. †

FREMONT, CLAUDE, univ. press dir.; b. Sainte-Foy, Que., Can., Aug. 18, 1922; s. Charles and Thais (Lacoste) F.; m. Gabrielle Duval, May 8, 1953; children—Jacques, Michèle, Claire. B.A., Coll. Garnier, 1943; B. Sci. Applied, Laval U., 1947, M.S., 1948. Lectr. physics and geophysics Laval U., Quebec, Que., 1948-52, asso. prof. electricity and magnetism, 1952-63, prof., 1963, asso. dir. physics dept., 1965-71, dir. ednl. TV service, 1965-70; gen. dir. Laval U. Press, from 1971. Mem. Institut Canadien de Quebec (pres. 1970-72, dir.), Association Québecoise des Presses Universitaires (pres.), Assn. Canadian Univ. Presses (pres.), Assn. Internationale des Presses Universitaires de Langue française (v.p.). Roman Catholic. Home: Sainte Foy PQ, Canada.

FRENCH, CHARLES AUGUSTUS, army officer; b. Sunol, Calif., Feb. 9, 1888; s. Henry Lathrup and Caroline Clarissa (Ballard) F.; B.S., in Elec. Engring. Ore. State Coll., 1911; grad. C.A. Sch., Field Officers Course, 1925, Command and Gen Staff Sch., 1926, Air Corps Tactical Sch., 1931, Chem. Warfare Sch., 1931. Commd. 2d lt., C.A., Mar. 1912; promoted through grades to brig. gen., Dec. 1943; served in Philippines, 1915-17; with A.E.F. in France, 1918-19; now comdg. gen. 68th Army Anti-Aircraft Brigade, in South Pacific Area. Home: Stockton, Calif. †

FRENCH, DEXTER, educator; b. Des Moines, Feb. 23, 1918; s. Raymond Albert and Minnie Emily (Ormerod) F.; A.B., U. Dubuque, 1938, D.Sc., 1960; Ph.D., Iowa State U., 1942; m. Mary Catherine Martin, June 17, 1939; children—Alfred, David, Walter, Barbara (dec.), Jean, Nancy, Carol. Research chemist Corn Products Co., 1945; mem. faculty Iowa State U., from 1946, prof. chemistry, from 1955, prof. biochemistry, from 1960, chmn. dept. biochemistry and biophysics, 1963-71. Postdoctoral fellow phys. chemistry Harvard Med. Sch., 1942-44; sr. postdoctoral fellow NSF, London and Paris, 1962-63. Mem. Am. Chem. Soc., Am. Soc. Biol. Chemists, Am. Assn. Cereal Chemists, Phi Beta Kappa (posthumously). Home: Ames, Iowa. Dec. Nov. 26, 1981. Interned Iowa State U. Cemetary, Ames.

FRENCH, LAFAYETTE, JR., lawyer; b. Austin, Minn., Oct. 10, 1887; s. Lafayette and Mary (Richards) F.; ed. Carlton Coll. and U. of Minn.; m. Mabel Kaufman, Oct. 10, 1912; children—Janet, Lafayette. Admitted to Minn. bar, 1911, and began practice at Austin; ex-city atty. of Austin, 1919-22; U.S. dist. atty., Dist. of Minn., by apptmt. of President Harding, from June 1, 1922. Capt. 130th Inf., A.E.F., 1917-19. Republican. Conglist. Mason. Clubs: Theta Delta Chi, Minnesota, Minneapolis Athletic. Home: St. Paul, Minn. †

FRENCH, WILL, prof. education; b. Burrton, Kan., Oct. 24, 1889; s. John B. and Altha M. (Morris) F.; A.B., U. of Kan., 1912, B.S., 1914; A.M., Teachers College, Columbia, 1922, Ph.D., 1933; m. Mary Alice Smith, June 5, 1914; children—Mary Elizabeth (Mrs. Woodring Pearson), John Eugene, William Cole. Teacher high school, Winfield, Kansas, 1912-14; principal high school, Abilene, Kansas, 1914-16; principal high school, Winfield, Kansas, 1916-22, supt. schs., 1922-25; prin. high sch., Lincoln, Neb., 1925-29, asso. supt. and supt. of schs., Tulsa, Okla., 1929-35; supt. of schs., Long Beach, Calif., 1935-37; prof. education Teachers Coll., Columbia, from 1937; on leave for academic years, 1942-43 and 1943-44 to serve as supt. of schs., Long Beach, Calif. Life mem. N.E.A. (dept. of superintendence); mem. Am. Assn. Sch. Adminstrs., Nat. Assn. Secondary Sch. Prins. (served on coms. 1923-43), Kan. Schoolmasters, Phi Delta Kappa, Kappa Delta Pi. Mem. Riverside Ch. Author: American High School Administration (with J. D. Hull and B. L. Dodds), 1950, others; articles ednl. mags. Address: New York, N.Y. †

FRESTON, HERBERT, lawyer; b. Kansas City, Mo., Apr. 3, 1890; LL.B., U. So. Cal., 1915. Admitted Cal. bar, 1914; now mem. Mitchell, Siberberg & Knupp, Los Angeles. Mem. Am., Los Angeles (pres. 1940) bar assns., State Bar of Cal. (gov. 1944-46), Delta Theta Phi. Order of Coif.†

FREUND, CLEMENT JOSEPH, mechanical engineer, college dean; b. Appleton, Wis., Aug. 7, 1895; s. Alois John and Ottilia (Lenz) F.; m. Mabelle Gertrude Ziegler, Aug. 21, 1926; children—Mary Elizabeth, Paul Clement (dec.), Louis James (dec.). A.B., Campion Coll., Prairie du Chien, Wis., 1916; M.E., Marquette U., 1922; D.Sc. (hon.), Catholic U. Am., 1962; D.Eng. (hon.), U. Detroit, 1977. With Falk Corp., 1922-32, ednl. dir., 1926-32; instr. evening tech. courses Milw. Vocat. Sch., 1924-32, supr. same, 1926-30; spl. lectr. Coll. Engring., Marquette U., 1930-32; dean Coll. Engring. U. Detroit, 1932-62, prof., 1962-84; cons. higher tech. edn., West Pakistan, 1958-60; cons. engring. edn. Pakistan Commn. on Nat Edn., 1958-60; cons. Minn. State Coll. Bd., S.W. Minn. State Coll.; Mem. conf. bd. Asso. Research Councils (Com. on Fulbright Awards in Engring.), 1955-58; Mem. Gov.'s Seaway Commn., Mich., 1954. Contbr. profl. jours. Served from 2d to 1st lt. U.S. Army, World War I. Fellow ASME (life), Engring. Soc. Detroit (distinguished mem. 1971—, past pres., Horace H. Rackham Humanitarian award 1978); mem. Am. Foundrymen's Soc. (hon.), Am. Soc. Engring. Edn. (past pres., past chmn. ethics com., rep. Am. Council on Edn. 1955-58), Engrs.' Council Profl. Devel. (chmn. com. on ethics 1955-58, engring. manpower com.), Mich. Soc. Profl. Engrs. (past chmn. long range planning com.), Mich. Engring. Soc. (hon.), Crown and Anchor, Tau Beta Pi, Alpha Sigma Nu, Pi Tau Sigma, Theta Tau. Roman Catholic. Home: Detroit, Mich. Died Apr. 1984.

FREY, ALBERT JOSEPH, pharm. and chem. co. exec.; b. Urnaesch, Switzerland, Apr. 23, 1927; s. Albert and Luise (Stieger) F.; m. Dora Braendli, Feb. 4, 1956; children—Monika, Juerg. B.S., State Coll. Trogen, 1947; B.S. Chem. Engr, Swiss Fed. Inst. Tech., Zurich, 1951, Ph.D., 1953. Research fellow Swiss Fed. Inst. Tech., 1953-55, Harvard U., 1955-56; research chemist, then group leader Sandoz Ltd., 1956-62; from dir. research to exec. v.p. Sandoz Pharms., E. Hanover, N.J., 1962-70; pres., chief exec. officer Sandoz, Inc., E. Hanover, 1970-81, chmn. bd., from 1981; dir. Sandoz U.S., Inc., Northrup King Corp. Author. Mem. Pharm. Mfrs. Assn. (dir.), Swiss Chem. Soc., Am. Chem. Soc., N.Y. Acad. Scis., N.J. Acad. Scis., Assn. Harvard Chemists, Presidents Assn. Club: Essex Fells Country. Patentee in field. Home: Essex Fells, NJ.

FREYHAN, FRITZ ADOLF, physician; b. Berlin, Germany, Nov. 24, 1912; came to U.S., 1937, naturalized, 1943; s. Max and Clara (Gottschalk) F. M.D., U. Berlin, 1937. Diplomate: Am. Bd. Neurology and Psychiatry. Pathol. tng. Sydenham Hosp., N.Y.C., 1939, rotating intern, 1939-40; mem. staff Del. State Hosp., Farnhurst, 1940-50, clin. dir., dir. research, 1950-60; dir. dept. psychiatry and neurology Del. Hosp., Wilmington, 1954-61; cons. psychiatry VA Hosp., Wilmington, Del., 1954-61; dep. chief charge clin. studies, clin. neuropharmacology research center NIMH, 1961-66; dir. clin. studies, clin. and behavioral studies center St. Elizabeths Hosp., Washington, 1961-66; from asso. to adj. asso. prof. psychiatry U. Pa. Sch. Medicine, 1950-61; clin. prof. psychiatry George Washington U. Sch. Medicine, 1960-66; mem. faculty Washington Sch. Psychiatry, 1962-66; dir. research dept. psychiatry St. Vincent's Hosp., N.Y.C., 1966-72; asso. clin. prof. psychiatry N.Y.U. Med. Center, 1966-72. Editor: Comprehensive Psychiatry, from 1960; editor: Internat. Pharmacopsychiatry, from 1967. Fellow Am. Coll. Neuropsychopharmacology, N.Y. Acad. Medicine, Am. Psychiat. Assn., AAAS; mem. AMA, Med. Soc. D.C., Am. Psychopath. Assn. (pres. 1969), Collegium Internationale Neuro-Psychopharmacologicum (councilor), Assn. Nervous and Mental Diseases, Soc. Biol. Psychiatry, Internat. Com. for Prevention and Treatment of Depression, U.S. Com. for Prevention and Treatment of Depression (chmn.), Soc. Medico-Psychologique (asso.), Deutsche Gesellschaft fur Psychiatrie und Nervenheikunde (corr.), Societa Italiana di Neuropsicofarmacologia (corr.), Societe Royale de Medecine Mentale de Belgique (hon.). Club: Cosmos (Washington). Home: Chevy Chase, Md. Died Dec. 9, 1982.

FRIDLUND, H(ILMER) MAURICE, ret. lawyer; b. Sioux City, Iowa, Apr. 11, 1896; s. Magnus and Hilma (Bergman) F.; A.B., Grinnell Coll., 1918, LL.D., 1970; J.D., (Perkins scholar), Harvard, 1921; Sheldon traveling fellow Faculte de Droit, Sorbonne, Paris, 1921-22; postgrad. Inst. Internat. Law, Paris, 1921-22, Berlin Law Sch., Germany, 1922-23; m. Edith St. John, Dec. 24, 1923 (dec. 1965); children—Elaine (Mrs. Roger Lester), Norman St. John, Alice (Mrs. Warren Hance). Admitted to N.Y. bar, 1923, since practiced in N.Y.C.; with Kirlin, Campbell & Keating, 1923-69, partner, 1934-69, sr. mng. partner, 1964-69, ret., 1970. Vis. prof. polit. sci. Grinnell Coll., 1968-70, Kans. Wesleyan U., 1970-71, 72-73. Pres. Tenafly (N.J.) Bd. Health, 1944-56, Bergen County Pub. Health and San. Assn., 1946-56, Commn. on World Service and Finance, Newark Conf. Methodist Ch., 1948-56; observer at World Council Chs. Amsterdam Assembly, 1948, Uppsala, 1968. Mem. Commn. on Interpretation and Support World Council Chs. in U.S., 1956-69. Mem. adv. council Grinnell Coll. Mem. Am., N.Y. State bar assns., Maritime Law Assn. U.S., Phi Beta Kappa. Republican. Clubs: Harvard, India House (N.Y.C.); Sarasota (Fla.) Yacht. Contbr. articles to profl. jours. Home: Sarasota, Fla. Deceased.

FRIED, LAWRENCE, photojournalist; b. N.Y.C., June 28, 1926; s. Charles and Thelma (Kosower) F.; m. Nancy Reed, Aug. 23, 1952; children—Lauren Ann, Patricia. B.A., U. Miami, Fla., 1950. Photojournalist, from 1950; pres. Am. Soc. Mag. Photographers, 1973-78; exec. v.p. Image Bank (picture agy.), from 1974; guest lectr. in field. Author numerous articles; photographer over 300 mag. covers. Served with inf. AUS, 1943-46, ETO. Decorated Purple Heart withoak leaf cluster; French, Belgian, and English combat citations; Presdl. combat citation with cluster; recipient Best Interpretations of Fgn. News award Overseas Press Club, 1960. Home: Tarrytown, N.Y. Died Sept. 11, 1983.

FRIED, MIRIAM, violinist; b. Satu Mare, Rumania, Sept. 9, 1946; d. Tibor and Lili (Jaeger) F.; m. Paul M. Biss, June 29, 1969; 1 son, Daniel. Tchr. diploma, performer certificate, Rubin Music Acad., Tel Aviv; student, Joseph Gingold at Ind. U. Sch. Music, Ivan Galamian at Juilliard Sch. Music. Appearances with maj. orchs. in, U.S. and Europe, including, N.Y. Philharmonic, Munich Philharmonic, Chgo. Symphony, Boston Symphony, Frankfurt Radio Symphony; performs in ensembles with, Paul Biss and Garrick Ohlsson, rec. artist, Deutsche Grammaphon and CBS Records. Winner 1st prize Paganini Internat. Competition, Genoa, Italy, 1968; 1st prize Queen Elizabeth Competition, Brussels, 1971. Home: Akron, OH. *

FRIEDBERG, ARTHUR LEROY, educator, ceramic engineer; b. River Forest, Ill., Mar. 25, 1919; s. Oscar and Fannie (Blumenthal) F.; m. Marian Davis, Feb. 4, 1944; children—Richard Charles, Anne. B.S. in Ceramic Engring, U. Ill., 1941, M.S., 1947, Ph.D., 1952; postgrad., U. Chgo., 1943-44. Mem. faculty U. Ill., Champaign-Urbana, 1946-79, prof. ceramic engring., 1957-79, prof. emeritus, 1979-84, head dept., 1963-79; adj. prof. ceramic engring. Ohio State U., 1979-84. Trustee Edward Orton, Jr. Ceramic Found., 1979-84. Served to lt. (s.g.) USNR, 1943-46. Mem. Am. Ceramic Soc. (exec. dir. 1979—), Nat. Inst. Ceramic Engrs. (exec. dir. 1979-84). Home: Columbus, Ohio. Died Oct. 13, 1984.

FRIEDLAND, SAMUEL, business exec.; b. Nov. 23 1896. Co-founder, chmn. bd. Food Fair Stores, Inc. chmn. bd. Lefcourt Realty Corp., 1959-85. Home: Miam Beach, Fla. Died Apr. 9, 1985.

FRIEDMAN, ARNOLD D'ARCY, publisher; b. Plumer ville, Ark., July 24, 1900; s. Saul and Ida (Adelman) F. m. Judith Scheinberg, Feb. 29, 1932; children—J. Roger Elisabeth, John. B.A., Columbia U., 1922. Co-founder 1925; since pub. Chain Store Age; pub. Drug Store News Discount Store News, Nat. Home Center News, Super market Sales Man, Nation's Restaurant News; pres Chain Store Pub. Corp., Business Guides, Inc.; chmn. bd Lebhar-Friedman Inc., Largo Music Inc.; founder Larg

Size Week, Multi-Unit Food Service Operators Conf., also seminars. Club: City Athletic (N.Y.C.). Home: New York, N.Y. Died July 29, 1981.

FRIEDMAN, MILTON, physician; b. Newark, Sept. 13, 1903; s. Samuel and Sarah (Goldberg) F.; M.D., George Washington U., 1926; m. Marian M. Mendelson, 1928 (div., 1946); 1 dau., Susan; m. 2d, Elna Linborg, 1947. Interne, Newark Hosp., 1926-28, resident Bellevue Hospital, New York City, 1928-29, research fellow, 1930-32, now vis. radiation therapist; asso. prof. radiology N.Y.U. School Medicine, now professor; attending radio-therapist Hospital for Joint Diseases, New York City; attending radiologist New York University Hospital. Cons. Nat. Bur. Standards on radiation protection also USPHS on supervoltage radiation; cons. Walter Reed Army Hosp.; area cons. VA; chmn. brachy-therapy radiation AEC; med. dir. Lila Motley Cancer Found.; consultant Israel-American Medical Center; member of executive com. N.Y.C. Cancer Adv. Com.; mem. com. for radiation therapy studies NRC; mem. Am. Joint Com. for Classification Tumors; chmn. Coop. Project for Chemotherapy plus Radiation; Am. delegate Internat. Congress of Radiology, 1965. Served as lt. col. U.S. Army, chief radiation therapy sect. Walter Reed Gen. Hosp., 1942-45. Decorated Legion of Merit; recipient awards and prizes for exhibits by various socs., and for research in supervoltage radiation in cancer of bladder and testis, cancer chemotherapy and enhancement. Diplomate Am. Bd. Radiology. Fellow Am. Coll. Radiology (com. on internat. affairs); mem. Am. Radium Soc. (treas. 1964, pres.-elect 1965, president 1966), Soc. Head and Neck Surgeons, N.Y. Roentgen Soc. (treas. 1964), radiol. socs. N.Am. (spl. lectr. refresher courses), N.J., N.Y. Cancer Soc. (pres. 1959-60), N.J. Assn. Tumor Clinics, Am. Assn. Cancer Research, Am. Assn. for Study Neoplastic Diseases, A.M.A., Am. Radiotherapy Soc. (pres. 1961-62), Soc. Nuclear Medicine, Sigma Xi. Author: Tumors of the Skin (with J. S. Eller); Gynecological Roentgenology (with J. Jarcho); Roentgens, Rads, and Riddles, A Report on Supervoltage and Gamma Beam Teletherapy; also monographs, other sci. papers. Editor: American Lectures in Radiation Therapy. Died Feb. 12, 1983.

FRIEDMAN, RAPHAEL NATHAN, architect, engr.; b. Warren, Ill., Mar. 10, 1890; s. Leopold Hirsch and Johanna (Barry) F.; B.S., Armour Inst. Tech., 1911; student Art Inst. Chgo., 1907-11; m. Gladys Glick, Apr. 2, 1914 (dec. Dec. 1937); children—Warren James, Tom Richard; m. 2d, Ruth Klauber, Sept. 9, 1939. Ind. practice architecture, 1911-16; prof. architecture Chgo. Tech. Coll., 1911-16; v.p. Alfred S. Alschuler, Inc., 1920-40; sr. partner Friedman Alschuler & Sincere, 1940—; chief architect Gary Armor Plate Plant, other projects include Bond Store (Chgo.), plants of Central Steel & Wire Co., Chgo., Milw., Detroit, Cin., U.S. Parcel Post Stas. and Bulk Mail Handling Unit, Cleve. Served as capt. C.E., U.S. Army, 1917-19. Licensed structural engr., Ill.; licensed architect Ill., 17 other states. Fellow A.I.A.; mem. Ill. Soc. Architects, Soc. Am. Mil. Engrs. Republican. Clubs: Cliff Dwellers, Standard (Chgo.). Home: Evanston, Ill. †

FRIEDMAN, SIDNEY, banker, lawyer; b. N.Y.C., Dec. 1, 1907; s. William and Sarah (Silver) F.; m. Blanche Banner, Apr. 6, 1930; children—Nancy (Mrs. Paul Friedman), Stuart, Susan Elaine (Mrs. Emilios Dimitris). LL.B., Yale, 1931; M.A., Brown U., 1931, Ph.B., 1928. Bar: N.Y. bar 1932. Asso. firm Kaufman, Weitzner & Celler, N.Y.C., 1931-33; asst. to justice N.Y. Supreme Ct., 1933; counsel RFC, Washington, 1933-36; partner firm Cole, Friedman & Deitz, N.Y.C., 1936-64; chmn. bd. Nat. Bank N. Am., N.Y.C., 1964-73; chmn. bd., pres. Farmers Bank State of Del., Wilmington, 1976-77; counsel firm Kronish, Lieb, Shainswit, Weiner & Hellman, from 1973; chmn. exec. com. Trust Co. N. Am., 1955-57, Comml. Bank N. Am., 1957-60, MeadowBrook Nat. Bank, 1960-64; dir. Nat. Bank N.Am., 1960-75, Graphic Scis., 1972-73, C.I.T. Financial Corp., 1966-73. Editor: Yale Law Jour, 1930-31. Bd. dirs. Mitchell Field Devel. Corp., Nassau Citizens Devel., 1967-72; asso. trustee North Shore Hosp., Manhasset, N.Y., from 1965; treas., mem. exec. com. United Fund L.I., 1965-68; chmn. bd. ethics, Nassau County, from 1967; trustee, sec. Hofstra U., 1971-75. Recipient Met. award Yeshiva U., 1966; Citizen of Year award Dowling Coll.; Tree of Life award Boys' Town, 1968; Fiance award Post Coll., 1972. Fellow Phi Beta Kappa Assos.; mem. Am., N.Y.C., Nassau County bar assns., County Lawyers Assn., Phi Beta Kappa, Order of Coif. Home: Great Neck, N.Y. Died Sept. 13, 1982.

FRIEDNER, RELNARD WALTER, ins. co. exec.; b. Chgo., June 24, 1911; s. Frank and Ellen (Anderson) F.; student Northwestern U., 1928-31; m. Marian A. Nelson, Aug. 11, 1934; children—Barbara (Mrs. Robert M. Stevens), Marilyn L. (Mrs. Richard P. Amundsen). Former vice chmn., dir. Washington Nat. Ins. Co., Evanston, Ill., Washington Nat. Corp. Mem. Ill., Evanston chambers commerce. Mason, Rotarian. Home: Wilmette, Ill. Died 1982.

FRIEDRICH, CARL JOACHIM, prof. govt.; b. Leipzig, Saxony, Germany, June 5, 1901; s. Paul Leopold and Charlotte (Baroness von Buelow) F.; student univs. of Marburg, Frankfurt, Vienna, Heidelberg (Ph.D., Heidelberg 1925, U.J.D., hon., 1951); hon. A.M., Harvard, 1941; LL.D., Grinnell Coll., 1952, Duke University, 1963, Washington University, 1968; L.H.D., Columbia Univ., 1954, Colby Coll.; Dr. rer. pol. U. Cologne, also U. Padua; Doctor of Laws, Washington University, 1968; married Lenore Pelham, Oct. 6, 1924; children—Paul William, Otto Alva, Elizabeth Charlotte (dec.), Matilda Cornwall, Dorothea Amanda. Came to U.S., 1922, naturalized, 1938. Lecturer in govt., Harvard, 1926-27, asst. prof., 1927-31, asso. prof., 1931-36, prof. govt., 1936-84, Eaton prof. science of govt., 1955-84; mem. faculty Grad. Sch. Pub. Adminstrn., Harvard, 1938-84; dir. Sch. of Overseas Adminstrn., 1943-46; prof. polit. science Juristische Fakultät, University Heidelberg, 1956-84; govtl. affairs adviser Office Military Government, 1946-49, Germany. First prize $5,000. Greater Boston Contest; knight comdr.'s cross German Order of Merit. Lecturer. Mem. Am. Polit. Sci. Assn. (pres. 1962). Internat. Polit. Sci. Assn. (president 1967-84), Inst. Internat. de Philosophia Politique (pres. elect), Hist. Assn., Am. Acad. Arts and Scis., Am. Soc. Polit. Legal Philosophy, Inst. Internat. Philosophy (vice president), Phi Beta Kappa (honorary). Episcopalian. Clubs: The Athenaeum (London); Harvard (N.Y.C., Boston). Author books including: Constitutional Government and Democracy, 1950, rev. edit., 1968; The Age of the Baroque, 1952, revised edition, 1962; The Philosophy of Hegel, 1953; (with Brzezinski) Totalitarian Dictatorship and Autocracy, 1956, rev., 1965; The Philosophy of Law in Historical Perspective, 1957, rev. edit., 1965; Constitutional Reason of State, 1958; Man and His Government, 1963; Transcendant Justice, 1964; An Introduction to Political Theory, 1967; The Impact of American Constitutionalism Abroad, 1967; Trends in Federalism, 1968; Europe; An Emergent Nation?, published 1969. Editor: Public Policy, from 1940-63; editor of Totalitarianism, 1954; Studies in Federalism, 1954; American Experiences in Military Government in World War II, 1947; Nomos-Yearbook of American Society Political and Legal Philosophy. Contbr. to mags. Home: Cambridge, Mass. Died Sept. 19, 1984.

FRIEDRICHS, KURT OTTO, mathematician, educator; b. Kiel, Germany, Sept. 28, 1901; s. Karl and Elisabeth (Entel) F.; Ph.D., U. Göttingen, 1925; Sc.D., U. Aachen, 1971; m. Nellie Bruell, Aug. 11, 1937; children—Walter, Elisabeth, David, Christopher, Martin. Came to U.S., 1937, naturalized, 1944. Privadozent Technische Hochschule Aachen, U. Göttingen, 1929; prof. math. Technische Hochschule Braunschweig, 1930-37; vis. prof. N.Y. U., 1937-39, asso. prof., 1939-43, prof. applied math., 1943-83. Distinguished prof. applied math., 1964, asso. dir. Courant Inst., 1966, dir., 1966-67. Fellow A.A.A.S.; mem. Nat. Acad. Scis. Author: (with Richard Courant) Supersonic Flow and Shock Waves, 1948; Mathematical Aspects of the Quantum Theory of Fields; From Pythagoras to Einstein; Perbutations of Spectra in Hilbert Space; also articles in profl. jours. Home: New Rochelle, N.Y. Died Jan. 1, 1983.

FRIEND, CURTIS LUDWIG, assn. exec.; b. Cottbus, W. Ger., Jan. 8, 1933; emigrated to Can., 1951, naturalized, 1955; s. Curt and Ida (Klostermann) F. Sr. matriculation Wittenburg U., 1951; Pub., pres. Agribus Ltd., Toronto, 1960-69, pres., 1969—, Canadian Feed Industry Assn., Ottawa, Ont., Can., 1969-74, from 1974; Dir. Canola Council of Can., from 1979; mem. Can. Grains Council, from 1969. Mem. Am. Soc. Assn. Execs. (planning com. 1979-81), Canadian Farm Writers Assn., Am. Feed Mfrs. Assn., Agrl. Assn. Exec. Council, Can. Egg Mktg. Agy., Can. Turkey Mktg. Agy., Can. Chicken Mktg. Agy. Home: Ottawa ON, Canada.

FRIES, CHARLES CARPENTER, educator; born Reading, Pa., Nov. 29, 1887; s. J. Howard and Caddie Corinne (Smith) F.; A.B., Bucknell U., 1909, A.M., 1911; grad. student U. Chgo., 1910, U. Mich., 1915, Ph.D., 1922; Litt.D., Bucknell U., 1946; m. Nala D. Webb, June 1911; m. 2d, Agnes Carswell, May 30, 1920; children—E. Corinne, A. Carolyn, Charles Carswell, Robert McMillan, Peter Howard. Instr., Bucknell U., 1911-15; asst. prof. English, 1915-17, prof., 1917-20; asst. prof. English, Univ. Mich., 1920-23, asso. prof., 1923-28, prof., 1928-58, emeritus professor of English, from 1958; editor in chief Early Modern English Dictionary, 1928-58, emeritus editor in chief, from 1958; dir. Linguistic Inst., 1936-40, 45-47, dir. English Language Institute, 1941-56, emeritus dir., from 1958. U.S. del. several internat. congresses. Cons. U.S., fgn. and internat orgns.; cons. linguistics and lang. teaching Poland, 1962. Mem. Modern Lang. Assn. Am. (1st v.p. 1958), Linguistic Society Am. (pres. 1939), Nat. Council Tchrs. English (past pres.; Hatfield award), Research Club U. Mich., Mich. Acad. Sci., Arts and Letters, Philol. Soc. of England, Phi Delta Kappa, Phi Kappa Phi, Phi Beta Kappa. Author numerous books of research studies on English syntax and on teaching English, 1925, the latest one: Foundations for English Teaching (with Agnes C. Fries), 1960; Linguistics and Reading, 1963; Linguistics: The Study of Lang., 1964. Contbr. Modern Lang. Assn., Language, Eng. Journal, Lang. Learning. Home: Ann Arbor, Mich. †

FRIES, VOLLMER WALTER, mfg. executive; b. Pleasant Valley, N.Y., July 17, 1902; s. William Christian and Lona A. (Vollmer) F.; E.E., Rensselaer Poly. Inst., 1924; Doctor of Engineering, Fenn College, 1965; m. Ruth Dudley Wick, July 17, 1928; children—William Vollmer, Carole Wick. With The White Motor Co., Cleve., 1924-56, became v.p., dir., 1943, resigned as exec. v.p., dir. 1955; chmn. bd. White Consol. Industries, Inc., (formerly known as White Sewing Machine Corp.), Cleveland, 1955-85. With conservation division W.P.B., 1940-41; mem. W. Averell Harriman Mission, U.S. Embassy, London, 1942-43. Mem. bd. trustees Fenn Coll., Rensselaer Polytechnic Institute, Troy, N.Y. Mem. Society Automotive Engineers. Clubs: Union, Country; Mid Day (Cleve.); Engineers (N.Y.C.). Home: Cleveland, Ohio. Died Jan. 9, 1985.

FRINK, RUSSELL L., lawyer; b. Jasper, Fla., Mar. 1, 1889; s. John Solon and Leila Clarice (Bell) F., student Jasper Normal Inst., 1905; LL.B., Washington and Lee Univ., Lexington, Va., 1910; m. Ruth Knight, June 30, 1915; children—Eloise (Mrs. Robert L. Cleveland), Russell L. Admitted to Florida state bar, 1910; in gen. practice of law, High Springs, Fla., Aug.-Oct., 1910, Jasper, Fla., 1910-24, Jacksonville, Fla., from 1924; general counsel asso. Flagler System Cos. 1953-59; genreal counsel Fla. East Coast Ry. 1939-59; dir., sec. Atlantic & East Coast Terminal Co. 1939-59. dir., Florida Pub. Co. Chmn. Fla. R.R. Assn. 1945-59. Member city council, Jasper, Fla., 1921-24, N.R.A. Compliance Bd., Duval Co., 1933-34, legal adv. bd. Duval Co. Selective Service, 1941-45. Mem. Fla. Council for the Blind, 1942-46, Jacksonville (past pres.), Fla., Am. bar assns., Jacksonville, and Fla State Chamber of Commerce, S.A.R. (past pres. Jacksonville chapter, past chancellor, vice pres. and pres. Fla. State Soc.), Fla., Jacksonville hist. socs. (director). Democrat. Baptist. Mason. Clubs: Florida Yacht, Ye Mystic Revelers, Traffic, Civitan (past pres. and lt. gov.). Home: Jacksonville, Fla. †

FRISBIE, ROBERT T., machinery exec.; b. Hartford, Conn., June 4, 1889; s. Charles Gillette and Bell (Welles) F.; B.S., Yale, 1912; m. Dorothy Pease Frisbie, Sept. 26, 1914; children—Barbara (Mrs. Miller), Robert Taylor, Herbert Sawyer. Pres., dir. New Britain Machine Co. now chmn. exec. com., dir.; dir. Storms Drop Forging Co. Dir. New Britain Gen. Hosp. Mem. New Britain C. of C. (dir.), Mfrs. Assn. Hartford Co. (dir.). Republican. Club: Shuttle Meadows, Inc. †

FRITCH, HOWARD F., street ry. exec.; b. Livingston, N.J., Sept. 24, 1888; s. Wilson and Jennie V. (Fowler) F.; B.S. in E.E., Worcester Poly. Inst., 1910; m. Ethel Gifford, 1914; 1 son, Ralph G. Began with Boston & Northern St. Ry. and Old Colony St. Ry., 1910; asst. gen. mgr. Eastern Mass. St. Ry., 1919-24; asst. to chmn. exec. com. B. & M. Ry., 1924-26, passenger traffic mgr., Boston, 1926-30, dir. budgets, 1930-48; pres. B. & M. Transportation Co., 1925-48; became asst. to pres. N.Y.N.H. & H. Ry., 1948, also pres., N.E. Transportation Co. and Conn. Co.; pres. Berkshire St. Ry. Co., Pittsfield, Mass. Mem. Assn. Am. R.R.'s (chmn. motor transport div.), Sigma Xi, Tau Beta Pi, Alpha Tau Omega. Republican. Address: Pittsfield, Mass. †

FRITZE, GERARD MARIA, bus. exec.; b. Rostock, Mecklenburg, Oct. 14, 1890; s. Paul and Lucca (Clement) F.; ed. pub. schs.; m. Margarete Illgner, Nov. 24, 1917; 1 dau., Lucca (Mrs. Rudolph Felix Werdmuller von Eigg). Came to U.S., 1940, naturalized, 1946. Employee Banco Aleman Trans-Atlantico, Buenos Aires, Argentina, 1909-14; chief of documentary credits Mendelssohn & Co., Berlin, 1922-23; a founder N.V. Hollandsche Koopmansbank, Amsterdam, 1923, and served as mng. dir., 1923-47, dir. since 1947; pres. and dir. Holland Am. Merchants Corp., N.Y. City, from 1940. Served as brevet lt. Army, 1914-18. Decorated Officer of Order of Orange-Nassau (Netherlands), 1947, Officer of Order of Vasa (Sweden), 1939. Lutheran. Clubs: India House (N.Y. City); Richmond County Country (S.I., N.Y.). Home: Staten Island, N.Y. †

FROHOCK, WILBUR MERRILL, ret. educator; b. South Thomaston, Maine, June 20, 1908; s. Horatio Wilbur and Sarah (Merrill) F.; Ph.B., Brown U., 1930, M.A., 1931, Ph.D., 1935; m. Natalie Barrington, Aug. 16, 1938; children—Natalie, Sarah. Instr. French, Brown U., 1935-37; instr. French, Columbia, 1937-42, asst. prof., 1945-48, asso. prof., 1948-53; prof. romance langs. Wesleyan U., 1953-56; prof. romance langs. and gen. edn. Harvard, 1956-59, prof. romance langs., 1959, emeritus, 1976; Bacon Exchange prof., Lille, 1959. Author: The Novel of Violence in America, 1950; Andre Malraux and the Tragic Imagination, 1952; Strangers to This Ground, 1962; Rimbaud's Poetic Practice, 1963; Style and Temper, 1967. Home: Cambridge, Mass. Died July 31, 1984.

FROME, WESTON GEORGE, business exec.; b. Pen Argyl, Pa., May 1, 1888; s. William R. and Jenny (Young) F.; student Lehigh U., Bethlehem, Pa.; m. Hazel E. Johnson, Oct. 12, 1913; 1 dau., Mada M. (wife of Lt. Col. Robert A. McGill). Successively gen. mgr. explosives dept., chemist, plant supervisor, plant mgr., sales mgr., gen. mgr. sales and operations (west coast branch), vice pres., mem. exec. com., mem. bd. dirs., Atlas Powder Co. Mem. Wilmington C. of C., U.S. Ordnance Assn. Republican. Presbyterian. Mason, Elk. Clubs: Wilmington, Wilmington (Del.) Country. Home: Wilmington, Del. †

FROMM, EDWARD, silver fox breeder; b. Hamburg, Wis., Mar. 6, 1890; s. Fred and Alvina (Nieman) F.; grad. County Normal, 1906, State Tchrs. Coll., 1909; m. Alice Frederick, June 25, 1919; children—Lenore (Mrs. Chester Wade), Doris (Mrs. Jack Tead), Johanna (Mrs. Thomas Alger). Pres. Fromm Bros., Inc., growers Am. ginseng and breeders of silver foxes and minks. Address: Hamburg, Wis. †

FROMME, ALEX M., justice Kans. Supreme Ct.; b. Hoxie, Kans., Mar. 11, 1915; s. Joseph H. and Frances (Morgan) F.; m. Ruth Marie Kesler, Sept. 16, 1939. A.B., LL.B., Washburn U. Bar: Kans. bar 1939. Practiced in, Hoxie, individual practice, 1939-48; partner firm Fromme & Fromme, 1949-66; county atty. Sheridan County, 1941-48; justice Kans. Supreme Ct., from 1966; partner Fromme Ins. Agy., Hoxie; dir. First Nat. Bank Hoxie. Contbr. articles to legal jours. Instl. rep. local council Boy Scouts Am., 1948-49; home service chmn. Sheridan County chpt. ARC, 1941-47; pres. Sheridan County Community Fund, 1964-65. Mem. Am., Kans. (pres. 1961-62), N.W. Kans. (past mem. council) bar assns., Nat. Conf. Bar Presidents. Club: Rotary (local pres. 1947-48). Home: Topeka, Kans.

FROST, CHARLES SYDNEY, business exec.; b. Argyle, N.S., Can., 1893. President, dir. The Bank Nova Scotia, Toronto; dir. Imperial Life Assurance Co. of Can., Cosmos Imperial Mills, Toronto Gen. Trusts Corp. Home: Toronto, Ont., Can. Died May 6, 1985.

FROST, HAROLD MAURICE, physician; b. Bowdoinham, Me., June 25, 1888; s. John Maurice and Jeanette (Dunlap) F.; A.B., Brown U., 1909; M.D., Harvard, 1915; m. Lucy Maria Church, Feb. 2, 1915; children—Harold Maurice, Richard John. Intern Mass. Gen. Hosp., Boston, 1913-15; asst. supt. Mass. Charitable Eye and Ear Infirmary, 1919-21; practice, specializing in surgery, Boston, 1921-28; with New Eng. Mut. Life Ins. Co. from 1924, med. dir. from 1931. Trustee New Eng. Bapt. Hosp. Served as capt. M.C., B.E.F. and U.S. Army, 1915-18. Mem. A.M.A., Assn. Life Ins. Med. Dirs., Mass. Med. Soc., Phi Beta Kappa, Alpha Omega Alpha. Mason. Club: Harvard. Home: Wellesley Hills, Mass. †

FROVA, MANLIO, mfg. exec.; b. nr. Caneva, Italy, Feb. 28, 1889; s. Antonio and Mary (Chiesa) F.; student Tech. Inst. of Textiles, Como, Italy, 1906, Bicconi U., Milano, 1908; m. Julia Hadro, Nov. 16, 1935; children—Carl, Jean. Came to U.S., 1912, naturalized, 1918. Textile mfr., Europe; with Warren (R.I.) Textile and Machinery Co., from 1935, pres., from 1944; joined Berkshire Fine Spinning Assn., Providence, 1935, becoming v.p., 1948; following merger of cos., became v.p., dir. Berkshire-Hathaway, Inc., Providence. Home: Attleboro, Mass. †

FRY, J(ACOB) M(ARTIN), coll. adminstr.; b. Ephrata, Pa., Feb. 20, 1887; s. Samuel Curtis and Catherine Rebecca (Kline) F.; B.S., Pa. State Coll., 1917; m. Mary Mabel Allison, May 1, 1919. Agrl. agt., Northumberland, Co., Pa., 1917-24; asst. dir., agrl. extension, Pa. State Coll., 1924-42, dir. of agr. and home economics extension, from 1942. Mem. Pa. Farm Show Commn.; mem. Nat. 4-H Club Found. Mem. Am. Farm Economics Assn., Acacia, Gamma Sigma Delta, Epsilon Sigma Phi, Phi Kappa Phi. Lutheran. Mason, Odd Fellow. Kiwanis Internat.(past gov., Pa. Dist.). Home: State College, Pa. †

FRYE, JOHN CHAPMAN, geologist; b. Marietta, Ohio, July 25, 1912; s. Harley Edgar and Maude Vesta (Chapman) F.; m. Ruth L. Heizer, Aug. 29, 1936; children—Sally Jean, John Douglas (dec.), Terri Ruth. A.B., Marietta Coll., 1934, D.Sc., 1955; postgrad., Ohio State U., 1935; M.S., U. Iowa, 1937, Ph.D., 1938. Geologist U.S. Geol. Survey, 1938-42; asst. dir. Kans. State Geol. Survey, 1942-45, exec. dir., 1945-54, asst. state geologist, 1942-45, state geologist, 1952-54; asst. prof. U. Kans., 1942-45, asso. prof., 1945-52, prof. geology, 1952-54; chief Ill. State Geol. Survey, 1954-74; prof. geology U. Ill., 1963-74; exec. dir. Geol. Soc. Am., from 1974; spl. research geologist Bur. Econ. Geology, U. Tex., summers 1955-64, N.Mex. Bur. Mines and Geology, NMIT, Socorro, summers from 1971; Adv. com. to sec. interior for U.S. Geol. Survey, 1960-66; sci. adv. council to gov., Ill., 1964-74; adv. com. health physics Oak Ridge Nat. Lab., 1959-72, adv. com. on environ. studies, 1972-77; del. to 19th Internat. Geol. Congress, Algiers, 1952; mem. div. earth scis. NRC, 1958-70, mem. div. exec. com., 1961-64, 72-75, mem. com. geologic aspects radioactive waste disposal, 1955-64, chmn., 1962-64; mem. adv. com. on earth resources remote sensing to U.S. Geol. Survey, 1966-70, chmn., 1966-69; mem. com. on mineral sci. and tech., adv. to U.S. Bur. Mines, 1966-69; chmn. com. on Radioactive Waste Mgmt., 1970-75; mem. bd. on energy studies NRC, 1974-77, mem. bd. mineral resources, 1974-78; mem. U.S. Nat. Commn. UNESCO, 1967-72, exec. com., 1970-72; mem. exec. com. Ill. Water Resources Center, 1963-74; mem. nat. adv. bd. Desert Research Inst., U. Nev., 1970-79; mem. exec. adv. com. future oil prospects Nat. Petroleum Council, 1968-70. Contbr. sci. articles to profl. jours. Recipient U.S. Dept. Interior Pub. Service award, 1972. Fellow Geol. Soc. Am. (councilor 1958-61, bd. asso. editors 1962-73), AAAS; mem. Nat. Acad. Engring., Ill. Geol. Soc., Am. Inst. Mining. Metall. and Petroleum Engrs., Am. Assn. Petroleum Geologists, Soc. Econ. Geologists, Ill. Acad. Sci. (pres. 1962-63), Soc. Econ. Paleontologists and Mineralogists (hon. mem., v.p. 1965-66), Am. Geol. Inst. (pres. 1966), Assn. Am. State Geologists (editor 1956-57, sec.-treas. 1957-58, pres. 1960), Am. Inst. Profl. Geologists, Am. Geophys. Union, Ill. Mining Inst., Sigma Xi, Sigma Gamma Epsilon, Alpha Sigma Phi. Clubs: Mason (Washington), Rotarian. (Washington), Cosmos (Washington). Home: Boulder, CO.

FRYE, ROYAL MERRILL, physicist; b. Milford, N.H., May 27, 1890; s. Frank Barton and Elsie Wiletta (Merrill) F.; m. Louise Alexander, June 11, 1915 (dec. Apr. 1969); m. Virginia May Brigham, May 7, 1970. A.B., Boston U., 1911, A.M., 1912, Ph.D., 1934; student, New Eng. Conservatory Music, 1906-08, Harvard Grad. Sch., 1912-13, Mass. Inst. Tech.; part-time, Am. Inst. Normal Methods, 1928; Sc.D. (hon.), Belknap Coll., 1968. Instr. physics Boston U., 1913-14, chemistry, 1914-16; instr. physics Mass. Inst. Tech., 1915-31, Worcester Poly. Inst., 1926-27, Lincoln Inst., Boston, 1930-46, 52-61; mem. staff grad. div. Coll. Engring., Northeastern U., 1951-60; instr. physics Boston U., 1931-36, asst. prof., 1936-42; prof., and chmn. dept. physics Boston U. (Grad. Sch.), 1942-50; prof. physics, head dept. Simmons Coll., 1950-59; prof. physics, dean (Coll. Advanced Sci.), Canaan, N.H., 1959-63; pres. Belknap Coll., Center Harbor, N.H., 1963-69, chancellor, from 1969; Wood Products Chem. Co., Inc., 1970-75; sci. cons. Operation Crossroads, Bikini, 1946; cons. AAF, AMC, Watson Labs., C.F.S. in connection with V-2 firing, 1946. Author: (with Robert E. Hodgdon) Practical Physics, 1935, Graphical Mathematics, 1941, Graphical Introduction to the Harmon, (with Esther W. Tipple), 1942, Essentials of Applied Physics, 1947, Significant Advances in Science for the Layman, 1978; Editor monthly letter: Significant Advances in Science, from 1960; Contbr.: also 60 articles to sci. jours. and govt. publs. Torch mag. Pres. Coop. Service, Inc., 1944-49, Boston Center Adult Edn., 1950-53; mem. bd. aldermen, Waltham, Mass., 1916-17; selectman Town of Royalston, Mass., from 1976, chmn. bd., 1978-79, 81-82; deacon 1st Congl. Ch. of Royalston, from 1973. Mem. AAAS, AAUP (nat. councillor 1950-53), Boston U. Alumni Assn. (v.p. 1954-56), Village Improvement and Hist. Soc. of Royalston (pres. 1976-78), Phi Beta Kappa. Club: Torch (Boston). Died Oct. 15, 1981.

FU, KING-SUN, electrical engineer; b. China, Oct. 2, 1930; s. Tzao-jen and Tzao-wen (Hsiang) F.; m. Viola Ou, Apr. 7, 1958; children: Francis, Thomas, June. B.S., Nat. Taiwan U., 1953; M.A.Sc., U. Toronto, 1955; Ph.D., U. Ill., 1959. Research engr. Boeing Airplane Co., 1959-60; mem. faculty Purdue U., 1960-85, prof. elec. engring., 1966-85, Goss disting. prof., 1975-85. Author: Sequential Methods in Pattern Recognition and Machine Learning, 1968, Syntactic Methods in Pattern Recognition, 1974, Statistical Pattern Classification using Contextual Information, 1980, Syntactic Pattern Recognition and Applications, 1982. Guggenheim fellow, 1972. Fellow IEEE; mem. Nat. Acad. Engring., Academia Sinica, Am. Soc. Engring. Edn., Assn. Computing Machinery. Home: West Lafayette, Ind. Died Apr. 29, 1985.

FUCHS, RALPH F(OLLEN), prof. law; b. St. Louis, March 8, 1899; s. Walter Herman and Paula (Follenius) F.; A.B., LL.B., Washington U. (St. Louis), 1922; Ph.D., Robert Brookings Grad. Sch. (Wash.), 1925; J.S.D., Yale, 1935; research fellow, Columbia school of law, 1937-38; married Gladys Alexander, Sept. 22, 1922 (died 1934); m. 2d Annetta Gross Zillmer, June 7, 1939; children—Martha (Mrs. John H. Ferger), Hollis Alexander. Admitted to bar in state of Mo., 1922; research asst., Inst. of Econs., Washington, 1922-25; staff, war transactions sect., U.S. Dept. of Justice, 1925-26; practiced law, St. Louis, 1926-27; asst. prof., prof. law Washington U. (St. Louis), 1927-41; asst. sec., sec., bd. legal examiners, U.S. Civil Service Commn., 1941-44; spl. asst., U.S. Atty. Gen., Solicitor-General, 1944-46; cons. Fed. agys.; mem. U.S. Atty. Gen.'s com. on administrative procedure, 1938-41; prof. law, Ind. U., since 1945; mem. Nat. Enforcement Commn., Econ. Stablzn. Agy., 1951-53; adviser Indian Law Inst., New Delhi, 1960-61. Chmn. Mo. N.R.A. Labor Compliance Bd., 1933-35; commr. Mo., Nat. Conf. of Commrs. on Uniform State Laws, 1936-45. Served as pvt., field arty., U.S. Army, 1918-19; 2d lt., field arty. res., 1919-29. Mem. Am. Bar Assn., Am. Econs. Assn., Am. Assn. University Professors (1st v.p. 1950-52, pres. 1960-62, gen. secretary 1955-57), Phi Beta Kappa. Unitarian. Editor: vol. IV, Selected Essays on Constitutional Law, 1938; Co-editor: Cases and Materials on Introduction to Law, 1952; contbd. prof. jours. Home: Bloomington, Ind. Died Feb. 7, 1985.

FUESLER, JOHN PETER, exec.; b. Hartington, Neb., June 11, 1887; s. Sigmund and Elizabeth (Fuessler) F.; student pub. schs.; m. Sue L. Couch, Aug. 9, 1915. With Anderson, Clayton & Co., Houston, 1905-48, v.p., 1942-48, dir. from 1942. Address: Hunt, Tex. †

FULCHER, GEORGE AVIS, bishop; b. Columbus, Ohio, Jan. 30, 1922; s. George Avis and Mary Munson (Lennon) F. A.B., St. Charles Coll., Columbus, 1944; Th.B., Mt. St. Mary Sem., Norwood, Ohio, 1948; Th.D., Pontifical U. St. Thomas, Rome, 1951. Ordained priest Roman Catholic Ch., 1948, asst. pastor in, Columbus and Newark, Ohio, 1948-75, editor of diocesan newspaper, 1958-67; part-time instr. moral and pastoral theology Pontifical Coll. Josephinum, Worthington, Ohio, from 1956; pastor St. Joseph Cathedral, Columbus, from 1975; aux. bishop Cath. Diocese of Columbus, from 1976; mem. Met. Area Ch. Bd., Columbus. Democrat. Home: Columbus, Ohio. Died Jan. 25, 1984.

FULLER, FRED ELLSWORTH, lawyer; b. Bedford, Iowa, Sept. 26, 1901; s. Ren Herman and Bess M. (Smith) F.; A.B. cum laude, Ohio Wesleyan U., 1923; J.D. summa cum laude, Ohio State U., 1926; m. Mary Isabelle Beetham, Sept. 1, 1923; children—Anne (Mrs. Alan C. Boyd), Fred Ellsworth, Bess (Mrs. Robert D. Brownell), Margaret (Mrs. Trygve J. Sandberg). Admitted to Ohio bar, 1926, practiced in Toledo; partner law firm Fuller, Henry, Hodge & Snyder, 1926-74, counsel, from 1974. Dir. Toledo Edison Co., 1949-73, now dir. emeritus. Corp. trustee from alumni Ohio Wesleyan U., 1953-63, trustee-at-large, 1964-70; trustee Ohio Wesleyan Assos. (1st chmn.); trustee Am. Cancer Soc. Lucas County. Fellow Am. Coll. Trial Lawyers, Ohio Bar Found. (life), Am. Bar Found. (life mem.; mem. U.S. Atty. Gen.'s nat. com. to study anti-trust laws); mem. Am. (former chmn. anti-trust sect., mem. com. on restrictive trade practices fgn. 1966-67), Ohio (former chmn. com. antitrust law), N.Y., Toledo, Inter-Am., Internat. bar assns., Assn. Bar N.Y.C., Am. Law Inst. (life), Internat. Assn. Ins. Counsel (def. research inst. liaison com.), Ohio Hist. Soc. (trustee 1966-75), Newcomen Soc. N. Am., Ohio Soc. N.Y., Order of Coif, Chi Phi, Phi Delta Phi, Delta Sigma Rho. Republican. Methodist. Clubs: Toledo, Inverness, Rotary, Skytop (Skytop, Pa.). Home: Toledo, Ohio. Died Oct. 8, 1981.

FULLER, LEONARD FRANKLIN, elec. engr.; b. Portland, Ore., Aug. 21, 1890; s. Franklin Ide and Anna Jessie (Parrish) F.; M.E., Cornell U., 1912; Ph.D., Stanford, 1919; m. Lucretia Robinson Strong, June 22, 1912 (she died 1943); children—Franklin Ide, Leonard Franklin, Mary Esther; married 2d, Eleanor Pearl Rideout, September 15, 1944. Began as electrical engineer with the National Electric Signaling Co., Brooklyn, N.Y., 1912; chief elec. engr. Federal Telegraph Co., 1913-19; designed, superintended mfr. and installation high power transoceanic radio telegraph transmitters for U.S. Navy in various parts of world, 1914-19; mem. anti-submarine group of Nat. Research Council, 1917-19; cons. practice, 1919-22; designed carrier current telephone equipment installed on 165 kilovolt lines, Great Western Power Co., 1921, and 220 kilovolt lines Pac. Gas and Electric Co., 1922; elec. engr., General Electric Co., 1923-24; cons. practice, 1924-26; elec. engr., General Electric Co., 1926-28; executive v.p. and chief engineer Federal Telegraph Company, 1928-32; prof. electrical engineering and chairman department, University of California, and in consulting practice, 1930-43; consultant on carrier current installations Hoover Dam power lines, City of Los Angeles, 1936; consulting engr. Joshua Hendy Iron Works 1943, chief engr., 1944-45; acting prof. elec. engring. and coordinator of Contract Research Stanford U., 1946-54; engaged in private consulting practice, from 1954. Fellow Am. Inst. E.E., Inst. Radio Engrs., A.A.A.S.; mem. Sigma Xi, Eta Kappa Nu, Tau Beta Pi. Awarded Morris Liebmann prize, Inst. Radio Engrs., 1919. Club: Sierra. Patentee radio telegraph apparatus. Contbr. tech. papers. Home: Palo Alto, Cal. †

FULLER, RICHARD BUCKMINSTER, geometrician, educator, architect-designer; b. Milton, Mass., July 12, 1895; s. Richard Buckminster and Caroline Wolcott (Andrews) F.; m. Anne Hewlett, July 12, 1917; children—Alexandra Willets (dec.), Allegra Fuller Snyder. Student, Milton Acad., 1904-13, Harvard, 1913-15, U.S. Naval Acad., 1917; student recipient 47 hon. doctorates in design arts, sci., humane letters, laws, fine arts, lit., engring. and archtl. engring. from, N.Am. univs., 1954-80; fellow, St. Peter's Coll., Oxford (Eng.) U., 1970. Apprentice machine fitter Richards, Atkinson & Haserick (cotton mill machinery importers), Sherbrooke, Que., Can., 1914; various apprentice positions Armour & Co., N.Y.C., 1915-17, asst. export mgr., 1919-21; nat. account sales mgr. Kelly-Springfield Truck Co., 1922; pres. Stockade Bldg. System, 1922-27; founder 4-D Co., Chgo., 1927, pres., 1927-32; asst. dir. research Pierce Found.-Am. Radiator-Standard San. Mfg. Co., 1930; founder Dymaxion Corp., Bridgeport, Conn., 1932, dir., chief engr., 1932-35; asst. to dir. research and devel. Phelps Dodge Corp., 1936-38; tech. cons. Fortune Mag., 1938-40; v.p. chief engr. Dymaxion Co., Inc., Del., 1941-42; chief mech engring. sect. Bd. Econ. Warfare, 1942-44; spl. asst. to dir Fgn. Econ. Adminstrn., 1942-44; chmn. bd., adminstrv engr. Dymaxion Dwelling Machines, 1944-46; chmn. bd trustees Fuller Research Found., Wichita, Kans., 1946-54 pres. Geodesics, Inc., Forest Hills, N.Y., from 1949 Plydomes, Inc., Des Moines, from 1957; chmn. bd Tetrahelix Corp., Hamilton, Ohio, 1959; Charles Elio Norton prof. Harvard, 1961-62; vis. prof., lectr., criti Cornell U., Yale, Mich. U., M.I.T., Princeton, U. Minn Washington U., U. Calif. at Berkeley, U. Ill., others distinguished univ. prof. So. Ill. U., from 1959; now univ prof. emeritus; world fellow in residence University Cit Sci. Center, from 1972, Bryn Mawr, Haverford, Swarth more colls.-U. Pa., Phila., 1972-78; prof. emeritus U. Pa Jahawarlal Nehru lectr. Nehru Meml. Fund, New Delh India, 1969; hon. royal designer for industry Royal Soc Arts, Eng., 1980; numerous lectures, exhibits at ma instns. throughout world. Author: 4D Timelock, 192 Nine Chains to the Moon, 1938, (with Robert Marks Dymaxion World of Buckminster Fuller, 1960, No Mor Second Hand God, 1962, Education Automation, 196 Untitled Epic Poem on the History of Industrializatio poetry, 1963, Ideas and Integrities, 1963, (with Joh McHale) World Resources Inventory, 1963-67, Operatin Manual for Spaceship Earth, 1969, Utopia or Oblivio 1969, Buckminister Fuller Reader, 1970, I Seem to be Verb, 1970, Intuition, 1972, Earth Inc, 1973, Synergetic 1975, And It Came to Pass, 1976, Synergetics II, 1979, O Education, 1979, Critical Path, 1981; contbr., editor (wi John McHale) several mags.; Inventor: (with Joh McHale) Dymaxion House, Chgo., 1927, Dymaxic

3-wheeled automobile, 1932-34; designer (with John McHale) Dymaxion deployment unit steel igloo, Kansas City, 1940, geodesic structure for Ford Motor Co. rotunda dome, Dearborn, Mich., USMC, advance base shelters, Dept. Commerce Internat. Trade Fair dome pavillions, 1956—, all D.E.W. Line radomes, USN geodesic storage domes, Antarctica, 1956, Union Tank Car repair shop domes, Baton Rouge, also Wood River, Ill., 1958-59, Kaiser Aluminum domes, Hawaii, 1957, Virginia Beach, Va., 1958, Oklahoma City, Borger, Tex., Abilene, Kans., Okla. Bank, 1959, golden dome Am. exhibit, Moscow, USSR, 1959, geodesic dome, nat. hdqrs., Am. Soc. Metals, climatron for, Mo. Bot. Gardens, St. Louis, 1960, domes for U.S. sci. malls, Boeing Co. spaceorama dome, Ford Motor dome, Ency. Brit. dome, all at Seattle Worlds Fair, 1962, Sports Palace, Paris, France, 1960, Cinerama Theatre, Hollywood, Cal., 1963, Yomiuri Star dome, Tokyo, Japan, 1964, also dome for, N.Y. World's Fair Pavilion, 1964, U.S. Pavilion, Montreal World's Fair, 1967. Recipient award of merit USMC, 1954; Gran Premio Trienniale de Milano, Italy, 1954, 57; Centennial award Mich. State U., 1955; Gold medal scarab Nat. Archtl. Soc., 1958; Frank P. Brown medal Franklin Inst., 1960; Plomado de Oro award Soc. Mexican Architecture, 1963; 1st Dean's award SUNY, Buffalo, 1980; honored with Buckminster Fuller Recognition Day U. Colo., 1963, Buckminster Fuller Recognition Day State of Mass., 1977, Buckminster Fuller Recognition Day Cities of Boston and Cambridge, 1977, Buckminster Fuller Recognition Day State of Minn., 1978, Buckminster Fuller Recognition Day State of Ill., 1980, Buckminster Fuller Recognition Day City of Buffalo, 1980, Buckminster Fuller Recognition Day City of Austin, 1981; Benjamin Franklin life fellow Royal Soc. Arts, Eng., 1960; named Humanist of Year Am. Assn. Humanists, 1969; named to Housing Hall of Fame, 1981. Fellow AAAS (life), Royal Inst. Brit. Architects (hon., gold medal 1968), Inst. Gen. Semantics (hon. trustee), Bldg. Research Inst. of Nat. Acad. Scis., World Acad. Art and Sci., Lincoln Acad. Ill., Inst. Advanced Philosophic Research, AIA (hon. life, award of merit N.Y. chpt. 1952, gold medal Phila. chpt. 1960, Allied Professions gold medal 1963, gold medal 1970, honor award U.S. pavilion Expo 67 1968); mem. Nat. Inst. Arts and Letters (academician, life, gold medal architecture 1968), Mensa (internat. pres. 1975—), World Soc. for Ekistics (internat. pres. 1975-77), Am. Acad. Arts and Letters (academician 1980), Harvard Engring Soc., Am. Soc. Profl. Geographers, Archtl. League N.Y., AAUP, Soc. Archtl. Historians, N.A.D., Phi Beta Kappa (hon.), Alpha Rho Chi (life). Clubs: Somerset (Boston); Century Assn. (N.Y.C.), Coffee House (N.Y.C.); Authors (London, Eng.). Inventor-discoverer synergetic geometry, geodesic structures, tensegrity structures; patentee Dymaxion world map, 1942. Address: Philadelphia, Pa. Died July 1, 1983.

FULLER, TRUMAN S., engr.; b. Saratoga Springs, N.Y., Apr. 23, 1888; s. Walter S. and Abigail R. (Harris) F.; B.S., Syracuse U., 1911; m. Flora Field Vosburgh, Sept. 8, 1917; children—Truman S., Lydia (Mrs. William Kruesi). Chemist Edison Lamp Works, Harrison, N.J., 1911; metallurgist research lab. Gen. Electric Co., 1911-38, engr. materials works lab., 1938-43, asst. engr., 1943-45, engineer, 1945-53; consulting engineer, 1953—. Member of the Am. Soc. Metals, Am. Soc. Testing Materials (pres. 1951-52), Am. Inst. Mining and Metall. Engrs. (chmn. inst. metals div. 1933), Brit. Inst. Metals, Brit. Iron and Steel Inst., Psi Upsilon. Republican. Presbyn. Clubs: Mohawk Golf, Mohawk (Schenectady). Address: Schenectady, N.Y. †

FULTON, WILL HUSTON, judge; b. Bardstown, Ky., Aug. 8, 1888; s. John Anderson and Brooke (Gore) F.; B.L., U. of Va., 1909; m. Belle McCandless, Nov. 3, 1921; children—John A., Will H., Jr., Betty Brooke. Admitted to Ky. bar, 1909; began practice of law, 1909; later with Internal Revenue Service; circuit court judge, 1931-39; judge, Ky. Court of Appeals, 1939-44; chief justice, Jan. 1, 1943-Oct. 15, 1944. Resigned to practice law (Louisville) with firm of Woodward, Dawson, Hobson & Fulton. First lt., 327th F.A., 84th Div., A.E.F., 1918-19. Mem. Pi Kappa Alpha. Democrat. Presbyterian. Mason. Home: Louisville, Ky. †

FUNSTEN, BENJAMIN REED, merchant; b. St. Louis, Nov. 3, 1887; s. James Johnston and Amelia (Moore) F.; ed. pub. schs. of Mo.; m. Gladys Little, Dec. 7, 1921. With Rice Stix Dry Goods Co., St. Louis, 1904, Ralston Purina Co., 1905, Moore Watson Dry Goods Co., 1906, dept. head, 1915-17; 2d v.p. Walton N. Moore Dry Goods Co., San Francisco, 1917-21, 1st v.p., 1921-26, pres. 1926-57; pres. B. F. Schlesinger & Sons, 1932-33; pres. City of Paris Dry Goods Co., 1932; pres., dir. B. R. Funsten & Co., Smith & Lang, Inc.; dir. Baker & Hamilton. Standard Realty and Development Company; director Wells Fargo Bank, Laurentide Financial Corp., Payne Bolt Works, Cal. Trustee, Children's Hosp. Clubs: Bohemian, San Francisco Golf, Pacific Union. †

FURRY, WENDELL HINKLE, physicist, educator; b. Prairieton, Ind., Feb. 18, 1907; s. John Henry and Effie (Hinkle) F.; A.B., DePauw U., 1928; A.M., U. Ill., 1930, Ph.D. (fellow in physics), 1932; A.M. (hon.), Harvard, 1941; m. Elizabeth Josephine Sawdey, Dec. 27, 1931; children—Ellen Jane (Mrs. William F. Brewer, Jr.), Mary Susan. Asst. physics U. Ill., 1928-31; instr. physics Harvard U., 1934-37, asst. prof., 1937-40, assoc. prof., 1940-62, prof., 1962-77, emeritus, 1977-84, chmn. dept., 1965-68; research assoc. radiation lab., MIT, 1943-45; research in relativistic quantum theory, cosmic rays, kinetic theory, quantum theory of measurement. NRC fellow U. Calif., Calif. Inst. Tech., 1932-34; Guggenheim fellow, Copenhagen, Denmark, 1950. Fellow Am. Phys. Soc., AAAS, Am. Acad. Arts and Scis.; mem. Am. Assn. Physics Tchrs., Sigma Xi, Phi Beta Kappa. Author: Physics for Science and Engineering Students (with E. M. Purcell and J. C. Street), 1952; also articles sci. jours. Home: Belmont, Mass. Dec. Dec. 17, 1984. Interned Mt. Auburn Cemetery, Cambridge, Mass.

GABRIEL, RALPH HENRY, prof. history; b. Watkins Glen, N.Y., Apr. 29, 1890; s. Er Cleveland and Alta (Monroe) G.; prep edn., Starkey Sem. and Watkins High Sch.; B.A., Yale, 1913, M.A., 1915, Ph.D., 1919; Litt.D., Bucknell U., 1952, Williams Coll., 1958; D.H.L. (hon.), Colgate University, 1963; married Christine Davis, Aug. 18, 1917; children—Robert Todd, John Cleveland, Susan. With Yale U., 1915-58, asso. prof. of history, 1925-28, prof., 1928-58; fellow Trumbull College, from 1933; prof. Am. civilization School International Service, American University, Washington, 1958-64; Phi Beta Kappa visiting scholar, 1963-64; visiting professor Tokyo U., spring 1964. George Washington U., summer 1965, New York Univ., summer, 1933; acting prof. Leland Stanford Univ., summer, 1934, visiting prof. Univ. of Colorado, summers, 1941, 1942, Univ. of Sydney (Australia), 1946, Stanford University, 1949, Cambridge University, 1951-52; Gina Speranza lecturer Columbia Univ., 1955. U.S. del. to 10th UNESCO Conf., Paris, 1958; member of U.S. National Commission for UNESCO. Collaborator educational program 2d Army, 1942; mem. faculty War Dept. Sch. Mil. Govt., Charlottesville, Va., 1943-46. Dir. Yale studies for ex-servicemen, 1944-46. Served as 2d and 1st lt. inf., U.S. Army, World War. Trustee Colleges of Yale (China). Mem. Am. Hist. Society, Newcomen Society, Graduate Club, Aurelian Society, American Studies Assn. (president 1962-63), Phi Beta Kappa, Sigma Xi and Beta Theta Pi, Berzelius. Congregationalist. Club: Cosmos (Washington). Author books, latest are: The Course of American Democratic Thought, revised edition in 1956; Religion and Learning at Yale, 1958; Traditional Values in American Life, 1959; also joint author of The School of the Citizen Soldier, 1942. Gen. Editor Library of Congress Series in American Civilization, Pageant of America (15 vols.). Home: New Haven, Conn. †

GADDUM, LEONARD W(ILLIAM), univ. prof.; b. Cincinnati, Jan. 18, 1889; s. Alexander William and Aliene (Lambert) G.; A.B., U. of Mo., 1921, Ph.D., 1924; m. Louise Babb, Jan. 26, 1918; children—Florence Marian (Mrs. Richard H. Gaylord), Jerry William, Joseph Glenn, Elizabeth Louise, Shirley Anne. Research worker pectins and glucosides U. of Fla. Agr. Expt. Sta., 1926-34, development of spectrographic methods in agrl. research, 1935-39, development of materials and methods for cultural edn. in phys. scis., from 1935. Mem. Am. Assn. Univ. Profs. Home: Gainesville, Fla. †

GAEBELEIN, FRANK ELY, educator; b. Mt. Vernon, N.Y., Mar. 31, 1899; s. Arno Clemens and Emma Fredericka (Grimm) G.; m. Dorothy Laura Medd, Dec. 8, 1923 (dec. Nov. 1980); children—Dorothy Laura (Mrs. Clyde R. Hampton), Donn Medd, Gretchen Elizabeth (Mrs. Philip G. Hull). B.A., N.Y. U., 1920; A.M., Harvard U., 1921; Litt.D., Wheaton (Ill.) Coll., 1931; D.D., Ref. Episcopal Theol. Sem., 1951; LL.D., Houghton (N.Y.) Coll., 1960. Organizer Stony Brook Sch., 1921, headmaster, 1922-63, headmaster emeritus, from 1963, also trustee; Griffith Thomas Memorial lectr. Dallas Theol. Sem., 1944, 52; Bauman lectr. Grace Theol. Sem. and Coll., 1962; Lilly lectr. Eastern Bapt. Coll., 1969; dir. faculty seminar on faith and learning Wheaton (Ill.) Coll., 1969-72; Bible conf. speaker and guest preacher in chs., colls., and univs. Co-editor: Christianity Today, 1963-66; Author: Down Through the Ages, 1924, A Brief Survey of Scripture, 1929, Exploring the Bible, 1929, The Hollow Queen, 1933, Facing the Fact of Inspiration, 1934, Philemon, the Gospel of Emancipation, 1939, Looking Unto Him, 1941, The Christian Use of the Bible, 1946, The Servant and the Dove, 1946, Christian Education in a Democracy, 1951, The Pattern of God's Truth, 1954, The Practical Epistle of James, 1955, A Varied Harvest, 1967, Four Minor Prophets: Their Message for Today, 1970, From Day to Day, 1975; Editor: A Christianity Today Reader, 1967; gen. editor: Expositor's Bible Commentary, from 1971. Deacon R.E. Ch., 1940, Presbyter, 1941; emeritus trustee Council for Religion in Ind. Schs. Commd. 2d lt. inf. U.S. Army, 1918. Mem. Headmasters Assn., Am. Acad. Religion, Soc. Bibl. Lit. and Exegesis, Evang. Theol. Soc., Phi Beta Kappa, Kappa Sigma. Democrat. Clubs: Harvard of N.Y, Andiron, Am. Alpine, Alpine of Can, Cosmos. Home: Arlington, Va. Died Jan. 19, 1983.

GAGE, PHILIP STEAMS, army officer; b. Detroit, Mich. Nov. 13, 1885; s. William Tenny and Elizabeth (Godwin) G.; student Trinity Coll., Hartford, Conn., 1904-05; B.S., U.S. Mil. Acad., 1909; m. Irene Julia Toll, Apr. 17, 1911; children—Betty Whistler (Mrs. Devereux H. Lippitt), Philip S. Commd. 2d lt., Coast Arty. Corps, June 11, 1909; promoted through grades to col., Aug. 1, 1938; apptd. brig. gen., Apr. 6, 1941. Mem. Psi Upsilon, Gamma Delta Psi. Episcopalian. Died Jan. 13, 1982.

GAGER, LESLIE TRACY, M.D.; b. Norwich, Conn., Aug. 27, 1890; s. John Austin and Luella (Tracy) G.; A.B., Yale, 1915; M.D., Johns Hopkins, 1918; m. Josephine Willoughby Chapman, of Towson, Md., June 15, 1919; children—John Chapman, Margaret Tracy, Jane Chatterton. Interne, Sloane Hosp. for Women, N.Y. City, 1919; resident phys., New York Hosp., 1920-21; instr. in medicine, Cornell Univ. Med. Coll., 1921-27; also adj. prof. medicine, New York Polyclinic Hosp. and Med. Sch., 1923-27; clin. asso. in medicine, George Washington U., 1927-28, clin. prof., 1929-32; prof. medicine and head of dept., Howard U., from 1931. Mem. Johns Hopkins Hosp. Unit, A.E.F., Evacuation Hosp. No. 12, Army of Occupation, 1917-19; maj. Med. Reserve Corps. Fellow N.Y. Acad. Medicine and asso. fellow Harvey Soc., 1924-27; mem. A.M.A., American Heart Association, Association of Military Surgeons (life mem. by Wellcome prize award), Med. Soc. D.C. (chmn. sect. internal medicine, 1929-30), Washington Pathological Soc. (president 1929-30), Biological Soc., Phi Beta Kappa, Sigma Xi. Congregationalist. Clubs: Yale Cosmos, Clinical. Author: Hypertension, 1930. Contbr. to Jour. Am. Medical Association, Am. Heart Journal, Am. Jour. Med. Sciences, Am. Jour. Syphilis, Archives Internal Medicine, etc., on internal medicine, especially diseases of circulation. Home: Washington, D.C. †

GALAMIAN, IVAN ALEXANDER, musician, educator; b. Tabriz, Persia, Jan, 23, 1903; s. Alexander J. and Sarah (Khounoutz) G.; grad. Philharmonic Sch., Moscow, USSR, 1923; Mus.D., Curtis Inst., 1954, Cleve. Inst. Music, 1968; hon. degree Oberlin Coll., 1966; m. Judith Johnson, Nov 22, 1941. Came to U.S., 1937, naturalized, 1944. Mem. violin faculty Russian Conservatory, Paris, France, 1925-39, Ecole Normale de Masique, Paris, 1936-39, Curtis Inst. Music, 1944-81, Julliard Sch. Music, N.Y.C., 1946-81; dir. Meadowmount Sch. Music, Westport, N.Y., 1952-81. Pres. Soc. for Strings, Inc., 1952. Hon. mem. Royal Acad. Music. Author: Principles of Violin Playing and Teaching, 1962. Home: New York, N.Y. Died Apr. 14, 1981.

GALBRAITH, VIRGINIA LEE, educator; b. Boise, Idaho; d. Eugene Robert and Ione (Atkinson) G. A.B., U. Calif. at Berkeley, 1941, Ph.D., 1954. Instr. Vassar Coll., 1945-47, U. Calif. at Berkeley, 1949-50; prof. econs. Mt. Holyoke Coll., from 1950; Vis prof. U. Minn., summers 1959, 61. Author: World Trade in Transition, 1965; Contbg. author: South of the Sahara, 1973; Contbr. articles to profl. jours. Mem. Consumer Council Mass., 1958-63; Trustee Arthur D. Little Mgmt. Edn. Inst. Mem. Am. Econ. Assn. Democrat. Home: South Hadley, Mass. Died Mar. 24, 1984.

GALE, RICHARD NELSON, Brit. army officer; b. Wandsworth, London, Eng., July 25, 1896; s. Wilfred and Helen Webber Ann (Nelson) G.; student Royal Mil. Coll., Sandhurst, Army Staff Coll., Camberley, Eng.; m. Ethel Maude Larnack Kleene, 1924 (dec. 1952); m. 2d Daphne Mabelle Eveline Blick, 1953. Commd. 2d lt. Worcestershire Regt., British Army, 1915, advanced through grades to gen., 1952; raised and commanded 1st Parachute Prigade; comdr. 6th Brit. Airborne Div.; dep. comdr. 1st Allied Airborne Army, 1945, 1st Brit. Airborne Corps, 1945, 1st Inf. Div., 1946-47; gen. officer comdg. Brit. Troops, Egypt and Mediterranean Command, 1948-49; dir.-gen. Mil. Tng. War Office, 1949-52; comdr.-in-chief No. Army Group, Allied Land Forces Europe, and Brit. Army of Rhine, 1952-57; a.d.c. to the Queen, 1954-57; dep. Supreme Allied Comdr. Europe, 1958-60. Decorated Legion of Merit (U.S.); Legion of Honor, Croix de Guerre with palm (France); Knight Grand Cross of Bath, Knight Comdr. Brit. Empire, Companion Distinguished Service Order, Military Cross. Mem. Royal Central Asian Soc. Clubs: Army and Navy; Royal Thames Yacht (London). Home: London, Eng. Died June 10, 1982.

GALITZINE, NICHOLAS, utility executive; b. Smolensk, Russia, May 8, 1903; s. Paul and Alexandra (Mestctersky) G.; came to U.S., 1923, naturalized, 1938; student Northwestern U., evenings 1933-36; m. Josephine Dennehy, Apr. 2, 1932; children—Alexandra (Mrs. Bruce Sherman), Marina (Mrs. Peter Carney), Josephine. With Commonwealth Edison Co., Chgo., 1923-68, asst. to chmn., 1950-61, v.p., 1961-68; ltd. ptnr. Bacon, Whipples' Co., Chgo.; dir. Hartford Plaza Bank, Chgo. Bd. dirs. Chgo. Better Bus. Bur. Vice pres., dir. Passavant Memorial Hospital, Chgo.; member board directors Sears Roebuck Foundation, also Lyric Opera, Chgo. Clubs: Chicago; Onwentsia (Lake Forest, Ill.). Home: Lake Forest, Ill. Died Dec. 19, 1981.

GALL, EDWARD B., physician, surgeon; b. Cleve., Aug. 24, 1905; s. Edward and Emma (Schmidt) G.; A. B., Ohio State U., 1933, M.D., 1933; m. Janet M. Laudick, Sept. 16, 1935; 1 dau., Penny Lee. Intern, Meml. Hosp., Lima, Ohio, 1933-35; resident Louisville City Hosp., 1938-40; asst. chief surgery Brown Hosp., Dayton, Ohio, 1946-49, chief thoracic surgery, 1949-52; pvt. practice, Dayton, 1952-80; thoracic surgery staff Good Samaritan Hosp., St. Elizabeth Hosp., Miami Valley Hosp., Kettering Meml. Hosp.; cons. thoracic surgery; instr. thoracic surgery Coll. Medicine, Ohio State U., 1954-80. Served surg. staff USPHS, USCG, USN, 1941-46. Diplomate Am. Bd. Surgery, Am. Bd. Thoracic Surgery. Fellow A.C.S. Home: Dayton, Ohio. Died Nov. 8, 1980.

GALLAGHER, HAROLD JOHN, lawyer; b. Clinton, Iowa, Dec. 29, 1894; s. James A. and Ella (Walsh) G.; LL.B., U. Iowa, 1916; postgrad. Harvard U., 1916-17;

LL.D., St. John's U., 1954; m. Alicia Schnoebelen, Sept. 26, 1917; children—Alicia Ellen, Harold John (dec.), Katherine E. (Mrs. W. Voelker) (dec.), Mary L. (Mrs. James Cremins). Admitted to Iowa bar, 1916, to N.Y. bar, 1919, since practiced in N.Y.C.; entered office of Hornblower, Miller and Garrison, 1917, became mem. firm, 1925, later successor firm of Willkie Farr & Gallagher; ret. gen. counsel S.A.L. Ry. Pres., Am. Bar Assn. Endowment, 1949-50. Fellow Am. Bar Found. (dir.), Am. Coll. Trial Lawyers; mem. Am. Bar Assn. (chmn. standing com. pub. utility sect., 1934-35, chmn. standing com. commerce, 1935-38, 48-49, mem. N.Y. State Council, 1931-36, former mem. bankruptcy com., mem. ways and means com., chmn. pub. utility sect., 1938-39, chmn. com. on resolutions, 1946, N.Y. State del. 1948-49, pres. 1949-50, recipient Gold Medal 1972), N.Y. State Bar Assn. (50th Year award), Assn. Bar City of New York, New York County Lawyers' Assn., Am. Law Inst., Am. Judicature Soc., Order of Coif. Republican. Roman Catholic. Clubs: Blind Brook, American Yacht, Siwanoy. Home: Bronxville, N.Y. Died Sept. 26, 1981.

GALLEN, HUGH J., gov. N.H.; b. Portland, Oreg., July 30, 1924; s. Hugh J. and Mary (O'Kane) G.; m. Irene Carbonneau, Oct. 16, 1948; children—Kathleen A., Michael J., Sheila M. Hon. degree, Dartmouth Coll., 1979, N.H. Vocat.-Tech. Coll., 1979. Pres., treas. Hugh J. Gallen, Inc.; founder, dir., chmn. bd. People's Nat. Bank, Littleton, N.H.; gov. State of N.H., Concord, 1978—. Mem. N.H. Ho. of Reps., 1973; Chmn. Democratic State Party, 1971-72; del. Dem. Conv., 1972; mem. Littleton Planning Bd., 1962-65, N.H.-Vt. Devel. Council, 1969-72; bd. dirs. White Mountain Community Services, 1967-70; mem. nat. adv. council SBA, 1967. Roman Catholic. Home: Bridges House Mountain Rd Concord NH 03301 Office: State House Concord NH 03301*

GALLMEYER, ERNEST JOHN, sales exec.; b. Ft. Wayne, Ind., June 29, 1890; s. Conrad W. and Wilhelmina (Geye) G.; LL.D., Valparaiso University, 1950; m. Selma E. Hoppe, January 7, 1913 (deceased August 10, 1962); children—Robert E., Marybelle (Mrs. Richard C. Stauffer), Richard D.; m. second, Helen Haefling, January 30, 1964. Successively file clk., collection corr., sales corr., territorial salesman, sales supt., dist. mgr., asst. to sales mgr., editor of house organ, S. F. Bowser & Co., Louisville, N.Y.C., Ft. Wayne, 1908-17; asst. dist. mgr. Wayne Pump Co., Memphis, 1917, successively dist. mgr., gen. sales mgr., Ft. Wayne, 1918-24, 34-45, v.p., dir., 1935-51; with North & Gallmeyer, 1924-30, Blitz, O'Keeffe & Gallmeyer, 1930-31; postmaster Ft. Wayne, Ind., 1931-34; v.p., dir. Indiana Bank & Trust Company (formerly known as Dime Trust & Savs. Co.), from 1947; counsellor Culligan, Inc., Northbrook, Illinois; sales consultant; member board of directors Summit Laboratories, Indpls. Chmn. Bd. of Pub. Works, City Fort Wayne, 1959. Active Community Chest, YMCA, other civic affairs. Dir. Luth. Ch., Mo. Synod 1935-56; founder, trustee Valparaiso U.; pres. Luth. Ch. Found., Mo. Synod, 1959. Mem. Internat. Luth. Laymen's League (bd. 1934-46, pres. 1936-48), Internat. Walther League (dir. 1919-37, pres. 1932-36), Am. Soc. Sales Execs. (chmn. 1947-48). Clubs: Quest, Rotary, Ft. Wayne Country (Ft. Wayne, Ind.); Lake Shore (Chgo.). Author: Making Ourselves Acceptable (sales course); booklets on salesmanship; lectr. sales subjects. Home: Ft. Wayne, Ind. †

GALLOWAY, ALEXANDER H(ENDERSON), corp. exec.; b. Winston-Salem. N.C., Dec. 27, 1907; s. Alexander H. and Mamie (Gray) G.; student Woodberry Forest Sch., Orange, Va., 1921-25; A.B., U. N.C., 1929; m. Martha Erckman, May 10, 1930; children—Alexander Henderson, Robert Galloway, James G. With R.J. Reynolds Tobacco Co. since 1929, asst. treas., 1937-51, treas. and dir., 1951-55, vice president, treasurer, 1955-59, exec. vice pres., 1959-60, president, 1960-82, chairman of board, 1969-82, also chief exec. officer. chmn. exec. com., dir., formerly chief financial officer: director and mem. Winston-Salem bd. Wachovia Bank & Trust Co.; dir. sified Share of Security Life & Trust Co. Mem. Grocery Mfrs. of America (director). Business Council, Washington. Mem. Phi Beta Kappa, Beta Theta Pi. Democrat. Episcopalian. Clubs: Rotary, Twin City, Old Town, Country of North Carolina, Augusta Nat. Home: Winston-Salem, N.C. Died June 11, 1982.

GALT, ERROL FAY, former banker; b. Myrtle, Minn., Oct. 2, 1889; s. William Wylie and Emma Retta (Robinson) G.; grad. So. Minn. Normal Coll., 1906; m. Florence E. Johnson, Aug. 28, 1916 (dec. Sept. 1973); children—Fay, Edna Ann, William Wylie, Gwen, Jack, Patricia. Office boy Eclipse Lumber Co., Belle Plaine, Ia., 1907; various positions with lumber cos., Toeterville, Ia., 1908-09, hardware bus., Stanford, Mont., 1910-16; organizer First Nat. Bank, Geyser, Mont., 1916-32; asst. to pres. First Nat. Bank of Great Falls (Mont.), 1932, v.p., 1934, pres., 1946-54, chmn. bd., 1954-68. Mem. Mont. Senate from Judith Bosin County, 1930-34. Bd. regents Coll. Great Falls. Home: N Great Falls, Mt. †

GALVES, JUAN MANUEL, President of Republic of Honduras; b. 1887. Address: Tegucigalpa, Honduras. †

GAMBRELL, BARMORE PEPPER, lawyer; b. Belton, S.C., Jan. 27, 1894; s. Enoch Pepper and Macie (Latimer) G. A.B., Furman U., 1915; student, Washington and Lee U., 1916; LL.B., Georgetown U., 1918. Bar: D.C. bar 1919, Ga. bar 1920. Clk. office of sec. U.S. Senate, 1917-18; practicing lawyer, Atlanta, 1920-84; mem. Arnold & Gambrell (and predecessors), 1930-57. Served as chief petty officer USN, World War I. Recipient Distinguished Alumnus award Furman U., 1968. Fellow Am. Bar Found.; mem. Am., Atlanta bar assns., State Bar Ga., Am. Legion (comdr. Atlanta post 1922-23). Democrat. Baptist. Clubs: Capital City (Atlanta), Piedmont Driving (Atlanta), Lawyers (Atlanta). Home: Atlanta, Ga. Died May 10, 1984.

GAMBRELL, CHARLES GLENN, former banker; b. Belton, S.C., Sept. 27, 1902; s. Enoch Pepper and Macie Amanda (Latimer) G.; m. Sarah Walkup Belk, Nov. 21, 1952; 1 dau., Sarah. Student, U. S.C., 1918-19; A.B., Furman U., 1922; M.B.A., Harvard U., 1925; LL.D., Presbyn. Coll., 1962. Clk. Wilmington (N.C.) Saving and Trust Co., 1923; Clk. Irving Trust Co., N.Y.C., 1925-29, asst. sec., 1929-34, asst. v.p., 1934-46, v.p., 1946-67; now hon. chmn. pension fund Belk Stores, Charlotte, N.C.; Mem. adv. council Furman U.; life trustee Converse Coll. Served to lt. col. USAAF, 1942-45. Mem. Harvard Bus. Sch. Alumni Assn. N.Y. (past pres.), Sigma Alpha Epsilon (life trustee). Presbyn. (life elder). Clubs: Union (N.Y.C.), University (N.Y.C.), Harvard (N.Y.C.); Charlotte City (Charlotte, N.C.), Charlotte Country (Charlotte, N.C.). Home: New York, NY.

GAMMON, JOSEPH ALLAN, diversified co. exec.; b. Bowling Green, Ky., Apr. 1, 1922; s. Lelie S. and Lela (Bray) G.; student pub. schs., Bowling Green; m. JoAnn Glenn, Sept. 20, 1974; 1 son by previous marriage, John Scott. Propr. retail liquor bus., Indpls. 1944-47; pres., co-owner Service Transport Co., Bowling Green, 1948-52; exec. v.p. Gasoline Transport Co., Louisville, 1953-56; pres. So. Tank Lines, Louisville, 1957-66, Ala. Tank Lines, Birmingham, 1957-64; pres. Yellow Cab-Atlanta, 1957-66, Yellow Cab-Tampa (Fla.), 1957-66; pres. Yellow Cab Co. of Louisville, 1957-75, chmn. bd., 1975-82; exec. v.p. So. Atlantic Co., 1962-66; v.p. transp. Nat. Industries, Louisville, 1967-70, exec. v.p., chief operating officer, 1971-75, chmn. bd.; chmn. bd. TSC Industries, Inc., Chgo. Served with USNR, 1942-44. Home: Louisville, Ky. Died 1982.

GANDHI, INDIRA, prime minister of India; b. Allahabad, India, Nov. 19, 1917; d. Jawaharlal and Kamala (Koul) Nehru; student schs. Switzerland, Shantiniketan Univ., India; Somerville Coll., Oxford (Eng.) U.; D.Litt. (hon.), Andrha U., 1963; m. Feroze Gandhi, 1942 (dec.); children—Rajiv, Sanjay. Disciple of Gandhi; formed children's orgn. to help Indian Nat. Congress during non-cooperation movement; worked among untouchables popularizing hand-spun cloth and Indian made goods; active student movement India, Eng.; mem. Indian Nat. Congress, from 1938, mem. working com., central election com., central parliamentary bd., from 1955, pres. Congress, 1959; minister of information and broadcasting Govt. of India; prime minister of India, 1966-84. Ofcl. hostess Prime Minister Nehru, 1947. Hon. pres. Adv. Council of Edn. Centre for Southeast Asia Internat. Coop. Alliance; chmn. Citizens' Central Council, 1962; exec. com. Nat. Def. Fund, 1962; sec. Jawaharal Nehru Meml., 1964. Pres. Indian Council Child Welfare; v.p. Internat. Union Child Welfare. Mem. Indian Delegation, UNESCO, 1960, mem. exec. bd. UNESCO, mem. central adv. bd. edn. Chmn. Nat. Integration Com., Indian Nat. Congress, Nat. Inst. Women, Kamala Nehru Vidayalaya, Bal Bhavan, Bal Sahyog; also several other social welfare orgns. Mem. governing body Himalayan Mountaineering Inst., Tebetan Homes Found. Recipient Mother's award, U.S.A., 1953; Yale U. Howland Meml. prize, 1960. Mem. Fed. Film Socs. India (v.p.). Died Oct. 31, 1984.

GARBARINO, JOSEPH JOHN, chem. co. exec.; b. N.Y.C., Jan. 21, 1929; s. Joseph John and Amilia E. (Tosi) G.; m. Anita Murphy, Sept. 3, 1955; children—Joseph, John, Maryann, Joan. B.S. in Chemistry, St. John's U., 1950, M.S., 1956; M.B.A., N.Y. U., 1962. With Am. Cyanamid Co., Wayne, N.J., from 1956, v.p. agrl. div., 1976-78, pres., from 1978. Served to capt. USCGR. Mem. Am. Chem. Soc., Comml. Devel. Assn., Res. Officers Assn. Home: Wayne, NJ.

GARBER, JAMES RHODES, obstetrician; b. Pueblo, Colo., May 26, 1889; s. James Rhodes and Katherine LaMotte (Morgan) G.; A.B., Springhill Coll., Mobile, Ala., 1909; M.D., Jefferson Medical Coll., Phila., 1913; m. Elizabeth Taylor Evans, July 15, 1915; children—Katherine LaMotte (Mrs. Mortimer Harvie Jordan), Mary Charlotte (Mrs. John Barratt Rudulph). Interne, obstetrician, Johns Hopkins Hosp., 1913-14; private practice, Birmingham, Ala., from 1914. Prof. obstetrics, and chmn. dept. obstetrics Medical Coll. of Ala.; obstetrician-in-chief, La. Div. of U. of Ala. Univ. Hosp.; chmn. bd. dirs. and medical director The Physician's National Life Insurance Co., Birmingham. Mem. bd. Jefferson Co. Dept. Welfare. Lt. col. on staff of Gov. of Ala., 1939-43. Mem. Am., So., State med. assns., Jefferson Co. Med. Soc., Ala. Acad. Science, Sigma Nu. Democrat. Clubs: Kiwanis, Birmingham Country. Author Handbook on Obstetric Nursing, 1925. †

GARBER, RALPH JOHN, agronomist; b. Apr. 24, 1890; s. John and Lena (Oswald) G.; B.S., Coll. of Agr., U. of Ill., 1912; M.S., Coll. of Agr., U. of Minn., 1917, grad. student, 1916-17, Ph.D., 1922; m. Mildred Evelyn Fitschen, July 19, 1917; children—John Douglas, Joy Marie. On farm in Central Ill., June 1912-Aug. 1913; instr. Morgan (Minn.) High Sch., 1913-15, Monticello (Minn.) High Sch., 1915-16; asst. prof. agronomy, U. of Minn., 1917-20; asso. prof., prof. and head of dept. of agronomy and genetics, Coll. of Agr., W.Va. U., 1920-36; dir. United States Regional Pasture Research Lab., 1936-52; chief agrl. institutions and services Food and Agr. Orgn. of United Nations, Rome, from 1952. Fellow A.A.A.S. (vice president and chairman Section O., 1944); fellow American Society of Agronomy (president 1938-39), member Am. Genetics Assn. Genetics Soc. America, Am. Soc. Naturalists, National Research Council, Sigma Xi, Alpha Zeta, Gamma Sigma Delta, Acacia. Presbyn. Club: Centre Hills Country. Author: Breeding Crop Plants (with H. K. Hayes), 1921, rev. edit., 1927; also many scientific articles and bulletins. Home: New York, N.Y. †

GARDINER, ALEXANDER (ANDREW), editor; b. South Hadley Falls, Mass., Nov. 21, 1889; s. John and Agnes (MacDonald) G.; student Williams Coll., 1907-09, Brown U., 1911-14; m. Nan Skliba, Nov. 4, 1916; 1 son, John Richard. Reporter, Springfield (Mass.) Republican, 1915-16; with Savannah (Ga.) Morning News, Atlanta (Ga.) Constitution, Waterbury (Conn.) Republican, Providence (R.I.) Journal, 1916, Hartford (Conn.) Times, 1917-19; teacher, Pinkerton Acad., Derry, N.H., 1920-21; mng. editor, Poughkeepsie (N.Y.) Star, 1921-22; news editor, Worcester (Mass.) Gazette, 1922-24; with American Legion Magazine from 1924, editor, 1940-49, advisory editor from 1949. Served as private, Battery B., 41st Arty., C.A.C., U.S. Army, 1918. Mem. Delta Tau Delta, Am. Legion. Conglist. Mason, Lion. Clubs: Touchdown, Brown University (New York). Author: Canfield, the True Story of the Greatest Gambler. Home: Fairfield, Ct. †

GARDNER, JOHN CHAMPLIN, JR., educator, author; b. Batavia, N.Y., July 21, 1933; s. John Champlin and Priscilla (Jones) G.; m. Joan Louise Patterson, June 6, 1953 (div.); children—Joel, Lucy; m. Liz Rosenberg, Feb. 14, 1980. Student, DePauw U., 1951-53; A.B., Washington U., St. Louis, 1955; M.A., State U. Iowa, 1956, Ph.D., 1958. Mem. faculty Oberlin Coll., 1958-59, Chico State Coll., 1959-62, San Francisco State Coll., 1962-65; prof. English So. Ill. U., Carbondale, 1965-76, Bennington Coll., 1974-76, Skidmore Coll., 1975-77, Williams Coll., 1976-77, George Mason U., Fairfax, Va., 1977-78, SUNY, Binghamton, from 1978; vis. prof. U. Detroit, 1970-71, Northwestern U., 1973, Salzburg seminars, 1977. Author: The Forms of Fiction, 1961, The Complete Works of the Gawain Poet, 1965; novel The Resurrection, 1966, The Wreckage of Agathon, 1970, Grendel, 1971, The Alliterative Morte Arthure and Five Other Middle English Poems, 1971, The Sunlight Dialogues, 1972; epic poem Jason and Medeia, 1973; novel Nickel Mountain, 1973, The Construction of the Wakefield Cycle, 1974, The King's Indian, 1974, Dragon, Dragon, and Other Tales, 1975, Gudgkin, and Other Tales, 1976, October Light, 1976, King of the Hummingbirds, 1977, Construction of Christian Poetry in Old English, 1975, The Poetry of Chaucer, 1976, The Life and Times of Chaucer, 1967, Child's Bestiary, 1977, In the Suicide Mountains, 1977, On Moral Fiction, 1978; plays Death and the Maiden, 1978, The Latest Word from Delphi, 1978, Helen at Home, 1978; libretti Rumpelstiltskin, 1978, William Wilson, 1978, Frankenstein, 1978, Samson and the Witch, 1978, The Pied Piper of Hamlin, 1978; radio plays The Temptation Game, 1978, The Waterhorse, 1978, The Angel, 1978; poems Poems, 1978; novel Freddy's Book, 1980; short stories The Art of Living, 1981. Recipient NEA award, 1972; Nat. Book Critics award, 1976; Woodrow Wilson fellow, 1955-56; Danforth fellow, 1970-73; Guggenheim fellow, 1973-74. Mem. MLA, PEN, AAUP. Died Sept. 14, 1982.

GARDNER, RUSSELL EUGENE, JR., mem. Reinholdt & Gardner; b. Humboldt, Tenn., July 18, 1890; s. Russell Eugene and Annie (Cathey) G.; B.S., Princeton, 1912; m. Enid Ridgley Simpkins, Sept. 18, 1917; children—Russell Allan, John Ridgley, David Lee. Began with Banner Buggy Co. of St. Louis (firm reorganized as Chevrolet Motor Co. of St. Louis, 1916), 1912, v.p. in charge sales, 1916-17; one of organizers, v.p., 1919-24, Gardner Motor Co., pres., 1924-29; gen. partner Reinholdt & Gardner, mem. N.Y. Stock Exchange; pres., dir. Urban Redevelopment Corp.; member board directors St. Louis Insurance Corporation; formerly state dir. in Missouri, Office of Price Adminstrn.; dist. chief, St. Louis Ordnance District; dir. St. Louis Fire and Marine Ins. Company, La-†

GARGES, HERBERT KELLY, business exec.; b. Nortonville, Kansas, July 24, 1888; s. William Lewis and Alice Emma (Kelly) G.; grad., Savannah (Ohio) Acad.; m. Eunice L. Roasberry, Aug. 7, 1916; children—Herbert Kelly, Robert L., Betty L. (Mrs. Tom Patton). Mgr. trainee, W. T. Grant Co., 1914-17, store mgr., 1917-26, dist. mgr., headquarters Atlanta, Ga., 1926-41, regional mgr. headquarters Atlanta, 1941-48, vice pres., 1944, mem. bd. of dirs. from 1948; dir. Citizens Bank, from 1952, Southern Emory Bank, from 1945. Trustee Young Harris Coll. Address: Atlanta, Ga. †

GARIBI, RIVERA JOSÉ, archbishop; b. Guadajara, Jalisco, Mexico, Jan. 30, 1889; s. Miguel and Joaquina (Rivera) G.; ed. Seminario Menor (Guadalajara), Pontifical Latin Am. Coll. (Rome); Th.D., Pontifical Gregorian U., Rome, 1916. Ordained priest, Guadalajara, 1912; tchr. and prefect of discipline Seminario Menor, 1911-13; asst.

vicar, Totatiche parish, 1916; tchr. Seminario Auxiliar, 1916; asst. vicar, parishes of Atotouilco el Alto and Jess, 1917; chaplain Ch. of Nuestra Senora del Carmel and ofcl. of ecclesiastical court, 1917; canon of the cathedral, 1924; chancellor of ecclesiastical court, 1925; titular bishop of Rosso and asst. bishop, Guadalajara, 1929; dean of cathedral and vicar gen., 1933; titular arch-bishop of Bizya and asst. to bishop, Guadalajara, 1934; became archbishop of Guadalajara, 1936. Address: Guadalajara, Mexico. †

GARMAN, WILFORD OLDEN HIGGETT, clergyman; b. Phila., Aug. 15, 1899; s. Samuel and Bertha Rodgers (Plant) G.; grad. Phila. Sch. Bible, 1922; Th.B., Pitts. Theol. Sem., 1925; D.D., Burton Coll., 1953; Th.M., Bible Bapt. Sem., 1955; D.D., Bob Jones U., 1970; m. Josephine Pearl Hill, June 26, 1931; children—Joyce Esther, Paul Wilford, Linda Ruth. Ordained to ministry U.P. Ch., 1925, ind. 1939; pastor, Indiana County, Pa., 1925-29, Altoona, 1929-39, Callender Meml. Ch., Wilkinsburg, Pa., 1939-73; organizer, dean Altoona Sch. Bible, 1933-40; pres. Immanuel Coll. Bible, 1953-59; instr. Christian Crusade's Anti-Communist U., Manitou Springs, Colo.; asso. tour dir. Christian Crusades yearly Holy Land Tours, 1965-69; pastor Grace Fundamental Chapel, Monroeville, Pa., from 1974. Past pres. Fundamental Chs. Am.; tours of Europe, 1947, Germany, 1948, Far East, 1953 at invitation of fed. govt.; attended 1st plenary congress, Internat. Council Christian Chs., Amsterdam, Holland, 1947, 2d plenary congress, Geneva, 1950, regional congress, Scotland, 1952; participant World Congress Fundamentalists, Edinburgh, 1976; engaged world missionary tour, 1949; visited S. Africa, Rhodesia and Greece, 1967; chmn. Wilkinsburg Citizens for Law and Order, from 1968; mem. Chaplain (capt.) Dep. Sheriffs Res. Mem. bd. United Congl. Appeal, Am. Security Council; bd. regents Am. Christian Coll.; bd. policy Liberty Lobby, 1970. Recipient citation, chief of staff USAF, 1956; Congress of Freedom award, 1959, 68, 70, 72, 74, 75, 76; named to Fundamentalist Hall of Fame, 1978. Fellow Royal Geog. Soc.; mem. Asso. Gospel Chs. (pres., chmn. commn. chaplains 1958-79), Am. Ordnance Assn., U.S. Navy League, Mil. Chaplains Assn., Am. Council Christian Chs. (past pres., chmn. commn. edn., mem. exec. com.), Nat. Sheriff's Assn. Author: The Life and Teachings of Christ; Communist Infiltration In The Churches, 3d edit.; numerous religious pamphlets. Editor: A.G.C. Reporter. Home: Pittsburgh, Pa. Died July 2, 1983.

GARRATT, GEORGE ALFRED, educational consultant; b. Bklyn., May 7, 1898; s. Henry Masters and Rebecca (Kerr) G.; B.S., Mich. State U., 1920, LL.D., 1972; M.F., Yale, 1923, Ph.D., 1933; D.Sc., U. of South, 1957; m. Barbara Julia Lillie, July 28, 1922; (dec. 1976); children—Stephen Masters, Rowland Masters. Instr. forestry Mich. State Coll., 1920-22; prof. forestry and engring. U. of South, Sewanee, Tenn., 1923-25; asst. prof. forest products Yale, 1925-31, asso. prof., 1931-39, Mfrs. Assn. prof. lumbering, 1939-55, asst. dean Sch. Forestry, 1936-39, dean, 1945-65, dean emeritus, 1965—, Pinchot prof. forestry, 1955-66, emeritus, 1966—, part-time leave to serve as chief div. tech. service tng. U.S. Forest Products Lab., Madison, Wis., 1942-45; dir. Canadian Forestry Edn. Study, 1965-71. Mem. Conn. State Park and Forest Commn., 1949-71, chmn., 1951-71; mem. Conn. Council Agr. and Natural Resources, 1959-71, chmn., 1961-64. Fellow Soc. Am. Foresters (pres. 1958-59), Forest History Soc. (dir., pres. 1970-74); mem. Soc. Wood Sci. and Tech., Forest Products Research Soc. (pres. 1948), Am. Forestry Assn. (dir.), Sigma Xi, Xi Sigma Pi. Author: The Mechanical Properties of Wood, 1931; (with Geo. M. Hunt) Wood Preservation, 1938, rev. edit., 1967; Forestry Education in Canada, 1971. Home: Hamden, Conn. Died May 1, 1984.

GARRETT, HOMER L(YCURGUS), prof. edn.; b. Tallassee, Ala., June 5, 1888; s. Jesse Sanford and Martha Drusilla (Canady) G.; diploma, La. State Normal Sch., 1908; A.B., La. State U., 1914; student, summers, U. of Wis., 1915, U. of Chicago, 1916-20; A.M., Teachers Coll., Columbia, 1921; Ed.D., Stanford U., 1932; m. Hattie Cutrer, May 18, 1917; children—Martha Lee, Bowman Staples, Mary Adele. Teacher, prin., La. pub. schs., 1908-16; asst. prin., Univ. High Sch., La. State U., 1916-18, prin., 1918-20, prof. secondary edn., 1920-35, prof. edn., dir. grad. studies in edn., since 1935, acting dean, grad. sch., 1931-32, chmn. grad. council, 1932-44. Mem. So. Assn. of Colls. and Secondary Schs. (commn. on secondary schs., 1920-36, from 1940), N.E.A., Nat. Soc. for Study of Edn., Nat. Vocational Guidance Assn., Nat. Soc. of Coll. Teachers of Edn., Nat. Assn. of Secondary Sch. Prins., La. Edn. Assn., Phi Kappa Phi, Phi Delta Kappa, Kappa Delta Pi. Democrat. Baptist. Mason, K.P. Home: Baton Rouge, La. †

GARRETT, RAY, lawyer; b. Murphysboro, Ill., Sept. 17, 1889; s. Anderson Barker and Georgia (Williams) G.; student U. Ill., 1906-08; LL.B., Ill. Wesleyan U., 1916; student Northwestern U., 1924-25; m. Mabel Marian May, Aug. 1, 1916; children—Glenn May, Ray, Martha Ann. Ofcl. stenographer Supreme Ct. Ill., Springfield, 1910-17; admitted to Ill. bar, 1916; law asso. A. M. Fitzgerald, Springfield, 1916-17; atty. Chgo. Mill & Lumber Co., 1919-21; counsel A. W. Swayne & Co., 1921-23; asso., partner Cooke Sullivan & Ricks, Chgo., 1923-34; partner Lawyer & Garrett, 1934-39; pvt. practice, 1939-42; asso., partner Sidley, Austin, Burgess & Smith, Chgo., from 1942. Pres. Midland Subsidiary Corp., 1937-39, Chgo., South Shore & South Bend R.R., 1938-39; pres., trustee Indiana R.R., 1941-51; counsel to bd. D.& R.G.W., R.R. Co., from 1947; dir. Denver and Rio Grande Western R.R. Served from lieutenant to major, infantry, U.S. Army, 1917-19; AEF. Fellow American Bar Foundation; member American Law Inst., Am. Bar Assn. (former chmn. corp. banking and bus. law), Ill., Chgo. bar assns., Newcomen Soc., Phi Delta Phi. Methodist. Clubs: Mid-Day, Univ., Law (Chgo.); Mich. Shores (Wilmette, Ill.). Co-author: Illinois. Business Corporation Act, Model Business Corporation and Non-Profit Corporation Acts. Contbr. articles legal jours. Home: Evanston, Ill. †

GARROWAY, DAVE, TV personality; b. Schenectady. Emcee: Dave Garroway Show, NBC radio network, 1947-49; TV program Garroway at Large, 1949-51, Pontiac TV Show, 1953-54; NBC radio Friday with Garroway, 1954-56; narrator: NBC radio Wide Wide World, 1955-59, segment on, NBC (radio) Monitor; star: Dave Garroway Today Show, NBC-TV Network, 1952-61, Exploring the Universe, Nat. Ednl. TV, 1961-62, Garroway AM and PM, CBS, 1964-65, Tempo-Boston TV Show, 1969-70, show in, Los Angeles, 1970-71; host: CBS Newcomers, summer 1971. Asso. with USIA, 1961; Bd. dirs. Fed. Union. Served as ensign USNR, 1942-45. Mem. Nat. Acad. TV Arts and Scis. (gov. 1968). Died July 21, 1982.

GARY, THEODORE SAUVINET, communications exec.; b. Kansas City, Mo., Dec. 23, 1912; s. Hunter L. and Lamora (Sauvinet) G.; m. Laura Avritt Brown, July 23, 1934 (dec.); children—Theodore Sauvient, Laura Castleman Gary Thorne; m. Patricia Murrill Du Vivier, Aug. 22, 1958; children—Jerome S., Tracy DuVivier; m. Anna Gary, Apr. 1972; children—Alexander, Hunter Clark. Student, Yale U., 1932-33, Northwestern Bus. Sch., 1933-34. Asst. to chmn. bd. Automatic Electric Co., 1934-36, v.p., 1936-45, vice chmn. bd., 1955, dir., 1955-57; pres., dir. Automatic Electric Sales Corp., 1945, dir., 1956-57; pres., dir. Theodore Gary & Co., 1955; (co. merged into Gen. Telephone Corp.), 1955; v.p., dir. Gen. Telephone & Electronics Corp. (formerly Gen. Telephone Corp.), 1966, Gen. Telephone Services Corp., 1955-75. Mem. Armed Forces Communications Assn. (exec. com., past pres.). Clubs: Chgo. (Chgo.), Racquet (Chgo.); Brook (N.Y.C.), Racquet (N.Y.C.); Surf (Miami Beach, Fla.), Bath (Miami Beach, Fla.), Indian Creek Country (Miami Beach, Fla.). Home: Miami Beach, Fla. Died Feb. 11, 1983.

GAST, GUSTAV CARL, copy editor; b. Detroit, Michigan, July 11, 1888; s. Friederich Julius and Ottilie (Preuss) G.; A.B., Capital University, Columbus, O., 1908, D.D., 1929; A.M., U. of Mich., 1919, B.D., Augustana Sem., Rock Island, Ill, 1929; m. Alma May Young, Aug. 26, 1914; children—Paul Frederick, Robert Henry, Naomi Marie. Ordained to ministry Evang. Luth. Ch., 1911; pastor Grace Luth. Ch., Hubbard, Ohio, 1911-14; prof. of German, Luther Sem., St. Paul, Minn., 1914-17, pres. 1917-18; prof. of theology, Capitul U., Columbus, OH., 1918-41; copy editor, Wartburg Press, Columbus, OH., from 1941. Mem. Uniting Com. of United and Am. Luth. Churches, 1937. Author of brochure, The Oxford Group Movement, 1934; Interpretation of Gospel according to Saint Luke, 1940. Contbr. to Luth. Standard. Home: Columbus, Ohio †

GATES, EDWARD DWIGHT, coll. pres.; b. Wauwatosa, Wis., Mar. 26, 1921; s. Perez Dickinson and Delia (Dousman) G.; m. June Elizabeth Rowell, Sept. 10, 1944; children—Pamela Gates Tressler, Geoffrey, James. B.A., Beloit Coll., 1943; student, U. Chgo., 1943; B.D., Pacific Sch. Religion, 1945; Ph.D., Bradley U., 1953; LL.D., Hiram Scott Coll., 1969. Ordained to ministry, 1945; asst. minister First Presbyn. Ch., Peoria, Ill., 1947-48, minister, 1948-54; ministerial staff First Congl. Ch., Los Angeles, 1954-56; gen. sec. Macalester Coll., St. Paul, 1956-60; pres. Beaver Coll., Glenside, Pa., from 1960; mem. exec. com. Commn. for Ind. Colls. and Univs., Pa., 1972-75; vice chmn. Found. for Ind. Colls. Pa., 1972-73. Co-chmn. 1964 nat. and sch. awards jury Freedoms Found. at Valley Forge, chmn., 1974; bd. Christian edn. U.P. Ch. U.S.A., 1968-72; chmn. Delaware Valley Regional Planning Council for Higher Edn., 1973-78, Council Protestant Colls. and Univs., 1965-66; bd. dirs. Delaware Valley NCCJ, from 1972, Area Council for Econ. Edn., from 1980. Served as chaplain USNR, 1944-47. First pl. winner Freedoms Found. award, 1950, 2d pl., 1951, 52; others, 53-55. Mem. Presbyn. Coll. Union (exec. com. 1964-71, 76-80), Assn. Am. Colls. (commn. on coll. adminstrn. 1964-67), Pa. Assn. Colls. and Univs. (govt. relations com. 1975, chmn. 1977). Home: King of Prussia, Pa. Died Jan. 9, 1983.

GATES, THOMAS S(OVEREIGN), JR., ex-secretary of def.; b. Germantown, Phila., Apr. 10, 1906; s. Thomas Sovereign and Marie (Rogers) G.; A.B., U. of Pa., 1928; LL.D., Univ. of Pa., Yale, Columbia; m. Millicent Anne Brengle, Sept. 29, 1928; children—Millicent Anne, Patricia S., Thomas S. (dec.), Katharine Curtin. Asso. with Drexel & Co., Phila., 1928; partner Drexel & Co., Phila., 1940-53; pres., dir. Morgan Guaranty Trust Co., 1961-65, chairman of the board, chief executive officer, 1965-83, also chairman of the executive committee; dir. Gen. Electric Co., Scott Paper Co., Campbell Soup Co., Ins. Co. N.Am., Smith, Kline & French Labs., Cities Service Co.; under sec. navy, 1955-57, sec.navy, 1957-59; dep. sec. def., 1959-60, sec. def., 1960. Trustee Foxcroft Sch.; life trustee U. Pa. Served as comdr. USNR, 1942-45; overseas. Mem. Acad. Polit. Sci., Council Fgn. Relations, Navy League, Pa. Soc., Colonial Soc. of Pa., Phi Beta Kappa. Clubs: Philadelphia, Racquet (Philadelphia, Pa.); Gulph Mills Golf, Chevy Chase, Metropolitan, Links (Washington); Economic (N.Y.C.). Home: Devon, Pa. Died Mar. 25, 1983.

GAUMNITZ, ERWIN ALFRED, university adminstr.; b. St. Cloud, Minn., Feb. 24, 1907; s. August H. and Ada H. (McNeal) G.; B.B.A., U. Minn., 1929, M.A., 1934, Ph.D., 1935; m. Evelyn E. Kenney, Sept. 5, 1928; children—Jane (Mrs. Kieth F. Johnson), Roger K. Jack E., Thomas W. Prof., U. Minn., 1929-35, Coll. of St. Thomas, 1934-36; dir. research Minn. Unemployment Compensation Dept., also U.S. Bur. Labor Statistics, St. Paul, 1937-38; with U. Wis., 1938—, from asst. prof. to asso. prof., 1941-45, prof. econs., 1945—, asst. dean Sch. Commerce, 1946-50, dean Sch. Commerce, 1955-73, dean Grad. Sch. Bus. Adminstrn., until 1973. Economist OPA, 1942-44; regional price exec. OPS, 1951; cons. research, mgmt. for bus. firms; Arthur H. Eliott lectr., Gt. Britain, 1968; seminar lectr. U.S. Africa, 1971; Bombay, New Delhi, Calcutta, Madras, 1973. Vice pres. Wis. Council of Chs., 1957-71, Madison YMCA, 1956-69. Fellow Royal Econ. Soc. (Eng.); mem. Am. Statis. Assn. (life), Am. Econ. Assn., Am. Risk and Ins. Assn. (past pres.), Beta Alpha Psi, Beta Gamma Sigma, Phi Kappa Phi. Author: Social Security and Life Insurance, 1941; Life Insurance Mathematics, 1951; Futures Trading Seminar, 1966; Life Insurance Mathematics (Formosa), 1970; also articles. Home: Madison, Wis. Died June 9, 1982.

GAYE, MARVIN, singer, songwriter; b. Washington, Apr. 2, 1939. Grad., Cardoza High Sch. Began singing in, 1950's with vocal group, The Rainbows; co-founder group, The Marquees (later became The Moonglows), 1957, later became soloist, rec. artist, Tamla records, from 1962; first hit Stubborn Kind of Fellow, 1962; has also recorded with first hit, Tammi Terrell, Mary Wells, and, Kim Weston; albums include In Our Lifetime; songs written include Inner City Blues; TV appearances include The Tonight Show. Served with USAF. Died Apr. 1, 1984.*

GAYLORD, FAY CLAUDE, horticulturist; b. Lafayette, Ind., Mar. 19, 1889; s. George C. and Julia S. (Shaw) G.; B.S.A., Purdue, 1917; m. Ethel O. Dyer, Aug. 2, 1918; 1 son, James D. Extension horticulturist Purdue, 1918-26, hort. marketing, specialist, Purdue Univ. Agrl. Expt. Sta., 1926-35, asst. chief in charge marketing hort. crops, hort. dept. Purdue from 1935; exec. sec.-treas. Agrl. Alumni Seed Improvement Assn., Inc., from 1938; pres., treas. Klondike Canners, Incorporated, Lafayette. Recipient Certificate of Distinction, Purdue Agricultural Alumni Association, 1955. Member Indiana State Vegetable Growers Assn. (sec.-treas. since 1926), Purdue Agrl. Alumni Assn. (pres. 1925-27), Nat. Assn. Marketing Officials (vice pres. 1945-46, pres. 1947), Vegetable Growers Assn. of Am., Am. Soc. Hort. Sci., Sigma Xi, Alpha Zeta. Republican. Methodist. Mason (Scottish rite), Elk. Club: Kiwanis. Home: Lafayette, Ind. †

GAYMAN, HARVEY ELLISON, educator; b. Doylestown, Pa., Apr. 15, 1890; s. Harvey and Sarah (Gross) G.; B.S., Cornell, 1916; A.M., Columbia, 1933; Sc.D. in edn. (hon.), Temple U., 1953; m. Hazel Bennett, June 12, 1918; children—Sara E. (Mrs. Philip J. Shaw), Anne B. (Mrs. Sylvan Sheely), Deborah W. (Mrs. E. H. Kofke). Tchr., adminstr. schs., Jenkintown, also Richboro, Pa., 1909-12; tchr. vocational agr., Porter Twp., 1916-17; mem. staff rural edn. Cornell, 1917-18; staff agrl. div., bur. vocational edn. Dept. Pub. Instrn., Harrisburg, 1918-23, dir. statis. research, 1923-29; dir. research Pa. State Edn. Assn., 1929-39, exec. sec. from 1939; editor Pa. Sch. Jour. from 1939; dir. N.E.A. from 1939, exec. sec., 1952-53. Mem. exec. com. Pa. State Com. Pub. Edn., 1939-41. Mem. Nat. Assn. Secs. State Edn. Assns., Pub. Service Inst., Horace Mann League, Phi Delta Kappa, Phi Sigma Sigma. Club: Pa. Schoolmen's. †

GAYNOR, JANET, actress; b. Chicago, Ill., Oct. 6, 1906; ed. Lake View High Sch., Chicago; m. Lydell Peck, Sept. 11, 1929, divorced 1934; m. 2d, Gilbert Adrian, Aug. 14, 1939. Voted year's most popular actress, 1929; listed among five leading stars in a poll of 6,000 theater owners, 1934. Has stared in "Seventh Heaven" "Street Angel" "State Fair," "Servants Entrance," "The Farmer Takes a Wife," "A Star is Born," "Three Loves Has Nancy," "The Young in Heart,"Died Sept. 14, 1984.*

GAZIANO, JOSEPH SALVATORE, mfg. co. exec.; b. Waltham, Mass., Apr. 2, 1935; s. Salvatore and Carmela (Ganzi) G.; m. Anne Marie Bradley, Sept. 8, 1962; children—Christopher, Cara, Mary Elizabeth. B.S.E.E., M.I.T., 1956. Mgr. maj. space systems Raytheon Co., Lexington, Mass., 1960-67; v.p., gen. mgr. Allied Research Assos., Concord, Mass., 1967-69; pres. Prelude Corp., Westport, Mass., 1969-73; chmn. bd., pres. Tyco Labs., Inc., Exeter, N.H., from 1973; dir. Mobil Tyco Solar Energy Corp., New Boston Garden Corp., Muirhead Ltd. Trustee Berwick Acad., St. Anselm's Coll. Republican. Roman Catholic. Home: Epping, N.H. Died, 1982.

GEARHART, HARRY A(LONZO), coll. prof., clergyman; b. Templeton, Pa., Nov. 27, 1889; s. Owen Wagner and Alvira Virginia (Patton) G.; student Dayton (Pa.) Acad. 1908-11; A.B., Grove City (Pa.) Coll., 1915; B.S.T., Western Theol. Sem., 1918; Ph.D., Edinburgh Univ., Scotland, 1924; m. Elizabeth Grace Davis, June 5, 1918; 1 d., Nancy Louise Rural sch. teacher near Templeton, Pa., 1090-10; salesman Aluminum Co. of Am., New Kensington, Pa., 1916; ordained to ministry of Presbyn. Ch., 1918, and served as asst. pastor, E. Liberty Ch., Pittsburgh, 1918-20, pastor, Bakerstown, 1920-22, supply-pastor Middlebie Ch., Scotland, 1928; pastor Aspinwall Ch., Pittsburgh, 1924-30, Beaver, Pa., 1930-37; prof. of Bible, Grove City (Pa.) Coll. from 1937. Trustee Grove City Coll., 1934-37; dir. Boys Club, North Side, Pittsburgh, 1915-17. Served as U.S. Chaplain, Govt. Hosp. 108, Aspinwall, Pa., 1925-30. Mem. Nat. Assn. Biblical Instrs., Western Pa. Assn. Liberal Arts Colls., Independent Mason (Scottish rite). Interested in Christine edn. on the coll. level. Home: Grove City, Pa. †

GEHMAN, HENRY SNYDER, Orientalist, clergyman; b. Ephrata Twp., Lancaster County, Pa., June 1, 1888; s. Christian Eberly and Amanda Minerva (Snyder) G.; A.B., Franklin and Marshall Coll., 1909 (first honors); A.M., 1911, Litt.D., 1947; Ph.D., University of Pennsylvania (Philadelphia, Pa.), 1913; student Dropsie Coll., 1921-26; S.T.B., Div. Sch. of P.E. Ch., Phila., 1926, S.T.D., 1927; student Divinity Sch., U. of Chicago, summer 1922; m. Bertha W. Lausch, Aug. 30, 1917; children—Amanda Elizabeth (wife of Rev. Samuel E. Kidd), Henry Nevin. Teacher rural sch. and prin. high school, Pa., 2 yrs.; ordained ministry Reformed Ch. in U.S., 1917; organized Tabor Ref. Ch., Phila., and pastor, July 1917-Feb. 1921; univ. research fellow, 1920-29, and assistant in Sanskrit, University of Pa., 1920-21; instr. in Semitic langs., Princeton U., 1929-35, lecturer in Semitic languages since 1935; instr. in New Testament Greek, Princeton Theol. Sem., 1930-31, acting prof. Old Testament, 1931-34, prof. Old Testament literature from 1934, chmn. dept. Biblical Studies, from 1942; representative American Schools of Oriental Research, from 1937; visiting professor of Old Testament and Theology, Presbyterian Theological Seminaries. Awarded John Simon Guggenheim Found. Fellowship, 1954. Mem. Am. Oriental Soc., Soc. Bibl. Lit. and Exegesis, Linguistic Society America, Pa. German Folklore Soc. (pres. 1947-48), Archaeol. Inst. Am., Phi Beta Kappa, Phila. Oriental Club (president 1929-30, 46-47). Minister Presbyn. Ch., U.S.A.; mem. Presbytery of New Brunswick, N.J.; commr. to Presbyn. Gen. Assembly, 1943; mem. council on theol. edn. Presbyn. Ch., U.S.A., 1947-50. Author several books since 1914, also translation Peta-Vatthu into English, in the Minor Anthologies of the Pali Canon, Part IV, London, 1942. Rewrote and revised Westminster Dictionary of the Bible, 1944. Mem. editorial com., Jour. Biol. Lit., 1948-55. Mem. editorial com. and editor-in-chief O.T. sect. Westminster Study Edit. of Holy Bible, 1948. Spl. editor of etymologies for 2d edition of Webster's New International Dictionary. Contributing editor Am. Jour. of Archaeology, 1932-47; mem. editorial council, Theology Today; editor: A Critical and Exegetical Commentary on The Book of Kings, by J.A. Montgomery, 1951; contbr. to periodicals. Home: Princeton, N.J. †

GEIGER, JOSEPH ROY, prof. philosophy; b. Ocala, Fla., Oct. 10, 1887; s. Lorenzo Dow and Martha (Anderson) G.; B.A., Furman U., Greenville, S.C., 1909; M.A., John B. Stetson U., DeLand, Fla., 1912; M.A., U. of Chicago, 1914, Ph.D., 1916; m. Dorothy Osborn Milchrist, of Chicago, July 28, 1918. Prof. philosophy Coll. of William and Mary, from 1916, also head of dept. Mem. Am. Philos. Assn., Va. br. Acad. of Science, Am. Assn. Univ. Profs., Sigma Nu, Phi Beta Kappa, Omicron Delta Kappa, Phi Gamma Mu. Democrat. Baptist. Author: Religious Implications of Pragmatism, 1919. Contbr. to Internat. Jour. of Ethics, Jour. of Philosophy, etc. Home: Williamsburg, Va. †

GEISER, KARL FREDERICK, lawyer; b. New Hampton, Iowa, June 6, 1903; s. Mathias Edgar and Belle (Rowe) G.; m. Jane Schoentgen, June 6, 1928; children: Karl Frederick, Gretel (Mrs. George E. Stephens, Jr.). Student, Oberlin Coll., 1921-22; A.B., State U. Iowa, 1925, J.D., 1927. Bar: Iowa 1927, Calif. 1946, U.S. Supreme Ct. 1946. Ptr.firm Geiser, Donohue & Geiser, New Hampton, 1927-29; exec. v.p. E.H. Lougee, Inc., 1929-30; partner firm Tinley, Mitchell, Rosa, Everest & Geiser, Council Bluffs, Iowa, 1930-42, pvt. practice, Beverly Hills, Calif., 1945-78, ret., 1978. Served to comdr. USNR, 1942-45. Mem. Am., Iowa, Calif. bar assns., Order of Coif, Phi Delta Phi, Sigma Alpha Epsilon. Republican. Home: Los Angeles, Calif. Died Feb. 1984.

GEISER, SAMUEL WOOD, biologist; b. at Independence, Ia., June 11, 1890; s. Matthäus and Maria Ann Lucas (Wood) G.; A.B., Upper Ia. Univ., Fayette, 1914, hon. A.M., 1919, hon. Sc.D., 1934; Bruce fellow in zoölogy, Johns Hopkins, 1921-22, Ph.D., 1922; m. Bessie Adella Teeple (A.B., Upper Iowa Univ.), Dec. 28, 1916; children—David Teeple, Phyllis Elizabeth. Prof. biology, Guilford (N.C.) Coll., 1914-16; prof. biology, Upper, Ia. U., 1917-19; temp. asst., U.S. Bur. Fisheries, 1920-21; asst. prof. zoölogy, Washington U., St. Louis, 1922-24; prof. biology and head of dept. Southern-Meth. U., Dallas, from 1924. Fellow A.A.A.S., Iowa Academy Science, Oklahoma Academy of Science, Texas Academy of Science (honorary life fellow), Texas State Historical Association; mem. Biol. Soc. Washington, N. Tex. Biol. Soc. (pres. 1927-28), Am. Soc. Zoölogists, Am. Micros. Soc., History of Science Soc. (council, 1946-48), Am. Assn. University Professors, Philosophical Society of Texas (dir.), Phi Beta Kappa, Sigma Xi, Gamma Alpha, Lambda Chi Alpha. Methodist. Mason. Clubs: Thirteen, Town and Gown. Author: Lecture Outlines in General Biology (9th edit.), 1926; Laboratory Manual and Notebook in General Biology (8th edit.), 1925; Invertebrate Micrology, 1934; Amphibian Micrology, 1935; Naturalists of the Frontier (2d edit.) 1937; Scientific Study and Exploration in Early Texas, 1939; Horticulture and Horticulturists in Early Texas, 1945; Men of Science in Early Texas, 1948. Editor Field and Laboratory; contrbg. editor Southwest Review. Contbr. to tech. jours. and Dictionary of Am. Biography. Home: Dallas, Tex. †

GEISLER, RICHARD MARCUS, manufacturing executive; b. Abilene, Kans., May 14, 1925; s. August E. and Clare E. (Taylor) G.; m. Barbara J. Bernas, Aug. 4, 1971; children: Deborah, Michael, Michelle. B.S. in Acctg, Kans. State Tchrs. Coll., 1951; M.B.A., Tex. Christian U., 1964. Pres. Am. LaFrance div. A.T.O., Elmira, N.Y., 1969-71; pres. Spalding div. Questor, Chicopee, Mass., 1971-79; pres., chief exec. officer Champion Products Inc., Rochester, N.Y., from 1979, chmn. bd., from 1981. Trustee Springfield Coll., 1976; bd. dirs. Basketball Hall of Fame., 1973; trustee emeritus Basketball Hall of Fame, 1984; bd. dirs. Nat. Golf Found., 1976. Served with U.S. Army, 1946-48. Mem. Sporting Goods Mfg. Assn., Athletic Inst., Nat. Sporting Goods Assn., Am. Apparel Mfrs. Assn. (dir. 1981), Nat. Knitwear Mfrs. Assn. (dir. 1981), Rochester C. of C. (dir. 1981). Home: Rochester, N.Y. Died June, 1984.

GELDARD, FRANK ARTHUR, psychologist; b. Worcester, Mass., May 20, 1904; s. Arthur and Margaret Hardy (Gordon) G.; m. Jeannette Manchester, June 20, 1928; 1 dau., Deborah Rea. A.B., Clark U., 1925, A.M., 1926, Ph.D., 1928, Sc.D. (hon.), 1978; Sc.D. (hon.), Washington and Lee U., 1969. Assoc. prof. psychology U. Va., 1928-37, prof. psychology, dir. psychol. lab., 1937-60, chmn. dept., 1946-60; dean Grad. Sch. Arts and Scis., 1960-62; Stuart prof. psychology Princeton U., 1962-72, prof. emeritus, 1972-84, sr. research psychologist, 1972-84; Green Honors prof. Tex. Christian U., 1977; Served as col. U.S. Army Air Corps, chief field service and liaison sect., psychol. br. Office of Air Surgeon, hdqrs. Army Air Forces, 1942; chief psychol. sect. Office of Surgeon, hdqrs. Army Air Forces Tng. Command, 1942-45; comdg. officer, psychol. mission to P.I. and Japan, 1945; col. USAF Res., 1946-57; Cons. research and devel. bd. Nat. Mil. and Office of Naval Research, U.S. Navy Dept., 1947-58; research chief human resources div., research and devel. directorate Hdqrs. USAF, 1949-50; chmn. human resources com. Office Sec. of Def., 1950-56; sci. liaison officer Office Naval Research, London br., 1956-57. Author: The Human Senses, 2d edit, 1972, Fundamentals of Psychology, 1962, Sensory Saltation, 1975; Editor: Defense Psychology, 1962, Communication Processes, 1965, Cutaneous Communication Systems and Devices, 1974; Contbr. numerous articles to psychol. and ednl. jours. Chmn. NATO Adv. Group on Human Factors, 1959-65; chmn. Mil. Psychology Comm.; mem. Com. Internat. Relations in Psychology; NRC Vision Com., com. on biol., med. scis. NSF, 1953-59. Decorated Legion of Merit; recipient Distinguished Teaching award Am. Psychol. Found., 1974; Disting. Contbn. to Psychology award Va. Psychol. Assn., 1979. Fellow Am. Psychol. Assn. (past pres. div. exptl. psychology and div. mil. psychology), Royal Soc. Medicine (Gt. Brit.), AAAS (v.p. sect. I 1957-58); mem. AAUP, Soc. Exptl. Psychologists, So. Soc. for Philosophy and Psychology (past pres.), Internat. Brain Research Orgn., UNESCO, Eastern Psychol. Assn., Raven, Gryphon, Phi Beta Kappa, Sigma Xi, Phi Sigma, Kappa Phi, Omicron Delta Kappa. Democrat. Clubs: Colonnade (Princeton), Nassau (Princeton); Cosmos (Washington); Princeton (N.Y.C.). Home: Princeton, N.J. Died Dec. 8, 1984.

GELSINGER, MICHAEL GEORGE HOWARD, educator, clergyman; b. Reinhold, Pa., Jan. 14, 1890; s. John W. and Effie H. (Griffin) G.; A.B., Muhlenberg Coll., 1910; A.M., Harvard, 1914, Ph.D., 1929; m. Mary A. Orr, June 7, 1919; children—John H., Mary A. (wife of Rev. George P. Lambros). Prof. Carthage Coll., 1914-18, Collegiate Sch., N.Y.C., 1919-21, Coll. William and Mary, 1921-28; prof. Greek and Latin, U. Buffalo, from 1929, Andrew V. V. Raymond prof. classics, from 1955, chmn. dept. classics, 1954-58; priest Eastern Orthodox Ch., 1922, mitred archpriest, 1947. Trustee Am. Orthodox Cath. Alliance, Orthodox Cath. Frontier. Served with U.S. Army, 1918-19. Mem. Am. Philol. Assn., Am. Assn. U. Profs., Phi Beta Kappa. Republican. Author: Orthodox Hymns in English, 1939; Prayer Book for Eastern Orthodox Christians, 1944; also (with wife) graded series of lesson books; contbr. articles Byzantine hymnology and liturgics. †

GEMMILL, PAUL FLEMING, author; b. Muddy Creek Forks, York County, Pa., May 30, 1889; s. William James and Sue Mary (Jamison) G.; prep. edn., York County Acad.; A.B., Swarthmore Coll., 1917; Ph.D., U. of Pa., 1925; m. Jane Pancoast Brown, Mar. 29, 1920; children—Robert Fleming, Jean McAllister (Mrs. John G. H. Halstead). Began as cashier McClellan & Gotwalt Company, York, Pennsylvania, 1902; stenographer York Printing Co., 1905-08; asst. sec. Y.M.C.A., York, 1908-09; pub. entertainer (—magician—), 1909-11, also summers 1911-17; with U. of Pa., 1919-59, successively instr. in industry, 1919-21; asst. prof. economics, 1922-28, prof. economics, 1928-59, professor emeritus of economics, from 1959, chairman grad. group in economics, 1938-54. Made survey of British National Health Service in England, Scotland and Wales, Feb. to Sept., 1956. Entertainer in France, under direction of Nat. War Council, 1918; pvt. Gas Defense Div. of Chem. Warfare Service, Aug. 1918-Jan. 1919. Member Kappa Sigma, Phi Beta Kappa, (president Swarthmore chapter, 1942-45). Delta Sigma Rho, Pi Gamma Mu. Author many books from 1926, later ones: The Economics of Defense Mobilization, 1951; Current Introductory Economics, 1955; Britain's Search for Health, 1960, rev., 1962 Fundamentals of Econ., 6th edit., 1960. Editor, pub. Magic Without Apparatus, 1945; Sleight-of-Hand, 1946; Our Magic, 1946; The Fine Art of Magic, 1948. Contbr. to magazines and scientific journals. As —Paul Fleming, the Magician,— has appeared throughout the U.S. with his own company for many years. Home: Swarthmore, Pa. †

GENDRON, JOHN WILBROD, oil executive; b. Washington, July 30, 1919; s. Ulric Joseph and Louise M. (Nash) G.; m. Mary Sullivan, Mar. 5, 1946; children: John Michael, Robert Patrick, David Andrew. B.A., U. Oreg., 1940; postgrad., U. San Francisco Law Sch., 1946-48, Georgetown U. Law Sch. With Tidewater Oil Corp., 1946-59, asst. gen. mgr. Eastern div., N.Y.C., 1958-59; gen. mgr. transp. and supply Richfield Oil Corp. (merger Atlantic Refining Co. and Richfield into Atlantic Richfield Co. 1966), Los Angeles, 1959-62, v.p., gen. mgr. mfg. and transp., 1962-66, sr. v.p. public affairs, 1966-84, also dir. Bd. dirs. Am. Heart Assn.; bd. govs. Arthritis Found.; bd. dirs., chmn. allocations com. U. So. Calif. Bldg. Funds. Served to lt. comdr. USN, 1942-46. Mem. Western Oil and Gas Assn. (pres.), Petroleum Club Los Angeles, Am. Petroleum Inst., Twenty-Five Year Club Petroleum Industry, Delta Upsilon. Clubs: Calif. (Los Angeles); Internat. (Washington), Pisces (Washington). Home: Santa Barbara, Calif. Died June 14, 1985. *

GENGRAS, E. CLAYTON, ins. co. exec.; b. W. Hartford, Conn., Aug. 21, 1908; s. Alfred J. and Elizabeth (Doyle) G.; ed. pub. schs.; m. Elizabeth Hutchins, Feb. 11, 1936; children—Elizabeth (Mrs. Peter O. Kilbourn), Judith (Mrs. E. Merritt McDonough), Merrily, E. Clayton, Guy, John, Richard, Mark, James, Joel. Pres. Gengras Motors, Inc., Hartford, Conn., 1949-83; president then chairman bd., treas. Security-Conn. Ins. Group, New Haven, 1957-83; pres. Fire & Casualty Inc. Co., Hartford, 1950-57, chmn. bd., 1957-83; chmn. board, chief executive officer New Amsterdam Casualty Company, Baltimore, Maryland; director Newton Co., Manchester, Conn. Past mem. parole bd. Conn. State Prison, now dir., chmn. bldg. com.; adv. bd. Hartford Girl Scouts Am., Greater Hartford Community Chest; adv. bd., chmn. fund and planning com. St. Joseph Coll., also chmn. spl. gifts com. St. Joseph Cathedral Bldg. Fund; corporator Inst. of Living; bd. dirs. St. Francis Hosp.; chmn. Jesuit Shadowbrook Bldg. Fund; pres. Gengras Found., Inc.; hon. mem. Hartford Assn. Help of Retarded Children. Clubs: Hartford Golf (dir.), Hartford; Wampanoag Country; Carlouel Yacht (Clearwater, Fla.). Home: West Hartford, Conn. Died June 27, 1983.

GEORGE, COLLINS CRUSOR, music critic; b. Washington, June 30, 1909; s. John S. and Margaret (Crusor) G.; A.B., Howard U., 1929; M.A. in Anthropology, Harvard, 1932; A.M. in French, U. So. Calif., 1939. Tchr. English, A. and T. Coll., Greensboro, N.C., 1932-33; tchr. French and German, Langston (Okla.) U., 1933-35, Lemoyne Coll., Memphis, 1935-42; with Pitts. Courier, 1944-53, mng. editor Detroit edit., 1946-53; with Detroit Free Press, 1953-80, music critic, 1960-80; condr. classical music program Sta. WQRS-FM; music columnist Birmingham (Mich.) Eccentric, 1968-80. Mem. Am. Newspaper Guild, Music Critics Assn., Detroit Hist. Soc., Sigma Delta Chi, Omega Psi Phi. Club: Detroit Press. Home: Detroit, Mich. Died Feb. 14, 1980.

GEORGE, CHIEF DAN, actor; b. 1899; m. Amy; 6 children. Former stevadore; Indian Chief; actor, 1953-81; film appearances include: Smith!, 1969, The Ecstasy of Rita Joe, Little Big Man (Acad. award nominee 1970), Harry and Tonto, 1974, Cancel My Reservation, 1972, The Bears & I, 1974, The Outlaw Josey Wales, 1976, Shadow of the Hawk, 1976, Americathon, 1979; TV guest appearances include Cariboo Country (Can.), High Chaparral, Bonanza, Cade's County, The Peach Gang, 1975, mini-series Centennial, 1978-79. Recipient N.Y. Film Critics award, 1970, Nat. Soc. Film Critics award, 1970 (both for Little Big Man). Author: My Heart Soars, 1975. Died Sept. 23, 1981.*

GEORGE, NEWELL A., lawyer; b. Kansas City, Mo., Sept. 24, 1904; s. Adolphus K. and Ida (Scobee) G.; m. Jean Hannan, Apr. 16, 1934. Student, Park Coll., Parksville, Mo., Kansas City U.; LL.B., Nat. U., 1934, M.P.L., LL.M., 1935. Bar: D.C. 1935, Kans. 1943. Mem. staff U.S. Senator George McGill of Kans., 1933; regional atty. Bur. Employment Security, also FSA, 1935-52; chief legal counsel War Manpower Commn., 1942-44, pvt. practice law, Kansas City, Kans., from 1943, 1st asst. atty., Wyandotte County, Kans., 1952-58; mem. 86th Congress, 2d Dist. Kans., U.S. atty. for Kans., 1961-68; Mem. Gov.'s Com. on Criminal Adminstrn., Interstate Oil Compact Commn., Kans. Govt. Ethics Commn., Gov.'s

Criminal Justice Adv. Panel; mem. commn., mem. rules and personnel coms. Kans. Govtl. Commn. (name now Kans. Pub. Disclosure Commn.). Author: articles Kans. Law Rev. Trustee U. Mo. at Kansas City Law Found.; mem. Kansas City (Kans.) CSC; pres. Kans. Assn. Hi-12 Clubs; bd. dirs. for Kans., Nat. Multiple Sclerosis Soc. Recipient Outstanding Service award Am. Assn. Criminology; Law Enforcement Man of Year Rockne Club Am.; named adm. Nebr. Library, 1960; others. Hon. fellow Harry S. Truman Library; Mem. Am., Kans., Wyandotte County bar assns., Am. Judicature Soc., Am. Acad. Polit. and Social Sci., Supreme Ct. Hist. Soc., Nat. Ctr. for State Cts., L.B. Johnson Library, John F. Kennedy Meml. Library, Kansas City (Kans.) C. of C., Assn. U.S. Army, Delta Theta Phi. Democrat. Presbyn. Clubs: Mason (Kansas City, Kans.) (past master, trustee, Shriner), Optimist (Kansas City, Kans.), Hi-12 (Kansas City, Kans.), Top O'the Morning (Kansas City, Kans.) (past pres.). Sponsor legislation to create Agr. Hall of Fame, Wyandotte County, Kans. Home: Kansas City, Kans. Deceased.

GEORGE, NICHOLAS APOSTOLOS, labor arbitrator; b. Decatur, Ill., Oct. 10, 1908; s. Apostolos Nicholas and Helen (Kastanas) G.; m. Jacoba K. Benton, June 8, 1963. Student, Wash. U., 1925-27, U. Minn., 1944, U. Mich., 1949-50. Muskegon dir. indsl. relations Brunswick-Balke-Collender Co., 1941-49, Murray Corp. Am., 1949-54; v.p. Ohio Boxboard Co., Rittman, Ohio, 1954-59, Brunswick Corp., Chgo., 1959-64; pres., dir. Muskegon Paper Box Co., 1964-75; labor arbitrator, from 1976; mem. state adv. council SBA, 1975-77; Mem. Muskegon Area Devel. Council.; Vice pres. Brunswick Found., 1960-64. Bd. dirs. Muskegon County United Way, 1972-74. Mem. AIM, Am. Mgmt. Assn., Am. Arbitration Assn., Paperboard Packaging Council. Greek Orthodox. Clubs: Mason (32 deg., Shriner), Muskegon Country, Muskegon Century, Muskegon Yacht, Marco Island (Fla.) Country, Riviera Yacht. Address: Muskegon, Mich.

GEORGE, ROBERT HUDSON, educator; b. Brookline, Mass., Dec. 25, 1889; s. Andrew Jackson and Alice Nelson (Vandt) G.; A.B., Amherst Coll., 1911; A.M., Harvard, 1913, Ph.D., 1916; m. Katharine Hunt Ames, Jan. 29, 1914; children—Eleanor Ames (Mrs. William Loris Mather), Katharine Nelson (Mrs. Charles Burgess Ayres), Instr. in history, Harvard, 1915-16, Yale, 1916-17; asst. prof., 1919-22; asso. prof. of history, Union Coll., 1922-23; asso. prof. of history, Brown U., 1923-39, prof. of history from 1939. Mem. Am. Commn. to Negotiate Peace, Paris, 1919. Served as capt., Inf., U.S. Army, 1917-19, lt. col., U.S. Army Air Force, 1942-45, historian Ninth Air Firce, 1943-45, Awarded Bronze star, 1947. Mem. Am. Hist. Assn., Chi Psi. Fellow Royal Hist. Soc. Club: Providence Art Contbr. of monographs on 17th Century English history to hist. revs. Home: Providence, R.I. †

GEORGE, W(ESLEY) C(RITZ), biologist, educator; b. Yadkin County, N.C., Aug. 20, 1888; s. Thomas Millard and Mary Henrietta (Critz) G.; A.B., U. of N.C., 1911, A.M., 1912, Ph.D., 1918; Hinton Maule fellow, Princeton, 1917-18; m. Wilma Kirk Green, February, 27, 1926; one daughter, Patricia Ann (Mrs. John Dortch). Began as instructor zoology U. of N.C., 1912-16; prof. biology Guilford Coll., N.C., 1916-17; adjunct prof. zoology U. of Ga., 1919; asso. prof. histology and embryology U. of Tenn. Med. Sch., 1919-20, asso. prof. U. N.C., 1920-24, prof., 1924-59, emeritus, head dept. anatomy 1940-49; investigator in marine biology during summers, U.S. Fisheries Biol. Sta., Beaufort, N.C., Bermuda Biol. Sta., Bass Biol. Sta., Fla. Served as sergt., M.C., U.S. Army 1918-19. Fellow A.A. A.S.; mem. Am. Assn. Anatomists, Am. Soc. Zoologists, Am. Soc. Human Genetics, Elisha Mitchell Science Society (co-editor journal), North Carolina Acad. Sci. (pres. 1952) Sigma Xi, Sigma Chi, Sigma Upsilon, Phi Chi. Democrat. Episcopalian. Author articles on development of man and other vertebrates, comparative hematology, philosophy of sci. Home: Chapel Hill, N.C. †

GEPPERT, OTTO EMIL, ednl. pub., sch. map and globe cons.; b. Chgo., July 17, 1889; s. Julius and Wilhelmina (Simmons) G.; student Lewis Inst., 1906-07, YMCA Coll., 1908-09, Northwestern U., 1915-16; m. Margaret Masley, Apr. 28, 1920; children—David Frederick, Robert Roundsville. Clk. law office Dent, Whitman & Eaton, Chgo., 1903; with A. J. Nystrom & Co., ednl. publishers, 1905-16; sec.-treas. Denoyer-Geppert Co., Chgo., 1916-64, pres., 1964-68, chairman of the board, from 1968, general manager, from 1947. Director of Chicago YMCA; exec. com. Chgo. Auditorium Restoration; trustee Roosevelt U. Served with intelligence div., U.S. Army, 1918-19; AEF in France. Mem. A. Assn. Sch. Adminstrs., Assn. Am. Geographers (life), National Education Association (life), Institute Internat. Edn. Northwestern Univ. Alumni Assn. (life), Eleanor Assn. (dir.), Acad. Polit. Sci. (life), Am. Civil Liberties Union, Am. Hist. Assn. Mason (Shriner). Rotarian. Home: Wilmette, Ill. †

GERAGHTY, JAMES, art editor; b. Spokane, Wash., Apr. 22, 1905; s. James Michael and Nora (Toolen) G.; student Gonzaga U., 1924-27; m. Eva Elizabeth Carr, Oct. 3, 1931; children—James Michael, Sarah Ann. Radio writer, 1930-38; art editor New Yorker mag., 1939-83. Clubs: Century Assn., Grolier (N.Y.C.). Home: Weston, Conn. Died Jan. 16, 1983.

GERAGHTY, JOHN JAMES, lawyer; b. Weehawken Heights, N.J., Feb. 12, 1908; s. James and Martha (Andrews) G.; m. Ruby Tyson, July 23, 1945. A.B., Columbia, 1933, LL.B., 1935. Bar: N.Y. and N.C. bars. With firm Duke and Landis, N.Y.C., 1937-42, 46-51, Poyner, Geraghty, Hartsfield and Townsend, Raleigh, N.C., from 1951; lectr. law N.Y. U. Sch. Finance, 1946-51. Served to maj. AUS, 1941-46. Decorated Legion of Merit. Home: Raleigh, N.C. Deceased.

GERETY, PIERCE JOSEPH, lawyer, bus. exec.; b. Shelton, Conn., Mar. 6, 1914; s. Peter Leo and Charlotte U. (Daly) G.; m. Helen Martin, June 8, 1940; children—Pierce, Peter Leo, Thomas Richard, Miles Stephen. LL.B. cum laude, Fordham U., 1942. Bar: N.Y. bar 1942, Conn. bar 1942, D.C. bar 1957. Asso. firm Wilkie, Owen, Otis, Farr, Gallagher and Walton, N.Y.C., 1942-43, 44-47; partner firm Curtis, Trevethan and Gerety, Bridgeport, Conn., 1947-57; chmn. Internat. Orgns. Employees Loyalty Bd., Washington, 1953-55; gen. counsel U.S. Civil Service Commn. and legal adviser to the Pres.'s asst. on personnel, Washington, 1954-55; dep. adminstr. Refugee Relief Program, Dept. of State, 1955-57; gen. counsel Fed. Housing Adminstrn., 1957-58; N.Y. partner Wolf, Bloch, Schorr and Solis-Cohen, Phila., 1959-61; partner Wolf and Gerety, N.Y.C., 1961-63, Royall, Koegel and Rogers, N.Y.C., 1963-66; v.p., counsel Ogden Corp., N.Y.C., 1966-68; chmn. bd., dir. Gould, Cargill & Co., Inc., 1968-70; counsel Whitman & Ransom, 1971-73; sr. v.p. Ogden Corp., N.Y.C., 1970-77; chmn. bd. Barkey Internat. Corp., Fairfield, Conn.; dir. Enrique C. Welbers (S.A.), Buenos Aires, Argentina; pres., dir. Sasco Creek Corp., Fairfield; partner firm Gerety and Gerety, Fairfield, from 1978. Town counsel, Fairfield, 1945-55; Chmn. Am. Immigration and Citizenship Conf., 1964-65; Mem. Rep. State Central Com. Conn., 1948-54. Mem. Am., N.Y. State, Conn., Bridgeport bar assn. Home: Southport, Conn. Died Dec. 4, 1983.

GERMAIN, EDWARD BENNETT, mfr.; b. Buffalo, N.Y., June 2, 1890; s. Charles B. and Mary (Begges) G.; M.E., Mass. Inst. Tech., 1913; m. Bennette Craig, Sept. 17, 1913; 1 son, Edward Bennett. With Aberthaw Constrn. Co., Boston, as contracting engr. and gen. mgr., 1913-17; with Bethelhem Shipbuilding Corp., Ltd., 1917-22, as gen. mgr. various periods, Moore plant, Buffalo plant, Providence plant and Harlan plant, and as gen. sales mgr. of the corp.; pres. from Dec. 1, 1922, of Dunlop Tire & Rubber Corp., Dunlop Tire & Rubber Co., Utica Spinning Co.; dir. Marine Midland Corp., Marine Trust Co., Niagara Share Corp., Buffalo Ins. Co., Rubber Mfgrs. Assn., Dunlop Tire & Rubber Goods Co., Ltd., Dunlop Tire & Rubber Corp. Mem. Phi Beta Epsilon, Republican. Episcopalian. Clubs: Buffalo, Cherry Hill Country, Buffalo Canoe, Country. Home: Buffalo, N.Y. †

GERNREICH, RUDI, designer; b. Vienna, Austria, Aug. 8, 1922; came to U.S., 1938, naturalized, 1943; s. Siegmund and Elisabeth (Mueller) G. Student, Los Angeles City Coll., 1938-41, Los Angeles Art Center Sch., 1941-42. founder, pres. GR Designs, Inc. (name changed to Rudi Gernreich, Inc. 1964), Los Angeles, 1960-85; mem. internat. designer adv. council Montgomery Ward, 1967-85. Modern dancer, Lester Horton Dance Theatre, 1942-48, free-lance designer, N.Y.C., Los Angeles, 1948-51, designer, Walter Bass, Inc., Beverly Hills, Calif., 1951- 59, swimwear designer, Westwood Knitting Mills, Los Angeles, 1953-59, shoe designer, Genesco Corp., 1958-60, underwear and sleepwear for, Lily of France, 1975-77, decor and costumes for, Bella Lewitzky Dance Co.'s Inscape, 1976-77, dance wear for, Capezio-Ballet Makers, 1977, swimwear for, Berlei-Hestia, U.K., 1977 (Recipient Designer of Year award Sports Illustrated mag. 1956, Sporting Look award 1963, spl. award for swimming design Coty Am. Fashion Critics 1960, Winnie award 1963, award for creative achievement women's knitwear industry Wool Knit Assos. 1960, 62, Hall of Fame award 1964, Am. Fortnight trophy Nieman-Marcus Co. 1961, London Sunday Times Internat. Spl. award 1965, Filene's Design award 1966, Coty Am. Fashion Critics Return award 1966, named to Hall of Fame 1967, Fenit-Industria Textil Trophy, San Paolo, Brazil 1967, Mare Moda-Tiberio D'Oro award (Italy) 1967, Production Design award for bedspreads and pillows Am. Resources Council Inc. 1972, Knitted Textile Assn. Design award 1975, Robinson's Creative Spirit award 1976); knitwear, swimwear designer, Harmon Knitwear, Marinette, Wis., 1960-72, Quilts for Knoll Internat., 1972. Home: Hollywood, Calif. Died Apr. 21, 1985.

GERSHON, RICHARD KEVE, pathologist; b. N.Y.C., Dec. 24, 1932; s. Murray Huda and Juliette G.; m. Robyn Randice Mione, June 10, 1975. B.A., Harvard U., 1954; M.D., Yale U., 1959. Pathology intern Yale U., 1960-61, asst. resident in pathology, 1963-64; mem. faculty Yale U. Med. Sch., from 1964, prof. pathology, immunology and biology, from 1976, chief lab. div. immunology, from 1976; dir. lab. cellular immunology Howard Hughes Med. Inst., from 1977; prin. investigator NIH grants, from 1966; civilian dir. lab. virology U.S. Army Med. Gen. Hosp. 406, Japan, 1962-63. Contbr. articles to profl. publs. Mem. AAAS, Am. Soc. Exptl. Pathology, Am. Assn. Immunologists, Brit. Soc. Immunology, Nat. Acad. Sci. Home: New Haven, Conn. Died July 11, 1983.

GERSHWIN, IRA, lyricist; b. N.Y.C., Dec. 6, 1896; s. Morris and Rose (Bruskin) G.; m. Leonore Strunsky, Sept. 14, 1926. Student, Townsend Harris Hall, 1910-14, Coll. City of N.Y., 1914-16, Columbia U. Extension, 1918; D.F.A., U. Md., 1966. Wrote lyrics for music written by his brother George Gershwin; stage plays A Dangerous Maid, 1921, Lady, Be Good, 1924, Primrose, (with Desmond Carter), 1924, Tell Me More, (with B. G. DeSylva), 1925, Tip Toes, 1925, Oh, Kay, 1926, Funny Face, 1927, Rosalie, (with P. G. Wodehouse), 1927, Treasure Girl, 1928, Strike Up The Band, 1929, Show Girl, (with Gus Kahn), 1929, Girl Crazy, 1930, Of Thee I Sing, 1932 (won Pulitzer prize), Pardon My English, 1932, Let 'Em Eat Cake, 1933, Porgy and Bess, (with DuBose Heyward), 1935; motion pictures Delicious, 1930, Shall We Dance? , 1936, A Damsel in Distress, 1937, Goldwyn Follies, 1937; also wrote: (music by Youmans and Lannin) lyrics for Two Little Girls in Blue, 1921, Be Yourself, (with Kaufman and Connelly; music by Gensier and Schwartzwald), 1924, That's a Good Girl, (music by Charig and Meyer), 1928, Life Begins at 8:40, (with Harburg and Arlen), 1934, Ziegfeld Follies (music by Duke), 1936, Lady in the Dark (music by Weill), 1940, North Star (music by Copland), 1943, Cover Girl (music by Kern), 1943, Where Do We Go From Here? (music by Weill), 1944, Firebrand of Florence (music by Weill), 1945, Park Avenue (music by Schwartz), 1946, The Shocking Miss Pilgrim (posthumous music, George Gershwin), 1946, The Barkleys of Broadway (music by Warren), 1948, An American in Paris (music by Gershwin), 1952, Give A Girl A Break (music by Lane), 1952, A Star Is Born (music by Arlen), 1954, The Country Girl (music by Arlen), 1954, Kiss Me, Stupid. (posthumous music Gershwin), 1964; Author: Lyrics on Several Occasions, 1959. Awarded Coll. City N.Y. Townsend Harris Medal, 1952; James K. Hackett award, 1972. Mem. ASCAP, Dramatists Guild. Died Aug. 17, 1983.*

GESCHWIND, NORMAN, physician, educator; b. N.Y.C., Jan. 8, 1926; s. Morris and Anna (Blau) G.; B.A., Harvard, 1946, M.D., 1951; m. Patricia Dougan, Sept. 8, 1956; children—Naomi, David, Claudia. Moseley Travelling fellow Nat. Hosp., London, Eng., 1952-53, USPHS research fellow, 1953-55; resident in neurology Boston City Hosp., 1955-56; research fellow Mass. Inst. Tech., 1956-58; staff neurologist Boston VA Hosp., 1958-62, chief neurology service, 1962-66; asso. prof. neurology Boston U., 1962-66, prof., chmn. dept., 1966-68; James Jackson Putnam prof. neurology Harvard Med. Sch., 1969-84. Fellow Am. Acad. Neurology; mem. Acad. Aphasia, Am. Neurol. Assn. Research, publs. on anat. basis higher functions nervous system, explanation disturbances higher function on basis damage to pattern cortico-cortical connections in animals and man. Died Nov. 4, 1984.

GESELL, WILLIAM H., corp. exec.; b. Jersey City, June 8, 1890; s. William J. and Laura (Thomas) G.; Ph.C., Columbia, 1908; B.Chem. Engring., U. Mich., 1911, Ll.D.; m. Violet Hoehn, June 4, 1913; children—William Hance, Ruth (Mrs. F. Channing Soule). Chem. engring., gen. mgr. Hamersley Mfg. Co., Garfield, N.J., 1913-20; v.p., dir. Lehn & Fink Products Corp., pharm. specialists, Bloomfield, N.J., from 1920. Rep. Nat. Research Council, Warsaw and The Hague, 1927-28; rep. Dept. State as Am. del. 60th Internat. Management Congress, London, 1935, v.p., Washington, 1938; cons. W.P.B., 1943-45. Mem. adv. bd. N.Y.U. from 1941. Served as maj. San. Corps. U.S. Army, 1926-28. Recipient Taylor Key, 1939. Licensed profl. engr. N.Y. Mem. Soc. Advancement of Management (pres. 1935-39), Nat. Management Council (chmn. 1936-38). Home: Montclair, N.J. †

GESSNER, JAMES WALTER, railroad exec.; b. Monroe, Mich., Sept. 6, 1930; s. Allan Earl and Margaret Marie (Keehn) G.; m. Joy Layne Wahl, Jan. 8, 1955; children—James, Julie, Jeffrey. B.S. in Engring, U. Mich., 1952, M.S. in Civil Engring, 1955. With So. Ry. Co., 1955-69; div. supt. Macon, Ga., Greensboro, N.C., 1960-64, mktg. mgr. customer service engring., Washington, 1964, dir. transp. engring., Atlanta, 1965-67, dir. planning and devel., 1967-69; asst. to v.p. ops. Mo. Pacific R.R., St. Louis, 1969-71, gen. mgr., Little Rock, 1971-72, gen. mgr. transp., St. Louis, 1972-74, v.p. ops., 1974-76, exec. v.p., 1976-78, pres., 1978-79, pres., chief exec. officer, from 1979, also dir.; dir. Commerce Bankshares, Mo. Pacific Corp., Mo. Improvement Co., MP Truckline, Am. Refrigerator Transit Co. Served with U.S. Army, 1952-54. Mem. Assn. Am. Railroads (dir.), Am. Assn. R.R. Supts., U.S.-Mex. C. of C. (dir.). Republican. Lutheran. Clubs: Union League (Chgo.); Media (St. Louis); Bellerive Country. Home: Ballwin, Mo. Died May 24, 1982.

GETMAN, ARTHUR KENDALL, agrl. educator; b. Richfield Springs, N.Y., June 20, 1887; s. Arthur R. and Carrie (Goodier) G.; grad. Richfield Springs High Sch., 1906; B.S., Cornell U., 1911; D.Sc., Alfred (N.Y.) U., 1934; post grad. study in edn. and economics, Columbia, 1918, Harvard, 1921; m. Fredella E. Babcock, 1912; 1 son, Kendall G. Head of dept. agrl. teacher training, State Normal and Training Sch., Cortland, N.Y., 1911-15; specialist in agrl. edn., N.Y. State Dept., Edn., 1915-17; prof. agrl. edn., Rutgers U., New Brunswick, N.J., 1917-19, chief of Agrl. Edn. Bur. N.Y. State Dept. Edn., 1919-47; asst. commr. for vocational edn., 1947; special lecturer at various college summer sessions; instr. professional classes, Cornell U., summer sessions 1919. Mem. war finance com. U.S. Dept. of Agr., War Bd.; mem. trade council War Manpower Commn.; mem. salvage com., W.P.B. Author: Teaching Agrl. Vocations (with R. M. Stewart), 1927; Future Farmers in Action, 1929; The Church School in Action, 1931; The Young Man in Farming (with P. W. Chapman), 1933; bulletins. Editor: (with others) Wiley Farm Series, 14 technical texts for schs. and colls. Mem. bd. trustees Green Mountain Jr. Coll., Poultney, Vt.; mem. Am. Vocational Assn. (v.p. 1930-36, pres. 1936-38), N.Y. State Council Churches and Religious Edn. (v.p.), N.E.A., N.Y. State Teachers Assn., N.Y. State Vocational Assn., Alpha Zeta, Phi Delta Kappa. Methodist. Club: Albany University. Home: Albany, N.Y. †

GETTS, CLARK H., public relations counsel; b. Whitehall, Wis., Aug. 5, 1893; s. Edmund Cyrus and Pearl (Sherwood) G.; m. Osa Johnson, Feb. 3, 1941 (dec.); m. Dorothy Raphun Jones, Dec. 30, 1955. A.B., U. Wis., 1914; LL.B., Columbia, 1916. Rep. Am. and Brit newspapers, China, 1920-26, writer for mags., lectr. on China and Manchuria, 1927-30; with NBC (promoting tours for Paderewski, Rachmaninoff and others), 1930-32; established ind. lecture and radio prodn. bur., 1933; inc. as Clark H. Getts, Inc., 1937, inc. pub. relations bus., 1940. Asso. in prodn.: radio shows, including Heinz Mag. of Air, 1937, Army-Navy-Red Cross show, 1944, John T. Flynn's Behind the Headlines, 1947, John Tasker Howard's Our American Music, 1950; TV programs Chronoscope, 1951 (both received Freedoms Found. and TV gold medal awards), Men and Ideas, 1952, others; Mgr. and condr. Johnson expdn. to Africa, making Stanley and Livingstone feature film for, 20th Century-Fox; arranged nat. tours for numerous artists, speakers, internat. figures, including, Harold Stassen., C. J. Hambro, Esequiel Padilla, Grand Duchess Marie, Alexander Wollcott, Eleanor Roosevelt, William Lyon Phelps, Rajan Nehru, Mme V. L. Pandit, Maj. Alexander P. de Seversky, Gen. Leslie R. Groves, Gen. Robert L. Eichelberger, Adm. Blandy, Marquis of Donegal, Gen. George C. Kenney, Prince Peter and Princess Irene of Greece, concert prodns. including, Nat. Tipica Orchestra of Mexico, Chinese Cultural Theatre, Mia Slavenska and her Ballet, Dublin Players, Gay Tyroliers, Fiesta Mexicana, London Players. Pres. Clark H. Getts Assos., Transat Inc., Am. Inst. for Civic Edn. Methodist. Clubs: Mason (Shriner), Dutch Treat. Address: Clemson, SC.

GETZ, OSCAR, distilling company executive; b. Chgo., Nov. 20, 1897; s. Meyer Philip and Jennie (Mann) G.; m. Emma Dorothy Abelson, Jan. 9, 1923; children: Constance Joy (Mrs. Otto Bresky, Jr.), William Murray. Student, Northwestern U. Sch. Commerce, 1918-19. With William D. McJunkin Advt. Agy., Chgo., 1920-23; owner Radio Doctors, Inc., Chgo., 1924-27; pres. Steinite Radio Corp., Chgo., 1927-30; with Arlington Time Labs. (Fluorescent Lighting Co.), 1930-33; gen. partner Barton Brands, Ltd., Chgo., from 1933, also dir.; v.p., dir. Barton Western Distilling Co., Barton Internat. Corp., Barton Distillers Import Corp. Author: Whiskey-An American Pictorial History, 1978. Founder Barton Mus. Whiskey History, Bardstown, Ky.; gen. chmn. Lyric Opera Fund initial fund raising campaign, 1955; co-chmn. Auditorium Theatre Restoration Council, Chgo.; mem. Mayor Chgo. All Citizens Com., 1958; bd. dirs. World Rehab. Fund, Inc., N.Y.C., Lyric Opera, Chgo., Rehab. Inst., Internat. Film Festival, Chgo. Symphony Soc., Gastro-Intestinal Research Found. U. Chgo.; nat. trustee City of Hope; trustee Lincoln Acad. Ill.; bd. govs. Ford's Theatre, Washington; founding mem. Council Biol. Scis., Pritzker Sch. Medicine, U. Chgo.; v.p. Chgo. chpt. Brandeis U.; bd. dirs. PACE Inst.; chmn. Com. 100; bd. govs. Israel Bond Orgn., Variety Club Ill.; bd. mgrs. Old Town Chgo. Boys Club; fellow Brandeis U., Waltham, Mass. Named Liquor Industry Man of Yr., 1957; recipient City of Hope Torch award, 1966; Jewish Sem. Am. Nat. award, 1970; Shimer Coll. Angel award, 1971; PACE Inst. Exemplary Citizenship award, 1972; Cook County Sheriff Certificate Pub. Service, 1972; Retailers award of merit Ill. Liquor Stores Assn., 1975; Humanitarian of Year award Am. Jewish Com., 1975; Internat. Humanitarian award B'nai B'rith, 1977; Oscar Getz Fellowship created by World Rehab. Found., 1977. Mem. Chgo. Hist. Soc. (life), Stephen A. Douglas Assn. (founding), Manuscript Soc., Art Inst. Chgo. (life), Ill. State Hist. Soc. (past v.p.), Civil War Round Table. Clubs: Standard (Chgo.), Executives (Chgo.); Briarwood Country (Deerfield, Ill.); Racquet (Palm Springs, Calif.); Met. (Chgo.); Le Mirador Country (Vevey, Switzerland). Home: Chicago, Ill. Died July 7, 1983.

GEWEHR, WESLEY MARSH, prof. of history; b. Chicago, Ill., May 3, 1888; s. Fred and Phoebe (Arch) G.; grad. Evansville (Wis.) Sem., 1908; Ph.B., U. of Chicago, 1911; A.M., 1912, Ph.D., 1922; m. Mae Sansom, Sept. 3, 1913; 1 son, Hamilton Dodd. Instr. of history, Baker U., Baldwin, Kan., 1912-13; instr. of history, Ohio Wesleyan U., 1913-15, asst. prof., 1915-17; fellow in history, U. of Chicago, 1917-18; prof. Ia. State Teachers Coll., 1918-19, Morningside Coll., 1919-22, Denison U., 1922-29; prof. of history, Am. Univ., 1929-40; prof. and chmn. dept. history U. of Maryland from 1940; head of history, Army U., Shrivenham, Eng., 1945-46; professor in U.S. Army Univ., Biarritz, France; attached to Army Lecture Bureau in Germany, 1945-46. exchange prof. of history, Tsing Hua Coll., Peking, China, 1924-25. Mem. Am. Hist. Assn., Miss Valley Hist. Assn., Southern Hist. Assn., Am. Assn. Univ. Professors, Middle States Council for Social Studies (president 1942-43), National Council for Social Studies, Pi Gamma Mu, Phi Alpha Theta. Methodist. Club: Federal Schoolmen's (pres. 1948-49). Author several books, from 1929; contbr. articles; editor, contbr. American Civilization, 1957. Home: Washington, DC. †

GEZORK, HERBERT, clergyman, educator; b. Insterburg, Germany, June 15, 1900; s. Friedrich and Anna (Schirrmann) G.; student Bapt. Div. Sch., Hamburg, Germany, 1921-24, U. Berlin, 1925-28; Ph.D., So. Bapt. Theol. Sem., 1930; D.D., Colby Coll., 1942, Bucknell U., 1956, Colgate U., 1957, Brown U., 1964, Ottawa U., 1977; LL.D., Emerson Coll., 1956, Anderson-Broaddus Coll., 1968; D.S.O., Curry Coll., 1970; m. Ellen Markus, May 22, 1937; children—Herbert Peter, Thomas Edward, James William (dec.), Janet Ellen. Came to U.S., 1936, naturalized, 1943. Ordained to ministry Bapt., Ch., 1927; asso. pastor First Bapt. Ch., Berlin, Germany, 1925-28; gen. sec. German Bapt. Youth Movement, 1931-34; asst. prof. religion Furman U., 1937-38; interim pastor First Bapt. Ch., Clarksburg, W.Va., 1939; asst. prof. Bibl. history Wellesley Coll., 1939-43, lectr. social ethics, 1943-50; prof. social ethics, Christian world relations Andover Newton Theol. Sch., 1939-50, pres. sch., 1950-65, pres. emeritus, 1965-84; vis. lectr. Brown U., 1965-66; vis. prof. Harvard Div. Sch., 1965-68, Assumption Coll., 1968, Kanto Gakuin U., Japan, 1968-69; dir. dept. religion Chautauqua Instn., 1968-72; acting chaplain Middlebury Coll., 1973. Mem. U.S. Strategic Bombing Survey in Germany, 1945; chief Protestant affairs U.S. Mil. Govt. for Germany, 1946-48; cons. U.S. high commr. in Germany, 1950. Mem. Mass. Council Chs., chmn. com. on legislation, 1948-49; mem. com. on internat. justice and goodwill Nat. Council Chs., del. World Conf. on Faith and Order, Lund, Sweden, 1952, Montreal, 1963; v.p. Am. Bapt. Conv., 1954- 55, pres., 1959-60; mem. Christian Deputation to Russia, 1956; del. World Council Chs., Evanston, 1954, New Delhi, 1961. Mem. bd. preachers Harvard, 1956-72. Recipient Am. Legion Outstanding Fgn. Born Citizen award, 1969. Fellow Am. Acad. Arts and Scis. Mason. Author: Die Gottlosenbewegung, 1932; So Sah Ich Die Welt (in German, Finnish, Dutch), 1933; contbr. to Unity of the Faith, 1960. Contbr. articles and essays to various publs. Home: Natick, Mass. Dec. Oct. 21, 1984. Interned Newton Center, Mass.

GIAUQUE, WILLIAM FRANCIS, educator; b. Niagara Falls, Ont., Can., May 12, 1895; s. William Tecumseh Sherman and Isabella Jane (Duncan) G. (parents U.S. citizens); m. Muriel Frances Ashley, July 19, 1932; children—William Francis Ashley, Robert David Ashley. B.S., U. Calif., 1920, Ph.D., 1922, LL.D., 1963; D.Sc. (hon.), Columbia, 1936. Instr. chemistry U. Calif., 1922-27, asst. prof., 1927-30, assoc. prof., 1930-34, prof. chemistry, 1934-77, emeritus, 1962. Berkeley fellow (hon.).; Recipient prize for discovery (with H.L. Johnston) oxygen isotopes Pacific div. AAAS, 1929; Chandler medal Columbia, 1936; Elliott Cresson medal Franklin Inst., 1937; Nobel Prize for Chemistry, 1949; G.N. Lewis medal, 1956. Fellow Am. Phys. Soc., Am. Acad. Arts and Scis.; mem. Am. Chem. Soc. (Gibbs medal 1951), AAUP, Nat. Acad. Scis., Am. Philos. Soc., Sigma Xi, Phi Lambda Upsilon (hon.). Clubs: Faculty (Berkeley); Contbr. (numerous articles to profl. jours.). Home: Berkeley, Calif. Dec. Mar. 28, 1982.

GIBBONS, EDWARD F., retail co. exec.; b. Boston, 1919; (married). Grad., Bentley Coll., 1948. With McCord Corp., 1965-66; v.p. finance United Brands Co., 1966-73; v.p. finance F. W. Woolworth Co., N.Y.C., 1973-74, exec. v.p., 1974-75, pres., 1975-77, chief exec. officer, from 1977, chmn., from 1978, also dir. Died Oct. 26, 1982.

GIBBONS, WILLIS ALEXANDER, chemist; b. Long Island, N.Y., Nov. 1, 1888; s. Samuel George Naylor and Mary Garland (Graham) G.; A.B., Wesleyan U., Middletown, Conn., 1910, M.A., 1911, Sc.D., 1942; Ph.D., Cornell, 1916; spl. student, Columbia, 1913-14; m. Stella Louise Hopewell, June 21, 1913; children—Virginia Graham, Dorothy Hopewel Cooke. Research chemist, U.S. Rubber Co., New Brunswick, N.J., 1912-17, 1919-22, in charge research dept. gen. labs., 1922-27, dir. gen. labs., 1928, dir. development, 1930-38, dir. gen. development div., 1939-46, asso. dir. research and development dept. from 1946, Executive secretary sci. adv. com. O.D.M., 1951. Mem. Am. Rubber Mission to U.S.S.R., 1942-43, Trustee Wesleyan U. from 1943 (v.p. Bd. 1950). Served as 1st lt., Coast Arty. Res. Corps. capt. Inf., U.S. Army, 1917, capt. ordnance, 1918; asst. military attache. Am. Embassy, London, 1917-18; hon. disch. 1919. Mem. Nat. Research Council, chmn. adv. bd. Q. M. Research and Development, 1948-52, chmn. div. engineering and industrial research, 1952. Fellow American Assn. Advancement Sci.; Am. Inst. Chemists, London Chem. Society, Institute of Rubber Industry; mem. American Chemical Soc. (chmn. rubber div.); Am. Phys. Soc., Soc. Chem. Industry, New York Academy of Sciences (pres. 1931), Franklin Institute, Phi Beta Kappa, Alpha Delta Phi, Sigma Xi, Republican. Episcopalian. Clubs: Army and Navy (Washington, D.C.); University (New York); Gatineau Fish and Game, Upper Montclair Country (Montclair, N.J.). Author: Rubber Industry, 1839-1939, 1939; Careers in Research, 1940. Inventor number of processes relating to vulcanization of rubber, applications of latex, mfr. of rubber thread, etc. Home: Montclair, N.J. †

GIBBS, JULIAN HOWARD, coll. pres.; b. Greenfield, Mass., June 24, 1924; s. Howard Brown and Judith Martha Bassett (Hemenway) G.; m. Cora Lee Gethman, July 27, 1946; children—James Hemenway, Judith Maxwell, Jeffrey Stephen, Jonathan Myles. B.A., Amherst Coll., 1947, Sc.D., 1971; M.A., Princeton, 1949, Ph.D., 1950. Instr. phys. chemistry U. Minn., 1951-52; with research lab. Gen. Electric Co., 1952-55, Am. Viscose Corp., 1955-60; mem. faculty Brown U., 1960-79, prof. chemistry, 1963-79, chmn. dept., 1964-73; pres. Amherst (Mass.) Coll., from 1979; mem. solid state scis. panel NRC, from 1975; mem. corp. Woods Hole Oceanographic Inst., from 1981. Editor: Biophys. Chemistry; mem. editorial bd.: (1970-75) Jour. Statis. Physics; mem. adv. bd.: Biopolymers, 1963-74; Author articles in field. Served with USNR, 1944-46. Fulbright fellow Cambridge (Eng.) U., 1950-51; Guggenheim fellow, 1967-68; Fulbright research scholar Max Planck Inst. for Phys. Chemistry, 1967-68; NATO fellow U. Essex, Colchester, Eng., 1975. Fellow Am. Phys. Soc. (chmn. high polymer physics 1963, exec. com. div. 1963-66, High Polymer Physics prize 1967), Am. Inst. Chemists; mem. Am. Chem. Soc. (exec. com. div. phys. chemistry 1978), Phi Beta Kappa, Sigma Xi, Theta Delta Chi. Died Jan. 20, 1983.

GIBSON, DANIEL ZACHARY, college president; b. Middlesboro, Ky., Jan. 26, 1908; s. Daniel Z. and Mellie (Rice) G.; A.B., Ky. Wesleyan Coll., 1929, LL.D., 1956; A.M., U. Cin., 1931, Ph.D., 1939; L.H.D., Washington Coll., 1970; m. Helen Katharine Schaefer, Aug. 12, 1936; children—Linda (Mrs. Thomas Haag), Daniel Douglas, Mary Laurent, Helen Clark. Instr. English, Cin. Conservatory Music, 1931-40; Taft teaching fellow U. Cin., 1934-35; asst. prof. English, The Citadel, 1940-43; asso. prof. English, Franklin and Marshall Coll., Lancaster, Pa., 1946-50, dean coll., 1946-50; pres. Washington Coll., Chestertown, Md., 1950-70, pres. emeritus, 1970-84; acad. dean Salisbury (Md.) State Coll., 1970-84. Mem. Md. State Scholarship Bd.; mem. exec. com. Middle States Assn. Colls., Md. Fulbright com.; community council Wye Inst.; chmn. Rhodes Scholarship Com. for Md., D.C., 1965-68. Served as lt. USNR, 1943-46. Mem. Am. Council for Pharm. Edn. (bd. grants), Phi Mu Alpha, Omicron Delta Kappa. Episcopalian. Home: Chestertown, MD. Died Apr. 23, 1984.

GIBSON, FOYE GOODNER, clergyman, gerontologist; b. Bristol, Tenn., Oct. 5, 1903; s. Blair T. and Virginia (Leftwich) G.; m. Doris Aldrich, Apr. 19, 1925; children—Marita (Mrs. Fred N. Sesler), Helen (Mrs. Robert O. Duncan), Eleanor (Mrs. David L. Via). A.B., Emory and Henry Coll., 1927, L.H.D., 1960; student, Vanderbilt U., 1927, 29-30; D.D., Randolph-Macon Coll., 1944. Mem. Holston Conf. Meth. Ch., ordained elder, 1931, apptd. to, White Pine, Tenn., 1928-29, English Congregation, Warszawa, Poland, 1930, Instl. Ch., Katowice, Poland, 1931-32; pastor, Lake City, Tenn., 1933; finance dir. Central Ch., Knoxville, Tenn., 1934-37; pastor First Ch., Pulaski, Va., 1937-41; pres. Emory and Henry Coll., 1941-56, Scarritt Coll., Nashville, 1956-59; adminstr. Asbury Acres, Holston Meth. Home for Ret., Maryville, Tenn., 1959-72, exec. dir. emeritus, 1972-81. Sec. Polish Meth. Mission, 1931-33; del. Meth. Gen. Conf., Jackson, Miss., 1934; mem. Gen. Council on World Service and Finance Meth. Ch., 1944-56, 64-72, exec. com., 1952-56, 68-72; Evangelism, 1956-60; del. Meth. S.E. Jurisdictional Conf., Columbia, S.C., 1948; Former mem. Va. Adv. Com. on Schs. and Colls.; chmn. Ch. Related Colls. of South, 1953; pres. Tenn. Assn. Homes for Aging, 1961-66. Recipient DeFriece award for Service to Humanity, 1967; named Meth. Health and Welfare Adminstr. of Yr., 1972. Mem. Soc. Tenn. Mountain Men, Gerontological Soc., Tau Kappa Alpha, Kappa Phi Kappa, Theta Phi, Blue Key. Club: Rotarian. Address: Maryville, Tenn. Died Nov. 16, 1981.

GIBSON, PHIL SHERIDAN, chief justice Supreme Ct. of Cal.; b. Grant City, Mo.; s. william Jesse and Mollie (Huntsman) G.; A.B. and LL.B., U. Mo.; LL.D., Coll. of

Pacific, Southwestern University, McGeorge College of Law, University of Missouri, U. So. Cal.; m. Victoria Glennon; 1 son, Blaine Alan. Has been dir. finance State of Cal., chmn. Bd. Control, chmn. Lands commn., mem. Emergency Council, Water Project Authority, Gov.'s Council, and asso. justice of Supreme Ct.; chief justice Cal. Supreme Ct. since 1940; chmn. Jud. Council, chmn. Commn. on Judicial Appointments. President board of dirs. Hastings Coll. Law, U. of Cal. Served as 1st lt., U.S. Army, 137th Inf., A.E.F., World War I. Mem. Am. Bar Assn., American Law Institute, Conf. of Chief Justices, Order of the Coif. Clubs: Bohemian (San Francisco); Sutter (Sacramento); Los Angeles Athletic; Pasadena Athletic. Home: Atherton, Calif. Died Apr. 28, 1984.

GIBSON, RALPH EDWARD, phys. chemist, educator; b. Kings Lynn, Norfolk, Eng., Mar. 30, 1901; came to U.S., 1924, naturalized, 1940; s. John and Jane (Ferry) G.; m. Elizabeth Burnham Derby, Apr. 4, 1927; children—John D. Southmayd, Anne K. (Mrs. W.H. Kumm), Ronald Malcolm Eustace. Student, George Watson's Boys' Coll., Edinburgh, 1914-19; B.S., U. Edinburgh, 1922; Ph.D. (Carnegie Research scholar), 1924; M.D. (hon.), Johns Hopkins, 1972. Mem. staff Geophys. Lab., Carnegie Instn., Washington, 1924-46; lectr. in chemistry George Washington U., 1929-39, adj. prof., 1932-45; vice chmn. section H div. 3 NDRC, 1941-44; dir. research Allegany Ballistics Lab., 1944-46; mem. Applied Physics Lab., Johns Hopkins, from 1946, acting dir., 1947-48, dir., 1948- 69, dir. emeritus, 1969-83, prof. biomed. engring., 1969-83. Recipient Crum Brown chem. medal, 1920, Hope prize in chemistry, 1921, Hillebrand prize Chem. Soc. Washington, 1939, Pres.'s certificate of Merit, 1948; Navy Distinguished Pub. Service award, 1958; Capt. Robert Dexter Conrad award, 1960; Dept. Def. Distinguished Pub. Service medal, 1969; decorated hon. comdr. Most Excellent Order Brit. Empire, 1965; Edward Orton Jr. fellow lectr. Am. Ceramic Soc., 1947. Fellow Am. Inst. Aeros. and Astronautics; mem. Am. Chem. Soc. (chmn. Chem. Soc. Washington 1931, councilor 1932, 33, 35-36, 38-41, chmn. div. phys. and inorganic chemistry 1942-43, councilor 1942-43), Am. Phys. Soc., Washington Acad. Scis. (pres. 1956), Armed Forces Chem. Assn. (v.p. 1953-56), Philos. Soc. Washington (pres. 1940), Sigma Xi (hon.), Sigma Tau (hon.). Episcopalian (organist, choir dir. 1935-75). Club: Cosmos (Washington) (pres. 1956). Home: Chevy Chase, Md. Died Feb. 16, 1983.

GIBSON, RALPH MILTON, psychology educator; b. Cleve., Oct. 5, 1923; s. Samuel Milton and Audrey Ethel (Day) G.; m. Rose Cleland Campbell, Dec. 31, 1947; children—Ralph Milton, John Samuel. B.S., U. Mich., 1945, M.S., 1947, Ph.D. (USPHS fellow), 1959. Counselor Cuyahoga County (Ohio) Child Welfare Bd., Cleve., 1947; psychologist Cleve. Guidance Center, 1947-49, chief psychologist, 1949-51; instr. dept. pediatrics U. Mich. Med. Sch., Ann Arbor, 1953-63, asst. prof., 1963-66, assoc. prof., 1966-70, prof., from 1970, dir. counseling, 1972-83, asst. dean student affairs, 1975-83, assoc. dean, from 1983; assoc. staff mem. Wayne County Gen. Hosp., Eloise, Mich., 1963-72; mem. Human Relations Commn. Ann Arbor, 1957-58, Mich. Adv. Commn. on Certification of Psychologists, 1962-64. Author: The Role of Audition in the Development of the Object Concept in the Congenitally Blind Infant, 1966, Trauma in Early Infancy and Later Personality Development, 1965. Trustee Greenhills Sch., Ann Arbor, 1966-79, pres. bd. trustees, 1973-74. Fellow Am. Orthopsychiat. Assn. (life); mem. Am., Mich. psychol. assns., AAAS, Alpha Kappa Delta, Phi Sigma, Psi Chi, Phi Delta Kappa, Alpha Phi Alpha. Home: Ann Arbor, Mich.

GIBSON, RUSSELL, univ. prof.; b. St. Louis, Mo., Oct. 21, 1887; s. James Boyd and Bessie (Hensey) G.; A.B., Washington Univ., 1920; A.M., Univ. Colo., 1922; Ph.D., Harvard, 1929; m. Katharine Brookes, Apr. 11, 1922; children—Jean Burrowes, Mark, Seth. Bank clerk and teller, 1901-11; constn. work, 1912-16 instr., asst. prof. geol., University of Colo., 1920-26; lecturer in geology Wellesley Coll., 1928-53; instr., asst. prof., asso. prof. econ. geol., Harvard, 1927-54, emeritus, from 1954; prof. geology U. Peshawar, West Pakistan, 1962-63; Fulbright prof. geology Ain Shams U., Cairo, 1965; field geologist or cons. geologist, Mo. Bur. Geology and Mines, 1918, Okla. Producing & Refining Corp., 1920, Colo. Geol. Survey, 1921-24, Homestake Mining Co., 1927, U.S. Geologic Survey, 1928-36, Mexican Government, 1938, Union Carbide Corp., 1944-46, M. Hochschild, Bolivia, 1947-48, AEC, 1951-52, 56; USOM, Iran 1953-55, India, 1956, Chile, Costa Rica, 1957, Brazil, 1959; geologist UN, Pakistan, 1958. Fellow Geol. Society of America, American Academy Arts and Sciences. Member Society Econ. Geologists, Am. Inst. Mining and Metall. Engrs., Sigma Xi, Tau Beta Pi. Mason. Presbyn. Home: Belmont, Mass. †

GIDEONSE, HARRY DAVID, university chancellor; b. Rotterdam, Netherlands, May 17, 1901; came to U.S., 1904; s. Martin Cornelius and Johanna Jacoba Helena Magdalena (de Lange) G.; m. Edmee Koch, June 15, 1926; children—Hendrik, Martin. B.S., Columbia U., 1923, M.A., 1924, LL.D., 1954; Diplome des Hautes Etudes Internationales, U. Geneva, 1928; LL.D., Bklyn. Law Sch., St. Lawrence U., 1943, Western Res. U., 1946, Lake Forest U., 1962; L.H.D., Hebrew Union Coll., 1953, U. Hawaii, 1955, Bklyn. Coll., 1966; Litt.D., L.I. U., 1966, Denison U., 1967. Chem. research Eastman Kodak Co., 1919-21; lectr. econs. Barnard Coll., Columbia U., 1924-26; dir. internat. students' work, Geneva, 1926-28; asst. prof. econs. Rutgers U., 1928-30; assoc. prof. econs. U. Chgo., 1930-38; prof. econs. Columbia U.; chmn. dept. econs. and sociology Barnard Coll., 1938-39; pres. Bklyn. Coll., City U. N.Y., 1939-66; chancellor New Sch. Social Research, N.Y.C., from 1966; mem. exec. com. Chgo. Council Fgn. Relations, 1936; mem. N.Y. Council Fgn. Relations; exec. v.p. Economist's Nat. Com. on Monetary Policy, 1937-46; pres. U. Chgo. chpt. AAUP, 1936-38; chmn. youth div. com. Nat. Social Welfare Assembly, 1946-48; mem. Nat. Commn. Ednl., Sci. and Cultural Co-operation, 1946; chmn. Commn. of Inquiry into Forced Labor, 1948-50. Author: Transfert des Reparations et Plan Dawes, 1928, The International Bank, 1930, The Higher Learning in a Democracy, 1937, The Economic Foreign Policy of the United States, 1953, Against the Running Tide, 1967; Editor: Pub. Policy Pamphlets, U. Chgo., 1932-42. Bd. dirs. Woodrow Wilson Found.; chmn. bd. dirs. Freedom House, 1942—. Decorated King Christian X Order of Liberation Denmark; knight comdr. Order of Orange-Nassau Netherlands; chevalier Legion of Honor France). Mem. Am. Econ. Assn., Phi Beta Kappa, Kappa Delta Pi. Address: East Setauket, N.Y. Died Mar. 12, 1985.

GIDNEY, DEAN ROBERT, chemical company executive; b. Washington, Sept. 15, 1915; s. Ray M. and Jean (Brock) G.; m. Olive Milbrandt, July 28, 1941. A.B., Dartmouth Coll., 1936; M.B.A., N.Y. U., 1940. With U.S. Trust Co., 1936-37; v.p., sales mgr. U.S. Potash Co., 1937; v.p., gen. mgr., dir. U.S. Borax & Chem. Corp., 1956-59; v.p. sales Potash Co. Am. div. Ideal Basic Industries, Inc., N.Y.C., 1960-73, exec. v.p., 1973-75, pres., from 1975, also sr. v.p., dir. parent co. Served as lt. comdr. USNR, 1941-46. Mem. Phi Beta Kappa. Clubs: St. Andrews Golf, Bridgehampton, Shinnecock Hills Golf; Mid-Ocean Golf (Bermuda). Home: New York, NY.

GIEG, L. FREDERICK, mfr.; b. Millville, N.J., Feb. 7, 1890; s. Harry J. and Ellen M. (Reeves) G.; student Pennington Sem., 1907-09; B.S., Swarthmore Coll., 1909-13; m. Marie Wall, Apr. 14, 1914; children—Charles Frederick, Louis, Jr., Dorothy, Margaret. Sales rep. David Lupton's Sons Co., 1913-20; pres. Acme Can Co., 1920-36, Crown Can Co., 1936-41; pres. and dir. Nat. Can Corp. from 1941. Mem. Kappa Sigma. Republican. Presbyterian. Clubs: Union League, Racquet, Pine Valley (Phila.); Cloud, Siwanoy (New York); Philadelphia Country. Home: Rosemont, Pa. †

GIES, THOMAS GEORGE, educator; b. Detroit, Jan. 12, 1921; s. Charles G. and Jane E. (Sturman) G.; m. Thelma Irene Young, Sept. 6, 1941; children: Laurie Hollis, Thomas Michael, Joseph Christopher. A.B., U. Mich., 1946, M.A., 1948, Ph.D., 1952. Instr. econs. U. Mich., 1948-51; fin. economist Fed. Res. Bank Kansas City, Mo., 1951-57; lectr. econs. U. Colo., 1955, 57, 70; lectr. fin. U. Mo., Kansas City, 1956-57; faculty U. Mich., Ann Arbor, 1957-85, prof. fin., 1960-85, chmn. fin. dept., 1977-85; lectr. Netherlands Sch. Econs., 1964; cons. in field, 1957-85; Chmn. Gov. Mich. Com. Revision Fin. Code, 1964-65; mem. Gov. Mich. Com. Econ. Growth, 1959-60, 61-62; vice chmn. Gov. Mich. Council Financial Advisers, 1965-69. Author: Consumer Installment Credit, 1957, Portfolio Policies and Regulations of Private Financial Institutions, 1962, Consumer Finance Companies in Michigan, 1960, Public Utility Regulations: New Directions in Theory and Policy, 1966, Legislating for Economic Expansion, 1970, Banking Markets and Financial Institutions, 1971, Investor Experience With Municipal Bond Ratings, 1974, Public Utility Regulation, 1975, Regulation in Further Perspective, 1974, Inflation in Wholesale Distribution, 1981, Deregulation-Appraisal Before the Fact, 1982; Contbr. articles to profl. jours. Served with AUS, USAAF, 1941-46. Mem. Am. Econ. Assn., Midwest Fin. Assn. (pres. 1971-72), Am. Fin. Assn., Phi Kappa Phi. Home: Ann Arbor, Mich. Died July 23, 1985.

GIFFEN, ERNEST CLYDE, state supt. schs.; b. New Castle, O., Jan. 24, 1888; s. Orange Harrison and Ella (Scott) G.; B.S. in Edn., Northern State Teachers Coll., Aberdeen, S.D., 1924; m. Lillian Clara Trousil, of New Effingham, S.D., Sept. 1, 1915 (died Dec. 25, 1924); 1 son, Edward Dean; m. 2d, Frieda A. Moeller, of Parkston, S.D., Dec. 6, 1930. Teacher, rural schs., Coshocton Co., O., Buffalo Co., Neb., Roberts Co., S.D., 1905-12; prin. high sch., Verdon, S.D., 1912-14, Eagle Butte, S.D., 1915-17; supt. pub. schs., Java, S.D., 1919-23; county supt. schs., Walworth Co., S.D., 3 months, 1920 (resigned); mem. faculty, Northern State Teachers Coll., 1923-24; state supervisor rural edn., S.D. State Dept. Pub. Instrn., 1924-26; state supt. pub. instrn., S.D., 1928-33. Attended Motor Transport Corps Training Camp, 1918-19. Dir. of Americanization, northern S.D., 1919-22; organizer, 1925, state sec., 1928-29, state chmn. S.D. Young Citizens League to 1933; mem. N.E.A., S.D. Edn. Assn. Republican. Mason. Kiwanian. Author of Young Citizens League Manual; contbr. to S.D. Edn. Assn. Journal. Inaugurated and supervised construction of first integrated unit social studies course of study for rural, elementary and secondary schs. for S.D., 1929-33. Home: Parkston, S.D. †

GIKOW, RUTH, artist; b. Ukraine; came to U.S., 1922, naturalized, 1928; d. Boris and Lena (Pohoriles) G.; m. Jack Levine, Oct. 4, 1946; 1 dau., Susanna. Student, Cooper Union Art Sch., 1932-35. Former tchr. New Sch. Social Research. Illustrator: History of Jews in America; Author: Ruth Gikow-Paintings, Prints and Drawings, 1970; One-man shows, Weyhe Gallery, 1946, Grand Central Moderns, 1948, 50, Ganso Gallery, 1952, 53, 54, Rehn Gallery, 1956-58, Nordness Gallery, 1961, Forum Gallery, 1967, 70, Kennedy Galleries, 1976, group shows at, Whitney Gallery, Corcoran Gallery, Washington, others; represented in permanent collections, Colby Coll., Springfield Mus., Nat. Acad. Arts and Letters, Brandeis U., Nat. Gallery Fine Arts, Smithsonian Instn., Whitney Mus., Kennedy Galleries, print collections, Met. Mus. Art, Mus. Modern Art, Phila. Art Mus., others; represented by, Kennedy Galleries. Nat. Inst. Arts and Letters grantee, 1959. Address: New York, N.Y.

GILBANE, THOMAS FREEMAN, bldg. co. exec.; b. Providence, Nov. 4, 1911; s. William Henry and Frances Virginia (Freeman) G.; m. Jean Ann Murphy, Sept. 12, 1946; children—Thomas Freeman, Robert Vincent, Richard Thompson, Jean Marie, John Damien, James Manning. Ph.B., Brown U., Providence, 1933, A.M. (hon.), 1958. Supt. Gilbane Bldg. Co., Providence, 1933-39, sec., 1933-50, pres., treas., 1939-75, chmn. bd., chief exec. officer, treas., 1975-81; exec. v.p., treas. B.T. Equipment Co., Providence, 1943-75, pres., treas., 1975-81; pres. Gilbane Internat. Corp., Ltd., 1958-81, Downtown Realty Corp., Providence, 1964-81, Gilbane-McShain Hotel Corp., 1964-81; trustee HNC Mortgage and Realty Investors, 1971-81, Westport Co., 1977-81; head varsity football coach Westminster Coll., New Wilmington, Pa., 1935; head coach freshman football Brown U., 1936-40. Mem. editorial adv. bd.: Bldg. Design and Constrn, 1974-81. Chmn. parents com. Harvard, 1972-73; past chmn. New Eng. region, mem. nat. exec. bd. Boy Scouts Am.; mem. Narragansett council, 1924-81, past Area I pres. Northeast region, chmn. sustaining membership enrollment campaign Northeast region, 1974-75; trustee emeritus Brown U., past mem. athletic council; mem. corp. Emma Pendelton Bradley Hosp., Sophia Little Home, Roger Williams Gen. Hosp., Women and Infants Hosp.; bd. govs. R.I. Commodore Commn.; mem., past trustee Indsl. Found. R.I.; voting mem. R.I. Soc. Prevention of Blindness, 1972-73, 78-79; bd. dirs. R.I. affiliate Am. Heart Assn., 1974-80; past bd. dirs. Butler Hosp.; mem. friends com. Pine Manor Jr. Coll., 1972-73; mem. Coast Guard Acad. Found. Recipient Silver Antelope award Boy Scouts Am., 1972, Distinguished Eagle award, 1975; award of merit R.I. dept. Jewish War Vets. U.S.A., 1956; Honor award Nat. Jewish Hosp. and Research Center, Denver, 1975; Silver Buffalo award Nat. Boy Scouts Am., 1979; elected Brown Football and Track Hall Fame, 1971. Mem. Asso. Gen. Contractors Am. (past pres. R.I. chpt.), Am. Soc. Concrete Constrn. (dir. 1974-75), Brown Football Assn. (dir. 1973-74), Nat. Eagle Scout Assn. (chmn. nat. com. 1974-76), Providence C. of C. (past pres.). Roman Catholic. Clubs: Knight of Malta, Knight of Holy Sepulchre, K.C. (4th deg., Providence council), University, Turks Head, Brown of R.I. (past pres.), Serra, Providence Gridiron (founding pres.), Point Judith Country, Dunes; Brown of Palm Beach (Palm Beach) (past pres.), Beach (Palm Beach); Saunderstown Yacht Home: Providence, R.I. Died Nov. 7, 1981.

GILBERT, CARL JOYCE, retired business exec.; b. Bloomfield, N.J., Apr. 3, 1906; s. Seymour Parker and Carrie Jennings (Cooper) G.; A.B., U. Va., 1928; LL.B., Harvard, 1931; m. Helen Amory Homans, June 27, 1936; 1 son, Thomas Tibbals. Admitted to Mass. bar, 1931, practiced in Boston as asso. Ropes, Gray, Boyden & Perkins, 1931-38, mem. firm, 1938-48; treas., v.p. The Gillette Co. (formerly Gillette Safety Razor Co.), Boston, 1948-56, pres. 1956-58, became chmn. bd., 1958, then chmn. exec. com., dir.; spl. rep. for trade negotiations Exec. Office Pres., 1969-71; trustee Mass. Investors Trust; dir. Mass. Investor Growth Stock Fund, Mass. Financial Devel. Fund, Mass. Income Devel. Fund, Mass. Capitol Devel. Fund. Pres. Assn. Ind. Coll. and Univs. Mass.; past pres. Boston Dispensary. Trustee Carnegie Instn.; trustee, mem. exec. com. Tufts Coll. Served with AUS, 1941-46; lt. col., F.A. Decorated Silver Star, Bronze Star. Clubs: Somerset Dedham Country, Polo (Boston). Home: Dover, Mass. Died 1983.

GILBERT, DALE WINSTON, educator; b. Jefferson, Iowa, July 10, 1926; s. Vernie Merle and Jessie May (Gaer) G.; m. Lois May Talbot, Aug. 6, 1949; children: Jay Warren, Carol Ann. Mem. faculty dept. music U. Wis.,

Madison, 1955-84, prof. music, 1965-84; dir. U. Wis. (Sch. Music), 1974—; choral dir., profl. singer, 1950-84. Bd. dirs. Madison Civic Symphony Orch., Wis. Youth Symphony Orch. Served with USNR, 1945-46. Mem. Nat. Assn. Tchrs. Singing, Chgo. Singing Tchrs. Guild, Nat. Assn. Schs. Music, Music Educators Nat. Conf., Nat. Assn. Music Execs. in State Univs., Assn. Wis. Coll. and Univ. Music Adminstrs., Phi Kappa Phi (hon.). Lodge: Rotary. Home: Madison, Wis. Died May 19, 1984.

GILBERT, DOUGLAS, author; b. Rochester, N.Y., Sept. 17, 1889; s. Andrus L. and Elizabeth Ann (Lester) G.; ed. Moorestown (N.J.) High Sch. and Pratt Inst., Brooklyn, N.Y.; m. Marguerite Snyder, Apr. 19, 1914; children—George Arthur, Ethel Joyce (Mrs. G. Everett Hill, 3d). Began journalism, 1917; served on N.Y. Evening Post, Daily News and World; became drama critic World-Telegram, later feature writer; specialized in English lit. of Victorian period; collector of 1st edits. of Victorian period authors. Episcopalian. Club: The Players (N.Y. City). Author: American Vaudeville, Its Life and Times, 1940; Lost Chords, the Diverting Story of American Popular Songs, 1942. Home: New York, N.Y. Deceased.*

GILBERT, KENNETH, author; b. Chetek, Wis., June 10, 1889; s. Franklin Henry and Clara Louisa (Tait) G.; ed. Chetek high sch.; m. Melissa Tschabold, Nov. 29, 1913; children—June Marie, Jane Louise. Telegrapher for ry. and commercial cos., 1906-09, for U.S. Navy, 1909-13 (in Asiatic waters during Chinese Rebellion 1910-11); mem. staff Seattle Post-Intelligencer, 1913-22, successively reporter, city editor, news editor, spl. writer; author from 1922. Mem. Am. Soc. Mammalogists, Am. Ornithol. Union, Authors' League of America, Free Lances (an organizer, 1916, 1st pres.). Republican. Club: Washington State Press (Seattle). Author: Fighting Hearts of the Wild, 1928; Red Meat Country, 1929; Boru, Wolf Dog, 1929. Contbr. fiction to various mags. in U.S. and Europe; Arctic Venture, Bird Dog Bargain, Smoke Over Skygak, Challenge of the Wild. Has been rated as a leading writer of animal stories.†

GILBREATH, FREDERICK, army officer; b. Dayton, Wash., Feb. 21, 1888; s. Samuel Love and Margaret Hannah (Fanning) G.; student Whitman Coll.; B.S., U.S. Mil. Acad., 1911; grad. School of the Line, 1922. Gen. Staff Sch., 1923, Army War Coll., 1927; m. Edna Brown, Dec. 21, 1916. Commd. 2d lt., Cavalry, June 13, 1911; promoted through grades to maj. gen. Army of U.S., Sept. 7, 1942; mem. Gen. Staff Corps, 1925-32; ret. 1946. Decorated Philippine Campaign, Mexican Border and World War (with 5 brown stars) medals; Purple Heart; Chevalier Polonia Restituta; Germany; American Continent; Asiatic; D.S.M. Mem. Master Fox Hounds Assn., Vets. Fgn. Wars. Episcopalian. Home: Austin, Tex. †

GILCHRIST, GIBB, engineer; born Wills Point, Tex., Dec. 23, 1887; son Angus Jackson and Katherine (Douglass) G.; student Southwestern U., 1905-06, LL.D., 1945; C.E., Texas U., 1909; D.Sc., Austin College, 1939; LL.D., Baylor U., 1946, Southwestern University, Georgetown, Texas, 1946; married Vesta Weaver, March 29, 1920; 1 son, Henry. Engr. Santa Fe Ry. Co., 1910-17; resident and div. engr. Tex. State Highway Dept., 1919-23, state highway engr., 1924; cons. practice, Dallas, 1925-27; again state highway engr., 1928-37; dean engring., A.&M. Coll. of Tex., 1937-44, pres., 1944-48; chancellor, Tex. A. & M. Coll. Systm, 1948-53, emeritus, 1953, civil engring. research, 1953-57; cons. engr. Served as 1st lieut., capt., Engr., Corps, U.S. Army, 1918-19. Mem. Am. Soc. Civil Engrs., Tex. Soc. Professional Engrs., Am. Soc. for Engring Edn., Philos. Soc. of Tex., Tex. State Hist. Soc., Newcomen Soc. Democrat. Methodist. Mason (32 deg., Shriner; past Grand Master of Tex.). Home: College Sta., Tex. †

GILDERSLEEVE, THOMAS ARTHUR, hotel executive; b. Seattle, Oct. 26, 1903; s. Maro Davis and Eva L. (Dodds) G.; m. Anne Clarice Walken, Mar. 16, 1929; 1 child, Lynn Marie. Student pub. schs. corr. courses. Dir. Olympic, Inc., Am. Underwriters Corp.; asso. with Leopold Hotel, Bellingham, Wash., Mt. Baker Lodge, Wash., New Washington Hotel, Benjamin Franklin Hotel, Seattle, 1925-30; mgr. Roosevelt Hotel, 1930-43; mng. dir. Davenport Hotel, Tennis, Broadmoor Country, Washington Athletic, Spokane, Robert Treat Hotel, Newark, 1945-47; v.p., gen. mgr. Olympic Hotel, 1943-57, gen. mgr., 1957-60, mng. dir., 1960-82; v.p. Seattle Olympic Hotel Co., 1960-64, pres., 1964-68; now with William Lockwood Saunders (Corporate Counsel), Seattle; dir. Franklin Savs. & Loan Assn. Bd. dirs. Wash. State Internat. Trade Fair, Broadmoor Maintenance Commn.; bd. dirs., mem. exec. com. Greater Seattle. Mem. Am., Wash. State hotel assns., Seattle C. of C. (trustee), Navy League U.S. (sec. Seattle council), Urban League (dir.). Clubs: Rotarian, Rainier (trustee), Seattle Tennis, Broadmoor Country, Washington Athletic (sec., mem. exec. com.). Home: Seattle, Wash. Dec. May 1, 1982.

GILES, BARNEY MCKINNEY, army officer; b. Mineola, Tex., Sept. 13, 1892; grad. Air Corps Tactical Sch., 1935. Command and Gen. Staff Sch., 1938; Dr. Aero Science (hon.) Pennsylvania Mil. Coll. rated command pilot, combat observer, tech. observer, Began as pvt., Aviation Sect., Signal Corps. Sept. 1917; commd. 2d lt., Aviation Sect., Apr. 1918, and advanced through the grades to lt. gen., Apr. 1944; Comd. 20th Bombardment Squadron, Langley Field, Va., 1935-36; operations officer 2d Bombardment Group, 1936-37; Office, Chief of Air Corps. 1938-40; comdg. gen. 4th Bomber Command and comdg. gen., 4th Air Force, 1940-42; asst. chief Air Staff, Apr.-July 1942, chief, Air Staff. July 1943, and dep. comdr. Army Air Force, May 1944; apptd. dep. comdr. U.S. Strategic Air Forces in Pacific, July 1945; comdg. gen., Pacific Ocean Area, Air Forces, Apr. 1945; retired as lt. gen., July 1946. Awarded Distinguished Flying Cross, 1936; D.S.M. with two Oak Leaf Clusters; Navy D.S.M.; D.F.C. with Cluster; Air Medal with one Cluster; Most Excellent Order Knight Comdr. British Empire; Cloud Necklet Banner, Chinese Govt.; Medal of Mil. Merit Mexican Govt. Home: San Antonio, Tex. Died May 6, 1984.

GILFILLAN, S(EABURY) COLUM, sociologist; b. St. Paul, Minnesota, April 5, 1889; s. Rev. Joseph A. and Harriet Woodbridge (Cook) G.; A.B., University of Pennsylvania, 1910; A.M., Columbia, 1920, Ph.D., 1935; m. Louise H. Wenzel, Sept. 15, 1922; children—Barbara Wenzel (Mrs. J. C. Crowley), Marjorie W. Acting associate professor of social sciences, University of the South 1921-24; instr. sociology and economics, Grinnell Coll., 1924-26; curator of transportation and social sciences, Museum of Science and Industry, Chicago, 1928-29; asst. prof. of sociology, Purdue U., 1937-38; researcher, President's Research Com. on Social Trends Nat. Resources Com., Nat. Indsl. Conf. Board; research asso., U. of Chicago, on social aspects of invention and patents, and cultural prediction. Lecturer Roosevelt Coll., 1948-49. Mem. Am. Sociol. Soc., Soc. for Social Study of Inventin (sec.), Phi Beta Kappa. Author: Inventing the Ship, 1935; The Sociology of Invention, 1935. Address: Chicago, Ill.†

GILKEY, JAMES GORDON, clergyman; b. Watertown, Mass., Sept. 28, 1889; s. James Henry and Mary Lottie (Johnson) G.; A.B., Harvard, 1912, A.M., 1913; studied univs. of Berlin and Marburg; B.D., Union Theol. Sem., 1916; D.D., Colgate U., 1925, Colby Coll., 1934, U. of Vt., 1935; LL.D., Am. Internat. Coll., 1935; Litt.D., Marietta Coll., 1937; m. Calma Wright Howe, June 7, 1916; children—James Gordon, Margaret Howe, Edith Brigham. Ordained Presbyn. ministry, 1916; asst. minister, Bryn Mawr (Pa.) Ch., 1916-17; pastor South Ch., Springfield, Mass., from 1917; professor Biblical literature, Amherst, 1923-30. Trustee, Springfield College preacher at Eastern colleges, Republican. Rotarian. Mem. Delta Upsilon, Phi Beta Kappa. Author books including: When Life Gets Hard; Gaining the Faith You Need; Here is Help for You. Home: Springfield, Mass. †

GILL, MURRAY FRANCIS, gas and elec. exec.; b. Paris, Tex., Oct. 4, 1888; s. William Francis and Miriam (Fort) G.; E.E., U. of Tex., 1910; m. Mildred E. Wellington, Nov. 17, 1921; children—James William, Barbara Jane. Gen. supt. Phoenix Utility Co., Allentown, Pa., 1928-35; coordinator Pa. Power & Light Co., 1935-37; asst. to pres. Kan. Gas & Electric Co., Wichita, 1937-38, v.p., 1938-39, chmn. bd. to 1956, dir.; dir. First National Bank in Wichita, Central States Fire Insurance Co.; cons. Ebasco Services Incorporated, N.Y.C. Mem. Am. Inst. E.E. Republican. Presbyn. Clubs: Wichita, Wichita Country (Wichita, Kan.); Crestview Country, Home: Wichita, Kans. †

GILLESPIE, DAVID JOSEPH, advertising agency executive; b. N.Y.C., Mar. 9, 1915; s. David Joseph and Catherine (Mitchell) G.; B.A., Manhattan Coll., 1936; m. Jane Louise Reynolds, Sept. 5, 1949; 1 child, Patricia Jane. With Kenyon & Eckhardt Advt., Inc., from 1936, v.p., 1954-72, dir., from 1957, mgmt. supr., head Detroit Office, 1966-72, sr. v.p., 1972-75, chmn. bd., 1975-80. Mem. spl. gifts com. Detroit Round Table NCCJ, 1956-79; adv. mem. Nat. Cath. Office for Radio and TV, from 1961; chmn. advt. adv. com. Northwood Inst., 1968-73; chmn. promotion United Found. Torch Drive, 1975. Served with AUS, 1942-46. Decorated Bronze Star medal. Mem. Am. Assn. Advt. Agys. (gov. Central region, past gov. Mich. region), Adcraft Club Detroit (dir., pres. from 1973). Clubs: Detroit Athletic, Grosse Pointe Yacht, Grosse Pointe Hunt, Renaissance, Fairlane. Home: Grosse Pointe, Mich. also Vero Beach, Fla. Dec. Dec. 12, 1984. Interned Crestlawn Cemetery, Vero Beach, Fla.

GILLESPIE, ROBERT GILL, ret. judge; b. Madison, Ala., Sept. 17, 1903; s. Philander M. and Flora (Gill) G.; m. Margaret Griffith, June 30, 1930 (dec.); children—Robert Gill, Virgil Griffith; m. Alice Wells McIlwaine, May 29, 1975. Student, Huntsville Jr. Coll., 1923-24, U. Ala., 1924-26. Bar: Miss. bar 1927. Practiced in, Meridian, 1927-33; spl. agt. FBI, 1934-35; partner Bailey & Gillespie, 1939-43, Gillespie & Minniece, 1945-48, Gillespie, Huff & Williams, 1948-54; chancellor 2d Chancery Ct. Dist. Miss., 1939; justice Miss. Supreme Ct., Jackson, 1954-65, presiding justice, 1966-71, chief justice, 1971-77; vis. prof. law Miss. Coll., 1977-81. Mem. Miss. Council State Govts., 1944-48; mem awards jury Freedoms Found., 1959; bd. dirs. Southwestern Coll., Memphis. Mem. Am., Miss. bar assns., Am. Judicature Soc., Delta Tau Delta. Presbyterian. Home: Jackson, Miss.

GILLFILLAN, SOLON JOHN, ret. pub. exec.; b. Brazil, Ind., Oct. 21, 1889; s. Dennis C. and Nancy A. (Miller) G.; student U. Ind., 1909-12; m. Ethel E. Leitch, Aug. 4, 1914; children—James H., Thomas L., Judith. With F. E. Compton & Co., Chgo., 1912-61, successively salesman, sec., exec. v.p., pres., exec. dir., 1952-61. Mem. Delta Tau Delta. Democrat. Methodist. Clubs: Athletic (Chgo.); Skokie Country (Glencoe). Home: Evanston, Ill.†

GILMAN, ALEXANDER GEORGE, paper mfr.; b. Kingsley Falls, Quebec, Can., Dec. 17, 1887; s. Ernest Hayes and Annie Shaw (Grosset) G.; ed. Newburgh (N.Y.) Free Acad. and Cleary Business Coll., Ypsilanti, Mich.; m. Sadie M. MacGuffin, of Memphis, Mich., Apr. 1909; children—Betty Lee, Jean Alexandria, Marianna, Ernest John. Began as sec. Monarch Paper Co., Kalamazoo, Mich., 1909, pres. from 1918; 1st v.p. Allied Paper Mills, Kalamazoo, 1921, pres. and gen. mgr. from 1922. Ex-pres. Mich. Paper Mills Traffic Assn., Kalamazoo; ex-mem. and ex-v.p. com. Am. Paper & Pulp Assn., New York; mem. exec. com. Book Paper Mfrs. Assn. (chmn. merchants contact com.); mem. nat. council of National Economic League. Served as private Co. A, Signal Corps, Michigan N.G.; 2d lieutenant inf., Indiana N.G., Elkhart; chmn. Am. Red Cross, Elkhart, 1917. Republican. Presbyn. Mason (K.T., Shriner), Elk, Rotarian. Clubs: Park (dir.), Kalamazoo Country (ex-pres.); Gull Lake Country (ex-pres.); Battle Creek Country; Chicago Country Club of Valparaiso, Fla.; Hamilton (Chicago); Nat. Republican, Fine Arts (New York). Patentee of methods for finishing paper and apparatus for same. Home: Richland, Mich. †

GILMAN, ALFRED, educator, pharmacologist; b. Bridgeport, Conn., Feb. 5, 1908; s. Joseph and Frances (Zack) G.; m. Mabel J. Schmidt, Jan. 11, 1934; children—Joanna, Alfred Goodman. B.S., Yale U., 1928, Ph.D., 1931; 1D.Sc. (hon.), Dartmouth Coll., 1979. Research fellow biochemistry Yale, 1931-32, research asso., asst. prof. pharmacology, 1933-43, lectr. in pharmacology Med. Sch., 1973—; asso. prof. pharmacology Columbia, 1946-48, prof., 1948-55; prof. pharmacology, chmn. dept. Yeshiva U. Albert Einstein Coll. Medicine, 1956-73, asso. dean grad. edn., 1964-69, prof. emeritus, 1976-84; vis. prof. pharmacology U. Va. Sch. Medicine, 1974-84; spl. cons. USPHS; mem. sci. and edn. council Am. Found. Allergic Disease; exec. com. med. div. NRC; mem. panel on chem. agts. Presdl. Sci. Adv. Com., 1970-84; mem. drug research bd. NRC, chmn., 1971-84, Author: (with L.S. Goodman) Pharmacological Basis of Therapeutics, 1941; Editorial bd.: (with L.S. Goodman) Pharmacol. Rev. Served as maj. CWS; Served as maj. AUS, 1943-46. Fellow Am. Acad. Allergy (hon.), N.Y. Acad. Sci.; mem. Am. Physiol. Soc., Am. Soc. Pharmacology and Exptl. Therapy (pres. 1960), Harvey Soc., Nat. Acad. Sci., Am. Acad. Arts and Scis., Soc. Exptl. Biology and Medicine, N.Y. Acad. Medicine (asso.), Conn. Acad. Sci. and Engring., Sigma Xi, Alpha Omega Alpha. Home: New Haven, Conn. Died Jan. 13, 1984.

GILMAN, CHARLES, JR., paper co. exec.; b. N.Y.C., Nov. 16, 1930; s. Charles Seymour and Sylvia (Phillips) G.; m. Sondra Minette Golden, Aug. 19, 1960; children—Hadley Rowena, Charles Evan. A.B. (Rufus Choate scholar), Dartmouth Coll., 1952; M.S. Mass. Inst. Tech, 1954. Vice pres. Gilman Paper Co., N.Y.C., 1956-64, exec. v.p., 1964-67, pres., co-chief exec. officer, dir., from 1967; pres., dir. St. Marys' R.R., St. Marys' Timber Co., Gilman Internat., Inc. Chmn. bd. Gilman Found., Inc.; Trustee Collegiate Sch. Served with AUS, 1954-56. Mem. Am. Paper Inst. (dir.), Inst. Paper Chemistry (trustee), Phi Beta Kappa. Club: Univ., Dartmouth. Home: New York, NY.

GILMORE, GRANT, educator; b. Boston, Apr. 8, 1910; s. Ernest Augustus and Louise (Beerbohm) G.; m. Helen Richter, Mar. 26, 1934; children—Nancy Hubbard, David Creighton. B.A., Yale, 1931, Ph.D., 1936, LL.B., 1942. Bar: N.Y. bar 1943. With firm Milbank, Tweed & Hope, N.Y.C., 1942-44; instr. French Lehigh U., 1936-37; instr. French Yale, 1937-40, prof. law, 1946-65, William K. Townsend prof., 1957-65; prof. law U. Chgo., 1965-73, Harry E. Bigelow prof., 1967-73; Sterling prof. law Yale, 1973-78; prof. law U. Vt. Law Sch., from 1978; vis. prof. U. Chgo., 1949, 57, U. Calif., 1951, Columbia, 1953-54, Harvard, 1962-63. Author: (with C.L. Black, Jr.) The Law of Admiralty, 1957, 2d edit., 1975, Security Interests in Personal Property, 2 vols, 1965 (Ames prize 1966, Coif award Assn. Am. Law Schs. 1967), The Death of Contract, 1974, The Ages of American Law, 1977; Contbr. (with C.L. Black, Jr.) articles to legal publs. Served to lt. USNR, 1944-46. Mem. Am. Law Inst. Home: Norwich, VT.

GILPATRICK, RALPH BENJAMIN, JR., banker; b. McKeesport, Pa., Mar. 26, 1924; s. Ralph Benjamin and Katherine J. (Smith) G.; m. Dorothy Olga Werlinich, Sept. 3, 1955; 1 son, David A. B.A., Amherst Coll., 1949; M.B.A., Harvard U., 1951. With Mellon Bank (N.A.), Pitts., 1951-83, asst. cashier, 1954-58, asst. v.p., 1958-60, v.p., 1960-73, sr. v.p., 1973-78, exec. v.p., 1978-80, vice-chmn., 1980-83; dir. Pennzoil Co., Dravo Corp., RIDC Indsl. Devel. Fund, Pitts. Trustee Shadyside Hosp., Pitts., 1978; bd. dirs. Pitts. Regional Planning Assn.,

1979. Served with USAAF, 1942-45. Decorated Air medal with 2 oak leaf clusters, Purple Heart. Mem. Am. Bankers Assn., Assn. Res. City Bankers, Robert Morris Assos. Clubs: Duquesne (Pitts.), Long Vue (Pitts.); Rolling Rock (Ligonier, Pa.), Laurel Valley Golf (Ligonier, Pa.). Home: Pittsburgh, Pa. Died May 24, 1983.

GIMBEL, SOPHIE HAAS, designer; m. Adam Long Gimbel; 1 son, Jay Rossbach. Mgr. Women's modern dress div., designer Saks Fifth Av. Home: New York, N.Y. Died Nov. 28, 1981.

GIMMESTAD, VICTOR EDWARD, educator; b. Galesville, Wis., Aug. 13, 1912; s. Lars Monsen and Amalie (Anderson) G.; m. Lucille Gray, Aug. 26, 1937; children—Carole Kay (Mrs. Larry Johnson), Vickie Gail (Mrs. Milford Hofius), Gary Gene. B.A., St. Olaf Coll., 1934; postgrad., U. So. Cal., summer 1940; M.A., U. Wis., 1940, Ph.D., 1950. Tchr. pub. high schs., Minn., Wis., 1934-41, C.Z. 1941-42; grad. asst. U. Wis., 1945-47; asst. prof. English St. Olaf Coll., 1947-48; faculty Ill. State U., Normal, from 1948, prof. English, 1957-80, head dept., 1960-67, on leave, 1968-69; chmn. dept. Calif. Lutheran Coll., Thousand Oaks, 1968-69; Mem. adv. com. faculty salaries, other benefits Ill. Commn. Higher Edn., 1957-58. Author: John Trumbull, 1974, also articles in profl. jours. Mem. youth commn. Central Conf. Augustana Luth. Ch., 1956-58; mem. Luth. Student Found. Bd., U. Ill., 1956-58. Mem. NEA, Ill. Edn. Assn., Nat. Council Tchrs. English, Norwegian Am. Hist. Assn., Modern Lang. Assn., Midwest Modern Lang. Assn., Internat. Platform Assn., Blue Key. Lutheran (dir. Evangelism, past bd. adminstrn., council). Home: Normal, Ill.

GINASTERA, ALBERTO, composer; b. Buenos Aires, Argentina, Apr. 11, 1916; grad. Nat. Conservatory Music, Argentina, 1938. Pro., Nat. Conservatory Music, 1953. Guggenheim fellow, U.S., 1946-47. Composer: (ballets) Panambi, 1937, Estancia, 1941; Sinfonia elegiaca for orchestra, 1944; (motel) Lamentation for the Prophet Jeremiah, 1946; Pampeana No. 1 for violin and piano, 1947, No. 2 for cello and pianoforte, 1950, No. 3, a pastoral symphony, 1953; Variaciones Concertantes, 1953; Concerto for Piano and Orch., 1961; Concerto for Harp, 1957, rev., 1968; Cantata para America magica, 1961; also dances, songs, chamber music, overtures. Died June 25, 1983.*

GIROUARD, ROBERT LOUIS, journalist; b. Providence, Jan. 15, 1942; s. Fernand Louis and Anita Evelyn (Cloutier) G.; m. Nancy Elizabeth How, Aug. 29, 1964; children—Robert James, Mark Jared. A.B., Tufts U., 1962; M.A., Johns Hopkins U., 1963; Ph.D., Brown U., 1971. Tchr. English Westport (Conn.) Schs., 1964-65; teaching asst., asso. Brown U., 1965-68, admissions officer, lectr. English, 1968-70, asst. dir. admissions, lectr., 1970-72; asso. and editorial page editor Free Press, Mankato, Minn., 1972-78, exec. editor, 1978-79; opinion page editor Mpls. Star, from 1979; cons. in field, from 1967; mem. Brown U. Alumni Secondary Schs. Program. Author poems and articles in mags., jours. and quars. Recipient 1st pl. editorial writing William Allen White Found., 1978; numerous others. Mem. Am. Soc. Newspaper Editors, Minn. Newspaper Assn., Colonial Soc. Mass. Unitarian. Clubs: Minn. Press, Minn. Alumni; 6 O'Clock (Mpls.); Brown of Minn. Home: Golden Valley, Minn.

GLAIR, HARRY FRANKLIN, oil company executive; b. Chicago, August 28, 1888; s. Louis C. and Emma (Olsey) G.; B.S., U. of Ill., 1912; m. Hortense Oliver, Nov. 10, 1915; 1 dau., Jacquelyn. Began with Standard Oil Co. as clerk at Whiting refinery, 1906, draftsman Wood River refinery, 1907; with Curtis & Co., St. Louis, July-Oct. 1912; became engr. Whiting refinery Standard Oil Co., 1912, asst. supt. paraffin dept., 1914, supt., 1920, asst. gen. supt. Whiting refinery, 1921, gen. supt., 1927, mgr. refinery, 1929, asst. gen. mgr. mfg. dept., 1931, gen. mgr. mfg. dept., 1933, elected dir. Standard Oil Co., 1934, dir. of purchases since 1951. Pres. bd. trustees Whiting Community Service; dir. Ill. Found. from 1949, pres. since 1952. Mem. Zeta Psi. Conglist. Mason. Clubs: Flossmoor Country; Executives (Chgo.). Home: Flossmoor, Ill.†

GLASER, EVA SCHOCKEN, publisher; b. Ger., Sept. 30, 1918; came to U.S., 1938, naturalized, 1946; d. Salman and Lilli (Ehrman) Schocken; m. T. Herzl Rome, 1941 (dec. 1965); children—Nathan, David I., Dan H., Abigail; m. Julius S. Glaser, 1968. B.S., Columbia U., 1949; M.A., CCNY, 1963. Instr. remedial reading Edenwald Sch., Bronx, N.Y., 1962-66; instr. Grad. Sch. Edn., CCNY, 1967; edn. editor Schocken Books Inc., N.Y.C., 1968-75, pres., 1975—. Jewish. Address: New York, NY.

GLASGOW, LOWELL ALAN, physician, educator; b. Cin., Aug. 28, 1932; s. Russell Lowell and Glenna (Wheeldon) G.; m. Mary Ann Lewis, June 16, 1956; children—Russell, Lauren, Scott. A.B., U. Rochester, 1954, M.S., 1958, M.D., 1958. Diplomate: Am. Bd. Pediatrics. Intern sch. medicine U. Rochester, N.Y., 1958-59, resident, 1959-60, mem. faculty, 1962-70, asst. prof. microbiology and pediatrics, 1965-67, asso. prof. microbiology and asst. prof. pediatrics, 1968-70, also asso. pediatrician, 1965-70; research asso. Nat. Inst. Allergy and Infectious Disease NIH, Bethesda, Md., 1960-62; prof., chmn. microbiology Coll. Medicine, U. Utah, Salt Lake City, 1970-73, prof., chmn. pediatrics, from 1972; med. dir. Primary Childrens Med. Center, from 1977; asso. dir. clin. microbiology labs Strong Meml. Hosp., also Monroe County Health Dept., both Rochester, 1964-70; mem. staff U. Utah Med. Center; cons. antiviral substances NIH, from 1970, NIH (virology study sect.), 1970-74, NIH (virology and rickettsia study group), 1974-78, mem. virology task force, 1976-77; mem. Basil O'Conner research adv. com. Nat. Found., from 1977. Mem. editorial bd.: Pediatric Research Jour, 1970-72, Pediatrics, from 1978; contbg. editor: Pediatrics in Rev, 1978-80; contbr. numerous articles to profl. jours.; Speaker several sci. meetings. Recipient Mead Johnson Pediatric Research grant Am. Acad. Pediatrics, 1963-64; Townsend Found. Pediatrics Research award, 1970; student microbiology fellow U. Rochester, 1955-56, 57-58; Wyeth Pediatric fellow, 1959-61; spl. USPHS fellow, 1963-64. Mem. Am. Soc. Microbiology, Soc. Pediatric Research (v.p. 1977-78), Am. Soc. Pediatrics, Am. Assn. Immunology, Infectious Diseases Soc. Am. (Squibb award 1977), Am. Soc. Pediatrics Dept. Chairmen (exec. council 1975-78), Western Soc. Pediatric Research (exec. council 1978-80, pres. 1981), Utah Med. Assn., Sigma Xi, Alpha Omega Alpha. Home: Salt Lake City, UT.

GLATFELTER, PHILIP HOLLINGER, business exec.; b. Spring Grove, Pa., Mar. 30, 1889; s. William Lincoln and Katherine (Hollinger) G.; grad. Hill Sch., 1910; Doctor of Laws, Lawrence College, 1959; married Cassandra McClellan, June 1, 1911; children—Mary E. (Mrs. Joseph L. Rosenmiller), Philip H., William L. (dec.), Theodore McC., George H. With P. H. Glatfelter Company, Spring Grove, Pa., from 1908, P. H. Glatfelter Co., Spring Grove, secretary-treasurer, 1914-30, pres., 1930-54, chairman bd. dirs., from 1954; dir. Dentists Supply Co. N.Y. Western Md. Ry. Co. Commd. 1st lt. O.R.C., 1917; served overseas as capt., 1918-19. Mem. Am. Forest Products Industries, Inc. (bd. govs., treas., 1949-50), Tech. Assn. Pulp and Paper Industry (pres., 1929), Am. Paper and Pulp Assn. (v.p., 1940-47), Mfrs. Assn., York (dir.), Printing Paper Mfrs. Assn. (chmn. 1939, treas., 1940-47). Mason (32 deg., Shriner). Clubs: Union League (N.Y. City); Lafayette, Country (York).†

GLEESON, FRANCIS DOYLE, bishop; b. Carrollton, Mo., Jan. 17, 1895; s. Charles and Mary Alice (Doyle) G.; A.B., Santa Clara Univ., 1917; A.M., Gonzaga Univ., 1920; theology student, St. Francis Xavier's Coll., Spain, 1923-27, Manresa Hall, Port Townsend, Wash., 1927-28; hon. Ph.D., Gregorian U., 1931. Ordained priest (S.J.) R.C. Ch., 1926; instr., Seattle Coll. Prep. (Wash). 1917-20, Bellarmine High Sch., Tacoma, Wash., 1928-32; pres., Bellarmine High Sch., 1933-39, Jesuit Sem., Sheridan, Ore., 1939-42; consecrated bishop of Vicariate of Alaska, Apr. 5, 1948, installed as 1st bishop of Fairbanks, 1963, ret., 1968; now titular bishop of Cuicul (Numidia). Home: Fairbanks, Alaska. Died Apr. 30, 1983.

GLENN, BENJAMIN DUKE, JR., electronics co. exec.; b. N.Y.C., Sept 23, 1936; s. Benjamin Duke and Florence (Smith) G.; B.A., Yale U., 1958; M.B.A., Harvard U., 1962; m. Lynn W. Knight, July 10, 1965; children—Heather, Laura, Benjamin Duke, III. Mgr. corp. finance dept. R.W. Pressprich & Co., N.Y.C., 1962-68; pres., chmn. bd. Arrow Electronics Inc., Greenwich, Conn., 1968-80; chmn. bd. Fla. Capital Corp., 1970-80; adv. com. SBA. Served to lt. (j.g.) USNR, 1958-60. Club: Coral Reef Yacht (Coconut Grove, Fla.). Home: Greenwich, Conn. Died Dec. 4, 1980.

GLENN, FRANK, surgeon; b. Marissa, Ill., August 7, 1901; s. Charles and Minnie (McMurdo) G.; M.D., Washington U., 1927; advanced study tching., surgery, Scotland, Eng., Germany, Austria, Orient, 1931-32; m. Esther Child, Jan. 15, 1938; children—Gardner, Prudence, Frank. Intern medicine Strong Meml. Hosp., Rochester, N.Y., 1927-28; first asst. resident surgeon N.Y. Hosp., 1932-33, surgeon-in-chief, 1947-67, cons. in surgery, 1967-82, asst. surg. Cornell U. Med. Coll., 1932-33, asso. prof., 1941-47, prof. surgery, 1947-67, prof. emeritus, 1967-82, adv. cons. surg. V.A., N.Y. Br., 1948-50, cons. gen. surg. V.A. since 1946; editorial cons. med. dept. Macmillan Co., N.Y. City. Served with U.S. Army M.C., 1942-46, as surg. cons. 6th Army, advancing from maj. to lt. col.; also surg. cons. 8th Service Command, Chgo. Awarded Bronze star, 1945. Diplomate Am. Bd. Surgery (past vice chmn.). Fellow A.C.S. (pres.); mem. A.M.A., Am. Geriatrics Soc. (editor Jour.), Am. Heart Assn. (exec. com.), Am. Soc., N.Y. surg. assns., N.Y. Soc. Thoracic Surgery New York Medical Society, New York Academy of Medicine (president 1961-82), Soc. University Surgeons, Harvey Soc., Soc. Clin. Surgery, N.Y. Clin. Soc., N.Y. Gastroenterol. Assn., N.Y. Med., Surgical Society, Society Experimental Biology, Medicine, New York Soc. Cardiovascular Surgery (president), Soc. U.S. Med. Cons. World War II, Alpha Home: Manhattan, N.Y. Died Jan. 12, 1982.

GLICKSMAN, FRANK LEONARD, TV producer, writer; b. N.Y.C., June 29, 1921; s. Jack Gordon and Ann (Davidson) G.; m. Pearl Lerner, July 6, 1948; 1 dau., Susan Gail. B.A., UCLA, 1942. Publicist MGM, 1942-46, story analyst, 1947-55; story editor CBS West Coast, 1955-60, 20th Century Fox, 1960-64. Producer: TV series 12 O'Clock High, 20th Century Fox, 1964-65, Long Hot Summer, 1965-66, Custer, 1967; exec. producer, co-creator: TV series Medical Center, 1969-76; exec. producer, co-developer: TV series Trapper John M.D, 1979-84; Co-author: novel Unicorn Affair, 1980. Mem. Screen Writers Guild. Home: Beverly Hills, Calif. Died Jan. 19, 1984.

GLIDDEN, WILLIAM ROY, engineer; b. Boston, Mar. 7, 1889; s. William Meyers and Sarah Elizabeth (Grant) G.; B.S., Mass. Inst. Tech., 1912; m. Helen Louise Hansen, Aug. 17, 1912; 1 son, Robert Thorwald. Engr. B.&M. R.R., Mass. Highway Commn., Met. Water and Sewerage Board, 1912-16; asst. bridge engr. Va. Dept. Highways, 1916, bridge engr., 1917-52, asst. chief engr. from 1952; faculty dept. engring. Va. Mechanics Inst., Va. Poly. Inst., U. Va., 1918-44. Mem. Hwy. Research Bd.; chmn. adv. com. Va. Council Hwy. Investigation and Research. Mem. Am. Soc. C.E. (v.p. 1951-52, pres. 1955), Nat. Soc. Profl. Engrs., Am. Concrete Inst., Am. Assn. State Hwy. Ofcls., Southeastern Assn. State Hwy. Ofcls., Va. Soc. Profl. Engrs. (founder), Sigma Xi. Unitarian. †

GLOCKLER, GEORGE, phys. chemist; b. Munich, Germany, Sept. 7, 1890; s. George and Margaret (Feucht) G.; came to U.S., 1907, naturalized, 1913; B.S., U. of Wash., 1915, M.S., 1915; Ph.D., U. of Calif., 1923; m. Ruby Moser Clift, June 24, 1916; children—Margaret Ellen, Ruby Frances. Power sta. operator, Seattle Electric Co. and City of Seattle, 1912-16; traffic mgr. Horne Co., Ltd., Tokyo, 1916-21; analytical and cons. chemist, Yokohama, 1916-21; teaching fellow, U. of Calif., 1921-23; nat. research fellow, Calif. Inst. of Tech., Pasadena, 1923-26; research asso. Am. Petroleum Inst., of Minn., 1926-29; asso. prof. U. of Minn., 1929-36, prof. of phys. chem., 1936-40; head dept. chemistry and prof. phys. chemistry, U. Ia., 1940-52; dir. chem. sci. div. Office: Ordnance Research, Durham, N.C., 1952-53, dep. chief scientist, 1953-54, chief scientist, 1954-57, chief research investigator, from 1959; visiting lecturer Duke, 1952-59; research asso. Naval Research Lab., Wash., 1929-30. Mem. subcom. elec. insulation Nat. Research Council. Consultant of War Prodn. Bd., 1943-48. Recipient Ia. gold medal award Am. Chem. Soc., 1952, citation for meritorius service U.S. Army, 1958. Mem. fellowships board AEC. Fellow Am. Phys. Soc., A.A.A.S. (vice president 1948); mem. New York Acadamy of Science, Franklin Inst., Am. Chem. Soc. (exec. com., phys. and inorganic chemistry div.), Am. Electrochemical Soc., Faraday Soc. (London), Phi Beta Kappa, Sigma Xi, Phi Lambda Upsilon, Alpha Chi Sigma. Clubs: Cosmos (Wash.); Faculty (Duke); Triangle (U. of Iowa). Author: The Electrochemistry of Gases and Other Dielectrics (with S. C. Lind), 1939. Chemistry in Our Time (with Ruby C. Glockler), 1947. Asso. editor Jour. Phys. Chem. Contbr. numerous articles to professional jours. Mem. editorial bd. Ann. Rev. Phys. Chemistry, 1950-52. Home: Durham, N.C. †

GLOVER, JOHN DESMOND, educator, cons.; b. Australia, Feb. 15, 1915; Ph.B., Brown U., 1936; M.B.A., Harvard U., 1939, A.M., 1942, Ph.D., 1947; m. Ruth Eleanor Adams, Sept. 12, 1938; children—Elizabeth Trías, Katherine, Margaret. Mem. staff U.S. C. of C., 1936-37; instr. and tutor econs. dept. Harvard U., 1939-42, faculty Grad. Sch. Bus. Adminstrn., 1942-81, successively instr., asst. prof., asso. prof., 1949-54, prof. bus. adminstrn., 1954-81, Learned-Lovett prof., 1970-81, mem. faculty Law Sch., 1974-76; chmn. bd. dirs. Cambridge Research Inst.; spl. cons. USAF, 1943-52; secretariat U.S. Strategic Bombing Survey, 1945, civilian rank of col.; chmn. internat. seminars corp. and govt. policy, Rotterdam, Barcelona, Bizerte; dir. Allied Chem. Corp.; cons. Hon. fellow U. Tel Aviv, 1970-81. Author: Public Loans to Private Business, 1948, 79; The Attack on Big Business, 1954; (with R.M. Hower and Renato Tagiuri) The Administrator, Cases on Human Relations in Business, 5th edit., 1973; (with Gerald A. Simon) Chief Executives Handbook, 1975; The Corporate Revolution, 1979. Clubs: Harvard (N.Y.C. and Boston); Cosmos (Washington). Home: Cambridge, Mass. Died Feb. 16, 1981.

GLYNN, WILLIAM EDWARD, lawyer; b. Schenectady, July 7, 1923; s. William Albert and Marie Veronica (Fitzgerald) G.; m. Jacquelyn Mullaney, June 8, 1957; children: J. Garrett Tilton, William E., Sarah M., Mary Elizabeth, Molly Ann. B.S., U.S. Mil. Acad., 1945; LL.B., Harvard U., 1953. Bar: Conn. 1954. Mem. firm Day, Berry & Howard, Hartford, Conn., 1953-84, ptnr., 1959-84. Commr. Hartford Housing Authority, 1958-61; mayor City of Hartford, 1961-63, 63-65; mem., chmn. Hartford Found. Pub. Giving, 1968-83. Served to 1st lt. Signal Corps U.S. Army, 1945-50. Mem. ABA, Conn. Bar Assn., Hartford County Bar Assn. Democrat. Roman Catholic. Died Aug. 5, 1984.

GOBBI, TITO, baritone, stage dir.; b. Bassano del Grappa, Italy, Oct. 24, 1915; s. Giovanni and Enrica (Weiss) G.; m. Matilde de Rensis, Apr. 10, 1937; 1 dau., Cecilia. D.honoris causa, Rosary Coll., 1981. Dir. Opera Workshop, Villa Schifanolia, Rosary Coll., Florence, Italy, 1974; also master classes, lectr. world-wide. Debut in opera as Germont Pere in: La Traviata, Teatro Adriano, Rome, 1937; appeared throughout world in 27 complete operas; recorded numerous albums; stage dir. throughout world; Author: My Life. Named Commendatore and Grand Officiale of Italy, 1960, Grand Officiale Sant Jago Portugal, 1970. Mem. Dante Aligheri (hon.), Lyons (hon.), Art Club (London) (hon.), Royal Acad. Music (hon.). Home: Rome, Italy. Died Mar. 5, 1984.

GODBER, FREDERICK, Lord 1st Baron Godber of Mayfield, business exec.; born Dulwich, London, Eng., Nov. 6, 1888; s. Edward and Marion Louise (Peach) G.; m. Violet Ethel Beatrice Lovesy, Aug. 29, 1914; children—Joyce (Mrs. Andrew Agnew), Daphne (Mrs. Ian Debenham). With Asiatic Petroleum Co., 1904-19; pres. Roxana Petroleum Corp., St. Louis, 1919-29; dir. Shell Union Oil Corp., 1919-29; mng. dir. Royal Dutch Shell Group, 1929-46; chmn., mng. dir The Shell Transport & Trading Co., Ltd., 1946-61; chmn. The Anglo-Saxon Petroleum Co. and The Shell Petroleum Co. Ltd., 1946-61; chmn. Commonwealth Devel. Finance Co. Ltd., 1953. Chmn. overseas supply com. Petroleum Bd. World War II; chmn. exec. com. Help Holland Council. A trustee Churchill Coll. Trust Fund, Cambridge, 1958. Hon. bencher Middle Temple, 1954; hon. liveryman Leathersellers Co., 1962. Decorated Grand Officer, Order of Oranje Nassau, 1947; knighted, 1942; created baron, 1956. Hon. fellow Inst. of Petroleum. Home: Sussex, England. †

GODDARD, DAVID ROCKWELL, educator; b. Carmel, Calif., Jan. 3, 1908; s. Pliny Earle and Alice (Rockwell) G.; m. Doris Martin, Aug. 21, 1933 (dec.); children—Alison G. Elliott; Robert Martin; m. Katharine Evans, Feb. 2, 1952. A.B., U. Calif., 1929, A.M., 1930, Ph.D., 1933. NRC fellow Rockefeller Inst. Med. Research, 1933-35; instr. to prof. U. Rochester, 1935-46, chmn. dept., 1938-46; prof. botany U. Pa., 1946-58, chmn. dept., 1952-57, dir. div. biology, 1957-61, provost, 1961-70, emeritus provost, 1973-85, Gustave C. Kuemmerle prof. botany, 1958-64, prof. biology, 1964-71, univ. prof. biology, 1972-75, emeritus, 1975-85; univ. prof. sci. and pub. policy, 1971-72; home sec. Nat. Acad. Scis., Washington, 1975-79; Walker-Ames prof. U. Wash., 1955; vis. prof. Rockefeller U., 1956-64; Guggenheim fellow U. Chgo., 1942-43, U. Cambridge, 1950. Author: (with Höber) Physical Chemistry of Cells and Tissues, 1945; also articles sci. periodicals.; Contbg. author: (with Höber) Treatise of Plant Physiology (Steward), Vol. 1A, 1960; Mem. editorial bd.: (with Höber) Ann. Rev. Plant Physiology, 1948-54; asso. editor: (with Höber) Quar. Rev. of Biology, 1950-75; editor-in-chief: (with Höber) Plant Physiology, 1953-57; asso. editor (with Höber), 1958-63; bd. trustees: (with Höber) Biol. Abstracts, 1950-56; pres. (with Höber), 1955-56. Mem. nat. adv. council health research facilities NIH, 1962-67, mem. health scis. advancement award rev. com., 1965-66, 67-70; cons. to President's spl. asst. for sci. and tech., cons. President's Sci. Adv. Com., 1961-63; chmn. ad hoc panel on drug abuse White House, 1962; Trustee Wistar Inst. Anatomy and Biology, 1971-85. Recipient Stephen Hales award Am. Soc. Plant Physiology, 1948. Fellow Am. Acad. Arts and Scis.; mem. Am. Philos. Soc., Nat. Acad. Sci. (chmn. com. on USSR and Eastern Europe 1964-68), AAAS (bd. dirs. 1963-68), Bot. Soc. Am., Am. Soc. Plant Physiology (pres. 1958), Soc. Study Growth and Devel. (pres. 1953), Soc. Gen. Physiologists (pres. 1948). Club: Franklin Inn (Phila.). Home: Philadelphia, Pa. Died July 9, 1985.

GODDARD, GEORGE W(ILLIAM), air force officer; b. Tunbridge Wells, Eng., June 15, 1889; s. George William and Ellen Jane (Le Strange) G.; grad. U.S. Officers Sch. Aerial Photography, Cornell, 1918; D.Sc. Boston U., 1952; LL.D., Keuka Coll., 1956; m. Elizabeth Hayes, May 8, 1943; 1 dau., Diana H. Enlisted as pvt., aviation sect. Signal Corps, 1917 and advanced through grades to brig. gen. U.S.A.F.; chief photog. officer Wright Field, Dayton, pioneering field of night photography, color, high altitude, stereoscopic photography, 1936, chief research and development engring. sect. Aerial Photog. Lab., 1945; apptd. photog. disarmament officer, Germany, 1945; duty with E.T.O.U.S.A., Eng., 1944; temp. duty in Korea, 1950; assigned dir. reconnaissance, Allied Air Forces Central Europe, Fontainebleau, France, 1952; retired 1953; asst. to pres. of Itek Corp., Lexington, Mass. Decorated Legion of Merit with oak leaf cluster, Distinguished Service Medal, Croix de Guerre (France). Awarded Thurman H. Bane award for outstanding development in low-altitude high speed night photography, Inst. Aero. Scis., 1950; Hon. Master Photographer, Am. Photographers Assn., 1951; Progress medal, Photog. Soc. Am., 1951; George Harris award for outstanding conbn. to photography 1951, Fellowship award Soc. Photog. Scientists and Engrs., 1962, Mem. Am. Soc. Photogrammetry (hon.). Clubs: Tavern (Chgo.); Army Navy (Washington); U.S. Air Force Bolling Field (all hon.). Address: Chevy Chase, Md. †

GODDARD, ROY WILLIAM, dean jr. coll.; b. Putney, S.D., Dec. 26, 1889; s. William Henry and Minnie (Roffey) G.; student Knox Coll., 1911-13; B.Ph., U. of Chicago, 1916; M.Ph., U. of Wis., 1933; m. Nellie Boardman, Nov. 27, 1913; children—Rosalee Evelyn, Dorothy Rolline Macarty. Teacher rural sch., Daviess County, Mo., 1909-11; teacher history and govt. high sch., Virginia, Minn., 1916-21, jr. coll., 1921-25; dean Rochester (Minn.) Jr. Coll. since 1925. Mem. charter com. City of Rochester since 1932 (pres. 1936-39); mem. advisory bd. St. Mary's Sch. Nursing, 1939-43, chmn. Nat. Peony Show, 1940. Pres. Minn. Jr. Coll. Deans Assn., 1928-32; chmn. jr. coll. sect., Minn. Ednl. Assn., 1942-44; vice pres. Am. Assn. Jr. Colls., 1943, pres., 1944; mem. executive com. of Am. Assn. of Jr. Colls., 1944-48; mem. N.E.A., Pi Gamma Mu. Unitarian. Odd Fellow. Chmn. editorial bd., Jr. Coll. Jour., 1947-48. Contbr. to ednl. and hort. jours. Home: Rochester, Minn. †

GODFREY, ALFRED LAURANCE, lawyer; b. Lima, Wis., Jan. 8, 1888; s. Thomas G. and Mary (Dickson) G.; A.B., U. of Wis., 1914, J.D., 1919; m. Helen Humphrey, Apr. 24, 1918; children—Thomas Grant, Richard Laurance. Prin. Westby (Wis.) High Sch., 1910-12, Stevens Point High Sch., 1914-15; admitted to Wis. bar, 1919, engaging in practice of law at Milwaukee, at Elkhorn since 1921; on legal staff Soo Line Ry., 1919-21; dir. and gen. counsel State Long Distance Telephone Co.; dist. atty., Walworth County, Wis., 1922-26; chmn. Walworth County Rep. Com., 1926-29; chmn. Rep. Congressional Com., 1st Dist. of Wis., 1931; sec. State Rep. Com. of Wis., 1932-34. Commd. 1st lt. 1917, resigned, 1919; later commd. capt. and maj., Reserve Corps. Chmn. Central Walworth Co. chpt. Am. Red Cross; mem. bd. govs. Wis. State Bar, 1948-51, pres. 1951-52. Fellow American Bar Found.; mem. American (house of delegates 1952-60, Wis. (past president), Walworth Co. (pres.) bar assns. Phi Delta Phi, Am. Legion. Republican. Conglist. Mason. Club: Kiwanis, Big Foot Country. †

GODFREY, ARTHUR, radio and TV entertainer; b. N.Y.C., Aug. 31, 1903; s. Arthur H. and Kathryn (Morton) G.; m. Mary Bourke, Feb. 24, 1938; children—Richard, Michael, Patricia. Ed. grammar school and 1 1/2 years high sch., Hasbrouck Heights, N.J.; various home study and correspondence courses; grad., Naval Radio Sch., Great Lakes, Ill., 1921, Naval Radio Materiel Sch., Bellevue, D.C., 1929. Announcer and entertainer, Sta. WFBR, Balt., 1930, NBC, Washington, 1930-34, free-lance radio entertainer, 1934-83, artist, Columbia records; nat. program Arthur Godfrey Time; radio, 1960-83, various TV programs.; Appeared in: films Four for Texas, 1963, Where Angels Go . . . Trouble Follows, The Glass Bottom Boat, 1966. Internat. trustee World Wildlife Fund.; mem. State N.Y. Council Environ. Advisors, Citizen's Adv. Com. on Environ. Quality, 1970-83, Nat. Adv. Com. on Oceans and Atmosphere.; Trustee N.Y. Ocean Sci. Lab. Served in USN, 1920-24; Served in USCG, 1927-30; commd. comdr. USNR, 1939; comdr. 1951. Mem. AFTRA, ASCAP, Soc. Illustrators, Musicians Protective Union, Explorers Club. Clubs: N.Y. Yacht, Sky, QB'S. Died Mar. 16, 1983.*

GOETHALS, ROBERT JOSEPH, retail company executive; b. San Francisco, Dec. 15, 1924; s. Gustave Cosmos and Veronica Elizabeth (Fogarty) G.; m. Bernice Corvello, Dec. 10, 1949; children—Lee Ann, Glenn. B.A., U. San Francisco, 1950. Reporter San Francisco Chronicle, 1950-56; dir. public relations Kaiser Steel Corp., 1956-61; dir. communications IBM, 1961-70; v.p. communications RCA Corp., Marlborough, Mass., 1970-75; v.p. creative services Federated Dept. Stores, Inc., Cin., from 1975. Editor: A Treasury of Popular River Songs, 1980; Contbr. articles to nat. mags., jours. State coordinator Common Cause, Ohio, 1974-78. Served with USN, 1942-46. Home: Cincinnati, OH.

GOFF, BRUCE, architect, educator, painter; b. Alton, Kan., June 8, 1904; s. Corliss Arthur and Maude Rose (Furbeck) G.; student pub. schs. Tulsa. Apprentice, Rush, Endacott & Rush, architects, Tulsa, 1916-26; mem. Rush, Endacott & Goff, 1926-33; tchr. Chicago Acad. Fine Arts, 1935-41; pvt. practice, Chicago, 1934-41; N.J., Pa., Fla., Md., Chicago and Calif. from 1944; design dir., show room Libbey Owens Ford Glass Co., Chicago; designer Boston Av. M.E. Ch., Page Warehouse, Tulsa Bldg., Guaranty Laundry, Tulsa, houses. Chicago, structures Aleutian Islands (Navy), camp parks, Calif., bldg. projects U. Okla.; prof. and chmn. sch. architecture U. Okla. from 1946. Served with U.S.N., Sea Bees, 1941-44. Mem. Tau Sigma Delta. Author articles in profl. jours. and fgn. mags. Home: Norman, Okla.

GOFF, CHARLES RAY, clergyman; b. Dallas, Ia., May 7, 1889; s. Samuel J. and Mary Ellen (James) G.; B.S., Northwestern Univ., 1923, B.D., Garrett Biblical Inst., 1926, D.D., 1934; m. Ruth Maddy, Oct. 11 1911; children—Dorothy Evelyn (Mrs. Frank Satten), Margaret Louise (Mrs. Donald G. Bate), Charlotte Jean (Mrs. Donn Fowler). Served as pastor, Elmhurst, Illinois, 1924-28, Oak Park, Illinois, 1928-33, Rockford, Illinois, 1933-42; Chicago, Illinois, from 1942; instructor religion, Rockford Coll., 1935-42; pastor, Chicago Temple, from 1942; preacher Nat. Methodist Men's Hour Radio Network. Received Alumni merit award, Northwestern U., 1935. Trustee Garrett Biblical Inst., Evanston, Ill.; Rockford (Ill.) Coll. Clubs: Builders, Union League, Chicago, Rotary. Author: A Better Hope, 1951; Anyone for Calvary, 1958; Invitation to Commune, 1959; Chapel in the Sky, 1960; Shelters and Sanctuaries, 1961.†

GOFFMAN, ERVING, educator, sociologist; b. Manville, Alta., Can., June 11, 1922; came to U.S., 1945; m. Angelica Schuyler Choate, 1952 (div. dec. 1964); 1 son, Thomas Edward. A.B., U.Toronto, Ont., Can., 1945; M.A., U. Chgo., 1949, Ph.D., 1953, L.H.D., 1979; LL.D., U. Man., Can., 1976. Mem. Shetland field research U. Edinburgh, Scotland, 1949-51; vis. scientist Nat. Inst. Mental Health, 1954-57; asst. prof. dept. sociology U. Calif. at Berkeley, 1958-59, asso. prof., 1959-62, prof., 1962-68; Benjamin Franklin prof. anthropology and sociology U. Pa., Phila., 1968-82. Author: Presentation of Self in Everyday Life, 1956, Encounters, 1961, Asylums, 1961, Behavior in Public Places, 1963, Stigma, 1964, Interaction Ritual, 1967, Strategic Interaction, 1969, Relations in Public, 1971, Frame Analysis, 1974, Gender Advertisements, 1979, Forms of Talk, 1981. Recipient MacIver award, 1961; In Medias Res award, 1978. Fellow Am. Acad. Arts and Scis., Am. Sociol. Soc. (pres. 1981-82). Home: Philadelphia, Pa. Died Nov. 19, 1982.

GOLD, AARON MICHAEL, newspaper columnist; b. Chgo., Aug. 4, 1937; s. Ben and Anne (Silver) G.; m. Judith Ann; children—Tracy, Sharon, Andrea. Student, Northwestern U., 1955-56. With news prodn. dept. CBS-TV, Chgo., 1956-63; owner, mgr. Aaron Gold & Assos., Chgo., 1963-73; entertainment columnist Chgo. Tribune, 1973-83. Asso. producer, Ivanhoe Theatre, Chgo., 1969-73; co-producer on Broadway for: Status Quo Vadis, 1973. Bd. dirs. Chgo. Heart Assn., Chgo. Lung Assn., Little City, Palatine, Ill., Spl. Children's Charities. Named Communications Man of Yr. Israel Bonds, 1979; Humanitarian of Yr. Easter Seals Soc., 1981. Club: Variety. Home: Chicago, Ill. Died May 23, 1983.

GOLDBLATT, JOEL, business exec.; b. Chicago, Ill., August 12, 1907; s. Simon and Hannah (Diamond) Goldblatt; married Lynne C. Walker, December 31, 1948 (div. Nov. 1962); children—Jan Hannah, Jody Lou, Joel. Began as buyer, Goldblatt Bros., Inc., later in active mgmt. of co., v.p., operating dir., 1928-46, pres. from 1945, vice chmn., 1963-81, co-chmn. 1946 Red Cross Drive; chmn. Trades and Industries Div. 1946 Community Fund Drive; trustee Goldblatt Brothers foundation. Pres. State St. Council, 1948-49, chmn. bd. 1950-51, dir., 1952-53; dir. Michael Reese Hosp.; mem. Chgo. Plan Commn. Major Q. M. Corps. U.S. Army, World War II disch., 1945. Died Aug. 10, 1982.

GOLDBLATT, MAURICE, bus. executive; b. Strashov, Poland, Dec. 17, 1893; s. Simon and Hannah (Diamond) G.; ed. pub. schs.; m. Sylvia Gottstein, June 22, 1924 (div. 1935); chidlren—Noel Lyman, Gloria Hope; m. 2d, Bernice Mendelson, Jan. 7, 1935; children—Merle Ann, Stanford Jay. Salesman, E. Iverson & Co., 1912-14; pres. Goldblatt Bros., Inc., dept. stores, Chicago, 1914-45; chairman bd. since 1945. Chmn. bd. trustees Goldblatt Bros. Found.; 1945. Chmn. bd. U. Chgo. Cancer Research Found., Cancer Research Found., Inc., Heart Research Found., Inc.; past dir. Mount Sinai Hosp., Chicago, La Rabida Jackson Park Sanitarium B'nai B'rith; hon. dir. Cancer Prevention Center of Chgo. Past pres. Marks Nathan Hall; former exec. dir. Am. Cancer Soc., past dir. Am. Heart Assn.; past member National Advisory Cancer Council, USPHS. Mem. citizens bd. Loyola Univ., Univ. of Chgo. Awarded Rosenberger Medal for 1951. Member Chicago Heart Association (dir.), Am. Hosp. Assn. (hon.). Mason. Elk. Clubs: Standard, Bryn Mawr Country (Chgo.). Home: Chicago, Ill. Died July 17, 1984.

GOLDBLOOM, ALTON, educator; b. Montreal, Can., Sept. 23, 1890; s. Samuel and Bella (Goldstein) G.; student Manitoba Coll., Winnipeg, 1908; B.A., McGill U., 1913, M.D.C.M., 1916; m. Annie Esther Ballon, May 21, 1918; children—Victor C., Richard B. Intern Royal Victoria Hosp., Montreal, 1916-17; assistant demonstrator pediatrics McGill University, 1920-25, prof. pediatrics from 1948; chmn. dept. and phys. in chief Children Meml. Hosp., Montreal, 1947-53, ret.; cons. pediatrician Montreal Gen., Jewsih Gen. and Shriners hosps. since 1945; chief pediatrics Jewish Gen. Hosp., 1934-37, Champlain Valley Hosp., Plattsburgh, N.Y. from 1930, Placid Meml. Hosp., Lake Placid, N.Y. Hon. fellow A.M.A.; mem. Am. Acad. Pediatrics (state chairman), American Pediatric Soc., Canadian Soc. for Study Diseases Children (past pres.), Canadian Med. Assn., Montreal Medico-Chirurg. Soc. Alpha Omega Alpha, Sigma Xi, Pediatric Travel Soc. Author: The Care of the Child, 1945, Le Soin de l'enfant (French edit.), 1948, De Zorg voor Het Kind (Dutch edit.), 1947; also articles on pediatrics Mem. editorial bd. Pediatrics. Home: Montreal, Canada. †

GOLDEN, HARRY, editor, pub., writer; b. N.Y.C., May 6, 1903; s. Leib and Anna (Klein) Goldhirsch; student Coll. City N.Y., 1919-22; L.H.D., Belmont Abbey Coll., 1962, Johnson C. Smith U., Charlotte, N.C., 1965; m. Genevieve Gallagher, Apr. 20, 1926; children—Richard, Harry, William, Peter. Editor, pub. The Carolina Israelite, Charlotte, N.C., 1942-81. Named Man of Year, Carver Coll., 1957, Johnson C. Smith Coll., 1958, Temple Emanu-El, N.Y.C., 1958. Mem. Am. Jewish Congress (mem. bd.), N.A.A.C.P. (life), Shakespeare Soc. Am., Cath. Interracial Council. Mem. B'nai B'rith. Author: Only in America, 1958; For 2 Cents Plain, 1959; Enjoy, Enjoy, 1960; Carl Sandburg, 1961; You're Entitle', 1962; Forgotten Pioneer, 1963; Mr. Kennedy and the Negroes, 1964; So What Else is New, 1965; A Little Girl Is Dead, 1965; Eat, Eat, My Child, 1966; The Lynching of Leo Frank, 1966; The Right Time, 1968; So Long as You're Healthy, 1969; The Israelis, 1970; The Greatest Jewish City in the World, 1972; Golden Book of Jewish Humor, 1972; Our Southern Landsman, 1974; Long Live Columbus, 1974. Home: Charlotte, N.C. Died Oct. 2, 1981.

GOLDMANN, NAHUM, b. Wischnewo, Poland, July 10, 1894; s. Salomon and Rebecca (Kwini) G.; J.D., U. of Heidelberg, 1920; student U. of Marburg, 1914, U. of Berline, 1915; m. Alice Gottschalk, Dec. 19, 1934; children—Michael, Guido. Came to U.S., 1940. Founder Eshkol Pub. Co., Berlin, 1920; an editor Encyclopedia Judaica, 1929; rep. Jewish Agency for Palestine, League of Nations, Geneva, 1935. mem. exec. com., 1935, rep. in U.S.A., 1940-46, chmn. Am. sect. from 1949; chmn. administrative com., World Jewish Congress, 1936, chmn. executive committee from 1945, acting president 1949-77.

Author: Reisebriefe von Erez Israel, 1913. Home: New York, N.Y. Died Aug. 29, 1982.

GOLDMANN, SIDNEY, lawyer, ret. judge; b. Trenton, N.J., Nov. 28, 1903; s. Samuel and Stella (Reich) G.; m. Beatrice Corosh, Nov. 20, 1938; 1 son, Donald Alan. B.S. magna cum laude in Math, Harvard, 1924, LL.B., 1927. Bar: N.J. bar 1928. City atty., acting city mgr., Trenton, 1935-39; exec. clk. Gov. Charles Edison, 1942-44; N.J. state librarian, 1944-47; head archives and history bur. Div. N.J. Library, 1947- 48; standing master N.J. Supreme Ct., 1949-51; became judge N.J. Superior Ct., 1951; presiding and adminstrv. judge N.J. Superior Ct. (Appellate Div.), until 1971; of counsel Katzenbach, Gildea & Rudner, Trenton, N.J.; Served 1947, N.J. Constl. Conv. as historian and archivist, and chmn. Gov.'s Com. Prep. Research; chmn. N.J. Election Law Enforcement Com., Edn. Law Center. Author: (with Thomas J. Graves) The Organization and Administration of the N.J. Highway Dept, 1942; Contbr. to: (with Thomas J. Graves) A History of Trenton, 1679-1929, 1929; Editor: (with Thomas J. Graves) Proc. N.J. Constnl. Conv. of 1947 (5 vols.). Pres. Trenton Free Public Library; chmn. Trenton Bicentennial Com.; Bd. dirs. Trenton Jewish Community Center, Trenton Jewish Fedn. (pres., 1936-40, life mem.), Trenton Jewish Family Service (life mem., past pres.), Greenwood House, Helene Fuld Med. Center, Trenton, Trenton Council Social Agys. (pres. 1951-53), Am. Jewish Com. (life. mem. bd. of gov.), Council Jewish Fedn. and Welfare Funds, Jewish Welfare Bd., Am.-Jewish Tercentenary Commn. Mem. Mercer County Bar Assn. (past pres.), N.J. Bar Assn., ABA., Trenton Hist. Soc. (past pres.), Trenton Jewish Hist. Soc. (past pres.), Am. Judicature Soc., Inst. Jud. Adminstrn., N.J. Constl. Conv. Assn., Harvard Law Sch. Assn. of N.J. (past pres.), NCCJ. Democrat. Jewish. Clubs: Harvard of N.J, Trenton Symposium. Home: Trenton, NJ.

GOLDSTON, ROBERT CONROY, author; b. N.Y.C., July 9, 1927; s. Philip Henry and Josephine (Conroy) G.; m. Marguerite Garvey, Jan. 16, 1956; children—Rebecca, Gabrielle, Sarah, Francesca, Maximilian, Theresa. Student, Columbia, 1946-48, Sch. Gen. Studies, 1948-51. Author: novels The Eighth Day, 1956, The Catafalque, 1957, The Shore Dimly Seen, 1963, The Last of Lazarus, 1966; non-fiction The Soviets, 1967, Communism: A History, 1971; juveniles Tales of the Alhambra Retold, 1962, The Legend of the Cid, 1963, The Song of Roland, 1964, The Russian Revolution, 1966, The Civil War in Spain, 1966, The Life and Death of Nazi Germany, 1967, 71, The Rise of Red China, 1967, Spain, 1967, The Negro Revolution, 1968, Great Depression, 1971, Barcelona: The Civic Stage, 1969, London: The Civic Spirit, 1969, New York: Civic Exploitation, 1970, Suburbia: Civic Denial, 1970, The Vietnamese Revolution, 1972, Next Year in Jerusalem, 1978, The Road between the Wars, 1978, Sword of the Prophet, 1979; numerous others; writer of: TV documentary films The Bullfight, 1960, Bjorn's Inferno, 1964, Running Away Backwards, 1965, all for CBC. Guggenheim fellow, 1957-58. Address: New York, NY.

GOMULKA, WLADYSLAW, Polish polit. ofcl.; b. Krosno. Lwów, Poland. Feb. 6, 1905; married: 1 son Profl. organizer Communist party, promoter Polish working youth movement following World War I, also sec. several trade union orgns.; mem. underground resistance movement Polish Communists, 1941; sec. Warsaw group Polish Workers party, 1942, mem. central com., sec. Polish workers party 1943-49; prin. organizer Cominform (Communist-Information Bur.), 1947; mem., 1st sec. Polish United Workers party, 1956-82, dep. premier Poland, 1944, minister recovered Western areas, 1945-49, vice minister Supreme Nat. Control Chamber, 1949-51; mem. Council of State, 1957-82. Home: Warsaw, Poland. Died Sept. 1, 1982.

GOOCH, JAMES THOMAS, lawyer; b. Vanndale, Ark., Dec. 10, 1913; s. Samuel Amos and Augustus (Halk) G.; children—Edris Johanna Gooch Quinn, Marilyn Kay Gooch Peterson. Student, Ark. State U., 1937, Ark. Law Sch., 1940. Bar: Ark. bar 1940. Practiced in, Wynne, 1940-46, Arkadelphia, 1954-84; mem. firm Gooch & Gooch, 1940-46; U.S. atty. Eastern Dist. Ark., 1946-54; partner firm Lookadoo, Gooch & Lookadoo, 1954-75, Lookadoo, Gooch & Ashby, 1975-84; Vice pres., dir. Elk Horn Bank & Trust Co.; Pres., U.S. Atty.'s Conf., 1948-50; Pres. Ark. Trial Lawyers Assn., 1971-73. Mem. War Meml. Stadium, Little Rock, 1946-67, Ark. Senate, 1940-44; chmn. Clark County Democratic Com., 1960-72. Served to lt. USNR, 1942-45. Mem. Am. Judicature Soc., Am., Ark., S.W. Ark., Clark County bar assns., Am. Trial Lawyers Assn., Ark. Trial Lawyers Assn. (pres. 1971-73). Home: Lake Hamilton, Ark. Died Oct. 23, 1984.

GOOCH, ROBERT KENT, univ. prof.; b. Roanoke, Va., Sept. 26, 1893; s. William Stapleton and Mary Stuart (Anderson) G.; B.A., U. of Va., 1914, M.A., 1915; B.A., Oxford U., 1920, M.A., 1922, Ph.D., 1924; married Florine Kinney Holt, July 31, 1928; step-children—Nancy Holt (Mrs. Samuel P. Preston), Jacqueline Ambler Holt. Professor of government, College of William and Mary, 1920-22; asso. prof. political science U. of Virginia, 1924-26; prof. from 1926, on leave of absence to act as chief of Western European Section, Branch of Research and Analysis, Office of Strategic Services, Washington, D.C., 1941-43, Div. Polit. Studies, Dept. of State, Aug. 1943-May 1944. Alternate mem. bd. appeals on visa cases, 1944-45. Served as capt. Battery B, 60th Artillery, Coast Artillery Corps. A.E.F., 1917-19. Awarded Rhodes scholarship, 1914. Member American Polit. Science Assn., Acad. Polit. Science, Am. Soc. Pub. Adminstrn., Southern Polit. Science Assn., Va. Social Science Assn., Phi Beta Kappa. Democrat. Clubs: Serpentine, Colonnade, Author books. Editor: Source Book on the Government of England, 1939. Contbr. articles and revs. to mags. Mem. adv. bd. Va. Quarterly Rev. Home: Charlottesville, VA. Died May 22, 1982.

GOODDING, T(HOMAS) H(OMER), univ. prof.; b. Macon, Mo., Apr. 9, 1890; s. Thomas Simpson and Henrietta (Dale) G.; B.Sc., Univ. of Neb.; 1916, M.Sc., 1923; Ph.D., Cornell U., 1933; m. Laura Birdie Sleuman, June 2, 1917; children—George Vernon (lt., A.A.F., killed at Pantelleria, June 10, 1943), Richard Dale, John Alan, Barbara Belle. Teacher science, high sch., Glidden, Ia., 1916-17, extension specialist U. of Neb., 1917-19; instr. Cornell U., 1930-33; supervisor short courses U. of Neb., 1933-36, prof. agronomy (corps) from 1933. Fellow Am. Soc. of agronomy; mem. Univ. Religious Welfare Council, Agronomy Coll. Pub. Relations Bd., Sigma Xi, Alpha Zeta, Gamma Sigma Delta. Democrat. Methodist. Home: Lincoln, Nebr. †

GOODE, DELMER MORRISON, editor; b. Rose Creek, Minn., May 18, 1889; s. Horatio Fitch and Ella (Kirby) G.; advanced diploma Moorhead State U., 1909; B.A. with distinction, U. Minn., 1916; M.A., Oreg. State U., 1938; m. Gladys Whipple, Sept. 18, 1926; 1 son, Kirby Whipple. Tchr. rural schs., N.D., 1907-08; prin. pub. schs., Omemee, N.D., 1909-11; supr. schs., Pine River, Minn., 1912-15, Clarkfield, Minn., 1916-18; editor publs. Oreg. State U., Corvallis, from 1919, dir. publs., 1943-55, prof. higher edn., 1935-83, coordinator studies in coll. and univ. teaching and curriculum Grad. Sch., 1955-73, dir. summer workshop coll. and univ. teaching Grad. Sch., 1956-73; editor Jour. Improving Coll. and Univ. Teaching, from 1953. Sec.-treas., editor Pacific N.W. Conf. Higher Edn., 1949-76, cons., from 1976. Vice pres. Oreg. Trail council Boy Scouts Am., 1948-50, recipient Silver Beaver award, 1947; moderator Congl. Conf. Oreg., 1948-49, bd. dirs., 1947-51, mem. conf. and nat. com. world missions, 1949-54. Served with U.S. Army, 1918-19; AEF in France. Recipient Distinguished Alumni award Moorhead State U., 1975. Mem. Internat. Platform Assn., Triad Club, Phoenix Soc., Phi Kappa Phi, Phi Eta Sigma, Phi Delta Kappa, Kappa Delta Pi, Alpha Phi Omega, Epsilon Sigma Phi, Owls, Acacia (Nat. award merit 1956, nat. historian 1975). Democrat. Mason. Author articles, editorials, pamphlets. Co-author: College and University Teaching, 1964. Home: Corvallis, Oreg. Died Apr. 16, 1983.

GOODE, JOHN CHAMBERS, JR., newspaper exec.; b. Boydton, Va., May 12, 1920; s. John Chambers and Lucille (Pleasants) G.; m. Aurelia Virginia Wyland, July 23, 1944. Ed. public and bus. schs. With Richmond Newspapers Inc., Va., from 1942, bus. mgr., 1973-78, v.p., gen. mgr., from 1978. Pres. United Way Greater Richmond, 1981; bd. dirs. Richmond YMCA, Richmond Jr. Achievement. Mem. Am. Newspaper Pubs. Assn., Internat. Circulation Mgrs. Assn., So. Newspaper Pubs. Assn., Mid-Atlantic Circulation Mgrs. Assn. (past pres.), West Richmond Bus. Men's Assn. Episcopalian. Clubs: Bull and Bear (Richmond); Masons, Shriners. Home: Richmond, Va. Died Apr. 29, 1984; buried Forest Lawn Cemetery, Richmond.

GOODLING, GEORGE A., congressman; b. Loganville, Pa., Sept. 26, 1896; grad. Pa. State U.; LL.D., York Coll., 1975; 6 children. Fruit grower; chmn. bd. Peoples Bank of Glen Rock, White Rose Motor Club; mem. Pa. Ho. of Reps. 14 yrs.; mem. 87th-88th, 90-96th congresses from 19th Dist. Pa. Exec. sec. Pa. Hort. Assn.; pres. York County chpt. Ducks Unlimited. Mem. Civil War Centennial Commn. Recipient Distinguished Alumni award Pa. State U., 1970. Mem. Am. Legion, Pa. Farmers Assn., Grange, Gamma Sigma Delta. Republican. Mason (33 deg.), Elk. Address: Loganville, Pa. Dec. Oct. 17, 1982.

GOODMAN, CLARK DROUILLARD, nuclear physicist; b. Memphis, Sept. 9, 1909; s. J. Alma and Naomi (Clark) G.; m. Mary Ellen Hohiesel, Aug. 8, 1933 (dec. 1969); children—Gaye Ellen, Alan Clark; m. Deni D. Seinfeld, Jan. 12, 1970. B.S., Calif. Inst. Tech., 1932; Ph.D., Mass. Inst. Tech., 1940. Tech. aide div. 16 and 17 OSRD, 1942-45; sr. physicist Oak Ridge Nat. Lab., 1945-46; asso. prof. physics Mass. Inst. Tech., 1947-58; asst. dir. div. reactor devel. AEC, Washington, 1955-58; v.p. technique Schlumberger Ltd., Houston, 1958-62; v.p., tech. dir. Houston Research Inst., 1962-69; prof. physics U. Houston, 1963-74, prof. emeritus, from 1974, chmn. physics dept., 1966-68; sec. com. radio-activity NRC, 1939-47; cons. Joint Congl. Com. Atomic Energy, 1961-62; mem. NASA Lunar and Planetary Missions Bd., AEC Licensing and Regulations Panel; chmn. com. radioactive waste disposal Nat. Acad. Scis.; mem. Three Mile Island-2 Safety Adv. Bd., from 1981. Author: Science and Engineering of Nuclear Power, vols. I and II, 1947, 48, Introduction to Nuclear Power, 1955, Atomic Energy (in Japanese), 1957, Science and Technology of the Environment, 1972. Fellow Am. Phys. Soc., Geol. Soc. Am.; mem. Sigma Xi, Tau Beta Pi. Address: Coronado, Calif.

GOODMAN, MARTIN WISE, newspaper exec.; b. Calgary, Alta., Can., Jan. 15, 1935; s. Aaron and Rosalind (Wise) G.; m. Janis Ripstein, Aug. 28, 1960; children—Jonathan, Lauren. B.A., McGill U., 1956; M.Sc., Columbia U., 1957; D.C.L. (hon.), King's Coll., 1981. With McGill Daily, Montreal, 1952-53, Monitor Pub. Co., Montreal, 1953-56; financial reporter Calgary Herald, 1957; reporter Canadian Press, Toronto, 1957-58; with Toronto Star, 1958-81, beginning as reporter, successively city hall bur. chief, Washington bur. chief, Ottawa bur. chief, city editor, mng. editor, 1968-71, editor-in-chief, 1971-78, pres., 1978-81; dir. Torstar Corp., Toronto Star Newspapers Ltd.; hon. pres., dir. Canadian Press. Decorated Order of Can.; Nieman fellow Harvard U., 1961-62. Mem. Canadian Daily Newspaper Pubs. Assn. (dir.). Jewish. Home: Toronto, Ont., Can. Died Dec. 20, 1981.

GOODMAN, STEVEN BENJAMIN, singer, guitarist; b. Chgo.; s. Joseph Bayer and Minnette (Erenburg) G.; m. Nancy Pruter, Feb. 6, 1970; children—Jessie, Sarah, Rosanna. Student, U. Ill., Lake Forest Coll. Singer, guitarist clubs and concert halls, throughout U.S., 1967—; producer phonograph records.; Composer: City of New Orleans. Office: 4121 Wilshire Blvd Los Angeles CA 90010

GOODRICH, FOREST JACKSON, educator; b. Norfolk, Neb., Jan. 23, 1889; s. Lee Jesse and Hannah (Gibbs) G.; Ph.C. and B.S., U. of Wash., 1914, M.S., 1917, Ph.D., 1926; m. Robin Wilkes, Aug. 20, 1923; children—Forest Gail (dec.), Carolyn Jean. Began as pharmacist, 1914; asst. chemist, State of Wash. Dept. of Agr., 1914-17; instr. U. of Wash. Coll. of Pharmacy, 1919-25; asst. prof., 1925-29, asso. prof., 1929-35, prof. pharmacognosy, from 1935, dean Coll. of Pharmacy, 1939-56, dean emeritus. Served in C.W.S., 1917-19. Pres. Am. Assn. Colleges of Pharmacy, 1943-44. Mem. U.S. Pharmacopoeia Revision Com., 1940-50. State Chemist for Department of Agriculture. Member American Pharm. Assn., Wash. State Pharm. Assn., Kappa Psi, Rho Chi, Sigma Xi, Tau Kappa Epsilon. Methodist. Mason (Shriner). Clubs: Seattle Yacht, Rainier (Seattle). Home: Seattle, Wash. †

GOODRICH, FRANCES, author; b. Belleville, N.J.; d. Henry Wickes and Madeleine Christy (Lloyd) G.; m. Robert Ames, 1917 (div.); m. Hendrik Willem Van Leon, 1927 (div.); m. Albert M. Hackett, Feb. 7, 1932. B.A., Vassar Coll., 1912; student, Sch. Social Service, N.Y.C., 1912-13. Actress, Vassar Theatre; writer stage and cinema; collaborator (with Albert Hackett); stage plays Up Pops the Devil, 1930, Bridal Wise, Great Big Doorstep, 1943, Diary of Anne Frank, 1955; motion pictures include Thin Man, Naughty Marietta, Oh Wilderness, Father of the Bride, Easter Parade, Seven Brides for Seven Brothers, Five Finger Exercise, 1962; collaborator others. (Recipient Pulitzer prize (with Albert Hackett), for play Diary of Anne Frank 1956, also, Antoinette Perry award 1956, N.Y. Drama Critics award 1956, Screen Writers Guild award, Laurel award 1956); Author: The Third Adam, 1967. Mem. Dramatists Guild, Authors League. Clubs: Vassar (N.Y.C.), Cosmopolitan (N.Y.C.). Died Jan. 29, 1984.*

GOODRICH, PAUL W., ret. business exec.; b. Oskaloosa, Iowa, Sept. 2, 1906; s. Harry and Stella (Guthrie) G.; A.B., Drake U., 1928; LL.B., Chgo. Kent Coll. Law, 1931; M.B.A., U. Chgo., 1947; m. Virginia Davis, Feb. 6, 1932; children—William D., James W., Carolyn. Joined Chgo. Title & Trust Co., 1931, pres., 1953-69, chmn. bd., 1967-71; hon. dir. Chgo. Title & Trust Co. Trustee Field Mus. Natural History; hon. trustee Northwestern Meml. Hosp. Mem. Am., Ill., Chgo. bar assns., Chgo. Assn. Commerce and Industry (pres. 1959-60), Am., Ill. title assns. Republican. Methodist. Clubs: Univ., Mid-Am., Econ., Chgo., Commercial (Chgo.); Indian Hill Country. Home: Kenilworth, Ill. Died Aug. 27, 1982.

GOODSON, LOUIS HOFFMAN, biochemist; b. Liberty, Mo., Apr. 5, 1913; s. William Hammack and Luella (Hoffman) G.; m. Dorothy Elizabeth Hoffman, Feb. 14, 1940; children—Eleanor, Marilyn, Cynthia. B.A., U. Mo., 1935; M.A., Harvard U., 1938, Ph.D., 1940. Chemist Maltbie Labs., Newark, 1940-44; asst. lab. dir. George A. Breon Co., Kansas City, Mo., 1944-47; with Midwest Research Inst., Kansas City, 1948-82, prin. biochemist, 1964-69, sr. advisor for biology, 1969-77, prin. advisor for biology, 1977-82. Author. Recipient Sci. award Council Prin. Scientists, 1974; grantee Nat. Cancer Inst., 1948-62; co-recipient IR-100 award, 1972, 76, 77. Mem. Am. Chem. Soc. (chmn. Kansas City 1956, nat. councilor 1957-60), Mo. Acad. Sci., Am. Def. Preparedness Assn., Kansas City Movie Makers, Nat. Assn. Watch and Clock Collectors, Clay County Mus. Assn. (dir. 1979-81), Sigma Xi. Baptist. Patentee immobilized enzymes for monitoring toxic materials in air and water. Home: Kansas City, Mo. Died Dec. 9, 1982; buried Liberty, Mo.

GOODSON, MAX REED, educator; b. Garrett, Ill., Feb. 5, 1911; s. Otis Richard and Eva (Reed) G.; B.A., U. Ill., 1933, M.A., 1936, Ed.M., 1942, Ed.D., 1949; m. Margaret Catherine Schnapp, June 5, 1935; children—Nancy Kay, Charles Robert. Tchr. elementary sch., Tuscola, Ill., 1933-34; sci. tchr. Community High Sch., Mason City, Ill., 1934-35; prin. Dana Twp. High Sch., Ill., 1935-36; sci. tchr. Univ. High Sch., U. Ill., 1936-43, coordinator student teaching Coll. Edn., 1943-44; curriculum cons. Community High Sch., Blue Island, Ill., 1940-41; instr. edn., asst. prin. Univ. Sch., Ind. U., 1944-45; coordinator curriculum and instrn. Horace-Mann Lincoln Sch., N.Y.C., 1945-46, prin., 1946-47; asst. dean. coordinator research and service Ohio State U., 1947-57, prof. edn., 1949-57, asso. dean Coll. Edn., 1957; dean, prof. sch. edn. Boston U., 1957-62; editor-in-chief high sch. div. Ginn & Co., Boston, 1962-65; prof. ednl. policy studies U. Wis., Madison, 1965-77, prof. social work, 1969-77, emeritus prof., 1977-84; dir. Wis. Research and Devel. Center for Cognitive Learning, 1965-67, prin. investigator planned ednl. change, 1965-70; trustee Corp. Upper Midwest Regional. Ednl. Lab., Mpls., 1965—, pres., 1967-68; fellow Midwest Group for Human Resources, Kansas City, Mo.; prof. edn. U. Fla., summers 1948-50; prof. U. Va., summers 1951-53; policy com., staff Nat. Tng. Labs., Bethel, Maine, 1949-60; dir. Midwest Center Human Relations Tng., 1954-57. Cons. Am. Cancer Soc., A.R.C., Lago Oil & Transport Co., Aruba, Dutch West Indies. Bd. govs. Human Relations Center, Boston U. Mem. N.E.A. (commn. on safety edn. 1955-59, Nat. Tng. Labs. Inst. for Applied Behavioral Scis. fellow), Mass. Council for Pub. Schs., Mass. Com. for Children and Youth, Am. Assn. Sch. Adminstrs., Phi Delta Kappa, Kappa Phi Kappa. Democrat. Unitarian. Author: (with Gale E. Jensen) Formal Organization in School Systems, 1956; 1960 Yearbooks of Nat. Soc. Study Edn.; (with others) Organization Development in Schools, 1971; Humanistic Considerations in Graduate Education and Research, 1977; Human Foresight and Moral Re-Education, 1978; also tech. reports, articles. Home: Green Valley, Ariz. Died July 31, 1984.

GOODSPEED, GEORGE EDWARD, univ. prof.; b. Boston, Mass., Apr. 16, 1887; s. George Edward and Isabel Sprague (Goddard) G.; grad. Roxbury Latin Sch. Boston, 1906; S.B., Mining Engring., M.I.T., 1910; m. Ludella Miriam Whittlesey, Dec. 31, 1916; children—Isabel Penelope (Mrs. George L. Poor), Josephine Whittlesey (Mrs. Gordon W. Dick). Asst. to Professor Robert H. Richards, Mass. Inst. Tech., 1910, asst. in dept. of geology, 1911-12; asst. geologist Oregon State Bureau of Mines and Geology, 1912-19; became instr. in geology, Oregon State Coll., Corvallis, 1912, advancing to prof., 1918-19; asst. prof. geology, U. of wash., 1919-28, prof. from 1934. and exec. officer dept. of geology 1936-52; cons. geologist Cornucopia Gold Mines, 1933-40; cons. mineral technologist U.S. Bureau of Mines, 1922-43; geologist U.S. Geol. Survey, summers 1943-45. Served as 1st lt., Corps of Engrs., U.S. Army, 1916-17; chief bomb reconnaissance agent for Seattle on staff of chief air raid warden, civilian protection div., Seattle War Commn., 1942-45, Mem. Geol. Soc. America, Am. Inst. Mining and Metall. Engrs., Am. Mineral. Soc. (v.p. 1957), Soc. Econ. Geologists, A.A.A.S., Research Soc. U. Washington, Northwest Sci. Assn., Seismological Society of America, American Association of Univ. Professors, Am. Geophys. Union, Am. soc. Mil. Engrs., Nat. Rifle Assn., Sigma Xi, Theta Xi. Episcopalian. Clubs: Faculty Men's, Kiwanis, Clankers (Seattle). Contbr. numerous tech. articles, especially on petrogenesis and granitization, to scientific publs. Home: Seattle, Wash. †

GOODWIN, FREDERICK DEANE, bishop; b. Cismont, Va., Nov. 5, 1888; s. Edward Lewis and Maria L. (Smith) G.; A.B., B.S. and A.M., William and Mary College, 1912, LL.D., 1951; B.D., Virginia Theological Seminary, 1917, Doctor of Divinity, 1928; LL.D., Hampden-Sidney Coll., 1935; studied Columbia University; m. Blanche Elbert Moncure, Oct. 16, 1917; children—Frederick Deane, Elbert Moncure, Edward Le Baron. Deacon, 1917, priest, 1918, P.E. Ch.; asst. minister Grace Ch.; Richmond, Va., July-Oct. 1917; rector Cople, Lunenburg and North Farnham parishes, Warsaw, Va. 1917-30; sec. for rural work Nat. Council P.E. Church, 1924-26; bishop coadjutor Diocese of Virginia, 1930-44, bishop of Virginia since 1944. Chairman bd. Church Schools of Diocese of Virginia, Episcopal High School (Alexandria, Va.), Virginia Theol. Sem. Mem. Kappa Sigma, Phi Beta Kappa. Mason. Author: Beyond City Limits, 1926. Compiler: Centennial Address of the Diocesan Missionary Society, 1929. Home: Richmond, Va. †

GOODWIN, GUY SPENCER, educator; b. Concordia, Kan., Jan. 3, 1887; s. John Charles and Lucy Margaret (Spencer) G.; A.B., Coll. of Emporia, Kan., 1911; student U. of Chicago, summer 1911, Harvard Grad. Sch., 1913-14; unmarried. Teacher prep. dept. Coll. of Emporia, 1911, and at Abbott Sch., Farmington, Me., 1914-17; headmaster Madison (Wis.) Day Sch., 1920-22; organizer, and head of Jr. Country Day Sch., Kansas City, Mo., 1922-25; founder, 1925, and headmaster Pembroke Sch. for Boys, Kansas City. Mem. Hdqrs. Co., 353d Inf., 89th Div., U.S.A., with A.E.F. in France, 1918. Mem. Headmasters' Assn., Country Day Sch. Assn. Republican. Presbyn. Clubs: Cooperative, Kansas City Athletic Club, Kansas City Chamber of Commerce. Travels abroad summers in charge school boys. Home: Concordia, Kan.†

GOODWIN, LEO, SR., ins. exec.; b. Lowndes, Mo., Dec. 30, 1886; s. Dr. Edward E. and Mary Ann (Smith) G.; ed. public schools, Mo. State Normal, home study accounting course; married Lottie Z. Evelsizer, Oct. 15, 1911 (dec.); 1 son, Leo; m. 2d, Lillian E. Sargent Wilson, Jan. 5, 1936. Underwriter, office mgr. United Services Automobile Assn. San Antonio, 1925-35; one of founders Govt. Employees Ins. Co., exec. v.p., 1936-48, pres., 1948-58, chmn., 1956-57; pres. Govt. Employees Corp., 1949-58; founder chmn., mem. exec. com., dir. Govt. Employees Ins. Co., Govt. Employees Life Ins. Co., Govt. Employees Corp., from 1958; (all Washington); dir. Riggs Nat. Bank, Washington; past pres. Nat. Assn. Independent Insurers, Chgo.; mem. adv. bd. Washington Mut. Investors Fund. Mem. Washington Bd. Trade, Clubs: Congressional Country (Washington); Coral Ridge Country, Phillips 66 (Ft. Lauderdale, Fla.). Home: Washington. †

GORDON, DONALD EDWARD, fine arts educator; b. N.Y.C., May 13, 1931; s. Edward and Ethel Cecelia (Branner) G.; m. Anne Elizabeth Waterson, Aug. 24, 1957 (div. 1973); children: Richard Edward, Thomas Hale; m. Joan Berend Morse, Sept. 9, 1979. B.A. cum laude, Harvard, 1952, M.A., 1953, Ph.D., 1960; postgrad., U. Hamburg, 1953-54, Art Students League, 1958-59. Asst. prof. fine arts Dickinson Coll., 1960-63, asso. prof. fine arts, 1963-69, chmn. dept. fine arts, 1960-69; prof. fine arts U. Pitts., from 1969; chmn. dept., dir. Henry Clay Frick Fine Arts Bldg., 1969-74; vis. prof. art history Columbia U., N.Y.C., 1981-82; Dir. Kirchner exhbn. displayed at Seattle Art Mus., Pasadena Art Mus., Mus. Fine Arts, Boston, 1968-69; cons. Fine Arts Inventory, U.S. Govt., 1972. Author: Ernst Ludwig Kirchner, 1968, Modern Art Exhibitions 1900-1916: Selected Catalogue Documentation, 1974; cons. editor: Art Exhbn. Catalogues on Microfiche, from 1976. Served with USN, 1955-57. Recipient Arthur K. Porter prize Coll. Art Assn. Am., 1967; Fulbright grantee U. Hamburg, 1953-54; Fulbright sr. research grantee U. Marburg, 1964-65; Humboldt grantee Inst. for Art History, Munich, 1967-68; Thyssen Found. research fellow, 1970-73; Am. Council Learned Socs. fellow, 1973-74. Mem. Coll. Art Assn. Am., Soc. Art, Religion and Contemporary Culture (dir.), Art Students League (life), AAUP (chpt. v.p. 1966-67), C.G. Jung Center for Analytical Psychology.

GORDON, JACK MURPHY, judge; b. Lake Charles, La., Feb. 13, 1931; s. Lawrence Raymond and Jewel Evangeline (Murphy) G.; m. Dianne Louise Weiss, May 26, 1956; children—Kathryn Ann, Jack Murphy. B.S., La. State U., 1951, J.D., 1954. Bar: La. bar. Asso. Phelps, Dunbar, Marks, Claverie & Sims, New Orleans, 1954-58, partner, 1958-71; U.S. dist. judge Eastern Dist. La., New Orleans, from 1971; Faculty mem. Practicing Law Inst. Seminars, 1973-74. Mem. Republican State Central Com. of La., 1966-71; chmn. Jefferson Parish Rep. Exec. Com., 1966-71. Served to lt. JAG Corps USAF, 1954-56. Mem. Am., La., New Orleans bar assns. Presbyn. Club: Stratford (New Orleans). Address: New Orleans, LA.*

GORDON, MORTIMOR S., lawyer, mfg. exec.; b. N.Y.C., June 21, 1905; s Jacob and Rose (Stiefel) G.; A.B., Columbia Coll., 1925, LL.B., 1927; m. Helen Roth, June 11, 1931 (dec. Feb. 1972); children—Barbara Jane, Elaine; m. 2d, Sydnée Davidson, May 1978. Admitted to N.Y. bar, 1927, since practiced in N.Y.C.; admitted to U.S. Supreme Ct., also other Fed. Cts.; dir., Continental Copper & Steel Industries, Inc., 1945-84, pres., dir., 1956-84, chmn. bd., chief exec. officer, 1970-77; counsel firm Hall, Dickler, Lawler, Kent & Howley. Trustee Fedn. Jewish Philanthropies, N.Y.C., Police Athletic League; trustee Congregation Emanu-El, chmn. law com., chmn. investment com. bd. visitors Columbia U. Sch. Law; adv. bd. Robert A. Taft Inst. Govt.; mng. dir. Met. Opera Assn., Inc.; pres. Gordon Found., Inc. Mem. Am., N.Y. State bar assns., N.Y. Co. Lawyers Assn., Am. Iron and Steel Inst., Navy League U.S. (life mem.). Home: New York, N.Y. Died Feb. 21, 1984.

GORDON, ROBERT DONALDSON, business exec.; b. La Crosse, Wis., Mar. 25, 1888; s. George H. and Stella (Goddard) G.; grad. Lake Forest Acad., 1908; LL.B., Cornell, 1911; m. Louise Gund, Dec. 29, 1917 (dec.); four children—m. 2d, Norma H. Bosworth, Aug. 21, 1936. Admitted to Wis. bar, 1911; practiced, La Crosse, 1911-17; investment banker, 1921-38; dir. Ashland Oil & Refining Co., Bowser, Incorporated, Johnson Farebox Company, also dir. Economy Portable Bldg. Co., Ky. Boon Coal Co. Served as lt. col., C.W.S., 1918-21. Mem. Chi Phi. Clubs: Univ., Attic (Chgo.). Home: Winnetka, Ill. †

GORDON, ROBERT S., multi-industrial corporation executive; b. Atlanta, Oct. 30, 1923; s. Nathan Morton and Dora G.; student U. So. Calif.; 1940-42; m. Jacqueline Gordon, May 11, 1953; children. Sales mgr. Community Rental Services, Los Angeles, 1947-53, exec. v.p., 1953-60; gen. partner Nathan M. Gordon Co., Beverly Hills, Calif., 1960-67; pres. Environmentals, Inc., Beverly Hills, 1967-72; corp. v.p. Angelica Corp., St. Louis, 1969-72, sr. v.p., 1972-78, pres., chief operating officer, 1978, pres., chief exec. officer, 1979-80, also dir. Served to lt. AC, U.S. Army, 1942-45. Republican. Office: Saint Louis, Mo. Dec. Oct. 1980. Interned, Calif.

GORDON, ROBERT WINSLOW, specialist in Am. folk-song; b. Bangor, Me., Sept. 2, 1888; s. Elijah Winslow and Harriet Adeline (Ewer) G.; grad. Phillips Exeter Acad., 1906; A.B., Harvard, 1910; m. Roberta Porter Paul, of Darien, Ga., Dec. 26, 1912; 1 dau., Roberta Paul. Asst. in English, Harvard, 1912-18; asst. prof. English, U. of Calif., 1918-25; Seldon fellow, Harvard, 1925-26; spl. consultant in music, Library of Congress, from 1927, also in charge Archive of Am. Folk-Song, Library of Congress, from Jan. 1929. Mem. Am. Folk-Lore Soc., Ky. Folk-Lore Soc., Am. Folk Dance Soc. (hon.), Folk-Song Soc. of the Northeast (hon.), Soc. for Preservation of Spirituals (hon.), Am. Dialect Soc., Modern Lang. Assn. America, Internat. Commn. of Popular Arts (U.S. sect.) Club: Harvard (Washington). Extensive contbr. on folk-song. Home: Washington, D.C. †

GORDON, RUTH, actress; b. Quincy, Mass., Oct. 30, 1896; d. Clinton and Annie Tapley (Ziegler) Jones; m. Gregory Kelly, 1918; 1 son, Jones Harris; m. Garson Kanin, Dec. 4, 1942. Ed. Quincy Schs. Made first appearance, Empire Theatre, N.Y.C., 1915; as Nibs in: (with Maude Adams) Peter Pan; other appearances include Seventeen, 1917-19, Saturday's Children, 1928, Serena Blandish, 1929, Hotel Universe, 1930, The Church Mouse, 1930-31, Ethan Frome, 1935, The Country Wife, 1936-37; Nora in: other appearances include A Doll's House, 1938; Natasha in: other appearances include The Three Sisters, 1942-43, Over Twenty-One, 1943-45, The Leading Lady, 1948, The Smile of the World, 1949, The Matchmaker, London and Berlin, 1954, N.Y.C., 1955, The Good Soup, 1960, A Time to Laugh, in London, 1962, My Mother, My Father and Me, 1963, The Loves of Cass McGuire, 1966; Dreyfus in: other appearances include Rehearsal, 1974, Mrs. Warren's Profession, 1976, films; Mary Todd in: Abe Lincoln in Illinois, 1939; Mrs. Ehrlich in: Dr. Ehrlich's Magic Bullet, 1939, Two Faced Woman, Action in the North Atlantic, Edge of Darkness, Inside Daisy Clover, 1965, Lord Love a Duck, 1966, Rosemary's Baby, 1968 (Acad. award Best Supporting Actress), Whatever Happened to Aunt Alice? , 1969, Where's Poppa? , 1970, Harold and Maude, 1971, The Big Bus, 1976, Every Which Way But Loose, 1978, Brighton Beach, 1979, Any Which Way You Can, 1980; TV films Isn't It Shocking, 1973, Prince of Central Park, 1975, Rosemary's Baby II, 1976, The Great Houdini, 1976, Perfect Gentlemen, 1978, Scavenger Hunt, 1979; guest appearance: TV shows Kojak, 1975, Rhoda, 1975, Medical Story, 1975; playwright, star: TV shows A Very Rich Woman, 1965, Ho! Ho! Ho!, 1976; TV Mommy in The American Dream, 1963, Madame Arcati in Blithe Spirit; Author: plays The Leading Lady; (with Garson Kanin) screenplays Pat and Mike; Myself Among Others, 1971; autobiography My Side, 1976, An Open Book, 1980, Shady Lady, 1981; Contbr. to: (with Garson Kanin) autobiography N.Y. Times (Winner Emmy award for appearance on Taxi 1979). Gold medal Holland Soc., 1980. Address: PO Box 585 Edgartown MA 02539 Office: 200 W 57th St Suite 1203 New York NY 10019

GORDON, SETH, (EDWIN GORDON) wildlife cons., writer; b. Richfield, Pa., Apr. 2, 1890; s. G.B.M. and Caroline (Wochley) G.; m. Dora Belle Silverthorn, Jan. 29, 1910; children—Seth Edwin (dec.), Phyllis Rowena Gordon Stephenson. Student, New Bloomfield Acad., 1907, Pa. Bus. Coll., 1911; D.Sc. (hon.), U. Mich., 1953. Pub. sch. tchr., Pa., 1907-11; stenographer-clk. Pa. Steel Co. (now Bethlehem Steel), 1911-13; game protector Pa. Game Commn., 1913-15, asst. sec., 1915-19, sec., chief game protector, 1919-26, exec. dir., 1936-48; conservation dir. Izaak Walton League Am., Chgo., 1926-31; pres. Am. Game Assn. N.Y.C., Washington, 1931-35; wildlife cons., writer, from 1948; cons. Calif. Wildlife Conservation Bd., 1948-51; dir. Calif. Dept. Fish and Game, 1951-59; founder, sec. Am. Wildlife Inst., 1935; Mem. migratory bird adv. bd. U.S. Biol. Survey, 1932-35; mem., sec. Nat. Com. Wildlife Legislation, 1928-38; mem. forestry research adv. com. U.S. Dept. Agr., 1952-62, mem. Pres.' water pollution control adv. bd. to surgeon gen. U.S., 1958-61. Trustee N. Am. Wildlife Found., 1948-75, v.p., 1948-73; pres. Keystone (Pa.) council Boy Scouts Am., 1946, mem. conservation com., 1956-64. Recipient Aldo Leopold award Wildlife Soc., 1967; Seth Gordon award Internat. Assn. Fish and Wildlife Agys., 1970; Spl. Cons. award Nat. Wildlife Fedn., 1978. Mem. Internat. Assn. Fish and Wildlife Agys. (hon. life mem., past pres., gen. counsel 1963—), Western Assn. State Game and Fish Commrs. (hon. life), Am. Fisheries Soc. (hon. life mem., past sec. and pres.), Am. Forestry Assn. (past v.p.), Nat. Rifle Assn. (dir. 24 years, endowment mem., mem. hunting and conservation com. 1958-69, 71-77), Wildlife Mgmt. Inst., Outdoor Writers Am., Wildlife Soc. (hon. life mem.), Izaak Walton League Am. (Founders award 1959, hon. nat. pres. 1961-62, Hall of Fame 1969, nat. life mem. 1978). Republican. Lutheran. Clubs: Cosmos (Washington); Wilderness (Phila.) (hon.); Camp Fire (N.Y.C.) (hon.). Home: Sacramento, CA.

GORE, GEORGE WILLIAM, JR., educator; b. Nashville, July 11, 1901; s. George William and Emma Joe (Hambrick) G.; A.B., DePauw U., 1923, LL.D., 1966; student U. Chgo., 1924; M.Ed., Harvard, 1928; Ph.D., Columbia, 1940; LL.D., U. Miami, 1969; Litt.D., U. Fla., 1969; m. Pearl M. Winrow, Sept. 4, 1927; 1 child, Pearl Mayo. Sec. colored br. YMCA, Marion, Ind., 1923; head dept. English, Agrl. and Indsl. State Coll., Nashville, 1923-27, dean instrn., 1927-50; pres. Fla. A. and M. U., 1950-68, emeritus, 1968-82; lectr. George Peabody Coll. Tchrs., Nashville, 1969-82; interim pres. Fisk U., 1976-77, cons. to pres., 1978-82; chmn. Conf. on Coll. Projects, 1957-58; dir. Citizens Savs. Bank, Nashville. Vice chmn. Fla. Civil Def. Council, 1966-82; chmn. Council Former Presidents of Black Colls., 1977-82. Trustee Nashville Kent Coll. Law, Fla. Meml. Coll.; rep. Nat. Bapt. Conv. Am., div. religious edn. Nat. Council Chs. Christ; mem. bd. control So. Regional Edn., 1950—; mem.-at-large nat. council Boy Scouts Am. Recipient DePauw U. Alumni citation, 1952; Distinguished Service award Nat. Newspaper Pubs. Assn., 1963; Medal of Honor, Alpha Phi Alpha, 1966; Disting. Service award Nat. Assn. Equal Opportunities in Higher Edn., 1979. Mem. Assn. Coll. Honor Socs. (exec. com., v.p. 1957-61), Nat. Soc. Coll. Tchrs. Edn.,

Nat. Soc. Study Edn., Nat. Assn. Coll. Deans and Registrars (pres. 37-38), Am. Tchrs. Assn. (pres. 1949-51), NEA (v.p. 1952-53, vice chmn. nat. commn. of def. of democracy through edn. 1954-58), Fla. Council Pres. (chmn. 1953-58), Agora Assembly, Assn. Colls. and Secondary Schs. (pres. 1950-51), Nat. Conf. Pres. Land Grant Colls. (exec. com. 1951-54), Alpha Kappa Mu (founder, pres. 1944-46, exec. sec., treas. 1946-82), Fla. Assn. Colls. and Univs. (mem. exec. com. 1962-63, recipient Distinguished Service certificate and medallion 1969), Delta Phi Delta, Sigma Pi Phi (grand sire archon 1954-56), Alpha Phi Alpha, Kappa Delta Pi (Service Key 1956), Beta Kappa Chi, Alpha Phi Omega, and Scabbard and Blade. Mason, Elk, K.P. Author: Negro Journalism, 1923; In-Service Improvement of Public School Teachers in Tennessee, 1940. Contbg. editor Quarterly Rev. Higher Edn. Among Negroes, 1935—. Home: Nashville, Tenn. Dec. Sept. 10, 1982. Interned Nashville.

GORE, JACK WORTER, editor, publisher; b. Evansville, Ind., Aug. 8, 1916; s. Robert Hayes and Lorena (Haury) G.; B.S., John B. Stetson U., 1939; m. Bettylou Stickrod, Nov. 19, 1941; children—John Christopher Richard Stewart, David Stephen, Laurence Douglas. Bus. mgr. Daytona Beach (Fla.) Sun-Record, 1939-40; with Ft. Lauderdale (Fla.) News, 1945-76, columnist, cashier, sports editor, 1945-47, editor, 1947-69, editor, pub., 1969-76; ret., 1976; dir. Chgo. Tribune, N.Y. News Syndicate, N.Am. Co., Ft. Lauderdale. Served with USNR, 1941-45. Recipient First Place Editorial award Freedom Found., 1953, Distinguished Service award, 1969; Med. Journalism award A.M.A., 1971; named Citizen of Year, Fraternal Order of Police, 1972. Mem. C. of C., Sigma Delta Chi, Sigma Nu. Club: Coral Ridge Country (Fort Lauderdale). Home: Fort Lauderdale, Fla. Died May 15, 1982.

GORKIN, JESS, editor; b. Rochester, N.Y., Oct. 23, 1913; s. Barnett and Bessie (Berk) G.; m. Dorothy Kleinberg, June 23, 1940; children: Michael, Brett, Scott. B.A., U. Iowa, 1936. Editor-in-chief Daily Iowan, Iowa City, 1936-37; assoc. editor Look Mag., N.Y.C., 1937-41; originated and edited picture mag. for distbn. in friendly and occupied countries Photo Review, OWI, 1942-46; mng. editor Parade, N.Y.C., 1947-49, editor, 1949-79, cons. editor, 1983-85; editor 50 Plus, N.Y.C., 1979-85. Recipient Christopher Award, 1956, citation Overseas Press Club, 1955, editorial award Nat. Comdr. Am. Legion. Mem. Overseas Press Club, Sigma Delta Chi. Club: Dutch Treat. Home: Longboat Key, Fla. Died Feb. 19, 1985.

GORMLEY, ROBERT EMMETT, banker; b. Cuthbert, Ga., Sept. 25, 1889; s. Patrick Henry and Ellen Celeste Gormley; M.A., St. Mary's Coll., Belmont, N.C.; m. Rebecca Graham, Nov. 27, 1918; children—Celeste (Mrs. J. T. Greer), Gloria (Mrs. R. C. Weston). Banker, Cuthbert, 1910-11, 12-30; supt. banks State of Ga., 1931-39; v.p. Ga. Savs. Bank & Trust Co., Atlanta, from 1939. Mem. Independent Bankers Am. (pres. 1958), Ga. Bankers Assn. (pres. 1946). Club: Rotary of Atlanta. †

GORNITZKA, ODD, religious educator; b. Tistedalen, Norway, Apr. 2, 1887; s. Karl Peter Waldemar and Julie (Haagaas) G.; student St. Olaf Coll., Northfield, Minn., 1908-11; C.T., Luth. Sem., St. Paul, 1914; m. Anna Sophie Monson, of Eleva, Wis., June 12, 1915; children—Rolf Orlando, Arnold Ruben, Hjordis Sylvia, Elsa Valborg. came To U.S., 1908, naturalized, 1913. Ordained to ministry Norwegian Luth. Ch., 1914; pastor Seattle, Wash., 1914-22, Farwell, Minn., 1922-25; prof. Luth. Bible Inst., Minneapolis, 1925-31, dean same from 1931. Dir. Gateway Gospel Mission, Minneapolis. Editor of The Bible Banner; contbr. religious publs. Home: St. Paul, Minn. †

GORNOWSKI, EDWARD JOHN, research co. exec.; b. Wilmington, Del., Feb. 27, 1918; s. Stanley and Kathryn (Zieniewicz) G.; m. Dorothy M. Galvin, Aug. 15, 1942; children—Edward J., Thomas A., Dorothy Sue, David P. B. Ch.E., Villanova Coll., 1938; Ph.D., U. Pa., 1942. Sr. engr. Exxon Research Labs, Baton Rouge, 1942-45, sr. devel. engr. devel. div., Linden, N.J., 1945-54, dir. petroleum devel., 1954-62, dep. to v.p., 1962-64; mgr. chem. products Bayway Refinery, Exxon Co. U.S.A., Linden, 1964-65; mgr. coordination and planning dept. Exxon Corp., N.Y.C., 1965-66; v.p. Esso Europe Inc., London, 1966-69; exec. v.p. Esso Research & Engr. Co., Florham Park, N.J., 1969-83. Mem. Nat. Acad. Engrs., Am. Inst. Chem. Engrs., Am. Chem. Soc., Am. Petroleum Inst., Sigma Xi, Alpha Chi Sigma. Patentee petroleum processing. Home: Scotch Plains, N.J. Died Dec. 19, 1983; buried Fairview Cemetery, Westfield, N.J.

GOSHEY, FRANK JOSEPH, retired govt. ofcl.; b. Holder, Ill., Oct. 12, 1887; s. John and Katherine (Compas) G.; student pub. schs. of Minn. and Wis.; m. Genevieve B. Miller, June 21, 1916; children—Katherine (Mrs. Alban W. Ruhland), Mary E. (Mrs. Eugene F. Barrett). Rural sch. tchr., Minn., 1907-08; prin. schs., Chandler, Minn., 1908-09, 10-11; ry. postal clk. Post Office Dept., 1910-11, 12-19, post office insp., St. Louis, St. Paul divisions, 1919-53, dist. operations mgr., Indpls., 1953, regional operations manager, Minneapolis, 1954-55, regional director, 1956-57. Recipient of the 1st Annual Distinguished Service Award, Minnesota Chpt. Am. Soc. for Pub. Adminstrn., 1956. Mem. Cath. Order Foresters. Catholic. K.C. Clubs: Serra (Mpls.); St. Lukes Mens' (St. Paul). †

GOSHORN, R. C., newspaper publisher; b. Winterset, Ia., May 8, 1890; s. Arthur and Kate (Shriver) G.; student Ia. State U., 1909-11; m. Lenore Rhyno, Dec. 11, 1920; 1 dau., Betty Goshorn Handy. Pub. weekly newspaper in Winterset, Ia., 1912-17, Eagle Grove, Ia., 1920-26; pub. two daily newspapers in Jefferson City, Mo., from 1926. Served in armed forces in World War I. Pres. Tribune Printing Co., New Tirbune Co., Capital Broadcasting Co. Past pres. Assn., C. of C.; mem. Sigma Delta Chi. Mason (Shriner); Elk. Club: Rotary (Jefferson City, Mo.). Home: Jefferson City, Mo. Died Apr. 14, 1953.†

GOSSETT, CHARLES C., senator; b. Pricetown, O., Sept. 2, 1888; s. Wyatt Henry and Maggie (Finnegan) G.; ed. public schools; m. Clara Louise Fleming, Nov. 28, 1916; children—James Wyatt, Robert Milton, Charles Elmer. Served in Ida. Ho. of Reps. (from Canyon County), 1933-36; lt. gov. of Idaho, 1937-38, 1941-42, became gov., 1945; apptd. to U.S. Senate Nov. 1945, to fill vacancy caused by death of John Thomas. Mem. Chamber of Commerce. Democrat. Mem. Christian Church. Mason, Elk, Eagle, Grange. Club: Countrymen's (Boise). Address: Boise, Idaho. Deceased.

GOTT, PHILIP PORTER, pub. relations cons.; b. La Grange, Ohio, Dec. 11, 1889; s. Charles W. and Laura (Lincoln) G.; A.B., Oberlin Coll., 1915; A.M. Columbia U., 1917; m. Ethel Hastings, June 26, 1919; children—Porter Hastings, Laura Jane. Research work, Bureau of Municipal Research, N.Y. City, 1915-16; sec. C. of C., Berlin, New Hampshire, 1917; with Akron Builders Exchange and Ohio State Builders Assn., 1919-28; asst. mgr. and mgr. Trade Assn. Dept., U.S. C. of C., 1928-41; pres., Nat. Confectioners' Assn., 1941-58; v.p. in charge pub. relations August Burghard, Inc., 1959-61; public relations consultant, college visitor, director American Viewpoint, Incorporated, from 1961; speaker and lecturer National Institute for Commercial and Trade Assn. Execs., summer conf., Northwestern U., 1930-48; del. Internat. Cocoa Conf., London, Eng., Sept. 1949. Mem. Washington, D.C. Bar. American Trade Assn. Execs., Washington Trade Assn. Execs., Pub. Relations Soc. of Am., Trade Assn. Execs. Forum Chgo., Greater Ft. Lauderdale C. of C., Oberlin College Alumni Assn. (pres. 1955-58), Mason (Shriner, K.T.). Club: Coral Ridge Yacht. Co-author, editor: All About Candy and Chocolate, 1958. Contbr. articles to numerous trade publs. Home: Ft. Lauderdale, Fla. †

GOTTSHALL, RALPH K(ERR), mfg. exec.; b. Lansdale, Pa., Dec. 31, 1965; s. Harvey S. and Alice (Kerr) G.; B.S. magna cum laude, Lafaytete Coll., 1927, D.Sc. (honorary), 1959; was married to Lorraine Lively, September 4, 1929. With Atlas Chemical Industries, Inc., since 1927, dir. sales, 1943-48, asst. gen. mgr., explosives dept., 1948-50, v.p. and dir. 1951-52, exec. v.p., dir., 1952, president, 1953-58, chmn. bd., pres., 1958-66, chmn. bd., 1966-83; dir. Mfrs. Hanover Corp., Mfrs. Hanover Trust Co., The Phila., Balt. & Washington R.R., Balt. & Eastern R.R. Co., Alleghany Corp., Alan Wood Steel Co., Diamond State Telephone Co., The News-Jours. Co. Mem. Nat. Indsl. Conf. Bd. Bd. dirs. Nutrition Found.; pres. bd. trustees Wilmington (Del.) Med. Center; life trustee, pres. bd. trustees Lafayette Coll. Mem. Mfg. Chemists Association (member of the board of directors, past chmn.), Am. Mining Congress (director mfg. sect.), N.A.M., Phi Beta Kappa, Alpha Chi Sigma, Kappa Phi Kappa, Kappa Delta Rho. Clubs: University, Pinnacle (N.Y.C.); Wilmington, Wilmington Country. Home: Wilmington, Del. Died Sept. 11, 1983.

GOTTWALD, FLOYD DEWEY, chem. co. exec.; b. Richmond, Va., May 22, 1898; s. William H. and Mary A. Gottwald; student William and Mary Coll.; m. Anna Cobb, Nov. 17, 1919; children—Floyd Dewey, Bruce Cobb. Asst. paymaster Richmond Fredericksburg & Potomac R.R. Co., 1917-18; with Ethyl Corp. (formerly Albemarie Paper Mfg. Co.), Richmond, 1918-82, successively export mgr., asst. sec., sec., prodn. mgr., v.p., exec. v.p., pres., chmn. bd., chief exec. officer, chmn. exec. com., vice chmn. bd., vice chmn. exec. com., also dir. Trustee U. Richmond. Mem. Richmond C. of C. Baptist. Mason. Clubs: Commonwealth, Country of Virginia. Home: Richmond, Va. Died July 31, 1982.

GOTTWALD, FLOYD DEWEY, JR., chem. co. exec.; b. Richmond, Va., July 29, 1922; s. Floyd Dewey and Ann (Cobb) G.; B.S., Va. Mil. Inst., 1943; M.S., U. Richmond, 1951; m. Elisabeth Morris Shelton, Mar. 22, 1947; children—William M., James T., John D. With Albemarle Paper Co., Richmond, 1943-82, sec., 1956-57, v.p., sec., 1957-62, pres., 1962-82, also dir.; exec. v.p. Ethyl Corp., 1962-64, vice chmn., now chmn.; dir. Seaboard Coast Line Industries Inc. Trustee V.M.I. Found., Inc., U. Richmond. Served to 1st lt. U.S. Army Res., 1943-46. Decorated Bronze Star medal, Purple Heart. Mem. Va. Inst. Sci. Research (trustee), Am. Petroleum Inst. (dir.). Home: Richmond, Va. Died July 31, 1982.

GOUGE, SIR ARTHUR, aero. engr.; b. Northfleet, Kent, Eng., July 3, 1890; s. George and Elizabeth (Wickham) G.; student Ch. of Eng. Sch., Gravesend Tech. Sch.; B.Sc., Woolwich Poly., 1922; m. Margaret Ellen Cook, Sept. 1918 (dec.); children—James Arthur, Margaret Kathleen. Mechanic Short Bros., Ltd., 1915, became chief designer, 1926, gen. mgr., 1929, vice chairman, 1939-43; vice chairman, chief executive Saunders-Roe, Limited, from 1943; research in flying boat hull form and metal aircraft since 1920; Wilbur Wright Meml. lectr., 1948. Freeman, City of Rochester, 1937. Created knight, 1948. Awarded British Gold Medal for Aeronautics, 1937; Musick Meml. Trophy, 1939. Honorary fellow Royal Aero. Soc. (pres. 1942-44); fellow Institute of Aeronautical Sciences; member Institution Mechanical Engrs., Soc. Brit. Aircraft Constructors (pres. 1945). Clubs: Royal Aero, Royal Automobile (Eng.). Home: Wootton, Isle of Wight. †

GOUGH, HAROLD ROBERT, business exec.; b. Somerset, Eng., Dec. 15, 1889; s. Robert and Annie (Ralph) G.; student Merchant Venturer's Tech. Coll., Bristol, Eng., 1901-05; m. Barbara Tait, Apr. 30, 1941. With Brit.-Am. Tobacco Co., Ltd., London, from 1905, pres., from 1950; with Tobacco Securities Trust Co., Ltd., London, from 1948, chmn. Home: London, Eng. †

GOULD, CHESTER, cartoonist; b. Pawnee, Okla., Nov. 20, 1900; s. Gilbert R. and Alice M. (Miller) G.; m. Edna Gauger, Nov. 6, 1926; 1 dau., Jean. Student, Okla. A. & M. U., 1919-21; grad., Northwestern U., 1923. Cartoonist Hearst Publs., 1924-29, Chgo. Tribune, 1931-77, ind. cartoonist, 1977-85. Creator: cartoon Dick Tracy, 1931; appearing in cartoon, Chgo. Tribune-N.Y. News Syndicate, Inc., and syndicated newspapers. Mem. Nat. Cartoonists Soc., Lambda Chi Alpha. Clubs: Tavern, Lake Zurich Golf, Woodstock Country. Home: Woodstock, Ill. Died May 11, 1985.

GOULD, FREDRICK G., lawyer; b. Chgo., Aug. 22, 1943; s. Benjamin Z. and Shirley (Handleman) G. B.A., Washington U., St. Louis, 1965; J.D. cum laude, Northwestern U., 1968. Bar: Ill. bar 1968. Asso. firm Gould & Ratner, Chgo., 1968-74, partner, from 1974; dir., v.p., gen. counsel and sec. Feinberg Group, Inc., Feinberg Devel. Corp., Queensway Devel. Corp., Dana Assos.; sec. 208 Liquidating Co.; gen. counsel Queensway Hilton Hotel, Port of Long Beach, Calif.; v.p., asst. sec. Standard Forgings Corp., Century-Am. Corp., Century Steel Corp., Dave Hokin Found., Red Eagle Marine Inc., S.T.W. Inc. Editorial bd.: Northwestern U. Law Rev. Bd. dirs. Hebrew Theol. Coll., Lincoln Park/Lake View Jewish Community Center.; Mem. Navy Found. Children's Therapeutic Edn. Mem. Navy League U.S., Am., Ill. State, Chgo. bar assns., Chgo. Council Lawyers, Alpha Epsilon Pi. Jewish (dir.). Clubs: Standard, Chicago Yacht. Home: Chicago, Ill.

GOULD, GLENN HERBERT, pianist, composer; b. Toronto, Can., Sept. 25, 1932; s. Russell Herbert and Florence (Greig) G.; student Royal Conservatory of Music, Toronto, 1943-52; sr. matriculation, Malvern Collegiate, Toronto, 1951. Profl. debut as soloist Toronto Symphony Orch., 1947; U.S. debut in recital, Washington, 1955; concert tours U.S., 1956-59, Europe, 1958; European debut as soloist Moscow Philharmonic Orch., 1957; recorded Bach's Godberg Variations, Columbia Records, 1956, Beethoven Sonatas, Opus 109, 110, 111, Bach Concerto in D and F minors, Beethoven Concerto in B flat and C majors, Bach Partitas Nos. 5, 6, Haydn Sonata in E Flat major, Mozart Sonata C major; composer: A String Quartet (world premiere Canadian Broadcasting Corp., 1956; first pub. performance Stratford (Ont.) Mus. Festival 1956). Home: Toronto, Ont., Canada. Died Sept. 6, 1982.

GOULD, HARLEY NATHAN, prof. biology; b. W. Springfield, Pa., Oct. 17, 1887; s. William Nathan and Mabel (DeWolf) G.; A.B., Allegheny Coll., Meadville, Pa., 1910; A.M., Princeton, 1914, Ph.D., 1916; m. Mary Raymond (M.D.), of New Orleans, La., June 9, 1922; children—Mary Louise (dec.), Alfred Raymond. Instr. zoölogy, U. of Calif., 1916-17; asst. prof. anatomy, W.Va. U., 1917-18, U. of Pittsburgh, 1918-19; prof. biology, Wake Forest Coll., 1920-22; asst. prof. anatomy, Med. Sch., Tulane U., 1922-24; prof. biology, Newcomb Coll. (Tulane U.), since 1924. Mem. Am. Assn. Anatomists, Soc. Exptl. Biology and Medicine, Am. Assn. of Phys. Anthropologists. Episcopalian. Contbr to zoöl., anat. and anthrop. publs. Home: New Orleans, La. †

GOURLEY, JAMES EDWIN, librarian; b. Birmingham, Ala., June 13, 1908; s. Ed and Addie (Ozena) G.; A.B., Howard Coll., Birmingham, 1930; B.S., Columbia, 1931; postgrad. U. Tulsa; m. Virginia B. Ewing, Nov. 10, 1934; children—Dorothy Ewing, James Edwin. Page, jr. library asst. Birmingham Pub. Library, 1922-30; reference asst. N.Y. Pub. Library, 1930-37; dir. Pub. Library, Charlotte, N.C., 1937-39; asst. to librarian Racquet and Tennis Club, N.Y., 1933-37; librarian Tulsa Pub. Library, 1939-62; chief of Aero Center Libraries FAA, 1962-73. Served as lt. USNR, 1942-45. Mem. A.L.A., Oklahoma Library Assn. (past pres.), Sigma Nu, Kappa Phi Kappa. Democrat. Methodist. Compiler: (with Robert M. Lester) The Diffusion of Knowledge, 1935; Regional American Cookery, 1936; Eating Round the World, 1937. Contbr. articles profl. jours. Home: Gainesville, Fla. Died Jan. 26, 1983; buried Birmingham, Ala.

GOWAN, SISTER M. OLIVIA, nursing edn.; b. Stillwater, Minn., Mar. 15, 1888; d. William and Margaret (Lawler) Gowan; R.N., St. Mary's Sch. of Nursing, Duluth, Minn., 1912; Novitiate, Villa Scholastica, Duluth, Minn., 1912-14; B.S., Coll. of St. Scholastica, Duluth,

Minn., 1925; A.M. Columbia, 1932; Doctor of Laws (honorary), Boston College, 1948. Instructor, St. Mary's School for Nursing, 1914-15; supervisor, operating room, St. Joseph's Hosp., Brainerd, Minn., 1915-16; supt. St. Mary's Hosp., Duluth, Minn., 1916-26; prin. St. Gertrude's Sch., Washington D.C., 1926-32; dir. div. of nursing edn. Catholic U. of America, 1932-35, dean of sch., from 1935, prof. nursing edn.; v.p. St. Gertrude's Sch., Washington; cons. training committee in Psychiatric Nursing, USPHS, on Hospitals and Nursing, to Sisters of Saint Benedict, Duluth, Minn., 1956-57. Member advisory council Nursing Service VA; hon. civilian cons. Bur. Medicine and Surgery, USN. Hon. fellow Am. Hospital Assn.; mem. Nat. League for Nursing (collegiate bd., accrediting service), Grad. Nurses Assn. Nat. Cath. Edn. Assn. (mem. edn. com. on nursing). Author: Institutes and Workshops. Editor of Studies in Nursing Edn., from 1934. Contbr. profl. jours. Made survey Cath. schs. of nursing Brazil, S.A.; attended Internat. Council Nurses, Rome, 1957. Home: Washington, D.C. †

GOYEN, CHARLES WILLIAM, author; b. Trinity, Tex., Apr. 24, 1915; s. Charles Provine and Mary Inez (Trow) G.; m. Doris Roberts, Nov. 10, 1963. B.A., Rice U., 1937, M.A., 1939. Instr. English New Sch. for Social Research, N.Y.C., 1955-60; asso. in English Columbia, 1964-66; sr. editor trade dept. McGraw Hill, 1966-71; vis. prof. English Brown U., 1973—; lectr. writing program Princeton U., 1976-78; writer in residence Hollins Coll., 1979; vis. writer U. Houston, 1981, U. So. Calif., 1981, 82, 83. Author: (novels) The House of Breath, 1950, 25th anniversary edit., 1975; In a Farther Country, 1955, The Fair Sister, 1963, Come The Restorer, 1974, Wonderful Plant, 1980, Arcadio, 1983; (short stories) Ghost and Flesh, 1952; The Faces of Blood Kindred, 1960, Selected Writings, 1974, The Collected Stories, 1975, O. Henry Prize Stories, 1976; (non-fiction) A Book of Jesus, 1973; (plays) The House of Breath, 1956; The Diamond Rattler, 1960, Christy, 1964, House of Breath, Black/White, 1971, Aimee, 1973; also critical pieces in N.Y. Times, 1950—; Translator: The Lazy Ones (Albert Cossery). Recipient mus. awards (words and music) A.S.C.A.P., 1964, 65, 68, 70, 71, award Tex. Inst. Arts and Letters, 1950; Distinguished Alumnus award Rice U., 1977; Guggenheim fellow, 1950, 52; Ford Found. grantee, 1963-64. Died Aug. 29, 1983.

GRABACH, JOHN ROBERT, artist; b. Greenfield, Mass.; s. John Robert and Genevefa (Asam) G.; m. Anna Thompson. Student, Art Students League, N.Y.C. Instr. Newark Sch. Fine and Indsl. Art, from 1930. Author: Drawing and Painting the Human Figure, 1956; one man shows include, Art Inst. Chgo., 1930, Grand Central Galleries, N.Y.C., 1952, Montclair (N.J.) Art Mus., 1950, Meml. Art Gallery, Rochester, N.Y., 1935, Nat. Collection Fine Arts, Washington, 1980, retrospective, Graham Gallery, N.Y.C., 1981, group exhbns. include, Springfield (Mass.) Art Mus., Audubon Artists, Pa. Acad. Fine Arts, N.A.D., Detroit Inst. Arts, Corcoran Gallery Art, Art Inst. Chgo., Carnegie Inst., Los Angeles Mus., Buffalo Fine Arts Acad., Pan Am. Exhbn., Los Angeles, Panama Pacific Internat. Exposition, San Francisco, Old White Art Colony, White Sulphur Springs, W. Va., Richmond (Ind.) Pub. Art Gallery, Art Club Phila., Montclair Art Mus., Gallery Sci. and Art, N.Y. Worlds Fair 1940, Meml. Art. Gallery, Rochester, J.B. Speed Meml. Mus., Louisville, Cin. Mus., Art Assn. Indpls., City Art Mus., St. Louis, Toledo Mus. Art, Columbus (Ohio) Gallery Fine Arts; represented in permanent collections, Phila. Art Alliance, Art Inst. Chgo., Vanderpoel Art Assn., Chgo., John Herron Art Inst., Indpls., Corcoran Gallery Art, IBM Gallery, Norton Mus., Fla., Sea Isle, Fla., Newark Mus., Smithsonian Instn., also pvt. colls. Recipient Peabody prize Art Inst. Chgo., 1930, Sesnam gold medal Pa. Acad. Fine Arts, 1927, Preston Harrison prize Los Angeles Mus., 1928, 2d William A. Clark prize and silver medal Corcoran Gallery Art, 1932, IBM medal N.Y. World Fair, 1940, R. Stern prize Audubon Artists, 1953, hon. mention Salmagundi Club, 1961, hon. mention Herman Wick prize, 1961, Seley Purchase prize, 1963, gold medal of honor Am. Artists Profl. League, 1965, gold medal of honor Knickerbocker Artists, N.Y., 1965; named N.J. Artist of Yr., 1968. Mem. Audubon Artists, Salmagundi Club. Address: Irvington, NJ.

GRABAU, RICHARD FRED, educator; b. Buffalo, Sept. 4, 1926; s. Alexander August and Anna Ernestine (Welkner) G.; B.A., Capital U., 1949; M.A., Yale, 1951, Ph.D., 1953; m. Frances E. Wildermuth, Feb. 3, 1951; children—Elizabeth, Kathryn, Charlotte, Susan. Instr. Yale, New Haven, 1952-53; asso. prof. Hanover Coll., 1953-58; vis. lectr. Williams Coll., Williamstown, Mass., 1958; mem. faculty Purdue U., West Lafayette, Ind., 1958-80, prof. philosophy, 1968-80, head dept., 1972-80. Served with AUS, 1946-47. Fulbright research fellow, Heidelberg, Germany, 1968-69. Mem. Am. Philos. Assn., AAUP, Soc. Phenomenology and Existential Philosophy, Metaphys. Soc. Am. Author trans. and introduction The Philosophy of Existence (Karl Jaspers), 1968. Home: West Lafayette, Ind. Died Sept. 15, 1980.

GRABB, WILLIAM CLARENCE, plastic surgeon; b. Rochester, N.Y., July 10, 1928; s. Clarence Frederick and Frances (Watley) G.; m. Cozette Aleen Tweedie, Aug. 25, 1951; children: Betsy Grabb Suits, David William, Anne Cozette. B.S. cum laude, Mich. State U., 1950; M.D., U. Mich., 1953. Diplomate: Am. Bd. Plastic Surgeons (dir. from 1978, vice chmn. residency rev. com. from 1980). Intern Ohio State U. Hosp., 1953-54; resident in gen. surgery U. Mich. Hosp., 1954-55, 57-59; resident in plastic surgery St. Joseph Mercy Hosp., Ann Arbor, 1959-61; mem. faculty U. Mich. Med. Sch., 1961-82, prof. plastic surgery, head sect., 1976-82. Co-editor: Plastic Surgery, 3d edit, 1979, Cleft Lip and Palate: Surgical, Dental and Speech Aspects, 1971, Skin Flaps, 1975, Reconstruction and Rehabilitation of the Burned Patient, 1979; contbr. articles to profl. jours., chpts. to books. Served to capt. M.C. USAF, 1955-57. Mem. Am. Soc. Plastic and Reconstructive Surgeons (dir. 1974-75, assoc. editor jour. 1973-79, pres. ednl. found. 1974-75, Robert H. Ivy award 1966, essay prize 1969), Am. Assn. Hand Surgeons (dir. 1969-73), Am. Soc. Surgery Hand (essay prize 1968), Am. Assn. Plastic Surgeons, Plastic Surgery Research Council, Am. Fedn. Clin. Research, Internat. Soc. Aesthetic Plastic Surgery, Am. Cleft Palate Assn. (co-editor jour. 1969-73), Am. Burn Assn., A.C.S., AMA, Turkish Soc. Plastic Surgeons (hon.), Balloon Fedn. Am. (pres. 1971-73). Home: Ann Arbor, Mich.

GRABER, LAURENCE FREDERICK, agronomist; b. Mineral Point, Wis., Mar. 5, 1887; s. Louis and Salome (Engels) G.; B.S., U. of Wisconsin, 1910, M.S., 1912; Ph.D., University of Chicago, 1930; married Frankie A. Trainor, October 25, 1926. Asst. in agronomy, U. Wis. 1910-12, instr. 1912-16, assistant prof., 1917-18, asso. prof., 1918-20, prof. from 1921, chmn. dept. of agronomy, 1941-50. Member Fourth Internat. Grassland Congress, Oxford, Eng., and Aberysthwyth, Wales, 1937. Chmn. Com. on Internat. Crop Improvement Assn. on Development of Alfalfa Seed Certification in U.S., 1917-18; chairman of the seed practices committee of the North Central States, 1947-51. Member Committee, Agricultural Board, National Research Council, 1945, Nat. Found. Seed Stock Project since 1950. Fellow A.A.A.S., Am. Soc. Agronomy (pres. 1949-50); mem. Am. Soc. Plant Physiologists, Wis. Acad. Sciences, Arts and Letters, Am. Assn. U. Prof., Wis. Alumni Assn. (dir. life mem), Alpha Zeta, Sigma Xi, Phi Sigma, Epsilon Sigma Phi. Club: University (Madison). Cons. editor Jour. of Am. Society of Agronomy. Author of Laboratory Manual for Students of Agronomy; Agronomy, Principles and Practices. Contbr. to Ency. Brit., 1944; also contbr. numerous papers on research to various publs. Home: Madison, Wis. †

GRACE, PRINCESS OF MONACO b. Phila., Nov. 12, 1929; d. John Brendan and Margaret (Majer) Kelly; m. Rainier III (Prince of Monaco), Apr. 19, 1956; children—Caroline Louise Marguerite, Albert Alexandre Louis Pierre, Stephanie Marie Elizabeth. Student, Acad. Assumption (Ravenhill), Phila., Stevens Sch., Phila., Am. Acad. Dramatic Arts, N.Y.C.; student hon. degree, Duquesne U. Dir. Twentieth Century Fox Film Corp., 1976-81. Actress in plays, TV and motion pictures, 1949-56; Broadway debut in: The Father, 1949; Films include High Society; (recipient Acad. award for role in Country Girl 1954). Pres. Monegasque Red Cross, Princess Grace Found., Garden Club Monaco; chmn. organizing com. Centennial of Monte Carlo; hon. pres. Monaco-U.S.A., Girl Guides of Monaco, A.M.A.D.E., Irish-Am. Cultural Inst. Decorated Order St. Charles; lady Equestrian Order of Holy Sepulchre of Jerusalem; named Disting. Dau. Pa. Address: Monaco. Died Sept. 14, 1982.

GRAF, JOHN E(NOS), fellow of Smithsonian Instn.; b. Banning, Calif., May 28, 1889; s. Conrad and Mary (Frey) G.; A.B., Pomona Coll., 1910; m. Dorothy Wilks, Sept. 26, 1931. Entomologist U. S. Bur. Entomology, Dept. of Agr., 1911-15, 16-31, assistant chief, 1928-31; mem. Fed. Hort. Bd., U.S. Dept. Agr., 1926-31; asso. dir. U.S. National Museum, 1931-45; asst. secretary Smithsonian Instn. 1945-57, fellow, from 1957; mem. Nat. Arboretum Adv. Council, from 1958. Fellow A.A.A.S.; mem. Entomol. Soc. of America, Entomol. Soc. of Wash. (pres. 1929-30), Biol. Soc. Washington, Wash. Acad. (pres. 1945), Am. Assn. Museums, Sigma Xi (pres. Wash. chapter, 1947-48). Club: Cosmos (Washington; pres. 1943). Author of publs. on Truck Crop entomology. †

GRAF, SAMUEL HERMAN, cons. engr.; b. Portland, Ore., Aug. 4, 1887; s. Samuel E. and Frederika Emille (Schlueter) G.; B.S., Elec. Engring., Oregon State Coll., 1907, E.E., 1908, B.S., Mech. Engring., 1908, M.E., 1909, M.S., Elec. Engring., 1909; D.Sc. in Engineering, Linfield College, 1959; m. Blanche Ann Edlefsen, Aug. 24, 1920 (dec.); children—Thomas Rexford, Ralf Stefan, Therese Ann, Samuel Edlefsen; married 2d, Violet Fliess, Dec. 5, 1952. Began as teacher, and successively instructor and asst. prof. mech. and exptl. engring., Oregon State Coll., 1908-12; head dept. exptl. engring., 1912-20, prof., 1914-54; prof. mechanics and materials, 1920-34, prof., head dept. mech. engring., 1934-50, dir. engring. research 1927-44; dir. Engring. Expt. Station, 1944-54; consultant; research engineer Portland Gas & Coke Co.; research in safety of appliances, Am. Gas Assn. Testing Lab., Cleveland; consulting engineer, Willamette Valley Project from 1936. Mem. bd. trustees Linfield Research Institute, from 1955, Linfield Coll., from 1959. Recipient Award of Merit by American Gas Association, 1959. Member State Bd. Engring. Examiners, 1927-49 (representing mech. engring.), pres. 1939-49; Nat. Coun. State Bd. Engring. Examiners (dir. Western Zone 1934-36; v.p. 1936-37; pres. 1937-38). Recipient distinguished service citation, American Society of Mechanical Engineers, 1954. Member American Society Mech. Engrs. (past chmn. Ore. sect., mgr. 1934-46, v.p. Region VII, 1949-53), American Soc. for Testing and Materials (vice president Northwest district 1961-64); American Society, for Metals (past president of the Oregon chapter), Pacific Coast Gas Assn., Professional Engrs. of Ore., Northwestern Soc. of Highway Engrs. (past v.p.), Tau Beta Pi, Sigma Tau, Pi Tau Sigma, Eta Kappa Nu, Sigma Pi Sigma, Sigma Xi, Phi Kappa Phi, Phi Sigma Kappa. Mason (32 deg., Shriner). Clubs: Triad, Corvallis Engineers (past pres.). Co-author book; editor, Gas Engineers' Handbook, 1934. Contbr. articles to tech. jours. Home: Corvallis, Ore. †

GRAHAM, PALMER HAMPTON, educator; b. Jonesville, Va., Dec. 11, 1887; s. Robert L. and Phoebe O. (Parsons) G.; A.B., Emory and Henry Coll., Emory, Va., 1909; M.A., U. of Va., 1914; m. Kathleen Knight, Dec. 30, 1919; children—Jean K. Steel, Phoebe Lee. Teacher, Prep. sch., Dublin, Va., 1909-11; fellow in astronomy, U. of Va., 1911-16, instr. mathematics, 1912; prof. physics and astronomy, Agnes Scott Coll., Decatur, Ga., 1916-17 and 1919-20; instr. mathematics, New York U., 1920-22, asst. prof., 1922-26, asso. prof., 1926-28, prof., 1928-53. chmn. dept., 1931-47, asst. dean, 1932-35, asso. dean, 1935-45, 47-51, acting dean, 1945-47, 1951-52, asso. dean prof. emeritus, 1953; lectr. So. Meth. U., 1954-55. Served as pvt., 1st lt. A.E.F., U.S.A., 1918-19. Member Math. Assn. Am., Am. Math. Soc., Phi Beta Kappa, Pi Mu Epsilon, Raven Soc. Author textbooks including: (with H.R. Cooley, F. W. John, A. Tilly) Trigonometry, 1942. Home: Dallas, Tex. †

GRAHAM, WILLIAM HUGH, electronics co. exec.; b. Dayton, Ohio, Jan. 11, 1919; s. Charles Walter and Katherine (Ernst) G.; student mech. engring., U. Dayton, 1942; m. Mary Emerson Glotfelter, Oct. 26, 1940; children—John W., Barbara A. (Mrs. Richard Corman). Spl. asst. to works mgr. Nat. Cash Register Co., Dayton, 1937-47; gen. mgr. Crosley div. Avco Mfg. Corp., Cin., 1947-55; exec. v.p. Magnavox Co. of Tenn., Greeneville, 1955-59; pres. Metals Engring. Co., Greenville, 1959; pres., dir. North Electric Co., Galion, Ohio, 1959-79. Named to Exec. Order Ohio Commodores. Mem. exec. bd. Johnny Appleseed Area council Boy Scouts Am., also mem. nat. council; trustee, pres. Galion Community Center. Mem. Ohio Mfrs. Assn. (trustee), Armed Forces Communication and Electronics Assn. (dir.), Newcomen Soc. Home: Galion, Ohio. Died 1979.

GRAHAME, GLORIA, actress; b. Los Angeles, Nov. 28, 1924; d. Michael and Jean (McDougall) Hallward; m. Stanley Clements, 1945 (div.); m. 2d, Nichoas Ray, 1948 (div. 1953); 1 son, David. Recent films: Oklahoma, 1955; Not As a Stranger, 1955; Man Who Never Was, 1956; Odds Against Tomorrow, 1959. Nominated for academy award for supporting actress in Crossfire, 1944; received Academy Award for supporting actress in The Bad and the Beautiful, 1952. Home: West Los Angeles 49, Calif. Died Oct. 5, 1981.

GRAMLICH, HOWARD JOHN, animal husbandry; b. South Omaha, Neb., Jan. 26, 1889; s. John N. and Joanna M. (Gramlich); G.; B.S., U. of Neb., 1911; m. Mabel Cassandra Daniels, June 16, 1915; children—Herbert Howard (dec.), Lois Alice. Asst. dir. of agr. extension, U. of Neb., 1911-13; prof. animal husbandry, U. of Neb., 1913-16, head of dept., 1916-38; sec. Am. Shorthorn Breeders' Assn. since 1938. Special adviser on feed, U.S. Dept. Agr., 1934-35, collaborator, 1936-37. Vice-pres. Lincoln Chamber of Commerce; dir. Am. Royal Live Stock Expn., Kansas City, Ak-Sar-Ben Live Stock Show, Omaha. Mem. Am. Soc. of Animal Production (pres. 1929), Alpha Zeta, Gamma Sigma Delta, Acacia. Republican. Conglist. Mason (32 deg., Shriner). Club: Rotary (Chicago). Contributor to journals of animal husbandry. Home: Oak Park, Ill. †

GRAMM, DONALD, opera singer; b. Milw., Feb. 26, 1927; s. Rinold H. and Victoria (Danneker) Grambsch. Student piano and organ, Wis. Coll. Music, Wis. Conservatory, 1935-44; student, Chgo. Mus. Coll., 1944-49. Faculty Yale U. Radio singer, Chgo. Theater of the Air, Hymns of All Churches, Club Time, Best of All, 1947-55; soloist recitals, U.S., Alaska, Can., 1945-47, Hollywood Bowl, Tanglewood, Ravinia (Chgo.), May festivals, Ann Arbor, Mich., Cin, Alaska Festival, Anchorage, 1959, 60, 61, Santa Fe Opera Assn., 1960-83, Stratford (Ont.) Festival, 1963, Miami Opera, 1965, also Met. Opera Co., 1964-83, Glyndebourne (Eng.) Festival, 1976; singer with symphony orchs., N.Y.C., Boston, Phila., Pitts., Chgo., San Francisco, Los Angeles, others; leading bass baritone, N.Y.C. Opera, 1952-83, Orleans Opera Assn., 1957-58; roles include Boheme; others; appeared as Moses in: Am. premiere of Moses and Aron, 1966; singer, NBC-TV Opera Theatre, Tulsa opera, 1963, Berlin Festwochen, 1961, Opera Nacional, Mexico City, Mexico, 1965, The Festival of Two Worlds, Spoleto, Italy, 1967, Aix-en-Province Festival, France, 1969, Chgo. Lyric Opera, 1968, Glyndebourne Festival, 1975, San Francisco Opera Co., 1975, Miami Opera, 1978, Houston Grand Opera, 1978, Royal Opera House, Covent Garden, 1978, 79, Santiago (Chile) Opera, 1981, appeared, Am. Die Jacobsleiter, Santa Fe, 1968, world premiere, Wilderness Journal, John Lamontaine, Nat. Symphony, Washington, 1972, Songfest, 1977, Am. premiere, Britten's Owen Wingrave, Santa Fe, 1973, Prokofiev's War and Peace, Boston, 1974; soloist, Wolf Trap Festival, Washington, 1973; stage dir.: Marriage of Figaro, 1981; (Recipient award Chicagoland Music Festival 1943, Oliver Ditson scholarship 1945-46, Paul LaValle award 1947, Ford Found. program for solo artists 1962). Mem. Am. Guild Mus. Artists, AFTRA, Santa Fe (N.Mex.), Opera Assn. Club: Forty (Chgo.). Died June 2, 1983.*

GRANGER, JEFFREY SOLON, stockbroker; b. N.Y.C., June 21, 1891; s. David and Minnette (Neuburn) G.; m. Carolyn Sears, Apr. 5, 1921; children—Ann (Mrs. Andrew Laszlo), Jeffrey Sears (dec.). Ph.B., Brown U., 1913; J.D., Columbia, 1916. Mng. and sr. partner Granger & Co., 1919-81; chmn. Granger Div., Seligman Securities, Inc., 1981-83; pres., chmn. bd. Fed. Match Corp., 1928-29; chmn. bd. Harvill Corp., Los Angeles, 1944-56; mgr. and partner Granger Ranches, Ennis, Mont.; pres. Indian Creek Ditch Co., Cameron Ditch Co., Mont. Served as 2d lt. U.S. Army, 1917-19. Mem. Am. Stock Exchange, Am. Arbitration Assn. (arbitrator), Mil. Order World Wars, N.E. Soc., St. George's Soc. N.Y., Phillips-Exeter Alumni Assn. Clubs: Brown U. (N.Y.C.) (pres.), Regency (N.Y.C.), Touchdown (N.Y.C.), Church (N.Y.C.), Bankers Am. (N.Y.C.); Riverside Country (Bozeman, Mont.); Turf and Field. Home: New York, N.Y. Died 1983.

GRANOVSKY, ALEXANDER A., professor; b. Berezcy, Ukraine, Nov. 4, 1887; s. Anastacy J. and Emily (Sichnievich) G.; came to U.S., 1913; student of Kiev Inst. Economic and Social Studies, 1909-10; Sorbonne Univ., Paris, 1919; B.S., Colorado Agrl. Coll., 1918; M.S., Univ. of Wis., 1923, Ph.D., 1925; Dr. Agrl. Scis. honaris causa, Ukranian Poly. Inst., Regensburg, Germany, 1949; m. Irene V. Thorpe, Aug. 7, 1928; children—Sandra R., Robcert A., Philip A., Natalie A., Theodore A. Asst. manager estate in Ukraine, 1906-07; asso. prof. entomology and econ. zool., Univ. of Minn., 1920-43, prof. from 1943; dir. forestry and biol. sta., Univ. of Minn., Itasca Park, 1935-40; entomologist, Minn. Agrl. Expt. Sta. from 1930. Mem. bd. of dirs. Internat. Inst. of St. Paul, Minn. since 1934, chmn. public com., 1937; chmn. training com., Boy Scouts, St. Paul; pres. Orgn. for Rebirth of Ukraine; mem. exec. com. Ukrainian Congress Com. of Am. (rep. Peace Conf., Paris, France, 1946); del. Am. Citizens of Ukrainian Descent to San Francisco U.N. Conf., 1945; mem. Ukrainian Congress Com. of Am. (del. to Peace Conf., Paris, 1946, mem. political council); Pan Am. Ukrainian Conf., 1947. Fellow A.A.A.S., Entomological Soc. of Am.; mem. Am. Assn. of Economic Entomologists, Entomological Soc. of Ontario, Entomological Soc. of Wash., Am. Phytopathological Soc., Ecological Soc. of Am., Potato Assn. of Am., Wisconsin Acad. of Sciences, Arts and Letters, Minn. Acad. of Science, Alpha Zeta, Phi Sigma, Gamma Alpha, Sigma Xi, Phi Kappa Phi, Gamma Sigma Delta. Mem. Ukrainian Orthodox Ch. Mason. Clubs: Campus, Biological (U. of Minn.). Author books including: Free Ukraine Is Vital to Lasting Peace, 1945. Contbr. sci. articles, 3 volumes of Ukrainian poems, 1910-14. Home: St. Paul, Minn. †

GRANT, BEN JOSEPH, editor; b. Dothan, Ala., July 20, 1909; s. Ben Joseph and Ethel (Dowman) G.; B.S., U. Fla., 1931; m. Elizabeth Brubaker, Aug. 9, 1938; children—William Dowman, Richard Martin, Martha Watts (Mrs. Mark Bedner). Staff writer Jacksonville (Fla.) Jour., 1932-35; staff writer A.P., Fla. Bur., 1935-36, Washington Bur., 1936-42; asso. editor U.S. News and World Report, Washington, 1946-52, asst. exec. editor, 1952-65, asso. exec. editor, 1965-67, mng. editor, 1968-70, exec. v.p., 1970-75. Served from 1st lt. to maj. USAAF, 1942-46. Decorated Legion of Merit; recipient citation of merit as distinguished alumnus U. Fla., 1953; named to Sigma Delta Chi Hall Fame, 1975. Clubs: Nat. Press (past pres.), Internat. (Washington); Sea Pines (Hilton Head Island, S.C.). Home: Hilton Head Island, S.C. Died June 24, 1982.

GRANT, CHAPMAN, biologist, editor, army officer (ret.); b. Salem Center, N.Y., March 22, 1887; s. Jesse Root and Elizabeth (Chapman) G.; student Thacher Sch., Ojai, Cal., 1903-05, Morristown Sch., Morristown, N.J., 1906; A.B., Williams Coll., Williamstown, Mass., 1910; m. Mabel Glenn Ward, Nov. 21, 1917; children—Ulysses S., Mabel (Mrs. Bruce R. Hazard). Pres., Lyceum Nat. History, Williams Coll., 1907-10. Commd. U.S. Army in competitive examination from civil life, 1913, served until 1935; disch. as major. Asst. dir. New York Aquarium, 1910-13; scientist, espdn. of Am. Mus. to Yucatan and Mexico, 1910; dir. Detroit Aquarium, 1920; scientist U.S. Navy and Bishop Mus. U.S.S. Tanager expdn. to Leeward Islands (Hawaiian group), 1923; real estate operator, San Diego, Calif., 1935-45; avacado grower, Escondido, Calif., 1939-46; founder Herpetologica, 1936, and served as editor and pub.; founded Herpetologists League 1946. Fellow A.A.A.S., Herpetologists League. Mem. Am. Soc. Icthyologists and Herpetologists, Am. Ornithol. Union, Cooper Ornithol. Club, Indiana Acad. Sci., San Diego Soc. Nat. History (dir., life mem.), Ark. Valley Hist. Soc. (dir. 1928-30), San Diego Aquarium Soc. (dir.), San Diego Audubon Soc. (dir.). Republican. Contbr. about 100 tech. papers on biology and geology to various publs. Home: San Diego, Calif.

GRANT, GEORGE MCINVALE, congressman; b. Louisville, Ala., July 11, 1897; s. Benjamin Giles and Lannie Gholson (Stephens) G.; LL.B., U. of Ala., 1922; m. Matalie Carter, Dec. 5, 1938. Admitted to Ala. bar, 1922, and practiced in Troy, 1922-38; County solicitor, 1927-38; member 75th-79th Congresses (1939-47), 2d Alabama District Chmn. Pike County, Ala., Dem. Exec. Com., 1927-38; mem. State Dem. Com., 1935-38. Served in U.S. Army, 1918-19. Mem. Am. Legion (state comdr. 1929), Pi Kappa Phi (nat. sec. 1922-25). Democrat. Methodist. Mason (Shriner), Woodmen of World. Home: Troy, Ala. Died Nov. 4, 1982.

GRANT, HUGH GLADNEY, diplomatist, journalist, lecturer; b. Birmingham, Ala., Sept. 2, 1888; s. William Curtis and Minnie Becket (Gladney) G.; A.B., Howard Coll., Birmingham, 1910, A.M., 1916, LL.D., 1935; A.B., Harvard, 1912; A.M., George Washington University, 1931; m. Cora Dean Hibbs, August 9, 1916; 1 dau., Louise Esther. Correspondent for Birmingham News and other southern newspapers, 1910-13; with Birmingham Board of Education, 1913-17. Served in United States Army, 1918. With Federal Board for Vocational Education, 1919-21; mem. staff, Ala. State Dept. of Edn., 1921-23; asso. prof. polit. science and head of dept. of journalism, Ala. Poly. Inst., Auburn, 1923-27; sec. to U.S. Senator H. L. Black of Ala., 1927-33; in div. of western European affairs, Dept. of State, Washington, D.C., 1933-35; E.E. and M.P. of U.S. to Albania, 1935, until closing of Legation, Sept. 27, 1939; Dept. of State, 1939-40; E.E. and M.P. to Thailand (Siam), 1940-41. Mem. Alabama Soc. of Washington (pres. 1934-35), The American Platform Guild, N.Y. Am. Legion, Pi Gamma Mu, Pi Kappa Alpha. Lecturer on political subjects; author governmental publs. Contbr. to newspapers. In accordance with authorization of Dept. of State made tour of Balkan countries, 1937, studying political and economic trends. In charge Am. Legation, Tirana, Albania at time of Italian invasion, 1939. Had last audience granted to any foreign rep. by King Zog, the day before Italian invasion. Following return from Thailand late in 1941, made nation-wide lecture tour, speaking on the "Far Eastern Situation." Also speaker for War Dept. in orientation lecture program for soldiers and aviators in U.S. Army camps and aviation fields, organized ednl. program for disabled veterans of World War II in State of Oregon, 1943-44. Deceased.

GRANT, JOHN FRANCIS, banker; b. East Machias, Maine, July 25, 1918; s. Arthur J. and Sarah (McDonald) G.; m. Margaret Wells Libby, June 8, 1947; children—John E., Robert A., Richard A. A.B., U. Maine, 1948. With Merrill Trust Co., Bangor, Maine, 1937-83, asst. treas., 1948-54, v.p., 1954, exec. v.p., 1955-58, dir., 1958, pres., 1959-83, chmn., 1969-83; dir. Cole's Express, Bangor, Bangor Hydro Electric Co., Hannaford Bros. Co. Trustee Bangor Pub. Library; dir., v.p. Bangor Humane Soc. Served to lt. col. USAF, World War II, Korea. Mem. Phi Beta Kappa, Phi Kappa Phi. Home: Bangor, Maine. Died 1983.

GRANTGES, WILLIAM FIDELAS, insurance exec.; b. New Cambria, Mo., Jan. 9, 1889; s. John Peter and Elizabeth (Fulton) G.; student pub. schs., Macon, Mo.; m. Geraldine Rohan, Nov. 7, 1928; children—Richard F., David R. Bookkeeper, teller State Exchange Bank, 1906-08; cashier, asst. sec. Internat. Life Ins. Co., 1908-17, successively asst. sec, sec., v.p., supt. agencies, exec. v.p., 1917-28; agy. dir. Northwestern Nat. Life Ins. Co., 1928-49, 2d v.p., agy. dir., 1949-51, v.p., agy. dir., from 1951. Dir. Mpls. Aquatennial Assn., 1944-46. Served as ensign USN, 1917-19. Mem. Isaac Walton League, Nat. Assn. Life Underwriters. Roman Catholic. Elk. Home: Minneapolis, Minn. †

GRAVELY, WILLIAM S., army officer; b. Martinsville, Va., Mar. 30, 1888; s. William Seymour and Elizabeth Leigh (Hairston) G.; grad. Va. Poly. Inst., Blacksburg, Va., 1911; grad. Air Service Pilots Sch. and Bombardment Sch., 1921, Air Corps Tactical Sch., 1931, Command and Gen. Staff Sch., 1936; m. Ada Colson, Sept. 24, 1919. Commd. 1st lt., F.A., 1917, on active duty to 1920; commd. 1st lt., Air Service, 1920, advancing through the grades to brig. gen., 1944. Home: Roanoke, Va.†

GRAVES, LESTER HERBERT, engr., corp. exec.; b. Milwaukee, Wis., June 19, 1889; s. Herbert George and Luella E. (Morse) G.; B.S. in E.E., U. of Ill., 1912; m. Helena Mann, June 15, 1915 (deceased); 1 son, Lester Herbert; m. 2d, Marie B. Gundlach, June 17, 1950. Worked in repair shops, Gen. Electric Co., Chicago, 1907-08; with Curtis Lighting, Inc., Chicago, 1912; with Curtis Lighting, Inc., N.Y. City, from 1912, v.p. from 1936. Trustee Village of Pelham Manor, 1929-33, mayor, 1933-35. Fellow Illuminating Engring. Soc. (pres. 1930-40); mem. Zeta Psi (trustee 1933-34; corr. sec. 1935), Eta Kappa Nu. Republican. Presbyterian. Mason (Wilmete (Ill.) Lodge 931). Clubs: Pelham Country (Pelham, N.Y.). Author articles, papers on lighting practice for Illuminating Engring. Soc. Home: Pelham Manor, N.Y. †

GRAVES, ROGER COLGATE, urologist; b. Buffalo, June 23, 1889; s. Roger W. and Emma (Mabie) G.; A.B., Syracuse U., 1913, M.D., 1918; m. Hazel Moore, June 22, 1918; children—Roger Colgate, Sarah Mabie, Charles Moore. With Peter Bent Brigham Hosp. and Harvard Med. Sch., 1918-23; pvt. practice, Boston, from 1923; clin. prof. urology, Tufts U. Med. Sch., from 1937; urologist-in-chief to Carney Hosp., from 1938; genito-urinary surgeon, Pondville State Hosp.; urologist New England Deaconess Hosps.; consultant at Carney Hospital, Boston. Diplomate Am. Bd. Urology. Fellow A.C.S.; mem. A.M.A., Am. Assn. Genito-Urinary Surgeons, Am. Urol. Assn., Boston Surg. Soc., N.E. Cancer Soc. Baptist. Club: Harvard (Boston). Contbr. Lewis Practice of Surgery, also med. jours. Home: Brookline, Mass. †

GRAY, AUGUSTINE HEARD, naval officer; b. Boston, Mass., Nov. 10, 1888; s. Russell and Amy (Heard) G.; student, Groton Sch., 1901-06; B.S., U.S. Naval Acad., 1910; student Naval War Coll., 1933-35; m. Elizabeth DuBois Jordan, Apr. 17, 1933; children—Russell (dec.), Augustine Heard, Peter Russell, Robert Molten, Russell, Elizabeth Jordan. Entered U.S. Navy, 1906, and advanced through the grades to commodore, 1944; commands include submarines D-1 and L-2, submarine divisions 9 and 10, U.S.S. Bruce (destroyer), U.S.S. New Orleans (cruiser), Amphibious Transport Div. 5, and Service Squadron 8; foreign service includes duty European and Asiatic stations and in South America. Decorated Commendation Ribbon, Legion of Merit with gold star, Retired as rear adm., 1947. Club: Army and Navy (Washington). Home: Coronado, Calif. †

GRAY, G. CHARLES, clergyman; b. St. Georges, Delaware, Nov. 23, 1889; s. Montgomery Johns and Mary Rebecca (Sutton) G.; A.B., Dickinson Coll., Carlisle, Pa., 1909, hon. A.M., 1913; S.T.B., Boston U. Sch. of Theology, 1912; D.D., Park Coll., 1935; m. Elizabeth Maud Collins, Mar. 23, 1919; 1 son, James Collins. Entered M.E. ministry, 1908, ordained, 1908; pastor First M.E. Ch., Hummelstown, Pa., 1908-09; asso. minister Old South Congl. Ch., Boston, 1911-15; pastor First M.E. Ch., Newton, Mass., 1915-18; chaplain (capt.) U.S. Army, 1918-20; asso. dir. Am. Red Cross, U.S. Army Base Hosp., Ft. Riley, Kan., 1920-21; editorial and promotion work, religious motion pictures, New York, 1922-29; pastor Westminster Congl. Ch., Kansas City, Mo., since 1929; state dir. Am. Campaign for China Famine Relief, 1921-22; guest radio preacher, Station WDAF, Kansas City Star, 1929-40; radio preacher Columbia nat. chain, summer, 1936. Member Kansas City Com. National Housing Board. Mem. bd. for examining chaplaincy candidates, U.S. Army, Central West Div., 1919-20; pioneer in organizing with A.L.A., first circulating libraries for training camps and hosps., 1919. Trustee Mo. Conf. Congl. Chs.; del. Nat. Council Congl. Chs., 1935, 1948; chaplain Military Order of World Wars since 1948; pres. bd. trustees Volunteers of Am.; chmn. dept. of inter-goodwill, Kansas City Council of Chs.; chmn. Kansas City Pub. Affairs Forum. Mem. Alpha Chi Rho, Wranglers Club. Mason. Chaplain Mil. Order of World Wars; mem. bd. trustees Friends of Democracy (New York). Clubs: University, Blue Hills Country; Co-operative. Home: Kansas City, Mo.

GRAY, GILES WILKESON, univ. prof.; b. Shelbyville, Ind., Dec. 11, 1889; s. Isaac Redding and Lucy Abigail (White) G.; A.B., De Pauw U., 1914; A.M., U. of Wis., 1923; Ph.D., U. of Ia., 1926; student U. of Ill., 1921-24; m. Helen Harris Clark, Aug. 30, 1924; children—Helen Clark (Mrs. Frank C. Crawford, Mary Lucy (Mrs. Wyeth A. Read), Edmund Wright. Assistant in speech, University of Illinois, 1921-24; associate, speech, University of Ia., 1924-26, asst. prof. 1926-32; asst. prof. Speech, La. State U., 1932-34, asso. prof. 1934-37, prof. since 1937; U. of Ga., summer 1929, St. Louis U., summer 1946, University of California (Berkeley), summer 1949. Mem. Speech Assn. of Am. (editor, Quarterly Jour. of Speech, 1939-41), So. Speech Assn. (pres. 1937), Acoustic Soc. of Am., International Phonetic Assn., Sigma Xi, Pi Kappa Delta, Tau Kappa Alpha, Delta Upsilon. Mem. Meth. Episcopal Ch. Author: The Bases of Speech (with C. M. Wise), 1934, 1946; Public Speaking; Principles and Practice (with W. W. Braden) 1951; editor: Studies in Experimental Phonetics, 1936. Home: Baton Rouge, La. †

GRAY, GORDON, broadcasting co. exec.; b. Balt., May 30, 1909; s. Bowman and Nathalie Fontaine (Lyons) G.; m. Jane Boyden Craige, June 11, 1938 (dec. July 1953); children—Gordon, Burton Craige, Boyden, Bernard; m. Nancy Maguire Beebe; step-children—Cameron, Alexandra, Schuyler Beebe. A.B., U. N.C., 1930; LL.B., Yale U., 1933. Bar: N.Y. bar 1934, N.C. bar 1936. Asso. Carter, Ledyard & Milburn, 1933-35, Manly, Hendren & Womble, 1935-37; pres. and pub. Piedmont Pub. Co. (Winston-Salem Jour.), Piedmont Pub. Co. (Twin City Sentinel); also operator radio sta. WSJS, 1935-47; asst. sec. Army, Dept Def., 1947-49; sec. Army, 1949-195O; spl. asst. to Pres. U.S., Apr.-Nov. 1950; pres. U. N.C., Feb. 1950, asst. sec. def. for internat. security affairs, 1955-57, dir. office def. moblzn., 1957-58, spl. asst. to Pres. for nat. security affairs, 1958-61, chmn. bd. Piedmont Pub. Co., 1961-69, Triangle Broadcasting Co., 1969-75, Summit Communications, Inc., 1975-82; dir. Am. Security & Trust Co., Media Gen. Trustee Fed. City Council; mem. Pres.'s Fgn. Intelligence Adv. Bd., 1961-77; Chmn. emeritus Nat. Trust for Historic Preservation; trustee emeritus Corcoran Art Gallery.; Dir. Psychol. Strategy Bd., July-Dec. 1951; mem. N.C. State Senate, 1938-42, 46-47. Served as pvt. U.S. Army; commd. 2d lt., Inf., discharged as capt., Inf. 1942-45. Mem. Phi Beta Kappa, Delta Kappa Epsilon, Phi Delta Phi. Episcopalian. Clubs: Alibi (Washington), Burning Tree (Washington), Met. (Washington). Home: Washington, D.C. Died Nov. 26, 1982.

GRAY, HAMILTON, educator, civil engr.; b. Gardiner, Maine, July 26, 1910; s. Charles Henry and Grace Duncan (Hamilton) G.; B.A., Harvard, 1933, M.S. in Engring., 1934, Sc.D., 1938; m. Prudence M. Jones, Sept. 5, 1936 (dec. Oct. 1965); children—Faith Harriet, Priscilla Hamilton (Mrs. David D. Platt); m. 2d, Barbara J. Bidwell, Oct. 21, 1966; 1 son, Charles Hamilton. Asst. civil engring. Harvard Grad. Sch. Engring., 1934-36; soil technician Moran & Proctor, N.Y.C., 1936-40; asst. prof. civil engring. N.Y. U., 1940-45; prof. U. Maine, soils engr. Maine Hwy. Commn., 1945-55; prof. Ohio State U., Columbus, 1955-76, chmn. civil engring., 1955-71. Cons. civil engr., 1942-84, Fellow ASCE (A.M. Wellington award 1958); mem. Asso. Hwy. Research Bd., Sigma Xi, Phi Kappa Phi, Tau Beta Pi. Home: Columbus, Ohio. Died July 11, 1984.

GRAY, PHILIP F., bank exec.; b. Chicago, 1889; s. Philip H. and Emma G.; U. Ill., 1913; m. Marion K., 1912; children—Helen G. Dean, Philip F. Senior v.p., dir. Irving Trust Co., N.Y. City from 1950. Mem. Theta Delta Chi. Clubs: Union League (N.Y. City); Ridgewood (N.J.) Country. Home: Ridgewood, N.J. †

GRAY, RICHARD GEORGE, journalist, educator; b. Tacoma, Feb. 24, 1932; s. Leo James and Olive (Masterman) G.; m. Ida Ruth Higgins, Aug. 5, 1956; children—Christopher Devin, Grant Allen. A.B., Whitworth Coll., 1954; M.A., U. Minn., 1956, Ph.D., 1964. News editor Tacoma Star, 1955; teaching asst. U. Minn., 1957-58; asst. prof. Northwestern U., 1961-66, assoc. prof. journalism, 1966-68; nat. dir. Project Pub. Information, U.S. Office Edn., 1966-68; prof., dean Sch. Journalism, also dir. mass communication program Ind. U., Bloomington, 1968-84; mem. Accreditation Council for Edn. in Journalism; cons. Gannett Found., Scripps-Howard Found., Hearst Found., 1959-61; Chmn. com. on fed. role in sci. edn. for non-specialists Nat. Research Council. Reporter, rewrite man, feature writer, St. Louis Post-Dispatch, 1958-61, corr., Life mag., 1959-61. Author: Freedom of Access to Government Information, 1965, Education and Communication in a Dynamic Society, 1969, Public Relations in State Departments of Education, Education in the States: Nationwide Development since 1900, 1969; Editor: Research in Journalism: Past, Present and Future; editorial bd.: Journalism Quar; contbr. articles to profl. jours. Danforth fellow, 1954-59; Lincoln scholar, 1950-51. Mem. Am. Soc. Newspaper Editors (edn. com.), Assn. Collegiate Presses (judge 1955-65), Assn. Edn. in Journalism (pres. 1979-80), AAUP, AP Mng. Editors Assn. (freedom of info. com.), Soc. Religion in Higher Edn., Inland Daily Press Assn. (editorial com.), Sigma Delta Chi. Democrat. Methodist. Home: Bloomington, Ind. Died Nov. 20, 1984; interred Parkdale, Oreg.

GRAY, WILLIAM STEELE, JR., chem. co. exec.; b. N.Y.C., Sept. 21, 1924; s. William Steele and Margaret (Dunlop) G.; m. Anne Sweetser, June 29, 1946; children—Margaret Anne, Susan Nichols Gray Townsend, William Steele, III, John Stuart. LL.B., NYU, 1950. Bar: N.Y. 1951. With Union Carbide Corp., 1950-83; exec. v.p. Union Carbide Corp. (Linde div.), N.Y.C., 1966-73, dir. mgmt. info. and acctg. services, 1973-75, v.p., 1975-83, chief fin. officer, 1978-83; dir. Putnam Trust Co., Greenwich, Conn.; mem. Manhattan east adv. bd. Mfrs. Hanover Trust Co. Past pres. bd. trustees Greenwich Country Day Sch. Served with USMC, 1944-46. Mem. Am. Bar Assn., Phi Delta Phi. Republican. Episcopalian. Clubs: Round Hill (Greenwich); Ivy (Princeton, N.J.); Board Room (N.Y.C.). Home: Greenwich, Conn. Died Dec. 1983.

GREAVES, DONALD CRITCHFIELD, educator, physician; b. Minot, N.D., June 26, 1924; s. John Perce and Adelaide (Hamilton) G.; student Mont. State U., 1942-43, 44-45, Yale, 1943-44; M.D., Washington U., St. Louis, 1949; B.S., U. Mont., 1959; children—Mary McGregor, Donald Critchfield. Intern, Salt Lake City Gen. Hosp., 1949-50; from jr. asst. resident psyciatrist to resident psychiatrist Payne Whitney Psychiat. Clinic, N.Y.C., 1950-54, asst. attending psychiatrist, 1954-55; asst. in psychiatry, then instr. psychiatry Cornell U. Med. Coll., 1951-55; asso. prof. psychiatry, neurology, behavioral scis. U. Okla. Sch. Medicine, 1955-58; prof. psychiatry, head dept. U. Kan. Sch. Medicine, 1958-74; chief in-patient psychiatry service U. Okla. Hosps., 1955-58; attending psychiatrist VA Hosp., Oklahoma City, 1955-58; cons. psychiatrist student health service Okla. State U., 1955-58, VA hosps., Kansas City, Mo., Wadsworth, Kan., 1958-74, Winter VA Hosp., Topeka, 1958-63. Spl. asst. to dir. Nat. Inst. Mental Health, 1968-69. Mem. Gov. Kan. Adv. Commn. State Instl. Mgmt., 1958-63, 66. Diplomate Am. Bd. Psychiatry and Neurology (examiner from 1957). Mem. A.A.A.S., A.M.A., Am. Psychiat. Assn., Assn. Am. Med. Colls., Am. Psychosomatic Soc., N.Y. Acad. Sci., Acad. Psychoanalysis. Contbr. articles to profl. jours. Home: Shawnee Mission, Kans. Died Jan. 9, 1983.

GREBE, JOHN JOSEF, chem. research; b. Uerzig, Rhineland, Germany, Feb. 1, 1900; s. Carl and Gertrude (Erbes) Grebe; B.S., Case School of Applied Science, 1924, M.S., 1927, D.Sc., 1935; married Hazel Amanda Holmes, March 2, 1929; children—Ruth Elaine (Mrs. Jos. T. Davis), Joanne Hazel (Mrs. Dwight T. Hendricks), John Holmes, Carolyn Louise, James Carl. Came to United States, 1914, naturalized citizen, 1921. With Dow Chemical Company from 1924 as director Physical Research Laboratory; on loan from Dow Chem. Co. to Oak Ridge Nat. Lab., Oct. 1946-July 1947; on loan to Army Chem. Corps as chief tech. adivser, Aug. 1948, July, 1949; research counselor Dow Chemical Company, 1949-53, dir. nuclear research and development, 1953-58, director of nuclear and basic research, 1958-65; developed electrometric control. Awarded certificate of merit for development of sun screen. Franklin Inst., 1942; Chem. Ind. medal, 1943; John Wesley Hyatt award, 1947. V.p. and dir. Dowell; director Ewing Development Co. Civilian observer Bikini bomb tests, 1946. Felllow A.A.A.S., American Instutite of Chemists; mem. American Chem. Society, Am. Inst. Chem. Engrs., Am. Physical Soc., Am. Soc. of Mechanical Engineers, Engineering Soc. of Detroit, Mich. Acad. Science, Society of Chemical Industry, Found. Study of Cycles, Atomic Industrial Forum, Am. Nuclear Soc., Am. Ordnance Assn., Armed forces Chem. Assn., Franklin Inst., N.Y. Acad. Sci., Sigma Xi. Lutheran. Clubs: Kiwanis, Midland Country, Saginaw Valley Torch (Midland), Contbr. articles sci. jours. Home: Midland, Mich. Died Feb. 4, 1984.

GREEN, BEN CHARLES, judge; b. Cleve., Jan. 4, 1905; s. Isadore and Rose (Mailman) G.; m. Sylvia E. Chappy, Nov. 20, 1940; 1 dau., Rosemary A. A.B. cum laude, Western Res. U., 1928; LL.B., 1930, J.D., 1968. Bar: Ohio bar 1930. Practiced in, Cleve., 1930-61; atty. Fed. Land Bank, Louisville, 1933-35; spl. counsel to atty. gen., Ohio, 1937-38; mem. law dept., real estate cons. City of Cleve., 1944-50; mem. bd. elections, 1950-61; U.S. dist. judge No. Dist. Ohio, 1961-76, sr. judge, from 1976; chmn. Bd. Elections Cuyahoga County, Ohio, 1952-55, 59-61; trustee Ohio Assn. Elections Ofcls., 1955-61. Treas. Cuyahoga County Democratic Com., 1948-61; del. Dem. Nat. Conv., 1948, 52; trustee NCCJ, from 1963. Mem Ohio, Cleve., Fed., Cuyahoga County bar assns., Nat. Lawyers Club, Order of Coif. Club: Beechmont Country (Cleve.). Home: Beachwood, OH.

GREEN, DAVID EZRA, educator; b. N.Y.C., Aug. 5, 1910; s. Herman and Jennie (Marrow) G.; m. Doris Cribb, Apr. 15, 1935; children—Rowena (Mrs. Larry Matthews), Pamela (Mrs. Joseph Baldwin, Jr.). B.A., N.Y. U., 1930, M.A., 1932; Ph.D., Cambridge (Eng.) U., 1934. Beit Meml. Research fellow Cambridge, Eng., 1934-40; fellow Harvard, 1940-41; with enzyme lab. Coll. Phys. and Surg., Columbia, 1941-48; asso. prof. biochemistry Columbia, 1947; co-dir. Inst. Enzyme Research, U. Wis., 1948—, prof. enzyme chemistry, 1948—. Author: Mechanisms of Biological Oxidations, 1939, Molecular Insights into the Living Process, 1967. Recipient Paul-Lewis Labs. award enzyme chemistry, 1946. Fellow Am. Acad. Arts and Scis.; fgn. fellow Royal Flemish Acad. Arts and Scis.; mem. Am. Soc. Biol. Chemists, Nat. Acad. Scis., Am. Chem. Soc., Harvey Soc., Biochem. Soc., Am. Soc. Cell Biology, Phi Beta Kappa, Sigma Xi. Home: Madison WI

GREEN, RICHARD CALVIN, utility co. exec.; b. Kansas City, Mo., Dec. 12, 1925; s. Ralph Jerome and Nell (Shroer) G.; m. Ann Gabelman, May 10, 1952; children—Suzanne, Cassandra, Richard Calvin, Pamela, Robert. Student, U. Mo., 1942-43, B.S. in Bus. Adminstrn, 1950; student, Mich. State U., 1944. With Mo. Public Service Co., Kansas City, 1941-82, pres., chmn., 1963-72, pres., gen. mgr., 1972-82; pres. Green Securities, Inc.; dir. United Mo. Bank, Kansas City. Pres. Heart of Am. council Boy Scouts Am., 1970-72, mem. exec. com., 1959-82, chmn. bd., 1972-74; pres. Kansas City Crime Commn., 1967-69, bd. dirs., from 1966, chmn. bd., 1969-71; v.p., dir. Starlight Theatre Assn., Kansas City; mem. Civic Council of Greater Kansas City. Recipient Citation of Merit award U. Mo. Sch. Bus. and Public Adminstrn., 1963; named Outstanding Boss. Mo. Jaycees, 1954; named to Eagle Scout Ct. of Honor Boy Scouts Am., 1966; recipient Silver Beaver award, 1969. Mem. C. of C. of Greater Kansas City (pres. 1965-66), Missouri Valley Electric Assn. (pres. 1960-61), Nelson Gallery Soc. Fellows. Mem. Christian Ch. (Disciples of Christ). Clubs: River, Kansas City, Kansas City Country; Eldorado Country (Indian Wells, Calif.); Garden of Gods (Colorado Springs, Colo.); La Coquille (Palm Beach, Fla.); John's Island (Vero Beach, Fla.). Home: Kansas City, Mo. Died May 7, 1982.

GREEN, THOMAS HENRY, army officer; b. Cambridge, Mass., April 11, 1889; s. Jeremiah and Emeline (Louise) G.; LL.B., Boston U., 1915; LL.M., George Washington U., 1923; m. Ruth Cooper Tuthill, Jan. 25, 1921. Commd. 2d lt., Cav., U.S. Army, October 24, 1917, and advanced through the grades to maj. gen., Dec., 1945; appointed asst. judge advocate general, Apr. 14, 1943; judge advocate gen., Dec. 1, 1945. Home: Winthrop, Mass.

GREEN, WILLIAM PAUL, finance educator, corporation executive; b. Rayne, La., Sept. 7, 1930; s. Murphy Joseph and Verl Russia (Butler) G.; m. Margaret Phyllis Lapleau, July 9, 1961; children: Philip Lee, Larre Paul, Sara Margaret. B.S. in Bus. Adminstrn, U. Colo., 1963, M.B.A. in Fin, 1964; Ph.D. in Bus. Adminstrn, U. N.C., 1968. Mgmt. trainee Johns-Manville Corp., Denver, 1951-52; owner, mgr. Green's Hardware and Machinery Co., Inc., Crowley, La., 1952-63; prof. fin. U. Tex., Arlington, 1967-81; chmn., chief exec. officer Teltek Corp.; Mem. adminstrv. bd. ch. Mem. Am., So., Southwestern fin. assns., Fin. Mgmt. Assn., Am. Inst. Decision Scis., Fin. Execs. Inst., M.B.A. Assn., Beta Gamma Sigma. Home: Arlington, Tex. Dec. July 5, 1981.

GREENBAUM, EDWARD S., army officer, lawyer; b. New York City, N.Y., Apr. 13, 1890; s. Samuel and Selina G.; grad. Horace Mann Sch., 1907, Williams Coll., Williamstown, Mass., 1910, Columbia Law Sch., 1913; LL.D., Williams Coll., 1946; research asso. Johns Hopkins Univ.; m. Dorothea R. Schwarcz, Oct. 21, 1920; children—David S., Daniel W. In practice of law, N.Y. City, 1913-17, 1919-40 and from 1946; mem. firm Greenbaum, Wolff & Ernst from 1915; D.C., 1933; special asst. to atty. gen., 1938 counsel, Long Island Railroad Commn., 1952-53. Mem. N.Y. Judicial Conf., 1st dept., 1956-67; mem. United States delegation to UN 1956-57. Mem. N.J. Commn. on Dept. Instns. and Agys., 1958. Served in U.S. Army, 1917-19 and 1940-46; commd. lt. col., 1940, col. 1941, brig. gen., 1943-46. Awarded Distinguished Service Medal, 1945. Mem. American Academy of Arts and Letters, American, City of New York and N.Y. State bar assns., N.Y. County Lawyers Assn. Clubs: Army and Navy (Washington); Williams. Democrat. Jewish religion. Author: The King's Bench Masters (with Leslie I. Reade), 1932; A Lawyer's Job, 1968. Home: Princeton, N.J. †

GREENBERG, CARL, journalist; b. Boston, Aug. 19, 1908; s. Harry and Fannie (Herman) G.; m. Gladys Bilansky, July 12, 1930; 1 son, Howard Allan. Student extension div., UCLA, 1927. Reporter Los Angeles Evening Express, 1926-28, City News Service of Los Angeles, 1928-33; Reporter Los Angeles Examiner, 1933-43, polit. editor, 1943-62; polit. writer Los Angeles Times, 1962-66, 68-73, polit. editor, 1966-68, mem. editorial bd., 1962-68. Disaster acting gov., Calif., 1959-67; past bd. dirs. 8-Ball Welfare Found. Served as coxswain USCGR, World War II. Recipient 1st prize for best news story So. Calif. Newspaper Writers, Los Angeles chpt. Theta Sigma Phi, 1944; Silver award Calif.-Nev. Asso. Press, 1957; co-recipient Pulitzer prize for gen. local reporting, 1966. Mem. Order of Hound's Tooth (charter), Coast Guard League, Eureka (Ill.) Community Assn. (hon. life), Soc. Profl. Journalists, Sigma Delta Chi, Kappa Tau Alpha., B'nai B'rith. Club: Greater Los Angeles Press (hon. life). Home: Culver City, Calif. Died Nov. 13, 1984.

GREENBERG, FRANK, lawyer; b. Chgo., July 21, 1910; s. Samuel and Sophie (Nowosenitz) G.; m. Bernice Jenks, Nov. 12, 1938 (dec.). Ph.B., U. Chgo., 1930; J.D. cum laude, 1932. Bar: Ill. bar 1932. Since practiced in, Chgo.; ptnr. firm Greenberg, Keele, Lunn & Aronberg (and predecessors), 1938-84; dir. Oppenheimer Casing Co. (and subs.); Chmn. spl. inquiry Commn. Ill. Supreme Ct., 1969; mem. Ill. Jud. Inquiry Bd., 1971-79. Served to lt. comdr. USNR, 1942-45. Recipient Public Service citation U. Chgo. Alumni Assn., 1979. Mem. ABA, Ill. Bar Assn., Chgo. Bar Assn. (chmn. grievance com. 1963, inquiry com. 1959-60, bd. mgrs. 1964-67, bd. mgrs. 70-71, pres. 1969-70), Am. Judicature Soc. (adv. council Center Jud. Conduct Orgns., Herbert Harley award 1980), Chgo. Council Lawyers, Law Club Chgo., U. Chgo. Law Sch. Alumni Assn. (pres. 1976-78). Club: Standard (Chgo.). Home: Chicago, Ill. Died Mar. 3, 1984.

GREENE, CHARLES JEROME, journalist; b. Conway, Ark., Oct. 6, 1910; s. Charles Jerome and Euella (Pettus) G.; m. Helen Ford Curwood, Oct. 29, 1938. B.A., Hendrix Coll., Conway, 1929. With B.E. Vaughan Advt. Agy., 1929-30; reporter Ark. Gazette, Little Rock, 1930-35, A.P., Washington, 1935-36, Chgo. Daily News, 1936-39; editor Fawcett Publs., N.Y.C., 1939-40; reporter Time, Inc., Washington, 1940-41; reporter, mil. editor New York Daily News, 1945-69; columnist, chief New York Daily News (Washington bur.), 1969-75; polit. columnist Bradenton (Fla.) Herald, from 1976. Served to col. USMCR, 1942-45. Decorated Bronze Star medal with combat V. Mem. Sigma Delta Chi. Democrat. Methodist. Club: Gridiron (Washington). Home: Sun City Center, Fla.

GREENE, RICHARD LEIGHTON, English language educator emeritus; b. Rochester, N.Y., Jan. 18, 1904; s. James Gereau and Ruth (Leighton) G.; m. Eleanor Foulkes Curtiss, June 5, 1944 (dec. 1950); stepsons: Stephen Alan Curtiss, Peter Andrew Curtiss. A.B., U. Rochester, 1926; A.M., Princeton U., 1927, Ph.D., 1929; A.M. (hon.), Wesleyan U., 1956. Instr. English U. Rochester, 1929-30, asst. prof., 1930-34, prof., 1934-42, Joseph H. Gilmore prof., chmn. dept. English, 1942-46; pres. Wells Coll., Aurora, N.Y., 1946-50; vis. prof. English Purdue U., 1951-52, U. Calif., Berkeley, 1952-53, Calif. Inst. Tech., 1953-54; Frank B. Weeks vis. prof. English Wesleyan U., Middletown, Conn., 1954-56, prof., 1956-60, Wilbur Fisk Osborne prof. English, 1960-72, emeritus, 1972-83; Research fellow Am. Council Learned Socs., 1931-32; vis. fellow Princeton, 1963-64, 68; asso. fellow Silliman Coll., Yale, 1972-83. Editor: The Early English Carols, 1935, 2d edit., 1977, A Selection of English Carols, 1962, The Lyrics of The Red Book of Ossory, 1974; Contbr. articles and revs. to philol. jours. Mem. Am. Musicological Soc., Modern Humanities Research Assn., MLA, Medieval Acad. Am., Medieval Acad. Ireland, Conn. Acad. Arts and Scis., AAUP, Johnsonians, Phi Beta Kappa, Alpha Delta Phi (Samuel Eells award 1963, pres. 1946-47). Republican. Presbyn. Clubs: University (Rochester) (hon.); Princeton (N.Y.C.); Graduates (New Haven); Nassau (Princeton). Died Dec. 24, 1983.

GREENE, WILLIAM CHASE, teacher, writer; b. Brookline, Mass., June 14, 1890; s. Herbert Eveleth and Harriet Savage (Chase) G.; A.B., Harvard, 1911, A.M.,

1916, Ph.D., 1917; Rhodes Scholar from Mass., at Balliol College, Oxford University, England, 1911-14, B.A., 1914; married Margaret Weed Eckfeldt, 1917; children—Herbert Thomas, Margaret Chase (Mrs. Albert S. Watson), Anne Marston (deceased). Instructor English, Harvard, U., 1914-17; master, Groton Sch., 1917-20; instr., Latin and Greek, Harvard, 1920-23, asst. prof., 1923-27, asso. prof., 1927-43; prof. from 1943, chmn. dept. classics, 1946-51; annual prof. Am. Academy in Rome, 1931-32; visiting professor University of Chicago, summer, 1938. Trustee Radcliffe Coll., 1927-33, Anatolia Coll., Thessaloniki, Greece, from 1952. Fellow American Acad. Arts and Sciences (editor 1936-37); mem. Am. Philol. Assn. (pres. 1950-51), N.E. Classical Assn. (pres. 1950-51), Phi Beta Kappa (sec., Harvard Chapter, 1944-45). Club: Faculty (Cambridge), Author: Moira: Fate, Good, and Evil in Greek Thought, 1944. Editor: Scholia Platonica, 1938. Contbr. numerous articles, etc., in periodicals. Home: Cambridge, Mass. †

GREENFIELD, ALFRED M., condr., educator; b. St. Paul, Mar. 14, 1902; s. Joseph William and Edith Mary (Stripe) G.; m. Elsie Holbrook Learned, June 15, 1925 (dec. Feb. 1967); 1 son, William Edward; m. Nancy Ann Harris, May 19, 1970. Student, Inst. Musical Art, N.Y.C., 1922-25, David Mannes Sch., N.Y., 1925-26, N.Y. U, 1924-27. Organist Virginia Avenue Ch. (Swedenborgen), St. Paul, 1920, First Ch. Christ Scientist, St. Paul, 1921-22, Calvary P.E. Ch., N.Y.C., 1923-24, Fifth Ch. Christ Scientist, N.Y.C., 1924-41; condr. Oratorio Soc. of N.Y.C., 1943-55, hon. condr., 1955-83; Instr. N.Y.U., 1925-29, asst. prof., 1929-34, asso. prof., 1934-46, prof. music, 1946-68; adminstr. chmn. dept. music U. Coll., 1930-59; tchr. oratorio interpretation and conducting Union Theol. Sem., Sch. of Sacred Music, 1945-55; vis. prof. various ednl. instns., summers; prof. choral music U.S. Dept. State specialist program, Colombia, S. Am., 1962-63, U.S. specialist, Dominican Republic, 1969; Fulbright lectr. Nat. U., Bogota, Colombia, 1961, 64; dir. Nat. Choral Home: Winston-Salem, N.C. Univ. Choruses, Bogota, 1971; condr. Messiah seminar Emory U. Concert Series, 1972; Prof. honorario Universidad de Cartagena, 1962; Dir. Army Specialist Tng. Unit Glee Club, Air Cadet Singers, N.Y.U., World War II. Condr. of, Bach Festival Choir, Rollins Coll., 1946, Handel's Messiah, Salt Lake Oratorio Soc., Mormon Tabernacle, 1947, 1948, also with, Shreveport Civic Chorus, Dallas Symphony Orch., Shreveport, La., Twin City Chorus and Mpls. Symphony Orch. for Nat. Conv. Am. Guild Organists, 1954, Mozart Club Chorus and Orch., Winston-Salem, N.C., 1958, 65, 66, 67, 77, 78, 82, in, Carnegie Hall with Oratorio Soc. N.Y. and Orch., 1958; condr.: with chorus and orch. Messiah, Ridgecrest, N.C. and Glorietta, N.M., 1965; Composer: anthems Here, O My Lord; solos The Hem of His Garment; organ Prelude in Olden Style; solo Here, O My Lord, 1948, The Earth Is the Lord's; Anthem, 1950, Quodlibet; for organ, 1959; Editor: University Glee Club series, 1931—. Decorated Camilo Torres Colombia).; Hon. asso. N.Y. Hist. Soc. Mem. Am. Guild Organists, Juilliard Alumni Assn., Music Library Assn., Phi Kappa Tau. Clubs: Andiron (Heights), Saint Wilfrid (Heights), New York Univ. Faculty (Heights); Bohemians (N.Y.). Home: Winston-Salem, N.C. Died Jan. 14, 1983.

GREENMAN, FRANCES CRANMER, portrait painter; b. Aberdeen, S. Dakato, June 28, 1890; d. Simeon Harris and Emma A. (Powers) Cranmer; grad. Wisconsin Acad., Madison, 1906; studied Art Students League (N.Y.), Boston Museum School, Corcoran School of Art, Wash., D.C., winner Corcoran Gold Medal 1908; Academie de la Grande Chaumiere, Paris; pupil of William Chase, Frank Vincent Du Mond, and Robert Henri; m. John Wolcott Greenman, Oct. 26, 1915; children—Patricia (Mrs. Earl Plant), Coventry. Began career as professional painter, 1912; studios in Minneapolis, New York and Hollywood; twice winner of First award at Minneapolis Inst. of Arts and Gold Medal, Minnesota State Fair Art Exhibit. Guest instructor Art Inst. of Chicago Art School (summer), 1943; instructor, Protrait and Still-Life Minneapolis School of Art, 1941, 1942, 1943; represented by portraits Minneapolis Institute of Art, Neville Museum. Green Bay, Wisconsin, Neenah (Wis.) Public Library, and many private collections, Art critic and columnist of Minneapolis Tribune with column entitled, Frances Greenman Says. Mem. Wash. Soc. of Artists, Cor Ardens, Whitney Studio Club, Minnesota Artists Assn. Address: Minneapolis, Minn. †

GREENMAN, WILLIAM GARRETT, naval officer; b. Utica, N.Y., Aug. 26, 1888; s. Byron Scott and Carrie Vosse (Pierce) G.; B.S., U.S. Naval Acad., 1912; m. Marion Frances Pierce, Dec. 21, 1912; children—Franklin Pierce, William G., Mary Nelson (Mrs. William C. Rae, Jr.). Commd. ensign U.S. Navy, June 1912; and advanced through the grades to commodore, Nov. 2, 1945; served on U.S.S. North Dakota, 1912-13, U.S.S. Sacramento, 1914-15, U.S.S. Nevada, 1915-18, U.S.S. Florida, Jan.-Sept. 1919; on duty Navy Dept., Washington, D.C., 1919-21; exec. officer U.S.S. Shawmut, 1921-23; aide and flag sec., staff vice adm. McCully, 1923-24; sec. academic bd., U.S. Naval Acad., 1924-27; comd. U.S.S. Preston, 1928; aide and flag sec. staff Adm. Wiley (comdr. in chief, U.S. Fleet), 1928-29; comd. U.S.S. Brooks, 1930; in exec. dept. U.S. Naval Acad., 1930-33; 1st lt. and damage control officer, U.S.S. Ranger, 1934-36; insp. Naval Petroleum Reserves in Calif., 1936-39; comdr. destroyer div. 10 and 27, 1939-40; chief of staff and aide to comdr. destroyers, Atlantic Squadron, 1940-42; commd. U.S.S. Astoria, cruiser (Battle of Savo Island), 1942; attached to 1st Marine div. on Guadalcanal as 1st comdr. naval bases in Solomon Islands, 1942; comdr. Service Force, Pacific Fleet, later duty h.q. comdr.-in-chief, Pacific Fleet, 1943-44; Chief of Staff to Comd., Marshall and Mariannas Islands, 1944; dir. naval petroleum reserves, Office Sec. of Navy, Washington, D.C., since Apr. 1944. Recipient Legion of Merit, Purple Heart medal, Presidential Unit Citation ribbon, Mexican Service medal, Haitian Campaign medal, Victory medal, Grand Fleet and Atlantic Fleet clasp, Am. Defense Service medal, Fleet clasp, Asiatic-Pacific Area Campaign medal, Am. Area Campaign medal, World War II Victory medal. Episcopalian. Home: Arlington, Va. †

GREENSON, RALPH ROMEO, physician; b. Bklyn., Sept. 20, 1911; s. Joel O. and Katherine (Goldberg) G.; student Columbia U., 1928-30; M.D., U. Berne (Switzerland), 1934; m. Hildegard Troesch, July 14, 1935; children—Daniel, Joan (Mrs. Andreas Aebi). Intern, Cedars of Lebanon Hosp., Los Angeles, 1934-35; resident U. Vienna, Austria, 1935-36; practice medicine specializing in psychiatry, Beverly Hills, Calif., 1936-42, 46-79; tng. analyst Los Angeles Psychoanalytic Inst., Beverly Hills, 1947—; clin. prof. psychiatry UCLA Med. Sch., 1951-79. Chmn. sci. adv. bd. Found. for Research in Psychoanalysis, 1964-79. Served to maj. M.C., AUS, 1942-46. Mem. Am. Psychoanalytic Assn., Los Angeles Psychoanalytic Soc. (pres. 1951-53). Author: The Technique and Practice of Psychoanalysis, vol. I, 1967; Explorations in Psychoanalysis, 1978. Contbr. articles to profl. jours. Home: Santa Monica, Calif. Died Nov. 24, 1979; buried Hillside Cemetery, Los Angeles.

GREENWOOD, FREDERICK, banker; b. LaCrosse, Wis., Apr. 21, 1889; s. Marcellus Bixby and Clara Eliza (Bradish) G.; A.B., U. of Montana, 1909; M.C.S., Amos Tuck Sch. of Adminstrn. and Finance, Dartmouth Coll., 1910; m. Grace Mildred Tucker, Nov. 11, 1925; 1 son, Robert Earl. Clerk, Old Nat. Bank, Spokane, Wash., 1910-17; with Spokane branch Federal Reserve Bank of San Francisco, 1917-18, cashier Portland branch, 1919-20, mgr. Portland branch, 1920-25; asst. mgr. The Bank of California, N.A., Portland, Ore., 1925-35, mgr., 1935-47, vice president and mgr. from 1947. Served with U.S. Army, 1918-19. Trustee and treasurer Good Samaritan Hospital; trustee, Gabel Country Day School. Member Oregon Bankers Association (president (1934-35), American Bankers Association (member executive com. 1935-38), Sigma Chi. Republican. Conglist. Clubs: Arlington (dir.), University (pres. 1930-31), Waverly Country (Portland). Home: Portland, Oreg. †

GREENWOOD, JAMES A., lawyer; b. Franklin, Neb., Apr. 22, 1887; s. James and Ruth (Kenyon) G.; B.A., Grinnell Coll., 1913; m. Margaret Goshen, Feb. 8, 1920; 3 children. Admitted to Wyo. bar, 1917, and began practice in Sheridan; county atty. Weston County, 1923-25; dep. atty. gen. Wyo., 1927-31, atty. gen., 1931-33; resigned, 1933, and from practiced law in Cheyenne. Served with the U.S. Army, World War I. Member Cheyenne C. of C. (pres. 1945). Republican. Conglist. Mason (32 deg.), Lion (pres. Newcastle 1943-44). Club: Cheyenne Country (dir.). †

GREER, EVERETT, lawyer; b. Mountain City, Tenn., May 26, 1890; s. Ben W. and Martha (Gentry) G.; ed. Carson Newman Coll., Washington and Lee Univ., U. of London and Inns of Court, London; m. Elizabeth Brickey; 4 children. Admitted to Tenn. bar, 1914, and began practice at Newport. U.S. dist. attorney, Eastern Tenn. Dist., 1928; gov. Veterans Home, Johnson City, Tenn., 1931-34; with Veterans Adminstrn., legal dept., 1934-41. Served as lt. F.A. and Air Service, U.S. Army, 1917-18. Rep. presdl. elector, Tenn., 1920. Methodist. Address: Newport, Tenn.†

GREER, MARSHALL RAYMOND, naval officer; b. Riverside, N.C., Mar. 1, 1896; s. George Washington and Emily Elizabeth (Yates) G.; grad. Pikeville Collegiate Acad. 1912, U.S. Naval Acad., 1918 (class of 1919); m. Elizabeth Brooks, Nov. 30, 1922 (dec. 1927); 1 dau. Grace Emily (Mrs. Fred A. Richards, Jr.); married Katherine Sherburne French, Mar. 30, 1932; childlren—Elinor, Marshall Raymond, Jr. Commissioned ensign, U.S.N., 1918, and advanced through grades to rear adm., 1945; served on U.S.S. North Dakota, 1918-21; flight trainee, Pensacola, Fla., and designated naval aviator, Dec. 1921; various assignments at sea and ashore with naval aviation, including naval aviation adviser, Argentine Naval War Coll., 1939-42; commanded successively U.S.S. Wright, U.S.S. Core, U.S.S. Bunker Hill, during World War II; comdr., Aircraft S. Pacific, Jan.-May 1945; placed in commn. Fleet Air Wing 18, May 1945, serving as comdr. to Dec. 1945; chief Pan Am. Affairs and U.S. Naval Missions, Navy Dept., Washington, 1946-48; comdr. Carrier, Division 3, from Jan. 1948, additional duty as mem. Inter-Am. Defense Bd., Joint Brazil-U.S. Defense Bd., Joint Mex.-U.S. Defense Bd., Permanent Joint Bd., Canada-U.S.; naval advisor to Sec. of State at Rio Conf., 1947; comdr. Carrier Div. 3, Jan. 1948-April 1949; comdr. Fleet Air Wing 2 and comdr. Fleet Air Hawaii, May 1949-Sept. 1950; comdr. Carribbean Sea Frontier and 10th Naval Dist. since Oct. 1950. Methodist. Died Sept. 2, 1981.

GREGG, DONALD CROWTHER, educator; b. Marlboro, N.H., June 25, 1913; s. Arthur E. and Ida May (Crowther) G.; m. Florence Bentley Green, May 29, 1943 (dec. 1973); children—Bentley Crowther, Fulton Mills; m. Elizabeth Moulton, Dec. 21, 1974. B.S., U. Vt., 1935; M.S., U. N.H., 1937; Ph.D., Columbia, 1941. Asst. chemistry U. N.H., 1935-37, Columbia, 1937-39; research chemist Wallace & Tiernan Products, Belleville, N.J., 1940-41; faculty Harvard, 1940; vis. lectr., summer 1946; instr., asst. prof. Amherst (Mass.) Coll., 1941-46; prof. U. Vt., 1952-84, Pomeroy prof. chemistry, 1963-78; vis. prof. U. Fla., 1962-63; sci. faculty fellow NSF, 1962-63. Author: Principles of Chemistry, 3d edit, 1968, College Chemistry, 2d edit, 1965, Chemistry in the Laboratory, 1966. Trustee Fletcher Free Library, 1964-84, Pine Ridge Sch., 1972-84, St. Johnsbury Acad., Vt. Inst. Community Involvement. Fellow Am. Inst. Chemists, Vt. Acad. Arts and Scis. (trustee); mem. Am. Chem. Soc. (chmn. Western Vt. sect. 1953), AAUP (pres. Vt. chpt. 1953-55), New Eng. Assn. Chemistry Tchrs. (hon.), New Eng. Acad. Sci. (pres. 1965-66), Vt. Library Trustees Assn. (pres. 1968-69), Sigma Xi (pres. Vt. chpt. 1952-53), Alpha Chi Sigma, Phi Lambda Upsilon, Sigma Delta Psi, Sigma Alpha Epsilon. Clubs: Sagamore Beach Colony, Burlington Tennis (v.p., dir. 1959-62). Home: Hyde Park, Vt. Died Aug. 17, 1984.

GREGORY, CHRISTOPHER, educator; b. Cleve., June 6, 1916; s. Thomas and Katherine (Schwan) G.; m. Rose Ching, Aug. 11, 1942; children—Cheryl (Mrs. Forrester T. Johnson), Christopher Thomas, Charles Michael, Christina (Mrs. Gregory Broughton), Deeling Catherine-Rose. B.S., Calif. Inst. Tech., 1938, M.S., 1939, Ph.D., 1941. Physicist Nat. Bur. Standards, 1944-45; instr. math., physics and engring. U. Hawaii, Honolulu, 1941-43, asst. prof., 1944-50, asso. prof. math., 1950-52, prof., 1952-80, dept. chmn., 1951-57, 1961-63, chmn. grad. dept., 1961-65, emeritus prof., 1980-83. Mem. Am. Phys. Soc., Am. Math. Soc., AAAS, Sigma Xi. Research on relativity and quantum theory, extra-dimensionality in gen. theory of relativity and theory of spaceons, Doppler effects and hypervelocities for Quasar sources. Home: Honolulu, Hawaii. Died May 3, 1983.

GREGORY, DAVID ALBERTUS, M.D.; b. Nashville, Tenn., June 27, 1887; s. David Lee and Phoebe Jane (Knapp) G.; grad. Fogg High Sch., Nashville, 1905; M.D., Vanderbilt, 1916; grad. Army Med. Sch., Washington, 1918; m. Mary L. Williams, Nov. 18, 1917; 1 son, David. Asst. in pathology, Vanderbilt, 1916-17; pathologist Macon Hosp., 1920; pathologist Sioux Falls (S. D.) Clinic, 1920-24; surgeon Miller (S.D.) Hosp., from 1926. Served in 3d U.S. Cav., 1905-08, and in Hosp. service, U.S.N., 1908-12; commd. 1st lt. M.R.C., 1917; 1st lt. M.C., U.S.A., 1918; capt., 1918-20. Mem. A.M.A., A.A.A.S., Am. Assn. Bacteriologists, Am. Urol. Assn. Unitarian. Mason (32 deg.). Club: Golf and Country. Home: Miller, S.D. †

GREGORY, H. W., univ. prof.; b. Sedan, Kan., Aug. 11, 1889; s. Elliott B. and Louise (Wiley) G.; B.S., Agrl. and Mech. Coll., Stillwater, Okla., 1912; M.S., Purdue U., 1918; m. May Kilpatrick, Dec. 25, 1914; children—Edith (Mrs. Ralph Baur), Winifred (Mrs. William Troyer). Instr., South Dakota State Coll., 1912-16; grad. asst. in dairy husbandry, Purdue U., 1916-17, asst. prof., 1917-19, asso. prof., 1919-20, prof. dairy husbandry and head dairy dept. from 1920. Mem. Am. Dairy Science Assn. (pres. 1937-38). Phi Kappa Phi. Lambda Gamma Delta, Sigma Xi, Scabbard and Blade. Home: West Lafayette, Ind. †

GREGORY, HORACE VICTOR, poet, critic; b. Milw., Apr. 10, 1898; s. Henry Bolton and Anna Catherine (Henkel) G.; m. Marya Zaturenska, Aug. 21, 1925; children—Joanna Elizabeth, Patrick Bolton. Student, German-English Acad., Milw., 1914-19, Milw. Sch. Fine Arts, 1913-16; B.A., U. Wis., 1923, D.Litt. (hon.), 1977. Lectr. poetry and critical theory Sarah Lawrence Coll., Bronxville, N.Y., from 1934; editor New Letters in Am., 1937. Free-lance writer, 1923-34; contbr. to: Poetry mag, Chgo., New Verse, London, others; Translator.; Author: verse Chelsea Rooming House, 1930, several books, 1930—, including, A History of American Poetry, 1900-1940, (in collaboration with Marya Zaturenska), 1946, Selected Poems, 1951, Amy Lowell; Portrait of the Poet in Her Times, 1958, The World of James McNeil Whistler, 1959, Medusa in Gramercy Park (new poems), 1961, The Dying Gladiators and Other Essays, 1961, (with Marya Zaturenska) The Crystal Cabinet, 1962, Collected Poems, 1964, Love Poems of Ovid, new English version, 1964, Dorothy Richardson: An Adventure in Self-Discovery, 1967, The House on Jefferson Street: A Cycle of Memories (autobiography), 1971, Another Look (poems), 1976; Editor: (with Marya Zaturenska) The Triumph of Life, 1943, Selected Poetry of Robert Browning, 1956, The Mentor Book of Religious Verse, 1957, The Crystal Cabinet: An Invitation to Poetry, 1962, The Silver Swan, 1966, Henry Wadsworth Longfellow: Evangeline and Other Tales and Poems, 1964, Selected Poems of E.E. Cummings, 1965, Spirit of Time and Place: Collected Essays of Horace Gregory, 1973; asso. editor: (with Marya Zaturenska) The Tigers Eye; editor: (with Marya Zaturenska) The Portable Sherwood Anderson, 1949-71, The Selected Poems of George Gordon Lord Byron, 1969. Recipient Lyric prize Poetry mag., 1928, Helen Haire Levinson prize, 1934; Russell Loines award for poetry Am. Inst. Arts and Letters, 1942; fellowship award Acad. Am. Poets, 1961; Bollingen prize in poetry, 1965; Guggenheim fellow, 1951. Mem. Nat. Inst. Arts and Letters. Address: Shelburne, Mass. Died Mar. 11, 1982.

GREGORY, THORNE, banker; b. Halifax, N.C., Dec. 25, 1928; s. Fletcher Harrison and Boyd (Thorne) G.; m. Hester Lockett, Feb. 23, 1957; children—Hester Elizabeth, Boyd Wynn, Ann Harrison, Thorne. A.B. in History, U. N.C., 1952, grad. Sch. Banking, 1960. Vice pres., dir. Bank of Halifax, N.C., 1960-68; sr. v.p., dir. Br. Banking & Trust Co., Wilson, N.C., 1968-73, pres., chief exec. officer, 1973-82; dir. Coastal Lumber Co., Weldon, N.C. Mem. N.C. Ho. of Reps., 1961-69, chmn. com. on fed. and interstate cooperation, 1963-69, chmn. com. banks and banking, 1965, chmn. com. on fin., 1969; mem. Com. on Nat. Hwy. Policy, N.C. Com. on Aviation, N.C. Adv. Budget Com., N.C. Bd. Higher Edn., Rex Hosp. Found., Atlantic States Marine Fisheries Commn.; bd. dirs. N.C. Citizens Assn., Med. Found. N.C., Bus. Found. N.C.; trustee Blue Cross and Blue Shield of N.C. Served to 1st lt. USAF, 1952-56. Mem. N.C. Bankers Assn. (dir., chmn. govt. relations council 1975-82, pres. 1981-82), Wilson C. of C. (dir.), Order of Gimghoul, Zeta Psi, St. Andrews Soc. Democrat. Episcopalian. Clubs: Country of N.C. (Pinehurst); Carolina Country (Raleigh); Wilson Country, Kiwanis. Home: Wilson, N.C. Died Feb. 13, 1982.

GRENIER, PIERRE, chemical engineering educator, university dean; b. Quebec, Que., Can., Aug. 15, 1922; s. Joachim and Corinne (Koenig) G.; B.A., Coll. Garnier, Quebec, 1942; B.Sc.A., U. Laval, Quebec, 1946; M.S., Columbia U., 1947; m. Therese Vallee, Sept. 3, 1949; children—Lucie (Mrs. Jean Turcotte), Ivan P., Francois M. Asst. prof. chem. engring. U. Laval, 1947-50, assoc. prof., 1950-55, prof., 1955-85, chmn. dept. chem. engring., 1965-69, dean Faculty Sci., from 1969; vis. prof. U. Nancy, France, 1963-64. Centre hospitalier U. Laval. Decorated officer Order Can. Mem. Engring. Inst. Can., Order Engrs. Que., Chem. Inst. Can. (pres.). Home: Ste-Foy, Que., Can. Died July 18, 1985.

GRESSETTE, LAWRENCE MARION, state senator; b. St. Matthews, S.C., Feb. 11, 1902; s. J. T. and Rosa (Wannamaker) G.; m. Florence Howell, Aug. 18, 1927. J.D., U. S.C., 1924, LL.D., 1977; LL.D., Clemson U., 1980, The Citadel, 1981. Bar: S.C. 1924. Practiced in, St. Mathews, 1924-84; mem. firm Gressette & Gressette, 1959-80, Gressette and Prickett, 1980-84; mem. S.C. Senate, 1937-84, pres. pro tem, 1972-84, chmn. com. on judiciary, 1953-84, com. hwys., 1970, vice chmn. com. on edn., 1967-84, vice chmn. S.C. Reorgn. Commn., 1972-76, chmn. Commn. on Interstate Coop., 1972-84; mem. governing bd. Council State Govts., 1972-84. Chmn. S.C. Sch. Com., 1951-66; mem. S.C. Democratic Exec. Com., 1948-84, chmn., 1953-54; del. at large Nat. Dem. Conv., Chgo., 1956, Los Angeles, 1960, Atlantic City, 1964. Fellow Am. Coll. Trial Lawyers; mem. Blue Key, Phi Kappa Phi. Baptist. Club: Masons. Address: Saint Matthews, S.C. Died Feb. 2, 1984.

GRIBBIN, GEORGE HOMER, advt. exec.; b. Nashville, Mich., Aug. 13, 1907; s. George Ward and Anna Laura (Downing) G.; A.B., Stanford, 1929; m. Barbara McBride, Oct. 24, 1941 (dec. May 4, 1952); 1 son, Andrew Downing; married second, Jane Lindon, July 21, 1953; children—Laura, Peter, Sarah, Susan, James, Mary. Advt. copywriter J.L. Hudson Co., L. Bamberger, Macy's, 1929-35; copywriter Young & Rubicam, Inc., 1935-42, copy supr., 1942-51, v.p., head radio-TV commercials, 1951-58, copy director, 1954-58, senior vice president, 1956-58, pres., 1958-63, chmn. bd., 1963-65, chief executive officer, adviser, 1965-81. Served from pvt. to capt. AUS, 1943-45. Home: Greenwich, Conn. Died Aug. 26, 1981.

GRIBBIN, ROBERT EMMET, bishop; b. Windsor, S.C., Feb. 21, 1887; s. John and Rebecca (Moore) G., B.S., Mil. Coll. of S.C., 1906; B.A., Coll. of Charleston, S.C., 1909; student Gen. Theol. Sem., New York, 1909-12, S.T.D., 1934, D.D., Univ. of the South, 1934; m. Emma Manigault Jenkins, June 30, 1915; children—Robert Emmet, Josephine Manigault, John Hawkins, Deacon, 1912, priest, 1913, P.E. Ch.; asst. minister Grace Ch., Charleston, 1912-15, St. Luke's Ch., Atlanta, Ga., 1915-16; rector St. John's Ch., Wilmington, N.C., 1916-21, St. Paul's Ch., Winston-Salem, N.C., 1921-34; consecrated bishop of Western N.C., Jan. 25, 1934; Chaplain 3d Pioneer, Inf., 1918-19, 105th Med. Regt., N.C. Nat. Guard, 1931-40; entered active service for one year as chaplain of the 105th Med. Regt., with rank of lt. col., at Fort Jackson, S.C., 1940-41. Mem. Am. Legion. Democrat. Mason, Elk. Home: Asheville, N.C. †

GRIER, ROBERT CALVIN, clergyman, educator; b. Due West, S.C., Oct. 12, 1889; s. Paul Livingston and Effie Lillian (Pressly) G.; A.B., Erskine Coll., Due West, 1910; grad. Erskine Theol. Sem., 1914; studied Princeton Sem., 1919-20; D.D.; Presbyn. Coll. S.C., 1922; LL.D., University S.C., 1932; Litt. D., Furman University, 1951; married Gladys Victoria Patrick, November 17, 1915; children—Robert C. (dec.), Barbara Moffatt, Gladys Patrick, Robert Calvin. Ordained ministry Associate Ref. Presbyn. Ch., 1914; pastor Louisville, Ky., 1914-18, Columbia, S.C., 1918-21; pres. Erskine Coll. from Sept. 1, 1921; apptd. mem. Bd. of Edn., S.C., 1946; moderator Gen. Synod, Asso. Reformed Presbyn. Ch., 1950-51; mem. exec. com. Western sect. Alliance of Reformed Chs. Holding Presbyn. System. Mem. Phi Beta Kappa. Dem. Home: Due West, S.C. †

GRIERSON, ELMER PRESLEY, attorney; b. Manchester, O., Dec. 18, 1888; s. John Hendron and Dora May (Scott) G.; A.B., U. of Mich., 1912, law student, 1912-13; LL.B., Detroit Coll. of Law, 1915; m. Phyllis Evers Murray, June 18, 1914; children—Margaret Eleanor (Mrs. Theron F. Gifford), John Murray. Former Pub. The American Boy, Detroit. Dir. U. of Mich. Alumni Assn., 1939-42. Commr. Dept. of Water Supply, City of Detroit, 1940-42; mem. bd. of assessors, City of Detroit, 1942-47; chmn. Detroit panel Seventh Regional Loyalty Board. Dir. Medical Science Center, Wayne University, Detroit. Republican. Episcopalian (former vestryman). Clubs: Detroit, Players (Detroit). Home: Detroit, Mich. †

GRIFFENHAGEN, EDWIN O., cons. mgmt. engr.; b. Chgo., Ill., Jan. 14, 1886; s. Oscar Fred and Anna Maria (Kleinhans) G.; B.S. in C.E., Ill. Inst. Tech., 1906, C.E., 1909; m. Christine A. Gloeckler, Jan. 7, 1909; children—Ruth Christine (Mrs. Newton Du Puy), Elinor Jane (Mrs. David B. Truman). Mining engring., Alaska, 1906; bldg. engr., C.M. & St. P. Ry., 1907-09; archtl. engr. Chgo., 1909, orgn. tech. work, Civil Service Commn., 1910; head indsl. engring. dept., Arthur Young & Co., Chgo., N.Y.C., 1911-19, with colleagues took over business of indsl., engring. dept. 1920, and since practiced as Griffenhagen & Assos. cons. mgmt. engrs.; cons. Griffenhagen-Kroeger, Inc., from 1959. Reorganized Canadian Gov't. depts., 1918- ret. naval officer; b. Phila., Jan. 12, 1906; s. Joseph Richard and Maude (Spicknall) G.; B.S., U.S. Naval Acad., 1927; M.S. in Aero. Engring., U. Mich., 1937; grad. Nat. War Coll, 1951; m. Camilla Yvonne Ganteaume, Sept. 14, 1935 (dec.); children—Linda (Mrs. Harry Collins II), Charles Donald; m. 2d., Marion Hopkins Schaefer, Nov. 21, 1964. Commd. ensign USN, 1927, advanced through grades to adm., 1963; designated naval aviator; duty in battleships, destroyers, 1927-30; attached U.S.S. Enterprise, 1937-40; flight test officer Naval Air Sta., Anacostia, 1940-42; comdr. Carrier Air Group 9, U.S.S. Essex, 1942-43; operations officer T.F. 58 Pacific, 1943; mem. Joint War Plans Com. Joint Chiefs Staff, 1944; comdg. officer U.S.S. Croatan, 1945-46; plans officer U.S. Atlantic Fleet, 1946-47; strategic plans div. Operations Navy, 1948-50; plans officer U.S. Pacific Fleet, 1951-53; comdg. officer U.S.S. Oriskany, 1953-54; spl. asst. to chmn. Joint Chiefs of Staff, 1955-56; comdr. Carrier Div. 4, 1947-48; dir. strategic plans Navy Dept., 1959-60; comdr. Seventh Fleet, 1960-61; dep. chief naval operations, 1962-63; comdr. in chief USN Forces Europe, 1963-65; comdr. in chief allied forces So. Europe, 1965-68. Decorated D.S.M. with gold star, Bronze Star medal, Presdl. citations; supreme comdr. Order of George the First (Greece); knight Grand Cross Order of Republic (Italy); comdr. Philippine Legion Honor; Order Mil. Merit with silver star (Korea); Order of Double-Rays of Rising Sun (Japan); Medal of Pao-Ting (China). Episcopalian. Clubs: Chevy Chase (Md.); Army and Navy, Metropolitan, Tavern Association (Washington); Army and Navy Country (Arlington, Va.); American (London, Eng.); Circolo dell'Unione (Naples, Italy); Royal and ancient Golf of St. Andrews (Scotland); New York Yacht (N.Y.C.). Home: Washington, DC. †

GRIFFIN, NORVAL BURRIS, mfg. exec.; b. Fredericksburg, O., Nov. 17, 1887; s. Albert Sidney and Laura (Lytle) G.; student Muskingum Coll., 1905-07; LL.D., Muskingum College, 1954; B.S., Case Institute of Technology, 1911, M.E., 1916; m. Terese Kennedy, April 18, 1917; children—John K., Marjorie (Mrs. O. F. Apel, Jr.). With Selby Shoe Co. since 1914, prodn. mgr., 1915-31, div. sales mgr., 1926-34, asst. gen mgr., 1931-34, dir. from 1934, v.p., gen. mgr., 1934-46, pres., 1946-53, ret., 1953. Member Ohio White House Conference Com. on Edn., Capitol Planning, Improvement Bd. State Ohio. Trustee Muskingum Coll. Served as 2d lt. A.S., U.S. Army, World War I. Profl. indsl. engr., Ohio. Mem. Ohio Engrs. Soc., C. of C., Sigma Alpha Epsilon. Presbyn. (elder). Mason (K.T., Shriner), Elk. Club: Portsmouth Reading. Home: Portsmouth, Ohio. †

GRIFFIN, ROBERT MELVILLE, ret. naval officer; b. Washington, May 23, 1890; s. Robert Stanislaws and Helena (Laube) G.; student Swavely Prep. Sch., 1906-07, B.S., Naval Acad., 1911, post-grad. work, 1916-17; m. Mary McKay Hemming, Dec. 16, 1924; children—Patricia Hemming (Mrs. Frank Gum Sterrett), Mimi, Robert. Commd. and advanced through the grades to v. adm. as comdr. Naval Forces Far East; ret. 1951; exec. v.p. Pa. Hosp., Phila., from 1951. Awarded Navy Cross, World War (service overseas); Legion Merit with star for second award. Officer, Order of the Crown (Belgium). Club: Chevy Chase. Home: Overbrook, Pa. †

GRIFFIN, S. MARVIN, former gov. of Ga.; born Bainbridge, Ga., Sept. 4, 1907; son E. H. and Josie (Butler) G.; A.B., The Citadel, 1929; m. Elisabeth Smith; 1 son, Samuel Marvin. Owner and editor, Post Searchlight, Bainbridge, Ga.; pres., Radio Sta. WMGR, Bainbridge. Mem. Ga. Gen. Assembly, 1935-36; exec. sec. to gov. of Ga., 1940; adjutant gen. of Ga., 1944-47, lt. gov., 1948-54, gov. of Ga., 1955-59. Presbyn. Mason. Home: Bainbridge, Ga. Died June 13, 1982.

GRIFFITH, LOUIS EUGENE, business exec.; b. Columbus, Miss., Jan. 31, 1889; s. Louis Eugene and Charlotte (Hatfield) G.; student Lafayette Coll., 1908-10; m. Mary Kenaston, May 29, 1917; 1 son, Robert Kenaston. Various engring. positions since 1910; with Riley Stoker Corp., Worcester, from 1924, v.p., dir., 1929-49, gen. mgr., from 1924, then president, chairman, v.p., general manager; president and dir. A.W. Cash Co., Badenhausen Corp.; Cash-Stacon Corporation; chairman board Union Iron Works, Erie, Pa. Member American Boiler Mfrs. Assn. (pres., dir.), Am. Soc. M.E., Newcomen Soc. Eng., Knights of Round Table, Delta Upsilon. Republican. Episcopalian. Clubs: Calumet, Engineers (N.Y.C., Boston); University. Home: Worcester, Mass. †

GRIFFITH, THEODORE BARTON, business exec.; b. Indianapolis, Nov. 11, 1888; s. Claude T. and Lizzie Belle (Stone) G.; A.B., Williams Coll., 1910; m. Helen M. Wheelock, June 1, 1918; children—Helen (Mrs. Daniel Reagan), Sylvia (Mrs. John E. D. Peacock). With Potter Hat Co., 1910-15, Griffith Bros., 1915-19; with L. S. Ayres & Co., from 1920, dir., from 1923, pres., 1940-54, chairman of the board, 1954-59, ret. Trustee of the Committee for Fundamental Edn. Mem. Kappa Alpha. Clubs: University, Columbia, Athenaeum, Dramatic, Literary (Indpls.); Williams (N.Y.C.). Episcopalian. †

GRIFFITTS, CHARLES HURLBUT, psychologist; born Ozawkie, Kan., Jan. 5, 1889; s. Alvin and Mary (Hurlbut) G.; A.B., Campbell Coll., Holton, Kan., 1913; A.M., U. of Kan., 1914; Ph.D., U. of Mich., 1919; m. Blanche Kuhman, Sept. 7, 1912; children—Charles Hurlburt, Alice Genevieve (Mrs. Ralph H. Danhof), Wallace Rush. Instr. Park Coll., Parkville, Mo., 1914-16; mem. faculty U. of Mich. from 1917, prof. psychology from 1936; organized and dir. Psychol. Clinic of Inst. for Human Adjustment, 1938-45. Served as 1st lt., Air Service, U.S. Army, 1918-19. Fellow A.A.A.S.; mem. Am. Psychol. Assn., Sigma Xi. Author: Fundamentals of Vocational Psychology, 1925. Contbr. to psychol. periodicals. Home: Ann Arbor, Mich. †

GRIMM, EDITH RAMBAR, merchandising/marketing consultant; b. Seneca Falls, N.Y., Jan. 17, 1908; d. Mitchel J. and Florence (Kutner) Rambar; m. Emery G. Grimm, Aug. 31, 1929 (dec. Mar. 19, 1959). Ph.B., U. Chgo., 1927; postgrad., U. Mich., 1927-28. Tchr. math. Detroit pub. schs., 1927-29; supr. personal shopping service Marshall Field and Co., Chgo., 1935; with Carson Pirie Scott and Co., Chgo., 1935—, asso. gen. mdsg. mgr., 1958-63, v.p. gen. merchandising, 1963-73; chmn. retail adv. bd. Bride's mag., 1946-48; Regional dir. Chgo. Fashion Group, 1949-50; mem. adv. council Tobé-Coburn Sch., 1965—; dir. seminars on retailing Am. Mgmt. Assn. Chmn. gen. mdse. div. Chgo. Heart Fund, 1964; Mem. U. Ill. Citizens Com., 1972—, Nat. Home Fashions League Found. Com., 1969—. Recipient Victory award and citation for war bond sales, 1945; YWCA award for outstanding Chgo. woman in bus. and industry, 1972; named one of ten outstanding women bus. and community leaders in Chgo., 1959. Mem. Home Fashions League, Am. Inst. Decorators (nat. jury mem. for design competition 1953, design awards jury 1964), U. Chgo. Alumni Assn. (exec. bd. and senate 1952-53, chmn. improved activities com. 1954), Fashion Group. Clubs: Arts (Chgo.), Economic (Chgo.). Home: Dallas TX.

GRIMM, HAROLD JOHN, history educator; b. Saginaw, Mich., Aug. 16, 1901; s. Henry Frederick and Ella Emelie (Lepien) G.; m. Thelma Jayne Rickey, Aug. 29, 1931; 1 dau., Jane (Mrs. H.S. Minton). A.B., Capital U., 1924; grad., Evang. Luth. Theol. Sem., Columbus, Ohio, 1927; M.A., Ohio State U., 1928, Ph.D., 1932; student, U. Leipzig, 1929-30, U. Hamburg, summer 1930; Litt.D., Carthage Coll., 1965; D.H.L., Ohio Wesleyan U., 1971; D.Humanities, Capital U., 1978. Instr. history Capital U., 1925-29, asst. prof., 1930-33, asso. prof., 1933-36, prof., chmn. dept., 1936-37; asst. prof. history Ohio State U., 1937-42, asso. prof., 1942-47, prof., 1947-54, prof. history, 1958-72, prof. emeritus, from 1972, chmn. dept., 1958-66, regents' prof., 1968-72; prof. history, chmn. dept. Ind. U., 1954-58; Fulbright teaching fellow U. Freiburg i. Br., 1954; Bd. dirs. Found. for Reformation Research. Author: Martin Luther as a Preacher, 1929, Western Civilization, (with Tschan and Squires), 2 vols.), 1942, The Reformation Era, 1954, 73, Luther and Culture, (with G.W. Forell and T. Hoelty Nickel), 1960, Lazarus Spengler: Lay Leader of the Reformation, 1978; Editor: Luther's Works, Vol. 31, 1957; Am. editor: Archiv fuer Reformationsgeschichte, 1949-62; editorial bd., from 1962; Contbr. articles to profl. publs. Mem. bd. edn. Bexley pub. schs. Recipient Distinguished Tchr. award Ohio State U., 1978. Fellow Royal Soc. Arts (Gt. Britain), Royal Hist. Soc. (Gt. Britain); mem. Am. Hist. Assn., Ohio Hist. Soc. (past pres.), Am. Soc. Ch. History (past pres.), Am. Soc. Reformation Research (past pres.), Hansischer Geschichtsverein, Am. Assn. U. Profs., Phi Beta Kappa, Phi Alpha Theta (hon. life 1965). Lutheran. Clubs: Rotarian, Ohio State University Faculty. Home: Columbus, OH.

GRINNELL, ROBERT LOUIS, banker; b. Bay City, Mich., Apr. 9, 1890; s. Joseph and Emily (Fox) G.; B.A., Yale, 1915; m. Mary King, June 30, 1917; children—Mrs. Mary Grinnell Gordon, Joseph F. With First Nat. Bank of Chicago from 1919, vice pres. to 1950. Mem. Chicago bar assns. Clubs: University (Chicago).†

GRISDALE, JOHN THOMAS, ret. architect; b. Mpls., Sept. 30, 1904; s. Charles and Frances Ruth (Orvis) G.; student U. Minn., 1923-26, U. Pa., 1927-28; m. Catherine Johnston Hanford, Jan. 31, 1931; 1 son, Hanford Gillespie. With Mellor, Meigs & Howe, Phila., 1928-38; architect in firm of Paul P. Cret, Phila., 1941-44; partner

Carroll, Grisdale and Van Alen, Phila., 1946-72. Pres., Child Study Center, Phila., 1957-58. Recipient various awards for architecture. Fellow AIA; mem. Phila. Art Alliance. Works include: college bldgs., schs., airport terminal, libraries, courthouses, offices bldgs., residences. Home: Radnor, Pa. Died July 19, 1985; buried St Martins Ch., Radnor.

GRIZZELL, E(MIT) DUNCAN, univ. prof.; b. Alexandria, Ky., Apr. 28, 1887; s. William Franklin and Margaret (Rees) G.; A.B., Yale, 1915; A.M., U. of Pa., 1919, Ph.D., 1922; m. Ethyl Blackerby, Aug. 3, 1911. Asst. prof. secondary edn. U. of Pa., 1922-29, professor since 1929, dean, School of Education, 1948-56. emeritus from 1957; vis prof. Am. U., Cairo, 1957-58; staff survey public and independent schools, 1925-56, chairman schoolmen's week, 1941-48. visiting prof. (summer), U. Wis., 1928, U. Mich., 1930, Wash., 1932; Ohio State U., 1935; U. Va., 1937, 38, 40, 42, 46; U. Colo., 1951, 56; distinguished visiting prof. So. Ill. U., 1959; spl. lectr. Leeds, 1929. Chmn. commn. secondary schools Middle States Assn. Colls., Secondary Schs., 1926-46; dir. com. on implementation studies in secondary edn., Am. Council on Edn.; mem. com. Assn. Am. Schs. in Latin-Am., mem. com. for study of teaching materials on inter-Am. subjects; chmn. com. on Inter-Am. Schools Service, 1944-57; chmn. exec. com. Co-op. Study Secondary Sch. Standards, 1933-49, chmn. gen. com. 1950-56; mem. commn. on human resources and advanced tng. Asso. Research Councils, 1948-53. Dir. Dela. State School Survey, 1946. Mem. com. on language teaching. Am. Council Learned Societies; planning com. Nat. Asso. Secondary Sch. Prins., consultative com. Nat. Com. coordination in Secondary Edn.; com. on modern lang. Am. Council on Education com. on trends in edn. Modern Language Assn.; mem. U.S. Commn. for survey of Bolivian Schs., 1944, mem. adv. com. Secondary Edn., Internat. Ednl. Relations. U.S. Office Edn., 1945. Mem. Com. Am. Council Edn., Study Teaching Materials, Intergroup Relations in schs. and colls., 1945; Commn. Edn., Internat. Affairs. Mem. reviewing staff, Quarterly Book List, Library of Congress. Member Am. Assn. Colls. for Tchrs. of Edn. (mem. accrediting com.), Am. Ednl. Research Assn., American Historical Association, National Society for Study Education, Historical Society of Pennsylvania, Kentucky Civil War Round Table. Author: Origin and Development of the High School in New England Before 1865, 1923; Education: Principles and Practices, 1928; American Secondary Education, 1937; Principles of Unit Construction (with A. J. Jones and W. J. Grinstead), 1939. Mem. editorial bd. Jour. Ednl. Research; editor-in-chief: Ednl. Outlook, 1952-56. Home: Lexington, Ky. †

GRONCHI, GIOVANNI, pres. of Italy; B. Pontedera, Pisa, Italy, Sept. 10, 1887; m. Carla Bissantini, 1941; children—Mario, Maria Cecilia. Elected to Parliament, Partito Popolare party, 1919; leader Confederazione Italiana dei Lavoratori, the White Confederation, 1920; served as Under-Sec. for Industry, 1922-24; salesman, Indsl. cons., Northern Italy, 1924-44; active in partisan underground, World War II; served as Demo-Christian, Central Com. Nat. Liberation; served as minister of Commerce and Industry, Bonomi Govt., 1944-45, Parri govt., 1945, first De Gasperi Govt., and also as Speaker, Chamber of Deputies, 1948-55; elected Pres. of Italy, for seven yr. term, Apr. 1955. Served in Italian Army, World War I. Address: Rome, Italy. †

GRONDAL, BROR LEONARD, prof. of forestry; b. Round Rock, Tex., May 15, 1889; s. Bror Gustaf and Sara Margaret (Noyd) G.; A.B., Bethany Coll., 1910. Sc.D., 1943; M.S.F., University of Wash., 1912; Ph.D. (hon.), Crown-Zellerbach Paper Sch., 1953; m. Florence Armstrong, Apr. 8, 1912; children—Eloise (Mrs. Don James Robbins), Bror Philip. With U. of Wash. since 1913, as instr. in forestry, 1913-16, asst. prof., 1916-25, asso. prof., 1925-29, prof. since 1929; Walker-Ames research prof., 1936, sec. engring. expt. sta., 1927-49; cons. engr. Moore Dry Kiln Co. from 1928, Red Cedar Shingle Bur. since 1932, also other orgns. Associated Forest Products Technologists (pres. 1945-46); chmn. organizing com., Nat. Forest Products Research Soc., 1946-47. Member Cedar River Watershed Commission, 1944. Fellow A.A.A.S.; mem. Soc. Am. Foresters, Swedish Soc. of Foresters (life), Am. Chem. Soc., Am. Wood Pres. Assn., U. of Wash. Alumni Assn. (pres.1950-51, award, 1950), Phi Sigma, Sigma Xi, Xi Sigma Pi (national pres. 1938-39), Swedish Lutheran. Contbr. articles on forest products to mags. Specializes in forest products research and photo-micrography. Licensed professional engr., state of Wash. Home: Seattle, Wash. †

GRONERT, BERNARD GEORGE, editor; b. Prairie du Chien, Wis., June 22, 1920; s. George M. and Irene J. (Kimball) G.; m. Laura Cahalan, Dec. 2, 1942; children: Paula Gronert Hayes, John, Monica. A.B., Wabash (Ind.) Coll., 1942; M.A., U. Wis., 1948. Reporter Dayton Herald, 1946-47; Field editor Ronald Press, N.Y.C., 1950-61; history editor Macmillan Co., 1961-63; exec. editor Columbia U. Press, N.Y.C., 1964-85. Served with USAF, 1942-46. Home: Little Silver, N.J. Died May 15, 1985.

GROSS, CHESTER H(EILMAN), congressman; b. near Manchester, Pa., Oct. 13, 1888; s. Tachirias and Laura Jane (Heilman) G.; ed. public sch., business coll. and Short Course in Agr., Pa. State Coll., 1909; m. Carrie May Hykes, Jan. 10, 1912; children—Esther Elizabeth (Mrs. Oran Yeager), Kathryn Romaine (Mrs. John Row); Marion Ruth (dec.), Harold Tachirias, Nellie Ada, Louise Laura, Stanley Robert, Samuel Hykes. Has farmed from 1912 on the farm where he was born; auditor Emigsville Grange Corpn., former dir. Inter-state Mill Producers Assn.; pres. Pa. State School Dirs. Assn.; served as school dir. 9 years, also pres. of bd.; town supervisor 7 years; mem. 76th Congress (1939-41), 22d Pa. Dist. Awarded Master Farmer. Republican. Lutheran. Mem. Grange, Patriotic Order Sons of America, K.P., York County Rep. Club. Home: Manchester, Pa. †

GROSS, COURTLANDT SHERRINGTON, aircraft corp. exec.; b. Boston, Nov. 21, 1904; s. Robert H. and Mabel (Bell) G.; student St. George's Sch., 1919-23; A.B., Harvard, 1927; m. Alexandra van R. Devereux, July 18, 1939; children—Alexandra Devereux (dec.), Courtlandt Devereux, Mary L. Wanamaker Watriss (step-dau.). Clk., salesman Lee Higginson & Co., Boston, 1927-29; buyer, dir. Viking Flying Boat Co., New Haven, 1929-32; Eastern rep. Lockheed Aircraft Corp., N.Y.C., 1932-40, v.p., gen. mgr., dir., Burbank, 1943-52, exec. v. p., dir., 1952-56, pres., dir., 1956-61, chmn. bd., chmn. exec. com., 1961-67; pres., dir. Vega Aircraft, Burbank, 1940-43. Contributionship for Ins. Houses from Loss by Fire. Episcopalian. Home: Villanova, Pa. Died July 25, 1982.

GROSS, ERWIN GEORGE, educator; b. Merrimac, Wis., May 12, 1892; s. George A. and Frances (Roick) G.; B.S., U. of Wisconsin, 1917, M.S., 1919, Ph.D., 1921; student Yale, 1920-21 and 1927-29; M.D., State U. of Iowa, 1930; m. Eva Lee, Oct. 27, 1921; children—Robert Erwin, Richard Lee. Assistant, U. of Wisconsin, 1917-20; fellow Yale Grad. Sch., 1920-21; instr. Yale Med. Sch., 1921-24; asst. prof., 1924-29; asso. prof., State U. of Iowa, 1929-37; prof. from 1937, head dept. of pharmacology from 1940. Mem. Am. Phys. Soc., Am. Soc. Biochemistry, Soc. for Pharmacology and Therapeutics, Soc. Exptl. Biology and Medicine, A.A.A.S., A.M.A., Phi Chi, Alpha Omega Alpha, Sigma Xi. Mason. Home: Iowa City, Iowa. Died Nov. 26, 1981.

GROSS, NEAL, sociologist, educator; b. San Antonio, Dec. 9, 1920; s. Ely and Lillian (Hochman) G.; m. Pan Dale, Mar. 10, 1948; children—Sandra Jill, Linda Lorrie, Richard Conant. Ph.B., Marquette U., 1941; M.S., Ia. State U., 1942, Ph.D., 1946; student, U. Chgo., 1945-46; M.A. (hon.), Harvard, 1956. Tchr., researcher Iowa State U., 1941-42, 46-48, U. Minn., 1948-51; faculty Harvard, 1951-68, prof. edn., 1958-62; prof. edn. and sociology, research asso. Harvard (Center Internat. Affairs), 1959-68, prof. sociology, 1962-68; dir. Harvard (Sch. Exec. Studies), 1952-57, Harvard (Nat. Principalship Study), 1959-68; also research asso. Harvard (Center for Edn. and Devel.); prof. sociology, prof. edn. U. Pa., Phila., from 1968; dean U. Pa. (Grad. Sch. Edn.), 1968-74; Vis. fellow Wolfson Coll., Oxford (Eng.) U., 1974; cons. OECD, Paris, 1974; Ford Found. spl. travel and research fellow, Western Europe, 1974-75; vis. prof. U. Ife, Nigeria, 1979-80. Author: Who Runs Our Schools, 1958, The Schools and the Press, 1955; Co-author: Explorations in Role Analysis, 1958, Staff Leadership in Public Schools, 1965, Implementing Organizational Innovations, 1971, The Sex Factor and The Management of Schools, 1976; co-editor: The Dynamics of Planned Educational Change, 1979. Served with USNR, 1943-45. Recipient Demblzn award Social Sci. Research Council, 1945, postdoctoral fellowship, 1948; Outstanding research award Am. Personnel and Guidance Assn., 1953; fellow Center Advanced Study in Behavioral Scis., 1957-58; Ford Found. Spl. awards for travel and study in Europe and Africa, 1963-64, Western Europe, 1974. Fellow Am. Sociol. Assn. (chmn. com. on social studies curriculum in Am. secondary schools, mem. exec. council 1967-70); mem. Eastern Sociol. Soc., Am. Ednl. Research Assn., Sociol. Research Assn. Address: Philadelphia, PA.

GROSS, SPENCER, lawyer; b. Hartford, Conn., Dec. 22, 1906; s. Charles Welles and Hilda Frances (Welch) G. A.B., Yale, 1928, LL.B., 1931. Bar: Conn. bar 1931. Since practiced in, Hartford; with Gross, Hyde & Williams, 1931-82, partner, 1936-82; asso. judge City Ct. of Hartford, 1945-47; dir. Nat. Fire Ins. Co. of Hartford, Transcontinental Ins. Co.; corporator Mechanics Savs. Bank.; Mem. Adv. Council on Banking, 1957-77. Mem. Met. Dist. Commn., 1940-54; mem. Bd. Park Commrs., 1939-48, City Plan Commn., 1936-45; Mem. Distbn. Com. Hartford Found. Pub. Giving, 1936-68; Vice pres. Children's Mus. of Hartford, 1948-55; sec. Wadsworth Atheneum, 1942-66; trustee Howard and Bush Found., YMCA Met. Hartford; corporator Hartford Hosp., St. Francis Hosp. Fellow Am. Coll. Probate Counsel; mem. Zeta Psi, Phi Delta Phi. Congregationalist. Clubs: University (Hartford), Wampanoag Country (Hartford), Twentieth Century (Hartford). Home: Hartford, Conn. Died Mar. 1, 1982.

GROSVENOR, MELVILLE BELL, editor; b. Washington, Nov. 26, 1901; s. Gilbert Hovey and Elsie May (Bell) G.; m. Helen North Rowland, Jan. 4, 1924; children—Helen Rowland (Mrs. Richard Lemmerman), Alexander Graham Bell (dec. 1978), Gilbert Melville; m. Anne E. Revis, Aug. 12, 1950; children—Edwin Stuart, Sara Anne. B.S., U.S. Naval Acad., 1923; Sc.D., U. Miami, 1954; LL.D., George Washington U., 1959; Litt.D., Boston U., 1970; D.Sc., U. N.B., Can., 1975. Asst. chief illustrations div. Nat. Geog. mag., 1924-35, asst. editor, 1935-51, sr. asst. editor, 1951-54, asso. editor, 1954-57, editor, 1957-67, editor-in-chief, 1967-77, editor emeritus, 1977-82; v.p. Nat. Geog. Soc., 1954-57, pres., 1957-67, chmn. trustees, 1967-77, chmn. emeritus, 1977-82; adv. dir. Riggs Nat. Bank; mem. Nat. Parks Adv. Council. Author: numerous articles in Nat. Geog. mag; Editor-in-chief: numerous articles in Greece and Rome, Builders of Our World. Trustee emeritus Miami (Fla.) U., George Washington U., Jackson Hole Preserve, Inc., White House Hist. Assn.; hon. v.p. Am. Forestry Assn., 1970-82. Ensign in USN, 1923-24. Decorated Mil. Order of Christ Portugal; commendatore del ordine al Merito della Republica Italiana; recipient gold medal, Bradford Washburn award Boston Mus. Sci., 1964, Nat. Park Service Conservation award, Distinguished Service award Am. Forestry Assn., 1969, Horace Albright Conservation award, Eisenhower medal People to People, Inc., 1970, Internat. Oceanographic Found. Gold medal Rosenstiel Sch. U. Miami, 1975; Parks Can. Nat. Heritage award for devel. Alexander Graham Bell Nat. Historic Park, Baddeck, N.S. Govt. of Can., 1980. Clubs: Cosmos, National Press, Chevy Chase, Overseas Writers, Gibson Island, Cruising Club of Am, Metropolitan; Bath (Miami, Fla.). Home: Bethesda, Md. Died Apr. 22, 1982.

GROVER, CHARLES STRAUDER, patent lawyer; b. Frankfort, Ind. Mar. 25, 1888; s. James H. and Carrie (DeVault) G.; B.S., Purdue U., 1910; LL.B., George Washington U., 1916; m. Mary Hedgcock, July 2, 1911; children—James, Stuart. Engr., Gen. Electric Co., 1910-11; examiner U.S. Patent Office, 1911-16; admitted to D.C. bar, 1915, Mass. bar, 1916; with Boston patent firm from 1916, formerly Roberts, Roberts & Cushman, now Roberts, Cushman & Grover; dir. Technicolor Motion Picture Corp. Mem. bd. appeals City of Newton. Trustee Garland Sch. Mem. Am., Mass., Boston bar assns., Am. Patent Law Assn., Tau Beta Pi. Clubs: St. Botolph (Boston); Brae Burn Country (Newton, Mass). Home: Auburndale, MA. †

GROVES, HERBERT LAWRENCE, foreign service officer; b. Coudersport, Pa., Jan. 21, 1888; s. John R. and Charlotte Elizabeth (Dowse) G.; grad. Hotchkiss Sch., Lakeville, Conn., 1908; A.B., Harvard, 1912; m. Ethel Julia Falconer, Aug. 14, 1914; 1 dau., Carolyn. With Internat. Harvester Co., Chicago, 1913-16; with Chicago office of Paine, Webber & Co., of Boston, 1916-19; U.S. Dept. of Commerce, fgn. service, 1919-33, serving in the principal countries of Europe; exec. sec. Drug Inst. of Am., Inc., 1933-35; asst. dir., Bur. of Fgn. and Domestic Commerce, Washington; chief of Fgn. Commerce Service, 1936-38; in U.S. fgn. service from 1939 as commercial attaché and econ. counselor, successively in Belgium, China, Venezuela, Norway and Greece; U.S. consul general, Montreal, Canada. Author: numerous economic, financial, and commercial studies on various countries. Home: Coudersport, Pa. †

GRUBB, H. DALE, aerospace consultant; b. Henryetta, Okla., Apr. 23, 1925; s. Hiram D. and Buena Vista (Troth) G.; B.A. in Journalism, U. Okla., 1951; m. Martha Ann Ports, July 8, 1967. With U.S. Secret Service, 1951, NASA, 1959-60, Avco Corp., 1960-68; spl. asst. to Pres. Nixon, 1969-70; asst. adminstr. legislative affairs NASA Hdqrs., Washington, 1970-73; cons. Rockwell Internat., 1974; asst. dep. adminstr. VA, Washington, 1975-77; cons. to aerospace industry, 1977-81. Served as pilot USAAF, World War II. Mem. U. Okla. Alumni Assn. (pres. Washington chpt. 1962), Delta Tau Delta. Clubs: Nat. Space (pres. 1965-66) (Washington); Burning Tree (Bethesda, Md.). Home: Arlington, Va. Dec. Apr. 21, 1981. Interned Arlington Cemetary, Washington.

GRUBER, CHARLES MICHAEL, physician, teacher; b. Hope, Kan., Mar. 11, 1887; s. John Nicholas and Barbara (Ehrsam) G.; A.B., U. of Kan., 1911, A.M., 1912; Ph.D., Harvard, 1914; M.D., Washington U., St. Louis, 1921; m. Hermione Archer Sterling, June 6, 1912; children—Barbara (Mrs. Joseph Wrigley), Charles M. Austin teaching fellow Harvard, 1912-14; instr. physiology U. Pa., 1914-15; prof. pharmacology and physiology Albany Med. Coll., 1915-17; asso. prof. pharmacology and physiology U. of Colo., 1917-18, prof. pharmacology and physiology, 1918-20; asso. in physiology Washington U. St. Louis, 1920-21, asso. prof. pharmacology, 1921-32; prof. pharmacology Jefferson Med. Coll., Phila., 1932-53, emeritus; prof. pharmacology and exptl. therapeutics Coll. of Med. Evangelists, Loma Linda, Cal. Fellow A.M.A. (chmn. sect. on pharm. and exptl. therapeutics, 92d ann. conv., 1941); mem. Soc. for Pharm. and Exptl. Therapeutics (pres. 1954), Soc. for Exptl. Biology and Medicine, Philadelphia (president, 1947-48) physiol. socs., Phila. Coll. Phys., Pa. Acad. Sci., Pa. State Phila. County med. socs., Sigma Xi, Phi Beta Pi, Alpha Omega Alpha. Author: Handbook of Treatment, 1948-49, also articles in scientific jours. Asso. editor Cyclopedia of Medicine, Surgery, and Specialties, 1944-49. Home: Redlands, Cal. †

GRUBER, WILLIAM R., army officer; b. Cincinnati, O., Dec. 17, 1890; s. Edmund and Genevieve (Keene) G.; student Germany, 1911-12; Field Artillery School, Fort Sill, Oklahoma, 1924; hon. graduate Command and General Staff School, Fort Leavenworth, Kansas, 1925; Army War College, Washington D.C. 1929; Naval War Coll., Newport, R.I., 1936; m. Helen L. Drennan, June 16, 1919. Commd. Nov. 30, 1912 and advanced through grades to brig. gen., Feb. 1942; served in Panama, 1913-17; World War I, batn. and regt. comdr., 17th F.A. 2d Div., Soissons, Aisne-Marne, St. Mihiel, Champagne and Meuse-Argonne operations; instr. Comd. and Gen. Staff Sch., 1925-28; comdr. 7th F.A., 1929-30; asst. to 3 secs. of war on affairs of Panama Canal, Inland Waterways Corp., army engr. projects, War Dept. negotiations on treaty with Panama. Dir. Panama R.R. & S.S. Co., 1930-38; commander 36th F.A., 1936-38; G.A., chief of staff, Hawaiian Division, 1938-41; army housing construction, Hawaii, 1940; commander 26th F.A. Brigade, Camp Roberts, Calif., 1941; artillery commander Burma, India, China, 1942, 38th Div., 1943, 24th Div., S.W. Pacific, New Guinea and Philippine operations, 1944-45; asst. Army-Navy Fgn. Liquidation Commr., State Dept., Europe, 1945. Clubs: Aero, Army and Navy, Army and Navy Country (Washington, D.C.). Home: Carmel, Calif.

GRUENEWALD, WENDELL LEROY, educator; b. Stewardson, Ill., July 17, 1916; s. William LeRoy and Bertha Ethel (Harrington) G.; m. Emma Jane Ross, Dec. 24, 1939; children—Dorothy Jean (Mrs. Richmond Thom Downie II), Roger Wendell, Beth Ellyn. B.Ed., Eastern Ill. U., 1938; M.A., U. Ill., 1943; Ph.D., Syracuse U., 1950. Tchr. Newton (Ill.) Community High Sch., 1938-43, 46-47; asst. prof. Eastern Ill. U., 1947-48; asst. mem. faculty Ball State U., Muncie, Ind., 1950-81, prof. polit. sci., 1958-81, chmn. dept., 1965-81; cons. pub. schs. in social studies. Co-author: Civics for Americans, 1965; Editor: Ind. Social Studies Quar, 1958-59, 61. Contbr. articles profl. lit. Served with AUS, 1944-46. Mem. Ind. Council Social Studies (pres.), Ind. Acad. Social Sci. (dir.), Am., Midwest polit. sci. assns., Am. Soc. Pub. Adminstrn. Home: Muncie, Ind. Dec. Dec. 7, 1981.

GRULLEMANS, JOHN JAMES, hort. executive; born Noordwyk, Holland, May 1, 1890; s. Cornelius Marinus and Katriena Berta (Van Konynenberg) G.; student pvt. schs. Europe; m. Evelyn Crosby, May 15, 1915; children—Katrina, Winslow. Came to U.S., 1904, naturalized, 1918. U.S. rep. J.J. Grullemans, bulb growers of Lisse, Holland, 1906-17; operated Grullemans Co., Avon Lake, O., 1917-22; sect. treas. Wayside Gardens Co., Mentor, O., 1920-44, pres. from 1944. Recipient gold medal Mass. Hort. Society, 1958. Mem. Am. Assn. Nurserymen, All Am. Rose Selections. Home: Cape Cod, Mass. †

GRUMMAN, LEROY RANDLE, aircraft engring. exec.; b. Huntington, N.Y., Jan. 4, 1895; s. George T. and Grace E. (Conklin) G.; M.E., Cornell U., 1916; grad. student Mass. Inst. Tech., 1918-19; D.Eng., Poly Inst. Bklyn., 1949; LL.D., Adelphi Coll., 1961; m. Rose Marion Werther, Mar. 19, 1921; children—Marion Elinor (Mrs. Ellis L. Phillips, Jr.), Florence Werther (Mrs. Florence Hold), Grace Caroline (Mrs. A.C. Nelson), David Leroy. Engring. dept. N.Y. Telephone Co., 1916-17; aero. engr. Loening Aero. Engring. Corp., N.Y.C., 1920-29; pres. Grumman Aircraft 66, hon. chmn., 1966-82. Died Oct. 4, 1982.

GRUNAUER, MORTIMER, real estate exec.; b. N.Y.C., June 3, 1889; s. Reuben and Delia (Abrahams) G.; B.S. in Civil Engring., N.Y.U., 1910. With Bing & Bing, Inc., N.Y.C., from 1912, dir., from 1931, exec. v.p., 1955-56, pres., 1956-67, vice chmn. bd., 1967-70, chmn., 1970-73, pres., from 1973; v.p. Bijur Lubricating Co. Served with U.S. Army, 1918-19. Fellow ASCE (life). K.P. Home: New York, N.Y. Deceased.

GRUNEBAUM, ERNEST MICHAEL, investment banker; b. London, Eng., Dec. 26, 1934; came to U.S., 1941, naturalized, 1947; s. Erich Otto and Gabrielle (Neumann) G.; m. Marjorie Bleetstein, Aug. 20, 1957; children: Edward, Lauren, David. B.A. in Liberal Arts, Dartmouth Coll., 1956; M.A. in Liberal Arts, Brown U., 1958. With N.Y. Hanseatic Corp. (investment bankers), N.Y.C., 1956-73, pres., 1973-74; gen. partner Stuart Bros., N.Y.C., 1974-81; exec. v.p., mgr. Hanseatic div. The Securities Groups, N.Y.C., from 1981; dir. Miltons Inc. Mem. exec. com. Self-Help Community Services, Inc.; mem. exec. bd. N.Y. Fedn. Reform Synagogues, v.p. Mem. Money Marketeers (bd. govs., pres.). Jewish (pres., trustee temple). Home: Chappaqua, NY.

GRUNEBAUM, KURT H., corp. exec.; b. Essen, Germany, Aug. 11, 1905; came to U.S., 1941, naturalized, 1947; s. Ernst and Agathe (Hirschl) G.; m. Anneliese Eichwald, Dec. 27, 1929; 1 son, Peter K. Joined N.Y. Hanseatic Corp., N.Y.C., 1941, exec. v.p., 1947-59, pres., 1959-73, chmn. bd., 1973-74; partner Stuart Bros., 1974-78, ltd. partner, 1978-81; chmn. bd. Panta Inc.; with Unified Securities Corp., N.Y.C.; dir. United Stockyards Corp., Greater N.Y. Mut. Ins. Co., Ins. Co. Greater N.Y. Home: Harrison, N.Y. Died Dec. 1982.

GRUNER, JOHN W., mineralogist, geologist; b. Neurode, Germany, July 12, 1890; s. Robert and Minna (Wolf) G.; came to U.S., 1912, naturalized, 1921; A.B., U. of N.M., 1917; M.S., U. of Minn., 1919, Ph.D., 1922; student (in sabbatical leave) U. of Leipzig, Germany, 1926-27; m. Opal Garrett, Apr. 4, 1920; children—Wayne Robert, Hazel (Mrs. Don Hudson), Garrett. Asst. prof. of geology Ore. Sch. of Mines, 1919-20; instr. U. of Minn., 1920-23, asst. prof. geology and mineralogy, 1923-28, asso. prof., 1928-43, prof. from 1943; geologist State geol. Survey of Minn., summers 1919-43 (except 1927, 38); cons. mineralogist and geologist to indsl. concerns and U.S. Signal Corps; consulting mineralogist to Atomic Energy Commission. Fellow Geol. Soc. Am., Mineral. Soc. Am. (vice pres. 1943, pres. 1948), Soc. Econ. Geologists; mem. Crystallographic Soc. Am. (pres. 1947-48), Geophys. Union, Am. Gem Soc., Sigma Xi. Contbr. tech. papers to sci. publs. †

GUERTIN, ALFRED N., actuary; b. Hartford, Conn., Mar. 11, 1900; s. N. P. and Mary L. (Belanger) G.; m. Rhoda R. Thomas, Jan. 28, 1933 (dec. Dec. 1980); children—A. Thomas, Robert P. B.S., Trinity Coll., 1922, M.S. (hon.), 1951. Mem. actuarial dept. Conn. Mut. Life Ins. Co., Hartford, 1922-29; chief asst. actuary N.J. Dept. Banking and Ins., Trenton, 1929-32, actuary, 1932-45, Am. Life Conv., Chgo., 1945-65, actuarial cons., 1965-81; pres. Scholarships for Ill. Residents, Inc., Chgo., 1951-65, hon. chmn., from 1965; spl. adviser taxation life ins. cos. U.S. Treasury Dept., 1955; Chmn. spl. com. Nat. Assn. Ins. Commrs. (whose recommendations resulted in widespread enactment of standard non-forfeiture and valuation laws), 1937-42. Contbr. articles in actuarial and ins. publs. Recipient Elizur Wright Ins. Lit. award, 1945, Alumni medal of Excellence Trinity Coll., 1973, alumni award of achievement, 1978; named to Internat. Ins. Hall of Fame at Ohio State U., 1967. Fellow Soc. Actuaries (bd. govs. 1960-63); asso. Inst. Actuaries of Eng., Casualty Actuarial Soc.; mem. Am. Acad. Actuaries, Old Guard Princeton, Sigma Nu. Clubs: Union League (Chgo.); Nassau (Princeton). Home: Princeton, NJ.

GUETTEL, HENRY ARTHUR, producer; b. Kansas City, Mo., Jan. 8, 1928; s. Arthur Abraham and Sylva (Hershfield) G.; student Wharton Sch. of U. Pa., 1944-47, U. Kansas City, 1947-48; 1 dau. by previous marriage, Laurie C.; m. 2d, Mary Rodgers, Oct. 14, 1961; children—Matthew Rodgers (dec.), Adam Arthur, Alexander Burton. Stage mgr. on Broadway and TV, also stock cos., 1949-60; gen. mgr. Royal Ballet Canada, 1953-54; producer nat. touring cos. The Best Man, Sound of Music, Camelot, Oliver, then also gen. mgr. Music Theatre of Lincoln Center, touring cos. The Merry Widow, Kismet, Carousel, Annie Get Your Gun, Show Boat, 1964-67; mng. dir., then v.p. Am. Nat. Opera Co., 1967-68; prodn. supr. exploratory music theatre prodns., forum Vivian Beaumont Theater and theatre concerts Music Theatre, Lincoln Center, 1966-69; lectr. in field. Asso. Kaplan Veidt, Ltd., 1970-72; v.p., prodn. asso. Cinema 5, Ltd., 1972-78; v.p. creative affairs Columbia Pictures, from 1978. Mem. theatrical advisory panel N.Y. State Council of Arts, 1965-70; cons. theatre to State U. N.Y., 1969-70; bd. dirs. Chelsea Theatre Center, N.Y.C., 1966-72; bd. dirs. Performing Arts Repertory Theatre, N.Y.C., from 1971. Served with AUS, 1954-56. Mem. League N.Y. Theatres, Internat. Assn. Concert Mgrs. Deceased.

GUGGENHEIM, HARRY F., found. and bus. exec.; b. at West End, N.J., Aug. 23, 1890; s. Daniel and Florence (Shloss) G.; student in Yale, 1907, Pembroke Coll., Cambridge, End., 1910-13, B.A., 1913, M.A., 1918; D.Sc., Ga. Sch. Tech., 1931; LL.D., Clark U., 1949, Columbia U., 1962, Hofstra U., 1967; D.Eng., N.Y.U., 1950; L.H.D., L.I. U., 1965; m. Helen Rosenberg, Nov. 9, 1910; children—Joan Florence (Mrs. Albert Van de Maele), Nancy (Mrs. Nancy Williams); m. 2d, Caroline Morton, Feb. 3, 1923; dau., Diane (Mrs. Diane Meek); m. 3d, Alicia Patterson, July 1, 1939 (dec.). Began with Am. Smelting & Refining Co., Aguascalientes, Mexico, 1907; member Guggenheim Brothers, 1916-23, now senior partner; past chairman board of Anglo-Lautaro Nitrate Corporation (nitrate properties Chile), ret., 1961; pres., editor in chief of Newsday, newspaper. U.S. del. com. aviation, 3d Pan-Am. Conf., Wash., 1927; U.S. del Internat. Conf. on Civil Aeros., Wash., 1928; A.E and P. to Cuba, 1929-33. Served from lt. to lt. comdr., USN aviation, World War I, AEF, lt. comdr. to capt., 1942-45. Awarded Commendation Ribbon (twice), Grand Cross National Order Carlos Manuel de Cespedes (Cuba), 1935; recipient Wright Bros. Meml. trophy Nat. Aero Assn., 1964. Mem. nat. and local civic coms. Pres. and dir. The Daniel and Florence Guggenheim Found.; chmn. found. commn. The Daniel and Florence Guggenheim jet propulsion centers at Princeton U. and Cal. Inst. Tech., sion centers at Princeton U. and California Institute Technology; pres. The Solomon Guggenheim Found. Hon. fellow Am. Inst. Aeros. and Astronautics, Am. Soc. Internat. Law, Am. Inst. Mining, Metall. and Petroleum Engrs., Nat. Aero. Assn. (dir.), Sigma Delta Chi. Clubs: Yale (N.Y.C.); Metropolitan (Washington); Jockey. Home: Washington, N.Y. †

GUILD, DOUGLAS SCOTT, telephone co. exec.; b. Honolulu, July 28, 1907; s. John and Mary (Knox) G.; student Armour Inst. Tech., 1928-29; m. Janet Carter, Aug. 15, 1936; 1 son, Robert C. With Hawaiian Telephone Co., 1922-81, v.p. ops., 1950-62, pres., 1962-72, chmn., 1972-78; dir. Hawaiian Western Steel Ltd. Bd. dirs. Queen's Med. Center. Mem. Armed Forces Communications and Electronics Assn., Assn. U.S. Army, Air Force Assn. (Oahu chpt.), Navy League U.S., Hawaii Kennel Club (dir.). Home: Honolulu, Hawaii. Died Aug. 23, 1981.

GUILFOYLE, MERLIN JOSEPH, bishop; b. San Francisco, July 15, 1908; s. John Joseph and Teresa (Bassity) G. Student, St. Joseph's Coll., Mountain View, Calif., 1925-27, St. Patrick's Sem., Menlo Park, Calif., 1927-33; Dr. Canon Law, Cath. U., 1937. Ordained Priest Roman Cath. Ch., 1933; designated monsignor Domestic Prelate, by Pope Pius XI, 1949, consecrated aux. bishop, San Francisco, 1950; pastor Mission Dolores Basilica, 1950-70; mil. vicar Armed Forces, 1948, bishop of Stockton, Calif., 1970-80. Home: Stockton, Calif. Died Nov. 20, 1981.

GUILLEN, JORGE, educator, poet; b. Valladolid, Spain, Jan. 18, 1893; s. Julio and Esperanza (Alvarez) G.; B.A., Instituto de Valladolid, 1909; Licenciado en Letras, Granada, 1913; Ph.D., U. Madrid, 1924; m. Germaine Cahen, Oct. 17, 1921 (dec. 1947); children—Teresa (Mrs. Stephen Gilman); Claudio. Came to U.S., 1938. Lectr. Sorbonne, France, 1917-23; prof. Spanish lit. U. Murcia, 1926-29; lectr. Oxford U., Eng., 1929-31; prof. U. Seville, 1931-38, Middlebury Coll., 1938-39, McGill U., Montreal, Que., 1930-40; faculty Wellesley Coll., 1940-57, prof., 1943-57; vis. prof. U. Cal., 1950, Ohio State U., 1951; Charles Elliot Norton prof. Harvard, 1957-58; retired, 1958. Author: Cantieo, 4th edit., 1950; Maremagnum, 1958. Died Feb. 6, 1984.

GULLEN, GEORGE EDGAR, JR., former univ. pres.; b. Detroit, Mar. 6, 1914; s. George Edgar and Alice Maud (Scruton) G.; J.D., Wayne State U., 1936; LL.D., U. Mich., 1972, No. Mich. U., 1975; L.H.D., Olivet Coll., 1972; m. Mary Ruth Gullen, Jan. 9, 1937; children—Nancy (Mrs. Gerald Scheffler), George Edgar III, Gail (Mrs. Paul Fitzsimmons), Kathryn (Mrs. Luis Jauregui), Carolyn (Mrs. Neil Spink), Christopher, Frederick, John. Admitted to the Mich. bar, 1936; asst. sec. Detroit Motors Corp., 1940-45, dir., 1945-55; dir. labor relations Am. Motors Corp., Detroit, 1955-63, v.p. indsl. relations, 1963-66; v.p. univ. relations Wayne State U., Detroit, 1966-71, acting pres., 1971-72, pres., 1972-78; profl. arbitrator, mediator. Commr. Mich. Civil Rights Commn., 1967-71. Vice pres., exec. com. Mich. United Fund; bd. dirs. YMCA's North Am.; pres. Nat. Council YMCA's, 1966-68; trustee Olivet Coll., 1978-82, Detroit Inst. Tech., 1978-82; mem. advisory bd. Detroit Inst. Arts, 1978. Recipient Alumni award Wayne State U., 1962. Mem. Indsl. Relations Research Assn., Am. Arbitration Assn. Congregationalist. Mason. Home: Lake Orion, Mich. Died Jan. 8, 1982.

GUNNISON, RAYMOND M., pub. exec.; b. Brooklyn, Apr. 14, 1887; s. Herbert F. and Alice (May) G.; B.S., St. Lawrence U., 1909; m. Olive Mason, Oct. 19, 1912. On staff N.Y. World, 1909; v.p. Brooklyn Daily Eagle, 1929; pres. and dir. R.H. Donnelley Corp., N.Y. City office, 1929-51, chmn. bd. since 1951. Trustee St. Lawrence U. Clubs: University, Municipal, Bankers, Scarsdale Golf, Quaker Hill Country. Home: Pawling, N.Y. †

GUNTHER, ARTHUR GORDON, restaurant exec.; b. Dunkirk, N.Y., Mar. 18, 1936; s. Truman Arthur and Ella Katherine (Kenny) G.; m. Rebecca Mae David, June 8, 1960; children—Michael, Lisa, Kathleen. B.A., Gannon U., 1958. Asst. v.p. mktg. services McDonald's Corp., Oakbrook, Ill., 1973-76; sr. v.p. ops. and mktg. Sambo's Restaurants, Inc., Santa Barbara, Calif., 1976-79; sr. v.p. mktg. Jerrico, Inc., Lexington, Ky., 1979-80; pres., chief operating officer Pizza Hut, Inc., Wichita, Kans., from 1980; Mem. bd. incorporators Gannon U. Mem. steering com. Crest, Inc., 1978-80. Served to 1st lt. U.S. Army, 1958-60. Home: Wichita, Kans.

GUNTHER, FRANK ALEXANDER, corp. exec.; b. N.Y.C., Feb. 3, 1908; s. Alexander K. and Barbara (Hertel) G.; student Columbia, 1925-26, Wagner Coll., 1939-40; m. Lillian Marie Madden, Sept. 17, 1930; children—Frank M., Robert C. With Radio Engring. Labs. div. Dynamics Corp. Am., L.I. City, N.Y., 1927-82, asst. radio engr., radio engr., chief engr., v.p., 1927-59, exec. v.p., 1959-60, pres., 1960-82; exec. v.p. Dynamics Corp. of Am., since 1962-82. Mem. nat. industry adv. com. FCC, 1962-69. Mem. Richmond County Grand Jurors Assn., 1946-82. Bd. dirs. Armstrong Meml. Research Found. (pres. 1968-82). Served to maj. USAAFR, 1941-46. Recipient Distinguished Service award Armed Forces Communications and Electronics Assn., 1969; DeForest Audion award Vet Wireless Operations Assn., 1969. Fellow I.E.E.E., Radio Club Am. (pres. 1956-58); mem. Armed Forces Communications and Electronics Assn. (pres. 1961-63 bd. dirs.), U.S. Air Force Assn., Am. Radio Relay League. Episcopalian. Clubs: Richmond County Country, Richmond County Yacht (S.I., N.Y.), N.Y. Yacht. Contbr. articles profl. jours. Home: Dongan Hills, N.Y. Died June 8, 1982.

GURFEIN, MURRAY IRWIN, judge; b. N.Y.C., Nov. 17, 1907; s. Louis and Rose (Feld) G.; m. Eva Hadas, Aug. 6, 1931; children—Abigail (Mrs. Robert Hellwarth), Susan Hadas (Mrs. Arthur Rosett). A.B., Columbia U., 1926; LL.B. magna cum laude, Harvard U., 1930; LL.D., Bard Coll., 1972. Bar: N.Y. bar. Law clk. to U.S. Circuit Judge Julian W. Mack, 1930-31; asst. U.S. atty. So. Dist. N.Y., 1931-33; pvt. practice law, N.Y.C., 1933-35; chief asst. investigation organized crime to Hon. Thomas E. Dewey, 1935-38; asst. dist. atty. N.Y. County, 1938-42;

partner Judd and Gurfein, N.Y.C., 1946-54, Goldstein, Judd and Gurfein, 1955-68, Goldstein, Gurfein, Shames & Hyde, 1968-71; judge U.S. Dist. Ct., So. Dist. N.Y., 1971-74, U.S. Ct. Appeals 2nd Circuit, from 1974; chmn. Multi-dist. Litigation Panel, from 1979; Mem. N.Y. State Temporary Commn. Cts., 1953-58. Former pres. United Hias Service, Internat. Council Jewish Social and Service Orgns. Served as lt. col., chief intelligence Psychol. Warfare Div., Supreme Hdqrs. Allied Expeditionary Force OSS and AUS, 1942-45; asst. to Hon. Robert H. Jackson, U.S. Chief Counsel in Nuremberg Trials 1945. Decorated Legion of Merit; hon. officer Order of Brit. Empire; Croix de Guerre France). Fellow Am. Coll. Trial Lawyers, Am. Bar Found.; mem. Am., N.Y. State bar assns., Assn. Bar City N.Y., Harvard Law Sch. Assn. N.Y. (pres. 1977-78), Council Fgn. Relations, Phi Beta Kappa. Club: Harmonie (N.Y.C.). Home: New York, NY.

GUSTAFSON, FELIX G(USTAF), educator; b. Forsby, Finland, Jan. 8, 1889; s. Gustaf and Anna (Hendrickson) Källman; came to U.S., 1903, naturalized, 1911; student Northland Coll., Ashland, Wis., 1911-13, Marine Biol. Lab., Woods Hole, Mass., 1912; A.B., U. Wis., 1915; A.M., Harvard, 1919, Ph.D., 1921; m. Beulah E. Lewis, Mar. 25, 1916; children—Philip Felix, Lawrence Allan. Botanist Marine Biol. Lab., Woods Hole, 1915-20; teaching asst., Harvard, 1917-20; mem. faculty U. Mich. from 1920, prof. of botany from 1943; instr. U. Wis., summer 1927; spl. lectr. plant physiology, Universidade Rural, Rio de Janeiro, 1946. Fellow A.A.A.S.; mem. Am. Soc. Plant Physiologists, Bot. Soc. Am., Torrey Bot. Club, Mich. Acad. Sci., Sigma Xi. A pioneer in producing seedless fruits by chemical means. Home: Ann Arbor, Mich. †

GUSTAFSON, JOHN KYLE, mining co. exec.; b. Chgo., Mar. 13, 1906; s. Lewis and Irene Stoddard (Baker) G.; A.B., Washington U., St. Louis, 1927, D.Sc., 1977; A.M., Harvard U., 1928, Ph.D., 1930; D.Sc., Mich. Coll. Mining and Tech., 1963; m. Elizabeth Brigham, June 11, 1930; children—Lewis Brigham, Judith (Mrs. Milde), Andrew Baker. Geologist with various cos. Can., Australia, 1930-39; in charge Toronto (Ont., Can.) office, Hollinger Exploration Ltd., 1939-42, 1st expdn. to Labrador and Ungava, 1942; adviser Metals Res. Co., Washington, 1942-44; chief geol. Newmont Mining Corp., Magma Copper Co. and affiliated cos., 1944-49; cons. Zinc Corp. Ltd., New Broken Hill Consol. Ltd., Australia, 1947; cons. geologist M.A. Hanna Co., 1950-56, dir. explorations, 1956-60; v.p. Hanna Mining Co, and predecessor corp., 1953-60; pres. Homestake Mining Co., 1961-70, chief exec. officer, 1962-70, chmn., 1970-76, cons. to bd., 1976-77; dir. Pacific Indemnity Group. Dir. raw materials AEC, 1947-48, mgr. raw materials operations, 1948-49, mem. adv. com. raw materials, 1950-59; mem. NSF advisory panel mineral exploration research, 1952-59; mem. adv. council Inst. Geophysics and Planetary Physics, U. Calif., 1961-68; mem. pres. council Calif. Inst. Tech., 1968-69. Mem. overseers com. to visit dept. geol. scis. Harvard, 1961-67; trustee Washington U., St. Louis, 1962-70. Fellow Geol. Soc. Am. (mem. council 1957-60), Soc. Econ. Geologists (councilor 1949-51, v.p. 1961-62, pres. 1966-67); mem. Am. Inst. Mining, Metall. and Petroleum Engrs. (Daniel C. Jackling award 1971), Canadian Inst. Mining and Metall., Mining. Metall. Soc. Am., Am. Mining Congress (bd. govs. 1962-67), Phi Beta Kappa, Sigma Xi, Sigma Chi, Alpha Chi Sigma. Republican. Clubs: Stock Exchange, Golden Gate Angling and Casting, Pacific Union (San Francisco); Claremont Country (Oakland, Cal.). Home: Berkeley, Calif. Died June 1, 1982.

GUSTAFSON, STANLEY WENDELL, auto company executive; b. Lansing, Mich., Feb. 18, 1930; s. Palmer L. and Erma (Washburn) G. B.A., Mich. State U., 1957, M.A., 1958. C.P.A., Ohio. With Dana Corp., Toledo, 1958-66, 68-83, audit mgr., 1965, controller, 1968-70, v.p., treas., 1970-71, v.p. finance, treas., 1971-74, sr. v.p. finance, 1974-80, pres., dir., 1980-83; sec.-treas. Victor Mfg. & Gasket Co., Chgo., 1966-68; dir. Linbeck Constrn. Co., N.W. Ohio Med. Indemnity Mut. Corp.; bd. dirs. Hwy. Users Fedn., Automotive Info. Council. Served with AUS, 1951-53, Korea. Decorated UN Service medal, Bronze Star medal.; Recipient Mich. P.T.A. Distinguished Service award, 1963. Mem. Fin. Execs. Inst., Beta Alpha Psi. Club: Sertoma. Died Dec. 1983.

GUTE, GEORGE GAYLORD, lawyer; b. Portland, Oreg., July 21, 1922; s. Roy John and Virginia (Gaylord) G.; m. Marion Carstarphen, May 1, 1949; children—Virginia, Frederick Gaylord, Catherine. A.B. with great distinction, Stanford, 1946, J.D., 1948. Bar: Calif. bar 1949, U.S. Supreme Ct. bar 1966. Practiced law, Los Angeles, from 1949; partner firm Darling, Rae & Gute, Los Angeles, from 1955. Trustee Clifford Willard Gaylord Found. Mem. Am., Los Angeles County bar assns., State Bar Calif., San Marino City Club, Univ. Club Los Angeles, Phi Kappa Sigma. Home: San Marino, Calif.

GUTH, SYLVESTER KARL, physicist; b. Milw., Dec. 31, 1908; s. Alexander C. and Laura (Kiesslich) G.; B.S., U. Wis., 1930; E.E., 1950; D.Ocular Sci., No. Ill. Coll. Optometry, 1953; m. Beryl K. Van Deraa, May 2, 1931. With Gen. Electric Co., Cleve., 1930-73, with lighting research lab., 1930-54, mgr. radiant energy effects lab., 1955-68, mgr. applied research, 1969-73; lighting cons., 1974-85. Del. Commn. Internationale de l'Eclairage, 1951, 55, 59, 63, 67, 71, 75, 79, v.p., 1971-75, pres., 1975-79; lectr. Case Inst. Tech., 1950-64; mem. com. on vision Armed Forces Nat. Research Council, 1957-84; cons. various instns. Fellow A.A.A.S., Illuminating Engring. Soc. (medal 1967), Am. Acad. Optometry (Charles F. Prentis award 1980); mem. Optical Soc. Am., Ohio Acad. Sci., Inter-Soc. Color Council, Assn. Research Ophthalmology. Research and publs. on psychol. and physiol. aspects of light, vision and seeing; also effects of radiant energy on man, animals and plants. Address: Euclid, Ohio. Died June 5, 1985.

GUTHE, ALFRED KIDDER, anthropologist, educator; b. Detroit, Apr. 30, 1920; s. Carl Eugen and Grace Ethel (McDonald) G.; m. Lois Frances Kuhlman, Sept. 2, 1944; children: Carol Jean, Nancy Lee, Janet Tate, Philip Bruce, Martin Eugene, Donald Edward. Student, U. N.C., 1937-39; A.B., U. Mich., 1941, Ph.D., 1956; M.A., U. Chgo., 1948. Jr. anthropologist, then curator anthropology Rochester (N.Y.) Mus. Arts and Scis., 1949-61; lectr. anthropology U. Rochester, 1949-61; prof. U. Tenn., Knoxville, from 1961, head dept. anthropology, 1961-71; dir. Frank H. McClung Mus., 1961-78; archaeol. research Eastern U.S. Treas. N.Y. State Archaeol. Assn., 195O-58, v.p., 1958-62; mem. archaeol. adv. council Tenn. Dept. Conservation, 1970-82. Editor: Tenn. Archaeologist, 1961-72; asst. editor (N.E.): Am. Antiquity, 1952-61, N.E., Abstracts of New World Archaeology, 1959-62; Contbr. articles to profl. jours. Served with USNR, 1942-45. Fellow Am. Anthrop. Assn.; mem. Soc. Am. Archaeology, Tenn. Assn. Museums (pres. 1963-65), Southeastern Archaeol. Conf. (treas. 1973-78), Sigma Xi. Unitarian. Club: Kiwanis. Home: Knoxville, Tenn.

GUTHRIE, S(EYMOUR) ASHLEY, lawyer; b. Chgo., June 20, 1889; s. Seymour and Martha G. (Greene) G.; student Mass. Inst. Tech., 1907-11; LL.B., Northwestern, 1915; m. Annie Laurie Rainey, Aug. 22, 1917. Admitted to Ill. bar, 1915, from practiced in Chgo.; with Dent, Dobyns & Freeman, 1919-21; with Tenney, Harding & Sherman and successor firms, now Tenney, Bentley, Guthrie, Askow & Howell, from 1922, partner from 1928. Village atty., Riverside. Served as 1st lt. 346th Machine Gun Bn., U.S. Army, 1917-19. Mem. Am., Ill. State, Chgo. bar assns., Chgo. Law Inst., Phi Alpha Delta, Order of Coif. Republican. Presbyn. Clubs: Law, Univ., Legal (Chgo.); Riverside Golf. Home: Riverside, Ill. †

GUYER, TENNYSON, congressman; b. Findlay, Ohio, Nov. 29, 1913; B.S., Findlay Coll., 1934; m. Edith Mae Reuter, 1944; children—Sharon Mae, Rosetta Kae. Ordained minister; pub. speaker; mayor, Celina, Ohio, 1940-44; pub. affairs dir. Cooper Tire & Rubber Co., Findlay, 1950-72; mem. 93d-95th congresses from 4th Ohio Dist. Mem. Ohio Republican Central Com., 1954-66; mem. Ohio Senate, 1959-72. Mem. Internat. Platform Assn. Mason (Shriner), Rotarian, Elk, Lion. Author: The Church-Institution or Destitution; Blueprints for Youth. Home: Findlay, Ohio. Died Apr. 12, 1981.

GUYTON, GRADY, economist; b. West, Miss., July 6, 1888; s. David Thomas and Susie Sevannah (Ellington) G.; B.S., Miss. State Coll., 1909; student U. of Chicago, 1914-15; A.M., Columbia 1925; m. Alma Sullivant, June 2, 1919; children—Erin Rosamond (dec.), Thomas Grady. Public sch. teacher, Hamilton, Miss., 1909-10, Greenwood, Miss., 1916-17; fellow Miss. State Coll., 1912-13, instr., 1917., asst. prof. economics and history, 1918, asso. prof., 1919-24; asso. prof. economics U. of Miss., 1925-26; prof. sociology, 1926-27, prof. economic from 1937. Dir. Bank of Oxford, Miss. Served as cpl., U.S. Army, World War I. Mem. So. Econ. Assn., Miss. Ednl. Assn. Sigma Chi, Delta Sigma Pi, Beta Gamma Sigma, Democrat. Baptist. Author: Mississippi's General Sales Tax-How it Works (with J. W. Bell and R.L. Sackett), 1933; Methods of Tax Equalization in Mississippi, 1925. Home: University, Miss. †

GWINN, WILLIAM PERSONS, aircraft executive; b. N.Y.C., Sept. 22, 1907; s. Frederick W. and Clare (Persons) G.; student Gunnery Prep. Sch., Washington, Conn., 1923-25; D.Eng. (hon.), Rensselaer Poly. Inst., 1956; D.Sc. (hon.), Trinity Coll., 1961; m. Joyce Clark, Nov. 29, 1934 (dec. 1957); children—William Clark, Linda Clare, Michael; m. 2d, Mary Berry Devoe, 1958 (dec. 1969); m. 3d, Rachel Coleman Witman, 1970. Joined Pratt & Whitney Aircraft div. United Aircraft Corp., East Hartford, Conn., 1927, engr., 1929-34, West Coast rep., Los Angeles, 1934-39, asst. sales mgr., 1939-42, asst. gen. mgr., 1942, acting gen. mgr., 1943, gen. mgr. 1944-56, v.p. United Aircraft Corp., 1946-56, pres., dir., chief administrv. officer, 1956-67, chmn., chief exec. officer, dir. company and various subsidiaries 1968-72; dir. The F & M Schaefer Corp., Shell Oil Co., Conn. Mut. Life Ins. Co., Nat. chmn. U.S. Indsl. Payroll Savs. Com., 1968; mem. def. industry adv. council Dept. Def. Trustee Trinity Coll. (life), Rensselaer Poly. Inst. Conn., Marine Hist. Assn., Mystic Seaport. Mem. Aerospace Industries Assn. (gov.). Clubs: Hartford Golf; Conquistadores del Cielo, N.Y. Yacht, Essex Yacht, Fishers Island Yacht, Key Largo Anglers, Fishers Island Country; La Coquille; Country of Florida; Delray Beach Yacht, Everglades. Home: Palm Beach, Fl. Died Dec. 25, 1981.

GWYNNE, JOHN WILLIAMS, govt. ofcl.; b. Victor, Ia., Oct. 20, 1889; s. Thomas Williams and Katherine (McGilway) G.; A.B., State U. of Ia., 1912, LL.B., 1914; m. Myrtle Nash, June 1, 1921; children—Mary Myrtle, John Williams. Admitted to Ia. bar, 1914; in practice; Waterloo, Ia., 1915-20; judge Municipal Ct., Waterloo, 1920-27; county atty. Blackhawk County, Ia., 1929-35; mem. 74th to 80th Congresses, 3d Ia. Dist.; chmn. FTC, from 1955. Served as 2d lt., 88th Division U.S. Army, World War. Republican. Episcopalian. Home: Waterloo, Ia. †

HAASE, CARL ALVIN, former ins. co. exec.; b. Mpls., June 19, 1915; s. Alvin and Helen (Peterson) H.; B.B.A., U. Minn., 1938; postgrad. U. Man., 1948-50; m. Patricia Mary Graff, Nov. 15, 1944; 1 dau., Mary Beth. Asst. actuary N. Am. Life & Casualty Co., Mpls., 1937-48; v.p. Nelson & Warren, Consulting Actuaries, Kansas City, (Mo.), 1950-58; chief actuary I.D.S. Life Ins. Co., Mpls., 1958-70, pres., 1970-79; v.p. ins. operations Investors Diversified Services, Inc., Mpls., 1970-79. Served with USAAF, 1942-46. Fellow Soc. Actuaries; mem. Am. Acad. Actuaries (charter), Phi Sigma Kappa. Home: North Oaks, Minn. Died Jan. 5, 1983; buried Ft. Snelling, Mpls.

HABERKORN, CHRISTIAN HENRY, JR., banker; b. Detroit, May 24, 1889; s. Christian Henry and Frances Harriette (Ruehle) H.; grad. Detroit Univ. Sch., 1908, A.B., Harvard, 1912, A.M., 1913; m. Charlotte Madeleine Beck, Sept. 17, 1913; children—Frances Madeleine (Mrs. J. Frank Durham), Christian Henry III, Charlotte Elizabeth (Mrs. William Court), Mary Margaret (Mrs. J. Christy Conner), Constance Adelaide, (Mrs. William B. Nichols), George Beck. Sec., treas. C. H. Haberkorn & Co. (founded by father), 1912-15, pres. from 1915; dir. Bank of Detroit, 1919-30, v.p., 1921-23, chmn. bd., 1923-30; vice pres. and sec. Guardian Detroit Union Group, 1931-33; mgr. trust dept. Nat. Bank of Detroit, 1933-36, vice pres. and trust officer from 1936. Dir. and sec. Mech. Handling system, Inc., Canadian Mech. handling Systems, Ltd.; dir. Friends of Detroit Public Library, Inc. Mem. Phi Beta Kappa, Sigma Alpha Phi, Republican. Conglist. Clubs: Detroit, Bankers, Harvard of Mich. (dir.), Country Club of Detroit. Home: Grosse Pointe Farms, Mich. †

HACKETT, JOAN, actress; b. N.Y.C., Mar. 1; d. John and Mary (Esposito) H.; m. Richard Mulligan, Jan. 3, 1966 (div. dissolved 1973). Grad. high sch.; studied with, Mary Welch, Lee Strasberg, 1958-63. Broadway debut in: A Clearing in the Woods, 1959; stage appearances include: Park, Night Watch; TV appearances include: series Another Day; TV movies include Stonestreet; appeared in: TV series Young Doctor Malone, 1959-60, The Defenders, 1961-62; films include Will Penny, 1968, Support Your Local Sheriff, 1969, Assignment to Kill, 1969, The Rivals, 1972, The Last of Sheila, 1973, The Terminal Man, 1974, Mackintosh and T.J, 1976, Treasure of Matecumbe, 1976, Mr. Mike's Mondo Video, 1979, The North Avenue Irregulars, 1979, One Trick Pony, 1980; also nightclub appearances. films include, Recipient (Obie award Village Voice 1961, Vernon Rice award 1961, Theatre World award 1961). Mem. AFTRA, Screen Actors Guild, Actors Equity Assn. Died Oct. 9, 1983.*

HACKETT, RAYMOND E., lawyer; b. New Haven, Sept. 6, 1889; LLB., Yale. Admitted to N.Y. bar, 1912, Conn. bar, 1914; mem. firm Cummings & Lockwood, Stamford; asst. U.S. atty., 1916-19. Mem. Am., Stamford bar assns., State Bar Assn. Conn., Corbey Court, Phi Delta Phi.†

HADDON, WILLIAM, JR., professional institute executive, physician; b. Orange, N.J., May 24, 1926; s. William and Anna (Herrstrom) H.; m. Gene Billo, June 16, 1956; children—Jonathan, Charles, Robert. S.B., Mass. Inst. Tech., 1949; M.D., Harvard, 1953, M.P.H. magna cum laude, 1957. Research fellow microbiology, postdoctoral fellow Nat. Found. Infantile Paralysis, Harvard Sch. Pub. Health, 1954-55, research asso., 1955-56; dir. driver research center N.Y. Dept. Health, 1957-61, dir. epidemiology residency program, 1961-65, acting asst. commr. pub. health research, devel. and evaluation, 1963-64, assoc. dir. div. chronic disease services, 1964-66; asst. prof., then assoc. prof. epidemiology Albany (N.Y.) Med. Coll., Union U., 1960-66; spl. asst. for traffic safety planning to undersec. transp. Dept. Commerce, 1966; adminstr. Nat. Hwy. Safety Agy., also; Nat. Traffic Safety Agy., Dept. Commerce, 1966-67; dir. Nat. Hwy. Safety Bur., Dept. Transp., 1967-69; pres. Ins. Inst. Hwy. Safety, Washington, 1969-85, Highway Loss Data Inst., Washington, 1972-85; Mem. com. mil. accidents Armed Forces Epidemiological Bd., 1965-69; mem. U.S. delegation com. on challenges of modern society North Atlantic council NATO, 1969; mem. com. emergency med. services Nat. Acad. Sci./NRC, 1970-73. Author: (with E. A. Suchman and D. Klein) Accident Research, Methods and Approaches, 1964; also articles. Served with USAAF, 1944-45. Recipient Modern Medicine award for distinguished achievement, 1969; Bronfman prize Am. Pub. Health Assn., 1969; Stone award Am. Trauma Soc., 1977. Mem. Am. Pub. Health Assn. (council on environment 1970-72, chmn. reference com. on resolutions on environment 1972), Sigma Xi, Delta Omega. Home: Bethesda, Md. Died Mar. 4, 1985.

HADLEY, EGBERT CHARLES, engr.; b. Burlington, Ia., Nov. 16, 1888; s. Harry Clifton and Caroline Augusta (Starr) H.; grad. Gunnery Sch., Washington, Connecticut, 1906; A.B., Middlebury (Vt.) College, 1910; student, Grad. Sch. Arts and Sciences, Harvard, 1910-11; B.S.,

Mass. Inst. Tech., 1914; Dr. Engring., Norwich U., Northfield, Vt., 1949; m. Marjorie Finch, June 16, 1917; 1 son, Egbert Starr. Laboratorian, New York Navy Yard, 1914-15; engr. Remington Arms Co., Inc., Bridgeport, Conn., 1915-48, ballistic engineer, 1919-30, asst. to pres., 1930-31, tech. director, 1931-39, 1940-43, asst. to vice pres. and asst. gen. mgr., 1943-48; corporator Southport (Conn.) Savs. Bank, 1929-51; dir. Middlebury Hotel Corp., Middlebury Nat. Bank. Mem. Co. L. First Training Regt., Plattsburgh, N.Y., 1915. Chmn. bd. trustees Middlebury (Vt.) Coll.; alumni mem. of corp. Mass. Inst. Tech. 1940-45. Chmn. zoning commn. Town of Fairfield, Conn., 1939-47, Town Plan and Zoning Commn., Town of Fairfield, 1947-49; director Conn. Fedn. Planning and Zoning Agencies, 1948-49. Chmn. Small Arms Ammunition Engring. Adv. Com. of Ordnance Dept., 1942. Mem. Sporting Arms and Ammunition Mfrs. Inst. (pres.), Am. Ordnance Assn. (exec. bd. ammunition div.), Wildlife Mgmt. Inst. (chmn. bd.), C. of C. (dir. Bridgeport 1947-48); Vt. S.A.R., Phi Beta Kappa Assos., Newcomen Soc. of Eng., Delta Kappa Epsilon, Phi Beta Kappa. Clubs: University (past pres.) (Bridgeport); University, Delta Kappa Epsilon, Century, Mass. Inst. Tech. (N.Y.C.). Home: Middlebury, Vermont. †

HAESSLER, F. HERBERT, physician, educator; b. Milwaukee, Dec. 15, 1890; s. Rudolph and Louise (Wagner) H.; A.B., U. Wis., 1913; M.D., Johns Hopkins, 1916; m. Bertha Torchiani, M.D., May 29, 1917; children—Louise (Mrs. J. Knight), Herbert. Intern Children's Meml. Hosp., Chicago, 1916-17; resident pathology, Louisville, 1917-18; asst. Rockefeller Inst., 1918-20; pvt. practice ophthalmology, Milwaukee, 1922-48; mem. faculty dept. ophthalmology Marquette U. Med. Sch. from 1949, prof. ophthalmology from 1949, also dir. dept. ophthalmology from 1949. Mem. Am. Acad. Medicine, Am. Ophthalmol. Soc., Phi Beta Kappa, Alpha Omega Alpha. Episcopalian. Author: A Primer of Ophthalmology, 1953; Ophthalmologic Diagnosis, 1953. Abstract editor Am. Jour. Ophthalmology from 1945. †

HAFNER, CHARLES ANDREW, sculptor, painter; b. Omaha, Neb., Oct. 28, 1888; s. Charles and Louisa (Hintzpeter) H.; student sch. of the Museum of Fine Arts, Boston, 1905-10, Art Students League, New York, 1913-14, Beaux Arts Inst. of Design, 1914-17; asst. student in studios of Daniel Chester French, Charles Henry Niehaus, Herman McNeil and Albert Jaegers; m. Isa MacGuire, Sept. 22, 1922; 1 son, Gair Hamlin. Dir. of Adult Art Classes, Univ. State of New York, 1933; instr. in sculpture, N.Y. Industrial Sch. of Art, 1936; instr. N.Y. Evening Industrial Sch. of Art since 1925. Works include "Peter Pan" fountain in lobby of Paramount Theatre, N.Y. City; "Golden Age" fountain in lobby of Albee Theatre, Brooklyn; busts of Thomas A. Edison, Daniel Carter Beard, Maude Adams, Richard Strauss. Represented in exhbns. at Nat. Acad. of Design, Phila. Acad. of Fine Arts, Archtl. League of N.Y., Brooklyn Museum of Art, Albright Galleries, Reinhardt Galleries. Exhibited paintings at Scranton (Pa.) Museum of Art, Nat. Acad. of Design (N.Y. City), Ogunquit (Me.) Art Center, etc. Awarded bronze medal Olympiade Art Exhbn., Holland, 1928; popularity prize, 1st Municipal Art Exhbn., N.Y. City, 1934. Served as yeoman, 2d class, Dept. of Camouflage, Hdqrs. Third Naval Dist., 1918. Founder mem. Am. Vets. Soc. of Artists, Inc. (New York). Mem. Nat. Sculpture Soc. Democrat. Protestant. Home: New York, N.Y. †

HAGAN, CLARENCE W(ESTERVELT), dentist, educator; b. Pitts., Apr. 4, 1889; s. Luman R. and Estelle E. (Evans) H.; D.D.S., U. Pitts., 1911; m. Norma E. Miller, June 14, 1921; 1 son, John E. Gen practice dentistry, Wilkinsburg, Pa., 1911-25, pedodontics. 1925-47; faculty Sch. Dentistry, U. Pitts., 1921-59, organized dept. pedodontics, 1925, prof., chmn. dept. pedodontics, 1925-59, emeritus; chief dental dept. Children's Hosp., Pitts., 1927-59, emeritus; consultant Heart House, Pitts., from 1940; staff Western State Psychiat. Hosp., Pitts., from 1956. Fellow Am. Coll. Dentists; mem. Am. Acad. History Dentistry, Am. Dental Assn., Am. Soc. Dentistry for Children, Am. Acad. Pedodontics, S.A.R., Hist. Soc. Western Pa., Delta Sigma Delta, Omicron Kappa Upsilon. Presbyn. Home: Pittsburgh, PA. †

HAGEL, WILLIAM, business exec.; b. Wilkes Barre, Pa., Oct. 15, 1897; s. Charles G. and Caroline (Hagel) H.; student Wilkes Barre Mining Inst., 1915-16; Pa. State Coll. Extension Sch., 1916-17; Diploma, Carnegie Inst. Technol., 1923, post grad. work, 1923-24, 1929-30; m. Mabel F. Geary, Aug. 15, 1923; 1 son, William Carl. Mine surveyor Delaware & Hudson Coal Co., Scranton, Pa., 1915-17; insp., Pittsburgh Steel Foundry, 1917; estimator United Engring. & Foundry Co., Pittsburgh, 1917-28, asst. chief estimator, 1928-33, chief estimator, 1933-43, machinery sales mgr., 1943, vice pres. charge machinery sales 1944-46, v.p. sales, 1946-54, v.p., exec. asst., mem. exec. com., 1954-57; v.p. operations, 1957-63, cons., from 1963, also dir.; v.p. Adamson United Co., Akron, O., 1945-63, director, from 1945; v.p. Lobdell United Co. (Wilmington, Del.) from 1949, dir. and mem. exec. com. from 1953. Mem. Assn. Iron and Steel Engrs., Engrs. Soc. Western Pa., Ordnance Assn., Pa. and Pittsburgh C.'s of C. Republican. Lutheran. Clubs: Duquesne, Rotary (Pittsburgh); St. Clair Country (Bridgeville, Pennsylvania). Home: Pittsburgh, PA. †

HAGER, DORSEY, geologist and oil operator; b. St. Paul, Minn., June 7, 1887; s. Frederick Dorsey and Sarah Scott (Dilworth) H.; prep. edn., Manual Training Sch., St. Louis, Mo.; student Washington U., St. Louis, 1905-08, Columbia, 1909-10; m. Adelaide Tyler Myer, May 1913 (died 1914); 1 son, Franklin Tyler; m. 2d, Mary Hathaway Taber, June 1917 (divorced 1923); children—Dorsey, Mary Hathaway; m. 3d, Jane Ruston, 1924. In employ Kern Trading and Oil Co. (now Pacific Oil Co.), 1910-12; cons. practice in N.Y. City, Tulsa, Okla., Los Angeles, Calif., 1913-22; vice-pres. Sunburst Oil and Gas Co., Montana, 1922-24; mgr. Garber-Hager Syndicate, Seattle, Wash., Associated Syndicate Oil Co., Rochester, N.Y. Mem. Soc. Econ. Geologists, Am. Inst. Mining and Metall. Engrs., Am. Petroleum Inst., Sigma Alpha Epsilon. Unitarian. Mason (32 deg., Shriner). Author: Practical Oil Geology; Oil Field Practice; also numerous technical and scientific papers. Home: Beverley Hills, Calif. †

HAGER, LAWRENCE WHITE, SR., newspaper pub.; b. Louisville, May 28, 1890; s. Samuel Wilber and Bessie Woods (White) H.; A.B., Centre Coll., Danville, Ky., 1909, A.M., 1910; Litt.D., Ky. Wesleyan Coll., 1965; m. Martha Augusta Brown, June 25, 1921; children—Lawrence White, John Stewart. With Owensboro (Ky.) Inquirer 1910—, Consol. Messenger and Inquirer, 1929—, editor and pres. of both, chmn. bd., 1967—; postmaster Owensboro, 1935-41; pres. Owensboro Broadcasting Co., 1938—. Pres. Ky. Press Assn., 1933, Ky. Postmasters Assn., 1935-36; established Goodfellows Christmas Club for Needy Children, 1916, dir. club activities, 1916—. Chmn. County War Finance Com., 1942-45. Mem. Am. Legion Publs. Commn., 1939-50, vice chmn., 1949-50. Del. Democratic Nat. Conv., 1956. Trustee Centre Coll., 1950; mem. bd., chmn. finance com. Ky. Wesleyan Coll., 1951-56. Served as officer F.A., U.S. Army, in Argonne offensive, World War I. Mem. C. of C. (charter, dir. 1911), Ky. Hist. Soc. Democrat. Methodist. Mason (K.T.). Clubs: Rotary (charter mem., pres. 1922-23; dist. gov. 1938-39); Filson (Louisville). Home: Owensboro, Ky. Died Dec. 25, 1982.

HAGERTY, JAMES C., ret. radio-TV exec.; b. Plattsburg, N.Y., May 9, 1909; s. James A. and Katherine S. (Kearney) H.; grad. Blair Acad., 1928; A.B., Columbia, 1934; m. Marjorie Lucas, June 15, 1937; children—Roger C., Bruce C. Mem. staff N.Y. Times, 1934-42, legis. corr., Albany bur. 1938-42; exec. asst. to Gov. Thomas Dewey, 1943-50, sec. to gov., 1950-52; press sec. to the President, 1953-61; v.p. ABC, 1961-75. Mem. Delta Kappa Epsilon. Roman Catholic. Home: Bronxville, N.Y. Died Apr. 11, 1981.

HAILER, FLORIN J., drug co. exec.; b. Switzerland, Aug. 20, 1889; s. Joseph and Maria C. (Luzio) H.; m. Florence H. Cleary, Feb. 5, 1917; children—Florin J., Janet (Mrs. C. D. McGrath), Robert C., Clare A. (Mrs. Richard J. Dennis), Donald G. Joined Rexall Drug Co., Boston, 1912, v.p. from 1940. Roman Catholic. Home: Newton, Mass. †

HAINES, RICHARD, painter, muralist; b. Marion, Iowa, Dec. 29, 1906; s. Fred C. and Hattie (Carver) H.; m. Leonora Stevens, Mar. 12, 1938; children—Steven Carver, Brock Ashlock. Student, Mpls. Sch. Art, 1933-34, Ecole des Beaux Arts, Fontainbleau, France, 1934. Head dept. painting Chouinard Art Inst., Los Angeles, from 1954, Otis Art Inst., Los Angeles. (Recipient numerous exhibit awards throughout U.S.), One-man shows, Am. Contemporary Gallery, Los Angeles, 1944, Hatfield Gallery, Los Angeles, 1948, 54, 58, 62, 64, Scripps Coll. Art Galleries, 1956, Santa Barbara Art Mus., 1959, Pasadina Art Mus., 1960, Santa Monica Art Gallery, 1961, Ventura County Forum of Arts, 1966, Adele Bednarz Galleries, 1967, 69, 70, 73, 75, Palas Verdes Mus., 1978, Abraxas Gallery, Newport Beach, 1978, 79, 80, 81; exhibited in group shows, Corcoran Biennial, Washington, 1951, Met. Mus. Art, 1950, 52, U. Ill., 1950, 51, 61, Carnegie Internat., 1954, Pa. Annual, 1955, others, retrospective exhbn., Brand Library, Glendale, Calif., 1981, meml. exhbn. Los Angeles Art Assn., 1985, paintings represented in permanent collections, including, Met. Mus. Art, N.Y.C., Corcoran Gallery, Los Angeles County Mus., San Francisco Mus., Dallas Mus., Santa Barbara Mus., murals, Mayo Clinic, Rochester, Minn., Minn. Mining & Mfg. Co., St. Paul, Med. Center U. Ky., Music and Physics bldg. UCLA, Fed. Bld., Los Angeles, Los Angeles Civic Center and, many U.S. post offices. Home: Los Angeles, Calif. Died Oct. 9, 1984.

HAKE, DON FRANKLIN, psychologist; b. St. Louis, June 28, 1936; s. Wesley Franklin and Flora Haline (Sechrest) H.; m. Elaine Bicknell, Sept. 18, 1960; children—Lisa, Holly. B.A., DePauw U., Greencastle, Ind , 1958; M.A., So. Ill. U., 1962, Ph.D., 1963. Research scientist IV State of Ill., 1962-74, State of Md., 1974-76; prof. psychology, W.Va. U., Morgantown, 1976-82. Author articles in field, chpts. in books.; mem. editorial bds. profl. jours. Fellow Am. Psychol. Assn. (exec. com. div. 25 1979-81); mem. Assn. Behavior Analysis (exec. com. 1979-81, asso. editor Jour. Exptl. Analysis of Behavior 1973-77), Psychonomic Soc., Eastern Psychol. Assn. Home: Morgantown, W.Va. Died Aug. 1, 1982.

HALAS, GEORGE STANLEY, former professional football coach; b. Chgo., Feb. 2, 1895; s. Frank and Barbara (Poludna) H.; m. Minnie S. Bushing, Feb. 18, 1922 (dec. Feb. 1966); children—Virginia Marion (Mrs. Edward W. McCaskey), George Stanley, Jr. (dec.). B.S., U. Ill., 1918; LL.D., St. Joseph's Coll., Ind., 1958, Lake Forest Coll., 1980. Player Gt. Lakes team in Rose Bowl Game (Most Valuable Player), 1919; semi-pro football player, Hammond, 1919; with bridge dept. Burlington R.R., 1919-20; played profl. baseball with N.Y. Yankees and St. Paul Club, 1919; profl. football with Chgo. Bears, 1920-29, coach, 1920-29, 33-42, 46-55, 58-67; pres. Chgo. Bears Football Club, 1920-64, chmn., 1964-68, now pres.; chmn. and chief exec. officer.; Pres. Nat. Football Conf. of NFL. Author: (with Gwen Morgan and Arthur Veysey) Halas By Halas, 1979; Contbr. (with Gwen Morgan and Arthur Veysey) articles to mags. Bd. dirs. Chgo. Heart Assn., Eye Rehab. and Research, NFL Charities, Rehab. Inst. Chgo., Met. Fair Expn. Authority, Crime Detection Inst.; trustee St. Joseph's Coll.; citizens com. U. Ill.; bd. lay trustees Loyola U.; mem. soc. fellows, bd. assos. De Paul U., Chgo. Served as ensign USN, 1918-19; capt. USNR, 1942-46. Decorated Bronze Star; recipient Navy distinguished pub. service award; named Coach of Year AP, Coach of Year UP, Coach of Year Sporting News, 1963, 65; Outstanding Profl. Coach of Year Washington Touchdown Club, 1963; recipient Acad. Sports Editors award, 1963; J.F. Kennedy Meml. trophy Chgo. Mayor and City Council, 1963; named Chicagoan of Year Chgo. Press Club, Chicagoan of Year Jr. Assn. Commerce and Industry; recipient Alumni Achievement award U. Ill., 1965; Horatio Alger, Jr. award, 1968; Bert Bell Meml. award Phila., 1968; Great Humanitarian award Mentally Retarded Olympian Program, 1975; Frank Leahy award U. Notre Dame, 1976; Chicagoan of Year award Chgo. Boys Clubs, 1976; Outstanding Humanitarianism and Service to Youth Through Athletics award Loyola U., Chgo., 1976; Varsity I award of yr., 1977; Outstanding Chicagoan of Today award, 1977; Mother Cabrini award, 1977; Semper Fidelis award, 1978; Order of Leather Helmet, 1978; Father of Year award, 1978; 1st Sportsman award Easter Seal Soc., 1978; Armed Forces Disting. Service award, 1979; Ill. Legislature citation, 1979; Sword of Loyola, 1979; VFW Hall of Fame award, 1980; Britannica Achievement in Life award, 1980; USO award, 1980; Disting. Am. award Walter Camp Found., 1981. Mem. Nat. Profl. Football Hall of Fame (charter mem.), Mil. Order World Wars, Hundred Club Cook County, Mawan-da, Sachem, Navy League of U.S. (nat. v.p., dir., adv. council), Tau Kappa Epsilon, Sigma Tau, Theta Nu Epsilon. Roman Catholic. Clubs: K.C, Hundred of Cook County, Chgo. Athletic Assn, Tavern, Carlton, Execs, Mid-Am, Bob O'Link Golf. Home: Chicago, Ill. Died Oct. 31, 1983.

HALAS, GEORGE STANLEY, JR., profl. football exec.; b. Chgo., Sept. 4, 1925; s. George Stanley and Minnie (Bushing) H.; B.S. in Commerce, Loyola U. Chgo., 1950; m. Therese Leona Martin, Apr. 20, 1963; children—Christine, Stephen. Gen. mgr. May-Halas, mail order house, Chgo., 1951-59; treas. Chgo. Bears Football Club, 1953-63, pres., gen. mgr., 1963-74, pres., 1974-83, Bd. dirs. Chgo. Assn. Retarded Children, United Cerebral Palsy. Served with USNR, 1944- 46. Fellow St. Joseph's Coll., Rensselaer, Ind., 1964-83. Roman Catholic. Clubs: Chgo. Athletic Assn., Ridgemoor Country (Chgo.). Died Dec. 16, 1979.

HALDIMAND, LOIS DEFORREST, business exec.; b. N.Y. City, June 8, 1889; s. John Croydon and Louise (DeForrest) H.; B.C.S., New York U., 1914; m. Edith R. Davis, Nov. 18, 1915; children—Marjorie (Mrs. Harold Haldeman), Madeleine (Mrs. Robert Johnson), Joan (Mrs. Robert Seaman), Lois E. With Wall St. firm, 1905-14; cost accountant Nathan Mfg. Co., N.Y. City, 1914-16; comptroller, Lancaster, Pa., 1916-21; mem. staff Lybrand Ross Bros. and Montgomery, pub. accountants, N.Y. City, 1921-24; with Ward Baking Co. of N.Y. from 1924, trustee estate of William B. Ward since 1929, now dir. and mem. exec. com.; vice pres. and dir. United Markets, Inc., Boston; treas. and dir. Ward Foundn. Corp., N.Y. City; trustee Robert Boyd Ward Fund. Former chmn. bd. trustees Hitchcock Memorial Ch., Scarsdale, N.Y.; mem. Ward Manor Com. of Community Service Soc. Republican. Presbyterian. Clubs: American Yacht (Rye, N.Y.); Scarsdale Golf, Fox Meadow Tennis (Scarsdale). Home: Scarsdale, N.Y. †

HALE, J. A., utilities exec.; b. Calloway, Va., Sept. 18, 1888; s. R. E. and Mary (Callaway) H.; B.S., Civil Engring., Va. Poly. Inst., 1911; m. Lael Irvine, Apr. 2, 1918; children—Joanne, J. A. With Utah Power & Light Co., from 1913, v.p., dir., from 1937; v.p., dir., Western Colo. Power Co., from 1937. Mem. Navy League. Mason. Address: Salt Lake City, Utah. †

HALE, WILLIAM WETHERLA, railroad exec.; b. Solomon, Kan., Mar. 15, 1887; s. Louis William and Alice (Adams) H. ed pub. schs.; m. Clara May Loring, Mar. 30, 1908; 1 son, Howard Loring. With Southern Pacific Lines from 1901, filled various positions in operating and traffic depts., San Francisco, Calif., 1901-17, car service agent, Chicago, 1917, asst. mgr. refrigerator car sect., U.S. Railroad Adminstrn., Chicago, 1918, became gen. agent, Detroit, 1920, asst. to freight traffic mgr., San Francisco, 1929-32, freight traffic mgr., Portland, Ore., 1932-34, gen. freight traffic mgr., Houston, Tex., 1934-38, gen. traffic mgr., Chicago, 1938-42, vice pres. system freight traffic, San Francisco, from 1942. Mason. Clubs: Chicago, Pacific-Union, Family, Commercial (San Francisco); Arlington (Portland); Traffic (New York); California (Los Angeles, Calif.). Home: San Francisco, Calif. †

HALEY, JAMES ANDREW, former congressman; b. Jacksonville, Ala., Jan. 4, 1899; s. Andrew Jackson and Mary Lee (Steveson) H.; student U. Ala., 1919-22; m. Aubrey B. Ringling. Accountant, Sarasota, Fla., 1925-33; gen. mgr. John Ringling estate, 1933-43; lst v.p. Ringling Circus, 1943-45; pres., dir. Ringling Bros. Barnum & Bailey Circus, Sarasota, 1946-48; mem. 83d to 92d congresses from 7th Fla. Dist., 93d-94th congresses from 8th Dist. Fla. Mem. Fla. Ho. of Reps., 1948-52. Chmn. Democratic exec. com., Sarasota, 1935-52. Served U.S. Army, World War I. Mem. Am. Legion, V.F.W., S.A.R. Methodist. Mason, Elk. Clubs: Sarasota Yacht, Sun and Surf, 40 and 8. Home: Sarasota, Fla. Dec. Aug. 6, 1981.

HALEY, JOHN LESLIE, pub. utilities; b. Ada, O., Aug. 25, 1887; s. Patrick R. and Josephine (McQuown) H.; B.S. in E.E., U. of Colo., 1914; m. Rose L. Wilson, 1918; 1 son, John L.; m. 2d, Harriet H. Sluus, 1930; 1 dau., Shirley M. With Henry L. Doherty orgn., 1914-22; v.p. Adirondack Power & Light Corp., 1922-27, N.Y. Power & Light Corp., 1927-36; pres. Central N.Y. Power Corp. since 1937 (dir.); pres. and dir. Oswego Canal Co., St. Lawrence Power Co., Ltd., Cornwall, Ont.; v.p. and dir. Niagara Mohawk Power Corp. since 1950; v.p. and dir. Frontier Corp. Member and director American Gas Association. Clubs: Technology, Century, Onondaga Golf and Country (Syracuse). Home: Syracuse, N.Y. †

HALEY, MOLLY ANDERSON (MRS. FRANK LEROY HALEY), author; b. Waterford, Saratoga Co., N.Y., Jan. 19, 1888; d. Richard Knill and Sarah A. (Hill) Anderson; B.A., Elmira Coll., 1909, M.A., 1912; m. Frank LeRoy Haley, M.D., of Mobile, Ala., Sept. 14, 1916. Organized first child welfare agency of Yates County, N.Y., 1913-14; state insp. alms-houses and pub. hosps., N.Y. Bd. Charities, 1911-16. Mem. League Am. Pen Women, Order of Bookfellows, N.Y. Craftsmen's Group in Poetry. Republican. Episcopalian. Clubs: Plandome Women's, Elmira Coll. Club of New York. Author: Heritage and Other Poems, 1925; Gardens and You, 1925; The Window Cleaner and Other Poems, 1931. Winner of one of two annual prizes of Poetry Soc. America, 1928, also of Forum Mag. prize for best transl. of L'Enfant Jésus de Prague (by Paul Claudel), 1928. Contbr. verse to mags., also articles on social service. Home: Manhasset, L.I., N.Y. †

HALL, CHAFFEE E(ARL), lawyer; b. Oakland, Cal., Mar. 5, 1888; s. Samuel Pike and Charlotte Whipple (Spear) H.; B.L., U. Cal., 1910; m. Emmy Marie Lemcke, Apr. 6, 1915; children—Chaffee Earl, Marie Hall (Mrs. Penry Griffiths). Admitted to Cal. bar, 1912, practiced in San Francisco, partner Hall, Henry & Oliver, from 1944; dir. Pacific Lighting Corporation, San Francisco and Napa Valley Railroad. Mem. Sigma Nu. Phi Delta Phi. Republican. Unitarian. Clubs: Bohemian. Cercle de L'Union (San Francisco); Pacific-Union. Home: Piedmont, Cal. †

HALL, CORNELIUS A(LOYSIUS), pres., borough of Richmond, N.Y.; b. S.I., N.Y., June 19, 1888; s. John Francis and Agnes (Barr) H.; grad. Curtis High Sch., 1907; pvt. tutor; m. Edith Mildred Milo, Nov. 23, 1934; 1 dau. (adopted), Patricia Ann. With Allis Chalmers Mfg. Co., 1907-22; partner, Hall Bros. (real estate development), 1922-26; supt. of public bldg. and offices, 1926-30; asst. commr. public works in charge of constrn., borough of Richmond, 1930-40, commr. of borough works, 1940-45; pres., borough of Richmond, N.Y. City, since 1946. Trustee, S.I. Civic Symphony Orchestra; dir., S.I. Inst. of Arts and Sciences, S.I. Zoolog. Soc. Decorated Distinguished Citizenship award, Wagner Coll., S.I., 1946. Mem. Municipal Engrs. of City of N.Y. Democrat. Roman Catholic. Clubs: Rotary, Elks. Home: Eltingville, N.Y. †

HALL, DONALD KEITH, lawyer; b. Ely, Nev., Aug. 24, 1918; s. Edward Clyde and Mabel Louise H.; m. Alla T. Puchalsky, Apr. 27, 1947; children—Melanie, Matthew, Natalie, Kristina, Theodore. B.S., U. Calif. at Los Angeles, 1940; J.D., U. So. Calif., 1949. Bar: Calif. bar 1949. Since practiced in, Los Angeles; law clk. U.S. Ct. Appeals 9th Circuit, Los Angeles, 1949-50; staff atty. Western Air Lines Inc., Los Angeles, 1950-52; mem. firm Darling, Hall, Rae & Gute, Los Angeles, 1953-79; sr. v.p., gen. counsel, sec. Western Air Lines, Inc., Los Angeles, 1979-81; mem. firm. Darling, Hall & Rae, Los Angeles, from 1982. Pres. South Pasadena Unified Sch. Dist., 1964. Served to capt. AUS, 1942-47. Mem. Los Angeles County Bar Assn. (pres. 1972-73), ABA, State Bar Calif., Order of Coif, Phi Kappa Phi. Home: South Pasadena, Calif. Deceased.

HALL, FREDERICK WILSON, ret. state justice, lawyer; b. Pitts., Feb. 22, 1908; s. Peter B. and Rachel (Crispin) H.; Litt.B., Rutgers U., 1928, LL.D., 1960; LL.B. cum laude, Harvard U., 1931; m. Jane R. Armstrong, July 18, 1936; 1 son, Peter W. Admitted to N.J. bar, 1932; asso. Arthur T. Vanderbilt, Newark, 1931-41; mem. Wharton & Hall, and successors, Somerville, N.J., 1941-53; judge Superior Ct. of N.J., 1953-58, appellate div. Superior Ct., 1958-59; asso. justice Supreme Ct. of N.J., 1959-75; counsel to Wharton, Stewart & Davis, Somerville, 1975-84. Mem. State Univ. Bicentennial Commn., 1966. Mem. bd. edn., Bound Brook, N.J., 1934-49, pres., 1946-49. Past bd. mgrs. N.J. State Village for Epileptics. Fellow Am. Bar Found.; mem. Am. (adv. commn. on housing and urban growth), N.J., Somerset County (past pres.) bar assns., Am. Judicature Soc., Am. Law Inst., Inst. Jud. Adminstrn., Phi Beta Kappa, Chi Psi. Democrat. Presbyterian. Clubs: Raritan Valley Country (Somerville); Rutgers Alumni Faculty (New Brunswick, N.J.). Home: Bound Brook, N.J. Died July 7, 1984.

HALL, J. FRANK, oral surgeon, educator; b. Quaker City, Ohio, Apr. 1, 1899; s. Lewis Walton and Lucretia Margaret (Lowery) H.; student Muskingum Coll., New Concord, O., 1927-28; D.D.S., U. Pitts., 1934, B.S., 1935; m. Roberta Cain, Nov. 21, 1927. dental intern U. Pitts. Med. Center, 1934-35; Carnegie fellow in pathology U. Rochester Med. Center, 1935-36; postgrad. in gen. anesthesia U. Pitts., 1938, in oral surgery, Northwestern U., 1940, oral diagnosis and pathol., Ohio State U., 1946; pvt. practice oral surgery (part time), from 1947; bus. mgr. Jour. Dental Research, 1936-58; instr. oral surgery and anesthesia Med. Coll. Va., 1936-38, asst. prof., 1938-42, assoc. prof., 1942; prof. oral surgery Ind. U. Sch. Dentistry, Indpls., from 1942. Diplomate Am. Bd. Oral Surgery. Mem. Am. Assn. Dental Schs. (chmn. oral surg. sect. 1943- 49), Am. Dental Assn. (organizer council hosp. dental service), Am., Ind., Indpls. Dist. (editor jour. 1955-60) dental socs., Am. Acad. Oral Pathology, Am., Ind., Great Lakes socs. oral surgeons, Am., Ind. socs. anesthesiologists, Internat. Assn. Dental Research, Pierre Fauchard Acad., Fedn. Dentaire Internat., Omicron Kappa Epsilon, Psi Omega. Republican. Methodist. Clubs: Columbia, Atheneum (Indpls.). Home: Indianapolis, Ind. Died Apr. 22, 1981.

HALL, JAMES H(USST), music educator; b. Cohoes, N.Y., Feb. 3, 1890; s. James Marvin and Mary (Husst) H.; A.B., Oberlin Coll., 1914, Mus.B., 1915, A.M., 1922; student Schola Cantorum, Paris, 1926-27; in Edinburgh and Paris, 1937-38; m. Florence Belle Jenney, June 28, 1919; 1 son, James Truman (died 1943). Successively instr., asst. prof. pianoforte and history of music Coll. of Wooster (Ohio), 1915-21; asst. prof. history and criticism of music Oberlin Coll., 1922-27, prof., 1927-55, emeritus, from 1955, vis. lectr. Richmond U. Area Center (John Hay Whitney Found.), 1956; organist-dir. Calvary Presbyterian Ch., Cleve., 1921-27; Plymouth Church, Shaker Hts., 1930-35, and other churches; dir. 1st Church (Cong.), Oberlin, 1939-40, organist, 1943-47, from 56. Served with U.S.N.R.F., 1919. Mem. Pi Kappa Lambda. Republican. Conglist. Author: The Art Song, 1953. Contbr. criticism and reviews various journals. Composer: (anthems) Lord of Love, Light of Lights, Sleeping the Christ Child Lay, I Know not Where, Come Unto Me, The Troubadors, In Flanders Field, The Child. Home: Oberlin, OH. †

HALL, JOHN LEWIS, lawyer; b. Woodville, Fla., July 26, 1904; s. Thomas Milton and Ola (Page) H.; m. Martha Buford, Aug. 24, 1927; children—John Lewis, Thomas Munroe. A.B. in Edn, U. Fla., 1927. Bar: Fla. bar 1936. Tchr. pub. schs., Fla., 1927-35, practiced law, Tallahassee; mem. Fla. Capitol Center Planning Commn., Tallahassee, 1972-77; county atty. Leon County, 1939-66; atty. Fla. Assn. County Commrs., 1941-64; Mem. Fabisinski Com. of Fla., 1956-57; Adv. Commn. Revision Fla. Constn., 1957-59, Fla. Gov.'s Adv. Com. Race Relations, 1957-58. Bd. dirs. Tallahassee Symphony Assn. Mem. ABA, Tallahassee Bar Assn. (pres. 1946), Fla. Bar (gov. 1954-60, pres. 1959-60), Fla. County Attys. Assn. (pres. 1942), Blue Key, Beta Theta Pi, Sigma Delta Chi. Methodist (pres. legal adv. council Fla. conf. United Meth. Ch. 1973). Clubs: Mason (grand master Fla. 1958), Lions (pres. 1945). Home: Tallahassee, Fla. Died Oct. 16, 1984.

HALL, JOYCE CLYDE, greeting card publisher; b. David City, Nebr., Aug. 29, 1891; s. George N. and Nancy (Dudley) H.; m. Elizabeth Dilday, Mar. 25, 1922 (dec. Mar. 15, 1976); children—Elizabeth Ann, Barbara, Donald. Student pub. schs., David City and Norfolk, Nebr.; LL.D., U. Mo., 1963, Kans. State U., 1963, U. Nebr., 1968. Founder, pres., chmn. bd. Hallmark Cards, Inc., 1910-66, chmn., 1966-82; dir. First Nat. Bank of Kansas City. Bd. dirs., hon. pres. People-to-People; bd. dirs. Eisenhower Found., Midwest Research Inst. Decorated knight Order of Leopold; hon. comdr. Order Brit. Empire; recipient Dr. Lee DeForest award Nat. Assn. Better Radio and TV, 1953; Horatio Alger award Am. Schs. and Colls. Assn., 1957; Mr. Kansas City C. of C. award, 1961; Trustees' Sponsors award Nat. Acad. TV Arts and Scis., 1961; Trustees citation Midwest Research Inst., 1972; Named to Bus. Hall of Fame award Fortune/Jr. Achievement, 1977. Mem. Am. Assn. French Legion Honor. Home: Kansas City, Mo. Died Oct. 29, 1982.*

HALL, KENT BRUCE, lawyer; b. New Martinsville, W.Va., June 14, 1888; s. Samuel Bruce and Kate E. (Hornbrook) H.; A.B. and A.M., Washington and Jefferson Coll., 1910; LL.B., Harvard, 1913; grad. work, Oxford U., 1913-14; m. Mary Ellen Hazlett, May 23, 1917; children—Ellen Hall (Mrs. Kenneth A. Pennington), Robert Bruce, Kent Hazlett. Admitted to W.Va. bar, 1914; former chmn. bd. dirs. M. Marsh & Sons (cigars); mem. trust com., exec. com., dir. Wheeling Dollar Savs. & Trust Co. Served as lt. AC, World War I. Mem. Wheeling Park Commn.; sec. mem. exec. com., dir. Ohio Valley Gen. Hosp.; past dir. Episcopal High Sch., Alexandria, Va.; past pres. Fresh Air Farm, Inc. Mem. Am., W.Va., Ohio County (past pres.) bar assns., Newcomen Soc., Kappa Sigma. Republican. Episcopalian. Clubs: Harvard (N.Y.C.); Rotary (past pres., Wheeling); Fort Henry. Home: Wheeling, W.Va. †

HALL, LYNN THOMPSON, physician; born Davenport, Ia., July 10, 1887; s. Charles E. and Lora Helen (Thompson) H.; student Drake U.; M.D., U. of Ia., 1911; spl. study internal medicine, Harvard Post Grad. Med. Sch.; m. Ida Mae Garlock, Mar. 30, 1918. Interne, Ia. Methodist Hosp., Des Moines, 1911-12; mem. staff Bishop Clarkson Memorial, Creighton Memorial and St. Joseph's hosps.; mem. staff Immanuel Deaconess Inst., Neb. Methodist Episcopal and Deaconess Home, Neb. Univ. Hosp. Prof. clin. medicine U. of Neb. Fellow Am. Coll. Physicians; mem. A.M.A., Omaha, Douglas County and Mid-West med. socs. Republican. Presbyterian. Mason. Club: Omaha. Home: Omaha, Nebr.†

HALL, PAUL, labor union ofcl.; b. Ala., Aug. 21, 1914; m. Rose Hall; 2 children. Mem. Seafarers Internat. Union N. Am., 1938—, sec.-treas. Atlantic, Gulf, Great Lakes and In Land Waters dists., 1948-81, 1st v.p., 1948-57, pres., 1957-81; pres. maritime trades dept. AFL-CIO, 1957-81, nat. v.p., mem. exec. com., 1962-81. Mem. Nat. Com. Immigration, Citizens Com. Free China; former mem. Nat. Commn. for Indsl. Peace; former mem. Pres.'s labor mgmt. adv. com. Cost of Living Council; mem. Labor Mgmt. Adv. Com. on Econ. Matters. Bd. dirs. Am. Immigration and Citizenship Conf.; a founder, mem. nat. council Eleanor Roosevelt Found.; trustee George Meany Found.; sponsor, trustee Coordinating Council Edn. to Disadvantaged; v.p. Civic Center Clinic, N.Y.C. Recipient Humanitarian award Civic Center Clinic; citation of honor Nat. Com. Rural Address: Brooklyn, N.Y. Died 1981.*

HALL, PAYSON, broadcasting co. exec.; b. Oil City, Pa., July 6, 1915; s. Samuel Payson and Marie (Howe) H.; A.B., Cornell U., 1936; M.S., Columbia, 1945; m. Milnore Hoel; 1 son, Samuel. Staff accountant Hurdman & Cranstoun, C.P.A.'s, N.Y.C., 1936-40; financial sec. N.Y. State Vet. Coll., Cornell U., 1940-41; sr. credit analyst Chase Nat. Bank, N.Y.C., 1941-42; exec. accountant U.S. Army Engrs., Iran, 1942-43; chief accountant Bridgeport Brass Co., 1944-45; indsl. engr., mgr. reports and budgets Trans World Airlines, Kansas City, Mo., 1945-47; controller Meredith Corp., Des Moines, 1947-50; asst. sec., dir. radio-TV, 1950-60, treas., 1953-60, exec. v.p., 1960-65; v.p. McCall Printing, Inc., 1965; v.p. finance and planning, mem. exec. com. King Broadcasting Co., Seattle, from 1965, also dir.; v.p., dir. Cowilitz Cableview Co., 1966-73; treas., dir. King Videocable Co., from 1966. Mem. adv. bd. accounting dept. Drake U., 1949-52, sec., 1951-52; mem. TV com. Brotherhood Week, 1947-58, NCCJ. Mem. Nat. Assn. Accountants (past pres.), Quad-Cities and Seattle Financial Execs. Insts. (past pres.), (chmn. nat. corp. accounting procedures and reports 1951-53, chmn. pub. industry conf. 1952), Nat. Assn. Broadcasters (dir.), TV Bur. Advt. (dir.), TV Pioneers (charter), Broadcast Pioneers, Internat. Radio and TV Soc., Planning Execs. Inst. (dir., treas. Puget Sound chpt. 1972—), Newcomen Soc., Beta Gamma Sigma. Congregationalist. Club: Rainier (Seattle). Home: Seattle, Wash. Died 1985.

HALL, ROBERT BRUCE, bishop; b. Wheeling, W.Va., Jan. 27, 1921; s. Kent Bruce and Mary Ellen (Hazlett) H.; m. Dorothy Varner Glass, Jan. 26, 1949; children—Ellen Lynn, Kent Bruce II, Elizabeth Hazlett, Anne Louise, Susan Glass. B.A., Trinity Coll., Hartford, Conn., 1943, D.D., 1967; S.T.B., Episcopal Theol. Sem., Cambridge, Mass., 1949; D.D., Seabury Western Theol. Sem., 1966, Va. Theol. Sem., 1967, Kenyon Coll., 1969. Ordained to ministry Episcopal Ch., 1949; asso. minister, Huntington, W.Va., 1949-53, rector, Huntington, 1953-58, St. Chrysostom's Ch., Chgo., 1958-66; bishop coadjutor Episcopal Diocese Va., 1966-74, bishop of Va., 1974-85. Trustee Va. Theol. Sem., 1967-85, Blue Ridge Sch., Dyke, Va., 1968-85. Served with AUS, 1943-46. Fellow Coll. of Preachers; mem. Delta Phi, Pi Gamma Mu. Home: Richmond, Va. Died May 27, 1985.

HALL, ROBERT HOWELL, U.S. district judge; b. Soperton, Ga., Nov. 28, 1921; s. Instant Howell, Jr. and Blanche (Mishoe) H.; m. Janice Kay Wren, July 15, 1982; children: Carolyn C., Patricia A., Howell A. B.S. in Commerce, U. Ga., 1941; LL.B., U. Va., 1948; LL.D. (hon.), Emory U., 1973. Bar: Ga. bar 1948, also U.S. Supreme Ct 1948. Prof. law Emory U., 1948-61; asst. atty. gen., Ga., 1953-61; head criminal div. Ga. Law Dept., 1959-61; judge Ga. Ct. Appeals, Atlanta, 1961-74; justice Ga. Supreme Ct., Atlanta, 1974-79; judge U.S. Dist. Ct. (No. Dist. Ga.), 1979—; Chmn. Jud. Council Ga., 1973-74, Gov.'s Commn. on Jud. Processes, 1971-73. Author 3 legal texts, also articles. Served with AUS, 1942-46; lt. col. Res. ret. Recipient Leadership award Harvard Law Sch. Assn. Ga., 1971; Golden Citizenship award Fulton Grand Jurors Assn., 1975. Fellow Am. Bar Found.; mem. Am. Bar Assn. (ho. dels. 1971-73, chmn. com. Nat. Inst. Justice 1976-80), Am. Judicature Soc. (dir. 1964—, pres. 1971-73, Harley award 1974), Nat. Center State Cts. (adv. council 1971—, dir. 1977-79), Inst. Ct. Mgmt. (trustee 1976—), Am. Acad. Jud. Edn. (gov. 1964-71), Atlanta Lawyers Club, Delta Tau Delta, Delta Sigma Phi, Phi Delta Phi.

HALL, SPENCER GILBERT, lawyer; b. Harrisburg, Pa., May 13, 1910; s. Francis J. and Harriet Spencer (Gilbert) H.; m. Josephine McCreight, Jan. 15, 1946 (dec. May 1974); children—Spencer Gilbert (dec.), W. Maclay, Harriet G., Josephine McC.; m. Julia Ann Storey, July 14, 1976. Grad., Lawrenceville (N.J.) Sch., 1928; A.B., Princeton U., 1932; LL.B., Dickinson Sch. Law, 1936. Bar: Pa. bar 1937. City solicitor, Harrisburg, 1949-68; mem. firm Nauman, Smith, Shissler & Hall, Harrisburg, 1937-79; dir. Commonwealth Nat. Bank, 1949-83, chmn. exec. com., 1964-83, chmn. bd., 1979-83; dir. Harrisburg Hotel Co., 1949-71, v.p., 1963-67, pres., 1967-71; dir. W.O. Hickok Mfg. Co., Penn-Harris Hotel Co. Trustee Harrisburg Acad., 1952-83, past pres.; bd. mgrs. Harrisburg Hosp., 1939-83, chmn. med. com., 1948-83; trustee Harrisburg State Hosp. Served to lt. comdr. USNR, 1942-46. Mem. Scotch Irish Soc. (past pres.), Delta Psi. Presbyterian (trustee). Clubs: Rotarian, Philadelphia, Harrisburg Country; Ivy (Princeton). Home: Dillsburg, Penn. Died Apr. 1983.

HALL, STANDISH, finance, trusteeships and warehousing exec.; b. Chgo., Sept. 30, 1891; s. Harry Newbury and Anne (Russell) H.; m. Helen Brooks, June 5, 1920 (dec. Dec. 1961); children—Brooks, Wolcott (dec.), Bradford; m. Margaret Bailey Echols, Dec. 12, 1962. A.B., Harvard U., 1916. With W.R. Grace & Co., Peru, 1916-17; with credit dept. Union Trust Co., Chgo., 1919-20, mgr. new bus. dept., 1920-21, advt. dir., 1921-22, asst. sec., 1922-23; v.p., dir. Union Nat. Bank, Wichita, 1923-28; v.p., dir. Guarantee Title & Trust Co., 1928-29, pres., dir., 1929-30, Yellow Van & Storage Co., 1931-52, Met. Warehouse Co., 1931-63; operator Standish Hall Co. (gen. ins. and investments), 1930-63, trustee ct. apptd. oil royalty syndicates. Dir. civil def., State of Kans., 1950-54. Served from seaman to ensign USNR, 1917-19; comdr. 1941-46. Awarded Commendation medal. Mem. Nat. Assn. State Civil Def. Dirs. (pres. 1951-52), Wichita Art Assn. (pres. 1962-63). Republican. Episcopalian. Clubs: University (Chgo.); Army and Navy (Washington). Address: Houston, Tex.

HALL, WILLIAM CHARLES, former assn. exec.; b. St. Louis, Mar. 21, 1909; s. William Antoine and Grace (Caldwell) H.; student Washington U., St. Louis, 1927; B.S., U.S. Mil. Acad., 1931; M.S. in Civil Engring., U. Calif. at Berkeley, 1938; student Nat. War Coll., 1955-56; m. Elizabeth Pleasants Brooke, Nov. 2, 1940; 1 son, Edward Brooke. Commd. 2d lt. U.S. Army, 1931, advanced through grades to brig. gen., 1959; chief map and photo br. Dept. of Army, 1950-53; army engr. 2d Army, 1953-55; chief logistics div. Alaskan Command, 1956-59; asst. chief engrs. for personnel Office Chief Engrs., 1959-61, acting chief mil. constrn., 1960-61, dir. research and devel., 1961-62; dep. chief logistics div. European Command, 1962-63; exec. sec. Soc. Am. Mil. Engrs., Washington, 1965-78. Decorated Legion of Merit with oak leaf cluster, Bronze Star medal; Croix de Guerre with palm (France). Registered profl. engr., D.C. Clubs: Army-Navy, Army-Navy Country (Washington). Author: A Medal for Horatius, 1955. Contbr. articles to tech. mags. Home: Washington, D.C. Died May 22, 1984; interred Arlington Nat. Cemetery, Arlington, Va.

HALLADAY, DANIEL WHITNEY, university chancellor; b. Santa Ana, Calif., Oct. 13, 1920; s. Harlow Monroe and Marion (Winans) H.; B.A., Pomona Coll., 1942; M.A., Claremont Grad. Sch., 1947; postgrad. U. So. Calif., 1949; Ed.D., Columbia, 1955; m. Elaine Owings, Aug. 21, 1941 (dec.); children—Whitney Sue (Mrs. Ernest Whitelaw), Steven Owings, m. Cherie Longeway, May 19, 1972. Athletic coach Pomona Coll., Claremont, Calif., 1946-47; assoc. prof. phys. edn. and health U. Fla., Gainesville, 1947-51; lectr. health edn. Columbia, N.Y.C., 1953-54, asst. provost Tchrs. Coll., 1954-55; prof. of edn., dean of students U. Ark., Fayetteville, 1955-66; pres. East Tex. State U., Commerce, 1966-72; pres. Tex. A. and I. U. at Corpus Christi, 1972-76; acting chancellor, pres. Tex. A. and I. U. System, 1976-77; chancellor Univ. System of South Tex., 1977-80; pres. Council of Presidents State Sr. Colls., 1967-68; mem. adv. com. on formulas for sr. colls. and univs., coordinating bd. Tex. Coll. and Univ. System; mem. spl. adv. com. to commr. higher edn. State of Tex. Bd. visitors U.S. Mil. Acad., 1970-73. Served to capt. AUS, 1942-46, to maj., 1951-53, now lt. col. Res. Decorated Silver Star, Bronze Star with two clusters, Purple Heart with cluster. Mem. U.S. (edn. and manpower devel. coms.), South Tex. (dir.) chambers of commerce, Am. Assn. State Colls. and Univs. (dir.), Tex. Assn. Colls. and Univs. (chmn. commn. on ednl. policy), Corpus Christi Area Conv. and Tourist Bur., Center for Econ. Studies (chmn. bd.), Kappa Delta Pi, Phi Delta Kappa. Methodist. Kiwanian. Home: Corpus Christi, Tex. Dec. July 2, 1980. Interned Corpus Christi.

HALLADAY, HENRY EARNEST, lawyer; b. Battle Creek, Mich., Mar. 27, 1915; s. Ivor Ronald and Augustine (Earnest) H.; A.B., U. Mich., 1936, J.D., 1937; m. Soramae Greenberg, Oct. 19, 1967. Admitted to Minn. bar, 1938, since practiced in Mpls.; trial and labor relations atty. Dorsey, Windhorst, Hannaford, Whitney & Halladay and predecessors, from 1937; dir. Assoc. Industries Mpls., from 1957. Chmn. Minn. Supreme Ct. Rules Adv. Com., 1965-72, also adv. com. Jury Instrn. Guides; mem. com. to study standards for fed. practice U.S. Supreme Ct. Sponsor, Minn. Symphony, Mpls. Art Inst., Walker Art Inst. Fellow Am. Coll. Trial Lawyers; mem. ABA. Home: Excelsior, Minn. Deceased.

HALLER, JOHN, geology educator; b. Basel, Switzerland, Mar. 6, 1927; s. Hans and Frieda (Meyer) H.; m. Susanna Margaretha Weisskopf, June 4, 1952; children: Daniel Urs, Patrick Renato. Ph.D., U. Basel, 1952, venia docendi, 1957. Geologist Lauge Koch's East Greenland Expdns., Greenland Dept., Copenhagen, Denmark, 1949-62; lectr. U. Basel, 1958-64; vis. lectr. Harvard U., Cambridge, Mass., 1964-65, assoc. prof., 1965-69, prof. geology, 1969-84. Author: Geology of the East Greenland Caledonides, 1971. Recipient Steno medal Geol. Soc. Denmark, 1974. Fellow Geol. Soc. Am., Arctic Inst. N.Am.; mem. Swiss Mineral. Soc. Home: Belmont, Mass. Died May 1, 1984.

HALLORAN, GEORGE MATTHEW, army officer; b. Fort Abraham Lincoln, N.D., Jan. 19, 1889; s. Capt. James and Mary (Keane) H.; student Pa. State Coll., 1908-10; grad. Chem. Warfare Service Sch., 1921, Army War Coll., 1926, Army Indsl. Coll., 1927; m. Loretta Boyd Hunter, Nov. 1, 1915; 1 son, James Paul Stacy. Commd. 2d lt., Inf., Oct. 7, 1911, and advanced through the grades to brig. gen., Oct. 27, 1942; prof. mil. science, U. of Wyo., 1936-40; asst. exec., 1st Mil. Area, Knoxville, 1940-41; acting chief of staff, 81st Div., July-Dec. 1941; comdg. officer, Camp Shelby from Dec. 1941.†

HALLQUIST, EINAR GUSTAVE, business exec.; born Norrkoping, Sweden, Mar. 13, 1887; s. Andrew Gustave and Axeline (Peterson) H.; ed. pub. schs., St. Louis and Edwardsville, Ill., and LeClaire Coll.; m. Alma S. Amman, June 27, 1914; children—Ralph Fred, Alma Marie (Mrs. George Ross Wolf). Began as draftsman Commonwealth Steel Co., 1909, chief draftsman, 1915, mech. engr., 1919, chief mech. engr., 1925; with Gen. Steel Castings Corp. since 1929, vice pres., 1938, special rep., Chicago, 1943, vice pres. from 1946. Republican. Presbyterian. Home: University City, Mo. †

HALLS, JAY CLARENCE, lawyer; b. River Falls, Wis., Dec. 1, 1889; s. Oluff O. and Anna (Sather) H.; student U. Wis.; LL.B., Georgetown U., 1913; m. Ruth Norman, Mar. 26, 1945. Admitted to Minn. bar, 1915, Ill. bar, 1923; practice of law, Chgo., from 1923; mem. firm Hopkins, Sutter, Halls, Owen & Mulroy (and predecessors), from 1923. Spl. atty. Office Solicitor Internal Revenue, 1921-22. Mem. Am., Ill., Chgo. bar assns. Club: Legal, Law, Union League, Midday, Lake Shore (Chgo.); Glenview Country; Valley (Santa Barbara). Home: Santa Barbara, Calif. †

HALLSTEIN, WALTER, German statesman; b. Mainz, Germany, Nov. 17, 1901; s. J. and Anna (Geibel) H.; student Bonn U., Muenchen U., 1920-23; LL.D., U. Berlin, 1925, Georgetown U., Washington, U. Padua, Italy, Tufts U., Medford, Mass., Colby Coll., Waterville, Me., Adelphi Coll., Garden City, N.Y., Harvard, John Hopkins University, Univ. of Liege, Belgium. Prof. Rostock Univ., 1930-41; prof., dir. Inst. Comparative Law, Frankfurt, 1941-44; rector Frankfurt U., 1946-48; vis. prof. Georgetown U., Washington, 1948-49; chmn. German com. UNESCO activities, 1949-50; head German Schuman Plan delegation. Paris, 1950; state's sec. Fed. Chancellery, 1950, German Fgn. Office, 1951-58; pres. Commn. European Econ. Community, 1958-67. Internat. European Movement, 1968-82. Mem. Deutsche UNESCO Commn. Served as lt. German Army, WWII (U.S. prisoner of war 1944); head Camp U., Como. Miss. Recipient Charlemagne prize, 1961; recipient of the Robert-Schuman-Preis. 1969. Mem. Deutsche Gesellschaft für Vôlkerrecht, Deutsche Gesellschaft für Rechtsvergleichung (pres.), Deutsche Vereinigung für Internationales Recht (pres.), Deutscher Juristentag, Deutsche Parlamentarische Gesellschaft, Presidency Deutsche Gesellschaff für Auswärtige Politik. Author: Die Aktienrechte der Gegenwart, 1931; Die Berichtigung des Gesellschaftskapitals, 1942; Wiederherstellung des Privatrechts, 1946; Wissenschaft und Politik, 1949; United Europe Challenge and Opportunity, 1962; also articles in encys. and periodicals. Home: Bonn, Germany. Died May 11, 1982.

HALPER, ALBERT, author; b. Chgo., Aug. 3, 1904; s. Isaac and Rebecca H.; m. Lorna B. Howard; 1 child by previous marriage, Thomas. Student, Northwestern U., 1924-26. Writer, 1929-84; Author: novels including Union Square, 1933, The Foundry, 1934, On The Shore, 1934, The Chute, 1937, Only an Inch from Glory, 1943, This is Chicago, 1952, The Golden Watch, 1953, Atlantic Avenue, 1956, The Fourth Horseman of Miami Beach, 1966; memoir Good-Bye, Union Square, 1970; non-fiction Chicago Crime Book, 1967; ink drawings Post War, 1975; novels translated into French, Spanish, Swedish, Russian, Danish, Czechoslovakian, Norwegian, Polish, Finnish.; contbr. articles and stories to Atlantic Monthly, New Yorker, Harper's, Yale Rev., Commentary, others. Guggenheim fellow for creative writing, 1934. Mem. Authors League Am., P.E.N. Address: Pawling, N.Y. Died Jan. 18, 1984.

HALPERN, HARRY, clergyman; b. N.Y.C., Feb. 4, 1899; s. David and Dora (Saratchek) H.; B.A., Coll. City N.Y., 1919; student Rabbi Isaac Elchanan Sem., 1920-24; LL.B., Bklyn. Law Sch., 1925, J.D., 1926; M.A., Columbia, 1925; M.H.L., Jewish Theol. Sem., Am., 1929, D.H.L., 1951, D.D., 1958; m. Mollie Singer, Mar. 27, 1941 (dec.); 1 dau., Deborah; m. 2d, Jean Rosenhaus, June 19, 1967. Rabbi, 1929; rabbi Jewish Communal Center of Flatbush, 1919-29, East Midwood Jewish Center, 1929-77; vis. prof. homiletics Jewish Theol. Sem. Am., 1957, now adj. prof. pastoral psychiatry. Pres. N.Y. Bd. Rabbis, 1961-62. Chmn. bd. edn. Yeshivah of Flatbush; Kings County adv. council N.Y. State Commn. on Discrimination; commr. N.Y.C. Commn. on Human Rights; chmn. Bklyn. div. State of Israel Bonds; exec. com. Bklyn. Cancer Soc. Trustee Jewish Chronic Disease Hosp., Pride of Judea Children's Home, Fedn. Jewish Philanthropies; co-chmn. nat. planning com. Jewish Theol. Sem. Fellow Herbert Lehman Inst. Ethics; mem. Zionist Orgn. Am. (exec. com.), Rabbinical Assembly Am. (pres.). Home: Southbury, Conn. Dec. June 10, 1981.

HALPERN, SHELDON WILLIAM, lawyer, consultant; b. N.Y.C., Dec. 16, 1935; s. Joseph and Bertha (Zins) H.; children: Joel Michael, Paul Benjamin. B.A., Cornell U., 1957, LL.B., 1959. Bar: N.Y. 1959, Minn. 1973. Mem. law firms, N.Y.C., 1959-73; v.p., gen. counsel, sec. Fingerhut Corp., Minnetonka, Minn., 1973-79; partner firm Robins, Davis and Lyons, Mpls., 1979-80; v.p., gen. counsel, sec. Viacom Internat., N.Y.C., 1980-82; tchr. U. Minn. Sch. Social Work, 1976. Editor: Cornell Law Rev. Bd. dirs. Jewish Community Relations Counsel, Anti-Defamation League Minn. and the Dakotas, Cricket Theatre. Mem. Assn. Bar City N.Y., Minn., N.Y. State bar assns., Corporate Counsel Assn. Minn., Phi Beta Kappa, Phi Kappa Phi, Order of Coif.

HALSTED, JAMES ADDISON, physician; b. Syracuse, N.Y., Apr. 19, 1905; s. Thomas Henry and Charlotte (Palmer) H.; m. Isabella Hopkinson, Nov. 30, 1930 (div. Oct. 1952); children—Elinor, Thomas Addison, Charles H., Isabella; m. Anna Roosevelt, Nov. 11, 1952 (dec. 1975); 1 adopted son, John R. Boettiger; m. Diana Hopkins, Aug. 28, 1976 (div. 1983). B.A., Harvard U., 1926, M.D., 1930. Diplomate: Am. Bd. Internal Medicine. Intern Mass. Gen. Hosp., Boston, 1930-32; resident Lakeside Hosp., Cleve., 1932-33, practice medicine, specializing in internal medicine, Boston and Dedham, Mass., 1934-50, Los Angeles, 1950-55, Syracuse, N.Y., 1955-58, Shiraz, Iran, 1958-60, Lexington, Ky., 1960-61, Detroit, 1961-64, Washington, 1964-70; chief med. service Faulkner Hosp., Boston, 1946-50; chief gastroenterology sect. VA Hosp., Los Angeles, 1950-55; dir. profl. services Syracuse VA Hosp., 1955-60; chief med. service Met. Hosp., Detroit, 1961-63; asso. chief staff for research Allen Park (Mich.) VA Hosp., 1962-64; dep. asst. chief med. dir. for research and edn. VA Central Office, Washington, 1964-66; asso. chief staff for research VA Hosp., Washington, 1966-71, cons., 1971-80; attending gastroenterologist Albany (N.Y.) Med. Center Hosp.; mem. staff Columbia Meml. Hosp., Hudson, N.Y.; chief med. service Nemazee Hosp., Shiraz, 1958-60; asso. clin. prof. medicine U. Calif., 1950-55; asso. prof. medicine SUNY, Syracuse, 1955-60; prof. medicine Wayne State U. Sch. Medicine, 1961-64; prof. epidemiology and environ. health George Washington U. Sch. Medicine, Washington, 1966-68; prof. clin. medicine U. Pa., Phila., 1968-71; Fulbright vis. prof. Pahlavi U., Iran, 1958-60; dir. nutrition research project, Iran, 1966-70; clin. prof. medicine Albany Med. Coll., 1970-83, dir. nutrition program, 1973; mem. nat. adv. council arthritis and metabolic diseases NIH, 1965-69; mem. ad hoc coms. Nat. Acad. Sci., Nat. Library Medicine, NIH, 1969-70. Author: (with B.B. Wells) Clinical Pathology, (1967); contbr. articles to profl. jours.; editor: The Laboratory in Clinical Medicine, 1976; sr. editor, 2d edit., 1981. Served to lt. col. U.S. Army, 1942-46. Decorated Legion of Merit; Fulbright grantee, 1958-60; USPHS grantee, 1963-68; Rockefeller Found. grantee, 1976-77. Mem. Am. Soc. Clin. Nutrition, Am. Gastroent. Assn., Am. Clin. and Climatological Assn., A.C.P., Am. Inst. Nutrition. Address: Brookline, Mass. Died Mar. 2, 1984.

HAMILTON, CHARLES WALTER, oil executive; b. Ithaca, Mich., Apr. 8, 1890; s. Edward D. and Ella (Weidman) H.; grad. Ithaca Pub. Sch., 1908; student Alma (Mich.) Coll., 1908-09, Mil. Sch., Highland Falls, N.Y., 3 mos., 1909; A.B., U. of Okla., 1912; post-grad. study U. of Chicago, Colombian-Am. dir. Pan-Am. mos., 1915; m. Irene Lucile Stroup, Oct. 26, 1916; children—Robert Dyer, Irene Elizabeth, Charles Walter (Jr.), Jean. With U.S. and Okla. Geol. Survey in Northeastern Okla., summer 1910; U.S. Geol. Survey, N.D. and Mont., summer, 1911; asst. in Okla. Geol. Survey offices, 1910-12; geologist Cia Mexicana de Petroleo, El Aguila, S.A., 1912-15. Roma Oil Co., Okla. and Kan., 1915-16; chief geologist Mexican Gulf Oil Co., Mexico, 1916-17, gen. agt., 1917-22; asst. to vice pres. Gulf Oil Companies, New York, 1923-40; v.p. Gulf Oil Corp. from 1940; chmn. Gulf Eastern Co., from 1954; officer various Am. cos. operating Eastern Hemisphere wholly or party owned by Gulf Oil; dir. Kuwait Oil Co., Ltd., Eastern Gulf Oil Co., Ltd. Iranian Oil Participants, Ltd., Iranian Oil Services, Ltd.) mem. bd. mgrs. Montclair Savings Bank, 1949-54. Dir. Inter-Am. Safety Council, 1943-45, v.p., dir., 1946-47; dir., v.p. Montclair YMCA, 1949-54; mem. Montclair Housing Authority, 1949-51. Dir. Venequelan C. of C., N.Y., 1943-45, pres., dir. 1945-46; dir. Colombian-Am. C. of C., N.Y., 1946-49; dir. Pan-Am. Soc., Inc. Mem. U.S. C. of C., Am. Petroleum Inst., Bolivarian Soc. U.S., Inc., Am. Inst. Mining and Metall. Engrs., 25 Year Club of Petroleum Industry, Am., Royal geog. socs., Inst. Petroleum London, Am. Soc. London, English Speaking Union. Clubs: Whitehall, University (N.Y.); Duquesne (Pitts.); American, Ends of Earth, Monday Lunch (London), Home: Upper Montclair, N.J. †

HAMILTON, CLARENCE OTIS, bus. exec.; b. Flint, Mich., May 27, 1913; s. Bertis F. and Nell (Pruitt) H.; m. Dorothy V. Fitzpatrick Gallahue, Aug. 2, 1975; children—George O., Elaine Hamilton Jacobson, Louise Hamilton Kruger, Charles L. Co-founder Cosco, Inc., Columbus, Ind., 1935, pres., 1961-69, chmn. bd., 1969-79, cons., 1980-82; dir. Irwin Bank & Trust Co. Home: Columbus, Ind. Died 1982.

HAMILTON, DUNCAN ALEXANDER, business exec.; b. Rio Vista, Calif., July 10, 1889; s. Alexander and Helen (McCormack) H.; student McGill Univ. 1910-12; m. Hazel Keddy, July 31, 1912; 1 dau. Helene. Clerk, C. F. Jackson Co., Ltd., Vancouver, B.C.; pres. D. A. Hamilton & Co., Ltd., Vancouver, B.C., Can., from 1931, pres. Vancouver News Herald from 1938, Liberal. Mason. Clubs: Rotary, Terminal City, Shaughnessey Heights Golf (Vancouver, Can.). Home: Vancouver, B.C., Can. †

HAMILTON, EDWARD JOSEPH, fastener manufacturing company executive; b. Port Chester, N.Y., Nov. 9, 1928; s. Joseph Edward and Louise Mary (Shaugnessy) H.; m. Barbara Jane Barr, Apr. 29, 1978. Bus. Adminstrn. degree, N.Y. U., 1951; postgrad., Northeastern U., Boston, 1968-69. With Russell, Burdsall & Ward Corp., Mentor, Ohio, from 1945, controller, then v.p., 1971-77, v.p. fin., 1977-82, exec. v.p., from 1982, also dir. Bd. dirs. Lake County YMCA, from 1976. Served with AUS, 1951-52. Mem. Nat. Assn. Accountants. Republican. Roman Catholic. Clubs: University (Cleve.); Elks (Willoughby, Ohio). Home: Wickliffe, OH.

HAMILTON, EDWIN S., physician; b. Emington, Ill., July 30, 1890; s. Edwin C. and Emma Jane (Stump) H.; A.B., U. Ill., 1911; S.B., U. Chicago, 1912; M.D., Rush Med. Coll., 1913; m. Zona Clark, Dec. 1, 1939; children—Edwin Clark, Helen Jane. Interne Cook County Hosp., Chicago, 1913-15; pvt. practice medicine, Kankakee, Ill., from 1915; chief of staff, St. Mary Hosp., 1924-59; v.p. City Nat. Bank, Kankakee, from 1932; pres. Kankakee County Title & Trust Co. from 1939. Served as capt., M.C., U.S. Army, 1918-19. Mem. adv. bd., Ill. Selective Service, 1940-45, chmn. adv. bd., 1951. Trustee 1943, chmn., 1948; chmn. bd. trustees Interstate Post Grad. Medical Assembly, 1951. Mem. med. examining com. state Ill., from 1943, chmn. 5 yrs. Mem. World Med. Association (council), A.M.A. (mem. House Dels., 1938-48, trustee 1948-58, sec. bd. 1948-58), Ill. and Kankakee County med societies, Am. Legion (past comdr.), Ill. State Med. Assn. (president from 1961), N.Y. Central Railroad Surgeons, Kankakee C. of C. (dir.), Phi Beta Pi, Alpha Omega Alpha. Methodist (trustee). Mason (Shriner), Elk (trustee 1925-28). Clubs: Kiwanis, Kankakee Country (Kankakee); Chicago Athletic Association (Chicago). Home: Kankakee, Ill. †

HAMILTON, FOWLER, lawyer; b. Kansas City, May 7, 1911; s. Eugene Paul and Emily Rhodelle (Fowler) H.; B.A., U. Mo., 1931; B.A., B.C.L., M.A. (Rhodes scholar), Oxford U., 1934; m. Helen Katherine Miller, Sept. 15, 1934; children—Helen Dudley, Emily Katherine (Mrs. Valerian L. Puskar), Milo Charles. Admitted to Mo. bar, 1935, D.C. bar, 1945, N.Y. bar, 1947; asso. Watson, Ess, Groner, Barnett & Whittaker, 1935-38; spl. asst. to atty. gen. U.S., 1938-42. Died June 7, 1984.

HAMLIN, WALTER BERGEN, state justice; b. New Orleans, Mar. 13, 1898; s. Charles Hector and Henrietta Mary (Bergen) H.; student Soule Coll., New Orleans, 1914-16; LL.B., Loyola U., New Orleans, 1919; m. Stella Malynn, Apr. 3, 1923. Admitted to La. bar, 1919; gen. practice, New Orleans, 1919-48; judge Civil Dist. Ct., Orleans Parish, 1948-58; asst. city atty. New Orleans, 1943-46; asso. justice Supreme Ct. of La., 1958-73. Democratic candidate for atty. gen., La., 1932. Served with U.S. Army; World War I.; mem. USNR, 1935-42. Home: New Orleans, La. Died Jan. 1, 1984.

HAMMOND, WALTER WILLIS, lawyer; b. Elgin, Neb., Jan. 9, 1890; s. Willis F. and Elizabeth J. (Campbell) H.; B.A., Beloit Coll., 1913; J.D., U. of Chicago, 1916; m. Mary Iva Reid, Oct. 28, 1916; children—Willis R., Roger M. Admitted to Wis. bar, 1916, and since practiced at Kenosha; asst. dist. atty., Kenosha County, 1927, pub. administrator, 1927-35; pres. Kenosha County Bar Assn., 1937; v.p. State Bar Assn. of Wis., 1940-41, pres., 1941-42. Mem. Am. Bar Assn., Phi Delta Theta, Phi Alpha Delta. Republican. Conglist. Mason, Elk. Home: Kenosha, Wis. †

HAMMOND, WILLIAM PHIN, engr., power co. exec.; b. Atlanta, Aug. 11, 1889; s. Charles Phin and Cornelia Alice (Moreland) H.; B.S., Ga. Sch. Tech., 1913; m. Emily Moreland Roberts, June 30, 1930. Stenographer, engring. asst. to elec. engr. No. Contracting Co., Atlanta, 1913-15; distbn. engr. Ga. Ry. & Power Co., 1915-16, asst. to chief engr., designing hydro-electric plants and high voltage transmission sub-stas. and trans lines, 1916-27; engr., gen. plant div. Southeastern Engring. Co., Birmingham, Ala., 1927-31; gen. engr. Ga. Power Co., Atlanta, 1931-44, v.p. charge maj. engring. projects from 1944, designed or supervised design of Burton, Tugalo, Yonah, Terrora and Nacoochee hydro-electric plants, and Atkinson Arkwright, Mitchell, Yates and Hammond steam-electric plants on Georgia Power Co. System, (last one named in his honor); also rebuilt Morgan Falls; designer hydro-plants for Habersham Mills, Bibb Manufacturing Company, R.C. Camp; consultant engr. several cos. constructing hydroelectric or steam generating plants S.E. Fellow Am. Inst. E.E.; mem. Ga. Engring. Soc., Ga. Soc. Profl. Engrs., Newcomen Soc., Phi Kappa Phi. Presbyn. (elder). Home: Atlanta, Ga. †

HAMPTON, HARRY HORTON, v.p. Nickel Plate R.R.; b. Columbus, O., Feb. 18, 1887; s. Howard and Helen (Kelley) H.; ed. Ohio State U., 1904-08; m. 2d, Virginia Taylor, 1947 1 dau., Floranell (Mrs. James Richard Loughry). Mining engr., 1908, then entered indsl. real estate field, and later engaged in indsl. railroad work; v.p., Nickel Plate R.R. from 1928; v.p. Buffalo Properties Co.; pres. Nickel Plate Development Co.; v.p. Cuyahoga Savings & Loan Co.; dir. Northern Ohio Food Terminal. Served as capt., Ordnance Dept. U.S. Army during World War. Mem. Ohio Development and Publicity Commn. Mem. Phi Kappa Psi. Republican. Episcopalian. Clubs: Shaker Heights Country, Union (Cleve.). Home: Shaker Heights, Ohio. †

HAMPTON, WILEY BISHOP, govt. ofcl.; b. Fordyce, Ark., Oct. 2, 1888; s. George Minor and Mary Anna (Hall) H.; B.A., Washington and Lee U., Lexington, Va., 1909; m. Baronice Chisolm, Jan. 31, 1912; children—Mary (Mrs. Pearson), Jean (Mrs. Vaughan), Wade. Lumber mfr., Ark., Miss., Ala., 1909-36; ofcl. soil conservation service U.S. Dept. of Agr., Spartanburg, S.C. since 1936. Served as pvt. U.S. Army, World War I. Mem. Soil Conservation Soc. of Am. (nat. sec. 1948). Democrat. Presbyterian. Mason. Home: Spartanburg, S.C. †

HANCOCK, HARRY D(AVID), engr., business exec.; b. Higginsville, Mo., Apr. 22, 1890; s. David Henry and Betty Shelby (Moran) H.; B.S., U. of Mo., 1912; m. Margaret Shewan Robertson, July 20, 1959. Junior engineer, Denver Gas & Electric Light Co., 1912; engr. City Light and Water Co., Amarillo, Tex., 1913, Lincoln (Neb.) Gas & Electric Light Co., 1914; gen. supt. Bristol (Tenn.-Va.) Gas & Electric Light Co. and Watauga Power Co., 1915; supt. gas and ice depts. City Light & Traction Co., Sedalia, Mo., 1916; gas efficiency engr. Henry L. Doherty & Co., N.Y. City, 1917-19; supt. gas distbn. dept. Empire Gas & Fuel Co., Bartlesville, Okla., 1920-24; chief engr. The Gas Service Co., Kansas City, Mo., 1925-26; chief engr. or asso. mgr. natural gas and natural gasolene div., Henry L. Doherty & Co., Cities Service Co., N.Y. City, 1927-37; pres. and dir. Gas Advisers, Inc., 1938-54, Cities Service Gas Company, 1956-58; president, director Cities Service Gas Producing Co., 1956-58. Recipient Distinguished Service award by American Gas Assn., 1947. Mem. Am. Gas Assn. (past chmn.).†

HAND, CLIFFORD JAY, univ. ofcl.; b. Center Point, Iowa, Apr. 9, 1922; s. Milton J. and Eva S. (Ring) H.; m. Doris Dahlin, Jan. 2, 1946. B.A., Cornell Coll., 1945; M.A., Harvard, 1949; M.A. Fulbright fellow, Sorbonne, 1949-50; Ph.D. (Univ. fellow), U. Chgo., 1957. Instr. Cornell Coll., 1947-49, Valparaiso U., 1952-53, U. Ill., 1953-54; lectr. U. Chgo., 1953-56, dir. undergrad. studies, 1956-57; asso. prof. dept. English Coll. of Pacific, 1957-64, asso. dean, 1969-72, dean, 1972-74; prof. English Raymond Coll., 1964-69; acad. v.p. U. of Pacific, Stockton, Calif., 1974-83, acting pres., 1981-83; Asso. dir. NDEA Summer English Inst., Miles Coll., 1965-67, Paine Coll., 1969; cons., mem. adv. com. Calif. Bd. Edn., 1966-67. Served with USAAF, 1943-45. Recipient Tully C. Knoles award, 1961-62; Fulbright vis. prof. U. Caen and U. Grenoble, 1962-63; Fulbright vis. prof. U. Morocco, 1967-68. Mem. Am. Assn. for Higher Edn., AAUP, Internat. Assn. U. Profs. English, Phi Beta Kappa, Phi Kappa Phi. Home: Stockton, Calif. Died Sept. 27, 1983.

HANDY, THOMAS T., army officer; b. Tenn., Mar. 11, 1892; B.S., Va. Mil. Inst., 1914; grad. battery commanders course, F.A. School, 1920, F.A. School Advance Course, 1926; hon. graduate Command and Gen. Staff Sch., 1927; grad. Army War Coll., 1935. Naval War Coll., 1936. Commd. 2d lt. F.A., Nov. 1916 and advanced through the grades to brigadier general, March 1942, major gen., July 1942; lt. gen., Sept. 1944; gen., Mar. 1945; served as 2d lieut. to major, World War I; mem. Gen. Staff, 1929-31; comdg. officer 78th F.A. Batn. (armored), Ft. Benning, 1940-42; dep. chief of operations, War Dept. Gen. Staff, Mar.-May 1942; asst. chief of staff, operations, War Dept., June 1942-October 1944; Deputy Chief of Staff, War Dept., Oct. 1944-Aug. 1947, comdg. gen. 4th Army, San Antonio, Tex., from Aug. 1947. Awarded Distinguished Service Cross, Croix de Guerre with gilt star Comdr. of Legion of Honor (Fr. govt.), Distinguished Ser. Medal with oak leaf cluster, Legion of Merit, Abdon Calderon Star. Died Apr. 14, 1982.

HANFT, FRANK W(ILLIAM), univ. prof.; b. Brainerd, Minn., Dec. 21, 1899; s. Frank William, Sr., and Jennie Maud (Fox) H.; LL.B., U. of Minn., 1924, A.B., 1929, LL.M., 1929; S.J.D., Harvard, 1931; completed course, Sch. of Mil. Govt., U. of Va., 1943; m. Jennie Ensio Wall, Aug. 26, 1924; 1 son, John Wall. Admitted to Minn. bar, 1924, and practiced in Minneapolis, 1924-29; staff atty. League of Minn. Municipalities, 1929-30; asst. in polit. sci. U. of Minn., 1928-29, part time instr. in law, 1929-30; asso. prof. law U. of N.C., 1931-37, prof. of law, 1937-65, Graham Kenan prof. law, 1965-84; vis. prof. Duke Law Sch., 1963; asso. utilities commr., N.C., part time, 1934-41, mem. gen. statutes commn., 1946-84, chmn. 1961-67. Served S.A.T.C., United States Army, 1918; served to lt. col., U.S. Army, 1943-45; with Ninth Air Force, overseas 20 mos., 1944-45. Awarded Croix de Guerre (France), Bronze Star Medal (U.S.). Fairchild research fellowship in the law of railroads and other public utilities, Harvard Law School, 1930-31. Member North Carolina Bar Association, North Carolina State Bar, Order of Coif, Delta Sigma Rho, Phi Beta Kappa, Golden Fleece. Democrat (mem. Minn. Central Com., 1928). Methodist. Author: You Can Believe: A Lawyer's Brief for Christianity, 1952. Presented series pub. lectrs. at U. N.C. on Essentials of Christianity, 1947, 48. Contributor of numerous articles to legal pubs., particularly on adminstrv. and pub. utility law and jurisprudence. Home: Chapel Hill, N.C. Died Oct. 7, 1984.

HANKS, GEORGE RAYMOND, steel exec.; b. McConnellsburg, Pa., Oct. 29, 1889; s. Albert Barton and Mary Jeannette (Hays) H.; student Pierce Sch., Phila., 1907, Mercersburg Acad., 1911; C.E., Princeton, 1915; m. Jeannette Probasco, Oct. 2, 1919. With 4th St. Nat. Bank, Phila., 1907-09; with Taylor-Wharton Steel Co., 1915-55; pres. Am. LaFrance, 1951-56; adminstrative consultant for the National-U.S. Radiator Corp., from 1957. Pres. bd. mgrs. N.J. Sanatorium, Glen Gardner, N.J.. Mem. Am. Soc. M.E., Am. Inst. Metals and Metall. Engrs. Clubs: Princeton (N.Y.C.); Cap and Gown (Princeton); Northampton Country. Address: Clinton, N.J. †

HANKS, NANCY, arts organization administrator; b. Miami Beach, Fla., Dec. 31, 1927; d. Bryan Cayce and Virginia (Wooding) H. Student, U. Colo., 1946, Oxford (Eng.) U., 1948; A.B. magna cum laude, Duke U., 1949; D.H.L., Princeton U., 1971; D.F.A., U. Mich., 1971, U. Pa., 1972; D.L., U. So. Calif., 1973; D.H.L., Yale U., 1978; numerous others., Yale U. Mem. staff ODM, Washington, 1951-52; mem. staff Pres.'s Adv. Com., Govt. Orgn., 1953; asst. to undersec. HEW, 1953-54; spl. asst. Spl. Projects Office, White House, 1955; asst. to Nelson A. Rockefeller, N.Y.C., 1956-59; assoc. Laurance S. Rockefeller, 1959-69; also exec. sec. Spl. Studies Project, Rockefeller Bros. Fund, project coordinator The Performing Arts: Problems and Prospects, staff coordinator Prospect for America, 1956-69; chmn. Nat. Endowment for Arts, Washington, 1969-77; also chmn. Nat. Council on the Arts; dir. Equitable Life Assurance Soc. U.S., Conoco, Scholastic. Bd. dirs. Salzburg Seminar in Am. Studies; mem. Nat. Com. for Urban Recreation, Indo-U.S. Subcommn. on Edn. and Culture, White House Conf. on Aging; trustee Duke U., Jackson Hole Preserve, Inc., Conservation Found.; vice chmn. Rockefeller Bros. Fund. Recipient 3d Ann. Cultural award Rec. Industry Assn. Am., 1971; Nat. citation Arts and Bus. Coop. Council N.Y. Bd. Trade, 1971; Golden Baton award Am. Symphony Orch. League, 1974; Distinguished Achievement award The Links, 1974; Nat. Humanitarian award Nat. Recreation and Park Assn., 1975; Woman of Conscience award Nat. Council of Women of U.S., 1977; Catalyst award, 1979. Mem. Am. Council for the Arts (pres. 1968-69), Am. Assn. Museums, mem. council (1969), A.I.A. (hon.), Am. Soc. Landscape Architects (hon.), Phi Beta Kappa, Phi Kappa Delta, Kappa Alpha Theta, Sigma Alpha Iota. Clubs: Cosmopolitan (N.Y.C.); Capitol Hill (Washington), City Tavern (Washington). Home: Washington, DC.

HANLEY, EDWARD JAMES, steel co. exec.; b. Whitman, Mass. Feb. 27, 1903; s. Francis J. and Mary Ellen (McGovern) H.; grad. Mass. Inst. Tech., 1924, Harvard Sch. Bus., 1927; D.Sc., Duquesne U. 1951; LL.D., St. Vincent Coll., 1956; m. Dorothy Ward Hanley, 1930 With Gen. Electric Co., 1927-36; sec. Allegheny Ludlum Steel Corp. 1936, treas., 1941, v.p., 1946, dir., 1947-82, pres., 1951-67, chief exec. officer, 1951-68, chmn., 1962-72, chmn. finance com., 1972-82; dir. Duquesne Light Co., Mine Safety Appliances Co. (emeritus). Bd. dirs. Duquesne U., Pitts. Symphony Soc.; mem. corp. Mass. Inst. Tech. Mem. Am. Iron and Steel Inst., Nat. Assn. Accountants. Clubs: Duquesne, Rolling Rock, Fox Chapel Golf (Pitts.). Home: Allison Park, Pa. Died Mar. 13, 1982.

HANNA, CHARLES GEORGE, ex-mayor; b. Syracuse, N.Y., Apr. 27, 1889; s. Charles Fred and A. Maude (Hungerford) H.; grad. high sch., Syracuse; student Mass. Inst. Tech., 1917-18; m. Florence Brezee, of Syracuse, Apr. 10, 1912; 1 dau., Florence Virginia. Began as automobile dealer, Syracuse; pres. Charles G. Hanna, Inc.; pres. Fireproof Bldgs., Inc. Served as pvt., later lt. Aviation Corps, U.S.A., 1917-19; major Air Corps, Pres. Common Council, Syracuse, 1924-25; mayor of Syracuse, 1926-29; chmn. advisory council N.Y. State Bur. Municipal Information, 1926-27; pres. N.Y. State Aviation Conf., 1928-29. Mem. Quiet Birdmen. Trustee Syracuse U. Republican. Baptist. Clubs: Commodore, Syracuse Yacht and Country. Inventor of a selfstarter, automatic gear shift and vacuum horn. Home: Syracuse, N.Y. †

HANNA, FOREST W., lawyer; b. Burlington Junction, Mo., Jan. 29, 1887; s. Orr C. and Lettie (Walker) H.; A.B., Northwestern, 1909; LL.B., 1913; m. Mary E. Robinson, Sept. 30, 1930; children—Forest W., Robert Orr, John R. Admitted to Mo. bar, 1913, practiced in Kansas City; mem. firm Hanna, Hurwitz & Goodman; 1st asst. pros. atty., Jackson County, Mo., 1921-22, pros. atty., 1925-26; asst. city counselor, Kansas City, from 1946. Served as capt. Co. C 47th Heavy Arty., U.S. Army, World War I. Mem. Am., Mo. and Kansas City bar assns. Candidate for Congress, 5th Dist. Mo., 1940. Home: Kansas City, Mo. Deceased.

HANNAFORD, MARK WARREN, business executive; b. Woodrow, Colo., Feb. 7, 1925; s. William Townsend and Ina (Owen) H.; m. Sara Jane Lemaster, Apr. 20, 1948; children: Mark William, Kim Karl, Robert Owen. B.A., Ball State U., 1950, M.A., 1955; postgrad. (John Hay fellow), Yale, 1961-62. Tchr. Lakewood (Calif.) High Sch., 1956-67; tchr. polit. sci. Long Beach (Calif.) City Coll., 1967-77; mem. 94th and 95th Congress from 34th Calif. Dist.; White House coordinator internat. trade policy U.S. Dept. Commerce, 1978; sr. assoc. Martin Haleey Co., Washington, 1980; pres. Bankcard Holders of Am., 1980, Window on Washington, Inc., 1983-85. Mem. planning commn., Lakewood, 1960-61, councilman, 1966-68, mayor, 1968-70, 72, 74; mem. Los Angeles County Dem. Central Com., 1962-67, Calif. State Dem. Central Com. Served with USAAF, 1943-46. Address: Lakewood, Calif. Died June 2, 1985.

HANNAH, JOHN DONALD, accountant; b. Spokane, Oct. 18, 1920; s. Dan and Margaret (Hindley) H.; B.A., U. Wash., 1942; m. Mary King, Dec. 8, 1945; children—Dan, Richard. With Price Waterhouse & Co., C.P.A.s, 1946-81, ptnr., from 1962. Commr., Hennepin County Park Dist., 1979-81. Served with AUS, 1942-45. Mem. Mpls. C. of C., Minn. Soc. C.P.A.'s, Am. Inst. C.P.A.'s, Am. Accounting Assn. Club: Kiwanis. Home: Excelsior, Minn. Dec. July 5, 1981.

HANNAY, ALLEN BURROUGHS, judge; b. Hempstead, Tex., Feb. 14, 1892; s. Robert Edwards and Katherine Donaldson (Allen) H.; m. Frances Edna Johnson, July 16, 1918; children—Helen Johnson, Allen Burroughs. Student, Agrl. and Mech. Coll. Tex., 1907-09; LL.B., U. Tex., 1913. Bar: Tex. bar 1913. Practiced law, Hempstead and Houston, Tex., 1913-30, Waller County judge, 1915-17; dist. judge 113th Dist. of Tex., 1930; U.S. dist. judge, Houston, from 1942, now sr. U.S. dist. judge. Served with U.S. Army, 1917-19. Mem. Am., Houston bar assns., Tex. State Bar, Phi Delta Phi, Delta Sigma Phi. Clubs: Mason (Houston) (32, Shriner), Elk (Houston) (past pres. Tex. chpt), River Oaks Country (Houston). Died Oct. 22, 1983

HANNOCH, HERBERT J., lawyer; b. Newark, 1890; LL.B., N.Y. U., 1911. Admitted to N.J. bar, 1911; mem. firm Hannoch, Weisman, Stern and Besser, Newark. Chmn. Legislative Commn. for Revision of Eminent Domain Law, from 1962. Mem. Am. (mem. coms. municipal law and eminent domain from 1959), N.J. State, Essex County (pres. 1934) bar assns.†

HANNUM, JOSHUA EYRE, engring. educator; b. Concord Township, Delaware County, Pa., May 5, 1890; s. Howard and Margaretta (Bishop) H.; B.S. in Industrial Engring., Pennsylvania State Coll., 1915, M.E., 1920; m. Amy Marie Welch, Dec. 26, 1916; children—Wallace Howard, Mary Eleanor. Machine shop foreman, Skinner Engine Co., Erie, Pa., 1915-16; various postitions 1918-26; editor, Engineering Index, N.Y.C., 1927-36, office mgr., Am. Soc. Mech. Engrs., 1931-36; research engr., div. of engring. research, Assn. of Am. Railroads, Chicago, Ill., 1936-37; research engr., Crane Co., Chicago, Ill., 1938; asst. dean of engring. and prof. engring., Ala. Poly. Inst., 1938-43, dean Sch. of Engring., and prof. engineering from 1943. Member American Society M.E., Am. Society for Engring. Edn., Alabama Edn. Assn., Tau Beta Pi, Omicron Delta Kappa, Phi Kappa Phi, Pi Tau Sigma. Contbr. professional papers, reports and articles to tech. periodicals. Home: Auburn, Ala. †

HANSEN, ELWOOD LESLIE, savs. and loan exec.; b. San Francisco, Apr. 23, 1917; s. Leslie Walter and Alma Caroline (Bansemer) H.; m. Lynnea Jo Stankevich, Nov. 1, 1975; children by previous marriage—Joyce T. Hansen Scott, Robert N. Ed., MacMaster-Paine Bus. Coll., Am. Savs. and Loan Inst. With Bay View Fed. Savs. & Loan Assn., San Francisco, 1936-84, pres., 1954-67, chmn. bd., chief exec. officer, 1967-84; vice chmn. bd. Fed. Home Loan Bank of San Francisco, 1961. Chmn. bd. trustees Cogswell Coll., San Francisco; mem. San Francisco Sheriffs Air Squadron; legal custodian Western States Assn. Sheriffs Air Squadrons; v.p. San Mateo County Devel. Assn., 1977-84; bd. dirs. Govtl. Research Council San Mateo, San Francisco Opera Assn.; pres. Better Bus. Bur., 1965. Recipient pub. service awards Better Bus. Bur., pub. service awards Am. Bus. Women's Assn., pub. service awards YMCA, pub. service awards Nat. Aid to Visually Handicapped, pub. service awards Fed. Home Loan Bank. Mem. Calif. Savs. and Loan League (pres. 1965-66, pub. service award), Bay Cities Savs. and Loan League (past pres.), Am. Savs. and Loan Inst. (past pres.), U.S. League Savs. Assns., San Francisco C. of C. (dir.). Clubs: Peninsula Golf and Country, Masons. Home: Hillsborough, Calif. Died July 13, 1985.

HANSEN, ERLING W., ophthalmologist; b. Minneapolis, Minn., May 22, 1890; s. Martin and Maren O. (Field) H.; B.S., U. of Minn., 1913, M.D., 1915; graduate work at New York City, Paris and Vienna; m. Anna Ruth Eddy, June 4, 1924; children—Gordon Eddy, Mary Elizabeth. Intern, University Hosp., Minneapolis, 1914-15, grad. work and asst., 1916-17; asso. with Dr. Horace Newhart in pvt. practice diseases of eye, ear, nose and throat, 1919-44, also part time teacher, med. sch., U. of Minn.; work confined to ophthalmology from 1930; clin. prof. opthalmology, head dept. ophthalmology, med. sch. U. Minn., 1944-58, emeritus. Served 1st lt. capt., Med. Corps, U.S. Army, 1917-19; with 1st Div., France, and with Army of Occupation, Germany. Decorated Croix de Guerre (France), Silver Star. Recipient honor society key Am. Acad. Ophthalmology and Otolaryngology. Fellow Am. Coll. Surgeons (mem. board of governors); mem. A.M.A. (chmn. sect. on ophthalmology 1955), Minn. Soc. for Prevention of Blindness, Am. (pres. 1956-57), Minn. acads. of ophthalmology and otolaryngology, Hennepin County and Minn. State med. assns., Minn. and Minneapolis acads. of medicine, Am. Opthmol. Soc., A.A.A.S., Alpha Kappa Kappa, Am. Legion. Clubs: Kiwanis, Athletic, Campus (Minneapolis). Contbr. articles to med. jours. Home: Minneapolis. †

HANSEN, HARRY JAMES, naval officer; b. Freesoil, Mich., Mar. 24, 1888; s. Harry and Myrtina (Hanson) H.; student Naval War Coll., 1924-25; m. Mary Jane Hunt, Apr. 28, 1909 (div. 1934); 1 dau., Madeleine Dorothy; m. 2d, Edna Bartzen, Mar. 23, 1935 (dec. Oct. 1951); 1 son, Harry James (USN); m. 3d, Nona Ann Bartzen, Dec. 28, 1952. Enlisted in U.S. Navy, 1905, commd. ensign, 1917, promoted through grades to rear adm.; served with Amphibious Forces, Western Pacific to end of War with Japan. Decorated Bailey medal, 1905, Mexican Service medal, World War I medal and campaign medals Cuba, Hayti and Santo Domingo, Am. Def., Am. sector, Asiatic sector, Philippine Liberation, World War II Occupation, Bronze Medal. Mem. Naval Inst. Elk, Moose. Club: Commonwealth of Cal. Contbr. verse and articles on govt., economy, social welfare and profl. mil. subjects to mags. Home: Glendale, CA. †

HANSEN, JAMES ROGER, musician; b. Joliet, Ill., Sept. 22, 1908; s. James and Minnie (Petersen) H.; m. Rita Ellen Williams, Aug. 30, 1947; children—Jane, Susan, Mary Joan. Mus.B., Cosmopolitan Sch. Music, Chgo., 1952; Mus.M., Chgo. Conservatory Music, 1955; student, Loyola U. at Chgo. chmn. Chgo. Symphony Orch. mems'. com., 1970-71, 71-72; faculty Chgo. Conservatory Music. Violinist, Kansas City Philharmonic Orch., 1935-42, Pitts. Symphony Orch., 1945-46, Chgo. Symphony Orch., 1946-83. Served with USAAF, 1942-45. Mem. Chgo. Fedn. Musicians (shopsteward 1970-71, 71-72). Club: Cliff Dwellers (Chicago). Home: Evanston, Ill. Died Feb. 10, 1985.

HANSEN, RASMUS, business exec.; b. Odense, Denmark, Jan. 30, 1888; s. Hans and Bertha Marie (Nielsen) H.; grad. (highest honors) U. of Copenhagen, 1905, Commercial Coll., Copenhagen, 1907; LL.B., La Salle U., 1936; m. Evangeline Shearer Cooper, Aug. 25, 1920. Came to U.S., 1916, naturalized citizen, 1925. Asso. with East Asiatic Co., Ltd., of Copenhagen and affiliated cos., Copenhagen, Bangkok, Singapore, Libau, Leningrad, Archangel and New York until 1925; with Am. Export Lines, Genoa, Alexandria and New York, and on comml. and shipping missions in Europe, 1926-36; dir. in charge operations Gdynia America Line, New York, 1936-40; pres. and dir. the East Asiatic Co., Inc., and chmn. bd. dirs. West Indian Co., Ltd., St. Thomas, V.I., from 1940; mem. board of dirs. Re-insurance Co., —Constituion,—N.Y. City from 1943, Johnson Walton Steamships, Ltd., Vancouver, B.C., from 1946; chmn. Eighth St. Pier Co., Hoboken, from 1948. Awarded Knight of Dannebrog by King of Denmark, 1948. Mem. Riverside Church, New York (non-sectarian). Club: Whitehall. Home: New York, N.Y. †

HANSEN, VICTOR RUSSELL, lawyer; b. Mpls., Mar. 12, 1904; s. Hans A. and Gina (Ericksen) H.; student U. Calif. at Los Angeles, 1923-25; J.D., U. So. Calif., 1928; grad. U.S.A. Command and Gen. Staff Sch., 1943; m. Lillian Clausen, May 7, 1932; children—Marlene Adrianne (Mrs. Peterson), Victor Russell, Robert Arthur. Admitted to Calif. bar, 1928, since practiced in Los Angeles; partner Hansen & Sweeney, 1931-51; judge Superior Ct., 1951-56; asst. atty. gen. U.S. charge antitrust div. Dept. Justice, 1956-59; partner firm Hansen & Dolle, Los Angeles until 1970; now in pvt. practice. Adj. gen. of Calif., 1944-46; brig. gen. Calif. N.G., from 1944. Regent U. Calif., 1946-62; v.p., dir. Braille Inst. Am. Adv. bd. Am. Inst. Fine Arts. Mem. Recipient Dickson Alumnus of Yr. award U. Calif. at Los Angeles, 1950, Medal of Merit State Cal., 1952, award of merit Luth. Hosp. Soc. So. Calif. Mem. Res. Officers Assn. (past pres. Los Angeles), Am., Los Angeles, Calif. bar assns., Mil. Order World Wars (past comdr.), Am. Legion (past comdr. allied post), Phi Delta Theta, Phi Delta Phi. Mason (32 deg., Shriner). Club: Sertoma. Author: History of State Guard of California, 1946; Tortuous Path of a Fiduciary; Preparation of Condemnation Cases for Trial; The Antitrust Laws in a Changing Economy. Home: Flintridge, Calif. Dec. July 31, 1980.

HANSLOWE, KURT LOEWUS, educator; b. Vienna, Austria, Oct. 15, 1926; came to U.S., 1940, naturalized, 1948; s. Ernst and Leopoldine (Olbrich) Loewus; m. Nannette Reese, Dec. 20, 1948; children—David, Nicholas, Theodora. B.A., Yale U., 1947; J.D., Harvard U., 1951. Bar: Mich. bar 1952. Asst. gen. counsel UAW, Detroit, 1951-58; prof. law, indsl. and labor relations Cornell U., Ithaca, N.Y., from 1958; labor arbitrator; cons., mediator N.Y. Public Employment Relations Bd., from 1968. Author: (with Oberer) Labor Law: Collective Bargaining in a Free Society, 1972; editor: (with Oberer) Indsl. and Labor Relations Rev, 1962-65. Pres. Am. Unitarian Youth, 1948-49; mem. Unitarian-Universalist Council of Liberal Chs., Boston, 1954-56. Sr. Fulbright-Hays scholar Vienna, 1977-78. Home: Ithaca, N.Y. Deceased. *

HANSON, ADOLPH MELANCHTON, surgeon; b. St. Paul, Minn., Sept. 11, 1888; s. Martin Gustav and Caroline (Runice) H.; student Red Wing (Minn.) Sem., 1903-07, Hamline U., 1907-08, U. of Minn., 1908-09; M.D., Northwestern U., 1911; grad. study, School of Neurosurgery, University of Pennsylvania, 1917; A.B., St. Olaf College, Northfield, Minn., 1922, M.A., 1923, honorary D.Sc., 1943; married Marie Lucile Boxrud, Nov. 26, 1914; children—Jane Lucile, Anne Marie, Adolph Martin, Patricia. Began practice at Red Wing, 1911; 1st house surgeon City Hosp., Seattle, Wash., 1912; in practice at Faribault, Minn., since Aug. 1912; formerly condr. Hanson Research Laboratory; research in glands of internal secretion since 1922; neurosurgeon. Served as neurosurgeon, Evacuation Hosp. S. A.E.F., World War I; in active service as colonel, Medical Corps, United States Army, Aug. 1942-Aug. 1943; retired for disability in line of duty, as colonel Medical Reserve Corps; formerly commanding officer, 76th Station Hospital. Member A.M.A., American Chemical Society, Assn. Mil. Surgeons U.S., Assn. for Study Internal Secretions, Am. Med. Editors and Authors Assn. Awarded 1st prize for work on parathyroid gland, Minn. Soc. Internal Medicine, 1927. Author: Practical Helps in the Study and Treatment of Head Injuries, 1925; also chapter, Management of Gunshot Wounds of the Head and Spine, in Vol. XI, The Med. Dept. of The U.S. Army in the World War. Contbr. numerous articles on parathyroid and thymus glands, head, spine and superficial nerve surgery, etc. Discoverer of the parathyroid thymus and pineal active extracts; inventor of dural separator and bone elevator used in brain surgery. Donated scientific equipment of Hanson Research Lab. to chemistry dept., St. Olaf Coll., Northfield, Minn., July 1942, to be perpetuated as special lab. for advanced students.†

HANSON, CLARENCE BLOODWORTH, JR., publisher; b. Augusta, Ga., Nov. 7, 1908; s. Clarence Bloodworth and Harriet (Pinkham) H.; m. Elizabeth Fontaine Fletcher, Sept. 9, 1929; 1 child, Victor Henry II. B.S., U. Va., 1930; D.Litt. (hon.), U. Ala. Advt. dept. Indpls. Star, 1929- 30; advt. dept. Birmingham News, Ala., 1930-34, nat. advt. mgr., 1934-37, asst. advt. dir., 1937-42, pub., 1945-83; chmn., dir., mem. exec. com. The Birmingham News Co. (pubs. Birmingham News, Huntsville Times Huntsville News, Agent, Birmingham Post-Herald); v.p., dir. Mercury Express, Inc.; dir., mem. exec. com. First Nat. Bank of Birmingham, Amsouth Bancorp.; dir. chmn. exec. com. Royal Crown Cola Co. Bd. dirs. Birmingham Mus. of Art; trustee Eye Found. Hosp. Served to maj. USAAF, 1942-45. Mem. Asso. Press (v.p. 1952-56), Am. Newspaper Publishers Assn., So. Newspaper Publishers Assn. (pres. 1950), Ala. Press Assn. (pres. 1951), Newcomen Soc. N. Am., Phi Gamma Delta. Episcopalian. Clubs: Mountain Brook Country (Birmingham), Birmingham Country (Birmingham), Shoal Creek (Birmingham), Relay House (Birmingham); Honorable Company Edinburgh Golfers (Muirfield). Home: Mountain Brook, Ala. Died May 14, 1983.

HANSON, HOWARD, composer, condr., educator; b. Wahoo, Nebr., Oct. 28, 1896; s. Hans and Hilma (Eckstrom) H.; student Luther Coll., Wahoo, U. Nebr. Sch. of Music, Inst. Musical Art, N.Y. City; Mus. B., Northwestern U., 1916; Mus.D. honoris causa, Northwestern U., Syracuse U., Horner Inst., Augustana Coll. and Theol. Sem., U. Nebr., Am. Conservatory Mus., Columbia, Capital U., Shurtleff Coll., Hartt Coll., of Music, New Eng. Conservatory, Temple U., Newcomb Coll. of Tulane U., U. Mich., Mus. Fund Soc. Phila., N.Y. State Bd. Regents, U. Ariz., Gustavus Adolphus Coll., Boston U.; LL.D., U. Ky., Ill. Wesleyan U., Coll. of the Pacific, Ball State Tchrs. Coll., St. John Fisher Coll.; Litt.D., Keuka Coll., Wooster Coll.; L.H.D., Drury Coll., Valparaiso U., Ohio State U., Midland Luth. Coll., Denison U., D.F.A., Drake U., 1966, U. Portland, 1968; D.Sacred Music, Kenyon Coll., Youngstown U.; m. Margaret Elizabeth Nelson, July 24, 1946. Mem. staff theory dept. Coll. of the Pacific, San Jose, Calif., 1916, dean Conservatory Fine Arts, 1919-21, dir. Eastman Sch. Mus., U., Rochester, 1924-64, dir. Inst. of Am. Music, 1964-81; Phi Beta Kappa visiting scholar, 1964-65. Cons. U.S. Dept. of State; adv. com. arts Nat. Cultural Center, Washington; mem. exec. com. of UN-ESCO. Served as guest condr. major cities both U.S. and fgn.; works have been performed by major fgn. and U.S. orchs. and bands. Winner several awards 1921-81, including Pulitzer Prize, 1944, George Foster Peabody Award, 1946, Huntington Hartford Found. award, 1959, and several others. Fellow Am. Acad. Rome, 1921-24, Royal Acad. Music in Sweden, 1938; mem. N.Y. State Council Arts (concert adv. panel), Am. Acad. Arts and Scis., Am. Acad. and Inst. Arts and Letters, Am. Philos. Soc., Newcomen Soc., Phi Beta Kappa. Lutheran. Composer wide variety musical compositions, including 7 symphonies, symphonic poems, symphonie operas, mixed choruses, male choruses, instrumental selections for particular instruments, including among many others: Dies Natalis, Laude, Two Yule-tide Pieces, Opus 19; Concerto in G Major, Opus 36 for piano and orchestra; "Vermeland" from Scandinavia Suite, Opus 13, for organ; Chorale and Alleluia for symphonic band; oratorio New Land, New Convenant; Concerto for organ, strings and harp, Opus 22; Sea Symphony for chorus and orch.; opera Merry Mount; also Harmonic Materials of Modern Music. Clubs: Country of

Rochester; Century Assn., Bohemians (N.Y.C.); Cosmos (Washington). Home: Rochester, N.Y. Died Feb. 26, 1981; buried Bold Island, Maine.

HANSON, JOSEPH OSGOOD, meat packing; b. Chicago, Ill., Dec. 23, 1888; s. Albert Hoit and Josephine (Osgood) H.; B.A., Williams Coll., 1909; m. Sally McMullin, Sept. 30, 1915; children—Joseph Osgood, Carol. Credit dept. Swift & Co., Chicago, 1909-10, foreign plant dept., 1910-18; when Compania Swift Internacional was segregated from Swift & Co., 1918, went with new Co.; v.p., dir., 1930, pres. from Mar. 1942. Mem. bd. trustees, Sunday Evening Club. Mem. Delta Kappa Epsilon. Clubs: The Chicago, University, Commercial, Executives Quadrangle (Chicago); Chikaming Country (Lakeside, Mich.). Home: Hinsdale, Ill. †

HANWAY, EARL EDWIN, publisher; b. Topeka, Kan., Dec. 7, 1890; s. J. Edwin and Effie Emma (Grace) H.; student pub. schs., Topeka and Denver; m. Sunshine Perry, June 20, 1915; children—Charlene, Earl Perry, Lois Marie. News editor Casper Tribune-Herald, 1915-18, bus. mgr., 1918-30, co-pub., 1930-46, pub., 1946-53, chmn. bd.; pres. Sunshine Realty Co., 1944-48, Wyo. Weekly Review Corp., Casper, from 1946; pub. Star, Casper, v.p., dir. Casper Nat. Bank, 1st Nat. Bank of Riverton (Wis.). Mem. Wyo. State Bd. Edn., 1922-24; chmn. Wyo. Commerce and Industry Com., from 1950. Mem. Wyo. Press Assn. (past pres.), Greater Wyo. Assn. (pres. 1935), C. of C. (pres. 1940), Better Casper Assn. (pres. 1939). Mason (32 deg.), Elk. Clubs: Rotary, Nat. Press (Washington). Home: Casper, Wyo. †

HARDAWAY, FRANCIS PAGE, army officer; b. St. Louis, Mo., Apr. 26, 1888; s. William Augustus (M.D.) and Lucy Nelson (Page) H.; A.B., Washington U., 1909; grad. Coast Guard Arty. Sch., 1914, advanced course, same, 1924, Command and Gen. Staff Sch., 1925; Army War Coll., 1936; m. Lucille Mullanphy Cates, Nov. 25, 1911; children—Francis Page (dec.), John Mullanphy; m. 2d, Harriet Lane Cates, Apr. 8, 1932. Commd. 2d lt., Coast Arty. Corps, 1909; comd. 3d Batt., 42d Coast Arty., A.E.F., World War I; prof. mil. sci. and tactics, Washington U., 1919-23; instr. dept. of tactics, Coast Arty. Sch., Ft. Monroe, Va., 1925-29; served in office of chief of Coast Arty., 1933-35; comdg. officer Harbor Defenses of Chesapeake Bay, Ft. Monroe, Va., 1939-40; promoted to brig. gen., Apr. 6, 1941; organized and commanded Anti-Aircraft Arty. Replacement Training Center, Camp Callan, Calif., 1940-43; commanded 37th A.A.A. Brigade, 1943-44, Panama Coast Artillery Command, 1945-46; comd. Pacific Sector, Panama Canal Dept., 1946-47. Retired as brig. general, U.S. Army, Apr. 1948. Home: Ferguson, Mo. †

HARDEEN, THEODORE, JR., lawyer; b. London, Eng., Dec. 20, 1905; s. Theodore and Elsie (Parsons) H.; m. Elizabeth Brett, Nov. 1, 1952; 1 son, Theodore Brett. LL.B., U. Va., 1930. Bar: Ill. bar 1930, Va. Bar 1964. Practiced in, Chgo., 1930-53; adminstr. Def. Air Transp., Dept. Commerce, Washington, 1953-64; gen. counsel Va. Trailways, 1964-67; v.p. Western Sales, Ltd., Geneva, 1967-70; counsel Export-Import Bank U.S., Washington, 1970—; Chmn., U.S. rep. NATO Civil Aviation delegation, 1958, 59, 60, 61, 62; Dir. Universal Motor Co., Universal Foundry Co., Lantana Aero Corp., Dr. Peter Fahrney & Sons Co., Palm Beach Aero Corp.; Bd. dirs., v.p. Chgo. Blackhawk Hockey Team. Served as maj. Air Transport Command USAAF, 1942-46. Decorated Air medal, Commendation medal. Mem. Chgo. Bar Assn., Phi Sigma Kappa. Clubs: Everglades (Palm Beach, Fla.); Tavern (Chgo.); Farmington Country (Charlottesville, Va.), Farmington Hunt (Charlottesville, Va.), Boar's Head (Charlottesville, Va.); University (Washington). Home: Charlottesville, Va. Died June 18, 1984.

HARDEN, CECIL MURRAY (MRS. FROST R. HARDEN), mem. Republican Nat. Com.; b. Covington, Ind.; d. Timothy and Jennie (Clotfelter) Murray; ed. Ind. U.; m. Frost R. Harden, Dec. 22, 1914; 1 son, Murray Harden. Mem. Republican Nat. Com. for Ind., from 1964; mem. 81st-86th congresses. Mem. D.A.R.; charter mem. Bus. and Profl. Women's Club. Home: Covington, Ind. Died Dec. 7, 1984.

HARDIE, THORNTON, lawyer; b. Montgomery, Ala., Sept. 15, 1890; s. Bradford and Mary B. (Thornton) H.; student Starke's U. Sch., 1902-06; LL.B., U. Tex., 1913; m. Mabelle Bryan, Aug. 25, 1915. Admitted to Tex. bar, 1913, practiced in El Paso, Tex.; v.p. El Paso Nat. Bank; v.p., dir. Rio Grande, El Paso & Santa Fe R.R.; dir. So. Union Gas Co. Mem. bd. regents U. Tex., 1957-63, chmn., 1961-62. Mem. Am., El Paso (pres. 1932) bar assns., State Bar Tex., Chancellors, Philos. Soc. Tex., Tex. Hist. Assn., Sigma Alpha Epsilon, Phi Delta Phi. Clubs: Headliners (Austin, Tex.); El Paso, Internat. Home: El Paso, Tex. †

HARDIGG, CARL A., army officer; b. Uniontown, Ky., June 28, 1890; s. William Leopold and Annie Bracey (Johnson) H.; student Evansville (Ind.) High Sch., 1903-07; grad. Q.M.C. Subsistence Sch., 1921, Command and Gen. Staff Sch., 1925, Army War Coll., 1929; m. Mary O'Brien, June 30, 1915; 1 son, James Sutton. Commd. 2d lt., Inf., Mar. 3, 1913, 1st lt., Inf., July 1, 1916, capt. Q.M. Corps, Nov. 5, 1917, and advanced through grades to Major General, November 8, 1944; served on War Dept. Gen. Staff, 1929-33; Office of Q.M. since Aug. 1936; now Director, Subsistence Division. Home: Washington, D.C. †

HARDIN, RICHARD LYNN, educator; b. Oskaloosa, Ia., June 19, 1923; s. James O. and Marie (Ensor) H.; B.A., Washington U., St. Louis, 1948; Ph.D., Ind. U., 1952; m. Mildred Musick, Sept. 14, 1944; children—Judith, Richard, Jill, Randolph. Instr. biochemistry, U. Louisville, 1952-54; asst. prof., Med. Coll. Va., 1954-56; prof. chemistry, Lomar State Coll. Tech., Beaumont, Tex., 1956-60; prof., head dept. chemistry, Western Ill. U., Macomb, 1960-83. Served with USMCR, 1941-45. Mem. Am. Chem. Soc. Home: Macomb, Ill. Died May 15, 1983.

HARDY, ALLSTER CLAVERING, zoologist, educator; b. Nottingham, Eng., Feb. 10, 1896; s. Richard Hardy; ed. Oundle Sch., Exeter Coll., Oxford; M.A., D.Sc., Oxford U.; LL.D., U. Aberdeen; D.Sc., Southampton, Hull; m. Sylvia Lucy Garstang, 1927; 1 son, 1 dau. Christopher Welch biol. research scholar, 1920; Oxford biol. scholar Stazione Zoologica, Naples, Italy, 1920; asst. naturalist fisheries dept. Ministry Agr. and Fisheries, 1921-24; chief zoologist Discovery Expdn., 1924-28; prof. zoology and oceanography Univ. Coll., Hull, Eng., 1928-42; Regius prof. natural history U. Aberdeen, 1942-45 Gifford lectr., 1963-65; Linacre prof. zoology Oxford U., 1946-61, prof. emeritus, hon. fellow Merton Coll., 1961-85. Created knight, 1957. Recipient Sci. medal Zool. soc., 1939, Templeton prize, 1985. Fellow Royal Soc. Author: The Open Sea, Part I, The World of Plankton, 1956, Part II, Fish and Fisheries, 1958; Memoirs on Biological Oceanography; The Living Stream, 1965; The Divine Flame, 1966; Great Waters, 1967; (with others The Challenge of Chance, 1973. Joint editor Bulls. Marine Ecology. Club: Athenaeum. Died May 23, 1985.

HARDY, OSGOOD, univ. prof.; b. San Bernardino, Calif., June 9, 1889; s. William Prescott and Lill Jane (Adams) H.; A.B., Pomona Coll., 1910; A.B., Yale, 1911, A.M., 1913; Ph.D., U. of Calif., 1925; m. Amy Berlin Mead, Nov. 25, 1918. Interpreter, quartermaster, Yale Peruvian Expeditions, 1912, 1914-15; publicity work, Mercantile Bank of Am., New York City and Lima, Peru, 1919-20; office mgr., Am. Finance and Commerce Co., Lima, Peru, 1921; prof. Am. history, Occidental College, Los Angeles, since 1923; on leave, 1942-45; Norman Bridge professor Latin American Hist., 1946; sr. econ. analyst, Bur. of Fgn. and Domestic Commerce and principal economic analyst, Bd. Econ. Warfare, 1942; senior econ. analyst and cultural relations attaché, U.S. Embassy, Panama, 1943-44; attaché, U.S. Embassy, Ciudad Trujillo Dominican Republic, 1944-45. Regt. supply sergt., 10th Conn. F.A., U.S.A., 1916; pvt. U.S. Army, assigned to Col. House Inquiry, Latin-Am. Research Section, 1918. Mem. Am. Hist. Assn., Pacific Coast Branch of Am. Hist. Assn., Phi Beta Kappa, Alpha Tau Omega. Club: Kiwanis (Eagle Rock, Calif.). Co-author: March of Industry, 1929; East and West; a History of the Pacific Area, 1949. Home: Los Angeles, Calif. †

HARGER, ROLLA NEIL, chemist, toxicologist; b. Decatur Co., Kan., Jan. 14, 1890; s. William Delashmutt and Margaret Elizabeth (Neil) H.; A.B., Washburn College, 1915, Doctor of Science (hon.), 1960; A.M., Kansas University, 1917; Ph.D., Yale, 1922; m. Helen Harriet Dick, June 6, 1917; children—Elizabeth Ann (Mrs. John W. Stalcup), Robert William, Susan Margaret (Mrs. C. R. Stanley). Began as laboratory instructor in chemistry Washburn Coll., 1913-15; instr. Kan. U., 1915-17; asst. biochemist U.S. Dept. of Agr., Washington, D.C., 1917-20; Nat. Research Council fellow, Yale, 1920-22; asst. prof. biochemisry and toxicology sch. medicine Ind. U., 1922-29, asso. prof., 1929-33, prof. 1933-60, prof. emeritus biochemistry and toxicology, from 1960, chmn. dept., 1933-56; guest lectr. poisons and alcohol before various tech. groups. Prof. biochemistry, U.S. ICA, Indiana U. Sch. Medicine, Basic Med. Sci. Inst., Karachi, 1958-59. Research, cons. on poisons, alcohol, ether, vitamins; inventor —drunkometer— for testing intoxication, 1931; served as expert witness and consultant in many notable cases. Member committee on driver intoxication National Safety Council from 1938, chairman traffic com. Indianapolis Safety Council, 1941-58, consultant traffic division, from 1960. Member American Chem. Soc., Am. Society Biological Chemists, Ind. Chem. Soc., A.A.A.S., Am. Soc. Pharmacol. and Exptl. Medicine, Am. Soc. Forensic Scis. (pres. 1953), Sigma Xi. Presbyn. Contbr. sci. publs. Home: Indianapolis. †

HARGIS, ANDREW BROADUS, engr.; b. Oxford, Miss., Aug. 1, 1889; s. Rev. William Iverson and Laura Adeline (Adair) H.; B.E., U. of Miss., 1910; C.E., 1919; m. Alma Mae Newman, Dec. 14, 1913; children—Annie Laurie (Mrs. Thos. Lang Harvey), James Cawood. Civil engring. student, U. of Miss., 1910; resident constrn. engr. on municipal works, Tex. and Tenn., 1910-12; asst. engr. City of Birmingham, Ala., 1912-15, spl. engr., 1915-17; office div. engr., dep. chief engr. and chief engr., constrn. of Camp McClellan, Ala., 1917-19; sr. asst. and project engr. Morris Knowles, Inc., Pittsburgh, 1919-21; city engr. and supt. waterworks Jellico, Tenn., pvt. consulting business, 1921-32; acting dean, prof. civic engring., U. of Miss., 1932-34, dean and prof. civil engring., 1934-37, supervising engr. physical plant and prof. civil engring., 1937-47, prof. civil engring. (1947-1951). Chmn. disaster com., local Am. Red Cross, mem. local employment com., Jellico, Tenn., 1923-25; mem. Am. Soc. for Engring. Edn., Am. Road Builders Assn. (ednl. div., faculty rep.), Miss. Soc. Professional Engrs. (past pres.), Chi Epsilon (faculty adviser). Democrat. Baptist. Clubs: Faculty (past pres.), Kiwanis (past pres.). Counsellor Eno Foundation. Editor: Final Construction Report for constructing q.m., Camp McClellan, Ala., 1919 (War Dept. Records); Industrial Housing (with Morris Knowles), 1920. Holder patents of automatic drain valve for waterworks use. Home: University, Miss. †

HARGRAVE, WILLIAM WALTER, naval med. officer; b. Tazewell, Va., Sept. 6, 1887; s. Alfred Frontis and Bettie Louise (Woolwine) H.; student, Washington Lee U., 1905-07; M.D., Med. Coll. of Va., 1912; m. Harriet Hopkins Whaley, Dec. 14, 1922; children—Bettie Louise (Mrs. Byron M. Burbage), Grace (Mrs. Henry D. Cox), William Walter, Louis Whaley. Commd. lt. (j.g.), U.S. Navy, 1914, and advanced through grades to commodore, 1945; served as pub. health officer, Am. Samoa, 1930-31; chief, diagnostic clinic, U.S. Naval Med. Sch., 1931-35; fleet med. officer, Atlantic Fleet, 1941-42; med. officer, comdg. 3 major naval hosps., World War II; chief, div. of personnel, bur. of medicine and surgery, Navy Dept., 1945-46; capt., sr. med. officer, head dept. of hygiene, U.S. Naval Acad. Med. Corps. 1947-50. Diplomate Am. Bd. of Internal Medicine. Fellow Am. Coll. Physicians. Recipient Legion of Merit, 1945, for citation by comdr. in chief, Pacific Ocean Area, for duties in connection with bldg. Advance Base Hosp. 128, and med. officer in command, U.S. Naval Hosp., Aiea Heights, Pearl Harbor, T.H. Episcopalian. Home: Rustburg, Va. †

HARINELL, TIMOTHY V., corp. exec.; b. Brooklyn, N.Y., Dec. 14, 1890; s. Cornelius and Mary (O'Donnell) H.; student St. Vincent de Paul Sch., Brooklyn, 1897-1904; Sch. of Commerce, 1904-06; m. Margery Berteau, Apr. 25, 1918; 1 son, Timothy V., Jr. With British Am. Tobacco Co., New York, N.Y., 1906-14; mgr. Imperial Tobacco Co., St. John's Newfoundland, 1914-29; sales exec. Imperial Tobacco Co., Montreal, Que., 1929-30; v.p. Brown & Williamson Tobacco Corp., Louisville, Ky., 1930-36, exec. v.p., 1936-41, pres. and dir. 1941-54; chmn. Tobacco Industry Research Com., from 1954; pres. Campbell Co., Inc., from 1955. Served as Am. vice counsul, St. John's, Newfoundland, 1919-20. Democrat. Roman Catholic. Knight of St. Gregory. Clubs: Pendennis, Louisville Country. †

HARKNESS, REBEKAH WEST, composer, philanthropist, foundation executive; b. St. Louis, Apr. 17, 1915; d. Allen T. and Rebekah (Semple) West; m. Dickson Pierce, 1938; children—Allen West, Anne Terry; m. William Hale Harkness, 1947 (dec. 1954); 1 child, Edith Hale; m. Benjamin Harrison Kean, 1961 (div. 1965). Composition student with, Nadia Boulanger, Fontainebleau, France; student of, Fred Werele, Mannes Coll. Music, Dalcroze Sch., N.Y.C.; studied orchestration with, Lee Holby; D.F.A., Franklin Pierce Coll., Rindge, N.H., 1968; Hum.D., Lycoming Coll., 1970. Founder Rebekah Harkness Found. (sponsors ballet and dance programs throughout U.S.), pres., 1959-82; founder Harkness Ballet, 1964, pres., 1964-82, artistic dir., 1970-82; opened Harkness House for Ballet Arts, 1965; pres., dir. William Hale Harkness Found. (supporting med. research.). Composer: tone poem Safari, 1955, Mediterranean Suite, 1957, Musical Chairs, 1958; ballet Journey to Love, 1958, Barcelona Suite, 1958, Gift of the Magi, 1959, Letters to Japan, 1961, Elements, 1965; orch. suite Macumba, 1965; orchestrated: orch. suite Six Etudes in the Form of a Canon (Schumann), 1964, Suite 1 (Rachmaninoff), 1967, Variations in B Flat (Schubert), 1967, Adantino Varié and Two Marches (Schubert), 1967, Cello Sonata (Rachmaninoff), 1969. Bd. dirs. Soc. More Beautiful Nat. Capitol, President's Council Youth Opportunity; trustee John F. Kennedy Center for Performing Arts. Recipient bronze medal appreciation N.Y.C., 1965; Marquis de Cuevas prize U. de la Dance, Paris, France, 1965; Congl. Record citation, 1965-66; Handel award N.Y.C., 1 967; Shield award Am. Indian and Eskimo Cultural Found., 1967; citations White House, 1968; citations D.C. Dept. Correction, 1969; Two Thousand Women of Achievement award, 1970; Ann. award Ballet Des Jeunes, Phila., 1975; named officer Mérité Culturel et Artistique France, 1966. Clubs: River (N.Y.C.), Colony (N.Y.C.). Address: New York, N.Y. Died June 17, 1982.

HARLOW, AGNES VIRGINIA, educator; b. Auburn, N.Y., Sept. 20, 1890; d. Stephen Bedford and Lillian (Smith) H.; A.B., Mt. Holyoke Coll., 1913; A. M., U. Cal., 1923; resident U. Edinburgh, 1926, King's Coll., London, 1927; Ph.D., Duke, 1946. Tchr. English and Latin, Rockville (Conn.) High Sch., 1914-17; tchr. English Shippensburg (Pa.) State Normal Sch., 1917-19; instr. DePauw U., Greencastle, Ind., 1919-23, asst. prof., 1923-33, asso. prof., 1933-46, prof. from 1946. Mem. Am. Assn. Univ. Profs., Am. Assn. U. Women, Modern Lang., Assn., Nat. Council Tchrs. English, Phi Beta Kappa. Author: Thomas Sergeant Perry with Letters of Henry James, 1950; also articles in scholarly jours. Home: Greencastle, Ind. †

HARLOW, HARRY F., educator; b. Fairfield, Iowa, Oct. 31, 1905; s. Lon H. and Mable (Rock) Israel; student Reed Coll., 1923-24; A.B., Stanford, 1927, Ph.D., 1930; m. Clara Mears, 1932 (div. 1946); children—Robert M., Richard F.; m. Margaret Kuenne, 1948 (dec. 1971); children—Pamela Ann, Jonathan; m. 3d, Clara Mears, 1972. Asst. prof. psychology U. Wis., 1930-38, assoc. prof., 1938-44, prof., 1944-50, 1952-56, George Cary

Comstock prof. psychology, dir. primate lab., 1956-74, emeritus, 1974, dir. regional primate center, 1961-71; research prof. psychology U. Ariz., from 1974. Chief human resources research U.S. Army, 1950-52; chmn. d.v. anthropology and psychology NCR, 1954-56. Recipient Nat. Medal of Sci., 1967. Fellow Am. Acad. Arts and Scis.; mem. Am. (pres. div. exptl. psychology 1950-51, pres. 1957-58), Midwest (pres. 1947-48) psychol. assns., Am. Philos. Soc., Nat. Acad. Scis., Gamma Alpha, Sigma Xi. Editor Jour. Comparative and Physiological Psychology, 1951-63. Home: Tucson, Ariz. Dec. Dec. 6, 1981.

HARLOW, VIRGINIA, coll. prof., writer; b. Throopsville, N.Y., Sept. 20, 1890; d. Stephen Bedford and Lillian (Smith) Harlow; A.B., Mount Holyoke Coll., 1913; A.M., U. of Calif., 1923; Ph.D., Duke U., 1946; student U. of Edinburgh, 1926, Kings Coll., London, 1927. Teacher of English and Latin. Rockville (Conn.) High Sch., 1914-17; teacher English, Shippensburg (Pa.) State Teachers Coll., 1917-19, instr. English, DePauw U., 1919-23, asst. prof., 1923-33, asso. prof., 1933-46, prof. English from 1946. Mem. Assn. Univ. Profs., Assn. Univ. Women, Modern Lang. Assn., Phi Beta Kappa. Author: Thomas Sergeant Perry: A Biography, 1950. Contbr. to Collier's Ency. and scholarly jours. Home: Greencastle, Ind. †

HARMS, HERM, clergyman; b. nr. Celle, Germany, June 10, 1888; s. Henry and Marie (Rabe) H.; student Concordia Coll. and Sem., Uelzen, Germany, 1902-08, Concordia Theol. Sem., 1909, D.D., 1947; m. Marie Mueller, July 12, 1911; children—Beata (Mrs. James Blaylock), Vera (Mrs. Lawrence K. Mason), Erhard H., Lota (Mrs. Robert J. Niemand), Elda (wife Dr. Richard E. Bennett). Came to U.S., 1908, naturalized, 1922. Ordained to ministry Luth. Ch. (Mo. Synod), 1909, pastor, Elkton, Mich., 1909-11, Standish, 1911-12, Batavia, Ill., 1912-19, Davenport, Ia., 1919-51; pres. Ia. Dist. Luth. Ch. (Mo. Synod), 1927-38, nat. v.p., 1938-59, hon. v.p. from 1959. Address: Waukegan, Ill. †

HARNED, HERBERT S(PENCER), phys. chemist; b. Camden, N.J., Dec. 2, 1888; s. Thomas Biggs and Augusta Anna (Traubel) H.; student William Penn Charter Sch., 1898-1905; A.B., U. of Pa., 1909, B.S., 1910, Ph.D., 1913; m. Dorothy Elizabeth Foltz, Sept. 8, 1917; children—Julia (Mrs. Pardee), Herbert S., Louise, Eleanor. Instr. chemistry U. of Pa., 1913-16, asst. prof., 1916-26, prof., 1926-28; prof. chemistry Yale, 1928-57, prof. emeritus, from 1957; Spiers Meml. lectr. Faraday Society, 1959; Harkins Meml. lectr. University of Chicago, 1959. Cons. Union Carbide Nuclear Co., Oak Ridge, Tenn. Consultant Department, Health Pa., 1920-21; mem. bd. healing arts Conn., from 1949. Served as capt. C.W.S., U.S. Army, 1918-19; cons. ofcl. investigator O.S.R.D., 1941-43, group leader Manhattan Project, 1943-45. Mem. Am. Chem. Soc., Faraday Soc. Gt. Britain, Nat. Acad. Scis., Sigma Xi, Phi Beta Kappa, Delta Kappa Epsilon. Author: The Physical Chemistry of Electrolytic Solutions, 1943; also articles in chem. publs. Home: New Haven, Conn. †

HARNESS, EDWARD GRANVILLE, soap products manufacturing company executive; b. Marietta, Ohio, Dec. 17, 1918; s. Lewis Nye and Mary (McKinney) H.; m. Mary McCrady Chaney, Aug. 7, 1943; children: Frances Ann (Mrs. Daniel J. Jones), Edward Granville, Robert R. A.B., Marietta Coll., 1940. With Procter & Gamble Co., Cin., 1940—, v.p. paper products div., 1963-66, v.p.-group exec., dir., 1966-70, exec. v.p., 1970-71, pres., 1971-81, chmn. bd., chief exec. officer, 1972-81, chmn. exec. com., 1981-83; dir. Caterpillar Tractor Co., Exxon Corp. Chmn. bd. trustees Marietta Coll.; trustee Ohio Found. Ind. Colls.; trustee, vice chmn. Conf. Bd. Served with USAAF, 1942-46. Mem. Bus. Council, Conf. Bd. Clubs: Commercial (Cin.), Carmargo (Cin.), Queen City (Cin.), Commonwealth (Cin.). Home: Cincinnati, Ohio. Died Nov. 15, 1984. *

HARNSBERGER, HARRY SCOTT, state judge, lawyer; b. Decatur, Ill., Dec. 25, 1889; s. William Henry and Lenore Calista (Thomas) H.; LL.B., Georgetown U., 1914; m. Evelynn Alice McCoy, Dec. 22, 1929; children—William Robert, Harry Scott, Evelynn Belle. Admitted to Wyo. bar, 1914; co. and pros. atty., Fremont Co., 1930-42; gen. counsel First Nat. Bank, Lander, Wyo., 1943-51, v.p., from 1945; v.p. Central Trust Co., Lander, from 1945; stockman; atty. general State of Wyoming, 1950-53; justice Supreme Court, Wyoming, from 1953; chief justice, from 1967. Chairman of Wyoming Republican State Conv., 1944, Wyo. delegation Rep. Nat. Conv., 1948. Chmn. adv. bd. Selective Service, 1941-47; chmn. Nat. War Fund, Inc., 1944. Capt. cav., Wyo. N.G. Mem. Am. (mem. ho of dels. 1943-44), Wyo. (pres. 1941-42), Laramie County, Fremont County (pres.) bar assns., Internat. Com. Jurists. Mason (32 deg.); past grand commander Knights Templar Shriner, (Jester). K.P., Kiwanian. Club: Cheyenne Literary. Author legal articles. Home: Cheyenne, Wyo. †

HARNWELL, GAYLORD P., educator, business executive; b. Evanston, Ill., Sept. 29, 1903; s. Frederick William and Anna Jane (Wilcox) H.; B.S., Haverford Coll., 1924; student Cambridge U. (Eng.), 1924-25; M.A., Princeton, Ph.D., 1927, LL.D., 1955; LL.D., U. Pa., 1953, Ursinus Coll., 1954, Dropsie Coll., 1955, U. Pitts. and Columbia U., 1957; D.Sc., Temple U., Haverford Coll., Hahnemann Med. Coll., 1954, Franklin and Marshall Coll., 1956, U. So. Calif., 1959, Drexel Inst., 1961; LL.D., Washington Coll., 1957, Northwestern U., 1958; Brown U., 1959, Swarthmore, 1959, Coll. William and Mary, 1960, Duke, St. Andrews (Scotland), 1963, U. Calif. at Los Angeles, Occidental Coll., 1964, Harvard, 1965, Hahnemann Med. Coll., Yale, 1970; Ph.D., Pahlavi U. (Iran), 1970; Pd.D., LaSalle Coll., 1957; C.L.D., The Div. Sch. in Phila., 1957; Sc.Ped.D., Elizabethtown Coll., 1959; L.H.D., Wilkes Coll., 1965, Jewish Theol. Sem. Am., 1965, Yeshiva U., 1966, Loyola U. Chgo., 1970; A.H.D., St. Joseph's Coll., 1969; m. Mary Louise Rowland, June 18, 1927; children—Mary Jane Wallace, Ann Wheeler Ashmead, Robert Gaylord. NRC fellow Calif. Inst. Tech., 1927-28, Princeton, 1928-29; asst. prof. physics Princeton, 1929-36, asso. prof., 1936-38; prof. physics, chmn. dept. and dir. Randal Morgan Lab., U. Pa., 1938-53, pres., prof. physics, 1953-70, pres. emeritus, 1970-82, emeritus Univ. prof. physics, 1974-82; leave absence, 1942-46, to act as dir. U. Calif. div. war research, U.S. Navy Radio and Sound Lab., San Diego; past dir. Rorer-Amchem Co., 1st Pa. Bank, N.Y. Stock Exchange, Penn Central Co. chmn. bd. emeritus West Phila. Corp. Bd. dirs. University City Sci. Center; bd. mgrs. emeritus Haverford Coll.; trustee, chmn. Phila. com. United World Colls., 1974-77; chmn. Am. Council on Edn., 1959-60. Awarded medal for Merit; Distinguished Pub. Service award Dept. Navy; hon. comdr. Order Brit. Empire; comdr. Nat. Order Republic Ivory Coast. Fellow Royal Soc. Edinburgh (hon.), Am. Phys. Soc., Accoustical Soc.; mem. Am. Philos. Soc., Sigma Xi, Phi Beta Kappa, Sigma Pi Sigma, Alpha Epsilon Delta, Alpha Phi Omega. Club: Merion Cricket (Phila.). Cons. editor, Internat. Series in Physics, McGraw-Hill Book Co., 1946-53. Author: Principles of Electricity and Electromagnetism, 1929; Experimental Atomic Physics (with John J. Livingood), 1939; Atomic Physics (with W.E. Stephens) 1955; Russian Diary, 1960; Educational Voyaging in Iran, 1962; (with G.J.F. Legge) Physics: Matter, Energy, and the Universe, 1967. Home: Haverford, Pa. Died Apr. 18, 1982.

HARPER, JAMES WRIGHT, clergyman; b. Providence, Tex., Sept. 27, 1890; s. George and Harrett (Allen) H.; student Draughans Bus. Coll., Southwestern Baptist Sem.; m. Hattie Robertson, Nov. 6, 1910. Ordained to ministry Baptist Ch., 1923; asso. editor Baptist Monotor, Henderson, Tex., from 1929. Bus. mgr. Tex. Bapt. Orphanage, 1929-34; moderator Bapt. Missionary Assn. Tex., 1934-37; corr. sec., 1937-39; pres. Am. Bapt. Assn., from 1956; corr. sec. Missionary Bapt. Assn., from 1951. Mem. Tex. legislature, 1925-29. Mason. Home: Gallatin, Tex. †

HARPER, JOHN, physician, naval officer; b. Phila., Pa., Aug. 15, 1890; s. James and Mary Emma (Patterson) H.; grad. Central High Sch., Phila., 1907; Ph.G., Medico-Chirurgical Coll., Phila., 1909, M.D., 1913; grad. U.S. Naval Med. Sch., Washington, D.C., 1916; m. Henrietta Elizabeth Berens, June 2, 1921; children—John Henry Robert, Richard Harris, James Robert, Mary Elizabeth. Commissioned lt. (j.g.) Med. Corps U.S. Navy, 1916; promoted through grades to rear adm., 1945; teacher pathology and med. zoölogy, U.S. Naval Med. Sch., 1919-23; chief of med. service and in charge Municipal Hosp., St. Thomas, Virgin Islands, 1923-25; former dir. labs., U.S. Naval Med. Sch. and prof. preventive medicine and teacher med. zoölogy, George Washington U.; later in charge div. of publs., Bur. Medicine and Surgery, U.S. Navy, editor Naval Medical Bulletin; chief Medical Service, U.S. Naval Hosp., Washington, D.C.; general inspector and chief of research division, Bureau of Medicine and Surgery, Navy Dept.; district medical officer, 3d Naval Dist., staff comdr. Eastern Sea Frontier. Fellow A.M.A., A.C.P. Home: Brooklyn, N.Y. †

HARPER, JOHN DICKSON, aluminum manufacturing company executive; b. Louisville, Tenn., Apr. 6, 1910; s. Lafayette Rodgers and Mary Alice (Collier) H.; m. Samma Lucille McCrary, Oct. 21, 1937; children: Rodgers McCrary, John Dickson, Thomas William.; m. Mary Lee Lawson, May 27, 1982. B.S., U. Tenn., 1933; D.Eng., Maryville Coll., 1964, Lehigh U., Rensselaer Poly. Inst., Carnegie-Mellon U., 1982; LL.D., U. Evansville; Sc.D., Clarkson Coll. Tech.; D. Comml. Sci. (hon.), Widener Coll. With Aluminum Co. of Am., 1933-75, successively elec. engr., Alcoa, Tenn., asst. dist. power mgr., works mgr., Rockdale, Tex., gen. mgr. smelting div., Pitts., asst. prodn. mgr., 1933-60, v.p., 1960, v.p. prodn., 1962, exec. v.p., 1962-63, pres., 1963-75, chief exec. officer, 1965-75, chmn. bd., 1970-75, chmn. exec. com., 1965-78; chmn. bd. Communications Satellite Corp., 1979-83, chmn. fin. com., 1979-84, dir., 1973-84; chmn. bd. Coke Investors, Inc., 1979-85; dir. Am. European Assocs., Inc., Crutcher Resources Corp. Mem. nat. council, nat. exec. com. Boy Scouts, past pres. N.E. region; trustee Com. Econ. Devel.; hon. mem. Bus. Council, Bus. Com. for Arts, Inc.; past chmn. Nat. Alliance Businessmen, Bus. Roundtable; councillor Conf. Bd.; mem. Pres.'s Export Council, Pres.'s Commn. on Personnel Interchange, Pub. Oversight Bd.; hon. trustee, past vice chmn. Carnegie-Mellon U.; mem. devel. bd. U. Tenn.; past chmn., hon. mem. Internat. Primary Aluminum Inst.; founding mem. Rockefeller U. Council. Recipient Silver Quill award Am. Bus. Press, Inc.; Gold medal Pa. Soc.; Invest in Am. Spokesman award; Nathan W. Dougherty award U. Tenn.; decorated knight's cross Order St. Olav (Norway). Fellow ASME (Gantt medal), IEEE (past v.p.); mem. Engrs. Soc. Western Pa., Metcalf award, Newcomen Soc., Aluminum Assn. (hon. mem., past chmn.), Am. Soc. for Metals (life), Am. Soc. Metals (Bryce Harlow award 1982), Nat. Acad. Engring., Tau Beta Pi, Eta Kappa Nu, Beta Gamma Sigma. Clubs: Duquesne (Pitts.), Harvard (Pitts.), Yale (Pitts.), Princeton (Pitts.), Allegheny (Pitts.), Fox Chapel (Pitts.), St. Clair Country (Pitts.); Rolling Rock (Ligonier, Pa.); Internat. (Washington), F St. (Washington), Met. (Washington); Links (N.Y.C.), Sky (N.Y.C.); Seminole Golf, Jonathan's Landing. Home: Pittsburgh, Pa. Died July 26, 1985.

HARRAR, J. GEORGE, ret. found. exec.; b. Painesville, Ohio, Dec. 2, 1906; s. E.S. and Lucetta (Sterner) H.; m. Georgetta Steese, Jan. 193O; children—Cynthia Ann (Mrs. Alvin Wilson), Georgetta Louise (Mrs. David T. Denhardt). A.B., Oberlin Coll., 1928, LL.D. (hon.), 1962; M.S., Iowa State Coll., 1929; Ph.D., U. Minn., 1935; LL.D., U. Calif., 1963, U. Nebr., 1969; D.Sc., U. Fla., 1964, W.Va. U., 1964, Ohio State U., 1964, Emory U., 1966, Clemson (S.C.) U., 1967, U. Ill., 1968, U. Ariz., 1968, Utah State U., 1971, Columbia U., 1971, Rockefeller U., 1968, Washington U., 1969, Ripon Coll., 1975; Dr. honoris causa, Central U., Quito, 1966, U. Andes, Colombia, 1966, Agrarian U., Lima, Peru, 1964. Prof. botany Coll. Agr., U. P.R., 1929-3O, chmn. dept., 1930-33; instr. plant pathology U. Minn., 1934-35; prof. biology Va. Polytech. Inst., 1935-41; chmn. dept. plant pathology Wash. State Coll., 1941-43; dir. Mexican Agrl. Program, 1943-51; field dir. for agr. Rockefeller Found., N.Y.C., 1952-55, dir. for agr., 1955-59, v.p., 1959-61, pres., 1961-72, pres. emeritus, life fellow, cons., 1972-82; Andrew D. White prof.-at-large Cornell U., 1971-77; hon. prof. U. San Carlos, Guatemala City, Cath. U. Chile; chmn. Internat. Agrl. Devel. Service, 1975-82. Author: (with E.S. Harrar) Guide to Southern Trees, 1945, (with E. C. Stakman) Principles of Plant Pathology, 1967, Strategy for the Conquest of Hunger, 1967; Contbr. (with E. C. Stakman) publs. on phytopathology and mycology to profl. jours. Trustee Gen. Edn. Bd., 1960-72, pres., 1961-71, chmn., 1971-72; trustee Nutrition Found., N.Y.C., 1964—, chmn., 1972-78; trustee Acad. Natural Scis., Phila., 1972-75; bd. dirs. Near East Found., 1972-78; chmn. nat. adv. council Monell Chem. Senses Center, U. Pa., 1968-82; mem. council Rockefeller U., 1973-79; hon. chmn. Population Crisis Com., 1973; chmn. governing council Rockefeller Archive Center, 1973-79; trustee Oberlin Coll., 1962-73. Decorated knight comdr. Crown of Thailand; recipient Certificate of Merit for service to agr. U. Fla., 1950; Medal Agrl. Merit Coll. Agr., Saltillo, Mexico; Medal Agrl. Merit Govt. Mex., 1952; Cruz de Boyaca Govt. Republic Colombia, 1954; Chilean Order of Merit, 1958; Pub. Welfare medal Nat. Acad. Scis., 1963; Order Golden Heart Govt. Philippines, 1964; Rafael Uribe Order of Merit in Agr. Govt. of Colombia, 1973; Outstanding Achievement award U. Minn., 1953; Elvin Charles Stakman award, 1969; citation of merit U. Ariz., 1960; Distinguished Achievement citation Iowa State U., 1970; Edward A. Browning award Am. Soc. Agronomy, 1971; Wilbur O. Atwater medal, 1974; Americas award, 1974; Underwood-Prescott Meml. award, 1975; citation Diplomatic Corps in Honduras, 1961; Caballero decoration Govt. of Ecuador, 1963; Aztec Eagle award Mex., 1980; Presdl. award Am. Public Health Assn., 1962; Ohio Gov.'s award, 1965; J. George Harrar Research award Nutrition Found., 1979. Fellow AAAS, Am. Phytopath. Soc., Royal Soc. Arts (London); mem. Japan Acad. Sci. (hon.), Am. Acad. Arts and Scis., Nat. Acad. Scis., Brazilian Soc. Geneticists (hon.), Am. Philos. Soc., Italian Nat. Acad. of Agr. Am. Phytopath. Soc. Club: Century Assn. (N.Y.C.). Home: Scarsdale, N.Y. Died Apr. 18, 1982.

HARRELL, EUGENE FLOWERS, prison official; b. Carrolton, Miss., Mar. 27, 1889; s. Charles Franklin and Isabelle Sabrina (Belear) H.; ed. pub. schs.; m. Maude Fry, of Marceline, Mo., July 9, 1914; children—Calvin Eugene, Annie Christine. Traffic officer, Paris, Tex., 1913-19, chief of police, 1919-25; mem. firm Upton & Harrell, real estate and loans, Paris, 1926; Tex. state ranger, Fort Worth, 1927; warden, Tex. Penitentiary, from 1928. Asst. sergt. at arms, Dem. Nat. Conv., 1928. Democrat. Baptist. Mason, K.P. Address: Huntsville, Tex. †

HARRELL, LUTHER ALONZO, clergyman; b. nr. Hawkinsville, Ga., Dec. 31, 1888; s. William Levi and Margaret Winnifred (Daniel) H.; Ph.B., Emory U., 1913, D.D., 1956; m. Mary Elizabeth Quillian, Nov. 28, 1913; children—Margaret Elizabeth (wife of Rev. Ralph Miller), Maria Lilias, Luther Alonzo (dec.), William Asbury. Ordained to ministry Meth. Ch., 1916; prof. mathematics Sparks Coll., 1916-17; pastor, Butler, Ga., 1917-21, Lee Street Ch., Americus, Ga., 1922-24, Cherokee Heights Ch., Macon, Ga., 1924-29, First Ch., Dublin, Ga., 1929-30; supt. Columbus Dist., 1930-34; pastor First Ch., Brunswick, Ga., 1934-38, Valdosta, Ga., 1938-42; supt. Americus dist., 1942-45; pastor First Ch., Albany, Ga., 1945-51; supt. Macon dist., 1951-56; dir. Ga. Meth. Commn. higher Edn., 1956-58; mem. Gen. Conf. Commn. on Higher Edn., 1956-58. Dir., v.p. S. Ga. Found. for Conf. Claimants, from 1942; mem. gen. bd. edn. Meth. Ch., 1940-48. Active dist. councils Boy Scouts Am., 1934-51. Trustee Emory U., from 1945. Home: Albany, Ga. †

HARRILL, PAUL EUGENE, cotton coop. exec., univ. regent; b. Forest City, N.C., Aug. 1, 1889; s. Samuel Floyd and Mary Jane (Walker) H.; student Mars Hill (N.C.) Coll., 1908-10; m. Bonnie Mae Pruitt, Mar. 5, 1924; 1 son, Paul Eugene. Vice pres., gen. mgr. Okla. Cotton Coop. Assn., now dir.; v.p. Am. Cotton Coop. Assn., from 1934; mem. N.Y. Cotton Exchange, from 1956; producer del.

Nat. Cotton Council Am., from 1939. Bd. regents Okla. State U., also seven affiliated agrl. and mech. colls. of Okla., 1944-62. Mem. Christian Ch. Address: Oklahoma City, Okla. †

HARRINGTON, ROBERT STUCKEY, lawyer; b. Lathrop, Mo., Oct. 10, 1913; s. Robert Montgomery and Mae (Stuckey) H.; B.A., U. Mo., 1935; LL.B., U. Mich., 1938; m. Rose Elizabeth Nelson, Aug. 12, 1939. Admitted to Mo. bar, 1938, Calif. bar, 1947; dist. atty. Clinton County, Mo., 1939-43; spl. agt. FBI, 1942-44; trial atty. Parker, Stanbury, Reese & McGee, Los Angeles, 1947-53; sr. partner Harrington, Foxx, Dubrow & Canter, Los Angeles, from 1953. Seminar lectr. trial techniques Calif. State Bar/U. Calif., 1960-83. Served to capt. USMCR, 1944-46; judge adv. 9th Marine Air Wing. Diplomate Am. Bd. Trial Advocates. Fellow Internat. Acad. Trial Lawyers, Am. Coll. Trial Lawyers; mem. Internat. Assn. Ins. Counsel, Am. Trial Lawyers Assn., Calif. Trial Lawyers Assn., Def. Research Inst., Assn. Dist. Attys., Soc. Former Spl. Agts. FBI, Am. Judicature Soc., Law-Sci. Acad., Am., Los Angeles County bar assns., Calif. State Bar (disciplinary com.), Beta Theta Pi, Phi Delta Phi. Democrat. Methodist. Clubs: Annandale Golf (Pasadena, Calif.); California, Jonathan (Los Angeles). Author, lectr. Preparing and Examining Witnesses, videotapes for Calif. State Bar and U. Calif. on trial techniques, 1968, 75; author: (with others) California Book of Approved Jury Instructions, 1975. Contbr. articles, lectr. on art of Bonsai. Home: Flintridge, Calif. Died Mar. 27, 1983.

HARRIS, ARTHUR RINGLAND, army officer; b. Norfolk, Neb., Aug. 1, 1890; s. Edmund Coleman and Anna Rosa (Mulholland) H.; student St. Paul's Sch., Concord, N.H., 1906-08, U. of Nev., 1908-10; B.S., U.S. Mil. Acad., 1914; m. Helen Curtice Abbott, Jan. 27, 1934. Commd. 2d lt., F.A., U.S. Army, June 12, 1914, and advanced through the grades to brig. gen., March 14, 1943; served as capt. and maj., asst. chief of staff, G-3, of 87th and 80th Divs., 1917-18, sec. of gen. staff, Third Army, Coblenz, Germany, 1919-20; mil. attaché, Central Am. Republics, 1931-35; prof. mil. science and tactics, Harvard, 1935-39; War Dept. gen. staff, 1939-41; asst. chief of staff, G-2, Eastern Defense Command, and First Army. Governors Island, N.Y., 1942; mil. attaché, Am. Embassy, Mexico City, 1943, Argentina, 1945-46; pres. Inst. of Inter-Am. Affairs and Inter-Am. Ednl. Foundation, 1946-48; mem. mil. com. U.S. Delegation United Nations, 1949; chmn. adv. council Jonathon Dickinson State Park. Decorated Order Condor of Andes (Bolivia); Order of Merit of Juan Pablo Duarte (Dominican Republic); Order of Abdel Calderon (Ecuador), Legion of Merit (U.S.). Mason. Clubs: Army and Navy, Chevy Chase Country (Washington); Jupiter Island (Hobe Sound, Fla.). Mem. Am. Olympic Polo Team, 1920. Home: Hobe Sound, Fla. †

HARRIS, DAVID BULLOCK, oil exec., cons.; b. Dallas, Aug. 9, 1888; s. Frederick and Elizabeth (Dabney) H.; B.S. in Civil Engineering, Agricultural and Mechanical College of Texas, 1909, LL.D., 1954; married Eugenia Dabney Kendall, Aug. 16, 1941. With South Texas Commercial Nat. Bank, 1909-17; with Humble Oil and Refining Co., Houston, Tex., from 1919, beginning as laborer and advancing through various positions to div. supt., 1919-34, mgr. indsl. relations, 1934-46, dir. treas., from 1942, v.p. and treas., 1947-53; cons., from 1953. Served as pvt., advancing to capt., U.S. Army, in A.E.F., 1917-19. Chmn. industry members Nat. War Labor Bd., Region VIII (Tex., Okla., La.), during entire period World War II. Adm. Texas Navy (honorary). Councilor Tex. A. & M. Research Foundation. Member national advisory council, Junior Achievement, Inc., N.Y. Mem. Air Force Survey Adv. Com., Houston East, South and West Texas C.'s of C., Am. Petroleum Inst., Mid-Continental Oil and Gas Assn., Mus. Fine Arts, Am. Legion, Newcomen Soc., Va. Hist. Soc., Houston Symphony Soc., Petroleum Club, S.A.R., Soc. Cincinnati, Tau Beta Pi. Episcopalian. Clubs: Bayou, HoustonCountry, Ramada.Home: Houston,Tex. †

HARRIS, DAVID TAYLOR, banker; b. N.Y.C., Mar. 1, 1923; s. Victor and Catherine (Richardson) H.; m. Joan A. Tompkins, Jan. 24, 1974; children—David Taylor, Catherine. A.B., Princeton U., 1944. With U.S. Trust Co., N.Y.C., 1947-82, asst. sec., 1955-57, asst. v.p., 1957-60, v.p., 1960-66, sr. v.p., 1966-72, exec. v.p., 1972-82. Trustee Cultural Instns. Retirement Systems. Served to lt. (j.g.) USNR, 1943-46. Mem. Nat. Inst. Social Scis. Republican. Episcopalian. Clubs: Field (Greenwich), Round Hill (Greenwich); Union (N.Y.C.), Pilgrims of U.S. (N.Y.C.); Rockaway Hunting (Lawrence, N.Y.), Lawrence Beach (Lawrence, N.Y.). Home: Greenwich, Conn. Died Feb. 23, 1982.

HARRIS, GUY M., univ. regent; b. Nashville, Ill., Apr. 5, 1887; s. Francis and Allie (Ayers) H.; student Bus. Coll., Sulphur, Okla. Buick automobile dealer, Ardmore, Okla.; 1963; rancher, Johnson County, also Carter County. Organizer Ardmore Community Chest. Bd. regents Higher Edn. State Okla. Mem. Ardmore C. of C. (past pres.), Am. Automobile Assn. Presbyn. (elder, deacon). Mason, Elk, Rotarian. Home: Ardmore, Okla. †

HARRIS, JOHN BLACK, corp. exec.; b. Bklyn., Apr. 17, 1918; s. John Black and Helen (Woodman) H.; m. Elizabeth Moody, Nov. 29, 1941; children—Pamela Preston (Mrs. William O. McClure), Lee Woodman (Mrs. David K. Volckhausen), Holly Stetson (Mrs. John C. Huntress), John Black. A.B., Bard Coll., 1939; postgrad. in econs, Columbia, 1939-42. Financial, research staff Chase Nat. Bank, 1939-42, fgn. credit depts., 1946-50; asst. to treas. W.R. Grace & Co., N.Y.C., 1950-51, asst. to pres., 1951-52, asst. project mgr. chem. devel., 1951-52, dir. personnel, 1953-55, v.p. mgmt. orgn. and planning, 1955-56, v.p., gen. mgr. operations West Coast S.Am. and C.Am., 1956-61; v.p. indsl. operations United Fruit Co.; v.p. United Fruit & Food Corp., 1961-64; v.p. gen. devel. div. W.R. Grace & Co., 1964-68; v.p. W.R. Grace & Co. (Frozen Foods div.), 1969-73; devel. officer New Eng. Fish Co., Seattle, 1973-80; v.p., dir. Alaska Food Co., Inc., Seattle, Anchorage and Kodiak, Alaska, from 1980. Dir., chmn. exec. com. Alaska Fisheries Devel. Found., Anchorage, 1977-80; Trustee, treas. Bard Coll., 1946-49. Served as maj. USAAF, 1942-46. Home: Seattle, Wash.

HARRIS, MICHAEL MARCUS-MYERS, architect; b. Newark, Sept. 8, 1907; s. Bernhardt and Josephine (Myers) H.; m. Rosalind Wright, Mar. 8, 1946; children—Alison, Peter Quincy. B.Arch., Cornell U., 1930. Mem. staff Office John Russell Pope, 1935-39; designer Office Alfred Easton Poor, 1939-40; asst. project designer Shreve, Lamb & Harmon, 1941-42; architect Abramovitz-Harris-Kingsland (architects), N.Y.C., 1942-82, partner, 1962-82; adj. prof. architecture Columbia, 1965-82; Pres. N.Y. Bldg. Congress, 1972-82. Principal works include; asst. dir. planning: UN Hdqrs, 1950; partner-in-charge: UN Library, 1962, Time and Life Bldg, 1963, McGraw-Hill World Hdqrs, 1969, Celanese Corp. Bldg, 1970, Standard Oil of N.J, 1968, all N.Y.C. Mem. adv. com. constrn. N.Y.C. Bd. Edn., 1964-69. Fellow A.I.A. (treas. N.Y. chpt. 1961-64, exec. com. 1960-65); mem. Nat. Inst. Archtl. Edn. (bd. dirs.), Century Assn. Home: New York, N.Y. Died Aug. 16, 1982.

HARRIS, PATRICIA ROBERTS, cabinet member, lawyer, educator; b. Mattoon, Ill., May 31, 1924; d. Bert Fitzgerald and Hildren Brodie (Johnson) Roberts; m. William Beasley Harris, Sept. 1, 1955. A.B. summa cum laude, Howard U., 1945; J.D. (with honors), George Washington U., 1960; postgrad., U. Chgo., 1945-47, Am. U., 1949-50; LL.D., Lindenwood Coll., Morgan State Coll., 1967, Russell Sage Coll., Tufts U., Dartmouth Coll., 1970, Johns Hopkins, MacMurray Coll., U. Md., Williams Coll., Ripon Coll., 1972, Brown U., 1972, Wilburforce U., Aquinas Coll., Brandeis U., Colby Coll., No. Mich. U.; D.H.L., Miami U., 1967, Newton Coll. of the Sacred Heart, 1972, U. Mich., 1973, Smith Coll., Wittenberg U., 1974; D.C.L., Beaver Coll., 1968; P.Sc.D., Rollins Coll., 1974. Bar: D.C. 1960, U.S. Supreme Ct 1960. Program dir. YWCA, Chgo., 1946-49; asst. dir. Am. Council Human Rights, 1949-53; exec. dir. Delta Sigma Theta, 1953-59; research assoc. George Washington U. Sch. Law, 1959-60; trial atty. Dept. Justice, 1960-61; asso. dean students, lectr. law Howard U., 1961-63, prof. law, 1963-65, 67-69; dean Howard U. (Sch. of Law), 1969; ptnr. Fried, Frank, Harris, Shriver & Kampelman, Washington, 1970-77; sec. HUD, Washington, 1977-79, HEW, 1979-81, HHS, 1980-81; prof. law George Washington U., Washington, 1981-85; dir. Scott Paper Co.; mem. U.S.-P.R. Commn. Status P.R., 1964-66; U.S. ambassador to, Luxembourg, 1965-67; alternate del. of U.S. to 21st-22d Gen. Assemblies of UN, 1966-67. Mem. exec. com. Nat. Citizens Com. Community Relations, 1964-65; co-chmn. Nat. Women's Com. Civil Rights, 1963-64; chmn. D.C. Law Revision Commn., 1975-77; vice chmn. Nat. Capitol Area Civil Liberties Union, 1962-65; exec. bd. D.C. chpt. NAACP, 1958-60; bd. dirs. Legal Def. Fund, 1967-77; chmn. welfare com. Urban League D.C., 1953-55; Del. Democratic Nat. Conv., 1964, chmn. credentials com., 1972; mem.-at-large Dem. Nat. Com., 1973-76, Dem. nat. committeewoman from D.C., 1976-77, presdl. elector, D.C., 1964; Bd. dirs. ACLU, 1964-65, YWCA of U.S., 1958-59, Am. Council Human Rights, 1953-55, Nat. Capitol area YWCA, 1963-65, Family and Child Services D.C., 1962-65, Home Rule Com. D.C., 1965-66, Com. on Admissions and Grievances U.S. Dist. Ct. for D.C., 1970-77; mem. Adminstrv. Conf. U.S., 1967-71; nat. adv. com. Reform Fed. Criminal Laws, 1967-70; mem. Nat. Com. on Causes and Prevention Violence, 1968-69, Carnegie Commn. on Future Higher Edn., 1969-73; Bd. dirs. Georgetown U., 1970-77, Nat. Merit Scholarship Found., 1975-76; trustee Twentieth Century Fund, 1969-85; bd. govs. Atlantic Inst., 1967-77; adv. council Marshall Scholarship Program, 1973-77. Decorated Order of Oaken Crown Luxembourg; recipient Distinguished Achievement award Women's Com., Yeshiva U., 1968; Distinguished Alumni award Howard U., 1966; Distinguished Service award Washington Alumnae chpt. Delta Sigma Theta, 1963; Aquinas award Aquinas Coll., 1972; One Nation award Phila. br. NAACP, 1972; named Woman of Year Women's Aux. Jewish War Vets., 1968, Woman of Year in Bus. and Professions Ladies Home Jour., 1974; Achievement award in professions Black Enterprise, 1976; award in honor women dirs. of corps. Catalyst, 1976. Mem. Council on Fgn. Relations, Fed. Bar Assn., ABA, Order of Coif, Phi Beta Kappa, Delta Sigma Theta, Kappa Beta Pi. Club: Cosmopolitan (N.Y.C.). Home: Washington, D.C. Died Mar. 23, 1985.

HARRIS, REED, writer, government foundation official; b. N.Y.C., Nov. 5, 1909; s. Tudor Reed and Lois Estella (Jones) H.; m. Martha Margaret Tellier, Aug. 2, 1931 (dec. 1966); children—Robert Reed, Ann Shapleigh, Donald Reed; m. Mary Mateer West, Dec. 27, 1966. Student, Staunton (Va.) Mil. Acad., 1928, Columbia U., 1932, George Washington U., 1947. With Washington County Post, Cambridge, N.Y., 1925-27; editor Columbia U. Daily Spectator, 1932; with N.Y. Times, 1931-32, N.Y. Jour., 1932; reporter Newspaper Enterprise Assn., N.A. Newspaper Alliance, King Features Syndicate and others, 1932-33; advt. Robert Mack, Inc. and Badger, Browning & Hersey, Inc., N.Y.C., 1933-34; exec. editor Fed. Emergency Relief Adminstrn., WPA, Washington, 1934-38; travel book editor Europe on Wheels, Inc., N.Y.C., 1938-39; N.Y. State dir., then regional supr. Nat. Emergency Council, Office Govt. Reports, O.W.I., 1939-42; chief mgmt. planning O.W.I., Washington, 1942-44; chief div. of communications and records U.S. Dept. State, 1945-48, chief pubs. div., 1949-50; dep. adminstr. U.S. Internat. Info. Adminstrn., 1950-53; pres. Publ. Services, Inc., 1953-61, Reinforced Learning, Inc., 1958-62; exec. asst. to dir. USIA, Washington, 1961-64; asst. dir. Info. Centers, 1964-66, agy. asst. dir. for policy and plans, then research and assessment, 1966-73; pres. Freedoms Found. at Valley Forge, 1974-75, pres. emeritus, 1975-82; Mem. Army-State Dept. survey mission to Germany, 1948; dir. Nat. Self Govt. Com., Inc.; Poynter fellow Vassar Coll., 1974. Author: King Football, 1932, Travelers' Windfall, (with J.S. Robbins), 1938, (with Lewis Robins) Living Method Typing Course, 1958, Rider FCC Code Course, 1958, Instant French, 1959, Instant Russian, 1960, also other langs; Contbg. editor: (with Lewis Robins) Concerning Government Benefits, 1935, American Guide Series, 1935-38, New Frontiers of Knowledge, 1958. Served USAAF, 1944-45. Recipient Edward R. Murrow award pub. diplomacy Tufts U., 1966; Silver Helmet award, civil servant of year AMVETS, 1968. Mem. New Directions, Common Cause, AMVETS (life mem. D.C. dept. comdr. 1959-60, nat. exec. com. 1960-62), Phi Gamma Delta. Democrat. Methodist. Clubs: Mason. (Washington), Internat. (Washington) (dir., v.p. 1971-73). Home: Crestview, Md. Died Oct. 15, 1982.

HARRIS, ROBERT SAMUEL, educator; b. Brookline, Mass., May 10, 1904; s. William and Ann Ellen (Bell) H.; B.S., Mass. Inst. Tech., 1928, Ph.D., 1935; hon. degree, U. Havana, 1953; children—Richard, Donald. Research asst. Mass. Inst. Tech., 1928-31, research asso., 1931-37, asst. prof., 1937-41, asso. prof., 1941-46, prof. nutritional biochemistry, 1946-70, emeritus, 1970—, dir. oral sci. research lab.; guest prof. U. Minn., 1970-71, U. Cal. at Los Angeles, 1971-72; field rep. Pan-Am. San. Bur., 1943-52; sci. dir. Nat. Inst. Nutrition, Ecuador, 1950-54, Laboratorios FIM de Nutricion, Havana, 1952-58; hon. prof. U. Havana, 1953. Expert nutrition cons. to sec. war, 1943-46, U.S. Bd. Econ. Warfare, 1943-46; mem. sci. adv. com. Inst. Nutrition C.Am. and Panama, 1946-54; spl. cons. to sec. of health and assistance, Mexico, 1943-47; mem. grants com. NIH, 1965-69; cons. Miralin Corp., 1972—. Decorated by presidents Ecuador, Cuba, Guatemala. Fellow A.A.A.S. (v.p. 1969), Am. Acad. Dentists, Am. Pub. Health Assn., N.Y. Acad. Sci.; mem. Internat. Soc. Dental Research, Am. Inst. Nutrition, Brit. Nutrition Soc., Am. Chem. Soc., Am. Gerontol. Soc., Acad. Phys. Med., Am. Oil Chem. Soc., Am. Dental Assn. (asso.), Sigma Xi, Delta Omega, Theta Delta Chi, Omicron Kappa Upsilon. Editor: The Vitamins (7 vols.), 2d edit., 1968; Nutritional Evaluation of Food Processing, 1960, 2d edit., 1975; also numerous sci. articles. Editor: Vitamins and Hormones, vols. I-XXXII. Home: Newton, Mass. Died Dec. 24, 1983.

HARRIS, THOMAS LEWIS, surgeon; b. Hedgeville, W.Va., Feb. 28, 1889; s. James Trone and Ruth Lewis (Martin) H.; B.S., W.Va. U., 1910, D.Sc. (hon.), 1960; M.D., Jefferson Med. Coll., Phila., 1912; Sc.D. (hon.), Marietta (O.) Coll., 1942; m. Caroline M. Neal, June 28, 1922 (dec.); children—Caroline (Mrs. William A. Goebel), Ruth Neal (Mrs. Frank L. Gillis); m. 2d, Elizabeth W. Moran, Apr. 17, 1948. Resident Surgery Pa., Children's Hosps., Phila., 1912-15; chief resident Louisville City Hosp., 1915-16; chief surgeon St. Joseph's Hosp., Parkersburg, W.Va.; pres. Wood Co. Home Corp.; dir. Consol. Natural Gas Co., N.Y.C. Mem. President's Com. Employment Handicapped; mem. Emergency Resource Planning Com., Com. Higher Edn. W.Va., Gov.'s Com. Phys. Rehab.; mem. Pres.' Com. Crime and Delinquency Bd. dirs. Boys' Clubs Am.; bd. govs. W.Va. U. Served as surgeon U.S. Army, 1917-19. Diplomate Am. Bd. Surgeons (founders group). Fellow A.C.S., Internat. Coll. Surgeons; mem. World Med. Assn. (U.S. Com.); Med. Rehab. Assn.; Pan Am. Med. Assn., Southeastern, So Surg. socs., Acad. Polit. Sci., N.Y. Acad. Sci., Am. Assn. R.R. Surgeons, Am. Assn. Trauma, A.M.A., Newcomen Soc. London, W.Va. Med. Assn. (pres. 1940-41, 45-46), W.Va. Hosp. Assn. (pres. 1938-39), Va., N.C., S.C. hosp. assns. (pres. 1940-41), Beta Theta Phi, Phi Rho Sigma. Elk, Mason (32, Shriner). Clubs: Parkersburg Country, Williams Country (Weirton, W.Va.); Everglades, Bath and Tennis (Palm Beach, Fla.). Contbr. tech., articles surg. jours. Home: Parkersburg, WV. †

HARRIS, WILLIAM BLISS, author, business cons.; b. Denver, Aug. 17, 1900; s. Robert E. and Anna (Bliss) H.; m. Jane Grant, June 3, 1939. Mem. bd. editors Fortune magazine, N.Y. City, 1937-61; gen. partner Laidlaw & Co., 1960—. Home: Litchfield, Conn. Died June 21, 1981.

HARRISON, FRED NASH, tobacco exec.; b. Amelia County, Va., June 18, 1887; s. John Hartwell and Anna Mayo (Carrington) H.; student Washington and Lee U.,

1905-06; C.E., U. of Va., 1911; m. Virginia L. Robertson, Jan. 23, 1919; children—Fred Nash, Jacquelin Marshall, Virginia Carrington. Engr., sanitary dept., Isthmus of Panama, 1911; engr., Mackay Copper Process Co., 1912-14; buyer for Export Leaf Tobacco Co., 1914-16; for W. H. Winstead Co., 1916-23, v.p. from 1919, also dir; pres., dir. Universal Leaf Tobacco Co., 1924-46, chmn. bd., 1946-51, chmn. finance com., from 1951; dir. Canadian Leaf Tobacco Co., Ltd., J.P. Taylor, Inc., Southwestern Tobacco Co., Mut. Assurance Soc. Va., Va. Trust Co., Seaboard Air Line R.R. Dir. Sheltering Arms Hosp.; member board trustees Hampden Sydney College. Business supervisor Air Nitrate Corp., U.S. Nitrate Plant, Muscle Shoals, Ala., 1918. Knight of the Royal Order of Vasa, First Class, Sweden. Mem. Phi Delta Theta. Democrat. Presbyn. Clubs: Commonwealth, Country, Richmond German. Home: Richmond, Va. †

HARRISON, W. SPENCER, corporate executive; b. Yorktown, Ind., Apr. 30, 1917; s. William Henry and Myrtle (Decker) H.; A.B., Ind. U., 1939, LL.B., 1941; m. Margie Leonard, Apr. 25, 1950. Admitted to N.Y. bar, 1947; joined C.B.S. TV, 1942, sr. atty., 1951-52, v.p., 1952, later v.p., bus. mgr. talent and contract properties; v.p. Ashley Famous Agy., Inc., 1962—. Home: Greenwich, Conn. Died Oct. 12, 1983.

HARRISON, WALLACE KIRKMAN, architect; b. Worcester, Mass., Sept. 28, 1895; s. James Henry and Rachel (Kirkman) H.; L.H.D., Dartmouth, 1950; A.F.D., Rollins Coll., Oberlin Coll., New Sch. Social Research; LL.D., Harvard, 1958, Clark U., 1960; LL.D., U. Mich., 1968; m. Ellen Milton, Feb. 13, 1926; 1 child, Sarah Moore. Co-architect Rockefeller Center; architect Met. Opera Lincoln Center, Nelson Rockefeller-Empire State Plaza, Albany, N.Y., Museum of Sci. N.Y., Empire State Plaza, Albany; dir. planning hdqrs. UN; former dir. Office Inter-Am. Affairs. Recipient gold medal A.I.A., 1967. Episcopalian. Clubs: Century Assn., Knickerbocker (N.Y.C.). Archtl. works include: 3 new skyscrapers for Rock Center Exxon, McGraw Hill, Celenese. Home: New York, N.Y. Dec. Dec. 2, 1981.

HARRISON, WILLIAM HENRY, real estate broker, appraiser; b. Cape Girardeau, Mo., Aug. 1, 1910; s. Charles Luce and Maude (Rozier) H.; m. Mina Mary Cohan, June 30, 1945; children—Mary Rozier Harrison Bland, William Henry, John Valle, Robert Sverdrup. B.A., U. Mo., 1932, M.A., 1933. Vice pres., sec. Housing Service, Inc., 1935-40; prin. William H. Harrison (realtor), St. Louis, 1946-60, reopened office, 1975; with 1st Nat. Bank in St. Louis, 1960-75, exec. v.p., 1969-75; also sec. bd. dirs.; pres., dir. Valle Mining Co., 1968-83, Rozier Investment Co., 1968-83; treas., dir. Val-U-Line Liquids, Inc. Mem., treas. Bd. Police Commrs. Met. St. Louis, 1964-68; v.p., dir. Downtown St. Louis, 1961-74; mem. City Plan Commn. St. Louis, 1955-65, vice chmn., 1959-61, chmn., 1961-65; chmn. Mayor St. Louis Community Adv. Com., 1965-67, Citizens Adv. Com. to Modernize and Improve Mo. State Legislature, 1973-75, Mayor's Task Force to Develop an Hist. Preservation Ordinance for St. Louis, 1978-79; mem. army gen. staff com. Army Res. and N.G. Affairs, 1957-62; mem. res. forces policy bd. Dept. Def., 1960-63; chmn. Am. Bankers Assn. Nat. Mortgage Conf., 1972; Trustee Jefferson Nat. Expension Meml. Assn.; bd. dirs., dist. chmn. St. Louis council Boy Scouts Am.; bd. dirs. St. Louis Bi-State chpt. A.R.C., St. Louis council U.S.O. Served to col. AUS, 1940-46; maj. gen. Res. ret. Decorated Legion of Merit with oak leaf cluster U.S.; Croix de Guerre France; Order Leopold; Croix de Guerre Belgium; recipient Alumni Citation U. Mo. Coll. Adminstn. and Pub. Affairs, 1973. Mem. St. Louis Met. C. of C., St. Louis Real Estate Bd., Am. Inst. Real Estate Appraisers, Soc. Indsl. Realtors (pres. St. Louis chpt. 1960, 78), Mil. Order World Wars, Phi Delta Theta, Alpha Kappa Psi. Clubs: Rotary (St. Louis), Round Table (St. Louis), Bellerive Country (St. Louis), Noonday (St. Louis), Racquet (St. Louis); Wings of St. Albans. Home: Saint Louis, Mo. Died Aug. 10, 1983; buried Jefferson Barracks, St. Louis.

HART, DONN VORHIS, univ. adminstr.; b. Anaheim, Calif., Feb. 15, 1918; s. Edgar Manton and Iva (Vorhis) H.; A.B., U. Calif., Berkeley, 1941; M.A., Harvard U., 1942; Ph.D., Syracuse U., 1954; m. Harriett Elizabeth Colegrove, May 31, 1954; 1 dau., Susan Elizabeth. Asst. prof. anthropology U. Denver, 1951-54; vis. prof. anthropology U. Philippines, Quezon City, 1956-57; research asso. Yale U., 1956-57, Syracuse U., 1957-71; prof. anthropology, dir. Center S.E. Asian Studies, No. Ill. U., DeKalb, 1971-81; Fulbright research fellow, Philippines, 1950-51, 54-56, 64-65; cons. in field; chmn. Com. Research Materials S.E. Asia, 1971-74; exec. sec. Philippine Study Com., 1975-81; mem. S.E. Asia Region Council, 1970-72. Served with USAAF, 1942-46. Mem. Assn. Asian Studies, Am. Anthrop. Assn., Am. Folklore Assn., Sigma Nu. Author: (with H.E. Wilson) The Philippines, 1946; Riddles in Philippine Folklore: An Anthropological Analysis, 1965; Compadrinazgo: Ritual Kinship in the Philippines, 1977. Home: DeKalb, Ill. Died July 10, 1983.

HART, GEORGE LUZERNE, JR., U.S. judge; b. Roanoke, Va., July 14, 1905; s. George Luzeren and Lavela (Slicer) H.; m. Louise Neller, Oct. 12, 1935; 1 child, George Luzerne III. A.B., Va. Mil. Inst., 1927; LL.B., Harvard, 1930. Bar: D.C. bar 1930, Va. bar 1936. Practice law with firm Lambert & Hart, 1930-40, Lambert, Hart & Northrop, 1946-58; judge U.S. Dist. Ct. D.C., 1958-84, chief judge, 1974-75; pres. judge U.S. Fgn. Intelligence Surveillance Ct., 1979-84. Home: Washington, D.C. Died May 21, 1984.

HART, WILLIAM A., advt. exec.; b. Fredonia N.Y., Aug. 1, 1890; s. William L. and Reca (Gould) H.; student Teacher Coll., Fredonia, N.Y.; A.B., U. of Mich., 1914; m. Leone Winifred Riorden, Apr. 26, 1916; children—William A., Winifred Jean (Mrs. Henry Davis, Jr.). Asst. to advt. mgr. Burroughs Adding Machine Co., Detroit, 1914-16; western dist. advt. mgr., San Francisco, 1916; advt. mgr. Detroit Steel Products Co., 1917; advt. agency Frank Seaman, Inc., N.Y. City, 1918, mgr. marketing div., 1919-23; dir. marketing and prodn. Elliott Service Co., 1923; dir. advt. E.I. duPont de Nemours & Co., 1924-55; pres. Advt. Research Found., Inc., 1955-59, dir. 1953-59. Dir. Audit Bur. of Circulation, 1927-55, 1st vice chairman, 1950-52, chairman 1952-54. Mem. Del. War Finance Com. (chmn. publicity com.), United War Fund of Del. (dir. and mem. exec. com.). Mem. Assn. Nat. Advertisers (dir. 1924-26, 1929-39 pres., 1928), Advt. Fedn. Am. (dir. 1939-45), Nat. Better Bus. Bur. Phi Gamma Delta, Alpha Delta Sigma (profl. mem.), Druids. Clubs: University (N.Y.); Wilmington Country. Address: Wilmington, Del. †

HARTECK, PAUL, educator, research chemist; b. Vienna, Austria, July 20, 1902; s. Josef and Gabriele (Schattenfroh) H.; student U. Vienna, 1921-23; Ph.D., U. Berlin (Germany), 1925; D.Natural Sci. (hon.), U. Bonn (Germany), 1966; m. Marcella Piccino-Hay, Sept. 27, 1948; children—Claudia, Lawrence Paul. Came to U.S., 1951, naturalized, 1957. Asst. to Prof. Eucken, U. Breslau (Germany), 1926-28; asst. to Geheimrat Haber, Kaiser Villhelm Inst., 1928-33; Rockefeller fellow Cavendish Lab., Cambridge, Eng., 1933-34; prof., dir. Inst. Phys. Chemistry, Hamburg, Germany, 1934-51; rector U. Hamburg, 1948-50; Disting. Research prof. phys. chemistry Rensselaer Poly. Inst., from 1941. Recipient Jean Servaois Stas medal Soc. Chimique de Belgique, 1957; Wilhelm Exner medal Vienna, Oester. Gewerbeverein, 1961; William H. Wiley Distinguished Faculty award Rensselaer Poly. Inst., 1977; Alfred Krupp von Bohlen und Halbach prize, Wiber., 1977; Pioneer award of Am. Chemists, 1979; decorated Grand Decoration of Honor in Gold (Austria). Mem. Joachim-Jungius Gesellschaft der Wissenschaften (v.p. 1949); fgn. sci. mem. Max Planck Soc.; hon. mem. Soc. Chimique de Belgique. Research on ortho-para hydrogen-photo- chemistry-nuclear physics. Deuterium-Deuterium reaction producing Tritium and Helium III, radiation chemistry, planetary atmospheres, nitrogen fixation. Home: Santa Barbara, Calif. Dec. Jan. 21, 1985.

HARTIGAN, JOHN PATRICK, judge; b. Providence, R.I., Dec. 29, 1887; s. John J. and Ellen (Smith) H.; A.B., Brown U., 1910; grad. study, Harvard, 1910-11; A.M. and LL.B., Columbia, 1913; married Alice F. Carroll, October 25, 1920; 1 daughter, Alice Mary (Mrs. James J. Brady). Admitted to Rhode Island bar, 1912, and began practice at Providence; asst. attorney general of R.I., 1923-24, attorney gen., 1933-39; apptd. judge U.S. Dist. Court, R.I., Feb. 1940; apptd. U.S. Circuit Judge, First Circuit, 1951. Chmn. Dem. State Com. Served as 2d lt. 151st Depot Brig., U.S. Army, 1917-18. Mem. Am. and R.I. bar assn., Am. Legion (past dept. comdr. R.I.). Democrat. Catholic. Elk. Home: Edgewood, R.I. †

HARTLINE, HALDAN KEFFER, educator, physiologist; b. Bloomsburg, Pa., Dec. 22, 1903; s. Daniel Schollenberger and Harriet Franklin (Keffer) H.; m. Mary Elizabeth Kraus, Apr. 11, 1936; children—Daniel Keffer, Peter Haldan, Frederick Flanders. B.S., Lafayette Coll., Easton, Pa., 1923, D.Sc. (hon.), 1959; M.D., Johns Hopkins, 1927, LL.D. (hon.), 1969; Sc.D. (hon.), U. Pa., 1971; M.D. (hon.), U. Freiburg i/B, 1971; Sc.D. (hon.), Rockefeller U., 1976, U. Md., 1978, Syracuse U., 1979; Eldridge Johnson traveling research scholar, U. Leipzig and Munich, 1929-31. Nat. Research fellow med. scis. Johns Hopkins, 1927-29; fellow in med. physics Eldridge Johnson Research Found., U. Pa., 1931-36, asst. prof. biophysics, 1936-40, 41-42, asso. prof. biophysics, 1943-48, prof., 1948-49; asso. prof. physiology Cornell Univ. Med. Coll., N.Y.C., 1940-41; prof. biophysics, chmn. dept. Johns Hopkins, Balt., 1949-53; prof. Rockefeller U., N.Y.C., 1953-74, emeritus, 1974-83. Recipient William H. Howell award physiology, 1927; Howard Crosby Warren medal exptl. psychology, 1948; A.A. Michelson award Case Inst., 1964; Nobel prize in physiology or medicine, 1967; Lighthouse award N.Y.C., 1969. Mem. Nat. Acad. Scis., Am. Physiol. Soc., Am. Philos. Soc., Am. Acad. Arts and Scis., Royal Soc. (fgn. mem; London), Biophys. Soc., Optical Soc. Am. (hon.), Physiol. Soc. (U.K.) (hon.), Phi Beta Kappa, Sigma Xi. Address: Hydes, Md. Died Mar. 17, 1983.

HARTMAN, CARL HENRY, paper mfr.; b. Woodville, O., Nov. 27, 1889; s. Louis H. and Minnie L. (Bruns) H.; m. Clara M. Kortier, Sept. 2, 1914; children—Robert L., John A. Office mgr. Valve Bar Co., Toledo, 1910, successively in charge factory operation, asst. mgr. and asst. sec., asst. mgr. and sec., dir., v.p. and sec., dir., sec. and gen. mgr., dir., v.p. and gen. mgr., 1927-45, co. absorbed by St. Regis Paper Co., v.p. St. Regis Sales Corp., N.Y.C., 1945, v.p. St. Regis Paper Co., from 1951; cons. on packaging. Club: Camp Fire of America. Home: Eustis, Fla. †

HARTMAN, IRVIN H., b. Balt., 1887. Hon. chmn. Leath & Co. Address: Chicago, Ill. †

HARTMAN, JOHN ADAMS, JR., internat. communications exec.; b. Windber, Pa., July 10, 1911; s. John Adams and Fanny (Shook) H.; A.B., Dickinson Coll., 1932; LL.B., George Washington U., 1936; m. Denise Cary, Aug. 19, 1958 (dec.); m. 2d, Thora Lawson, Sept. 13, 1961. Admitted to D.C. bar, 1935; atty. FCC, 1936-41; atty. Am. Cable & Radio Corp., 1946-57, v.p., gen. counsel, 1957-83, dir., 1961-83; dir. All Am. Cables & Radio, Inc., Commercial Cable Co., Press Wireless Incorporated, ITT World Communications, Inc., Globe Wireless, Ltd.; gen. counsel ITT Communications Operations. Served lt. col. USAAF, 1942-46. Mem. Am. Bar Assn., U.S. Supreme Ct. Bar Assn., Phi Kappa Sigma, Phi Delta Phi. Dutch Ref. Home: New York, N.Y. Died July 8, 1983.

HARTMAN, JOHN JACOB, sociology educator; b. Kansas City, Mo., June 5, 1931; s. Jacob Benjamine and Helen Elizabeth (Jones) H.; m. Norma Jean Coffman, Mar. 8, 1954. B.S. Ed. in Sociology, S.W. Mo. State Coll., 1961; M.S. in Sociology, U. Mo., 1963, Ph.D., 1966. Instr. U. Mo., 1964-65; asst. prof. Iowa State U., 1965-68; prof. sociology Wichita (Kans.) State U., 1968-83; Cons., tchr. Urban Tchr. Edn. Program. Served with USNR, 1951-55. Mem. Am. Sociol. Assn., Midwest, Rural sociol. socs., S.W. Social Sci. Assn., Alpha Kappa Delta, Gamma Sigma Delta, Alpha Phi Zeta, Phi Kappa Phi. Home: Wichita, Kans. Died Sept. 15, 1983.

HARTMAN, JOHN MAURICE, jazz singer; b. Chgo., July 3, 1923. Student, Chgo. Musical Coll., 193. Singer with Earl Hines, 1947, Dizzy Gillespie, 1947-48, solo performer, from 1948. Appeared at jazz festivals, London, 1959, Japan, 1963, Australia, 1968, Newport Jazz Festival, 1974; albums include Voice That Is; others. Address: Melville, NY.

HARTSFIELD, WILLIAM BERRY, lawyer, cons.; b. Atlanta, Mar. 1, 1890; s. Charles Green and Victoria (Dagnall) H.; educated in public schools and business college, Atlanta; studied law in law office; married Pearl Williams, August 2, 1913; children—William Berry, Mildred; m. 2d, Mrs. Tollie Tolan, July 11, 1962; one adopted son, Carl Hartsfield. Admitted to Georgia State bar, 1917, from in practice in Atlanta; cons. Ford Foundation, also various Atlanta Corporations. Member of City Council, Atlanta, 1923-28, State Legislature, Georgia, 1933-36; mayor Atlanta, 1937-61; mem. Am. (past pres.), Ga. (past pres.) municipal assns., U.S. Conf. Mayors, Ga. State Bar Assn., Atlanta Lawyers Club, S.E. Fair Assn. (pres.). Mason. Baptist. Club: Capital City. †

HARTSUCH, PAUL JACKSON, editor; b. Kendallville, Ind., Sept. 17, 1902; s. George Wesley and Agnes Isabella (Ritter) H.; m. Lucile Grover, July 2, 1925; children—Grover Paul, George Lynn. B.S. in Chem. Engring, Mich. State U., 1924; M.S., U. Chgo., 1930, Ph.D. in Phys. Chemistry, 1935. Instr. chem. engring. Case Sch. Applied Sci., Cleve., 1927-33; Seymour Coman fellow St. Luke's Hosp., Chgo., 1934-38; mem. chemistry faculty Central YMCA Coll., Chgo., 1938-45, chmn. dept., 1944-45; supr. Lithographic Tech. Found., Chgo., 1945-50; lithographic cons. printing ink div. Inmont Corp., Chgo., 1950-59; asst. to research dir. Graphic Arts Tech. Found., Chgo., 1959-65; editor Graphic Arts Monthly, Chgo., 1965-76, editorial cons., 1976-82. Author: Chemistry of Lithography, 1960, Think Metric Now!, 1974, Chemistry for the Graphic Arts, 1980. Mem. Soc. Fellows of Graphic Arts Tech. Found.; mem. Internat. Assn. Printing-House Craftsmen (Printing Week award 1981), Tech. Assn. Graphic Arts (pres. 1955-56, Honors award 1976), Lithographers Club Chgo. Home: LaGrange, Ill. Died Oct. 3, 1982.

HARVEY, MOSE LOFLEY, educator; b. Friendship, Ga., Nov. 25, 1910; s. Mose Lofley and Pearl (Wells) H.; Ph.B., Emory U., 1930, M.A., 1931; Ph.D., U. Cal., 1938; m. Mary Ruth Vaughn, Aug. 11, 1931; 1 son, Dodd Lofley. Grad. fellow Social Sci. Research Council, 1932-33, grant for research USSR, 1939; spl. Rockefeller fellow for advanced research USSR, 1941-42; asst. prof. history Emory U., 1933-41; research sec. Council Fgn. Relations, 1941-42; chief economist WPB, 1942-43, dep. dir. fgn. div., 1943-46; dir. Bur. Internat. Supply, Civilian Prodn. Adminstrn., 1946-47; dir. U.S. staff, dep. U.S. mem. Combined Prodn. Resources Bd., 1946; cons. Soviet affairs Dept. State, 1947-48, chief div. research and intelligence USSR and Eastern Europe, 1948-55, cons. and sec. in Diplomatic Service, 1955; assigned as instr. Nat. War Coll., 1955, dir. polit. affairs div., 1955-57; mem. policy planning staff Dept. State, 1957; dep. chief mission, counselor embassy Am. embassy, Helsinki, Finland, 1957-59; consul gen., FS01 Diplomatic Service, 1959; dep. U.S. rep. Internat. Atomic Energy Agy., 1959-61; sr. mem. Policy Planning Council, 1961-64; prof. history, dir. Center Advanced Internat. Studies, U. Miami (Fla.), 1964-85. Cons. to adminstr. NASA, 1965-69, U.S. Dept. State, 1964-70; lectr. on Soviet history Johns Hopkins, 1947-48, Soviet affairs Sch. Advanced Internat. Studies, 1951-57; guest lectr. Nat. War Coll., Indsl. War Coll., 1947-65; commentator internat. affairs radio sta. WSB, Atlanta, 1940-42. Mem. Am. Hist. Assn., Phi Beta Kappa, Omicron Delta Kappa. Methodist. Author: Focus on the Soviet Challenge, 1963; East-West Trade and United States Policy, 1966; Science and Technology as

Instrument of Soviet Policy, 1972; Soviet Strategy for the Seventies, 1972. Contbr. articles to profl. jours. Chmn. bd. editors Jour. Inter-Am. Studies, from 1968; editor Soviet World Outlook. Home: Miami, Fla. Died Feb. 25, 1985.

HARVEY, ROBERT OTTO, educator; b. Bloomington, Ind., Dec. 12, 1923; s. Paul and Amy (Arnett) H.; m. Margaret Johnson, Aug. 28, 1948; children—David W., Robert Otto (dec.), John P. B.S., Ind. U., 1947, M.B.A., 1949, D.B.A., 1951. Asst. prof. real estate Ind. U., 1948-52; vis. lectr. U. Calif. at Berkeley, 1952-53; mem. faculty U. Ill., 1953-63, prof. finance, 1959-63, dir. exec. devel. center, 1961-63; dean Sch. Bus. Adminstrn., U. Conn., Storrs, 1963-73, prof. bus., 1973-76, prof. emeritus, 1976-81; dir. Research Center for Real Estate and Econ. Studies, 1973-76; prof., chmn. real estate and regional sci. So. Meth. U., Dallas, 1976-81; also dir. Costa Inst. Real Estate Finance; trustee Henry S. Muller Realty Trust; econ. cons. Dallas Fed. Savs.; dir. Hartford Fund Inc., Am. Nat. Financial Corp., Am. Nat. Ins. Co.; separate account com. Hartford Variable Annuity Life Ins. Co. Author: Land Uses in Bloomington, Indiana, 1818-1950, 1951. Mem. Gov.'s Commn. on Tax Reform.; Trustee Heitman mortgage investor. Served to 1st lt., inf. AUS, 1943-46. Mem. Am. Savs. and Loan Inst. (hon.), Newcomen Soc., Beta Gamma Sigma (nat. pres. 1972-74), Lambda Alpha, Delta Sigma Pi, Omicron Delta Kappa, Sigma Iota Epsilon, Sigma Alpha Epsilon, Tau Kappa Alpha, Theta Alpha Phi. Home: Dallas, Tex. Died July 1981.†

HARWICK, HARRY JOHN, business exec.; b. Sherburne County, nr. Elk River, Minn., Sept. 2, 1887; s. John and Effie (Spickerman) H.; ed. pub. schs., Winona, Minn.; m. Margaret Graham, Nov. 16, 1910; children—John William, Margaret Esther (Mrs. W. E. Herrell), Mary Anne (Mrs. C. L. Sundberg). Bookkeeper, First Nat. Bank, Rochester, Minn., 1906-08; bookkeeper, Mayo Clinic, 1908-10, bus. mgr., 1910-20, sec.-treas., 1920-47, exec. officer, 1947-52; sec.-treas. Mayo Assn., 1919-39, chmn. 1939-53; trustee and mem. exec. com. Northwestern Mutual Life Ins. Co., Milwaukee; dir. First National Bank of Rochester, Weber & Judd Drug Co. Chmn. Rochester Cemetery Assn., C. of C. Mem. Am. Hosp. Assn., Am. Coll. Hosp. Adminstrs., Am. Museum Natural History, Nat. Inst. Social Sci. Conglist. Mason (K.T.) Clubs: Rochester Golf and Country, Rochester University; Milwaukee; Minnesota (St. Paul); Minneapolis; Lake Francis Shooting Assn. (Can.). †

HASSENFELD, MERRILL LLOYD, mfg. co. exec.; b. Providence, Feb. 29, 1918; s. Henry J. and Marion L. (Frank) H.; B.S. in Econs., Wharton Sch., U. Pa., 1938; m. Sylvia Kay, Oct. 15, 1940; children—Stephen D., Ellen Hassenfeld Block, Alan G. With HASBRO Industries, Pawtucket, R.I., vice chmn. bd., chief exec. officer; v.p., dir. Mallard Pen & Pencil Co., Blue Ribbon Pen and Pencil Co.; dir. Jerusalem Pencil Co. (Israel), Narragansett Electric Co. Trustee Miriam Hosp., Providence, Jewish Home Aged of R.I.; life trustee United Israel Appeal; hon. pres., bd. dirs. Jewish Fedn. R.I.; vice chmn. United Way Southeastern New Eng.; exec. com., hon. chmn. United Jewish Appeal. Served with AUS, 1945. Home: Providence, R.I. Died 1979.

HASTINGS, WALTER SCOTT, prof. modern langs.; b. Snow Hill, Md., Jan. 17, 1890; s. Laurence Hastings and Emma (Scott) H.; A.B., Princeton Univ., 1910, M.A., 1911; Ph.D., Johns Hopkins, 1916; unmarried. Instr. French, Union Coll., Schenectady, N.Y., 1911-13; Johns Hopkins, 1915; instructor French, Princeton, 1920-35, professor modern languages, 1935-42. Served as 1st lt. inf., World War; asst. mil. attaché, Am. Legation, Berne, Switzerland, 1919. Mem. Modern Lang. Assn., Assn. Am. Coll. Profs. Author: The Drama of Honoré de Balzac, 1917; Balzac and Souverain, 1927. Editor: Balzac's Cromwell, 1925; French Prose and Poetry (1850-1900), 1926; Balzac's Letters to His Family, 1934; The Student's Balzac, 1937. Contbr. articles. Home: Snow Hill, Md. †

HASTY, FREDERICK EMERSON, physician; born Ball Ground, Ga., Aug. 21, 1888; s. John Terrell and Harriet (Cockran) H.; grad. Reinhardt College, Waleska, Ga., 1912; M.D., Vanderbilt, 1917; m. Mary Ethel Washburn, Apr. 19, 1917; children—Frederick Emerson, Marian Francis; m. 2d, Bessie N. Vaughan, September 6, 1943. Student instructor in anatomy, Vanderbilt, 1916-17; resident physician, City View Sanitarium, Nashville, 1917-18; asst. and house surgeon, Manhattan Eye and Ear Hosp., N.Y. City, 1918-20; began practice as ear, nose and throat specialist, Nashville, 1920; asst., eye, ear, nose and throat dept., Vanderbilt Med. Sch., 1922-38; mem. visiting staff Nashville Gen. Hosp., Protestant Hosp., St. Thomas Hosp. Fellow A.M.A. (com. for study of hygienic swimming), Am. Coll. Surgeons; mem. Southern Med. Assn. (chmn. eye, ear, nose and throat sect.), Am. Laryngol., Rhinol and Otol. Soc., Tenn. State Med. Soc., Tenn. State Eye, Ear, Nose and Throat Soc. Baptist. Mason (Shriner). Home: South Miami, Fla. †

HATCH, RICHARD ALLEN, clergyman; b. Monroe City, Mo., Mar. 13, 1890; s. Rev. Wm. Allen and Martha (Thomas) H.; A.B., Washington U., St. Louis, Mo., 1913; grad. Gen. Theol. Sem., New York, 1916; student Columbia, 1914, U. of Poitiers, France, 1919; m. Mildred Mack, of St. Louis, Mo., Aug. 10, 1930. Ordained deacon and priest, P.E. Ch., 1916; rector Palmyra, Mo., 1919, Ottawa, Kan., 1921, Ada, Okla., 1922; rector St. Andrews Ch., Clearfield, Pa., 1923-24, then rector St. Luke's Ch., Altoona, Pa., and now Grace and St. Peters Ch., Baltimore, resigned, 1936; temporary work in dioceses of N.J. and Newark while taking grad. work at Columbia; now rector at Woodcliff, N.J. Sabbatical yr. spent at Good Shepherd Ch., Jacksonville, Florida. Chaplain U.S.A. during World War, serving with 35th Division in Argonne and Meuse. Chmn. Diocesan Bd. Religious Edn.; mem. Diocesan Council (Harrisburg, Pa.). Hon. canon St. Stephens Cathedral (Harrisburg). Mason. Address: Woodcliff, N.J. †

HATHAWAY, STARKE R(OSECRANS), clinical psychologist; b. Central Lake, Mich., Aug. 22, 1903; s. Martin Walter and Bertha Bell (Rosecrans) H.; A.B., Ohio U., 1927, A.M., Ohio State U., 1928; Ph.D., University of Minnesota 1932; L.H.D., Ohio University, 1966; m. (Mary) Virginia Riddle, Aug. 25, 1928. Instr., Ohio U., 1927-29, asst. prof., 1929-30; lecturer in psychology U. of Minn., 1930-37, asst. prof. psychiatry and clin. psychologist, 1937-40, asso. prof., 1940-47, prof. clin. psychology since 1947, dir. div. clin. psychology since 1951; vis. porf., Thomas Wilton research fellow Stanford, 1952-53. Served as expert, Adjutant General Office, 1943-45; chief clin. psychologist Vets. Administrn., Fort Snelling, St. Paul, 1946-47, cons. in psychology V.A., St. Paul. Fulbright prof., Nat. U. of Mexico, 1964-65. Certified psychologist Minnesota State Board Examiners of Psychologists. Diplomate in clin. psychology, Am. Bd. Examainers in Profl. Psychology. Fellow Am. Psychol. Assn. (scientific contbn. award 1959); mem. Midwestern, Minnesota psychological associations, Sigma Xi, Phi Beta Kappa. Author books including: Atlas for the Clinical Use of the MMPI (with P.E. Meehl), 1951; Analyzing and Predicting Delinquency with the MMPI (with E.D. Monachesi), 1953; Adolescent Personality and Behavior, 1963. Home: Minneapolis, Minn. Died July 5, 1984.

HATTERSLEY, J(OHN) F(RANK), co. exec.; born Brooklyn, Dec. 10, 1889; s. John Thomas and Emily Maude (Rice) H.; student pub. schs. of Newark; m. Gertrude B. Riley, Apr. 7, 1915; 1 son, Robert Frank. Engring. dept. Crocker-Wheeler Co. of Ampere (N.J.), 1907-16; chief draftsman Reliance Electric & Engring. Co., Cleveland, 1916-20; joined Hoover Co. North Canton, Ohio, 1920, president and director, 1951-53; chairman of the board of Gussett Boiler & Welding, Inc., Canton; pres., dir. Hoover Company, Limited, Hamilton, Ont., 1951-54; past pres., director Am. Die Casting Inst. Member Canton C. of C. (director 1940-42). Methodist. Mason (32 deg.). Club: Canton. Home: North Canton, Ohio. †

HATTSTAEDT, JOHN ROBERT, educator; b. Chgo., Aug. 21, 1887; s. John James and Kate May (Castle) H.; student Princeton, 1905-08; m. Maren G. Johansen, July 18, 1930; children—John James II, Jane Ann; married second, Ethel Beck, September 29, 1956. Advertising dept. George Kleine Co., motion picture importers, Chgo., 1910-14; sec. Am. Conservatory Music, 1914-24, asst. mgr., 1924-31, v.p., mgr., 1931-35, pres., mgr. from 1935; pres. Ellencourt Bldg. Corp. Chgo., from 1938. Republican. Lutheran. Clubs: Cliff Dwellers, University, Princeton (Chgo.); Skokie Country (Glencoe, Ill.). Home: Chicago, Ill. †

HAUGAN, RANDOLPH EDGAR, publisher; b. Martel, Wis., July 31, 1902; s. Torgier H. and Hilda (Ehrhardt) H.; A.B., St. Olaf Coll., Northfield, Minn. 1924; LL.D., Luther Coll., Decorah, Iowa, 1944; m. Mildred Kathryn Knudson, Aug. 5, 1924; children—Mary, James. Gen. mgr. Augsburg Pub. House, Mpls., 1929-70; dir. Marquette Nat. Bank, Mpls., Luth. Brotherhood (Legal Res. Life Ins.), Mpls., 1947-59; v.p. Graphic Arts Industry, Mpls. 1939-54; nat. pres. Pubs. Adv. Sect. of Internat. Council Religious Edn., 1941-42; mem. Charter Commn., Mpls. 1944. Chmn. bd. trustees St. Olaf Coll., 1950-54; bd. mem. United Hosp. Fund, Minn. Coll. Fund Assn.; past mem. Selective Service Bd., Hennepin County; state chmn. Am. Relief for Norway; v.p. bd. dirs. Fairview Community Hosp., Mpls.; past adv. bd. Minn Poll; mem. joint polity and orgn. com. formation Am-Luth. Ch.; bd. mem. bd. Protestant Ch.-Owned Pubs. Assn., from 1952; exec. dir. div. publs. Am. Luth. Ch., 1961-70. Mem. joint polity and orgn. com. formation Evang. Luth. Church of Can.; councillor Nat. Luth. Council, 1945-54, 61. Decorated knight first class Royal Order of St. Olaf (Norway), 1948. Republican. Kiwanian. Clubs: Minneapolis Athletic. Editor: Christmas in Many Lands, Vols. 1-3, 1936-38; Yuletide in Many Lands, Vols. 4-7, 1939-42; Christmas, An American Annual. Home: Minneapolis, Minn. Died Feb. 18, 1985.

HAUSER, EMIL DANIEL WILLIAM, orthopedic surgeon; b. Freeland, Pa., Feb. 22, 1897; s. Karl and Wilhelmina (Volkert) H.; m. Mary Frances Thomas, July 28, 1930; children: Joan Thomas Hauser Gately, Emil David William, Constance Hauser Tresch, Mary Hauser Dunn, Kevin. Student, Concordia Coll., St. Paul, 1911-15; B.S., U. Minn., 1918, M.S., 1921, M.D., 1922, M.S. in Orthopedic Surgery, 1927; postgrad. study, others. Diplomate: Am. Bd. Orthopedic Surgeons. Postgrad. fellow in surgery U. Minn., 1923; fellow orthopedic surgery, mem. staff Mayo Clinic, 1924-25; Am.-Scandinavian fellow in orthopedic surgery, 1926; asso. Dr. H.B. Thomas, Chgo., 1927-29; staff med. sch. Northwestern U., from 1930, assoc. prof. bone and joint surgery, from 1949, med. dir. course in phys. therapy, 1950-54; also Poliomyelitis Epidemic Aid Unit, 1945-53; attending orthopedic surgeon (pres. med. staff 1959-60) Passavant Meml. Hosp., Chgo.; dir. Winnetka Med. Center. Author: Curvatures of the Spine, 1962, Congenital Clubfoot, 1966; Contbg. author: Surgical Treatment of the Motor Skeletal System; Contbr. articles to med. jours. Served as hosp. apprentice U.S. Navy, World War I. Mem. Am. Acad. Orthopedic Surgeons, Am. Orthopedic Assn., A.C.S., AMA, Clin. Orthopedic Assn., Chgo. Orthopedic Soc., Ill. Med. Soc., Am. Assn. Railway Surgs., Inst. Medicine Chgo., Société Internationale de Chirugie Orthopedique et de Traumatologie, Société Belge d'Orthopedic et de Chirurgie de l'Appariel Moteur, Sociedad Latino-Americana de Ortopedia Y Traumatologia, Pan-Am. Med. Assn., Alpha Sigma Phi, Nu Sigma Nu. Republican. Lutheran. Clubs: Med-Am. (Chgo.); Indian Hill (Winnetka, Ill.). Home: Sun City, Ariz. Died Nov. 18, 1982.

HAVERSTICK, EDWARD EVERETT, JR., investment banker; b. St. Louis, June 30, 1907; s. Edward Everett and Laura (Krenning) H.; m. Doris Emily Briggs, Aug. 26, 1942 (dec. Feb. 1981); children—Doris Mather, Laura Krenning, Sarah Vinyard. A.B., Washington U., St. Louis, 1926; LL.B., Benton Coll., 1935. Chartered fin. analyst. With Graham Paper Co., 1927-28, R.H. Cobb & Co., 1928-30, First Nat. Co., 1930-32, E.E. Haverstick & Co., 1933-41; with Smith, Moore & Co., St. Louis, 1946-83, gen. partner, 1951-83; pres., dir. Radio St. Louis, Inc. (Sta. KSTL). Pres., bd. dirs. Neighborhood Assn., 1960-62, Childrens Home Soc. of Mo., 1965-67; bd. dirs. Neighborhood Assn., 1934-83. Served to comdr. USNR, 1942-46. Mem. St. Louis Soc. Fin. Analysts (pres. 1967), Mo. Bar, Bar Assn. Met. St. Louis, Sigma Alpha Epsilon. Episcopalian. Clubs: Noonday (St. Louis), St. Louis Country (St. Louis). Home: Saint Louis, Mo. Died 1983.

HAWES, HENRY QUINBY, advt. exec.; b. Westbrook, Me., Oct. 4, 1888; s. Henry Hill Boody and Ellen Catherine (Quinby) H.; A.B., Bowdoin Coll., 1910; M.A., Columbia, 1911; m. Corinne M. White, June 8, 1925. Mgr. Mechanics Inst., Rumford, Me., 1911-13; with McCann-Erickson, Inc., N.Y.C., 1913-14, San Francisco, from 1914, sr. v.p., Pacific Coast regional mgr., dir., from 1921; dir. Am. Trust Co. Chmn. publicity campaign, exec. com. San Francisco Community Chest, 1929-35; chmn. fund raising Golden Gate Internat. Expn., 1939-40; chmn. budget com. War Chest of San Francisco, 1945. Trustee, mem. finance com. Mills Coll., 1938-48. Served as 1st lt. F.A., U.S. Army, 1917-19. Mem. San Francisco Stock Exchange Club, Phi Beta Kappa, Theta Delta Chi. Clubs: Pacific Union, Bohemian (San Francisco). Breeder purebred registered Herefords. †

HAWKES, ANNA L. ROSE, ednl. administrator; b. Mansfield, Pa., May 18, 1890; d. James Emerson and Margaret Burns (Everett) Rose; A.B., George Washington U., 1912, A.M., 1924; Ph.D., Teachers Coll. (Columbia), 1932; m. Herbert Edwin Hawkes, Feb. 17, 1934. Teacher of German, Mansfield (Pa.) State Normal Sch., 1912-19; ednl. dir. Y.W.C.A., Washington, D.C., 1919-21; registrar George Washington U., 1921-24, dean of women, 1924-29; staff asst. Carnegie Foundation for Advancement of Teaching, 1929-39. Secretary to Finch Junior College, New York, N.Y., 1944-45; dean of students Mills Coll., 1945-55. Member U.S. delegation UNESCO Conf., 1958, U.S. Nat. Commn. for UNESCO, 1959-65; U.S. Adv. Commission Educational Exchange, Dept. of State. Mem. Am. Assn. U. Women (pres. from 1955), Nat. Assn. Deans Women, A.C.P.A., Chi Omega, Kappa Beta Pi. Republican. Episcopalian. Author books incldg.: Through The Dean's Open Door (with late husband Herbert E. Hawkes), 1945. Contbr. to various publs. Home: Orleans, Vt. †

HAWKINS, BERTRAM SPENCE, cotton textile mfg.; b. New York, N.Y., Jan. 5, 1888; s. William Spence and Harriet Mellisa (Roberge) H.; student N.Y. City pub. sch. and high sch.; m. Ethel Belle Coombs, Jan. 13, 1933. Accountant Am. Locomotive Co., N.Y. City, 1905-10; traveling auditor Gen. Electric Co., 1910-12; sec. and gen. mgr. Phillips Wire Co., Pawtucket, R.I., 1916-23; financial and official sec. to Senator Jesse H, Metcalf, R.I., 1923-26; comptroller Wanskuck Co., Providence, R.I.; pres. and treas. Guerin Mills, Inc., Woonsocket, R.I., 1926-36; pres., treas. and dir. Merrimack Mfg. Co., Boston, from 1937. Baptist, Clubs: Manhattan (N.Y.C.); Noon Day, Algonquin. Union League (N.Y. City). Home: Wellesley Hills, Mass. †

HAWKINS, ROBERT BRUCE, laywer; b. Phila., Dec. 12, 1928; s. Harry Linton and Jessica Loretta (Cutlip) H.; B.A., Amherst Coll., 1951; postgrad. Harvard, 1953-54, U. Pa. Grad. Sch. Econs., 1954-56; J.D., U. Minn., 1960; m. Nancy Jane Perry, Aug. 30, 1954; children—Philip, Mike, Martha. Asst. personnel mgr. Esterbrook Pen Co., 1954-56; advt. rep. Phila. Bull., 1956-57; admitted to Minn. bar, 1960; asso. firm Oppenheimer, Wolff, Foster, Shepard & Donnelly, Mpls., 1960-63, partner, 1964-74; v.p., gen. counsel, sec. Control Data Corp., 1974-80. Atty., Village of North Oaks, 1963-76. Mem. Am., Minn. bar assns., Order of Coif, Alpha Delta Phi, Phi Delta Phi. Clubs: Minneapolis, North Oaks Golf, Decathlon, St. Croix Yacht. Home: Saint Paul, Minn. Died Jan. 27, 1980.

HAWKINS, ROBERT MARTYR, clergyman, educator; b. Boonville, Mo., Feb. 21, 1887; s. Charles Martyr and Mary Agnes (Mathews) H.; A.B., Washington U., 1906; M.A., Central Coll., 1907; B.D., Vanderbilt U., 1910;

Ph.D., U. Edinburgh, 1927; D.D., Birmingham-So. Coll., 1923; grad. study Yale, 1926-27; m. Reuben Mastin Clarke, Dec. 7, 1916. Ordained to ministry Meth. Ch., deacon, 1912, elder, 1914; minister S.W. Mo. Conf., 1910-18; pastor Cleveland Av. Ch., Kansas City, Mo., Independence, Springfield, and Warrensburg, Mo.; prof. philosophy and Bibl. lit. Birmingham (Ala.)-So. Coll., 1918-23, registrar, 1919-23; prof. Bibl. lit. and religious edn. Southwestern Coll., Winfield, Kan., 1923-28; prof. O.T. Vanderbilt U., Nashville, 1928-32, prof. Bibl. literature, 1933-38, professor New Testament, 1939-55, emeritus professor, from 1955, registrar, 1929-34; Jeanette Miriam Goldberg lectr. Hebrew Union Coll., 1950. Mem. S.W. Mo. Conf. Meth. Ch., 1910-18, 1923-28, N. Ala. Conf., 1918-23, Tenn. Conf. since 1928. Mem. Soc. Bibl. Lit. and Exegesis, Pi Gamma Mu. Author: The Recovery of the Historical Paul, 1943; also articles in profl. jours. and religious publs. Home: Nashville, Tenn.†

HAWKINS, SION BOONE, army officer; b. Americus, Ga., Aug. 19, 1887; student U. of Ga. Enlisted as private, 4th Regiment, Ga. Nat. Guard, 1904; sgt. 5th Inf., 1912-14; entered 7th Provincial Training Regt., Ft. McPherson, Ga., 1917; commd. 2d lt., Officer's Res. Corps, 321st Machine Gun Batt., 1st lt., 82d Div., in France, 1918; honorably discharged, Camp Gordon, Ga., June 14, 1919; commd. major, Ga. Nat. Guard, 1926, lt. col., 1933, brig. gen., 1941; adjutant gen. of Ga., 1941; dir. Selective Service System, Atlanta, Ga., from May 20, 1941.†

HAWLEY, CHARLES ARTHUR, author, college prof.; b. Verona, N.Y., Dec. 3, 1889; s. Charles Andrew and Clara Elizabeth (Russell) H.; A.B., Hamilton Coll., Clinton, N.Y., 1916; S.T.B., Union Theol. Sem., N.Y. City, 1919 S.T.M., 1920; Ph.D., Columbia, 1922; student U. of Basel, Switzerland, 1920-21, also U. of Halle, Germany, Am. Sch. Archaeology, Jerusalem, Palestine; m. Barbara Kimball, June 25, 1924; children—Mary Barbara, Bernard Russell, Charels Dickinson. Ordained to Presbyn. ministry, 1918; pastor of the First Presbyterian Ch., Atchison, Kan., 1941-48; professor, head department language and literature, Ottawa U., Kan., from 1948. Moderator of the Synod of Kan., 1944-45. Mem. Palestine Oriental Soc., Archaeol. Inst. Am., State Hist. Soc. Kan., Am. Soc. of Ch. Hist., Am Oriental Soc., Phi Beta Kappa. Rep. Mason (32 deg.). Author books including: Duncan Chambers Milner: Militant Idealist, 1945, Contbr. sects., articles, book revs. to religious jours.†

HAWLEY, JEAN H., hydrographic and geodetic engr.; b. Colton, N.Y., Sept. 11, 1887; s. Morris B. and Lucia (Hodgkins) H.; B.S. in Civil Engring., Clarkson Coll. Tech., Potsdam, N.Y., 1907; m. Fannie L. Hopkins, Nov. 2, 1915; 1 dau., Lucia Frances (wife of Lt. James H. Starkey, Jr., U.S.N.R.). With Coast and Geodetic Survey from 1907, comd. ships Onward, Wenonah, Explorer, Lydonia, 1920-24, chief, coast pilot section, Washington, D.C., 1924-30, dir. coast surveys, Philippine Islands, 1930-32, asst. dir., Washington, D.C., 1932-49, rank of rear adm. from 1942, ret., 1949. Mem. Soc. Am. Military Engrs., Am. Geophys. Union. Club: Columbia Country (Chevy Chase, Md.). Author: Construction and Operation of the Wire Drag, 1919; Construction and Operation of the Wire Drag and Sweep, 1925; Hydrographic Manual, 1931. Home: Washington, D.C. †

HAWTHORN, HORACE BOIES, sociologist; b. Castana, Iowa, Dec. 4, 1889; s. William Franklin and Annie (Masters) H.; student State U. Iowa, 1907; B.S., Iowa State Coll., 1914, M.S., 1915; Ph.D., U. Wis. (fellow in econs. 1920), 1922; m. Hazel Waples, Sept. 21, 1916; children—Miriam (Mrs. John Nye), Clarice (Mrs. Donald Watson), Horace Duane. Asst. prof. sociology Iowa State Coll., 1921-26; asso. prof. sociology, Municipal U. Akron, 1926-30; prof. sociology Morningside Coll., Sioux City, Iowa, 1931-58, prof. emeritus and research sociologist, from 1958; rural sociologist Iowa Agrl. Expt. Sta., 1925-26; research sociologist Better Akron Fedn., 1926-30; lectr. Civic and Welfare Assn., 1928. Recipient Merit award for distinguished Service in writing a world record book on immortality Editors Dictionary Internat. Biography, 1970. Mem. Am. Sociol. Soc., AAUP, Nat. Writers Club, Alpha Kapps Delta, Phi Kappa Phi, Delta Sigma Rho, Gamma Sigma Delta, Pi Gamma Mu. Methodist. Author: Outlines of Sociology, 1923; Sociology of Rural Life, 1926; Sociology of the World Crisis, 1947; Efficiency of Akron Welfare Agencies Board, 1928; Sociology of the United Nations World, 1952; Culture of Sioux City Youth, bull., 1936; Sociology of Personality Functioning, 1954; The Immortal Survival of the Human Personality, 1959, enlarged edit., 1967, popular edit., 1975; A Case Study of Iowa School Reorganization, 1966; Social Factors In a Scholastic Writing Career, 1968; Scientific Evidence of Man's Power to Survive into a Future Life, 1977. Research in personality adjustment in rural and urban communities. Home: Sioux City, Iowa. Deceased.

HAYES, ALBERT J(OHN), labor union exec.; b. Milw., Feb. 14, 1900; s. Albert and Augusta (Wolter) H.; student pub. schs.; m. Lilliam M. Fink, Feb. 25, 1921; 1 dau., Jane (Mrs. E. Blankenship). Apprentice and machinist C., M., St.P. & P. R.R., 1917-21; gen. machinist C.& N.W. Ry., 1921-34; gen. chmn. dist. 7 Internat. Assn. Machinists, 1924-34, grand lodge rep., 1934-44, gen. v.p., 1944-49, internat. pres., 1949-1981; vice pres. AFL, 1952-55, v.p. AFL-CIO, 1955-1981; chairman AFL-CIO Ethieal Practices Committee. Served as labor mem. War Labor Bd. from 6th region, 1942-44; co-chmn. United Labor Policy Com., 1951; asst. to Asst. Sec. Def., 1951-52; mem. Pres.'s Commn. on Health Needs of Nation, 1952, Nat. Manpower Council of Columbia U., labor-management manpower policy com. O.D.M., Pres.'s Com. on Nat. Enploy the Physically Handicapped; mem. Nat. Security Tng. Commn., Nat. Citizens Commn. for Pub. Schs., White House Conf. on Edn. Labor chmn. Am. Nat. Red Cross, 1952; dir. Am. Heart Assn.; trustee Nat. Planning Assn. Lutheran. Eagle. Home: Silver Spring, Md. Died Aug. 16, 1981.

HAYES, HOYT E., corp. exec.; b. St. Louis, Feb. 27, 1890; s. Harry E. and Grace L. (Green) H.; grad. Sheffield Sci. Sch., Yale, 1911; m. Dorothy Barber, Dec. 10, 1924; m. 2d, Marie H. Holdgate Oct. 24, 1941. With Indsl. Brownhoist Corp., Bay City, from 1912, European rep., v.p. sales, pres., 1939-54; pres. dir. Green Foundry Co., St. Louis; dir. Peoples Nat. Bank, Bay City, Resistance Welder Co., Bay City. Home: Bay City, Mich. †

HAYES, JAMES JUVENAL, coll. prof.; b. San Jose, Calif., Dec. 14, 1889; s. Doremus Almy and Hester (Juvenal) II.; A.B., Harvard, 1911, A.M., 1912; Ph.D., State Univ. of Ia., 1938; grad. study U. of Chicago, 1912-14; m. Margaret Brand, Sept. 1, 1915; children—Hester Juliet (Mrs. Paul K. Perkins), Dorothy Margaret (Mrs. Lyman W. Riley), James Brand. Head of English dept. Morningside Coll., Sioux City, Ia., 1914-32, head English dept. Oklahoma City U. from 1932, chmn. div. gen. edn. from 1952. Mem. Modern Lang. Assn. Okla. State Writers, Puppeteers of Am. Stereoescoic Soc. Am., Lambda Chi Alpha. Methodist. Club: Camera (past pres.). Author: Old English for Beginners, 1947; Shortype, a system of shorthand based on English letters, 1946. Home: Oklahoma City, Okla. †

HAYES, JOHN W., osteo. surgeon; b. Chillicothe, Ohio; grad. Kirksville Coll. Osteo. and Surgery, 1928; married; 1 dau. Began practice osteo. medicine, 1928. Mem. adv. bd. Am. Profl. Practice Assn., 1967-82. Trustee Eastern Ohio chpt. Am. Heart Assn., pres. Columbiana County chpt.; permanent chmn. Columbiana County Bd. Mental Health and Retardation; trustee Columbiana County Mental Health Clinic. Diplomate Am. Osteo. Bd. Surgery. Fellow Am. Coll. Osteo. Surgeons; mem. Am. Osteo. Assn. (pres. 1966-67, chmn. chpt. bus. affairs; chmn. bur. comprehensive health planning 1967-69), Ohio Osteo. Assn. Physicians and Surgeons (trustee, past pres.; mem. ho. dels.), Columbiana County Mental Health Assn. (pres. 1968-69), C. of C., Psi Sigma Alpha (exec. sec.-treas.). Lutheran. Mason (32 deg., K.T., Shriner), Elk. Home: East Liverpool, Ohio. Died Feb. 16, 1982.

HAYES, REGINALD CARROLL, pub. co. exec.; b. Richmond, Va., Apr. 1, 1928; s. Frank and Willie Cloria (Henry) H.; m. Carmen Bontemps; children—Jacquelyn, Jocelyn, Reginald, Nicole. B.S., Va. State Coll., 1952; M.S. in Edn, Chgo. Tchrs. Coll., 1964; postgrad., U. Chgo., 1965-67; LL.D. (hon.), St. Paul's Coll., 1980. Lang. arts tchr. Chgo. Pub. Schs., 1958-66, TV producer and dir., 1966-70; columnist, bus. editor Chgo. Courier, 1966-70; v.p. public affairs and promotion Johnson Pub. Co., Chgo., from 1970. Contbr. articles to popular mags. Served to 1st lt. AUS, 1952-55; maj. Res. Mem. U.S. C. of C., Chgo. United, Chgo. Public Relations Clinic, Mag. Pubs. Assn., Econ. Club Chgo., Omega Psi Phi. Episcopalian. Address: Chicago, Ill.

HAYES, THOMAS JAY, army officer; b. Ironton, O., Sept. 18, 1888; s. Thomas J. and Susanna (Davis) H.; B.S., U.S. Mil. Acad., 1912; grad. Army Industrial Coll., 1931, Army War Coll., 1932; m. Mary Louise Ringwalt, Nov. 12, 1913; children—Thomas J., III, Theodore R., Mary Louise (Mrs. William Peek Brett). Commd. 2d lt., U.S. Inf., June 12, 1912; promoted thourgh grades to major gen., U.S. Army, February 1942; with 4th Inf., Ft. Crook, Neb., Galveston, Tex., Vera Cruz, Mex., and Ft. Brown, Tex., 1912-15; instr. Ordnance and Gunnery, West Point, Dec. 1915-July 1917; capt. Ordnance Dept., San Antonio Arsenal, July 1917-Jan. 1918; maj. ordnance officer 5th Div., Camp Logan, Tex. and A.E.F., Jan.-Oct. 1918; asst. chief of staff, 4th Div., Jan.-May 1919; exec. officer Ordnance Sch. of Application, Aberdeen Proving Ground, Md., June 1919-Oct. 1920; transferred to Ordnance Dept. with rank of major, July 1, 1920; ordnance officer 7th Corps Area, Ft. Crook, Nov. 1920-Jan. 1922; chief of mil. Personnel Div., Office of Chief of Ordnance, Jan. 1922-July 1925; ordnance officer 9th Corps Area, Presidio of San Francisco, Aug. 1925-May 1928, 8th Corps Area, Ft. Sam Houston, Tex., June 1928-July 1930; exec. officer Chief of Ordnance, 1932-33; prof. Ordnance and Science of Gunnery, U.S. Mil. Acad., July 1933-July 1938; works mgr. Springfield (Mass.) Armory, July 1938-Dec. 1940; in production div., Industrial Service, Office of Chief of Ordnance, Washington, Dec. 1940-July 1941; div. of production branch. Office of the Under Sec. of War, July 1941-Mar. 1942; chief, production branch, Hdqrs. S.O.S., Mar.-May 1942; chief, Industrial Service, Ordnance. Dept., June 1942-Apr. 1945; retired as major general; September 1945. Awarded Legion of Merit, Distinguished Service Medal. Mem. Army Ordnance Assn. Episcopalian. Clubs: Army and Navy (Washington); Army and Navy Country (Arlington, Va.). Author: Elements of Ordnance, 1938. Home: Falls Church, Va. †

HAYES, THOMAS MICHAEL, railroad official; b. Morrisonville, Ill., Oct. 9, 1887; s. Michael and Mary Ellen (Bray) H.; ed. pub. sch., Morrisonville, Ill.; St. Teresa's Acad., Decatur, Ill., 1900-03; m. Marie Van Leunen, April 15, 1913; children—John Joseph Francis (commander, U.S. Navy), Thomas Michael (lt. comdr., U.S.N.R.). Sect. hand, Wabash Ry., 1903; successivley sec. to supt., sec. to supt. transportation, sec., then asst. to pres., asst. gen. mgr., asst. passenger traffic mgr., mgr. from 1939. Mem. Pub. Relations Assn. of Am. R.R.'s (advisory com.). Republican. Catholic. K.C. Clubs: Missouri Athletic Club, Rotary (St. Louis); various traffic and transportation clubs: Home: Saint Louis, Mo. †

HAYES, WILLIAM PATRICK, prof. entomology; born Leadville, Colo., June 26, 1887; s. John and Sarah (Doonarr) H.; B.S.; Kan. State Coll., 1913, M.S., 1918; Ph.D., Cornell U., 1923; m. Louise Jacobs, Nov. 13, 1914; children—Mary Louise, William (dec.), John Charles, Jean Margaret. Asst., Kan. Agrl. Expt. Sta., 1914-18; asst. prof. Kan. State Coll., 1918-24; instr. Cornell U., 1922-23; asst. prof. U. of Ill., 1924-27, also prof., 1927-39, prof. entomology from 1939, acting head dept., 1947-49, head of dept. from 1949. Mem. Am. Entomol. Soc., Am. Assn. Econ. Entomology, Sigma Xi. Contbr. to entomol. jours. Home: Urbana, Ill. †

HAYS, BROOKS, former congressman, lawyer, educator; b. Russellville, Ark., Aug. 9, 1898; s. Adelbert Steele and Sallie (Butler) H.; m. Marian Prather, Feb. 2, 1922; children—Betty Brooks (Mrs. William E. Bell), Marion Steele. A.B., U. Ark., 1919; J.D., George Washington U., 1922; LL.D., U. Ark., Coll. of Ozarks, Clarksville, Ark., Salem (W.Va.) Coll.; LL.D. hon. degrees, Mercer U., William Jewell Coll., U. of Pacific, Stetson U., Belmont Abbey Coll., also others. Bar: Ark. bar 1922. Mem. Hays, Priddy & Hays, Russellville, 1922-25, asst. atty. gen., Ark., 1925-27, mem., Hays & Turner, Little Rock, 1928-33; Mem. Democratic Nat. Com., 1932-39; Directed surveys, chmn. Ark. Rural Ch. Commn., 1928-29, Pulaski County Hosp. Com., 1929-30; apptd. labor compliance officer for Ark. NRA, 1934, spl. asst. to adminstr. of resettlement, 1935; later asst. dir. rural rehab. Farm Security Adminstrn.; resigned 1942 to become congrl. candidate; mem. 78th-85th congresses from 5th Dist. Ark.; bd. dirs. TVA, 1959-60; asst. sec. state for congl. relations. Dept. State, 1961; spl. asst. to Pres. of U.S., 1961-63; presdl. cons., 1963-66; Arthur T. Vanderbilt prof. pub. affairs Rutgers U., 1963-65; vis. prof. pub. affairs U. Mass., 1966; dir. Ecumenical Inst., Wake Forest U., 1969-72. Author: (with John E. Steely) Hotbed of Tranquility, 1968, Politics Is My Parish, 1981. Chmn. N.C. Human Relations Commn., 1970-74; U.S. del. to 10th gen. assembly UN, 1955; Bd. dirs. Ark. Tb Assn.; Bd. dirs. Ark. Children's Home and Hosp., pres., 1928-29; pres. Ark. State Conf. Social Work, 1932-35; Trustee George Peabody Coll., George Washington U. Recipient Silver Buffalo award Boy Scouts Am., Charles Evans Hughes award NCCJ. Mem. Am. Bar Assn., Former Mems. of Congress (co-founder 1970), Am. Legion, Council Fgn. Relations, Phi Beta Kappa, Sigma Chi, Phi Alpha Delta, Tau Kappa Alpha, Omicron Delta Kappa. Baptist (pres. So. Bapt. Conv. 1957-59). Clubs: Mason (33 deg.), Cosmos. Home: Chevy Chase, Md. Died Oct. 11, 1981.

HAYS, DONALD C., lawyer; b. N.Y.C., Apr. 30, 1911; s. Walter E. and Mary (Lansing) H.; m. Ann P. Hays; 1 dau., Viviane J. B.A., U. Colo., 1932, LL.B., 1935. Bar: N.Y. bar 1937. Since practiced in, N.Y.C.; partner firm Gifford, Woody, Carter & Hays, 1942-78; firm Sage, Gray, Todd & Sims, from 1978; sec., dir. Arthur H. Lee & Jofa Inc., John J. McMullen Assos., Inc. Served with AUS, 1943-46. Mem. Assn. Bar City N.Y., Am. Bar Assn., N.Y. County Lawyers Assn., N.Y. C. of C. and Industry, JAG Assn., Vets. of OSS, Assn. Former Intelligence Officers, Phi Delta Phi, Phi Delta Theta (sec. N.Y.C.). Republican. Presbyn. Clubs: Players (N.Y.C.), Met. (N.Y.C.). Home: New York, NY.

HAYS, GEORGE OMAR, publisher; b. Marion, Ind., Apr. 11, 1887; s. William E. and Harriett (Witherow) H.; B.S. in Civil Engring., Purdue U., 1912; m. Agnes T. Finnegan, Feb. 17, 1914; children—Mary Marjorie (Mrs. Robert J. Saggau), George Omar. With Universal Portland Cement Co., Chgo., 1912; with Penton Pub. Co., Cleve., from 1913, successively editor, advt. sales staff, bus. mgr., v.p. and gen. mgr., 1913-49, treas., 1950-56, pres., 1949-58, chmn., from 1958. Trustee, past chmn. Indsl. Advt. Research Inst.; mem. lay bd. Fenn Coll. Mem. Am. Iron and Steel Inst., Triangle, Iron Key, Sigma Delta Chi, Tau Beta Pi. Clubs: Union, Canterbury Golf (Cleve.). Home: Cleveland, Ohio. †

HAYS, PAUL R., judge; b. Des Moines, Apr. 2, 1903; s. Everett Hollingsworth and Fae Susan (Hatch) H.; A.B., Columbia, 1925, M.A., 1927, LL.B., 1933; m. Eleanor K. Williams, Feb. 1, 1924 (div. Dec. 1943); 1 child, Rhys Williams (dec.); m. Elinor Rice, Nov. 19, 1949. Instr. Greek and Latin, Columbia, 1926-32; associated with law firm, Cravath, de Gersdorff, Swaine & Wood, N.Y.C., 1933-34, 1935-36; counsel Nat. Recovery Adminstrn., Resettlement Adminstrn., Washington, 1934-35; asst. prof. law, Columbia, 1936-38, asso. prof. law, 1938-43, prof. law, 1943-57, Nash prof. law, 1957-61, prof. law, 1961-71, emeritus, 1971-80; U.S. Circuit judge, second circuit, 1961-80. Mem. N.Y. State Bd. Mediation, 1940-44, U.S. Bd. Legal Examiners, 1941-44; legal cons.

N.Y. State Banking Dept., 1936-37, N.Y. State Law Revision Com., 1937, 45, U.S. Dept. Justice, 1944, 45, labor arbitrator and impartial chmn. many industries, 1940-61; mem. N.Y.C. Bd. Health, 1954-60. Chmn. gov.'s com. on welfare funds, 1957-60. Chmn. Liberal Party, 1960-61; presidential elector, 1960. Mem. Am. (sec. sect. on labor relations law 1959-60), N.Y. State bar assns., Assn. of Bar of City of N.Y., Phi Beta Kappa. Club: Century. Author: The Judicial Function in Federal Administrative Agencies (with Jos. P. Chamberlain and Noel T. Dowling), 1942, 2d edit., 1970; Cases and Materials on Civil Procedure, 1947; Cases on Labor Law (with Milton Handler), 1950, rev. edit., 1963; Labor Arbitration: A Dissenting View, 1966; also articles in periodicals. Home: New York, N.Y. Dec. Feb. 13, 1980.

HAYWARD, EDWARD BEARDSLEY, librarian; b. Rutland, Vt., Jan. 21 1916; s. James E. and Rita (Beardsley) H.; m. Ruth Kelley, Aug. 15, 1940; children—James Kelley, John Linn, Dana Beardsley. B.S., Middlebury Coll., 1938; postgrad., Columbia, 1939; M.A., Bread Loaf Sch. of English, 1940; B.L.S., Ill. U., 1947. Inst. library sci. U. Wis., 1950; asst. librarian Racine (Wis.) Pub. Library, 1951-53; dir. Hammond (Ind.) Pub. Library, from 1953. Served with CIC AUS, 1943-46. Mem. Ind. Library Assn., A.L.A., Hammond C. of C., Sigma Phi Epsilon. Club: Kiwanian. Home: Hammond, Ind.

HAYWOOD, THOMAS HOLT, banker; b. Raleigh, N.C., July 31, 1887; s. Alfred Williams and Louise Moore (Holt) H.; Ph.B., U. N.C., 1903-07; m. Mary Louise Bahnson, Oct. 22, 1914; children—Mary Louise (Mrs. Archie K. Davis), Thomas Holt, Emma Pauline. Designer cotton goods Frederick Vietor & Achelis, N.Y.C., 1909-15, mgr. T. Holt Haywood dept., 1915-29; formed Haywood, Mackay & Valentine, 1929, former chmn. bd., Winston-Salem, N.C.; v.p., dir. So. Steel Stampings, Inc., Haywood Real Estate Co., Inc., Raleigh, N.C.; mem. bd. directors Washington Mills, Inc., Leward Cotton Mills, Inc. Former mem. N.C. State Bd. Agr.; former mem. Internat. Com. of Y.M.C.A. Former dir. N.C. Symphony Soc., Inc.; former trustee Salem Coll.; former v.p. Assn. for the Blind in Forsyth Co.; former chmn. bd. trustees Home Moravian Ch. Mem. N.C. Guernsey Breeders Assn. (past pres.). Zeta Psi, National Grange. Clubs: Union League, Merchants (N.Y.C.); Forsyth Country, Old Town (Winston Salem, N.C.). Address: Clemmons, N.C. †

HAYWORTH, DON, former congressman, educator; b. Toledo, Iowa, Jan. 13, 1898; s. Charles LeRoy and Mae Estelle (Wilkinson) H.; m. Frances Margaret Knight, June 17, 1934; children—Donna Lou, Francene Mae, Barbara. A.B., Grinnell Coll., 1918; M.A., U. Chgo., 1921; Ph.D., U. Wis., 1928. High sch. tchr., Oskaloosa, Iowa, 1921-23; head speech dept. Penn Coll., 1923-27, U. Akron, 1928-37, Mich. State Coll., 1937-42, prof. speech, 1944-54, 57-63; cons. U.S. Dept. Agr., 1963-64; mem. 84th Congress, 6th Dist. Mich.; In charge of speakers' activities Office Civilian Def., Washington, 1942-43. Author: (with Robert Capel) Oral Argument, 1933, Public Speaking, 1935, Introduction to Public Speaking, 1940, A Research into the Teaching of Public Speaking; mimeographed, 1941, It's the Family That Counts!; Contbr. articles to profl. jours. and lit. mags. Promotion of speakers' activities for fund raising campaign A.R.C, Washington, 1944; in charge of relations with states on fuel conservation Dept. of Interior, 1944-46; chmn. Mich. Victory Speakers Bur., 1941-42; cons. Social Security Adminstrn., 1965-67. Mem. Speech Assn. Am., AAUP, NAACP, Pi Kappa Delta. Democrat. Clubs: Kiwanian, Torch. Home: Washington, D.C. Dec. Feb. 29, 1982.

HAZAM, LOUIS JOSEPH, television producer; b. Norwich, Conn., Jan. 3, 1911; s. George John and Afifi (Habeeb) H.; B.A. in Journalism, Columbia, 1933; m. Ruby Gene Hymer, Oct. 30, 1939; children—Nancy Lynn, Chad Thomas. Script writer U.S. Dept. Interior, 1938-45; freelance writer for radio and TV, 1945-59; TV producer, writer NBC News, Washington, 1959-74. Bd. dirs. Council Internat. Nontheatrical Events, Washington. Recipient Christopher award, 1960, George Foster Peabody award, 1961, Bronze award Venice Film Festival, 1962, 1st place documentary, 1963, Golden Gate award San Francisco Internat. Film Festival, 1963, 64, 66. Mem. Acad. TV Arts and Scis. (recipient Emmy 1961, 71), Writers Guild. Producer, writer: Way of the Cross, 1960; Vincent Van Gogh, 1961; US #1, 1962; River Nile, 1963; Shakespeare; Soul of an Age, 1963; Greece: The Golden Age, 1964; Michelangelo, The Last Giant (Part I), 1965, (Part II), 1966; The National Gallary of Art, 1967; The Art Game, 1968; Sahara, La Caravane Du Sel, 1969; Venice Be Damned, 1971; Blanchard Springs Caverns, The Amazing World Below. Died Sept. 6, 1983.

HAZEN, BEN H., savs. and loan assn. exec.; b. Davenport, Ia., Aug. 22, 1890; s. Dr. Edward II and Sarah (Freeman) H.; student Drake Univ.; m. Dana Willcox, June 29, 1914; children—Elizabeth, Jeanne M., Robert H., Frances Ann. Treas., Douglas Fir Lumber Co., 1914-23; partner Lovejoy & Hazen Ins. Co., 1923-25; organized Beni Franklin (Fed.) Savs. & Loan Assn., Portland, Ore., 1925, became president, 1942, chairman of the board; president of Ben Hazen Insurance Agency, Portland, Insured Accounts Fund, Inc. (Boston), Home Loan Assos. Past pres. Pacific N.W. Savings & Loan Conf. Chairman Portland Community Chest campaign, 1947, pres., 1948-50; director YMCA, 1948-50; dir. Better Business Bur., from 1951; campaign dir. United Fund, Inc., Portland, 1954; dir. Nat. Thrift Com.; pres. Portland Rose Festival, 1947. Named first citizen of Portland, 1954. Mem. U.S. (pres. 1952) and Ore. (past pres.) savs. and loan leagues. Kiwanian (dist. gov. 1948, internat. trustee 1957-59). Home: Portland. †

HAZEN, HAROLD LOCKE, educator; b. Philo, Ill., Aug. 1, 1901; s. Wirt Mandeville and Elta Belle (Brewer) H.; S.B., Mass. Inst. Tech., 1924, S.M., 1929, Sc.D., 1931; m. Katherine Pharis Salisbury, Sept. 5, 1928; children—Stanley Seamans, Martha Locke (Mrs. William Liller), Nathan Lord, Anne Webb (Mrs. John G. Bowen). With Mass. Inst. Tech., 1925—, research asst. in elec. engring., 1925-26, instr., 1926-31, asst. prof., 1931-35, asso. prof., 1935-38, prof., head dept. elec. engring., 1938-52, dean Grad. Sch., 1952-67, fgn. study adviser, 1967-72; mem. adv. council dept. elec. engring. Princeton, 1948-56; chief div. 7. Nat. Def. Research Comm., 1942-46, exchange prof. elec. engring. Ohio State U., 1934-35; cons. on engring. edn. Robert Coll. Istanbul, 1955, interim pres., 1961; cons. engring. edn. Am. U. Beirut, 1957, Ministry of Edn., Iceland, 1958. Mem. U.S. Naval Weapons Lab. adv. council, 1953-65; chmn. edn. com. Engrs. Council for Profl. Devel., 1954-56, exec. com., 1954-58; chmn. Engring Edn. Mission to Japan, 1951, cons. engring. edn. UN Mission to U. Brasilia, 1962. Trustee Robert Coll. Bebek, Istanbul, Turkey, 1956-72, Coll. of Petroleum and Minerals, Dhahran, Saudi-Arabia, 1965-72; bd. visitors U.S. Air U., 1956-59. Recipient Levy medal of Franklin Inst., 1935; Lamme Gold medal Am. Soc. Engring. Edn., 1962; Presdl. Certificate of Merit, 1948; L.E. Grinter award Engrs. Council Profl. Devel., 1975, Rufus Oldenburger medal ASME, 1977. Served as 2d lt. Air Service, 1924-29; lt. comdr. USNR, 1936-49. Fellow I.E.E.E. (life), Am. Acad. Arts and Scis. (council), Franklin Inst. (life); mem. Am. Soc. Engring. Edn. (life mem.; chmn. com. devel. engring. faculties), Inst. Elec. Engrs. Japan (hon.), Sigma Xi, Tau Beta Pi, Eta Kappa Nu. Contbr. articles on instrumental calculation, automatic control devices, engring. edn., accreditation. Home: Belmont, Mass. Died Feb. 21, 1980.

HEAD, EDITH, costume designer; b. Los Angeles; A.B., U. Calif.; M.A., Stanford; student Otis Art Sch., Chouinard Art Sch. (Los Angeles). Began as tchr. French, Spanish and art, Hollywood Sch. for Girls, and Bishop's Sch., La Jolla; chief designer Paramount Pictures Corp., now with Universal City Studios. Recipient (with Gile Steele) Acad. Award for black and white costume design (The Heiress), 1949, Acad. Award (in collaboration) (All About Eve), 1950, (Samson and Delilah), 1951; award for costume design (Place in the Sun), 1952, (Roman Holiday), 1954, (The Sting), 1973; Acad. Award black and white costume design (Sabrina), 1954, (The Facts of Life), 1960. Author: The Dress Doctor; How to Dress for Success. Address: Universal City, Calif. Dec. Oct. 24, 1981.

HEALD, KENNETH CONRAD, geologist; b. Bennington, N.H., Mar. 14, 1888. s. Josiah Heald and Mary Katharine (Pike) H.; U. N.M., 1907-08; B.S. in Engring., Colorado Coll., 1912; studied Yale, 1912-14; D.Sc., U. Pitts., 1928; LL.D., Colo. Coll., 1955; m. Mary Marguerite Drach, Dec. 26, 1914; children—Mary Katherine (dec.), Kenneth Conrad. Field work, summers, U.S. Geol. Survey, until 1914, and full time, 1914-24, except 1918; chief of Sect. of Oil Geology, U.S. Geol. Survey, 1919-24; asso. prof. petroleum geology, Yale, 1924-25; geologist with Gulf Oil Cos. 1925-53, v.p. 1945, dir. 1950; and v.p. various Gulf Oil subsidiaries; now owner Heald & Heald, geology and engring. cons.; petroleum cons Lectured on petroleum geology, U. Chicago and Johns Hopkins, 1923, 24, U. of Pitts. 1926-53; spl. lecturer, Texas Christian University, Director of Texas Christian U. Research Found. Director Goodwill Industries, Ft. Worth. Capt. engrs., U.S. Army, unattached, staff geologist, 1918. Awarded certificate of appreciation by Am. Petroleum Inst., 1952; Sydney Powers Meml. Award by Am. Assn. Petroleum Geologists, 1952; Metcalf award Engrs. Soc. Western Pa., 1966. Member at large Nat. Research Council, 1925-26; member American Assn. Petroleum Geologists hon. mem.; rep. NRC 1921-25), Geol. Soc. Can., Geol. Society Am. (rep. Nat. Research Council 1927), Soc. Economic Geologists, Am. Inst. Min. and Metall. Engrs., Geol. Soc. Washington, Engrs. Soc. Western Pa., American Petroleum Institute; fellow Am. Association Advancement of Sci., Geological Soc. of Fort Worth. Conglist. Clubs: Cosmos, Mid-River (Washington, D.C.); Fort Worth, Petroleum (Ft. Worth). Author: (bulls.) Geologic Structure of the Pawhuska Quadrangle, Okla., 1918; Structure and Oil and Gas Resources of Osage Reservation, Okla., 1922; Healdton Oil Field, Oklahoma, 1915; Eldorado Oil Field, Arkansas, 1925; Geology of Ingomary Anticline, Mont., 1926. Contbr. papers dealing with geology, geophysics and oil field technology. †

HEALY, KENT TENNEY, univ. prof.; b. Chicago, Ill., Feb. 2, 1902; s. William and Mary Sylvia (Tenney) H.; A.B., Harvard, 1921; B.S. in E.E., Mass. Inst. of Tech., 1923; student Harvard Law Sch., 1923-24; M.A., Yale, 1945; m. Ruth Emily Allen, Nov. 3, 1928; children—Ruth Tenney, William Kent, Kent Allen, Sylvia Kent. Switchboard operator, N.Y., N.H. & H. R.R., 1922, insp., 1924-25, cost engr., 1925-26; studying transportation in Europe, 1926-27; asst. prof. transportation, Yale U., 1928-35, asst. prof. econs., 1935-40, asso. prof., 1940-45, T. Dewitt Cuyler Prof. transportation, 1945-85, chairman committee on transportation 1943-85, chmn. econs. dept., 1945-51, director division of social scis., 1956-59; cons. Connecticut Commn. on Reorganization of State Depts., 1935: transportation consultant Nat. Resources Planning Bd., 1940, Bituminous Coal Div., Dept. of Interior, 1941; to administrator of Lend-Lease, 1942-44, F.E.A., 1944-45; also at various times to private transportation agencies; mem. Conn. Highway Adv. Commn., 1943-45; chmn. Conn. Savings Bank R.R. Investment Committee, 1945-64; mem. Reorganization Com., dir. N.Y. N.H. & H. R.R. Co., 1947-48; dir. Conn. Co. 1947-64; Mem. Transportation Council for Dept. of Commerce, 1952-57. Chmn. bd. finance, Killingsworth, Conn., 1959-65, chmn. planning and zoning commission, 1965-85. Mem. Am. Econ. Assn., Royal Econ. Soc., Am. Econ. Hist. Assn., Sigma Xi, Delta Psi. Club: Graduate (New Haven, Conn.). Author: Steam Railroad Electrification. 1929; Economics of Transportation in America, 1940; The Effects of Scale in the Railroad Industry, 1961. Home: Killingworth, Conn. Died Jan. 9, 1985.

HEALY, PAUL FRANCIS, newspaperman; b. Chgo., Mar. 1, 1915; s. Waldo and Julia (Henzie) H.; m. Constance Maas, Jan. 2, 1943 (div.); children: Kevin, Julie, Monica, Jane, Kathleen. Ph.B., Loyola U., Chgo., 1938. Reporter Chgo. Tribune, 1938-43; assoc. editor Popular Mechanics mag., 1943-45; mem. Chgo. bur. Time, Inc., 1945; civilian info. officer War Dept., 1945; Washington corr. N.Y. Daily News, 1945-77, ret., 1980. Author: (with B. K. Wheeler) Yankee From The West, 1962, Cissy, A Biography of Eleanor M. Patterson, 1966; Contbr. to nat. periodicals. Mem. White House Corrs. Assn. (pres. 1977-78). Roman Catholic. Clubs: Washington Press (Washington), Gridiron (Washington). Home: Washington, D.C. Died Oct. 14, 1984.

HEALY, THOMAS JEFFERSON, lawyer; b. Bennington, Vt., Aug. 10, 1890; s. John Martin and Sarah Jane (Corbett) H.; B.S., Colgate U., 1913; LL.B., Columbia, 1916; m. Leila Volk, Feb. 26, 1921; children—Michaelanne (Mrs. Samuel Edward Walters), Jean Margot (Mrs. Harry A. McMillin), Joan Audrey. Admitted to D.C. bar, 1918, N.Y. bar, 1921; asso. Duncan & Mount, N.Y.C., 1920-23; counsel to German agt., mixed claims com. U.S. and Germany, 1923-31; counsel Austrian and Hungarian agts. Tripartite Claims Commn., U.S., Austria, Hungary, 1927-30; asso. Mendes & Mount, N.Y.C., gen. counsel in U.S. for underwriters at Lloyd's, London, Eng., 1937-65. Mem. Am., N.Y. County bar assns., Internat. Assn. Ins. Counsel. Clubs: Lawyers (N.Y.C.); Echo Lake Country (Westfield, N.J.). Home: Mountainside, N.J. †

HEARN, THOMAS G, army officer; b. Tuskegee, Ala., Nov. 14, 1890; s. Andrew Hamilton and Martha Elizabeth (Grimmett) H.; student Ala. Poly. Inst., 1911; B.S., U.S. Mil. Acad., 1915; m. Charlotte Frances Jadwin, Dec. 19, 1917; children—Thomas G., Jean Elizabeth. Commd. 2d lt., Inf., U.S. Army, June 1915, and advanced through the grades to major gen., 1943; served in Mexican campaign, 1916-17; with A.E.F., in France, 1918-19; now serving in China as chief of staff of China, Burma, India Theater. Mason. Home: Tuskegee, Ala.†

HEATH, EDWARD CHARLES, biochemist, educator; b. St. Louis, Mar. 29, 1926; s. Glenn Garrison and Edna M. (Fluchel) H.; m. Patricia L. Nolan, Jan. 29, 1947; children—Justin P. (dec.), Paula J., Dana J. B.S., St. Louis U., 1949; A.M., U. Mo., 1951; Ph.D., Purdue U., 1955. Instr. to asso. prof. microbiology U. Mich., 1957-63; assoc. prof. physiol. chemistry Sch. Medicine Johns Hopkins U., Balt., 1963-66, prof., 1966-71; prof., chmn. dept. biochemistry U. Pitts. Sch. Medicine, 1971-76; prof., head dept. biochemistry U. Iowa Coll. Medicine, 1976-84; cons. USPHS, NRC, Cystic Fibrosis Research Found., Nat. Bd. Med. Examiners; mem. biochemistry tng. com. NIH. Exec. editor: Archives Biochemistry and Biophysics; Editorial bd.: Analytical Biochemistry, Jour. Biol. Chemistry, Biochemistry; Contbr. articles sci. jours. Served with USNR, 1944-46. Mem. Am. Soc. Biol. Chemists, Am. Chem. Soc., Am. Soc. Microbiology, Sigma Xi, Phi Lambda Upsilon. Home: North Liberty, Iowa. Died Oct. 24, 1984.

HEATON, LEONARD D(UDLEY), army surgeon gen.; b. Parkersburg, W.Va., Nov. 18, 1902; s. George and Emma Gertrude (Dudley) H.; student Denison U., 1919-22; M.D., U. of Louisville, 1926, D.Sc., 1959; D.Sc., Denison U., 1959, West Va. U., 1962; Doctor of Humane Letters, Brandeis U., 1964; m. Sara Hill Richardson, June 30, 1926; one dau., Sara Dudley (Mrs. Preston B. Mason Junior). Interne, Letterman Gen. Hosp., San Francisco, 1926-28; entered M.C., U.S. Army, 1926, commd. 1st lt., 1927, and advanced through grades to lt. gen., 1959; asst. to chief, surgical services, William Beaumont Gen. Hosp., El Paso, Tex., 1929-30, Tripler Gen. Hosp., Honolulu, T.H., 1930-32, Brooke Gen. Hosp., San Antonio, 1932-37; chief, surgical services, Fort Warren, Wyo., 1937-40, North Sector Gen. Hosp., Hawaii, 1940-42; exec. officer, Woodrow Wilson Gen. Hosp., Staunton, Va. 1942-44; comd. 160th Gen. Hosp. and 802d Hosp. Center, Blandford, Eng., 1944-45; comdg. gen., Letterman Gen. Hosp., 1946-53; comdg. gen. Walter Reed Army Med. Center, Washington, 1953-59; surgeon gen. Dept. of Army, 1959-83. Decorated Legion of Merit with 2 oak leaf clusters, D.S.M. with 2 oak leaf clusters. Diplomate Am. Bd. Surgery, 1948. Fellow A.C.S., Am. Surg. Assn.,

Southern Surg. Assn.; member Internat. Soc. Surg., Halstead Soc., A.M.A., Alpha Omega Alpha, also mil. orgns. Baptist. Home: Washington, D.C. Died Sept. 10, 1983.

HEATTER, GABRIEL, news commenator; b. New York, N.Y., Sept. 17, 1890; s. Henry and Anna (Fishman) H.; ed. Brooklyn Boys High Sch. and New York U.; m. Saidie Hermalin, May 23, 1915; children—Maida (Mrs. Ellis Gimbel), Basil. Began as reporter N.Y. American, 1907, later with Brooklyn Eagle; became pub. and owner small Brooklyn paper; then advertising salesman and feature writer for Forest and Stream; editor Shaft from 1927; radio news commentator, news analyst, Mutual Broadcasting System. Author: Come Let Us Walk Together; Whom Are You Leaning On.†

HECHT, HAROLD, motion picture producer; b. N.Y.C., June 1, 1907; s. Joseph and Rose (Lowey) H.; student Am. Lab. Theatre; m. Gloria J. Buzzell, Nov. 1, 1947; children—Steven, Duffy, Alma Virginia; m. 2d, Margaret Truefitt, 1962; 1 son, Harold W. Asst. to Richard Boleslavky; actor in N.Y. Theatre, 1923-30; dancer, choreographer, N.Y.C., 1926-31; motion picture dance dir. Paramount Pictures, Warner Bros., MGM, Los Angeles, 1931-36; established lit. agy., Goldstone Agy., later Hecht-Rantz Agy., Hollywood, Calif., 1938-41; partner with Burt Lancaster, Norma Prodns., 1945-53; pres. Hecht-Lancaster Cos., 1954-85. Recipient of year award Look mag., 1955; recipient Acad. Award for prodn. Marty, 1955. Mem. Screen Producers Guild, Acad. Motion Picture Arts and Scis. Films include: The Flame and the Arrow, Ten Tall Men, Apache, Marty, Trapeze, Bachelor Party, Run Silent, Run Deep, Separate Tables, Bird Man of Alcatraz, Taras Bulba, Cat Ballou, The Way West, others. Died May 25, 1985.

HECHTMAN, ROBERT AARON, educator, structural engr.; b. Spokane, Apr. 22, 1911; s. Abe and Maren (Olson) H.; B.S. in Civil Engr., U. Wash., 1938, M.S. in Civil Engring., 1939; student Lehigh U., 1939-41; Ph.D., U. Ill., 1948; m. Sarajane Furman; children—Geoffrey Kier, Paul Randall. With Dravo Corp., 1941-44, adminstr. asst., 1944-45; research engr. civil engring. U. Ill., 1945-49; asso. prof. structural research U. Wash., 1949-53, prof., 1953-55; prof. civil engring. George Washington U., 1955-64, chmn. dept. 1955-62; vis. prof. U. Chile, 1959; pres. Planning, Analysis & Design Corp., Kensington, Md., 1964-65; pres. R.A. Hechtman & Assos., 1965-74; adj. prof. civil engring. Howard U., 1967-71; professorial lectr. George Washington U., 1972-73; prof., dir. environ. systems labs. Coll. Architecture and Urban Studies, Va. Poly. Inst. and State U., Blacksburg, 1974-85. Cons. engr. failure ship and land structures, concrete structures, fire protection, archtl. design for disabled Column Research Council, from 1951, project dir., 1963-64; mem. Nat. Bur. Standards, 1959-69, chmn. adv. panel to bldg. research div., 1964-69. Mem. Nat. Commn. on Fire Prevention and Control, 1970-73. Fellow Am. Soc. C.E. (chmn. com. on fire protection 1974); mem. Am. Concrete Inst., Prestressed Concrete Inst., Nat. Fire Protection Assn., Sigma Xi, Tau Beta Pi. Author research publs., reports. Died Feb. 12, 1985.

HECK, CHARLES VOISIN, orthopaedic surgeon, association executive; b. Collinsville, Ill., Aug. 17, 1918; s. Charles John and Ada (Voisin) H.; m. Susan Virginia Jones, July 4, 1948; children: Charles Chandler and Helen Kay (twins). A.B., U. Ill., 1939, B.S., M.D., 1943. Diplomate: Am. Bd. Orthopaedic Surgery. Intern Ill. Research and Ednl. Hosps., Chgo., 1943-44; resident St. Luke's Hosp., Chgo., 1945-46, preceptor, 1948-50, practice medicine specializing in orthopaedic surgery, Chgo., 1948-68; dir. Am. Acad. Orthopaedic Surgeons, Chgo., 1968-71, exec. dir., 1976-84, cons., 1984-85; research asst. U. Ill. Coll. Medicine, Chgo., 1948-50, asst. prof. orthopaedic surgery, 1950-58, assoc. prof., 1958-71, Rush Med. Center, 1971-72, prof., 1972—; mem. staff Rush Presbyn.-St. Luke's Med. Center; dir. Services By Satellite, Inc., Washington.; Bd. dirs. Pub. Service Satellite Consortium, Washington, 1975—. Author: Fifty Years of Progress; Contbr. articles on spine and hip to med. publs. Co-trustee Hulbert Fund, Chgo. Served with M.C. AUS, 1946-48, 50-51. Mem. ACS, Am. Acad. Orthopaedic Surgeons, Internat. Soc. Orthopaedics and Trauma, Clin. Orthopaedic Soc., Inst. Medicine Chgo., Am. Orthopaedic Assn., Mid-Am. Orthopaedic Assn., Assn. Ret. Physicians Am. (dir. 1975-77). Presbyterian. Club: Oak Park (Ill.) Country. Home: Oak Park, Ill. Died May 8, 1985.

HECK, FRANK HOPKINS, educator; b. Racine, Wis., Oct. 18, 1904; s. Victor and Ruth Alice (Perham) H.; A.B., Lawrence Coll., 1925; M.A., U. Minn., 1929, Ph.D., 1938; m. Edna Drill, Oct. 3, 1945; 1 son, Edward V. Tchr. high sch., Rice Lake, Wis., 1926-27, Faribault, Minn., 1928-29; asst. prof. history Nebr. State Tchrs. Coll., Peru, 1929-33, asso. prof., 1933-38; asst. prof. Miami U., Oxford, Ohio, 1938-46, asso. prof., chmn. integrated studies, 1946-48; prof. history Centre Coll., Danville, Ky., 1948-71, Matton prof. history, 1971-74, prof. emeritus, 1974-83, dean 1955-65. Served to capt. AUS, 1942-46. Mem. Am., So. hist. assns., Orgn. Am. Historians, Phi Beta Kappa, Beta Theta Pi. Democrat. Episcopalian. Author: The Civil War Veteran in Minnesota Life and Politics, 1941; Proud Kentuckian: John C. Breckenridge, 1821-1875, 1976. Home: Danville, Ky. Died Mar. 30, 1983; buried Bellevue Cemetery, Danville.†

HECKER, ARTHUR ORR, physician, hosp. supt.; b. Pitts., Aug. 14, 1910; s. Arthur Walter and Carrie (Orr) H.; M.D., U. Pitts., 1933; m. Sarah Johnson, Feb. 22, 1936; children—Carolyn Ann, Sarah Atlanta, Deborah Lee; m. 2d, Eleanore Reidell Wright, Feb. 11, 1956; children—Eleanor Helen Wickersham Wright, Curtis Wright IV (foster children). Intern U. Pitts. Med. Center, 1933-34; resident C. H. Buhl Hosp., Sharon, Pa., 1934-35; practice medicine, specializing in psychiatry, Downington, Pa., 1953-54; staff psychiatrist Pa. State Hosp. System, 1935-41; chief profl. services, dir. profl. tng. VA Hosp., Coatesville, Pa., 1945-53; clin. dir. Friends Hosp., Phila., 1954-55; supt. Embreeville (Pa.) State Hosp., 1955-70, ret. Served from capt. to col., M.C., AUS, 1941-45; ETO. Decorated Bronze Star medal. Fellow A.C.P., Am. Psychiat. Assn.; mem. Chester County Med. Soc. (past pres.), Phila. Psychiat. Soc. (past pres.). Died Nov. 17, 1982.

HECKERLING, PHILIP EPHRAIM, lawyer; b. N.Y.C., May 17, 1921; s. Israel and Rose (Burg) H.; m. Ruth Kaufman, Aug. 29, 1942; children: Dale Anthony, Stephanie Ria. J.D., U. Fla., 1949; LL.M., U. Miami, Fla., 1963, N.Y. U., 1964. Bar: Fla. 1949. Practiced law, Miami, 1949-67; counsel firm Greenberg, Traurig, Hoffman, Lipoff & Quentel, Miami, 1967-78, Schwartz, Nash, Heckerling, Tescher & Kantor, Miami, 1978-83; prof. law U. Miami, 1967-83; dir. U. Miami (Inst. Estate Planning), 1967-83, dir. grad. program in estate planning, 1975-83, fed. taxation, 1973-78; v.p., trust counsel Pan Am. Bank of Miami, 1967-80. Co-author: Workbook for Florida Estate Planners, 1968; editor: U. Miami Inst. Estate Plannings, vols. 1-17; editorial bd.: Estates and Gift Trusts Jour; contbr. numerous articles to profl. jours. Fellow Am. Coll. Probate Counsel; mem. Am. Law Inst., Internat. Acad. Estate and Trust Law, Fla. Bar (chmn. com. estate and gift taxes tax sect.). Home: Miami, Fla. Died Nov. 30, 1983.

HEDERMAN, THOMAS MARTIN, JR., b. Jackson, Miss., May 23, 1911; s. Thomas Martin and Pearl (Smith) H.; m. Bernice Flowers, May 11, 1938; children: Thomas Martin III (dec. USAF), Bernice Hederman Hussey. B.A., Miss. Coll., 1932, LL.D. (hon.), 1967; postgrad., Columbia U., 1932-33. Assoc. editor Clarion-Ledger, Jackson, Miss., 1948, editor, co-pub., from 1948; pres. Miss. Publs. Corp., Capitol Broadcasting Co.; owners KNAZ, Flagstaff, Ariz.; former dir. First Magnolia Fed. Savs. & Loan Assn., Jackson. Contbr. to: World Book ency. Trustee, chmn. bd. Miss. Coll.; past mem. exec. com. Miss. Research and Devel. Commn.; past pres., now bd. dirs. Central Growth Found. Named Outstanding Alumnus of Year Miss. Coll.; recipient Silver EM award Miss. Scholastic Press Assn. and Miss. Journalism Assn., 1970. Mem. Miss. Press Assn. (past pres.), Am. Soc. Newspaper Editors, Am. Newspaper Pubs. Assn., So. Newspaper Pubs. Assn. (dir. 1947-49), Am. Press Inst., Internat. Press Inst., C. of C. (v.p., pres.). Home: Jackson, Miss. Died Jan. 6, 1985.

HEDLUND, FLOYD FREDERICK, agrl. mktg. cons.; b. Valparaiso, Nebr., July 4, 1911; s. Claus Oscar and Hulda (Lundquist) H.; m. Delia M. Roth, May 18, 1963. B.S., U. Nebr., 1933; Ph.D., Cornell U., 1937. Asso. Mktg. Adminstrn. and Agrl. Mktg. Service, Dept. Agr., 1946-61; dir. fruit and vegetable div. Mktg. Adminstrn. and Agrl. Mktg. Service, Dept. Agr. (Agrl. Mktg. Service), 1961-79, individual practice agrl. mktg. cons., Washington, from 1979. Served to maj. USAAF, 1942-46; lt. col. Res. Mem. Am. Agrl. Econs. Assn., Internat. Assn. Agrl. Economists, Nat. Assn. Mktg. Ofcls., Farm House Frat., Nebr. U. Alumni Assn., Alpha Zeta, Gamma Sigma Delta, Phi Kappa Phi. Lutheran. Clubs: Cornell (Washington), Congressional Country (Washington), Nat. Press (Washington); Palmetto Dunes Golf (Hiltonhead, S.C.). Home: Washington, DC.

HEDMAN, MARTHA, actress; b Ostersund, Sweden, Aug. 12, 1888; d. Johan and Ingrid (Kempe) H.; studied for stage under first wife of August Strindberg, Siri von Essen; m. Henry Arthur House, 1921. Début, as the Prince in one of Hans Andersen's fairy tales, at Alexander Theatre, Helsingfors, Finland, Feb. 1905; later appeared in leading parts in plays and for 3 yrs. under Albert Ranft, principally at Vasa Theatre, Stockholm; came to U.S., 1912, and appeared as Renée de Rould in "The Attack," at Garrick Theatre, New York, Sept. 19, 1912; played in same rôle at St. James Theatre, London, 1914, also "The Two Virtues" at same theatre; has appeared in "Liberty Hall," "Indian Summer," "Half an Hour," "The Heart of a Thief," "The Trap," "The Boomerang," "The Dancer," "Three for Diana," "Forbidden," "The Hole in the Wall," "Transplanting Jean," "The Romantic Young Lady," etc. Co-Author with Henry Arthur House of comedy "What's The Big Idea?" and other plays. Home: Springdale, Conn. †

HEDRICH, ARTHUR WILLIAM, b. Chicago, Ill., July 7, 1888; s. Louis F. A. and Augusta (Neunuebel) H.; B.S., Northwestern U., 1914; C.P.H., Harvard-M.I.T. Pub. Health Sch., 1919; Sc.D., Sch. of Hygiene, Johns Hopkins, 1928; m. Helen Chandler Dyer, 1921; children—Arthur William, Lefa Cordelia, Nancy Louise. Assistant city chemist, and bacteriologist, Evanston, Illinois, 1912-14; city chemist and deputy health officer, East Chicago, Indiana, 1914-16; editorial assistant Am. Jour. Pub. Health, Boston, 1916-17; sec. Am. Pub. Health Assn., and editor Am. Jour. Pub. Health, 1917-23; dir. of surveys, Dept. of Health, Chicago, 1924-26; instr., later lecturer in vital statistics and epidemiology, Sch. of Hygiene, Johns Hopkins U., Baltimore, from 1927; consultant in vital statistics and epidemiology, U.S. Public Health Service, 1928-34; regional supervisor, chronic disease survey, 1934-35; consultant Social Security Bd., 1939-42; chief Bur. of Vital Statisitcs, Md. State Dept. of Health, Baltimore, from 1936; chmn. Nat. Council Vital Records and Vital Statistics, 1946-50. Mem. Alpha Chi Sigma, Phi Beta Kappa, Delta Omega. Home: Stoneleigh, Md. †

HEDRICK, LAWRENCE HYSKELL, army officer; b. Warren County, Ind., Nov. 22, 1880; s. Scott and Ada (Pollock) H.; grad. Black Hills (S.D.) Coll., 1897; LL.B., cum laude, Univ. of Missouri, 1905; m. Lurline Logan, Sept. 7, 1905; 1 dau., Lois Lurline (Mrs. John M. Willem, Jr.). Employed variously on ranches, railroads, and as traveling salesman to 1902; admitted to Mo. bar, 1905. S.D. bar, 1907, U.S. Supreme Court, 1919, Florida bar, 1945; began law practice, Hot Springs, S.D., 1907; served as city atty., 4 years, states atty., 4 years. Capt., 4th Inf., S.D. Nat. Guard, 1908-16, major, 1916-17; major, 147th F.A., 1917-18; lt. col. Army of U.S., 1918-20; major, Judge Advocate General's Dept., Regular Army, 1920, advancing through the grades to brig. gen. June 1942; served on Mexican border, 1916-17; with 147th and 121st F.A., France, Jan.-Aug. 1918; asst. dir. gunnery dept. Sch. of Fire, Fort Sill, Okla. Sept. 1918 to May 1919; with atty. gen. 1919-20; Judge Advocate General's Dept., 1920-45; distinguished graduate School of Line; graduate Staff School; grad., Army War Coll.; War Dept. Gen. Staff, 1931-35, Hawaiian Dept., 1935-37; asst. judge advocate gen. in charge branch Judge Adv. General's Office, European Theater of Operations, England, 1942-43; air judge advocate, Army Air Forces, July 1943-Oct. 1945; gen. law practice since Oct. 1945. Mem. Kappa Sigma, Phi Delta Phi. Mason. Elk. Episcopalian. Address: Miami, Fla.†

HEFFERNAN, JOSEPH LAWRENCE, lawyer; b. Youngstown, O., Feb. 8, 1887; s. John and Rose Ann (Flynn) H.; ed. Valparaiso (Ind.) U. and Ohio State U.; m. Catherine O'Connor, Oct. 27, 1914 (died 1917); 1 son, Joseph Lawrence; m. 2d, Beatrice Mary Jones, May 8, 1920; children—Martha, David. Mem. editorial staff successively Youngstown Telegram, Youngstown Vindicator, Ohio State Jour., Cleveland Leader, 1910-13; newspaper corr., Europe, 1913-14; admitted to Ohio bar, 1915, and began practice at Youngstown. Served as pvt., later sergt., U.S. Army, assigned to Stars and Stripes, official Army newspaper, World War. Apptd. municipal judge, Youngstown, Mar. 1923, elected to same office, Nov. 1923, for term 1923-27; mayor of Youngstown, term 1927-31; apptd. legal counsel Federal Communications Commission, May 9, 1935, and assigned to investigation of interstate telephone business and particularly Am. Telephone and Telegraph Co. and associated Bell interests, which was largest investigation ever made under authority of Congress; asst. atty. gen. of Ohio, 1937-39; also acted as special counsel in the statewide rate litigation with the Ohio Bell Telephone Co.; legal counsel Bur. of Internal Revenue, Northern Dist. of Ohio, from 1940; resumed private practice of law, with gen. and corp. practice, and specialization in matters before government bureaus, Treasury Dept., and Tax Court of the U.S., 1942; asst. director law City of Youngstown, from 1954. Democrat. Roman Catholic. Home: Youngstown, OH. †

HEFFNER, HUBERT CROUSE, educator; b. Maiden, N.C., Feb. 22, 1901; s. Sylvanus Lafayette and Lily (Crouse) H.; A.B. with honors in Lang. and Lit., U. N.C., 1921, M.A., 1922; student U. Chgo., 1930-34, 44; L.H.D., Ill. Wesleyan U., 1964; Litt.D., U. N.C., 1969; m. Ruth Penny, Apr. 8, 1922; 1 son, Hubert Heffner. Instr. English, dir. dramatics U. Wyo., 1922-23; instr. English, dir. dramatics U. Ariz., 1923-26; asst. prof. English, asso. dir. The Carolina Playmakers, U. N.C., 1926-30; prof. dramatic lit. Northwestern u., 1930-39; prof. dramatic lit., exec. head dept. speech and drama, Stanford, 1939-54; Rockefeller grand in aid for research and study in France and Eng., 1951-52; Folger Shakespeare Library grant in aid, 1952; Fulbright award, 1954-55; prof. speech, theatre, and dramatic lit. Ind. U., 1954-61, Distinguished Service prof. dramatic lit., 1961-85, chmn. div. theatre, 1970-71; vis. prof. summers Northwestern U., 1930, Stanford, 1937, U. Cal., 1939, Cornell U., 1948, U. Colo., 1950, 65, U. Denver, 1962; Carnegie vis. prof. drama U. Hawaii, 1958, U. Bristol, 1954-55, U. Denver, summer 1962, U. Colo., summer 1965. Commd. capt., Spl. Res., U.S. Army, 1943; grad Sch. of Mil. Govt., U. Va., 1943; inactive status in charge of mil. govt. instrn. Civil Affairs Training Sch., Stanford, 1943-44; research project Provost Marshal Gen's. Office, 1944; head Theatre and Radio Arts Br., chief Fine Arts sect. Biarritz Am. U., 1945-46. Fellow Am. Edn. Theatre Assn. (pres. 1949, editor Jour. 1955-56); mem. Am. Assn. U. Profs., Speech Assn. Am., Modern Lang. Assn., Nat. Theatre Conf., ANTA (bd. dirs. 1953-56, 60-85). Author several publs. Editor: (with Isaac Goldberg) Davy Crockett and Other Plays, 1940. Asso. editor Quarterly Jour. of Speech, 1947-50; dir. number of theatrical prodns. for U. Wyo., U. Ariz., The Carolina Playmakers, Northwestern U. and Stanford. Home: Bloomington, Ind. Died Apr. 17, 1985.

HEFFRON, ROBERT JAMES, ex-premier of New South Wales; b. Thames, New Zealand, Sept. 10, 1890; s. Michael and Ellen (Heath) H.; D.Litt. (hon.), U. Sydney (Australia), 1952, U. New Eng., New South Wales, 1956; D.Sc. (hon.), New South Wales U. Tech., 1954; hon. fellow Sydney Tech. Coll., 1960; m. Jessie Bjornstadt, Dec. 29, 1917; children—Maylean (Mrs. Peter Cordia), June. Organizer, Gen. Workers Union, Auckland, 1915-17, Fed. Clothing Trade Union, Melbourne, 1919-21; sec. Marine Stewards Union, Sydney, 1921-30; Australian Labor Party candidate for Botany, New S. Wales, 1927; mem. Legislative Assembly for Botany, 1930-50, for Maroubra, from 1950; minister nat. emergency services, New S. Wales, 1941-44, for edn., 1944-60; dep. premier S. Wales, and minister for edn., 1952-59, premier, from 1959. Home: Maroubra, New South Wales. †

HEFLEBOWER, RICHARD BROOKS, economist; born at Milliken, Colorado, October 4, 1903; son of Ernest and Etna Tabitha (Brooks) H.; student Fresno State Coll., 1921-23; A.B., U. of Calif., 1925, Ph.D., 1929; m. Velma Harris, June 2, 1926; children—Ellen, Louise, Jean, Linda. Instr. economics, U. of Ida., 1928-29; asst. prof. economics. State Coll. of Wash., 1929-34, asso. prof., 1934-36, professor and dean, 1936-45, School of Business Administration. Various positions, including Economic Advisor to Deputy Adminstrator, Office of Price Adminstrn., 1943-46; econ., Brookings Instn., Washington, 1946-49; prof. econs. Northwestern U. since 1949, chairman of the department, 1951-59; visiting professor, Harvard, 1962-63. Member of the Midwest Economics Association (president 1967-68), Econometric Soc., American Economic Assn., Royal Economic Society. Author of book: Economics with Applications to Agriculture (with E.F. Dummeier and T. Norman), 1934; also articles. Asso. editor of Jour. Indsl. Econs. since 1952. Home: Wilmette, Ill. Died June 10, 1982.

HEFNER, FRANK KARL, inst. adminstr.; b. Vienna, Austria, Nov. 10, 1917; s. Frank and Leopoldina (Koziste) H.; brought to U.S., 1921, naturalized, 1936; B.A., Westminster Coll., Fulton, Mo., 1939; M.A., U. Mo., 1942; postgrad. Yale U.; m. Annadell Pegram, Nov. 10, 1939; children—Cynthia Lee, Paul Douglas. Instr. Fulton (Mo.) High Sch., 1939-42, Conn. Coll. Pharmacy, New Haven, 1942-44; indsl. engring. staff Winchester Repeating Arms Co., New Haven, 1942-44; budget examiner Bur. Budget, Exec. Office of the Pres., Washington, 1944-49; mgmt. analyst, budget staff sec. commerce, Washington, 1949-50; fgn. mgmt. analyst bur. European affairs Dept. State, 1950-52, exec. dir. bur. German affairs, 1952-54; dep. exec. dir. U.S. High Commn. for Germany, Bonn, 1954-55, exec. dir., 1955-56; consul, sec. Diplomatic Service, 1955; counselor for adminstrn. Am. embassy, Bonn, Germany, 1956-57; dir. exec. staff bur. econ. affairs Dept. State, 1957-59, chief econ. devel. div., 1959-60, dep. dir. Office Internat. Financial and Devel. Affairs, 1960-61, dep. dir. Office Internat. Adminstrn., 1961-62, dir., 1962-63; dep. U.S. rep. Internat. AEC, Vienna, Austria, 1963-66; dir. mgmt. reports staff Dept. State, 1966-68; adminstr. Crowell Collier Inst., Arlington, Va., 1968-81. Mem. Fgn. Service Assn. Home: Old Lyme, Conn. Dec. June 12, 1981.

HEGRE, THEODORE A., clergyman; b. Woodville, Wis., Mar. 17, 1908; s. Adolph and Maria (Bodsberg) H.; m. Lucile Alta Conley, Oct. 1, 1935; children: Jean Marie Hegre Mikkelson, Joane Carol Hegre Brooks. Ordained to ministry, 1944; pastor Bethany Missionary Ch., Mpls., 1943—; pres. Bethany Fellowship Inc., Mpls., 1945-83; prin. Bethany Fellowship Missionary Tng. Center, Mpls., 1948-80; internat. sec. Bethany Fellowship Missions, from 1962. Author: The Cross and Sanctification, 1960, How to Find Freedom from the Power of Sin, 1961, Creative Faith, 1980; contbr. articles to numerous jours. Home: Minneapolis, Minn. Deceased.

HEIDBREDER, EDNA FRANCES, psychologist; b. Quincy, Ill., May 1, 1890; d. William Henry and Mathilda Emelie (Meyer) Heidbreder; A.B., Knox Coll., 1911; A.M., U. of Wis., 1918; Ph.D., Columbia, 1924; student of U. of London, 1930; unmarried. Instr. psychology, U. of Minn., 1924-26, asst. prof., 1926-28, asso. prof., 1928-34; prof. Wellesley from 1934; prof. psychology U. Cal., summer 1950. Recipient Knox Alumni award, 1942. Fellow A.A.A.S. (v.p. 1947), N.Y. Acad. Sci., Am. Psychol. Assn. (council 1939-49, 42-44; rep. Nat. Research Council 1944-47, 1952-55), Eastern Psychol. Assn. (pres. 1944, bd. dirs. 1944-47); mem. Phi Beta Kappa, Sigma Xi, Author several books including: Seven Psychologies, 1932; also articles. Editor: book review sect., Jour. Abnormal and Social Psychology, 1937-47. Asso. editor Psychological Monographs. Home: Wellesley, Mass. Died Feb. 19, 1985.

HEIDELBERGER, CHARLES, educator; b. N.Y.C., Dec. 23, 1920; s. Michael and Nina (Tachau) H.; m. Judith Werble, Dec. 22, 1943; children—Nina, Philip, Lisa; m. Patricia Boshell, June 8, 1975. S.B., Harvard U., 1942, M.S., 1944, Ph.D., 1946. Instr. chemistry Harvard U.,

1946; research chemist Radiation Lab., U. Calif. at Berkeley, 1946-48; mem. faculty U. Wis., 1948-76, prof., 1958-76, Am. Cancer Soc. prof. oncology, 1960-76; prof. biochemistry and pathology U. So. Calif., 1976-81, disting. prof. biochemistry and pathology, 1981-83; dir. for basic research Los Angeles County-U. So. Calif. Comprehensive Cancer Center, 1976-83; cons. Nat. Cancer Inst., 1958-83. Recipient Teplitz award cancer research Langer Meml. Fund, 1958; award of merit Am. Cancer Soc., 1965; Lucy Wortham James award James Ewing Soc., 1969; G.H.A. Clowes award Am. Assn. Cancer Research, 1970; Nat. Ann. award Am. Cancer Soc., 1974; Lila Gruber award Am. Acad. Dermatology, 1976; Papanicolaou award, 1978. Mem. Nat. Acad. Sci., Am. Chem. Soc., Am. Soc. Biol. Chemists, Am. Assn. Cancer Research (dir. 1960-62, 66-68, 75-78). Synthesized, devel. tumor inhibitory drug 5-fluorouracil, 1956; pioneered studies chem. carcinogenesis in tissue culture. Home: Pasadena, Calif. Died Jan. 18, 1983.

HEIL, WALTER, mus. dir.; b. Oppenheim, Germany, Nov. 10, 1890; s. Georg and Elisabeth (Lautenberger) H.; student Technische Hochschule, Munich, 1909-13, diploma engring.; student U. Munich, 1913-14, Ph.D., 1922; student Sorbonne, 1914, U. Frankfurt, 1919; m. Katherine W. Buttrick, Apr. 24, 1928; 1 dau., Barbara Ellen. Came to U.S., 1926, naturalized, 1932. Asst. curator Bavarian State Galleries, Munich 1922-24; fellow at Inst. Art History, Florence, Italy, 1924-26; curator of European art, Detroit Inst. Art, 1926-1933; dir. Calif. Palace of the Legion of Honor, San Francisco, 1933-40, M. H. de Young Memorial Mus., San Francisco since 1933; dir. div. European art, Fine Arts Dept.; Golden Gate Internat. Exposition, 1937-40; regional dir. Pub. Works of Art Project, 1933-34; chmn. San Francisco com., sect. of painting and sculpture, Pub. Work br., U.S. Treasury Dept.; regional dir. Treasury Relief Art Project; mem. Fine and Applied Arts Com. on Works Progress Adminstrn. of Fed. Govt. Decorated Chevalier Legion of Honor (France), 1937; Stella, della Solidarieta Italiana (Italian Govt.); Officer's Cross, Order of Merit, Fed. Republic, Germany, 1957. Club: Bohemian Club (San Francisco). Contbr. articles to mags. Home: San Francisco. †

HEILMAN, ERNEST A., univ. prof.; b. Watertown, Wis., Apr. 17, 1887; s. Henry John and Martha (Gibb) H.; A.B., Northwestern Coll., 1905; A.B., U. of Minn., 1906; A.M., U. of Wis., 1908, Ph.D., 1919; student U. of Berlin, 1911, U. of Munich, 1912; m. Elsa Baumann, Aug. 9, 1915; children—Ruth, Margaret Lois (Mrs. Frank C. Larimore), Instr., U. of Ia., 1914-18, U. of Mich., 1918-19; asst. prof. of accounting Drake U., 1919-20, asst. prof. accounting U. of Minn., 1920-23, asso. prof., 1923-39, prof. of accounting from 1939. Mem. Am. Accounting Assn. (pres. 1938), Nat. Assn. Cost Accountants, Am. Assn. Univ. Profs. Contbr. to Accountants Handbook, 1932 and 1943, also articles to Accounting Rev. Home: Minneapolis, Minn. †

HEINZE, ROBERT HAROLD, author, religious publisher; b. Ashland, Pa., Feb. 26, 1920; s. Edward Lewis and Marian (Goyne) H.; m. Elizabeth Lee Kohler, May 15, 1948 (div. Oct. 1979); children—Carolyn, Timothy, Jonathan; m. Nancy Ann Battye, Nov. 17, 1979. A.B., Lafayette Coll., 1941; B.D., Princeton Theol. Sem., 1944; D.D. (hon.), Waynesburg Coll., 1953. Ordained to ministry United Presbyn. Ch., 1944; pastor Immanuel Presbyn. Ch., Harrisburg, Pa., 1944-47; gen. mgr. Presbyn. Life mag., Phila., 1947-72, pub., 1972-73, A.D. mag., N.Y.C., 1972-76; writer United Presbyn. Ch., 1976-80, ret., 1980; Trustee United Presbyn. Found., 1954-73, chmn. joint com. worship, 1958-73; Sec. Pa. Presbyn. Com. on Colls., 1958-69. Author: After Five Years. Home: Fort Lee, N.J. Died Aug. 13, 1984.

HEINZERLING, LYNN LOUIS, foreign correspondent; b. Birmingham, Ohio, Oct. 23, 1906; s. Louis and Grace (Lawrence) H.; m. Agnes C. Dengate, July 21, 1934; children—Lynn Louis (dec.), Larry. Student, Akron U., 1924-25, Ohio Wesleyan U., 1925-27. Reporter Cleve. Plain Dealer, 1928-33; editor Asso. Press, Cleve. and N.Y.C., 1934-38, fgn. corr. in, Berlin, Danzig, Helsinki, 1938-41, N.Y.C., 1942, London and Cairo, Egypt, 1943; with British 8th Army and U.S. 5th Army, Italy and Austria, 1943-45, chief bur., Vienna, Austria, 1945-46, Corr., Berlin, 1947-48, chief bur., Geneva, Switzerland, 1948-57, Johannesburg, S. Africa, 1957-61, asst. chief bur., London, Eng., 1961-63, chief of bureau, Columbus, Ohio 1963-64; chief of British 8th Army and U.S. 5th Army (Africa Operations), 1964-72, free lance writer, lectr., 1972-83. Recipient Pulitzer prize internat. reporting, 1961; Overseas Press Club award for best reporting from abroad, 1961. Mem. UN Corr. Assn., fgn. corr. assns. Bern and S. Africa, Phi Delta Theta. Club: Overseas Press (N.Y.C.). Home: Elyria, Ohio. Died Nov. 21, 1983.

HEISKELL, AUGUSTUS LONGSTREET, lawyer; b. Memphis, Nov. 4, 1890; s. Frederick Hugh and Augusta (Lamar) H.; student U. Tenn., 1909-13, U. Va., 1913-14; m. Ardeane McNeil, June 15, 1918; children—Ann Longstreet (Mrs. Albert C. Rickey), Ardeane McNeil (Mrs. Warren Lee Smith). Admitted to Tenn. bar, 1914, since practiced in Memphis; sr. partner firm Heiskell,

Donelson, Adams, Williams & Wall, from 1964; with legal dept. City Memphis, 1916-20, 29-41; gen. counsel Dixie Greyhound Lines, 1938-54; instr. med. jurisprudence U. Tenn., 1938-42. Commr., mem. council Chickasaw council Boy Scouts Am., 1921-26, del. nat. council, 1925. Trustee Gooch Found., 1943, 46, from 1969. Served with U.S. Army, 1916. Fellow Am. Coll. Trial Lawyers; mem. Am., Tenn., Memphis and Shelby County (sec., treas. or bd. dirs. 1920-32) bar assns., Kappa Alpha. Democrat. Presbyn. (elder 1935). Home: Memphis, Tenn. †

HEISLER, CHARLES HARRINGTON, foreign service officer; b. Milford, Del., July 20, 1888; s. Charles Cornelius and Minnie Warfield (Watson) H.; B.S., U. of Del., 1911; m. Ingeborg Elisabet Tornquist, Sept. 16, 1927. Served in consular capacity, successively, Johannesburg, Cape Town, Kovno, Riga, Malmo, Warsaw, Danzig, Hamilton (Bermuda), Hamilton (Ont.), Tunis, 1914-42; consul at Newcastle-on-Tyne, Eng., 1942-49. Served with Del. Nat. Guard, 1908-11. Rotarian. Home: Milford, Del. †

HELEN MADELEINE, SISTER ednl. adv.; b. Saxonville, Mass., Nov. 29, 1887; dau. W. Henry and Kathleen (Kirby) Ingraham; A.B., Trinity College, Washington, 1918; A.M., Emmanuel Coll., Boston, 1926; LL.D. (hon.), Boston Coll., 1940, Regis Coll., Weston, Mass., 1950. Entered Order Sisters of Notre Dame, 1905; teacher academies of Notre Dame in Mass., 1908-19; dean of Emmanuel Coll., 1919-50 (dean emeritus); educational adviser for sisters of Notre Dame, Waltham Province. Hon. mem. Eugene Field Soc., Mark Twain Soc. Author: With Heart and Mind, 1937; Strength Through Prayer, 1938; Peace Through Prayer, 1940; Translation from French of Vol. II. of L'Heure de Jésus. Address: Waltham, Mass. †

HELLEGERS, ANDRE E., physician, educator; b. Venlo, Netherlands, June 5, 1926; s. Clement A. and Jane (Boland) H.; student Stonyhurst (Eng.) Coll., 1940-44; L. Royal Coll. Physicians, Edinburgh (Scotland) U., 1951; M.D., Belgian Central Jury, 1952; diploma in aviation medicine Paris U., 1953; D.H.L. (hon.), Wheeling Coll., 1974; m. Charlotte Lindsay Fraser Sanders, June 17, 1957; children—Paul, Caroline, Desiree, Renee. Intern, Johns Hopkins U., 1953-54, resident in ob-gyn, asst. prof. ob-gyn, asso. prof., until 1967; Macy Found. fellow in physiology Yale U., 1956-57; prof. ob-gyn Georgetown U., from 1967; prof. physiology-biophysics, from 1969, dir. Kennedy Inst. Ethics; mem., dep. sec. Pope Paul VI Commn. on Population and Birth Control, 1966; mem. Pres. Johnson's Com. on Population and Family Planning, 1968; mem. nat. adv. com. Child Health and Human Devel. Council, 1969-72. Mem. Soc. Clin. Investigation, Perinatal Research Soc. (past pres.), Am. Gynecol. Soc., Soc. Gynecologic Investigation (past pres.), Sigma Xi, Alpha Omega Alpha. Roman Catholic. Author: books; contbr. numerous articles on obstetrics, fetal physiology, population and bioethics to profl. publs.; editor bd. Am. Jour. Ob-Gyn, European Jour. Ob-Gyn, Concilium. Home: Potomac, Md. Dec. May 1979.*

HELLER, ROBERT G., retired food co. exec.; b. Czechoslovakia, Jan. 12, 1890; s. Simon and Emma (Lobel) H.; widower; children—Muriel (Mrs. Howard Weinberger), Doris (Mrs. Ralph J. Tasch). Past vice chmn., treas. Vita Food Products, Inc., N.Y.C. Home: New York City, NY. †

HELLMAN, LILLIAN, playwright; b. New Orleans, June 20, 1907; d. Max B. and Julia (Newhouse) H.; m. Arthur Kober. Ed., NYU; Litt. D, NYU, 1974; ed., Columbia U.; M.A., Tufts U., 1940; Litt.D., Wheaton Coll., 1961, Rutgers U., 1963, Brandeis U., 1965, Smith Coll., 1974, Yale, 1974, Franklin and Marshall Coll., 1975, Columbia U., 1976. With Horace Liveright, Inc., N.Y.C., 1924-25; book reviewer for Herald Tribune, 1925-28. Theatrical play-reader, 1927-30, writer, 1926-84, scenario writer, 1935-84; Author: The Children's Hour, 1934, Days to Come, 1936, The Little Foxes, 1939, Watch on the Rhine, 1941, The Searching Wind, 1944, Another Part of the Forest, 1946; adapted: Roble's Montserrat, 1949, The Autumn Garden, 1951; Dramatized: for movies The Dark Angel, 1935, These Three, 1935-36, Dead End, 1937, The Little Foxes, 1940, The North Star, 1943, The Searching Wind, 1945; author: a memoir An Unfinished Woman, 1969, Pentimento: A Book of Portraits, 1973, Scoundrel Time, 1976, Maybe, 1980; Editor: The Letters of Anton Chekhov, Farrar, Straus, 1955; musical version of Voltaire's Candide, 1955; Adaptation of Anouilh's play. The Lark, 1955, Toys in the Attic, 1960; Adaptation My Mother, My Father and Me, from Burt Blechman's How Much, 1963; Author: motion picture The Chase; Editor: motion picture The Big Knockover (Dashiell Hammett), 1966, The Collected Plays, 1972; Contbr. to mags. Recipient Gold medal for drama Nat. Inst. and Acad. Arts and Letters, 1964. Fellow Am. Acad. Arts and Scis.; mem. Am. Acad. Arts and Letters, Dramatists Guild. Home: New York, N.Y. Died June 30, 1984.*

HELLMAN, MORTON J., mathematician, educator; b. N.Y.C., Jan. 28, 1918; s. Jacob and Bess (Frank) H.; B.S., Coll. City N.Y., 1938, M.S., 1942; Ph.D., N.Y. U., 1954;

m. Martha Dorothea Kaufman, Dec. 31, 1942; children—Paul Victor, Charles David, George Edward. Mem. faculty Newark Coll. Arts and Scis., Rutgers State U., 1946-66, assoc. prof., 1958-65, prof., 1965-66; prof. math. L.I. U., Bklyn., 1966-80, chmn. dept., 1966-79, dir. NSF coop. coll.-sch. sci. program grant, 1972-73, dir. NSF pre-coll. tchr. devel. in sci. project grant, 1978-79 Served to lt. USNR, 1943-46. Recipient Outstanding Tchr. award Newark Rutgers U., 1966; NSF grantee, 1979-80. Mem. AAUP, Am. Math. Soc., Math. Assn. Am. (vice chmn. met. N.Y. sect. 1969-71, chmn. 1971-73), Nat. Council Tchrs. Math., Phi Beta Kappa, Sigma Xi. Author: College Algebra, 1956, rev. edit., 1963. Contbr. articles to profl. jours. Home: New York, N.Y. Died Oct. 15, 1980.

HELM, CHARLES ALTON, univ. prof.; b. Sheldon, Mo., Feb. 4, 1889; s. Charles and Elizabeth (Sullins) H.; B.S., U. of Mo., 1913; A.M., U. of Neb., 1916; m. Nelle Mae McGehee, June 2, 1914; 1 dau., Connie Cordelia (Mrs. Robert Southen). Prof. field crops, U. of Mo., from 1916. Sec.-treas. Mo. Seed Improvement Assn.; mem. Columbia City Council, 6 yrs. Served as personnel officer, U.S. Army, World War I. Mem. Farm House, Sigma Xi, Alpha Zeta. Democrat. Baptist. Mason (32 deg., Shrine). Home: Columbia, Mo. †

HELM, EBE WALTER, JR., ins. co. exec.; b. Phila., Aug. 9, 1890; s. Ebe Walter and Mary Helm; student Brown Prep Sch., Balt. Law Sch.; m. Margaret V. Buck, Dec. 20, 1911; children—Ebe Walter III, Margaret (Mrs. Younghusband), Dean T. With Philadelphia Casualty Co., 1905-11, Fidelity & Deposit Co. (merged with Phila. Casualty Co., Balt.), 1911-13, Am. Fidelity Co., Montpelier, Vt., 1913, Zurich Ins. Co., 1914-30, Southern Surety Co., 1930-32; with New Amsterdam Casualty Co., from 1932, v.p., dir.; with E. Walter Helm, Jr., Inc., Media, Pa., from 1963; dir. Am. Indemnity Co. Chmn. Ednl. Ins. Adv. Council. Pres. boro council School Dist. Alden, Pa. Presbyn. (presiding elder). Clubs: Union League, Down Town (Phila.); Merchants (Balt); Country of Md.†

HELMER, HUGH JOSLIN, former banker; b. Pontiac, Mich., Dec. 10, 1909; s. Arthur J. and Genevieve (Weston) H.; B.A., U. Wis., 1932, grad. Grad. Sch. Banking, 1947; m. Jane E. L. Stratton, Nov. 23, 1932; children—Louise Baumert, Frederick, James. Clk., First Nat. Bank & Trust Co., Pontiac, 1925-32; asst. examiner Wis. Banking Dept., 1932; examiner Fed. Deposit Ins. Corp., 1938; with Fed. Res. Bank Chgo., 1933-70, v.p., 1958-62, 1st v.p., 1962-70; dir. Mt. Rushmore Ins. Co., Rushmore Mut. Life Ins. Co., Rapid City. Mem. Chgo. Com. Mem. Alpha Kappa Psi, Phi Kappa Sigma. Clubs: Bankers, Union League (Chgo.). Home: Wilmette, Ill. Died Aug. 7, 1985.

HELSTEIN, RALPH L., lawyer; b. Duluth, Minn., Dec. 11, 1908; s. Henry and Lena (Litman) H; B.A., U. Minn., 1929, LL.B., 1934; m. Rachel Brin, Jan. 2, 1939; children—Nina, Toni. Admitted to Minn. bar, 1936, pvt. law practice, Mpls., 1936-43; labor compliance office for Minn. N.R.A., 1934-35; gen. counsel Minn. Council C.I.O., 1939-43; United Packinghouse Workers Am., 1942-46, internat. pres., 1946-68; spl. counsel, v.p. Amalgamated Meat Cutters and Butcher Workmen of North America, 1968-72, pres. emeritus, 1972-85; pres. emeritus United Food and Comml. Workers, AFL-CIO; v.p. indsl. union dept. AFL-CIO, 1961-65, v.p., mem. exec. council, 1965-69, v.p. emeritus, 1969-85; lectr. labor history Roosevelt U. Mem. pension research council U. Pa., 1972; bd. dirs. Chgo. Inst. Psychoanalysis; bd. dirs. Indsl. Areas Found., 1972-85. Home: Chicago, Ill. Dec. Jan. 14, 1985.

HEMKE, PAUL EMIL, college official; b. Petersburg, Ill., May 22, 1890; s. Emil Adolph and Hedwig (Keller) H.; A.B., Central Wesleyan Coll., Warrenton, Mo., 1909; A.M., U. of Chicago, 1911; Ph.D., Johns Hopkins U., 1924; m. Edith Helen Kriege, Sept. 2, 1914; children—Harold Paul, Marjorie Helene, Emily Doris. Began as teacher mathematics, Sheboygan (Wis.) High Sch., 1909; instr. mathematics and physics, Central Wesleyan College, 1912-14; instr. mathematics, Ga. Sch. Tech., Atlanta, 1914-19, Northwestern U., 1919-20; instr. mathematics and mechanics, U.S. Naval Acad., 1920-24; analyst in mathematics and physics, Langley Meml. Aeronautical Lab., Hampton, Va., 1924-27; professor aeronautics and mathematics, U.S. Naval Academy Post-Grad. Sch., 1927-31; prof. fluid mechanics, Case Sch. Applied Science, 1931-35; prof. and head aeronautical engring. dept., Rensselaer Poly. Institute, from 1935, dean of faculty, 1949-57, vice president, 1954. Consultant for Pratt & Whitney Aircraft Co., East Hartford, Conn., and Gen. Electric Co., Schenectady, N.Y. Awarded Daniel Guggenheim fellowship in aeros., Eng., 1929-30. Asso. fellow Inst. Aero. Scis.; fellow A.A.A.S.; member Am. Society for Engring. Edn., Newcomen Soc., Sigma Xi. Republican. Methodist. Club: Professional Men's (Troy). Author: Chaper on fluid mechanics in Handbook of Engineering Fundamentals, 1936; Elementary Applied Aeronautics, 1946; also various tech. reports and govt. bulls. Contbr. to mags. Home: Troy, N.Y. †

HEMPHILL, ROBERT WITHERSPOON, dist. judge; b. Chester, S.C., May 10, 1915; s. John McLure and Helen (Witherspoon) H.; m. Forrest Isabelle Anderson, June 29, 1942; children: Forrest Richardson, Harriet Witherspoon, Robert Witherspoon. A.B., U. S.C., 1936, LL.B., 1938. Bar: S.C. 1938. Assoc. firm Hemphill & Hemphill, Chester, 1938-64; solicitor 6th S.C. Jud. Circuit, 1950-56; practice before VA, U.S. Civil Service Comm., ICC, 4th Circuit Ct. of Appeals U.S. Supreme Ct.; mem. S.C. Ho. of Reps., 1947-48, 85th-88th Congresses, 5th S.C. Dist.; U.S. dist. judge Eastern, Western dists. S.C., 1964-83; judge Temporary Emergency Ct. Appeals, 1981-83. Served with USAAF, 1941-45; mem. USAF Res. Recipient Algernon Sidney Sullivan award U. S.C., 1969; Jud. award of merit Am. Trial Lawyers Assn., 1973; Distinguished Pub. Service award Am. Legion, 1976. Mem. Am. Judicature Soc., Am., S.C., Chester County bar assns., Am. Law Inst., Am. Legion, 40 and 8. Democrat. Presbyn. Club: K.P. Home: Chester, S.C. Died Dec. 25, 1985.

HENCKEN, HUGH O'NEILL, archaeologist; b. N.Y.C., Jan. 8, 1902; s. Albert Charles and Mary Creighton (O'Neill) H.; grad. Hill Sch., Pottstown, Pa., 1920; B.A., Princeton, 1924; B.A., Cambridge U., 1926, M.A., 1930, Ph.D., 1929, Sc.D., 1972; hon. D.Litt., Nat. U. Ireland, 1937; m. Mary Thalassa Alford Cruso of Pirbright, Surrey, Eng., Oct. 12, 1935; children—Ala Mary, Sophia, Thalassa. Carried out archaeol. excavations in Eng., 1928, 30, 31; dir. Harvard Archaeol. Expdn. in Ireland, 1932-36; curator European Archaeology, Peabody Mus., Harvard, 1932-72; dir. Am. Sch. of Prehistoric Research, 1945-72 (directed excavations in Morocco 1947, Algeria 1949), chmn., 1959-72; Monro lectr. Edinburgh U., 1959; lectr. Lowell Inst., 1942; spl. univ. lectr. London and Oxford univs., 1947; hon. fellow St. John's Coll., Cambridge U., 1968. Recipient Erie Soc. Gold medal, 1951. Fellow Soc. Antiquaries London, Soc. Antiquaries Scotland (hon.), Royal Irish Acad., British Acad. (corr.), Prehistoric So. Eng. (hon. corr.), Archaeol. Inst. Am. (hon. pres.), Am. Acad. Arts and Scis.; mem. Société des Antiquaries de l'Quest, Instituto de Estudios Ibéricos (corr. mem.), Com. Honor Internat. Congress Prehistoric Scis., Royal Archaeol. Inst. Great Britain, German Archaeol. Inst., German Soc. for Prehistory, Jutland Archaeol. Soc. (corr.), Instituto di Studi Italici ed Etruschi (corr.), Istituto Intaliano di Preistoria, Phi Beta Kappa (hon.). Democrat. Episcopalian. Clubs: United Oxford and Cambridge (London, England); Somerset, Odd Volumes (Boston); Harvard Faculty (Cambridge, Mass.); University (N.Y.); Country of Brookline. Author: Archaeology of Cornwall, 1932; Cahercommaun, 1938; Lagore Crannog, 1950; Tarquinia, Villanovans and Early Etruscans, 1968; Tarquinia and Etruscan Origins, 1968; The Earliest European Helmets, 1972. Contbr. Tech. articles. Home: Boston, Mass. Died Aug. 31, 1981.

HENDEE, SEARLE, advt. exec.; b. Omaha, Neb., Sept. 14, 1890; s. Joseph Watkins and Laura Etta (Searle) H.; student U. Wichita, 1907-09, Valpariso U., 1909-11; m. Ruth Hunter, May 6, 1915; 1 son, Hunter Hendee. Reporter Wichita Eagle, summers 1908-10, telegraph editor, 1911-12; city hall reporter Chicago Inter-Ocean and Chicago Record-Herald, 1912-14; asso. editor Popular Mechanics mag., 1914-19; advt. mgr. Winnipeg Tribune, 1919-20; editor, mgr. Detroit Motor Times, 1921; v.p., creative dir. George M. Savage Advt. Agy., Detroit, 1922-27, also director; v.p. Maxon, Inc., Detroit. Mem. Advt. Fedn. Am. Mason. Club: Detroit Boat. Home: Grosse Pointe Farms, Mich. †

HENDEL, CHARLES WILLIAM, educator; b. Reading, Pa., Dec. 16, 1890; s. Charles William and Emma Leininger (Stolz) H.; B.Litt., Princeton, 1913; student Marburg U. (Germany), 1913-14, College de France, 1914; Ph.D., Princeton, 1917; M.A. (hons.), Yale, 1940; m. Elizabeth Phoebe Jones, Sept. 23, 1916; children—James Norman, Charles William. Tchr., Princeton Prep. Sch., 1919; instr. Williams Coll., 1919-20; asst. prof. Princeton, 1920-26, asso. prof., 1926-29; MacDonald prof. moral philosophy, chmn. dept. McGill U., 1929-40, dean faculty Arts and Scis., 1937-40; prof. moral philos. and metaphysics, chmn. dept. Yale, 1940-59, Clarke prof. moral philosophy and metaphysics emeritus, 1959-82; Gifford lectr. natural theology U. Glasgow, 1962-63. Mem. Am. Philos. Assn. (pres. Eastern div.), Am. Soc. Polit. and Legal Philosophy (pres. 1959-61), Institut Internationale de Philosophie. Democrat. Lutheran. Author several books, the latest: Studies in the Philosophy of David Hume, 1963; Jean Jacques Rousseau, Moralist, 1963. Co-author; Philosophy in American Education, 1945; Preface to Philosophy, 1945; Goals for American Education, 1950; Freedom and Authority, 1953; The Philosophy of Kant and our Modern World, 1959; John Dewey and the Experimental Spirit in Philosophy, 1959. Home: Brandon, Vt. Died Nov. 18, 1982.

HENDERSON, HARRY ORAM, univ. prof.; b. Elders Ridge, Pa., Nov. 5, 1889; s. Joseph Henry and Jennie Prudence (Telford) H.; B.S., Pa. State Coll., 1915, M.S., 1916; Ph.D., U. of Minn., 1928; m. Marian Clark Saltsman, May 29, 1918; 1 son, Robert Eugene. Employed as county agrl. agt., Crawford County, Pa., 1916-18; dairy extension specialist, W.Va. Univ., 1919-20, asst. prof. dairy husbandry, 1920-24, asso. prof., 1924-28, prof. dairy husbandry, from 1928; head dairy dept., 1928-56. Sec.-treas. W.Va. Westminster Found. Recipient Dairy Prodn. Teaching award, Am. Dairy Sci. Assn., 1958. Fellow A.A.A.S.; mem. Am. Dairy Sci. Assn., Internat. Assn. Milk Sanitarians, Am. Soc. of Animal Prodn., W.Va. Acad. Sci., Alpha Gamma Rho, Lambda Gamma Delta, Alpha Zeta, Phi Kappa Phi, Sigma Xi. Republican. Presbyterian. Author: Dairy Cattle Feeding and Management, rev. edit., 1954. Home: Morgantown, W.Va. †

HENDERSON, ZACH SUDDATH, educator; b. Gillsville, Ga., Jan. 24, 1902; s. Hollis and Onieda (Suddath) H.; B.S., Piedmont Coll., 1922, LL.D., 1948; A.M., Columbia Tchrs. Coll., 1928, postgrad., 1930-31; postgrad. U. Chgo., 1940-41; LL.D., LaGrange Coll., 1967; m. Marjorie Clark, July 2, 1927; children—Gene, Mary, Ann. Sci. tchr. Piedmont Coll. Demonstration Sch., 1922-23; sci. tchr., coach Plant City (Fla.) High Sch., 1923-24; prin., coach Eastman (Ga.) High Sch., 1924-26; supt. pub. schs., Eastman, 1926-27; dean Ga. So. Coll., 1927-48, pres., 1948-68, pres. emeritus, also cons. tchr. edn. to univ. system chancellor, 1968-85. Chmn. Ga. High Sch. Accrediting Commn., 1946-55; Meth. Conf. lay leader of South Ga. Conf., del. to gen. and jurisdictional confs., 1944, 48, 52, 56, 60, 64, 68, 72; council, exec. com. Southeastern Jurisdiction. Trustee Piedmont Coll., 1928-30. Recipient Distinguished Alumni award Piedmont Coll., 1971. Mem. Boy Scouts Am. (Silver Beaver award), C. of C. (past pres. Stateboro), N.E.A. (dir. 1966-72), Ga. Assn. Colls. (pres. 1966-67), Am. Assn. Sch. Adminstrs., Soc. Advancement Edn., Ga. Edn. Assn. (pres. 1965-66), Phi Delta Kappa, Kappa Delta Phi. Methodist. Club: Rotary (past pres., dist. gov. 1958-59). Contbg. editor Wesleyan Christian Advocate, 1942-45; contbr. articles to Ga. Edn. Assn. Jour., Meth. Laymen. Home: Statesboro, Ga. Died Jan. 6, 1985.

HENGST, RAYMOND GUTHRIE, lawyer; b. Columbus, Ohio, Aug. 2, 1898; s. George C. and Myrta (Guthrie) H.; A.B., Oberlin Coll., 1920; J.D. Harvard, 1925; m. Fanny S. Lister, Sept. 5, 1933; children—Barbara Snow (Mrs. Ernest L. Hartmann), William Guthrie. Admitted to Ohio bar, 1925; asso. with Hauxhurst, Inglis, Sharp & Cull, and predecessors, Cleve., 1925-35, partner, 1935-55; counsel, sec. Eaton Mfg. Co., Cleve., 1955-56, gen. counsel, sec., 1956-63; v.p., gen. counsel Eaton, Yale, & Towne, Inc., 1963-67; counsel Arter & Hadden, from 1967. Mem. Am., Ohio, Cleve. bar assns., Phi Beta Kappa, Phi Delta Theta. Conglist. Clubs: Union, Court of Nisi Prius (Cleve.). Home: Cleveland, Ohio. Died Feb. 27, 1983; buried Brecksville Cemetery, Ohio.

HENION, JOHN QUINT, army officer; b. San Antonio, Oct. 3, 1922; s. Karl and Elizabeth (Schmitt) H.; m. Helen Jean Mickelsen, Mar. 11, 1947; children—Mrs. Ralph E. Janes, Nancy Cagle, John Quint, Thomas E. Student, U. Wash., 1940-43; B.Gen.Edn., Omaha U., 1962; grad., Nat. Def. Coll., 1967. Commd. officer U.S. Army; advanced through grades to lt. gen.; bn. ops. officer, exec. officer U.S. Army (3d Inf. Div.), 1950-52; asst. sec. gen. staff Office of Chief of Staff, Dept. Army, 1953-57; comdr. (3d Armored Rifle Bn., 3d Armored Div.), Germany, 1963-64, (G-3, 3d Armored Div.), 1964-66, (3d Brigade, 2d Inf. Div.), Korea, 1967-68; chief of combat ops. and analysis br. (Ops. Directorate, Jt. Chiefs of Staff), 1968-69; asst. div. comdr. (1st Inf. Div.), Vietnam, 1969-70; dir. tng. and spl. asst. to comdr. (U.S. Mil. Assistance Command), Vietnam, 1970-71; comdr. (Army Recruiting Command), 1971-74; comdg. gen. (9th Inf. Div. and Fort Lewis), Wash., 1974-75; chief of staff (Army Forces Command), Fort McPherson, Ga., 1975-77; comdr. U.S. Army Japan/IX Corps, 1977-80, ret., 1980. Decorated D.S.M. with oak leaf cluster, Legion of Merit, D.F.C., Bronze Star with Oak Leaf Cluster and V, Meritorious Service medal, Air medals (5).; Named to Inf. Officers Hall of Fame Fort Benning, Ga. Mem. Mil. Order World Wars, Assn. U.S. Army. Address: Austin, Tex.

HENLINE, HENRY HARRISON, elec. engr.; b. Colfax, Ill., Mar. 12, 1889; s. Henry Calvin and Sarah Lucinda (Wiley) H.; B.S. in E.E., U. of Ill., 1914; student Chicago Central Station Inst., 1915-16; m. Adele Letts Poole, Jan 26, 1918; 1 son, Henry Harrison, Jr. Instr. science and mathematics, Oktaha (Okla.) High Sch., 1914-15; commercial engring. dept. Ill. Maintenance Co., Chicago, 1916-17; instr. in elec. engring., Stanford U., 1917-20, asst. prof., 1920-24, asso. prof., 1924-26. Fellow Am. Inst. Elec. Engrs. (chmn. San Francisco Sect., 1922-23; chmn. Dist. 8 com. on student activities, 1926; asst. nat. sec. 1927-32; acting nat. sec., June-Dec. 1932, sec. from 1933; sec. Edison Medal com. 1932-50, Lamme Medal com. 1928-53; secretary nominating, planning and coordination coms.), Engineers Joint Council (sec. 1952). Commissioned 2d lt., Field Arty., Oct. 1918; hon. disch., Dec. 1918. Mem. Am. Society Engring. Education, Eta Kappa Nu, Sigma Xi. Republican. Club: Engineers (New York). Writer of papers on engineering education; standard frequency radio station and high voltage power transmission. Home: Scarsdale, N.Y. †

HENNESSY, JOHN JAMES, motion picture producer; b. Chgo.; s. John J. and Eleanor Marie (Burke) H.; m. Ruth Miriam Wagner, Mar. 4, 1944; children—Mildred Elaine Hennessy Heffner, Ruth Gay. B.S. magna cum laude in Chemistry, Loyola U., Chgo., 1936; M.B.A. magna cum laude, Harvard U., 1940. Asst. advt. mgr. Elgin Nat. Watch Co., 1941-42; account exec., gen. mgr. West-Marquis Advt. Agy., Los Angeles, 1947-54; pres., exec. producer John J. Hennessy Motion Pictures, South Pasadena, Calif., from 1954; tchr. mktg. and advt. UCLA, 1946-50. Writer, Pubs. Prodns., Chgo., 1937-38, (Recipient Grand Prix, Internat. Indsl. Film Festival, London, for film 23/28 1976, numerous other film awards.); Producer: films And Then There Were Four (both considered Am. classics). Commr. City of South Pasadena Freeway, 1969-77; gov.'s appointee Calif. Motion Picture Council, from 1974; bd. dirs. San Gabriel Valley region Camp Fire Girls, 1956, Ernest Thompson Seton award, 1959. Served to lt. comdr. USNR, 1943-46. Baker scholar Harvard U. Bus. Sch., 1940. Mem. Internat. Quorum of Motion Picture Producers (pres. from 1976), Info. Film Producers Am. (exec. v.p., past pres. Los Angeles chpt.), Authors Club Los Angeles (pres. from 1960), Soc. Motion Picture and TV Engrs., Public Relations Soc. Am., Nat. Press Club, Navy League, World Affairs Council Los Angeles. Republican. Roman Catholic. Clubs: Harvard (N.Y.C.); Army-Navy (Washington). Home: Pasadena, Calif.

HENNEY, RICHARD BERNARD, foundation executive; b. Upper Montclair, N.J., June 21, 1918; s. David Simonds and Stella Caroline (Bruggeman) H.; B.A., U. Va., 1950; M.B.A., Hofstra Coll., 1957. With First Nat. City Bank N.Y., 1937-41, 50-53, ofcl. asst., 1950-53; with Duke Endowment, 1953-79, treas., 1961-66, sec., 1966-73, exec. dir., 1971-79; treas. Doris Duke Trust, 1961-66, sec., 1966-73, exec. dir., 1971-79; sec. Angier B. Duke Meml., Inc., 1966-73, v.p., 1970-79; asst. treas. Duke Power Co., 1961-67, chmn. finance, 1967-74, also dir.; mem. adv. bd. Rockefeller Center office Chem. Bank, 1973-79. Served to capt. AUS, 1941-47; PTO. Mem. Newcomen Soc. N.Am., Assn. Ex-Mems. Squadron A, Am. Legion, Phi Beta Kappa, Phi Eta Sigma, Phi Kappa Psi, Alpha Kappa Psi. Elk. Clubs: Hemisphere, Rockefeller Center Luncheon (N.Y.C.). Home: Merrick, N.Y. Dec. May 30, 1979.

HENNING, O(SCAR) A(DAM), teacher; b. Cottleville, Mo., Sept. 15, 1887; s. Michael and Katharine Elisabeth (Rueffer) H.; student Elmhurst (Ill.) Coll., 1903-05, 1906-07; A.B., Central Wesleyan, Warrenton, Mo., 1913, A.M., 1915; student Culver-Stockton, Canton, Mo., 1911-13; grad. work Mo. Univ., summer 1916, 30, U. of Wis., 1916-17, summer 1917, Northwestern 1926-27, summers 1921, 22, 26, 29; m. Elizabeth C. Mackey, Dec. 25, 1913; children—O(scar) A(dam) Jr., Michael Mackey, Elizabeth (Mrs. F. M. Kiburz), Paul. Asst. prof. of German, Culver-Stockton, 1912-13; became instr. German and English, Mo. Sch. of Mines and Metallurgy, Rolla, 1920-21, asst. prof., 1921-24, assoc. prof., 1924-31, head of modern language department. 1931-46, prof. of modern fgn. lang., 1946-48; professor of modern languages and head of department Culver-Stockton College from 1949. Member Phi Kappa Phi. Mem. Evangelical Reformed Ch. Mason. Home: Florissant, Mo. †

HENRICKS, NAMÉE (MRS. WALTER A HENRICKS), "Sah-nee-weh." lecturer, sponsor Indian benefits; b. Harrington, Del., Nov. 12, 1890, d. Rev. Thomas Lambert and Eva (Bogardus). Price; grad. Adelphi Kindergarten Normal Sch., 1910; m. Rev. Walter A. Henricks, pastor First Presbyn. Ch. Penn Yan, N.Y., June 12, 1912; children—Walter Abraham, Lambert Price (dec.), Helen Namée, Eva Bogardus, Susan Kunitz. Kindergarten teacher, N.Y. City kindergarten Assn., 1910, and Los Angeles Girls Collegiate Sch.; in community service in war camps during World War; lecturer on Indian history, arts, crafts and legends; secured the appropriation from Works Progress Adminstrn. for erection of first Indian community house in N.Y. State; persuaded Am. Tract Soc. to reprint Seneca Hymnal, first written record of Seneca lang.; adopted by Tonawanda Seneca Indians, given name "Sah-nee-weh," and attends many secret ceremonies. Mem. Yates County Defense Council, chmn. mobilization, Oct. 1941-May 1942; mem. War Council since May 11, 1942; dir. Yates County War Council Office; chmn. Red Cross Blood Bank for Yates County. Chairman advisory board Tonawanda Indian Reservation Association, Inc., Nat. vice-chairman. D.A.R. Indians, 1942-44; N.Y. State chmn. C.A.R. Indians, 1937-43; senior case worker and children's agent, Department Public Welfare, Yates county, since 1944. Member D.A.R. (New York chmn. Am. Indian com.), Colonial Daughters of 17th Century, N.Y. State Hist. Soc., Am. Museums Assn., Am. Assn. Univ. Women. Compiled: (with Sidney Ayres) Romance Map of Finger Lakes, 1934; (with Arthur C. Parker) Indian Episodes of N.Y. State (map), 1935; (with Jesse Cornplanter) Legends of the Long House (book), 1938. Contbr. articles of Indian interest. Home: Penn Yan, N.Y. †

HENRY, CHARLES DANIEL, II, athletic conference executive; b. Conway, Ark., Sept. 25, 1923; s. Charles C. and Mary F. (Bush) H.; B.A., Philander Smith Coll., 1946; M.A., U. Iowa, 1948, Ph.D., 1954; m. Jeanette Therese Mouton, Aug. 12. 1957; children—Charles Daniel III, Nannette Therese. Asst. coach, dir. athletics Philander Smith Coll., Little Rock, 1949-53; faculty, head phys. edn. dept. Grambling (La.) State U., 1955-74, prof., 1958-74; asst. commr. Big Ten Conf., Chgo., 1974-82; vis. prof. summers SUNY-Cortland, 1973, SUNY-Buffalo, 1974. Served with AUS, 1943-45. Mem. Nat. Assn. Intramural Athletics (sec., exec. officer Southwestern Athletic Conf. 1958-73, exec. sec. nat. athletic steering com. 1959-75), Nat. Coll. Athletic Assn. (com. on reorgn. 1972-73, spl. com. on womens athletics 1974-75), AAHPER (chmn. nat. fin. com. 1974-75, TV promotional and income com., Ethnic Services Com. Honor award 1975), Am. Coll. Sports Medicine, AAUP, La. Assn. for Health, Phys. Edn. and Recreation (past pres., Phys. Educator of Year 1967, So. Dist. Honor award 1974, Dist. Omega Man of Year award 1966, 70), Ill. Alliance for Health, Phys. Edn. and Recreation, Ark. Alliance for Health, Phys. Edn. and Recreation, Omega Psi Phi (nat. sec. 1970-76), Phi Epsilon Kappa, Sigma Delta Psi. Roman Catholic. Club: Lions. Office: Schaumburg, Ill. Dec. Dec. 14, 1982. Interned River Valley Meml. Gardens, Dundee, Ill.

HENRY, HARRY DEWITTE, clergyman; b. Van Meter, Ia., July 3, 1890; s. Benjamin Franklin and Florence May (Lanning) H.; A.B., Simpson Coll., Indianola; Ia., 1916, D.D., 1931; B.D., Garrett Bible Inst., Evanston, Ill. 1922; m. Edyth C. Allensworth. June 30, 1918; children—James DeWitte, Gene Turner. Ordained ministry M.E., Ch., 1919; pastor Beaver, Ia. 1917-18. Maxwell, Ia., 1918-19, Dundee, Ill., 1919-22. Hillsdale, Mich., 1922-26, Burton Heights M.E. Ch. Grand Rapids, Mich., 1926-30. Iowa City, Ia., 1930-35; pres. Ia. Wesleyan Coll. Mt. Pleasant, 1935-38; pastor Central Meth. Ch., Winona, Minn., 1938-48; ret. 1948. Mem. Kappa Theta Psi. Kiwanian. Home: Clearwater, Fla. †

HENRY, JAMES BUCHANAN, lawyer; b. Balt., July 25, 1919; s. James B. and Mary (Mc Claughry) H.; m. Eleanor C. Nixon, Dec. 22, 1945; children—James B., Mary C., Elizabeth E. B.S. summa cum laude, U. Ariz., 1939; LL.B. cum laude, Harvard, 1948. Bar: N.Y. bar 1949. Asso. Cahill, Gordon, Sonnett, Reindel & Ohl, N.Y.C., 1948-61; mem. firm Kaye, Scholer, Fierman, Hays & Handler, N.Y.C., 1962-67, counsel, 1974-81; v.p., gen. counsel, sec. Am. Electric Power Service Corp., N.Y.C., 1968-74, also dir. and sec. affiliates. Spl. asst. atty. gen., N.Y., 1952-54. Served to capt. C.E. AUS, 1941-46. Mem. Am. Bar Assn., Assn. Bar City N.Y., Harvard Law Sch. Assn., Phi Beta Kappa, Phi Kappa Phi, Phi Delta Phi, Phi Lambda Upsilon. Home: Montclair, N.J. Died Aug. 24, 1981; buried Tucson, Ariz.†

HENRY, JOHN MARTIN, educator; b. Junction City, O., Dec. 9, 1889; s. Levi H. and Isabel (Bowland) H.; A.B., Ohio U., 1913; A.M., U. Wis., 1922; student U. Ia., 1927-28, 42; m. Ada Sprague, Sept. 11, 1920. Instr. U. N.D., 1913-16; asst. prof. Miss. A. and M. Coll., 1918-19; instr. econs. Coe Coll., 1919-22, asst. prof., 1922-28, Austin N. Palmer prof. commerce and finance, from 1928, bus. mgr., 1938-42, head dept., 1952-54. Mem. Am. Accounting Assn., Am. Econ. Assn., Am. Assn. U. Profs. Presbyn. (trustee). Home: Cedar Rapids, Ia. †

HENRY, PHINEAS MCCRAY, lawyer; b. Des Moines, Apr. 9, 1889; s. George Farnum and Rose (Casady) H.; A.B., Harvard, 1909; LL.B., Drake U., 1911; m. Mildred Hippee, Jan. 14, 1914 (dec. 1944); children—Phineas McCray (dec.), Patrick; m. 2d, Caroline Keck Bridge, Aug. 24, 1945 (dec. 1949); m. 3d, Elizabeth R. O'Connor, Mar. 28, 1951. Admitted to Ia. bar, 1911, since practiced law in Des Moines. Served as 1st lt., F.A., AEF, 1918. Mem. Am., Ia., Polk County bar assns. (pres. 1949), Assn. Life Ins. Counsel (pres. 1943-45). Clubs: American Alpine (N.Y.C.); Des Moines. Home: Des Moines, IA. †

HENRY, WILLIAM M., columnist, war corr., radio analyst; born at San Francisco, August 21, 1890; s. John Quincy Adams and Margaret (Weddell) H.; ed. various schools in U.S. and abroad; grad. Los Angeles High Sch., 1909; student Sydney U., Australia, 1910, A.B., Occidental Coll., Los Angeles, 1911-14, Litt.D., 1947; Litt.D., University of Redlands, 1957; married Corinne Stanton, 1914; children—Margaret (Mrs. Fred Stichweh), Patricia (Mrs. Yeomans), Mary Virginia (Mrs. Blum). With Los Angeles Times, from 1911; Times and CBS war corr. with R.A.F. in France, 1939; war corr., South Pacific, 1942; now news analyst on NBC. Adminstrv. Aide to V.P. Nixon on round-the-world Goodwill trip, 1956, spl. asst. to Nixon on African tour, 1957; member President's Com. Fitness for Youth, 1956. Pres. Radio Corr. Assn., Washington, 1947. Chmn. Radio-TV Arrangements Com. for Rep.-Dem. polit. convs., 1948, 52, 56, 60, 64. Mem.-at-large U.S. Olympic Com., 1962; pres. So. Cal. Com. for Olympic Games, 1962-66. Recipient Nat. Headliners Award for 1943 as outstanding columnist; received Headliners Award for radio reporting in 1948; Freedoms Found. Spl. Achievement Award, 1951-52; The Olympic Diploma by Internat. Olympic Com., Helsinki, Finland, 1952. Fellow Sigma Delta Chi for outstanding service to journalism, 1954; Printers Devil award, Theta Sigma Phi, 1957; M and M award for outstanding contbn. to pub. understanding of U.S. Econ. and Political System, 1964. Author: An Approved History of the Olympic Games, 1948. †

HENRY-HAYE, GASTON, French ambassador; b. Wissous, France, Feb. 6, 1890; married; 1 son, Pierre. Entered French Army, 1914; saw service at Champaigne, Somme, Verdun; wounded, cited five times for bravery and decorated with Legion of Honor and Croix de Guerre; also decorated Comdr. of British Empire, Grand Cross of Lebanese Cedar; sent to the United States as instructor to United States Army, 1917; promoted to major, Morrocan Troops, French Army, 1918, and returned to France to fight in the Argonne campaign; lectured in U.S. after World War; became engr. in charge indsl. research and a patent bureau, France; elected deputy, Versailles dist., 1928; founded Republican Reformist party, 1932; elected to Senate, 1935; mem. Senatorial Commn. on Foreign Affairs (believed direct negotiations with Hitler could avert war); became mayor of Versailles; apptd. ambassador to U.S., July 30, 1940. Speaks French and English. Made his first visit to U.S., 1908. Address: Washington, D.C.†

HENSHAW, MARSHALL B., lawyer; b. Downey, Cal., Nov. 24, 1889; A.B., Stanford, 1912. Admitted to Cal. bar, 1916, Hawaii bar, 1916; mem. firm Henshaw, Conroy & Hamilton, Honolulu. Mem. Am. Bar Assn., Bar Assn. Hawaii.†

HEPLER, ALEXANDER BRENNER, M.D.; b. Reading, Pa., Apr. 28, 1889; s. Dr. Harry and Adele (McDowell) H.; M.D., New York U., 1912; Hooper Research Foundation, 1922-24; m. Carolyn Shoemaker, 1921; children—Margaret, Barbara, Alexander Brener, William Rawle Shoemaker. Intern Jersey City Hosp., 1912-14; resident Physician Seaview Hosp. Staten Island, 1914-15; practice of medicine and surgery, Newark, N.J., 1915-17; lt. comdr. Med. Dept., U.S. Navy, 1917-21; instr. in dept. of urology, U. of Calif. Med. Sch., 1922-24; urologist, Seattle, Wash., from 1924. Fellow Am. Coll. Surgeons; diplomate Am. Bd. Urology; mem. Am. Assn. Genito-Urinary Surgeons, Société Internationale d'Urologie, Am. Urol. Assn., Pacific Coast Surg. Assn. (past pres.), North Pacific Surg. Soc., Seattle Surg. Soc. (past pres.), Am. Med. Editors and Authors Assn., Nu Sigma Nu. Clubs: Seattle Golf and Country, University (past pres.) (Seattle). Contbr. to Archives of Surgery and other med. jours. Home: Port Blakely, Wash. †

HERBER, ELMER CHARLES, educator; b. New Tripoli, Pa., Jan. 26, 1900; s. Alfred James and Amanda (Sieger) H.; A.B., Ursinus Coll., 1925; M.A., U. Pa., 1929; Sc.D., Johns Hopkins, 1941; m. Verna Rosa Weiss, June 15, 1929; 1 child, Charles Joseph. Instr. to asso. prof. biology Dickinson Coll., 1929-50, prof. 1950-84, head dept., 1955-65; parasitologist Stream Control Commn., Mich., 1940, 41; head biology dept. Evening Coll., Harrisburg, Pa., 1946-47; mem. commn. Schistosome Dermatitis Investigation, El Salvador, 1960; vis. prof. biology Messiah Coll., 1968-70. Hon. collaborator Smithsonian Instn., 1957-84. Recipient Darbaker prize in microbiology, 1954, 61. Fellow A.A.A.S.; mem. Pa. Acad. Sci. (pres. 1954), Am. Soc. Parasitology, Sigma Xi. Methodist. Rotarian. Author articles on parasites; Baird-Agassiz Letters. Home: Carlisle, Pa. Died May 12, 1984.

HERBERT, FRANK MARION, mag. exec.; b. Brooklyn, N.Y., Dec. 27, 1887; s. Hugh J. and Sarah (Moore) H.; ed. pub. schs. of Brooklyn; m. Florence Hartung, June 11, 1919. Asst. circulation sales mgr. The Literary Digest, 1919-21; direct mail sales mgr. Colliers, American mag., Woman's Home Companion, 1921-26; circulation mgr. Popular Science Monthly, 1929-39; with the Reader's Digest, from 1939, circulation sales promotion mgr., from 1939; dir. S-M News Co., O. E. McIntype, Inc.; former spl. lectr. advt. and marketing, N.Y.U. Mason. Home: Bedford Village, N.Y. Deceased.

HERBERT, HAROLD HARVEY, prof. of journalism; b. Freeport, Ill., Dec. 30, 1888; s. Edwin Day and Anna (Mitchell) H.; A.B., U. of Ill., 1912; M.A., U. of Wis., 1918, grad. study, 1923-27; m. Mary Elizabeth Baird, Sept. 4, 1923. Reporter Freeport Daily Jour., 1907-08; office asst. Freeport Daily Bulletin, 1909; reporter Freeport Daily Journal, 1910; editor Daily Illini, U. of Ill., 1911-12; city editor Freeport Daily Journal, 1912; telegraph editor Peoria (Ill.) Evening Journal, 1912-13; with U. of Okla. from 1913, prof., dir. Sch. of Journalism, 1917-45, prof., from 1945, David Ross Boyd prof. journalism, 1948-59, now emeritus chmn. publ. bd., 1915-45; editor U. of Okla. Mag., 1916-19; editor, part owner Norman (Okla.) Daily Transcript, 1918; established Sooner State Press, U. of Okla., 1920; prof. journalism, U. of Kan., summer 1921, Tex. State Coll. for Women, summer 1929; vis. prof. U. Tex., summer 1946, Oklahoma City U., from 1959; pres. Journalism Press, U. Okla., 1930-45. Dir. University Okla. Y.M.C.A., 1919-42, 1947-56, chairman of the board, 1947-49, 52-53. Consultant Ednl. Policies Commn., N.E.A., 1936-47. Awarded Gold Key, Columbia Scholastic Press Assn., Columbia, 1954; Okla. Hall of Fame, 1959. Mem. American Assn. Schs. and Depts. of Journalism (sec.-treas. 1929-40, v.p. 1940-41), Am. Assn. Teachers of Journalism (sec.-treas. 1929-40), Am. Assn. Univ. Profs. (pres. Okla. chapter, 1934-35, 1946-47, Southwestern Journalism Congress (pres. 1935-36), Press Congress of World, Nat. Editorial Assn., Okla. Press Assn., Phi Beta Kappa (triennial council, 1940, 46, 49, 52, 55, 58), Sigma Delta Chi, Kappa Tau Alpha, Chi Beta (Chi Psi). Presbyn. (elder). Club: Faculty. Contbr. to Journalism Quarterly, etc. Home: Norman, Okla. †

HERBERT, PAUL M., lt. gov. Ohio; b. Marseilles, O., Dec. 2, 1889; s. Lemuel Groves and Laura Jane (Kissell) H.; A.B., Ohio State U., 1912; law student Ohio State U., U. Mich., 1915-16; m. Ruby Fahn Thomas, Aug. 14, 1924; children—Patricia Jane (Mrs. Edward F. Lannigan), Thomas Morgan. Admitted to Ohio bar, 1917, practiced in Columbus, from 1920; asst. city atty., Columbus, 1921-22; lt. gov. Ohio, 1939-44, 46-48, from 1956. Chmn. Ohio Postwar Program Commn., 1943-44. Mem. Ohio Ho. of Reps., 1923-26, state senatory, 1926-30. Served as capt. Co. C., 324th Machine Gun Bn., U.S. Army, 1917-18; AEF. Mem. Am., Ohio, Columbus bar assns., Ohio Archcol. and Hist. Soc., Am. Legion (past mem. nat. exec. com.). Methodist. Mason. Clubs: Athletic, University, Brookside Country, Exchange (pres. 1926). Home: Columbus, Ohio. †

HERDMAN, MARGARET M., librarian; b. Chicago, Ill., Apr. 27, 1888; d. Frank E. and Mary Tilden (Victor) Herdman; A.B., U. of Ill., 1910, B.L.S., 1915; Ph.D., U. of Chicago, 1941. Librarian, philosophy, psychology, education seminar, U. of Ill., 1911-16, Rockford Coll., 1916-17; dir. reference and claim files, Law Bur., Alien Property Custodian, Washington, D.C., 1918-19; personnel and office mgr., Nat. Bd. Y.W.C.A., N.Y., 1919-23; dir. Chicago Collegiate Bur. 1923-25; organized Library and Files, Ecole de Bibliothercaires, Paris, France, 1926-27; asst. prof., McGill U. Library Sch., Montreal, Can., 1927-31; prof., La. State U. Library Sch. since 1931 (directed orgn. and adminstrn. of sch. 1931-39). Chmn. finance com. and faculty discussion group, Episcopal Students Center. Mem. A.L.A., Assn. Am. Library Schs., Am. Assn. Univ. Women, Kappa Kappa Gamma, Delta Kappa Gamma. Democrat. Episcopalian. Club: Baton Rouge Library. Editor; Louisiana Library Association Bulletin (quarterly); contbr. articles to library and education jours. etc. Author: Classification, an introductory Manual, 1934. Home: Baton Rouge, La. †

HERGET, PAUL, astronomer, educator; b. Cin., Jan 30, 1908; s. Conrad Fred and Clara Louise (Brueckner) H.; A.B., U. Cin., 1931, M.A., 1933, Ph.D., 1935; D.Sc. (hon), Edgecliff Coll., 1969; m. Harriet Louise Smith, July 27, 1935 (dec. Mar. 1972); 1 dau., Marilyn Jean; m. 2d, Anne Vallery Lorbach, Sept. 20, 1972. Instr. astronomy U. Cin., 1931-40, asst. prof., 1940-43, prof., 1943-78, Distinguished Service prof., 1965-78; Morrison fellow Lick Obs., U. Calif., 1935-36; scientist Navy Dept., U.S. Naval Obs., 1942-46; dir. Cin. Obs., 1943-78, Minor Planet Center of Internat. Astron. Union, 1947-78; cons. Manhattan Project, Oak Ridge, AEC, Argonne Nat. Lab., Chgo., USAF Project Atlas, NRL Project Vanguard, Project Mercury; staff Watson Sci. Computing Lab., 1951-52. Recipient Engr. of Year award Tech and Sci. Socs. Council of Cin., 1957; Taft medal U. Cin. Alumni Assn., 1965; Gov's award State Ohio, 1972; Rieveschl award U. Cin., 1974. Mem. Nat. Acad. Scis. (recipient James Craig Watson gold medal 1965), Am. Astron. Soc. (council 1952-55), A.A.A.S., Engring. Soc. Cin. (hon.), Am. Assn. U. Profs., Internat. Astron. Union (pres. commn. 20 1961-67), Phi Beta Kappa, Sigma Xi. Author: The Computation of Orbits, 1948. Home: Cincinnati, Ohio. Died Aug. 27, 1981.

HERMANN, GROVER MARTIN, industrialist; b. Callicoon, N.Y., July 21, 1890; s. Martin and Mary Elizabeth (Wizemann) H.; student pub. schs. of Callicoon; LL.D. (hon.), Manhattan College, N.Y.C., Ill. Inst. Technology; L.H.D. (honorary), Marietta Coll.; LL.D., Mo. Valley Coll., Marshall, Mo., 1965; m. Hazel Hessinger, Jan. 30, 1914; children—Grover Martin (dec.), Shirley, Robert; m. 2d Sarah Thurmond, Oct. 27, 1945. Founder, Am. Asphalt Paint Co., Chicago, 1913, pres., dir., 1913-40, corp. name changed to Am.-Marietta Co., 1940, pres., dir., 1940-50, chmn. bd., dir., 1950-61, merged into Martin-Marietta Corp., hon. chmn. bd., 1965-66, dir.; director Coleman Cable & Wire Company, Sovereign Life Ins. Co. Cal., Mercury Casualty Co., Consol. Freightways. Member bd. govs. Research Triangle Inst., adv. council Alfred P. Sloan Sch. of Management, Mass. Inst. Tech.; trustee Ill. Inst. Tech. Presbyn. Clubs: Tavern, Arts (Chgo.); Stock Exchange (San Francisco); Carmel Valley Golf and Country. Home: Chicago, Ill. †

HERMLE, LEO DAVID, Marine Corps officer; b. Hastings, Neb., June 30, 1980; s. William Adam and Dosia (Stauffer) H.; A.B., U. of Calif., 1914, J.D., 1917; graduate Marine Corps Schools; Army War Coll., 1939; m. Venepha A. Plass, Sept. 29, 1917; 1 son, Robert Lee, Commd. 2d lt., U.S., Marine Corps, 1917, advancing through the grades to lt. gen., 1949; comdg. officer 74th Co., 6th Marines, 2d. Div., A.E.F., France and Germany, 1918-19; col. Garde d' Haiti, Republic of Haiti, 1931-34; commanding 6th Marines, Iceland; 1941; chief of staff, second Marine Davision, Guadalcanal, 1943, asst. div. comdr., Tarawa, 1943; asst. div. comdr. 5th Div., 1945; landed Iwo Jima, D-Day; island comdr. Guam, 1946; comdg. gen. Marine Corps Recruit Depot, San Diego, to 1949; vice pres. McCune Motors Inc., National City. Decorated, Navy Cross; D.S.M. (Navy), Distinguished Service Cross, Legion of Merit, Silver Star (2), Bronze Star, Purple Heart (2), Presidential Citation (U.S.), Legion of Honor, Croix de Guerre with 2 palms, French Fourrigere, Honor and Merit (Haiti). Distinguished Service Medal (Haiti), Navy Commendation Ribbon, Navy Unit Citation, Member Kappa Alpha, Southern, Phi Delta Phi. Mason (32 deg., Shriner). Clubs: Army and Navy, Army Navy Country (Washington); Cuyamaca, San Diego (San Diego). Home: El Cajon, Calif. †

HERNDON, FRED E., coop. exec.; b. Macomb, Ill., June 5, 1887; s. Elijah C. and Elizabeth L. (Clark) H.; grad. high sch.; m. Helen E. Marrs, Sept. 20, 1922; 1 dau., Mary Ellen (Mrs. Walker R. Robb, Jr.). Farm owner and operator, Macomb, Ill.; mgr. agrl. estates; pres. Ill. Farm Supply Co., Chgo., from 1931, Pana (Ill.) Refinery, from 1948, Loudon Pipeline Co., Chgo., from 1948; dir. Farm Bur. Milling, Hammond, Ind., United Coops., Alliance, O., Central Farmers Fertilizer Co., Chgo., Coop. Plant Foods, Inc., Schererville, Ind., Premier Petroleum, Longview, Tex. Exec. sec. Wis. Farm Bur. Fedn., 1937. Bd. govs., mem. development bd. Agrl. Hall Fame. Mem. citizens com. U. Ill. Mem. C. of C. (dir.). Mem. Christian Ch. Mason. Home: Chicago, Ill. †

HEROLD, DON, writer, artist; b. Bloomfield, Ind., July 9, 1889; s. Otto F. and Clara (Dyer) H.; grad. high sch., Bloomfield, 1907; studied Art Inst. Chicago, 1908; A.B., Indiana U., 1913; m. Katherine Porter Brown, Aug. 12, 1916; children—Doris, Hildegarde. Staff The Commentator. Mem. Phi Delta Theta. Club: Players (New York). Author: So Human!, 1923; Bigger and Better, 1925; There Ought to Be a Law, 1926; Our Companionate Goldfish, 1927; Strange Bedfellows, 1930; Doing Europe—and Vice Versa, 1931. Home: New York, N.Y. †

HERRICK, H.T., labor arbitrator; b. N.Y.C., Apr. 24, 1920; s. Horace Terhune and Elinore (Morehouse) H.; B.S., Hamilton Coll., 1942; LL.B., Cornell U., 1948; m. Virginia Boardman Leigh, Oct. 6, 1945 (dec. 1964); children—Christine Terhune, David Morse; m. 2d, Allison Butler, May 1, 1965. Admitted to N.Y. bar, 1949; asso. firm Paul, Weiss, Wharton & Garrison, N.Y.C., 1948-50; atty. NLRB, 1950-57; labor atty. Westinghouse Electric Corp., 1957-61; asst. to asst. sec. labor, 1961-63; gen. counsel Fed. Mediation and Conciliation Service, 1963-65; dir. div. of labor relations ERDA, AEC, Dept. Energy, 1966-78; labor arbitrator, 1978-80; adj. prof. Georgetown U. Sch. Law, 1965. Served with USAAF, 1942-45. Mem. Am., Fed. bar assns. Unitarian. Home: Washington, D.C. Died Feb. 1980.

HERRICK, HAROLD EDWARD, lawyer; b. Lawrence, N.Y., Apr. 17, 1890; s. Harold and Annie T. (Lawrence) H.; B.A., Yale, 1912; LL.B., Columbia, 1915; m. Pauline Bacon, Nov. 9, 1918; children—Harold Edward, Elanor (Mrs. Albert Stickney), Adeline (Mrs. J.M.A. Bird). Admitted to New York bar, 1915, practiced in N.Y.C.; mem. firm Sowers, Herrick & Black, 1925-66. Dir. Home Life Ins. Co. Trustee St. Pauls Episcopal Ch., Rome, Italy, St. James Episcopal Ch., Florence, Italy. Home: Woodmere, N.Y. †

HERRIDGE, WILLIAM DUNCAN, diplomat; b. Ottawa, Can., Sept. 18, 1887; s. William Thomas and Marjorie (Duncan) H.; student Collegiate Inst., Ottawa; A.B., U. of Toronto, 1909; grad. in law, Osgood Hall, Toronto, 1912; m. Mildred Marion Bennett, Apr. 14, 1931. In practice of law, specializing in patent and corporation law, at Ottawa from 1913; was mem. firm Henderson, Herridge & Gowling; appt. king's counsel, 1928; now minister to U.S., Washington D.C. Served Canadian E.F., May 1915-19, advancing to brigade maj. Decorated Distinguished Service Order, Mil. Cross, and bar to Mil. Cross; mentioned in dispatches 3 times. Mem. Kappa Alpha. Mem. United Ch. of Can. Clubs: Rideau Country, Royal Ottawa Golf (Ottawa); University (Montreal).†

HERRING, ROBERT RAY, utility company executive; b. Childress, Tex., Feb. 11, 1921; s. Lonnie Ray and Clara (Wolford) H.; m. Sylvia Carmen Grant, Oct. 27, 1945; children—Sylvia Diane, Robert Ray, Randolph W.; m. Joanne Johnson King, May 6, 1973; stepchildren—Beauford King, Robin King. B.A., Tex. A. and M. Coll., 1941. Vice pres. Fish Engring. Corp., 1950-52; pres. Fish Service Corp., 1952-58, Valley Gas Prodn., Inc., 1958-63; v.p., gen. mgr. Houston Pipe Line Co., 1963-65; sr. v.p. Houston Natural Gas Corp., 1965-67, pres., 1967-74, chmn. bd., chief exec. officer, 1967-81; dir. Tex. Commerce Bancshares, Inc., Proler Internat., Cameron Iron Works, Inc. Pres. Tex. Heart Inst.; exec. bd. Sam Houston Area council Boy Scouts Am.; chmn. bd. govs. Rice U.; bd. dirs. Salvation Army. Served to lt. col. USAAF, World War II, PTO. Decorated Legion of Merit, Silver Star, Air Medal with clusters; recipient Gold Citizenship medal SAR; U.S. Treasury medal of merit; Disting. Alumnus awards Tarleton State Coll., 1970; Disting. Alumnus awards Tex. A and M. U., 1974; Disting. Citizen award Goodwill Industries, 1981; Silver medal Chief Exec. Officer of Yr. awards Fin. World, 1981; Outstanding Service to Mankind award Tex. Gulf Coast chpt. Leukemia Soc. Am., 1981; named Interpipeliner of 1981. Mem. Inst. Mining, Metall. and Petroleum Engrs., Houston C. of C. (past pres.). Clubs: Ramada (Houston) (dir.), River Oaks Country (Houston), Petroleum (Houston); Met. (N.Y.C.), Sleepy Hollow Country (N.Y.C.); Pisces (Washington); 1001 (Nassau, Bahamas), Lyford Cay (Nassau, Bahamas); Annabel's (London); Travellers (Paris); Links (Boca Grande, Fla.); Augusta Nat. Golf, Houston City. Home: Houston, Tex. Died Oct. 11, 1981.

HERRMANN, CARL STRAUSS, pub. utility exec.; b. Worcester, Mass., July 11, 1890; s. Charles and Emma (Strauss) H.; ed. Worcester pub. schs., Becker Coll. Bus. Adminstrn. and Secretarial Sci.; m. Bertha Irene Bates, July 14, 1909; children—Marion Emma Hemeon, Carl Bates, Allen Milton, Richard, Barbara Davidson. Typist, clk. stenographer Am. Steel & Wire Co., 1906-12; with New Eng. Electric System, from 1912, pres., 1935-41, chmn. bd., 1941-55; dir. Liberty Mut. Ins. Co. Mem. Panel of Arbitrators of Arbitration Com. N.Y. Stock Exchange. Mem. chambers commerce of Boston and Worcester. Mason (32, Shriner), Elk. Club: Algonquin (Boston). Home: Wellesley Hills, MA. †

HERSCHER, IRENAEUS JOSEPH, archivist, ret. librarian; b. Guebviller, Alsace, France, Mar. 11, 1902; came to U.S., 1913, naturalized, 1921; s. Jean-Baptiste and Josephine (Hugendobler) H. B.A., St. Bonaventure U., 1929, M.A., 1930; S.T.B., Cath. U. Am., 1931; M.L.S., Columbia, 1934; Litt.D. (hon.), St. Bonaventure U., 1969. Joined Order of Friars Minor, 1920; ordained priest Roman Cath. Ch., 1931, master of clerics, Croghan, N.Y., 1932-33, prof. philosophy, 1932-33; prof. ancient langs. St. Bonaventure U., 1934- 38, asst. librarian, 1934-37, librarian, 1937-71, librarian emeritus, from 1971, univ. archivist, from 1971, art curator, from 1971; initiated Union Catalog of Franciscan Lit., 1952-58, Franciscan Bibliog., from 1934. Mem. A.L.A., Cath. Library Assn., U.S.-Cath. Hist. Soc., Cath. Hist. Assn., O-Pa-Hi Hist. Assn. Franciscan Ednl. Conf., Western N.Y. Cath. Library Conf., InterAm. Bibliog. and Library Assn. Spl. research Franciscan history, printing.

HERTER, CHRISTIAN ARCHIBALD, editor, congressman; born Paris, France, March 28, 1895, of American parents; son of Albert and Adele (McGinnis) H.; prepared education École Alsatienne, Paris, 1901-04, Browning School of New York City, 1904-11; A.B., cum laude, Harvard Univ., 1915; married Mary Caroline Pratt, Aug. 25, 1917; children—Christian A., Frederic Pratt, Adele, Eliot Miles. Attaché Am. Embassy, Berlin, 1916-17; spl. asst., U.S. Dept. State, 1917-18; sec. Am. Commn. to Negotiate Peace, Paris, 1918-19; asst. to Sec. of Commerce Herbert Hoover, 1919-24, and exec. sec. European Relief Council, 1920-21; editor The Independent, 1924-28; asso. editor The Sportsman, Boston, Mass., 1927-36; lecturer on internat. relations, Harvard, 1929-30. Rep. in Mass. Legislature, 1931-43, speaker 1939-43; mem. 78th-80th Congresses (1943-49), 10th Mass. Dist. Director Commn. for Relief of Belgium Ednl. Foundation; chmn. bd. trustees Foreign Service Educational Foundation: trustee World Peace Foundation. Boston Library Society; overseer Harvard Univ., 1940-44. Decorated Order of Crown (Belgium); Order of Polonia Restituta (Poland). Clubs: Century, Harvard (New York); Somerset, Tavern (Boston); Essex Country (Manchester, Mass.); Metropolitan (Washington). Home: Boston, Mass. †

HERTZOG, DONALD PAUL, lawyer, oil co. exec.; b. Washington, Apr. 25, 1926; s. Rudolph Paul and Helen (McGraw) H.; B.A. cum laude, Georgetown U., 1948, LL.B., 1951; LL.M., N.Y.U., 1963; m. Jeanne Gail O'Malley, June 29, 1957; children—Donald (dec.), John, Mary, Matthew. Admitted to D.C. bar, 1951, N.Y. bar, 1958; spl. atty. Office of Chief Counsel IRS, Washington, 1951-52; spl. asst. to atty. gen. Dept. Justice, Washington, 1952-57; tax atty. Texaco Inc., N.Y.C., 1957-62, sr. tax atty., 1962-63, gen. tax atty., 1963-71, asso. gen. tax counsel, 1971-72, asso. gen. counsel, 1972-75, dep. tax counsel, 1975-76, gen. tax counsel, 1976-80; tax advisory bd. Tax Mgmt., 1971, Tax Found. Inc., 1976. Served with U.S. Army, 1944-46. Mem. Am., N.Y. bar assns., N.Y. County Lawyers Assn. Republican. Roman Catholic. Clubs: Cloud (bd. govs. 1973-77), Pelham Country (bd. govs. 1977). Home: Pelham, N.Y. Died Nov. 29, 1980.

HERZ, MARTIN FLORIAN, educator, former ambassador; b. N.Y.C., July 9, 1917; s. Gustave L. and Edith (Flammerschein) H.; m. Elisabeth Kremenak, Apr. 6, 1957. B.S., Columbia, 1937. Entered U.S. Fgn. Service, 1946, 3d sec., Vienna, Austria, 1946-48, Washington, 1949-50, 2d sec., Paris, France, 1950-54, Phnom Penh, Cambodia, 1955-56, 1st sec., 1956-57, Tokyo, Japan, 1957-59; spl. asst. Bur. African Affairs, Washington, 1960-63, polit. counselor, Tehran, Iran, 1963-67; country dir. Laos, Cambodia Dept. State, Washington, 1967-68, counselor with rank minister, Saigon, Vietnam, 1968-70, dep. asst. sec. state internat. orgn. affairs, Washington, 1970-74; ambassador People's Republic of Bulgaria, Sofia, 1974-77; Oscar Iden research prof. diplomacy, dir. Inst. for Study Diplomacy, Georgetown U., Washington, 1977-83. Author: (with Zack Hanle) The Golden Ladle, 1945, A Short History of Cambodia, 1958, Beginnings of the Cold War, 1966, How the Cold War Is Taught, 1978, The Prestige Press and the Christmas Bombing, 1970, 1980; editor: Decline of the West? George Kennan and his Critics, 1978, The Modern Ambassador, 1983; Contbr. numerous articles to profl. jours. Served from pvt. to maj. AUS, 1941-46, ETO, NATOUSA. Decorated Purple Heart, Bronze Star U.S.; Medal City of Paris; Grand Silver Insignia with star Austria; Horseman of Madara 1st class Bulgaria; recipient Commendable Service award, 1960, Superior Honor award, 1970; both U.S. Dept. State).; Woodrow Wilson vis. fellow, 1978-80. Mem. Am. Fgn. Service Assn. (dir. 1960-63, 67-68), Freedom House, DACOR. Home: Washington, D.C. Died Oct. 6, 1983.

HERZBERGER, MAXIMILLAN JAKOB, optical research exec.; b. Charlottenburg, Germany, Mar. 7, 1899; s. Leopold and Sonja (Behrendt) H.; B.S., Schiller Real Gymnasium, 1917; M.S., Ph.D. in Math., Berlin U., 1922; student Jena U., 1923-24; m. Edith Kaufman, May 31, 1925; children—Ruth (Mrs. Roy A. Rosenberg), Ursula (Mrs. Ed Klima), Hans George. Came to U.S., 1935, naturalized, 1940. Lens designer, Emil Busch, Bathenow, Germany, 1923-25; charge lens computing dept. Leitz Co., Wetzlar, Germany, 1925-27; mathematician, personal asst. to dir. C. Zeiss Co., Jena, 1927-34; lectr. optics Delft U., 1934; lens designer Scophony TV Co., London, Eng., 1935; sr. research asso. charge geometrical optical research Eastman Kodak Co., Rochester, N.Y., 1935-65; mem. Inst. Advanced Study, Princeton, 1946; research on designing lenses, theory optical image, gen. field theory, theory of microscope, gen. math. problems; guest professor Eidgenossische Technische Hochschule, Zurich, Switzerland, 1965-68, lectr., 1968-82. Mem. bd. dirs. Jewish welfare, 1942, 53-57, 60-64. Recipient Cressy Morrison prize math. N.Y. Acad. Scis., 1945; Ives medal, Optical Soc. Am., 1962. Fellow Optical Soc. Am. (lectr. 1962-63), Am. Association, Advancement Sci.; mem. Am. Math. Soc., Deutsche Optische Gesellschaft, American Chess Association (life member), N.Y. State Chess Assn. (president 1949, v.p. 1949-82, Rochester Optical Soc. (program chmn.), Swiss Optical Soc., Swiss Phys. Soc., German Math. Soc., Zuircher Schachgesellshaft. Sigma Xi (chpt. pres. 1964-65); corr. mem. Bavarian Acad. Scis. Jewish religion (charge adult edn. 1963-64). Clubs: Swiss American, American. Author: Strahlenoptik, 1932; Modern Geometrical Optics, 1958. Contbr. Handbook of Physics, Condon and Odishaw, 1958; McGraw-Hill Ency. of Science and Technology, 1960. Home: Zurich, Switzerland. Died Apr. 9, 1982.

HESS, SEYMOUR LESTER, educator; b. Bklyn., Oct. 27, 1920; s. Morris J. and Rose B. Hess; B.A., Bklyn. Coll., 1941; M.S., U. Chgo., 1945, Ph.D., 1949; m. Eugenia E. Legrande, Dec. 18, 1966; children—Stephen B., Robert N., Barbara L. Research asso., instr. U. Chgo., 1946-48; research meteorologist Lowell Obs., Flagstaff, Ariz., 1948-50; asso. prof., prof., assoc. dean Fla. State U., Tallahassee, 1950-82, Disting. prof., 1978-79; liaison scientist U.S. Office Naval Research, London, Eng.; vis. prof. N.Y. U.; vis. scientist Nat. Center for Atmospheric Research; leader meteorology team Project Viking, NASA; Fulbright-Hays lectr. Leningrad (USSR) U., 1978. Trustee Nat. Center for Atmospheric Research, Boulder, Colo. Served to 1st lt. USAAF. Recipient Spl. award Am. Meteorol. Soc., medal for exceptional sci. achievement NASA. Fellow Am. Meteorol. Soc. (councilor 1964), AAAS; mem. Am. Geophys. Union, Am. Astron. Soc., Royal Meteorol. Soc., Sigma Xi. Author: Introduction to Theoretical Meteorology, 1959. Home: Tallahassee, Fla. Dec. Jan. 15, 1982.

HESS, WALTER NORTON, prof. zoölogy; b. Great Valley, N.Y., May 1, 1890; s. Charles Fremont and Florence Dell (Norton) H.; A.B., Oberlin, 1913; A.M., Cornell U., 1916, Ph.D., 1919; student and investigator, various periods, Marine Biol. Lab., Woods Hole, Mass. and Tortugas Lab. of Carnegie Inst.; also investigator Johns Hopkins U., as Johnson scholar, 1923-24; m. Rachel Victoria Metcalf, July 31, 1924; children—Wilmot Norton, Carroll Norman. Instr. in zoölogy, Pa. State Coll., 1913-15; asst. in entomology, Cornell U., 1915-17; prof. zoölogy and head of dept., DePauw U., 1917-28, also sec. of faculty; prof. biology and head of dept., Hamilton Coll., Clinton, N.Y., from 1928. Served as bacteriologist, U.S. Army, 1918-19; teacher Biarritz (France) Am. Univ. (U.S. Army), 1945-46; lecturer Information and Edn., U.S. Army, Germany, 1946. Fellow A.A.A.S.; mem. Am. Soc. Zoologists (sec. 1948-51); rep. bd. govs. Am. Inst. Biol. Scis., 1952-56), Am. Assn. Univ. Profs., Society Exptl. Biology and Medicine, Gamma Alpha, Sigma Xi. Presbyn. Contbr. to World Book Ency., and various zoöl. jours. Asso. editor Jour. of Morphology, 1940-43. Home: Clinton, N.Y. †

HESSEY, JOHN HAMILTON, lawyer; b. Worton, Md., Aug. 18, 1890; s. John Hamilton and Emma (Nicholson) H.; A.B., Washington Coll., Chestertown, Md., 1910, A.M., 1913; LL.B., U. Md., 1913; LL.D., Washington Coll., 1963; m. Gladys E. Messersmith, June 1, 1921; children—John Hamilton, Mahlon W. Admitted to Md. bar, 1912, since practiced in Balt.; lectr. U. Balt., 1928-59, asst. dean Sch. of Law, 1935-46, dean, 1946-69; lectr. corps., 1959-66. Chmn. appeal bd. SSS, 1940-67, Pub. Service Commn. Md., 1948-55; mem. 4th Regional Loyalty Bd., 1948-52; mem. loyalty review bd. U.S. Civil Service Commn., 1952-53; mem. Council Chs. and Christian Edn. Md., 1944-63. Trustee U. Balt., Wesley Theol. Seminary; chmn. trustees South Baltimore Gen. Hosp.; bd. visitors and govs. Washington Coll., Chestertown, Md., from 1943, chmn., 1952-63; pres. George Washington Masonic Nat. Meml. Assn., Alexandria, Va. Served as 2d lt. A.S., U.S. Army, W.W. I; with A.S. Md. N.G., 1919-22. Mem. Assn. Ind. Colls. of Md. (treas.), Md. Bible Soc. (mem. bd. from 1929, pres. 1960), Am., Md. bar assns., Am. Judicature Soc., Am. Meth., Md. hist. socs. Methodist (trustee). Elk, Mason (past grand master). Club: Merchants (Balt.). Home: Baltimore, MD. †

HESTER, HUGH BRYAN, army officer; b. Hester, N. C., Aug. 5, 1895; s. William Alexander and Marietta (Bullock) H.; A.B., U. of N.C., 1916. LL.B., 1917; grad. Arty. Sch., Saumur, France, 1917, F.A. Sch., 1923, Cav. Sch., 1932. Chem. Warfare Sch., 1938, Army Industrial Coll., 1939, Babson (Mass.) Inst., 1938; m. Paula Hester Green, Jan. 18, 1935. Commd. 2d lt., U.S. Army, 1917, and advanced through grades to brig. gen., 1944; exec. to dir. procurement Office of Sec. of War, 1939-41; chief of procurement control Office of Q.M.G., 1941-42, dep. chief quartermaster Southwest Pacific Theater, 1942-43, chief of subsistence depot, Jan.-Sept. 1943. dir. procurement, 1943-44; comdg. gen. Australian Base Sect., U.S. Army Services of Supply. 1944-45; dir. food and agr. Office of Mil. Gov., U.S. Army, Germany, 1945-47; mil attaché, Australia. 1947-48; with Gen. Staff Corps, 1944-48; comdg. gen. Phila. Q.M. Depot since 1948. Decorated D.S.M., Silver Star (U.S.), Legion of Honor, Croix de Guerre, Fourragère (France). Mem. Kappa Alpha, Scabbard and Blade. Mason (32 deg.), Elk, Presbyterian. Home: Asheville, N.C. Dec. Nov. 24, 1983.†

HETZEL, FREDERICK JOSEPH, newspaper exec.; b. S.I., N.Y., Feb. 27, 1928; s. Frederick J. and Anna (Steers) H.; m. Sue M. Casper, Sept. 2, 1950; children—Patricia Ann, Frederick John, Michael. B.B.A., Pace Coll., 1959. With Dow Jones & Co., Inc., Princeton, N.J., from 1953, asst. treas., 1960-70, treas., from 1970. Served with AUS, 1948-50, 50-52. Mem. Nat. Assn. Accountants, Inst. Newspapers Controllers and Finance Officers. Home: Trenton, NJ.

HEUER, SCOTT, JR., lawyer, former govt. ofcl.; b. St. Louis, Mar. 3, 1925; s. Scott and Maurine (Barnes) H.; m. Ann Foster Lynch, Dec. 29, 1956; children—Scott Casilear, Catherine Ann, Charles Edwin, Amanda Hollins. Student, Princeton, 1942-43; B.S., Cornell U., 1945; J.D., Columbia, 1949; postgrad., Sch. Advanced Internat. Studies, Johns Hopkins, 1961. Bar: Mo. bar 1949, D.C. bar 1954, Supreme Ct. bar 1964. Mem. firm McDonald & Wright, St. Louis, 1949-51; atty. adviser Office Sec. Def., Washington, 1954-55; asst. gen. counsel USIA, Washington, 1955-59; exec. officer USIS, Rio de Janeiro, Brazil, 1959-61, individual practice, Washington, 1961-69, from 71; insp. gen. fgn. assistance with rank of asst. sec. Dept. State, Washington, 1969-71; dir. various petroleum corps. Vice chmn. Washington Republican. Finance Com., 1968; Pres. bd. trustees Barney Neighborhood House, Washington, 1969-75. Served to lt. USNR, 1943-46, 51-53. Mem. Am. Bar Assn., D.C. Bar Assn., Internat. Bar Assn. Republican. Episcopalian. Clubs: Congressional Country (Washington); Federal City, Marlboro (Md.) Hunt; Princeton (N.Y.C.); New Orleans Country (New Orleans), Boston (New Orleans). Home: Washington, DC.

HEUSSLER, ROBERT WILLIAM, educator; b. Buffalo, Aug. 11, 1924; s. Herman K. and Carlotta (Morgan) H.; m. Ten Broeck Jackson, Jan. 12, 1957; children—Morgan Ten Broeck, Lowry Elizabeth, Sarah Stuyvesant, Ann Bayard. B.A., Dartmouth, 1948; student, Coll. Chinese Studies, Peking, 1948, Woodrow Wilson Sch. Pub. and Internat. Affairs, Princeton, 1950-52; Fulbright scholar, St. Antony's Coll., Oxford (Eng.) U., 1959-61; Ph.D. in Politics, Princeton, 1961. Aviation exec. Standard Oil Co., Far East, 1948-50; overseas rep. Lowell Thomas, 1952-55; dir. Africa-Asia program U.S. univs. Syracuse U., 1961-62; Ford Found. exec. Latin Am. program, 1962-64; research appointments Ahmadu Bello U., Nigeria, 1965, Univ. Coll., Tanzania, 1968; pres. Trenton (N.J.) State Coll., 1968-70; vis. fellow Center Internat. Studies, Princeton U., 1970-71; Nat. fellow Hoover Instn. Stanford U., 1971-72; research asso. St. Antony's Coll., Oxford, 1972-73; prof. history State U. N.Y., Geneseo, 1973-83, chmn. dept., 1973-75. Author: Yesterday's Rulers: The Making of the British Colonial Service, 1963, The British in Northern Nigeria, 1968, British Tanganyika, 1971, Interlude in the Forties, 1980, British Rule in Malaya, 1981, British Malaya, 1981, Completing a Stewardship: The Malayan Civil Service, 1942-57, 1983. Served to 1st lt. USAAF, World War II, ETO. Decorated D.F.C., Air medal with 3 oak leaf clusters. Fellow Royal Commonwealth Soc. (London). Address: Sharon, Vt. Died Feb. 18, 1984.

HEWARD, BRIAN, stock broker; b. Brockville, Ont., Can., July 15, 1900; s. Arthur Richard Graves and Sara Efa (Jones) H.; m. Anna Barbara Lauderdale Logie, Dec. 28, 1925; children—Barbara, Chilion F.G., Efa (Mrs. Donald Greenwood), Faith (Mrs. William Berghuis). Grad., Lower Can. Coll., 1915; M.A., St. John's Coll., Cambridge (Eng.) U., 1921. Accountant P.S. Ross & Sons, 1921-22, Oswald & Drinkwater, 1922-25; partner Jones Heward & Co., 1925-64, sr. partner, 1945-64, co. inc., 1965; pres. Jones Heward & Co., Ltd., 1965, chmn. bd., 1966, all Montreal, Que., Can.; chmn. bd. Consumers Glass Co., Ltd., Montreal, Toronto, Ont., from 1960. Served as midshipman Royal Canadian Navy, 1918. Home: Westmount PQ, Canada.

HEWITT, ARTHUR WENTWORTH, clergyman; b. West Berlin, Vt., June 22, 1883; s. Arthur Lee and Florence Elnora (Eddy) H.; grad. Montpelier (Vt.) Sem., 1904; D.D., Middlebury Coll., 1923; Litt. D., Norwich U., 1956; L.H.D., U. Vt., 1968; m. Nina A. Battles, Sept. 18, 1907; 1 dau., Hilda (dec.). Ordained M.E. ministry, 1904; pastor, Glover, Vt., 1904-08, Plainfield, 1908-33, Moretown and South Duxbury, 1933-35, Northfield, 1939-56; pastor Riverton (Vt.) Ch., from 1956. Supt. schs., Glover, 1905-06, Plainfield, 1910-11; lectr., U.S., Can.; Slover lectr. on preaching Southwestern U., 1952; preacher Middlebury Coll., 1927-37; headmaster Montpelier Sem., pres. Vt. Jr. Coll., 1935-38. Mem. Vt. Ho. of Reps., 1912-17; mem. Vt. State Bd. Edn., 1915-35, chmn., 1923-35; Vt. rep. Nat. Conf. on Vocational Edn., Indpls., 1917, Nat. Conf. on Rural Edn., Washington, 1918. Mem. Gen. Conf. M.E. Ch., 1920, 28, 32, 36; pres. Vt. Council Religious Edn., 1933-36; mem. Fed. Council Chs., 1932-39; rep. Vt. Conf. M.E. Ch., Boston Area Council, 1933-37; mem. U. Senate M.E. Ch., 1936-38. Pres. trustees Montpelier Sem., 1921-36; chaplain Vt. State Grange 6 years. Recipient Quadrennial award honor Nat. Meth Town and Country Conf., 1959. Mem. Vt. State Tchrs. Assn., Poetry Soc. Vt. (pres. 1959-67). Democrat. Mason (32 deg.). Author: Harp Of the North, 1916; Bubbles, 1920; Songs of the Sea, 1923; Steeples Among the Hills, 1926; The City of Joy, 1926; Highland Shepherds, 1939; God's Back Pasture, 1941; The Shepherdess, 1943; Jerusalem the Golden, 1944; The Bridge, 1948; The Mountain Troubadour, 1962; The Old Brick Manse, 1966. Contbr. articles to theol. mags. Home: VT. †

HEWITT, ROBERT RUSSELL, physicist, educator; b. Los Angeles, Oct. 28, 1923; s. Claude Nathan and Lillie Christina (Anderson) H.; m. Carol La Verne Heins, Sept. 9, 1951; children—Robin Lee, Catherine Anne, Tammy Lynne. B.A. in Physics, U. Calif. at Berkeley, 1951, Ph.D., 1956. Instr. U. Calif. at Berkeley, 1956-57; asst. prof. U. Calif. at Riverside, 1957-62, asso. prof., 1962-68, prof. physics, from 1968, asso. dean research, 1966-68; dean Grad. Div., 1968-73; Cons. Aerospace Research Assos., West Covina, Cal. Contbr. articles physics jours. Served with USNR, 1944-46. A.P. Sloan postdoctoral fellow U. Calif. at Berkeley, 1958-59. Mem. Am. Phys. Soc., Am. Physics Tchrs. Assn., A.A.A.S., Phi Beta Kappa, Sigma Xi. Home: Riverside, Calif.

HEWLETT, FRANK WEST, newspaperman; b. Pocatello, Ida., Dec. 30, 1910; s. Albert J. and Annie (Neaf) H.; student Ida. State U.; Nieman fellow Harvard; m. Virginia Bryant, June 23, 1939; 1 dau., Norma Jean Petty. Reporter, editor newspapers Ida., Cal., Hawaii, Japan: fgn. corr. United Press, 1941, mgr., Manila, 1941, war corr., World War II, covering fall and recapture of P.I., Merrill's Marauders in Burma, Papuan and New Georgia campaigns in So. Pacific; Washington corr. Salt Lake Tribune and Seattle Times. Mem. Corregidor-Bataan Meml. Commn., 1958, 62, 66; mem. standing com. corrs. covering U.S. Congress, 1970-71, chmn. com., 1971. Recipient Nat. Headliners award for series of articles on Fall of Bataan, Corregidor, 1942. Mem. Sigma Delta Chi. Roman Catholic. Club: Nat. Press (Washington). Home: Arlington, Va. Died July 7, 1983.

HEXTER, RICHARD MARTIN, investment company executive; b. Cleve., Nov. 6, 1933; s. Samuel J. and Helen (Apple) H.; B.S., U. Calif.-Berkeley, 1954; M.B.A. (Baker scholar) Harvard, 1956; m. Anne Maren Glasoe, Mar. 7, 1966; children—Douglas Owen, Elizabeth Page, Russell Anthony. With TRW, Inc., Los Angeles, 1956-59; exec. v.p. Ovitron Corp., N.Y.C., 1959-61; exec. v.p. Donaldson, Lufkin & Jenrette, Inc., N.Y.C., 1961-75; chmn. bd., pres. Ardshiel Assoc., Inc., N.Y.C., 1976-81; chmn. bd. New Sources for Funding, Inc., N.Y.C.; dir. Arcata Corp., Menlo Park, Calif., Clopay Corp., Cin., Advanced Micro Devices, Inc., Sunnyvale, Calif., Burndy Corp., Norwalk, Conn., Wavetek, Inc., San Diego, Mind, Inc., Norwalk; adj. prof. bus. Columbia U., 1976-78; disting. faculty fellow Sch. Orgn. and Mgmt., Yale U., 1979-80. Trustee, 1st v.p. Lexington Sch. for Deaf, Kennecott fellow; Kraft scholar; chartered fin. analyst. Mem. Manuscript Soc., Internat. Wine and Food Soc., Tau Beta Pi, Phi Eta Sigma. Clubs: Harvard, Harvard Bus. Sch. (dir.), Whipporwill. Author numerous articles on investment banking, also lectr. Home: Armonk, N.Y. Dec. Mar. 23, 1981.

HEYMAN, DAVID M., foundation executive; born New York City, August 29, 1891; s. Simon and Bella (Heinsheimer) H.; student Mohegan Lake Mil. Acad., 1905-09, Cornell, 1909-10; A.B., Columbia, 1912; L.H.D., Columbia, 1954; LL.D., N.Y. Univ., 1960; m. Ruth Stein, July 3, 1921; children—David John, Thomas M., Kenneth L. Entered investment banking bus., 1912; partner Lewisohn & Co., 1933-47; member board of directors Tennessee Corporation; dir., mem. exec. com. Cities Service Co. Pres. New York Found.; pres., chmn. Pub. Health Research Inst. City N.Y., 1949-61; hon. chmn. bd. Health Ins. Plan Greater N.Y.; mem. N.Y.C. Bd. Health, 1938-50; mem. N.Y.C. Bd. Health, 1938-50; mem. N.Y.C. Bd. of Hosps., 1950-1984; mem. Health Research Council, N.Y.C.; trustee World Rehabilitation Fund, Conservation Found. Mem. nat. adv. health council USPHS, 1951-55; chmn. Commn. on Health Services N.Y.C., 1959-60; chmn. Task Force on Orgn. Med. Services, 1961-63. Mem. Columbia Coll. Council, 1959-63. Bd. govs. Pinchot Found. Clubs: Explorers, City Midday, Bankers of Am., Lotos (N.Y.C.). Home: New York, N.Y.

HEYWOOD, CHESTER DODD, civic worker; b. Worcester, Mass., Oct. 12, 1887; s. Frank Everett and Harriet Dodd (Jennings) H.; grad. Blair Acad., 1907; B.A., Williams Coll., 1911; m. Rachel Wallace, Oct. 10, 1925. With Heywood Boot & Shoe Co., Worcester, 1911-47, pres., 1940-45, chmn. bd., 1946-47; dir. Mechanics Nat. Bank, Worcester, from 1929, State Mut. Life Assurance Co., Worcester, from 1938, Providence and Worcester R.R. Co., from 1929; trustee Peoples Savs. Bank, Worcester, from 1921. Mem. Worcester City Sch. Com., 1920-23; civilian aide to sec. of war, 1934-40; liaison with U.S. Army and civilians Worcester City Govt., 1919-24. Trustee Worchester Art Museum, from 1955, chmn. members council, 1953-54; chmn. bd. Travelers Aid Soc. Worcester, from 1955; bd. dirs. Nat. Travelers Aid Assn., Mass. Soc. Prevention Cruelty to Children; trustee Williams Coll., 1932-36, Blair Acad., from 1930. Served to capt., inf., U.S. Army, World War I; AEF in France. Decorated Croix de Guerre with palm. Clubs: Worcester (past pres.), University (past pres.), Tatnuck Country (past pres.) (Worcester); Williams (N.Y.C.). Author: Negro Combat Troops in the World War, 1928; Playlets, Papers and Poems, 1957; also several one act plays. Address: Worcester, Mass. †

HIBBARD, HOWARD, art historian, educator; b. Madison, Wis., May 23, 1928; s. Benjamin Horace and Margaret M. (Baker) H.; m. Shirley Irene Griffith, Sept. 14, 1951; children: Claire Alexandra, Susan Giulia, Carla Costanza. B.A., U. Wis., 1949, M.A., 1952; Ph.D., Harvard U., 1958; M.A., Oxford (Eng.) U., 1977. Research fellow Am. Acad. in, Rome, 1956-58; vis. instr. U.

Calif., Berkeley, 1958-59; mem. faculty Columbia U., N.Y.C., 1959-84, prof. art history, 1966-84, chmn. dept. art history and archaeology, 1978-81; vis. disting. scholar CCNY, 1973-74; vis. prof. Yale U., 1976; Slade prof. fine art Oxford U., 1976-77. Author: The Architecture of the Palazzo Borghese, 1962, Bernini, 1965, Bernini e barocco, 1968, Carlo Maderno and Roman Architecture, 1580-1630, 1972, Poussin: The Holy Family on the Steps, 1974, Michelangelo, 1975, Masterpieces of Western Sculpture, from Medieval to Modern, 1977, The Metropolitan Museum of Art, 1980, Caravaggio, 1983; also exhbn. catalogue; book rev. editor: Art Bull., 1961-65, editor-in-chief, 1974-78. Fulbright fellow Paris, 1949-50; fellow Am. Council Learned Socs., 1962-63; fellow Guggenheim Found., 1965-66, 72-73; fellow Nat. Endowment Humanities, 1967, 79-80. Fellow Am. Acad. Arts and Scis.; mem. Assn. Art Historians Gt. Britain, Coll. Art Assn. Am., Renaissance Soc. Am., Soc. Archtl. Historians (dir. 1963-65). Home: Scarsdale, N.Y. Died Oct. 29, 1984.

HIBBEN, SAMUEL GALLOWAY, engr. elec. illumination; b. Hillsboro, O., June 6, 1888; s. Joseph M. and Henriette (Martin) H.; B.Sc., Case Institute Tech., 1910, E.E. (hon.), 1915, D.Eng., 1952; student U. of Paris, Sorbonne, France, 1918; m. Ruth Rittenhouse, April 14, 1923; children—Eleanor Rittenhouse, Stuart Galloway, Barry Cummings, Craig Rittenhouse. Began as electrician, 1906; illuminating engineer Macbeth Evans Glass Company, Pittsburgh, Pennsylvania, 1910-15; consulting engr., Pittsburgh, 1915-16; with Westinghouse Lamp Co. from 1916, dir. of lighting from 1933. Served as 2d and 1st lt. U.S. Army, searchlight design Washington, D.C., and capt. sound ranging, A.E.F., World War I; U.S. Strategic Bombing Survey, Germany, World War II. Mem. Am. Inst. E.E., Soc. Am. Mil. Engrs., Illuminating Engring. Soc. (p. pres.), Am. Soc. Agrl. Engrs., Illuminating Engrs. London, Sigma Nu. Republican. Presbyn. Clubs: Engineers, Ohio Soc. of New York. Contbr. tech. articles. Home: Montclair, N.J. †

HICKS, GRANVILLE, author; b. Exeter, N.H., Sept. 9, 1901; s. Frank Stevens and Carrie Weston (Horne) H.; A.B., Harvard, 1923, A.M., 1929; L.H.D., Skidmore Coll., 1968, Ohio U., 1969; Litt.D., Siena Coll., 1971; m. Dorothy Dyer, June 27, 1925; 1 dau., Stephanie. Instr. Smith Coll., 1925-28; asst. prof. English, Rensselaer Poly. Inst., 1929-35; counsellor Am. civilization Harvard, 1938-39; editorial staff New Masses Mag., 1934-39; chmn. radio program Speaking of Books, 1941-43; dir. Corp. of Yaddo, from 1942. Lectr. Pacific Northwest Writers' Conf., 1948; lit. cons. New Leader mag., 1951-58; instr. novel writing New School, N.Y.C., 1955-58; McGuffey prof. Am. lit. Ohio U., 1967-68; contbg. editor Saturday Rev., 1958-69. Recipient Clarence Day award A.L.A., 1968. Author: The Great Tradition-An Interpretation of American Literature since the Civil War, 1933, rev. edit., 1935; (with Lynd Ward) One of Us, 1935; John Reed-The Making of a Revolutionary, 1936; I Like America, 1938; Figures of Transition, 1939; The First to Awaken, 1940; Only One Storm, 1942; Behold Trouble, 1944; Small Town, 1946; There Was a Man in Our Town, 1952; Where We Came Out, 1954; Part of the Truth: An Autobiography, 1965; James Gould Cozzens, 1967; Literary Horizons, 1970; Granville Hicks in the New Masses, 1973. Co-editor Proletarian Literature in the United States, 1935; The Letters of Lincoln Steffens (with Ella Winter), 1938; editor The Living Novel, 1957. Home: Grafton, N.Y. Died June 18, 1982.

HIGBEE, JOHN MORRIS, veterinarian; b. Albert Lea, Minn., May 18, 1917; s. Myrtle Rice and Blanche (Holbrook) H.; D.V.M., Iowa State U., 1939; m. Lucille Ann Roberts, Aug. 11, 1977; children—Tamra Ann, John Dwight. Gen. practice vet. medicine, Albert Lea, 1939-57; asst. prof. vet. medicine U. Minn., Mpls., 1957-60, prof., from 1960, dir. vet. diagnostic labs., 1960-79. Recipient award of merit Gamma Sigma Delta, 1979. Mem. AVMA, Minn. Vet. Med. Assn., Am. Assn. Vet. Lab. Diagnosticians, Am. Animal Hosp. Assn., Am. Assn. Avian Pathologists, Phi Zeta. Republican. Mem. Wesleyan Ch. Address: Saint Paul, Minn. Dec. Oct. 30, 1981.

HIGGINS, CHARLES ALFRED, business exec.; b. Gillingham, Kent, Eng., July 2, 1888; s. George and Elizabeth Eleanor (Wheeler) H.; ed. pvt. schs., England; m. Marion Dunham, June 4, 1921. Came to U.S., 1915, naturalized, 1931. Chemist New Explosives Co., Ltd., Eng., 1910-15; chief chemist Union Powder Corp., Parlin, N.J., 1915-16; asso. with Hercules Powder Co., Wilmington, Del., from 1916, as manager development dept. then vice president and pres., 1939-53, also chmn. bd., 1944-53, mem. bd. dirs. Mem. Acad. Polit. Sci. Episcopalian. Clubs: Wilmington, Wilmington Country, Hercules Country (Wilmington); The Pilgrims (N.Y.C.). Address: Wilmington, Del. †

HIGGINS, HOWARD, gas company executive; b. Reynoldsville, Pa., Aug. 19, 1916; s. Howard Lee and Alice Marie (Fenstamaker) H.; m. Genevieve Dale Betz, July 20, 1941; children—William R., Thomas F. Student, U. Akron, 1937-39; grad., Command and Gen. Staff Sch., Fort Leavenworth, Kans. Various operating and mgmt. positions Ohio Fuel Gas Co., Elyria, 1936-41; dist. mgr. Ala. Gas Corp., Birmingham, 1946-65, v.p., 1965-67, sr. v.p., 1967-73, pres., dir., 1973-76, chmn. bd., pres., chief exec. officer, 1976-77, chmn. bd., chief exec. officer, 1977-84, Alagasco, Inc. (and subsidiaries), 1979-84; dir. 1st Ala. Bank of Birmingham, Am. Gas Assn., 1980-84; trustee Inst. Gas Tech., 1978-84, So. Research Inst., 1978. Mem. adv. com. on natural gas Fed. Energy Adminstrn. Organizer; chmn. Birmingham-Jefferson Regional Planning Commn., 1965-67; Bd. dirs. United Appeal, Birmingham, 1967-69, Associated Industries Ala., 1976-84; pres. Met. Devel. Bd., 1976-77. Served to maj. AUS, 1941-45. Mem. So. Gas Assn. (dir. 1963-66, pres. 1976), Jr. Achievement Lee and Chambers County (pres. 1954), Jr. Achievement Jefferson County (chmn., pres. 1964-66), Birmingham C. of C. (dir., exec. com.), Ala. C. of C. (dir. 1976-84), Newcomen Soc. N.Am. Methodist. Clubs: Kiwanian, Relay House, Downtown, The Club, Birmingham Country, Vestavia Country. Home: Birmingham, Ala. Died Feb. 2, 1984.

HIGHT, EUGENE STUART, cons. engr.; b. Green Valley, Ill., Aug. 22, 1888; s. James Stuart and Bertha Julia (Troll) H.; B.S., U. Ill., 1910, M.S., 1911, E.E., 1915; m. Beatrice Felicitas Staab, Feb. 28, 1938. Operating and chief engr. Ill. Traction Co., Peoria, Ill., 1916-23; gen. operating engr. N.A. Light & Power Co., Chgo., 1924-27, asst., v.p., 1927-33; dir., chief engr. Ill. Terminal R.R. Co., 1928-39; pres. Central Terminal Co., St. Louis, 1932-45; v.p. Ill. Ia. Power Co., Monticello, Ill., 1933-39; v.p., dir. Ill. Power Co., Decatur, Ill., 1947-54, gen. mgr. 1951-54. Mem. Am. Inst. E.E., A.A.A.S., Sigma Xi. Republican. Clubs: University (Chgo.); Creve Coeur (Peoria Ill.). Home: Delavan, Ill. †

HILDEBRAND, FRANCIS BEGNAUD, educator; b. Washington, Pa., Sept. 1, 1915; s. Frank Alonzo and Inez (Patin) H.; m. Eleanor Maclaren Jenkins, Sept. 18, 1943; children—Susan Lee (Mrs. John Wayne France), Robert Craig, Jean Ellen. B.S., Washington and Jefferson Coll., 1936, M.A., 1938; Sc.D. (hon.), 1969; Ph.D., Mass. Inst. Tech., 1940. Mem. faculty Mass. Inst. Tech., Cambridge, from 1938, asso. prof. math., 1950-67, prof., from 1967. Author: Advanced Calculus for Applications, 1949, 62, 76, Methods of Applied Mathematics, 1952, 65, Introduction to Numerical Analysis, 1956, 74, Finite-Difference Equations and Simulations, 1968. Mem. Am. Math. Soc., Math. Assn. Am., Sigma Xi, Phi Beta Kappa, Phi Delta Theta. Home: Wellesley, Mass.

HILDEBRAND, JOEL HENRY, chemist; b. Camden, N.J., Nov. 16, 1881; s. Howard Ovid and Sarah Regina (Swartz) H.; m. Emily J. Alexander, Dec. 17, 1908; children—Louise, Alexander, Milton, Roger Henry. B.S., U. Pa., 1903, Ph.D., 1906, D.Sc. (hon.), 1939; student, U. Berlin, 1906-07; LL.D., U. Calif., 1954; Sc.D., Eastern Mich. U., 1972. Instr. chemistry U. Pa., 1907, asst. prof. chemistry, 1913, assoc. prof., 1917, prof., 1918-52, prof. emeritus, 1952, dean of men, 1923-26, faculty research lectr., 1936; dean Coll. Letters and Sci., 1939-43; chmn. dept. chemistry U. Calif., 1941-43; dean Coll. Chemistry, 1949-51; cons. chemist U.S. Bur. Mines, 1924-26; liaison for OSRD, Am. embassy, London, 1943-44. Author: Principles of Chemistry, 1918, 7th edit, 1964, (with R.E. Powell) Solubility of Non-electrolytes, 1924, 36, 1951, Reference Book of Inorganic Chemistry, (with W. M. Latimer), 1929, 40, Camp Catering, (with Louise Hildebrand), 1938, 41, Science in the Making, 1956, An Introduction to Molecular Kinetic Theory, 1963, Is Intelligence Important? , 1963, Regular and Related Solutions, (with J.M. Prausnitz and R.L. Scott), 1970, Viscosity and Diffusivity: A Predictive Treatment, 1977; also numerous papers on chemistry, edn., skiing. Mgr. U.S. Olympic Ski Team, 1936, Joel Henry Hildebrand Hall dedicated by U. Calif, 1966. Mem. citizen's adv. commn. to Joint Com. on Edn. of Calif. Legislature, 1958-60; mem. adv. com. to Calif. Bd. Edn., 1966. Commd. capt. O.R.C., 1917; maj. Chem. Warfare Service 1918; lt. col. 1919; dir. C.W.S. lab. nr. Paris; later comdt. Hanlon Field, nr. Chaumont, which included exptl. field and A.E.F. Gas Def. Sch.; Mem. chem. referee bd. War Prodn. Bd., 1942-43; expert cons. mil. planning div. Q.M.C., 1942-45. Decorated D.S.M., World War I; King's Medal Brit., 1948; Citation by Army and Navy for OSRD service, World War II; Nichols medal, 1939; Guthrie lectr. Phys. Soc. London, 1944; Walker Meml. lectr., 1944; Romanes lectr., 1953; both U. Edinburgh; Remsen Meml. lecture and award, 1949; Am. Chem. Soc. award in chemistry edn., 1952; Priestley medal, 1962; James Norris Flack award New Eng. sect., 1961; S.C. Lind lectr. Eastern Tenn. sect., 1974; Spiers Meml. lectr. Faraday Soc., 1953; Bampton lectr. Columbia U., 1956; Willard Gibbs medal Chgo. sect. Am. Chem. Soc., 1953; William Proctor prize Sci. Research Soc. Am., 1962; Am. Chem. Soc. Centenial lectr., 1976; Hildebrand professorial chair named in his honor, 1981; bronze bust and tapestry presented in his honor Am. Chem. Soc., 1981. Fellow AAAS (v.p. Pacific div. 1924-27, pres. 1933-34, mem. exec. com. 1929-35), Am. Phys. Soc.; hon. fellow Royal Soc. Edinburgh, Calif. Acad. Sci.; mem. Am. Philos. Soc., Am. Chem. Soc. (pres. 1955), Nat. Acad. Scis., Faraday Soc. (hon. life), Am. Inst. Chemists (hon.), Phi Beta Kappa, Sigma Xi. Clubs: Faculty, Sierra (pres. 1937-40). Home: Berkeley, Calif. Died Apr. 30, 1983.

HILEMAN, DONALD GOODMAN, college dean; b. Anna, Ill., Sept. 8, 1925; s. Turner Clifford and Mary (Goodman) H.; m. Shirley Ann Rau, Aug. 28, 1948; children: David, Mark, Mike, Kathryn. Student, Carthage Coll., 196-48; B.S. in Journalism, U. Ill., 1949, M.S. in Journalism, 1951, Ph.D. in Mass Communications, 1955. Instr. U. Ill., 1949-52; asst. prof. bus. adminstrn. Wash. State U., Pullman, 1952-55; assoc. prof. journalism So. Ill. U., 1955-69; chmn. dept. advt. U. Tenn., 1969-70, dean Coll. communications, 1970-84; vis. prof. U. S.C., fall 1980. Author: (with Billy I. Ross) Towards Professional in Advertising, 1969; Editor: Linage, 1963-70; Contbr. articles profl. jours. Mem. synod ethics com. Presbyn Ch. Ill., 1960-62; mem. Council pub. relations Boy Scouts Am., 1958-68; Bd. dirs., asso. Danforth Found.; pres. Helen Ross McNabb Mental Health Ctr., 1982-83. Served with USNR, 1943-46. Recipient spl. awards U. Ill., 1967, spl. awards Tex. A. and M. Coll., 1969; Distinguished Service award Am. Motel Assn. Ill.; Phi Eta Sigma Outstanding Tchr. award U. Tenn., 1980. Fellow Am. Assn. Advt. Agys., Direct Mail Advt. Assn., Splty. Advt. Assn., Advt. Age Creative Workshop; mem. Am. Advt. Fedn. (silver medal), Assn. Schs. Journalism and Mass Communication (nat. pres. 1983-84), Assn. Edn. in Journalism, Am. Marketing Assn., AAUP, Am. Acad. Advt., Alpha Delta Sigma (exec. dir. 1961-70, recipient 6th Key, spl. awards). Home: Knoxville, Tenn. Died Dec. 5, 1984.

HILL, CLARENCE EDWIN, banker; b. Minneapolis, Minn., Jan. 15, 1887; s. William H. and Nellie (Bigelow) H.; A.B., Univ. of Minn., 1909; m. May Boyd, Apr. 21, 1917; children—Barbara, Robert Boyd. With Minneapolis Nat. Bank, 1910-22; vice pres. Northwestern Nat. Bank, Minneapolis, 1922-45, past chmn. bd. directors; with Harris Upham Co.; dir. Mpls., St. Louis R.R., Fed. Res. Bank of Mpls., Northwest Bankcorp. Consul for Belgium, Minn., N.D., S.D.; Foreign Operations Mission, Germany and Italy, 1954, 55, U.S. Department of Commerce, Turkey, 1956. Treas., mem. bd. trustees Minn. Masonic Home: mem. bd. trustees Shriners Crippled Children Hosp.; pres. Community Fund of Mpls. Mem. Alpha Tau Omega. Republican. Conglist. Clubs: Minikahda (past pres.), Minneapolis, Woodhill Country, Chicago, Bankers (New York). Home: Minneapolis, Minn. †

HILL, EDWARD W., engraver; b. Chgo., 1888. Chmn. Jahn & Ollier Engraving Co., Chgo.†

HILL, EUGENE DUBOSE, business exec.; b. Washington, Ga., Mar. 2, 1889; s. William Merriwether and Susan Montgomery (Stokes) H.; B.S., Ga. Inst. Tech., 1911; m. Lila Robinson, Oct. 6, 1921; children—Lee Robinson, Eugene DuBose, William Speed. With So. Bell Tel. & Tel. Co., Atlanta, 1911-22, now dir.; asst. sales mgr. Louisville Cement Co., 1922-29, v.p., dir., 1929-39, president, mem. board of directors, from 1939, chairman board dirs., from 1958; dir., mem. exec. com. Fed. Chem. Co., Louisville Textiles, Inc., First Nat. Bank, Cave Hill Cemetery Co. (all in Louisville). Dir. Indsl. Found., Louisville. Mem. board trustees University of Louisville. Served as 1st lt. signal corps, U.S. Army, World War I. Home: Louisville, KY. †

HILL, JAMES DANIEL, lawyer; b. Phoenix, June 27, 1913; s. Daniel Peters and Anna Held (Jacoby) H.; m. Nancy Ellinor Griffin, July 30, 1939; children: James Daniel, Martha Ellinor, George Denman. B.A., U. Iowa, 1936, J.D., 1938. Bar: Iowa 1938, D.C. 1964, U.S. Supreme Ct 1952. Practice in, Cedar Rapids, Iowa, 1938-42; spl. asst. to atty. gen. Justice Dept., 1946-48, chief alien property litigation br., 1948-54; gen. counsel Office Alien Property Custodian, 1954-59; asso. gen. counsel, then dep. gen. counsel FAA, 1959-63, pvt. practice, Washington, 1964-83; professorial lectr. transp. law George Washington U. Law Sch., 1964-74; Exec. dir. Nat. Fedn. Profl. Orgns., from 1968. Contbr. articles to legal jours. Served to lt. (j.g.) USNR, 1943-45. Mem. Iowa Bar Assn., Bar Assn. D.C. (chmn. aviation law com. 1962-65, chmn. civil service law com. 1973-74), Am. Legion (nat. exec. com. 1950-52, 56-58), Order of Coif. Presbyn. (chmn. bd. deacons 1965). Clubs: Metropolitan (Washington); Kenwood Golf and Country (Bethesda, Md.) (chmn. bd. govs. 1966, chmn. exec. com. 1970, 73). Home: Harwood, MD.

HILL, JOHN D(OWNING), lawyer; born Castleberry, Alabama, September 4, 1890; s. William Arthur and Alice Moselle (Downing) H.; student, Vanderbilt Univ., 1912; LL.B., Univ. of Ala., 1915; grad. student, Northwestern U., 1921; m. Carrilee Heflin, June 13, 1914; children—Carolyn Heflin (Mrs. C. Dozier Carr), Alice Moselle (wife of Dr. Edward V. Schaffer). Admitted to Ala. State bar, 1915, practiced in Birmingham, Ala. from (with absence for mil. service); U.S. atty. for northern dist. of Ala., 1946-53. Commd. 2d lt., U.S. Army, and advanced through grades to maj., 1916-21; served with Inf., World Wars I and II; rank of col., O.R.C. Democrat. Episcopalian. Contbr. articles on delinquency to various publs. Home: Birmingham, Ala. †

HILL, JOHN M(CMURRY), language educator; b. Dresden, Tenn., Sept. 3, 1887; s. Henry Leake and Nancy (McMurry) H.; B.A., Vanderbilt U., 1908, M.A., 1910; Ph.D., U. of Wis., 1912; studied U. of Madrid, 1914-15, U. of Paris, 1915-16; unmarried. Fellow and Asst. in Romance langs., Vanderbilt U., 1909-10; same, U. of Wis., 1910-12; Markham memorial traveling fellow, U. of Wis., 1914-15; asso. prof. Spanish, Ind. U., 1915-22, prof. since 1922. Mem. Modern Lang. Assn. America, Modern Humanities Research Assn., Am. Assn. Teachers of Spanish, Alpha Tau Omega, Phi Beta Kappa; corr. mem. Hispanic Soc. America. Author: several Spanish books: Cuatro comedias (with M. M. Harlan), 1941; Poesias germanescas, 1945; Voces germanescas, 1949. Address: Bloomington, Ind.†

HILL, JOHN WARREN, judge; b. Ogden, Utah, June 20, 1889; s. John Wesley (D.D., LL.D.) and Nora (Holmes) H.; grad. Bordentown (N.J.) Mil. Inst., 1907; A.B., Columbia University, 1911, LL.D., 1914; married Charlotte G. Shrady, 1917; 1 son, Archibald Shrady; married 2d, Paula Helene Raparlier, 1947; one son, John Warren, Jr. Admitted to New York bar, 1914; assistant district attorney N.Y. County under Chas. S. Whitman, 1914-16; mem. firm Carr, Hill & Koenig, 1916-26, Hill & Koenig, 1926-34; appointed temporary justice, May 12, 1934, justice, November 1, 1934, presiding justice Domestic Relations Court, City of N.Y., Dec. 10, 1934; reappointed from, and term expired 1964. Govt. Appeal agt., Draft Bd., 1917; enlisted in N.A. 1917; honorably discharged as 2d lt., 1918. Commissioned major, U.S. Army, June 17, 1942; promoted lt. col., Apr 26, 1943, col., April, 1946; served two yrs. European Theater; col Judge Adv. Gen. Res., 1946-50. Republican candidate for justice City Ct., N.Y.; 1924, for justice N.Y. Supreme Ct., 1929. Chmn. Inter-Dept. Coordinating Bd. for Child Welfare of City of N.Y., 1936-69; mem. bd. dirs. Nat. Com. Mental-Hygiene, 1939-42; mem. exec. com. Grant Monument Assn. of N.Y., from 1942; mem. adv. com. Joint Legislative Com. on Interstate Coop., 1946-59; mem. adv. council American Child Guidance Foundation, 1954-59; member New York City Youth Commn. from 1947, N.Y.C. Commn. for Foster Care of Children from 1946, N.Y. State Citizens Com. of One Hundred for Children and Youth, 1950, Mid-Century White House Conf. on Children and Youth, 1950, Mayor's Adv. Com. on Aid to Dependent Children, 1950; mem. exec. com. Bd. Christian Edn., Protestant Council of City of N.Y., 1946-48; mem. bd. Fedn. Prot. Welfare Agencies from 1948. Mem. sect. on correctional and allied services Welfare and Health Council of New York, 1952-55; member central coordinating committee Community Council of Greater New York, 1956-58; member New York State Assn. Judges Children's Cts. (pres. 1951; chmn. exec com. 1951-58); trustee Nat. Probation and Parole Assn., 1949-56. Mem. Am. Bar Assn., Nat. Council Juvenile Ct. Judges (dir. from 1958, exec. com. 1958-59), Interstate Conf. on Reciprocal Support Laws (executive com. 1958-59), Mil. Order Fgn. Wars (N.Y. State comdr. 1948), Pilgrims Soc. of U.S., Am. Legion, 40 and 8, Res. Officers Assn., Assn. Bar, City of N.Y. (chmn. com. on lectures 1930-32), Phi Delta Theta. Espicopalian. Mason. Clubs: N.Y. Young Republican (a founder), Park Republican (past pres.), Union League. Received Columbia U. Medal for Excellence, for rendering able pub. service 1943. Home: New York, N.Y. †

HILL, JOHN WILEY, pub. relations counsel; b. Shelbyville, Ind., Nov. 26, 1890; s. T. Wiley and Katherine (Jameson) H.; student Ind. U., 1911-12, LL.D., 1971; L.H.D., Boston U., 1950; m. Elena K. Hill, 1917-27; instituted Monthly Bus. Bull. of Cleve. Trust Co., 1920; contbr. syndicated newspaper column and author many bus., econ. articles and studies; entered field of pub. relations as counsel Union Trust Co., other large firms, 1927; became pub. relations counsel Am. Iron and Steel Inst., 1933; formed firm Hill & Knowlton, 1933, chmn. policy com. Hill & Knowlton, Inc.; formed H & K, Internat., 1952; pub. relations counsel indsl. corps. and assns. Clubs: Sleepy Hollow; Pinnacle (N.Y.C). Author: Corporate Public Relations, 1957; The Making of a Public Relations Man, 1963 Contbr. articles on pub. relations. Home: New York City, NY. †

HILL, KARL ALLEN, educator; b. Littleton, N.H., Feb. 22, 1915; s. Allen F. and Lyle K. (Morse) H.; student Worcester Acad., 1932-34; A.B. cum laude, Dartmouth, 1938; M.C.S. with distinction, Amos Tuck Sch., 1939; LL.D., Drury Coll., 1968; m. Phyllis A. Mann, Oct. 16, 1938; children—Allen C., George F. Instr. bus. adminstrn. Nichols Jr. Coll., 1940-43; dir. purchases Holtzer-Cabot div. First Indsl. Corp., 1943-46; prof. indsl. mgmt. Amos Tuck Sch., Dartmouth Coll., 1946-68, asso. dean Amos Tuck Sch., 1953-57, dean, 1957-68; dean Sch. Bus., Washington U., St. Louis, 1968-76, dean emeritus, prof. bus. adminstrn., 1976-83; dir. Wehr Corp., Milw. Mem. Sphinx, Delta Kappa Epsilon, Republican. Home: Durham, N.H. Died May 7, 1983.

HILL, LISTER, former senator; b. Montgomery, Ala., Dec. 29, 1894; s. Luther L. (M.D.) and Lilly (Lyons) H.; grad. Stark Univ. Sch., Montgomery, 1911; A.B., U. Ala., 1914, LL.B., 1915; LL.B., Columbia, 1916; spl. course, U. Mich.; LL.D., U. Ala., Ala. Polytech. Inst., Nat. Univ., Woman's Med. Coll., Columbia U., Washington U., St. Louis, U. Pa., Phila., 1965; Sc.D., Hahemann Med. Coll., N.Y. Med. Coll. Gallaudet Coll., also Jefferson Medical Coll.; m. Henrietta Fontaine McCormick, Feb. 20, 1928; children—Mrs. Charles Hubbard, Luther Lister. Began practice at Montgomery, 1916; mem. 68th Congress from 2d Ala. Dist. (to fill unexpired term of dec. Hon. John R. Tyson), mem. 69th-75th Congresses; elected U.S. senator to fill unexpired term of Hugo L. Black, 1938, reelected 1939-45, 45-51, 51-57, 57-63, 63-69; majority Whip Senate, 77th-79th Congresses. Served with U.S. Army, 1917-19. Recipient Albert Lasker award med. research, 1959, 68; award of honor Am. Hosp. Assn., 1966; award Nat. Acad. Scis.; award Assn. Am. Phys. Edn.; Dean's award U. Ala. Sch. Law; Alumnus of Year, Univ. of Ala.; Statesmen in Medicine Airlie Found., also awards Parkinson's Disease Found., Nat. Assn. Phys. Handicapped, Nat. Acad. Sci., Armed Forces Inst. Pathology, Am. Assn. Hosp. Planning, Ala. Hosp. Assn., So. Council Optometrists, Sidney Farber Cancer Research Found., Assn. Research in Ophthalmology, Am. Legion, U. Ala. Sch. Law, numerous others. Ann. Lister Hill lecture U. Ala. Sch. Dentistry and Dental Sch. Alumni Assn. Hon. fellow Am. Coll. Hosp. Adminstrs., Am. Coll. Dentists, Am. Psychiat. Assn., Internat. Coll. Surgeons; mem. A.C.P. (hon.), A.C.S. (hon.), Nat. Ophthalmology Assn. (hon.), Internat. Med. Club. (hon.), Am. Dental Assn. (hon.), Am. Pub. Health Assn., Nat. Conf. Christians and Jews, Phi Beta Kappa. Democrat. Mem. M.E. Ch. Mason. Home: Montgomery, Ala. Died Dec. 20, 1984.

HILL, LON CARRINGTON, public utilities; b. Manor, Tex., Mar. 14, 1889; s. Lon Carrington and Eustacia (Dabney) H.; student U. of Tex., 1909-11; m. Georgiana Owsley, July 29, 1918; children—Georgette (Mrs. K. F. Burgess, Jr.), Lon Carrington, Owsley. Land developer in the Rio Grande Valley of Tex., later becoming asso. with A. C. Allyn & Co., Chgo.; pres. Central Power & Light Co., Corpus Christi, Tex., from 1939; chmn. bd., from 1954; chmn. board First State Bank of Corpus Christi. Democrat. Club: Country (Corpus Christi). Home: Corpus Christi, Tex. †

HILL, ROBERT BURNS, army officer; b. N.C., Nov. 28, 1890; B.S., Davidson (N.C.) Coll., 1910, A.M., 1911; M.D., U. of Md., 1915; grad. Army Med. Sch., 1917. Commd. 1st lt., M.C., U.S. Army, 1917, and advanced through grades to brig. gen. Decorated Bronze Star Medal. Home: Washington, D.C. †

HILL, ROBERT WHITE, publisher, editor; b. Richmond, Va., Sept. 12, 1919; s. Dudley Jeffries and Mary Etta (Banks) H.; m. Barbara Whitall, Oct. 20, 1956; children—Matthew Banfield, Elizabeth Brinton, Anthony Whitall. B.A., Haverford Coll., 1944, M.A., 1947. Book salesman, editorial reader, trade dept. Harcourt, Brace & Co., N.Y.C., 1948-53; mem. editorial dept., spl. sales mgr. E.P. Dutton Co., N.Y.C., 1954; mng. editor John Day Co., N.Y.C., 1955-66, v.p., sec., dir., 1961-66; editor-in-chief J.B. Lippincott Co., N.Y.C., 1967-68; dir., editor-in-chief Assn. Press, N.Y.C., 1969-77; editor-in-chief Assn. Press/Follett Pub. Co., 1978-81, New Century Pubs., Inc., 1981-82; Founding mem. Wilton (Conn.) Land Trust; chmn. home selection com. Am. Field Service, Wilton, Conn., 1963-64. Author: What Colonel Glenn Did All Day, 1968, What The Moon Astronauts Do, 1971, The Chesapeake Bay Bridge-Tunnel, 1972, Workbook: The New Science of Skin and Scuba Diving, 1980. Served to lt. (j.g.) USNR, 1943-46. Recipient Nat. Council for Coop. in Aquatics award, 1976; Distinguished Service award Nat. YMCA, 1977. Mem. Beta Rho Sigma. Episcopalian. Clubs: Saunderstown (R.I.) Yacht (bd. govs. 1970-82, rear commodore 1976-77, vice commodore 1978-79, commodore 1980-81), Wilton (Conn.) Kiwanis and Rotating Lunch, New York City, Publishers Lunch. Home: Wilton, Conn. Died Sept. 25, 1982.

HILL, SAMUEL S., college pres.; b. Halifax County, Va., April 1, 1890; s. Sterling Price and Eldora James (Stowe) H.; grad. Hargrave Mil. Acad., 1913; A.B., U. of Richmond, 1917, D.D., 1943; Th.M., Southern Bapt. Theol. Sem., 1924, Th.D., 1926; m. Mary L. Brown, June 23, 1926; children—Samuel S., Mary Jane. Ordained to ministry of Baptist Church, 1924; pres. Georgetown (Ky.) College from 1942. Trustee Ky. Bapt. Hosp. Moderator Gen. Assn. of Baptists in Ky., 1942-44. Mason. Club: Rotary. Address: Georgetown, Ky. †

HILL, THEODORE ALBERT, psychiatrist; b. Denver, June 12, 1908; s. Albert Lyon and Helen (Brown) H.; m. Eva Grace Harris, June 30, 1934; children—Helen Julia Felicia, Grace Lorraine, Theodora Susan. B.A., U. Calif. at Los Angeles, 1930; M.A., Stanford, 1931; M.D., Loma Linda U., 1947. Diplomate: Am. Bd. Psychiatry and Neurology, Nat. Bd. Med. Examiners. Adminstrv. analyst Div. Research, County of Los Angeles, 1937-40; adminstrv. analyst personnel div. Treasury Dept., Washington, 1940, adminstrv. analyst procurement div., 1940-41; adminstrv. insp. Bur. Reclamation, Dept. Interior, Washington, 1941-42; intern, resident psychiatry Los Angeles County Gen. Hosp., 1946-50; dir. St. Joseph County Adult and Child Guidance Clinic, South Bend, Ind., 1952-56, pvt. practice medicine specializing in psychiatry, 1956-68, Long Beach and Michigan City, Ind., 1972-82; supt. Dr. Norman M. Beatty Meml. Hosp., Westville, Ind., 1968-72; instr. psychiatry Sch. Medicine, Ind. U., 1967-73, asso. prof., 1973-82; Psychiat. cons. Peace Corps, 1962, LaPorte County Comprehensive Mental Health Center, 1973, Ind. State Prison, Michigan City, 1973-82, also Mennonite Ch. Bd. Missions, Diocese No. Ind. Episcopal Chs., Nat. Missionary Bd. Meth. Chs. Served to maj. M.C. AUS, 1950-52. Fellow Am. Psychiat. Assn. (del. Assembly Dist. Brs. to 1977), Am. Orthopsychiat. Assn., Am. Group Psychotherapy Assn.; mem. No. Ind. Psychiat. Soc. (past pres.). Episcopalian. Address: Michigan City, Ind. Died Aug. 11, 1982.

HILL, THOMAS BOWEN, JR., lawyer; b. Montgomery, Ala., Nov. 11, 1903; s. Thomas Bowen and Lida Tunstall (Inge) H.; m. Mildred Ellen Abrams, Sept. 22, 1925; children: Thomas Bowen, III, Mildred Inge, Luther Abrams, William Inge, II. A.B., U. Ala., 1922, LL.B., 1924, LL.D. (hon.), 1978. Bar: Ala. 1924. Assoc. prof. German U. Ala., 1923-24; practiced law, Montgomery; sr. mem. firm Hill, Hill, Carter, Franco, Cole & Black (and predecessor firm), 1947-84; spl. chief justice Supreme Ct. Ala., 1966, 67, 68; Chmn. bd. Union Bank & Trust Co., Montgomery., 1954-76, chmn. emeritus for life, 1976-84, also dir. Former mem. bd. dirs. Montgomery YMCA, Children's Protective Home; vice chmn. U. Ala. Found.; bd. dirs. U. Ala. Law Sch. Found. Recipient George Washington Honor medal Freedoms Found., 1970, Daniel J. Meador Outstanding Alumnus award U. Ala. Sch. Law, 1975; named to Ala. Acad. of Honor, 1977. Fellow Am. Coll. Trial Lawyers, Internat. Acad. Trial Lawyers, Am. Bar Found.; mem. ABA (ho. of dels.), Ala. Bar Assn. (v.p. 1951-52, pres. 1952-53, mem. bd. commrs. 1953-80), Montgomery County Bar Assn. (past pres.), Farrah Law Soc. (charter), Ala. Bible Soc. (dir.), Ala. C. of C. (dir.), Am. Judicature Soc., Ala. Motorists Assn. (dir.), Phi Beta Kappa, Phi Alpha Delta. Episcopalian (vestryman, sr. warden). Clubs: Mason (Shriner), Kiwanian (past pres. Montgomery). Home: Montgomery, Ala. Died Aug. 24, 1984.

HILL, THOMAS FOSTER, utilities exec.; b. Anderson, S.C., Dec. 3, 1889; s. Thomas F. and Ottie (Latimer) H.; B.A., Wofford Coll., 1909; m. Marie Seybt, Oct. 12, 1914. With Duke Power Co. and predecessor firms, from 1909, beginning as clk., successively supt. street ry., supt. meters and contracts, asst. mgr., then mgr. Anderson (S.C.) Dist., mgr., Winston-Salem, supr. branches, Charlotte Gen. Offices, 1909-50, v.p., 1950-59, also dir. Trustee Duke Endowment, from 1956. Methodist (trustee). Clubs: Charlotte Country; Rotary (past pres.) (Anderson, S.C.; Winston-Salem, N.C.); Anderson Country. Home: Charlotte, N.C. †

HILLEBOE, GERTRUDE MIRANDA, educator; b. Willmar, Minn., Mar. 18, 1888; d. Hans S. and Antonilla (Ytterboe) Hilleboe; student Benson High Sch., 1902-04, Willmar Sem., 1904-06, State Teachers Coll., St. Cloud, Minn., summer 1906, U. of Minn., summer 1907; A.B., St. Olaf Coll., 1912; grad. study U. of Minn., 1913-14, U. of Wis., summers 1917, 18; A.M., Columbia, 1922; LL.D. Augustana Coll., Sioux Falls, S.D., 1949; Teacher, grade sch., New London, Minn., 1906-07, Willmar Sem., 1907-08, Benson, Minn., 1910-11; was teacher of English and of Latin and preceptress, Waldorf Coll., Forest City, Ia., 1914-15; dean of women, St. Olaf Coll., from 1915. Mem. N.E.A., Nat. Assn. Deans of Women, Am. Assn. Univ. Women, Norwegian Am. Hist. Soc., Minn. Hist. Soc., Minn. Assn. Deans of Women, Business and Professional Women's Club, Am. and Minn. United Nations Assn. Lutheran. Lecturer. Home: Northfield, Minn. †

HILLENKOETTER, ROSCOE HENRY, business executive; b. St. Louis, May 8, 1897; s. Alexander and Olinda (Deuker) H.; m. Jane E. Clark, Nov. 21, 1933; 1 child, Jane G. B.S., U.S. Naval Acad., 1920. Commd. ensign U.S. Navy, 1919, advanced through grades to vice adm., 1956, ret., 1957; Dir. Central Intelligence Agy., 1947-50; comdt. Third Naval Dist., 1952; Vice chmn., v.p., treas. Hegeman-Harris Co., Inc., 1962-82. Decorated comdr. Legion of Honor France). Mem. U.S. Naval Inst. Home: Weehawken, N.J. Died June 18, 1982.

HILLHOUSE, JAMES T(HEODORE), coll. prof.; b. Willimantic, Conn., Feb. 17, 1890; s. James William and Annie Laura (Niles) H.; A.B., Yale, 1911, M.A., 1912, Ph.D., 1914; m. Mildred Lambert, June 14, 1928; children—Anne Lambert, Margaret Lambert. Instr. in English, U. of Minn., 1914, successively asst. prof. and asso. prof., prof. from 1945. Mem. Modern Lang. Assn., Am. Assn. Univ. Profs., Phi Beta Kappa. Editor: Fielding's Tragedy of Tragedies, 1918. Author: The Grubstreet Journal, 1928; The Waverley Novels and Their Critics, 1936; also various articles and reviews in professional jours. Home: Minneapolis, Minn. †

HILLMAN, ARTHUR, educator; b. Nevada City, Calif., June 26, 1909; s. Adolph and Mary (Forsman) H.; A.B., U. Wash., 1931, A.M., 1934; Ph.D., U. Chgo., 1940; m. Stina Eklund, Aug. 17, 1936 (dec. Feb. 1956); m. 2d, Marie Salomaa, August 30, 1958. Tchr. high sch., Elma Wash., 1931-32; teaching asst., grad. student U. Wash., 1932-35; grad. study, research asst. U. Chgo., 1935-38, C.R. Henderson fellow sociology, 1937-38; asst. prof. sociology Bucknell U., 1936; instr., asst. prof. Central YMCA Coll., Chgo., 1938-45; asso. prof. Roosevelt U., 1945-48, prof., 1948-74, chmn. dept. sociology, 1946-55, 62-64, dean coll. arts and scis., 1955-60, chmn. urban studies program, 1969-74; cons. various programs, 1974-85. With office community war services FSA, 1943-45; dir. social work-labor project Council Social Agys. of Chgo., 1945-46. Fulbright research scholar sociology U. Oslo, Norway, 1950; participant 1st World Congress Sociology and Polit. Sci., Zurich, 1950; dir. survey neighborhood goals project Nat. Fedn. Settlements and Neighborhood Centers, 1958-59; dir. Tng. Center, 1960-71. mem. bd. civic and social agys. Pres., Hyde Park Co-op. Soc., 1941-43. Mem. Am. Sociol. Assn., Soc. for Study Social Problems, Am. Scandinavian Found., AAUP. Lutheran. Author: Unemployed Citizens League of Seattle, 1934; Community Organization and Planning, 1950, Italian edit., 1953; Tomorrow's Chicago (with R.J. Casey), 1953; Sociology and Social Work, 1956; (with W. Kloetzli) Urban Church Planning, 1958; (with T.D. Eliot) Norway's Families, 1960. Home: Chicago, Ill. Died Apr. 10, 1985.

HILLMAN, CHARLES CLARK, army officer, physician, hospital administrator; born at Almyra, Arkansas, August 27, 1887; son of Charles M. and Laura (Molonson) H.; B.S., U. of Ark., 1907; student Tulane U. Med. Sch., 1907-08, U. of Chicago, 1908; M.D., Rush Med. Coll., 1911; m. Martha Wood, February 13, 1911. Served as intern Cook County Hosp., Chicago, 1911-12; contract surgeon, U.S. Army, Sept.-Oct., 1912; Med. Reserve Corps, October 1912-May 1913; commd. 1st lt. Med. Corps, U.S. Army, May 12, 1913, and advanced through the grades to brig. general, Jan. 29, 1942; served as lt. col., World War I; chief of professional service, Surgeon General's Office, War Dept. 1939-44; comdg. gen. Letterman Gen. Hosp., San Francisco, 1944-46; retired 1947; cons. in community hosp. planning, hosp. design. Citations: Legion of Merit with Oak Leaf Cluster (army); Comdr. Order of Brit. Empire; Grand Official Order of Southern Cross (Brazil). Recipient Distinguished Alumnus award, U. Ark., 1944. Mem. bd. dirs. Fla. Blue Cross. Diplomate Am. Board Internal Medicine. Fellow Am. College Physicians; mem. So. Med. Adminstrs., Soc. Med. Consultants to the Armed Forces, A.M.A., A.A.A.S.; Am. Association Hospital Consultants, Sigma Chi. Mason (Shriner). Clubs: Army and Navy, Army and Navy Country (Washington); Coral Gables (Fla.) Country; Biscayne Bay Yacht (Miami, Fla.); Rotary. Home: Coral Gables, Fla. †

HILLS, ELMER WALKER, educator; b. Sidney, Ia., Sept. 19, 1887; s. Lewis and Ellen (Kimsey) H.; A.B., U. Neb., 1909; student U. Mich., 1911; J.D., U. Chgo., 1914; m. Ione Bellamy, Feb. 20, 1915; children—William Bellamy, Richard Lewis. Prin. Fairbury (Neb.) High Sch., 1909-13; head commerce dept., also prin. Caldwell (Ida.) High Sch., 1914-15; instr. commerce Jefferson High Sch., Portland, Ore., 1915-17; prof. commerce, head dept. Ore. State Coll., 1917-19; asst. prof. commerce State U. Ia., 1919-22, asso. prof., exec. sec. of coll., 1922-28, prof. since 1928, head dept. gen. bus. form 1948; limited practice law. Pres. Ia. River Valley Council Boy Scouts Am., 1936-40, Ia. City Community Chest, 1939-43; chmn. Co. chpt. A.R.C., 1950-52; dir. Ia. City C. of C. Served as 2d lt., personnel adj., U.S. Army, 1918-19. Mem. Nat. Assn. Coll. Honor Socs. (council 1946-50). Mem., Ia. bar assns., Phi Delta Phi, Phi Alpha Tau, Delta Sigma Pi, Phi Omega Pi, Beta Gamma Sigma (nat. sec., treas. 1936-50), Order of Artus, Acacia. Democrat. Baptist. Mason. Clubs: Lions (past pres.), Univ. Faculty (past pres.). Author artilces law, accounting. Home: Iowa City, Ia. †

HILLS, GEORGE BURKHART, b. Chgo., May 5, 1890; s. George Adelbert and Louise (Burkhart) H.; B.S., Armour Inst. of Tech., Chgo., 1911, C.E., 1918; m. Anna Donna McEnery, 1912 (dec. Jan. 1941); children—Mace Banta (Mrs. Philip M. Travis), Mary Ann, George Burkhart, John Robert, Thomas Marion; m. 2d, Beatrix M. Riley, Dec. 1942. Member Reynolds Smith and Hills, architects and engrs., cons., from 1969. Mem. Newcomen Soc. N.A., Am. Soc. C.E., Am. Inst. Cons. Engrs., Nat. Soc. Profl. Engrs., Tau Beta Pi. Presbyn. Home: Jacksonville, FL. †

HILTON, JAMES H., coll. ofcl.; b. Hickory, N.C., Nov. 20, 1899; s. Henry Monroe and Alice (Clampitt) H.; student N.C. State Coll., 1918-19; B.S., Ia. State Coll., 1923; M.S., U. Wis., 1937; D.Sc., Purdue U., 1945, Cornell 1953, N.C. State Coll., 1955; m. Lois Baker, Dec. 31, 1923; children—Elinor (Mrs. Carl M. Thomas), Helen Ann (Mrs. Richard Bryant), James G. Instr. animal husbandry Iowa State University, 1923; county agricultural agt., Greene County, Ia., 1923-26; dairy extension service Purdue U., 1926-27, prof. dairy husbandry charge daily prodn. teaching and research, 1927-45; head dept. animal industry N.C. State Coll., 1945-48, dean Sch. agr., dir. N.C. Agrl. Expt. Sta. 1948-53; pres. Ia. State U., Ames, 1953-65; dir. univ. devel., 1965-67; exec. dir. Z. Smith Reynolds Found., from 1967. Dir. Northwestern Bell Telephone Co., Quaker Oats Co., Fed. Res. Bank of Chgo. Mem. Sigma Xi, Alpha Zeta, Phi Kappa Phi. Author sci. publs. Home: Winston-Salem, N.C. Died Jan. 14, 1982.

HIMES, CHESTER BOMAR, author; b. Jefferson City, Mo., July 29, 1909; s. Joseph Sandy and Estelle (Bomar) H.; m. Lesley Packard. Student, Ohio State U., 1926-27. (Rosenwald fellow creative writing 1944-45); Author: If He Hollers Let Him Go, 1945, Lonely Crusade, 1947, Cast The First Stone, 1952, The Third Generation,, The Primitive, 1956, Pinktoes, 1965, Cotton Comes to Harlem, 1968, The Heat's On, 1968, Run Man Run, 1968, Blind Man With a Pistol, 1969, French edit., 1982, Hot Day, Hot Night, Pinktoes, 1961, A Rage in Harlem, All Shot Up, 1960, The Real Cool Killers, 1969, The Crazy Kill, Quality of Hurt: The Autobiography of Chester Himes (1st vol.), 1972, 2d vol, My Life of Absurdity, U.S.A, 1976, Black on Black-Baby Sister: A Black Greek Tragedy and Selected Writings, 1973, A Case of Rape, U.S.A, 1980, also numerous articles. Home: Alicante, Spain. Died Nov. 12, 1984.

HINCKS, EDWARD WINSLOW, educator; b. Hyde Park, Mass., Mar. 8, 1890; s. William Sylvanus and Elizabeth (Robinson) H.; Ph.B., Brown U., 1915; Ed.M., Harvard, 1927; m. Arline Louise Shoemaker, Nov. 26, 1917; children—Edward Winslow, William Harvey (dec.), Richard Shoemaker (dec.), Roger Robinson, Barbara Jean, Dorothy Arline. Instructor in physical education, Brown Univ., 1915-17; dir. of athletics, Nichols Sch., Buffalo, N.Y., 1918-20; instr. in English and mathematics, dir. of athletics, and senior master Thayer Acad., South Braintree, Mass., 1920-29; headmaster Kents Hill (Me.) Sem. from 1929; pres. Kents Hill Junior Coll. from 1941. Y.M.C.A. worker, Camp Bartlett and Camp Gordon, 1917. Mem. N.E.A., Me. Teachers' Assn., Grange, Phi Delta Theta. Mason. Methodist. Address: Kents Hill, Maine. †

HINES, EARL KENNETH, (FATHA HINES) pianist, jazz band leader; b. Duquesne, Pa., Dec. 28, 1905. Studied piano with Pitts. area tchrs. Leader trio performing in clubs while in high sch., Pitts.; pianist with band leader-singer, Lois B. Deppe, Chgo., 1922; toured, played with, Carroll Dickerson, Sammy Stewart, Jimmie Noone, Louis Armstrong, band leader, 1924-48, mainly at, Grand Terrace, Chgo., 1928-40, mem., Armstrong's All Stars, 1948-51, moved to, San Francisco; played with small bands on, West Coast; performed with, Jack Teagarden in, Europe, 1957, at, Little Theatre, N.Y.C., 1964, Village Vanguard, N.Y.C., 1965, in Europe, 1965; featured in weekly broadcasts from, U.S. Treasury Dept.; artist on, Capitol, Columbia, RCA Victor, Focus, Fantasy records, numerous TV appearances.; helped establish (through his band), musicians including, Dizzy Gillespie, Charlie Parker, Billy Eckstine, Sarah Vaughan.; Composer: Pianology. Recipient Esquire Silver award, 1944; named to Down Beat Mag. Hall of Fame. Leading influence in devel. large swing band and jazz piano styles. Died Apr. 22, 1983.*

HINES, HAROLD H., JR., insurance company executive; b. Chgo., Nov. 21, 1924; s. Harold H. and Babette (Schnadig) H.; m. Mary Pick, Jan. 23, 1954; children: William H., Anne, David F. B.A., Yale, 1948. Exec. v.p., dir. Combined Internat. Corp.; pres., chief exec. officer Rollins Burdick Hunter Co., 1980-84; dir. Unibanc Trust Co., Midland Bancorp, Corcom Inc., Stone Conlainee Corp.; Lectr. profl. ins. groups, assns., 1957-84. Contbr. articles to ins. jours. Bd. dirs. Adler Planetarium, Local Initiatives Support Corp., Newberry Library, U. Chgo., United Way of Chgo.; mem. vis. com. Harvard Med. Sch.; trustee Michael Reese Hosp. and Med. Center, Research and Edn. Trust. Served with AUS, 1943-46. Mem. Am. Soc. Property and Casualty Underwriters (bd. dirs.), Chgo. Council on Fgn. Relations (dir.); Coll. of Ins. (dir.). Clubs: Chicago, Commercial, Standard, Mid-Am, Metropolitan (mem. bd. govs. Chgo.); Lake Shore Country (Glencoe, Ill.); University (N.Y.C.). Home: Winnetka, Ill. Died June 14, 1984.

HINES, J. F., educator; b. Oral, S.D., April 11, 1889; s. William and Mary (McLaughlin) H.; grad. Spearfish (S.D.) Normal, 1912; A.B., Yankton (S.D.) College, 1914, LL.D., 1937; A.M. Univ. of South Dakota, 1924; m. Alice McConnell, August 1, 1917; children—Alice Kathryn Carlson, Frances Emily (Mrs. Robert E. Bigelow). Rural teacher, 1906; superintendent schs., Custer, South Dakota, 1914-16; instr. Spearfish Normal, 1916-17; prin., Sidney, Mont., 1917-18. Mobridge, S.D., 1921-22; supt. St. Lawrence, S.D., 1921-24, Wolsey, S.D., 1924-28, Plankinton, S.D., 1928-33; dep. supt. pub. instruction, 1933-35, state supt. from 1935. Mem. Nat. Edn. Assn., S.D. Edn. Assn., State Hist. Soc. Mason (Shriner). Contbr. articles to jours. Home: Plankinton, S.D. †

HINES, MARION, neurologist; b. Carthage, Mo., June 11, 1889; d. Frank Bristow and Laura Maria (Saunderson) H.; A.B., Smith Coll., 1913, hon. Sc.D., 1943; Ph.D., U. of Chicago, 1917; student, Drury Coll., 1909-11. Univ. Coll., London, Eng., 1920-21, Cambridge U., Eng., 1923-24, U. Of Wurzburg, Germany, 1930. Asst., U. of Chicago, 1915-17, asso., 1917-18, instr., 1918-24, asst. prof. anatomy, 1924-25; asso. sch. of medicine, Johns Hopkins, 1925-30, asso. prof., 1930-47; prof. exptl. anatomy Emory University, Georgia, from 1947, acting chmn., 1956-57. Member of American Association of Anatomists (2d v.p., 1946-48, rep. on Nat. Research Council, 1948-54), Am. Physiol. Soc., Am. Neurol. Assn. (asso.), Assn. Research in Nervous and Mental Diseases. Phi Beta Kappa, Sigma Xi. Conglist. Club: Hamilton St. (Baltimore) (pres., 1936-38, 1945-47). Bd. of collaborators: Jour. of Nervous and Mental Diseases, Jour. of Neurophysiology. Home: Atlanta, Ga. †

HINKLE, SAMUEL FORRY, chocolate mfg. exec.; b. Columbia, Pa., June 9, 1900; s. Samuel W. and Elizabeth (Forry) H.; B.S., Pa. State Coll., 1922; m. Margaret Joseph, June 14, 1935; children—Samuel F., James E. Lab. chemist Norton Co., Chippawa, Ont., Can., 1922-23; chief chemist Nat. Abrasive Co., Niagara Falls, Ont., 1923-24; chief chemist and dir. research Hershey (Pa.) Chocolate Corp., 1924-47, plant mgr., 1947-56, president, from 1956, director, from 1948; director Hershey National Bank, Hershey Trust Co., Pa. Mfrs.' Assn. Casualty, Ins. Co., Pa. Mfrs.' Assn. Fire Ins. Co. Mem. bd. mgrs., Milton Hershey Sch., M. S. Hershey Found.; gov. Harrisburg Hosp., Hershey Hosp.; dir. Tri-Co. Heart Assn., Tri-County United Fund. Recipient Distinguished Alumnus award Pa. State U. Mem. Nat. Confectioners Assn., Am. Assn. Candy Technologists, Nat. Planning Assn. (nat. council), Pa. Mfrs. Assn. (gov.), Newcomen Soc. N.A., Pa. (dir.), Harrisburg, Lebanon County C.'s of C., A.A.A.S. Grocery Mfrs. Am., Inc. (dir.), Pa. Soc., N.Y. Cocoa Exchange, Inc., Am. Chem. Soc., Inst. Food Technologists (charter), Ams. Competitive Enterprise System (dir.), Phi Kappa Phi, Phi Lambda Upsilon, Alpha Chi Sigma. Republican. Presbyn. (elder). Mason, Rotarian. Contbr. to trade jours. Home: Hershey, Pa. Died Apr. 19, 1984.

HINKS, KENNETT WEBB, government consultant; b. Mpls., Sept. 3, 1897, William Herbert and Florence Mary (Webb) H.; A.B., U. Minn., 1920; m. Elizabeth Porter Dial, Nov. 2, 1946 (dec.); step-children—Nathaniel Victor, Diana. With J. Walter Thompson Co., N.Y.C., 1921-64, Pacific Coast mgr., 1925-28, Central European mgr., 1929-32, v.p., 1936-61, sr. v.p., 1961-63, dir., 1949-64; dir. Caribbean and Canadian subsidiaries of J. Walter Thompson Co. until 1964; cons. U.S. Fgn. Agrl. Service, 1963—. Council Assn. for Aid of Crippled Children, 1948; dir. The Advt. Council, N.Y.C., 1958-70. Served to 2d lt., inf., U.S. Army, World War I; to lt. comdr. USNR, World War II; mem. planning group, chief of planning staff, OSS, 1942-45. Mem. Nat. Planning Assn. (trustee), English-Speaking Union (nat. dir., exec. com.), Phi Beta Kappa, Chi Psi, Phi Delta Phi. Episcopalian. Clubs: University (N.Y.C.); Army and Navy Metropolitan (Washington); Farmington Hunt, Farmington Country, Greencroft (Charlottesville, Va.). Home: Ivy, Va. Died July 22, 1982.

HINSHAW, CLIFFORD REGINALD, educator; b. Randleman, N.C., Jan. 16, 1890; s. Zeno and Annie Martha (Allred) H.; A.B., Guilford Coll., 1916; A.M., U. of N.C., 1924; A.M., Columbia, 1927; Litt. D., Western Md. Coll., 1932; m. Lucile Garnett Walton, June 29, 1918 (now deceased); children—Clifford Reginald, Lucile Garnett (Mrs. Clifford H. May); m. 2d, Kathleen Spain, Aug. 25, 1934. Supt. of schs., Aberdeen, N.C., 1916-17, Ahoskie, N.C., 1917-18, Gates Co., N.C., 1918-19, Battleboro, N.C., 1919-21, Aulander, N.C., 1921-26; prof. of edn. and psychology, High Point (N.C.) Coll. from 1927, dir. of summer sch. from 1927, dean of instrn., 1938-55; prof. of edn., Womans Coll. of Univ. of N.C., summer 1927. Mem. N.E.A., N.C. Edn. Assn. Methodist (sec.-treas. bd. of edn. of Meth. Protestant Ch. in N.C., Inc.). Mason. Home: High Point, N.C. †

HINSHAW, WILLIAM RUSSELL, microbiologist; b. Traverse City, Mich., Dec. 20, 1896; s. William Russell and Lucy May (Core) H.; D.V.M., Mich. State U., 1923; M.S., Kans. State U., 1926; Ph.D., Yale, 1939; m. Edna Florence Bangs, June 19, 1926; children—David William, Robert Frederick. Instr. to asst. prof. Kans. State U., 1923-27; chief animal health control lab. U. Mass., 1927-29; asso. prof. to prof. vet. sci. U. Calif. at Davis, 1929-49; supervisory microbiologist U.S. Biol. Labs., Ft. Detrick, Md., 1949-54, chief virus and rickettsia lab., 1954-58, liaison officer animal diseases, 1958-66; ret., 1966; cons. Nat. Acad. Scis.-NRC, 1967-84, AID, 1971-84; exec. sec. U.S. sect. Argentine-U.S. Joint Commn. on Foot and Mouth Disease, 1967-74. Served with U.S. Navy, 1918-19. Diplomate Am. Coll. Vet. Microbiology, Am. Bd. Pub. Health Vets. Fellow A.A.A.S., Am. Acad. Microbiology (charter); mem. Poultry Sci. Assn. (pres. 1950), Am. Vet. Med. Assn. (life), Am. Soc. Microbiology, Am. Inst. Biol. Scis., Am. Assn. Avian Pathologists, Am. Poultry Hist. Soc., N.Y. Acad. Scis., U.S. Animal Health Assn., Sigma Xi, Phi Kappa Phi, Gamma Sigma Delta. Contbr. numerous articles to sci. jours. Asso. editor avian diseases Poultry Sci., 1942-46, Vet. Medicine, 1948-59; mem. editorial adv. bd. Animal Care Panel, 1962-64; mem. adv. bd. Advances in Vet. Sci. and Comparative Medicine, 1961-78. Research in salmonellosis, gen. poultry diseases, turkey diseases, virus and rickettsial diseases. Home: Frederick, Md. Died Apr. 18, 1984.

HINTON, FANNY DARLING, librarian; b. New Orleans, La., Feb. 23, 1890; d. Eugene Henry and Josephine Pierson (Solomon) H.; student Randolph Macon Woman's Coll., Lynchburg, Va., 1907-09, Library Sch., Carnegie Library of Atlanta, 1916-17. Asst. in reference dept., Carnegie Library, Atlanta, 1917-18, head dept., and instr. in library sch., 1918-30, asst. librarian, 1930-39, librarian, 1939-49. Mem. Am., Southeastern, and Georgia library assns., Atlanta Art Assn., Atlanta Hist. Soc., Randolph Macon. Alumnae Assn., Emory Alumni Assn., Delta Delta Delta. Home: Atlanta, Ga. †

HINTON, WALTER, aviator; b. Van Wert, O., Nov. 10, 1889; s. Millard Madison and Edle (Garrison) H.; ed. high sch., Van Wert County, Ohio; grad. U.S. Naval Flying Sch., Pensacola, Fla., 1916; m. Carrie Susan Muller, Dec. 30, 1931. Entered U.S. Naval Service Feb. 12, 1908; commd. Naval Aviator, 1917, lt., 1918. Served as flight instr., U.S. Naval Sta., at Pensacola, Fla., 1917-18; sr. flight officer, U.S. Navy Air Sta., Halifax, N.S., Aug.-Dec. 1918; assigned to test and exptl. duty, Jan.-Apr. 1919, pilot of NC-4 on 1st trans-Atlantic flight, landing at Plymouth, Eng., May 31, 1919; also pilot of NC-4 on its 10,000 mile trip around U.S., Sept. 1919-Jan. 1920; Navy free-balloon flight, Rockaway to Hudson's Bay, 1921; resigned from U.S. Navy, 1922; made Friendship Flight (New York to Rio de Janeiro, Brazil, 8,500 miles), for New York World, 1922; aircraft pilot, Dr. A. Hamilton Rice Exploration Expdn. to Brazil (flew over and mapped from the air, 12,000 sq. miles unexplored Amazon jungle), 1924. Awarded Congl. Medal of Honor, presented by Pres. Hoover. Decorated U.S.N. Cross and Service medal; service stars for Haitian Campaign, Mexican Punitive Expdn., World War (U.S.); British Air Cross; Cavalier, Tower and Sword of Portugal; Knight of Portugal; also many medals, plaques, etc., presented by State of N.J., Brazilian and French govts., chambers of commerce, clubs and assns. Protestant. Mason. Clubs: Adventurers, Explorers. Lecturer, writer and editor. Former treas. Northwest Realty Corp. Home: New York, N.Y. Died Oct. 28, 1981.

HIPP, HERMAN NEEL, life insurance company executive; b. Spartanburg, S.C., Nov. 2, 1913; s. William Frank and Eunice Jane (Halfacre) H.; m. Jane Fishburne, Nov. 25, 1950; children—Herman Neel, Mary Ladson, William Franklin, Edward Fishburne, Jane Gage. B.S., Furman U., 1935; LL.D. (hon.), Furman U. With Liberty Life Ins. Co., Greenville, S.C., 1954-84, exec. v.p., then pres., 1968-77, chmn. bd., 1977-84; pres. Liberty Corp., 1977-84; dir. Cosmos Broadcasting Corp., Greenville bd. S.C. Nat. Bank. Past chmn. bd. trustees Greenville Hosp. System; adv. council Furman U.; trustee Converse Coll., Greenville United Way. Mem. Greater Greenville C. of C. (past dir.), Am. Life Conv., Life Ins. Mktg. and Research Assn., Life Insurers Conf. (exec. com.), Life Underwriters Tng. Council (past dir.), Phi Kappa Phi. Episcopalian. Clubs: Green Valley Country, Poinsett, Summit, Paletto, Greenville Country. Home: Greenville, S.C. Died Nov. 30, 1984.*

HIRAMOTO, MASAJI, painter, sculptor; b. Fukui, Japan, Dec. 8, 1888; son of Yoshitaka and Hayako (Imadate) H.; studied Art Sch. of Pa. Mus.; B.S., Columbia, 1918, M.A., 1919; hon. mention Art Sch. of Pa. Mus., 1914, Columbia, 1919. Served as asst. to Profs. A. Dow and C. Upjohn, Columbia, 1918, 20. Prin. works: The Daibutsu (Great Buddha), sculpture, Columbia Univ.; mural work, residence of Frank A. Vanderlip; represented in Nat. Acad. Design, Pa. Acad. Fine Arts, Conn. Acad. Fine Arts, Buffalo Acad. Fine Arts, Waldorf Astoria, Am. Mus. Natural History, etc. Mem. Soc. Independent Artists, Japanese Artists Assn., Japan Soc. Clubs: Nippon, Entre Nous. Home: New York, N.Y. †

HIRSCH, FELIX EDWARD, historian, librarian; b. Berlin, Germany, Feb. 7, 1902; came to U.S., 1935, naturalized, 1941; s. Felix and Stephanie (Szamatolski) H.; m. Elisabeth Feist, Nov. 6, 1938; children—Roland Felix, Thomas Feist. Ph.D., U. Heidelberg, 1923; B.S. in L.S, Columbia, 1940. Polit. editor German newspapers, 1924-34; librarian Bard Coll., Annandale-on-Hudson, 1936-54, asso. in German, 1937-42, asst. prof. history, 1942-45, asso. prof., 1945-46, prof., 1946-54; chmn. area tng. program A.S.T.P., 1943-44; librarian, prof. history Trenton State Coll., 1955-72, prof. emeritus, from 1972; Lecture tour, Western Germany, (sponsored Am. Mil. Govt.), univs. Göttingen, Heidelberg, Munich, summer 1949; lecture tour, Can., (sponsored by Canadian Inst. Internat. Affairs), 1951; vis. lectr. history Tech. U., Karlsruhe, Germany, 1954-55, vis. prof. history, 1962; vis. prof. history U. Heidelberg, 1965; Mem. N.Y. State Bd. Regents Commn. to Study Integration Coll. and Univ. Library Resources, 1952-54. Author: Germany Ten Years After Defeat, 1955, Biography of Gustav Stresemann, 1964, Stresemann: Ein Lebensbild, 1978; Editor: (Hermann Oncken), 5th edit.) Lassalle Biography, 1966; Contbr. to: Studies in Diplomatic History and Historiography in Honor of G.P. Gooch, 1961, Bibliotheca Docet, 1963, Memorial to Federal President Theodor Heuss, 1964, Gegenwart im Rueckblick, 1970, Wilhelm Sollmann in Rheinische Lebensbilder, vol. VI, 1975, others; Contbr. articles to profl., gen. publs. Research fellow Am. Philos. Soc., 1954-55; Recipient Bard medal for distinguished service Bard Coll., 1961; decorated comdr.'s cross Order Merit German Fed. Republic, 1972. Mem. Assn. Coll. and Research Libraries (chmn. com. on standards 1957- 63), A.L.A. (council 1953-57, chmn. history sect. 1967-68), N.J. Council State Coll. and U. Librarians (chmn. 1968-69), N.J. Library Assn. (exec. bd. 1958-61, 2d v.p. 1962-63, pres. coll. and univ. sec. 1959-60), Am. Assn. U. Profs., Am. Council on Germany (dir. 1952-56), Am. Hist. Assn., Soc. Friends. Home: Trenton, NJ.

HIRSCH, JOSEPH, artist; b. Phila., Apr. 25, 1910; s. Charles S. and Fannie (Wittenberg) H.; student Phila. Coll. Art, 1927-31; m. Ruth L. Schindler, Oct. 30, 1938; children—Charles, Paul; m. 2d, Genevieve Baucheron, July 19, 1955; 1 son, Frederic Henri-Joseph. Paintings exhibited in prin. museums, galleries of U.S., 1934-81; one-man shows, N.Y.C., Paris, Phila., Chgo., Beverly Hills, 1934-81; also represented permanent collections. Instr. painting Art Students League, 1959-67, 76-81, N.A.D., 1974-81; vis. artist at U. Utah, 1959, Dartmouth, 1966, Brigham Young U., 1971. War artist corr. AUS, USNR, 1943-44. Woolley fellow in Paris, Inst. Internat. Edn., 1935; Guggenheim fellow, 1942, 43; Nat. Inst. Arts and Letters grantee, 1947; Fulbright research fellow in France, 1949; Distinguished Bicentennial prof. as artist-in-residence U. Utah, 1975-81. Recipient 4th prize Met. Mus. Art, 1951; Altman prizes figure painting N.A.D., 1959, 66, 78; Purchase prize Butler Inst., 1965; Carnegie prize N.A.D., 1968; Purchase awards Davidson Coll. Nat. Print Competition, 1972, 73; Print Purchase award Oklahoma Art Center, Oklahoma City, 1974; Purchase award Minn. Mus. Art, 1980. Artists Equity Assn. (founder; 1st treas.), N.A.D., Century Assn., Nat. Inst. Arts and Letters (life). Address: New York, N.Y. Dec. Sept. 21, 1981.

HIRSCH, MAURICE, lawyer; b. Houston, Jan. 13, 1890; s. Jules and Theresa (Meyer) H.; m. Winifred Busby, Jan. 25, 1947. B.A., M.A., U. Va., 1910; J.D., Harvard U., 1913; LL.M., U. Tex., 1914; LL.D. (hon.), Northwood Inst., 1971. Practiced in, Houston, 1914-17, 18-42, 47-83; of counsel firm Hirsch and Westheimer; chmn. bd. Wald Transfer & Storage Co.; chmn. emeritus Republic Bank, Houston.; Chmn. City of Houston Civil Service Commn., 1915-17; sec. priorities com. War Industries Bd., 1917-18; expert cons. War Dept. Price Adjustment Bd., 1942, chief settlements div., 1942; mem., vice chmn. Price Adjustment Bd.; dep. dir. renegotiation div. Hdqrs. ASF, 1943; dir. renegotiation div. and chmn. War Dept. Price Adjustment Bd., 1944-1947; mem., chmn. Joint Price Adjustment Bd. (War, Navy and Treasury Depts., RFC, Maritime Commn. and War Shipping Adminstrn.), 1944-47; mem. War Contracts Price Adjustment Bd. (War, Navy and Treasury Depts., etc.), 1945-47, chmn., Feb. 1945-47. Hon. life mem. exec. bd. Sam Houston Area council Boy Scouts Am., hon. Eagle Scout, Silver Beaver award.; Life trustee Salesmanship Club Camp for Children; mem. internat. council Mus. Modern Art, N.Y.C.; past chmn., hon. life mem. U.S.O. Council Houston and Harris County; mem. emeritus bd. govs. Shrine Hosps. Crippled Children; mem. Met. Opera Nat. Council N.Y.; hon. life trustee Mus. Fine Arts Houston; bd. dirs. Houston Soc. for Performing Arts, Houston Lyric Theatre Found., Tex. Arts Alliance; mem. governing council Shepherd Sch. Music, Rice U.; mem. governing bd., vice chmn. Houston Grand Opera; hon. mem. dirs. com. Orpheus Soc., U. Houston Sch. Music; hon. mem. bd. dirs. Citizens for Animal Protection. Served as col. AUS, 1944; detailed in Judge Adv. Gen.'s Dept. 1944; Gen. Staff Corps 1944-47; brig. gen. AUS, 1946-50. Decorated D.S.M. U.S.; Stella Della Solidariata Italiana; Order of Sacred Treasure (Japan); recipient Disting. Service medal Tex. Heritage Found.; Brotherhood award NCCJ; Disting. Citizen award Goodwill Industries; Disting. Citizen award Sheltering Arms; Cultural Leader award Houston Youth Symphony and Ballet; medal of grand order Dr. Mazzei of Unico Nat. Honor Soc. Mem. Jr. C. of C. (hon. life), Am., Tex., Houston, Harris County bar assns., Houston Bar Found., Houston Symphony Soc. (pres. 1956-70, pres. emeritus 1971—), Navy League U.S. (life mem., Houston council), Com. Fgn. Relations, Confrerie des Chevaliers du Tastevin, Confrerie de la Chaine Des Rotisseurs, Rice U. Assos. (life), Japan-Am. Soc. Houston (past pres., pres. emeritus), Am. Legion, Houston C. of C. (mil. affairs com., cultural com., bus. com. for arts, 1st Gen. Maurice Hirsch award), Ret. Officers Assn., Raven Soc. U. Va., Phi Beta Kappa, Delta Sigma Rho; mem. B'nai B'rith (past pres. dist.). Clubs: Mason (32 deg., Shriner), Kiwanian (life), Rotarian (hon.; Disting. Citizen award 1978), Elk (hon. life); Houston (Houston), Heritage (Houston), Salesmanship (Houston) (hon. life), Houston Press (Houston) (hon. life), Petroleum (Houston), Coronado (Houston), Allegro (Houston), Ramada (Houston), Houston City (Houston), Houston Center (Houston), Inns of Ct. (Houston), Lakewood Yacht (Houston), River Oaks Country (Houston), Plaza (Houston), University (Houston); Army and Navy; Nat. Aviation (Washington); Commodore. Home: Houston, Tex. Died Aug. 5, 1983.

HIRSCH, MONROE JEROME, optometrist, educator; b. N.Y.C., Mar. 6, 1917; s. Stanley and Anna (Mandell) H.; m. Winifred Maud Wilson, May 4, 1940; 1 son, Geoffrey Alan. Student, Coll. City N.Y., 1934-37; A.B., U. Calif., Berkeley, 1940; Ph.D., Stanford U., 1947; D.O.S. (hon.), Ill. Coll. Optometry, 1979. Pvt. practice optometry, Oakland, Calif., 1940-45; clin. instr. U. Calif. at Berkeley, 1942-66, lectr., 1967-69, prof. optometry and physiol. optics, 1969-78, dir. clinics, 1969-73, dean, 1973-78; research asst. and asso. Stanford U., 1943-47, asst. prof. physiology, 1948-49; asst. prof. Ohio State U., 1947-48; asso. prof. Los Angeles Coll. Optometry, 1949-51, prof., 1951-53; faculty Pacific U., summer 1946; refractionist Alameda County Hosp., 1941-44; First Thomas H. Peters Meml. lectr. Sch. Optometry, U. Calif. at Berkeley, 1956; First George Cox Meml. lectr. U. Auckland, New Zealand, 1969; First Squarebriggs Meml. lectr. U. Waterloo, Can., 1972; mem. adv. com. Calif. Dept. Pub. Health, 1961-63; optical aids adv. com. Am. Found. for Blind, 1952-59; adv. com. on problems of health Calif. Dept. Edn., 1960-62; chancellor's adv. com. on med. edn. U. Calif., 1970-74; mem. com. on vision NRC, from 1974. Author: (with Ralph E. Wick) Vision of the Aging Patient, 1960, Vision of Children, 1963, The Optometric Profession, 1968, Refractive State of the Eye, 1966; Asso. editor: (with Ralph E. Wick) Archives of Am. Acad. Optometry, 1953-67; editor (with Ralph E. Wick), 1968-79; contbr. (with Ralph E. Wick) articles to profl. jours. Councilman, Ojai, Calif., 1956-60, 66-70, mayor, 1958; mem. County Democratic Central Com., 1960-64, Calif. Dem. Central Com., 1962-64. Recipient Silver medal Distinguished Service Found. in Optometry, 1960; Distinguished Service award U.S. C. of C., 1967; Berkeley Optometry citation, 1978; Prentice medal Am. Acad. Optometry, 1978. Fellow Am. Acad. Optometry (exec. council from 1956, pres. 1966-68), AAAS; mem. Am. Optometric Assn., Calif. Optometric Assn. (Optometrist of Year 1969, citation 1979), AAUP, U. Calif. Optometry Alumni Assn. (Alumnus of Year 1962), Sigma Xi. Home: Ojai, Calif.

HIRST, CLAUDE MARVIN, government official; born Nevada County, Arkansas, September 5, 1889; son of Jesse Joseph and Susan A. (Alsobrooks) H.; B.A., U. of Ark., 1912; M.A., George Peabody Coll. for Teachers, 1924; m. Ruth Sutton, Sept. 13, 1914; children—Ruth Sutton, Claude M. Prin. high sch., Sutton, Ark., 1912-15; supt. pub. schs., Prescott, Ark., 1915-23; dir. school plant div. Ark. Dept. of Edn., 1924-29; state supt. pub. instrn., Ark., 1929-31; commr. of edn., Ark., 1931-33; dir. Sch. Building Survey and Indian Edn., Calif., 1934-36; dir. Indian edn. for Alaska, 1936-38; gen. supt. for Alaska Indian Service, 1938-44; conference manager, U.S. Civil Service Commn., 1944-46; dir. Real Property Disposal, U.S. Office of Edn., from Mar. 1946. Mem. N.E.A., Ark. Edn. Assn., Am. Council on School House Constrn., Nat. Congress of Parents and Teachers, Civil Service Assembly, Soc. for Personnel Adminstrn., Phi Delta Kappa, Kappa Delta Pi. Presbyterian. Mason. Address: Arlington, Va. †

HISE, HARLEY, business exec.; b. Houston, Ind., Jan. 26, 1890; s. James Martin and Sarah Ann (Brown) H.; ed. high sch., bus. coll., spl. work in accounting and law; m. Grace Greenlaw, July 24, 1915. Clk. in auditing div., Dept. Justice, Washington, 1913-18; land bank examiner, then chief examiner bd., Fed. Farm Loan Bd., 1919-22; v.p., mgr. Pacific Coast Joint Stock Land Bank of San Francisco (later merged with Pacific Coast Joint Stock Land Bank of Los Angeles), 1922-38; v.p., mgr. Merc. Mortgage Co., v.p., mem. exec. com. real estate loan dept. Am. Trust Co., San Francisco, 1927-29; v.p., dir. Pacific Coast Mortgage Co., Bankamerica Co., Golden Gate Ferry Co.; pres., dir. Western Lands Securities Co., No. Cal. Mortgage Co.; dir. Gen. Metals Corp., San Francisco; v.p., dir. Reclaimed Island Lands Co., Sears Point Toll Road Co., Vallejo and Marin Cos.; trustee, Reclamation Dists. 2058 and 2062, San Joaquin Co., Cal., 1925-40; apptd. custodian in receivership of Pacific States Savings & Loan Co., State Bldg. and Loan Commr. of Cal., 1940-43; apptd. mem. bd. dirs. Reconstrn. Finance Corp., 1947, chmn. 1949, term expired 1950. Del. at large Dem. Nat. Conv., 1948, 52. Mason (32, Shriner). Presbyn. Home: San Francisco, CA. †

HISLOP, JOSEPH, operatic tenor; b. Edinburgh, Scotland, Apr. 5, 1887; s. Joseph Dewar and Mary (Lunn) H.; ed. Edinburgh and London; studied singing in Stockholm, Milan and Naples; studied acting and stage deportment, Sch. of Opera, Royal Opera, Stockholm; m. Karin Elizabeth Asklund, May 26, 1915. Début at Royal Opera House, Stockholm, Sept. 12, 1914; has sung leading tenor roles at Covent Garden, London, and in Stockholm, Christiania, Copenhagen, Naples, etc.; joined Chicago Opera Assn., 1920. Repertoire includes leading tenor parts in "La Boheme," "Tosca," "Butterfly," "Aida," "Rigoletto," "Romeo and Juliet," "Pagliacci," "Faust," etc. Address: New York, N.Y. †

HITCHCOCK, FRED A(NDREWS), physiologist, educator; b. Akron, O., Oct. 30, 1889; s. George E(lisha) and Florence M. (Tucker) H.; Ph.B., U. Akron, 1912; grad. study U. Chicago, 1916, Cambridge U., 1919, Carnegie Instn. Nutrition Lab., 1933; M.S., Ohio State U., 1923, Ph.D., 1926; m. Mary Alice Rines, 1917. Chemist, photographer various cos., also actor Charles Coburn Players, 1912-15; instr. high schs., Ohio, 1915-16, Western Mil. Acad., 1916-17, high schs., Columbus, Ohio, 1919-23; faculty mem. Ohio State U., from 1923, asst. prof., 1928-35, asso. prof., 1935-40, prof. physiology, 1940-60, prof. physiology emeritus, from 1960, chmn. dept. physiology, 1947-49, organizer, dir. Lab. Aviation Physiology; adj. prof. physiology, Pahlevi U., Shiraz, Iran, 1963-64; cons. Auco Corp., from 1959; research under contract Wright Field Aero-Med. Lab. (Air Force Research and Development Command), Office Naval Research, Office Surgeon Gen. Army, Nat. Safety Council; chmn. com. orgn. Inst. Research in Vision, Ohio State U. Cons. aviation physiology and medicine Civil Aeronautics Adminstrn.; dir. research program in cooperation with Civil Aeronautics Adminstrn. and comml. airlines; civilian Office Sci. Research and Development, com. med. research, 1941-46. Mem. Internat. Physiological Congress, England, 1947, Denmark, 1950, Brussels, 1956, Buenos Aires, 1960; rep. Am. Physiol. Society on council of A.A.A.S. Served as 2d lt. 323d F.A., U.S. Army, Army of Occupation, France, Germany, 1917-19. Recipient Arnold D. Tuttle Meml. award, 1955. Fellow A.A.A.S., American Astronautical Soc.; member New York Academy of Science, also American Rocket Soc., Brazilian Interplanetary Soc. (scientific council), American Physiological Soc. (council), Aero-Med. Assn., Space Medicine Soc. (pres. 1955-56), N.Y. Acad. Sci., Am. Astronautical Soc., Soc. Exptl. Biology and Medicine, Am. Soc. Zoologists, Am. Inst. Nutrition, Sigma Xi. Author articles sci. jours.; also chpt. explosive decompression. Mem. editorial bd. Jour. Nutrition, 1942-47, Jour. Astronautics. Translator: Bert's Barometric Pressure (with Mary Alice Hitchcock), 1943. Home: Columbus, OH. †

HITCHMAN, ROBERT BRUCE, assn. exec., ins. co. exec.; b. Denver, Oct. 28, 1908; s. Herbert Samuel and Hazel (Chamberlin) H.; m. Helen Marie Evens, Oct. 1, 1967. B.A., U. Wash., 1929. With Unigard Mut. Ins. Co. (formerly Northwestern Mut. Ins. Co.), Seattle, 1928-78, sr. v.p., 1968-69, pres., 1969-73, also dir.; dir. Unigard Ins. Co., Unigard Olympic Life Ins. Co. Pub.: booklist Sighted From The Crow's Nest, 1953-79; editorial bd.: The American West, 1968-80. Mem. adv. bd. King Co. Council on Alcoholism, Seattle, 1959-62; bd. curators Wash. Hist. Soc., 1952-81, pres., 1976-81; regional adv. bd. Nat. Archives, 1969-73; sec. for domestic correspondence, bd. councillors Am. Antiquarian Soc., 1970-81; Trustee Seattle Found., 1969-78; pres. 1975-77; bd. dirs. Pacific Search press, 1973-81, Pacific NW Grantmakers Forum, 1977-81; mem. nat. council Mus. of Am. Indian (Heye Found.), 1979-81. Served to col. AUS, 1942-46, ETO. Decorated Bronze Star. Mem. Champlain Soc., Hakluyt Soc. Clubs: Rotarian. (Seattle), Rainier (Seattle), The Monday (Seattle). Home: Seattle, Wash. Died Apr.

17, 1981; interred Chapel of Resurrection, St. Mark's Cathedral, Seattle.

HITE, OMAR, newspaper man; b. Smithton, W.Va., Jan. 11, 1890; s. Rev. Raymond M. and Mary S. (Cochran) H.; grad. high school, 1907; student Campbell Coll., Holton, Kan., 3 yrs.; A.B., U. of Kan., 1913; m. June R. Barker, July 19, 1919; children—Howard Omar, Lois Elizabeth (Mrs. Hessel E. Yntema, Jr.). Member of the editorial staff, Fort Worth (Tex.) Record, fall of 1913; telegraph editor Arkansas Gazette, Little Rock, Ark., 1914-15; editorial staff St. Louis Republic, 1915-17; with St. Louis Star, 1917; editorial staff and asst. day city editor, New York Herald, 1917-20; asso. editor Christian Herald, 1920-25, editor, 1925-28; mem. editorial staff New York Times from 1929. Served as 2d lt. inf., Camp Pike and Camp Funston, World War I. Presbyn. Home: Glen Rock, N.J. †

HITT, FRANCIS GUY, business executive; b. DuQuoin, Illinois, June 11, 1890; s. Francis Marion and Olivia L. (Harriss) H.; graduate DuQuoin Twp. High School and Graduate School of Banking, Rutgers Univ.; m. Martha Lee Provart, May 15, 1917; children—Frances Lee (Mrs. Harry K. Sandhagen), Marian Louise (Mrs. Harry T. Maltby), Robert, Lela Jeanne (Mrs. C. A. Helzer), Martha Suzanne. Served as assistant postmaster in city of Du-Quoin, 1914-20; asst. cashier First Nat. Bank, Christopher, Ill., 1921-26; pres. First Nat. Bank Zeigler, Ill., 1927-37; chmn. bd., pres. Bank of Zeigler, from 1951, chmn. bd., 1957-64, chairman of the executive committee, from 1964; dir. of Bank of St. Louis; pres. Bank of Benton, Ill., 1951-57, chmn. bd., from 1957; dir. So. Ill., Inc., General Bancshares Corporation, St. Louis; dir. Fed. Res. Bank of St. Louis, 1932-37, 1st vice pres., 1937-51; conservator First National Bank, East St. Louis, Illinois, 1933-34. Vice chairman of U.S. Treasury War Finance Company, 8th Fed. Res. Dist., 1943. Mem. Com. on Higher Education State of Ill., 1959. Trustee Shurtleff Coll., 1950-54; mem. bd. dirs. St. Louis Conv. and Publicity Bureau, 1938-51. Mem. Benton C. of C. (pres. 1951-52, bd. dirs. 1951-53). Mason (32 deg., Shriner). Clubs: Benton Country, Rotary (president of chapter of St. Louis 1948-49; gov. Dist. 216 Internat. 1952-53), Benton, Saint Louis, Mo. Athletic. Home: Benton, Ill. †

HITZIG, WILLIAM MAXWELL, physician; b. Austria, Dec. 15, 1904; s. Maier and Jeannette (Kreisberg) H.; brought to U.S., 1914, naturalized, 1926; A.B., Columbia U., 1926; M.D., Cornell U., 1929; children—Candis, Rupert, Saartje, Pietr, William Maxwell, Myron S. Hall and Elizabeth Topping (twins). Intern Mount Sinai Hosp., N.Y. City, 1929-32, asso. physician in medicine, after 1946; practice of medicine, N.Y. C., after 1934; specializing in internal medicine and cardiovascular diseases, after 1936; instr. medicine Columbia, 1938-50, asst. clin. prof. medicine, after 1959; prof. clin. medicine, then prof. emeritus; Mt. Sinai Sch. Medicine, N.Y. Med. cons. Ravensbrueck Lapins Project, 1958. Med. officer N.Y.C. Fire Dept., 1942-43, physician Police Dept., after 1943; med. observer, atomic bomb tests at Bikini, 1946. Citation and Alumni medal for conspicuous service to Columbia U., 1951; Dean's award Columbia Coll. 1968; hon. mem. Honor Legion, Police Dept. N.Y. City. Diplomate Am. Bd. Internal Medicine. Fellow A.C.P., Acad. of Medicine N.Y.; mem. Am. Fedn. for Clin. Research, Pilgrims U.S., Phi Beta Kappa, Mu Sigma, Phi Sigma Delta, Phi Delta Epsilon, Alpha Omega Alpha. Club: City Athletic (N.Y. City). Author sci. articles. Book reviewer Sat. Rev. Lit., 1946-50. Sponsor (with Norman Cousins) of Hiroshima Maidens Project which brought 25 Japanese girls disfigured by atom bomb to U.S. for plastic surgery and reconstructive surgery. Home: New York, N.Y. Died Aug. 27, 1983.

HIXSON, A(RTHUR) NORMAN, educator, chem. engr.; b. Iowa City, Ia., July 30, 1909; s. Arthur Warren and Edetha Mary (Washburn) H.; B.A., Columbia, 1931, B.S., 1932, Chem.E., 1933, Ph.D., 1941; m. Clara E. Sherwin, Sept. 2, 1939; children—Gwen E., Stephen S., Arthur Norman. Chem. engr. research Intermetals Corp., Newark, 1933-36; chem. engr. development nylon E. I. duPont de Nemours, 1936-38; instr. chem. engring. U. Pa., 1938-41, asst. prof., 1941-44, asso. prof., 1944-52, prof., 1952-84, asst. v.p., 1954-84; cons. raw materials div. Bethlehem Steel Co., 1943-61; vis. prof. Univ. College London, 1960-61. Member Am. Inst. Chemical Engrs. (editorial bd. jours.), American Chemical Society, A.A-.A.S., also Sigma Xi, Tau Beta Pi, Phi Lambda Upsilon, Sigma Chi, Theta Chi. Contbr. tech. jours. Home: Moylan, Pa. Died Nov. 23, 1984.

HJELLE, JOHN ORLO, editor; b. Mercer, N.D., Nov. 15, 1913; s. Ole S. and Ella T. (Myrah) H.; A.B., Luther Coll., 1936; m. Alice Marie Driver, Dec. 19, 1943; children—Ann Marie, Kathryn Lynn, Barbara, Kristin. Reporter, sports editor, telegraph editor Bismarck Tribune, 1936-41, city editor, 1941-45, editor, 1948-79, exec. sec., adminstrv. asst. to U.S. Senator M.R. Young, Washington, 1945-48. Bd. dirs. Upper Midwest Council of Mpls. Mem. Am. Soc. Newspaper Editors, N.D. Newspaper Assn. (pres. 1969-70). Lutheran. Elk. Mason (Shriner), Rotarian. Contbr. articles to profl. publs. Home: Bismarck, N.D. Dec. Apr. 16, 1982.

HNIZDO, JAROSLAV, Czechoslovak counsul gen.; b. Nemceves, Czechoslovakia, Dec. 20, 1890; s. Anton and Anna (Vanickova) H.; student Real Sch., 1902-09; mil. training, 1909-10; Export Acad., Vienna, 1910-12; unmarried. Consular rep. Czechoslovak govt., Shanghai and Peking, China, 1919-30; with Ministry of Foreign Affairs, Praha, Czechoslovakia, 1930; consul, Montreal, 1931-42; consul gen., Chicago, from 1942. Served as lt. Austro-Hungarian Army, 1914-15; taken prisoner in Russia; joined Czechoslovak polit. orgn. for liberation of his country; served in Serbian Army in Russia, 1916, Czechoslovak Army, Kiev, Ukraine, 1917-19; promoted to major, comdr. 12th Inf., 1918. Awarded Czechoslovak and Yugoslav mil. decorations. Mem. Arts Club (Chicago). Home: Chicago, Ill. †

HOADLEY, FRANKLIN ROGERS, business exec.; b. Ansonia, Conn., Apr. 1, 1890; s. Frank Edgar and Jenny (Rogers) H.; B.A., Yale, 1914; m. Esther B. Schmitt, 1913. Began with Farrell-Birmingham Co. in 1914, mgr. of foundries, 1927, v.p., 1930-36; pres. and treas. Atwood Machine Co., Stonington, Conn., 1937-45; pres. Gray Iron Founders Society, 1934-35; pres. National Founders Assn., 1937-39; pres. Farrel-Birmingham Co., Inc.; dir. South New England Telephone Co., 1st Nat. Bank and Trust Co. New Haven, Conn.). Clubs: Yale, New Haven Country, Quinnipiack, The Graduate Club (New Haven). Home: New Haven, Conn. †

HOBART, EDWARD A., mfg. exec.; b. Middletown, Ohio, Dec. 25, 1888; s. Charles Clarence and Lou E. (Jones) H.; m. Martha L. Lantis, Oct. 12, 1921. E.E., Ohio State U., 1912; D.Sc. (hon.), 1969. With Hobart Bros. Co., Troy, 1917—, pres., 1932-70, chmn. bd., 1970-85; v.p. Welded Products Co.; v.p., dir. First Troy Nat. Bank; dir. Fla. Minerals Co., Continental Minerals Co. Mem. Miami Valley Conservancy Bd. Honored by City of Troy, 1976. Fellow I.E.E.E.; mem. Newcomen Soc., Am. Welding Soc., Am. Inst. E.E., Engrs. Club, Ordnance Assn., Eta Kappa Nu. Presbyn. Clubs: Moraine Country (Dayton, Ohio), Engineers (Dayton, Ohio); Troy Country; Queen City (Cincinnati); Rio Mar Yacht (Vero Beach, Fla.). Home: Troy, Ohio. Died July 26, 1985; interred Troy, Ohio.

HOBART, HAROLD PECKHAM, oil company consultant; b. Cleveland, Aug. 22, 1888; s. M. Montague and Elizabeth W. (Peckham) H.; Ph.B., Yale, 1910; M. Mildred Painter, Apr. 15, 1914 (died 1938); children—Agnes Clarke (Mrs. Edwin N. Hower, dec.), Edward Painter; married 2d, Frances Lyndon, August 9, 1941; 2 stepdaughters—Frances Lyndon (Mrs. E. P. Snyder, Jr.), Louis Lyndon (Mrs. Robert E. Noble, Jr.). With Gulf Oil Corp., Pitts., 1919-54, mgr. lubricants sales, 1920-32, gen. mgr. lubricants sales, 1933-47, v.p., 1947-53, ret.; v.p. Gulf Refining Co., 1947-54, ret.; formerly v.p. and dir. Gulf Research and Development Co., Gulf Trie and Supply Co., Goodrich-Gulf Chems., Inc.; trustee Dollar Savings Bank, Pitts. Served as capt., Ordnance Dept. AUS; World War I. Mem. C. of C. (past dir.), Soc. Automotive Engrs., Am. Petroleum Inst. (chmn. lubrication com. 1947). Nat. Lubricating Grease Inst. (dir.; pres. 1947). Nat. Petroleum Assn. (past trustee), Mil. Order World Wars (past comdr. Pitts.). Presbyn. Clubs: Duquesne, Pittsburgh Golf (Pitts.); Rolling Rock (Ligonier); Yale (N.Y.C.); The Beach, Lawn, Graduates (all of New Haven). Home: Greenwich, Conn. †

HOBART, HARRISON CLAYTON, union ofcl.; b. Fairchild, Wis., Sept. 6, 1888; s. James and Mary Elizabeth (MacLyman) H.; student U. Minn., 1932-33; m. Bessie Louise Ryder, 1908; children—Jean (Mrs. Henry Brewer), Lois (Mrs. Claire Hendricks), Harrison Samuel; m. 2d. Mrs. Martha Buske Barrow, 1947; 1 son, Richard Winston Barrow. Fireman C., St.P., M.& O. Ry., 1905-10; with Brotherhood Locomotive Engrs. from 1915, chief engr. Div. 241 until 1924. gen. chmn. 1924-42, alternate asst. grand chief engr., 1942-44, asst. grand chief engr., 1944, 55-57; charge Chgo. office, 1945-46; labor coordinator, Minn., 1942, charge labor State Civilian Def. Program until 1944, served various commns. in connection state labor relations law; served spl. bds. adjustment, various railroads Southwest, West, 1947-53; staff Dept. Labor, Washington, 1953, asst. sec. of labor, 1953-54. Mem. pres.'s adv. com. Coll. Bus. Adminstrn., U. Houston; board govs. U. Houston, 1957. Republican. Lutheran. Mason (K.T., Shriner). Home: Houston, TX. †

HOBBS, CLARK SIMPSON, assn. exec.; b. Baltimore, Md., July 1, 1888; s. Rev. Gustavus Warfield and Jeannette (Richardson) H.; ed. Baltimore pub. schs.; m. Janet Septima Tustin, Dec. 5, 1914; 1 dau., Pauline. Began career as a reporter in 1907; editor, Baltimore Municipal Journal, 1914-17; contact officer between State Dept. and War Trade Bd. for Latin Am., 1917-19; columnist and asso. editor, Evening Sun, 1919-45; trustee, Goucher Coll. from 1933, v.p., 1945-51; dir. civic development bur., Balt. Assn. Commerce, from 1951. Chmn., Land Redevelopment Commission; chairman, advisory com. on sanitation, Baltimore City Dept. of Health; trustee, Kelso Home for Girls, and Home for Aged of Meth. Ch.; mem. Bd. of Child Care of Meth. Ch. and Baltimore Annual Conf. of Meth. Ch.; pres. Baltimore Goodwill Industries, Inc.; chmn. med. care sect. Baltimore Council Social Agencies. Mem. Nat., Assn. Housing Ofcls. Author: numerous articles on city planning, slum clearance and housing. Home: Baltimore, Md. †

HOBBS, NICHOLAS, educator, psychologist; b. Greenville, S.C., Mar. 13, 1915; s. Caswell Owen and Albirta Judson (Jones) H.; m. Mary Madeline Thompson, May 21, 1949; 1 son, Nicholas Thompson. A.B., The Citadel, 1936, D.Litt., 1973; M.A., Ohio State U., 1938, Ph.D., 1946; D.Sc., Louisville, 1972; D. (h.c.), U. Paul Valery-Montpellier, 1978. Tchr. Riverside Mil. Acad., 1936-37, Spartanburg (S.C.) High Sch., 1937-38; asso. prof., dir. tng. clin. psychology Columbia Tchrs. Coll., 1946-50; chmn. dept. psychology La. State U., 1950-51; chmn. div. human devel. Peabody Coll., 1951-65; dir. Kennedy Center Research on Edn. and Human Devel., 1965-70; provost Vanderbilt U., 1967-75, prof. psychology, 1975-80, prof. emeritus, from 1980; dir. Center for Study of Families and Children, 1976-80; dir. selection, research Peace Corps., 1961-62; lectr. Inst. Humanistic Studies for Execs., U. Pa., 1956-60; Dir. So. Regional Edn. Bd. Mental Health Tng. and Research Project, 1954-55; vice chmn. So. Regional Council Mental Health Tng. and Research; vice chmn., trustee Joint Commn. on Mental Illness and Health; mem. President's Panel on Mental Retardation, Nat. Advisory Council Child Health and Human Devel., Nat. Advisory Mental Health Council; v.p. Joint Commn. Mental Health Children; mem. U.S. Nat. Commn. UNESCO; mem. adv. com. child devel. Nat. Acad. Scis., 1971-73, dir. project on classification exceptional children, 1972-75; mem. commn. on mentally disabled Am. Bar Assn., from 1973; mem. Nat. Inst. Medicine, Nat. Acad. Scis., from 1976; coordinator panel on the family Pres.'s Commn. on Mental Health, from 1977; mem. select panel on promotion of child health HEW, 1979-81. Author: The Futures of Children, 1975, The Troubled and the Troubling: Reeducation in Mental Health Programs for Children, 1982. Trustee Fisk U., from 1976. Served with USAAF, 1941-46. Fellow Center Advanced Study Behavioral Scis., 1966-67. Mem. Am. Psychol. Assn. (dir. 1952-55, pres. 1965-66, pres. div. clin. psychology), Southeastern Psychol. Assn. (pres. 1956-57), A.A.A.S., Nat. Inst. Medicine, So. Soc. Philosophy and Psychology (treas. 1954-55), Sigma Xi. Club: Cosmos. Home: Nashville, Tenn.

HOBLER, ATHERTON W., advt. exec.; b. Chgo., Sept. 2, 1890; s. Edward and Harriet (Wells) H.; A.B., University of Illinois, 1911; married Ruth Windsor, March 30, 1914; children—Edward Windsor, Wells Atherton, Virginia (dec.), Herbert Windsor. With Appleton Mfg. Co., Batavia, Ill., successively as credit mgr., advt. mgr. and sales mgr., 1911-17; account exec. and v.p. Gardner Advt. Co., St. Louis, 1917-25; v.p. and partner Erwin, Wasey & Co., advt., N.Y. City, 1925-32; pres. Benton & Bowles, Inc., advt., New York City, 1932-42, chairman bd., 1942-52, chmn. exec. com., 1952-62, founder chmn., from 1962. Elected chairman board of American Association of Advertising Agencies, 1940. Republican. Clubs: Union League, University (N.Y.C.); Bedens Brook (Princeton, N.J.); Everglades, Bath and Tennis (Palm Beach, Fla.). Address: New York, N.Y. †

HOBSON, ASHER, agrl. economist; b. Quenemo, Kan., Nov. 26, 1889; s. Felix and Ida May (Harr) H.; B.A., U. of Kan., 1913; studied U. of Wis., 1913-16, M.A., 1915; Dr. Polit. Sci., U. of Geneva (Switzerland), 1931; m. Thea Dahle, June 26, 1917; children—Merk, Marcelaine. Research asst. in agr. economics, U. of Wis., 1914-16; state dir. markets, State of Wash., 1917-19; asst. chief Office of Farm Management, U.S. Dept. Agr., 1919-20; asso. prof. economic agr., Columbia, 1920-22; Am. del. at Internat. Inst. Agr., Rome, 1922-29; cons. economist Federal Farm Bd., 1929-30; chief of Div. of Foreign Agrl. Service, U.S. Dept. Agr., Washington, 1930-31; prof. agrl. econs., since 1931, head, Dept of Agrl. Econs., U. of Wis., 1932-48. Mem. agrl. com. C. of C. of the U.S.A. since 1948. Mem. Am. Econ. Assn., Am. Farm Econ. Assn. (sec., treas., 1931-46, pres. 1947), Internat. Conf. of Agrl. Economists (Am. mem. of council, 1930-48), Am. Inst. of Cooperation (mem. bd. of trustees, exec. com. since 1944, chmn. trustees since 1949), Phi Kappa Phi, Delta Sigma Rho, Acacia. Clubs: Cosmos (Washington, D.C.); University (Madison, Wis.). Home: Madison, Wis. †

HOBSON, KATHERINE THAYER, sculptress, poet; b. Denver, Apr. 11, 1889; d. Henry Wise and Katherine S. (Thayer) Hobson; student law U. Leipzig, Koenigsberg, Goettingen; student sculpture Dresden, Paris, Athens; m. Herbert Kraus, Dec. 2, 1911 (div. Dec. 1938); m. 2d, Diether Thimme, Feb. 21, 1939 (div. Dec. 1948). Exhibited in group shows galleries in Berlin, Dresden, Hamburg, Koenigsberg, Paris Salon, Hudson Valley Art Assn., NAD, Audubon Artists, Nat. Assn. Women Artists, Pen and Brush, Nat. Sculpture Soc., others; important works include statue Bahnhofs Platz, Goettingen; busts Univs. Goettingen, Koenigsberg, Sch. Tech., Dresden, U. Library and Gymnasium, Goettingen; 8-foot war meml. St. James Episcopal Ch., N.Y.C.; tchr. occupational therapy Halloran Gen. Hosp., World War II. Recipient awards Catherine Lorrilard Wolfe Club, 1953, 54, 68, 73, 1st prize Womens Nat. Republican Club, 1964, medal Nat. Arts Club, 1967, Newington award Hudson Valley Art Assn., 1968, 73, 1st prize sculpture Cooperstown Art Assn. Ann. Exhbn., 1968. Fellow Nat. Sculpture Soc. (mem. council); mem. Pen and Brush (chmn. sculptor sect. 1953, 54, 62-64, 66, 75-76, recipient Founders prize 1955, Gold medal 1965, Silver medals, 1964-66), Am. Artists Profl. League (v.p., asst. treas. Pres.'s prize 1962, 66), Am. Artists Soc. (mem. council), Fine Arts Fedn. N.Y. (sec. 1952-69), Allied Artists Am. Hudson Valley Art Assn. (Gold medal 1963, Archer Milton Huntington award 1963, 64), Contemporary Arts Club, Women Geographers, Poetry Soc., Am. Cath. Poetry Soc. Mem. editorial bd. Nat. Sculpture

Rev. Contbr. poetry to newpapers and mags. Died Sept. 10, 1982.

HODGE, JAMES CAMPBELL, engring., mfg. exec.; b. Falkirk, Scotland, Sept. 3, 1902; s. James and Anne (Campbell) H.; came to U.S., 1916, naturalized, 1941; B.S., Case Sch. Applied Sci., 1923; D.Sc., Harvard, 1933; D.Eng., Fenn Coll., 1965, Cleve. State U., 1968; m. Emma C. Meinke, June 12, 1926; children—Jean Elizabeth (Mrs. Harold C. Colley), Carol Anne (Mrs. Donald L. Poe), Emily Jane (Mrs. Philip H. Brasfield). A cons. metallurgist Bennett & Christensen, Cleve., 1923-27; metallurgist Babcock & Wilcox Co.. Barberton, O., 1927-32, chief metallurgist, 1932-40; v.p., dir. Wellman Engring. Co., Cleve., 1940-44, exec. v.p., dir., 1944-54, pres., dir., 1954-55; v.p. Warner & Swasey Co., Cleve., 1956, exec. v.p., 1956-62, pres., 1962-69, chmn. bd., 1969-72, chmn. exec. com., 1973-74, also dir.; chmn. bd., dir. Digital Gen. Corp.; dir. Wang Lab., Inc. Trustee Case Inst. Tech., 1964-67, Case Western Res. U., 1967-75, Fenn Coll., 1952-65, Cleve. Community Fund, 1964-68, Kolff Found., 1974-76; vice chmn. bd. trustees Fenn Ednl. Found., 1965-71; vice chmn. Fenn Ednl. Fund of Cleve. Found., 1971-72, chmn., 1972-74; bd. govs. Asso. Industries Cleve., 1965-71, v.p., 1967-68, pres., 1970-71; mem. Greater Cleve. adv. bd. Salvation Army, 1951-82, chmn., 1955-57; mem. exec. bd. Greater Cleve. council Boy Scouts Am.; vice chmn. bd. trustees John Carroll U. Corp., 1969-71, chmn., 1971-74; bd. dirs. Greater Cleveland Growth Assn., 1968-72; mem. adv. bd. lay trustees John Carroll U., 1968-69; hon. corp. mem. Dyke Coll., 1973-75. Recipient Hon. Alumnus Membership award Cleve. State U., 1966, Pres.'s Achievement award Case Inst. Tech., 1966, Silver Knight award as Mgmt. Man of Year, Mgmt. Club of Greater Cleve., 1967, Alumni citation Case Western Res. U., 1968, Gold Medal award Case Alumni Assn., 1968, Distinguished Service award Cleve. Tech. Socs. Council, 1970; Distinguished Aux. Service award Salvation Army, 1974. Mem. Am. Inst. Mining and Metall. Engrs., N.A.M. (state dir. 1966-68), Machinery and Allied Products Inst. (exec. com. 1964-73), Am. Soc. Metals (Sauveur Meml. lectr. Cambridge 1954), Am. Soc. Testing Materials, Am. Welding Soc., Assn. Iron and Steel Engrs., Profl. Engrs. Soc., Cleve. Engring. Soc. (past bd. govs.), Cleve. Astron. Soc., Am. Ordnance Assn. (pres. dir.), U.S. C. of C. (mem. policy com. 1966-67), Newcomen Soc., Sigma Alpha Epsilon, Tau Beta Pi. Clubs: Pepper Pike, Union, Hillbrook (Cleve.). Home: Cleveland, Ohio. Died Feb. 12, 1982.

HODGES, JOSEPH HOWARD, bishop; b. Harpers Ferry, W.Va., Oct. 8, 1911; s. Joseph Howard and Edna Belle (Hendricks) H. Student, St. Charles Coll., Catonsville, Md., 1928-30, North Am. Coll., Rome, Italy, 1930-36; D.D. (hon.), North Am. Coll., Rome, Italy, 1952. Ordained priest Roman Cath. Ch., Rome, 1935; asst. Sacred Heart Ch., Danville, Va., 1936-39, St. Andrew's Ch., Roanoke, Va., 1939-45; adminstr. St. Mary's Ch., Richmond, Va.; also dir. Diocesan Missionary Fathers, 1945-55; pastor St. Peter's Ch., Richmond, 1955-61; consecrated Titular Bishop of Rusadus, and Aux. Bishop of the Cath. Diocese of Richmond, 1952; vicar gen. Diocese of Richmond, 1958-61; coadjutor bishop and vicar gen. Diocese of Wheeling-Charleston, W.Va., 1961, bishop, 1962-85. Home: Wheeling, W.Va. Died Jan. 27, 1985.

HODGKINSON, HAROLD DANIEL, merchant; b. Wallingford, Conn., May 8, 1890; s. Samuel and Sara LaVerne (Averill) H.; Ph.B., Yale, 1912; D.C.S. Boston U., 1951; L.H.D., Suffolk U., 1956; m. Laura White Cabot, June 22, 1929; 1 dau., Charlotte Anne. Chmn. exec. com. William Filene's Sons Co., Boston, Mass.; vice president, dir. Federated Dept. Stores, Cin. and N.Y., 1944-65; chmn., dir. Federal Res. Bank of Boston, 1947-56; dir. Liberty Mutual Ins. Co., Nat. Life Ins. Co.; hon. dir. Asso. Merchandising Corp., N.Y., Liberty Mut. Fire Ins. Co. Mem. council for ednl. station WGBH; trustee Boston Symphony Orch.; v.p. Mass. Com. of Caths., Protestants and Jews; mem. nat. adv. com. A.R.C., 1945; trustee Plimoth Plantation; mem. corp. Mass. Gen. Hosp. Mem. corp. Simmons Coll.; trustee Northeastern U. Trustee Boston U., Essex Inst. Served as lt. (j.g.) USNRF, 1917-21. Decorated Legion of Honor (France); Order of Merit (Italy). Fellow Am. Acad. Arts and Scis. (v.p.); mem. Am. Retail Fedn. (pres. 1962-63). Clubs: Somerset, Union, Harvard, Club of Odd Volumes (Boston); Eastern Yacht (Marblehead); Yale (N.Y.C.); The Country (Brookline, Mass.). Home: Boston, Mass. †

HODGSON, JAMES FLINN, business counselor; b. Haddonfield, N.J., May 26, 1890; s. William W. and Clara R. (Flinn) H.; student Friends Central School, Philadelphia; grad. U.S. Mil. Acad., 1914; m. Theodora J. Morgan, Dec. 19, 1914; 1 son, James Morgan. Commd. 2d lt., U.S. Army, 1914; promoted through grades to major, 1918; in charge famine operations Am. Relief Administration. Odessa and Rostov. Russia, 1921-23; comml. attaché Am. Legation, Warsaw, Poland, 1924, Prague, Czechoslovakia, 1925-26, Cairo, Egypt, 1927-23, at large, 1929-33; compliance dir. (N.Y. Dist.) NRA, 1933-35. Lecturer dept. economics, Coll. City of N.Y., from 1933; lecturer on marketing, New York U. Served during World War II with F.A., U.S. Army as lt. col. Gen. Staff Corps, U.S. Army; col., U.S. Army Res. Corps. Mem. govt. delegation Internat. Navigation Congress, 1926; official Am. observer Internat. Cotton Congress, 1927. Clubs: University (Washington, D.C.); Bankers (New York). Home: New York, N.Y. †

HOFER, PHILLIP, librarian, trustee; b. Cin., Mar. 14, 1898; s. Charles Frederick and Jane (Arms) H.; A.B. cum laude, Harvard, 1921, A.M., 1929, L.H.D., 1967; D.Arts, Bates Coll., 1962; m. Frances L. Heckscher, Nov. 1, 1930; 1 son, Myron Arms. Asso. with coal-mining firm W. H. Warner Co., Cleve., 1922-27, asst. to pres., 1922-26; partner financial firm Philip Hofer & Co., Cleve., 1924-27; apptd. adviser to Spencer collection N.Y. Pub. Library, 1929-34; asst. dir. Pierpont Morgan Library, 1934-37; founder and curator dept. printing and graphic arts Harvard Library, 1938-67, emeritus, 1968-84; asst. dean Harvard Bus. Sch., 1942-44; sec. Fogg Art Mus., Harvard, 1952-64, hon. curator; hon. curator Peabody Mus., Salem, Mass.; hon. mem. Gutenberg Mus., Germany. Lyell lectr. in bibliography Oxford U., 1962; resident scholar Am. Acad. in Rome, 1958. Trustee emeritus Corning Glass Mus., Mass. Hist. Soc.; trustee Boston Mus. of Fine Arts, 1943-71, emeritus trustee, 1971-84; adv. bd. Mus. of China Trade, Boston; adv. com. Princeton Art Mus., 1970-84; overseer Boys Club of Boston, Boston Athenaeum, Am. Sch. Classical Studies. Fellow Soc. Antiquaries (London); mem. Council Fgn. Relations, English-Speaking Union (trustee Boston br., v.p. 1965-72), Order St. John of Jerusalem (asso. officer), Signet Soc. Harvard (grad. pres. 1960-61). Clubs: Athenaeum (London, Eng.); Somerset, Wednesday Evening, Tavern, Winter's Night, Odd Volumes (pres. 1960-63, v.p. 1972—) (Boston); Century Assn., Grolier (hon.) (N.Y.C.). Home: Belmont, Mass. Died Nov. 9, 1984.

HOFF, EBBE CURTIS, educator; b. Rexford, Kans., Aug. 12, 1906; s. Hans Jacob and May (Knudson) H.; B.S. summa cum laude, U. Wash., 1928; B.A. with honors in Physiology, Oxford (Eng.) U., 1930, Ph.D., 1932, B.M., B.Ch., 1941, M.D., 1953; m. Phebe Margaret Flather, June 2, 1934; children—Phebe May (Mrs. Leigh Van Valen), David Christiansen. Sterling research fellow Yale, 1932-33, Coxe research fellow, 1933-34, instr. physiology, 1934-36, resarch fellow, 1940-43; prof. psychiatry, chmn. psychiat. research Med. Coll. Va., 1962-85, dean Sch. Grad. Studies, 1956-66, med. dir. Bur. Alcohol Studies and Rehab., 1948-85, also mem. adminstrv. council; cons. to surgeon gen. U.S. Army, NIMH. Served from lt. comdr. to comdr. M.C., USNR, 1943-46. Fellow N.Y. Acad. Scis., Royal Soc. Medicine; mem. AMA, Am. Physiol. Soc., Am. Psychiat. Assn. (asso.), Am. Acad. Neurology (asso.), AAAS, Brit. Med. Assn., History Sci. Soc., Soc. Exptl. Biology and Medicine, Phi Beta Kappa, Sigma Xi, Alpha Omega Alpha. Contbr. articles profl. jours. Home: Richmond, Va. Died Feb. 17, 1985; interred St. Mary's Episcopal Ch., Richmond, Va.

HOFFER, ERIC, author; b. N.Y.C., July 25, 1902; s. Knut and Elsa (Goebel) H. Migratory worker, Calif., 1920-43, longshoreman, 1943-83. Author: The True Believer, 1951, The Passionate State of Mind, 1955, The Ordeal of Change, 1963, Temper of Our Time, 1967, Working and Thinking on the Waterfront, 1969, First Things Last Things, 1970, Reflections on the Human Condition, 1972, In Our Time, 1976, Before The Sabbath, 1979, Between the Devil & the Dragon: Thoughts of Men & Nature, 1983, Truth Imagined, 1983. Address: San Francisco, Calif. Died May 21, 1983.*

HOFFMAN, JAMES HARVEY, lawyer; b. Mansfield, Ohio, Aug. 29, 1911; s. Charles and Sarah Estelle (Phillips) H.; m. Ruth Johnson, Sept. 4, 1972; children by previous marriage: James Harvey, Philip Newton, Virginia Ann. Grad., Culver Mil. Acad., 1929; B.S., Lafayette Coll., 1933; LL.B., Western Res. U., 1936. Bar: Ohio 1936. Practice in, Mansfield; asst. sec., gen. counsel Mansfield Tire & Rubber Co., 1938-40, sec., gen. counsel, 1940-45, v.p., gen. counsel, 1945-51, exec. v.p., gen. counsel, 1951-52, pres., 1952-78, chmn. bd., 1978—; pres., dir. Chas. Hoffman Co., from 1951; dir. Madras Rubber Factory, Ltd., India, Brit. Molded Fiber, Reading, Eng.; chmn. exec. com., dir. Denman Rubber Mfg. Co. Bd. Advisors Mansfield Friendly House; life bd. dirs. Mansfield YMCA; trustee, chmn. exec. com. Ashland (Ohio) Coll.; trustee, vice-chmn. bd. emeritus Lafayette Coll., Easton, Pa. Served from 2d lt. to capt. AUS, 1942-45. Mem. Mansfield C. of C., Rubber Mfrs. Assn., Am. Legion, Alpha Chi Rho, Phi Delta Phi. Clubs: Ashland Country, Westbrook Country, Windermere Golf. Lodges: Masons; Shriners; Elks; Moose. Home: Mansfield, OH.

HOFFMAN, JULIUS J., judge; b. Chgo., July 7, 1895; s. Aaron and Bertha H.; m. Eleanor H. Greenebaum, Sept. 20, 1928 (dec.). Student, Lewis Inst., Chgo.; Ph.B., Northwestern U., 1912, LL.B., 1915, LL.D., 1955. Bar: Ill. bar 1915. Practiced in, Chgo., 1915-47; past v.p., gen. counsel, dir. Brunswick Corp.; mem. faculty Northwestern U. Law Sch.; asso. editor Am. Jour. Criminal Law and Criminology; judge Superior Ct. of Ill., Cook County, 1947-53; judge U.S. Dist. Ct. for No. Dist. Ill., 1953-72, sr. judge, 1972-83. Past editor: Am. Jour. Criminal Law and Criminology; Contbr. numerous articles to law jours. Former mem. Ill. State Housing Bd. Recipient award merit, service award Northwestern U.; gold good citizenship medal SAR; gold medal of merit VFW; numerous others. Fellow Am. Bar Found.; mem. Northwestern U. Alumni Assn. (past pres.), Am. Law Inst., Fed., Am., Ill., Chgo. bar assns., Bar Assn. 7th Jud. Circuit, Am. Judicature Soc., Northwestern U. Assos., Wigmore Club. Northwestern U. Republican. Clubs: Standard (Chgo.), Tavern (Chgo.), Union League (Chgo.), Mid-Day (Chgo.), Law (Chgo.); Lake Shore Country (Glencoe, Ill.). Presided numerous civil and criminal trials, including Krebiozen, Chicago 7 cases. Home: Chicago, Ill. Died July 1, 1983.

HOFFMAN, RALPH MUELLER, business executive; b. Mpls., Oct. 12, 1888; s. Charles A. and Mary E. (Mueller) H.; B.S., U. Minn., 1911; m. Esther Davis, Aug. 10, 1916; children—Mary (Mrs. Charles A. Hamilton), Howard. With Link-Belt Co., Chgo., since 1923, v.p. in charge sales, 1940-43, pres. Pacific div. from 1943. Republican. Episcopalian. Clubs: Family, Rotary, Bohemian (San Francisco). Home: Atherton, Calif. †

HOFFMAN, THOMAS GLENN, mfg. exec.; b. near Leipsic, O., June 9, 1889; s. Andrew Jackson and Mary Ellen (Edwards) H.; student Berea (Ky.) Coll.; B.S., O. Wesleyan U., 1911; C.P.A., N.Y., 1925; m. Ruth Ripton, Dec. 23, 1918; children—Mary Eleanor, Thomas Ripton. With Bradley Contractiing Co., subway builders, N.Y. City, 1911-13; with Gen. Electric Co., Schenectady, N.Y., 1913-17; with Hurdman & Cranstoun certified public accountants, 1917-18, 1919-27; treas. and dir. Foster Wheeler Corp. since 1927, also of affiliated cos. Dir. White Plains, Y.M.C.A. Mem. Am. Inst. of Accountants, Am. Legion, Southern N.Y. Fish & Game Assn., Westchester Co. Hist. Soc., Berea Coll. Alumni Assn., O. Wesleyan U. Alumni Assn., Alpha Sigma Phi, Delta Beta Xi, Phi Beta Kappa Assos., O. Soc. of N.Y. Methodist (trustee). Mason, Shriner. Clubs: University, Westchester Hills Golf. Home: White Plains, N.Y. †

HOFFMAN, WILLIAM STAMM, registrar Pa. State Coll.; b. Pottstown, Pa., Feb. 24, 1889; s. Jacob Smith and Harriet (Lingle) H.; B.S., Pa. State Coll., 1911, M.S., 1919; m. Margaret Hess, Jan. 2, 1917; children—Mary Dorman, Margaret Susan. Instr. engring., Pa. State Coll., 1911-13; instr. at Am. U. of Beirut, Syria, 1913-16; instr. engring., Pa. State Coll., 1916-19; asst. registrar Pa. State Coll., 1919-23, registrar from 1923. Mem. ex officio Pa. Com. on Secondary (accrediting) of the Middle States Assn.; mem. Am. Assn. Collegiate Registrars (pres. 1939-40); mem. Nat. Puzzlers' League under name of "Cryptox"; mem. Lambda Chi Alpha, Scarab, Pi Delta Epsilon. Republican. Lutheran. Contbr. papers on selective admissions to ednl. jours. Editor, Bulletin Am. Assn. of Collegiate Registrars, 1929-32. Home: State College, Pa. †

HOFFMANN, SAL B., labor ofcl.; b. Aversa, Italy, Apr. 25, 1899; s. Leopoldo and Anna (Tornicaso) H.; ed. at high sch.; m. Frances Zeichner, June 2, 1920; children—Mrs. Jackie Toll, Benjamin, Richard. With Bell Telephone Co. and Western Electric Co., 1917-18; joined Phila. Wholesale Upholsters' Union, 1920; formed Upholsterers' Internat. Union regional dist. council, 1935, exec. sec., 1935-37, elected internat. pres. at Cleve. conv., 1937, 39, 40, 43, 44, 46, 48, 50, 53, 56, 59, 62-66, 70, 74, 78. Mem. community services com. AFL-CIO, 1956-81; del. White House Conf. on Aging, 1961. Chmn. bd. trustees Health and Welfare Fund, 1944-77, Retirement Plan, 1950-81, chmn. bd. govs. Nat. Pension Plan, 1953-77; chmn. bd. mgrs. Salhaven Found., 1957-71, Gerontol. Retirement Village, Jupiter, Fla. Mem. Furniture Labor Adv. Bd., WPB; panel mem. Nat. War Labor Bd.; adv. mem. Furniture Industry Com. in drafting of Wage and Hour Law, 1941. Author: Trade Unions under War Conditions (pamphlet), 1943; Work Of A Business Agent (pamphlet), 1942. Contbr. articles to various periodicals. Home: Philadelphia, Pa. Died June 9, 1981.

HOFFSOMMER, HAROLD CHARLES, educator, sociologist; b. Roxbury, Kan., Dec. 8, 1898; s. John Adam and Rose Ida (Manshardt) H.; grad. Bethany Acad., Lindsborg, Kan., 1914-16; student Bethany College, 1917-19; B.S., Northwestern U., 1921, A.M., 1923; student U. Chicago, summer 1923; Ph.D., Cornell U., 1929; m. Ruth Andrews, May 28, 1930; children—John Charles, Elizabeth Andrews. Acting prof. sociology Rockford (Ill.) Coll., 1921-22; prof. sociology Ala. Polytech. Inst., 1929-35; dir. cotton area rural research, also Ala. supr. rural research, 1934-35; sr. research supr. WPA, Washington, 1935-36; rural sociologist La. State U., 1936-42; leader area VI div. farm population and rural welfare Dept. Agr., 1939-40; dir. regional land tenure research project, Fayetteville, Ark., 1942-45; prof., chmn. div. social scis. U. Md., 1945-66, head dept. sociology, 1945-66, emeritus prof.; cons. Ford Found. community devel., India, 1961. Mem. Am., D.C. (pres.) Rural (past pres.) sociol. socs., Alpha Kappa Delta, Phi Delta Kappa, Phi Mu Alpha-Sinfonia. Presbyn. (elder). Author: Regional Research Cooperation: The Sociology of American Life, 1958. Co- author, editor and project dir.: The Social and Economic Significance of Land Tenure in the Southwestern States; also agr. expt. sta. bulls. Editor-in-chief Rural Sociology. Contbr. articles sociol. jours. Home: College Park, Md. Died July 24, 1982.

HOFFSTROM, PIERCY J. (P. J. HOFF), cartoonist, weatherman; b. Mounds, Okla., Jan. 11, 1896; s. Frank Henry and Emma Jane (Marshall) H.; student U. Wash., 1915-16; m. Sue Virginia Miller, Jan. 11, 1917 (dec. Aug. 1972); 1 child, Virginia. Engr., Pacific Tel. & Tel. Co., Seattle, 1917-23; with St. Paul Dispatch, 1923-54, as polit., topical cartoonist, also daily column under signature as Hoff; tchr. cartooning St. Paul Inst., 1923-24, YMCA, 1938; conducted two daily TV programs over sta. KSTP-TV, using cartoons; weatherman as P.J. Hoff for

WBBM-TV radio, Chgo., 1954-68; staff writer Ga.'s Coastal Illus., St. Simon's Island; lectr., freelance writer on weather and photomicrography. Served with Co. F, 2d Inf., Mexican Border, 1916. Mem. Am. Meteorol. Soc., Am. Soc. Cartoonists, Chgo. Exec. Club, Delta Phi Lambda, Sigma Delta Chi. Clubs: Headline: Brunswick (Ga.) Press. Home: Saint Simons Island, Ga. Dec. May 7, 1981.

HOFLEY, BERNARD C., lawyer; b. Winnipeg, Man., Can., Dec. 16, 1928; s. Roy and Leocadie (Viller) H.; m. Micheline Fournier, Feb. 18, 1958; children—Bernard Charles, Charles Viller, Marc Arthur. B.A., St. Paul's Coll., Winnipeg, 1951; LL.B., Man. Law Sch., 1955. Bar: Called to Man. bar 1955, created Queen's counsel 1980. Legal officer Dept. Justice, Ottawa, Ont., Can., 1955-58; pvt. Sec. to minister of nat. def., 1958-60; with Fournier, Papillon Ltee, Quebec, 1960-64; exec. asst. to gen. mgr. Can. Corp. for World Exhbn. (Expo '67), 1964-67; gen. mgr. Schweppes-Powell Ltd., 1967-69; asst. dep. solicitor gen. for research and systems devel. Govt. of Can., Ottawa, 1969-78; registrar Supreme Ct. of Can., Ottawa, 1978-85. Bd. dirs. Ottawa Boys and Girls Club; founding mem. Le Cercle Universitaire, Ottawa. Recipient Centennial medal. Home: Ottawa, Ont., Can. Died Jan. 29, 1985.

HOGAN, BARTHOLOMEW WILLIAM, physician, orgn. exec.; b. Quincy, Mass., 1901; M.D., Tufts Coll., 1925, D.Sc.; LL.D., Mt. St. Mary's Coll., Emmitsburg, Md., Vilanova U.; D.Sc., Boston Coll., Marquette U., Tufts U.; married; children—Bartholomew William, Thomas F. III, Mary Ledie. Rear adm. M.C., USN; surgeon gen. U.S. Navy, 1955-61; chief of medicine and chief of psychiatry various naval hosps.; asso. prof. psychiatry Georgetown U. Sch. Medicine; dep. med. dir. Am. Psychiat. Assn. Mem. Pres.'s Com. on Employment of Handicapped. Decorated Silver Star, Purple Heart, Navy and Marine Corps medal, D.S.M., six battle stars on ribbons; Médaille d'Honneur (France); Cross of Merit (Peru); Royal Swedish Armed Forces medal. Diplomate and examiner Am. Bd. Psychiatry and Neurology. Fellow A.C.P., Am. Psychiat. Assn.; mem. AMA (ex.-mem. ho. of dels.), Am. Hosp. Assn. (past trustee), Am. Psychiat. Assn., John Carroll Soc. (pres.). Club: Army-Navy (pres.) (Washington). Home: Lake Wales, Fla. Died Mar. 17, 1983.

HOGAN, JOHN ARTHUR, educator, arbitrator; b. Boise, Idaho, Aug. 11, 1909; s. Michael and Olive (McConnell) H.; A.B., U. Wash., 1932, A.M., 1934; law student Denver U., 1938; Ph.D., Harvard, 1952; m. Rhoda Doyle, 1936. Economist, Bur. Labor Statistics, 1935; asst. prof. econs. U. Denver 1935-39; teaching fellow Harvard, 1940-41; instr. Tufts Coll., 1942; disputes dir. Nat. War Labor Bd., New Eng. region, 1945-46; pub. mem. Nat. Wage Stblzn. Bd., 1946-47; part-time lectr. mgmt. tng. program Radcliffe Coll., 1946-53; asso. prof., prof. econs. and bus. U. N.H., 1947-63, Carter prof. econs. Whittemore Sch. Bus. and Econs., 1963-74; vice chmn., pub. mem. Wage Stblzn. Bd., New Eng., 1951-53. Impartial umpire collective bargaining agreements. Mem. New Eng. Gov.'s Textile Commn., from 1957. Mem. Am. Arbitration Assn. (labor arbitration panel), Nat. Acad. Arbitrators, Am. Econ. Assn., Indsl. Relations Research Assn., Sigma Alpha Epsilon. Author: (with others) The New England Economy, 1952. Contbr. articles profl. jours. Home: Durham, N.H. Died Feb. 27, 1981; buried Durham Cemetery.

HOGAN, RALPH M(ONTAGUE), personnel research administr.; b. Glasgow, Mo., June 5, 1890; s. Edgar LeRoy and Hattie Hutchinson (Sallsbury) H.; Pd.B., N.E. Mo. State Teachers Coll., 1911; S.B., U. of Chicago, 1915, A.M., 1916, Ph.D., 1927; Certificate in Chinese, Coll. of Chinese Studies at Peiping, China, 1921; m. Mary Love Powell, Aug. 17, 1910; children—Edgar Powell (dec.), Ralph M., Douglas LeRoy. Pub. sch. tchr., principal Mo., tchrs. coll. instn., 1908-18; sec. for tng., YMCA personnel, Tsinan and Shanghai, China, 1918-34; head training and supt. edn., T.V.A., Norris Dam, 1934-36; personnel methods cons. Social Security Bd., Washington, 1936-39; chief of training Railroad Retirement Bd., Washington, 1939-40; prin. training adviser U.S. Civil Service Commn., Washington, 1940-45; field rep., Office of Strategic Services, Chungking, China, 1945-46; head manpower research Office Naval Research, Washington, from 1946. Mem. A.A.A.S., Soc. for Personnel Adminstrn., Am. Statis. Assn., Am. Sociol. Soc., Am. Psych. Assn., Phi Delta Kappa. Author: YMCA Program Making (in Chinese), 1929. Home: Alexandria, Va. †

HOGUE, FRED CALVIN, railway executive; b. Burlington Junction, Mo., Sept. 6, 1889; s. George C. and Lucinda (Maple) H.; ed. pub. sch. Tarkio, Mo.; m. Blanche Thayer, Jan. 26, 1911; 1 son, Walter Robert; m. 2d, Florence Uridge, March 24, 1933. Station helper C.B.&Q. R.R., Tarkio, Mo., 1905, telegraph operator and station agt., 1907-09; with D.&R.G.W. R.R. from 1909, asst. traffic mgr., Chicago, 1933-40, gen. traffic mgr., Denver, from 1940; dir. Rio Grande Motorway. Mason. Clubs: Union League, Traffic (Chicago); Traffic, Denver, Cherry Hills, Denver Athletic (Denver, Colo.). Address: Denver, Colo. †

HOLBROOK, DAVID STEARNS, steel co. exec.; b. St. Louis, July 17, 1912; s. Harold L. and Lucy (Styring) H.; B.S., U. Pitts., 1932; LL.D., Laurentian U.; m. Marguerite Somes, Nov. 14, 1931; children—Diane (Mrs. Hugh H. Hansard), David Stearns, Richard Lyman. Steam engr. Carnegie Steel Co., Youngstown, Ohio, 1933-35; project engr. Carnegie-Ill; Steel Corp., 1935-40, asst. chief engr. Homestead works, 1940-44; asst. gen. mgr. Algoma Steel Corp., Ltd., Sault Ste. Marie, Ont., Can., 1944-45, exec. asst. to pres., 1945-46, v.p. 1946-49, exec. v.p., 1949-56, pres., 1956-75, chmn., 1962-81; co-dir. DuPont of Can., Royal Bank of Can.; dir. Dominion Bridge Co., Ltd. Registered profl. engr., Ont., Pa. Mem. Am., Internat. iron and steel insts., Assn. Iron and Steel Engrs., Conf. Bd., Sigma Alpha Epsilon. Presbyn. Clubs: York (Toronto); Mount Royal (Montreal). Home: Toronto, Ont., Canada. Died Mar. 15, 1981.

HOLBROOK, HOLLIS HOWARD, educator, painter, sculptor; b. Natick, Mass., Feb. 7, 1909; s. Goldwin P. and Jessie (Underwood) H.; m. Vivian Alma Nicholas, June 26, 1937; children: Ferris, Nicholas (dec.), Peter W. Student, Boston U. Evening Sch., 1928-30, Mass. Sch. Art, 1930-34; B.F.A., Yale U., 1936. Designer, Dennison Mfg. Co., Framingham, Mass., 1929-30; illustrator AP, N.Y.C., 1943; designer Warren Telechron Co., 1943; tchr. art U. Fla., 1938, successively instr., asst. and assoc. prof., prof., 1947-48, 51-79, head prof., 1948-51; instr. Penland (N.C.) Sch. Art, summer 1971-78, artist-scholar, 1975. One-man show, Shillard Smith Art Center, Clearwater, Fla., 1975, Daytona (Fla.) Mus. Arts and Scis., 1980; exhibited in group shows, Pa. Acad. Ann., 1961, Ill. Biennial, 1961, Delgado Mus., 1963, Corcoran Bienniel, 1965, Norton Gallery, Palm Beach, Fla., 1971, Bklyn. Mus. Art, 1980; represented in collections including, Canton (Ohio) Art Inst., Sheldon Swope Art Gallery, U. Ga. Mus., Richmond (Va.) Library, Norfolk (Va.) Mus. Arts and Scis., U. Fla., Coll. William and Mary, Walter Chrysler Jr., So. Coll., Lakeland, Fla., Clemson U., Daytona Mus. Arts and Scis., frescoes in, Biblioteca Michoacan, Mexico, murals, Fountain of Youth Mus., St. Augustine, Fla., Library of U. Fla., murals (awarded by govt. in competitions) in post offices, Natick, Mass., Haleyville, Ala., Jeanerette, La., mural series, adminstrn. bldg., R.I. Coll. Edn., Providence, 18 panels in Post Office, Ocala, Fla., 1963; John Eliot mural in pub. library, Natick. Mem. Gainesville Cultural Commn., 1973-76. Served USN, 1944-45. Recipient Honor award Columbia Mus. Art, 1960, Atwater Kent award Soc. Four Arts, 1964, 1st award for painting Southeastern Ann., 1967; U. Fla. Grad. Sch. grantee for creative work, 1965. Fellow Royal Soc. Arts; mem. Fla. Edn. Assn. (art sect. sec. 1943), So. States Art League (dir. 1946-48), Fla. Fedn. Art (pres. 1947), Fla. Artists Group (pres. 1948-51), Nat. Soc. Mural Painters. Home: Gainesville, Fla. Died Aug. 18, 1984.

HOLCOMBE, OSCAR FITZALLEN, mayor; born Mobile, Ala., Dec. 31, 1888; s. Robert Slough and Sarah King (Harrell) H.; ed. pub. schs., San Antonio, Tex.; m. Mary Grey Miller, May 3, 1912; 1 dau., Elisabeth Adelaide. In lumber and millwork business, later engring. and constrn.; mayor Houston, Tex., 1921-29, 1933-37, 1939-41, 1947-50; re-elected mayor Oct. 14, 1950. Democrat. Baptist. K.P., Elk. Clubs: Democratic (New York); Country, Houston. Home: Houston, Tex. †

HOLCOMBE, THOMAS HULL, headmaster; b. Ft. Branch, Ind., Mar. 20, 1889; s. A. G. and Alice (Hull) H.; LL.B., U. of Ga., 1908; student Yale Law Sch., 1909; m. Sarah Whittemore, Dec. 16, 1914. Formerly mem. Philippine Constabulary; commd. 2d lt. N.A., Jan. 1918; 1st lt., Oct. 1918; commd. in regular army, July 1, 1920; retired, Dec. 15, 1922; headmaster and comdt. Kearney Mil. Acad. Mem. Kappa Alpha. Democrat. Episcopalian. Address: Kearney, Neb. †

HOLDER, CALE JAMES, Judge U.S. Dist. Ct.; b. Lawrenceville, Ill., Apr. 5, 1912; s. John Wesley and Martha (Glaser) H.; m. Martha Mae Stanton, Apr. 16, 1942; 1 child, Martha Sue. LL.B., Benjamin Harrison Law Sch., 1934; J.D., Ind. Law Sch., 1938. Bar: Ind. bar 1934. Practiced in, Indpls., 1934-54; judge U.S. Dist. Ct. So. Dist. Ind., 1954-83; dep. prosecutor 19th jud. circuit Marion Co. (Ind.) Criminal Ct., 1940-42; spl. counsel Ind. State Personnel Bd., 1946-49; dep. atty. gen., Ind., 1953. Chmn. Rep. State Central Com., Ind., 1949-52; mem. Rep. Nat. Com., 1952. Served as lt. USNR, 1942-46; comdg. officer naval base, island comdr. Wallis Islands; also legal officer, judge adv., gen. ct. martial bd. New Hebrides Islands. Mem. Marion Co. Rep. Vets. World War II (pres. 1946- 47, dir. 1947-54), Lawyers Assn., Indpls. Legal Soc., Am. Legion, VFW, ABA, Ind. Bar Assn., Indpls. Bar Assn. (sec. 1948-52, exec. com. 1953-54), Sigma Delta Kappa. Died Aug. 23, 1983.*

HOLDSWORTH, ROBERT POWELL, forester, educator; b. East Lansing, Mich., Jan. 7, 1890; s. William Sanders and Adelaide Kirtland (Smith) H.; B.S., Mich. State Coll., 1911; M.F., Yale, 1928; student Royal Coll. of Forestry, Stockholm, Sweden, 1928-29; m. Mildred Hoit Curtis, Oct. 21, 1912; children—Robert Powell, Mary Virginia, Wiliam Curtis, James R. L. Employed in U.S. Forest Service, 1911-14; engaged in business in Boston, 1915-27; fellow Am.-Scandinavian Found., 1928-29; prof. forestry, U. Ark., 1929-30, head dept., U. Mass., 1930-56, prof. forestry, 1956-58, professor emeritus from 1958. Trustee of Jones Library, Inc., 1947-58, pres., 1956-58; mem. alumni bd. Yale, 1957-62; mem. Massachusetts State Board Natural Resources, 1953-63, chairman, 1953-54, chairman special advisory committee, 1964-65. Served as captain 74th Infantry, U.S. Army, 1917-19; maj. AC, AUS, 1942-44, in Africa, Italy; maj. USAF, ret. 1956; hon. mem. USAF Res. Head dept. forestry, Shrivenham Am. U. Eng., 1945. Mem. Am. Legion, Mich. Hist. Soc., Alumni Council Yale School of Forestry (president 1959-61), Society of American Foresters, Phi Kappa Phi, Sigma Xi. Episcopalian. Author tech. articles and bulls. Home: East Dennis, Mass. †

HOLE, WILLIAM EDWARD, SR., business exec.; b. Versailles, Ohio, Aug. 25, 1899; s. Harrison B. and Ottillie (Engelken) H.; m. Dorothy Coppock, June 25, 1925; children—Jean Louise (Mrs. W.I. Thieme), William Edward Jr., Susan Jane (Mrs. R.L. Brewer), Barbara Kell (Mrs. W.D. Brewer). Student, Mercersburg Acad., 1917-18; A.B., Princeton, 1922; student, Harvard Law Sch., 1924-25. With Am. Aggregates Corp., 1927, successively gen. counsel, sec., sec.-treas., exec. v.p., 1932-51, dir., 1945-84, pres., 1951-64, chmn. bd., 1964-69, chmn. exec. com., 1969-84, mem. exec. com., 1950-84; pres. Greenville Nat. Bank, 1957-74. Hon. trustee Wayne Hosp. Mem. Nat. Sand and Gravel Assn. (past dir., past exec. com.), Ohio Sand and Gravel Assn. (past pres.), Am., Ohio, Darke County bar assns., Ohio C. of C. (dir. 1959-84, life dir. 1971-84, exec. com. 1964). Home: Greenville, Ohio. Died Nov. 30, 1984; buried Greenville Cemetery, Greenville, Ohio.

HOLLAND, JEROME HEARTWELL, relief organization official; b. Auburn, N.Y., Jan. 9, 1916; s. Robert Howard and Viola (Bagby) H.; m. Laura Mitchell; children: Jerome, Pamela, Lucy, Joseph. B.S., Cornell U., Ithaca, N.Y., 1939, M.S., 1941; Ph.D., U. Pa., 1950; Ph.D. hon. degrees; L.H.D., Northeastern U., 1965, Hobart and William Smith Colls., 1965, Hamilton Coll., 1967, St. Paul's Coll., Lawrenceville, Va., 1978; Litt.D., Union Coll., 1966; LL.D., U. Cin., 1966, Colgate U., 1969, Washington U., St. Louis, 1970, Del. State Coll., 1970, Rider Coll., N.J., 1971, Washington and Lee U., 1971, Columbia U., 1972, Eastern Mich. State U., 1972, Va. Union U., 1973, U. Pa., 1973, Adelphi U., 1973, Lincoln U., 1973, Am. Internat. Coll., Mass., 1975, Villa Maria Coll., Erie, Pa., 1976, Tuskegee Inst., 1977, Morehouse Coll., 1979; D.Public Service, Ohio No. U., 1973. Pres. Del. State Coll., Dover, 1953-60, Hampton (Va.) Inst., 1960-70; U.S. ambassador to, Sweden, 1970-72; chmn. bd. govs. ARC, since 1979—; dir. AT&T, Chrysler Corp., The Continental Corp., Culbro Corp., Gen. Foods Corp., Federated Dept. Stores, Inc., Mfrs. Hanover Corp., Union Carbide Corp., Pan Am. Bancshares, Inc., Zurn Industries, Inc. Author: Black Opportunity, 1969. Vice-chmn. N.E. region NCCJ, 1975; vice-chmn. N.Y. adv. bd. Salvation Army, 1974; trustee Inst. Internat. Edn., 1973; trustee emeritus Cornell U.; bd. dirs. United Negro Coll. Fund, 1976—, The Johnson Found., 1973-85. Carnegie Corp. grantee, 1964; Danforth Found. grantee, 1968. Fellow Am. Acad. Arts and Scis.; mem. Nat. Geog. Soc. (dir.), Fgn. Policy Assn. (dir.), Am. Arbitration Assn. (dir.), N.Y. C. of C. and Industry (dir.), Econ. Devel. Council (dir.), Council Fgn. Relations (dir.). Clubs: Alfalfa, Century Assn. Home: Bronxville, N.Y. Died Jan. 13, 1985.

HOLLAND, NORMAN NORWOOD, lawyer; b. Princess Anne, Md., Feb. 19, 1896; s. John A. and Elizabeth (Powell) H.; m. Harriette Breder, Oct. 22, 1924; 1 son, Norman Norwood. B.E., Johns Hopkins, 1920; LL.B., Fordham U., 1923; postgrad., Columbia, 1923. Bar: N.Y. bar 1924. Sr. partner Holland, Armstrong, Carlson & Wilkie (and predecessor firms), 1926-67, Holland, Armstrong, Wilkie & Previto, N.Y.C., from 1967; Lectr., cons. Practising Law Inst. on Patent and Trademark Law, 1956-67. Mem. Am. Bar Assn. (chmn. sect. patent trademark copyright law 1951, mem. council 1946-49, 51-54), Bar City N.Y. (chmn. patent com. 1959-61), Am. Patent Law Assn. (bd. mgrs. 1955-58), N.Y. Patent Law Assn. (pres. 1954-55), Internat. Patent and Trademark Assn. (sec. 1949-52, exec. com. 1960-68), Johns Hopkins Alumni Assn. N.Y., N.J. and Conn. (pres. 1951-53), Scabbard and Blade, Tau Beta Phi, Omicron Delta Kappa. Republican. Clubs: N.Y. Athletic (N.Y.C.), Downtown Athletic (N.Y.C.), Johns Hopkins (N.Y.C.) (pres. 1942-46). Home: New York, N.Y.

HOLLAR, GORDON C., army officer; b. Sioux City, Ia., Dec. 7, 1887; s. Frank Pierce and Emilie Louise (Falkenhainer) H.; m. Grace Margaret James, Apr. 14, 1915; children—Mary Marjorie (Mrs. John S. Young). Employee, T. S. Martin Co., Sioux City, Ia., 1907-10, N.W. Bell Tel. Co., 1910-13, F.P. Hollar & Son, 1913-16; sales dept., Tolerton & Warfield, 1919-25, Headington-Hedenbergh, 1925-28, Inter. Bus. Machines Co., 1928-30; Sioux City chief of police, 1930-34; with Iowa Tax Commn., 1931-35; commr. public safety, 1935-38; again with Iowa Tax Commn., 1939-41. Enlisted Ia. Nat. Guard, 1907; commd. 2d lt., 1913, and advanced through the grades to brig. gen. of the line, 1940; federal service, Mexican Border 1916-17, Camp Cody, N.Mex., and overseas, 1917-19; comdg. gen., Camp Claiborne, La., 1941; asst. div. comdr., 1942; provost marshal, Hdqrs. Service of Supply, European Theater of Operations, from 1942. Mason (Consistory, Shrine). Home: Sioux City, Iowa. †

HOLLENDER, SAMUEL SYLVAN, optometrist, business exec.; b. Chgo., Dec. 8, 1900; s. Joseph and Mary (Koss) H.; m. Sylvia Vivian Jacobson, July 26, 1922; children—Elaine Ann Kaplan, Caryl Rose Susman. Dr. Optometry, No. Ill. Coll. Ophthalmology and Otology, 1923; L.H.D. (hon.), Hebrew Union Coll., 1956, Jewish

Inst. Religion, Lewis Inst., Ill. Inst. Tech., Northwestern U., John Marshall Law Sch. Gen. merchandise mgr. The Fair, exec. v.p. dept. store, Chgo., 1930-32; gen. partner S. S. Hollender Ltd. (Consultants.). Bd. dirs. Mt. Sinai Hosp., 1934-39; bd. govs. Chgo. Opera Co., 1935; bd. dirs. Jewish Fedn. Chgo., 1941, treas., 1947-50, v.p., 1951, pres., 1956, gen. chmn. bldg. campaign, 1963; a founder Roosevelt U.; mem. bd. Jewish Braille Inst.; bd. dirs. Jewish Vocational Service and Employment Service, 1938-40; chmn. Met. Chgo. war records com. Nat. Jewish Welfare Bd., 1954-55, mem. nat. council; pres. Chgo. Fedn. Union Am. Hebrew Congregations, 1944-45, mem. nat. exec. bd., 1944, v. chmn. exec. bd., 1946-51, chmn., 1951, pres. 42d Biennial Assembly, 1953; mem. bd. World Union for Progressive Judaism; nat. chmn. Combined Appeal Union of Am. Hebrew Congregations, Hebrew Union Coll., and Jewish Inst. Religion, 1948-54; bd. dirs. Nat. Joint Distbn. Com., 1947; gen. chmn. Combined Jewish Appeal, Chgo., 1951, pres., 1952; bd. dirs. United Jewish Bldg. Fund, 1946; trustee Hebrew Union Sch. of Edn. and Sacred Music; bd. govs. Hebrew Union Coll., Cin.; mem. nat. bd. Chgo. Med. Sch.; hon. chmn. Million Dollar Endowment Fund, 1976-80, 100th Centennial Celebration, 1980 (both Emanuel Congregation). Recipient award of merit Chgo. Fedn. Reform Synagogues, 1948, Man of Valor award Union of Am. Hebrew Congregations, 1955, Julius Rosenwald Meml. award Jewish Fedn. Met., Chgo., Bibl. Breastplate award, 1963; named to Golden Age Hall of Fame Jewish Community Center of Chgo., 1967; honoree grove of 1000 trees planted in Leo Baeck Forest La hav, Israel, 1980; recipient Award of Merit Emanuel Congregation, 1981. Mem. Art Inst. Chgo. (life), Ill. Inst. Tech. (life; mem. bd. 1955-56), Alumnus Lewis Inst. (life), Zeta Beta Tau. Jewish (pres. Emanuel Congregation 1939). Clubs: Mason (Chgo.) (32, Shriner), B'nai B'rith. (Chgo.), Bryn Mawr (Chgo.) (pres. 1950-51), Convenant (Chgo.) (pres. 1935-37), Standard (Chgo.) (bd. mgrs. 1950-56), Chgo. Executives (Chgo.); Harmonie (N.Y.C.). Home: Chicago, Ill. Died Oct. 17, 1984.

HOLLIDAY, HOUGHTON, dentist; b. Sanborn, N.D., July 9, 1889; s. William and Marilla (Hancock) H.; A.B., U. of Minn., 1915, D.D.S., 1917; hon. D.D.S., U. Montreal, 1944; grad. work Columbia, U. of Chicago, New York U.; m. Ellen Hope Wells, Dec. 8, 1917 (dec. June 29, 1945); children—Paul Houghton, Robert William; m. 2d Irmgard Oesterreich Menke, Mar. 9, 1950. Fellow Mayo clinic, 1918-19; supt., Sch. of Dental and Oral Surgery, Columbia, and instr. in x-ray and periodontia, in charge x-ray div., 1928-30, associate dean, 1936-45, prof. of dentistry from 1936; head of the radiology division, Columbia, from 1928; attending dental surgeon Presbyn. Hospital from 1930; engaged in private practice, New York City, from 1929. Served as 1st lieutenant Army dental reserve corps, 1918; lt. comdr. U.S.N.R. from 1932. Mem. bd. dirs. Am. Bur. Med. Aid to China, Inc.; mem. of dental advisory com. of Community Service Soc. of New York; mem. of Dean's Screening Com. for Navy V-12 program; consultant on dental admissions com. of Army Specialized Training Program. Fellow Am. Coll. of Dentists; mem. First District Dental Soc., N.Y. Acad. of Dentistry, N.Y. State Dental Soc., Am. Dental Assn., A.A.A.S., Internat. Assn. of Dental Research, N.Y. Acad. of Science, Am. Acad. Periodontology, Federation Dentaire Internationale, Sigma Xi, Omicron Kappa Upsilon. Protestant. Author: Dental Radiology Handbook, 1935. Contbr. to dental jours. Home: New York, N.Y. †

HOLLIDAY, RAYMOND MIDDLETON, tool co. exec.; b. Winfield, Tex., Aug. 14, 1914; s. Charles Calvin and Carrie Roan (Middleton) H.; B.S., E. Tex. State Coll., 1935; grad. student Tex. A. and M. Coll., 1937-38; LL.B., S. Tex. Coll. Law, 1949; m. Mary Frances McCulloch, Oct. 1, 1938. With Hughes Tool Co., Houston, from 1938, v.p., sec., 1955-63, exec. v.p., 1963-74, chief exec. officer, 1974-79, chmn., from 1974, also dir.; admitted to Tex. bar, 1949; asst. dist. atty. Harris County, 1949; chmn. Hughes Tool Co. of Australia, Ltd.; v.p., dir. Hughes Tool Co. S.A.C.I.F.I., Hughes de Mexico, S.A. de C.V., Hughes Tool Co. de Mex., S.A. de C.V.; chmn. bd. Hughes Tool Co. Ltd., BJ-Hughes, Inc.; dir. Tex. Commerce Bank, Houston, Hughes-Mechas Venezolanas C.A., Tex. Commerce Bancshares, Inc., Regan Offshore Internat., Inc., Byron Jackson Inc., Great So. Corp., Borg-Warner Corp. Bd. regents East Tex. State U. Served to lt. USNR. 1943-45. C.P.A. Tex. Mem. Am. Inst. C.P.A.'s, Tex. Soc. C.P.A.'s, Am. Mgmt. Assn., Houston, C. of C. Methodist. Mason (Shriner). Clubs: Lakeside Country, Petroleum, Houston. Deceased.*

HOLLINGER, HARVEY H., business exec.; b. North Lawrence, O., Aug. 6, 1889; s. Martin L. and Sarah II. (Eschliman) H.; m. Bessie B. Clapper, May 21, 1911. Auditor Firestone Tire & Rubber Co., 1922-28, comptroller, 1928-43, sec., 1943-48, treas., 1948-56; v.p., 1956-60, dir., 1930-62; dir. Firestone Bank. Trustee Akron Gen. Hosp. Clubs: Portage Country; Mayflower (Akron); Coral Ridge Yacht (Ft. Lauderdale, Fla.). Home: Akron, OH. †

HOLLIS, STANLEY E(RNEST), fgn. trade and credit service; b. Sydney, Australia, Dec. 18, 1889; s. Robert and Alice (Turton) H.; ed. pub. schs., New South Wales; m. Margaret L. McFadden, Aug. 21, 1920; 1 dau., Jean Ann. Came to U.S., 1919, naturalized, 1936. Formerly engaged in exporting, importing and related activities in Calif., Australia and Canada; devoted full time to fgn. trade and credit service with Am. Fgn. Credit Underwriters Corp., N.Y.C., 1920-59, pres., mng. dir., 1957-59; pub. Exporters' Digest and Internat. Trade Rev., 1926-61, The Market Guide for Latin American, 1921-61, The Market Guide for the Pacific Area, 1941-61, asso. dir. internat. div. Dun & Bradstreet, Inc., N.Y.C., 1959-61; pub. Internat. Trade Rev., 1959-61; cons. internat. bus. and finance, Ridgewood, N.J., from 1961; cons. Fgn. Credit Ins. Assn., N.Y.C., from 1962. Bd. dirs. Mexico Pilgrims Found. Mem. Am. Arbitration Assn., Internat. Trade Assn. New Eng. Rotarian. Clubs: Southern Cross; Overseas Automotive (dir.). Author: Guide to Export Credit Insurance. Address: Ridgewood, N.J. †

HOLLISTER, SOLOMON CADY, civil engineer; b. Crystal Falls, Mich., Aug. 4, 1891; s. Solomon Davis, Jr. and Mary Eliza (Runkel) H.; m. Ada R. Garber, June 2, 1919; children—John G., Mary G. (dec.), David G., Elizabeth Hollister Zimmerman. Student, State Coll. Wash., 1909-11, 13-14; B.S., U. Wis., 1916, C.E., 1932, D.Sc. (hon.), 1952; D.Eng. (hon.), Stevens Inst. Tech., 1942, Purdue U., 1958, Lehigh U., 1958. Chief design engr. U.S. Shipping Bd., 1918-20; cons. engr., Phila., 1920-30; prof. structural engring. Purdue U., 1930-34; dir. civil engring. Cornell U., 1934-37; dean Cornell U. (Coll. Engring.), 1937-59, cons. engr., Ithaca, N.Y., 1959-82; cons. Babcock & Wilcox Co., 1932-36; mem. Commn. on Orgn. Exec. Br. Govt. (Hoover Commn.), 1953-55; chmn. bd. cons. Isthmian Canal studies to Ho. of Reps. Com. Mcht. Marine and Fisheries, 1957-60. Author books; contbr. engring. articles to profl. jours. Trustee Cornell U., 1959-64. Recipient Lamme medal Am. Soc. Engring. Edn., 1952. Fellow AAAS; mem. ASCE (hon. mem., dir. 1944-47), ASME (hon.), Am. Ry. Engring. Assn., ASTM, Am. Concrete Inst. (past pres., dir., hon. mem., Wason Research medal 1928, Turner medal 1979), AIA (hon.), Am. Acad. Engring., Internat. Assn. Bridge and Structural Engrs., Soc. Promotion Engring. Edn. (hon. mem., dir., past pres.). Clubs: Masons; Cosmos (Washington); Conn. Soc. of Cincinnati. Home: Ithaca, N.Y. Died July 6, 1982.

HOLLOMON, JOHN HERBERT, educator; b. Norfolk, Va., Mar. 12, 1919; s. John Herbert and Pearl (Twiford); m. Margaret Knox Wheeler, Aug. 12, 1941 (dec.); children—Jonathan Bradford, James Martin, Duncan Twiford, Elizabeth Wheeler Vrugtman, Peter Heinz Richter; m. Nancy Elizabeth Gade, Dec. 27, 1970. Grad., Augusta Mil. Acad., Ft. Defiance, Va., 1936; B.S., M.I.T., 1940, Sc.D., 1946; hon. doctorates, Worcester Poly. Inst., 1964, Mich. Tech. U., 1965, Rensselaer Poly. Inst., 1966, Carnegie-Mellon U., 1967, Northwestern U., U. Akron, 1967. Instr. Harvard U. Grad. Sch. Engring., 1941-42; research asso. Gen. Electric Research Lab., Gen. Electric Co., 1946-49, asst. mgr. metallurgy research dept., 1949-52, mgr. metallurgy and ceramics research dept., 1952-60; gen. mgr. Gen. Electric Research Lab., Gen. Electric Co. (Gen. Engring. Lab.), 1960-62; asst. sec. for sci. and tech. Dept. Commerce, 1962-67; also acting under sec.; pres. U. Okla., 1967-70; cons. to pres. and to provost M.I.T., 1970-72; dir. Center Policy Alternatives, 1972-85, 1st Japan Steel Industry prof., 1975-85; adj. prof. Rensselaer Poly. Inst., 1950-62; dir. Bell & Howell Corp.; cons. Pres.'s Sci. Adv. Com.; also chmn. Atmospheric Scis. Com., 1963-67; Mem. Commerce Tech. Adv. Bd., 1962-67. Author: (with Leonard Jaffe) Ferrous Metallurgical Design, 1947; Contbr. articles to profl. jours. Served as maj. AUS, 1942-46; chief phys. metallurgy sect. Watertown (Mass.) Arsenal. Decorated Legion of Merit; recipient Rossiter W. Raymond award AIME, 1946, Alfred Nobel prize Combined Engring. Socs., 1947, Rosenhain medal Brit. Inst. Metals, 1958. Fellow Am. Phys. Soc., Am. Inst. Chemists, AAAS; mem. Soc. for History of Tech., Am. Acad. Arts and Scis., Am. Soc. Metals (trustee 1957), Royal Swedish Acad. Engring. Sci. (fgn.), Mid-Am. State Univs. (pres. 1969), Acta Metallurgica (sec.-treas.), Nat. Acad. Engring. (a founder), Nat. Planning Assn. (bus. adv. council), Sigma Xi, Kappa Sigma. Clubs: Harvard (Boston); Cosmos (Washington). Address: Brookline, Mass. Died May 1985.

HOLLOWAY, STANLEY, actor; b. London, Eng., Oct. 1, 1890; s. George and Florence (Bell) H.; grad. Worshipful Company of Carpenter's Sch., London, 1905; m. Violet Marion Lane, Jan. 2, 1939. Boy Choirister, 1903-06; student singing, Milan, Italy, 1914; appeared musical comedies London including Hit the Deck, 1927; an original mem. Co-Optimists (concert party), 1921-27; motion pictures include Hamlet, 1947, Lavender Hill Mob, 1950, Brief Encounter, 1945, This Happy Breed, 1943, The Way Ahead, 1943; appeared Met. Opera Co. prodn. Midsummer Nights Dream, 1954; originated role of Mr Doolittle in My Fair Lady, 1956, same role in film version; TV series Blandings Castle, 1967; films Mrs. Brown You Have a Lovely Daughter; Run A Crooked Mile, 1969, The Private Life of Sherlock Holmes, 1969, The Flight of the Doves, 1970; played in Bernard Shaw Festival, Canada, 1970; played Burgess in Candida. Decorated Order Brit. Empire. Author: Wiv A Little Bit of Luck, 1967. Home: East Preston, Sussex, England. Died Jan. 30, 1982.

HOLMAN, CLARENCE HUGH, educator, writer; b. Cross Anchor, S.C., Feb. 24, 1914; s. David Marion and Jessie Pearl (Davis) H.; m. Verna Virginia McLeod, Sept. 1, 1938; children—Margaret McLeod Strowd, David Marion. B.S., Presbyn. Coll., 1936, A.B., 1938, Litt.D., 1963; Ph.D., U. N.C., 1949; L.H.D., Clemson U., 1969. Dir. public relations Presbyn. Coll., 1936-39, dir. radio, 1939-41, instr. English, 1941-45, acad. dean, 1945-46; instr. English U. N.C., 1946-49, asst. prof., 1949-51, asso. prof., 1951-56, prof., 1956-59, Kenan prof. English, from 1959, chmn. div. humanities, 1959-62, 74-77, chmn. dept. English, 1958-62; chmn. U. N.C. (Coll. Arts and Scis.), 1954-55; dean U. N.C. (Grad. Sch.), 1963-66, provost, 1966-68, spl. asst. to chancellor, 1972-78. Author 5 detective novels, 1942-47, (with others) The Development of American Criticism, 1955, (with W. F. Thrall and A. Hibbard) A Handbook to Literature, 4th edit, 1980, (with others) The Southerner as American, 1960, Southern Writers Appraisals in Our Time, 1964, Seven Modern American Novelists, 1964, Thomas Wolfe, 1960, John P. Marquand, 1965, The Am. Novel Through Henry James, A Bibliography, 1966, 2d edit., 1979, Three Modes of Modern Southern Fiction, 1966, Southern Fiction Today, 1969, Roots of Southern Writing, 1972, The Loneliness at the Core, 1975 (Mayflower Cup award 1975, S.C. Excellence in Writing award 1976), The Immoderate Past, 1977, Windows on the World, 1979, also articles in field.; Editor: (with others) Short Novels of Thomas Wolfe, 1961, The Yemassee (W.G. Simms), 1961, The World of Thomas Wolfe, 1962, The Thomas Wolfe Reader, 1962, Simms's View and Reviews, 1962, Garretson Chronicle (G.W. Brace), 1964, Of Time and the River (Thomas Wolfe), 1965, Tucker's Partisan Leader, 1971; co-editor: (with others) The Letters of Thomas Wolfe to His Mother, 1968, Southern Literary Jour, 1968—, Southern Writing, 1585-1920, 1970, (with L.D. Rubin) Southern Literary Study, 1975. Publicity dir. S.C. Council Nat. Def., 1942-44; trustee, chmn. exec. com. Triangle Univs. Center for Advanced Study, from 1975; trustee, v.p. Nat. Humanities Center, from 1975. Acad. coordinator 2199th BU. USAAF, 1943-45. Recipient Thomas Jefferson award, 1975; recipient O. Max Gardner award, 1977; Guggenheim fellow, 1967-68. Fellow Am. Acad. Arts and Scis.; mem. N.C. Univ. Press (chmn. bd. govs. 1957-73), Coll. English Assn., S. Atlantic Modern Lang. Assn., Modern Lang. Assn. (chmn. Am. lit. sect. 1970), Am. Studies Assn., Nat. Council Tchrs. English, Phi Beta Kappa, Alpha Sigma Phi. Democrat. Presbyterian. Home: Chapel Hill, NC.

HOLMBERG, LAWRENCE OSCAR, advertising agency executive; b. Sac City, Iowa, July 29, 1908; s. Bror Frichoff and Ruth Sophia (Greenwall) H.; m. Lura Phillips Schreiner, Apr. 26, 1941; 1 son, Lawrence Oscar. B.C.S., Drake U., 1929. Traffic mgr. Yellow Cab Airways, Des Moines, 1929; field service Campbell-Ewald Co., Detroit, 1929-30; asst. advt. mgr. Vacuum Oil Co., Chgo., 1930-32; owner L. O. Holmberg Advt., 1932-36; Chgo. mgr. J. Stirling Getchell, Inc., 1936-43; Chgo. mgr. Compton Advt., Inc., 1943-59, v.p., 1948-59; propr. Lawrence O. Holmberg Co., Chgo., 1959-62, pres., 1962-84. Bd. dirs. Union League Found., Boys Clubs, Central YMCA Coll.; Trustee Shimer Coll. Mem. Nat Outdoor Advt. Bur. (dir. 1951-60), Traffic Audit Bur. (dir., v.p. 1958-59), Am. Assn. Advt. Agys. (dir. 1955-56). Clubs: Chicago, Indian Hill. Home: Wilmette, Ill. Died June 20, 1984; buried Rosehill Cemetery, Chgo.

HOLME, PETER HAGNER, JR., lawyer; b. Denver, June 5, 1918; s. Peter Hagner and Jamie (Sexton) H.; A.B., Yale, 1939; postgrad. Harvard, 1939-41; LL.B., U. Colo., 1942; m. Lena Phillips, Aug. 20, 1940; children—Richard Phillips, Howard Kelley, Peter Hagner. Admitted to Colo. bar, 1942; asso. firm Dines, Dines & Holme, Denver, 1942, 46-48, ptnr., from 1948 (firm now Holme, Roberts & Owen); dep. dist. atty., Denver, 1944-46. Vice chmn. Legal Aid Soc., from 1960, pres., 1963-65; bd. dirs. Nat. Inst. Trial Advocacy, from 1971. Bd. dirs. U. Colo. Alumni Fund; trustee U. Denver, 1968-76. Served with USAAF, 1942-44. Fellow Am. Coll. Trial Lawyers (bd. regents 1962-65, sec. 1964), Am. Bar Found.; mem. Am. Judicature Soc., Nat. Legal Aid and Defender Soc., Am. Law Inst. (council 1968-72), Am. (ho. dels. 1957-60, 72-73, chmn. legal edn. and admissions to bar sect., chmn. mng. com. fund for legal edn. 1964-68), Colo. (gov. 1952, 66-70, pres. 1968-69), Denver (award of merit 1966, trustee) bar assns., Law Club Denver (pres. 1952), Phi Delta Phi. Clubs: Cactus, University, Mile High, Denver Country. Home: Denver, Colo. Dec. Feb. 21, 1981.

HOLMES, JAMES ALBERT, shoe company exec.; b. Plympton, Mass., May 22, 1887; s. James H. and Clara A. (Bryant) H.; m. Carrie E. Chamberlain, Sept. 16, 1911; children—Richard Bradford, Philip Dearborn. With Regal Shoe Co., Whitman, Mass., 1905-32, dir., mem. exec. com. from 1939, v. chmn. bd., chmn. exec. com. since 1948; sales dir. W.L. Douglas Shoe Co., Brockton, Mass., 1932-39; v.p., dir., mem. exec. com. Mut. Fed. Savs. & Loan Assn. of Whitman; incorporator Whitman Savings Bank. Republican. Conglist. Mason. Home: Whitman, Mass. †

HOLMES, OLIVER WENDELL, archivist, historian; b. St. Paul, Feb. 2, 1902; s. Henry Anderson and Charlotte (Benson) H.; m. Dorothy Behner, Sept. 14, 1927; children—Benson Venables, Helena Victoria (Mrs. Charles E. Morrison). B.A., Carleton Coll., 1922; Ph.D., Columbia, 1956. Asst. in history Mont. State U., 1923-24; staff asst.

reference br. N.Y. Pub. Library, 1926-28; editorial asst. Ency. Brit., 1928-29, Columbia U. Press, 1929-30, 32-35; research specialist Inst. Social and Religious Research, 1930-31; assoc. archivist, chief div. Interior Dept. archives; dir. research and record description, program adviser, chief archivist Interior Dept. archives (Nat. Resources Records div.); chief archivist social and econ. records div. Nat. Archives, Washington, 1936-61; exec. dir. Nat. Hist. Pubs. Commn., 1961-72; cons. Rep. on Interdeptl. Com. on Sci. and Cultural Coop., 1944-49, to Nat. Council Historic Sites and Bldgs., 1948-52; Adj. prof. archives adminstrn. Am. U., Washington, 1957-64. Author: Lifeline of Empire, 1969, Shall Stagecoaches Carry the Mail? , 1972; Editor: Handbook of Federal World War Agencies and Their Records, 1917-1921, 1943, Records of the Columbia Historical Society, 2 vols, 1955, 59; Contbr. articles to profl. jours. Fellow Soc. Am. Archivists (council mem. 1948-50, del. to 1st Internat. Congress Archivists, Paris 1950, pres. 1958-59); hon. mem. Internat. Council Archives; mem. Inst. Early Am. History and Culture (council 1963-66), Am., Western, So. hist. assns., Orgn. Am. Historians, Agrl. History Soc., Columbia History Soc., Am. Assn. State and Local History, Am. Antiquarian Soc., Md., Minn., Mass., Mont., Nev., Utah, Va. hist. socs., The Westerners (sheriff Potomac Corral 1959-60). Club: Cosmos (Washington). Home: Washington, D.C. Died Nov. 25, 1981.

HOLMES, URBAN TIGNER, III, clergyman, ednl. adminstr.; b. Chapel Hill, N.C., June 12, 1930; s. Urban Tigner and Margaret Allan (Gemmell) H.; m. Jane Wiley Neighbours, Aug. 24, 1951; children—Jane Teresa, David Thomas, Janet Reid Holmes Haws, Allan Tigner. B.A., U. N.C., 1950, M.A., 1954; M.Div., Phila. Div. Sch., 1954; S.T.M., U. of South, 1962; Ph.D., Marquette U., 1973; D.D., Nashotah House, 1974. Ordained priest Episcopal Ch.; curate St. Luke's Parish, Salisbury, N.C., 1954-56; chaplain La. State U., Baton Rouge, 1956-66, spl. lectr. in Greek, 1959-65; prof. pastoral theology Nashotah (Wis.) House, 1966-73; priest-in-charge St. Simon's Episc. Ch., Port Washington, Wis., 1966-73; dean Sch. Theology, U. of South, Sewanee, Tenn., 1973-81; lectr. Marquette U., 1971; mem. exec. council Episc. Ch., 1976-81. Author: The Future Shape of Ministry, 1971, Young Children and the Eucharist, 1972; To, Speak of God, 1974, Confirmation: The Celebration of Maturity in Christ, 1975, Ministry and Imagination, 1976, The Priest in Community, 1978, Praying with the Family of God, 1979, A History of Christian Spirituality, 1980, Turning to Christ: A Theology of Renewal and Evangelization, 1981; co-author: The Sexual Person, 1970, Christian Believing, 1979; co-editor: To Be a Priest, 1975, Male and Female, 1976, Realities and Visions, 1976; editor: Medieval Man, 1980; contbr. articles to profl. jours. Mem. Phi Beta Kappa, Alpha Tau Omega. Democrat. Home: Sewanee, Tenn. Died Aug. 6, 1981.

HOLMES, WALTER RICHARD, surgeon; b. Macon, Ga., Dec. 10, 1887; s. Walter Richard and Leila (Burke) H.; A.B., U. of Ga. 1909; M.D., Johns Hopkins 1913; m. Idelle Palmour, Sept. 28, 1922; children—Palmour Holmes (Mrs. Pope McIntire), Kate (Mrs. Ellis Murphy). Interne, Johns Hopkins Hosp., Baltimore 1913-14, asst. resident in gynecology 1914-16, resident 1917 instr. in gynecology Johns Hopkins U., 1917; pvt. practice, Atlanta from 1920; visiting gynecologist Emory U. Hosp., Grady Memorial Hosp. from 1930; consulting gynecologist Henrietta Egleston Hosp. for Children; mem. faculty Emory U. Med. Sch. since 1921 as instr. in gynecology, 1921-22, asso., 1922-41, asso. prof., 1941-45, prof. clin. gynecology, 1945-62, emeritus prof. clin. gynecology, from 1962. Served as first lieutenant, M.C., U.S. Army 1917-18. Diplomate Am. Bd. Obstetrics and Gynecology, 1939. F.A.C.S. (bd. govs.). Mem. A.M.A., So. Med. Assn. So. Soc. of Clin. Surgeons (pres. 1933), So. Surg. Assn., S. Atlantic Assn. of Obstetricians and Gynecologists, S. Eastern Surg. Assn., Am. Assn. Obstetricians, Gynecologists and Abdominal Surgs., Ga. Obstet. and Gynecol. Soc., Phi Beta Kappa, Alpha Omega Alpha. Phi Delta Theta, Phi Chi. Democrat. Methodist. Clubs: Piedmont Driving, Capital City, Fifty. Contributor to surg. jours.; chapter on endometriosis, Progress in Gynecology, 1946. Home: Atlanta, GA. †

HOLMES, WILLIAM M., business exec.; b. Ireland, 1887. Chmn. bd. Jacqueline Cochran, Inc.; chmn., dir. Jacqueline Cochran-Charbert; trustee Emigrant Indsl. Savings Bank; director of New York Board of Trade. Lily of France Corsets. Clubs: Westchester Country (Rye, N.Y.); Everglades (Palm Beach, Fla.).†

HOLSTEIN, EDWIN JOSEPH, educator, economist; b. Utica, N.Y., Apr. 17, 1921; s. Clarence E. and Elizabeth (Linfoot) H.; m. Katherine Jean Hansen, Jan. 31, 1948; children—John Joseph, Lynn Marie, Ann Judith. B.A., State U. N.Y. at Albany, 1942, M.A., 1947; Ph.D., N.Y. U., 1957. Instr. history and sociology State U. N.Y. at Cortland, 1946-47; mem. faculty Rensselaer Poly. Inst., from 1947, prof. econs., from 1963, chmn. dept., 1968-79; dir. NSF Inst. Econ. Analysis Applied to Urban Problems, 1971; prof. Gen. Electric Co. Edn. Found. Fellowship program, from 1959; vis. prof. State U. N.Y. at Albany, Russell Sage Coll., Union Coll., Schenectady; cons. in field, from 1958. Author: (with E. J. McGrath) Liberal Education and Engineering, 1960; also articles. Mem. study com. Eastern Mohawk Valley Devel. Council, 1961; mem. study group Charles Kettering Found., from 1964; ordained permanent deacon Albany Diocese, Roman Catholic Ch., 1976. Served to lt. USNR, 1942-46. Recipient Founder's Day award N.Y. U., 1957. Mem. Am. Econs. Assn., N.Y. State Econs. Assn. (pres. 1970-71), AAUP, Pi Gamma Mu, Kappa Phi Kappa, Kappa Delta Rho. Home: Troy, N.Y.

HOLT, DOCTOR DILLON, college president, clergyman; b. Albermarle, N.C. July 20, 1899; s. David Alexander and Elizabeth Sophronia (Rummage) H.; A.B., Duke, 1927, B.D., 1933; D.D., Wesley Coll., 1960. U. N.D., 1960; m. Grace Elizabeth Sanders, Jan 4, 1936; children—David Dillon, John Sanders. Instr. Bible and psychology Rutherford (N.C.) Coll., 1927-30; ordained to ministry Methodist Ch., 1930; minister in Charlottesville, Va., 1936-40, Lynchburg, Va., 1940-44, Portsmouth, Va., 1944-45, Durham, N.C., 1945-52; exec. dir. Meth Coll. Found., N.C., 1952-56; dir. financial promotion quardrennium Commn. Christian Higher Edn., Meth. Ch., 1956-60; pres. Scarritt Coll. for Christian Workers, Nashville, 1960-70; acting pres. Pfeiffer Coll., Misenheimer, N.C., 1971-72; lectr. ecumenical movements, before assemblies, commencements, others; pres. Internat. Prayer Fellowship, 1973—. Active Council of Chs.; counselor family life and vocational guidance, higher edn., fund raising. Mem. Nashville C. of C. Mason, Rotarian. Contbr. articles religious periodicals. Home: West Jefferson, N.C. Died June 27, 1983.

HOLT, DON S., textile company consultant; b. Graham, N.C., Mar. 7, 1908; s. Seymour S. and Glenanna (Shaw) H.; A.B., U. N.C., 1929; LL.D., Elon Coll., 1972, Livingstone Coll., 1974; m. Margaret McConnell, 1932. Exec. v.p. Travora Mfg. Co., 1938-49; v.p. Cannon Mills Co., 1951-58, exec. v.p., 1959-61, pres., 1962-73, chmn. bd., 1971-74, cons., 1974-82, also dir.; dir. Cabarrus Bank & Trust Co. Mem. U.S. bd. Anglo-Am. Textile Mission to Japan, 1950; dir. N.C. Textile Mfrs. Assn., Inc., 1952. Served to lt. comdr. USNR, 1942-45. Named 1973 Textile Man of Year, Phi Psi. Mem. Am. Textile Mfrs. Inst. (past dir.). Methodist. Club: Rotary (hon.). Home: Charlotte, N.C. Dec. Mar. 20, 1982.

HOLT, JOSEPH FRANK, justice Ark. Supreme Ct.; b. 1910. LL.B., U. Ark. Bar: Ark. bar 1937. Justice Ark. Supreme Ct. Died Oct. 30, 1983.

HOLTER, NORMAN JEFFERIS, biophysicist; b. Helena, Mont., Feb. 1, 1914; s. Norman B. and Florence (Jefferis) H.; m. Miss Wheeler, Sept. 1941 (div. Jan. 1952); children—Troy Jefferis, Marian; m. Joan Treacy, July 18, 1952; children—John Treacy, Anton Jeffery. A.B., U. Calif. at Los Angeles, 1937, M.A., 1940; M.S., U. So. Calif., 1939; postgrad., U. Heidelberg, Germany, 1937, U. Chgo., 1939, Oak Ridge Inst. Nuclear Studies, 1949, Med. Sch., U. Oreg., 1956; D.Sc. (hon.), Mont. State U., 1965; LL.D. (hon.), Carroll Coll., 1978. Chemist Calif. Consumers Corp., Los Angeles, 1937-38; teaching asst. U. Calif., 1940-41; sr. scientist U. Calif.-Navy Dept. Capricorn Expdn., 1952; asst. physicist Nat. Def. Research Com., San Diego, 1941; asst. physicist Navy Dept., 1941-42, asso. physicist, 1942-44, physicist, 1944-45, sr. physicist, 1946-47; mem. tech. staff Bikini Atomic Bomb Expdn., 1946-47; participant Eniwetok Hydrogen Bomb Tests, 1952; specialist in physics Inst. Geophysics and Planetary Physics, U. Calif. at San Diego, La Jolla, 1964-65, asst. to the chancellor, 1965-66; Pres. Holter Research Found. Inc., Helena and La Jolla, from 1947; past pres. Bozeman State Coll. Research Found.; past adv. med. physics Western Found. Clinic Research; past pres. Rancho Calif. Corp., Holter Realty Co., A. M. Holter Hardware Co.; past v.p. N Bar Ranch Co., Park Ave. Apts. Corp., Helena, Angus Sales Co.; past dir., mem. exec. com. Ind. Coal & Coke Co., Salt Lake City; past dir. First Nat. Bank & Trust Co., Helena. Past editorial bd.: Jour. Nuclear Medicine; now editorial bd.: Jour. Internat. Soc. Biotelemetry; Contbr. to profl. and govtl. jours. Past adv. council Sch. Bus., U. Mont.; past trustee, v.p., pres. St. Peter's Hosp.; past mem. adv. bd. Mont. Crippled Children's Home and Hosp.; past cons. biophysics VA Hosp., Ft. Harrison, Mont.; past mem. adv. com. sci. activities SSS; past trustee La Jolla Country Day Sch., La Jolla Mus. Art. Recipient Order of Grizzly U. Mont.; Harold Laufman Found. award for outstanding contbn. to med. instrumentation, 1979; USPHS grantee (12). Fellow AAAS; mem. Explorers Club (N.Y.C.), Am. Phys. Soc., Soc. Nuclear Medicine (founder, past pres.), Am. Assn. Physics Tchrs., Mont. Med. Assn. (hon.), Biophys. Soc., N.Y. and Mont. acads. scis., AMA (asso.), Sigma Xi, Phi Kappa Sigma. Clubs: Mont, La Jolla Beach and Tennis; Cosmos (Washington). Home: Helena, MT.

HOLTZ, FREDERICK C(ARL), pub. utility exec.; b. Wahoo, Neb., May 6, 1888; s. Charles A. and Martha (Gumfer) H.; B.S., U. of Neb., 1913, hon. Dr. Engring., 1947; m. Margaret Norval, Apr. 18, 1916; children—Frederick C., Helen Margaret. Gen. engr. Gen. Electrice Co., Schenectady, 1913-16, v.p. and chief engr. Sangamo Electric Co., Springfield, Ill., from 1919. Served as 1st lt. U.S.S.C., World War I. Mem. Am. Inst. E.E., A.A.A.S., Ill. Acad. Sci., Sigma Xi. Home: Springfield, Ill. †

HOLWAY, WILLIAM REA, consulting engineer; b. Sandwich, Mass., Apr. 29, 1893; s. Jerome Richardson and Ella (Ellis) H.; B.S. in San. Engring., Mass. Inst. Tech., 1915; m. Frances Hope Kerr, July 28, 1916 (dec.); children—Donal Kerr, Charlotte Holway Meagher, William Nye; m. Helen Annette Thayer, Mar. 31, 1970. Asst. engr. City of Providence, 1915-17; water plant engr. City of Tulsa, 1918-20; owner, pres. W.R. Holway and Assocs., cons. engrs., Tulsa, 1920-73, cons., 1973-81. Pres. All Souls Unitarian Ch., Tulsa, 1922-23. Recipient Outstanding Achievement award Mass. Inst. Tech., 1957. Mem. Am. Inst. Cons. Engrs., ASCE, ASME, Am. Water Works Assn., Am. Cons. Engrs. Council. Democrat. Club: Masons. Author: History of the Grand River Dam Authority, 1968. Home: Tulsa, Okla. Dec. Apr. 23, 1981.

HOLZWORTH, C. E., business exec.; b. Rochester, N.Y., Apr. 19, 1890; s. Christopher J. and Katherine (Heck-Roth) H.; m. Cecile Wendover, Sept. 18, 1916; children—Beverly (Mrs. Clover), Wendover. With S. S. Kresge Co. from 1908, mgr. several stores, 1910-27, dist. mgr., Chicago, 1928-34, in charge store management, Detroit, 1934, dir. of co. since Oct. 1934, v.p. charge store mgmt., 1935-54, ret.; dir., exec. rep. Pepsi-Cola Co.; dir. Standard Tube Co., Higbie Mfg. Co. Republican. Clubs: Detroit Athletic, Bloomfield Hills Country, The Recess. Home: Bloomfield Hills, Mich. †

HOLZWORTH, JOHN MICHAEL, lawyer, explorer, author; b. Cleve., May 28, 1888; s. Frederick and Ella (Degnon) H.; B.S., Columbia, 1910; LL.B., N.Y. U., 1912; m. Sarah Haight Slater, Feb. 1, 1914; children—Jean, Betty. Admitted to N.Y. bar, 1912; mem. firm Delafield, Thorne & Rogers, N.Y.C., 1912-19; asst. dist. atty. Westchester County, 1925-26; organizer, and served as treas., Griffin & Howe, Inc., N.Y.C., 1921-29; pres. Yukon Engring. Co. Placed markers of Lewis and Clark expn. from Lolo Pass to Columbia River, 1914-15; led sci. expdns. in B.C. and Alaska for U.S. Biol. Survey and Nat. Mus., collecting speciments of large mammals and mapping unexplored territory, 1923, 24, 25, 28-29; pioneer navigator Salmon River, Ida. (later known as River of No Return) to Snake River; head of movement for Admiralty Island Alaska Wildlife Sanctuary and Nat. Park; pioneer in motion pictures of big game in America; discoverer new and largest, species of grizzly bear (ursus holzworthi). Served as capt., FA, U.S. Army, AEF, World War I, Staff speaker for N.A.M. in war plants, World War II, Pres. Nat. Assn. Wild Life Conservationists, Inc. Mem. N.Y. Bar Assn. (pub. defender com. 1932-35). Sigma Chi. Republican. Roman Catholic. Author: Wild Grizzlies of Alaska, 1930; Twin Grizzlies of Admiralty Island, 1932; Woof, the Half-Pint Bear Chaser, 1934; The River of No Return, 1936; Blue Book of Dogs, 1938; The Fighting Governor, 1938; The Wild Animals of North America, 1938; Bears, Judges and Politicians, 1957. Address: Portland, Oreg. †

HONEGGER, HERMAN CHARLES, philanthropist, author, industrialist, sportsman; b. Vienna, Austria, (Swiss origin), June 10, 1890; s. Herman and Rosalie (Engel-Baur) H.; economics degree U. Neuchâtel, Switzerland, 1912; m. Corinne Baumann, Feb. 19, 1926; children—Ursula, Peter. Came to U.S., 1922, naturalized, 1927. Pres. Helvetic Importers and Mfrs. Corp., N.Y. City from 1922, Ursula, Inc., N.Y. City from 1945. A founder Universal Pestalozzian Movement, 1939, Pestalozzi Found. Am., 1942 (hon. president from 1949; chairman executive board of directors), Pestalozzi World Foundation American, 1948. Recipient Médaille de la Reconnaissance française, 1946; Chevalier of the Legion Honor, 1949; Stella della Solidarieta Italiana, 1949; hon. citizenship City of Sempach, 1949; first world prize for Help to Youth from Switzerland, 1949; Medal of Honor from Austria, 1950; Officier de L'Ordre de Leopold II, Belgium, 1951; candidate Nobel Peace Prize, Feb. 1951; Union Internationale de Protection de l'Enfance Ordre de Mérite, Switzerland, 1952; Stella della Solidarieta prima classe Italiano, 1952; Médaille de l'Ordre de Mérite de l'Union internationale de l'Enfance, 1952; Officer of la Santé Publique et la Population, France, 1952; La Crofix de Commandeur de la Courónne de Chêne, Luxembourg, 1953; Officier in de Ordre van Orange-Nassau, Netherlands, 1953; Verdienstkreuz de Verdienstordens, German Fed. Rep., 1956. Mem. Am. Soc. Friendship with Switzerland (dir.), Conglist. Clubs: Grasshopper (Zurich, Switzerland); West Side Tennis (Forest Hills, N.Y.); River (N.Y.C.). Author: Religious Significance of Vincent van Gogh, 1937; Antigone, 1938; Essay on LeComte du Nouy's books, The Road to Reason, and Human Destiny, 1948; Henry George, an Orthodox American, 1935; St. Stephen's Cathedral in Vienna, 1940; Death of the Dragon Fly. Home: Sandy Hook, Conn. †

HONG, CHARLES JUAY, b. Swatow, China, July 10, 1908; came to U.S., 1925, naturalized, 1942; s. Liong Siu and Sue Kee (Wong) H.; m. Maye Jung, Nov. 15, 1945; children—Suzanne C., Charles B. A.B., Albion Coll., 1934; M.D., U. Mich., 1937, M.S., 1939; postgrad., U. So. Calif., Stanford, 1960-81, U. Calif. at Los Angeles and San Francisco, 1960-81, Loma Linda U., 1960-81. Diplomate: Am. Bd. Abdominal Surgery. Intern U. Mich. Med. Sch. and Hosp., Ann Arbor, 1937-38, resident in surgery, instr., 1938-42, practice gen. surgery, Bakersfield, Calif., 1945-81; sr. attending surgeon Mercy, Bakersfield Meml., Kern Med. Center, San Joaquin, Bakersfield community hosps.; Owner Hong Oil Co., Hong Assos., Hong Farms

Assos.; Owner Hong Oil Assos., Hongville Land Devel. Co.; pres. Kerncot Fibre Corp. Contbr. articles to med. jours. Served as maj., M.C. AUS, 1942-46, CBI. Decorated Bronze Star; Order of Yun Hui China). Fellow Pan-Pacific Surg. Assn., Internat. Coll. Surgeons, Am. Soc. Abdominal Surgeons; mem. AMA, Mich. Acad. Sci. and Arts, U.S. Mil. Surgeons, Res. Officers Assn. U.S., World Med. Assn., Kern County Med. Soc., Calif. Med. Assn., Am. Legion, VFW, Sigma Xi, Phi Sigma. Club: Optimist. Home: Bakersfield, Calif. Died 1981.

HOOD, GEORGE WILLIAM, forester; b. Lancaster, O., July 30, 1888; s. James Theodore and Elizabeth (Hodgison) H.; B.Sc., in Horticulture and Forestry, Ohio State U., 1910, M.Sc., 1914; m. Mildred May Neimeier, July 7, 1915; children—Helen Elizabeth (Mrs. O. L. Jenkins), Kenneth James. Instructor in horticulture, Ohio State University, 1907-09, also in charge conservatories; assistant in United States Department of Agriculture, 1910-11; instr. horticulture, Mich. Agrl. Coll., East Lansing, Mich., 1911-13; asso. prof. horticulture, U. of Neb., 1913-22; commercial practice, 1922-23; supt. Forest Lawn, Omaha, 1923-30; supt. park dept., City of Omaha, 1930-34; forester Soil Conservation Service of U.S. Dept. of Agr., 1934-36, regional forester, 1936-43; Research specialist cooperating with the University of Arkansas, 1943-49; Soil Conservation Nurseries, Waterloo, Neb., from 1946, investigations, reclamation of eroded land, Ozarks, 1949. Mem. Soc. Hort. Science, Society of American Foresters, Ohio Academy Science, Michigan Academy Science, Neb. State Hort. Soc., Omaha and Salina chambers of commerce. Sigma Kappa Zeta (national pres.), Gamma Sigma Delta. Presbyterian. Clubs: Continental Commercial, Kiwanis, Carter Lake, Prettiest Mile Club. Author: Laboratory Manual of Horticulture, 1915; Practical School and Home Gardens, 1916; Farm Horticulture, 1918, 20; Horticulture, 1929; Viability and Germination of Tree Seeds, 1938; Planting of Woody Plants for Erosion Control, 1939; Seed Collecting of Woody Plants, 1940; Use of Structures in Gully Control, 1947. Contbr. to soil conservation jours. Mason, Elk. Home: Waterloo, Nebr. †

HOOD, GILBERT HENRY, JR., dairy products mfg. company executive; b. Derry, N.H., Aug. 19, 1899; s. Gilbert Henry and Helen (Davis) H.; A.B., Harvard U., 1920, M.B.A., 1922; m. Margaret Barr Allan, June 9, 1928; children—Emily C., Elizabeth Hood Wilson. With H.P. Hood, Inc., Boston, 1922-75, pres., 1962-66, chmn. exec. com., 1966-70, chmn. bd., 1970-75, now dir.; dir. Loomis-Sayles Capital Devel. Fund, Boston, 1965-74, dir. emeritus The Fidelity Group Funds, (Boston), 1966-76. Pres. N.E. Council Econ. Devel., 1969-70, Greater Boston YMCA, 1968-69; trustee Mus. Sci. Boston, 1964-85, v.p., 1975-85; trustee Boston Hosp. Women, Winchester (Mass.) Hosp., Wheaton Coll., Norton, Mass., Andover-Newton (Mass.) Theol. Sch.; bd. overseers Crotched Mountain Sch., Greenfield, N.H. Served with U.S. Army, 1918. Mem. Milk Industry Found. (past pres.), Greater Boston C. of C. (pres. 1964-65), Sigma Alpha Epsilon. Republican. Congregationalist. Clubs: Masons, K.T., Harvard; Winchester Country; Eastern Yacht (Marblehead, Mass.); Royal Poincianna Golf (Naples, Fla.). Home: Winchester, Mass. Dec. Mar. 24, 1985.

HOOKER, DAVENPORT, anatomist; b. Brooklyn, N.Y., May 13, 1887; s. Henry Daggett and Mary Theodora (Davenport) H.; A.B., Yale Coll., 1908; A.M., Yale U., 1909, Ph.D., 1912; Scott Hurtt Fellow of Yale at Bonn and Naples, 1911-12; D. Sc., U. of Pittsburg, 1939; m. Helen Millington Ferris, Apr. 14, 1917; 1 daughter, Elizabeth Bradford (Mrs. Benjamin A. Gjenvick). Assistant in biology, Yale. 1908-09, instructor in anatomy, 1909-14; assistant professor histology, U. of Pittsburg, 1914-15; asst. prof. anatomy, Yale, 1915-19; prof. anatomy U. Pitts., 1919-57, chmn. dept. 1919-56; emeritus from 1957; Harry Burr Ferris lectr. in anatomy, Yale, 1935-36, lecturer in anatomy, from 1958; university lecturer U. Mich., 1943, 58; asso. fellow Trumbull Coll., Yale, from 1946; Porter lectr. Kan. University, 1951. Served as capt., Field Artillery Reserves, 1919-23; major, Sanitary Reserves 1923-42. Mem. Am. Assn. Anatomists (mem. exec. com. 1922-25; 2d vice president, 1940-42, president, 1958-59), American Physiological Society, Association Research Nervous and Mental Disease (pres. 1953), Phi Beta Kappa, Sigma Xi, Alpha Omega Alpha, Nu Sigma Nu. Club: Graduate (New Haven). Mem editorial bd. Jour. of Comparative Neurology from 1931, mng. editor, 1932-50; mem. adv. bd. Jour. of Neurophysiology from 1938. Author of scientific articles relating to development and regeneration of nervous system, nerve-muscle relationships, and development of human fetal activity. Home: New Haven, Conn. †

HOOKER, SANFORD BURTON, physician; b. Peacham, Vt., Apr. 23, 1888; s. Burton Sanford and Clara (Dow) H.; student Bradford Acad., 1900-04; A.B., Dartmouth, 1909; Ch.B., Boston U., 1912, M.D., 1913; student med. sch., Harvard, 1914, U. Pa., 1915; M.A. (fellow), U. Cal., 1916; m. Lillian A. Osgood, Oct. 11, 1919; children—Burton Sanford, Janet (Mrs. Donald Ross Bishop), Robert Osgood. Intern Mass. Homeopathic Hosp., 1911-12; resident physician Evans Meml. Hosp., Boston, 1913-14, research asso., 1914-20, mem. staff, 1921-52, emeritus from 1952; instr. phys. diagnosis, pharmacology Boston U., 1913-14, instr. preventive medicine, 1916-18, asst. prof. immunology, 1920-24, asso. prof., 1924-32, prof., 1932-52, prof. emeritus from 1952; immunologist Mass. Meml. Hosp., 1920-52; cons. Nat. Research Council, 1924-26, Nat. Insts. Health, 1949-53. Served as 1st lt. M.C., U.S. Army, 1917-19, A.E.F., France, 1918-19. Recipient 1st Distinguished Service citation Alumni Assn. Boston U. Sch. Medicine, 1954. Member Am. Academy Allergy (pres. 1935-36, chmn. research council 1946-52), Am. Assn. Immunologists (pres. 1936-37), Soc. Am. Bacteriologists, Am. Pub. Health Assn., A.A.A.S., Am. Coll. Allergists, A.M.A., Mass. Med. Soc., N.Y. Acad. Sci., Soc. Exptl. Biology and Medicine (editorial bd. Proc. 1935-42), Am. Acad. Arts and Sci., Phi Beta Kappa, Sigma Chi, Alpha Kappa Kappa, Alpha Omega Alpha. Mason (32 deg.). Republican. Co-editor: Yearbook Pathology and Immunology, 1940-41. Editorial bd. Jour. Immunology from 1935, Jour. Investigative Dermatology from 1940, Jour. Allergy, 1944-52, Internat. Archives Allergy from 1947. Contbr. articles profl. publs. Home: Bradford, Vt. †

HOOPER, FRANK ARTHUR, judge; b. Americus, Ga., Apr. 21, 1895; s. Frank Arthur and Helena (Callaway) H.; student Ga. Inst. Tech.; LL.B., LL.M, LL.D., Atlanta Law Sch.; LL.D., Mercer U.; m. Carolyn Newton, June 29, 1926; children—Frank A. III, Charles N., Ellis C. Admitted to Ga. bar, 1916; sec. to judge Ga. Ct. Appeals, 1917, judge, 1932; practiced in Atlanta, 1919-43; instr., Atlanta Law Sch., 1934-43; asst. city atty., Atlanta, 1940-43; judge Superior Ct., Atlanta Jud. Circuit, 1943-49; U.S. dist. judge No. dist. Ga., 1949-67, U.S. sr. dist. judge, 1967-77. Rep. Ga. Legislature, 1925-28. Served as lt. (j.g.) U.S.N.R.F., 1918-19. Mem. Am., Ga., Atlanta bar assns., Am. Legion, Ga. Tech. Nat. Alumni Assn. (pres. 1945-47), Sigma Alpha Epsilon. Democrat. Baptist. Mason (32 deg.), Kiwanian. Home: Atlanta, Ga. Dec. Feb. 11, 1985.

HOOPER, LIONEL E(LCAN), U.S. Pub. Health Service; b. Farmville, Va., Feb. 15, 1887; s. Benjamin Stephen and Sarah William (Holman) H.; student Hampden Sidney (Va.) Coll., 1902-04, Washington and Lee U., 1904-05, U. of Va., 1905-08; M.D., Georgetown U., 1911; m. Lucile White Rogers, Apr. 15, 1916 (she died May 1938); 1 daughter, Alice Rogers; m. 2d, Ruth Wallace, September 23, 1941. Comd. asst. surgeon, U.S.P.H.S., 1913, passed asst. surgeon, 1917, surgeon, 1921, sr. surgeon, 1933; med. dir., 1939; served at Quarantine Sta., Honolulu, 1913-20; med. officer in charge. U.S. Marine Hosp., Norfolk, Va., 1920-22; duty at Am. consulate gen., Rotterdam and Antwerp, 1922-26; exec. officer U.S. Marine Hosp., Stapleton, N.Y., 1926-27; med. officer in charge Quarantine Sta., Galveston, 1927-28; chief quarantine officer, Puerto Rico, 1928-32; med. officer in charge U.S. Marine Hosp., Seattle, 1932-36, Stapleton, N.Y., 1936-37; chief quarantine officer Hawaiian Islands, 1937-39; med. officer in charge U.S. Marine Hosp., New Orleans, 1939-44. Med. Officer in Charge, U.S. Marine Hosp., and Chief Quarantine Officer, Galveston, Tex., 1944-45; med. officer in charge U.S.P.H.S. Relief Sta. and Quarantine Sta., Phila., 1945-47; Dist. Coast Guard med. officer, 1946-47; med. officer in charge U.S. Marine Hosp., Ellis Island, N.Y., 1947-49, U.S. Quarantine Sta. and Outpatient Clinic, Miami, Fla., 1949-50; ret. Dec. 1, 1950. mem. A.M.A., Assn. Mil. Surgeons, Phi Chi. Home: Fort Lauderdale, FL. †

HOOPER, MALCOLM PITTS, foreign service officer; b. Baltimore, Md., Oct. 26, 1890; s. James Albert, Jr. and Alice Evans (Herring) H.; student Baltimore City Coll.; m. Mary Ellen Elliott July 28, 1915 (now deceased); 1 dau., Elizabeth Duane (Mrs. Bruce Learned). Asst. to nat. bank examiner in Md. and S.C., 1908-10; auditor-solicitor, Commercial Credit Co., Baltimore, 1910-14; rep. Am. cotton interests in Japan, China and Russia, 1915-16, Italy, 1916-24; banking and brokerage, 1924-34; trade commr. in Italy, 1935; asst. commercial attache, Rome, 1936-41; U.S. fgn. service officer as consul in Panama, 1942, Palestine and Trans-Jordan, from 1943. Rep. gen. purchasing agent, A.E.F., Italy, 1917-18; co-founder Am. Relief Soc. for Italy, 1916-18; officer in charge British interests in Italy, 1940-41. Delegate 1st annual conf., Internat. C. of C., Paris, 1920; pres. Am. C. of C. for Italy in Milan, 1920; dir. Jerusalem Y.M.C.A. Mason. Clubs: Maryland (Baltimore, Md.); Sports (Jerusalem); Union (Rome). Home: Baltimore, Md. †

HOOVEN, FREDERICK JOHNSON, mechanical engineer; b. Dayton, Ohio, Mar. 5, 1905; s. Claude Caldwell and Elizabeth (Johnson) H.; m. Martha Galloway Kennedy, Apr. 28, 1928; children—John, Peter, Michael, Martha Hooven Richardson. S.B., M.I.T., 1927. Engr. DayFan Radio, 1925; jr. engr. Gen. Motors Research, 1927-28; engr. Dayton Rubber Mfg. Co., 1929-30, Am. Loth Corp., 1932; civilian aero. engr. USAAC, Dayton, 1930-31; chief engr. Radio Products Co., 1933-34; v.p., chief engr. Radio Products div. Bendix Aviation, 1935-37; cons. product devel., Dayton, 1938-56; with Ford Motor Co., Dearborn, Mich., 1956-67, dir. research planning, 1963-65, spl. cons. to gen. mgr. Ford div., 1966-67; adj. prof. engring. Thayer Sch. Engring., Dartmouth Coll., 1967-75, prof. engring., 1975-85; cons. in field; vis. lectr. Antioch Coll., 1938-56; vol. research assoc. in psychophysiology Fels Inst. for Human Devel., Yellow Springs, Ohio, 1946-56; Mem. ednl. council M.I.T., 1958-67, mem. vis. com. dept. mech. engring., 1959-65, mem. devel. com., 1961-68; mem. tech. adv. bd. Dept. Commerce, 1969-72. Contbr. articles to profl. jours. Mem. Oakwood (Ohio) Bd. Edn., 1949-56; trustee Antioch Coll., 1952-64, Miami Valley Hosp., Dayton, 1952-56, Charles F. Kettering Found., 1959-77, Hitchcock Meml. Hosp., Hanover, N.H., 1968-75, Hitchcock Found., Hanover, 1968-73. Mem. AAAS, Dartmouth Soc. Engrs., Dayton Engrs. Club (Deeds Kettering Meml. award 1968), Exptl. Aircraft Assn., Fedn. Am. Scientists, Nat. Acad. Engring., Sigma Xi. Patentee aircraft radio direction-finders, receivers, navigation, blind-landing and guidance systems, automotive and aircraft high-energy and high-frequency ignition systems and components, electronic computing, control, measurement and switching systems, others Home: Norwich, Vt. Died Feb. 5, 1985.

HOOVER, H. EARL, appliance mfg. co. exec.; b. Kansas City, Dec. 12, 1890; s. Frank Kryder and Effie Laura (Phelps) H.; B.S. in Engring., U. Mich., 1912; m. Miriam F. Ulvinen, Oct. 2, 1951; children—Gorden, Robert, John, H. Earl II. Engr. phosphate mines, Mt. Pleasant, Tenn., 1912-13; engring. asst. Hoover-Mason Phosphate Co., Chgo., 1913-18, pres., treas., 1935-52; v.p. Hoover Co., Chgo., 1915-53; vice chmn., 1953-54, chmn., 1954-56; v.p., dir. Hoover Co., Ltd., Hamilton, Ont., Can., 1915-56; chmn. Ruhm Phosphate & Chem. Co., 1946-53. Pres. bd. edn., Glencoe, Ill., 1924-25. Trustee, v.p. Highland Park (Ill.) Hosp. Assn., 1935-43; founder dir., fellow Palm Springs (Cal.) Desert Museum; founder, life mem. Living Desert Assn., Palm Desert, Cal.; founder, trustee The (H. Earl) Hoover Found.; adv. exec. bd. Chgo. council Boy Scouts Am.; voting trustee Chgo. YMCA: v.p., bd. dirs. Bishop McLaren Center, Sycamore, Ill.; adv. bd. Chgo. Salvation Army, Chgo. Orchestral Assn. Hon. Cooley fellow U. Mich., 1953; recipient Silver Beaver award Boy Scouts Am., 1937. Mem. Am. Soc. M.E., A.A.A.S., Indsl. Research Inst. (pres. 1940-41), Phi Delta Theta. Episcopalian (vestryman, treas.). Clubs: University, Farmers (Chgo.); Sunset Ridge (Northfield, Ill.). Address: Glencoe, IL. †

HOPE, ASHLEY GUY, educator, writer; b. Norfolk, Va., Sept. 8, 1914; s. William Frank and Anne Elizabeth (Guy) H.; LL.B., U. Va., 1936, J.D., 1970; postgrad. Worcester Coll. (Oxford U., Eng.), 1936, Columbia U., 1936-37, Princeton U., 1944-45, Stanford U., 1945, Nat. War Coll., 1955-56; M.A. in Internat. Affairs, George Washington U., 1964; Ph.D., Syracuse U., 1967; m. Janet Barker, June 1, 1949 (dec. 1973), children—Anne (Mrs. Richard M. Hamrick) and Jean (Mrs. Robert N. Nye) (twins); m. 2d, Myda Weaver Price, Sept. 10, 1977. Admitted to Va. bar, 1935; practiced in Richmond, 1937-39; atty., later clk. spl. congl. com. for investigation NLRB, 1939-40; atty. D.C. Unemployment Compensation Bd., 1940-41; asst. dir. securities div. Va. State Corp. Commn., 1941; fgn. service officer, 1946-64, assigned successively Shanghai, Dairen, Brussels, Tel Aviv, 1946-49, staff, Office Chinese Affairs, 1950-55; consul, Istanbul, 1956-58; office-in-charge Turkish affairs, 1958-60; dep. dir. Office Near Eastern and So. Asian Regional Affairs, 1960-61, dir., 1961-62; dep. chief of mission Am. embassy, Abidjan, Ivory Coast, 1962-63; dir. multilateral policy planning staff Bur. Ednl. and Cultural Affairs, 1963-64; acting dir. South Asia program Syracuse U., 1964-65, lectr. polit. sci. Maxwell Grad. Sch., 1965-67; prof. govt. Western Ky. U., 1967-69; prof. politics, dir. social and behavioral scis. program St. Andrews Presbyn. Coll., 1969-71; lectr. polit. sci. Va. Commonwealth U., 1971-72, prof. polit. sci., 1972-73. Cons. State Dept. Fgn. Service Inst., Washington, 1966-67; adviser U.S. del. UN Gen. Assembly, 1960-61. Served from ensign to comdr., USNR, 1941-45. Mem. Am. Fgn. Service Assn., Phi Alpha Delta. Episcopalian. Clubs: Va. Writers; Dacor (Washington). Author: American and Swaraj, 1968; (with Mrs. Hope) Symbols of the Nations, 1973. Journal of a Journey, 1976. Contbr. articles to profl. jours. Home: Kill Devil Hills, N.C. Died Sept. 14, 1982.

HOPKINS, EDWARD JURIAN, business exec.; b. Austin, Tex., Feb. 10, 1888; s. Eugene and Martha (Mattingly) H.; grad. Austin High Sch.; m. Edmee Frankel, June 13, 1914; children—Jean (Mrs. Jean Gallagher), Edward John, Marjory May. With Internat. Shoe Co. since 1913, beginning as credit mgr., dir. from 1932. Episcopalian. Home: St. Louis, Mo. †

HOPKINS, HAROLD DANA, assn. exec.; b. Gratiot County, Ashley, Mich., 1887; s. William R. and Mabel (Urania) H.; B.A., U. of Mich., 1917, M.A., 1926; LL.D., Heidelberg College; married Florence Michaels, 1920; children—Margarete (wife of Lt. col. Edward Buhrer), Robert A., Richard. Teacher at the East Side High School, in Saginaw, Michigan, 1916-23; head, department of speech, Heidelberg Coll., 1923-43; pres., Defiance (Ohio) College, 1943-51; nat. exec. sec. Accrediting Commn. Bus. Schs., Washington, 1956-62, cons. Dir. leader Chattanooga Co. Exptl. Center Adult Civic Ednl. Forum, 1935. Exec. sec. Perry Meml. and Peace Commn., 1937. Mem. Council Nat. Orgns. (mem. exec. com.), Pi Kappa Delta (past nat. pres.). Address: Columbia City, Ind. †

HOPKINS, L(EVL) THOMAS, educator; b. Truro, Cape Cod, Mass., Apr. 1, 1889; s. Ezra Rogers and Charlotte (Crallee) H.; A.B., Tufts, 1910, A.M., 1911; studied Hyannis (Mass.) Normal Sch., Teachers Coll. (Columbia); Ed.D., Harvard, 1922; m. 2d, Hester Sherman Rich, Mar. 31, 1935. Teacher pub. sch., 1908-10; asst. in history, Tufts, 1910-11; high sch. prin., 1911-13; supt. schs., Mass., 1913-21; asst. in edn., grad. sch. of edn., Harvard, 1921-22; prof. edn. U. of Colo., 1922-29; became professor of education Teachers Coll. Columbia University, 1929, professor emeritus. Member bd. trustees Dean Academy and Junior College. Member N.E.A. National Society for Study of Education, Progressive Edn. Assn., Soc. for Curriculum Study, A.A.S.A., Phi Beta Kappa, Phi Delta Kappa, Kappa Delta Pi. Author: Interaction—The Democratic Process, 1941; The Emerging Self, 1954; and many others between 1924-38; also articles. Address: Truro, Mass. †

HOPKINS, MILO BRANCROFT, business exec.; b. Brooklyn, Wis., 1901. Grad., U. Wis., 1923. Formerly chmn. fin. com., dir. Wean United, Inc.; formerly chmn. fin. com., dir. Schenley Industries, Inc. Home: Fort Lauderdale, Fla. Died 1981.†

HOPKINS, SAM, blues musician; b. Centerville, Tex., Mar. 15, 1912; s. Abe and Frances Sims H.; m. Antoinette Charles. Appeared in major clubs and folk festivals throughout world including, U. Calif. Folk Festival, Ann Arbor Blues Festival, Festival of Am. Folk Life, Washington, New Orleans Jazz and Heritage Festival, Rotterdam Jazz Festival, Dortmund Jazz Festival; recorded for, Folkways, Tradition, World Pacific and Arhoolie Record cos.; songs include Morning Blues, Slavery, Katie Mae, Walkin' Blues, Abilene. Died Jan. 30, 1982.*

HOPPENSTEIN, JOEL MANUEL, lawyer; b. Waco, Tex., Mar. 17, 1910; s. Zorach and Ronie (Dalkowitz) H.; m. Stella Mosesman, July 7, 1935; children—Jay Marshall, Linda Carol. Student, U. Tex., 1927; B.A., Baylor U., 1930, J.D., 1933. Bar: Tex. bar 1933. Practiced in, Dallas, asst. city atty., 1935-39; partner firm Hoppenstein & Prager, Dallas, from 1966, Pres. S.W. Film Lab. Inc. Bd. dirs., v.p. Jewish Welfare Fedn. of Dallas. Mem. Am., Dallas bar assns., State Bar Tex. Jewish (pres. synagogue, dir.). Clubs: Columbian Country of Dallas, Masons, Shriners. Home: Dallas, Tex.

HOPPER, GEORGE DUNLAP, foreign service; b. Stanford, Ky., July 13, 1889; s. George Dunlap and Katherine (Higgins) H.; grad. high sch., Stanford, 1907; A.B., Centre Coll., Danville, Ky., 1913; LL.B., U. of Louisville, 1916; m. Minnie Parker Durham, June 23, 1920; 1 dau., Virginia Lee; m. 2d, Sue Cushing Hayes, July 8, 1939. Admitted to Ky. bar, 1916, and practiced at Danville, 1916-17; U.S. consul, Stockholm, Sweden, 1917-20; detailed to Dept. State, 1920; consul at Rotterdam, The Netherlands, 1920-23, Hamburg, Germany, 1923, Dunkirk, France, 1924-25, Antofagasta, Chile, 1925-28, Montreal, Can., 1929-34; consul and judge U.S. Consular Court, Casablanca, Morocco, 1934-37; consul gen. Winnipeg, Can., 1937-41, St. John's Newfoundland, 1941-45; consul gen., Hong Kong, 1945-49; detailed to Dept. of State, ret. from fgn. service 1950. American delegate to Inter-Allied Blockade Com., Stockholm, 1919; represented Dept. State at Pacific Foreign Trade Conv., Los Angeles, Calif., 1938. Mem. Kappa Alpha. Presbyterian. Mason. Home: Asheville, N.C. †

HOPPER, W(ILLIAM) W(ESLEY), banker; b. Ione, Cal., Apr. 14, 1887; s. Benjamin and Adda Belle (Stevens) H.; ed. in public schs. and high sch., Ione; m. Almeda Eloise Brown, Oct. 5, 1910; 1 son, Robert Edwin. With agrl.-reclamation development Alameda Sugar Co., West Sacramento Co., Netherlands Farms Co., Woodland and Sacramento, Calif., 1909-16; branch mgr. First National Bank of Woodland, 1916-22, mgr. Bank of Italy, Woodland, 1922-27; became asst. vice pres. as supervisor of credits, head office, Bank of Italy, San Francisco, 1927; v.p. Bank of America Nat. Trust & Savings Assn., San Francisco, 1931-37; v.p. and dist. mgr. Bank of America North Coast Branches, 1931; v.p. Bankitaly Agrl. Credit Corp., 1929-31, pres., 1931-37; asst. sec. Nat. Bankitaly Co., 1929-31; dir. Calif. Joint Stock Land Bank, San Francisco, 1928, v.p., 1930, pres., 1935-38; v.p. Corp. of America, 1933-48; became v.p. Bankitaly Mortgage Co., 1930; dir. Calif. Lands, 1935-43, Capital Co., San Francisco, 1935-43; pres. and dir. First Nat. Bank of Nev., Reno, Nev., 1937-52, chmn. bd., 1952-58, 62-65, mem. exec. com., 1958-65; mem. adv. com. San Francisco Loan Agy., Reconstrn. Finance Corp. Chmn. Housing Authority City Reno; chmn. nat. adv. com. State Nev. N.Y. World's Fair; chmn. Nev. commn. Golden Gate Internat. Exposition; chmn. Nev. citizens com. Navy Relief Soc.; Nev. chmn. United Def. Fund, Inc.; state campaign treas. Am. Heart Assn.; rep. in Nev. for Arthritis and Rheumatism Found.; mem. Pacific Coast Transportation Bd., San Francisco. Mem. Am. (exec. council finance and nominating coms.; state chmn.), Nevada (pres.) bankers assns., Am. Inst. Banking, Nev. Econ. Conf., Atomic Power Utilization Com., Cal. Wool Growers Assn., Nev. Hereford Assn., N.A.M. (mem. com.), C. of C., Newcomen Soc. (Nev. chmn.). Rotarian. Mason (Shriner). Elk. Club: Prospectors (Reno). Home: Menlo Park, Calif. †

HOPSON, DAN, law educator, educational administrator; b. Phillipsburg, Kans., Sept. 23, 1930; s. Daniel Ashton and Ruth (Whitaker) H.; m. Phyllis Ann Gray, Nov. 23, 1956; children: Daniel Gray, Christopher Paul, Bruce Edward. Student, La. State U., 1947-48; A.B., U. Kans., 1951, LL.B., 1953; LL.M., Yale U., 1954; postgrad., Cambridge U., 1954-55. Bar: Kans. 1953. Asst. prof. law U. Kans., Lawrence, 1955-59, assoc. prof., 1959-63, prof., 1963-67; research assoc. Yale U., New Haven, 1959-60; prof.law Ind. U., Bloomington, 1967-80, asoc. dean faculties, 1974-789; dean, prof. law So. Ill. U., Carbondale, 1980-85; arbitrator Am. Arbitration Assn. and Fed. Mediation and Conciliation Service, 1963-85. Author: (with Quintin Johnstone) Lawyers and Their Work, 1967; contbr. articles to law jours. Mem. ABA, Ill. Bar Assn., Jackson County Bar Assn., Council Juvenile Ct. Judges (assoc.), Order of the Coif, Phi Beta Kappa, Pi Sigma Alpha, Phi Alpha Delta, Phi Delta Theta. Episcopalian. Home: Carbondale, Ill. Died June 16, 1985.

HORAN, JAMES EDWARD, chemical company executive; b. Chgo., May 20, 1928; s. Lawrence James and Louise M. (Schevers) H.; m. Barbara Patch, Jan. 24, 1953; children: Julia, James, Michael. B.S., St. Procopius Coll. (now Ill. Benedictine Coll.), Lisle,, 1950; Ph.D., Pa. State U., 1955. Chemist Amoco Chem. Corp., Chgo., 1955-83; v.p. Amoco Chems. Corp., 1977-84. Mem. Am. Chem. Soc., AAAS. Roman Catholic. Home: Glen Ellyn, Ill. Died June 25, 1984.

HORD, STEPHEN Y., banking and investment service company executive; b. Indpls., Nov. 7, 1897; s. Francis T. and Eleanor (Young) H.; ed. Phillips Acad., Andover, Mass., 1913-17; B.A., Yale U., 1921; m. Catharine Norcross, Oct. 29, 1926; children—Stephen Y., Frederic N., Catharine Brent. With No. Trust Co., Chgo., 1921-27; asso. Lee, Higginson & Co., Chgo., 1927-32; with Brown Bros., Harriman & Co., from 1932; gen. ptnr. 1945-81; dir., exec. com. Ill. Central Industries, Inc., 1962-72, I.C.R.R. Co., 1945-72; dir. Abex Corp., 1968-72. Trustee Cowles Commn. Bd. dirs. Northwestern Meml. Hosp.; trustee emeritus Phillips Acad. Mem. Sr. Soc. (Yale). Clubs: Onwentsia (Lake Forest); Chicago, Commercial, Attic (Chgo.); Old Elm (Ft. Sheridan). Home: Lake Forest, Ill. Dec. Oct. 12, 1981.

HORINE, J(OHN) S(HERMAN), univ. prof.; born Nicholasville, Ky., Jan. 24, 1887; s. John Henry and Virginia Washington (Overstreet) H.; student Threlkeld Select Sch., Nicholasville, 1904-05; B.M.E., U. of Ky., 1909, M.E., 1912; m. Nannie Rhodes Wallace, Nov. 26, 1913; children—John Sherman, (killed in World War II), Wallace Rhodes. Exptl. engring. Fairbanks-Morse Co., Beloit, Wis., 1909-10; instr. steam engring. U. of Ky., 1910-16, instr. mech. drawing, 1916-17, asst. prof. drawing, 1917-21, asso. prof. drawing, 1921-46, prof. engring. drawing and coordinator for engring. freshmen from 1946. Mem. Am. Soc. Engring. Edn., Am. Assn. Univ. Profs., Tau Beta Pi, Phi Eta Sigma, Pi Tau Sigma, Triangle. Mem. Christian Ch. (trustee). Club: University Kentucky Faculty. Home: Lexington, Ky. †

HORN, ANDREW HARLIS, educator, librarian; b. Ogden, Utah. July 22, 1914; s. Edward Cooper and Cora (Harlis) H.; student Santa Monica City Coll., 1932-35, Am. U., 1951; A.B., U. Cal. at Los Angeles, 1937. M.A., 1940, Ph.D., 1943, B.L.S., U. Cal. at Berkeley, 1948; m. Mary Amelia Baier, Jan. 4, 1948. Lab. asst. Santa Monica City Coll., 1933-35; teaching asst. U. Cal. at Los Angeles, 1937-40, 42-43, research asst., 1940-41, Hattie Hellar scholar history, 1941, lectr. European history, extension div., 1941-42; tech. writer Douglas Aircraft Co., 1942-43; asst. prof. history Johns Hopkins, 1946-47; asst. head dept. spl. collections U. Cal. at Los Angeles Library, 1948-49, univ. archivist, 1950-54, head dept. spl. collections, 1950-51, asst. librarian, 1951-52, asso. librarian, 1952-54; univ. librarian, prof. librarianship U. N.C., 1954-57; librarian Occidental Coll., Los Angeles, 1957-59, asst. dean Sch. Library Service, U. Cal. at Los Angeles, 1959-66, dean, after 1966, then dean emeritus, asso. prof., 1959-63, prof., 1963-83. Served as sgt. AUS, 1943-46. Mem. Am., Cal. library assns., A.A.U.P., Soc. Cal. Archivists, Biblog. Soc. (London), Printing Hist. Soc. (London), Medieval Acad. Am., Bibliog. Soc. Am., Phi Beta Kappa, (London), Medieval Acad. Am., Bibliog. Soc. Am., Phi Beta Kappa, Phi Delta Kappa, Pi Gamma Mu, Phi Eta Sigma, Blue Key, Kappa Alpha. Club: Rounce and Coffin (Los Angeles). Home: Glendale, Calif. Died May 25, 1983.

HORN, STANLEY FITZGERALD, editor, publisher; b. nr. Nashville, May 27, 1889; s. Williamson Williams and Sadie Ashby (Graves) H.; grad. Fogg High Sch., Nashville, 1906; Litt. D. (hon.), U. Chattanooga; m. Alice Beryl Williams, June 12, 1913; children—Stanley Fitzgerald, Ruth. With J.H. Baird pub. Co., pubs. So. Lumberman, Nashville, from 1908, (except short period on Phila. Eve. Ledger 1914); editor, part owner So. Lumberman, from 1917; pres. J. H. Baird Pub. Co. Chmn. Tenn. Civil War Centennial Commn. (state historian), mem. Tenn. Hist. Commn. Mem. Tenn. Hist. Soc. (past pres.), Phi Beta Kappa. Democrat. Episcopalian. Clubs: Coffee House, Cumberland, Belle Meade Country, Round Table. Author: Boy's Life of Robert E. Lee, 1935; The Hermitage: Home of Andrew Jackson, 1938; Invisible Empire, 1939; the Army of Tennessee, 1941; This Fascinating Lumber Business, 1943; Gallant Rebel, 1947; Robert E. Lee Reader, 1949; The Decisive Battle of Nashville, 1957. Editor, compiler: Tennessee's War, 1965. Home: Nashville, TN. †

HORNBEAK, MACK HAYNES, banker; b. Hornbeak, Tenn., June 23, 1906; s. Pleas and Ada (Haynes) H.; m. Barbara Thomas, June 5, 1958; 1 dau., Anne Haynes. B.S. in Commerce, U. Tenn., 1929; M.A., La. State U., 1933, Ph.D., 1937. Mem. faculty La. State U., 1932-41; with City Nat. Bank, Baton Rouge, from 1949, pres., from 1957, chmn. bd., 1972-80, chmn. emeritus, from 1980, also dir. Served to lt. col., inf. AUS, 1942-45, ETO. Decorated Legion of Merit, Bronze Star with 1 oak leaf cluster; Croix de Guerre with palm France and Belgium; Croix de Guerre Luxembourg). Mem. Baton Rouge C. of C. (pres. 1958-59), Sigma Nu, Phi Kappa Phi. Clubs: Boston (New Orleans); Baton Rouge Country (Baton Rouge) (pres. 1953-54), City (Baton Rouge), Rotary (Baton Rouge). Home: Baton Rouge, LA.

HORNE, JOHN E., insurance company executive; b. Clayton, Ala., Mar. 4, 1908; s. John Eli and Cornelia (Thomas) H.; m. Ruth F. Kleinman, July 27, 1938; children: Linda (Mrs. Richard Clark), Susan (Mrs. James K. Ewart). Normal certificate, Troy State U., 1928; A.B. with honors, U. Ala., 1933, M.A. (fellow in history 1933-35), 1941, LL.D., 1970; LL.D., Troy State U., 1982. Tchr., Pike County, Ala., 1925-26, Columbiana, Ala., 1928-31; rep. Macmillan Pub. Co., 1935-39, Row, Peterson Pub. Co., 1939-42, 46; adminstrv. asst. to Senator John J. Sparkman of Ala., 1947-51, 53-61; adminstr. Small Def. Plants Administrn., 1951-53; staff dir. Democratic Senatorial Campaign Com., 1954; asst. campaign mgr. to Adlai E. Stevenson, 1956; exec. dir. Nat. Citizens Com. Kennedy-Johnson, 1960; adminstr. Small Bus. Administrn., 1961-63; mem. Fed. Home Loan Bank Bd., 1963-68; chmn., 1965-68; pres. Investors Mortage Ins. Co., 1969-70, chmn., 1970-78; pres. John E. Horne Assocs., 1979-85; dir. Continental Investment Corp., Boston, Tiger IMI, Boston, Midwest Fed. Savs. & Loan Assn., Mpls.; mem. adv. com. FNMA; mem. adv. council Fed. Home Loan Bank Bd.; Disting. vis. prof. Troy State U., 1978-85, Adams-Bibby Chair Free Enterprise, 1983-85. Pres. Pi Kappa Alpha Meml. Found., 1967-69; trustee Coop. Housing Found., 1976-85, Nat. Small Bus. Assn., 1979-85; treas. Nat. Housing Conf., 1978-85. Served from lt. (j.g.) to lt. (s.g.) USNR, 1943-46; capt. Res.; ret.). Recipient Letter of Commendation for meritorious Navy service, Outstanding D.C. Alumnus award U. Ala., 1965, Outstanding Troy State U. Alumnus award, 1967; named one of 50 outstanding contbrs. to better housing in Am. Nat. Housing Conf., 1981. Mem. Fla. Jr. C. of C., Am. Legion, SCV, VFW, Newcomen Soc., Ala. Hist. Soc., Phi Beta Kappa, Omicron Delta Kappa, Phi Delta Kappa, Kappa Delta Pi, Pi Kappa Alpha (chmn. nat. conv. 1958, chmn. distinguished achievement award com. 1961-62, distinguished achievement award 1966, nat. treas. 1966-68, chosen among 200 most famous alumni 1976). Episcopalian. Clubs: Nat. Press, Nat. Capital Democratic (dir.), Congl. Staff, Post Mortem, Burro; Internat. (Washington), Metropolitan (Washington); Algonquin (Boston); Elks.

HORNER, H. MANSFIELD, aircraft exec.; b. New Haven, Conn., Sept. 12, 1903; s. Leonard S. and Julia Stuyvesant (Barry) H.; B.S., Yale, 1926; D. Eng. (hon.) Renssalaer Polytechnic, 1948; D.Sc. (hon.), Hillyer Coll., 1956, Trinity Coll., 1959; m. Lela Thomas Shumate, June 25, 1926; children—Leonard M., Lela Burwell. Pres., dir. United Aircraft Corporation, East Hartford, Connecticut, 1943-56, chairman and chief executive officer, 1956-83; chairman board, director United Aircraft of Canada Ltd.; dir. First Nat. City Bank (N.Y.), So. N.E. Telephone Co., Travelers Ins. Co., Hartford National Bank & Trust Co. Member bd. trustees Hartford YMCA, Rensselaer Poly. Inst. Recipient Pres.'s Certificate of Merit, 1948; Chevalier French Legion Honor. Member Nat. Indsl. Conference Board, Conn. Pub. Expenditure Council. Aerospace Industries Assn. (chmn. 1955, 61). Home: Hartford, Conn. Died May 9, 1983.

HORNER, WILLIAM LUDWIG, consulting engineer, oil and gas producer; b. Stroudsburg, Pa., May 29, 1908; s. Ludwig and Irene (Lander) H.; B.S., U. Pitts., 1928, Petroleum Engr., 1934, Geol. Engr., 1951; m. Elizabeth Berghane, June 24, 1929; children—William B., David L., Richard A. Student engr. Standard Oil Co. of N.J., 1928-29; petroleum prodn., reservoir and water flood research Humble Oil Co., Forest Oil Corp., 1929-36; developed core analysis, co-founder, dir. Core Labs., Inc., 1936-42; with Barnsdall, Sunray Oil Corps. (now Sun Oil Co.), 1943-54, chief engr., v.p., 1952-54; with Core Labs. Inc., 1954-60, v.p. engring. and cons. dept.; coordinator, mgr. Citronelle, Ala. Oil Field Unit, 1960-64; oil producer, partner Horner & Smith, Inc., 1964—. Past chmn. of numerous oil operators and engring. coms., 1943-54; mem. secondary recovery adv. and engring. coms. Interstate Oil Compact Commn. Recipient Distinguished Engring. Alumnus award U. Pitts., 1974. Registered profl. engr., Tex., Ala. Mem. Ind. Petroleum Assn. Am. (dir. 1961-64), Am. Inst. Mining, Metall. and Petroleum Engrs. (Anthony F. Lucas gold medal 1974), Am. Assn. Petroleum Geologists, Sigma Tau, Sigma Gamma Epsilon, Sigma Chi. Presbyterian. Club: Pine Forest Country (Houston). Contbr. articles in field. Patentee in field. Home: Katy, Tex. Dec. Sept. 23, 1983. Interned Memorial Oaks Cemetery, Houston, Tex.

HORSEY, OUTERBRIDGE, former fgn. service officer; b. N.Y.C., Oct. 1, 1910; s. Outerbridge and Mary Digges (Lee) H.; student Downside Sch., Eng., 1921-28; B.A., Trinity Coll., Cambridge (Eng.) U., 1931; S.B., Mass. Inst. Tech., 1933; m. Mary Hamilton Lee, Jan. 2, 1946; children—Mary Lee, Sarah R., Anita C., Outerbridge. Spl. asst. Nat. Emergency Council, 1934-36; sales engr. Autocar Co., Ardmore, Pa., 1936-37; fgn. service officer, 1938-70; vice consul, Naples, Italy, 1938, Budapest, Hungary, 1940-41; 3d sec. Am. embassy, Madrid, Spain, 1942-44; asst. chief div. Western European affairs Dept. State, 1944-48; assigned Am. embassy, Rome, Italy, 1948-52; staff European affairs Dept. State, 1953-56; minister Am. embassy, Tokyo, Japan, 1956-59, Am. embassy, Rome, 1959-62; ambassador to Czechoslovakia, 1963-66; consul gen., Palermo, Italy, 1968-70 Clubs: Metropolitan (Washington); Chevy Chase (Md.). Home: Washington, D.C. Died Aug. 18, 1983.

HORSLEY, THOMAS A., business exec.; b. Cedartown, Ga., Feb. 1, 1890; s. George C. and Annie (Costley) H.; grad. Samuel Benedict Memorial High Sch., Cedartown, Ga.; student bus. adminstrn. Rome (Ga.) Bus. Coll.; m. Alma Kirkpatrick, Dec. 23, 1919; children—George C., Thomas A., Jr. Bookkeeper, 1909-11; mgr. plantation and farm credits, 1912-21; gen. mgr. and dir. Selma (Ala.) Creamery and Ice Co., 1921-26, co. acquired by Southern Dairies, Inc., 1926, zone mgr. and dir. gen. office, Washington, from 1926, also mem. bd. dirs. and v.p. subsidiaries. Mem. Internat. Assn. Milk Dealers, Internat. Assn. Ice Cream Mfrs., Asso. Industries of Ala. (dir. 1940-41). Democrat. Mem. Ind. Presbyterian Ch. Mason (K.T.). Clubs: Rotary (dir. two terms), Birmingham Country. Home: Birmingham, Ala. †

HORTENSTINE, RALEIGH, civil engineer, consultant; born at Abingdon, Va., July 12, 1887; s. Joel Wilson and Mary Virginia (Campbell) H.; B.S. in C.E., Va. Poly Inst., 1906; grad. student Cornell U., 1906-07; m. Helen Buchanan Grant, June 26, 1912; 1 son, Raleigh. Engr. and supt. Penn Bridge Co., Beaver Falls, Pa., 1907-12; contracting engr. Va. Bridge & Iron Co., Dallas, Tex., 1912-18, plant mgr. Memphis, Tenn., 1918-23; v.p., gen. mgr. Wyatt Industries, Inc. (formerly Wyatt Metal & Boiler Works), Dallas, 1923-38, pres. 1938-55, chmn. bd., 1955-61, sr. chmn. bd., 1961-68; consultant Wyatt division U.S. Industries, Inc., from 1968; dir. Lone Star Steel Co., Dallas; dir. Republic Nat. Bank of Dallas. Mem., past chmn. bd. trustees Tex. A amd M Research Found. Mem. N.A.M. (past dir.), Am. Soc. C.E., Tau Beta Pi. Presbyn. Clubs: Country, Petroleum. Home: Dallas, TX. †

HORWITT, WILL, sculptor; b. N.Y.C., Jan. 8, 1934. Student, Art Inst. Chgo., 1952-54. One-man exhbns. include, Stephen Radich Gallery, N.Y.C., 1963, 65, 67, Lee Ault & Co., N.Y.C., 1972, 74, 77, 79, Vanderwoude Tananbaum, N.Y.C., 1983, numerous group shows, including, Open Air Mus. Sculpture, Antwerp, Belgium, 1971, Whitney Mus. Am. Art, N.Y.C., 1973, Mus. Art, Oqunquit, Maine, 1973, Tanglewood, Lenox, Mass., 1973, Van Dam Park, Paramus, N.J., 1974, Gruenebaum Gallery, Ltd., N.Y.C., 1975, Keene (N.H.) State Coll., 1975, SUNY, Purchase, 1976, Indpls. Mus. Art, 1976, Weathespoon Art Gallery, N.C., 1982, U. N.C., Greensboro, 1982; represented in permanent collections, Indpls. Mus. Art, Boston Mus. Fine Arts, Wadsworth Arheneum, Hartford, Conn., Yale U. Art Gallery, Smith Coll. Mus. Art, Guggenheim Mus., Amherst Coll., Cornell U., Collection N.Y. State, Stephens Coll., Columbia, Mo., Chase Manhattan Bank, N.Y.C., Tokyo, Rome, Geneva, State U. N.Y. at Purchase, Albright Knox Art Gallery, Buffalo., Nelson A. Rockefeller Collection, Nat. Trust for Historic Preservation. Guggenheim fellow, 1965; grantee Louis Comfort Tiffany Found., 1968-69; grantee Hereward Lester Cooke Found., 1979. Address: New York, N.Y. Died 1985.

HOSMER, CRAIG, lawyer, former congressman; b. Brea, Calif., May 6, 1915; s. Chester Clevel and Mary Jane (Craig) H.; m. Marian Caroline Swanson, Feb. 12, 1946; children—Susan Jane, Craig Larkin. A.B., U. Calif., 1937; postgrad., U. Mich., 1938, U.S. Naval Acad., 1941; J.D., U. So. Calif., 1940. Bar: Calif. bar 1940, Supreme Ct. bar 1953. Practiced in, Long Beach, 1946-47, 49-74; spl. asst. U.S. dist. atty. for AEC, Los Alamos, 1948; mem. 83d-93d congresses from 32d Dist. Calif.; ranking minority mem. interior and insular affairs and joint com. on atomic energy; adviser U.S. Atoms-for-Peace Del., Geneva, 1958, 63, 71; Congl. adviser 18 Nation Disarmament Conf., UN Conf. Com. on Disarmament; mem. U.S. del. IAEA, 1959-75; pres. Am. Nuclear Energy Council, 1975-78, bd. dirs., 1978-82, energy cons., 1978-79; of counsel firm Doub & Muntzing, Washington, 1979-82. Editor: U. So. Calif. Law Rev, 1939-40. Bd. dirs. Inst. for Congress, 1975-78; v.p., bd. dirs. Oceanic Ednl. Found., 1972-82. Served to rear adm. USNR, 1941-73. Recipient Oliver Townsend award for disting. service Atomic Indsl. Forum, 1978. Mem. Am. Nuclear Soc., AAAS. Home: Washington, D.C. Died Oct. 11, 1982.

HOSTETTLER, GORDON FLOYD, educator; b. Kent, Ohio, Mar. 17, 1918; s. Clyde O. and Ocala (Feigert) H.; m. R. Joyce Kirsch, Sept. 24, 1943; children—Margaret Gail, Barbara Joyce (twins). A.B., Kent State U., 1940, B.S., 1940; M.A., State U. Iowa, 1942, Ph.D., 1947. Instr. speech State U. Iowa, 1942-44, Coe Coll., 1944-45; instr. speech, dir. forensics Temple U., 1945-47, asst. prof., 1947-52, asso prof., 1952-58, prof. speech, 1958-64, chmn. dept. speech and dramatic arts, 1952-64; prof. speech Ohio State U., 1964-66; prof. speech Colo. State U., 1966-81, prof. emeritus, 1981-83, chmn. dept. speech, 1966-75. Author articles in field. Mem. Pa. Speech Assn. (exec. sec. 1949-52, pres. 1963-64), Speech Assn. Eastern States (exec. sec. 1952-54). Home: Kent, Ohio. Died July 29, 1983.

HOUGH, WILLIAM JARRETT HALLOWELL, architect; b. Ambler, Pa., July 19, 1888; s. Charles B., M.D., and Mary Paul (Hallowell) M.D., H.; B.S. in Architecture, U. of Pa., 1911, M.S., 1913; fellow Am. Acad. in Rome, 1914-17; m. Mae Shoemaker, Oct. 8, 1924; children—Charles Shoemaker, William Jarrett Hallowell. Began practice of architecture, 1913; partner in firm Harbeson, Hough, Livingston and Larson, architects. Mem. Am. Red Cross in Italy. Mem. Ambler Borough Council. Ambler Borough Sch. Bd. Winner Stewardson travelling scholarship. Fellow A.I.A.; mem. Psi Upsilon. Sigma Xi. Home: Fort Washington, Pa. †

HOUGHTON, AMORY, former ambassador, glass mfg. co. exec.; b. Corning, N.Y., July 27, 1899; s. Alanson Bigelow and Adelaide Louise (Wellington) H.; m. Laura DeKay Richardson, Oct. 19, 1921; children—Elizabeth, Amory, Alanson Bigelow II, James Richardson, Laura DeKay. Ed., St. Paul's Sch., Concord, N.H., 1913-17; A.B., Harvard, 1921; LL.D., Hobart and William Smith Colls., Geneva, N.Y., 1947, Alfred (N.Y.) U., 1948, N.Y. U., 1961, Colgate U., 1961, Ohio State U., 1969; D. Eng. (hon.), Rensselaer Poly. Inst., 1949. With Corning Glass Works, from 1921, asst. to pres., 1926-28, exec. v.p., 1928-30, pres., 1930-41, chmn. bd., 1941-61, chmn. exec. com., 1961-64, hon. chmn. bd., 1964-71, chmn. emeritus, 1971; dir. emeritus Dow Corning Corp., ambassador to, France, 1957-61; Councillor Nat. Indsl. Conf. Bd.; mem. adv. council State U. N.Y.; Bd. dirs. Atlantic Council U.S., Inc.; Asst. dep. dir. materials div. OPM, 1941-42; dep. chief, bur. industry brs. WPB, 1942, dir. gen. operations, 1942; dep. chief Mission for Econ. Affairs, 1943-44. Trustee, mem. Corning Glass Works Found.; trustee Eisenhower Coll., Eisenhower Exchange Fellowships, Corning Mus. Glass, Houghton Found., Inc., French Inst.; hon. v.p., mem. nat. exec. bd. Boy Scouts Am. Decorated Order Merit Bernardo O'Higgins Chile; grand croix Legion de Honneur France). Mem. Internat. C. of C. (exec. com., trustee, mem. U.S. council), France Am. Soc. (chmn. bd.). Republican. Episcopalian. Clubs: University (N.Y.C.), Harvard (N.Y.C.), Links (N.Y.C.); Elmira Country, Corning Country; Rolling Rock (Ligonier, Pa.); Metropolitan (Washington); Eldorado Country (Calif.). Home: Corning, N.Y. Deceased.

HOUGHTON, WALTER EDWARDS, educator; b. Stamford, Conn., Sept. 21, 1904; s. Walter Edwards and Nancy (Acheson) H.; Ph.B., Yale 1924, M.A., 1927, Ph.D., 1931; D.L.H. (hon.), Wellesley Coll., 1976; m. Esther Lowrey Rhoads, June 22, 1929; children—Nancy Acheson, Esther Edwards. Instr., Hill Sch., Pottstown, Pa., 1924-25, Phillips Andover Acad., 1927-29; instr., tutor in history and lit. Harvard, Radcliffe Coll., 1931-38, asst. prof., tutor history and lit., 1938-41; asso. prof. English lit. Wellesley Coll., 1942-48, prof. English lit., 1948-69, Sophie C. Hart prof. English, 1957-69. Active in Civil Def., Cambridge and Wellesley, Mass., World War II. Fellow Am. Acad. Arts and Scis.; mem. Conf. Brit. Studies, Modern Lang. Assn. Author: The Formation of Thomas Fuller's Holy and Profane States, 1938; The Art of Newman's Apologia, 1945; The Victorian Frame of Mind, 1830-70, 1957; The Poetry of Clough, 1963. Editor: (with Spencer, Ferry, Barrows) British Literature from 1800 to the Present Day, 1952, 3d edit., 1974; (with G. Robert Stange) Victorian Poetry and Poetics, 1959, 2d. edit., 1968; The Wellesley Index to Victorian Periodicals, 1824-1900, vol. 1, 1966, vol. II, 1972. Adv. editor Victorian Studies, 1960-69, Victorian Poetry, 1963-76. Home: Wellesley, Mass. Died Apr. 11, 1983.

HOUSE, HOWARD HENRY, educator; b. Brooksville, Kan., Nov. 13, 1888; s. Henry and Zella (Roberts) H.; B.P.E., Springfield Coll., 1917; A.M., Clarke U., 1922; Ph.D., N.Y. Univ., 1936; m. Blythe H. Schee, Aug. 22, 1933. Profl. baseball, summers 1909-22; dir. Rawlins (Wyo.) Athletic Club, 1911-12; asst. prof. phys. edn., Ohio Wesleyan U., 1917-21, A. and M. Coll., Tex., 1922-26; asst. prof. phys. edn., State Coll., Wash., 1926-36, became prof., 1936, chmn. dept. phys. edn. for men, 1944, professor and chairman, dept. emeritus; director of Alaska Exploration and Mining Co. Vet. of World Wars I and II; lt. col., Fellow Am. Assn. Health, Phys. Edn. and Recreation (bd. dirs.); mem. Wash. Edn. Assn., Phi Epsilon Kappa, Pi Gamma Mu, Phi Delta Kappa, Sigma Delta Psi. Democrat. Prsbyn. Contbr. articles on health, phys. edn. and recreation in various profl. jours. Address: Asotin, WA. †

HOUSER, HAROLD A(LEXANDER), navy officer; b. Ft. Valley, Ga., Mar. 31, 1897; s. Emmett and Mary (Mathews) H.; student Marion Inst., 1916-17; grad. U.S. Naval Acad., 1921; LL.B., George Washington U., 1931; m. Vera Allen, Aug. 2, 1924; children—Noradee (Mrs. C. J. Haak), Bradford Carr, David Allen. Commd. ensign U.S. Navy, 1921 and advanced through ranks to brig. gen., 1950; gov. Am. Samoa, 1945-47; comdr. Naval Base, Key West, Fla., 1947, comdr. South Pacific, dir. Office Legislative Liaison, Dept. Def. 1949-55. Decorated Bronze Star medal (Navy), Fleet Clasp with star, 2d Nicaraguan Campaign medal, Am. Def. Service medal, Am. Campaign medal, Asiatic-Pacific Campaign medal, Victory medal. Clubs: Officers (Bethesda, Md.); Army-Navy Country (Washington). Home: Washington, D.C. Died Sept. 3, 1981.

HOUSTON, CHARLES BOONE, co. exec.; b. Chester, Pa., Aug. 14, 1890; s. Howard H. and Nellie (Maitland) H.; student Swarthmore Coll., 1914; m. Pauline V. Smith, Oct. 14, 1914; 1 dau., Margaret M. (Mrs. C. Stuart Brown). Pres. Tug River Lumber Co., 1921-50; sec. Houston Coal & Coke Co., 1914-21; sec., treas. Allburn Collieries Co., 1942-49; breeder Angus cattle and farmer; dir. Eastern Gas & Fuel Assos., Phila. Nat. Bank (Chester, Pa. branch). First National Bank, Flat Top Insurance Agy. (both Bluefield, West Virginia); vice president, director First Clark Nat. Bank, Northfork, W.Va. Chmn. adv. com. Welch (W.Va.) Salvation Army, 1938-50. Mem. Phi Kappa Psi. Episcopalian (vestryman, sr. warden). Mason (32 deg.). Clubs: Union League (Phila.); Sky Top (Pa.); Springhaven (Wallingford, Pa.); Gulf Stream Bath and Tennis(Delray Beach, Fla.). Home: Woodstock, Va. †

HOUSTON, JOHN M., govt. official; b. Formosa, Kan., Sept. 15, 1890; s. Samuel J. and Dora (Nieves) H.; ed. Fairmount Coll., Wichita, Kan., 1906; m. Charlotte Stellhorn, May 28, 1920; chidlren—Patricia Mary Jane, Robert Allan. Appeared as actor, 1912-17; engaged in retail lumber business at Newton, Kan., from 1919; mayor of Newton, Kan., 2 terms, 1927-31; mem. 74th to 77th Congresses (1935-43), 5th Kan. Dist.; mem. Nat. Labor Relations Bd. from Mar. 1943. Served in U.S.M.C., World War. Mem. Kan. Lumbermen's Assn. (pres. since 1926), Am. Legion, Vets, Fgn. Wars. Democrat. Episcopalian. Mason (Shriner); mem. Elks (pres. Kan. Assn.). Home: Washington, D.C. †

HOVDE, FREDERICK LAWSON, former univ. pres.; b. Erie, Pa., Feb. 7, 1908; s. Martin Rudolph and Julia Essidora (Lawson) H.; m. Priscilla Boyd, Aug. 23, 1933 (dec.); children—F. Boyd, Jane (Mrs. D. R. Price), Linda (Mrs. Louis Buehler II). B.Chem. Engring., U. Minn., 1929, LL.D., 1956; Rhodes Scholar from N.D., Oxford U., 1929-32, B.A., B.Sc., 1932, M.A., 1942, D.C.L., 1957; D.Sc., Hanover Coll., 1946, Case Inst. Tech., 1948, Tri-State Coll., 1967; LL.D., Wabash College, 1946, N.D. Agrl. Coll., 1949, N.Y. U., 1951, Mich. State U., 1955, Northwestern U., 196O, U. Notre Dame, 1964, Ball State U., 1965, Ind. State U., 1966, Ind. U., 1969, Purdue U., 1975; D.Ed., Valparaiso U., 1967; D.Eng., Rose-Hulman Inst. Tech., 1948; L.H.D., U. Cin., 1956; Pd.D., Findlay Coll., 1961; Dr. Honoris Causa, U. Rural do Estado de Minas Gerais, Brazil, 1965; D.Hum., Northwood Inst., 1969. Asst. to dir. Gen. Coll., U. Minn., 1932-36; asst. to pres. U. Rochester, N.Y.; also exec. sec. U. Rochester (Rochester prize scholarships), 1936-41; head London mission OSRD, 1941-42; exec. asst. to chmn. Nat. Def. Research Com., 1942-43, chief div. 3, 1943-45; pres. Purdue U., 1946-71, pres. emeritus, 1971-83; Chmn. guided missiles com. Research and Devel. Bd., 1947-49; chmn. bldg. research adv. bd. NRC, 1950-52; mem. bd. fgn. scholarships Dept. State, 1951-55, chmn., 1953-55; cons. Nat. War Coll., 1953-55; Dir. Gen. Electric Co., Investors Mut., Inc., Investors Stock Fund, Inc., Investors Selective Fund, Inc., Investors Variable Payment Fund, Inc., IDS Bond Fund, Inc., Inland Steel Co. Bd. dirs. Culver Ednl. Found., 1962-68, Ednl. Facilities Labs., 1957-69; trustee Carnegie Fund for Advancement of Teaching, 1955-71; mem. President's Com. on Edn. Beyond High School, 1956-57; chmn. Pres.'s Task Force Com. on Education, 1961; mem. sci. adv. panel Dept. of Army, 1952-6O, chmn., 1956-58; mem. study com. on fed. aid to agr. Commn. Intergovtl. Relations, 1954; bd. visitors U.S. Naval Acad., 1946, Air U., 1949-51, Air Force Acad., 1961-63, U.S. Mil. Acad., 1965-67; mem. adv. bd. Air Tng. Command, 1953-54. Decorated comdr. Order So. Cross Brazil; recipient President's Medal for Merit, King's Medal for Service in Cause of Freedom; Washington award Western Soc. Engrs., 1967; Gold Medal Nat. Football Found. and Hall of Fame, 1967; Ednl. award Govt. Taiwan, 1968; Theodore Roosevelt award Nat. Coll. Athletic Assn., 1970; Distinguished Pub. Service medal Dept. Def., 1970; others. Mem. Assn. Land-Grant Colls. and Univs. (pres. 1953-54), A.A.A.S., Ind. Acad., Phi Delta Theta, Phi Lambda Upsilon, Tau Beta Pi, Sigma Xi. Home: Lafayette, Ind. Died Mar. 1, 1983.

HOWARD, BUSHROD BRUSH, former oil co. exec.; b. Annapolis, Md., Nov. 18, 1889; s. Thomas Benton and Anne Jacob (Claude) H.; student St. John's Coll., 1905-06; B.S., U.S. Naval Acad., 1911; m. Esther Margaret Green, Apr. 23, 1913 (dec.); children—Thomas Benton, Margaret (Mrs. David L. Roscoe, Jr.), Bushrod Brush, Peter; m. 2d, Mrs. Margaret Cobb Perkins, July 28, 1939. Joined marine dept. Standard Oil of N.J., 1920, apptd. fgn. rep., Paris, France, 1922, mng. operator Societe Auxiliare de Transports, 1925, dir. L'Economique and Bedford Petroleum Co., Paris, 1926, London rep. Standard Shipping Co., 1929, asst. to gen. mgr. marine dept., N.Y.C., 1934, asst. gen. mgr., 1938, gen mgr., 1939, dir. co., 1945-54. Served to lt. comdr. U.S. Navy, 1907-19. Episcopalian. Club: University (N.Y.C.). Address: Charleston SC. †

HOWARD, DAVID AUSTIN, bus. exec.; b. Washington, May 1, 1889; s. Samuel Theodore and Ellen (Patterson) H.; C.E., Cornell, 1911; m. Margot Doye, July 8, 1933. Engr., engring. dept., City of Washington 1911-16; asst. to v.p., Cities Service Gas Co., Bartlesville and Okla. City, 1943-45; v.p. Rep. Natural Gas Co., Dallas, 1945-50; oil and gas consultant. Registered profl. engr., states of Okla., Kan., Tex. Admitted to Okla. state bar, 1942. Trainee engr., Officers Training Sch., 2nd lt. (Reserves), 1918. Mem. Am. Legion, Okla. Bar Assn.; Delta Upsilon. Republican. Club: Dallas Petroleum. Home: Dallas, Tex.

HOWARD, JOHN EAGER, physician, educator; b. Baltimore County, Md., Aug. 27, 1902; s. John Duvall and Mary Greenwood (Smith) H.; grad. Hill Sch., 1920; A.B., Princeton, 1924; M.D., Johns Hopkins, 1928; m. Lucy James Iglehart, June 30, 1928; children—John Eager (dec. 1971), William James, Lucy Anne Calhoun. Intern, Mass. Gen. Hosp., Boston, 1928-30; asst. resident Johns Hopkins Hosp., 1930-32, mem. staff; practice medicine, Balt., 1934-85; chief medicine Union Meml. Hosp., 1957-71; prof. medicine Johns Hopkins, 1960-68, prof. emeritus, 1968-85. Recipient Distinguished Achievement award Modern Medicine 1964; Passano award, 1968. Mem. Assn. Am. Physicians, Endocrine Soc. (pres. 1960-61), Md. Soc. Internal Medicine (pres. 1961-62), Am. Clin. and Climatol. Assn. (pres. 1973), Balt. City Med. Soc., Interurban Clin. Club. Home: Lutherville, Md. Died Feb. 27, 1985.

HOWARD, KARL S., business exec.; b. Wood River, Neb., July 28, 1887; s. George E. and Frone (Kautz) H.; student Manual Training Sch., Washington U., St. Louis 1902-05; B.S., Washington U., 1909. M.E., 1949; m. Helene Bolland McLaughlin, Jan. 18, 1936; 1 dau., Hila Curtice (Mrs. William S. McGinness). Plant engr. Commonwealth Steel Co., Granite City, Ill., 1909-18, mech. supt., 1918-31; mech. supt. Gen. Steel Corp., Eddystone, Pa., 1931-34, works mgr., 1934-42, at Madison, Ill., plant, 1942-44, gen. mech. supt., Eddystone, 1944-46, vice pres. from 1946; dir. Main Belting Co.; mem. N.Y. adv. bd. Mutual Boiler Ins. Co. of Boston. Registered professional engr., Commonwealth of Pa. Fellow Am. Soc. M.E.; mem. Franklin Inst., Am. Foundrymens Soc., Kappa Sigma. Republican. Episcopalian. Mason (32 deg. Shriner). Clubs: Merion Golf (Ardmore, Pa.); Aviation Country (Ambler, Pa.). Home: Haverford, Pa. †

HOWARD, LEON, educator; b. Talladega, Ala., Nov. 8, 1903; s. Percy L. and Georgia (Heacock) H.; A.B., Birmingham-So. Coll., 1923; A.M., U. Chgo., 1926, L.H.D., 1961; Ph.D., Johns Hopkins, 1929; Ph.D. (hon.), Abo Akademi, Finland, 1968; m. Henrietta Starr, Mar. 6, 1931; children—Mary Morris, Charles Malone, Kathleen. Newspaper work, tchr. prep. schs., Ala., Ga., 1923-26; instr. English, Johns Hopkins, 1927-30; instr. English, Pomona Coll., 1930-32, asst. prof., 1932-37; Internat. Research fellow Henry E. Huntington Library, 1937-38; asso. prof. English, Northwestern U., 1938-43, prof., 1943-50, Morrison prof. English, 1945-50; prof. English, U. Calif. at Los Angeles, 1950-71. Vis. prof. Tokyo U., summers 1951, 54, Centre Universitaire Mediterranean, summer 1957, U. N.M., Albuquerque, 1972-82. Fulbright lectr. U. London, 1956-57, U. Copenhagen, 1960, Australia, 1963, Germany and Switzerland, 1964; Guggenheim fellow, 1944-45; sr. research fellow Newberry Library, 1966. Mem. Am. Acad. Arts and Scis., Modern Lang. Assn. Am., Am. Studies Assn., Phi Beta Kappa. Democrat. Episcopalian. Author: The Connecticut Wits, 1943; Herman Melville: a Biography, 1951; Victorian Knight-Errant: A Study of the Early Literary Career of James Russell Lowell, 1952; Literature and the American Tradition, 1960; The Mind of Jonathan Edwards, 1963. Contbr. articles to profl. publs. Home: Albuquerque, N.Mex. Died Dec. 21, 1982.

HOWARD, ROBERT BOARDMAN, sculptor, painter; b. N.Y.C., Sept. 20, 1896; s. John Galen and Mary Robertson (Bradbury) H.; m. Adaline Kent, 1930; children: Ellen Kent, Galen H. Student, Art Students League, N.Y.C., 1916-17; D.F.A. (hon.), Calif. Coll. Arts and Crafts, 1977, San Francisco Art Inst., 1977; study, travel in, Europe, 1919-22. Mem. San Francisco Art Commn., 1950-54. Designer, executor murals, sculpture, 1922-83; sculpture in wood, stone and iron, murals, Yosemite Nat. Park, 1929-36, murals, sculpture, San Francisco Stock Exchange, 1938-39, ann. shows, San Francisco Mus. Art, Whitney Mus. Am. Art, one-man shows, Mills Coll., 1945, Legion of Honor, San Francisco, 1946, U. Calif. at Berkeley, 1947, Calif. Sch. Fine Arts Gallery, 1956, Salon de Mai, Paris, France, 1962, 63, Seattle Expn., 1962, San Francisco Mus. Art, 1963, U. Calif. at Santa Cruz, 1968, San Francisco Art Commn., 1971 (award), sculpture, Acad. Scis., San Francisco, IBM, San Jose, one-man shows, Sculpture San Francisco Art Inst., 1973, U. Santa Cruz, 1973; (Recipient awards, painting or sculpture, San Francisco Art Inst., 1923, 24, 37, 41, 43, 44, 46, 51, San Francisco Art Festival, 1952, Chgo., 1947-48, Crocker prize 1955). Served with U.S. Army in, 1918-19, France. Mem. San Francisco Art Inst. Home: San Francisco, Calif. Died Feb. 18, 1983.

HOWARD, STANLEY EDWIN, univ. prof.; b. Sherbrooke, P.Q., Sept. 29, 1888; s. George Henry and Hannah Bertha (Lambly) H., citizens of U.S.; A.B., Bates Coll., Lewiston, Me., 1910; A.M., Princeton U., 1913, Ph.D., 1916; m. Ethel Mae Chapman, June 24, 1913 (died 1923); children—Esther Caroline (Mrs. Robert Roswell Palmer), Marshall Chapman; m. 2d, Helen Sibley, June 29, 1925; 1 son, Charles Sibley (died 1943). Instr. Latin, Greek and pub. speech, Pennington (N.J.) schs., 1910-12; instr. econs. and sociology, Mount Holyoke Coll., South Hadley, Mass., 1913-14; instr. econs., Princeton U., 1916-17, Dartmouth Coll., Hanover, N.H., 1917-18; asst. prof. econ., Princeton U., 1918-23, asso. prof., 1923-40, prof. from 1940, chmn. dept. econ. and social instns., 1934-48. With U.S. shipping bd., Washington, 1918. Mem. bd. overseers Bates Coll., Lewiston, Me. Mem. Am. Econ. Assn., Am. Accounting Assn., Am. Finance Assn., Econ. Hist. Assn., Am. Assn. Univ. Profs., Phi Beta Kappa. Contbr. articles in field of econs. Home: Princeton, N.J. †

HOWELL, MARION GERTRUDE, dean; b. Freeport, O., Sept. 26, 1887; d. John Gilmore, M.D., and Mary Jane (Knox) H.; Ph.B., Coll. of Wooster, O., 1912, LL.D., 1942; diploma in nursing, Lakeside Hosp. Sch. of Nursing, Cleveland, Oh., 1920; M.Sc., and certificate in pub. health nursing, Western Reserve U., 1921, L.H.D., 1948. Sch. nurse, instr. English and pub. health nursing, 1912-23, asst. prof., asso. prof., prof. pub. health nursing, Sch. Applied Social Scis. Western Reserve University, acting dir., and dir. Univ. Pub. Health Nursing Dist., 1923-32; dir. of Nursing Service, Univ. Hosps., 1932-38, prof. of pub. health nursing, dean, Sch. of Nursing, 1932-46, dean emeritus. Mem. American Nurses Association, National Orgn. for Pub. Health Nursing, Nat. League of Nursing Edn., Am. Assn. of Univ. Women, Delta Delta Delta, Phi Beta Kappa. Home: Beaver Falls, Pa. †

HOWERY, BILL NELSON, railway exec.; b. Cherokee, Iowa, May 6, 1915; s. Robert Richard and Ossie Margaret (Nelson) H.; m. Geraldine Louise Francisco, June 6, 1937; children—Judith, William, Sandra, Nancy, Robert. Grad., Advanced Mgmt. Program, Harvard, 1956. With C.G.W.R.R., 1936-60, beginning as brakeman, successively condr., asst. trainmaster, trainmaster, asst. supt., asst. gen. mgr., 1936-57, gen. mgr., 1957-60; v.p., gen. mgr. St. Paul Union Depot & Minn. Transfer Ry. Co., 1960-64, Mpls., Northfield & So. Ry., 1964-80. Clubs: Masons, Mpls. Athletic. Home: Deerwood, Minn. Deceased.

HOWLEY, LEE CHRISTOPHER, lawyer; b. Cleve., June 16, 1910; s. Christopher J. and Emily A. (Smith) H.; m. Jean H. Hauserman, June 5, 1937; children—Tim (dec.), Dan, Kate, Lee, Tom. B.A., Wittenberg Coll., 1932; LL.B., Western Res. U., 1935. Bar: Ohio bar 1935. Practiced in, Cleve., 1935-39, asst. U.S. dist. atty., 1939-45, law dir., City of Cleve., 1945-51; v.p., gen. counsel Cleve. Electric Illuminating Co., 1951-75; partner firm Weston, Hurd, Fallow, Paisley & Howley, 1975-83; chmn. bd. Elyria Spring & Splty. Co.; dir. E.F. Hauserman Co., Wright Airlines, Inc., Wenham Trucking Co.; chmn. bd. Revco, D.S., Inc., 1969-83; trustee U.S. Realty Investments. Past pres., dir. Catholic Charities Corp.; mem. exec. com., past pres., past dir. Cleve. Conv. and Visitors Bur.; past bd. dirs. Kaiser Found. Health Plans, Hosps.; past chmn. bd. dirs. Kaiser Community Health Found. Recipient certificate of recognition for achievements in field of good govt. Cleve. U.S. Jr. chambers commerce, 1954; named hon. commr. Cleve. Mounted Police; hon. bn. chief City of Cleve. Fire Dept. Mem. Am., Ohio, Cuyahoga County, Cleve. bar assns., Ohio C. of C., Ducks Unlimited (past pres.), Phi Gamma Delta, Delta Theta Phi. Clubs: Cleveland Athletic, City, Union, Vermilion Yacht. Home: Vermilion, Ohio. Died Jan. 7, 1983.

HOY, WILLIAM EDWIN, prof. biology; b. of Am. parents, Sendai, Japan, Aug. 23, 1890; s. William Edwin and Mary Belle (Ault) H.; stud. Mercersburg (Pa.) Acad., 1905-07; A.B., Franklin and Marshall Coll., 1911; Ph.D., Princeton U., 1917; m. Mabel Elizabeth George, Nov. 2, 1918; children—William Edwin, Mary Camilla. Instr. biology, U. of Rochester, N.Y., 1915-18; prof. biology, Presbyterian Coll., Clinton, S.C., 1919-29; prof. biology and head of dept., U. of S.C., from 1929. Served in Med. Dept., U.S. Army, 1918-19. Fellow A.A.A.S., S.C. Acad. Science (pres. 1927); mem. Am. Soc. Zoölogists, Am. Assn. Anatomists. Editor: U.S.C. Series III, Biology. Home: Columbia, S.C. †

HOYT, GILE CALVERT, business exec.; b. Ida Grove, Ia., August 28, 1889; s. C. L. and Ida (Bowland) H.; ed. high school and business courses; m. Constance Furlonge, 1922. With Internat. Harvester Co. and affiliated companies since 1916. Protestant. Home: Chicago, Ill. †

HOYT, HOMER, cons., real estate economist; b. St. Joseph, Mo., June 14, 1895; m. Gertrude O'Neill, Aug. 13, 1941; 1 son, Michael. A.B., U. Kans., 1913, A.M., 1913; J.D., U. Chgo., 1918, Ph.D. in Econs, 1933; LL.D. (hon.), Marymount Coll. Va., 1981. Bar: Ill., D.C., U.S. Supreme Ct. bars. Instr. econs. Beloit Coll., 1917-18; economist War Trade Bd., Washington, 1918-19; prof. econs. U. Del., 1919-20; statistician Am. Tel. & Tel. Co., N.Y.C., 1920-21; asso. prof. econs. U. N.C., 1921-23, U. Mo., 1924-25; real estate broker, economist, Chgo., 1925-34; prin. housing economist FHA, 1934-40; dir. research Chgo. Plan Commn., 1941-43; dir. econ. studies Regional Plan Assn., N.Y.C., 1943-46; pres. Homer Hoyt Assos., Washington, 1946-84; Vis. prof. land econs. Mass. Inst. Tech., Columbia, 1944-46. Author: One Hundred Years of Land Values in Chicago, 1933, Structure and Growth of Residential Neighborhoods in American Cities, 1939, World Urbanization, 1962, According to Hoyt, 1966, rev., 1970, (with Arthur M. Weimer) Real Estate, 1939, rev., 1948, 54, 60, 66, (with Arthur M. Weimer and George F. Bloom), 1972, 78, Urban Land Use Requirements 1968-2000, 1968, People, Profits, Places, 1969; Cons. editor: Land Econs; Contbr. numerous articles to profl. jours. Recipient award Nat. Assn. Ind. Fee Appraisers, 1974, Distinguished Service citation U. Kans., 1976, Distinguished service award Internat. Frat. Land Econs., 1976; Ind. U. Inst. Real Estate and Applied Urban Econs. fellow, 1976. Mem. Am. Inst. Real Estate Appraisers (George L. Schmutz award 1964), Am. Econ. Assn., Am. Statis. Assn., Am. Hist. Assn., Washington Real Estate Bd., Fairfax C. of C., Phi Beta Kappa, Lambda Alpha (Urban Affairs award 1971), Delta Sigma Rho. Address: Washington, D.C. Died Nov. 29, 1984; buried Chgo.

HOYT, VANCE JOSEPH, author, naturalist and motion picture dir.; b. Arkansas City, Kan., Apr. 27, 1889; s. Edward and Ella (Hoyt) Blubaugh; father killed during opening of Okla.; adopted by maternal grandfather, Edw. Jonathan Hoyt ("Buckskin Joe"); student Southwestern Coll., Winfield, Kan., 1 yr.; musician (band and theatre orchestra), 1906-14; Coll. of Osteopathic Physicians and Surgeons, Los Angeles, Calif., 1910-14, D.O., 1914; M.D., Pacific Med. Coll., 1915; married to Ruth Luella Ulm; one son, Albert Jonathan. Practicing physician, 1916-32. Author of nature features, Los Angeles Times, 1930-31; conductor of column, "Walks and Talks with Nature," in Los Angeles Illustrated News, 1931-32; nature column, Rob Wagner's Script, 1930-39. Mem. Iota Tau Sigma, Screen Writer's Guild, Sierra Club. Author nature-novels, latest: Monarch of The Sierra, 1945; Whispering Giants, 1953. Author and tech. dir. of motion picture Sequoia, 1935, Bar-Rac's Night Out, 1936, etc. Platform and radio lecturer on nature and North Am. wild-life; teacher nat. defense subjects for Los Angeles Bd. of Edn., 1940-45; asso. with William R. Lasky in writing, producing and directing nature and wild animal films for theaters, TV, schs., 1949-50; with Douglas Aircraft Co., Inc., 1943; med. dir., safety engr. Mar Vista Engring. Co., Los Angeles, 1950-52; freelance author short stories and articles in Sat. Eve. Post, Coronet, This Week, Esquire, Argosy, Nature Mag., etc., from 1943. Author: The Doctor Goes Wild (biography), 1957. Home: West Los Angeles, CA. †

HUBBARD, ORVILLE LISCUM, city ofcl.; b. Union City, Mich., Apr. 2, 1903; s. Ralph Star and Sylvia Elizabeth (Hart) H.; student Ferris State Coll., 1925-26; LL.B., Detroit Coll. Law, 1932; extension courses Henry Ford Community Coll., U. Mich.; m. Fay Velma Cameron, July 20, 1927; children—James, Frank, Nancy Anne, John Jay, Henry Ford. Admitted to Mich. bar, 1932; stenographer Ford Motor Co., 1925; reporter Wall Street Jour., 1929-34; U.S. Army reserve officer, 1930-37; Mich. state trooper, 1942-45; asst. Atty. Gen. Mich., 1939-40; mayor of Dearborn, Mich., 1942-74. Republican precinct del., from; mem. Wayne County Bd. Suprs., 1942-68; del. Rep. Nat. Conv., 1952, alternate del., 1940. Served as sgt. USMCR, 1922-25. Recipient Distinguished Citizen award Dearborn C. of C., 1962. Mem. Dearborn Bar Assn. (pres.). Republican. Club: Dearborn Exchange. Holder nat. record longest full-time mayor. Founder first out-of-state apt. bldg. for retirees, Dearborn Towers, Clearwater, Fla., also Camp Dearborn. Home: Dearborn, Mich.

HUBENKA, LLOYD JOHN, educator; b. Omaha, Jan. 1, 1931; s. Lloyd John and Emma (Dobrovolny) H.; B.A., Creighton U., 1952, M.A., 1959; Ph.D., U. Neb., 1966; m. Beverly Ann Conkling, Feb. 14, 1953; children—Jayne, Evan, Naomi, Sara. Faculty, Creighton U., Omaha, from 1958, asso. prof., 1966-68, prof., from 1968, chmn. English dept., from 1966; pres. Harcum Jr. Coll. Served to col. U.S. Army, 1952-54; Korea. Decorated Commendation medal. Fellow Nat. Endowment for Humanities, 1968. Mem. Modern Lang. Assn., Nat. Council Tchrs. English, Assn. Depts. English, A.A.U.P. Editor: Unto This Last (John Ruskin), 1968; (with R. Garcia) The Design of Drama, 1973; (with R. Garcia) The Narrative Sensibility, 1975; Practical Politics (Bernard Shaw), 1976. Home: Omaha, Nebr. Died Aug. 18, 1982.

HUBERT, ERNEST E., chief pathologist; b. Philipsburg, Mont., Sept. 17, 1887; s. Henry and Marie H.; student U. of Calif., 1906-08, Mont. State Sch. of Mines, 1909; B.S. in Forestry and Botany, U. of Mont., 1912, M.S., 1918; Ph.D., U. of Wis., 1923; m. Bess Ann Rhoades, Oct. 13, 1915; children—Douglas E., David L. Lab. asst. Botany and Forestry Dept., 1911-12, prof. forestry, charge forest products lab., Sch. of Forestry, U. of Ida., 1925-35; research technologist Western Pine Assn., 1935-42; chief pathologist, I. F. Laucks, Incorporated, from 1942, Monsanto Chemical Company, from 1945; research pathologist University of Idaho from 1949. Editor Northwest Science, 1930-35. Mem. A.A.A.S., Soc. Am. Foresters, Northwest Scientific Assn., Sigma Xi, Phi Sigma, Xi Sigma Pi, Sigma Chi. Winner of C.A. Duniway prize in forestry, U. of Mont., 1911. Author: Outline of Forest Pathology, 1931. Contbr. numerous papers and bulls. on forest pathology. Home: Moscow, Idaho. †

HUBSHMAN, HENRY MARTIN, factor and comml. banker; b. N.Y.C., May 26, 1888; s. Bernard and Sara (Polock) H.; ed. City Coll. N.Y.; m. Sylvia J. Cohn, June 24, 1919; children—Jeanne D. (Mrs. Arnold M. Bergson), Henry Martin. Founder, chmn. Hubshman Factors Corp., N.Y.C., 1915-61; company merged with Canteen Corp. Am., 1961; acquired from Canteen Corp. by First Nat. City Bank N.Y., 1965, cons. Hubshman factors dept. Founder, pres. Henry and Sylvia Hubshman Found.; founder factors group Fedn. Jewish Philanthropies Socs.; past chmn. factors group Gt. N.Y. Fund. Hon. mem. Phila. Textile Coll. Civilian Service award U.S. Army. Chief contract re-negotiation sect. Price Adjustment Bd., 1942-43. Mem. Am. Arbitration Soc., Carolina Yarn Assn., Nat. Fedn. Textiles, Nat. Knitted Outerwear Assn., N.Y. Credit and Financial Mgmt. Assn., Uptown Credit Group. Clubs: Harmonie, Manhattan (N.Y.C.); Metropolis Country. Home: New York, N.Y. †

HUDDLESTON, CLARENCE J., banker; b. Ontonagan County, Mich., July 2, 1889; s. John H. and Anna (Johnston) H.; LL.B., Detroit Coll. of Law, 1916; m. Helen Adele Crotty, Oct. 16, 1918 (dec.); 1 son, James P. With Calumet & Hecla Mining Co. (Mich.), 1910-12, chem. lab., Dollar Bay, Mich., 1912-13; staff law office W. H. Wetherbee, A. M. Henry & Burns Henry, Detroit, 1913-16, Wasey, Christie & Martz, Detroit, 1916; with Anderson, Wilcox, Lacy, Detroit, 1916-43, mem. firm Anderson, Wilcox, Lacy & Lawson, 1927-43; exec. v.p. Wabeek State Bank of Detroit, 1943-55, also dir.; exec. v.p. Detroit Wabeek Bank & Trust Co., 1955-56, also dir.; sr. v.p. Detroit Bank & Trust Co., from 1956; dir. Parker Rust Proof Co., Detroit. Chmn. indsl. com. Detroit Tomorrow Com. Dir. Oakland Housing Corp. Mem. Am., Mich., Detroit bar assns., Judicature Soc. Clubs: Detroit Golf, Detroit, Hundred, Recess, Economic (Detroit). Home: Detroit, Mich. †

HUDDLESTON, ERIC TREVOR, architect; b. Winchester, Ind., Feb. 5, 1888; s. Albert Fausdick and Laura Belle (Green) H.; B.Arch., Cornell, 1910; m. Mabel Sprague, June 14, 1913; children—John Sprague, Eric Trevor. Various positions archtl. offices, Chgo., Dayton, O., 1910-14; head dept. drawing U. N.H., 1914, established archtl. dept., 1919, mem. faculty archtl. dept. from 1919, coll. architect, 1919-49, mem. campus planning bd.; assn. I.W. Hersey Asso., Durham, from 1935; projects include Durham Post Office block, Dunfey block, schs. and pub. bldgs. throughout N.H.; asst. treas. Durham Realty Co., 1948-53; dir. Durham Trust Co., 1948-53. Fellow A.I.A. (1st pres. N.H. chpt. 1948); mem. N.H. Soc. Architects (1st pres. 1935), Phi Kappa Phi. Gargoyle. Mason (Shriner). Home: Durham, N.H. †

HUDELSON, EARL, professor edn.; b. Princeton, Ind., Oct. 16, 1888; s. William Crawford and Nancy Virginia (McClure) H.; B.A., Ind. U., 1911, M.A., 1912; Ph.D., Columbia, 1923; m. Helena Houf, Feb. 24, 1915; children—Virginia Louisa, William Henry. Instr. in English, Ind. U., 1911-12, Tome Sch., Port Deposit, Md., 1912-14; critic in English, Univ. High Sch., Bloomington, Ind., 1914-18; asst. in English, Teachers' Coll. (Columbia), 1918-19; prof. secondary edn., W.Va., U., 1920-23; prof. edn., U. of Minn., 1923-30; dean of Coll. of Edn., West Va. Univ., 1930-45, prof. edn. from 1946; U.S. War Dept. ednl. consultant, European Theater of Operations, 1945-46; teacher, summers, Indiana Univ., Teachers' Coll. (Columbia), univs. of Mich., Chicago and Minn., etc. Mem. N.E.A., Nat. Soc. for Study of Edn., Phi Beta Kappa, Phi Delta Kappa, Kappa Delta Pi. Author, collaborator, editor: latest publ.: Manual on Thesis Writing, 1949. Home: Morgantown, W.Va. †

HUDNUT, WILLIAM HERBERT, JR., clergyman; b. Youngstown, Ohio, May 29, 1905; s. William Herbert and Harriet (Beecher) H.; m. Elizabeth Kilborne, Nov. 21, 1931; children: William Herbert III, Robert Kilborne, David Beecher, Stewart Skinner, Harriet Hudnut Halliday, Thomas Cushman. A.B., Princeton U., 1927, D.D., 1967; B.D., Union Theol. Sem., 1930; D.D., Blackburn Coll., 1940; LL.D., Huron Coll., 1960; L.H.D., Pikeville Coll., 1964. Dir. religion The Hill Sch., Pottstown, Pa., 1930-32; pastor Glendale Presbyn. Ch., Cin., 1932-40, 1st Presbyn. Ch., Springfield, Ill., 1940-46, 3d Presbyn. Ch., Rochester, N.Y., 1946-64; nat. chmn. Presbyn. 50 Million Fund, 1964-67; interim pastor Chevy Chase (Md.) Presbyn. Ch., 1967-69, 1st Presbyn. Ch., Evanston, Ill., 1970, Brick Ch., N.Y.C., 1970-72, 2d Presbyn. Ch., Indpls., 1972-74; interim pastor 1st Presbyn. Ch., Phoenix, 1975-76, Hastings, Nebr., 1977, Brick Ch., N.Y.C., 1977-78, 1st Presbyn. Ch., Glens Falls, N.Y., 1978-80; Dir. McCormick Theol. Sem., Chgo., 1942-49. Pres. Westminister Found. N.Y., 1947-53; mem. nat. student com. YMCA, 1946-57; mem. Presbyn. U.S.A. Gen. Council, 1950-58, 64-67; Bd. dirs. Union Sem., N.Y., 1957-75; mem. bd. Nat. Missions Presbyn. Ch. U.S.A., 1962-64; trustee Ill. Coll., 1943-46, Wilson Coll., 1967-70. Clubs: Princeton (N.Y.C.); Rochester City (pres. 1952-53). Home: North Creek, N.Y. Died May 31, 1985.

HUDSON, HERBERT EDSON, JR., environ. engr.; b. Chgo., Sept. 21, 1910; s. Herbert Edson and Etta May (Dow) H.; m. Annabelle Woods, May 28, 1932; children—Herbert Edson, Kenneth Alan. Jr. B.S., U. Ill., 1931. San. engr. Chgo. Water Dept., 1931-41, designer, 1941-42, filtration engr., 1945-46; research asso. U. Ill., 1942-44; head engring. subdiv. Ill. Water Survey, 1946-55; asso. Hazen and Sawyer Engrs., Detroit, 1955-57, partner, 1957-71; pres. Water and Air Research, Inc., Gainesville, Fla., 1971-83; adj. prof. U. Fla. Author: Water Clarification Processes, 1981. Served with C.E. U.S. Army, 1944-45. Recipient Water Resource, Water Quality Research award Am. Water Works Assn., 1966, Diven medal, 1967, Fuller award, 1943, Research award, 1976. Fellow ASCE, Am. Inst. Chemists; mem. Nat. Acad. Engring., Am. Acad. Environ. Engrs. (diplomate, pres. 1968-69), Am. Water Works Assn. (hon. mem., dir. 1961-73, chmn. water resources div. 1955-56, chmn. water quality div. 1961-62), Am. Geophys. Union, Asociacion Interamericana de Ingenaria Sanitaria, Sigma Xi, Tau Beta Pi. Unitarian. Home: Gainesville, Fla. Died Sept. 13, 1983.

HUDSON, HINTON GARDNER, lawyer; b. Smithfield, N.C., Nov. 1, 1896; s. James Buchanan and Sarah Agnes (Woodall) H.; A.B., U. N.C., 1916; LL.B., Harvard, 1919; m. Margaret Baggs, Aug. 6, 1927; children—Margaret (Mrs. John M. Blades), Hinton Gardner, Gordon L. Admitted to N.C. bar, 1919, since practiced in Winston-Salem; sr. partner firm Hudson, Petree, Stockton, Stockton & Robinson, 1958-79; of counsel, 1979; lectr. law Wake Forest Coll., 1963. Mem. N.C. Gen. Statutes Commn., 1960-70, chmn., 1967-70. Rep. Gen. Assembly N.C., 1943. Trustee Lees-McRae Coll., 1966-70. Served with USN, 1918. Recipient spl. resolutions of commendation for 10 years service on N.C. Gen. Statutes Commn. (including rewriting of Rules Civil Procedure 1st time since 1868), from N.C. Gen. Assembly, N.C. State Bar and N.C. Bar Assn., 1970. Mem. Am., N.C., Forsyth County (past pres.), Forsyth County Jr. (a founder, past pres.) bar assns., N.C. State Bar (councillor 1959-68), Phi Beta Kappa. Democrat. Methodist. Clubs: Forsyth Country (pres. 1957), Twin City, Winston-Salem Torch. Home: Winston-Salem, N.C. Died July 7, 1979.

HUDSON, JOHN ALLEN, librarian; b. Beaumont, Tex., May 14, 1927; s. Walter Byron and Bessie (Aman) H.; m. Genevieve Lynch, Jan. 3, 1948; 1 dau., Lourdes Marie. B.A., U. Tex. at Austin, 1951, M.A., 1954; M.L.S., Case Western Res. U., 1957. Librarian journalism and newspaper collection U. Tex. at Austin, 1951-54; state dir. library extension Tex. State Library, Austin, 1954-56; univ. librarian U. Tex. at Arlington, 1957-84, dir. Ctr. Mesoam. Studies, 1982-84, project dir. micro-filming of Yucatecan archives, 1976-83, project dir. preservation of archives of Honduras, 1981-84. Author: (with George Wolfskill) All but the People: Franklin D. Roosevelt and His Critics, 1933-39, 1969. Trustee Arlington Pub. Library. Served with USNR, 1944-45. Mem. Am., Southwestern, Tex. library assns.; mem. Texas Council State Coll. Librarians (pres. 1968-84); Mem. Am. Hist. Assn., Southwestern Social Sci. Assn. Home: Arlington, Tex. Died May 23, 1984.

HUDSON, ROBERT ANGELO, merchant; b. Portland, Ore., July 27, 1887; s. Robert Milton and Emma (Johnson) H.; m. Daisy Ferry, Dec. 15, 1926; children—John Henry, Patricia (Mrs. John Misko). With Hudson House, Inc., from 1907, chmn. bd., from 1964; dir. Hudson Stores Co., Gray Co., Irish Stores Co., Patty Dau Co. Mem. adv. bd. Profl. Golfers Assn.; v.p. Profl. Golfers Assn. Great Britain; mem. Com. Twenty Five, Palm Springs, Cal. Named Golfer of Year, 1947; recipient Walter Hagen award, 1966. Mem. Pacific Northwest Golf Assn. Elk, Mason (Shriner). Clubs: Portland Golf; Thunderbird Golf and Country (Palm Springs, Cal.); Oswego (Ore.). Home: Portland, Ore. †

HUDSON, WILLIAM NOEL, educational administrator; b. Taylorville, Ill., Oct. 7, 1912; s. William and Lillie (Freeman) H.; B.A., James Millikin U., 1938; postgrad. George Williams Coll., 1939, Columbia, 1944; m. Margaret Ann Waldron, July 24, 1939; children—Judith Ann (Mrs. Glenn T. Dallas), Joda Sue (Mrs. David F. Marano). Sec., Decatur (Ill.) YMCA, 1933-38; gen. supt. Chgo. Boys Clubs, 1938-42; dir. operations U.S.O., N.Y.C., 1942-45; exec. v.p., asst. treas. Fedn. Protestant Welfare Agys., N.Y.C., 1945-54; exec. v.p. Protestant Childrens Service, N.Y.C., 1946-48; exec. dir. Protestant Fund Greater N.Y., 1947-48; acting exec. dir. Welfare Council N.Y.C., 1950-51; adminstrv, v.p. Tamblyn & Brown, Inc., pub. relations, N.Y.C., 1954-60, v.p. for devel. Rensaelaer Poly. Inst., 1960-64; dir. devel. Colgate U., 1964-68; v.p. devel. and relations Niagara (N.Y.) U., from 1968. Pres., N.Y. State Welfare Conf., 1952-54; mem. N.Y.C. Commn. Foster Care Children, 1947-54, Greater N.Y. Fund Distbn. Com., 1947-54, Mayor N.Y.C. Com. Pub. Assistance, 1948-49; reconstrn. com. Welfare Council N.Y.C., 1949-50; dir. federated hosp. campaign, Camden, N.J., 1956-57, program for united engring. center at UN Plaza, 1957-58. Mem. Pub. Relations Soc. Am., Nat. Assn. Social Workers, Sigma Alpha Epsilon, Alpha Omega. Rotarian. Clubs: Engineers' Bankers, N.Y., Athletic (N.Y.C.); Niagara Falls Country, Niagara. Home: Lewiston, N.Y. Deceased.

HUESTON, ETHEL, author; b. Southeastern Ia., Dec. 3, 1887; d. Rev. C. W. and Julia Anne (Buell) Powelson; Ph.B., Ia. Wesleyan Coll., Mt. Pleasant, Ia., 1909; m. Rev. William J. Hueston, 1910 (died 1915); 1 daughter, Buell; m. 2d, Lieut. E. J. Best, of 115th U.S. Engineers Corps, August 13, 1917 (died April 30, 1919); m. 3d, Randolph Blinn (died February 4, 1943). Member Authors' League of America, Pi Beta Phi. Presbyterian. Clubs: Woman's Press, Woman's College (San Diego, Calif.); Ia. Press and Authors' Club. Author: Prudence of the Parsonage, 1915; Prudence Says So, 1916; Sunny Slopes, 1917; Leave It to Doris, 1919; Eve to the Rescue, 1920; Merry O, 1923; Prudence's Daughter, 1924; Coasting Down East, 1924; Swedey, 1925; Idle Island, 1926; Ginger Ella, 1927; Ginger and Speed, 1928; The People of This Town, 1929; Birds Fly South, 1930; For Ginger's Sake, 1930; Rowena Rides the Rumble, 1931; Good Times, 1932; That Hastings Girl, 1933; Blithe Baldwin, 1933; Beauty for Sale, 1934; Star of the West, 1935; Man of the Storm, 1936; A Roof Over Their Heads, 1937; Calamity Jane of Deadwood Gulch, 1937; High Bridge, 1938; The Honorable Uncle Lancy, 1939; Uncle Lancy for President, 1940; Preacher's Wife, 1941; This One Kindness, 1942; Drink to Me Only, 1943; Mother Went Mad on Monday, 1944; No Shortage of Men, 1945; Heaven and Vice Versa, 1946; Please, No Paregoric, 1947; All About Marriage, 1948; The Reverend Mister Red, 1949; The Family Takes A Wife, 1950; Brotherly Love, Unlimited, 1951. Home: (winter) 88 North Brook Street, Geneva, N.Y.; (summer) Fayson Lakes, N.J. Home: New York, N.Y. †

HUFF, ABNER, hosp. exec.; b. Harlan, Ky., June 12, 1937; s. Briscoe S. and Letha E. H.; m. Mary Louise Gutierrez, June 11, 1960; children—Andrea Louise, Jason Abner. B.S., Ariz. State U., 1963; M.B.A., U. Chgo., 1964. Resident Ohio State U. Hosp., 1964-65, adminstrv. asst., 1965-66; asst. adminstr. Southside Hosp., Mesa, Ariz., 1966-67, adminstr., 1967-68, Notre Dame Hosp. and Med. Center, Phoenix, 1968-70, St. Joseph's Hosp. and Med. Center, Phoenix, 1970-72, exec. dir., adminstr., 1972-76, pres., from 1976, dir., from 1973; bd. dirs. Central Ariz. Health Systems Agy., 1975-76; mem. Ho. of Reps. Adv. Commn. on Health Care Delivery, 1977; mem. ad hoc com. health care cost Ariz. Med. Assn., 1977. Served with U.S. Army, 1956-58. Mem. Health Execs. Group of Sisters of Mercy (chmn. 1977), Phoenix Regional Hosp. Council (pres. 1976), Am. Hosp. Assn. (alt. del. regional adv. bd.), Ariz. Hosp. Assn. (dir. from 1973, chmn. bd. 1978, pres.-elect from 1977, chmn. budget com. 1976-77, treas. 1976-77), Am. Coll. Hosp. Adminstrs. (Mead Johnson award 1965). Club: Ariz. Biltmore Golf. Home: Phoenix, Ariz.

HUFF, CLAY G., scientist; b. Cory, Ind., Sept. 10, 1900; s. Howard and Estella May (Coble) H.; student Ind. State Tchrs. Coll., 1918-21; A.B., Southwestern (Kan.) Coll., 1924; Sc.D., Johns Hopkins, 1927; m. Florence May Clark, Sept. 1, 1927; children—Eskin, Elaine. NRC fellow Harvard Med. Sch., 1928-83; asso. prof. zoology, U. Ga., 1927-28; asst. prof. parasitology U. Chgo., 1930-36, asso. prof., 1936-41 prof., 1941-47; dir. dept. parasitology Naval Med. Research Inst., Bethesda, 1947-69, ret., 1969; sci. writer, from 1969. Recipient Distinguished Civilian service awards Navy, Dept. Def., 1958. Fellow Royal Soc. Tropical Medicine and Hygiene (hon.); mem. Nat. Malaria Soc. (v.p. 1945-46), Am. Acad. Tropical Medicine (Theobald Smith award 1947, sec. 1949-52), Am. Soc. Tropical Medicine and Hygiene (pres. 1962-63, Le Prince award 1973 A.A.A.S., Sigma Xi. Author: Parasitology (with Hegner, Root, Augustine), 1938; A Manual of Medical Parasitology, 1943. Home: Charlottesville, Va. Died June 26, 1982.

HUFF, JOHN AMOS, clergyman; b. Ala., Mar. 29, 1887; s. Joshua Alexander and Elmira (Witt) H.; prep. edn., Scottsboro (Ala.) Inst., 1905-08; Howard Coll., Birmingham, Ala., 1909-14; D.D., Oklahoma Baptist Univ., Shawnee, 1937; m. Gertrude Boynton, Nov. 23, 1916; 1 dau., Helen. Ordained ministry Southern Bapt. Ch., 1907; student pastor, 1907-09; pastor successively at Haileyville, Ala., Kingfisher, Okla., and Oklahoma City until 1926, First Ch., New Orleans, 1926-37, First Ch., Chattanooga, Tenn., from 1937. Democrat. Mason. Home: Chattanooga, Tenn. †

HUFF, WILBERT JAMES, chemist, chem. and gas engr.; b. Butler, Pa., Oct. 4, 1890; s. Leonidas Martin and Mary Ann (Weidhas) H.; A.B., Ohio Northern U., 1911, D.Sc., 1927; A.B., Yale, 1914, Ph.D., in Chemistry, 1917; m. Rachel Smith, May 11, 1918. With Barrett Co. Research Lab., N.Y. City, 1917-18; research chemist U.S. Bur. Mines, 1919-20; in charge research div. Koppers Co., Labs., Pittsburgh, 1920-24; fellow Mellon Inst. Indsl. Research, 1921-24; prof. gas engring., Johns Hopkins U., 1924-37; prof. of chem. engring. and chmn. dept. chem. engring. U. of Md., from 1937, chmn. div. phys. scis., from 1938, mem. gen. adminstrv. bd., 1938-56, dir. engring. expt. station, from 1940; cons. practice; consulting chem. engr. Fuels and Explosives Div., Bur. of Mines, 1946-50, chief chemist explosives div., Bureau Mines 1935-57; consultant United States Dept. of Commerce, 1946-47, Army Chemical Corps from 1949, Served as lt. Chemical Warfare Service, comdg. Princeton Research Detachment, U.S. Army, 1918-19. Chairman Army-Navy Bureau of Mines Board on Storage of Smokeless Powder; member major disaster panel, safety and security div., Army Ordnance, dir. research for explosives div., Bureau of Mines, during World War II. Member of American Chemical Soc. (chmn. gas and fuel div. and mem. council, 1935), Am. Inst. Chem. Engrs. (chmn. Md. sect. 1935), Am. Gas Assn. (chmn. chem. com. 1931), Am. Assn., University Profs. (president, Maryland chpt. 1945-47), Am. Soc. Engring. Edn. (pres. nat. capitol area sect. 1956-57), Sigma Xi, Alpha Chi Sigma, Tau Beta Pi, Phi

Kappa Phi. Contbr. reports on researches to tech. publs. Home: Silver Spring, Md. †

HUFF, WILLARD LOUIS, corp. exec.; b. Rutledge, Mo., April 6, 1889; s. John and Catherine (Chapler) H.; student DePauw U., 1912; m. Lucretia Ross, Aug. 30, 1917; children—Ellen (Mrs. Samuel L. Powers), John R. Sec.-treas., dir. Honeywell Heating Specialties Co., Wabash, Ind., 1916-27; treas., dir Minneapolis-Honeywell Regulator Co. from 1927, treas., 1927-47, v.p., 1934-45, executive vice pres. from 1945; dir. First Nat. Bank of Minneapolis. Soo Line R.R. Co. Republican. Methodist. Clubs: Minneapolis, Minikahda, Woodhill. Home: Wayzata, Minn. †

HUFFMAN, ROBERT OBEDLAH, hosiery mfr.; b. Morganton, N.C., May 15, 1890; s. Samuel and Martha Ann (Hildebrand) H.; A.B., University of North Carolina, 1913, LL.D. (honorary), 1954; married Pearl Trogdon, Nov. 4, 1915; children—Pearl Trogdon, Anne Lancaster, Martha Roberta. Pres. Drexel (N.C.) Knitting Mills, 1935-56, chmn. board, 1956-59; pres. Drexel Enterprises, Inc. (formerly Drexel Furniture Co.), 1935-61, chmn., pres., from 1961; treas. Morganton Full Fashioned Hosiery Co., 1927-44, pres., 1944-58; pres. Huffman Full Fashioned Mills, Morganton, 1938-58; pres. Burke Farmers Cooperative Dairy, 1949-61; mem. exec. com. Jefferson Standard Life Ins. Co.; dir. all foregoing and other cos. Dir. Fed. Reserve Bank, Richmond, Va., 1955-60. Chief Men's Hosiery Unit, textile division, W.P.B., 1943; consultant on hosiery, OPA, 1944; chief hosiery and underwear section OPA, 1944; price executive manufactured articles branch, OPA, 1944; assistant director consumer soft goods division, OPS, 1951. Dir. Grace Hospital, Morganton. President Business Found. U.N.C., 1950-51. Mem. Nat. Assn. Hosiery Mfrs. (v.p. 1939), So. Hosiery Mfrs. Assn. (pres. 1933-34), Phi Beta Kappa. Republican. Baptist. Mason (32 deg., past master, Shriner). Clubs: Kiwanis; Biltmore Forest Country (Asheville, N.C.); Mimosa Hills Golf (Morgantown, N.C.). Home: Morgantown, N.C. †

HUFFMAN, WILLIAM PHILLIPS, business exec.; b. Dayton, O., June 26, 1890; s. Torrence and Annie Eliza (Beckel) H.; B.S., Denison U., 1911; m. Elizabeth M. Kiet, July 1, 1969. Accountant, Dayton Engring. Labs. Co., 1912-15; head order dept. Domestic Engring. Co., Dayton, 1916; sec.-treas. Buckeye Iron & Brass Works, Dayton, 1917-36, pres., 1936-65; pres. State Fidelity Fed. Savs. & Loan Assn., 1949-64, vice chmn., 1964-71; dir. City Transit Co., Midwest Securities Investment, Inc., Home Av. R.R. Co. Trustee, Woodland Cemetery Assn. Mem. Dayton C. of C., Sigma Chi. Clubs: Dayton City, Dayton Country,Moraine Country. Home:Dayton,OH. †

HUGGETT, GEORGE WILLIAM, chem. mfr.; b. Sutton, Eng., Sept. 1, 1889; s. William George and Turrell (Watts) H.; m. Elizabeth Cox Blanken, Apr. 4, 1923; 2 sons, Jr. clk., London, Eng., 1905-11; various positions Nobel's Explosives Co., Ltd., Glasgow, Scotland and affiliated firms (now Imperial Chem. Industries Ltd., London), 1911-28; with Canadian Industries, Ltd., 1928-54, v.p., treas., 1934-41, dir., 1938-51, mng. dir., 1941-49, pres., chmn., 1949-51, chmn., 1951-54; chmn. DuPont of Canada Securities, Ltd., DuPont Co. of Can., Ltd., from 1955. Clubs: Mount Royal Kanawaki Golf; St. James's; Forest and Stream, St. Andrew's Country. Home: Montreal, Can. †

HUGGINS, MALLOY ALTON, denominational exec.; b. Dillon Co., S.C., Oct. 5, 1890; s. A. R. F. and Alice (Lundy) H.; A.B., Wake Forest Coll., 1912, A.M., 1915, LL.D., 1949; A.M., University of North Carolina, 1929; graduate work Columbia, summers, 1916, 1922 and 1923; University of Paris, France, 1919; married Katiebet Morris, July 13, 1918; children—Minnie Morris, Katherine Elizabeth. High sch. prin., 1912-13; prof. of Latin and Greek, Union U., 1913-15; supt. of Clayton (N.C.) Schs., 1915-17; Scotland Neck (N.C.) Schs., 1919-24; sec. of edn. Bapt. State Conv. of N.C., 1924-29; gen. sec. and treas. since 1932; prof. of edn. Meredith Coll., Raleigh, N.C., 1929-32. Served as pvt. Machine Gun Co., 324th Inf., A.E.F., U.S. Army, World War. Ind. Democrat. Baptist. Clubs: History (Raleigh). Home: Raleigh, N.C. †

HUGHES, ARTHUR MIDDLETON, petroleum exec.; b. Holland, Texas, Apr. 7, 1889; s. Samuel Alexander and Mary Lula (Smith) H.; ed. pub. schs., Temple, Tex.; m. Elsie Tyson, June 6, 1921; children—Sara Beth, Anna Marie, Robert Samuel, John Frederick. Employed by Southwestern Oil Co., 1904-06, Watters Pierce Oil Co., 1906-18, Cities Service Oil Co., 1918-28; with Phillips Petroleum Co. from 1928, at Amarillo, Tex., 1928-32, Bartlesville, Okla., from 1932, vice pres. in charge of sales from 1937, mem. bd. dirs. from 1938. Served with U.S. Army, World War I. Mason (32 deg.). Clubs: Hillcrest Country (Bartlesville); Petroleum Industry. Home: Bartlesville, Okla. †

HUGHES, BERNARD J., financial editor; b. East Boston, Mass., Dec. 3, 1890; s. Peter Francis and Catherine Agnes (Brannan) H.; ed. parochial and pub. schs., East Boston, Clark Shorthand and Bus. Sch., Boston U., and Boston Conservatory of Music (Dept. of Dramatics); m. Gertrude Louise Glynn, Sept. 18, 1931; children—Muriel, Bernard, Gertrude. Began as financial service mesenger Boston News Bureau, 1903, filling positions as stenographer, sec., and cub financial reporter to 1914; asst. financial editor Boston Post, 1920-31, financial editor from 1931. Served in Adj. Gen.'s Office, Washington, 1914-17; with U.S. Army, 1919-20; with 1st Army Arty., France. Mem. Am. Legion, Izaak Walton League. Roman Catholic. K.C., Elk. Clubs: Wampatuck, Sportsmen's (Hingham). Home: Hingham, Mass. †

HUGHES, CHARLES E., III, architect; b. N.Y.C., Mar. 14, 1915; s. Charles E., Jr. and Marjorie Bruce (Stuart) H.; m. Gladys Christine Lindseth, Nov. 19, 1949 (div. 1960); m. 2d Kimberly Jean Wiss, Dec. 19, 1964. B.A. magna cum laude, Brown U., 1937; M.Arch., Harvard U., 1940. Designer Caribbean Archtl.-Engring., N.Y.C., 1941-42; Designer Skidmore Owings & Merrill, N.Y.C., 1946-53, assoc. ptnr., 1953-60; prin. Charles E. Hughes, AIA, N.Y.C., 1961-75; mng. Hughes, Cecil, Goodman, N.Y.C., 1975-82; prin. Charles E. Hughes, FAIA, N.Y.C., 1982-85; designers Manufacturers Trust, N.Y.C., 1954, Citybank, Kennedy Airport, 1959; v.p. N.Y. Bldg. Congress, N.Y.C., 1979-80. Trustee Corp.-Brown U., Providence, from 1955, later trustee emeritus; pres. Mcpl. Arts Soc. N.Y., 1968-70; v.p. Fine Arts Fedn. N.Y., 1971-73. Served to lt. USNR, 1942-46, PTO. Decorated Battle Star (12). Fellow AIA (chpt. pres. 1978-79); mem. Soc. Archtl. Historians, Phi Beta Kappa, Alpha Delta Phi. Club: Brown of N.Y. (past pres.). Home: New York, N.Y. Died Jan. 7, 1985.

HUGHES, CLAIR BRINTON, lawyer; b. Ashland, O., Mar. 7, 1889; s. Charles Z. and Berta (Brinton) H.; A.B., U. of Mich., 1912; J.D., 1914; m. Emma Stephenson, Nov. 12, 1921; children—Thomas Leland, Susanna Stephenson. Admitted to bar in Ohio and Mich., 1914, N.Y., 1920, to Supreme Court of U.S., 1921; practiced, Toledo, 1915-18, N.Y. City, from 1919. Asst. sec. clearance com. of War Industries Bd., 1918; asst. counsel War Finance Corpn., 1920-21; sec. Ry. Loan Advisory Com. to Federal Reserve Bd., 1921. Mem. Order of the Coif, Phi Gamma Delta, Phi Delta Phi. Republican. Clubs: Phi Gamma Delta (New York); University (Washington); Larchmont (N.Y.) Yacht. Home: Bronxville, N.Y. †

HUGHES, DANIEL THOMAS, anthropology educator; b. N.Y.C., Feb. 7, 1930; s. Thomas Joseph and Josephine (Rogers) H.; m. Violeta Cantos Peralta, June 20, 1969; 1 son, Eric. A.B., Bellarmine Coll., 1953, Licentiate in Philosophy, 1955, M.A. in Edn., 1956; S.T.B., Woodstock Coll., 1962; Ph.D., Cath. U. Am., 1967. Research assoc. Inst. Philippine Culture, Manila, 1967-68; asst. prof. dept. sociology and anthropology Ateneo de Manial, 1967-69; acting chmn. dept. Ateneo de Manila, 1968; research assoc. NRC-Nat. Acad. Sci., Washington, 1969-70; mem. faculty Ohio State U., Columbus, 1970-85, prof., chmn. dept. anthropology, 1976-85. Author: Political Conflict and Harmony on Ponape, 1970, (with Sherwood G. Lingenfelter) Political Development in Micronesia, 1974; editor: (with James A. Boutilier and Sharon W. Tiffany) Mission, Church and Sect in Oceania, 1978; contbr. articles to profl. jours. NIH grad. fellow, 1964-67; NIH research grantee, 1966; Nat. Endowment of Humanities research grantee, 1973; Ohio State U. research grantee, 1975, 83. Fellow Am. Anthrop. Assn., Assn. for Social Antropology in Oceania; assoc. Current Anthropology; mem. Assn. for Polit. and Legal Anthropology, Pacific Asian Studies Assn. Democrat. Roman Catholic. Home: Columbus, Ohio. Died Feb. 18, 1985.

HUGHES, EMMET JOHN, author, journalist, educator; b. Newark, Dec. 26, 1920; s. John L. and Grace (Freeman) H.; A.B. summa cum laude, Princeton, 1941; children by previous marriages John, Mary, Kathleen, Caitlin, Johanna. Press attache Am. embassy, Madrid, 1942-46; fgn. corr., chief Rome bur. Time-Life, 1946-48, chief Berlin bur., 1948-49; articles editor Life mag., 1949-52; speech writer nat. campaign Dwight D. Eisenhower, 1952; adminstrv. asst. to Pres. Eisenhower, 1953; spl. European corr. Life mag., 1954-56; speech writer Eisenhower campaign, 1956; mem. bd. editors Fortune mag., 1956-57; chief fgn. corr. Time-Life, 1957-60; sr. adviser pub. policy to Rockefeller Family, 1960-63; columnist Newsweek, 1963-68; spl. asst. to Gov. Nelson Rockefeller, N.Y.C., 1968-70; prof. politics Eagleton Inst., Rutgers U., 1970-82. Roman Catholic. Author: The Church and The Liberal Society, 1943; Report From Spain, 1947; America the Vincible, 1959; The Ordeal of Power, 1963; The Living Presidency, 1973. Home: Princeton, N.J. Died Sept. 19, 1982.

HUGHES, IVOR W., tobacco company executive; b. Porth, Eng., 1925. Student, Birmingham U., Oxford U. Chmn. bd., chief exec. officer Brown & Williamson Tobacco Corp., Louisville, until 1985. Home: Louisville, Ky. Died Mar. 22, 1985.

HUGHES, JIM, state ofcl.; b. Lehigh, Indian Ty., Mar. 27, 1890; s. Richard and Annie (Manley) H.; student, Wilburton Sch. Mines, 2 yrs.; m. Cena Banks, Aug. 9, 1924. Coal miner, 15 yrs.; state legislative rep. United Mine Workers of Am., 1918; factory insp. Okla. State Dept. of Labor, 1919, chief factory insp., 1926, asst. commr. labor, 1928, state commr. labor from 1946. Mem. Internat. Assn. Govt. Labor Ofcls. (dir.), Am. Soc. Safety Engrs. K.P. Home: Oklahoma City, Okla. †

HUGHES, JOSEPH P., grocery company executive; b. Atlantic City, N.J., 1906. Chmn. Hughes Markets Inc.; pres. Hughes Market No. 2, Inc.; Hughes Coldwater, Sherman Oaks, Calif.; dir. Certified Grocers of Calif. Ltd., Los Angeles, Spartan Grocers Inc., Hughes Realty, Inc. Bd. dirs. Los Angeles Beautiful. Mem. Food Employers Council (dir.). Died Dec. 24, 1982.

HUGHES, SARAH TILGHMAN, judge; b. Balt., Aug. 2, 1896; d. James Cooke and Elizabeth (Haughton) Tilghman; m. George E. Hughes, Mar. 13, 1922. A.B., Goucher Coll., 1917, LL.D., 1950; LL.B., George Washington U., 1922, LL.D., 1977; LL.D., So. Meth. U., Ind. State U., 1967, Wesleyan Coll., 1969, Mary Hardin-Baylor Coll., 1974; L.H.D., Clarkson Coll., 1975. Bar: Tex. 1922. Tchr. Salem Acad. and Coll., Winston-Salem, N.C., 1917-19; police woman Met. Police Dept. Washington, 1919-22; practiced in, Dallas, 1922-35; mem. Tex. Legislature, 1931-35; judge 14th Dist. Ct. of Tex., 1935-61; judge U.S. Dist. Ct., No. Dist. Tex., 1961-85, sr. judge. Active Nat. Fedn. Bus. and Profl. Women's Clubs, 1931-84, 1st. v.p., 1948-50, pres., 1950-52; v.p. Internat. Fedn. Bus. and Profl. Women, 1953-59; Past trustee Goucher Coll., Bishop Coll. Mem. State Bar of Tex., Am., Dallas bar assns., Am. Judicature Soc., Nat. Assn. Women Lawyers, AAUW, Phi Beta Kappa, Delta Sigma Rho, Kappa Beta Pi, Delta Gamma, Delta Kappa Gamma (hon.). Democrat. Episcopalian. Home: Dallas, Tex. Died Apr. 23, 1985. *

HUGHSTON, HAROLD VAUGHAN, lawyer; b. Tuscumbia, Ala., Aug. 15, 1915; s. Hubert H. and Lutie (Vaughan) H.; m. Lucy Caroline Allison, Sept. 18, 1948; children—Lutie Caroline, Lucy Ann, Harold Vaughan, James Dowlen. LL.B., U. Ala., 1940. Bar: Ala. bar 1940. Practiced in, Tuscumbia, 1940-42, 46-81; mem. firm Smith, Hughston & Tompkins, 1946-47; judge Colbert Law and Equity Ct., 1947; circuit judge 11th Jud. Circuit and 31st Jud. Circuit, 1948-55; mem. firm Kirk, Rather & Hughston, 1955-81; dir. Valley Fed. Savs. & Loan Assn., chmn. bd., 1977-81; dir. New Southland Nat. Life Ins. Co., Nat. Telephone of Ala., Inc.; Solicitor, Colbert County, 1942, city atty., Tuscumbia, 1965-81; atty. Colbert County Sch. Bd., 1965-73, Colbert County Commn., 1970-81. Mem. pres.'s cabinet U. Ala., chmn., 1977; chmn. Tuscumbia Bd. Edn., 1967-70, mem., 1970-73; v.p. U. Ala. Law Sch. Found., 1977-78, pres., 1979-81. Served to capt. Judge Adv. Gen. Corps AUS, 1942-46, ETO, MTO. Recipient Disting. Alumnus award U. Ala., 1978, Tutwiler Service award, 1979. Mem. ABA, Ala. Bar Assn., Colbert County Bar Assn., 31st Jud. Circuit Bar Assn. (pres. 1971), Ala. State Bar (bd. commrs., pres.-elect 1980-81), Farrah Law Soc., U. Ala. Law Sch. Alumni Assn. (pres. 1975-76), Nat. Alumni Assn. U. Ala. (pres. 1970-71), Newcomen Soc. N.Am., Bench and Bar, Kappa Alpha, Phi Delta Phi, Omicron Delta Kappa. Presbyn. (elder, trustee). Club: Kiwanian (dist. gov. 1955). Home: Tuscumbia, Ala. Died Nov. 20, 1981.

HUGO, RICHARD FRANKLIN, author, educator; b. Seattle, Dec. 21, 1923; s. Franklin James and Esther Clara (Monk) Hogan; m. Margaret Ripley Schamm, July 12, 1974; stepchildren—Matthew Ferdinand Hansen, Melissa Merrifield Hansen. B.A., U. Wash., 1948, M.A., 1952. With Boeing Co., 1951-63; prof. English, dir. creative writing U. Mont., from 1964. Author: A Run of Jacks, 1961, Death of the Kapowsin Tavern, 1965, Good Luck In Cracked Italian, 1969, The Lady in Kicking Horse Reservoir, 1973, What Thou Lovest Well, Remains American, 1975 (Theodore Roethks Meml. prize 1976), 31 Letters and 13 Dreams, 1977, The Triggering Town: Lectures and Essays on Poetry and Writing, 1979. Served with AC AUS, 1943-45. Decorated Air medal, D.F.C. Rockefeller Creative Writing grantee, 1967-68. Address: Missoula, Mont.

HULBURT, EDWARD OLSON, physicist; b. Vermilion, S.D., Oct. 12, 1890; s. Lorrain Sherman and Elizabeth (Dorey) H.; prep. edn., Boys' Latin Sch. and Jefferson Sch. for Boys, Baltimore, Md.; A.B., Johns Hopkins, 1911, Ph.D., 1915; m. Charlotte Teresa Howell, Jan. 31, 1920; children—Edward Macpherson, Elizabeth Anne. Carnegie research asst., Johns Hopkins, 1915-16; instr. in physics, Western Reserve U., 1916-17, Johns Hopkins, 1919-21; asst. prof. physics, State U. of Ia., 1921-23, asso. prof. 1923-24; physicist, supt. physical optics div. Naval Research Lab., 1924-49, dir. research, 1949-55. Sr. sci. U.S. Nat. Com. Internat. Geophys. Yr., 1956-58. Member eclipse expdns. Brazil, 1940, 47, Khartoum, 1952, Sweden, 1954. Lt. Signal Corps, A.E.F., France, 1917-18, capt., 1918-19. Fellow Am. Phys. Soc., Optical Soc., Am., A.A.A.S.; mem. Washington Philos. Soc., Am. Geophysical Union, Phi Beta Kappa, Ives Medal of Optical Society of America, 1955. Democrat. Episcopalian. Clubs: Portland (Me.) Yacht, West River (Md.) Yacht. Contbr. to Physical Rev., Jour. Optical Soc. of America, Science. Home: Alexandria, Va. †

HULL, HENRY WATTERSON, actor; b. Louisville, Ky., Oct. 3, 1890; s. William Madison and Elinor (Vaughn) H.; ed. pub. schs. of Louisville and N.Y. City, Cooper Inst. and Columbia U.; m. Juliet Fremont, Nov. 30, 1913; children—Henry F., Shelley F., Joan F. Actor since Oct. 10, 1911; appeared in (plays) The Man Who Came Back, Cat and the Canary, Grand Hotel, Tobacco Road, 39 East, Lulu Belle, The Ivory Door, Michael and Mary, Masque of Kings; (motion pictures) Great Expectations, Werewolf of London, Three Comrades, Boys Town, The Great Waltz, Jesse James, High Sierra, Deep Valley,

Fighter Command, Fountainhead, Colorado Bound. Home: Old Lyme, Conn. †

HULL, OSMAN RANSOM, prof. edn.; b. Fallbrook, Calif., Aug. 21, 1890; s. Linn Ransom and Mary Frances (Keith) H.; B.S., U. of Calif., 1913, M.S., 1914, Ph.D., 1925; student Columbia U., summer 1927; m. Evelyn May Huston, July 22, 1914; children—Evelyn Augusta (dec.), Osman Huston, Florence Eva, Frances Edith. Asst. instr. in physics, U. of Calif., 1912-14; prin. County High Sch., Crescent City, Calif., 1914-18; supt. schs., Sebastopol, Calif., 1918-20, Napa, 1920-24; asst. prof. edn., U. of Southern Calif., 1924-26, asso. prof., 1926-28, prof. ednl. adminstrn. from 1928, also chmn. dept. of edn. from 1926, dean sch. edn., 1946-53. Mem. N.E.A., Am. Assn. Sch. Adminstrs., Nat. Soc. for Study Edn., Am. Assn. Univ. Profs., Nat. Soc. Coll. Teachers of Edn., Calif. Teachers' Assn., Assn. Pub. Sch. Business Officials, Sigma Xi, Phi Delta Kappa (nat. pres.), Phi Kappa Phi. Presbyterian. Mason (K.T.). Clubs: University Faculty, Kiwanis. Writer on sch. topics, dir. school surveys. Home: Los Angeles, CA. †

HULL, THOMAS GORDON, educator; born in Southington, Conn., Dec. 21, 1889; s. Lewis Caleb and Frances Reynolds (Hinman) H.; Ph.B., Yale, 1913, M.S., 1915, Ph.D., 1916; m. Edna Louise Crittenden, June 16, 1917; 1 son, Gordon Crittenden. Asst., Am. Museum of Natural History, New York, N.Y., 1916-17; dir. of exhibits, U.S. Food Adminstrn., Washington, D.C., 1917-18; bacteriologist, Mass. Experiment Station, Amherst, Mass., 1919; dir. laboratories, Ill. State Dept. of Pub. Health, Springfield, Ill., 1920-30; dir. The Scientific Exhibit and sec. of council on the Scientific Assembly, Am. Med. Assn., Chicago, 1930-59; lecturer preventive medicine U. of Ill. College of Medicine, Chicago, 1927-60, asso. prof.; exec. dir. med. exhibits, Chicago Mus. Sci. and Industry, 1947-60; chmn. adv. com. Hinsdale Health Mus. 1958-60. Served as 1st lt., Sanitary Corps, U.S.A., 1918-19; lt., later capt., then major, Sanitary Reserve Corps, U.S. Army, 1920-37. Mem. nat. advisory com. Cleveland Health Museum; consultant Smithsonian Museum, Washington. Fellow American Public Health Assn. (affiliate) A.M.A.; mem. socs. of Am. and Ill. bacteriologists, Am. Vet. Med. Assn. (hon.), Sigma Xi. Mason. Club: Cummaquid Golf. Recipient gold medal for contbn. to Am. Medicine, 1946. Author: Diseases Transmitted from Animals to Man, 1930, rev. edit., 1961; Health Education of the Public (with Dr. William W. Bauer), 1937, rev. edit. 1942, Portuguese edit. 1943. Home: Yarmouth Port, Mass. †

HULSART, C. RAYMOND, newspaper exec.; b. N.Y.C., July 12, 1912; s. C. Raymond and Rosemarie (Reilley) H.; B.A., Dartmouth, 1934; LL.B., Harvard, 1937; m. Shirley L. Crandall, Feb. 7, 1942; children—Elizabeth Sharon, Barbara Jane, Asst. gen. counsel N.Y.C. R.R., 1937-47; sec. Amalgamated Textiles, Ltd., 1947-53; dir. labor relations and personnel N.Y. Times Co., N.Y.C., 1953-68, sec., 1968-77. Admitted to N.Y. bar, 1937. Served to lt. USNR, 1942-45. Mem. N.Y. Pubs. Assn. (chmn. 1964-65). Home: New York, N.Y. Died June 15, 1982.

HUNGERFORD, CYRUS COTTON, cartoonist; b. Manilla, Ind.; s. Addison J. and Florence (Cotton) H.; Dr. Arts, Washington and Jefferson Coll., 1945; m. Dorothy Evans, Nov. 29, 1966. Newspaper cartoonist Pitts. Sun, 1912-27, Pitts. Post-Gazette, 1927-77; European cartoon news assignments, 1923, 37, 47, 53. Recipient Nat. Headliners award, 1947; Freedoms Found award, 1953; Lincoln Nat. Life Found. award, 1957; Pitts. Jr. C. of C. award, 1957; award for excellence in journalism Gov.'s Com. 100,000 Pennsylvanians, 1970. Hon. mem. Omicron Delta Kappa, Sigma Delta Chi. Club: University. Home: Pittsburgh, Pa. Died May 25, 1983.

HUNSAKER, JEROME CLARKE, aeronautical engineer; b. Creston, Ia., Aug. 26, 1886; s. Walter J. and Alma (Clarke) H.; grad. U.S. Naval Acad., 1908; M.S., Mass. Inst. Tech., 1912, D.Sc., 1916; D.Sc., Williams College, 1943, Adelphi Coll., 1955; Doctor of Engineerng, Northeastern University, 1945; married Alice Porter Avery, June 26, 1911 (deceased 1966); children—Mrs. Sarah P. Swope, Jerome Clarke, James (dec.), Mrs. T.A. Bird. Officer, later advancing to comdr., Construction Corps, United States Navy, 1909-26; instructor of aeronautic engineering, Mass. Inst. Tech., 1912-16; in charge aircraft design, Navy Dept., Washington, D.C. designed airship Shenandoah, and flying boat NC4, (1st to fly Atlantic), 1916-23; asst. naval attaché, London, Paris, Berlin, Rome. 1923-26; asst. vice pres. Bell Telephone Laboratories (wire and radio services for airways), 1926-28; vice pres. Goodyear-Zeppelin Corp., 1928-33; head depts. aero. engring. and mech. engineerng MIT, 1933-51, then professor emeritus. Member of Guggenheim Medal Bd., Sperry Medal Bd. Regent Smithsonian Instn. Captain, USNR (ret.) Chmn. Nat. Adv. Com. Aeros., 1941-56. Awarded Navy Cross, Medal for Merit (U.S.); Legion on Honor (France); Daniel Guggenheim medal, Franklin medal; Wright Brothers medal; Godfrey L. Cabot Trophy, 1950; Langley Medal, 1955; Gold Medal of Royal Aeronautical Society (Great Britain), 1957; Navy award for distinguished public service, 1958. Fellow American Physical Society, American Academy Arts and Scis.; hon. fellow Inst. of Aero. Scis., Royal Aero. Soc. of Britain, Imperial Coll. of Sci. (London); hon. mem. Am. Soc. Mech. Engrs., Inst. of Mech. Engrs. (London); mem. Am. Soc. Naval Architects and Marine Engrs., Am. Soc. Automotive Engrs., Nat. Acad. of Scis., Am. Philos. Soc., Delta Kappa Epsilon, Sigma Xi. Clubs: Century (N.Y.C.); Army and Navy (Washington); St. Botolph (Boston). Contbr. to journals of profl. socs. Home: Boston, Mass. Died Sept. 10, 1984.

HUNT, ALFRED MORTIMER, aluminum company executive; b. Pitts., Apr. 2, 1919; s. Roy Arthur and Rachel McMasters (Miller) H. Grad., St. Paul's Sch., 1938; A.B., Yale U., 1942. With Massena (N.Y.) works Aluminum Co. Am., 1942-45, Massena (N.Y.) works Aluminum Co. Am. (New Kensington (Pa.) works), 1945-47, Massena (N.Y.) works Aluminum Co. Am. (Alcoa (Tenn.) works), 1948; With Massena (N.Y.) works Aluminum Co. Am. (Cleve. works), 1948-50, dir., 1949-84, asst. sec., 1950-52, sec., 1952-84, v.p., 1963-84; also mem. retirement bds.; dir. Alcoa Properties, Inc., Allendale Mut. Ins. Co. Mem. Carnegie Hero Fund Commn.; mem. sponsoring com. Allegheny Conf. on Community Devel.; Trustee Carnegie Inst., also chmn. finance com.; trustee emeritus Duke U.; trustee Roy A. Hunt Found., Hunt Found., Helen Clay Frick Found.; bd. dirs., v.p. Pitts. Regional Planning Assn.; bd. dirs. Alcoa Found., Pitts. History and Landmarks Found., Bishop's Fund; vice chmn. fin. and endowment com. Ch. of the Ascension, Pitts. Recipient F. Ambrose Clark Meml. award in steeplechasing, 1977. Mem. Masters of Foxhounds Assn. Am., Nat. Steeplechase and Hunt Assn. (sr.), Am. Inst. Mining and Metall. Engrs. (jr.), Newcomen Soc. Eng., Engrs. Soc. Western Pa., Pa. Horse Breeders Assn., Pa. Soc., Am. Soc. Metals, Am. Soc. Corp. Secs., Pitts. Bibliophiles, Berzelius, Rolling Rock Hunt Racing Assn. (co-chmn.), Chi Psi. Episcopalian. Clubs: Pitts. Golf (Pitts.), Fox Chapel Golf (Pitts.), Rolling Rock (Pitts.) (gov.), Duquesne, University (Pitts.), Allegheny Country (Pitts.), Harvard-Yale-Princeton (Pitts.); Brook (N.Y.C.), Yale (N.Y.C.); Chagrin Valley Hunt (Cleve.); Rolling Rock-Westmoreland Hunt (ex-master fox hounds). Home: Pittsburgh, Pa. Died Oct. 31, 1984.

HUNT, ARTHUR BILLINGS, baritone; b. Fargo, N.D., Feb. 2, 1890; s. Charles Joseph and Mary Electa (Perkins) H.; B.A., Macalester Coll., St. Paul, 1911; Mus.D., U. of Tenn., 1933; Mus.D., Macalester College, St. Paul, Minnesota, 1943; studied voice under masters; unmarried. Made début in St. Paul, 1911; teacher of voice; lecture-recitalist at Brooklyn Inst. Arts and Sciences, 1922-24; toured in U.S., Can. and Great Britain, 1921-26; dir. music Greater New York Fedn. of Chs., 1923-33; organizer of first radio choir, and radio singer WEAF, New York, from 1923; dir. music, Browning School for Boys, N.Y. City, 1933, 1934; musical dir. for weekly program, Nat. Broadcasting Co.; musical dir. First Presbyn. Ch., Forest Hills, L.I.; head of Voice Dept., Missionary Training Inst., Nyack, N.Y.; exec. sec. Nat. Hymn Sing Assn., Laymen's Nat. Fellowship (New York); dir. of music Friendly Hour, weekly, Old First Ref. Ch., Brooklyn. Teacher Y.M.C.A. war work sch., Silver Bay, Lake George, N.Y., 1917; building sec. Camp Upton Y.M.C.A., 1917; served 13 mos. overseas with Base Hosp. No. 37. Capt., Army of the U.S., since Nov. 1942, serving as music officer for European Theater of Operations. Citation and medal, Brit. Gen. Hosp., Glasgow, Scotland. Mem. Dutch Ref. Ch. Clubs: New York Musicians (The Bohemians), Town Hall. Folksong editor of "Singing"; founder of Hunt Library of first editions of music. Deceased.

HUNT, DANIEL, naval officer; b. Ripley, Miss., Oct. 4, 1889; s. Enoch Newton and Elizabeth (Murry) H.; student U. of Miss., 1905-09, Tulane U., 1910-11, Jefferson Med. Coll., 1911-12; m. Dorothy Chantler, Mar. 12, 1919; children—Daniel, Alfred Chantler. Entered Navy as med. officer, 1913; promoted through grades to rear adm., 1941, ret. 1950. Home: Tacoma, Wash. †

HUNT, EVERETT LEE, college prof.; b. Colfax, Ia., Oct. 14, 1890; s. Charles Reeve and Anna Belle (Johnson) H.; A.B., Huron (S.D.) Coll., 1913; M.A., U. of Chicago, 1921; m. Dorothy Rossman, June 24, 1919; 1 son, Alan Reeve. Instr. in debate and oratory, Huron Coll., 1913-18; asst. prof. public speaking, Cornell U., 1918-26; prof. rhetoric and oratory, Swarthmore Coll., from 1926; visiting prof, pub. speaking, U. of Ill., summer 1922, U. of Colo., summer sessions, 1928-31. Editor Quarterly Journal of Speech, 1927-30. Pres. Eastern Pub. Speaking Conf., 1922-24; mem. Nat. Assn. Teachers of Speech, Modern Lang. Assn. America, Am. Assn. Univ. Profs. Quaker. Club: Colorado Mountain (Boulder). Editor: (with A. M. Drummond), Persistent Questions in Public Discussion, 1924. Home: Swarthmore, Pa. Died Apr. 30, 1984.

HUNT, H(ARRISON) R(ANDALL), zoölogist; b. Conneaut, O., Mar. 7, 1889; s. Henry Harrison and Agnes Estelle (Howard) H.; B.S., summa cum laude, Allegheny College, Meadville, Pennsylvania, 1912; A.M., Harvard University, 1913, Ph.D., 1916; married Jane Myrtle Fisher, August 12, 1916; children—Howard Francis, Herve Henry, Althea Inez (Mrs. Hugh Sheehan), Edward Laurence, Margaret Agnes. Inst. zoölogy, W. Va. U., 1916-18, asst. prof., 1918-19, prof. biology and head dept. biol., teacher of embryology, Med. Sch., U. of Miss., 1919-23; prof. zoölogy and head zoölogy dept., head zoology sect. Mich. State U. Agr. Expt. Sta., 1923-54, prof. emeritus, 1954; tooth decay researcher USPHS. Chmn. finance com. Peoples Ch., East Lansing, Mich., 1925-30; pub. affairs com. Lansing Council of Chs., 1942-45; com. on diffusion of knowledge, Mich. Acad., 1927-32, com. on pub. welfare, Mich. Acad., 1932-48; mem. com. on human heredity, Nat. Research Council, 1935. Centenary Award, Michigan State U., 1955. Fellow American Assn. for Advancement of Science (former mem. council); mem. Am. Soc. Naturalists, Am. Soc. Zoölogists, Genetics Soc. Am., Central District Dental Society of Mich. (hon.), Internat. Assn. Dental Research, Human Genetics Soc., Mich. Acad. Sci., Arts, and Letters (chmn. zoology sect., 1926, v.p. 1927, pres. 1943), Sigma Alpha Epsilon, Phi Beta Kappa, Sigma Xi, Delta Sigma Rho, Phi Kappa Phi (pres. Mich. State Coll. chap., 1938, del. to nat. conv., 1938-40, Phi Sigma. Club: Inter-City Wranglers (pres. 1939). Author: A Laboratory Manual of The Anatomy of The Rat, 1924; Some Biological Aspects of War, 1930; also sci. papers tech. jours. Co-author of one chpt.: Advances in Experimental Caries Research (AAAS) 1955; A Symposium on Preventive Dentistry (Mosby), 1956; Genetics and Dental Health, 1962. Home: East Lansing, Mich. †

HUNTER, EDWIN RAY, coll. dean; b. New Salem, Pa., June 20, 1890; s. Alison and Mary Ellen (Wood) H.; student Greenville (Ill.) Coll., 1910-11; A.B., Maryville (Tenn.) Coll., 1914; A.M., U. of Chicago, 1917, Ph.D., 1925; m. Elva Grace Watkins, Aug. 10, 1916; children—Robert Alison, William Harold. Teacher East St. Louis (Ill.) High Sch., 1917-18; prof. English, Maryville (Tenn.) Coll. from 1918, dean curriculum 1930-56, chmn. division languages and literature, 1940-61. Member Modern Language Assn. of America, Shakespeare Assn. of America, Assn. Deans Southern Colls., Tenn. Folklore Soc. Democrat. Presbyn. Author: Shakspere and Common Sense, 1954. Home: Maryville, Tenn. †

HUNTER, FRANK O'DRISCOLL, army officer; b. Savannah, Ga., Dec. 8, 1894; s. John Heard and Fanny (O'Driscoll) H.; ed. Hitchkiss Sch., 1909-13; unmarried. Sergt., 1st lt., Aviation Sec., Officers' Res. Corps, 1917; commd. 1st lt., Aviation Sec., Signal Corps, regular army Nov. 28, 1920, advanced through grades to maj. gen., Nov. 30, 1943; served with 103d Aero Squadron, A.E.F., May 1917-Jan. 1919; officially credited with destruction of 8 enemy aircraft; wounded in action, June 2, 1918; 3 time member of Caterpillar Club; mil. observer and asst. air attache, Am. Embassy, Paris, and Am. Embassy, London, May-Oct. 1940. Comdg. gen., VIII Fighter Command. European Theater of Operations, May 1942-Aug. 1943; comdg. gen., First Air Force, Sept. 1943-Nov. 1945; retired as major gen. Mar. 1946. Decorated D.S.C. with 4 oak leaves, D.S.M., Legion of Merit, Silver Star, D.F.C., Purple Heart, Croix de Guette with palm (France), C.B.E. (British). Mem. Soc. of the Cincinnati (hon.). Clubs: Army and Navy (Washington, D.C.), Oglethorpe (Savannah, Ga.). Home: Savannah, Ga. Died June 12, 1982.

HUNTER, JAMES M., architect; b. Omaha, Nebr., Apr. 19, 1908; s. Edgar William and Ida L. (Bogue) H.; m. Madelyn J. Engleman, Feb. 5, 1937; children—John David, Janet Diane Hunter Powers. Student, Iowa State Coll., 1927-30; B. Arch., U. Ill., 1936. Registered architect, Colo., Wyo., Nebr. Practice architecture, 1940-76, cons., 1976—; firm James M. Hunter and Assos., Boulder, Colo., 1945-78; cons. architect, 1978—; planner, architect Colo. State U., Ft. Lewis Coll., Tarkio (Mo.) Coll., Regis Coll., Denver; architect in residence Am. Acad., Rome, 1963; vis. prof. architecture U. Colo.; Mem. adv. bd. Assn. Applied Solar Energy, U. Colo. Sch. Architecture; mem. pub. adv. panel on archtl. services GSA, 1965; chmn. archtl. jury HEW, 1966; profl. advisor to State Colo. in competition for Supreme Ct. and Heritage Bldgs. complex, 1975-76. Served as lt. (j.g.) USNR, World War II. Recipient award of merit AIA, 1955, regional awards, 1954, 55, 56, 57, 58, 60, 62, 65, 67; award N.Y. Archtl. League, 1954, 55; Church Archtl. Guild Am., 1956, 58. Fellow AIA (2d v.p. 1960-61, past nat. chmn. com. on edn., nat. chmn. com. on profession, regional dir. Rocky Mountain region 1964-67, past pres. Colo. chpt.), Am. Acad. in Rome; mem. Colo. Bd. Examiners of Architects (past pres.), Colo. Soc. Architects (past pres.). Club: Masons. Address: Boulder CO

HUNTER, JOHN ANDERSON, ret. univ. pres.; b. Donner, La., Apr. 23, 1914; s. John Anderson and Minnie Lee (Steinwinder) H.; B.S., Davidson Coll., 1934; M.A., La. State U., 1947, Ph.D., 1949; m. Doris Paine, June 12, 1937; children—David M., John Anderson. Tchr.-coach Gulf Coast Mil. Acad., 1934-37; geophysicist Stanolind Oil & Gas Co., 1937-39; ednl. adviser Civilian Conservation Corps., 1939-41; comdt. cadets Gulf Coast Mil. Acad., 1941-43; dir. classified personnel La. State U., 1947-49; supr. La. Dept. Edn., 1949-51; registrar La. State U., 1951-56, dean jr. div., 1956-59, dean student services, 1959-62, pres., 1962-72, prof. edn., 1959. Dir. Atlanta bd. Fed. Reserve Bank, 1964-69. La. coordinator So. Regional Edn. Bd., exec. com., 1962-66, commn. on higher ednl. opportunity in South, 1966-85; mem. Cabot Corp. Scholarship Com.; mem. Nat. Citizens Com. for Community Relations, 1964-85. Adv. bd. Our Lady of Lake Hosp., Baton Rouge. Served with USNR, 1943-46. Mem. Council So. Univs., So. Assn. Colls. and Schs. (pres. 1963-64), Am. Assn. Collegiate Registrars and Admissions Officers, So. Assn. Land-Grant Colls. and State Univs. (pres. 1964-65), La. Hist. Assn., La. Registrars Assn. (past pres.), S.A.R., Am. Council on Edn., Nat. Assn. State Univs. and Land Grant Colls., Southeastern Conf. (pres. 1968), La. Beta Club Council, La. Sch. Bds. Assn. (hon.), N.E.A., La. Tchrs. Assn., La. Fulbright Scholarship Com., So. Assn. Coll. and Univ. Registrars (past pres.),

Am. Radio Relay League, Am. Legion, Omicron Delta Kappa, Phi Kappa Phi, Phi Delta Kappa, Kappa Phi Kappa, Kappa Delta Pi, Phi Eta Sigma, Sigma Phi Epsilon, Gamma Beta Phi, Alpha Sigma Lambda, Phi Mu Alpha. Democrat. Episcopalian. Mason (33 deg., Shriner). Clubs: Camelot (gov. 1967-85), Pickwick, Internat. House (New Orleans), Moose (supreme gov. 1975-76). Author: A Handbook for Louisiana School Board Members, 1949; Teacher Welfare Laws of Louisiana, 1956; School Board Service, 1961; Progress and Promise, 1967. Contbr. articles to prof. jours. Home: Baton Rouge, La. Died Feb. 5, 1985.

HUNTER, STANLEY ARMSTRONG, clergyman; b. Orangeville, Ont., Aug. 23, 1888; s. Rev. William Armstrong and Eliza (Chambers) H.; student Denver U., 1905-06; A.B., Princeton, 1910; A.M., Columbia, 1914; grad. Union Theol. Sem., 1916; D.D., Occidental Coll., Los Angeles, 1925; m. Elizabeth, d. Harold Peirce, Mar. 21, 1918; children—Stanley Armstrong (dec.), William Armstrong III, Charlotte (dec.), Converse P. Prof. English and philosophy, Ewing Christian Coll., Allahabad, India, 1910-12; pastor North Church, Pittsburgh, 1916-24, St. John's Presbyterian Church, Berkeley, Calif., 1924-54. Secretary Western Pa. Com. Near East Relief, 1917-24. Mem. Bd. of Temperance and Moral Welfare Presbyn. Ch. Religious work dir. Y.M.C.A., League Island Navy Yard, June-Sept. 1918; mem. Charities Commn. City of Berkeley; chmn. Foreign Missions Com., Synod of Calif., 1925-29 and 1937-41; moderator of Synod, 1939-40. Clubs: Princeton Terrace, Faculty. Compiler and editor: Various religious works. Contributor to religious press. Home: Berkeley, Cal. †

HUNTZICKER, HARRY NOBLE, chemist, mfr.; b. Omaha, June 29, 1906; s. Albion Clinton and Annabelle (Noble) H.; m. Mildred Harriet Carlson, Aug. 14, 1934; children—Jon Noble, James Frederick. B.S., Macalester Coll., 1927; M.S., U. Wis., 1930, Ph.D., 1932. Sr. teaching asst. chemistry dept. U. Wis., 1930-32; tchr. high sch. chemistry, Rockford, Ill., 1932-35; with U.S. Gypsum Co., Chgo., 1935-56; research chemist, research supr. gypsum and lime products, tech. products mgr., prodn. mgr. lime plants, mgr. research and devel. labs., dir. research and devel., v.p. charge research and devel.; exec. v.p. Am.-Marietta Co., 1956-61, dir., 1961; v.p., dir. Martin Marietta Corp., 1961-66, pres. constrn. materials div., 1962-66; pres. Portland Cement Assn., Skokie, Ill., 1966-72; dir. Gen. Portland Inc., 1973-80, chmn. bd., 1975-80; Mem. bldg. research adv. bd. NRC, Nat. Acad. Scis., 1953; bd. govs. Bldg. Research Inst., 1954. Trustee Macalester Coll., St. Paul. Mem. Am. Standards Assn., Am. Chem. Soc., ASTM, Am. Soc. Engring. Edn., Am. Concrete Inst., Sigma Xi, Phi Lambda Upsilon, Alpha Chi Sigma. Republican. Presbyterian. Club: Westmoreland Country (Wilmette, Ill.). Patentee in field Home: Evanston, Ill. Died Oct. 28, 1984.

HURD, FREDERICK WILLIAM, traffic engineer, association official; b. Troy, Mo., Aug. 24, 1907; s. Fred Arthur and Mary Emelie (Howing) H.; B.S., C.E. in Civil Engring., U. Mo., 1934; certificate traffic engring. Bur. St. Traffic Research, Yale, 1939; m. Ida Mae Richmond, June 23, 1933; children—Marilyn Helen (Mrs. James F. Roach), Frederick William. Engr., traffic engr. safety bur. Mo. Hwy. Dept., 1927-42; asst. safety engr. Wayne County (Mich.) Rd. Commn., 1942; asst. to dir. Mich. Safety Commn., 1942-43; traffic engr. Mich. Hwy. Dept., 1943-45; assoc. prof. Bur. Hwy. Traffic, Yale, 1945-55, dir. bur., 1955-68; prof., dir. Bur. Hwy. Traffic, Pa. State U., 1968-72; tech. editor, dir. research Eno Found. for Transp., Westport, Conn., 1972-78, cons., 1978-84. Pres., Inst. Traffic Engrs., 1964; chmn. dept. traffic and operations Hwy. Research Bd., Nat. Acad. Scis., 1961-63; chmn. Conn. Safety Commn., 1966-67; mem. accident prevention study sect. NIH, 1962-65; adv. com. Pres.'s Com. Traffic Safety, 1964-66. Recipient T.M. Matson Meml. award for outstanding contbn. to advancement traffic engring., 1969, Burton W. Marsh award for distinguished service Inst. Traffic Engrs., 1973. Mem. Tau Beta Pi, Phi Kappa Phi, Phi Gamma Delta. Co-author: Traffic Engineering, 1955. Contbr. articles to profl. jours. Home: Trumbull, Conn. Died Feb. 29, 1984.

HURLEY, THOMAS DREUX, army officer; b. Arkansas, Feb. 15, 1890; M.D., U. of Arkansas, 1911; grad. Army Med. Sch., 1917, Med. Field Service Sch., 1921. In federal service as 1st lt., Med. Corps, Okla. Nat. Guard, 1916; 1st lt., med. sect., O.R.C., 1917 capt. Am. Ambulance Service, Nat. Army, 1917-18; commd. 1st lt., Med. Corps, U.S. Army, 1917, and advanced through the grades to brig. gen., 1945. Address: Washington, D.C. Deceased.

HURLIN, RALPH GIBNEY, statistician; b. Antrim, N.H., Sept. 30, 1888; s. Henry Albert and Mary Mernetta (Gibney) H.; grad. Colby Acad., New London, N.H., 1908; A.B., Brown U., 1912, Ph.D., 1915; m. Helen Humphry Wood, of Providence, R.I., June 14, 1916; children—Barbara Starr, Mary Wood. Asst. in biology, Brown U., 1911-15; instr. in biology, Clark U., 1915-16, asst. prof., 1916-18; chief of reports sect., statistics br., Gen. Staff U.S.A., rank of 1st lt., later capt. and maj. Washington, D.C., June 1918-Oct. 1919 (maj. O.R.C. 1919-29); statistician, Russell Sage Foundation, 1919-20, dir. dept. of statistics since 1920. Consultant in social statistics, U.S. Children's Bur., since 1932; chmn. advisory com. on statistics, N.Y. State Department of Social Welfare, 1931-35; director, division of statistics, New York City Emergency Relief Bureau, 1934-35. Fellow A.A.A.S., American Statis. Assn. (v.p. 1928-29); mem. Am. Econ. Assn., Am. Sociol. Soc., Academy of Polit. Science, Am. Genetic Assn., Am. Assn. Social Workers, Phi Beta Kappa, Sigma Xi, Delta Upsilon. Baptist. Club: Brown University. Co-Editor: Employment Statistics for the United States (with W.A. Berridge), 1926. Contbr. statis., econ. and social articles. Home: Jackson Heights, N.Y. †

HURWITZ, ABRAHAM, journalist, editor; b. Brooklyn, N.Y., Jan. 3, 1888; s. Morris and Esther Rachel (Malakoff) H.; student U. of Wash., 1906-09; admitted to Wash. bar, 1910, but did not practice; m. Charlotte Lippert, Apr. 20, 1918. City editor Seattle Star, 1914-16, 1916-22; editor Jacksonville (Fla.) Journal, 1922-24. Reading (Pa.) Times, 1924-40. Western Newspaper Union Chicago, 1940-42; editor Seattle Star, 1942-43; editor in chief John H. Perry Newspapers, incl. Jacksonville Journal, Pensacola Jour. Pensacola News, Ocala Star-Banner, Panama City News-Herald, Deland Sun-News, in Fla., and the Frankfort (Ky.) State Jour., 1943-46; Phila. Record, 1946; editorial writer and columnist (as "Elmer Pickney"). Miami (Fla.) Herald, from 1946; northwest corr. for Newspaper Enterprise Association representative and special writer for Kansas City (Missouri) Star, New York World, etc., various times. Helped draft first workmen's compensation act held constitutional in U.S. (Wash. state act); active in fight against convict leasing and flogging, Fla., 1922-23. Office: Ithaca, N.Y.†

HUSE, HOWARD RUSSELL, univ. prof.; b. Omaha, Neb., July 20, 1890; s. Jesse Benjamin and Mary Josephine (Wearne) H.; ed. U. of Dijon, France, 1909-10; Ph.B., U. of Chicago, 1913, Ph.D., 1930; m. Charlotte Jeanne Vulliémoz, Aug. 16, 1920; children—Mary-Louise, Henri; m. 2d, Mary Kathleen Martin, August 18, 1946. Asst. instructor Romance langs., U. of Chicago, 1914-16; asst. prof. Romance langs., Newcomb Coll., Tulane U., 1916-18; asst. U.S. trade commr., Athens, Greece, and Constantinople, Turkey, 1919; asst. prof. Romance langs., University of N.C., 1920, professor, from 1931. Private, later second lieutenant infantry, U.S. Army, World War I. Member Alpha Tau Omega. Editor: Contes et Récits, 1932. Author: Essentials of Written and Spoken French, 1928; Psychology of Foreign Language Study, 1931; Illiteracy of the Literate, 1933; Reading and Speaking Foreign Languages, 1945. Transl.: Dante's Divine Comedy, 1954. Home: Durham, N.C. †

HUSSEY, GEORGE FREDERICK, JR., retired naval officer; b. Brookline, Mass., June 15, 1894; s. George Frederick and Kate Willard (Nash) H.; grad. with distinction U.S. Naval Acad., 1916, student ordnance, Postgrad. Sch., 1921-23; m. Phebe Nell Tidmarsh, Mar. 23, 1929; children—George Frederick III (dec.), William Tidmarsh. Commd. ensign USN, 1916, advanced through grades to vice adm., 1945; served in U.S.S. Pennsylvania 1916-20; comdr. Destroyer Div. 24, 1939-41, Mine Squadron 3, 1941-42, Offshore Patrol of Pearl Harbor, 1941-42; dir. prodn. div. Bur. Ordnance, 1942-43, asst. chief, 1943, chief, 1943-47, ret.; mng. dir., sec. Am. Standards Assn., Inc., 1948-61, hon. mem., 1961; v.p. Internat. Orgn. for Standardization, 1958-61. Mem. adv. council on devel. Norwalk (Conn.) Hosp.; mem. adv. bd. New Eng. Inst. Med. Research, 1963-69; adv. bd. Community Coll., Norwalk, 1961-67, regional council, 1967-83; dir. Sr. Personnel Placement Bur., 1966-83; mem. exec. com. Conn. Red Cross Blood Program, chmn., 1967-69; chpt vice chmn., chmn. blood program com. Norwalk-Wilton chpt. A.R.C. Decorated D.S.M., hon. comdr. mil. div. Order Brit. Empire; recipient Blandy gold medal, 1958, Distinguished Service to Def., 50th Anniversary Gold medal, 1969 (both Am. Ordnance Assn). Fellow Standards Engrs. Soc. (Leo B. Moore medal 1972); mem. Am. Ordnance Assn. (pres. 1955-56), Naval Acad. Assn. N.Y. (pres. 1950-51), U.S. Naval Acad. Alumni Assn. (pres. 1953-55), ASME, Am. Soc. Assn. Execs., Chartered Assn. Execs. Republican. Episcopalian. Clubs: Army and Navy, Army-Navy Country (Washington); N.Y. Yacht (N.Y.C.). Spl. editor naval terms Websters' Internat. Dictionary, 2d edit., 1st printing, 1934. Home: Laguna Hills, Calif. Dec. Apr. 17, 1983. Interned at sea.

HUSSEY, HUGH HUDSON, physician, editor, educator; b. Washington, Nov. 12, 1910; s. Hugh Hudson and Laura (Klinge) H.; m. Wilhelmina Catherine Gude, July 27, 1935; 1 son, John Christopher. B.S., Georgetown U., 1932, M.D. magna cum laude, 1934, L.H.D., 1964. Diplomate: Am. Bd. Internal Medicine. Rotating intern Georgetown U. Hosp., 1934-35, fellow medicine, 1935-36, vis. physician, 1946-62, chmn. dept. medicine, physician-in-chief, 1956-58; instr. clin. medicine Georgetown U. Sch. Medicine, 1936-41, asso. clin. prof. medicine, 1941-47, asso. prof. medicine, 1948-56, prof., chmn. dept. preventive medicine and pub. health, 1953-56, prof. medicine, 1956-62, dean, 1958-62; dir. div. sci. activities A.M.A., 1963-69, dir. div. sci. publs. and editor jour., 1970-73; editor emeritus Jour. AMA, 1973-76; asso. physician Georgetown (div. D.C. Gen. Hosp.), 1936-39; vis. physician, chief Georgetown Med. div., 1940-58; asso. editor Continuing Edn. for Family Physicians, 1976-78; prof. internal medicine, prof. biomed. communications U. Tex. Health Scis. Center at Dallas, from 1977. Med. editor, GP, 1951-59; asso. editor: Med. Annals D.C, 1940-56. Mem. (rep. AMA) div. med. scis. NRC, 1960-74, mem. exec. com., 1963-73, drug research bd., 1963-76, policy adv. com. of drug efficacy study, 1966-69; Bd. regents Georgetown U., 1967-73. Fellow A.C.P.; mem. A.M.A. (trustee 1956-62, chmn. bd. trustees 1961-62), Georgetown Clin. Soc. (emeritus), Am. Heart Assn., Nat. Soc. Med. Research (dir.), So. Soc. Clin. Research (emeritus), Alpha Omega Alpha. Episcopalian. Home: Dallas, Tex.

HUSSEY, RUSSELL CLAUDIUS, educator; b. Mendon, O., Oct. 31, 1888; s. Elroy Edward and Mary Isabelle (Griffin) H.; A.B., U. of Mich., 1911; Ph.D., 1923; m. Minnie Simmons, Nov. 4, 1922. Cons. geologist Colo. and Calif., 1912-18; mem. faculty, dept. of geology, U. of Mich., from 1920, prof. of geology and lecturer in organic evolution from 1923. Mem. Geol. Soc. Am., Paleontol. Soc. Am., Am. Assn. Petroleum Geologists, Geophys. Union, Mich. Acad. of Sci., Mich. Geol. Soc. (academic counselor, U. of Mich., 1931-36), Sigma Xi, Phi Sigma, Pi Kappa Alpha, Gamma Alpha, Sigma Gamma Epsilon. Club: Rotary (past pres.; Ann Arbor). Author: Historical Geology, 1947; Geology and Man (with K. K. Landes), 1948. Contbr. articles on invertebrate paleontology and stratigraphy in Collier's Ency., 1950; contbr. articles in geol. jours. Home: Ann Arbor, Mich. †

HUTCHENS, FRANCIS CASE, lawyer; b. Pender, Nebr., Dec. 27, 1903; s. Frank B. and Helen (Case) H.; A.B., Stanford U., 1923; LL.B., Harvard U., 1926; m. Kathleen Shuman, Dec. 27, 1935; children—Sara C., Susan M. Admitted to Calif. bar, U.S. Supreme Ct. bar, 1932; practiced in San Francisco; mem. Morrison & Foerster (formerly Morrison, Foerster, Holloway, Shuman & Clark), 1944-68. Hon. trustee Starr King Sch. of Ministry, from 1967; trustee Calif. Acad. Scis., 1961-72. Mem. Phi Beta Kappa. Republican. Unitarian. Club: Bohemian (San Francisco). Home: San Francisco, Calif. Dec. Sept. 5, 1981.

HUTCHENS, RAYMOND PAUL, educator, lawyer; b. Ohio, Jan. 29, 1913; s. John Harvey and Nellie (Prine) H.; m. Rachel Emily Gieringer, 1938; children—Paula Rae, James Ray. Student, Ohio State U., 1931-32; B.S. in Edn, Wilmington Coll., 1936; M.A., Miami U., 1942; J.D., Salmon P. Chase Coll., 1948; Ph.D., U. Ottawa, Can., 1960; postgrad., Sorbonne, Paris, U. Cin.; LL.D., No. Ky. State Coll., 1974. Bar: Ohio bar 1948, Ala. bar 1971. Tchr. pub. schs., Warren County, Ohio, 1934-35, tchr., adminstr. pub. schs., Butler County, 1935-39, Hamilton County, Ohio, 1939-42, 46-47; mem. faculty Salmon P. Chase Coll. Sch. Commerce, summer 1947, dir., dean adminstrn., 1947-50, dean coll., 1950-51, pres., 1951, hon. pres., dean, prof. law, 1952-68; vis. prof. Cumberland Sch. Law, Samford U., Birmingham, Ala., 1967-68, asst. dean, prof. law, 1968-71, asso. dean, prof. law, 1971-75, prof. law, 1975-82, prof. emeritus, 1982-83. Served with AUS, 1942-45; with USNR, 1948-61. Mem. Am., Ala. bar assns., Birmingham Bar (asso.), V.F.W., Delta Sigma Phi, Kappa Delta Pi, Phi Alpha Delta, Phi Delta Kappa, Phi Delta Phi (hon.). Club: Mason. Home: Birmingham, Ala. Died May 26, 1984; buried Miamitown, Ohio.

HUTCHINS, JOHN SELLERS, business executive; b. Arlington, Mass., Dec. 30, 1904; s. Horace C. and Elizabeth (Sellers) H.; grad. Lawrenceville Sch., 1923 Yale. 1927; m. Belle Brockenbrough, Oct. 18, 1934; children—John Brockenbrough, Coleman Sellers, Harley, Brown Brockenbrough. With Am. Brake Shoe Co., N.Y.C., 1925-66, dir., 1955-66, exec. v.p., 1956-63, pres., 1963-66; dir. Templeton, Kenly & Co. (Chgo.), Western Union Telegraph Co., N.Y.C. Pres., Passavant Memorial Hosp., Chgo. Member of the Western Society Engrs., Chi Psi. Clubs: Chicago, Indian Hill, Glen View, Commonwealth, Old Elm. Commercial (Chgo.); Farmington (Charlottesville, Va.); Sky (N.Y.C.). Home: Winnetka, Ill. Died Aug. 4, 1983.

HUTCHINS, ROBERT MAYNARD, fund exec.; b. Bklyn., Jan. 17, 1899; s. William James and Anna Laura (Murch) H.; m. Maude Phelps McVeigh (div.); children—Frances Ratcliffe, Joanna Blessing, Clarissa Phelps; m. Mrs. Vesta Sutton Orlick. Student, Oberlin Coll., 1915-17; A.B., Yale, 1921, A.M. (hon.), 1922, LL.B., 1925; LL.D., W.Va. U., Lafayette Coll., Oberlin Coll., 1929, Williams Coll., 1930, Berea Coll., 1931, Harvard, 1936, Tulane U., 1938; hon. doctoral degrees, U. Copenhagen, 1946, U. Ill., 1947; LL.D., U. Frankfurt, 1948, U. Stockholm, 1949, Rollins Coll., 1950, U. Chgo., 1951, Colby Coll., 1956, U. Rochester, 1958, Lewis and Clark Coll., 1967; D.Litt., Georgetown U., 1964, Hebrew Union Coll., 1964. Master English, history Lake Placid (N.Y.) Sch., 1921-23; sec. Yale, 1923-27; lectr. Yale Law Sch., 1925-27, acting dean, 1927-28, dean, 1928-29, prof. law, 1927-29; pres. U. Chgo., 1929-45, chancellor, 1945-51; asso. dir. Ford Found., 1951-54; chief exec. officer Fund for Republic, 1954-74; chief exec. officer Center for Study Democratic Instns., 1954-74, life fellow, 1974—, pres., 1975—, Fund for the Republic, 1975-79; dir. Ency. Brit., Inc., 1947-74, Ency. Brit. Films, Inc., 1947-74. Author: No Friendly Voice, 1936, The Higher Learning in America, 1936, Education for Freedom, 1943, St. Thomas and the World State, 1949, Morals, Religion and Higher Education, 1950, The Democratic Dilemma, Some Questions about Education in North America, The Great Conversation, 1951, The Conflict in Education, 1953, The University of Utopia, 1953, Freedom, Education and The Fund, 1956, Some Observations On American Education, 1956, The Learning Society, 1968, Dr. Zuckerkandl, 1968; Bd. editors: Ency. Brit, 1946-74.

Served in ambulance service U.S. Army, 1917-19; Served in ambulance service Italian Army, 1918-19. Decorated Croce di Guerra Italian, 1918; officer Legion, 1969; Honor, 1938; recipient Goethe medal, 1948; Aspen Founders award, 1960. Mem. Chgo. Bar Assn., Order of Coif, Phi Beta Kappa. Clubs: University (Chgo.), Tavern (Chgo.) (hon.). Address: Washington DC †

HUTCHINS, ROSS ELLIOTT, entomologist; b. Ruby, Mont., Apr. 30, 1906; s. Elliott J. and Helen M. (Pierce) H.; B.S., Mont. State Coll., 1929; M.S., Miss. State Coll., 1931; Ph.D., Iowa State Coll., 1935; m. Annie L. McClanahan, June 5, 1932. Mem. faculty Miss. State U., 1929-68, prof. entomology emeritus, 1968-81; entomologist, exec. officer Miss. Plant Bd., 1951-68. Served to lt. comdr. USNR, 1943-45. Mem. Miss. Entomol. Soc., Am. Entomol. Assn., Sigma Xi, Phi Kappa Phi. Author: Insects: Hunters and Trappers; Strange Plants and Their Ways; Insect Builders and Craftsman; Wild Ways; This Is a Leaf; This is a Flower; This is a Tree; The Amazing Seeds; Travels of Monarch X; Insects; Plants Without Leaves; Caddice Insects; The Last Trumpeters; The Ant Realm; Island of Adventure: The World of Dragonflies and Damselflies; Adelbert The Penguin, Galls and Gall Insects; Little Chief of the Mountains; The Mayfly; Hop, Skim and Fly; Insetti Cacciatori; Saga of Pelorus Jack; Scaley Wings; The Cicada; Hidden Valley of the Smokies; The Carpenter Bee; Insects in Armour; Grasshoppers and Their Kin; Paper Wasps; Tonka, The Cave Boy; The Bug Clan; Trails to Nature's Mysteries. Home: Columbus, Miss. Died Oct. 14, 1983.

HUTCHINSON, EDWARD, congressman; b. Fennville, Mich., Oct. 13, 1914; s. Marc C. and Wilna (Leland) H.; A.B., U. Mich., 1936, J.D., 1938; m. Janice Eleanor Caton, Sept. 19, 1959. Admitted to Mich. bar, 1938; mem. Mich. Ho. of Reps. from Allegan County, 1946-50, Senate from 8th Senatorial Dist., 1951-60; del., v.p. Mich. Constl. Conv., 1961-62; mem. 88th-94th congresses from 4th Dist. of Mich. Served with AUS, 1941-46. Republican. Home: Fennville, Mich. Died July 22, 1985.

HUTCHINSON, JAMES HERBERT, coll. dean; b. Fayetteville, Tenn., Nov. 5, 1889; s. Thomas L. and Mettie Lou (Baird) H.; B.S., George Peabody College, 1917, M.A., 1927; LL.D., Arkansas A. and M. College, 1959; also L.H.D. (honorary), Sioux Empire College; m. Elva B. Batchelor, June 12, 1918; children—Jo (Mrs. Charles E. Jackson), James Herbert, William B. Tchr. langs. Paducah (Ky.) High Sch., 1915-19; prin. Murray (Ky.) High Sch., 1919; supt. city schs., Murray, 1919-25, head tchr. tng., 1924-25; dean Ark. A. and M. Coll., 1927-59; emeritus, from 1959; manager of Monticello Chamber of Commerce, from 1963. Served as 2d lt. AUS, World War I; AEF; from pvt. to lt. col., AUS, World War II. Mem. N.E.A., Ark. Tchrs. Assn., Ark. Edn. Assn. (pres. coll. sect.), Ford Expt. Tchr. Ark. (exec. com.), Nat. Registrars Assn., Monticello C. of C., Vets. Fgn. Wars, Phi Delta Kappa, Sigma Tau Gamma, Methodist. Mason, Rotarian. Author corr. courses psychology, ednl. psychology, reading, technique of teaching. Home: Monticello, Ark. †

HYATT, HARRY MIDDLETON, clergyman; b. Quincy, Ill., Feb. 21, 1890; s. Samuel Segar and Sarah Francis (Miller) H.; student Culver-Stockton Coll., Canton, Mo.; grad. Bexley Hall (Kenyon Coll.), Gambier, O., 1920; B.A., U. of Oxford, Eng., 1926, M.A., 1930; D.D., Culver-Stockton Coll., 1928; m. Mrs. George Altenberg, dau. Thomas P. Egan, Jan. 28, 1924. Deacon, 1920, priest, 1921, P.E. Ch.; served as asst. rector Ch. of The Advent, Walnut Hills, Cincinnati, and rector St. James Ch., Columbus; rector Christ Ch., Yonkers, 1927-30; asso. rector Ch. of the Holy Spirit, N.Y. City, since 1930. Del. to Conf. European Chs., Basle, Switzerland, 1929; mem. Am. Com. to Aid Faculté Libre de Théologie Protestante de Paris. Mem. bd. trustees St. Bernard's Sch., Gladstone, N.J. Decorated Officier d'Academie (France), 1933. Fellow Royal Geog. Soc., Soc. of Oriental Resrch. (sec.-treas. 1926-29). Officier de l'Ordre de la Couronne Royale (Belgium). Clubs: Cincinnati Country, Cincinnati Riding. Author: The Church of Abyssinia, 1928; The Millers of Millersburg, Kentucky, 1929; A Pioneer's Estate, 1931; Folk-lore from Adams County, Illinois, 1935. Arranged "Root Doctor" (a folklore work concerning negro healer known as a root doctor, root worker, or hoodoo doctor). Asso. editor Jour. Society Oriental Research, 1927-32, also of Ethiops (oriental mag.), Paris, 1928-32. Pres. bd. of dirs. Alma Egan Hyatt Foundation (scholarly jours.) since 1932. Home: New York, N.Y. †

HYDE, DORSEY WILLIAM, JR., b. Plainfield, N.J., Jan. 25, 1888; s. Dorsey William and Katherine (Clarke) H.; Student Rutgers Coll., 1905-07; A.B., Cornell, 1910; Sorbonne and Collège de France, Paris, 1910-13; m. Sybil Marjorie Cox, July 1, 1915; stepson, Anthony. On editorial staff The American City, 1915; mgr. research bureau same and Am. City Bureau, 1916-18; librarian, New York Municipal Reference Library. 1918-20; organized motor truck research bureau of Packard Motor Car Co., Detroit, 1920; chief of nat. civics bureau, civic development dept., Chamber of Commerce of U.S., 1921-26; sec. Chamber of Commerce, Washington, 1926-34; dir. Archival Service Nat. Archives of U.S., 1934-42, spl. asst. to Archivist of U.S., 1942; chief, Document Security Service. War Production Bd., 1943-45. Lecturer on civic research, Summer Sch. for Organization Secretaries, sessions at Lake Cayuga, N.Y., Eaglesmere, Pa., Madison, Wis., Evanston, Ill., 1916-22; lecturer on community orgn., George Washington U., 1926-28. Mem. adv. com. research information service, Nat. Research Council, 1923-26; official del. to former Pan Am. Comml. Congresses. Washington; del. to 2d Gen. Assembly Pan Am. Inst. of Geography and History, 1935; del. to 8th Am. Scientific Congress, 1940. Chmn. nat. archives com., W.P.A. Survey of Fed. Archives. Fellow A.A.A.S., Founding mem. Society American Archivists; American Assn. for Pub. Adminstrn., Inter-Am. Bibliog. and Library Assn., Am. Assn. for State and Local History; mem. British Pub. Records Assn., Soc. for Advancement of Management, Am. Statis. Assn. (past dist. sec.), Am. Polit. Science Assn., Am. Hist. Assn., Nat. Municipal League (past mem. editorial bd.), Special Libraries Assn. (pres. 1920-22, 1st v.p.), A.L.A. (former mem. council), Pub. Affairs Information Service (mem. publ. com.), Middle Eastern Library Assn. (pres. 1937), N.Y. Special Libraries Assn. (pres. 1918). D.C. Library Assn. (ex-pres.), Cornell Alumni Assn. of Washington (ex-pres.), Washington Council of Social Agencies (former mem. bd.), Columbia Hist. Soc. (mem. bd. govs.), D.C. Family Service Assn. (mem. bd. dirs.), D.C. Travelers Aid Soc. (mem. bd. dirs.), Monday Evening Club (ex-pres.). Citizens Relief Assn. (former mem. bd.), Zeta Psi. Episcopalian. Club: Torch (former bd. mem.). Editor: Special Libraries Directory, 1921; Washington Library Directory, 1928; Washington Educational Directory, 1932; also articles on municipal govt., library and archival science. Home: Washington, D.C. †

HYDE, HENRY VAN ZILE, assn. exec., physician; b. Syracuse, N.Y., Mar. 3, 1906; s. Henry Neal and Madeleine (Van Zile) H.; m. Ellen Sedgwick Tracy, June 24, 1933; children—Henry, Susan Sedgwick, Thomas Prentice. M.D., Johns Hopkins, 1933; diploma, Trudeau Sch. Tb, 1938. Diplomate: Am. Bd. Internal Medicine, Am. Bd. Preventive Medicine. Pvt. practice internal medicine, Syracuse, 1936-41; dir. bur. pneumonia control N.Y. State Dept. Health, 1941; commd. sr. surgeon USPHS(R), 1941; med. dir. USPHS, 1950; dir. med. div. Middle East Supply Center, Cairo, Egypt, 1944-45; chief health div. UNRRA Balkan Mission, 1945; chief Middle East office UNRRA, 1945; asst. chief health services br., div. internat. labor, social and health affairs Dept. State, 1945-48; dir. div. health and sanitation Inst. Inter-Am. Affairs, 1950-52; dir. health and sanitation staff Tech. Coop. Adminstrn., 1952-53; asst. chief div. internat. health USPHS, 1948-49, chief, 1953-58, asst. to surg. gen. for internat. health, 1958-62; dir. div. internat. med. edn. Assn. Am. Med. Colls., 1962-72; exec. dir. World Fedn. Med. Edn., 1972-82; U.S. rep., exec. bd. WHO, 1948-62, chmn., 1954-55; v.p. U.S. citizens com.; bd. dirs. Nat. Health Council; tech. bd. Milbank Meml. Fund; mem. USPHS Mission to USSR, 1957; U.S. del. 1st-14th, 20th World Health assemblies, 1948-61. Contbr. numerous med. articles to profl. jours. Mem. Phi Beta Kappa, Alpha Omega Alpha. Club: Cosmos (Washington). Home: Bethesda, Md. Died Nov. 5, 1982.

HYETT, EARL JESSE, railway executive; b. Neoga, Ill., Nov. 30, 1889; s. Charles Britton and Charity Elizabeth (Hanna) H.; student pub. schs.; m. Irene Denman, Nov. 28, 1912 (died May 26, 1926); 1 son, Robert Denman; m. 2d. Marian McCormick, 1928 (died Oct. 12, 1949); children—Donna Elizabeth (Mrs. Milburn Carter), Margaret Karen; m. 3d Virginia Octavia Wheeler, June 7, 1952. Traffic dept. Pa. R.R., St. Louis, 1905-12, C.M.& St.P. R.R., Seattle, 1912-21; traffic dept. C.,M., St.P. & P. R.R., Chgo., since 1922, freight traffic mgr. since 1951. Mem. U.S., Ill. C.'s of C., Nat. Def. Transportation Assn. Mason. Club: Chicago Traffic. Home: Northbrook, Ill. †

HYMAN, ORREN WILLIAMS, med. edn.; b. Tarboro, N.C., Dec. 21, 1890; s. Aquilla Pierce and Margaret (Williams) H.; A.B., U. of N.C., 1910, A.M., 1911; Ph.D., Princeton U., 1921; LL.D., Southwestern Coll., Memphis, Tenn., 1938; m. Jane Johnston, Sept. 3, 1921; children—Margaret, Orren Williams, Rufus Johnston. Prin. Salisbury, N.C., Pub. Sch., 1911-12; asst. prof. biology, U. of Miss., 1912-13; asst. prof. of histology and embryology, U. of Tenn., 1913-17, asso. prof., 1917-19, prof., from 1921; vice pres. U. Tenn. in charge Med. Units, Memphis. Presbyterian. Contbr. articles to med. jours. Home: Memphis, Tenn. †

HYNEMAN, CHARLES S., emeritus political science educator; b. Gibson County, Ind., May 5, 1900; s. Willis Smith and Hattie (Ford) H.; m. Frances Virginia Tourner, Aug. 31, 1926; children: Richard Frank, Ruth Anne, Elizabeth Harriet. A.B., Ind. U., 1923, A.M., 1925; postgrad., U. Pa., 1925-26; Ph.D., U. Ill., 1929; L.H.D. (hon.), Ohio No. U., 1960; LL.D. (hon.), Wabash Coll., 1971, Ind. U., 1980. High sch. tchr., univ. prof., 1923-41; prin. adminstrv. analyst U.S. Bur. Budget, 1942-43; chief tng. br. Mil. Govt. Div., Office Provost Marshal Gen., 1943-44; dir. Fgn. Broadcast Intelligence Service, FCC, 1944-45, asst. to chmn. commn., exec. officer, 1945-47; prof. polit. sci. Northwestern U., 1947-56; prof. govt. Ind. U., Bloomington, 1956-61, Distinguished Service prof. govt., 1961-71, prof. emeritus, 1971-85; adj. scholar Am. Enterprise Inst. for Policy Research, Washington, 1971-85; Fellow Woodrow Wilson Internat. Center Scholars, 1973-75; Mem. UN Monitoring Com., 1944-45, Social Sci. Research Council, 1944-47, NRC, 1963-65, Chgo. San. Dist. Civil Service Bd., 1952-56. Author: The First American Neutrality, 1935, Bureaucracy in a Democracy, 1950, The Study of Politics, 1959, The Supreme Court on Trial, 1963, Popular Government in America, 1968, (with C. Richard Hofstetter and Patrick F. O'Connor) Voting in Indiana, 1979; Editor: (with George W. Carey) A Second Federalist, 1967, (with Donald S. Lutz) American Political Writing During the Founding Era, 1760-1805, 1983; Contbr. articles to profl. jours. Mem. Am. Polit. Sci. Assn. (pres. 1961-62). Address: Bloomington, Ind. Died Jan. 20, 1985.

ICE, HARRY TREESE, lawyer; b. Paulding, Ohio, Oct. 17, 1904; s. Henry J. and Senna (Treese) I.; m. Elizabeth McIntyre, July 9, 1932; 1 dau., Marabeth. A.B., Butler U., 1926; LL.B., Harvard, 1929; LL.D. (hon.), Ind. Central Coll., Indpls., 1966, Butler U., 1978. Bar: Ind. bar 1929. Asso. Ice Miller Donadio & Ryan, Indpls., 1929-82, partner, 1934-82; vice chmn. bd. Am. United Life Ins. Co., Union City Body Co.; dir. Fairbanks Broadcasting Co. Mem. Bd. dirs. Greater Indpls. United Fund; mem. Bd. dirs. Greater Indpls. Progress Commn., Crossroads of Am. council Boy Scouts Am., Christian Ch. Found., Community Hosp. Found.; mem. adv. com. Holcomb Research Inst., Asso. Colls. of Ind.; emeritus trustee Butler U.; past trustee Ind. Boys Sch., Ind. Reformatory; hon. dir. Central Ind. council Boy Scouts Am., YWCA; past mem. Constl. Revision Commn., Ind. Commn. on Higher Edn., Commn. on State Taxation and Financing Policy; past chmn. Ind. Ethics and Conflict of Interests Commn. Served to lt. comdr. USNR, 1943-45. Mem. Ind. C. of C. (dir.), Indpls. C. of C. (dir.), Ind. Acad. Mem. Christian Ch. (trustee Found.). Club: Econ. (Indpls.) (dir.). Home: Indianapolis, Ind. Died Sept. 8, 1982.

IDRIS, I (MOHAMMED IDRIS EL SENUSSI), King of Libya; b. 1890; m. Emira Fatima. As Emir of Cyrenaica, 1949, was chosen to be king of Libya, by constituent assembly, which decided the country's form of govt. should be a constitutional monarchy, 1950; monarchy proclaimed, 1951. Home: Tripoli, Libya. Died May 25, 1983.

IGLEHART, LOUIS TILLMAN, former publishing exec.; b. Dawson Springs, Ky., Mar. 2, 1915; s. Volney Cicero and Agnes Norine (Rich) I.; A.B. in Journalism, U. Ky., 1940; m. Dixie Lynn Gower, June 30, 1947; children—Louis Tillman, Bruce Lee. Reporter, Lexington (Ky.) Herald-Leader, 1940-41, 46; tng. officer VA, 1947; editor, mgr. Campbellsville (Ky.) News-Jour., 1948-49; editor news bur. U. Tenn., Knoxville, 1949-56, dir. univ. publs. and U. Tenn. Press, 1957-78. Bd. dirs. Assn. Am. Univ. Presses, 1968-69; adv. bd. Appalachian Consortium, 1972-78. Served to maj. USAAF, 1941-46; PTO. Mem. Council Advancement and Support Edn. (dir. Southeastern dist. predecessor group 1960-61), Omicron Delta Kappa. Democrat. Mem. Christian Ch. Home: Knoxville, Tenn. Died May 29, 1981.

IGLEHEART, AUSTIN SMITH, bus. exec.; b. Evansville, Ind., Oct. 25, 1889; s. John L. and Belle (Smith) I.; grad. U. of Wis., 1912; m. Suzanne Bridwell, Nov. 2, 1915; children—Austin S., Evaline (Mrs. Wesley D. Hamilton), James. B., John David. Began with Igleheart Bros. Inc., (est. 1856) 1912; mgr. Swans Down Cake Flour dept., 1915; advtg. and sales promotion until 1926 (firm joined Gen. Foods, Inc., 1926); vice pres. Gen. Foods (mfg., transportation), 1929; v.p. (sales), 1935, exec. v.p. 1938, pres., 1944, chief exec. officer, 1953, chairman of bd., 1954, now dir., mem. exec. com.; dir. Mead Johnson & Co., Grocery Mfrs. Am., Comml. Solvents Corp., C.&E.I. R.R.; mem. trust adv. board Chase Nat. Bank. Mem. bus. adv. council Dept. Commerce. Clubs: Racquet and Tennis, Union League, Round Hill (Greenwich, Conn.); Clove Valley Rod and Gun. Home: Greenwich, Conn. †

ILG, FRANCES L., educator; b. Oak Park, Ill., Oct. 11, 1902; d. Joseph and Lennore (Peterson) Ilg.; A.B., Wellesley Coll., 1925; M.D., Cornell, 1929; 1 adopted dau., Tordis Kristin. Intern St. Mary's Hosp. for Children, N.Y.C., 1930, Bellevue Hosp., 1930-31, N.E. Hosp. Women and Children, Boston, 1931-32; vis. pediatrician Clinic of Child Development, Yale, 1932-33, research asst., 1933-36, asst. prof. child development, 1937-50; child health work, Stockholm, 1936-37; dir. Gesell Inst. Child Development, New Haven, 1950-70. Author: (with Arnold Gesell, others) The First Five Years of Life, 1940; Infant and Child in the Culture of Today, 1943; The Child from Five to Ten, 1946; Youth: The Years from Ten to Sixteen, 1956; School Readiness. Home: New Haven, Conn. Died July 26, 1981.

IMIRIE, JOSEPH SCOTT, diversified industry exec.; b. Washington, July 11, 1916; s. Austin S. and Augusta G. (Maddox) I.; m. Mildred F. Klinke, May 10, 1940; 1 son, Timothy D. B.S., Cath. U., 1938. Adminstrv. asst. Dept. Interior, 1938-41; adminstr., orgn. planner War Dept., 1941-43; various positions, also dep. to under-sec. Dept. Air Force, 1946-51; asst. to pres. Carborundum Co., Niagara Falls, N.Y., 1952-54, gen. mgr. electro minerals div., 1955-63, v.p., 1956-61; asst. sec. USAF, 1961-63; exec. v.p. profl. services, equipment group Litton Industries, Inc., Beverly Hills, Calif., 1963-67, sr v.p., 1967-71, exec. v.p., 1971-84. Served as maj. Air Transport Command AUS, 1943-46. Clubs: Los Angeles Country; Congressional Country (Washington). Home: Beverly Hills, Calif. Died Feb. 19, 1984.

IMRIE, NORMAN ALLAN, editor, lecturer; b. London, Ont., Can., Mar. 12, 1887; s. Rev. Andrew Bertram and Elizabeth (Grey) I.; B.L., Berea (Ky.) Coll.; Ph.B., U. of

Chicago; grad. student U. of Calif.; m. Gwendoline Copeland. Head of English dept. Berea Coll. Acad., 1910-13; head of history dept., high sch., Everett, Wash., 1913-15; prof. history and pub. speaking Culver (Ind.) Mill. Acad. 1920-22, 1926-34; chautauqua and lyceum lecturer, 1922-26; lecturer and pub. speaker; asso. editor Columbus Dispatch, 1934-40; pub. relations counsel Ohio State Highway Dept., 1940-42; program dir. Gov.'s State Fire Safety Com., also asst. state fire marshal, 1948-49; special field representative Ohio Forestry Association since 1949; conservation editor and lecturer Zanesville (O.) Signal and Times-Recorder from 1951. Served with Canadian Army, advancing from pvt. to rank of capt., 1915-19; spl. lecturer attached to U.S. Army of Occupation, Coblenz, Germany; maj., U.S. Reserve, 1925-42; on spl. staff Army Air Force, 1942-45; lecturer and pub. relations counsel on staff 2d Army Hdqrs., Ft. Hayes, O., and Ft. Meade, Md., 1946-48. Mem. Am. Legion Good Will Tour of Europe, 1927. Episcopalian. Mason (32 deg., Shriner), Rotarian. Clubs: Forty (Chicago); Columbus Athletic; Ohio Society of New York. Home: Columbus, Ohio. †

INGERSOLL, CHARLES EDWARD, hospital executive; b. Phila., Mar. 3, 1922; s. R. Sturgis and Marion B. (Fowle) I.; m. Vivian Martin, June 6, 1964; children—Patricia (Mrs. Douglas Adams), Charles Jared II; stepchildren—Harriet (Mrs. Morton Saunders), Joan Martin (Mrs. Charles A. Hunt), Sydney Martin III. Grad., Millbrook Sch.; student, Princeton, 1940; LL.B., U. Pa., 1949. Bar: Pa. bar 1950. With Kan., Okla. & Gulf Ry. Co., Midland Valley R.R. Co., and Okla. City-Ada-Atoka Ry. Co., 1949-64, chmn. bd., 1954-64; pres. Muskogee Co., 1954-66, Sebastian County Coal & Mining Co., 1954-64; asst. v.p. staff Pa. R.R. Co., 1965-66, asst. v.p. passenger service contracts, 1967-70, exec. rep. pub. affairs, 1970-71; exec. dir. Coll. Physicians Phila., 1971-72; pres. Children's Hosp., Phila., 1972-80, assoc. chmn., bd. mgrs., 1980-82; dir. Beneficial Mut. Savs. Bank, Provident Mut. Life Ins. Co. Bd. mem. Phila. Redevel. Authority, 1967-68. Bd. mgrs. Home Merciful Savior for Crippled Children. Served from pvt. to 1st lt., pilot USAAF, World War II. Republican. Club: Philadelphia. Home: Penllyn, Pa. Died Feb. 2, 1982.

INGERSOLL, HAROLD G., corporation exec.; born Sandoval, Ill., Aug. 18, 1888; s. Stephen Abraham and Cordelia (Gaylord) I.; A.B., Knox Coll., 1911; m. Florence Shephard, June 20, 1922; children—Judith, Harold Gaylord, Richard, William, John, Charles, Stephen, Edward. Joined Borg-Warner Corp., Chicago, 1928, dir. from 1929, v.p., dir. Ingersoll steel div., from 1918, president, 1950-56. Chmn. Ind. State Indsl. Savs. Bond Av. Com. Trustee Knox Coll. from 1951. Mem. Ind. Mfrs. Assn. (pres. 1950), Phi Gamma Delta. Republican. Presbyn. Club: Elk, Rotary. Home: New Castle, Ind. †

INGERSOLL, RALPH MCALLISTER, editor, author, publisher; b. New Haven, Dec. 8, 1900; s. Colin Macrae and Theresa (McAllister) I.; m. Mary Elizabeth Carden, 1925 (div. 1935); m. Elaine Brown Keiffer, Aug. 9, 1945 (dec. Apr. 1948); children: Ralph McAllister II, Ian Macrae; m. Mary Hill Doolittle, Nov. 25, 1948 (div. 1963); 1 adopted son, Brooks; m. Thelma Bradford, 1964. Student, Hotchkiss Sch., Lakeville, Conn., 1917-18; B.S., Yale, 1921; postgrad., Columbia, 1922. Mining engr.; reporter New Yorker mag., 1925, mng. editor, 1925-30; asso. editor Fortune, 1930, mng. editor, 1930-35; v.p., gen. mgr. Time, Inc. (pub. Time, Life, Fortune and Archtl. Forum, sponsoring radio and cinema prodns. 'The March of Time), 1935-38; pub. Time mag., 1937-39; organizer, finance co. to publish PM (N.Y. daily evening newspaper), 1939-40; pres. R.J. Co., Inc., 1948-59, R.J. Co., Inc. (investments, principally newspapers), Gen. Pubs., Inc. (newspaper mgmt.), 1959-75, Ingersolls Publs. Co., 1975-85. Author: In and Under Mexico, 1924, Report on England, 1940, America Is Worth Fighting For, 1941, Action on All Fronts, 1941, The Battle is the Payoff, 1944, Top Secret, 1946, The Great Ones, 1948, Wine of Violence, 1951, Point of Departure, 1961. Served from pvt. Engr. Amphibian Command to lt. col. Gen. Staff Corps AUS, 1943-45. Decorated Legion of Merit; officer Order of the Crown Belgium). Episcopalian. Club: Brook (N.Y.C.). Home: Cornwall Bridge, Conn. Died Mar. 8, 1985.

INGERSOLL, STUART HOWE, naval officer; b. Springfield, Mass., June 3, 1898; s. Arthur and Bernice (Howe) I.; B.S., U.S. Naval Acad., 1920; Doctor of Laws, University of Rhode Island; m. Josephine Sprigman, 1931; children—Mary Josephine (Mrs. Verne H. Jennings, Jr.), Sally Anne, Stuart Howe. Commd. ensign, U.S. Navy, 1920, and advanced through grades to vice adm., 1955; comdr. U.S. Seventh Fleet, also U.S. Taiwan Def. Command, 1955-57; pres. U.S. Naval War Coll., 1957-60, ret. 1960 and recalled active duty Office Sec. Def., 1960. Decorated Order British Empire; Grand Comdr. Royal Order Phoenix (Greece); Order Merit 1st Class (Portugal); Grand Cordon Precious Tripod (China); Order Naval Merit Grande Official (Peru); Ordem No Merito Naval Grande Official (Brazil). Mem. Soc. Colonial Wars, Soc. Cincinnati. Clubs: Army and Navy (Washington); N.Y. Yacht, Brook, Nickerbocker (N.Y.C.); Newport Clambake. Home: Newport, R.I. Died Jan. 29, 1983.

INGOLS, ROBERT SMALLEY, ret. educator; b. Newark, Mar. 5, 1911; s. George A. and Nellie (Smalley) I.; B.Sc. in Biology, Bucknell U., 1931, D.Sc. (hon.), 1969; M.A. in Biochemistry, Columbia U., 1934; Ph.D. in Sanitation, Rutgers U., 1939; m. Dorothy Ohlson, Nov. 4, 1939; children—Marcia R. Ingols Batchelor, Cynthia A., George A. Research asst. Rutgers U., 1935-41; chemist sewage treatment plant, Hackensack, N.J., 1941-43; research fellow Fla. Citrus Commn., 1943-44; instr. Sch. Pub. Health, U. Mich., 1944-47; asso. prof. Ga. Inst. Tech., 1947-50, prof., 1950-57, prof., head dept. applied biology, 1957-60, prof., dir. Sch. Applied Biology, 1960-65, prof. Engring. Expt. Sta., 1965-80; chmn. Joint Com. on Standard Methods for Water Exam.; mem. nat. tech. adv. com. Fed. Water Pollution Control Adminstrn. on Indsl. Water Supplies, 1967-68; research participant Oak Ridge Inst. Nuclear Studies, 1950; Fulbright lectr. Instituto Politecnico di Milano, Italy, 1956-57. Named Mr. Pollution Control, Inst. Plant Engrs., 1971. Fellow Am. Inst. Chemists; mem. AAAS (v.p. sect. C 1955), Am. Chem. Soc. (councillor 1955-58, chmn. water and wastes div. 1959; chmn. Ga. sect. 1967-68), Am. Water Works Assn. (life), Water Pollution Control Fedn. (life), Sigma Xi. Baptist. Home: Atlanta, Ga. Died Oct. 24, 1980.

INGRAHAM, EDWARD, corp. official; b. Bristol, Conn., Dec. 20, 1887; s. William Shurtleff and Grace Ella (Seymour) I.; grad. Phillips Andover Acad., 1906; B.A., Yale U., 1910; m. Alice Patti Pease, Sept. 21, 1918 (dec.); children—Alice Edward, William Shurtleff, Grace Seymour, Ellen Jane, Faith Allen; m. 2d, Ethel Leishman Beach, Jan. 16, 1952. Entered employ of The E. Ingraham Co. (founded by great-grandfather, Elias Ingraham, 1831), 1910, held various positions until 1927, president, from 1927, chmn. bd., from 1954; officer or dir. other cos. Pres. Bristol Clock Mus., Inc. Served in Coast Arty. Corps Fortress Monroe, 1918. Past pres. Bristol Boys Club; mem. bd. dirs. Boys Club Am.; past pres. Clock Mfrs. Assn. of Am. Mem. Beta Theta Pi. Republican. Conglist. Mason. P.p. Mfrs. Assn. Conn. Home: Bristol, Conn. †

INGRAHAM, MARY SHOTWELL, educator; b. Bklyn., Jan. 5, 1887; d. Henry Titus and Alice Wyman (Gardner) Shotwell; A.B., Vassar Coll., 1908; L.H.D., Wesleyan U., 1952, Columbia, 1961; m. Henry Andrews Ingraham, Oct. 28, 1908; children—Mary Alice (Mrs. Henry Bunting), Henry Gardner Winifred Andrews (Mrs. Harold L. Warner, Jr), David. Mem. Dept. Edn., Bklyn. YWCA, 1908-15, chmn., 1915-22; pres. Bklyn. YWCA, 1922-39, v.p., 1939; pres. nat. bd. YWCA, 1940-46; vice chmn., dir. N.Y. Council Adult Edn., 1933-37; vice chmn. Bklyn. Council for Social Planning, 1933-38; mem. Bd. Higher Edn., N.Y.C., 1938-68, chmn. exec. com., 1944; v.p. United Service. Orgns., 1941-48; exec. com. Nat. Budget and Consultation Com., from 1946; bd. dirs. Nat. War Fund. Trustee Bklyn. Coll., 1938-68, chmn., 1943-52; mem. Nat. Isnt. Social Scis., from 1930; mem. rep. council Vassar Coll.; mem. bd. dirs., exec. com. Community Chest, Council of U.S., 1946-52; v.p. Asso. Youth Serving Orgn., 1944-48. Chmn. Nat. Social Welfare Assembly, 1949-52, v.p., from 1960; mem. Nat. Assembly for Social Policy and Devel.; mem. internat. com., pub. affairs com., mem. leadership devel. com. Nat. YWCA. Mem. Jr. League, Bklyn. Recipient Medal of Merit from Pres. of U.S., 1946. Republican. Mem. Society of Friends. Clubs: Civitas. (Bklyn.); Brooklyn Heights Garden. Writer on edn. and social work. Home: Brooklyn, N.Y. †

INGRAM, FRANCES, operatic contralto; b. Liverpool, Eng., Nov. 5, 1888; d. William and Alice (Doyle) I.; brought to U.S., 1897; ed. Erasmus Hall High Sch., and Teachers' Training Sch., Brooklyn, N.Y. Début with Chicago Opera Co. at Phila., 1912; joined Met. Opera Co., 1919; sang principal rôles in Carmen, Il Trovatore, Butterfly, Aida, Hoffman; widely known as concert singer.†

INZER, JOHN WASHINGTON, clergyman; b. Hico, Tex., Jan. 6, 1890; s. Perry Monroe and Margaret (Marie Smith) I.; student Peacock Mil. Sch., San Antonio, Tex., 1906-07, Southwest Tex. Normal Sch., 1907-08, Simmons Coll., Abilene, Tex., 1908-11, D.D., 1921; student Southwestern Bapt. Theol. Sem., Fort Worth, Tex., 1911-13; m. Marie La Mitis Smith, Dec. 31, 1918. Ordained ministry Bapt. Ch., 1909; pastor churches, 1913-17; chaplain with rank of 1st lt., U.S. Army, Mar. 1918-Mar. 1919; nat. organizer Am. Legion, May-Nov. 1919, nat. chaplain, 1920; pastor 1st Baptist Church, Asheville, N.C., 1938-43; interim pastor among Southern Baptist Churches. Trustee Tenn. Baptist Coll.; mem. Home Mission Bd., Southern Bapt. Ch., Tenn. Bapt. State Mission Bd.; pres. Gen. Pastors Assn. of Chattanooga, 1928-29; chmn. exec. bd. Ala. Bapt. State Conv.; pres. Montgomery Pastors Assn.; past nat. chaplain Sons of Confed. Vets.; nat. chaplain Soc. of The Founders of Am. Legion. Democrat. Mason (Shriner), K.P. Club: Rotary International (gov. 164th dist., 1945-46). Former mem. Ala. State Bd., NRA. Address: Sylacauga, Ala.†

IREDELL, ROBERT, engr.; b. Akron, O., Aug. 26, 1887; s. Robert and Mary A. (Terrass) L.; B.S., Buchtel Coll., 1909; Chem.E., U. Pa., 1911; m. Helen Knight, Sept. 18, 1912; children—Robert, Helen K. Gulick. With Firestone Tire & Rubber Co., Akron, 1910-15; chief engr. Gen. Tire & Rubber Co., Akron, 1915-41, dir. engr., 1941-52; retired 1952, still a dir. Trustee Akron City Hosp. Mason. Clubs: Portage Country, City, Univ. Home: Akron, Ohio. †

IRELAND, CLARENCE LEO, lawyer; b. Littleton, Colo., Dec. 5, 1889; s. Frederick and Clara Jennie (Ball) I.; A.B., U. of Colo., 1913, LL.B., 1916; m. Bess Low, Jan. 26, 1918; children—Elizabeth, Edith Alice. Began practice at Denver, 1916; asst. U.S. dist. atty., 1922-26; pvt. practice, 1926-31; atty. gen. of Colo., 1931-33; mem. Ireland & Ireland; officer or dir. various corps. Served in U.S. Army, 1917-19; instr. in aviation, Scott Field, Belleville, Ill., 1918. Mem. Denver, Colo. State and Am. bar Assns. Am. Legion, Phi Gamma Delta, Phi Delta Phi. Republican. Episcopalian. Clubs: Kiwanis Luncheon, Denver Club. Home: Denver, Colo. †

IRENAY, METROPOLITAN, (JOHN BEKISH) bishop; b. S.W., Russia, Oct. 2, 1892; came to U.S., 1952, naturalized, 1957; s. Dimitry and Agnia (Saltrukovich) Bekish. Grad., Theol. Sem., Kholm, Russia, 1914. Ordained priest Russian Orthodox Ch., 1916; asst. rector Cathedral of Lublin, Poland, 1916-19; mem. Polish consisitory Diocese of Pinsk, 1935-47, also chmn. missionary com.; dean, Counties of Sarna, Kamen-Kashursk and Pinsk, 1938-44, displaced person, Germany, 1944-47; rector Russian Orthodox Ch., Charleroi, Belgium, 1947-52, Holy Trinity Ch., McAdoo, Pa., 1952-53, bishop of, Tokyo and, Japan, 1953-60, archbishop of, Boston and, New Eng., 1960-65, archbishop of N.Y., Met. all, Am. and Can., 1965-70; primate Orthodox Ch. Am., 1970-77; vicar bishop Russian Orthodox Ch. in Home: New York, N.Y. Died Mar. 24, 1984.

IRISH, EDWARD SIMMONS, sports promotion executive; b. Lake George, N.Y., May 6, 1905; s. Clifford and Madeleine (Lancaster) I.; B.S. in Econs., Wharton Sch., U. Pa., 1928; 1 son, Ned. Sports writer Phila. Record, also N.Y. World Telegram, 1924-34; engaged in sports promotion, 1934-40; with Madison Sq. Garden Corp., N.Y.C., 1940-74; acting pres., 1941-45, exec. v.p., 1945-60, pres., 1960-74; hon. chmn. N.Y. Knickerbockers. Named to Basketball Hall of Fame, 1964. Home: New York, N.Y. Died Jan. 21, 1982.

IRONS, EVELYN CHRISTINE, govt. ofcl.; b. Wilmington, Del., May 31, 1921; d. Harry Samuel and Edith May I.; 1 son, Lane L. McVey. Student, Beacom Bus. Coll., Wilmington, Del., 1940. Secretarial asst. to asst. sec. Dept. Army, Washington, 1950-60; staff asst. to chmn. Internat. Joint Commn., 1960-63; secretarial asst. to spl. asst. Sec. Def., 1964-65; secretarial asst. to spl. asst. to Pres., 1965-69; secretarial asst. to asst. dir. Bur. Budget, 1969-71; staff asst. to chmn. AEC, 1971-73; staff asst. to dir. CIA, 1973; staff asst. to Sec. Def., 1973-75; staff asst. to asst. to Pres., 1976-78; exec. asst. to sec. Dept. Energy, Washington, 1978-79. Methodist. Home: Arlington, VA.

IRVIN, JOSEPH LOGAN, biochemist, educator; b. Jacksonville, Fla., Nov. 24, 1913; s. Joseph Logan and Eva (Hawkins) I.; m. Elinor Moore, Dec. 26, 1941. B.S., U. S.C., 1934; Ph.D., U. Pa., 1938. Instr. Wayne U. Coll. Medicine, 1938-41; instr. Johns Hopkins Sch. Medicine, 1941-43, asst. prof., 1943-50; asso. prof. biochemistry U. N.C., 1950-56, prof., chmn. dept., 1957-78, Kenan prof., from 1970. Editorial bd.: Biol. Bull, 1960-66. Mem. Middle Atlantic Regional Heart Com., 1969-73; mem. instl. research grant com. Am. Cancer Soc., 1976-79. Guggenheim fellow, 1956. Mem. Am. Chem. Soc., Am. Soc. Biol. Chemists, Soc. Exptl. Biology and Medicine, Am. Assn. Cancer Research, N.C. Heart Assn. (chmn. bd. dirs. 1967-69), Am. Heart Assn. (finance com. 1968-71, regional-nat. research com. 1973-75), Phi Beta Kappa, Sigma Xi. Home: Chapel Hill, NC.

IRWIN, DAVID D., business exec.; b. Chicago, May 4, 1887; s. Charles David and Hettie D. (Duryea) I.; Ph.B., Yale, 1908, E.M., 1911; m. Dorothea C. Baldwin, May 4, 1915; 1 son, David Baldwin. Various positions with various mines, Ariz. and N.M., 1911-17; gen. supt. Kennecott Copper Corp., Alaska, 1918; gen. supt. Phelps Dodge Corp., Ariz. and Mexico, 1918-28; gen. mgr. Roan Antelope Copper Mine, North Rhodesia, 1928-33; in charge transportation and supply, Pure Oil Co., Chicago; pres. and dir. Pure Oil Pipe Line Co., Pure Transportation Co. since 1934; pres. and dir. Mountain State Gas Co., Detroit Southern Pipe Line Co.; v.p. and dir. Sabine Transportation Co., Ajax Pipe Line Co.; dir. Roan Antelope Copper Mine, Mululira Copper Mine, Ltd. since 1930, Am. Metal Co., Ltd. from 1944, Great Lakes Pipeline Co.; retired from active business. Apptd. asst. to mobilization director, Charles E. Wilson, June 1951. Mem. Blackburn Dist. Sch. Bd., Kennecott, Alaska, 1918, Winnetka Village Caucus Com., 1939, advisor Metals Res. Co., Washington, 1941-42, vice chmn. dist. 2 transportation com. under Petroleum Coordinator. Mem. Am. Inst. Mining and Metall. Engrs., Chem., Metall. and Mining Society (South Africa), Am. Petroleum Inst., Sigma Xi, Delta Psi. Clubs: University (Chicago); Indian Hill, Sky Line. Home: Winnetka, Ill. Deceased.†

IRWIN, HARRY H(ARRISON), educator; b. Colfax, Wash., Sept. 16, 1890; s. DeLance J. and Delila J. (Buson) I.; A.B., Wash. State Coll., 1915, M.A., 1926; m. Alma E. Phillips, July 26, 1916; 1 dau., Almarose (Mrs. Robert J. Bartow). Teacher high sch. mathematics, Kelso, Wash., 1916-18; prof. mathematics Washington State College from 1920. Member American Institute of Electrical Engrs., Am. Math. Assn., Am. Assn. U. Profs., N.W. Sci. Assn., Phi Kappa Phi. Home: Pullman, Wash. †

IRWIN, HERBERT MILTON, railway exec.; b. Quenemo, Kan., Nov. 8, 1890; s. John Milton and Lillie May (Dougherty) I.; spl. courses Topeka Bus. Coll., 1912, Alexander Hamilton Inst., 1918, N.Y.U., 1919; m. Mildred Myers, June 7, 1913; children—Herbert Milton (dec.), Charlotte Helen. Sta. work C., R.I. & P. Ry., 1909-10, timekeeper in constrn., yard clk., 1910-11, roadmaster's clk., 1911-12, stenographer, sec. to supt., 1912-14, acct., 1914-17; statis. clk. D.&H. R.R., 1917-18, gen. acct., 1918-19, gen. bookkeeper, 1919-21, asst. to comptroller, 1921-28, asst. to pres., 1928-49, v.p., treas., 1949-52, v.p., sec., treas. to co. and subsidiaries, 1952-56, v.p., from 1957; dir. D.&H. Co., D & H R.R.; chmn. N.Y. State Business Development Corp. from 1959. President board education Port Washington, 1931-37. Mem. Assn. Am. R.R.'s, Kan. Soc., Newcomen Soc. Republican. Mason. Clubs: Mt. Stephen (Montreal, Can.); Ft. Orange (Albany, N.Y.); Canadian (N.Y.C.). Home: Port Washington, N.Y. †

IRWIN, JAMES WILLIAM, govt. ofcl., lawyer; b. Savannah, Tenn., Dec. 8, 1890; s. James W. and Cornelia (Broyles) I.; B.S., Vanderbilt U., 1914, LL.B., 1918; m. Gladys Marie Cornell, June 14, 1928. Instr. English, Sherman (Tex.) High Sch., 1914-16; instr. comml. law Hill Bus. Coll., Nashville, 1916-17; admitted to Tenn. bar 1917, Okla. bar, 1919; practiced in Okmulgee, Okla., 1919-35; litigation atty. Nat. Recovery Adminstrn., 1935-36; regional atty. ICC, 1936-41; chief hearing examiner Civil Service Commn., from 1941. Atty. Okmulgee (Okla.) County, 1928-32. Mem. Bar Supreme Ct. U. S., Am., Fed., Okla. bar assns., Am. Legion (designate mem. first state exec. com.), Order of Coif, Torch International (former president, director Washington), Trial Examiners Conference (member executive committee). Mason. Methodist. Club: Cosmos (Washington, D.C.). Author and compiler: Hatch Act Decisions of U.S. Civil Service Commission: A Text and Case Book, 1949. Home: Washington. †

ISAACSON, WILLIAM JOSEPH, lawyer; b. Gallitzin, Pa., Jan. 10, 1913; s. Louis and Anna (Kaufmam) I.; m. Bernice N. Kavinoky, Feb. 9, 1936 (dec. Feb. 1965); 1 son, Stephen S.; m. Edith Lipsig Hebald, May 19, 1975. A.B. with distinction, U. Mich., 1935, J.D., 1937. Bar: Mich. 1937, N.Y. 1948. Practiced law, Detroit, 1937-39; atty., trial examiner, regional dir. NLRB, 1939-48; gen. counsel Amalgamated Clothing Workers Am., N.Y.C., 1948-58; vis. prof. Cornell U., 1958, practiced law, N.Y.C., 1958-59, dep. indsl. commr., N.Y., 1959-60; partner Kaye, Scholer, Fierman, Hays and Handler, N.Y.C., 1960-84. Editor-in-chief: Employee Relations Law Jour; contbr. articles to profl. publs. Chmn. N.Y. State Grievance Appeals Bd., 1965-69; Vice pres. Lenox Hill Neighborhood House, 1967-81. Fellow Am. Bar Found.; mem. ABA (chmn. labor relations law com. 1958-59), N.Y. Bar Assn., Am. Law Inst., Assn. Bar City N.Y. (chmn. com. labor and social security legislation 1963-66, post admissions legal edn. com.), Am. Arbitration Assn. Home: Redding, Conn. Died May 27, 1984.

ISHIBASHI, SHOJIRO, tire co. exec.; b. Feb. 25, 1889; ed. Kurume Comml. Sch. Became pres. Bridgestone Tire Co. Ltd., 1931, chmn., from 1963; chmn. bd. Prince Motors Ltd., 1951; pres. Japan Synthetic Rubber Co. LTd., 1957, chmn. bd., 1965. Exec. dir. Nat. Fedn. Econ. Orgns., 1949, Japan Fedn. Employers' Assns., 1952. Pres. Bridgestone Gallery, 1952; councillor Nat. Mus. Modern Art, 1952, Soc. for Internat. Cultural Relations, 1957, Nat. Mus. Occidental Art, 1959, Nat. Mus. Tokyo, 1959; chmn. Ishibashi Found., 1956. Decorated Dark Blue Ribbon medal (4); Green Ribbon medal, Blue Ribbon medal, 2d Order Sacred Treasure (Japan); Legion of Honor (France); grand officer Order Merit (Italy), others. Address: Tokyo, Japan. †

ISHIDA, REISUKE, Japanese govt. ofcl.; b. Matsuzaki-machi, Kamo-Gun, Shizuoka Prefecture, Japan, Feb. 20, 1886; s. Fusakichi and Ichi (Yoda) I.; student Tokyo Coll. Commerce, 1904-07; m. Tsyu Nakamura, Feb. 2, 1913; children—Fusanosuke, Shizuko. With Mitsui & Co. Ltd., 1907-46, exec. mng. dir., 1939-41, rep. exec. dir., 1943-46; pres. Trade Corp., controlling export and import of Japan, 1956-62; chmn. inquiry and audit com. Japanese Nat. Rys., 1962-63, pres., from 1963. Mem. Met. Transp. Council, Japan Electric Power Survey Com., Ry. Constrn. Council, Civil Aero. Council; counselor Japan Productivity Center, Japan Atomic Indsl. Forum; recommended mem. Fedn. Econ. Orgns. Home: Kanagawa Prefecture, Japan. †

ISHIDA, TAIZO, automobile and textile machinery mfg. cos. exec.; b. Tokoname, Aichi-Ken, Japan, Nov. 16, 1888; s. Tokusaburo Sawada and Koh Takeuchi; ed. in Japan; m. Masao Kosugi, Nov. 11, 1944; 1 child, Ai. Mng. dir. Toyoda Automatic Loom Works, Ltd., Kariya, Aichi-Ken, 1941-45, sr. mng. dir., 1945, exec. v.p., 1945-48, pres. 1948; pres. Toyota Motor Co. Ltd. (Japan), 1950-61, chmn. bd., from 1961; chmn. bd. Aichi Steel Works, Ltd., Kariya, Aichi-Ken, from 1961, Toyoda Spinning & Weaving Co. Ltd., Kariya, Aichi-Ken, from 1967; pres. Towa Real Estate Co., Nagoya, Japan, 1964—; mng. dir. Toyota Central Research & Devel. Labs., Inc., Nagoya, 1960; auditor Toyota Motor Sales Co. Ltd., Nagova, 1963—, Toyoda Tsusho Kaisha Ltd., from 1956, counselor Iino Motor Co. Ltd., from 1967. Chmn. bd. Toyoda Med. Facilites. Decorated Second Order of Merit, other awards for indsl. devel. Mem. Japan Textile Machinery Mfrs. Assn. (chmn.), Japan Machinery Fedn. (vice chmn.), Fedn. Econ. Orgn. (mng. dir.), Japan Fedn. Employers Assn. (mng. dir.), Japan Automobile Mfrs. Assn. (dir.). Author: The Race in Life, 1961. Home: Kariya, Japan. †

ISRAEL, SAM, JR., coffee importer; b. New Orleans, July 7, 1910; s. Samuel and Edna (Shwartz) I.; m. Merryl Silverstein, Dec. 1, 1931; 1 son, Lawrence Joseph. Student, Tulane U., 1927-28; LL.D., Tulane U. With Leon Israel & Bros., Inc. (merger A.C. Israel Commodity Co. name now changed to ACLI Internat. Inc.), green coffee importers), New Orleans, 1928—, vice chmn. bd., chmn. exec. com., dir., 1971—; dir. Times-Picayune Pub. Co., Hibernia Nat. Bank New Orleans, Zapata Corp., New Orleans Pub. Service. Chmn. Bd. Liquidation City Debt New Orleans; former pres. Bd. Commrs. Port of New Orleans; mem. study assessment group Mayor New Orleans, Miss. Valley World Trade Council, Council Lower Miss. River Port Interests, Bur. Govt. Research, Council Better La., Met. New Orleans Crime Commn.; Bd. dirs. Internat. Trade Mart; chmn. fin. com., ednl. fund Tulane U. Served to lt. col. Transp. Corps AUS, 1942-45, ETO. Decorated Bronze Star with oak leaf cluster; French Medal Merit. Mem. Nat. Coffee Assn. (chmn. fgn. affairs com.), N.Y. Coffee and Sugar Exchange, New Orleans Bd. Trade, Mil. Order World Wars, Confererie de la Chaine des Rotisseurs, Confrerie des Chevaliers du Tastevin, Fgn. Relations Assn. New Orleans. Jewish. Clubs: Internat. House (New Orleans) (dir., exec. com., chmn. nominating com.), Lakewood Country (New Orleans). Home: New Orleans, La. Died Oct. 5, 1982.

IVAN, FRANKLIN BAKER, electric exec.; b. Cedar Rapids, Neb., Apr. 11, 1887; s. Frank N. and Etta I. (Baker nee Bowers) I.; B.S. in E.E., U. Neb., 1909; m. Lucile Atkinson, 1911; 1 dau., Helen Merle (Mrs. Robert A. Cushman). Apprentice engr. Westinghouse Electric & Mfg. Co., Pittsburgh, 1909-10, mgr. for Japan, later mng. dir. Westinghouse Electric Co. of Japan, and dir. Mitsubishi Electric & Engring. Co., 1919-27, mgr. far east Westinghouse Electric Internat. Co., N.Y. City, 1927-29, European sales mgr., European mgr., 1929-38, industry sales mgr., sales mgr., 1938-44, co. rep., Washington, 1942-43, asst. to pres., 1944-45, treas., 1945-47, v.p., treas., 1947, dir., from 1940; dir. Constructora Nacional de Maquinaria Electrica, Spain, 1930-39; cons. War Dept., 1943; mem. adv. com. comml. activities fgn. service Dept. State and Dept. Commerce since 1946; mem. adv. group internat. econ. relations com. Nat. Assn. Mfrs. from 1940. Mem. Am. Inst. E.E., N.Y. Credit Men's Assn., Am. Asiatic Soc., Pan Africa Soc. (dir.), Far East Council Commerce and Industry (dir.), Council Fgn. Relations, Inc. Clubs: Town Hall, Sales Execs., Downtown Athletic, India House, Shanghai Tiffin, India League (N.Y. City); Country (Richmond Co.). Home: New Brighton, N.Y. Deceased.†

IVES, ERNEST LINWOOD, b. Norfolk, Va., Oct. 17, 1887; s. Eugene and Sarah (Read) I.; ed. Norfolk Acad.; Va. Mil. Inst.; William and Mary Coll.; m. Elizabeth Davis Stevenson; 1 child, Timothy Read. Apptd. vice and deputy consul. Mannheim, Germany, 1909: same, at Magdeburg, 1910-14; vice and dep. consul gen., Frankfort-on-the-Main, 1914, later vice consul; vice consul Cologne, 1915, Frankfort, 1915. Erfort, 1916, Breslau, 1916, again at Frankfort, 1916, at Budapest 1917; apptd. counsular asst., 1917; vice consul, Paris, France, 1917, Nantes, 1917, again at Paris, 1918-23; consul at Alexandria, Egypt, 1923-25; first sec. Diplomatic Service, Am. Embassy. Constantinople, Turkey, 1925-30, first sec. Am. Legation, Copenhagen, Denmark, 1930; served as 1st sec. Am. Legation, Pretoria, Union of S. Africa; consul gen. at Lima, 1932, at Algiers, 1933-36, Stockholm, 1936, Belfast, 1937; retired as American foreign service officer, 1939. Mem. Kappa Alpha (Southern). Clubs: American (hon.; Paris); Virginia (Norfolk); Princess Anne (Virginia Beach, Va.); Bloomington Country. Home: Norfolk, Va. †

IVEY, CHARLES HERBERT, brass co. exec.; b. London, Ont., Can., 1889; s. Charles H. and Louise (Green) I.; B.Sc., McGill U., 1911; m. Ethel Jamieson, Feb. 15, 1916; children—Peter, Robert, Joanne. With Emco, Ltd., London, Ont., from 1911, pres., 1948-55, chmn., 1955-60, dir.; dir. London Life Assurance Co.; pres. Pumps & Softeners, Ltd. Served to capt. Canadian Army, 1916-18. Decorated Mil. Cross. Home: London, Can. †

JACK, WILLIAM HARRY, lawyer; b. Kaufman, Tex., Dec. 13, 1899; s. William Harry and Kosci (Snow) J.; m. Marian Price, Nov. 27, 1928 (dec. 1968); children—Robert William, Patricia Jack Porter, Marian Jack Jenkins; m. Josephine Hunley Dillon, Aug. 16, 1969. B.A., U. Tex., 1922, LL.B., 1923. Bar: Tex. bar 1923. Partner firm Jack & Jack, Corsicana, 1923-26; Partner firm Saner, Jack, Sallinger & Nichols, Dallas, 1926-79, of counsel, 1979-84; dir., gen. counsel Booth, Inc., Carrollton, Tex., from 1948. Pres. Blanche Mary Taxis Found., Dallas, from 1958; bd. dirs. Dallas Child Guidance Clinic, 1956-58. Served with U.S. Army, 1918; to maj. USAAF, 1942-44; lt. col. JAG Res. ret. Fellow Am. Bar Found., Southwestern Legal Found. (trustee 1966-84, vice chmn. 1970-75); mem. ABA (ho. dels. 1957-59, 68-70), Dallas Bar Assn. (pres. 1951), State Bar Tex. (dir. 1958-62, v.p. 1962-63, President's award 1964), Am. Coll. Probate Counsel (dir. 1959-63, pres. 1963-64), S.A.R., Phi Beta Kappa, Phi Delta Phi, Sigma Delta Chi. Presbyn. (ruling elder from 1938, mem. bd. Christian edn. 1951-57). Clubs: Masons (33 deg.), Shriner, Dallas, Dallas Country. Home: Dallas, Tex. Died Oct. 9, 1984.

JACKSON, CHARLES SHATTUCK, banker; b. Parkersburg, W.Va., Aug. 22, 1887; s. Andrew Gardner and Mary (Shattuck) J.; student Va. Mil. Inst., 1902-04; B.S., U.S. Mil. Acad., 1908; m. Edith Carroll Reeder, May 26, 1917; children—Charles Reeder (dec.), John Jay, Carroll Shattuck. Oil producer, Parkersburg, W.Va., 1911-14, Tulsa, Oklahoma, 1914-17, Baltimore, 1919-25; secretary of the Federal Land Bank of Baltimore, 1929-31, v.p. and sec., 1931-32, pres. 1932-42; sec. Fed. Intermediate Credit Bank of Baltimore, 1929-31, v.p. and sec., 1931-32, pres., 1932-33; vice pres., Boots Aircraft Nut Corp., Stamford, Conn., from 1944; dir. other cos. Ins. commr. state of Md., 1952-58. Served as 2d lt., 11th U.S. Cavalry, Camp Columbia, Cuba, May 1908-Mar. 1909, and Fort Oglethorpe, Ga., Mar. 1909-Jan. 1, 1911; capt. and adj. 2d Inf., W.Va. Nat. Guard, 1911-16; capt. Air Service, exec. officer Wilbur Wright Field, Dayton, O., July 1917-Jan. 1918; capt. Air Serv., Tours, France, and Aviation Acceptance Park, No. 1, Orly, France, Jan. 1918-Aug. 1918; maj. Air Service, Orly, France, Aug. 1918-Dec. 1918; resigned Feb. 17, 1919. Mem. Newcomen Soc. of England. Clubs: Maryland, The Elkridge (Baltimore). Home: Baltimore, Md. †

JACKSON, GLENN EDWARD, assn. exec.; b. Gilmore City, Ia., Apr. 25, 1889; s. Seymour Turnicliffe and Mary (Mann) J.; B.S., Coe Coll., 1913; grad. student Columbia, 1926-28; m. Vesta L. Wilson, Aug. 4, 1915; children—Eleanor Mary, Betty (Mrs. Ralph DeVries), Robert L. Exec. sec. community work YMCA, Honolulu, T.H., 1913-19, North Side YMCA, Mpls., 1919-25, sec. boys' work Nat. Council, 1925-29, assn. gen. sec., Rochester, N.Y., 1930-35; commr. Funeral Service Bur. of Am., 1929-30; dep. commr. N.Y. State Relief Adminstrn., 1935-37, exec. dir. bur. pub. assistance N.Y. Dept. Social Welfare, 1937-41; dir. community programs Fed. Office Civil Def., 1941-45; exec. dir. Orthopedic Appliance and Limb Mfrs. Assn., from 1946, exec. dir. Am. Bd. for Certification, from 1948. Instr. pub. welfare adminstrn. Smith Coll., summers 1936, 37; instr. Summer Inst. Assn. Execs., Yale, 1955, 56, 58, Mich. State U., 1957, 58. Mem. President's Com. Employment Physically Handicapped, from 1955. Exec. com. Social Planning Bd., Rochester, N.Y., 1933-35; mem. agency credentials com. Council Social Agencies, Washington, mem. Council for Aging. Served as capt. Hawaii N.G. 1919. Mem. Am. Soc. Assn. Execs. (chmn. ins. com. from 1954; dir. 1955; trustee retirement program), Nat. Inst. Assn. Mgmt. (bd. regents), Phi Beta Gamma. Mason. Author articles on trade assns., group dynamics. Home: Bethesda, Md. †

JACKSON, HAROLD PINEO, cons.; born Bar Harbor, Me., Feb. 18, 1889; s. Charles Augustus Goodrich and Ruby Mae (Pineo) J.; A.B., Dartmouth Coll., 1910; m. Grace Gillette Burnham, Dec. 1, 1917; children—Katherine Ruby, Charles Burnham, Ralph Pineo; m. 2d, Recardia McGuirk, Oct. 30, 1941. Newspaper reporter, 1910; in ins. bus., from 1911; pres., gen. mgr. Norwich Union Indemnity Co., 1927-30; pres. Bankers Indemnity Ins. Co. 1930-54; dir.; v.p. Am. Ins. Co. 1946-54, dir.; ret. 1954; cons. Center for Safety Edn., N.Y.U. Served as lt. Infantry, 42d (Rainbow) Div., in France and Germany, 1918-19. Fellow Ins. Inst. Am.; mem. Soc. Mayflower Descs., Huguenot Soc., Delta Tau Delta. Club: Montclair Golf. Home: Montclair, N.J. †

JACKSON, HENRY MARTIN, U.S. senator; b. Everett, Wash., May 31, 1912; s. Peter and Marine (Anderson) J.; m. Helen E. Hardin, Dec. 16, 1961; children—Anna Marie, Peter Hardin. LL.B., U. Wash., 1935. Bar: Wash. bar 1935. Asso. with Black & Rucker, 1935-38; pros. atty. Snohomish County, 1938-40; mem. 77th-82d Congresses from 2d Wash. Dist., U.S. senator from, Wash., 1953-83; ranking minority mem. com. on energy and natural resources, mem. Armed Services Com., chmn. strategic arms control subcom. Chmn. Democratic Nat. Com., 1960-61; bd. regents Smithsonian Inst.; bd. overseers Whitman Coll.; bd. advisors John F. Kennedy Inst. Politics, Harvard U. Mem. Wash. Bar Assn., Phi Delta Phi, Delta Chi. Presbyterian. Home: Everett, Wash. Died Sept. 1, 1983.

JACKSON, HEZEKIAH, college dean; b. Greensburg, La., Feb. 8, 1917; s. Harvey and Dicy (Lewis) J.; B.S., So. U., 1941; M.S., Mich. State U., 1947, Ph.D., 1952; m. Adele Martin, May 26, 1949; children—Reginald Jerome, Raymond Eugene, Ronald Keith. Prof. horticulture, head dept. So. U., Baton Rouge, 1947-56, dir. div. agr., 1956-58, dir. internat. program, dean Coll. Agr., 1958-79, also coordinator Coop. State Research Service programs; mem. nat. adv. com. Hort. Crops Research; mem. La. State adv. com. Agrl. Stblzn. Conservation Service. Mem. La. Small Bus. Adv. Council; vice chmn. African-Am. Scholars Council; mem. com. policy, program and role State Univs. and Land Grand Colls.; active local YMCA, United Givers Fund, Blundon Orphanage. Served to capt., inf. AUS, 1941-45. Mem. Am. Soc. Hort. Sci., Am. Soc. Plant Physiologists, Bot. Soc. Am., Phi Beta Sigma. Republican. Methodist (chmn. fin. commn.). Club: Masons (32 deg.). Home: Baton Rouge, La. Died Aug. 16, 1979.

JACKSON, ROBERT TILDEN, life ins. co. exec.; b. Barre, Vt., Sept. 18, 1917; s. Henry Hollister and Carrie Carlton (Bemis) J.; m. Edna Florence Otka, Sept. 21,

1946; children—Sherry Ann, Patricia Carrie, Henry Hollister. B.A., Yale, 1939; LL.B., U. Conn., 1952. Bar: Conn. bar 1952. With Phoenix Mut. Life Ins. Co., Hartford, Conn., 1939-83, v.p., actuary, 1960-68, exec. v.p., 1968-71, pres., 1971-78, chmn. bd., 1978-83, also dir. Served to maj. USAAF, 1942-46. Fellow Soc. Actuaries. Home: Hartford, Conn. Died 1983.

JACKSON, SAMUEL CHARLES, lawyer; b. Kansas City, Kans., May 8, 1929; s. James C. and Mattie (Webber) J.; m. Judith M. Bradford, Jan. 27, 1952; children—Marcia Lyn, Brenda Sue. A.B., Washburn U., 1951, LL.B., 1954, J.D., 1970. Bar: Kans. bar 1954. Pvt. practice, Topeka, 1957-65; dep. gen. counsel Kans. Dept. Social Welfare, 1963-65; commr. Equal Employment Opportunity Commn., Washington, 1965-68; v.p. Am. Arbitration Assn. Center Dispute Seattlement, Washington, 1968; asst. sec. met. devel. HUD, 1969-73; partner firm Stroock & Stroock & Lavan, 1973-82. Precinct committeeman Shawnee County Republican Com., 1960, 63; del. Rep. Nat. Conv., 1976. Served with USAF, 1954-57. Mem. Nat. (chmn. judiciary com. 1969-82), Am., Fed., Topeka bar assns., Kappa Alpha Psi. Republican. Home: Washington, D.C. Died Sept. 27, 1982.

JACKSON, THOMAS WOODROW, mechanical engineering educator and consultant; b. Chgo., Apr. 3, 1917; s. Thomas and Elizabeth (Slivka) J.; m. Dymitrea Alice Templeman, Feb. 7, 1943; children: Anita Louise Scavullo, Elizabeth Ann Brown. B.S. in Mech. Engring, U. Ill., 1941; M.S. in M.E, U. Calif., 1946; Ph.D. (XR fellow), Purdue U., 1949. Registered profl. engr., Ohio, Ga., Mo. Instr., designing engr. Standard Oil Co., Ind., 1941-42; aero. research scientist NACA Lewis Flight Propulsion Lab., 1949-51; air force officer (lt. col.) and civilian Aircraft Nuclear Propulsion Program, 1951-54; chief mech. scis. div. Engring. Expt. Sta., Ga. Inst. Tech., 1954-67, prof., 1954-70, assoc. dean engring. research, 1965-67, acting dean grad. div., 1966-67, prof. energy engring., 1974-78, emeritus prof. mech. engring., 1978-82, cons. engr., writer, 1978-82; dir. Skidaway Inst. Oceanography, Univ. System Ga., 1967-70; tech. dir. Pres.'s Nat. Indsl. Pollution Control Council, Dept. Commerce, 1970-73, Office Environ. Affairs, 1973-74. Co-author: Research and Development Management, 1966. Served from aviation cadet to lt. col. USAAF, 1942-46; col. Res. (ret.). Mem. ASME, Sigma Xi, Phi Kappa Phi, Tau Beta Pi, Pi Tau Signa, Sigma Pi Sigma. Home: Ava, Mo. Died Mar. 13, 1982.

JACKSON, WILL WOODWARD, former ins. co. exec.; b. Waynesboro, Tenn., Apr. 20, 1890; s. George Washington and Martha Mollie (Craig) J.; A.B., Southwestern U., Georgetown, Tex., 1916, Litt. D., 1940; M.A., U. Tex., 1928; postgrad. Yale, 1929-30; m. Ruth Goddard, Aug. 20, 1919; children—Leila Craig, Will Woodward. Supt. pub. schs., Normangee, Tex., 1916-17; sec. Student YMCA of Ark., 1919-21; pres. Wesleyan Inst., San Antonio, 1921-29, Westmoreland Coll., 1930-36, U. San Antonio, 1936-42; v.p., dir. pub. relations Trinity U., 1942-46; v.p. Am. Hosp. Life Ins. Co., San Antonio, 1946-60. Regional exec. USO, 1942-46; mem. USAF Community Council; mem. exec. com. jurisdictional conf. Meth. Ch., lay del. world-wide confs.; pres. Community Welfare Council, San Antonio, 1964-66; mem. Tex. State Bd. Edn., 1950-69, chmn. 1959-69; gov. St. Mary's U.; mem. bd. devel. So. Meth. U. Chmn. bd. dirs. San Antonio Heart Assn., 1954-61, Tex. Heart Assn., 1961; bd. dirs. YMCA, Nat. Travelers Aid Assn., A.R.C., Tex Council Econ. Edn., S.W. Ednl. Research Lab. Served with F.A., U.S. Army, 1917-19. Recipient Distinguished Alumnus award Southwestern U., 1961; Ann. Conf. award Christians and Jews for contbn. to human relations, 1962. Mem. San Antonio Council Chs. (pres.), San Antonio C. of C. (dir.), Am. Sociol. Soc., Am. Acad. Polit. and Social Scis., Alpha Chi. Methodist. Mason, Rotarian (dist. gov. 1943). Home: San Antonio, TX. †

JACKSON, WILLIAM THOMAS HOBDELL, educator; b. Sheffield, Eng., Apr. 2, 1915; came to U.S., 1948, naturalized, 1957; s. William A. and Harriet (Williams) J.; m. Erika Anna M. Noltemeyer, Aug. 23, 1945; children—Thomas C.H., Inge A.M., Christopher M.P. B.A., Sheffield U., 1935, M.A., 1938; Ph.D., U. Wash., 1951. Instr. U. Wash., 1948-50; asst. prof. Coe Coll., 1950-52; asst. prof. medieval lit. Columbia, 1952-55, asso. prof., 1955-58, prof., 1958-83, Villard prof. German and comparative lit., 1973-83, chmn. German dept., 1961-67; vis. prof. U. Chgo., 1955, Rutgers State U., 1962-83, Duke U., 1965, Yale U., 1966, City U. N.Y., 1975-77, Fordham U., 1977, SUNY, 1979; vis. lectr. Princeton, 1957; Phi Beta Kappa vis. scholar, 1965-66; Trustee Columbia Univ. Press, 1980-83. Author: The Literature of the Middle Ages, 1960, Essential Erasmus, 1964, Medieval Literature: A History and a Guide, 1965, (with P. Demetz) Anthology of German Literature to 1750, 1968, The Anatomy of Love-A Study of the Tristan of Gottfried von Strassburg, 1971, The Interpretation of Medieval Lyric, 1980, The Hero and the King: An Epic Theme, 1981; Contbr. (with P. Demetz) articles on medieval lit. to profl. jours.; Editor: (with P. Demetz) Germanic Rev, 1955-66, Columbia Records of Civilization Series, 1962-83. Served with Brit. Army, 1940-46. Guggenheim fellow, 1958-59, 67-68; grantee Am. Council Learned Socs. Fellow Medieval Acad. Am. (mem. council 1968—); mem. Acad. Literary Studies, Modern Humanities Research Assn. Home: New York, N.Y. Died May 7, 1983.

JACKSON, WILLIS CARL, librarian; b. Beverly, Mass., May 20, 1923; s. Willis Carl and Olive (McAllister) J.; m. Mary Elisabeth Lett, Aug. 13, 1948; 1 dau., Carla. A.B., Fla. State U., 1951, M.A., 1952. Asst. order librarian U. Tenn., 1952-54; head order dept., head acquistions State U. Iowa Library, 1954-57; chief acquistions librarian U. Minn., 1957-63; asso. dir. libraries U. Colo., 1963-65; dir. libraries Pa. State U., 1966-72; dean univ. libraries Ind. U., Bloomington, 1973-82; cons., lectr. in field, 1956-82; lectr. on sailing, 1978-82; adv. com. CIP program Library of Congress, 1970-82; adv. com. Aerospace Research Applications Center, 1973-82; bd. dirs., chmn. steering com., acting pres. MIDLNET, 1974-75, exec. com. of bd. dirs., 1975-82; vis. com. Lehigh U., 1970-76, Tufts U., 1976-82; pres., dir. LARC Assos.; trustee Educom. Author: The Log of the Carla Mia, 1980; contbr. articles to profl. jours. Mem. Benner Twp. (Pa.) Gen. Authority, 1966-72; bd. dirs. Incolsa, 1977-82. Served with AUS, 1942-45. Mem. ALA (pres., resources and tech. services div. 1970-71, council 1967, 69-72, 75-79), Pa. Library Assn. (Disting. Service award 1972), Ind. Library Assn., Am. Aviation Hist. Soc., Soc. World War II Aero. Historians, Air Power History Found., OX-5 Club, U.S. Power Squadron, Beta Phi Mu. Democrat. Methodist. Clubs: Rotary, Grolier, Elks, Caxton, Bloomington Yacht; Royal Cork Yacht (Crosshaven, Ireland). Solo sailing voyage across Atlantic Ocean, 1978. Home: Bloomington, Ind. Died May, 1982.

JACOBI, HERBERT J., patent lawyer, orgn. exec.; b. Washington, Dec. 25, 1888; s. Joseph W. and Esther R. (Pimes) J.; spl. engring. course George Washington U., 1909-10; LL.B., Georgetown U., 1914, M.P.L., 1914; m. Hermione Bennett, Nov. 20, 1920; children—Herbert, Robert B. Admitted to D.C. bar, 1914, practice in Washington, specializing in patents and trademark law; admitted bar Supreme Ct. U.S.; arguing Vets. Preference Legislation before coms. of Congress from 1946. Served as lt., U.S. Air Corps, A.E.F. and Army Occupation, World War I. Mem. Am. Legion (comdr. dept. D.C., 1945-46, nat. vice comdr., 1950-51), Am. Patent Law Assn., Am. and D.C. bar assns. Club: Post Mortem. Home: Washington, D.C. †

JACOBS, HAROLD, physicist; b. Port Chester, N.Y., Nov. 21, 1917; s. Maurice LeRoy and Lillian J.; m. Lydia S. Zarkower, Oct. 15, 1943; children—Suzanne L. Jacobs Miller, Glenn S., Steven M., Maura E. B.A., Johns Hopkins U., 1938; M.S., N.Y. U., 1940, Ph.D., 1946. Physicist RCA Corp., Lancaster, Pa., 1940-46; physicist Sylvania Electric Products, Inc., N.Y.C., 1946-49; physicist U.S. Army Electronics Lab., Fort Monmouth, N.J., from 1949, supervisory research physicist, from 1949, prof. dept. elec. engring. Monmouth Coll., West Long Branch, N.J., from 1957, chmn. dept., 1957-77; mem. N.J. State Panel Sci. Advisors, from 1981, N.J. State Council Engring. Deans, 1972-77. Contbr. articles to profl. jours. Recipient Harry Diamond award IEEE, 1973; Achievement award Dept. Army, 1978. Fellow IEEE; mem. Am. Phys. Soc., Am. Soc. Engring. Edn. Patentee in field. Home: West Long Branch, NJ.

JACOBS, JOSEPH BENJAMIN, linen service exec.; b. Russia, Dec. 25, 1887; s. Abraham and Rose Jacobs; brought to U.S., 1891; student pub. schs., Atlanta; m. Lena Jacobs, Aug. 19, 1913. Executive v.p. Linen Service Corp., Atlanta, from 1928. Jewish religion. Home: Atlanta, Ga. †

JACOBS, NORMAN ERNEST, clergyman; b. Johnson City, N.Y., July 9, 1925; s. Paul Sanford and Marian Charlotte (Locke) J.; m. Alice Ann Berry, Mar. 6, 1954; children—Martha Ann, Paul Errett. Student, La. Poly. Coll., 1944-45, U. Okla., 1945-46; A.B., Phillips U., 1948; M.Ed., U. Pitts., 1957, Ph.D., 1963. Ordained to ministry Christian Ch., 1948; pastor First Christian Ch., Scranton, Pa., 1949-54, Knoxville Christian Ch., Pitts., 1954-63; dean Coll. of Bible; v.p. for acad. affairs, dean of faculty Phillips U., 1963-75, prof. Christian edn., 1963-80, acting pres., 1972-73; pastor First Christian Ch., McPherson, Kans., from 1980; dir. Council of Chs., Pitts. area, 1955-63. Author: Christians Learning for Christian Living, 2 vols, 1961, The Church Alive and Perking, 1973; Contbr. numerous articles religious, scholastic jours. Bd. dirs. Pitts YMCA, 1956-63. Served with USNR, 1943-46. Mem. Assn. Christian Chs. Pa. (pres. 1962), Religious Edn. Assn., Disciples Hist. Soc., Theta Phi. Home: McPherson, Kans.

JACOBS, WALTER WILLIAM, educator; b. Newark, Sept. 26, 1914; s. Harry Simon and Beatrice (Kaplan) J.; m. Irene Ostreicher, Mar. 30, 1941. B.S., Coll. City N.Y., 1934; A.M., George Washington U., 1940, Ph.D., 1951. Analyst War Dept., 1945-47; chief prodn. and marketing sect. Dept. Commerce, 1947-51; dept. chief computation div. Hdqrs. USAF, 1951-57; dep. chief, office research Nat. Security Agy., 1957-65; comdt. Nat. Cryptologic Sch., 1966-69; chmn. dept. math. Am. U., Washington, 1969-73, prof., 1973-80, prof. emeritus, 1980-82. Author: (with Alain C. White) Variation Play, 1943. Served with AUS, 1943-46. Decorated Legion of Merit. Mem. Math. Assn. Am., Assn. Computing Machinery. Club: Cosmos. Home: Washington, D.C. Died Feb. 11, 1982.

JACOBSEN, ERNEST A., dean; b. Moroni, Utah, Sept. 22, 1890; s. Jacob and Anna (Simmonsen) J.; A.B., Brigham Young U., 1917, A.M., 1923; student U. of Utah, 1919, U. of Calif., 1928-29; Ed.D., U. of Ore., 1937; m. Eva Michaelson, June 5, 1912; children—Jewel (Mrs. B. D. Scott), Maurine (Mrs. M. F. Pulley), Eldon E. Teacher, 1910; prin., Uintah Acad., 1920-23; supt., North Summitt Sch. Dist., 1923-28; prof. of edn., Utah State Agrl. Coll., from 1929, dean, Sch. of Edn., from 1932. Fellow Utah Acad. of Sciences, Arts and Letters; mem. Phi Delta Kappa. Home: East Logan, Utah. †

JACOBSON, AVROHM, psychiatrist, educator; b. Toronto, Ont., Can., July 12, 1919; came to U.S., 1919, naturalized, 1944,; s. Morris and Tillie (Gorback) J.; m. Shirley S. Applebaum, Jan. 3, 1948; children: Debra Ann, Nancy Ellen, Aric Daniel. B.A., U. Mich., 1941; M.D., Tulane U., 1944. House physician Newark Beth Israel Hosp., 1944-45; resident in psychiatry State Hosp., Middletown, N.Y., 1945-46; fellow in psychiatry St. Elizabeths Hosp., 1948-49; trainee in psychoanalysis Washington-Balt. Psychoanalytic Inst., 1948-52; pvt. practice psychiatry and psychoanalysis, Monmouth County, N.J., from 1952; instr. psychiatry Georgetown U. Med. Sch., 1948-52; asso. clin. prof. psychiatry N.Y. Med. Coll., 1956-64; prof. clin. psychiatry Seton Hall Coll. Medicine, 1960-63; clin. prof. psychiatry Rutgers U. Med. Sch., from 1970; sr. attending psychiatrist Monmouth Med. Center, Long Branch; mem. med. bd. Monmouth County Heart Assn., 1956-58; Monmouth County Mental Health Bd. Councilman Borough of Interlaken, from 1966. Contbr. articles to profl. jours. Served with AUS, 1946-47, 50-52. Fellow A.C.P., Am. Psychiat. Assn., AAAS, Am. Acad. Polit. and Social Sci., Am. Acad. Psychosomatic Medicine; mem. Am. Soc. Psychoanalytic Physicians, Pan Am. Med. Assn., Eastern Psychoanalytic Assn., AMA, N.J. Psychiat. Assn. (pres. 1968-70, trustee 1963-66, del. to Am. Psychiat. Assn. 1970, Golden Merit award 1981), Monmouth County Med. Soc. (pres. 1969-70), Phi Delta Epsilon. Clubs: Mason, Kiwanis. Home: Interlaken, NJ.

JACOBSON, EDMUND, physician, physiologist; b. Chgo., Apr. 22, 1888; s. Morris and Fannie (Blum) J.; B.S., Northwestern U., 1907; A.M., Harvard, 1909, Ph.D., 1910; fellow Cornell U., Ithaca, N.Y., 1911; M.D., U. Chgo., 1915; LL.D., George Williams Coll., 1962; m. Elizabeth Ruth Silberman, Dec. 16, 1926; children—Ruth Frances, Edmund, Nancy Elizabeth. Practice medicine specializing in internal medicine, Chgo.; research asso. U. Chgo., 1926-30, asst. prof. physiology, 1930-36, dir. Lab. for Clin. Physiology, from 1936. Bd. dirs. Found. Sci. Relaxation. Recipient William G. Anderson merit award AAHPER, 1974, Northwestern U. merit award, 1975. Fellow Internat. Coll. Angiology, AAAS, ACP, St. Louis Med. Soc. (hon.); mem. AMA, Ill., Chgo. med socs., Am. Physiol. Assn., Am. Assn. Advancement Tension Control (dir.), Phi Beta Kappa, Sigma Xi. Club: Quadrangle (U. Chgo.). Author books including: Progressive Relaxation, 1929, rev. edit., 1938; You Must Relax, 1934, 5th rev. edit., 1976; The Peace We Americans Need, 1944; How to Relax and Have Your Baby, 1959; Tension Control for Businessmen, 1963; Anxiety and Tension Control, 1963; Tension in Medicine, 1967; Biology of Emotions, 1966; Modern Treatment of Tense Patients, 1969; Teaching and Learning, 1973. Contbr. articles to med. jours. Home: Chicago, Ill. Died Jan. 7, 1983.

JACOBUS, DONALD LINES, genealogist; b. New Haven, Oct. 3, 1887; s. John Ira and Ida Wilmot (Lines) J.; B.A., Yale, 1908, M.A., 1911. Sec. New Haven Bldg. & Loan Assn., 1912-17; editor, pub. Am. Genealogist, from 1932; genealogist Conn. Soc. Colonial Dames Am., 1949-53. Served as pvt. A.E.F., U.S. Army, World War I. Fellow American Genealogical Society; member New Haven Colony Historical Society (hon. dir.). Author: Genealogy as Pastime and Profession, 1930; Index to Genealogical Periodicals (3 vols.), 1932, 47, 53; also articles and verse in periodicals. Editor: Families of Ancient New Haven, 8 vols., 1922-32; Families of Old Fairfield, 1930-34; Bowen's History of Woodstock, Conn. (vols. 7 and 8, with W. Herbet Wood), 1943; The Hazen Family, 1947; Ancestry of Thomas Chalmers Brainerd, 1948; Deacon George Clark(e) of Milford, 1949; The Gilbert Family, 1953; The Waterman Family (3 vols.), 1939, 42, 54; The Ancestry of Rev. Grier Parke & His wife Ann Elizabeth Gildersleeve, 1959; The Early Daytons and Descendants of Henry Jr., 1959; The Ancestry of Lorenzo Ackley and his wife Emma Arabella Bosworth, 1960. Compiler geneal. vols., from 1922. Coordinator, Denison Genealogy, 1963. †

JACOBY, OSWALD, actuary, writer; b. Bklyn., Dec. 8, 1902; s. Oswald N. and Edith (Sondheim) J.; student Columbia; m. Mary Zita McHale, Apr. 25, 1932; children—James O., Jon P. With Met. Life Ins. Co., 1922-28; cons. actuary, Dallas, from 1937; writer syndicated newspaper column on bridge, from 1940. Served as corpl. U.S. Army, World War I; lt. USNR, World War II; comdr., Korean War; mem. original staff Pan Mun Jom armistice talks. Selected as No. 1 bridge player in Am., by Shepard Barclay, 1936-40. Fellow Soc. Actuaries; mem. Phi Kappa Sigma. Clubs: Dallas Country, Fort Worth. Author: Oswald Jacoby on Poker, 1940; How to Figure the Odds, 1946; Gin Rummy, 1946; How to Win at Canasta, 1949; Oswald Jacoby's Complete Canasta, 1950; Winning Poker, 1950; What's New in Bridge, 1953. Home: Dallas, Tex. Died.

JAEGER, EDMUND CARROLL, author; b. Loup City, Neb., Jan. 28, 1887; s. John Phillip and Catherine (Guenther) J.; Loma Linda Coll. of Med. Evangelists; B.Sc., Occidental Coll., Los Angeles, Calif., 1918; studied

Pomona Coll. Marine Lab., U. of Calif., and U. of Colo.; unmarried. Lecturer scientific temperance, W.C.T.U., 1910-12; spl. lecturer on natural history, pub. schs., Pasadena, Calif., 1913, 14; instr. zoölogy, Riverside Jr. Coll. and lecturer on natural history, Boys' Poly. High Sch., from 1921; spl. observer Calif. Acad. Sciences; extension lecturer in zoölogy, U. of Calif., 1924, 25. Spent nearly 12 yrs. in travel and exploration in deserts and mountains of the Southwest. Mem. Am. Soc. Mammalogists, Calif. Acad. Sciences, Western Soc. Naturalists (pres. San Jacinto Sect., 1928-29), Cooper Ornithol. Club. Author: The Mountain Trees of Southern California, 1919; Denizens of the Desert, 1922; Birds of the Charleston Mountains of Nevada, 1926; Report on the Flora of the Charleston Mountains of Nevada, 1926; Denizens of the Mountains, 1929. Home: Riverside, Calif. †

JAFFÉ, BERNARD FREDERICK VICTOR, electrical manufacturing executive; b. Posen, Germany, July 16, 1890; s. Maurice and Félicie (Schaps) J.; Dr. Law, U. Rostock, 1914; m. Garda Platen-Hallermund, May 7, 1931; 1 child, Bernard W. Naturalized Brit. citizen, 1945. Regular and res. service Royal Saxon Army, 1908-18; mem. German Peace Del., Versailles, France, 1919; engaged in bus., 1924-81, with ITT, N.Y.C., 1928-81; v.p., dir. subs. Internat. Standard Electric Corp., 1928-62; hon. chmn. bd. subs. Standard Elektrik Lorenz A.G., Stuttgart; vice chmn. Hanseatische Industrie Beteiligung GmbH, Bremen, Germany, 1928-48. Home: Bottmingen, Switzerland Dec. July 28, 1981.

JAFFE, SAM, actor; b. N.Y.C., Mar. 10, 1891; s. Bernard and Ada (Steinberg) J.; m. Lillian Taiz, 1926 (dec. 1941); m. Bettye Louise Ackerman, June 7, 1956. B.S., CCNY, 1912; L.H.D. (hon.), Drew U., 1983. Dean math. Bronx Cultural Inst., 1915-16; tour Washington Sq. Players Theatre, N.Y.C., 1917-18; Founder (with George Freedly), curator theatre sect. N.Y. Pub. Library, Equity Library Theatre, 1948. Founder (with George Freedly), 1948; plays include The Jazz Singer, 1927, Grand Hotel, 1930, The Eternal Road, 1937, A Doll's House, 1938, The Gentle People, 1939, Merchant of Venice, 1938, 71, King Lear, 1941, Storm in Summer, 1972, A Meeting by the River, 1979; films include The Scarlet Empress, 1933, Lost Horizon, Gunga Din, The Day The Earth Stood Still, Asphalt Jungle (Venice Internat. award for best male performance 1950), Ben Hur, Battle Beyond the Stars, 1980, Jayne Mansfield, An American Tragedy, 1981, Nothing Lasts Forever, 1983, On the Line, 1983; TV appearances include Ben Casey series (Dr. Zorba), 1961-65, Playhouse 90, Hitchcock Presents, Naked City, Bonanza, Daniel Boone, Alias Smith and Jones, The Snoop Sisters, The Oath '74, Hollywood TV Theatre, Streets of San Francisco, S.W.A.T, Harry O, Medical Story, Bionic Woman, 1976, Kojak, 1977, Flying High, 1978, Buck Rogers, 1980, Hour Mag, 1980, Good Morning America, 1981, Love Boat, 1983. Served with U.S. Army, 1919. Recipient Edgar Allen Poe award, 1950; recipient Acad. award nomination, 1950, Emmy award nomination, 1961-62, Townsend Harris award, 1962, James K. Hacket award, 1971, 125th Anniversary medal City Coll., CUNY, 1973, Paul Robeson award, 1978, spl. honor Equity Library Theatre, 1977. Home: Beverly Hills, Calif. Died Dec. 24, 1984.

JAHNS, RICHARD HENRY, geologist; b. Los Angeles, Mar. 10, 1915; s. Alfred H. and Cecelia (Schnackenbeck) J.; m. Frances M. Hodapp, Sept. 5, 1936; children: Alfred, Jeannette. B.S., Calif. Inst. Tech., 1935, Ph.D., 1943; M.S., Northwestern U., 1937. Teaching fellow Northwestern U., 1935-37; teaching fellow Calif. Inst. Tech., 1937-39, asst. prof. geology, 1946, asso. prof., 1946-49, prof., 1949-60; prof. geology Pa. State U., 1960-65, chmn. div. earth scis., 1960-62; dean Pa. State U. (Coll. Mineral Industries), 1962-65; prof. geology, dean Sch. Earth Scis., Stanford U., 1965-79, W. J. and M. L. Crook prof. geology and applied earth scis., 1977-83; jr. geologist U.S. Geol. Survey, Washington, 1937-40, asst. geologist, 1940-42, asso. geologist, 1942-44, geologist, 1944-48, sr. geologist, 1949-65, cons., 1967-83; nat. lectr. Sigma Xi, 1965; Mem. Calif. State Mining and Geology Bd., 1965-75, Gov.'s Sci. Adv. Bd. Calif., Calif. Seismic Safety Commn., 1975-83; mem. Calif. desert conservation area adv. com. U.S. Bur. Land Mgmt., 1977-81, Nat. Pub. Lands Adv. Council, 1979-81. Author: Hand Specimen Petrology; Editor: Geology of Southern California; asst. editor: Am. Minerologist and Engring. Geology; Contbr. numerous articles and reports on econ., glacial engring. and structural geology, and petrology to sci. publs. Recipient Disting. Alumnus award Calif. Inst. Tech., 197O, Ian Campbell Medal Am. Geol. Inst., 1981. Mem. AAAS, Am. Assn. Petrol. Geologists (Pub. Service award 1982), Am. Geophys. Union, Am. Inst. Mining and Metall. Engrs., Calif. Acad. Scis. (pres. 1978-81), Geol. Soc. Am. (pres. 197O-71), Geol. Soc. Washington, AAUP, Mineral. Soc. Am., Soc. Econ. Geologists, Seismol. Soc. Am., Geochem. Soc., Am. Inst. Profl. Geologists, Assn. Engring. Geologists (hon.), Nat. Assn. Geology Tchrs. Home: Menlo Park, Calif. Died Dec. 31, 1983.

JAKOBSON, ROMAN, linguist, lit. historian; b. Moscow, Russia, Oct. 11, 1896; came to U.S., 1941; s. Osip and Anna (Volpert) J.; m. Krystyna Pomorska, Sept. 28, 1962. A.B. with Silver medal, Lazarev Inst. Oriental Langs., Moscow, 1914; Diploma first degree, Moscow U.; Diploma first degree (Buslaev prize for study lang. North Russian Oral Epos 1916), 1918; Ph.D., Prague U., 1930; D.Litt., U. Cambridge (Eng.), 1960, univs. Chgo., Oslo, 1961, U. Uppsala, U. Mich., 1963, U. Grenoble, U. Nice, 1966, U. Rome, Yale U., 1967, Charles U., Prague, U. Brno, 1968, Zagreb U., 1969, Ohio State U., 1970, U. Louvain, 1972, U. Tel Aviv, Harvard U., 1975, Columbia U., 1976, U. Liège, 1979, Copenhagen U., 1979, Ruhr U., 1980, Georgetown U., 1980, Brandeis U., 1981, Oxford U., 1981; D.Sc., U. N.Mex., 1966, Clark U., 1969. Research asso. Moscow U., 1918-20; prof. Russian philology Masaryk U., Brno, 1933-39; prof. gen. linguistics and Czechoslovak studies Ecole Libre des Hautes Etudes, N.Y.C., 1942-46; vis. prof. linguistics Columbia U., 1943-46, T.G. Masaryk prof. Czechoslovak studies, 1946-49; S.H. Cross prof. Slavic lang. and lits. Harvard, 1949-67, also gen. linguistics, 1960-67; Inst. prof. Mass. Inst. Tech., 1957-67; Vis. prof. Yale U., 1967, 71, Princeton, 1968, Brown U., 1969-70, Brandeis U., 1970, Collège de France, 1972, Louvain U., 1972, N.Y. U., 1973, Bergen U., 1976, Wellesley Coll. Author: books including Kindersprache, Aphasie und allgem. Lautgesetze, 1941, (with G. Fant and M. Halle) Preliminaries to Speech Analysis, 1952, Fundamentals of Language, 1956, 71, Selected Writings I, 1962, II, 1971, III, 1981, IV, 1966, V, 1979, Essais de linguistigue générale I, II, 1963; 1973, Saggi di linguistica generale, 1966, Fonema e Fonologia, 1967, Child Language, Aphasia and Phonological Universals, 1968, Linguistica, Poetica, Cinema, 1970, Langage enfantin et aphasie, 1969, (with L.L. Hammerich) Low German Manual of Spoken Russian-16O7, I, 1961, II, 1970, (with L.G. Jones) Shakespeare's Verbal Art, 1970, Studies on Child Language and Aphasia, 1971, Questions de Poétique, 1973, Main Trends in the Science of Language, 1973, Form und Sinn, 1974, Aufsätze zur Linguistik und Poetik, 1974, Premesse di storia letteratura slava, 1975, Pushkin and His Sculptural Myth, 1975, N.S. Trubetzkoy's Letters and Notes, 1975, Six Leçons sur le son et le sens, 1976, Hölderlin, Klee, Brecht, 1976, Coup d'oeil sur le développement de la sémiotique, 1976, (with S. Rudy) Yeats' Sorrow of Love Through the Years, 1977, Bibliography of Publications, 1971, (with L. Waugh) The Sound Shape of Language, 1979, The Framework of Language, 1980, Brain and Language, 1980, (with K. Pomorska) Dialogues, 1980. Decorated chevalier de la Légion d'Honneur; recipient award Am. Council Learned Socs., 1960, award Am. Assn. Advancement Slavic Studies, 1970; Internat. Feltrinelli prize for Philology and Linguistics, 1980. Fgn. mem. Royal Netherlands, Polish, Norwegian, Danish, Serbian, Irish, Italian (Bologna), Brit., Finnish acads. sci., Bohemian Royal Soc. Sci., Royal Soc. Letters Lund (hon.), Finno-Ugric Soc. (hon.); mem. Am. Acad. Arts and Sci., N.Y. Acad. Scis. (hon.), Philol. Soc. (London, hon.), Mediaeval Acad., Acad. Aphasia (hon.), Tokyo Inst. for Advanced Studies Lang. (hon. pres.), Royal Anthrop. Inst. Gt. Britain and Ireland (hon.), Am. Anthrop. Assn., Soc. de Ling. de Paris, Linguistic Soc. Am. (pres. 1956), Internat. Com. Slavists (hon.), Cercle Ling. de Copenhague (hon.), Moscow Linguistic Circle (founder, chmn. 1915-20), Prague Linguistic Circle (co-founder, v.p. 1927-38), Linguistic Circle N.Y. (co-founder, v.p. 1943-49), Internat. Soc. Phonetic Sci. (v.p.), Acoustic Soc. Am., Internat. Phonetic Assn. (hon.), Slovak Acad. Sci. (Golden medal 1968). Home: Cambridge, Mass. July 18, 1982.

JALONICK, GEORGE WASHINGTON, III, business executive; b. Dallas, Oct. 10, 1913; s. George Washington, Jr. and Charlotte Katherine (Johnston) J.; student U. Tex., 1932-34; m. Dorothy Elizabeth Cockrell, Nov. 22, 1938; children—George Washington, Dorothy Aurelia, Sally Ann. With Southwest Airmotive Co., 1941-69, v.p., 1941-58, exec. v.p., then dir., pres., chmn. bd., 1958-69, ret., 1969. Mem. Dallas Planning Council, Dallas Crime Commn. (dir.), Tex. Aviation Adv. Council and Aviation Council of Texas, Aviation Legis. Com.; chmn. bd. Dallas Soc. Prevention Cruelty to Animals. Mem. Tex. Police Assn., Kappa Alpha. Clubs: Dallas Country; Northwood, Terpsichorian; Dallas; Headliners (Austin, Tex.). Home: Dallas, Tex. Died Dec. 13, 1981.

JAMES, CLIFFORD CYRIL, educator, mgmt. adviser; b. Timsbury, Somerset, Eng., Dec. 9, 1900; came to U.S., 1923, naturalized, 1942; s. George Thomas and Dora Elizabeth (Maggs) J.; m. Mae Laura Coleman, Dec. 27, 1941. Ed. in, U.S.; LL.D., U. Balt., 1980. Writer mags. and newspapers, also advt. exec., Can. and, Calif. 1920-25; internat. dir. Round Table Internat., 1925-29; advt. and pub. relations exec. and cons., N.Y.C. and Phila., 1929-40; mng. editor Econ. Forum, 1932-40; organizer, dir. engring., sci. and mgmt. war tng. program, also U.S. pilot tng. program U. Balt., 1940-45, founder, 1945; dean U. Balt. (Sch. Bus.), 1945-69, now dean emeritus; mgmt. and mktg. adviser, from 1940; Mgmt. devel. adviser Md. Comptroller's Office, from 1970; mem. Balt. Mayor's Prof. Adv. com. Author: syndicated articles Management Guideposts, from 1952. Chmn. pub. relations Community-Red Cross United Appeal, Balt., 1958-60; chmn. membership com. Balt. Assn. Commerce, 1959-61, mem. edn. com., chmn. edn.-bus. coordinating council, from 1954; dir. Advt. Club Balt., from 1961; Mem. Md. adv. council Small Bus. Adminstrn., from 1964; mem. export expansion council Dept. Commerce, from 1969; com. mem. Md. Council for Higher Edn., from 1964; mem. shock-trauma found. adv. bd. Md. Inst. Emergency Medicine, from 1979. Dean James chair disting. teaching established U. Balt., 1980. Fellow Soc. Advancement Mgmt. (internat. v.p., chmn. profl. mgmt. standards and recognition council 1975, Outstanding Mgmt. award 1956); mem. C. of C. of Met. Balt., Sales and Marketing Execs. Internat. Home: Baltimore, MD.

JAMES, HARRY HAAG, dance band leader; b. Albany, Ga., Mar. 15, 1916; s. Everette Robert and Maybelle (Stewart) J.; ed. grade and high school, Beaumont, Tex.; m. Louise Tobin, May 4, 1935; children—Harry Jeffery, Timothy Ray; m. 2d Elizabeth Grable, July 5, 1943 (div. 1965); children—Victoria Elizabeth, and Jessica; m. third, Joan Boyd. His parents were circus people and the early years were spent with the circus; his father taught him to play the trumpet and at age 14 he played in local dance bands, Beaumont; traveled with Joe Gale's orchestra at age 15; played with Ben Pollock's orchestra, 1935-36, with Benny Goodman's orchestra, 1937-39; organized his own orchestra, Jan. 1939, later adding a string quartet to usual instrumentation; made recording of "You Made Me Love You," spring 1941 (has sold over a million copies); went to Hollywood for motion pictures, spring 1942; played on Coca Cola Spotlight Saturday Show, 7 times, 1942; returned to N.Y. City and played at Hotel Astor and again on Spotlight Show; appearing TV, clubs in various cities. Numerous motion pictures. Received No. 1 rating for swing bands from Radio Daily Poll, 1942. Home: Beverly Hills, Calif. Died July 5, 1983.

JAMES, JOHN, educator, lawyer; b. Maple Hill, Pender Co., N.C., Feb. 3, 1888; s. Gibson and Anebelle (Murray) J.; A.B., Davidson (N.C.) Coll., 1909, A.M., 1922; U. of Va., summer 1913; LL.B., La Salle Extension U., 1923; m. Estelle Mott, July 19, 1911. Supt. various schs. in N.C., 1909-14; prof. Greek, Lincoln Memorial Univ., Cumberland Gap, Tenn., summer 1912; pres. Synodical Coll., Fulton, Mo., 1914-22; dean Chicora Coll., Columbia, S.C., 1922-3; in practice of law, Charlotte, N.C. from 1923. Exec. sec. campaign to raise $500,000 to endow ednl. instns. of Mo. Presbyn. Synod. Mem. N.E.A., Southern Ednl. Assn. Democrat. Presbyn. Mason (K.T., Shriner), K.P. Clubs: Commercial, Fulton Country. Home: Charlotte, N.C. †

JAMES, M(AZEY) STEPHEN, seminary pres.; b. Kirkville, Ia., May 4, 1889; s. Stephen and Anna (Mazey) J.; A.B., Mt. Union Coll., 1914, D.D., 1934; grad. student Harvard, 1917-18; S.T.B., Boston U., 1918; D. Litt., Central College (Pella, Iowa), 1959; m. Marjorie Alden Miller, Sept. 27, 1922; children—Ruth Marjorie (Mrs. William L. Forsythe, Jr.), Betty Alden (Mrs. David C. Beardslee). Ordained to ministry, Meth. Ch., 1918; pastor, Revere, Mass., 1917-21, First Ch., Pittsfield, Mass., 1922-32, First (Ref.) Ch., Albany, N.Y., 1932-42; faculty dept. homiletics, practical theology New Brunswick Theol. Sem., 1942-52, dean, 1952-53, pres. 1953-59, pres. Gen. Synod Ref. Ch. Am., 1944-45, mem. exec. com. bd. edn. Mem. Nat. Council Chs. Christ, Am. Assn. Theol. Seminaries. Home: Bklyn., N.Y. †

JAMES, NEWTON, bank ofcl.; b. Leakesville, Miss., Mar. 28, 1890; s. Philip Edward and Cynthia (Walley) J.; student S. Miss. Coll., Miss. Normal Coll., Clark's Bus. Sch.; m. Flora Byrd, Apr. 17, 1910; children—Van Owen, Daisy Belle (Mrs. H. C. Caulfield), Newton Haskin. High sch. supt., co. supt., Miss., 1912-20; bookkeeper and accountant, 1920-25; bond clk. State Treasurer's Office, Miss., 1929-35; dep. state treas. of Miss., 1935; state treas., 1936-40, 1944-48, 1952-56; v.p. Deposit Guaranty Bank & Trust Co., from 1956. Member Nat. Assn. State Auditors, Comptrollers and State Treasurers, Sons Confederate Vets. Democrat. Baptist. Mason (Shriner). Kiwanian. Home: Clinton, Miss. †

JAMES, WRIGHT ELWOOD, lawyer; b. Compton, Calif., Jan. 16, 1900; s. Edward M. and Lillie (Edwards) J.; m. Josephine Rush, Sept. 28, 1927; 1 son, William E. Student, Oreg. State Coll., 1919-20; A.B., Stanford, 1924, J.D., 1934. Bar: Calif. bar 1934. Geologist Gen. Petroleum Corp., 1924-31, practiced law, Bakersfield.; sec. Laymac Corp. Mem. Calif. Legislature, 1947-48; chmn. Kern County Republican Central Com., 1957-58. Served to lt. comdr. USNR, 1942-45. Mem. Am. Assn. Petroleum Geologists, Am. Bar Assn., State Bar Calif., Res. Officers Assn., Phi Gamma Delta. Clubs: Los Angeles Country, Los Angeles Athletic. Home: Bakersfield, Calif. Deceased.

JAMIESON, JOHN CALHOUN, educator; b. St. Joseph, Mo., Jan. 5, 1924; s. William Thomas and Glessie (McPike) J.; m. Ruth Virginia Lamb, Mar. 26, 1949; children—William Thomas, Virginia Anne, John Booth; m. Rita Marie Powell, Dec. 2, 1978. B.S., U. Chgo., 1947, M.S., 1951, Ph.D., 1952. Mem. faculty U. Chgo., 1953-83, prof. geophysics, 1965-83; With Calif. Research Corp., summer 1953, Stanford Research Inst., summers 1959-63, U.S. Geol. Survey, 1958-83; cons. Los Alamos Sci. Lab., 1964-83, Batelle Meml. Labs., 1969-70. Mem. editorial adv. bd.: Jour. High Temperatures-High Pressures, 1973-83, Physics and Chemistry of Minerals, 1977-83; Contbr. articles profl. jours. Recipient Quantrell award U. Chgo., 1969; NSF fellow, 1953. Mem. Am. Geophys. Union, Am. Phys. Soc., Sigma Xi. Home: Chicago, Ill. Died June 26, 1983.

JAMIESON, ROBERT ARTHUR, savings and loan executive; b. Nairn, Scotland, Dec. 20, 1908; came to U.S., 1924, naturalized, 1928; s. Alexander Lawrence and Jean Fleming (Smith) J.; m. Evelyn C. McNeil, Dec. 24, 1934; children: Richard, Robert, Kathleen. A.B., Knox Coll., 1932; M.A., U. Ill., 1940; LL.D. (hon.), Bradley U., 1981; postgrad., U. Colo. Athletic dir., social sci. tchr. Sparta Twp. High Sch., Wataga, Ill., 1933-35; supt. schs., Varna, Ill., 1935-41; staff FSA, 1941-43; employment mgr. R.G. LeTourneau, Inc., Peoria, Ill., 1943-48; asst. to pres.

Bradley U., 1948-50; dean Bradley U. (Coll. Commerce), 1950; arbitrator labor disputes, from 1948; v.p. Irions' Concrete Products Co., 1954-65; v.p. Security Savs. & Loan Assn., Peoria, 1966-67, pres., 1967-74, chmn. bd., from 1974; Bank for Savs. & Assns., from 1973; dir. Roosevelt Nat. Life Ins. Co. Author articles on personnel, labor relations, sch. bd. practices. Pres. bd. Ill. Lung Assn., 1971; dir. at large Am. Lung Assn.; pres. Ill. Assn. Sch. Bds., 1969-70, Crippled Childrens Center, 1971; mem. Peoria Bd. Edn., 1955-70, Ill. Bd. Edn., from 1974. Recipient Knox Coll. Alumni Disting. Service award, 1954; William Booth award Salvation Army, 1974; Alma Fringer award Ill. Lung Assn., 1974; Will Ross medal Am. Lung Assn., 1982. Mem. Tau Kappa Epsilon, Alpha Kappa Psi, Phi Delta Kappa, Omicron Delta Kappa. Clubs: Creve Coeur, Rotary; Union League (Chgo.). Home: Peoria, Ill.

JAMIESON, ROBERT GORDON, corp. exec.; b. Honolulu, June 18, 1920; s. William and Margaret (Quinan) J.; m. Virginia Dargel Leithead, Aug. 15, 1953; 1 stepson, Thomas William Leithead. A.B., Stanford, 1941; grad., Advanced Mgmt. Program, Harvard br. Hawaii, 1956. Asst. auditor Alexander & Baldwin, Inc., Honolulu, 1941-49, adminstrv. asst., 1949-60, asst. treas., 1960-61, treas., 1961-69, asst. treas., asst. sec., 1969-70, v.p., treas., 1970-82, also officer various subsidiaries. Served to lt. USNR, 1942-46. Mem. Nat. Assn. Accountants, Financial Execs. Inst., Chi Psi. Republican. Club: Oahu Country (Honolulu). Home: Honolulu, Hawaii. Died 1982.

JANSON, HORST WOLDEMAR, educator; b. St. Petersburg, Russia, Oct. 4, 1913; s. Friedrich and Helene (Porsch) J.; M.A., Harvard, 1938, Ph.D., 1942; m. Dora Jane Heineberg, Aug. 14, 1941; children—Anthony Frederick, Peter, Josephine, Charles. Asst. fine arts Harvard, 1936-37, vis. prof., 1967; lectr. Worcester Art Mus., 1936-38; instr., State U. Ia., 1938-41; asso. prof., curator of art coll. Washington U., St. Louis, 1941-48; prof. arts Washington Sq. Coll., N.Y. U., 1949-79, prof. emeritus, 1979-82, chmn. dept. fine arts, 1949-75. Andrew W. Mellon lectr. Nat. Gallery Art, Washington, 1974. Guggenheim fellow, 1948-49, 55-56; Mem. Coll. Art Assn. (editor-in-chief Art Bull. 1962-65, pres. 1970-72), Am. Studies Assn. Author: Apes and Ape Lore in the Middle Ages and the Renaissance; The Story of Painting for Young People; The Sculpture of Donatello; The Picture History of Painting; Key Monuments of the History of Art; History of Art. Cons. editor Time-Life Library of Art. Contbr. articles in fine arts publs. Home: New York, N.Y. Dec. Sept. 30, 1982.

JANTZEN, ALICE CATHERINE, occupational therapist, educator; b. Brookline, Mass., Aug. 17, 1918; d. Francis T. and Alice M. (Doyle) J. A.B., Wellesley Coll., 1939; diploma, Boston Sch. Occupational Therapy, 1952; M.S. in Edn, U. Pa., 1957; Ph.D., Boston Coll., 1971. Occupational therapist N.Y. State Rehab. Hosp., 1952-54; asst. prof. Western Mich. U., 1954-55; teaching fellow, instr. U. Pa., 1955-58; prof., chmn. dept. occupational therapy, dir. occupational therapy service, mem. grad. faculty U. Fla., 1958-76; prof., chmn. dept. occupational therapy, mem. grad. faculty Colo. State U., Fort Collins, 1976-78; dir. Jantzen Engring Inc. Author: Research-The Practical Approach for Occupational Therapy, 1981; Contbr. Articles to profl. jours. Pres. Am. Occupational Therapy Found., 1964-66. Served with USNR, 1943-46. Recipient Fla. Blue Key Distinguished Faculty award, 1971. Fellow Am. Occupational Therapy Assn. (chmn. com. grad. study 1962-64, bd. mgmt. 1962-64, v.p. 1964-66, exec. bd. 1964-66, 74-76, steering com. of commn. on edn. 1978-80, editorial bd. 1978-80, personnel com. 1979-82, Acad. award 1973, award of merit 1979); mem. Fla. Occupational Therapy Assn. (pres. 1971-72, mem. exec. bd. del. to Am. Occupational Therapy Assn. 1967-70), Md. Occupational Therapy Assn., World Fedn. Occupational Therapists, Phi Beta Kappa, Omicron Delta Kappa. Home: Columbia, Md. Died Oct. 21, 1983.

JANZEN, CORNELIUS CICERO, prof. economics; b. Lehigh, Kan., Nov. 9, 1887; s. Cornelius Jacob and Margaretha (Epp) J.; A.B., Tabor Coll., Hillsboro, Kan., 1913; A.M., U. of Kan., 1914; scholarship, U. of Chicago, 1915-17, Ph.D., 1926; m. Clara Belle Durbrow, June 18, 1927; 1 dau., Margaret Louise. Teacher rural schs., Kan. 1905-06, 1907-09; mem. faculties at U. Kan., U. Colo., Bethel Coll., U. Me., Lawrence Coll., Allegheny Coll., 1909-29; prof. econs. State Tchrs. Coll., Milw. 1929-56, head dept. econs., 1930-56; prof. econ. U. Wisconsin at Milwaukee, from 1956; lectr. Shorewood Opportunity Sch., 1932-45; vis prof. econs., U. Wis., summer, 1937. Member Am. Friends Service Com., France, 1918-19. Member of the American Economic Society, Knights of the Round Table, Phi Kappa Phi, Phi Delta Kappa, Lambda Chi Alpha. Republican. Episcopalian. Mason. Author books including: Everyday Economics, (with O. W. Stephenson), 1931, rev. edit., 1941; Everyday Problems in Economics, (with O. W. Stephenson), 1935, rev. edit., 1941; Everyday Terms in Economics, 1938, rev. edit., 1941. Home: Milw., Wi. †

JAQUES, FLORENCE PAGE, author; b. Decatur, Ill., Mar. 7, 1890; d. Henry Putnam and Anna (Farrell) Page; A.B., Millikin U., 1911; grad. student Columbia U.; m. Francis Lee Jaques, May 12, 1927. Mem. Soc. of Woman Geographers, Pi Beta Phi. Author: Canoe Country, 1938; The Geese Fly High, 1939; Birds Across the Sky, 1942, Snowshoe Country, 1944; Canadian Spring, 1947; As Far as the Yukon, 1951; There Once Was a Puffin, 1956. Recipient John Burroughs medal (with F. L. Jacques), 1946. Contbr. to Natural History, Am. Girl, Child Life, Flower Grower mags. Home: St. Paul, Minn. †

JARMAN, JOHN, congressman; b. Sallisaw, Okla., July 17, 1915; s. John H. and Lou Neal (Jones) J.; student Westminster Presbyn. Coll., Fulton, Mo., 1932-34; A.B., Yale, 1937; LL.B., Harvard, 1941; m. Ruth Virginia Bewley, Feb. 25, 1942 (dec. 1964); children—Jay, Susan, Steve; m. Marylin Grant, Feb. 10, 1968. Admitted to Oklahoma bar, 1941, since practiced in Oklahoma City. Mem. ho. of reps. Okla. State Legislature, 1947, mem. state senate, 1949; mem. 82d-91st Congresses, 5th Dist., Okla. Served as pvt. to master sgt., AUS, 1942-45. Democrat. Home: Oklahoma City, Okla. Died Jan. 15, 1982.

JARMAN, WALTON MAXEY, apparel co. exec.; b. Nashville, May 10, 1904; s. J.F. and Eugenia (Maxey) J.; ed. Mass. Inst. Tech.; LL.D., Stetson U., Georgetown Coll.; m. Sarah Anderson, Oct. 10, 1928; children—Franklin, Anne, Eugenia. Sec.-treas. Jarman Shoe Co., 1925-32, pres., 1932-33; pres. Gen. Shoe. Corp. (became GENESCO, Inc. 1959), 1933-47, chmn., 1947-69, chmn. exec. and finance com., 1969-73; dir. Nashville City Bank & Trust Co., Fin. Fedn.; trustee Mut. Life Ins. Co. N.Y., Genesco Retirement Fund. Mem. Tenn. Tax Commn., 1949; chmn. Gov's Study on Cost Control, 1971. Trustee Moody Bible Inst.; v.p. So. Bapt. Conv., 1950. Mem. Christian Bible Soc. (trustee), Pi Delta Epsilon, Theta Delta Chi, Theta Tau, Eta Mu Pi, Beta Gamma Sigma. Republican. Baptist. Clubs: Bellemeade Country; Everglades, Bath and Tennis (Palm Beach, Fla.). Author: A Businessman Looks at the Bible; O Taste and See. Home: Nashville, Tenn. Deceased.

JARNEFELT, EERO, diplomat; b. St. Petersburg (Leningrad), Russia, May 3, 1888; s. Arvid and Emmy (Parviainen) J.; m. Elma Ramstedt, of Helsinki, Finland, June 16, 1928. Began as journalist, 1914; entered Ministry for Fgn. Affairs, 1920, at Ministry, Helsingfors, 1923-24, chief of press bur., 1927-31, asst. chief polit. div., 1931-33, undersecretary of Ministry, 1933-34; attaché legation, Stockholm, 1920-21; sec. legation Copenhagen, 1921, Moscow, 1921-22, London, 1925, Paris, 1926; consul in Prague, 1927; minister of Finland to U.S., Washington, D.C., 1935-39, Rome since 1939. Decorated Knight Comdr. of Order of Vasa I and Knight Comdr. Order of St. Olof II (Sweden); Knight Comdr. Order of Merito Civil (Spain); Officer of Order of Three Stars (Latvia); Officer of the Crown (Italy); Knight Comdr. of II Class of Order of the White Rose (comdr. II class); Great Officer of Order of the Crown (Belgium); Comdr. of Order of Nat. Guard II (Esthonia). Lutheran. Address: Rome, Italy.†

JAWORSKI, LEON, lawyer; b. Waco, Tex., Sept. 19, 1905; s. Rev. Joseph and Marie (Mira) J.; m. Jeannette Adam, May 23, 1931; children—Joanie, Claire, Joseph. LL.B., Baylor U., 1925, LL.D., 1960; LL.M., George Washington U., 1926; LL.M. 15 hon. degrees. Bar: Tex. bar 1925. Counsel firm Fulbright and Jaworski, Houston, spl. asst. U.S. atty. gen., 1962-65, spl. counsel atty. gen. Tex., 1963-65, 72-73, presdl. adv., 1964-69; dir. Office Watergate Spl. Prosecution Force, 1973-74; spl. counsel House Com. on Standards of Ofcl. Conduct, 1977-78; adv. dir. Bank of S.W., Houston; dir., mem. exec. com. Southwest Bancshares Inc., Houston; dir. Anderson Clayton & Co., Houston; trustee Nat. Coll. Dist. Attys.; mem. Pres.'s Commn. on Law Enforcement and Adminstrn. of Justice, 1965-67; arbitration mem. Internat. Centre Settlement Investment Disputes, 1967-82; U.S. mem. Permanent (Internat.) Commn. of Arbitration, The Hague, Netherlands, 1965-69; mem. Commn. on Marine Sci., Engring. and Resources, 1967-69, Pres.'s Commn. on Causes and Prevention of Violence, 1968-69; past chmn. Gov.'s Com. on Pub. Sch. Edn. Author: After Fifteen Years, 1961, The Right and the Power (Watergate), 1976, Confession and Avoidance, 1979, Crossroads, 1981; contbr. articles to legal jours. Bd. dirs., past pres. Houston chpt. ARC; mem. Nat. Citizens Com. Community Relations; nat. trustee NCCJ, 1966-82; trustee United Fund, 1958-82; chmn. bd. trustees, trustee emeritus Southwestern Legal Found.; trustee emeritus Baylor Coll. Medicine; pres. Tex. Med. Center, Houston Soc., Leon Jaworski Found., Baylor Med. Found.; trustee M.D. Anderson Found. Served as col. JAGC U.S. Army, 1942-46; chief war crimes trial sect. JAGC, ETO. Decorated Legion of Merit; recipient numerous awards from civic and profl. orgns. Fellow Am. Coll. Trial Lawyers (regent 1958-66, pres. 1961-62), Am. Bar Found.; mem. Am. Law Inst., State Bar Tex. (pres. 1962-63), Am. Bar Assn. (pres. 1971-72, chmn. 2d Century Fund 1978-82), Houston Bar Assn. (pres. 1949), Can. Bar Assn. (hon.), Tex. Civil Jud. Council (pres. 1950-52), C. of C. (pres. 1960, dir.), Order of Coif (hon.), Phi Delta Phi (hon.). Presbyterian (elder). Clubs: Rotary (Houston) (hon.; pres. 1955-56), Houston (Houston), Houston Country (Houston); Coronado, Headliners; Met. (Washington). Home: Houston, Tex. Died Dec. 9, 1982.

JEAN, JOSEPH, solicitor general of Canada; b. St. Philippe de Néri, Que., Feb. 7, 1890; s. Théodule and Marie (Chamberland) J.; B.S., Coll. of St. Anne de la Pocatiere, 1910; LL.L., Laval Univ., 1913; m. Marie-Anna Roy, Jan. 10, 1916; children—Jean-Pierre, Paul-Andre, Therese and Etienne. Gen. practice of law, Montreal; 1913-46; legal adv. l'Union from 1919; mem. House of Commons, for Montreal-Mercier, since 1932; solicitor Gen. of Can., since 1945; mem. Privy Council since 1945; parliamentary asst., Minister of Justice, 1943-44. Bencher of Law Soc. of Upper Can. Liberal. Roman Catholic. K.C., Royal Arcanum. Clubs: Canadian, Reform. Home: Pointe-aux-Trembles, Que., Canada †

JEFFERS, LEWIS FRANCIS, mfg. co. exec.; b. Calera, Ala., Aug. 28, 1899; s. Henry Lewis and Sarah (Francis) J.; grad Marion Mil. Inst., 1917; m. Mimi Bell Haynes, Sept 26, 1923; children—Bell (Mrs. Henry Fowlkes), Jane (Mrs. Willis Hagan). Pres., Trustees Loan & Guaranty Co., Birmingham, Ala., 1920-50; with Hayes Internat. Corp., Birmingham, 1951-79, pres., 1954-65, chmn. bd., 1965-79; dir. City Investing Co., N.Y.C., Rheem Mfg. Co., N.Y.C. Chmn., Ala. Export Council, 1962-66; mem. exec. bd. Nat. Export Council, from 1964. Bd. dirs. Birmingham Community Chest, 1950; trustee Samford U., 1957-71, Crippled Children's Hosp., Birmingham, 1958, Southside Bapt. Ch., Birmingham; bd. advisers Ala. chpt. AIESEC, U. Ala. Served with U.S. Army, 1917-19; AEF in France. Named Golden Knight Mgmt., Nat. Mgmt. Club, 1957. Mem. Ala. (dir. 1960-66), Birmingham Area chambers commerce, Air Force Assn. (past pres. Birmingham chpt.), Army Aviation Assn. Assn. of U.S.A., N.A.M., Newcomen Soc. N.Am., Am. Ordnance Assn. (past pres. Birmingham chpt.), Beta Gamma Sigma (hon.). Rotarian (pres. 1957-58). Clubs: Birmingham Country, Mountain Brook Country, Relay House, The Club (Birmingham). Home: Birmingham, Ala. Died Jan. 22, 1979.

JEFFERSON, HOWARD B., former university president; b. Norwalk, Ohio, Sept. 28, 1901; s. George E. and Isabella Ann (Bonar) J.; B.A., Denison U., 1923, LL.D. (hon.), 1948; Ph.D., Yale U., 1929; LL.D. (hon.), Hillsdale Coll., 1952, Northwestern U., 1958, Emerson Coll., 1968; L.H.D. (hon.), Colgate U., 1951, Assumption Coll., 1956, Clark U., 1967; Litt.D. (hon.), Coll. Holy Cross, 1962, Anna Maria Coll., 1972; m. Genevieve Ruth Rowe, June 19, 1926 (dec. Nov. 1971); children—David R., William H.; m. Ruth Brown Radcliffe, Aug. 18, 1974; stepchildren—Anne (Mrs. W. Jennison), Jane Elizabeth. Dir. athletics, Hillsdale Coll., 1923-25; asst. prof. philosophy Colgate U., 1929-30, asso. prof., 1930-35, prof., 1935-46, dir. Sch. Philosophy and Religion, 1945-46, acting dir. admissions, 1943-45; pres. Clark U., Worcester, Mass., 1946-67; vis. prof. theology U. Chgo., 1937. Trustee Worcester County Instn. for Savs. Trustee Am. Antiquarian Soc., Old Sturbridge Village; asso., trustee Coll. Holy Cross. Fellow Am. Acad. Arts and Scis.; mem. Am. Philos. Assn. (sec., treas. Eastern div. 1943-45), Nat. Council on Religion in Higher Edn. (pres. 1956-60), Am. Antiquarian Soc., Phi Beta Kappa, Beta Theta Pi. Unitarian. Clubs: Worcester, Rotary. Author: The God of Ethical Religion, 1933; Experience and the Christian Faith, 1942. Co-author: Experience, Reason and Faith, 1940; The American Idea, 1942; The Vitality of the Christian Tradition, 1944; The Teaching of Religion in American Higher Education, 1951. Contbr. to Jour. of Religion and other religious and philos. jours. Home: Worcester, Mass. Dec. Oct. 1, 1983.

JEFFRESS, EDWIN BEDFORD, newspaper publisher; b. Canton, N.C., May 29, 1887; s. Charles James and Maria Love (Osborne) J.; A.B., U. of N.C., 1907; m. Louise Bond Adams, July 17, 1913; children—Rebecca Bond, Edwin Bedford, Carl Osborne, Mary Louise, Sarah Clark. Teacher Bingham Sch., Asheville, 1907-09; reporter Gazette News at Asheville, 1908-10. Raleigh corr., 1911; mgr. Greensboro Daily News, 1911; sec.-treas. Greensboro News Co., 1911-18, pres. since 1918; pres. North State Engraving Co.; mayor of Greensboro, term 1925-29; acting city mgr. Greensboro; pres. Greensboro Community Chest, 1930-31; mem. Commn. for Study of Prison Situation in N.C.; chmn. N.C. State Highway Commn., 1931-33; apptd. chmn. N.C. State Highway and Pub. Works Commn. (including State's prison system), July 1933, resigned, Jan. 1935. Mem. N.C. legislature, 1931. Mem. Am. Newspaper Publs. Assn., Southern Newspaper Pubs. Assn., N.C. Press Assn., Nat. Press Club, Greenboro Chamber Commerce (pres. 1921-22; dir.), Omicron Delta Kappa, Phi Beta Kappa. Awarded Loving Cup, 1923, for greatest civic service, Greensboro. Democrat. Episcopalian. Mason (K.T., Shriner). Elk, K.P. Clubs: Kiwanis, Merchants and Mfrs., Greensboro Country. Home: Greensboro, N.C. †

JENKINS, HARRY EARLE, coll. chancellor; b. Pittsburg, Kans., Aug. 23, 1899; s. Charles Benton and Minnie (Wade) J.; m. Iva Alice Willey, July 30, 1920; 1 son, Harry Earle. B.S., Kans. State Coll., 1924; M.S., U. Mo., 1939; Ph.D., U. Tex., 1942. Supt. schs., Kans., 1929-34; asst. supt. schs., dean Tyler (Tex.) Jr. Coll., 1934-46; chancellor Tyler Jr. Coll., 1946-83; Mem. fin. aid com. HEW, 1957-61; adv. com. VA, 1959-63. Recipient T.B. Butler Outstanding Citizen award Tyler C. of C., 1960. Mem. So. Assn. Colls. and Schs. (past pres., hon. life mem.), Tex. Assn. Colls. and Univs. (past pres.), Tex. Assn. Jr. Colls. (past pres.), Am. Assn. Jr. Colls. (past bd. dirs.). Methodist (chmn. bd stewards 1964-65). Clubs: Mason (33 deg., Shriner, K.T.), Kiwanian. Home: Tyler, Tex. Died Nov. 14, 1983.

JENKINS, OLAF PITT, geologist; b. Greencastle, Ind., Feb. 9, 1889; s. Oliver Peebles and Elizabeth (Hester) J.; A.B., Stanford, 1913, M.A., 1915, Ph.D., 1930; m. Dorothy Gunnell, 1914 (dec. Jan. 28, 1952); children—

Barbara, William, Nancy; m. 2d, Louise Matteson, Aug. 26, 1952. Asst. state geologist, Tenn., 1913-16; asst. prof. econ. geology State Coll. Wash., 1916-18, asso. prof., 1920-25; chief geologist Ariz. Bur. Mines, 1918-19; geologist Sinclair Corp., 1919-20, Standard Oil Co. N.J., Batavia, Java, 1925-28; chief geologist div. mines, Cal. State Dept. Natural Resources, 1929-47, state mineralogist, 1947-58; consultant Carroll E. Bradberry and Associates, Los Altos, California, from 1958. Professional petroleum engr., California Fellow Geol. Soc. Am., Cal. Acad. Sci.; mem. Am. Inst. Mining and Metall. Engrs., Am. Assn. Petroleum Geologists, Mining and Metall. Soc. Am. Assn. Geologica Argentina, Phi Beta Kappa, Sigma Xi, Theta Tau. Contbr. articles profl. publs. Home: Pacific Grove, Cal. †

JENNER, WILLIAM EZRA, senator, lawyer; born at Marengo, Indiana, July 21, 1908; son of L. Lenwood and Jane (MacDonald) J.; graduate Lake Placid (New York) Preparatory School, 1926; A.B., Indiana University, 1930; LL.B., 1932; m. Janet Cuthill, June 30, 1933; 1 son, William Edward. Admitted to Ind. bar, 1932, and practiced in Paoli and Shoals, Indiana, 1932-42 and in Bedford from 1944; state senator, 1934-42, serving as minority leader, 1937, 38 and 39, majority leader, 1941; elected to U.S. Senate to fill unexpired term of Frederick Van Nuys, 1944; elected U.S. senator from Ind., 1946 also 52. Served as 1st lt. to capt., U.S.A.A.F., 1942-44. State chairman Rep. State Gent. Com. of Ind. from Feb. 1945. Mem. Phi Delta Phi, Delta Tau Delta. Mason, Elk. Home: Bedford, Ind. Died Mar. 9, 1985.

JENNETT, WILLIAM ARMIN, mgmt. cons.; b. Chgo., Nov. 28, 1924; s. Clarence B. and Esther G. (Pinkel) J.; m. D. Patricia McCabe, Oct. 7, 1950; children—Robert, Janice, John, Mary. B.B.A., U. Mich., 1948; M.B.A. (Baker scholar), Harvard, 1950. Vice pres. A.T. Kearney & Co. (cons.), 1950-70, v.p., 1980-81; with Baxter Travenol Labs., Inc., Morton Grove, Ill., 1970-80, sr. v.p. finance, 1971-72, exec. v.p., 1972-74, pres., 1974-76, vice chmn., 1976-80; dir. AAR Corp., LaSalle Nat. Bank, Chgo. Served with USAAF, 1943-46. Mem. Financial Execs. Inst. Home: Chicago, Ill. Died Sept. 15, 1981.

JENNINGS, DUNCAN TALLMADGE, advertising executive; b. Summit, N.J., Nov. 6, 1911; s. Ralph Crawford and Inez (Tallmadge) J.; B.A., U. Wis., 1933; m. Dorothy Elton Cutting, Apr. 21, 1940; children—Tallmadge Poole, Felice Cutting, Christopher Duncan, Dorothy, Roy Crawford. Chmn. Jennings & Thompson Advt., Inc., Phoenix, 1948-81. Mem. Ariz. Acad., Beta Gamma Sigma, Phi Kappa Phi, Alpha Tau Omega. Republican. Episcopalian. Home: Phoenix, Ariz. Died Aug. 5, 1981.

JENNINGS, ELMER HAYWARD, paper mfg. exec.; b. Platteville, Wis., Aug. 28, 1890; s. William Thomas and Mathilda (Hayward) J.; grad. Evanston Acad.; A.B., Northwestern U., 1912; m. Marie Benton, June 4, 1913; children—Suzanne (Mrs. G. D. Beck), Margaret (Mrs. C. L. Dostal), Barbara (Mrs. B. T. Gunz). Clk.-teller First Nat. Bank, Sterling, Ill., 1912-16; part-time agt. Northwestern Mutual Life Ins. Co., 1916; with Thilmany Pulp & Paper Co., Kaukauna, Wis., 1916-61, successively sec., dir., v.p., pres., 1916-59, chairman of board, 1959-61; director First National Bank, Appleton, Wisconsin. Trustee Lawrence Coll., Appleton, from 1938, pres. bd. trustees, 1943-48, 59-62. Mem. Wis. Paper and Pulp Mfrs. Traffic Assn. (pres. 1942-44), Glassine and Greaseproof Mfrs. Assn. (pres. 1946-48), Appleton C. of C. (pres. 1926-27), Beta Theta Pi (past trustee, v.p.). Conglist. Mason, Elk. Clubs: University (Chgo.); North Shore Golf (Menasha, Wis.); Riverview Country (Appleton). Home: Appleton, Wis. †

JENNINGS, FRANK, clergyman; b. Island City, Mo., Sept. 6, 1887; s. Horace Lilburn and Mary (Alsop) J.; A.B., Ottawa U., Kan., 1912, D.D., 1930; A.M., U. of Chicago, 1916, B.D., 1917; m. Ruth Ethel Corle, May 20, 1914; children—Margaret Elizabeth (Mrs. John Harris), Francis Edith (Mrs. Harry Irwig), Audrey Eleanor (deceased). Ordained to ministry of the Baptist Church, August, 1912; pastor, Ch. of the Master, Cleveland, 1929-35; British-Am. interchange preacher, 1935; sec. Mass. Council of Chs. from 1935. Mem. exec. com., Fed. Council of Chs. Christ in America, 1940-44; mem. Commn. on Bases of Just and Durable Peace, Fed. Council of Churches; mem. bd. dirs. Washingtonian Hosp. (Boston), Greater Boston Community Fund. Served as sec. overseas Y.M.C.A., 1919. Clubs: Boston City, Theological, Circle (Boston); Alathian (Cleveland); Old and New (Lawrence, Kan.). Contbr. to religious papers. Home: West Newton, Mass. †

JENNINGS, FRANK LAMONT, physician; b. Moravia, N.Y., May 17, 1889; s. Clarence Mills and Elizabeth Jane (Story) J.; M.D., Syracuse U., 1913; m. Helen Katherine Germond, July 22, 1919; children—Frank Lamont, Elizabeth Jane, Eleanor Stark. Asst. supt. and asso. med. dir. Glen Lake Sanitarium, Minneapolis, Minn., 1917-38; instr., later asst. clin. prof. medicine U. of Minn., 1921-38; supt. and med. dir. Sunnyside Sanatorium, Indpls., Inc., 1938-53; chief profl. services VA Hosp., Indpls., 1953-57, chief of tuberculosis and pulmonary disease, from 1957; mem. faculty Ind. U., from 1940; clin. professor medicine, from 1952. Pres. Miss. Valley Trudeau Valley Soc., 1942. Diplomte Am. Bd. Internal Medicine. Fellow A.C.P.; mem. Nat. (v.p. 1948-49, dir. 1947-54), Ind. (pres. 1947), Marion County (president 1957-58) Tuberculosis associations, A.M.A., Indiana and Indianapolis med. socs., Am. Trudeau Soc. (vice pres. 1946), Nu Sigma Nu. Presbyn. Mason, Kiwanian. Contbr. to 33 med. jours. †

JENNINGS, LEWELLYN A., banker; b. Birch Tree, Mo., Dec. 1, 1906; s. Horace and Laura (Bodle) J.; student pub. schs. Silver Creek, N.Y.; m. Virginia Lee Cambell, June 28, 1941. With Silver Creek (N.Y.) Nat. Bank, 1924-29; asst. nat. bank examiner Office Comptroller of Currency, 2d Fed. Res. Dist., N.Y.C., 1929-35, nat. bank examiner, N.Y., N.J., Conn., 1935-37, examiner fgn. brs. nat. banks, Europe, S.A. and Caribbean area, 1937-39, asst. chief nat. bank examiner, Washington, 1941-50, 3d dept. comptroller, 1950-51, 2d dep. comptroller, 1951-52, 1st dep. comptroller of currency, 1952-60; on loan to Govt. of Haiti to make surveys and exams. of Central Bank, Republic of Haiti, part-time, 1938, 41, Guam and Samoa, for U.S. Navy Dept., 1948; sr. v.p., exec. com. Republic Nat. Bank Dallas 1960-61, exec. v.p. for adminstrn., 1961-63; chmn. bd., chief exec. officer Riggs Nat. Bank, Washington, 1963-73, chmn. exec. com., 1973-75, cons., 1975-83; dir. Potamac Electric Co. Trustee George Washington U. Served to capt. AUS, 1942-46, mil. govt. officer, ETO, 1944-46. Decorated Legion of Merit. Mem. Transp. Assn. Am. (hon. dir.). Clubs: Masons. Congressional Country, Alfalfa, Burning Tree, Metropolitan (Washington). Home: Chevy Chase, Md. Dec. May 23, 1985. Interned Silver Creek, N.Y.

JENNINGS, WILLIAM HOWARD, (HAROLD JENNINGS) lawyer; b. San Diego, Jan. 20, 1899; s. Frederick Merrick and Ida (Orrell) J.; m. Margaret Mary Donohue, Sept. 14, 1945; 1 son by previous marriage, Bill Henry. Student, U. Calif. at Berkeley, 1921; J.D., Los Angeles Coll. Law, 1930. Bar: Calif. 1930. With Calif. Legislative Counsel Bur., 1930-31; gen. practice, La Mesa, from 1931; mem. firm Higgs, Jennings, Fletcher & Mack, 1966-72, Jennings, Engstrand & Henrikson, from 1972; city atty., La Mesa, 1934-52, El Cajon, 1937-38; gen. counsel Helix Irrigation Dist., 1936-69; legal cons. Internat. Boundary and Water Commn. U.S. and Mexico, from 1952; tech. cons. Colorado River Bd., from 1946; gen. counsel San Diego County Water Authority, from 1944. Mem. Calif. Water Commn., from 1958, chmn., 1961, vice chmn., 1962-69; mem. Calif. adv. com. Western States Water Planning, 1966-69; mem. exec. com. legal coms. Calif. Irrigation Dists. Assn., 1938-69. Served with USNRF, 1918. Mem. Sigma Chi. Lodge: Rotary (pres. La Mesa 1935-36). Home: San Diego, Calif.

JENSEN, ALFRED JULIUS, artist; b. Guatemala City, Guatemala, Dec. 11, 1903; s. Peter and Anna (Shipke) J.; studied at Horsholn, Denmark, 1910-19, with Hans Hofmann, 1927-28; student Ecole Scandinave, Paris, 1929-34, Fine Arts Mus., San Diego, 1925-26; m. Regina Bogat, Nov. 12, 1963; children—Anna Bogat, Peter Bogat. Came to U.S., 1934. One-man shows: Tanager Gallery, 1955, Bertha Schaefer Gallery, 1957, Martha Jackson Gallery, 1959, 61, Guggenheim Mus., 1961, Graham Gallery, 1962, 64, 65, Fairleigh-Dickinson U., 1963, Kornfeld and Klipstein, Berne, Switzerland, 1963, 75, Kunsthalle, Basel, Switzerland, 1964, 75, Rolf Nelson Gallery, Los Angeles, 1964, Stedelijk Mus., Amsterdam, 1964, Royal Marks Gallery, 1966, Galerie Ziegler, Zurich, Switzerland, 1966, Cordier and Ekstrom, 1967, 69, Pace Gallery, 1972, 73, 84, Kestner-Gessellschaft, Hannover, Germany, 1973, Mus. Louisiana, Humbleback, Denmark, 1973, Kunsthalle, Baden Baden, Germany, 1973, Kunsthalle, Dusseldorf, Germany, 1973, Kunsthalle, Bern, 1973, Kunsthalle, Basel, 1975, Galerie Kornfeld, Zurich, 1977, Albright Knox Art Gallery, Buffalo, 1978, New Mus., N.Y.C., 1978, Guggenheim Mus., 1985; exhibited numerous group shows, from 1954, including Inst. Contemporary Art, Boston, 1960, St. Louis City Art Mus., 1960, Art Inst. Chgo., 1961, Guggenheim Mus., 1961, Corcoran Gallery Art, Washington, 1962, Whitney Mus. Am. Art, 1962, 63, 66, 71, San Francisco Mus. Art, 1963, Nat. Gallery Art, Washington, 1963, Los Angeles County Mus., 1964, Venice Biennale, 1964, 78, Brown U., 1965, Sao Paulo (Brazil) Biennial, 1977; represented in permanent collections: Mus. Modern Art, N.Y.C., Rose Art Mus., Brandeis, Dayton Art Mus., Whitney Mus. Am. Art, N.Y.C., Chase Manhattan Bank, N.Y.C., Time, Inc., N.Y.C., Am. Rep. Ins. Co., Des Moines, Galerie Beyeler, Basel, Hayes Galleries, N.Y.C., also numerous pvt. collections. Ford Found. grantee, summer 1965. Home: Glen Ridge, N.J. Died Apr. 4, 1981.

JENSEN, MERRILL MONROE, educator, historian; b. Elkhorn, Iowa, July 16, 1905; s. John Martin and Julia (Seymour) J.; B.A., U. Wash., 1929, M.A., 1931; Ph.D., U. Wis., 1934; m. Genevieve Margaret Privet, Dec. 24, 1929; 1 dau., Julanne (Mrs. David G. Pease). From instr. to asso. prof. history U. Wash., 1935-44; mem. faculty U. Wis., from 1944, prof. history, 1946-76, prof. emeritus, 1976-80, Vilas Research prof. of history, from 1964, chmn. dept., 1961-64; Harmsworth prof. history U. Oxford (Eng.), 1949-50; vis. prof. U. Tokyo (Japan), 1955, U. Ghent (Belgium), 1960; historian USAAF, 1944. Mem. Orgn. Am. Historians (pres. 1969-70), Mass. Hist. Soc. (corr.), Am. Antiquarian Soc., Colonial Soc. Mass. Author: The Articles of Confederation, 3d edit., 1959; The New Nation: A History of the U.S. During the Confederation, 1950; American Colonial Documents to 1776, 1955; The Making of the American Constitution, 1964; Tracts of the American Revolution, 1967; The Founding of a Nation; A History of the American Revolution 1763-1776, 1968; The American Revolution within America, 1974; The Documentary History of the Ratification of the Constitution, vols. I and II, 1976, vol. III, 1978; The Documentary History of the First Federal Elections, vol. I, 1976. Editor: Regionalism in America, 1951; Documentary History of the Ratification of the Constitution, from 1970. Editor Pacific Northwest Quar., 1935-42. Home: Middleton, Wis. Died Jan. 30, 1980.

JENSEN, MORONI LUNDBY, state senator; b. Ogden, Utah, Jan. 10, 1912; s. Hans Simon and Christine (Jensen) J.; grad. Snow Jr. Coll., 1932; B.S., Brigham Young U., 1946; M.A., Columbia U., 1950; m. Vivian Nelson, Mar. 8, 1934; children—M. Leon Jerold Tchr. elementary sch. Sevier (Utah) Sch. Dist., 1932-35, teaching prin., 1935-45; field dir. ARC Overseas PTO, 1945-46; supervising prin. Salina (Utah) Elementary Sch., 1946-49; prin. Richfield (Utah) Jr. High Sch., 1951-52, Valley Jr. High Sch., Salt Lake City, 1953-59, Cyprus High Sch., Magna, Utah, 1959-65, 70-72, Granger (Utah) High Sch., 1965-68; dir. continuing edn., prin. adult evening high sch. Granite Sch. Dist., Salt Lake City, 1968-70, dir. secondary edn., 1973-80; mem. Edn. Commn. of States, 1977-79; mem. Utah Ho. of Reps., 1965-71; mem. Utah Senate, 1971-80, pres., 1977-79. Active Boy Scouts Am.; mem. Utah Art Curriculum Com., 1956-80; pres., founder David Gourley Scholarship Fund Granite Sch. Dist.; councilman City of Salina, 1941-43, mayor, 1943-45; mem. Utah Central Republican Com., 1949-51. Recipient Distinguished Service award Salina Jr. C. of C., 1941. Mem. So. Utah (pres. 1938), Sevier (pres. 1937) tchrs. assns., Utah Elementary Prins. Assn. (pres. 1943), Utah Edn. Assn. (pres. 1961-63, pres. dept. adminstrs. and suprs. 1974-80), Nat. Council State Assn. Pres.'s (pres. 1962-63), NEA (dir. Utah chpt. 1965-69), Utah Secondary Prins. Assn. (pres. 1959-60). Mormon. Clubs: Rotary, Lions. Home: Salt Lake City, Utah. Died Nov. 8, 1980.

JENSON, THEODORE JOEL, educator; b. New Richmond, Wis., Oct. 9, 1905; s. John Gabriel and Tilla (Johnson) J.; m. Gertrude Beatrice Eberdt, June 7, 1930; children: Jon Eberdt, Karen Ann (Mrs. Daniel M. Voecks). Diploma, Wis. State Coll., River Falls, 1926; Ph.B., U. Chgo., 1928; M.S., U. Wis., 1930, Ph.D., 1952. Student sec. YMCA, 1928-30, supervising prin. schs., Wis., 1930-34, supt. schs., Delavan, Wis., 1934-40, Fond du Lac, 1940-46, Shorewood, Wis., 1946-57; instr. Wis. State Coll., Milw., summers 1953-54; cons., adviser Internat. Edn. Service, Hesse, Germany, 1954; lectr. U. Wis., 1954, instr., summer 1955; prof. edn. Ohio State U., 1957-62, chmn. dept., 1962-65; prof. Coll. Edn. Bowling Green (Ohio) State U., 1965-73, dean, 1965-71, trustee prof., 1971-73, prof. emeritus, 1973-84; also dir. Anderson Center for Personal Devel.; arbitor, cons., lectr., mediator, researcher, 1973-84; prof. U. So. Calif., summer 1961. Co-author: Educational Administration: The Secondary School, 1961, Elementary School Administration, 1963, Practice and Theory in Educational Administration, 1963, also articles. Del. White House Conf. on Edn.; Active Boy Scouts Am. Recipient Distinguished Alumnus award U. Wis.-River Falls, 1974. Mem. Am. Assn. Sch. Adminstrs., Am. Ednl. Research Assn., NEA, Nat. Soc. Study Edn., Ohio Sch. Adminstrs., Wis. Sch. Adminstrs. (past pres.), Classroom Tchrs. Assn., NCCJ, Ohio, Wis. edn. assns., Am. Acad. Polit. and Social Sci., Columbus Schoolmasters Club, Ohio Council Advancement Ednl. Adminstrn. (chmn.), Kappa Delta Pi, Phi Kappa Phi, Phi Delta Kappa. Clubs: Rotarian. (Fond du Lac, Wis.), Conservation (Fond du Lac, Wis.). Edn. auditorium at Bowling Green State U. named in his honor, 1983 Home: Leesburg, Fla. Died Nov. 12, 1984.

JERITZA, MARIA, soprano; b. Brünn, Austria, Oct. 6, 1887; studied piano, violin, cello and harp; studied voice under Prof. Auspitzer, of Brünn; m. Baron Leopold Popper de Podharagn (div.); m. 2d, Winfield Sheehan, Aug. 12, 1935. Début as Elsa, in "Lohengrin," at Olmutz, Austria, 1910. Mem. Imperial and Royal Opera, Vienna, 1913, Met. Opera Co., New York, 1921-32; Am. début as Marietta in "Die Tote Stadt," 1921; concert singer throughout the country; great performances with San Francisco and Los Angeles opera companies, etc. Author: Sunlight and Song (autobiography), 1924. Address: New York, N.Y. †

JEROME, F(RANK) J(AY), railroad exec.; born Painesville, O., May 26, 1890; s. Frank Joseph and Lucy Ella (Dingley) J.; A.B., Williams Coll., 1911; S.B., Mass. Inst. Technol., 1914; m. Grace Fraker, July 31, 1915; children—Mary (Mrs. H. G. Seyffert), Barbara (Mrs. G. B. Bradburn), Frank Jay. Transitman New York Central R.R., Elyria, O., 1914-15; instrumentman Toledo, 1915-17, asst. engr. Chicago, 1917-23, trainmaster Chicago, 1923-27, div. engr., 1927-38; engr. maintenance of way, Mich. Central R.R., Detroit, 1938-39; asst. chief engr. N.Y. Central R.R., Chicago, 1939-43, chief engr., 1943-45, asst. to exec. v.p., 1945-47, v.p. operations and maintenance N.Y. City, 1947, exec. v.p. Mason (Shrine). Republican. Home: New York, N.Y. †

JERRARD, JERRY, interior designer; b. Bakertown, Pa., Jan. 25, 1928; s. Bruno and Ann (Tortella) Simoncini. B.F.A., Carnegie Tech. U., 1949. Interior designer Kaufman Interiors, Hinsdale, Ill., 1952-58; designer, owner, mgr. Jerrard Interiors, Chgo., from 1958; with Trayner Murray Inc., from 1977; tchr. Chgo. Acad. Fine Arts, 1950. Designs include Arlington Towers Hotel. Served with USN, 1945-46. Fellow Am. Soc. Interior Designers; mem. Nat. Soc. Interior Designers (pres. Midwest chpt.

1966-68, gold key award 1967). Roman Catholic. Address: Fort Lauderdale, Fla.

JESNESS, OSCAR BERNARD, agrl. economist; b. Morris, Minn., Feb. 4, 1889; s. Ole L. and Bertha J.; B.S.A., U. of Minn., 1912, M.S., 1924, Ph.D., 1928; m. Ella Freeland, 1916 (died 1928); 1 son, Robert (dec.); m. 2d, Lulu Steiner, 1930. Instr. in agr., high sch., Winthrop, Minn., 1912-13; asst. in marketing, U. of Minn., 1914-15; specialist in coöp. orgn., U.S. Dept. Agr., 1915-20; head of dept. markets and rural finance, U. of Ky., 1920-28; head dept. agrl. econs., U. Minn., 1928-57, emeritus, from 1957; dir., dep. chmn., chmn. Fed. Res. Bank Mpls., 1955-60; chmn. of the board Experience, Incorporated; dir. Green Giant Co., LeSueur, Minn.; dir. Mpls. Grain Exchange. Pres., dir. Green Giant Foundation. Chmn. Minn. State Planning Board, 1936-37. Mem. Regional Export Expansion Council; adv. council, agr. com. Am. Bankers Assn.; mem. postwar agr. policy com., Land-Grant College Assn., 1944-46; U.S. Council mem. Internat. Assn. Agrl. Economists, 1949-51. Recipient Am. Farm Bur. Fedn. award, 1953. Fellow Am. Farm Economics Assn.; mem. of Council, Am. Assn. Univ. Profs., 1947-49; mem. Am. Econ. Assn., Am. Farm Econ. Assn. (pres. 1937), Farm House (hon.), Alpha Zeta, Gamma Sigma Delta. Methodist. Club: Informal (St. Paul). Author several books on agrl. econ.; also federal and state bulls. on agrl. economics. Editor of Jour. of Farm Economics, 1933-35. Home: St. Paul, Minn. †

JESSEN, HERMAN FREDRICK, Democratic nat. committeeman; b. Boel, Germany, July 29, 1887; s. John F. and Christine (Witt) J.; ed. pub. and art schs.; m. Eleanor Wait, Jan. 2, 1941; children—Grace Louise, Jewel Christine. Painter, 1905-14; editor weekly, daily newspapers, 1914-17; sales exec. Imperial Paper & Color Corp., Chgo., 1919-60; mink rancher, 1930-60; v.p., dir. State Bank of Phelps (Wis.), 1946-55. Chmn. Vilas County Dem. Com., from 1946; vice chmn. Wis. Dem. Party, 1951-54; mem. Dem. Nat. Com. for Wis., 1956-60. Served with U.S. Army, World War I. Mem. Am. Acad. Polit. and Social Scis., Fgn. Policy Assn. Mutation Mink Breeders Assn., Mink Breeders Association U.S. (pres.), Nat. Bd. Fur Farms Orgns. (exec. bd. 1944-55), Am. Wild Life Fedn., Adult Edn. Assn., Americans for Dem. Action, Civil Liberty League, Am. Legion. Clubs: Lions; City (Chgo.); Travel (N.Y.C.). Home: Phelps, Wis. †

JESSEPH, JOHN ERVIN, educator, surgeon; b. Pasco, Wash., Nov. 6, 1925; s. Harry Ervin and Eula Victoria (Ledgerwood) J.; m. Marley M.G. Austin, June 20, 1948; children—Steven A., Jerry M. A.B., Whitman Coll., 1949, D.Sc. (hon.), 1975; M.D., U. Wash., 1953, M.S., 1956. Diplomate: Am. Bd. Surgery (dir., chmn. 1978-80), Am. Bd. Family Practice. Intern King County Hosp., Seattle, 1953-54; resident in surgery U. Wash. Affiliated Hosps., Seattle, 1954-59; asst. prof. surgery U. Wash., Seattle, 1959-62; scientist Brookhaven Nat. Lab., 1962-65; faculty Ohio State U., Columbus, 1965-71, prof., 1967-71; prof. surgery, chmn. dept. Sch. Medicine, Ind. U., Indpls., 1971-82. Editor, contbg. author med. books; contbr. articles to profl. jours. Served with USMCR, 1944-46. USPHS research grantee, 1955-58, 66-70. Mem. Am. Surg. Assn., A.C.S., other orgns. Club: Mason. Home: Indianapolis, Ind. Died Mar. 29, 1982.

JEWELL, MARY FRANCES, educator; b. Berry, Harrison Co., Ky., Dec. 23, 1889; d. Asa H. and Elizabeth S. (Berry) J.; A.B., Vassar, 1913; M.A., Columbia, 1918; instr. and asst. prof. English, U. of Ky., 1915-23; dean of women same univ., from 1921. Mem. State Com. Child Welfare, 1922; mem. Council of Southern Div. Y.W.C.A.; mem. Ky. Child Labor Com.; 1st pres. Central Ky. br. Am. Assn. Univ. Women; organizer and 1st pres. Ky. Deans of Women; pres. Ky. Vassar Club, 1921-3. Presbyn. Home: Lexington, Ky. †

JILLSON, WILLARD ROUSE, geologist, engineer, author; b. Syracuse, N.Y., May 28, 1890; s. Willard Rogers and Anna Delle (Bailey) J.; B.S., Syracuse U., 1912; M.S., U. of Wash., 1915; Sc.D., Syracuse U., 1921; D.Sc., Berea Coll., 1925; m. Oriole Marie Gormley, Sept. 10, 1917; children—Mrs. Marie Jillson Sharpe, Mrs. Oriole Jillson Burlew, Willard Rogers, Mrs. Ann Jillson Overstreet. Began practice in Lake Temiscaming Region, Ontario, Can., 1912; instr. geology, U. of Wash., 1914-15; with U.S. Geol. Survey, mapping Mount St. Helens, 1915; fellow in geology, Univ. of Chicago, 1915-16, Yale, 1916-17; oil geologist, Okla., Tex., Kan. and Ky., 1916-17; prof. geology, U. of Ky., 1918-19, acting head department of geology, 1918-19, apptd. asst. state geologist, Ky., 1918, Ky. state geologist and commr. geology and forestry, Feb. 1919; oil and gas evaluation (geol.), U.S. Dept. of Treasury, 1918; apptd. dir. and state geologist (6th) Ky. Geol. Survey, term 1920-32; curator Ky. State Mus., 1924-32; chmn. Ky. Park Commn., 1924-28, mem to 1932; chmn. Ky. Geog. Council, 1927; prof. geology and head dept. Transylvania Coll., Lexington, Ky., 1947-51; lectr. Mem. Troop D, 1st Cav., N.G.N.Y. Recipient medal for merit and achievement, Lehigh University, 1959. Fellow A.A.A.S.; former member or member many professional, scientific and hist. assns. or orgns., Ky. Civil War Round Table (chmn. exec. com. 1953-57), Ky. Hist. Soc. (exec. vice pres. 1958-59). Republican. Presbyterian (historian Presbyn. Synod of Ky., 1961). Author numerous books, from 1919, primarily on Ky., including items on geology, topography, paleontology, lit., history, mining, including biographies; latest include: Early Times, 1952; A Bibliography of Mammoth Cave, 1953; A Glimpse of Old Bridgeport, 1956; Geology of Marion County, Ky., 1956; Kentucky Literature: 1900-1950, 1956; Geology of Green County, Ky., 1956; Rambo Flats, 1957; Geology of Barren County, Kentucky, 1958; Geology of the Pitman Oil Pool, Green County, Ky., 1959; A Tour Down Stream, 1959; Geology of the Goose Creek Dome, 1960; Bibliography of the Cumberland River Valley, 1960; Paul Sawyier: American Artist, 1961; Geology of the Mintonville Dome, 1962; Geology of the Mina Dome, 1963; Geology of Henry County, Ky., 1965; many pamphlets, sci. and hist. articles. Address: Frankfort, Ky. †

JIMENEZ, ENRIQUE A., president, Republic of Panama; b. Panama, Feb. 8, 1888; s. Adolfo and Felicidad Brin de Jimenez; ed. schools of Panama City; self educated in law; m. Beatriz Guardia, July 1898; children—Gladys, Martha, Aida, Eñrique, Jr. Began as private sec. to Pres. Porras of Republic of Panama; dep. to Nat. Assembly for 3 legislatures; became pres. of Assembly; del. to 3d Pan. Am. Commercial Conf., Washington, D.C., 1927, and to 3d Pan-Am., Conf. on Reciprocal Trade, Sacramento, Calif., 1930; dir. Panama Chamber of Commerce, 1938; served as mgr. Nat. Bank of Panama (pres. bd.), sec. of Treasury, mgr. Nat. Charity Lottery. Mem. Liberal party; founder and leader Partido Democrata and nominated as its candidate for pres., 1936. Ambassador of Republic of Panama to U.S., 1943-45; pres. of the Republic of Panama, 1945-48. Decorations: Chevalier, Legion of Honor; Medal of Merit (Ecuador); Grand Cordon of the Order of the Liberator of Venezuela; Grand Official of the Order of the Sun (Peru); Grand Cross Order of Balboa (Panama). Address: Panama, Republic of Panama. Deceased.

JOBE, MORRIS BUTLER, aerospace company executive; b. Princeton, Ia., Jan. 29, 1916; s. William H. and Irene (Butler) J.; B.A. in Edn., U. Akron, 1938; certificate Northwestern Inst. Mgmt., 1957; m. Maxine Gerber, Nov. 13, 1942; children—Barbara, Kathryn (Mrs. Gregory Steffy). With Goodyear Aerospace Corp., from 1938, pres., chief exec. officer, from 1968, also dir. Mem. Atomic Indsl. Forum (uranium enrichment policy); past chmn. U.S. del. NATO Indsl. Adv. Group. Trustee Mt. Union Coll., 1968-80. Mem. Nat. Security Indsl. Assn. (trustee, exec. com.), Aerospace Industries Assn. (bd. govs.), Am. Inst. Aero. and Astronautics, Am. Ordnance Assn., (dir. Cleve,), Phi Kappa Tau. Mason (32 deg.). Clubs: City, Portage Country (Akron). Home: Akron, Ohio. Dec. Mar. 26, 1981.

JOCHER, KATHARINE, professor sociology; b. Philadelphia, Pa., Sept. 22, 1888; d. John Conrad and Lillie Caroline (Reichle) Jocher; A.B., Goucher Coll., 1922; A.M., U. of Pa. (Univ. scholarship); Ph.D., U. of N.C., 1929. Social worker, Lutheran Settlement, Phila., 1914-17, Community Council, Ambler, Pa., Family Service Soc., Johns Hopkins Hosp., Baltimore, Polyclinic Hosp., Phila., 1920-24; instr., Sweet Briar Coll., 1923-24; research asst., Inst. for Research in Social Science, 1924-29, research asso., 1929-43, assistant director, 1927-57, associate director, 1957-59; research professor, University of North Carolina from 1943; professor State College of Washington, summer 1938, U. of Va., summer, 1941. Special research assignment, President's Research Com. on Social Trends, 1930-31. Member Governor's committee for revision of domestic relations laws in North Carolina, 1947-51; mem. N.C. Merit System Council, 1959-65. Member American Sociol. Assn. (2d v.p., 1942; exec. com. 1947-50, council 1952-55), So. Sociological Soc. (2d v.p., 1938-39; pres., 1942-44), N.C. Mental Health Assn., Nat. Conf. of Social Work, Am. Assn. Univ. Women (Nat. Social Studes Com., 1940-45), N.C. Conf. Social Service dir from 1947, president, 1952-53, v.p. 1959-60), Phi Beta Kappa, Alpha Kappa Delta (2d v.p. 1942-46, vice president 1959-60). Member of the Committee on Services for Children and Youth in N.C. (exec. com., from 1946). Author: (with Howard W. Odum) An Introduction to Social Research, 1929. Editor: (with Howard W. Odum) In Search of the Regional Balance of America (commemorating Sesquicent, N.C.), 1945. Mng. editor Social Forces, 1931-51, editor since 1951. Home: Chapel Hill, N.C. †

JOHANN, ALBERT EUGENE, physician, med. dir.; b. Eureka, Ill., May 13, 1888; s. Carl and Georgina (Callendar) J.; A.B., Culver-Stockton Coll., 1906; M.D., Johns Hopkins, 1910; m. Helen Kaylor, Oct. 28, 1916; children—Albert, Robert, William, Walter. Intern Boston Childrens Hosp., 1910-12; pediatrician, Minneapolis, 1912-18; asst. pediatrics U. Minn., 1917-18; with Office Surgeon Gen., Washington, 1918-19; asst. med. dir. Travelers Ins. Co., Hartford, Conn., 1919-22, 1922-36, asso. med. dir., 1936-38, med. dir., 1938-46; v.p., med. dir. Bankers Life Co., 1946-53, med. cons., 1953-55; med. rating specialist U.S. VA, from 1955. Member American Life Conv. (chmn. med. sect. 1938), Life Ins. Dirs. Am. (exec. council 1938-48). Mem. Disciples of Christ Ch. Home: Des Moines, Ia. †

JOHANSEN, FREDERICK ANDREW, physician, public health dir.; b. Burlington, Ia., May 30, 1889; s. Jorgen and Maren (Rasmussen) J.; student Carthage (Ill.) Coll.; M.D., Chicago Coll. Medicine and Surgery, 1911; m. Alma M. Morris, Mar. 25, 1913; 1 dau., Amy Josephine (Mrs. Clyde Brown). With Am. Med. Dispensary Assn., P.R., 1911-12; practice of medicine, Nauyoo, Ill., 1913-15, Kahoka, Mo., 1915-24; dep. state health commr. State of Mo., 1920-24; coroner Clark Co., Mo., 1920-24; exec. officer and clin. dir. U.S. Marine Hosp., U.S.P.H.S., Carville, La., 1924-47, med. officer in charge, from 1947; commd. officer, med. dir. Regular Corps, U.S.P.H.S.; mem. med. adv. bd. Leonard Wood Meml. (Am. Leprosy Foundn.). Served as 1st lt., U.S. Army Med. Corps, 1918-19; med. officer, World War II. Diplomate Am. Bd. Preventive Medicine and Pub. Health. Fellow A.C.P., A.M.A.; mem. Miss. Valley Dermatol. Assn., Internat. Leprosy Assn. (gen. councillor), Assn. Mil. Surgeons, Am. Coll. Hosp. Adminstrs., World Health Orgn. (expert adv. panel on leprosy), Am. Legion, 40 et 8 (Grand Medicin State of La.), N.Y. Acad. Sciences. Mason (32 deg., Shriner), Author and co-author articles pertaining to leprosy in med; jours. and pub. health reports. Contbg. editor to Internat., Jour. of Leprosy. Address: Carville, La.†

JOHANSON, PERRY BERTIL, architect; b. Greeley, Colo., May 9, 1910; s. Erik and Martina (Pehrson) J.; m. Jean Louise Peterson, Apr. 4, 1936; children—Peter Erik, Kristina Therese (Mrs. Bruce Peters). B.Arch. (traveling scholar 1931), U. Wash., 1934. Partner Smith-Caroll & Johanson, Seattle, 1935-50; Partner Naramore-Bain-Brady & Johanson, Seattle, 1943-80, cons. partner, from 1980; pres. Nat. Archtl. Accrediting Bd., 1955-57. Prin. works include VA Hosp, Seattle, U. Wash. Health Sci. Bldg, Swedish Hosp, Seattle, IBM Bldg, Seattle, Financial Center, Seattle, King County Stadium, Seattle, Seattle First Nat. Bank Bldg. Pres. Children's Soc. Wash., 1957-59; Mem. Plan Commn. King County, 1951-63, chmn., 1953-54, vice chmn., 1956-57; Trustee Wash. Roadside Council, from 1980, Wash. chpt. Nature Conservancy, from 1980, Downtown Seattle Devel. Assn., 1960-78, Jr. Achievement, 1966-75, Pacific Sci. Center, 1972-78. Fellow A.I.A. (pres. Wash. 1950-51), N.W. Ornamental Hort. Soc. (dir. from 1979, v.p. 1980), Seattle C. of C. (trustee 1972-75). Clubs: Monday, Rainier, College. Home: Bellevue, WA.

JOHNS, JAY WINSTON, bus. exec.; b. Uniontown, Pa., July 14, 1888. Former pres., Atlas Fuel Corp., Pittsburgh, Pa.; dir. Va. Electric & Power Co., Charlottesville, Va. Pres., dir. Stonewall Jackson Meml., Lexington, Va.; bd. visitors Va. Mil. Inst; trustee Va. Mus. Fine Arts, Richmond; pres. Va. Trust Historic Preservation. Clubs: Metropolitan (N.Y.C.); Collonnade; Commonwealth (Richmond). Home: Charlottesville, VA. †

JOHNS, WILLIAM FRANKLIN, newspaper mgr.; b. Baltimore, Md., Aug. 5, 1888; s. James Frank and Jennie (Houck) J.; ed. Tome Sch., Port Deposit Md., 1903-08, Amherst Coll., 1908-09; m. Penrose Hasgall, Oct. 29, 1916; children—Myles Hasgall, William Franklin. Began as salesman for trade paper, 1909; advertising dept. Burroughs, Welcome & Co., N.Y. City, 1 year; newspaper advertising rep. Omara & Ormsbee, Chicago, 5 years; Chicago office of Good Housekeeping, 2 years; Erwin Wasey Advertising Agency, Chicago, 1 year; advertising mgr. Minneapolis Jour., 1919-25; with St. Paul Dispatch-Pioneer since 1925, as advertising mgr., 1925-30, gen. mgr. 1930-42. Pres. Ridder-Johns, Inc.; part owner radio station WOSH. Republican. Clubs: Minnesota, St. Paul, Chicago Athletic Assn., Chicago, Bob-O-Link Golf. Home: Chicago, Ill. *

JOHNSON, A. THEODORE, educator; born Paris, Mo., Oct. 19, 1890; s. Peter and Christine (Petersen) J.; A.B., Westminster Coll., 1914; A.M., U. of Va., 1917; Ph.D., U. of N.C., 1925; m. Marie Mayo Long, Dec. 21, 1922; 1 son, William Theodore. Teacher of Latin, Randolph-Macon Acad., Front Royal, Va., 1914-16; instr. English, U. of N.C., 1922-26; asso. prof. of English, Southwestern at Memphis, 1926-30, prof., 1930-61, emeritus, from 1961, acad. dean, 1934-55; vis. prof. Lausanne Sch. for Girls, Memphis, 1961-64; vis. prof. English, Southwestern at Memphis, from 1964. Mem. Modern Language Association, Kappa Alpha, Omicron Delta Kappa and Phi Beta Kappa. Democrat. Presbyterian. Club: Executives. Author: (monograph) Aspects of the Supernatural in Shakespearean Tragedy, 1959. America Through the Essay, an anthology (with Allen Tate), 1938. Home: Memphis, Tenn. †

JOHNSON, ALBERT GARFIELD, clergyman; b. Liverpool, Eng., Jan. 4, 1887; s. Thomas and Jane (Kirkpatrick) J.; grad. engring., Liverpool, 1910; grad. Moody Bible Inst., Chicago, 1915; grad. Northern Bapt. Theol. Sem., Chicago, 1918, D.D., 1927; m. Mary Hannah Johnson, Feb. 23, 1910; children—Doreen Agnes (dec.), Dorothy Mary, Pearl Downes, Albert Garfield. Came to U.S., 1913, naturalized citizen, 1920. Ordained ministry Bapt. Ch., 1915; pastor Albany Park Ch., Chicago, 1915-24, Temple Ch., Detroit, Mich., from 1924. Trustee Northern Bapt. Theol. Sem. Republican. Home: Detroit, Mich. †

JOHNSON, CHARLOTTE BUEL, art historian; b. Syracuse, N.Y., July 21, 1918; d. Edward Sullivan and Mary Frances (Power) J.; m. Henry von Wodtke, Oct. 12, 1979. B.A. in Art History, Barnard Coll., 1941; M.A. in Art History, N.Y. U., 1951. Tchr. Vincent Smith Sch., Port Washington, N.Y., 1941-42; tchr. art and art history St. Mary's Sch. for Girls, Peekskill, N.Y., 1942-45, Calhoun Sch., N.Y.C., 1946-47; instr. art history Hollins Coll., 1947-48; instr., then asst. prof. charge art Maryville (Tenn.) Coll., 1948-52; mus. instr. Worcester (Mass.) Art

Mus., 1952-57; vis. lectr. art history Clark U., Worcester, summer 1957; lectr. Albright-Knox Art Gallery, Buffalo, 1957-80, curator edn., 1958-80; part-time lectr. Am. Studies U. Buffalo, 1957-68; Travel to European galleries, summers 1949, 50, 62, 68, 69, Mexico, summer 1961. Contbr. articles to profl. jours.; Contbg. editor: Sch. Arts Mag, 1963-70. Kinnicutt travel award to Greece, summer 1954; participant UNESCO Museums Seminar Athens, 1954. Mem. Coll. Art Assn. Am., Barnard Coll. Club Western N.Y. (past pres.). Address: Hamburg, N.Y.

JOHNSON, DAVENPORT, army officer; b. Tex., Mar. 28, 1890; B.S., U.S. Mil. Acad., 1912; grad. Air Service Field Officers' Sch., 1921, Command and Gen. Staff Sch., 1926, Army War Coll., 1929. Commd. 2d lt., inf. June 12, 1912; promoted through grades to maj. gen. (temp.), Oct. 2, 1940; asst. to chief of Air Corps, Washington, D.C., Oct. 1940-41; with Caribbean Defense Command, 1941-42; comd. 6th Air Force, Albrook Field, Canal Zone. Mar.-Nov. 1942; dir. mil. personnel, Army Air Forces, Washington, D.C., Nov. 1942-Feb. 1943; became comdg. gen. 2d Air Force, Ft. George Wright, Wash., Feb. 1943; then comdg. gen. 11th Air Force. Address: Washington, D.C.†

JOHNSON, ELDON V., business exec.; b. Gowanda, N.Y., May 11, 1889; s. August Theo and Jane Olivia (Totman) J.; student of business schools; LL.B. Springfield Coll., 1956; children—Betty, Theodore, Nancy and Barbara; m. 2d. Luella Thayer, Dec. 28, 1957. Started as stenographer with U.S. Envelope Co., Waukegan, Ill., 1906, now pres. and dir.; dir. Baystate Corporation, Boston, Mass. Trustee of Springfield College. Clubs: Colony (Springfield); Worcester (Mass.). Home: Wilbraham, Mass. †

JOHNSON, FRANK LUDWIG, business exec.; b. Chicago, Nov. 18, 1888; s. John Levin and Hulda Karoline (Faugust) J.; student Armour Institute Tech., Chicago; m. Florence Mabel Farr, July 3, 1912; children—Frank Ludwig, Florence Evelyn Johnson Laub. Asso. with Pullman Car Works, Chicago, 1902-06, working in various depts.; engring. dept. Western Steel Car & Foundry Co., 1906-09; connected with Pressed Steel Car Co., Inc., Chicago, from 1906 in various capacities, dir.; pres., dir. Roseland Standard Bldg. and Loan Assn.; dir. Pullman Trust and Savings Bank; director United States Industries Incorporated. Trustee, v.p. Roseland Community Hosp. Past chmn. bd. 111th St. YMCA. Clubs: Union League, Western Railway, South Side Swedish (Chgo.).†

JOHNSON, HALL, composer; b. Athens, Ga., Mar. 12, 1888; s. William Decker and Alice Virginia (Sansom) J.; grad. Knox Inst., Athens, 1903; student Atlanta U., 1 yr.; grad. Allen U., 1908; student Hahn Sch. of Music, Phila., 3 yrs.; grad. U. Pa. Music Sch., 1910; student Inst. Musical Art, N.Y.C., 1923-24; pvt. teachers for French and German; Mus. D. (hon.), Phila. Musical Acad., 1934; m. Celeste Corpening, Nov. 4, 1912 (dec. Dec. 1935). Studied and worked in Phila., 1908-14; went to N.Y.C., became mem. dance orchestra of Mr. and Mrs. Vernon Castle; toured the country with leading Negro attractions, including Shuffle Along (revue); organized the Hall Johnson Negro Choir, N.Y. City, 1925, gave concerts, appeared on radio and theater programs, 1925-35; went to Calif., 1935, with 50 singers to make motion picture of The Green Pastures; has since from worked with choir in motion pictures, including Lost Horizons; radio and concert work, with Hollywood as center; organized the Festival Negro Chorus of Los Angeles, 1941 (a tng. group with scholarships for young Negro talent); returned to N.Y. with choir, May 1943; organized The Festival Negro Chorus of N.Y. City to aid young Negro students, 1946. Recipient Simon Haessler prize for composition, 1910; Harmon award for music of The Green Pastures, 1931. Works include: Music for The Green Pastures, 1930; book and music for Run Little Children (produced N.Y.C. 1933; Los Angeles and San Francisco, 1938-39). Composer, Son of Man, a religious (full-length) cantata in Negro idiom; two N.Y. performances, 1946-1948. Has arranged and publ. numerous Negro spirituals and folk songs; has completed book and music for Fi-yer, a Negro operetta (still in manuscript). Contbr. articles on Negro music to mags. Address: N.Y.C. †

JOHNSON, HALLET, foreign service officer; b. N.Y. City, Nov. 26, 1888; s. J. Augustus and Fanny V. (Mathews) J.; A.B., Williams Coll., 1908; LL.B., Columbia, 1911; m. Katherine M. Steward, May 20, 1920; children—Katherine Beeckman, Priscilla Livingston, Hallett. Entered diplomatic service, 1912; served as sec. embassies in London, Constantinople, Santiago, and chargé d'affaires at Legation in La Paz; acting chief Div. of Latin Am. Affairs, Dept. of State, 1919; 1st sec. Legation, Oslo, 1927-29, embassies at Brussels, 1920-21, Paris, 1924-27; counselor of Legation and chargé d'affaires, The Hague, 1929-33, Madrid, 1933-36; in charge of Summer Embassy, Sebastian, Spain, at outbreak of Spanish Civil War, 1936; counselor of Embassy and chargé d'affaires, Warsaw, 1936-37; counsul gen. and counselor of Legation, Stockholm, 1937-41; asst. chief, Div. of Controls. Dept. of State, 1941-42; asst. chief, Div. of Defense Materials, 1942-45; ambassador to Costa Rica, 1945-49; retired. Member Co. K, 7th Reg., Nat. Guard of N.Y., 1909-12. Mem. Soc. of Colonial Wars, S.A.R., Delta Psi. Episcopalian. Clubs: Union, St. Anthony (New York); Metropolitan (Washington, D.C.); Travelers (Paris). Address: New York, N.Y. †

JOHNSON, HAROLD KEITH, ret. army ofcr.; b. Bowesmont, N.D., Feb. 22, 1912; s. Harold C. and Edna M. (Thomson) J.; B.S., U.S. Mil. Acad., 1933; grad. Command and Gen. Staff Coll., 1947, Armed Forces Staff Coll., 1950, Nat. War Coll., 1953; Doctor of Education (honorary), Park College, 1962; LL.D., Yankton Coll., 1963, Illinois Coll., 1965, U. Akron, 1968, Pa. Mil. Colls., 1968; H.H.D., N.D. State Univ., 1966; D.Sc., Norwich U., 1968; Dorothy Rennix, Apr. 13, 1935; children—Harold Keith, Ellen Kay, Robert James. Commd. 2d lt. United States Army, 1933, advanced through grades to general, 1964; assigned successively to the 3d Infantry, 28th Inf., Philippine Scouts, prior to World War II; survivor Bataan death march, prisoner of Japanese, 1942-45; bn., regt. comdr. 1st Cav. Div., also G-3 1st U.S. Corps, 1951; assigned G-3 Dept. of Army, asst. div. comdr. 8th Inf. Div., 1956-57; chief staff 7th Army, 1957-59, G-3 U.S. Army Europe, 1959; chief staff Central Army Group, Europe, 1959-60; comdt. U.S. Army, Command and Gen. Staff Coll., Ft. Leavenworth, Kan., 1960-63; dep. chief of staff for mil. operations, 1963-64; chief of staff United States Army, 1964-68, retired, 1968; president Herbert Hoover Presdl. Library Assn., 1969-83; dir. Genesco, Inc., Research Analysis Corp. Decorated Distinguished Service Cross, Legion of Merit with 3 clusters, Distinguished Unit citation with two clusters, Bronze Star medal, D.S.M. with cluster; Presdl. Unit citation (Republic of Korea) (P.I.); Legion of Honor (France) (P.I.); Order Mil. Merit (Brazil); Cross Venezuelan Ground Forces; Knight Grand Cross of Most Exalted Order White Elephant (Thailand); Order Mil. Merit Taeguk (Korea); White Cross Mil. Merit and Greatest Grade (Spain); Nat. Order, 2d Class (Republic of Vietnam); recipient Silver Beaver and Silver Buffalo awards Boy Scouts Am. Mason (33 deg.). Home: Washington, D.C. Died Sept. 24, 1983.

JOHNSON, IRVING HARDING (MRS. CURTIS B. JOHNSON), ret. bus. exec.; b. Davidson, N.C., Nov. 10, 1889; d. Richmond and Mildred (Berry) Harding; A.B., Queens Coll., 1909, LL.D., 1959; m. Rev. Dr. Archibald McGeachy, July 14, 1910 (dec. 1928); m. 2d, Curtis Boyd Johnson, May 1942 (dec. 1950). Editor syndicated problem column under name of Caroline Chatfield, 1932-42; chmn. bd. Observer Co., Charlotte, N.C., 1951-53; pres. Charlotte Observer, Charlotte Observer Transp. Co. Mem. bd. United Community Services. Trustee Queens Coll.; bd. visitors Davidson Coll. Democrat. Presbyn. Club: City, Charlotte Country. Home: Charlotte, NC. †

JOHNSON, JAMES H., army officer; b. Kentucky, May 12, 1887; B.S., U.S. Mil. Acad., 1912; grad. Coast Arty. Sch., advanced course, 1927, Command and Gen. Staff Sch., 1928, Q.M.C. Motor Transport Sch., 1929, Chem. Warfare Sch., field officers course, 1929, Army Indsl. Coll., 1935. Commd. 2d lt., U.S. Army, 1912, advanced through the grades to brig. gen., 1945. Address: Washington, D.C. Deceased.

JOHNSON, JOHN BURLIN, scientist; b. Olean, N.Y., May 31, 1890; s. John August and Emily Amanda (Burlin) J.; M.E., Cornell U., 1912; m. Marian Ochiltree, Sept. 20, 1922; children—Margaret, John Burlin. Spl. engr. N.Y.C. R.R., 1912-16; aero. mech. engr. Air Corps U.S. Govt., 1916-22, chief materials lab., 1922-49, chief sci. Air Development Center, 1949-58, consultant, from 1958. Recipient D.S.M., War Dept., 1946; Thurman Bane award Inst. Aero Scis., Morehead medal Internat. Acetylyne Assn. Mem. Am. soc. Metals, Soc. Automotive Engrs., NACA. Mason. Club: Engineers (Dayton, O.). Author: Aircraft Welding, 1929; Material and Welding, 1933. Home: Dayton, OH. †

JOHNSON, JOHN CHARLES, physicist, educator; b. Pike County, Ill., June 19, 1920; s. John Creston and Florence Ellen (Bradbury) J.; m. Lorraine Irene Ura, Oct. 14, 1950; children—John Anthony, James Andrew, William Dean. B.A., Culver Stockton Coll., 1942; postgrad., Ohio State U., 1942-43; M.A., U. Mich., 1947, Ph.D., 1950. Registered profl. engr., Pa. Tech. supr. Tenn. Eastman Corp., Oak Ridge, 1944-46; research asst., research physicist U. Mich., 1946-59; prof. engring research Pa. State U., from 1959; dir. Pa. State U. (Applied Research Lab.), from 1959, ex-officio mem. grad. program engring. acoustics; mem. USN Research and Devel. Tech. Council, 1959-76; mem. com. on fed. labs. Fed. Council for Sci. and Tech., 1969-75. Editor: Acoustics Engring. News for Mech. Engring. News, 1977-79; asso. editor: U.S. Navy Jour. Underwater Acoustics, 1964-68, from 74. Chmn. Nittany Mountain dist. Boy Scouts Am., from 1977; Bd. dirs. Inst. Noise Control Engring., 1974-77, pres., 1980; bd. dirs. Internat. Inst. Noise Control Engring., from 1975. Fellow Acoustical Soc. Am. (pres. 1971-72), AAAS; mem. Am. Soc. Engring. Edn., Am. Inst. Physics (sec. from 1980), N.Y. Acad. Scis., Marine Tech. Soc., Am. Def. Preparedness Assn., Sigma Xi, Sigma Pi Sigma. Presbyterian. Clubs: Masons, Centre Hills Country, Centre Squares Dance, Rotary Internat. Home: Boalsburg, PA.

JOHNSON, JOHN SEWARD, business executive; b. New Brunswick, N.J., 1895; s. Robert Wood and Evangeline (Armstrong) J.; student Yale; m. Esther Mead Underwood, 1939; children—Mary Lea (Mrs. William Ryan), Elaine (Mrs. Keith C. Wold), John Seward, Diana (Mrs. Richard G. Stokes), Jennifer (Mrs. Peter H. Gregg), James Loring. Vice Pres. Johnson & Johnson, New Brunswick, N.J., 1931-71; member board directors, 1921-71, also chairman of finance com. Republican. township committeeman. Tewksbury Twp., Hunterdon County, New Jersey. Trustee Hunterdon Co. Med. Center. Served as lt. (j.g.) U.S.N., 1917; comdr. subchaser 255 in Mediterranean. Clubs: Cruising of Am., N.Y. Yacht, Royal Thames Yacht, Kringl Svenske Saleskapt. Home: Oldwick, N.J. Died May 23, 1983.

JOHNSON, PAMELA HANSFORD (THE LADY SNOW), writer; b. London, Eng., May 29, 1912; d. Reginald Kenneth and Amy Clotilda (Howson) Johnson; educated Clapham County Sch., London; D.Litt. (hon.), Temple U., York U., m. Gordon Neil Stewart, Dec. 15, 1936; children—Andrew Morven, Lindsay Jean; m. 2d, Charles Percy Snow, July 15, 1950; 1 son, Philip Charles Hansford. Novelist, critic and broadcaster, 1945; mem. panel Brains Trust on BBC, from 1956, Critics on BBC, from 1953. Fellow Centre Advanced Studies, Wesleyan U., Middletown, Conn., 1961; Timothy Dwight fellow arts and letters Yale, 1961. Fellow Royal Soc. Lit.; mem. Societe Europeene de Culture. Author: (novels) This Bed Thy Centre, 1935; Too Dear for My Possessing, 1940; An Avenue of Stone, 1947; A Summer to Decide, 1948; Catherine Carter, 1952; An Impossible Marriage, 1954; The Last Resort (in U.S., The Sea and The Wedding), 1956; The Unspeakable Skipton, 1959; The Humbler Creation, 1959; An Error of Judgement, 1962; Night and Silence Who is Here?, 1963; Cork Street, Next to the Hatter's, 1965; (criticism) Thomas Wolfe, a Critical Study, 1947, (in U.S. as The Art of Thomas Wolfe, 1963), I. Compton-Burnett, 1953; Social Criticism: On Iniquity, 1967; (play) Corinth House, 1948; (radio series) Six Proust Reconstructions, 1948. Translator: (with Kitty Black) Anouilh's The Rehearsal, 1962; (novel) The Survival of the Fittest, 1968; The Honours Board, 1970. Died July 1, 1981.

JOHNSON, PYKE, automotive safety found. exec.; b. Denver, June 27, 1888; s. Joseph and Isabella Mary (Pyke) J.; student U. Denver, 1911; LL.D. (hon.), Kenyon (Ohio) University; married Mary Allen Green, June 11, 1913 (died Nov. 1941); children—Pyke, Thomas Lee, Elizabeth Ann, Allen MacTavish; m. 2d, Helen Davis Stibolt, Jan. 26, 1943. Newspaper writer Rocky Mountain News, Denver, 1910-16; with Colorado State Highway Dept., 1916-18; Washington rep. and v.p. Automobile Mfrs. Assn., 1918-39, exec. v.p., June 1939-Mar. 4, 1942; pres. Automotive Safety Found., Washington, from 1942. Mem. bd. govs., Dist. of Columbia div., A.A.A.; exec. sec., Highway Edn. Bd.; exec. dir., Pan-Am. Confederation for Highway Edn.; pres. Am. Trade Assn. Execs., 1935-36, chmn. advisory com. U.S. member Permanent Internat. Road Commission. Decorated Chevalier Legion of Honor (French), 1933. Mem. Sigma Delta Chi, Sigma Alpha Epsilon. Episcopalian. Clubs: Metropolitan, Burning Tree, National Press (Washington); Columbia Country (Chevy Chase, Md.); Detroit Athletic. Home: Washington, D.C. †

JOHNSON, ROY, farmer; b. Casselton, N.D., Sept. 12, 1889; s. Frank Gustaf and Fredrika (Hammergren) J.; B.S., U. of Minn., 1912; m. Wanda Gladys Cooper; children—Frank Cooper, Harry Roy, Ralph Douglas, Margaret Fredrika, Roy Henry. Began farming Mar. 1916, on farm homesteaded by father, 1877; county agrl. agt., 1912-14; mem. N.D. Ho. of Rep., 1919-23, speaker, 1923; pres. Cass Co. Farm Council; trustee Farm Foundation; dir. First Nat. Bank and Trust Co., Fargo. Rep. agr. before U.S. Chamber of Commerce, 1928; mem. of Township Bd. of Supervisors from 1917 (chmn. 20 years); mem. local school board from 1921 (chmn. 10 yrs.); mem. N.D. State Bd. of Higher Edn. Awarded Master Farmer, by Assn. of Standard Farm Papers, 1927. Mem. N.W. Farm Mgrs. Assn., Alpha Zeta. Republican. Methodist. Mason (Shriner), Kiwanian. Contbr. articles farm jours. Home: Casselton, N.D. †

JOHNSON, ROY IVAN, educator; b. Princeton, Mo., Nov. 9, 1889; s. Joseph E. and Ruth Ann (Covey) J.; A.B. and B.S. in edn., U. of Mo., 1909; A.M., U. of Chicago, 1917, Ph.D., 1923; m. Laura Maud Stuart, June 8, 1911; children—Joseph Stuart, Raymond Lewis; married 2d, Irmgard Grossmann, 1936; one daughter, Meredith. Instructor Kemper Military School, Boonville, Mo., 1909-11; instr. English, William Jewell Coll., Liberty, Mo., 1911-14, Northeast High Sch., Kansas City, Mo., 1914-17, Kan. City Jr. Coll., 1917-20; dir. dept. English, Stephens Coll., 1920-25; St. Louis pub. schs., 1925-32; Stephens Coll., 1932-49, U. Denver, chmn. grad. studies, Sch. of Edn., 1949-55; research cons. U. Fla., from 1956. Mem. Phi Delta Kappa. Baptist. Author, contbr. textbooks, latest publs. include: English for Your World, 1943; Explorations in General Education (gen. editor), 1947. Co-author: The Teacher Speaks 1954; Communication, 1956.†

JOHNSON, ROYAL KENNETH, musician; b. Beloit, Wis., July 28, 1906; s. Louis Paul and Jessie Mae (Morse) J.; m. Gertrude Elizabeth Boo, Jan. 3, 1954; children—Timothy, Kenneth. Student instrument and theory, New Eng. Conservatory Music, Berlin, Germany, 1930-32. Mem. Cremona String Quartet, Boston, 1932-34, WPA String Quartet, Chgo., 1935-38. Violinist, Chgo. Symphony Orch., from 1938. Home: Northbrook, Ill.

JOHNSON, WARREN C., educator; b. Otter Lake, Mich., Sept. 22, 1901; s. Grant W. and Elizabeth (Osborne) J.; m. Florence Louise Campbell, June 27, 1928 (dec. July 10, 1980); children—Barbara Ann, Margaret

Louise Johnson Levine, Mary Elizabeth. B.S., Kalamazoo Coll., 1922, D.Sc., 1946; M.A., Clark U., 1924; Ph.D., Brown U., 1925, D.Sc., 1960. Research instr. chemistry Brown U., 1925-27; instr. chemistry U. Chgo., 1927-28, asst. prof., 1928-32, asso., 1932-43, prof. chemistry, 1943-67, prof. emeritus, 1967-83, chmn. dept., 1945-55, dean div. phys. scis., 1955-58, v.p. univ., 1958-67, v.p. emeritus, 1967-83; Dir. chemistry div. Clinton Labs., Oak Ridge, 1943-45; bd. dirs. Oak Ridge Inst. Nuclear Studies (now Oak Ridge Asso. Univs.), 1952-59, 61-67, cons., 1967-83; chmn. mgmt. adv. council Oak Ridge Nat. Lab., 1962-70; mem. gen. adv. com. AEC, 1954-60, chmn., 1956-60; cons. NSF. Author: Qualitative Analysis and Chem. Equilibrium, 1937, latest rev. edit., 1966, Elementary Principles of Qualitative Analysis, 1938, Ionic Equilibria as Applied to Qualitative Analysis, 1941, 46, 54; An, Introduction to Qualitative Analysis, 1957, also articles. Trustee Mellon Inst., 1958-67, Kalamazoo Coll., 1950-83; trustee Inst. Def. Analysis, 1960-67, Chgo. Planetarium Corp. Recipient citation amd medal U.S. AEC, 1961. Fellow AAAS, Am. Nuclear Soc. (dir. 1961-64); mem. Am. Chem. Soc., Sigma Xi. Club: Quadrangle (Chgo.). Home: Grand Rapids, Mich. Died Oct. 17, 1983.

JOHNSON, WILFRID ESTILL, ret. govt. ofcl.; b. Whitley Bay, Eng., May 24, 1905; s. Arthur Nicholas and Edith (Peace) J.; came to U.S., 1920, naturalized, 1928; B.S., Oreg. State U., 1930, M.E., 1939, D.Sc. (hon.), 1959; m. Esther Taylor, Dec. 31, 1930; children—Anita Louise (Mrs. Clark B. McKee), Arthur Robert, Richard Beeson. Engr. refrigeration Gen. Electric Co., Schenectady, 1930-36, Ft. Wayne, Ind., 1936-40, mgr. engring. aircraft engines, Lynn, Mass. and Syracuse, N.Y., 1940-46, mgr. engring. air conditioning, Bloomfield, N.J., 1946-48; asst. gen. mgr. Hanford Atomic Works, Richland, Wash., 1948-52, gen. mgr., 1952-66; commr. AEC, Washington, 1966-72. Mem. Richland Community Council, 1966; mem. Wash. Citizens Council, 1953-58; mem. vis. com. Sch. Bus. Adminstrn. U. Wash., 1961-66. mem. Recipient Pi Tau Sigma award, 1938, AEC citation, 1965. Fellow ASME, Am. Nuclear Soc.; mem. Acad. Polit. and Social Scis., Am. Soc. for Engring. Edn. (asso. mem.), Nat. Acad. Engring., Sigma Xi, Phi Kappa Phi, Tau Beta Pi, Sigma Tau. Elk. Contbr. profl. jours. Patentee in field. Home: Richland, Wash. Died Feb. 10, 1985.

JOHNSTON, FRANK EVINGTON, church exec.; b. Wilkinsburg, Pa., Mar. 1, 1907; s. Frank Evington and Minnie Ruth (Campbell) J.; m. Mary Frances Stallings, Nov. 25, 1937 (dec. Aug. 1977); m. Mary C. Evans, 1978. B.A., Bucknell U., 1928; B.D., Colgate Rochester Div. Sch., 1935; D.D., Alderson Broaddus Coll., 1962. Ordained to ministry Bapt. Ch., 1935; asst. pastor Calvary Bapt. Ch., Washington, 1937-39; pastor 1st Bapt. Ch., Middletown, Ohio, 1939-43; nat. dir. ch. sch. adminstrn. Am. Bapt. Conv., Phila., 1943-51; pastor Calvary Bapt. Ch., Davenport, Iowa, 1951-53; exec. dir. Lucerne Bapt. Assembly, Calif., 1953-56; asso. pastor Central Bapt. Ch., Hartford, 1956-57; budget adviser Am. Bapt. Conv., N.Y.C., 1958-62, asso. gen. sec., Valley Forge, Pa., 1962-70, gen. sec., 1971-72; dep. exec. minister Am. Bapt. Chs. of West, Oakland, Cal., from 1973. Trustee Ellen Cushing Jr. Coll., Bryn Mawr, Pa., 1963-72, Am. Bapt. Sem. of West, Berkeley. Home: Santa Barbara, Calif.

JOHNSTON, HENRY RUST, b. Chicago, Ill., Feb. 13, 1888; s. James Wright and Bessie (Rust) J.; A.B., Wiliams Coll., 1909; LL.B., cum laude, New York Law Sch., 1912; m. Helen Earle, May 20, 1914; children—Douglas Earle, David Prince, Alexander Rust. Admitted to N.Y. bar, 1912, and began practice at N.Y. City; mem. Greene & Hurd until 1917; asst. to pres. Mercantile Trust Co., 1919-21; with Chatham Phenix Nat. Bank & Trust Co. (Mfrs. Trust Co.), 1921-33, was v.p. and dir.; v.p. and dir. Case, Pomeroy & Co., 1933-38, pres. 1938-41; retired, 1942. Dir. Lord, Abbett group Investment Trusts, since 1946. Treas., exec. dir. Com. for Econ. Development, 1943-49. Trustee, vice-president Citizens Budget Commission, New York City, 1946-50. Served in United States Navy Flying Corps, World War I. Chmn. National Iner-fraternity Conference, 1925-26, instituting system of annual surveys of scholarship of male students in 120 colleges and universities of United States. Member Borough Council of Essex Fells, N.J., 2 terms 1929-35, pres. 1935; mem. N.J. State Prison Bd., Trenton, 1934-48. Pres. Ponte Verda Community Association, 1951. Trustee Williams College, 1926-31; pres. Society of Alumni of Williams Coll., 1933-36. Mem. Council of Fgn. Relations, Delta Kappa Epsilon. Republican. Episcopalian. Clubs: University, Williams, Down Town Assn. (New York); Pine Valley Golf. Donor of Amherst-Williams Trophy of Trophies, 1919. †

JOHNSTON, RICHARD WYCKOFF, journalist; b. Eugene, Oreg., Mar. 21, 1915; s. Claude D. and Sarah (Wyckoff) J.; m. Laura M. Smith, July 5, 1939; children—Dana, Elisa. Student, U. Oreg., 1936-38. Sports editor Eugene Register-Guard, 1933-35; city editor Eugene Daily News, 1937-38; domestic corr. U.P., 1939-42, war corr., Pacific and Far East, 1943-45, freelance lectr., 1946; with Time mag., 1946-47, fgn. corr. and fgn. news writer, 1947; with Life mag., 1947-53, asst. copy editor, 1951-53; with Sports Illustrated mag., 1953-81, asst. mng. editor, 1954-63, exec. editor, 1963-70, spl. contbr., 1971-81; partner Johnston/Wood Assocs. (media consultants), 1976-81; lectr. mag. writing U. Hawaii, 1976-77. Author: Follow Me, 1948, (with Mrs. Johnston); juvenile Elizabeth Enters, 1952; Copy editor: juvenile Picture History of World War II, 1950. Recipient Nat. Headliners award, 1943. Mem. 2d Marine Div. Assn. (hon. life), Sigma Delta Chi. Clubs: Honolulu Press, Outrigger Canoe. Home: Honolulu, Hawaii. Died Aug. 4, 1981.

JOHNSTONE, ALAN, lawyer; b. Newberry, S.C., July 11, 1890; s. Alan and Lilla Rawl (Kennerly) J.; A.B., Newberry Coll., Newberry, S.C., 1910; A.M. and LL.B., U. of S.C., 1912; grad. student Harvard, 1912-13; m. Lalla Rook Simmons, 1914; children—Lalla Rook, Martha Ward. Admitted to S.C. bar, 1913; practiced in Columbia, 1913-17; asst. city atty., 1915-17; rep. Federal Res. Bank of Richmond, promoting Victory Loan, 1919; exec. officer Maryland Social Hygiene Soc., Baltimore, 1920-23; exec. dir. and organizer, Baltimore Criminal Justice Commn., 1923-29; exec. dir. Baltimore Fund, 1925-29; dir. Emergency Relief, S.C., 1932-33; gen. law practice in Newberry, 1920-38; field rep., S.E., states, Federal Emergency Relief Adminstrn., and Civil Works Adminstrn., 1933-35, Works Progress Adminstrn., 1935-37; counsel spl. com. of U.S. Senate to investigate unemployment and relief, 1937-38; gen. counsel Federal Works Agency, 1939-48; in practice of law, Newberry, S.C. Appointed by secretaries of War and Navy departments rep. law enforcement div. Commn. on Training Camp Activities, War and Navy depts., 1917-19. Mem. S.C. Legislature, 1915-16. Mem. Ga., S.C., Md. and Supreme Court of U.S. bar assns. Democrat. Episcopalian. Home: Newberry, S.C. †

JONAH, DAVID ALONZO, ret. librarian; b. Sackville, N.B., Can. Mar. 19, 1909; s. Alonzo Dow and Jennie (Cochran) J.; B.S., Mt. Allison U., 1929, LL.D., 1960; M.S., Brown U., 1931; postgrad. Columbia U., summer 1940; m. Elizabeth Rhodes Wright, Nov. 18, 1937. Came to U.S., 1929, naturalized, 1938. Instr. math. Brown U., Providence, 1932-34, 42-44, gen. asst. library, 1935-38, in charge phys. scis. library, 1938-43, 44-46, acting librarian, 1946-48, asso. librarian, 1948-49, librarian, 1949-60, librarian univ. library and dir. libraries, 1960-74, asst. prof., 1945-51, asso. prof. bibliography, 1951-53, John Hay prof. bibliography, 1953-74, prof. emeritus, librarian emeritus, dir. libraries emeritus, 1974-81. Mem. R.I. Library Assn. (pres. 1956-58, award in recognition for distinguished contbn. to library service in R.I. 1973), East Greenwich Free Library Assn. (pres. 1958-71), Bibliog. Soc. Am., Sigma Xi. Episcopalian. Home: East Greenwich, R.I. Died Feb. 10, 1981.

JONES, AARON EDWARD, army officer; b. Cincinnati, Sept 26, 1889; s. Edward Everett and Katherine (Leist) J.; B.D., Kenyon Coll., Gambier, O., 1912; spl. course A.C. officers, Mass. Inst. Tech., 1918; rated command pilot, combat observer, tech. observer; m. Lena Hardin Miller, May 10, 1923. Commd. 1st lt. A.C., 1917, and advanced through the grades to brig. gen., Oct. 31, 1942; asst. dir., Air Force Aid Soc. Home: Alexandria, Va. †

JONES, ALFRED WILLIAM, bus. exec.; b. Dayton, Ohio, 1902; s. Samuel Rufus and Mary Adele (Yost) J.; m. Katharine Houk Talbott, Sept. 6, 1928; children—Alfred, Marianna (Mrs. David L. Kuntz), Katharine (Mrs. Paul O'Connor), Howard. Student, Moraine Sch., Dayton, 1917-20, U. Pa., 1920-23. Mgr. Sapeloe Plantation, Ga., 1925-28; pres. Sea Island Co. (developers of resorts), 1928-44, chmn. bd., from 1944. Hon. mem. Bus. Council.; Mem. Phi Kappa Psi. Methodist. Home: Sea Island, Ga. Died June 9, 1982.

JONES, BURNIE EDWARD, lawyer; b. Frisco City, Ala., Feb. 8, 1889; s. James W. and Mary F. (Hughes) J.; B.S., U. Ala., 1911, LL.B., 1914; m. Mildred Rutland, June 27, 1925. Admitted to Ala. bar, 1914; mem. firm Hare & Jones, Monoreville, 1914-17; mem. faculty U. Ala. Law Sch., 1919-21; mem. firm Hamilton & Jones, Evergreen, Ala., 1922-49; pvt. practice, Evergreen, 1949-51; mem. firm B. E. Jones & R. L. Jones, Evergreen, from 1952; dir. Bank of Evergreen, Conecuh Development Corp. Dir. Indsl. Development Bd., City of Evergreen, Ala. Past chmn. Conecuh County Dem. Exec. Com. Served from pvt. to 1st lt., inf., U.S. Army, 1916-19; AEF, France. Decorated Purple Heart. Mem. Am., Ala. State (commr. from 1934, pres. 1957-58), bar assns., Phi Beta Kappa, Am. Legion (past post comdr.). Home: Evergreen, Ala. †

JONES, CAROLYN, actress; b. Amarillo, Tex., 1933; m. Herbert Greene. Stage appearances include Live Wire; also roles TV The Addams Family; series; films include Road to Bali, 1952, The Big Heat, 1953, Invasion of the Body Snatchers, 1955, The Opposite Sex, 1956, The Bachelor Party, 1957, Last Train from Gun Hill, 1958, A Hole in the Head, 1959, Ice Palace, 1960, Sail a Crooked Ship, 1962, A Ticklish Affair, 1963, Heaven with a Gun, 1969, Eaten Alive, 1977; appeared in TV movies Little Ladies of the Night, 1977, Roots, 1977, The French Atlantic Affair, 1979; Author: Twice Upon A Time, 1971, (with others) Diary of a Mad Eater, 1974. Died Aug 3, 1983.*

JONES, EDWARD COLE, meat packing co. exec.; b. Fort Atkinson, Wis., May 10, 1902; s. Edward C. and Charlotte W. (Brown) J.; m. Helen E. Schlosser, Jan 23, 1926; children—Frances Cole (Mrs. F.J. Paddock), Deborah Wells (Mrs. Malcolm Donaldson), Edward Cole. Student, Dartmouth, 1920-22, U. Wis., 1922-24. With Jones Dairy Farm, Ft. Atkinson, from 1922; pres., from 1966; Bd. dirs. Am. Meat Inst., from 1948, treas., 1964-68, chmn. bd., 1968-71; dir. Wis. Live Stock and Meat Council, from 1963. Pres. bd. trustees Ft. Atkinson Meml. Hosp., 1942-78; bd. dirs. Center for Study of Presidency. Recipient Community Relations award, 1958, award outstanding service and leadership Wis. Live Stock Breeders Assn., 1964; hon. recognition U. Wis., 1967; award distinguished community service Ft. Atkinson Lions Club, 1968; recognition and appreciation award Wis. Live Stock and Meat Council, 1969; Hon. Am. Farmer award Future Farmers Am., 1973; Distinguished Service award Am. Meat Inst. Mem. N.A.M. (past dir.), Wis. Mfrs. Assn. (past dir., recognition outstanding service to Am. bus. 1969), Def. Orientation Conf. Assn. (pres. 1978-80, dir.), Sigma Chi. Republican. Episcopalian. Clubs: University (Milw.); Madison; Chicago (Chgo.), Union League (Chgo.), Tavern (Chgo.); Rolling Rock (Ligonier, Pa.); Lake Zurich (Ill.) Golf. Home: Fort Atkinson, Wis.

JONES, EDWIN DONATUS, JR., lawyer; b. Washington, Sept. 19, 1919; s. Edwin Donatus and Kathryn (Sullivan) J.; m. Ann Ellen Harris, Feb. 17, 1945; children—Susan, Laura, Andrew, Sarah. A.B., Stanford, 1941, LL.B., 1950. Bar: Calif. bar 1950. With firm Betts, Ely & Loomis, Los Angeles, 1950-53; partner firm Hoge, Fenton, Jones & Appel, San Jose, 1953-85; Legal adviser Jr. League San Jose; past v.p., bd. dirs. Family Service Assn., San Jose. Past trustee San Jose Unified Sch. Dist.; past bd. dirs. Goodwill Industries, Santa Clara County. Served to lt. comdr. USNR, World War II. Fellow Am. Coll. Trial Lawyers; mem. ABA, Calif. Bar Assn., Santa Clara County Bar Assn. (trustee), Monterey County Bar Assn., Am. Trial Lawyers Assn., Santa Clara County Trial Lawyers Assn. (past pres.), Assn. Def. Counsel, Internat. Assn. Ins. Counsel, Am. Judicature Soc., Def. Research Assn., R.R. Trial Counsel, Am. Arbitration Assn. (nat. panel). Episcopalian (past sr. warden). Clubs: San Jose Country Sainte Claire (San Jose). Home: San Jose, Calif. Died June 9, 1985; buried Oak Hill, San Jose.

JONES, ELI SHERMAN (JACK), physician; b. Fairmont, Ind., Feb. 9. 1890; s. David and Sarah (Thomas) J.; B.S., Ind. U., 1914, M.D., 1916; m. Berta Herold, Nov. 18, 1916; 1 dau., Janet (Mrs. Julien McCall). Intern City Hosp., Indpls., 1915-16; practice of medicine, specializing in surgery, and indsl. medicine, Hammond, Ind., from 1916; staff St. Margaret Hosp., Hammond. Past mem. Lake County Bd. Health, Hammond Bd. Health; adv. bd. Norman M. Beatty Meml., Hosp. Diplomate Am. Bd. Preventive Medicine, Internat. Bd. Surg. F. A.C.S., Am. Coll. Preventive Medicine, Internat. Coll. Surgeons; mem. Am. Med. Association (past vice pres.), International Industrial Medical Association, Ind., Indsl. (past pres.), World med. Assns. Central States Soc. Indsl. Medicine and Surgery (past pres.), Am. Assn. Ry. Surgeons, Am. Fracture Assn., Internat. Acad. Proctology, American Geriatrics Soc., Am. Indsl. Hygiene Assn., C. of C. Mason (33 deg., Shriner; past potentate), Rotarian (past pres.). Home: Hammond, Ind. †

JONES, GORDON BURR, ins. co. exec.; b. Peabody, Mass., Sept. 10, 1918; s. Burr Frank and Helen (Robinson) J.; m. Geraldine A. Stefko, Sept. 12, 1942; children—Carol Jones Heil, Gordon Burr, David R., Valerie G. (Mrs. Stephen Roy), Allison G., Randall B. A.B., Colby Coll., 1940, LL.D., 1976; M.B.A., Harvard, 1942. Investment analyst Provident Mut. Life Ins. Co., Phila., 1945-48; investment analyst John Hancock Mut. Life Ins. Co., Boston, 1948-52, asst. treas., 1952-57, 2d v.p., 1957-66, v.p., 1966, sr. v.p., 1966-68, exec. v.p., mem. exec. com., 1968-82, chmn. finance com., 1970-82, also dir.; corporator, trustee Eliot Savs. Bank, Boston; dir. Seiler Corp., John Hancock Advisers, Inc., John Hancock Growth Fund, Inc., John Hancock Balanced Fund, Inc., John Hancock Tax-Exempt Income Trust, John Hancock Bond Fund, Inc., John Hancock Investors Inc., John Hancock Income Securities Corp., John Hancock Cash Mgmt. Trust, John Hancock Realty Devel. Corp., Jeffrey Co., Raytheon Co.; mem. cons. investment com. Arkwright-Boston Mfrs. Mut. Ins. Co., Waltham, Mass. Gen. campaign chmn. Ford Found. Challenge Campaign, Colby Coll., 1962-65; dir., mem. investment com. Mass. Soc. Prevention Cruelty to Animals; mem. corp., investment com. Boston Mus. Sci.; trustee, mem. nominating com., chmn. investment com. Colby Coll. Recipient Man of Yr. award Colby Coll. Club, 1955. Mem. Boston Econ. Club, Boston Security Analysts Soc., Phi Beta Kappa. Republican. Congregationalist. Clubs: Brae Burn Country; Boston Madison Square Garden (Boston), Union (Boston). Home: Needham, Mass. Died 1982.

JONES, HARRY LEE, II, ret. army officer; b. Kansas City, Mo., Oct. 27, 1918; s. Harry Lee and Hazel (Hixon) J.; student Washington U., St. Louis, 1937-40; A.B., George Washington U., 1950, M.A., 1963; M.B.A., Harvard, 1953; grad. Army War Coll., 1963; m. Gloria Carolyn Raeder, Mar. 26, 1947; children—Patricia (Mrs. Chris Sullivan), Harry Lee. Joined U.S. Army, 1940, commd. 2d lt., 1943, advanced through grades to maj. gen., 1970; finance officer 24th Inf. Div., 1942-46; mem. Gen. Staff, 1958-62; adv. to dir. finance and audit Ministry Def., Vietnam, 1963-65; chief finance and accounting Office Comptroller Army, 1967-70; asst. comptroller for information systems, Washington, 1969-70; chief Army Audit Agy., Washington, 1970-72; instr. U. Md., Heidelberg, Germany, 1953-56. Bd. dirs. Army Mut. Aid Assn., Fort Myer, Arlington, Va., 1967-75. Decorated D.S.M., Legion Merit with 2 oak leaf clusters, Bronze Star, Army Commendation medal with oak leaf cluster; Medal Honor 1st class (Republic Vietnam). Mem. Assn. U.S. Army,

Army Finance Assn. (nat. pres., 1967-70), Am. Soc. Mil. Comptrollers (nat. v.p.). Home: El Paso, Tex. Died Jan. 2, 1980.

JONES, HENRY L. C., army officer; b. Brokenbow, Neb., Aug. 20, 1887; B.S. in C.E., U. of Nev., 1906; hon. grad. Comd. and Gen. Staff Sch., 1924; grad. Army War Coll., 1931; m. Louise Crawford, Apr. 4, 1923; children—Barbara, Cornelia. Commd. 2d lt. cav., 1911, and advanced through the grades to maj. gen., 1942; served as lt. col., field arty., World War I; apptd. comd. gen. 38th Inf. Div., Camp Shelby, Miss., May 1942; participated in Leyte and Luzon campaigns, 1944-45. Home: Esparto, Calif. †

JONES, JAMES VICTOR, librarian; b. Willard, O., May 14, 1924 s. Harry D. and Hazel (Kuhn) J.; student Fenn Coll., 1942-43, U. Ala., 1943-44; B.S. magna cum laude, John Carroll U., 1949; M.S., Western Res. U., 1950; m. Elizabeth Jean Stillions, Aug. 17, 1946; children—Kathryn Lee, Kenneth James, Richard Joseph, Christopher John. Student library asst. Fenn. Coll., 1942-43, John Carroll U., 1947-48; student library asst. Western Res. U., 1948-49, reference asst., 1950; librarian Sch. Commerce and Finance St. Louis U., 1950-52, asst. dir. libraries, 1952-55, dir. libraries, 1955-66; dir. libraries Cleve. State U., 1966-68; dir. univ. libraries Case Western Res. U., Cleve., 1968-82. Asso. Leadership Tng. Project, North Central Assn. Colls. and Secondary Schs., 1962-63, examiner, cons., 1963-82. Bd. govs. Case Western Res. U., 1965-67, chmn. vis. com. Sch. Library Sci., 1966-68; bd. overseers Case Western Res. U., 1967-68; council Center Research Libraries, 1965-66; trustee Ohio Coll. Library Center, 1971-82, chmn., 1972-73, 73-75, rep. to Council on Computerized Library Networks, 1973-82. Mem. Ohio (nominating com. 1971-72), Cath. (pres. Greater St. Louis unit 1959-61, chmn. scholarship com. 1959-63), Am. (council 1959-61, com. on awards 1971-72, madge citation com. reference and adult service div. 1974-75) library assns., Spl. Libraries Assn. (conv. chmn. 1964), Assn. Coll. and Research Libraries (past chmn. com. liaison with accrediting agys.), Am. Soc. for Information Sci., St. Louis Library Club (past pres.), Ohio Coll. Assn. (pres. library sect. 1969-70), Tri-State Assn. Coll. and Research Libraries (v.p. 1970-71, pres. 1971-72), Library Council Greater Cleve. (pres. 1974), Beta Phi Mu. Roman Catholic. Adv. editor Manuscripta, 1957-66. Contbr. articles to profl. jours. Home: Cleveland Heights, Ohio. Died Feb. 27, 1982.

JONES, JOHN DAVID, JR., agriculturist; b. Mt. Pleasant, Wis., Jan. 4, 1887; s. John David and Katherine (Gittins) J.; student high sch., 1898-1902, and U. of Wis., 1904-10; m. Eleanor Chapman Day, of Wilmette, Ill., Feb. 15, 1915; children—David Day, Hugh Day, Sarah Day. Dairy and truck farmer, 1910-23; commr. of agr. State of Wis., 1923-27; exec. sec. Nat. Cheese Inst., 1927-30; agrl. advisor Wis. Bankshares Corpn., 1930-36; gen agt. Farm Credit Adminstrn., St. Paul, Minn., from 1936. Mem. Alpha Tau Omega. Mason. Club: Athletic (St. Paul). Home: Racine, Wis. †

JONES, JOHN PAUL, govt. ofcl.; b. Cin., June 12, 1916; s. Edward William and Lily (Morrissey) J.; m. Dorothy Hoffhouse, Apr. 27, 1944; children—Gerald Paul, Julia Ann. B.B.A., U. Cin., 1939. With Cin. Transit Co., 1937-72, successively traffic researcher, claim investigator, staff asst., asst. to pres., dir. pub. relations, 1937-55, pres., dir., 1956-72; assoc. adminstr. Urban Mass Transp. Adminstrn., U.S. Dept. Transp., Washington, 1972-81, ret., 1981. Served to 2d lt. AUS, 1941-45. Mem. Pub. Relations Soc. Am., Ohio Transit Assn. (pres. 1959-63, 70-71, exec. v.p. 1972), Young Presidents Orgn., Cincinnatus Assn., Cin. C. of C. (dir. 1967-72), Am. Transit Assn. (pres. 1969-70), Cin. Conv. Bur. (pres. 1962-64), Cin. Hist. Soc., Newcomen Soc., Ohio C. of C., Cin. Council World Affairs. Clubs: Univ. (Cin.), Queen City (Cin.), Cincinnati Country (Cin.); Literary; River Bend Country. Home: Cincinnati, Ohio. Died Mar. 30, 1984.

JONES, JUNIUS WALLACE, ret. USAF ofcr.; b. Jackson, La., Apr. 3, 1890; s. Dr. Philip Huff and Annabelle (Smith) J.; grad. Bingham Sch., Asheville, N.C., 1907; B.S., U.S. Mil. Acad., 1913; grad. Air Service Pilots Sch., 1920, Air Service Observers Sch., 1921, Air Corps Tactical Sch., 1928, Command and Gen. Staff Sch., 1929, Army War Coll., 1930, Naval War Coll., 1934; m. Mary Beirne Harman, Dec. 29, 1914; 1 dau., Mary Beirne (Mrs. Hugh H. Kerr); m. 2d, Josephine Stevens Lanier, Dec. 26, 1923; m. 3d, Martha Katherine Callahan, Nov. 25, 1936; 1 dau., Esther Marilynn (Mrs. Virgil A. A. Robinson, Junior). Commissioned 2d lieut., Coast Arty. Corps, June 12, 1913; promoted through grades to brig. gen., U.S. Army, Feb. 14, 1941; comdg. gen. 5th Air Support Command, Bowman Field, Louisville, Ky., Aug. 1941; exec. Technical Training Comd., Knollwood Field, N.C., 1942; comdg. gen. 1st Dist. Technical Training Command, Sedgefield, N.C., 1942; assigned as Air Inspector, Hdqrs. A.A.F., Washington, 1943-48; Maj. Gen. Feb. 20, 1944; Comdg. gen. Sacramento Air Materiel Area, McClellan Air Force Base, McClellan, Cal., 1948-52; chief aircraft sect. Internat. Staff, NATO, 1952-53; ret.; mem. Orleans Aviation Commn., 1954; aviation dir. New Orleans Aviation Bd., 1955-57, aviation cons., 1957. Decorated D.S.M. with oak leaf cluster, Legion of Merit, Air Medal. Mem. West Point Soc. (pres. Mid Gulf area, 1955-57), Air Force Assn. (comdr. La. wing 1958). Mason (Shriner). Clubs: Army and Navy, Army and Navy Country (Washington). Home: Culver City, Cal. †

JONES, MALCOLM GWYNNE, business exec.; b. Nanticoke, Pa., Sept. 17, 1902; s. Evan L. and Emma Jane (Edmunds) J.; m. Mary Woodford White, July 13, 1931 (dec. Oct. 1971); children—Malcolm Gwynne, Nancy Kent; m. Sarah Lillian Clements, July 15, 1972. B.S. in Chemistry, Bucknell U., 1926. Gen. engring. constrn., 1926-29; foreman acetate rayon plant E. I. duPont de Nemours, Waynesboro, Va., 1929-31, supr., 1931-37, chief supr., 1937-46, plant mgr., 1946-48, dir. prodn. acetate rayon, orlon acrylic fibers, Wilmington, Del., 1948-50, dir. nylon sales, 1950, dir. sales synthetic fibers, 1951-53; pres., dir. Robbins Mills, Inc., 1953-54; chmn. bd., pres., 1954; dir. Sidney Blumenthal & Co., Inc., 1954-56, also; mem. exec. com.; pres., dir. Shelton Looms Distbg. Corp., 1954-56; pres. Wayne Devel. Co., Inc., 1957-71; mgmt. cons. Hercules Powder Co., 1960-70; gen. partner The Centre for Shopping, from 1965; Chmn. bd. trustees Blue Ridge Community Coll., 1965-77. Mem. Phi Gamma Delta, Pi Delta Epsilon. Presbyn. Clubs: Mason. (Va.), Waynesboro Country (Va.). Address: Waynesboro, VA.

JONES, RALPH WALDO EMERSON, college president; b. Lake Charles, La., Aug. 6, 1905; s. John Sebastian and Maria (Morrison) J.; A.B., So. U., Baton Rouge, 1925; A.M., Columbia, 1932; LL.D., La. Tech. U., 1970; m. Mildred Shay, Apr. 11, 1937; children—Ralph, John Arthur. Tchr., Lampton Coll., Alexandria, La., 1925-26; instr. Grambling (La.) State U., 1926-27, dean, 1927-36, pres., 1936-77. Mem. Phi Beta Sigma Baptist. Mason (33 deg.). Home: Grambling, La. Died Apr. 9, 1982.

JONES, RICHARD LLOYD, JR., newspaper exec.; b. Jyack, N.Y., Feb. 22, 1909; s. Richard Lloyd and Georgia (Hayden) J.; m. Martha Meredeth Corder, Mar. 4, 1933; children—Richard, Dana. Ph.D., U. Wis., 1932; LL.D. (hon.), Oral Roberts U. With Tulsa Tribune, 1933-82, v.p., bus. mgr., from 1938, later pres., chmn. bd.; v.p., bus. mgr., then pres. Newspaper Printing Corp., Tulsa, 1941-76; v.p., treas. Hennepin Paper Co., Little Falls, Minn., 1953-56; dir. Brookside State Bank, Tulsa; past dir. Douglas Aircraft Co., McDonnell-Douglas Corp.; past bd. dirs., vice chmn. AP.; Chmn. bd. visitors U. Okla., 1976-78. Chmn. Tulsa Airport Authority, 1955-78; bd. dirs. Okla. State Fair and Livestock Exposition, Tulsa. Served to lt. USNR, World War II. Mem. Am. Newspaper Pubs. Assn. (chmn. bd. bur. advt. 1956-58), So. Newspaper Pubs. Assn. (pres. 1960-61), Aviation Writers Assn., Tulsa C. of C. (pres. 1960-61), Phi Gamma Delta. Unitarian. Clubs: Tulsa (Tulsa), Summit (Tulsa), So. Hills Country (Tulsa). Home: Tulsa, Okla. Died Jan. 27, 1982.

JONES, ROBERT ANTHONY, conductor, educator; b. Yorkshire, Eng., Aug. 6, 1936; s. Arthur and Mary (Dixon) J.; came to U.S., 1965, naturalized, 1976; B.A., King's Coll., Cambridge U., 1959, M.A., 1961. Mem. music staff Glyndebourne Festival Opera, 1962-64, Dallas Opera, 1970-71; mem. music staff Santa Fe Opera, 1965-70, chorus dir., 1971-74; musical dir. Tex. Opera Theatre, Houston, 1974; chorus dir. San Francisco Opera, 1975-76; prof. Manhattan Sch. Music, N.Y.C., 1977-80; head music staff, mus. cons. to gen. dir. Opera Theatre of St. Louis, 1978-80. Rec. artist. Home: New York, N.Y. Dec. June 13, 1980.

JONES, ROBERT IRWIN, accounting company executive; b. Oak Park, Ill., Jan. 20, 1920; s. Irwin Arthur and Helen Elizabeth (Henson) J.; B.S. in Commerce, Northwestern U., 1941; m. Lois Tehle, Aug. 29, 1941; children—Linda, Nancy, Barbara. With Arthur Andersen & Co., from 1941, vice chmn. internat. ops., 1970-75, mem. exec. bd., 1970-80, co-chmn. bd., San Francisco, 1975-78, sr. ptnr., 1978-80; dir. Heizer Corp., Del E. Webb Corp.; mem. exec. com. India-U.S. Bus. Council; mem. Adv. Council on Japan-U.S. Econ. Relations; mem. U.S.-USSR Trade and Econ. Council; mem. Nat. Council for U.S.-China Trade. C.P.A., Ill., Calif. Mem. Am. Inst. C.P.A.'s, Ill., Calif. socs. C.P.A.'s, Fgn. Policy Assn. (dir.), Internat. C. of C. (trustee U.S. Council). Republican. Presbyterian. Clubs: Union League (N.Y.C.); Chicago, Exmoor, University (Chgo.). Home: Lake Forest, Ill. Dec. Sept. 17, 1982.

JONES, ROBERT LETTS, retired publishing company executive; b. Oakland, Calif., Nov. 9, 1913; s. Madison Ralph and Carolyn (Oliver) J.; student U. Ariz., 1935; A.B., Stanford, 1936; m. Darlene Zahalka, 1977; stepchildren—Michelle, Christina. Editor, bus. mgr. Stanford Daily, 1935-36; war corr. Spanish Civil War, UPI, 1936; free lance writer League of Nations Session, Geneva, 1936; editorial side Chronicle, San Francisco, 1937-39; editor, pub. Vallejo (Calif.) Evening-News, 1939-42; asst. bus. mgr. Los Angeles Examiner, 1946-47; asst. pub. Salem (Oreg.) Capital Jour., 1947-53; asst. gen. mgr. Detroit News, 1953-57; dir. Inst. Newspaper Ops., 1955-56; dir. personnel Copley Press, Inc., La Jolla, Calif., 1957-59, v.p., dir., 1959-65, pres., 1965-75, also mem. exec. com.; hon. chmn. Copley Internat. Corp., 1968-74; mem. U.S. State Dept. Joint Com. on U.S.-Japan Cultural and Ednl. Cooperation, 1971-76; mem. adv. com. Stanford Profl. Journalism Fellowships Program. Pres. Calif. Newspaperboy Found., 1963-64, 1st v.p., 1962-63, chmn. bd., 1964-65; bd. dirs. Anita Oliver Lunn Found., 1961-81; trustee Scripps Clinic and Research Found., 1964-81. Served with USMCR, 1942-46. Decorated Bronze Star, Purple Heart; recipient Honor certificate Freedoms Found., 1965. Mem. Internat. Press. Inst., U.S. C. of C. (taxation com. 1959-63), Am. Council on Edn. for Journalism, Am. Newspaper Pub. Assn. (taxation com. 1959-63, labor relations com. 1969-75), Internat. Fedn. Newspaper Pubs., Stanford Assos., Stanford Alumni Assn., Marine Corps Res. Officers Assn., Soc. Calif. Pioneers, Wine and Food Soc. London, Navy League, Delta Upsilon, Sigma Delta Chi. Republican. Presbyterian. Clubs: Circumnavigators; La Jolla Beach and Tennis; Cuyamaca (San Diego); Confrerie de la Chaine des Rotisseurs; Adcraft (Detroit); Nat. Press (Washington); Explorers, Overseas Press (N.Y.C.); Bohemian (San Francisco). Home: Ramona, Calif. Died 1981.

JONES, ROBERT LYNN, bus. exec.; b. Mabank, Tex., Sept. 28, 1932; s. Mason and Lena (Dixon) J.; m. Arlene M. Scott, Mar. 9, 1957; children—Scott, Kevin. B.B.A., LL.B., Tex. U., 1956. Sr. v.p., sec., resident counsel Gulf & Western Industries, Inc., N.Y.C., from 1963. Methodist. Address: New York, N.Y.

JONES, THOMAS FRANKLIN, JR., electrical engineer, educational administrator; b. Henderson, Tenn., July 9, 1916; s. Thomas Franklin and Addye Mae (Moore) J.; m. Mary Katherine Butterworth, March 9, 1942; children—Thomas, James, Jonathan, Katherine, Andrew. B.S., Miss. State Coll., 1939; M.S., Mass. Inst. Tech., 1940, Sc.D., 1952; LL.D., The Citadel, 1966; D.Eng., Purdue U., 1971. Physicist underwater sound, harbor def. Naval Research Lab., 1941-47; instr. Mass. Inst. Tech., 1947, research assoc. guided missiles, analog computation and analysis, 1948-49, asst. prof., 1949-54, assoc. prof. charge circuits, electronics and measurements labs., 1954-58; head Purdue U. Sch. Elec. Engring., 1958-62; pres. U. S.C., Columbia, 1962-74, Distinguished prof. univ., 1974-77; vis. prof. Mass. Inst. Tech., 1974-77, v.p. for research, 1975-81, prof. engring., 1977-81; chmn. tech. adv. bd. Western Union Telegraph Co., 1967-70; spl. adviser NSF, 1960-64, mem. sci. info. council, 1964-66; mem. Nat. Sci. Bd., 1966-72; chmn. research applications policy adv. com., 1975-77, chmn. applied sci.-research applications adv. com., 1977-81, mem. exec. adv. council, 1977-81; participant Council on Higher Edn. in Am. Republics, Lima, Peru, 1968, Bogota, Colombia, 1969, Buenos Aires, Argentina, 1970, Lima, 1971, Rio de Janeiro, Brazil, 1972; bd. dirs. Nat. Electronics Conf., 1959-62. Recipient Meritorious Civilian Service award USN; named South Carolinian of Year, 1966, Columbia Ambassador of Year 1974. Fellow IRE (editor 1962), IEEE (mem. profl. group on edn., dir. 1963-66, exec. com. editorial bd. 1962, publs. bd. 1963-66, chmn. external awards com. 1969-70, fellow com. 1971-72, v.p. edn. 1975), AAAS, Radio Club Am.; mem. Engrs. Council Profl. Devel. (past dir.), Am. Soc. Engring. Edn. (v.p. public affairs 1980-82, Dist. Service award 1981), Newcomen Soc., Nat. Acad. Engring. (com. engring. manpower 1972), Sigma Xi, Phi Eta Sigma, Kappa Mu Epsilon, Tau Beta Pi, Eta Kappa Nu, Theta Xi, Phi Mu Alpha. Home: Arlington, Mass. Died July 14, 1981.

JONES, VIRGINIA LACY (MRS E.A. JONES), librarian; b. Cincinnati, O., June 25, 1912; dau. Edward and Ellen Louise (Parker) Lacy; B.S., Sch. of Edn., Hampton Inst., 1936, B.S. L.S., 1933; M.S. in L.S., Univ. of Ill. (Gen. Edn. Bd. fellow, 1937-38), 1938; Ph.D., Univ. of Chicago (Gen. Edn. bd. fellow, 1943-45), 1945; m. Dr. Edward Allen Jones, Nov. 27, 1941. Assistant librarian Louisville Municipal College, 1934-35, librarian 1936-37; assistant circulation dept., Hampton Inst. Library, 1935-36; dir. dept. library sci., Prairie View State Coll., Prairie View, Texas, summers, 1936-39; catalog librarian Atlanta (Ga.) Univ. 1939-41, instr. sch. of Library Service, 1941-43, dir., 1945-81. Mem. A.L.A., Assn. Am. Library Schs., Adult Edn. Assn., N.A.A.C.P., YWCA, Delta Sigma Theta, Beta Phi Mu. Democrat. Conglist. Home: Atlanta, Ga. Died Dec. 3, 1984.

JONES, WILBUR BOARDMAN, lawyer; b. St. Louis, Mo., Sept. 10, 1888; s. William Edward and Ada Anna (Jewett) Jones: A.B., magna cum laude, Amherst Coll., 1909; LL.B., cum laude, Washington U., St. Louis, 1912; m. Irene Clifford, Oct. 28, 1914; children—Wilbur Boardman (lt., U.S.N.R.), Alfred Clifford (lt. U.S. Naval Reserve). Admitted to bar 1911; engaged in practice of law since 1911; partner firm William E. and Wilbur B. Jones, 1912-17, Salkey & Jones, 1922-57 Husch Eppenberger, Donohue, Elson & Jones, from 1957. Served as 1st lt., Air Service, 1918. Civilian aide to sec. of war for Mo., 1940-52; adviser to industry War Manpower Commission, 1941-45; incident officer Civilian Defense of St. Louis, 1942-45. Sec. Bd. of Freeholders (New Charter Commn.), 1913-14; exec. sec. Citizens New Charter Campaign, 1914, Citizens Parkway Campaign, 1915; sec. and treas. Mo. Commn. for Blind, 1930-32; chmn. advance gifts com. United Charities Campaign, 1937. Trustee Iberia Jr. Coll., 1912-47, chmn. bd. trustees, 1937-47. Dir. St. Louis YMCA, 1914-59, pres., 1934-35. Nat. councillor U.S. Chamber of Commerce, 1940-41; dir. St. Louis Chamber of Commerce, 1935-36 and 1943-44; mem. exec. com. 1937-43, vice chmn. bd. dirs., 1938-39, chmn. bd. dirs., 1940-41; vice chmn. St. Louis com. of Pan American Soc., 1942-45. Trustee Missouri Hist. Soc., 1942-56, v.p. 1946-51. Mem. St. Louis Bar Assn. (exec. com., 1919-20; treas. 1920), Missouri Bar Assn., Phi Beta Kappa (v.p. men's club 1937-47), Psi Upsilon, Phi Delta Phi. Mason (33 deg.). Clubs: Log Cabin, Country, Noonday (St. Louis). Home: St. Louis, Mo. †

JONES, WILLIAM HUGH, newspaper editor; b. Marinette, Wis., May 23, 1939; s. Hugh Fred and Mildred (Festge) J.; m. Virginia Marie Murphy, Aug. 22, 1964; children—William Hugh, Michael Joseph, Megan Kathleen. B.S. in Journalism with sr. honors, U. Wis.-Milw., 1964; M.S., Northwestern U., 1965; student, Advanced Mgmt. Program, Harvard U., 1978. Mng. editor Chgo. Tribune, 1965-82. Served with USMC, 1958-61. Recipient Pulitzer prize for local reporting, 1971, Nat. Headline Club award, 1968, more than 20 other journalism awards; Civic award Civic Found. Northbrook, 1971; award of merit Northwestern U. Alumni Assn., 1972; Distinguished Alumnus award U. Wis.-Milw., 1975. Home: Glencoe, Ill. Died Nov. 23, 1982.

JORDAN, DANIEL C(LYDE), assn. exec., educator; b. Alliance, Nebr., June 2, 1932; s. Edward Davis and H. Melissa (Hartmann) J.; m. Nancy Crawford Blair, Sept. 27, 1956; children—Melissa Kathleen, Sara Margaret, Charlotte Blair. Mus.B., U. Wyo., 1954; B.A., Oxford (Eng.) U., 1956; M.A. (Rhodes scholar), 1958; M.A., Ph.D. in Human Devel, U. Chgo., 1960, Ph.D. in Human Devel, 1964. Dir. Inst. Research in Human Behavior, Ind. State U., 1965-68; dir. Center for Study Human Potential, U. Mass., 1968-80; exec. sec. Am. Nat. Insts. for Social Advancement, Vista, Calif., from 1969; dean Sch. Edn., Nat. U., San Diego, from 1980; mem. Nat. Task Force on Nutrition Edn., HEW, 1979. Author; composer: ballet Metamorphosis of the Owls, 1962. Served with Judge Adv. Gen. Corp. U.S. Army, 1956-58. Recipient Theodore Pressor award, various grants. Mem. Am. Psychol. Assn., Nat. Assn. Edn. Young Children, Am. Acad. Arts and Scis., Baha'i. Devel. ANISA, comprehensive ednl. system, 1969. Home: Escondido, Calif.

JORDAN, FRANK M(ORRILL), govt. ofcl; b. Alameda, Calif., Aug. 6, 1888; s. Frank C. and Emma Dudley (Morrill) J.; ed. pub. schs., Oakland, Calif.; m. Alice Kathryn Crossan, June 10, 1919; 1 dau., Mary Jane (Mrs. Robert E. Law). Engr., Clara Constrn. Mining Co., Ariz., 1906-11; engr., Auto Club of So. Calif., 1911-17; with Western Pipe & Steel Co., San Francisco, 1919-21; own contracting bus., Jordan-Archer Co., San Jose, Calif., 1922-33; sec. of state, 1935-40. Mem. 144th F.A., 1917-19. Mem. Nat. Assn. Secs. of State (pres., from 1949), Native Sons of Calif. Republican. Mason (32 deg.). Elk L.O.M. Club: Jonathan. Home: Carmichael, Calif. †

JORDAN, LEONARD BECK, U.S. senator; b. Mt. Pleasant, Utah, May 15, 1899; s. Leonard Eugene and Irene (Beck) J.; m. Grace Edgington, Dec. 30, 1924; children—Patricia Jean, Joseph Leonard, Stephen Edgington. A.B., U. Oreg., 1923. Mem. Idaho Legislature, 1947; gov. of Idaho, 1951-55; chmn. U.S. sect. Internat. Joint Commn., 1955-57, U.S. Senator from Idaho, 1962-73. Served as 2d lt., inf. U.S. Army, World War I. Mem. Phi Beta Kappa, Alpha Tau Omega. Republican. Methodist. Clubs: Masons (33 deg.), Shriners. Home: Boise, Idaho. Died June 30, 1983.

JORDAN, LEWIS, newspaperman; b. Pataskala, Ohio, Dec. 4, 1912; s. Elmer Webber and Blanche (Lewis) J.; A.B., Marietta (Ohio) Coll., 1934, Litt. D. (hon.), 1961; m. Elizabeth Lee, Dec. 15, 1959. Machinist, Winton Engine Co., Cleve., 1929-30; reporter, copy editor Detroit Free Press, 1934-40; mem. staff N.Y. Times, 1940-83, news editor, 1960-83; asso. journalism, asst. prof. Grad. Sch. Journalism. Columbia, 1946-57. Served with AUS, 1942-46; ETO. Author News-How It Is Written and Edited, 1960. Editor: The New York Times Style Book. Home: New York, N.Y. Died Nov. 17, 1983.

JORDAN, RUSH, coll. pres.; b. Valley Town, N.C., Oct. 16, 1888; s. James H. and Rachel C. (Trull) J.; B.S., U. Ida., 1923, A.M., 1929; grad. student U. Cal., 1932, 33, 38; m. Ollie A. Kinzer, Aug. 17, 1913; 1 dau., Margaret V. Tchr. rural schs., Ida., 1907-13; coach, high sch. instr., Kendrick, Ida., 1913; prin., Spalding, Ida., 1914; supt. Juliaetta, Ida., 1915-17; asst. jr. high sch. Lewistown Normal Sch., 1917; supt., Peck, Ida., 1918-21, Culdesac, Ida., 1921-23; asst. Am. history U. Ida., 1923; head social studies dept. Walla Walla (Wash.) High Sch., 1923-26; asso. prof. social studies State Normal, Dillon, Mont., 1926-38; president Western Montana College of Edn., 1946-56; vis. lectr. U. Ohio, summer 1941. Mem. N.E.A., Mont. Edn. Assn., Am. Assn. U. Profs., Mont. Adminstrs. Assn., Beaverhead C. of C. Mason, Elk. Contbr. verses Peoples Home Jour. Home: Berkeley, Cal. †

JOSEPH, BERTRAM LEON, educator; b. Maesteg, S. Wales, Gt. Britain, July 1, 1915; s. Barnett and Ella (Levy) J.; came to U.S., 1965; B.A., Univ. Coll. S. Wales and Monmouthshire, 1936; D.Phil., Magdalen Coll., Oxford (Eng.) U., 1946, B.A., 1947, M.A., 1947; m. Ada Emilie Goldschmidt, July 10, 1939; children—Hilary Margaret, Anthony. Fellow U. Wales, Cardiff, 1946-49; lectr. English, U. Bristol (Eng.), 1949-60, reader Renaissance English lit., 1960-64; vis. sr. prof. English U. Western Ont., London, 1964-65; prof. drama U. Wash., Seattle, 1965-70; prof. drama, chmn. dept. drama and theater Queens Coll., Flushing, N.Y., 1970-81; instr. acting Shakespeare, London Acad. Music and Dramatic Art, 1959-64, Bristol Old Vic Sch., 1957-64; asso. dir. Mermaid Theatre, London, 1951-53, Bristol Theatre Royal, 1961; dir. Shakespeare studies E.15 Theatre Sch., London, 1961-64. Served with Intelligence Corps, Royal Army Med. Corps, 1940-44. Author: Elizabethan Acting, 1951, 64; Conscience and the King: Study of Hamlet, 1953; Tragic Actor, 1959; Acting Shakespeare, 1960; Shakespeare's Eden, 1971; Shakespeare: An Actor's Workbook, 1978. Corp. Pub. Broadcasting grantee for Nest of Singing Birds, programs on English verse, U. Wash., 1969; research in audio-visual media, rec. films on teaching Shakespeare. Home: Glen Cove, N.Y. Died Sept. 3, 1981.

JOSEPH, JOHN J., lawyer; b. Marathon, Ohio, July 27, 1899; s. Frank A. and Ella Maria (Hensel) J.; A.B., Ohio Wesleyan U., 1920; LL.B., Western Res. U., 1928; LL.D., Bowling Green (Ohio) State U., 1943; m. Dorothy S. Griswold, Dec. 21, 1952; m. Martha M. Kenny, June 5, 1981. Several positions 1917-1928; admitted to Ohio bar, 1928, practiced in Cleve., 1928-29; instr. polit. sci. Western Res. U., instr. Law Sch., 1942-50; with Ohio Bell Telephone Co., from 1929, plant supr., 1929-33, directory advt. sales mgr., 1933-35, asst. to v.p., 1935-37, asst. v.p., 1937-48, v.p. charge pub. relations and pub. affairs, 1948-63; assoc. firm Claypool & Joseph, Columbus, Ohio, from 1983; owner Clermont Farms, Danville, Ohio, from 1949; dir. First State Bank & Trust Co. of Columbus, Ohio Farmers Ins. Co., Westfield Ins. Cos. Mem. Selective Service Bd., Cleveland, 1941-46. Bd. dirs. Ohio Council on Econ. Edn.; life trustee Ohio Wesleyan U. Mem. Am., Ohio bar assns., Am. Judicature Soc., Ohio C. of C., U.S. C. of C., Omicron Delta Kappa, Phi Delta Phi, Alpha Tau Omega (chmn. high council 1954-58, Province chief, Ohio, 1937-46). Republican. Methodist. Mason. Clubs: Athletic (Cleve.); Univ. (Columbus). Home: Danville, Ohio. Dec. Apr. 22, 1985. Interned Oak Grove Cemetery, Delaware, Ohio.

JOSLIN, CHARLES LERING, pediatrist; b. Sudlersville, Md., Nov. 10, 1887; s. Charles Lober and Anor (Gooden) J.; M.D., U. of Md., 1912; grad. student, Johns Hopkins, 1913-15; N.Y. Postgrad. Med. Sch., 1915; m. Hester Leavenworth Riddle, Mar. 2, 1918; children—Mary Margaret Leavenworth, Charles Loring, Blackburn Smith, Light Leavenworth, Interne James Walker Memorial Hosp., Wilmington, N.C., 1912-13; instr. in pediatrics, U. of Md., 1920-22, assoc. in pediatrics, 1922-24, asst. prof., 1924-27, assoc. prof., 1927-30, prof. of clin. pediatrics, 1930-34, prof. of pediatrics since 1934; pediatrists, Baltimore, since 1919. Commd. 1st lt. Med. Corps, U.S. Army, Aug. 1917, capt. Mar. 1918; served with 315th F.A., 80th Div.; with A.E.F. in active service in Meuse-Argonne. reserve at Chateau-Thierry. Fellow Am. Acad. Pediatrics; certified by Am. Bd. Pediatrics; mem. A.M.A., Southern Med. Assn., Med. and Chirurg. Faculty of Md., Baltimore City Med. Soc. Nu Sigma Nu. Democrat. Episcopalian. Contbr. to professional jours. Home: Baltimore, Md. †

JOSLYN, MAYNARD ALEXANDER, educator; b. Alexandrovsk, Russia, July 7, 1904; s. Alexander Leo and Anna (Kalutsky) J.; brought to U.S., 1913, naturalized, 1922; B.S. in Chemistry, U. Cal. at Berkeley, 1926, M.S. in Agrl. Tech., 1928, Ph.D. in Chemistry, 1935; m. Golda Fischer, Apr. 19, 1947. Supr. prodn. Nat. Juice Corp., Tampa, Fla., 1930-31; mem. faculty U. Cal. at Berkeley, 1927-84, successively research asst., instr., asst. prof., asso. prof., 1927-49, prof. dept. food tech., 1949-84; cons. Cal. Dept Health, 1958-84; food processing adviser, Australia, 1942-45, New Zealand, 1944, China, 1945, Israel, 1951, 58-59, 60, 64; vis. prof. food tech. Mass. Inst. Tech., 1960. Served from capt. to col., AUS, 1942-46. Decorated Legion of Merit (Australia); Bronze Star medal (China); special breast Order Yun Hai (Nat. Govt. of China); recipient prize for book on table wines Office Internat. du Vin, Paris, 1951; Internat. award Inst. Food Tech., 1961, Babcock-Hart award, 1963. Fellow A.A.A.S., Am. Inst. Chemists; mem. N.Y. Acad. Sci., Asso. Quartermasters, Food and Container Inst., Am. Soc. Encologists, Am. Chem. Soc., Am. Soc. Plant Physiologists, Inst. Food Tech. (pres.-elect), Am. Soc. Biol. Chemistry, Am. Soc. Microbiology, Soc. Ind. Microbiology, Plant Phenolics Group Gt. Britain. Asso. editor Advances in Food Research; editorial bd. Food Tech., Jour. Biochem. and Microbiol. Tech. Home: Berkeley, Calif. Died Nov. 28, 1984.

JOYCE, HARRY ALEXIS JONES, insurance company executive; b. Columbia, Tenn., Mar. 7, 1924; s. John Clarence and Watha Bess (Jones) J.; B.S., U.S. Naval Acad., 1946; m. Margaret Sinclair Henry, Sept. 22, 1951; children—Alexis Jones, Douglas Henry. Commd. ensign USN, 1946, advanced through grades to lt., 1953; ret., 1953; with First Am. Nat. Bank, Nashville, 1949-51, 53-54; v.p., treas. Nat. Life & Accident Ins. Co., 1973-81; treas. NLT Corp., Nashville, 1971-81; treas. NLT Computer Services Corp., NLT Mktg. Service Corp., NLT Capital Corp., WSM, Inc., Nat. Property Owners Ins. Co. Active YMCA, United Fund, Tenn. Bot. Gardens and Fine Arts Center; bd. dirs. Nashville Symphony Assn., Salvation Army, YMCA. Episcopalian. Clubs: Exchange, Cumberland, Belle Meade Country (Nashville); Linville (N.C.) Golf. Home: Nashville, Tenn. Dec. Mar. 26, 1981.

JOYCE, ROBERT PRATHER, fgn. service officer; b. Los Angeles, Oct. 17, 1902; s. William Henry and Josephine (Haskins) J.; student Deep Springs (Calif.) Sch., 1919-22; A.B., Yale, 1926; student Free Sch. of Polit. Sci., Paris, 1926-27; m. Jane Chase, Jan. 22, 1935. Entered U.S. Fgn. Service, 1928; first secretary, Havana, Cuba; 1941-43; with agencies under Joint Chiefs of Staff, Cairo, 1943, Barl, Italy, 1944, Allied Forces Mediterranean H.Q., Caserta, Italy, 1944-45; spl. asst. to minister, Bern, 1945-46; apptd. U.S. Consul Gen., 1947; U.S. Polit. adviser to comdr. of British-U.S. Zone, Free Ter. of Trieste, 1947-48; mem. policy planning staff Dept. of State, 1948-52; counselor of embassy, Paris, 1953-56; minister-counselor Am. Embassy, Rio de Janeiro, 1956-57, spl. asst. Bur. Intelligence and Research, Dept. of State, from 1957. Mem. Psi Upsilon. Episcopalian. Club: Yale. Home: Washington, D.C. Died Feb. 8, 1984.

JUDD, ARDON BERKELEY, corp. exec.; b. Nebraska City, Neb., Aug. 22, 1890; s. Homer Ardon and Minerva Douglass (Berkeley) J.; student Denison U.; LL.B., U. Tex., 1913; m. Sallie Reynolds Matthews, Oct. 20, 1920; children—Sally Ann (Mrs. R. C. Harrison), Susan Berkeley (Mrs. Jos. C. Brown Jr.), Ardon Berkeley. Admitted to Tex. bar, 1913; practiced in Ft. Worth, 1913-17, Tampico, Mex., 1920-22; sec. Republic Supply Co., a subsidiary of Republic Steel Corp., Houston, 1923-41, v.p., 1941-48, pres., 1948; pres. Southwest Fabricating & Welding Co., Inc., from 1952; dir. Tenn. Gas Transmission Co. Breeder of pure bred Santa Gertrudis cattle, Houston, from 1951. Founder, trustee, St. John's Sch., Houston. Mem. Nat. Petroleum Council, 1947-48, Am. Petroleum Inst., Beta Theta Pi. Clubs: Ramada, Tejas, Houston Country, River Oaks Country.†

JUDD, WILLIAM EDWARD, mfg. co. exec.; b. Chgo., Sept. 1, 1919; s. Frank and Frances (Meitz) J.; ed. U. Chgo., Loyola U. and Law Sch., Chgo., 1935-42; m. Dorothy R. Neunuebel, Aug. 1, 1942; children—Robert A., Patricia R. (Mrs. A.G. Brightman), Donald E. With firm Willians, Bradbury, McCaleb & Hinkle, patent law, 1936-42; with Stewart-Warner Corp., 1942-84, gen. mgr. heating and air conditioning div., 1956—, v.p. corp., 1960-84, gen. mgr. Thor Power Tool div., 1975-84. Bd. dirs. Nat. Oil Fuel Inst., chmn. bd., 1970-71; bd. dirs. United Fund Greater Indpls. Mem. Soc. Automotive Engrs., Nat. Warm Air Heating and Air Conditioning Assn. (pres. 1968, trustee), Am. Gas Assn., Nat. Petroleum Council, Am. Ordnance Assn., Newcomen Soc., Confederacy of Indian Sachems, Sagamore of Wabash. Clubs: Evanston (Ill.) Golf; Meridian Hills Country (Indpls.). Home: Evanston, Ill. Died Jan. 12, 1984; buried Rosehill Cemetery, Chgo.

JUDKINS, HENRY FOREST, assn. exec.; b. Kingston, N.H., Feb. 13, 1890; s. Arthur R. and Delia A. (Page) J.; B.S., University N.H., 1911. Doctor of Science (honorary), 1960; married to Alice Cecile Bates, Oct. 12, 1912; children—Forest H., Roger B. Tchr. dairy mfg. U. N.H., Conn. Agrl. Coll., Ia. State Coll., Mass. State Coll., 1911-25; research and prodn. mgr. Eastern Dairies, Inc., Springfield, Mass. 1925-31, merged with Gen. Ice Cream Corp., then Nat. Dairy Products Corp., dir. prodn. Nat. Dairy Products Corp., 1931-35; exec. v.p., then pres. Sealtest, Inc., 1935-49, became Nat. Dairy Products Co., Inc., v.p., dir. plant prodn. div., 1949-55; pres. Am. Dairy Sci. Assn., 1941-42, sec.-treas. from 1955. Mem. Old Guard of White Plains, Phi Kappa Phi, Alpha Zeta. Mason. Home: White Plains, N.Y. †

JULIAN, ANTHONY, judge; b. Italy, Mar. 25, 1902; came to U.S., 1913, naturalized, 1923; s. Francesco and Maddalena (Ventresca) Giuliani. A.B., Boston Coll., 1925, LL.D., 1961; J.D., Harvard, 1929. Bar: Mass. bar 1929. Practiced law, Boston, 1929-53, town counsel, Watertown, 1930-32, 41-43; faculty Boston Coll., 1934-37; U.S. atty. Dist. Mass., 1953-59; U.S. dist. judge Dist. of Mass., 1959-84, chief judge, 1971-72, sr. judge, 1972-84. Mem. Mass. State Legislature, 1937-38; Mem. adv. bd. Don Orione Home for Aged. Served as maj., JAGC U.S. Army, World War II, ETO. Decorated Bronze Star; knight Order Holy Sepulchre of Jerusalem; Star of Solidarity Italy). Home: Boston, Mass. Died Jan. 18, 1984.

JUNKIN, GEORGE BENN, investment co. exec.; b. Sterling, Kan., Nov. 23, 1889; s. John Evans and Susan Blair (Benn) J.; B.S., U.S. Naval Acad., 1913; m. Ruth Rea, Nov. 15, 1919. Vice pres. Wolf Summit Coal Co., Phila., 1925-27, pres., 1927-29; pres. Wilson Line, Inc., Phila., 1929-64; dir. Wellington Fund, Inc., Cord Meyer Development Co., John T. Dyer Quarry Co., Wellington Equity Fund. Served to lt. comdr. USN 1913-24. Mem. S.A.R. Republican. Presbyn. Clubs: Merion Cricket (Phila.); Rolling Rock (Ligonier, Pa.); Army and Navy (Washington). Home: Bryn Mawr, Pa. †

JURGENS, CURT, actor; b. Munich, Germany, Dec. 12, 1915; m. Lulu Bascar; m. Judith Holtzmeister; m. Eva Bartok; m. Simone Bicheron; m. Margie Schmitz. Stage actor in, Germany, began film career, 1939; films include The Devil's General, 1954, An Eye for an Eye, 1956, The Enemy Below, 1957, Inn of the Sixth Happiness, 1958, The Blue Angel, 1958, Lord Jim, 1964, The Threepenny Opera, 1965, The Assassination Bureau, 1968, Nicholas and Alexandria, 1971, Vault of Horror, 1973, The Spy Who Loved Me, 1977, Breakthrough, 1979, Golden Girl, 1979; toured Germany in: films include Clarence Darrow; played Ernest Hemingway in films include, Vienna, Austria.; Author: films include Sixty and Not Yet Wise. Address: Los Angeles, Calif. Died June 18, 1982.*

JUSTIN, BROTHER CORNELIUS Brennan Joseph **(JOSEPH M. BRENNAN),** educator; b. Bklyn., Jan. 21, 1901; s. John and Mary (Culleton) B. A.B., Manhattan Coll., 1925; M.A., Columbia, 1932. Mem. teaching order Bros. of Christian Schs.; founder, 1947; dir. Westchester Labor Sch., Yonkers, N.Y.; head dept.

labor-mgmt. Manhattan Coll., from 1947; Lectr. U.S. Dept. State, Venezuela, 1965, Colombia, 1966; Mem. N.Y.C. Mayor's Action Panel To Study Problems of Job Discrimination, from 1963, N.Y. State Pub. Employment Relations Bd. Recipient Quadragesimo Anno medal Assn. Cath. Trade Unionists, 1950; John Acropolis Found. award, 1957. Mem. Am. Arbitration Assn., Indsl. Relations Research Assn., Cath. Bus. Edn. Assn., Acad. Polit. Sci., Am. Mgmt. Assn., Am. Acad. Polit. and Social Home: New York, N.Y.

JUSTUS, ROY BRAXTON, cartoonist; b. Avon, S.D., May 16, 1901; s. Augustus Braxton and Eliza Jane (Ruch) J.; m. Ruth Eleanor Langley, Aug. 25, 1928 (dec. 1970); m. Jeanne Boehrer, 1973. Student, Morningside Coll., 1920-23, LL.D., 1956. Polit. cartoonist Sioux City (Ia.) Tribune, 1924-26, 27-41; editorial cartoonist Sioux City Jour., 1941-44, Mpls. Star & Tribune, 1944-75; engaged in polit. cartoon syndication from, Washington, 1927; mem. A.P. art staff, N.Y.C., 1927. Recipient Nat. Headliners' Club cartoon award; 1944 Freedoms Found. awards, 1949-56; Christopher award, 1955; Grenville Clark editorial page award, 1962, 65; Sigma Delta Chi award, 1965. Mem. Assn. Am. Editorial Cartoonists (pres. 1958-59). Club: Minn. Press (Mpls.). Home: Minneapolis, Minn.

KAC, MARK, educator, mathematician; b. Krzemieniec, Poland, Aug. 3, 1914; came to U.S., 1938, naturalized, 1943; s. Bencion and Chana (Rojchel) K.; m. Katherine Elizabeth Mayberry, Apr. 4, 1942; children—Michael Benedict, Deborah Katherine. Magister of Philosophy, U. Lwow, Poland, 1935, Ph.D., 1937; D.Sc. (hon.), Case Inst. Tech., 1966. Teaching asst. U. Lwow, 1935-37; jr. actuary Phoenix Co., Lwow, 1937-38; fellow Parnas Found., Johns Hopkins, 1938-39; instr. Cornell U., 1939-43, asst. prof., 1943-46, prof. math., 1947-61, Andrew D. White prof.-at-large, 1965-71; mem. Inst. Advanced Study, Princeton, 1951-52; prof. Rockefeller U., N.Y.C., 1961-81, U. So. Calif., Los Angeles, 1981-84; H.A. Lorentz vis prof. U. Lelden, Netherlands, 1963; vis. fellow Brasenose Coll.; sr. vis. fellow Oxford (Eng.) U., spring, 1969; Solvay lectr. U. Brussels, Belgium, 1971. Contbr. articles to profl. jours. Guggenheim fellow, 1946-47; recipient Chauvenet prize for paper Random Walk and the Theory of Brownian Motion Math. Assn. Am., 1950, Chauvenet prize for paper Can One Hear the Shape of A Drum, 1968; Alfred Jurzykowski Found. award in sci., 1976; Birkhoff prize Am. Math. Soc.-Soc. Indsl. and Applied Math., 1978. Mem. Am. Acad. Arts and Scis., Am. Philos. Soc., Am. Math. Soc., Math. Assn. Am., Nat. Acad. Scis., Inst. Math. Stats., Royal Netherlands Acad. Arts and Sci. (fgn.), Royal Norwegian Acad. (fgn.), Sigma Xi. Home: Culver City, Calif. Died Oct. 26, 1984.

KADAR, JAN, director; b. Budapest, Hungary, Apr. 1, 1918; ed. Charles U., Prague, Czechoslovakia. Asst. dir. and producer documentary films Bratislava Short Film Studio; writer, asst. dir. Berrandov Studio, Prague, after 1947; dir. first feature Katya, 1950; other films include: The Shop on Main Street (Acad. award for best fgn. film 1966), 1966, The Angel Levine, 1970, Adrift, 1971, Lies My Father Told Me (Golden Globe award for best fgn. film 1975), 1975; TV films: The Other Side of Hell, 1977, Freedom Road, 1978. Address: Beverly Hills, Calif. Deceased.

KAHAN, ARCADIUS, educator, economist; b. Lodz, Poland, Jan. 16, 1920; s. Boruch M. and Sophie (Stupel) K.; student law and econs. Stefan Batory U., Vilno, Poland, 1936-38, econs. Free U. Warsaw (Poland), 1938-39; M.A., Rugters U., 1955, Ph. D., 1959; m. Pearl Ellenbogen, Nov. 12, 1946; children—Vivian Sarah, Miriam Israela. Came to U.S., 1950, naturalized, 1955. Research asso. U. Chgo., 1955-57, mem. faculty, 1957-82, prof. econs., 1965-82, master social sciences collegiate division, associate dean of college of university; vis. prof. London (Eng.) School Econs., 1963; Fulbright prof. Hebrew U., 1967-68. Cons. RAND Corp., 1959, Nat. Bur. Econ. Research, 1963-66. Fellow Russian Research Center, Harvard, 1961; NSF grantee, 1963-66; Guggenheim fellow, 1964. Mem. Am. Econ. Assn., Econ. History Assn., Econ. History Soc., Am. Assn. Advancement Slavic Studies. Home: Chicago, Ill. Died Feb. 26, 1982.

KAHLER, WOODLAND, orgn. ofcl., author; b. Dallas, Feb. 6, 1895; s. Harry Adams and Beulah (Pace) K.; m. Baroness Olga Clewesahl-Steinheil, May 3, 1932 (dec.); m. Amy Lorton McKay, 1977. Grad., Phillips Acad., 1914; B.A., Yale, 1918; student, Faculte des Lettres, Paris, 1923; student hon. degree; Internat. Pythagorean Philos. Soc., London; L.H.D. (hon.), Nathaniel Hawthorne Coll., Antrim, N.H. Officer Am. Trust Co., N.Y.C., 1919-22; pub. relations exec. Alfred A. Knopf, 1928-29; Rep. UNESCO, Paris; pres. Council for World Govt., The Hague, Netherlands; Founder, 1st pres. Internat. Vegetarian Union; pres. World League for Protection of Animals; v.p. Beauty without Cruelty, Inc.; pres. World Orgn. Culture; adv. editor Voice of Ahinsa, Aliganj, India; hon. com. Terre Et Cosmos (1st interplanetary exhbn. in world). Author: Early to Bed, 1928, Smart Setback, 1930, False Front, 1937, Giant Dwarf, 1942, Portrait in Laughter, 1946, Almighty Possibility, 1958, Cravings of Desire, 1960; Contbr. newspaper, mags, books and art; translated into Swedish, French, German, Hebrew, Hindi, Spanish. Served with U.S. Army, World War I. Created marquis d'Orlier de St. Innocent; decorated Hon. Diploma Vie et Action, chevalier Order of Merit, Livre d'Or, France; chevalier San Juan Bautista, Heraldica, Madrid; chevalier Order St. John of Cross, Spain; recipient Prani Mitra gold medal Pres. of India. Fellow Am. Natural Hygiene Soc. (exec. com.), Indian Vegetarian Congress (life), Nilgiri Humanitarian League (exec. com.), All-Indian Animal Welfare Assn. (exec. com.), World Jain Mission (exec. com.), Men of the Trees (London), Friends of Buddhism (Paris), Millenium Guild (N.Y.C.); mem. S.R. (life N.Y. State), Vegetarian Soc. Eng. (v.p.), Authors League Am., S.A.R. (life), Psi Upsilon, Cercle de L'Union, Union Interalliée (Paris, France), Federación Vegetariana Española (hon. pres.). Clubs: Polo de Barcelona; Polo (Paris, France); Ootacamund (India); Everglades (Palm Beach, Fla.); Capitol Hill (Washington). Home: Palm Beach, Fla. Died June 31, 1981.

KAHN, HERMAN, defense analyst, author; b. Bayonne, N.J., Feb. 15, 1922; s. Abraham and Yetta K.; m. Rosalie Jane Heilner, Mar. 31, 1953; children: Deborah Yetta, David Joshua. Student, U. So. Calif., 1940-41; B.A., UCLA, 1945; M.S., Calif. Inst. Tech., 1948; Ph.D. (hon.), U. Puget Sound, 1976, Worcester Poly. Inst., 1976. Mathematician Douglas Aircraft Co., 1945; lab. analyst on project for RAND Corp., 1947-48; teaching asst. UCLA, 1946; mathematician Northrop Aviation, 1947; sr. physicist, mil. analyst RAND Corp., 1948-61; with assos., established Hudson Inst., Croton-on-Hudson, N.Y., 1961; now dir. Staff tech. adv. group AEC, 1950; cons. Oak Ridge Nat. Lab., 1950-52, Gaither Com. on Strategic Warfare, 1957, Stanford Research Inst. Non-Mil. Def., 1958; tech. adviser Boeing Aircraft, RCA; cons. design of mech. drum computers, reactor calculations; mem. computing council Nat. Bur. Econ. Research. Author: On Thermonuclear War, 1960, Thinking About the Unthinkable, 1962, On Escalation Metaphors and Scenarios, 1965, (with Anthony Wiener) The Year 2000, 1967, (with others) Can We Win in Viet Nam, 1968, Why ABM, 1969, The Emerging Japanese Superstate - Challenge and Response, 1970, (with B. Bruce Briggs) Things to Come, 1972, World Economic Development, 1979; Editor: (with B. Bruce Briggs) The Future of the Corporation, 1974, (with William Brown, Leon Martel) The Next 200 Years, 1976, (with Thomas Pepper) The Japanese Challenge: The Success and Failure of Economic Success, 1979, Will She Be Right? The Future of Australia, 1980, The Coming Boom: Economic, Political and Social, 1982; Contbr. numerous articles to sci. jours., popular mags. Served with AUS, 1942-45. Mem. Am. Phys. Soc., Council on Fgn. Relations, Center for Inter-Am. Relations, Am. Polit. Sci. Assn. Home: Chappaqua, N.Y. Died July 7, 1983.

KAHN, SIDNEY, physician; b. Paterson, N.J., Mar. 30, 1913; s. Jacob Moses and Bertha (Orleansky) K.; B.A., NYU, 1933, M.D., 1937; m. Henrietta Berger, Aug. 31, 1939; children—Barbara Kahn Pollack, Rhoda Kahn Nussbaum. Intern, Bronx Hosp., N.Y.C., 1937-39, resident in surgery, 1939-42; pvt. practice medicine specializing in surgery, N.Y.C., 1946-81; attending plastic surgeon Bronx Mcpl. Hosp. Center, from 1955; clin. prof. plastic surgery Mt. Sinai Sch. Medicine, N.Y.C., from 1968; chief plastic surg. services Beth Israel Med. Center, 1967-79, Bronx-Lebanon Hosp. Center, N.Y.C., 1958-79; cons. plastic surgeon N.Y. Rehab. Hosp., West Haverstraw, N.Y., 1953-66, Nyack (N.Y.) Hosp., 1953-79; pres. med. bd. Bronx-Lebanon Hosp. Center, 1970. Served with M.C., AUS, 1942-46. Diplomate Am. Bd. Surgery, Am. Bd. Plastic Surgery. Fellow A.C.S.; mem. AMA, Am. Soc. Plastic and Reconstructive Surgery, Am. Assn. Plastic Surgeons, N.Y. Acad. Medicine, Am. Cleft Palate Assn., Am. Soc. Surgery of Hand. Author: (with A. J. Barsky and B. E. Simon) Principles and Practice of Plastic Surgery, 1964; contbr. articles to profl. jours. Home: Englewood, N.J. Dec. June 8, 1981.

KAIER, EDWARD A., lawyer; b. Mahanoy City, Pa., July 26, 1908; s. Edward John and Catharine (Gorman) K.; A.B., Pa. State U., 1930; LL.B., U. Pa., 1933; m. Mary Patricia Crimmins, Apr. 15, 1940; children—Anne, Edward John. Admitted to Pa. bar, 1933; with Pa. R.R., 1933-70, law clk., Phila., asst. solicitor, asst. gen. solicitor, Chgo., 1935-44, asst. gen. counsel, Pitts., 1944-48, dir. pub. relations, Phila., 1948-49, gen. atty., Phila., 1949-58, gen. solicitor, Phila., 1958-69; gen. counsel Penn Central Co., Phila., 1969-70, v.p., 1970; pvt. practice, Phila., 1970—; chief counsel various r.r.'s nationwide on regional freight rate cases ICC; bd. mgrs. Beneficial Mut. Savs. Bank, Phila.; dir. Continental Bank, Phila. Mem. Pa., Phila. bar assns. Roman Catholic. Clubs: Racquet, Phila. Country. Died May 31, 1981.

KAISER, EDGAR FOSBURGH, corp. exec.; b. Spokane, July 29, 1908; s. Henry J. and Bess (Fosburgh) K.; student U. Calif., 1927-30; LL.D. (hon.), U. Portland, Pepperdine Coll., Mills Coll., Golden Gate U., U. of Pacific; L.H.D., U. Calif.; m. Sue Mead, Aug. 24, 1932 (dec. June 1974); children—Carlyn, Becky, Gretchen, Edgar Fosburgh, Henry Mead, Kim John; m. 2d, Nina McCormick, Feb. 1, 1975. Constrn. supt. natural gas line Kans. to Okla., 1930-32; shift supt. Boulder Dam, Nev., 1932-33; adminstrv. mgr. Columbia Constrn. Co., Bonneville (Oreg.) Dam, 1934-38, project mgr., Grand Coulee Dam, Wash., 1938-41; v.p., gen. mgr. Oreg. Shipbldg. Corp. and Kaiser Co., Inc., Portland, Oreg. and Vancouver, Wash., 1941-45; pres., dir. Kaiser Motors Corp., 1945-56; pres. Kaiser Industries Corp., 1956-67, chmn., dir.; chmn., dir. affiliated Kaiser cos. and subsidiaries, principally; Kaiser Steel Corp., Kaiser Aluminum & Chem. Corp., Kaiser Cement & Gypsum Corp., Kaiser Resources Ltd., Kaiser Found. Health Plan, Inc., Kaiser Found. Hosps.; dir. Nat. Steel & Shipbldg. Co., Bank Am. Corp., Hindustan Aluminium Co., Ltd., Volta Aluminium Corp., Mysore Cements Ltd. Past mem. Pres.'s Com. on Equal Employment Opportunity, Pres.'s Missile Sites Labor Commn., Pres.'s Adv. Com. Labor-Mgmt. Policy; past chmn. Pres.'s Com. on Urban Housing; past mem. adv. council Stanford U. Grad. Sch. Bus.; nat. chmn. UN Day, 1966; former mem. bus. leadership adv. council OEO; mem. Business Council; chmn. corp. support com. Nat. Urban League; past chmn. bd. incorporators Nat. Corp. for Housing Partnerships; vice chmn. U.S. sect. Bulgarian-U.S. Econ. Council; dir. U.S.-U.S.S.R. Trade and Econ. Council. Chmn. bd. dirs. Stanford Research Inst.; trustee, past chmn. Bay Area Council, San Francisco; trustee Council of The Americas, Henry J. Kaiser Family Found.; past mem. bd. incorporators Communications Satellite Corp.; v.p., dir. Oakland-Alameda County Coliseum; mem. adv. bd. Oakland Museum Assn.; chmn. bd. Oakland Symphony Orch. Assn.; mem. adv. bd. San Francisco Opera Assn. Recipient numerous honors and awards, including: Ann. Moles award for outstanding achievement in constrn. industry, 1962; Achievement award Bldg. and Industry Conf. Bd., 1968; Mgmt. Achievement award Loyola U., 1968; Hoover medal, 1969; Presdl. Medal of Freedom, 1969; 1st annual Internat. Key award Opportunities Industrialization Center, 1970; Golden Beaver award for Mgmt. The Beavers, 1975; Interat. Achievement award World Trade Club San Francisco, 1975; New Oakland Com. award City of Oakland, 1976; decorated grand officer (Republic of Ivory Coast), 1972; named Industrialist of Year, Calif. Mus. Sci. and Industry, 1966, Constrn.'s Man of Year, Engring., News-Record, 1968, Alunmus of Year, U. Calif., 1969, Bus. Statesman of Year Harvard Bus. Sch. No. Calif., 1971, Mfr. of Year, Calif. Mfrs. Assn., 1976. Fellow Am. Acad. Arts and Scis.; mem. Chi Psi. Clubs: Marco Polo, Links, Blindbrook (N.Y.); Moles, Pacific Union, Bohemian (San Francisco); Commonwealth of Calif.; International, F Street (Washington); Seattle Yacht; The Beavers; Claremont Country (Oakland); Cypress Point (Pebble Beach, Calif.); Lyford Cay (Nassau). Died 1982.

KAISER, FREDERICK HENRY, ret. exec.; b. Ontardoville, Ill., Sept. 21, 1887; s. Fred C. and Sophie (Thiemann) K.; student Walton Sch. Commerce, 1915-17; m. Ebba Mae Nelson, June 4, 1913; children—Arlyne, Betty, Joan. Office boy Crane Co., Chicago, 1902, clk., bookkeeper, 1902-12, chief clk., 1912-22, traveling auditor, 1922-28, asst. gen. auditor, 1929, gen. auditor, 1930-37, comptroller, 1938-53. Mem. Controllers Inst. Am. Methodist. Mason. Home: Park Ridge, Ill. †

KAISER, JOSEPH A., banker; b. Bklyn., June 14, 1906; s. Joseph A. and Elizabeth A. (Turner) K.; student Forham U., 1926, St. John's Law School, 1929; m. Marian M. Mullen, Oct. 22, 1932; children—Robert J., Patricia Ann. With Williamsburgh Savs. Bank since 1926, exec. v.p., 1945-53, trustee after 1950, president, 1953-81, chmn., 1974-81, also treasurer; member board of directors Savings Bank Trust Company. Chmn. N.Y. State Com. Real Estate and Mortgages. Trustee Savs. Bank Life Ins. Fund. Trustee Indsl. Home for Blind (Bklyn.). Dir. Bklyn. chpt. A.R.C., Bklyn. C. of C., Nat. Assn. Mut. Savs. Banks, Downtown Bklyn. Assos. Clubs: Union League (N.Y.C.); Garden City (N.Y.) Golf; Montauk (Bklyn.); Cherry Valley Country. Home: Garden City, N.Y. Died Oct. 10, 1982.

KALDERON, ALBERT ELI, pathologist; b. Istanbul, Turkey, July 27, 1933; came to U.S., 1961, naturalized, 1969,; m. Eli and Mary K.; m. Janet Louise Seuferer, Apr. 2, 1963; children: Mark, Steven. Baccalaureate Scis., Coll. St. Michel, Istanbul, 1952; M.S., Istanbul U., 1961. Diplomate: Am. Bd. Pathology. Intern Mercy Hosp., Des Moines, 1961-62; resident in pathology, instr. Albert Einstein Coll. Medicine-Bronx (N.Y.) Municipal Hosp. Center, 1962-66; research fellow in anatomy Sch. Medicine, McGill U., Montreal, Que., Can., 1966-67; asst. pathologist R.I. Hosp.-Brown U. Med. Sch., 1970-71; asst. prof. med. scis. Brown U. Med. Sch., 1971-75; prof. pathology Univ. Hosp., Little Rock, 1975, Grad. Sch., U. Ark. Med. Scis., Little Rock, from 1975; dir. anat. pathology Univ. Hosp., from 1975; cons. Little Rock VA Hosp.; mem. sarcoma panel, chmn. subcom. head and neck cancer S.W. Oncology Group. Contbr. articles to med. jours. Recipient Golden Apple award U. Ark. Med. Scis., 1978; grantee Brown Hazen Fund, 1971-73; grantee R.I. Cancer Soc., 1969-70; grantee NIH, 1974-77. Fellow Am. Coll. Pathology, Am. Soc. Clin. Pathology; mem. AAAS, Am. Thyroid Assn., Internat. Acad. Pathology, Am. Assn. Pathologists, Arthur Purdy Soc. Surg. Pathologists, N.Y. Acad. Scis., R.I. Soc. Pathologists (pres. 1971-72), Sigma Xi. Home: Little Rock, Ark.

KALINKA, JOHN ERNST, structural engr.; b. Tyrol, Austria, Dec. 16, 1888; s. Dr. Francis and Anna (Wolf) K.; student High School, Vienna, Austria, 1898-1906; Engr's. Diploma, Tech. U. Vienna, 1911; m. Dr. Margaretha Kalinka, Dec. 30, 1920; 1 son, Fred Otto; m. 2d, Dorothea von Mazanec Engelhardswall, Sept. 9, 1932; 1 son, Hans Sanford. Came to U.S., 1924, naturalized 1930. Engr. Austrian Southern R.R., 1911-15; capt. Austrian Engrs. Corps, 1915-18; cons. engr. for constrn. of railroads and bridges Jugoslavia and Austria, 1918-24; engr. Pa. R.R., Pitts., 1924-25; successively engr., chief engr., dir., exec. v.p. Roberts & Schaefer Co., Chicago, from 1925, chmn., from 1953; pres. Thompson Starrett Co.,

Inc., from 1954. Mem. Am. Railroad Engring. Assn., Am. Concrete Inst., Soc. of Mil. Engrs., Chicago Engrs. Club, Ill. C. of C. Club: Cornell (N.Y.C.). Home: Wilmette, Ill.†

KAMPMEIER, OTTO FREDERIC, med. educator; b. nr. Clarksville, Ia., Nov. 7, 1888; s. August and Mary (Ehrlicher) K.; A.B. with honors, State U. of Ia., 1909; fellow, Princeton, 1909-12, Ph.D., cum laude, 1912; grad. and med. study U. of Chicago, 1921, U. of Freiburg, Germany, 1922; M.D., summa cum laude, U. of Munich, Germany, 1924; m. Ruzena Tomek, September 7, 1912 (decased, 1952); 1 dau., Jacinta. Married Carolyn Riechers, 1953. Student assistant in biology, State U. of Ia., 1906-09; asst., U.S. Bur. of Fisheries, 1909; instr. in anatomy, U. of Pittsburgh, 1912-15; asst. prof., 1915-18; instr. in anatomy, U. of Ill. Coll. Medicine, 1918-19, asso. prof. 1920-22, 1924-28; prof. from 1928, head of department, 1929-51, professor of medical history, 1951-53; prof. emeritus anatomy U. Ill. Coll. Medicine, from 1953; prof. anat., head dept. Sch. Medicine, Coll. Med. Evangelists, Loma Linda, California, 1953-57. Member Am. Assn. Anatomists, Am. Soc. Naturalists, A.M.A., A.A.A.S., Chicago Inst. Medicine (v.p. 1949-50), Deutsche Medizinische Gesellschaft of Chicago, Sigma Xi, Alpha Omega Alpha. Club: Chaos. Author: (books) A Laboratory Textbook of Human Anatomy; Atlas: A Frontal Section Anatomy of the Head and Neck, 1957; (poetry) Curriculum Vitae, 1945; Madonna of the Rocks, 1949. Editor publs. Contbr. to jours. Home: Redlands, Cal. †

KANAGA, LAWRENCE WESLEY, JR., mfg. co. exec.; b. Indpls., June 22, 1913; s. Lawrence Wesley and Harriet (Wilson) K.; m. Virginia Honold, Feb. 19, 1938; children—Lawrence Wesley III, Jill Winn. B.S., U. Ill., 1934; student, Advanced Mgmt. Program, Harvard U., 1955; postgrad., Yale U., 1962-63. Sales mgr. Montgomery Ward Co., Chgo., 1934-41, mdse. mgr., Oakland, Calif., 1941-43, Hale Bros., San Francisco, 1943-47; v.p. RCA Distbg. Corp., Detroit, 1947-49; gen. mgr. RCA Victor, N.Y.C., 1949-55; v.p. RCA, 1955-57; pres., chief exec. officer Gen. Artists Corp., N.Y.C., 1957-62; pres. Electrographic Corp., N.Y.C., 1965-67; chmn. bd. Am. Corp., N.Y.C., 1967-69; sr. v.p. Bell & Howell Co., Chgo., 1969-80, dir., 1980-82; cons., 1980-82. Republican. Home: Northbrook, Ill. Died Oct. 11, 1982.

KANE, CLARENCE P(EYTON), air force officer; b. San Francisco, Calif., Apr. 9, 1890; s. Ellsworth Charles and Amy (Peyton) K.; student San Francisco Law Sch., 1913-16, Army Balloon Sch., 1920-21, Army Indsl. Coll., 1938; m. Helen Nickerson, Nov. 23, 1933; children—Elizabeth (Mrs. J.D. Slagle), Clarence P., Kimberlin J., Rosalind (Mrs. K.T. Rice). Promoted through grades to brig. gen., 1943; attaché Am. embassy, Japan, 1926-29; comdg. gen. Rome (N.Y.) Air Service Command; comdg. gen. ATSCE, 1944-45, Decorated D.S.M., Legion of Merit, Bronze Star Medal (U.S.), Comdr. Order Brit. Empire (Gt. Britain), Legion of Honor, Croix de Guerre with palm (France), Yun Hui 4th Class (spl. collar Oder of Yun Hui) (China). Home: Arlington, Va. †

KANE, HARNETT THOMAS, author critic; b. New Orleans, La., Nov. 8, 1910; s. William J. and Anna (Hiri) K.; B.A., Tulane U., New Orleans, 1931, grad. work in sociology, 1932-33; unmarried. Reporter with New Orleans Item-Tribune, 1928-43, assignments covered welfare, business, labor, politics; teacher of journaliam, Loyola U. (New Orleans), 1943-44. Del. of New Orleans Item-Tribune to Cities Investment Trust Foundation Safety Seminar, N.Y. City, 1937. Mem. Lyceum Assn. (mem. bd. dirs.). Authors Guild of Am., Soc. of Midland Authors, Am. Newspaper Guild, Sigma Delta Chi, Theta Nu, Kappa Delta Phi. Received Dorothy Dix journalism award, 1939. Guggenheim fellowship for study of southern problems, 1943-44, 1944-45. Democrat. Roman Catholic. Club: Arts and Crafts (New Orleans). Author: Louisiana Hayride: The American Rehearsal for Dictatorship, 1941; Bayous of Louisiana, 1943; Deep Delta Country; Planatation Parade—the Grand Mannet in Louisiana, 1945; New Orleans Woman, 1946; Natchez on the Mississippi, 1947; Bride of Fortune, 1948; Queen New Orleans, 1949; Pathway to the Stars, 1950. Articles in Colliers, Reader's Digest, American Mercury and articles and book reviews to newspapers and nat. mags.; also series of articles on leprosy in La. and history of New Orleans and Louisiana. Home: New Orleans, La. Died Sept. 4, 1984.

KANE, W. J., exec. v.p., then pres., to 1975. Great Atlantic & Pacific Tea Co. Address: New York, N.Y. Died Feb. 1, 1985.

KANN, ROBERT ADOLF, educator, historian; b. Vienna, Austria, Feb. 11, 1906; came to U.S., 1939, naturalized, 1944; s. Leo and Louise (Eisenschitz) K.; m. Marie Breuer, Jan. 26, 1937; children—Peter R., Marilyn B. Dr.Jur., U. Vienna, 1930; Ph.D., Columbia, 1946; Ph.D. honoris causa, U. Salzburg, Austria, 1972. Legal work Austrian cts., 1931-36, pvt. practice law, Vienna, 1936-38; mem. Inst. Advanced Study, Princeton, 1942-45; mem. faculty Rutgers U., 1947-76, prof. history, 1956-76; mem. faculty U. Vienna, 1976-81, hon. life mem., 1981; mem. faculty Diplomatic Acad., Vienna, 1978-79; vis. prof. Columbia, 1957, 62-64, 66-67, U. Vienna, 1973-74; research asso. Princeton, 1952-53, vis. prof., 1966. Author: The Multinational Empire, 2 vols, 1950, The Hapsburg Empire, 1957, A Study in Austrian Intellectual History, 1960, Die Sixtusaffaire, 1966, The Problem of Restoration, 1968, A History of the Habsburg Empire, 1526-1918, 1974, Franz Ferdinand Studien, 1976; co-author: Political Community and North Atlantic Area, 1957, Spectrum Austriae, 1957, Historica, 1965, Quantitative History, 1969; Editor: Theodor Gomperz, 1974, The Hapsburg Empire in World War I, 1977, (with F. Prinz) Deutsch-osterreichische Beziehungen, Vienna-Munich, 1980; Editorial bd.: (with F. Prinz) Austrian History Yearbook, 1965-70, Central European History, 1968-73, Canadian Rev. of Studies in Nationalism, from 1973. Rapporteur Internat. Congress Hist. Scis., 1965. Decorated Grosses Goldenes Ehrenzeichen Republic of Austria, Preis für Geisteswissenschaften Vienna).; Guggenheim fellow, 1949-50; Social Sci. Research Council fellow, 1960; recipient award for research Lindback Found., 1969. Mem. Am. Hist. Assn. (exec. sect. com. research Hapsburg monarchy 1968-70, chmn. conf. group Central European history 1964); life corr. mem. Austrian Acad. Home: Princeton, N.J.

KAO, SHIH-KUNG, scientist, educator; b. Foochow, China, Mar. 9, 1918; came to U.S., 1947, naturalized, 1965; s. T.C. and Kang-Yi (Cheng) K.; m. Yasuko Kao, Apr. 1, 1959; children—John Sterling, Stephanie Margaret. B.S., Nat. Tsing Hua U., 1939; M.A., UCLA, 1948, Ph.D., 1952. Lectr., research staff Aero. Research Inst., Nat. Tsing Hua U., China, 1939-46; univ. fellow UCLA, 1948-52, vis. asst. prof., 1956-57, research scientist, 1958-60; postdoctoral fellow Johns Hopkins U., 1953-55, vis. prof., 1964; prof. meteorology U. Utah, Salt Lake City, from 1960, chmn. dept. meteorology, from 1972; vis. prof. U. Calif., summer 1964; vis. scientist, sr. postdoctoral fellow Nat. Center for Atmospheric Research, 1963, 69-70; councilor, trustee, rep. U. Corp. for Atmospheric Research, from 1965; dir. Atmospheric Turbulence and Diffusion Project, from 1961; cons. NASA, Dept. Energy; asso. editor Plenum Pub. Corp. Research grantee AEC; Research grantee Dept. Energy; Research grantee EPA; Research grantee ERDA; Research grantee NASA; Research grantee NSF. Fellow AAAS (exec. com.); mem. Royal Meteorol. Soc. Gt. Britain, Am. Meteorol. Soc. (com. on atmospheric turbulence from 1979), Am. Geophys. Union, Sigma Xi, Phi Kappa Phi. Research and publs. on atmospheric circulation, air pollution, atmospheric turbulence and diffusion, wave motion in rotating fluids. Home: Salt Lake City, UT.

KAPITZA, PETER L(EONIDEVICH), Russian physicist; b. Kronshtadt, Russia, June 26, 1894; s. Leonid and Olga (Stebnitsckiy) K.; grad. Petrograd Polytechnic Inst., 1919; D.Ph., Cambridge U., 1923, fellow, 1923-24, fellow Trinity Coll., 1925-34; D.Sc. (hon.), Algiers University, 1944, Sorbonne (U. Paris), France, 1945; D.Ph. (hon.), Oslo U., 1946; Dr. Sc. hon. causa, Yagellonian U. Cracow, Poland, 1964, Technische Univ., Dresden, Germany, 1964, Karlova U., Czechoslovakia, 1965, Delhi U., 1966; m. Nedezhda Tschernovsvitova (dec.); m. 2d, Anna Krylova; 2 sons. Lectr. Petrograd Polytechnic Inst., 1919-21; asst. dir. magnetism research Cavendish Lab., Cambridge, Eng., 1924-32; dir. Royal Soc. Mond Lab., 1930-34, Inst. Physical Problems, Acad. Scis., Moscow, 1934-84; developer processes for liquifying helium, Decorated Order of Yugoslav Banner with ribbon. Recipient State prize, 1941, 43, Order of Lenin, 1943, 44, 45, 64, Hero Socialist Labour, 1945, Order Red Banner of Labour, 1954 (USSR); Faraday medal Inst. Elec. Engrs. (Eng.), 1942; Medal of Franklin Inst. (U.S.), 1944; diploma Royal Danish Acad., 1946; Sir Devaprasad Sarbadhikari gold medal (U. Calcutta), 1955; Kothenius Gold medal, Acad. Leopoldina, 1959; Lomonosov Gold medal, Acad. Sciences of USSR, 1960; Great Gold medal Exhbn. Econ. Achievements, USSR, 1962; medal for merits in sci. and to mankind Czechoslavak Academy of Sciences, 1964; Nils Bohr gold medal Danish Engrs. Soc., 1964; Rutherford medal Inst. Physics and Phys. Soc., Eng., 1966; Golden Kamerlingh Onnes medal Netherlands Soc. Refrigeration, 1968, Nobel prize, 1978. Hon. fellow Trinity Coll., Eng., 1966. Fellow Brit. Royal Soc., Inst. Physics (Eng.), Nat. Acad. Sci. India (hon.); fgn. hon. mem. Am. Acad. Arts and Scis.; hon. mem. Inst. Metals (Eng.), Franklin Inst., N.Y. Acad. Sci. (U.S.A.), Royal Irish Acad.; mem. Nat. Acad. Sci. U.S., Acad. Scis. USSR, Deutsche Akademie der Naturforscher, Leopoldiana, Internat. Acad. Astronautics; fgn. mem. Royal Netherlands Acad. Scis., Royal Acad. Science, Sweden; foreign member of Polish Academie of Science. Holder U.S. patent on turbine device for prodn. liquid air. Address: Moscow, USSR. Died Apr. 8, 1984.

KAPLAN, ALINE, organization executive; b. N.Y.C., June 23, 1923; d. Morris and Dora (Zeresky) K. B.A., Hunter Coll., 1943; LL.B., Columbia U., 1946; postgrad., Sch. Edn., Yeshiva U., 1959-62. Bar: N.Y. 1946. Pvt. practice, N.Y.C., 1946-52; dir. Nat. Jr. Hadassah, 1952-64; asst. dir. Hadassah Zionist Women's Orgn. Am., 1964-71, exec. dir., 1971-83; Hadassah rep. Am. Israel Pub. Affairs Com., 1971-83; Hadassah del. World Zionist Congress in Jerusalem, 1956, 64, 72, 78, 82, Convs. of World Fedn. United Zionists, 1956, 64, 72, 78, 82; mem. tribunal World Zionist Orgn., 1978, 82. Contbr. articles to Zionist ency. Bd. dirs. United Israel Appeal, 1971-83. Mem. Am. Zionist Fedn. (nat. bd. 1970-83), Delta Phi Epsilon. Jewish. Home: New York, N.Y. Died Sept. 29, 1983.

KAPLAN, HENRY SEYMOUR, educator, radiologist; b. Chgo., Apr. 24, 1918; s. Nathan M. and Sarah (Brilliant) K.; m. Leah Hope Lebeson, June 21, 1942; children—Ann Sharon, Paul Allen. B.S., U. Chgo., 1938, Sc.D. (hon.), 1969; M.D., Rush Med. Coll., 1940; M.S. in Radiology, U. Minn., 1944; Sc.D. (hon.), Hahnemann Med. Coll., 1973. Intern Michael Reese Hosp., Chgo., 1940-41, resident radiation therapy and tumor clinic, 1941-42; tng. fellow Nat. Cancer Inst., 1943-44; instr. radiology Yale Med. Sch., 1944-45, asst. prof., 1945-47; radiologist Nat. Cancer Inst., 1947-48; prof. radiology, chmn. dept. Sch. Medicine, Stanford U., 1948-72, dir. biophysics lab., 1957-64, Maureen (Lyles D'Ambrogio prof. oncology and dir. cancer biol. research lab.), 1972-84; mem. sci. adv. com. St. Jude's Children's Hosp., Memphis, 1970-74; chmn. sci. adv. com. Sharett Inst. Oncology, Hadassah Med. Center-Hebrew U., Jerusalem, 1977-84; mem. com. radiology NRC, 1950-56; gastrointestinal cancer com. Nat. Cancer Inst.; mem. panel path. effects radiation Nat. Acad. Sci.-NRC; adv. com. biology Oak Ridge Nat. Lab., 1969-75; subcom. radiation carcinogenesis (chmn. 1957-58), commn. on research Internat. Union Against Cancer; nat. adv. cancer council Nat. Cancer Inst., USPHS, 1959-63; advisor Cancer Council Calif., 1959-62, bd. sci. advisors div. cancer treatment, 1975-79; nat. panel cons. on cancer U.S. Senate, 1970-71; mem. council analysis and projection Am. Cancer Soc., 1972-76. Author: (with S.J. Robinson) Congenital Heart Disease: An Illustrated Diagnostic Approach, 1954, 2d edit, (with H. L. Abrams and S. J. Robinson), 1965, Angiocardiographic Interpretation in Congenital Heart Diseases, (with H.L. Abrams), 1955, Hodgkin's Disease, 1972, 2d edit., 1980; editor: (with P.J. Tsuchitani) Cancer in China, 1978, (with R. Levy) Malignant Lymphomas, 1978, (with S.A. Rosenberg) Advances in Malignant Lymphomas, 1981; editorial adv. bd.: Cancer, Proc. Nat. Acad. Sci, 1973-79, Current Topics Radiation Research Quar, 1971-77; editorial com.: Ann. Rev. Nuclear Sci, 1966-70; adv. editor: Internat. Jour. Radiation Oncology, Biology, Physics. Bd. govs. Weizmann Inst. Sci., Rehovoth, Israel, 1974-84, Ben Gurion U., Beersheba, Israel, 1974-84. Decorated Légion d'Honneur France; Order of Merit Italy; Shahbanou award Iran; recipient Lila Motley Cancer Found. award; Atoms for Peace award, 1969; Modern Medicine award for distinguished achievement, 1968; Lucy W. James award James Ewing Soc., 1971; R.R. de Villiers award Leukemia Soc., 1971; Commonwealth Fund fellow, vis. scientist NIH, 1954-55; David A. Karnofsky Meml. award Am. Soc. Clin. Oncology, 1971; Nat. award Am. Cancer Soc., 1972; Laureat, Prix Griffuel for cancer research France, 1975; G.H.A. Clowes Meml. award Am. Assn. Cancer Research, 1976; Erskine lectr. Radiol. Soc. N.Am., 1976; gold medal Am. Soc. Therapeutic Radiologists, 1977; medal of Honor Danish Cancer Soc., 1978; Ungerman-Lubin award Taubman Found., 1978; Lila Gruber Meml. award Am. Acad. Dermatology, 1978; Kettering prize Gen. Motors Cancer Research Found., 1979; Prentis award Mich. Cancer Found., 1980; Walker prize Royal Coll. Surgeons, 1981. Fellow Am. Coll. Radiology (chmn. commn. on cancer, bd. chancellors 1970-73, Gold medal 1981), Royal Coll. Radiologists (hon.); mem. Am. Soc. Exptl. Pathology, Assn. Univ. Radiologists (pres. 1954-55, Gold medal 1979), Radiol. Soc. N.Am., AAAS, Fedn. Am. Scientists, Soc. Exptl. Biology and Medicine, Radiation Research Soc. (pres. 1956-57), Western Soc. Clin. Research, Am. Assn. Cancer Research (dir. 1954-56, 64-67, pres. 1966-67), Am. Soc. Therapeutic Radiologists (pres. 1966-67, chmn. bd. dirs. 1967-68), Internat. Club Therapeutic Radiologists, Am. Soc. Biol. Chemists, Am. Acad. Arts and Sci., Harvey Soc. N.Y., Internat. Assn. Radiation Research (pres. 1974-79), Am. Roentgen Ray Soc., Am. Soc. Clin. Oncology, Nat. Acad. Scis., Inst. Medicine, Acad. Medicine Brazil (hon.), Swedish Soc. Med. Radiology (hon.), Acad. des Sciences, Institut de France (fgn. assoc.). Home: Stanford, Calif. Died Feb. 4, 1984.

KAPLAN, WALTER FRANCIS, management consultant; b. El Paso, Tex., July 29, 1900; s. Albert and Hannah (Kirske) K.; J.D., Golden Gate Coll., 1924; m. Margaret Jacob, Apr. 18, 1929; children—Margery, Charles. Controller, Emporium Capwell Co., San Francisco, 1930-42, sec.-treas., 1942-72; pres. San Francisco Downtown Parking Corp., Mgmt. Counselors Unltd., from 1972; dir., cons. Grodins of Calif. Chmn. San Francisco Redevel. Agy., 1966-77; treas., past pres. Goodwill Industries San Francisco; bd. dirs., treas. Hinkley and Griffen founds. Served to col. USAF, 1951-52. Mem. Retail Mchts. Assn. (past pres.). Mason. Contbr. articles to profl. jours. Home: San Francisco, Calif. Dec.

KAPP, ERNST, educator; b. Düsseldorf, Germany; Jan. 21, 1888; s. Wolfgang and Johanna (Haarmann) K.; student Gottingen and Berlin univs., 1906-13; Ph.D., U. Freiburg, 1912; m. Else Kapp, June 18, 1930. Came to U.S., 1939, naturalized, 1946. Privatdozent, U. Munich, Germany, 1920-27; prof. Greek lang. and lit., U. Hamburg, 1927-37; prof. Greek and Latin, Columbia, from 1948. Mem. Am. Philol. Assn. Author: Greek Foundations of Traditional Logic, 1942; Aristotle's Constitution of Athens and Related Texts (translated with Introducation and Notes by Kurt von Fritz and Ernst Kapp), 1950. Home: New York, N.Y. †

KAPPAUF, WILLIAM EMIL, JR., educator, psychologist; b. N.Y.C., Oct. 2, 1913; s. William Emil and Juliet Theodora (Bonnlander) K.; m. Catharine Anne Hamilton, June 16, 1945; children—Barbara, Charles, Katharine, William. A.B., Columbia, 1934; M.A., Brown U., 1935; Ph.D., U. Rochester, 1937. Instr. psychology U. Rochester, 1937-41; research projects under NDRC and OSRD, 1941-46; asso. prof. Princeton, 1946-51; prof. U. Ill., Champaign, 1951-80, asso. head dept. psychology, 1976-78; cons. Bell Telephone Labs.; cons., panel mem. Mil. Agys., NSF, NIH. Editor: Am. Jour. Psychology, 1971; Contbr. articles to profl. jours. Recipient Presdl. certificate of merit, 1948. Mem. Am., Midwestern psychol. assns., Soc. Exptl. Psychologists (sec.-treas. 1967-70), Am. Assn. U. Profs., A.A.A.S., Phi Beta Kappa, Sigma Xi. Home: Champaign, Ill. Deceased.

KAPPES, OSCAR TYLER, candy mfr.; b. Brooklyn, N.Y., Nov. 23, 1890; s. John Jacob and Louise (Miller) K.; student N.Y. Univ. Sch. of Commerce; married. Asso. with Life Savers, Inc. since 1929, started as asst. trea., and when Drug Inc. demerged, was made treas., pres. 1937-49; dir. Life Savers Corp. and its six subsidiaries. Dir. Washington Irving Trust Co., Arnold Brick Oven Bakers, Inc., Port Chester, N.Y. Dir. Y.M.C.A., Port Chester. Home: Port Chester, N.Y. †

KAPRIELIAN, ZOHRAB ARAKEL, educator; b. Aleppo, Syria, Sept. 23, 1923; came to U.S., 1949, naturalized, 1961; s. Arakel and Vartouhi (Lusigian) K. B.A., Am. U. in Beirut, Lebanon, 1942, M.A., 1943; Ph.D., U. Calif. at Berkeley, 1954. Research fellow, instr. Calif. Inst. Tech., 1954-57; asst. prof. elec. engring. U. So. Calif., Los Angeles, 1957-58, assoc. prof., 1958-62, prof., 1962-81, chmn. elec. engring. dept., 1962-70; acting dean U. So. Calif. (Sch. Engring.), 1969-70, dean, 1970-81, v.p. acad. adminstrn. and research, 1970-75, exec. v.p., 1975-81. Recipient Distinguished Faculty award U. So. Calif. Sch. Engring., 1965. Fellow IEEE; mem. Am. Phys. Soc., Sigma Xi, Tau Beta Pi, Eta Kappa Nu. Home: Los Angeles, Calif. Died Dec. 30, 1981.

KAPSTEIN, ISRAEL J., educator; b. Fall River, Mass., Jan. 16, 1904; s. Bernard and Fanny (Silver) K.; A.B., Brown U., 1926, A.M., 1928, Ph.D., 1933; m. Stella Cohen, Dec. 23, 1928; children—Judith Deborah (Mrs. David J. Drodsky), Jonathan. Faculty Brown U., from 1928, beginning as instr. English dept., successively asst. prof., asso. prof., 1928-50, prof. English, 1950-83. Trustee Miriam Hosp., Providence, Jewish Bd. of Edn., Providence, Providence Pub. Library; bd. dirs. Jewish Family and Children's Service R.I. Awarded Guggenheim, Sharpe fellowships. Smith-Mundt vis. prof. lit., U. Saigon, 1960-61. Mem. Modern Lang. Assn., Phi Beta Kappa. Home: Providence, R.I. Died Aug. 5, 1983.

KAPTAIN, STEPHEN PETER, paper products manufacturing company executive; b. Stamford, Conn., Mar. 20, 1925; s. Peter Achilles and Barbara (Pappas) K.; m. Mary Louise Ferguson, Sept. 13, 1949; children: Kathleen Barbara (Mrs. Charles Snowdon), Jocelyn Louise. B.A., U. Mich., 1948. With St. Regis Paper Co., from 1952, conservation engr. div., So. Woodlands, Fla., 1952-54; resident mgr. St. Regis Kraft, Jacksonville, Fla., 1954-65, gen. mgr. internat. div., N.Y.C., 1965-73, sr. v.p. internat. div., 1974-80; dir. S. K. Mencher Assocs., N.Y.C., Internat. Tech. Resources Inc., N.Y.C.; bd. advs. Energy for the Eighties, Washington. Vice chmn. Republican Nat. Finance Com., Fla., 1961-64; alt. del. Rep. Nat. Conv., 1964. Served to 1st lt. USAAF, 1943-45; Served to 1st lt. USAF, 1948-52. Decorated Air medal with four oak leaf clusters. Clubs: Metropolitan (N.Y.C.); Wee Burn Country (Darien, Conn.); The George Town (Washington). Home: Darien, Conn.

KARCH, GEORGE FREDERICK, banker; b. Barberton, Ohio, May 1, 1907; s. Charles Matthew and Nina (Close) K.; m. Mary Sargent, Aug. 2, 1932; children—George Frederick, Sargent, Mary K. Wilson, Jane K. Martin. Student, St. Lawrence U., 1924-26; also LLD.; LL.B., Cleve. Law Sch., 1930; grad., Rutgers U. Grad. Sch. Banking, 1940; LL.D., Cleve. State U.; L.H.D., Alliance Coll. With Cleve. Trust Co., from 1926, mem. officers exec. com., from 1954, exec. v.p., 1960-62, pres., 1962-66, chmn., pres., 1966-69, chmn. bd., 1969-73, hon. chmn., from 1973; dir., mem. audit com. Oglebay Norton Co.; dir., chmn. audit com., mem. exec. com. Brush Wellman Co., RPM, Inc. Trustee Cleve. Clinic Found., Ednl. Research Council Am., Coll. of Wooster, Cleve. Clinic Ednl. Found., Medusa Found., Southwaite Found., Oglebay Norton Found. Mem. Am. Heart Soc., Beta Theta Pi. Mem. United Ch. of Christ. Clubs: Canterbury Golf; Union (Cleve.), 50 (Cleve.); Princeton (N.Y.); Pepper Pike; Northport Point (Mich.). Home: Shaker Heights, OH.

KARDINER, ABRAM, psychiatrist; b. N.Y.C., Aug. 17, 1801; s. Isaac and Mildred (Wolff) K.; B.A., Coll. City N.Y., 1912; M.D., Cornell U., 1917; m. Ethel D. Rabinowitz, Dec. 3, 1948; 1 dau., Ellin A. Apprenticeship with Freud, 1921-22; faculty N.Y. Psychoanalytic Inst., 1922-44; instr. psychiatry Cornell U., 1923-29; asso. psychiatry Columbia, 1929-32, asso. dept. anthropology and sociology, 1939-52, asst. clin. prof. psychiatry, 1944-49, clin. prof., 1949-55, dir. psychoanalytic clinic, 1955-61; research prof. psychiatry, Emory Univ., from 1961. Mem. Am. Psychiatric Assn., Am. Psychol. Assn.; N.Y. Acad. Medicine. Author: The Individual and His Society, 1939; The Pscyhological Frontiers of Society (with others), 1945; The Mark of Appression (with L. Cvesey), 1951; Sex and Morality, 1954; They Studied Man (with Edward Preble), 1961, also numerous articles. Died July 20, 1981.

KARINSKA, BARBARA, costume designer; b. Kharkov, Russia, Oct. 1886; d. Andrei Zhmoudsky; m. 2d, Karinsky. Editor socialist paper, H Kharkov; owner embroidery and dress show, Moscow; exhibited paintings in group shows, Moscow; costume maker, Paris, 1932, U.S., 1938; costume designer Bourée Fantasque, N.Y. City Ballet Co., 1949, The Nutcracker, 1954, Liebeslider Walzer, 1960, Valses et Variations, 1961, Midsummer Night's Dream, 1962, Western Symphony, 1968; also made costumes for prodns. Met. Opera Co.; costumer for films Lady in the Dark, 1944, Gaslight, 1944, Frenchman's Creek, 1944, Kismet, 1944, Kitty, 1945. Recipient (with Dorothy Jeakins) Oscar for costumes Joan of Arc, Acad. Motion Picture Arts and Scis., 1948. Died Oct. 18, 1983.*

KARP, WILLIAM, mgmt. cons.; b. N.Y.C.; s. Harry and Sarah (Zemelman) K.; A.B., U. Ala., 1932; M.A., Columbia, 1953; m. Belle Allen, May 27, 1961; 1 son, Robert Alan. Formerly supr. N.Y. State Dept. Edn., youth worker N.Y. Bd. Edn., exec. dir. East Side Job Council; sr. officer charge planning readjustment, guidance, counseling services VA, Washington, 1946-47; dir. United Service for New Americans, N.Y.C., 1947-52; pres. William Karp Cons. Co., Inc., Chgo., 1952—, Am. Diversified Research Corp., Chgo., 1967-70. Mem. employment com. and Chgo. Commn. on Human Relations, 1956-64; chmn. employment and vocat. guidance agys. Welfare and Health Council, N.Y.C., 1949-51; exec. vice chmn. Mayor's Com. on Manpower Planning and Utilization, N.Y.C., 1949-51; chmn. com. to study vocat. guidance, employment coop. work study and distributive edn. Chgo. Bd. Edn., 1958-60; cons. Eastern European project Ford Fund, 1953-55, High Council Indsl. Mgmt. Inst., Ministry Economy Govt. Iran, 1965, HEW, 1962-79; mem. Ill. Gov.'s Employee Grievance Panel, 1963-79; mem., sec. Ill. Gov.'s Commn. to Study Automation and Technol. Progress in Ill., 1965-67; tech. cons., staff dir. Ill. Commn. on Technol. Progress, 1968-69; pub. mem. Ill. Commn. on Technol. Progress, 1969-71; participant founders group Key Personnel Obsolescence Conf., 1966, HEW Sec.'s Regional Conf. on Vocat. Edn., 1971; mem. com. on manpower and employment Bus. Research Adv. Council, U.S. Dept. of Labor, 1975-79, Bus. Research Adv. Council, 1978-79; mem. 3-mem. grievance panel Ill. Dept. Transp., 1975-79. Treas. Consumers League N.Y., 1949-57; pres. Cultural Arts Surveys, Inc., Chgo., 1965-70; founder Consumers League Found., 1955, mem. Necchi scholarship adv. com. Tchrs. Coll., Columbia U., 1949-51; nat. co-chmn. Nat. Conf. New Ams., 1949-50; pres. Chgo. Lighthouse for the Blind, 1978-79. Served to 2d lt. AUS, 1943-46. Mem. Am., N.Y., Ill. psychol. assns., Am. Mgmt. Assn., Indsl. Relations Research Assos., Soc. for Psychol. Study Social Issues, Am. Personnel and Guidance Assn. (mem. nat. steering com. on sex equality in guidance opportunities 1974-76), Nat. Vocat. Guidance Assn., Ill. C. of C. (labor relations com., indsl. labor legis. subcom.), Chgo. Assn. Commerce and Industry (chmn. merit employment com. 1959-62), Pub. Personnel Assn., N.Y. Acad. Scis., AAAS, Nat. Council Psychol. Aspects Disability, Soc. Applied Anthropology, Assn. Measurement and Evaluation in Guidance, Internat. Assn. Empirical Aesthetics (France), Nat. Assn. Intergroup Relations Ofcls. (chmn. resources and devel. com. 1958-60), Ill. Vocat. Guidance Assn. (chmn. program com. 1971-79). Clubs: Bagatelle, City (bd. govs.) (Chgo.). Author: Operations Research and the Management of Mental Health Systems, 1969; reports for Ill. commns., 1967, 69; contbr. articles in field to bus. and profl. jours. Home: Chicago, Ill. Died Apr. 28, 1979; interred Hillside Cemetery, Los Angeles, Calif.

KARPF, HENRY C., banker; b. Cin., July 22, 1890; s. Charles and Harriet Karpf; ed. pub. schs.; m. Lodiceo Babcock, Aug. 21, 1916; 1 son, Charles. Pres. 1st Nat. Bank, Morrill, Neb., also Live Stock Nat. Bank, Omaha, Neb.; vice chmn., dir. Omaha Nat. Bank; dir. Union Stock Yards Co., Mutual of Omaha Ins. Co. Regent Omaha Municiple U. Presbyn. Mason (32 deg., Shriner), †

KARSTEN, CHRISTIAN FRIEDRICH, banker; b. Assen, Netherlands, July 1, 1917; s. R. and M. (Graf) K.; master's degree, Netherlands Econ. U., 1940, doctor's degree, 1952; m. Carolina Johanna Wilhelmina van Waard, May 27, 1942; children—Peter, Cardina, Frederik, Roelof. Economist, Rotterdamsche Bank N.V., 1945-48, sec. to mng. dirs., 1948-52, asst. mng. dir., 1952-55, mng. dir., 1955-65, mng. dir. successor firm Amsterdam-Rotterdam Bank N.V., 1965-78, chmn. bd. until 1979. Decorated knight Order Dutch Lion. Home: Oost Laren, Netherlands. Died July 24, 1984.

KASE, NATHAN, obstetrician, gynecologist, educator; b. N.Y.C., Apr. 6, 1930; m. Judith Caryl Glass, July 8, 1956; 3 children. A.B., Columbia Coll., 1951; M.D., Columbia U., 1955; M.A. (hon.), Yale U. Diplomate: Am. Bd. Ob-Gyn (examiner, bd. mem., dir. exam. reproductive endocrinology subdiv.). Rotating intern Mt. Sinai Hosp., N.Y.C., 1955-56; asst. resident in Ob-Gyn, 1956-57, asso. resident in, 1960-61, chief resident in, 1961-62; USPHS trainee in steroid biochemistry Clark U. and Worcester Found. for Exptl. Biology, Worcester and Shrewsbury, Mass., 1959-60; instr. dept. Ob-Gyn, Sch. Medicine, Yale U., New Haven, 1962-63, asst. prof., 1963-66, asso. prof., 1966-69, prof., dept. chmn., 1969-78, prof., from 1978; attending physician Ob-Gyn, Yale-New Haven Hosp.; cons. Greenwich (Conn.) Hosp., Griffin Hosp., Derby, Conn., New Britain (Conn.) Gen. Hosp., St. Raphael Hosp., New Haven, Stamford (Conn.) Hosp., Norwalk (Conn.) Hosp., William W. Backus Hosp., Norwich, Brown U./Women and Infants Hosp., Providence, Emory U. Sch. Medicine, Atlanta; nat. cons. Dept. Air Force, 1974-77; mem. steering com. for five-year research plan Nat. Inst. Child Health and Human Devel., NIH, Bethesda, Md. Editorial bds.: Obstetrics & Gynecology, from 1979, Postgraduate Obstetrics and Gynecology; contbr. articles to med. textbooks and jours. Recipient Francis Gilman Blake award Yale U. Sch., 1967. Fellow Am. Coll. Obstetricians and Gynecologists, Sigma Xi; mem. Am. Fertility Soc., Conn. Soc. of Am. Bd. Obstetricians and Gynecologists, Endocrine Soc., New Haven Obstet. Soc., Soc. Gynecologic Investigation, Internat. Soc. for Research in Biology of Reprodn. Am. Gynecol. Soc./Am. Assn. Obstetricians and Gynecologists, Alpha Omega Alpha. Home: Woodbridge, Conn. *

KASHDAN, ISAAC, chess master; b. N.Y.C., Nov. 19, 1905; s. Isadore and Molly (Friedl) K.; m. Hadassah Cohen, June 3, 1933; 1 son, Richard L. B.A., Coll. City N.Y., 1926. Mem. U.S. Chess Fedn., 1925-85, life dir., 1945-85, master, 1926-85, internat. grandmaster, 1932-85; trainer, capt. teams Olympics, 1928, 30, 31, 33, 37, non-playing capt., 1960, 64; chess editor Los Angeles Times, 1955-85; internat. chess judge, 1948-85; statistician Jacques Coe & Co., 1941-49. Adminstrv. officer Jewish Fedn. Council Los Angeles, 1949-67. U.S. Chess champion, 1938, 42, 47 Home: Los Angeles, Calif. Died Feb. 20, 1985.

KASSABAUM, GEORGE EDWARD, architect; b. Atchison, Kans., Dec. 5, 1920; s. George A. and Dorothy (Gaston) K.; m. Marjory Verser, Jan. 22, 1949; children—Douglas, Ann, Karen. B.Arch., Washington U., St. Louis, 1947. Registered profl. architect, Mo., Kans., Pa., Ohio, Fla., D.C., Mass., N.Y., Alaska, Wis., Calif., Md., Colo., N.C., Tex., N.J. (pres. St. Louis chpt. 1964, nat. pres. 1968-69, chancellor 1978). Faculty Washington U., 1947-50; asso. firm Hellmuth, Yamasaki & Leinweber, St. Louis, 1950-55; prin. Hellmuth, Obata & Kassabaum, St. Louis, 1955-82; dir. Tower Grove Bank. Important works include Equitable Bldg, St. Louis, Smithsonian Air-Space Mus, Washington, Mobil Hdqrs, Fairfax, Va., MC Auto Computer Center, St. Louis, Dull Hosp, Durham, N.C., Conv. Center, San Francisco, U. Riyad, Riyadh, Saudi Arabia, Riyadh Airport, Exxon Research and Engring. Facilities, Clinton, N.J.; Contbr. articles to profl. jours. Bd. dirs. YMCA, St. Louis, 1970-82, Downtown St. Louis, Inc., 1976-82, St. Louis Symphony; trustee Washington U., 1976-82. Served with USAAF, 1945-46. Named Mo. Architect of Year, 1978. Mem. La Sociedad de Arquitectos Mexicanos (hon.), Sociedad Columbiana de Arquitectos (hon.), Royal Architects Inst. Can. (hon.), Sigma Chi. Clubs: Noonday (St. Louis), Media (St. Louis), Old Warson (St. Louis), St. Louis Country (St. Louis), Racquet (St. Louis), Bogey Country (St. Louis). Home: St Louis, Mo. Died Aug. 15, 1982.

KASTENDLECK, RAYMOND STONE, architect; b. Billings, Mo., Aug. 31, 1894; s. John Herman and Mary M. (Stone) K.; B. Archtl. Engring., Washington U., St. Louis, 1923; m. Marion E. Williams, Aug. 3, 1941. With archtl. firm William B. Ittner, St. Louis, 1923-33; propr. Raymond Stone Kastendleck, architect, Gary, Ind., 1933-83; projects include housing projects, schs., chs., including Andrean High Sch. and Residences, 1959, (assoc. architect) Ind. State Office Bldg., 1959-60. Past rep. Nat. council Sauk Trails council Boy Scouts Am., also mem. exec. bd. Calumet council; pres. N.W. Ind. Symphony Soc., 1971-73; treas. Lake Michigan Regional Planning Com., 1970-73. Bd. dirs. Gary YMCA; pres. AIA Found., 1968-71. Served to 1st lt., F.A., U.S. Army, World War I; AEF in France. Recipient Silver Beaver award Boy Scouts America. Fellow AIA (bd. dirs. Great Lakes dist. 1953-56, nat. treas. 1956-63, bursar Coll. of Fellows, 1964-68; advanced fellowship, 1959; mem. nat. jud. bd. 1963-68); mem. Ind. Soc. Architects (pres. 1948-50), Gary C. of C. (past bd. dirs.), No. Ind. Artists Assn. (past treas.), Am. Legion, Tau Beta Pi. Mason (Shriner, Jester), Rotarian (past gov. Dist. 224, Paul Harris fellow). Clubs: Gary Country, Gary University; Lake Shore (Chgo.). Home: Gary, Ind. Dec. Apr. 21, 1983.

KATAYAMA, TETSU, ex-premier of Japan; b. Wakayama-ken, Japan, July 28, 1887; s. Shozo Katayama; grad. Law Coll., Tokyo Imperial U., 1912; m. Kikuye Shimizu; 5 children. Practiced as lawyer, splzing. in labor cases; served in Imperial Diet as rep. from Kanagawa-ken, 3 terms; ret. from politics, 1940; returned as mem. of the Diet, 1946 and 1947; chosen premier by the Diet, May 1947; formed coalition govt.; resigned, Feb. 1948. Socialist. Home: Tokyo, Japan. †

KATES, EDGAR JESSE, cons. mech. engr.; b. N.Y.C., Aug. 1, 1889; s. Mark J. and Esther (Barasch) K.; B.A., Columbia, 1909, M.E., 1911; m. Josephine Warschauer, Mar. 16, 1920 (dec. 1949); children—Lillian (Mrs. Walter Kaghan), Richard; m. 2d, Edna R. Marx, Mar. 30, 1955. Engr., then chief engr. De La Vergne Machine Co., 1911-26; cons. engr., diesel engines, from 1926; lectr. diesel engines Bklyn. Poly. Inst., 1927-30, lectr. diesel and gas engines Columbia, 1949-57; cons. first fully automatic diesel electric plant, 1930; designed large bomb-proof diesel power plants for naval bases, World War II. Registered profl. engr., N.Y. Fellow Am. Soc. M.E. (chmn. oil and gas power div. 1925-29, 38, 46, dir.

1946-49, asst. treas. 1949-57, treas. 1957); mem. Engrs. Joint Council (dir., 1955, v.p. 1955-56). Author: Diesel-Electric Plants, rev. edit., 1945; Diesel and High-Compression Gas Engines-Fundamentals, rev. edit., 1965. Contbr. diesel engine sect. Kent's Mechanical Engineers Handbook, 1936. Contbr. articles tech. jours. Dir. Engineering Index, from 1963. Home: Bronxville, N.Y. †

KATZ, BENJAMIN JOSEPH, educator; b. Bklyn., July 13, 1923; s. Louis H. and Sarah (Golinsky) K.; m. Kaila Goldman, Aug. 11, 1957; children—Frederic M., Daniel L., Shira. A.B., Bklyn. Coll., 1946; A.M., Harvard, 1949, Ph.D., 1954. Asst. prof. econs. U. N.H., 1949-54, asso. prof., 1954-57, N.Y.U., 1957-65, prof., 1965-82, chmn. dept. econs., 1968-73, dir. undergrad. studies, dept. econs., 1973-82; Cons. N.H. Mfrs. Assn., 1954-55, Joint Council on Econ. Edn., 1958. Served with AUS, 1943-46. Mem. Phi Beta Kappa. Home: Oradell, N.J. Died Oct. 1, 1982.

KAUFFMAN, JAMES LAURENCE, ret. naval officer; b. Miamisburg, O., Apr. 18, 1887; s. James and Mary Laura (Hunt) K.; student Pa. Mil. Coll., Chester, Pa., 1902-03, Army and Navy Sch., 1903-04; B.S., U.S. Naval Acad., 1908 grad. Naval War Coll.; honorary Doctor of Naval Science, P.M.C.; honorary D. Eng., Drexel Inst.; L.H.D. (hon.), Temple U.; LL.D. (hon.), Jefferson Med. Coll.; m. Elizabeth Draper, Nov. 5, 1910; children—Draper Laurence (U.S. Navy), Elizabeth Louise Hunt (Mrs. Prescott S. Bush, Jr.). Commd. ensign, U.S. Navy, June 5, 1910; promoted through grades vice adm., Apr. 1945; comdr. Philippine Sea Frontier; comdt. 4th Naval District, Phila.; World War II; comdr. naval base Iceland, comdr. Gulf Sea Frontier, comdr. Pacific Destroyers; retired 1949; former pres. Jefferson Medical College and Corp.; trustee Eastern Pa. Psychiatric Institute. Chairman Central branch A.R.C. Awarded: Distinguished Service Cross D.S.M.; Legion of Merit (3); Navy .Cross; Commendation Ribbon; Mexican Campaign; World War I Medal with star; Defense, European, Atlantic and Pacific (3 stars) area ribbons; Philippine Distinguished Service Order; Philippine Liberation Ribbon with Star; Cuban Order of Merit; Belgian Order of Leopold; Knight Comdr. Order of the Falcom (Iceland) Brazilian Order Southern Cross. Episcopalian. Clubs: Army and Navy, Army and Navy Country (Washington); Gulph Mills Golf, Philadelphia, Racquet (Phila.). Home: Philadelphia, Pa. †

KAUFFMANN, JOHN HOY, newspaper executive; b. Washington, Jan. 21, 1925; s. Samuel H. and Miriam (Hoy) K.; grad. Choate Sch., 1943; A.B., Princeton U., 1947; m. Laura Allen, July 15, 1946 (div. 1958); children—Bruce Gordon, Louise Miriam, Margaret Ellen, Samuel Hay IV; m. 2d, Patricia Bellinger, Feb. 8, 1958; 1 son, John Hoy II. With Evening Star, Washington, 1949-75, v.p., bus. mgr., 1957-68, pres., dir., 1969-74; pres. Washington Star Communications, 1971-76, also dir.; pres., chmn. bd. John J. Enterprises Ltd., Washington and N.Y.C., 1976-79; dir. Columbia Planograph Co., Washington, N.Am. Philips Co., Peoples Life Ins. Co., Am. Finance System Inc.; bd. dirs. Met. Washington Bd. Trade, mem. exec. com. Greater Nat. Capital Com., bd. dirs. Downtown Progress; bd. dirs. mem. Mayor's Com. for Internat. Visitors; v.p.; dir. Health and Welfare Council Met. Washington; bd. dirs. D.C. chpt. ARC, blood recruitment chmn., 1955-58; bd. dirs. Nat. Symphony Orch., Jr. Achievement Met. Washington, Davis Meml. Goodwill Industries, Inc., Nat. Capital area United Way; mem. adv. bd. Boy Scouts Am.; trustee Am. Cancer Soc., crusade chmn., 1964. Served with USAAF, 1943-45. Decorated Air medal; recipient Community Service award. Clubs: Metropolitan, Variety, Alfalfa, Advertising (Washington); Chevy Chase (Md.). Home: McLean, Va. Dec. 1979.

KAUFMAN, ANDY, entertainer; b. N.Y.C., Jan. 17, 1949; s. Stanley L. and Janice T. (Bernstein) K. A.A., Grahm Jr. Coll., Boston. Comedian coll. coffee houses, later nightclubs; appeared on: TV series The New Dick Van Dyke Show; star: TV Series Taxi, 1978-84; other TV appearances include The Redd Foxx Show; star: TV spl. Andy's Fun House; appeared: in film Heartbeeps; sold-out appearance, Carnegie Hall, N.Y.C., 1979, profl. wrestling debut, Mid-South Coliseum, Memphis, 1981. Mem. Screen Actors Guild, AFTRA, Writers Guild Am. Died May 16, 1984.

KAUFMAN, FRANK B., real estate exec.; b. Mt. Pleasant, Ia., Sept. 30, 1887; s. Andrew J. and Ophelia (Bowman) K.; student pub. schs. Mt. Pleasant; m. Elsie Benjamin, June 21, 1911; children—Dan A., Jack B. Salesman Hibbard, Spencer, Bartlett Co., Evanston, Ill., 1906-32, v.p., 1932-46, pres. 1946-52. Republican. Presbyn. Elk, Mason. Clubs: Athletic Assn., Tavern, Execs. (Chgo.); North Shore Country. Home: Evanston, Ill. †

KAUFMAN, FREDERICK, chemist, educator; b. Vienna, Austria, Sept. 13, 1919; came to U.S., 1940, naturalized, 1946; s. Erwin and Else (Pollack) K.; m. Klari Simonyi, Nov. 2, 1951; 1 son, Michael Stephen. Student, Vienna Technische Hochschule, 1937-38; Ph.D., Johns Hopkins, 1948. With Ballistic Research Labs., Aberdeen (Md.) Proving Ground, U.S. Army, 1948-64, chief phys. chemistry sect., 1951-60, chief chem. physics br., 1960-64; lectr. Johns Hopkins U., Balt., 1948-64; prof. chemistry U. Pitts., 1964-85, chmn. dept., 1977-80, univ. prof. chemistry, 1980-85, dir. space research coordination center, 1975-85; mem. advisory bd. office of chemistry tech. Nat. Acad. Scis., 1975-77; cons. to govt. agys. and industry. Editorial bd.: Jour. Chem. Physics, 1971-74, Jour. Photochemistry, 1972-85, Internat. Jour. Chem. Kinetics, 1976—, Jour. Phys. Chemistry, 1980-85. Recipient Rockefeller Pub. Service award Woodrow Wilson Sch., Princeton, 1955; Kent award Ballistic Research Labs., 1958; Research and Devel. award U.S. Army, 1962. Fellow Am. Phys. Soc.; fellow AAAS; mem. Am. Chem. Soc. (Pitts. award 1977), Chem. Soc. Gt. Britain, Nat. Acad. Sci., Combustion Inst. (v.p. 1978-82, pres. 1982-85), AAAS, Nat. Acad. Scis., Phi Beta Kappa, Sigma Xi. Home: Pittsburgh, Pa. Died Dec. 7, 1985.

KAUFMAN, LEONARD, lawyer; b. N.Y.C., Apr. 30, 1913; s. Louis and Lillian (Brown) K.; m. Rita Dembitz, Aug. 9, 1940; children—Lawrence J., Robert I. Student, Coll. City N.Y., 1929-31; LL.B., Fordham U., 1936. Bar: N.Y. bar 1937, U.S. Supreme Ct. bar 1959. Staff law offices Nathan Burkan, N.Y.C., 1933-36, Schwartz & Frohlich, N.Y.C., 1936-49; legal staff Paramount Pictures Corp., N.Y.C., 1949-59, gen. house counsel, 1959-64, gen. counsel, 1964-67, pvt. practice of law, 1968-81; mem. firm Kaufman & Kaufman, 1969-75, 78-79, Kommel Rogers Kaufman Lorber & Shenkman, 1975-78; individual practice law, 1979-81; of counsel Weisberg, Sieven & Mammana, 1981. Served with AUS, 1943-45, CBI. Mem. Am., N.Y. State bar assns., Assn. Bar N.Y.C., Copyright Soc. U.S.A., Motion Picture Pioneers, Karet League for Child Care, Variety Clubs N.Y. (gen. counsel, trustee cinema-radio-TV unit). Club: B'nai B'rith. Home: Mamaroneck, N.Y. Died Dec. 9, 1981.

KAUFMANN, HELEN LOEB, author; b. New York, N.Y., Feb. 2, 1887; d. Herman Albert and Selina (Loeb) Loeb; A.B., Barnard Coll., 1908; m. Mortimer J. Kaufmann, Aug. 12, 1907; children—George Mortimer (killed World War II), Richard Edward, Ruth (Mrs. Russell Abbot Ames). Member board Henry St. Music Sch.; Met. Music Sch. Dir. music div. Am. Com. for Emigre Scholars from 1949. Mem. Internat. Soc. Contemporary Music, Beethoven Assn., Phi Beta Kappa. Club: Town Hall. Author books including: A Little Dictionary of Musical Terms, 1947; Little Book of Music Anecdotes, 1948; Little Guide to Music Appreciation, 1948; The Little History of Music, 1949. Contbr. to mags. Home: Hampton, N.J. †

KAWATA, SHIGE, business exec.; b. Japan, July 25, 1887; student Tokyo (Japan) U. With Nippon Kokan Kabushiki Kaisha (Japan Steel and Tube Corp.), Tokyo, 1918, auditor, from 1942, dir., from 1942, mng. dir., 1945-47, pres., 1947-63, chmn. bd., from 1963; pres. Nippon, Kokan Co., Ltd., Tokyo, Kokan Mining Industry, Co., Nippon Kokan Light Steel Co.; dir. Japan Usiminas Co., Arabian Oil Co.; mng. dir. Japan Iron and Steel Fedn. Recipient Blue Ribbon medal, 1958.†

KAYSER, CARL E., business exec.; b. Newark, N.J., May 20, 1889; s. Carl F. and Lillie Pauline (Eble) K.; A.B., Columbia U., 1909; m. Mildred Janet Leach, Jan. 6, 1915; children—Carl M., Frederick T., Janet M. With Am. Metal Co., Ltd., N.Y. City, 1909-12; pres. Smelter Gas Co., Bartlesville, Okla., 1912-21; pres. Miss. Valley Oil Gas Company, Bartlesville, 1921-27; independent oil and gas operator, Tulsa and Bartlesville, 1927-32; pres. Carbon Black Export, Inc., N.Y. City, 1933-45, sec. from 1946; exec. sec. Nat. Gas Products Assn., N.Y. City, 1933-45, treas. from 1946; asst. to pres. Columbian Carbon Co., N.Y.C., 1946-48, pres., 1948-58, chmn. bd., from 1958, apptd. mem. adv. com. for carbon black industry, War Prodn. Bd. and Nat. Prodn. Authority. Republican. Home: New York 28. †

KAYSER, ELMER LOUIS, educator, historian; b. Washington, Aug. 27, 1896; s. Samuel Louis and Susie Brown (Huddleston) K.; m. Margery Ludlow, Feb. 11, 1922; 1 dau., Katherine Ludlow (Mrs. Arthur Hallett Page III) (dec.). B.A., also Bachelor's Diploma in Edn., George Washington U., 1917, M.A., 1918, LL.D. (hon.), 1948; Ph.D., Columbia, 1932; L.H.D., Mount Vernon Coll., 1975. Asst. in history George Washington U., 1914-17, instr., 1917-20, asst. prof., 1920-24, asso. prof., 1924-32, prof., 1932-67, emeritus, 1967-85, asst. librarian, 1917-18, recorder, 1918, sec., 1918-29, dir. summer sch., 1925-29, dir univ. students, 1930-34, dean, 1934-62, dean emeritus, 1967-85, univ. historian, 1962-85, asso. chmn. sch. of govt., 1957-58; radio commentator on world affairs, 1940-45. Author: The Grand Social Enterprise, 1932, A Manual of Ancient History, 1937, The George Washington U., 1821-1966, 1966, Washington's Bequest to a National University, 1965, Luther Rice, Founder of Columbian Coll, 1966, Bricks Without Straw, 1970, A Medical Center, 1973; co-author: Contemporary Europe, 1941; Past mem. bd. editors: World Affairs. Sec.-treas. Gen. Alumni Assn., George Washington U., 1918-24, v.p., 1945-50, pres., 1950-53; vice-chmn. bd. trustees Mt. Vernon Sem., 1946-66; hon. bd. dirs. Mt. Vernon Coll., 1966-85; past chmn. com. improvement Adminstrn. Justice D.C.; historian Nat. Capital Sesquicentennial Commn., 1950; past bd. govs. Nat. Cathedral Sch.; past chmn. sec. navy's adv. com. naval history.; Historian Nat. Capital Sesquicentennial Commn., 1950. Served with F.A. O.T.S., World War I, Camp Zachary Taylor, Ky. Recipient Alumni Achievement award George Washington U., 1941, Alumni Service award, 1962, George Washington award, 1977; comdr. Nat. Order of Merit Ecuador). Mem. Inst. Jud. Adminstrn., Am. Hist. Assn. (treas. 1957-73), Columbia Hist. Soc. (v.p.), AAUP (council 1952-54), Am. Peace Soc. (dir.), Sigma Phi Epsilon (citation for distinguished service 1965), Pi Gamma Mu, Omicron Delta Kappa, Delta Phi Epsilon, Gate and Key. Club: Cosmos (past bd. mgrs.). Home: Washington, D.C. Died Apr. 28, 1985.

KAYSER, PAUL, business exec.; b. Tyler, Tex., Feb. 10, 1887; s. Albert and Mary Louise (Lawrence) K.; A.B., Baylor U., 1909, LL.D. (hon.), 1953; legal edn. by correspondence, U. Tex.; LL.D. (hon.), U. Ariz., 1957; m. Elizabeth Harris Clegg, Sept. 1, 1910; children—Betty and Jean (twins). Prin. high sch., Gatesville, Tex., 1909-11; admitted to Tex. bar, 1913; practice in Houston, 1913-29; mem. firm Huggins, Kayser & Liddell; pres. El Paso Natural Gas Co., Houston, Texas, 1929-60, chmn. and chief exec. officer, 1960-65, hon. chmn., 1965-66, dir., from 1966; pres. Western Natural Gas Co., 1935-63; mem. adv. bd. First Nat. Bank of San Antonio (Tex.), Tex. Nat Bank Commerce, Houston. Served as capt., 7th Cav., N.G., World War I. Mem. Ind. Natural Gas Assn. (pres. 1951-52). Episcopalian. Clubs: Houston, River Oaks Country (Houston); University (Chgo.); Recess (N.Y.C.). Contbr. articles profl. jours. Home: Houston, TX. †

KEALOHA, JAMES KIMO, orgn. exec.; born Pahoa, Puna, T.H., Apr. 29, 1908; s. Lee Chau and Alice K. Makanui; grad. high sch.; m. Miulan Pele Young, Oct. 13, 1929; children—Emma Leihulu (Mrs. William Cooper), Lillie Leiohu (Mrs. Sequeira). Rep., Territorial Ho. Reps., 1934-37, senator Territorial Senate, 1938-39, pres. pro-tem, 1938; supr. 1st Republican Dist., County of Hawaii, T.H., 1940-47, chmn, exec. officer, 1948-59; lt. gov. of Hawaii, 1959-62; exec. officer Hawaii N.Y. World's Fair Com., 1962-83. Hawaiian del. 1st Japanese-Pacific Coast Mayor's Conf., Tokyo, 1951; presiding officer U.S. Conf. Mayors, N.Y.C., 1952; ofcl. U.S. del. World Conf. Mayors, Rome, Italy, 1955; mem. adminstrv. and finance com. U.S. Civil Def. Council, 1958, 59; mem. U.S. Civil Def. and Def. Moblzn. Council; 50th State rep. Ga. State Fair, Salute to Hawaii, 1959; 50th State rep. Wash. State Daffodils Salute to Hawaii, 1960; mem. team sponsored U.S. Army to participate in goodwill tour of Taipei. Decorated officer Order of Kamehameha, officer Order Hale O Na Alii. Mem. Nat. Assn. County Ofcls., U.S. Conf. Mayors, Newcomen Soc. N.A., Hawaiian Bot. Gardens Found. Inc., Hawaiian Chinese Civic Assn., Hawaiian Assn. AAU (chmn. pub. relations com.). Republican. Clubs: Hawaiian Civic, Propeller of U.S. (Honolulu); Kuhio Lion, Optimist, Elk. Home: Hilo, Hawaii. Died Aug. 24, 1983.

KEAR, PAUL WINFRED, lawyer; b. Van Wert O., Nov. 2, 1887; s. Wiley M. and Malinda (Romig) K.; student U. of Mich. and Ohio Wesleyan U.; LL.B., U. of Va., 1908; unmarried. Admitted to Va. bar, 1908, and began practice at Norfolk; U.S. atty., Eastern Dist. Va., 1921-31; apptd. spl. asst. to atty. gen., Apr. 1, 1931; again apptd. U.S. atty., Apr. 11, 1932; spl. asst. to atty. gen. and to U.S. atty., 1933-35; clk. U.S. Dist. Court, Eastern Dist. Va., since 1936. Formerly mem. Ohio N.G.; joined Norfolk Light Arty., 1908, capt., 1915; served on Mexican border and with A.E.F.; maj., Jan. 1918 and assigned to 112th Heavy Field Arty., 54th Arty. Brigade, 29th Div.; assigned duty Peace Conf., in charge 1st Dist. line of communications; hon. discharged, Oct. 1919. Mem. Am. and Va. bar assns., 29th Div. Assn., Phi Gamma Delta. Methodist. Mason (Shriner). Clubs: Virginia, Norfolk Golf, Norfolk Yacht & Country (Norfolk); Army and Navy (Washington, D.C.). Home: Norfolk, Va.†

KEARNS, HENRY, international finance and business consultant; b. Salt Lake City, Apr. 30, 1911; s. Henry A. and Mary (Orilla) K.; m. Marjorie Harriett Prescott, Aug. 30, 1938; children: Patricia Kearns Hitchcock, Henry Timothy, Michael and Mary Kearns Rohe (twins). Student, U. Utah Sch. Engring., 1929-31; grad., Internat. Corr. Schs., 1935; D.Bus. Adminstrn. (hon.), Woodbury Coll., 1960; D.Econs. (hon.), Chung Aug U., Seoul, Korea, 1971. Salesman, Loesch & Osborne Motor Co., Pasadena, Calif., 1933-34; service sta. salesman Shell Oil Co., 1934-35; new car salesman Uptown Chevrolet Co., Pasadena, 1935-37, new car sales mgr., 1937-38, gen. sales mgr., 1938-39; partner David H. Lane Chevrolet Co., Pasadena, 1939-41; organizer, v.p., gen. mgr. Victory Mfg. Co., Los Angeles, 1942-43, pres., gen. mgr., 1943-46, established plastic devel. sect., 1943-47; asst. sec. internat. affairs U.S. Dept. Commerce, 1957-60, 60-69; now cons. internat. trade and finance; owner Kearns Car Rental, Orange Oaks Ranch; pres. San Gabriel Valley Motors, Rio Hondo Devel. Co., Policyholders Ins., Co., Sharder Water Co., Kearns Internat., Am. Capital Corp.; v.p., dir. Pike Corp. Am., 1966-67; pres., chmn. Export Import Bank U.S., 1969-73; pres. Kearns Internat., 1973-75, chmn., 1975-85; pres. Fin. Services Corp., Panama, 1975-85; pres. Nat. Sci. Engring. Co., 1966-67; adviser to bd. dirs. Philippine Investment Mgmt. Inc., Manila, 1964-66; dir., chmn. bd., chmn. adv. bd. Am. Asian Bank, San Francisco, 1974-79, chmn., 1979-85; dir. FMC Corp., Am. Internat. Group, Inc., Washington Fin. Center, 1977-78; mem. adv. council Brazil Inter Part, 1980-85; mem. Nat. Adv. Com. on Internat. Monetary and Fiscal Policy, 1969-73. Vice pres., dir. C. of C. U.S.; pres. Alhambra C. of C.; mem. nat. council cons. SBA; mem. spl. Pasadena War Meml. Com.; chmn. Pasadena Freedom Train Com.; exec. bd., com. for Young Men in Govt.; vice chmn. Task Force Intelligence Activities, Hoover Commn., 1965-66; Republican central committeeman Los Angeles County; pres. Pasadena Rep. Club, Pasadena Rep. Assembly; chmn. Eisenhower-Nixon campaign, So.

Calif., 1956; mem. exec. com. Calif. Rep. Central Com.; vice-chmn. Rep. Nat. Finance Com.; trustee Pasadena Boys Club; Trustee Hazel Hurst Found. Blind; bd. dirs. Pasadena Civic Music Assn., Am. Soc. Internat. Execs., Internat. Execs. Service Corps; trustee Woodbury U., Los Angeles. Decorated knight grand cross Most Exalted Order of White Elephant, Thailand; grand officer de l'Ordre Nat. Republic Ivory Coast; comandador de Mesma Ordem Nacional do Cruxeiro do Sul Brazil; Order Brillant Star Republic of China; Diplomatic Order Merit Korea; knight comdr. Ct. of Honor; recipient Disting. Service award City of Pasadena, 1943; capt. Robert Dollar award Nat. Fgn. Trade Council, 1971; award Phila. Fgn. Traders Assn., 1972; Disting. Service award San Francisco World Trade Club, 1973; Emeritus award U. Utah, 1976; Merit Honor award. Fellow AIM; mem. So. Calif. Sales Mgrs. Council (past pres.), Tournament of Roses Assn. (pres. 1966-67), Korean-Am. C. of C. (bd. dirs.), Nat. Indsl. Info. Com. Clubs: Masons (San Francisco), San Francisco Golf (San Francisco), Bohemian (San Francisco); Stock Exchange of San Francisco (pres., dir.); Burning Tree (Washington); St. Francis Yacht. Home: San Francisco, Calif. Died June 5, 1985.

KEATS, EZRA JACK, illustrator, author; b. Bklyn., Mar. 11, 1916; s. Benjamin and Augusta (Podgainy) K. Ed. pub. schs. Tchr. Workshop Sch., N.Y.C., 1955-57, Sch. Visual Arts, N.Y.C., 1947-48. Exhibited, Asso. Am. Artists Gallery, N.Y.C., 1950-54, mag., advt. illustrator, 1947-83; Author, illustrator: The Snowy Day, 1962 (Newbery-Caldecott medal 1963), Whistle For Willie, Peters Chair, John Henry, A Letter to Amy, Jennie's Hat, Goggles, 1970 (Caldecott honor award), Hi, Cat (Boston Globe-Horn book award 1970), Apt. 3, Pet Show, 1972, Psst! Doggie, 1973, Skates!, 1973, Dreams, 1974, Kitten for a Day, 1974, Louie, 1975; Editor, illustrator: God Is In The Mountain; illustrator Christmas card series, UNICEF, 1966, The King's Fountain, The Trip, 1978, Maggie and the Pirate, 1979, Louie's Search, 1980, Regards to the Man in the Moon, 1981; editor: Night. Mem. P.E.N., Author's Guild, Soc. Illustrators. Home: New York, N.Y. Died May 6, 1983.

KECK, GEORGE FRED, architect; b. Watertown, Wis., May 17, 1895; s. Fred George and Amalie (Henze) K.; student U. Wis., 1914-15; B.S., U. Ill., 1920; D.F.A., Lawrence U., 1950; m. Lucile Liebermann, Nov. 26, 1921. Designer various archtl. offices, Chgo., 1920-26; instr. design U. Ill., 1923-24; individual practice architecture, Chgo., 1926-80; ptnr. William Keck, 1937—; head dept. architecture Inst. Design, 1938-44; several one-man shows. Mem. Hyde Park-Kenwood Community Conf., Am. Civil Liberties Union. Bd. dirs. S.E. Chgo. Commn. Served to 2d lt. U.S. Coast Arty., 1917-19. Mem. Arts Club Chgo., Renaissance Soc. Contbr. articles to profl. jours. Painter watercolors. Important works include House of Tomorrow, Crystal House Chgo. Worlds Fair 1933-34, pub. housing projects Chgo. Housing Authority, Chgo. Child Care Soc. Bldg. Home: Chicago, Ill. Dec. Oct. 21, 1980. Interned Watertown, Wis.

KEEFE, DONALD FORAN, lawyer; b. New London, Conn., Mar. 12, 1917; s. Arthur T. and Mabel (Foran) K.; m. Kate Stevens Hemingway, Apr. 8, 1942; children—Sarah, Nicholas, Thomas. B.A., Yale U., 1938, LL.B. cum laude, 1946; postgrad., King's Coll., Cambridge (Eng.) U., 1938-39. Bar: Conn. bar. Since practiced in, New Haven; partner firm Tyler, Cooper, Grant, Bowerman & Keefe (and predecessor), 1949-84; dir. Colonial Bancorp Inc., Blue Cross and Blue Shield Conn., Inc. Pres. United Fund Greater New Haven, 1964-66, bd. dirs., 1961-67; mem. sch. bd. Cath. Archdiocese Hartford, 1966-69; Mem. adv. bd. Albertus Magnus Coll., New Haven. Served to comdr. USNR, 1941-45. Decorated knight St. Gregory. Mem. Am., Conn., New Haven County bar assns., Am. Judicature Soc., New Haven C. of C. (dir. 1966-72, v.p. 1971-72). Republican. Roman Catholic. Clubs: Quinnipiac (New Haven), Lawn (New Haven). Home: North Haven, Conn. Died June 28, 1984.

KEEGAN, JOHN JAY, educator, surgeon; b. Axtell, Kan., Jan. 8, 1889; s. John Andrew and Agnes Theresa (Graney) K.; student U. of Kan., 1907-08; A.B., U. of Neb., 1911, A.M., 1914, M.D., 1915; m. Grace Gilliland, Jan. 8, 1918; children—Nancy Jane, Norman Jay. Instr. in anatomy, U. of Neb. Coll. Medicine, 1915-17; path. house officer Peter Bent Brigham Hosp., Boston, Mass., 1917, surg. house officer, 1919-20; asst. prof. pathology, U. of Neb. Coll. Medicine, 1920-23, prof. clin. pathology, 1923-29, dean, 1925-29, sec. of faculty and dir. of clinics, 1923-25; prof. neurol. surgery same univ. from 1929, chmn. dept. of surgery, 1933-48, specializing in neurol. surgery. Served as lt. Med. R.C., U.S. Navy and dir. lab. U.S. Naval Hosp., Chelsea, Mass., 1917-19. Mem. A.M.A., Am. Soc. Neurol. Surgeons (pres. 1942), Western Surg. Assn., Harvey Cushing Society, Central Neuro-psychiatric Assn. Omaha Midwest Clinical Soc. (pres. 1945), Omaha Douglas County Med. Soc. (pres. 1936-37), Sigma Xi, Phi Rho Sigma, Alpha Omega Alpha. Club: Omaha. Home: Omaha, Nebr. †

KEEHN, GRANT, investment banker; b. Kenilworth, Ill., Oct. 11, 1900; s. George Washington and Jeannette Sophronia (Shipman) K.; m. Marjorie Elliott Burchard, July 30, 1923 (dec. Jan. 1961); children—Nora, Gretchen, Silas; m. Veronika Marietta Rona, Mar. 31, 1962; children—Dorka, Fruzsina. A.B., Hamilton Coll., Clinton, N.Y., 1921; M.B.A., Harvard, 1923; LL.D., Hamilton Coll., 1972. With Goldman Sachs and Co., 1923-31; partner, 1931; independent financial cons.; v.p. Kelsey Hayes Wheel Corp., Detroit, 1932-33; officer, dir. Equity Corp. (and asso. cos.), 1934-38; partner Grant Keehn & Co., 1939-42; v.p. 1st Nat. Bank City N.Y., 1945-50, exec. v.p., 1950-55, dir., 1951-55; exec. v.p. 1st Nat. City Bank N.Y., 1955-58; sr. v.p., dir. Equitable Life Assurance Soc. U.S., 1958-64, pres., dir., 1964-67, vice chmn. bd., dir., 1967-69, chmn. finance com., dir., 1965-71; ltd. partner Goldman Sachs & Co., N.Y.C., 1971-83. Trustee Hamilton Coll., 1948-83, chmn., 1963-69; trustee N.Y. Pub. Library. Served from maj. to col. AUS, 1942-45; liaison officer Army Service Forces Chgo. Mem. Phi Beta Kappa, Alpha Delta Phi. Clubs: Harvard (N.Y.C.), Links (N.Y.C.), N.Y. Athletic (N.Y.C.); Ranier (Seattle); Bellevue Athletic (Bellevue, Wash.), Overlake Golf and Country (Bellevue, Wash.). Home: Bellevue, Wash. Died 1983.

KEENAN, KEVIN WILLIAM, banker; b. N.Y.C., May 16, 1933; s. William Henry and Lillian (Fromm) K.; B.S. in Econs., U. Pa., 1955; LL.D., Cornell U., 1958; m. Barbara E. Belfield, Aug. 27, 1955; children—John Blakeley, Elizabeth Ann. Admitted to Pa. bar, 1960; mem. trust adminstrn. staff Personal Trust dept. First Pennsylvania Bank, Phila., 1958-66, v.p., mgr. Bus. Interest div., 1966-71, sr. v.p., chief operating officer Trust and Investment group, 1971-77, exec. v.p. and chief exec. officer Trust and Investment Group, 1977-81. Dir. KWM Cos., Inc., Easton, Pa., First Pa. Internat., Ltd., Fund Plan Services, Inc., Stock Clearing Corp. Phila., Philadep, Inc. Trustee, Abington (Pa.) Meml. Hosp., Morris Arboretum, U. Pa., Phila. Mem. Phila. Bar Assn., Pa. Bankers Assn. (chmn. trust div.), Am. Mgmt. Assn., Am. Hort. Soc., Delta Kappa Epsilon. Republican. Episcopalian. Clubs: Union League of Phila., Skytop, Huntingdon Valley Country, Wharton. Author: Closely-Held Businesses, 1970. Home: Huntingdon Valley, Pa. Dec. June 23, 1981.

KEENER, SIDNEY CLARENCE, dir. baseball Hall of Fame; b. St. Louis, Aug. 15, 1888; s. Edward and Martha (von Schoenpflug) K.; ed. St. Louis pub. schs.; m. Blanche Simmons, Sept. 21, 1918. Office boy St. Louis Star, 1901-05, sports reporter, 1906; sports reporter St. Louis Times, 1907-14, sports editor, 1914-29; sports editor St. Louis Star, 1929-32, and continued in position when St. Louis Star and Times merged, 1932; daily column on sports, 1914-51; apptd. dir. Nat. Baseball Hall Fame and Mus., Inc., Cooperstown, N.Y., 1952. Home: Cooperstown, N.Y. †

KEETTEL, WILLIAM CHARLES, JR., physician, educator; b. Lyons, Nebr., Apr. 30, 1911; s. William Charles and Eunice Una (Rohde) K.; m. Mary Helen Shinn, June 30, 1940; 1 son, William David. A.B., B.Sc., U. Neb., 1932, M.D., 1936. Rotating intern U. Ind., 1936-37; resident obstetrics and gynecology State U. Iowa, Iowa City, 1937-40, asst. prof., 1946-49, asso. prof., 1949-53, prof., from 1953, head dept. obstetrics and gynecology, 1959-77; postgrad. instr. State Dept. Health, U. Wis. Med. Sch., 1940-42; Mem. reviewing bd. maternal deaths in Iowa. Past dir. Am. Bd. Obstetrics and Gynecology. Contbr. articles to profl. jours. Fellow A.C.S. (past mem. tripartite residency review com. obstetrics and gynecology, residency rev. com.); mem. Am. Coll. Obstetricians and Gynecologists, Am., Central assns. obstetricians and gynecologists, Central Travel Club Obstetricians and Gynecologists, Ia. Obstet. and Gynecol. Soc., Am. Gynecol. Soc. Home: Iowa City, Iowa. Died July 28, 1981.

KEIGHLEY, WILLIAM J., motion picture director; b. Phila., Aug. 4, 1889; s. William Jackson and Mary (Hausel) K.; m. Genevieve Tobin, Sept. 19, 1938. Stage dir., N.Y.C., 1925-30; motion picture dir. Warner Bros., Burbank, Cal., 1930-42; films directed include: Green Pastures, Robin Hook, The Man Who Came to Dinner, Varsity Show, 1936, Each Dawn I Die, Easy to Love, 1938, Yes My Darling Daughter, 1939, The Fighting 69th, 1940, No Time for Comedy, 1941, George Washington Slept Here, 1942; dir. Street with No Name, 20th Century-Fox, also films Rocky Mountain Close to My Heart, Master of Ballantrae; prod. Lux Radio Theatre; prod., directed documentary Target for Today, selected by U.S. Treasury, 6th war loan drive; pioneer film selected for hist. library films U.S. Archives; compiled photog. documentation in color France's hist. monuments, serving base for lectures given ann., Musee des Arts Decoratifs, Paris. Served lt. col. to col., USAAF, 1942-45; chief motion picture div., organized combat camera units. Decorated Legion of Merit; Silver medal City of Paris; fellow in perpetuity Met. Mus. of Art, N.Y.C., 1959; Chevalier Des Arts et Lettres; Chevalier, de la Legion d' Honneur; Comdr. Legion de Merit (Spain). Address: Paris, France. Died June 24, 1984.

KEIGHLEY, WILLIAM J., motion picture dir.; b. Phila., Aug. 4, 1889; s. William Jackson and Mary (Hausel) K.; m. Genevieve Tobin, Sept. 19, 1938. Stage dir., N.Y.C., 1925-30; motion picture dir. Warner Bros., Burbank Cal., 1930-42; films directed include: Green Pastures, Robin Hood, The Man Who Came to Dinner, Varsity Show, 1936, Each Dawn I Die, Easy to Love, 1938, Yes My Darling Daughter, 1939, The Fighting 69th, 1040, No Time for Comedy, 1941, George Washington Slept Here, 1942; dir. Street with No Name, 20th Century-Fox, also films Rocky Mountain Close to My Heart, Master of Ballantrae; prod. Lux Radio Theatre; prod., directed documentary Target for Today, selected by U.S. Treasury, 6th war loan drive; pioneer film selected for hist. library films U.S. Archives; compiled photog. documentation in color France's hist. monuments, serving base for lectures given ann., Musee des Arts Decoratifs, Paris; lectr. Paris Serie on The Route to St. James de Compostelle. Served lt. to colonel, USAAF, 1942-45; chief motion picture div., organized combat camera units. Decorated Legion of Merit; Silver medal City of Paris, 1957; fellow in perpetuity Met. Mus. of Art, N.Y.C., 1959. Mem. Chevalier Des Arts et Lettres. Died June 26, 1984.

KELLEHER, PATRICK JOSEPH, art historian; b. Colorado Springs, Colo., July 26, 1917; s. Patrick and Mary (Devaney) K.; m. Marion Mackie, Mar. 14, 1948; 1 dau., Maria. A.B., Colo. Coll., 1939; M.F.A., Princeton, 1942, Ph.D. (Procter fellow), 1947; postgrad. fellow, Am. Acad. in Rome, 1947-49. Chief curator art Los Angeles County Mus., 1949; lectr. U. Buffalo, 1950-51; curator collections Albright-Knox Art Gallery, Buffalo, 1950-54; curator European art Nelson Gallery-Atkins Mus., Kansas City, Mo., 1954-59; dir. Art Mus., Princeton, 1960-72, prof. art and archeology, 1960-73. Served to maj. AUS, 1942-46. Mem. Phi Beta Kappa. Home: Princeton, N.J. Died June 16, 1985.

KELLER, FRANKLIN JEFFERSON, educator; b. N.Y. City, July 2, 1887; s. Martin Christian and Katie (Stetzer) K.; B.S., Coll. City of New York, 1906; M.A., Columbia, 1910; Ph.D., New York, 1916; m. Evelyn Miles, Sept. 1, 1914; children—Joan Miles, Geoffrey. Teacher pub. schs., N.Y. City, 1906-17; asst. prin., 1917-18; reporter New York Times, 1918-20; prin. Pub. Sch. No. 7, N.Y. City, 1920-25, Metropolitan Vocational High School (formerly East Side Continuation School) from 1920; exec. sec. Friedsam Commn. on Sch. Finance and Administrn., 1925-26; dir. Vocational Survey Commn., New York Bd. of Edn., 1930-33; dir. Nat. Occupational Conf. (Carnegie Corp.), 1933-36; head, vocational and tech. sect., Edn. and Religious Affairs Branch, Am. Mil. Govt. in Germany, 1946-47; technical director of the Edgar Starr Barney project of the Hebrew Technical Institute from 1948; member of faculty of summer school Harvard, 1926-32, 1936, and Stanford U., 1941; lecturer New York U., 1926-33, 37. Mem. governor's commn. on Education in Correctional Institutions, 1934-42. Mem. N.E.A., Nat. Vocational Guidance Assn. (pres. 1937-38), Am. Vocational Assn., Nat. Soc. Study Edn., Nat. Assn. of Secondary School Prins., Phi Delta Kappa. Quaker. Clubs: Propeller, Rotary, University Glee. Author: Day Schools for Young Workers, 1924; Vocational Guidance Throughout the World (with M.S. Viteles), 1937, Principles of Vocational Edn., 1948. Chmn. editoral com. and contbr. to 42d yearbook of Nat. Soc. for Study of Edn., Vocational Edn., 1943. Contbr. articles on edn. Home: New York, N.Y.†

KELLER, HARRISON, musician; b. Delphos, Kan., Oct. 8, 1888; s. Milton and Amanda (Thompson) K.; Bachelor Music, Bethany College, Lindsborg, Kansas, 1907, Doctor Music (honorary), 1954; student Stern's Conservatory, Berlin, Germany, 1907-11; studied with Anton Witek, Prague, 1912, Leopold Auer, St. Petersburg, Russia, 1913-14; m. Kathleen Geoghegan, June 24, 1924; children—Joan (Mrs. John Alden), Kathleen Angela. Concerts, U.S., 1914-17; head string dept. New Eng. Conservatory Music, 1922-46, dir., 1947-52, pres., 1952-58, vice chmn. exec. com. and trustee, from 1958; founder Boston String Quartet, 1925, leader, 1925-46. Trustee Paderewski Fund, Frank Huntington Beebe Fund. Served as lt. 301st F.A., U.S. Army, World War I. Decorated Legion of Honor (France). Fellow Am. Acad. Arts and Sci.; mem. Nat. Assn. Schs. Music (pres. 1952-55), Am. Musicol. Soc., Boston Opera Assn. (v.p.), Sinfonia, Pi Kappa Lambda. Club: Tavern. Home: Wellesley Hills, Mass. †

KELLER, JEAN HERMAN, graphic arts co. exec.; b. Stroudsburg, Pa., Apr. 2, 1925; s. Joseph and Louise (Ruckenbrod) K.; m. Elinor Margaret Mueckenheim, June 22, 1947; children—Peter Stephen, Paul Stuart, Deborah Lynn, Philip Scott. B.S., Parks Coll., 1949; M.S., Columbia U., 1953. Sr. asso. Stewart Dougall & Assos., N.Y.C., 1953-62; mgr. mktg. planning Curtiss-Wright Corp., Woodridge, N.J., 1962-65; corp. v.p. mktg. ITT, N.Y.C., 1965-75; owner, cons. J.H. Keller Assos., Upper Saddle River, N.J., 1975-77; pres. Conval Internat., Chgo., 1977-78, Brown & Bigelow (div. Saxon Industries, Inc.), St. Paul, 1978—. Served with USAAF, 1943-45.

KELLER, LUE ALICE, musician; b. Findlay, O. July 4, 1888; d. Capt. J. L. and Mary (Moorhead) Keller; grad. Cincinnati Conservatory of Music, 1905; studied Columbia. Concert pianist, organist and lecturer on mus. subjects; made 7 concert tours of U.S., beginning in 1908. Past activities: vice pres. Calif. Fedn. Music Clubs, chmn. course of study; pres. Tuesday Musicale of Pasadena; organized Tuesday Musicale Jrs., Pasadena. Pres. Fine Arts Club, Pasadena; mem. Soc. Native Am. Composers. Composer Larks and Lupines, The Swing, Raindrops, My Garden, The Music of Life, God Guide America, Hear Us, O Father, Book of Songs for Mother and Child, Garden Things, Vacation Time (piano duet book). Teacher piano, harmony and composition. Presbyn. Home: Pasadena, Calif. †

KELLEY, ARTHUR LIVINGSTON, banker; b. Providence, R.I., June 14, 1888; s. Arthur Livingston and Lotta Persia (Fuller) K.; prep. edn., St. George's Sch., Newport, R.I.; student Williams Coll., 1906-10; m. Olive Douglas

Maltby, May 18, 1911; children—Jean Maltby, Doris Read, Harriet Maltby, Olive Douglas. Treas. Mech. Fabric Co., 1912-17; pres. R.I. Textile Company, 1913-38; dir., Lloyd Mfg. Co.; chairman Providence Inst. for Savings; director Indsl. Nat. Bank, R.I. Textile Co., Ashworth Bros., Inc., Providence Gas Co., Providence-Wash. Ins. Co., also the Gorham Manufacturing Company, Title Guarantee Co. of R.I. Served as 2d lt. engrs., U.S. Army, 1917-19. Trustee Providence Lying-In Hospital. Mem. Alpha Delta Phi. Republican. Episcopalian. Clubs: Agawam Hunt, Art (Providence); Williams (N.Y.C.). Home: Saunderstown, R.I. †

KELLEY, VERNON EDWARD, ret. union leader; b. Tappen, N.D., Jan. 31, 1914; s. Charles Anthony and Helen Catherine (Dagen) K.; student trade union program Harvard U., 1957; m. Ruby Mae Hareleson, July 10, 1940; children—Charles R., Cynthia Claire Kelley Thornton. With Stone & Webster Engring. Co., Baton Rouge, 1940-44, Kaiser Aluminum Co., Baton Rouge, 1946-51; mem. staff AFL, 1951-53, officer Aluminum Workers Internat. Union, AFL-CIO, St. Louis, 1953-77, pres., 1975-77. Served with USMC, 1944-46; PTO. Democrat. Roman Catholic. Home: Zachary, La. Died Apr. 8, 1984.

KELLIN, MIKE, actor; b. Hartford, Conn., Apr. 26, 1922; s. Samuel and Sophie (Botuck) K.; m. Sally Moffet, Aug. 3, 1966; 1 dau., Shauna. Student, Bates Coll., 1939-40, Boston U., 1940-41; A.B., Trinity Coll., 1943; postgrad., Yale, 1947-48. Faculty performing arts Rockland Community Coll. Actor appearing in TV, stage, films; co-star: TV series The Wackiest Ship in the Army; appeared on: Broadway in Pipe Dream (Tony nominee); 25 others; films include The Jazz Singer; 30 others, regional theatre credits; appeared on Cable TV: King Lear; actor-in-residence, Buffalo, St. Louis, Utica and Providence Jewish Community Centers, 1978-81, (Recipient OBIE award for performance in American Buffalo 1976, Creative Artists Pub. Service fellow for mus. play Time (retitled Riffraff Revue) 1978); Composer, performer: record album And the Testimony's Still Comin' In, 1967; Composer: series of songs for Sierra Club Survival Songbook. Adv. bd. Fortune Soc., from 1968; mem. Rockland County Legislature Blue Ribbon Com. on Criminal Justice, 1973; dir. Rockland Arts Council; adv. bd. N.Y. Assn. Pretrial Service Agys., 1976. Served with USNR, World War II. Creative Artists Pub. Services fellow and ASCAP award Riffraff Revue. Home: Nyack, N.Y.

KELLOGG, CHARLES EDWIN, soil scientist; b. Ionia County, Mich., Aug. 2, 1902; s. Herbert Francis and Eunice Irene (Stocken) K.; B.S., Mich. State Coll., 1925, Ph.D., 1929; D.Sc., U. Gembloux (Belgium), 1960, U. Ghent (Belgium), 1963, N.D. State U., 1962; m. Lucille Jeanette Reasoner, Dec. 25, 1925; children—Robert Leland, Mary Alice. Fellow in soils Mich. State Coll., 1926-28; soil scientist Wis. Geol. Natural History Survey, 1928-30; asst. prof., then prof. soils N.D. Agrl. Coll., Fargo, 1930-34; chief soil survey U.S. Dept. Agr., from 1934, asst. adminstr., soil conservation service, 1953-63, dep. adminstr., 1963-71; freelance writer, cons. Del. 3d Internat. Congress Soil Sci., Oxford, Eng., 1935, gen. assembly Internat. Inst. Agr., Rome, 1938, 2d Inter-Am. Conf. Agr., Mexico City, 1942, 7th Pacific Sci. Congress, New Zealand, 1949; head U.S. delegation 4th Internat. Congress Sci., Amsterdam, 1950, 5th Internat. Congress Soil Sci., Leopoldville, 1954, 6th Internat. Congress Soil Sci., Paris, 1956; chmn. U.S. Mission on Soil Sci. to USSR, 1958; guest scientist India, 1958, 59, S. Viet Nam, 1959; Messenger lectr. Cornell U., 1945; Sigma Xi lectr., 1947; guest Acad. Scis. USSR for Jubilee Anniversary Sessions, Moscow and Leningrad, 1945; guest scientist, France, 1947, Belgian Congo, 1947, Britain, 1948, Ireland, Portugal and Iceland, 1950, Israel, 1952, Gold Coast, 1954. Recipient Distinguished Service award, gold medal U.S. Dept. Agr., 1950; Distinguished service citation Mich. State U., 1955. Fellow AAAS, Am. Soc. Agronomy; mem. Assn. Am. Geographers, Profl. Soil Classifiers Assn. N.D. (hon.), Internat. Soc. Soil Sci. (hon.), Soil Sci. Soc. Am. (pres. 1941, hon. recognition 1974), Royal Soc. New Zealand (hon.), Indian Soc. Soil Sci. (hon.), Sigma Xi, Phi Kappa Tau, Alpha Zeta. Mason. Club: Cosmos (Washington). Author: The Soils that Support Us, 1941; Soil Survey Manual; Our Garden Soils, 1952; (with D.C. Knapp) The College of Agriculture-Science in the Public Service, 1966; Agricultural Development: Soil, Food, People, Work, 1975. Contbr. numerous bulls. and papers to profl. lit. Home: Hyattsville, Md. Died Mar. 9, 1980; buried Palo, Mich.

KELLOW, WILLIAM F., university dean; b. Geneva, N.Y., Mar. 14, 1922; s. Robert Leo and Mary Loretta (Kelley) K.; B.S., U. Notre Dame, 1943; M.D., Georgetown U., 1946, D.Sc., 1979; D.Sc. (hon.), St. Joseph's Coll., 1967; L.H.D. (hon.), Hahnemann Med. Coll., 1978; m. Stella Margaret Toczylowski, Apr. 21, 1951; children—Suzanne, Joanne, Jennifer, Mary Jeanne, Kathleen. Intern D.C. Gen Hosp., 1946-47; resident internal medicine and pulmonary diseases D.C. Gen. Hosp., Georgetown U. Hosp., Walter Reed Med. Center, 1947-51; mem. faculty U. Ill. Coll. Medicine, 1953-61, assoc. prof. medicine, assoc. dean, 1959-61; prof. medicine, dean Hahnemann Med. Coll., Phila., 1961-67; prof. medicine, dean, v.p. Jefferson Med. Coll., Phila., 1967-81. Mem. gen. research adv. com. NIH, 1971-74. Trustee Eastern Pa. Psychiat. Inst., Ednl. Council Fgn. Med. Grads., 1968-79, Liaison Com. on Med. Edn., 1975-81. Served to capt. M.C., USAF, 1951-53. Recipient Sci. Achievement award U. Notre Dame, 1965; Schaffrey award St. Joseph's Coll., Calif., 1978; diplomate Am. Bd. Internal Medicine, Am. Bd. Pulmonary Diseases. Mem. A.C.P. (master 1977, regent 1968-75, treas. 1968-75), AMA (council med. edn. 1979-81), Am. Fedn. Clin. Research, Am. Thoracic Soc., Sigma Xi. Club: Union League (Phila.). Home: Wynnewood, Pa. Dec. Dec. 3, 1981.

KELLY, GEORGE LOMBARD, M.D., prof. anatomy; b. Augusta, Ga., Oct. 8, 1890; s. Jefferson Davis and Carrie Winslow (Lockwood) D.; A.B. (with honors), U. of Ga., 1911, B.S. in medicine, 1922, M.D., 1924; m. Adeline Mina Weatherly, Mar. 21, 1913 (died Oct. 18, 1918); m. 2d Ina Melle Todd Hoffman, June 9, 1920; children—Margaret Elizabeth (adopted stepdaughter, m. Nathan Massey DeVaughn), Georgia Anne, George Lockwood. Teacher of science, Academy of Richmond County, Augusta, Georgia, 1915-18; with Medical Coll. of Georgia since 1918, successively as instr. in anatomy, asst. prof., asso. prof., prof. since 1929; pres. from 1950; supt. Univ. Hospital, 1936-39; research asso. Cornell U. Med. Sch., dept of anatomy, N.Y. (on leave), 1926-27. Sec. Council on Medical Service and Public Relations, Am. Medical Assn. (on leave) Jan.-July, 1944. Awarded gold medal by Ga. Med. Assn. for paper read at annual meeting, 1932. Fellow American Medical Assn.; mem. Am. Assn. Anatomists, Georgia Academy of Science, Delta Tau Delta, Phi Rho Sigma, Phi Beta Kappa, Alpha Omega Alpha. Ind. Democrat. Author: Sexual Feeling in Woman, 1930; Sex Manual for Those Married or About to Be, 1945; Sexual Feeling in Married Men and Women, 1951. Contbr. to profl. jours. Home: Augusta, Ga. †

KELLY, JOHN BRENDEN, JR., constrn. company executive, sports association executive; b. Phila., May 24, 1927; s. John Brenden and Margaret (Majer) K.; m. Sandra Worley, May 28, 1981; children: Ann, Susan, Maura, Elizabeth, John Brenden III, Margaret. Grad., U. Pa., 1950. With John B. Kelly, Inc. of Pa., Phila., 1950-85, former pres., chmn. bd., 1979-85; pres., dir. Phila. Athletic Co.; dir. Phila., Geriatrics & Med. Centers, Inc.; Pres. Amateur Athletic Union, 1970-72; chmn. Greater Phila. Olympic Com., 1964-68, 72-76; v.p. U.S. Olympic Com., 1972—. Mem. Phila. City Council, 1968-70; Bd. dirs. Hero Scholarship Fund Police Athletic League Phila.; pres. John B. Kelly Found., 1961-85. Recipient Sullivan award Amateur Athletic Union, 1947, Phila. Zionist award, 1964; named Outstanding Young Man of Year Phila. Jr. C. of C., 1960, Outstanding Young Man of Year Pa. Jr. C. of C., 1961. Mem. VFW, Phila. Pres.'s Orgn., Schuylkill Navy Phila. (commodore 1963-64), Kappa Sigma (Man of Year 1975). Clubs: Phila. Country, Urban, Phila. Athletic (pres.), Vesper Boat (treas.), N.Y. Athletic; Seaview Country (Atlantic City). Died Mar. 2, 1985.

KELLY, PATSY (SARAH VERONICA ROSE KELLY), actress; b. Bklyn., Jan. 12, 1910. Appeared in plays Three Cheers, 1928, Earl Carroll's Sketchbook, Earl Carroll's Vanities, Wonder Bar, Flying Colors, Dear Charles, No No Nanette, 1971, Irene, 1973; appeared in motion pictures: Girl from Missouri, 1934, Go Into Your Dance, 1935, Thanks a Million, Kelly the Second, 1936, Nobody's Business, Pick a Star, Wake Up and Live, 1937, Merrily We Live, 1938, There Goes My Heart, The Cowboy and the Lady, Hit Parade of 1941, Topper Returns, 1941, Broadway Limited, In Old California, Danger-Woman at Work, The Crowded Sky, Please Don't Eat the Daisies, 1960, The Ghost in the Invisible Bikini, 1966, Rosemary's Baby, 1968, Freaky Friday, 1976, The North Avenue Irregular, 1979; appeared in TV series Valentine's Day, 1964, The Cop and The Kid, 1975-76; toured in Irene, 1974-75. Recipient Tony award for No, No, Nanette, 1971. Address: Beverly Hills, Calif. Dec. Sept. 24, 1981.*

KELLY, SAMUEL EDGAR, JR., lawyer; b. Blakely, Ga., Apr. 3, 1915; s. Samuel Edgar and Eleanor (Spier) K.; A.B., U. Ga., 1938, LL.B., 1942; m. Mary Coker, Apr. 19, 1946; children—Samuel E. III, Mary Ann, Frank B. Admitted to Ga. bar; mem. firm Kelly, Denney, Pease & Allison, and predecessors, Columbus, Ga., 1946-82; past exec. v.p., counsel Gas Light Co. of Columbus; dir., past mem. exec. com., counsel Am. Family Life Assurance Co., Columbus. Mem. Com. to Study City-County Govt. Merger, Columbus; past dir., pres. Girls Club of Columbus. Served with USN, 1942-45. Fellow Am. Coll. Trial Lawyers; mem. Am., Ga. bar assns. Baptist. Club: Lions (pres. Muscogee chpt.). Home: Columbus, Ga. Office: 233 12th St Columbus GA 31902 Died Sept. 23, 1982.

KELLY, WILLIAM TOLSON, JR., manufacturing executive; b. Mobile, Ala., June 5, 1907; s. William Tolson and Helen Rhodes (Prince) K.; grad. Phillips Acad., 1924; B.S., Yale, 1928; m. Mary Kelly Vizard, Sept. 17, 1929; children—William Tolson III, J. Douglas, Eugene V. With Am. Brake Shoe Co. (name changed to Abex Corporation), 1928—, asst. to the general purchasing agt., 1933-40, gen. purchasing agt., 1940-44, exec. v.p. Kellog div., 1944-45, pres. div., 1945-58, pres. engineered castings div., 1946-48, exec. v.p. Am. Brakeblok div., 1947-50, pres. 1950-53, pres. Sintermet div., 1954-55, vice pres. of corp., N.Y.C., 1946-64, first vice president, 1964-66, pres., chief operating officer, 1966-69, chairman, chief executive officer, 1969-74, member board directors, 1955-74; mem. of Midtown adv. bd. Chem. Bank N.Y. Trust Co.; mem. New York advisory board Liberty Insurance Company; dir. Abex Industries Can., Ltd., Chmn. industry adv. com. Iron and Steel Scrap Industry OPA, also mem. adv. coms. Ferrous Foundry and Iron and Steel Scrap, WPB, World War II. Mem. Am. Iron and Steel Institute, Berzelius Soc., Torch Honor Society, Society of Automotive Engineers, Episcopalian. Clubs: Yale, Sky (New York City); Wee Burn Country (Darien). Home: Naples, Fla. Died Jan. 21, 1982.

KELSH, HARRY THOMAS, precision instrument mfr.; b. Phila., Nov. 15, 1889; s. Harry Thomas and Emma (Fulmer) K.; B.S., Central High Sch., Phila., 1908; student U. Pa., 1908-11. With U.S. Coast & Geodetic Survey, 1911-17; with U.S. Soil Conservation Service, U.S. Geol. Survey, 1933-52; pres. Kelsh Instrument Co., Inc., from 1953. Served as 1st lt., air service, U.S. Army, 1917-18. Recipient Fairchild award for invention device for compilation of maps from aerial photographs, 1947; distinguished service award Dept. Interior, 1952. Mem. Am. Soc. Photogrammetry (past pres.), Internat. Soc. Photogrammetry, Photogrammetric Soc. Eng. Home: Washington, D.C. †

KEMBLE, EDWIN CRAWFORD, physics educator; b. Delaware, O., Jan. 28, 1889; s. Duston and Margaret Agnes (Day) K.; student Ohio Wesleyan U., 1906-07; B.S., Case Sch. Applied Science, 1911, hon. D.Sc., 1931; A.M., Harvard, 1914, Ph.D., 1917; Ed.D., R.I. College of Education, 1957; married to Harriet Mary Tindle, Sept. 8, 1920; children—Robert Day, Jean Allen. Asst. instr. in physics, Carnegie Inst. Tech., 1911-13; engring. physicist Curtiss Motor Corp., 1917-18; instr. in physics. Williams Coll., 1919; instr. in physics, Harvard, 1919-23, asst. prof., 1923-27, associate prof., 1927-30; professor 1930-57; professor of physics emeritus, 1957—, chairman of the department of physics, 1940-45. Guggenheim fellow, 1927. Fellow Am. Physical Soc., Am. Acad. Arts and Sciences, Nat. Acad. Sciences; mem. A.A.A.S., Sigma Xi, Tau Beta Pi, Phi Kappa Psi. Conglist. Author: Fundamental Principles of Quantum Mechanics, 1937; Physical Science: Its Structure and Development, Vol. I, 1966. Co-author: Report on Molecular Spectra in Gases, 1926. Contbr. to Physical Review. Home: Cambridge, Mass. Died Mar. 12, 1984.†

KENDALL, FREDERICK C(HARLES),, editor, b. London, Eng., Oct. 27, 1889; s. Edmund Ernest and Anna Blanca (Von Schmalensee) K.; student Stationers Co. Sch., London; m. Natalie Aldrich Cobb, Sept. 15, 1915; children—Aldrich Frederick, Bruce Cobb, David Arthur. Came to U.S., 1907, naturalized, 1918. Engaged in adv. and sales promotion work Sherwin-Williams Co., Cleveland, O., 1907-18; mng. editor Printers' Ink, New York, 1918-22; editor and pub. Advertising and Selling, New York, N.Y. 1923-48; vice president dir. Moore Publishing Co., New York City, since 1938. Exec. sec. annual advt. awards since 1935. Recipient gold medal, Harvard Advt. Awards, 1930. Mem. Alpha Delta Sigma. Episcopalian. Clubs: Dutch Treat. Art Directors, New York Advertising. Home: Short Hills, N.J. †

KENDRICK, PEARL L., bacteriologist; b. Wheaton, Ill., Aug. 24, 1890; d. Milton H. and Ella (Shaver) Kendrick; B.S., Syracuse U., 1914; Sc.D., Johns Hopkins Sch. of Hygiene and Pub. Health, 1932; unmarried. Science teacher, high sch. principal, New York State Schs., 1914-19; lab. asst. division of laboratories and research State Dept. of Health, New York, 1919-20; bacteriologist Bureau of Laboratories, Mich. Dept. of Health, 1929-51; asso. dir. of laboratories, in charge Western Mich. Div. 1926-51; resident lecturer school of public health, University of Mich. from 1951. Mem. bd. dirs. Council Social Agencies, Grand Rapids, Mich.; cons. to Dept. of Health Mexico, 1940, 1942, World Health Orgn., Eng., Colombia, Chile and Brazil, 1949-50. Fellow Am. Pub. Health Assn. (former v.p.; chmn. lab. sect., mem. exec. bd.) Mem. A.A.A.S., Soc. of Am. Bacteriologists, Mich. Acad of Science, Sigma Xi, Delta Omega. Protestant. Contbr articles to prof. jours. concerning pub. health laboratory procedures, serology of syphilis, bacteriophage, pertusis immunization. Home: Comstock Park, Mich. †

KENNEDY, FRANK BRITTAIN, investment banker; b Medford, Mass., May 29, 1904; s. Frank Alexander and Sadie (Brittain) K.; m. Kathryn James, June 12, 1926 children—Frank Brittain, Martha Burrage Fitch. Student Boston U., 1924-30. New Eng. mgr. C.F. Childs & Co 1925-31; treas., dir. Webster, Kennedy & Co., 1932-37 pres., dir. Kennedy, Spence & Co., 1937-40; propr. F Brittain Kennedy & Co., Boston, 1940-78; v.p. Moors & Cabo's, Inc., Boston, from 1978. Mem. adv. com. na council Boy Scouts Am.; Trustee Lahey Clinic Found Episcopalian. Clubs: Down Town (Boston); Cohasse (Mass.) Golf. Home: Cohasset, Mass.

KENNEDY, FREDRICK C., supermarket executive Head produce dept. Loblaw Grocerteria Co., Toronto Ont., Can., 1937-39; produce clk. Great Atlantic & Pacifi Tea Co. of Can., Ltd., 1939-40, head produce dept 1940-43, store mgr., 1943-44, asst. sales mgr. Toront office, 1944-51, sales and purchasing rep. Montreal offic 1951-66, v.p., 1966-69, gen. supt., 1969-70, pres. Can. div then chmn. bd., 1970-75, corp. pres., 1975-84; v.p., ge mgr. Great Atlantic & Pacific Tea Co. of Can., Inc Montvale, N.J., 1970-81, exec. v.p., 1981—, also di pres., dir. A & P Properties Ltd., A & P Drug Mart Lt Died 1984.*

KENNEDY, GERALD HAMILTON, bishop; b. Benzonia, Mich., Aug. 30, 1907; s. Herbert Grant and Marian (Phelps) K.; A.B., Coll. of Pacific, 1929, D.S.T., 1952; A.M., Pacific Sch. Religion, 1931, B.D., 1932; D.D., 1952; S.T.M., Hartford Theol. Sem., 1933, Ph.D., 1934; LL.D., Coll. of Puget Sound, 1949; Litt.D., Nebr. Wesleyan U., 1950; L. H.D., Beliot Coll., 1952; LL.D., Ohio Wesleyan U., 1952; D.D., Redlands U., 1954, Bucknell U., 1959; H.H.D., Bradley U., 1956; L.H.D., Calif. Western U., 1967; m. Mary Grace Leeper, June 2, 1928. Ordained ministry Methodist Ch., 1932; pastor First Congregational Church, Collinsville, Conn., 1932-36, Calvary Meth. Ch., San Jose, Calif., 1936-40, First Meth. Ch., Palo Alto, Calif., 1940- 42; acting prof. homiletics Pacific Sch. Religion, 1938-42; pastor St. Paul Meth. Ch., Lincoln, Nebr., 1942-48; bishop of Methodist Ch., Portland area, 1948; bishop Meth. Ch., Los Angeles area, 1952; dir. Wesley Found., Stanford U., 1940-42; lectr. in religion Nebr. Wesleyan U., 1942; radio preacher, KFAB and KFOR, Lincoln, Nebr., Sundays, 1945-48; book program, KEX, Portland, Oreg., Tuesday, 1949; Pilgrimage in World of Books, ABC, 1954; Earl lectr. Pacific Sch. Religion, 1946; Peyton lectr. So. Meth. U., 1949; Slover lectr. Southwestern U., 1950; Quillian lectr. Emory U., 1951; Mendenhall lectr. Depauw U., 1954; Beecher lectr. Yale, 1954; Ayer lectr. Colgate-Rochester, 1955; Grey lectr. Duke, 1957; Auburn lectr. Union Theol. Sem., 1957; Willson lectr. Southwestern Coll., 1964; sr. minister First Meth. Ch., Pasadena, Calif., 1969-73; Denman lectr. Perkins Sch. Theology, Dallas; Voigt lectr. McKendree Coll., 1968. Mem. exec. co. Community Chest, Lincoln, Nebr., 1945-48; pres. Council Social Agys., Lincoln, 1946-48; pres. Council of Bishops of Meth. Ch., 1960-61; mem. bd. trustees Pacific Sch. Religion, So. Calif. Sch. Theology; pres. Gen. Bd. Evangelism, Methodist Church, 1964-68; executive bd. Nat. Council Churches. Mem. Calif. State Bd. Edn. Clubs: University, Pasadena. Author: His Word Through Preaching, 1947; Have This Mind, 1948; The Best of John Henry Jowett (edited), 1948; The Lion and the Lamb, 1950; With Singleness of Heart, 1951; Go Inquire of the Lord, 1952; A Reader's Notebook, 1953; Who Speaks for God?, 1954; God's Good News, 1955; The Christian and His America, 1956; The Methodist Way of Life, 1958; I Believe, 1958; Readers Notebook, 2, 1959; The Parables, 1960; While I'm On My Feet, 1963; For Preachers and Other Sinners, 1964; Fresh Every Morning, 1966. Seven Worlds of the Minister, 1968; For Laymen and Other Martyrs, 1969; My Third Reader's Notebook, 1974. Home: Laguna Hills, Calif. Died Feb. 17, 1980.

KENNEDY, HAYES, lawyer; b. Joliet, Ill., Sept. 10, 1898; s. Martin Edward and Catherine Ann (Tuohy) K.; m. Mary Louise Lennon, May 24, 1926; children—Mary Frances, Helen (Mrs. Edwin J. Ryan), Hayes, Daniel, James. Ph.B., U. Chgo., 1922, J.D., 1924. Bar: Ill. bar 1924. Since practiced in, Chgo.; mem. firm Ryan, Condon & Livingston, 1948-64; gen. claims counsel, asst. gen. counsel Greyhound Corp., 1948-64; pres., counsel Ill. Comml. Men's Assn., Inc., Chgo., 1964-82; Tchr. Loyola U. Law Sch., Chgo., 1926-37; dir. Brach Candy Co., 1931-65. Trustee Lewis Coll., Lockport, Ill., 1960-73. Served with U.S. Army, World War I. Mem. Am., Ill., Will County bar assns., Am. Legion (founder Boys State program in Ill. 1935). Club: K.C. Home: Joliet, Ill. Died Oct. 3, 1982.

KENNEDY, PAUL A(LFRED), educator; b. Ware, Mass., Aug. 24, 1887; s. John and Mary Ann (Gleason) K.; B.S., Columbia, 1915, A.M., 1917; Ph.D., Fordham, 1927; m. Esther McKeown, Dec. 16, 1927; 1 son, Anthony. Teacher Longfellow Sch., Brooklyn, 1909; grade adviser Erasmus Hall High Sch., Brooklyn, 1920-24; prin. The Mapleton Sch. and Halsey Jr. High Sch., Brooklyn, 1925-35; head of methods dept. Fordham Univ. Grad. Sch. of Edn., 1927-30; asst. supt. schs., City of New York, since 1935, chmn. curriculum com. since 1947. Served as lt., Air Service, U.S. Army, 1918-19; researcher in aviation psychology and adminstrn. of altitude classification in tests. Mem. N.Y. Acad. Pub. Edn. (chmn. bd. dirs.; past pres.), Am. Legion, Assn. Asst. Supts. (past pres.). Roman Catholic. Knights of Columbus. Club: Cathedral. Home: Brooklyn, N.Y. †

KENNEDY, RIDGWAY, JR., dairy exec.; b. Philadelphia, Apr. 23, 1888; s. Samuel Ridgway and Lettitia Taylor (Jones) K.; student Spring Garden Ins., Phila., 1903; student N.Y. State Coll. Agrl., Cornell, 1905-07; m. Viola Gransback, Jan. 28, 1908; children—Evelyn (wife of Dr. Alfred G. Petrie), Viola (Mrs. John Lampey). With father in dairy bus., Phila., 1907-12; with Abbotts Dairies, Phila., from 1912, v.p. and gen. mgr., 1940-50, pres., from 1950, chmn., from 1956. Chmn. definitions and standards com. for the Ice Cream Industry, 1939-51. Mem. Internat. Assn. Ice Cream Mfrs. (pres. from 1950), Pa., Del. and N.J. Assn. Ice Cream Mfrs. (past pres.). Republican. Presbyn. Mason (32 deg.). Clubs: Union League, Kiwanis, Aronomink Golf. Home: Drexel Hill, Pa. †

KENNEDY, WILLIAM JESSE, III, insurance company executive; b. Durham, N.C., Oct. 24, 1922; s. William Jesse, Jr. and Margaret Lillian (Spaulding) K.; m. Alice Charlene Copeland, Jan. 29, 1949; 1 son, William Jesse IV. B.S. in Bus. Adminstrn, Va. State Coll., 1942; M.B.A., U. Pa., 1946; M.B.A. in Finance and Investments, N.Y. U., 1948. With N.C. Mut. Life Ins. Co., Durham, 1950-85, financial v.p., 1966-69, sr. v.p., 1969-72, pres., chief exec. officer, 1972-85, chmn., 1979-85; dir. J.A. Jones Constrn. Co., Charlotte, N.C., Mechanics & Farmers Bank, Durham, Urban Nat. Corp., Boston, Pfizer, Inc., Mobile Corp., N.Y.C., Quaker Oats, Chgo. Mem. Durham Com. Negro Affairs, NAACP, Durham Bus. and Profl. Chain; bd. dirs. N.C. Central U. Found., N.C. Citizens Assn.; trustee Triangle Univs. Center Advanced Studies; bd. overseers Wharton Sch., N.Y. U. Grad. Sch. Bus.; bd. visitors Fuqua Sch. Bus., Duke; trustee United Student Aid Funds, N.Y.C. Served with AUS, 1943-45. Charles E. Merrill Found. fellow Stanford Exec. Program, 1971. Mem. Durham C. of C., Conf. Bd., N.C. Soc. Fin. Analysts, Omega Psi Phi. Baptist (trustee 1950-85). Club: Kiwanian. Died July 8, 1985. *

KENNEY, GEORGE CHURCHILL, former air force officer; b. Yarmouth, N.S., Can., Aug. 6, 1889 (parents Am. citizens); s. Joseph Atwood and Louise (Churchill) K.; student Mass. Inst. Tech., 1907-11; LL.D., U. Notre Dame, 1947; m. Hazel Dell Richardson; 1 son, William Richardson; m. 2d, Alice Steward Maxey, June 5, 1922; 1 dau., Julia (Mrs. Edward C. Hoagland); m. 3d, Sarah Schermerhorn, Dec. 13, 1955; m. 4th, Jeanette C. Stehlin, 1971. Railroad surveyor, engr., 1911-14; pres. Beaver Contracting & Engring. Corp., Boston, 1914-17; commd. lt. AS, U.S. Army, 1917, advanced through grades to gen., 1945; comdr. 4th Air Force, 1942, Allied Air Force, S.W. Pacific, 1942-45, Pacific, 1945; sr. U.S. rep. mil. staff com. UN, 1946; comdg. gen. SAC, 1946-48, Air U., 1948-51; ret. 1951. Pres., Nat. Arthritis and Rheumatism Found., 1951-63. Decorated D.S.C. with oak leaf cluster, D.S.M. with two clusters, Silver Star, D.F.C., Legion Merit, Purple Heart, Bronze Star; knight comdr. Order Brit. Empire; Legion Honor, Croix de Guerre (France); Order Leopold, Croix de Guerre (Belgium); Order of Orange-Nassau with Swords (Netherlands); Order Mil. Merit (Guatemala); Philippine Star. Mem. Am. Legion, Mil. Order World Wars N.Y., V.F.W. Mason. Club: Lotus (N.Y.C.). Author: General Kenney Reports, 1948; The MacArthur I Know, 1951; The Saga of Pappy Gunn, 1959; Dick BongAce of Aces, 1960. Home: Bay Harbor Islands, FL. †

KENNY, DUMONT FRANCIS, ret. coll. pres.; b. N.Y.C., Dec. 3, 1914; s. Paul T. and Gertrude (Bandilla) K.; B.S., Fordham U., 1940; Ph.D., U. Chgo., 1953; L.H.D., Ia. Wesleyan U., 1967; m. Esther Mary Greenwood, Aug. 10, 1944; children—Marshall Francis, Jeremy Durbin, Pamela Anne, Terrence Paul, Rebecca Olive. Head dept. edn. P.K. Kenedy & Sons, publishers, N.Y.C., 1940-41; asst. prof., chmn. dept. philosophy Lewis Coll., Lockport, Ill., 1949-52; v.p. program devel. Nat. Conf. Christians and Jews, 1953-63; pres. Queensborough Community Coll. of City U. N.Y., Bayside, N.Y., 1963-66, York Coll., Flushing, N.Y., 1966-70, Colo. Women's Coll., Denver, 1970-76, emeritus, 1976-81. Mem. adv. council higher edn. N.Y. State Dept. Edn. and Bd. Regents, 1965-69; pres. Asso. Colls. of Colo., 1972-73, vol. dir., from 1976; adv. com. Colo. Commn. Higher Edn., from 1972. Chmn. community appeal N. Shore (L.I.) chpt. A.R.C., 1966-67. Bd. dirs. Queens chpts. Nat. Conf. Christians and Jews, 1963-70, Rocky Mountain region, 1970; chmn. bd. dirs. LaFarge Inst., N.Y.C., 1964; bd. dirs. Denver Execs. Club, 1973, Assoc. Seminaries of Colo., 1976; trustee Buckley Country Day Sch., Roslyn, N.Y., 1968-70. Served to capt. AUS, 1942-46; ETO. Mem. N.Y. Historical Soc., English Speaking Union, N.Y. Acad. Scis., Alpha Beta Kappa. Clubs: Denver, Cherry Hills Country, Rotary (Denver). Contbr. books, jours. Home: Denver, Colo. Died Dec. 31, 1981.

KENNY, JAMES DONALD, lawyer; b. San Francisco, Aug. 20, 1938; s. James B. and Claire (McDonald) K.; B.A., U. Santa Clara, 1960; J.D., U. San Francisco, 1965; m. Christine Carlson, Feb. 1, 1964; children—James Francis, John Joseph, Jeffrey Richard, Joseph Michael. Traffic rep. States Marine Lines, Inc., San Francisco, 1960-65, legal counsel, N.Y.C., 1965-67; admitted to Calif. bar, 1966; practice in San Francisco, 1967-81; resident ptnr. Galland, Kharasch, Calkins & Lippmann, 1967-69; asso. Loughran, Berol & Hagerty, 1969-70; corporate sec., legal counsel Am. Pres. Lines, Oakland, Calif., 1970-78, legal counsel, 1970-72, v.p. legal, 1972-74, v.p. adminstrn., 1974-77, v.p., gen. counsel, 1974-78; ptnr. firm Meadows, Finan, Kenny & Dorris, 1978-79; ptnr. firm Kenny & Finan, 1979-81. Bd. dirs. San Francisco Better Bus. Bur., 1971-76; trustee Redwood City Publ. Library, 1979-81. Served with Transp. Corps, AUS, 1960-61. Mem. Am. Inst. Mcht. Shipping (mem. legal com.), Maritime Law Assn. U.S., Maritime Aminstrv. Bar Assn., Am. Steamship Owners Protection and Indemnity Assn. (dir. 1974-78), Am., San Francisco bar assns., State Bar Calif. Clubs: Olympic, World Trade (San Francisco). Home: Redwood City, Calif. Dec. Apr. 14, 1981.

KENT, CARLETON VELNEY, JR., newspaperman; b. Northfield, Minn., June 13, 1909; s. Carleton Volney and Cecilia (Loizeaux) K.; A.B., U. of Kansas, 1932; m. Janet Hurd, Oct. 19, 1935; 1 son, Carleton Hurd. Newspaper reporter Lawrence (Kan.) Daily Journal-World, Daily Oklahoman, Okla. City, Kansas City Times, Okla. City Times; with Chicago Times (now Sun-Times) since 1939; war corr., Pacific and European theaters, 1942-4, Washington corr. since 1945. Mem. White House Corrs. Association (pres. 1950-51). Clubs: National Press, Overseas Writers (Washington D.C.); Gridiron; Burning Tree (Bethesda, Md.). Home: Cork, Ireland. Died Jan. 24, 1985.

KENT, EVERETT, ex-congressman; b. East Bangor, Pa., Nov. 15, 1888; s. Charles V. and Mary A. (Barnet) K.; grad. high sch., 1906; LL.B., U. of Pa., 1911; m. Daisy Allen Speer, of Bangor, Nov. 22, 1911; children—Sarah Elizabeth, Mary Louise, James Everett. Admitted to Pa. Bar, 1911, and began practice at Bangor; solicitor to Northampton County Prison Inspectors, 1912-16; county solicitor Northampton County, 1920-24; mem, 68th and 70th Congresses (1923-25 and 1927-29), 30th Pa. Dist. Democrat. Home: Bangor, Pa. †

KENYON, THEODORE STANWOOD, patent lawyer; b. N.Y. City, Jan. 17, 1890; s. William Houston and Maria Wellington (Stanwood) K.; A.B. cum laude Harvard, 1911; LL.B., Columbia, 1914 (editor Columbia Law Review 1912-14); m. Martha Tipton, July 2, 1919 (dec. 1935); children—Stanwood, Madge (Mrs. John W. Fisher), Edward Tipton; m. 2d, Helen Ward (dec. 1963); m. 3d, Sarah Whitney, 1969. Asso. Kenyon & Kenyon, N.Y.C., 1914-19, mem. 1919. Mem. Common Council, Summit, 1928-31. Pres. Overlook Hosp., 1951; trustee Kent Pl. Sch. for Girls, Summit, 1928-43, Pingry Sch., for Boys (Elizabeth, N.J.), 1935-48; adv. council Patent Trademarke and Copyright Foundation of George Washington U., 1950-62. Served with N.Y.N.G., 1912-17; capt. 306th inf. 77th Div., U.S. Army, 1918-19. Decorated D.S.C. (U.S.); Legion of Honor, Croix de Guerre (France). Mem. N.Y. Patent Law Assn. (pres. 1940-41), Am. Bar Assn., Am. Patent Law Assn. Clubs: Baltusrol Country, Monday Night (Summit, N.J.); Harvard of N.Y. Home: Short Hills, N.J. †

KEOSIAN, JOHN, educator, scientist; b. Armenia, Mar. 28, 1906; s. Hagop and Paris (Boyajian) K.; came to U.S., 1912, naturalized, 1932; B.S., N.Y. U., 1927, Ph.D., 1936; m. Jessie S. Levey, Nov. 4, 1933 (div. 1974); 1 dau., Julie. Asst. instr. N.Y. U., 1927-33; instr. U. Newark, 1933-37, asst. prof., 1937-42, asso. prof., 1942-46; asso. prof. Rutgers U., 1946-47, prof. biology, 1947-71, prof. emeritus, 1971-81, chmn. dept., 1952-57, dir. div. natural scis., 1957-64. Mem. Corp. Marine Biol. Lab., Woods Hole, Mass. Fulbright fellow to U.S. Ednl. Found. in Greece and Democritos Nuclear Research Center, Athens, 1969-71. Fellow N.Y. Acad. Sci.; mem. Internat. Soc. for Study of Origin of Life, Am. Astron. Soc. (div. planetary sci.). Author: The Origin of Life. Contbr. articles on cell physiology, biochem. genetics, origin of life to sci. jours. Home: Woods Hole, Mass. Died Nov. 26, 1981.

KEOWN, WILLIAM HAMILTON, educator; b. Madison, Wis., Dec. 24, 1914; s. Robert McArdle and Frances (Burnham) K.; B.A., U. Wis., 1936, M.B.A., 1947, Ph.D., 1954; m. Elizabeth Belle Seward, July 7, 1943; children—Allan Hamilton, David Wortham. Asst. exec. Four Lakes council Boy Scouts Am., Madison, Wis., 1936-38, exec. State Line council, Beloit, 1938-41; instr. commerce U. Wis., 1947-48; dir. indsl. relations Ry. Co., Louisville, 1948-49; mem. faculty U. Okla., Norman, from 1949, asst. prof., then asso. prof., 1949-56, David Ross Boyd prof. bus. mgmt., from 1958, chmn. dept. bus. mgmt., 1953-59. Served from pvt. to capt., AUS, 1941-46. Mem. Acad. Mgmt., Am. Econ. Assn., Indsl. Relations Research Assn., Am. Assn. U. Profs., Am. Acad. Polit. and Social Sci., Southwestern Mgmt. Assn. Episcopalian. Home: Norman, Okla. Died July 23, 1981; interred St. John's Episcopal Ch. Columbarium, Norman, Okla.

KERCHEVAL, ROYAL DICKSON, banker; b. St. Louis, Feb. 19, 1890; s. Robert and Louisa (Pettibone) K.; student U. Mo., 1909-12, Army and Navy Acad., 1912-13; m. Jane Shapleigh, Nov. 29, 1921. Sec. Kauffman Smith & Co., 1917-29; v.p. Boatmen's Nat. Bank, St. Louis, 1929-38, trust officer, 1938-53, dir., from 1947, sr. vice pres., 1954-57, vice chmn., 1958-60; v.p., dir. Washington Land & Mining Co., from 1941, Columbia Hotel Co.; dir. Southwestern Public Service Co., Missouri Utilities Co. Pres. St. Louis Children's Hosp., 1951-57, trustee, from 1958; dir. St. Louis Provident Assn., St. Louis Children's Aid Soc. Mem. Phi Gamma Delta. Clubs: St. Louis Country, Noonday, Missouri Athletic. Home: St. Louis, Mo. †

KERN, RICHARD ARMINIUS, physician; b. Columbia, Pa., Feb. 20, 1891; s. George and Wilhelmine (Maurer) K.; m. Donna A. Couch, Aug. 19, 1927 (div. dec. 1969); children—Richard Bradford, Donna Natalie; m. Ellen J. Hawkins, Oct. 22, 1976. A.B., U. Pa., 1910, M.D., 1914; LL.D., Lebanon Valley Coll., 1947; Sc. D., Franklin and Marshall Coll., 1947, Temple U., 1958, Bucknell U., 1959. Interne and sr. med. resident Univ. Hosp., 1914-17; instr. in medicine U. Pa., 1919-23, asso, 1923-28, asst. prof., 1928-34, prof. clin. medicine, 1934-46, Louis A. Godey fellow in medicine, 1927-31; prof. clin. medicine Grad. Sch. Medicine, U. Pa., 1934; vis. physician Grad. Sch. Medicine, U. Pa. (Hosp. of U. Pa.); also chief med. outpatient dept. and allergy sect.; prof. medicine, head dept. medicine Temple U. Sch. Medicine and Hosp., 1946-56, prof. emeritus, 1956-82; Vice res. Bd. of Health, Lower Merion Twp., 1934-54, pres., 1955-58; v.p. Phila. Bd. Health, 1960-61. Asso. editor: Am. Jour. Med. Scis, 1925-50; editor, 1951-67; Contbr. numerous articles to med. jours. Trustee Temple U., 1958-76; Grand Master of Masons in Pa., 1946-47; active mem. Supreme Council (33). Served as lt. M.C. U.S. Navy, World War I; capt. M.C. USNR; organizer N.R. Specialist Unit at U. Pa. on active duty 1942-44, South Pacific; U.S.S. Solace and Halsey Staff chief of medicine and rehab. officer Naval Hosp. 1944-46, Phila.; rank rear adm. 1952; ret. 1955;

med. officer in command, vol. Res. Div. 4-3. Chief div. gen. medicine VA 1946-47; cons. Surgeon Gen. Army 1947-82; mem. Armed Forces Epidemiology Bd. 1956-68; mem. Naval Research adv. com. 1957-69; cons. Surgeon Gen. Navy 1949-68; cons. Armed Forces Inst. Pathology 1962; mem. def. sci. bd. Dept. of Def. 1956-64; mem. nat. health resources adv. com. Office Emergency Preparedness mem. nat. adv. com. to SSS 1969-73; dir., trustee Research Found. Nat. Assn. Mental Health 1962; Chmn. com. naval med. research, Div. Med. Scis., NRC 1951-69. Master A.C.P. (sec. gen. 1951-55, pres. 1957-58, regent 1958-61); mem. Internat. Soc. Internal Medicine (pres. 1970-73), Pa. Med. Soc. (pres. 1964-65), AMA (chmn. sect. mil. medicine 1952-53), Soc. U.S. Med. Cons. (pres. 1954), Am. Assn. Advancement Sci., Assn. Am. Physicians, Soc. for Clin. Investigation, Am. Clin. and Climatol. Assn., Assn. Study of Allergy (ex-pres.), Soc. Study of Asthma and Allied Conditions (ex-pres.), Assn. Mil. Surgeons (pres. 1960), Phila. Medico-Legal Inst., Coll. Physicians Phila. (pres. 1952), Am. Acad. Allergy, Sigma Xi, Alpha Omega Alpha, Phi Chi, Phi Gamma Delta. Republican. Mem. United Ch. of Christ. Clubs: Union League (Phila.); Philadelphia Country (Bala-Cynwyd, Pa.); Army and Navy (Washington). Home: Wynnewood, Pa. Died July 26, 1982.

KERR, FLORENCE STEWART, government official; b. Harrimen, Tenn., June 30, 1890; d. Thomas James and Ruby (Ingersoll) Stewart; A.B., Grinnell (Ia.) Coll., 1912; LL.D., Grinnell (Ia.) College, 1943; m. Robert Young Kerr, September 1, 1915; 1 child, Elisabeth (dec.). Prin. Gladbrook (Ia.) High Sch., 1912-13; teacher of English and history Marshalltown (Ia.) High Sch., 1913-15; with Gulf Div. of Am. Red Cross, 1917-18; instr. English composition and lit., Grinnell Coll., 1921-26, 1931-32; regional dir. women's and professional div., Works Progress Adminstrn., Chicago, 1935-38; became asst. commr. Works Projects Adminstrn., Washington, D.C., 1939; asst. to adminstr. Fed. Works Agency, Washington, from 1942. Dir., Women's Dept., Traffic Promotion and Public Relations, Northwest Airlines, Inc., St. Paul, Minn., Jan. 1, 1945. Mem. Am. Assn. Univ. Women, League of Women Voters, P.E.O., Theta Sigma Phi, Phi Beta Kappa. Democrat. Conglist. Clubs: Business and Professional Women's Nat. Democratic Woman's Club of Washington, D.C., Am. Newspaper Women's Club, Women's City Club of St. Paul. Home: Saint Paul, Minn. †

KERR, JOHN FAY, educator, poet; b. Monette, Ark., May 28, 1930; s. Felix Washington and Mary Florence (Fay) K.; B.A., Ark. State U., 1953; M.A., U. Mich., 1956; postgrad., U. Iowa, 1956, U. Mo., Columbia, 1957-58; Ph.D., U. Tex., Austin, 1965. Tchr. speech and journalism Kennett (Mo.) High Sch., 1954-55; asst. prof. Am. lit. and fiction writing Westminster Coll., Fulton, Mo., 1956-57; instr. English U. Mo., Columbia, 1957-58, U. Tex., Austin, 1958-63; asst. prof. Am. lit. and fiction writing La. State U., Baton Rouge, 1965-67; asst. prof. English Calif. Poly. State U., San Luis Obispo, 1967-69, assoc. prof., 1969-74, prof., 1974-84, dir. grad. studies English, 1973-76; lectr., reader poetry, Calif. Author: Hemingway's Use of Physical Setting and Stage Props in His Novels: A Study in Craftsmanship, 1965; assoc. editor: Calif. State Poetry Quar, 1977-80; contbr. poetry to mags. and anthologies. Served with USMC, 1946-49. Recipient excellence in teaching award U. Tex., Austin, 1961, award for humorous poetry Calif. Fedn. Chaparral Poets. Mem. Calif. State Poetry Soc. (pres. 1975). Democrat. Home: Grover City, Calif. Died Aug. 28, 1984.

KERR, MALCOLM HOOPER, educator, political scientist; b. Beirut, Lebanon, Oct. 8, 1931; s. Stanley E. and Elsa (Reckman) K.; m. Ann C. Zwicker, Aug. 18, 1956; children—Susan Elizabeth, John Malcolm, Stephen Douglas, Andrew Stanley. A.B., Princeton, 1953; M.A., Am. U. Beirut, 1955; Ph.D., Johns Hopkins, 1958. Asst. prof. Am. U. Beirut, 1958-61; faculty UCLA, 1961-84, prof. polit. sci., 1967-84, chmn. dept., 1967-70, dean div. social scis., 1973-76; dir. U. Calif. at Los Angeles (Von Grunebaum Center for Near Eastern Studies), 1976-79; vis. prof. Am. U. Beirut, 1965-66, pres. until 1984. Author: Lebanon in the Last Years of Feudalism, 1840-1868, 1959, Islamic Reform, 1965, The Arab Cold War, 3d edit, 1971, (with others) The Economics and Politics of the Middle East, 1975; Editor: (with others) The Elusive Peace in the Middle East, 1975. Bd. dirs. Am. Friends of Middle East, 1969-84. Rockefeller fellow St. Antony's Coll., Oxford U., Eng., 1961-62; fellow Am. Research Center Egypt, 1964-65. Mem. Am. Polit. Sci. Assn., Middle East Studies Assn. (v.p. 1968-69, pres. 1971-72). Home: Pacific Palisades, Calif. Died Jan. 18, 1984; interred Beirut and Calif.

KERR, THOMAS, flour milling executive; b. Portland, Oreg., May 1, 1910; s. Thomas and Mabel (Macleay) K.; B.A., Yale U., 1932; m. Barbare Pooley Labbe, Jan. 26, 1948 (div. 1970); children—Edmund Randolph Labbe, Josephine Kerr Warren, Thomas. Various positions Kerr Gifford & Co., Inc., Portland, 1932-42, pres., 1949-55; chmn. Kerr Grain Corp., Portland, 1955-74; pres., now chmn. Hawaiian Flour Mills, Inc., Honolulu, 1964-82; chmn. bd. Kerr Pacific Corp., 1942-; pres. Kerr Land & Livestock Co., 1967-82, Port San Francisco Grain Terminal, Inc., 1957-67; partner Plateau Farms, 1948-82, Santosh Farms; pres. Smith-Murphy & Co., N.Y.C., 1949-55; dir. Fidelity Savs. & Loan Assn., San Francisco, Fidelity Financial Corp., San Francisco; past pres., dir. Portland Grain Exchange, Pacific Flour Millers Assn., Pacific N.W. Grain Terminal Assn., Pacific N.W. Grain Exporters Assn., N.Am. Export Grain Assn., Nat. Grain Trade Council; mem. White House Conf. Export Expansion, 1963-64; dir. Portland Met. Futures, Unlimited, 1963-82; mem. nat. council U.S.-China Trade. Chmn., Oreg. State Radio Free Europe and Crusade for Freedom, 1955; mem. Osaka Trade Conf., 1959; mem. Gov.'s Indsl. Devel. Mission, 1963. Trustee Reed Coll., 1952-82, Thacher Sch., 1948-66; bd. dirs. U.S. Olympic Equestrian Team, also chmn. Zone IX; bd. dirs. Oreg. Symphony Assn., Portland Opera Assn., Pacific N.W. Ballet Assn., Oreg. Roadside Council, Pacific Study Center; bd. dirs. Japanese Garden Soc., pres. 1975-77; bd. dirs. Portland Art Mus., pres., 1975-76; bd. dirs. Oreg. Museum Sci. and Industry, pres., 1952-54; nat. bd. dirs. NCCJ; bd. dirs. Nat. Council on Alcoholism, Good Samaritan Hosp. Found. Served as maj. AUS, 1942-45; PTO. Decorated Bronze Star. Mem. Portland (dir.), British-Am. (dir., v.p.) chambers commerce, Portland Freight Traffic Assn. (dir. 1948-82, chmn. 1954-56), Pacific Internat. Livestock Assn. (dir., pres. 1959-63, chmn. 1964-82), Oreg. Japan Soc. (pres. 1952-54, dir.), Yale Alumni Assn. Oreg. (pres. 1938-39), Order St. John, Japanese Garden Soc. Oreg. (pres. 1975-77), Zeta Psi. Clubs: Merchants Exchange (Portland and San Francisco); Rotary, Arlington, University, Multnomah Athletic, Waverly Country, Racquet, Portland Shipping (Portland); Pacific-Union, Burlingame Country (San Francisco); Rainier (Seattle); Vancouver, Capilano Golf and Country (Vancouver, B.C., Can.); Outrigger Canoe (Honolulu). Home: Portland, Ore. Died May 13, 1982.

KERR, WILLIAM JOHN, physician, prof. of medicine; b. Blencoe, Ia., Apr. 30, 1889; s. Burdette and Sarah Ellen (Daywalt) K.; B.S., U. Cal., 1912, LL.D., 1956; Master in Medicine, Am. Coll. Physicians, 1955; M.D., Harvard, 1915; m. Dorothy Campbell Fish, June 19, 1917; children—William John, Marjorie Simpson, Dorothy Campbell, Farnum Woodward. Interne Mass. Gen. Hosp., Boston, 1915-16; traveling fellow in medical research, Harvard, 1916-17 (working with Dr. George H. Whipple, Hooper Foundation for Med. Research, U. of Calif. Med. Sch.); with U. of Calif. Med. Sch., 1916-52, successively instr. in medicine, asst. prof., asso. prof. to 1927, prof. of medicine 1927-52, chairman of the division of medicine 1932-52; physician in chief U. of Calif. Hosp., 1925-52, retired 1952; cons. several govt. agencies 1927-52. Mem. com. med., Nat. Research Council, from 1947. Served successively as contract surg., 1st lt. Med. Corps, U.S. Army, capt. and maj., 1917-19; chief med. service, Base Hosp., Camp Lewis, Wash. Fellow Am. Coll. Physicians (pres. 1938-39); mem. A.M.A., other nat., state and local, gen. and specialized profl. orgns. Republican. Conglist. Mason (32 deg., Shriner). Clubs: William Watt Kerr, Bohemian (San Francisco). Contbr. of sects. to several med. books, also to med. jours. Home: Humboldt County, Cal. †

KERSHNER, RICHARD BRANDON, laboratory administrator; b. Cresline, O., Oct. 11, 1913; s. James Alexander and Eva Della (Shoemaker) K.; Ph.D. in Math., Johns Hopkins, 1937; m. Mary Amanda Brown, June 8, 1935; children—Richard Brandon, James Williamson. Instr. math. U. Wis., 1937-40; asst. prof. math. Johns Hopkins, 1940-42; with Geophys. Lab., Carnegie Instn., Washington, 1942-44, Allegany Ballistics Lab., Cumberland, Md., 1944-46; with Applied Physics Lab., Johns Hopkins U., Silver Spring, Md., 1946-78, head space devel. dept. 1958-78, asst. dir., 1972-78. Recipient Presdl. certificate of award, 1948; Norman P. Hayes Award citation Inst. Nav., 1969; Distinguished Pub. Service awards Navy Dept., 1958, 61, 67. Fellow Am. Inst. Aeros. and Astronautics; mem. A.A.A.S., Philos. Soc. Washington, Phi Beta Kappa, Sigma Xi. Author: The Anatomy of Mathematics, 1950. Inventor jet control by rotatable off-set nozzle; radar antenna positioning device. Home: Bryan's Road, Md. Died Feb. 15, 1982.

KERWIN, CHARLES CORNELIUS, investment company executive; b. Chgo., Feb. 5, 1892; s. Michael William and Catherine Camilla (Quinlan) K.; m. Mary Allen Gray, Sept. 4, 1926; children: Mary Catherine (Mrs. George J. Murphy, Jr.), Elizabeth Anne (Mrs. Oren Taft Pollock), Margaret Agnes (Mrs. William A. Crane). Student pvt., pub. schs.; LL.D. (hon.), U. Chgo., 1960, Loyola U., Chgo. Real estate sales Ballard, Rowe & Whitman, 1915-18; salesman Halsey, Stuart & Co., Inc. (name changed to Prudential-Bache Securities Inc.), 1919-26, 30-66, v.p., 1966-68, sr. v.p., 1968-76, hon. sr. v.p., 1976-84; pres. Kerwin & Co., 1929-30, Interstate Comml. Corp., 1942-84, Western Comml. Co. of Del., 1926-84; v.p. Locust Street Co., 1927-52, pres., 1952-84. Bd. dirs. Community Fund of Chgo., 1934-45, exec. com., 1939-45, v.p., 1941-45, dir., v.p., exec. com. war fund, 1945-46; treas. Cath. Ch. Extension Soc. U.S., 1926-64, v.p., 1944-64; pres. Cath. Charities, Archidiocese Chgo., 1939-44, dir., mem. exec. com.; Chmn. bd. lay trustees Loyola U., Chgo., 1960-66, mem. bd. lay trustees, 1948-84; treas. St. Vincent's Crib Soc., 1948-72; governing life mem. Art Inst. Chgo.; governing mem. John G. Shedd Aquarium, Orchestral Assn., Chgo. Served with Ordnance Dept. U.S. Army, 1918. Decorated knight comdr. Order of Pius IX, Pro Eclesia et Pontifice (Pope Pius XI), knight comdr. Order of Pius IX (Pope Pius XII); recipient Damen award Loyola U., 1968. Clubs: Chicago (Chgo.), Chicago Athletic (Chgo.), Attic (Chgo.); Onwentsia (Lake Forest, Ill.), Old Elm (Lake Forest, Ill.). Home: Lake Forest, Ill. Died Mar. 19, 1984.

KESSLER, JEAN BAPTISTE AUGUST, oil executive; b. The Hague, Holland, June 16, 1888; s. J. B. Aug. and M. (de Lange) Kessler; ed. High School at The Hague electro tech. engr., Coll. at Delft, Holland; m. Anna Stoop, July 13, 1911; children—5 dau., 1 son; married 2d, Thalia de Kempanaer, July 8, 1948. Employee of Royal Dutch Shell Subsidiaries in Russia, 1912-15. With Bataafsche Petroleum Maatschappij, The Hague, 1916-19. With Astra Romana in Bucharest, 1919. Mng. Dir. Royal Dutch Petroleum Co., 1924-47; dir. gen., 1947-49, chmn. bd., 1949-61; mng. dir. Royal Dutch Shell Subsidiaries, 1924-48; dir. Shell Transport & Trading Co., 1929-61. Home: Tucker's Town, Bermuda. †

KETCHAM, HOWARD, color engr.; b. N.Y.C., Sept. 4, 1902; s. Charles Belden and Suzanne (Brightson) K.; m. Lois R. Barrett (div. 1942); m. Mary L. Sauerbrun, Mar. 14, 1944 (dec. 1965); children—Suzanne Ketcham Rose, Marsha K. Bozarth, Mary K. de Lambea; m. Elisabeth T. Gardner, Dec. 1968. A.B., M.Sc., Amherst Coll., 1925; student, N.Y. Sch. Design, 1926-27, Columbia, 1939-40. Art dir. H. K. McCann Co. (advt.), 1925-27; dir. color adv. service E. I. duPont de Nemours, 1927-34; originated profession color-engring., 1935; chmn. Howard Ketcham, Inc., 1935-70; color cons. House & Garden mag. (developing color palette annually for use by mfrs. of house furnishings); cons. U.S. Steel Homes Inc., Goodrich Rubber Co.; Mobil Oil Co., Kroger Co., Pan Am, United Airlines, Am. Airlines, Inc., Walgreen Drug Co., Am. Cyanamid, Scripto, Inc., Grand Union Co., R.J. Reynolds Tobacco Co., S.S. Kresge, Borden Co., Nat. Homes, McCrory Stores, Masonite Corp., Pitts. Plate Glass Co., Coca-Cola Co., Asbestos & Vinyl Asbestos Tile Inst.; Lectr. Harvard, Ohio State, Northwestern U., San Francisco State U., U. Minn. Profiled in: New Yorker Mag, 1952; Author: Automobile Color Index, 1929-34, How to Use Color and Design in the Home, 1949 (Book of Month Club selection), Color-Its Theory and Application, 1952, Paint It Yourself, 1954, Color Planning for Business and Industry, 1958, also articles in periodicals.; Cons. and/or editor: Newsweek mags; works include: color-styled coaches for r.r.'s, supermarket chains, chains of gasoline stas.; interior and exterior styling jet airplanes; developed color styling for, Volvo, Volkswagen and all U.S. automobile mfrs., grading color lines for paints, plastics, fabrics; for USAF developed optimum lighting for all mil. aircraft; color-coordinator, Am. Enka Corp. Served as comdr. Sec. Navy's Office Research and Inventions, World War II. Recipient Gold medal Phila. Pub. Ledger exhibit, Wolf award for package design ingenuity; design awards Kidskin Guild; design awards Art Dirs. League; design awards and others; 1000 prize for Color Schemers in Readers Digest, 1936. Mem. Nat. Paint, Varnish and Lacquer Assn. (chmn. com. color surveys), Nat. Retail Dry Goods Assn., Illuminating Engring. Soc., Soc. Automotive Engrs., Soc. War 1812, Vet. Corps Arty., Soc. Am. Wars, Am. Indsl. Designers (dir.), Intersoc. Color Council, Am. Arbitration Assn., Am. Numis. Assn., Chi Psi. Republican. Episcopalian. Clubs: Univ. (N.Y.C.), Archtl. League (N.Y.C.); Interallié 0 (Paris); Huntington (N.Y.) Country; Beach (Palm Beach, Fla.), Four Arts Soc. (Palm Beach, Fla.). Pioneer in transmission of colors from Europe to Am. by wireless, Aug. 5, 1936; developed telephone colors for Bell Telephone Labs. Instigator of pioneer nationwide consumer surveys to predetermine color, texture and design preferences for manufactured articles. Colorstyled, created lighting for or designed more than 500 products, establishments and packages for Am. bus. Home: West Palm Beach, Fla. Died May 4, 1982.

KETCHUM, CARLTON GRISWOLD, retired public relations executive; b. Yankton, S.D., Feb. 17, 1892; s. Lester and Luna L. (Beard) K.; m. Mildred Caroline Storey, Oct. 8, 1914; 1 son, David Storey. Student, Oberlin Coll., 1910-11; B.S. in Econs, U. Pitts., 1916. Various positions, 1900-12; asst. to dir. univ. extension U. Pitts., 1912-14, asst. registrar, 1914-16, publicity, asso. campaign dir., campaign dir., 1916-19; pres., dir. Ketchum, Inc. (campaign direction, pub. relations), Pitts., 1919-66, chmn., 1966-78. Bd. dirs. YMCA; v.p., bd. dirs. Assn. for Improvement the Poor; v.p. 100,000 Pennsylvanians.; Finance dir. Republican Nat. Com., 1937-41, 49-57; mem. Rep. finance coms. Served from pvt. to 2d lt. U.S. Army, 1917-19; Served to 2d col. USAAF, 1942-45. Mem. Am. Legion (past comdr.), Western Pa. Hist. Soc. (exec. com. 1971-84, v.p., dir.), Omicron Delta Kappa. Presbyterian (nat. exec. com. Presbyn. Lay Com.). Clubs: Duquesne (Pitts.), Univ. (Pitts.); Masons. Home: Pittsburgh, Pa. Died July 24, 1984.

KEYES, GEORGE THURMAN, b. Sheyboygan, Wis., Dec. 17, 1889; s. Charles Henry and Nellie (Brown) K.; student Trinity Coll., Conn., 1907-10; B.S., Columbia, 1911; student Training Sch. for Pub. Service, New York Bur. Municipal Research, 1911-12; m. Phebe Hoffman, May 29, 1915. With Nat. Civ. Service Reform League from Jan. 1912, sec. from Oct. 1914; formerly editor Good Government (official publ. of the league). Mem. City Managers' Assn., Honest Ballot Assn., Civic Secretaries Assn., Alpha Delta Phi. Democrat. Clubs: City (New York), Ft. Orange (Albany), Nat. Press (Washington D.C.) Home: New York, N.Y. †

KEYS, DAVID ARNOLD, physicist; b. Toronto, Ont. Can., Nov. 4, 1890; s. David Reid and Erskine (McLean)

K.; student Upper Can. Coll., U. Munich, Germany, 1910-11; B.A., U. Toronto, 1915, M.A., 1916; Ph.D., Harvard, travelling fellow, 1920-21; Ph.D., Cambridge U., 1922; D.Sc. (hon.), McMaster U., Hamilton, Ont., 1947, McGill U., 1947, Toronto U., 1953, Ottawa U., 1957; hononary fellow, Trinity College, 1958; LL.D., Mount Allison University, 1958; L.H.D., Lawrence Inst. of Tech., 1959; married May Irene Freeze, 1921; one son, John David. Asst. physicist, later physicist antisubmarine div. Brit. Admiralty, 1918-19; teaching fellow Harvard, 1919; asst. prof. McGill U., 1922-26, asso. prof., 1926-29, professor, 1929-41, Macdonald prof. physics, 1941-47, dir. R.A.F. radio course, 1941-43, Army course, 1943-44; physicist U.S. Bur. Mines, 1927-28; cons. physicist Geol. Survey Can., 1929, geophysicist, 1929-30; mem. council Nat. Research Council Can., Ottawa, 1945, v.p. (sci.), 1947-55 in charge Atomic Energy project, Chalk River, Ont.; chmn. project coordinating com. Atomic Energy of Can. Ltd., 1952-53; sci. adviser to the pres., 1953-66, AECL Overseas rep., London, 1960-61. Canadian rep. on NATO Science Com., 1961-63. Recipient gold medal Canadian Assn. Physicists, 1964. Fellow Royal Soc. Can., Am. Phys. Soc., Chem. Inst. Can. (hon.), A.A.A.S.; mem. Engring. Inst. Can. (hon.). Author: Applied Geophysics (with A.S. Eve), 1929, rev. edit. 1954; Heat, Light and Sound, 1934; College Physics (with R. M. Sutton), 1944, rev. edit. 1955. Home: Deep River, Ont., Can. †

KHAN, FAZLUR RAHMAN, structural engr.; b. Dacca, Bangladesh, Apr. 3, 1929; came to U.S., 1952, naturalized, 1967; s. Abdur Rahman and Khadija (Khanum) K.; m. Liselotte A. Turba, Aug. 3, 1959; 1 dau., Yasmin Sabina. B.S., U. Dacca, 1950; B.S. Structural Engr, U. Ill., 1952, M.S. in Structural Engring, 1952, M.S. in Theoretical and Applied Mechanics, 1955, Ph.D., 1955; Sc.D. (hon.), Northwestern U., 1973; D.Tech. Scis. (hon.), ETH, Zurich, 1980; D.Engring. (hon.), Lehigh U., 1980. Lectr. U. Dacca, 1950-52; Fulbright scholar, 1952-53; project engr. Skidmore, Owings & Merrill, Chgo., 1955-57, sr. project engr., 1960-65, asso. partner, 1966-70, gen. partner, 1970-82; exec. engr. Karachi Devel. Authority, Pakistan, 1958-60; adj. prof. architecture Ill. Inst. Tech., 1966-82; mem. Chgo. Com. High Rise Bldgs., 1970; chmn. Internat. Council on Tall Bldgs. and Urban Habitat. Designer: structural system for 100-story John Hancock Center, Chgo., 110-story Sears Hdqrs. Bldg, Chgo., 52-story Shell Plaza Bldg, Houston; tent roof for Haj Terminal, King Abdul Aziz Internat. Airport, Saudi Arabia. Named among Constrn. Men of Year Engring. News Record, 1966, 69, 71, 80, Man of Year, Chicagoan of Year in Architecture and Engring., 1970, Man of Year Engring. News-Record, 1972; recipient Oscar Faber medal Instn. Structural Engrs., London, 1973; Alumni award U. Ill., 1972. Mem. Am. Inst. Steel Constrn. (J. Lloyd Kimbrough medal 1973), Nat. Acad. Engring., Am. Concrete Inst. (Alfred E. Lindau award 1973), Am. Welding Soc., Reinforced Concrete Research Council, ASCE (Middlebrooks award 1972, Ernest E. Howard award 1977, named Chgo. C.E. of Year 1972). Home: Chicago, Ill. Died Mar. 27, 1982.

KIBBEE, ROBERT JOSEPH, univ. chancellor; b. N.Y.C., Aug. 19, 1921; s. Guy B. and Helen (Shay) K.; m. Margaret Tracey Rockwitz, May 15, 1980; children—Robert Joseph, Katherine, Douglas Alan. A.B., Fordham U., 1943; M.A., U. Chgo., 1947, Ph.D., 1957; LL.D., Poly. Inst. Bklyn., 1972. Asst. dir. survey State Controlled Higher Edn. in Ark., Little Rock, 1949-50; asst. dean, dir. sr. coll. So. State Coll., Magnolia, Ark., 1950-52, dean coll., 1952-55; dean students Drake U., Des Moines, 1955-58; ednl. adviser Govt. Pakistan, Karachi; also assoc. prof. U. Chgo., 1958-61; asst. to pres. for planning Carnegie-Mellon U., Pitts., 1961-65, v.p. planning, 1965-68, v.p. adminstrn. and planning, 1968-71; chancellor City U. N.Y., N.Y.C., 1971-82. Trustee N.Y. State Higher Edn. Services Corp.; trustee Inst. Internat. Edn., N.Y. Interface Devel. Projects, Inc.; exec. com. trustees Assn. Colls. and Univs. N.Y.; v.p. Com. on Urban Program Univs.; Bd. dirs. Mt. Sinai Med. Center, Mt. Sinai Hosp., Mt. Sinai Sch. Medicine, Urban Acad. for Mgmt., Inc.; hon. adviser to nat. adv. bd. Exec. High Sch. Internships Am. Mem. Nat. Assn. State Univs. and Land Grant Colls. (exec. com. div. urban affairs and com. on fed. legis.), Am. Assn. State Colls. and Univs. (com. fed. relations). Home: New York, N.Y. Died June 16, 1982.

KIBRE, PEARL, educator, historian; b. Phila.; d. Kenneth and Jane (du Plone) K. Student, UCLA, 1920-22; A.B., U. Calif. at Berkeley, 1924, M.A., 1925; Ph.D., Columbia, 1936. Instr. history Pasadena (Calif.) Jr. Coll., 1925-28; research asst. Columbia, 1929-37; instr. history Bklyn., 1937-38; mem. faculty Hunter Coll., City U. N.Y., 1938-85, prof. history, 1957-71, prof. grad. sch., 1964-71, prof. emeritus, 1971-85; co-chmn. Columbia Seminar in History of Legal and Polit. Thought, 1972-74. Author: The Library of Pico della Mirandola, 1936, (with Lynn Thorndike) A Catalogue of Incipits of Mediaeval Scientific Writings in Latin, 1937, 2d edit., 1963, The Nations in the Mediaeval Universities, 1948, Scholarly Privileges in the Middle Ages, 1962 (Haskins gold medal 1964), Hippocrates Latinus: Repertorium of Hippocratic Writings in the Latin Middle Ages, 1975-82; Co-editor: Osiris, vol. XI, 1954; Contbr. to books, profl. jours. Research fellow N.Y. Acad. Medicine, Nyon, Switzerland, 1938-39; Guggenheim fellow, 1950-51. Fellow Medieval Acad. Am. (3d v.p. 1964-67, pres. of fellows 1975-78); mem. History Sci. Soc., AAUP, Medieval Club N.Y.C., Am. Hist. Assn., Renaissance Soc., Phi Beta Kappa; corr. mem. Acad. Internationale d'Histoire des Sciences. Home: New York, N.Y. Died July 17, 1985.

KIEB, ORMONDE ANTON, corp. exec.; b. Springfield, Mass., Aug. 17, 1901; s. August Anton and Harriet Augusta (Livingston) K.; m. Gladys Chandler, Nov. 14, 1928; 1 dau., Elizabeth Livingston (Mrs. Albert L. Diano). Student, Franklin and Marshall Coll., Lancaster, Pa., 1920-23. With real estate bus. E.J. Maier Corp., 1925-27; pres., sec. Kieb-Pasbjerg, Inc. and Kieb-Pasbjerg Agy., Inc., 1946-50; pres. The Kieb Co., Newark, from 1933; dir. Clinton Title & Mortgage Guaranty Co., 1945-48; asst. postmaster gen., 1953-59; pres. First Marketing Corp., from 1959, Kieb, Turnbull & Jewett Corp., Princeton, N.J., from 1967; pres. Property Mktg. Corp., from 1963, gen. mgr., from 1970, Homestead Enterprise, from 1970, Aladco, Inc., from 1970. Hon. mem. Planning Bd. Maplewood, N.J.; land use adv. com. N.J. Dept. Econ. Devel., 1945-48; mem. adv. com. on roadside improvement Hwy. Dept., 1944-47; mem. Gov.'s Com. on Housing, 1948; chmn. Commn. Efficiency and Economy in State Govt., 1964-68; Bd. dirs. Newark YMCA, 1950-54, v.p., 1951-53; v.p. Realtors Nat. Found. Inc., 1962, bd. dirs., 1962-68, pres., 1969; v.p. YM-YWCA Newark and vicinity, 1959-62; bd. dirs. South Monmouth Real Estate Bd.; mem. Newark adv. bd. Salvation Army. Recipient Disting. Service award by Govt.; Realtor Emeritus, 1979. Mem. Am. Soc. Real Estate Counselors, Inst. Real Estate Mgmt. (governing council 1943-55, pres. 1951, editorial bd. Jour. Property Management 1944-45), Nat. Assn. Real Estate Bds. (v.p. 1946-52, 60-61, 63-68), Nat. Inst. Land and Farm Brokers, Internat. Real Estate Fedn., Nat. Indsl. Realtors (charter), N.J. Shore, Nat. home builders assns., Phi Sigma Kappa. Episcopalian. Clubs: Mason, Rotarian, Manasquan River Golf, Downtown; Essex (Newark); Capitol Hill, Nat. Aviation (Washington) (Exec.). Home: Brielle, NJ.

KIEFER, JACK CARL, mathematician; b. Cin., Jan. 25, 1924; s. Carl J. and Marguerite (Rosenau) K.; B.S., M.S., Mass. Inst. Tech., 1948; Ph.D., Columbia, 1952; m. Dooley Sciple, Sept. 15, 1957; children-Sarah Elisabeth, Daniel Jonathan Baird. Instr. Cornell U., Ithaca, N.Y., 1951-52, asst. prof., 1952-55, assoc. prof., 1955-59, prof. math., from 1959; Horace White prof. math., 1973-79; prof. statistics U. Calif.-Berkeley, from 1979, Miller research prof., 1981-82; vis. prof. Oxford (Eng.) U., 1958-59; Guggenheim fellow Stanford, 1962-63. Vice Chmn. Tompkins County (N.Y.) Liberal Party, 1967—. Served to 1st lt. USAAF, 1943-46. Fellow Inst. Math. Statistics (Wald Meml. lectr. 1962, pres. 1969-70); mem. Nat. Acad. Scis., Am. Acad. Arts and Sci., Am. Math. Soc., Am. Statis. Assn., Mycol. Soc. Am., N.Am. Mycol. Assn. Author: (with others) Sequential Ranking Procedures, 1968. Asso. editor Zeitschrift Für Wahrscheinlichkeitstheorie. Contbr. articles on math. statistics and probability theory to profl. jours. Home: Ithaca, N.Y. Dec.

KIEKENAPP, ERNEST, optometrist; b. Faribault, Minn., May 13, 1889; s. Fredrick Henry and Mary (Kaiser) K.; student Minn. Business and Normal Coll., 1910; O.D., Stone Sch. of Optometry, 1913; post grad. student, O.D., De Mars Sch. of Optometry, 1914; m. Edna Kingsley, Oct. 17, 1917; dau., Audrey. Practice of optometry, Lake Benton, Minn., 1914, Faribault, 1920; elected sec. Am. Optometric Assn., 1922, assuming increased duties in Minneapolis, 1936. Appointed to Minn. State Bd. of Examiners in Optometry by Gov. Burnquist, 1919 (sec., 1919-36, pres. of bd., 1939-48). Fellow, Distinguished Service Foundn. of Optometry (dir.); mem. Am. Optometric Assn., Am. Optometric Found., Am. Acad. of Optometry, Internat. Assn. of State Bds. of Examiners in Optometry (dir.). Served in World War I, 1918-19. Awarded honorary O.D., D.O.S., No. Ill. Coll. of Optometry, 1949 Beta Sigma Kappa Gold Medal, distinguished service award Am. Optometric Assn. Mem. Beta Sigma Kappa, Phi Theta Upsilon, Am. Legion. Republican. Conglist. Club: Minneapolis Lions. Contbr. editorials on optometry, poetry anthologies. Home: South, Minneapolis. †

KIEKHOFER, BENJAMIN ALVIN, business exec.; b. Clintonville, Wis., Nov. 15, 1889; s. Gustavus F. and Christina (Gasser) K.; A.B., U. Wis., 1912; m. Elizabeth M. Turner, Dec. 30, 1915; 1 dau., Dorothy (Mrs. Allen P. Daniel). Acct. Wis. Bd. Pub. Affairs, 1912-15; sec., 1915-20; partner Elwell, Kiekhofer & Co., C.P.A.'s, 1919-39; sec. Union Refrigerator Transit Co. of Wis., 1921-29; with Gen. Am. Transp. Corp., from 1929, sec., 1951-61, sec. to exec. committee, from 1961. Member Wisconsin Soc. C.P.A.'s, American Institute of Accountants. Mason (32 deg.). Clubs: Kiwanis, University (Milw.); Attic (Chgo.). Home: Milwaukee, Wis. †

KIERAN, JOHN FRANCIS, writer; b. N.Y.C., Aug. 2, 1892; s. James Michael and Kate (Donohue) K.; student Coll. City N.Y.; B.S. cum laude, Fordham U., 1912; D.Sc., Clarkson Coll., 1941; M.A., Wesleyan U., 1942; m. Alma Boldtmann, May 14, 1919 (dec.); children—James Michael, John Francis, Beatrice; m. 2d, Margaret Ford, Sept. 5, 1947. With N.Y. Times sports dept., 1915-43; columnist on N.Y. Sun, 1943-44. Elector, Hall of Fame for Gt. Americans, N.Y.C., from 1945. Recipient John Burroughs medal, 1960. Author: Story of Olympic Games, 1936; Nature Notes, 1941; American Sporting Scene, 1941; Footnotes on Nature, 1947; Not Under Oath: Recollections and Reflections, 1964. Contbr. chpts. on sports to We Saw it Happen, 1938; America Now, 1938; Introduction to Nature, 1957; Natural History of New York City, 1959; contbr. articles to many mags., also articles on philology and natural history. Home: Rockport, Mass. Died Dec. 9, 1981.

KIESEWETTER, WILLIAM BURNS, educator, physician; b. Phila., Oct. 5, 1915; s. Otto Bismarck and Florence Miller (Burns) K.; m. Grace Virginia Johnston; children: Constance (Mrs. Thomas A. Elliott, Jr.), William Burns, Patricia. B.S., Davidson Coll., 1938; M.D., U. Pa., 1942. Diplomate: Am. Bd. Surgery. Intern Pa. Hosp., 1942-43; William Harvey Cushing fellow surgery Yale U., 1946-47, asst. resident, 1947-49, resident, 1950; resident surgery Children's Hosp., Phila., 1949-50; instr. surgery U. Pa., 1950-53, assoc. surgery, 1953-55; assoc. prof. surgery U. Pitts., 1955-59, prof. pediatric surgery, 1959-81; chief surg. services Children's Hosp., Pitts., 1955-81. Contbr. articles to profl. jours. Served with USAAF, 1943-46. Rockefeller sabbatical grantee, 1965. Fellow ACS; mem. Allegheny County, Pa. med. socs., Am. Acad. Pediatrics, AMA, Central, Pitts., Am. surg. assns., Pitts. Pediatric Soc., Soc. Univ. Surgeons, Pitts. Soc. Biol. Research, Brit. Assn. Pediatric Surgeons, Pan Am. Med. Assn., Am. Pediatric Surg. Assn., German Pediatric Surg. Soc., Internat. Soc. Surgery, Phi Beta Kappa, Sigma Xi, Phi Gamma Delta. Clubs: Fox Chapel Golf, Pitts. Golf. Home: Pittsburgh, PA.

KILBURN, LANE DIXON, ednl. adminstr.; b. Norton, Mass., Apr. , 1923; s. Winford Almon and Mary Elizabeth (Sampson) K. Ph.B., Laval U., Que., Can., 1948, Ph.L., 1950. Entered Congregation of Holy Cross, 1950; ordained priest Roman Catholic Ch., 1955; instr. philosophy King's Coll., Wilkes-Barre, Pa., 1955-56, 57-58, dean coll., 1958-64, pres. coll., 1964-74; adminstr. Ecumenical Inst. Theol. Research, Jerusalem, Israel, 1974-82. Author: The Role and Moral Value of Music, 1951, also articles. Mem. Am. Soc. Aesthetics, New Eng. Historic and Geneal. Soc., Pa. Soc., Wyoming Valley Hist. and Geol. Soc., Mayflower Soc., Alden Kindred Am. K.C. (4 deg.). Home: Jerusalem, Israel. Died Mar. 15, 1982.

KILCOYNE, FRANCIS PATRICK, educator; b. Lawrence, Mass., June 28, 1902; s. Patrick Henry and Sarah Gertrude (Hughes) K.; A.B., Boston Coll., 1924, A.M., 1926; Ph.D., N.Y.U., 1945; m. Eleanor Marie Dunn, June 17, 1939; 1 son, Francis Patrick. Dean of adminstrn., prof. English, Bklyn. Coll., 1945-67, president, 1967, president emeritus, 1967-85; ordained priest Roman Cath. Ch., 1980; parochial vicar Our Lady of Refuge Ch., Flatbush, N.Y. lectr.; vis. prof. Fordham U., St. Joseph's Coll., St. Michael's Coll. Mem. Cath. Commn. on Intellectual and Cultural Affairs, 1950—. Trustee Brentwood (N.Y.) Coll. Decorated Knight of Holy Sepulchre. Mem. John Henry Newman Hon. Soc., Kappa Delta Pi. K.C. Home: Brooklyn, N.Y. Died Jan. 19, 1985.

KILDARE, MRS. OWEN (LEITO OUIDA BOGARDUS), author, lecturer; b. Tarrytown, N.Y., Dec. 16, 1888; d. George Clinton and Marghetia Ainge Bogardus; ed. pub. and pvt. schs., and under tutor; studied medicine and law; m. Owen Fernald Kildare, Mar. 13, 1903 (died 1911); 1 dau., Lowen Loris Marghetia; m. 2d, Charles Albert Adams, May 2, 1911. Wrote verse and travel letters at age of 12; collaborated with husband writing books, plays, etc., 1903-10; organized Kildare System of Writing and Public Speaking, 1908; specialized in "personality development," on lecture platform, from 1904; active in war work, civic and social movements. Historian, Women Builders of America; publicist U.S. Flag Assn.; mem. Authors' League America, Am. Pen Women, Am. Woman's Assn., Professional Woman's League, Nat. Opera Soc., etc. (48 orgns. in all). Republican. Episcopalian. Clubs: Woman's Press. Author: (with Owen Kildare) Regeneration, 1903; Good of the Wicked, 1904; Wisdom of the Simple, 1905; My Old Bailiwick, 1906; Intermezzo, 1908; Golden Shares, 1910; Such a Woman, 1911; also writer of stories, verse, plays, and spl. articles. Editor Cyclopedia of American Women, 1922-23. Home: New Rochelle, N.Y. †

KILE, ELTON, state legislator, association executive; b. Kileville, Ohio, May 3, 1887; s. Fred and Elizabeth (Purdum) K.; A.B., Ohio State U., 1910, J.D., 1912; m. Edith Worthington, Sept. 30, 1912; children—Hazel (Mrs. Robert Fravel), James. Pres. Nat. Asso. Businessmen, Inc., since 1946. Mem. Ohio Gen. Assembly from Madison Co. from 1947. Served as 1st lt. Inf., U.S. Army, 1917-19. Mem. Ohio Grain, Mill and Feed Dealers Assn. (past pres.), Grain and Feed Dealers Nat. Assn. (dir.). Am. Legion, Vets. Fgn. Wars, Pi Kappa Alpha, Delta Sigma Rho. Methodist. Mason (Shriner). Club: Lions. Address: Plain City, Ohio. †

KILGALLEN, JAMES LAWRENCE, writer; b. Pittston, Pa., July 11, 1888; s. John Joseph and Mary (Cavanaugh) K.; grad. Graham Sch., Chgo.; m. Mae Ahern, July 10, 1912; children—Dorothy (Mrs. Richard Kollmar), Eleanor (Mrs. Wilbur Snaper). Reporter Chgo. Tribune, Chgo. Farmers and Drovers Jour.; editor Laramie (Wyo.) Daily Boomerang, 1914-16; mng. editor Indpls. Daily Times, 1917-19; staff Asso. Press, United Press, 1920-21; reporter, writer International News Service (now United Press International), New York City, from 1921, war corr. Pacific, Africa, Italy, France and Germany, World War II. Mem. The Salurians, Sigma

Delta Chi. K.C. Clubs: Overseas Press of N.Y.; Dutch Treat (N.Y.C.). Home: N.Y.C. 21. †

KILLICK, VICTOR W(ILLIAM EDWARD), statistician; b. Phila., Pa., July 20, 1889; s. Frederick Herbert and Annie Sutherland (Rabbits) K.; ed. public schs. of San Francisco and Los Angeles and U. of Calif., U. of Southern Calif.; m. Susie Marion Crump, May 11, 1923 (died Sept. 1, 1935); 1 dau., Phebe Ann; m. 2d. Leona Bailey Dolese, Aug. 1, 1942 (divorced). Mem. staffs of Los Angeles Times. Los Angeles Examiner, Los Angeles Herald, 1909-17; agent U.S. Dept. of Justice, 1917-19; chief statistician Independent Petroleum Marketers Assn. of Calif., 1919-23; statisician and dir. of public relations Sheriff Department, Los Angeles County, 1923-29; chief Bureau of Statistics, Department of Motor Vehicles and California Highway Patrol, State of California 1929-49; active in promotion state and national traffic safety campaigns and safety legislation; cons. service in statistical systems; lecturer and college instr. (hon.) on traffic engring and statistical technique, Certified statistician, State of Calif. Appointed by governor chairman California Population Commission, 1942-45; State Interdepartmental Coordinating Com. from 1945. Fellow Western Statis. Assn. (past pres.), American Inst. Genealogy; mem. Sacramento Statis. Assn. (dir., past pres.), Am. Statis. Assn., A.A.A.S., American Association Motor Vehicle Administrators, Western Government Research Association, Calif. Teachers Retirement, Sacramento Writers' Club, California Writers' Club, Astronomical Society of the Pacific. Author of "Can We Build Automobiles to Keep Drivers Out of Trouble," 1939; "Sherman Act and the Petroleum Industry," 1926; "Business Administration by Statistical Controls," 1928; a number of important contrbns. to Am. genealogy; also contbr. on sociology, economy and statistical technique; feature writer in mags. of U.S., Eng., Can., Mexico. Home: Sacramento, Calif. †

KILLION, GEORGE LEONARD, bus. exec.; b. Steamboat Springs, Colo., Apr. 15, 1901; s. James Abraham and Lydia Jane (Harris) K.; student U. So. Cal., 1920-21, U. Cal., 1921-22; m. Grace Ludora Harris, Dec. 25, 1922 (dec.); 1 son, James L.; m. 2d. Margaretha Rahneberg. Med. editorial staff various West Coast newspapers, 1925-30; pub. relations, financial cons., Oakland, Cal., 1930-35; pub. relations, legislative cons. Safeway Stores, Oakland, 1935-39; commr. Golden Gate Internat. Expdn., 1939; sec. Gov. Cal., 1939-40; dir. of finance, State Cal., 1940-43; asst. to petroleum adminstrn. for war, Washington, 1943; chmn. bd. Metro-Goldwyn-Mayer, 1957-63, 63-69, 70-71, vice chmn., 1969-70, dir., mem. exec. com., 1963-71; past pres. Am. President Lines, Ltd., San Francisco, also dir., cons.; dir. Prentice Electronics, World Airways, Communications Satellite Corp., First Western Bank. Ambassador U.S. Mission to UN, 1966-67. Asst. to treas., Dem. Nat. Com., 1944, treas., 1945-47; Bd. dirs. San Francisco chpt. Am. Cancer Soc.; trustee San Francisco Maritime Mus., John F. Kennedy Library Corp., United Seamen's Service; mem. adv. bd., dir. Pacific Am. S.S. Assn.; vice chmn. 11 western states March of Dimes, Nat. Found.; hon. fellow Harry S. Truman Library Inst. Served as maj. AUS, Staff of Allied Mil. Gov't., 1943. Mem. Am. Bur. Shipping (bd. mgrs.), Nat. Def. Transp. Assn. (life). Democrat. Clubs: Bohemian, Olympic, World Trade (pres. 1957-66), Eldorado Country (Palm Desert, Cal.). Home: San Francisco, Calif. Died Jan. 13, 1983.

KILPATRICK, MARTIN, chemist; b. New York, N.Y., Apr. 3, 1895; s. Martin and Martha (Anderson) K.; A.B., City Coll. of N.Y., 1915; A.M., Columbia, 1917; Ph.D., N.Y.U., 1923; m. Mary Lydston Johnson, Dec 25, 1921. Tutor, City Coll. N.Y., 1915-19; asst. prof. chemistry, Vassar Coll., 1919-23, Duke Univ., 1923-25; Nat. Research Council fellow, Johns Hopkins U., 1925-27, Univ. of Copenhagen (Denmark), 1927; research scientist under from Rask-Orsted Fund, U. of Copenhagen, 1927-28; asst. prof. asso. prof., prof., U. of Pa., 1928-47; asst. dir. of research and dev. dir. S.A.M., Laos., Manhattan Project, Columbia, U., 1943-46; consultant and coordinator of research and development program on hydrogen peroxide, bur. of ordnance, U.S. Navy, 1945-47; pres. and chmn., dept. of chemistry, Ill. Inst. Tech., 1947-60; sr. chemist emeritus Argonne Nat. Lab., Ill., 1960-82. Mem. Am. Chem. Soc. (chmn., dir. of phys. and inorganic chemistry). Sigma Xi. Presbyterian. Contbr. numerous papers to sci. jours. Walked Applachian Trail from Maine to Georgia. Home: Chicago, Ill. Died Feb. 10, 1982.

KIMBALL, SOLON TOOTHAKER, educator, anthropologist; b. Manhattan, Kans., Aug. 12, 1909; s. Charles Augustus and Matie (Toothaker) K.; m. Hannah Jackson Price, Dec. 24, 1935; children—Sally Makielski, John Price (dec.). B.S., Kans. State U., 1930, Sc.D., 1963; A.M., Harvard U., 1933, Ph.D., 1936. Sheldon fellow Harvard, 1933; head socio-economic surveys Navajo Reservation, Dept. Interior, 1936-42; vis. prof. anthropology and sociology Okla. U., summer 1940; head community orgn. War Relocation Authority, 1942-45; asso. prof. sociology and anthropology Mich. State Coll., 1945-48; head dept., prof. sociology and anthropology U. Ala., 1948-53; vis. prof. sociology U. Chgo., summer 1947; anthropology U. Calif., summer 1957; social anthropol. research in, Ireland, 1933-34; social anthropol. research in Navajo Indians, 1936-42, summer 1949, rural communities in, Michigan, 1945-48, Talladega Health Survey, 1951-53, sch. desegregation in, Fla., 1972-73, Wales summer 1978; prof. anthropology and edn. Columbia Tchrs. College, 1953-66; grad. research prof. anthropology U. Fla., 1966-80, emeritus, from 1980; vis. prof. Univ. P.R., summer 1954; UNESCO specialist Brazilian Center Ednl. Research, 1958-59; dir. summer seminar Nat. Endowment for the Humanities, 1975, 76, 79, dir. residential fellowship seminar, 1977-78. Author: (with C.M. Arensberg), rev. 2d edit.) Family and Community in Ireland, 1968, Community Government in War Relocation Centers, 1946, The Talladega Story, (with Marion Pearsall), 1954, Readings in the Science of Human Relations; editor, 1949, (with J.E. McClellan) Education and the New America, 1962, (with C.M. Arensberg) Culture and Community, 1965, Crossing Cultural Boundaries, (with James B. Watson), 1972, Learning and Culture, (with J. Burnett), 1973, Culture and the Educative Process, 1974, (with William Partridge) The Craft of Community Study, 1979. Social Science Research Council fellow, 1961-62; Guggenheim fellow, 1966-67; recipient Tchr./Scholar award U. Fla., 1981. Fellow Am. Anthrop. Assn. (nominations com. 1977-78), Soc. Applied Anthropology (pres. 1953), AAAS; mem. So. Anthrop. Soc. (pres. 1979-80), Am. Ethnol. Soc. (pres. 1970-71), Council on Anthropology and Edn., Phi Kappa Phi, Alpha Kappa Delta, Sigma Delta Chi, Beta Theta Pi. Home: Gainesville, Fla.

KIMBARK, EDWARD WILSON, elec. engr.; b. Chgo., Sept. 21, 1902; s. Edward Hall and Maude (Wilson) K.; m. Ruth Elizabeth Merrick, July 19, 1930 (dec. Nov. 1976); m. Iris Vera Tattersall, Aug. 25, 1977. B.S., Northwestern U., 1924, E.E., 1925; S.M., Mass. Inst. Tech., 1933, Sc.D., 1937. Substa. operator Pub. Service Co. No. Ill., Evanston, 1925-26; asst. testing lab., 1926-27; instr. elec. engring. U. Calif. at Berkeley, 1927-29; asst. curator div. power Chgo. Mus. Sci. and Industry, 1929-32; asst. prof. elec. engring. Poly. Inst. Bklyn., 1937-39; asst. prof. elec. engring. Northwestern U., 1939-41, asso. prof., 1941-45, prof., 1945-50, acting chmn., 1941-42; prof. elec. power Instituto Tecnológico de Aeronáutica, São José dos Campos, Brazil, 1950-55; dean Sch. Engring. Seattle U., 1955-62; elec. engr. Br. of System Engring. Bonneville Power Adminstrn. Author: Power System Stability, 3 vols, 1948-56, Electrical Transmission of Power and Signals, 1949, Direct Current Transmission, 1971; Editor: Principles of Radar, 1944, (with Richard T. Byerly) Stability of Large Electric Power Systems, 1974; Contbr. (with Richard T. Byerly) articles to profl. jours. Recipient Honor award, Gold medal U.S. Dept. Interior, 1974; Habirshaw award IEEE, 1980. Fellow IEEE (Best Paper prize IEEE Power Engring. Soc. 1977); mem. Nat. Acad. Engring., Conf. Internationale des Grands Reseaux Electriques à Haute Tension, Paris. Home: Portland, Ore.

KIMBELL, ARTHUR W., business exec.; b. Chicago, Ill., Mar. 20, 1890; s. Martin Nelson and Annie C. (Craigmile) K.; B.S. in C.E., U. of Ill., 1913; m. Alice Raymer, Apr. 22, 1914. Employed in real estate dept., Kimbell Trust & Savings Bank, Chicago, 1913-14; sec. Kimbell-Wheeler Brick Co., 1914-18; pres., treas., gen. mgr. Cinch Mfg. Corp., 1918-29; v.p., dir. and gen. mgr. United-Carr Fastener Corp., 1929-42, pres., gen. mgr., 1942, chmn., 1957-60, hon. chmn., from 1960; dir. Reed and Barton Co. Mem. Soc. Automotive Engrs., Phi Delta Theta, Sigma Xi. Clubs: Algonquin (Boston); Brae Burn Golf (West Newton, Mass.). Inventor numerous fasteners and mech. specialties. Home: Auburndale, Mass. †

KIMBER, HARRY HUBERT, educator; b. Indpls., May 12, 1903; s. Arthur Smith and Carrie (Echols) K.; A.B., U. Mich., 1925. M.A. 1928, Ph.D., 1932; m. Daisy Schulz, Mar. 3, 1928; children—Rebecca Cope, Caroline Echols, Katherine Spangler. Inst. history U. Mich., 1927-28; asst. prof. history and polit. sci. Bradley Coll., 1928-31; prof. history Mich. State Coll., from 1932, head of dept. humanities, dir. div. social sci., 1943-62, prof., head dept. religion, dir. residence instrn. Coll. Arts and Letters, 1964-70, prof. emeritus, 1970-83. Mem. Patriarchal Order St. Vladimir, Mich. Acad. Sci. and Arts, Mich. Coll. Assn. (pres. 1950-51, chmn. com. legislation 1952-55), All-Coll. Ednl. Research Com. (chmn. 1952-56), Phi Beta Kappa, Phi Alpha Theta, Pi Gamma Mu. Episcopalian. Mason. Co-author: The Teaching of Religion in State Universities, 1960. Co-editor: Readings in the History of Civilization. 1939. Contbr. articles to ednl. publs. Home: East Lansing, Mich. Dec. May 14, 1983.

KIMBROUGH, JAMES C., army medical officer; b. Madisonville, Tenn., Nov. 5, 1887; s. George Washington and Minnie (Williams) K., A.B., Hiawassee (Tenn.) Coll., 1909; M.D., Vanderbilt Univ., 1916; m. Pauline Damon, Oct. 3, 1929; 1 child, Mary Jane. Interne St. Thomas Hosp., Nashville, 1916-17; entered U.S. Army as 1st lt., July 1917, and advanced through grades to col. M.C., 1942; regimental surgeon, World War I; specialized in urology, 1919; chief, urology service, U.S. Station Hosp., Germany, 1919-21; Station Hosp., Ft. Sam Houston, Tex., 1921-25, Letterman Gen. Hosp., San Francisco, 1926-30, Walter Reed Hosp., Washington, 1930-34; Ft. Sam Houston, Tex., 1943-37, Sternberg Gen. Hosp., Philippine Islands, 1937-38; chief profl. services, E.T.O., World War II; chief of urology service, Walter Reed Army Hosp. from 1946. Awarded: Purple Heart, World War I; Bronze Star medal, Legion of Merit, World War II. Holder "A" rating as urological specialist, The Surgeon General's Office. Diplomate Am. Bd. Urology, Inc., 1947. Fellow Am. Coll. Surgeons; mem. A.M.A., Am. Urol. Assn., Washington Urol. Assn. (pres.), Royal Soc. of Medicine, London (hon. mem.), Acad. of Surgery, Paris, Alpha Omega Alpha. Democrat. Baptist. Mason (32 deg., Shriner). Club: Army and Navy (Washington). Home: Washington, D.C.†

KINCAID, JOHN FRANKLIN, scientist; b. Blackwell, Mo., Feb. 27, 1912; s. John Randall and Rose (Rich) K.; m. Nancy Virginia Ange, June 28, 1938 (dec.); children: James Randall, John Peter, Thomas Franklin (dec.); m. Marguerite Belair Hull, Oct. 30, 1971. A.B., Central Coll., Fayette, Mo., 1934; M.A., George Washington U., 1936; Ph.D., Princeton, 1938. Instr. chemistry U. Rochester, 1938-42; div. head explosives research lab. Carnegie Inst. Tech., 1942-45; research scientist Gen. Electric Co., 1945-46; head high pressure research dept. Rohm & Haas Co., 1946-49, research supr., 1949-58; head gen. sci. br., adv. research project div. Inst. Def. Analysis, 1958-59, dep. dir. advanced research projects div., 1959-60, dir. research and engring. support div., 1960-62, ind. cons., 1962-63; v.p. research and devel. Internat. Minerals and Chem. Corp., 1963-67; asst. sec. Dept. Commerce, 1967-69; cons., 1969-71; sr. scientist Applied Physics Lab., Johns Hopkins, 1971-84. Author articles. Recipient Naval Ordnance Devel. award, 1945, Presdl. cert. merit, 1948. Mem. AIAA (Wyld Propulsion award 1981), AAAS, Am. Def. Preparedness Assn. Clubs: Cosmos (Washington); Aviation (Princeton, N.J.). Inventor or co-inventor mil. and indsl. processes and products Home: Arlington, Va. Died Aug. 31, 1984.

KINDIG, RAYMOND, pub. utility exec.; b. Oberlin, Kan., Sept. 19, 1888; s. Raymond and Fanny (Kulp) K.; ed. pub. schs. of Denver; m. Irene Lucia Leahy, Apr. 29, 1915. Entire business career with Pacific Gas and Electric Co. from 1914, sec.; sec. and dir. Arlington Properties Co., Ltd., Valley Elec. Supply Co. Served in U.S. Navy, 1910-13. Mem. San Francisco C. of C. Republican. Roman Catholic. Elk. Home: San Francisco, Calif. †

KING, CYRIL BERNARD, newspaper editor; b. Tidioute, Pa., Aug. 10, 1905; s. Bernard Christy and Gertrude (Thomson) K.; m. Dorothea L. Brower, Nov. 29, 1934; children—Dorothy (Mrs. Daniel McCormick), Barbara Ann (Mrs. Hans Peter Lagoni). With Oil City (Pa.) Derrick, 1925-29; city editor Altoona (Pa.) Tribune, 1929-30; mem. staff Pitts. Press, 1930-34; 1930-34; news broadcaster radio sta. KDKA, Pitts., 1932-34; news analyst radio sta. WBEN, Buffalo, 1934-42; gen. mgr. radio sta. WEBR, Buffalo, 1942-52, v.p., from 1942; editor Courier-Express, Buffalo, 1952-70; v.p. Courier-Cable Co., 1970-77. Mem. N.Y. State Soc. Newspaper Editors (past pres.). Club: Mason (hon. 33 deg.). Home: Williamsville, N.Y.

KING, DONALD DEWOLF, technical laboratory executive; b. Rochester, N.Y., Aug. 7, 1919; s. James Percival and Edith (Seyerlen) K.; m. Mary Anne Henderson, June 21, 1944; children—Stuart DeWolf, Alison Anne, Mary Scotland, James Wyeth. B.A., Harvard Coll., 1942; M.A., Harvard U., 1944, Ph.D., 1946. Asst. prof. Harvard U., 1946-47; Vice pres. research Electronic Communications, Timonium, Md., 1956-64; dir. Electronic Research Lab., Aerospace Corp., Los Angeles, 1964-67; pres. Philips Labs., Briarcliff Manor, N.Y., from 1967. Author: Measurements at Centimeter Wavelensth, 1951. Fellow AAAS, IEEE; mem. Am. Phys. Soc., N.Y. Acad. Sci., Indsl. Research Inst., Dirs. Indsl. Research. Home: Chappaqua, N.Y.

KING, EDWARD BEVERLY, JR., publishing co. exec.; b. Roanoke, Va., Aug. 17, 1939; s. Edward Beverly and Gladys Ruth (Johnson) K. Student, Del. State Coll., 1957-58, Ky. State U., 1958-60, Va. Union U., summer 1962; B.S. in Edn, Wilberforce (Ohio) U., 1963; postgrad. U. Dayton, 1968, Hofstra U., 1969; Ed.D., Mt. Sinai U and Theol. Sem., 1971. Tchr. English and social studies high sch., Charlotte, N.C., 1963-64, Gary, Ind., 1964-66 counselor A-Team Program, Dept. Agr., Eaton Rapids, Mich., summer 1965; exec. dir. alumni affairs and editor jour. Wilberforce U., 1966-68; instr. Upward Bound Program, Purdue U., West Lafayette, Ind., summer 1966 vis. prof. coll. relations Chase Manhattan Bank, N.Y.C., 1968; with Voice of Am., 1968; asst. to pres. Hofstra U., Hempstead, N.Y., 1968-70; staff dir., sr. asso. Assn. Am Pubs. Inc., N.Y.C., 1970-75; edn. textbook pub. sales exec. Steck-Vaughn Pub. Co., Norfolk, Va., from 1975 Appearances on: TV documentary Our Times, 1960, Walk in My Shoes, 1961 (Emmy award); Author: TV documentary Student Frontier, 1961; contbr.: articles to Newsweek. Adminstrv. sec. Student Nonviolent Coordinating Com., Atlanta, 1960-61; Mem. student selection com pub. procedures program Radcliffe Coll., from 1972 Recipient Adminstrn. Improvement award Am. Alumni Council, 1967; Distinguished Alumnus of Year award Wilberforce U., 1968; New Career Opportunities award Talladega Coll., 1971; certificate of recognition Nat Alliance Businessmen, 1973. Mem. Am. Negro Commemorative Soc., Nat. Geog. Soc., N.E.A., Nat. Fedn. Tchrs Nat. Hist. Soc., Alpha Psi Omega. Home: Norfolk, VA

KING, FRANK L(ESTER), banker; b. Sparta, Ill., Aug. 5, 1897; s. John L. and Anna (Syar) K.; ed. Sparta High Sch., and Northwestern Sch. of Commerce, Evanston; m. Lucille Alhime, Aug. 30, 1924; children—Frank Lester, John Frederick, Robert Elexander. Asst. cashier 1st Nat. Bank, Sparta, 1916-18; nat. bank examiner, 1920-25; asst. cashier Mutual Nat. Bank, Chicago, 1926-27; joined Continental Nat. Bank and Trust Co. (now Continental Ill. Nat. Bank and Trust Co.), Chicago, 1928, comptroller, 1930; exec. v.p., dir. United Cal. Bank, Los Angeles, 1943, pres., dir., 1945-59, chmn. bd., 1959-73; dir. United California Bank Internat., 1962-73; director Automobile Club Southern California, United States Borax and Chemical Co., Pacific Indemnity Company, Pacific Mutual Life Ins. Co., Times Mirror Company, Cyprus Mines Corp., El Paso Natural Gas Co. Dir. Assn. Registered Bank Holding Cos. Trustee U. So. Cal. Mem. Assn. Reserve City Bankers. Clubs: Los Angeles Country, California, Stock Exchange (Los Angeles); Pacific Union (San Francisco); The Links (N.Y.C.). Home: Los Angeles, Calif. Died Nov. 23, 1982.

KING, FREDERIC RHINELANDER, architect; b. N.Y.C., Apr. 13, 1887; s. LeRoy and Ethel (Rhinelander) K.; A.B. cum laude, Harvard, 1908, Columbia Archtl. Sch., 1908-11, Ecole des Beaux Arts, Paris, France, 1912-14; m. Edith P. Morgan, Feb. 9, 1924; children—David Rhinelander, Jonathan LeRoy. With McKim, Mead and White, 1914-17; with Carrere and Hastings, 1919-20; asso. Marion S. Wyeth, 1920-32; partner Wyeth & King, 1932-64. Mem. A.R.C. Commn., 1917; constrn. div. W.P.B., N.Y.C. and Washington, 1942-43. Trustee Barnard Coll., 1933-57; former chmn. (bd. of trustees of N.Y. Soc. Library; trustee St. Luke's Hosp. (hon.). Served as 1st lt., U.S. Army, G2 AEF, 1918-19, Am. Commn. to Negotiate Peace; mem. Coolidge's Mission to Austria, 1919. Academician N.A.D. Fellow A.I.A.; mem. Soc. Beaux Arts. Republican. Clubs: Century Association, Harvard, Pilgrims of U.S. Church. Address: New York, N.Y. †

KING, GEORGE HAROLD, lumberman; b. Mt. Lebanon, La., Nov. 11, 1896; s. William L. and Julia C. (Baker) K.; ed. Gibsland High Sch.; m. French Freeman, Aug. 25, 1917; 1 child, George Harold. With Long Bell Lumber Co., Ludington, La., 1913-17; shipping clk. Forrest Lumber Co., Oakdale, La., 1917-21; supt. pine lumber operations Hillyer-Deutsch-Edwards, Oakdale, 1921-24; gen. mgr. Hillyer-Edwards-Fuller, Glenmora, La., 1924-36, v.p., 1936-41; organizer King-Edwards-Fuller, St. Francisville, La., mng. ptnr. 1941-45; pres. King Lumber Industries, Canton, 1946-58, chmn., 1958-81; pres. Canton & Carthage R.R. Co., 1946-81; dir. Am. Bank & Trust Co. Mem. La. Mineral Bd., 1952. Mem. So. Hardwood Producers (pres. 1951-52), N.A.M. (dir.), Nat. Hardwood Lumber Assn. (dir.). Home: Baton Rouge, La. Dec. Aug. 21, 1981.

KING, HARRY ORLAND, b. Chicago, Ill., Mar. 6, 1890; s. William James and Caroline (Concord) K.; grad. Lake View High Sch., 1908; m. Mildred L. Holmes, of Chicago, Dec. 11, 1915; children—Wendell Holmes (dec.), Barbara Lucile, Harry Orland, Saranne. With A. M. Castle & Co., Chicago, 1909-15; pres. H. O. King Co., Chicago, 1915-23; v.p. and gen. mgr. Bassick Co., Bridgeport, Conn., 1923-28; pres. Housatonic Co., Bridgeport, from 1928. Dep. administrator NRA, Washington, from 1933. Dir. Sikorsky Aviation Corpn., Bridgeport City Trust Co., Siemon Co. Episcopalian. Clubs: Mountain Lake (Fla.); Black Rock Yacht (Bridgeport, Conn.); Country (Fairfield, Conn.). Home: Washington, D.C. †

KING, HENRY, motion picture dir.; b. Christiansburg, Va., Jan. 24, 1896. With Norfolk & Western R.R., then toured in stock, circuses, vaudeville and burlesque; appeared N.Y. stage in Top O'the Morning; motion picture actor for Pathe Studios; exec. head Inspiration Co.; with Fox Film Co., remaining after merger with 20th Century Pictures Co.; producer motion pictures 23/Hours Leave, Tol'able David, Fury, White Sister; motion pictures directed include Stella Dallas, Romola, Winning of Barbara Worth, Woman Disputed, Over the Hill, Carolina, State Fair, Country Doctor, Ramona, Lloyds of London, In Old Chicago, Alexander's Ragtime Band, Jesse James, Little Old New York, Stanley and Livingstone, Maryland, Chad Hanna, Yank in the R.A.F., Black Swan, Song of Bernadette, Wilson, Bell for Adano, Margie, Captain from Castile, Deep Waters, Twelve O'Clock High, The Gun Fighter, I'd Climb the Highest Mountain, David and Bathsheba, Wait 'till the Sun Shines Nellie, Snows of Kilmanjaro, O. Henry's Full House, King of the Khyber Rifles, Untamed, Love is a Many Splendored Thing, Carousel, The Sun Also Rises, This Earth is Mine, Tender is the Night. Died June 29, 1982.*

KING, JAMES BERRY, lawyer; b. Harrison, Ark., May 29, 1888; s. Alfred La Fayette and Laura (McCormick) K.; ed. U. of Ark., 1903-07; B.L., U. of Va., 1910; m. Sadye Thompson, Apr. 21, 1923. Practiced at Tahlequah, Okla., with Congressman W. W. Hastings, 1910-17; practiced with Ramsey de Muelles, Rosser, Martin & King, Muskogee, Okla., 1919-25; apptd. asst. atty. gen. of Okla., 1925; apptd. atty. gen. of Okla. to fill vacancy, 1929, and elected to same office, 1931, for term ending 1935; practicing under firm J. Berry King & George J. Fagin. Enlisted in inf., U.S. Army, 1917; trans. to Judge Advocate Gen.'s dept.; commd. capt. and assigned as personal aide to Maj. Gen. E. H. Crowder; promoted to maj. and assigned as judge advocate 77th Div., in France; apptd. superior provost judge, after Armistice, and pres. of Spl. Court, Army Hdqrs., Coblenz, Germany, continuing 7 mos. Mem. Am. Legion, Vets. of Foreign Wars, Delta Chi, Kappa Sigma. Democrat. Mem. Christian Ch. Mason (32 degree, K.T., Shriner). Clubs: Oklahoma, Oklahoma City Golf and Country. Home: Muskogee, Okla. †

KING, JOSEPH H., banker; b. Fort Worth, Feb. 17, 1902; s. Silas Lee and Mary (Rayner) K.; student Columbia, 1921-23; m. Rosalee Speaker, Oct. 13, 1923 (div. Apr. 1960); children—Susan, Anthony S.; m. 2d, Gioconda Castro, Apr. 27, 1960. With Guardian Trust Co., N.Y., 1925-26, J. and W. Seligman & Co., N.Y.C., 1927-38. Union Securities Corp., 1938-56, pres.; merged with Eastman Dillon & Co., 1956; sr. partner Eastman Dillon, Union Securities & Co., 1956-71, chmn. bd., from 1971, merged to form Blyth Eastman Dillon & Co., 1972, chmn. mgmt. com., from 1972, also dir. Clubs: Blind Brook, Links (N.Y.C.); Brook Hollow (Dallas); Everglades, Bath and Tennis (Palm Beach, Fla.); Augusta (Ga.) Nat. Golf. Home: Palm Beach, Fla. Dec. Sept. 19, 1980.

KING, PHILIP COATES, coll. pres.; b. Oberlin, O., May 27, 1887; s. Henry Churchill and Julia (Coates) K.; A.B., Oberlin, 1910, B.D., 1915; studied Union Theol. Sem., 1912-13; A.M., Columbia University, 1913; D.D. from Oberlin College, 1932; m. Zoe Catherine Marts, December 1, 1917; children—Arno Marts, Barbara Lee. Dist. agt. Asso. Charities, Cleveland, O., 1910-12; ordained Congl. ministry, 1915; asso. pastor Washington Street Ch., Toledo, O., 1915-18; pastor Denison Av. Ch., Cleveland, 1920-24, Plymouth Ch., Columbus, O., 1924-29; asso. pres. Washburn Coll., Topeka, Kan., 1930-31, pres. from Sept. 1, 1931. Served as lt. (j.g.) chaplain U.S. Navy, on duty U.S.S. Pittsburgh, July 1918-Jan. 1920. Mem. Phi Beta Kappa (hon. Oberlin 1930). Ind. Republican. Mason. Rotarian. Home: Topeka, Kan. †

KING, THOMAS STARR, JR., transp. exec., ret. naval officer; b. Wilmington, Del., Dec. 7, 1914; s. Thomas Starr and Anne (Winchester) K.; B.S. in Mech. Engring., U.S. Naval Acad., 1936; M.S. in Elec. Engring., Mass. Inst. Tech., 1945; m. Jeanne Sanford Everett, Aug. 10, 1938; children—Thomas Starr IV, William Kimberly, Anne Stuart. Commd. ensign U.S. Navy, 1936, advanced through grades to rear adm., 1965; comdr. exptl. destroyer U.S.S. Winslow, 1948-49, Destroyer Div. 212, 1954-55, Destroyer Squadron 5, 1961-62, Destroyer Flotillas 5 and 11, 1962-63, 65-66; mem. staff comdr. Seventh Fleet, Korean War; comdr. U.S.S. Observation Island, Polaris exptl. test ship, 1960-61; grad. Naval War Coll. 1952; asst. chief Bur. Naval Weapons, 1964-65; mfg. officer Naval Gun Factory, 1955-58; comdr. joint navy-airforce task group that recovered Astronaut Shirra, 1962, Astronaut Cooper, 1963; comdr. Cruiser Destroyer Flotilla 11, 1965-66; asst. chief naval operations (tng.), Washington, 1966-70; gen. mgr. Tri Country Met. Transp. Dist. Ore., Portland, from 1970. Decorated Legion of Merit, Bronze Star with combat V. Mem. U.S. Naval Inst., Am. Ordnance Assn. Presbyn. Home: McLean, Va. Died May 28, 1981.

KINGHAN, CHARLES ROSS, artist; b. Anthony, Kans., Jan. 18, 1895; s. Robert E. and Sarah Frances (Edwards) K.; m. Ruth F. Weidler, Sept. 13, 1927; children: Donald Earl, Charles Bruce. Student, Acad. Fine Arts, Am. Acad. Art, Art Inst., Audubon Sch. Art, all Chgo. Asso. Stevens, Sundblom & Henry Studios, Chgo., 1926-30; free-lance, 1950-51; tchr. Am. Acad. Art, 1933-35; co-owner Huguenot Sch. Art, 1949-53; with Maxon Advt. Agy., 1952-53; art work Batten, Barton, Durstine & Osborn Advt. Agy., N.Y.C., 1954; now tchr. pvt. class in water color, mem. juries of award and selection Am. Water-color Soc., Allied Artists. Represented permanent collections, Smithsonian Instn., Washington, Phila. Mus. Art, U. Maine, also pvt. collections.; Author: Rendering Techniques for Commercial Art and Advertising, 1957, Ted Kautzky and How He Painted, 1959; also contbr. articles to art mags. Recipient gold medal All Ill. Soc. Arts, 1933, Ernest Quantrel award Hudson Valley Art Assn., 1951; 1st prize New Rochelle Woman's Club, 1951, 53; 1st prize Westchester Woman's Club, Bronxville, N.Y., 1954; 1st prize watercolor Westchester Fedn. Women's Clubs, 1956; Emily Lowe award Am. Watercolor Soc., 1957; John Newton Howitt award Hebrew Vets. Assn., 1959; Rudolph Lesch award, 1965; others. Mem. Am. Watercolor Soc. (v.p. 1969, 71), Phila. Watercolor Club, Allied Artists Hudson Valley Art Assn. (dir.), New Rochelle Art Assn. (past pres.), NAD, Allied Artists of Am., Hebrew Vets. Assn. (v.p. 1969), Salmagundi Club. Home: Pacific Grove, Calif. Died July 22, 1984.

KINGSBURY, B., dentist, educator, assn. exec.; b. Susanville, Cal., Dec. 7, 1889; s. Fred Fillmore and Dora Amanda (Gray) K.; D.D.S., Coll. Phys. and Surg., 1913; m. Florien D. Adair, July 1, 1915; children—Dr. Bernerd Cussick, Dr. Kenneth Adair. Gen. practice dentistry, San Francisco, from 1913; clin. prof. prosthetic dentistry, trustee, treas. Coll. Phys. and Surg., from 1920. With Manpower Service, U.S. Procurement and Assignment Service, 8th Corps Area, 1943-46. Fellow Am. Coll. Dentists (pres. San Francisco chpt.); mem. Am. (nat. pres. 1955-56), Cal. (dir. 1927-51, pres. 1946), dental assns., Cal. Acad. Periodontology, Am. Acad. Restorative Dentistry, Golden Gate Dental Congress (dir. 1947-39), San Francisco Dental Soc. (dir. 1927-50, pres. 1927). Mason (Shriner). Clubs: Olympic, Presidio Golf (San Francisco), Contbr. profl. jours. †

KINGSLEY, HAROLD M., clergyman and social worker; b. Mobile, Ala., Mar. 1, 1887; ed. Emerson Inst., Mobile, Ala., 1904; A.B., Talladega (Ala.) Coll, 1908; B.D., Yale, 1911; m. Dec. 25, 1911; children—Harold M., Anna Marie, Roy Edward. Asst. sec. Goffe St. Y.M.C.A., New Haven, Conn., 1908-09; sec. Dearborn St. Y.M.C.A., Mobile, Ala., 1909; ordained to ministry of Congregational Ch., 1911; pastor Union Congl. Ch., Newport, R.I., 1911-13; supt. Congl. ch. work, Tex. and Okla., also sec. Tillotson Coll., Austin, Tex., 1913-16; supt. Congl. Ch. work in Ala., Tenn., Ky. and Fla., 1916-20; dir. Negro work in the north, Congl. Bd. Home Missions, 1920-43. Organizer-pastor Ch. of the Good Shepherd, Chicago, 1927-43, dir. from 1943; organizer Pilgrim House Community, 1945; pastor Ch. of Christian Fellowship Los Angeles, 1948. Asst. moderator Nat. Council Congl. Chs., 1917; sec. Negro welfare, Joint Com. on War Prodn. Communities, 1918-19; special investigator Negro exodus to north. Home Missions Council, 1919-20; pioneer in racially integrated churches. Trustee Talladega College, Talladega, Alabama. Member Sigma Pi Phi. Republican. Clubs: Cleric, Town Hall (Los Angeles). Home: Los Angeles, CA. †

KINGSLEY, HIRAM WEBSTER, merchandising exec.; b. Madison, Wis., Aug. 1, 1888; s. Hiram A. and Cora Belle (Webster) K.; A.B., Washburn Coll., 1911; married Eloise Sargent; children—Carol (Mrs. Hoyt S. Pardee), Robert Sargent. Timekeeper, assistant superintendent, asphalt chemist, Kaw Paving Co., Topeka, Kan., 1911-13; with Sears Roebuck and Co. 1913-49, became mgr. billing dept., Chicago mail order plant, 1920, asst. to operating supt. Philadelphia mail order, 1920-25, operating supt. Kansas City mail order, 1925-28, operating supt. Phila. mail order, 1928, dist. mgr. eastern retail stores, 1929, territorial officer Pacific Coast, 1930-31, dist. mgr. Middle West retail stores, 1932-33, gen. mgr. Los Angeles mail order, 1934-42, regional mgr. Pacific Coast territory, 1942-45, vice pres. in charge Pacific Coast territory 1945-49. Served with U.S. Navy, 1918. Mason (Shriner), Kiwanian. Clubs: Los Angeles Country, Jonathan (Los Angeles). Home: Los Angeles, Calif. †

KINGSTON, MORGAN, operatic tenor; b. Staffordshire, Eng., Mar. 16, 1889; s. John and Jane (Williams) K.; father of English, mother of Welsh descent; ed. high sch.; studied music under Evelyn Hatteras, London; widower. Mem. ch. choir, at Nottinghamshire, at 8; played tenor horn in brass band at 14; studied mining engineering several yrs.; début as singer under auspices of Nat. Sunday League, at Queen's Hall, London, 1910; later appeared with festival socs. throughout British Isles and at The Hague; was tenor soloist at Wagner Centenary Festival, Albert Hall, London, 1912; New York début as Radames, in "Aida," with Century Opera Co., 1913; with Chicago Opera Co., 1916-17, Metropolitan Opera Co. since 1917. Toured U.S. with Chicago Symphony Orchestra, 1915, also toured with Metropolitan Opera Quartette. Repetoire includes leading tenor parts in Wagnerian operas and in "Carmen," "Samson," "Faust" in French; also entire Italian dramatic repetoire. Widely known as oratorio singer.†

KINNAIRD, CLARK, writer; b. Louisville, Ky., May 4, 1901; s. Charles Beck and Nellie (Clark) K.; m. Marian Gosnell, 1924; children—Kenneth, Laird. Employed on various papers and corr. in, Europe, 1921-24; mng. editor Central Press Assn., 1924-28; editor-pub. Edenton (N.C.) Daily News, 1928-30; assoc. editor King Features Syndicate, 1930-37, 39-70, now contbr.; syndicated columns, 1949-70, broadcaster, book reviewer. Author: 500 Americans, 1939, War Comes to Us, 1942, The Real F.D.R, 1945, This Must Not Happen Again, 1945, It Happened in 1945, 1946, It Happened in 1946, 1947, The Last Defense, (with H.J. Heinz and J. Iorgy), 1947); contbg. author: The College Anthology, 1949; author: George Washington: The Pictorial Biography, 1967, 75; Editor: Runyon Short Takes, 1947, Runyon Poems for Men, 1948, Runyon First and Last, 1949, A Treasury of Damon Runyon, 1959, 78, First Century and Forward, 1966, Rube Goldberg vs. The Machine Age, 1968, rev. edit., 1981, Milton Caniff: Rembrandt of the Comic Strips, 1981, Women: Inevitable Warriors, 1981; contbr. to: From Source to Statement, 1968, Harper Dictionary of Contemporary Usage, 1975. Served with USN, 1918-19. Recipient awards from Freedoms Found., 1949, 50, 53, 62, awards from Children Am. Revolution, 1960, awards from Dept. Def., 1966, awards from Am. Legion, 1968, awards from Pi Delta Epsilon, 1973, awards from U.S. Flag Found., 1975, awards from Sons and Daus. Pilgrims, 1977. Club: Dutch Treat (N.Y.C.). Home: Flemington, N.J. Died Nov. 4, 1983.

KIRBY, AMOS, radio commentator; b. Mullica Hill, N.J., Sept. 13, 1889; s. Clayton Gaunt and Deborah Fowler (Steward) K.; student George Sch., Pa., 1906-09; grad. short course in agr., Rutgers U., 1912; m. Ellen C. Conover, Feb. 11, 1915; children—Marjorie Conover (Mrs. Robert Lentz), Wenonah, Major Burton Moore Kirby. Asst. editor and treas. Monitor Register, Woodstown, N.J., 1923; farm editor Courier-Post, Camden, N.J., 1925-28; N.J. editor Am. Agriculturist, Ithaca, N.Y. from 1928; editor N.J. Grange Gleaner, 1932; farm program. dir. WCAU Broadcasting Co., Phila., 1937; farm and garden television dir. WCAU, 1948, farm consultant for WCAU Radio station; columnist Sunday Bulletin, Phila., 1948. Awarded citation from Edward B. Voorhees Agrl. Soc., Rutgers U., distinguished service to agr. as writer and editor, 1939; Amos Kirby Dahlia, 1948; citation Phila. Rose Soc., 1949; citations N.J. Editorial Assn. for agrl. contbns., 1923, 24, 25, 26; Asso. Press Pa. Broadcaster's Farm award, 1957. Mem. N.J. Agrl. Soc., Trenton, N.J., Grange, 7th degree (legislative com. State Grange, 1947), Pa. Hort. Soc., Phila., N.J. Hort. Soc., New Brunswick; N.J. Soc. of Pa., Phila. Soc. for Promoting Agr. Republican. Methodist. Mason (32 deg.). Clubs: Quaker City Farmers, Toastmasters. Home: Mullica Hill, N.J. †

KIRBY, GEORGE FRANCIS, petroleum company executive; b. Cheneyville, La., Dec. 7, 1916; s. George Francis and Vesta (Mason) K.; A.B., La. Coll., 1936; M.S., La. State U., 1938, Ph.D., 1940; postgrad. Harvard, 1952; m. Nannette Dutsch, Dec. 12, 1941; children—Michael E., John M. With Ethyl Corp., N.Y.C., 1940-69, v.p. research and devel., 1955-62, exec. v.p., 1963-64, pres., 1964-69, also dir.; dir., mem. exec. com. Tex. Eastern Corp., Houston, 1969-80, exec. v.p., 1970-71, pres., 1971-80, chief exec. officer, 1973-75, chmn. bd., 1975-80; dir. emeritus La. Nat. Bank, 1st City Nat. Bank. Bd. dirs. La. State U. Found., Inst. Gas Tech. Mem. Am. Chem. Soc., Am. Inst. Chem. Engrs., AAAS, Am. Petroleum Inst. (dir.), Gulf Research Inst. (trustee), Soc. Automotive Engrs., Gulf Univs. Research Consortium (trustee). Clubs: Pinnacle (N.Y.C.), Baton Rouge Country, Camelot (Baton Rouge); Houston, Petroleum, Ramada (Houston). Home: Houston, Tex. Dec. Sept. 29, 1980.

KIRCHHOFFER, RICHARD AINSLIE, bishop; b. Souris, Manitoba, Can., June 28, 1890; s. Richard Beresford and Mary Elizabeth (Young) K.; brought to U.S., Aug. 15, 1890, naturalized, 1893; A.B., University of Southern California, 1913; student General Theol. Sem., N.Y. City, 1913-16, hon. S.T.D., 1939; D.D., University of the South, 1939, Kenyon College, 1944; m. Arline L. Wagner, Sept. 7, 1918; children—Richard Ainslie, Donald, James Hawley. Ordained to ministry P.E. Ch., 1916; asst. All Saints' Church, Worcester, Mass., 1916-18; rector All Saints' Ch., Riverside, Calif., 1919-25, Christ Ch., Mobile, Ala., 1925-39; bishop of Indianapolis from Feb., 1939. Home: Indianapolis, IN. †

KIRCHMAYER, LEON KENNETH, electrical engineer; b. Milw., July 24, 1924; s. Henry F. and Clara (Zenker) K.; m. Olga Temoshok, Dec. 2, 1950; children: Karyn, Kenneth. B.E.E., Marquette U., 1945; M.S. in Elec. Engring. (Univ. fellow 1945-46), U. Wis., 1947, Ph.D. in Elec. Engring. (Tau Beta Pi fellow 1947-48), 1950; grad. sr. exec. program, M.I.T., 1975. Lab. instr. and research asst. Marquette U., 1944-45; exptl. research engr. Cutler-Hammer, Inc., Milw., 1945-46; instr. elec. engring. U. Wis., Madison, 1946-48; with Gen. Electric Co., Schenectady, from 1948, mgr. system generation analytical engring., 1958-63, mgr. system planning and control, 1963-77, mgr. advanced system tech. and planning, from 1977. Author: Economic Operation of Power Systems, 1958, Economic Control of Interconnected Systems, 1959, (with D.N. Ewart, H.J. Fiedler and H.H. Happ) Modern Dispatch Techniques of Interconnected Power Systems, 1969; co-editor: (with W. Morsch) Technology Trends: Communications, Computers, Electric Energy, Electric Components, Instrumentation, 1975, A Technology Assessment Primer, 1975; assoc. editor: (with W. Hafele) Modeling of Large-Scale Energy Systems, 1981; contbr. articles to profl. jours. Bd. dirs. Schenectady Light Opera Co., 1952-57, pres. co., 1955-56. Recipient Disting. Service citation U. Wis., 1972; Mgmt. award Gen. Electric Co., 1951. Fellow IEEE, ASME; mem. Nat. Soc. Profl. Engrs. (Schenectady chpt. Engr. of Yr. 1965), Schenectady Gen. Electric Engring. Assn., Internat. Fedn. Automatic Control, Am. Automatic Control Council, Ops. Research Soc. Am., Conf. Internat. des Grands Reseaux Electriques á Haute Tension, Nat. Acad. Engring., Marquette U. Alumni Assn., U. Wis. Alumni Assn., Sigma Xi, Tau Beta Pi (Fellow 1946-47), Pi Mu Epsilon, Eta Kappa Nu. Clubs: Glen Hills Swimming, Mohawk, Mayfield Yacht. Patentee in field Home: Rexford, N.Y. Deceased.

KIRK, ALEXANDER COMSTOCK, diplomat; b. Chicago, Ill., Nov. 26, 1888; A.B. Yale, 1909; diplome, Ecole Libre des Sciences Politiques, 1911; LL.B., Harvard, 1914. Admitted to bar of Ill. Private sec. to 3d asst. sec. of state, 1915, assigned to Berlin, 1915, The Hague, 1917. Am. Commn. to Negotiate Peace, Paris, 1918-19, Tokyo, 1920, Peking, 1922; became 1st sec., Mexico City, 1924; asst. to under sec. of state, 1925; vice chmn. bd. of review for efficiency ratings, 1927; assigned 1st sec., Rome, 1928, counselor, 1929, consul gen., 1936; cons. gen. and counselor of embassy, Moscow, 1938; counselor of Embassy, Berlin, 1939, Rome, Sept. 1940; minister counselor, Rome, Nov. 1940; E.E. and M.P. to Egypt, also to Saudi Arabia, 1941; ambassador extraordinary and plentpotentiary, near the govt. of the King of the Hellenes, 1943; became U.S. rep. on advisory counsil for Italy, Apr. 1944; U.S. Polit. adviser to Supreme Allied Comdr. in Chief, Mediterranean Theater, Sept. 1944; ambassador to Italy from 1944. Address: Washington, D.C. †

KIRK, JAMES, army officer; b. Jacksonville, Fla., Feb. 24, 1890; s. James Edgar and Eunice Louisa (Gladwin) K.; student Sewanee Mil. Acad., Tenn., 1903-05, U. of Fla., 1905-08; B.S., U.S. Mil. Acad., 1912; m. Mildred E. Collins, Aug. 8, 1912; 1 son, James Edgar. Commd. 2d lt. coast arty., U.S. Army, June 12, 1912, and advanced through the grades to maj. gen., 1944; ordnance proof officer, 1917-22; chief of maintenance, Ordnance Dept., 1927-31; works mgr. Watertown Arsenal, 1934-38; officer in charge Small Arms Ammunition Factory, Frankford Arsenal, 1938-42; chief Small Arms Branch. Ordnance Dept., 1942-46; assistant chief of Ordnance, U.S. Army. Mem. Army Ordnance Assn., Alpha Tau Omega. Club: Army and Navy Country (Arlington, Va.). Home: Alexandria, Va. †

KIRKPATRICK, MARTIN GLEN, editor, writer; b. South English, Ia., Dec. 18, 1889; s. Martin Van Buren and Frances Virginia (Beery) K.; student Central U., Pella, Ia., 1912; B.S., Ia. State Coll., 1917; m. Eloise A. Dalrymple, Aug. 14, 1919; children—Virginia Lois (Mrs. James Rathmell), Barbara Jean (Mrs. Carl Pedersen). Tchr. pub. schools, Ia., 1908-12; chautauqua supt., Jones Chautauqua System and Lincoln Chautauqua, 1912-14; farm editor Des Moines (Ia.) Daily Register, 1916-17; asso. editor The Farm Journal, 1917, managing editor, 1943. Advertising director Dr. Hess & Clark, Inc., Ashland, O., 1944-48; dir. pub. relations, 1948-54; free lance writer, from 1954. Member Rosscraggon Woods, Incorporated, Iowa Hort. Society, Agrl. Editors Assn., Iowa Hist. Soc., N.C. Literary and Hist. Assn., Nat. Geneal. Soc., Gamma Sigma Delta, Sigma Delta Chi. Republican. Baptist. Contbr. articles on farm management. Home: Asheville, N.C. †

KIRKPATRICK, MILO ORTON, former coll. pres.; b. Memphis, Mo., Oct. 13, 1898; s. Elmer Morton and Florence Oleva (Barnes) K.; student U. Mo., 1915-17; grad. Chillicothe Coll., 1921, Chillicothe Sch. Art, 1923; m. Zeitha Genevieve Patterson, Sept. 23, 1927; children—Milo Orton, Robert Calvin. Dean bus. adminstrn. Astoria (Oreg.) Bus. Coll., 1921-22; v.p. Cecil's Bus. Coll., Asheville, N.C., 1923-32, exec. v.p., dir., 1933-43; pres. King's Coll., Charlotte, N.C., 1943-68, chmn. exec. bd., 1968-70, pres. emeritus, 1970-81; pres. Kirkpatrick Realty Corp., 1968-70. Pres., N.C. Assn. Pvt. Bus. Schs., 1939-41, So. Bus. Edn. Assn., 1941-43, Nat. Bus. Tchrs. Assn., 1956-57, Bus. Edn. Research Assos. Am., 1958-60; mem. N.C. Adv. Com. for Bus. Edn., 1944-58, Pres.'s Commn. for Edn. Beyond High Sch., 1954-57. Chmn. coll. div. United Appeal, 1964-65. Recipient Southeastern Bus. Coll. Assn. Outstanding Young Man of Year award in bus. edn. in N.C., 1965. Paul Harris fellow Rotary Found., 1971. Mem. Nat. (regional dir. 1958-60), N.C. (pres. 1957-58) rehab. assns., Adminstrv. Mgmt. Soc. (pres. Charlotte chpt. 1948-49, area nat. dir. 1952-54, Merit award 1956, Diamond Merit award 1965), Execs. Club. Republican. Presbyn. (deacon, pres. Mens Fellowship Club 1946-47). Rotarian. Contbr. articles to profl. publs. Died May 13, 1981.

KIRKPATRICK, RALPH, harpsichordist; b. Leominster, Mass., June 10, 1911; s. Edwin Asbury and Florence May (Clifford) K. A.B., Harvard U., 1931; Harvard fellow, Paris, Berlin, Eng., 1931-33; Guggenheim fellow for study 17th and 18th century music, 1937; Mus.D. (hon.), U. Rochester, Oberlin, 1973; studied with, Nadia Boulanger, Wanda Landowska, Arnold Dolmetsch, Gunther Ranin, Heinz Tiessen. Faculty Salzburg Mozarteum Acad., summers 1933, 34; dir. festivals 18th century music, Williamsburg, Va., 1938-46; vis. lectr. Yale U., 1940, asso. prof., 1956-65, prof. music, 1965-76; Ernest Bloch prof. music U. Calif. at Berkeley, 1964. Recorded albums Scarlatti sonatas, 1948, 53, 55, 70, Bach Clavier Ubung, 1952, Bach's Complete Keyboard Works, 1956-67, Mozart concertos, 1951, 56, sonatas, 1945-52; Author: Biography of Domenico Scarlatti, 1953; Editor: Scarlatti sonatas; Pub. concert, Berlin, 1933, other cities Germany and Italy, pub. concerts, U.S., 1934-84, harpsichord, clavicord solo and chamber music concerts, throughout U.S., 1939-84; soloist with major orchs. in U.S. and Europe, ann. transcontinental trips, 1944-84, European tours, 1947-84. Decorated Knight Cross Order Al merito della Republica, Italy). Mem. Am. Acad. Arts and Scis., Am. Philos. Soc. Home: Guilford, Conn. Died Apr. 13, 1984.

KIRKWOOD, MARION RICE, prof. law; b. Colorado Springs, Colo., July 9, 1887; s. Thomas Carter and Sarah (Lord) K.; A.B., Stanford U., 1909, J.D., 1911; LL.D., U. of Southern Calif., 1926; m. Mary Morrow Tucker, July 2, 1912; children—Thomas Frederic, Robert Lord. Admitted to Calif. bar, 1911; asst. prof. law, U. of Okla., 1911-12; asst. prof. law, Stanford U., 1912-15, asso. prof., 1915-18, prof. since 1918, William Nelson Cromwell professor since 1947, also acting dean, 1922-23, dean Law School, 1923-45. Visiting prof. Duke U., 1930-31. Acting prof. during summers, Cornell U., 1927, U. of Chicago, 1930, U. of Mich., 1931, U. of Washington, 1935, U. of Southern Calif., 1939. Pres. of Assn. of Am. Law Schools, 1934. Member American and California bar associations, Am. Assn. Univ. Profs., Delta Upsilon, Delta Chi, Phi Alpha Delta, Phi Beta Kappa, Order of the Coif (nat. pres. 1922-25). Mem. bd. dirs. San Francisco Legal Aid Soc. since 1926, Am. Judicature Soc., 1938-39; exec. com. Assn. Am. Law Schs., 1929, 35; mem. Law Sch. Editorial Bd., Commerce Clearing House, Inc., 1930-33; same, Foundation Press, Inc., since 1933; expert examiner (Law) for U.S. Civil Service Commn., 1941-44; "public" member, 10th Regional Advisory Council to Nat. War Labor Board, 1942-43; "public" Member, 10th Regional War Labor Board, 1943-45; mem. Statewide Adv. Com. to revise Calif. Constitution since 1947; mem. Regional Loyalty Bd. (12th region) U.S. Civil Service Comn. since 1948; mem. adv. and editorial com. on bar examinations Nat. Survey of Legal Profession since 1948; chmn. adv. bd., Stanford U., 1946-49. Conglist. Author: Cases on Conveyances, 2d edit., 1941; Calif. Annotations to Restatement of Property, 5 vols. (with Lowell Turrentine), 1948. Club: Commonwealth (San Francisco). Home: Palo Alto, Calif. Deceased.

KISSOCK, ALAN, mining engr.; b. Summit, N.J., Dec. 8, 1888; s. John and Margaret Lockhart (McNeil) K.; E.M., Colo. Sch. of Mines, 1912; m. Ethel Brinkerhoff Wheeler, Apr. 18, 1917; children—Jean McNeil, Joyce Bradford. Engr. Twin Buttes Mining Co., Tuscon, Ariz., 1912-14; mgr. Molybdenum Products Co., Tucson, 1914-17; with Carbon Steel Co., Pittsburgh, Pa., for War Industries Bd., 1917-18; pres. Steel Alloys Co., Los Angeles, Calif., 1918-22; mgr. Federal Mining Co., Jackson, Calif., 1922-24; engr. and metallurgist Climax Molybdenum Co., N.Y. City, 1924-30, v.p. in charge of production, 1930-38; v.p. in charge mfg., v.p. and dir. Climax Molybdenum Co. of Pa., 1938 to Apr. 30, 1942; consultant mining and metallurgical engineer. Received Stoiber metall. award, Golden, Colo., 1912, distinguished service award Am. Soc. Metals, 1948, distinguished service medal Colo. Sch. of Mines, 1949. Inventor of simplified processes of making molybdenum steels and other metallurgical ore treatment processes. Member Mining and Metall. Soc. of America, Am. Inst. Mining and Metall. Engrs., Am. Electrochem. Soc., Am. Soc. Metals, Sigma Alpha Epsilon, Theta Tau. Republican. Presbyn. Clubs: Mining, Union League (N.Y.C.). Address: New York, N.Y. †

KISTIAKOWSKY, GEORGE BOGDAN, educator; b. Kiev, Russia. Nov. 18, 1900; s. Bogdan and Mary (Berenstam) K.; came to U.S., 1926, naturalized, 1933; student Kiev pub. sch., and high sch., to 1918; Ph.D., U. of Berlin, 1925; D.Sc., Harvard, 1955, Williams Coll., 1958. Oxford, 1959, U. Pa., Columbio, 1960, U. Rochester, Carnegie Tech., 1961, Princeton U., Case Inst. Tech., 1962; m. Hildegard Moebius, 1926; 1 dau., Vera; m. 2d, Irma E. Shuler, 1945; m. 3d, Elaine Mahoney, 1962. Internat. research fellow, Princeton, 1926-28, research asso., 1928-30; asst. prof. chemistry, Harvard, 1930-33, asso. prof., 1933-37, prof. chemistry, 1937-59, 61-71, emeritus, 1972-82; spl. asst. to The Pres. for sci. and tech., 1959-61; chmn. sci. bd., dir. Itek Corp., 1961-73. Mem. Pres.'s Sci. Adv. Com., 1957-63. Recipient Medal for Merit, 1946; Nichols medal, 1947; Brit. Medal for Service in Cause of Freedom, 1948; Priestly award, 1958; Willard Gibbs medal, 1960; Presdl. Medal of Freedom, 1961; Ledlie prize, 1961, Parsons medal, 1963; Nat. Medal of Sci. 1967; Richards medal, 1968; Peter Debye award in phys. chemistry, 1968; Priestley medal, 1972. Hon. fellow Chem. Soc. (London); fgn. mem. Royal Soc.; mem. Nat. Acad. Scis. (v.p. 1965-73), Am. Acad. Scis., Am. Chem. Soc., Am. Philos. Soc., Am. Phys. Soc. Died Nov. 11, 1982.

KITCHEN, DELMAS KENDALL, pharmaceutical company executive, physician; b. Ark., Nov. 16, 1906; s. Newton and Mary K.; m. Patricia Grubb, July 28, 1972. B.A., Little Rock Coll., 1928; B.S., U. Ark., 1932, M.D., 1932. Intern Gorgas Hosp., Panama, C.Z., 1932-33; resident Polyclinic Hosp., N.Y.C., 1934; pvt. practice of medicine, Ark., 1935-36; successively sales and promotion, asst. to sci. dir. lab. research, asst. to v.p. research and product devel. Parke, Davis & Co., 1936-45; med. dir. Bristol Labs., 1945-49; v.p. Bristol-Myers Co., chief med. counsel asso. cos., 1949-52; cons. USPHS, 1949-55; asst. clin. prof. dermatology and syphilology Bellevue Med. Center, N.Y.U. Postgrad. Sch., 1949-56; v.p. Cortez F. Enloe, Inc., advt. agy., 1952-56; assoc. Emerson Cook Co. (underwriting and security investments), 1955-57; with Chattem Drug & Chem. Co. (and affiliates), 1959-72; chmn. product devel. com., asst. advt. and sales, also med. dir., now cons.; spl. med. cons. Warner-Lambert Research Inst., Morris Plains, N.J., from 1967. Author numerous bus., research publs. Mem. nat. exec. com. chmn. disaster com. Hamilton County chpt. A.R.C.; Bd. dirs. Cleve. Regional Mental Health Center, 1973. Decorated Medal of Honor Haiti, 1948; also awards Mexico Ministry Health; also awards Greek Dermatol. Union; also awards Cuba Med. Lab. Clinician Soc.; also awards Inst. Prophylactique France; also awards Portugese Soc. Dermatology. Mem. Assn. Med. Dirs. N.Y. (pres. 1951), Pharm

Mfrs. Assn., Pharm. Advt. Club, Proprietary Assn., AIM, Am. Acad. Dermatology and Syphilology, AAAS, Am. Chem. Soc., Am. Found. Tropical Medicine, AMA (life mem.), Tenn. Med. Assn. (life mem.), Hamilton County Med. Assn. (life mem.), Am. Pub. Health Assn., Soc. Tropical Medicine and Hygiene, Am. Venereal Disease Assn., Endocrine Soc., N.Y. Acad. Medicine (life mem.), N.Y. Acad. Scis., Soc. Investigative Dermatology, World Med. Assn. (founder mem. U.S. com.), Internat. Acad. Law and Sci. (mem. council from 1963), Aerospace Med. Assn., Internat. Narcotic Enforcement Officers Assn.; hon. mem. of fgn. sci. socs. Episcopalian (mem. vestry). Clubs: Mason (32 deg., Shriner), Kiwanian (bd. dirs.), Explorers (life mem.); Torch (Chattanooga). Home: Cleveland, Tenn.

KITTAY, SOL, apparel company executive; b. London, Eng., Nov. 6, 1910; s. Abraham Isaac and Rose (Darer) K.; came to U.S., 1926, naturalized, 1926; student N.Y.U., 1926-29; m. Frieda Strauss, Nov. 6, 1938; children—Arlyne (Mrs. Jeremy Zimmermann), Jeffrey. Pres. Superior Mills, Piqua, O., 1945-51; pres., chmn. bd. B.V.D. Co., Inc., N.Y.C., 1951-82; chmn. bd. Phoenix Textiles Industries Ltd., Malta, 1965-82, La Preparacion Textile, Barcelona, Spain, 1965-82, Flexees Internat., London, 1965-82, Arosa Hosiery Mfg. Co. Ltd., Eng., 1965-82; chmn., pres., chief exec. officer KDT Industries, Inc.; dir. Fedn. Bank and Trust Co., N.Y.C. Gen. campaign chmn. United Jewish Appeal, 1964. Bd. dirs. Beth Israel Hosp., Hillside Hosp., Am. Friends Hebrew U., Westchester Urban League; trustee Horace Mann Sch.; mem. Father's Day Council, N.Y.C. Mem. So. Garment Mfrs. Assn. (bd. dirs.), Confrerie des Chevaliers du Tastevin, Commanderies de Bordeaux, Physicians Wine Appreciation Soc. (bd. dirs.). Clubs: Harmonie (N.Y.C.); Old Oaks Country (Purchase, N.Y.); Fenway Country (White Plains, N.Y.). Home: Port Chester, N.Y. Died June 11, 1982.

KITTREDGE, HENRY CROCKER, teacher, author; b. Cambridge, Mass., Jan. 4, 1890; s. George Lyman and Frances Evelyn (Gordon) K.; grad. Nobel and Greenough School, Boston, Mass., 1908; A.B., Harvard, 1912; M.A. (hon.) Trinity College, 1938; married Gertrude Livingston, November 28, 1917; children—Barbara Livingston, James Gordon. Teacher Adirondack-Florida Sch., Onchiota, N.Y., 1912-16, St. Paul's Sch., Concord, New Hampshire, from 1916, became vice rector, 1929-47, rector from June 1947. Served as 1st lt. inf., A.E.F., World War. Mem. New Hampshire Hist. Soc., Am. Antiquarian Soc., Phi Beta Kappa. Republican. Episcopalian. Club: Tavern (Boston). Author: Cape Cod, Its People and Their History, 1930; Shipmasters of Cape Cod, 1935; Mooncussers of Cape Cod, 1937. Address: Concord, N.H. †

KLAUS, KENNETH BLANCHARD, musician, educator; b. Earlville, Iowa, Nov. 11, 1923; s. Kenneth R. and Iris (Blanchard) K.; B.A., U. Iowa, 1947, M.A., 1948, M.F.A., 1949, Ph.D., 1950; m. Marian Ida Fyler, June 8, 1947; children—Kenneth Sheldon, Karl Sherman. Prof., La State U., Baton Rouge, from 1950, alumni prof., 1966-80; assoc. condr. Baton Rouge Symphony, from 1965, prin. viola, from 1950. Served with USAAF, 1942-45; ETO. Mem. Am. Soc. Univ. Composers, Am. Musicol. Soc., Internat. Webern Soc., Berg Soc., Shoenberg Soc., Am. Mus. Library Assn., Am. Dedn. Musicians, Am. String Tchrs. Assn. (state pres.), Phi Mu Alpha, Omicron Delta Kappa, Pi Kappa Lambda, Phi Kappa Phi, Delta Phi Alpha. Author: The Romantic Period in Music. Composer over 100 compositions, 1940—. Home: Baton Rouge, La. Dec. 1980.

KLEEMAN, RITA HALLE, author; b. Chillicothe, O., May 23, 1887; d. Charles A. and Rachel (Lewis) Sulzbacher; A.B., Wellesley Coll., 1907; m. Louis J. Halle, Sept. 23, 1908; children—Rita (Mrs. Frederic Wm. Wile, Jr.), Louis J., Joseph Charles (dec.), Roger; m. 2d, Arthur S. Kleeman, Sept. 29, 1934. Mem. Writers War Bd., 1941-45 (chmn. juvenile book com.); chmn. western hemisphere solidarity com. Nat. Council Women, 1941-45; mem. Can.-Am. Com. (ex-dir.), Union Mujeres Americanas (dir.), Womens Conf., Nat. Fedn. Bus. and professional Womens Clubs, Authors League Am. (fund bd.), Am. Assn. Univ. Women, Pan Am. Women's Assn. Clubs: P.E.N. (vice-pres.), Wellesley, Woman Pays (N.Y. City); Lyceum (London). Author: Which College?, 1928, 30, 34; Gracious Lady: The Life of Sara Delano Rossevelt, 1935; A "Bible" for Freshman, 1937; Young Franklin Roosevelt, 1946. Contbr. Saturday Evening Post, Collier's mag., Red Book and other nat. mags. Home: New York, NY. †

KLEIN, ALFRED, govt. ofcl.; b. Wolozin, Poland, Sept. 28, 1887; s. Louis and Rachel (Berman) K.; came to U.S., 1898, naturalized, 1910; LL.B., Nat. U., Washington, 1924; m. Pearl Bellman, Oct. 22, 1915 (died Mar. 2, 1952). Washington corr. The Day, N.Y.C., 1916-30; gen. practice of law, Washington, 1925-30; accounting Navy and Treasury depts., 1910-19; investigator, examiner, mem. bd. of appeals, U.S. Civil Service Commn., Washington, from 1930, chief law officer, from 1943. Club: Federal (Washington). Home: Washington, D.C. †

KLEIN, JULIUS, retired army officer, journalist, public relations counsel; b. Chgo., Sept. 5, 1901; s. Leopold and Regina (Schick) K.; m. Helen von Holstein, May 11, 1928. Ed. Sophien Coll., Berlin, 1919; Grad., Sch. Mil. Govt., U. Va. War corr., World War I; editor Hearst Newspapers, 1926-33; exec. R.K.O., Universal Pictures, Hollywood, Calif., 1934-39; nat. comdr. Jewish War Vets. of U.S.A., 1947-48, chmn. exec. com., 1952; Chmn. Julius Klein Pub. Relations, Inc., 1947-84; Served as field clk. U.S. Mil. Mission U.S. Army, 1918-19; joined (33d Inf. Div.), 1933, head, investigation of subversive activities in middle west, 1932-34, lt. col., 1941; active service (33d div., Ill. N.G.), 1941; comd. (23d T.C. regt.), 1943, service in, South Pacific, Philippines, in charge of 10,000 troops in active theater of, South Pacific and Philippine Islands, 1943, advanced to col., 1944, spl. asst. to sec. of war, 1946, separated from service, 1946; continued assn. with U.S. N.G. as comdg. officer (623d T.C. group and attached service troops); brig. gen. (109th anti-aircraft arty. brig.), 1948-51, nominated brig. gen. of line (N.G. U.S.), 1949, confirmed, 1950; maj. gen. U.S. Army Res., trans., ret. maj. gen., 1966; nat. def. cons. to U.S. Senate; mem. Ill. Armory Bd., 1954-84, acting chmn., 1972-84. Author: American Spy, Black Cargo-Windy City. Republican candidate for U.S. senate, 1954; Nat. pres. Nat. Shrine to Jewish War Dead, until 1970; trustee Adm. Nimitz Found., Fredericksburg, Tex.; hon. dir. Hebrew Theol. Coll., Chgo. Decorated Soldier's Medal for Heroism, Citation for Heroism, Philippine Distinguished Service Star, Legion of Merit (2 clusters), Bronze Star, ribbon of French Legion of Honor, Knight Order Johanis (Denmark); recipient Nat. Comdrs. citation Catholic War Vets U.S., 1950; award Am. Jewish Lt. Found.; Distinguished Service award VA; Fighters for State of Israel medal. Hon. fellow Truman Library.; Mem. Chgo. Council Fgn. Relations, Pub. Relations Soc. Am., Am. Ordnance Assn., Assn. U.S. Army, Am. Legion, DAV, Amvets, Jewish War Vets. Republican (del. nat. conv. 1940, 48, 56, 60). Clubs: Mason, mem. B'nai B'rith, Army and Navy, Nat. Press, others. Made fact finding mission to Europe for Armed Services sub-com. U.S. Senate Appropriations Com., 1954. Home: Chicago, Ill. Died Apr. 6, 1984.

KLETZER, VIRGINIA MERNES, parent-teacher leader; b. Plattsmouth, Neb., Sept. 7, 1887; d. Peter and Theresa (Engels) Merges; ed. Portland (Ore.) Acad., 1901-06; m. William Kletzer, June 27, 1911; children—William Merges, Constance Marcile (Mrs. Clark P. Spurlock), Kenneth Miles. Vice pres. Nat. Congress of Parents and Teachers, 1937-40, pres., 1940-43. Vice chmn. Ore. Child Welfare Commn., 1931-39; mem. State Legislative Interim Commn., 1935-37, 1943-45; chmn. State Surv. Pub. Welfare, 1935-37. Trustee Endowment Fund Nat. Congress Parents and Teachers; mem. Governor's Committee on Children and Youth. Comdr. Ore. Div. Am. Cancer Soc.; trustee Oregon Merit Council, 1940-47. Mem. American Legion Auxiliary, Pi Gamma Mu, Delta Kappa Gamma. Republican. Unitarian. Club: Sorosis (Portland). Contbr. to Nat. Parent-Teacher Mag., etc.; editor Ore. Cancer Control News. Home: Portland, Oreg. †

KLIEFORTH, ALFRED WILL, pub. relations cons.; b. Mayville, Wis., Oct. 10, 1889; B.A., U. Wisconsin, 1913; LL.D., University of Manitoba, Canada, 1944; m. Barbara Leslie, Feb. 20, 1918; children—Alexander A., Leslie A. Attaché Am. Legation, Stockholm, Sweden, 1916; asst. mil. attaché Am. Embassy to Russia, 1916-19; apptd. economic expert on Russia and Poland, Dept. of State, 1929, consul, Mar. 1, 1923; consul at Berlin, Germany, 1924-27, Riga, Latvia, 1927-29; sec. Am. Embassy, Berlin, 1929-33; sec. of Legation, Vienna, 1933-35; consul general, Cologne, Germany, 1935-41, Winnipeg, Canada, 1941-45; counselor of embassy, Prague, Czechoslovakia, 1945; consul gen., Halifax, Can., 1946-48, Vancouver, B.C., 1948-50; pres. Foothills Pub. Co., La Mesa, Cal., 1953-54; broker E. S. Hope & Co., San Diego, 1955-57. Vice pres. San Diego Symphony, 1955. Commd. 1st lt. inf., 1918, now ret. capt. U.S. Army, Mem. English Speaking Union (v.p. San Diego 1955-57). Catholic. Clubs: Army and Navy Country, (Washington); University (dir. 1956) (San Diego, Cal.) Founder of Klieforth Canadian-Am. History Prize. Address: San Diego 3, Cal. †

KLINE, CHARLES TALCOTT, newspaper executive; b. Chgo., Jan. 18, 1911; s. William Shinn and Elma Erwin (Talcott) K.; A.B., U. Mich., 1932; m. Velma Helene Case, Apr. 20, 1935 (dec. July 1955); children—Marion Suzanne, Charles Talcott; m. 2d, Janet Poulsen, July 3, 1956; children—Nan, Sue, George. With advt. dept. Chgo. Tribune, 1934-35, Chgo. Times, 1935-37; nat. newspaper rep., 1937-43; sales dept. Met. Sunday Newspapers, Inc., 1943-50, Western mgr., 1950-53, v.p. 1953-54, pres., 1954-76. Pres., Newspaper Comics Council; bd. dirs. Mus. Cartoon Art, N.Y.C. Mem. Sigma Delta Chi, Theta Delta Chi. Clubs: Union League (N.Y.C.); Patterson, Saugatuck Shores (Westport); Weston (Conn.) Gun. Home: Westport, Conn. Died Jan. 16, 1985.

KLINE, NATHAN SCHELLENBERG, educator, research psychiatrist; b. Phila., Mar. 22, 1916; s. Ignatz and Florence (Schellenberg) K.; m. Margot Hess, June 29, 1942 (div. 1976); 1 dau., Marna Brill Anderson. A.B., Swarthmore Coll., 1938; postgrad., Harvard, 1938-39, New Sch. Social Research, 1940-41; M.D., N.Y. U., 1943; postgrad., Princeton, 1946-47, Rutgers U., 1947-48; M.A., Clark U., 1951, postgrad., 1951-53. Diplomate: Am. Bd. Psychiatry and Neurology. Intern, resident St. Elizabeths Hosp., Washington, 1943-44; staff VA, Lyons, N.J., 1946-50; child psychiatrist Union County Mental Hygiene Soc. Clinic, 1946-47; assoc. Columbia Greystone, 1947-50, N.Y. State Brain Research Project, 1948-50; research asst. dept. neurology Columbia Coll. Physicians and Surgeons, 1948-50, research assoc., 1952-55, research assoc. dept. psychiatry, 1955-57, asst. clin. prof., 1957-69, assoc. clin. prof., 1969-73, clin. prof., 1973-80; clin. prof. psychiatry N.Y. U., 1980-83; dir. research Worcester (Mass.) State Hosp., 1950-52, Rockland State Hosp. Research Center, Orangeburg, N.Y., 1952-75, Rockland Research Inst., Orangeburg, 1975-83; dir. psychiat. services Bergen Pines County Hosp., Paramus, N.J., 1963-75; cons. Lenox Hill Hosp., N.Y.C., 1974-83; profl. adv. com. Manhattan Soc. Mental Health, Nat. Com. Against Mental Illness; clin. adv. panel NIMH, 1957-59; temporary adviser WHO, 1957, expert adv. panel, 1973-83; pres. Internat. Com. Against Mental Illness. Contbr. articles profl. publs.; contbg. editor: Excerpta Medica, 1955-83; adv. editorial bd.: Internat. Jour. Social Psychiatry, 1958, Fgn. Psychiatry, 1972-74. Served to sr. asst. surgeon USPHS, 1944-46. Decorated knight Great Cross Master's Grace Sanctae Mariae Serenissimus Militaris Ordo; Commandeur Ordre Touissant-Louverture; Grande Officeur Legion d'Honneur et Merite Republic of Haiti; knight grand comdr. Liberian Humane Order of African Redemption Republic of Liberia; recipient Page One award sci. N.Y. Newspapers Guild, 1956, Adolf Meyer award Assn. Improvement Mental Health, 1956, Albert Lasker award Am. Pub. Health Assn., 1957, Henry Wisner Miller award Manhattan Soc. Mental Health, 1963, Albert Lasker clin. research award, 1964. Fellow Royal Coll. Psychiatrists (hon.), ACP, AAAS, N.Y. Acad. Medicine, Am. Psychiat. Assn. (chmn. research com. 1956-57), Royal Soc. Medicine (Eng.); found. fellow Royal Coll. Psychiatrists (Eng.); mem. AMA, Am. Psychol. Assn., Soc. Biol. Psychiatry, Soc. Exptl. Biology and Medicine, Am. Coll. Neuropsychopharmacology (pres. 1966-67), Indian Psychiat. Assn. (corr. mem.), Assn. Research Nervous and Mental Disease, Med. Soc. County N.Y., Sigma Xi; hon. mem. La Sociedad Colombian de Psiquiatria Republica de Colombia. Club: Atrium. Died Feb. 11, 1983.

KLINE, REAMER, educator; b. San Jose, Calif., Dec. 2, 1910; s. Allen Marshall and Florence (Reamer) K.; m. Louise E. Brayton, June 17, 1933; children—Florence (Mrs. David Britton), Penelope (Mrs. William Bardel), Marcia (Mrs. Larry Sharp). B.A., Middlebury (Vt.) Coll., 1932, D.D. (hon.), 1955; M.A., U. Mich., 1936; B.D., Episcopal Theol. Sch., Cambridge, Mass., 1938; S.T.D., Gen. Theol. Sem., 1963; L.H.D. (hon.), Bard Coll., 1974. Asst. editor Lydonville (Vt.) Union Jour., Colebroke (N.H.) News and Sentinel, 1933-34; ordained to ministry Episcopal Ch., 1938, curate, Fitchburg, Mass., 1939, rector, Nashua, N.H., 1938-44, St. Mark's Ch., New Britain, Conn., 1944-60; pres. Bard Coll., Annandale-on-Hudson, 1960-74, pres. emeritus, prof. Hebrew, 1974-83. Pres. standing com. Diocese Conn., 1955-56, chmn. dept. Christian edn., 1945-60; del. gen. convs. Episcopal Ch., 1943, 55, 58, convenor nat. confs. ch. and city, 1958-61. Chmn. New Britain Civil Rights Commn., 1957-60; mem. New Britain Commn. Urban Redevel., 1951-57; Bd. dirs. Empire State Found. Liberal Arts Coll., Union for Experimenting Colls. Founding mem. Assn. Episcopal Colls. Home: Barrytown, N.Y. Died Mar. 9, 1983.

KLOAP, JOHN MELNICK, foundry exec.; b. Nanticoke, Pa., Jan. 25, 1929; s. Peter and Palazesia (Melnick) K.; m. Nancy Ramey, Mar. 27, 1954; children—Kathryn Jeanne, Carolyn Ann, Suzanne Audrey, Elizabeth Jane, Eileen Ruth. B.S., Carnegie Inst. Tech., 1953. Mfg. trainee Continental Can Co., Md., N.Y., 1953-55, dir. product planning metal div., plant mgr., asst. div. mgr. mfg., 1969-70; v.p. ops. Nat. Can Co., Chgo., 1970-74; pres. CWC Castings div. Textron, Inc., Muskegon, Mich., from 1974; dir. Muskegon Bank & Trust Co. Bd. dirs. United Way, gen. chmn., 1976; trustee Hackley Hosp., Muskegon County Community Found. Served with USAF, 1946-49. Mem. Mfg. and Employers Assn. (dir. from 1975), Cast Metals Assn., Foundry Ednl. Found. (trustee), Am. Foundry Soc., Ductile Iron Soc. (dir.), Nat. Foundrymen's Assn., Nat. Mgmt. Assn., Muskegon Area C. of C. (vice chmn. from 1977), Sigma Nu. Episcopalian. Club: Rotary Internat. Address: Muskegon, Mich.

KLONOWER, HENRY, dir. tchr. edn. and certification; b. Phila., Sept. 14, 1888; s. Oscar and Sophia (Heintz) K.; B.S., Central High School, Phila.; grad. Phila. Sch. of Pedagogy, Phila., 1910; B.S., U. of Pa., 1915, A.M., 1920; student Temple U., 1921, Columbia, summer, 1920; hon. Pd.D., Ursinus Coll., Collegeville, Pa., 1936; A.F.D., Moore Inst. of Art, Sci. and Industry, 1950; LL.D., Waynesburg Coll., 1951; m. Elizabeth Luburg Peddrick, 1915 (died 1916); m. 2d, Reba Wilson Riegner, 1940 (dec. 1962). Tchr. elementary schs., Phila., 1910-16, Sch. of Pedagogy, Phila, 1916-18, high sch., Radnor, Pa., 1918-20; dir. in charge secondary certification and placement, Dept. Pub. Instrn., Pa., 1920-25, dir. Teachers Bur., 1925-34, chief Teacher Div., 1934-36; dir. Teacher Edn. and Certification, Pa. Dept. Pub. Instrn., 1936-55. Sec. Bd. of Pres. of State Teachers Colls., 1925-55; sec. Nat. Assn. of State Dirs. of Teacher Training and Certification, 1932-33, pres., 1933-39, 1945-46; pres. interstate Conf. on Common Problems in Teacher Edn., Columbia, 1937-38; chmn. subcom. on tchr. edn. and visual instrn., Am. Council Edn., 1955; exec. dir. Pa. Conservation Lab. Tchrs., 1945-55; chmn. Fulbright Scholarship Com., 1953-55; mem. bd. mgrs. Moore Inst. of Art, Phila., chmn. edn. com.; mem. adv. bd. Polyclinic Hosp., Harrisburg, Pa. Mem. R.O.T.C., 1917; farm insp. Sch. Mobilization Com., 1918. Mem. Am. Assn. Pub. School Adminstrs.

(life), Nat., Pa. edn. assns., Phi Sigma Pi, Kappa Phi Kappa, Phi Delta Kappa (chapter historian). Mason. Clubs: Schoolmen's, University of Pa. Alumni Assn. (Phila.); Torch (Harrisburg). Compiler: Syllabi for State Teachers Colls. courses in Preparation of Elementary and Secondary School Teachers, 1932. Contbr. to Public Education and other publs. on tchr. edn. Home: Harrisburg, Pa.

KLUCKMAN, REVONE W., electronics co. exec.; b. Mound City, S.D., Feb. 28, 1929; s. Arthur A. and Rose (Bollinger) K.; m. Mary Senftner, Oct. 17, 1956; children—Jeffrey, Jane. Partner Arthur Andersen & Co., 1952-67; with Zenith Radio Corp., Glenview, Ill., 1967-83, sr. v.p., 1971-77, pres., chief operating officer, 1977-79, pres., chief exec. officer, 1979-83. Served with U.S. Army, 1946-48. Home: Northbrook, Ill. Died July 18, 1983.

KLUGER, SAMUEL B., mfg. co. exec.; b. N.Y.C., Nov. 6, 1907; s. Nathan David and Regina Ray K.; m. Jean Goodwin, Feb. 22, 1941; children—Neal W., Victoria Kluger Sommer, Lynne Kluger Altshuler. Student public schs. With Eagle Electric Mfg. Co., Inc., Long Island City, 1929-82, v.p., 1944-69, pres., 1969-82, also dir.; pres., dir. Eagle Electric Can. Ltd., Eagle Electric Internat. Corp.; v.p. dir. Eagle Plastic Corp., 24th St Plaza Realty Corp. Mem. Nat. Elec. Mfrs. Assn., NAM. Jewish. Club: Masons. Home: Great Neck, N.Y. Died 1982.

KNAPP, HALSEY B., dir. agrl. edn.; b. Port Byron, N.Y., Sept. 1, 1888; s. Halsey and Anna (Bowles) K.; B.S., Cornell U., 1912, M.S., in Agr., 1913; LL.D. (honorary), Hofstra University, 1949; married Sarah Gertrude Newkirk, Apr. 5, 1913 (died Nov. 13, 1929); children—Merrill Newkirk, Dorothy Halsey (dec.), Laura Sherman, Janet Elizabeth; married 2d Grace Van Nostrand, August 4, 1952. Instr. N.Y. State Coll. of Agr., Cornell, 1912-13, asst. prof., 1913-16; director of the New York School of Agriculture, Cobleskill, N.Y., 1916-33; dir. Agr., and Tech. Inst., Farmingdale, N.Y., 1923-56; leader Los Bahos project in P.I. for Internat. Co-operation Adminstrn. Dir. Farmingdale Federal Savings and Loan Assn. Dist. gov. Rotary Internat., 1932-33, director, 1952-54, 1st v.p. 1953-54, chairman program planning com., observer at UN; pres. N.Y. State Assn. Crippled Children, 1954-56, dir., 1956. Dir. Near East Found. Trustee Indsl. Home for Blind, 1939-40. Member American Vocational Assn., N.Y. State Vocational Assn. (pres. 1941), New York State Agricultural Society (pres. 1939, 40), N.Y. State Horticultural Society, 7th degree Patrons of Husbandry (Grange), Alpha Zeta, Gamma Alpha, Delta Sigma Rho. Methodist. Author: Orchard and Small Fruit Culture (with E. C. Auchter), 1929; Growing Trees and Small Fruits (with E. C. Auchter), 1929. Address: Stony Brook, N.Y. †

KNAPP, JOSEPH GRANT, economist; b. Loveland, Colo., Nov. 22, 1900; s. Mason E. and Florence Amy (White) K.; m. Carol Maud Freston West, Feb. 13, 1929; children—Sheila Margaret (Mrs. Woodard), John Laurence. Student, Colo. A. and M. Coll., 1918-19, U. Ill., 1920-21, U. Chgo., 1923-24; B.S., U. Nebr., 1922, M.A. (H.E. Sidles scholar), 1923, D.Sc., 1967; Ph.D., Stanford, 1929; D.Sc., N.C. State U., 1967. Research asst. U. Chgo., 1923-24; fellow Food Research Inst., Stanford, 1924-25, teaching asst., 1925-26; mem. staff Inst. Econs., Brookings Instn., 1926- 29, 44-46; asso. prof. charge agrl. marketing, asso. agrl. economist N.C. State Coll., 1929-34; sr. agrl. economist FCA, 1934-36, prin. agrl. economist, 1936-48, asso. and acting chief coop. research and service div., 1948-53; adminstr. Farmer Coop. Service, U.S. Dept. Agr., Washington, 1954-66, ind. writer, cons., from 1966. Author: (with Edwin Griswold Nourse) The Cooperative Marketing of Livestock, 1931, The Hard Winter Wheat Pools, 1933, E.A. Stokdyk—Architect of Cooperation, 1953, Seeds That Grew—A History of The Cooperative Grange League Federation Exchange, 1960, Farmers in Business-Studies in Cooperative Enterprise, 1963, An Appraisement of Agricultural Cooperation in Ireland, 1964, An Analysis of Agricultural Cooperation in England, 1965, (with others) Great American Cooperators, 1967, The Glen Haven Story, 1967, The Rise of American Cooperative Enterprise, 1969, The Advance of American Cooperative Enterprise, 1973, Capper-Vostead Impact on Cooperative Structure, 1975, Edwin G. Nourse-Economist for the People, 1979; Contbr. (with others) articles to various profl. jours. Recipient Pioneer award Am. Inst. Cooperation, 1964; Coop. Communications award, 1973; The Coop. Found. Ellerbe award, 1975; named to Coop. Hall of Fame, 1979. Mem. Am. Econ. Assn., Am. Farm Econs. Assn., Am. Mktg. Assn. (pres. Washington chpt. 1956-57), Phi Kappa Phi, Sigma Nu, Alpha Kappa Psi. Club: Cosmos (Washington). Home: Bethesda, MD.

KNEISLY, NATHANIEL MCKAY, publishing co. exec.; b. Omaha, Apr. 5, 1892; s. Charles Christian and Harriet Augusta (McKay) K.; m. Mary Eleanor Simpson, June 5, 1923 (dec. Dec. 6, 1977); m. Gretchen Elsie Rider, June 18, 1979. Student, U. Ill., 1914. Vice pres., gen. mgr. Mut. Motor Stores, Chgo., 1914-16; sales mgr. Equipment Co., Kansas City, Mo., 1919-21, pres., 1921-23; with Irving-Cloud Pub. Co., Chgo., 1926-, v.p., gen. mgr., 1941-50, pres., 1950-65, vice chmn. bd., from 1965; Chmn. Nat. Bus. Publs., 1956-57. Active U. Ill. Found. Served with U.S. Army, 1917-18. Mem. Theta Delta Chi. Club: President's of U. Ill. Home: Evanston, Ill.

KNERR, HUGH JOHNSTON, U.S.A.F. officer; b. Fairfield, Ia., May 30, 1887; s. Ellsworth Brownnell and Elizabeth (Barclay) K.; student Midland Coll., 1900-04, U.S. Naval Acad., 1904-08, U.S. Army Staff Sch., 1925-26, U.S. Army War Coll., 1930-31; various special schs. in Coast Arty. and Air Corps; m. Hazel Dow, Sept. 2, 1910; 1 son, Hugh S. Grad. U.S. Naval Acad., 1908; ensign, U.S. Navy, 1908-12; transferred to Coast Arty., U.S. Army, 1912-17; mil. aviator, U.S. Army Air Corps., 1917-39; served as air officer Hawaiian Dept., 1918-19; command 88th Observation Squadron, 2d Bombardment Group, chief of staff of G.H.Q. Air Force, 1935-38; air officer 8th Corps Area at time of retirement; retired as col. because of physical disability incident to mil. service, Mar. 21, 1939; became mil. advisor Sperry Gyroscope Co., 1939, returned to active service as dept. comdr., Hdqrs. Air Service Comd., Fairfield, O., Oct. 1942; brig. gen., July 1943; dep. comdr. VIII Air Service Comd., London, Eng.; comdg. gen. Hdqrs. Air Service Comd., U.S. Strategic Air Forces in Europe, and dep. comdg. gen. for adminstrn. (London), Jan. 1944; maj. gen., Mar. 1944; dep. comdg. gen. for adminstrn., Paris, Fr., Dec. 1944; comd. Hdqrs. Air Tech. Service Comd., Wright Field, Dayton, O., June 1945; inspector general of the U.S. Air Force, 1948-49; vice pres. Liberty Liners. Incorporated from 1950. An associate of Gen. William Mitchell and long a partisan to get air power recognized as the primary strategic weapon for U.S.; in collaboration with Gen. Andrews furthered doctrines of Air Forces in active service. Decorations: D.S.M., Legion of Merit, Bronze Star, War Dept. Commendation. Am. Defense with star, European Campaign with 3 stars. Liberty Medals both World Wars; French Legion of Honor, Croix de Guerre with palms; British Companion of the Bath. Mem. Soc. Naval Architects and Marine Engrs. Lutheran. Author: The Student Pilots Training Primer, 1941. Contbr. to Am. Mercury. Home: Annapolis, Md. †

KNIGHT, CLAUDE ARTHUR, biologist, educator; b. Petoskey, Mich., Oct. 17, 1914; s. Claude and Wilhelmina Ruth (Hedt) K.; m. May Marion Ferry, June 19, 1943; children—Thomas Arthur, Susan Knight Hamamura, Robert Stanley. B.S., Alma Coll., 1936; Ph.D., Pa. State U., 1940. Research fellow Rockefeller Inst. Med. Research, Princeton, N.J., 1940-48; prof. molecular biology U. Calif., Berkeley, from 1948, chmn. dept., 1976-78; dir. U. Calif. (Virus Lab.), 1976-78; dir. NSF Summer Inst. in Molecular Biology, 1964-73; cons. USPHS virology study com., 1965-69. Author: Chemistry of Viruses, 1975, Molecular Virology, 1974; asso. editor: Virology, 1963-65; contbr. articles to profl. jours. Recipient certificate of merit OSRD, 1948; USPHS research grantee, 1952-79. Mem. Am. Soc. Biol. Chemists, Am. Soc. Microbiology, AAAS, Sigma Xi. Home: Saint Helena, Calif.

KNIGHT, FRANCES GLADYS, former govt. ofcl.; b. Newport, R.I., July 22, 1905; d. Frederick and Fanni (Smolik) K.; ed. in France, Czechoslovakia, Monaco; student N.Y. U., Columbia U., Hunter Coll., N.Y.C.; L.H.D., Mo. Valley Coll., Marshall, 1963; m. Wayne W. Parrish, Sept. 15, 1935. Div. chief Nat. Indsl. Recovery Adminstrn., 1934-36; dep. dir. info. program WPA, 1936-39; pub. relations cons. White House Conf. on Children, 1940; spl. asst. to commr. Nat. Def. Adv. Com., 1941-42; pub. relations dir. U.S. Office Civilian Def., 1942-45; dir. pub. relations Am. Retail Fedn., 1945-47; congressional cons., 1947-48; info. specialist, dep. adminstr. security and consular affairs Dept. State, 1948-55, dir. Passport Office, 1955-77. Home: Washington, D.C. Deceased.

KNIGHT, FRANK BURKE, publisher; b. Lampasas, Tex., Aug. 15, 1928; s. Burke Charles and Ina Mae (Gunter) K.; m. Frances Watson Seaborn, June 23, 1951; children: David B. (dec.), Susan G., Sandra J., Nancy B., Philip M. (dec.), John P. Student, U. Tex., 1947-49. Advt. salesman Lampasas Dispatch, 1949; pub. Florence (Tex.) Post, 1949-52, Taylor (Tex.) Times, 1952-53; editor, advt. mgr. Winkler County News, Kermit, Tex., 1953-62; advt. dir. Coin World, Sidney, Ohio, 1962-69; pres. Collector's Media Inc., pubs. Am. Collector, Plate Collector, Kermit, 1969—; dir. Golden West Leasing Inc., Collectables Inc.; pub. cons. Mayor of Florence, 1952. Contbr. sect. to book; articles to publs. including Antiques USA. Mem. adv. bd. Kermit Community Ch., 1981-83, chmn., 1983. Served with USMC, 1950-52. Mem. Am. Ltd. Edit. Assn. (exec. dir.), Am. Numis. Assn. Clubs: Kermit Jaycees (pres., dir. 1954-61, Service award 1958), Kermit Rotary (dir. 1962). Died May 5, 1983.

KNIGHT, HARRY HAZELTON, entomologist; b. Koshkonong, Mo., May 13, 1889; s. Wells George and Emma E. (Lamb) K.; student State Teachers Coll., Springfield, Mo., 1908-10; B.S., Cornell U., 1914, Ph.D., 1920; m. Jessie Mae Kite, Aug. 4, 1919; children—Harold Kite (lt., died in action, 1945), Rolland Carl. Entomologist for Genesee County, N.Y., Fruit Growers' Association, 1914-16; investigator in entomology, experiment station, Cornell University, 1916-17; assistant prof. entomology and curator collections, U. of Minn., 1919-24; asst. prof. entomology, Ia. State Coll. Agr. and Mechanic Arts, 1924-25, asso. prof., 1925-35, prof. since from 1935. 2d lt. A.S., U.S. Army, 1918; c.o. 20th Aerial Photo Sect., 1918-19 Fellow A.A.A.S., Entomol. Soc. Am. (pres. 1948); mem. Am. Assn. Econ. Entomol., N.Y. Entomol. Soc., Société Entomologique de France, Société Entomologique de Belgique, Sigma Xi, Gamma Alpha, Phi Kappa Phi, Alpha Gamma Rho, Alpha Zeta, Gamma Sigma Delta; asso. mem. Am. Mus. Natural History. Author: (with Dr. W.E. Britton) Hemiptera of Connecticut, 1923; Miridae of Illinois, 1941. Editor Hemiptera sect. Biol. Abstracts. Home: Ames, Ia. †

KNIGHT, HARRY WALLACE, stock broker; b. Goderich, Ont., Can., May 26, 1887; s. William R. and Jennie (Saunders) K.; student pub. schs.; m. Grace E. Martin, Nov. 18, 1908; children—Grace Martin (Mrs. George W. Gooderham), Harry William. Vice pres. Service Station Equipment Co., Ltd., 1928-33; partner Draper Dobie & Co., from 1933; pres. Barvue Mines, Ltd., 1950-59; president Manitou Bar vue Mines Ltd., from 1959; pres. Will Roy Mines Ltd.; dir. John Wood Industries, Ltd., also American Zinc Lead & Smelting Co., Inc. †

KNIGHT, JOHN JAMES, grain merchant; b. Woonsocket, S.D., Nov. 28, 1888; s. Joseph and Anna (Richter) K.; student Dakota Wesleyan U., Mitchell, S.D., 1906-07, Drake U., 1909-11, Capital City Commercial Coll., Des Moines, Ia., 1911-12; A.B., Cornell Coll., Mt. Vernon, Ia., 1916; m. Josephine E. Hammels, of Glendale, Ariz., Sept. 25, 1916; children—John James, Elizabeth Josephine, Dorothy Lucille. Clk. and teller Citizens Nat. Bank, Woonsocket, 1907-09; dist. agt., Salina, Kan., Great Western Ins. Co., 1911-12; traveling salesman N. J. Heinz Co., 1914; dep. county treas., Palo Alto Co., Ia., 1917; stock dealer, Glendale, Ariz., 1918; instr. of mil. training, Wentworth Mil. Acad., Lexington, Mo., 1918-19; with Equity Union Grain Co., Kansas City, Mo., since 1919, sec.-treas. and gen. mgr. since 1921; sec.-treas. Equity Union Mercantile Co., Equity Union Auditing Assn.; mem. orgn. com. Farmers Nat. Grain Corpn., also dir., mem. exec. com. and mem. bd. of mgrs.; mem. orgn. com. Nat. Chamber Agrl. Coöperatives (now Nat. Coöperative Council); editor and mgr. The Kernel (assn. mag.). Mem. Izaak Walton League America, Zoöl. Soc. of Kansas City, Sigma Alpha Epsilon, Gamma Sigma Kappa. Republican. Methodist. Mason. Clubs: Kansas City Grain, Blenheim Fathers. Home: Kansas City, Mo. †

KNIGHT, JOHN SHIVELY, newspaper publisher; b. Bluefield, W.Va., Oct. 26, 1894; s. Charles Landon and Clara Irene (Scheifly) K.; student Tome Sch., Md., 1911-14, Cornell U., 1914-17; LL.D., U. Akron, 1945, Northwestern U., 1947, Kent State U., 1958, Ohio State U., 1961, U. Mich. 1969, Oberlin Coll., 1969, Colby Coll., 1969; m. Katharine McLain, Nov. 21, 1921 (dec. 1929); children—John Shively (dec. 1945), Charles Landon, Frank McLain (dec.); m. 2d, Beryl Zoller Comstock, Jan. 24, 1932 (dec. Aug. 1974); 1 dau., Mrs. Kenneth Hewitt; m. 3d, Elizabeth Good Augustus, Jan. 6, 1976. Newspaper reporter and exec., 1920-25; mng. editor Akron (Ohio) Beacon Jour., 1925-33; editor 1933-71, editorial chmn., 1971-76, editor emeritus, 1976-81; editorial dir. Springfield (Ohio) Sun, 1925-27; editorial dir. Massilion (Ohio) Ind., 1927-33, pres., 1933-37; chmn. bd., pub. Miami (Fla.) Herald, 1937-67, editorial chmn., 1967-76, editor emeritus, 1976-81; pres. Beacon Jour. Pub. Co., Knight Newspapers, Inc., to 1966, editorial chmn., 1966-76, editor emeritus, 1976-81; purchased and discontinued Miami (Fla.) Tribune, Nov. 30, 1937; purchased Detroit Free Press, 1940, pres. and editor, 1940-67, editorial chmn., to 1976, editor emeritus, 1976-81; owner, editor and pub. Chgo. Daily News, 1944-59; v.p. Charlotte (N.C.) Observer, 1954, Charlotte News, from 1959, also Tallahassee Democrat. Chief liaison officer between U.S. and Brit. censorship, London, Eng., 1943-44; v.p., dir. Asso. Press. Trustee emeritus Cornell U., U. Miami. Served with 113th Inf., AAC and AEF, 1917-19. Recipient Frank M. Hawks Meml. trophy, 1947, citation of merit from Poor Richard Club, 1946, gold medal of achievement, 1972; Honor award distinguished service journalism U. Mo. 1949; Brotherhood of Children award, 1946; medal for achievement in journalism Syracuse U., 1946; La Prensa award, 1954, Am.'s Found. award, 1959, John Peter Zenger award, 1967, Pulitzer prize for distinguished editorial writing, 1968; Carr Van Anda award Ohio U., 1970; William Allen White award of journalistic merit, 1972; Fourth Estate award Nat. Press Club, 1976; others; cited Outstanding Chicagoan in Inter-Am. relations U.S.-Uruguay alliance, 1952. Established Knight Meml. Fund commemorating his father; La Prensa Scholarship furthering Inter-Am. understanding. Mem. Am. Soc. Newspapers Editors (past pres.), V.F.W., Am. Legion, A.P. (past dir., chmn. finance com., mem. exec. com.), 40 and 8, Phi Sigma Kappa, Sigma Delta Chi. Episcopalian. Clubs: Portage Country (Akron); Tin Whistles (Pinehurst, N.C.); Bath, Indian Creek (Miami); Union (Cleve.); Detroit, Detroit Athletic, Detroit Economic, Country Grosse Pointe (Detroit); Burning Tree Golf (Washington); Tavern, Casino, Commercial (Chgo.); Old Elm (Ft. Sheridan, Ill.); Kirtland Country (Willoughby, Ohio). Home: Akron, Ohio. Died June 16, 1981.

KNIGHT, RICHARD BENNETT, educator, cons. engr.; b. Cin., Oct. 11, 1914; s. Harry C. and Helen (Van Horn) K.; B.S., U. Md., 1935; M.S., U. Ill., 1939; m. Sara Kelso Wooten, May 27, 1944 children—Barbara Ann, Richard Bennett. Grad. research asst. Am. Soc. Heating and Ventilating Engrs.; fellow in mech. engring. U. Ill., Urbana, 1937-39; air conditioning engr. Md. Refrigeration Co., Balt., 1940, York-Shipley, Inc., York, Pa., 1946; mech. engr. Army Chem. Center, War Dept., Md., 1940-42; vibrations engr. Glenn L. Martin Co., Middle River, Md., 1942-45; asso. prof. heating and ventilating U Ky., Lexington, 1946-52; L.L. Vaughan prof. mech engring. N.C. State U., Raleigh, 1952-83; Fulbright vis lectr. Alexandria (Egypt) U., 1951; UNESCO lectr., Lebanon, Syria, Iraq, 1951; heating and air conditioning cons. to architects and engrs., from 1952; heat transfer and air conditioning cons. Convair, Ft. Worth, Martin Co., Balt., 1953-57; research participant Oak Ridge Inst. Nuclear Studies, 1958-59; heat transfer cons. Oak Ridge Nat. Lab., 1958—; chief scientist P.R. Nuclear Center, Mayaquez, 1961-62, heat transfer cons., 1962; AEC lectr. in univs. and atomic energy labs., Brazil, Argentina, Bolivia, Peru, Columbia, 1962. Mem. N.C. Bd. Refrigeration Examiners, from 1968, chmn. bd., 1970. Bd. dirs. N.C. State Coll., Raleigh YMCA. Recipient Outstanding Tchr. award N.C. State U., 1969-70, Outstanding Extension Service award, 1976-77. Registered profl. engr., N.C., Ky. Mem. Am. Soc. Engring. Edn., Am. Soc. Heating, Refrigerating and Air Conditioning Engrs., Pi Tau Sigma. Presbyn. Lion. Club: Raleigh Engineers. Home: Raleigh, N.C. Died Aug. 31, 1983.

KNIGHT, TELFAIR, maritime service officer; b. Jacksonville, Fla., July 12, 1888; s. Raymond Demeré and Katherine Varina (Telfair) K.; student Sewanee Mil. Acad., 1901-03; A.B., U. of the South, Sewanee, Tenn., 1907; LL.D., University of Miami (Fla.), 1950; married Cecil Mayfield Grimme, February 1, 1909; 1 son, Telfair. Pres. Knight Crockery and Furniture Co., Jacksonville, Fla., 1908-15; practiced law, Jacksonville, 1915-23; gen. mgr. Coral Gables (Fla.) Corp., 1923-28, George E. Merrick Coral Gables Co., 1928-30; gen. mgr. Peacock Motion Picture Co., Shanghai, China, 1930-34, pres., New York City, 1934; counsel for Textile Labor Relations Bd. and Nat. Steel Labor Relations Bd., 1934-36; gen. counsel Bituminous Coal Labor Bd., 1935-36; sec. U.S. Maritime Commn., 1936-37, asst. to Rear Adm. H. A. Wiley, retired, mem. of the commn., 1937-40, acting dir., div. of training, 1940, dir. of div., 1940-42; asst. deputy administr., training organization, War Shipping Administrn., 1942-46; director Training Organization U.S. Maritime Commission, 1946-48; chief bur. Maritime Service. U.S. Maritime Commn. and Commandant U.S. Maritime Service, 1948-50; chief division of maritime training, Maritime Administration. Dept. of Commerce from 1950; connected with program for training personnel for Merchant Marine. United States Marchant Marine Cadet Corps and U.S. Maritime Service since 1938; rank of commodore U.S. Maritime Service, 1944, became comdt. of the service, 1945, rear admiral, 1946. Served with F.A., U.S. Army, 1918. Mem. Soc. Safety Engrs., Am. Legion, Kappa Alpha. Democrat. Episcopalian. Mason (32 deg.). Club: Propeller (Washington). Home: Merrifield, Va. †

KNIPE, JAMES LAUNCELOT, econ. cons.; b. Marshall, Ill., Mar. 31, 1904; s. Henry Hedges and Mabel (Graham) K.; m. Danielle Rolin, June 14, 1930; children—James Graham, Peter Rolin. Ph.B., Yale U., 1926, M.A., 1934; Ph.D., 1940. Organizer, financier telephone utilities, Chgo., 1926-32, own investment counsel firm, New Haven, 1932-41; research dir. Hawaii Employers' Council, Honolulu, 1946-47; asst. to pres. to v.p., dir. Union Bag & Paper Corp., N.Y.C., 1947-51; v.p., gen. sales mgr., dir. Ball Bros. Co., Inc., Muncie, Ind., 1952; exec. v.p., dir. C.E. Hooper, Inc., 1953, pres., chmn. bd., 1954-57; cons. to chmn. bd. govs. Fed. Res. System, 1959-62, financial and econ. cons., 1962-81; vis. prof. finance U. N.C., Chapel Hill, 1965-67; prof. econs. East Carolina U., Greenville, 1967-72; financial cons., writer, 1972-81. Author: (with Alexander Calder) The Guaranteed Annual Wage, 1948, The Federal Reserve and the American Dollar, 1965, Inflation in the United States: How It Happened, How to Stop It, 1978. Served to comdr. USNR, 1941-46. Clubs: Yale (N.Y.C.); Chevy Chase (Md.); Nassau, Princeton. Home: Sea Girt, N.J. Died Nov. 23, 1981.

KNOCH, WIN G., judge; b. Naperville, Ill., May 24, 1895; s. William and Adolphine C. (Boecker) K.; m. Irene Mae Fauth, June 30, 1926; children—Marjorie Ann (Mrs. Kenneth Schaller), Marion Jean (Mrs. Donald Wehrli), Doris Marie (Mrs. Warren Wood), Joanne (Mrs. James Strong). LL.B., DePaul U., 1917; LL.D., North Central Coll., St. Procopius Coll., Lisle, Ill.; , DePaul U., 1968. Bar: Ill. bar 1917. Since practiced in, Naperville; partner firm Reed, Knoch & Keeney, 1922-30, asst. state's atty., DuPage County, 1922-30, county judge, 1930-39; circuit judge 16th Jud. Circuit Ill., 1939-53; U.S. dist. judge, 1953-58; judge U.S. Ct. Appeals, 1958-67; sr. circuit judge U.S. Ct. Appeals 7th circuit, 1967-83. Gen. chmn. Naperville Centennial Celebration, 1931, DuPage County Centennial, 1939. Served as lt. inf. U.S. Army, AEF, 1917-19. Recipient Silver Beaver Boy Scouts Am. Mem. ABA, Ill. Bar Assn., DuPage County Bar Assn. (past Pres.), Ill. County and Probate Judges Assn. (past Pres.), Ill. Circuit and Superior Judges Assn. (past pres.), Am. Legion (past comdr. city, county, dist.), 40 and 8. Republican. Roman Catholic. Clubs: K.C, Elk, Moose, Naperville Country. Home: Naperville, Ill. Died May 23, 1983.*

KNOTT, J. PROCTOR, educator; b. Lebanon, Ky., Oct. 15, 1890; s. Joseph McElroy and Mattie Taylor (Rubel) K.; A.B., Princeton, 1913. A.M., 1914; Ph.D., U. Wis., 1933; student Univs. of Clermont-Ferrand and Montpellier, France, 1921-22. Instr. French Northwestern, 1916-21; asst. prof. French Coll. Wooster, 1922-26; acting head fgn. lang. dept. State Coll. Wash., 1926-28, asso. prof. French, 1928-30; instr. French U. Wis., 1930-33; mem. faculty Center Coll. from 1933, prof. French from 1936, head dept. from 1942. Mem. Modern Lang. Assn. Am., Phi Beta Kappa. Democrat. Presbyn. Home: Lebanon, Ky. †

KNOTT, J(OSEPH) C(ARLTON), agrl. educator; born Tipton, Ia., May 25, 1893; s. Carlton Joseph and Ida McKee (Lupton) K.; B.S., State Coll. of Wash., 1920; M.S., 1930; Ph.D., U. of Minn., 1941; m. Bess E. Sleater, June 21, 1922 (dec.); 1 son, Robert Joseph; m. 2d, Rae Russell, July 26, 1947. Herdsman, State Coll. of Wash., 1920-26, instr. dairy husbandry, 1926-30, asst. prof., 1930-36, asso. prof., 1930-40, prof., 1940-42, dir. of agrl. extension service, 1942-46, dir. Inst. Agrl. Scis., 1946-55, prof. dairy science, 1955-58; technical consultant to Foreign Agricultural Service in several Latin American countries, from 1958. Mem. dairy research and marketing adv. com. U.S. Dept. Agriculture. Served with U.S. Army, 1917-19. Mem. Am. Dairy Sci. Assn., Soc. of Animal Prodn., Am. Farm Econ. Assn., A.A.A.S., Am. Legion, Sigma Xi, Phi Kappa Phi, Phi Sigma, Phi Eta Sigma, Alpha Gamma Rho. Mason. Methodist. Club: Kiwanis. Contbr. to bulletins, sci. and popular jours. Home: Pullman, Wash. Died Nov. 19, 1975.

KNOTT, LAURA A., academy prin.; A.B., Hamline U., 1887; A.M., Radcliffe Coll., 1897; unmarried. Head dept. of English, Lowell (Mass.) Normal Sch., 1897-1901; prin. Bradford (Mass.) Acad., 1901-1918. Author: Teaching of English in Normal Schs., 1900 (publ. for Paris Expn.); Vesper Talks to Girls, 1916. Home: Brookline, Mass. †

KNOWLES, RICHARD, educator; b. Boston, Jan. 1, 1889; s. Charles Sumner and Nina (Adams) K.; student St. Mark's Sch. Southboro, Mass., 1901-05; A.B., Harvard, 1908; LL.B., 1911, Ph.D., 1930; A.M., U. of Pa., 1936; m. May Ashley, Sept. 23, 1916; children—Mary, Hope, Nina, Charles Sumner, Sylvia. Admitted to Mass. bar, 1911, and practiced in New Bedford; mem. New Bedford Common Council, 1912-13, pres. 1913; mem. Mass. Ho. of Rep., 1914-15, Senate, 1916-17; master St. Mark's Sch., 1918-31; headmaster Great Neck N.Y.) Prep. Sch., 1931-35; became headmaster William Penn Charter Sch. (country day school for boys), Philadelphia, 1935, then head of English department Avon (Conn.) Sch. Republican. Unitarian Clubs: Germantown Cricket, Phila. Cricket, New Bedford Yacht. Address: Philadelphia, Pa.†

KNOX, WALTER EUGENE, III, medical educator; b. Norcatur, Kans., July 21, 1918; s. Walter Eugene and Lucy (Frewen) K.; m. Olga Halpert, Oct. 6, 1967; children—Phebe Lee (Mrs. William E. Whitehead), Tamsin Ann, Walter Eugene IV. A.B., U. Nebr., 1939; M.D., Harvard U., 1943. Intern, then asst. physician Presbyn. Hosp., N.Y.C., 1943-48; spl. research fellow USPHS, U. Cambridge (Eng.) and Nat. Inst. Med. Research, London, 1949-52; asso. prof. biochemistry Tufts U. Med. Sch., 1953; prof. biochemistry Am. U., Beirut, 1961-62; mem. faculty Harvard Med. Sch. and New Eng. Deaconess Hosp., Boston, from 1953, prof. biol. chemistry, from 1969; Chmn. metabolism study sect. NIH, 1962-65. Author papers in field.; Editor: Enzyme; co-editor: Research in Medical Science. Served to capt., M.C. U.S. Army, 1944-47. Recipient Claude Bernard medal U. Montreal, 1970. Fellow N.Y. Acad. Sci.; mem. Am. Assn. Cancer Research, Am. Chem. Soc., Am. Soc. Biol. Chemistry, Am. Soc. Human Genetics, Biochem. Soc., Harvey Soc., Japanese Biochem. Soc. (hon.). Home: Brookline, Mass.

KNOX, WILLIAM CARROLL, JR., lawyer; b. Winchester, Tenn., Oct. 13, 1916; s. William Carroll and Laura (Mason) K.; A.B., Harvard U., 1938, LL.B., 1941; m. Inge Madsen, July 17, 1948; children—John William, Peter Erik. Admitted to N.Y. bar, 1942; asso. firm White & Case, 1946-55, partner, 1955-81. Served in U.S. Army, 1942-46. Mem. Assn. Bar City N.Y., N.Y. State Bar Assn., Am. Bar Assn., Internat. Bar Assn., Am. Law Inst., Nat. Bankruptcy Conf., Am. Soc. Internat. Law. Clubs: Down Town Assn., Board Room, Manhattan. Home: Ridgewood, N.J. Died Mar. 14, 1981; interred Washington Meml. Park, Paramus, N.J.

KNOX, WILLIAM WALLACE, U.S. judge; b. Erie, Pa., June 18, 1911; s. Wallace John and Edna (Wallace) K.; A.B., U. Mich., 1932, J.D., 1935; m. Agnes Ruth Graham, Sept. 5, 1936; children—Virginia M., Wallace John, Charles Graham, Katherine Elizabeth. Admitted to Pa. bar, 1935, practice in Erie, 1935-70; partner Knox, Graham, Pearson & McLaughlin, to 1970; judge U.S. Dist. Ct. Western Dist. Pa., 1970-81. Past pres. Erie County Lawyers Title Co.; past, sec., dir. Lyons Transp. Co.; past dir. Worster Motor Lines, Inc. Solicitor, Erie Sch. Dist., 1943-46, Harborcreek Twp. Sch. Dist., 1955-70, Millcreek Sch. Dist., 1959-70, Erie County Sch. Bd., 1961-70, Union City Sch. Bd., 1963-70, Erie Met. Transit Authority, 1966-70, Pa. Transp. Assistance Authority, 1968-70. Mem. bd. pub. assistance Erie County, 1955. Bd. dirs., pres. Family and Child Service of Erie; mem. com. of visitors Mich. Law Sch., 1972-81. Served to 1st lt. Pa. State Guard, 1941-46. Recipient certificate of Merit, Family and Child Service, 1956. Mem. Am., Pa., Erie County (pres.) bar assns., Am. Judicature Soc., Erie C. of C. (dir.), Pa. Citizens Assn. (dir. 1955-64, v.p. 1957-61), Order of Coif, Phi Beta Kappa. Republican. Presbyterian (trustee). Mason. Home: Erie, Pa. Dec. Aug. 30, 1981.

KNUDSEN, ARTHUR MILLER, clergyman; b. St. Paul, Minn., June 30, 1887; s. William Martin and Bertha Gurine (Thori) K.; B.A., Red Wing Sem., 1910, B.D., 1913; D.D., Midland Coll., Fremont, Neb., 1938; m. Elna Annette Jorgensen, May 14, 1913 (died 1928); 1 son, Arthur Miller; m. 2d, Ethel Grace Petersen, June 10, 1930; children—Grace Dorcas, Donald Peters, Carol Elizabeth, Alice Margaret. Ordained Lutheran ministry, 1913; pastor Trinity Lutheran Ch., Boulder, Colo., 1913-18, St. Paul's Ch., Albuquerque, N.M., 1918-30, Trinity Ch., Longview, Wash., 1930-36; sec. of English missions Bd. of Am. Missions, United Lutheran Ch. in America, 1936-55; dir. Midland Coll. Appeal, Fremont, Neb., 1955-58; asst. pastor Our Savior's Luth. Ch., Omaha, Neb., from 1959. Pres. Rocky Mountain Synod, 1919-21, Pacific Synod, 1934-36. Republican. Home: Omaha, Neb. †

KOCK, WINSTON EDWARD, scientist, corp. exec.; b. Cin., Dec. 5, 1909; s. Henry Edward and Olivia (Hoffman) K.; m. Kathleen Redmond, June 24, 1939; children—Winston Edward, Robert Marshall, Kathleen Redmond. E.E., U. Cin., 1932, M.S., 1933, D. Sc. (hon.), 1952; Ph.D., U. Berlin, 1934; postgrad. Inst. Advanced Study, Princeton, 1935-36. Fellow Indian Inst. Sci., Bangalore, India, summer 1936; Teaching fellow U. Cin., 1934-35; research engr. Baldwin Piano Co., 1936-38, dir. electronic research, 1938-42; research engr. microwaves Bell Telephone Labs., 1942-51, dir. acoustics research, 1951-55, dir. audio and video systems research, 1955-56; chief sci. systems div. Bendix Corp., 1956-57; dir., gen. mgr. Bendix Corp. (Bendix research labs. div.), Southfield, Mich., 1958-62, v.p. corp., Detroit, 1962-64; dir. Electronics Research Center, NASA, Cambridge, Mass., 1964-66; v.p., chief scientist Bendix Corp., Detroit, 1966-72; acting dir. Herman Schneider Lab., U. Cin., from 1972; dir. Roanwell Corp., Hadron Corp.; Mem. Hartwell com. Nat. Acad. Sci., summer 1950, Teota com., 1952, Lamplight com., 1953, Nobska com., 1956, ARDC-Nat. Acad. Sci. com., 1957, Atlantis com., 1960; cons. Sec. Def., from 1958, U.S. Def. Dept. adv. panel on electronics, from 1959; mem. reactor devel. Com., bd. dirs. Argonne Univs. Assn., 1967-73; bd. dirs. Atomic Indsl. Forum; chmn. space nuclear com.; mem. com. on undersea warfare Nat. Acad. Scis.; mem. research and devel. task group Def. Sci. Bd.; Mem. U.S. del. NSF U.S.-Japan Holography Seminar, 1967, co-chmn., 1969, 73; co-chmn. U.S.-USSR Seminar, 1975, NSF Seminar, 1976. Author: Sound Waves and Light Waves, 1965, Lasers and Holography, 1969, 2d edit., 1972, Heinemann edit. (Brit.), 1973, Seeing Sound, 1971, Radar, Sonar and Holography, 1973, 2d edit., 1978, Engineering Applications of Lasers and Holography, 1975, 2d edit., 1977, The Creative Engineer, 1978, numerous papers.; Co-editor: Optical Information Processing, 1976, vol. 2, 1978. Trustee Western Coll. for Women, 1962-72, chmn., 1968-70; adv. com. U. Cin., from 1957; bd. dirs. Wayne State Rehab. Found., from 1976. Recipient Outstanding Young Engr. award Eta Kappa Nu, 1938, award of merit, 1959; eminent mem., 1966; Naval Ordnance award, 1946; U.S. Navy Distinguished Pub. Service medal, 1964; George Washington medal Engrs. Club, 1966; Confere award Worcestor Jr. Coll., 1965. Fellow IEEE (chmn. of profl. group on audio), Am. Phys. Soc., Am. Acoustical Soc. (mem. exec. council 1952-56), AAAS, Am. Inst. Aeros. and Astronautics (asso); hon. fellow Indian Acad. Scis.; mem. Am. Inst. Physics (mem. governing bd. 1956-62), NAM, Indsl. Research Inst., Am. Ordnance Assn., Nat. Security Indsl. Assn. (Weakley award 1975), Am. Orchid Soc., Sigma Xi, Tau Beta Pi, Eta Kappa Nu (nat. chmn. 1946, dir. 1960-63). Presbyterian (ruling elder 1960—). Clubs: Cosmos, Harvard Faculty, U. Cin. Faculty. Inventions and research Baldwin Electronic organ, waveguide microwave lens, underwater sound, speech analysis, narrow band TV, holography. Home: Ann Arbor, Mich.

KOENIG, ROBERT P., mining co. exec.; b. N.Y.C., Apr. 26, 1904; s. F. Otto and Margarette (Purington) K.; m. Angela Pow, Feb., 16, 1946; children—Robert Julian, Harold Otto, Margarette Whittemore, Rosalie Angela, John Lauriston. A.B. magna cum laude, Harvard U., 1924; D.Eng. (hon.), Sch. Mines, Mont. U., 1958. Asst. geologist Cerro de Pasco Copper Corp. (now Marmon Group), 1925-27; engr. New Verde Mines Corp., 1927-30, Internat. Mining Corp., 1930-32, Lehman Bros., 1935-36; v.p., gen. mgr. Montezuma Corp., 1933-35; v.p., pres., dir. Elec. Shovel Coal Corp., 1936-39; pres., dir. Ayrshire-Patoka Collieries Corp., 1939-50; pres., dir. Cerro Corp., 1950-70, chmn., 1970-72, Compania Minera Andina (S.A.), 1960-70, dir., 1960-84; dir. Foote Mineral Co., Bancroft Convertible Fund, Cheapside Dollar Fund.; Mem. Nat. Bituminous Coal Adv. Council, 1948-50; chmn., then acting dir. industry div. ECA, 1948. Author: An American Engineer Looks at British Coal (Foreign Affairs), 1948, Ore, Avalanches and Water, 1968, Vertical Integration in Mining Industry, 1964. Bd. dirs. Daniel and Florence Guggenheim Found.; trustee emeritus Mystic Seaport. Served to col. C.E. AUS; staff Gen. Eisenhower SHAEF, 1942-45. Decorated Order of Brit. Empire; Croix de Guerre with palms Belgium; Croix de Guerre; Legion Honor France; Legion of Merit U.S.; Order de Bernardo O'Higgins Chile; recipient Rand award Am. Inst. Mining, Metall, and Petroleum Engrs., 1962. Mem. Am. Inst. Mining and Metall. Engrs. (hon.), Mining and Metallurgy Soc. Am. (hon., pres.), Instn. Mining and Metallurgy (hon.) (London), Harvard Engring. Soc., Soc. Econ. Geologists, Lead Devel. Assn. (chmn. 1969-71), N.Am. Chilean C. of C. (pres.). Clubs: Harvard (N.Y.C.), N.Y.

Yacht (N.Y.C.); Mining, Cruising of Am. Home: Oyster Bay, N.Y. Died Feb. 1984.

KOENKER, ROBERT HENRY, college dean; b. Mankato, Minn., Mar. 4, 1913; s. Frank H. and Hattie (Roos) K.; B.E., Mankato State Tchrs. Coll., 1935; M.A., U. Minn., 1937, Ph.D., 1941; m. Jeanette Bandelin, June 7, 1943; children—Susan, Frank, Jeffrey. Dir. grad. studies, prof. edn. Ball State Tchrs. Coll., 1946-64, dean grad. program, 1964-66, prof. edn., psychology, 1964-, dean Grad. Sch., 1966-79, dean emeritus, 1979-81; examiner, cons. North Central Assn. Colls. and Secondary schs.; cons., mem. com. preparation coll. tchrs. Council Grad. Schs. U.S.; cons.-expert Bur. Postsecondary Edn.; examiner Nat. Council Accreditation Tchr. Edn. Chmn. Delaware County (Ind.) Selective Service Bd., 1950-70. Served with USCG, 1941-45. Mem. Midwest Assn. Grad. Schs. (past chmn.), Am. Assn. State Colls. and Univs. (grad. studies com.), Council Grad. Schs., NEA (nat. com. on D. Arts degree), Phi Delta Kappa, Kappa Delta Pi, Blue Key. Methodist. Author: Row Peterson Arithmetic Books, Grades 3-8, 2d edit., 1959; Simplified Statistics for Students in Education and Psychology, 1971; also research, publs. on specialists in edn. and D. Arts degree. Home: Muncie, Ind. Dec. Nov. 2, 1981.

KOESTLER, ARTHUR, author; b. Budapest, Hungary, 1905; s. Henry and Adele Koestler; student Univ. and Polytech. High Sch., Vienna, Austria, 1922-26; m. Mamaine Paget, 1950; m. Cynthia Jefferies, 1965. Began as the Middle East corr., 1926-29, Paris corr., 1929-30, fgn. corr. in Berlin, U.S.S.R., etc., 1930-38, corr. Spanish Civil War, 1931; participated in Arctic expdn., traveling on Graf Zeppelin. Served in the French Army, 1940, in the British Army, 1941. Author of The Spanish Testament, 1938; Gladiators, 1939; Darkness at Noon (Book of the Month Club selection), 1941; Scum of the Earth, 1941; Arrival and Departure 1943; The Yogi and the Commissar 1945; Twilight Bar 1945; Thieves in the Night 1946; Insight and Outlook, 1949; Promise and Fulfillment, 1949; The Age of Longing, 1951; Arrow in the Blue, 1950; The Invisible Writing, 1952; The Trail of the Dinosaur, 1955; Reflections on Hanging, 1957; The Sleepwalkers, 1959; The Lotus and the Robot, 1960; Suicide of a Nation, 1963; The Act of Creation, 1964; The Ghost in the Machine, 1968. Address: London, England. Died Mar. 3, 1983.

KOGAN, LEONLD, violinist; b. 1924; ed. Moscow Conservatory. Concert tours Europe, U.S.A., Canada, China; instr. Moscow Conservatory, 1952-82. Recipient 1st prize Internat. Youth Festival. Prague, 1947, internat. music competition, Brussels, 1951. Address: Moscow, USSR. Died Dec. 17, 1982.*

KOHLER, ARTHUR W., business executive; b. Lansing, Mich., Dec. 13, 1890; s. George J. and Christine Katherine (Baier) K.; A.B., U. of Mich., 1914; m. Lucile Marr Titus, Dec. 12, 1914; children—Arthur W., Robert T. Seedsman. D.M. Ferry & Co., Detroit, Mich., 1913-15; asso. with Woods Motor Vehicle Co., Chicago, 1915-19; William H. Wise & Co., publishers, Chicago, 1921-24; joined Curtis Publishing Co. as advt. solicitor The Saturday Evening Post, Philadelphia, 1925, mgr. Ladies' Home Journal, Phila. branch office, 1926, mgr., Phila. office, 1927, mgr., New York Advt. office, 1937, mgr. The Saturday Evening Post, Phila., 1943, vice pres. and advertising dir. The Curtis Pub. Co., 1947-54; senior vice president and dir. advt., 1954-57; director N.Y. & Pa. Co., N.Y.C. Mem. Advt. Council (dir.) Advt. Fedn. Am. (dir.), Periodical Pubs. Assn. (dir.), Pubs. Information Bur. (dir.), Mag. Advt. Bureau (dir.), Delta Upsilon. Clubs: Merion Cricket; Merion, Golf (Ardmore, Pa.); Pine Valley Golf (Clementon, N.J.); The Midday, Down Town, Poor Richard (Philadelphia). Home: Rosemont, Pa. †

KOHUT, HEINZ, psychoanalyst, psychiatrist; b. Vienna, Austria, May 3, 1913; came to U.S., 1940, naturalized, 1945; s. Felix and Else (Lampl) K.; m. Elizabeth Meyer, Oct. 9, 1948; 1 son, Thomas August. Grad., Döblinger Gymnasium, Vienna, 1932; M.D., U. Vienna, 1938; D.Sc. (hon.), U. Cin., 1973. Diplomate: in neurology and psychiatry Am. Bd. Psychiatry and Neurology. Resident neurology U. Chgo. Hosps., 1941-42, asst. neurology, 1942-43, instr. neurology, 1943-44, instr. neurology and psychiatry, 1944-47, asst. prof. psychiatry, 1947-50; lectr. U. Chgo. Hosps. (Sch. Social Service Adminstrn.), 1952-53, professorial lectr. dept. psychiatry, 1975-81; vis. prof. U. Cin., 1972-81; mem. Inst. Psychoanalysis, Chgo., 1953-81. Author: essays Die Zukunft der Psychoanalyse, 1975, Introspektion, Empathie und Psychoanalyse, 1977, The Search for the Self, 2 vols, 1978; contbr.: articles to profl. jours., chpt. Concepts and Theories of Psychoanalysis (in Concepts of Personality), 1963, The Analysis of the Self, 1971; chpt. to Freud: the Fusion of Science and Humanism, 1976, The Restoration of the Self, 1977; contbr. to: chpt. to The Psychology of the Self—A Casebook, 1978, Advances in Self Psychology, 1980. Recipient Austrian Cross of Honour for sci. and art, 1977. Mem. Internat. Psychoanalytic Assn. (v.p. 1965-73), Am. Psychoanalytic Assn. (pres. 1964-65, editorial bd. jour. 1955-58, 60-63, 66-69), Chgo. Psychoanalytic Soc. (pres. 1963-64), Am. Psychiat. Assn., Chgo. Med. Soc., AMA, Sigmund Freud Archives, Inc. (v.p.), Austrian Acad. Scis. Home: Chicago, Ill. Died Oct. 8, 1981.

KOKOMOOR, FRANKLIN WESLEY, prof. and mathematician; b. Dale, Ind., June 10, 1890; s. Henry Frederick Charles and Mary Sophia (Wedeking) K.; B.S., Valparaiso (Ind.) U., 1915; A.M., U. of Mich., 1924, Ph.D., 1926; m. Flora Mae Weller, Nov. 1, 1917; children—Marvin LaVon, Gretchen Weller (Mrs. Brill), Donald Franklin. Part-time instr., Valparaiso (Ind.) U., 1914-15; instr. Ga. Normal Coll. 1915-16; prin. and supt. Edgerton (O.) High Sch., 1916-22; asst. prof. U. of Fla. 1927-29, asso. prof. 1929-31, prof. from 1931, chmn. comprehensive course from 1935, head of department of mathematics from 1951. Member Math. Assn. of Am. (past chairman Southeastern section, member of the board of governors, 1955-58), National Council Teachers of Mathematics (state rep.), Am. Assn. U. Profs. (past pres. U. of Fla. chapter), Am. Math. Soc., History of Sci. Soc. Methodist. Club: Kiwanis. Author: Mathematics in Human Affairs (Prentice-Hall, Inc., 1942), Popular Matematik (Meijels Bokindustri, Halmstad, Sweden, 1948); numerous text books; contbr. articles to prof. jours. Home: Gainesville, Fla. †

KONES, RICHARD JOSEPH, physician; b. N.Y.C., Apr. 8, 1941; s. Joseph I. and Ruth Murphy (Winkler) K.; m. Sandra Lee Morrissey, Dec. 28, 1969; children—Kimberly Susan, Robin Melissa (dec.), Melanie Ann, Sabrina Lee. B.S. in Chem. Engring. (N.Y. State Regents scholar 1958-60, Eshborn scholar 1960), N.Y. U., 1960, M.D. (Arthritis and Rheumatism Found. scholar, Physiology honors program scholar), 1964. Diplomate: Am. Bd. Internat Medicine, Nat. Bd. Med. Examiners. Fellow in physiology N.Y. U. Sch. Medicine, 1961-62, in biochem. surgery, 1963, in biochemistry, 1964-65; intern in medicine Kings County Hosp., Bklyn., 1964-65; resident in surgery Albert Einstein Coll. Medicine-Bronx Mcpl. Hosp., 1965-66; resident in medicine Lenox Hill Hosp., N.Y.C., 1966-68; teaching fellow in cardiology, physician in charge intensive care unit Arthur Logan Meml. Hosp. and Knickerbocker Hosp., N.Y.C., 1968-69; fellow in cardiology, acting chief resident VA Hosp., New Orleans, 1969-70; instr. internal medicine Tulane U., 1969-71, USPHS-Nat. Blood, Heart, Lung Inst. fellow in cardiology, 1970-71, vis. physician sec. cardiology, 1972—; asst. prof. clin. cardiology N.Y. Med. Coll., 1971-76, practice medicine specializing in cardiology, Houston, 1969—, N.Y.C., 1971—, Bridgeport, Conn., 1976-78; dir. med. edn., chief ECG and Noninvasive Lab. N. Westchester Hosp.-Cornell Med. Ser., 1972-75; lectr. dept. physiology, cons. Westchester County Med. Center-Med. Sch., Valhalla, N.Y.; mem. staffs Park East Hosp., Park West Hosp., N.Y. U. Med. Center-Midtown Hosp., Logan Meml. Hosp., Madison Ave. Hosp., Parkchester Gen. Hosp., Kings Hwy. Hosp., Community Gen. Hosp., Westchester Square Hosp., Lefferts Gen. Hosp., Leroy Hosp., Kings Hwy. Hosp., Mt. Eden Gen. Hosp., Flatbush Gen. Hosp., all N.Y.C., Park City Hosp., Yale New Haven Med. Center, Bridgeport; also chief intensive and coronary care units Leroy Hosp., Osteo. Hosp., Trafalgar Hosp., Rosewood Hosp., Meml. Hosp., others; cons. N.Y. and Conn. burs. disability determinations Social Security Adminstrn.; medicolegal cardiopulmonary cons. Tech. Advisory Service for Attys.; lectr. in field. Author: The Molecular and Ionic Basis for Altered Myocardial Contractility, 1973, Cardiogenic Shock, 1974, Glucose, Insulin, Potassium and The Heart, 1975, Shocko Cardiogenico, Barcelona, Spain, 1977; editor: Controversies in Cardiology, Vols. 1-5, 1980-81; contbr. numerous articles to profl. jours.; contbg. editor: Chest, Am. Hosp. Formulary Service, Current Prescribing. Recipient Freshman Chemistry Achievement award N.Y. U. Dept. Chemistry, 1958, Continuing Edn. awards AMA, 1969, 71, 76, 78. Fellow Am. Coll. Chest Physicians, Am. Coll. Cardiology, Am. Coll. Clin. Pharmacology, Royal Soc. Medicine, Royal Soc. Health (London), Am. Coll. Angiology, Am. Geriatrics Soc. (founding charter), Am. Bariatrics Soc., Internat. Coll. Angiology, N.Y. Cardiological Soc., Am. Soc. Echocardiography, Am. Acad. Law and Sci., Am. Coll. Legal Medicine, Soc. Advanced Med. Systems; mem. A.C.P., Am. Physiol. Soc. (asso. charter mem.), Am. Zoological Soc., Soc. Gen. Physiologists, Am. Fedn. Clin. Research, Am. Soc. Exptl. Biology in Medicine, Am. Acad. Clin. Toxicology, Am. Soc. Internal Medicine, Am. Cancer Soc., Am. Heart Assn. (council on basic sci., cardiopulmonary diseases, circulation, thrombosis, clin. cardiology), N.Y., La., Conn., Tex., Westchester heart assns., Am. Chem. Soc. (award in chemistry achievement), Am. Soc. Clin. Pharmacology and Exptl. Therapeutics, French Cardiological Soc., French Soc. Advancement Soc., Am. Med. Writers Assn., Am. Coll. Emergency Physicians (charter fellow), AAAS, Am. Diabetes Assn., Am., Conn., La. thoracic socs., Am. Statis. Assn., Am. Inst. Biol. Scis., Am. Acad. Social and Polit. Soc., Am. Pub. Health Assn., Laennec Soc., Biophys. Soc., Biomed. Engring. Soc., Am. Math. Soc. Engring. in Biology and Medicine Group, Audio Engring. Soc., Am. Lung Assn., Am. Assn. Advancement Med. Instrumentation, Belgian Soc. Cardiology, Am. Acad. Polit. and Social Sci., Soc. Critical Care Medicine, Med. Electronics and Data Soc., Internat. Study Group Research Cardiac Metabolism, Internat. Soc. Heart Research, Microcirculatory Soc., Internat. Soc. Thrombosis Haemostasis, Internat. Soc. Internal Medicine, Internat. Soc. Cardiology, Internat. Union for Pure & Applied Biophysics, Internat. Soc. Cardiology, Nat. Research Council, Internat. Diabetes Fedn., Internat. Union Physiol. Scis., U.S. Bioenergetics Group, Internat. Union Pure and Applied Biophysics, Societe Francaise de Cardiologie, So. Med. Assn., N.Y. Acad. Scis., N.Y. Trudeau Soc., N.Y. Lung Assn., N.Y. Allergy Soc., Am. Soc. Zoologists, N.Y. State Soc. Internal Medicine, Musser-Burch Soc., Am. Med. Tennis Assn., U.S. Lawn Tennis Assn., Albert Einstein Coll. Medicine Alumni Assn., Am. Mus. Natural History, East African Wildlife Soc. (Kenya), Nat. Geog. Soc., Nat. Wildlife Fedn., Tulane Med. Alumni Assn., N.Y. U. Med. Alumni Assn. Home: Houston TX

KONO, FUMIHIKO, corporate executive; b. Japan, 1896; ed. Tokyo U. Formerly fuselage designer Mitsubishi Internal Combustion Engine Mfg. Co., now exec. v.p. Nagoya Airplane Factory, Mitsubishi Heavy Industries Ltd.; dir., gen. mgr. Kawasaki Engring. Works, East Japan Heavy Industries, Ltd. (now Mitsubishi Nippon Heavy Industries), 1952-62, pres., 1961—; dir. Mitsubishi Atomic Power Industries, Inc. Died Aug. 11, 1982.

KOO, VI KYUIN WELLINGTON, judge international court of justice; born in China, 1887; student St. John's, Shanghai; B.A. and M.A. (in 3 yrs.), Columbia University (called most brilliant student in the history of Columbia Univ.; ran debating team, edited Columbian and Spectator); LL.D., Yale, Columbia, St. John's, Aberdeen, Birmingham, Manchester Univs., D.C.L., Miami U., L.H.D., Rollins Coll. Beagan as English sec. to President of China; sucessively chinese minister to Mexico, then U.S. and Cuba, beginning at age 27, 1915; served as Chinese rep. on Council of League of Nations, 1920-22, and brought China into League of Nations; acting prime minister and minister of foreign affairs of China, Peking, 1922-24; finance minister, 1926; prime minister and minister foreign affairs, 1926-27; mem. Internat. Court of Arbitration, The Hague, 1927 and 1933; again minister foreign affairs, 1931; Chinese rep. on Commn. of Inquiry into Manchurian Crises, 1932; Chinese rep. on Council League of Nations, 1932-34, del. 13th and 14th assemblies and to special assembly, 1932-33, World Monetary and Econ. Conf., London, 1933, and Conf. for Reduction and Limitation of Armaments, Geneva, 1933; chief del. to assemblies of League of Nations, 1935-36 and 1938; ambassador to France, 1936-40; pres. 96th session of League of Nations Council, 1937, and del. to sessions, 1937-39; chief del. to Brussels Conf., 1937; special envoy to consecration of His Holiness Pius XII, 1939; Chinese Chief delegate to Dumbarton Oaks Conf., 1944, and Chinese delegate to San Francisco Conf., 1945; ambassador to Great Britain 1941-46; ambassador to United States, 1946-56; chairman Chinese delegation UN Assembly, 1946, acting chmn., 1947; sr. adviser to Pres. of China, Gen. Chiang Kai-Shek judge Permanent Court Arbitration at Hague, 1928-57; judge Internat. Ct. Justice, from 1957. Author: Status of Aliens in China, 1912. Home: Holland. †

KOOLSBERGEN, HEIN ISAAC, corp. exec.; b. Maassluis, Netherlands, Jan. 13, 1923; came to U.S., 1950, naturalized, 1956; s. Hein Isaac and Pietertje (Van Rossen) K.; m. Maureen Wendy Maggs, Feb. 1, 1968; children—Sarah Elizabeth, Jonas Michael. M.Sc., Royal Netherlands Mcht. Navy Coll., 1948. Engaged in marine ops. Royal Dutch Shell Co., 1948; mgr. fgn. marine ops. Cities Service Oil Co., 1951-56; asst. to chmn. So. Natural Gas Co., 1956-58; coordinator oil ops. Newmont Mining Co., 1958-61; pres., chmn. bd., chief exec. officer Oil Shale Corp., 1961-76; owner H.I. Koolsbergen firm (investments in energy and minerals industries), Los Angeles, 1976-80; chmn. bd., chief exec. officer U.S. Ethanol Corp., Del., 1980-82. Trustee Curtis Sch. Found., Los Angeles, 1977-82. Mem. Soc. Mining Engrs. of AIME, Am. Petroleum Inst., Mining Club N.Y.C. Home: Beverly Hills, Calif. Died July 18, 1982.

KOONTZ, HAROLD, management educator, consultant; b. Findlay, Ohio, May 19, 1908; s. Joseph Darius and Harriett (Dillinger) K.; m. Mary Learey, June 16, 1935; children: Karen Kathryn (Mrs. Gene Dickinson), Jean Carol (Mrs. Erling Gullixson). A.B., Oberlin Coll., 1930; M.B.A., Northwestern U., 1931; Ph.D., Yale U., 1935. Asst. prof. econs. Colgate U., 1935-41; chief traffic br. WPB, Washington, 1942-44; asst. to v.p. Assn. Am. R.R.s, 1944-45; asst. to pres., dir. planning Trans-World Airlines, 1945-48; dir. comml. sales Consol. Vultee Aircraft Corp., 1948-50; prof. bus. policy and transp. Grad. Sch. Mgmt., UCLA, 1950-62, Mead Johnson prof. mgmt., 1962-84; dir. Found. Adminstrv. Research, Inc., 1965-84, pres., 1965-71; chmn. bd. Genisco Tech. Corp., 1957-72; dir., cons. Farr Corp., Dust Control. Inc., 1950-80, Student Aid Found.; mgmt. cons. to various cos.; world wide lectr. on mgmt. subjects. Author: Government Control of Business, 1941, (with Cyril O'Donnell) Principles of Management, 1955, 6th edit., 1976 (also translated in 15 langs), (with Heinz Werhrich), Management, 8th edit., 1984, (with R. W. Gable) Public Control of Private Enterprise, 1956, Readings in Management, 1959, Requirements for Basic and Professional Education for Management, 1964, Management; A Book of Readings, 5th edit, 1980, Toward a Unified Theory of Management, 1964, Board of Directors and Effective Management, 1967, Appraising Managers as Managers, 1971, (with Cyril O'Donnell) Essentials of Management, 1974, (with Heinz Werhrich) Essentials of Mangement, 3d edit., 1982; 3d edit., 1982; (with R.M. Fulmer) A Practical Introduction to Business, 4th edit., 1984; also numerous articles. Mem. Los Angeles Bd. Airport Commrs., 1961-65. Recipient Mead Johnson award, 1962; USAF Air Univ. award, 1971; Taylor Key award, 1974; Fort Findlay award, 1975; Dean Conley award, 1977; Chung Hsing Mgmt. award Taiwan, 1978. Fellow Am. Acad. Mgmt. (pres. 1963), Internat. Acad. Mgmt. (bd. govs., Paccios chmn. 1964-70, world chancellor 1975-82); mem. Am. Mgmt Assn., Am. Soc. Traffic and Transp., Inst. Mgmt. Scis., Soc. for Advancement Mgmt., Conf. Bd., World Future Soc., Alpha Kappa Psi, Beta Gamma Sigma (Distinguished Scholar award 1976). Home: Encino, Calif. Died Feb. 11, 1984.

KOOPMAN, HENRY E., oil exec.; b. Pittsburg, Kan., June 17, 1889; s. Fred and Helen (Drunagel) K.; ed. Pittsburg (Kan.) Business Coll.; m. Lillian Dachtler, June 16, 1919; 1 dau., Mary Louise (Mrs. C. H. Armstrong). Began career in association with Frank Phillips, 1911-16; sec., treas. Phillips Petroleum Co., Bartlesville, Okla., 1917-26, v.p. and dir. from 1927; dir. First Nat. Bank, Bartlesville, First Investment Co. Mem. Mid Continent Oil and Gas Assn., Independent Petroleum Association of America, American Petroleum Inst., C. of C., Bartlesville. Club: Hillcrest Country. Home: Bartlesville, Okla. †

KOOPMANS, TJALLING CHARLES, economist; b. s'Graveland, Netherlands, Aug. 28, 1910; came to U.S., 1940, naturalized, 1946; s. Sjoerd and Wijtske (van der Zee) K.; m. Truus Wanningen, Oct. 1936; children: Anne W., Henry S., Helen J. M.A. in Physics and Math, U. Utrecht, Netherlands, 1933; Ph.D., U. Leiden, Netherlands, 1936; Ph.D. hon. doctorate econs, Netherlands Sch. Econs., 1963, Catholic U. Louvain, Belgium, 1967; D.Sc. (hon.), Northwestern U., 1975; LL.D. (hon.), U. Pa., 1976. Lectr. Netherlands Sch. Econs., Rotterdam, 1936-38; specialist fin. sect. League of Nations, Geneva, 1938-40; research asso. Princeton, 1940-41; spl. lectr. Sch. Bus., N.Y.U., 1940-41; economist Penn Mut. Life Ins. Co., 1941-42; statistician Combined Shipping Adjustment Bd., Washington, 1942-44; research asso. Cowles Commn. Research Econs., U. Chgo., 1944-55, asso. prof. econs., 1946-48, prof. econs., 1948-55; dir. research Cowles Commn., 1948-54; prof. econs. Yale, 1955—; dir. Cowles Found. for Research in Economics, 1961-67, Alfred Cowles prof. econs., 1967-81, Alfred Cowles emeritus prof. econs., 1981-85 Frank W. Taussig prof. econs. Harvard, 1960-61. Author: Three Essays on the State of Eonomic Science, 1957; Editor: Statistical Inference in Dynamic Economic Models, 1950, Activity Analysis of Production and Allocation, 1951; co-editor: Studies in Econometric Method, 1953; Contbr. articles to profl. jours. Recipient Alfred Nobel Meml. prize in econs., 1975. Fellow Econometric Soc. (v.p. 1949, pres. 1950, council 1949—); mem. Am. Acad. Arts and Scis., Nat. Acad. Scis., Am. Econ. Assn. (pres. 1978), Royal Netherlands Acad. Arts and Scis. (corr.), Am. Mathematical Soc., Inst. Mgmt. Scis., Ops. Research Soc. Am. Home: Hamden, Conn. Died Feb. 26, 1985.

KOOTZ, SAMUEL MELVIN, art dealer; b. Portsmouth, Va., Aug. 23, 1898; s. Louis and Ann (Persky) K.; LL.B., U. Va., 1921; m. Jane Ogden, Sept. 25, 1937 (dec. Mar. 1970); m. Joyce Lowinson, Aug. 22, 1972. Former owner Kootz Gallery, N.Y.C., specializing in modern American and European painting and sculpture. Author: Modern American Painters, 1928; New Frontiers in American Painting, 1944; Puzzle in Paint, 1943; Puzzle in Petticoats, 1944; (play) Home is the Hunter, 1946. Address: New York, N.Y. Died Aug. 7, 1982.

KOPP, GEORGE WILLIAM, educator; b. Fredonia, N.Y., July 27, 1920; s. George William and Hazel (Smith) K.; B.S., State U. N.Y., Fredonia, 1951, M.S., 1953; Ed.D., Syracuse U., 1958; m. Earline Rae Ellis, Sept. 26, 1946; children—Thomas William, Timothy Raymond. Elementary sch. tchr. Westfield Central Sch., 1951-52; campus sch. tchr. State U. N.Y., Fredonia, 1952-55; grad. asst., instr., asst. prof. Syracuse U., 1955-60; dean grad. studies State U. N.Y., Oswego, 1960-72, prof. edn. tchr. preparation program, from 1972. Served with USAAF, 1942-46. Mem. N.E.A., Kappa Delta Pi, Pi Delta Kappa. Republican. Presbyn. (elder). Clubs: Masons, Rotary. Home: Oswego, N.Y. Dec. Mar. 5, 1980.

KOPROWSKI, EUGENE JOSEPH, management educator; b. Chgo., Aug. 29, 1930; s. Matthew G. and Katherine Lorraine (Hendzel) K.; m. Laurel T. Etkin, Jan. 7, 1983; children by previous marriage: Michael, Kathy, Kris. B.S., U. Wis., 1952; M.A., U. Denver, 1953, Ph.D., 1963. Mgr. personnel and labor relations Nat. Farmer Union, Denver, 1953-63; mgmt. cons. McMurry Co., San Francisco, 1963-64; corp. dir. Manpower Planning and Devel., Kaiser Alume Chem. Corp., Oakland, Calif., 1964-66; asst. prof. mgmt. and orgn. U. Colo., Boulder, 1966-68; asso. dean U. Colo. (Bus. Sch.), 1968-72, prof. mgmt. and orgn., from 1972; pres. Koprowski & Assos. Author: (with John C. Buechner) Public Administration, 1976, Source Book for Mental Health Administrators, 1976. Mem. Am. Psychol. Assn., Am. Acad. Mgmt. Home: Boulder, Colo.

KORDUS, HENRY, landscape architect; b. Warsaw, Poland, Apr. 20, 1922; came to U.S., 1958, naturalized, 1964; s. Michal and Jadwiga (Zarzycka) K.; m. Juanita Bruns, July 26, 1961; children—Maria, Marcela. B.S., State Coll., Warsaw, 1944; M.S., U. Agr., Warsaw, 1951, Ph.D., 1972; M.A., U. Warsaw, 1957; postgrad., N.Y. U., 1961-63. Landscape designer Flora Forestry Co., Warsaw, 1939-45; landscape architect State Planning Bd., Warsaw, 1951-56, Andrews & Clark (cons. engrs.), Pomona, Calif., 1964-80; faculty fellow multidisciplinary program 1973; lectr. Polish Acad. Scis., Soc. Eng., 1971, U. Agr., 1972, Zagreb (Yugoslavia) U., 1972; field dir. Jagiellonian U., Cracow, Poland, 1971-72. Author: (with others) Siedem Wiekow Zamku Warsawskiego, 1972; contbr. to (with others) profl. jours. Vice chmn. Chino (Calif.) Planning Commn., 1967-71. Recipient medals Ministerswo Obrony Narodowej, London, 1949, 67, 69; cert. of appreciation City of Chino, 1966; cert. of merit City of Montclair; Calif., 1967; grantee Bur. Cultural Affairs, Dept. of State, 1971; grantee Kosciuszko Found., 1971. Mem. Soc. Landscape Architects, Gamma Sigma Delta. Home: Chino, Calif. Died June 2, 1980.

KORN, RICHARD, symphony condr.; b. N.Y.C.; A.B., Princeton, 1928; LL.B., Yale, 1931; student Juilliard Grad. Sch., 1937-39; m. Peggy Lashanska Rosenbaum (Mrs. Peter G. Lehman), Nov. 14, 1945; children—Penelope (Mrs. Stanley Karp), Wendy (Mrs. Stephen Lash), Lehman. Mem. Nat. Symphony Orch. (clarinet), Washington, 1939-40; asst. condr. Nat. Orchestral Assn., N.Y., 1940-42; founded Alumni Orch. of Nat. Orchestral Assn., conducted it in N.Y. concert and R.C.A. Victor record albums, 1941; fellowship in conducting with Serge Koussevitzky, 1941; asst. condr. N.Y. City (Center) Opera Co., 1945-46; condr. Original Ballet Russe, 1947; mus. dir. Orch. of Am., 1959-65; guest condr. Boston Pops Orch., Lewisohn Stadium Concerts, Czech. Philharmonic (Prague), philharmonic orchs. of Stockholm, Copenhagen and Oslo, Conservatoire Orch. of Paris, Carnegie Hall Pops London Symphony Orch., etc. 1945-50, New Orleans summer concerts 1949, NBC Symphony, Buffalo Philharmonic Orch., 1951-52, Lena concerts, also 1962 Montreal summer concerts; condr. Baton Rouge Symphony Orch. 1950-51; Cin. Symphony Orch., 1956, Asahi Broadcasting Symphony Orch. Japan, 1957, Phila. Dell Concerts, Kol Yisroel, Israel, Haifa Symphony, Israel, 1958, Carl Schurz Park concerts, 1962; condr. on records, notably Am. Music. Mem. faculty New York Coll. Music, 1965-81. Mem. exec. com. Nat. Music Council; pres. Am. Council Judaism, 1966-68. Chmn. Music School Com. Henry St. Settlement. Bd. dirs. Hosp. for Joint Diseases, N.Y.C., Musicians Found.; bd. govs. Bohemians, 1964-72; trustee Temple Emanu-El, N.Y.; mem. adv. com. to dept. astrophysics Princeton U.; mem. Hayden Planetarium com. N.Y. Mus. Natural History. Served as lt., USCG, 1942-45. Fellow World Acad. Arts and Scis. Author: Orchestral Accents. Clubs: Lotos, Century Assn., Princeton (N.Y.C.); Century Country. Home: New York, N.Y. Died Apr. 27, 1981.

KORSTIAN, CLARENCE FERDINAND, university dean, educator; b. Saline County, Neb., June 26, 1889; s. John Weber and Mary Emma (Trout) K., B.S.F., U. of Neb., 1911, M.F., 1913; M.A., Southeastern Christian Coll., 1924; research fellow, Yale Univ., 1925-26, Ph.D., 1926; m. Catherine Dick, Nov. 25, 1914; children —Kenneth Clarence, Robert John, Grace K. Graham. Asst. in dendrology and silviculture, U. of Neb., 1909-10; field asst. in Forest Service, U.S. Dept. Agr., 1910-11; asst. pathologist Pa. Chestnut Tree Blight Commn., 1912; forest asst. Forest Service, U.S. Dept. Agr., 1912-13, forest examiner, 1913-22, asso. silviculturist, Appalachian Forest Expt. Sta., 1922-27, silviculturist, 1927-28, sr. silviculturist, 1928-30; dir. Duke Forest and prof. silviculture, Duke U., from 1930, dean Sch. of Forestry since 1938. Mem. Nat. Research Council (adv. rep. div. biology and agr., 1935-41; mem. exec. com. 1939-40; vice chmn. 1944-45). Chmn. of the City Tree Commission of Durham, North Carolina, 1931-53, commission on forestry and related tng. So. Regional Edn. Bd. Fellow A.A.A.S. (mem. council, 1933-46); mem. Soc. American Foresters (sec. Intermountain sect. 1916-20; sec. Appalachian sect. 1921-25, chmn. 1928, 35; mem. exec. council, 1932-35; pres., 1938-41; Fellow, 1942), Utah Acad. Sciences (v.p., 1919-20; pres., 1920-21), Am. Forestry Assn. (vice-pres. 1939, 41), N.C. Forestry Assn. (pres., 1943-47), N.C. Forestry Council (chmn. 1949-51), N.C. Acad. Sci. (pres., 1949-50), Ecolog. Society of America (vice president 1942), Southern Association Science and Industry (v.p. 1949-51), Xi Sigma Pi (honorary), Phi Sigma, Sigma Xi, Acacia. Presbyterian. Mason, Rotarian. Author: Seeding and Planting in the Practice of Forestry, 3d edit. (with James W. Toumey), 1941; Foundations of Silviculture Upon an Ecological Basis (with James W. Toumey), revised edit. 1947. Co-editor: Naturalist's Guide to the Americas, 1926. Contbr. bulls., reports and articles on forestry. Mem. editorial bd. Ecology, 1923-30, 33-49; editor Ecological Monographs, 1933-49. Home: Durham, N.C. †

KOTSCHNIG, WALTER MARIA, govt. ofcl., writer; b. Judenburg, Austria, Apr. 9, 1901; came to U.S., 1936, naturalized, 1942; s. Ignaz and Therese (Huber) K.; m. Elined Prys, Dec. 10, 1924; children—Enid Maria Ileana, Christopher Hans Owen (dec.), John W. Student univs. of Graz, Austria) and Kiel (Germany), 1920-24; Dr. Polit. Sci., Inst. World Econs., Kiel, 1924; LL.D. (hon.), Rockford (Ill.) Coll., 1945. First asst. Inst. World Econs., Kiel, 1924-25; sec. gen. Internat. Student Service, Geneva, Switzerland, 1925-34; dir. High Commn. for Refugees Coming from Germany, League of Nations, Geneva, 1934-36; prof. comparative edn. Smith Coll. and Mt. Holyoke Coll., 1937-44; asso. chief Div. Internat. Orgn. Affairs, Dept. State, Washington, 1944, charge specialized orgn. br., 1945, acting chief, 1947-49; dir. Office UN Econ. and Social Affairs, 1949, Office Internat. Econ. and Social Affairs, 1954-62; spl. adviser Bur. Internat. Orgn. Affairs, 1962-65, minister, 1962, dep. asst. sec. state, 1965-71, ret., 1971; Adviser Friends. Home: Newtown, Pa. of Planning, Afghanistan, 1959; sec. U.S. delegation conf. to establish UNESCO, London, 1945; acting exec. sec. Prep. Commn. (on loan from State Dept.), 1946; adviser U.S. delegation, 1st gen. conf., Paris, 1946, 2d gen. conf., Mexico City, 1947; asso. exec. sec., cons. UN Subcommn. Econ. Reconstrn. Devastated Areas (on loan from State Dept.), 1946; asst. sec. U.S. Group, Dumbarton Oaks Conf. Internat. Orgn. Washington, 1944; tech. expert U.S. Delegation, San Francisco, 1945; adviser Internat. Labor Conf., Paris, 1945, U.S. alt. del., Geneva, 1950; U.S. alt. del. governing body ILO, Mysore, India, 1951; adviser to U.S. reps. on UN econ. and social council, 2d to 6th sessions; dep. U.S. rep. Econ. and Social Council, 7th to 50th sessions, Lake Success, N.Y., Geneva, and; Santiago, Chile; U.S. alternate delegate to UN Conf. Tech. Assistance, Lake Success, 1950; to 7th Gen. Conf. UNESCO, Paris, 1952; sr. adviser 8th Gen. Conf., Montevideo, 1954; adviser U.S. delegation to UN Gen. Assembly, 1950; sr. adviser U.S. delegation UN Gen. Assembly, 1955-56; dep. U.S. rep. UN Econ. Commn. for Asia and the Far East, Rangoon, Burma, 1952, Bangalore, India, 1956, Bangkok, 1957, Kuala Lumpur, 1958; U.S. observer at 1st session UN Econ. Commn. Africa, 1959, 3d session, 1961, 5th session, 1963; dep. U.S. rep. UN Econ. Commn. Latin Am., 1959; chmn. U.S. delegation Industry, Trade Com. ECAFE, Bangalore, 1956, Com. Industry and Resources, Bangkok, 1962, U.S. del., Wellington, New Zealand, 1965; chmn. U.S. delegation UN Econ. Com. for Europe, Geneva, 1962, 63, 64; vice chmn. U.S. delegation UN Conf. Trade and Devel., Geneva, 1964, 65; U.S. del. Gen. Conf. UNESCO, 1962, 64; U.S. dep. rep. UNESCO exec. bd., Istanbul, 1962; chmn. U. S. del. UNIDO Indsl. Symposium, Athens, 1967; spl. adviser U.S. del. Internat. Middle Level Manpower Conf., P.R., 1962; U.S. del. UN Slavery Conf., Geneva, 1956; rapporteur UN Com. on Program Appraisal, 1959-60; spl. UN cons. drug abuse control, 1971-73. Author: Unemployment in Learned Professions, 1937, Slaves Need No Leaders, 1943; co-author: Toward the General Welfare, 1957, The United Nations and Promotion of the General Welfare; Editor: The University in a Changing World, 1932. Trustee Inst. Internat. Edn., 1946-52. Decorated St. Sava Order Yugoslavia, 1926, officers cross Civil Service Order Bulgaria, 1929; recipient Distinguished Honor award State Dept., 1971. Mem. Council on Fgn. Relations, Com. To Study Orgn. Peace. Mem. Soc. of Friends. Home: Newton, Pa. Died July 23, 1985; buried Friends Cemetery, Sandy Spring, Md.

KRAFT, ARTHUR CARL, tenor; b. Buffalo, N.Y., Feb. 18, 1888; s. Oscar Hermann and Cacelia (Schotte) K.; LL.B., Kent Coll. Law, 1913; studied music Chicago and New York; m. Clara Mallen, May 2, 1932. Admitted to Ill. bar, 1913. Concert tenor; pres. Columbia Sch. of Music, Chicago. Served as pvt. U.S.A., World War. Mem. Symphonia Soc., Phi Alpha Delta. Mason (32 deg., K.T., Shriner). Clubs: Cliff Dwellers, Chicago Athletic; Bohemian (New York). Home: Oak Park, Ill. †

KRAMER, MARTIN S., retail store executive; b. 1920; B.S., U. Pitts., 1942; married. Methods engr., mgr. system control dept. Kaufmann's, Pitts., 1945-47; mgr. mdse. dept., asst. buyer, buyer Macy's, N.Y.C., 1947-52; div. mdse. mgr., gen. mgr. br. store, dir. research and planning, asst. to pres. Gimbels, Pitts., 1952-63; dir. long-range planning Federated Dept. Store, Cin., 1963-66; with Maas Bros., Allied Stores Corp., Tampa, Fla., 1966, v.p. in charge stores and future store devel., 1966-69, exec. v.p. store, 1969-70, pres., mng. dir., 1970-71, exec. v.p., dir. stores parent co., 1971-74, also dir.; chmn., chief exec. officer Gimbel Brothers Inc., N.Y.C. Served to capt. USAAF, 1942-45. Office: New York, N.Y. Dec. Oct. 25, 1983.

KRAMER, MILTON A., clothing mfg. co. exec.; b. Butte, Mont., Oct. 19, 1915; s. Benjamin and Sarah Kramer; B.A., U. Mich., 1936, J.D., 1938; m. Charlotte Rosenthal, July 3, 1941; 1 son, Mark. Admitted to Ohio bar, 1938; pvt. practice, Cleve., 1938-42; with Work Wear Corp., Cleve., from 1946, sr. exec. v.p. mfg., sec. Served with USCGR, 1942-46. Died.

KRANTZ, FRED ALFRED, horticulturist; b. Westphalia, Ia., Nov. 10, 1890; s. Peter Joseph and Christinia (Wachendorf) K.; B.S., U. of Minn., 1918, M.S., 1921. Ph.D., 1924; m. Katherine Leahy, Sept. 15, 1919; children—Fred, Katherine, Mary, Margaret, Alice, Ann, Josephine. Instr., U. of Minn., 1919-23, asst. prof., 1925-34, asso. prof., 1934-36, prof. from 1937. Served as 2d lt., U.S. Army, 1918. Recipient Bronze medal Minn. State Hort. Soc., 1943. Mem. Potato Assn. of Am. (pres. 1938), Am. Soc. for Hort. Sci., Sigma Xi, Alpha Zeta, Gamma Sigma Delta. Roman Catholic. Developed and introduced 7 varieties of potatoes; major contbns. potato breeding methods outlined in Minn. Agrl. Expt. Sta. Tech. Bulls. Home: Saint Paul, Minn. †

KRANTZ, JOHN CHRISTIAN, JR., educator; b. Balt. Oct. 8, 1899; s. John Christian and Johanna Fredericka (Steinmann) K.; Pharm. B., U. Md., 1923, M.S., 1924, Ph.D., 1928, Ph.M., hon. Sc.D., 1931; m. Helen King, June 15, 1921; 1 dau., Margaret Claire. Asso. prof. chemistry U. Md. Sch. Pharmacy and Dentistry, Balt., 1921-26, prof. chemistry, 1926-27; dir. pharm. research, Sharp & Dohme, Balt., 1927-30; chief Bur. Chemistry Md. Dept. Health, 1930-35; prof. pharmacology U. Md. Sch. Medicine, 1933-65, emeritus prof., 1965-83. Mem. Revision Com. U.S. Pharmacopoeia (sec. 1940-50); cons. toxicologist U.S. Services Forces, from 1943; spl. cons. USPHS, from 1949; mem. NRC, 1959-62; chmn. adv. council environmental hygiene Md. Bd. Health, 1964-68; dir. Scope, USP, 1968; med. sci. cons. Huntingdon Research Center, 1965-69; dir. pharmacologic research Md. Psychiat. Research Center, 1969-73. Served in S.A.T.C., 1918. Mem. Am. Coll. Cardiology (v.p.), Am. Therapeutic Soc., Am. Pharm. Assn., Am. Assn. Univ. Profs. Am. Soc. History Medicine, Am. Chem. Soc. (mem. council), Parmacol. Soc. (mem. council 1946, v.p. 1949-50), Soc. for Exptl. Biology and Medicine, A.A.A.S., Md. Acad. Sci., Md. Soc. for Med. Research (mem. exec. com.), N.Y. Acad. Sci., Soc. for Cancer Research, Sigma Xi. Recipient Simon medal, Ebert prize in chemistry, 1929; Rho Phi Honor award, 1955, U.Md. alumni award, 1958; distinguished service award Young Men's Christian 1958. Presbyn. Clubs: Gibson Island; Torch (pres. 1940-46); Grachur (Balt.); L'Hirondelle (Ruxton). Author: (textbook) Pharmacologic Principles of Medical Practice, 1949, 7th edit., 1967; The Art of Eloquence, 1951; A Portrait of Medical History and Current Medical Problems, 1962; Profiles of Medical Science and Inspired Moments, 1966; Historical Medical Classics Involving New Drugs, 1974. Home: Gibson Island, Md. Died Nov. 19, 1983.

KRASNA, NORMAN, writer; b. N.Y.C., Nov. 7, 1909; s. Benjamin and Beatrice (Mannison) K.; student N.Y.U., Columbia, Law Sch. St. John's U.; m. Erle Galbraith, Dec. 7, 1951. Film critic N.Y. World, 1928; dramatic editor N.Y. Evening Graphic, 1929; writer screen plays for films, from 1932, including Richest Girl in the World, Fury, Bachelor Mother, Devil and Miss Jones, Princess O'-Rourke (winner Academy award 1943), Ambassador's Daughter, Indiscreet; also writer-producer, dir., author stage plays, including Louder Please, 1931, Small Miracle, 1934, Dear Ruth, 1944, John Loves Mary, 1947, Time for Elizabeth (with Groucho Marx), 1948, Kind Sir, 1953, Who Was That Lady I Saw You With?, 1958; Sunday in New York, 1961; Love in E Flat, 1967. Died Nov. 7, 1984.

KRASNER, LEE, painter; b. Bklyn.; m. Jackson Pollock. Ed., Cooper Union, Art Students League, N.A.D., CCNY; studied with, Hans Hofmann. Selected group shows include, Palazzo Graneri, Turin, Italy, 1959, Galerie Beyeler, Basle, Switzerland, 1961, Laing Art Gallery, Newcastle-upon-Tyne. Eng., 1961, Marlborough Fine Art, London, Eng., 1961, Yale Art Gallery, 1961-62, Mt. Holyoke Coll., 1962, Wadsworth Atheneum, Hartford, Conn., 1962, Mary Washington Coll., U. Va., Fredericksburg, 1962, Queens Coll., N.Y.C., 1962, Howard Wise Gallery, 1962, Guild Hall, East Hampton, N.Y., 1963-64, 73-74, 80, 81, Guggenheim Mus., N.Y.C., 1964, 79, Gallery of Modern Art, N.Y.C., 1965, Southampton Coll. of L.I. U., 1965, Mus. Modern Art for Am. Embassy, 1963-65, White House traveling exhbn., 1967, selected group shows include, Jewish Mus., N.Y.C., 1967, 70, Mus. Modern Art, N.Y.C., 1969, 77, 78, Palazzo Reale, Milan, 1971, Lakeview Center, Peoria, Ill., 1972, Whitney Mus. Am. Art, N.Y.C., 1973, 75, 77, 78, Phila. Civic Center, 1974, Kunsthalle Dusseldorf and Staatlichen Kunsthalle, Baden-Baden, Germany, 1974-75, Los Angeles County Mus. Art, 1977, Bklyn. Mus., 1977, Phila. Coll. Art, 1978, Albright-Knox Art Gallery, Buffalo, 1978, Met. Mus. Art, N.Y.C., 1979, Corcoran Gallery Art, 1979, Wildenstein Gallery, N.Y.C., 1980, Nassau County Mus. Fine Art, 1981, Grey Art Gallery, N.Y. U., 1981, Robert Miller Gallery, N.Y.C., 1982, Contemporary Art Mus., Houston, 1982, Carnegie Inst., Pitts., 1982, Phila. Coll. Art, 1983, exhibited in solo shows, Betty Parsons Gallery, N.Y.C., 1951, Stable Gallery, N.Y.C., 1955, Martha Jackson Gallery, N.Y.C., 1958, Signa Gallery, East Hampton, 1959, Howard Wise Gallery, 1960, 62, Whitechapel Gallery, London, 1965, Arts Council of Gt. Britain, London, 1966, U. Ala. Gallery, 1967, Marlborough-Gerson Gallery, N.Y.C., 1968, 69, Reese Paley Gallery, San Francisco, 1969, Marlborough Gallery, N.Y.C., 1973, Whitney Mus. Am. Art, 1973, 74, Pace Gallery, N.Y.C., 1977, Susan Hilberry Gallery, Mich., 1977, Miami-Dade Community Coll., 1974, Beaver Coll., 1974, Gibbes Art Gallery, 1974, Corcoran Gallery Art, Washington, 1975, Pa. State Mus. Art, 1975, Brandeis U., 1975, Janie C. Lee Gallery, Houston, 1978, 81, Pace Gallery, N.Y.C., 1979, 81, Tower Gallery, Southampton, N.Y., 1980, others., Robert Miller Gallery, 1982, retrospective, Houston Mus. Fine Arts, San Francisco Mus. Fine Arts, Mus. Modern Art, N.Y.C., Centre Nat. d'Art et de Culture Georges Pompidou, Paris, 1983-85; represented in permanent collections. Address: East Hampton, N.Y. Died June 19, 1984.

KRAUS, SIDNEY M., naval officer; b. Peru, Ind., July 16, 1887; son Charles J. and Hannah (R.) K.; B.S., U.S. Naval Academy, 1908; grad. U.S. Navy Post Grad. Sch., 1915, M.S., Columbia, 1916; m. Harriet Langdon, Nov. 21, 1932. Commd. ensign U.S. Navy, and advanced through the grades to rear adm.; assigned to aeronautical duties from Oct., 1918. Decorated Legion of Honor (France). Fellow Inst. of the Aeronautical Sciences; mem. Am. Soc. of Naval Engrs., Am. Legion. Mason. Club: Army and Navy (Washington, D.C.). Home: St. Petersburg, Fla. †

KRAUSS, PAUL H(ARTZELL), clergyman; b. Homestead, Pa., Nov. 16, 1890; s. Elmer Frederick and Irene Elizabeth (Hartzell) K.; student Northwestern U., 1909-10; A.B., Muhlenberg Coll., 1912, D.D., 1932; graduate Chicago Luth. Theol. Sem., 1912-15; U. of Chicago, summer 1911; D.D., Wittenberg Coll., 1932; m. Helen Avery Hitchcock, Dec. 31, 1914; 1 dau., Constance Avery; m. 2d, Mary Adams Winter, June 15, 1965. Ordained to ministry of Lutheran Ch., June 11, 1915; pastor Mt. Zion Ch., Pittsburgh, Pa., 1915-18; chaplain U.S. Navy, 1918-19; sec. for student work Bd. of Edn., United Luth. Ch., 1919-20; pastor Trinity Ch., Ft. Wayne, Ind., from 1920. Dir. Luth. Sch. Theology, Chgo.; exec. bd. United Luth. Ch. Am., 1938-46, now mem. bd. theol. edn. Mem. Phi Kappa Psi. Clubs: Quest, Fortnightly, Fort Wayne Chamber of Commerce. Author: A Lamb of Burnished Gold, 1941; A Goodly Fellowship, 1949; A Hallelujah In Stone. Contbr. to Epistle Messages, and other periodicals. Home: Fort Wayne, Ind. †

KREMER, ETHEL MACKAY, hon. exec. dir.; b. N.Y.C., Apr. 28, 1887; d. James Woodworth and Josephine E. (Laurence) MacKay; student Hunter Coll., 1903, Art Students League, 1905; studied art abroad, 1907; m. Walter V. Kremer, Feb. 4, 1911 (dec.), Asso. editor Home Furnishings Good Housekeeping mag., 1920; stylist for various companies mfg. home furnishings products, 1920-22; research work on art in France and Italy in connection with work as sytle advisor to mfrs., 1924-28; exec. dir. The Fashion Group, Incorporated, N.Y. City, 1931-53, honorary director from January 1, 1953. dir. yearly Fashion Training Course from 1932. Served with Y.M.C.A. as canteen worker, Service of Supply, France, 1918. Mem. Am. Com. for Devastated France, 1916-17. Collector 1st editions relative to history of costume design, also editions on textile furniture and architecture.†

KREPS, THEODORE JOHN, economist; born Prinsburg, Minn., Jan. 13, 1897; s. Peter and Grace (Phelpher) K.; A.B., U. of Colo., 1920; A.M., Harvard, 1924, Ph.D., 1928; LL.D. (hon.), Univ. of Colorado, 1957; married Esther Elvira Corsberg, Aug. 7, 1919; children—Estalyn, Theodora, Donald, Allyn Overton, Rodney Emerson, Susan Eileen. Instr. history and economics. Colorado State Preparatory Sch., Boulder, 1920-23; tutor history, govt. and econs., instr. econs. Harvard U. and Radcliffe Coll., 1925-30; Frederick Sheldon fellow. Harvard U., summer 1926; Laura Spellman. Rockefeller fellow, 1928-29; asso. prof. statistics. Grad. Sch. of Bus., Stanford U., 1930-35, asso. prof. bus. econ., 1935-40, prof. bus. econ., 1940-81; Ford Found. exchange prof. Free Univ., Berlin, 1954; econ. adviser Temporary Nat. Econ. Com., 1939-41; chief econ. adviser Bd. of Econ. Warfare, 1942-44; staff director joint econ. com., U.S. Congress, 1949-51; trustee No. Cal. Council on Econ. Edn.; has served various govtl. agencies in adv. capacity, Intermittently. U.S. del. various internat. confs. Served as 1st lt., A.E.F., France, 1917-19. Life fellow Royal Econ. Soc.; mem. Am. Econ. Assn., Am. Acad. Polit. and Social Sciences, Assn. Harvard Chemists, Am. Legion. Methodist. Mason. Clubs: Cosmos, Kiwanis. Author several books, latest being: Taxes and the Human Factor, 1951. Co-author: Economic Problems in a Changing World, 1939. Home: Palo Alto, Calif. Died May 6, 1981.

KRESGE, STANLEY SEBASTIAN, found. exec.; b. Detroit, June 11, 1900; s. Sebastian Spering and Anna Emma (Harvey) K.; m. Dorothy Eloise McVittie, Oct. 2, 1923; children—Walter H., Stanley Sebastian, Bruce Anderson. A.B., Albion (Mich.) Coll., 1923. With S.S. Kresge Co., 1923-77, store mgr., 1927-28, various positions in main office, 1930-45, dir., 1950—; trustee Kresge Found., Troy, Mich., 1931-85, pres., 1952-66, chmn. bd., 1966-78. Author: S.S. Kresge, 1979. Del. Republican Nat. Conv., 1948, 52; emeritus trustee Albion Coll.; hon. dir. Detroit YMCA. Methodist. Clubs: Detroit, Detroit Athletic. Home: Pontiac, Mich. Died June 30, 1985.

KREUSSER, OTTO THEO, b. N.Y. City, Apr. 20, 1889; s. Julius A. and Julia E. (Fox) K.; ed. Pratt Inst. Tech.; m. Emma Larson, Dec. 1, 1921; children—Carolyn Louise, Richard Theodore. With Brooklyn Rapid Transit System, 1908-12; asst. engr. of car design, New York Municipal Ry. Corp., 1913-18; engr. of aviation ignition, Dayton (O.) Engring. Labs. Co., 1917; in charge Liberty engine sch., U.S. Bur. Aircraft Production, Detroit, Mich., 1918; asst. sales mgr. Dayton Engring. Labs. Co., 1919; ednl. dir. in charge apprentices, foremen's exec. training courses and spl. machine operators' sch., Delco Dayton, 1920-21; head of tech. data sect. Gen. Motors Research Labs. and chmn. Gen. Motors new devices com., 1922-24; dir. Gen. Motors Proving Ground, Milford, Mich., 1924-29; dir. engring. tests, Fisher Body Corp. Div. of Gen. Motors, 1930-31; dir. Mus. of Sciences and Industry, Chicago, 1931-36; asst. dir. General Motors Research, 1936-37, pres. and gen. mgr. Allison Engring. Co., Indianapolis, 1937-40; dir. of service and training Allison Div. of Gen. Motors Corp. 1940-45; Engring. Adminstr. 1946-52; asst. to gen. mgr. from 1952. Mem. Soc. Automotive Engrs. (chmn. Dayton Sect. 1922-24, Detroit Sect. 1930-31), Newcomen Soc., Inst. of aero. Sciences, Engring. Soc. of Detroit. Mason. Clubs: Recess (Detroit); Columbia (Indianapolis). Home: Indianapolis, Ind. †

KRIDA, ARTHUR, orthopedic surgeon; b. Lodz, Poland, Jan. 6, 1888; s. John Krida and Johanna (Kunkel) K.; brought to U.S., 1893; M.D., Albany, (N.Y.) Med. Coll. 1911; m. Marta Barkowska December 28, 1914; children—Arthur, Robert; m. 2d, Elise Munn Hasbrouk, Nov. 29, 1935. Adjunct prof. physiology, Albany Med. Coll., 1914-16, demonstrator of anatomy, 1917; asst. orthopedic surgeon, Hosp. for Ruptured and Crippled, New York, N.Y., 1922-24, chief of clinic and asso. orthopedic surgeon, 1925-32; dir. orthopedic surgery, Bellevue Hosp., New York, N.Y., 1930-50; prof. orthopedic surgery, New York U. Coll. of Medicine, 1930-50, emeritus professor from 1950; cons. orthopedic surgeon Bellevue Hospital, Hospital for Ruptured and Crippled, Knickerbocker, Luth., U. Manhattan Gen. (N.Y.C.), Tuxedo (N.Y.) Meml., Dobbs Ferry (N.Y.), St. Luke's (Newburgh, N.Y.), St. Agnes (White Plains, N.Y.), N. Hudson (Weehawken, N.J.), Beth Israel, St. Francis (Port Jervis, N.Y.), hosps., South Nassau Communities Hosp. (Rockville Centre, N.Y.). Served as capt., Med. Corps, U.S. Army, 1917-19. Diplomate Am. Bd. of Orthopedic Surg. Fellow Am. Coll. Surgeons, N.Y. Acad. Medicine; mem. Am. and Internat. orthopedic assns., Am. Acad. Orthopedic Surgeons, A.M.A., N.Y. County and State societies, Soc. of Alumni of Bellevue Hosp. (pres.); mem. bd. govs. Am. Acad. Compensation Med., adv. com. greater N.Y. chpt. Nat. Found. Inf. Paralysis. Clubs: University. Member editorial board Am. Jour. Surgery. Contbr. articles and essays to med. lit. Home: New York, N.Y. †

KRIEGER, HERBERT WILLIAM, museum curator, ethnologist; b. Des Moines County, Ia., Dec, 8, 1889; s. Frederick and Rieke (Schaele) K.; M.A., U. of Ia., 1908; m. Louise Krapf, Dec. 1, 1922; 1 dau., Eleanor Louise. Curator of enthnology, U.S. Nat. Museum, Washington, from 1925. Decorated with Order Heraldica de Cristobal Colon of the Dominican Republic. Fellow, Am. Geog. Soc., N.Y. Mem. Sociedad Colombista Panamericana, Havana, Cuba, Junta Nacional de Arquelogia y Etnologia, Cuba, American Anthropologist Association, Anthropologist Assn. of Washington, Washington Acad. of Sciences. Clubs: Cosmos. Author: Material Culture of the People of Southeastern Panama, 1926; The Collection of Weapons and Armor of the Philippine Islands, 1926; The Aborigines of the Ancient Island of Hispaniola, 1930; Island Peoples of the Western Pacific, 1943; The People of Taiwan (Formosa), 1952. Home: Arlington, Va. †

KRILL, WALTER R., veterinarian; b. Edgerton, O., Apr. 13, 1902; s. Frederick P. and Christiana (Weber) K.; B.S., Ohio State U., 1923, D.V.M., 1927, D.Sc., 1974; m. Gladys P. Nesser, June 30, 1927. Vet. practice, Lima, O., 1927-29; instr. Coll. Vet. Medicine Ohio State U., 1929-35, asst. prof., 1935-40, asso. prof., 1940-43, prof. from 1943, dean Coll. Vet. Medicine 1946-67; cons. Surg. Gen. USAF, 1950-53, from 1963; cons. to Spl. Fund Div. UN 1963 for service in Mexico; cons. Biol. Labs., Camp Detrick, Md.; cons. AID, India, 1967. Chmn. com. Regulatory Edn.; mem. gov's com. Peacetime uses Atomic Energy. Adv. com. Animal Industry Quarantine Div. U.S. Dept. Agr. Recipient Gamma award, 1960, Distinguished Alumni award Ohio State U. Coll. Vet. Medicine; name to Ohio Agrl. Hall Fame, 1975. Mem. Am. Assn. Deans Vet. Colls., Ohio State Vet. Med. Assn. (exec. com.), U.S. Livestock Loss Prevention Association, Research Workers Animal Disease in North America, U.S. Livestock Sanitary Assn. Regional Health Service Adv. Com. (Region IV), Am. Dairy Sci. Assn., Am. Vet. Med. Assn. (exec. bd. 1944-49, 50-54, chmn. bd. 1948-49, chmn. emergency adv. com.; com. on vet. splty. board), Nat. Assn. Standard Med. Vocabulary, Nat. Bd. Vet. Med. Examiners (pres.), Healing Arts Edn. Adv. Com. to Selective Service, A.A.A.S., Land-Grant Coll. Assn. (senate; centennial com.), Omega Tau Sigma, Alpha Psi, Phi Zeta. Methodist. Mason (Shriner), Rotarian. Home: Columbus, Ohio. Died Mar. 30, 1983.

KROC, RAYMOND A., restaurant co., baseball club exec.; b. Chgo., Oct. 5, 1902; m. Jane Dobbins. Ed., Oak Park (Ill.) pub. schs. With Lily Tulip Cup Co., 1923-41, sales mgr., until 1941; with Mult-A-Mixer Co., 1941-55; pres. McDonald's Corp., Chgo., 1955-68, chmn., 1968-77, sr. chmn., 1977-84; chmn. San Diego Padres Baseball Team, 1974-84, treas., 1974-78, pres., 1979-84. Author: Grinding It Out: The Making of McDonalds, 1977. Served in Ambulance Corps, World War I. Died Jan. 14, 1984.

KROEHLER, DELMAR LEROY, furniture manufacturing executive; b. Naperville, Ill., Mar. 6, 1902; s. Peter Edward and Josephine Lucille (Stephens) K.; U. of Ill. 1924; m. Dorothy Jane Hughes, Jan. 22, 1927; children—Rodney Stuart, Jane Ann. Began as machine operator Kroehler Mfg. Co., mfrs. furniture, Naperville, Ill., 1922, engring. dept., 1923-25, mgr. plants at Kankakee, Ill., 1925-27, production mgr. all plants, 1927-38, pres., from 1938. Mem. Nat. Assn. Furniture Mfrs. (pres. 1956), Psi Upsilon. Evangelican. Clubs: Lake Shore Athletic (Chgo.); Hinsdale (Ill.) Golf. Home: Hinsdale, Ill. Dec. Oct. 16, 1982.

KROLL, HARRY HARRISON, author, educator; b. nr. Hartford City, Ind., Feb. 18, 1888; s. Darius Wesley and Caroline (Cripe) K.; B.S., Peabody Coll. for Teachers, Nashville, Tenn., 1923, M.A., 1925; m. Nettie Heard, May 12, 1911; children—Harry Harrison II, Robert Torrey, Danny Wesley. Rural sch. teacher and high sch. prin., Ala., 1911-21; prof. English and head dept., Lincoln Memorial U., Harrogate, Tenn., 1925-27; prof. journalism, Ia. Wesleyan Coll., Mt. Pleasant, 1928-29; instr. in journalism and publicity, Peabody Coll., summers 1925-31, asso. prof., head English dept., U. of Tenn. Jr. College (Martin, Tenn.), prof. emeritus, from 1958; free lance writer, 1930-35; fiction adv. editor Southern Literary Messenger, 1940-43. Book reviewer, Comml. Appeal

(Memphis) and Nashville Tennesseean (Nashville), New York Times Book Section. Member Am. Dialect Soc. Meth. Mason. Author: Comparative Study Southern Folk Speech, 1925; The Mountainy Singer, 1928; The Cabin in The Cotton, 1931 (filmed by Warner Bros., starring Bette Davis and Richard Barthelmess, 1932); Three Brothers and Seven Daddies, 1932; The Ghosts of Slave Driver's Bend, 1937; I Was a Share-Cropper, 1937; (play) No Romance, 1938; The Keepers of the House, 1940; The Usurper, 1941; The Rider on the Bronze Horse, 1942; Perilous Journey (with Clifford Sublette), 1943; Rogues' Company, 1943; Waters over the Dam, 1944; Fury in the Earth, 1945; Witches' House, 1945; Their Ancient Grudge, 1946; Darker Grows the Valley, 1947; Mem. of Empire, 1949; Lost Homecoming, 1950; The Long Quest, 1953; Barbara's Farm, 1955; The Medicine Man, 1955; Summer Gold, 1955; Smoldering Fire, 1955; My Heart's in The Hills, 1956; Cloi, 1957; For Cloi, With Love, 1958; books pub. fgn., countries, overseas edits. Contbr. short stories, verse and illustrations to mags.; short stories in numerous anthologies. Home: Martin, Tenn. †

KROLL, WILLIAM, violinist; b. N.Y.C., Jan. 30, 1901; s. Adolph and Fanny (Braham) K.; student Royal Acad., Berlin, Germany, 1911-14; grad. with highest honors Inst. Mus. Art, N.Y.C., 1917-22; m. Pearl Friedman, June 7, 1922; 1 dau., Barbara. Debut in N.Y.C., 1915; violinist with Elshuco Trio, 1923-29; 1st violinist with Coolidge Quartet, 1935-45; founder Kroll Quartet, 1945; tchr. violin and chamber music Mannes Coll. Music, N.Y.C., 1943-76, Peabody Conservatory, Balt., 1947-65; chamber music Tanglewood, Berkshire Music Center, 1949-79; head string dept. Cleve. Conservatory Music, 1965-68; prof. violin Queens Coll., 1969-76; teaching asso. in music Boston U., 1977-79; soloist with orchs., U.S., Europe; soloist with Nat. Symphony Orch., White House, 1966. Recipient Coolidge medal Library of Congress, 1942. Club: Bohemians (N.Y.C.). Composer violin and chamber music. Address: Boston, Mass. Died Mar. 10, 1980.

KRONHEIM, MILTON STANLEY, corp., exec.; b. Washington, Oct. 2, 1888; s. Jacob and Judith (Benzinger) K.; ed. pub. schs., Washington; m. Meryl Goldsmith, Oct. 3, 1909; children—Milton Stanley, Judith E. Pres. Milton S. Kronheim & Co. Inc., Washington, The Kronheim Co., Balt.; dir. Madison Nat. Bank, Washington, Bd. dirs. Washington Better Bus. Bur. Bd. dirs. Boys Club, Big Brothers, Mt. St. Agnes Coll., Linwood Children's Center. Recipient Man of Year award Nat. Conf. Christians and Jews, 1960, Heart of Gold award Variety Club, 1962. Democrat. Mason (Shriner), Elk. Club: Optimist. Home: Washington, D.C. †

KRUSE, CORNELIUS WOLFRAM, educator, sanitary engr.; b. College Station, Tex., Feb. 19, 1913; s. Samuel Andrew and Geraldine (Eilts) K.; B.S., Mo. Sch. Mines, 1934, C.E., 1939; M.S., Harvard, 1940; Dr.P.H., U. Pitts., 1961; m. Adele Reeburgh, Feb. 1, 1939; children—Judith Philippides, Carol Steil, Christina Ricklen, Cornelia. Resident san. engr., health and safety dept. TVA, 1935-46; asso. prof. san. engring. Sch. Hygiene and Pub. Health, Johns Hopkins, 1946-61, prof., head dept. environmental health, 1961-82; vis. prof., head dept. pub. health engring. Inst. Hygiene, U. Philippines, Manila, 1953-55; cons. TVA, WHO, Rockefeller Found., AID. Mem. Md. Bd. Health and Mental Hygiene; chmn. subcom. animal reservoirs and vectors NRC San. Engring. and Environment, 1951-53; tech. mem. Md. Air Pollution Study Commn., 1950-51; mem. Commn. Environmental Hygiene Armed Forces Epidemiological Bd., from 1963. Mem. Am. Acad. Environmental Engrs., Am. Soc. C.E., Am. Water Works Assn., Am. Indsl. Hygiene Assn., Am. Pub. Health Assn., Am. Soc. Tropical Medicine and Hygiene. Contbr. articles to profl. jours. Home: Baltimore, Md. Died Jan. 17, 1982.

KUECHLE, BENNO ERNST, ins. exec.; b. Sheboygan, Wis., July 3, 1889; s. Theodore A. and Clara (Jung) K.; A.B., U. Wis., 1912; m. Edna Luchsinger, Sept. 8, 1914; children—John, Mary Ann (Mrs. R. L. Dudley), David. Instr. accounting U. Wis., 1912; chief statistician Wis. Indsl. Commn., 1913; dir. Employers Mutuals (Employers Mut. Liability Ins. Co. of Wis., Employers Mut. Fire Ins. Co.), Wausau. Spl. cons. Mem. Pres.'s Com. Employment Handicapped. Mem. Wis. Tb Assn. Universalist. Elk. Home: Wausau, Wis. †

KUHLMAN, AUGUSTUS FREDERICK, librarian; b. Hubbard, Ia., Sept. 3, 1889; s. Henry and Anna (Wickman) K.; B.S., Northwestern Coll., Naperville, Ill., 1916; A.M., University of Chicago, 1922, Ph.D., 1929; married Katharine Edmonstone Jones, Apr. 25, 1922; (died November 17, 1944); children—Clara Ann, Clementina Katharine; married 2d, Virginia Wood Walker, Sept. 18, 1946. Director social surveys American Red Cross, 1919-20; asst. prof. sociology, U. of Mo., 1920-24, asso. prof., 1924-29; asso. dir. U. of Chicago libraries, 1929-36; dir. joint Univ. libraries (Vanderbilt U. and George Peabody and Scarritt colls.), Nashville, from 1936; library bldg. consultant Tex. Christian U., 1949, Miss. State Coll., 1949-50, Southwestern U., Memphis, 1950-51, Tenn. State Library and Archives bldg., 1950-51, Jackson (Mississippi) State College, 1957-58. Served as Y.M.C.A. war service sec. Great Lakes Naval Sta., 1917-18; asst. sec. Ill. War Recreation Bd., 1918; in U.S. Army, 1918-19. Sec. Bd. Pub. Welfare Sec., Columbia, Mo., 1921-28; pres. Mo. Conf. for Social Work, 1923; asst. dir. Mo. Crime Survey, 1925; dir. Survey of Research on Crime and Criminal Justice, Social Science Research Council, 1927-28. Mem. Am. Library Assn.; mem. Council, 1932-36; chmn., Com. on Public Documents, 1932-36; chmn. Com. on Archives and Libraries, 1936-1940; chmn. Steering Com. Univ. and Reference Librarians Round Table, 1938; chmn. Assn. of Coll. and Reference Libraries com. on publs., 1939-41; joint chmn. Conf. Grad. Deans and Librarians on Development of Library Resources and Grad. Work in coop. U. Centers of South (editor Proc.). Fellow Am. Library Inst.; mem. Phi Beta Kappa of Tenn. Rotarian. Episcopalian. Editor: Papers A.L.A. Com. on Public Documents, 1933-36; Papers of A.L.A. Com. on Archives and Libraries, 1937-40; Coll. and Univ. Library Service—Trends, Standards, Appraisals, Problems, (A.L.A.), 1938; Coll. and Research Libraries, 1939-41; The Development of Univ. Centers in the South, 1942. Co-author: A Survey of the U. of Florida Library (A.L.A.), 1940; A Survey of the U. of Mississippi Library, 1940. Author: Social Survey of City of Jackson, Tenn., 1920; Paroles and Pardons, Missouri Crime Survey, 1926: A Guide to Material on Crime and Criminal Justice, 1929; The North Texas Regional Libraries (survey), 1943; Survey of four St. Paul Coll. Libraries, 1952; Survey of seven Libraries of Ark. Found. of Asso. Colls., 1958. Contbr. of articles to profl. publs. †

KUHN, ALFRED, educator; b. Reading, Pa., Dec. 22, 1914; s. Alvin Boyd and Mary (Leippe) K.; m. Nina Marguerite deAngeli, Oct. 18, 1941; children—J. David, Jeffrey P., Henry T. B.A., Albright Coll., 1935; M.A. in History, U. Pa., 1941, Ph.D. in Econs, 1951. Tchr. pub. schs., N.J. and Pa., 1935-41, various indsl. positions, 1941-45; with WLB, Phila., 1945-46; instr. industry U. Pa., 1946-49; prof. econs. U. Cin., from 1949, David Sinton prof., from 1968, prof. sociology, from 1980, fellow Grad. Sch., from 1968, disting. service prof., from 1981. Author: Study of Society: A Unified Approach, 1963, Labor: Institutions and Economics, 1967, The Logic of Social Systems, 1974, Unified Social Science, 1975, (with Edward Herman) Collective Bargaining and Indsl. Relations, 1981. Mem. panel arbitrators Fed. Mediation and Conciliation Service, from 1952, Am. Arbitration Assn., from 1947; Pres., chmn. bd. Fulmer Heights Home Ownership Assn., 1946-49. Served with USNR, 1945. Mem. ACLU (chmn. Cin. chpt. 1968-76, bd. dirs. Ohio affiliate from 1966), AAUP (Distinguished Service award acad. freedom 1968), Soc. Gen. Systems Research, Am. Sociol. Assn., Social Sci. Edn. Consortium, AAAS, Acad. Mgmt., Assn. for Integrative Studies, Acad. Ind. Scholars. Home: New Richmond, OH.

KUHN, LLOYD WILSON, banker; b. Adams County, Pa., Apr. 22, 1898; s. Lloyd E. and Mary (Smith) K.; m. Mary E. Garretson, July 31, 1922; children—Charles E. (dec.), Ronald B., Jean M. (Mrs. Justin J. Horick), Joyce L. (Mrs. Richard L. Swope). Grad., Pa. Bus. Coll., Lancaster, 1919. Tchr., Adams County, 1918-19; with Bendersville Nat. Bank, Pa., from 1919, pres., from 1954; pres., dir. Penn Products Corp., Bendersville, from 1952; dir. Fed. Res. Bank Phila.; Chmn. banking div. War Savs. Bond Com. Adams County, from 1962. Bd. dirs. Annie M. Warner Hosp., Gettysburg, Pa. Mem. Pa. Bankers Assn. Club: Elk. Home: Bendersville, PA.

KUHN, REINHARD, educator; b. Berlin, Germany, Sept. 6, 1930; s. Helmut and Kaethe (Lanke) K.; came to U.S., 1938, naturalized, 1942; A.B., Princeton, 1952, M.A., 1954, Ph.D., 1957; M.A. ad eundem, Brown U., 1965; m. Ira Astride Ameriks, June 15, 1963; children—Bernhard Helmut, Nicholas Peter. Asst. prof., then assoc. prof. U. Kans., 1958-63; prof. U. Buffalo, 1963-64; prof. French, Brown U., 1964-77, prof. French and comparative lit., 1977-80, chmn. dept., 1967-76; mem. adv. com. Sweetbriar Jr. Year in France, 1968-80. Mem. tech. com. on R.I. Coastal Zone. Fulbright research scholar France, 1964-65; sr. fellow Nat. Endowment for Humanities, France, 1972-73, cons.-panelist, 1976—; fellow John Carter Brown Library, 1973, Camargo Found., 1978-79, Inst. Advanced Study, Princeton, N.J., 1979-80. Served with AUS, 1954-56. Fellow Am. Council Learned Socs.; mem. Modern Lang. Assn., Am. Assn. Tchrs. French, Modern Humanities Research Assn., Acad. Lit. Studies (sec.-treas.), Assn. Study Dada and Surrealism, AAUP, Pawtuxet-Edgewood Preservation Soc. (sec.). Author: The Return to Reality, 1962; Correspondence de Francis Jammes et de Francis Viele-Griffin, 1966; L'Esprit Moderne dans la Litterature Francaise, 1972; The Demon of Noontide: Ennui in Western Literature, 1976; co-author: Panorama du Theatre Nouveau, 4 vols., 1966-67. Translator: New Ways of Ontology, 1952; Dying we Live, 1957. Assoc. editor: Novel. Home: Edgewood, R.I. Dec. Nov. 6, 1980.

KULP, BENJAMIN, chairman board, Wilson-Jones Co.; b. Clinton, Ia., Mar. 15, 1890; s. Leo and Flora (Gordon) K.; ed. private sch. and Jewish Orphan Home, Cleveland, O.; m. Lillian Goldman, Aug. 15, 1911. Began with DeRode, Faulkner & Ettelson, ins., 1904, as stenographer; exec. v.p. Madison-Kedzie State Bank, 1911-19; pres. Wilson-Jones Co., Chicago, 1919-40, chmn. board, from 1940. Home: River Forest, Ill. †

KUNKEL, HENRY GEORGE, immunologist; b. N.Y.C., Sept. 9, 1916; s. Louis O. and Johanna C. K.; m. Betty Jean Martens, Jan. 8, 1949; children—Louis M., Henry G., Ellen L. A.B., Princeton U., 1938; M.D., Johns Hopkins U., 1942, Uppsala U., Sweden. Intern Bellevue Hosp., N.Y.C., 1942-43; mem. faculty dept. immunology Rockefeller U., N.Y.C., 1946-83, Abby Rockefeller Mauzé prof., 1976-83; adj. prof. medicine Cornell U. Med. Sch., 1971-83; bd. councilors Arthritis Inst., NIH, Sloan Kettering Inst., Brookhaven Labs., Cancer Center Columbia Med. Sch. Editor: Advances in Immunology, Jour. Exptl. Medicine. Served with USNR, 1945-46. Recipient Lasker award; Gairdner award; Hazen award; Waterford award; Pasteur medal; Avery-Landsteiner award; Kovalenko medal; medal N.Y. Acad. Medicine. Mem. Nat. Acad. Scis., Assn. Am. Physicians, Am. Soc. Clin. Investigation (pres. 1963), Am. Assn. Immunologists (pres. 1975), Harvey Soc. (lectr. 1965). Clubs: Princeton, Interurban Clin. Home: New York, N.Y. Died Dec. 14, 1983.

KUNZIG, ROBERT LOWE, judge; b. Phila., Oct. 31, 1918; s. Robert Weiss and Hilda Elsa (Lowe) K.; children—Kim Chappell, Robert Lowe, Jr. B.A., U. Pa., 1939, J.D., 1942. Bar: Pa. bar 1942, Minn. bar 1961. Co-prosecutor Buchenwald concentration camp case, Germany, 1947; asso. firm Clark, Ladner, Fortenbaugh & Young, Phila., 1948-69; dep. atty. gen., Pa., 1948-53; counsel U.S. Congl. Com., 1953-54; exec. dir. CAB, 1955-58; mem. U.S. Fgn. Claims Settlement Commn., 1958-61; v.p. E.G. Clinton Co., Mpls., 1961-62; adminstrv. asst. to U.S. Senator Hugh Scott, 1963-67; exec. dir. Pa. Gen. State Authority, 1967-69, Pa. Hwy., Bridge and Transp. Authorities, 1967-69; mem. cabinet Gov. Pa., 1967-69; adminstr. Gen. Services U.S., Washington, 1969-72; asso. judge U.S. Ct. Claims, 1972-82; Chmn. Task Force for Minority Businessman, 1969-72; spl. asst. to Pres. for coordination 1976 Washington bicentennial, 1970-72; mem. Cabinet Com. on Constrn., 1969-72, U.S. Property Rev. Bd., 1969-72, Commn. on Govt. Procurement, 1969-72, Regulations and Purchasing Rev. Bd., 1969-72; mem. com. on ct. facilities and design U.S. Jud. Conf., 1972-75, mem. ad hoc com. on records disposition, 1978-82. Contbr. articles nat. mags.; lectr. in field. Del. Republican Nat. Conv., Chgo., 1952; dir. GOP Truth Squad campaigns Rep. Nat. Com., 1956, 60, 68; mgr. Hugh Scott Senatorial Campaign, 1964, mgr. Phila. dist. atty. campaign, 1965, mgr. Pa. Rep. gubernatorial campaign, 1966, Rep. candidate atty.-gen. Minn., 1962; chmn. Phila. Young Reps., 1948-50, Young Reps. Pa., 1951-52. Served to capt. AUS, 1942-46. Decorated Army Commendation medal with oak leaf cluster; named to Pa. Young Rep. Hall of Fame; recipient 2 awards for distinguished service govt. CAB, 1956, 58; Award for Excellence and Outstanding Performance Gen. Services Adminstrn., 1972; cited by Pres.'s Eisenhower and Nixon. Mem. ABA (adminstrv. law sect., litigation sect., judicial adminstrn. div.), Pa. Bar Assn., Phila. Bar Assn., Minn. Bar Assn., Phi Beta Kappa, Phi Sigma Kappa, Pi Gamma Mu, Mask and Wig (dir. Phila.). Episcopalian. Clubs: Union League (Phila.); Metropolitan (Washington). Home: Washington, D.C. Died Feb. 21, 1982.

KU PEI-MOO, research institute executive, phys. scientist; b. Sian, China, Feb. 3, 1915; s. Yi-Nung and Shiang-Yun (Yun) K.; B.S., Chiao Tung U. (Shanghai, China), 1935; D.I.C., Imperial Coll. (London, Eng.), 1939; m. Anlin Wang, June 14, 1942; children—June, Warren, Leighton. Asst. prof. Mass. Inst. Tech., Cambridge, 1945-47; prof., head dept. aero. engring. Tsinghua U., Peiping, China, 1948-49; chief engines and lubrication sect. Nat. Bur. Standards, Washington, 1954-56; dir. depts. aerospace propulsion and fluids and lubrication tech., v.p. Southwest Research Inst., San Antonio, 1956-78; adviser Center for Engring. Research, Republic of China, 1965-78; lectr., cons. in field. Fellow Am. Soc. Lubrication Engrs. (hon. mem.; pres. 1969-70, Nat. award 1973), ASME (chmn. research com. lubrication 1966-68), Instn. Mech. Engrs. Gt. Britain; mem. ASTM, Coordinating Research Council. Author papers in fields of tribology and applied thermodynamics. Asso. editor Applied Mechanics Rev., 1956-52, Am. Soc. Lubrication Engrs. Trans., 1962-72; editor, chmn. steering com. NASA Interdisciplinary Lubrication Symposia, 1966-73. 1966-73. Home: San Antonio, Tex. Died July 5, 1978.

KUPFERMAN, LAWRENCE EDWARD, artist; b. Boston, Mar. 25, 1909; s. Samuel and Rosa (Maysles) K.; m. Ruth Cobb, Apr. 29, 1937; children—Nancy, David. Student, Sch. of Museum of Fine Arts, Boston, 1929-30; B.S. in Edn, Mass. Sch. Art, 1935. Asso. prof. of drawing and painting, also screen Mass. Coll. Art, Boston, 1941-58, prof. painting, from 1958, also head dept. One man shows include, Boris Mirski Gallery, 1944, 45, 46, 47, Mortimer Brandt Gallery, N.Y.C., 1946, Swetzoff Gallery, Boston, 1956, Ruth White Gallery, N.Y.C., 1958, Pace Gallery, Boston, 1950, 51, 63, DeCordova Mus., Lincoln, Mass., 1961, Galerie Irla Kert, Montreal, Que., Can., 1962, Art Unltd., Providence, 1963, Horizon Gallery, Rockport, Mass., 1968, Greenfield Gallery, N.Y.C., 1970, Horizon West, Los Angeles, 1971, Brockton (Mass.) Art Center, 1974, group shows include, Art Inst. Chgo., Whitney Mus. Am. Art, N.Y.C., Internat. Biennial, Venice, Pa. Acad. Fine Arts, Met. Mus. Art, N.Y.C., Butler Inst. Am. Art, Youngstown, Ohio, Balt. Mus. Art, City Mus. of St. Louis, Wadsworth Atheneum, Hartford, Conn., Petit Palais, Paris, Carnegie Inst., Pitts., works represented in permanent collections of, Boston Mus. Fine Arts, Met. Mus. Art, Mus. Modern Art, N.Y.C., Fogg Art Mus., Cambridge, Mass., Library of Congress, Washington, N.Y. U. Art Collection, Boston Public Library, Walker Art Center, Mpls., numerous others. Recipient numerous awards and prizes, from 1938; latest being First prize for painting for Odysseus Rhode Island Arts Festival, 1961. Home: Newton Centre, Mass.

KURAZ, RUDOLF, counsul general of Czechoslovakia; b. Praha, Czechoslovakia, April 8, 1888; s. Jan and Anna (Vacikarova) K.; ed. Coll. in Rakovnik, 1906; U. in Praha, 1910; Doctorate, 1911; m. Pavla Scheinerova. April 26, 1913; children—Eva Havlickova, Dagmar Reichova. Entered Czechoslovak Ministry of Fgn. Affairs, 1918; 1st sec. Czechoslovak Legation, Washington, 1920-25; study of conditions of Czechoslovak immigrants in Can., 1926; consul gen. of Czechoslovakia in Sydney, Australia. 1927-35; chief Anglo-Saxon div., econ. dept., Ministry of Fgn. Affairs, Praha, 1935-38, Participated in negotiations for the trade treaty between U.S. and Czechoslovakia, 1937-38; chief trade treaties div., Dept. of Commerce, Praha. 1939-45. Chief territorial div. Ministry of Fgn. Affairs. Praha, 1945-46, special envoy, minister plenipotentiary heading the Czechoslovak Trade and Monetary Del. to United Kingdom, 1945, headed del. in same capacity for Trade Agreement negotiations with Norway, 1945, Ireland, 1946; consul gen. of Czechoslovakia in N.Y. City, from 1946. Hon. mem. Czechoslovak Acad. of Agr. (Praha); mem. Czechoslovak Econ. Assn. (Praha). Roman Catholic. Home: New York, N.Y. †

KURTZ, WILLIAM FULTON, banker; b. Philadelphia, Pa., Aug. 17, 1887; s. William B. and Margaret (Fulton) K.; A.B., Harvard, 1908; m. Anita Downing, Oct. 8, 1910. Clerk Kurtz Bros., brokers, 1908, partner, 1913; pres. The Colonial Trust Co., 1918-30; v.p. and dir. The Pa. Co., named changed to The First Pa. Co. for Banking and Trusts, 1930-34, exec. v.p., 1934-38, pres., 1938-52, chmn. bd., 1952-55, ret.; trustee Penn Mut. Life Ins. Co.; director Reading Company, The Pennsylvania Insurance Company, Proctor-Silex Corporation, Reliance Insurance Co., Western Saving Fund Soc. Clubs: Philadelphia, Racquet, Rabbit; Harvard (N.Y.C.). Home: St. Martins, Pa. †

KURTZWORTH, HARRY MUIR, art director; b. Detroit, Mich., Aug. 12, 1887; s. William John and Helen (Miller) K.; ed. Central High Sch., Detroit; studied Detroit Acad. Fine Arts, Art Museum Sch. and in Paris, Munich, Rome, Museum Sch. of Art, Phila.; graduate in fine arts, Columbia Univ., 1911; A.F.D. Andhra Univ., British South India, 1937; m. Constance E. Kienzle, May 15, 1922; 1 dau., Constance (Mrs. Rowland Harris Crocker). Director art work, Muskegon, Mich., 1911-16; founder and director School of Art, Grand Rapids, 1916-20; made director Mich. Art Institute, 1917; associate dir. Chicago Acad. Fine Arts, 1920-21, and 1926-30; curator of art, Los Angeles Museum, 1931-32; dir. Kansas City Art Inst. and Art Sch., 1921-25; prof. Western Reserve, summer, 1926; dir. Modern Homes Bur., 1927-30; art dir. Los Angeles Art Assn., 1933-38, Calif. Inst. of Fine Arts, 1938. Founded first state owned art collection, State of Michigan, 1921. Painter, designer and lecturer on art; exhibited in Chicago, Detroit, Philadelphia and throughout western circuit; paintings exemplify the emotional aspects of life. Recipient Medaille d'Honneur du Merite Francais, 1939; Commander Cross, Grand Prix Humanitaire, Belgium, 1939. Member Eastern Arts Assn., Western Arts Assn., Am. Fedn. Arts, Am. Inst. Architects (hon.), Detroit Soc. Arts and Crafts, Art Mus. Dirs. Assn., Am. Assn. Museums, Western Assn. Art Mus. Dirs., Alpha Chi Rho, Phi Omega, Delta Phi Delta (hon.); del. 4th Internat. Art Congress, Dresden. Republican. Mason. Club: Calif. Art (hon.). Author: Industrial Art—a National Asset, 1918; Western Arts Annual, 1922; How to Use Your Talent, 1923; Genius, Talent, Ability or Mediocrity, 1924. International Design 1936; Designer 10th Olympiad official diploma of award. Chairman econ. progress com. Engrs. and Architects Inst. Creator of Lucideum. Secretary, Golden-Age Society, art dir. treas. Am. Art Soc.; treasurer Coordinating Com. for Traditional Art; contbr. World Book Ency. Art dir. Cal. Missions Pictorial. Studio: Los Angeles, Calif. †

KUTAK, ROBERT JEROME, lawyer; b. Chgo., Oct. 7, 1932; s. Jerome Frank and Jessamine Mary (Geagan) K. A.B., U. Chgo., 1952, J.D., 1955. Bar: Nebr. bar 1955, Ind. bar 1955. Asso. firm Robinson, Hruska, Crawford, Garvey & Nye, Omaha, 1955-56; law clk. to Hon. Richard E. Robinson, chief judge U.S. Dist. Ct., Omaha, 1956-59; legis. asst. to Senator Roman L. Hruska, Washington, 1959-62, adminstrv. asst., 1962-65; partner firm Kutak Rock & Huie, Omaha, 1965-83; dir. Guarantee Res. Life Ins. Co., Hammond, Ind., S & B Brokerage Service Corp., White Plains, N.Y.; partner Municipal Issuers Service Co., White Plains; bd. dirs. Legal Services Corp., 1975-83; mem. Pres.'s Task Force on Prisoner Rehab., 1969-70; mem. U.S. del. to 4th and 5th UN Congress on Prevention Crime and Treatment of Offenders, 1970, 75; mem. Nat. Advisory Commn. on Criminal Justice Standards and Goals, 1971-73; mem. advisory bd. Nat. Inst. Corrections, 1973-83; mem. Nebr. Jail Standards Bd., 1978-81. Trustee Joslyn Art Museum, Omaha, 1978—. Served to maj. Judge Adv. Gen. Corps. USAR, 1956-66. Mem. Am. Bar Assn. (chmn. sect. on individual rights and responsibilities 1974-75, chmn. spl. com. on coordination fed. jud. improvements 1974-77, chmn. Commn. on Evaluation Profl. Standards 1977-83, mem. council sect. on legal edn. 1976-83), Nebr. Bar Assn., Ind. State Bar Assn., Omaha Bar Assn., Am. Law Inst. Republican. Unitarian. Home: Omaha, Nebr. Died Jan. 23, 1983.

KUTZ, HARRY R., army officer; b. Pottstown, Pa., Jan. 29, 1889; s. Charles Miller and Rebecca Boltz (Koble) K.; B.S., U.S. Mil. Acad., 1911; grad. Army Indsl. Coll., 1939;. Commd. 2d lt., Inf., U.S. Army, 1911, and advanced through the grades to brig. gen., 1942; chief of the Military Plans and Training Service Ordnance Dept. Served as lt. col. in France with A.E.F., World War I. Decorated Purple Heart Mexican Border, Victory and War Dept. Gen. Staff medals. Mason (Shriner, York and Scottish Rites). Clubs: Chevy Chase (Md.); Army and Navy (Washington, D.C.); Army and Navy Country (Arlington, Va.). Home: Washington, D.C. †

KUTZ, SALLY E., hygiene educator., b. New York, N.Y., Dec. 26, 1888: dau. Gabriel S. and Caroline Kutz; B.A., Hunter Coll., 1909; C.P.H., New York Univ., 1915, M.S., 1916, Ph.D., 1932. With Elizabeth Tuberculosis Assn., 1912-14; teacher of hygiene, Hunter Coll., 1914-30; Brooklyn Coll. from 1930, prof. and chmn. dept. hygiene (women) from 1933. Fellow Am. Pub. Health Assn Mem. Women in Pub. Health, Am. Student Health Assn., Health and Phys. Edn. Assn., Nat. Cancer Assn., Brooklyn Assn. for Care of Blind, A.A.A.S., New York City Nutrition Com., Lay Bd. of Kingston Av. Hosp., Bell Island Assn. Bd., Pi Lambda Theta, Kappa Delta Pi. Republican. Unitarian. Home: New York, N.Y. †

KUZELL, CHARLES R., copper co. exec.; b. Cleve., Nov. 1, 1889; s. Charles A. and Mary A. (Evans) K.; B.S., Case Sch. Applied Sci., 1910, Metall. Engr., 1914; D.Sc. (honorary), University of Arizona, 1960; m. Theresa A. O'Leary, Oct. 15, 1913; children—William C., Ralph E. (officer U.S. Army), Mary C., Charles E. (officer U.S. Navy). Testing engr. Anaconda Copper Mining Co., Great Falls, Mont., 1910-14, supt. reverberatory smelting, Anaconda, Mont., 1914-18; from smelter supt. to gen. supt. United Verde Copper Co., Clarkdale, Ariz., 1918-35; with Phelps Dodge Corp., Douglas, Ariz., from 1935, beginning as mgr. United Verde br., successively dir. labor relations and cons. metallurgist, gen. mgr., 1935-55, v.p. charge Western activities, 1955-58, dir., from 1956; pres. Apache Powder Co., Benson, Ariz. Mem. Am. Inst. Mining and Metall. Engrs. (chmn. com. reduction and refining copper, 1933-34; chmn. Ariz. sect. 1946-47; dir. 1955-59; James Douglas gold medal 1955), Mining and Metall. Soc. Am., Am. Mining Congress (chmn. labor relation and labor legislation com. 1946-53; gov. Ariz. chpt. 1946-47, dir. 1940-60), Am. Chem. Soc., Electrochem. Soc. Address: Phoenix, Ariz. †

KUZNETS, SIMON, economist; b. Kharkov, Russia, Apr. 30, 1901; s. Abraham and Pauline (Friedman) K.; m. Edith H. Handler, June 5, 1929; children: Paul, Judith. B.S., Columbia, 1923, M.A., 1924, Ph.D., 1926, D.H.L. (hon.), 1954; D.Sc. (hon.), Princeton, 1951; D.Sc. in Econs. (hon.), U. Pa., 1956, LL.D., 1976; D.Sc., Harvard, 1959; Ph.D. (hon.), Hebrew U. Jerusalem, 1965; LL.D., U. N.H., 1972; D.H.L., Brandeis U., 1975. Social Sci. Research Council Fellow, 1925-27; mem. staff Nat. Bur. Econ. Research, 1927-61; asst. prof. econ. statistics U. Pa., 1930-34, asso. prof., 1934-35, prof., 1936-54; prof. polit. economy Johns Hopkins, 1954-60; Frank W. Taussig research prof. econs. Harvard, 1958-59, prof. econs., 1960-71; Asso. dir. Bur. Planning and Statistics, WPB, 1942-44. Author: Cyclical Fluctuations, 1926, Secular Movements in Production and Prices, 1930, Seasonal Variations in Industry and Trade, 1933, National Income and Capital Formation, 1938, Commodity Flow and Capital Formation, 1938, National Income, 1941, National Product in Wartime, 1945, National Income: A Summary of Findings, 1946, National Product since 1869, 1946, Shares of Upper Income Groups in Income and Savings, 1953, Six Lectures on the Economic Growth, 1959, Capital in the American Economy, 1961, Postwar Economic Growth, 1964, Economic Growth and Structure: Selected Essays, 1965, Modern Economic Growth, 1966, Economic Growth of Nations, 1971, Population, Capital, and Growth, 1973, Growth, Population, and Income Distribution, 1979; Contbr. articles to econ. jours. Recipient Nobel prize in econs., 1971. Fellow Royal Statis. Soc., Am. Statis. Assn. (pres. 1949), A.A.A.S., Econometric Soc., Brit. Acad. (corr.); mem. Am. Econ. Assn. (pres. 1954), Royal Acad. Scis. Sweden, Am. Philos. Soc., Internat. Statis. Inst., Am. Acad. Arts and Scis., U.S. Acad. Scis. Jewish. Home: Cambridge, Mass. Died July 9, 1985.

KVERNLAND, JACK THEODORE, insurance company executive; b. Portland, Oreg., Apr. 12, 1917; s. John Theodore and Dagmar (Magnussen) K.; B.A., Reed Coll., 1940; grad. Exec. Program, Columbia, 1960; m. Jeanne Audrey Steenburgh, June 2, 1945; children—Sally Jane, John Bruce. With Prudential Ins. Co. Am., 1940-83, exec. gen. mgr. Jacksonville, Fla., 1955-57, v.p., Mpls., 1957-65, sr. v.p., Newark, 1965-66, sr. v.p., chief actuary, 1966-77; pres. Prudential Property & Casualty Co., also Prudential Reins. Co., 1977-83; instr. Life Office Mgmt. Assn. exams., 1948-51. Active United Fund, v.p. spl. gifts sect., Mpls.; active Boy Scouts Am., Citizens League Hennepin County. Bd. dirs. Alliance Am. Insurers, Aquatennial Assn., Mpls., Kiwanis Found., Minn.; trustee Essex County (N.J.) Blood Bank, Monmouth Med. Center, Reed Coll. Fellow Soc. Actuaries; mem. Actuaries Club N.Y., Southeastern Actuaries Club, Twin Cities Actuary Club, C. of C. Presbyn. Rotarian, Kiwanian (pres. 1964). Clubs: River, Revelers, Ponte Vedra, San Jose Country (Jacksonville, Fla.); Athletic, Edina Country (v.p. 1965) (Mpls.); Essex, Morris County Country, Rumson Country (N.J.); Lard Sound Golf, Ocean Reef (Key Largo, Fla.). Home: Monmouth Beach, N.J. Dec. Sept. 22, 1983.

KYLE, PETER EDWARD, mech. engr., educator; b. Lakeport, N.H., Feb. 10, 1908; s. Edward McKenzie and Lydia Mary (Plant) K.; student Carnegie Inst. Tech., 1927-29, Lehigh U. (James Ward Packard research fellow), 1933-34; M.E., Cornell U. (Westinghouse War Meml. scholar), 1933; M.S., M.I.T., 1939; m. Fanny E. Sly, July 8, 1933; 1 son, James Peter; m. 2d, Mary Savage Wells, Nov. 27, 1953; children—James Savage, Robert Seth, Richard Edward. Research engr. Westinghouse Elec. Corp., E. Pittsburgh, 1929; research fellow Lehigh U., 1933-34; mem. faculty mech. engring. Mass. Inst. Tech., 1934-46, asso. prof., 1944-46; instr. Lowell Inst. Sch. Machine Design, 1937-43; mem. faculty Cornell U., 1946-54; former v.p. Lessells & Assos., Inc.; cons. indsl. concerns on mech. and metall. problems, 1954-59; mgr. materials dept. Allied Research Assos., Inc., Boston, 1959-61, chief engr. aero/mech. engring. dept., 1961-62, chief materials tech. sect., Concord, Mass., 1962-68; prof. mech. engring. Norwich U., Northfield, Vt., 1968-79, prof. emeritus, 1979—; exec. sec. Vt. State Bd. Registration for Profl. Engrs., Norwich U., 1978—. Staff war metallurgy com. Nat. Acad. Scis., Washington, 1943-44. Registered profl. engr., Mass., Vt. Mem. ASME, Am. Soc. Metals, Sigma Xi, Tau Beta Pi. Home: Northfield, Vt. Died Dec. 6, 1984.

LA BINE, GILBERT A., business exec.; b. Westmeath, Ont., Can., 1890. Pres., dir. Gunnar Gold Mines, Ltd., Toronto; v.p. Shawkey Gold Mining Co., Toronto; dir. Howey Gold Mines, Ltd., Toronto, Polymer Corp. Ltd., Teck Hughes Gold Mines, Ltd., East Malartic Mines, Ltd. Gov. U. Toronto. Address: Toronto, Ont., Canada. †

LABOON, JOHN FRANCIS, engr.; b. Pitts., Mar. 8, 1890; s. Frank William and Catherine (Netcavage) L.; B.S., Carnegie Inst. Tech., 1914. C.E., 1919; m. Catherine Agnes Reilly, Jan. 29, 1917; children—Mary Jane (Mrs. James D. Allen), Patrice (Sister M. de Lellis), Rev. John F., S.J., Katherine, Claire (Mrs. Hugh J. Maloy, Jr.), Thomas A., Rosemary (Sister M. Anne), Joan (Sister Joan of Arc), Reverend Joseph D. Began as an assistant engr. Chester & Fleming, 1912-15; chief engr. Pitts. Filter Mfg. Co., 1915-18; partner The Chester Engrs., 1918-35; with Commonwealth of Pa., as dir. state work relief, dir. W.P.A., Allegheny Co., 1935, dir. Dept. Pub. Works, 1936-43; chmn. bd. Allegheny Co. San. Authority, 1946-55, exec. dir., chief engr., from 1955; cons. san. engr., Pitts., 1946-55. Mem. supervisory com. Bellefield Boiler Plant. Trustee, exec. com., athletic bd. Carnegie Inst. Tech., from 1935, v.p. adv. bd. Mercy Hosp., from 1952; trustee DePaul Inst., from 1949. Served from lt. col. to col. AUS, 1943-45, ETO. Cavalier Order of Crown of Italy; Cavalier Order of Concordia; Knight in the Order of St. Gregory. Mem. Am. Soc. C.E., Am. Soc. Testing Materials, Engrs. Soc. Western Pa., Am. Pub. Works Assn., Pa. Sewage and Indsl. Wastes Assn., Fedn. Sewage and Indsl. Wastes Assns. Clubs: Ligonier Country, Serra (Pitts.). Home: Mt. Lebanon, Pitts. †

LA DUE, JOHN SAMUEL, physician; b. Minot, N.D., Sept. 6, 1911; s. Samuel and Edith Woodsworth (Mann) La.D.; A.B., U. Minn., 1932, S.M. in Medicine, 1940, Ph.D. in Medicine, 1941; M.D., Harvard, 1936; m. Margaret Ruth Stokes, Apr. 24, 1937. Intern L.I. Hosp., 1936-37; resident Mpls. Gen. Hosp., 1937-40, adj. staff physician, 1940-41; asst. vis. physician Charity Hosp., New Orleans, 1941-43, vis. physician, 1943-45, dir. lung sta., 1943-45; clin. asst. Meml. Hosp., N.Y.C., 1945-46, asst. attending physician, 1946-48, asso. attending physician, 1948-80; physician to outpatient dept. N.Y. Hosp., 1946-47, asst. attending physician, 1948-80; tchr. fellow U. Minn. Med. Sch., 1937-40, instr. medicine, 1940-41; instr. La. State U. Sch. Medicine, 1941-43, asst. prof. medicine, 1943-44, asso. prof. clin. medicine, 1944-45; clin. asst. Cornell U. Med. Coll., 1945-46, faculty, 1946-80, asso. prof. clin. medicine, 1958-80; dir. heart sta. Meml. Center, N.Y.C., 1955-57; dir. cardiovascular sect. Meml. Center and Sloan Kettering Inst., 1957-66; sr. attending cardiologist St. Barnabas Hosp. Chronic Diseases. Bd. dirs., sec., past pres. med. staff Doctors Hosp., N.Y.C. Recipient Hektoen medal A.M.A., 1955; Alfred P. Sloan award clin. investigation, 1955; Cummings Humanitarian award, 1963, 64. Diplomate Nat. Bd. Med. Examiners, Am. Bd. Internal Medicine. Mem. Am. Coll. Cardiology (pres. 1962-63), Academia Nacional de Medicina do Brazil, Am. Fedn. Clin. Research (past pres.), A.M.A., A.C.P., Am. Coll. Chest Physicians, Harvey Soc., Soc. Exptl. Biology and Medicine, Am., N.Y. heart assns., N.Y. Acad. Med., N.Y. Acad. Sci., James Ewing Soc., N.Y. Cardiological Soc. (past pres.), N.Y. State Soc. Internal Medicine (past pres.), Harvard Med. Soc. N.Y., Academia Nacional de Medicina de Peru (hon.), Sigma Xi, Sigma Chi. Episcopalian. Contbr. articles to profl. jours., sects. several med. text books. Home: New York, N.Y. Died Apr. 18, 1980; buried Minneapolis, Minn.

LADUE, RALPH ELLSWORTH, business exec.; b. Stillwater, N.Y., Aug. 13, 1890; s. William Seward and Emma (Dugas) L.; A.B., Colgate U., 1911; LL.B., Albany Law Sch., 1913; m. Mary Elizabeth Gaffney, June 15, 1916; children—Ralph Ellsworth, James Warren. Mdse. mgr. De Pinna, N.Y.C., 1913-16, B. Altman, 1916-19; v.p. John David, Inc., 1919-37, pres., 1937-64, chmn. bd., dir., from 1964; pres., dir. R.E. Ladue Corp. Dir. 5th Av. Assn., Better Bus. Bur., N.Y.C. Served as capt. Co. A., 11th M.G. Bn., 4th Div., U.S. Army, AEF, World War I; col., AUS, 1942-46. Decorated D.S.C., Legion of Merit,

Silver Star, Purple Heart with palm, Mexican Border Medal, World War Medal with 4 battle clasps; French Legion of Honor, Croix de Guerre with gold star (France); Knight of Malta. Mem. Am. Legion, 7th Regt. N.G., N.Y. Vets. Assn., 4th Div. Assn. (pres. 1942). Roman Catholic. Clubs: American Yacht, Army and Navy, University, Metropolitan Union League. Home: New York, N.Y. †

LA FOLLETTE, SUZANNE, editor; b. Pullman, Wash.; d. William LeRoy and Mary (Tabor) La Follette; student Wash. State Coll., 1911-13; B.L., Trinity Coll., Washington, D.C., 1915; unmarried. Sec. to late Senator Robert M. La Follette, Sr., 1916-17, William L. La Follette (congressman), 1917-19; asst. editor The Freeman, 1920-24, The New Freeman, 1930-31; Guggenheim fellow, 1935; sec. and editor of publs., commn. of inquiry into charges made against Leon Tretsky in Moscow trials, 1937-38; mng. editor Am. Mercury 1940. Mem. Kappa Alpha Theta. Author: Concerning Women, 1926; Art in America, 1929. Editor: The Case of Leon Trotsky, 1937; Not Guilty, 1938; Balkan Firebrand, 1943. Contbr. articles and verse to periodicals. Died Apr. 23, 1983.

LAGINESTRA, ROCCO MICHAEL, marketing executive; b. N.Y.C., July 1, 1926; s. Michael and Caroline L.; children—Carolyn, Michael, Rochelle, Charles, Ann Marie. B.S. in Acctg, L.I. U., 1950, postgrad., 1951. Controller, gen. mgr. Curtiss-Wright Corp., River Edge, N.J., 1951-59; controller Univac div. Sperry Rand Corp., N.Y.C., 1959-63; dir. fin. planning and budgets, v.p. NBC, N.Y.C., 1963-68, v.p. fin. and treasury ops., 1968-69; exec. v.p. record div. RCA, N.Y.C., 1979, pres. div., 1979; staff v.p. ops. analysis and study RCA Corp., N.Y.C., 1974-75; staff v.p. ops analysis and bus. planning Electronics and Diversified Bus. Group, 1975-77, v.p. planning and mktg., 1977-80, sr. v.p. planning, mktg. and internat., 1980-83. Active Boy Scouts Am.; dir. Little League Baseball and Basketball. Served with AUS, World War II, ETO. Mem. Fin. Execs. Inst., Nat. Assn. Accts. Clubs: Indian Trail Country (Franklin Lakes, N.J.); Rockefeller Center Luncheon (N.Y.C.); K.C. Home: Franklin Lakes, N.J. Died Mar. 21, 1983.

LAIRD, HELEN CONNOR, lumber co. exec.; b. Wisconsin Rapids, Wis., Aug. 22, 1888; d. W. D. and Mary B. (Witter) Connor; student Milw. Downer Coll.; B.A., U. Wis.; m. Melvin R. Larid, Apr. 16, 1913; children—Connor, Richard, Melvin R., David. Mem. board regents University of Wisconsin, 1952-61. Secretary, member board directors Connor Lumber & Land Co. Pres. Marshfield (Wis.) Bd. Edn., Marshfield Library Bd.; mem. Wis. Coordinating Commn. on Higher Edn. Mem. Gen. Fedn. Woman's Clubs (past pres. 7th dist. Wis.), P.E.O., Pi Beta Phi, Theta Sigma Phi. Republican (del. conv. 1948). Presbyn. Address: Marshfield, Wis. †

LAIRD, LINNIE, nursing exec.; b. Norristown, Pa., Feb. 3, 1890; s. Lindsay G. and Sarah Ann (Jones) Ellington; grad Chester (Pa.) Hosp. Sch. of Nursing, 1912; certificate pub. health nursing, U. of Ore., 1926; m. John Alexander Laird, Dec. 2, 1912; children—Helen, John Alexander. Practice as nurse (registered), Ore., Cal., Pa., from 1921. Pres. Ore. State Orgn. Pub. Health Nursing, 1934-36; 1st v.p. and dir. Ore. State Nurses Assn., 1932-36, exec. sec., 1936-48; member com. on nominations, Am. Nurses Assn., 1944, sec., 1946-50, dir., 1950. Chief nurse Civil Defense, Portland, 1951; dir. Portland Conf. Social Work. Hon. spl. agent U.S.P.H.S.; hon. chmn. Emergency Med. Nursing Service, Portland; hon. sec. State Nursing Council War Service; hon. nurse dep. Ore. State Defense Council; hon. mem. hosp. survey and constrn. adv. council to State Bd. Health. U.S. del. Internat. Council Nurses, Stockholm, 1949. Mem. Chester Hosp. Sch. of Nursing Alumnae Assn. (sec. 1912-15), Met. Opera Assn. Guild (N.Y. City), Alpha Tau Delta. Dem. Baptist. Club: Stanford Mothers of Cal. Home: Redwood City, Calif. †

LAKE, FORREST U(NNA), naval officer (ret.), univ. adminstr.; b. Florence, S.C., Oct. 8, 1890; s. Fred Unna and Hattie (Parrott) L.; B.S., U.S. Naval Acad., 1912; hon. LL.D., Tulane U., 1945; m. Rosamond Tonkin, Oct. 27, 1914. Commd. ensign U.S. Navy, June 1912, advanced through grades to capt., 1940; served in U.S.S. North Dakota, 1912-17, U.S.S. New Hampshire, 1917-18; aide and flag sec. to comdr. of battleship dev., Atlantic fleet, 1918-19; administrative sec. to mil. gov., Santo Domingo 1919-22; gunnery officer, U.S.S. Wyoming, U.S.S. Trenton, 1922-25; with bur. of ordnance, Navy Dept., 1926-28; gunnery officer, U.S.S. Tennessee, 1928-31; instr., U.S. Naval Acad., 1931-34; comdg. officer, U.S.S. Borie and destroyer div., 1934-36; in charge naval officer training, Navy Dept., 1936-40, dir. naval training, 1940-43; prof. naval sci. and comdg. officer Navy V-12 unit, Tulane U., New Orleans, 1943-45; ret. from active duty, Oct. 26, 1945; dean of admissions, Tulane U., since 1945, gen. asst. to pres., faculty chmn. of athletics, adviser on mil. and selective service, also prof. emeritus, since 1945. Awarded Mexican Service medal, 1914 Navy Expeditionary medal, 1917, World War I Victory medal with fleet clasp, letter of commendation from Navy Dept., 1918, spl. commendations from Sec. of Navy, 1940-45. Mem. Kappa Sigma, Omicron Delta Kappa. Clubs: Boston, Army Navy (both New Orleans), Army Navy (Washington). Home: New Orleans, La. †

LAL, GOBIND BEHARL, editor, lecturer, author; b. Delhi, India, Oct. 9, 1889; s. Bishan and Jagge (Devi) L.; student St. Stephen's High Sch., Delhi, 1900-03; B.Sc., St. Stephen's Coll., U. of the Punjab, 1907, M.A., 1908; post grad. research fellow in social sciences, U. of Calif., 1912-17; unmarried. Came to U.S., 1912. Asst. prof. gen. science, Hindu Coll., U. of Punjab, 1909-12, also contbg. to jours. in Delhi; feature writer San Francisco Examiner, 1925-30; science editor Universal Service, Internat. News Service and American Weekly; sci. editor emeritus Hearst Newspapers, 1954-82; Watumull Foundation Research Fellow in history Indian science, Columbia University, 1946-48. Co-winner Pulitzer Prize for Scientific Journalism, 1937; winner George Westinghouse Distinguished Sci. Writers Award, A.A.A.S., 1946. Guggenheim fellow, 1956; A.M.A. citation, 1958; Taraknath Das Found. prize, Columbia, 1958. Mem. Nat. Assn. Science Writers (pres. 1940-41; hon. life) Author: Joseph Mazzini as a Social Reformer, 1915; Politics and Science in India, 1920; Chemistry of Personality, 1932. Has written numerous articles on physics, chemistry, astronomy, medicine, biology, psychology and other sciences, pub. daily in Hearst and other papers. Lecturer on scientific culture. Contbr. to mags. Home: San Francisco, Calif. Died Apr. 29, 1982.

LAMARSH, JOHN RAYMOND, nuclear engineering educator; b. Hartford, Conn., Mar. 12, 1928; s. Euclid Wilfred and Lillian (Brogan) L.; m. Barbara Arden Glaser, Oct. 11, 1958; 1 dau., Michele. B.S., MIT, 1948, Ph.D., 1952. Group leader United Aircraft Corp., 1952-53; asst. prof. physics U. Ky., 1953-54; asso. physicist Brookhaven Nat. Lab., 1954-56; asst. prof. N.Y. U., 1956-57, Cornell U., 1957-62; mem. faculty N.Y. U., 1962-73, prof. nuclear engring., chmn. dept., 1966-73, adj. prof. environ. medicine, from 1973; prof., chmn. dept. nuclear engring. Poly. Inst. N.Y., Bklyn., from 1973; adminstrv. law judge U.S. Nuclear Regulatory Commn., from 1981; mem. adv. com. engring. sci. N.J. Inst. Tech., from 1976; cons. in field. Author: Nuclear Reactor Theory, 1966, Introduction to Nuclear Engineering, 1975, 2d edit., 1983. Mem. Environ. Task Force, Mamaroneck, N.Y., 1970-73; mem. Mayor's Tech. Adv. Com. on Radiation, N.Y.C. Fellow Am. Nuclear Soc. (chmn. N.Y. Met. sect. 1977-78, chmn. edn. div. 1978-79, Arthur Holly Compton award 1980). Home: Boston, Mass.

LAMAS, FERNANDO, actor, director, writer; b. Buenos Aires, Argentina, Jan. 9, 1925; came to U.S., 1950, naturalized, 1955; m. Esther Williams, Dec. 31, 1969. Ed. schs., Europe. Star numerous motion pictures, Hollywood, Calif., Europe, S.Am.; dir. several films, numerous TV shows and several stage plays. (Recipient Broadway's Tony award 1957, Drama Critics award 1959, numerous other awards.). Mem. Acad. Motion Picture Arts and Scis., Dirs. Guild, Screen Actors Guild, AFTRA, Actors Equity. Died Oct. 8, 1982.*

LAMASTER, SLATER, author; b. Big Bone Springs, Ky., June 25, 1890; s. John T. and Fannie (Slater) L.; grad. high sch., Campbellsburg, Ky.; student Centre Coll. (Danville, Ky.), Columbia U. and New York Law Sch.; also student U. of Cincinnati, 1907-11; m. Anna Schooner, Apr. 25, 1917 (divorced); m. 2d, Dorothy Millicent Mellard, Jan. 20, 1934. Served as cadet U.S. Merchant Marine, summer 1908; admitted to bar, 1911 and began practicing at Louisville, Ky.; in stock brokerage business, 1919-25; devoted attention to writing since 1925. Democrat. Author: Luckett of the Moon, 1927; The Phantom in the Rainbow, 1928; The Bigot (play), 1930; Memory Lane—Life Story of Gus Hill, 1933; Cupid Napoleon, 1934; The Trillionaire of the Pit, 1936; also many articles in mags.†

LAMBERT, HENRY LEWIS, jeweler; b. N.Y.C., Aug. 23, 1903; s. August V. and Betty (Schiele) L.; student Franklin Sch., N.Y.C.; m. Marion Lissberger, Dec. 27, 1933; children—Henry L., Benjamin V. With Lambert Bros. Jewelers, Inc., N.Y.C., from 1912, chmn. bd., 1960-77. Pres. N.Y. Bd. Trade, 1962-65. Member board directors Greater New York Safety Council. Pres. Manhattan council Boy Scouts Am., 1957-60. Trustee Emergency Shelter: past bd. dirs. men's com. N.Y. Lighthouse. Recipient Star Italian Solidarity. Mem. Empire State C. of C., Newcomen Soc. N.Am., Sales Execs. Club, Am. Soc. Italian Legions of Merit, Confrerie des Chevaliers du Tastevin, Commanderie de Bordeaux, St. Hubert Soc. Clubs: Harmonie, Adventurer's (N.Y.C.). Home: New York, N.Y. Dec. Dec. 31, 1982.

LAMBIE, MORRIS BRYAN, polit. science; born Northampton, Mass., Mar. 29, 1888; s. Jasper Eadie and Henrietta Elizabeth (Bryan) L.; B.A., Williams Coll., 1910; M.A., Harvard, 1920, Ph.D., 1924; student London Sch. of Economics and Polit. Science, 1921-22; hon. L.H.D., Williams Coll., 1936; m. Adeline Richardson Williams, Dec. 30, 1916; children—Morris Williams, James Wood. With George LaMonte & Son, paper mfrs., Holyoke, Mass., and N.Y. City, 1911-14; staff New York Bur. Municipal Research, 1914-16; dir. personnel investigations, State of Mass., 1916-17; staff N.Y. State Reconstruction Commn., 1919; asst. prof. polit. science U. of Minn., 1921-24, asso. prof., 1924-25, prof., 1925-35; prof. govt., Harvard, from 1935. Chief of Municipal reference bur. and exec. sec. League of Minn. Municipalities, 1921-25; coordinator of relief and welfare, State of Minn., 1932-34; chmn. State Planning Bd., Minn., 1935; chmn. advisory council Div. of Employment Security, State of Mass., 1939-44, chmn. Mass. Commn. on Employment Problems of Negroes, 1940-43; mem. Governor's Commn. on Taxation and Revenue, Mass., 1947. Trustee Williams Coll. from 1938. Mem. Am. Polit. Science Assn., Nat. Municipal League, Phi Delta Theta. Unitarian. Home: Cambridge, Mass. Deceased.

LAMPRON, EDWARD JOHN, state justice; b. Nashua, N.H., Aug. 23, 1909; s. John P. and Helene (Deschenes) L.; m. Laurette L. Loiselle, Sept. 22, 1938; children—Norman E., J. Gerard. A.B., Assumption Coll., 1931, LL.D., 1954; J.D., Harvard, 1934. Bar: N.H. bar 1935. Practice in Nashua, 1935-47, city solicitor, 1936-46; justice N.H. Superior Ct., 1947-49; justice N.H. Supreme Ct., 1949—, chief justice, to 1979. Mem. adv. bd. St. Joseph's Hosp., Nashua. Mem. ABA, Nashua Bar Assn. (past pres.). Club: Exchange (hon.).

LAND, FRANCIS LAVERNE, physician, educator; b. Carrington, N.D., June 24, 1920; s. Harold L. and Lena (White) L.; m. Dorothy Julia Andrews, Sept. 1, 1946; children: Judith Ruth, Cynthia Andrews, Wendolyn White. Student, Ball State U., 1938-41; A.B., Ohio State U., 1946; M.D., Ind. U., 1950. Intern Milw. County Hosp., 1950-51; individual practice medicine, Fort Wayne, Ind., 1952-66; cons. to commn. of welfare HEW, 1966-67, commr. med. service adminstrn. social and rehab. services, 1967-69; chmn. dept. family practice U. Nebr. Med. Sch., 1969-74; assoc. dean clin. affairs U. Nebr. Med. Sch. (Coll. Medicine), 1972-74; assoc. dean clin. affairs, med. dir. Bernallio County Med. Center, U. N.Mex. Coll. Medicine, Albuquerque, 1974-77, prof. family and community medicine, 1974-77, dir. continuing med. edn., 1976-77; prof., dir. div. family practice Georgetown U. Sch. Medicine, Washington, 1977-82; cons. surgeon gen. USAF, 1962-82; surgeon gen. USPHS, 1960-65. Bd. dirs. Fine Arts Planning Center, United Chest Council, Retarded Childrens Soc., Cancer Soc. Served with USAAF, 1941-46; Served with USAF, 1950-52. Mem. AMA, Allen County Med. Soc. (pres. 1963-64, del. to AMA 10 yrs.), Am. Acad. Gen. Practice (v.p. 1965-66), Ind. Acad. Gen. Practice (pres. 1960). Home: McLean, Va. Died Aug. 20, 1982.

LANDAUER, JERRY GERD, journalist; b. Stuttgart, Germany, Jan. 16, 1932; came to U.S., 1938, naturalized, 1943; s. Adolph and Meta (Marx) L. B.A., Columbia, 1953. Reporter Washington Post, 1956-60, U.P.I., 1960-62, Wall St Jour., Washington, 1962-81. Recipient Distinguished Service award Sigma Delta Chi, 1963; Raymond Clapper Meml. award, 1963; Drew Pearson prize, 1973; Worth Bingham prize for investigative reporting, 1974. Club: Nat. Press. Home: Washington, D.C. Died Feb. 27, 1981.

LANDER, MAMIE STUBBS, orgn. exec.; b. Sandersville, Ga., Aug. 20, 1890; d. Jasper Newton and Susan (Peddy) Stubbs; A.B., U. Ga. Teachers Coll., 1908; student Wesleyan Coll., 1908-09; m. Thomas Henry Lander, May 14, 1911 (died 1940); children—David Luther, Ella Maude (Mrs. Lawrence W. Brady). Teacher pub. schs., Dexter, Ga., 1909-11, Sulphus, La., 1911-12, Bradenton, Fla., 1913. Mem. Order of Eastern Star since 1917, worthy grand matron, Fla., 1929-30, right worthy grand trustee, gen. grand chapter, 1934-37, most worthy grand matron, gen. grand chapter, 1943-46, right worthy grand sec., gen. grand chapter since 1946. Presbyn. P.E.O. Clubs: Fortnightly, Womans (Avon Park, Fla.); Sorosis (pres.), Womans (Lakeland, Fla.). Author: Concise History of the Order of Eastern Star, 1949. Home: Washington, D.C. Deceased.

LANDER, TONI (TONI PIHL PETERSEN), ballerina; b. Copenhagen, 1931; dance tng. Royal Danish Ballet, Copenhagen; m. Harold Lander (div. 1965); m. 2d, Bruce Marks, 1966. Mem. Royal Danish Ballet Co., 1948-50, solo dancer, 1950; guest ballerina Original Ballet Russe, London, 1951-52, London Festival Ballet, 1954-59; ballerina Am. Ballet Theatre, 1960-61, 63; guest ballerina London Festival Ballet, summer 1962, Am. Ballet Theatre, San Antonio, 1964. Created knight of Dannebrog. Died May 19, 1985.

LANE, FREDERIC CHAPIN, univ. prof., historian; b. Lansing, Mich., Nov. 23, 1900; s. Alfred Church and Susanne Foster (Lauriat) L.; A.B., Cornell U., 1921; M.A., Tufts Coll., 1922; student U. of Bordeaux, 1923-24, U. of Vienna, 1924, Harvard, 1925-26; John Thornton Kirkland Fellow for research in Italy, Harvard, 1927-28; Ph.D., Harvard, 1930; m. Harriet Whitney Mirick, June 4, 1927; children—George, Jonathan, Alfreda. Instr. in history, U. of Minn., 1926; instr. in history, Johns Hopkins, 1928-31, asso., 1931-35, associate professor, 1935-46, professor, 1946-66, professor emeritus history, from 1966; visiting prof. Brandeis U.; asst. director div. social scis. Rockefeller Found., 1951-53; historian U.S. Maritime Committee, 1946-47. Fellow Am. Acad. Arts and Scis., Medieval Acad.; mem. Am. Hist. Assn. (council 1959-62; pres. 1964-65), Soc. Italian Historical Studies (pres. 1961-63), Economic Hist. Assn. (pres. 1956-58), Internat. Econ. History Association (president 1966-68), American Philos. Soc., Istituto Veneto. Unitarian. Clubs: Hamilton Street (Baltimore, Md.); Cosmos (Washington). Editor of Jour. of Econ. History, 1943-51. Author: Venetian Ships and Shipbuilders of the Renaissance, 1934; Andrea Barbarigo, Merchant of Venice, 1418-1449, 1944; Venice and History, 1966; Venice: A Maritime Republic, 1973. Co-author: The World's History, 1947; Ships for Victory, 1951. Home: Westminster, Mass. Died Oct. 14, 1984.

LANE, REMBRANDT PEALE, corp. exec.; b. Washington, Oct. 11, 1927; s. Rembrandt Peale and Mabel Audrey (Herron) L.; m. Shirley Grace Meecham, Nov. 15, 1975; children—Russell F., Linda J. B.A., Duke U., 1950; M.B.A., N.Y. U., 1953. Asst. treas. Chase Manhattan Bank, N.Y.C., 1950-57; v.p. fin. and treas. N.E. Airlines, Boston, 1957-63; v.p. fin., dir. N.Am. Car Corp., Chgo., 1963-67, Rohr Industries, Inc., Chula Vista, Calif., 1967-71; exec. v.p., dir. Larwin Group, Beverly Hills, Calif., 1971-73; exec. v.p. Republic Corp., Los Angeles, 1973-80, 1980-84, also dir.; dir. Butler Aviation Co., 1964-68. Bd. dirs. San Diego Opera Co., 1967-71. Served with U.S. Army, 1945-47. Mem. Fin. Execs. Inst., Phi Beta Kappa. Republican. Club: Los Angeles Country. Home: Los Angeles, Calif. Died July 8, 1984.

LANE, THOMAS HENRY, marketing consultant; b. Hartford, Conn., Nov. 13, 1913; s. Thomas H. and Grace (O'Brien) L.; A.B., Dartmouth Coll., 1935; m. Virginia Chalmers, Mar. 31, 1937; children—Christopher Thomas, Nia. Reporter, N.Y. Herald Tribune, 1935; pub. relations, radio sta. WOR, 1936; account exec., copywriter Young & Rubicam, N.Y.C., 1937-42; dir. advt., press and radio, war finance div. U.S. Treasury, 1942-45; dir. sales promotion and advt. Rexall Drug Co., Los Angeles, v.p., 1945-49; then v.p., dir. McCann-Erickson, Inc., N.Y.C.; sr. v.p. Lennen & Newell, Inc., N.Y.C., until 1966; sr. v.p. J. Walter Thompson Co., 1966-76; v.p. pub. affairs N.Y. C. of C. and Industry, 1977-78; pres. Tom Lane Assocs. Inc., mktg. cons., Quechee, Vt., 1978-80. Dir. adv. bd. Salvation Army N.Y.; trustee Loomis Sch., Quechee Lake Landowners Assn. Clubs: Dartmouth, Sales Executives, University, N.Y. Yacht (N.Y.C); Nat. Press (Washington); American Yacht; Apawamis (Rye, N.Y.). Home: Quechee, Vt. Died Dec. 24, 1980.

LANG, JOHN JACOB, educator, C.P.A.; b. St. Louis, May 9, 1890; s. John J. and Marie (Luethi) L.; student St. Louis U., 1917-21; m. Angela F. Van Iseghem, June 24, 1932; 1 son, John Joseph. C.P.A., Mo., Ill., Ia.; mem. faculty Sch. Commerce and Finance St. Louis U., 1921-43, prof., dir. dept. accounting, 1943-56, dir. emeritus, from 1956; apptd. G. K. Klausner chair accounting research, 1956, prof. accounting grad., from 1957. Partner Lybrand, Ross Bros. & Montgomery, from 1962. Pres. Mo. State Bd. Accountancy. Served as chief petty officer, U.S.N., 1918-19. Recipient St. Louis Univ. Alumni Merit Award, 1957. Mem. Am. Inst. Accountants (mem. bd. of examiners, 1948-51; mem. nat. council, 1952-58; mem. nat. trial bd., 1957-60), Nat. Assn. Cost Accounts (v.p.), Mo. Soc. Certified Public Accountants (pres.), Am. Accounting Assn., Am. Assn. U. Profs., Am. Management Assn., Am. Acad. Polit. and Social Sci., Delta Sigma Pi. Club: Missouri Athletic. Author tax articles profl. jour. Mem. editorial bd. Management Handbook, 1933. Home: Clayton, Mo. †

LANG, MARGARET RUTHVEN, composer; b. Boston, Nov. 27, 1867; d. Benjamin Johnson L. and Frances Morse (Burrage) Lang; began writing music when 12 years old; studied pianoforte under her father, violin under Louis Schmidt, Boston, and 1886-87, under Drechsler and Abel, Munich; also studied composition with Victor Gluth, Munich; studied orchestration, 1887, under G. W. Chandwick and E. A. MacDowell. Composer pianoforte solos, songs, choruses and orchestral works, of which her "Dramatic Overture" (opus 12) has been performed by the Boston Symphony Orch., and her overture "Witichis" (opus 10) performed several times at Chgo. under leadership of Theodore Thomas; Heavenly Noël, a Christmas cantata, and many choral works in general performance. Home: Boston, MA. †

LANGENDORF, STANLEY S., bakery exec.; b. Chgo., July 30, 1890; s. Bernard and Sarah (Judesberg) L.; grad. Wilmerding Sch. of Indsl. Arts, San Francisco, 1909. Vice-pres., dir. Langendorf Baking Co., 1915-26, pres., dir., 1926-28; pres., dir. Langendorb United Bakeries, Inc., San Francisco, Cal., from 1928, chmn. of the board, 1963-64. Clubs: Commonwealth, Concordia. Author: Idle Men and Idle Money Spell Depression, 1932. Home: San Francisco, Calif. †

LANGER, LAWRENCE, producer; b. Swansea, Wales, May 30, 1890; student patent law Burbeck Coll., m. Estelle Roege, 1916 (div.); 1 dau., Phyllis; m. 2d, Armina Marshall, 1924; 1 son, Philip. Patent lawyer from 1913. Organized Theatre Guild, 1918; founder mem. Am. Shakespeare Festival at Stratford, Conn. Author: (play; with Armina Marshall) The Pursuit of Happiness, 1933; The Magic Curtain, 1951; The Importance of Wearing Clothes, 1959. Home: New York, N.Y. †

LANGER, SUSANNE KNAUTH, educator; b. N.Y.C., Dec. 20, 1895; d. Antonio and Else M. (Uhlich) Knauth; A.B., Radcliffe Coll., 1920, A.M., 1924, Ph.D., 1926; student U. Vienna, 1921-22; D.Litt. (hon.), Wilson Coll., 1954, also Western, Wheaton, Mt. Holyoke colls., 1962; LL.D., Columbia, 1964; D.F.A., Philadelphia Coll. Fine Arts, 1966; L.H.D., Clark Univ., 1968; m. William L. Langer, Sept. 3, 1921 (div. 1942); children—Leonard C.R., Bertrand W. Tutor philosophy Radcliffe Coll., 1927-42; asst. prof. philosophy U. Del. 1943; lectr. philosophy Columbia, 1945-50; vis. prof. N.Y.U., 1945, New Sch. Social Research, Northwestern U., Ohio U., U. Wash., U. Mich.; prof. philosophy Conn. Coll., 1954-62, prof. emeritus, research scholar, from 1962; research grant Edgar Kaufmann Found., 1956-58, 58-63, 63-65. Recipient Radcliffe Alumnae Achievement medal, 1950, Rockefeller Found. grant to Columbia for philos. research, 1946-49. Mem. American Academy of Arts and Sciences, also Phi Beta Kappa. Author: The Practice of Philosophy, 1930; Philosophy in a New Key, 1942; An Introduction to Symbolic Logic, 1953; Feeling and Form, 1953; Problems of Art, 1957; Philosophical Sketches, 1962; Mind: An Essay on Human Feeling, Vol. 1, 1967. Co-editor: Structure, Method and Meaning—Essays in Honor of Henry M. Sheffer, 1951. Editor: Reflections on Art, 1958. Home: Old Lyme, Conn. Died July 17, 1985.

LANGSAM, WALTER CONSUELO, university president emeritus; b. Vienna, Austria, Jan. 2, 1906; came to U.S., 1906; s. Emery Bernhardt and Angela Virginia Bianca (Mûnz-Kleinert) L.; m. Julia Elizabeth Stubblefield, Dec. 10, 1931; children: Walter Eaton, Geoffrey Hardinge. B.S., CCNY, 1925; M.A., Columbia U., 1926, Ph.D., 1930; LL.D., Gettysburg Coll., 1950; Bucknell U., Loyola U., Chgo., 1965, Xavier U., Cin., 1966, U. Cin., 1975; Litt.D., Wagner Coll., 1955, St.Thomas Inst., 1974; Sc.D., Northeastern U., 1960; L.H.D., Hebrew Union Coll., 1961, Miami U., Oxford, O., 1965; Sc.D. Edn., Midland Coll., 1963; D.C.L., Youngstown (O.) U., 1965. Tutor history CCNY, 1926-27, instr. history, Columbia U., 1927-35, asst. prof., 1935-38, vis. prof. history, 1942; prof. history Union Coll., 1938-45; on leave to OSS, 1944-45; pres. Wagner Coll., 1945-52, Gettysburg Coll., 1952-55; pres. U. Cin., 1955-71, pres. emeritus, Disting. Service prof. emeritus, 1971-85; vis. prof. summers Duke, Ohio State U., N.Y.U., U. B.C., U. Colo.; radio news commentator Sta. WGY, Schenectady, 1941-43; Chmn. bd. Cin. br. Fed. Res. Bank Cleve., 1964-66; dir. Diamond Internat. Corp., 1969-83, So. Ohio Bank, Western-So. Life Ins. Co.; Civilian aide to sec. army, 1962-66; chmn. hist. adv. com. Dept. of Army, 1967-72; chmn. exec. bd. commn. on colls. and univs. North Central Assn., 1968-70; pres. Ohio Coll. Assn., 1965-66; bd. cons. Nat. War Coll., 1972-76. Author: The Napoleonic Wars and German Nationalism in Austria, 1930, The World since 1914, 6th edit, 1948, Major European and Asiatic Developments since 1935, 1939, In Quest of Empire: the Problem of Colonies, 1939, Documents and Readings in the History of Europe Since 1918, 1939, Since 1939: A Narrative of War, 1941, Francis the Good, the Education of an Emperor (1768-1792), 1949, The World Since 1919, 8th edit, (with O.E. Mitchell, Jr.), 1971, Franz der Gute. Die Jugend eines Kaisers, 1954, Historic Documents of World War II, 1958, World History since 1870, 1963, Where Freedom Exists, 1967, An Honor Conferred, A Title Awarded, A History of the Commercial Club of Cincinnati, 1880-1972, 1973, The World and Warren's Cartoons, 1977, Cincinnati in Color, with Photographs by Julianne Warren, 1978, Centennial History of the Commercial Club of Cincinnati, 1981; Editor: Lippincott Hist. Series, 1934-50; Contbr.: The Shadow of War (L. Dodson, editor), 1934, War in the Twentieth Century (W. Waller, editor), 1940, War As a Social Institution (J.D. Clarkson, T. Cochran, editors), 1941, Nationalism and Internationalism: Essays Inscribed to Carlton J.H. Hayes (E.M. Earle, editor), 1950, Virtute Fideque, Festschrift für Otto Von Habsburg, 1965; profl. jours. U.S. del. Internat. Congress Peace and Christian Civilization, Florence, 1958; Trustee Hamma Sch. Theology, 1967-70, Endicott Coll., U. Cin. Found.; v.p. bd. theol. edn. Luth. Ch. Am., 1963-72; chmn. bd. Cin. Ballet Co., 1975-77. Recipient Townsend Harris medal, 1952; Outstanding Civilian Service medal with 2 laurel leaf clusters Dept. Army; Alumni medal City Coll. N.Y., 1972; comdr's. cross Order Merit W. Germany, 1970; hon. consul of Finland, 1967-76. Mem. Cin. Hist. Soc. (v.p. 1972-82), Phi Beta Kappa, Phi Gamma Delta. Clubs: Commercial (Cin.), Cincinnati Country (Cin.), Queen City (Cin.), Literary (Cin.). Died Aug. 14, 1985.

LANGSTAFF, JOHN BRETT, clergyman; b. Brooklyn, N.Y., Mar. 22, 1889; s. John Elliot (M.D.) and Sarah Josephine (Meredith) L.; A.B., Harvard, 1913; B.Litt., Magdalen Coll., Oxford, 1916; Gen. Theol. Sem., 1913-14; unmarried. Deacon and priest, P.E. Ch., 1917; asst. dean St. Mary and St. John Cathedral, Manila, P.I., 1917-18; served as pvt. Artists' Rifles, British Army, 1918 (invalided out same yr.); asst. vicar St. Mark's Ch., N. Audley St., London, 1918-20; head of Magdalen Coll. Mission, Oxford, 1920-22; pres. Children's Libraries Movement, Eng.; lecturer on liturgics, Berkeley Div. Sch., Conn., 1924; rector St. Andrew's Ch., Walden, N.Y., from 1924. Established David Copperfield Library, London, and The Children's Cathedral, Walden. Mem. Walkill Valley Ministers' Assn. Mason, K.P. Clubs: Harvard (New York); Royal Socs. (London). Author: Harvard of To-day, 1913; The Holy Communion in Great Britain and America, 1919; David Copperfield's Library, 1924; From Now to Adam, 1928. Home: Walden, N.Y. †

LANHAM, BENJAMIN TILLMAN, JR., coll. adminstr.; b. Edgefield, S.C., Apr. 5, 1917; s. Benjamin Tillman and Mary (Shaw) L.; m. Margaret Bernice Arnold, June 29, 1941; children—Benjamin Tillman III, Betty Anne. B.S., Clemson U., 1937; M.S., U. Tenn., 1938; postgrad., Ia. State U., 1938-39; Ph.D., Mich. State U., 1960. Mem. faculty Auburn (Ala.) U., from 1939, prof., head dept. agrl. econs., 1956-64; asso. dir. Agr. Expt. Sta., asst. dean agr., 1964-66, v.p. for research, 1966-72, v.p. for adminstrn., from 1972. Past chmn. edit. bd.: Jour. Ala. Acad. Sci; Contbr. profl. jours. Chmn. Ala. Water Resources Research Inst. Council; mem. council grad. edn. agrl. scis. So. Regional Edn. Bd.; mem. adv. com. Ala. Program Devel. Office. Served to maj., inf. AUS, 1942-46. Mem. A.A.A.S., Am. Farm Econ. Assn., Am. Econ. Assn., Am. Marketing Assn., Am. Acad. Polit. and Social Sci., Am. Sociol. Soc., Assn. So. Agrl. Workers, So. Econ. Assn., Internat. Conf. Agrl. Economists, Ala. Acad. Sci., Ala. Edn. Assn., Nat. Council U. Research Adminstrs., Land-Grant Coll. Assn., Sigma Xi, Gamma Sigma Delta, Omicron Delta Epsilon, Phi Delta Kappa, Omicron Delta Kappa. Baptist. Club: Kiwanian. Home: Auburn, Ala.

LANIER, MONRO BANISTER, shipbldg. exec.; born Huntsville, Ala., Dec. 9, 1886; s. Sterling Sidney and Mary (Banister) L.; spl. work U. Ala., 1903-06, spl. scientific course, 1904-07; post grad. work U. South, 1908; m. Katherine Beverly Leach, Apr. 20, 1910; one daughter, Katherine Beverly (Mrs. Joseph D. Wilson). Sales manager and combustion engineer, Monro-Warrior Coal & Coke Co., Birmingham, Ala., 1908-14, became v.p., 1914, pres., 1918; also v.p. Norton Coal Corp., 1914, pres., 1918; also pres. asso. mining cos.; v.p., dir. Freeport Sulphur Co., Freeport Transportation Co. and Cuban-Am. Manganese Corp., 1930-37; pres. Cuban Mining Co., 1936-37; became exec. v.p. Ingalls Iron Works Co. and subsidiaries, Birmingham, 1936, dir., vice chmn. bd., 1957-61; pres. Ingalls Shipbldg. Corp., 1938-56; vice chmn. bd. Ingalls Shipbldg. Corp. div. Litton Industries, from 1962. Mem. bd. dirs. Warrior-Tombigbee Devel. Assn. Pres. W. Ky. Coal Bur., 1922, mem. exec. com. to 1930; mem. shipbldg. stblzn. com., also shipbldg. commn., WPB, 1942-45; mem. bd. mgrs. Am. Bur. Shipping. Pres. Gulf Shipbuilders Assn., 1940-48. Mem. Am. Welding Soc., Soc. Naval Architects and Marine Engrs. (member council 1950, vice pres. 1962, hon. life v.p.), Navy League U.S., Am. Soc. Naval Engrs., Am. Waterways Operators, Inc., shipbuilders Council Am. (dir.), Phi Delta Theta. Clubs: Redstone, Downtown, The Club, Mountain Brook (Birmingham); Boston, Internat. House (New Orleans). Home: Pascagoula, Miss. †

LANIGAN, JAMES VINCENT, railway official; b. St. Louis, Mo., Sept. 29, 1887; s. John and Mary Lanigan; ed. high sch.; m. Frances Moltz, of Wellsville, Mo., June 1909; clk. passenger dept., C., B. & Q.R.R. until 1904; with passenger dept. M.,K.&T. Ry., 1904-06; rate clk. passenger dept. I.C.R.R., 1906-08, chief rate clk., 1908-11, asst. gen. passenger agt., 1911-21, gen. passenger agt., 1921-27, passenger traffic mgr. since 1927. Clubs: Union League, South Shore Country, Olympia Fields Country. Home: Chicago, Ill. †

LANNAN, J. PATRICK, financial consultant; b. Sterling, Ill., June 30, 1905; s. Patrick Henry and Kathryn (Killen) L.; m. Ora Mary Pelham, Aug. 20, 1924; children—Patricia Mary (Mrs. John H. Campbell), Michael Joseph, Lawrence Patrick, Colleen Margaret (Mrs. James L. Dillon), Sharon Ann (Mrs. Harve A. Ferrill), J. Patrick. Ed. pub. schs., Duluth, Minn.; LL.D., Duquesne U., 1955. With Ford Motor Co., Iron Mountain, Mich., 1924-26; indsl. cons., 1926-29; with Leight & Co. (finance), Chgo., 1929-32; industrialist, partner Kneeland & Co.; mems. Midwest Stock Exchange, Chgo., 1932-57; dir. Lannan & Co., ins. brokers, Chgo.; ins. brokers Advance Ross Corp., Chgo.; mem. exec. com., dir. Internat. Tel. & Tel., Macmillan, Inc., N.Y.C.; chmn. bd., dir. JPL Enterprises, Inc.; dir. Gt. Falls Gas Co., Mont. Contbr. articles to jours. Bd. dirs. New Mus., N.Y.C.; bd. dirs., pres. Lannan Found., Palm Beach, Fla.; Served as Dollar-a-Year man on WPB, World War II; spl. asst. to sub-com. Com. on Edn. and Labor of U.S. Congress which traveled throughout Europe, fall 1947; Chmn. bd. trustees Mag. Poetry; trustee Cancer Research Found. Roman Catholic. Clubs: Bondmen's (Chgo.); Rolling Rock (Pitts.). Home: Palm Beach, Fla. Died Sept. 25, 1983.

LANSING, CHARLES BRIDGEN, b. Colorado Springs, Colo., Nov. 3, 1889; s. Charles A. and Sarah (Macklin) L.; student schools in France; Phillips Acad., Andover; Yale, Sheffield Scientific Sch.; m. Alice Scott, 1911; children—Charles B., Jr., Alice Josephine, Gerrit Yates. Began with Denver & Rio Grande Railroad, Simplex Auto Company; mgr. Colo. Concrete Co., 1913-15; from 1915-22 was pres. Van Briggle Tile & Pottery Co., and dir. Granite Gold Mines, First Nat. Bank of Colo. Springs, and Intermountain Ry. Light & Power Co. Served in France with 12th Engrs., 1917-19. Pres. Strang Garages, 1921-25; vice chmn. Colo. Highway Commn., 1921-26; mgr. Murray Radiator Co., 1926-27; pres., dir. (chmn. bd.) Nat. Tile Co.; dir. and consultant S.F. Bowser & Co., 1928-30; v.p. Cleveland Storage Co., 1939-40, Billings-Chapin Co.; chmn. bd., dir. Indiana Limestone Corp. 1937-44; cons. engr. Cleveland Trust Co., 1936-46; pres. and dir. Ilco Ordnance Corp. 1942-44; v.p. and dir. The Arco Co., 1935-53, Bendix Westinghouse Automotive Air Brake Co., 1949-53; limited partner firm of Prescott & Company; dir. Motch & Merryweather Machinery Co., Miller Co., S.P. Mfg. Co. Trustee Western Res. U.; mem. Foundation for Study of Cycles. Fellow American Soc. M.E.; mem. Newcomen Soc. Clubs: Union (Cleve.); Yale (N.Y.); Cruising of America. Home: Chagrin Falls, OH. †

LANTZ, C(YRUS) W(ILLIAM), educator; b. Brooklyn, Ill., June 27, 1889; s. Thomas A. and Clara (Horney) L.; grad. Western Ill. State Tchrs. Coll., 1909; A.B., U. Ill., 1913, A.M., 1914, Ph.D., 1925; m. Myra Armstrong, 1919. Tchr. pub. schs., Ill., 1909-11, 14-17; asst. prof.

botany U. Nev., 1917-21; prof. biology Ia. State Tchrs. Coll., from 1921, head dept. sci., from 1948. Served as sgt. M.C., U.S. Army, 1919. Fellow A.A.A.S.; mem. Sigma Xi, Phi Kappa Phi, Kappa Delta Pi. Conglist. Rotarian. Contbr. articles sci., ednl. jours. Home: Cedar Falls, Ia. †

LAPE, ESTHER EVERETT, writer; b. Wilmington, Del.; dau. Henry and Esther E. (Butler) L.; student Bryn Mawr, 1901-02; A.B., Wellesley, 1905; unmarried. Instr. in English composition, Univ. of Ariz., 1907-08. Swarthmore Coll., 1908-10, Columbia and Barnard, 1911-13; writer and student of problems of govt., particularly the judicial settlement of internat. disputes; mem. in charge and dir. Am. Found. Studies, from 1924. Mem. A.A.A.S. Club: Cosmopolitan. Author: The United States and The Soviet Union, 1933. Editor and author: (introductory sect.) Ways to Peace, 1924; American Medicine-Expert Testimony out of Court, 1937; Medical Research: A Mid-Century Survey, 2 vols., 1955. Address: Westbrook, Conn. Died May 17, 1981.

LAPHAM, MAXWELL EDWARD, government official; b. Newfane, N.Y., Dec. 25, 1899; s. Edward and Pearle Lapham; M.D., U. of Pa., 1925; unmarried. Obstetrician, Lying in Hospital of Phila., 1929-32; instr. in obstetrics, U. of Pa. Med. Sch., 1929-32; practiced medicine specializing in obstetrics, Phila., 1929-32; post grad. extension teaching and field clinician, U. of Va., 1932-34; field clinician Com. on Post Grad. Med. Edn. in Miss., 1935-36; asst. prof. of obstetrics and dir. of extension grad. med. teaching, Tulane U. Sch. of Medicine, since 1937, dean sch. of medicine and prof. obstetrics, 1940-63, provost Tulane U., 1963-66, assoc. with School of Medicine, 1967-83; director of academic adminstrn. internship program Am. Council on Edn., 1966-67, Served in M.C., USN, 1941-46. Fellow A.C.S.; mem. Southern Med. Assn., A.M.A., Delta Kappa Epsilon. Author of numerous articles in professional mags. on obstet. and med. ednl. subjects. Address: New Orleans, La. Died Sept. 24, 1983.

LARET, ALFRED N(OEL), ret. r.r. exec.; b. Crawford Co., Kan., Oct. 11, 1890; s. Jules and Marie (Lecomte) L.; grad. Pittsburg Bus. Coll., 1906; m. Harriett A. Jones, 1914; children—Philip Alfred, Mary Alice (Mrs. Glen Dial, Jr.). Stenographer, sec. stores dept. K.C.S. Ry., Pittsburg, Kan.; and A.T.&S.F. Ry., Topeka, 1906-13; asst. chief clk., chief clk., asst. to and asst. chief purchasing officer St.L.-S.F. Ry. Co., St. Louis, 1913-46, chief purchasing officer, 1946-47, gen. purchasing agt., 1947-51, v.p. purchases and stores, 1951-58, v.p. exec. dept., 1958. Mem. Assn. Am. R.Rs. (chmn. purchases and stores div.). Home: St. Louis, Mo. †

LARKIN, FREDERICK, govt. official; b. N.H., Mar. 31, 1887; s. John and Mary (Lane) L.; student of archtl. design Atelier Masqueray, New York, 3 yrs.; travel and study, Europe, 2 yrs.; m. 1917 (divorced); children—Frederick, Jane, Lawrence. Began as constrn. engr., New York, 1910; pres. Realty Constrn. Co., engring. and financing corp., operating in U.S. and abroad, 1915-33; special inspection engr., public bldgs. branch, U.S. Treasury, 1935-36; chief Foreign Bldgs. Office, Dept. of State, with rank of minister; exec. sec. Foreign Service Bldgs. Commn. of Congress since 1937. Clubs: Congressional Country, Columbia Country (Washington, D.C.); American (London). Home: Washington, D.C. †

LARMON, WILLIAM ALEXANDER, physician; b. Sunnyvale, Calif., Oct. 23, 1916; s. William A. and Eleanor (Bradford) L.; student San Jose State Coll., 1933-36, Stanford U., 1936-37; B.S., Northwestern U., 1941, M.B., M.D., 1942; m. Irene Traska, Oct. 13, 1945 (dec. Oct. 1976); m. Jane Alderson, Mar. 14, 1977. Intern, Harper Hosp., Detroit, 1941-42, asst. resident pathology, 1942; Kemper fellow bone and joint dept. Northwestern U. Hosp., 1942-45, fellow bone and joint dept., 1945-46; faculty Northwestern U. Med. Sch., 1947-80, prof. bone and joint surgery, 1974, acting chmn. dept. orthopedic surgery, 1971; pvt. practice, Chgo., 1947-80; chief staff Northwestern Meml. Hosp., 1974, bd. dirs., 1974-80; attending staff VA Hosp., Hines, Ill. Orthopaedic rep. Adv. Bd. Med. Specialists, 1962—; chmn. nat. adv. com. orthopaedic surgery VA, 1969—. Bd. dirs. Nat. Interne and Residency Program. Diplomate Am. Bd. Orthopaedic Surgery (sec.-treas. 1962-68). Fellow A.C.S. (gov. 1968—); mem. AMA, Ill., Chgo. med. socs., Am. Acad. Orthopaedic Surgery, Clin-Orthopaedic Soc., Am. Rheumatism Soc., Chgo. Rheumatism Assn., Chgo. Orthopaedic Soc. (pres. 1961-62), Chgo. Surg. Soc., Am. Assn. Ry. Surgeons, Hines Surg. Assn., Assn. Bone and Joint Surgeons, Am. Orthopaedic Assn., Alpha Kappa Kappa. Contbr. articles to profl. jours., chpts. to books. Editor instructional course vol. 15, Am. Acad. Orthopaedic Surgeons, 1958. Home: Chicago, Ill. Dec. July 17, 1980.

LAROM, IRVING HASTINGS, rancher; b. Bklyn., June 3, 1889; s. Frank W. and Elizabeth E. (Shute) L.; grad. Lawrenceville (N.J.) Sch., 1908; Princeton, class 1913; m. Irma E. Dew, Oct. 20, 1920. Partner in purchase Valley Ranch, Wyo., 1915, inc., 1922, pres., treas., from 1922; engaged in live stock, farming, dude ranching; dir. Shoshone Power Co., dir., headmaster Valley Ranch Sch. Mem. Wyo. Bd. Commerce and Industry, 1929-33. Vice-pres. Am. Forestry Assn., 1945; chmn. Fed. Elk Commn. Bd. dirs. Buffalo Bill Meml. Museum, Am. Wild Life Inst. Served in O.T.C. and 12th Div., U.S. Army, 1918. Mem. Izaak Walton League, Dude Ranchers Assn. (founder, pres. 1925-44), Wyo. Game and Fishing Commn., Newcomen Soc. Eng., Am. Legion. Republican. Episcopalian (vestry). Mason (K.T.), Elk, Lion. Clubs: Cody (Wyo.); Camp Fire, Princeton, Racquet and Tennis, Church (N.Y.C.); Univ. Cottage (Princeton). Active devel. West for recreation, promoting game conservation. Address: Cody, Wy. †

LARRABEE, CARROLL BURTON, former publisher; b. Coudersport, Pa., June 21, 1896; s. Leon E Eugene and Louise (Berfield) L.; m. Kathryn White, May 25, 1921; children—Donna Louise Rigali, Elizabeth Ann Nelson. Student, Peddie Sch., 1913-14, Brown U., 1914-17, 19-20, Univ. Coll., London, Eng., 1919. Reporter Bradford Daily Era, 1920; editorial writer Printers' Ink Pub. Co., Inc., 1920-23, asso. editor, 1923-33, mng. editor, 1932-42, dir., 1941-55, pres., 1942-44, pres., pub., 1944-54, chmn. bd., 1954-55; dir. publs. Applied Jours., Am. Chem. Soc., 1955-62, ret.; Dir. Mag. Pubs. Assn., 1942-55; Pres. Peddie Alumni Assn., 1927-28. Author: (with R.B. Franken) Packages that Sell, 1928, How to Package for Profit, 1935, (with H.W. Marks) Tested Selling of Ideas, 1936, Check List of Advertising, Selling and Merchandising Essentials, 1937, Tested Display Ideas, 1938, (with E.B. Weiss) How to Sell Through Wholesalers, 1937; Editor: (with E.B. Weiss, F.C. Kendall) Handbook of Advertising, 1938. Dir. Nat. Com. for Edn. Alcoholism, 1948-50; bd. dirs. Delta Upsilon, 1927-47, editor quar., 1926-47. Served as pvt. Battery A, 103d F.A. U.S. Army, 1918-20; with AEF. Decorated Purple Heart; recipient medal for spl. service to journalism U. Mo., 1953; Golden Fifty award Alpha Delta Sigma, 1963. Mem. Advt. Club N.Y.C. Home: Annandale, Va. Died June 15, 1983.

LARREMORE, THOMAS ARMITAGE, law tchr., writer, choral condr.; b. July 20, 1889, N.Y. City; s. Wilbur and Susie Barratt (Armitage) L.; A.B., Yale, 1911; LL.B., Columbia, 1916; M.A., 1922; B.Mus., Syracuse U., 1931; M. Sacred Music, Union Theol. Sem., 1932; summer student Westminster Choir Sch., 1933-34; student Rutgers U., 1943; m. Amy Helen Hopkins, Aug. 2, 1917 (deceased September 26, 1962); children—Frank Wilbur, John (twins, dec.). Instr. law Leland Stanford, Jr. University, 1916-19; prof. law U. Ore., 1919-21, Tulane U. La., 1921-22, U. Kan., 1922-28, Washburn Coll. of Law, 1932-33; dean, prof. law Hartford Coll. of Law, 1933-34; vis. prof. law Columbia, U. Penn., U. Colo., U. Kan., Ohio State U., George Washington U. Legal consultant Am. Soc. Hygiene Assn., Inc. from 1943. Dir. Men's Glee Clubs Stanford U., 1916-17, Tulane U., 1921-22, U. Kan., 1923-28; dir. Am. Legion Posts Glee Clubs at Syracuse, N.Y., 1930-31, Rockville Center, N.Y., 1931-32, Lawrence and Topeka, Kan., 1932-33, West Hartford, Conn., 1939-31; dir. Washburn Coll. Choir, 1932-33, Chorus Am. Legion Auxiliary, West Hartford, Conn., 1939-41. Served as 1st lt. sanitary Corps, U.S. Army, 1917-19. Pres. Am. Legion Choruses Assn., 1938-49, v.p. 1937-38; pres. Mo. Valley Intercollegiate Glee Club Contest Assn., 1923-28; mem. bd. dirs. Intercollegiate Musical Council, 1926-52; hon. life mem. Am. Social Hygiene Assn., from 1950; mem. adv. council Pestalozzi Found. Am., from 1943, dir., 1959-60 (recipient silver medal 1950); dir. Bide-A-Wee Home Association, from 1962. Mem. Am. Assn. U. Profs., Am. Legion (40 et 8), N.Y. Hist. Soc., Am., Fed., Cal. bar assns., Assn. Am. Law Schs. (mem. exec. com. 1921-22), Am. Assn. Watch & Clock Collectors, Bibliog. Soc. Am., Nat. Speleological Soc., S.R., Steamship Hsit. Soc. of America (director from 1954), Knickerbocker Greys Veteran Corps of N.Y. City (secretary from 1952), Phi Beta Kappa, Phi Mu Alpha Sinfonia, Phi Delta Phi, Alpha Delta Phi, Order of the Coif. Clubs: Elizabethan (Yale); Conductors (treas. from 1943), Gotham Cat (treas., dir. from 1957), St. Nicholas Society, University Glee, Grolier, Players, Yale, Mendelssohn Glee (New York); Plainfield Mendelssohn Glee, Kiwanis, Author: The Duodecimos, 1937; An American Typographical Tragedy, 1949; Compiler: Cases on Personal Property, 1928. Editor: Last Lyrics, by Wilbur Larremore, 1930; composer and arranger various part songs and hymns; contbr. articles to various publs. Home: Flemington, N.J. †

LARRIMER, WALTER HARRISON, forester; b. nr. Bloomingburg, O., Feb. 23, 1889; s. Henry Thomas and Rachel Ann (Roebuck) L.; B.S. in Forestry, Ohio State U., 1913, Ph.D., 1925; M.S. in Biology, Purdue, 1921; m. Cheslye Long, Nov. 18, 1918; children—Cheslye Ann, Walter Harrison, Mary Elizabeth. Entomologist with U.S. Bureau Entomology, 1913-35; research staff assistant U.S. Forest Service from 1935; research on insect pests of cereal and forage crops. Served in U.S. Army, 1918-19; capt. F.A. (Res.). Fellow A.A.A.S.; mem. Am. Assn. Econ. Entomologists, Entomol. Soc. America, Entomol. Soc. of Washington, Gamma Alpha, Sigma Xi. Presbyterian. Spl. researches on application of statis. methods to biol. research. Specialized in research orgn. and adminstrn. Home: Washington, D.C. Deceased.

LARSEN, ARNOLD, energy co. exec.; b. Lakeview, Mich., July 12, 1917; s. Niels Otto and Julia (Peterson) L.; m. Maxine Patricia Delaurante, June 23, 1951; children—Jon Lawrence, Gregg Thomas, Mark Andrew, Rande William, Julie Catherine. B.Econs., U. Mich., 1947. C.P.A., Wyo. Office clk. Atlantic Commn. Co., 1936-38; jr. accountant White, Bower & Prevo (C.P.A.'s), 1947-48; intermediate accountant Congdon, O'Hara & Becker (merged with Peat, Marwick, Mitchell & Co. 1952), 1948-52, successively supr., mgr., mgr. area office, 1952-53; v.p. finance, treas., asst. sec., dir. Husky Oil & Refining, Ltd., 1953-61; also its successor co. Canadian Husky Oil, Ltd., 1962-64; sr. v.p. Husky Oil Co., Husky Oil Ltd., 1964-67, exec. v.p., 1967-73, sr. v.p., asst. sec., 1973-75; past v.p. Husky Petroleum Corp.; past sr. v.p. Husky Oil Operations Ltd.; past v.p., dir. No. Natural Gas Co. Ltd., Husky Oil, Alta., Lloydminster Pipeline Ltd., Husky Pipeline, Ltd., other subsidiaries; past dir. Husky Leasebacks, Ltd., Gate City Steel Corp., Peace Pipe Line Co., Ltd.; past v.p. Husky Oil Exploration, Inc.; past mng. dir. Husky Finance Co. N.V.; past v.p. Alta. Energy Co. Ltd., now corp. advisor; chmn., dir. Fossil Resources Ltd., AEC Power Ltd., Steel Alta. Ltd.; dir. Interprovincial Steel & Pipe Co. Ltd., Brit. Canadian Resources, Maynard Exploration Co., Mont. Internat. Resources. Served to capt. AUS, 1941-46. Mem. Ind. Petroleum Assn. Can. (dir. 1963-67, 72-75), Can. Petroleum Assn. (dir. 1972-75), Wyo. Inst. C.P.A.'s. Methodist. Home: Calgary, Alta., Can. Deceased.

LARSEN, HARRY IRGENS, shipping co. exec.; b. Trondheim, Norway, Apr. 13, 1908; s. Arne and Aagot (Myhre) L.; grad. Trondheim Merc. Coll., 1927; m. Patricia Constance Pike, July 9, 1942; children—Siri (Mrs. Stanley G. Mortimer III), Rikk, H. Peik, Per, Leif. Came to U.S., 1940, naturalized, 1951. Shipbroker firms, Oslo, Norway, 1930-40; exec. Norwegian Govt. Shipping Agy., N.Am., 1940-45; co-founder Gotaas-Larsen, Inc., N.Y.C., 1946, pres., 1956-63; vice chmn. IU Internat. Corp., Wilmington, Del., 1971-77; dir. IU Overseas Capital Corp., Eastern Steamship Lines, Inc., Gotaas-Larsen A/S, Christiania Gen. Ins. Corp. N.Y. Clubs: River Sky (N.T.C.). Home: Armonk, N.Y. Died Aug. 3, 1982.

LARSEN, JAMES BERKELEY, state govt. ofcl.; b. Mt. Pleasant, Utah, Feb. 27, 1889; s. Andrew and Christena (Mathiasen) L.; student Snow Coll., Ephrim, Utah, 1904, U. Utah, 1908-09; m. Florence B. Tingey, May 4, 1910; children—Geraldine (Mrs. Eldro J. Reid), Maxine (Mrs. John Jowers), James Berkeley, Allan F., Naida (Mrs. D. L. Goodman), Reid K. Engaged in farming, from 1953; mem. Idaho Legislature, 1951-53; lt. gov. Ida., from 1954. Past dir. Latter Day Saints Hosp., Idaho Falls, Ida., Firth (Ida.) Sch. Bd. Mem. Ida. Beet Growers Assn. (dir.), Eastern Ida. Grazing Assn. (past dir.), Ida. Potato Growers Assn. (fieldman), Ida. Farm Bur. Fedn. Mem. Ch. of Jesus Christ of Latter Day Saints (supt. Shelly Stake Young Men's Mutual Improvement Assn. 1916-24; pres. Shelly Stake, 1924-54). Home: Firth, Ida. †

LARSON, CLARE LINN, Red Cross worker; b. Sherbrooke, N.D., Dec. 25, 1889; dau. Samuel Levin and Karen (Domholdt) Linn; student Pacific Lutheran Coll., 1906-09; grad. Park Region Luther College, Fergus Falls, 1910; m. Dr. Ludwig P. Larson, Jan. 1, 1913; children—LaVaughn, Kathlinn (Mrs. B. K. Kunny), Phyllis Gwendolinn (wife of James H. Robinson, D.D.S.). Teacher, public speaker, dental asst. Served as N.D. State Hosp. and Rehabilitation Chmn. Active Am. Red Cross from 1917, Steel co. chpt. first supply and prodn. chmn., 1917, volunteer in prodn., nursing service and roll call chmn., 1918-33, chpt. chmn., Steele Co., 1934-51; spl. roll call chmn. over several chpts., 1937; completed advanced instructors course, 1st aid, State Tchrs. Coll., Maville, N.D.; mem. Midwestern area adv. council, since 1948; attended Red Cross Conventions and Regional Confs. from 1934; mem. Nat. Am. Red Cross Bd. Govs., 1949-52. Mem. Am. Cancer Soc. (chpt. Steele Co., 1941-51), Nat. Foundn. Infantile Paralysis (sec. Steele Co., 1939-41), Public Health Com. of Dental Auxiliary (state chmn. 1948-49), Nat. Church Pocket Testament Assn. (sec. N.D., 1932-42), Am. Legion Auxiliary (state pres. N.D., 1926-27, nat. com. woman, 1927-28), N.D. Conf. Welfare and Social Service, Sr. and Jr. League (pres. 1928-48), Finley P.T.A. (pres.), Republican. Lutheran (church organist; supt. ch. sch., 1928-51; pres. Ladies Aid). Clubs: Study, N.D. Federation Women's. Speaker on flag of U.S., flag code lecturer to schs. Recipient Nat. Flag medal, 1927; pres. Nat. Flag Assn. Address: Finley, N.D. †

LARSON, HENRIETTA MELIA, educator, author; b. Ostrander, Minn., Sept. 24, 1894; d. Hans Olaf and Karen Maria (Norgaarden) Larson; B.A., St. Olaf Coll., 1918, Litt.D., 1943; postgrad. U. Minn., 1922-24; Ph.D., Columbia U., 1926; M.A. (hon.), Harvard U., 1960. Instr., So. Ill. U., 1926-28; with Harvard Grad. Sch. Bus. Adminstrn., from 1928, successively, research asso., asst. prof., 1938-42, assoc. prof., 1942-59, prof., 1960-61, prof. emerita, 1961-83. Trustee Bus. History Found., from 1947; cons. Ford Found., Indian Inst. Mgmt., Ahmedabad, 1966. Mem. Am., Norwegian-Am., Econ. (v.p.) hist. assns., Econ. History Soc., Am. Assn. U. Women, Phi Beta Kappa. Lutheran. Author: Farmer and the Wheat Market, 1926; Jay Cooke, Private Banker, 1936; (with N.S.B. Gras) Casebook in American Business History, 1939; Guide to Business History, 1948; (with K.W. Porter) History of Humble Oil and Refining Company, 1959; (with E.H. Knowlton and C.S. Popple) History of Standard Oil Company (New Jersey), vol. 3, 1971. Editor, Harvard Studies in Bus. History, 1950-64. Home: Northfield, Minn. Died Aug. 26, 1983.

LARUS, JOHN RUSE, insurance exec.; b. Baltimore, Md., Aug. 4, 1890; s. John Ruse and Mary Chilton (Atkinson) Larus; A.B., Yale Univ., 1912; m. Elizabeth Taft, of Hartford, Conn., Apr. 26, 1917; 1 son, Charles Taft. Engaged in life ins. business since 1913; asst. actuary Phoenix Mutual Life Ins. Co., Hartford, Conn., 1918-28, actuary, 1928-34, v.p. and actuary from 1934, dir. from 1944. Member board trustee Hillyer College. Fellow Soc. Actuaries (pres. 1952-53); mem. International Congress Actuaries (permanent com.), Am. Math. Soc., Am. Statis. Assn., Am. Acad. Polit. and Social Science, Beta Theta Pi, Phi Beta Kappa. Episcopalian. Clubs: Bridge, Drama (Hartford). Home: West Hartford. †

LA SALLE, JOSEPH PIERRE, mathematician; b. State College, Pa., May 28, 1916; s. Leo Joseph and Aline (Mistric) LaS.; m. Eleanor Seip, June 12, 1942; children—Nannette Maria, Marc Joseph. B.S., La. State U., 1937; Ph.D. (Henry Laws fellow), Calif. Inst. Tech., 1941. Instr. U. Tex., 1941-42, Radar Sch., Mass. Inst. Tech., 1942-43; research asso. Princeton, 1943-44, Cornell U., Ithaca, N.Y., 1944-46; mem. faculty U. Notre Dame, 1946-47, 48-58, prof. math., 1951-58; asso. dir. Math. Center Research Inst. for Advanced Studies, Balt., 1958-64; prof., dir. Lefschetz Center for Dynamical Systems, Brown U., Providence, 1964-81, prof. emeritus, 1981-83, chmn. div. applied math., 1968-73. Author: (with N. Haaser, J. Sullivan) Introduction to Analysis, Vol. 1, 1959, (with S. Lefschetz) Stability by Liapunov's Second Method with Applications, 1961, Recent Soviet Contributions to Mathematics, 1962, (with S. Lefschetz and L. Cesari) International Symposium on Nonlinear Differential Equations and Nonlinear Mechanics, 1963, (with N. Haaser, J. Sullivan) Intermediate Analysis, Vol. 2, 1964, (with Jack K. Hale) Differential Equations and Dynamical Systems, 1967, (with Henry Hermes) Functional Analysis and Time Optimal Control, 1969, (with L. Cesari and J.K. Hale) Dynamical Systems, Vols. I and II, 1976, The Stability of Dynamical Systems, 1976, also articles.; Editor-in-chief: (with L. Cesari and J.K. Hale) Jour. Differential Equations; editor: (with L. Cesari and J.K. Hale) Nonlinear Analysis: Theory, Methods and Applications. Guggenheim fellow, 1975. Fellow A.A.A.S., Am. Acad. Mechanics; mem. Soc. for Indsl. and Applied Math. (past pres.), Am. Math. Soc., Math. Assn. Am. (Chauvenet prize 1965). Pioneered devel. modern theory of optimal control; contbr. to theory of differential equations, dynamical systems and theory of stability. Home: Little compton, R.I. Died July 7, 1983.

LASDON, WILLIAM STANLEY, foundation exec.; b. Bklyn., Mar. 14, 1896; m. Mildred D. Silverman, May 30, 1922; children: Nanette L. (Mrs. Laitman), Robert Steven. LL.D., Nat. U. Ireland, 1954; L.H.D., Yeshiva U., 1969; D.C.S., Pace U., 1981. With research dept. Stanley Securities, N.Y.C., 1914-26; sec.-treas. Pyridium Corp., 1926-36, pres., chmn. bd., 1936-50; pres. Anahist Co., Inc., 1949-55; pres., chmn. bd. Nepera Chem. Co., 1950-56; dir. Nepera Internat. Corp., 1946; dir. Warner-Lambert Pharm. Co., Inc., Morris Plains, N.J., 1956—, chmn. exec. com., 1960-72, vice chmn. bd., 1973-80, cons., 1973—; dir. Capital Cities Communications Inc.; Pres. Lasdon Found., 1946—; bd. overseers Albert Einstein Coll. Medicine, 1954—. Bd. dirs. Cerebral Palsy Assn.; bd. dirs. Boys Clubs Am.; mem. adv. com. John F. Kennedy Center for Performing Arts, 1970—; patron Lincoln Center Performing Arts, Mus. Modern Art. Clubs: Harmonie (N.Y.C.), Sky (N.Y.C.), Metropolitan (N.Y.C.); Rockrimmon (Conn.), Country, Palm Beach (Fla.) Country. Office: Lasdam Found Inc 45 Rockefeller Plaza New York NY 10111*

LASKIN, BORA, chief justice Can.; b. Ft. William, Ont., Can., Oct. 5, 1912; s. Max and Bluma (Singel) L.; m. Peggy Tenenbaum, 1938; children—John, Barbara. B.A., U. Toronto, 1933, M.A., 1935, LL.B., 1936; postgrad., Osgoode Hall Law Sch., 1933-36; LL.M., Harvard U., 1937; hon. LL.D., D.Phil., D.H.L., D.C.L., numerous univs. Bar: called to bar Ont 1937, created Queen's counsel 1956. Read law with W.C. Davidson, 1933-36; lectr. in law and asst. prof. U. Toronto, 1940-45, prof., 1949-65; lectr. in law Osgoode Hall Law Sch., 1945-49; labor arbitrator and conciliator, 1942-65; asso. editor Dominion Law Reports and Canadian Criminal Cases, 1943-65; justice Ont. Ct. Appeal, 1965-70; Puisne judge Supreme Ct. Can., 1970-73, chief justice, 1973—; chancellor Lakehead U., 1971-80. Author: Canadian Constitutional Law, 3d edit, 1966, Cases and Notes on Land Law, new edit, 1964, The British Tradition in Canadian Law, 1969, The Institutional Character of the Judge, 1972, also articles. Chmn., mem. bd. govs. Ont. Inst. Studies in Edn., 1965-69; bd. govs. York U., 1967-70, Carleton U., 1970-73. Recipient Milner award; Canadian Assn. Univ. Tchrs., 1971. Mem. Assn. Canadian Law Tchrs. (pres. 1953-54), Canadian Assn. Univ. Tchrs. (pres. 1964-65), Nat. Acad. Arbitrators; fellow Royal Soc. Can., Brit. Acad. (corr.). Died Mar. 26, 1984.

LASSETTER, WILLIAM CASPER, editor; b. Villa Rica, Ga., Aug. 31, 1887; s. John George Washington and Mary (Barnett) L.; B.S. in Agr., U. of Wis., 1909; m. Irma Lee Hamby, of Prescott, Ark., Dec. 16, 1916; 1 dau., Helen Elizabeth. Asst in agronomy, Ohio State U., 1909-10; instr. in agronomy, U. of Ark., 1910-12, asst. prof., 1912-14, prof., 1914-15; asst. dir. of extension, same univ., 1915-17, dir., 1917-20; mng. editor The Progressive Farmer, 1920-34, asso. adv. mgr. from 1934. Mem. Alpha Zeta, Phi Lambda Upsilon. Democrat. Methodist. Club: Civitan. Home: Birmingham, Ala. †

LASTFOGEL, ABE, talent representative; b. N.Y.C., May 17, 1898; m. Frances Arms, Apr. 6, 1927. Assoc. with William Morris Agy., from 1912, pres. from 1952, chmn. bd., 1969-76, co-chmn. bd., Beverly Hills, Calif., from 1976-84. Bd. govs. USO; pres. St. Jude Hosp.; bd. dirs. Nat. Jewish Welfare Bd., Big Bros. Greater Los Angeles; assoc. Calif. Inst. Tech.; hon. life mem. Am. Theatre Wing. Recipient medal of Freedom and Presdl. certificate of merit from Pres. Truman, 1945. Home: Los Angeles, Calif. Died Aug. 25, 1984.*

LASZLO, ERNEST, director motion picture photography, photographer; b. Szabadka, Yugoslavia, Apr. 23, 1905; came to U.S., 1923, naturalized, 1928; s. Max and Gizella (Steiner) L.; m. Rose Ellen Nelson, July 3, 1925; 1 child, Joan Ellen. Grad., Gymnasium, Budapest, Hungary, 1922. Camerman Paramount Studios, until 1943, dir. motion picture photography, 1943-49, free-lance, 1949-84; v.p. Am. Soc. Cinematographers Holding Corp., Hollywood, 1961-84. (Recipient Acad. award for best photography 1965); Photog. dir.: Inherit the Wind, 1960, Judgement at Nuremberg, 1961, Mad, Mad, Mad World, 1963, Ship of Fools, 1965, Fantastic Voyage, 1966, Star, 1968, Airport, 1970, Logans Run, 1977. Mem. Acad. Motion Pictures Arts and Scis. (bd. govs.), Am. Soc. Cinematographers (pres. 1972-74). Club: Mason (Shriner, 32 deg.). Home: Los Angeles, Calif. Died Jan. 6, 1984.

LATIMER, JONATHAN WYATT, author; b. Chgo., Oct. 23, 1906; s. Jonathan Guy and Evelyn (Wyatt) L.; m. Ellen Baxter Peabody, Dec. 11, 1937; children—Ellen Jane, Jonathan, Nicholas; m. Jo Ann Hanzlik, Dec. 18, 1954. Ed., Mesa (Ariz.) Ranch Sch., 1922-25; A.B., Knox Coll., 1929. Began as newspaperman, 1929; reporter Chgo. Herald-Examiner, later Chgo. Tribune, 1930—35; writer Paramount, Metro-Goldwyn-Mayer, 1940-41, RKO, Paramount, 1946-47. Author: Murder in the Madhouse, 1935, Headed for a Hearse, 1935, The Lady in the Morgue, 1936, The Dead Don't Care, 1937, Red Gardenias, 1939, Dark Memory, 1940, Topper Returns, 1941, Night in New Orleans, 1942, The Glass Key, 1942, The Fifth Grave, Nocturne, 1946, They Won't Believe Me, 1947, The Big Clock, 1947, Sealed Verdict; Beyond Glory, 1948, Night Has A Thousand Eyes; Alias Nick Beal, 1949, Copper Canyon, 1950, The Redhead and the Cowboy; Submarine Command, 1951, Botany Bay, 1952, Plunder of the Sun, 1955, Sinners and Shrouds; The Strange Case of the Cosmic Rays; Back from Eternity, 1956, The Lady and the Prowler, 1957, The Unchained Goddess, 1957, The Whole Truth, 1958, Tiger by Night, 1959, Black Is the Fashion for Dying, 1959, The Mink- Lined Coffin, 1960, CBS, Perry Mason Series, 1960-65. Served with USNR, 1942-45. Mem. Screen Writers Guild, Acad. Motion Picture Arts and Scis., Phi Beta Kappa, Phi Delta Theta. Club: Beach and Tennis (La Jolla, Calif.). Home: La Jolla, Calif. Died June 23, 1983.

LATTIMORE, RICHMOND, educator; b. Paotingfu, China, May 6, 1906 (parents U.S. citizens); s. David and Margaret (Barnes) L.; A.B., Dartmouth Coll., 1926; A.B., Oxford (Rhodes scholar from Ind. at Christ Ch., 1929-32), 1932; Ph.D., U. Ill., 1935; fellowship, Am. Acad. in Rome, 1934-35; Litt.D., Dartmouth, 1958; M.A., Oxford, 1964; m. Alice Bockstahler, August 31, 1935; children—Steven, Alexander. Asst. in classics, English, U. Ill., 1926-28, asst. in philosophy, 1933-34; asst. prof., Wabash Coll., 1928-29; mem. faculty Bryn Mawr (Pa.) Coll. since 1935, prof. of Greek since 1948. Rockefeller post war fellowship, 1946; vis. lecturer, U. Chicago, 1947, Columbia, 1948, 50; Turnbull lectr. Johns Hopkins, 1956; Lord Northcliffe lectr. U. College; London, 1961. Recipient Fulbright research fellowship, Greece, 1951-52; Fulbright lecturer Oxford, 1963-64. Recipient award, Nat. Inst. Arts and Letters, 1954; award American Council Learned Societies, 1959; award Acad. Am. Poets, 1984. Served from lt. (j.g.) to lt. USNR; 1943-46. Member American Philosophical Society, National Institute of Arts and Letters, also mem. Archeological Institute of America, American Academy of Arts and Scis., P.E.N. Phi Beta Kappa. Club: Merion Cricket. Author: Themes in Greek and Latin Epitaphs, 1943; The Odes of Pindar, 1947; The Iliad of Homer, 1951; The Oresteia of Aeschylus, 1953; Greek Lyrics, 1955; Poems, 1957; The Poetry of Greek Tragedy, 1958; Hesiod, 1959; Sestina for a Far-Off Summer, 1962; Story Patterns in Greek Tragedy, 1964; The Stride of Time, 1966. Author (translator); The Frogs of Aristophanes, 1962 (recipient Bolligen Translation Prize); The Revelation of John, 1962. Editor: (with David Greene) The Complete Greek Tragedies. Contbr. ednl. and lit. jours. Home: Rosemont, Pa. Died Feb. 26, 1984.

LATZER, ROBERT LOUIS, milk company exec.; born Highland, Ill., May 18, 1887; s. Louis and Eliza (Leuhm) L.; B.S., U. Ill., 1908; M.S., Cornell, 1909; m. Cora Wells Owiett, Oct. 7, 1915; children—Ruth Ellen (Mrs. John L. Donnell), Jane Elizabeth (Mrs. Charles G. Schott), Roberta Wells (Mrs. Frederick R. Keydel). Pres. Highland (Ill.) Milk Condensing Co., 1911-22; v.p. Pet Milk Co., St. Louis, 1922-52, pres., 1952-64, chmn. bd., from 1959. Member Gamma Sigma Delta, Sigma Psi. Conglist. Clubs: M.A.A.A., Bellerive Country (St.L.). Home: St. Louis, Mo. †

LAUB, DESMOND KENNETH, journalist; b. Washington, D.C., Mar. 9, 1887; s. Ditlev Christian Ernst and Catherine Ann (Gaynor) L.; Georgetown U., 1904-05; m. Gertrude Rutgers Osburn, of Grosse Ile, Mich., Sept. 22, 1913; children—Elizabeth Osburn, Anne Gaynor, Desmond Kenneth (dec.), Wallace Osburn. Sec. to Maurice Francis Egan, U.S. minister to Denmark, at Copenhagen, 1909-11. Commd. 1st lt. inf. 2d O.T.C., Ft. Sheridan, Ill., Nov. 15, 1917; aide to Brig. Gen. Andrews, Camp Grant, Ill., until July 1918; assigned to 318th Inf., 80th Div., A.E.F.; wounded at Sivry-les-Buzancy, Nov. 3, 1918; hon. discharged, June 5, 1919. Awarded Order of Purple Heart by U.S. War Dept., 1935. Club: The Islanders (Grosse Ile). Contbr. to mags. Home: Grosse Ile, Mich. †

LAUDER, ANDREW B., manufacturing company executive; b. Bklyn., Oct. 19, 1927; s. Andrew and Emily P. L.; m. Sue Ann Walner, May 13, 1978; children—Janine L., Andrew Scott. B.S., Lebanon Valley Coll., 1951; postgrad., U. Pa., 1953. C.P.A., D.C., Ohio. With Ernst & Whinney, 1953-60; with The Black Clawson Co., Middletown, Ohio, 1960-81, sec.-treas., to 1981. Mem. Am. Inst. C.P.A.s, N.Y. State Soc. C.P.A.s. Home: Monroe, Ohio. Died Oct. 24, 1981.

LAUGIER, HENRI, U.N. ofcl.; b. Mane, France, Aug. 5, 1888; s. Albert and Marie (Coulomb) L.; Docteur en Medecine, Faculty of Medecine, Sorbonne, Paris, France, 1913, Docteur es Sciences, Faculty of Sciences, 1922. Prof. physiology of work, indsl. hygiene, vocational guidance, Conservatoire National des Arts et Metiers, Paris, 1929-38; dir. Nat. Center of Sci. Research, 1938-40; co-dir. Nat. Inst. Vocational Guidance, Paris, 1929-49; prof. physiology, Faculte des Sciences, Sorbonne, since 1938; dismissed from all functions by Petain govt., became refugee in Eng., U.S. and Can., 1940-43; prof. physiology U. of Montreal, 1940-43; chancellor U. of Algiers; 1943-44; dir. cultural relations Ministry Fgn. Affairs, Paris, 1944-46; asst. sec. gen. U.N., Lake Success, N.Y., from 1946. Chmn. Internat. League for Human Rights, N.Y. City, 1941-43. Exchange prof., Rio de Janeiro and Sao Paulo, Brazil, Lima, Peru, Mexico City. Made Comdr. Legion of Honor, 1938. Recipient Croix de Guerre, World War I. Author: Service de France au Canada, 1942; Combat de l'Exol, 1943. Contbr. numerous articles to sci. publs. Home: Paris, France. †

LAVELY, HORACE THOMAS, educator, clergyman; b. Petersburg, O., Mar. 8, 1890; s. John A. and Hannah R. (Foster) L.; A.B., Allegheny Coll., 1912; S.T.B., Boston U., 1916; Th.D., 1936; m. Gertrude Hillman, June 18, 1915; children—John H., Horace Thomas, William H., Henry C. Ordained to ministry of Meth. Ch., 1916; pastor, Prairie City, Ia., 1916-18, Stuart, 1919-20; missionary, Central China, 1920-26; prof. philosophy Allegheny Coll. from 1928, dean of men, 1942-47. Served as 1st lt., chaplain corps, 127th Inf., U.S. Army, 1918-19. Mem. Am. Philos. Assn., Am. Assn. U. Profs., Delta Tau Delta, Kappa Phi Kappa. Home: Meadville, Pa. †

LAVENTURE, WILLIAM BURROWS, lawyer; b. Davenport, Iowa, Jan. 29, 1905; s. William Mason and Bessie (Burrows) LaV.; m. Barbara Walton, Nov. 5, 1938. Grad., Asheville (N.C.) Sch., 1922; Ph.B., Yale, 1926, LL.B., 1928. Bar: N.Y. bar 1928. Practiced law, N.Y.C.; partner firm Reynolds, Richards, LaVenture, Hadley & Davis (and predecessors), from 1944. Mem. Am. Bar Assn., Assn. Bar City N.Y. Clubs: Down Town Association (N.Y.C.), University (N.Y.C.). Home: Irvington, N.Y. Died July 4, 1984.

LAVERTY, ROGER MONTGOMERY, business exec.; b. Pitts., Apr. 23, 1890; s. Charles Edward and Helen Senter (Flanders) L.; student pub. schs., Pitts.; m. Mae Lyle, Feb. 10, 1919; children—Robert Edward, Roger Montgomery, Nancy Jane. Store mgr. A. & P. Tea Co., Pitts., 1912-14. 1st v.p. Central div., 1928-31; pres. Fitzsimmons Stores, Ltd., Los Angeles, from 1931, Market Equities, Lankershim Center Development Co.; dir. Hody's Restaurants. Mem. A.I.M. Presbyn. Mason (Shriner). Club: Los Angeles Country. Home: Beverly Hills, Calif. Deceased.

LAVES, WALTER HERMAN CARL, educator; b. Chicago, May 11, 1902; s. Kurt and Luise (Moshagen) L.; Ph.B., U. of Chicago, 1923, Ph.D., 1927; grad. work, U. of Berlin and U. of Chicago, 1923-27; LL.D., Washington and Jefferson Coll., 1966; m. Ruth Wilson, September 16, 1926; two daughters-Ruth Anne (Mrs. Eiji Hashimoto), and Margaret Joan. Asst. political science, University of Chicago, 1926-27; prof. polit. science and chmn. of dept., Hamilton Coll., Clinton, N.Y., 1927-37; visiting prof. polit. science, U. of Chicago, 1936-37, lecturer in polit. science, 1937-38, asso. prof. and chmn. of social sciences in the college, Univ. of Chicago, 1938-46; on leave of absence, Dec. 1941-46, to act as dir. Div. of Inter-Am. Activities in U.S., Office of Coordinator of Inter-Am. Affairs, Washington, D.C., 1941-42; chief Organizations Service Div., Office of Civilian Defense, 1942-43; cons. on Internat. Affairs, exec. office of the President, Bur. of the Budget, 1943-47; on spl. mission for secretary of State, 1945; adviser U.S. dels. to San Francisco UN Conf., 1945; UN Assembly, Lond., 1946; I.L.O., 1946; UNESCO, 1946; ECOSOC, 1946; dep. director gen. UNESCO, 1947-50, chmn. U.S. Nat. Commn. for UNESCO, 1952-54, alternate delegate UNESCO Conference, 1964; cons. U.N. Tech. Assistance Bd., U.S. Dept. State also E.C.A., and Mut. Security Agency, UN, 1967, UN Ednl. Scientific and Cultural Orgn., 1967; vice chmn. U.S. delegation to UNESCO Gen. Conf., 1952; mem. Governing bd. UNESCO Social Sci. Inst., Germany, 1951-60; v.p. Governmental Affairs Inst., Washington, 1952-54; prof. dept. govt. Ind. U., Bloomington, after 1954, then prof. emeritus, chmn. dept., 1954-66. Mem. Am. sect. Internat. Inst. Adminstrv. Scis., Brussels, Belgium. Vis. prof. U. Mich., 1951. Decorated Order of the Crown Thailand, also Order of White Elephant. Mem. Am. Polit. Sci. Assn.,

Internat. Studies Association, (v.p. 1958-59), Am. Council on Edn. (chmn. internat. ednl. policies com.), Midwest Polit. Sci. Assn., Internat. Studies Assn., Am. Soc. Pub. Adminstrn., Ind. Acad. Social Scis., Fgn. Policy Assn., Am. Assn. U. Profs., Am. Council Learned Socs. (past dir.), Soc. Internat. Develop. Club: Cosmos (Washington, D.C.). Co-author (with Charles A. Thomson): UNESCO: Purpose, Program, Prospects, 1957; Cultural Relations and U.S. Foreign Policy, 1963. Editor: International Security, 1939; Foundations for a Stable World Order, 1940; Inter-American Solidarity, 1941 (all Harris Found. lectures). Contbr. articles to numerous profl. jours. Home: Bloomington, Ind. Died Oct. 6, 1983.

LAWFORD, PETER, actor; b. London, Eng., Sept. 7, 1923; s. Sir Sidney and Lady L.; m. Patricia Kennedy (div. 1966); children: Christopher, Sydney, Victoria, Robin; m. Mary Ann Rowan, Nov. 2, 1971 (div. 1973). Ed. pvt. tutors. pres. Chrislaw Prodns., Inc. TV series Dear Phoebe, 1956-57; role of Nick Charles: series Thin Man, NBC-TV, 1957-59; recent films include: The Longest Day, 1962, Advise and Consent, 1962, Sargeants Three, 1961, Dead Ringer, 1963, Harlow, The Oscar, Skidoo, Hook, Line and Sinker, Buona Serra Mrs. Campbell, April Fools, One More Time, They Only Kill Their Masters, That's Entertainment, 1974, Rosebud, 1975, Won Ton Ton, 1976, Angels Brigade, 1980, Body and Soul, 1981; TV prodn.: Ellery Queen, 1971. Died Dec. 24, 1984.*

LAWLER, JOSEPH CHRISTOPHER, engineering executive; b. Lynn, Mass., May 3, 1920; s. Joseph Christopher and Clara Mae (Emerson) L.; children—Susan Vivian, Joseph Christopher III, William Douglas. B.S. cum laude (Desmond Fitzgerlad scholar 1943), Northeastern U., 1943, D.Eng. (hon.), 1972; M.S., Harvard, 1947. Diplomate: Am. Acad. Environ. Engrs.; Registered profl. engr., N.H., Vt., R.I., Conn., Maine, Mass., N.Y., Calif., Va. Project engr. Camp Dresser & McKee Inc., Boston, 1947-52, partner, 1952-83, pres., 1970-78, chmn. bd., 1970-83, chief exec. officer, 1978-83. Contbr. to: Handbook of Applied Hydraulics (Davis), 1969, articles to profl. jours. Mem. North Reading Pub. Sch. Bldg. Com., 1956-60, North Reading Sch. Com., 1960-61; Trustee Northeastern U., 1977-83, mem. corp., 1965-83. Served to lt. (j.g.) C.E.C. USN, 1944-46. Recipient New Eng. Engr. of Year award, 1972; named Alumni Man of Yr. Northeastern U., 1972, Outstanding Civil Engring. Alumnus, 1979; recipient Gordon Maskew Fair award, 1979. Fellow ASCE, Water Pollution Control Fedn. (dir. at large 1972-75, exec. com. 1972-73), Am. Cons. Engrs. Council; mem. Nat. Acad. Engring., Northeastern U. Alumni Assn. (dir. 1958-60, v.p. 1960-62), Engring. Socs. New Eng. (pres. 1962-63), Nat. Council Profl. Services Firms (dir. 1972—, pres. 1976), New Eng. Water Pollution Control Assn. (pres. 1970), Am. Water Works Assn., Nat. Soc. Profl. Engrs. (Profl. Engrs. in Pvt. Practice award 1977), Tau Beta Pi, Chi Epsilon (hon.). Home: Reading, Mass. Died Nov. 18, 1983.

LAWLER, RICHARD H(AROLD), physician, surgeon, educator; b. Chicago, Aug. 12, 1895; s. James and Margaret (Griffin) L.; student U. Wis., 1928, U. Mich., 1927; B.S., Loyola U., 1929, M.D., 1930; m. Charlotte Andersen, Sept. 29, 1937; children—Christine, Rosemary. Asst. prof. surgery Stritch Sch. Medicine, Loyola U., 1940-51; prof. surgery Cook Co. Grad. Sch. from 1940. Served as lt., U.S. Naval Aviation, 1917-19; lt., U.S.N.R.F., 1919-33. Fellow A.C.S., Internat. Coll. Surgeons, Am. Coll. Chest Physicians. Mem. Bd. Surgery. Clubs: South Shore Country, Beverly Country (Chicago). Author articles med. jours. Performed first human kidney transplant, 1950. Home: Chicago, Ill. Died July 24, 1982.

LAWLER, THOMAS NEWMAN, lawyer; b. N.Y.C., Apr. 18, 1908; s. Thomas B. and Margaret A. (Brennan) L.; A.B., Princeton, 1929; LL.B., Harvard, 1932; m. Martha E. Reynolds, Nov. 15, 1934; children—Ann (Mrs. Thomas E. Dewey, Jr.), Martha Elisabeth (Mrs. David T. Schiff). Admitted to N.Y. bar, 1932, since practiced N.Y.C.; asso. Breed, Abbott & Morgan, 1932-34, O'Brien, Driscoll & Raftery, 1934-44; partner firm O'Brien, Driscoll, Raftery & Lawler, 1944-51, Lawler & Rockwood, N.Y.C., 1951-66, Lawler, Sterling & Kent, 1966-74, Hall, Dickler, Lawler, Kent & Howley, from 1974. Dir. Philip Morris, Inc., Bank of Commerce, Wheelock Signals, Inc., Irving Berlin Music Corp. Trustee Irving Berlin Charitable Fund, Fred C. Gloeckner Found. Mem. Am. (chmn. copyright com. 1946-48), N.Y. bar assns. Club: Sleepy Hollow Country (Scarborough, N.Y.). Home: New York, N.Y. Died July 12, 1985.

LAWTON, ROBERT OSWALD, educator; b. Greenwood, S.C., Dec. 28, 1924; s. Robert O. and Anne (Simpson) L.; student Wofford Coll., 1941-43, Litt. D., 1969; A.B., Duke, 1946, M.A., 1947, Ph.D., 1953; m. Elise Bates Nicholson, Aug. 15, 1945; children—Robert O., Elise Bates. Mem. faculty Fla. State U., Tallahassee, 1949-80, prof. English, 1964-80, dean Coll. Arts and Scis., 1966-72, v.p. acad. affairs, 1977-80. Profl. cons. So. Assn. Colls. and Secondary Schs., 1960-80. Served with AUS, 1943-45. Decorated D.S.C. Mem. S. Atlantic Modern Lang. Assn., Shakespeare Assn., So. Conf. Acad. Deans, Am. Assn. Acad. Deans, Council Arts and Scis., Omicron Delta Kappa. Home: Tallahassee, Fla. Died Oct. 8, 1980.

LAY, HERMAN WARDEN, ret. soft drink co. exec.; b. Charlotte, N.C., June 3, 1909; s. Jesse N. and Bertha Erma (Parr) L.; m. Amelia Harper, Dec. 28, 1935; children—Linda (Mrs. Henry Chambless, Jr.) (dec.), Susan Lay-White, H. Ward, Dorothy (Mrs. James Rutledge). Student, Furman U., 1926-28, LL.D., 1967; LL.D., Drury Coll., Springfield, Mo., 1966; , Furman U., 1967. Founder, pres., chmn. H. W. Lay & Co., Inc., 1939-61; pres. Frito-Lay, Inc., 1961-62, chmn. exec. com., chief exec. officer, 1962-65, chmn. bd., 1964-65; chmn. bd., chmn. finance com. Pepsi Co. Inc., 1965-71, chmn. exec. com., 1971-80; dir. Braniff Internat. Corp.; adv. dir. Third Nat. Bank of Nashville. Pres. Potato Chip Inst. Internat., 1949; vice chmn. Baylor U. Med. Center Found.; bd. dirs. Dallas chpt. Am. Cancer Soc., Dallas Civic Opera; former dir. Am. Mgmt. Assn.; mem. adv. council to trustees Furman U. Named Alumnus of Year Furman U., 1965; recipient Golden Plate award Am. Acad. Achievement, 1975; Horatio Alger award, 1969. Mem. Chief Execs. Forum. Clubs: Piedmont Driving (Atlanta); Preston Trl. Golf (Dallas), Petroleum (Dallas), Brook Hollow Golf (Dallas). Home: Dallas, Tex.

LAYTON, WARREN K(ENNETH), educator; b. Potomac, Ill., Oct. 27, 1889; s. John and Luella (Copeland) L.; A.B., Northwestern, 1911; A.M., U. of Ill., 1918; Ph.D., U. of Mich., 1931. Research asst., Nat. Research Council, U. of Mich., 1919-20; psychol. examiner and statistician, psychol. clinic, Detroit Pub. Schs., 1920-23; counselor, Jefferson Intermediate Sch., 1923-25; asst. prin. Foch Intermediate Sch., 1925-1930, asst. dir., div. of guidance and placement, dir., div. dir. Served as 1st lt., U.S. Army, 1918-19. Mem. bd. Detroit Council Boy Scouts of Children's Aid Soc., Council for Youth Service and Y.M.C.A. Mem. N.E.A., Mich. State and Detroit Edn. Assns., Nat. Soc. Study Edn., Council of Guidance and Personnel Assns. (past pres. and trustee, 1948-49), Nat. Vocational Guidance Assn. (past. com. chmn., treas. and vice pres.; pres., 1947-48, 1948-49), Phi Delta Kappa, Phi Kappa Sigma. Republican. Methodist. Reviser: The Seven Laws of Teaching (with Wm. Chandler Bagley) by John Milton Gregory, 1918. Contbr. articles in various prof. jours. and Yearbooks of Nat. Soc. for Study of Edn., N.E.A. Home: Dearborn, Mich. Deceased.

LAZARON, MORRIS SAMUEL, rabbi; b. Savannah, Ga., Apr. 16, 1888; s. Samuel Louis and Alice (De Castro) L.; B.A., U. of Cincinnati, 1909, M.A., 1911; studied Hebrew Union Coll., Cincinnati, 1905, 1914; Litt.D., Rutgers University, 1936; married Pauline Horkheimer, on May 1, 1916 (died April 25, 1933); children—Morris, Samuel, Harold Victor, Clementine; married 2d Hilda Rothschild Rosenblatt, July 23, 1945. Rabbi Congregation Leshem Shomayim, Wheeling, W.Va., 1914, Baltimore Hebrew Congregation, 1915-47, emeritus since 1947; vis. prof. religion and sociology, Rollins College. Chaplain during World War I; then major chaplain, O.R.C., Am. Merchant Marine Library Assn.; member Central Conference American Rabbis; bd. dirs. Am. Assn. for the United Nations. Democrat. Mason (33 deg.). Clubs: Suburban Country, Woodholme Country; Blowing Rock Country (Blowing Rock, N.C.); Winter Park Golf, University (Winter Park, Fla.). Author: Religious Services for Jewish Youth; Side Arms; Consolations of Our Faith; Seed of Abraham; Ten Jews of the Ages, 1930; Common Ground, 1938; various booklets and pamphlets. Contbr. to Jewish and gen. mags. Home: Pikesville, Md. Deceased.

LAZARUS, MARVIN PAUL, lawyer, photographer; b. Albany, N.Y., June 1, 1918; s. Louis and Eva (Goldberg) L.; m. Roberta Ann Fast, June 29, 1947; children—Edward Fast, Jonathan Fast. B.A. magna cum laude, Union Coll., Schenectady, 1940; LL.B., Harvard U., 1943. Bar: N.Y. State bar 1943. Asst. atty.-gen. State of N.Y., Albany, 1943-50; counsel Eagle Water Corp., N.Y.C., 1950-62; free-lance photographer, 1962-74; resident counsel Martin E. Segal Co., N.Y.C., from 1974; lectr. group legal plans; lectr. photography and the artist. Exhibited in one-man shows, East Hampton Gallery, N.Y.C., 1963, Marilyn Pearl Gallery, N.Y.C., 1976, group shows, including, Fogg Art Museum, Cambridge, Mass., 1967, Mabel Brady Garvan Gallery, Yale U., 1973, Mus. Modern Art, N.Y.C., 1974, M.I.T., 1975; represented in permanent collections, including, Mus. Modern Art, Chrysler Mus., Provincetown, Mass., also, numerous pvt. collections; contbr. photographs to periodicals including, Harper's Bazaar, Fortune, Seventeen, Art Voices, Art in Am., Time, Show, Popular Photography, Popular Photography Ann., Art News, photographs to books, Stuart Davis (Goosen), 1959, Purposes of Art (Albert E. Elson), 1975, The World of Marcel Duchamp, 1966, Documents of 20th Century Art, Dialogues with Marcel Duchamp (Pierre Cabanne), 1971, Milton Avery (Hilton Kramer), 1960; also, Mus. Modertn Art and Whitney Mus. Am. Art catalogs. Mem. Assn. Bar City N.Y., Am. Prepaid Legal Inst., Nat. Resource Center for Consumers Legal Services, Phi Beta Kappa. Home: White Plains, NY.

LEAKE, ARTHUR CYRUS, railway exec; b. Monett, Mo., Mar. 31, 1889; s. James Cyrus and Mary Katherine (Miller) L.; student pub. schs. Mo.; m. Lucille Rutherford, Mar. 25, 1921; 1 dau., Peggy Ann. Clk. to city passenger agt. St.L.-S.F. R.R., 1904-28; traveling agt. to traffic mgr. M.& St. L. R.R., 1928-48, v.p. traffic from 1948; dir. Hocking Coal Co., Ry. Transfer Co. Mem. Am. Legion, Army Transportation Assn. Mason. Clubs: Bankers, Metropolitan (N.Y.C.); Union League (Chgo.); Minneapolis, Minikahda, Athletic (Mpls.). Home: Minneapolis, Minn. †

LEATHAM, CHARLES H(ENRY), foundation exec.; b. Frostburg, Md., Jan. 13, 1889; s. Charles H. and Ruth (Hicks) L.; grad. Allegheny Co. Acad., 1907; m. Lillian Sloan Skidmore, June 29, 1911 (dec. 1956); 1 son, Charles Henry; m. 2d, Celia Burnside Smith, Dec. 21, 1957. Student Westinghouse Elec. & Mfg. Co., East Pitts., Pa., 1907-09; in charge substation maintenance Uniontown (Pa.) dist. West Penn Power Co., 1909-11; dist. mgr. Frostburg district Potomac Edison Co., 1911-19, various positions, including comml. mgr., 1919-32; in charge indsl. research West Penn Electric Co., Pitts., 1932-35; comml. mgr. Monongahela Power Co., Fairmont, W.Va., 1935-37, v.p., 1937-50, exec. v.p., 1950-55, dir., 1938-56; exec. dir. W.Va. Found. Ind. Colls., from 1956; dir. Statton Furniture Co. (Hagerstown, Md.). Chmn. rural electrification sect. Edison Elec. Inst., 1942-45. Registered engr., W.VA. Mem. Am. Inst. E.E., Pub. Utilities Assn. Virginias (pres. 1947). Methodist. Elk. Home: Fairmont, W.Va. †

LEAVELL, BYRD STUART, physician; b. Washington, Dec. 29, 1910; s. Byrd and Lucie (Browning) L.; B.S., Va. Mil. Inst., 1931; M.D., U. Va., 1935; m. Nancy Butzner, Oct. 7, 1939; children—Anne Leavell Reynolds, Lucie Leavell Vogel, Byrd Stuart, Jr. Intern, N.Y. Hosp., N.Y.C., 1935-36, asst. resident, 1936-38; practice medicine specializing in internal medicine, Charlottesville, Va., from 1946; fellow U. Va., 1938-39, asst. dir. student health, 1939-40, instr. medicine Sch. Medicine, 1940-42, asst. prof., 1946-54, prof., from 1954, chmn. dept. internal medicine, 1966-68, asst. dean Sch. Medicine, 1958-61, head div. hematology, 1945-70. Served to maj., M.C., AUS, 1942-46. Decorated Bronze Star. Mem. AMA, A.C.P., Internat., Am. socs. hematology, AAAS, So. Soc. Clin. Investigation, Am. Clin. and Climatol. Assn., Kappa Alpha, Alpha Omega Alpha, Omicron Delta Kappa. Episcopalian. Clubs: Colonnade (pres. 1960), Farmington Country (Charlottesville). Author: The 8th Evac., 1970; (with O.A. Thorup) Fundamentals of Clinical Hematology, 4th edit., 1976. Home: Charlottesville, Va. Died Nov. 5, 1979.

LEAVITT, MILO DAVID, JR., physician, govt. ofcl.; b. Beloit, Wis., June 24, 1915; s. Milo David and Helen (Hubner) L. B.A., U. Wis., 1938; M.D., U. Pa., 1940; M.Sc., U. Minn., 1948; M.P.H., Harvard, 1959. Rotating intern Phila. Gen. Hosp., 1940-42; fellow internal medicine Mayo Clinic, Rochester, Minn., 1945-49; clin. asst. prof. medicine Woman's Med. Coll. Pa., Phila., 1949-58; with NIH, Bethesda, from 1959, asst. chief perinatal research br., 1960-62; head spl. internat. programs sect. Office Internat. Research, 1962-66; dep. asst. sec. for sci. and population HEW, 1966, dep. dir., acting dir. office program planning, 1967-68; dir. Fogarty Internat. Center, 1968-78; spl. asst. to dir. Nat. Inst. Aging, NIH, from 1978; cons. VA, Phila., 1954-58; mem. U.S. del. 25th-27th, 29th World Health Assemblies. Contbr. articles to profl. jours. Bd. dirs. Gorgas Meml. Inst. Tropical and Preventive Medicine. Served to capt. M.C. AUS, 1942-45. Mem. A.M.A., Indsl. Med. Assn., Am. Geriatrics Soc., Gerontol. Soc., Phila. County Med. Soc., Am. Diabetes Assn., Assn. Am. Med. Colls., N.Y. Acad. Scis., A.A.A.S., Alumni Assn. Mayo Found., Am. Heart Assn., Am. Pub. Health Assn., Am. Soc. Pub. Health Adminstrs., Phila. Coll. Physicians, Sigma Xi, Kappa Sigma, Alpha Mu Pi Omega. Episcopalian. Home: Silver Spring, MD.

LEAVITT, STURGIS ELLENO, coll. prof.; b. Windham, Me., Jan. 24, 1888; s. William Hooper and Mary Ellen (Sturgis) L.; grad. high sch., Gorham, Me., 1904; A.B., Bowdoin, 1908; M.A., Harvard University, 1913, Ph. D., 1917; Litt.D., Davidson College, 1941; Litt.D., Bowdoin College, 1943; LL.D., University of North Carolina, 1965; Sheldon traveling fellow, in Peru, Bolivia, Chile, Argentina and Uruguay, 1919-20; m. Alga Webber, June 29, 1916. Instr. foreign langs., Jackson (Mo.) Mil. Acad., 1908-09; in French, Cushing Acad., Ashburnham, Mass., 1909-12; in Romance langs., Northwestern U., 1913-14, Harvard, 1915-17; asst. prof. Romance langs., U. of N.C., 1917-18, asso. prof., 1918-21, prof. Spanish, 1921-45, Kenan prof. Spanish, 1945-60, Kenan professor emeritus, from 1960; director, Institute of Latin-American Studies, U. of N.C., 1940-59. Member general advisory committee, U.S. Office of Edn., 1941-45. Alcalde Perpetuo Hon. Zalamea de la Serena (Spain), 1959. Mem. several profl. and scientific socs.; corr. mem. Spanish socs. Presbyterian. Mason. Author several books, lastest being: Revistas Hispano-americanas. Indice bibliográfico, 1843-1935, 1960. Bibliog. compiler Bolivian, Chilean, Colombian, Peruvian and Uruguayan lits. Editor works of several Spanish authors. Has served as editor profl. mags. Contbg. editor: Handbook of Latin American Studies, 1935-46. Home: Chapel Hill, N.C. †

LEBOUTILLIER, PHILIP, merchant; born in New York, N.Y., Oct. 22, 1887; s. John and Fannie (Goodman) LeB.; A.B., Princeton; m. Gertrude Havens Tifft, May 19, 1909 (divorced 1936); children—Peggy, Philip, Jr., Gertrude (Mrs. William A. Wood, Junior), Peter; married 2d, Mrs. Florence H. Bachman, Feb. 2, 1944. Began with Sibley, Lindsay & Carr, Rochester, N.Y., then with Jordan Marsh, Boston; supt., gen. mgr. LeBoutillier Brothers, 1911-13; with John Wanamaker (New York), 1914; gen. asst., later sec., gen. mgr. and dir. Best & Co. (New York), 1917-24, v.p., gen. mgr. and dir., 1924-27, pres., gen. mgr., dir., 1927-55, chmn. board, dir., from 1957; dir. 2 E. 70th St. Corp. Originator, developer of the Suburban Branch Store Idea. Chevalier, French Legion of

Honor; Commendatore, Order of the Crown of Italy. Mem. American Society of Royal Italian Order, Am. Soc. of French Legion of Hon., Huguenot Soc., Magna Charta Barons (Somerset chapt.), Soc. Colonial Wars in State of N.Y., S.A.R. (Empire State Soc.), Ancient and Hon. Arty. Soc. of Mass. Soc. of Cincinnati (N.J.), St. Nicholas Soc. Episcopalian. Clubs: University, Lake Placid (New York); Royal Ocean Racing (Eng.), Long Island Country, Westhampton Golf, Quantuck Beach. Home: New York, N.Y. †

LECLERG, ERWIN LOUIS, biometrician; b. St. Louis, Feb. 16, 1901; s. Charles F. and Lillian (Dunn) LeC.; B.S., Colo. State U., 1924; M.S., Ia. State Univ., 1925; Ph.D., U. Minn., 1932; m. Phylis M. Robertson, Aug. 10, 1926; 1 son, Robert E. Jr. plant pathologist U.S. Dept. Agr., 1924-25, asst. plant pathologist, 1930-39, pathologist. 1939-46, research coordinator, 1948-54, dir. biometrical services Agrl. Research Service, Beltsville, Md., 1954-64, chmn. dept. biol. scis. Grad. Sch. Dept. Agr., 1955-64, mem. Grad. Sch. council, 1949-64; collaborator Agr. Research Service, United States Dept. of Agr., Washington, 1965-64; assistant plant pathologist Colo. Agrl. Expt. Sta., 1925-30; prin. budget examiner Bur. Budget, 1946-48. Recipient Profl. Achievement award Colo. State U., 1960. Fellow A., Am. Statis. Assn., Washington Acad. Scis. Royal Statis. Soc. London: member Cmo. Sci. Soc., Bot. Soc. Wash., Am. Phytopathological Soc., Posto Assn. America, Am. Soc., Agroomy. Biometrics Soc., Sigma Xi, Gamma Alpha, Sigma Chi. Club: Cosmos (Washington). Home: Silver Spring, Md. Died Aug. 3, 1981.

LEDBETTER, G. EDWARD, investment banker; b. McLeansboro, Ill., 1890. Partner, Merrill Lynch, Pierce, Fenner & Beane. †

LEDDEN, WALTER EARL, theol. educator; b. Glassboro, N.J., Mar. 27, 1888; s. Joseph Jackson and Miriam Risden (Higgins) L.; grad. Pennington (N.J.) Sem., 1907; Ph.B., Dickinson Coll., Carlisle, Pa., 1910, A.M., 1913; B.D. Drew Theol. Sem., 1913; grad. study, Drew U., 1913-14; D.D., Syracuse University, 1927, Lycoming College, 1957; LL.D., Dickinson Coll., 1944; m. Mary Lida Iszard, July 2, 1913 (dec.); children—Howard (dec.), Joseph (dec.), Jean Virginia (Mrs. Bruce R. Gordon); m. 2d, Henrietta Gibson, January 25, 1964. Ordained ministry M.E. Church, 1914; pastor Goodwill M.E. Ch., Rumson, N.J., 1910-14; First M.E. Ch., Belmar, N.J., 1914-19; State St. M.E. Church, Camden, 1919-20; Broadway M.E. Church, Camden, N.J., 1920-26; Richmond Av. M.E. Church, Buffalo, N.Y., 1926-30; Mathewson St. M.E. Ch. Providence, R.I., 1930-38; Trinity Methodist Ch. Albany, N.Y., 1938-44. Elected bishop of the Methodist Church, 1944; resident bishop Syracuse area of Meth. Ch., 1944-60, prof. Christian worship Wesley Theol. Sem., Am. U., Washington, from 1960. Pres. N.Y. State Council Chs., 1945-49, Council of Bishops of Meth. Ch., 1956-57, ret. 1960. Mem. Newcomen Soc., Phi Beta Kappa, Alpha Chi Rho, Theta Phi. Mason. Club: Torch, University. Home: Washington, D.C. †

LEDERER, ALBRECHT MISA, mgmt. cons.; s. Richard M. and Helen (Leod) L.; m. Eileen Farrell, 1931. Ed. privately in chem. engring. Engr., mgmt. cons. Morris & Van Wormer, N.Y.C., 1924-58, gen. partner, 1934-58, offices, Rio de Janeiro, Caracas, Lima, Santiago, Washington; pres. Am. Lederer & Co., Inc., N.Y.C., from 1958; Sr. adviser to adminstr. UN Devel. Programme, N.Y.; cons. to ECA; mem. commerce mission to Europe, cons. Mut. Security Agy.; adv. group on European productivity; v.p. Nat. Mgmt. Council U.S., 1945-51, pres., 1951-60; v.p., trustee, exec. com. China Inst. in Am., 1949-55; rep. Com. Econ. Devel.; adv. com. to State, Commerce depts. comml. activities of fgn. service; adviser on mgmt. to Ministry of Finance Brazil; bd. councilors Rock Island (Ill.) Arsenal, 1955-63; cons. to bd. adviser, dir., former mem. exec. com. Internat. Exec. Service Corps; chmn. bd., mem. exec. com. Technoserve, Inc.; mem. Seminar Orgn. and Mgmt. Colo. U. Author: World Business Education: An Investment Opportunity. Past pres., chmn. bd. Council Internat. Progress Mgmt., Inc., also dir.; pres. World Council Mgmt., 1960-63; Bd. dirs. Inst. Mgmt. Consultants. Decorated knight comdr. Order Lion, Finland; recipient Gold medal award Internat. U., Rome, Italy, 1957; Mgmt. Man of Year award Nat. Mgmt. Assn., 1963; Wallace Clark award, 1964; Mgmt. Cons. award for Excellence, 1977. Fellow Internat. Acad. Mgmt. (past vice chancellor); mem. Nat. Sutures Corp. (past pres.), ASME, Bombay Mgmt. Assn. (hon.), Assn. Mgmt. and Indsl. Engrs. P.I. (hon.), Malaysian Inst. Mgmt. (hon.), Soc. Prof. Mgmt. Cons.'s (hon.), ASME. Club: Downtown Athletic (N.Y.C.). Home: New York, NY.

LEDERLE, ARTHUR F., judge; b. Leland, Mich., Nov. 25, 1887; s. John Edward and Christina Marie (Dunkelow) L.; grad. Eastern Mich. Coll., 1909. Ed.M. (hon.), 1936, LL.D., 1953; LL.B., Detroit College of Law, 1915. LL.M., University of Detroit, 1923; LL.D., Wayne State U., 1952; m. Margaret Bailie Matthews. Mich., Jan. 3, 1911. Sch. teacher, Sherman, 1909-10. Traverse City, Mich., 1914-23; admitted to Mich. bar, 1915; asst. city atty., Detroit, 1923-33, and 1934-36; spl. asst. atty. gen. Mich. 1933-34; judge U.S. Dist. Court, Eastern Dist. of Michigan from 1936, chief judge from 1948; mem. faculty Wayne State U. Law Sch., 1927-46. Fellow Am. Bar Found; mem. Am., Mich., Detroit bar assns., Am. Judicature Soc. Democrat. Mason, K.P. Clubs: Detroit Athletic, Detroit Golf. †

LEE, CALVIN BOW TONG, ins. co. exec.; b. N.Y.C., Feb. 18, 1934; s. George G. and Lin (Hong) L.; m. Beverly Song, June 8, 1957 (div.); children—Christopher, Craig; m. Audrey A. Evans, Sept. 11, 1971. A.B., Columbia, 1955, LL.B., 1958; LL.M., N.Y.U., 1965, J.S.D., 1968; LL.D. (hon.), Montclair State Coll., 1980. Bar: N.Y. bar 1959, U.S. Supreme Ct. bar 1959. Gen. mgr. Lee's Restaurant, N.Y.C., 1951-58; atty. Emmet, Marvin & Martin, N.Y.C., 1958-61; asst. dean, dir. Citizenship Program; lectr. polit. sci. Columbia, 1961-65; Am. Council Edn. fellow in acad. adminstrn. Bryn Mawr Coll., 1965-66; staff asso. Am. Council on Edn., 1966-67; asst. dir. div. of coll. support Bur. Higher Edn., U.S. Office Edn., 1967-68; dean Coll. Liberal Arts, Boston U., 1968-70, acting pres., 1970, exec. v.p., 1971; chancellor U. Md., Baltimore County, 1971-76; v.p. Prudential Ins. Co. Am., Newark, 1976—. Author: Chinese Cooking for American Kitchens, 1958, Chinatown, U.S.A, 1965, One Man, One Vote, 1967, The Campus Scene: 1900-1970, 1970; co-author: The Invisible Colleges, 1972, The Gourmet Chinese Regional Cookbook, 1976; Editor, contbr.: Improving College Teaching, 1967; co-editor, contbr.: Whose Goals for American Higher Education, 1968. Mem. Authors Guild, Phi Alpha Delta. Home: Chatham Township, N.J. Died Mar. 13, 1983.

LEE, CHARLES HENRY, lawyer, internat. exec.; b. Santiago, Chile, June 28, 1909; s. Charles Henry and Ellen Scott (Wilson) L.; student Columbia, 1927-28; Ph.B. cum laude, Georgetown U., 1931; postgrad. George Washington, Columbia, 1932-33; LL.B., Fordham U., 1937; m. Lulu Vargas-Vila, Aug. 20, 1938; children—Patricia Ellen (Mrs. Lars Schonander), Charles Henry III (dec.), Elizabeth (Mrs. John D. Sevier). Asst. to arbitrator Guatemala-Honduras Boundary Arbitration Tribunal, Washington, 1931-33; admitted to N.Y. bar, 1938, D.C. bar, 1946; pvt. practice, N.Y.C., 1937-41; atty. Coordinator Inter-Am. Affairs, Washington, 1941; atty. Tex. Co., N.Y.C., 1941-46; spl. asst. to asst. sec. state Inter-Am. affairs Dept. State, Washington, 1946-47; mng. dir. E.R. Squibb & Sons Argentina, Buenos Aires, 1947-49; asst. v.p., asst. to pres. E.R. Squibb & Sons, N.Y.; dir. Brazilian subsidiary, 1949-56; mng. dir. internat. practice McKinsey & Co., mgmt. cons., N.Y.C., 1956-58; mng. partner Lee, Altieri, Sisto & Assos., mgmt. cons., Mexico City, 1958-61; partner Rado & Lee, attys., N.Y.C., 1958-61; dir. U.S. Econ. Mission to Chile, Santiago, 1961-64; v.p., chmn. bd. Hooker Mexicana S.A. de C.V., v.p. Hooker Internat. Corp., 1972-82; partner Sintemex. Mem. Council on Fgn. Relations N.Y., 1951-82; hon. mem. faculty Cath. U. Chile. With Inter-Am. Def. Bd., Washington, 1942; mil. attache Div. G-2 War Dept., Washington, 1942-43; asst. mil. attache Am. embassy, Argentina, 1943-45. Bd. dirs., v.p. Mexican-N.Am. Cultural Inst. Decorated comdr. Order al Merito (Chile). Mem. Am. C. of C. Mexico (dir., past pres., chmn. bus. adv. council), Am. Chamber of Mex., Assn. Am. Chambers Commerce Latin Am. (v.p.), Mexican Acad. History and Geography, Am. Bar Assn. (past sec., chmn. Latin Am. law com.), Assn. Bar City N.Y., Pan Am. Soc. U.S. Roman Catholic. Clubs: University (Washington, N.Y.C. and Mexico City); Campestre Churubusco (Mexico City). Internat. relations editor: Handbook of Latin Am. Studies, 1941. Home: Mexico, Mexico. Died Dec. 5, 1982.

LEE, FRANK HERBERT, educator; b. Mansfield, Ohio, Dec. 13, 1900; s. Howard Edgar and Helena (Frank) L.; m. Carolynn Lampson, Sept. 15, 1923; children—Mary Emilie, Frank Lampson; m. Lorraine A. Leland, Apr. 6, 1958. A.B., Miami U., Oxford, Ohio, 1923; A.M., Columbia, 1932; D.Sc. (hon.), Marlboro Coll., 1956; LL.D., Hendrix Coll., 1962. Asst. dept. drawing Miami U., 1922-23; teaching fellow Ohio State U., 1923-24; instr. drafting Columbia, 1924-34, asso., 1934-42, asst. prof., 1942-46, asso. prof., 1946-52, prof., 1952-69, prof. emeritus, 1969-83; dir. spl. projects Henry Krumb Sch. Mines, Sch. Engring. and Applied Sci., 1969-83, chmn. dept. graphics, 1952-69; asst. to dean Columbia Coll., 1942-83, adminstrv. asst. to dean engring., 1952-83; co-founder faculty childrens tuition remission plan, co-founder, chmn. bd. Tuition Exchange; chief draftsman Peele Co., Bklyn., 1929; cons. Richmond Fireproof Door Co., N.Y.C.; mem. scholarship com., tng. cons. Grumman Aircraft, 1942-83. Recipient Great Tchr. award Soc. Older Grads., 1961. Mem. ASME, Am. Soc. Engring. Edn., Sigma Chi. Ind. Democrat. Episcopalian. Clubs: Men's Faculty (N.Y.C.), Columbia University (N.Y.C.). Home: Roslyn, N.Y. Died May 26, 1983.

LEE, GEORGE HAMOR, scientist, educator; b. Oakmont, Pa., June 3, 1908; s. Alfred McClung and Edna (Hamor) L.; m. Dora Maye Raymo, Oct. 12, 1929 (div. 1963); 1 son, George Hamor II; m. Lola Frances Madagan, Sept. 19, 1963. B.S., U. Pitts., 1936; M.S. in Engring. (Westinghouse Research asso.), Cornell U., 1937, Ph.D. (McMullen research scholar), 1940. With Aluminum Research Labs., New Kensington, Pa. and; Massena, N.Y., 1927-33; instr. mechanics Cornell U., 1937-40, asst. prof., 1941-45, asso. prof., 1945, coordinator, supr. math. and mechanics for engring., sci. and mgmt. war tng. program, 1941-45; instr. mechanics Carnegie Inst. Tech., 1940-41; asso. prof. mech. engring. U.S. Naval Postgrad. Sch., 1945-50, prof., 1950-51; prof. mechanics Rensselaer Poly. Inst., 1951-61, asso. head dept., 1952-53, head dept., 1953-55, dir. div. research, 1954-60; chief scientist, dir. research and devel. Office Chief Ordnance, U.S. Army, 1960-62; chief ground warfare tech. Mpls.-Honeywell Regulator Co., Washington, 1962-63; prof. aerospace engring. U. Cin., 1963-74, emeritus, from 1974; adminstr. univ. research, asso. dean U. Cin. (Grad. Sch.), 1963-67, asst. v.p. for research (scis. and engring.), 1967-74, cons. to exec. v.p. for acad. affairs, from 1971; Cons. Babcock & Wilcox Co., 1942, Naval Ordnance Lab., 1949-51; chmn. sci. adv. com. KDI, Inc., Cin., 1963-64; mem. adv. com. Eglin AFB, U. Pa.; dir. Center Study Aging, Inc., Albany, N.Y.; Mem. exec. com. Nat. Conf. Adminstrn. Research, 1958-59; mem. Nat. Miniturization Awards Com., from 1957. Author: An Introduction to Experimental Stress Analysis, 1950; Contbr.: articles to profl. jours. Am. Civil Engring. Practice. Fellow A.A.A.S.; mem. ASME (sponsor exptl. stress analysis applied mech. div. 1952-54, research com. mech. pressure responsive elements from 1953), A.A.U.P., Am. Soc. Engring. Edn., Am. Ordnance Assn., Assn. U.S. Army, Sigma Xi, Sigma Chi, Atmos. Clubs: University (pres. 1950-51); Annapolis (Md.); Engineers (N.Y.C.); Troy (N.Y.) Country, Albany Camera. Home: Cincinnati, OH.

LEE, HAROLD, lawyer; b. Grand View, Ind., Feb. 11, 1889; s. Otto V. and Sabina R. (May) L.; grad. Mo. Mil. Acad., Mexico, Mo., 1907; student U. of Kan., law, 1908-10, LL.B., Epworth U., Oklahoma City, 1911; special student Columbia, 1920; m. Helen Mitchell, Dec. 18, 1912. Admitted to Okla. bar, 1912, N.Y. bar, 1920, bar of U.S. Supreme Court, 1932, U.S. Court of Appeals for D.C., 1939; clerk of Superior Court, Oklahoma City, 1913-14; mem. law firm Paul & Lee, 1915; judge of Municipal Court, 1916-17; mem. law firm Choate & Lee, N.Y. City, 1920-31; asst. solicitor N.Y. Title & Mortgage Co., New York, 1931-34; dep. gen. mgr. Home Owners Loan Corp., Washington, D.C., 1934-39; gen. counsel Fed. Home Loan Bank Adminstrn., Fed. Savings & Loan Ins. Corp., Home Owners' Loan Corp., Wash., D.C., 1939-46; Gov. Federal Home Loan Bk. System, Washington, D.C., 1946-48; spl. asst. to atty. gen. of U.S. in charge overseas Branch, U.S. Dept. Justice, Munich, Ger., from 1948. Served as capt. Okla. Nat. Guard on Mexican border, 1916-17; capt., maj. U.S. Army, 1917-19; served with 162 F.A. Brig. A.E.F.; asst. judge adv., Dist. of Paris, after Armistice; later lt. col. F.A., U.S. Reserves. Mem. ABA, Fed. (pres. 1947) and Okla. State bar assns., Phi Gamma Delta, Phi Delta Phi. Democrat. Mason (32 deg.). Club: Belle Haven (Alexandria, Va.). Home: Alexandria, Va. Deceased.

LEE, JOSEPH A., business exec.; b. Chicago, Nov. 8, 1887; s. Allen and Lydia (Hargrave) L.; student, Yale, 1909; m. Barbara Senseney, Apr. 14, 1919; 1 son, Joseph A. Sales mgr. Fleischman Co., N.Y.C., 1912-1929; 1st v.p. and dir. Standard Brands, Inc., N.Y.C., 1929-30, became v.p., 1930, 1st v.p., gen. sales mgr. and dir. Trustee Am. Bakers Foundn., Chicago; treas. and dir. Am. Inst. of Baking, Chicago. Republican. Episcopalian. Clubs: Yale (New York); Round Hill (Greenwich). Home: Greenwich, Conn. †

LEE, M. O., textile co. exec.; b. Indianola, Nebr., Nov. 11, 1911; s. Rual O. and Mayme (Mann) L.; m. Rosalie Hakel, Nov. 27, 1935 (dec.); children—William Frank, Regina Ann, Mary Sylvia, John Manford. With VF Corp. (formerly Vanity Fair Mills, Inc.), Reading, Pa., from 1942, v.p., 1948-59, pres., 1959-82, dir., chmn. bd., 1965-69, chmn., 1969-82, chief exec. officer, 1969-75; dir. Nat. Central Bank, First Nat. Bank Mobile. Mem. adv. com. Profl. Golf Assn. Clubs: Athelstan, Lakewood Golf (Mobile); Country of N.C. (Pinehurst) Berkshire Country (Reading); Dunes (Cal.) Country; Hemisphere, Metropolitan (N.Y.C.); Kansas City (Mo.). Home: Wyomissing, Pa. Died Mar. 5, 1982.

LEE, MAURICE WENTWORTH, economics educator, consultant; b. Chgo., Mar. 30, 1912; s. Judson F. and Jesse R. (Bacon) L.; m. Florence Quinn, June 9, 1936 (dec. Jan. 1972); children: Denis W., Sally M.; m. Nancy Mearns, Mar. 7, 1973; children: Terry Elizabeth, Laura Kathryn, Matthew Wentworth. Student, Denison U., 1929-32; B.S., Ill. Inst. Tech., 1933; Ph.D., U. Chgo., 1939. Instr. U. Chgo., 1936-38; asst. prof., then assoc. prof. Utah State U., Logan, 1938-41; exec. asst. adminstr. Office Price Adminstrn., Washington, 1941-46; dean, prof. econs. Wash. State U., Pullman, 1946-56, U. N.C., Chapel Hill, from 1956; dir. Nat. Bur. Econ. Research, N.Y.C., 1958-78, Joint Council Econ. Edn., N.Y.C., 1959-70; cons. to bd. govs. Fed. Res. System, Dept. treasury, 1960—. Author: Macroeconomics: Economic Fluctuations, 1955, Toward Economic Stability, 1966. Fellow Royal Econ. Soc.; mem. Am. Econ. Assn., So. Econ. Assn., Am. Assn. Coll. Schs. of Bus. (pres. 1961-62). Home: Chapel Hill, N.C. Died Mar. 16, 1985.

LEE, WALLACE ORISON, utility exec.; b. Edgefield, S.C., Nov. 8, 1889; s. Orison Perry and Rosa Ada (Whittle) L.; spl. student Butler U., 1920; m. Faye Elizabeth Springer, June 14, 1911; children—Virginia Luana (dec.), Mary Louise, Wallace Orison, Nancy Yvonne. Salesman Indpls. Power & Light Co., 1910-28, personnel dept., 1929, v.p. in charge personnel and pub. relations, 1936-50, senior vice pres., from 1950, dir., from 1937; president Hoosier Engring. Co., Inc. (Columbus, Ohio), Louisville Postal Realty Co., Northwestern Postal Realty Company. Director A.R.C. Day Nursery, Flanner House, C. C. Fairbanks Meml. Assn.; mem. bd. mgrs., trustee YMCA; mem. bd., dean Boy Scout Commrs.;

mem. adv. com. Juvenile Ct.; trustee Central State Hosp.; mem. athletic adv. bd. Butler U. Served as 1st lt. 2d Inf., U.S. Army. Decorated Order of Crown (Romania). Mem. Nat. Assn. Power Engrs., Elec. League, Edison Inst., Ind. C. of C., Elec. Assn., Ind. Hist. Soc., Ind. Personnel Assn., Alpha Phi Omega, Blue Key. Republican. Mem. Christian Ch. Mason. Clubs: Athletic, Columbia, Woodstock Country, Ulen Country, Indianapolis Country, Athenaeum, Riviera, Gyro (Indpls.). Home: Indianapolis, IN. †

LEECH, GEORGE L., bishop; b. Ashley, Pa., May 21, 1890; s. William Dillon and Helen Mary (Simons) L.; educated St. Charles Seminary, Overbrook, Pa., 1913-20; J.C.D., Cath. U. of America, 1922. Ordained priest R.C. Ch.; sec. Apostolic Delegation, Washington, 1923-29; rector S. Patrick's Church, Pottsville, Pa., 1929-35; apptd. titular bishop of Mela and auxiliary bishop of Harrisburg, Pa., July 6, 1935; bishop of Harrisburg 1935-71. Address: Harrisburg, Pa. Died Mar. 1985.

LEEDY, HALDON A., research executive; b. Fremont, O., Apr. 15, 1910; s. A. Earl and Alta Mae (Stull) L.; B.A., N. Central Coll., Naperville, Ill., 1933; M.A., U. of Ill., 1935, Ph.D., 1938; m. Margaret Raynor, Aug. 17, 1940; children—Marilyn, Haldon, Barbara. Assistant in physics, University of Illinois, 1933-38; physicist, Armour Research Foundation, in Chicago, Illinois 1938-44, co-chmn. physics research, 1944-45. chmn., 1945-48, dir., 1948-50, exec. v.p., dir. 1950-63; pres., chief exec. officer Nuclear-Chicago Corp. (a subsidiary of G. D. Searle & Co.), Des Plaines, 1963-67, also dir.; v.p. G. D. Searle & Company; member of board of dirs. Signode Corp., Stewart-Warner Corporation, Link-Belt Co., Business Capital Corp.; v.p. adminstrv. affairs U. Ill., 1971-72. Mem. Atomic Power Investigating Commn., State Ill. Trustee Chgo. Planetarium Soc., Chgo. Theol. Sem., N. Central Coll. Chgo. Theol. Sem. Fellow I., A., Acoustical Soc. Am.; mem. Midwestern Air Pollution Prevention Assn. (pres. 1951-60), Am. Standards Assn., Chgo. Assn. Commerce and Industry, Am. Phys. Soc., Inst. Am. Strategy (dir.), Am. Inst. Physics, Ill. Acad. Scis., Am. Soc. Testing Materials (chmn. com. C-20 on acoustical materials, 1949-58), North Central Coll. Alumni Assn. (pres. 1960-62), Physics Club Chgo., Sigma Xi, Sigma Pi Sigma, Tau Beta Pi. Clubs: University (N.Y.C.); Cosmos (Washington); Executives, University, Economic (Chgo.) Contbr. jours. Home: LaGrange, Ill. Died Mar. 14, 1983.

LEEDY, PAUL FRANCIS, former educator; b. Battle Creek, Mich., May 10, 1903; s. Francis I. and Loretta (Dunne) L.; m. Thelma Farlin, Sept. 6, 1925. A.B., U. Mich., 1930, A.M., 1931, Ph.D., 1940, A.B. in L.S, 1946; LL.D., Bowling Green State U., 1971. Asst. English U. Mich., 1930-31, teaching fellow, 1932-38, 39-40; faculty Bowling Green (Ohio) State U., 1938-69, prof. English, 1946-69, librarian, 1943-56, dir. library, 1956-61, prof., chmn. dept. library sci., 1946-61, provost, 1961-68, trustee prof. English, 1968-69, provost emeritus, prof. emeritus, 1969-83. Mem. Modern Lang. Assn. Am., A.L.A., A.A.U.P., Ohio Library Assn. (chmn. coll. and univ. sect. 1960-61), Ohio Coll. Assn. (chmn. library sect. 1953-54), Phi Kappa Phi, Alpha Tau Omega, Omicron Delta Kappa. Club: Torch (Toledo) (pres. 1965-66). Home: Bowling Green, Ohio. Died May 11, 1983; interred Meml. Park, Battle Creek, Mich.

LEEK, SYBIL, astrologer, author; b. Stroke-Upon-Trent, Eng. Author: numerous books including Diary of a Witch, 1968, Complete Art of Witchcraft, 1971, Reincarnation, The Second Chance, 1974, Driving Out the Devils, 1975, Herbs, Medicinal and Mystical, 1975, (with Stephen B. Leek) Ring of Magic Islands, 1976, (with Bert Sugar) The Assassination Chain, 1976, Moonsigns, 1977; columnist: (with Bert Sugar) numerous books including Palm Beach Life mag. Address: Melbourne Beach, Fla. Died Oct. 26, 1982.

LEEN, WALTER VICTOR, lawyer; b. Chgo., Jan. 13, 1911; s. Harry and Sadie (Izaks) L.; m. Molly S. Sheras, June 26, 1948; 1 dau., Barbara Ellen. Student, U. Mich., 1928-31; Ph.B., U. Chgo., 1933, J.D., 1934. Bar: Ill. bar 1934. Asso. firm Sidney J. and Arthur Wolf, Chgo., 1934-39; spl. atty. Ill. Dept. Revenue, 1939-41; legal counsel Golan Wine, Inc., Los Angeles, 1942; individual practice, Chgo., 1946-47; staff asst. Law Sch., U. Chgo., 1947-48; legal counsel Spl. Constrn. Staff, 1948-50, mem. legal dept., 1950-53, asso. legal counsel, 1953-62, sec. bd. trustees, gen. counsel, 1962-77, spl. asst. to pres., 1977-78, individual practice, Chgo., from 1979. Bd. editors: U. Chgo. Law Rev, 1933-34. Bd. dirs., officer Country Home Convalescent Children, 1962-78; trustee Chgo. Sinai Congregation, from 1976, treas., from 1979. Served with USAAF, 1942-46. Mem. Am. Bar Assn., Fed. Bar Assn., Nat. Assn. Coll. and Univ. Attys. (a founder), Ill. Bar Assn., Chgo. Bar Assn., Order Wig and Robe, Zeta Beta Tau, Phi Sigma Delta. Club: Quadrangle (Chgo.). Address: Chicago, Ill.

LEFFEL, CHARLES POAGUE, elec. appliances co. exec.; b. Evanston, Ill., May 30, 1928; s. Philip Clark and Catherine Smith (Poague) L.; m. Grace Ann Hartnett, June 2, 1962; 1 dau., Kay. A.B., Amherst Coll., 1950. Salesman Goodbody & Co., Chgo., 1950-51, Internat. Paper Co., Cleve., 1951-54; exec. v.p. No. Electric Co., 1957-67, pres., 1967-72; v.p., pres. non-Sunbeam domestic consumer products group Sunbeam Corp., Oak Brook, Ill., 1974-76, exec. v.p. parent co., 1976-77, pres. domestics consumer products group, 1976-77, pres. corp., from 1977, also dir. Bd. mgrs. Chgo. Boys Club Camps, Robert E. Wood Boys Club. Served with AUS. Clubs: Metropolitan (Chgo.), Racquet (Chgo.); Glen View (Golf, Ill.); Deke (N.Y.C.). Home: Chicago, Ill.

LEFKOWITZ, NAT, talent agency executive; b. Bklyn., July 24, 1905; s. Henry and Rose (Berkowitz) L.; m. Sally Feigelman, Feb. 27, 1932; children: Dorothy Beth (Mrs. Burton L. Litwin), Rona Carol Lefkowitz Pinkus, Helene Andrea (Mrs. Robert D. Nachtigall). Diploma, Coll. City N.Y., 1922-26; LL.M., Bklyn. Law Sch., 1938. Bar: N.Y. bar 1938; C.P.A., N.Y. Accountant Gottheimer, Getz & Co., 1924-26; comptroller, treas., exec. v.p., treas. William Morris Agy., Inc., N.Y.C., 1927-69, pres., 1969-76, co-chmn., 1976-81, chmn. emeritus, 1981-83, also dir. Active amusement and entertainment divs. United Jewish Appeal and Fedn. Jewish Philanthropies, 1945-83, chmn. television industry's campaign for fedn., 1968, recipient award in honor entertainment div., 1975; Trustee Will Rogers Hosp., O'Donnell Meml. Research Labs.; Mem. Arts and Entertainment Bd. N.Y.C. Partnership, Inc. Recipient Human Rights award Anti-Defamation League, 1969; Man of Year award Variety Club Found., N.Y., 1978. Mem. Motion Picture Pioneers, Nat. Acad. TV Arts and Scis., Variety Clubs Internat, B'nai B'rith. Jewish. Clubs: City Athletic, Friars, Dellwood Country. Home: New York, N.Y. Died Sept. 4, 1983.

LEGAULT, MAURICE JEAN, holding co. exec.; b. Montreal, Que., Can., May 31, 1926; s. Adolphe and (Georgette); m. Francoise Bastien, June 1, 1946; children—Monique, Robert, Normand. Student, Fortin Bus. Coll., 1940-41, Sir George Williams U., 1942-43; M.M.C., Western U., 1959, M.T.C., 1964. Mgr. Pure Spring Bottling Co., L'Epiphanie, 1952-54; sales supr. for Montreal, La Brasserie Labatt Limitee, 1954-56, sales mgr., 1956-58, territorial sales mgr., 1958-62, gen. sales mgr., 1962-65, v.p. mktg., 1965-69, v.p., gen. mgr., 1969-71, pres., gen. mgr., 1971-75, pres., 1975-77; sr. v.p. John Labatt Ltd., Montreal, from 1977; dir. Urgel Bourgie Ins. Co., La Brasserie Labatt Ltee, Ogilvie Mills Ltd. Bd. dirs. Canadian Cancer Soc., Forum for Young Canadians, Found. Hautes Etudes Commerciales, Theatre de Marjolaine; Exec. Can. Safety Council. Served with RCAF, 1944-45. Mem. Found. Maisonneuve-Rosemont (bd. dirs.), World Citizens Que. (mem. govs. com.), Traveling Salesmen Assn. Montreal C. of C. Roman Catholic. Clubs: de Golf Laval sur-le-lac, de Golf Longchamp, St. Denis, Hunting and Fishing of Lac d'Argent, K.C, Kiwanis, Profl. Golfers Assn. Home: Verdun PQ Canada.

LEH, JOHN HENRY, banker; b. Allentown, Pa., May 24, 1899; s. John and Irene (Keck) L.; A.B., Princeton U., 1921; m. Dorothea Backenstoe, Sept. 8, 1921 (dec. 1955); 1 dau., Jean Robinson Graham; m. 2d, Eleanore Bear Pope, Feb. 16, 1957; stepchildren—Robert Bear, William Henry, Richard Warren, James Webster. Dir. Second Nat. Bank, Allentown, 1928-54, v.p., 1941-54; with First Nat. Bank, Allentown, 1954-85, v.p., mem. exec. com., 1954-75, chmn. bd., 1968-75, chmn. emeritus, 1975-85; partner H. Leh & Co., 1921-78, Leh Bros., from 1932; dir., sec. Internat. Film Found., 1946-71. Treas., Allentown Redevel. Authority, 1956-73; mem. Lehigh-Northampton Airport Authority, 1946-72, chmn., 1955-70, chmn. emeritus, 1970-85; pres. Great Valley council Girl Scouts U.S.A., 1961-64, mem. nat. equipment com., 1960-70; mem. bd., exec. com. Pa. div. Am. Cancer Soc., 1962-63, Pa. crusade chmn., 1962. Trustee, Cedar Crest Coll., 1963-71, mem. exec. com., treas., 1965-71. Served with U.S. Army, 1917-18. Recipient Distinguished Aviation Citizens award, 1964; Founders award Lehigh U., 1963; Distinguished Service award Allentown C. of C., 1967; We Point With Pride award FAA, 1972; Service award Princeton Alumni Council, 1973. Lutheran (past deacon, elder). Kiwanian. Home: Allentown, Pa. Died June 6, 1985.

LEHMAN, BENJAMIN HARRISON, prof. English, writer; b. Mullan, Ida., Oct. 20, 1889; s. Abraham and Hannah (Levinger) L.; B.A., Harvard, 1911, A.M., 1918, Ph.D., 1920; m. Gladys Collins, Dec. 31, 1915 (div. 1928); children—Hal, Collins (dec.); m. 2d, Judith Anderson, May 18, 1937 (div. 1939). Asst. prof. English, U. of Idaho, 1911-14, Wash. State Coll., 1914-17; instr., Harvard, 1917-20; asso. prof. English, U. of Calif., 1920-28, prof. from 1928, chmn. dept. dramatic art, 1941-44, chmn. dept. English, 1944-49. Lecturer, Sch. Pacific and Oriental Affairs, U. of Hawaii, summer, 1933, U. of Hawaii, summer, 1935. Mem. Phi Beta Kappa. Awarded Sohier prize, 1911, Bowdoin prize, 1920 (both from Harvard). Author: Wild Marriage (novel), 1925; The Lordly Ones (novel), 1927; Carlyle's Theory of the Hero, 1928. Contbr. fiction and articles to mags. and scholarly journals and series. Home: Berkeley, Calif. †

LEHMAN, HARVEY CHRISTIAN, educator; b. Allen Co., Kan., Mar. 13, 1889; s. John S. and Mary A. (Kistler) L.; A.B., U. of Kansas, 1912, M.A., B.S., 1913; Ph.D., U. of Chicago, 1925; m. Vera Marjorie Simmons, Dec. 21, 1927 (died Aug. 9, 1939); children—Paul Robert, Helen Joyce; married second Lydia Meisel Class, Aug. 20, 1949. Began as teacher, Reno County (Kan.) high sch., 1910-11; prin., Hiawatha (Kansas) high school, 1913-14; teacher, Mayville (N.D.) State Normal Sch., 1914-16; teacher, Hibbing (Minn.) Junior Coll., 1916-23; asst. prof. edn., U. of Kan., 1923-27; asso. prof. psychology, Ohio U., Athens, OH., 1927-35, prof. psychology, from 1935, Fellow A.A.A.S.; mem. Am. Psychological Assn., Nat. Soc. for Study of Edn., Am. Ednl. Research Assn., Midwestern Psychol. Assn., Am. Asso. Advancement Edn. Served as cpl., Battery E, 62d Regiment C.A.C., San Francisco, World War I. Author: The Psychology of Play Activities (written in collaboration with P. A. Witty), A.S. Barnes & Co., 1927; numerous articles in the fields of psychology and education; recent publications deal with man's creative achievement in relation to chronological age. Home: Athens, Ohio. †

LEHMAN, IRVING GEORGE, artist; b. Russia, Jan. 1, 1900; s. Aaron and Pearl (Feller) L.; student Nat. Acad.; m. Martha Weingard, June 26, 1934. Painter, sculptor; exhibited ACA Gallery, 1934, Uptown Gallery, 1938, 39, 40 Seattle Mus., Chgo., Art Inst., Albany Inst. History and Art, Bklyn. Museum's Internat. water-color shows and sculpture shows, Harry Salpeter Gallery, 1947, 48, wood sculpture Whitney Mus., 1949, New Sch. Social Research, 1948-49, Riverside Mus., N.Y.C., 1948, 49, Bklyn. Mus. Water Color Show, 1949, oils Am. Abstract Artists, 1950, woodcut and sculpture Nebr. Art Assn., 1950, Bibliotheque Nationale, Paris, 1951; one-man shows: Phila. Art Alliance, 1950, Harry Salpeter Gallery, 1950, 54, 55, Oxford U., 1950, Mus. of Columbia (S.C.), 1958, The Gallery Ten, Mt. Vernon, N.Y., 1959, Gladstone Galleries, Woodstock, N.Y., 1961-64, 66, Berkshire Playhouse Gallery, Stockbridge, Mass., 1963, Knapnick Galleries, N.Y.C., 1962, Gallery One, Hillsdale, N.Y., 1966, 67, Atelier 5, Canaan, N.Y., 1969, 70, Gallery at Shelter Rock Library, Albertson, N.Y., 1973, Simon's Rock, Great Barrington, Mass., 1973, Red Rock Gallery, East Chatham, N.Y., Cordy Gallery, N.Y.C., 1977; exhibited Nocturne, Worship, Evening Traffic, Mardi Gras, Fog, Evening, at Harry Salpeter Gallery, 1947, Paris, Denmark, Belgium, Italy, Munich, 1951; Italy, Japan, 1955; exhibited at Berkshire Mus., Pittsfield, Mass., 1977, Union Carbide Gallery, N.Y.C., 1977, Parsons Sch. Design, N.Y.C., 1977, Patterson (N.J.) Coll., 1977, Pittsfield Community Arts Ctr., 1985; works included U.S. internat. traveling show in Europe, 1951-83; metal sculpture Passing Forms in Kaback collection, 1968. Recipient Water Color Soc. Ala. award, 1948, Kate W. Arms Meml. prize for print in miniature sec. 33d ann. exhbn. Soc. Am. Etchers, Gravers, Lithographers and Woodcutters Am., 1947; hon. mention Washington Watercolor, 1949; Terry Art Inst. award for oils, 1952; Victor Wyler Found. award for oils, 1958, Mary and Gustave Kellner award sculpture Bklyn. Soc. Artists, 1959; Bklyn. Soc. Artists 44th Ann. award for oils, 1961. Mem. Am. Abstract Artists, Audubon Artists, Am. Soc. Contemporary Artists. Home: East Chatham, N.Y. Died Sept. 18, 1983; interred Red Rock, East Chatham, N.Y.

LEHMANN, LOTTE, soprano; b. Perleberg, Germany, February 27, 1888; d. Carl and Marie (Schuster) Lehmann; m. Otto Krause, Apr. 28, 1926 (died January 22, 1939). Opera and concert singer; visited United States, 1930 and 31; member Metropolitan, San Francisco and Chicago civic opera companies; made debut Met. Opera Co., Jan. 11, 1934, as Sieglinde in "Die Walkuere," scored notable success as Eva, in "Die Meistersinger," Die Marschallin in "Der Rosenkavalier," and other standard operas. Awarded hon. membership State Opera, Vienna; Chevalier Legion of Honor (France); Medal of Art (Sweden); Ring of Honor (Vienna Philharmonic Orchestra). Author: Eternal Flight, 1937; Midway in My Song, 1938; More Than Singing; My Many Lives, 1948.†

LEHMKUHL, JOAKLM, manufacturing executive; b. Bergen, Norway, Sept. 22, 1895; s. Kristofer and Magdalene (Michelsen) L.; grad. Bergen Tekniske Skole, 1915; B.S., Harvard, 1918, Mass. Inst. Tech., 1919; m. Marie Butenschon, 1931; children—Kristofer Joakim, Brita Marie. Came to U.S., 1940. Pres., dir. U.S. Timex Corp., Waterbury, 1942-73, chmn. bd., 1957-73. Lutheran. Clubs: Cotton Bay; University (N.Y. C.); Round Hill Country (Greenwich, Conn.). Home: Nassau, Bahamas. Died Oct. 15, 1984.

LEIB, KARL ELLAS, educator; b. Marengo, Ia., Dec. 15, 1888; s. Joseph Creighton and Laura (Buriff) L.; A.B., Stanford, 1916, J.D., 1923; m. Rachel Smith, Dec. 28, 1917; children—Laura Louise (Mrs. Martine Petersen), Evelyn Eileen (Mrs. John McFaul). Mem. faculty U. Wash., 1924-29; prof. commerce U. Ia., 1929-57, emeritus, head dept. labor and mgmt., 1950-57, acting dir. Bur. Labor Mgmt., 1950-54; vis. prof. mgmt. Univ. of Illinois, 1957-59, sch. of bus. Southern Illinois University, 1959-61. Mem. Nat. Collegiate Athletic Assn. (pres. 1946-49), Soc. Advancement Mgmt., Acad. Mgmt., Am. Econ. Assn., Beta Alpha Psi, Beta Gamma Sigma, Delta Sigma Pi. Elk, Rotarian.†

LEICHLITER, VAN HANDLIN, retired manufactured executive; b. Mt. Braddock, Pa., Sept. 9, 1906; s. Braden Boyd and Nana (Handlin) L.; B.S., Pa. State Coll., 1930; m. Helen Rodgers, Nov. 26, 1936; 1 son, Van Handlin. Mill metallurgist Am. Steel & Wire Co., Worcester, Mass., 1930-34, metallurgist, Cleve., 1934-35, dist. metallurgist, 1935, asst. supt. Newburgh works, Cleve., 1936-39, supt. wire mills Cuyahoga works, 1939-41, supt. wire mills So. works, Worcester, 1941-44, div. supt., 1944, gen. supt., 1945-50, asst. v.p. ops., Cleve., 1950-53, v.p. ops., 1953-56, pres. Am. Steel and Wire div., Cleve., 1956-64; v.p. wire ops. U.S. Steel Corp., Pitts., 1964-70. Hon. v.p. Boy Scouts Am., Cleve.; bd. dirs. Cleve. Mus Arts Assn.; v.p., trustee Coronary Club, Inc.; hon. trustee John Carroll U.; trustee Lake Erie (Ohio) Coll., Coll. Wooster,

Ednl. Research Council Am., Fenn Ednl. Found. Recipient David Ford McFarland award Pa. State U., 1956, Distinguished Alumnus award, 1959; Distinguished Service award Cleve. C. of C., 1964. Mem. Am. Iron and Steel Inst., Am. Soc. Metals, Penn State Alumni Assn., Alpha Phi Sigma, Delta Chi. Clubs: Masons (33 deg.); Union, Fifty (Cleve.); Pepper Pike. Home: Shaker Heights, Ohio. Dec. Dec. 9, 1983.

LEIDY, PAUL ALLEN, educator; b. Detroit, Sept. 5, 1888; s. Clarence Fruit and Emma (Brown) L.; A.B., U. of Mich., 1909, A.M., 1911, J.D., 1924; m. Kathryn Breymann, Oct. 16, 1915; children—Barbara (Mrs. James H. Mulchay), John Breymann. Asst. sec., Toledo Commerce Club, 1911-12; sec. Jackson (Mich.) C. of C., 1913-15; sec.-treas., Mich. Drop Forge Co., Pontiac, 1916-22; admitted to Mich. bar, 1924, and Ohio bar, 1925; associated, Miller & Brady, attys., Toledo, 1924-25, partner Miller, Brady, Yager & Leidy, 1925-26; prof. of law and sec., law sch., U. of Mich., 1926-45, prof. of law and placement dir., from 1945; asso. law dept. The Quaker Oats Co., Chicago, 1943-45. Mem. Am., Mich. and Chicago bar assns., Phi Delta Phi, Order of the Coif. Republican. Conglist. Clubs: Rotary (Ann Arbor); Union League (Chicago). Author: Cases on Torts, 1935; Cases on Torts (with M. L. Plant), 1949. Home: Ann Arbor, Mich. †

LEIGH, THOMAS WATKINS, lawyer; b. Winnsboro, La., Apr. 8, 1903; s. Benjamin Watkins and Olive (Buckingham) L.; m. Louise Grisham Kellogg, July 7, 1942. LL.B., La. State U., 1924. Bar: La. bar 1924. Pvt. practice, 1924-29; mem. firm Theus, Grisham, Davis & Leigh, Monroe, La., from 1929; dir. First Nat. Bank West Monroe. Mem. La. Gov.'s Spl. Commn. to Study Needs Higher Edn. La., 1954-56; mem. Pub. Affairs Research Council; del. La. Constl. Conv., 1973; mem. Gov. La. Spl. Tidelands Adv. Com., 1964-72; chmn. La. Mineral Bd., 1966-72; Bd. dirs. Council for Better La.; mem. bd. suprs. La. State U., 1940-60, chmn., 1948-50. Served as lt. comdr. USNR, 1942-45. Fellow Am. Bar Found.; mem. ABA (ho. of dels. 1958-80, bd. govs. 1975-78), La. Bar Assn. (pres. 1954-55, gov.), Am. Counsel Probate Attys., Am. Coll. Trial Lawyers, Scribes, Am. Law Inst., La. Law Inst. (council, v.p.), Internat. Assn. Ins. Counsel, Am. Judicature Soc., Order of Coif, Stair Soc. (Edinburgh), Gamma Eta Gamma, Theta Xi. Episcopalian (vestryman). Clubs: Army and Navy (Washington); Boston (New Orleans), Internat. House (New Orleans), Pickwick (New Orleans). Home: Monroe, LA.

LEIGHTON, PHILIP ALBERT, univ. prof.; b. Los Angeles, Calif., Aug. 9, 1897; s. Charles Albert and Marie (Plattenburg) L.; A.B., Pomona Coll., 1920, A.M., 1923; A.M., Harvard, 1925, Ph.D., 1927; Univ. Munich, 1927-28; London U., 1937; m. Susan Case, July 6, 1922; 1 son, Philip Doddridge; m. 2d, Maria Blaisdell, Aug. 11, 1940. Instr. chemistry, Harvard, 1927; Sheldon traveling fellow abroad, 1927-28; instr. chemistry, Stanford, 1928-29; asst. prof., 1929-32, asso. prof., 1932-37, prof. 1937-54, dept. head 1939-51; chmn. sch. physical sciences, 1941-42, dean, School Physical Sciences, 1946-49. Lalor fellow, London U., 1937; lieut. col., Chem. Warfare Service, 1943, col., 1945. Dir. of operations Dugway Proving Grounds. Awarded Legion of Merit, 1945. Mem. Am. Chem. Soc., A.A.A.S., Optical Soc. America, Armed Forces Chemical Association (dir. at large). Alpha Chi Sigma, Phi Lambda Upsilon, Sigma Xi, Phi Beta Kappa. Club: Bohemian (San Francisco). Mason. Author: The Photochemistry of Gases (with W. A. Noyes, Jr.), 1941. The Determination of the Mechanism of Photochemical Reactions, 1938. Home: Palo Alto, Calif. Died Aug. 2, 1983.

LEIGHTON, RALPH WALDO, educator; b. Ida Grove, Ia., Apr. 27, 1888; s. John Harrington and Abbie (McPhillips) L.; A.B., Coll. of Idaho, 1925; Ph.D., U. of Ore., 1931; D. Sc. (hon.), Coll. of Ida., 1941; m. Lucia Marie Strub, Nov. 21, 1914; 1 son, Jack Richard. Sch. prin. Idaho City, Ida., 1914, Bruneau, Ida., 1915; supt. of schs., Kuna, Ida., 1916-22, supt. Council, Ida., 1922-24; faculty mem., athletic coach Coll. of Ida., 1926-28; exec. sec. research U. of Ore., 1931-38; prof. edn., U. of Ore., since 1934; dean and dir. physical edn., Ore. State System of Higher Edn. 1937-46; dean Sch. Physical Edn., U. of Ore., since 1937. State dir. physical fitness, Office of Civilian Defense, 1941-45; dir. physical training, Army specialized training, 1942-44. Chmn. Ore. Edn. Policies Commn. for pub. sch. and higher edn., 1938-43; Ore. State Joint Com. on Health and Phys. Fitness; adv. bd. ednl. problems of parks. Dir. Crater Lake Sch. of Appreciation of Nature, 1947. Mem. N.E.A., Am. Assn. for Health, Phys. Edn. and Recreation (state, sect., and nat. divs.). Republican. Elk. Club: Kiwanis. Author: Studies of Laboratory Methods of Teaching (part I), 1935; Studies to Determine Relative Achievement of Students at Different Potentiality Levels, 1933; (with B. W. DeBusk) A Study of Pupil Achievement and Attendant Problems, 1931; Studies of Appreciation of Nature at Crater Lake National Park, 1939; Samuel Alexander's Doctrine of Value as Emergent in Nature, contbr. to Studies in Philosophical Naturalism, 1931. Editor: Studies in Appreciation of Art, 1934. Engaged in research in physical performance. Home: Eugene, Oreg. †

LEINBACH, FREDERICK HAROLD, merchant; b. Irving, Ill., Apr. 22, 1901; s. Rev. Samuel and Edith Beatrice (Luick) L.; B.S., Ia. State Coll., 1926; M.S., Colo. State Coll., 1927, Ph.D., Cornell U., 1940; m. Alice Virginia Curry, Oct. 9, 1927; children—F. Harold, Paul Curry, Mary Edith. Instr. animal husbandry, Colo. State U., 1927-28, asst. prof., 1928-31, asso. prof., 1931-36; instr. and fellow in agr., Cornell, 1936-37; asso. prof. Colo. State, 1937-38; prof. animal husbandry, U. Md., 1938-40, prof. and head dept., 1940-46, asst. dean agr. and head animal husbandry dept., 1946-Jan. 1947; pres. S.D. State Coll. of Agr. and Mech. Arts, Brookings 1947-51; sr. partner Leinbach Equipment. Dir. Nat. Livestock Conservation Program, Chgo., 1943-44, Trustee Westminster Found. Minn. Fellow A.A.A.S., mem. Buffalo Assn. Commerce (pres. 1955-56), Minn. Implement Dealers Assn. (chmn. legislative com. 1959). Delta Chi, Alpha Zeta, Gamma Sigma Delta, Lambda Gamma Delta, Phi Kappa Phi, Sigma Xi, Scabbard and Blade, Pi Kappa Delta. Presbyn. (synod com. on christian edn.). Mason (Shriner, K.T.). Clubs: Rotary (pres. 1954-56), Block and Bridle (past nat. pres.). Home: Buffalo, Minn. Died June 26, 1984.

LEISURE, GEORGE STANLEY, lawyer; b. Slater, Mo., Aug. 14, 1889; s. Joseph A. and Nancy A. (Keeton) L.; Ph.B., U. Chgo., 1914; LL.B., Harvard, 1917; LL.D., Friends U., 1937; m. Lucille E. Pelouze, Oct. 27, 1923; children—George S., David B., Peter K., Michael W. Law practice office Charles E. Hughes, N.Y.C., 1919; asst. U.S. atty. So. Dist. N.Y., 1925-27; was chief criminal div. Office U.S. Atty.; spl. dept. atty. gen. N.Y. in prosecution election frauds, 1928, chief asst. bankruptcy inquiry, conducted by Assn. Bar City N.Y., County Lawyers' Assn. and Bronx County Bar Assn., 1929-30; mem. firm Donovan, Leisure, Newton & Irvine, N.Y.C. Washington, Paris, France and London; chief asst. in case U.S. vs. Harry M. Daugherty, former atty. gen. U.S. and Thomas W. Miller, former alien property custodian, 1927; def. counsel Waialua Agrl. Co. in Christian vs. Waialua, Honolulu, 1929; asso. with Clarence Darrow in def. Fortescue-Massie case, Honolulu, 1932; def. counsel Joseph W. Harriman, pres. Harriman Nat. Bank, N.Y.C., 1934; of def. counsel E.I. du Pont de Nemours & Co. and Remington Arms Co. munitions investigation, Washington, 1934, U.S. vs. RKO Distbg. Corp., Warner Bros. and Paramount motion picture cos., St. Louis, 1935-36, U.S. vs. Standard Oil Co. and 23 other oil cos., 1937; chief def. counsel FTC vs. Cement Inst. and 75 cement cos., Washington, 1937-41, ICC vs. C. & O. Ry., Nickel Plate Ry. and Pere Marquette Ry., 1944; of counsel State of Ga. vs. Pa. R.R., et. al., Supreme Ct., Washington, and Mo. Pacific R.R. Reorgn., St. Louis, 1945. Chmn. bd. Children's Village; trustee Mo. Valley Coll.; past trustee Choate School. Served as pilot U.S. Army, World War I. Fellow, regent Am. Coll. Trial Lawyers; mem. Harvard Law Sch. Assn. N.Y.C. (past pres.), Choate Fathers Assn. (pres.), Am., N.Y. State, N.Y. County, N.Y.C. bar assns., Am. Legion, Sigma Alpha Epsilon. Republican. Episcopalian. Mason. Clubs: Harvard, Downtown Assn., River, Harvard Law, Downtown Athletic, N.Y. Athletic, N.Y. Yacht, India House, Creek (N.Y.C.); Manursing Island; Sleepy Hollow; Camp Fire Am.; Sakaigan Shooting Lodge (Can.); Everglades (Fla.). Home: New York City, N.Y. †

LEITHAUSER, DANIEL JAMES, general surgeon; b. Defiance, O., Oct. 11, 1887; s. Peter and Theresa (Blaser) L.; M.D., Ohio State U., 1915; m. Irene Paulson, Jan. 22, 1900; children—Gail Irene, Daniel James, Thomas Robert. Fellow Am. Coll. Surgeons. Author of scientific articles relating to field of work. Home: Grosse Pointe, Mich. †

LELAND, AUSTIN PORTER, publisher; b. St. Louis, Jan. 31, 1907; s. Frederick Austin and Henrietta (Brolaski) L.; m. Dorothy Lund, Apr. 24, 1935; children—Mary Talbot (Mrs. John Peters MacCarthy), Irene Austin (Mrs. Joseph H. Barzantny). A.B., Princeton, 1928. With investment firm, 1928-31; sec.-treas. Sta. List Pub. Co., St. Louis, 1931-39, pres., 1939-75; foreman Fed. Grand Jury for Eastern dist., Mo., 1952-53. Alumni trustee Princeton, 1950-54, hon. mem. alumni council, 1950-75, pres. class, 1928, 1963-68, mem. exec. com., from 1968; chmn. bd. Mary Inst. (country day sch. for girls), 1947-49; v.p. bd. trustees St. Louis Country Day Sch., 1960-62; trustee Nat. Trust Historic Preservation, also chmn. pub. affairs com., trustee nominating com.; trustee Jefferson Nat. Expansion Meml. Assn. Recipient Distinguished Service award for preservation Landmarks Assn. St. Louis, 1974. Mem. AIA (hon. asso. St. Louis chpt.), Def. Orientation Conf. Assn. (dir.), Landmarks Assn. St. Louis (chmn. Old Post Office landmark com.). Clubs: Traffic (N.Y.C.); Traffic (St. Louis), Princeton (St. Louis) (past pres., chmn. Princeton schs. and scholarship com.), Noonday (St. Louis), Press (St. Louis), St. Louis Country (St. Louis), University (St. Louis); University Cottage (Princeton, N.J.); Princeton (N.Y.C.); Belvedere (Charlevoix, Mich.) (trustee); Nassau (Princeton). Home: Ladue, Mo. Died Jan. 24, 1975; buried Bellefontaine Cemetery, St. Louis.

LE MAIRE, CHARLES, O'Guns, designer; b. Chgo., Apr. 22, 1898; s. Charles Frank and Lillian Margarete (Joneese) LeM.; student pub. schs.; m. Beatrice Hayman Goetz, Nov. 17, 1943. Vaudeville actor, 1915-17; costume designer Florenz Zeigfeld, 1919, Arthur Hammerstein operattas Wild Flower, Rosemarie, Sweet Adeline, 1919-25, George White Scandals, Earl Carroll Vanities, musicals Sons O'Guns, New Moon, Princess Charming, Fine and Dandy, Flying High, Hot Cha; exec. designer Brooks Costume Co., 1924-29, LeMaire Studios Designs, 1931-39. LeMaire Originals, 1940-41; dir. wardrobes 20th Century Fox Studio, 1943-59; designed for motion pictures and wholesale dress mfg.; watercolor represented permanent collection Los Angeles County; paintings exhibited Hammer Galleries, N.Y.C., 1958. Raymond Burr Galleries Beverly Hills, California, 1963, Gallery Five, Santa Fe, 1965. Curator fashion and costume department Los Angeles County, Hollywood Museum. Served as sgt., U.S. Army, World Wars I and II. Recipient 3 Oscars. Acad Motion Picture Arts and Scis., 3 awards Photoplay mag. Mem. Costume Designers Guild, United Scenic Artgeles Art Assn. bd. mem.), Am. Fedn. Television and Radio Artists. Died June 8, 1985.

LEMBECK, HARVEY, actor; b. N.Y.C., Apr. 15, 1923; s. Irving H. and Hannah (Reisner) L.; student U. Ala., 1940-41, Muhlenberg Coll., 1941-42; B.A., N.Y. U., 1947; m. Caroline Dubs, June 22, 1944; children—Michael Roberts, Helaine Jo. Actor appearing in motion pictures, television, and theatre; these credits include Mr. Roberts, Stalag 17, Wedding Breakfast, Phoenix 55; appeared in revivals of Oklahoma, South Pacific on Broadway; mem. stock cos. for Bells Are Ringing, Oliver; mem. nat. co. of Man of LaMancha; television credits include Sgt. Bilko show, Ensign O'Toole series; appeared in about 40 movies including Stalag 17, View from the Bridge, The Unsinkable Molly Brown, Love With a Proper Stranger, 7 beach films; dir. road co. of Mr. Roberts, Stalag 17. Flush revue for Las Vegas; creater, dir. free comedy workshop Harvey Lembeck Comedy Workshop; exec. J.J.H. Prodns. staff producer Bedford Prodns.; author movie scripts Why Do You Need Such Big Potatoes?. Why Me All the Time?. Make Mine Manila; with Richard Kiley performed scenes from Man of LaMancha for President Lyndon Johnson and Pres. of Italy at White House, 1967; producer, dir. A Nite at the Mark, San Francisco Revue; entertainment coordinator Eddie Cantor Charitable Found., Sugar Ray Robinson Youth Found. Served with AUS, USMCR, USNR, World War II. Recipient 2 Laurel awards for Stalag 17, 1953, Debut award Mr. Roberts, 1948. Mem. B'nai B'rith. Home: Beverly Hills, Calif. Died Jan. 6, 1982.

LEMCKE, NORMAN ROHDE, lawyer; b. N.Y.C., Dec. 3, 1894; s. Albert William and Dora (Rohde) L.; m. Elizabeth Bouteiller, Sept. 3, 1918 (dec.); 1 son, Norman Rohde. B.S., Amherst Coll., 1917; LL.B., N.Y. Law Sch., 1924, J.D., 1970. Bar: N.J. bar 1924. Asso. firm Smith & Slingerland, Newark, 1924-27; with Prudential Ins. Co. of Am., 1927, br. office atty., Montreal, 1927-28, regional appraiser, supr., Newark, 1928-34, mgr. regional office, Phila., 1934-35, N.Y.C., 1935-37, supr., West Coast, 1937-44, East Coast, 1944, asst. sec., Newark, 1944-46, gen. mgr., 1946-47, v.p., 1962-63, ret., 1963; mem. firm Eisner & Lemcke, Newark, 1964-68; dir. govt. sponsored Housing Enterprises Can., 1945-47. Served as ensign USN, 1917-19. Mem. Am., N.J. State bar assns., Phi Beta Kappa, Alpha Delta Phi, Delta Theta Phi. Methodist. Address: Mequon, Wis.

LEMMON, CLARENCE EUGENE, clergyman; b. Seward County, Neb., Feb. 2, 1888; s. Orion Augustus and Louverne (Houser) L.; A.B., Cotner Coll., Lincoln, Neb., 1913, D.D., 1926; U. of Neb., 1913-14; D.D., Culver-Stockton College, Canton, Missouri, 1925; m. Constance Harlan, June 10, 1913; 1 daughter, Bernice Allean (Mrs. Mark Hale). Ordained to the ministry of Disciples of Christ Church, 1913; pastor Ashland, Nebraska, 1913-14; Hastings, Nebraska, 1914-21, Hamilton Avenue Christian Church, St. Louis, Mo., 1921-30, Columbia, Mo., from 1930. Trustee Christian Coll., Columbia; trustee Pension Fund, Disciples of Christ Ch., from 1930. Mem. exec. com. United Christian Missionary Society, 1927-29; pres. Ministerial Alliance, St. Louis, 1927; del. to Universal Christian Conf. on Life and Work, Stockholm, 1925; dir. Ministers Life and Casualty Union, 1941. Chmn. Mo. Centennial Commn., Disciples of Christ, 1933-37; president Mo. State Conv., Disciples of Christ, 1939; pres. Internat. Conv. of Disciples of Christ, 1942-44. Trustee, Disciples Divinity House, Chicago, 1944. Author: The Art of Church Management, 1933; Religion Helps, 1941. Mason (32 degree), Kiwanian. Contbr. to World Call and Christian Evangelist. Home: Columbia, Mo. †

LEMMON, FRANK DAVIDSON, railroad exec.; b. N.Y. City, May 15, 1889; m. Hazel Mildeberger, Mar. 30, 1920; 1 dau., Barbara Evelyn. With Atlantic Coast Line R.R. Co. from 1903, now vice pres. and dir.; v.p., dir. Charleston & Western Carolina Ry. Co., Columbia, Newberry & Laurens R.R. Co., S.C.-Pacific Ry. Co., Atlantic Land & Improvement Co.; dir. Atlantic Coast Line Co., Fort Myers So. R.R. Co., Tampa So. R.R. Co., Peninsular & Occidental S.S. Co., Baltimore Steam Packet Co., Charleston Union Station Co., North Charleston Terminal Co., Columbia Union Station Co. Episcopalian. Club: Bankers (N.Y.C.). Home: Scarsdale, N.Y. †

LEMMON, GUY, executive; b. Shawnee, Kan., Mar. 5, 1889; A.B., Indiana University, Bloomington, Ind., 1912. President Hecker Products Corp. from 1937; dir. Best Foods, Inc. Served as 2d lt., 325th F.A., A.E.F., 1917-19. Mem. Phi Gamma Delta. Clubs: Executive, Westchester Country, Scarsdale Golf (New York, N.Y.). Home: Scarsdale, N.Y. Deceased.†

LEMMON, MARK, retired architect; b. Gainesville, Tex., Nov. 10, 1889; s. William Leonard and Cosette (Lipscomb) L.; B.A., U. Tex., 1912; B.S., Mass. Inst.

Tech., 1916; m. Maybelle Reynolds, Nov. 14, 1922; children—Mark Leonard, George Reynolds. Pvt. practice architecture, Dallas, from 1923; designs executed include Highland Park Presbyn Ch., 22-story Corrigan Tower, Perkins Sch. Theology for So. Meth. U., U. Tex. Southwestern Med. Sch., Southland Center (cons.), Sheraton Dallas Hotel (cons.); one of two architects Fed. Courthouse and Office Bldg., Dallas; sole architect St. Luke's Meth. Ch., Houston, pub. schs. in Marshall, Longview, Terrell, Grand Prairie, Port Arthur, Sherman and Dallas, Tex.; archtl. cons. Dallas Ind. Sch. Dist., So. Meth. U.; dir. Nat. City Bank of Dallas. Adv. com. Greater Dallas Planning Council; past mem. council, Highland Park. Served as 1st lt., C.E., U.S. Army, World War I; chmn. contract renegotiations bd. Southwestern div. C.E., AUS, 1943-44. Mem. Newcomen Soc. N.A., Tex. Philos. Soc., Dallas Hist. Soc., Am. Legion, Sigma Chi. Presbyn. Clubs: City, Dallas Country; Friars. Home: Dallas, TX. †

LEMON, A(SA) B(ERTRAM), educator; b. Hartford, Ont., Can., Sept. 3, 1889; brought to U.S., 1910; s. W(illiam) E(dgar) and Mary Elizabeth (Jacques) L.; Ph.G., U. of Buffalo, 1913; Phar.D., Brooklyn Coll., 1915; m. Gretta Edith Moore, June 14, 1919; children—Edgar Rothwell, James Dixon. Asst. in materia medica, U. of Buffalo, 1916-18, instr., 1918-21, prof. from 1921, dean Sch. of Pharmacy from 1936. Recipient Gregory Memorial Award, 1948; Samuel Paul Capen Award, 1950. Member New York Bd. Pharmacy Examiners. Mem. A.A.A.S., Am. Pharm. Assn., Rho Chi, Kappa Psi. Independent Republican. Presbyterian. Mason. Co-author: Basic Material for a Pharmaceutical Curriculum, 1927. Home: Buffalo, N.Y. †

LEMON, ERWIN BERTRAN, coll. dean; b. Grass Valley, Ore., July 15, 1889; s. Isaac Newton and Irena (Hawley) L.; B.S., Ore. State Coll., 1911; student U. of Calif. at Berkeley, summers 1913-15; m. Lora Hansell, Dec. 20, 1911; children—Berlan, Mardis. Statistician, Ore. Statis. Bur. at Corvallis, 1911-12; instr. in accounting, Ore. State Coll., 1912-18, asst. prof., 1918-20, assoc. prof., 1920-22, prof., 1922-43, registrar (prof. and dean), 1922-43, dean of adminstrn. from 1943. Mem. Corvallis Sch. Bd., 1932-38. Recipient First Citizen award Benton County, 1959. Mem. Nat. Collegiate Players, Am. Assn. Collegiate Registrars, Am. Personnel Assn., C. of C. (pres.), Phi Kappa Phi, Alpha Kappa Psi, Beta Alpha Psi, Phi Eta Sigma, Delta Sigma Rho, Delta Chi. Republican. Presbyn. Rotarian (district gov. international 1959-60). Contributor to professional journals. Home: Corvallis, Ore. †

LEMPERLY, CHARLES M., business exec.; b. Cleveland, Sept. 19, 1888; s. Paul and Emma (Warner) L.; student Williams Coll., 1910; m. Eva Brainerd, Sept. 20, 1913; children—Charles Loring, Joan. Clerk advt. dept., Sherwin-Williams, Cleveland, 1907-08, editor advt. dept., 1908-09, 10, advt. mgr. and dir. publicity, 1914-43, dir. sales, 1943, vice pres. and dir. sales 1943-52, dir., 1943-52, vice pres. and dir. public relations from 1952. Asst. advt. mgr. Am. Multigraph Sales Co., Cleveland, 1910-13; dir. Nat. Screw & Mfg. Company. Member Central Y.M.C.A. Mem. Cleveland C. of C., Zeta Psi. Clubs: Advertising, Mid-Day, Union, Clifton. Home: Rocky River, Ohio. †

LENESS, GEORGE JOHN, investment banker; born Springfield, Mass., May 17, 1903; s. George and Ellen McInnerney L.; S.B., Mass. Inst. Tech., 1926; A. B., Harvard, 1927; m. Christine Gibbs, Apr. 19, 1933; children—John Gibbs, George Crawford, Anthony Vanderneth. Mem. buying dept., Harris Forbes & Co., N.Y. City, 1927-31, later Chase Harris Forbes Corp., 1931-34; with First Boston Corp., 1934-43, v.p., 1939-43; pres. Merrill Lynch, Pierce, Fenner & Smith, Inc., 1961-65, chmn., chief exec. officer, 1965—; dir. of Sinclair Oil Corporation. Bd. dirs. Beekman Downtown Hosp.; member corp. Mass. Institute of Technology. Mem. Delta Tau Delta, Tau Beta Phi. Clubs: Harvard, Mass. Inst. Tech., University, Down Town Assn., Brook (N.Y.C.), Nat. Golf Links (Southampton, L.I.). Home: New York, N.Y. Died Aug. 17, 1983.

LENGYEL, EMIL, educator, author; b. Budapest, Hungary, Apr. 26, 1895; s. Joseph and Johanna (Adam) L.; student Budapest secondary schs., 1901-13; LL.D., Royal Hungarian U., 1918; m. Livia Delej, July 16, 1938; 1 son, Peter. Came to U.S., 1921, naturalized, 1927. Journalist, Budapest, 1919; editor in Vienna 1920-21; corr. various European newspapers in U.S., 1922-30; adj. prof. history and econ. Bklyn. Poly. Inst., 1935-42; staff lectr. N.Y.U. Sch. Edn., 1939-43, asst. prof., 1943-47, asso. prof., 1947-51, prof., 1951-60, prof. emeritus, 1960-85; prof. history Fairleigh Dickinson U. 1960-75, prof. emeritus, 1975-85, chmn. social sci. dept., from 1963; corr. Star Weekly, Toronto, Can.; book reviewer Sat. Rev. N.Y.; mem. Columbia Seminar Pre-Indsl. Areas, Columbia U. Seminars, 1976-85. Served with Austro-Hungarian Army, World War I; prisoner in Siberia 20 months. Mem. Acad. Polit. Scis., Authors League Am., AAUAP, NEA, Am. Econ. Assn., Am. Hist. Assn., Fgn. Policy Assn., Am.-European Friendship Assn. (pres., recipient citation), Hungarian Student Orgn. Am. (hon.). Am. Assn. Middle East Studies, Mongolia Soc., Kappa Delta Pi (hon.). Clubs: P.E.N.; Overseas Press. Author numerous books from 1931; latest being: The Middle East Today, 1954; The Soviet Union: The Land and Its People, 1956; Egypt's Role in World Affairs, 1957; 1000 years of Hungary, 1958; The Changing Middle East, 1960; India, Pakistan, Ceylon, 1961; Krishna Menon: A Biography, 1962; Scenario: World in Revolt; From Prison to Power, 1964; Mahatma Ganhdi: The Great Soul, 1966; Jawaharlal Nehru: The Brahman from Kashmir, 1968; Nationalism, 1969; Ignace Paderewski, 1970; Modern Egypt, 1973; The Congress of Vienna, 1973; The Colony of Pennsylvania; The Colony of New Hampshire; And All Her Paths Were Peaceful: The Life of Bertha Von Suttner,1975; co-author, translator other books and film scenarios. Home: New York, N.Y. Died Feb. 12, 1985.

LENT, WILMAR FRANCIS, mfr. elec. controls; b. Washington, Oct. 8, 1889; s. Ernst and Mary J. (Simons) L.; B.S., U. Wis., 1910, E.E., 1911; m. Mildred W. Wright, July 2, 1924; children—Laura Jane (Mrs. Robert W. Spinti), Robert Wright, James Wright. Research asst. elec. labs. U. Wis., 1911; supt. mfg. Passaic Metal Ware Co. (N.J.), 1912; with Cutler Hammer, Inc., Milw., 1912-18, from 22, succesively control and sales engr., mgr. molded products dept., prodn. mgr., asst. supt., works mgr., 1912-56, v.p. mfg., 1956-59, sr. v.p., 1959; prodn. supr. Winchester Repeating Arms Co., New Haven, 1917-18; mfg. engr. Greist Mfg. Co., New Haven, 1918-22. Mem. Am. Inst. E.E. (life; chmn. Milw. 1932-33), Soc. Advancement Mgmt. (chmn. Milw. 1934). Home: Colgate, Wis. †

LENYA, LETTE (KAROLINE BLAMAUER), singer; b. Hitzing, Vienna, Austria, 1905; m. Kurt Weill, 1925 (dec. 1950); m. 2d, George Davis, 1951 (dec. 1958). Came to U.S., 1935. Dancer neighborhood circus, became tight-rope walker at age 8; with corps de ballet Zurich Stadttheater; appeared various theaters in Berlin. Little Mahoganny music festival, Baden-Baden, 1926; in Threepenny Opera, adaptation John Gay's Beggar's Opera, Berlin, then other European capitals, 1928; singer premier performance of opera Rise and Fall City of Mahoganny, Leipzig, 1930; appeared as Annie in dance-drama Seven Deadly Sins, N.Y. City Center, 1958; recordings include Threepenny Opera, Lotte Lenya Sings Berlin Theatre Songs, 1955. Seven Deadly sins, 1957. Died Nov. 27, 1981.*

LEON, RUIX, consul, physician; b. Les Caves, Haiti, Dec. 2, 1890; s. Ludovic Léon and Angèle (Moraille) L.; Ecole des Frères, 1900; Séminaire Coll. (St. Martial), 1910; M.D., Faculté de Médecine d'Haiti, 1915; Rockefeller Foundation scholarships, 1927, 1930, Hôpital Brodeloque, Paris, 1930, Cuba; m. Octavie de Valenton, Apr. 9, 1920; children—Josette, Maxime, Adeline, Gérard. Began practice 1915, Les Cayes; hygiene officer Quarantine Service, 1920-22; physician Cap Haitien Hosp., 1922-26; adminstr., Hosp. Port de Paix, 1926-27; maternity ward, Gen. Hosp. (Port au Prince), 1927-31; prof., Faculty Medicine, Haiti, 1927-31; Haitian del. to Congress Hygiene Services Dirs., Washington, D.C., 1936, Pan-Am. San. Conf., Bogota, 1938, 6th Congress Internat. Hosps. Assn., Toronto, 1939, Internat. Meeting Caribs, Ciudad Trujillo, 1940, Conf. Am. San. Assn., 1941; gen. dir. Nat. and Pub. Welfare Services, Haiti, 1931-41; undersec. hygiene, 1940-41; consul gen. for Haiti in New York, 1941. Comdr. Honneur et Mérite of Haiti, Comdr. Order of Duarte, Dominican Republic, Comdr. Cuban Red Cross. Mem. Am. Pub. Health Assn., Assn. Mil. Surgeons of U.S. Author: La Pratique Medicale Saint Domingue, 1927, Mèdecins et Naturalistes de la Colonie Franenise de Saint Domingue, 1939, la Législation de l'Hygiene, de l'Enseignement et de l'Exercice de la Medecine en Häiti, 1933-38 (3 vols.), Propos d'histoire d'Haiti, 1945. Home: Port-au-Prince, Haiti. Deceased.

LEONARD, GEORGE EDMUND, savs. and loan assn. exec.; b. Brookline, Mass., Sept. 1, 1912; s. George E. Leonard and Theresa (Carroll) L.; m. Evelyn S. Fairbank, May 18, 1951; children—George E., Marsha Ann; 1 stepson, Leigh C. Fairbank III. A.B., Columbia, 1935. With First Fed. Savs. of Phoenix, 1936-52, 60-82, pres., 1961-63, pres., chmn. bd., 1963-73, chmn. bd., chief exec. officer, 1973-82, also dir.; pres. San Diego Fed. Savs., 1952-54; financial v.p. Coast Fed. Savs., Los Angeles, 1954-56, Great Western Savs., Los Angeles, 1957-60; dir. Fed. Home Loan Bank, San Francisco, 1964, 67-72, vice chmn., 1969-71; dir. MGIC Investment Corp., MGIC.; Mem. fed. adv. council Fed. Home Loan Bank Bd., 1965-82; adv. council on govt. sect. for savs. and loan assns. Treasury Dept.; Mem. Phoenix Com. of Forty. Pres. Phoenix United Fund, 1975, 76; chmn. bd. dirs. Barrows Neurol. Inst., 1975; mem. exec. com. Ariz. Heart Inst. Found., Jr. Achievement Met. Phoenix, 1964-66, Goodwill Industries Phoenix, 1966-69; chmn. dean's adv. council Coll. Bus. Adminstrn., Ariz. State U., 1975; treas. Fiesta Bowl; pres. bd. trustees Camelback Mental Health Found., 1979-80. Served to lt. USNR, 1942-46. Mem. U.S. Savs. and Loan League, Ariz. Savs. and Loan League (pres. 1964), Nat. League Insured Savs. Assns. (bd. govs. 1946-52, pres. 1964-65), U.S. League Insured Savs. (dir., exec. com.), Newcomen Soc., Navy League, Beta Theta Pi, Beta Gamma Sigma (hon.). Republican. Episcopalian. Clubs: Phoenix Country (Phoenix), Kiwanis (Phoenix) (bd. dirs., pres.), Paradise Valley Country (Phoenix), Arizona (Phoenix). Home: Phoenix, Ariz. Died Apr. 27, 1982.

LEONARD, GEORGE KINNEY, engr.; b. Lincoln, Neb., July 17, 1889; s. George Bergen and Emma Amelia (Kinney) L.; B.C.E., U. Neb., 1912, C.E., 1939; m. Charlotte Marion Calder, Feb. 18, 1914; children—George Kinney, Thomas Calder. Bridge designer, resident engr., chief draftsman, chief office engr. Neb. State Highway Dept., 1912-20; asst. state engr. State of Neb., 1920-23; promotion, sales engr. Woods Bros. Constrn. Co., Lincoln, 1923-25, gen. supt. constrn., asst. chief engr., in charge constrn. Starved Rock Lock and Dam, Ottawa, Ill., and other heavy constrn. projects, 1925-31; cons. engr. highway transportation U.P. R.R., 1931-33; with TVA from 1933, asst. constrn. engr. Wheeler Dam, constrn. engr. Guntersville, Watts Bar, Cherokee Dams, project mgr. Apalachia, Ocoee, Chatuge, Nottely, Watauga, South Holston, Boone, Ft. Patrick Henry Dams, 1933-49, chief constrn. engr. charge steam, hydro-electric power constrn., 1950-56, chief engr., 1957-59; cons. engr., Knoxville, Tenn., from 1959. Licensed profl. engr. Fellow Am. Soc. C.E.; mem. Sigma Tau, Tau Beta Pi. Rotarian. Author articles in field. Home: Knoxville, Tenn. †

LEONARD, HAROLD JUDSON, dentist; born in Minneapolis, Minn., Nov. 24, 1887; s. Leon D. (dentist) and Mary (Judson) L.; D.D.S., U. of Minn., 1912, B.A., 1915; m. Marion Slater, Sept. 8, 1915; children—Edwin Slater, Judson Greer, William Francis, Robert Donham. Teacher oral hygiene, oral pathology and periodontology, Sch. of Dentistry U. of Minn. 1913-26, resigning as asst. prof.; research asst. Univ. Hosp., 1913-15, dir. Sch. for Dental Nurses, 1917-26; chief of Dental Dept. Students' Health Service, 1922-26; chief dental service Minneapolis Gen. Hosp., 1920-21; ednl. dir. and prof. oral pathology, Marquette U. Dental Sch., 1926-27; asso. prof. dentistry, Columbia U. Sch. of Dental and Oral Surgery, 1927, prof., 1928-47, chairman Div. of Oral Diagnosis, 1927-35, Div. of Periodontology, 1936-47; chief dental service Presbyterian Hosp., New York, 1933-37; spl. lecturer Tufts Coll. Dental Sch., from 1947. Sec.-treas. Am. Bd. of Periodontology and Advisory Bd. for Dental Specialities from 1939. Served as 1st lt. Dental Officers Res. Corps, 1917-21. Took part in the Assn. of Cosmopolitan Clubs, 1914-26, gen. sec., 1918-20, 1921 and 1922, pres. 1920-21. Fellow Am. Acad. Periodontology (pres. 1931-32). A.A.A.S.; mem. Am. Dental Assn. (mem. com. on dental practice, 1928-30, chmn. periodontia sect. 1947-48). Internat. Assn. Dental Research, 9th Dist. Dental Soc. Sigma Xi. Delta Sigma Delta, Omicron Kappa Upsilon. Politics: Independent Democrat. Chmn. Pelham Dist. Com., Boy Scouts of America, 1943-44; mem. Scarsdale Dist. Boy Scouts of America, (chmn. health and safety com. Fenimore Cooper Council, since 1947). Writer of many articles on dental subjects. Home: Scarsdale, N.Y. Died July 5, 1981.

LEONARD, JOHN WALTER, petroleum company executive; b. Washington, Pa., Jan. 30, 1904; s. John Walter and Caroline (McCollum) L.; m. Ruth Snellenberger, Mar. 22, 1940; children: John Walter III, William McCollum, Caroline Marie, Linda L., Dorothy J. Student, Culver (Ind.) Mil. Acad.; B.S., U. Pitts., 1927. Treas. S.Am. Oil Co., Pitts., 1926-27; mgr. Big Horn Petroleum Co., Cody, Wyo., 1927-29; treas. Motembo Basin Petroleum Co., Havana, Cuba, 1930-48; pres. Meridian Drilling Co., Inc., Oklahoma City, 1950-59; chmn. bd. Leonard Refineries, Inc., Alma, Mich., 1937-70, Leonard Crude Oil Co., 1956-68; pres. Rowmor Corp., 1934-47, Leonard Oil, Inc., 1947-71; past chmn. bd., chief exec. officer Am. Security Bank; dir. Peoples Banking Corp.; Mem. Small Bus. Adv. Council, 1954-67. Past chmn. bd., exec. com. Mich. Accident Fund; past bd. dirs. Mt. Pleasant Community Hosp. Mem. Ind. Petroleum Assn. Am. (past v.p., past mem. exec. com.), Oil and Gas Assn. Mich. (past pres., now hon. bd. dirs.), Sigma Alpha Epsilon. Methodist. Clubs: Elk, Detroit Athletic. Home: Mount Pleasant, Mich.

LEONARD, JOHN WILLIAM, army officer; b. Toledo, O., Jan. 25, 1890; s. Dennis William and Anastasia (Sheahan) L.; B.S., U.S. Mil. Acad., 1915; grad. F.A. Sch., 1927, Command and Gen. Staff Sch., 1928; M.M.S., Pa. Mil. Coll., 1931; m. Eileen O'Brien, April 5, 1918; children—Eileen, Natalie, John William. Commd. 2d lt., U.S. Army, 1915, and advanced through the grades to major gen., 1942, assigned to 4th Armored Div., June 1942, comd. 9th Armored Div., 1942-45; comdt. The Armored Sch., Ft. Knox, Ky., July 1946; mil. attache Am. Embassy, London, Eng., from July 1948. Decorated D.S.C., D.S.M., Legion of Merit, Silver Star, Bronze Star, Purple Heart; Victory Ribbon with 3 battle Stars, World War I, Army of Occupation, World War I; Army commendation ribbon with oak leaf cluster; Army of Occupation, World War II, Am. Defense and Am. Theatre ribbons; ETO ribbon with 3 battle stars, Victory ribbon World War II; Mexican Campaign; Legion d'Honneur, Croix de Guerre (France) World War I; Legion d'Honneur, Croix de Guerre with Palm (France) World War II; Belgian Croix de Guerre with Palm (Belgium) World War II; Czechoslovakian Croix de Guerre. Home: Fort Bragg, N.C. †

LEOPOLD, ALDO STARKER, educator; b. Burlington, Ia., Oct. 22, 1913; s. Aldo and Estella (Bergere) L.; B.S. in Agr., U. Wis., 1936; student Yale Forest Sch., 1936-37; Ph.D. in Zoology, U. Cal. at Berkeley, 1944; m. Elizabeth Weiskotten, Aug. 6, 1938; children—Frederic Starker, Sarah Pendleton. Field biologist Mo. Conservation Com., 1939-44. Pan-Am. Union, Mexico, 1944-46; instr. Mus. Vertebrate Zoology, U. Cal., at Berkeley, 1946-52, asso. prof., 1952-57, prof. zoology, after 1957, then prof. emeritus. asst. to chancellor univ., 1960-63. Pres. Cal. Acad. Sci., 1958-66. Recipient medal Nat. Audubon Soc., 1966. Guggenheim fellow, 1947-48. Mem. Wildlife Soc.

(pres. 1957). Am. Ornithologists Union. Am. Soc. Mammalogist, Am. Soc. Range Mgmt., Wilderness Soc., Nature Conservancy. Club: Sierra (San Francisco). Author: Wildlife in Alaska (with F. F. Darling), 1952; Wildlife of Mexico the game birds and mammals, 1959. Co-author: The Desert, 1961. Home: Berkely, Calif. Died Aug. 23, 1983.

LEOPOLD, MORTON F., safety engr.; b. Duluth, Minn., Apr. 25, 1889; s. Henry F. and Carrie (Nirdlinger) L.; student U. of Pa. 2 yrs., U.S. Sch. Submarine Defense, 1 yr., U.S. Engr. Sch. 1 yr.; m. Ilma Wolff, Sept. 26, 1916. With U.S. Bur. of Mines from 1911, now safety engr.; organizer and mgr. various expns., and producer of motion picture films of an ednl. nature, dealing with the mining industry; lecturer on safety and welfare work at colleges, meetings of mining socs., etc. Served in U.S. Army 5 yrs. Mason. Home: Washington, D.C. †

LEPOW, IRWIN HOWARD, immunologist; b. N.Y.C., Sept. 2, 1923; s. Herman and Mollie (Rutchik) L.; m. Martha Josephine Lipson, Feb. 7, 1958; children—Lauren Ethel, David Andrew, Daniel Joseph. B.S., Pa. State U., 1942; Ph.D., Case Western Res. U., 1951, M.D., 1958. From instr. to prof. Case Western Res. U. Sch. Medicine, 1951-67; prof., head dept pathology U. Conn. Health Center, 1967-73, prof., head dept. medicine, 1973-78; pres. Sterling-Winthrop Research Inst., Rensselaer, N.Y., from 1978; v.p. research ops. Sterling Drug, Inc., Rensselaer, N.Y., from 1982; pres. Sterling Research Group, from 1983; chmn. allergy and immunology study sect. NIH, 1970-73; mem. Bd. Health Sci. Inst. Medicine/Nat. Acad. Scis., 1982; adv. mem. commn. immunization Armed Forces Epidemiol. Bd., 1969-74; chmn. research com. Conn. Heart Assn., 1970-72; chmn. Conn. Commn. Medicolegal Investigations, 1969-71. Contbr. articles to profl. jours. Trustee Trudeau Inst., 1972-78, Albany Coll. of Pharmacy of Union U., 1981; Bd. dirs. Albany Symphony Orch., 1982, Capital Repertory Theatre, 1981. Served with USAAF, 1943-45. Recipient Distinguished Alumnus award Case Western Res. U., 1968; Research career award NIH, 1962-67; grantee for research, 1955-78. Fellow A.C.P.; mem. Am. Assn. Immunologists (council 1974-80, pres. 1979-80), Am. Soc. Clin. Investigation, Am. Soc. Exptl. Pathology, Fedn. Am. Socs. Exptl. Biology (v.p. 1979-80, pres. 1980-81), Infectious Diseases Soc. Am., Assn. Am. Physicians. Home: Albany, N.Y. Deceased.

LERCH, FRANK H., JR., business exec.; b. Easton, Pa., Mar. 27, 1888; s. Frank H. and Jeannette (Beldler) L.; B.S., Lafayette Coll,, Easton, Pa., 1909; m. Reba H. Quick, Oct. 7, 1915. With Empire Steel & Iron Co., Catasauqua, Pa., 1909-14; gen. contracting T. A. Gillespie Co., Inc., New York City, 1914-19; War Contract Claims Settlement, U.S. Army Ordinance Dept., New York City, 1919-20; engring. and management, Ford, Bacon & Davis, Inc., N.Y. City, 1920-33; natural gas exec., Standard Oil Co. (N.J.), New York, 1933-43; pres. and dir. Consolidated Natural Gas Company, 1943-51, chairman of the board 1951-53, dir., 1953-55, cons., 1953-63. Life trustee Lafayette Coll., Pa. Republican. Clubs: University. Home: Jackson Heights, N.Y. †

LERNER, ABBA PTACHYA, economist; b. Bessarabia, Russia, 1903; came to U.S., 1937, naturalized, 1949; s. Morris Isaac and Sofie (Buchman) L.; m. Alice Sendak, 1929; children—Lionel John, Marion; m. Daliah Goldfarb, 1960. B.Sc. in Econs, U. London, 1932, Ph.D. in Econs, 1943. Instr. London Sch. Econs., 1935-39; asst. prof. U. Kansas City, 1940-42; prof. New Sch. Social Research, N.Y.C., 1942-47, Roosevelt U., Chgo., 1947-59, Mich. State U., 1959-65, U. Calif. at Berkeley, 1965-71; distinguished prof. econs. Queens Coll., City U. N.Y., 1971-78, Fla. State U., 1978-82; vis. prof. Columbia U., U. Va., Amherst Coll., Hebrew U. Jerusalem, Johns Hopkins U., U. Hawaii, U. Calif. at Los Angeles, U. Tel Aviv, U. Rio de Janeiro, Fla. State U.; cons. RAND Corp., 1949, Econ. Commn. for Europe, Geneva, 1950-51, Inst. Mediterranean Affairs, N.Y.C., 1958-59; econ. adviser Govt. Israel, Jerusalem, 1953-55; adviser to treasury Govt. of Israel and Bank of Israel, 1955-56. Author: Economics of Control, 1944, Economics of Employment, 1951, Essays in Economic Analysis, 1953, Everybody's Business, 1962, Flation, 1973, (with Ben Shachar) The Efficient Economy, 1974, The Economics of Efficiency and Growth, 1975, (with David Colander) MAP—A Market Anti-Inflation Plan, 1980; contbr.: (with David Colander) articles to profl. jours. Ency. Brit. Leon fellow, 1934-35; Rockefeller fellow, 1937-39; Center for Advanced Study in Behavioral Scis. fellow, 1960-61; NSF grantee, 1975-76; fellow Villa Serbelloni Rockefeller Found., 1976. Fellow Am. Econ. Assn. (past v.p.), Econometric Soc., London Sch. Econs. (hon.); mem. Nat. Acad. Scis. Atlantic Econ. Soc. (pres. 1980), Western Econ. Assn. (v.p. 1980), Royal Brit. Acad. Pres., Univ. Centers for Rational Alternatives, 1975-77. Home: Tallahassee, Fla. Died Oct. 27, 1982.

LERNER, DANIEL, social scientist, educator; b. N.Y.C., Nov. 3, 1917; s. Louis and Yetta (Swiger) L.; A.B., N.Y.U., 1938, M.A., 1939, Ph.D., 1948; m. Jean Weinstein, May 16, 1947; children—Louise, Thomas, Amy. Instr. modern European history and lit., 1939-42; European rep. Library of Congress Mission, 1946-47; exec. sec. and research dir. internat. studies project, 1947-53; acting prof. sociology Stanford, 1951-53; vis. prof. sociology Columbia, 1951; prof. sociology Mass. Inst. Tech., 1953-79, Ford prof. sociology and internat. communications, 1958-79, chmn. polit. and social sci. dept., 1963- 64; dir. Institut de Recherches Sociales, Paris, France, 1955-65; vis. prof. U. Paris (Sorbonne); adj. prof. sociology U. Calif., Santa Cruz, 1979. Served to capt. AUS, 1942-46; chief editor intelligence br. Psychol. Warfare Div., SHAEF; chief intelligence Info. Control Div., Office of Mil. Govt. U.S. Decorated Bronze Star, Purple Heart; Palmes Academiques, officier d'Academie (France). Fellow Conf. Sci., Philosophy and Religion; mem. Am. Sociol. Soc., Am. Polit. Sci. Assn., World, Am. assns. pub. opinion research, Am. Psychol. Assn. Author: Psychological Warfare Against Nazi Germany, 1949; Propaganda in War and Crisis, 1951; (with H.D. Lasswell) The Policy Sciences, 1951; The Nazi Elite, 1951; (with Raymond Aron) LaQuerelle de la CED, 1956; France Defeats E.D.C., 1957; The Passing of Traditional Society, 1958; The Human Meaning of the Social Sciences, 1959; Evidence and Inference, 1960; Quantity and Quality, 1961; Parts and Wholes, 1963; Cause and Effect, 1965; (with H.D. Lasswell) World Revolutionary Elites, 1965; (with Wilbur Schramm) Communication and Change in the Developing Countries, 1967; (with Morton Gorden) Euratlantica; Changing Perspectives of The European Elites, 1969; (with Wilbur Schramm) Communications and Change: The Last Ten Years-and the Next, 1976; Values and Development: Appraising Asian Experience, 1976; (with L.M. Nelson) Communication Research-A Half-Century Appraisal, 1977, Propaganda and Communication in World History, 3 vols., 1979; editor: M.I.T. Studies in Comparative Politics, 1965-75. Home: Santa Cruz, Calif. Died May 1, 1980 buried N.Y.C.

LERNER, LOUIS ABRAHAM, former ambassador, newspaper publisher; b. Chgo., June 12, 1935; s. Leo Alfred and Deana (Duskin) L.; m. Susan Winchester, July 22, 1957; children: Lucy Alix, Jane Chelsea. Student, U. Chgo., 1951-54; Scandinavian seminars, Copenhagen, 1956-57; B.A., Roosevelt U., 1960. Reporter North Town News, Chgo., 1954-56; corr. Accredited Home Newspapers Am., Chgo., Copenhagen, 1956-58; exec. Lerner Home Newspapers, Chgo., 1959-77, pub., 1969-77, 80-84, U.S. ambassador to Norway, 1977-80; pres. Lerner Suburban Communications, 1970-77; editor, pub. Lerner Newspapers, Inc.; dir. Myers Pub. Co., Lincoln-Belmont Pub. Co.; Commr. Nat. Commn. on Libraries and Info. Scis., 1972-77; mem. Ill. Adv. Com. on State Library, 1969-77. Mem. citizen's bd. Catholic Interracial Council, 1964-69, Walker Art Center., Mpls., 1969-77, Chgo. Mus. Contemporary Art, 1965, Stedjelik Mus., Amsterdam, 1960; bd. dirs. Surburban Newspapers Am., Chgo. Better Bus. Bur., Lyric Opera Guild; bd. dirs. Pub. Library, also v.p.; mem. Nat. UN Day Com., 1972-74; spl. mem. U.S. delegation Human Rights Talks, Madrid, 1980-81; mem. spl. com. on cable tech. Suburban Newspapers Am., 1981-84; trustee Am. Scandinavian Found., Planned Parenthood Fedn. Am., Council for U.S. and Italy, 1983-84; del. Dem. Nat. Conv. Decorated grand cross Order St. Olav, Norway; grand cross Order Prince Henry, Portugal; recipient Service award Accredited Home Newspapers Am., 1960; spl. award CIA, 1980. Mem. Newspaper Soc. (Eng.), North Town C. of C. (dir. 1963-65), Am. Acad. Polit. and Social Sci., ALA, Chgo. Council on Fgn. Relations, Sigma Delta Chi. Democrat. Clubs: Headline (Chgo.), Econ. (Chgo.), City (Chgo.) (bd. govs. 1966-69). Home: Chicago, Ill. Died Nov. 14, 1984.

LESLIE, DONALD S., manufacturer; b. Minneapolis, Minn., Mar. 2, 1895; s. John and Bessie May (McAfee) L.; grad. Shattuck Sch., Faribault, Minn., 1914; student Princeton, 1914-17; m. Dorothy Rogers, Jan. 11, 1921; children—Nancy R., Donald S. Jr., Joan R. With Hammermill Paper Co. since 1928, 1st v.p., gen.mgr., 1940-52, pres., general mgr., 1952-63, chairman, 1963-69, hon. chmn., 1969-83, also dir.; dir. Rayonier, Inc., 1st Nat. Bank Erie. Served with United States Army, World War I. Mem. bd. govs. Hamot Hosp., Erie. Mem. U.S. Pulp Producers Assn. (exec. bd.), Am. Paper and Pulp Asnn. Clubs: Erie, Kahkwa (Erie); Sky (N.Y.). Home: Erie, Pa. Died Apr. 12, 1983.

L'ESPERANCE, WILFORD LOUIS, III, economist, educator; b. N.Y.C., Dec. 9, 1930; m. Barbara Manochio, May 4, 1957 (dec. d. Jan. 1977); children—Annette, Suzanne, Claire, Wilford IV. A.B., Columbia Coll., 1951; M.S., Columbia U., 1952; Ph.D., U. Mich., 1963. Math. analyst Ordnance Corps., U.S. Army Guided Missile Devel. Div., Huntsville, Ala., 1953-55; lectr. Ind. U., 1956-60; mktg. research analyst Gen. Electric Co., N.Y.C., Ft. Wayne, Ind., 1952-53, 55-60, cons., 1965; research asst. dept. econs. U. Mich., 1961-63; economist Bur. Comml. Fisheries, Dept. Interior, Ann Arbor, Mich., 1962-63, cons., Sandusky, Ohio, 1963-65; asst. prof. econs. Ohio State U., 1963-66, asso. prof., 1966-70, prof., from 1970, instr. exec. devel. program div. continuing edn., 1970-75; pres. M.W. Econometrics, Inc., Columbus, Ohio, 1973-79; cons. in field; mem. Ohio Gov.'s Task Force on Lake Erie Fishery, 1973-74, Population Study Group, Environ. Health Com., Office Comprehensive Health Planning, Ohio Dept. Health, 1973-76; mem. panel econ. adviser for John Glenn, Ohio Democratic candidate for U.S. Senate, 1974; mem. tech. adv. group Columbus Mayor's Econ. Devel. Council, 1975. Author: (with others) Columbus Area Economy-Structure and Growth, 1950-1985, 1966, Modern Statistics for Business and Economics, 1971, The Structure and Control of a State Economy, 1981; asso. editor: (with others) Jour. Regional Sci, from 1978; contbr. (with others) articles on econs. to profl. jours. Dept. Interior Bur. Comml. Fisheries grantee 1963-64; Coll. Research Com., Coll. Commerce and Adminstrn. grantee, 1965-66; Ohio Dept. Devel. grantee, 1967-68; Coll. Research Com., Coll. Social and Behavioral Scis. grantee, 1969, 76. Mem. Am. Econ. Assn., Am. Statis. Assn. (pres. Columbus chpt. 1968), Regional Sci. Assn., N.Y. State Soc., Cin., Ohio, Worthington hist. socs. Clubs: Hoover Yacht (trustee), Columbus Metropolitan (trustee). Home: Columbus, OH.

LE TELLIER, LOUIS SHEPHERD, cons. profl. engr.; b. nr. Charlottesville, Va., Feb. 8, 1887; s. William Wertenbaker and Ida (Davis) Le T.; student U. of Va., 1905-06; M.S., Coll. of Charleston (South Carolina), 1920; LL.D. (honorary), The Citadel, 1954; Dr. of Engr. Sci., Clemson College, 1954; married Ella Tobias, Nov. 11, 1913; m. 2d, Vivian Nance, June 19, 1924; children—Louis Shepherd, Carroll Nance. Began as draftsman Alberene Stone Co., Va., 1906; instr. engring., The Citadel, Charleston, S.C., 1908-16, asst. prof., 1916-19, prof. 1919-54, head engring. dept., 1920-54; dir. constrn., 1935-54, acting pres. 1953-54, consulting engineer. Part time engring. practice on roads, bridges, concrete design and constrn., 1913-35; consultant to Charleston County on construction projects. Served as lt. U.S. Army, 1918. Mem. S.C. Bd. Archtl. Examiners, 1917-22; mem. and chmn. S.C. Bd. Engring. Examiners since 1922; mem. Water Power Investigating Com., S.C., 1933. Mem. regional committee on engring., Schs. of Engring. Council for Professional Development, 1948. Recipient Algernon Sydney Sullivan award, 1942; Engr. of Year award, S.C. Soc. Profl. Engrs., 1958. Mem. S.C. Society of Engrs. (cofounder, 1928, pres., 1937-38), Am. Soc. C.E. (chmn. com. on engring. edn., 1942; pres. S.C. sect. 1943), Am. Concrete Inst., Am. Soc. Engring. Edn. (chmn. Civil Engring. div. 1942-43, mem. gen. council 1946-47), Nat. Council State Bds. of Engring. Examiners (chmn. conv. com., 1940; Distinguished Service Certificate, 1943). Democrat. Episcopalian. Academic visitor, Army Specialized Training Program, 1943-45. Address: Charleston, S.C. †

LETSCHE, J. HARRY, business exec.; b. Pittsburgh, Sept. 8, 1888; s. John Harry and Ella (Berkebile) L.; A.B., Cornell U., 1912; m. Catharine Brocas, May 8, 1920; children—Catharine (Mrs. John Watson Cummins), Mary Ann (Mrs. John Walter Yockey). With H. J. Heinz Co. from 1913, vice pres. and dir. from 1944. Served as capt. and adj., 326th Inf., 82d Div., World War I. Awarded Silver Star, Purple Heart. Mem. Grocery Mfrs. of Am. (dir.), Am. Legion, Kappa Sigma. Republican. Presbyterian. Clubs: Duquesne, University (Pitts.); Cornell (New York). Home: Ben Avon, Pa. †

LÉVECQUE, MARCEL AMÉDÉE, manufacturing company executive; b. Paris, July 15, 1922; s. Anatole Louis and Marguerite Adéle (Robineau) L.; Engring. degree Conservatoire National des Arts et Métiers, 1945; m. Régine Louise Lardeux, Mar. 11, 1944; children—Aliette, Jean-Luc, Marc. Asst. dir. metals lab. Laboratoire du Bâtiment et des Travaux Publics, Paris, 1941-42; asst. to tech. dir. Manufacture Nationale de Porcelaine de Sèvres (France), 1942-44, chief chemist, 1944-47; research engr. L'Office National d'Etudes et de Recherches Aéronautiques, Paris, 1947-50; research engr. Saint-Gobain Industries, Neuilly-sur-Seine, France, 1950-52, head research group, 1952-56, dir. devel. dept. for glasses, 1956-60, dir. research and devel. dept. of plate glass div., 1960-63, tech. mgr. Société d'Etude pour le Développement de la Fibre de Verre, 1963-68, tech. and research and devel. dir. of insulation, strand and asbestos-cement div., 1969-76; sr. v.p., chief technology CertainTeed Corp., Valley Forge, Pa., 1976-77, exec. v.p., 1977-78, pres., chief exec. officer, 1978-79, chief of technology, 1977-78, chmn. operating com., 1978-79, also dir. Recipient Prix du Cercle Republicain, 1945, Prix de la Société d'Encouragement pour l'Industrie et le Commerce, 1957; decorated chevalier du Mérite Industriel et Commercial, 1962, chevalier du Mérite National, 1974; prix de l'Energie, 1975. Patentee fiber glass insulation (30). Address: Valley Forge, Pa. Died March 1979.

LEVEN, STEVEN ALOYSLUS, bishop; b. Blackwell, Okla., Apr. 30, 1905; s. Joseph J. and Gertrude (Conrady) L.; student St. Benedict's Coll., Atchison, Kan., St. Mary's Sem., LaPorte, Tex.; student philosophy and theology Cath. U. Louvain (Belgium), 1922-28; Ph.D., Institut Superieur de Philosophie, Louvain, 1938; LL.D. honoris causa, St. Edwards's U., Austin, Tex., 1957. Ordained priest Roman Cath. Ch., 1928; consecrated bishop, 1956; asst. pastor St. Joseph's Old Cathedral, Oklahoma City, 1928-32; pastor St. Joseph's Ch., Bristow, Okla., 1932-35; vice rector Am. Coll., Louvain, 1935-38; pastor St. Joseph's Ch., Tonkawa, Okla., 1938-48, St. Francis Xavier Ch., Enid, Okla., 1948-56; auxillary bishop of San Antonio, after 1956. Home: San Antonio, Tex. Died June 28, 1983.

LEVIN, SAMUEL M., economics; born, Poland, Ju 6, 1888; son of Judah L. and Esther Rhoda L.; A.B., U. of Michigan, 1912; A.M., U. of Chicago, 1925; m. Lillian Keidan, Aug. 25, 1914; children—Joseph Harmon, Miriam Elizabeth (Mrs. Stanley Bertram Friedman), Herbert George, Judith Leonora (Mrs. Bernard J. Cantor). Instructor in history and economics, Detroit (Michigan) Junior College, 1915-19; head of com. to revise social science curriculums in Detroit Pub. Schs., 1920-22; prof. economics, Coll. of City of Detroit, 1925; professor econ., Wayne U., from 1933, chmn. dept., 1933-53. Member of the mayor's unemployment com., 1931, mayor's com. on labor, 1931; mem. budget review com. Detroit Community Fund, 1936-39. President, Jewish Social Service Bureau, 1936-39. Member Am. Econ. Assn., Mich. Acad. Science, Arts and Letters (chmn. econ. sect. 1936 and 1937), Am. Assn. Univ. Profs., A.A.A.S. Hon. mem. Scholarship Honor Soc., Coll. of Liberal Arts, Wayne U., Detroit, Mich. Contbr. tech. articles to professional publs. Home: Detroit, Mich. †

LEVINTHAL, ISRAEL HERBERT, rabbi; b. Vilna, Russia, Feb. 12, 1888; s. Rabbi Bernard L. and Minna (Kleinberg) L.; A.B., Columbia, 1908, M.A., 1910; Rabbi, Jewish Theol. Sem. of Am., 1910, D.H.L., 1920, D.D. (hon.), 1940; J.D., N.Y.U., 1914; D.J.T. (hon.) Jewish Inst. of Religion, 1948; m. May R. Bogdanoff, Aug. 12, 1908; children—Helen Hadassah Lyons, Lazar E. Rabbi Temple B'nai Sholom, Bklyn., 1910-15, Temple Petach Tikvah, Bklyn., 1915-19, Bklyn. Jewish Center, 1919-82. Founder and dir. Inst. Jewish Studies for Adults. Mem. adv. com. burial survey Met. Life Ins. Co., 1926-28. Lectr. in homiletics Jewish Theol. Sem., 1937-38, vis. prof. homiletics, 1948-62; mem. adv. council Jewish Information Bur.; mem. exec. council United Synagogue of Am.; hon. chmn. Bklyn. region Zionist Orgn. of Am.; trustee Israel Matz Found. for Hebrew Writers; chmn. bd. sponsors Hadoar (Hebrew weekly); mem. N.Y. Bd. of Jewish Ministers; nat. chmn. Jerusalem Synagogue Center Campaign, 1928-30; nat. chmn. Com. for Advancement of Hebrew Culture; mem. council Jewish Agy. for Palestine, 1929-33; mem. Brooklyn Citizen's Com. for Racial and Religious Amity; pres. Bklyn. Jewish Community Council, 1940-44, hon. pres., 1944-82; bd. dirs. Bklyn. chpt. A.R.C. Del. of United Synagogue of Am., N.Y. Bd. of Jewish Ministers and Bklyn. Jewish Center, at dedication of Hebrew U. in Jerusalem. Mem. exec. com. Bklyn. Tb and Health Assn. of Bklyn. Bur. of Charities. Mem. Am. Schs. of Oriental Research, Jewish Acad. of Arts and Scis., Am. Acad. Jewish Research, Rabbinical Assembly of Am. (pres. 1930-32), Bklyn. Jewish Ministers Assn. (1st pres. 1929-31). Mem. Joint Prayer Book Commn. of Rabbinical Assembly and United Synagogue of Am. Winner Curtis medal (oratorical), Columbia, 1908. Club: The Judaeans. Author: The Jewish Law of Agency, 1923; Steering or Drifting Which?, 1928. Compiler: Song and Praise for Sabbath Eve (with Israel Goldfarb), 1920; Judaism-An Analysis and an Interpretation, 1935, Yiddish translation 1949; A New World Is Born, 1943; The Hour of Destiny, 1949; Point of View-An Analysis of American Judaism, 1958; Judaism Speaks to the Modern World, 1963; Selected Sermons in Hebrew, 1968; The Message of Israel, 1973. Contbr. articles to Jewish Quarterly Rev., etc. Home: New Rochelle, N.Y. Dec. Oct. 31, 1982. Interned Montifiore Cemetery, N.Y.C.

LEVIT, BERT WILLIAM, lawyer; b. San Francisco, Feb. 16, 1903; s. Morris and Fannie (Jacobs) L.; A.B. magna cum laude, Stanford, 1924, J.D., 1925; m. Thelma Clumeck, May 10, 1928 (dec. 1970); children—Victor Bert, Roger Clumeck; m. 2d, Edith I. Garland, Oct. 4, 1972. Admitted to Calif. bar, 1925; sr. partner firm Long & Levit, San Francisco and Los Angeles, from 1927, gen. counsel, from 1977; lectr. Stanford Law Sch., 1932-45. Spl. asst. to U.S. atty. gen., Washington, 1925-26; chief asst. dist. atty. San Francisco, 1944-45; chief dep. atty. gen. Calif., 1951; dir. finance State of Calif., 1959. Commr. edn. San Francisco pub. schs., 1948-58; charter mem. Calif. Law Revision Com., 1953-58, Calif. Scholarship Com., 1955-58; Calif. del. White House Conf. on Edn., 1955; pres. Calif. Sch. Bds. Assn., 1956-57; chmn. Gov.'s Com. on Calif. Govtl. Reorgn., 1959-60; pub. mem. Calif. Coordinating Council for Higher Edn., 1962-67. Pres. San Francisco br. Am. Cancer Soc., 1968-70, bd. dirs. Calif. div., 1971-74, recipient Pres.'s Gold award, 1978; legal counsel San Francisco Conservatory Music, from 1971, bd. dirs., 1971-77; bd. govs. Internat. Ins. Seminars, from 1976. Fellow Am. Coll. Trial Lawyers; mem. World Assn. Lawyers (founding mem.), Order of Coif, Phi Beta Kappa, Delta Sigma Rho. Clubs: Bankers, San Francisco Comml. Home: San Rafael, Calif. Deceased.

LEVY, B. J., investment securities; b. N.Y. City, May 7, 1888; s. Morris and Sarah (Drezner) L.; ed. pub. schs. of N.Y. City; m. Anna E. M. Cohn, Feb. 18, 1911; children—Maurice, Rudnick, Bernice. Clerk, Ferd Salomon, 1903-09, Salomon Bros., 1910; with Salomon Bros. & Hutzler, from 1910, partner 1919, senior partner, from 1951. Member Committee Jewish Theological Seminary; founder, member board overseers Albert Einstein College. Medicine. Mem. Fedn. Jewish Philanthropics Soc., Acad. Polit. Sci., N.Y. State C. of C. Jewish religion (trustee, Cong. B'Nai Jeshurun). Clubs: Fresh Meadow Country, The Economic, Bond, Harmonie. Home: New York, N.Y. †

LEVY, GEORGE MORTON, race track exec.; b. Seaford, L.I., June 26, 1889; s. Adolph and Anna (Katz) L.; LL.M., N.Y.U.; 1 son by former marriage, George Morton; m. 2d, Elise Huelle, Dec. 31, 1948; children—Elise Vandervoort, Robert Vandervoort. Admitted to N.Y. bar; practice of law, Mineola, N.Y. Development, advancement, promotion Roosevelt Raceway, harness race track, from 1940, chairman of the exec. com. and gen. counsel. Prin. founder cerebral palsy aid, Nassau County. Mem. N.Y., Nassau County bar assns. Elk, Mason. Clubs: Friars (N.Y.C.); Rotary; Glen Head; Glen Oaks; Diplomat Golf. Home: Westbury, N.Y. †

LEWIS, ANNA, prof: history; b. Poteau, Indian Ty., Oct. 25, 1887; d. William Ainsworth and Bettie Anne (Moore) L.; A.B., U. of Calif., 1915, A.M., 1917; Ph.D., U. of Okla., 1930. Prof. history, Okla. Coll. for Women, since 1917. Mem. Am. Hist. Soc., Okla. Hist. Soc., Am. Assn. Univ. Women, Pi Gamma Mu. Baptist. Author: Syllabus of Lectures, American History and Government, 1924; Outlines of Oklahoma History, 1926; The Early History of the Arkansas River Region. Contbr. to Chronicles of Okla., Miss. Valley Dist. Review. Home: Chickasha, Okla. †

LEWIS, BURTON O., army officer; b. Apr. 1, 1889; B.S., U.S. Mil. Acad., 1910; grad. Ordnance Sch. of Technology, 1915, Ordnance Sch. of Application, 1916, Army Industrial Coll., 1929, Army War Coll., 1939. Commd. 2d lt., Field Arty., June 15, 1910; promoted through grades to brig. gen. (temp.), Oct. 2, 1940; served as lt. col. Ordnance Dept., World War. Decorated Purple Heart. Deceased.

LEWIS, CHARLES ELBERT, lawyer; b. Manchester, Mich., June 12, 1889; s. Charles E. and Frances A. (Case) L.; A.B., U. Mich., 1912, LL.B., 1913; m. Mabel E. Wilson, July 15, 1921; children—Charles W., Richard C. Admitted to Mich. bar, 1913; mem. firm Hill, Lewis, Andrews, Adams, Goodrich & Power and predecessor firms, 1921-66, of counsel, from 1967. Secretary, director Detroit Michigan Stove Company, 1947-55; secretary Detroit Can. Tunnell Corp., 1927-55; mem. Birmingham and Ferndale adv. coms. The Detroit Bank & Trust Co., from 1956. Mem. Bd. Zoning Appeals, 1960-63. Served as 1st lt. inf., U.S. Army, 1917-19. Mem. Am. Judicature Soc., Am., Mich., Detroit bar assns. Republican. Episcopalian. Mason. Clubs: Detroit Athletic, Detroit. Home: Birmingham, Mich. †

LEWIS, CHARLES FLETCHER, foundation executive; b. at Gibsonton, Pa., January 8, 1890; son of William Henry and Maria (Fletcher) L.; A.B., Allegheny Coll., Meadville, Pa., 1909; grad. study, U. of Pittsburgh, 1911-12, LL.D. 1934; LL.D., Chatham Coll., 1959, Allegheny Coll., 1962; m. Jessamine DeHaven, June 12, 1915. Instr. in Latin and history, Alden Acad., Meadville, 1909-11; newspaper work, 1912-28; became connected with Pittsburgh Sun, 1916, chief editorial writer, 1919-27; editor Pittsburgh Record, 1928; dir. The Buhl Found., 1928-56, cons., from 1956; pres. Chatham Village Co., 1931-56; mem. com. on large scale operations, Pres.'s Conf. on Home Bldg. and Home Ownership, 1931; mem. Housing Adv. Council of Federal Housing Adminstrn., 1934-35; mem. Planning Commn., City of Pittsburgh, 1934-45; president Buhl Planetarium, 1939-56; trustee, Dollar Savings Bank; pres. Western Pa. Conservancy; mem. bd. Recreation, Conservation and Park Council; member board Chatham College, Cook Forest Association; member of sponsors committee Allegheny Conf. on Community Development. Awards, Am. Assn. State and Local History, 1955, Pitts. Newspaper Guild, Allegheny Coll. Alumni, 1956; lit. award Pittsburgh Jr. C. of C., 1958; American Motors National Conservation award, 1961. Mem. Delta Tau Delta, Sigma Delta Chi, Omicron Delta Kappa. Mason. Clubs: Duquesne, University (Pittsburgh). Author: pamphlets. Home: Pittsburgh, Pa. †

LEWIS, CHARLES WILLIAM, JR., urologist; b. Greensboro, N.C., May 13, 1921; s. Charles William and Ida (Hodgkin) L.; m. Gene Harlow, Nov. 10, 1945; children—Charles William III, Allan McDonald, Lloyd Arthur, Richard Harlow. B.S., Guilford Coll., 1942; M.D., Duke, 1945. Commd. ensign M.C. USN, 1943, advanced through grades to capt., 1960; sr. med. officer (U.S.S. Orion), 1946-48; sr. med. officer (Naval Hosp.), Pensacola, 1948-50, resident urology, San Diego, 1950-53, chief urology naval hosps., Guam, 1953-54, Jacksonville, Fla., 1955-58, St. Albans, N.Y., 1958-66, M.C. detail officer, 1966-69; comdg. officer (Naval Hosp.), Jacksonville, 1969—72; dep. dir. (Navy Regional Med. Center), Portsmouth, Va., 1972-73; chief urology U. Hosp. of Jacksonville, from 1973; asso. prof. U. Fla. Sch. Medicine, from 1973; Mem. Mayor's Health Adv. Bd., Jacksonville, 1969-72; Bd. dirs. Mental Health Clinic Duval County, Fla., pres., 1979. Decorated Navy Commendation medal, Meritorious Service medal. Mem. A.M.A., Am. Urol. Assn., Duval County Med. Soc. (v.p. 1979), Fla. Urol. Soc. (pres. 1983), Nu Sigma Nu, Alpha Omega Alpha. Home: Orange Park, Fla.

LEWIS, DAVID THOMAS, Judge; b. Salt Lake City, Apr. 25, 1912; s. Thomas David and Ettie (Ellerbeck) L.; m. Marie Stewart, Sept. 10, 1938; children—Kent, David, Frank. B.A., U. Utah, 1934, LL.B., 1937, LL.D., 1971. Bar: Utah bar 1938. Practiced, Salt Lake City, 1938-50, state dist. judge, 1950-56, U.S. circuit judge 10th Circuit, 1956-83, chief judge, 1970-77, sr. judge, 1977-83; Chmn. Circuit Chief Judges Conf., 1974-75. Mem. Utah Legislature, 1947-48. Served with criminal investigation div. AUS, 1944-45. Mem. Am., Fed., Utah bar assns., Maritime Law Assn., Order of Coif, Phi Delta Phi. Club: Salt Lake Country. Home: Salt Lake City, Utah. Died Sept. 9, 1983.

LEWIS, EARL RAMAGE, congressman; b. at Lamira, O., Feb. 22, 1887; s. William Duff and Nanna Laura (Ramage) L.; B.S., Muskingum Coll., 1911; LL.B., Western Reserve Univ., 1914; m. Hazel Jane Neff, Sept. 28, 1916; children—Capt. Robert Neff, U.S.A. M.C.R., Elizabeth Jeanette (Mrs. Paul M. Spurrier), Richard Earl. Admitted to Ohio bar, 1914, and began practice in St. Clairsville; mem. firm Thornburg & Lewis; mem. Ohio State Senate, 1927-28, 1931-34, pres. pro tem of Senate, 1931-32, Rep. floor leader, 1931-34; member 76th Congress (1939-41), 78th to 80th Congresses (1943-49), 18th Ohio District. Chmn. Ohio State Republican campaign, 1930. Member Interstate Commission on Conflicting Taxation of Am. Legislators Assn., 1931-35. Mem. bd. trustees Muskingum Coll. from 1922. Mem. Am., Ohio State and Belmont County bar assns., Phi Delta Phi, Tau Kappa Alpha. Republican. Mem. United Presbyn. Ch. Mason (Shriner), Elk, K.P. Author of Annotations Ohio State Mining Code, 1933. Home: St. Clairsville, Ohio. †

LEWIS, GEORGE (MATHEWS), educator; b. Washington, D.C., Apr. 12, 1888; s. William Henry and Eleanor Veronica (Craig) Mathews; A.B., LaSalle Coll., Phila., 1917; A.M., Univ. of Pa., 1922; Sc.D., Duquesne U., 1925. Entered Order of Brothers of the Christian Schs., 1904; asst. prof. physics and mathematics, LeSalle Coll., 1917-22; vice pres., dean, prof. of mathematics, St. Thomas Coll., Univ. of Scranton, 1922-25; pres., dean, St. Thomas Coll., 1925-31; prof. of mathematics, LaSalle Coll., Phila., from 1934, dean of coll., 1938-44, v.p. since 1944. Fellow A.A.A.S.; mem. Am. Math. Soc.; Alpha Epsilon Delta. Home: Philadelphia, Pa. †

LEWIS, JOHN E., army officer; b. Emporia, Kan., Apr. 27, 1887; grad. U.S. Mil. Acad.; commd. 2d lt. Cav., June 1912; and advanced through the grades to brig. gen., Feb. 1942; became instr. Army Industrial Coll., June 1938, asst. commandant, July, 1938, commandant, Nov. 1940; on duty with Armored Force, Ft. Knox, Ky., Feb. 1941; with 90th Inf. Div., Camp Barkley, Tex., 1942. Deceased.

LEWIS, JOSEPH, author; b. Montgomery, Ala., June 11, 1889; s. Samuel and Ray (Levy) L.; ed. pub. schs.; m. Ruth Stroller Grubman, July 15, 1952. Responsible for election of Thomas Paine to Hall of Fame, 1946; dedicated Borglum statue of Thomas Paine, Paris, France, 1948, statue of Thomas Paine, Morristown, N.J., 1950, made address at unveiling of plaque at burial site of Thomas Paine, New Rochelle, N.Y., 1953; ded. as pub. meml. the house in which Robert Ingersoll was born, 1954; dedicated Thomas Paine statue, Stratford, Eng., 1964. Instituted legal proceedings to stop reading of Bible in pub. schs. of N.Y., to prevent dismissal of N.Y. pub. sch. children to receive religious instr., to prevent use of pub. sch. buses in N.Y. State to transport children to parochial schs., to prevent formation of sectarian clubs in pub. ednl. instns. Founder, sec. Thomas Paine Found., Robert G. Ingersoll Meml. Assn., Am. League for Separation Ch. and State; founder, pres. Freethinkers of Am. Mem. A.A.A.S. (life). Author: The Tyranny of God, 1921; The Bible Unmasked, 1926; Voltaire: The Incomparable Infidel, 1929; Burbank: The Infidel, 1930; Spain: Land Blighted by Religion, 1933; The Ten Commandments, 1945; Thomas Paine, Author of the Declaration of Independence, 1947; In the Name of Humanity, 1949; Inspiration and Wisdom from the Writings of Thomas Paine, 1954; The Tragic Patriot, 1954; Ingersoll the Magnificent, 1957; An Atheist Manifesto, 1954; The Serpents of Religion, 1959; The Fable of Jesus Christ, 1969. Founder, editor: The Age of Reason mag. Home: Miami Beach, Fla. †

LEWIS, NORMAN, educator, author; b. N.Y.C., Dec. 30, 1912; s. Herman and Deborah (Nevins) L.; m. Mary Goldstein, July 28, 1934; children: Margery, Debra. B.A., City Coll. N.Y., 1939; M.A., Columbia U., 1941. Instr., lectr. City U. N.Y., 1943-52; asso. prof. English N.Y.U., 1955-64; instr. Compton (Calif.) Coll., summers 1962-64, U. Calif. at Los Angeles extension, 1962-69; prof. English Rio Hondo Coll., Whittier, Calif., from 1964, chmn. communications dept., 1964-75. Author: (with Wilfred Funk) Thirty Days to a More Powerful Vocabulary, 1942, rev., 1970, Power with Words, 1943, How to Read Better and Faster, 1944, rev. edit., 1978, The Lewis English Refresher and Vocabulary Builder, 1945, Better English, 1948, Word Power Made Easy, 1949, rev. edit., 1978, The Rapid Vocabulary Builder, 1951, rev. edit., 1980, How to Get More Out of Your Reading, 1951, Twenty Days to Better Spelling, 1953, The New Roget's Thesaurus in Dictionary Form, 1961, rev. edit., 1978, Dictionary of Correct Spelling, 1962, Correct Spelling Made Easy, 1963, Dictionary of Modern Pronunciation, 1963, New Guide to Word Power, 1963, The New Power with Words, 1964, Thirty Days to Better English, 1964, The Modern Thesaurus of Synonyms, 1965, RSVP-Reading, Spelling, Vocabulary, Pronunciation, elementary texts I-III, 1966, coll. edit., 1977, rev. and enlarged edits., 1982-83, See, Say, and Write!, Books I and II, 1973, Instant Spelling Power, 1976, R.S.V.P. for College English Power, Book II, 1978, Book III, 1979, R.S.V.P. with Etymology, Book I, 1980, Book II, 1981, Book III, 1982, Instant Word Power, 1981, rev. edit., 1982, RSVP, Book A, 1984; also numerous articles in nat. mags. Address: Whittier, Calif.

LEWIS, OTTO O., sales exec.; b. Larned, Kan., Feb. 4, 1887; s. Americus B. and Celina E. (Thompson) L.; student Rose Poly. Inst., 1905; m. Ruth E. Reif, June 3, 1908; children—Ruth Elizabeth, Robert O. Asso., Fairbanks, Morse & Co., from 1908, mgr. Atlanta br. house, 1932-43, asst. sales mgr., 1943-48, sales mgr., 1948-50, dir. and v.p. charge sales, Chicago, from 1950; dir. Canadian Fairbanks, Morse Co., Ltd., Clinton (Ia.) Mfg. Co., Chicago Municipal Acceptance Corp. Mem. Am. Soc. M.E., Soc. Naval Architects and Marine Engrs. Mason

(Shriner). Clubs: Propeller of America; Atlanta Athletic, Union League (Chicago). Home: Evanston, Ill. †

LEWIS, READ, orgn. exec.; b. Oak Park, Ill., May 19, 1887; s. John and Isadel H. (Read) L.; A.B., U. Wis., 1909; LL.B., Columbia, 1914. Admitted to N.Y. bar, 1915, and began practice in N.Y.C.; apptd. spl. asst. to Am. ambassador to Russia, and as such administered relief funds in Kursk and Voronezh, 1916-17, and directed Am. publicity in Moscow and Archangel, 1918-19; exec. dir. Common Council for Am. Unity and its successor orgn., Am. Council Nationalities Service, 1922-66, chmn. bd., 1966-69, chmn. nat. com., from 1969. Home: New York, N.Y. †

LEWIS, SAMUEL J., orthodontist; b. Kalamazoo, Mich., June 2, 1887; D.D.S., Wayne U., 1907; student Kalamazoo Coll., 1908-09; Angle Sch. of Orthodontia, New London, Conn., 1911; m. Marion E. Hecht, June 30, 1920; children—Carol L. (wife of Lt. I. Sackman Marx, Army Air Corps), Elizabeth Brock (Mrs. Howard F. Marx). Practicing orthodontist since 1911; professor orthodontics U. of Detroit, 1932-46, head of post graduate orthodontics, 1946-49; head of orthodontic research, Mich. Children's Fund, 1928-33; research consultant Merrill-Palmer Sch., Detroit, from 1944; director post graduate orthodontics School Dentistry, St. Louis Univ., from 1956. Served with Base Hosp. No. 102, A.E.F., Italy, 1918-19. Decorated Garibaldi Medal. Fellow Am. Coll. Dentists; mem. Am. Dental Assn., Am. Soc. Orthodontists, A.A.A.S., Omicron Kappa Upsilon, Xi Psi Phi, Alpha Omega. Mason. †

LEWIS, THOMAS E., army officer; b. Milwaukee, Wis., Oct. 16, 1890; s. Maj. Gen. Edward M. and Harriet R. (Balding) L.; student St. John's Mil. Acad., Delafield, Wis., Columbia Prep. Sch., Washington, D.C.; B.S., U.S. Mil. Acad., 1912; grad. Field Arty. Sch., battery officers course, 1931, advanced horsemanship course, 1932, advanced equitation course, Cav. Sch., 1934. Command and Gen. Staff Sch., 1937; m. Lucile O. Witherspoon, Dec. 26, 1925; children—Nancy Joan, Ann Witherspoon. Commanding 2d lt. Inf., June 1922, and advanced through the grades to brig. gen. 1943; transferred to Field Arty., 1923, then with 5th U.S. Army. Awarded Purple Heart, Legion of Merit. Deceased.

LEWIS, TRACY HAMMOND, advertising; b. Richfield, O., Nov. 30, 1890; s. William E. and Frances (Oviatt) L.; A.B., Yale, 1912; m. Esther Tufts, Oct. 16, 1920; children—William E. (dec.), Nancy, Anne, Patricia. Began as reporter for New York Times; editor Sunday Morning Telegraph, New York, 1912-15; on Mexican border, summer of 1916; admitted to Officers' Training, Gunnery Sect., Signal Corps., Dec. 1917; 1st lt., Air Service, 1917-18; on discharge from service apptd. maj., Ordnance Dept., N.Y., on staffs of Gov. Smith and Gen. O'Ryan. Washington polit. corr., New York Morning Telegraph, 1916-17; became asso. editor Morning Telegraph, New York, 1919; with Smith, Sturgis & Moore (advertising). Clubs: Yale, Manhasset Bay Yacht, North Hempstead Country, N.Y. Athletic, Nat. Press, Monches Bay Gun (pres.), Lands Point Casino (pres.). Author: Along the Rio Grande, 1916. Home: L.I., N.Y. †

LEWIS, WILLARD POTTER, librarian; b. Watertown, N.Y., Aug. 10, 1889; s. Benjamin Morgan and Jennie Noa (Potter) L.; B.A., Wesleyan U., Conn., 1911, M.A., 1912; B.L.S., New York State Library Sch., Albany, N.Y., 1913; m. Harriet Edna Stillman, Apr. 9, 1914; children—Robert Stillman, Barbara Evelyn, Walter Morgan, Donald Richey. Asst. N.Y. State Library, 1912-13; librarian, Albany (N.Y.) Y.M.C.A., 1913-14, Baylor U., 1914-19; organizer and librarian, Camp McArthur Library, Waco, Tex., Oct.-Dec. 1917; librarian U. of N.H., 1919-29, Wesleyan U., Conn., 1929-31, Pa. State Coll., 1931-48, asso. librarian from 1948, resident dir. N.H. Summer Library Sch., 1920-26; lecturer Conn. Pub. Library Summer Sch., 1926-30; dir. Pa. State Coll. Summer Library Sch., 1932-48. Member A.L.A. (chmn. agrl. libraries sect. 1927-28; sec., treas. coll. and reference sect. 1935-38; sec., Assn. of College and Reference Libraries, 1938-41), N.H. Li- Inst. Am., Phi Beta Kappa, Sigma Chi, Beta Gamma Sigma, Beta Alpha Psi, Alpha Kappa Psi. Republican. Conglist. Clubs: Rockefeller Center Luncheon (N.Y. City); Riverside (Conn.) Yacht. Home: Riverside, Conn. Deceased.

LEWIS, WILMARTH SHELDON, author, editor; b. Alameda, Calif., Nov. 14, 1895; s. Azro Nathaniel and Miranda (Sheldon) L.; student Thacher Sch., 1910-14; B.A., Yale, 1918, hon. M.A., 1937, LL.D., 1965; Litt.D., Brown U., 1945, U. Rochester, 1946, Nat. U. Ireland, 1957, U. Del., 1961, U. Cambridge (Eng.), 1962, U. Melbourne, 1972; L.H.D., Trinity Coll., 1950, Bucknell U., 1958; LL.D., U. Hartford, 1972; m. Annie Burr Auchincloss, Jan. 25, 1928 (dec. 1959). Assoc. Yale U. Press, 1920-22; research assoc. Yale U., 1933-38; chief info. div. OSS, 1941-43. Chmn. John Carter Brown Library Assocs., 1944-47, mem. bd. mgmt.; chmn. Yale Library Assocs., 1933-45; hon. fellow Pierpont Morgan Library; trustee Inst. Advanced Study, Watkinson Library, Hartford, Redwood Library, Newport, Thacher Sch. Ojai (Calif.), Henry F. DuPont Mus., Winterthur, Historic Deerfield (Mass.), John F. Kennedy Library; mem. Nat. Portrait Gallery Commn., Nat. Collection Fine Arts; founder chmn. librarians council Library of Congress, 1942-46. Served as 2d lt., 144th F.A., U.S. Army, 1917-19. Fellow Yale, 1938-64. Recipient Yale medal, 1965, Donald F. Hyde award Princeton, 1968; Gleeson Library Assos. medal U. San Francisco, 1969; Benjamin Franklin gold medal Royal Soc. Arts, 1975; Nathan Hale award Yale Club Hartford, 1975; Nat. Portrait Gallery gold medal, 1978. Fellow Am. Philos. Soc., Am. Acad. Arts and Scis., Royal Soc. Lit.; mem. Soc. Colonial Wars, Soc. Cin (hon.), Soc. Antiquaries, Royal Soc. Arts, Holland Soc. N.Y., Phi Beta Kappa (hon.), Beta Theta Pi, Scroll and Key. Clubs: Pacific Union (San Francisco); Athenaeum (London); Century, Grolier, Yale (N.Y.C.); Tavern (Boston); Metropolitan (Washington). Author: Tutor's Lane, 1922; Three Tours Through London in the Years 1748, 1776 and 1797 (Colver lectures Brown U.), 1941; The Yale Collections, 1946; Collector's Progress, 1951; Horace Walpole's Library (Sandars lectures Cambridge U.), 1957; Horace Walpole (Mellon lectures), 1960; One Man's Education, 1967; See For Yourself, 1971; Read As You Please, 1977; Rescuing Horace Walpole, 1978. Editor: A Selection of Letters of Horace Walpole, 1926, 1951, 73; Horace Walpole's Fugitive Verses, 1931; Private Charity in England, 1947-57 (with Ralph M. Williams), 1938; Yale edition of Horace Walpole's Correspondence, 39 vols., 1937-73. Contbr. Atlantic Monthly, Am. Scholar, Va. Quar., Yale Rev., other mags. Home: Farmington, Conn. Died Oct. 7, 1979.

LEY, KATHERINE LOUISE, educator; b. Prairie du Sac, Wis., Dec. 6, 1919; d. Ivan Herman and G. Louise (Conger) L. B.S., U. Wis., 1941; M.S., UCLA, 1947; Ph.D., U. Iowa, 1960. Tchr. pub. schs., Platteville, Wis., 1941-43; instr. Iowa State Coll., Ames, 1943-45; instr., asst. prof., asso. prof. U. Colo., Boulder, 1946-61; asso. prof. U. Mich., Ann Arbor, 1961-66; vis. prof. U. So. Calif., Los Angeles, summer, 1959, U. Wash., Seattle, summer 1961, U. N.C., 1971, Tex. Women's U., 1973; Distinguished vis. prof. U. Bridgeport, Conn., 1974, Bowling Green State U., 1978; prof., chmn. women's phys. edn. dept. State U. N.Y., Coll. at Cortland, 1966-78; prof., chmn., athletic dir. Capital U., Columbus, Ohio, 1978-81; Cons. Ednl. Testing Service, Princeton, N.J., from 1968; chmn. Nat. Com. on Standards for Girls and Women's Sports, 1954-56; mem. governing council U.S. Track and Field Fedn., 1962-65; U.S. Gymnastics Fedn., 1962; 1st chmn. Commn. on Intercollegiate Athletics for Women, 1966-69; bd. cons. U.S. Olympic Com., from 1969; bd. dirs. U.S. Sports Acad., from 1979. Co-author: Team and Individual Sports for Women, 1955; Editor, cons., Addison Wesley Pub. Co., Reading, Mass.; Contbr. articles to profl. jours. Recipient merit award Eastern Assn. Phys. Edn. Coll. Women, 1974, merit award Assn. Intercollegiate Athletics for Women, 1979; M. Gladys Scott award U. Iowa, 1975; Varsity C Faculty award, 1979; Honor Fellow award Nat. Assn. Girls and Women in Sport, 1979; named to Hall of Fame Nat. Assn. Collegiate Dirs. Athletics, 1981. Mem. AAHPER (life, v.p. 1961, mem. exec. council phys. edn. div. 1972, pres. from 1974, honor award Eastern dist. 1976), Nat. Assn. Phys. Edn. Coll. Women, Am. Acad. Phys. Edn., Am. Coll. Sports Medicine, Nat. Found. for Health, Phys. Edn. and Recreation, Phi Kappa Phi, Delta Kappa Gamma., Order Eastern Star. Home: Granville, OH.

LIBBY, WILLIAM CHARLES, artist, educator; b. Pitts.; s. Isaac and Elizabeth (Ochs) L.; 1 son, William Charles II. Student, U. Pitts., 1936-37; B.A., Carnegie-Mellon U., 1941; postgrad., U. Tex., 1944, Colorado Springs Fine Arts Center, 1948, L'Academie de la Grande Chaumier, France, 1951, Atelier 17, France, 1941. Mem. faculty dept. art Carnegie-Mellon U., Pitts., from 1945, prof., from 1967; vis. prof. U. Ga., 1967-68, U. Wis., 1981; lectr. Western Pa. Edn. Assn. Conf., Pitts., 1959; lectr. color and structural sense Oglebay Inst., W.Va., 1970, Youngstown (Ohio) U., 1978, Seton Hill Coll., Greensburg, Pa., 1979, U. Wis., Madison, 1981. Author: Color and the Structural Sense, 1974; illustrator: (by Stefan Lorant) The Story of An American City, 1957; contbg. editor: Am. Artist, 1970-73; contbr. articles to profl. publs.; One man shows include, Cleve. Inst. Art, retrospective exhbn., Arts and Crafts Center Pitts., Carnegie Mus. Art, Ind. U., Allegheny Coll., group exhbns. include, Pa. Acad. Art, Phila., Cin. Mus. Art, Phila. Print Club; represented in permanent collections, Met. Mus. Art, N.Y.C., Bklyn. Mus. Art, Library of Congress, Carnegie-Mellon U. Recipient graphic arts research grantee Carnegie-Mellon U., 1963. Mem. Soc. Am. Graphic Artists, NAD. Home: Pittsburgh, PA.

LICHTENWALNER, NORTON LEWIS, congressman; b. Allentown, Pa., June 1, 1889; s. Fred H. and Jennie H. (Seiple) L.; student Lehigh, 1906-08; m. Anna E. Koch, Oct. 15, 1912. With E. Naumburg & Co., bankers, Wall St., New York, 7 yrs.; in furniture business, Allentown, until 1922; dealer in motor cars as Lichtenwalner Motor Co. from 1922; dir. Allentown Industrial Loan Corpn., Lehigh Valley Finance Co. Mem. 72d Congress (1931-33), 14th Pa. Dist. Mem. U.S. Naval Res., Warld War. Mem. Internat. Rotary Club, Am. Legion. Democrat. Mason (32 deg., Shriner), Elk. Clubs: Lehigh Valley Motor (sec.), Livingston (Allentown); Bethlehem (Pa.). Home: Allentown, Pa. †

LICHTY, GEORGE M., cartoonist; b. Chgo., May 16, 1905; s. Julius and Ella (Hirsch) Lichtenstein; m. Eleanor Louise Fretter, Jan. 5, 1931; children—Linda Louise, Susan Emory. Student, Chgo. Art Inst., 1924-25; A.B., U. Mich., 1929. Sports cartoonist, Chgo. Daily Times, 1930-32; created: feature Grin and Bear It, 1932; syndicated by feature, United Features Syndicate, N.Y.C., 1934-40, Chgo. Sun-Times, 1947-67, Field Newspaper Syndicate, Chgo., 1967-83. Mem. Nat. Cartoonists Soc. Democrat. Clubs: Press (San Francisco), Bohemian (San Francisco). Home: Santa Rosa, Calif. Died July 18, 1983.

LIEBERMAN, SAUL, educator, rabbi; b. Motol, Poland, May 28, 1898; s. Moses and Luba (Katzenellenbogen) L.; Rabbi, Slobodca Theol. Sem., 1916; M.A., Hebrew U., Jerusalem, 1931; D.H.L. (hon.), Jewish Theol. Sem., 1942; Ph.D. (hon.), Hebrew U., 1962; Litt.D. (hon.), Harvard, 1966; LL.D. (hon.), Dropsie U., 1969, Bar Ilan U., Israel, 1971. Came to U.S. 1940, naturalized, 1953. Tchr. of Talmud, Hebrew U., 1931-36; dean Harry Fischel Inst., Jerusalem 1935-40; prof. Palestinian lit. and instns. Jewish Theol. Sem. Am., N.Y.C., 1940-66, Distinguished Service prof., 1966-83, dean grad. dept., from 1949, rabbi congregation, dean Rabbinical Sch., from 1954, also rector. Recipient State of Israel prize, 1972; Internat. Harvey prize, 1976. Fellow Am. Acad. Jewish Research (pres. 1950-58), Am. Acad. Arts and Scis., Israel Acad. Scis. and Humanities, State of Israel Acad. Hebrew Lang. (fgn.). Author: A Commentary on the Palestinian Talmud, 1934, A Commentary on the Tosefta, vols. I-IV, 1937-39; The Talmud of Caesarea Jerusalem, 1931; Greek in Jewish Palestine, 1942; Roman Legal Institutions in Early Rabbinica and Acta Martyrum, 1944; The Martyrs of Caesarea, 1944; Hellenism in Jewish Palestine, 1950; Tosefta Commentary, vols. 1-12, 1955-73. Editor: The Louis Ginsberg Jubilee Vols., 1954; The Laws of the Jerushalmi by Maimonides, 1947; The A. Marx Vols., 1950. Contbr. to Harry A. Wolfson Jubilee Vols., 1965; Salo W. Baron Jubilee Vols., 1974; also articles to jours. Home: New York, N.Y. Died Mar. 23, 1983.

LIEBHAFSKY, HERMAN ALFRED, educator; b. Zwittau, Austria-Hungary, Nov. 18, 1905; s. Hugo and Aurelia (Demel) L.; B.S., Tex. A. and M. Coll., 1926; M.S., U. Nebr., 1927; Ph.D., U. Calif. at Berkeley, 1929; m. Sybil Small, Nov. 30, 1935; childrn—Douglas, Alison (Mrs. Roger Van Vranken Des Forges). Came to U.S., 1912, naturalized, 1921. Instr. chemistry U. Calif. at Berkeley, 1929-34; with Gen. Electric Co., Schenectady, 1934-67, mgr. electrochem. br., 1964-67; prof. chemistry Tex. A. and M.U., College Station, 1967-72, prof. emeritus, 1972-82. Mem. Soc. Applied Spectroscopy (hon. life), Am. Chem. Soc. (Fisher award 1961). Club: Mohawk Golf (Schenectady). Sr. author: X-ray Absorption and Emission in Analytical Chemistry, 1960, Fuel Cells and Fuel Batteries, 1968; X-Rays, Electrons, and Analytical Chemistry, 1972; author: William David Coolidge: A Centenarian and His Work, 1974. Contbr. articles to profl. jours. Patentee in field. Home: Bryan, Tex. Died July 24, 1982.

LIEBMAN, MAX, TV producer-dir.; b. Aug. 5, 1902; s. Harry and Sara (Glazer) L.; student Boys High Sch., Bklyn.; m. Sonia Veskova, Aug. 10, 1932. Producer mus. shows, from 1938; dir. Tamiment Summer Playhouse, Stroudsburg, Pa., 1934-41; producer Broadway Rev., 1949; producer, dir. Your Show of Shows, WNBT, N.Y.C., 1950-54; producer Bob Hope TV show, 1951, NBC-TV color spectaculars 1954-56, NBC-TV Stanley Comedy series, from 1956, Jackie Gleason spl., CBS, The Politician; producer From the Second City, Broadway, 1961, Chrysler World's Fair Show-Go-Round, 1964-65; producer-dir. feature film Ten from Your Show of Shows, 1973. Recipient numerous awards in TV. Mem. A.S.-C.A.P., Authors League Am. Jewish. Home: New York, N.Y. Died July 21, 1981.

LIEFERANT, HENRY, editor and author; b. Poland, Jan. 30, 1892; s. Maximilian and Cecilia (Engel) L.; ed. through high school, Poland; came to U.S. 1910, naturalized, 1918; m. Sylvia Saltzberg, June 27, 1924. With fashion magazine of May Manton Pattern Co., 1910-15; engaged in free-lance short story writing, 1915-17 and 1919-27; with Macfadden Publications, N.Y. City, 1927-46; editor-in-chief True Story Mag., also supervising editor of 3 other magazines. Served as corpl., U.S. Army, World War I. Mason. Author: (all in collaboration with Sylvia Saltzberg Lieferant) Doctors' Wives, 1930; Grass on the Mountain, 1938; Charity Patient, 1939; United They Stand, 1940; One Enduring Purpose, 1941; Hospital—Quiet, Please, 1941; Teacher's Husband, 1941; They Always Come Home, 1942; Heavenly Harmony, 1942; Seven Daughter, 1947; Fields White Harvest (England only), 1947. Home: New York, N.Y.

LIGGITT, EARLE O., ednl. adminstr.; b. Knoxville, OH., July 19, 1890; s. Charles and Loretta (Culp) L.; B.S. cum laude, Muskingum Coll., 1917; A.M., U. of Pittsburgh, 1927, Ph.D., 1942; student Teachers Coll. Columbia U., summer 1929; extension courses, Pa. State Coll., 1923-24; m. Anna Rose Kingan, Aug. 14, 1917; children—William A., Loretta Jane, Robert C., Mary Lois. Teacher elementary and high sch., 1910-14; supt. schs., Quaker City, OH., 1917; instr. edn. (summer terms), State Teachers Coll., Slippery Rock, Pa., 1921-24; supervising prin. schs. Washington Twp. (Butler County), Pa., Freeport, Pa., 1922-28, Bridgeville, Pa., 1928-30; supt. schs., Crafton, Pa., 1930-38; supt. schs., Munhall, Pa., since 1938; lecturer in ednl. adminstrn. (part-time), U. of Pittsburgh, 1946-48; mem. exec. com. local Boy Scouts. Served with U.S. Army, 1918. Mem. Pa. state and Allegheny county Supts. assns., Nat. and State Edn. Assns., Am. Assn. Sch. Adminstrs., Pittsburgh Council on Adult Edn., Am. Legion (bd. dirs.), Xi chap. Phi Delta

Kappa (nat. sec. 1942-44, nat. vice pres., 1944-48; nat. pres. 1948-50). Presbyterian (trustee). Mason (Shriner, Consistory). Club: Homestead Kiwanis. Home: Munhall, Pa. †

LILIENFELD, ABRAHAM MORRIS, epidemiologist; b. N.Y.C., Nov. 13, 1920; s. Joel and Eugenia (Kugler) L.; A.B., John Hopkins, 1941, M.P.H., 1949; M.D., U. Md., 1944; m. Lorraine Zemil, July 18, 1943; children—Julia, Saul, David. Intern, resident obstetrics Lutheran Hosp., Balt., 1944-46; asso. pub. health physician N.Y. State Dept. Health, 1949-50; dir. So. health dist. Balt. Health Dept., 1950-52; asst. prof. epidemiology Johns Hopkins, 1952-54, prof. chronic diseases, chmn. dept., 1958-84, dir. gamma globulin evaluation center USPHS, 1952; chief dept. statistics and epidemiology Roswell Park Meml. Inst., 1954-58. Member of National Advisory Heart Council, 1962-66; chairman of NIH joint council subcommittee on cerebrovascular disease, 1966-68; research adv. council Am. Cancer Soc., 1964-84; staff dir. President's Commn. Heart Disease, Cancer and Stroke, 1964-67; chmn. adv. council preventive medicine Md. Dept. Health, 1964-68. Trustee Md. Heart Assn.; exec. bd. Md. div. Am. Cancer Soc.; recipient Bronfman award pub. health achievement, 1968. Research Career awardee NIH, after 1962. Fellow Am. Pub. Health Assn. (recipient Bronfman prize 1968), American College Preventive Medicine; mem. Am. Epidemiol. Soc., A.A.A.S., Am. Statis. Assn., Am. Sociol. Assn., Am. Soc. Human Genetics. Home: Baltimore, Md. Died Aug. 6, 1984.

LILLEHEI, RICHARD CARLTON, surgeon, med. researcher, educator; b. Mpls., Dec. 10, 1927; s. Clarence I. and Elizabeth L. (Walton) L.; B.A. magna cum laude, U. Minn., 1948, B.S., 1949, M.D., 1951, Ph.D., 1960; m. Betty Jeanne Larsen, Dec. 20, 1952; children—Richard Carlton, Theodore J., John C., James L. Intern, Hennepin County Gen. Hosp., Mpls., 1951-52; resident surgeon U. Minn. Health Scis. Center, Mpls., 1952-54, 56-59, resident cardiovascular surgeon, 1959-60, asst. prof. surgery, 1960-62, asso. prof., 1962-66, prof., 1966-81. Served as capt. M.C., AUS, 1954-56. Recipient Hektoen gold medal AMA, 1964, Irving S. Cutter gold medal Phi Rho Sigma, 1976; named Man of Year, Minn. Jr. C. of C., 1962. Mem. Phi Beta Kappa, Sigma Xi, Alpha Omega Alpha. Contbr. articles to profl. jours., chpts. in books. Finished Boston Marathon, 1972-79. Home: Minneapolis, Minn. Died Apr. 1, 1981.

LILLEY, TOM, organization executive; b. Bluefield, W.Va., Aug. 13, 1912; s. Charles Ellis and Minnie Alice (Holl) L.; m. Nancy Clegg, Dec. 27, 1936; children: Anne, Cynthia, Susan. B.A., Harvard U., 1934, M.B.A., 1936. Indsl. dept. Lehman Bros., N.Y.C., 1936-40; staff Burlington Mills, Greensboro, N.C., 1941-42; asso. prof., asst. dir. research Harvard Bus. Sch., 1942-48; successively mem. controller's office Ford div., product planning mgr., asst. gen. mgr. internat. div. Ford Motor Co., v.p. internat. staff, 1948-65; dir. Export-Import Bank of U.S., 1965-72; treas. Population Crisis Com., Washington, 1974-81; dir. Huyck Corp., 1974-80; Past mem. Internat. Road Fedn., Nat. Fgn. Trade Council, Nat. Export Expansion Council, U.S. Council Internat. C. of C. (trustee). Presbyn. Home: Washington, D.C. Died Nov. 16, 1981.

LILLY, JOHN FRANCIS, banker; b. Cape Girardeau, Mo., Oct. 11, 1889; s. Edward S. and Mary (Albert) L.; student pub. schs.; m. Emily Kimball, July 7, 1923; children—Mary Jean (Mrs. Robert C. Ausbeck), John K., Douglas R. Mng. officer Sturdivant Bank, Cape Girardeau, Mo., 1915-28; nat. bank examiner 8th Fed. Res. Dist., 1928-33; exec. v.p. Clayton Nat. Bank (Mo.), 1933-40, pres., 1940-46; pres. St. Louis County Nat. Bank, Clayton, 1946-64, chmn. bd., from 1951; dir. Clayton Fed. Savs. & Loan Assn. Mem. St. Louis County C. of C. (chmn. bd.). Clubs: Racquet, Missouri Athletic (St. Louis); Bellerive Country. Home: University City, Mo. †

LINCOLN, VICTORIA, writer; b. Fall River, Mass., Oct. 23, 1904; d. Jonhathan Thayer and Louise Sears (Cobb) Lincoln; A.B., Radcliffe, 1926; m. Isaac Watkins, 1927; 1 dau., Penelope Thayer (Mrs. Paul Williams); m. 2d, Victor Lowe, Apr. 3, 1934; children—Thomas Cobb, Louise Lincoln Kittredge. Author: The Swan Island Murders, 1930; February Hill, 1934; Grandmother and the Comet, 1944; The Wind at My Back, 1946; Celia Amberley, 1949; Out From Eden, 1951; The Wild Honey, 1953; A Dangerous Innocence, 1958; Charles, 1962; Desert Water, 1963; (juvenile) Everyhow Remarkable, 1967; A Private Disgrace; Lizzie Borden by Daylight (Mystery Writers Am. award), 1967; also articles, short stories, novelettes in The New Yorker, Harpers, Atlantic, McCalls, Ladies Home Jour., others. Home: Baltimore, Md. Died June 13, 1981.

LINDAMAN, EDWARD BENJAMIN, coll. pres.; b. Davenport, Iowa, May 6, 1920; s. Benjamin and Lillian (Hammerand) L.; A.S., Mesabi Community Coll., 1939; L.H.D. (hon.), Tarkio Coll., 1966; Sc.D. (hon.), Chapman Coll., 1970; m. Geraldine Metcalf, Apr. 26, 1944; children—David William Susan, Brian Edward, Merrilee. Prodn. control and project scheduling N.Am. Aviation, Inc., Los Angeles, 1940-50; asst. to pres. Am. Helicopter Co., Inc., Manhattan Beach, Calif., 1951-53; mgmt. reporting specialist Hughes Aircraft Co., Culver City, Calif., 1954-56; with autonetics div. N.Am. Aviation, Inc., Los Angeles, 1956-62; mgr. master program planning, def. div. Otis Elevator Co., Santa Ana, 1962-64; asst. to v.p. mgmt. planning and controls, mgr. configuration mgmt., dir. program control Apollo Spacecraft, N.Am. Rockwell Corp., Downey, Calif., 1964-69; pres. Whitworth Coll., Spokane, Wash., 1970-80. Pres. Nat. Council Presbyn. Men, 1967; ofcl. del. 4th Assembly World Council Chs., Uppsala, 1968; chmn. nat. goals steering com. Nat. Council YMCA's, 1976; chairperson Gov.'s Task Force on Alternatives for Wash. 1985, 1974-75; nat. chairperson Environmental Symposium series Expo '74 World's Fair, Spokane, 1974. Trustee San Francisco Theol. Sem. Mem. AFTRA. Author: Space: A New Direction For Mankind, 1969; (TV program) Rebels with a Cause, ABC, Los Angeles, 1967-69. Home: Spokane, Wash. Died Aug. 26, 1982.

LINDBERG, WILLIAM J., judge; b. Minot, N.D., Dec. 17, 1904; s. Carl and Elizabeth (Beran) L.; LL.B., Gonzaga Law Sch., 1927; LL.M., Georgetown U., 1928; m. Josephine Byrd Poe, July 24, 1937; children—Josephine Poe, Elizabeth Beran, William J., John F. Admitted to Wash. bar, 1927; clk. Senator C.C. Dill, Washington, 1928; assoc. law firm Cannon, McKevitt & Frazer, Spokane, 1928-33; prof. law Gonzaga Law Sch., 1928-33; sec. Wash. State Senate, 1933; asst. atty. gen., Olympia, 1933-34; mem. Wash. State Liquor Control Bd., 1934-41; individual practice law, Olympia, 1941-44, Seattle, 1944-51; apptd. U.S. Dist. Judge for Eastern and Western dists. Wash., 1951-61; chief judge Western Dist. Wash., 1959-71, sr. judge (ret.), 1971-81. Dist. Ct. rep. 9th Circuit to U.S. Jud. Conf., 1960-63. Mem. Am., Wash. State, Seattle bar assns. Home: Seattle, Wash. Died Dec. 15, 1981.

LINDEMANN, CARL, JR., broadcasting company executive; b. Hackensack, N.J., Dec. 15, 1922; s. Carl and Dorothy (O'Connor) L.; m. Marguerite Darmour Williams, Apr. 8, 1951; children: Catherine Darmour, Sarah C., Frances C., Mary A., Carl III. Grad., Phillips Exeter Acad., 1940; S.B., Mass. Inst. Tech., 1947. With Foote, Cone & Belding, 1947; with NBC, 1948-77; v.p. NBC-TV, 1959-77, v.p. program sales, 1960-77, charge daytime programs TV network, 1957-77, v.p. programs Calif. nat. programs, 1960-77, v.p. spl. projects, news, 1962-64, v.p. sports, 1963-77; cons. N.Y. Olympic Project, 1977; exec. producer Nat. Hockey League Network, 1977-78; v.p. programs CBS Sports div. CBS Inc., N.Y.C., 1978-80, v.p. and asst. to pres., 1980-85. Mem. nat. council Boy Scouts Am.; Mem. vis. com. Mass. Inst. Tech. Served to 1st lt. AUS, 1942-46. Home: New York, N.Y. Died June 3, 1985.

LINDHOLM, WILLIAM LAWRENCE, retired telephone company executive; b. Mountain Grove, Mo., May 27, 1914; s. Lawrence E. and Elizabeth (Mitchell) L.; m. Eleanor Lane Davis, June 16, 1939; 1 son, Robert Kenneth. Student, U. Ala., 1933-34; B.A. in Bus. Adminstrn, U. Mo., 1936; LL.D., Bethany Coll., 1972. With Southwestern Bell Telephone Co., 1936-65, gen. mgr. South Tex. area, Houston, 1959-63, v.p. for Tex., Dallas, 1963-65; pres., chief exec. officer Chesapeake & Potomac Telephone Cos., 1965-70; exec. v.p. Am. Tel. & Tel. Co., N.Y.C., 1970-72, vice chmn. bd., 1972-76, pres., 1976-77; dir. Shell Oil Co., InterFirst Bank of Austin, N.A. Methodist. Home: Austin, Tex.

LINDLEY, DENVER, editor; b. N.Y.C., 1904; s. Charles Newton and Mary Louise (Denver) L.; grad. Hotchkiss Sch., 1922; B.A., Princeton, 1926; m. Jane Hastings Hickok, 1928 (dec.); 1 son, Denver Lindley; m. 2d, Frances Smyth, 1948 (div.); 1 son, Charles Robert; m. 3d, Helen K. Taylor, 1963 (div.). Instr. Princeton U., 1926-27; article and fiction editor Collier's Weekly, 1928-44; editor Appleton-Century Co., 1944-46, Henry Holt & Co., 1946-48; editor Harcourt, Brace & Co., N.Y.C., 1949-55, exec. editor, 1955-58; sr. editor Viking Press, N.Y.C., 1958-68, cons., 1968-82. Mem. Phi Beta Kappa. Club: Century Assn. Translator books by André Maurois, Erich Maria Remarque, Thomas Mann, Hermann Hesse, Jean Dutourd. Author articles, short stories. Home: Tucson, Ariz. Died Feb. 11, 1982.

LINDSAY, CHARLES ROGERS, III, chem. mfr.; b. Chgo., July 10, 1903; s. Charles Rogers, Jr. and Dorothea (Gilman) L.; m. Isabella Woods Walsh, May 15, 1926; children—Dorothea Gilman (Mrs. Jurgen W. Heberle), Katherine Bingham. Grad., St. Albans Sch., Washington.; A.B., Williams Coll., 1925. Vice pres., dir. Lindsay Chem. Co., West Chicago, Ill., 1926-37, chmn. bd., pres., 1937-58; v.p., dir. Am. Potash & Chem. Corp., Los Angeles, 1958-68; Mem. personnel security bd. AEC, 1950-70. Precinct committeeman Republican Party, St. Charles, Ill., 1954-80, presdl. elector for Ill., 1956; chmn. St. Charles Rep. Central Com., 1966-70; Mem. exec. com. County Bd., Kane County, Ill., from 1972; mem. exec. com. Kane County Forest Preserve, from 1972; Adv. bd. Salvation Army; life trustee Delnor Hosp., St. Charles, Ill. Mem. Masters Fox Hounds Assn. Am., Sigma Phi Soc. Congregationalist. Clubs: Chevy Chase (Washington); Williams (N.Y.C.); University (Chgo.), Tavern (Chgo.); Mill Reef (Antigua, B.W.I.); Dunham Woods Riding (Wayne, Ill.), Wayne-DuPage Hunt (Wayne, Ill.) (master fox hounds 1935-45). Home: St Charles, Ill.

LINDSAY, INABEL BURNS, univ. dean; b. St. Joseph, Mo., Feb. 13, 1900; d. Joseph Smith and Margaret L. Hartshorn (Hawkins) Burns; A.B. cum laude, Howard U., 1920; Urban League fellow N.Y. Sch. Social Work, 1920-21; M.A. (Univ. fellow), U. Chgo., 1937, postgrad. Sch. Social Service Adminstrn., summers 1938, 40; Dr. Social Work, U. Pitts., 1952; m. Arnett G. Lindsay, June 27, 1925. Asst. to exec. Cleve. Urban League, summer 1922; tchr. Lincoln High Sch., Kansas City, Mo., 1922-25; social case work, Pub. Welfare Adminstrn., 1926-36; instr., asst. charge div. social work Howard U., 1937-42, acting dir., asst. prof., 1943-45, asso. prof., dean Sch. Social Work, 1945-51, prof., dean 1951-83; vis. prof. U. Coll. West Indies, Jamaica, 1960-61. Mem. adv. council nat. orgns. planning White House Conf. on Children and Youth, 1950, chmn. work group on minorities, 1960; cons. div. tech. tng. Dept Health, Edn. and Welfare, 1960, also mem. exam. rev. bd. state merit systems Bur. Pub. Assistance, nat. adviser U.S. Children's Bur. Bd. dirs. Bur. Rehab., Washington, Mental Health Assn. Recipient tng. specialist grant for study and lecture, Norway and Sweden, 1958. Mem. Council Social Work Edn. (council dels. 1952), Nat. Assn. Social Workers, Nat. Conf. Social Welfare (chmn. com. social research and social studies, mem. nat. bd.), Nat. Council Negro Women Edn. Found. (exec. com.), Nat. Urban League (del.-at-large). Contbr. numerous articles profl. publs.; author monograph. Home: Washington, D.C. Died Sept. 20, 1983.

LINDSAY, JOHN RALSTON, physician, educator; b. Renfrew, Ont., Can., Dec. 23, 1898; s. John M. and Christena (Wright) L.; M.D., McGill U., 1925; M.D. (hon.), Uppsala, Sweden, 1963; m. Elizabeth Wood, Feb. 6, 1937 (div. 1955); children—Christena W., Anne S., Elizabeth W.; m. 2d, Dorothy Morrison, Mar. 1, 1962 (div.); m. 3d. Marguerite Glynn, Aug. 6, 1969 (dec.). Came to U.S., 1928, naturalized, 1936. Intern Ottawa Civic Hosp., 1925-26; resident otolaryngology Royal Victoria Hosp., Montreal, 1927-28, Hosp. for Sick Children, Toronto, 1926-27; postgrad. tng. Zurich and Vienna, 1931; splst. otolaryngology, from 1928; faculty U. Chgo., 1928-81, prof. otolaryngology, from 1941, Thomas D. Jones prof. surgery, 1963-81, head otolaryngology sect., 1929-66. Fellow A.C.S.; mem. A.M.A., Am. Acad. Ophthalmology and Otolaryngology (pres. 1964), Am. Laryngol., Rhinol. and Otol. Soc. (past pres.). Am. Broncho-Esophagological Assn., Am. Otol. Soc. Inc. (past pres.), Am. Laryngol. Assn., Collegium Oto-Rhinolaryngologicum Amicitae Sacrum (pres. 1967), Ill., Chgo. med. socs., Inst. Medicine Chgo., Chgo. Laryngol. and Otol. Soc. (past pres.). Home: Chicago, Ill. Died Dec. 20, 1981.

LINDSAY, KENNETH, mfg. exec.; b. Dubuque, Ia., June 23, 1890; s. James Rodgers and Florence (Trout) L.; B.S., U. Chgo., 1912; m. Ida Lyman, May 6, 1914; children—George Lyman, Kenneth. Gen. mgr. Wapsie Power & Light Co., Mt. Vernon, Ia., 1912-17; sales mgr. Terry Durin Co., Cedar Rapids, Ia., 1917-30; v.p., sales mgr. Ia. Mfg. Co., 1930-48, exec. v.p., from 1948; pres. Ia. Mfg. Export Sales Co. Past pres. Social Welfare League. Mem. overall adv. com. constrn. machinery industry, adv. com. portable rock crusher mfrs. WPB. Mem. Am. Road Builders Assn. (dir.), Internat. Rd. Fedn. (dir.), Nat. Resources Development Assn. (dir.), U.S. C. of C. (mem. conservation com.), Ia. State Golf Assn. (past pres.), Constrn. Industry Mfrs. Assn. (dir.). Mason, Elk. Clubs: Kiwanis (past pres.), Cedar Rapids Country. Home: Cedar Rapids, Ia. †

LINEY, JOHN JOSEPH, JR., cartoonist; b. Phila., May 9, 1912; s. John Joseph and Mary Elizabeth (Manderfield) L.; m. Rosa E. Acquesta, Apr. 9, 1938; 1 dau., Muriel Elise. Syndicated cartoonist: strip, Henry. Democrat. Roman Catholic. Deceased.*

LINK, ROGER PAUL, veterinarian, educator; b. Woodbine, Iowa, Jan. 24, 1910; s. Walter George and Jennie (Fornia) L.; m. Marjorie Haines, Apr. 16, 1938; 1 son, Ronald Charles. D.V.M., Iowa State U., 1934; student, U. Chgo., 1934; M.S., Kans. State U., Manhattan, 1938; Ph.D., U. Ill., 1951. Instr. physiology and pharmacology Mich. State U., 1934-35; instr., then asst. prof. vet. physiology Kans. State U., 1935-45; instr. Northwestern U. Med. Sch., 1946; mem. faculty U. Ill., 1946—, prof. vet. physiology and pharmacology, 1955—, head dept., 1961—; vis. prof. vet. pharmacology Chas. Pfizer & Co., 1955; Cons. div. health manpower Bur. Health Manpower, HHS; cons. Bur. Vet. Medicine, FDA; chmn. revision com. vet. drugs Nat. Formulary, 1960-65; mem. U.S. Pharmacopeia Conv., 1960-70, 75—; adv. bd. Morris Animal Found. Active Little League, Babe Ruth Baseball. Recipient Spl. Service award U. Ill. Alumni Assn., 1982, citation for outstanding service to univ. and state Ill. Gen. Assembly. Fellow Am. Soc. Vet. Toxicology; disting. fellow Am. Coll. Vet. Pharmacology and Therapeutics; mem. AVMA (chmn. council biol. and therapeutic agts. 1961-62, pres. 1972, mem. council on edn. 1975, com. on animal technicians 1976-81, mus. com. 1972-74), Ill. Vet. Med. Assn. (pres. 1966, recipient service award 1968, 50 yr. Disting. Service award 1984), Am. Soc. Exptl. Pharmacology and Therapeutics, Am. Soc. Vet. Physicians and Pharmacologists, Am. Chem. Soc. (medicinal chemistry), Sigma Xi, Phi Kappa Phi, Gamma Sigma Delta, Phi Zeta, Phi Sigma, Sigma Phi Epsilon. Methodist. Home: Urbana IL

LINKLETTER, JOHN AUSTIN, editor; b. Winnipeg, Man., Can., Feb. 11, 1923; s. Isaac Ernest and Edna Mae (Stamy) L.; m. Joan Helen Otterman, Aug. 18, 1950; children: Gayle Joan, Scott Douglas, John Stewart. B.A., U. Iowa, 1947, M.A., 1948. Reporter-photographer, then city editor Newton (Iowa) Daily News, 1950-54; mng.

editor book dept. Better Homes & Gardens, Des Moines, 1954-59; assoc. editor, then mng. editor Popular Mechanics mag., Chgo., also N.Y.C., 1959-74, editor-in-chief, N.Y.C., 1974-85. Served with USN, 1943-46. Mem. Am. Soc. Mag. Editors, Soc. Illustrators, Sigma Delta Chi. Republican. Unitarian. Clubs: N.Y. Athletic, Wings. Home: Old Greenwich, Conn. Died Apr. 18, 1985.

LINTHICUM, FRANK HARMAN, b. Baltimore, Md., Mar. 7, 1887; s. Frank and Mary Ann (Jackson) L.; B.S. in engring., U. of Mich., 1910; post-grad. work same univ.; m. Mary Elizabeth, d. Andrew Douglas Robertson, of Ridley Park, Pa., Apr. 7, 1915 (died Feb. 1920); m. 2d, Evelyn Hope Sparling, d. Mrs. Joseph Sparling, of Detroit, Michigan, June 28, 1921. Began as apprentice American Steel Foundries, Chester, Pa., 1911; supt. Chicago plant, same company, 1918; sales engr., later asst. mgr., Nat. Steel Foundries, Milwaukee, Wis., 1914-16; sales mgr. Am. Manganese Bronze Co., Phila., 1916-17; organized and propr. F. H. Linthicum Bronze Foundry, Baltimore, Md., 1917-22. Dir. cooperative work, Drexel Inst., Phila., 1919, dean, 1920-22; gen. mgr. Benedict Stone Corpn., N.Y. City, 1922-24; pres. and gen. mgr. Linthicum Stone Corpn., Baltimore, 1924-28; apptd. engr. Am. Manganese Bronze Co., Phila., 1928; engr. and asst. to pres. Am. Manganese Bronze Co., Phila., 1928-30; engr. Bartlett-Hayward Co., Baltimore, 1930-32, sales mgr. since 1932. Mem. Delta Tau Delta. Republican. Presbyn. Clubs: Maryland, Elkridge Kennels (Baltimore); Art (Phila.); Springhaven Country (Chester, Pa.); City (New York); Gibson Island Club (Md.). Home: Baltimore, Md. †

LINTNER, JOHN, educator, economist; b. Lone Elm, Kans., Feb. 9, 1916; s. John Virgil and Pearl (Daily) L.; m. Sylvia Chace, June 17, 1944 (dec.); children—John Howland, Nancy Chace Molvig; m. Eleanor J. Hodges, June 8, 1963; 1 stepson, Allan Hodges. A.B., U. Kans., 1939, M.A., 1940; M.A., Harvard U., 1942, Ph.D., 1946. Instr. U. Kans., 1939-40; staff Nat. Bur. Econ. Research, 1941; teaching fellow Harvard U., 1941-42; faculty Harvard U. (Grad. Sch. Bus. Adminstrn.), 1945-83, prof. bus. adminstrn., 1956-64, Gund prof. econs. and bus. adminstrn., 1964-83; Dir. U.S. & Fgn. Securities Corp.; trustee, dir. Chase of Boston Mut. Funds, 1975—1975-83; trustee Cambridge Savs. Bank, 1950-83; Cons. govt. agencies, pvt. founds., bus. firms; sr. cons. to Sec. of Treasury, 1975-78; asso. editor, mem. exec. com. Review of Economics and Statistics, 1950-83. Author: (with J. K. Butters) Effect of Federal Taxes on Growing Enterprises, 1945, Mutual Savings Banks in the Savings and Mortgage Markets, 1948, Corporate Profits in Perspective, 1950, (with J. K. Butters and W. L. Cary) Effect of Taxation on Corporate Mergers, 1951; Asso. editor: (with J. K. Butters and W. L. Cary) Jour. Fin. Econs, 1973-79; contbr. (with J. K. Butters and W. L. Cary) articles to profl. and bus. jours. Fellow Am. Acad. Arts and Scis., Econometric Soc.; mem. Am. Econ. Assn., Am. Fin. Assn. (pres. 1974), AAAS, Soc. of Fellows (Harvard), Phi Beta Kappa. Home: Belmont, Mass. Died June 8, 1983.

LINTON, CLARENCE, educator; b. Emden, Ill., Feb. 19, 1890; s. Charles E. and Minnie Linton; A.B., Neb. State Teachers Coll., 1919; A.M., U. Of Neb., 1921; Ph.D., Columbia, 1927; m. Hattie Baker, July 6, 1910; children—Mildred, Merle. Teacher rural sch., Little Sioux, Ia., 1909-10; farmer, Carroll, Neb., 1910-12; supt. schs., Dakota City, Neb., 1915-18, Lyons, Neb., 1918-21; instr. Neb. State Teachers Coll., summer 1922; supervising prin. Lawrence (N.J.) Twp. pub. schs., 1922-25; sec., Teachers Coll., Columbia, 1925-37, asst. prof. edn., 1928-34, asso. prof., 1934-37, prof. from 1937, asso. director placement, 1936-37, dir. 1937-38, dir. div. guidance and student personnel, 1938-42. Dir. inquiry of relation of religion to pub. edn., for com. on religion and edn. Am. Council on Edn. Served as lt. col., edn. officer, U.S. Army, 1942-45; assisted in planning and inaugurating army information and edn. program in European theater, and as ednl. advisor in China theater. Awarded Bronze Star, Croix de Guerre, Hon. Order British Empire. Fellow A.A.A.S.; life mem. N.E.A.; mem. Am. Assn. Sch. Administrators, Am. Assn. U. Prof., Nat. Soc. Coll. Teachers Edn., Prog. Edn. Assn., Nat. Soc. for Advancement Edn., Am. Coll. Personnel Assn., Nat. Vocational Guidance Assn., Phi Delta Kappa, Kappa Delta Pi. Presbyterian. Author: A Study of Problems Arising in the Admission of Students as Candidates for Professional Degrees in Education (Teachers Coll.), 1927. Contbr. ednl. jours. and yearbooks. †

LINVILL, WILLIAM KIRBY, elec. engr.; b. Kansas City, Mo., Aug. 8, 1919; s. Thomas Grimes and Emma Kirby (Crayne) L.; A.B. in Math. and Physics, William Jewell Coll., 1941; A.B./S.M. Elec. Engring., M.I.T., 1945, Sc.D. in Elec. Engring., 1949; m. Bessie Blythe Burkhardt, June 28, 1942; children—Barbara, Mary Lou, Thomas, Anne, Carl. Asst. prof. elec. engring. M.I.T., 1949-53, asso. prof., 1953-56; project leader Inst. Def. Analysis, Pentagon, Washington, 1956-58; sr. staff mem. electronics Rand Corp., Santa Monica, Calif., 1958-60; prof. elec. engring. Stanford U., 1960-64, chmn., prof. Inst. in Engring.-Econ. Systems, 1964-67, then prof., chmn. dept. engring. econ. systems; Battelle fellow, Columbus, Ohio, 1971-72; mem. vis. com. Nat. Bur. Standards, Dept. Commerce; mem. adv. com. on space and terrestrial applications NASA; mem. Westinghouse Electronics Research Adv. Council, Pitts.; vis. prof. elec. engring. U. Tex., Austin. Fellow IEEE; mem. Nat. Acad. Engring., AAAS. Democrat. Home: Portola Valley, Calif. Dec. Aug. 17, 1980.

LIPMAN, JOSEPH CARROLL, banker; b. San Francisco, May 22, 1887; s. Louis and Regina (Hauser) L.; student Cal. Sch. Mech. Arts, 1901-05; m. Lydia Reinstein, Apr. 7, 1912; children—Jack Carroll, Tom Arthur. With Bank of San Francisco, 1905-10, Bank of Italy (Bank of Am.), San Francisco, 1910-20; with Union Bank, Los Angeles, from 1920, director, 1920-59, vice president, 1920-50, sr. v.p. 1950-56, now hon. vice chmn. exec. com. Former chmn., mem. exec. com. Better Bus. Bur.; v.p. Municipal Art Patrons; exec. com., trustee Los Angeles Art Association; dir. Downtown Businessmen's Assn.; exec. com., treas. Nat. Found.; dir., treas. Los Angeles area council Boy Scouts Am. Dir., treas. Independent Colls. So. Cal., Inc. Member California Bankers Assn. (past pres.). Republican. Clubs: Jonathan, Hillcrest Country, Stock Exchange. Home: Los Angeles, Calif. †

LIPPARD, VERNON WILLIAM, physician; b. Marlboro, Mass., Oct. 4, 1905; s. William Charles and Lucy Maria (Balcom) L.; B.S., Yale, 1926, M.D. cum laude, 1929; D.Sc., U. Md., 1955; m. Margaret Isham Cross, Aug. 29, 1931; 1 dau., Lucy Rowland. Intern New Haven Hosp., 1929-30; asst. resident and resident pediatrician N.Y. Nursery and Child's Hosp., 1930-32; resident pediatrician N.Y. Hosp., 1932-33; instr. pediatrics Cornell U. Med. Coll., 1933-37, asso. pediatrics, 1937-38; dir. study commn. Study Crippled Children, N.Y.C., 1938-39; asso. dean Coll. Phys. and Surgs., Columbia, 1939-46; dean, prof. pediatrics Sch. Medicine, La. State U., 1946-49. Sch. Medicine, U. Va., 1949-52; dean, prof. pediatrics Sch. Medicine, Yale, 1952-67, asst. to pres. for med. devel., prof. pediatrics, 1967-71, dean emeritus, 1971-84; bd. med. cons. Oak Ridge Inst. Nuclear Studies, 1948-52, Brookhaven Nat. Lab., 1955-60; mem. bd. counsellors Smith Coll., 1959-64; cons. Josiah Macy Jr. Found., 1967-75. Pres. Assn. Am. Med. Colls., 1954-55. Bd. dirs. Grant Found., 1967. Founds. Fund for Research in Psychiatry, 1953-67, World Edn., 1973-75, Gaylord Hosp., 1972. Nat. Fund for Med. Edn., 1975. Served to col., M.C., AUS. 1942-45; overseas in Australia, New Guinea, Netherlands E. Indies, P.I. Diplomate Am. Bd. Pediatrics. Mem. Soc. Pediatric Research, Assn. Am. Physicians, Sigma Xi, Alpha Omega Alpha. Episcopalian. Author: The Crippled Child in New York City, 1940; A Half Century of American Medical Education, 1974. Contbr. numerous articles on immunology in childhood and med. edn. to med. jours. Home: New Haven, Conn. Died Dec. 22, 1984.

LIPPINCOTT, BERTRAM, pub.; b. Philadelphia, Nov. 18, 1897; s. Joshua Bertram and Joanna (Wharton) L.; student Episcopal Acad., Phila., 1906-16, Penn Charter Sch., 1917, Princeton, 1919-20; m. Elsie Hirst, Jan. 7, 1922; children—Bertram, Elsie (Mrs. Theodore Chadwick), Barton Hirst, Joanna Wharton (Mrs. Richard Sorlien). Dir. J. B. Lippincott Co., 1923-85, sec., 1926-40, 2d v.p., 1942-47, v.p., 1947-50. Mem. bd. mgrs. U. of Pa. Veternary Hosp., 1931-55, mem. council on veterinary med. edn. and research, from 1956, pres. bd., 1940-42. Mem. Pa. Soc. Mayflower Descendents (governor, 1953-56). Clubs: Racquet, Princeton (Philadelphia); Sunnybrook (Flourtown, Pa.); Conanicut Yacht (commodore 1952, 53). Author: Indians, Privateers, and High Society, 1961. Home: Penllyn, Pa. Died Apr. 28, 1985.

LIPSNER, BENJAMIN BERL, aviation historian; b. Chgo., Sept. 15, 1887; s. Mordecal and Sara Rachel (Lipsner) L.; student premed. div. U. Valparaiso, Chgo. Coll. Medicine and Surgery, 1903; M.E., Armour Inst., 1905; m. Rose Evelyn Grichter, Aug. 31, 1905; children—Milton Arthur, Jerry Sheldon, Charlotte Louella, Shirley Muriel. Capt. aviation sect. Signal Corps., U.S. Army, 1917-18; exec. sec. Chgo. Aero. Commn., from 1922. Recipient Winged Am. Trophy awarded by Adm. Perry, 1919. A founding dir. Air Mail Pioneers, 1939; mem. and hon. life mem. various leading engring., philatelic and aero. socs. Mem. Chgo. Assn. Commerce (ex officio aviation com.), Am. Legion (past comdr. aviation post, detachment comdr. and adviser Ill. Dept. Sons Am. Legion 1964, adv. dir. Cook County council). Organizer, supt. world's first regular airmail service, 1918. Author: Air Mail Jennies to Jets, 1951; Story of Flight, 1953. Contbr. documentary aviation information to mags. and newspapers. Address: Chicago, Ill. †

LISSER, HANS, physician; b. San Francisco, Apr. 12, 1888; s. Louis Lisser; A.B., U. of Calif., 1907; M.D., Johns Hopkins, 1911; m. Enid M. Turner, Aug. 28, 1918; children—Alan Chapman, Gordon Turner. Resident house officer Johns Hopkins Hosp., 1911-12; visited clinics in Japan, Ceylon, Italy, Switzerland, Germany and England, 1912-13; asst. resident and asst. phys., Washington Univ. Hosp., St. Louis, and asst. in medicine, med. sch., 1913-14; in pvt. practice medicine, San Francisco, after 1914; specialist in endocrinology; asst. in medicine U. of Calif., 1914-17, instr., 1917-20, asst. clin. prof., 1920-27, asso. clin. prof., 1927-31, clin. prof., 1931-52, clin. prof. medicine and endocrinology, from 1952, professor emeritus, from 1955, also chief of endocrine clinic University Hospital, chief of the ductless gland clinic, Out Patient Department, 1920-29, chief D-Unit., after 1930; visiting physician Univ. Hosp.; former chief ductless gland and metabolic div. Franklin Hospital. Director The Emporium. Trustee The William and Alice Hinckley Fund. Patron San Francisco Symphony Orchestra. Awarded Gold-headed Cane, med. dept., U. Cal., 1955, Mem. A.M.A., Assn. Am. Physicians, Am. Coll. Physicians, Assn. Study Internal Secretions (past pres.), Calif. Acad. Medicine (past pres.), Phi Beta Kappa, Sigma Xi, Alpha Delta Phi, Alpha Omega Alpha, Nu Sigma Nu. Unitarian (past trustee). Clubs: Presidio Golf (past pres.), St. Francis Yacht, The Family (past dir.), Pacific Interurban Clin. (past chmn.). Co-author: Endocrinology-Including Text of Diagnosis and Treatment, 1957. Co-editor: Endocrinology in Clinical Practice, 1953. Contributed to medical books; articles on clinical endocrinology in med. publs. Lectr. sci. and lay orgns. Home: San Francisco, Calif. Deceased.

LISSIM, SIMON, painter, designer; b. Kiev, Russia, Oct. 24, 1900; came to U.S., 1941, naturalized, 1946; s. Michel and Anna Maria (Schorr) L.; m. Irene Zalchoupine, 1925 (dec. 1945); m. Dorothea Howson Waples, January 25, 1946. Student, Art Sch. of Alexander Monko; grad., Naoumenko Sch., 1919; student, Sorbonne, Ecole du Louvre. head art edn. project N.Y. Pub. Library, N.Y.C., 1942-66; faculty French Lycee, N.Y.C., 1943-49, Horace Mann-Lincoln High Sch., Columbia, Coll. City N.Y., 1944, art. supr. adult edn. program, 1945-47, asst. prof. art, 1947-54, asso. prof., 1954-60, prof., 1960-71, prof. emeritus, 1971, asst. dir. evening session charge adult edn. program, 1948-50; asst. dir. Coll. City N.Y. (Sch. Gen. Studies, div. adult edn.), 1950-64; faculty French Summer Sch., McGill U., 1949; Chmn. nat. selection com. Fulbright awards (in painting, sculpture, graphic arts), 1956. Stage designer, Theatre de l'Oeuvre, 1923, Theatre de L'Atelier, Theatre National de l'Opera Comique, Theatre des Nouveautes, Paris, 1931, Theatre Michel, Theatre Antoine, 1932; Conbtr. articles to books, periodicals.; works include painting, stage designs, ceramics, gouaches, china, works permanently exhibited, N.Y. Pub. Library, Bklyn. Mus. Art, Hyde Park Library, Met. Mus. of Art, Boston Mus. Fine Arts, Fogg Mus. Art, Cleve. Mus. Fine Arts, Santa Barbara Mus. Art, Cooper Mus., Columbus (Ohio) Gallery Fine Arts, Fla. So. Coll., Va. Mus. Art, Phila. Mus. Art, Victoria and Albert Mus., London, Eng., Shakespeare Meml. Mus., Stratford-on-Avon, Eng., Nat. Gallery of Can., Ottawa, Musee Nat. du Jeu de Paume, France, Nat. Collection Fine Arts, Washington, Calif. Palace Legion Honor, San Francisco, others, museums in, Eng., France, Prague, Holland, Austria, Can., Denmark, Switzerland, Italy, Portugal, Spain, Belgium, Latvia, Norway; traveling exhbn. The World of Simon Lissim, Internat. Exhbns. Found., 1979-81; illustrator several books; over 80 one-man shows in various countries. Served as vol. French Army, World War II. Recipient silver medal Internat. Exhbn., Paris, 1925, gold medal Barcelona, 1929; two grand Diplome d'honneur Paris, 1937. Hon. fellow Am.-Scandinavian Found. U.S.A., Royal Soc. Arts (v.p. council); mem. Société du Salon d'Automme, Société des Artistes Decorateurs (Paris), Royal Acad. Fine Arts St. George (Barcelona, Spain) (hon. corr.), AAUP, Coll. Art Assn., Am., Theatre Library Assn. Am., Royal Soc. Miniature Painters (hon.), Audubon Artists. Club: Century (N.Y.C.). Home: Naples, Fla. Died May 31, 1981.

LIST, EUGENE, pianist; b. Calif., 1921. Ed., Los Angeles and Phila.; studied with Olga Samaroff, Phila. Conservatory of Music and Juilliard Sch. N.Y.C. Began pub. appearances as pianist in early years profl. debut with, Phila. Symphony Orch. under Leopold Stokowski, N.Y. debut with, N.Y. Philharmonic under Otto Klemperer; has appeared as guest with leading orchs. and in recitals, throughout U.S. and abroad; also played over radio; currently performs with, Vermont Festival Players. Home: New York, N.Y. Died Mar. 1, 1985.*

LIST, ROBERT STUART, bus. exec.; b. Wheeling, W.Va., Jan. 31, 1903; s. Daniel Carter and Clara Cunningham (Fisher) L.; grad. Shenandoah Mil. Inst., 1920; m. Claire Perry Wrightson, July 3, 1924; children—Nancy Lloyd (Mrs. Jerome Davis Green, II), Claire. Mem. staff Washington Times, 1920-23; advt. dir. Rochester (N.Y.) Journal-Am., 1923-35; gen. mgr. Pitts. Sun-Telegraph, 1935-53; pub. Chgo.'s Am., 1953-69; pres. Chgo. Am. Pub. Co., 1956-69; v.p. for pub. affairs ARA Services, Inc., Chgo., from 1969. Home: Chicago, Ill. Died May 10, 1983.

LITHGOW, JAMES HECTOR, life ins. exec.; b. Bobcaygeon, Ont., Can., Sept. 7, 1890; s. James and Mary (Long) L.; student Trinity Coll. Sch., 1905-08; m. Mizpah Sussex, June 11, 1919; children—Charles H., Janet, Marni. Clk. actuarial dept. Mfrs. Life Ins. Co., 1908, assistant actuary, 1919, actuary, 1924, asst. gen. mgr., actuary, 1930, gen. manager, actuary, 1931, general manager, 1935, vice president 1944, president, 1951, chairman board, also director; director Corporation Investors, Limited, Sentinel Securities of Can., Ltd., Chartered Trust. Served with Canadian F.A., 1916-19. Fellow Actuarial Soc. Am.; mem. Canadian Life Ins. Officers Assn. (pres. 1932-33, 33-34), Ins. Inst. Toronto (pres. 1935-36), Life Ins. Inst. Can. (pres. 1936-37), Dominion Mortgage and Investment Assn. (pres. 1936-37), Inst. Actuaries Gt. Britain (asso.), Delta Chi. Clubs: Toronto, Toronto Golf, Granite (Toronto, Can.). Home: Toronto, Ont., Can. †

LITTELL, GALE PATTERSON, telephone co. exec.; b. Pekin, Ind., Oct. 6, 1917; s. Harold Crawford and Ethel Vanita (Whitson) L.; m. Justine Delores Davis, Dec. 20, 1945; children—Jane Ann (Mrs. Philip Meyer), John

Harold. A.B., Ind. U., 1938. Sunday editor Indpls. Star, 1948-52; with Ind. Bell Telephone Co., 1952-61, gen. mgr. comml. dept., 1960-61; v.p. pub. relations N.J. Bell Telephone Co., 1961-63, v.p. met. area, 1963-66, v.p. revenue and bus. research, 1966-71; asst. v.p. AT & T Co., 1971-75; v.p. pub. relations So. Bell Telephone Co., from 1975. Served to maj., 101st Airborne Div. AUS, World War II. Mem. Sigma Delta Chi. Methodist. Clubs: Commerce, Cherokee Town and Country. Home: Dunwoody, GA.

LITTLE, DILLON ALVA, petroleum company executive; b. Corsicana, Tex., Mar. 6, 1887; s. Thomas P. and Henrietta (Megarity) L.; student Southwestern Univ. (Georgetown, Tex.), 1903-04; m. Evelyn Haslam, Mar. 17, 1910; children—Sara Lee (Mrs. Ray L. Miller), Louise (Mrs. William R. Barbeck). Clerk, U.S. Post Office, Corsicana, Tex., 1909-14; clerk Magnolia Petroleum Co., and Magnolia Pipe Line Co., 1914-23; asst. treas., 1923-29; dir. and asst. gen. mgr., 1929-30; v.p., 1930-33; pres. 1933-46; mem. exec. com. Tex. Centennial Expn., 1934-36; re-elected dir. C. of C., 1937-40, 1941-45; dir., Community Chest, Citizens' Council (Dallas), 1937-40, 1941-45; bd. fellows Dallas Hist. Soc. Democrat. Methodist. Clubs: Dallas, Petroleum, Lakewood Country, City. Home: Dallas, Tex. †

LITTLE, EVELYN (AGNES) STEEL, librarian; b. Portland, Ore., May 29, 1890; d. Thomas and Evelyn Annie (Willis) Steel; A.B., U. of Calif., 1913, A.M., 1914; A.M. in Library Science, U. of Mich., 1933, Ph.D., 1936; m. Thomas Gavin Steel Little, Dec. 13, 1922 (died Feb. 25, 1927). Senior asst. library, U. of Calif., 1914-16; librarian, Oakland (Calif.) Tech. High Sch., 1916-22; asst. prof. library sci., Emory U., Atlanta, Ga., 1935-36; reference librarian, Mills Coll., Oakland, Calif., 1936-37, librarian and asso. prof. bibliography, 1937-39, librarian and prof. comparative lit., 1940-55, emeritus librarian, dean faculty, 1945-50; asst. dir. Am. Library in London, O.W.I., 1943-44; lecturer in book selection, U. of Calif. Sch. of Librarianship, 1938-40; asso. prof., U. of Calif. at Los Angeles, summer session 1938, 1940. Mem. Calif. Library Assn., Am. Library Assn., Assn. of Coll. and Research Libraries, Am. Assn. Univ. Profs., Phi Beta Kappa. Author: Backgrounds of World Literature from Homer to Tolstoy, 1935; Instruction in the Use of Books and Libraries in Colleges and Universities, 1935. Editor: Quintus Horatius Flaccus, a check list of editions in U.S. and Can., 1938; Twenty-Six Lead Soldiers, 1939; Homer and Theocritus in English Translation: a critical bibliography, 1941; Books Under Fire, 1945. Address: Berkeley, Cal. †

LITTLEFIELD, ROBERT CRANDALL, savs. and loan exec.; b. Monterey, Calif., Jan. 18, 1930; s. Glenn Crandall and Mary (Hill) L.; A.A., Monterey Peninsula Coll., 1950; student Stanford, 1951; B.A., San Jose State Coll., 1953; m. Mary Ortman, Feb. 28, 1954 (dec.); 1 dau., Susan Marie; m. 2d, Patricia R. Hodgson, Oct. 24, 1976. Pres., dir. Monterey Savs. and Loan Assn., 1948-80; pres., dir. First Monterey Co., 1954-80; pres., dir. Bessemer Oil Co., 1948-80. Sec.-treas., dir. United Fund Monterey Peninsula, 1955-75; vice chmn. Monterey City Planning Commn., 1961-72; bd. dirs. Monterey History and Art Assn., 1970-80; trustee Eskaton Monterey Hosp., 1977-80. Served with AUS, 1951-53. Named Young Man of Year, Jr. C. of C., 1961. Mem. Monterey Peninsula C. of C. (treas., dir. 1955-80, named citizen of year 1977), Calif. Savs. and Loan League (dir. 1976-80). Republican. Methodist (treas.). Elk, Kiwanian (treas.). Home: Monterey, Calif. Died Oct. 10, 1980.

LITTLEJOHN, ROBERT MCGOWAN, army ofcr. ret.; b. Jonesville, S.C., Oct. 23, 1890; s. Samuel and Catharine (McGowan) L.; student Clemson Coll., 1906-07; B.S., U.S. Mil. Acad., 1912; student Q.M. Corps Subsistence Sch., 1921. Command and Gen. Staff Sch., 1925-26. Army War Coll., 1929-30; m. Mary A. Lambert, July 24, 1918. Commd. 2d lt., 1912, promoted through grades to major gen. 1943; served as lt., later capt., Cav., 1912-17, major Inf., France and Germany with A.E.F., 1917-19; asso. with Q.M. Corps from 1920; mem. War Dept. Gen. Staff, 1930-34; quartermaster U.S. Mil. Acad., 1934-38; asst. quartermaster Philippine Dept., 1938-39; quartermaster Philippine Dept. and supt. Army Transport Service, 1939-40; became chief Clothing and Equipage Div., Office of Q.M. Gen., 1940; chief Q.M. for the European Theater, June 1942; became War Assets Adminstr., 1946. Mem. bd. dirs. Community Chest, Arundel Co., Md. Awarded D.S.M. with oak leaf cluster; Legion of Merit; Bronze Star; French Foreign Legion; French Legion of Honor, Croix de Guerre with Palm; Comdr. of the Bath, British Empire; Order of Comml. Merit, France. Comdr. Order of the Crown, Belgium. Mem. vestry Christ's Ch., Owensville, Md. Clubs: Army and Navy (Washington). Contbr. articles on subsistence to tech. publs. Home: Harwood, Md. Died May 6, 1982.

LITTLETON, LEONIDAS ROSSER, educator; born Belle Haven, Va., Aug. 1, 1889; s. Jesse Talbot and Louisa (Rosser) L.; A.B., Birmingham-Southern Coll., 1907; A.M., Tulane, 1910; Ph.D., U. of Ill., 1912; m. Alice Scott, June 17, 1916; children—Rachel (Mrs. G. W. Jones), Louisa Chandler, Leonidas Rosser. Instr. in science, Southern U., 1907-08; teaching fellow in mathematics, Tulane, 1908-10; fellow in organic chemistry, U. of Ill., 1910-12; instr. in chemistry, Grinnell (Ia.) Coll., 1912-13; prof. chemistry, Emory (Va.) and Henry Coll., 1913-17; asst. chemist Ordnance Dept., U.S. Army, Picatiny Arsenal, Dover, N.J., 1917-18; chief chemist Mathieson Alkali Works, Saltville, Va., 1918-19; research chemist Nat. Aniline & Chem. Co., Buffalo, N.Y., 1919-22; dir. and dean summer session, Emory and Henry Coll., 1915, 28, prof. chemistry, Emory and Henry Coll., 1922-41; principal chem. engr., Research Engineering, Office of Quartermaster Gen., U.S. Army, May-July 1941, principal Chemist Ordnance Dept., July 1941-June 1943; head engr. Ordnance Dept., 1943; chief explosive sect. research and development, 1947-57; director of science, head of department of chemistry Emory and Henry Coll., Emory, Va., from 1957. cons. chemist on high explosives, filtration, etc. Mem. spl. com. on high explosive storage, Va., 1928. Mem. Washington County (Va.) Sch. Trustee Electoral Bd., 1928-30; clk. Washington County (Va.) Sch. Bd., 1936-41. Fellow A.A.A.S.; mem. Am. Chem. Soc. (com. on labels, com. on naming and scope of coms.; councillor 1934; chmn. N.E. Tenn. Sect. 1936), Va. Acad. Science, Sigma Xi, Phi Lambda Upsilon, Alpha Epsilon Delta. Democrat. Methodist. Mason. Club: Faculty (pres.). Home: Emory, Va. †

LITTLEWOOD, GEORGE, publisher, editor; b. Barrow-in-Furness, Eng., Feb. 3, 1917; s. George Francis and Jane Elizabeth (Wilkinson) L.; came to U.S., 1921, naturalized, 1943; student Columbia U. Sch. Gen. Studies, 1951-56; m. Evelyn Lucia Lindner, June 19, 1942; children—George Frederic, Deborah Mary. Mktg. dir. Indl. Press, Inc., N.Y.C., 1965-72; v.p. Gordon Publs.; pub. Metalworking Digest, Mining/Processing Equipment, Morristown, N.J., 1972—. Welfare dir. Kinnelon, N.J., 1965-71; v.p. Fayson Lakes Assn., 1960, 64; sec. Zoning Bd., Cresskill, N.J., 1953-56. Served with AUS, 1942-45. Republican. Presbyn. Home: Kinnelon, N.J. Died Feb. 20, 1981.

LIVESAY, EDWARD ALEXANDER, educator; b. Frankford, W.Va., Oct. 22, 1889; s. John Granville and Elizabeth (Robinson) L.; B.S., Va. Poly. Inst., 1912, M.S., 1916; M.A., U. Mo., 1917; M.S., Harvard, 1925, D.Sc., 1928; m. Helen Hungate, Dec. 27, 1919; children—Betty Jane, Virginia Lee, Alice Marie, Nelle Maxine. Tchr. agr., Va. Poly. Inst., 1914-16; asst. county agt. leader, U. Mo., 1917-19; head dept. animal husbandry, W.Va. U. from 1919. Chmn. Monongalia (W.Va.) County Red Cross, 1939-43; mem. Monongalia County civilian def. orgn. during World War II. Mem. A.A.A.S., Am. Soc. Animal Production, Sigma Xi, Alpha Zeta, Gamma Alpha. Alpha Gamma Rho. Presbyn. Mason, Kiwanis. Author of Expt. Station bulletins and contbr. sci. papers to profl. jours. Home: Morgantown, W.Va. †

LIVINGSTON, ROBERT LOUIS, chemist, educator; b. Ada, Ohio, Nov. 15, 1918; s. Ralph and Ruth (Sink) L.; m. Virginia Capron, May 30, 1943 (div. 1973); children—Douglas, Roy, Margaret, Bruce; m. Jean Moriarty, Aug. 25, 1979. B.S., Ohio State U., 1939; M.S., U. Mich., 1941, Ph.D., 1943. Asso. chemist Naval Research Lab., Ann Arbor, Mich., 1944-46; faculty Purdue U., Lafayette, Ind., 1946—, prof. chemistry, 1954—, asst. dept. head, 1960-68; dir. NSF-URP Program, 1969-72; Cons. Coll. Entrance Exam. Bd., 1972—. Author: (with F.D. Martin) General Chemistry, pub. annually 1952-64; Contbr. to (with F.D. Martin) profl. jours. Recipient Standard Oil Teaching award, 1968. Mem. Am. Chem. Soc. (sec. div. chem. edn. 1963-68, mem. exec. com. 1968-71), Sigma Xi, Phi Lambda Upsilon, Phi Delta Kappa, Phi Eta Sigma, Gamma Alpha. Research on molecular structure of gaseous molecules by electron diffraction. Home: West Lafayette, Ind. Died Aug. 21, 1983.

LLEWELLYN, RICHARD, author: ed. St. David's Cardiff and London; studied painting and sculpture, Venice. Apprentice in hotel mgmt., Italy; with Italian film unit; joined ranks of H. M. Regular Army, serving both home and abroad; became capt. Welsh Guards, 1939; bit player motion pictures, later became reporter on a penny film paper; scenarist MGM, Hollywood, 1946-47. Author: (mystery play) Poison Pen; How Green Was My Valley; None but the Lonely Heart, 1943; A Few Flowers for Shiner; Sweet Witch; Fire Over Hercules; Warden of The Smoke and Bells; Mr. Hamish Gleave; A Flame for Doubting Thomas; Chez Pavan; Up, Into the Singing Mountain; Sweet Morn of Judas' Day; Down Where the Moon is Small, 1966; End of the Rug, 1968; But We Didn't Get The Fox, 1969. Died Nov. 30, 1983.

LLEWELLYN-THOMAS, EDWARD, physician; b. Salisbury, Eng., Dec. 15, 1917; s. Hugh and Beatrice Caroline (Carre) Llewellyn-T.; m. Ellen Wise Buford, Sept. 25, 1947; children: Caroline, Roland, Edward Jr. B.S.c., U. London, 1950; M.D., McGill U., 1955. Engr., BBC, London, 1935-39; controller Tellecommunications, Singapore, 1945-50; research asso. dept. psychiatry Cornell U. Med. Sch., 1956-60; physician scientist Def. Research Bd. Can., Toronto, Ont., 1958-61; prof. pharmacology U. Toronto, 1961-84, also asso. dean medicine. Served to capt. Brit. Army, 1939-45. Fellow Royal Soc. Can., Inst. Elec. Engrs.; mem. Human Factors Assn. Can. (pres. 1969-70). Club: Univ.

LLOYD, FRANK W(ILLIAM G.), motion picture producer and dir.; b. Glasgow, Scotland, Feb. 2, 1888; s. Edmund Taylor and Jane (Newman) L.; ed. schools of London; m. Alma Haller, July 11, 1913; 1 dau., Alma. Came to U.S., 1912, naturalized, 1921. Began as actor in London, 1903; actor for Universal in motion pictures, 1913, later began writing and directing 1-reel pictures; directed for Morosco, Pallas Pictures, Fox, Goldwyn, Joseph M. Schenck, Sol Lesser; organized Frank Lloyd Productions and produced Oliver Twist, Black Oxen, Sea Hawk, Splendid Road, Winds of Chance, The Wise Guy; dir. for First National; became producer-dir. Paramount Pictures, Inc., 1937, now same for Frank Lloyd Productions, Inc. Directed prodns. for various Hollywood studios, and later for Frank Lloyd Prodns., Inc. Mem. Acad. Motion Picture Arts and Scis. Mem. Bel Air Country Club.†

LLOYD, LYNN, banker; b. Big Springs, Neb., May 14, 1888; s. Lowell C. and Sara Catherine (Little) L.; A.B., U. Neb., 1911, student Law Sch., 1911-12; m. Josephine Sanford, Dec. 29, 1913; 1 son, Rodney Sanford. Newspaper reporter, Neb. State Jour., 1909-11; engaged in advt. bus. Lincoln, Neb., 1911-17; retail merchant, 1918-24; mgr. property and investments, 1924-29; asst. sec., Harris Trust and Savs. Bank, Chicago, 1929-37, v.p., 1937-54, head trust dept. 1951-54, sr. vice pres. Valley National Bank, Phoenix. Mem. Phi Kappa Psi, Phi Delta Phi. Republican. Presbyterian. Clubs: University, Bankers, Executives, Skokie Country. Address: Phoenix, Az. †

LLOYD, NORMAN, musician, foundation executive; b. Pottsville, Pa., Nov. 8, 1909; s. David and Annie Sarah (Holstein) L.; B.S., N.Y. U., 1932, M.A., 1936; Mus.D., Phila. Conservatory Music, 1963, New Eng. Conservatory, 1965, Peabody Inst., 1973; grad. piano study with Abbey Whiteside; study in music composition with Vincent Jones, Aaron Copland; m. Ruth Dorothy Rohrbacher, Apr. 10, 1933; children—David Walter, Alex. Instr., Ernest Williams Band Sch., 1935-37; lectr. NYU, 1936-45; faculty Sarah Lawrence Coll., 1936-46, condr. chorus, 1945-49; dir. edn. Juilliard Sch. Music, 1946-49, faculty, 1949-63; dean Oberlin Coll. Conservatory Music, 1963-65; dir. arts program Rockefeller Found., 1965-72, cons., 1973-75; cons. Nat. Assn. Schs. Music, 1973-76, Mary Flagler Cary Charity Trust, 1974-80; composer, condr. dance scores for Martha Graham, 1935, Hanya Holm, 1937, Doris Humphrey, 1941-46, 49, José Limón, 1949; composer, condr. numerous music scores for exptl. and documentary films OWI, Internat. Film Found., Shirley Clarke-Halcyon Films, Mus. Modern Art, others; compositions include Song for Summer's End, 1951, Nocturne for Voices, 1953, 3 Pieces for Violin and Piano, 1957, A Walt Whitman Overture for Band, 1962, Sonata for Piano, 1963, Three Scenes from Memory, 1963, Episodes for Piano, 1964; Rememories for Wind Orchestra, 1974. Mem. vis. com. humanities Mass. Inst. Tech., 1973-75; vis. com. arts Tufts U., 1976-80; bd. dirs. Nat. Music Council. Mem. ASCAP, Am. Fedn. Musicians, Pi Kappa Lambda. Compiled: (with M. Boni) Fireside Book of Folk Songs, 1947, Fireside Book of American Songs, 1952, Fireside Book of Love Songs, 1954, Favorite Christmas Carols, 1957, Songs of the Gilded Age, 1960; (with Arnold Fish) Fundamentals of Sight Singing, 1963 (with Ruth Lloyd) The American Heritage Songbook, 1969; Creative Keyboard Musicianship, 1975. Author: Golden Ency. of Music, 1968. Home: Greenwich, Conn. Died July 31, 1980; buried Pottsville, Pa.

LOCKEY, STEPHEN DANIEL, physician; b. East Pikeland Twp., Pa., Apr. 29, 1904; s. Stephen and Elizabeth (Demeter) L.; B.S., Franklin and Marshall Coll., Lancaster, Pa., 1928; M.D., Temple U., 1932; m. Anna Bair Funk, Nov. 30, 1933; children—Doris Anne Lockey Bock, Stephen Daniel, Richard Funk, James Edward. Rotating intern Lancaster Gen. Hosp., 1932-33, founder, chief dept. allergy, 1935-70, chief emeritus, 1970-85, founder, chief dept. inhalation therapy and ventilation studies, 1952-55, asso. chief, 1955-70; gen. practice medicine, East Petersburg, Pa., 1933-45, specializing in allergy, Lancaster, 1945—; mem. staff, allergist St. Joseph Hosp., Lancaster. Cons. allergist Community Meml. Hosp., West Grove, Pa.; allergist Student Infirmary, Franklin and Marshall Coll.; cons. in allergy Armstrong Cork Co., Lancaster, 1940-50, De Walt, Inc., Lancaster, 1940-45, B.F. Goodrich Rubber Co., Oaks, Pa., 1940-50; lectr. U. Tex., Southwestern Sch. Medicine, Dallas, 1969-72. Vice pres., co-founder Citizens Scholarship Found. of Lancaster County, 1963, bd. dirs., 1963—, pres., 1964; pres. Allergy Found. of Lancaster County; bd. dirs. Lancaster County Council for Sr. Citizens, Phoebe-Devitt Homes for Aged, United Ch. of Christ, 1963-72, Salvation Army; mem. exec. bd. United Ch. of Christ Retirement Homes, 1962-64, Boy Scouts Am. and Girl Scouts Am., Lancaster County; mem. parents com. Ursinus Coll., Collegeville, Pa. Recipient awards Pa. Allergy Assn., 1949, 58, Pa. Med. Soc., 1962, 66, AMA, 1969, 73; award for outstanding contbns. to allergy and medicine Am. Coll. Allergists, 1970; Jonathan Forman award Soc. Clin. Ecology, 1974; Abraham Lincoln award, 1974; Alumni citation Franklin and Marshall Coll., 1979. Diplomate Am. Bd. Clin. Immunology and Allergy. Fellow Am. Assn. Clin. Immunology and Allergy, Am. Coll. Allergists (past 2d v.p., chmn. sect. tech. 1944-80, Disting. Service award 1976, award of merit 1977); mem. Am., Pan Am. (lectr.) med. assns., Pa. Allergy Assn. (past pres., life mem., past chmn. bd. regents), Pa. (chmn. splty. sect. in allergy), Lancaster City and County (trustee) med. socs., Soc. for Clin. Ecology, Am. Assn. Med. Writers, Internat. Assn. Allergology, Am. Med. Writers Assn. Clubs: Elks, Kiwanis, Hamilton, Temple U. Alumni of Lancaster County (pres. 1965-66). Contbr. articles to profl. jours. Home: Lancaster, Pa. Died Apr. 8, 1985.

LOCKRIDGE, RICHARD, author; b. St. Joseph, Mo., Sept. 26, 1898; s. Ralph David and Mary Olive (Notson) L.; student Kansas City Jr. Coll., 1916-18, U. Mo., 1920; m. Frances Davis, Mar. 4, 1922 (dec.); m. 2d Hildegarde Dolson, May 26, 1965. Reporter, Kansas City Kansan, 1921-22. Kansas City Star, 1922; reporter New York Sun, 1923-29, became drama critic, 1929; co-pres. Mystery Writers Am., Inc., from 1960. Served as seaman USNRF, 1918; lt. USNR, 1942-45. Mem. P.E.N., Authors League Am, Players. Author: Darling of Misfortune Edwin Booth, 1932; Mr. and Mrs. North, 1936; The Empty Day, 1965; Encounter in Key West, 1966; Murder Roundabout, 1966; Die Laughing, 1969; Death in a Sunny Place, 1971; One Lady, Two Cats, 1967; Write Murder Down, 1972; Not I, Said The Sparrow, 1973; Death on the Hour, 1974; (with Frances Lockridge) The Norths Meet Murder, 1940; Murder Out of Turn, 1941; A Pinch of Poison, 1941; Death on the Aisle, 1942; Hanged for a Sheep, 1942; Killing the Goose, 1944; Payoff for the Banker, 1945; Cats and People, 1950; The Faceless Adversary, 1956; Show Red for Danger, 1960; others. Home: Tryon, N.C. Died June 19, 1982.

LOCKWOOD, LEE, financier; b. Waco, Tex., Nov. 11, 1900; s. James H. and Gussie (Doss) L.; student U. Tex., 1918-22; LL.D., Baylor U.; m. Marie Coates, Oct. 3, 1923; children—Ann Marie (Mrs. Duncan C. Howard), Laurine Lockwood Dosher. Chmn., Waco Mortgage Co., First Waco Co., Inc., Waco Savs. & Loan Assn.; owner Waco Lumber Co.; vice chairman Farm & Home Savs. Assn.; dir. Citizens Nat. Bank Waco, Merc. Nat. Bank Dallas. Past chmn. Commn. Higher Edn. Tex.; mem. Tex. com. on church and state Baylor U. Del. Democratic Nat. Conv., 1940, 44, 48, 52. Pres. Masonic Home and Sch. Tex., 1951-60; chmn. emeritus Scottish Rite Found. Tex., Scottish Rite Ednl. Assn. Tex., Scottish Rite Hosp., Dallas; bd. dirs. Community Chest, Waco, Waco Boys Club, Waco Growth Found.; dir. George Washington Nat. Meml. Assn.; bd. regents U. Tex., 1953-59; trustee Freedoms Found., Valley Forge. Recipient George Washington award. Mem. Waco C. of C., S.A.R. (gold citizenship medal Tex. chpt.), Soc. Colonial Wars. Mason (33 deg.; past dep. grand comdr., mem. emeritus Supreme Council); mem. Order De Molay (past grand master), Order Red Cross of Constantine (past grand sovereign). Home: Waco, Tex. Died Aug. 6, 1980; buried Oakwood Cemetery, Waco, Tex.

LODGE, HENRY CABOT, former senator, former government official, author, lectr.; b. Nahant, Mass., July 5, 1902; s. George Cabot and Mathilda Elizabeth Frelinghuysen (Davis) L. (g.s. of late U.S. Sen. Henry Cabot Lodge); m. Emily Sears, July 1, 1926; children: George Cabot, Henry Sears. Grad., Middlesex Mass. Sch., 1920; A.B., Harvard U., 1924; LL.B., Northeastern U., 1938; D.C.L., Bishop's U., 1953; LL.D., Clark U., Norwich U., 1951, Hamilton Coll., Franklin and Marshall Coll., Boston U., 1953, Harvard, 1954, N.Y. U., Fordham U., Rensselaer Polytechnic Inst., 1955, Lehigh University, U. Pa., 1956, also Williams Coll., Union Coll., Boston Coll., Princeton, Adelphi U., Columbia, U. N.H., Notre Dame U., U. Mass., Am. U., Holy Cross U., 1978, Georgetown U., 1979; Docteur es Lettres, Laval Univ. With Boston Evening Transcript, 1923, N.Y. Herald Tribune, 1924; mem. Mass. Gen. Court, 1933-36; elected to U.S. Senate from Mass., 1936, for term ending 1943, reelected, 1942, resigned to go into U.S. Army; reelected, Nov. 5, 1946, for term ending Jan. 1953; U.S. rep. UN, 1953-60; director gen. The Atlantic Inst., 1961-62, U.S. ambassador to, South Viet Nam, 1963-64, 65-67, ambassador at large, 1967-68, ambassador to, Germany, 1968-69; personal rep. to head U.S. delegation to Vietnam Peace Talks, Paris, 1969; spl. envoy to visit, Vatican, 1970-77; vis. prof. Gordon Coll., 1977; Chmn. Presdl. Commn. for Observance of UN 25th Anniversary, 1970-71; mem. nat. council Salvation Army, 1976; campaign mgr. for nomination Gen. Dwight D. Eisenhower, 1952; nominated for v.p. Republican Party, 1960; bd. overseers Harvard. Author: The Storm Has Many Eyes, 1973, As It Was, 1976. Active Res. Officer from 1925; maj. U.S.A., with 1st Am. Tank Detachment in Brit. 8th Army, 1942, Libya; maj. U.S.A., with 1st Am. Tank Detachment in Brit. 8th Army, 1944, Italy; lt. col. 1944-45, So. France, Rhine and So. Germany; ret. maj. gen. Res. Decorated Bronze Star, Legion of Merit medal, 6 battle stars; Legion of Honor; Croix de Guerre (with palm) France; Chevalier's cross Order of Polonia Restituta; Humane Order African Redemption Liberia; Grand Cross of Merit Malta; Nat. Order Republic Viet Nam; recipient Distinguished Honor award State Dept.; Sylvanus Thayer medal West Point; Pres. Eisenhower's Gold Medal; unanimously thanked by U.S. Senate for Vietnam service, 1967; others. First senator since Civil War to resign to enter U.S. Army Address: Beverly, Mass. Died Jan. 27, 1985.

LOEB, WILLIAM, publisher; b. Washington, Dec. 26, 1905; s. William and Katharine W. (Dorr) L.; m. Nackey Scripps, July 15, 1952; children—Edith, Elizabeth. A.B., Williams Coll., 1927; postgrad., Harvard Law Sch., 1929-31. Pres., publisher Saint Albans (Vt.) Daily Messenger, 1941-82, Vt. Sunday News, 1942-62, Manchester Union Leader, 1946-82, N.H. Sunday News, 1948-82; publisher Haverhill (Mass.) Jour., 1957-65, Conn. Sunday Herald, 1964-74; Bd. dirs. Am. China Policy Assn., pres., 1941-43; chmn. Council Profit Sharing Industries, 1949-52. Trustee Lahey Clinic, Boston. Decorated comdr. Cross Polonia Restituta; Knight of Malta. Mem. Nat. Rifle Assn. (dir.), Zeta Psi. Baptist. Clubs: Seawanhaka Corinthian Yacht (Oyster Bay, L.I., N.Y.); Harvard (Boston); Prospectors (Reno). Home: Carson City, Nev. Died 1982.

LOESCHE, WILLIAM HERMAN, banker; b. Phila., Dec. 22, 1888; s. Charles and Sophia (Hoeffleman) L.; student Franklin Inst. Pa., 1904-07; L.H.D., Temple University, Phila., 1958; married Minnie Elizabeth Jetter, June 16, 1909; 1 son, William Herman. Ret. v.p. Girard Trust Corn Exchange Bank (formerly Girard Trust Company); director Collins & Aikman Corp., Fire Assn. of Phila., Eureka Casualty Ins. of Phila., Reliance Ins. Co. of Phila. Keystone Portland Cement Company. Served as mem. and v.p. Bd. Pub. Edn. of Phila.; trustee Abington (Pa.) Meml. Hosp. Mem. Pa. Bankers Assn. Presbyn. (trustee, elder). Mason. Clubs: Union League (Phila.); Old York Road Country (Jenkintown, Pa.). Home: Philadelphia, Pa. Deceased.

LOFTS, NORAH, author; b. Shipdham, Norfolk, Eng., Aug. 27, 1904; dau. Isaac and Ethel (Garner) Robinson; student Bury St. Edmund's England; m. Geoffrey Lofts, Dec. 29, 1933; 1 son, Geoffrey St. Edmund Clive. Author: I Met a Gypsy, 1935; Here Was a Man, 1936; White Hell of Pity; 1934; Requiem for Idols, 1938; Colin Lowrie, 1938; Blossom Like the Rose, 1939; Hester Room, 1940; The Brittle Glass, 1942; The Golden Fleece, 1943; Jassy, 1945; To See a Fine Lady, 1946; Road to Revelation (pub. in Eng. only), 1941; Silver Nutmeg, 1947; A Calf for Venus, 1949; Women of the Old Testament, 1949; Esther, 1950; The Luteplayer, 1951; Bless This House, 1954; Winter Harvest, 1955; Afternoon of An Autocrat, 1956; Scent of Cloves, 1957; The Town House, 1959; Heaven In Your Hand; The House At Old Vine, 1961; The House at Sunset, 1962; The Concubine, 1963; How Far to Bethlehem, 1965; (with Margery Weiner) Eternal Flame, 1968; The Lost Queen, 1969; The King's Pleasure, 1969. Home: Bury St. Edmonds, England. Died Sept. 10, 1983.

LOGAN, PAUL P., trade assn. exec.; b. Red Oak, Ia., Oct. 7, 1889; s. George Rankin and Lucy Caroline (Gibson) L.; student Army Subsistence Sch., Army Inf. Sch., Army Indsl. Coll., Am. Inst. Baking, Sch. Food Tech., Mass. Inst. Tech.; m. Valentine McNally, Apr. 23, 1912; children—Helen Vivian (Mrs. Nuel Pazdral), Mary Jane (Mrs. L. Martin), Margaret Pauline (Mrs. Gordon Riddick), Carolyn Ann (Mrs. Harry L. Morris). Commd. capt. U.S. Army, 1917, and advanced through grades to col., 1942; inf. capt., 1917-31; student, instr. and commandant Quartermaster Subsistence Sch., 1931-36; chief of subsistence office, Q.M. Gen., Washington, 1936-38; maj., student and instr., Army Indsl. Coll., chmn. food com. Office Under Sec. of War, 1938-40; lt. col., col., dept. dir. Subsistence div., chief of food service Office of Q.M. Gen., Washington, 1940-46; dir. food research Nat. Restaurant Assn., Chicago, from 1946. Awarded Legion of Merit. Chmn. provisions com. Fed. Specification Bd., 1940-46; rep. Armed Forces Presidential War Meat Bd., 1943-45; mem. fisheries com. Dept. Interior, 1942-45. Mem. Inst. Food Technologists, Quartermaster Assn. (pres. 1951). Chicago, Ill. †

LOGAN, RAYFORD W., historian, educator; b. Washington, Jan. 7, 1897; s. Arthur and Martha (Whittingham) L.; m. Ruth Robinson, Aug. 2, 1927 (dec. June 1966). A.B., Williams Coll., 1917, A.M., 1929, L.H.D. (hon.), 1965; A.M., Harvard, 1932, Ph.D., 1936; LL.D., Howard U., 1972. Prof. history Va. Union U., 1925-30; asst. to editor Jour. Negro History, 1932-33; head dept. history Atlanta U., 1933-38; prof. history Howard U., 1938-65, prof. emeritus, 1965; reapptd. prof. history and historian Centennial History of Howard U., 1965-69, reapptd. prof. history, 1971, disting. prof., 1972-74, head dept., 1942-64; acting dean Centennial History of Howard U. (Grad. School), 1942-44, mem. program African studies, 1954-65; fgn. affairs editor Pitts. Courier, 1945-48; accredited corr. San Francisco Conv. UN, 1945; Adv. com. Coordinator Inter-Am. Affairs, 1941-43; sec. Pan-African Congress, Paris, 1921, London and Lisbon, 1923, N.Y.C., 1927; cons. UN for N.A.A.C.P., 1949; mem. U.S. Commn. for UNESCO, 1947-50; dir. Assn. Study Negro Life and History, 1950-51; accredited observer N.A.A.C.P. at UN Gen. Assembly, Paris, 1951-52. Author: The Diplomatic Relations of the U.S. with Haiti, 1776-1891, 1941, The Operation of the Mandate System in Africa, with an Introduction to the Problem of the Mandates in the Post-War World, 1942, The Senate and the Versailles Mandate System, 1945, The Negro and the Postwar World: A Primer, 1945, The African Mandates in World Politics, 1948, The Negro in American Life and Thought: The Nadir, 1877-1901, 1954, The Negro in the United States, 1957, The Betrayal of the Negro, 1965, The American Negro: Old World Background and New World Experience, (with Irving S. Cohen), 1967, 70, Haiti and the Dominican Republic, 1968, The Negro in the United States, Vol. I: A History to 1945, 1970, Howard University: The First Hundred Years, 1867-1967, 1969, The Negro in the United States, vol. II: Ordeal of Democracy, (with Michael R. Winston), 1971; Editor: What the Negro Wants, 1944, Jour. Negro History, 1950-51, Negro History Bull, 1950-51, Memoirs of a Monticello Slave, 1951, W.E.B. Du Bois: A Profile, 1971; Bd. editors: Hispanic Am. Hist. Rev, 1949-55. Served as 1st lt. U.S. Army, 1918-19, AEF. Decorated comdr. Nat. Order Honor and Merit Haiti; Fulbright research fellow France, 1951-52; State Dept. leaders grant West Africa, summer 1953; recipient Spingarn medal NAACP, 1980. Mem. Authors League Am., Phi Beta Kappa. Club: Cosmos (Washington). Home: Washington, D.C. Died Nov. 5, 1982.

LOGAN, WALTER SETH, lawyer; b. Washington, Conn., July 8, 1888; s. Walter S. and Eliza (Kenyon) L.; A.B., Yale, 1910; LL.B., Harvard, 1913; m. Verna McCutcheon, June 21, 1916. Gen. counsel Federal Reserve Bd., Washington, D.C., 1920-22; admitted to New York bar, 1913, Conn. bar, 1955; vice-pres. and gen. counsel Federal Reserve Bank of N.Y., 1928-53; mem. Reynolds, Richards, McCutcheon & Ely.†

LOHMAN, VICTOR JOHN, (GUS LOHMAN) food company executive; b. Houghton, Iowa, Dec. 11, 1928; s. Joseph G. and Kathryn (Sanders) L.; m. Verla Mae Schultz, June 5, 1964; children—David, Bruce, Michael, Brenda. Student bus. adminstrn, Bradley U., 1948-52. Founder, partner Lohman Bros. Agy., Geneseo, Ill., 1953-83; pres. Lohman Bros. Inc. (real estate devel.), Geneseo, 1958-83; also dir.; pres., chmn. bd. Illini Beef Packers, Inc., Geneseo, 1968-83. Served with USNR, 1946-47. Mem. C. of C. Club: Moose. Home: Geneseo, Ill. Died 1983.

LOHNES, GRANVILLE (RAY), business exec.; b. Donelsville, OH.; Jan. 25, 1889; s. Charles Young and Cora May (Fetter) L.; student pub. schs.; m. Stella E. Peterson, Oct. 23, 1912; children—Alice Maxine (Mrs. William F. Oblinger), Beverly May (Mrs. David G. Perry); m. 2d, Mrs. Rosemond K. Ball Bolenbaugh, 1949. Clk. accounting dept. Nat. Cash Register Co., Dayton, 1910-16, head fgn. accounting dept., 1916-20, asst. to comptroller, 1920-26, comptroller, 1926-31, treas. from 1931, mem. bd. dirs., exec. com. from 1945; dir. Cin. br. Fed. Res. Bank of Cleve. from 1951, chmn. bd. from 1952. Chmn. campaign com. A.R.C., 1946; pres. Community Chest Assn. Dayton and Montgomery Co., 1949, mem. adv. com. from 1950. Trustee Dayton Boys Club. Mem. Nat. Assn. Cost Accts. (pres. Dayton chpt. 1927-28; past nat. dir., nat. pres. 1935-36), Dayton C. of C. (bd. dirs.), Comptrollers Inst. Am., Beta Alpha Psi. Club: Moraine Country (treas., bd. govs.). Home: Dayton, Ohio. †

LOHR, WILLIAM SHANNON, educator, civil engr.; b. Centre Hall, Pa., Oct. 29, 1887; s. James Hale and Annie J. (Welsh) L.; B.C.E., U. Pa., 1909, C.E., 1925; m. Frances Hubbard, Dec. 27, 1911; children—Dorothy Hubbard (Mrs. Robert H. Woolston), Audrey Frances (Mrs. Evan L. Roberts, Jr.). Draftsman Am. Bridge Co., Pencoyd, Pa., summer, 1909, L. F. Shoemaker & Co., summer 1911; instr. civil engring. U. Pa., 1909-12; 15-16; instr. civil engring. Lafayette Coll., 1912-15, asso. prof., 1920-30, prof. from 1930, head dept., 1912-53, prof. emeritus from 1953; cons.; engr. John H. Wickersham, Lancaster, Pa., 1916-17, 19-20; concrete engr. Austin Co., Phila., 1917-19; designing engr. State Highway Commn., Augusta, Maine, summers 1926, 28-29, 31. Registered profl. engr., Pa. Mem. Nat., Pa. socs. profl. engrs., ASCE, Am. Soc. Metals, Am. Soc. Engring, Edn., AAUP, ASTM, Sigma Xi, Tau Beta Pi. Republican. Presbyn. Co-inventor encased columns. Home: East New Market, Md. Deceased.

LOHWATER, A.J., educator; b. Rochester, N.Y., Oct. 20, 1922; s. Arthur A. and Florence (Wagner) L.; m. Marjorie Anne White, May 28, 1949; children—Susan, Sarah, Karl. A.B., U. Rochester, 1942, M.S., 1947, Ph.D., 1951; postgrad., Columbia, 1947-49. Instr. math. U. Rochester, 1942-44; from instr. to asso. prof. U. Mich., 1949-59; prof. Rice U., 1959-65; research asso. Brown U., 1961-65; exec. editor Math. Rev., 1961-65; prof. math. Case Inst. Tech., 1965-82, chmn. math. dept., 1967-82, chmn. math.-statistics dept., 1970-75, vice provost, 1969-70; dir. NSF summer inst. So. Univ., 1965; cons. editor Addison-Wesley Internat. Series, 1960-82; exec. editor Math. Systems Theory, 1966-75. Author: Russian-English Dictionary of Mathematical Sciences, 1961, (with Sir Edward Collingwood) Theory of Cluster Sets, 1966, Boundary Behavior of Analytic Functions, 1973, also articles.; Adv. bd.: (with Sir Edward Collingwood) Internat. Library Rev. Served to lt. (j.g.) USNR, 1944-46. Recipient medal of honor Jyväskylä U., Finland, 1973; AEC fellow, 1948-49; Guggenheim fellow, 1955; Fulbright research grantee, 1955-56. Mem. N.Y. Acad. Sci., London, Finnish math. societies, Inst. Math. Statistics, AAAS, Math. Assn. Am., Am. Math. Soc. (spl. citation), Soc. Indsl. and Applied Math., Phi Beta Kappa, Sigma Xi. Home: Cleveland Heights, Ohio. Died June 10, 1982.

LOMBARD, MARION SUNSARI, U.S. Pub. Health Service; b. Broken Bow, Neb., Sept. 7, 1888; s. Vincent and Josephine (Sunsari) L.; prep. edn. high sch. dept. of Creighton U.; M.D., Creighton U., Sch. of Medicine, 1910; m. Mary Steiner, Oct. 25, 1916; children—Mary Josephine (Mrs. W. D. Walsh), Vivian Lee (Mrs. Martin Downey), Marion Ann (Mrs. Leo Newcombe), Robert Marion. Med. officer, 1st lt. M.R.C., U.S. Army, 1911-14; commd. asst. surgeon, U.S. P.H.S., 1914, passed asst. surg., 1918, surg., 1922, sr. surgeon, 1934, med. dir. from 1940. Served as surgeon U.S.S. Tampa in Internat. Ice Patrol, 1916; U.S. quarantine officer, Tampico, Mex., 1917; med. officer in charge plague eradication, New Orleans, 1919; med. officer in charge Quarantine Sta., Mobile, Ala., 1922; clin. dir. Marine Hosp., Chicago, 1923; med. officer in charge Marine Hosp., Key West, 1927, Memphis, Tenn., 1933; med. dir. Region F, Am. Red Cross, Ohio and Miss. Valley floods, 1937; med. officer in charge U.S. Marine Hosp. and Med. Inspection of Aliens, Buffalo, N.Y., 1937-41; dist. med. dir. alien detention camps, Hdqtrs. Spokane, Wash., 1941-43; dist. Coast Guard Medical Officer 13th Naval Dist., 1944-45; med. officer in charge U.S. Marine Hosp. Pittsburgh, 1945-50. Fellow A.M.A., Am. Coll. Surgeons, Southeastern Surg Congress; mem. Assn. Mil. Surgeons of U.S., Am. Coll. Hosp. Adminstrs., Pi Gamma Mu. Catholic. K.C. Address: New Orleans, La. †

LOMMEL, W(ALTER) E(RNEST), univ. prof.; b. Lawrenceburg, Ind., June 9, 1890; s. George Fred and Luella Amelia (Leiendecker) L.; B.S.A., Purdue U., 1914; student U. of Wis., 1921, 22, U. of Chicago, 1929; m. Thelma Jane Warrick, Aug. 28, 1926; children—Phyllis Mignon, Anne Warrick. Asst. in horticulture Purdue U., 1914, instr., 1915-17, asst. prof., 1917, asso. prof., 1918-35, prof. horticulture from 1935. Mem. Am. Soc. for Hort. Sci., Ind. Hort. Soc., Acacia (pres. Acacia Bldg. Assn.). Republican. Presbyterian. Mason. Home: West Lafayette, Ind. †

LONDON, GEORGE, opera and concert singer; b. Montreal, Que., Can., May 30, 1920; s. Louis Samuel and Bertha (Broad) Burnstein; m. Nora Sheldon, Aug. 30, 1955; children—Marina, Mark. Student, Los Angeles City Coll., 1937-39; Mus. D. (hon.), Cleve. Inst. Music, 1976. Artistic adminstr. John F. Kennedy Center for Performing Arts, Washington, 1968-71; exec. dir. Nat. Opera Inst., 1971-77; gen. dir. Opera Soc. of Washington, 1975-80, ret., 1980; Mem. performing arts adv. com. 1976 Bicentennial Commn. With, Am. Music Theater, Los Angeles, also Pasadena, Calif., 1940; profl. opera debut as Dr. Grenvil in La Traviata, Hollywood Bowl, 1941; singer profl. opera debut as, Los Angeles and San Francisco civic light opera assns., 1942-44; San Francisco Opera debut in Rigoletto, 1943; baritone soloist: world premiere Hindemith's composition When Lilacs Last in the Dooryard Bloomed, 1946; Vienna State Opera debut in Aida, 1949; singer Vienna State Opera debut in, Glyndebourne Opera, 1950, Bayreuth Festival, 1951-53, 56, 57, 59, 61-64, Salzburg Festival, 1952; Met. Opera debut Aida, 1951; LaScala debut, 1952, San Francisco, 1959; sang: title role Boris Godunov, Moscow, 1960; title role: Am. premiere The Last Savage, 1963-64; Contbr. articles on music Am. publs.; Recorded: (with Bolshoi Ensemble.) title role of Boris Godunov. Bd. dirs. N.Y.C. Center. Apptd. Austrian Kammersaenger (court singer) by pres. of Austria, 1955; decorated Cross of Honor 1st class for arts and letters Austria). Mem. Am. Guild Mus. Artists (pres. 1967-71). Home: Armonk, N.Y. Died Mar. 14, 1985.

LONG, AVON, actor; b. Balt., June 18, 1910; s. Charles and Bertha (Minnes) L.; student pub. schs.; m. Gretchen Cotton, Feb. 20, 1937; children—Janice, Gretchen, Ellyn. Broadway appearances include: Very Warm For May, 1938, Porgy and Bess, 1938, Don't Play Us Cheap, 1972, Bubbling Brown Sugar, 1976; film appearances include The Sting, 1973, Harry and Tonto, 1974. Named Actor Most Likely to Succeed, Variety Poll, 1942; Man of Year in Balt., by Mayor of Balt., 1976; recipient award Dance Educators Am., 1976. Mem. Actors Equity, Screen Actors Guild, AFTRA, Am. Guild Variety Artists, ASCAP, Holy Name Soc. Roman Cath. Club: K.C. Composer musical: Dear Harriet Tubman, 1977. Died Feb. 15, 1984.

LONG, GILLIS W., congressman, lawyer, investment banker, soybean farmer; b. Winnfield, La., May 4, 1923; s. Floyd H. and Birdie (Shumake) L.; m. Catherine Small; children—George Harrison, Janis. B.A., La. State U., 1949, J.D., 1951. Legal counsel select com. small bus. U.S. Senate, 1951-53; chief counsel spl. com. campaign expenditures (elections) U.S. Ho. of Reps., 1952, 56, 58, 60; mem. 88th, 93d-98th Congresses from 8th Dist. La.; chmn. 88th, 93d-98th Congresses from 8th Dist. La. (Democratic caucus, mem. rules com.), 1973—; chmn. subcom. on legis. process, Joint econ. com. 88th, 93d-97th Congresses from 8th Dist. La. (Democratic caucus, mem. rules com.), 1975—; chmn. subcom. on internat. trade, fin., security econs.; asst. dir. Office Econ. Opportunity, 1964-65; Legis. counsel Spl. Com. hist. Preservation, Spl. Com. Urban Growth Policy. Chmn. La. Superport Task Force, pres., 1972; commr. La. Offshore Terminal Authority, 1973; pres. Lower Mississippi Flood Control Assn., 1973-74; vice chmn. United Dems. of Congress, 1973-74, chmn., 1975—, exec. bd., 1977; co-founder Congl. Rural Caucus, 1973, mem. exec. bd., 1973—; mem. Dem. nat. com., congl. campaign con., 1980—, Congl. Caucus for Women's Issues. Served to capt., inf. AUS, World War II, ETO. Decorated Bronze Star, Purple Heart. Mem. Am., La., Alexandria bar assns., La. Wildlife Fedn., V.F.W., Am. Legion, Omicron Delta Kappa, Delta Kappa Epsilon, others. Baptist.

LONNQUEST, THEODORE CLAYTON, naval officer; b. Lynn, Mass., Apr. 10, 1894; s. David Emmanuel Theodore and Carrie Belle (Thurston) L.; B.S., Dartmouth, 1917; student U.S. Naval Postgrad. Sch., 1922-24; M.S., Mass. Inst. Tech., 1924; m. Alice Marie Born, Sept. 15, 1923; children—Theodore Clayton, Dorothy Elaine. Commd. ensign U.S. Navy, 1917, and advanced through the grades to rear adm., 1946; served at Naval Air Stas., World War I; designated naval aviator, 1919; naval aviator on U.S.S. Langley, Pennsylvania, Saratoga, 1924-32; comdg. officer Scouting Squadron 2, U.S.S. Saratoga, 1932-34; head power plant design br. Bur. Aeronautics, Washington, D.C., 1934-37; comdr. Naval Aviation Sta., Norfolk, 1937-41; dir. engring. Bur. of Aeronautics in charge of design and development of Navy's wartime aircraft, 1941-45; duty on staff Comdr. Joint Task Force I, serving during Operation Crossroads, atom bomb tests at Bikini atoll, 1946; on duty under Sec. of Navy in connection with aviation applications of atomic energy, Washington, D.C., 1946; asst. chief research and development. Bur. of Aeronautics, Navy Department, 1947-48; deputy chief of Bureau of Aeronautics from 1949. Recipient Nat. Air Council Award, 1948. Decorated: Legion of Merit. Sec. Navy Commendation Ribbon. Navy Unit Commendation Ribbon, Victory Medals (World War I and II), Am. Defense Medal, Am. Campaign Medal, Asiatic-Pacific Area Campaign Medal. Pistol Expert Medal. Fellow Inst. Aeronautical Scis.; mem. Nat. Adv. Com. for Aeronautics. Am. Inst. Engrs. Phi Beta Kappa, Lambda Chi Alpha. Episcopalian. Mason. Club: Cosmos. Home: Chevy Chase, Md. Died Mar. 9, 1982.

LONNQUIST, JOHN HALL, agronomist, educator; b. Ashland, Wis., May 22, 1916; s. James Oscar and Ethel Selma (Hall) L.; m. Betty Claire Hanson, July 27, 1942; children—John Hall, Ladd, George, Tom, Kathleen, Kristine, Margaret Anne, Ken. B.S., U. Nebr., 1940, Ph.D., 1949; M.S., Kans. State Coll., 1942; postgrad., Ohio State U., 1942-43, Iowa State Coll., 1948. Grad. asst. Kans. State Coll., 1940-42, Ohio State U., 1942; instr. Pa. State Coll., 1943; asst. agronomist U. Nebr., 1943-49, asso. agronomist, 1949-53, prof. agronomy, 1953-61, C. Petrus Peterson prof. agronomy, 1961-67; also head corn breeding and genetics investigations; project specialist agr. Ford Found.; assigned Internat. Center for Maize and Wheat Improvement as; dir. internat. maize program, Mexico, 1967-70; prof. agronomy, head corn investigations U. Wis. at, Madison, from 1970; Mem. agrl. panel AID; cons. vis. lectr. plant breeding, Argentina, Brazil; adviser Rockefeller Found. agrl. programs, Central and S.Am. Contbr. numerous sci. papers on corn breeding and genetics. Recipient Distinguished Service to Agr. award radio sta. KMMJ, Grand Island, Neb., 1962. Fellow Am. Soc. Agronomy (Crop Sci. award 1961); mem. Am. Genetic Assn., AAAS, Am. Inst. Biol. Scis., Sociedade Brasileira de Genetica (corr.), São Paolo State Acad. Scis. (fgn. asso.), Sigma Xi, Gamma Sigma Delta, Alpha Zeta. Home: Middleton, Wis.

LOOMIS, ARTHUR KIRKWOOD, educator; b. Battle Creek, Mich., Oct. 25, 1888; s. Merritt Francis and Lydia Hoxie (Kirkwood) L.; A.B., Baker U., Kan., 1909, L.H.D., 1944; A.M., U. Kan., 1917; Ph.D., Columbia, 1926; Ph.D., (hon.), Nihon U., Tokyo, Japan, 1954; m. Ethel Morgan, June 17, 1914; children—Robert Kirkwood, Edward Warren, Richard Morgan; m. 2d, Kate Wood Ashley, June 13, 1938. Supt. schs., Oswego, Kan., 1909-12, Peabody, Kan., 1912-16; prin. County High Sch., Wellington, Kan., 1917-21; supt. schs., Hiwatha, Kan., 1921-23; dir. curriculum Denver Pub. Schs., 1925-31; prin. Univ. High Sch., asso. prof. edn., asso. dean Coll., U. Chgo., 1931-36; supt. schs., Shaker Heights, Cleve., 1936-44; dir. sch. Edn., prof. edn. U. Denver, 1944-47; adviser ednl. reorgn., 1947-49; chief ednl. div. Civil Information and Ednl. Sect., Gen. Hdqrs., Supreme Comdr. for Allied Powers, Tokyo, 1949-52; ednl. adviser J-5 Hdqrs., Far East Command, 1952-57; post doctoral Harvard, 1958; curriculum cons. Centennial Scholars Program, U. Denver, 1962-63. Chief specialist curriculum Nat. Survey Secondary Edn., Office Edn., 1930-31; mem. Nat. Com. on Reorgn. Community Services, 1945. Mem. Am. Ednl. Research Assn., Am. Assn. Sch. Adminstrs. (Yearbook com. 1946), Nat. Soc. for Study Edn. (Yearbook com. 1945), N.E.A., Phi Delta Kappa, Kappa Delta Pi. Author: Estimating School Equipment Costs, 1926; School Equipment Costs, a Method of Estimating, 1927; (with Edwin S. Lide) The Program of Studies, 1932. Editor series Courses of Study, (Denver Pub. Schs.), 1925-31. Contbr. articles to profl. jours. Address: Claremont, CA. †

LOOMIS, JOHN PUTNAM, govt. ofcl.; b. Englewood, N.J., Feb. 9, 1889; s. Chester and Sarah (Dana) L.; A.B., Williams Coll., 1911; m. Eleanore Gilbert, Oct. 2, 1936. Traffic mgr., asst. sales mgr. Lamont Corliss Co., N.Y., 1911-17; exec. several businesses, 1919-32; personnel exec. State and Nat. work relief agencies, 1932-37; food adminstr. for occupied areas Dept. of Army, 1948-52; chief Office of Materials Specialists, Munitions Bd. Dept. Def., 1952-53. Served as 2d lt. to capt. U.S. Army, 1917-19, major to col., 1941-47. Decorated Bronze Star, Commendation Ribbon, European Campaign medal with 3 stars, Occupation medal World War II. Mem. Delta Psi. Club: University. Home: Washington, D.C. Deceased.

LORD, MILTON EDWARD, librarian; b. Lynn, Mass., June 12, 1898; s. William Delbert and Eliza Anna (Bishop) L.; A.B., Harvard, 1919, postgrad., 1921-24, Ecole des Sciences Politiques, Paris, 1925-26; m. Rosamond Lane, Sept. 8, 1928; children—Peter, Joan (Mrs. Ernest B. Johnston, Jr.), Mary (Mrs. John G. Van Dusen), Anne (Mrs. Conrad H. Malicoat), Sarah Peabody (Mrs. Walter H. Corson II). Asst., Harvard Coll. Library, Cambridge, Mass., 1919-25; librarian Harvard Union, 1919-23, Am. Acad. in Rome, 1926-30, librarian-in-residence, 1971-72, 73-74, dir. library, 1975-76; prof., dir. Univ. Libraries and Library Sch., State U. Iowa, 1930-31; dir. Boston Pub. Library, 1932-65, emeritus, 1965-85; dir. Am. Library, Paris, 1945. Mem. Commn. of Five Am. Librarians in Recataloging Vatican Library, 1928; U.S. del. Internat. Congress of Libraries and Bibliography, Rome-Naples-Venice, 1929, Madrid-Seville-Barcelona, 1935; chmn. Council Nat. Library Assns., 1944-45, Joint Com. on Books for Devastated Libraries, 1944-54; chmn. bd. Am. Book Center for War Devastated Libraries, 1945-54; pres. bd. U.S. Book Exchange, Inc., 1948-52; mem. U.S. Nat. Commn. for UNESCO, 1949-53; cons. Internat. Council of Monuments and Sites, Paris, 1969-78, hon. mem., 1978-85, mem. Am. com., 1970-85, pres. internat. com. for documentation, 1970-85. Attended Heavy Arty. Sch., Fort Monroe, Va., 1918-19; Served as 2d lt. Heavy Arty. R.C., 1919-24. Trustee Simmons Coll., from 1947, chmn. corp., 1957-65; chmn. bd. trustees Boxford Town Library, 1966-71. Decorated chevalier Legion of Honor (France). Benjamin Franklin fellow Royal Soc. Arts. Fellow Am. Acad. Arts and Scis., Royal Soc. Arts; mem. A.L.A. (pres. 1949-50), Mass. Hist. Soc., Mass. Library Assn. (pres. 1965-66), Old Cambridge Shakespeare Assn. (past pres.), Dante Soc. Am., Phi Beta Kappa. Clubs: Odd Volumes, Examiner (Boston). Home: Boxford, Mass. Died Feb. 12, 1985.

LOREE, JAMES TABER, corp. official; b. Logansport, Ind., Apr. 6, 1888; s. Leonor Fresnol and Jessie (Taber) L.; B.A., Yale, 1909; m. Miriam G. Collins, Mar. 23, 1927. Began as file clerk, K.C.S. Ry., 1909; became traveling auditor and chief traveling auditor, same road; signal department Pa. Lines west of Pittsburgh, 1910-11; head of party on constrn. and location S.P. Lines in Ore., Feb.-June 1911; chief tunnel insp. same rd., June-Sept. 1911; draftsman for construction engr. D.&H., at Colonie, N.Y., Sept.-Nov. 1911; spl. mission studying English railroad practices, Dec. 1911-June 1912; asst. div. engr., S.P. Co., 1912-13; with D.&H. Co. from July 1913, successively as asst. trainmaster, trainmaster to 1914, supt. Susquehanna div., 1914-15, asst. gen. supt. transportation, 1915-16, gen. mgr., 1917-23, became v.p. in charge of operation, 1923; officer or dir. many cos. Served as enlisted man, 2d lt., 1st lt. and capt. N.Y.N.G., 1915-17; maj., lt. col. and col. U.S. Army, 1917-20; served on Mexican border; later with 27th Div. and 80th Div. in France and as chief of staff Am. Mission, Interallied Mil. Mission to Hungary and as dep. U.S. commr. Decorated D.S.M. (U.S.); Legion of Honor and Croix de Guerre (French); Order Crown of Roumania; Order Crown of Italy; Order of Leopold (Belgian); Order of Simon Bolivar; Order of Danilo. Mem. Beta Theta Pi. Republican. Catholic. Clubs: University, Ft. Orange, Albany Country, Schuyler Meadows (Albany); Mohawk Golf (Schenectady); University, Yale (New York). Home: Albany, N.Y.†

LORIMER, GRAEME, author, editor; b. Wyncote, Pa., Feb. 9, 1903; s. George Horace and Alma Viola (Ennis) L.; m. Sarah Moss, Oct. 2, 1926; children—Sarah Lee (Mrs.Daniel I. Morris), Belle Burford (Mrs. Henry B. Robb III), George Horace II, Anna Hunter (Mrs. A. John P. Sirna). Grad., William Penn Charter Sch., Phila., 1919; B.A., U. Pa., 1923. Asst. editor Country Gentleman, 1926; asso. editor Ladies' Home Jour., 1930-31, Sat. Eve. Post, 1932-38; article and fiction editor Ladies' Home Jour., 1939-44; dir. Girard Bank, Phila., 1938-73. Author: (with wife) Men Are Like Street Cars, 1932, Stag Line, 1934, Heart Specialist, 1935, Acquittal, 1938, First Love, Farwell, 1940. Mem. distbn. com. Phila. Found., 1958-70, chmn., 1961-65; Trustee Phila. Mus. Art, 1939-70; hon. trustee, from 1970; trustee Phila. Award, 1947-70. Mem. Psi Upsilon. Episcopalian. Clubs: Franklin Inn, Merion Cricket. Home: Paoli, PA.

LOSEY, JOSEPH, film director; b. LaCrosse, Wis., Jan. 14, 1909; s. Joseph Walton and Ina (Higbee) L.; m. Patricia Mohan; 2 sons by previous marriage, 2 stepchildren. B.A., Dartmouth Coll., 1929, L.H.D., 1972; L.H.D., U. Wis.-Madison, 1983. Freelance journalist, 1931; jury pres. Cannes Film Festival, 1972; guest prof. Dartmouth Coll., 1970, 75. Stage mgr., theatre producer Broadway, 1932-40; writer, producer, editor radio documentaries, 1938-84; film dir., 1938-84; dir. films including: A Child Went Forth, 1941, A Gun in His Hand, 1945, The Boy With Green Hair, 1948, The Lawless, 1949, The Prowler, 1950, M, 1950, The Big Night, 1951, Stranger on the Prowl, 1951, The Sleeping Tiger, 1954, A Man on the Beach, 1955, The Intimate Stranger, 1955, Time Without Pity, 1956, The Gypsy and the Gentleman, 1957, Blind Date, 1959, The Criminal, 1960, The Damned, 1961, The Servant, 1963, King and Country, 1964, Modesty Blaise, 1965, Accident, 1966, Boom, 1967, Secret Ceremony, 1968, Figures in a Landscape, 1969, The Go-Between, 1970 (Gold Palm of Cannes Film Festival), The Assassination of Trotsky, 1971, A Doll's House, 1973, Galileo, 1974, The Romantic English Woman, 1974-75, Monsieur Klein, 1976 (French César awards for Best Picture and Best Dir.), Les Routes du Sud, 1978, Don Giovanni, 1979, La Truite, 1982; dir.: Boris Godunov, Paris Opera, 1980. Decorated chevalier de L'Ordre des Arts et des Lettres; recipient numerous film awards. Died June 22, 1984.

LOUCKS, DANIEL K(YLE), lawyer; b. Clear Lake, S.D., Mar. 4, 1887; s. Henry L. and Florence I. (McCraney) L.; student S.D. State Coll., Brookings, 1905-07; m. Frances Norris, Sept. 2, 1913; children—Marguerite N. (Mrs. Willard J. Dye), William N. Proprietor Watertown (S.D.) Times, 1909-14; collection agt., 1914-16; admitted to S.D. bar, 1916, since practiced in Watertown; mem. firm Loucks, Oviatt & Bradshaw, from 1952; states atty. Codington County, S.D., 1919-23; mem. S.D. Ho. of Reps., 1927-30, speaker of ho., 1929; city atty., Watertown, 1932-42, 46-48. Mem. Am., S.D. (chmn. real property and probate law com. 1941-47, 49-53, 56-57; pres. 1954-55) bar assns. Republican.

Methodist. Mason, Kiwanian, Elk, K.P., Modern Woodman. Home: Watertown, S.D. †

LOUGEE, NORMAN ARTHUR, engr.; b. Salem, Mass., Apr. 30, 1890; s. Arthur L. and Annah (Call) L.; B.S., M.S., Mass. Inst. Tech., 1907-12; m. Gladys Mae Smith, Dec. 26, 1916; children—Aristine (wife of Col. S. Y. Coker), Norman Arthur, David F. Cons. engring. lab. Gen. Electric Co., assisted in building lighting generator, patent and development pellet lighting arresters, 1912-22; cons. engr. Stone & Webster Engring. Corp., N.Y.C., 1922-38; v.p. Ulen & Co., N.Y.C., 1938-40; sr. partner N. A. Lougee & Co., N.Y.C., from 1947, chmn., from 1951; trustee Eastern Gas & Fuel Assos., Boston, 1956-57. Mem. Am. Gas Assn., Newcomen Soc., Am. Inst. E.E. Episcopalian. Home: Bronxville, N.Y. †

LOUTTIT, THOMAS ROBLEY, ins. co. exec.; b. Providence, Feb. 24, 1909; s. William Easton and Sophia (Robley) L.; student Brown U., 1928-29; m. Charlotte Anne Gies, Sept. 8, 1930; children—Lee Anne (Mrs. Tauck), Thomas Robley. Chmn. bd. Louttit Corp., Providence; dir., mem. exec. com. Allendale Mut. Ins. Co., Providence; dir. Appalachian Ins. Co., Providence, Union Mut. Ins. Co., Providence, Affiliated FM Ins. Co., New Providence Corp. Mem. Theta Delta Chi. Club: Turks Head (Providence). Home: Bristol, R.I. Died Jan. 28, 1980.

LOUW, ERIC HENDRICK, diplomat; b. Jacobsdal, S. Africa, Nov. 21, 1890; s. Jan Albertus and Margeretha (De Villiers) L.; B.A., Stellenbosch U., Stellenbosch, S. Africa, 1911; LL.B., Rhodes U., Grahamstown, 1916; m. Anna Snyman, of East London, Cape Province, S. Africa, July 6, 1918; children—Jan Albertus, Martin Snyman, Anna Snyman (dec.). Admitted to bar, 1917; mem. Ho. of Assembly, Union of S. Africa, 1924-25; 1st trade commr. Union of S. Africa to U.S. and Can., 1925-29; high commr., London, Eng., 1929; 1st E.E. and M.P. from Union of S. Africa to U.S. from Nov. 5, 1929. Del. Internat. Immigration Conf., Havana, Cuba, 1928; del. Internat. Red Cross and Prisoner of War Conf., Geneva, 1929. Del. League of Nations Assembly, Geneva, 1929.†

LOVETT, ISRAEL HERRICK, univ. prof.; b. Council Bluffs, Ia., Mar. 1, 1890; s. Israel and Nettie Florence (Herrick) L.; S.B., Mass. Inst. Tech., 1914; E.E., Mo. Sch. Mines, 1924; M.S., Univ. Mich., 1928; m. Alma A. Love, June 5, 1955. Graduate students course, Commonwealth Edison Co., Chicago, 1914-15; staff switchboard engring. div., Westinghouse Elec. Corp., Pittsburgh, 1915-16; chief elec. designer, New England Power Co., Worcester, Mass., 1916-20; instr. in elec. engring., Worcester Polytechnic Inst., 1920-21; instr. elec. engring. U. Mo. at Rolla, 1921, asst. prof., 1921-24, asso. prof., 1924-31, prof. elec. engring., from 1931. Fellow I.E.E.E.; mem. Mo. Soc. Profl. Engrs. Methodist. Specializing in electric power systems analysis. Home: Rolla, Mo. †

LOVETT, RALPH BRUNDIDGE, army officer; b. Altoona, Kan., Oct. 16, 1890; s. Andrew J. and Estelle A. (Brundidge) L.; student U. of Kan., 1908-10, Okla. Bapt. Coll., 1910-12, U. of Mo., 1931-32, army schs.; m. Florence P. Colburn, Aug. 2, 1919; 1 son, Colburn B. Newspaper reporter, 1914; professional writer, 1915-17; commd. capt. First Officers Training Camp, 1917; regular army, 1920, and advanced through the grades to brig. gen., Aug. 1942; on loan to Bur. of Budget as asst. chief coordinator participating in first govt. reorgn. plan, 1921-23; Gen. Staff Corps and dep. dir. Bur. Pub. Relations, War Dept., 1939-42; dir. operations (army classification system, personnel accounting, adminstrn. schs.) Office Adj. Gen., 1942-43; adj. gen. E.T.O., 1943-46; dir. Army Postal Service, 1946; ret., 1947. Adviser to adminstr. Vets. Affairs, 1947; mgr. Vets. Affairs, Philippines, 1948-53. Historian Dept. of Army. Decorated 15 various U.S. and fgn. service medals. Clubs: Nat. Press, Army and Navy, Army-Navy Country (Washington); Overseas Press, Wack-Wack, Army-Navy (Manila). Contbr. Am. and fgn. mags. on mgmt., pub. relations, various features. Home: Blackwell, Okla. Deceased.

LOW, EDMON, librarian; b. Kiowa, Okla., Jan. 4, 1902; s. Foster LaFayette and Katherine (Horton) L.; m. Mayme Frances Castleberry, Aug. 14, 1929; children: Frances Kathryn, Donald Foster, Marc Edmon. A.B., E. Central State Coll., Ada, Okla., 1926; B. L.S., U. Ill., 1930; A.M., U. Mich., 1938; Litt.D., Eastern Mich. U., 1967. Asst. librarian E. Central State Coll., 1926-37; librarian Bowling Green (O.) State U., 1938-40; librarian Okla. State U., Stillwater, 1940-67, dean, 1946-67; also head librarian, prof.; lectr. summer sessions U. Mich. Library Sch., 1939-46, 50-66, prof. library sci., 1967-72; librarian New Coll., Sarasota, Fla., 1972-75, U. South Fla., Sarasota Campus, 1975-80; chmn. Okla. Council Libraries, 1965-66. Mem. Assn. Coll. and Research Libraries (pres. 1960-61), ALA (v.p. 1962-63), Southwestern Library Assn. (pres. 1950-52), Okla. Library Assn. (pres. 1949), Phi Kappa Phi, Phi Delta Kappa. Democrat. Methodist. Home: Tulsa, Okla.

LOW, V. THEODORE, co. ofcl.; b. Mobile, Ala., 1905; A.B., Princeton, 1926. Ltd. partner Bear Stearns & Co. Trustee George Jr. Republic, Freeville, N.Y., Montefiore Hosp. and Med. Center; bd. dirs. Westchester County Golf Assn. Caddie Scholarship Fund, Inc. Clubs: Century Country, Blind Brook (Purchase, N.Y.); Princeton, Recess, Regency Whist, University (N.Y.C.); Tower (Princeton); Tryall Golf (Sandy Bay, Jamaica, W.I.). Home: New York, N.Y. Died 1979.

LOWE, BOUTELLE ELLSWORTH, author, educator; b. Marion, N.Y., Mar. 24, 1890; s. Ralph and Clara (Ellsworth) L.; A.B., Denison U., Granville, O., 1911; A.M., U. of Rochester, 1912; Ph.D., Columbia, 1918; m. Louise Alberta Caroline Klein, June 28, 1926. Prin. high sch., Machias, N.Y., 1912-14; dept. social science, East High Sch. and Washington Jr. High Sch., Rochester, 1914-16, Evander Childs High Sch., N.Y. City, 1916-17; vol. war service, 1917-18; teacher Courtney Sch. (pvt.), N.Y. City, 1919-20; Hackensack High Sch., 1920-54, head dept. of social sciences, 1929-37, prin., 1937-54; prin. Hackensack Summer Sch., 1933-36; pres. of Language Inst., Inc., N.Y. City, 1918-34; prof. economics, Jr. College Bergen Co., Teaneck, 1933-42. Mem. N.J. State adv. com. for secondary schs. 1944-52. Mem. Acad. Polit. Sci., Society Advancement Education, Phi Beta Kappa, Alpha Delta Tau, Lambda Chi Alpha. Club: Rotary. Author: Representative Industry and Trade Unionism of an American City, 1912; Internatl. Aspects of the Labor Problem, 1918; Historical Survey of International Action Affecting Labor (jointly), 1920; The International Protection of Labor, 1921 (enlarged edit., 1935); International Education for Peace, 1929. Contributor to N.Y. Sun, School and Society, the Compendum of American Genealogy, Vol. IV, 1930, Vol. VII, 1942; Vol. VIII, 1953, University of Pennsylvania Law Review, 1938, Bulletin National Association of Secondary Sch. Prins., 1940, School Activities, 1948, etc. Home: Hasbrouck Heights, N.J. †

LOWENS, IRVING, educator, musicologist, critic; b. N.Y.C., Aug. 19, 1916; s. Harry and Hedwig (Abramovich) L.; m. Margery Louise Morgan, Feb. 1, 1969. B.S., Columbia, 1939; M.A., U. Md., 1957, postgrad., 1957-59. Contbg. music critic Washington Evening Star, 1953-60, chief music critic, 1961-78; dean, asso. dir. Peabody Inst., Johns Hopkins U., Balt., 1978-83; reference librarian for sound recs., music div. Library of Congress, Washington, 1959-61, asst. head reference sect. music div., 1961-66; chmn. bd. dirs. Am. Mus. Digest, 1967-70; research cons. Moravian Music Found., 1956-83; sr. research fellow, vis. prof. Inst. Studies Am. Music, Bklyn. Coll., City U. N.Y., 1975-76; mem. advisory bd. Inter-Am. Inst. Mus. Research, Tulane U., 1961-76, Oral History of Music in Am. project City U. N.Y., 1974-83, Terrace Theater, Kennedy Center Performing Arts, 1979-83; Bd. dirs. Am. Music Center, 1966-72, People-to-People Music Com., 1973-83; trustee Robert O. Lehman Found., 1964-66, Inter-Am. Music and Arts Festivals Found., 1976-83; bd. govs. WJHU-FM, 1978-83. Author: Music and Musicians in Early America, 1964, A Bibliography of Songsters Printed in America Before 1821, 1976, Music in America and American Music, 1978, Haydn in America, 1979, other books and monographs, also numerous articles on history, bibliography and lit. early Am. music.; Music editor: We Sing of Life, 1955; book rev. editor: American Music, 1981-83. Recipient Moramus award for distinguished service to Am. music, 1960; ASCAP-Deems Taylor award for best newspaper articles on music, 1973, 77; Am. Council Learned Socs. travel grantee Germany, 1962; research grantee, 1965; Martha Baird Rockefeller Fund travel grantee Austria, 1964; Martha Baird Rockefeller Fund travel grantee Romania, 1967; State Dept. travel grantee Venezuela, 1968; State Dept. travel grantee Greece and Cyprus, 1970; Nat. Endowment for Arts research grantee, 1969. Fellow Am. Antiquarian Soc.; mem. Am. Musicol. Soc. (council 1956-59, 1961-64, 68-71, exec. bd. 1964-65), Internat. Musicol. Soc., Am. Studies Assn., Coll. Music Soc., Inter-Am. Assn. Music Critics (v.p. 1973-83), Sonneck Soc. (chmn. pro tem 1974-75, pres. 1975-81), Manuscript Soc., Am. Liszt Soc. (advisory bd. 1977-83), Hymn Soc. Am., Soc. Ethnomusicology, Internat. Assn. Music Libraries, Music Library Assn. (exec. bd. 1962-64, v.p. 1964-65, pres. 1965-66), Music Critics Assn. (treas. 1962-69, v.p. 1969-71, pres. 1971-75, exec. bd. 1975-77). Clubs: Johns Hopkins Faculty (Balt.); Cosmos (Washington). Home: Baltimore, Md. Died Nov. 14, 1983.

LOWENSTEIN, LEAH MIRIAM HILLER, physician; b. Milw., June 17, 1930; d. Abraham and Sarah (Lucoff) Hiller; m. John M. Lowenstein, Oct. 20, 1926; children: Charles, Andrew, Marc. B.S., U. Wis., 1950, M.D., 1954; D.Phil., Oxford (Eng.) U., 1958, postgrad. in biophysics, 1955-58. Intern U. Wis. Hosps., 1954-55; research asso. dept. anatomy Oxford U., 1955-58; instr. medicine Tufts U., 1961-64; research asso. Harvard U., 1964-65, asst. in medicine, 1965-68, asso. medicine, 1969-70, med. dir. alcohol research unit dept. psychiatry, 1967-70; asst. prof. medicine Boston U., 1968-71, asso. prof., 1971-76, prof., from 1976, asso. prof. biochemistry, 1971-76, prof. medicine and biochemistry, from 1976, acting dean Sch. Medicine, 1973, asst. dean, 1974-79, asso. dean, 1979-82; dean Jefferson Med. Coll., from 1982; vis. renal cons. VA Hosp., Boston, from 1964; med. adviser Office Asst. Sec. Health, HEW, from 1978; mem. rev. com. artificial kidneychronic uremia program NIH, also mem. gen. medicine B study sect.; mem. exptl. models of aging com. Nat. Inst. Aging, from 1974. Author: Becoming a Physician, 1979; contbr. articles tech. jours. USPHS grantee, from 1963; NIH spl. fellow, 1966-67; Mass. Heart Assn. grantee, 1968-69. Fellow AAAS (sec. med. sci. sect.); mem. Soc. Exptl. Biology (Eng.), Royal Soc. Medicine (Eng.), Inst. Medicine of Nat. Acad. Sci. (governing council), Am. Fedn. Clin. Research, Am. Assn. Study Liver Disease, A.C.P., Tissue Culture Assn., Mass. Med. Soc., Internat. Soc. Nephrology, Am. Soc. Nephrology, Nat. Kidney Found., Am. Physiol. Soc., Council in Kidney in Cardiovascular Disease (pres.), Am. Heart Assn., Am. Med. Women's Assn., Am. Med. Soc. on Alcoholism, Salt and Water Club, Phi Beta Kappa, Alpha Omega Alpha. Home: Wellesley Hills, Mass.

LOWERY, DOANE MCKENDRY, educator; b. Toledo, O., Apr. 4, 1888; s. Robert Gavin and Carrie (Norton) L.; m. Marguerite Frances Stough, Oct. 2, 1915; 1 dau., June Elizabeth (Mrs. Robert Tashian Lamson). Asst. in phys. edn., Y.M.C.A., Toledo, O., 1903-13, head physical edn. dept., Elyria, Ohio, 1913-17, Hartford, Conn., 1917-22; pres. Employed Officers Assn. of Conn., 1921-22; head dept. phys. edn., The Carl Curtis Sch., Los Angeles, Calif., 1925-33; pres., Flintridge Prep. Sch. for Boys, Pasadena, Calif., 1933-65; lecturer on boy development. Member of the faculty Y.M.C.A. summer school of physical edn., Lake Geneva, 1916, Lake Couchiching, Canada, 1919, 20, 21. Mem. Flintridge Chap. of Cum Laude Soc., Phys. Dirs. Soc. of N. Am. (awarded title dir. phys. activities, 1922), S.A.R., Cal. Assn. Independent Schools (v.p., 1955-57). Presbyterian. Club: Kiwanis (Pasadena. Co-author: Gymnastic Dancing. Contbr. to mag. Physical Education. Home: La Canada, Calif. †

LOWERY, MARTIN JOSEPH, college dean; b. Chgo., Dec. 23, 1919; s. Martin Joseph and Mary (Hession) L.; B.Ed., Chgo. Tchrs. Coll., 1941; A.M., Loyola U., Chgo., 1947. Ph.D., 1951; m. Margaret Shanahan, Dec. 3, 1943; children—Martin, Linda, David, Cynthia, Martha, Loretta, Christopher. Employee, spl. agt. FBI, 1940-43; assoc. prof. history DePaul U., Chgo., 1950-77, chmn. dept. history and polit. sci., 1955-77, became associate dean Coll. Liberal Arts, 1961, dean of DePaul College, 1967-77. Chmn. bd. edn. Catholic Diocese Chgo., after 1968. Served to lt. (s.g.) USNR, 1943-46. Mem. Am., Miss. Valley, Am. Cath. hist. assns., Latin Am. Conf., Am. Assn. U. Profs., Soc. Former Spl. Agts. FBI, Chgo. Council Fgn. Relations, Historian Met. Chgo., Blue Key, Sigma Delta Pi. Author article. Home: Chicago, Ill. Died Mar. 21, 1983.

LOWRANCE, JOHN WITHERSPOON, educator; b. Kansas City, Mo., Feb. 27, 1887; s. John W. and Samantha Antoinette (du-Pre-dillard) L.; grad. Webb Sch., Bellbuckle, Tenn., 1904; A.B., Yale, 1909; m. Ione Reid, June 24, 1910. Engaged in teaching from 1911; mng. dir. Roxbury Prep. Sch. (Short Beach, Conn.), Roxbury Tutoring Sch., Inc. (New Haven, Conn.), Roxbury Tutoring Sch. for Harvard, Inc. (Cambridge, Mass.). Mem. Kappa Alpha (Southern), Phi Delta. Republican. Presbyterian. Clubs: Graduates', Lawn, Yacht (New Haven); Yale (New York). Home: New Haven, Conn. †

LOWREY, LAWRENCE TYNDATE, coll. pres.; b. Blue Mountain, Miss., Aug. 14, 1888; s. Booth and Patti Elizabeth (Lowry) L.; grad. Miss. Heights Acad., Blue Mountain, 1905; B.S., Miss. Coll., Clinton, Miss., 1909, A.M., 1913, LL.D., 1959; studied U. Va., summer 1911, U. Chgo., summer 1914; A.M., Columbia, 1914, Ph.D., 1918; LL.D., Baylor U., 1957; m. Elizabeth Veeve Crockroft, September 2, 1919 (deceased December 23, 1950); children—Robert Booth, Jean; married second, Mrs. Ernestine Higdon Eastland, March 28, 1952. Principal high sch., Fair River, Miss., 1909-11; v.p. Hillman Coll., Clinton, Miss., 1911-13; fellow in Am. history, Columbia, 1915-16; instr. history, Smith Coll., 1916-18; asso. prof. history, U. of Southern Calif., 1919-20, prof., 1920-25; asst. prof. history, U. of Calif., Southern Br., 1921-22; pres. Blue Mountain Coll. since June 1, 1925. Served as lt. F.A., U.S. Army, 1918. Pres. Miss. Assn. of Colls., 1927-28; Miss. Bapt. Sunday Sch. and B.Y.P.U. conv., 1927-28; mem. Southern Bapt. Edn. Commn., 1928-40, 1943-49; mem. Fed. Alien Enemy Hearing Bd., 1941-45; pres. Miss. State Bapt. Conv., 1938-40. Trustee Tri-State Bapt. Hosp., 1937-49, 50-53 (pres. 1944-49); pres. Miss. Found. Independent Colls., from 1956; mem. bd. dirs. Southeastern Bapt. Theol. Sem. Wake Forest, N.C. Mem. Southern Assn. Colleges for Women (pres. 1930-31), Phi Alpha (U. of Southern Calif.), Sigma Sigma. Democrat. Baptist. Gov. Dist. 140, Rotary Internat., 1944-45. Wrote: Northern Opinion of Approaching Secession (Smith Coll. Studies in History), 1918. Home: Blue Mountain, Miss. †

LOWRY, GEORGE MAUS, investment banker; b. Erie, Pa., Oct. 27, 1889; s. Ricardo St. Philip and Annie (Maus) L.; B.S., U.S. Naval Acad., 1911; m. Caroline Coleman, Aug. 17, 1920; children—Ritchie Peter, Ann (Mrs. Alexander H. Brawner, Jr.). Ensign, U.S. Navy, 1912; comd. U.S.S. Niagara, original flagship of Com. Oliver Hazard Perry, on historic cruise, Great Lakes, 1913, commemorating 100th anniversary of Battle of Lake Erie, War of 1812; duty in U.S. ships North Dakota, Florida, North Carolina, O'Brien, Jenkins, O'Bannon, Coghlan; comd. U.S. Ringold and MacDonough, W.W. I; resigned from service, 1927; reentered active duty, U.S.N.R., Dec. 10, 1940; operations officer on staff comdr. Western Sea Frontier, World War II; advanced through grades from lt. comdr. to rear adm.; retired as rear adm., 1946; gen. partner Sutro & Co., investment brokers, Los Angeles, San Francisco, N.Y., 1930-56, spl. partner. Mem. San Francisco (Armed Forces com.), Carmel Valley C.'s of C., Naval Acad. Alumni Assn., Def. Orientation Conf. Assn., Naval Res. Assn., U.S. Naval Inst., Newcomen Society,

Congl. Medal of Honor Soc. Decorated Congressional Medal of Honor, Legion of Merit, Victory medals of World War I and World War II, Mex. Service, Am. Defense and Am. Area Campaign medals (U.S.), Merito Naval (Mexico). Episcopalian. Clubs: Burlingame, Burlingame Country; Marines Memorial and the Bohemian (San Francisco); Army-Navy (Washington); Chevy Chase (Md.); Pebble Beach (Cal.). Home: Carmel, Cal. †

LOWRY, RALPH, civil engr.; b. Bevier, Mo., Apr. 18, 1889; s. Edward James and Sarah (Humphrey) L.; B.S., Wash. State Coll., 1913, C.E., 1917; m. Gladys Waller, June 7, 1917; children—Robert James, Ralph, Jr. With United States Bur. of Reclamation as engr. on constrn. power and pumping projects, Yakima Valley, Wash., 1914-18; engr. on design, Denver Office, 1918-23; resident engr., McKay Dam, Ore., 1923-26; constrn, engr., Gibson Dam. Mont., 1926-29; field and constrn. engr., Boulder Dam, 1929-38; constrn. engr. Shasta Dam, Calif., 1938-45, asst. chief engr. from 1945. Mem. Am. Soc. Civil Engrs. Home: Denver, Colo. †

LOZZIO, BISMARCK BERTO, med. researcher, hematologist, oncologist; b. Patagones, Buenos Aires, Argentina, Jan. 27, 1931; came to U.S., 1965, naturalized, 1974; s. Bartolo and Haydee Angela (Piucill) L.; m. Carmen Irene Bertucci, Mar. 10, 1955; 1 dau., Graciela Irene. B.S., Bernardino Rivadavia Coll., Buenos Aires, 1949; Physician, U. Buenos Aires, 1955, M.D., 1957. Asso. gastroenterologist, instr. internal medicine Torn Hosp., U. Buenos Aires, 1955-58; asso. hematologist NIH, Buenos Aires, 1958-65; research asso. U. Tenn. Meml. Research Center, Knoxville, 1965-67, asst. prof., 1968-71, asso. prof., 1971-75, prof., from 1975; lectr. dept. microbiology U. Tenn., from 1971; mem. faculty Inst. Radiol. Biology, from 1971; cons. Oak Ridge Asso. Univs. Served with Argentine Marine Corps, 1952-53. Nat. Council for Sci. and Tech. Research fellow, 1958-60; Career award, 1961-65; NSF grantee, 1966; Am. Heart Assn. grantee, 1966, 74-76; NIH grantee, from 1968; Am. Cancer Soc. grantee, 1970-78. Mem. Reticuloendothelial Soc., Internat. Soc. Hematology, Am. Soc. Hematology, Am. Soc. Lab. Animal Sci., AAAS, Soc. Exptl. Biology and Medicine, Am. Fedn. Clin. Research, Internat. Soc. Exptl. Hematology, N.Y. Acad. Scis., Am. Assn. Immunologists, Am. Assn. Cancer Research, Southeastern Cancer Research Assn., Asociación Médica Argentina, Sociedad Argentina de Biología, Sociedad Argentina de Immunología, Sociedad Argentina de Investigación Clínica, Sociedad Argentina de Hematología y Hemoterapia, Sigma Xi. Home: Concord, Tenn.

LUBERG, LEROY EDWARD, ret. univ. dean; b. River Falls, Wis., Mar. 3, 1908; s. Frank Robert and Alice (Nelson) L.; B.S., Wis. State Coll., River Falls, 1930; M.Ph., U. Wis., 1936, Ph.D., 1963; m. Juliana Jane Smith, Nov. 29, 1942. Tchr., prin. West Jr. High Sch., Madison, Wis., 1930-42; specialist U.S. Office Edn., 1942; asst. to pres. U. Wis. System, Madison, 1946-57, became dean students, 1958. Univ. dean pub. services, 1964-73, dean emeritus, 1973-82, v.p., 1969-71; exec. sec. Gov. Wis., 1957; co-editor Democracy Charts, Nystrom Co. Mem. gov.'s ednl. adv. com.; chmn. Wis. Merit Award Com. Chmn. Dane County chpt. Cancer Soc., 1957; chmn. govtl. div. United Givers, Madison. Bd. dirs. Kidney Found. Wis., Wis.-Nicaragua Partners of Ams. Served from pvt. to maj. OSS, AUS, 1942-46. Decorated Bronze Star; recipient Distinguished Alumnus awards U. Wis., River Falls, 1967, Madison, 1973. Mem. Madison Edn. Assn. (pres.), Phi Delta Kappa, Phi Kappa Phi, Phi Eta Sigma. Conglist (moderator 1956-57). Clubs: University (Madison); Kiwanis (lt. gov. for Wis. 1953). Contbr. articles to ednl. publs. Home: Madison, Wis. Died Aug. 16, 1982.

LUCAS, G(ERALD) BRINTON, ins. exec.; b. Phila. Sept. 9, 1889; s. Samuel and Anna Hickman (Arnold) L.; student Episcopal Acad., 1907; m. Adelaide L. Loughead, Nov. 2, 1912; children—Nancy B. (Mrs. Charles M. Kirkland), Gerald Brinton, Barbara Brooke (Mrs. W. Burlings Cocks), Joan (Mrs. Morris H. Dixon, Jr.). Began as clk. Ins. Co. of N.A., Phila., 1909, became asst. sec., 1924, marine sec., 1937, v.p. from 1943; v.p. Phila. Fire & Marine Ins. Co., 1943. Chmn. exec. com. Inland Marine Underwriters Assn. and Inland Marine Ins. Bur., 1945-46; Am. com. Lloyd's Register of Shipping from 1939. Republican. Episcopalian. Clubs: India House (N.Y. City); Radnor Hunt (Malvern, Pa.). Home: Unionville, Pa. †

LUDWICK, WILLIAM R., insurance company executive; b. Warren, Ohio, Oct. 22, 1923; s. Frederick F. and Mary (Franks) L.; m. Willie Lee Horton, Nov. 20, 1946; children—Deborah, Candace, Karen. Student, Berea Coll., 1942-43, Murray State Tchrs. Coll., 1943, U. Ga., 1944-45; B.S.Commerce, U. N.C., 1946. Group ins. field rep. Travelers Ins. Co., 1946-48; with Pilot Life Ins. Co., Greensboro, N.C., 1948-83, 2d v.p. securities investment dept., 1965-68, v.p., 1968-75, sr. v.p., 1975-83, treas., 1968-83; dir. Pilot Life Ins. Co., Pomona Corp. Mem. endowment investment bd. and univ. investment com. U. N.C., Greensboro; bd. dirs. Home Econs. Found.; bd. regents Life Officers Investment Seminar, U. Chgo. Mem. N.C. Soc. Financial Analysts (pres. 1969-70), N.Y. Soc. Security Analysts, Am. Council Life Ins. (chmn. investment sect.). Presbyterian. Clubs: Greensboro Country, Greensboro City. Home: Greensboro, N.C. Died Mar. 12, 1983.

LUDWIG, LOUIS, business exec., inventor; b. Russia, Mar. 9, 1899; s. David and Fanny (Swedarsky) Grushevsky; student Columbia, 1916-20; m. Miriam F. Fischer, Sept. 20, 1953; children by previous marriage—Melvin S., Doris. Pres., Eagle Electric Mfg. Co., Inc., Long Island City, N.Y., 1920-69, chmn. bd., 1969-79; pres. Eagle Plastics Corp., 1938-69, chmn. bd., 1969-79; pres. 24th St. Plaza Corp., 1938-69, chmn. bd., 1969-79; pres. Eagle Electric Mfg. Co., Ltd. Can.; v.p. charge Israel industrialization Ampal-Amer Israel Corp., N.Y.C., 1953-79, also chmn. exec. com.) treas.; sec. Israel Mineral Devel. Corp., 1953-79; dir. Israel Am. Indsl. Devel. Bank, Ltd. Bd. dirs. N.Y. United Jewish Appeal, Israel Bond Drive; bd. dirs., v.p. Am. Com. for Weizmann Inst. Sci.; bd. govs. Weizmann Inst., Rehovot, Israel. Home: Hallandale, Fla. Died Dec. 2, 1979; buried L.I., N.Y.

LUHMAN, GEORGE BURTON, banker; b. Belvidere, Ill., Mar. 28, 1888; s. Henry E. and Elizabeth Jane (Burton) L.; A.B., U. of Wis., 1910, LL.B., 1912; m. Amarynthia J. Smith, July 5, 1919; children—Elizabeth Jane, George B., A. Susan, Mary Pressley, Katherine Townsend. Practicing law, Milwaukee, 1912-21; trust co. business from 1921; director First Wisconsin Trust Co. of Milwaukee; pres., dir. Title Guaranty Co. of Wis.; director Wis. Bankshares Corp. Vice pres., dir. Aquaterra Co., Wis. Securities Co. (Del.); dir. Milwaukee Forge & Machine Company Mississippi Valley Public Service Company, (Del.), Ben-Hur Mfg. Co. Past pres. and dir., Goodwill Industries; dir. Univ. of Wis. Found. Served as second lieutenant Field Artillery, U.S. Army, World War I. Mem. Am., Wis. State and Milw. bar assns., Newcomen Soc., Phi Alpha Delta. Republican. Conglist. Mason (32 deg., Shriner). Clubs: Rotary, Milwaukee, University, Milwaukee Country; Home: Oconomowoc, Wis. †

LUKKEN, ALBERT, educator; b. Worthing, S.D., Feb. 25, 1890; s. Peter J. and Margaret Annie (Urdahl) L.; B.S., Fremont (Neb.) Coll. 1911; B.M., Am. Cons. of Music, Chicago, 1916; M.M., 1926; m. Florence Moehlenbrock, May 30, 1923; children—Robert M., Albert E. Romayne F. Teacher of voice, Univ. S.D., 1913-15; head music dept., Univ. Wyo., 1916-17; Aborn Opera Sch., N.Y., 1917; teacher of voice, Univ. Ore., 1919-20. Am. Sch. of Opera, Chicago, 1921-22; dean Coll. Fine Arts, U. Tulsa, 1922-56, dean emeritus, professor of music, from 1956. Served in USN, 1918-19. Mem. Nat. Assn. Teachers Singing (gov. Southwest states), National Assn. Schools of Music (examiner; vice president 1951-52), Okla. Music Teachers Assn. (pres.), Kappa Kappa Psi, Phi Mu Alpha (province gov., vice pres. 1942-46 national president, 1946-50, became national hon. mem. 1952, v.p. 1950), Pi Kappa Alpha; hon. mem. Tulsa Music Tchrs. Assn., Phi Eta Sigma, Pi Gamma Mu. Presbyn. Choral conductor. Contbr. articles music publs. Home: Tulsa, Okla. Deceased.

LULL, GEORGE FAIRLESS, army officer, physician; b. Scranton, Pa., March 10, 1887; s. Charles Walter and Margaret (Fairless) L.; M.D., Jefferson Med. Coll., 1909, LL.D., 1949; M.P.H., Harvard, 1921; Dr. P.H., U. Pa., 1922; LL.D., Jefferson Med. Coll., 1949; D.Sc. (honorary), Woman's Medical Coll. Pa., 1953; m. Margaret R. Orr, Oct. 29, 1912 (dec.); children—George Fairless, Charles Orr (dec.); m. 2d, Janet Kuhn Love, Feb. 19, 1926 (dec. Feb., 1949); married third, Mildred L. Beckman, Sept. 10, 1952. Interne Jefferson Hosp., 1909-10, demonstrator morbid anat., 1910-12; commd. ofc. Med. Corps, U.S.A., 1912, and advanced through grades to maj. gen., 1943; sec. and gen. mgr. Am. Med. Assn., 1946-58, secretary and assistant to the president, 1958-59; med. dir. Cook County Dept. Pub. Aid, from 1960. Decorated Purple Heart, D.S.M. (U.S.); Legion of Honor (France), Order Carlos Finlay, (Cuba). Fellow American College of Chest Physicians (honorary), American College of Surgeons, Am. Coll. of Physicians; International College of Surgeons (honorary); mem. A.M.A., Am. Hosp. Assn. (hon.) Assn. Mil. Surgeons. Am. Pub. Welfare Assn., Alpha Omega Alpha, Phi Rho Sigma. Club: Army and Navy (Washington). Home: Chicago, Ill. †

LUND, JOSEPH WHEELOCK, former real estate exec.; b. Boston, Aug. 31, 1905; s. Fred Bates and Zoe Meriam (Griffing) L.; m. Margaret Covode, Sept. 18, 1926; children—John C., Lydia (Mrs. Robert D. Hale), Elizabeth (Mrs. A.G. Bullock, Jr.). A.B., Harvard, 1926. With firm Hayes and Read, 1926-29; investment broker Tucker Anthony & Co., 1929-34; with R.M. Bradley & Co., 1934-81, exec. v.p., 1947-61, pres., 1961-81, chmn. bd., 1970-81; trustee real estate trusts Bradley Real Estate Trust, Chgo., 1943-82; hon. trustee Suffolk Franklin Savs. Bank. Past chmn. Boston Redevel. Authority; pres. Urban Land Inst., 1961-62; past pres. Beacon Hill Civic Assn.; Trustee, v.p. Manomet Bird Obs.; mem. corp. Mass. Gen. Hosp. Mem. Nat. Assn. Real Estate Investment Funds (pres. 1961-63), Am. Soc. Real Estate Counsellors, Nat. Assn. Real Estate Boards (pres. 1952), Internat. Fedn. Real Estate Counselors (v.p. 1952-53), Boston Real Estate Bd. (pres. 1948), Am. Inst. Real Estate Appraisers, Greater Boston C. of C., Mass. Hort. Soc. (past pres.). Clubs: St. Botolph's (Boston); Duxbury Yacht; Harvard (Boston). Home: Duxbury, Mass. Died Mar. 13, 1982.

LUNDEEN, ARTHUR, business exec.; b. Moline, Ill., May 28, 1888; s. Elof and Hilda Lundeen; ed. pub. schs., Moline; m. Rosida Jacques, Apr. 19, 1943. With Otis Elevator Co., N.Y. City, since 1904, gen. service mgr., 1932-45, gen. zone mgr. from 1945, vice pres. from 1937; dir. Otis-Fensom Elevator Co., Ltd., Can. Served as lt., Air Service, World War I. Mem. N.Y. State C. of C. Republican. Mason. Clubs: Sleepy Hollow Country (Scarborough, N.Y.); Union League (New York). Home: New York, N.Y. †

LUNDEGARDH, HENRIK GUNNAR, educator; b. Stockholm, Sweden, Oct. 23, 1888; s. Johan and Katarina (Norman) L.; D.Sc., U. Stockholm, 1912; m. Sigrid Svenson, Dec. 28, 1916; 1 son, Per Henrik; m. 2d, Kraka Liljefors, Oct. 16, 1944; 1 dau., Katarina. Reader botany U. Stockholm, 1913-15, prof., head dept. botany, 1926-35; reader botany U. Lund, 1916-25, prof. plant physiology Upsala U., 1935-55; research plant physiology, biochemistry. Mem. Swedish Acad. Sci., Swedish Acad. Engring., Swedish Acad. Agr.; hon. mem. Vlaamse Acad. (Brussels), Sci., Lit. and Arts, Am. Acad. Arts and Scis., Am. Soc. Plant Physiologists, bot. socs. Am., Japan, Poland, Czecholslovakia, Acad. Scis. (Paris, hon.). Home: Penningby, Sweden. †

LUNDEN, LAURENCE RAYMOND, business educator; b. Watertown, S.D., Apr. 5, 1907; s. Hans and Gertrude Bertine (Peterson) L.; m. Anne Elizabeth Stub, June 21, 1941 (dec. Oct. 1967); children: Laurence Raymond, John Peter. B.A., Grinnell Coll., 1929; postgrad., U. Minn., 1929-34; LL.D., Luther Coll., 1940. Instr. Sch. Bus. Adminstrn., U. Minn., 1929-39, assoc. prof., 1939-57, prof., from 1957, investment counsel bd. regents, 1936-46, asst. comptroller, 1941-43, asst. sec. bd. regents, 1941-52, comptroller, 1943-59, treas. bd. regents, 1952-59, v.p., 1959-72, sec. bd. regents, from 1959; faculty, mem. adminstrv. com. Grad. Sch. Banking, U. Wis., from 1944; trustee Farmers & Mechanics Savs. Bank.; Mem. neurology program project com. NIH; cons. tng. contracts USAAF, 1941-42; gov.'s adv. com. on state trust funds, 1946-63; mem. Little Hoover Commn. State Minn., 1952; cons. NSF, from 1965. Also editor: Financial and Investment Rev, 1932-43; Author: (with R. A. Stevenson, others) A Type Study of American Banking, 1934; Contbr. articles profl. publs. Trustee Luther Coll., 1940-52; bd. dirs., exec. com. North Star Research and Devel. Inst.; trustee, chmn. budget com. Argonne Univs. Assn., 1966-70, cons., from 1970; dir. U. Minn. Found.; trustee Fairview Hosp. Mem. Central Assn. Coll. and Univ. Bus. Officers (treas., v.p., pres. 1947-52), Nat. Fedn. Assns. Coll. and Univ. Bus. Officers (dir., v.p. from 1953), Am. Council Edn. (chmn. com. taxation and fiscal reporting 1949-57), Assn. Land-Grant Colls. and Univs., Nat. Assn. State Univs., Midwestern Univs. Research Assn. (dir., sec. from 1954, pres. 1965-71), Am. Econ. Assn., Norwegian-American Hist. Assn., Phi Beta Kappa, Sigma Delta Chi, Alpha Kappa Psi. Clubs: University (Mpls.), Athletic (Mpls.). Home: Minneapolis, Minn.

LUNEBURG, WILLIAM V., automobile co. exec.; b. N.Y.C., 1912; grad. N.Y.U., 1934, Harvard Bus. Sch., 1936. Pres., chief operation officer, dir. Am. Motors Corp., Detroit; dir. Maccabees Mut. Life Ins. Co. Mem. Automobile Mfrs. Assn. (dir.), Soc. Automotive Engrs. Home: Ann Arbor, Mich. Died Jan. 21, 1982.

LUNSFORD, HARRY EARL, accountant; b. Cairo, Ill., Sept. 27, 1887; s. Albert L. and Eva (Mueller) L.; m. Grace M. Bomgardner, June 14, 1913; children—Harry Earl, Mary J. (wife of capt. Dick F. Tedford). Partner Smith, Lunsford & Wright, C.P.A.'s, 1918-25; sr. partner Lunsford, Barnes & Co., C.P.A.'s, 1925-50; partner Arthur Young & Co., C.P.A.'s, 1950-53. Dir. William Volher Fund. Served as capt. U.S. Army, 1917. C.P.A., 1917. Mem. Am. Soc. C.P.A.'s (pres. 1925-26), Am. Inst. Accountants (ex-officio mem. council). Mason. Address: Hartville, Mo. †

LUSBY, RALSTON NEWELL, credit card co. exec.; b. Washington, Apr. 24, 1914; s. James A. and Martha (Mansfield) L.; A.B., George Washington U., 1935, LL.B., 1937; m. Eileen Lenore Steward, Dec. 24, 1938; children—Penelope (Mrs. Joseph F. Viar Jr.), James S., Pamela (Mrs. Scott R. Christensen). Admitted to D.C. bar, 1937; with Fidelity & Casualty Co., N.Y.C., 1938-53; asst. sec. cos. Am. Fore Group, 1953-54, sec., 1954-57, v.p., 1957-60, v.p. Continental Ins. Cos. (formerly Am. Fore-Loyalty Group), 1960-64, v.p., mgr. Southeastern div., Atlanta, 1964-66, v.p., mgr. Pacific div., San Francisco, 1966-69; v.p., mgr. Western div., Chgo., 1969-71; chmn. bd., pres., chief exec. officer Diners Club, Inc., N.Y.C., 1971-79. Served to col. AUS, 1940-46. Decorated Legion of Merit, Bronze Star (U.S.); Croix dep Guerre, officier de l'Instruction Publique (France); Couronne de Chene (Luxembourg). Mem. Am. Bar Assn., Internat. Assn. Ins. Counsel. Home: Suffern, N.Y. Died 1979.

LUSH, HAROLD VICTOR, mfg. exec.; b. Newmarket, Ont., Can., May 26, 1889; s. John Thomas and Drusilla (Doan) L.; student pub. schs.; m. June 4, 1913; children—Lorraine, Sheldon, Jack, Donald, Mildred, Glen. Pres. Supreme Aluminum Industries, Ltd., Supreme Anodizing, Ltd. Toronto, Canada. Chmn. of the board of governors Toronto Eastern Gen. and Orthopedic Hosp. Mem. Council of Profit Sharing Industries of Chgo. (chmn. 1954-56), Canadian Exporters Assn. (pres. 1948), Canadian Mfrs. Assn. (chmn. tariff com., 1st v.p.). †

LYET, JEAN PAUL, diversified manufacturing company executive; b. Phila., May 6, 1917; s. Louis F. and Elizabeth (Fortune) L.; m. Dorothy Lillian Storz, Sept. 29, 1945. Grad., U. Pa. Sch. Accounts and Fin., 1941. Pub.

accountant Ernst & Whinney (C.P.A.s), Reading, Pa., 1940-43; with New Holland (Pa.) div. Sperry Corp. (and predecessor), 1943-84, v.p., sec.-treas., 1947-67; v.p., gen. mgr. New Holland (Pa.) div. Sperry Corp. (N. Am. div.), 1967-69; pres. New Holland (Pa.) div. Sperry Corp. (New Holland div.), 1969-84; asst. treas. Sperry Rand Corp., 1955-67, v.p., 1970, exec. v.p., 1970-71, pres., 1971-72, chmn. bd., chief exec. officer, 1972-82, dir., 1970-84; dir. Armstrong World Industries, Inc., Continental Group, Eli Lilly & Co., NL Industries, Consol. Edison, Hershey Trust Co., Eastman Kodak.; Chmn. Pres.'s Export Council, 1981-84; mem. Bus. Council, Bus. Roundtable, Emergency Com. for Am. Trade. Bd. mgrs. Milton Hershey Sch.; trustee U. Pa., Lancaster Country Day Sch., Elizabethtown Coll. Mem. Machinery and Allied Products Inst. (exec. com.). Episcopalian (vestryman 1955-84). Clubs: Lancaster Country (Lancaster), Hamilton (Lancaster); Blind Brook (Port Chester, N.Y.); River (N.Y.C.), Links (N.Y.C.), Economic (N.Y.C.); Siwanoy (Bronxville, N.Y.); Augusta (Ga.) Nat. Died June 7, 1984.

LYLE, ALEXANDER G, naval officer; b. Gloucester, Mass., Nov. 12, 1889; s. James Joseph and Mary MacFarlane (Duncan) L.; D.D.S., Baltimore Coll. Dental Surgery, 1912; Army Sanitary Sch., 1918; Army Indsl. Coll., 1936-37; m. Ruth Findlay Haire, Aug. 6, 1923; children—Alexander Gordon, Mary MacFarlane. Practiced dentistry 1912-15; entered Navy as lt. (j.g.) Dental Corps, 1915; advanced through grades to rear admiral; dental advisor for procurement supplies and materials for Navy; ret. with rank of vice adm., Aug. 1, 1948. Decorated Congressional Medal of Honor, Silver Star (with palms), Italian War Cross. Home: Newport, R.I. †

LYLE, RICHARD H., govt. ofcl., lawyer; b. Brownsville, Tenn., Jan. 16, 1889; s. George W. and Lula (Hotchkiss) L.; B.S., LL.B., Vanderbilt U., 1914; married Susan Beesley, February 9, 1928; 1 daughter Susan Beesley (Mrs. James Carson Warters). Admitted to Tennessee bar, 1914, practiced in Brownsville, 1914-17, partner Bond & Lyle, 1920-27; commr. Instns. of Tenn., 1927-33, also chmn. Pardon and Parole Bd., tenn.; dir. Tenn. State Industries, 1937-40; regional dir. Social Security Bd., 1940-48 Office Community Facilities, 1942-45, Fed. Security Agy., Atlanta, 1948-53; regional director Department Health, Edn. and Welfare, from 1953. Exec. dir. Nashville Community Chest, 1933-37. Pres. Tenn. Conf. Social Work, 1930. Served as 1st lt. to capt. Inf., 3d Div., AUS, overseas 1917-19, participating in 4 major battles. Mem. Phi Delta Phi, Kappa Alpha. Presbyn. Rotarian. Kiwanian. †

LYNCH, KEVIN, city planner, educator; b. Chgo., Jan. 7, 1918; s. James Joseph and Laura (Healy) L.; m. Anne Macklin Borders, June 7, 1941; children: David, Laura, Catherine, Peter. Sti dent, Yale U., 1935-37; apprenticeship with, F.L. Wı ight, 1937-39; student, Rennselaer Poly. Inst., 1940; B.City Planning, MIT, 1947; Dr.-Ing., U. Stuttgart, 1978. With Schweikher, Elting and Lamb (architects), Chgo., 1940-41; asst. dir. Dept. City Planning, Greensboro, N.C., 1947-48; instr. to prof. city planning MIT, Cambridge, 1948-78; partner Carr Lynch Assos. (environ. design), 1977-84; cons., Boston, Cleve., Balt., Los Angeles, Mpls., P.R., San Salvador, Columbia, Md., Venezuela, Town Gay Head, Mass.; cons. UNESCO, Vineyard Open Land Found., Martha's Vineyard, Mass., Dallas, San Diego, Ottawa, Ont., Can., Fez, Morocco, Washington, Lewiston, Maine, Burlington, Vt., Massport, Boston., Phoenix, Detroit. Author: The Image of the City, 1960, Site Planning, 1962, 72, (with others) The View From the Road, 1964, What Time Is This Place, 1972, Managing the Sense of a Region, 1976, Growing Up in Cities, 1977, A Theory of Good City Form, 1981. Chmn. Watertown Planning Bd., 1962-65; Trustee Palfrey St. Sch., Watertown, 1964-70, Conway Sch. Design, 1980—. Served with C.E. AUS, 1941-46. Decorated Bronze Star; recipient 50th Anniversary award Am. Inst. Planners, 1967; Allied Professions medal AIA, 1974. Home: Watertown, Mass. Died Apr. 25, 1984.

LYNCH, VINCENT DE PAUL, pharmacology educator; b. Niagara Falls, N.Y., May 27, 1927; s. Arthur John and Phoebe (Tooker) L.; m. Vivian Tamburrino, Aug. 21, 1954; children—Michael, Stephen, Richard, Laura Anne. B.S., Niagara U., 1950; B.S. in Pharmacy, St. John's U., 1954; M.S., U. Conn., 1956, Ph.D., 1959. Mem. faculty St. John's U., Jamaica, N.Y., from 1961, chmn. dept. pharmacognosy, pharmacology and allied scis., 1961-73, prof., from 1966, dir. div. toxicology, from 1969, chmn. dept. pharm. scis., 1973-83; Cons. N.Y. State Legislature Subcom. on Drug Abuse, from 1969, N.Y. State Narcotic Addiction Control Commn., from 1969. Served with USNR, 1944-46. Mem. Am. Assn. Colls. Pharmacy, Internat. Soc. Psychoneuroendocrinology, Internat. Narcotics Officers Enforcement Assn., Soc. Forensic Toxicology, Soc. Toxicology ((Mid Atlantic chpt.)), Sigma Xi, Rho Chi. Research and publs. on drug abuse, alcohol and marijuana. Home: Laurel Hollow, NY.

LYNN, CHESTER BERNARD, industrial distribution company executive; b. Niagara Falls, N.Y., June 3, 1914; s. Ralph Bell and Stella Frances (Connors) L.; m. Marian Rose Paskert, May 2, 1942; children—Michael Ralph, Mary Ann, Patricia Ann. B.A. magna cum laude, John Carroll U., 1936. Sales corr. Linde Air Products Co., Cleve., 1936-42; sales mgr. Cleve. Ignition Co., 1946-54, asst. to pres., 1949-54; dir. sales tng. Premier Indsl. Corp., Cleve., 1954-58, sales adminstrv. mgr., 1956-58; with Lawson Products, Inc., Chgo., 1958—, exec. v.p. sales, 1965-74, pres., 1974-77, chmn. bd., 1977—, chief exec. officer, 1977—, mem. exec. com., 1977—, also dir. and dir. various subs's. Served to capt. AC U.S. Army, 1942-46; to maj. USAF, 1950-52, PTO; to maj. USAF, ETO. Mem. Sales Mktg. Execs. Club Chgo., Execs. Club Chgo., Am. Mgmt. Assn., Res. Officers Assn. Republican. Roman Catholic. Clubs: Mission Hills Country, One Hundred of Cook County. Home: Northbrook, Ill. Died Aug. 31, 1983.

LYNN, WILBERT, greeting card co. exec.; b. Berwick, Pa., Aug. 2, 1927; s. Wilbert G. and Hazel (Levan) L.; m. Margaret T. Ferguson, July 1, 1951; children—Craig, Sharon. B.B.A., Pace U., 1950. C.P.A., N.J. Auditor Seidman & Seidman, N.Y.C., 1950-58; controller Union Bldg. & Investment Co., Passaic, N.J., 1958-59; in various auditing positions Curtiss Wright Corp., Woodridge, N.J., 1959-62; controller Hayden Pub. Co., N.Y.C., 1962-63; ops. controller Gen. Foods Corp. Post Div., Battlecreek, Mich., 1963-65; exec. v.p. Norcross-Rust Craft div. Windsor Communications Group Inc., West Chester, Pa., from 1965. Pres. Woodland Acres Community Assn., Westwood, Mass., 1970; troop com. chmn. Boy Scouts Am., 1974-75. Served with USN, 1945-46. Episcopalian. Club: Masons (Ridgewood, N.J.). Home: Westchester, PA.

LYON, HARVEY WILLIAM, dentist, research cons.; b. Chgo., May 20, 1920; s. Harvey Cady and Christina (Brown) L.; m. Margaret Ann Siggelkow, Apr. 26, 1946; children—Mark, Leslie, Karin. B.S., Marquette U., 1942, D.D.S., 1945; M.S., Georgetown U., 1951, Ph.D., 1956. Commd. lt. (j.g.) Dental Corps USN, 1943, advanced through grades to capt., 1960, ret., 1965; dir. clin. research, also sec. Council Dental Research, ADA, Chgo., 1965-79; cons., from 1979, U.S. Naval Dental Research Inst., from 1966; research asso. Northwestern U. Dental Sch., 1968-76; mem. exec. com., div. med. scis. NRC, 1968-76. Contbr. articles to profl. jours. Fellow Am. Coll. Dentists, AAAS (council); mem. ADA, Fedn. Dentaire Internat. (research cons., editorial bd.), Electron Microprobe Soc. Am., European Soc. Caries Research, Internat. Assn. Dental Research, Odontographic Soc. Chgo., Alpha Chi, Psi Omega. Republican. Club: Dad's (Glenbrook, Ill.). Home: Stoughton, Wis.

LYON, ROGER ADRIAN, banker; b. Phillipsburg, N.J., June 28, 1927; s. Howard Suydam and Mildred (Derry) L.; m. Mary Woodford, June 17, 1950; children—Nancy Carol, Roger Adrian. B.A., Princeton, 1950; M.B.A., Rutgers U., 1954; postgrad., Stonier Grad. Sch. Banking, 1959. With Chase Nat. Bank (now Chase Manhattan Bank), N.Y.C., 1950-76, ofcl. staff, 1954-76, sr. v.p. bank portfolio group, 1969-72, exec. v.p. instl. banking dept., 1972-76; exec. v.p. Chase Manhattan Corp., 1972-76; pres. Valley Nat. Bank, Phoenix, 1976-83; mem. adv. bd. Mountain Bell, 1979; instr. Stonier Grad. Sch. Banking, 1960-72. Author: Commercial Bank Investment Portfolio Management, 1960. Pres. East Jersey Bd. Proprs., 1972-76; chmn. Phoenix Pvt. Industry Council, 1979; met. Phoenix chmn. Nat. Alliance of Bus., 1979; trustee Nat. YMCA, 1964-76, mem. adminstrv. com., exec. com. fin. and budget, 1966-76, nat. treas., 1973-76; trustee Am. Grad. Sch. Internat. Mgmt.; bd. dirs. Heard Mus.; chmn. bd. Western Regional Council. Served with USMCR, 1945-46, 51, 52. Mem. Am. Bankers Assn. (chmn. corr. bank div. 1973-75, treas. 1975-77, mem. govt. borrowing com.), Internat. Monetary Conf., Pacific Basin Inst., Council Fgn. Relations. Home: Paradise Valley, Ariz. Died Apr. 1983.

LYON, TOM, consulting engr., geologist; b. Quincy, Ill., Aug. 11, 1888; s. Thomas Theron and Elizabeth (Bailey) L.; E.M., Mont. Sch. of Mines, 1916; m. Forence Marks, Nov. 9, 1916; 1 son, Tom. Geologist Anaconda Copper Mining Co., Butte, Mont., 1916-22; geologist, Internat. Smelting & Refining Co., Salt Lake City, 1922-27, chief geologist from 1927, asst. to mgr., Jan. 1944-Mar. 1951; dir. Supply Div. of Defense Minerals Adminstrn., Jan. 1951; dir. domestic expansion div. of Defense Materials Procurement Agency, Washington, Oct. 1951-53, acting dep. adminstr., May to July 1953; cons. engr. Mem. Am. Inst. Mining and Metall. Engrs., Am. Petroleum Inst. Republican. Episcopalian. Address: Washington, D.C. †

LYONS, EUGENE, author, mag. editor; b. Uzlian, Russia, July 1, 1898; s. Nathan H. and Minnie (Privin) L; came to U.S., 1907, naturalized, 1919; ed. Coll. City of N.Y., 1917-18, Columbia, 1918-19; m. Yetta Siegel, Sept. 6, 1921; 1 dau., Eugenie Rose (Mrs. Joseph A. Haimes). Employee, Erie (Pa.) Dispatch, 1920, Boston Telegram, 1922; editor Soviet Russia Pictorial, 1922-23; asst. dir. Tass Agy., 1923-27; U.P. corr. in Russia, 1928-34; mem. Ames and Norr, pub. relations, 1935-39; editor The Am. Mercury, 1939-44; editor Pageant, 1944-45; roving editor, The Readers Digest, 1946-52, sr. editor, 1952-68. Served as pvt. U.S. Army, 1918. Pres., Am. Com. for Liberation of the Peoples of Russia, 1951-52. Club: Overseas Press, Dutch Treat. Author: The Life and Death of Sacco and Vanzetti, 1927; Moscow Carousel, 1935; Assignment in Utopia, 1937; Stalin, Czar of all the Russias, 1940; The Red Decade, 1941; Our Unknown Ex-President, a Portrait of Herbert Hoover, 1948; Our Secret Allies: The Peoples of Russia, 1953; The Herbert Hoover Story, 1959; Herbert Hoover: a Biography, 1964; David Sarnoff: a Biography, 1966; Workers' Paradise Lost: 50 Years of Soviet Communism: a Balance Sheet, 1967. Editor: We Cover the World, 1937; Six Soviet Plays, 1934. Contbr. to leading mags. Home: New York, N.Y. Died Jan. 7, 1985.

LYONS, LOUIS MARTIN, educator; b. Boston, Sept. 1, 1897; s. Jacob Frederick Meade and Alice M. (Fitzmaurice) L.; B.S., Mass. Agrl. Coll., 1918, L.H.D., 1948; m. Margaret Wade Tolman, Aug. 6, 1921 (dec. 1949); children—Richard, Margaret, John, Thomas; m. 2d Catherine F. Malone. Reporter Boston Globe. 1919-20; extension editor Mass. Agrl. Coll., 1920-23; reporter Springfield Republican, summer 1923; reporter, spl. writer Boston Globe, 1923-46; Nieman fellow Harvard, 1938-39, curator Nieman Fellowships from 1939, chmn. exec. com. from 1946. As curator Nieman Fellowships, acted as coordinator of work of newspapermen awarded fellowships at Harvard; chmn. com. on selection of fellows; news commentator Lowell Broadcasting Inst., Sta. WBGH (TV-FM), 1951-78. Served as 2d lieutenant 363d Machine Gun Bn., U.S. Army, 1918. Mem. A.A.A.S., Acad. Soc. Mass. State Coll. (hon.). Phi Beta Kappa (hon.). Sigma Delta Chi (hon.). Clubs: Faculty, Four Tynes; Harvard (Boston). Author: Our Fair City (with others), 1947; The Nieman Fellows Report, 1948; also various articles. Editor: Nieman Reports. Home: Cambridge, Mass. Died Apr. 11, 1982.

LYONS, WILLIAM ALOYSIUS, utility executive; b. Bklyn., May 29, 1908; s. Samuel J. and Anna (McAuliffe) L.; m. Fern N. Kels, Aug. 18, 1934; children—Anna Clare Lyons Corkery, Nona Marie Lyons Livingston. Student, N.Y. U., 1928, Fordham U., 1929, Harvard Advanced Mgmt. Program, 1954. Accountant Utility Mgmt. Corp., 1929-34, asst. to comptroller, 1934-40, asst. to pres., 1940-41; comptroller NYPA-NJ Utilities Co., 1941-44; asst. to pres. N.Y. State Electric & Gas Corp., Binghamton, 1944-51, v.p., 1951-62, exec. v.p., 1962-66, pres., 1966-73, chief exec. officer, 1968-73, chmn. bd., chief exec. officer, 1973-77, dir., chmn. exec. and fin. com., 1977-83; dir. Utilities Mut. Ins. Co., Raymond Corp., Greene, Gt. Am. Industries, Inc.; Dir. allocations br. WPB, Office of War Utilities, 1942-44. Chmn. bd. trustees Ithaca Coll. Clubs: Sky (N.Y.C.); Binghamton City and Country. Home: Binghamton, N.Y. Died Mar. 15, 1983.

LYTLE, CLYDE FRANCIS, college dean; born Harrisburg, Pa., Apr. 9, 1890; s. Charles Henry and Catherine Louisa (Wise) L.; student Millersville (Pa.) State Normal Sch., 1913; Phila. Sch. of Pedagogy, 1915; A.B., Coll. of William and Mary, 1921; A.M., Middlebury Coll., 1929; Ed.D., N.Y. Univ., 1942; m. Clara Fenner, Sept. 3, 1921 (dec.); children—Clyde F., Richard Dudley, Thomas Fenner, Roane Clark, George Wellington Haynes. Teacher, Phila. Public Schs., 1915-18; head, English dept, Newport News (Va.) High Sch., 1918-22; prof. of English, State Teachers Coll., Kutztown, Pa., 1922-49, dean of instruction, 1949-56; prof. of speech, Wagner Coll., S.I., N.Y., 1956-58; associate dean State Univ. of N.Y., 1958-60; dean Ricker College, Houlton, Maine, 1960-63; prof. Shaw U., Raleigh, N.C., from 1963. Educational director, Camp Stuart, Va., 1918. Member Nat. Council Teachers of English, Shakespeare Assn. of Am., American Assn. Univ. Professors, Phi Delta Kappa, Kappa Delta Pi. Club: Torch. Author: State Supplement to Instruction in Shakespearean Drama, 1942; Pennsylvania in Song and Story, 1930; Leaves of Gold (anthology), 1938. Home: Kutztown, Pa. †

LYTLE, W(ILBERT) VERNON, educator; b. in Hockingport, Ohio, April 7, 1889; s. Harry Orville and Malinda Alice L.; A.B., Bethany (W. Va.) Coll., 1915; B.D., Yale, 1919, Ph.D., 1927; studied Columbia, summer 1929; m. Maude Schultz (M.A., Yale), Aug. 31, 1915; children—Clare Eleanor, Marylin Worth, Wilbert Vernon, Glenara Dawn, Star Gervinnes, Strohm Wentworth. Ordained ministry Disciples Church, 1915; successively pastor West Union, W.Va., Stony Creek, Conn., Grand Av. Ch., New Haven, until 1919; sec. N.E., Congl. Edn. Soc., Boston, 1919-22; prof. edn. and psychology and head of dept. of edn., Doane College, Crete, Neb., 1925-26; professor psychology and head of dept., De Pauw Univ., 1927-31; pres. and trustee Defiance (Ohio) Coll., 1931-32; founder Woman's Coll., New Haven, pres. and trustee 1933-39; organizer and pres. W. Vernon Lytle and Co., ednl. and financial counselors, New York City, from 1939. Fellow in psychology, Inst. of Human Relations, Yale, 1930-31; fellow in edn., Yale, 1932-33. Mem. Conn. Council of Deliberation; mem. Nat. Council of Nat. Economic League to represent state of Conn. Mem. Second Company, Gov.'s Foot Guard. Fellow A.A.A.S.; mem. Nat. Geog. Soc., Tau Kappa Alpha, Epsilon Phi Sigma. Republican. Conglist. Mason (32 deg., Shriner), K.T. Clubs: Rotary, Green Castle Country. Contbr. and lecturer on ednl. and psychol. subjects. Home: New Haven, Conn. †

MAC CORKLE, STUART ALEXANDER, author; b. Lexington, Va., Sept. 1, 1903; s. John Gold and Mattie Ella (Swink) MacC.; m. L. Lucile Emerson, Sept. 26, 1942. A.B., Washington and Lee U., 1924, LL.D., 1964; M.A., U. Va., 1928; Ph.D., Johns Hopkins, 1931. Instr. govt. U. Tex., 1930-31; asso. prof. govt. Southwestern Coll., 1931-32; instr. govt. U. Tex., 1932-34, asst. prof., 1934-37; asso. prof., dir. Bur. Municipal Research, 1937-41, prof., dir., 1941-50, Inst. Pub. Affairs, 1950-67; now pvt. cons. Chief adviser pub. adminstrn. Seoul Nat. U., 1958-60; Fulbright lectr. Coll. Europe, Bruges, Belgium, 1964; vis. ednl. counselor Nat. Inst. Pub. Affairs, 1941-42; lectr. Nat. U. Mexico, summer 1944, 68; mem. summer session staff U. Ill., 1946; spl. cons. USAAF, 1942. Author: The American Recognition Policy Toward Mexico, 1933, Police and Allied Powers of Municipalities in Texas, 1938, Municipal Administration, 1942, American Municipal Government and Administration, 1948, (with Dick Smith) Texas Government, 1949, rev., 1974, 8th edit. (with Janice C. May), 1980, Austin's Three Forms of Government, 1973, Cities from Scratch, 1974, (with Dick Smith, Thomas P. Yoakum) Texas Civics, 1955; Editorial bd.: (with Dick Smith, Thomas P. Yoakum) Public Administration Rev, 1942-44; Contbr. (with Dick Smith, Thomas P. Yoakum) articles to profl. Jours., newspapers. Prin. civilian mblzn. adviser Office of Civilian Def., 1942-43; chmn. Tex. Tax Commn., 1949; exec. dir. Tex. Economy Commn., 1951-52; mem. Austin City Council, 1949-51, 69-71, mayor pro tem, 1951-53, 69-71. Mem. Southwestern Social Sci. Assn. (sec.-treas. 1934-37), Am. Polit. Sci. Assn., Am. Soc. for Pub. Adminstrn., Internat. (hon. life), Tex. (hon. life) city mgrs. assns., Phi Beta Kappa, Pi Sigma Alpha, Kappa Sigma. Clubs: Rotarian. (Washington), University (Washington); Headliners (Austin). Home: Austin, Tex.

MACDONALD, DWIGHT, author; b. N.Y.C., Mar. 24, 1906; s. Dwight and Alice (Hedges) M.; m. Nancy Rodman, 1935 (div. 1950); children—Michael, Nicholas; m. Gloria Lanier, 1950; stepchildren—Day, Sabina. Grad., Phillips Exeter Acad., 1924; B.A., Yale, 1928; Litt.D. (hon.), Wesleyan U., Middletown, Conn., 1964. Staff writer Fortune, 1929-36; asso. editor Partisan Rev., 1937-43; editor and pub. Politics, 1944-49; staff writer New Yorker mag., 1951-71; movie critic Esquire mag., 1960-66; vis. prof. Northwestern U., 1956, Bard Coll., 1960, U. Tex. at Austin, 1966, U. Calif. at Santa Cruz, 1969, Hofstra U., 1969-70, U. Wis. at Milw., 1970, U. Mass. at Amherst, 1971, Yale, 1971, State U. N.Y. at Buffalo, 1973-74, John Jay Coll., 1974-76, U. Calif. at San Diego, 1977. Author: Henry Wallace: The Man and the Myth, 1948, The Root is Man, 1953, The Ford Foundation, 1956, Against the American Grain: Essays on the Effects of Mass Culture, 1962, Dwight Macdonald on Movies, 1969, Politics Past, 1970, Discriminations: Essays & Afterthoughts, 1938-74; Editor: Parodies, an Anthology from Chaucer to Beerbohm-and After, 1960, Selected Poems of Edgar Allan Poe (with hist. and critical intro.), 1966, My Past & Thoughts An Annotated Abridgment of the Memoirs of Alexander Herzen, 1973. Chmn. Spanish Refugee Aid, 1968-82. Guggenheim fellow, 1966; fellow Ezra Stiles Coll., Yale, 1967-82. Mem. Am. Acad. Arts and Scis., Am. Inst. Arts and Letters, Hedonists, Psi Upsilon. Home: East Hampton, N.Y. Died Dec. 19, 1982.

MACDONELL, JAMES JOHNSON, foundation official; b. Calgary, Alta., Can., Sept. 13, 1915; s. Archibald Joseph and Lillian Catherine (Johnson) M.; m. Audrey Mary Grafton, May 15, 1941; 1 child, Audrey Anne. D.Admin. (hon.), U. Ottawa, 1980. Chartered Accountant, Que. Partner-in-charge mgmt. cons. services Price Waterhouse & Co., Montreal, Que., Can., 1945-68; sr. partner Price Waterhouse Assos., Montreal, 1968-73; auditor gen. Can., Ottawa, 1973-80; chmn. Canadian Comprehensive Auditing Found., Ottawa, 1980-83. Fellow Mgmt. Cons.'s Que., Chartered Accountants Ont.; founding mem. Can. Assn. Mgmt. Cons. (pres. 1965-66). Clubs: Mount Royal (Montreal); Rideau (Ottawa); Met. (N.Y.). Home: Ottawa, Ont., Can. Died Mar. 30, 1983.

MACDONNELL, ROBERT GEORGE, government official; b. Spokane, Wash., May 10, 1911; s. John Grant and Marguerite (Crane) MacD.; m. Harriett Virginia Burks, Nov. 16, 1935; children: Robert Irwin, Richard Burks, Marguerite. B.S., U.S. Mil. Acad., 1934; M.S. in Civil Engring, U. Calif. at Berkeley, 1938; grad., Army War Coll., 1952. Registered profl. engr., La., Miss., Wash. Commd. 2d lt. U.S. Army, 1934, advanced through grades to maj. gen., 1962, served in, New Guinea, So. Philippines, Leyte and Luzon, World War II; asso. prof. engring (U.S. Mil. Acad.), 1947-51; assigned (VII Corps), Germany, 1952-55; mem. faculty (Army War Coll.), 1955-56; asst. comdt. (U.S. Army Engr. Sch.), 1956-58; div. engr. S. Pacific div., also pres. Calif. Debris Commn., 1958-61, dir. supply C.E., 1961-62, dir. civil works, 1962-63, dep. chief engrs., 1963-67; chmn. U.S. Bd. Engrs. Rivers and Harbors, 1962-69; mem. staff U.S. Senate, 1969—; pres. U.S. Beach Erosion Bd., 1962-63; assoc. prof. engring. U.S. Mil. Acad.; mem. faculty Army War Coll.; asst. commandant Engr. Sch. Chmn. Am. sect. Permanent Internat. Assn. Nav. Congresses, Brussels, 1962-63; pres. Mississippi River Commn., 1967-69; chmn. Red River Commn., 1967-69. Decorated Legion of Merit, D.S.M. (2), Bronze Star medal, Army Commendation ribbon. Home: Arlington VA

MACDOUGALL, RODERICK MARTIN, banker; b. N.Y.C., Mar. 27, 1926; s. Albert Edward and Ina M. (Brown) MacD.; m. Barbara Park, Oct. 31, 1952; children—Douglas E., Gordon P., Harriet H. and Susan B. (twins). B.A., Harvard U., 1951. Vice pres. Morgan Guaranty Trust Trust Co., N.Y.C., 1951-57; exec. v.p. Marine Midland Bank, Rochester, N.Y., 1967-68, pres., chief exec. officer, 1968-73; pres. New Eng. Mchts. Nat. Bank, Boston, 1974-76, 1976-78, chief exec. officer, 1976-84, chmn., 1978-84, chmn. exec. com., from 1948; chmn., pres., dir. New Eng. Mchts. Co., Inc.; chmn., dir. New Eng. Enterprises Capital Corp., New Eng. Investment Services Corp., New Eng. Mchts. Leasing Corp.; dir. New Eng. Mchts. Bank Internat., New Eng. Mchts. Realty Corp., EG&G, Inc., Arkwright-Boston, Mfrs. Mut. Ins. Co., New Eng. Mut. Life Ins. Co., Schlegel Mfg. Co. Trustee Boston Symphony Orch., Northeastern U., Boston; mem. corp. Babson Coll., Mass. Gen. Hosp., Mus. of Sci.; bd. dirs., v.p. Urban League Eastern Mass., United Way Mass. Bay. Served with USNR, 1943-46. Mem. Assn. Res. City Bankers, Mass. Bankers Assn., Greater Boston C. of C. (dir.). Clubs: Country (Brookline, Mass.); Somerset (Boston), Commercial (Boston), Merchants (Boston). Home: Weston, Mass. *

MACEACHRAN, CLINTON EDSON, b. Beverly, Mass., Dec. 27, 1887; s. James Lefavor and Eleanor (Marshall) MacE.; ed. Tufts College and Georgetown U.; m. Grace McDevitt, Aug. 1921 (dec.). Stenographer, Boston, 4 1-2 yrs.; apptd. clk. Dept. of State, Oct. 21, 1910; pvt. sec. to asst. sec. of state, 1911-13, to ambassador to Mexico, 1913, and to spl. rep. of the President in Mexico, 1914; chief clk. Am. Commn. to Am.-German prisoner of war conf., Berne, Switzerland, 1918; spl. asst. to counselor Dept. of State, 1919; spl. drafting officer to Am. Mission to Negotiate Peace, July-Dec. 1919; asst. to undersecretary of state, Dec. 1919-June 1921; apptd. consul June 1921; mem. Bd. of Efficiency, Dept. of State, 1921-22; consul, Antwerp, 1922, Ghent, 1924-26, Madrid, 1926-27; asst. chief Commercial Office, Dept. of State, 1931; chief clk. and administrative asst. Dept. of State, 1932-37; foreign service officer since 1934; consul gen. at Halifax, N.S., 1937-41; spl., agent, Dept. of State, 1943-45. Mem. Am. Foreign Service Assn. Home: Washington, D.C. †

MACHLUP, FRITZ, economist; b. Wiener Neustadt, Austria, Dec. 15, 1902; came to U.S., 1933, naturalized, 1940; s. Berthold and Cecile (Hayman) M.; m. Mitzi Herzog, Mar. 3, 1925; children—Stefan, Hanna. Dr. rer pol., U. Vienna, 1923; LL.D., Lawrence U., 1956, Lehigh U., 1967, La Salle Coll., 1968; Dr. Sc. Pol. h.c., U. Kiel, 1965; L.H.D., Case Inst. Tech., 1967; Dr. oecon. h.c., U. St. Gallen, 1972. Partner, dir. Timmersdorfer Holzstoff und Pappenfabrik Emerich Kren and Co., Vienna, 1922-33; partner, mng. dir. Ybbstaler Pappenfabriken Adolf Leitner und Bruder, Vienna, 1924-33; dir. First Hungarian Card Board Mfg. Corp., Budapest, 1924-48; mem. council Austrian Cardboard Cartel, Vienna, 1929-31; lectr. Volkshochschule, Vienna, 1929-33; research fellow Rockefeller Found., 1933-35; vis. lectr. Harvard, 1935, summer 1936, 38-39; Frank H. Goodyear prof. econs. U. Buffalo, 1935-47; Abram G. Hutzler prof. polit. economy Johns Hopkins, 1947-60; Walker prof. econs. and internat. finance, dir. internat. finance sect. Princeton, 1960-71; prof. econs. N.Y. U., 1971-83; vis. prof. Cornell U., 1937-38, Northwestern U., summer 1938, U. Calif., summer 1939, Stanford, summers 1940, 47, U. Mich., summer 1941, Am. U., 1943-46, Columbia, summer 1948, U. Calif. at Los Angeles, summer 1949, Kyoto U., Doshisha U., Japan, 1955, Osaka U., 1970, U. Melbourne, 1970, U. Vienna, 1973; chief div. research and statistics Office of Alien Property Custodian, Washington, 1943-46; cons. U.S. Treasury Dept., 1965-77; pres. Internat. Econ. Assn., 1971-74, hon. pres., 1974—. Author books, 1925—, including, The Stock Market, Credit, and Capital Formation, 1940, International Trade and the National Income Multiplier, 1943, The Basing Point System, 1949, The Political Economy of Monopoly, 1952, The Economics of Sellers' Competition, 1952, An Economic Review of the Patent System, 1958, Production and Distribution of Knowledge in the U.S, 1962, Essays on Economic Semantics, 1963, International Payments, Debts, and Gold, 1964, Involuntary Foreign Lending, 1965, Remaking the International Monetary System, 1968, Education and Economic Growth, 1970, The Alignment of Foreign-Exchange Rates, 1972, International Monetary Systems, 1975, Selected Economic Writings of Fritz Machlup, 1976, A History of Thought on Economic Integration, 1977, Methodology of Economics and Other Social Sciences, 1978, Information through the Printed Word: Books, Journals, Libraries, Bibliographic Services, 4 vols, 1978-80, Knowledge and Knowledge Production, 1980. Decorated comdr. Star of Africa, Liberia; Gt. Silver Medal of Honor with star Austria). Fellow Am. Acad. Arts Scis., AAAS.; mem. Am. Philos. Soc., Am. Econ. Assn. (bd. editors 1938-41, acting mng. editor 1944-45, pres. 1966), So. Econ. Assn. (pres. 1959-60), Royal Econ. Soc., AAUP (1st v.p. 1960-62, pres. 1962-64), Nat. Acad. Edn., Nationalökonomische Gesellschaft, Vienna (treas., sec. 1927-33), Accademia Nazionale dei Lincei (fgn.), Phi Beta Kappa (hon.). Home: Princeton, N.J. Died Jan. 30, 1983.

MACKAY, JOHN ALEXANDER, clergyman, educator; b. Inverness, Scotland, May 17, 1889; s. Duncan and Isabelle (Macdonald) M.; M.A. with 1st class honors in philosophy, U. Aberdeen, Scotland, 1912; B.D., Princeton Theol. Sem., 1915; U. Madrid, 1915-16; D.Litt., U. Lima, Peru, 1918; U. of Bonn, Germany 1930; D.D., Princeton, LL.D., Ohio Wesleyan U., 1937, Albright Coll., 1938, Coll. of Wooster, 1952; D.D., Aberdeen U., 1939, Debrecen U. Hungary, 1939, Presbyn Coll., Montreal, 1942, Serampore Coll., India, 1953; L.H.D., Boston U., 1939, Lafayette Coll., 1939; hon. fellow Stanford, 1941; m. Jane Logan Wells, Aug. 16, 1916; children—Isobel Elizabeth (Mrs. Bruce M. Metzger), Duncan Alexander Duff, Elena Florence (Mrs. Sherwood H. Reisner), Ruth (Mrs. Robert M. Russell). Prin., Anglo-Peruvian Coll., Lima, 1916-25; prof. philosophy Nat. U. Peru, 1925; lectr., writer under S.Am. Fedn. YMCA's, 1926-32; named lectr. numerous colls., sems., univs.; sec. Presbyn. Bd. Fgn. Missions, 1932-36; pres. Princeton Theol. Sem., prof. ecumenics, 1936-59, pres. emeritus; adj. prof. Hispanic thought Am. U. Washington, 1961-64. Mem. adv. council, dept. philosophy Princeton, 1941-62. Pres. Am. Assn. Theol. Schs., 1948-50; mem. central com. World Council Chs., 1948-54; chmn. Internat. Missionary Council 1947-59, hon. chmn., 1959-61; chmn. joint com. Internat. Missionary Council and World Council Chs., 1948-54, pres. Presbyn. Bd. Fgn. Missions 1945-51; chmn. Commn. of Universal Ch. and World of Nations, Oxford Conf. on Ch., Community and State, 1937; moderator Gen. Assembly Presbyn. Ch. in U.S.A., 1953-54. Decorated comdr. Palmas Magisteriales (Peru). Author numerous books in Spanish, English, from 1927, including Christianity on the Frontier, 1950; Gods Order: The Ephesian Letter and this Present Time, 1953; The Presbyterian Way of Life, 1960; His Life and Our Life, 1964; Ecumenica: The Science of the Church Universal, 1964; Christian Reality and Appearance, 1969, Realidad e Idolatria, 1970. Editor: Theology Today, 1944-51, chmn. editorial council 1951-59. Club: Cosmos (Washington); Nassau (Princeton). Home: Hightstown, N.J. Died June 9, 1983.

MACKAY, JOHN KEILLER, judge High Court Ontario; b. Plainfield, Pictou County, N.S., July 11, 1889; s. John Duncan and Bessie (Murray) M.; B.A., St. Francis Xavier Univ., 1912; LL.B., Dalhousie University, 1922; married Katherine Jean MacLeod, July 14, 1943; children—Ian Reay, Donald Alastair. Called to Nova Scotia bar, 1922, Ontario bar, 1923; created King's counsel, 1933; apptd. justice of the Supreme Court of Ont., 1935. Commd. lt. Canadian Field Arty., 1909, capt. 1913; apptd. lt. 6th Brigade, C.F.A., C.E.F., World War I; maj. in command of 22d Batn. 6th Brigade, C.F.A., 1915; lt. col. 7th brigade, C.F.A., Sept. 1916, in command 6th brigade, 1917. Awarded D.S.O. and bar; mentioned in dispatches three times. Mem. St. Andrew's (life mem.), Clan MacKay (life mem.), Celtic Historical. Clubs: Halifax, Ashburn Golf and Country, Waegwoltic Yacht (Halifax); Albany, Canadian Mil. Inst. (Toronto); Empire, Royal Canadian Yacht. Mason. Mem. Presbyterian Ch. Home: Toronto, Ont., Can. †

MACKAY, LOUIS ALEXANDER, educator; b. Hensall, Ont., Can., Feb. 27, 1901; s. William and Martha (Smallacombe) MacK.; B.A., U. Toronto, 1923; M.A., Balliol Coll., Oxford (Eng.) U., 1948; m. Constance Charlesworth, June 29, 1928; children—Pierre Antony, Katherine Camilla (Mrs. Arne Jensen). Came to U.S., 1948, naturalized, 1954. Instr., then asst. prof. U. Toronto, 1928-41; from asst. prof. to prof. U. B.C., 1941-48; prof. Latin, U. Cal. at Berkeley, 1948-68, prof. emeritus, 1968-82. Rhodes scholar, 1926; Guggenheim fellow, 1945. Mem. Am. Philol. Assn. (pres. 1960), Archaeol. Inst. Am., Philol. Assn. Pacific Coast, Canadian Classical Assn. Home: Kensington, Calif. Died June 24, 1982.

MACKELVIE, JAY WARD, army officer; b. Esmond, S. D., Sept. 23, 1890; s. Francis and Janette (Gibb) MacK.; grad. of U.S. Army service schs., and Army War Coll.; m. Ethel Leonard, April 11, 1924; children—Jay Ward, Philip Allen. Private 7th Cav., 1913; commd. 2d lt., U.S. Army, 1917, through the grades to maj. gen. Mason. Home: Washington, D.C. †

MACKENZIE, IAN ALISTAIR, Canadian government official; b. Assynt, Scotland, July 27, 1890; s. George and Anne (McRae) Mackenzie; M.A., Edinburgh U., 1911, honors in classics, 1912, LL.B., 1914. Began practice of law in Canada, 1919; elected to legislative assembly of British Columbia as member for Vancouver, 1920; re-elected 1924 and 1928; mem. Provincial Executive for B.C., 1919-22, Dominion Executive, 1921-23, Dominion vice-pres., 1924-25; apptd. provincial sec., B.C., 1928; held portfolios of Immigration, Colonization, Soldiers' Settlement and Indian Affairs in fed. govt.; mem. Federal Parliament, 1930, re-elected, 1935, 1940, 1945; apptd. Minister of National Defense, 1935; Minister of Pensions and Nat. Health, 1939; Minister of Veterans Affairs, 1944. Served as lieut., Seaforth Highlanders, C.E.F., 1915; with 72d at Ypres, Somme, and elsewhere, 1916, capt. on hdqrs. staff of Gen. J. W. Stewart, until 1919. Pres. Vancouver Command Great War Veterans, 1920, 1922. Presbyterian. Mem. Liberal Party. Clubs: Vancouver, Jericho Country, Royal Vancouver (Yacht) (Vancouver). Author: Songs and Buchanan (Gaelic) (with others); contbr. articles on old Celtic subjects to European jours. Address: Ottawa, Ont., Can.

MACKENZIE, OSSIAN, ednl. cons.; b. Hampden, Me., July 26, 1907; s. L. Robert and Evangeline Marion (Taylor) MacK.; B.A., U. Mont., 1928; postgrad. Harvard, 1928-31; J.D., Fordham U., 1938; LL.D., Rider Coll., 1962; m. Kyle Habberton, June 16, 1934; 1 dau., Robin (Mrs. Lucien E. Ferster). Estate supr. Guaranty Trust Co. of N.Y., 1931-39; admitted to N.Y. bar, 1938; head state and local tax dept. Allied Chem. & Dye Corp., N.Y.C., 1939-43; head tax dept. West Penn Electric Co., N.Y.C., 1946-47; univ. devel. officer Columbia, 1947-50; asst. dean Grad. Sch. Bus., asst. to exec. dir. Am. Assembly, 1950-53; dean Coll. Bus. Adminstrn., Pa. State U., 1953-73, asst. to pres., 1956-57, v.p., 1957-58, ednl. cons., 1977-80, prof. mgmt., chmn. dept. bus and econs. Rutgers U., Camden, N.J., 1973-77. Cons., Dept. of State, 1955-57, U. Costa Rica, 1964-65, Dept. of Health, Edn. and Welfare, 1967, Comptroller Gen. U.S., 1968-74, Ala. A. and M. U., 1968-80, Esan U., Lima, Peru, 1971-80; dir. Corr. Edn. Research Project, 1964-68. Served with USMCR, 1943-46. Recipient Disting. Alumnus award U.

Mont., 1979. Mem. Middle Atlantic Assn. Colls. Bus. Adminstrn. (pres. 1961), Am. Assembly Collegiate Schs. Bus. (pres. 1973), Council for Profl. Edn. for Bus. (pres. 1962), Verband der Hochschullehrer fur Betriesbswirtschaft, Beta Gamma Sigma (pres. 1966-70), Pi Gamma Mu, Sigma Delta Chi, Sigma Chi. Republican. Protestant. Mason. Clubs: Harvard (N.Y.C.); Pa. State Faculty. Author books, articles in field. Home: State College, Pa. Died July 25, 1980.

MACKIN, CATHERINE, broadcast journalist; b. Balt.; grad. with honors U. Md.; Nieman fellow Harvard U. Corr. Washington bur. Hearst Newspapers, 6 years; with NBC News, 1969-77, anchorwoman news program, investigative reporter WRC-TV, Washington, 1969-71, gen. assignment reporter NBC TV, 1971-73, corr. Los Angeles bur., 1973-74, Congl. corr., Washington, 1974—, TV floor reporter (1st woman) at nat. polit. convs., 1972, 76; with ABC News, from 1977. Died Nov. 20, 1982.

MAC LEAN, DONALD DREW, lawyer; b. Seattle, Oct. 11, 1923; s. James Matthew and Julia Agnes (Drew) MacL.; m. Joan Mary Rogers, May 1, 1954; children: Jane, Margaret Mary, Mary Denise, Drew, James, Peter, Sarah Susan. B.S., U.S. Merchant Marine Acad., 1943; B.S.L., U. Wash., 1949, J.D., 1950. Asst. to dean U. Wash. Sch. Law, 1950-52; practice law, Seattle, 1952-62; partner firm McMicken, Rupp & Schweppe, Seattle, 1959-62; gen. atty. Pacific N.W. Bell Telephone Co., Seattle, 1962-75, v.p., gen. counsel, sec., from 1975. Bd. dirs., vice chmn. Seattle Urban League, from 1975; trustee Pacific N.W. Indian Center, Mus. Native Am. Cultures, Spokane, from 1976; chmn. bd. trustees Matteo Ricci Coll., from 1976; v.p., bd. dirs. J. Homer Butler Found., from 1975; mem. vis. com. U. Wash. Law Sch.; regional co-chmn. NCCJ; ordained permanent deacon Archdiocese of Seattle, Roman Catholic Ch., 1975. Served with USNR, 1943-46. Recipient Bus. achievement award U.S. Merchant Marine Acad., 1963. Mem. ABA, Wash. State Bar Assn., Seattle-King County Bar Assn., Am. Judicature Soc., Mcpl. League. Clubs: Rainier, Harbor, Wash. Athletic, Central Park Tennis. Home: Bellevue, Wash.

MACLEAN, JOHN ALLAN, mfg. exec.; b. Maxton, N.C., Mar. 29, 1912; s. Sylvester Brown and Florence (Wooten) MacL.; B.S., U. N.C., 1933, M.S., 1936; D.Sc., Tri-State Coll., 1972; m. Gladys Wilkie, July 4, 1930; children—Jane Sherrill, Ann Wilkie. Instr. mech. engring. U. N.C., 1934-36; asst. prof. aero. engring. U. Notre Dame, 1936-40; successively sr. engr., quality mgr., asst. aircraft mgr., dir. indsl. relations, gen. mgr. automotive products Bendix products div. Bendix Aviation Corp., South Bend, Ind., 1940-57, asst. group exec., 1957-59; dir. Dodge Mfg. Corp. (merged with Reliance Electric Co. 1967 and now a div.), Mishawaka, Ind., 1956-57, pres., 1959-74; v.p., dir. Reliance Electric Co., 1967-74; dir. 1st Bank & Trust Co., South Bend, Ind. Bell Telephone Co., Aro Corp., Gladding Corp., Sibley Machine & Foundry Corp., No. Ind. Pub. Service Co., J.H. Fenner & Co., Hull, Eng. Mem. Ind. C. of C. (pres. 1970-71, dir.), Phi Beta Kappa, Tau Beta Pi. Presbyn. Contbr. articles aero. jours. Home: South Bend, Ind. Died 1982.

MACLEAN, JOSEPH BROTHERTON, cons. actuary; b. Glasgow, Scotland, Mar. 30, 1889; s. Hugh and Isabella (Brotherton) M.; ed. Glasgow pub. schs.; m. Marjorie MacLean, June 18, 1918; children—Hugh Norman, Elizabeth Cameron. Came to U.S., 1911. With Scottish Temperance Life Assurance Co., Glasgow, Scotland, 1905-11, with Mutual Life Ins. Co. of New York from 1911, vice president and actuary, 1941-47, Enlisted Scottish Rifles, infantry, active service in France and Belgium, British Army 1914-18; disch. as capt. Awarded Mil. Cross Oct. 1918. Fellow The Actuarial Soc. of Am. (past pres., mem. council), The Am. Inst. of Actuaries, The Faculty of Actuaries in Scotland (mem. council), The Inst. of Actuaries, London, Teachers Life Ins. and Annuity Assn. (trustee), Am. Arbitration Assn. (panel mem.). Presbyterian. Author: Life Insurance, 1924; (with E. W. Marshall) Distribution of Surplus, 1935; Introduction to Life Insurance, 1948. Home: Yarmouthport, Mass. †

MAC LEISH, ARCHIBALD, poet; b. Glencoe, Ill., May 7, 1892; s. Andrew and Martha (Hillard) Mac L.; m. Ada Hitchcock, June 21, 1916; children—Kenneth (dec.), Brewster Hitchcock (dec.), Mary Hillard, William Hitchcock. A.B., Yale U., 1915, Litt.D. (hon.), 1939; LL.B., Harvard, 1919, Litt.D. (hon.), 1955; M.A. (hon.), Tufts Coll., 1932; Litt.D. (hon.), Wesleyan U., 1938, Colby Coll., 1938, U. Pa., 1941, U. Ill., 1946, Washington U., 1948, Columbia, 1954; L.H.D. (hon.), Dartmouth, 1940; LL.D., John Hopkins, 1941, U. Calif., 1943, Queens U., Ont., 1948, Carleton Coll., 1956, Amherst Coll., 1963; Litt.D. (hon.), Rockford Coll., 1953, U. Pitts., 1959, Brandeis U., 1959; D.C.L. (hon.), Union Coll., 1941, U. P.R., 1953; L.H.D. (hon.), Princeton, 1965; D.H.L. (hon.), Williams Coll., 1942. Rede lectr. Cambridge (Eng.) U., 1942; Boylston prof. Harvard, 1949-62; Simpson lectr. Amherst Coll., 1963-67; Librarian of Congress, 1939-44; also dir. U.S. Office Facts & Figures, 1941-42; asst. dir. OWI, 1942-43, asst. sec. state, 1944-45. Author: verse The Happy Marriage, 1924, The Pot of Earth, 1925; verse play Nobodaddy, 1925; verse Streets in the Moon, 1926, The Hamlet of A. MacLeish, 1928, New Found Land, 1930, Conquistador, 1932, Frescoes for Mr. Rockefeller's City, 1933, Collected Poems, 1924-33, Union Pacific; a ballet, 1934, Panic; verse play, 1935, Public Speech; verse, 1936, The Fall of the City; verse play for radio, 1937, Land of the Free; verse, 1938, Air Raid; verse play for radio, 1938, America Was Promises; verse, 1939, The Irresponsibles; prose, 1940, The American Cause, 1941, A Time to Speak, 1941, A Time To Act, 1942, American Opinion and the War, 1942, American Story; broadcasts, 1944, Act Five; verse, 1948, Poetry and Opinion; prose, 1950, Freedom is the Right to Choose, 1951, Collected Poems, 1917-52, Songs for Eve; verse, 1954, J.B; verse play, 1958, Poetry and Experience; prose, 1961, Eleanor Roosevelt Story; book, 1965, motion picture, 1965 (Academy award 1966), Herakles; verse play, 1967, Magic Prison; libretto, 1967, An Evening's Journey to Conway Massachusetts; play, 1967; prose A Continuing Journey, 1968; verse The Wild Old Wicked Man and Other Poems, 1968, Scratch; prose play, 1971, The Human Season; selected poems, 1972, The Great American Fourth of July Parade; verse play for radio, 1975, New & Collected Poems, 1917-1976, 1976; prose Riders on the Earth, 1978, Six Plays; verse plays for radio, 1980. Am. del. Conf. Allied Ministers of Edn., London, 1944; chmn. Am. delegation London Conf. to draw up constn. for UNESCO, 1945, Am. delegation 1st Gen. Conf. UNESCO, Paris, 1946; first Am. mem. exec. council UNESCO. Served from pvt. to capt. U.S. Army, 1917-19, overseas, France; Served from pvt. to capt. U.S. Army, 1917-18, overseas, France. Decorated comdr. Legion of Honor France; Encomienda Order el Sol del Peru; recipient Bollingen prize in poetry, 1953, Nat. Book Award in poetry, 1953, Pulitzer prize in poetry, 1932, 53, Pulitzer prize in drama, 1959, Antoinette Perry award in drama, 1959, Presdl. Medal of Freedom, 1977, Nat. Medal for Lit., 1978, Gold medal for poetry Am. Acad., 1979. Mem. Am. Acad. Arts and Letters (pres. 1953-56). Clubs: Century (N.Y.C.); Tavern (Boston). Address: Conway, Mass. Died Apr. 20, 1982.

MACLEOD, JOHN HOLMES, marketing cons.; b. Boston, Oct. 12, 1890; s. John Holmes and Elizabeth Ann (Beal) M.; A.B., Harvard, 1914; m. Caro Kingman, Aug. 18, 1917; children—Caro (Mrs. A. B. Turner), John Holmes, Roderick Kingman, Elizabeth (Mrs. John Hagan). Salesman Dennison Mfg. Co., Framingham, Mass., 1915-17; investment banker Otis & Co. and McDonald & Co., 1920-26 (both Cleveland); v.p. Hinde & Dauch Paper Co., Sandusky, O., 1926-50; cons. containers div., chief paperboard br. N.P.A., 1951-52; spl. rep. containers div. Robt. Gain Co., Inc., N.Y.C., from 1952. Served as major, inf., U.S. Army, 1917-1919. Mem. Am. Management Assn., Marketing Execs. Soc., Rutland (Vt.) C. of C. Episcopalian. Clubs: University (Chicago); Union (Cleveland); Harvard, Canadian (N.Y. City); Royal Canadian Yacht (Toronto). Home: Wallingford, Vt. †

MACNAUGHT, J. WATSON, lawyer; b. Coleman, P.E.I., Can., June 19, 1904; s. Robert C. and Emily (Moreshead) MacN.; B.A., Dalhousie U., 1928, LL.B., 1930; m. Eva Palmer, May 11, 1932; children—John William, David Alexander. Called to Canadian bar, created King's counsel, 1942; law clk. Prince Edward Isle Legislative Assembly, 1935-41, clk. of assembly, 1941-45; crown prosecutor Prince County, 1942- 45; mem. Ho. of Commons, 1945-47, 63-65; Parliamentary asst. to minister fisheries, 1948-57; solicitor gen. Can., 1963-65; minister mines and tech. surveys, 1965; chmn. of Dominion Coal Bd., 1966-69; now mem. firm J. Watson & John W. MacNaught, P.E.I. Sec., P.E.I. br. Commonwealth Parliamentary Assn., 1941-45, del. conf., Wellington, New Zealand, 1950; adviser Canandian delegation Tokyo meeting, 1955; head Canadian delegation orgn. Internat. N. Pacific Fisheries Commn., Washington, 1953; Canadian rep. inauguration pres. of Mexico, 1964. Mem. Canadian Assn. Retarded Children, P.E.I., N.S. bar assns., Phi Delta Phi. Rotarian. Home: Summerside, Prince Edward Island, Canada. Interned United Ch. Cemetery, Brae, Prince Edward Island, Canada.

MACNICOL, ROY VINCENT, artist; b. New York, N.Y., Nov. 27, 1889; s. Archibald and Consuela MacNicol; early art training at U. of Ill.; later studied at Paris and Toledo, Spain; m. Fay Courtney, singer, Jan. 26, 1920 (died Feb. 14, 1941). Began as an actor, then took up art, 1st recognition in art, 1931, doing decorative screens, murals and panels; later land and sea scapes and character portrait studies; water colorist. Has exhibited at Chicago Art Inst., Nat. Acad., Archtl. League and museums of U.S. and Europe, Palace of Fine Arts, Mexico City, has held 29 one-man exhbns. Represented in museums in Palm Beach, Fla., Mexico City, Beverly Hills, Calif., Chicago, N.Y. City, Paris, London, China, S. America and Brit. West Indies. Has traveled in many parts of the world to complete his Round the World collection; living in Mexico from 1942. Address: New York, N.Y. †

MACOMBER, ALLISON RUFUS, sculptor; b. Taunton, Mass., July 5, 1916; s. Allison Rufus and Rose Anne (Williams) M.; m. Kathleen Mary Fripp, Oct. 2, 1944; children—Daphne Mary, Philip Allison. Student, Mass. Coll. Art, 1934-38; studied with, Cyrus Dallin, 1934-38, Raymond Porter, 1934-38, Henry Kitson, 1937-40. mem. Mass. State Senate Art Commn., 1975-79. Designer: Radiation Lab, Mass. Inst. Tech., 1940-42; sculptor portraits, coins, medals, memls., archtl. works in bronze and stone throughout, U.S., other countries; artist in residence, Boston Coll., 1963-79. Served with USAAF, 1942-45. Decorated D.F.C., Air medal with 4 oak leaf clusters. Mem. Fall River Art Assn. (hon.). Episcopalian. Home: Segregansett, Mass.

MAC QUEEN, LAWRENCE INGLIS, college prof.; b. Milledgeville, Ga., Jan. 26, 1889; s. Donald and Martha Jones (Windsor) M.; A.B., Centre Coll., Danville, Ky., 1909; student Lane Theol. Sem., Cincinnati, O., 1911; A.M., U. of Cincinnati, 1912; m. Madge Blount, Feb. 6, 1912. Prof. ancient langs., Fredericksburg (Va.) Coll., 1910; pres. Mo. Synodical Coll., Fulton, Mo., 1912-14; prof. polit. and social science, Southwestern Presbyn. U., Clarksville, Tenn., from 1914. Mem. Am. Hist. Assn., Am. Sociol. Soc., Sigma Alpha Epsilon. Democrat. Presbyn. Mason. Home: Clarksville, Tenn. †

MACRAE, JOHN, JR., publishing company executive; b. The Plains, Va., Dec. 17, 1898; s. John and Katherine (Green) M.; m. Anne McCrory Hinton, Oct. 12, 1926; children—Pamela Anne (Mrs. E.L. Bermingham), Jill Allison (Mrs. John Witherbee), John III. B.S., U. Va., 1919. Supr. U.S. Shipping Bd., 1921; with E.P. Dutton & Co., Inc., N.Y.C., 1928-83, chmn. bd., pres., 1970-83, also mem. exec. com. Author: Best From Yank. Served to capt. U.S. Army, 1917-19. Mem. Sigma Chi. Clubs: American Yacht; Field (Greenwich, Conn.); Nantucket (Mass.) Yacht, University. Home: Naples, Fla. Dec. Oct. 7, 1983.

MACRUM, GEORGE HERBERT, artist; b. Pittsburgh, Pa., Aug. 24, 1888; s. Nathaniel G. and Millie E. (Everson) M.; ed. Art Students' League, New York and in Paris, France; m. Grace Fallow Norton, 1914. Landscape painter; exhibited at Salmagundi Club, 1914, Nat. Acad. Arts and Letters, Soc. Independent Artists, Allied Artists America, all N.Y.C., Pa. Acad. Fine Arts, Phila., Salon de Beaux Arts, Paris. Awarded Trumbull prize. San Francisco Expn., 1915. Mem. Allied Artists America. Phila. Art Club, Salmagundi Club. Address: New York, N.Y. †

MACVANE, JOHN FRANKLIN, news analyst; b. Portland, Maine, Apr. 29, 1912; s. William Leslie and Bertha (Achorn) MacV.; m. Lucy Maxwell, Dec. 17, 1937 (div.); children—Ian (dec.), Myles Angus, Sara Ann Andrew, Matthew Chattan, Fiona Ellen; m. Henriette Butler Kidder, May 27, 1969. Grad., Phillips Exeter Acad.; B.A., Williams Coll., 1933; B.Litt., Exeter Coll. Oxford U., 1936. Reporter, ship news columnist Bklyn. Daily Eagle, 1935-36; reporter N.Y. Sun, 1936-38; sub-editor London Daily Express, 1938-39, Continental Daily Mail, Paris, 1939; corr. Exchange Telegraph Agy., Internat. News Service covering Fall of France; reporter, war corr. assigned Brit. Army, NBC, London, 1940-42, North African campaign Morocco-Algeria-Tunisia, 1942-43, Brit. and Am. Armies; covered Casablanca Conf., 1943; UN corr. NBC covering UN Security Council, 1946; Berlin air lift, 1948, UN Gen. Assembly, Paris, 1948; producer moderator weekly radio, TV panel; United or Not show, ABC, 1950-52; with UN Gen. Assembly, Paris, 1951-52; UN corr. ABC, 1953-78, Photo Communications Co., 1978-84. Writer-commentator documentary: TV film series Alaska: The New Frontier, for, Nat. Ednl. Television, 1960; Author: Journey into War, 1943, War and Diplomacy in North Africa, 1944, Embassy Extraordinary; The United States Mission to UN, 1961, On the Air in World War II, 1979. Decorated Purple Heart medal; chevalier and officer Legion of Honor Medaille de la France Libérée France; recipient Nat. Headliners award, 1947; Am. Assn. for UN award, 1960. Mem. Assn. Radio-TV News Analysts (pres. 1948-49, 55, 56, sec. 1954), St. Andrews Soc. N.Y., UN Corrs. Assn. (pres. 1964), Pilgrims of U.S., France-Am. Soc., Gargoyle Soc., Soc. of Silurians (gov.), Am. Soc. French Legion of Honor, France Am. Soc., Sigma Delta Chi, Sigma Phi (trustee Williams chpt. 1968-73). Clubs: Williams; Press (London, Eng.). Landed with 16th Inf. Regt. U.S. 1st Inf. Div., Normandy on D-Day; later U.S. 1st Army, 1944-45, French Deuxieme Div. Blindé Paris, 1944. Home: Portland, ME. Died Jan. 28, 1984.

MADDEN, CLIFFORD JOHN, computer company executive; b. Bessmer, Mich., Feb. 16, 1936; s. Boris and Mary M.; m. Mary E. Smaltz, Sept. 5, 1959; children: Todd, Derk. B.S. in Bus. Adminstrn; Miami U., Oxford, Ohio, 1961; J.D., U. Mich., 1963. Bar: Colo. 1964, Wis. 1965; C.P.A., Wis. Asso. gen. counsel Security Life & Accident Co., Denver, 1963-65; v.p., gen. counsel Gateway Foods, Inc., LaCrosse, Wis., 1965-69; dir. internat. fin. Pillsbury Co., Mpls., 1969-72; v.p. fin. Rucker Co., Oakland, Calif., 1972-74; sr. v.p. fin., sec. Amdahl Corp., Sunnyvale, Calif., 1975-80; pres. Trilogy Ltd., Santa Clara, Calif., from 1980. Served with AUS, 1954-57. Mem. Am. Bar Assn., Am. Inst. C.P.A.'s, Phi Beta Kappa, Beta Gamma Sigma. Home: Cupertino, Calif.

MADDEN, HENRY MILLER, educator; b. Oakland, Calif., June 17, 1912; s. Henry Joseph and Martha Ann (Miller) M. A.B., Stanford, 1933; student, U. Budapest, 1936-37; A.M., Columbia, 1944, Ph.D., 1948; B.L.S., U. Calif., 1947. Instr. history Stanford, 1937-42; acting asst. prof. history State U. Wash., 1948; ofcl. Internat. Refugee Orgn., Linz, Austria, 1948-49; univ. librarian Calif. State U., Fresno, 1949-79, adj. prof. bibliography, from 1979; Fulbright lectr. Austrian Nat. Library, 1953-54. Author: Xantus, Hungarian Naturalist in the Pioneer West, 1949, German Travelers in California, 1958, From Kapuvár to California, 1893, 1979; Editor: California Librarian, 1963-66; Contbr. profl. publs. Served as lt. comdr. U.S.N.R., 1942-46; sec. Tripartite Naval Commn. 1945-46, Berlin, Germany. Mem. Am. Hist. Assn., Calif. Library Assn. (past pres.), U.S. Naval Inst., A.L.A., Phi Beta Kappa. Club: Roxburghe (San Francisco). Home: Fresno, Calif.

MADDOCK, SYDNEY DEAN, finance ofcl.; b. Chgo., Jan. 31, 1889; s. Horace Herbert and Margaret A. (Thompson) M.; student pub. schs., Kenosha, Wis.; m. Leola Mae Havens, Aug. 6, 1914; children—Janet Ruth (Mrs. Dan C. Kelliher), Sydney Dean. Claims mgr. Simmons Co., Kenosha, Wis., 1912-17; dir. adminstrn. War Trade Bd., Washington, 1917-19; rep. Internat. Steel Co., China, Japan, 1920-21; pres. Sanford Narrow Fabric Co., 1922-26; v.p. New Amsterdam Credit Corp., 1926-29; with Comml. Investment Trust Inc., N.Y.C., 1929-56, v.p., 1933-56, dir., 1937-56; pres. Holtzen, Cabot Electric Co., Boston, 1943-45; pres., dir. C.I.T. Corp., N.Y.C., 1949-56, chmn. exec. com., dir., from 1957; v.p., dir. C.I.T. Financial Corp., N.Y.C., from 1952. Presbyn. Clubs: Sales Executives (N.Y.C.); Scarsdale (N.Y.) Golf. Home: Scarsdale, N.Y. †

MADSEN, MATTIAS, fishing vessel owner; b. Bjornerem, Midsund, Norway, Sept. 15, 1890; s. Mads Trulsen and Maria Ivasdötre (Midsund) B.; student schs. of Norway; student Columbia Coll., Everett, Wash., 1915-16; m. Inga Olea Petterson Ringen, June 2, 1923; children—Mattias Arnold, Ilene Margaret (Mrs. William Harry Taylor); came to U.S., 1911, naturalized, 1916. Fisherman, Norway, 1905-11, Seattle, from 1913. Mem. Internat. Pacific Halibut Commn., from 1955; chmn. Marine Protection Fund, 1930-40, 1952-53, dir., 1949-53, 55; dir. Halibut Producers Coop., 1941-42. Mem. Fishing Vessels Owners Assn. (dir., pres. 1940), Sons of Norway, Norwegian Male Chorus. Lutheran. Mason. Club: Norwegian Commercial. Home: Seattle. †

MADSON, BEN A(DOLPH), prof. of agronomy; b. Jewell, Ia., Mar. 19, 1887; s. Nels C. and Johana (Jepson) M.; B.S.A., Ia. State Coll., 1907; grad. student U. of Ill., Jan.-June, 1910, U. of Chicago, 1925-26; m. Mary Ellen Quane, June 12, 1912. Asst. chemist, Ia. Expt. Sta., 1907-09; with Coll. of Agr., U. of Calif., from 1910, successively asso. in agronomy, instr., asst. prof., asso. prof. to 1934, prof. of agronomy from 1934, head of div. of agronomy, 1927-48; dir. Field stations from July 1948. Fellow Am. Soc. Agronomy; member American Soc. Range Management, Alpha Zeta, Sigma Xi, Gamma Sigma Delta, Alpha Gamma Rho. Club: Commonwealth (San Francisco). Home: Davis, Calif. †

MAFFRY, AUGUST, banker, economist; b. Macon, Mo., July 22, 1905; s. August Fritz and Jessie Fremont (Williams) M.; m. Alice Mary Henry, June 8, 1929; children—Alice Mary (Mrs. William Silas Talbot), August. A.B., U. Mo., 1926, A.M., 1928, Ph.D., 1930; exchange student, U. Tübingen, Germany, 1926-27. Instr. U. Mo., 1929-30, Dartmouth, 1930-34; ofcl. U.S. Dept. of Commerce, 1935- 45; v.p., econ. adviser Export-Import Bank, Washington, 1945-47; v.p. Irving Trust Co., N.Y.C., 1948-61, sr. v.p., 1961-68; dep. gen. mgr. Internat. Comml. Bank Ltd., London, 1967-68; Sec. Am. sect. Mexican-Am. Commn. for Econ. Cooperation, 1943; tech. adviser U.S. delegation Internat. Monetary and Financial Conf., Bretton Woods, 1944; tech. officer Inter-Am. Conf. on Problems of War and Peace, Mexico City, 1945; tech. adviser, inaugural and 1st meetings Internat. Monetary Fund and Internat. Bank for Reconstrn. and Devel., Savannah, 1945, Washington, 1946; cons. ECA, 1948-68; Internat. Devel. adv. bd., 1950-51. Co-author: Process of Inflation in France, 1914-27, 1928; Contbr. numerous reports, pamphlets, articles to U.S. govt. publs. Decorated Sitara-i-Quaid-i-Azam Pakistan; comdr. Order of Merit Italy; comdr. Order of Phoenix Greece; Nat. Order of Merit France). Mem. Council Fgn. Relations, Kappa Sigma, Phi Beta Kappa. Presbyn. Club: Metropolitan (Washington). Home: Shaker Heights, OH.

MAG, ARTHUR, lawyer; b. New Britain, Conn., Oct. 11, 1896; s. Nathan Elihu and Rebecca (Goldberg) M.; m. Selma Rothenberg, Nov. 7, 1925 (dec. Oct. 1930); children—Josephine Selma Randall, Helen Louise Wolcott; m. Charline Weil, Nov. 24, 1932. A.B., Yale, 1918, J.D., 1920; LL.D., U. Mo.-Kansas City, 1974. Bar: Conn., Mo. bars 1920. Since practiced in, Kansas City; with Stinson, Mag & Fizzell, 1924-81; chmn. exec. com. Host Internat., Inc., Los Angeles; chmn. Schutte Lumber Co.; dir. Price Candy Co., Rival Mfg. Co., Hereford Redevel. Corp., First Nat. Bank of Kansas City, 1st Nat. Charter Corp., Standard Milling Co., L.B. Price Merc. Co., St. Louis, Rothschild's B & M, Oklahoma City, Helzberg's Diamond Shops, Z Bar Cattle Co. Author: Trusteeship, 1948. Pres. Greater Kansas City Mental Health Found., 1952-56; mem. nat. adv. council Mental Health, 1955-59; chmn. Greater Kansas City liaison com. Regional Med. Programs, 1952-66; mem. Gov.'s Citizens Com. on Delinquency and Crime, 1966-68, Mo. Com. for White House Conf. on Aging, Mayor's Commn. on Civil Disorder, 1968, Citizens Study Com. on Kansas City-Jackson County Health Services, 1968; co-chmn. Gov.'s Task Force on Role of Pvt. Higher Edn. in Mo., 1970; Hon. chmn. bd. dirs. Menorah Med. Center; mem. bd. curators Stephens Coll., 1967-72; trustee, v.p. Mo. Bar Found.; trustee U. Mo. at Kansas City, Frederic Ervine McIlvain Trust, Carrie J. Loose Fund, Harry Wilson Loose Fund, Sadie Danciger Trust, Edward F. Swinney Trust, Kansas City Assn. Trusts and Founds., Carl W. Allendoerfer Meml. Library Trust, Menninger Found., Topeka, Menorah Found. Med. Research; exec. com. Midwest Research Inst.; Hon. mem. exec. com. Yale Law Sch. Assn. Served with USN, 1918. Recipient Pro Meritis award Rockhurst Coll., 1960; Mr. Kansas City award, 1964; Brotherhood citation Nat. Conf. Christians and Jews, 1965; Law Day award U. Mo. at Kansas City, 1966; Chancellor's medallion U. Mo. at Kansas City, 1965; Civic Service award Hebrew Acad. Kansas City, 1975; award Kansas City Mental Health Found., 1976; Hall of Fame award Jr. Achievement, 1980. Hon. fellow Am. Coll. Hosp. Adminstrs.; mem. Am., Mo., Kansas City bar assns., Lawyers Assn. Kansas City, Assn. Bar City N.Y., Mo. Acad. Squires, Order of Coif, Delta Sigma Rho. Republican. Clubs: Yale (N.Y.C.); Kansas City (Kansas City), Oakwood Country (Kansas City); Reform (London, Eng.); Standard (Chgo.); Graduate (New Haven). Home: Kansas City, Mo. Died Oct. 21, 1981.

MAGDSICK, HENRY HERBERT, illuminating engr.; b. Van Dyne, Wis., Jan. 18, 1888; s. the Rev. G. F. and Minnie (Frevert) M.; B.S. in E.E., Univ. of Wis., 1910; m. Rachel Davis, 1917; 1 son, Charles Davis. With Lamp Dept., Gen. Elec. Co., 1910-53; dir. of coml. engring., National Lamp Works, 1919; exec. engr. Nela Park Engring. Dept., 1930-53; designed pioneer floodlighting installations including Woolworth Tower and Statue of Liberty; conducted 1st Internat. Lighting Mission, 1923; helped organize European lighting edn. centers, 1923; del. Internat. Commn. on Illumination, The Netherlands, 1939, Zurich, 1955. Fellow Illuminating Engring. Soc. (pres. 1929-30; gold medal 1952); member U.S. Nat. Com., Internat. Commn. on Illumination (pres. 1955-59), Cleveland Engring. Soc., Tau Beta Pi. Republican. Methodist. Directed basic studies in requirements of motor vehicle and street lighting and in the technology of architectural lighting; author of papers in these fields and that of light projection. Home: Cleve. †

MAGEE, ELIZABETH STEWART, social worker; b. Des Moines, Ia., June 29, 1889; d. William Archibald and Lizzie (Dysart) Magee; A.B., Oberlin Coll., 1911; A.M., Columbia, 1925. Teacher pub. schs., Altoona, Pa., 1911-16; asso. with Y.W.C.A.s, Denver, Colo., Detroit, Mich., and New York City, 1917-25; dir. summer sch. for workers in industry, U. of Wis., 1925; exec. sec., Consumers' League of Ohio, 1925-32, and from 1933; dir. Ohio Commn. on Unemployment Insurance, 1932-33; gen. sec., Nat. Consumers' League, from 1943. Delegate Women's Joint Congressional Com.; mem. advisory com., Protection of Young Workers of U.S. Children's Bur., Cleveland (Ohio) Urban League; member of the President's Commission on the Health Needs of Nation; mem. Gov.'s Com. on Migrant Labor (Ohio); mem. bd. Nat. council for Agrl. Life and Labor. Recipient special merit award U.S. Dept. Labor. Member Am. Assn. Social Workers. Club: Woman's City (Cleveland). Editor of report of Ohio Commn. on Unemployment Ins., 1933. Home: Cleveland, OH. †

MAGINN, EDWARD JOSEPH, clergyman; b. Glasgow, Scotland, Jan. 4, 1897; came to U.S., 1904, naturalized, 1917; s. Edward and Agnes (Keenan) M. Student, St. Mary's Acad., 1911-13, Holy Cross Coll., 1914-16, St. Joseph's Sem., Yonkers, N.Y., 1916-22. Ordained priest Roman Catholic Ch., 1922; chancellor Cath. Diocese of Albany, N.Y., 1924-36, vicar gen., 1936-84; pastor Ch. of St. Vincent de Paul, Albany, N.Y., 1944-72; vice chancellor Coll. St. Rose, Albany, 1936-84; Appointed Domestic Prelate by Pope Pius XI with title Rt. Rev. Monsignor, 1936; titular bishop of Curium and aux. bishop of Albany, N.Y., June 1957; consecrated bishop, Sept. 1957; apostolic adminstr. Diocese of Albany, 1966-69, aux. bishop, 1969-72, titular bishop of curium, 1957-84. Home: Albany, N.Y. Died Aug. 21, 1984.

MAHAN, BRUCE ELLIS, educator, author; b. Bedford, Ia., Nov. 25, 1890; s. Thomas Shelton and Luvira U. (Titus) M.; B.A., State U. of Ia., 1914, M.A., 1920, Ph.D., 1927; m. Edna M. Rohret, Apr. 22, 1914; children—Louis Frank, Thomas Patrick. Supt. schs., Cascade, Ia., 1914-18; asst. to prin. and head of dept. history Iowa City High Sch., 1918-23; asso. editor Ia. State Hist. Soc., 1923-29; lecturer in history, State U. of Ia., 1923-29, prof. and dir. extension div., 1929-47; exec. sec. State U. of Ia. Alumni Assn., 1935-47; dean Univ. of Iowa Extension division from 1947. Motion picture chmn. Nat. Congress Parents and Tchrs., 1946-52; dir. Motion Picture Previews, 1946-52. Mem. N.E.A., American Hist. Assn., Miss. Valley Hist. Assn., Ia. State Historical Society, Iowa State Teachers Association, National University Extension Association (pres. 1938-39), Phi Delta Kappa. Democrat. Catholic. Clubs: Rotary, Triangle. Author: Old Fort Crawford and the Frontier, 1926; Stories of Iowa for Boys and Girls (with R. A. Gallaher), 1929; also hist. booklets, extension bulls. Collaborator on Dictionary of Am. Biography, 1928. Adv. editor National Parent-Tchr. mag., 1952. Contbr. to hist. jours. Home: Iowa City, Ia. †

MAHAN, BRUCE HERBERT, chemist; b. New Britain, Conn., Aug. 17, 1930; s. Arthur Embury and Clara Blanche (Gray) M.; A.B., Harvard U., 1952, M.A., 1954, Ph.D., 1956. Mem. faculty U. Calif., Berkeley, from 1956, prof. chemistry, 1966-82, chmn. dept., 1968-71; vis. fellow joint Inst. Lab. Astrophysics, U. Colo., 1972. Sloan fellow, 1963-67; recipient Distinguished Tchr. award U. Calif., Berkeley, 1961. Fellow Am. Phys. Soc.; mem. Nat. Acad. Scis., Am. Chem. Soc. (award Calif. sect. 1968), Chem. Soc. London, AAAS. Author: Elementary Chemical Thermodynamics, 1964; College Chemistry, 1966; University Chemistry, 3d edit., 1975; also articles. Home: Berkeley, Calif. Died Oct. 12, 1982.

MAHLER, HENRY RALPH, educator, biochemist; b. Vienna, Austria, Nov. 12, 1921; came to U.S., 1938, naturalized, 1944; s. Hans and Elly (Schulhof) M.; m. Annemarie Ettinger, Feb. 2, 1948; children—Anthony J., Andrew M., Barbara A. A.B., Swarthmore Coll., 1943; Ph.D., U. Calif. at Berkeley, 1948. Sr. chemist Tex. Research Found., 1948-49; research asso. U. Wis., Madison, 1949, 50, asst. prof., 1950-55; faculty Ind. U., Bloomington, 1955-83, prof. chemistry, 1957-66, research prof., 1966-83; Rockefeller Found. Spl. fellow, vis. prof. U. Sao Paulo, Brazil, 1966; vis. investigator Centre de Génétique Moléculaire, Gif-sur-Yvette, France, 1962-63, 69-70, 77; vis. prof. U. Paris, 1970, University Coll., London, 1976, U. Vienna, 1977; vis. investigator, mem. corp. Marine Biol. Lab., Woods Hole, Mass., 1960-83. Mem. biochemistry study sect. NIH, 1967-71, mental retardation research tng. com., 1971-74, phys. biochemistry study sect., 1980-83; sci. adv. bd. Max Planck Inst. Exptl. Medicine, Goettingen, W. Ger., 1981-83. Author: (with E.H. Cordes) Biological Chemistry, 2d edit, 1971, Basic Biological Chemistry, 1968, also numerous articles; mem. editorial bd.: (with E.H. Cordes) Plasmid. Recipient Research Career award NIH, USPHS, 1962-83, NSF Travel award, 1955, 61. Fellow AAAS; mem. Am. Soc. Biol. Chemists, Biochem. Soc. (London, Eng.), Am. Chem. Soc., Biophys. Soc., N.Y. Acad. Scis., Soc. Cell Biology, Internat., Am. socs. neurochemistry, Sigma Xi. Research on isolation, modes action, biosynthesis respiratory enzymes, formation, integration in respiratory particles, control and mechanisms mitochondrial mutations, nucleic acids, structure, organization, modification and biosynthesis of macromolecules in synapses of the vertebrate central nervous system. Home: Bloomington, Ind. Died July 6, 1983.

MAHLSTEDT, WALTER, insurance executive; b. N.Y.C., Sept. 20, 1910; s. Frederick and Catherine (Buell) M.; m. Catherine Hoffman, June 5, 1937; children: Frederick, Robert. Student pub. schs., N.Y.C. With Tchrs. Ins. and Annuity Assn. Am., N.Y.C., 1929-79, exec. v.p. investments, 1967-75, trustee, 1970-79, chmn. finance com., 1972-79; dir. Heitman Realty Fund, 1975-76; mem. investment adv. panel Pension Benefit Guaranty Corp., 1975-80. Trustee, chmn. investment com. Devereux Found., Devon, Pa. Fellow Life Office Mgmt. Assn. Home: East Orleans, Mass.

MAHON, JAMES SAMUEL, lawyer; b. Eastland, Tex., Apr. 18, 1920; s. Ralph Dominic and Nora (Hefley) M.; B.B.A., U. Tex., 1943, J.D., 1948; m. Judy French, Jan. 20, 1962; children—Erin, Lorin, Kevin. Admitted to Tex. bar, 1948; asst. dist. atty., Dallas, 1949-50; atty. OPS, Dallas, 1951-53; pvt. practice, Dallas, 1953-84; partner firm Mahon, Fitzgerald & Winston, 1970-84; lectr. S.W. Inst. Grad. Studies in Banking, 1974-84. Served with AUS, 1942-46. Mem. Am., Tex., Dallas bar assns. Democrat. Methodist. Home: Dallas, Tex. Died Mar. 10, 1984; interred Sparkman-Hillcrest Meml. Park, Dallas, Tex.

MAHONEY, JAMES BONAPARTE, business exec.; b. Boston, Sept. 12, 1889; s. Patrick Francis and Delia (Gillegan) M.; student pub. schs. Boston; m. Margaret G. Donahue, June 25, 1916. With Stone & Webster, Inc., Boston, 1906-24, mgr. various ice properties, Charleston, S.C., 1924, pres., dir. properties, 1928; pres., dir. Woodstock Mfg. Co., Inc., Charleston, from 1931, So. Ice Co., City Ice Co.; dir. S.C. Electric & Gas Co., S.C. Nat. Bank, Ft. Sumter Hotel. Chmn. township commrs., Sullivan's Island, S.C. Chmn. bd. commrs. City Orphan Home (Charleston); mem. bd. govs. Charleston Municipal Airport; mem. exec. com. Charleston Development Bd. Mem. Nat. Assn. Ice Industries (pres., 1934-36), Charleston C. of C. (past pres.). Elk. Club: Rotary. Home: Charleston, S.C. †

MAHONEY, LOUIS A., investment banking; b. Lawrence, Mass., Nov. 16, 1888; s. John D. and Ellen E. (Regan) M.; graduate, Phillips Andover Acad., 1906; A.B. cum laude, Harvard Coll., 1910; unmarried. Vice president, director Halsey, Stuart & Company, Incorporated. Member Phi Beta Kappa. Democrat. Roman Catholic. Clubs: Harvard, Bond, University (New York), City Midday. Home: New York, N.Y. †

MAHONEY, TOM, (JOHN THOMAS MAHONEY) writer, editor; b. Dallas, Dec. 3, 1905; s. James Owen and Lacy (Braden) M.; m. Grace Dooley, 1930 (div.); 1 dau., Grace (Mrs. William Graves); m. Caroline Bird, Jan. 5, 1957; 1 son, John Thomas. B.J., U. Mo., 1927. With Dallas News, 1925-26; city editor El Paso Post, 1927-30; with UP, 1930-34, Buffalo Times, 1934-36; editor Mechanix Illus., 1936-37; asso. editor Look mag., 1937-39; with Gen. Electric Co., 1939-43; with overseas O.W.I., 1943; asso. editor Fortune mag., 1943-45; with Ben Sonnenberg, 1945-47, Young & Rubicam, Inc., 1948-56, Dudley-Anderson-Yutzy, 1956-68; Cons. ECA. Author: (with L. Sloane) The Great Merchants, 1974, The Merchants of Life, 1959, The Story of George Romney, 1960, (with George Schuster) The Longest Auto Race, 1966, (with Barry Sadler) I'm a Lucky One, 1967, FDR, The Great Collector, 1980; Contbr. (with Barry Sadler) articles to leading mags. Mem. Nat. Assn. Sci. Writers, Soc. Journalists and Authors, Authors League, P.E.N., Am. Philatelic Soc., Manuscript Soc., Am. Aviation Hist. Soc., AAAS, Psywar Soc., History of Sci. Soc., Dutchess County Hist. Soc., Sigma Delta Chi. Clubs: Overseas Press (Washington), Collectors (Washington), Nat. Press

(Washington); Baker Street Irregulars. Home: New York, N.Y. Died July 17, 1981.

MAIER, WILLIAM MORRIS, lawyer; b. Phila., June 11, 1909; s. Paul D.I. and Anna (Shinn) M.; m. Margaret Clarke Waterman, Aug. 14, 1943; children—James Hollingsworth, Anthony Morris. A.B., Haverford Coll., 1931, LL.D., 1972; LL.B., U. Pa., 1935. Bar: Pa. bar 1936. With Internat. Grenfell Assn., Labrador, 1931-32; partner firm Cahall & Maier, Phila., 1936-42, 45-48; with Am. Friends Service Com., Hawaii, 1942-45; asso. William Nelson West 3d, Phila., 1948-54, MacCoy, Evans and Lewis, 1954-82; Dir. Friends Fiduciary Corp. Trustee Phila. Friends Yearly Meeting, Westtown Sch.; bd. mgrs. Haverford Coll., 1938-82, treas., 1949-75; trustee Cheyney State Coll., 1941-68, chmn., 1947-68; treas. Ludwick Inst., 1956, Univ. Settlements, 1945-82, Friends Freedmens Assn., 1954-82; bd. mgrs. Am. Friends Service Com., 1953-69, Am. Sunday Sch. Union, 1937-69; trustee Internat. Grenfell Assn., 1948-82, vice chmn., 1963-67, chmn., 1967-75; pres. Friends Edn. Fund. Mem. Am., Pa., Phila. bar assns. Mem. Soc. of Friends. Clubs: Philadelphia Skating (Phila.), Rittenhouse (Phila.); Merion (Pa.) Cricket. Home: Bryn Mawr, Pa. Died Mar. 11, 1982.

MAINS, EDWIN BUTTERWORTH, botanist; b. Coldwater, Mich., Mar. 31, 1890; s. Benjamin William and Mary Ann (Butterworth) M.; student Mich. State Coll., 1909-11; A.B., U. of Mich., 1913, Ph.D., 1916; m. Mary Esther Elder, Aug. 16, 1917. Asst. botanist Agr. Expt. Sta., Purdue U., 1916-17, asso. botanist, 1917-30; asso. prof., Purdue U., 1925-30; prof. botany, U. of Mich., since 1930, acting dir. of Herbarium, 1930-31, dir. from 1931; agt. cereal investigations U.S. Bur. Plant Industry, 1918-30. Mem. scientific expedition British Honduras, 1936. Fellow A.A.A.S., Ind. Acad. Science; mem. Bot. Soc. America, Am. Bryol. Soc., Am. Phytopathological Soc., Am. Mycol. Soc. (pres. 1942), Torrey Botanical Club, Botanical Society of Cal., Michigan Academy Science, Sigma Xi. Republican. Contbr. to Plant Rusts, by J. C. Arthur and others, 1929; also many articles to bot. jours. Home: Ann Arbor, Mich. †

MAITLAND, JAMES W(ILLIAM), investment exec.; b. N.Y.C., Apr. 7, 1890; s. Thomas A. and Helen (Van Voorhis) M.; student Cloyne Sch., Holbrook School; Doctor of Philosophy, Yale, 1911; m. Sylvia Wigglesworth, February 16, 1927; children—Helen (Mrs. Robert F. Corroon), Sylvia (Mrs. Martin McG. Horner), Andree (Mrs. Howard B. Deane). Supt. Tuohy Bros., 1913-15, Flynn O'Rourke, 1916; with Turnes Constrn. Co., 1917-21, Bonbright & Co., investment bankers, 1921-35; exec. com., dir. Me. Central Railroad; dir. Portland Terminal Co.; trustee N.Y. Savs. Bank. Served to capt. 11th C.E. and 1st Army Staff, France, 1917-19. Clubs: Union (N.Y.C.); Rockaway Hunting (Lawrence, L.I.); Southside's Sportsman (L.I.). Home: Lawrence, L.I. †

MAKEN, NORMAN J(OHN) O(SWALD), diplomat; b. Petersham, New South Wales, March 31, 1889; s. John Hulme and Elizabeth (Yates) M.; LL.D. (honoris causa), U. of Syracuse, Ohio Wesleyan U., 1947; m. Ruby Florence Jennings, Nov. 16, 1912; children—Harry Arnold, Lloyd John. Rep. South Australian Electorate of Hindmarsh in Parliament as mem. Labor Party, 1919-45 (temp. chmn. coms., 1923-29, speaker Ho. of Reps., 1929-31); minister, navy and munitions, 1941-46, aircraft prodn., 1945-46; ambassador to U.S. since 1946. Mem. Australian delegation to Gen. Assembly, first pres. Security Council, 1946, also pres., 1947; leader Australian delegation to I.L.O. Conf., 1948; Australian gov. Internat. Bank for Reconstruction and Development and Internat. Monetary Fund, 1948; leader Australian delegation to F.A.O., 1949-50. Methodist. Author: A Progressive Democracy, 1917. Home: Washington, D.C. †

MALCOLM, OLA POWELL, home economist; b. Plainview, Tex., Dec. 19, 1889; d. Robert F. and Laura (Tisdel) Powell; ed. Friends' Central Sch., Phila.; domestic science course State Coll., Columbus, Miss.; grad. Drexel Inst., Phila., 1913; m. Dr. Robert Cummings Malcolm, Oct. 6, 1925. Assisted father in directing vacant lot gardening in Phila. and Cleveland; dir. domestic science dept., Sch. of Organic Edn., Fairhope, Ala., 1910-11; teacher domestic science and sch. gardens, summer schs., Cleveland, 1911, 12; asst. state agt. in charge extension work for women and girls, La. State U., 1913, 14; with U.S. Dept. of Agr. from 1914, in charge home demonstration work in 15 Southern states and Puerto Rico, with title of senior home economist; head of the extension's Food Production and Food Conservation Program from 1943. Presbyterian. Author: (book) Successful Canning and Preserving, 1917; home economics bulletins, U.S. Department Agriculture. Sent to France, summer 1921, to direct unit of workers on food preservation, under auspices French minister agr. and Am. Com. for Devastated France; also sent by U.S. Dept. Agr., to Spain and Italy, to study methods used in preserving and utilizing Spanish pimientos and other fruits and vegetable products and to secure other information to use in home demonstration work; sent again to France, 1922, for purpose of organizing and establishing home demonstration work in France. Assisted many yrs. planning study and travel for agts. of foreign governments sent to U.S. to study home demonstration work. Mem. Epsilon Sigma Phi. Home: Bethesda, Md. †

MALIK, ADAM, foreign minister Indonesia; b. 1917. Ambassador of Indonesia to USSR, 1959-63; minister of trade, 1963-66, of fgn. affairs, 1966-82. Died Sept. 5, 1984.

MALLETT, JANE DAWSON, actress, script writer; b. London, Ont., Can., Apr. 18, 1899; d. Clifford Benjamin and Emily Isabel (Daly) Keenleyside; m. Frederick John Mallett, Apr. 14, 1925; 1 son, John Christopher Aldworth. B.A., Victoria Coll., U. Toronto, 1921. Regular mem. Empire Stock Co., Toronto, 1927-28. Appeared in first radio plays; first Trans Can. Network series, 1930; writer, producer, actress satirical rev., Town Tonics, 1934-44, troop shows, 1939-45, Spring Thaw rev. and dramas, 1944-55; began filmwork, 1951; appeared on CBC-TV, from 1952; founder, Jane Mallett Assocs. Ltd., 1955. Active mem. South Rosedale Ratepayers Assn.; mem. Actors Fund of Can. Decorated Order of Can.; recipient John Drainie award for distinguished contbn. to broadcasting, 1976. Mem. Assn. Can. TV and Radio Artists (life mem., past exec. councillor), Can. Actors Equity (life mem., past councillor). Club: Toronto Heliconian. Home: Toronto Ont., Can. Died Apr. 14, 1984.

MALLON, HENRY NEIL, industrial executive; b. Cincinnati, O., Jan. 11, 1805; s. Guy Ward and Hannah (Neil) M.; student Taft Sch., Watertown, Conn., 1909-13; A.B., Yale, 1917; m. Anne Wrightson Thayer; children —Stephen C. Thayer, Jr., Francis W. Thayer, Elise Thayer. With U.S. Can Co., Cincinnati, as factory worker, later gen. mgr. and dir., 1920-29; pres., gen. mgr. Dresser Industries, Inc., Dallas, and predecessor cos., 1929-58, now chmn. executive com., dir.; dir. nummerous subsidiaries in U.S., Canada, South and Cent. Am., Europe, Gulf-Southwest Capital Corporation, Producing Properties, Inc., Wallas Investments. Mem. Com. Alliance for Progress, Dept. Def. Trustee Southwest Research Inst., Southwestern Legal Found. adv. com. So. Meth. U. Grad. Research Center; founder, dir. Dallas Council Fgn. Affairs; mem. Dallas Citizens Council; member board of Directors Greater Dallas Planning Council. Enlisted U.S. Army, 1917; capt. 323 F.A.; maj. 11th Arty. Brigade, overseas. France. Decorated Chevalier of Order of Crown (Belgium). Episcopalian. Clubs: Cloud, Sky, Yale, Pinnacle (N.Y.C.); Tex., Petroleum, City, Dallas, Brook Hollow Golf, Chapparal, Kiwanis (Dallas); Metropolitan (Washington). Home: Farmers Branch, Tex. Died Mar. 1, 1983.

MALLORY, VIRGIL S(AMPSON), mathematics; b. Union City, N.J., Aug. 14, 1888; s. Eugene Lester and Adele May (Reeder) M.; A.B., Columbia U., 1914, A.M., 1919, Ph.D., 1939; m. Lauris Baum, Sept. 22, 1914; children—Ruth Adele, Virgil Standish. Instr. in mathematics, Wright Oral Sch., N.Y. City, 1908-11; asst. prin. high sch., Dumont, N.J., 1914-18; head of math. dept., high sch., East Orange, N.J., 1918-28; also instr., extension courses, Columbia, 1918-27, spl. lecturer, 1918-29; asso. prof. mathematics, State Teachers Coll., Montclair, N.J., 1928-34; prof. and head math. dept. 1934-54, prof. emeritus, from 1954. Past mem. various coms. and commns. on study of mathematics. Fellow A.A.A.S.; mem. nat., state, and local ednl. and math. socs., past officer several. Presbyterian. Author and co-author many textbooks, manuals and tests in field of mathematics, from 1929. Contbr. to profl. publs.; also to Ency. Brit., Jr., 1942. Home: Montclair, N.J. †

MALONE, JOSEPH LAWRENCE, linguist; b. N.Y.C., July 2, 1937; s. Joseph Timothy and Katherine Veronica (O'Connor) M.; m. Pamela Joan Altfeld, Jan. 31, 1964; children: Joseph Timothy, II, Otis Taig. B.A., U. Calif., Berkeley, 1963, Ph.D., 1967. Mem. faculty Barnard Coll., N.Y.C., from 1967, prof. linguistics, from 1975, chmn. dept., from 1967; part-time vis. lectr. U. Pa., spring and fall 1970; linguistics adviser Grolier Pub. Co.; also editor, contbr. co. Acad. Am. Ency. Author articles in field. Served with U.S. Army, 1957-60. Grad. fellow U. Calif., Berkeley, 1965-66; Grad. fellow Am. Council Learned Socs., 1966-67. Mem. Linguistics Soc. Am., Am. Oriental Soc., AAUP, N. Am. Conf. Afro-Asiatic Linguistics, Phi Beta Kappa. Democrat. Address: Leonia, NJ.

MALONE, RICHARD HENRY, hospital administrator; b. Logansport, La., June 15, 1925; s. James Drew and Mary Amanda (Bryant) M.; m. Betty Jane Tucker, Feb. 12, 1950; children—Richard, Tucker, Jay, Drew. B.S. in Chemistry, La. State U.; M.B.A., U. Chgo., 1958. Asst. adminstr. Baton Rouge Gen. Hosp., 1952-58; adminstr. Jefferson Davis Meml. Hosp., Natchez, Miss., 1958-64; pres., chief exec. officer Hinds Gen. Hosp., Jackson, Miss., 1964-74; asso. exec. dir. Baylor U. Med. Center, 1974-77; exec. dir. Baptist Med. Center, Jacksonville, Fla., 1977-84. Contbr. articles to trade jours. Bd. dirs. Estes Park Inst., Englewood, Calif.; bd. dirs. Commn. on Profl. and Hosp. Activities, Ann Arbor, Mich. Served with USAAF, 1943-45, ETO. Fellow Am. Coll. Hosp. Adminstrs.; mem. Am. Hosp. Assn., Fla. Hosp. Assn., Am. Protestant Hosp. Assn. Baptist. Club: Rotary. Home: Jacksonville, Fla. Died Jan. 6, 1984.

MALONE, RICHARD SANKEY, journalist, publisher; b. Owen Sound, Ont., Can., Sept. 18, 1909; s. Willard Park and Mildred Villiers (Sankey) M.; m. Helen Mary Cook, Sept. 9, 1936; children: Robert Nesbit, Richard Cook, Deirdre Louise; m. Ioana Soutzo, 1981. Student, Bishop Ridley Coll., St. Catherines, Can., 1928. With Toronto Star, 1928-30, Regina Leader-Post, 1930-36, Saskatoon Star-Phoenix, 1933; pub. Winnipeg Free Press, 1960-74; publisher Globe & Mail, Toronto, 1974-78; chmn. F.P. Publs. Ltd., 1959-79; founder Canadian Army newspaper, Maple Leaf, 1941; hon. mgr. Imperial Press Conf., 1950. Author: Missing From the Record, 1947, A Portrait of War, 1983. Bd. dirs. Dafoe Found., Max Bell Found. Served to brig. Canadian Army, 1939-45. Decorated Order Brit. Empire. Mem. Internat. Inst. Strategic Studies, Winnipeg C. of C. (pres. 1956-57). Mem. Ch. of Eng. Clubs: Toronto (Toronto), York (Toronto), Royal Can. Mil. Inst. (Toronto). Home: Toronto, Ont., Can. Died June 24, 1985.

MALONEY, FRANK EDWARD, legal educator; b. Niagara Falls, N.Y., Mar. 27, 1918; s. Frank E. and Florence (Bielman) M.; B.A., U. Toronto (Can.), 1938, grad. student philosophy, 1938-39; LL.B., U. Fla., 1942; m. Lucille Tinker, Feb. 20, 1943; children—Frank Edward, Jo Ann, Elizabeth. Admitted to Fla. bar, 1942, also Supreme Ct. U.S.; with firm Jordan, Lazonby & Dell, Gainesville, Fla., 1942; asso. prof. law U. Fla., 1946- 50, prof. law, 1950-58, acting dean Law Sch., 1958-59, dean Law Sch., 1959-70, dean emeritus, 1970-80, prof. law, from 1959, dir. Eastern Water Law Center, from 1965; grad. fellow Sch. Law, Columbia, 1950-51; vis. prof. NYU Law Sch., 1957-58, Vanderbilt Law Sch., 1970-71, George Washington Law Center, summers 1968, 69, Tex. Tech. U., summer 1971; cons. internat. water law problems U.S. Dept. State. Served to maj. USAAF, 1942-46; CBI; col. USAF Res. ret. Fellow Am. Bar Found.; mem. Am. Law Inst., Am. Bar Assn., Fla. Bar, Assn. Am. Law Schs. (chmn. com. fed. legislation 1964-70), Internat. Assn. Water Law, U. Fla. Law Center Assn. (vice chmn. 1961-70), Bar Assn. 8th Jud. Circuit Fla., Nat. Conf. Bar Examiners (chmn. torts com. multistate bar exam.), Fla. Soc. Profl. Land Surveyors (hon. life), Phi Beta Kappa, Order of Coif, Fla. Blue Key, Phi Kappa Phi, Phi Alpha Delta, Pi Kappa Phi. Rotarian. Co-author: Water Law and Adminstration, 1968; A Model Water Code, 1972; drafted Fla. Water Resources Acts, 1957, 72, Tenn. Water Quality Act, 1971. Contbr. numerous articles to profl. jours. Home: Gainesville, Fla. Died 1980.

MALTBY, DAVID CAMPBELL, banker; b. Guelph, Ont., Can., Mar. 16, 1938; s. John Albert and Flora Irene (Page) M.; m. Clara Elizabeth Lowes, Aug. 8, 1958; children—Kirk, Ward, Paul. Grad., Guelph Collegiate Vocat. Inst. With Royal Bank Can., from 1954, exec. officer charge comml. mktg., 1974-79; v.p. Royal Bank Can. (Alta. dist.), Calgary, from 1979. Clubs: National (Toronto, Ont.); Calgary Petroleum. Home: Calgary AB Canada.

MALTZ, ALBERT, author; b. Bklyn., Oct. 28, 1908; s. Bernard and Lena (Sherry) M.; m. Margaret Larkin, 1937 (div. 1963); children: Peter, Katherine; m. Rosemary Wylde, 1964 (dec. 1968); m. Esther Engelberg, 1969. A.B., Columbia U., 1930; student, Yale U. Sch. Drama, 1930-32. Instr. Playwrighting Center, Sch. Adult Edn., N.Y.U., 1937-41; instr. playwriting Writers Conf. Rocky Mountains, 1939, 40; mem. exec. bd. Theatre Union, 1933-37; former arbitrator Am. Arbitration Soc.; editor Equality, 1939, 1940. Author: (with George Sklar) play Merry Go Round, 1932; plays Peace on Earth, 1933, Black Pit, 1935; short stories The Way Things Are, 1938, Afternoon in the Jungle, 1971; novels The Underground Stream, 1940, The Cross and The Arrow, 1944, The Journey of Simon McKeever, 1949, A Long Day in a Short Life, 1957, A Tale of One January, 1966; essays The Citizen Writer, 1950; films This Gun for Hire, 1942, Destination Tokyo, 1943, Pride of the Marines, 1945, The House I Live In (spl. award Acad. Motion Picture Arts and Scis.), The Naked City, 1948, Two Mules for Sister Sara, 1970; Contbr. to: magazines including Scholastic, New Yorker, So. Rev., Time & Tide, Scribner's, Harper's, New Masses; Short stories have appeared in Best Short Stories, 1936, 39, 41, O'Henry Memorial Award Prize Stories (1st award), 1938, 41, Best American Short Stories, 1914-39; and other anthologies. Mem. Authors League Am. (mem. council 1936-41), Phi Beta Kappa. Oral history housed in Dept. Spl. Collections, Research Library, UCLA Died Apr. 26, 1985.

MAMBERT, STEPHEN BABCOCK, business executive; b. Kingston, N.Y., July 31, 1887; s. Albert H. (M.D.) and Fannie (Derrich) M.; C.E., Cornell, 1907; m. Carrie J. Mambert, Sept. 1, 1911; 1 dau., Gladys Madelaine. Began with Westinghouse Electric & Mfg. Co., 1907; with McArthur Bros.-Winston & Co. (Ashokan Reservoir, Bd. of Water Supply City of New York), 1908-10; Nat. Cloak & Suit Co., 1910-12; Consolidated Gas and New York Edison cos., 1912-13; actively identified with Thomas A. Edison, 1913-24; now alone in business. Home: South Orange, N.J. †

MANAHAN, JOHN LEVI, univ. prof.; b. Logan County, O., Feb. 12, 1887; s. William Henry and Amanda (Pickering) M.; B.S., Ohio Northern U., 1912; A.M., Harvard Univ., 1914, Ph.D., 1918; m. Lucile Becker, Sept. 1, 1917; 1 son, John Eacott. Teacher rural schs., Hardin County, O., 1908-10; asst. in govt., Harvard U., 1913-14; asst. in edn., Radcliffe Coll., 1914-15; prof. history of edn., Miami U., 1915-16; state high sch. insp., Ohio, 1915-16; prof. ednl. administration, U. of Va., from 1916, dean Dept. of Education, 1920-49, professor emeritus, from 1957; professor educational administration, Ohio State U., summers, 1922-23. Lt. Sanitary Corps, U.S. Army, July 1918-Mar. 1919; chief ednl. service, Gen. Hosp. No. 17, Markleton, Pa., and No. 19, Oteen, N.C. Mem. N.E.A.,

Nat. Soc. for Study of Edn., Assn. Coll. Teachers of Edn., Assn. Deans Dept. of Edn. of State Univs. and Land Grant Colleges, Va. Acad. Science, Assn. of Va. Colls., Va. Education Association, Phi Delta Kappa, Sigma Phi Epsilon. Democrat. Presbyterian. Clubs: Colonnade, Farmington Country. Home: Scottsville, Va. †

MANAHAN, STEWART ALLAN, naval officer; b. Chicago, Ill., Mar. 1, 1887; s. Frank James and Julia May (Pinkney) M.; B.S., U.S. Naval Acad., 1909; m. Alice Herbert McCauley, Oct. 25, 1916; 1 dau., Alice Herbert. Commd. ensign, U.S. Navy, 1911, and advanced through grades to commodore, 1945; service on naval vessels, Nebraska, Celtic, Flusser, Tonopah, Severn (comdg. 1913-15), Arkansas, Connecticut, Lenape (exec. officer), and Drayton, 1909-19; stationed at Navy Yard, Charleston, S.C., 1915-17; fleet radio officer and aide on staff of Admiral Hugh Rodman, Comdr. in Chief Pacific Fleet, 1919-21; with radio div., Bur. of Engring., Navy Dept., Washington, D.C., 1921-23, 1928-29 and 1931-33; in command destroyers Parrott, 1923-25, Humphreys, 1929-30; Asiatic communication officer and mem. Philippines Radio Bd., 1925-27; 1st lt. cruiser San Francisco, 1933-34; exec. officer light cruiser Marblehead, 1934-36; sub-chief and sec., U.S. Naval Mission to Brazil, 1936-38; comdr. cruiser Memphis, 1939-40; marine supt., Panama Canal, 1940-46. Awarded Legion of Merit, Victory medal, Navy Expeditionary medal, Defense medal, Am. Area medal; Order of Leopold (Belgium); Grand Officer, Order of Vasco Nuñez De Balboa (Panama); Comdr. Order of the Southern Cross (Brazil). Clubs: Army and Navy, Army and Navy Country (Washington); Yacht (New York). Home: Washington, D.C. †

MANATOS, MIKE, retired corporate executive; b. Gunn, Wyo., Aug. 30, 1914; s. Nick and Anna (Anezakis) M.; B.S., Strayer's Coll., 1941; student George Washington U.; m. Dorothy Varanakis, July 3, 1938; children—Ann (Mrs. George Hatsis), Andrew, Kathleen (Mrs. Bruce Shand). Adminstrv. aide U.S. Senator Schwartz Wyo., 1937-43, U.S. Senator O'Mahoney Wyo., 1943-52; administrv. asst. to U.S. Senators Hunt, O'Mahoney and Hickey, all Wyo., 1953-61; adminstrv. asst. to Pres. Kennedy, 1961-63, Pres. Johnson, 1963-69; dir. for nat. govt. relations Procter & Gamble, Washington, 1969-79; ret. 1979. Democrat. Home: Sumner, Md. Died May 27, 1983; interred Gate of Heaven Cemetery, Silver Spring, Md.

MANCHESTER, ROBERT ASA, II, lawyer; b. Canfield, Ohio, Dec. 14, 1901; s. Josiah Isaac and Gertrude (Stitle) M.; m. Mary Barber, Feb. 6, 1931; children—Robert Asa III, James Russell. A.B., U. Mich., 1925, LL.B., H1J.D., 1927. Bar: Ohio bar 1927. Practiced law, Youngstown; partner Harrington, Huxley & Smith, from 1927; solicitor, Canfield, Ohio, 1938-41; Sec. dir. Research Cons.; formerly treas., dir. Manchester Co. Mem. Mahoning County Bd. Health, 1932-39, Mahoning County Charter Commn., 1934-35; mem. exec. bd. Mahoning Valley council Boy Scouts Am., 1934-71, pres., 1948-54; mem. exec. bd. region IV Nat. council, 1948-73, vice chmn., 1949-54; mem. Mahoning County Bd. Edn., 1950-55, pres., 1950-55; mem. Mahoning County chpt. Nat. Found., 1932-74, pres., 1952-65; mem. Ohio Bd. Edn., 1956-67, pres., 1956-57; mem. exec. bd. Nat. Assn. State Bds. Edn., 1957-65, pres., 1961-63, chmn., 1963-65; pres. Youngstown Area Council Chs., 1964-66, Mahoning County Soc. for Crippled Children and Adults, 1972-74; bd. dirs. Ohio Soc. Crippled Children and Adults, 1973-82, Mayor, Canfield, 1928-37. Recipient Silver Beaver award Boy Scouts Am., 1941, Silver Antelope award, 1949, disting. Eagle Scout award, 1976; named Man of Yr. Orgn. Protestant Men, 1964. Mem. Am., Ohio, Mahoning and Columbiana County bar assns., Youngstown C. of C. (chmn. youth com. 1957-65), Orgn. Protestant Men (pres. 1949), Pi Kappa Alpha, Delta Theta Phi. Presbyn. Clubs: Mason (33 deg.), Rotary International (pres. 1976-77). Home: Canfield, Ohio. Died Feb. 11, 1982.

MANDEL, ARCH, social worker; b. Hungary, July 17, 1888; s. Morris and Fanny (Goldberg) M.; brought to U.S., 1891; A.B., Coll. City of New York, 1909; grad. Training Sch. for Pub. Service of New York Bur. Municipal Research, 1912; m. Almedia Isabel Beatty, Nov. 28, 1916; 1 dau., Sarah Beatty. Teacher pub. schs., N.Y. City, 1910; spl. agt., U.S. Tariff Bd., 1911; with Training Sch. for Pub. Service, 1912; with New York Globe, 1913, Dayton (O.) Bur. Municipal Research, 1913-16; asst. dir. Detroit Bur. Governmental Research, 1916-23; dir. Dayton Research Assn., 1923-26; exec. sec. Dayton Bur. of Community Service, 1926-38; on leave, Jan. 1934-June 1935, as field representative Federal Emergency Relief Adminstrn. Asst. exec. dir. The Greater New York Fund, 1938-42; exec. dir. Russian War Relief, Inc., 1942-43; asso. exec. dir. Community Chests and Councils of Am., Inc., 1943-54; exec. sec. Nat. Com. on Community Founds.; now exec. sec. Mass. Community Orgn. Service. Mem. Nat. Assn. Social Workers, Nat. Conf. Social Work (treas. from 1937), Ohio Welfare Conf. (pres. 1938), Pi Gamma Mu. Author articles and monographs on profl. topics. Home: Boston. †

MANGHUM, MASON, lawyer; b. Prince George Co., Md., Apr. 12, 1890; s. Thomas Henry and Leon May (Lowe) M.; student Columbian (now George Washington) Univ., 1906-07, Georgetown Univ., 1908-11; m. Mildred Josselyn, of Portland, Ore. Admitted to Ore. bar, 1911, and practiced in Ore., Va. and D.C.; atty. for Interstate Commerce Commn., Washington, D.C., 1915-18; mem. New Eng. Dist. Freight Traffic Com. of R.R. Administration, 1919-20; commerce council Va. State Corpn. Commn., 1920-26; chmn. Va. State NRA Bd., 1933-35; chmn. regional NRA Bd. for Md., Va., N.C. and D.C.; planned NRA reemployment campaign machine for Gen. Hugh S. Johnson's office; chmn. Va. State Transportation and Utility Advisory Commn. Pres. Citizens Home Insurance Co., Va. Pres. Va. Turkey Breeders Assn. Clubs: Country of Va., Deep Run Hunt, etc.†

MANHART, GEORGE BORN, educator; b. Phila., June 14, 1890; s. Frank P. and Catharine (Born) M.; A.B., Susquehanna U., Selinsgrove, Pa., 1910; A.M., U. Pa., 1914, Ph.D., 1923; m. Florence M. Heritage, June 14, 1923; children—Catharine (Mrs. Ervan E. Walton), Joseph II. Prin. high sch., Strawberry Ridge, Pa., 1910-11; instr. history Baker U., 1914-17, asst. prof., 1917-19; instr. history DePauw U., 1919-20, asst. prof., 1920-23, asso. prof., 1923-26, prof., from 1926, acting dean, 1947-48; faculty summer schs. Susquehanna U., 1924, 1928, Ind. U., 1929-30, 34, Miami U., 1931. Served with A.L.A. War Service, 1918-19; from 2d lt. to capt. USAAF, 1943-46. Mem. Am. Hist. Assn., Ind. Hist. Soc. Presbyn. Author: Alliance and Entente, 1932, others. Contbr. year book World Scope Ency. from 1948; contbr. book revs. profl. jours. Home: Greencastle, Ind. †

MANHEIM, EDWARD, advt. co. exec.; b. Cleve., Jan. 12, 1926; s. Harry Sol and Belle (Speiser) M.; m. Suzanne Ellen Uberstine, Mar. 20, 1949; 1 son, Kenneth L. B.A., Northwestern U., 1948. Vice pres. sales L. Manheim Fish Co., Cleve., 1948-59; v.p. Howard Marks Advt., Cleve., 1959-65; v.p. Marcus Advt., Cleve., 1965-72, exec. v.p., 1972-79; pres. Manheim Advt., Inc., from 1979; mem. pub. relations bd. Fedn. for Community Planning; keynote speaker Am. Drycleaners Conv., 1967. (Recipient Gold medal for Best of Show TV Spot 1966, Drycleaning Advt. awards (9), internat. broadcasting award 1970, 71, outstanding achievement award Nat. Acad. TV Arts and Scis. 1971, CLIO Radio award 1976, Emmy award 1976, N.Y. Film Festival award 1979); Columnist: Am. Dry Cleaner, 1966-67. Bd. dirs. Bellefaire Foster Parents Program. Mem. Am. Advt. Fedn. (recipient 48 5th dist. awards), Cleve. Advt. Club. Jewish. Home: Cleveland, OH.

MANION, CLARENCE E., lawyer; b. Henderson, Ky., July 7, 1896; s. Edward and Elizabeth (Carroll) M.; m. Virginia O'Brien, Aug. 3, 1936; children—Marilyn, Carolyn, Daniel, Diana, Christopher. A.B., St. Mary's (Ky.) Coll., 1915; A.M., Ph.M., Cath. U. Am., 1917; J.D., Notre Dame U., 1922; J.U.D., Boston U., 1942. Bar: Ind. bar 1922. Tchr. history and govt. U. Notre Dame, 1919; practice in, Evansville, until 1925; prof. constl. law U. Notre Dame, 1925-52; dean U. Notre Dame (Coll. Law), 1941-52; mem. firm Doran, Manion, Boynton, Kamm & Esmont, South Bend; dir. Manion Forum radio network, St. Joseph Bank & Trust Co., South Bend. Author: American History, 1926, What Price Prohibition, 1927, Liberty and the Police Power, 1928, Catholics in Our Country's Story, 1929, Lessons in Liberty, 1939, Cases and Materials on the Law of the Air, 1950, The Key to Peace; Let's Face It, 1956, The Conservative American, 1964, Cancer in the Constitution, 1972. Pres. Commn. on Intergovtl. Relations.; Mem. Ind. Bd. Edn., 1956-60. Recipient 3d ann. Notre Dame Faculty award, 1950; Nat. Gold Medal award D.A.R., 1974; Nat. Man of Year award Am. Religious Town Hall Meeting, Inc., 1979. Mem. Am., Ind., St. Joseph County bar assns., Am. Legion. Clubs: K.C, Indianapolis Athletic. Home: South Bend, Ind. Died July 28, 1979.

MANLEY, JOHN, farming; b. Halls Summit, Kan., Apr. 14, 1888; s. Edwin and Lottie (Dudley) M.; grad. University Prep. Sch., Tonkawa, Okla., 1908; studied medicine, U. of Okla., 1909-10; m. Arlie B. Crabb, of Liberty, Mo., May 12, 1912 (died Apr. 2, 1921); children—Jessie J., Harvey A.; m. 2d, Bertha Bittle, of Covington, Okla., Apr. 5, 1922. Engaged in farming, Kay Co., Okla, 1910-21; sec.-treas. orgn. com. Okla. Wheat Growers' Assn., 1921-26, gen. mgr. same assn, and Okla. Wheat Pool Elevator Corpn. from 1926; gen. mgr. Tex. Wheat Growers' Assn. from 1929; mgr. Farmers National Grain Corpn. from 1930; dir. Panhandle Farms, Inc. Mem. Com. of 16 to organize Farmers' Nat. Grain Corpn. Chmn. Nat. Com. U.S. Wheat Pools; mem. Internat. Com. of Wheat Pools. Democrat. Methodist. Mason (32 degree, Shriner). Home: Enid, Okla. †

MANLEY, LOUIS KENNETH, dean Sch. of Business Administration, U. of Pittsburgh; b. East Liverpool, O., Jan. 2, 1888; s. Rev. Jason Brookes and Jane (Gardner) M.; grad. high sch., East Liverpool, 1905; A.B., Ohio Wesleyan University, 1908; Ph.D., University of Pittsburgh, 1918; m. Sarah Brown Mitchell, June 27, 1912; children—Barbara Mitchell (dec.), Sarah Jane, David Mitchell. Teacher secondary schs., and grad. student until 1918; with University of Pittsburgh from 1918, successively instr. polit. science, asst. prof., prof. from 1921, dean sch. of Business Administration and Bureau of Business Research from 1923. Dir. war issues course, S.A.T.C., U. of Pittsburgh, 1918; citizenship sec. Civic Club of Allegheny Co., 1920-22; press credentials to Washington Conf. on Limitation of Armament, 1921; del. of U.S. to Internat. Congress for Commercial Edn., Amsterdam, Holland, Sept. 1929. Mem. Am. Economic Assn., Am. Polit. Science Assn., Am. Acad. Polit. and Social Science, Am. Assn. Univ. Profs. (hon.), Phi Kappa Psi, Delta Mu Delta, Beta Gamma Sigma, Jesters. Methodist. Clubs: Faculty, Junta, University. Author: (pamphlet) Outline of the Covenant of the League of Nations, 1920; (with A.B. Wright) Good Citizenship, 1921. Home: Pittsburgh, Pa. †

MANN, DONALD NATHANIEL, radio exec.; b. Chgo., Dec. 15, 1920; s. Henry J. and Rose (Bonner) M.; m. Rhoda Fiener, Nov. 8, 1952; children—Gary Kevin, Eric Scott, Holly Jada. B.S., Northwestern U., 1943; M.A., Columbia U., 1946; J.D., John Marshall Law Sch., 1948. Program dir., asst. communications mgr. KWWL, Waterloo, Iowa, 1948-49; gen. mgr. communications mgr. WKNK, Muskegon, Mich., 1949-51; account exec. WBBM Radio & TV CBS, Chgo., 1951-54; gen. mgr. WOKY-TV, Milw., 1954; mgr. spl. projects, account exec. WBBM Radio, 1954-85; prof. communications Columbia Coll., Chgo., 1967; dir. Cosmopolitan Nat. Bank, Chgo.; pres. Am. Coll. Radio Arts, Crafts and Scis., Chgo., 1961-85. Co-author: Pvt. Droop Has Lost the War, 1944; author: History of Sault St. Marie, 1942, How to Become Your Company's Top Salesman thru Showmanship. Asst. chmn. communications div. Combined Jewish Appeal, Chgo., 1959-69; mem. Chgo. Crime Commn., 1974; dir. Niles Twp. (Ill.) Community Concerts, 1961-85; co-chmn. Red Feather drive, Chgo., 1960; pres. Timber Ridge Home Owners, Skokie, Ill., 1957-60; mem. Chgo. Council Fgn. Relations, 1965-85; pres. Bus. and Profl. Men City of Hope, Chgo., 1961; chmn. Bike-A-Thon, Am. Diabetes Assn.; pres. Skokie Caucus Party, 1957-64; master Chancery Village Ct. of Skokie, 1962; bd. dirs. Edward T. Lee Found., 1978, Easter Seal Soc., 1978; chmn. Sportsman of Yr. award, 1978; police and fire commr., Skokie, 1965; pres. Deere Park, 1970-85; trustee, chmn. 50th Ann. com. Mt. Sinai Hosp.; trustee Columbia Coll., John Marshall Law Sch., Chgo. chpt. Am. Diabetes Assn. Served with AUS, 1942-46. Recipient Distinguished Alumni award John Marshall Law Sch., 1968; named Radio Man of Year Am. Coll. Radio, 1964, Most Successful Media Person, 1972. Mem. Am., Ill., 7th Fed. Dist., Chgo. bar assns., Am. Fedn. Musicians, Am. Judicature Soc., Sales Exec. Club, Alpha Sigma Iota, Grocery Sales Mfg. Execs., John Marshall Alumni Assn. (pres. 1971-73), Decalogue Soc., Am. Legion, Jewish War Vets., Sales Exec. Club, Merchandising Exec. Club. Democrat. Jewish (trustee temple). Clubs: B'nai B'rith, Elk; Standard (Chgo.), Variety (Chgo.). Home: Highland Park, Ill. Died Jan. 13, 1985.

MANN, KARL MOWRY, publisher; b. Milw., Nov. 27, 1888; s. Charles L. and Mary B. (Mowry) M.; student Milw. Acad.; B.A., U. Wis., 1911; m. Louise Virginia Dickbrader, Mar. 1, 1930; children—Cynthia, Marcia, Roger Mowry. With United Publishers Corp., N.Y.C., 1912-18; advt. mgr. Fire and Water Engring., 1920-22, v.p., 1922-25; pres. Case-Shepperd-Mann Pub. Corp., N.Y.C., 1925-55; with Case-Shepperd-Mann dept., Reuben H. Donnelley Corp., from 1955; dir. Asso. Bus. Publs., from 1951; v.p., dir. Lakeside Pub. Co., N.Y.C., 1926-52. Rep. Am. Bus. Press, Internat. Advt. Conf., London, Eng., 1952; mem. nat. alumni bd. U. Wis., 1925-26. Mem. spl. gift com. Community Chest, A.R.C.; chmn. print com. Montclair (N.J.) Art Mus. Mem. Water Works Mfrs. Assn. (pres. 1940-41), S.A.R. (chmn. scholarship funds), Am. Pub. Works Assn., Nat. Indsl. Advt. Assns., Am. Water Works Assn., Am. Pub. Health Assn., Kappa Sigma, Sigma Delta Chi, Scabbard and Blade. Republican. Unitarian (chmn. service com.). Clubs: University, Engineers, Advertising, Railroad Machinery (N.Y.C.); Montclair (N.J.) Golf; Lake Placid (N.Y.), University Wisconsin Alumni. Home: Upper Montclair, N.J. †

MANN, STANLEY JAY, lawyer; b. Chattanooga, July 15, 1929; s. Lester and Lee (Baras) M. B.A., Hobart Coll., 1949; J.D., Harvard U., 1953. Bar: N.J. bar 1953, N.Y. bar 1966, Fla. bar 1972, Calif. bar 1973. Also U.S. Supreme Ct., U.S. Ct. Mil. Appeals; mem. firm Frederick M. Adams, Woodbridge, N.J., 1957-60, Stanley J. Mann, Woodbridge, 1960-65; staff atty. Levitt and Sons., Inc., Lake Success, N.Y., 1965-68, sec., asst. gen. counsel, 1968; sec., v.p., gen. counsel, dir. ITT Community Devel. Corp., Miami, Fla., 1968-72; assoc. counsel Larwin Group, Inc., Beverly Hills, Calif., 1972-74; ptnr. firm Mann & Dady, Miami, 1974-80, Mann Dady Corrigan & Zelman, 1980-84; Fla. chmn. HUD Equal Opportunity Com., 1974—; mem. Miami Human Resources Commn., 1976—; bd. dirs. Nat. Land Council, Miami, 1970-84; Senator Jr. Chamber Internat. Trustee Coconut Grove Playhouse, 1979—. Served to lt. USNR, 1953-57. Mem. Am., N.J., Fla., Los Angeles, Dade County bar assns. Jewish. Club: Mason. Home: Key Biscayne, Fla. Died May 3, 1984.

MANN, WILLIAM RICHARD, ret. univ. dean; b. Battle Creek, Mich., Apr. 29, 1916; s. Alexander Richard and Mary Amelia (Williams) M.; m. Margaret Alice Limberg, Sept. 16, 1940; 1 son, Alexander William. D.D.S., U. Mich., 1940, M.S., 1942; Sc.D. (hon.), Mich. State U., 1973. Mem. faculty U. Mich. Sch. Dentistry, 1940-82, prof., 1955-82; dean U. Mich. Sch. Dentistry (Sch. Dentistry); dir. W. K. Kellogg Found. Inst. Grad. and Postgrad. Dentistry, 1962-81; Instr. dental seminars, cons. in field, 1956-82; dir. sect. dental edn., survey dentistry in U.S. Am. Council Edn., 1958-60; mem. expert com. dental edn. WHO, 1962, expert adv. panel dental health, 1962-81; mem. dental research adv. com. Med. Research and Devel. Bd., Office Surgeon Gen., Dept. Army,

1954-62; mem. dental tng. com. Nat. Inst. Dental Research, USPHS, 1961-63; dental adv. com. W. K. Kellogg Found., 1963-67, Latin Am. study com., 1964-65, Latin Am. adv. com., 1966-67; adv. com. dental tng. USPHS, 1963-66; med. adv. bd. FDA, 1965-70; hon. prof. dental sci. Yonsei U., Seoul, S. Korea, 1970-82; Bd. dirs. Am. Fund Dental Edn., 1956-73; bd. dirs. Mich. Health Council, 1973-82, pres., 1977. Author articles, chpts. in books.; Editor: (with K. A. Easlick) Practice Administration for the Dentist, 1955. Mem. Am., Mich. dental assns., Washtenaw Dist. Dental Soc. (past pres.), Internat., Am. colls. dentists, Am. Assn. Dental Schs. (pres. 1970-71), Fedn. Dentaire Internat., Internat. Assn. Dental Research, Mich. Assn. Professions, Pierre Fauchard Acad., Sigma Xi., Omicron Kappa Upsilon (nat. pres. 1958-59), Phi Eta Sigma, Phi Kappa Phi, Phi Kappa Sigma, Delta Sigma Delta; hon. mem. Am. Acad. Periodontology, Assn. Latinoamericana de Facultades de Odontologia, Detroit Dental Clinic Club, Korean Dental Assn., Soc. Odontologica Antioquena. Home: Ann Arbor, Mich. Died June 5, 1982.

MANNE, SHELLY, musician, band leader, composer, jazz club owner; b. New York City, June 11, 1920; s. Max Harold and Anna (Cozlin) M.; student pub. schs., N.Y.C.; m. Florence Butterfield, Aug. 26, 1943. Alto saxophonist, 1938, drummer, 1939—; played on boats to Europe, 1939; with Bobby Byrne Band, 1939, Bob Astor Band, 1940, Jo Marsala Band, 1940, Raymond Scott Band, 1941, Will Bradley Band, 1941-42, Les Brown Band, 1942; musician NBC, CBS Studios, 1945, 52d Street Jazz Clubs, 1945-46, Stan Kenton Band, 1946-47, 47-48, 49-52, Charlie Ventura, 1947, Jazz at Philharmonic and Woody Hermann Orch., 1948-49; free lance musician, Los Angeles, 1952-55; organized own band, 1955; recordings for Capitol Records from 1954; owner The Manne-Hole, Hollywood, Cal., from 1960; tech. adviser motion picture Man with the Golden Arm; actor motion pictures I Want to Live, The Five Pennies, The Gene Krupa Story; music scored movie The Proper Time; guest star numerous TV shows; composer score for TV series Daktari, motion pictures Trial of Catonsville Nine, 1972, Trader Horn, 1973. Served with USCGR, 1942-45. Recipient pollwinner plaque Down Beat mag., 1947-51, 54, 56-60; poll winner Metronome mag., 1949-50, 52-53, 55-59; silver medal Playboy mag., 1957-62, spl. award All Stars All Star, 1959, 60; award internat. poll Melody Maker mag., Eng., 1957-59. Died Sept. 26, 1984.

MANNING, JOHN HALL, govt. ofcl.; b. Durham, N.C., Sept. 27, 1889; s. James Smith and Julia Tate (Cain) M.; A.B., U. N.C., 1909; Law, 1913; m. Jane Stillman, Nov. 23, 1920; children—Jane Stillman (Mrs. Charles A. McKenney Jr.), Richard De Yarman. Tchr. Horner Mil. Sch., 1909-10. Durham Pub. Schs., 1910-11; coach Stetson U. Football Team, 1912; asst. U.S. atty., 1934-46; U.S. atty., from 1946; asso. Manning & Fulton, Attorneys, Raleigh, N.C. Commnr. World War Vets, Loan Fund (N.C.), 1929-34; trustee U. N.C., 1921-31. Served as capt., maj., inf., 1916-19; retired maj. gen. AUS. lt. gen. N.C.N.G., 1951. Awarded Legion of Merit; N.C. distinguished service medal. Member Nat. Guard Assn. of U.S. (exec. council, 1946-49). Am. Legion. Mason (Shriner). Democrat. Episcopalian. Home: Raleigh. †

MANNING, MARGARET RAYMOND, editor; b. Omaha, Sept. 1, 1921; d. Annan and Florence (Hostetler) Raymond; m. Robert J. Manning, Dec. 28, 1944; children: Richard, Brian, Robert. A.B. cum laude, Vassar Coll., 1943. Book editor Boston Globe; v.p. Hostetler Land and Investment Co. Office: Boston MA

MANTEY, JULIUS ROBERT, educator; b. Gannett, Ida., Mar. 17, 1890; s. Julius and Emilie (Springer) M.; A.B., William Jewell College, Mo., 1916; M.Th., Southwestern Bapt. Theol. Sem., Ft. Worth, Tex., 1920; D.Th., Southern Bapt., Theol. Sem., 1921, Ph.D., 1931; D.D., Union U., Jackson, Tenn., 1925; m. Mary Ethyl Caldwell, Sept. 20, 1916. Pastor Tekamah, Neb., 1916-18; asst. prof. Greek New Testament, Southwestern Bapt. Theol. Sem., 1921-22; prof. Greek, Union U., 1922-25; prof. N.T., Northern Bapt. Theol. Sem., Chicago, from 1925. Mem. Am. Research Soc. (pres. 1923-24), Soc. Biblical Literature and Exegesis, Chicago Society Biblical Research (pres. 1947-48), National Association of Biblical Instructors, The Gnosis (president 1939-40), Alpha Tau Omega, Republican. Author: (with H. E. Dana) Manual for the Study of the Greek New Testament, 1923; A Manual Grammar of the Greek New Testament (with same), 1927; (with Ernest Cadman Colwell) A Hellenistic Greek Reader with Vocabulary, 1939; Was Peter a Pope?, 1946. Home: Chicago, Ill. †

MANVILLE, (HIRAM) EDWARD, JR., fiduciary; b. N.Y.C., Feb. 14, 1906; s. Hiram Edward and H. Estelle (Romaine) M.; student St. Paul's Sch., Concord, N.H., 1920-25; Ph.B., Yale, 1929; m. Ethel Schniewind, June 11, 1929 (div. 1940); children—Ethel Long, Hiram Edward, III, Maria Helene; m. 2d, Virginia A. Calvert, Mar. 8, 1946 (div. 1952); m. 3d, Loret Hawkins, Dec. 6, 1952 (div. 1959); m. 4th, Doris Hawn, Oct. 25, 1960. Credit dept. manager J.P. Morgan & Co., 1929-35; asst. to v.p. charge mfr., mfg. div. Johns-Manville Corp., N.Y.C., 1935-40, dir., 1940-60. Pres. United Fund Washoe County, Nev., 1966-67. Trustee Judge Baker Guidance Center, Boston, Hiram Edward Manville Found. Served as capt. USAAC, 1942-45. Republican. Episcopalian. Clubs: Yale (N.Y.C.). Home: Reno, Nev. Died Nov. 23, 1982.

MAPEL, WILLIAM, writer, editor; b. Osborn, Mo., July 24, 1902; s. Frank Joseph and Ada Louise (Latta) M.; m. Evelyn Edith Raines, Oct. 17, 1925; children—Evelyn Louise, William M.R. Student, N.W. Mo. State U., Maryville, 1920-23; B.J., U. Mo., 1925; LL.D., Lincoln Coll. of James Millikin U., 1950. Editorial work Democrat-Forum, Maryville, 1920-23; corr. Kansas City Star, 1923-25; asso. editor Sentinel, Edina, Mo., 1925; sports editor and city editor Forum, Maryville, 1926; dir. information N.W. Mo. State U., 1926-27; head dept. pubs. and publicity Kent (O.) State Coll., 1927-28; asst. prof. journalism Washington and Lee U., Lexington, Va., 1928-30; dir. Washington and Lee U. (Sch. Journalism), 1930-34; asst. editor Am. Boy Mag., Detroit, 1931; pres. Virginian Pub. Co., 1930-34; exec. editor, dir. Wilmington (Del.) Morning News and Evening Jour., 1934-37; with Inst. Pub. Relations, 1937; pres. William Mapel Assos., 1938-40; co-founder, gen. mgr. Newsday, Nassau County, N.Y., 1940-42; exec. sec. Pubs. Assn. N.Y.C., 1942-44, vice chmn., 1944, pres., 1952-58, cons., 1958-61; adminstrv. v.p. Am. Soc. Prevention Cruelty to Animals, 1961-72, emeritus, 1972-84; editor Anglers' Club Bull., 1973-75. Author: Legend of a Family. Mem. adv. com. N.Y. State Conservation Dept., 1968-84. Capt. specialized res. U.S. Army, 1932-37. Recipient medal for distinguished service to journalism U. Mo.; Oberlaender traveling fellow German univs., summer 1934. Mem. Am. Assn. Tchrs. Journalism (v.p. 1931-33, pres. 1934), S.R., Huguenot Soc. S.C., Alpha Delta Sigma, Phi Gamma Delta, Pi Delta Epsilon, Kappa Tau Alpha, Sigma Delta Chi (nat. treas. 1931-33). Clubs: Anglers (N.Y.C.) (dir.); Mill Reef (Antigua, West Indies); DeBruce Fly Fishers (Catskills). Home: Bronxville, N.Y. Died Mar. 30, 1984.

MARCHER, ROYAL, costume jewelry mfr.; b. N.Y.C., Sept. 25, 1889; s. Charles Albert and Sophie (Van Raalte) M.; student high sch.; m. Clara White, Oct. 3, 1923; children—Royal, Jane. With Coro, Inc., N.Y.C., from 1909, sec.-treas., sales mgr., 1929-49, dir., from 1929, exec. v.p., from 1949. Home: N.Y.C.; also Palm Beach, Fla.†

MARCUS, WILLIAM ARTHUR, banker; b. San Francisco, Aug. 29, 1889; s. Morris and Jean (Douglas) M.; m. Ruth Finn, July 10, 1920; children—Eva Jean (Mrs. R. P. Barker), Anita (Mrs. Paul B. Fay, Jr.), William John. Salesman, Gas & Electric Appliance Co., San Francisco, 1907-08; teller Metropolis Trust & Savs. Bank, 1909-11, American Trust Co., San Francisco, 1911-13, asst. cashier, 1914-19, asst. v.p., 1920-22, cashier, 1922-23, v.p., 1923-47, sr. v.p., 1947-58, cons.; pres. Shasta Iron Co. Bd., Goodwill Industries, San Francisco. Pres. Marin Municipal Water District. Served as lt. U.S.N.R.F., 1917-19. Former chmn. bd. Mill Valley Sch. Dist. Mem. Am. (pres. savs. div., 1948-49) and Calif. (pres. 1947-48) bankers assns., Mortgage Bankers Assn. Am. (past gov.). Clubs: Commonwealth, Bohemian. Home: Kentfield, Cal. †

MARCUSSEN, WILLIAM HENRY, business exec.; born Hoboken, N.J., May 28, 1887; s. William Jess and Louise Georgina (Bremer) M.; B.S.A., Cornell U., 1910; m. Freda Alzena Starkweather, July 9, 1913; one son, William Marvin. Bacteriologist and dairy specialist for the Lederle Laboratories, N.Y. City, 1910-11; bacteriologist New Jersey State Bd. Health, Trenton, 1911-12; bacteriologist in charge prodn. of spl. milk The Borden Co., Nichols, N.Y., 1912-15, specialist in quality control, Bonghamton, N.Y., 1915-17, dist. supt. in up-state N.Y. country milk plants, 1917-18, dir. labs., N.Y. City, 1918-22, asst. mgr. prodn. fluid milk div., 1922-29, vice pres. Bordens Farm Products Co., Inc., 1929-36, pres. Met. N.Y. Dist. fluid milk operations, 1936-44, v.p. in charge fluid division, parent company, N.Y. City, 1944-52; has been advisor on executive matters from 1953. Served as co. tech. rep. on research on time and temp. standards for pasteurization of milk with U.S.P.H.S. and state health depts., 1922-23. Mem. adv. com. N.Y. State Commn. Agr., 1936-37; dir. Milk Industry Foundation; mem. adv. com. N.Y. State Milk Control Bd., 1934-35. Mem. fluid milk industry adv. com. War Food Adminstrn., to dir. 1944-45; mem. dairy industry adv. com. O.P.S., 1951. Fellow American Public Health Assn. (member finance com.); mem. Internat. Assn. Milk Dealers (dir.), Internat. Assn. Milk Sanitarians, Soc. Am. Bacteriologists, Am. Dairy Sci. Assn. Republican. Methodist. Clubs: Union League, Cornell, (New York); Maplewood (N.J.) Country. Home: Maplewood, N.J. †

MARCY, MILTON ASA, clergyman; b. Mandan, N.D., Dec. 4, 1888; s. Joseph Edwin and Laura Lalinda (Andrews) M.; A.B., Willamette U., Salem, Ore., 1915, D.D., 1929; B.D., Kimball Sch. of Theology, Salem, Ore., 1915; m. Nellie Rickson, Sept. 6, 1911; children—Carl Milton, Donald Eugene, Helen Mildred, Bernice Lillian, Carol Barbara. Ordained to ministry of Meth. Ch., 1913; pastor, Falls City, Ore., 1913-15, Dayton, 1915-21, McMinnville, 1921-22, Hillsboro, 1922-25, Forest Grove, 1925-29; supt. Salem Dist., 1929-33; pastor, Sunnyside Ch., Portland, Ore., 1933-39; supt. Portland Dist., 1939-41; pastor First Church, Tacoma, Wash., 1911-51; supt. Forest Grove Dist. from 1951. Secretary Oregon Council of Churches, 1933-39; member Board of Home Missions, 1931-32; director Good-Will Industries; registrar and dean. Portland Area Summer Sch., 1943-47. Trustee Willamette U., 1925-42. College of Puget Sound from 1942. Dir. Tacoma Community Chest, 1942-48; president Tacoma Council of Churches, 1943-45, director Tacoma Council, Boy Scouts of America (30-year veteran Scouter). Director Oregon Anti-Liquor League, 1930-42. President Washington Temperance Association since 1942. Pres. bd. ministerial training and qualifications, from 1945; exec. com., P.N.W. annual conf.; trustee bd. conf. claimants; trustee Wesley Gardens. Republican. Mason (32 deg., Scottish Rite). Rotarian. Home: Portland, Ore. Deceased.

MARDAGA, THOMAS JOSEPH, bishop; b. Balt., May 14, 1913; s. Thomas J. and Agnes (Ryan) M. B.A., St. Charles Coll., Catonsville, Md., St. Mary's Sem., Balt., 1936; S.T.L., St. Mary's Sem., 1940; LL.D., Mt. St. Mary's Coll., 1968. Ordained priest Roman Catholic Ch., 1940; asst. pastor in, Balt., 1940-62; archdiocesan dir. Cath. Youth Orgn., 1946-55; dir., archdiocesan Confraternity of Christian Doctrine, also exec. sec. Cath. Charity Fund Appeal, Balt., 1955-68; mem. archdiocesan bd. consultors, Balt., 1966; rector Basilica of Assumption, Balt., 1965-67, aux. bishop of Balt., 1967-68, vicar gen., 1967-68, bishop of Wilmington, Del., 1968-84; mem. U.S. Cath. Bishops' Adv. Council, 1973; mem. nominating com. Nat. Conf. Cath. Bishops, 1972, univ. com., 1972, com. on budget and finance, 1972, adviser to com. on doctrine, 1973, mem. bishops com. on priestly life and ministry, 1974, chmn. region IV, 1974; alt. adminstrv. com. and bd.; mem. Nat. Hon. Com. for Black Catholics Concerned, 1972; chmn. Delmarva Ecumenical Agy., 1975; trustee Mount Saint Mary's Coll., Emmitsburg, Md.; bd. dirs. Cath. Diocese Found., Greater Wilmington Devel. Council, Cath. Relief Services, Inc., 1979; Episcopal adv. Region II, Cursillo Movement.; regional rep. Am. Coll. Immaculate Conception Cath. U. Louvain, Belgium, 1970-84. Mem. Nat. Conf. Cath. Bishops (adminstrv. com. 1970-84, mem. com. doctrine). Office: Wilmington, Del. Died May 28, 1984.

MARGARET, SISTER PATRICIA, coll. pres.; born Holyoke, Mass., Dec. 21, 1887; d. Patrick John and Mary (Carroll) Herbert; A.B., Trinity Coll., Washington, 1926. A.M., 1930; grad. certificate in library sci. Catholic U. of Am., 1934. Teacher elementary and secondary schs., Notre Dame de Namur. Mass., 1907-26; asst. librarian Trinity Coll., Washington, 1925-29; librarian Emmanuel Coll., Boston, 1929-46, mem. bd. trustees from 1930, pres. since 1946. Roman Catholic. Home: Boston, Mass. †

MARGETTS, WALTER THOMAS, JR., corporate executive, lawyer, former state treas.; b. N.Y.C., Jan. 23, 1905; s. Walter and Edith Pearl (Lawson) M.; m. Josephine Sharon, July 18, 1935; children—Sharon McLean Margetts Doremus, Cynthia Margetts Robinson, Walter Thomas, Susan Meredith Margetts Connell. Student, Am. Inst. Banking, 1923-25, N.Y. U., 1925-26; advanced agronomy, Columbia U., 1936; LL.B., St. Lawrence U., 1928, LL.M., 1930; LL.D., Fairleigh Dickinson U., 1953. With Bklyn. Trust Co., 1923-29; asso. Beekman, Bogue & Clark, N.Y.C., 1929-35; partner law firm Bainton, McNaughton & Douglas, 1935-43; asso. McLanahan, Merritt & Ingraham, 1943-54; past chmn. bd. Laythan Foundry Inc., Paterson, N.J.; chmn. exec. com., dir. Franklin Bank, Paterson; pres. Holly Hill Corp.; past dir., chmn. pension-fin. exec. com. U.G.I. Corp.; now cons.; pres., treas., dir. Hudson Rapid Tubes Corp., Hudson and Manhattan Corp., Washington Valley Farms, Inc.; dir., chmn. audit fin. com. Kayser-Roth Corp., N.Y.C.; mem. N.Y. adv. bd. Am. Mut. Ins. Co.; dir. SFM Corp., Plainfield, N.J., Tech-Torch Co., Carlstadt, N.J.; chmn. Komline Sanderson Engring. Corp., Peapack, N.J.; dir., v.p., treas. Found. Life Ins. Co. Am., Chatham, N.J.; cons. Vornado Inc., Garfield, N.J.; dir. Automatic Data Processing Corp., Clifton, N.J. Trustee N.J. Dental Service Plan, Inc.; Industry mem. Nat. War Labor Bd., 1943-45; treas. State of N.J., 1949-54; chmn. N.J. Mediation Bd., 1945-49, N.J. Commn. Intergovtl. Relations; pres. N.J. Citizen's Transp. Council; mem. adv. bd. on econ. devel. U.S. Dept. Commerce, Washington, 1970-83; past chmn., treas. N.J. Republican Fin. Com.; N.J. del. Rep. Conv.; presdl. elector from N.J., 1964; dir., former pres. Passaic Taxpayers Assn.; bd. dirs. Tax Found., Inc.; bd. govs. Passaic Gen. Hosp., N.J.; chmn. bd. trustees, dir. N.J. Camp Blind Children, Inc.; pres., trustee Frost Valley Assn.; trustee Margetts Found. Fellow Fairleigh Dickinson U. (vice chmn. bd.), Wroxton Coll.; Mem. Patrolmen's Benevolent Assn. (hon. life), Spring Valley Hunt Assn., Am., N.Y. State, Ariz. bar assns., N.J. Foundrymen's Assn. (pres., dir.), N.J. Taxpayers Assn. (past pres.), Am. Arbitration Assn. (panel arbitrators), N.Y. Zoology Soc. (life), St. Andrews Soc. (life), Alpha Chi Epsilon, Delta Theta Phi. Clubs: Downtown Athletic (life); Met., Nat. Press (Washington), Capitol Hill (Washington); Essex (Newark); Morristown (Morristown, N.J.), Morris County Golf (Morristown, N.J.); Elks (life mem.), Masons. Home: Morristown, N.J. Died Mar. 26, 1983.

MARGOLIES, JOSEPH AARON, bookseller; b. Brest-Litovsk, Russia, Dec. 25, 1889; s. David and Bella (Bergman) M.; m. Bertha Neft, June 30, 1914; children—Helen (Mrs. Leo Rifkin), Peter. Employed as book store mgr., Rand Sch. Social Science, 1906-12; book buyer, Brentano's, Inc., 1912-28; sales mgr. Covici-Friede, Inc., 1929-38; with Brentano's 1938-51, vice pres., gen. mgr. and dir., 1943-51, exec. v.p. Wilfred Funk, Inc. 1951. Member Am. Booksellers Assn. (chmn. bd. dirs., 1946-48); dir. Council of Books in Wartime, 1944-47.

Editor Strange and Fantastic Stories, 1946. Home: New York, N.Y. †

MARINO, PASQUALE AUGUSTINE, coll. dean; b. Boston, Oct. 8, 1933; s. Joseph and Maria A. (Percudco) M.; m. Audrey Jennings, Jan. 20, 1963; 1 child, Patricia. B.S., Northeastern U., 1956, M.S., 1961; Ph.D., U. Conn., 1965. Project engr. Badger Co., 1956-59; instr., asst. prof., asso. prof. mech. engring. Northeastern U., Boston, 1959-67; asso. prof. chem. engring. U. R.I., Kingston, 1967-68; asso. prof. chem. engring. U. Lowell, Mass., 1968-76, asst. dean grad. sch., 1972-76; pres. Norwalk (Conn.) State Tech. Coll., 1976-80; dean Sch. Engring., Manhattan Coll., Riverdale, N.Y., 1980-82. Reviewer, EPA. Treas. bd. dirs. Norwalk YMCA; bd. dirs. Norwalk/Wilton chpt. ARC, Ridgefield Arts Council; trustee Wooster Sch., Danbury, Conn. NSF Sci. Faculty fellow, 1963-64; recipient Western Electric award for outstanding teaching, 1972. Fellow Am. Inst. Chem. Engrs.; mem. Am. Soc. Engring. Edn. (editor, sec.-treas. grad. studies div., chmn. grad. studies div.). Died May 10, 1982.

MARION, JERRY BASKERVILLE, educator, author, physicist; b. Mobile, Ala., Dec. 10, 1929; s. Lester L. and Virginia (Hensel) M.; m. Adelia I. Macnab, May 31, 1952; children—Forrest Lee, Kathryn Ann. B.A., Reed Coll., 1952; M.A., Rice U., 1953, Ph.D., 1955. Research asso. Rice U., 1955; NSF fellow Calif. Inst. Tech., 1955-56, vis. asso. in physics, Guggenheim fellow, 1965-66; faculty U. Rochester, 1956-57; physicist Los Alamos Sci. Lab., 1957; mem. faculty U. Md., College Park, 1957-81, prof. physics, 1962-81; sr. staff scientist Convair/San Diego, 1960-61; Com. mem. Nat. Acad. Sci.-NRC; cons. govt. agys., indsl. firms. Author: Nuclear Reaction Graphs, 1960, Classical Dynamics of Particles and Systems, 1965, Classical Electromagnetic Radiation, 1965, Principles of Vector Analysis, 1965, Nuclear Reaction Analysis, 1968, Physics and the Physical Universe, 1971, Mathematical Preparation for General Physics, 1972, Mathematical Preparation for General Physics with Calculus, 1973, Physics—The Foundation of Modern Science, 1973, Mathematical Review for the Physical Sciences, 1974, Energy in Perspective, 1974, Physical Science in the Modern World, 1974, Physics in the Modern World, 1976, Essential Physics in the World Around Us, 1977, Our Physical World, 1978, General Physics with Bioscience Essays, 1979, Mathematical Methods for General Physics with Calculus, 1980; Editor: (with J.L. Fowler) Fast Neutron Physics, 1960, (with G.C. Phillips, J.R. Risser) Progress in Fast Neutron Physics, 1963, (with D.M. Van Patten) Research with Low Energy Accelerators, 1967, A Universe of Physics, 1970; Mem. internat. editorial bd.: (with D.M. Van Patten) Nuclear Data, 1965-81. Recipient Sci. Teaching award Washington Acad. Scis., 1973. Fellow Am. Phys. Soc., AAAS. Research, numerous publs. on structure of light nuclei, especially effects relative to isobaric spin, single particle states, configuration mixing. Home: Central City, Pa. Died Aug. 2, 1981.

MARKEVITCH, IGOR, composer, conductor; b. Kiev, Russia, July 27, 1912; s. Boris and Zola (Pokitonoff) M.; student Coll. Vevey, Music Coll., Paris, France; student piano with Alfred Cortot, mus. composition with Nadia Boulanger, orch. conducting with Hermann Scherchen; M. Kyra Nijinsky, Mar. 1936; 1 son, Vaslav; m. Topazia Caetani, July 1946; children—Allegra, Nathalie, Oleg. Orch. conductor, 1939—; leader orch. of Florence and of Mai florentin, 1944-46; charge internat. courses orch. conducting Salzburg, 1947-54, Mex., 1955-57, Santiago de Compostela, 1966; leader Havana Philharmonic Orch., 1957-59; conductor orchs. through Europe, Asia, Australia, N. and S. Am.; permanent conductor Lamoureux Orch., Paris, 1957-61, Spanish Radio Television Orch., 1965—; mus. dir. Symphonic Orch. Montreal, 1955-60; artistic director Monte-Carlo Opera, 1968—; condr. emeritus Japan Philharmonic Orch. Decorated knight Legion of Honor, comdr. Arts and Lit. (France). Composer: Piano Concerto, 1929; Lost Paradise: Icare; Rebus; cantata on words by Jean Cocteau; Lawrence the Magnificent; also chamber music. Author: Introduction to Music; Organ Point; Made in Italy. Address: Saint Cezaire-sur-Saigne, France. Died Mar. 7, 1983.

MARKEY, LUCILLE PARKER, thoroughbred breeder and owner; b. Maysville, Ky., Dec. 14, 1896; d. John W. and Sarah B. (Owens) Parker; m. Warren Wright, Mar. 26, 1919 (dec. Dec. 1950); 1 child, Warren (dec. 1978); m. Gene Markey, Sept. 27, 1952 (dec. May 1980). Ed., Weston Sch. Owner, propr. Calumet Farm (breeding establishment and racing stable), Lexington, Ky., 1950-82. 8 winners Ky. Derby; 2 triple crown winners: Whirlaway, 1941, Citation, 1948. Address: Miami Beach, Fla. Died July 25, 1982.

MARKHAM, JOSEPH LEO, newspaperman; b. Holyoke, Mass., Apr. 30, 1887; s. John and Margaret (O'Connell) M.; ed. St. Jerome's Parochial Sch., Holyoke, Mass.; m. Martha Mary Spurling, Aug. 27, 1912. Began as printer, Holyoke, 1902; supt. Billings (Mont.) Gazette, 1912-17, advertising mgr., 1917-22; also athletic dir. Mont. State Coll., Nov. 1913-May 1914; mgr. Anaconda Standard from 1922. Butte Standard, 1928-49; mem. staff Holyoke Transcript-Telegram from 1949. Home: Holyoke, Mass. †

MARKLEY, HERBERT EMERSON, bearing co. exec.; b. Elmore, Ohio, Oct. 5, 1914; s. Henry J. and Amelia (Wilde) M.; m. Nancy Mulligan, June 22, 1946; children—Sheila, Herbert James, Maura, Noreen. B.S. in Bus. Adminstrn, Miami U., Oxford, Ohio, 1938; LL.B., William McKinley Sch. Law, Canton, Ohio, 1943. Bar: Ohio bar 1943. With Timken Co., Canton, 1938-83, exec. v.p., 1959-68, pres., 1968-79, chmn. exec. com., 1979-83; dir. Firestone Tire & Rubber Co., Am. Electric Power Co. Trustee Case Western Res. U. Served with AUS, 1943-46. Mem. NAM (dir. 1967-83, chmn.), Conf. Bd. (sr.). Republican. Methodist. Clubs: International (Washington); Congress Lake (Hartville, Ohio); Union (Cleve.); Downtown Athletic (N.Y.C.); Canton Brookside Country (Canton); Ocean Reef (Fla.). Home: Canton, Ohio. Died Mar. 10, 1983.

MARKS, BARRY ALAN, educator; b. N.Y.C., Feb. 1, 1926; s. Eric Henry and Beatrice Sara (Hecht) M.; A.B., Dartmouth Coll., 1948; M.A., U. Minn., 1949, Ph.D., 1957; m. Gale Holman, Sept. 18, 1948; children—Stephen, Pamela, Dana. Instr. gen. studies U. Minn., 1949-53, Dartmouth, 1953-54; from instr. to asso. prof. English, Brown U., 1955-68; prof., chmn. dept. lit. Am. U., 1968-74; dean Coll. Arts and Scis., U. R.I., 1974-83. Mem., chmn. R.I. Adv. Com. U.S. Commn. Civil Rights, 1959-65; chmn. R.I. Commn. Human Rights, 1965-68. Mem. exec. com. R.I. Republican State Central Com., 1965-68. Served with USMC, 1943-46. Fulbright lectr. Am. lit. and civilization U. Lille (France), 1963-64. Mem. Modern Lang. Assn., Nat. Council Tchrs. English, AAUP. Author: Mark Twain's Huckleberry Finn, 1959; E.E. Cummings, 1964. Home: Jamestown, R.I. Died July 18, 1983.

MARKS, EDWIN HALL, army officer; b. Wilmington, Del., July 2, 1887; s. Rev. Lafayette and Elizabeth (Nevin) M.; B.S., U.S. Mil. Acad., 1909; grad. Engr. Sch., 1912; honor grad. Command and Gen. Staff Sch., 1926; grad. Army War Coll., 1929; m. Margaret Ainsworth, Sept. 29, 1917 (died Oct. 4, 1940); children—Edwin Hall, Willard Ainsworth; m. to Josephine Gaibraith, November 15, 1941. Commd. 2d lt. Corps of Engrs., U.S. Army, 1909, and advanced through grades to brig. gen., 1941; served successively at Detroit, Canal Zone, Rock Island, Ill., Pittsburgh and Washington Barracks, as 2d lt., 1909-12; at Island of Guam, Marianas Islands, Philippines, as 1st lt., 1912-15; at Detroit and as instr. U.S. Mil. Acad. and O.T.C. as capt., 1915-17; lt. col., command 20th Engrs., in charge forestry sect. of Div. of Constrn. and Forestry, France, with A.E.F., 1918; col. in Office of Chief of Engrs., Washington, D.C., 1918-21; as major at Duluth, Minn. and St. Paul, Minn., in charge engr. dists., 1921-24; comd. 13th Regt. Engrs., Ft. Humphreys, Va., 1926-28; mem. Gen. Staff Personnel Div., War Dept. Gen. Staff, 1929-33; dist. engr., Galveston, 1933-37, Buffalo, 1937-38; as col. Ohio River Div., 1938-41; as brig. gen. commd. Engr. Replacement Training Center and Post, Ft. Belvoir, Va., after May 1, 1941. Mem. Am. Soc. Engrs., Soc. Am. Mil. Engrs. Clubs: Cincinnati Country; Army and Navy (Manila); Army and Navy, Army and Navy Country (Washington, D.C.). Deceased.

MARLEY, JOHN, actor, dir.; b. N.Y.C., Oct. 17; m. Sanra Ulusevich; 1 dau., Alexis; children by previous marriage—Peter, Julia, Ben. Student, Coll. City N.Y. Appeared in: numerous motion pictures, including Faces (Best Actor award Venice Film Festival), A Man Called Sledge, 1970, The Godfather, 1972, Love Story, Framed, 1975, W.C. Fields and Me, 1976, The Car, 1977, The Greatest, 1977, Hooper, 1978, Oliver's Story, 1978, Tribute, 1980; dir. numerous motion pictures, including, Cleve. Playhouse, Center Stage, Balt., Civic Playhouse, Calif., Pasadena (Calif.) Playhouse; producer, dir. summer stock.; (Recipient Oscar nomination for best supporting actor for Love Story, Golden Globe nomination for Love Story.). Served with Armed Forces, World War II. Home: Los Angeles. Died May 22, 1984.*

MARLOWE, SYLVIA, (MRS. LEONID BERMAN) harpsichordist; b. N.Y.C.; d. Harry and Anna (Riklan) Sapira; m. Leonid Berman, Jan. 6, 1948. Student, Ecole Normale de Musique, Paris, 1929-32. Faculty Mannes Coll. Music, N.Y.C., from 1953. First harpsichordist to tour Asia sponsored by U.S. govt. under, ANTA, concert tours, U.S., Europe, Asia; rec. artist, Decca Gold Label Records; appeared radio and TV stas. including, NBC, CBS, ABC, BBC, Can. Broadcasting Co.; Recs. include Bach Goldberg Variations, RCA Gold Label. Decorated chevalier Arts et Des Lettres France; recipient Handel medallion N.Y.C. Mem. The Harpsichord Music Soc. (mus. dir.). Home: New York, N.Y. Died Dec. 10, 1981.

MARQUIS, WILLIAM BELL, landscape architect; b. Rock Island, Ill., Apr. 27, 1887; s. William Stevenson and Adelaide Mary (Bell) M.; A.B., Lake Forest Coll., 1909; M. Landscape Arch., Harvard, 1912; m. Martha Weare Ely, Feb. 14, 1922; children—Anne (Mrs. Prescott D. Stevenson), Gordon Ely. Staff P. J. Berckmans Co., Augusta, Ga., 1912-17; prin. asst. Olmsted Bros., landscape architects, Brookline, 1919-37, partner, from 1937. Served as civilian U.S. Army, engr. constrn. div., Washington, 1917-19. Fellow Am. Soc. Landscape Architects; mem. Mass. Forest and Park Assn. (exec. com.). Presbyn. Home: Waban, Mass. †

MARRIOTT, JOHN WILLARD, restaurant and motel exec.; b. Marriott, Utah, Sept. 17, 1900; s. Hyrum Willard and Ellen (Morris) M.; m. Alice Sheets, June 9, 1927; children—John Willard, Richard Edwin. Grad., Weber Coll., Ogden, Utah, 1922; A.B., U. Utah, 1926; LL.D. (hon.), Brigham Young U., 1958. Franchise holder A. & W. Root Beer Co., Washington, 1926-28; pres. Marriott Corp. (formerly Hot Shoppes, Inc.), 1928-64, now chmn., dir.; dir. Riggs Nat. Bank, Chesapeake & Potomac Telephone Co., Washington Bd. Trade. Biography: The J. Willard Marriott Story, 1977. Mem. commrs. adv. planning bd. Fed. City Council.; Bd. govs. United Service Orgns.; chmn. Presdl. Inaugural Com., 1969, 73, Honor Am. Com. Recipient Hall of Fame award Am. Restaurant Mag., 1954; Achievement award Advt. Club, 1957; award Am. Marketing Assn., 1959; U. Utah, 1959; Chain Store Age award, 1961; Businessman of Yr. award Religious Heritage Am., 1971; Capt. of Achievement award Am. Acad. Achievement, 1971; Horatio Alger award, 1974. Mem. N.A.M. (dir.), Com. for Econ. Devel. (trustee), Nat. Restaurant Assn. (pres. 1948), Washington Restaurant Assn. (pres. 1939, 43). Mem. Ch. of Jesus Christ of Latter-Day Saints (pres. Washington stake 1948-57). Clubs: Burning Tree (Bethesda, Md.); Indian Creek Country (Miami Beach, Fla.); Bald Peak Colony (Melvin Village, N.H.); Columbia Country (Chevy Chase, Md.); Paradise Valley Country (Ariz.); Washington Admirals (Washington), Capitol Hill (Washington). Home: Washington DC

MARRON, JOSEPH FRANCIS, librarian; b. Helena, Mont., Feb. 27, 1888; s. James Edward and Anna (Sullivan) M.; student Kan. State Coll., 1905-10, Washington U., 1912; m. Muriel Lindley, June 9, 1914; children—Elizabeth (Mrs. F. A. Wynhausen), Mary (Mrs. William Dally), James Lindley, Joseph Jeffery, John Carlos. Librarian Sch. Social Economy, 1910-12; legislative reference librarian Mo. Library Commn., 1912-13, Tex. State Library, 1913-17; chief librarian Jacksonville, Fla., 1920-58; library adviser Barnett National Bank, from 1963. Served as army camp librarian, Camp Travis, Tex., 1917-19. Mem. War Price and Rationing Bd., Jacksonville Def. Council, World War II. Past president of Tuberculosis Association. Member Council Social Agencies (president 1951-52), Civic Music Association (pres. 1951-53), A.L.A., Southeast, Fla. (past pres.) library associations, Ye Mystic Revellers. Democrat. Roman Catholic. Club: Torch (president 1942-43, secretary from 1959). Author: Legislative Reference Bureau as Bill Revising Agency. Home: Jacksonville, Fla. †

MARSCHNER, ROBERT FREDERIC, oil co. exec.; b. Wilkinsburgh, Pa., Aug. 17, 1908; s. Fred and Martha Josephine (Jaeger) M.; Ph.B., Brown U., 1928, Sc.M., 1929; Ph.D., Pa. State U., 1936; m. Ida Allenson Noble, July 14, 1934; children—Frederic Robert, Richard Glenn. Research chemist Dow Chem. Co., Midland, Mich., 1929-31; research chemist Am. Oil Co., Whiting, Ind., 1934-71, sr. research asso., 1951-71, asst. dir. research and devel. dept., 1960-63. Trustee Homewood (Ill.) Park Dist., 1948-54; mem. bd. edn. Homewood-Flossmoor High Sch., 1957-67, pres., 1958-59. Bd. dirs., asst. sec. Standard Oil Found., 1951-60. Recipient Silver Beaver award Boy Scouts Am., 1961; award merit Chgo. Tech. Socs. Council, 1963. Mem. Am. Chem. Soc. (chmn. Chgo. sect. 1951, div. petroleum chemistry 1961, councillor 1947-66). Contbr. articles to profl. jours. Patentee in field. Home: Homewood, Ill. Died Nov. 22, 1984.

MARSH, THAD NORTON, hosp. exec.; b. Wichita, Kans., Aug. 25, 1926; s. Paul Norton and Ethel (Reaugh) M.; A.B. (Summerfield scholar 1943-48), U. Kans., 1948; B.A. (Rhodes scholar), U. Oxford (Eng.), 1951, M.A., 1955, B. Litt., 1957; m. Patricia Anne Cunningham, Dec. 23, 1955; children—Anne Catherine, Alice Jean, Paul Norton. Instr. English, U. Kans., 1948-49, Kans. State Coll., 1951-52; asst. prof. English, Rice U., 1954-62, asst. to pres., 1959-61; dean coll., prof. English, Muhlenberg Coll., Allentown, Pa. 1962-66; dean of coll., prof. English, Centenary Coll. of La., Shreveport, 1966-73; provost, v.p., lectr. English, U. of South, Sewanee, Tenn., 1973-77, prof. English, 1977-78; v.p. Meth. Hosp., Tex. Med. Center, 1978-81; mem. Rhodes Scholarships Selection Com., Tex., 1955-61, 78—, Pa., 1962-65, La., 1966-76, Mo., 1977, sec., 1970-73; asso. adv. council The Danforth Found., 1964-67. Mem. bd. higher edn. United Luth. Ch. Am., 1960-62; mem. nat. selection bd. Harbison award for gifted teaching, 1965-68. Fellow Royal Geog. Soc.; mem. So. Conf. Acad. Deans (pres. 1969), Renaissance Soc. Am., Assn. Am. Rhodes Scholars, Nat. Soc. Fund-Raising Execs., Nat. Assn. for Hosp. Devel., Phi Beta Kappa. Democrat. Club: Doctors (Houston). Contbr. articles on 16th century English lit. to profl. jours.; editor: (with Wilfred S Dowden) The Heritage of Freedom, 1962. Home: Houston, Tex. Died May 24, 1981.

MARSHALL, EDWARD WAYNE, insurance exec.; b. Lumberton, N.J., Feb. 24, 1889; s. William B. and Anna B. Marshall; grad. Haddonfield High Sch., student U. of Pa.; m. Viola B. Craig; children—Virginia C., Dr. E. Wayne, William B., David L. Actuarial dept. Penn Mutual Life, 1909-11, Provident Life & Trust, 1911-17; asst. actuary Fidelity Mutual Life, 1917-20; with Provident Mutual Life Ins. Co. from 1920, successively asst. actuary, 1920-24, asso. actuary, 1925-28, actuary, 1928-30, vice pres. and actuary from 1931. Mem. actuorial advisory com., Veterans Adminstrn. Former pres. Actuarial Soc. Am.; fellow Society of Actuaries; dir. permanent com. Internat. Congresses of Actuaries; corr. mem. Institute Actuaries (England); member American Statistical Assn. Mem. Soc. of Friends. Club: Ozone Golf. Home: Haddonfield, N.J. †

MARSHALL, JAMES FREDERICK, educator; b. Indpls., Aug. 15, 1912; s. James Harrison and May (Weaver) M.; m. Sarah Elizabeth Shinn, June 3, 1943. A.B., Ind. U., 1937; M.A., U. Ill., 1939, Ph.D., 1948. Asst. prof. French U. Ariz., Tucson, 1948-49; prof. French and Spanish Whittier (Calif.) Coll., 1949-58; prof. French U. Wis.-Milw., 1958-75, prof. emeritus, 1975-84, chmn. dept. French and Italian, 1958-63, 68-70. Editor: Stendhal Henri III, 1952, Victor Jacquemont, Letters to Achille Chaper, 1960, De Stael-du Pont Letters, 1968; Contbr. to: Stendhal Madame de Stael et l'Europe, 1970; Contbr. articles profl. jours. Vice pres. orgn. com. to celebrate bicentennial of birth of Madame de Stael, Coppet, Switzerland, 1966. Served with AUS, 1942-46. Recipient Research grants U. Wis., 1959, 63, 64, Research grants Ford Found., 1955-56, Research grants Eleutherian Mills-Hagley Found., 1964, Am. Council Learned Socs., 1953. Mem. Modern Lang. Assn., Phi Beta Kappa. Home: Milwaukee, Wis. Died Oct. 3, 1984.

MARSHALL, JOHN SEDBERRY, philosophy educator; b. Fullerton, Calif., May 25, 1898; s. John Lundy and Emma Elizabeth (Gawley) M.; A.B., Pomona Coll., 1921; Ph.D., Boston U., 1926; student Harvard U., 1924-25, U. Basel (Switzerland), 1923-25, U. Calif., 1928, Russ. U. Prague (Czechoslovakia), summers 1935-36; m. Elizabeth Southard, May 26, 1923; 1 son, James Edward. Instr. philosophy Syracuse (N.Y.) U., 1926-29; prof. philosophy Albion Coll., 1929-46; prof. philosophy U. of the South, Sewanee, Tenn., 1946-68, prof. emeritus, 1968-79, prof. grad. sch. theology, 1950-62. Editor, Anglican Theol. Rev., 1959-65. Mem. Am. Philos. Assn., AAAS, AAUP, Brit. Inst. Philosophy, So. Soc. for Philosophy of Religion (past pres.), Guild of Scholars (past pres.), Realist Soc., Phi Beta Kappa, Lambda Chi Alpha. Democrat. Episcopalian. Author: (with N.O. Lossky), Value and Existence 1935; Hooker's Polity in Modern English, 1948; The Genius and Mission of the Episcopal Church, 1949; The Word Was Made Flesh, 1949; Hooker's Theology of Common Prayer, 1953; Hooker and the Anglican Tradition, 1963; contbr. various articles to The Anglican Theol. Review, The Sewanee Review, The Monist, The Personalist, The Review of Politics, Ency. Brit. Home: Sewanee, Tenn. Died Nov. 21, 1979.

MARSHALL, LAURENCE KENNEDY, pres. Raytheon Mfg. Co.; b. Newton, Mass., May 18, 1889; s. George Francis and Mary Elizabeth (Kennedy) M.; B.S., Tufts Coll., 1911; m. Lorna Jean McLean, June 21, 1926; children—Elizabeth, John Kennedy. Former chmn. bd. Raytheon Mfg. Co., now retired; director Metals & Controls Corp. Trustee Tufts Coll., Waltham Hospital. Served as 2d lt., 302d F.A., A.E.F., World War I. Mem. Alpha Tau Omega. Clubs: Algonquin (Boston); Faculty (Cambridge); Metropolitan (Washington). Home: Cambridge, Mass. †

MARSHALL, LAURISTON CALVERT, educator, physicist; b. Canton, China, June 27, 1902 (parents Am. citizens); s. George Washington and Edmonia Bell (Sale) M.; A.B., Park Coll., 1923; Ph.D. (Whiting fellow), U. Calif. at Berkeley, 1929; postgrad. (NRC fellow) Princeton, 1929-31; m. Lucie Welsh Sewell, Aug. 20, 1949; children—Clarice Sewell, Katherine Stow, Lauriston Calvert. With U.S. Dept. Agr., 1928-37; mem. faculty U. Calif. at Berkeley, 1937-54, prof. elec. engring., 1945-54, dir. microwave power lab., 1946-52; dir. phys. research lab. Link-Belt Co., Indpls., 1952-59; asso. tech. dir. microwave power lab. Varo, Inc., Garland, Tex., 1959-61; prof., chief office sci. personnel, dir. materials research div. S.W. Center for Advanced Studies, Dallas, 1961-67; vis. prof. U. So. Ill., Carbondale, 1967-73, prof. emeritus, adj. prof., 1973-79. Cons. U. Calif. Lawrence Livermore Labs., 1972-73. Mem. staff, div. head Radiation Lab., Mass. Inst. Tech., 1941-46, OSRD, 1944-46; staff Lawrence Radiation Lab., U. Calif., Berkeley, 1946-54, cons., 1956. Vice pres., sec. Leonardo Acad. Arts and Scis., from 1972; chmn. projects com., bd. dirs. North Coast Inst., from 1973. Recipient citations War Theater, 1945, OSRD, 1946, Presdl., 1948, Distinguished Alumnus award Park Coll., 1952; Guggenheim fellow, 1950-52. Fellow Am. Phys. Soc., IEEE (life); mem. Inst. Physics, Am. Geophys. Union, AAUP, AAAS, Sigma Xi, Eta Kappa Nu. Clubs: Faculty (Berkeley); Bohemian (San Francisco). Contbr. articles profl. jours. Home: Gualala, Calif. Died Nov. 9, 1979.†

MARSHALL, LYCURGUS LUTHER, congressman; b. Bucyrus, O., July 9, 1888; s. Daniel and Mary (Gerster) M.; B.S., Ohio Wesleyan U., 1909; LL.B., Western Reserve U., 1915; m. Minnie Martin, Aug. 14, 1911; children—Hubert Martin, Edward L. Admitted to Ohio bar, 1915; practiced law, Cleveland; mem. Ohio House of Reps., 1920-21, Ohio Senate, 1921-34. Mem. 76th Congress (1939-41), at large, Ohio. Mem. Euclid Sch. Bd. 8 years. Mem. Cuyahoga Bar Assn. Republican. Lutheran. Home: Euclid, Ohio. †

MARSHALL, RICHARD MATHER, business exec.; b. Langhorne, Pa., Nov. 13, 1890; s. Alfred and Florence Virginia (Mather) M.; student U. of Pa., 1910-14; grad. Wharton Business Adminstrn., 1914; m. Elizabeth C. Taylor, Sept. 1, 1915; children—Richard, John Ashby (killed World War II), Jaquelin, Clarence Taylor. Gen. mgr. Am. Manganese Mfg. Co., Dunbar, Pa., 1921-32; chmn. Kerchner, Marshall and Co., Pittsburgh, Pa. from 1923; v.p. and gen. mgr. Sloss-Sheffield Steel and Iron Co., Birmingham, Ala., 1932-34; v.p. and sec. Woodward (Ala.) Iron Co., 1934-41; exec. v.p. Pittsburgh (Pa.) Coke and Chem. Co., 1941-47, pres., 1947-55, chmn. bd., 1955-61; adv. dir. Pitts. Nat. Bank; dir. Pitts. Steel Co., Pitts. Coke & Chem. Co. Vice president Allegheny council Boy Scouts Am. Exec. vice pres., dir. Ohio Valley Hosp.; trustee U. Pa. Served as 1st lt., U.S. Army Tank Corps, 1918. Clubs: Duquesne, Pittsburgh Golf (Pitts.); Sewickley Hunt, Allegheny Country (Sewickley, Pa.); Racquet (Phila.); University of Pa. (N.Y.C.). Home: Pittsburgh, PA. †

MARSHALL, SARAH CATHERINE WOOD, (CATHERINE MARSHALL) author; b. Johnson City, Tenn.; d. John Ambrose and Leonora (Whitaker) Wood; m. Rev. Peter Marshall, Nov. 4, 1936; 1 son, Peter John; m. Leonard Earl LeSourd, Nov. 14, 1959. B.A., Agnes Scott Coll., 1936; D. Litt. (hon.), Cedar Crest Coll., 1954, Westminster Coll., 1979; L.H.D. (hon.), Taylor U., 1973. Faculty Nat. Cathedral Sch. for Girls, Washington, 1949-50; partner Chosen Books Pub. Co., Ltd. Author: A Man Called Peter, 1951 (became motion picture 1955), To Live Again, 1957, Beyond Ourselves, 1961, Christy, 1967, Something More, 1974, Adventures in Prayer, 1975, The Helper, 1978, (with Leonard LeSourd) My Personal Prayer Diary, 1979, Meeting God at Every Turn, 1981; Author, compilor: (with Leonard LeSourd) God Loves You, 1953, Friends with God, 1956, juveniles; Editor: (with Leonard LeSourd) Mr. Jones, Meet the Master, 1949, Let's Keep Christmas, 1953, The Prayers of Peter Marshall, 1954, The Heart of Peter Marshall's Faith, 1956, The First Easter, 1959, John Doe, Disciple, 1963; Woman's editor: (with Leonard LeSourd) Christian Herald mag, 1958-60; roving editor: (with Leonard LeSourd) Guideposts mag, from 1960. Trustee Agnes Scott Coll. Mem. Authors Guild, Nat. League Am. Pen Women, Phi Beta Kappa. Presbyn. Home: Boynton Beach, Fla.

MARSHALL, THOMAS OLIVER, JR., educator; b. Buffalo, Dec. 17, 1907; s. Thomas Oliver and Cynthia (MacNaughton) M.; m. Evelyn Glade, Aug. 10, 1936 (dec. Nov. 1977); children—Anthony Glade, Robert Glade. A.B., Colgate U., 1929; Ed.M., U. Buffalo, 1932; Ed.D., Harvard, 1941. Tchr., organizer Buffalo Adult Edn. Center, 1932; dir. adult edn., Genesee County, N.Y., 1934; research asso. Regents' Inquiry, Albany, N.Y., 1936-37; instr., asst. prof. U. Rochester, 1938-42; dir. student personnel Colo. A. and M. Coll., 1942-45, dir. summer session, 1942-45, acting dean vocat. edn., 1942-45; dean Coll. Arts and Scis., Am. U., Washington, 1945-46, prof., chmn. dept. edn., 1946-47, dir. summer sch., 1946-47; prof., chmn. dept. edn. U. N.H., 1947-59, prof., 1959-73, prof. emeritus, 1973-80; v.p. Center for Constructive Change, 1972-80, chmn. div. tchr. edn., 1947-59; on leave as spl. asst. to dean Grad. Sch., Harvard U., 1955-56; chmn. N.H. Council for Tchr. Edn.; pres. N.H. Dept. Higher Edn.; dir., mem. exec. com. N.H. Council Better Schs.; coordinator N.H. regional center New Eng. Sch. Devel. Council; chmn. steering com., inter-univ. coop. com. Coop. Program in Ednl. Adminstrn., Center for Field Studies, Harvard; cons. Ednl. Systems Corp., Ednl. Projects Inc.; migrant farm workers program Office Econ. Opportunity. Del. N.H. Dem. Conv., 1966, 68, 70, 72. Author: (with Ruth E. Eckert) When Youth Leaves School, 1939, Teaching Time: A Study of Teacher Load in N.H. Public Schools, 1961; editor: (with Ruth E. Eckert) Resource Persons in the New Eng. Area on Various Aspects of Ednl. Adminstrn, 1952; assoc. editor: (with Ruth E. Eckert) Jour. Constructive Change, 1979-80; contbr. (with Ruth E. Eckert) articles to ednl. publs. Ford Found. grantee London, 1965-66. Mem. N.H. Edn. Assn. (chmn. study tchrs. load 1959-61), Nat. Soc. Study Edn., AAUP, NEA, Soc. Advancement Edn., Kappa Delta Pi, Theta Chi, Gamma Delta Psi. Home: Durham, N.H. Died 1980.

MARSHALL, WALTER VANCLEVE, educator; b. Helena, Mont., Mar. 29, 1890; s. Franklin Pierce and Mary (Smith) M.; B.Arch. Eng., U. of Mich., 1915; m. Edith Stanley, Oct. 15, 1924; children—Marvin Stewart, Ross Donald. Archtl. draftsman, Mont., Colo., Ore. and Calif., 1915-25; teacher U. of Mich. from 1925, prof. architecture, asst. dean, coll. arch. and design from 1947; draftsman, structural designer Smith, Hinchman & Grylls, Detroit, summers 1928, 1941. Sec., treas. Barton Hills Maintenance Corp., and Improvement Assn. from 1949. Served as 2d lt., inf. U.S. Army, 1917-18. Mem. A.I.A. Methodist. Clubs: University, University of Michigan (Ann Arbor). Author archtl. articles. Home: Ann Arbor, Mich. †

MARTIN, BERNARD, educator; b. Seklence, Czechoslovakia, Mar. 13, 1928; naturalized, 1939; s. Benjamin Adam and Helen Hersh (Kowitz) M.; m. Nancy Louise Platt, June 30, 1955; children—Rachel, Joseph Louis. B.A., U. Chgo., 1947; M.H.L., Hebrew Union Coll., 1951; Ph.D., U. Ill., 1961. Ordained rabbi, 1951, rabbi in, Champaign, Ill., 1951-57, assoc. rabbi, Chgo., 1957-61, sr. rabbi, St. Paul, 1961-65; Abba Hillel Silver prof. Jewish studies Case Western Res. U., 1966-82, chmn. dept. religion, 1967-82; Chmn. com. theology Central Conf. Am. Rabbis, 1965-71. Author: The Existentialist Theology of Paul Tillich, 1963, Prayer in Judaism, 1968, Great Twentieth Century Jewish Philosophers, 1969, (with Daniel J. Silver) A History of Judaism, 1974; novel That Man from Smyrna, 1978; Translator: (with Daniel J. Silver) novel Athens and Jerusalem (Lev Shestov), 1966, Potestas Clavium, 1968, History of Jewish Literature, 12 vols. (Israel Zinberg), 1972-78, When All is Said and Done (David Bergelson), 1978, Speculation and Revelation (Lev Shestov), 1981; Editor: (with Daniel J. Silver) novel Contemporary Reform Jewish Thought, 1968, A Shestov Anthology, 1970, Issues and Movements in American Judaism, 1978, Jour. Central Conf. Am. Rabbis, 1975-77, Jour. Reform Judaism, 1977-82. Bd. dirs. Cleve. chpt. NCCJ, 1966-71; trustee Cleve. Jewish Fedn., 1967-74. Served with AUS, 1953-55. Mem. Acad. Jewish Philosophy, Am. Acad. Jewish Research, Am. Philos. Assn., Am. Acad. Religion, Central Conf. Am. Rabbis, Nat. Assn. Profs. Hebrew. Home: University Heights, Ohio. Died Jan. 14, 1982.

MARTIN, ERLE, ret. aircraft mfg. co. exec.; b. Tullahoma, Tenn., July 7, 1907; s. Eric and Goldie (Carroll) M.; student Pennington (N.J.) Prep. Sch., 1924-25; B.S., Pa. State U., 1929; m. Angenette Louise Vail, 1934; children—Erle, Steven Thornton, Angenette Carroll. With Kreider-Reisner div., Hagerstown, Md., 1929. Air Propellers, Inc., 1929-31; chief engr. Hamilton Standard. Windsor Locks, Conn., 1931-39, engring. mgr., 1939-46, gen. mgr., 1946-58; v.p. United Aircraft Corp., Hartford, Conn., 1952-60, v.p. research and devel., 1960-68, vice chmn., 1968-72, also dir.; Conn. Bank & Trust Co., Conn. Gen. Life Ins. Co., Aetna (Fire) Ins. Co., Mechanics Savs. Bank; cons. United Techs. Corp. Trustee. Greater Hartford YMCA. Hartt Coll. Music, Hartford Grad. Center, Inst. Living Pub. TV. Fellow Am. Inst. Aeros. and Astronautics; mem. Soc. Automotive Engrs. Home: West Hartford, Conn. Died Dec. 12, 1981.

MARTIN, HELEN M., geologist; b. Fargo, N.D., Nov. 20, 1889; d. Lawrence Mathew and Mary (Mandeville) Martin; A.B., U. of Mich., 1908, M.S., 1917; unmarried. Teacher physiography and geology, Battle Creek, Mich., 1908-16; teaching asst. dept. geology U. of Mich., 1916-17; geologist and editor Mich. Geol. Survey, Lansing, Mich., 1917-23; Roxana Petrol Co., Ardmore and Tulsa, Okla., 1923-24; subsurface geologist Carter Oil Co. (Standard of N.J.), 1924-32; cons. geologist on petroleum in Mich., 1933-35; research geologist, editor, lecturer, Geological Survey Div. Mich. Dept. Conservation, 1935-58, also teach and conduct field trips in training sch.; intensive work in pub. edn. in geology and in conservation edn. Recipient award contbn. to conservation education, American Association Conservation Education. Fellow Geol. Soc. Am., A.A.A.S. Life mem. Am. Assn. U. Women, mem. U. of Mich. Alumni Assn., Am. Assn. Petroleum Geologists, Mich. Acad. Sci. and Arts (chmn. geology sect., 1924), Am. Mus. Natural History, Nat. Geographic Soc., Am. Forestry Assn., Mich. Geol. Soc. Compiler: Centennial Geologic Map of Mich. (Mich. Dept. Conservation), 1936; Rev. Surface Geology Map So. Peninsula Mich. Author: Ne-Saw-Je-Won Story of the Great Lakes (Cleveland iron cos.), 1939; Rocks and Minerals of Michigan (with O. F. Poindexter and S. G. Bergguist) (Mich. Dept. Conservation), 1938; They Need Not Vanish (co-editor, co-author) (Mich. Dept. Conservation), 1942, rev. 1952. Author chpt. in Typical American Oil Fields (Am. Assn. Petrol. Geol. 1933) and chapters in Mineral Resources of Michigan: Non Metallic (several vols.) 1917-23. Contbr. to sci. publs. Author over 80 items on Michigan geology. †

MARTIN, JOHN FLETCHER, lawyer, former student adminstr.; b. Greencastle, Pa., Oct. 16, 1889; s. John Funk and Mary (Fletcher) M.; A.B., Princeton, 1911, A.M., 1914; J.D., U. Fla., 1949; m. Marta Amunategui, Mar. 29, 1924; children—James Watson, John, George Frederick, Martha Ellen (Mrs. Mangold). Instr. modern langs., Princeton U., 1914-15; mem. U.S. diplomatic service, 1915-29, assigned to following; 3d sec., Santiago, Chile and Buenos Aires; 2d sec., Havana, Mexico City and Bogotá, Columbia; 1st sec., London and Rome; 1st sec. and charge d'affairs, San José, Costa Rica, Panama, La Paz, Bolivia, Santiago, Chile, and Madrid; mgr. Standard Oil Co., Bolivia, 1929-31; admitted to Fla., Bar, 1933; gen. comml. supr. Chilean br., Internat. Telephone and Telegraph. 1935-41; acting dir., Inst. Inter-Am. Affairs, U. of Fla., 1942-45, dir., 1945-50, dir. Latin Am. student affairs, 1950-52; lawyer from 1952; asso. prof. in Spanish, U. Fla., 1946-48. Decorated Comdr. Chilean Order Al Mérito; Cross of Eloy Alfaro, 1949. Mem. Fla. Bar Assn., S.A.R., St. Augustine Hist. Soc., Kappa Alpha. Republican. Roman Catholic. Clubs: Princeton (N.J.) Campus; Newman (Gainesville, Fla.). Home: St. Augustine, FL. †

MARTIN, JOHN JOSEPH, dance critic; b. Louisville, June 2, 1893; s. William Joseph and Cora (Steinberg) M.; ed. pub. schs., Louisville; m. Hettie Louise Mick, Aug. 17, 1918. Actor, 1912-15; with Chgo. Little Theatre, 1915-17; press agt. Stuart Walker, 1922; editor Dramatic Mirror, N.Y., 1919-22; dramatic dir. Swarthmore Chautauqua, 1923; exec. sec. Richard Boleslavsky's Lab. Theatre, 1924-26; dance editor, critic N.Y. Times, 1927-62; dir. summer theatre prodns., Johnstown, Pa., 1929, Locust Valley, N.Y., 1933, New Rochelle, N.Y., 1934; mem. faculty New Sch. Social Research, N.Y.C., 1930-40, Bennington Coll. Sch. of Dance, 1934-38; lectr. on dance history and criticism, 1930-45; lectr. dance U. Calif. at Los Angeles, 1965-71. Served with Signal Corps, A.C., U.S. Army, World War I. Author: Yniard, 1922; The Modern Dance, 1933; America Dancing, 1936; Introduction to the Dance, 1939; The Dance, 1945; World Book of Modern Ballet, 1959; Book of the Dance, 1963; Ruth Page, An Intimate Biography, 1977; also long and short plays prod. various companies including Wife of Usher's Well, Hynd Horn, Yesterday's Husband, Strictly Incognito, Sketches from a County Poor Farm. Contbr. encys. various periodicals. Home: Saratoga Springs, N.Y. Died May 19, 1985.

MARTIN, JOSEPH J., chem. engr.; b. Anita, Iowa, Dec. 23, 1916; s. Joseph Wesley and Merle (Baker) M.; m. Merrylin Louise Baxter, Aug. 30, 1941; children—Judy, Joseph, Jacque, Jon. B.S. in Chem. Engring, Iowa State U., 1939; M.S., U. Rochester, 1944; D.Sc., Carnegie Mellon U., 1948, U. Nebr., 1971. Chem. engr. Eastman Kodak Co., Rochester, N.Y., 1939-41; from instr. to asst. prof. U. Rochester, 1940-45; instr. Carnegie Mellon U., Pitts., 1945-47; mem. faculty U. Mich., Ann Arbor, from 1947, prof. chem. engring., from 1956; asso. and acting dir. U. Mich. (Inst. Sci. and Tech.), from 1965; cons. to govt. and industry, from 1942; mem. NRC, 1966-72. Contbr. articles in field to profl. jours. Div. head Ann Arbor United Fund, 1966; pres. bd. Ann Arbor Hills Assn., 1950; mem. Ann Arbor Republican City Com., 1961, Ann Arbor Housing Commn., 1968-78. Recipient award for teaching Phi Lambda Upsilon, 1955; Distinguished Service award U. Mich., 1966; award N.Y. Acad. Sci., 1962. Fellow AAAS, Am. Inst. Chem. Engrs. (dir., pres. 1971, Founders award 1973); mem. Am. Chem. Soc. (chmn. div. nuclear tech.), Am. Soc. Engring. Edn. (v.p. 1968-70, pres. from 1978), Engrs. Joint Council (dir., pres. 1973-75), Am. Nuclear Soc., Engrs. Council Profl. Devel., Assn. for Cooperation in Engring. (founder, 1st chmn. 1975-76), Sigma Xi, Alpha Chi Sigma, Tau Beta Pi. Home: Ann Arbor, Mich.

MARTIN, LAURENCE JANNEY, business and govt. exec.; b. Aldie, Va., Sept. 27, 1888; s. William Thornton and Cornelia (Janney) M.; student Jefferson Sch., Charlottesville, Va., 1898-1903, Randolph-Macon Coll., Ashland, Va., 1905-06, U. of Va., 1907-11; m. Josephine Marshall, of Charlottesville, Va., Apr. 17, 1917; children—Marcella, Lilian Paige, Jane Wyndham. Athletic coach Richmond (Va.) Coll., 1912, U. of Wash., 1914-15; with Chesley Towing Co., Seattle, 1913-14, Drummond Lighterage Co., Seattle, in charge waterfront operations, 1915-21; exec. for Mayhew Steel Products Corpn., Hopewell, Va., 1921-27, for Tubize-Chatillon Corpn., mfrs. textile products, 1927-32; with NRA, Washington, D.C., 1933-36, deputy administrator in charge heavy machinery and fabricated metals codes, 1933-34, chief of compliance div., 1934-35, exec. officer, June-Aug. 1935, acting administrator, Aug. 1935-Jan. 1, 1936; asst. to pres. Thomas A. Edison, Inc., from Jan. 1, 1936. Served in 1st Wash. Cav., 1916-17. Mem. Phi Delta Theta. Democrat. Episcopalian. Home: East Orange, N.J. †

MARTIN, STANLEY HUBERT, college president; b. Edina, Mo., 1912; s. Ellis and Alice Gertrude (Marble) M.; A.B., Quincy Coll., 1936; S.T.B., Boston U., 1939, M.A., 1939, Ph.D., 1954; D.D., Adrian Coll., 1954; Doctor of Laws (hon.), Concord State Coll., 1967; m. Glenadene L. Parkin, Sept. 9, 1939; children—William Lee L., (dec.), Dawn Marie, Marc Edwin. Dir. Wesley Found., U. Ia., 1941-42; chaplain, instr. Simpson Coll., 1942-44; prof. religious edn., univ. chaplain Boston U., 1945-50, dir. univ. campaign, 1946-47; dir. student loans, scholarships and personnel Gen. Bd. Edn. Meth. Ch., 1950-57; pres. W.Va. Wesleyan Coll., after 1957. Bd. dirs. Found. Ind. Colls. W.Va. Mem. Nat. Assn. Schs. and Colls. United Meth. Ch. (pres. 1968). Rotarian. Home: Buckhannon, W.Va. Died Jan. 30, 1985.

MARTIN, TOWNSEND BRADLEY, sports executive; b. N.Y.C., Dec. 27, 1907; s. Bradley and Helen Margaret (Phipps) M.; m. Irene Redmond, May 7, 1948; children by previous marriage—Michael, Alan. Student pvt. schs., N.Y. and R.I. Officer Bessemer Securities Corp., N.Y.C., 1948-70; owner, dir. N.Y. Jets Football Team, 1963-82; dir. Monmouth Park Jocky Club. Republican. Episcopalian. Clubs: Rumson, Ocean, Quoque Field, Jockey. Home: Bedford, N.Y. Died Oct. 22, 1982; buried Quogue Cemetery, Long Island, N.Y.

MARTINDALE, DON ALBERT, educator; b. Marinette, Wis., Feb. 9, 1915; s. Don Lucien and Elsie Caroline (Tetzloff) M.; B.A., U. Wis., 1939, M.A., 1940, Ph.D., 1948; D.Litt. (hon.), Meml. U. Nfld., 1971; m. Edith Plotkin, Feb. 2, 1943. Instr. sociology U. Wis., Madison, 1945-48; from asst. prof. to prof. sociology U. Minn., Mpls., 1948—. Served to capt. AUS, 1942-46. Mem. Am. Sociol. Assn., Am. Assn. U. Profs., Am. Acad. Polit. and Social Sci., Phi Beta Kappa. Author: Nature and Types of Sociological Theory, 1960; American Society, 1960; American Social Structure, 1960; Community Character and Civilization, 1963; Social Life and Cultural Change, 1963; Institutions, Organizations and Mass Society, 1967; Small Town and the Nation, 1969; Sociological Theory and the Problem of Values, 1974; Prominent Sociologists Since World War II, 1975; The Romance of a Profession, 1976; editor: Sociology Monograph Series; Ideals and Realities: Some Problems of Professional Social Science, 1979, The Monologue: Hans Gerth (1908-1978) A Memoir, 1982. Home: Saint Paul, Minn. Died May 17, 1985.

MARTINDALE, JAMES VAUGHAN, publisher; b. Chgo., Oct. 16, 1894; s. George Boyd and Martha (Vaughan) M.; m. Ruth Helen McDermott, Sept. 1, 1960. Student, Bklyn. Poly. Prep. Sch., 1911. Vice pres., sec. Martindale-Hubbell, Inc., Summit, N.J., 1930-46, pres., treas., 1947-57, dir., from 1930, chmn. bd. dirs., 1943-46, 57—; pres. Bar Register Co., Inc., Summit, 1947-57, dir., from 1935; cons. to Survey Legal Profession, 1949-52. Served as yeoman USNRF, 1917-18. Club: Sports Car of Am. Home: Brooklyn, NY.

MARTZ, CHARLES E., ednl. journalist; b. Shenandoah, Pa., Jan. 8, 1890; s. William Henry and Matilda (Morgan) M.; grad. West Chester (Pa.) State Tchrs. Coll., 1908; A.B., Yale, 1915, A.M., 1917; student Harvard, 1934-35; m. Edith Nissley Freed, Dec. 8, 1915; 1 dau., Mary (wife of Rev. Robert B. Weaver). Tchr. in high schs. in Pa., 1908-12; prof. West Chester State Tchrs. Coll., 1918-21, Sch. of Edn., Western Reserve U., 1921-37; editor, Our Times current events weekly for high sch. students 1937-58, emeritus, from 1958, lectr. Wesleyan U., Middletown, Conn., from 1958. Mem. Hadam Bd. Edn., 1957-62; mem. Haddam Sch. Bldg. Com., 1958-63. Chmn. Columbus Fgn. Policy Assn., 1945-48; mem. program com. Columbus Town Meeting, 1948-50, moderator, 1945-52; sec.-treas. Jr. Town Meeting League, 1952-60; chmn. speakers bureau Columbus Community Chest, 1949-50. Mem. Haddam Pub. Health Nursing Assn. (dir.), Phi Beta Kappa, Sigma Xi, Beta Theta Pi. Member Presbyterian Church (elder). Clubs; Torch (president 1958-59); University (pres. 1960-61) (Middletown, Connecticut). Author: Social Science for Teachers (with John A. Kinneman), 1921. Home: Higganum, Conn. †

MARTZ, WILLIAM EDWARD, lawyer, chess master; b. Detroit, Mar. 21, 1945; s. Edward V. and Ellen (Legerat) M.; m. Norma Buth, June 15, 1981. B.A., U. Wis., 1965; J.D., Marquette U., 1970. Bar: Wis. bar 1970. Since practiced in, Hartland., Chess tchr., exhibitor, lectr., 1965—, rep. of U.S. in internat. chess competition, 1967-76. Contbr. to ofcl. state chess publs., Wis., Minn., N.D., Ill., Mich. Mem. U.S. Chess Fedn. (life master), Waukesha Chess Club, Wis. Chess Assn., Milw.Mcpl.Chess Assn. (pres. 1972-74). Wis. chess champion, 1964, 65, 66, 69, 70, 74, 75; Wis. del. U.S. Chess Fedn., 1968-79; internat. chess master, 1975; twice participant U.S.A. team World Chess Olympics. Home: Wauwatosa, Wis. Died Jan. 17, 1983.

MARX, HENRY MOSLER, lawyer; b. Birmingham, Ala., Mar. 18, 1908; s. Otto and Agnes (Mosler) M.; m. Peggy Esberg, Mar. 19, 1937 (dec.); children: Henry E., Otto III; m. Anna Duval, Dec. 24, 1969 (dec.); m. Rasma Svede, Dec. 15, 1980. A.B. cum laude, Princeton U., 1930; LL.B. cum laude, Harvard U., 1933. Bar: N.Y. 1933, Conn. 1954. Asso. firm White & Case, N.Y.C., 1933-41, 45; partner Kramer, Marx, Greenlee and Backus (and predecessor firms), 1946-74, Windels & Marx, 1974-77; partner Windels, Marx, Davies & Ives, 1978-83, counsel, from 1983; dir. Thyssen Inc., Chromasco Ltd., Am. Investment Trust N.V., Birmingham Corp. Town rep. Greenwich, Conn., 1949-51; coordinator atomic devel. activities State of Conn., 1955-68; mem. Conn. Research Commn., 1965-71; former mem. AEC Adv. Commn. of State Ofcls., Conn.; Patron, mem. nat. council Met. Opera Assn.; bd. dirs. Am. Friends of Covent Garden and Royal Ballet, Inc., N.Y.C. div. Am. Cancer Soc. Served from 1st lt. to maj. AUS, 1942-45. Decorated Bronze Star medal. Mem. Am. Bar Assn., Assn. Bar City N.Y., N.Y. County Lawyers Assn., Conn. Bar Assn., Am. Arbitration Assn. (mem. nat. panel). Clubs: Met. Opera (N.Y.C.), Hemisphere (N.Y.C.), Princeton (N.Y.C.), Wings (N.Y.C.), New York Yacht. (N.Y.C.); Byram Yacht (Conn.); Royal Norwegian Yacht, Royal Scandinavian Yacht, Nylandska Jaktklubben, Princeton Yacht, Wharf Rat, Storm Trysail; Mount Royal (Montreal). Home: New York, NY.

MASIKO, PETER, JR., emeritus coll. pres.; b. Vera Cruz, Pa., Mar. 18, 1914; s. Peter and Sophia (Baker) M.; m. Anna E. Fetterolf, July 9, 1932; children—Elaine Irene (Mrs. James Salapatas), Peter III. B.A. with highest honors, Lehigh U., 1936; M.A. (fellow), U. Ill., 1937, Ph.D., 1939. Instr. U. Ill., 1936-39; with Wright Jr. Coll., Chgo., 1939-56, successively instr., chmn. social sci. dept., asst. dean, dean, 1939-56; exec. dean Chgo. City Jr. Coll., 1956-62; pres. Miami (Fla.)-Dade Community Coll., 1962-80, pres. emeritus, 1980-81; economist Bd. Investigation and Research, Washington, summer 1942; mem. adv. com. on edn. U.S. Dept. Def., 1963-66; mem. steering com., mental health tng. and research So. Regional Edn. Bd.; mem. Fla. Post-Secondary Planning Com.; trustee Ednl. Testing Service. Author: (with Atteberry, Auble and Hunt), rev. edit., 1951.) Introduction to Social Science; Editorial bd.: Edn. Digest. Bd. dirs. South Fla. Comprehensive Health Planning Council, Am. Council Edn., Pub. TV Sta., Miami; mem. adv. com. Dade County Oceanographic Sci. Park, Internat. Oceanographic Found.; mem. adv. com. marine scis. Oceanographic Activities and Devel. Virginia Key; bd. dirs. United Way, Greater Miami. Mem. Am. Econ. Assn. (adv. com. on structure of profession), Am. Council on Edn. (commn. fed. relations, dir. from 1972, sec. 1973-74), Am. Assn. Sch. Adminstrs. (commn. on founds.), Am. Assn. Community and Jr. Colls. (dir. from 1969, chmn. from 1973), Am. Council Edn., Commn. on Women in Higher Edn., Ill. Assn. Jr. Colls. (sec.-treas. 1951-52), North Central Assn. (commr. commn. on colls. and univs. 1956-60), Phi Beta Kappa, Phi Kappa Phi. Lutheran. Home: Richland, WA.

MASON, CHARLES WALTER, judge; b. Stafford, O., Dec. 11, 1887; s. Frank and Mary O'Ella (Shankland) M.; student Grant U., Chattanooga, Tenn., 1908 to 1909; LL.B., Washington and Lee U., Va., 1911; m. Ruth Ethel Cobbs, Dec. 24, 1914. Admitted to Okla. bar, 1911, and began practice at Nowata; city attorney Nowata, 1913-14; county atty. Nowata County, 1914-16; dist. judge 2d Jud. Dist. of Okla., by appmt. of gov., to fill unexpired term, 1919-22, and elected Nov. 1922, for 4-yr. term; apptd. justice Supreme Court of Okla., Apr. 1923, to fill unexpired term, and elected to same office, Nov. 1924, for term ending Jan. 1931; elected vice chief justice, Jan. 12, 1925, chief justice, Jan. 14, 1929; v.p. Victory Nat. Bank; president Title Abstract Company, (both Nowata, Oklahoma). Enlisted in U.S. Army, Aug. 25, 1917; commd. 1st lt. inf., Nov. 25, 1917; capt., June 30, 1918; hon. disch. Dec. 16, 1918; col. Air Corps and inspector general Hdqrs. Third Army, U.S. Army, Dec. 1940-Apr. 1943; insp. gen., 6th U.S. Army, Australia, New Guinea and SW Pacific areas, Apr. 1943-Dec. 1944; office, the Insp. Gen., Washington, D.C., Jan. 1945-Aug. 1946. Awarded Legion of Merit by Gen. Douglas MacArthur. Mem. Okla. State Bar (mem. bd. govs. and 1st v.p. 1938-39), U.S. 169 Hwy. Assn. (pres.), Vets. Foreign Wars, Sigma Phi Epsilon, Delta Theta Phi, Am. Legion, Forty and Eight. Democrat. Mem. Christian (Disciples) Ch. Mason (Shriner), K.P., Elk. Clubs: Nowata, Rotary. Home: Nowata, Okla. †

MASON, CLYDE WALTER, educator; b. Watertown, S.D., June 17, 1898; s. George Walter and Cora Almira (Pitt) M.; A.B., U. Ore., 1919; Ph.D., Cornell U., 1924; m. Elizabeth Mandana Peterson, Aug. 2, 1920; children—George William, Phoebe Jane. Instr. chemistry U. Ore., 1919-20; instr. chem. microscopy Cornell U., 1920-28, asst. prof., then prof., 1928-83, Emile M. Chamot prof. chem. microscopy, professor of metallography School Chem. Engring., 1942-83. Tech. rep. chem. warfare agts., nat. def. research com. OSRD, 1943-45. Fellow N.Y., Micros. Soc.; mem. Am. Chem. Soc., Am. Soc. Metals, Am. Soc. Testing Materials, N.Y. Acad. of Sciences, Sigma Xi, Tau Beta Pi, Phi Kappa Phi, Alpha Chi Sigma. Author: Introductory Physical Metallurgy, 1946; (with E.M. Chamot) Handbook of Chemical Microscopy (2 vols.), 1931, 38, 58. Home: Ithaca, N.Y. Died Dec. 8, 1983.

MASON, HAROLD CARLTON, educator, lecturer; b. Kunkle, Ohio, Nov. 9, 1888; s. Rev. Emmet Carlton (D.D.) and Virginia Elizabeth (Munson) M.; B.S., Huntington (Ind.) Coll., 1907, A.B., 1913, D.D., 1924; A.B., Adrian (Mich.) Coll., 1916; M.A., U. of Mich., 1924, grad. study, 1925-27; LL.D., Houghton Coll., 1940; Ed.D., Ind. U., 1945; m. Alta Elvida McFate, Dec. 25, 1909; children—Robert Emmet, Wendell Dwight. Ordained ministry U.B. in Christ (Old Constn.), 1907; successively teacher Chesbrough Sem., North Chili, N.Y., prin. schs., Whitmore Lake, Mich., supt. schs., Horton, Mich., until 1911; pastor U.B. Ch., Adrian, Mich., 1911-12; instr. Huntington Coll. and pastor Ch., 1912-13; pastor Blissfield, Mich., 1913-18, Central Ch., Montpelier, Ohio, 1918-21; bishop Pacific Coast Dist., U.B. Ch., term of 4 yrs., 1921-25; prof. philosophy and rhetoric, and dean of the coll., Adrian Coll., 1925-29; supt. of schs. and Lenawee County Normal Sch., 1929-32; pres. Huntington (Ind.) Coll., 1932-39; prof. philosophy of Christianity, Winona Lake Sch. Theol., 1938; pastoral supply, Free Meth. Ch., Winona Lake, 1939-43; spl. lecturer Christian Philosophy, Grace Theol. Sem., Winona Lake, 1943; prof. Christian edn., Northern Baptist Theol. Sem., 1943-48; prof. christian philosophy, Houghton College, summer 1944, Christian education, Winona Lake Sch. Theology after 1947; prof. Christian edn. Asbury Theol. Sem. after 1948, Gen. sec. edn. U.B. Ch. (Old Constrn.), 1932-39. Some time mem. Mich. State Com. Y.M.C.A., Mich. Sch. Masters' Club, Mich. Coun. of Teachers of Eng. (sec.-treas.). Lenawee Co. School Masters' Club (pres.), Mich. State Tchrs. Assn., Lenawee County Brotherhood of Christian Laymen (pres.); Modern Lang. Assn. Am., Am. Acad. of Polit. and Social Science, A.A.A.S., Ind. Hist. Assn., Pi Gamma Mu, N.E.A., mem. Society of Biblical Research, Nat. Assn. & Biblical Instns., Soc. of Biblical Lit. and Exegesis. Club: Rotary (hon., Warsaw, Ind.). Author: (booklets) Commencement Meditations; Reclaiming the Sunday School. Contbr. Light and Life Press; Am. S.S. Union pubs.; Sunday Sch. Times. Editor: Light and Life Graded Lesson Series, Winona Lake, Ind., since 1952. Deceased.

MASON, LOWELL BLAKE, lawyer, former government official; b. Chgo., July 25, 1893; s. William E. and Edith J. (White) M.; m. Grace F. Gilbert, 1916; children—William E., III, Barbara Grace, Nancy Gilbert, Lowell B., Jr.; m. Rose d'Amore, 1938; children—Jimilu, Bianca. LL.B., Northwestern U., 1916, LL.D., 1954. Bar: Ill. bar 1916, D.C. bar 1936. Practiced in, Chgo. and Washington, asst. corp. counsel, City of Chgo., 1916; mem. Ill. Senate, 1922-30; gen. counsel Nat. Industry Recovery Bd. (Darrow Bd.), 1934; counsel U.S. Senate Judiciary subcom. investigating NRA, 1935; counsel U.S. Senate Interstate Commerce subcom., 1936; mem., later chmn. FTC, 1945-56; Mem. 1st Ill. State Aviation Commn., 1927. Author: Changing Forms of Government. Bruno Leoni fellow Inst. Humane Studies, Menlo Park, Calif. Mem. Bar Assn. D.C. Republican. Unitarian. Club: Mason (32 deg., Shriner). Address: Oak Park, Ill. Dec. July 11, 1983.

MASON, MARTIN ALEXANDER, ret. coll. pres.; b. Washington, Apr. 23, 1907; s. Alexander Kemp and Elizabeth (Arenz) M.; B.S. in Engring., George Washington U., 1931; postgrad. (John R. Freeman scholar in hydraulics 1937), Johns Hopkins, 1936-37; Ingenieur-Docteur, U. Grenoble (France), 1938; m. Winnifred Maupin Meade, Nov. 5, 1932; children—Ann Winnifred, Martin Everard. Hydraulic engr. Nat. Bur.

Standards, 1925-40; chief engr. Beach Erosion Bd., 1940-51; dean engring. George Washington U., 1951-67; pres. Capital Inst. Tech., 1967-71; also cons. engr. Mem. ASCE, ASME, Washington Soc. Engrs. (Outstanding Engr. award 1966), Washington Acad. Sci. (Outstanding Engr. award 1947), Am. Geophys. Union, Sigma Xi, Sigma Tau, Tau Beta Pi. Club: Cosmos (Washington). Home: Chevy Chase, Md. Died Jan. 12, 1982.

MASSER, HARRY L., public utilities; b. Los Angeles, Calif., Jan. 2, 1890; s. William H. and Sara L. (Wiegand) M.; B.S. in Chemical Engineering, University of California, 1914; married Mildred F. Lantz, August 20, 1921; children—Harry L., Jr., Rose G. Draftsman and shop supt. Keller Thompson Co., mfrs. of hydraulic appliances, 1914-15; draftsman and office engr., Southern Calif. Gas Co., Los Angeles, 1915-18; ensign, U.S.N.R., Bur. Ordnance, stationed at Sperry Gyroscope Co., Brooklyn, N.Y., and Ford Instrument Works, New York City, 1918-19; gas engr., Calif. R.R. Commn., for establishment of rates and standards of gas service, as well as gas adminstr., 1919-24; gas engr., Los Angeles Gas and Elec. Corp., 1924-28, v.p. and exec. engr. since 1928; exec. v.p., dir. Southern Calif. Gas Co. (merger of Los Angeles Gas & Electric Corp. and Southern Calif. Gas Co.) after 1937; in charge of constrn. and operation of Govt. Synthetic Rubber Plant S.R. No. 44. Dir. Los Angeles Gas and Electric Corp., Los Angeles Lighting Co., Jas. H. Knapp Co., industrial gas furnaces. Regent U. Cal.; president Los Angeles Orthopedic Hospital and Found.; treas., dir. Calif. Institute Cancer Research; member Los Angeles County Welfare Relief Commn., Los Angeles Citizens Com. on Coop. Self-Help Relief Unit; chmn., Los Angeles area War Chest, 1942; pres. Welfare Fedn. Los Angeles Area; vice chmn. Calif. Civil Defense for Utilities. Mem. bd. engrs. U. of Calif. Pres. Pacific Coast Gas Assn., 1945 (gold medalist); pres. U. of Calif. Alumni Assn. Awarded Carnegie medal. Mem. Phi Kappa Sigma (exec. bd.). Clubs: California, University Electric (pres.), (Los Angeles); Rotary. Home: Los Angeles, Calif. Deceased.

MASSEY, LOUIS MELVILLE, prof. plant pathology; b. West Point, Ia., Aug. 25, 1890; s. Milton and Anna May (Rose) M.; A.B., Wabash Coll., Crawfordsville, Ind., 1912; Ph.D., Cornell U., 1916; m. Margery Wheldon Leonard, June 21, 1921; children—Louis Melville, Ann Wheldon. Asst. in plant pathology, Cornell U., 1912-14, instr. in plant pathology, 1914-16, asst. prof., 1916-18, 1919-22, prof. from 1950, head department, 1922-50; pathologist U.S. Dept. Agr. (on leave), 1918-19. Mem. Am. Bot. Soc., Am. Soc. Plant Physiologists, Am. Phytopathol. Soc., Canadian Phytopathol. Soc., Mycol. Soc. of Am., Société Linnéenne de Lyon, Am. Rose Soc. (pres. 1940, 41; gold medal 1947); Fellow, Am. Assn. for Advancement of Science, Phi Beta Kappa, Phi Kappa Phi, Sigma Xi, Gamma Alpha. Contbr. to scientific publs. Home: Ithaca, N.Y. †

MASSEY, RAYMOND, actor, director, producer; b. Toronto, Ont., Can., Aug. 30, 1896; naturalized, 1944; s. Chester D. and Anna (Vincent) M.; m. Margery Hilda Fremantle, 1921; ((dissolved)), 1921; 1 child, Geoffrey; m. Adrianne Allen, 1929; ((dissolved)), 1929; children—Daniel, Anna; m. Dorothy Ludington, 1939. Ed., Appleby Sch., Oakville, Ont., Toronto U., Balliol Coll., Oxford U., Eng.; D.Litt. (hon.), Lafayette U., 1939, Hobart and Smith Colls., 1952; LL.D., Queens U., 1949; A.F.D., Northwestern U., Ripon Coll.; Dr. Humanics, Am. Internat. Coll., 1960; L.H.D., Coll. of Wooster, 1966. Acted in: many plays on London stage, including I Never Sang for My Father, 1970, St. Joan, Spread Eagle, The Shining Hour, Idiot's Delight, The Man in Possession, Five Star Final; dir.: 35 plays including The Silver Tassie, The Rats of Norway, Grand Hotel, Five Star Final, Idiot's Delight; N.Y. stage debut as Hamlet, 1931; starred in: 11 Broadway prodns. including J.B, Ethan Frame, Candida, The Doctor's Dilemma, Pygmalion, Abe Lincoln in Illinois; Night of the Iguana, Los Angeles; appeared in: over 60 motion pictures including Abe Lincoln in Illiois, The Scarlet Pimpernel, Things to Come, Hurricane, The Prisoner of Zenda, East of Eden; TV series Dr. Kildare as Dr. Gillespie; Author: play The Hanging Judge, produced in London, 1952; autobiography When I Was Young, 1976, A Hundred Different Lives, 1979. Served as lt. Canadian F.A., 1915-19, in France (wounded); Served as lt. Canadian F.A., 1916, in France (wounded); in U.S. as instr. in field arty., Yale and Princeton 1917, in Siberia; in U.S. as instr. in field arty., Yale and Princeton 1918, in Siberia; maj. on staff adj. gen. Canadian Army, 1942; officer in Res. 1943. Clubs: Garrick (London); Century (N.Y.C.); Pilgrims of U.S. Home: Beverly Hills, Calif. Dec. July 29, 1983.

MASTERS, JOHN, author; b. Oct. 26, 1914; s. John and Ada (Coulthard) M.; m. Barbara Allcard; 2 children. Student, Royal Mil. Coll., Sandhurst, Eng. Author: Nightrunners of Bengal, 1951, The Deceivers, 1952, The Lotus and the Wind, 1953, Bhowani Junction, 1954, Coromandel, 1955, Bugles and a Tiger, 1956, Far, Far The Mountain Peak, 1957, Fandango Rock, 1959, The Venus of Konpara, 1960, The Road Past Mandalay, 1961, To The Coral Strand, 1962, Trial at Monomoy, 1964, Fourteen Eighteen, 1965, The Breaking Strain, 1967, The Rock, 1969, Pilgrim Son, 1971, The Ravi Lancers, 1972, Thunder at Sunset, 1974, The Field Marshall's Memoirs, 1975, The Himalayan Concerto, 1976, Now, God Be Thanked, 1979, Heart of War, 1980. Served with Indian Army, 1934-48; active service in 1936-37, N.W. Frontier; active service in 1941, Iraq, Syria, Persia; active service in 1944-45, Burma. Decorated companion Disting. Service Order, officer Order Brit. Empire. Address: New York, N.Y. Dec. May 7, 1983.*

MASTERSON, WILLIAM HENRY, educator; b. Houston, Mar. 16, 1914; s. Leigh C. and Aileen (Sharp) M.; B.A., Rice U., 1935; M.A., U. Pa., 1946, Ph.D., 1950; m. Orvetta T. Weston, Aug. 18, 1945; children—David Glen (dec.), Amanda Roane, Aileen Talbott. Instr. history Bavlor Sch., Chattanooga, 1935-41, 47-48; asst. instr. history U. Pa., 1945-47; faculty Rice U., 1948-66, prof. history, 1955-66, asst. to pres., 1951-55, master Hanszen Coll., 1957-66, dean humanities, 1959-66; pres. U. Chattanooga, 1966-69, chancellor, 1969-73, prof. history, 1973-83, Guerry prof., 1977-83; vis. prof. U. Wis., 1957; chmn., Tenn. com. to relate humanities to pub. policy. Trustee St. Stephens Sch., Austin, Tex. Served to capt. AUS, 1941-45. Mem. Am., Mississippi Valley, So., Tex. Gulf Coast (pres. 1957-60, v.p. 1960) hist. assns., Houston Philos. Soc., C. of C. (met Council), Newcomen Soc., Phi Beta Kappa. Episcopalian. Rotarian. Author: William Blount, 1950. Editor: John Gray Blount Papers; editor Jour. So. History, 1959-61. Died Mar. 3, 1983.

MATE, HUBERT EMERY, coll. dean; b. Lima, N.Y., Sept. 2, 1917; s. Joseph Simeon and Inez Louise (Butler) M.; A.B. cum laude, Samford U., 1937; M.A., U. Ala., 1938; Ph.D., Northwestern U., 1949; m. Agnes Eileen Eddleman, June 3, 1937; children—Janet (Mrs. David W. Parr), Carolyn (Mrs. D. Randall Williams). Research asso. Rockefeller Found., Brazil, 1941-42; instr. Spanish, Ind. U., 1946-49; mem. faculty U. Ala., University, 1949-81, prof. Romance langs., 1958—, dean admissions and records, 1961-74, dir. curriculum studies, 1974-81; cons. So. Assn. Colls. and Schs., 1964-81. Chmn. So. Humanities Conf., 1969-70. Mem. Devel. Program Bur., Tuscaloosa, 1966—, Police Adv. Com., 1964-81. Trustee Wesley Found., 1962-81. Served to capt. USNR, 1942-46. Decorated Ordem do Cruzeiro do Sul (Brazil); Pi Kappa Phi scholar, 1937; recipient Distinguished Service award Theta Chi, 1970. Mem. Omicron Delta Kappa, Sigma Delta Pi, Phi Sigma Iota, Pi Tau Chi, Delta Kappa. Author: Handbook of Brazilian Studies, 1954; Conferencias Sobre O Ventura, 1943; Dicionario de Termos Tecnicos De Aviacao, 1944; Manual de Fornecimento de Aviacao, 1947; Guide to Equivalence and Transfer of Junior College Credits, 1976. Home: Tuscaloosa, Ala. Died Aug. 6, 1981.

MATEER, JOHN GASTON, physician; b. Wooster, O., Feb. 14, 1890; s. Horace Nelson and Elizabeth O. (Gaston) M.; A.B., Coll. of Wooster, 1911; M.D., Johns Hopkins Med. Sch., 1918; D.Sc., Wooster Coll., 1933; m. Gladys Keay, Jan. 1, 1921; children—William Gaston (dec.), Mary Keay. Instr. ZoÖlogy, Huron (S.D.) Coll., 1911-13; teaching fellow, physiology, Harvard Med. Sch., 1913-14; interne and asst. resident phys., Johns Hopkins Hosp., 1918-20; phys. in charge gastro-intestinal div., Henry Ford Hospital, Detroit, 1920-52, physician in chief, 1952-63, senior consultant in medicine, from 1963. Member of the Selective Service Medical Advisory Board No. 3, Detroit area. President board trustees Det. University School and Grosse Pointe Country Day School Corp., 1942-45; mem. bd. trustees Wooster Coll. Fellow A.C.P.; mem. Am. Clin. and Climatol. Assn., Am. Gastro-Enterol. Assn. (pres. 1950-51), Central Soc. for Clin. Research, Am. Med. Assn., Phi Beta Kappa, Alpha Omega Alpha, Nu Sigma Nu, Beta Theta Pi. Episcopalian. Clubs: Detroit Country, Detroit, Witenagemote (Detroit). Author med. articles. Home: Grosse Pointe, Mich. †

MATHESON, LILY GRACE, ofcl. W.C.T.U.; b. Neenah, Wis., June 25, 1888; d. Nels and Anna Louise (Jasperson) Matheson; student Lawrence Conservatory of Music, Appleton, Wis., 1906-07; grad. Moody Bible Inst., Chicago, 1915, grad. course, 1919-20; unmarried. Dist. supt. Jr. and Intermediate Christian Endeavor, Wis., 1905-07, state supt., 1908-12; children's and young peoples specialist and pianist, Interdenominational Evangelistic work, 1916-18, 1919-22, 1929; Y.W.C.A. religious edn. dir., Toledo, O., 1918-19; Y.W.C.A. club activities sec., later gen. sec., Green Bay, Wis., 1923-27; with Nat. W.C.T.U. from 1929, as field sec., 1929-42, corr. sec., 1942-48; instr. alcohol edn. in 48 summer youth confs., winter religious edn. schools, 4-H Camps, Youths Temperance Council encampments. Accredited teacher in alcohol edn. Internat. Council of Religious Edn., from 1938. Presbyterian. Republican. Club: Business and Professional Women; League of Woman Voters; Women's Republican Club of Evanston (Evanston, Ill.). Contbr. to temperance jours. Home: Chicago, Ill. Deceased.

MATHEUS, JOHN FREDERICK, coll. prof.; b. Keyser, W. Va., Sept. 10, 1887; s. John William and Mary (Brown) M.; A.B., cum laude, Western Reserve U., 1910; A.M., Columbia, 1921; student Sorbonne, Paris, summer 1925, U. of Chicago, 1927; m. Maude A. Roberts, Sept. 1, 1909. Teacher of Latin, Fla. A. and M. Coll., Tallahassee, 1911-13; prof. of modern langs., 1913-22. prof. and head of dept. of Romance languages West Virginia State College, 1922-53, professor emeritus, 1953; also professor Romance langs. Dillard U., 1954-57; professor fgn. langs. Md. State Coll., 1953-54; asso. prof. German, Spanish, Morris Brown Coll., 1958-59; asst. professor foreign languages and lits. Texas Southern U. Houston, 1959-61; vis. prof. German and French, Hampton Inst., 1961-62, romance langs., Ky. State Coll. from 1962. Sec. Am. mem. commn. apptd. by League of Nations to investigate forced labor in Liberia, 1930. Dir. English teaching in Haiti under Inter-Am. Ednl. Found., 1945-46. Awarded Officer d l'ordre Nationale Honneur et Merite (Haiti). Past president W.Va. Fgn. Lang. Assn. Mem. Modern Lang. Assn., Am. Assn. Teachers French, Spanish and Italian, American Assn. Univ. Profs., Coll. Language Association, Alpha Phi Alpha, Sigma Pi Phi. Mason. Edited (with W.N. Rivers) "Georges" by Dumas Père. Contbr. fiction and poems to Opportunity, The Crisis, Journal of Negro History, Poet Lore, etc., contributing editor to "Color"; also to anthologies. Home: Charleston, W.Va. †

MATHEWS, GRADY F., commissioner of health; b. Collins Co., Tex., Oct. 3, 1889; s. J. N. and Susan (Riley) M.; A.B., B.S., M.D., Univ. of Okla.; m. Lillian F. Norman, Oct. 18, 1917; children—Grady F., Charles R., Eugene H. Teacher pub. schs., 1910-17; high sch. coach and supt. of schs., 1919-21; with State Health Dept., 1926-33; mem. staff Mont. Hosp., 1933-36; dir. dist. No. 1 health dept., Okla., 1936-39; Okla. State commr. of health from 1939. Mem. Commn. on Cancer Control, Commn. Crippled Children, State Bd. Mental Hygiene. Served in World War I. Mem. Am. Pub. Health Assn., Am., Okla., Okla. County med. assns., Okla. Clin. Soc., Am. Legion, Farmers Union, Alpha Kappa Kappa. Democrat. Methodist. Mason. Contbr. to Okla. Farmer Stockman, Okla. Health Bull. Home: Oklahoma City, Okla. †

MATHEWS, MITFORD MCLEOD, SR., editor, author; b. Jackson, Ala., Feb. 12, 1891; s. James Waldrum and Frances Isabella (McLeod) M.; A.B., So. U., 1915; A.M., U. Ala., 1917, Harvard, 1934, Ph.D., 1936; m. Georgia Jane Garrett, Aug. 7, 1919; children—Mitford McLeod, George Garrett. Instr. English, Scarritt-Morrisville (Mo.) Coll., 1915-16; prin. high schs., Ala., 1919-25; instr. English, U. Chicago, 1926-31, mem. staff Dictionary Am. English, 1925-44, professorial lectr. dept. linguistics, 1951-57; editor dictionary dept. U. Chicago Press, 1944-56; became member of the editorial staff Webster New World Dictionary, 1957, then engaged as consultant. Served as ensign USNRF, 1918-22. Recipient of a first Loubat Award, 1953. Author: The Beginnings of American English, 1931; A Survey of English Dictionaries, 1933; Some Sources of Southernisms, 1948; A Dictionary of Americanisms, 1951; Words: How to Know Them, 1956; American Words, 1959; Dictionary of Selected Americanisms, 1966; Teaching to Read Historically Considerd, 1966. Home: Chicago, Ill. Died Feb. 14, 1985.

MATHEWS, ROBERT ELDEN, ret. educator, labor arbitrator; b. Waterville, Maine, Apr. 17, 1894; s. Shailer and Mary Philbrick (Elden) M.; A.B., Yale U., 1915; J.D. cum laude, U. Chgo., 1920; m. Grace Greenwood Caie, Dec. 30, 1922; 1 son, Craig. Admitted to Ill. bar, 1921; gen. practice with Frederick A. Brown, Chgo., 1920-22; instr. U. Chgo. Law Sch., 1922; asso. prof. U. Mont., 1922-24; prof. law Ohio State U., Columbus, 1924-64, prof. emeritus, 1964; prof. law U. Tex., Austin, 1966-72; vis. prof. law Columbia U., 1928-29; vis. prof. Indian Law Inst., cons. on legal studies, New Delhi, 1961-62; vis. prof. Harvard Law Sch., 1963-64; mem. faculty orientation program Am. law Princeton U., 1965. Mem. Office of Gen. Counsel Bd. Econ. Warfare and Fgn. Econ. Adminstrn., Washington, 1942-44 (on leave from Ohio State U.); mem. U.S. Labor Mission to Bolivia, 1943; asso. gen. counsel Nat. War Labor Bd., 1944-45, pub. mem. and co-chmn. appeals com., 1945. Chmn. Boulder Conf. Edn. for Pub. Responsibility, 1956. Chmn. local bd. No. 18, Selective Service Adminstrn., Columbus, 1940-42. Pres. League Ohio Law Schs., 1947; chmn. Nat. Conf. Tng. Law Students in Labor Relations, 1947, pres. Assn. Am. Law Schs., 1952; mem. U.S. Nat. Commn. for UNESCO, 1951-55. Served as capt. Adj. Gen's Dept., Hdqrs. 33d Div. and G.H.Q., AEF, 1917-19. Decorated Silver Star, Purple Heart. Mem. Internat. Soc. Labor Law and Social Legislation (chmn. U.S. nat. com., 1958-61; mem. internat. exec. com. 1958-61, nat. exec. com. 1958, Nat. Acad. Arbitrators (mem. labor law group 1947, chmn. 1947-58), Am. Bar Assn. (council sect. legal edn. 1953-61), A.C.-L.U. (nat. com. 1955-70), AAUP (nat. council 1936-39), World Peace through Law Center (exec. com. sect. legal edn. 1972), Soc. Am. Law Tchrs., Order of Coif (hon.), Elihu (Yale), Phi Beta Kappa (hon.), Beta Theta Pi, Phi Delta Phi. Congregationalist. Clubs: Faculty (Ohio State U.); Faculty Center (Austin); Chicago Literary Club. Compiler: Mathews' Revision of Mechem's Cases on Partnership, 1935; Mathews' Cases on Agency and Partnership, 1958. Editor in chief: Labor Relations and the Law, 1953; Readings on Labor Law, 1955; The Employment Relation and the Law, 1955; editor Legal Edn. and Public Responsibility, 1960; contbg. editor Labor Relations and the Law, 1965; Labor Relations and Social Problems, 1971-74. Author: Problems Illustrative of the Responsibilities of Members of the Legal Profession, 1955, 6th edit., 1974. Contbr. to Ohio Jurisprudence, also legal publs. Home: Austin, Tex. Died Nov. 4, 1983.

MATHIS, HAROLD FLETCHER, educator; b. Wichita Falls, Tex., July 19, 1916; s. Henry Fletcher and Annie Martha (Petty) M.; m. Lois Reno, June 6, 1942; children—Robert, Betty. B.S., U. Okla., 1939, E.E., 1954; M.S., Tex. A. and M. U., 1941, E.E., 1952; Ph.D., Northwestern U., 1953, Case Western Res. U., 1961. Research asso. Northwestern U., 1946-49; asso. prof. elec. engring. U. Okla., 1949-54; research specialist Goodyear, Akron, O., 1954-60; prof. elec. engring. Ohio State U.,

Columbus, 1960-85; Cons. N.Am. Rockwell Corp., 1962-70. Contbr. articles to profl. jours. Served with USNR, 1942-46, 51-53. Mem. IEEE, Am. Soc. Engring. Edn., Am. Bell Assn., Sigma Xi, Phi Eta Sigma, Sigma Tau, Eta Kappa Nu, Kappa Delta Pi. Home: Columbus, Ohio. Died May 12, 1985.

MATLOCK, CHARLES RUBEIN, clergyman; b. Beech Bluff, Tenn., Feb. 5, 1888; s. Rev. Charles Nick and Caroline (Buck) M.; student Bethel Coll., McKenzie, Tenn., 1905-07; Union U., Jackson, Tenn., 1907-11; N.Y. Bibl. Sem., 1921; D.D., Peoples Nat. U., Atlanta, Ga., 1922, LL.D., 1923; m. Mary Francis Douglass, Dec. 6, 1911; 1 son, Charles R.; m. 2d Mrs. Lucille Wallace Allen, June 27, 1952. Ordained ministry Cumberland Presbyn. Ch., 1908; pastor successively Beech Bluff, Tenn., Odessa, Mo., Evansville, Ind., and Cleveland, Tenn., until 1924; pastor Central Ch., Memphis, Tenn., 1924-31, First Ch., Knoxville, Tenn., 1931-34, 1st Church, Columbus, Miss., 1934-36; pastor First Ch., South Pittsburg, Tenn., 1936-43, Edgefield Church, Nashville, Tennessee, from 1943. Moderator General Assembly, 1946. Organizer, 1924, Young People's General Assembly Cumberland Presbyterian Ch.; editor of first young people's literature adopted by the Assembly. Mason (K.T.); mem. Order Eastern Star, Rotarian. Writer for 2 S.S. quarterlies of Cumberland Presbyn. Ch. Home: Nashville, Tenn. †

MATSUSHITA, SADAMI, geophysicist; b. Ehime, Japan, Feb. 12, 1920; came to U.S., 1955, naturalized, 1977; s. Kiyomi and Taka (Taniguchi) M.; m. Kyoko Nakajima, Mar. 23, 1946; children—Hiromi, Hidemi. M.S., Kyoto U., 1944, D.Sc., 1951. Asst. in geophysics Kyoto U., 1945, lectr., 1945-54; research staff physics U. Coll., London, 1954-55; sr. research staff High Altitude Obs., U. Colo., Boulder, from 1955, prof. astrophysics and atmospheric physics, 1962-84; researcher Nat. Bur. Standards, Boulder, 1955-84, Nat. Center Atmospheric Research, Boulder, 1961-84; cons. NOAA, Boulder, 1955-84. Author 3 books in field; contbr. articles profl. jours.; editor: Jour. Geomagnetism and Geoelectricity, 1949-56; editorial bd.: Brit. Jour. Planetary and Space Sci, from 1969. Recipient Tanakadate award, 1950, award Research Soc. Am., 1963. Fellow AAAS; mem. Am. Geophys. Union, Am. Meteorol. Soc., AAUP, Research Soc. Am., Sigma Xi, Internat. Soc. Equatorial Aeronomy (pres.), Internat. Sci. Radio Union, Internat. Assn. Geomagnetism and Aeronomy. Home: Boulder, Colo. Died Mar. 15, 1984; interred Kyoto, Japan.

MATTHEWS, EDWARD JOSEPH, JR., food company executive; b. N.Y.C., Oct. 20, 1935; s. Edward Joseph and Regina Theresa (Taylor) M.; m. Michelle McQueeny; children—Edward Joseph, IV, Peter M., Paul T., Margot Lynn. B.A. in Econs, Dartmouth Coll., 1957; M.B.A. in Finance and Acctg., Amos Tuck Sch., 1959. C.P.A. Sr. acct. Haskins & Sells (C.P.A.'s), N.Y.C., 1959-64; v.p. fin. Strawberry Hill Press Inc., N.Y.C., and Asheville, N.C., 1964-69; asst. controller Inmont Corp., N.Y.C., 1969-70; v.p., gen. mgr. Inmont Confections Co., N.Y.C., 1970-71; asst. treas. Inmont Corp., N.Y.C., 1971-73; asst. treas. Nabisco, Inc., N.Y.C., 1973-75, treas., 1975-78, v.p. corporate devel., 1978-82; sr. v.p. Nabisco Foods, Inc.; dir. Morris County Savs. Bank. Served with USMCR, 1959-60. Mem. Am. Inst. C.P.A.s, N.Y. State Soc. C.P.A.s, Fin. Execs. Inst., Morris County C. of C. (chmn.), Beta Theta Pi. Republican. Clubs: Mendham Golf and Tennis, Mantoloking Yacht; Yale (N.Y.C.). Address: East Hanover, N.Y. Dec. 1982.

MATTHIAS, EDWIN CLARK, railway exec.; b. Galion, O., Sept. 9, 1887; s. Winfield Scott and Amelia (Mann) M.; A.B., Stanford U., 1911; m. Ida Jamieson, Sept. 24, 1919; children—Marian Amelia, Edwin Clark, Jamieson, Roger Howard. Law clerk Great Northern Ry., 1912-13; in gen. practice of law, Spokane, Wash., 1914-20; attorney Great Northern Ry., Seattle, Wash., 1920-26, for Western Washington Great Northern Ry., 1926-37, gen. atty. for western lines, 1937-45, vice pres. and gen. counsel, St. Paul, Minn., from 1945; dir. and pres. St. Peter Co.; gen. counsellor Spokane Coeur d'Alene & Palonce Ry.; dir. and vice pres. Eastern Ry. Co. of Minn., Duluth & Superior Bridge Co.; general counsel, director Glacier Park Company; dir. St. Paul, Minn. & Manitoba Ry. Co., Brandon, Saskatchewan and Hudson Bay Ry. Co., Washington and Great Northern Townsite Company. Served as 1st lt., Judge Advocate Gen. Dept., U.S. Army World War I. Mem. Am., Wash. and Minn. bar assns., Phi Kappa Psi, Phi Delta Phi. Clubs: Minnesota, University, Athletic (St. Paul); University, Washington Athletic (Seattle); Union League (Chicago). Home: St. Paul, Minn. †

MATTHIAS, RUSSELL HOWARD, lawyer; b. Milw., Aug. 7, 1906; s. Charles G. and Lena (Martin) M.; m. Helene Seibold, Dec. 28, 1932; children—Russell Howard, William Warrens, Robert Charles. A.B., Northwestern U., 1930, J.D., 1932. Bar: Ill. bar 1933, D.C. bar 1947, Okla. bar 1947, Fla. bar 1979. Spl. asst. to atty. gen. U.S. R.R. Retirement Act, 1934-35; sec. Ill. Fraternal Congress, 1935-40, 45-60; partner firm Meyers & Matthias, Chgo., 1951-78; pres., treas. Meyers & Matthias, P.C., 1978-80; partner Matthias & Matthias, from 1980; chmn. bd., dir. Old Orchard Bank & Trust Co.; dir., gen. counsel United Founders Life Ins. Co. of Ill., United Founders Life Ins. Co. of Okla., Wesco Inc.; gen. counsel Nat. Ind. Statis. Service Chgo.; Drafting com. Ill. Ins. Code, 1938, annotating com., 1940; mem. drafting com. La. Ins. Code, 1948. Trustee Valparaiso U. Law Sch. Served from capt. to lt. col. AUS, 1942-46. Recipient Alumni award Northwestern U., 1973. Mem. Luth. Brotherhood (dir., gen. counsel), Internat. Assn. Life Ins. Counsel, Phi Delta Theta. Republican. Lutheran. Clubs: Indian Hill Country; Mid-Day (Chgo.), University (Chgo.); Kenilworth, Minneapolis; Citrus (Orlando, Fla.), Country (Orlando, Fla.). Home: Wilmette, Ill.

MATTSON, HENRY ELIS, artist; b. Gothenburg, Sweden, Aug. 7, 1887; s. Johan Emil and Augusta (Petterson) M.; student Sch. of Worcester (Mass.) Art Museum, 1912-13; m. Daphne Sawyer, Sept. 19, 1924. Came to U.S., 1906, naturalized, 1913. Represented in permanent collections of White House (Washington) and galleries and museums of U.S. Recipient various prizes and awards. N.A., 1951. Home: Woodstock, N.Y. †

MATZ, JOHN EDWIN, life insurance company executive; b. Hamburg, Pa., Sept. 2, 1916; s. Harry L. and Florence (Smith) M.; m. Phoebe Land, July 4, 1941; children—Susan Eugenia, John Edwin. M.A., Pa. State U., 1939. With John Hancock Mut. Life Ins. Co., Boston, 1949-81, v.p., 1961-65, sr. v.p., 1965-67, exec. v.p., 1967-72, sr. exec. v.p., 1972-73, pres., chief ops. officer, vice chmn. bd., 1974-78, chmn., chief exec. officer, 1979-81, also dir.; dir. Shawmut Bank Boston N.A., Shawmut Corp. Trustee Am. Coll.; mem. corp., trustee Northeastern U., Tax Found., Inc., 1978-81; bd. dirs. Council Fin. Aid to Edn., 1976-81; trustee, bd. govs. New Eng. Med. Center Hosp., New Eng. Colls. Fund; vis. com. Harvard Grad. Sch. Bus. Adminstrn.; mem. nat. bd. Jr. Achievement, Inc. Fellow Soc. Actuaries; mem. Am. Council Life Ins. (dir. 1980-81), Phi Beta Kappa. Clubs: Weston Golf; Bald Peak Colony (N.H.). Home: Weston, Mass. Dec. Oct. 17, 1983.

MAUGHAN, RICHARD JOHNSON, judge; b. Logan, Utah, Nov. 13, 1917; s. Heber Chase and Ragna (Johnson) M.; B.S., Utah State U., 1948; J.D., U. Utah, 1951; grad. Appellate Judges Seminar Sch. Law, NYU, 1975; m. Laura Dell Torgeson, July 12, 1946; children—Margith, Joyce, Eloise, Richard, Mary. Admitted to Utah bar, 1951, Fed. Dist. Ct. bar, 1951, Circuit Ct. Appeals bar, 1962, U.S. Supreme Ct. bar, 1967; asst. to Atty. Gen. for Utah, 1951-52; practice law, Salt Lake City, 1951-74; justice Supreme Ct. Utah, 1975-81. Mem. Utah State Bd. Regents, 1969-75; exec. com. Western Interstate Commn. for Higher Edn., 1969-75; Democratic candidate for Congress, Utah, 1968; chmn. Dem. Central Com., Davis County, 1967-71; pres. Peter Maughan Family Orgn., 1964-74; trustee Utah State U., 1965-69, chmn. bd., 1968-69. Served with U.S. Army, 1942-45. Mem. Utah State (chmn. continuing legal edn. com. 1966-69, mem. profl. competence com. 1974, mem. judiciary com. 1975-81), Davis County (pres. 1961-62) bar assns., Utah Jud. Council, Newcomen Soc. N.Am., Pi Sigma Alpha, Phi Alpha Delta. Mormon. Contbr. articles to jours. Home: Bountiful, Utah. Dec. July 8, 1981.

MAVITY, NANCY BARR, author; b. Lawrenceville, Ill., Oct. 22, 1890; d. Granville Walter and Annabelle (Applegate) Barr; A.B., Western Coll., Oxford, O., 1911; studied Wellesley, 1911-12; M.A., Cornell University, 1913, Ph.D., 1914; m. Arthur Benton Mavity, Dec. 25, 1917 (died in 1931); children—Nancy (Mrs. George Nye), John Barr; married 2d, Edward A. Rogers, June 18, 1938. Instructor English and psychology, Connecticut College, New London, 1915-17; editorial work, George H. Doran Co., New York, 1917-18; lit. editor San Francisco Chronicle, 1920-24; editorial and feature writer, Oakland Tribune, from 1925, literary editor since 1943. Member The American Association University Women, Nat. Woman's Party, Alameda County Mental Hygiene Society (director). Phi Beta Kappa. Democrat. Unitarian. Club: College Women's (Berkeley, Calif.). Author: Responsible Citizenship (with Arthur Benton Mavity), 1923; A Dinner of Herbs (verse), 1923; Hazard (novel), 1924; The Tule Marsh Murder, 1929; The Body on the Floor, 1929; The Other Bullet, 1930; The Case of the Missing Sandals, 1930; Sister Aimee, 1931; The Modern Newspaper (textbook), 1931; The Man Who Didn't Mind Hanging, 1932; The Fate of Jane McKenzie, 1933; State Versus Elna Jepson, 1937; Child Crime in California, 1946. Contbr. to mags. Home: Oakland, Calif. †

MAXCY, EVERETT HESELTINE, lawyer; b. Gardiner, Me., Sept. 8, 1888; s. William Everett and Ida Jeanette (Heseltine) M.; A.B., U. of Me., 1911; LL.B., Harvard, 1914; m. Ethel M. Blair, Dec. 28, 1914. Admitted to Me. bar, 1914, and practiced in that state; counsel for Central Me. Power Company, Augusta, from 1920; director of Central Me. Power Co.; dir., officer Central Securities Corp., Skowhegan Water Power Co., Cumberland Securities Corp. Served as 2d lt., C.A.C., World War I. Mem. Am. Legion, Am., Me., Kennebec bar assns., Sigma Alpha Epsilon. Republican. Mason (Shriner). Clubs: Union (Boston); Augusta Country. Home: Augusta, Me. †

MAXEY, CHESTER COLLINS, writer, lecturer; born Ellensburg, Wash., May 31, 1890; s. Morton M. and Leota (Collins) M.; B.A., Whitman Coll., 1912, L.H.D., 1959; A.M., U. Wis., 1914; Ph.D., Columbia, 1919; LL.D., Lewis and Clark Coll., 1950; m. Elnora Campbell, June 17, 1915; children—Marilyn, Aurel. Instructor and assistant professor polit. science, Ore. Agrl. Coll., 1914-18; mem. staff and supervisor Training Sch. for Public Service, New York Bur. Municipal Research, 1918-20; asso. prof. polit. science, Western Reserve U., 1920-25; M.C. Moore prof. polit. science, Whitman Coll., from 1925, dean social sciences, 1931-48, pres., 1948-59, emeritus, from 1959; writer and lectr. Mem. Am. Polit. Sci. Assn., Beta Theta Pi, Phi Beta Kappa. Rep. Clubs: University (Spokane); Inquiry. Author: County Administration, 1919; An Outline of Municipal Government, 1924; The Problem of Government, 1925; Urban Democracy, 1929; You and Your Government, 1931; The American Problem of Government, 1934, 5th ed., 1949; Political Philosophies, 1938, 2d ed. 1948. Editor: Readings in Municipal Government, 1924. Home: Walla Walla, Wash. †

MAXEY, DAVID ROY, editor, communications consultant; b. Boise, Idaho, Oct. 22, 1936; s. Roy Gess and Dott Elizabeth (Brown) M.; m. Francisca Juliana Guenther, Apr. 15, 1966; children: Brian Guenther, Elizabeth Elba. B.S., U. Idaho, 1958; M.B.A., Harvard U., 1961. Researcher, asst. editor Look mag., N.Y.C., 1961-63, sr. editor, 1964-66, adminstrv. editor, asst. mng. editor, 1967-69; mng. editor Careers Today mag., Del Mar, Calif., 1969; Washington editor Look, 1969-70, mng. editor, N.Y.C., 1970-71; staff writer Life mag., N.Y.C., 1971-72; editor Psychology Today mag., Del Mar, 1972-75, N.Y.C., 1975-77, Sports Afield mag., N.Y.C., 1977-78; communications cons., editor, writer, 1978-80; editor, v.p. GEO mag., from 1981. Served to 2d lt. Arty. U.S. Army, 1958-59. Home: New York, NY.

MAXFIELD, J. P., scientist, engr.; b. San Francisco, Dec. 28, 1887; s. Joseph Elwin and Harriett Whitemore (Mansfield) M.; S.B., Mass. Inst. Tech., 1910; m. Milicent Arnold Harrison, June 20, 1914; children—Katherine Hayward (Mrs. Robert Gibney), Eleanor Taylor (Mrs. Chas. Weis). Instr. physics and electro-chemistry Mass. Inst. Tech., 1910-14; research physicist Western Electric Co., N.Y.C., 1914-19, dept. head (Later Bell Telephone Labs.), 1919-26; mgr. engring. and research Victor Talking Machine Co., Camden, N.J., 1926-29; cons. engr. Electrical Research Products, Inc., N.Y.C., 1929-33, staff engr., 1933-36, dir. comml. engring., 1936-41; supt. comml. engring. Western Electric Co., Inc., 1941-42; prof., dir. div. phys. war research Duke, 1942-46, Bell Telephone Labs., Murray Hill, N.J., 1946-47; superintending scientist USN Electronics Lab., 1948-53; 1953-56; cons. Navy Air Missile Test Center, Point Mugu, Cal., from 1956, acting chief scientist, from 1957. Recipient meritorious civilian service award U.S. Army, 1947, USN, 1953; John Potts Meml. award for achievement in audio engring., 1953. Fellow Am. Inst. EE., Am. Phys. Soc., Accoustical Soc. Am.; mem. Sigma Xi. Mem. Ch. of Religious Science. Author: (with Douglas Stanley) The Voice, Its Production and Reproduction, 1933, also papers in sci. jours. Home: Escondido, Cal. †

MAXFIELD, J(OSEPH) P(EASE), scientist, engr.; b. San Francisco, Calif., Dec. 28, 1887; s. Joseph Elwin and Harriett Whitemore (Mansfield) M.; S.B., Mass. Inst. Tech., 1910; m. Milicent Arnold Harrison, June 20, 1914; children—Katherine Hayward (Mrs. Robert Gibney), Eleanor Taylor (Mrs. Chas. Weis). Instr. physics and electro-chemistry, Mass. Inst. Tech., 1910-14; research physicist, Western Electric Co., at New York, 1914-19, dept. head (later Bell Telephone Labs.), 1919-26; mgr. engring. and research Victor Talking Machine Co., Camden, N.J., 1926-29; cons. engineer Electrical Research Products, Inc., New York, 1929-33, staff engr., 1933-36, dir. comml. engring., 1936-41; supt. comml. engring. Western Electric Co., Inc., 1941-42; Prof. dir. div. phys. war research, Duke U., 1942-46; Bell Telephone Labs., Murray Hill, N.J., 1946-47; superintending scientist U.S. Navy Electronics Lab. from 1948. Fellow Am. Inst. Elec. Engrs., Am. Phys. Soc., Accoustical Society of America, Soc. Motion Picture Engineers (fellow), Am. Geog. Society; senior member Institute of Radio Engineers; member Sigma Xi. Member Society of Friends. Club: Wyoming Field (Milburn, N.J.). Author: (with Douglas Stanley) The Voice, Its Production and Reproduction, 1933, also numerous papers in scientific journals. Home: San Diego, Calif.

MAXWELL, ALICE FREELAND, physician; b. San Francisco, Calif., July 16, 1890; d. Thomas Joseph and Elizabeth (Leahy) Maxwell; B.S., U. of Calif., 1912, M.D., 1915; unmarried. Interne, Univ. Calif. Hosp., San Francisco, 1915-16; gen. practice of medicine, San Francisco, 1918-47; asso. clin. prof. dept. obstetrics and gynecology, Univ. of Calif. Med. Sch., San Francisco, from 1943. Fellow A.M.A., Am. Coll. Surgeons, Pacific Coast Soc. Obstetrics and Gynecology (pres. 1939); mem. Calif. Med. Assn. Author (with F. W. Lynch, M.D.): Pelvic Neoplasms (monograph), 1922. Contbr. med. articles to various jours. Home: Los Altos, Calif. †

MAXWELL, FRED(ERICK) R(ICHARD), JR., elec. engr., univ. prof.; b. Tuscaloosa, Ala., June 15, 1889; s. Frederick Richard and Lucy (Cockrane) M.; B.S. in M.E., U. of Ala., 1911, M.E., 1912, E.E., 1923; m. Kathleen Hobson Searcy, Jan. 30, 1924; children—Camille Searcy, Alfreda Tunstall. Engr. Tuscaloosa Ry. and Utilities Co., 1912-17, asst. gen. mgr., 1919-20; asso. prof. elec. engring., U. of Ala., 1920-35, consultant engr., 1922-41, prof. elec. engring., 1935-41, dir. of aeronautics, 1939-41, prof. and cons. engr. for U. of Ala. bldg. program, from 1945. Licensed engr., Ala. Mem. Army Adv. Com., 3d Army. Served as lt. (j.g.) (Naval aviator), U.S. Naval Res.

Force, 1917-19; comdr. U.S. Naval Res., officer in charge, Ground Sch. for Aviation Cadet Flight Training Program; ednl. officer, N.A.T.B., Pensacola, Fla., 1941-45; disch. as capt. Mem. Am. Inst. E.E. (v.p. 1937-39; dir. 1939-43; chmn. Ala. sect. 1938-39), Am. Legion, Res. Officers Assn., Am. Assn. U. Profs., Tau Beta Pi, Theta Tau, Chi Beta Phi, Phi Gamma Delta. Democrat. Episcopalian. Clubs: Country (Tuscaloosa); Faculty (U. of Ala.); Officers (Pensacola, Fla.). Home: Tuscaloosa, Ala. †

MAXWELL, GROVER EDWARD, educator; b. Rockvale, Tenn., June 21, 1918; s. John Edward and Jane Ashby (Jackson) M.; B.S. in Chemistry, U. Tenn., 1941, Ph.D., 1950; m. Mary Lou Canton, Oct. 28, 1960; children—Russell, Stephen. Chemist, TVA, 1941-43, 46; instr. chemistry U. Minn., 1950, faculty philosophy of sci., 1954-81, prof. philosophy, 1961-81, dir. Minn. Center for Philosophy Sci., 1971-81; mem. faculties U. Conn., 1951, Adelphi Coll., 1953. Vis. prof. U. Cal. at Berkeley, 1965, London Sch. Econs., 1966-67, U. Hawaii, 1970. Cons. NSF, 1962-64. Peace candidate for U.S. Congress, 1968. Served with USNR, 1943-46. NSF grantee, 1964-67, 72, 74. Mem. Sigma Xi. Editor: (with H. Feigl) series of vols. Minnesota Studies in the Philosophy of Science, 1958-74. Contbr. articles to profl. jours., numerous anthologies. Home: Minneapolis, Minn. Died June 14, 1981.

MAY, DAN, hosiery mfr.; b. Nashville, Dec. 25, 1898; s. Jacob and Rebecca (Weingarten) M.; m. Dorothy Fishel, June 14, 1927; children—Joseph Leserman, Elizabeth (Mrs. Walter P. Stern). A.B., Vanderbilt U., 1919. Partner Bloch Clothing Co., 1924-27; with May Hosiery Mills, from 1927, treas., 1933-46, chmn. bd., 1946-59, 64-65, pres., 1959-63, chmn. exec. com., 1965-75, ret., 1975; dir. Wayne Gossard Corp., 1966-75; Cons. WPB Office Civilian Requirements, 1945. Former mem. bd. edn., Nashville, pres., 1950-53; v.p. Tenn. Council Econ. Edn.; pres. Nashville Jewish Community Council, 1953-56; magistrate, Davidson County, Tenn., 1954-66; chmn. sch. com. County Ct., 1955-62; councilman-at-large Met. Govt. of Nashville and Davidson County, 1962-66; chmn. met. action com. Office Econ. Opportunity, 1967-69; pres. Mid-Cumberland Comprehensive Health Council, 1969-74; Trustee Vanderbilt U., from 1951; bd. dirs. Fisk U., 1950-59, vice chmn., 1959-61; mem. bd. Joint Univ. Library. Recipient Distinguished Citizenship award City of Nashville, 1970. Mem. Zeta Beta Tau. Republican. Jewish. Clubs: Rotary, Shamus, University, Thursday. Home: Nashville, Tenn.

MAYER, ALBERT, architect, town planner; b. N.Y.C., Dec. 29, 1897; s. Bernhard and Sophia (Buttenwieser) M.; A.B., Columbia, 1917; B.C.E., Mass. Inst. Tech., 1919; m. Phyllis Carter, Aug. 20, 1925 (div. 1961); children—Stella, Kerry; m. 2d, Marion Mill Preminger, Mar. 21, 1961 (dec. 1972); m. 3d Magda Wilhelm Pastor, Jan. 9, 1975. Mem. firm Mayer Whittlesey & Glass, N.Y.C., 1935-61; now engaged in private practice; planner of new city of Maumelle, Ark., 1966-68; cons. urban renewal devel. East Harlem N.Y.C. for Drug and Hosp. Workers Union, 1969-70; projects include Manhattan House, N.Y.C., new city for Alumnium Co. of Can., Kitimat, B.C., housing, bldgs. Standard Vacuum Oil Co. Refinery, Bombay, also Bataan, Philippines, Ft. Greene Housing Project, N.Y.C., master plans Greater Bombay, New Punjab capital city, Chandigarh, Delhi-New Delhi region, Gujrat University, Allhabad Agricultural Inst., Ashdad new seaport in Israel and the Etawah Rural Development Projects, India, housing, shops, community facilities, Belimawr, N.J.; planning advisor United Provinces Govt., India; also projects in other foreign countries; vis. prof. urban planning Columbia, 1967-71. Cons. Pub. Housing Adminstrn.; lectr. architecture and planning various univs. including Mass. Inst. Tech., Ohio State U., Columbia, U. Wis.; condr. regional seminars New Approaches in Pub. Housing Design. Dir. Nat. Housing Conf.; Served as 2d lt. AUS, 1918, lt. col., 1942-45. Received Apt. House Medal, N.Y. chpt. AIA, 1940, 1952, Medal of Honor, 1952, citation for ct. New Sch. Social Research, 1963; Certificate of Merit Municipal Art Soc., 1961, Honor award Am. Soc. Landscape Architects, 1962 (both for design E. Harlem Plaza, N.Y.C.); Spl. award Bd. Govs. Nat. Assn. Housing and Redevel. Ofcls., 1964, N.Y. chpt. Man of Year, 1969; Citizens Union City of N.Y. award for promoting city's aesthetic interests, 1965; 240 Central Park S. named one of N.Y.C.'s 10 best apt. houses, 1977. Felow AIA (chmn. com. urban design, housing 1950-52, Pioneer in Housing award N.Y. chpt. 1973), Soc. Applied Anthropology (hon.); mem. Am. Inst. Planners, ASCE, Housing Study Guild (co-founder), Regional Devel. Council Am., Regional Plan Assn. N.Y. (dir.), ASCE, N.Y. State Citizens' Council (past dir.), Phi Beta Kappa. Club: Technology (N.Y.C.). Author: Pilot Project; India, 1958; re-pub., 1973; The Urgent Future: People, Housing, City, Region, 1967; (monograph) Greenbelt Towns Revisited, 1968; sect. Urban Planning in the United States, in Ency. Urban Planning, 1973. Home: New York, N.Y. Died Oct. 14, 1981.

MAYER, CARL G., retired food co. exec.; b. Chgo., 1902; ed. U. Wis., 1925. Formerly sr. v.p., dir. Oscar Mayer & Co. Home: Madison, Wis. Died Oct. 1, 1982.

MAYER, FERDINAND LATHROP, foreign service; b. Indianapolis, Ind., May 25, 1887; s. Ferdinand L. and Katharine (Lathrop) M.; B.A., Princeton, 1909, M.A., 1916; LL.B., Harvard, 1913; m. Katharine Alex. Duer, Jan. 10, 1927; children—John Duer, Katharine (Mrs. J. F. Aimers), Lucie B. (Mrs. Donald McKee), Elizabeth L. Sec. embassy or legation of class 4, 1916; assigned to Port au Prince, 1916, to Dept. of State at Washington, D.C., 1917-19, 20-22, London, 1919; mem. secretariat and tech. staff Am. delegation, Conf. of Limitation of Armament, Washington, 1921-1922; assigned to Tangier, 1922, Peking, later Tokyo, 1923; counselor of legation at Peking, 1925; sec. Am. delegation Spl. Conf. Chinese Customs Tariff, 1925; counselor legation at Ottawa, 1928, Lima, 1929, Brussels and Luxembourg, 1930; adviser Gen. Disarmament Conf., Geneva, 1933-35; counselor of legation at Berne, 1933; unofficial observer spl. com. League of Nations Tech. CoÖperation with China, 1934; became counselor of embassy, Berlin, 1935; E.E. and M.P. to Haiti, 1935-Dec. 1940; retired from U.S. Foreign Service in 1940; with Office of Strategic Services, Washington, D.C., 1942-45. Presbyterian. Clubs: University (N.Y.); Metropolitan (Washington, D.C.); Cap and Gown (Princeton). Address: Bennington, Vt. †

MAYER, FREDERICK, lawyer; b. Seeheim, Germany, Aug. 16, 1890; s. Loesermann and Karoline (Hirsch) M.; brought to U.S., 1904, naturalized, 1912; LL.B., Chgo.-Kent Coll. of Law, 1912; m. Lelie Samish; Feb. 16, 1921; children—Richard J. (killed in action in Germany, Nov. 1944), Janet. Admitted to Ill. bar, 1912, practiced in Chgo.; various positions Greenebaum Sons Bank & Trust Co., 1906-12, atty., 1912-29; partner Johnston, Thompson, Raymond & Mayer, and predecessors, from 1929; sec., dir. Continental Grain Co. Served as sgt., U.S. Army, 1918-19; with A.E.F., Siberia. Mem. Am., Ill. State Chgo. bar assns., Am. Legion, Chgo. Law Inst. Jewish religion. Mason. Club: Standard (Chgo.). Home: Chicago, Ill. †

MAYER, MANFRED MARTIN, microbiology educator; b. Frankfurt on Main, Germany, June 15, 1916; s. Gustav and Julie (Sommer) M.; m. Elinor S. Indenbaum, Dec. 6, 1942; children: Jonathan Marnin, David Michael, Dan Ellis, Matthew Jared. B.S., Coll. City N.Y., 1938; Ph.D., Columbia U., 1946; Dr. Med. Sci. (hon.), Johannes Gutenberg U., Mainz, Germany, 1969. Sci. staff OSRD, Columbia, 1942-45, instr. biochemistry, 1946; asst. prof. bacteriology Sch. Hygiene and Pub. Health, Johns Hopkins, 1946-48, assoc. prof. microbiology, 1948-61; prof. microbiology Sch. Hygiene and Pub. Health, Johns Hopkins (Sch. Medicine), 1961-84; cons. USPHS, NSF, U.S. Dept. Agr., Office Naval Research. Author: (with Elvin A. Kabat) Experimental Immunochemistry, 1948, rev. edit., 1960; editorial bd.: Jour. Immunology. Recipient Kimble award methodology, 1953; Karl Landsteiner award Am. Assn. Blood Banks, 1974; Albion O. Bernstein award Med. Soc. State N.Y., 1976; Internat. award Gairdner Found., 1982. Fellow AAAS; mem. Am. Chem. Soc., Am. Assn. Immunologists (councillor 1971, pres. 1976), Soc. Exptl. Biology and Medicine, Internat. Coll. Allergists, Nat. Acad. Sci., Am. Soc. Biol. Chemists, Biochem. Soc., Phi Beta Kappa, Sigma Xi. Home: Baltimore, Md. Died Sept. 18, 1984.

MAYFIELD, CHARLES HERBERT, banker; b. Oilton, Okla., Jan. 14, 1924; s. Harmon Dodson and Bertha Odell (Smith) M.; m. Mary Ellin Voizin, Sept. 20, 1947; children—Charles David, Martha Ann. Student, U. Southwestern La., 1944-45; B.B.A., Tulane U., 1947; cert., La. State U. Sch. Banking of South, 1952. Sr. v.p. First Nat. Bank of Commerce, New Orleans. Vice chmn. mil. affairs com. City of New Orleans. Served with USN, World War II; rear adm. USNR. Fellow Nat. Inst. Credit; mem. La. Bankers' Assn., Am. Inst. Banking, Tulane Assn. Bus. Alumni, New Orleans C. of C., Naval Res. Assn., Res. Officers' Assn., Navy League Council New Orleans, Supply Corps Assn. Greater New Orleans, Naval Order, Mil. Order World Wars, U.S. Naval Inst., Navy Supply Corps Assn. and Found., Info. Council Ams., Internat. House, Kappa Alpha. Home: New Orleans, LA.

MAYFIELD, FRANK MCCONNELL, merchant; b. Cleveland, Tenn., May 8, 1887; s. Pearson B. and Elizabeth Caroline (McConnell) M.; student Vanderbilt U., 1905-08; m. Juanita Wilkinson, Jan. 28, 1918; children—Frank McConnell, Phoebe Wilkinson, Elizabeth. Pres., Scruggs-Vandervoort-Barney, dry goods. St. Louis, 1925-63, vice chmn. bd., 1963-70; past pres. Mermod, Jaccard & King Jewelry Co.; past chmn. bd. Denver Dry Goods Co., Emery-Bird-Thayer Co, Kansas City, Mo. Clubs: Racquet Noonday, St. Louis Country (Kansas City). Home: St. Louis, Mo. †

MAYFIELD, SAMUEL MARTIN, educator, geologist; b. Houston, Mo., Mar. 23, 1888; s. Jacob Nelson and Mary (Smotherman) M.; B.S., Berea Coll., 1914, B.A., 1923; Ph.D. in Geology, U. Chgo., 1932; m. Flora Sweeney, June 29, 1916; children—Darwin Lyell, Lois (Mrs. Grahama C. Wilson). Tchr. rural schs. of Ky., 1908-10; supt. city schs., Newbern, Tenn., 1914-16; in bus., merchandising, coal mining, lumbering, 1916-19; prin. high sch., Somerset, Ky., 1919-20; employed in bank, 1920-21; instr. Berea Coll., 1922-32; asst. state geologist of Ky., summers 1923-31; prof. geology Intermountain Union Coll., Helena, Mont., 1932-34; jr. engr. U.S. Geol. Survey, summers, 1934, 35; prof. geology Linfield Coll., 1934-36; prof. geology, chmn. dept. Bowling Green State U., 1936-58; prof. of geology Univ. Redlands (Cal.), from 1959. Fellow Ohio Acad Sci.; mem. A.A.A.S., Geol. Soc. Am., Am. Assn. Petroleum Geologists, Assn. Geology Tchrs., Am. Assn. U. Profs., C. of C., Sigma Xi, Phi Kappa Phi. Presbyn. Club: Kiwanis. Author articles in field. Home: Bowling Green, OH. †

MAYHEW, JOSEPH HOWARD, mfg. co. exec.; b. Mpls., Oct. 28, 1889; s. George Skaats and Nellie Fay (Brown) M.; night student U. Minn., 1908-11; m. Annalou McCracken, June 28, 1917; children—Joseph Howard, Nellie Adelaide (Mrs. David C. Prillaman), Barbarajane (Mrs. Beverly R. Howerton). Die and tool maker, 1912-18; organizer, developer, mgr., v.p. Carter-Mayhew Mfg. Co., Mpls., 1919-27; v.p. Hart-Carter Co., Mpls., 1928-31, became chmn. bd., 1963, dir.; developer Tyresoles Ltd., subsidiary Henry Simon Ltd., 1932-49; organizer retreading bus., Fla., 1938-42; engaged in treading tires for fighter planes U.S. Navy, 1942-45; organized, developed mfg. companies for labor saving indsl. equipment, 1945-56. Rep., Gov. Minn. on S. Am. trade tour, 1925. Home: Excelsior, MN. †

MAYNOR, HAL WHARTON, JR., educator; b. Nashville, Oct. 5, 1917; s. Hal Wharton and Ophelia Abbigail (Hill) M.; B.S., U. Ky., 1944, M.S., 1947, D.Eng., 1954; m. Marjorie Mae Baker, Mar. 16, 1946; children—Sandra Maynor Averhart, Susan Maynor Bromberg. Hal Wharton III. X-ray technician, lab asst. Henry Vogt Machine Co., Louisville, 1936; lab. asst. Jones Dabney Co., Louisville, 1936-39; asst. prof. mech. engring., asso. engr. atomic research inst. Iowa State Coll., 1947-51; research engr. major appliance div. Gen. Electric Co., Louisville, 1954-57; prin. investigator scaling of titanium and titanium base alloys USAF contract, U. Ky., 1951-54, asso. prof., 1957-59; prof. mech. engring. Auburn (Ala.) U., 1959-78, prof. emeritus, 1978-82; project leader fracture of high strength materials Army Missile Command, 1959-70. Chmn., Auburn High Sch. Kiwanis Career Day, 1961; bd. dirs. Friends Auburn Library. Served with USNR, 1943-46. Decorated Bronze Star (6), Silver Star. ASTM grantee, 1967-68; registered profl. engr., Ala., Ky. Fellow Am. Inst. Chemists; mem. Ala. Acad. Sci., Ky. Acad. Sci., AIME, Am. Soc. Engring. Edn., Nat. Soc. Profl. Engrs., Ala. Soc. Profl. Engrs. (pres. Auburn chpt. 1964-65), ASME, Sci. Research Soc. Am., Sigma Xi, Alpha Chi Sigma, Tau Beta Pi, Pi Tau Sigma. Mem. Christian Ch. (elder, bd. dirs., past chmn. ofcl. bd.). Reviewer papers and books Applied Mechanics Revs.; contbr. articles to profl. jours. Home: Auburn, Ala. Died Mar. 3, 1982.

MAYO, SELZ CABOT, sociologist, educator; b. Mesic, N.C., Sept. 20, 1915; s. Sebastian Cabot and Cora Ethel (Gaskins) M.; m. Anna Fay Hall, Sept. 11, 1940; 1 dau., Ann Tremayne. A.B., Atlantic Christian Coll., Wilson, N.C., 1935; M.S., N.C. State Coll., 1938; Ph.D., U. N.C., 1942. Mem. faculty N.C. State Coll., 1939-81, prof. sociology, 1955-81, prof. emeritus, 1981-83, head dept. rural sociology, from 1960, head dept. sociology and anthropology, from 1963. Author articles, bulls. in field. Mem. Am. Sociol. Assn., So. Sociol. Soc. (pres. 1963-64), Rural Sociol. Soc. Home: Raleigh, N.C. Died Nov. 16, 1983.

MAYO, THOMAS TABB, IV, educator, physicist; b. Radford, Va., June 15, 1932; s. Thomas Tabb and Martha (Lavinder) M.; m. Elna Ann Wilson, June 22, 1957; children—Thomas Tabb, Ann Burgess, Chester Wilson. B.S. in Physics, Va. Mil. Inst., 1954; M.S. in Physics, U. Va., 1957; Ph.D. in Physics, 1960. Sr. scientist Research Lab. for Engring. Scis., Charlottesville, Va., 1960-61; asst. prof. physics Hampden-Sydney (Va.) Coll., 1962-64, asso. prof., 1964-67, prof., from 1967, asst. acad. dean, 1971-73, asso. acad. dean, 1973-75, 76-77, acting acad. dean, 1975-76; research asso. Quantum Theory Project, U. Fla. at Gainesville, 1969-70. Served to 1st lt. Chem. Corps AUS, 1961-62. Mem. Am. Phys. Soc., Am. Assn. Physics Tchrs., Sigma Xi, Lambda Chi Alpha. Democrat. Presbyn. (deacon from 1967, elder 1980). Home: Hampden-Sydney, VA.

MAYS, BENJAMIN ELIJAH, emeritus college president; b. Epworth, S.C., Aug. 1, 1894; s. S. Hezekiah and Louvenia (Carter) M.; m. Sadie Gray, Aug. 9, 1926. A.B. with honors, S.C. State Coll., 1916, Bates Coll., Lewiston, Maine, 1920; D.D., Bates Coll., Lewiston, Maine, 1947; M.A., U. Chgo., 1925, Ph.D., 1935; LL.D., Denison U., Granville, Ohio, 1945, Virginia Union U., 1945, Centre Coll. Ky., 1970; D.D. (hon.), Howard U., 1945, Bucknell U., 1954, Berea Coll., 1955, Kalamazoo Coll., 1959, Morris Coll., Sumter, S.C., 1966, Ricker Coll., 1966, Interdenominational Theol. Center, Atlanta, 1974; LL.D., U. Liberia, Monrovia, 1960, Lincoln U., 1965, Alderson-Broaddus Coll., 1972; Litt.D., S.C. State Coll., 1946; L.H.D., Shaw U., Raleigh, N.C., 1966, Keuka Coll., 1962, Morehouse Coll., 1967, N.Y. U., 1968, Emory U., 1970, Brandeis U., 1970, Yeshiva U., 1971, Coe Coll., 1972, Pratt Inst., 1971, Edward Waters Coll., Jacksonville, 1974, Duke, 1975, Dillard U., New Orleans, 1975, Kean Coll., Union, N.J., 1975, Bethune Cookman Coll., Daytona Beach, Fla., 1976, SUNY, Old Westbury, 1981, U. D.C., 1981, Paine Coll., 1983; LL.D., St. Augustine's Coll., Raleigh, 1963, Harvard, 1967, Morgan Coll., Balt., 1967, Mich. State U., 1968, Dartmouth Coll., 1975, Bishop Coll., Dallas, 1977; Ed.D., St. Vincent Coll., Latrobe, Pa., 1964, Eastern Mich. U., 1982; Litt.D., Grinnell Coll., 1967, U. Ife, Nigeria, 1971; H.H.D., Boston U., 1950, Benedict Coll., 1970, Lander Coll., 1974, Talladega (Ala.) Coll., 1978, U. S.C., 1978; D.C.L., Middlebury (Vt.) Coll., 1969, Atlanta U., 1979; D.S.T., Olivet (Mich.) Coll., 1974, others. Tchr. higher math. Morehouse Coll., 1921-24; pastor Shiloh Bapt. Ch., Atlanta, 1921-24; instr. English State Coll. S.C., Orangeburg, 1925-26; exec. sec. Tampa (Fla.) Urban League, 1926-28; nat. student sec. YMCA, 1928-30; dir. study of

Negro chs. in U.S. for Inst. of Social and Religious Research, N.Y., 1930-32; dean Sch. of Religion, Howard U., Washington, 1934-40; pres. Morehouse Coll., Atlanta, 1940-67, pres. emeritus, 1967-84; vis. prof., adviser to pres. Mich. State U., 1968-69; Cons. Office Edn., HEW, Washington, 1969, Ford Found., 1970, United Bd. Coll. Devel. Author: The Negro's Church, 1933, The Negro's God, 1938, 2d edit., 1968, Seeking to be Christian in Race Relations, 1957, Disturbed About Man, 1969, Born to Rebel, 1971, Lord, The People Have Driven Me On, 1981, Quotable Quotes of Benjamin E. Mays, 1983; Contbr. to encys., books, mags. and newspapers.; Weekly columnist: Pitts. Courier; Compiler: A Gospel for the Social Awakening, 1950. Pres. United Negro College Fund, 1958-61, now bd. dirs.; v.p. Fed. Council Chs. Christ in Am., 1944-46; rep. U.S. at Oxford Conf. on Church, Community and State, Oxford (Eng.) U., 1937, YMCA of U.S. at Plenary Session of World Com., Stockholm, 1938; leader Youth Conf., Amsterdam, 1939; mem. U.S. del. World Conf. of YMCA, Mysore, India, 1937; del. to 1st assembly World Council Chs., 1948, mem. central com., 1949-54; del. Commn. on Ch. Amidst Racial and Ethnic Tensions, Geneva, 1953; del., leader Baptist World Alliance Assembly, Cleve., 1950; mem. U.S. Adv. Com. for UN, 1959; U.S. nat. commn. UNESCO, 1962; mem. nat. adv. council to Peace Corps, 1961; mem. Atlanta Bd. Edn., 1969-81, pres., 1970-81; v.p. World Student Service Fund; co-chmn. Citizens Crusade Against Poverty; Peace Corps rep. All-African Conf. on Edn., Addis Abada, 1961; Chmn. bd. trustees Benedict Coll.; past trustee Danforth Found., Nat. Fund for Med. Edn.; chmn. bd. dirs. Nat. Sharecropper Fund; bd. dirs. Inst. Internat. Edn. N.E. Region, Butler St. YMCA, Atlanta, Paine Coll., Religious Heritage Am., Martin Luther King, Jr. Center for Social Change; past bd. dirs. Nat. YMCA. Recipient Alumnus of Year award U. Chgo. Div. Sch., 1949; 2d Ann. Tex. State Fair Negro Achievement award, 1950; Christian Culture award Assumption U., Windsor, Ont., Can., 1961; Religious Leaders award NCCJ, 1970; Amistad award Am. Missionary Assn., 1968; Merrick-Moore-Spaulding award N.C. Mut. Life Ins. Co., 1968; Man of Year award Soc. Advancement of Mgmt., Greenville, S.C., 1968; Myrtle Wreath award Atlanta chpt. Hadassah, 1969; Achievement award Black Ednl. Services, Chgo., 1970; Russwurm award Nat. Newspapers Pubs., Chgo., 1970; citation Am. Bapt. Chs. of South, 1971; 1st recipient Dorie Miller award Dorie Miller Found., Chgo., 1971; Nat. Freedom Day award Phila., 1972; James Bryant Conant award Edn. Commn. of the States, 1977; Top Hat award The Chgo. Defender, 1978; Disting. Am. Educator award U.S. Office of Edn., 1978; Roy Wilkins award NAACP, 1977; Spingarn medal NAACP, 1982; Hale Woodruff award United Negro Coll. Fund, 1978; award Nat. Black Child Devel. Inst., 1978; Nat. Leadership award Nat. Assn. Equal Opportunity in Higher Edn., 1978; Alumni medal U. Chgo., 1978; Humanitarian award Internat. New Thought Alliance, 1978; recipient Meritorious Pub. Service medallion State of Ga., 1982, Meritorious Pub. Service medallion Nat. Assn. Secs. of State, William Booth award Salvation Army, 1982, Hall of Fame award Ga. Sch. Bd. Assn., 1982, Nat. Sch. Bd. Assn. award, 1982, Jefferson award, Atlanta Community Service award Sta. WXIA-TV, 1982, Hall of Fame award Nat. Dem. Black Caucus, 1982; Kent fellow Nat. Council Religion in Higher Edn.; numerous others. Mem. U. Chgo. Alumni Assn. (dir., mem. cabinet), Phi Beta Kappa, Kappa Delta Pi, Delta Sigma Rho (Distinguished Service award), Delta Theta Chi, Omega Psi Phi. Democrat. Baptist. Home: Atlanta, Ga. Dec. Mar. 28, 1984.

MAYS, PAUL KIRTLAND, artist; b. Cheswick, Pa., Oct. 4, 1887; s. Dallas and Lucy Hall (Kirtland) M.; student Art Students League, 1907-10, Hawthorne Sch. of Provincetown, Mass., 1911; studied at Newlyn Sch. of Painting, London and Colarossi Acad., Paris, 1923-24; m. Eleanor Moore, 1916; 1 dau., Lucy Kirtland; m. 2d, Margaret Pendleton Cooper, 1926; 1 son, Jared Potter Kirtland. Represented by painting —Monterey,— Cleveland Women's Club; —Jungle,— The White House (Washington, D.C.); —Taos,— U. of Pa.; —Harvest,— Oberlin College; murals, —Indian Legends,— Gallery of Contemporary Art (Phila.); murals U.S. P.O., Norristown, Pa., mural Bryn Athyn Acad., 1951. Paintings exhibited at Corcoran Gallery, Washington, D.C.; Whitney Museum, N.Y. City; Pa. Museum, Phila.; Stendahl's, Los Angeles. Grand Central Art Galleries, N.Y., 1946; Evanston, Ill., 1948. Pa. Acad. Fine Arts, 1951, Artists Guild of Am. (Carmel Art Gallery), 1952; exhbns. Pitts. and Carmel, Cal., 1953. Mem. Artists Equity, Carmel Art Assn., Nat. Soc. of Mural Painters. Address: Carmel, Calif. †

MAYTHAM, THOMAS NORTHRUP, museum ofcl.; b. Buffalo, July 30, 1931; s. Thomas Edward and Lorana Margaret (Northrup) M.; 1 son, Gifford. B.A., Williams Coll., 1954; M.A., Yale U., 1956. Asst., then head dept. painting Mus. Fine Arts, Boston, 1956-67; asso. dir., then acting dir. Seattle Art Mus., 1967-74; dir. Denver Art Mus., from 1974; mem. mus. adv. council Nat. Endowment Arts; bd. dirs. Colo. Celebration for Arts. Mem. Am. Fedn. Arts, Assn. Art Mus. Dirs. Home: Denver, Colo.

MC ALLISTER, DECKER GORDON, manufacturing executive; b. San Francisco, Aug. 19, 1900; s. Elliott and Alice (Decker) McA.; student Stanford, 1917-18; B.S. in Elec. Engring., Mass. Inst. Tech., 1921; m. Martha Ransome, Apr. 20, 1929; children—Decker Gordon, Bruce. With Pacific Sci. Co., San Francisco, 1925-84, pres., 1961-65, chmn. bd., 1965-73, hon. chmn. bd., 1973-84; with Pacific Sci. Aero Products, 1928-84, pres., 1954-84; vice chmn. bd. Oxford Labs.; dir. Varian Assos., Chemetal Corp. Chmn. trustees, fellow Calif. Acad. Scis.; trustee Internat. Sci. Found. Clubs: Pacific Union (San Francisco); Burlingame Country (Hillborough, Calif.). Home: Hillsborough, Calif. Dec. July 29, 1984. Interned Cypress Lawn, Colina, Calif.

MCALLISTER, SAMUEL WILSON, librarian; b. Conneaut, O., May 10, 1890; s. Alexander and Catherine (McFadden) McA.; student Antioch Coll., 1909-11; A.B., U. Mich., 1916. A.M., 1921; student Sorbonne, U. Paris, 1919; B.L.S., Columbia, 1928; m. Marguerite Lee Patterson, June 18, 1918; children—James Patterson, Nancy Wilson, Mary Lee. Dept. foreman Mazda Lamp Works, Conneaut, O., 1911-14; asst. in charge grad. reading room U. Mich. Library, 1916-17, 1919-21, asso. librarian, 1930-31, asso. dir. from 1941; librarian Ann Arbor (Mich.) Pub. Library, 1921-27, Central Mich. Coll. Edn., 1928-30. Served at 1st lt. Inf., U.S. Army, 1917-19, A.E.F., 1918-19. Mem. A.L.A., Assn. Coll. and Research Libraries, Mich. Library Assn. (pres. 1935-36), Mich. Acad. Sci. Arts. Letters. Presbyn. Clubs: University, Rotary. Home: Ann Arbor. †

MC ALLISTER, WALTER WILLIAMS, savs. and loan exec.; b. San Antonio, Mar. 26, 1889; s. Frank Williams and Lena (Stumberg) McA.; E.E., U. Tex., 1910; m. Lenora Alexander, Mar. 26, 1913 (dec. May 1969); children—Elizabeth McAllister Solcher, Walter Williams Jr., Gerald N. Founder, San Antonio Savs. Assn., 1921, chmn. bd., 1953-76, chmn. exec. com., 1976-84; chmn. bd. South States Oil Co., San Antonio, chmn. Fed. Home Loan Bank Bd., Washington, 1953-56; chmn. nat. advisory bond com. savs. and loan U.S. Treasury, 1958-63. Pres., Planning Bd. San Antonio and Bexar County, 1948-50; chmn. San Antonio City Mgr. Charter Revision Commn., 1951-84; mem. Tex. Finance Commn., 1952-53; mayor San Antonio, 1961-71, councilman, 1960. Bd. dirs. emeritus Ednl. TV Sta. KLRN, Austin, Tex.; pres. bd. trustees San Antonio Union Jr. Coll., 1946-60; chmn. bd. dirs. Witte Mus., 1952-53; trustee Internat. Union Bldg. Socs. and Savs. and Loan Assns. Recipient Golden Deeds award San Antonio Exchange Club, 1956, Outstanding Citizens award San Antonio Council Presidents, 1964. Mem. U.S. (legis. com., past pres.), Southwestern (past pres.), Tex. (past pres.) savs. and loan leagues, San Antonio C. of C. (past pres.), Phi Gamma Delta. Republican. Mason (33 deg., Shriner), Kiwanian. Clubs: San Antonio Country, Argyle. Home: San Antonio, Tex. Died Sept. 13, 1984.

MC BRIDE, LLOYD, union official; b. Farmington, Mo., Mar. 9, 1916; m. Dolores Neihaus, 1937; children—Larry, Sharon McBride Reynolds. Student, St. Louis pub. schs. Mem. Steelworkers Organizing Com., 1936; organizer Local 1295, Mo., 1936, pres., 1938-40, St. Louis Indsl. Union Council, CIO, 1940, Mo. CIO Indsl. Union Council, 1942-44; staff union rep. United Steelworkers Am., AFL-CIO, St. Louis, 1946-58, sub-dist. dir., 1958-65, dist. dir., 1965-77, pres., 1977-83; v.p. AFL-CIO, 1977-83, mem. exec. council indsl. union dept.; del. Internat. Metalworkers Fedn. meetings, Geneva. Bd. dirs. Nat. Soc. Prevention Blindness; bd. govs. United Way; mem. presdl. commn. to investigate accident at Three Mile Island; mem. Pay Adv. Bd.; trustee Human Resources Devel. Inst.; mem. Com. for Nat. Health Ins., Harry S. Truman Inst.; mem. steel tripartite com. Labor-Industry Coalition for Internat. Trade. Served with USN, 1944-46. Office: Pittsburgh, Pa. Dec. Nov. 5, 1983.

MC BRIDE, LLOYD MERRILL, lawyer; b. Corydon, Iowa, July 20, 1908; s. Ernest Eugene and Jeannie (Randolph) McB.; m. Alice Rowland, June 8, 1935; children: Patricia Ann, Barbara Jean. A.B. cum laude, Carleton Coll., Northfield, Minn., 1930, LL.D. (hon.), 1979; student, Harvard U. Law Sch., 1931-32; J.D., Northwestern U., 1934. Bar: Ill. 1934. Since practiced in Chgo.; with firm Stearns & Jones, 1934-41; ptnr. successor firms Stearns & McBride, 1941-43, McBride & Baker, 1943-58, 81-83, McBride, Baker, Wienke & Schlosser, 1958-81; sec., dir. SMI Investments Co., FRC Corp.; dir., chmn. exec. com. Wallace Computer Services, Inc.; sec., dir. Vermilion Corp., Bayou Corp. Sec., trustee Morton Arboretum, Lisle, Ill.; pres., dir. 1550 State Pkwy. Condominium Assn.; trustee Carleton Coll., Northfield, Minn. Mem. Phi Beta Kappa. Republican. Clubs: Racquet (Chgo.), Tower (Chgo.), Mid-Day (Chgo.), Mid-America (Chgo.). Home: Chicago, Ill. Died Dec. 26, 1983.

MCBRIDE, ROBERT H., former ambassador; b. Eng., May 25, 1918 (parents U.S. citizens); studen schs. in France; B.A., Princeton, 1940. Museum aide Nat. Gallery of Art, 1940-41; fgn. service officer 1941-74; vice consul, Habana, Cuba, 1941, 3d sec., vice consul, 1942-43; vice consul, Algiers, Algeria, 1943, sec., vice consul, 1944; temp. assignment, Corsica, 1943-44; sec. office U.S. rep. Adv. Council for Italy, 1944; 3d sec., vice consul, Rome, Italy, 1945; assigned fgn. service officer Dept. State, 1946; spl. asst. dir. Office Am. Republic Affairs, 1946-47; 1st sec., consul, Port-au-Prince, Haiti, 1947-49; consul, Rabat, Morocco, 1949-51; assigned Dept. State, Washington, 1951; formerly 1st consul, Paris, France, then asst. sec. European affairs Office European Regional Affairs, Dept. State; counsel, Madrid, Spain, 1961-69; later U.S. ambassador to Kinshasha. Dem. Republic of Congo, ambassador to Mexico, 1969-74. Died Dec. 26, 1983.

MCCABE, CHARLES RAYMOND, journalist; b. N.Y.C., Jan. 24, 1915; s. Peter Joseph and Mary Catherine (Kyne) McC.; m. Margaret Ellen Scripps, 1948 (div. 1955); children—Mary (Mrs. Peter Barmonde), Peter, Nini, Charles. B.A., Manhattan Coll., 1937. Reporter New York American, 1937-38; publicity rep. Steve Hannagan Assos., N.Y.C., 1939-42; corr. U.P.I., Washington, 1950-52; syndicated columnist San Francisco Chronicle and other papers, 1959-83; cons. Howard Gossage Assos., 1962-64. Author: Damned Old Crank, 1952, The Fearless Spectator, 1970, Tall Girls Are Grateful, 1973, The Good Man's Weakness, 1974. Mem. San Francisco Crime Commn., 1968-69. Served with USNR, 1942-45. Decorated Navy Commendation medal; recipient Munoz-Marin Journalism award San Juan, P.R., 1940. Mem. Newspaper Guild. Democrat. Roman Catholic. Club: Great Bedwyn Cricket (Witshire, Eng.) (pres. 1962-66). Home: San Francisco, Calif. Dec. May 1, 1983.

MCCABE, JAMES HARVEY, hotel exec.; b. Balt., Aug. 16, 1888; s. Lawrence B. and Mary Ellen (Keaveny) McC.; grad. Calvert Hall Coll., Balt.; student De La Salle Inst., N.Y.C., Old Point Comfort Coll., Phoebus, Va.; m. Eleanor Cather, July 1, 1923. Cashier, room clk. Hotel Belvedere, Balt., 1908-12; asst. mgr. Hotel Statler, Cleve., 1912-15, St. Louis, 1917-19, Hotel Pennsylvania, N.Y.C., 1919-21, Hotel Alexandria, Los Angeles, 1921-22, Providence (R.I.) Biltmore, 1922-23, Hotel Biltmore, Los Angeles, 1923-25; gen. mgr. Hotel Columbus, Miami, Fla., 1925-26, Hotel St. Francis, San Francisco, 1926-36, Hotel Statler, N.Y.C., from 1937; v.p., asst. to pres. Hilton Hotels Corp., Chgo. Mem. Am. N.Y., Cal., No. Cal. (pres.) hotel assns., Hotel Greeters of Am. Address: Chicago, Ill. †

MC CABE, THOMAS BAYARD, paper co. exec., banker; b. Whaleyville, Md., July 11, 1893; s. William Robbins and Beulah (Whaley) McC.; m. Jeannette Laws, Feb. 28, 1924; children—Thomas (dec.), Richard Whaley, James. Student, Wilmington Conf. Acad., Dover, Del., 1907-10; A.B., Swarthmore Coll., 1915; LL.D.; LL.D., Hahneman Med., Drexel Inst., Trinity Coll., 1949, Pa. Mil. Coll., U. Del., 1955, U. Maine, 1961, St. Joseph's Coll., 1962, U. Md., 1962; L.H.D., Temple U., 1959, Salisbury State Coll., 1979; L.H.D. hon. degrees, U. Pa., Colo. Coll., Jefferson Med. Coll., Colby Coll. With Scott Paper Co., Chester, Pa., 1916-80, salesman, 1916-17, asst. sales mgr., 1919-20, sales mgr., 1920-22, dir., 1921-80, sec., sales mgr., 1922-27, v.p., 1927, pres., 1927-62, chmn., 1962-68, chmn. finance com., 1969-72, chief exec., 1927-67, dir. emeritus, from 1980; dir. Fed. Res. Bank of Phila., 1938-48, chmn. bd., 1939-48; chmn. bd. govs. Fed. Res. System, 1948-51; Mem. bus. adv. council Dept. Commerce, from 1940; chmn., 1944-45; hon. chmn. Mktg. Sci. Inst.; with Council Nat. Def., 1940; dep. dir. div. of priorities Office Prodn. Mgt., 1941; dep. Lend-Lease Adminstrn., 1941-42; Public gov. N.Y. Stock Exchange, 1960-63. Trustee Com. for Econ. Devel., Army-Navy Liquidation Commn., Feb.-Sept. 1945; spl. asst. to sec. State and Fgn. Liquidation Commr., 1945-46; Trustee Eisenhower Exchange Fellowships, Inc.; bd. mgrs. Swarthmore Coll. Served from pvt. to capt. U.S. Army, 1917-19. Awarded Medal for Merit. Mem. Delta Upsilon. Presbyterian. Clubs: Rittenhouse (Phila.), Union League (Phila.), Pen and Pencil (Phila.) (hon. life); Corinthian Yacht. Home: Swarthmore, PA.

MCCAHEY, JAMES B., corp. exec.; b. Chicago, Apr. 19, 1890; student De LaSalle Inst.; m. Claire Miller, 1917; children—James B., Claire M., Anita R., Fred M., Carol Ann. Began in coal bus., 1907; trustee and executor Dunn Estate, 1910; pres. Dunn Coal Co. from 1920; pres. Morrison Hotel Corp.; dir. Nickel Plate R.R. Clubs: St. Charles (Ill.) Country; Chicago Golf, South Shore Country, Chicago Athletic, Country, Sky Line, Mid-Day (Chicago). Home: Chicago, Ill. †

MCCALL, HAROLD PERCY, newspaper editor; b. Cameron, La., Oct. 4, 1896; s. Milledge William and Martha Anne (Doland) McC.; student La. State u., 1914-16; certificate journalism and econs., AFF Univ. Beaune, France, 1919; m. Alice Athenia Rightor, May 18, 1927; 1 son, Malcolm Wetherill. Mem. staff New Orleans Times-Picayune, 1919-70, editorial writer, 1940-51, asso. editor, editor editorial page, 1952-70; past v.p. Times-Picayune Pub. Corp. Pres. New Orleans Round Table Club, 1966-68. Mem. Boswell Inst.; fellow Internat. Acad. Served U.S. Army, 1916-18; AFF in Mexico, France. Mem. Am. Soc. Newspaper Editors, New Orleans Fgn. Policy Assn. (chmn. bd. 1961-62), Pub. Affairs Research Council La. Episcopalian (sr. warden). Club: New Orleans Press (pres. 1926-27; best editorial award New Orleans area 1962). Home: New Orleans, La. Deceased.

MCCALL, MAX ADAMS, agronomist; b. Jamestown, Kan., Oct. 20, 1888; s. Andrew Rogers and Mary Pamelia (McKee) McC.; B.S.A., Ore. Agrl. Coll., 1910; M.S., Wash. State Coll., 1922; Ph.D., U. of Wis., 1932; m. Marjorie Sellers, Nov. 14, 1914 (died 1918); 1 dau., Marjorie Sellers; m. 2d, Bernadine Haller, Dec. 27, 1920; 1 dau., Maxine Adams. Instr. high sch., Davenport, Wash., 1910-11, Ore. Agrl. Coll., 1911-12, high sch. of Klamath County, Ore., 1912-14; county agrl. agt. Klamath County, 1914; dry farm specialist Wash. Agrl. Expt. Station and supt. Adams Branch Station, Lind, Wash., 1914-24; agronomist, sr. agronomist, prin. agronomist in charge cereal agronomy, div. of cereal crops and diseases, Bur. Plant Industry, Soils and Agr. Engineering, United States Department Agriculture, Washington, D.C., 1924-29, in charge of div. 1929-46; asst. chief of Bur. and head agronomist from 1935, in charge from 1946. Fellow A.A.A.S. (v.p. Dec. 10, 1946), American Society Agronomy (ex-pres.), Am. Soc. Plant Physiology. Am. Phytopathol. Soc., Am. Genetic Assn., Washington Botanical Society, Wash. Acad. Science, Gamma Sigma Delta, Phi Kappa Phi, Sigma Xi, Kappa Sigma. Club: Cosmos. Author official bulls. Home: Chevy Chase, Md. †

MCCALL, THOMAS LAWSON, governor of Oregon; b. Egypt, Mass., Mar. 22, 1913; s. Henry and Dorothy (Lawson) McC.; B.A. in Journalism, U. Oreg., 1936; LL.D., Linfield Coll., McMinnville, Oreg., 1965; m. Audrey Owen, May 20, 1939; children—Thomas Lawson, Samuel Walker III. Polit. news analyst radio and TV, 1944-64; adminstrv. asst. to Gov. Ore. McKay, 1949-52; secretary of the State of Oregon, 1965-66; gov. State of Oreg., 1967-74. Past. pres. Oreg. Prison Assn.; chmn. Portland Met. Youth. Commn. Pres. Oreg. Assn. Crippled Children and Adults; active NCCJ. Republican nominee for Congress, 1954. Served as corr. USNR, 1944-46. Recipient award outstanding TV documentary in U.S., Sigma Delta Chi, 1962; Golden Beaver award Izaak Walton League, 1959; Brotherhood award Oreg. Regional Conf. Christians and Jews, 1964. Mem. Phi Delta Theta, Alpha Delta Sigma. Episcopalian. Died Jan. 8, 1983.

MCCANKIE, REGINALD C., ins. exec.; b. Edinburgh, Scotland, May 6, 1890; s. James and Catherine (Henderson) McC.; student pub. schs. of Scotland; m. Olive Mary Hill, Oct. 5, 1918. Came to U.S., 1911, naturalized, 1928. Apprentice Scottish Met. Life Ins. Co., 1906-10; actuarial asst. Great So. Life Ins. Co., Houston, Tex., 1911-13; Shenandoah Life Ins. Co., Roanoke, Va., 1919-20; with Equitable Life Ins. Co. of Ia., Des Moines, from 1920, v.p. and actuary from 1948, mem. bd. of trustees since 1948. Fellow Soc. Actuaries of U.S. and Can. Served with British Army, 1914-19. Home: Des Moines, Iowa †

MCCANN, WILLIAM JAMES, mus. adminstr., city ofcl.; b. Pitts., Sept. 9, 1924; s. William James and Martha (Thomas) McC. B.S. in Comml. Edn, U. Pitts., 1948; postgrad., Pa. State U., 1949, UCLA, 1952. Tchr. Central High Sch., Pitts., 1949; head acctg. Blaw Knox Co., Pitts., 1949-52; controller Standard Steel Corp., Los Angeles, 1952-56; dir. Calif. Mus. Sci. and Industry, Los Angeles, from 1966; exec. sec. Calif. Mus. Found., Expn. Park, Calif., from 1966; exec. v.p. Imac, Inc. Co-founder City of Santa Fe Springs, Calif., 1957, mem. city council, from 1957, mayor, 1957-75. Named All Am. Mayor Look mag., 1960, One of Five Outstanding Young Men in Calif. Calif. Jr. C. of C., 1961. Mem. Nat. Assn. Accts., Nat. Acad. TV Arts and Scis., Am. Acad. Polit. and Social Sci., Calif. Soc. Assn. Execs., So. Calif. Industry-Edn. Council (exec. v.p. 1965-66), So. Calif. Assn. Govts., Hollywood Press Club. Home: Santa Fe Springs, Calif. *

MCCARTHY, EUGENE ROSS (LOUISE ROBLEE MCCARTHY), philanthropist; b. St. Louis, Oct. 7, 1888; d. Joseph H. and Florence (Allen) Roblee; grad. Mary Inst., St. Louis, Bradford Acad., Mass.; A.B., Vassar, 1912; H.H.D., Springfield Coll., 1953; m. Eugene Ross McCarthy, Dec. 13, 1913; children—Marjorie (Mrs. G. Kenneth Robins), Carol Louise (Mrs. H. Richard Duhme, Jr.), Roblee. Nat. dir. YWCA of U.S., 1939-64, hon., from 1965, v.p., 1949-55, chairman central region, 1946-52, vice president-at-large, 1952-55; vice president World YWCA. Geneva, Switzerland, 1955-59; American mem. World YWCA Council, 1949-64, exec. com., 1949-59; del. World Council, Beirut, Lebanon, 1951, Gt. Brit., 1955, Cuernavaca, Mex., 1959, Nyborg Strand, Denmark, 1963, del. membership conf., Whitby, Can., 1950; dir. St. Louis YWCA, from 1933, pres., 1938-40. Mem. Nat. USO Corp., 1941-47, 51-66, mem. Nat. bd., 1948-50, v.p. councils of St. Louis and Mo., 1941-47; nat. v.p. United Def. Fund, 1950-55; former mem. central budget and policy com. St. Louis Community Chest; mem. board of govs. United Fund of Greater St. Louis, from 1955; chmn. com. Mo. White House Conf. Com. on Children and Youth to study programs under religious auspices Missouri, 1949-50; member Missouri committee 1960 White House Conference Children and Youth; member Mayor's Race Relations Commn. St. Louis, 1943-49; dir. Nat. Conf. Christians and Jews, St. Louis, from 1945; v.p.-at-large, mem. gen. bd. Nat. Council Chs. Christ in USA, 1954-57, 60-63, mem. div. internat. affairs, 1960-66; exec. bd. Metropolitan Ch. Fedn. St. Louis, from 1938, v.p. from 1956. Trustee Vassar Coll., 1933-37, Springfield Coll., 1955-61. Recipient Woman of Achievement citation for nat. service St. Louis Globe Democrat, 1955; Ecumenical Woman of the year, Met. Ch. Fed. of Greater St. Louis, 1959, citation for notable achievement and service Bradford Jr. Coll., 1961, citation Women of Press, St. Louis, 1964. Mem. Nat. Soc. Colonial Dames Am., Mo. Historical Society, Am. Assn. U. Women (pres. St. Louis 1924-26), League of Women Voters. Clubs: Vassar (past pres.), Wednesday (hon.), Woman's (St. Louis); Vassar (N.Y.C.). Editorial bd. Am. Bapt. Conv., 1948-54. Home: St. Louis, MO. †

MCCARTY, GEORGE WEYMAN, corp. exec.; b. Atlanta, June 27, 1887; s. George W. and Sarah Elizabeth (Rucker) McC.; student Culver (Ind.) Mil. Acad.; M.E., Ga. Sch. of Tech., 1908; m. Passie May Ottley, July 9, 1915; children—George W., John Ottley. Salesman, A. D. Adair & McCarty Bros., Atlanta, 1909-11; owner Fertilizer Materials Co., 1911-15; dir. and officer, Ashcraft-Wilkinson Co., 1916-64, pres. 1942-52, chmn., 1953-64; dir. A & F Investing Co., Inc., Flag Sulphur & Chem. Co., Tampa, Fla.; hon. dir. Seaboard Air Line R.R. Co. Asst. chief, Nitrogen Unit, W.P.B., Washington, 1942-43. Mem. Ga. Tech. Nat. Alumni Assn. (past pres.), Ga. Tech. Alumni Found. (trustee), Mil. Order of World Wars, Soc. Colonial Wars, Newcomen Soc., Kappa Alpha. Baptist. Clubs: Capital City, Piedmont Driving. Home: Atlanta, Ga. †

MCCARTY, SAMUEL ELLSWORTH, naval officer; b. West Alexander, Pa., June 27, 1889; s. Samuel Ellsworth and Birdie (Bowman) McC.; degree in Bus. Adminstrn., Business Coll., Wheeling, W.Va., 1906; student Princeton, 1918, 1919; m. Gwendolyn Margaret Bowman, Oct. 30, 1924. Sports editor, spl. writer Pittsburgh Leader, 1912-15, polit. editor, 1915-17; entered U.S. Navy, 1917; commd. ensign, 1919, advanced through grades to rear adm., 1944; duty in Far East, 1921-24, serving 13 mos. in Vladivostok (Russia) area during part of Russian revolution, 1922, stationed at Yokohama, Japan, 1923-24, at time of earthquake which destroyed Yokohama and damaged Tokyo; served in North Atlantic area, 1942-43, Pacific area, 1944-46; aviation supply officer, U.S. Navy, responsible for support of naval air service 1947-51; gen. mgr. Martinolich Shipbldg. Co., San Diego, Cal. Mem. Cal. legislative harbor commn.; mem. overland mail commn.; chmn. Transportation and Facilities com., San Diego; trustee LaJolla town council; pres. San Diego Council Boy Scouts of America. Recipient medals World War I, two Secretary of Navy citations for duty in Pacific, medals for area occupation in European, Atlantic and Pacific Ocean areas during World War II (U.S.), 1 medal (France). Mem. Nat. Security Indsl. Assn., Mil. Order World War, Naval Acad. Athletic Assn. Republican. Mem. Christian Ch. Mason. Clubs: Union League, Eucalyptus (pres.). Home: La Jolla, Cal. †

MCCLELLAN, LESLIE NEWMAN, elec. engr.; b. Middleton, O., Mar. 27, 1888; s. James Rusk and Rose (Newman) McC.; B.S., in elec. engring., U. of Southern Cal., 1911; hon. Doctor engring. University of Colorado, 1949; m. Mary Jane Lair, June 18, 1919; 1 dau., Mary Elizabeth. With U.S. Bur. of Reclamation as jr. and asst. engr. Salt River project in Ariz., 1911-17, asst. elec. engr. in office of chief engr. at Denver, 1918-23; transmission engr., operating dept., So. Calif. Edison Co., 1923; chief elec. engr. U.S. Bur. Reclamation, 1924-48, now asst. commr., chief engr. Served as 1st lt. U.S. Army, 1918; capt, O.R.C., 1918-28. Recipient gold medal, Colo. Engring. Council, 1951; gold medal from U.S. Dept. of Interior, 1952. Fellow Am. Inst. Elec. Engrs. (v.p. 1938-39, life mem.); mem. American Society of Civil Engineers, International Commn. of Irrigation and Drainage, Colorado Soc. Engrs., Colorado Engring. Council, U.S. Nat. Com. of Internat. Conf. on Large Electric High-Tension Systems, Tau Beta Pi, Sigma Xi. Mason. Club: Denver University. Home: Denver, Colo. †

MCCLURE, DONALD C., utilities exec.; b. Coxsackie, N.Y., May 31, 1890; s. John C. and Anna (Collier) McC.; student N.Y. Mil. Acad.; E.E., Rensselaer Polytech. Inst., 1913; m. Agnes Clancy, Oct. 8, 1919; children—John Casper, Mrs. Richard L. Kerr. With Denver Gas & Electric Co., 1913-24; gen. supt. St. Joseph Ry., Light, Heat & Power Co. (Mo.), 1924-27; operating v.p. Central Pub. Service Co., Chgo., 1929-33; pres. Central Ill. Electric & Gas Co., Rockford, Ill., 1933-53, chmn., chief exec. officer, 1953-60, chairman of executive committee, from 1960; mem. bd. dirs. Ill. Nat. Bank & Trust Co., Rockford. Trustee, bd. counselors Rockford Coll.; trustee Rockford Meml. Hosp. Served as capt., 37th U.S. Engrs., U.S. Army, World War I. Mem. Delta Tau Delta. Presbyn. Elk. Clubs: University Rotary, Mid-Day, Rockford Country (Rockford); University (Chgo.). †

MCCLURE, WALLACE, educator; born in Knoxville, Tenn., July 30, 1890; s. William Kyle and Eliza Parsons (Lewis) McC.; A.B., U. of Tenn., 1910, LL.B., 1911; A.M., Columbia, 1915, Ph.D., 1924; m. Helen Mellen, Feb. 14, 1918; children—William Kyle, George Mellen, Wallace; married 2d, Anne Taylor, July 29, 1952. Admitted to the local bar of Knoxville, 1911, bar Dist. Court U.S., 1920; began practice at Knoxville, 1916; mem. firm Sansom & McClure, 1916-17; became teacher commercial policy and treaties, Sch. of Foreign Service, Georgetown U., 1925; co-founder and 1st sec. of bd. Acad. of World Economics, 1932; co-founder World Affairs Study Groups and founder of W. K. McClure Foundation for Study of World Affairs (Knoxville), 1941; lecturer public forums, Des Moines, 1935, Colorado Springs and Chattanooga, 1936; lecturer Johns Hopkins, 1936-37; officer, Dept. of State, Dec. 1920-Aug. 1951; was asst. to the economic adviser, thereafter assistant chief Treaty Div.; tech. adviser to Am. del. to 7th Internat. Conf. of American States, Montevideo, 1933; sr. econ. analyst Foreign Service Auxiliary, American Legation, Stockholm, 1942-46; Office of Spl. Polit. Affairs, 1946, later mem. of Commercial Policy Staff; member faculty Am. Internat. College, serving USAF, 1952-54; first assigned to Dhahran, later dean, overseas div., and prof.-in-charge Bermuda; vis. lectr. U. Va., 1954-55; Fulbright lectr. U. Dacca, East Pakistan, 1955-56; consulting dir. of World Rule of Law Center, 1958, vis. prof. law, Sch. Law, Duke U., 1958-61, lectr. law, 1961. Entered R.O.T.C., August 27, 1917; commissioned 2d lt., F.A., November 1917; honorably discharged, December 11, 1918. Hon. member of Internat. Law Association (Pakistan); mem. Phi Gamma Delta, Phi Kappa Phi. Democrat. Presbyterian. Clubs: Colonnade (Charlottesville); Cosmos (Washington). Author: State Constitution Making, 1916; A New American Commercial Policy, 1924; World Prosperity, 1933; International Executive Agreements, 1941; World Law, 1956; World Legal Order, 1960; rapporteur for study of U.S. in UN Commn. to study Orgn. of Peace, 1949-50; bd. editors UN League of Lawyres Rev., 1951-52. Home: Charlottesville, Va. †

MC CLUSKEY, ELLEN L., interior designer; b. N.Y.C.; d. Allan and Evelyn (Schiffer) Lehman; m. Richard McCluskey, 1942 (div. 1952); children: Maureen, Sharon, Orin; m. Preston Long, June 1957 (div. 1971). B.A., Vassar Coll., 1934; postgrad., Columbia U., 1934-36, N.Y. Sch. Interior Design, 1936-37. Asso. interior decorator with Adele Dewey, 1937-38, Franklin Hughes, 1938-42, Ruth Warburton Kaufman, 1942-43; prin. Ellen L. McCluskey Assos., Inc., 1948-84. Active Just One Break, Inc., N.Y. Infirmary; mem. acquisitions com. benefit auction Cooper Hewitt Mus.; chmn. Am. Soc. Interior Designers Edn. Found. Fellow Am. Inst. Interior Designers (past pres. N.Y. chpt.); mem. Am. Soc. Interior Designers (mem. working com. of nat. com. on historic preservation). Home: New York, N.Y. Died Oct. 21, 1984.

MCCLUSKY, HOWARD YALE, educator; b. Whitesboro, N.Y., Feb. 20, 1900; s. Frederick William and Lillian (Dean) McC.; student Blackburn Acad. 1913-17, Blackburn Coll., 1917-18, LL.D. 1959; A.B., Park Coll., 1921; Ph.D., U. Chgo., 1929; U. London, 1933-34; m. Helen Hazel Hartman, Aug. 26, 1930; children—Edith Lillian, William (dec.), Samuel (dec.), Frederick Yale, John Evans. Asso. prof. U. Mich., 1934-39, prof. since 1939, asst. to v.p. in charge of Univ. Relations in the Field of Adult Edn., 1938-45; vis. prof. ednl. psychology, Northwestern U., summer, 1937; asso. dir. Am. Youth Commn., Am. Council on Edn., 1940-42; chief Nat. Organizations Sect. and asso. dir. Civilian Mobilization Branch. Office of Civilian Defense, 1942; consultant to Office of War Information, 1943; com. chmn. White House Conf. on Rural Edn., 1944; post doctoral fellow Nat. Council Religion in Higher Edn., after 1945; mem. U.S. Nat. Commn, to UNESCO, after 1953; mem. adv. com. on edn. Dept. Def. after 1956; sr. cons. edn. U.S. Office Edn., 1963-66; mem. Mich. Gov.'s Panel on Ethics in Govt., after 1963; cons. Mich. Human Resources Council, after 1963; cons. Mott Found., after 1964. Recipient Delbert Clark award in adult edn., 1956; distinguished Faculty Achievement award U. Mich., 1958. Mem. Am. Psychol. Assn., Nat. Soc. for Study of Edn., Am. Ednl. Research Assn., Nat. Soc. Coll. Tchrs. Edn., Adult Edn. Assn. of U.S.A. (charter (first) pres., 1951-52, Nat. Edn. Association, Phi Beta Kappa, Phi Kappa Phi, Phi Delta Kappa, Alplha Kappa Lambda, Phi Kappa Delta. Club: University (Mich.). Author, editor Mental Hygiene and others. Recipient Delbert Clark award in adult edn., 1956. Home: Ann Arbor, Mich. Died Aug. 15, 1982.

MCCOARD, ALBERT BABCOCK, utilities exec.; born New Orleans, Oct. 26, 1889; s. David and Ida (Babcock) McC.; student pub. schs.; m. Virginia Kay Collette, Feb. 25, 1920. With New Orleans Pub. Service Inc. from 1903, gen. auditor, 1918, comptroller, 1926, exec. asst., 1933, v.p. from 1939; dir. from 1936. Mem. New Orleans C. of C., Internat. House, New Orleans Bd. Trade. Club: Louisiana (New Orleans). Home: New Orleans LA.†

MCCOLE, CORNELIUS (CON) J., business exec.; b. Glen Lyon, Pa., July 27, 1888; s. Cornelius and Sally (Mundy) McC.; ed. pub. schs., Wilkes-Barre; m. Arline Sweeney, Dec. 27, 1923; children—Cornelius E., John A., Sally. Began as ins. agent Mutual Life of N.Y., Wilkes-Barre, later asst. dist. mgr., mgr.; dir. Hudson Coal Co. Mayor, Wilkes-Barre, 1944-48. Roman Catholic. K.C., Elk, Moose, Eagle. Club: Kiwanis (hon. mem.). Home: Wilkes-Barre, Pa. Deceased.

MCCOLLOCH, CLAUDE, judge; b. Red Bluff, Calif., Jan. 14, 1888; s. Charles Henry and Mary Elizabeth

(Wooddy) McC.; ed. Stanford U., 1904-07, U. of Chicago, 1907-09 (Ph.B.); m. Erma Clifford, 1912. Admitted to Ore. bar, 1909; practiced at Baker, 1909-13, Portland, 1913-19, Klamath Falls, 1926-37; city atty., Baker, 1911-13; U.S. dist. judge, Dist. of Ore., from 1937. Mem. Ore. State Senate, 1911-13 sessions; former mem. Port of Portland Commn.; Dem. State chmn., 1936. Mem. Kappa Sigma, Phi Delta Phi. Democrat. Author: Notes of a District Judge, 1948, Part II, 1949. Home: Portland. †

MCCOMBS, NELSON WILBOR, librarian; born in Columbus, O., April 20, 1890; son of James and Antoinette Claypool (Flowers) McC.; student Ohio State U., 1912-16, Library Sch. of N.Y. Pub. Library, 1919; B.A., U. of Mich., 1932; m. Elizabeth Ross, Sept. 13, 1921; 1 dau., Janet (Mrs. E. W. Baldwin, Jr.). Asst. accessions dept., Ohio State U. Library, 1911-17; asst. Am. History Div., N.Y. Pub. Library, 1917-18, information desk, 1919; librarian Fed. Reserve Bd. Library, Washington, 1919-22; librarian N.Y.U., Washington Square Library from 1922. Served in U.S. Army World War I, 1918-19. Chmn., joint comm. of N.Y. Library Club and Special Libraries Assn., 1938-41, on Union Library Catalogue for N.Y. City. Mem. Bibliog. Soc. of Am. (permanent sec., editor, 1944-48), Am. Library Assn., N.Y. Hist. Soc., Assn. Coll. and Reference Libraries, Alumni Assn., Library Sch. of N.Y. Pub. Library (pres. 1924-25), Phi Kappa Tau. Episcopalian. Clubs: Grolier, D.C. Library (sec. treas., 1920-22, N.Y.C. Library (treas. N.Y. 1925-27, mem. council, 1934-38, pres. 1944-45). Home: Basking Ridge, N.J. †

MCCONAGHA, WILLIAM ALBERT, educator; b. Norwich, O., Aug. 4, 1890; s. David Hawthorne and Lida (Taylor) McC.; B.S., Muskingum Coll., 1917; A.M., U. Ill., 1922, Ph.D., 1925; m. Jessie Mae Pate, June 30, 1928; children—Alan Cameron, Margaret Jane. Asst. econs. U. Ill., 1922-25, instr., 1925-26, vis. prof. econs. summers, 1946-47; vis. instr. econs. Ill. State Normal, 1923-24; asso. prof. Lawrence College, 1926-30, professor from 1930. With Am. Expeditionary Forces, U.S. Marine Corps, during World War I. Mem. Am. Econ. Assn., Am Assn. U. Profs., Sigma Phi Epsilon. Methodist. Author: The Labor Movement in Great Britain, France and Germany, 1942. Home: Appleton, Wis. †

MCCONKEY, FREDERICK PAUL, clergyman; b. Grove City, Pa., Feb. 2, 1887; s. William James and Hetty Higby (Pringle) McC.; A.B., Grove City Coll., 1909, D.D., 1925; student Princeton Theol. Sem., 1909-12; M.A., Princeton U., 1912; m. Ruth Nash, Aug. 29, 1918; children—William James, Miriam Ella, Frederick Paul. Pastor Centre Presbyn. Ch., New Park, Pa., 1912-15, First Ch., Grove City, 1915-20, Gaston Ch., Phila., Pa., 1920-27, Immanuel Ch., Detroit 1927-41, First Ch., Seattle, Wash., after 1941. Mem. Bd. of Foreign Missions of Presbyn. Ch. Trustee, Whitworth College; trustee, San Francisco Theological Seminary. Home: Seattle, Wash. Deceased.

MCCONLEY, GEORGE E(LMER), lawyer; b. Sterling, Colo., Jan. 24, 1889; s. George Elvado and Mary Ann (Boyd) McC.; student U. of Colo., 1908-09; LL.B., U. of Mich., 1913; m. Mary Kathryn Batchelder, May 4, 1916; 1 dau., Jane Ellen (Mrs. Joseph Franklin Faner). Admitted to Mich. bar, 1913, Colo. bar, 1914; gen. practice Sterling, Colo., 1914-42, city atty., 1937-49, county atty., Logan County, 1925-27; specialized practice, Denver, 1942-43, counsel R.F.C., 1944-48, asst. gen. counsel 1948-53, gen. counsel, 1953-57; atty.-adviser Comptroller of Currency, 1957-58; asst. chief counsel Office of Def. Lending, after 1958. Admitted Supreme Ct., U.S., 1946. Mayor, Sterling, 1929-32. Served with F.A., U.S. Army, World War I. Mem. Am. Legion, Am., Fed., Colo., Northeastern Colo. (past pres.) bar assns., Phi Delta Theta. Presbyn. (elder). Elk (hon. life mem., past exalted ruler). Club: Rotary (Sterling). Home: Arlington, Va. Deceased.

MCCONN, WILLIAM FINNEY, clergyman, educator; b. Colony, Kan., Sept. 4, 1888; s. Cyrus Finney and Dora Augusta (Brown) McC.; Miltonvale (Kan.) Wesleyan Coll., 1916-17; B.O., Dillenbeck Sch. of Expression, Kansas City, Mo., 1919; A.B., Kansas City U., 1924; A.M., U. Kan., 1932; D.D., Houghton Coll., 1939; m. Viva Fern Ebling, June 12, 1919 (dec. 1953); children—Maynard, Dean Francis, Phyllis (dec.). Chautauqua work, 1914-17; field sec. Inter-Collegiate Prohibition Assn., 1917; Anti-Saloon League of Tex., 1918; asst. supt. Kansas City Dist. Anti-Saloon League of Mo., 1919, supt., 1920-24; pres. Miltonvale Wesleyan Coll. (jr. coll.), 1924-32; pres. Marion (Ind.) Coll., from 1932. Mem. World Methodist Council; mem. joint commn. Wesleyan Meth. and Free Meth. Churches. Member executive committee Ind. Council on Adult Education. Mem. Com. for the Consideration of Inter-Governmental Debts. Mem. Com. for Preservation of Constl. Government. Mem. Nat. Com. on Religion and Welfare Recovery; chmn. Ind. Commn. Alcohol Edn.; ex-chmn. United Dry Forces Ind.; mem. Nat. Commn. on Food for Small Democracies; trustee Temperance League Am.; pres. Edn. Found. of Nat. Temperance League; mem. exec. com. Nat. Temperance and Prohibition Council; pres. Temperance League of Ind.; trustee Washington Inst. for alcohol Studies. Member National Edn. Assn., Kan. Illustriana Soc., Ind. Hist. Soc., Phi Delta Kappa, Sigma Delta, Pi Gamma Mu. Ordained Wesleyan Methodist ministry, 1924. Lecturer on temperance edn. and social subjects. Ind. Republican. Club: Lions. Decorated King Christian X Medal of Honor (Danish). Home: Marion, Ind. †

MCCONNELL, BURT, editor; b. Port Norris, N.J., June 7, 1888; s. John (Sr.) and Mary (Burt) McC.; ed. Am. Sch. Physical Edn. (Chicago), Y.M.C.A. (business branches), Seattle and Los Angeles, also extension dept. Columbia; m. Gertrude M. Allen, of Riverside, R.I., Jan. 1, 1920; 1 son, Allen; m. 2d, Jane F. Tompkins, of N.Y. City, Feb. 6, 1927. Railroad survey, Ida., 1907-08; asst. cashier, Sanatorium, Battle Creek, Mich., 1908-10; supt. gold mine, Nome, Alaska, 1910-13; asst. to Comdr. Vilhjalmur Stefansson, Canadian Arctic Expdn., also meteorologist, 1913-14; newspaper and mag. writer; editorial staff Literary Digest, 1919-1929; editor Explorers Journal, 1932-36. Aviation Sect., U.S.A., May 1917; in France, July 1918-Apr. 1919; participated as squadron transp. sergt. in St. Mihiel and Argonne offensives; at Coblenz until July 1919. Republican. Methodist. Clubs: Explorers (New York); Nat. Press (Washington, D.C.). Took part in rescue of "Karluk" survivors from Wrangel Island, Siberia, 1914. Author: Mexico at the Bar of Public Opinion, 1939. Contbr. to Am. and fgn. mags. Address: New York, N.Y. †

MCCONNELL, FRANK CHARLES, army officer; b. Cicero, Ind., June 21, 1893; s. Charles M. and Mary Elizabeth (Burris) McC.; B.S., Purdue, 1920; grad. C.A.C. Sch., 1930. Command and Gen. Staff Sch., 1937; m. Paulena Scott, June 4, 1921; children—James Frank, Rodney David. Commd. 2d lt. C.A.C., 1921; promoted through grades to brig. gen., Sept. 1943; served in Canal Zone, Southwest Pacific, Hawaii, P.I., European Theater Hdqrs. Anti-aircraft Command Army Ground Forces, 1942-45; CG, 32AAA Brigade, Philippine- Command from 1945; Dep. Comdr., Philippine Ground Force Command since 1946; comdg. gen. 8th Inf. Div., since 1950. Mem. Sigma Nu. Mason. Clubs: Country (Richmond, Va.); Army-Navy (Manilla, P.I.). Died Aug. 21, 1981.

MC CORMICK, WILFRED, author; b. Newland, Ind., Feb. 8, 1903; s. Ivor B. and Nellie (Jordan) McC.; m. Eleanor Paddock, Nov. 2, 1935 (dec. Jan. 1952); children—Kathryn, Robert; m. Rebecca Fee, July 4, 1953 (dec. Oct. 1960); m. Helene Adele Huff, Aug. 1, 1962. Student, U. Ill., 1923-27. profl. lectr. on lit. and hist. subjects; instr. creative writing, extension div. U. N.Mex., 1949-76; pres. Bronc Burnett Enterprises, Albuquerque, from 1953; staff mem. Southwest Writers Conf., Corpus Christi, Tex., 1959-63; lectr. West Tex. State U. writing seminar, 1954; instr. Glorietta Writers Assembly, 1955; lectr. Nat. League Am. Pen Women, from 1959. Author numerous short stories and novels; moderator weekly TV show, Albuquerque, 1954-55; Author: The Three-Two Pitch, 1948, Legion Tourney, 1948, Fielder's Choice, 1949, Flying Tackle, 1949, Bases Loaded, 1950, Rambling Halfback, 1950, Grand-Slam Homer, 1951, Quick Kick, 1951, Eagle Scout, 1952, First and Ten, 1952, The Man on the Bench, 1955, The Captive Coach, 1956, The Hot Corner, 1958, The Bigger Game, 1958, The Big Ninth, 1958, The Proud Champions, 1959, Five Yards to Glory, 1959, The Last Putout, 1959, The Automatic Strike, 1960, Too Many Forwards, 1960, The Double Steal, 1961, One O'Clock Hitter, 1961, The Play for One, 1961, Man in Motion, 1961, Rebel with a Glove, 1962, Home-Run Harvest, 1962, Too Late to Quit, 1962, The Five Man Break, 1962, The Starmaker, 1962, The Phantom Short-stop, 1963, Once a Slugger, 1963, Rough Stuff, 1963, The Two-One-Two Attack, 1963, The Long Pitcher, 1964, The Pro Toughback, 1964, The Right-End Option, 1964, The Throwing Catcher, 1964, Seven in Front, 1965, The Go-Ahead Runner, 1965, Tall at the Plate, 1966, No Place for Heroes, 1966, Rookie on First, 1967, The Incomplete Pitcher, 1967, One Bounce too Many, 1967, Fullback in the Rough, 1969. Mem. armed forces adv. com. 4th Army Area, 1949—; Pres. N.Mex. Soc. Crippled Children, 1949-51, Friends of Library, Albuquerque, 1955-68; v.p. achievement and finance chmn. No. N.Mex. council Boy Scouts Am., 1953-55; Albuquerque chmn. Nat. Crusade for Freedom, 1951; N.Mex. co-chmn. Boys' Ranch expansion dir., 1949; Bd. dirs. Alburquerque Conf., NCCJ, 1954. Served to lt. col. AUS, 1942-46. Internat. Rotary Paul Harris fellow, 1973. Fellow Internat. Inst. Letters, Arts and Scis.; mem. Ret. Officers Assn., Assn. Former Mil. Intelligence Officers, Wisdom Hall Fame, Internat. Platform Assn., Am. Legion, Scabbard and Blade, C. of C., N.Mex. Com. Fgn. Relations (past chmn.), Delta Sigma Tau, Delta Alpha Epsilon. Mem. Christian Ch. Club: Rotarian (pres. Albuquerque 1952-53, Am. del. internat. conv. 1952, 67, 68, dist. gov. 1967-68, mem. world consultative group 1968-69). Address: Albuquerque, NM.

MC CORMICK, WILLIAM MORGAN, ret. naval officer; b. Perth Amboy, N.J., June 28, 1912; s. Edward Joseph and Mary Lloyd (Morgan) McC.; m. Lalla Jane Cary, June 9, 1936; children—Jane Cary (Countess Tristan du Parc Locmaria), James Watt, John Thomas. Student, Rutgers U., 1929-30; B.S., U.S. Naval Acad., 1934; student, Fgn. Service Inst., 1959-60. Commd. ensign U.S. Navy, 1934, advanced through grades to rear adm., 1961; assigned (battleships, destroyers, cruisers), 1934-42, (patrol squadrons), 1942-45, (aircraft carriers), 1945-49; comdr. (Naval Air Sta.), Miramar, Calif., 1949-50; assigned (aircraft carriers), Korean War, 1951-53; comdr. (U.S.S. Greenwich Bay), 1955-56, (U.S.S. Valley Forge), 1958-59; mil. asst. to dep. sec. def., 1960-61; dep. dir. (Def. Intelligence Agy.), 1961-64; comdr. (Carrier Div. 14), 1964-65; spl. asst. to (Joint Chiefs of Staff), 1965-67; comdr. (Fleet Air Wings, U.S. Atlantic Fleet), 1967-68; ret., 1968; v.p. Gen. Consultants Inc., 1968-69, Franklin Mint, Franklin Center, Pa., 1969-77; patent researcher Woolcott and Co., Arlington, Va., 1977-79; area rep. Earle Gear & Machine Co., 1979-81; participated AEC weapons tests, 1950-51; naval attache, attache for air, Rome, 1956-58. Author: The Silver Ships, 1971. Decorated Legion of Merit with 2 stars, Air medal; cavalier Order Mil. Merit Italy; others. Clubs: New York Yacht (N.Y.C.); Army-Navy Country (Washington). Home: Alexandria, VA.

MCCOY, CORNELIUS JOSEPH, educator; b. San Francisco, Calif., July 19, 1887; s. Michael and Honora (Sullivan) McC.; studied St. Ignatius Coll., San Francisco, 1900-05, Gonzaga U., Spokane, Wash., 1910-13, Colegio de S. Francisco Javier, Burgos, Spain, 1919-23. Joined Soc. of Jesus (Jesuits), 1905; ordained R.C. priest, 1921; prof. philosophy, Gonzaga U., Spokane, Wash., 1913-19; v.p. U. of Santa Clara, 1924-26, pres., 1926-31. Address: Los Angeles, Calif. †

MCCOY, LESTER, coll. regent; b. Lenox, Ia., May 19, 1889; s. Matthew S. and Nancy Louisa (Brown) McC.; ed. high sch.; m. Hazel Fay Millikan, June 14, 1917; 1 dau., Margaret M. (Mrs. Paul Masoner). Dept. comdr. Kan. dept. Am. Legion, 1927-28; propr. McCoy Motor Co., Garden City, Kan., from 1928. Mem. bd. regents Kan. State Coll., 1935-57, chmn., 1951-57. Congl. chmn. 7th Cong. Dist. of Kan., 1928-54. Served with USN, 1918. Presbyn. Mason, Elk. †

MCCOY, OLIVER RUFUS, physician; b. St. Louis, Aug. 1, 1905; s. William C. and Sarah Elizabeth (Wilson) McC.; A.B., Washington U., 1926, M.S., 1927; Sc.D., Johns Hopkins, 1930; M.D., U. Rochester, 1942; LL.D., Keio U., Tokyo, Japan, 1956; m. Julia Louise Large, Oct. 23, 1937; children—Caroline L. (Mrs. Paul E. White), William L. and Charles P. McCoy. Instructor of heiminthology Johns Hopkins, 1929-30; asst. prof. parasitology U. Rochester, 1930-42; field staff Rockefeller Found., France, 1946-48, Japan, 1948-56; asso. dir. China Med. Bd. of N.Y., Inc., N.Y.C., 1956-59, dir. 1959-73; cons. Gorgas Meml. Lab., Panama, 1934; vis. prof. Nat. Med. Coll. of Shanghai, 1936. Mem. N.Y. State Trichinosis Commn., 1939-41. Served from maj. to lt. col., M.C. AUS 1943-46. Decorated Legion of Merit (U.S.); third order Sacred Treasure (Japan). Fellow A.A.A.S., Am. Pub. Health Assn.; mem. Am. Soc. Tropical Medicine and Hygiene, Am. Soc. Parasitologists, Royal Soc. Tropical Medicine and Hygiene. Home: New Rochelle, N.Y. Died Apr. 10, 1982.

MC CRACKEN, HAROLD, author, explorer, mus. dir.; b. Colorado Springs, Colo., Aug. 31, 1894; s. James Owen and Laura Gladys (Crapsey) McC.; m. Angelyn Elizabeth Conrad, Oct. 23, 1924; children—Harold Conrad, Marjorie Angelyn. Ed., Drake U., 1911-13, Ohio State U., 1914-15; Litt.D., Hope Coll., 1957, U. Alaska, 1966; L.H.D., Colo. State U., 1972, St. Lawrence U., 1980; LL.D., U. Wyo., 1974. Ornithol. collector for Iowa State Mus., Des Moines, 1912; leader Ohio State U. expdn. to Alaska, 1915-17; mining in, Alaska, 1919-20; leader Ohio State Mus. photo-sci. expdn., to secure picture record of Alaska brown bear and other big game, 1922, 23, lectr. on Alaskan and Arctic wild life; regarded as authority on Alaska brown bear; dir.; Dir. Buffalo Bill Hist. Center, also Whitney Mus. Western Art, Cody, Wyo., 1958-74, dir. emeritus, from 1974. Author: 31 books including Iglaome (fiction), 1930, God's Frozen Children (travel), 1930, Pershing-The Story of a Great Soldier, 1931, Alaska Bear Trails (travel), 1931, Frederic Remington-Artist of the Old West, 1947, Caribou Traveler, 1949, The Flaming Bear, 1951, Portrait of the Old West, 1952, Pirate of the North, 1953, The Beast That Walks Like Man, 1955, Winning of the West, 1955, Story of Alaska, 1956, Hunters of the Stormy Sea, 1957, The Charles M. Russell Book, 1957, Hoofs, Claws and Antlers, 1958, George Catlin and the Old Frontier, 1959, Frederic Remington's Own West, 1960, The Frederic Remington Book, 1966, Roughnecks and Gentlemen, 1968, The American Cowboy, 1973, The Frank Tenney Johnson Book, 1974. Served as sgt. photog. sect. Signal Corps, and on spl. duty intelligence and aviation research divs., dept. physics Columbia U. World War I. Mem. Dutch Reformed Ch. Clubs: Douglaston (L.I.); Explorers (hon. life mem.). Leader Stoll-McCracken expdn. Am. Mus. Natural History for archeol. research in Aleutian Islands, discovering mummified bodies of Stone Age and collecting Arctic walrus group for museum's Hall of Ocean Life. Address: Cody, Wyo.

MCCREIGHT, ROBERT BAKER, stockyards executive; b. Wichita, Kans., Apr. 4, 1910; s. Robert Raymond and Mae (Baker) McC.; m. Gevene Shirk, Dec. 29, 1934. LL.B., U. Mo.-Kansas City 1932. Bar: Mo. bar 1932. Partner firm Borders, Wimmell & McCreight, Kansas City, Mo., 1934-42, Wimmell & McCreight, 1946-47; v.p., sec., dir. Kansas City Stock Yards Co., 1947-52; v.p., dir. St. Paul Union Stockyards Co., 1953-60, pres., dir., 1961-67; v.p., dir. Union Stockyards Co., Fargo, N.D., 1960-67, United Stockyards Corp., Chgo., 1967-68; pres., dir. Union Stock Yards Co., Omaha, 1968-75, S. Omaha Terminal Ry. Co., 1968-72, Am. Stockyards Assn., 1975-82; dir. Nat. Live Stock and Meat Bd., 1975-82, Omaha Livestock Market, 1976-82. Served with USAAF, 1942-46. Mem. Am. Judicature Soc. Club: Rotarian. Home: Omaha, Nebr. Dec. Mar. 17, 1982.

MCCULLOCH, EDGAR HASSELL, lawyer; b. Marianna, Ark., July 24, 1890; s. Edgar Allen and Harriet (Hassell) McC.; B.A., U. Ark., 1910; LL.B., Harvard, 1913; m. Georgia Eaken Miller June 5, 1920; children—Eva Jane (Mrs. Richard Mailey), Edgar Hassell. Admitted to Ark. bar, 1913, Mo. bar, 1921; practice in Little Rock, 1913-21, St. Louis, from 1921; mem. firm Thompson, Mitchell, Douglas & Neill, St. Louis, from 1929, partner, from 1946. Dir. Fulton Iron Works, St. Louis. Life bd. dirs. St. Louis Heart Assn. Mem. Mo. Bar, Kappa Alpha (So.). Clubs: Presbyn. Noonday. Home: St Louis, MO. †

MCCULLOCH, JOHN IRVIN BEGGS, association executive; b. St. Louis, Nov. 8, 1908; s. Richard and Mary Grace (Beggs) McC.; B.A., Yale, 1930; postgrad. New College Oxford, 1931; M.A., Stanford, 1937; m. Elizabeth Ten Broeck Jones, Sept. 9, 1934 (div. 1946); children—Mary Elizabeth, Keith, Roderick, Scott; m. 2d, Patricia Robineau, Nov. 15, 1956; children—Jeanne, Darcy, Catherine. Free-lance writer, 1931-83; editor, publisher Inter-American, Washington, 1939-45, English Around the World, 1969-83; pres. English-Speaking Union of U.S., N.Y.C., 1972-83. Mem. adv. bd. American-Hungarian Studies Found., N.Y.C., 1965—. Served to maj. OSS, AUS, 1943-45. Decorated comdr. Order Brit. Empire. Mem. Soc. of the Cincinnati. Clubs: Union, River, Yale (N.Y.C.); University (Washington); Maidstone (East Hampton, N.Y.). Author: Drums In the Balkan Night, 1936; Challenge to the Americas, 1938. Home: New York, N.Y. Died Aug. 15, 1983.

MCCULLOUGH, ROBERT DALE, osteo. physician; b. Terre Haute, Ind., Mar. 13, 1913; s. Francis Clarence and Bertha (Thompson) McC.; m. Roberta Maude Purdy, June 10, 1934; children—Robert Dale, Carol Joyce. Student, Kirksville Coll. Osteopathy and Surgery, 1931-33; D.O., Kansas City (Mo.) Coll. of Osteopathy and Surgery, 1935, D.Sc. (hon.), 1962. Intern Lakeside Hosp., Kansas City, Mo., 1935-36; surg. resident Conley Clinic Hosp., Kansas City, Mo., 1939-41; surgeon Eastern Okla. Hosp., Muskogee, 1941-43; gen. practice of surgery, Tulsa, from 1943; staff Okla. Osteo. Hosp., Tulsa, from 1944, chief of staff, 1950-51; pres. Okla. Bd. Osteo. Examiners, 1950-52; mem. Okla. Bd. Health, 1960-83, v.p., 1968-80, pres., 1980-83; chmn. Okla. Osteo. Cross, Blue Shield Com., from 1954; dir. Life Ins. Co. Minn., Mpls., Life Stocks of Minn., Inc.; trustee Okla. Blue Cross-Blue Shield. Chmn. bd. Tulsa Youth for Christ, 1954-71, chmn. emeritus, 1971-79; mem. bd. Internat. Youth for Christ, 1956-65; chmn. adv. bd. Frances Willard Home, Tulsa, 1955-58, Leader Dog for the Blind, Rochester, Mich.; Trustee Kansas City Coll. Osteopathy and Surgery, 1962-64; trustee Okla. Osteo. Hosp., 1944-83, chmn. bldg. com., 1962-77; trustee George Washington Boyhood Home, Ark. Enterprises for Blind, Little Rock, Mich. Osteo. Coll. Found.; trustee Lions Internat. Found., 1974-78, pres., 1974-78; mem. adv. bd. Southwestern Bapt. Theol. Sem., 1975-83. Recipient Distinguished Service award Am. Osteo. Assn., 1973. Mem. Am. Osteo. Assn. (trustee 1948-55, pres. 1956-57, Okla. del. ho. of dels. 1958-73, vice speaker from 1973, del. Nat. Health Council 1959-63, chmn. Assn's. com. on hosps. 1960-64), Okla. Osteo. Assn. (sec.-treas. 1938-39, jour. editor 1938-43, pres. 1943-44, trustee 1941-43), Am. Coll. Osteo. Surgeons (life), Am. Osteo. Coll. Proctology, Internat. Acad. Preventive Medicine (pres. 1972-73, trustee 1973-83), Soc. for Preservation and Encouragement Barber Shop Quartet Singing Am. (pres. Tulsa 1947-48), Assn. Internat. Champions, Tulsa C. of C., DeMolay Legion of Honor, Gideons Internat., Wycliffe Assos., Internat. Platform Assn., Psi Sigma Alpha, Alpha Phi Omega, Sigma Sigma Phi. Baptist (deacon). Clubs: Mason (32 deg., K.T., Shriner), Lion (pres. Tulsa 1946-47, internat. dir. 1963-65, exec. com. 1964-65, 67-71, internat. pres. 1970-71). Home: Tulsa, Okla. Died Feb. 17, 1983; buried Rose Hill, Tulsa.

MCCUNNIFF, DENNIS EDWARD, army officer; b. La Jara, Colo., Oct. 31, 1889; s. Thomas and Mary Alice (Stroud) McC.; B.S., U.S. Mil. Acad., 1913; grad. Inf. Sch., 1928, Command and Gen. Staff Sch., 1929. Army War Coll., 1938; m. Helen Tritch, Oct. 11, 1919; children—Thomas George, Carol, Nancy. Commd. 2d lt. U.S. Army, 1913, and advanced through the grades to brig. gen.; overseas assignment Dec. 1941. Decorated Legion of Honor (France); Abdon Calderon (Ecuador). Home: Denver, Colo. Deceased.

MCCURDY, ALEXANDER, JR., organist; b. Eureka, Calif., Aug. 18, 1905; s. Alexander and Lillie May (Ervin) McC.; m. Flora Bruce Greenwood, June 6, 1932; children: Xandra (Mrs. Robert L. Schultz), Alexander III. Studied piano, organ. harmony and counterpoint with, Wallace A. Sabin, Berkeley, Calif., 1919-24; piano with, Edwin Hughes; and organ with, Lynnwood Farnam, N.Y.C., 1924-27; grad. (scholar), Curtis Inst. of Music, Phila., 1934; Mus.D., Susquehanna U., 1936; Mus.D. (hon.), Curtis Inst., 1952. Organist Trinity Episcopal Ch., Oakland, Calif., 1919-21, First Congregational Ch., 1921-23; choirmaster, organist St. Luke's Episcopal Ch., San Francisco, 1923-24; Ch. of Redeemer, Morristown, N.J., 1924-27; dir. music Morristown Prep. Sch., 1925-27; head organ dept. Curtis Inst. Music, 1935-72; headmaster St. James Choir Sch. for Boys, 1937-40; head music dept. Episcopal Acad., Overbrook, Pa., 1937-40; head organ dept. Westminster Choir Coll., Princeton, N.J., 1940-65; Tchr. summers Occidental Coll., Los Angeles, and; Northfield Sch., East Northfield, Mass. Debut as concert organist, Town Hall, N.Y.C., 1926, choirmaster and organist, 1st Presbyn. Ch., Phila., 1927-71, comdr., Trenton Choral Art Soc., 1928-35, soloist, Am. Guild of Organist's convs., 1930, 32, 35, 37, recitals at, San Diego Expn., 1935; spl. recitalist, Swarthmore Coll., 1933-41; organist for: uncut performances St Matthew Passion (Bach) with, N.Y. Philharmonic Orch., Carnegie Hall, 1943; Contbr.: articles to others; Organ editor: articles to The Etude, 1946-57. Bd. dirs. Mus. Fund Soc. Phila., from 1962, chmn. music com., 1963-64. Mem. Art Alliance, Am. Organ Players Club (div.). Republican. Presbyn. (elder). Club: Mason. Home: Castine, ME.

MCCURDY, FRANCES LEA (MRS. WILLIAM E. MCCURDY), educator; b. Clifton Hill, Mo., Jan. 12, 1906; d. Ashley G. and Lillian (Pollard) Lea.; A.A., Stephens Coll., 1925; B.S., U. Mo., 1936, M.A., 1944, Ph.D., 1957; m. William Edward McCurdy, June 6, 1944; stepchildren—Patricia J., Mignon (Mrs. John Joseph Millin). Tchr., Mo., Okla. High schs., 1925-52; instr. U. Mo., Columbia, 1952-57, asst. prof., 1957-61, asso. prof., 1961-66, prof., 1966-73, prof. emeritus, 1973-81, chmn. dept. speech and dramatic art, 1968-70; vis. prof. U. Hawaii, 1967-68, U. Colo., summer 1972, Northwestern U., spring 1974. Mem. AAUP, Speech Communication Assn., Central State Speech Assn., Speech Assn. Mo. (pres. 1960), Pi Lambda Theta. Democrat. Author: (with others) Introduction to the Field of Speech, 1965; A guide for Speech, Dramatics, Radio and Television, 1959; Stump, Bar and Pulpit, 1969. Contbr. articles to profl. jours. Home: Columbia, Mo. Died Aug. 11, 1981.

MCCURRY, HARRY ORR, ex-dir. Nat. Gallery Can.; b. Ottawa, Ont., Can., Aug. 21, 1889; s. Henry and Margaret (Orr) McC.; ed. Lisgar Collegiate Inst., Ottawa; LL.D., Mount Allison University, 1951; married Dorothy Lampman Jenkins, September 10, 1925; 1 dau., Margot Lampman. With Nat. Gallery of Can., from 1919, dir. 1939-56. Served with C.E.F., 1918. Elected officier d'academie by French govt., 1948. Mem. Nat. Film Soc. of Can., Am. Museums Assn. Home: Kingsmere, P.Q., Can. †

MC CUTCHAN, JOSEPH WILSON, engring. educator; b. Pawnee, Okla., Dec. 24, 1917; s. Joseph E. and Grace (Shanks) McC.; m. Marie Schafer, Mar. 21, 1942; children—Joseph Gregory, Joella, Diane. Student, William Jewell Coll., 1935-36; B.S., U. Ark., 1939; M.S., UCLA, 1950. Surveyor, draftsman Midwestern Engring. & Constrn. Co., Tulsa, 1939-40; mech. engr. Douglas Aircraft Co., Inc., Santa Monica, Calif., 1940-46; lectr. engring. U. Calif., 1946-56, asso. prof., 1956-66, prof., from 1966; sabbatical leave Office of Saline Water, Dept. Interior, 1960-61, 67-68, Office Water Research and Tchn., 1975-76; sec. Com. to Evaluate Reverse Osmosis Process Research and Devel. Program, 1971. Contbr. articles to profl. jours. Mem. Am. Inst. Chem. Engrs., Am. Water Works Assn., Nat. Water Supply Improvement Assn., Am. Soc. Engring. Edn., ASME, Am. Chem. Soc., Sigma Xi, Tau Beta Pi. Home: Encino, Calif.

MC DAVID, RAVEN IOOR, JR., linguist, educator; b. Greenville, S.C., Oct. 16, 1911; s. Raven Ioor and Marie Louise (Henderson) McD.; B.A., Furman U., 1931, Litt.D., 1966; M.A., Duke, 1933, Ph.D., 1935, Litt.D., 1972; summer student Va. Mil. Inst., 1929, U. Mich., 1937, 38, 40, 48, 52, 56, 57, 58, U. N.C. 1941; student U. Mich., 1951-52, Yale, 1942-43; m. Elizabeth Lee Harris, Mar. 7, 1942 (div. 1945); 1 dau., Bettie McClain Mason; m. 2d, Virginia Ann Glenn, June 7, 1950; children—Glenn Truxtun, Raven Ioor III, Thomas Inglesby, Ann Hamilton. Instr. English, The Citadel, Charleston, S.C., 1935-38, Mich. State U., East Lansing, 1938-39; asst. prof. S.W. La. Inst., 1940-42, Western Res. U., Cleve., 1952-57; asso. prof. English, U. Chgo., 1957-64, prof. of English and linguistics, 1964-84; vis. summer prof. U. Colo., 1950, Mont. State Coll., 1951, U. Mich., 1952, 57, U. N.B., 1961, W.Va. State Coll., 1962, Mich. State U., 1964, Ill. Inst. Tech., 1967, 69; vis. prof. U. Ill., 1949-50, Cornell U., 1950-51, U. S.C., 1974, 76, La. State U., 1979; linguist lang. sect. U.S. Army, 1943-45, U.S. Bd. Geog. Names, 1947. Fellow Am. Council Learned Socs., 1942-44, 45, 50-51; Rosenwald fellow, 1941; Fulbright fellow, Mainz, 1965; sr. fellow Nat. Endowment for Humanities, 1975. Fellow Am. Anthrop. Assn., AAAS; mem. Nat. Council Tchrs. English (David Russell Research award 1969), Modern Lang. Assn. Am., Midwest Modern Lang. Assn., Linguistic Soc. Am., N.Y., Ill. acads. scis., Dutch Settlers Soc. Albany, Am. Dialect Soc. (pres. 1967-68), Internat. Assn. U. Profs. English, N.Y. Folklore Soc., Midwest Folklore Soc., Am. Oriental Soc., AAUP, Internat. Center Gen. Dialectology, Canadian Linguistic Assn., NAACP, SAR, Phi Beta Kappa. Democrat. Episcopalian. Club: Quadrangle (Chgo.). Author: Varieties of American English, 1979; co-author: Structure of American English, 1958; Pronunciation of English in the Atlantic States, 1961. Editor: (H.L. Mencken) The American Language, 1963; Linguistic Atlas of the North Central States, 1976; Linguistic Atlas of the Middle and South Atlantic States, 1979; co-editor: Lexicography in English, 1973. Field investigator, asso. editor Linguistic Atlas U.S. and Canada, 1941-64, editor, 1964—. Home: Chicago, Ill. Died Oct. 21, 1984.

MC DERMOTT, EDWARD H., lawyer; b. Cooperstown, N.D., Aug. 17, 1896; s. John H. and Anna (Arneson) McD.; m. Lucile Boso, May 29, 1924 (dec. Jan. 1965); children—Robert B., John H.; m. Mildred Wetten Kelly, Nov. 4, 1966. A.B., U. N.D., 1919; LL.B., Harvard, 1922. Bar: Mass. bar 1922. Asst. counsel and counsel Joint Congl. Com. Internal Revenue Taxation, 1927-29; cons. U.S. Treas. Dept., 1929; sr. ptnr. McDermott, Will and Emery (lawyers), Chgo., 1934-71, counsel, 1971-82. Cons. Office War Moblzn., Washington, 1944. Mem. Chgo., Ill., Am. bar assns. Presbyn. Clubs: Chicago (Chgo.), Legal (Chgo.), Mid-Day (Chgo.), Glen View (Chgo.). Home: Chicago, Ill. Dec. Nov. 15, 1982.

MCDERMOTT, JOHN FRANCIS, historian, educator; b. St. Louis, Apr. 18, 1902; s. John F. and Mary (Steber) McD.; A.B., Washington U., St. Louis, 1923, A.M., 1924; D.H.L., U. Mo., 1977; m. Mary S. Kendrick, Dec. 20, 1924; 1 son, John Francis IV. Instr. English, Washington U., St. Louis, 1924-36, asst. prof., 1936-49, asso. prof. English, 1949-61, asso. prof. Am. cultural history, 1961-63; research prof. humanities So. Ill. U., Edwardsville, 1963-71, research prof. emeritus, 1971-81; cons. early Western Am. history and 19th century Am. painting. Bd. dirs. Friends of Lovejoy Library, So. Ill. U., treas., 1976-81; mem. Gov. Bond's Bingham Sketches Com., 1975-76. Mem. Modern Humanities Research Assn., Bibliog. Soc. Am., Inst. Francais Washington (trustee 1958-81), Academie de Macon, Orgn. Am. Historians, Mo. Hist. Soc. (trustee 1950-59, 79-81, sec. bd. 1951-54, award of merit 1961, 78), Am. Name Soc., Am. Studies Assn., Am. Folklore Soc. (councillor 1958-60), Am. Antiquarian Soc., Nat. Folk Festival Assn. (pres. 1953-61; chmn. Wash. U. Folklore Conf., 1953, 55), N.Y., Kans., Ind., Ill., Minn., Mo. hist. socs., Am., Western (award of merit 1976) hist. assns., Am. Hist. Assn., Internat. Soc. for 18th Century Studies, Nat. Trust for Historic Preservation, William Clark Soc. St. Louis (pres. 1953-60), St. Louis Hist. Documents Found. (pres. 1948-78), St.Louis Westerners (pres. 1961), Instituto de Cultura Hispanica Madrid (hon.), Henry Shaw Meml. Assn. (pres. 1953-60). Served to capt. USAAF, 1942-45. Newberry Library Fellow in Midwestern Studies, 1947-48; Washington U. summer research appointments, 1950, 57, 60; Guggenheim Meml. Found. Fellow, 1954-55; research grants Am. Philos, Soc., 1939, 40, 54, 57, 58-59, 63, 64 (library research asso. 1959-62), Mich. State U., 1951, Am. Council Learned Socs., 1960, Pro-Helvetia Found., 1961, Henry E. Huntington Library, 1965, So. Ill. U., 1964-81; decorated chevalier Palmes Academiques, 1965, comdr., 1976; chevalier Ordre National du Merite, 1970. Chmn. Conf. France in Miss. Valley, Washington U., 1956; chmn. Conf. Research Opportunities in Am. Cultural History, 1959; chmn. Conf. (St. Louis Bicentennial) French in Miss. Valley, 1964, Conf. Trans. Miss. Frontier, So. Ill. U., 1965, Conf. French in Miss. Valley, 1967, Conf. Travelers on Western Frontier, 1968, Conf. Spanish in Miss. Valley, 1970. Author: Private Libraries in Creole Saint Louis, 1938; Glossary of Miss. Valley French, 1941; The Lost Panoramas of the Mississippi, 1958; The Art of Seth Eastman, 1959; George Caleb Bingham, River Portraitist, 1959; Seth Eastman Pictorial Historian of the Indian, 1961; Seth Eastman's Mississippi: A Lost Portfolio Recovered, 1973. Co-author: The Technique of Composition, 1931, latest rev. edit., 1960; English Communication, 1943. Editor: Collected Verse of Lewis Carroll, 1929; Modern Plays, 1932; The Russian Journal and other Selections from Works of Lewis Carroll, 1935, 77; Tixier's Travels on the Osage Prairies, 1940, 69; Western Journals of Washington Irving, 1944, 66; Old Cahokia, 1949; Travels in Search of the Elephant, The Wanderings of Alfred S. Waugh, Artist, 1951; Up the Missouri with Audubon; the Journal of Edward Harris, 1951; The Early Histories of St. Louis, 1952; Thaddeus Culbertson's Jour. of an Expedition to the Mauvaises Terres and the Upper Missouri in 1850, 1952; John Treat Irving's Indian Sketches, 1954; Washington Irving's Tour on the Prairies, 1956; Milford's Memoir of Travels in the Creek Nation, 1956; Research Opportunities in American Cultural History, 1961, 77; Robb's Streaks of Squatter Life, 1961; The Western Journals of Dr. George Hunter, 1796-1805, 1963; The World of Washington Irving, 1965; Audubon in the West, 1965; The French in the Mississippi Valley, 1965; The Frontier Reexamined, 1967; An Artist on the Overland Trail: The 1849 Diary and Sketches of James F. Wilkins, 1968; Before Mark Twain: A Sampler of Old, Old Times on the Mississippi, 1968; Frenchmen and French Ways in the Mississippi Valley, 1969; Travelers on the Western Frontier, 1970; The Spanish in the Mississippi Valley, 1973; Philip Pittman's The Present State of the European Settlements on the Mississippi, 1977. Co-editor: College Readings in Contemporary Thought, 1929; Contemporary Opinion, 1933; Matt Fields Prairie and Mountain Sketches, 1957; contbr. periodicals. Asso. editor French Am. rev., 1950. Gen.

editor Travels on Western Waters Series, So. Ill. U. Press; adv. bd. Papers on Language and Literature, 1965-81, Old Northwest Quar., 1974-79; publ. adv. com. Henry Francis duPont Winterthur Mus., 1968-71. Home: St Louis, Mo. Died Apr. 23, 1981.

MC DONALD, LAWRENCE P., congressman; b. Atlanta, Apr. 1, 1935; children—Tryggvi Paul, Callie Grace, Mary Elizabeth, Lawrence P., Lauren Aileen. Grad., Davidson (N.C.) Coll.; M.D., Emory U., 1957; Litt.D. (hon.), Daniel Payne Coll., Birmingham, Ala. Resident in gen. surgery Grady Meml. Hosp., Atlanta; resident in urology U. Mich., Ann Arbor; mem. 94th-98th Congresses from 7th Ga. Dist. Served with M.C. USNR, 1957-61. Mem. John Birch Soc. (nat. council), Am. Conservative Union (adv. bd.), Conservative Caucus (adv. bd.), Com. for Survival of a Free Congress (adv. bd.). Democrat. Methodist. Club: Rotary. Address: Washington, D.C. Dec. Sept. 1, 1983.*

MCDONALD, RICHARD A., corporation executive; born in Chicago, September 23, 1887; s. James H. and Honora (Collins) McD.; student public schs.; m. Cynthia Ann Fleming; 1 son, Richard A. Dir. Crown Zellerbach Corp.; cons. E. Tex. Pulp & Paper Co.; adminstr. Nat. Prodn. Authority, 1952. Clubs: Clarement, Sequoia Country (Oakland, California); Stock Exchange (San Francisco); Wild Goose Country (Live Oak, Cal.). Home: Oakland, Calif. †

MCDONNELL, JOHN CHILTON, army officer; b. Baltimore, Md., Nov. 9, 1887; s. Eugene and Ann Smith (Chilton) McD.; B.S., Loyola Coll., Baltimore, 1908; attended Air Corps Tactical Sch., 1932, Command and Gen. Staff Sch., 1933-34; m. Dorothy Cobbs, Nov. 18, 1933. Began in engr. corps Norfolk & Western R.R., 1909; commd. 2d lt., Cav., U.S. Army, 1912, rising to maj., during World War; commd. col., 1937, brig. gen., 1910; entered Air Service, U.S. Army, 1915; served with 1st Aero Squadron with Gen. Pershing in Mexico, 1916-17; comdr. Ellington Field, Houston, Tex., 7th Aviation Instrs. Center, Clermont-Ferrand, France, and Air Service comdr., 3d Corps, 3d Army, Coblenz, Germany, during World War; comdr. Phillips Field, Md., 1919-21; asst. prof. mil. science and tactics, Mass. Inst. Tech., 1921-23; comdr. Clark Field, P.I., 1923-25; chief of personnel, Office of Chief of Air Corps, 1926-30; comdr. Wheeler Field, Hawaii, 1935-37, 3d Attack Group, Barksdale Field, Shreveport, La., 1938-39, 3d Bombardment Group, Savannah, Ga., 1939-40; comdr. 7th Pursuit Wing, U.S. Army Air Corps, Mitchell Field, L.I., N.Y., Dec. 1940-Mar. 1941; comdg. gen. 1st Interceptor Command from Mar. 1941. Mem. Soc. of the Cincinnati, S. R. Catholic. Clubs: Metropolitan, Army and Navy (Washington); Rolling Rock (Ligonier, Pa.). Home: Warrentown, Va. †

MCDOWELL, C. BLAKE, lawyer; b. Orrville, O., July 21, 1890; s. Nathaniel and Emma (Snavely) McD.; LL.B., University of Mich., 1914; m. 2d. Mabel A. Smith, Dec. 27, 1957; children—Robert H. C. Blake, Edward R. Admitted to O. bar, 1914; pvt. practice of law, Akron, 1914-18 as mem. firm, Brouse, McDowell, May and Bierce; v.p., Treas., dir., Fed. Storage Co., from 1928; sec. and dir. Beacon Journal Publishing Company, Knight Newspapers, Inc., Knight Pub. Co., Charlotte, N.C.; chmn. Alsco, Inc., 1962-68; dir. Gt. Lakes Paper Co., Summit Radio Corp., Herberich-Hall-Harter Company, First National Bank, Akron, O., also director of Miami Herald Pub. Co., and others. Conglist. Mason (Shriner, Consistory, K.T., Jester), Clubs: University, Portage Country, City, Turner, Kiwanis (Akron); Union (Cleve.); Detroit (Mich.); Bal Harbour, Miami (Miami, Fla.). Home: Akron, OH. †

MC DOWELL, FRANK, plastic surgeon; b. Marshfield, Mo., Jan. 30, 1911; s. Hollie A. and Louise (North) McD.; m. Mary Elizabeth Neal, June 10, 1934; children—Robert Lawrence, George Edward, Carole Louise. A.B., Drury Coll., 1932; M.D., Washington U., St. Louis, 1936; Sc.D., Drury Coll., 1973. Diplomate: Am. Bd. Surgery, Am. Bd. Plastic Surgery (sec. 1955-60, vice chmn. 1960-61, chmn. 1961-62). Intern Barnes Hosp., St. Louis, 1936-37, asst. resident surgeon, 1937-39, attending surgeon, 1941-69; attending surgeon St. Louis Children's Hosp., cons. surgeon Shriners Hosp., Frisco, Mo. Pacific, St. Louis City hosps., 1941-69; pres. med. and surg. staff Barnes and Allied Hosps. Med. Center, 1958-59; mem. faculty Washington U. Sch. Medicine, 1939-69, asso. prof. clin. surgery, 1954-69; asso. prof. maxillofacial surgery Washington U. Sch. Medicine (Sch. Dentistry), 1940-69; surg. staff Queen's, Children's, Castle hosps., Honolulu, from 1967; surg. cons. Tripler Gen. Hosp., from 1967; exec. com. dept. surgery, prof. surgery U. Hawaii, from 1967; prof. clin. surgery Stanford, from 1974; v.p. Hawaii Med. Library, 1970-76; lectr. French Acad. Surgery, 1949, Hadassah U. Sch. Medicine, Jerusalem, 1954, U. Athens (Greece) Sch. Medicine, 1954, Nat. Inst. for Burned, Buenos Aires, Argentina, 1957; vice chmn. Am. Replantation Mission to, China, 1973; vis. prof. surgery UCLA, 1969, U. Utah, 1972, U. Mo., 1974; Mem. Adv. Bd. Med. Specialists, 1955-69; v.p. Am. Bd. Med. Specialists, 1970-71, chmn. surg. council, 1969-71; v.p. 3d Internat. Congress Plastic Surgery, 1963. Author: Skin Grafting, 3d edit, 1959, Plastic Surgery of the Nose, 2d edit, 1965, Surgery of Face, Mouth and Jaws, 1954, Neck Dissections, 1957, History of Plastic Surgical Societies, 1963, Surgical Rehabilitation in Leprosy, 1974, also numerous articles.; Asso. editor: Directory Med. Specialists, 1955-72, McDowell Indexes of Plastic Surgery Literature, 5 vols, 1977-81, The Source Book of Plastic Surgery, 1977; cons. editor: Lawyers Med, 1962-78, Stedman's Med. Dictionary, 1975-81, Current Contents, 1973-81, Internat. Dictionary Medicine and Biology, 1979-81, Biography of J.C. Carpue, 1981, Genealogy of McDowell Family, 1981; editor-in-chief: Jour. Plastic and Reconstructive Surgery, 1967-79; hon. editor, 1979-81. Trustee Drury Coll., 1956-78, chmn. bd. trustees, 1964-65. Recipient Disting. Alumni award Drury Coll., 1954; 1st Dow Corning Internat. award in plastic surgery, 1971; Honorary award Ednl. Found. ASPRS, 1978. Fellow A.C.S.; mem. Am. Assn. Plastic Surgeons (pres. 1962-63, hon. award 1978), Am. Soc. Plastic and Reconstructive Surgeons, Soc. Head and Neck Surgeons (founder), Am., Western surg. assns., Am. Assn. Surgery Trauma, Israel Assn. Plastic Surgeons (hon.), Société française de chirurgie reconstructive et plastique (hon.), Washington U. Med. Alumni Assn. (pres. 1960-61). Club: Pacific. Address: Kailua, HI.

MCDOWELL, WILLIAM RALSTON, lawyer, ry. exec.; b. Shreveport, La., Jan. 18, 1917; s. Milas R. and Mollie (Ayres) McD.; m. Fern Bronstad, Sept. 15, 1939; children—Rebecca Gail (Mrs. W. Lionel Craver), Mollye (Mrs. F.F. Bell Jr.). B.B.A., U. Tex., 1940, LL.B., 1940. Bar: Tex. bar 1940. Spl. agt. FBI, Washington, 1940-41, adminstrv. asst. to dir., 1941-45; asso. law firm McBride & Johnson, Dallas, 1945-47; asst. dist. atty., Dallas County, 1947-48; atty., gen. atty. T. & P. Ry., Dallas, 1948-58, v.p., gen. counsel, 1959-82; also dir.; gen. counsel So. Lines, M.P.R.R., Dallas, 1962-76, v.p., gen. counsel, 1976-82; dir. Weatherford Mineral Wells, Northwestern Ry. Co. Bd. dirs. Tex. Research League. Mem. Am., Dallas bar assns., State Bar Tex., Am. Judicature Soc., ICC Practitioners, Soc. Former Agts. FBI. Lutheran. Home: Dallas, Tex. Died Aug. 3, 1982; buried Dallas.

MCEACHRAN, JOHN NELSON, financial company executive; b. Montreal, Que., Can., Oct. 30, 1926; s. Flora Deschenes and McE.; m. Blanche Costello, Oct. 15, 1948; children—Gerald, Linda, Bruce, Joan, John, Susan. Ed., St. Joseph's Tchrs. Coll. Sch. tchr., 1945-48; with Imperial Tobacco Co., 1948-66, credit mgr., 1957-66; v.p. M. Loeb Ltd., Ottawa, 1966-84, corp. sec., 1969-84; past pres. Canadian Credit Inst. Author articles in field. Fellow Canadian Inst.; mem. Quebec C. of C., Assn. Canadian Franchisors, Ottawa Bd. Trade. Home: Ottawa, Ont., Can. Died Nov. 7, 1984.

MC ELIN, THOMAS WELSH, medical educator; b. Janesville, Wis., Aug. 27, 1920; s. Bertrand James and Evelyn (Welsh) McE.; m. Sylvia Dennison, June 30, 1945; children—Joan Dennison McElin Vogt, Thomas Welsh. A.B. summa cum laude, Dartmouth, 1942, postgrad. Med. Sch., 1941-42; M.D., Harvard, 1944; M.S. in Obstetrics and Gynecology, U. Minn., 1948. Diplomate: Am. Bd. Obstetrics and Gynecology (asso. examiner 1967-78). Intern Passavant Hosp., Chgo., 1944-45; resident Mayo Found., Rochester, Minn., 1945-48, 1st asst. gynecology and surgery, 1948-49, spl. 1st asst. obstetrics and gynecology, 1949-50, practice medicine, specializing in obstetrics and gynecology, Evanston, Ill., 1950-82; mem. faculty Med. Sch., Northwestern U., Chgo., 1950—, asso. prof. obstetrics and gynecology, 1960-67, prof., 1967-82, asst. chmn. dept. obstetrics and gynecology, 1974-82; chmn. dept. obstetrics and gynecology Evanston Hosp., 1965-82, pres. profl. staff, 1963-64; mem. editorial bd. Obstetrics and Gynecology Jour., 1973—. Contbr. articles to profl. jours. Fellow Am. Coll. Obstetricians and Gynecologists (founding fellow), A.C.S. (gov.); mem. Am. Assn. Obstetricians and Gynecologists (exec. council 1974-76, pres. 1977-78), Am. Fertility Soc., Central Assn. Obstetricians and Gynecologists (pres. 1970-71), Chgo. Gynecol. Soc. (pres. 1969-70), AMA, Central Travel Club Obstetricians and Gynecologists (pres. 1968), N. Am. Obstetrics and Gynecology Soc., Endocrine Soc., Inst. Medicine (Chgo.), Phi Beta Kappa, Sigma Xi, Alpha Kappa Kappa. Clubs: Dartmouth (Chgo.), Harvard (Chgo.); Glen View (Golf, Ill.). Home: Kenilworth, Ill. Dec. Oct. 19, 1982.

MCEWEN, ROBERT (STANLEY), prof. zoology; b. Cleveland, O., Jan. 6, 1888; s. William Cleaveland and Alice (Stanley) McE.; A.B., Western Reserve U., 1911; A.M., 1912; Ph.D., Columbia U., 1917; m. Mildred French Crane, Aug. 19, 1918; children—Robert Taylor, William Cleaveland. Instr., zoology, Oberlin Coll., 1917-19, asst. prof., 1919-25, associate prof., 1925-31, prof., 1931-41, head zoology dept., from 1941; summer instr., Woods Hole, 1922. Served in hosp. corp, U.S.N.R.F., 1917-18. Member Ohio Acad. Science (chmn.), zoology sect., 1936), A.A.A.S., Am. Soc. Zoologists, Am. Genetics Assn., Phi Beta Kappa, Sigma Xi. Conglist. Author: A Text Book of Vertebrate Embryology, 1923, rev., 1949. Contbd. papers to jours. Home: Oberlin, Ohio †

MCEWEN, WILLIAM ROBERT, educator; b. Duluth, Aug. 21, 1911; s. Alexander Murdoch and Alice Maude (Metcalfe) McE.; B.E., Duluth State Tchrs. Coll., 1935; M.A., U. Minn., 1939, Ph.D., 1946; m. Dorothy Larson, June 15, 1940; children—William Robert, Claudia, Audrey, Alice, Alexander, John. With U. Minn., 1937-82, with Duluth br., 1947-82, successively instr., asst. prof., assoc. prof., prof., 1949-82. Math. cons. Office Research Analysis, USAF. Mem. Am. Math. Assn., Math. Soc. Am. Home: Duluth, Minn. Dec. July 27, 1982. Interned Forest Hill Cemetery, Duluth.

MCFALL, WILLIAM BALLEY, lawyer, banker; b. Pitts., Oct. 11, 1890; s. William Bailey and Martha (Ramage) McF.; A.B., Washington and Jefferson Coll., 1912, LL.D., 1948; LL.B., U. Pitts., 1915; m. Ruth McKee, Sept. 23, 1919; children—Martha Frances, Sara Jane. Admitted to Pa. bar, 1915; chmn. Union Nat. Bank, Pitts.; dir. Union Title Guaranty Co., Theodore Markets, Inc., Mesta Machine Co. Bd. dirs. Pitts. Assn. Improvement of Poor. Clubs: Duquesne, University St. Clair Country. Home: Pittsburgh, PA. †

MCFARLAND, ANDREW JACKSON BRIGGS, army officer; b. Robinson Springs, Ala., May 7, 1887; s. William Archibald and Daisy Oneida (Briggs) McF.; grad. advanced course Inf. Sch., 1930, Command and Gen. Staff Sch., 1934, Army War Coll., 1936; m. Susan Hamlin, Sept. 5, 1924; 1 son, Andrew. Commd. lt., inf., U.S. Army, 1920, advancing through the grades to brig. gen., 1944; U.S. sec., Combined Chiefs of Staff, after 1944. Home: Fort Myer, Va. Deceased.

MCFARLAND, ERNEST WILLIAM, television executive; b. Earlsboro, Okla., Oct. 9, 1895; s. William Thomas and Keziah (Smith) McF.; m. Edna Eveland; 1 child, Jewell (Mrs. Delbert Lewis). B.A., Okla. U.; M.A., J.D., Stanford; LL.D. (hon.), U. Ariz., Ariz. State U. Asst. atty. gen., 1923-24, county atty., Pinal County, Ariz., 1925-30; judge Superior Ct. Pinal County, 1934-40, U.S. senator from Ariz., 1946-58, majority leader, 1951-52, gov., Ariz., 1955-58; justice, chief justice Supreme Ct. Ariz., 1965-70; pres. KTVK Ariz. Television Co., Phoenix, from 1970, then chmn.; dir. Fed. Home Loan Bank of San Francisco.; Mem. Pres.'s Commn. on Cause and Prevention Crime and Violence. Bd. dirs. Meml. Hosp., Phoenix. Served with USNR, World War I. Recipient Disting. Service award Am. Legion; Disting. Alumni award E. Central State Coll., Ada, Okla. Mem. Am. Legion, VFW. Clubs: Masons, Lions, Odd Fellows, Elks, KP. Home: Phoenix, Ariz. Dec. June 8, 1984.

MC GANNON, DONALD HENRY, broadcasting executive; b. N.Y.C., Sept. 9, 1920; s. Robert E. and Margaret (Schmidt) McG.; m. Patricia H. Burke, Aug. 22, 1942. B.A., Fordham U., 1940, LL.B., 1947, L.H.D., 1964; L.H.D., U. Scranton, 1963, Creighton U., 1965, Emerson Coll., 1966, Fordham U., 1964, Fairfield U., 1967; D.Sc. (hon.), St. Bonaventure U., 1965; H.H.D. (hon.), Georgetown U., 1980; D.Sc. (hon.), St. John's U., 1980. Bar: Admitted N.Y., Conn. bars 1947. Practiced in, N.Y.C., 1947-50, Norwalk, Conn., 1947-51; asst. to dir. broadcasting DuMont TV Network, 1951-52, gen. mgr., asst. dir. broadcasting, 1952-55; pres., chmn. bd. Westinghouse Broadcasting Co., Inc., Ind., Md., Del., 1955; chmn. bd. TV Advt. Reps., Inc., Radio Advt. Reps., Inc., Group W Prodns., Broadcast Rating Council, Inc.; Adviser to Pontifical Commn. for Communications Media; chmn. Conn. Commn. for Higher Edn.; mem. broadcasting adv. council Emerson Coll.; chmn. advt. council Coll. Liberal Arts U. Notre Dame; mem. communications com. N.Y. Urban Coalition. (Spl. Emmy award 1968). Trustee Georgetown U.; trustee Ithaca Coll., Nat. Urban League, N.Y. Law Sch., N.Y. U.; hon. Fordham U.; founder, dir. trustee Sacred Heart U.; mem. exec. com. council regents St. Francis Coll.; bd. dirs. Radio Free Europe, Acad. TV Arts and Scis. Found., Radio Advt. Bur.; past chmn. Advt. Council, Inc. Served as maj. CAC AUS, 1941-46. Recipient Disting. Service award Nat. Assn. Broadcasters, 1964; Trustees award Nat. Acad. TV Arts and Scis., 1967-68. Clubs: Duquesne (Pitts.); Union League (N.Y.C.). Home: Chester, Conn. Dec. May 23, 1984.

MCGEE, JOSEPH JOHN, ins. exec.; b. Kansas City, Mo., June 19, 1889; s. Thomas and Louise (Bannister: McG.; m. Margaret Elizabeth Cronin, Oct. 12, 1916; children—Mary Louise (Mrs. H. B. Miller), Joseph John, Martha Ann (Mrs. Bernard J. Duffy Jr.), Thomas Robert. Mem. Thomas McGee & Sons, Kansas City chmn. Old American Ins. Co.; director Commerce Trust Co., U.S. Supply Co., Kansas City Title Ins. Co. (Kansas City, Mo.), American Royal. Mem. C. of C. Clubs: Kansas City, Mission Hills Country, Saddle and Sirloin (Kansas City, Mo.). Home: Kansas City, Mo. †

MCGHEE, JAMES B., judge; born Vernon, Tex., Oct. 6, 1888; s. Franklin Pierce and Junita (Miller) McG.; ed. pub. schs. and law office; m. Glendora Lewis, May 28, 1910 (died Feb. 27, 1942). Court stenograher, 1912-20; admitted to New Mexico bar, 1919, and practiced in Carlsbad, Clovis and Roswell, N.M., 1920-33; apptd. judge 5th Judicial Dist., N.M., Jan. 16, 1933, elected to fill unexpired term, 1934, re-elected, 1936 and 1942; elected justice Supreme Ct. of N.M., 1946, reelected 1954. Mem. Am., N.M. bar assns. Democrat. Episcopalian. Mason, Elk. †

MC GHEE, ROBERT BARCLAY, scientist, educator; b. Cleveland, Tenn., Feb. 22, 1918; s. Charles McClung and Marion (Snavely) McG.; m. Ann Lewis Hinkle, Mar. 30, 1946; children—Nancy Stuart, Terence Barclay, Michael Bruce. A.B. in Biology, Berea Coll., 1940; M.S. in Zoology, U. Ga., 1940-42; Ph.D. in Bacteriology and Parasitology, U. Chgo., 1948. Asst. Rockefeller Inst. Med. Research, 1948-51, assoc., 1951-54; mem. faculty U. Ga., 1954-82, head dept. zoology, 1955-64, prof., 1958-82,

Alumni Found. Distinguished prof. zoology, 1964-82. Mem. study sect. tropical medicine and parasitology USPHS, 1965-71, chmn., 1970-71; mem. adv. sci. bd. Gorgas Meml. Inst., 1972-82. Author articles parastic protozoa. Served to capt. AUS, World War II. Decorated Bronze Star; recipient Michael award for research U. Ga., 1957. Fellow Am. Acad. Microbiology, Royal Soc. Tropical Medicine and Hygiene; mem. Am. Soc. Parasitologists (council 1960-64), Soc. Protozoologists (nominating com. 1961, sec. 1973-79, pres.-elect 1979-80, pres. 1980-81), Am. Soc. Tropical Medicine and Hygiene, Am. Inst. Biol. Sci., AAAS, Am. Soc. Naturalists. Club: Town and Gown (Athens) (pres. 1963-64). Home: Athens, Ga. Dec. Nov. 18, 1982.

MCGILLIVRAY, WILLIAM A., Can. provincial chief justice; b. Calgary, Alta., Can., Oct. 14, 1918. B.A., U. Alta., 1940, LL.B., 1941. Bar: Called to Alta. bar 1942, Sask. bar 1965, named Queen's counsel 1957. Partner firm Fenerty, McGillivray, Robertson & Co., Calgary, 1943-74, chief justice of Alta., 1974-84. Home: Calgary, Alta., Can. Died Feb. 16, 1984.

MCGINLEY, EDWARD FRANCIS, banker; b. Chester, Pa., Aug. 9, 1903; s. Edward F. and Elizabeth (McFadden) McG.; m. Georgiamary White, Feb. 9, 1968; children—Edward Francis III, Gerald Hayes, Richard Donald. B.S., U. Pa., 1925. With Nat. Bank of Commerce, N.Y.C., 1925-29, Guaranty Trust Co., 1929-30; with Chem. Bank & Trust Co., N.Y.C., 1929-51; pres., dir. Liberty Bank of Buffalo, 1951-56; v.p. Fidelity-Phila. Trust Co., Phila., 1957-61; pres., dir. Beneficial Mut. Savs. Bank, 1961-85, Del. & Bound Brook R.R. Co.; dir., mem. exec. com. Pittson Co. Investors Diversified Services, Inc.; dir. Phila. Life Ins. Co. Active Cath. Charities Appeal. Asso.; trustee U. Pa. Decorated knight Malta, knight St. Gregory. Mem. Pa. Soc. N.Y. (v.p., treas.), Wharton Sch. Alumni Soc. (past pres., dir.), Delta Tau Delta. Republican. Roman Catholic. Clubs: University of Pa. (N.Y.C.), Economic (N.Y.C.); University (N.Y.C.); Union League (Phila.), Racquet (Phila.); Spring Lake (N.J.) Bath and Tennis. Home: Sea Girt, N.J. Died Apr. 16, 1985.

MCGINN, HOWARD J., mfg. exec.; b. N.Y.C., May 13, 1888; s. John Henry and Sarah Jane (Gilmore) McG.; m. Arta Wheaton Scott, Oct. 1949. With Nat. Lock Washer Co., 1912, Reliance Mfg. Co., 1914-32; v.p. sales dir. Eaton Mfg. Co., Cleve., 1932-51, pres., 1951-56, chmn. 1956. Clubs: Detroit Athletic; Tavern, Pepper Pike, Kirtland Country, Cleveland, Union (Cleve.). Home: Mentor, Ohio. Deceased.

MCGINNIS, RAY E., ins. exec.; b. Nevada, Mo., Apr. 4, 1887; s. Hezekiah S. and Cynthia C. (Cash) McG.; LL.B., Kansas City Sch. Law, 1911; m. Clara B. Potter, June 2, 1909. Claim atty. Met. St. Ry. Co., 1911-14; mgr. claims dept. Kansas City Casualty Co., 1914-19; asst. sec. Employers Indemnity Corp., 1919-26; v.p. Central Surety & Ins. Corp., 1926-38, pres. and dir., 1938-56, vice chmn., 1956-61; pres. and dir. Central Surety Fire Corp., 1938-56. Mem. Nat. Assn. Casualty and Surety Execs. (pres. 1953-54). Home: Kansas City, Mo. †

MC GIVERN, WILLIAM PETER, novelist; b. Chgo., Dec. 6, 1922; s. Peter Frank and Julia Frances (Costello) McG.; m. Maureen Daly, Dec. 28, 1946; children—Megan, Patrick. Student, Birmingham (Eng.) U., 1946. Reporter Phila. Bull., 1947-49; guest lectr. U. N.C., 1961. Novelist, 1948-82; also writer screenplays, TV scripts and articles and short stories; co-owner sta., KOWN, Escondido, Calif.; author: The Big Heat, 1952, Rogue Cop, 1953, Odds Against Tomorrow, 1955, The Caper of the Golden Bulls, 1964, Choice of Assassins, 1965, Night of the Juggler, 1974, Soldiers of '44, 1979. Served with AUS, 1942-45, ETO. Decorated Soldiers medal. Mem. Writers Guild Am., Mystery Writers Am. (pres. 1980), Crime Writer Gt. Britain, TV Acad. Arts and Scis., Author League Am. Democrat. Clubs: Players (N.Y.C.); Indian Wells Country (Palm Desert). Address: Palm Desert, Calif. Dec. Nov. 18, 1982.

MCGOWAN, NORRIS COCHRAN, gas corporation executive; b. Chicago, Ill., Dec. 1, 1890; s. Edward J. and Rose Mary (Phee) McG.; grade and commercial sch. edn.; LL.D., Centenary Coll. La. and Spring Hill College, Mobile, Alabama; married Nelle Quigles, Dec. 12, 1917; children—Charley Nelle (Mrs. Claude G. Rives III), Norris Cochran. Accountant and yard man, Chicago & Northwestern R.R. local freight office, Chicago, 1908-10; successively with Globe Commission Co., David Palmer & Co., auditors and accountants, then with Audit Co. of N.Y., being assigned to properties in Shreveport, La., 1913-14; joined Atlas Oil Co., 1914, as accountant, handling gen. purchases, leasing, in charge of field development and pipe line construction and operation, from 1918 in gen. charge of properties as v.p. and gen. mgr., and head of various companies which merged into present orgn., pres., 1929-56; chmn. bd. directors United Gas Corporation, Union Producing Co., United Gas Pipe Line Company, 1956-66, hon. chmn. bd., director emeritus, from 1966. Mem. Petroleum Industry War Council, also as chmn. Natural Gas and Natural Gasoline Com., Dist. 3, during World War II. Pres. Am. Gas Assn., 1938; dir. several yrs. Mem. Knights of Holy Sepulchre of Jerusalem, Knights of St. Gregory (papal). Clubs: Boston (New Orleans); Shreveport (La.) Country, Shreveport; Ramada (Houston). Home: Shreveport, La. †

MCGRANE, REGINALD CHARLES, educator; born at Cincinnati, O., July 28, 1889; s. John J. and Laura J. (Lawhead) McG.; A.B., U. of Cincinnati, 1912, A.M., 1913; studied U. of Wis., 1914; Ph.D., U. of Chgo., 1915; m. Lenore R. Foote, 1916 (dec.) DAR fellow in Am. history, U. of Cincinnati, 1913; asst. in history, U. of Wis., 1914; fellow in history, U. of Chicago, 1915; with U. of Cincinnati from 1915, instr. history to 1917, asst. prof., 1917-19, prof., 1919-48, now emeritus, head dept. history, 1948-60. War Prodn. Bd., 1944-45; vis. prof. summer sessions, U. of Wyo., Northwestern U., American U., Univ. of Neb., U. of Tex., and prof. Am. history U. of Chicago 3 summers to 1930, Harvard U., summer 1951. Mem. Anthony Wayne State Highway Com. until 1956. Mem. Am. Hist. Assn., Am. Med. History Assn., Miss. Valley Historical Assn. (member exec. council), Phi Beta Kappa, Phi Alpha Theta, Tau Kappa Alpha, Omicron Delta Kappa, Pi Kappa Alpha. Methodist. Author: Panic of 1837, 1924; Life of William Allen, 1925 (honorable mention, Justin Winsor prize, 1925); Foreign Bondholders and American State Debts, 1935; also The Apologia of American Debtor States (essay), Essays in Honor of William E. Dodd, 1935; Economic Development of the American Nations, 1942, revised 1950; The Cincinnati Doctors' Forum, pub. 1957; The University of Cincinnati, published 1963. Editor: Correspondence of Nichols Biddle, 1919. Contributor historical articles to Ency. Americana and Dictionary Am. Biography; mem. editorial bd. Miss. Valley Hist. Rev., 1929, Historian, from 1952, Historical and Philosophical Society of Ohio, from 1954. John Simon Guggenheim research fellowship, 1930-31, renewed, 1931-32. Member of John H. Dunning Prize Committee, 1942-45; chairman 1945-47. Home: Cincinnati, OH. †

MCGRATH, MATHEW JOHN, govt. official; b. St. Charles, Minn., May 2, 1889; s. Mathew John and Fannie (Delmore) McG.; student U. of S.D., 1909-10, U. of Minn., 1910-11; m. Mary E. Wilson, Oct. 8, 1919. Bookkeeper to vice-pres. Citizens State Bank, St. Charles, Minn., 1912-32; examiner Reconstruction Finance Corp., Washington, 1932-34, asst. chief Examining Div., 1934-39, chief, 1939-47; regional manager for New England from 1949; exec. vice pres. and dir. Defense Homes Corp., 1940-42; v.p., dir. Defense Supplies Corp., 1940-47; v.p., dir. R.F.C. Mortgage Co., 1937-47; spl. asst. to bd. dirs. R.F.C., 1947-49. Served in U.S. Inf., 9 months, World War. Mem. Phi Delta Theta. Democrat. Catholic. Home: Boston, Mass. †

MCGUCKEN, JOSEPH THOMAS, clergyman; b. Los Angeles, Mar. 13, 1902; s. Joseph A. and Mary Agnes (Flynn) McG.; ed. U. Calif. at Los Angeles, St. Patrick's Sem., Menlo Park, Cal.; S.T.D., N. Am. Coll., Rome, Italy, 1928. Ordained priest Roman Cath. Ch., 1928; asst. St. Vibiana's Cath., Los Angeles, 1928; asst. Cathedral, Chapel Parish, Los Angeles, 1929-30; sec. to bishop, 1929; papal chamberlain to Pope Pius Xi, 1937; chancellor Archdiocese of Los Angeles, 1938; domestic prelate, 1939; consecrated titular bishop Sanavo, aux. bishop Los Angeles, 1941; pastor St. Andrew's Parish, Pasadena, Calif., 1944; vicar gen. Archdiocese Los Angeles, 1947; coadjutor bishop Sacramento, 1955, bishop, 1957-62; archbishop San Francisco, 1962-77. Decorated comdr. Order of Ysabella the Catholic (Spain). Home: San Francisco, Calif. Died Oct. 27, 1983.

MC GUIRE, EDWARD PERKINS, former govt. ofcl.; b. Boston, Oct. 22, 1904; m. Katherine Ward, Oct. 5, 1929 (dec. Dec. 19, 1980); m. Lillian Shapiro, June 7, 1981. Grad., Worcester Acad.; B.Textile Engring., Lowell Textile Inst., 1928; D.Sc., Lowell Technol. Inst., 1958. With Harris Forbes & Co., N.Y.C., 1928-29; Asso. Dry Goods Corp., 1929-31; with James McCreery & Co., N.Y.C., 1931-36, gen. mgr., 1937-39; divisional mgr. Montgomery Ward & Co., 1939-42; dir., pres. R.H. White Corp., Boston, and R.H. White Realty Corp., 1945-48; pres., mng. dir. Sterling-Lindner-Davis, Cleve., 1950-54; v.p., dir. Allied Stores of Ohio, 1952-54, dep. asst. sec. of def. for internat. security affairs, 1954-56, asst. sec. def. for supply and logistics, Washington, 1956-61. Chmn. Commn. on Govt. Procurement, 1970-73. Served to comdr. U.S. Navy, 1942-45. Decorated Legion of Merit; recipient Public Service medal Def. Dept., 1961. Mem. Phi Psi. Roman Catholic. Clubs: Knight of Malta (Washington), Knight Comdr. Holy Sepulchre. (Washington), Metropolitan (Washington), Chevy Chase (Washington). Organizer, supr. forward pricing and price revision activities, Navy Dept.; organizer negotiation group handling contracts of Bur. of Ordnance; dep. chief procurement br. of sec.'s office, chief of procurement br., 1945. Home: Washington, D.C. Died Mar. 30, 1982.

MC INTOSH, HARRIS, ret. business exec.; b. Cayuga, N.Y., July 25, 1904; s. John Esterley and Mary Luella (Witbeck) McI.; m. Elizabeth Ross Knight, June 24, 1939; children—Harris, John W., Daniel K., Elizabeth Ross. Ph.B., Yale, 1927. Prodn. mgr. Allen & Hills, Inc., Auburn, N.Y., 1928-30; securities analyst 5th Ave. Bank, N.Y.C., 1931-33; sales promotion Garrett & Co., Bklyn., 1933-34; asst. to pres., gen. mgr. Dura Co., Toledo, 1935-37; v.p., gen. mgr. Conklin Pen Co., 1937-38; prodn. mgr. Owen Dyneto div. Electric AutoLite Co., Syracuse, N.Y., 1938-40; pres. Fostoria Screw Co., Ohio, 1940-41; mgr. prodn. control Vega Aircraft Corp., Burbank, Calif., 1942-43; asst. to pres. Lockheed Aircraft Corp., 1943-45; v.p. charge mfg. Toledo Scale Corp., 1945-46, pres., 1946-68, Nicholas Corp., Toledo, from 1978, also dir.; hon. dir. Toledo Trust Co. Mem. Toledo Labor-Mgmt. Citizens Com., 1946-76; trustee Toledo Hosp.; past trustee Wells Coll., Aurora, N.Y. Club: Belmont Country (Perrysburg, Ohio). Home: Perrysburg, OH.

MC INTOSH, JAMES ALEXANDER, banker; b. Danbury, Conn., July 30, 1934; s. James Alexander and Margaret Helen (Brew) McI.; m. Elizabeth Ann McCarron, June 28, 1957; children—James Alexander, Mary E., Gregory W., Patricia A. B.S., Mt. St. Mary's Coll., Emmitsburg, Md., 1956. With Fed. Res. Bd., Washington, 1957-73; 1st v.p. Fed. Res. Bank, Boston, from 1973; dir. Mass. Higher Edn. Assistance Corp., New Eng. Edn. Loan Mktg. Corp. Fellow Nat. Inst. Public Affairs; mem. Am. Inst. Banking (adv. bd. Boston chpt.). Home: Marshfield Hills, Mass.

MC INTOSH, JAMES BOYD, life ins. co. exec.; b. Milton, Mass., Feb. 18, 1920; s. James A. and Margaret (Wilkie) McI.; m. Frances Glading, Feb. 20, 1943; children—Judith Boyd (Mrs. William C. Carr, Jr.), Gaye Glading, Linda Jane, James Boyd. B.B.A., Boston U., 1950. With New Eng. Mut. Life Ins. Co., Boston, 1945-67, asst. sec., asst. to pres., 1954-56, 2d v.p., asst. to pres., 1956-57, v.p., asst. to pres., 1957-59, adminstrv. v.p., 1959-64, exec. v.p., 1964-67; pres., dir. Midland Mut. Life Ins. Co., 1967-79, chmn., dir., 1980-84, dir. Lifetime Communities, Inc., Orange Co., Inc. Trustee Center Sci. and Industry, Columbus Symphony, Ohio Dominican Coll., Griffith Found., Boston U., Children's Hosp. Served as capt. USAAF, World War II. Mem. Life Office Mgmt. Assn. (dir., chmn.), Ohio C. of C. (dir.). Clubs: Columbus Country, University, Columbus, Columbus Athletic, Dedham (Mass.) Country and Polo. Home: Bexley, Ohio. Died Feb. 15, 1984; interred Vero Beach, Fla.

MCINTYRE, ALBERT CANNON, railroad exec.; born Hyde Park, Mass., Dec. 31, 1888; s. William F. and Mary (Cannon) McI.; student pub. schs. of Hyde Park; m. Ellen E. Hinckley, June 2, 1915; 1 son, Albert Hinckley. Clk, N.Y., N.Y. & H. R.R., Boston, 1904-06, rate clk., gen. freight office, 1906-10; joined Lehigh Valley R.R., as chief clk, N.E. freight agt., Boston, 1910, became asst. gen. freight agt., N.Y.C., 1921, gen. freight agt., 1925-30, asst. freight traffic mgr., 1930-36, freight traffic mgr., 1936-52, v.p. charge traffic, 1952); dir. Owasco River R.R. Mem. Nat. Freight Traffic Assn. Clubs: Downtown Athletic, Traffic (N.Y.C.). Home: East Orange, N.J. †

MCINTYRE, ELWOOD RICHARDS, editor; b. New London, Wis., Aug. 1888; s. George H. and Caroline (Richards) McI.; ed. pub. schs.; m. Alvina Kurz McIntyre, Apr. 1916; children—Margaret Ann, Jean Carol. Editor Wisconsin Farmer, 1917-29; in charge of dairy information A.A.A., Washington, D.C., 1933-35 former editor Wisconsin Agriculturist and Farmer. In charge of farm paper relations in U.S. Dept. of Agriculture. Writes essays under nom de plume, —Jeff McDermid,— for Better Crops. Mason. Home: Alexandria, Va. †

MCKEACHIE, WILLIAM EUGENE, advt. exec.; b. N.Y.C., Feb. 10, 1904; s. William Stevenson and Adelaide Anna (Theriault) McK.; B.S., Franklin and Marshall Coll., 1926; postgrad. New Sch. Social Research, Columbia; m. Anne Amelia Noble, Apr. 16, 1938; 1 son, William Noble. Reporter, feature writer, asst. Sunday editor Lancaster (Pa.) News Jour., 1922-26; copywriter Patterson-Andress Co., N.Y., 1926-28; exec. J. Walter Thompson Co., Paris and London, 1928-29; copywriter McCann-Erickson, Inc., N.Y.C., 1929-40, creative dir., 1940-52, v.p., dir., 1942-52, supr. European operations, 1952-60; pres., chmn. McCann-Erickson, S.A., Brussels, 1952-60; mng. dir. chmn. McCann-Erickson Advt., Ltd., London, 1952-60; sr. v.p., dir. McCann-Erickson Corp. Internat., N.Y.C., 1955-60; pres. McCann-Marchalk, 1960-61, cons. on European-Am. bus.; pres., dir. Adjunt-to-Mgmt., Inc., 1962-84; former chmn. and mng. dir. McCann-Erickson Europe S.A., Geneva; dir. McCann-Erickson Italiana S.A., Milan, Sodico, Sa., Paris, H.K. McCann Co., Frankfurt, Germany. Mem. Joint Com. on Grassland Farming, 1946-52. Mem. Internat. C. of C., Inst. Practitioners In Advt., Franklin and Marshall Met. Alumni Assn. (pres. 1940-52), Delaware Valley Protective Assn. (dir.), Farm Club of N.Y., Phi Sigma Kappa, Alpha Delta Sigma. Clubs: University (N.Y.C.); American, Farmers, Royal Automobile, Roehampton (London); New Cosmopolitan (Hamburg); American (Brussels). Address: Carversville, Pa. Died 1984.

MCKEE, CLYDE, agriculturist; born Mission Creek, Pawnee Co., Neb., June 8, 1889; s. Oliver and Lydia (Holt) McK.; B.S., Kan. State Coll., 1910, M.S., 1931; m. Clara L. Shofe, Feb. 17, 1911 (divorced July 10, 1933); children—Alan Eugene (dec.), Robert Thayer, Kenneth Charles, Donald Eugene; m. 2d, Ethel Myrtle McGriff, Nov. 28, 1935. Scientific asst. in agronomy U.S. Dept. Agr., 1911-13, dist. demonstration agt., 1913; asst. prof., acting prof. dept. of farm crops, Ia. State Coll., 1913-21; prof. of agronomy. Mont. State Coll., 1921-37, vice-dean of agr., 1927-37, dean of agr. and dir. Mont. Agrl. Exptl. Sta., 1937-52; chief agriculturist Fgn. Operations Adminstrn., Dept. of State, Beirut, Lebanon, 1952-56; cons. Office Personnel, ICA, Washington, from 1958. Served with Kan. Nat. Guard, 1907-11. Decorated Officer Nat. Order Cedars (Republic Lebanon). Fellow A.A.A.S.; mem. Alpha Gamma Rho, Gamma Sigma Delta, Phi

Kappa Phi, Alpha Zeta, Sigma Xi. Presbyn. Author and editor of exptl. station bulls. Home: Glendale, Ariz. †

MC KEE, EDWIN DINWIDDIE, geologist; b. Washington, Sept. 24, 1906; s. Edwin Jones and Ethel (Swope) McK.; student U.S. Naval Acad., 1924-27; A.B., Cornell U., 1929; postgrad. U. Ariz., 1930-31, U. Calif. at Berkeley, 1933-34, Yale, 1939-40; Sc.D. (hon.), No. Ariz. U., 1957; m. Barbara Hastings, Dec. 31, 1929; children—William Dinwiddie, Barbara (Mrs. John Lajoie), Edwin Hastings. Park naturalist Grand Canyon Nat. Park, 1929-40; asst. dir. charge research Museum No. Ariz., 1941-42, summers 1942-53; mem. faculty U. Ariz., 1942-53, prof. geology, 1950-53, chmn. dept., 1951-53; chief paleotectonic map sect. U.S. Geol. Survey, Denver, 1953-61, research geologist, 1962-84. Research investigator in field, vis. prof., participant numerous symposia, 1931-84; mem. U.S. Nat. Com. on Geology, 1968-72; vis. lectr. NRC of Brazil, 1970; USSR Acad. Scis., 1970; prin. investigator desert sand seas of world Earth Resources Tech. Satellite, 1972-73; discipline expert (deserts) sci. support team Skylab IV, 1973-74; leader expdn. to Namib Desert, 1977; cons. Research Inst., Dhahran, Saudi Arabia, 1978; geologist Nepal Inst. Ecotechnics, Kathmandu; cons. Research Inst., U. Petroleum and Minerals, 1978-79. Commr. Bow Mar (Colo.), 1962-63; trustee Mus. No. Ariz., 1953-84; bd. dirs. S.W. Parks and Monuments Assn., 1958—. Recipient Distinguished Service award Dept. Interior, 1962; nine fossil species (3 trilobites, 1 nautiloid, 2 brachiopods, 1 reptile, 1 foraminifer, 1 ammonoid) named mckeei in his honor, 1935-68; John Wesley Powell Centennial Guidebook of Four Corners Geol. Soc. dedicated to him, 1969. Mem. Grand Canyon Natural History Assn. (exec. sec. 1937-39), Tucson Natural History Assn. (pres. 1944), AAAS (Powell lectr. 1950), Ariz. Geol. Soc. (pres. 1952-53), Geol. Soc. Am. (councilor 1953-55), Am. Commn. Stratigraphic Nomenclature (chmn. 1957), Am. Assn. Petroleum Geologists (distinguished lectr. 1957), Rocky Mountain Assn. Geologists (hon.), Soc. Econ. Paleontologists and Mineralogists (hon.; pres. 1967-68, Twenhofel award 1975), Sigma Xi (pres. Ariz. chpt. 1950). Author books, monographs, articles in field. Home: Littleton, Colo. Dec. July 23, 1984. Interned Grand Canyon, Ariz.

MCKEE, GORDON NORFOLK, JR., business executive; b. Boston, July 18, 1930; s. Gordon Norfolk and G. Marion (Schneider) McK.; A.B. in Psychology and Sociology, Harvard U., 1951; m. Mary Brandt, July 21, 1951; children—Linda, Gordon, Pamela, Martha. With Texasgulf, Inc., Stamford, Conn., 1958-81, asst. treas., 1960-64, treas., 1964-81, v.p., 1972-81. Served to lt. (j.g.) USNR, 1951-55. Assoc. mem. Am. Inst. Mining Engrs. Clubs: Sky (N.Y.C.); Landmark (Stamford); Wee Burn (Darien, Conn.). Home: Darien, Conn. Died Feb. 11, 1981.

MCKEE, H. HARPER, geologist; b. Mpls., July 27, 1890; s. William Parker and Nettie (Hartley) McK.; B.Sc., U. Chgo., 1911, M.S., 1912; m. Mabel Hughes, Sept. 21, 1920; children—John Parker, Martha Hughes (Mrs. Thomas B. Keehn), Beatrice Ann (Mrs. Maynard J. Watson), William David, Margaret Sarah (Mrs. Edwin J. Seder). Instr. geology Drury Coll., Springfield, Mo., 1912; geologist Caribbean Petroleum Co., Venezuela, 1912-15; partner Brokaw, Dixon & McKee, from 1919; pres., dir. Venezuela Syndicate, Inc., 1935-55. Mem. Am. Inst. Mining and Metall. Engrs., Am. Assn. Petroleum Geologists. Conglist. Mason. Club: Explorers (N.Y.C.). Home: Forest Hills, N.Y. †

MCKEE, J(AMES) H(UGH), univ. prof.; b. Hagerstown, Md., Sept. 20, 1887; s. James Stanley and Fanny (Baker) McK.; Ph.B., Dickinson Coll., Carlisle, Pa., 1909; A.M., Columbia, 1915; m. Emma Elizabeth Hill, Sept. 3, 1917; children—Frances Stanley (Mrs. Richard Schlegel, Jr.), James Hugh, Emma Hill (Mrs. David Howard Bache). Instr., Conway Hall prep. sch., Carlisle, Pa., 1909-11, Ga. Sch. of Tech., Atlanta, 1912-19, Case Sch. of Applied Sci., Cleveland, 1919-21; prof. English, Purdue U., from 1921. Mem. Am. Assn. Univ. Profs., Nat. Council Teachers of Eng. (mem. com. on coll. reading), Phi Beta Kappa, Sigma Delta Chi, Phi Kappa Sigma, Phi Kappa Phi. Author: (with H. M. Baldwin and H. L. Creek) A Handbook of Modern Writing, 1930; (with G. S. Wykoff and H. H. Remmers) The Purdue Placement Test in English, 1931. Contbr. articles to English Journal, College English, from 1922. Home: West Lafayette, Ind. †

MC KEE, JOHN WILLIAM, business executive; b. Toronto, Ont., Can., Dec. 25, 1897; s. John Arnold and Christie Ann (McRae) McK.; m. Margaret Enid Phippen, Oct. 15, 1924; children—Margaret Ann (Mrs. Pattison), John Angus. Student, Univ. Schs., Toronto, 1912-16, Royal Mil. Coll., Kingston, Can., 1916-17, U. Toronto, 1920. Dir. Stone & Webster Can., Ltd., Toronto, 1950-82, chmn. bd. dirs., 1950-75, chmn. exec. com., 1975-82; dir. Stone & Webster, Inc., N.Y.C., 1950-70; dir., past pres. Royal Agrl. Winter Fair, Toronto; hon. dir., mem. adv. bd. Royal Trustco., Royal Trust Corp. Adv. bd. Salvation Army; dir. Canadian Geriatrics Soc. Served as lt. Royal Arty. RFC and RAF, World War I; exec. asst. Master Gen. of Ordnance, also mem. Nat. War Finance Com. and chmn. North York War Finance Com. World War II. Mem. Alpha Delta Phi. Presbyn. Clubs: Toronto (Toronto), York (Toronto), Rosedale Golf (Toronto), North York Hunt (Toronto); Knickerbocker (N.Y.C.); Ocean of Fla. (Delray Beach). Home: Toronto, Ont., Canada. Dec. 1982.

MCKEE, MARK THOMPSON, lawyer; b. Tipton, Ia., 1887; s. Samuel W. and Minnie (Thompson) McK.; J.D., Detroit Coll. Law, 1913; m. Angeline Fink, Nov. 20, 1908; children—Meredith Cody, Miles, Hugh, Rosemary Hathaway, Jane Leonard, Joan Guislain, Mark, Malcolm, Cynthia Schuknecht, Muir, Julian, Terry, Maurita; m. 2d, Millicent Lee, Nov. 30, 1952. Admitted to Mich. bar, 1913, from practiced in Detroit; v.p., dir. Sand Products Corp. from 1925; chmn. bd., dir. Wis.-Mich. S.S. Co., Milw., since 1934; dir. Pan-Am Airways Corp., N.Y. City from 1938. Dir. Steeprock Iron Mine Co., Atikokan, Ont., Can., W. Mich. Dock & Market Corp., Muskegon Dock & Fuel Co., Macomb Pub. Co., HCM Co., Guerdon Industries Inc., Hans Mueller Corp., Am. Family Life Assn.; chmn. Chatmar Inc., San Francisco. 1st lt. Chem. Warfare Service Reserve, U.S. Army, 1918, ret. as lt. col., 1942. Republican. Mason (Shriner). Clubs: Detroit Athletic; Union League (Chicago); Army-Navy (Washington); Metropolitan, Sky (N.Y.C.); Lawn (New Haven). Home: Oxford, CT. †

MCKEE, WILLIAM THOMAS, clergyman; b. N.Y.C., May 22, 1929; s. William Henry and Thelma Gertrude (Woltz) McK.; m. Rose Aiken, Aug. 20, 1960; children—William Thomas, Randall Steven. B.S., N.Y. U., 1957; M.Div., Colgate-Rochester Div. Sch., 1961; postgrad., Harvard U., 1970-71; D.D. (hon.), Bishop Coll., 1973, Ottawa U., 1975; LL.D. (hon.), Alderson-Broaddus Coll., 1974. Ordained to ministry Am. Bapt. Chs., U.S.A., 1960; chaplain N.Y. U., 1961-63; asso. dir. Ministers and Missionaries Bd., N.Y.C., 1963-73; exec. sec. Bd. Ednl. Ministries; assoc. gen. sec., then exec. dir. Am. Bapt. Chs. U.S.A., Valley Forge, Pa., 1973-83. Trustee Benedict Coll., Colgate-Rochester Div. Sch., Alderson-Broaddus Coll., Morehouse Coll.; active SCLC, NAACP, Urban League. Mem. Harvard U. Alumni Assn., Kappa Alpha Psi, Sigma Pi Phi. Home: Bala Cynwyd, Pa. Died Sept. 22, 1983; buried Cypress Hills Cemetery, Brooklyn.

MCKENNA, FRANK SHIRLEY, univ. adminstr.; b. Crafton, Pa., May 31, 1921; s. Charles Howard and Jennie (Elliott) McK.; B.S. in Metall. Engring., Lehigh U., 1942; M.A. in Psychology, Columbia U., 1948, Ph.D., 1951; m. Barbara St. Clair, June 19, 1943; children—Pamela St. Clair (Mrs. Harold Harwood II), Jenifer Elliott, Thomas St. Clair, Megan Carnegie. Lectr., then asst. prof. psychology Upsala Coll., East Orange, N.J., 1949-52; asst. prof., then asso. prof. psychology, then prof. DePauw U., 1952-66; prof. psychology, dean coll. Monmouth (Ill.) Coll., 1966-72; dir. univ. planning, then v.p. adminstrn. U. Evansville (Ind.), 1972-81. Bd. dirs. Evansville Day Sch. Served to lt. USNR, 1943-46. Mem. Am. Psychol. Assn., AAUP, Sigma Xi, Delta Upsilon. Author: Personnel Selection: A Self Instructional Program, 1967. Home: Evansville, Ind. Died Dec. 29, 1981.

MCKENNAN, ROBERT ADDISON, educator; b. Helena, Mont., Dec. 20, 1903; s. Samuel and Edith (Addison) McK.; student Mercersburg (Pa.) Acad.; A.B., Dartmouth, 1925, Ph.D., Harvard, 1933; m. Catherine Laycock, Dec. 20, 1928. Instr. sociology Dartmouth, 1930-34, asst. prof., 1934-38, prof., 1938-54, chmn. dept., 1937-41, chmn. div. social sci., 1947-51, prof. anthropology, 1954-69, prof. emeritus, research prof. anthropology, 1969-82, chmn. dept. sociology and anthropology, 1957-58, dir. No. Studies Program, 1953-58; anthrop. field work, Ariz., 1929, Alaska, 1929-30, 33, Canadian Arctic, 1958, Alaska, 1962, 66, 67, 69, 70, 71, 72. Served to lt. col. Air Corps, AUS, World War II. Mem. Am. Anthrop. Assn., Arctic Inst. N.A., Soc. for Am. Archaelogy, Canadian Archaeol. Assn., Current Anthropology Asso., Phi Beta Kappa, Psi Upsilon, Casque and Gauntlet. Democrat. Author monographs and articles on Am. Indians. Home: Norwich, Vt. Died Oct. 31, 1982.

MCKENZIE, VERNON, coll. prof., author; b. N.Y. City, Sept. 11, 1887; s. Bartholomew Edwin and Hattie Inez (Beebe) McK.; A.B., U. of Toronto, 1909, A.M., Harvard U., 1914; m. Edna Isobel Chapman, Nov. 5, 1915. Reporter and editor various daily newspapers in Can. and U.S., 1904-15; editor MacLean's Mag., Toronto, Can., 1919 and 1920-26; Canadian Trade commr. in Scotland and Ireland, 1920; European rep. Internat. Mag. Co., 1926-28; dir. Sch. of Journalism, University of Washington, 1928-43; professor journalism. Served in C.E.F. and Royal Air Force, 1915-19; in U.S. Army Air Corps, 1943-46. Awarded Bronze Star. Mem. Am. Assn. of Schs. and Depts. of Journalism (pres. 1939-41), Sigma Chi, Sigma Delta Chi, Alpha Delta Sigma. Methodist. Clubs: Seattle Tennis (Seattle); Harvard (N.Y.C.); Arts and Letters (Toronto); Savage (London). Author: War in Europe—1940, 1934; They Call This Peace, 1935; The Armament Road to Peace, 1936; Through Turbulent Years, 1937; Here Lies Goebbels, 1940. Editor: Behind the Headlines, 1931; These Stories Went To Market, 1935. Contbr. articles and fiction to mags. University of Washington, Seattle.†

MCKEON, RICHARD PETER, educator; b. Union Hill, N.J., Apr. 26, 1900; s. Peter Thomas and Mathilda (Hirschfeld) McK.; A.B., Columbia U., 1920, A.M., 1920; postgrad. U. Paris and Ecole des Hautes Etudes, 1922-25; Ph.D., Columbia U., 1928; Litt.D., Jewish Theol. Sem. Am., 1942; Dr. honoris causa, U. Aix, Marseilles, 1951; m. Clarice Muriel Thirer, July 10, 1930; children—Peter, Nora, Michael. Instr. philosophy Columbia U., 1925-29, asst. prof., 1929-35, instr. Greek and Latin, summer 1926; vis. prof. history U. Chgo., 1934-35, prof. Greek, 1935-47, prof. philosophy, 1937-47, dean div. humanities, 1935-47. Distinguished Service prof. Greek, philosophy, 1947-85, William H. Colvin research prof., 1965-66, now Charles F. Grey Distinguished Service prof. emeritus; mem. U.S. del. Gen. Conf. UNESCO, Paris, 1946, Mexico City, 1947, Beirut, 1948; U.S. counselor UNESCO affairs Am. embassy, Paris, 1947; pres. Internat. Inst. Philosophy, 1953-57; v.p. Internat. Fedn. Philos. Socs., from 1953. Apprentice seaman USN, 1918. Fellow Mediaeval Acad. Am., Am. Acad. Arts and Scis., AAAS; mem. Am. Philos. Assn. (pres. 1952), Am. Philol. Assn., History Sci. Soc., Inst. Internat. de Philosophie Politique, Am. Council Learned Socs. (vice chmn. 1939), Phi Beta Kappa, Kappa Alpha. Club: Quadrangle. Author: The Philosophy of Spinoza, 1928; Freedom and History, 1952; Thought, Action and Passion, 1954; (with R. K. Merton, W. Gellhorn) The Freedom to Read, 1957; co-author several books; editor: Introduction to Aristotle; Selections from Medieval Philosophers; editor, translator books; contbr. articles to sci. publs. Home: Chicago, Ill. Died Mar. 31, 1985.

MCKEOUGH, RAYMOND S., ex-congressman; b. Chicago, Apr. 29, 1888; s. Timothy and Catherine (Wiley) McK.; grad. De La Salle Inst., Chicago; m. Mary Ethel Ormsby, Jan. 3, 1911; children—Mary Margaret, Catherine. Began with Armour & Co. and the live stock commn. houses of Union Stock Yard, Chicago; in clerical and exec. depts. Elgin, Joliet & Eastern R.R. for 17 yrs.; began in investment securities business, Chicago, 1927; later with brokerage frim Babcock, Rushton & Co. Mem. 74th to 77th Congresses (1935-43), 2d Ill. Dist.; mem. Maritime Commn., 1945-50; mem. Internat. Claims Commn., 1950-53. Democrat. Home: Chicago, Ill. †

MC KEOWN, JAMES EDWARD, sociologist, educator; b. Detroit, Sept. 3, 1919; s. Francis Joseph and Grace Margaret (Ruddon) McK.; m. Mary Elizabeth McNamara, Aug. 6, 1955. B.A., Wayne U., 1941, M.A., 1945; Ph.D., U. Chgo., 1949. Instr. social sci. St. Xavier Coll., Chgo., 1945-48; asst. prof. sociology N.Mex. Highlands U., Las Vegas, 1948-52; asst. prof. sociology DePaul U., Chgo., 1952-55, asso. prof., 1955-57, prof. sociology, 1957-70, chmn. dept., 1962-70; prof. sociology U. Wis., Parkside, Kenosha, Wis., from 1970; vis. prof. sociology Emory U., summer 1952, Escuela Nacional de Asistencia Publica, La Paz, Bolivia, 1958, Northwestern U., 1965, Concordia Tchrs. Coll., River Forest, Ill., 1965, 66, Universidad Catolica, Santiago, Chile, 1968; fellow Fund Advancement Edn., summer 1954; Smith-Mundt lectr., Bolivia, 1958, Fulbright Hays lectr., Chile, 1968. Co-editor: The Changing Metropolis, 1964, 2d edit., 1971; Contbr.: articles to profl. jours., also to Britannica Book of Year, 1968-72. Social Sci. Research Council travel grantee, 1958. Mem. Am. Sociol. Soc., AAAS, Am. Acad. Polit. and Social Sci., AAUP, Pi Gamma Mu, Psi Chi, Phi Sigma Iota. Club: Quadrangle. Home: Kenosha, Wis.

MCKIBBEN, FRANK MELBOURNE, educator, clergyman; b. Conway Springs, Kan., Jan. 16, 1889; s. Samuel and Ida (Chenoworth) McK.; A.B., Southwestern Coll., 1914; S.T.B., Boston U., 1919; M.A., Northwestern U., 1924, Ph.D., 1929; m. Alma Palmer, June 14, 1916 (dec. 1935); 1 dau., Rita (Mrs. Everet Lothrop, Jr.); m. 2d, Helen M. Brown, Feb. 19, 1937; children—Jeanne Brown, Cathy, David. Ordained to ministry Methodist Ch., 1919; dir. youth work Methodist Bd. Sunday Schs., 1919-20; dir. religious edn., Evanston and Oak Park, Ill., 1920-23; dir. community program religious edn., S. Bend, Ind., 1923-25; dir. Balt. Council Religious Edn., 1925-27; prof. religious edn., head dept. U. Pitts., 1928-30, Northwestern U., 1930-42; prof. religious edn., academic exec. sec. to pres. Garrett Bib. Inst., Evanston, Ill., 1942; minister Central Meth. Ch., Phoenix, from 1958. Rep. Methodist Church Internat. Council Religious Edn., 1932-48, chmn. com. weekday religious edn., 1935-52; mem. commn. worship Fed. Council Churches, 1935-48. Dir. Religious Edn. Assn., 1945-53. Author: The Community Training School, 1920; Intermediate Method in the Church School, 1926; Studies in Youth, 1934-38; Improving Religious Education Through Supervision, 1929; Guiding Workers in Christian Education, 1954; Learning to Know God, 1936; Renaissance in Religious Education, 1929; Improving Your Teaching, 1937. Home: Phoenix, Ariz. †

MCKINLEY, CHARLES, educator; b. Fulton, S.D., Oct. 16, 1889; s. Charles Lincoln and Harriet Emma (Bull) McK.; B.A., U. Wash., 1913; M.A., U. Wis., 1916; Doctor of Laws (honorary), Reed Coll., 1960; married to Nellie Linda Higgins, Aug. 30, 1914; children—Donald, Hugh, Jean (Mrs. Don N. Johnson). Head history dept. Ogden (Utah) Sr. High, 1917-18; faculty Reed Coll., from 1918, successively instr., asst. prof., prof. polit. sci. dept., 1926-60, emeritus, from 1960. Cornelia M. Pierce prof. Am. polit. instns., 1958; part-time prof. polit. sci. Portland State Coll., 1960-64; vis. prof. Maxwell Sch. Citizenship & Pub. Affairs, 1925-26; research staff, com. on pub. adminstrn. Social Sci. Research Council, 1935-37. Mem. Portland City Planning Commn., 1934-64, pres., 1935-40; research staff Pres.'s com. on adminstrv. mgmt., summer 1936; mem. Alaska Resources Com., 1937; v.p. N.W. Regional Council, 1937-41; exec. sec. adminstrv. council U.S. Dept. Agr., 1940-42; spl. asst. adminstrv. officer W.P.B., 1942; regional adv. council Bonneville Power Adminstrn., 1945-52; has been cons. on natural resources to various govt. depts., commns. and planning bds. Recipient Bi-Centennial Silver Medallion, Columbia, 1954; sr. research fellowship Social Sci. Research Council, 1958-59. Mem. Am. (pres. 1954-55), Pacific N.W. (pres. 1950-51) polit. science associations, Nat. Municipal League, American Society of Public Administration, Phi Beta Kappa. Club: City of Portland. Author: Uncle Sam in the Pacific Northwest: Federal Management of Natural Resources in the Columbia River Valley, 1952. Contbr.: Federalism Mature and Emergent (editor Arthur W. Macmahon), 1955. Home: Portland, Ore. †

MCKINNEY, FRED, psychologist, educator; b. New Orleans, Apr. 4, 1908; s. William Henry and Clara Edna (Schneider) McK.; m. Margery Mulkern, Aug. 19, 1933; children—Megan (Mrs. Robert W. Whitfield, Jr.), Kent, Molly (Mrs. Carliss C. Farmer), Doyne (Mrs. William S. McKenzie). A.B., Tulane U., 1928, M.A., 1929; Ph.D., U. Chgo., 1931. Diplomate: Am. Bd. Examiners in Psychology. Clerk and advt. rep. Item-Tribune, New Orleans, 1923-29; instr. psychology John Marshall Law Sch., Chgo., 1930-31; psychologist Mo. Unemployment Compensation Com., Com. on Personnel, 1936; instr. psychology U. Mo., 1933-35, asst. prof., 1935-38, asso. prof., 1939-44, prof., 1944-78, emeritus, from 1978; chmn. dept. psychology, 1945-55; psychologist Student Health Service, 1938-58; vis. asst. prof. U. Ark., summer 1934; vis. prof. Miss. State Coll., summers 1948-49, U. Denver, summers 1950, 56, San Francisco State Coll., summer 1951, Tulane U., summer 1952; vis. lectr., cons. Stephens Coll., 1956-57; Fulbright prof. U. Ankara and Middle East U., Ankara, Turkey, 1958-59; prof. psychology U. Mid-Am., Ball State U. Overseas, 1978-79; prof. psychology, group therapist U.S.S. Eisenhower, 1980; VISTA vol. Mo. State Prison.; Chmn. Conf. of State Psychol. Assns., 1956-57; asso. editor Edn. and Psychol. Measurement; editor and rep. Am. Coll. Personnel Assn., 1947-58; asso. editor Jour. Cons. Psychol. Author: Psychology of Personal Adjustment, 1941, rev., 1960, You and Your Life, 1951, Counseling for Personal Adjustment, 1958, Understanding Personality: Cases in Counseling, 1965, Psychology in Action: Basic Readings, 1967, rev. edit., 1973, Effective Behavior and Human Developments, 1976; Contbr.: chpts. to Handbook for Child Guidance by E. Harms, 1947, An Introduction to Clinical Psychology by L.A. Pennington and I.A. Berg, 1948; Producer and performer: TV program Not in Our Stars; producer for, Stephens Coll.; 13 TV kinescopes (ednl.) Live Your Life, 1958; also produced 31 ednl. television video tapes on gen. psychology; 8 tapes for Psychology of Personality. Recipient Distinguished Faculty award Univ. Alumni Assn., 1966, Distinguished Teaching award in psychology Am. Psychol. Found., 1977, commendation Mo. Senate, 1977. Former asso. and fellow Am. Psychol. Assn. (pres. Div. 2, teaching psychology 1958-59); mem. Midwestern Psychol. Assn. (council mem. 1945-49), Mo. Psychol. Assn. (v.p. 1947-48, pres. 1948-49), AAUP, Mo. Assn. for Mental Hygiene (sec.-treas. 1936-38), Blue Key, U. of Mo. YMCA (chmn. faculty bd. advisors 1937-44), Midwestern Assn. Coll. Psychiatrists and Clin. Psychol. (sec.-treas. 1945-46, pres. 1946-47), Alpha Pi Zeta, Sigma Xi, Omicron Delta Kappa, Psi Chi (pres. Midwest div. 1930-32, nat. pres. 1932-34). Episcopalian. Research in psychotherapy, personality adjustment. Home: Columbia, MO.

MCKINNEY, HOWARD DECKER, univ. prof.; b. Pine Bush, N.Y., May 29, 1889; s. John Luther and Marianna (Decker) McK.; Litt.B., Rutgers Coll., 1913, hon. Mus.D., 1940; student Columbia U., 1914-15; unmarried. Instr. in music, St. Paul's Sch., Garden City, N.Y., 1914-16; organist and dir. of music, Rutgers Univ., 1917-22, asst. prof. of music, 1923-28, asso. prof. music, 1929-32, prof. of music from 1933. Mem. Delta Upsilon, Phi Beta Kappa, A.S.C.A.P. Clubs: University (N.Y. City), The Bohemians. Author: A Mystery for Christmas; The Three Marys; (with W.R. Anderson) Discovering Music, 1935, Music in History, 1940, and The Challenge of Listening, 1943; Music and Man, 1948. Editor The Rutgers Song Book; Fischer Edition News; musical editor J. Fischer & Brother, N.Y. City; contbr. on musical subjects. Address: New Brunswick, N.J. †

MCKNIGHT, WILLIAM LESTER, manufacturing corporation exec.; b. White, S.D., Nov. 11, 1887; s. Joseph and Cordelia (Smith) McK.; student pub. schs.; D.Sc., Macalester Coll., 1965; m. Maud Gage, Oct. 9, 1915; 1 dau., Virginia (Mrs. James H. Binger). Pres. Minn. Mining & Mfg. Co., St. Paul, 1929-49, chmn. bd., 1949-66, dir., from 1966, also hon. chmn. bd. directors, mem. exec., management and finance committees. Clubs: Minnesota, St. Paul Athletic, White Bear Yacht (St. Paul); Surf, Bath, Indian Creek Country (Miami Beach, Fla.); Union League (Chgo.). Home: St. Paul, Minn. †

MCKOWN, ROBERTA ELLEN, political scientist, educator; b. Endicott, N.Y., Mar. 26, 1932; d. Robert Edward and Rubina (Cunningham) McK.; children—Bruce Koplin, Mara Koplin Everett, Therese Koplin. B.A. in Econs, U. Oreg., 1953, M.A. in Polit. Sci, 1965, Ph.D., 1968. Inst. U. Oreg., 1967-68; asst. prof. polit. sci. U. Alta., Edmonton, 1968-72, asso. prof., 1972-77, prof., from 1977, chmn. dept., 1975-82. Contbr. articles to profl. jours. Can. Council Research grantee, 1971-72. Mem. Am. Polit. Sci. Assn., Can. Polit. Sci. Assn., Royal African Soc., Can. African Studies Assn., Internat. Studies Assn. Home: Edmonton, Alta., Can. Deceased.

MC LAIN, JOHN DAVID, JR., choreographer, educator, administrator; b. Brighton, Tenn., Dec. 29, 1931; s. John David and Elsie Leola (Burt) McL. B.S. in Edn, U. Ark., 1953; M.A., Wayne State U., Detroit, 1962. Asst. to dir. Robert Joffrey Ballet Co., N.Y.C., 1962-63; mem. faculty Am. Ballet Center, N.Y.C., 1962-63; ballet master Dayton (Ohio) Civic Ballet, also mem. faculty Schwarz Sch. Dance, Dayton, 1963-66; artistic dir. Cin. Ballet Co., also head dance div. and prof. ballet U. Cin. Coll.-Conservatory Music, 1966-84, New Orleans City Ballet, 1983-84; mus. adviser Detroit Severo Ballet, 1955-62; guest tchr. Sch. Pa. Ballet, Phila., 1963, Chgo. Nat. Dance Masters Assn., 1968, 70, 73; artist-in-residence Utah State U., 1970; mem. dance adv. panel Ohio Arts Council, 1969-71, Ky. Arts Commn., 1975-76; cons. in field. Choreographer: Ancient Dances and Airs, Lovers and Songs of Silence, 1967, Night Soliloquies, 1968, L'histoire du Soldat, 1968, Two x Two, 1968, Romanza, 1969, 12 x 9 in 5, 1969, Concerto, 1969, Morphosis and Clouds, 1971, Guitar Concerto, 1971, Winter's Traces, 1978, Lyric Waltz, 1972, Dilemmas Moderne, 1972. Named Outstanding Alumnus in Fine Arts U. Ark., 1962; recipient Dolly Cohen award U. Cin., 1971; Samuel and Rose Sachs award Cin. Inst. Fine Arts, 1975; citation Martha Kinney Cooper Ohioana Library Assn., 1980. Mem. Assn. Am. Dance Cos., MacDowell Music Soc. (v.p.), Phi Mu Alpha Sinfonia, Kappa Kappa Psi, Phi Delta Theta. Home: Cincinnati, Ohio. Died Dec. 15, 1984.

MC LAIN, JOSEPH HOWARD, college president; b. Wierton, W.Va., July 11, 1916; s. Howard Storer and Elizabeth Agnes (Gray) Mc L.; m. Margaret Ann Hollingsworth, Sept. 6, 1941; children: Elizabeth Ann, Susan Lynn. B.S., Washington Coll., Chestertown, Md., 1937; Ph.D., Johns Hopkins U., 1946. Tech. dir., sec. Kent Mfg. Corp., Chestertown, 1946-54; research liaison mgr. Olin Mathieson Corp., N.Y.C., 1954-55; prof. chemistry Washington Coll., 1946-73, pres., from 1973; dir. Balt. br. Fed. Res. Bank of Richmond; chmn. adv. bd. Md. Nat. Bank, Chestertown, 1963-78. Author: Pyrotechnics (From the Viewpoint of Solid State Chemistry), 1980; contbr. articles on solid state chemistry to profl. jours. Chmn. Water Pollution Control Commn., Annapolis, Md., 1947-53; mem. Kent County Bd. Edn., 1958-64, Gov.'s Sci. Adv. Council, from 1974, Bay Bridge Commn., 1966, Chesapeake Bay Grasses Com., from 1975. Served in U.S. Army, 1941-46. Mem. Am. Chemistry Soc., Am. Ordnance Assn., Am. Rocket Soc. (sr.), Faraday Soc., Chem. Soc. (London), N.Y. Acad. Sci., Combustion Inst., Phi Beta Kappa, Sigma Xi, Phi Lambda Upsilon. Democrat. Episcopalian. Club: Chester River Yacht Country. Home: Chestertown, Md. Died July 26, 1981.

MCLARIN, W(ILLIAM) S(ANFORD), JR., pres. Fed. Reserve Bank of Atlanta; b. Fairburn, Ga., Sept. 28, 1889; s. William Sanford and Lily (Howard) McL.; grad. Southern Bus. Coll., Atlanta, 1907; m. Dorothy Bodwell Melson, Jan. 17, 1925. Served with Federal Reserve, from 1916; managing dir. Jacksonville Branch, 1928-31; with Fed. Reserve Bank of Atlanta, from 1931, as 1st v.p., 1939-41, pres., 1941-51. Served as 1st lt. A.E.F. and in Army of Occupation, 1917-19. Mason, Rotary, Am. Legion. Home: Atlanta, Ga. Deceased.

MCLAUGHLIN, CHARLES HEMPHILL, educator; b. Little Rock, Oct. 17, 1908; s. William Wilson and Harriet Gertrude (Ritchie) McL.; A.B., U. Denver, 1929, M.A., 1934; student Westminster Law Sch., Denver, 1931-32; J.D., Harvard, 1935; student Grad. Sch., Columbia, 1939-40, 46; m. Mary Smilanich, Sept. 22, 1939; children—Mary Deborah (Mrs. H.M. Krider), John Wilson. Admitted to Colo. bar, 1935; from instr. to asso. prof. U. Minn., 1936-56, prof. dept. polit. sci., 1956-83, chmn. dept., 1961-66, dir. Center Internat. Relations and Area Studies, 1948-65; lectr. pub. law Columbia, 1946; vis. asso. prof. polit. sci. U. Calif. at Berkeley, 1955-56; vis. prof. polit. sci. U. Hawaii, 1966-67. Research dir. Minn. Com. against Bricker Amendment, 1953-55; radio commentator Mpls. Fgn. Policy Assn., 1954-55; regional dir. legal research Atty. Gen.'s Survey of Release Procedures, 1936-37. Served from 2d lt. to capt. USAAF, 1942-46. Recipient Regents award U. Minn., 1976. Mem. Am. Assn. UN (dir. Minn. 1948-68, v.p. 1950-55, chmn. constl. com. 1954, chmn. policy com. 1955-66), Internat. Law Assn., Am. Bar Assn., Minn. Atlantic Union, Am. Soc. Internat. Law, Am. Polit. Sci. Assn., Midwest Polit. Sci. Assn. Author: (with Robert J. Devenish) Historical and Genealogical Records of the Devenish Families, 1948; (with Lennox A. Mills) World Politics in Transition, 1956. Contbr. articles to profl. jours. Home: Saint Louis Park, Minn. Died Nov. 3, 1983.

MC LAUGHLIN, DONALD HAMILTON, mining geologist and engr.; b. San Francisco, Dec. 15, 1891; s. William Henry and Katherine (Hamilton) McL.; B.S., U. Calif. (with honorable mention for U. Calif. medal), 1914; A.M., Harvard U., 1915, Ph.D., 1917; D.Eng. (hon.), S.D. Sch. Mines and Tech., 1950, Mich. Coll. Mines and Tech., 1950, Mont. Sch. Mines, 1950, Colo. Sch. Mines, 1955; LL.D., U. Calif. at Berkeley, 1966; m. Eleanor Eckhart, Sept. 12, 1925; children—Donald Hamilton, Charles Capen; m. 2d, Sylvia Cranmer, Dec. 29, 1948; children—Jean Katherine, George Cranmer. Chief geologist Cerro de Pasco Copper Corp., Oroya, Peru, 1919-25; mem. faculty Harvard, 1925-41; dean Coll. Mining, U. Calif. at Berkeley, 1941-42, prof. mining engring., 1941-43, dean Coll. Engring., 1942-43, prof. emeritus, 1967-84, Berkeley fellow, from 1968; pres. Homestake Mining Co., 1944-61, chmn., 1961-70, chmn. exec. com., from 1970, also dir.; dir. emeritus Western Air Lines; chmn. adv. com. on raw materials AEC, 1947-52, mem. plowshare adv. com., 1959-72; trustee Com. for Econ. Devel., 1960-62; mem. advisory com. U.S. Geol. Survey, 1950-65. Regent U. Calif., 1951-66, chmn. bd., 1958-60; mem. nat. sci. bd. NSF, 1950-60; mem. earth scis. advisory bd. Stanford U., from 1969; mem. overseers com. to visit dept. geol. scis. Harvard, 1972-79; trustee San Francisco Conservatory Music, 1964-73. Served as 1st lt., inf. U.S. Army, 1917-19. Rand medalist Am. Inst. Mining, Metall. and Petroleum Engrs., 1961; Monell medal and prize Columbia U., 1964; Golden Plate award Am. Acad. Achievement, 1972. Fellow Geol. Soc. Am. (councilor 1934-36), Am. Acad. Arts and Scis. (councilor 1939-42), Calif. Alumni Assn. (mem. council 1972-76, Alumnus of Year award 1977); mem. and sometime officer several profl. assns., Phi Beta Kappa, Sigma Xi, Tau Beta Pi, Kappa Sigma, Theta Tau. Clubs: Pacific Union, Bohemian, Engineers' (San Francisco); University, Century, (N.Y.C.); Cosmos (Washington). Contbr. articles to profl. jours. Home: Berkeley, Calif. Died Dec. 31, 1984.

MCLAUGHLIN, GEORGE VINCENT, banker; b. Brooklyn, N.Y., May 20, 1887; B.C.S., New York Univ.; LL.B., Brooklyn Law Sch.; C.P.A., State Board of Regents; LL.D., St. Lawrence U., 1937; m. Hazel K. Sullivan, Oct. 1919; children—Jeanne, Kathleen. Admitted to N.Y. bar; examiner, State Banking Dept., 1911-17, dep. supt. of banks, 1917-20, supt., 1920-26; police commr., N.Y. City, 1926; exec. v.p. Mackay Cos., 1927 pres., trustee Brooklyn Trust Co., 1927-50; hon. dir. Mfrs. Hanover Trust Co.; dir. Equitable Life Assurance Soc.; vice chmn. Triborough Bridge & Tunnel Authority. Trustee L.I. Coll. Med., St. Johns U., Brooklyn Bur. Social Service, Brooklyn Inst. of Arts and Sciences; dir. Roman Catholic Orphan Asylum Society; member of advisory committee Brooklyn chapter, American Red Cross; mem. Brooklyn Chamber of Commerce (dir. to May 1950). Mem. Delta Sigma Pi, Phi Delta Phi (life). Dem. Elk (life). Clubs: Bankers of America, Brooklyn, Manhattan, New York Athletic, Economic, Pinnacle. Home: New York, N.Y. †

MCLAUGHLIN, WALTER WYLIE, profl. farm. mgr. and rural appraiser; b. Salem, Ill., Sept. 4, 1890; s. Joseph Knox and Terza Elvira (Morton) McL.; student Southern Ill. Normal U., 1909-11, U. of Ill., 1913-20; m. Kate S. Slightam, Dec. 16, 1925; children—Mary McLaughlin Green, Shirley Ann McLaughlin. Profl. farm mgr., Mich., 1920; farm adviser LaSalle County Ill., 1921-28; farm mgr., Citizens Nat. Bank, Decatur, Ill., 1928-31; dir. Ill. Dept. of Agr., 1933-37; profl. farm mgr. and appraiser, Decatur, from 1937; mgr. farm service dept. of Citizens Nat. Bank, Decatur. Served as 2d lt., inf., U.S. Army, World War I. Mem. bd. trustees, U. of Ill., 1945-51. Mem. agronomy advisory com. Coll. of Agr. Awarded title Accredited Farm Mgr. by Am. Soc. Farm Mgrs. and Rural Appraisers. Democrat. Presbyn. Mason. Club: Decatur. Home: Decatur, Ill. †

MCLEAN, LESLIE ALEXANDER, banker; b. Pittsburgh, Pa., Mar. 28, 1890; s. Leslie Alexander and Margaret Helen McL.; ed. U. of Pittsburgh; m. Hazel Kirkpatrick, June 29, 1910; children—Gladys Helen (Mrs. Edward W. Monroe), Leslie Cameron, Hazel Jacqueline. Clk. Union Savs. Bank of Pitts., 1907; banking business, Louisville, Kentucky, president and director Southern Trust Company of Louisville, Louisville Real Estate and Investment Company, First Mortgage Corp. of Louisville; pres. and director Real Estate Developers, Inc.; owner Southern Ins. Agency of Louisville Mem. Mortgage Bankers Assn. Am. (dir.). Presbyn. Home: Louisville, KY. †

MCLEAN, NOEL B., mfg. co. exec.; b. Watertown, Conn., 1906; married. With Bendix Aviation Corp., 1929-46; exec. v.p. Edo Corp., Colleg Point, N.Y., 1946-50, pres., 1950-62, chmn. bd., 1962-72, dir., 1962-84; dir. Edo Can. Ltd., Edo Western Corp., Elec. Indicator Co. Inc., Edo Comml. Corp. Home: New Hope, Pa. Died Sept. 17, 1984.

MC LEOD, JAMES CURRIE, clergyman, educator; b. Buffalo; s. Dugald and Mary Holmes (Currie) McL.; m. Emily Louise Johnson, Aug. 24, 1929; children—Mary Louise (Mrs. James S. Aagaard), Adrienne (Mrs. Craig Heatley), James Currie. B.S., Middlebury Coll., 1926, D.D., 1950; B.D., Yale U., 1929; D.D., Alfred U., 1941. Ordained to ministry Presbyn. Ch., 1929; univ. chaplain Alfred (N.Y.) U., 1929-40; minister to students Ohio State U., Columbus, 1940-43; univ. chaplain, prof. history and lit. of religion Northwestern U., 1946-50, prof., 1950-71, prof. emeritus, from 1971, dean students, 1952-67; research fellow Yale Div. Sch., 1963-64; vis. scholar Colgate-Rochester Div. Sch., 1967-68; guest preacher Presbytery of Glasgow, Scotland, 1950, also at; Syracuse, Chgo., Rutgers, Lake Forest, Middlebury, Stanford, Howard, others. Author: symposium Fruits of Faith, also articles various jours. Pres., trustee Evanston (Ill.) Pub. Library; bd. dirs. Vis. Nurses Assn., Evanston. Served as lt. comdr., chaplain USNR, 1943-46. Mem. Nat. Acad. Religion, Nat. Assn. Student Personnel Adminstrs. (pres. 1963-64), Religious Edn. Assn. (v.p. 1963-64), Presbytery of Chgo., Delta Upsilon (internat. pres. 1972-73). Republican. Clubs: Mason, Rotary (pres.), St. Andrew Soc. (pres. 1973-74); Yale (Chgo.). Home: Wilmette, Ill.

MCLURE, JOHN RANKIN, dean college of education; b. Troy, Ala., Nov. 6, 1888; s. Richard Umphrey and Sarah Elizabeth (Hamil) McL.; B.Pd., State Normal Coll., Troy, 1907; B.S., U. of Ala., 1911; M.A., Columbia, 1914, Master's diploma as supt. schs., 1916, Ph.D., 1925; m. Sallie Le Boyd, Aug. 28, 1924. Teacher training sch., State Normal Coll., Troy, 1907-08; teacher Disque High Sch., Gadsden, Ala., 1908-09; supt. schs., Troy, 1911-21; prof. ednl. administration, U. of Alabama, from 1924; dir. Summer Sch., 1926-43, and Div. Field Studies, U. of Ala., 1928-43; dir. Bur. Ednl. Research, 1939-43; dean Coll. Edn. from Oct. 1942. Governor 164th Dist., Rotary International, 1944-45. Mem. Nat. Educational Assn., Ala. Edn. Assn., Phi Beta Kappa, Sigma Alpha Epsilon, Phi Delta Kappa, Kappa Delta Pi. Democrat. Presbyn. Mason. K.P. Rotarian. Wrote: The Ventilation of School Buildings (thesis for Ph.D.), 1925. Home: Tuscaloosa, Ala. †

MCMAHON, JOHN E., JR., army officer; b. West Point, N.Y., Sept. 11, 1890; s. Gen. E. McMahon; grad. U.S. Mil. Acad.; commd. 2d lt. F.A., June 1913, and advanced through the grades to brig. gen., Feb. 1942; became asst. exec. Office of the Asst. Sec. of War, 1933; assigned to 76th Field Arty., Presidio of Monterey, Calif., July 1938, assumed command, Jan. 1940; assigned hdqrs. 7th Div., Fort Ord, Calif., July 1940; with 77th Inf. Div., Fort Jackson, S.C., after 1942. Deceased.

MCMILLAN, DONALD, ex comdr. Salvation Army; b. Middlesbrough, Eng., June 8, 1887; son Brig. Alexander McMillan; grad. Salvation Army Officers Training Coll., New York, 1906; m. Harriet Ruth Blackman, Oct. 1914; children—Donald Blackman, Harriet Elizabeth (Mrs. Harriet Gorlin), Margot Carol (Mrs. John Lawes). Served as officer Salvation Army in finance, men's soc. and field depts., as mem. Chgo. Tng. Coll. staff, gen. sec., divisional commander, chief sec. Eastern Territory; became territorial comdr. Western Territory, 1939, nat. sec., 1944, Eastern Territorial comdr., 1947-53, national comdr. Salvation Army in United States, 1953-57. Awarded Medal fo Merit for war time activities (U.S.); Medaille de la Reconnaisance in recognition of rehabilitation work (France); King's Medal for Service (Great Britain); medal of City of N.Y. for public service. †

MCMILLIN, GEORGE JOHNSON, naval officer; b. Youngstown, O., Nov. 25, 1889; s. Charles Pollock and Addie (Johnson) M.; B.S., U.S. Naval Acad., 1911; student Naval War Coll., Newport, R.I., 1935-36; m. Annabel Parlett, Oct. 23, 1912; children—Adda Louise (dec.), Ruth George (wife lt. W. P. Mack, U.S. Navy), Annabel Parlett, George Johnson, Jr. Commd. Ensign, U.S. Navy, 1911, advanced through ranks to capt.; served on U.S.S. Delaware, Sacramento, New Mexico, Conner, Hopkins, Saratoga, Black Hawk, Luzon, Idaho, Medusa, successively on duty at Navy Yard, Mere Island, Navy Dept., Washington, D.C., U.S. Naval Acad., Naval War Coll.; served as gov., Guam; also dir. edn., Guam. Awarded Mexican Campaign, Dominican and World War medals. Presbyterian. Deceased.

MC MILLIN, MILES JAMES, editor, publisher; b. Crandon, Wis., Mar. 12, 1913; s. Rolland James and Lillian (Lutsey) McM.; m. Elsie Rockefeller, Aug. 16, 1955; children—Nancy, Miles James. LL.D., U. Wis., 1941. Bar: Wis. bar 1941. Writer Progressive Pub. Co., 1941-45; editorial page editor Capital Times, Madison, Wis., 1945-66, asso. editor, 1966-67, exec. pub., 1967-70, editor, pub., 1970-78; pres. Capital Times Co., 1970-79; chmn. bd. Madison Newspapers, Inc., 1970-80; v.p. Badger Broadcasting Co., 1970-78. Vice pres. William T. Evjue Found., Madison Kiddie Camp.; Trustee William T. Evjue Charitable Trust. Mem. Am. Bar Assn., Wis. Bar Assn., Am. Newspaper Pubs. Assn. Club: Madison. Home: Paul Smith's, NY.

MC MURRY, ROBERT NOLEMAN, mgmt. cons.; b. Chgo., Dec. 19, 1901; s. Oscar Lincoln and Sadie (Adelaide) McM.; Ph.B., U. Chgo., 1925, M.S. in Psychology, 1932; Ph.D. (fellow Inst. Internat. Edn.), U. Vienna, 1934; m. Doris Baird, Oct. 3, 1936 (dec. Oct. 1965); children—Michael Baird, Sara Lou; m. 2d, Katherine Miller, Apr. 29, 1966. With Fed. Electric Co., Chgo., 1925-27, Yellow Cab Co., 1927-28, Transit Mixers, Inc., Chgo., 1928-31; charge Chgo. office Psychol. Corp., 1935-43; cons. service personnel, indsl. relations, market research Robert N. McMurry & Co., Chgo., 1943-53, McMurry, Hamstra & Co., Chgo. (name changed to McMurry Co., Oct. 1958), from 1943; chmn. John Wareham Internat., N.Y.C., 1978. Diplomate Am. Bd. Examiners Profl. Psychology. Fellow Am Psychol. Assn.; mem. Indsl. Relations Research Assn., Am. Mgmt. Assn., Am. Statis. Assn., Chgo. Psychoanalytic Assn., Am. Marketing Assn., Inst. Mgmt. Scis. Author: Handling Personality Adjustment in Industry, 1944; Tested Techniques of Personnel Selection, 1955; McMurry's Management Clinic, 1960; How to Recruit, Select and Place Salesmen, 1964; How to Build a Dynamic Sales Organization, 1968; 101 Business Problems and their Solutions, 1973; The Maverick Executive, 1974. Home: Chicago, Ill. Died Mar. 29, 1985.

MCNAB, ALLAN, museum dir., artist; b. Swaythling, Eng., May 27, 1901; came to U.S., 1938, naturalized, 1943; s. Duncan K. and Florence S. (McLeod) McN.; m. Dorothy Cumming, 1933 (div. 1949); m. Marjorie Kreilick, 1973. Grad., Westminster, London, 1917, Royal Mil. Coll., Sandhurst, 1918; M.A., Royal Coll. Art, London, 1929; student, Ecole des Beaux-Arts, Paris, France, 1929-30. Art dir. Gaumont Brit. Pictures Corp., 1930-38; design dir. Norman Bel Geddes, 1939-41; art dir. Life mag., 1941-48; dir. Lowe Gallery, U. Miami, 1949-55, trustee, 1950-55; tech. adviser Nat. Mus., Havana, Cuba, 1955-59; dir. Soc. Four Arts, Palm Beach, Fla., 1955-56; asst. dir. Art Inst. Chgo., 1956-57, asso. dir., 1957-58, dir. adminstrn., 1959-66; dir. Telfair Acad., Savannah, Ga.; chmn. trustees Miami Art Center; trustee Miami Arts Council, also mus. cons., from 1966; cons. on bldg. mus., City of Oakland, Calif., from 1962; art cons. Mayo Found., from 1967; art adv. panel Internal Revenue Service, 1966-69; Trustee Minn. Mus. Art, Allentown Mus. Art; cons. Met. Mus. of Manila, 1977-78, Wustum Mus. Art, Racine, Wis., from 1979, Lauren Rogers Library and Mus. Art, from 1980; hon. trustee Allentown Art Mus., Lincoln Acad. Ill. Exhibited paintings, Beaux Art Gallery, London, 1930, St. Georges Gallery, London, 1932, Print Club, Phila., 1932, Royal Acad., London, 1928-31, English Soc. Wood Engravers, 1929-31, Royal Soc. Painter-Etchers, 1929-31, Royal Scottish Acad., 1930, Art Inst. Chgo., 1930, City Art Gallery, Leeds, Eng., 1931, Melbourne (Australia) Mus., 1930, works in permanent collections, Brit. Mus., Nat. Gallery, Edinburgh, City Art Gallery, Leeds, Rosenwald Collection, Balt. Mus.; also collections Frank Crowinshield. Chmn. bd. suprs. Town La Pointe, from 1967. Decorated Order Vasa 1st class. Mem. So. Art Mus. Dirs. Assn. (chmn. emeritus), S.E. Mus. Conf. (council 1953-54), Assn. Art Mus. Dirs., Am. Assn. Mus., Am. Inst. Decorators. Clubs: Tavern (Chgo.), Arts (Chgo.). Address: Madison, Wis.

MCNAB, JOHN, clergyman; b. No. Ireland, Apr. 3, 1887; s. John A. and Jane (Harvey) McN.; B.A., Queen's U., Kingston, Ont., Can., 1914, B.D., 1920; M.A., Columbia, 1920; S.T.B., Union Theol. Sem., N.Y.C., 1920; D.D., Queens U., 1946, Presbyn. Coll., 1959; m. Margaret W. Adams, Sept. 8, 1915; children—John, Margaret W. (Mrs. Douglas Puddy), Norah (Mrs. Bruce Carruthers). Ordained to ministry Presbyn. Ch., 1918; minister Knox Ch., Midland, Ont., 1920-27, High Park Presbyn. Ch., Toronto, 1927-38; moderator Presbyn. Ch. in Can., 1958-59. Convener, Bd. Christian Edn., Presbyn. Ch. in Can., 1932-35, convener com. on history, 1936-40. Served as chaplain Canadian Army, World War I; dir. chaplain services Royal Canadian Air Force, World War II. Mason. Club: Canadian (Toronto). Author: They Went Forth, rev. edit., 1957; In Other Tongues, 1938; Our Heritage and Our Faith, 1950. Editor: What Do Presbyterians Believe, 1957; editor-in-chief: The Presbyterian Record, 1946-58. Address: Toronto , Ont., Can. †

MCNAMARA, JOHN ARTHUR, editor; b. Binghamton, N.Y., June 7, 1888; s. John Andrew and Catherine (Keenan) McN.; prep. edn., Staunton (Va.) Mil. Acad., 1904-05, and Swarthmore (Pa.) Prep. Sch., 1905-07; student Cornell U., 1907-09; unmarried. Mng. editor Hardware Age, New York, 1919-21; asst. editor Am. Machinist, New York, 1922-24; exec. editor The Modern Hospital and Modern Hospital Year Book from 1925; exec. editor The Nation's Schools from 1926. Served as 1st lt. Inf., U.S.A., World War. Mem. Am. Hosp. Assn., Catholic Hosp. Assn., Protestant Hosp. Assn., Western Hosp. Assn., Hosp. Assn. State of Ill., Tenn. Hosp. Assn., Chicago Editors' Assn. (pres.), Dept. of Superintendence N.E.A., Rotary Internat., Delta Chi. Democrat. Catholic. Club: Cornell. Author: What the Hospital Trustee Should Know. Home: Chicago, Ill. †

MCNARY, WILLIAM SELWYN, cons.; b. Wilkinsburg, Pa., Feb. 4, 1904; s. William Oscar and Martha (Chalfant) McN.; B.B.A., U. Colo., 1926; m. Marion Holly Delzell, Aug. 15, 1929; children—William D., Sidney (Mrs. Harlan D. Roedel). Bus. mgr. U. Colo. Sch. Medicine and Hosps., Denver, 1929-38; exec. dir. Colo Hosp. Service (Blue Cross), Denver, 1938-47, Colo Med. Service (Blue Shield), 1942-47; exec. v.p. Mich. Hosp. Service (Blue Cross), Detroit, 1947-62, pres., 1962-69, cons., from 1969; chmn. bd., pres. Health Service, Inc., Chgo., 1952-66; gov., mem. exec. com. Blue Cross Assn., 1956-65, gov., chmn. exec. com., 1966-69; exec. dir. Greater Detroit Area Hosp. Council, 1969-71, comprehensive Health Planning of S.E. Mich., 1971. Mem. Gov.'s Adv. Council on Comprehensive Health Care Planning, 1968-73; spl. cons. on prepayment programs Australian Minister for Health, 1953; mem. profl. adv. com. Detroit Mayor's Com. to Study Med. Care of Indigent and Medically Indigent and Hosp. Emergency Service, 1969-70; mem. Mayor's Health Care Adv. Commn., 1970, Mich. Hosp. Finance Authority, 1972; mem. health ins. benefits adv. council to sec. HEW, 1971-74. Trustee, mem. exec. com. Mich. Health Council, 1954, pres., 1962. Recipient Outstanding Alumnus award U. Colo. Bus. Sch., 1955, Justin Ford Kimball award Am. Hosp. Assn., 1963; Tri State Hosp. Assn. award, 1964; George Norlin Achievement award U. Colo., 1969. Fellow Am. Coll. Hosp. Adminstrs. (hon.); mem. Greater Detroit Area Hosp. Council (dir., exec. com.), Am. Hosp. Assn. (life mem.), Blue Cross Commn. chmn. 1951-53), Colo. (past pres.), Midwest (past pres.) hosp. assns., Mich. Assn. for Regional Med. Programs (regional adv. group, dir. 1970-71), Phi Delta Theta, Delta Sigma Pi. Republican. Rotarian. Clubs: Detroit Athletic, Detroit Economic; Orchard Lake (Mich.) Country; Palmbrook (Ariz); Gyro. Home: Sun City, Ariz. Died Nov. 3, 1982; buried Sun City, Ariz.†

MC NEIL, GOMER THOMAS, engineer; b. Kingston, Pa., Nov. 27, 1917; s. Roy Leslie and Elizabeth (Thomas) McN.; B.Civil Engring., Syracuse U., 1939; m. Myrtie Mae Erwin, Sept. 28, 1940; children—Myrtie Mae (Mrs. James B. Cummins), Dianne Leslie (Mrs. R. Wayne Loekle). Staff asst. Bell Aircraft Corp., 1943-44; civil engr. TVA, 1946-48; head photogrammetry dept. U.S. Naval Photog. Interpretation Center, 1948-52; pres. Photogrammetry, Inc., Rockville, Md., 1952-69, Photogrammetry div. Data Corp., Rockville, 1969-72, Mitchell Photogrammetry, Inc., Rockville, 1972, McNeil Engring., 1953-85; Mass. Inst. Tech. cons. to Navy Deep Submergence, 1973, 74, Naval Photog. Center for underwater optical imaging systems, 1974-85. Served with USNR, 1944-46. Registered profl. engr., Md., D.C. Mem. Am. Soc. Photogrammetry (pres. 1965; Talbert Abrams award 1969, Fairchild Photogrammetric award 1971; hon. mem. award 1975), Nat. Soc. Profl. Engrs., Soc. Photo-Optical Instrumentation Engrs., Soc. Photog. Scientists and Engrs., Explorers Club. Lodge: Mason (32 deg.). Author: Photographic Measurements, 1953; Optical Fundamentals of Underwater Photography, 1968, Underwater Photography Handbook for U.S. Navy, 1983, also articles. Patentee in field. Home: Bethesda, Md. Died Feb. 23, 1985; interred Gate of Heaven Cemetery, Silver Spring, Md.

MC NEIL, HENRY SLACK, pharmaceutical company executive; b. Phila., Apr. 22, 1917; s. Robert Lincoln and Grace F. (Slack) McN.; m. Lois A. Fernley, Oct, 4, 1941; children—Henry Slack, Barbara Joan McNeil Jordan, Marjorie Fernley McNeil Findlay, Robert Douglas. B.Sc., Yale U., 1939; LL.D. (hon.), Phila. Coll. Pharmacy and Sci. Dir. McNeil Labs., Inc., Phila., 1940-79, pres., 1955-60; pres., dir. McNeil Labs. (Can.) Ltd., Toronto, 1956-61; v.p., dir. Johnson & Johnson, 1959-77; chmn. bd. Penguin Industries, Inc., Claneil Enterprises, Inc.; pres. Claneil Found., Inc.; partner Bluebell Assocs.; dir. South Eleuthera Properties, Remington Rand Corp. Mem. Nat. Multiple Sclerosis Adv. Council; mem. fine arts com., chmn. fin. com. Dept. State Diplomatic Reception Rooms; mem. adv. council BIPAC; mem. Nat. council Boy Scouts Am.; trustee Pa. Acad. Fine Arts, pres., 1977-80, recipient Gold medal; mem. Yale Devel. Bd.; trustee Nat. Trust for Hist. Preservation, Henry Francis du Pont Winterthur Mus.; asso. trustee U. Pa., 1972-78; mem. Pa. Council on Arts; mem. adv. com. Gov.'s Mansion, Pa.; mem. council Am. Mus. in Britain. Mem. St. Andrew's Soc. Phila., Hist. Soc. Phila., Am. Pharm. Assn. (life), Clan Macneil Assn. Am. (pres. 1962-72), Newcomen Soc. N.Am., Confrerie des Chevaliers du Tastevin, Omicron Delta Kappa (hon.). Clubs: Racquet (Phila.), Yale (Phila.), Philadelphia (Phila.), Sunnybrook (Phila.), Union League (Phila.), Aviation Country (Phila.), Corinthian Yacht (Phila.); St. Elmo (New Haven); Met. (N.Y.C.); Met. (Washington), Capitol Hill (Washington); Wilmington (Del.); Royal Danish Yacht (Copenhagen). Home: Plymouth Meeting, Pa. Dec. 1983.

MC NEIL, NEIL VENABLE, educator; b. Houston, Oct. 24, 1927; s. Marshall and Blanche (Venable) McN.; m. Doris Rounder Matthews, Sept. 9, 1950; children—Jenny, Pitt Taylor Nieman. Student, U. Tex., 1945; A.B. with distinction, George Washington U., 1948; postgrad., Columbia U., 1948-49; M.A., Northwestern U., 1965. Reporter El Paso (Tex.) Herald-Post, 1949-52; reporter, desk man Washington Daily News, 1952-56; Washington corr. El Paso Herald-Post, Houston Press, Ft. Worth Press (Scripps Howard Newspapers), 1956-61; instr. Medill Sch. Journalism, Northwestern U., Evanston, Ill., 1961-62, asst. prof., 1962-68, asso. prof., 1968-81; founder, dir. Medill News Service, 1966-81. Author articles, revs. Nieman fellow, 1959-60. Mem. Nat. Assn. Profl. Bureaucrats (v.p., acad. chmn.), Am. Acad. Polit. and Social Sci., Nat. Aero. Assn., AAUP, Assn. Edn. in Journalism, Phi Beta Kappa. Clubs: Nat. Press, Harvard; Nat. Liberal (London). Home: Washington, DC.

MCNEILL, WINFIELD IRVING, management cons.; b. Wakefield, Mass., Nov. 21, 1890; s. Henry and Helen (Wilder) McN.; B.S., Mass. Inst. Tech., 1917; m. Carolena Nelson, Oct. 9, 1918; 1 dau., Ruth Carolyn (Mrs. E. B. Knauft). Accounting supervisor Procter & Gamble Mfg. Co., Cin., 1922-27; asst. to v.p. Colgate-Palmolive Peet Co., Jersey City, 1927-43; v.p., controller Gen. Aniline & Film Corp., N.Y.C., 1943-53; management cons. from 1953. Mem. controller's Inst., Nat. Assn. Cost Accts. Clubs: Mass. Inst. Tech. (past treas. N.Y. chpt., past pres., sec. N.J., past sec. Chgo.); University (N.Y. City). Contbr. articles profl. publs. Home: Summit, N.J.

MC NICHOLAS, JOSEPH ALPHONSUS, bishop; b. St. Louis, Jan. 13, 1923; s. Joseph Alphonsus and Mary Blanche (Tallon) McN.; B.A., Cardinal Glennon Coll., St. Louis, 1945; student Kenrick Theol. Sem., St. Louis, 1949; M.A. in Social Work, St. Louis U., 1957. Ordained priest Roman Cath. Ch., 1949, consecrated bishop, 1969; parish priest, St. Louis, 1949-69; sec. Cath. Charities, St. Louis, 1957-75; Roman Cath. chaplain St. Louis Juvenile Ct., 1957-70; aux. bishop Archdiocese St. Louis, 1969-75; bishop of Springfield, Ill., 1975-83. Vice chmn. Human Devel. Corp. Met. St. Louis, 1967-75. Named Mo. Citizen of Year, Mo. Assn. Social Welfare, 1968. Mem. Acad. Certified Social Workers, Nat. Assn. Social Workers, Child Welfare League Am. (v.p.).

MCPHEETERS, JULIAN C., pres. Asbury Theol. Sem.; b. Oxley, Mo., July 6, 1889; s. William Garland and Edna (Greer) McP.; Ph.B., Marvin Coll., Fredricktown, Mo.,

1909; student Meridian Male Coll., Miss., 1910-11, Southern Meth. U., Dallas, Tex., 1916; D.D., Asbury Coll., 1931; LL.D., John Brown U., 1940; m. Ethel Chilton, Jan. 28, 1914; children—Chilton Claudius, Virginia Wave. Student pastor, Oran, Mo., 1909; evangelist for 5 yrs.; pastor Meth. chs. in Mo., Mont., Ariz., and Calif.; pastor Glide Memorial Meth. Church, 1930-48; pres. Asbury Theol. Sem. from 1942; v.p. Glide Foundation. Mem. Calif. Temperance Fedn. (ex-pres.), Evang. Fellowship (mem. bd. dirs.; ex-pres.), Calif. Ch. Council (ex-pres. Northern Area). Democrat. Editor of Pentecostal Herald, Louisville, Ky. Author: Sons of God, 1929; Sunshine and Victory, 1931; Life Story of Lizzie II. Glide, 1936; The Power That Prevails, 1938; Religious Trends of ToDay, 1938; Faith for Men in Arms, 1943. Home: San Francisco. †

MCQUILLIN, RAYMOND E(UGENE), army officer; b. Britton, S.D., Dec. 24, 1887; s. Edward and Jennie (Peckins) McQ.; B.S. in Elec. Engring., U. of Minn., 1911; grad. student Yale (Sheffield), 1919-1920; grad. Cav. Sch., 1923; honor graduate, Command and Gen. Staff Sch., 1925; graduate Army War Coll., 1931; married Marion S. Webster, August 23, 1947. Commissioned second lt. U.S.; Cav., 1912; advanced through grades to brig. gen., 1942; served on Mexican border, 1912-16; Hawaii (cav.), 1917-18; Signal Corps, 1918-21; mil. aide at White House, 1927-31; Gen. Staff duty, 1934-36; instr., Command and Gen. Staff Sch., 1936-40; with 1st Armored Div., N. African Campaign; Insp. Gen. Fifth Army, 1946-47; ret. Decorations: Silver Star, Officer's Cross Polonia Restituta; Medal of Military Merit, 1st class (Mexican). Mem. Sigma Chi. Clubs: Army and Navy, Marine Corps. Home: Creve Coeur, Mo. Deceased.

MCQUISTON, IRVING MATTHEW, naval officer; born Waltham, Mass., June 27, 1895; s. James and Catherine (Havey) McQ.; student Allen Sch. Boys, 1915; Mass. Inst. Tech. Naval Aviation Sch., 1917-18; m. Fay Emerson, Sept 27, 1935; 1 son, Robert Emerson. Vice pres., gen. mgr. Alfred Hale Rubber Co., Quincy, Mass., 1918-22; gen. supt. Cotton Mill, Boston, 1922-29; Served as lt. (j.g.), U.S.N., 1917-18; naval aviator U.S.N. from 1929; mem. naval res., 1919-29; active naval service from 1929, rank of rear admiral, 1942; dir. aviation progress, Navy Dept. 1943-46; adv.-coordinator to chief naval operations for Naval Reserve Program, 1946-50. Vice chmn. Reserve Forces Policy Bd., Office Sec. of Defense. Mem. Am. Society Naval Engineers, Naval Order of U.S. Died Apr. 10, 1984.

MC QUOWN, O. RUTH, educator; b. Lexington, Ky., July 28, 1920; d. Elam Boles and Omega (Smith) McQ. B.A., U. Ky., 1942; M.A. (Hagin fellow), 1951; M.A. Fulbright scholar, Manchester (Eng.) U., 1954-55; Ph.D. (Arts and Scis. fellow 1958-59, So. Fellowship Fund fellow 1959-60), U. Fla., 1961. Legis planning analyst Dept. Agr., Washington, 1943-45; economist OPA, 1945-48; instr., research asso. polit. sci. U. Ky., 1948-61; asst. prof. U. Fla., Gainesville, 1961-65, asso. prof., 1965-74, prof., 1974-84; asst. dean U. Fla. (Coll. Arts and Scis.), 1971-76, assoc. dean, 1976-84; cons. Legis. Research Com. State Ky., 1948-50; gov. Ky., Emergency Orgn. State Govt., 1957-58; vice chancellor SUNY, 1970, Conservation Found., 1972-73; vis. evaluator for accrediting of Boston U., New Eng. Assn. Schs. and Colls., 1979. Author: (with J. B. Shannon) Presidential Politics in Kentucky, 1953, (with J. E. Reeves) Legislative and Congressional Redistricting in Kentucky, 1959, (with G. Kammerer) The City Consultant, 1959, (with W. Hamilton and M. Schneider) The Political Restructuring of a Community, 1964, (with C. Feiss) A Study of the Social, Political and Administrative Setting of the Rookery Bay Ecosystem, 1973; contbr. (with C. Feiss) articles to profl. jours. Dept. Agr. grantee, 1962-63; Social Sci. Research Council grantee, 1965-66. Fellow AAUW; mem. Am. Polit. Sci. Assn., So. Polit. Sci. Assn. (sec.), Phi Beta Kappa, Phi Kappa Phi. Democrat. Episcopalian. Home: Gainesville, Fla. Died Aug. 22, 1984; buried Gainesville.

MCRAE, FLOYD WILLCOX, physician, surgeon; b. Atlanta, Ga., Apr. 2, 1889; s. Floyd Willcox and Fannie (Collier) McR.; student Ga. Sch. of Tech. Atlanta, Ga., 1905, 06, 07; Ph.D., Yale, 1911; M.D., Johns Hopkins, 1915; m. Eleanor Deming Stout, Nov. 1, 1919; 1 son, Floyd Willcox. Interne Lakeside Hosp., Cleveland, O., 1915-16; in practice of medicine, Atlanta, Ga., from 1919. Served as lt. then major, A.E.F. adj., surgeon, Comdg. officer Base Hosp. 116, advance sector, France, Apr. 1917-Sept. 1919. Chmn. bd. dir. Piedmont Hosp., Atlanta. Dir. Boy Scouts. Mem. A.M.A., Fulton County Med. Soc., Southern Med. Assn., Southern Surg. Assn., Southern Soc. Clin. Surgeons, Eastern Surg. Soc., Chi Phi, Alpha Kappa Kappa. Clubs: Piedmont Driving, Atlanta Athletic. Home: Atlanta, Ga. †

MCRUER, JAMES CHALMERS, chief justice; b. Oxford County, Ontario, Can., Aug. 23, 1890; s. John and Mary (Chalmers) Mc.; student U. of Toronto, 1907-08; student Law Sch. of Law Soc. of Upper Canada, Osgoode Hall, Toronto, Ont., 1910-13; LL.D., Laval University, 1947, University of Toronto, 1962; m. Mary R. Dow, Sept. 27, 1919, children—Mary Louise (wife of Dr. John R. Gaby), Katherine R. (wife of Dr. Alex McIntyre), John Dow. Barister and solicitor, 1914-44; assistant crown attorney for City of Toronto and County of York, 1921-25; created Kings Counsel, 1929; lecturer in law school, Osgoode Hall, 1930-35; elected Bencher of the Law Society, Upper Canada, 1936; chmn. Legal Edn. Com., 1944; justice, Court of Appeal of Supreme Court of Ontario, 1944, chief justice, High Ct. of Justice, Ontario, 1945; president Canadian Bar Assn., 1946-47; mem. Royal Commn. Investigating the Penal System of Can., 1937-38; chairman of Royal Commission on defense of insanity in criminal cases; chairman Royal Commission on the law relating to sexual offenders. Member of the bar of British Columbia and Alberta; honorary member American Bar Assn. Served as lieutenant Canadian Artillery, overseas, World War I, 1916-19. Author: Evolution of the Judicial Process. †

MCSHANE, RALPH E(DWARD), naval officer; born Baltimore, Feb. 4, 1899; s. James Francis and Nettie May (Brannan) McS.; B.S., U.S. Naval Acad., 1920; M.S., Mass. Inst. Tech., 1924; m. Ruth Elizabeth Johnson, Aug. 18, 1927. Commd. ensign U.S. Navy, 1920, and advanced through grades to rear admiral, 1950; trans. to constrn. corps. 1924; duty in naval indsl. and allied activities, 1924-43; service E.T.O. (Normandy invasion), 1943-44, planning and occupation, Germany, 1944-45; comdr. Portsmouth Naval Shipyard, also dir. planning, Bur. of Ships, Washington, from 1945. Mem. Soc. Naval Architects and Marine Engrs., Am. Soc. Naval Engrs., Delta Kappa Epsilon. Club: Army-Navy (Washington). Died May 3, 1982.

MCWHORTER, ROGER BARTON, cons. engineer; b. Riverton, Ala., July 31, 1888; s. George Tilghman (M.D.) and Mary Susan (Terry) McW.; B.S. in Civil Engring., Ala. Poly. Inst., 1909, C.E., 1913; m. Katherine Beaufort Tweedy, Oct. 25, 1916 (died 1936); 1 son, Robert Tweedy; m. 2d, Anne Lane Martin, Feb. 19, 1947. Rodman and inspector, Tenn. River improvements, Colbert Shoals Canal, 1908; with Corps of Engineers on construction Hales Bar Dam (Tenn.) surveys of Tenn. River, and Muscle Shoals (Ala.) investigations, 1909-16; asst. engr. and div. engr. Miami Conservancy Dist., Dayton and Hamilton, O., 1916-23; gen. supt. construction Wilson Dam hydroelectric development, Muscle Shoals, 1923-25; U.S. engr. St. Lawrence Waterway Project, 1925-26; cons. engr. Orleans Levee Dist., New Orleans and Washington, D.C., 1926-28; prin. Corps of Engineers on Mississippi River flood control work, New Orleans, 1928-30; prin. engr. Great Lakes Div., U.S. Engr. Dept., 1930-31; chief engr. Federal Power Commn. from 1931. Mem. Internat. Joint Commn., United States and Canada, from 1939, acting chairman United States sect., 1944; mem. Bonneville adv. bd., 1938-46; mem. Internat. Com. of engrs. in charge of constrn. of submerged weir in Niagara River above Niagara Falls, 1942-46. Lt. col. Engineer Reserves, U.S. Army. Mem. Am. Society C.E., Society Am. Mil. Engrs., Washington Engring. Soc. Club: Cosmos. Home: Decatur, Ala. †

MC WILLIAMS, CAREY, writer; b. Steamboat Springs, Colo., Dec. 13, 1905; s. Jerry and Harriet (Casley) McW.; LL.B., U. So. Calif., 1927; m. Iris Dornfeld, Sept. 10, 1941; children—Wilson Carey, Jerry Ross. Admitted to Calif. bar, 1927, practiced in Los Angeles, 1927-38, mem. firm Black, Hammack & McWilliams; commr. immigration and housing State of Calif., 1938-42; contbg. editor The Nation, N.Y.C., 1945-51, assoc. editor, 1951-52, editorial dir., 1952-55, editor, 1955-75. Author: Ambrose Bierce: a Biography, 1929; Factories in the Field, 1939; Ill Fares the Land, 1942; Brothers Under the Skin, 1943; Prejudice, 1944; Southern California Country: An Island on the Land, 1946; A Mask for Privilege: Anti-Semitism in America, 1948; North from Mexico: The Spanish-Speaking People of the United States, 1949; California: The Great Exception, 1949: Witchhunt: The Revival of Heresy, 1950. Editor: The California Revolution, 1968; The Education of Carey McWilliams, 1979; contbr. to Dictionary of Am. Biography, numerous mags. Home: New York, N.Y. Died June 27, 1980.

MEACHAM, EDGAR D., coll. dean; b. Smithfield, Tex., Aug. 22, 1887; s. George Allison and Roxanna Josephine (Smith) M.; student S.W. State Teachers Coll., Weatherford, Okla., 1907-10; A.B., U. of Okla., 1914; A.M., Harvard, 1917; Ph.D., U. of Chicago, 1922, sr. fellow, 1931-32; m. Ray Ferrell, Dec. 3, 1910; children—John Ferrell, Martha Rae. Instr. in mathematics, U. of Okla., 1914, asst., 1919, asso. prof., 1922, prof. 1926, asst. dean Coll. of Arts and Sciences, 1926, dean 1910. Trustee Okla. Memorial Union Bldg. (mem. bd. mgrs.). Mem. Am. Math. Soc., Phi Beta Kappa, Sigma Xi, Sigma Delta Chi, Phi Eta Sigma, Pi Mu Epsilon, Kappa Sigma. Club: Lions (Norman, Okla.). Home: Norman, Okla. †

MEAD, FRANK SPENCER, author; b. Chatham, N.J., Jan. 15, 1898; s. Frank and Lillie (Spencer) M.; m. Judy Duryee, Oct. 24, 1927; children—Donald Duryee, Judy Spencer. A.B., U. Denver, 1922; student, Episcopal Theol. Sem., Va., 1922-23; M.Div., Union Theol. Sem., 1927; Litt.D., Dickinson Coll., 1948. Sec. 23d St. YMCA, N.Y.C., 1923-24; asst. pastor Reformed Ch., Harlem, N.Y., 1925-27; pastor Grace M.E. Ch., Newark, N.J., 1927-31, Kearny (N.J.) Ch., 1931-34; editor Homiletic Rev., 1934; exec. editor Christian Herald, 1942-48; editor-in-chief Fleming H. Revell Co., 1949-82. Author: The March of Eleven Men, 1932, 250 Bible Biographies, 1934, See These Banners Go, 1935, The Ten Decisive Battles of Christianity, 1937, Right Here at Home, 1939, The Handbook of Denominations, 1952 (rev. and pub. every 5 years), Rebels With A Cause, 1964, An Encyclopedia of Religious Quotations, 1965, (with Dale Evans Rogers) Let Freedom Ring, 1975, Hear the Children Crying, 1978, Talking With God, 1976; Editor: (with Dale Evans Rogers) Tarbell's Teacher's Guide. Served in U.S. Army, 1917-18. Mem. Phi Beta Kappa, Beta Theta Pi. Home: Nutley, N.J. Dec. June 16, 1982.

MEADE, RICHARD ANDREW, educator; b. Sutherland, Va., Dec. 13, 1911; s. John Andrew and Cora (Spain) M.; m. Mildred Broocks Lipscomb, June 9, 1937; children—Betsy Barrington, Andrew Lipscomb. A.B., Randolph-Macon Coll., 1931; M.A., U. Va., 1936, Ph.D., 1941; postgrad., U. Chgo., summers 1935, 39. Tchr. English Greensville County High Sch., Emporia, Va., 1931-34; tchr. English Lane High Sch., Charlottesville, Va.; asst. prof. secondary edn. and teaching of English U. Va., 1934-50, asso. prof. edn., Charlottesville, 1950-57, prof. edn., from 1957, chmn. curriculum and instrn. dept., 1967-71; cons. Va. Dept. Edn. Chmn. Charlottesville sch. Bd., 1962-63. Author: Better English, 1945, Effective English, 1961, Fifth-Year and Five-Year Programs for the Education of Teachers of English, 1965, Literature for Adolescents: Selection and Use, 1973; Contbr. to: National Interest and the Teaching of English, 1961, Ends and Issues, 1966; Contbr. articles to profl. jours. Recipient Distinguished Achievement award Alpha Beta chpt. Phi Delta Kappa, 1947; Outstanding Prof. award Sch. Edn., U. Va., 1980. Mem. Nat. Council Tchrs. English (past mem. commn. on English curriculum), Conf. on English Edn. (past mem. exec. com.), Va. Assn. Tchrs. English (mem. exec. com., Disting. Service award 1980), Phi Beta Kappa, Phi Delta Kappa, Omicron Delta Kappa, Tau Kappa Alpha, Sigma Phi Epsilon. Clubs: Colonnade (U. Va.); Greencroft Country (Charlottesville). Home: Charlottesville, VA.

MEADER, GEORGE FARNHAM, opera singer; b. Minneapolis, Minn., July 6, 1888; s. William Francis and Jane Birdsal (Stephens) M.; student U. of Minn., 1904-08, LL.B., 1908; m. Maria Karrer, of Stuttgart, Germany, Aug. 22, 1914; 1 dau., Jane Helene Marianne. Debut as Lionel, in "Martha," Civic Opera House, Leipzig, 1910; joined Metropolitan Opera Co., 1920; principal rôles: Ferrando in "Cosi Fan Tutte"; David in "Meistersinger"; Max, in "Freischütz"; Mime, in "Siegfried"; Almaviva, in "Barbe 4500 eville." Mem. Phi Kappa Psi, Phi Delta Phi. Republican. Episcopalian.†

MEAKER, SAMUEL RAYNOR, gynecologist; b. Carbondale, Pa., Nov. 14, 1890; s. Cyrus Truman and Frances Sayre (Raynor) M.; A.B., Princeton, 1911; M.D., Harvard, 1915; A.M., Boston U., 1937; m. Kathleen Edda Ford, April 4, 1918; children—Lawton Stephen Ford, Alan Francis (dec.), Samuel Raynor. Interne Boston City Hosp., 1915-16; practicing physician, specialist in obstetrics and gynecology from 1919; instr., asst. prof., later asso. prof. of gynecology, Boston U. Sch. of Medicine, 1922-30, prof. since 1930; staff gynecologist Mass. Memorial Hosps. from 1922. Served with Royal Army Med. Corps, 1916-19. Fellow Am. Coll. of Surgeons, Am. Med. Assn., Royal Coll. of Obstetricians and Gynecologists; mem. Royal Coll. of Surgeons, British Med. Assn., Alpha Kappa Kappa. Republican. Presbyn. Club: Harvard (Boston). Author: Mother and Unborn Child, 1927; Human Sterility, 1934. Contbr. to med. jours. Home: Wellesley, Mass. †

MEANS, LEWIS M., army officer; b. Camden County, Mo., July 15, 1890; s. Andrew C. and Rebecca Ann (Holder) M.; ed. Central Coll., Fayette, Mo.; m. Evangeline Boggs, Aug. 19, 1917; children—Mrs. Frank D. Waddell and Mrs. Philip N. Jones. Asst. in orgn. of Mo. State Highway Patrol, 1931, served as troop comdr. and exec. officer with rank of maj. until 1937; apptd. adj. gen. Mo. N.G., 1937-41; resigned for active duty World War II. Commd. 2d lt. Inf., 1917, 1st lt., 1918; served with 89th and 18th Divs.; commd. capt., O.R.C., Inf., 1922, maj., 1924; brig. gen., A.G.D. 1937, brig. gen. of the line, 1938; fed. service 1940 as comdg. gen. 70th Inf. Brigade, 35th Inf. Div.; assigned to organize anti-sabotage activities in N. Calif. sect. under 7th Army Corps, 1941; organized, commander Northern Defense Area, 1942; provost marshall at Presidio at San Francisco and Ft. Douglas, Utah until 1944; dir. security U.N. conf., San Francisco, 1945, also mem. U.S. secretariat; May 26, 1946. Decorations: World Wars I and II medals, Am. Theatre, Pre-Pearl Harbor, Asiatic Theatre, Army Commendation Ribbon, Legion of Merit. Mem. Officers Assn., Hon. Order of Ky. Cols., C.A.A. Mason. Club: Rotary. Home: Fayette, Mo. †

MEARSON, LYON, writer; b. Montreal, Can., Dec. 6, 1888; s. Joseph and Ethel (Marks) M.; came to U.S. with parents, 1893; student DeWitt Clinton High Sch., N.Y. City; student New York Law Sch., 1909; m. Rose Mary Cone. Art critic N.Y. Evening Mail, 1914-15; theatrical mgr., 1916; editor for Street & Smith, 1916-17; editor Metropolitan Mag., 1923-26; was acting editor, International Digest. Enlisted in 8th C.D., New York, at outbreak of World War I; served 17 months in heavy artillery. Author: (novels) The Whisper on the Stair, 1924; Footsteps in the Dark, 1927; Phantom Fingers, 1928; (plays) The French They Are a Funny Race, 1931. Co-author: (plays) People Don't Do Such Things, 1927; Our Wife, 1933; Love Costs Money, 1933; Murder by Appointment, 1936; The Vulture in the Parlor, 1947; Class Reunion, 1948. Contbr. numerous short stories and verse to national magazines. Home: New York, N.Y. †

MECKLENBURGER, ALBERT F., lawyer; b. Okolona, Miss., Apr. 2, 1888; s. Marcus and Dora (Feibelman) M.; B.S., U. Miss., 1907; J.D., U. Chgo., 1911; m. Josephine Pollak, June 2, 1917; children—Jerome Walter, Martha Dora, Alvin F. Admitted to Ill. bar, 1911; asso. Jones, Addington, Ames & Seibold, specializing patents, trademarks, copyrights, unfair competition, 1911-19, mem. firm 1919-37; mem. firm. Ames, Thiess, Olson & Mecklenburger, 1937-39, 1940-52, Thiess, Olson, Mecklenburger, von Holstand. Mem. Nat. Coltman from 1953, Fedn. Temple Brotherhoods (pres. 1939-41), Am., Ill. State, Chgo. bar assns., Patent Law Assn. Chgo., Union Am. Hebrew Congs. (exec. bd.), Delta Sigma Rho. Jewish religion. Mason, B'nai B'rith. Clubs: Standard, Northmoor Country. Home: Highland Park, Ill. †

MECKSTROTH, JACOB ADOLF, editor; b. New Knoxville, Ohio, May 28, 1887; s. Charles Adolf and Anna (Lammers) M.; A.B., Ohio State U., 1912; m. Adeline Hoelseher, Sept. 7, 1915; children—Gretchen (Mrs. R. H. Angerman), Rachel. (Mrs. G.R. Hoeflinger), Charles Victor, Jacob (deceased), Teacher public schools, New Knoxville, 1906-08; reporter Dayton Journal and Canton Repository, 1912-13; reporter and political writer Ohio State Journal, 1913-23; private secretary to Governor Vic Donahey of Ohio, 1923-29; editor Ohio State Jour., after 1929. Mem. O. Sesquicentennial Commn.; trustee Dennison University Research Found.; president, bd. trustees Columbus Pub. Library; vice chmn. James W. Faulkner Meml. Fund. Mem. Ohio Hist. Soc. (trustee), Sigma Delta Chi. Mem. Evangelical and Reformed Ch. of U.S. Home: Columbus, Ohio. Deceased.

MECOM, JOHN WHITFIELD, independent oil porducer; b. El Paso, Tex., Jan. 13, 1911; s. Harvey Mercer and Louise (Elam) M.; student Rice U., 1927, student U. Okla., 1928-31; m. Mary Elizabeth Withers, May 14, 1937; children—John Whitfield, Betsy, Lannie. Propr. John W. Mecom. ind. oil producer, Houston, 1938-81; owner Cardwell Mfg. Co., Wichita, Kan. 1954-81, U.S. Oil of La., Houston and New Orleans, 1954-81, Boonton Pastie Co. (N.J.). 1954-81, Gran Hotel, Bolivar, Lima, Peru, 1961-81, Warwick Hotel, Houston, 1962-81, Keystone Drug Co., Houston, 1960-81, Maple Room Restaurant, Houston, 1960-81, part owner Reed Roller Bit Co., Houston, 1961-81; dir. Nat. Bank Commerce, Houston. Gov. adviser Rice U. Mem. Sigma Alpha Epsilon. Democrat. Episcopalian. Clubs: Houston Country, River Oaks Country. Ramada (Houston); Boston (New Orleans). Home: Houston, Tex. Died Oct. 12, 1981.*

MECOM, PHILIP HENRY, lawyer; b. Arcadia, Bienville Parish, La., May 13, 1889; s. William Hardy and Caroline Arledge M.; student La. State Univ., 1904-05; m. Virginia Pullen, Oct. 3, 1916 (divorced, 1935); 1 son, Philip Henry; remarried Mrs. Minnie Brown Sherman of Haynesville, Louisiana, Nov. 3, 1944. Deputy clerk District Court, Columbia, La., 1913-15, same, and clerk Local Board, 1917-19; studied law while serving as minute clerk of court at Columbia and under private tutors in law offices in new Orleans and Columbia; admitted to bar in 1919; assistant U.S. attorney, Western. Dist. of La., Shreveport, La., 1921-22; U.S. atty., same dist., 1922-36; clerk, U.S. Dist. Court, Western Dist., La., from July 1, 1941. Mem. Am., La. and Shreveport bar assns., La. Hist. Soc. Chmn. Rep. State Central Com., 1936-41; alternate del. Rep. Nat. Conv., 1924, del., 1928 and 1932. Chmn. legal adv. bd. Local Bd. No. 2, Caddo Parish, La. Episcopalian. Club: Shreveport Golf and Country (Shreveport). Home: Shreveport. †

MEDEIROS, HUMBERTO SOUSA, archbishop; b. Arrifes, São Miquel, Azores, Oct. 6, 1915; came to U.S., 1931, naturalized, 1940; s. Antonio Sousa and Maria de Jesus Sousa Massa (Flor) M. M.A., Catholic U. Am., 1942, S.T.L., 1946, S.T.D., 1952; LL.D., Stonehill Coll., Mass., 1959. Ordained priest Roman Catholic Ch., 1946; asst. St. John of God Parish, Somerset, Mass., 1946, St. Michael's Parish, Fall River, Mass., 1946-47, Our Lady of Health Parish, Fall River, 1947, St. Vincent de Paul Health Camp, 1948-49, Mt. Carmel Ch., New Bedford, Mass., 1949; research N.Am. Coll., Rome, 1949-50; asst. Holy Name Ch., Fall River, 1950-51; sec., asst. chancellor, chaplain Sacred Hearts Acad. and Vicar for Religious, 1951-53; vice-chancellor, chancellor Fall River (Mass.) Diocese, 1953-66; named domestic prelate, 1958; pastor St. Michael's Parish, 1960-66; consecrated bishop, 1966; bishop Diocese Brownsville, Tex., 1966-70; archbishop archdiocese Boston, 1970-73, elevated to cardinal, 1973. Mem. U.S. Cath. Conf., Nat. Conf. Cath. Bishops. Address: Brighton, Mass. *

MEDINA, WILLIAM A., govt. ofcl.; b. Washington, Oct. 28, 1935; B.A., M.A., George Washington U.; Ph.D., Am. U., 1976. With C.E., 1960; staff personnel office NASA; with CSC, 1963-71; chief exec. devel. and tng. Office of Mgmt. and Budget. Washington, to 1977; asst. sec. for adminstrn. HUD, 1977-81; mem. faculty Willamette U., Salem, Oreg. Trustee Nat. Acad. Pub. Adminstrn., United Black Fund. Mem. Am. Soc. Pub. Adminstrn. (pres. Nat. Capital Area chpt.; nat. council), Fed. Exec. Inst. Alumni Assn. (treas., pres.). Founder, asso. editor Bureaucrat. Address: Portland, Ore. Died July 28, 1985.

MEEK, HARRY E., lawyer; b. Camden, Ark., Dec. 10, 1890; ed. Washington and Lee U.; LL.B., U. Ark., 1914. Admitted to Ark. bar, 1916; mem. firm Rose, Barron, Nash, Carroll & Clay, Little Rock. Recipient Ark. Outstanding Lawyer award, 1962. Mem. Am., Ark., Pulaski County (pres. 1940) bar assns.†

MEEK, JOSEPH HENRY, state market exec.; b. Rural Retreat, Va., Feb. 22, 1890; s. Charles J. and Mollie E. (Buck) M.; A.B., Roanoke Coll., 1912; grad. student U. of Wis., 1916; m. Mary W. Biscoe, Sept. 11, 1926. Prin. high sch., Stephens City, Va., 1912-13, Dinwiddie, Va., 1913-17; agrl. agt. Pulaski Co., Va., 1917-20; dir. div. markets Va. Dept. Agr. after 1920. Prin. organizer Va. Food Council, 1947; chmn., instigator, com. for trading on basis weight instead measure. Nat. Conf. Weights and Measures, 1941; leader in establishing standards and providing ofcl. inspections on foods and farm products. Mem. Nat. Assn. Marketing Ofcls., (pres. 1950-51), Mayflower Soc. Va., Gideons (past pres. Va.). Baptist. Home: Richmond, Va. Deceased.

MEEK, SAMUEL WILLIAMS, bus. exec.; b. Nashville, Sept. 22, 1895; S. Samuel W. and Williea (Pierce) M.; m. Priscilla Mitchel, Oct. 14, 1921; children—Elizabeth, Samuel, Priscilla, Susan. Student, Phillips Exeter Academy, 1913; A.B., Yale, 1917. With J. Walter Thompson Co., 1925-63; vice chmn., dir.; chmn. bd. Walker Pub. Co., 1962-81; pres., dir., pub. Rome Daily Am., Italy, 1964-69; dir. Time, Inc., 1922-70, adv. dir., 1970-74; chmn. bd. Walker & Co., N.Y.C., 1975-81; dir. emeritus State Nat. Bank Ct.; dir. Greenwich Pub. Co.; former publisher Brussels Times, Brussels, Belgium; dir., treas. Episcopalian mag. Trustee Empire Savs. Bank, N.Y., 1932-68; bd. govs. Yale U. Press.; Nat. gov. A.R.C., 1959-65; hon. trustee Presbyn. Hosp., Am. Hosp., Paris; trustee Sch. Advanced Internat. Studies, Johns Hopkins; bd. dirs. Seabury House of P.E. Ch. in U.S., Episcopal Ch. Found.; mem. Yale Council and Yale devel. bd. Yale U.; former pres. bd. trustees Greenwich Country Day Sch. Served as capt. USMC, 1917-19; mem. Navy civilian adv. com., World War II. Decorated Croix de Guerre with palm, Silver Star, Purple Heart with oak leaf cluster.; Recipient of the Medal for Merit, Navy Distinguished Pub. Service award, World War II. Mem. English-Speaking Union (dir.), Atlantic Council (dir.), Am. Order St. John of Jerusalem (treas.). Republican. Episcopalian. Home: Greenwich, Conn. Died Aug. 15, 1981.

MEEM, JOHN GAW, architect; b. Pelotas, Brazil, Nov. 17, 1894; s. John Gaw and Elsa (Krischke) M.; m. Faith Bemis, May 20, 1933; 1 child, Nancy (Mrs. John Wirth). Sc.B., Va. Mil. Inst., 1914; M.A. hon, Colo. Coll., 1936; A.F.D. (hon.), U. N.Mex. Began practice, 1924, specializing in Spanish pueblo architecture, ret. from active practice. Designer: La Fonda Hotel and Anthropology Lab, Santa Fe; numerous bldgs., U. N.Mex., Albuquerque, Colorado Springs Fine Arts Center (Silver medal 5th Pan-Am. Congress Architects), 1st Presbyn. Ch, Santa Fe, Santa Fe County Ct. House Municipal Bldg, Mus. Internat. Folk Art, St. Vincent Hosp; cons. architect: St. John's Coll, Santa Fe. Served as capt. inf. World War I. Fellow Sch. Am. Research. Fellow AIA; assoc. mem. NAD. Episcopalian. Home: Santa Fe, N. Mex. Dec. Aug. 4, 1983.

MEESE, WILLIAM GILES, utility co. exec.; b. Rugby, N.D., Aug. 27, 1916; s. William Gottlieb and Emma (LaPierre) M.; m. Mary Edith Monk, Apr. 4, 1942; children—Elizabeth Ann, Stephen William, Richard Edward. B.S. in Elec. Engring, Purdue U., 1941, D.Eng. (hon.), 1972. Registered prof. engr., Mich. With Detroit Edison Co., from 1941, asst. v.p., 1967, v.p., 1967-69, exec. v.p. prodn., 1969-70, pres., 1970-75, chief exec. officer, 1971-81, chmn., chief exec. officer, 1975-81, now dir.; dir. Eaton Corp., Ex-Cell-O Corp., Mfrs. Nat. Bank Detroit, Mfrs. Nat Corp. Served to maj. F.A. AUS, 1941-45. Decorated Bronze Star medal; recipient Distinguished Alumnus award Purdue U., 1969; Internat. B'nai B'rith Humanitarian award, 1977. Fellow Engring. Soc. Detroit, IEEE; mem. Tau Beta Pi, Eta Kappa Nu. Home: Atlantis, Fla.

MEHEGAN, JOHN FRANCIS, jazz musician; b. Hartford, Conn., June 6, 1920; s. John James and Margaret (Egan) M.; m. Doris Crowley, Dec. 3, 1940 (div. July 1956); children—Carey, Gretchen; m. Terry Adelstein, Feb. 17, 1957 (div. 1961); m. Gay Griscom, June 27, 1961 (div. Nov. 1978); children—Tara, Sean, Eben. Student, Hartford Fed. Coll., 1937-38, Julius Hartt Music Sch., Hartford, 1938-39. Asst. to Teddy Wilson Met. Mus. Sch., N.Y.C., 1945-46, head jazz dept., 1946-56; instr. jazz Juilliard Sch. Music, 1947-64, Columbia Tchrs. Coll., 1958-62, U. Bridgeport, Conn., 1968-77; lectr. jazz Brandeis U. Art Festival, 1952, Union S. Africa, 1959, Music Educators Nat. Conf., Atlantic City, 1960, Yale U., 1974-84; jazz critic N.Y. Herald Tribune, 1957-60; founder Sch. Jazz, 1963; conducted Jazz Seminar Syracuse U., summer 1964; jazz clinics in, Denmark, Sweden and Norway, 1974, 75. European jazz tour sponsored by, State Dept., 1961, recs. for, Savoy, Perspective, Victor, T.J., Epic records.; Author: Jazz Improvisation, 1959, vol. II, 1960, vol. III, 1963, vol. IV, 1964, jazz study books for children, 1962; contbr.: articles to Saturday Rev. Address: Westport, Conn. Died Apr. 3, 1984.

MEHOS, CHARLES ARTHUR, consumer products company executive; b. Malden, Mass., Oct. 14, 1920; s. Arthur J. and Stella (Booras) M.; m. Rita Zoukee, May 10, 1959; children: Harris, Arthur, Stephen, Lia. B.A., Boston U., 1942; I.A., Harvard U., 1943. With Loomis-Sayles & Co., Boston, 1946-50; with Am. Brands, Inc., N.Y.C., 1950-85, treas., 1967, v.p., v.p. finance, 1973-79, exec. v.p., 1979-83, vice chmn., 1983-85, also mem. exec. com., dir. Home: Darien, Conn. Died Jan. 14, 1985.

MEHRTENS, WILLIAM OSBORNE, district judge; b. Savannah, Ga., Jan. 24, 1905; s. Leo W. and Cornelia (Millen) M.; J.D., U. Fla., 1932; m. Jaime H. Hancock, Nov. 4, 1936; 1 son, William Osborne. Admitted to Fla. bar, 1932; mem. firm Mershon, Sawyer, Johnston & Simmons, 1933-42, partner Mershon, Sawyer, Johnston, Dunwody, Mehrtens & Cole, and predecessor, Miami, Fla., 1942-65; U.S. dist. judge, 1965-80. Mem. permanent adv. com. on appellate rules Fla. Supreme Ct., 1958—. Bd. dirs. Miami Heart Inst. Served from lt. (j.g.) to lt. comdr. USNR, 1942-45. Fellow Internat. Acad. Trial Lawyers, Am. Coll. Trial Lawyers, Acad. Fla. Trial Lawyers; mem. Fla. Bar (bd. govs. 1955-65, past pres. jr. sect., past dir.), Am., Fed., Internat., Dade County bar assns., Internat. Law Assn., Am. Trial Lawyers Assn., Internat. Oceanographic Assn. (dir.), Phi Beta Kappa, Sigma Alpha Epsilon, Phi Kappa Phi, Phi Delta Phi, Blue Key. Clubs: Riviera Country (Coral Gables, Fla.); Coral Reef Yacht (Miami); Palm Bay; Bermuda Anglers; Miami Beach Rod and Reel; Panama Marlin. Home: Miami, Fla. Dec. July 16, 1980. Interned Woodlawn Cemetery, Miami, Fla.

MEINBERG, CARL HERMAN, clergyman; b. Keokuk, Ia., Jan. 11, 1889; s. Francis Joseph and Mary Elizabeth (Brinkman) M.; student St. Ambrose Coll., Davenport, Ia., 1905-11, A.B.; St. Mary's (Kan.) Coll., 1908-09; S.T.B., St. Mary's Sem., Baltimore, 1914; A.M., Cath. U., Washington, D.C., 1924; student summers U. of Ia. and Columbia. Ordained priest R.C. Ch., 1914; instr., St. Ambrose Acad., Davenport, 1914-20; instr., St. Ambrose Coll., 1920-26, prof. of history, 1926-37, pres., 1937-40; pastor St. Mary's Church, Iowa City, Ia. Title, Right Rev. Monsignor. Mem. N. Am. Hist. Soc. Contbr. to hist. jour. Home: Iowa City, Iowa. †

MEISEL, EMANUEL GEORGE, dentist, educator; b. Carrolltown, Pa., Jan. 20, 1890; s. Cornelius W. and Margaret (Dishart) M.; D.D.S., U. Pitts., 1915; m. Caroline H. Dean, Nov. 15, 1916; children—Caroline Margaret (Mrs. James R. Hall), George Edward, Robert Gnam; m. 2d, Gula Gale Gordon Boyd, June 15, 1946. Pub. sch. tchr., 1906-12; instr. histology and pathology Sch. Dentistry, U. Pitts., 1915-18, prof., head dept. oral medicine and oral pathology, from 1933; pvt. practice dentistry, Pitts., from 1920. Served as 1st lt. U.S. Army, World War I. Fellow A.A.A.S., Am. Coll. Dentists (past pres.); mem. Internat. Assn. Dental Rseearch, Odontological Soc. Western Pa., Am. (trustee 1932-44), Pa. (chmn. trustees 1931-37) dental assns., Delta Sigma Delta, Omicron Kappa Upsilon. Club: University (Pitts.). Contbr. articles profl. publs. Home: Pittsburgh, Pa. †

MELCHER, LEROY, JR., food co. exec.; b. Brenham, Tex., Nov. 8, 1938; s. LeRoy and Lucile (Birmingham) M.; children—Frank Dodd, LeRoy, Pierre Schlumberger, Marc Carroll. Student, U. Tex., 1956-58, U. Houston, 1958-59. With UtoteM Co., Houston, from 1957, store mgr., 1959-67; co. merged with Fairmont Foods Co., 1967; corp. sr. v.p., pres. Fairmont Foods Co. (UtoteM div.); partner Helicopters United. Address: Houston, Tex. *

MELLEN, J. GRENVILLE, govt. official; b. New Orleans, Sept. 18, 1888; ed. Rugby Acad. and Dixon Acad., Covington, La., Tulane U.; married. Began career as mech. and engring. researcher, also bus. advisor to various concerns; commd. by trade bds. and civic orgns. to gather and present tech., econ. and financial data concerning nat. program, Minn. Valley flood control, 1927-28; founder Miss.-Gulfport (Miss.) Compress and Warehouse, Inc., 1932, and since served as pres.; pres. Gulfport Port Commn., 1936-46; apptd. commr. U.S. Maritime Commn., 1946, present term expiring in 1950. Nat. councilor U.S. C. of C. since 1938; dir. Gulfport C. of C.; co-founder Nat. Cotton Council of Am. Mem. Gulf Ports Assn. (past dir. and v.p.), Am. Ports Cotton Compress and Warehouse Assn. (past pres.), Nat. Cotton Compress and Cotton Warehouse Assn. (co-founder), Internat. House (New Orleans), Delta Kappa Epsilon. Club: Rotary International. Home: Washington, D.C. †

MELLETT, JOHN CALVIN, author; b. Elwood, Ind., Aug. 4, 1888; s. Jesse and Margaret (Ring) M.; A.B., Ind. U., 1912; m. Harriett Brooks, Nov. 17, 1913; children—Jesse Brooks, Harriett Sue. Formerly in newspaper, publicity and advertising work, Indianapolis, Ind., N.Y. City and Washington, D.C. Mem. Indiana Flood Control Commission, 1944-49. Mem. Alpha Tau Omega. Author (under pen name): High Ground, 1928; Jimmy Makes the Varsity, 1928; Chains of Lightning, 1929; Ink, 1930; Pigskin Soldier, 1931; Varsity Jim, 1939. Contbr. to Collier's American Mag., Liberty, Cosmopolitan, Saturday Evening Post, Blue Book, Public Utilities Fortnightly, New Republic. Jour. of the Am. Water Works Assn. Home: Indianapolis, Ind. †

MELSON, CHARLES LEROY, naval officer; b. Richmond, Va., May 25, 1904; s. Elijah Zenith and Edith (Allen) M.; student U. Richmond, 1922-23; B.S., U.S. Naval Acad., 1927; m. Vedah Lee Jenkins, Oct. 1, 1932; children—Arthur Howard Cummings, James Atkinson Cummings (foster sons), Nancy Lee Melson. Commd.

ensign USN, 1927, advanced through grades to rear adm., 1955; assigned various ships, also tour of duty China Sta., 1927-41; assigned destroyers, World War II; comdr. U.S.S. New Jersey, Korean waters, 1952-53; staff Comdr.-in-Chief Atlantic Fleet, 1954-57; supt. Naval Acad., 1958-60. Decorated Silver Star Medal, Legion of Merit with gold stars, Bronze Star. Mem. Pi Kappa Alpha. Died Sept. 14, 1981.

MELTON, OLIVER QUIMBY, newspaper pub.; b. Chepultipec, Ala., Nov. 17, 1890; s. Wightman Fletcher and Oliver (Keller) M.; student Baltimore (Md.) City Coll.; B.S., Emory U., Oxford, Ga., 1912; m. Mary Davenport, Sept. 10, 1919; children—Oliver Quimby, Fred Davenport. Began as reporter Baltimore American, 1906; reporter Birmingham (Ala.) Ledger, 1912; editor Americus Times-Recorder, 1913-14; city editor Atlanta Constitution, 1915-16; mng. editor, later gen. mgr. Birmingham Ledger, 1919; pub. Fla. Metropolis, Jacksonville, 1920-21; southern rep. Scripps-Howard Neswpapers, 1922; adv. mgr. Internat. Proprietaries, Inc., 1923-24; owner and pub. Griffin (Ga.) Daily News from 1924; pres. Griffin Daily News Co. Past state comdr. Am. Legion, Ga.; past nat. vice comdr. of same, 1935; founder The Georgia Legionnaire; nat. exec. committeeman from Ga., Am. Legion, 1933-37; first chmn. Ga. State Vets. Service Bd., 1946. Delegate to Ga. State Dem. Conv., 1912-31; del. to Democrat Nat. Conv., 1932, 44. Democratic presidential elector, 1936-48. Served as captain, later major inf., U.S. Army, in 4 major offensives, World War. Division and corps citations; awarded U.D.C. Service Cross of Honor. Named Griffin (Ga.) Man of the Year, 1955. Democrat. Methodist. Mason (Shriner). Red Man, Woodman of World, Odd Fellow. Club: Exchange. Home: Griffin, Ga. †

MELVIN, CRANDALL, lawyer, banker; b. Euclid, N.Y., April 6, 1889; s. Asel J. and Mae (Soule) M.; A.B. Syracuse U., 1911, LL.B., 1913; m. Elizann Hunter, June 14, 1923 (died 1926); m. 2d, Gertrude Christman, Sept. 29, 1927; 1 son, Crandall. Admitted N.Y. bar, 1913; practised in Syracuse from 1913, Melvin & Melvin from 1921; instr. law of torts, Syracuse Coll. Law, 1915-17, 1919-25; chmn. Mchts. National Bank & Trust Company of Syracuse; director Companion Life Insurance Company. Member Judicial Council N.Y. State. Director N.Y. State Council Churches, Syracuse Chapter Red Cross, Technology Club, Salvation Army, Onondaga Hist. Assn. (pres. 1947), Boy Scouts of Am. (pres. Onondaga Council 1941, Region II exec. com., nat. council); trustee, Syracuse U., Charlton Farm Sch. for Boys; nat. treas. United Cerebral Palsy Assn., Inc. Mem. Syracuse C. of C.; chairman Onondaga County Emergency Work Bureau (1931-3), N.Y. State U.S.O. War Fund Campaign 1942, Local American Social Hygiene Campaign 1942, S. U. Alumni Drive Onondaga County 1942, S. U. Law College Fund Drive 1946, Local Greek War Relief 1947, Local Cancer Drive, 1949; treas. Syracuse Centennial, 1948; nat. treas. S.U. Fund Drive from 1949; treas. U.S.O. campaign Upper N.Y. State from 1949. Chmn. N.Y. State Bar Assn. Comm. on Auto. Accident Prevention from 1934; drafted N.Y. State Safety-Responsibility Act. Second lt. Field Artillery, United States Army World War I. Member American Bar Association, N.Y. State Bar Assn., Onondaga County Bar Assn. (pres. 1933-34), N.Y. State Bankers Assn. (pres. 1958-59), Am. Arbitration Assn. Panel, S.A.R., Newcomen Soc. N.A., Am. Bankers Assn. (econ. adv. council), Phi Gamma Delta (nat. treas.), Phi Delta Phi, American Legion, 40 & 8, Scabbard & Blade, Rotary. Republican. Mason. Clubs: Onon Golf and Country, University, Citizens, Century, Liederkranz. Home: North Syracuse, N.Y. †

MENDELSOHN, ALBERT, mining engr.; b. Chgo., Mar. 13, 1889; s. Joseph and Natalie (Steinberg) M.; student Collegiate Sch., 1903-04, DeWitt Clinton, 1905-07; E.M., Columbia, 1911; m. Dorothy Sheldon Bowling, June 30, 1916 (dec.); children—Dorothy Sheldon (Mrs. Barton Sproule), Mary Jane (Mrs. A. V. Williams); m. 2d, Gertrude Barnett, Dec. 11, 1926; 1 dau., Gertrude (Mrs. Elmer Spaw). Supt. Baltic Mine (Mich.), 1915-20; gen. supt. Copper Range Co., Painesdale, Mich., 1921-37, dir., 1934-37; dir. Cananea Consol. Copper Co. S.A., Cananea, Sonora, Mexico, from 1937, pres., gen. mgr., from 1938; v.p., dir. Greene Cananea Copper Co., N.Y.C., from 1954. Address: Cananea Sonora, Mexico. †

MENDES FRANCE, PIERRE, French politician; b. Paris, Jan. 11, 1907; ed. Faculte deDroit and Ecole des Sciences Polítiques, U. Paris; Docteur en Droit, 1928; m. Lily Cicurel, Dec. 26, 1933; children—Bernard, Michel. Admitted to the bar, 1928; mayor of Louviers, Normandy, from 1935-58; deputy of the National Assembly, 1932-40, 45-58; minister of nat. economy, provisional govt. of Gen. Charles de Gaulle, 1944-45; permanent rep. of France on ECOSOC, 1947-50; prime minister, minister fgn. affairs, France, 1954-55; minister of state without portfolio, 1956. Served as lt., French Air Forces, arrested and imprisoned by Vichy government, 1940, escaped and joined French Resistance Movement. Decorated officer Legion of Honor, Rosette de la Résistance, Médaille des Evades (France); grand officer Order of Leopold (Belgium). Author: (with Gabriel Airdant) Economics and Action, 1955; A Modern French Republic, 1963. Editor in chief Le Courrier de la Republique. Address: Paris, France. Died Oct. 18, 1982.

MENDEZ, PEREIRA OCTAVIO, educator, author, diplomat; b. Aguadulce, Panama, Aug. 30, 1887; s. Joaquin and Micaela (Pereira) M.; grad. Normal Sch. of Panamá, 1908; U. of Chile, 1913; Dr. honoris causa, U. of San Marcos, Lima, Faculty of Law and Polit. Science, of Panamá; U. of So. Calif., Nat. U. of Colombia; certificate of U. of London; m. Luz Amalia Guardia; children—Luz Amalia, Octavio, Manuel José, Alicia. Prof. Spanish, Nat. Inst., asst. sec. pub. instrn., rector, 1918-23 and after 1933; sec. pub. instrn., 1923-27; M.P. to Chile, France, Great Britain, 1927-30; founder U. of Panamá(pres., 1935-40); pres. Inter-Am. Univ. after 1943; Panamanian del. to League of Nations, Internat. Labor Conf., Conf. at San Francisco, 1st Gen. Assembly, U.N., New York. Decorated Comdr. Legion d'Honneur, official French Acad. (France); Grand Cross Order of Liberator of Venezuela; Grand Cross Order of Chile, Medal Pub. Instrn. of Chile; Grand Cross Order of Vasco Ññez de Balboa; Grand Offical Order Carlos Manuel de Céspedes; Comdr. Order Charles III of Spain; Comdr. Order of Aztec Eagle; Grand Official Order Sun of Per; Medal of Merit (1st class) Ecuador and Chile; Medal of Solidarity of Panamá; Grand Official Order of Boyacá. Mem. Acad. Panamena de la Lengua, Acad. Panamena de la Historia, Unión Iber-Americana of Panamá, Sociedad Bolivariana, Sociedad Panamiciña de Defecho Internacional, Asoclacion de Maestros (hon.), Comite France-Amerique; corr. mem. Acad. de la Lengua, Acad. de Historia, Union Ibero-Americana (Madrid); Am. Philos. Soc.; Societé des Américanistes de Paris; Instituto Sanmartiniano de Columbia; Sociedad Bolivariana de Colombia y del Ecuador; Centro de Sciencias, Letras e Artes of Brasil; Sociedad de Geografía e Historia of Guatemala; Centro Valle-Caucano; Acad. de la Historia of Carracas, Havana, Cartagena, Bogota, Santander, Quito, Santiago de Chile; Sociedad de Artes y Letras of Havna; Sociedad Cientificia Chilena; Sociedad de Folklore Chileno; Ateneo of Lima and Guatemala. Clubs: Unión, Rotary. Author: Higiene del Estudiante, 1912; Elementos de Instrucción Civica (5th edition); Parnaso Panameno, 1916; Ejerclcios de Lenguaje (New York); Dante, 1922; El Canal de Panamá; En el Surco, 1925; Emociones y Evocaciones (Paris) 1928; El Tesoro del Dabaibe, 1933; Historia de Ibero-America, 1936; Tierra Firme, 1940; and other hist. works. Founder Estudios, El Educador, Antena and other newspapers and periodicals; dir. rev. Universidad de Panama. Home: Panama, Republic of Panama. Deceased.

MENGER, CARL S., mfg. co. exec.; b. Tex., Dec. 12, 1909; s. Rudolph A. and Adella M.; children by previous marriage—Carl S., Joanne; m. Eleanor McAuliffe, 1945; children—John, Eugene, Adella. Student, U. Iowa, St. Mary's U. With Triangle Conduit & Cable, Inc. (name later changed to Triangle Industries, Inc.), Holmdel, N.J., from 1945, pres., 1960-70, chmn. bd., chief exec. officer, from 1965, chmn. exec. com., from 1965; chmn. bd. Plastic Wire & Cable Corp., from 1965, Rowe Internat., Inc., from 1968; chmn., pres. Triangle Exploration, Inc., from 1968; dir. First Nat. State Bank N.J., Newark; gov. La Coquille Club Villas Inc., Palm Beach, Fla. Trustee Wardlaw Country Day Sch., Plainfield, Franklin Coll., Switzerland, Middlesex Gen. Hosp., New Brunswick, N.J.; trustee, mem. exec. com. N.J. Safety Council. Mem. Am. Mgmt. Assn., Nat. Indsl. Conf. Bd., NAM, Nat. Elec. Mfrs. Assn., Am. Soc. Naval Engrs., U.S. C. of C., N.J. C. of C. Clubs: Baltusrol Golf, Bay Head (N.J.) Yacht; Everglades (Palm Beach, Fla.), La Coquille (Palm Beach, Fla.); Little (Gulfstream, Fla.); Williams Country (Weirton, W.Va.). Home: Manalapan, Fla.

MENNIN, PETER, composer, music conservatory adminstr.; b. Erie, Pa., May 17, 1923; m. Georganne Bairnson, Aug. 28, 1947; children—Felica, Mark. Student, Oberlin Conservatory, 1940-42; Mus.B., Mus.M., Eastman Sch. Music, 1945, Ph.D., 1947; studied with, Howard Hanson; studied conducting with, Serge Koussevitsky at, Tanglewood, Mass., 1946. Tchr. composition Juilliard Sch. Music, 1947-58, pres., 1962-83; dir. Peabody Conservatory Music, Balt., 1958-62; Mem. adv. panel USIA, 1961; adv. com. arts State Dept., 1963—; mem. exec. com. Internat. Music Council, Paris, 1956, Nat. Fedn. Music Clubs Commn., 1957. (First Gershwin Meml. award, Koussevitsky award, Dallas Symphony Commn., Juilliard Found. commn., Collegiate Chorale commn., NBC Radio commn., League of Composers commn., Prot. Radio commn., Columbia Record's Chamber Music award 1952, Naumburg Found. Am. Composition award 1952, Elizabeth Sprague Coolidge Found.-Library of Congress Chamber Music commn. 1952, Nat. Fedn. Music Clubs commn. 1956, Cleve. Symphony commn. 1957, others.); Composer: First Symphony, 1942, String Quartet, 1942, Concertino for Flute, Strings and Percussion, 1945, Second Symphony, 1945, Folk Overture, 1945, Fantasia for Strings (Canzona and Tocata), 1946, Third Symphony, 1946; for piano Divertimento, 1947, Partita; 5 movements, 1949; for mixed chorus Song of the Palace, 1948; for women's chorus Bought Locks, 1949, Fourth Symphony for Chorus and Orch, 1949, A Christmas Cantata for Chorus, Soloists and Chamber Orch, 1949, Second Quartet, 1950, Fifth Symphony, 1950, Concertato for Orch. (Moby-Dick), 1952, Sixth Symphony, 1953, Cello Concerto, 1955, Sonata Concertante for Violin and Piano, 1956, Piano Concerto, 1957, Canto for Orch, 1957, Symphony No. 7, 1964, Piano Sonata, 1964, Sinfonia for Orch, 1971, Cantata de Virtute, 1969, Symphony No. 8, 1973, Voices for Soprano and Chamber Ensemble, Reflections of Emily for Treble Voices and Ensemble, 1979, Symphony No. 9, 1981; others., Works performed by, N.Y. Philharmonic Soc., NBC Symphony Orch., Columbia Broadcasting Orch., Boston, Chgo., San Francisco, Nat., Cin. WOR, Rochester (N.Y.), Mpls., Dallas, Houston, Los Angeles, Phila., Pitts., Detroit orchs., Götesburg Symphony Orch. of Sweden, orchs. in, Europe, S.A., Orient and Far East; in music festivals, Rochester, N.Y., Tanglewood, Mass., Yaddo (Saratoga Springs, N.Y.), Colorado Springs and, Seattle. Bd. dirs. Walter W. Naumburg Found. Served with USAAF, 1943. Recipient award Am. Acad. Arts and Letters; Guggenheim award; Bearns prize Columbia. Mem. League Composers (bd. dirs.), Composers' Forum (dir.), Nat. Music Council (pres. 1968—), Nat. Inst. Arts and Letters, Am. Music (dir.), Am. Soc. Composers, Authors and Pubs. (dir.), Phi Mu Alpha. Home: New York, N.Y. Dec. June 17, 1983.

MENNINGER, CHARLES AUGUST, ry. ofcl.; b. Tell City, Ind., June 12, 1890; s. August and Caroline (Obrecht) M.; student Marion (Ind.) Normal Coll., 1910-11; m. Agda Hassing, June 5, 1915; children—Mary Janet (Mrs. R.A. Corder, Jr.), Charles Norman. Clk. A.T. & S.F. Ry. Co., Topeka, 1911-16, asst. cashier treasury dept., Chicago, 1916-18, asst. paymaster, Topeka, 1918-29, chief clk. sec. dept., 1929-37, asst. treas., 1937-51, sec.-treas. from 1951; sec.-treas. the A.T.&S.F. Hosp. Assn., Haystack Mt. Development Co., Ill. Northern Ry., Kansas S.W. Ry. Co., Wichita Union Terminal Ry. Co., Dodge City Cimarron Valley Ry. Co., N.M. Central Ry. Co., Garden City, Gulf & Northern Railway Company; director Shawnee Federal Savings & Loan Assn., Topeka. Member Topeka, Kansas State C.'s of C. Rep. Mem. Evangelical Ch. Mason. Clubs: Rotary, Shawnee Country, Traffic (Topeka). †

MENTSCHIKOFF, SOIA, lawyer, university dean; b. Moscow, USSR, Apr. 2,1915; d. Roman S. and Eugenia A. (Ossipov) M. (parents Am. citizens); m. Karl N. Llewellyn, 1946. B.A., Hunter Coll., 1934; LL.B., Columbia, 1937, LL.D. (hon.), 1978; LL.D. (hon.), Smith Coll., 1967, Lafayette Coll., 1974, Boston Coll., 1974, Boston U., 1974, Syracuse U., 1974, U. Puget Sound, 1976, Bard Coll., 1978, Columbia U., 1978, Georgetown U., 1980, New Eng. Sch. of Law, 1980, Villanova U., 1981. Bar: N.Y. State bar 1937. Practiced in, N.Y.C., 1937-49; asso. firm Scandrett, Tuttle & Chalaire, 1937-41; assoc. mem. firm Spence, Windels, Walser, Hotchkiss & Angell, 1944-45; mem. firm Spence, Hotchkiss, Parker & Duryee, 1945-49; assoc. chief reporter Uniform Comml. Code, 1944-54; vis. prof., cons. Harvard Law Sch., 1947-49, U. Chgo. Law Sch., 1951-74; dean U. Miami Law Sch., Coral Gables, Fla., 1974-82; U.S. del. Hague Conf., 1964; commr. Uniform State Law, State of Ill., 1965-70; trustee Rand Corp., 1972—. Author: (with Katzenbach) International Unification of Private Law, 1961, Commercial Transactions, 1970, (with Stotzby) The Theory of Craft of American Law—Elements, 1981; Contbr. (with Stotzby) articles to profl. publs. Mem. Commn. on Rights, Liberties and Responsibilities of Am. Indians, 1962-66; panel of arbitrators Internat. Center for Settlement of Investment Disputes, 1963-69, 81—; mem. exec. com. Council for Study Mankind, 1965-69. Mem. ABA, Am. Law Inst., Am. Judicature Soc., Am. Soc. Internat. Law, Internat. Faculty Comparative Law, Assn. Am. Law Schs. (pres. 1974). Home: Coral Gables, Fla. Dec. June 18, 1984.

MENZIES, DUNCAN CAMERON, refrigeration and air conditioning mfg. exec.; b. Gonnell Ferry, Scotland, Feb. 3, 1902; s. Robert B. and Catherine (Cameron) M.; ed. in Eng. and Scotland; post grad. studies in Can.; m. Honor Elizabeth Schaab, June 29, 1926; children—Alister C., Rogene. Sales exec., Can., U. S.A., Eng., Scott-Bathgate Co., Ltd., Winnepeg, Can., 1924-32; field sales mgr. U.S.A. and Can., Lamont-Corliss Co., N.Y.C., 1932-37; v.p. sales-advt., flour milling div., gen. mgr. flour and cereal div. Hecker Products Corp., N.Y.C., 1937-42; v.p. Johnson & Johnson Research Found., asst. to pres. Johnson & Johnson, U.S.A. and fgn. subsidiaries, New Brunswick, N.J., and dir. Johnson & Johnson, Johnson Suture Corp., chmn. bd. Mersons, Ltd., Scotland, 1942-50; exec. v.p., gen. mgr. Ball Bros. Co., Inc., Muncie, Ind., also subsidiaries, 1950-54; pres., chief exec. officer, director Servel, Inc., Evansville, Ind., 1954-65; mem. bd. dirs. Fansteel Metallurgical Corporation, Langley Corporation. Clubs: Wall Street (New York City); Union League (Chgo.); Nassau (Princeton, N.J.). Home: Byram, Conn. Died Nov. 9, 1982.

MERCER, JOHNNY (JOHN H.), musician; b. Savannah, Ga., Nov. 18, 1909; student Woodbury Forest Sch., Orange, Va.; m. Ginger Meehan; children—Amanda, John. Actor, bit player, N.Y.C., 1927-29; vocalist, master ceremonies, writer mus. sketches Paul Whiteman orch.; singer Benny Goodman orch. CBS network, 1938, Bob Crosby orch. NBC, 1939-40; master ceremonies Army-sponsored program Mail Call, also master ceremonies, singer Lucky Strike Hit Parade; organizer Capitol Records, Inc. (with Glenn Wallichs, Buddy DeSylva), 1942, pres.; founder Heritage Music, Inc., 1970. Writer lyrics for songs including: Pardon My Southern Accent, Jeepers Creepers, You Must Have Been a Beautiful Baby, Too Marvelous for Words, Angels Sing, Blues in the Night, You Were Never Lovelier, Accentuate the Positive, Laura, Skylark, Lazybones, Fools Rush In, Autumn Leaves, Goody Goody, Day In, Day Out, One for My Baby, I Wanna Be Around, Come Rain or Come Shine, Satin Doll, I Remember You, That Old Black Magic, others; writer lyrics, music Something's Gotta Give, GI

Jive, Dream, I'm An Old Cowhand; writer lyrics for motion pictures including: Daddy Long Legs, Here Comes the Waves, Star Spangled Rhythm, Ready Willing and Able, Harvey Girls, others; plays St. Louis Woman, Li'l Abner, Foxy, Life is What You Make It for film Kotch (Golden Globes award 1972). Recipient Acad. Award for lyrics Atchison, Topeka, and Santa Fe, 1946. Pres., Songwriter's Hall of Fame, 1967-76. Mem. A.S.-C.A.P. Address: Hollywood, Calif. Died June 25, 1976.

MERCER, MARION EVERETT (MRS. CHARLES D. MERCER), social work volunteer; b. Providence, R.I., Mar. 25, 1888; d. Walter Goodnow and Harriet Mansfield (Cleaveland) Everett; grad. Mary C. Wheeler Sch., Providence, R.I., 1906; student Wellesley Coll., 1906-09; m. Charles Douglas Mercer, Apr. 27, 1910; children—Harriet Elizabeth (Mrs. Whitman Knapp), George Everett, Douglas. Teacher of English, Mary C. Wheeler Sch., Providence, R.I., 1909-10. Trustee Miss Dickinsons' Sch., Sewickly, Pa., 1920-23. Mem. Young Women's Christian Assn. (pres. Boston, 1930-34, mem. nat. bd., New York, since 1932, nat. v.p., 1943-49, chmn. community div. nat. bd., mem. bd. dir. chmn. endowment com., Boston), Mass. Soc. for Social Hygiene (sec. exec. com.), Marriage Study Assn. of Mass. (dir.), Planned Parenthood Assn. of Mass., Boston U. Womens Council, Wellesley Coll. Alumnae Fund Com., Summer Inst. for Social Progress at Wellesley (exec. com.), member of corporation United Service Organization. Episcopalian. Club: Cosmopolitan (N.Y.). Chmn. pubs. dept. and editorial bd., Womans Press. Home: Brookline, Mass. Deceased.

MERKLE, EDWARD ARROL, fin. exec.; b. Weehawken, N.J., May 12, 1909; s. Alfred and Laura (Arroll) M.; B.S., N.Y. U., 1929; m. Dorothy Osborn, Jan. 21, 1934; children—Edward O., Jane A. From analyst to head research Callaway, Fish & Co., N.Y.C., 1929-40; research, sales, G.M.P. Murphy Co., N.Y.C., 1940-42, Sherarson, Hammill & Co., N.Y.C., 1942-47, Mitchell, Hutchins & Co., N.Y.C., 1947-48; with Madison Fund, Inc. (formerly Pennroad Corp.), N.Y.C., from 1949, v.p. 1951-57, dir., 1953-84, pres., chmn., 1957-84; chmn. Mo.-Kan.-Tex. R.R. Co.; mem. adv. bd. Chem. Bank N.Y. Trust Co., dir. First Nat. Store, Union Dime Savs. Bank, Orange & Rockland Utilities. Clubs: Links (N.Y.C.); Arcola Golf and Country (Paramus, N.J.); Oyster Harbors (Osterville, Mass.). Home: Haworth, N.J. Died Mar. 13, 1984.

MERMAN, ETHEL, singer, actress; b. Astoria, N.Y., Jan. 16, 1909; d. Edward and Agnes Zimmerman; m. William B. Smith, Nov. 16, 1940 (div. Oct. 1941); m. Robert D. Levitt (div.); m. Robert F. Six (div. 1961); m. Ernest Borgnine, July 1964. Student pub. schs., Long Island City, N.Y. Sec. to pres. B.K. Vacuum Booster-Brake Co. Night club singer, also singing with, Jimmy Durante, Clayton and Jackson; made: Broadway debut in Girl Crazy, 1930; other theatre appearances include George White's Scandals, 1931-32, Take a Chance, 1932, Anything Goes, 1934, Red, Hot and Blue, 1936, Stars in Your Eyes, 1939, Dubarry Was a Lady, 1939, Panama Hattie, 1940, Something for the Boys, 1943, Annie Get Your Gun, 1946, Call Me Madam, 1950, Happy Hunting, 1956, Gypsy, 1959, Hello, Dolly!, 1970; radio program Rhythm at Eight, 1935; appearances in: motion pictures include Kid Millions, 1934, We're Not Dressing, The Big Broadcast, 1935, Strike Me Pink, 1936, Anything Goes, 1936, Happy Landing, 1938, Alexander's Ragtime Band, Straight, Place and Show, Stage Door Canteen, 1943, Call Me Madam, 1953, No Business Like Show Business, 1954, Gypsy, It's a Mad, Mad, Mad, Mad World, 1963, Won Ton Ton, 1976; numerous TV appearances, including Merv Griffin's Salute to Irving Berlin, 1976 (Winner N.Y. Drama Critics award 1943, 46, 59, Donaldson award 1947, Tony award 1951, 72, Barter Theatre of Va. award 1957, Drama Desk award 1969-70); Author: numerous TV appearances, including Merman, An Autobiography, 1978. Address: Los Angeles, Calif. Dec. Feb. 15, 1984.*

MÉRO, YOLANDA (MRS. HERMANN IRION), pianist; b. Budapest, Hungary, Aug. 30, 1887; d. T. and R. (Pick) M.; began studying piano under father; diploma Nat. Conservatory of Budapest, also hon. prof.; m. Hermann Irion, of Steinway & Sons, New York, Dec. 16, 1909; 1 dau., Elizabeth. Came to U.S., 1909; has appeared in concerts throughout U.S., and with the principal orchestras, and played in Europe, S. America, Mexico, etc. Founder and chmn. Woman's National Radio Com. Exec. dir. Musicians Emergency Fund of New York. Mem. Sigma Alpha Iota (hon.). Home: New City Rockland County, N.Y. †

MERRILL, DANIEL ROY, newspaper exec.; b. Wallaceburg, Ont., Can., Aug. 20, 1889; s. Frederick and Margaret Isabel (Shepley) M.; grad. Windsor Collegiate Inst., 1905; m. Lottie Marie Dumond, June 6, 1914; children—Jack Russell, Betty Marie (wife of Rev. Norman S. Rice), Robert Walter. Came to U.S., 1914, naturalized, 1926. Joined Detroit News, 1906, successively cashier, auditor, bus. mgr., gen. mgr., 1945, v.p., gen. mgr., dir., 1949-58, exec. vice president, dir., from 1958; mem. conf. board and operating com. This Week Mag., from 1957. Mem. bd. govs. Am. Newspapers Pubs. Assn., Bur. Advt., 1947-51. Mem. Bd. of Commerce, Met. Sunday Newspapers (bd. dirs. 1931-35, 47-53, 57). Clubs: Athletic, Golf, Economic, Adcraft, Detroit (Detroit). Home: Detroit, Mich. †

MERRILL, HAMILTON, mfg. exec.; b. Albany, N.Y.; Dec. 21, 1890; s. Frederick James Hamilton and Winifred (Edgerton) M.; B.S., Mass. Inst. Tech., 1912; m. Phyllis Galetine Gordon, Oct. 12, 1921; children—Nancy, Winifred Elizabeth. Held various positions, 1912-17; supt. Herf & Frerichs Chem. Co., 1919-20; asst. works mgr. Am. Steam Gauge & Valve Mfg. Co., 1920-22; gen. mgr. Tower Mfg. Co., 1922-26; works mgr. Am. Schaeffer & Badenburg Corp., 1926-28; works mgr. and dir. Consol. Ashcroft Hancock Co., 1928-36; v.p. and works mgr., Manning, Maxwell & Moore, Inc., Bridgeport, Conn., 1937-47; v.p. in charge mfg. Consol. Ashcroft Hancock Div., 1947-50; pres. and dir. Manning Maxwell & Moore, Inc., 1950-56, ret.; director City Trust Co. Mem. board of trustees University of Bridgeport, Conn. Served as captain, C.W.S., AEF, 1917-19. Mem. C. of C. (dir.), Mfrs. Assn., Delta Psi. Republican. Episcopalian. Clubs: University, Brooklawn Country; St. Anthony (N.Y.C.). Home: Bridgeport, Conn. Deceased.

MERRILL, HARWOOD FERRY, editor, association executive; b. Parkersburg, W.Va., Aug. 2, 1904; s. Dana True and Edith Claire (Ferry) M.; B.A., Cornell U., 1926; M.B.A., Harvard, 1928; m. Dorothy Merrill, Mar. 20, 1931; children—Anne Blossom (Mrs. William Webb Fancher), Dana True II. Research asst. Harvard Bus. Sch., 1928-30; asst. dir. advt. Curtiss-Wright Corp., 1930-32; indsl. editor Forbes mag., 1932-36, mng. editor. 1936-40; co-founder, editor Modern Industry mag., 1940-59; v.p., editorial dir. Magazines of Industry, 1948-49; v.p. Eagle-Picher Sales Co., gen. mgr. paint and varnish div., 1949-53, asst. to pres., 1953-56; editor-in-chief Am. Mgmt. Assn., 1956-57, v.p., editor, 1957-59, v.p. membership and publs., 1959-67; also dir. Vice pres. Jr. Achievement Greater Cin., 1955-56. Mem. alumni council Harvard Bus. Sch., 1946-49. Mem. N.Y. Bus. Paper Editors (chmn. 1945-47), Harvard Bus. Sch. Assn., Am. Found. Mgmt. Research (pres. 1961-62, 65—, trustee), Internat. Mgmt. Assn. (dir. 1957—), Harvard Bus School (v.p. N.Y.C. 1947-48; pres. Cin. 1955-56). Author: Case Studies in Commercial Aviation, 1931. Editor: The Responsibilities of Business Leadership, 1949: (with Elizabeth Marting) Developing Executive Skills, 1958; Classics in Management, 1960. Author numerous articles, reports. Home: Katonah, N.Y. Died Nov. 23, 1984.

MERRILL, JOHN PUTNAM, internist; b. Hartford, Conn., Mar. 10, 1917; s. Arthur Hodges and Olive (Grinnell) M.; m. Suzanne N. Strauss, Sept. 17, 1942; children: John Putnam, Stephen G., Anne L. A.B., Dartmouth Coll., 1938; M.D., Harvard U., 1942; D.Sc. (hon.), Colby Coll., 1969, U. Paris, 1974. Diplomate: Am. Bd. Internal Medicine. Intern Peter Brigham Hosp., Boston, 1942-43, house officer in medicine, 1942-43, asst. resident physician, 1947-48; instr. medicine Harvard U., 1950-52, prof., 1970—; nat. adv. council Nat. Inst. Arthritis, Metabolic and Digestive Diseases of NIH, 1975. Author: Treatment of Renal Failure, 1955, (with Hampers) Uremia, 1972, Present Status of Kidney Transplantation, 1974; editor-in-chief: Harvard Med. Alumni Bull., 1954-56; contbr. articles on kidney disorders and hypertension to profl. jours., chpt. to book. Served with USAAF, 1943-47. Recipient Alvarenga prize Phila. Coll. Physicians, 1960, Amory prize Am. Acad. Arts and Scis., 1962, Disting. Achievement award Modern Medicine, 1965, Gairdner Found. award, 1969, Valentine award N.Y. Acad. Medicine, 1970, Rosenthal Found. award ACP, 1978, Disting. Sci. Achievement award Kidney Found. Mass., 1978, Hume award Nat. Kidney Found., 1979, Dedication award Internat. Transplantation Soc., 1980. Mem. Aesculapian Club (pres. 1964-65), Internat. Soc. Nephrology (pres. 1966-69), Am. Acad. Arts and Scis. (pres.), Am. Soc. Artificial Internal Organs (pres. 1970), Internat. Soc. Artificial Organs (pres. 1978), Assn. Am. Physicians, Am. Soc. Clin. Investigation (pres. 1962), Harvard Med. Alumni Assn. (sec. 1975), Phi Beta Kappa, Alpha Omega Alpha; fellow Nat. Acad. Sci. (France). Home: Boston, Mass. Dec. Apr. 4, 1984.

MERRILL, JOSEPH L., investment banker; b. Boston, Sept. 27, 1889; s. John L. Merrill; A.B., Harvard, 1910; m. Kathleen Cushman, June 10, 1920; children—Arthur Cushman, Robert Gordon. With W. H. McElwain & Co., Boston, 1910-20; partner Merrill Lynch & Co., 1920-40; pres. and dir. Sterling Holding Corp., Wilmington, Del., from 1940; vice pres. in charge finance and dir. Melville Shoe Corp., N.Y. City, since 1940; dir. J. F. McElwain Co. Past dir. A. S. Beck Shoe Co., Diamond Shoe Corp., G. R. Kinney Co., Feltman & Curme Shoe Stores, Central Shoe Co., Waldorf System, Inc., Lane Bryant Inc., Adams-Hills Corp., Struthers Wells, Inc., Beechvale Investments, Ltd., Bird Grocery Stores, Daniel Reeves, Inc., Nat. Tea Co., Safeway Stores, Inc. Served as capt., U.S. Army, World War I. Owner of "Feather," winner championship Yacht Racing Assn. of L.I. Sound, 1940, 41, 46, 47; and Royal Bermuda Yacht trophy. Clubs: New York Yacht, American Yacht, Southampton Yacht; Meadow (Southhampton); Harvard (New York); Piping Rock, National Golf Links of America. †

MERRILL, MAUD AMANDA, psychologist; b. Owatonna, Minn., Apr. 30, 1888; d. Galen Allen and Estella Amanda (Ogden) Merrill; A.B., Oberlin Coll., 1911; A.M., Stanford U., 1920, Ph.D., 1923; m. William Francis James, May 10, 1935. Research asst., Minn. State Dept. of Research, 1913-19; instr. in psychology, Stanford U., 1920-24, asst. prof., 1924-31, asso. prof., 1931-47, prof. from 1947. Felow A.A.A.S., Am. Psychol. Assn.; mem. Sigma Xi, Pi Lambda Theta. Author: Measuring Intelligence (with Lewis M. Terman), 1937; Studies in Personality (with Q. McNemar), 1942; Problems of Child Delinquency, 1947. Home: Stanford, Calif. †

MERRILL, ROBERT TAYLOR, govt. ofcl.; b. Mine La Motte, Mo., July 29, 1888; s. George S. and Eliza B. (Bushnell) M.; B.S., U.S. Naval Acad., 1910; m. Marguerite S. Mason, June 19, 1916. Commnd. ensign U.S. Navy, 1910, advanced through grades to lt. comdr., 1919; resigned, 1919; v.p., gen. mgr. various steamship companies, 1919-21, 25-42; dir. research U.S. Shipping Bd., 1921-25; joined Dept. of State, 1950, assigned as shipping adviser, 1950-53, shipping officer, Tokyo, 1953-55, chief shipping div., from 1955. Served as capt. USCGR, 1942-50. Decorated Navy Cross, Legion of Merit, Commendation Ribbon. Mem. Retired Officers Assn. (dir.), Soc. Naval Architects and Marine Engrs. Home: Chevy Chase, Md. †

MERRIMAN, DANIEL, educator; b. Cambridge, Mass., Sept. 17, 1908; s. Roger Bigelow and Dorothea (Foote) M.; student Groton Sch., 1921-27, Harvard U., 1927-30; B.S., U. of Wash., 1933, M.S., 1934; Ph.D., Yale U., 1939; m. Mary Wieland, Sept. 18, 1934 (dec. Feb. 1968); m. 2d, Jean E. Lynch, May 8, 1971; children—Sydney Elizabeth Lynch, Alexander Robert Lynch. With U.S. Bur. of Fisheries, Portland Trawling Co., and Woods Hole Oceanograpic Instn., 1930-32; aquatic biologist, in charge striped bass investigation, Conn. Bd. Fisheries and Game, 1936-38; instr. biology Yale U. 1938-42, asst. prof., 1942-46, asso. prof., 1946-76, prof., 1976-77, prof. emeritus, 1977-84; dir. Bingham Oceanographic Lab., 1942-66, master of Davenport Coll., 1946-66; dir. Sears Found. Marine Research, 1966-77; research asso. fishes and aquatic biology Am. Mus. Natural History, N.Y.C., 1945-62. Commr. Conn. Bd. Fisheries and Game, 1953-56; chmn. com. food resources of coastal waters NRC, 1943-46; adv. com. biology office Naval Research, 1949-52; cons. NSF, 1951-54; adv. com. Susquehanna Fisheries Study, 1957-60; cons. President's Sci. Adv. Com., 1960-61. Trustee Bermuda Biol. Sta., 1944-64, Woods Hole Oceanog. Instn., 1944-64; dir. Conn. River Ecol. Study, Conn. Yankee Atomic Power Co., 1965-74. Fellow N.Y. Zool. Soc.; mem. Soc. Ichthyologists and Herpetologists, Am. Fisheries Soc., Am. Soc. Zoologists, History Sci. Soc., Conn., N.Y. acads. arts and scis., AAAS, Am. Soc. Limnology and Oceanography, Sigma Xi. Club: Century Assn. Editorial bd. Jour. Marine Research, 1943-60, Limnology and Oceanography, 1962-65, Fishes of W. N. Atlantic, from 1961; hon. editorial adv. bd. Deep-Sea Research, 1961-73. Contbr. numerous articles on marine biology, ichthyology, history oceanography and related subjects. Home: Bethany, Conn. Died Aug. 6, 1984.

MERRING, HARRY LLOYD, naval officer (ret.); b. Rathbone, N.Y., Nov. 25, 1888; s. Henry C. and Adelaide (Lloyd) M.; B.Sc., U.S.N. Acad., 1911; student Harvard, 1917; m. Virginia Costinett, Sept. 22, 1914; 1 son, Harry L(loyd). Commd. as ensign and promoted through grades to capt.; retired 1939; re-ordered to active duty, 1939; port dir. naval transportation service, Seattle, 1939-40; contracting officer bur. ordinance, Navy Dept., 1940-44; promoted to rear adm., 1944; chief navy contract settlement orgn., 1944-46; inactive duty since 1946. Awards: Legion of Merit, Army Commendation Ribbon for work in contract settlement; gold star in lieu of 2d Legion of Merit for work, bur. of ordnance. Mem. U.S. Naval Inst. (Annapolis, Md.). Club: Chevy Chase (Md.). Home: Washington, D.C. †

MERRITT, HIRAM HOUSTON, neurologist, educator; b. Wilmington, N.C., Jan. 12, 1902; s. Hiram Houston and Dessie (Cline) M.; A.B., Vanderbilt U., 1922; M.D., Johns Hopkins, 1926; A.M. (hon.) Harvard, 1942; Sc.D. (hon.), N.Y. Med. Coll., 1967, Columbia, 1971; m. Mabel Carmichael, Aug. 2, 1930. Intern New Haven Hosp., 1926-27; various hosp. and univ. assignments, study and fellowships, 1927-42; assoc. prof. neurology Harvard Med. Sch. 1942-44; vis. neurologist Boston City Hosp., 1934-42; cons. neurologist Peter Bent Brigham Hosp., 1939-44; cons. in neuropsychiatry U.S. Marine Hosp., 1937-44; dir. neuropathol. labs. Boston Psychopathic Hosp., 1943-44; mem. med. adv. bd. No. 12 SSS, 1940-44; prof clin. neurology Columbia Med. Sch., 1944-68, chmn. dept., 1948-68, Moses prof. neurology, 1963-70, emeritus, 1970-79, dean faculty medicine, v.p. charge med. affairs, 1958-70, dean, v.p. emeritus, 1970-79; chief neuropsychiat. service Montefiore Hosp., 1944-48; dir. service of neurology Neurol. Inst., Presbyn. Hosp., 1948-68; cons. various govtl. agys. Decorated grand officer Portuguese Order of Santiago; recipient George W. Jacoby award Am. Neurol. Assn., 1965; Bronze Hope Chest award Nat. Multiple Sclerosis Soc., 1967; Lennox award Am. Epilepsy Soc., 1967; North Carolina award, 1967; Golden Anniversary medal Assn. for Research in Nervous and Mental Disease, 1970; Thomas W. Salmon Distinguished Service award in psychiatry and mental hygiene, 1973. Diplomate Am. Bd. Psychiatry and Neurology (dir. 1942-50, pres. 1950). Mem. A.M.A., various other gen. and spl. med. and profl. assns. and orgns. Author: Cerebrospinal Fluid, 1937; Neurosyphillis, 1946; also textbooks; articles in profl. jours. Home: Bronxville, N.Y. Died Dec. 9, 1979.

MERSHEIMER, WALTER LYON, surgeon, educator; b. N.Y.C., Mar. 25, 1911; s. Christian Henry and Catherine (Vogel) M.; B.S., Norwich U., 1933, D.Sc. (hon.), 1962; M.D., N.Y. Med. Coll., 1937, M.Med. Sc. in Surgery, 1942; m. Janet Angeline Stanley, Dec. 26, 1941; children—Carol Janet (Mrs. Werner J. Roeder), Walter Henry, Joan Elizabeth (Mrs. Charles A. Taylor), Chris Lyon. Intern Flower and Fifth Av. Hosps., N.Y.C., 1937-39; resident surgery Met. Hosp., N.Y.C., 1940-42; fellow surgery N.Y. Med. Coll., 1939-40, mem. faculty, 1942-82, coordinator cancer edn. program, 1948-61, 62-72, prof. surgery, 1962-82, chmn. dept., 1962-76; dir. surgery Flower and Fifth Ave. Hosps., also Met. and Bird S. Coler Hosps., 1962-76, attending surgeon, 1950-82; attending surgeon Westchester County Med. Center, Valhalla, N.Y., 1970-82, chmn. div. surgery, 1970-76; cons. U.S. Naval Hosp., St. Albans, N.Y., 1947-59, VA Hosp., Lyons, N.J., 1951-64, Bronx VA Hosp., 1956-66, Yonkers Gen. Hosp., 1966-82, Victory Meml. Hosp., 1966-82, Holy Name Hosp., Teaneck, N.J., 1967-82, Italian Hosp., N.Y.C., 1967-82, S.I. Hosp., 1967-82, Hackensack (N.J.) Hosp., 1969-82, Lawrence Hosp., Bronxville, N.Y., 1969-82, Mt. Vernon Hosp., 1971-82, Stamford Hosp., 1974-82, VA Hosp., Castle Point, N.Y., 1976-82, St. John's Riverside Hosp., Yonkers, N.Y., 1976-82. Dir. N.Y.C. cancer com. Am. Cancer Soc., 1966-82; mem. results com. Nat. Cancer Inst., 1956-82. Trustee Pace U., N.Y., Norwich U., Northfield, Vt. Served to capt. M.C., USNR, 1942-46. Decorated Bronze Star; recipient Alumni medal N.Y. Med. Coll., 1960, 72. Diplomate Am. Bd. Surgery. Fellow A.C.S., Am. Coll. Gastroenterology; mem. AMA, N.Y. State, N.Y. County med. assns., N.Y. Acad. Medicine, N.Y. Acad. Sci., Harvey Soc., N.Y. Cancer Soc., N.Y. Surg. Soc., Assn. Am. Med. Colls., AAAS, Soc. Exptl. Biology and Medicine, Am. Assn. Surgery Trauma, Allen O. Whipple Surg. Soc., Soc. Surgery Alimentary Tract, Soc. Surg. Chmn., Am. Assn. Cancer Edn., Assn. Med. Schs. Greater N.Y. (mem. regional med. program), Westchester Acad. Medicine, Westchester Surg. Soc., Med. Soc. County Westchester, Sigma Alpha Epsilon, Alpha Kappa Kappa, Alpha Omega Alpha. Contbr. med jours. Home: Rye, N.Y. Died July 26, 1982.

MERSKEY, CLARENCE, physician; b. South Africa, July 20, 1914; s. Bernard and Hilda (Solomon) M.; came to U.S., 1959, naturalized, 1965; B. Med., B. Surgery, U. Capetown (S.Africa), 1937, M.D., 1947; m. Marie G. Fine, Oct. 8, 1939; children—Hilary Pamela Nathe, Susan Heather Sinistore, Joan Margaret Schneiderman. Intern, Groote Schuur Hosp., Capetown, 1938, City Hosp. for Infectious Diseases, Capetown, 1939; gen. med. practice, Tabankulu, Cape Province, Union South Africa, 1939-40; 1st asst. dept. medicine, vis. asst. physician Groote Schuur Hosp., 1947-48, vis. asst. physician, 1951, vis. physician, cons. hematologist, 1951-59; part-time lectr. physiology U. Capetown, 1947-48, 1st asst., sr. lectr. medicine, 1951-59; vis. fellow hematology Radcliffe Infirmary, Oxford, Eng., 1949-50; practice internal medicine, Capetown, 1951; fellow in biochemistry Harvard U. Med. Sch., Boston, 1957; asst. prof. medicine Albert Einstein Coll. Medicine, N.Y.C., 1959-66, assoc. prof., 1967-72, prof. medicine, 1972-82, asst. prof. pathology, 1966-68, assoc. prof., 1968-74, prof. lab. medicine, 1974-82. Served to capt. M.C., South African Army, 1940-46. Fellow mem. Royal Coll. Physicians London (Eng.); Am., N.Y., Bronx County med. assns., Coll. Physicians and Surgeons South Africa, Am. Physiol. Soc., Soc. Exptl. Biology and Medicine, Assn. Am. Physicians, Internat. Com. Thrombosis and Haemostasis, Am., Internat. socs. hematology, Soc. Study Blood. Contbr. articles to profl. jours. Home: Mamaroneck, N.Y. Died Nov. 10, 1982; buried Valhalla, N.Y.

MERTZKE, ARTHUR JOHN, economist; b. North Freedom, Wis., May 20, 1890; s. August Gustave and Bertha (Schramm) M.; A.B., U. of Wis., 1916; student U. of Chicago, 1916, Cambridge (Eng.) U., 1919; Ph.D., U. of Wis., 1926; m. Virginia Dearborn, July 16, 1920 (divorced 1938); children—Arthur John, Genevieve. Instr. economics, Pomona Coll., Claremont, Calif., 1916-18, U. of Wis., 1919-25; asst. prof. econs., Northwestern U., 1925-27; dir. edn. and research, Nat. Assn. Real Estate Bds., 1927-31; econ. analyst U.S. Bur. of Standards, 1931-32; chief economist Federal Home Loan Bank Board, 1933-34; instr. in economics, Coll. of the City of N.Y., 1936-40. Lecturer on real estate Cornell Univ., 1939-42. Sub-editor, Standard & Poor's Corp., publishers, 1942-43; research dir. Jos. W. Hicks, pub. relations, 1943-44; dir. of media, Batten, Barton, Durstine & Osborn, 1944-46; lecturer on marketing Northwestern U., from 1946. First sergt. U.S. Army at Base Hosp., Savenay, France, 1918-19. Mem. Am. Statis. Assn., Am. Marketing Assn., Am. Land Econs. Assn., Artus. Unitarian. Author: Real Estate Appraisals, 1927. Contbr. articles to real estate and econ. jours. Home: Chicago, Ill. Deceased.

MERWIN, BRUCE WELCH, educator; b. Iola, Kan., Feb. 27, 1889; s. Charles Edwin and Lydia Ella (Welch) M.; A.B., U. of Kan., 1911, B.S. in Edn., 1911, A.M., 1924, Ph.D., 1929; m. Helen Hinkle, 1914 (dec. 1939); 1 dau., Helen (Merwin); m. 2d, Blanche Cline, June 8, 1940. Teacher, Paris, Tenn., 1911-12, Jerome, Ida., 1912-13; supt. schs., Savonburg, Kan., 1913-15; curator University Museum, Phila., 1915-19; supt. schs., Republic, Kan., 1921-22; prin. county high sch., Sharon Springs, Kan., 1922-26; instr. edn., U. of Kan., 1926-27; instr. edn. Southern Illinois University, 1927-29, dir. training schs., 1929-46, professor of education from 1946, acting president 1944. Dir. and one of founders Jackson County Teachers' Credit Union, Ill. State Archael. Soc.; mem. Ill. Edn. Assn. (2d v.p.; mem. tenure com. and auditing com.; ex- pres. Southern Div.; also mem. other coms.). Am. Assn. School Adminstrs., Soc. Coll. Teachers of Edn.; Nat. Edn. Assn., Nat. Council Schoolhouse Constrn., N.E.A. (dept. higher edn.), So. Ill. Custodian Engr. Assn. (chmn. bd.), Ill. Schoolmasters Club, Ill. Elementary Sch. Prins. Assn., Kappa Phi Kappa (pres.), Phi Delta Kappa, Kappa Delta Phi, Acacia. Methodist. Contbr. articles to mags. Co-author: Illinois, Cross-Roads of a Nation (historical reader for elmentary schools). Home: Carbondale, Ill. †

MESERVE, SHIRLEY EDWIN, lawyer; b. Los Angeles, Oct. 7, 1889; s. Edwin A. and Helen (Davis) M.; U. Calif., 1912; U. So. Calif., 1914; m. Edith Porter, June 5, 1913 (dec. 1917); children—Edwin Abel, John Robert; m. 2d Leigh Whittemore, June 1, 1918. Admitted to Calif. bar, 1914; pres. Flour Corp., Ltd., engrs. and constructors, 1947, dir., chmn. bd. from 1949; dir., sec. Brock & Co., jewelers, from 1940, Filtex Corp., mfrs. vacuum cleaners, from 1948. Dir. Welfare Fedn. of Los Angeles Area. Trustee Harvard Mil. Sch., 1924-29; trustee, sec. Albert Soiland Cancer Found. Mem. Am., Calif. State, Los Angeles bar assns., Calif. State, Los Angeles Cs. of C., Phi Kappa Psi (nat. pres., 1924-26), Phi Delta Phi. Mason (Shriner, 32 deg.). Clubs: Newport, Harbor Yacht (Newport Beach, Calif.); California, University (Los Angeles); The Family (San Francisco). Home: Los Angeles, Calif. †

MESTRES, RICARDO ANGELO, univ. adminstr.; b. Tampico, Mexico, Jan. 8, 1910; s. Ricardo A. and Ema (Haymond) M.; diploma Hill Sch., Pottstown, Pa., 1926; A.B., Princeton, 1931; student Law Sch. Columbia, 1932-34; m. Anita McKim Gwynne, Aug. 13, 1932 (dec. 1961); children—Ricardo Angelo, Lee Gwynne. Came to U.S., 1913, naturalized, 1918. Real estate mgmt., N.Y.C., 1931-41; spl. rep. Western Union Telegraph Co., 1941-42; dir. Princeton Fund, 1947-53; asst. treas. Princeton, 1951-53, treas., 1953-72, fin. v.p., 1959-72; trustee Princeton U. Press. Dir. Mut. Benefit Life Ins. Co., Amerada Hess Corp., Baker Fentress & Co. Trustee Geraldine R. Dodge Found., Hill Sch., Whitehall Found. Served to lt. Air Combat Intelligence, USNR, 1942-46. Clubs: University, Princeton, Century Assn. (N.Y.C.); Nassau, Springdale Golf (Princeton). Home: Princeton, N.J. Died.

METCALF, JOHN THOMAS, lawyer; b. Pineville, Ky., June 23, 1890; s. Charles W. and Nettle L. (Gray) M.; A.B., Centre College, Danville, Kentucky, Law Sch., Centre Coll., 1911-12. Admitted to bar, 1912; practiced law, Pineville, 1912-17, Winchester, Ky., 1912-44, U.S. atty. Eastern Dist. Ky., 1937-44; gen. solicitor L.&N. R.R. Co. Past dist. gov. Rotary; chmn. Ky. Crippled Children Comm., from 1956. Hon. mem. Omicron Delta Kappa. Address: Louisville, KY. †

METCALF, KEYES DEWITT, library consultant; b. Elyria, Ohio, Apr. 13, 1889; s. Isaac Stevens and Harriet (Howes) M.; m. Martha Gerrish, June 16, 1914 (dec. 1938); children—Margaret (Mrs. Maxwell M. Small), William Gerrish; m. Elinor Gregory, July 12, 1941. A.B., Oberlin Coll., 1911, Litt.D., 1939; cert. and diploma, Library Sch., N.Y. Pub. Library, 1914; L.H.D., Yale U., 1946; LL.D., Harvard U., 1951, U. Toronto, 1954, Marquette U., Milw., 1958, St. Louis U., 1959, Grinnell Coll., 1959, U. Notre Dame, 1964, Ind. U., 1974; Litt.D., Brandeis U., 1959, Bowdoin Coll., 1965, Hamilton Coll., 1972. Student asst. Oberlin Coll. Library, 1905-11, exec. asst., 1912, acting librarian, 1916-17; chief of stacks N.Y. Pub. Library, N.Y.C., 1913-16 17-18, exec. asst., 1919-27, chief reference dept., 1928-37; librarian Harvard Coll. and dir. Harvard U. Library, 1937-55, prof. bibliography, 1945-55, librarian emeritus, 1955-83; adj. prof. library service Rutgers U., 1955-58, cons. library adminstrn. and bldg. planning, 1955-83; library cons. Australian univs., 1958, 61, 63, 65, 68, India, S. Africa, 1959, Ireland, 1960, Japan, 1961, Can., 1960-83, Costa Rica, 1964, U.K., 1972-83, Venezuela, 1973, Libya, Abu Dhabi, Saudi Arabia, 1975, Iran, 1976; cons. Nat. Capital Devel. Commn., Canberra, Australia, 1961-68; Fulbright lectr. to, Australia, 1958-59; lectr. Inst. Advanced Archtl. Studies, York, Eng., 1966; exec. sec. Assn. Research Libraries, 1938-41; v.p. New Eng. Deposit Library, 1942-55. Author: Planning Academic and Research Libraries, 1965, Library Lighting, 1970, Random Recollections of an Anachronism, 1980; contbr. numerous articles to profl. publs. Trustee Radcliffe Coll., 1939-45, Mass. State Library, 1942-60; mem. Com. to Aid Nat. Library of Peru, 1943-50. Decorated Knight first class Order St. Olav (Norway); Recipient 50th Anniversary medal N.Y. Pub. Library, 1961, Lippincott and Scarecrow Press award, 1967, Academic/Research Librarian of Year award, 1978, citation Boston Archtl. Center, 1982; Fulbright scholar Queen's U., Belfast, 1966. Mem. ALA (pres. 1942-43), Am. Library Inst., Bibliog. Soc. Am., Am. Antiquarian Soc., Mass. Hist. Soc., Bibliog. Soc. (London), Am. Acad. Arts and Scis. Congregationalist. Clubs: Century (N.Y.C.); Odd Volumes (Boston). Home: Belmont, Mass. Dec. Nov. 3, 1983.

METCALF, THOMAS NELSON, prof. phys. edn.; b. Elyria, Ohio, Sept. 21, 1890; s. Isaac Stevens and Harriet (Howes) M.; A.B. and A.M., Oberlin Coll., 1912; student Harvard, summer 1912, Columbia U., 1914-17, New York U., summer 1928; m. Helen Margaret Waller, Dec. 23, 1915; children—Jean (Renfro), Alan Wilder. Instr. in physical edn., coach of football and track, Oberlin Coll., 1912-14, asso. prof., also coach, 1918-22; asso. in phys. edn., also coach, Columbia U., 1915-18, prof. and coach, track and freshman football. U. of Minn., 1922-24; dir. athletics and prof. phys. edn., Iowa State Coll., 1924-33, U. Chgo., after 1933. Comdr. U.S.N.R. 1912-16. Sec. Am. Olympic Track and Field Com., 1929-36, asst. mgr. Am. Olympic Track and Field Team, 11th Olympiad, 1936; chmn. adminstrn. U.S. Olympic Teams, 1948, 52. Fellow, Am. Assn., Health, Phys. Edn. and Recreation. Mem. Central Assn. Amateur. Athletic Union (pres. 1952-53), College Phys. Edn. Assn. (sec.-treas. 1920-29, pres. 1930). Conglist. Club: Quadrangle. Home: Chicago, Ill. Deceased.

METZGER, EARL H., army officer; b. Steelton, Pa., Aug. 14, 1889; s. Joseph Miller and Fannie (Kaylor) M.; B.S. in Elec. Engring., Pa. State Coll., 1911; grad. Army War Coll., 1935; m. Dorothy McKaye, Dec. 5, 1916; children—Earl H., Jr. (capt.), Donald McKaye (1st lt.). Commd. 2d lt., U.S. Army, 1912, and advanced through the grades to brig. gen., Feb. 13, 1942; comd. Anti-aircraft Training Center, Camp Stewart, Ga., Feb. 13, 1942-Feb. 18, 1943. Mason. Home: Newport, R.I. Deceased.

METZLER, HARRY RANCK, ins. exec.; b. Paradise, Twp., Pa., Oct. 2, 1887; s. Isaac Eby and Mary Ann (Ranck) M.; student pub. schs., Pa.; diploma Pa. Bus. Coll.; m. Mary G. Leaman, Feb. 6, 1913 (dec.); children—Elsie, Albert, Dorothy (Mrs. E. Earl Walton), Henry (killed in action, France, World War II); married second, Miriam Mann Barton, May 13, 1949; 1 adopted son, Philip R. Clk. Phila. and Reading R.R., 1910; mem. Pa. State Police 1911-13; dir. Poultry Producers Coop. Exchange, 1932-43; mgr. Lancaster County Farm Bur. Coop. Assn., 1934-40, sec.-treas., from 1940; chmn. Peoples Mortgage Co., from 1955; county commr. Lancaster County, 1939-55; dir. Farm Bur. Mut. Automobile Ins. Co., Farm Bur. Fire Ins. Co., Farm Bur. Life Ins. Co., Peoples Development Co., Peoples Broadcasting Co., Peoples Research & Mfg. Co., Approved Finance Co., Mut. Income Fund, Nationwide Corp. (all Farm Bur. ins. cos.) from 1955; mem. finance com. all Nationwide Ins. cos. and subsidiaries. Road supr. Paradise Twp., 1926-40; mem. Lancaster Airport Commn., 1948-52. Recipient Master Farmer degree Pa. Farmer, 1931. Mem. Lancaster County Agrl. Extension Assn. (trustee 1926-40, treas. 1934-40). Home: Lancaster, Pa. †

MEYER, ALBERT JULIUS, economics educator; b. Hawarden, Iowa, May 14, 1919; s. Albert Julius and Susan (French) M.; m. Anne Avantaggio, Dec. 23, 1950; children: Barbara, Peter, Stephen. A.B., UCLA, 1941, M.A., 1942; Ph.D., Johns Hopkins U., 1951; M.A. (hon.), Harvard, 1960. Assoc. prof. econs., exec. asst. to pres. Am. U., Beirut, Lebanon, 1947-55; mem. faculty Harvard, 1955-83, prof. Middle Eastern studies, 1964-83, lectr. econs., 1955-83; assoc. dir. Harvard (Center Middle Eastern Studies), 1956-83, cons. corps., philanthropic founds., govt. agys., 1955-83; Dir. Indsl. Bank of Japan Trust Co.; Head spl. U.S. econ. mission to Saudi Arabia, 1962. Author: Middle Eastern Capitalism; Nine Essays, 1959, The Economy of Cyprus, 1962. Trustee Rhinelander Found., 1964—, Near East Found., 1970—. Served to lt. USNR, 1942-45. Fulbright-Hays vis. scholar Middle East, 1966-67. Mem. N.Y. Council Fgn. Relations, Middle East Inst. Home: Cambridge, Mass. Dec. Oct. 31, 1983.

MEYER, EUGENE, III, physician, educator; b. N.Y.C., June 7, 1915; s. Eugene and Agnes (Ernst) M.; grad. Taft Sch., 1932; A.B., Yale, 1937; M.D., Johns Hopkins, 1941; m. Mary A. Bradley, Dec. 27, 1940; children—Eugene Bradley, Ruth Emery, Anne, Elizabeth Ernst. Intern Johns Hopkins Hosp., 1941-42, resident, 1946-49; asso. prof. medicine and psychiatry Johns Hopkins Med. Sch., 1955-66, prof. psychiatry, 1966-82, prof. medicine, 1970-82; practice medicine specializing in psychiatry, Balt., 1946-82. Dir. Washington Post Co. Mem. Gov's. Commn. on Law Enforcement and Adminstrn. Justice, 1967; pres. adv. bd. Md. Childrens Center Bd. dirs. Eugene and Agnes E. Meyer Found., Washington; trustee William Alanson White Psychiat. Found. Served to capt. M.C., USAAF, 1942-45. Mem. Am. Psychiat. Assn., Am. Psychosomatic Soc., Am. Psychoanalytic Soc., A.M.A., A.C.P. Home: Baltimore, Md. Died Feb. 24, 1982.

MEYER, HARRY W(ILLIAM), assn. consultant; b. Chicago, Ill., Jan. 29, 1889; s. Henry F. and Emma (Holtz) M.; student Lewis Inst. of Chicago, 1903-07; student Ill. Wesleyan U., 1915; m. Pauline Ann Kiesling, Feb. 9, 1915; 1 son, Harold W. Chmn. of bd. Liquinet Corp., Chgo.; cons. Nat. Assn. Retail Druggists. Member Ill. C. of C., Chicago Drug & Chem. Assn., Phi Gamma Delta. Rep. Lutheran. Clubs: North Shore Country (Glenview, Ill.); Dunedin Isles Country (Dunedin, Fla.), Carlouel Yacht. Home: Chicago, Ill. †

MEYER, HENRY HAROLD, business exec.; b. Hodgeman County, Kan., Aug. 30, 1888; s. Edwin Carlos and Ida May (Chapman) M.; grad. Bryant-Stratton Coll., Buffalo, N.Y.; m. Hallie Rouse, Nov. 25, 1914. Bookkeeper, cost accountant, salesman and office mgr. for various firms in Buffalo, N.Y., 1908-14; mgr. Welch Grape Juice Co., Ltd., St. Catherine, Ont., Can., 1914; in exec. capacity Welch Grape Juice Co., Westfield, N.Y., 1915-18; examining auditor Fed. Trade Commn., Washington, D.C., 1918-19; office mgr. and asst. gen. mgr.,

Harvard Products Co., Brocton, N.Y., 1919-22; gen. mgr., dir., treas., Keystone Cooperative Grape Assn., North East, Pa., 1922-26; sec., treas., gen. mgr., dir. H.H. Meyer Packing Co., Cin., 1926-32, pres. and dir., 1932-64, chmn. bd., from 1964; v.p. John Morrell & Co., from 1964; dir. Mohawk Provision Co. Cons. War Meat Bd., U.S. Dept. Agr., Washington, 1943-46. A founder Am. Meat Inst. Found., Chgo., 1944, mem. found. bd. dirs. 14 yrs., also served as sec. and treas., vice chmn. and chmn. Mem. bd. dirs. Bethesda Hosp., Cin., Emanuel Community Center, Cin. Mem. City Council North East, Pa., 1925-26. Mem. Midwest Meat Packers Assn. (dir. 1933-37), Am. Meat Inst. (treas. dir. 1931-64). Methodist. Mason (Shriner), Elk. Clubs: Cincinnati, Maketewah Country; Chicago (Ill.) Athletic Assn.; Everglades (Palm Beach, Fla.). Home: Cincinnati, OH. †

MEYER, JOHN DIEDRICH ERNEST, lawyer; b. Charleston, S.C., Aug. 27, 1890; s. J. D. Ernest and Mary R. S. (Reils) M.; B.S., The Citadel, 1912; LL.B., U. of S.C., 1915; unmarried. Admitted to S.C. bar, 1915, and began practice at Charleston; U.S. atty. Eastern Dist. of S.C., by apptmt. of President Harding, from May 16, 1922. Capt. and adj. 2d S.C. Inf., Mexican border service, 1916; maj., asst. gen. staff officer, 30th Div., also 30th Div. ammunition officer, A.E.F., World War; participated in all engagements of 30th Div. Mem. S.C. Bar Assn. Republican. Lutheran. Mason, Moose, Elk. Club: Charleston Rifle. Home: Charleston, S.C. †

MEYER, VINCENT, army officer; b. N.Y. City, Aug. 29, 1889; s. Daniel Charles and Emily (Doyle) M.; B.S., U.S. Naval Acad., 1911; grad. Command and Gen. Staff Sch., 1930, Army War Coll., 1937; m. Agnes Beattle Stewart, Aug. 12, 1919; children—Stewart Canfield, Vincent. Commd. 2d lt., Field Arty., U.S. Army, 1911, and advanced through the grades to brig. gen. (temp.), Oct. 31, 1941; served as major, A.E.F., World War I; Italian campaign, 1943-44; European Adv. Com., 1944-45; Allied Control Council, Berlin, 1945; retired as brig. gen., Dec. 31, 1945; dep. chief operations, U.N.R.R.A., Germany, 1946-47; special commr. Internat. Refugee Orgn., for Venezuela, Colombia, Ecuador, Peru, Bolivia, Chile, 1947; chief mission Venezuela for Internat. Refugee Orgn., 1947-50. Awarded Distinguished Serv. Medal, Victory medal with 5 battle clasps, E.T.O. ribbon with 2 battle clasps. Episcopalian. Clubs: Army and Navy (Washington); Country Club of Virginia (Richmond). Address: Richmond, Va. †

MEYER, WILLIAM WALTER, lawyer; b. Ada, O., Aug. 15, 1887; s. William Henry and Harriet Coit (Grafton) M.; A.B., Ohio Northern U., 1911; A.M., Yale, 1912, LL.B., 1915; unmarried. Began as asst. atty. N.Y., N.H.&H. R.R., 1915, and advanced through grades to gen counsel, 1935; counsel for bd. of trustees, 1935-43; retired Aug. 15, 1943. Served as mem. Conn. Gen. Assembly from Clinton, 1933. Lt. 145 Inf., U.S. Army, World War. Republican. Episcopalian. Mason. Club: Graduate (New Haven). Home: Clinton, Conn.†

MEYER, ZOE, author; b. Metamora, Ill., Apr. 26, 1888; d. Peter and Cora B. (Gibson) M.; ed. Bradley Inst., Peoria. Teacher pub. schs. Author: Under the Blue Sky, 1917; Orchard and Meadow, 1919; The Little Green Door, 1921; The Garden of Happiness, 1923; Followers of the Trail, 1926; Sunshine Farm, 1927; The Sunshine Book, 1932. Home: Peoria, Ill. †

MEYERHOFF, JOSEPH, philanthropist; b. Russia, Apr. 8, 1899; came to U.S., 1906, naturalized, 1913; s. Oscar and Hannah (Gurewitz) M.; m. Rebecca Witten, Aug. 21, 1921; children: Peggy Meyerhoff Pearlstone (dec.), Harvey M., Eleanor Meyerhoff Katz. LL.B., U. Md., 1920; D.H.L. (honoris causa), Balt. Hebrew Coll., 1970; D.H.L., Dropsie U., 1974, Towson State U., 1980, U. Md., 1981, Johns Hopkins U., 1983; Ph.D. (hon.), Tel Aviv U., 1973, Hebrew U., Jerusalem, 1977, Weizmann Inst., 1979. With Monumental Properties, Inc. (formerly Joseph Meyerhoff Corp.), Balt.; With Monumental Properties, Inc. (and predecessor cos.), 1933—, pres., 1933-72, chmn. bd., 1972-75, chmn. exec. com., 1973-78; trustee Monumental Properties Trust, 1978-81; chmn. bd. Magna Properties, Inc., 1979-85; dir. PEC-Israel Econ. Corp. (formerly Palestine Econ. Corp.), N.Y.C., 1950-85, pres., 1957-63, chmn. bd., 1963-85; dir. IDB Holding Co., Discount Bank Investment Corp. Mem. Md. Bd. Pub. Welfare, 1953-57; bd. dirs. Technion-Israel Inst. Tech., Hebrew U. Jerusalem, Tel Aviv U., U. Negev, Weizmann Inst., Tel Aviv Mus.; chmn. Md. Planning Commn., 1957-63; gen. chmn. United Jewish Appeal, 1961-64; pres. Balt. Symphony Orch., Inc., 1965-85, Jewish Welfare Fund of Balt., 1951-53; pres. Asso. Jewish Charities of Balt., 1959-62, bd. dirs., 1953-85; bd. dirs. Balt. Mus. Art, Balt. Opera Co.; exec. com. Peabody Conservatory of Music. Mem. Nat. Assn. Home Builders U.S. (pres. 1946-47, dir.). Club: Center (Balt.) (pres. 1964-74). Home: Baltimore, Md. Died Feb. 2, 1985.

MEYEROWITZ, WILLIAM, artist; b. Russia, July 15, 1893; s. Gershon and Sophia (Midleman) M.; came to U.S., 1905; art edn. N.A.D.; m. Theresa F. Bernstein, Feb. 1918. Painter, etcher; work rep. numerous pub., pvt. collections. Recipient Modern Jury first prize and gold medal for painting Exodus; 1st prize for etching N.Y., Am. Color Print Soc., 1950; 1st anonymous prize Audubon Artists, 1955; best painting prize N. Shore Arts Assn., 1957, 1st prize, 1968; Peterson Allied Arts prize, 1958; hon. mention for still life Ogunquit Art Assn., 1959; Eric Hudson prize for painting Cavalcade, 1960; Layton prize Allied Artists, 1962; Vavana Meml. Painting prize, 1965; H. Register prize Rockport Art Assn., 1964, Rothenberg prize 1967; Ellin P. Speyer prize N.A.D.; 1965; Nat. Acad. prize for paintiing, 1965; W.F. Schrafft award for best painting exhbn. Rockport Art Assn., 1965, prize, 1967, gold medal honor award painting, 1970; Vayana Meml. award Ogonquit Art Center, 1973; Carl Matson meml. prize portrait painting, 1964, Iver Rose Meml. award Rockport Art Assn., 1975, E. Schllem award for excellence in painting North Shore Arts Assn., 1976. Mem. arts council Gloucester Arts Festival; v.p., hon. life mem. N. Shore Art Assn. N.Am. Mem. Bklyn, Soc. Etchers, Conn. Acad. Fine Arts, Gloucester Soc. Art, Phila. Soc. Etchers, Cape Ann Art Soc., Boston Print Makers, Soc. Am. Etchers, Audubon Soc. Artists, Rockport Summer Artists, Internat. Inst. Arts and Letters, Allied Artists Am., Rockport Art Assn. Home: New York, N.Y. Died June 4, 1981.

MEYEROWITZ, WILLIAM, artist; b. Russia, July 15, 1887; s. Gershon and Sophia (Midleman) M.; came to U.S., 1905; art edn. N.A.D.; m. Theresa F. Bernstein, Feb. 1918. Painter, etcher; work rep. numerous pub., pvt. collections; posthumous exhbns: Summit Gallery, N.Y.C., 1981, Bethesda Art Gallery, Md., 1981, Cayuga Mus. History and Art, Auburn, N.Y., 1983, Rockport Art Assn., Mass., 1983, N.Y. Hist. Soc., 1983-84, Patterson Pub. Library, N.J., 1984, Shore Rd. Gallery, Boston, 1984, Smith Girard Collection, Standford, Conn., 1984. Recipient Modern Jury first prize and gold medal for painting Exodus; 1st prize for etching N.Y., Am. Color Print Soc., 1950; 1st anonymous prize Audubon Artists, 1955; best painting prize N. Shore Arts Assn., 1957, 1st prize, 1968; Peterson Allied Arts prize, 1958; hon. mention for still life Ogunquit Art Assn., 1959; Eric Hudson prize for painting Cavalcade, 1960; Layton prize Allied Artists, 1962; Vavana Meml. Painting prize, 1965; H. Register prize Rockport Art Assn., 1964, Rothenberg prize 1967; Ellin P. Speyer prize N.A.D.; 1965; Nat. Acad. prize for painting, 1965; W.F. Schrafft award for best painting exhbn. Rockport Art Assn., 1965, prize, 1967, gold medal honor award painting, 1970; Vayana Meml. award Ogonquit Art Center, 1973; Carl Matson meml. prize portrait painting, 1964, Iver Rose Meml. award Rockport Art Assn., 1975, E. Schllem award for excellence in painting North Shore Arts Assn., 1976, Gold medal honor Rockport Art Assn., 1978, Gold medal Academia Italia delle Arti e del Lavoro; recipient posthumous awards Butler Inst. Art, 1983, Academico D'Europa Parma, Italy, Internat. Exhbn. for Peace, 1984. Mem. arts council Gloucester Arts Festival; v.p., hon. life mem. N. Shore Art Assn. N.Am. Mem. Bklyn. Soc. Etchers, Conn. Acad. Fine Arts, Gloucester Soc. Art, Phila. Soc. Etchers, Cape Ann Art Soc., Boston Print Makers, Soc. Am. Etchers, Audubon Soc. Artists, Rockport Summer Artists, Internat. Inst. Arts and Letters, Allied Artists Am., Rockport Art Assn. (Gold medal of honor 1978). Home: New York, N.Y. Died May 28, 1981; interred New Montefiore Cemetery, L.I., N.Y.

MEYERS, CECIL KENNETH, church official; b. Calcutta, India, Aug. 28, 1887; s. Herbert Benjamin and Ellen (Hunt) M.; ed. in India and Burma, and at Theol. Coll. Seventh Day Adventists, London, Eng.; m. Ethel Winnifred Hoopes, of Redcloud, Neb., Oct. 14, 1907; children—Kenneth Lewis, Dorothy Winifred Helen. Missionary Seventh Day Adventists Ch. in South Sea Islands, Australia and New Zealand, 1908-21; came to U.S., 1921; asso. sec. Gen. Conf. Seventh Day Adventists, 1921-26, sec. since 1926, making annual tours of foreign missionary stations; sec. Internat. Med. Service Foundation, Inc., since 1932. Home: Washington, D.C. †

MICHAUD, JOSEPH ENOLL, ex-minister transport, Can.; b. St. Antonin, Teminsconata County, Que., Sept. 26, 1888; s. Joseph and Eugénie (Bernier) M.; B.A., Laval Univ., 1910, hon. LL.D., 1940; LL.B., Dalhousie Law Sch., 1913; m. Nelida Ringuette, Sept. 22, 1914; 9 children. Called to bar of N.B., 1914; King's counsel, 1935; practiced in Edmundston, N.B.; mayor of Edmundston, 1919-36; mem. N.B. Hydro-Elec. Commn., 1922-25. Elected to N.B. Legislature, 1917, 20, 25, 30; minister without portfolio, N.B., Foster adminstrn., 1921-23, Veniot adminstrn., 1923-25; elected to House of Commons, Can., at by-election, 1933, re-elected at gen. election, 1935; sworn to Privy Council and minister of fisheries, Canada. 1935-42; minister of transport October 7, 1942-Apr. 1945; chief justice, King's Bench Div. Province of New Brunswick, since April, 1945. Roman Catholic. Address: New Brunswick, Can. †

MICHAUX, HENRI, author and painter. Works include Barbarian in Asia; Ecuador: A Travel Journal, 1969; Miserable Miracle, 1963; Selected Writings, 1968. Address: New York, N.Y. Died Oct. 18, 1984.*

MICHEL, MAXIMIN, business executive; b. Barcelonnette, France, Aug. 1888; s. Henri and Virginie (Marcel) M.; student Coll. de Barcelonnette, Lazaristes, Bawden Coll.; m. Bertha S. Michel, Sept. 16, 1925; children—Renee (Mrs. Guichard), Madeleine, Max. With El Puerto de Liverpool, S.A., since 1905, dir. gen.; pres. Banco de Londres y México, S.A., La Provincial Cía. Gral. de Seguros, S.A.; mem. bd. dirs. several corps., Mexico City. Mem. La Nacional Ins. Co. Club: Bankers (Mexico). Home: Mexico D.F., Mexico. †

MICHELBACHER, GUSTAV FREDERICK, ins. exec.; b. Riverside Co., Calif., Dec. 26, 1890; s. Ezra and Ida (Baumann) M.; B.S., U. of Calif., 1912, M.S., 1913; m. Winifred Bowen, June 22, 1915; children—Winifred, Barbara. Statistician Workmen's Compensation Service Bur., N.Y. City, 1915-16; actuary Nat. Workmen's Compensation Service Bur., 1916-19; sec. Nat. Council on Workmen's Compensation Ins., 1919-21; sec.-treas. Nat. Bur. Casualty & Surety Underwriters, 1921-26; v.p. Great Am. Indemnity Co., N.Y. City, 1926-47, pres. from 1947. Mem. Casualty Actuarial Soc., Ins. Soc. N.Y., Ins. Inst. Am., Sigma Xi. Club: Drug and Chemical (N.Y. City), Author Workmen's Compensation Insurance (with Thomas M. Nial), 1925; Casualty Insurance Principles (with others), 1930. Home: White Plains, N.Y. †

MICHELMAN, HERBERT, publishing company executive; b. Harrisburg, Pa., Mar. 26, 1913; s. David I. and Sara (Robbin) M.; B.A., Bklyn. Coll., 1934; m. Blanche Krainin, May 14, 1941; children—Faith Michelman Lennon, Frances. With Gimbel Bros. Co., N.Y.C., 1929-41, book buyer, 1938-41; asst. to pres. World Pub. Co., Cleve., 1941-43; with Crown Pubs. Inc., N.Y.C., 1943-79, v.p., editor-in-chief, 1952-59; pub. Herbert Michelman Books, N.Y.C., 1952-79; lectr. adult edn. City Coll. N.Y. Editor, Laurelton (N.Y.) Civic News. Served with U.S. Army, 1943-46. Jewish. Co-author: Body Control, 1964; International Guide to Physical Fitness, 1973. Home: East Hills, N.Y. Dec. Nov. 11, 1980.

MICKELSON, PETER PALMER, ret. educator; b. Tracy, Minn., May 27, 1904; s. Alfred Paul and Tolena (Holen) M.; A.B., Mayville State Coll., 1935; A.M., U. Colo., 1939, Ph.D. (Grad. fellow), 1941; m. Inger H. Thompson, Dec. 31, 1927. Tchr., prin., supt. pub schs., N.D., 1921-36; supr. Mayville (N.D.) State Coll., 1936-39; research fellow U. Colo., 1939-41; pres. State Jr. Coll., Trinidad, Colo., 1941-46, Western State Coll., Gunnison, Colo., 1946-60; prof. ednl. adminstrn. U. Hawaii, 1960-64; prof. U. Wis., Madison, 1964-68, prof. ednl. adminstrn., dir. internat. programs Sch. Edn., 1967-74, asso. dean, 1970-74. Chief of party No. Nigeria Tchr. Edn. Project. Kaduna, Nigeria, 1964-66; mem. Airport Commn. Gunnison, 1948-60; chmn. Gunnison Nat. Forest Council, 1955-60. City Planning Commn. Gunnison, 1956-60. Recipient Key Man award Trinidad Jr. C. of C., 1945; Distinguished Alumni award Mayville State Coll., 1970; named Man of Year, Gunnison C. of C., 1959. Fellow Wilton Park Conf., Eng., 1969. Mem. N.E.A., Am. Assn. Sch. Adminstrs., Hawaii, Wis. edn. assns., Wis. Assn. Sch. Dist. Adminstrs., Phi Delta Kappa. Author: (with Kenneth Hansen) Elementary School Administration, 1957. Home: St. Petersburg, Fla. Died June 24, 1982.

MIDDELDORF, ULRICH ALEXANDER, art educator; b. Stassfurt, Germany, June 23, 1901; s. Hans and Meta (Zuckschwerdt) M.; student U. of Giessen, 1918-19, Univ. of Munich, 1919-20, Univ. of Berlin, 1921-24 (Ph.D.); Litt.D. (honorary), University Florence, 1965; m. Gloria Greenhut, Sept. 9, 1938. Came to U.S., 1935. Fellow, Kunsthistorisches Institut, Florence, Italy, 1926; travel and study in Italy and U.S., 1927-28; curator Kunsthistorisches Institut, 1928-35; asst. prof. of art, U. of Chicago, 1935-38; asso. prof. and acting chmn. of dept. of art, 1938-40; asso. prof. and chmn., dept. of art, 1940-41; prof. and chmn. dept. art, 1941-53; dir. Kunsthistorisches Inst., Florence, Italy, 1953-83. Decorated Silver medal (City Florence); great cross Order of Merit (Germany), comdr. Order of Merit (Italy). Mem. Societa Colombaria (corr.), Accademia del Disegno (hon. academician), Coll. Art Assn. of Am. (pres. 1939-40), Verband Deutscher Kunsthistoriker, Deutsche Verein fur Kunstwissenschaft. Author: Catalog of Morgenroth Collection of Italian Medals and Plaquettes (with O. Goetz), 1944; Raphael's Drawings, 1945. Mem. editorial bd., Art Bull. Contbr. U.S., European art jours. Home: Florence, Italy. Died Feb. 20, 1983.

MIDDLETON, EDWIN GHEENS, mem. Republican Nat. Com., lawyer; b. Louisville, June 11, 1920; s. Charles G. and Anita (Gheens) M.; B.A., U. Va., 1941; LL.B., U. Louisville, 1948; m. Mary Jane Lampton, July 11, 1942; children—Edwin Gheens, Anita G., Huntley L. Admitted to Ky. bar, 1948; partner firm Middleton, Reutlinger & Baird, Louisville, 1948-79; gen. counsel, dir. Am. Life & Accident Ins. Co.; vice chmn., dir. Capital Projects Corp., 1978-79. Mem. Republican Nat. Com. for Ky., 1965-79, state central com., 1972; chmn. Rep. county exec. com., 1958-63; del., mem. platform com. Rep. Nat. Conv., 1964, chmn. com. contests, 1972, vice-chmn. site selection com., 1976; chmn. bd., dir. Louisville and Jefferson County Children's Home, 1952-62, Louisville Park Theater Assn., 1956-68; trustee, sec. Louisville Country Day Sch., 1957-64; trustee Louisville Collegiate Sch.; chmn. bd. trustees U. Louisville, 1964-74, bd. overseers, 1975-79. Served to maj. USMC, 1941-46. Decorated Bronze Star with V, Purple Heart; recipient Faculty Senate Disting. Service award U. Louisville Middleton Theatre, 1975, John Sherman Cooper award Lincoln Club, 1979. Mem. Am., Ky., Louisville bar assns. Episcopalian. Clubs: Filson, Salmagundi, Pendennis, Louisville County (pres. 1966-68, dir. 1964-69). Home: Harrods Creek, Ky. Deceased.

MIDDLETON, RAY, actor, singer; b. Chgo., Feb. 8, 1907; s. Almor C. and Lela (Owens) M.; B. Mus., U. Ill., 1930; postgrad. Juilliard Sch. Music, 1935. Debut as John Kent in Roberta, N.Y.C., 1933, later played Washington

Irving in Knickerbocker Holiday, 1938, appeared George White's Scandals, 1939, American Jubilee, 1940, played Frank Butler in Annie Get Your Gun, 1946, Sam Cooper in Love Life, 1948; succeeded Ezio Pinza in South Pacific, 1949; appeared in Too Good to be True, 1963 (all Broadway); toured U.S. as lectr. in America in Song and Story, 1957, 63; appeared in films including Gangs of Chicago, 1940; I Dream of Jeannie, 1952; Road to Denver, 1955. Served with USAAF, 1942-45. Mem. Actors Equity Assn., A.F.T.R.A., Screen Actors Guild, Am. Guild Variety Artists. Address: New York, N.Y. Died Apr. 12, 1984.*

MIDKIFF, FRANK ELBERT, former govt. ofcl., trustee; b. Anna, Ill., Nov. 15, 1887; son James Jesse and Bertha (Wilson) M.; student Shurtleff Acad. and Coll., Upper Alton, Ill., 1905-08; A.B., Colgate University, 1912; Ph.D., Yale Univ., 1935; m. Ruth Richards, June 29, 1917; children—Mary W. (dec.), Robert Richards, Frances Elizabeth. Teacher English, coach football, baseball, Peddie Inst., Hightstown, N.J., 1912-13; teacher English and science and dir. athletics Punahou Sch., Honolulu, 1913-18; capt. inf., U.S. Army, in charge O.T.S., Schofield Barracks, T.H., and post adj., 1918-19; islands business for Lewers & Cooke, Ltd., lumber and building materials, 1919-23; pres. The Kamehameha Schs., 1923-34. Trustee, Punahou school from 1940; director of the Community Assn. of Hawaii; trustee Bernice P. Bishop Estate, from 1939, now president of the trustees; also trustee of the Bishop Mus., U.S. high commr. of Pacific Trust Ty., 1953-54; civilian aide Sec. Army for Hawaii, 1955-63; former mem. of U.S. Loyalty Review Board; chairman T. H. Full Employment Committee; mem. Pacific War Memorial Commn. Past president Chamber of Commerce of Honolulu; pres. Barstow Found. Am., Samoans; past Royal Danish Consul at Honolulu, Hawaii. Decorated Knight of Danneborg (by King of Denmark). Member Am. Historical Association, American Geographical Society, Beta Theta Pi, Phi Beta Kappa. Republican. Conglist. Mason (K.T.). Clubs: Social Science, University, Pacific, Oahu Country. Co-editor: Ancient Hawaiian Civilization. Co-author: Textbook in Hawaiian Language 1929; Survey of Education in American Samoa; also articles on edn. Home: Honolulu, HI. †

MIEDÉL, RAINER, conductor; b. Regensburg, West Germany, June 1, 1938; came to U.S., 1970; s. Karl and Marga (Zippelinski) M.; m. Cordelia Wikarski; 1 child, Florian. Prin. cellist, Stockholm Philharmonic, 1965, music dir., Gavleborg (Sweden) Symphony Orch., 1968, asst. condr., Stockholm Philharmonic, 1968, Balt. Symphony Orch., 1969, asso. condr., 1970-73, music dir., Seattle Symphony Orch., 1976—. German Govt. grantee, 1962; Swedish Govt. scholar, 1965. Mem. Nordiska Råd. Home: Seattle, Wash. Dec. Mar. 25, 1983.

MIHALIK, EMIL JOHN, bishop; b. Pitts., Feb. 7, 1920; s. William and Mary (Jubic) M. Student, Catholic Inst. Pitts., 1938-40, St. Procopius Sem., 1940-45. Ordained priest Roman Catholic Ch., 1945, bishop, 1969; pastor Sts. Peter and Paul Chs., Struthers, Ohio, 1945-55, Endicot, N.Y., 1955-61, St. Thomas Ch., Rahway, N.J., 1961-69; dir. vocations Diocese of Passaic; mem. Diocesan Tribunal, chancellor of Diocese, 1968; mem. Diocesan Bd. Consultors, 1968, bishop of, Parma, Ohio, 1969-84. Mem. Nat., Ohio confs. Cath. bishops. Home: Parma, Ohio. Died Jan. 27, 1984. *

MIKKELSEN, HENNING DAHL, cartoonist; b. Skive, Denmark, Jan. 9, 1915; came to U.S., 1948, naturalized, 1954; s. Jens Peder and Thora (Dahl) M.; m. Jessie Anna Andersen, Oct. 2, 1949; children—Betty Ann, Mary Louise, Sally Jean, Eric Dahl. Creator animated cartoons for films, 1933-35; chief animator, Anglia Films, London, 1935-36; creator comic strip: Ferd'nand, 1937-82, also comic strip based on old Nordic myths in Danish weeklies, 1940-45. Home: Hemet, Calif. Dec. June 1, 1982.

MILES, CATHARINE COX (MRS. W. R. MILES), psychologist; b. San Jose, Calif., May 20, 1890; d. Charles Ellwood and Lydia Shipley (Bean) Cox; grad. Washurn Sch., San Jose, 1907; A.B., Stanford, 1912, A.M., 1913, Ph.D., 1925; student U. of Calif., 1912, U. of Jena, 1913-14, U. of Berlin, 1914; m. Prof. Walter Richard Miles, Sept. 9, 1927; children—Anna Mary, Elwood Morris (dec.). Assistant in phys. education, Stanford Univ., 1912-13; asst. prof. German, College of the Pacific, San Jose, 1914-15, prof., 1915-20; instr. in German, Stanford, 1920-23, fellow, 1923-24; dir. Calif. Bur. Juvenile Research, Whittier, 1924-25; psychologist, Central Mental Hygiene Clinic, Cincinnati, OH., 1925-27; also asst. attending psychologist, Gen. Hosp., 1925-27, psychologist, Children's Hosp., 1926-27, and U.S. Vet's Bur. Diagnostic Center No. 1, 1926-27; research asso. in psychology, Stanford, 1927-30; clin. prof. psychology, Yale, from 1931; attending psychologist, New Haven Hosp. and Dispensary since 1932. In charge child feeding, Am. Friends Service Com., Berlin Dist., 1919-20. Chairman Home Service Division American Red Cross, New Haven, 1942-45; lecturer at U.N.E.S.C.O. Training Center, 1945. Consultant in clin. psychology Vet. Administration since 1946. Fellow American Assn. Advancement of Science: mem. American Psychol. Association, Phi Beta Kappa, Sigma Xi, Tau Psi Epsilon. Mem. Soc. of Friends (Quakers). Author: Early Mental Traits of Three Hundred Geniuses, 1926; Sex in Social Psychology, 1935; Sex and

Personality (with L. M. Terman), 1936. Contbr. to psychol. jours. Home: New Haven, Conn. †

MILES, JOSEPHINE, educator, poet; b. Chgo., June 11, 1911; d. Reginald Odber and Josephine (Lackner) M. B.A., UCLA, 1932; M.A., U. Calif.-Berkeley, 1934, Ph.D., 1938; D.Litt., Mills Coll., 1965. Mem. faculty dept. English, U. Calif.-Berkeley, 1940-85, prof. English, 1952-85, Univ. prof., 1973-85. Author: Lines at Intersection, 1939, Poems on Several Occasions, 1941, Local Measures, 1946, The Vocabulary of Poetry (3 studies), 1946, The Continuity of English Poetic Language, 1951, Prefabrications, 1955, Eras and Modes in English Poetry, 1957, rev. edit., 1964, Renaissance, Eighteenth Century and Modern Language in Poetry, 1960, Poems 1930-60, 1960, House and Home (verse play), 1961, Emerson, 1964, Style and Proportion, 1967, Kinds of Affection, 1967, Civil Poems, 1966, Fields of Learning Poems, 1968, To All Appearances: Poems New and Selected, 1974, Poetry and Change, 1974, Coming to Terms, 1979, Working Out Ideas, and Other Essays on Composition, 1980, Collected Poems, 1983; co-editor anthology: Criticism, Foundations of Modern Judgment, 1948, Idea and Experiment, 1950-54; editor: The Poem, 1959, The Ways of the Poem, rev. edit., 1972, Classic Essays in English, rev. edit., 1965; Contbr.: Fifteen Modern American Poets, 1956, Poets' Choice, 1963, Modern Hindi Poetry, 1965, Voyages, 1968, Norton Anthology of Modern Poetry, 1975, Epoch, 1981; contbr. articles, poems to critical revs.; recs 12 Contemporary Poets, 1966, Todays Poets, vol. II, 1967. Recipient Shelley Meml. award for poetry, 1935; Nat. Inst. Arts and Letters award for poetry, 1956; award for poetry Nat. Commn. Arts, 1966; MLA Lowell award for literary scholarship., 1974; Phelan fellow, 1937-38; AAUW fellow, 1939-40; Guggenheim fellow, 1948-49; Am. Council Learned Socs. fellow, 1965; Acad. Am. Poets fellow, 1978; Berkeley fellow, 1979; Nat. Endowment for Arts fellow, 1980-81. Mem. MLA, Am. Acad. Arts and Scis., Am. Acad. and Inst. Arts and Letters, Am. Soc. Aesthetics, Phi Beta Kappa, Chi Delta Phi. Home: Berkeley, Calif. Died May 12, 1985.

MILGRAM, STANLEY, social psychologist; b. N.Y.C., Aug. 15, 1933; s. Samuel and Adele (Israel) M.; m. Alexandra Menkin, Dec. 10, 1961; children: Michele Sara, Marc Daniel. B.A., Queens Coll., N.Y.C., 1954; Ph.D., Harvard U., 1960. Asst. prof. psychology Yale U., 1960-63; asst. prof. social psychology Harvard U., 1963-67, exec. dir. comparative internat. program dept. social relations, 1966-67; faculty Grad. Center, City U. N.Y., N.Y.C., 1967-84, prof. psychology, 1967-79, Disting. prof. psychology, 1980-84; cons. Polaroid Corp., 1977. Author: Obedience to Authority, 1974 (Nat. Book award nomination 1975); Television and Antisocial Behavior, 1973, The Individual In A Social World, 1977; films Obedience, 1965, The City and the Self, 1974, Conformity and Independence, 1974, Invitation to Social Psychology, 1974, Human Aggression, 1976, Nonverbal Communication, 1976. Guggenheim fellow, 1972-73. Fellow AAAS (Ann. Socio-Psychol. prize 1965), Am. Psychol. Assn., Am. Acad. Arts and Scis. Died Dec. 20, 1984.

MILITZER, WALTER ERNEST, educator; b. Arlington Heights, Ill., Aug. 20, 1906; s. Theodore and Caroline (Demmerle) M.; m. Clementine Newman, Aug. 20, 1939; children—John W., Susan A. B.A. in Chemistry, U. Wis., 1932, Ph.D. in Biochemistry, 1936. Mem. faculty U. Nebr., 1936-84, prof., 1948-84; dean U. Nebr. (Coll. Arts and Scis.), 1952-67. Author articles biochemistry bacteria. Mem. Am. Soc. Biol. Chemists, AAAS, Phi Beta Kappa, Sigma Xi, Alpha Chi Sigma, Sigma Alpha Epsilon. Methodist. Club: Sertoma. Home: Lincoln, Nebr. Deceased.

MILLAR, KENNETH (ROSS MACDONALD), author; b. Los Gatos, Calif., Dec. 13, 1915; s. John M. and Anne (Moyer) M.; m. Margaret Ellis Sturm, June 2, 1938; 1 child, Linda Jane (Mrs. Joseph J. Pagnusat) (dec.). B.A., U. Western Ont., 1938; postgrad., U. Toronto, 1938-39; M.A., U. Mich., 1942, Ph.D., 1951. Tchr., English and history Kitchener (Ont.) Collegiate Inst., 1939-41; fellow, spl. instr. English dept. U. Mich., 1941-44, free lance writer, 1946-83. Author: The Dark Tunnel, 1944, Trouble Follows Me, 1946, Blue City, 1947, The Three Roads, 1948, The Moving Target, 1949, The Drowning Pool, 1950, The Way Some People Die, 1951, The Ivory Grin, 1952, Meet Me at the Morgue, 1953, Find a Victim, 1954, The Name is Archer, 1955, The Barbarous Coast, 1956, The Doomsters, 1958, The Galton Case, 1959, The Ferguson Affair, 1960, The Wycherly Woman, 1961, The Zebra-Striped Hearse, 1962, The Chill, 1964, The Far Side of the Dollar, 1965, Black Money, 1966, The Instant Enemy, 1968, The Goodbye Look, 1969, The Underground Man, 1971, Sleeping Beauty, 1973, The Blue Hammer, 1976. Served to lt. (j.g.) USNR, 1944-46. Mem. Mystery Writers Am. (pres. 1965, recipient Edgar A. Poe scrolls 1962, 63, Grand Master award 1974), Crime Writers Assn. London (Silver Dagger award 1965, Golden Dagger award 1966), Writers Guild of Am., Authors League, ACLU, Phi Beta Kappa. Clubs: Sierra (Santa Barbara), Coral Casino (Santa Barbara). Home: Santa Barbara, Calif. Dec. July 11, 1983.

MILLARD, MARK JACOB, investment banker; b. Kiev, Russia, June 14, 1908; came to U.S., 1938, naturalized, 1944; s. Jacob Mark and Cecile (Paperno) M.; m. Liselotte Von Falkenhayn; 1 dau., Marsha Antonia.

Student, U. Berlin; Ph.D., U. Heidelberg, 1932. Fin. editor Pester Lloyd, Budapest, Hungary, 1933-38; assoc. Loeb, Rhoades & Co., N.Y.C., 1941-85, partner, 1944-85; sr. mng. dir. Shearson/Am. Express Inc., N.Y.C.; trustee Fla. Gulf Realty Trust; chmn. Gulf Applied Technologies Inc., Appalachian Co.; dir. Biotechnica, Madison Fund, Norsk Hydro N.A. Mem. Am. Econ. Assn., N.Y. C. of C. Clubs: Meadow (N.Y.C.), Southampton (N.Y.C.), Sky (N.Y.C.), Doubles (N.Y.C.), Grolier (N.Y.C.); Ramada (Houston).

MILLDYKE, JOHN WILLIAM, broadcasting company executive; b. Kearney, Nebr., Apr. 10, 1937; s. John William and Myra Irene (Dow) M.; m. Doris Helen Evans, Aug. 28, 1960; children—Sonja Lynne, Michelle Marie. B.A., Nebr. State Coll., 1958; postgrad, U. Nebr., 1959-60. News dir. Sta. KHGI-TV, Kearney, 1960-62; news dir. Sta. WOI-AM-FM-TV, Ames, Iowa, 1962-68; asso. prof. journalism Iowa State U., 1963-68; assignment editor, producer news ABC, Washington, 1968-71, producer news, London, 1971-77, mgr. news coverage, Europe, 1977-83. Mem. Assn. Am. Corrs. in London (dir. 1977-81); mem. (pres. 1983); Mem. Brit. Acad. Film and TV Arts, Overseas Press Club Am., Internat. Press Inst., Radio-TV News Dirs. Assn., Sigma Delta Chi. Club: Reform (London). Home: London, England. Dec. Oct. 26, 1983.

MILLER, ADA HOLDING (MRS. ALBERT HELRCY MILLER), music assn. exec., musician; b. New Bedford, Mass., Oct. 5, 1889; d. Robert Stowe and Mary Ann (Dunn) Holding; student Normal Sch. Me., 1908, R.I. Coll. Edn., 1909; M.A. (hon.), Bates Coll., 1952; M.A. (honorary), Brown University, 1953; married Dr. Albert Miller, Mar. 30, 1910 (dec. 1959); children—Elizabeth Eunice (Mrs. Jonathan Barlow Richards), Kathleen Louise (wife of Dr. Alexander Barry), Janice (Mrs. Clayton Talmadge Koelb). Soprano soloist ch., light opera, concerts; pianist, harpist, performer on glass armonica (mus. glasses); past pres. Nat. Fedn. of Music Clubs. Nat. chmn. war service National Fedn. Music Clubs, 1941-46, v.p., 1947-51; pres. R.I. Fedn. Music Clubs, 1938-41, N.E. Dist. Nat. Fedn. Music Clubs, 1941-43, 51-55; exec. com. opera dept. Nat. Music Camp; hon. mem. com. friends Berkshire Music Center; trustee N.E. Conservatory of Music; corporate member Mac Dowell Assn. Recipient Hadley medal National Assn. Am. Composers and Condrs., 1954. Mem. A.S.C.A.P. (hon.). Clubs: Musicians Am. (Coral Gables, Fla.); Musicians (past pres., hon. mem.) (N.Y.C.). Home: Providence, R.I. †

MILLER, ALTON LOMBARD, b. Somerville, Mass., Apr. 10, 1890; s. Charles Nahum and Lula Elizabeth (Lombard) M.; A.B., Harvard, 1911, A.M., 1913, Ph.D., 1916; grad. study U. of Turin (Italy), 1915-16; m. Mary Evangeline Mason, Dec. 23, 1911; children—Ruth M. Gates, Mary E. Dietrich. Tchr. chemistry Browne-Nichols Sch., Cambridge, Mass., 1911-12; instr. math. Harvard, 1911-13, 1917-18, U. Mich., 1913-17; pres., treas. Charles N. Miller co., mfg. confectioners. Treas. Stevens Machine Co.; trustee Home Savs. Bank; dir. Pilgrim Trust, Boston, 1932-52. Bd. dirs. New Hampshire Music Festival; trustee, treas. Wheelock Coll.; trustee Gen. Theol. Library, Andover Newton Theol. Sch.; trustee, pres. emeritus Mass. Bible Soc. Pres. Northern Baptist Conv., 1929; v.p. Boston Baptist Bethel City Mission Soc., 1934-35; v.p. Laymen's Missionary Movement; chmn. bd. mgrs. Am. Bapt. Fgn. Missionary Soc., 1935-51. Mem. Am. Math. Soc., Am. Assn. Math. A.A.A.S., N.E. Mfg. Confectioners Assn. (pres. 1926-28), N.E. Confectioners Club (pres. 1940-42), Boston Bapt. Social Union (pres. 1928-29). Republican. Mason (K.T., Shriner, 32). Clubs: University (past pres.), Harvard, Harvard Musical Association, (N.Y.C.); Harvard Faculty, Laconia Country, Woodland Golf. Home: Babson Park, MA. †

MILLER, ARNOLD RAY, labor union ofcl.; b. Leewood, W.Va., Apr. 25, 1923; s. George Matt and Lulu (Hoy) M.; student pub. schs., Leewood; m. Virginia Ruth Brown, Nov. 26, 1948; children—Larry Allen, Vickie Lynn. Bituminous coal miner, 1939-42, 50-70; pres. Black Lung Assn., 1970-72; v.p. spl. projects Designs For Rural Action, Inc., 1970-72; pres. United Mine Workers Am., Washington, 1972-79, co-organizer Miners for Democracy, 1969; v.p. Miners Internat. Fedn., 1975. Bd. dirs. Appalachian Research and Def. Fund, 1970-72; trustee United Mine Workers Am. Welfare and Retirement Fund. Served with AUS, 1942-46. Decorated Purple Heart. Democrat. Died July 12, 1985.

MILLER, BURKETT, lawyer; b. Nashville, June 8, 1890; s. White Burkett and Mary Lua (Gibson) M.; grad. McCallie Sch., 1908; student U. of South, 1908-10, LL.B., U. Va., 1914; m. Willie Davenport Fred, Mar. 28, 1931. Admitted to Tenn. bar, 1914; mem. Miller, Martin, Hitching & Tipton, Chattanooga, from 1914; dir. Tonya Corp., Volunteer State Life Ins. Co.; hon. dir. Am. Nat. Bank & Trust Co., Coca-Cola Bottling Co. N.Y.; exec com. Greater Chattanooga Downtown Devel. Com. Organizer Tonya Meml. Found., 1950; trustee William Minor Lile Fund, Community Found. Greater Chattanooga, Inc Served as capt., inf. U.S. Army, 1917-19, AEF. Mem. Am Tenn. bar assns., Sigma Alpha Epsilon, Phi Delta Phi Clubs: Bankers (N.Y.C.); Mountain City, Fairyland Lookout Mountain Golf (Chattanooga); Indian Creek Bath, Biscayne Bay Yacht, Key Largo Anglers (Miami Beach, Fla). Home: Lookout Mountain, TN. †

MILLER, CARL NICHOLAS, JR., stock broker; b. Montclair, N.J., Mar. 5, 1926; s. Carl Nicholas and Madeline (Shoemaker) M.; student U. Va., 1950; m. Joy Whitmore, June 30, 1951; children—Carl Nicholas III, Edward W., Stacy K. With Neergaard, Miller & Co., N.Y.C., 1950-58; with Shirmer, Atherton & Co., Boston, 1958-60; partner, v.p. Bache & Co., Inc., N.Y.C., after 1960; also dir; mem. Illus. Properties Realty, Inc., North Palm Beach, Fla. dir Oberly & Newell. Bd. govs. N.Y. Stock Exchange. Served with USNR, 1944-46. Home: Jupiter Hills Village, Fla. Died Aug. 12, 1983.

MILLER, CAROLIN HOPKINS, Democratic Nat. committeewoman; b. Lorain, O., Aug. 10, 1889; d. Francis Theodore and Josephine Ella (Higgins) Hopkins; student Seattle Bus. Coll.; m. Bert H. Miller, July 6, 1916; children—Lee Francis, Patricia Ann (Mrs. James H. Hawley Jr.). Mem. Democratic Nat. Com. Mem. D.A.R. Episcopalian. Clubs: Tuesday Musicale; Senate Ladies (Washington). Home: Boise, Ida. †

MILLER, CLARENCE ROSS, hosp. supt., physician; b. Navasota, Tex., Jan. 17, 1893; s. Ross Joseph and Minnie Lee (Teague) M.; M.D., U. Tex., 1913; m. Bertha George Fouts, Nov. 14, 1918. Intern, Scott and White Hosp., Temple, Tex., 1913; mem. staff Austin (Tex.) State Hosp., from 1957, supt., 1965-67; neurol. physician USPHS, also VA hosps. at Greenville, S.C., Sheridan, Wyo., Northport, L.I., N.Y., Boston, N.Y.C., Chgo., Ft. Lyon, Colo., Lyons, N.J., Coatesville, Pa., Jackson, Miss., Marlin, Tex.; cons. Tex. Rehab. Commn., from 1969. Mil. service, World War I. Diplomate Am. Bd. Psychiatry and Neurology. Fellow Am. Psychiat. Assn. (life); mem. AMA, Tex. Med. Assn., Travis (Tex.) County Med. Soc. Episcopalian. Rotarian (dist. gov. 1955-56). Home: Temple, Tex. Died Apr. 23, 1982.

MILLER, CLYDE RAYMOND, cons. community edn., public opinion, educator; born Columbus, Ohio, 1888; s. Charles E. and Sarah J. (Ketter) M.; A.B., Ohio State U., 1911; grad. work Ohio State U., Columbia U.; Ed.D. (hon.), Am. Internat. Coll., 1937; m. Lotta MacDonald, 1919; 1 son, Robert M. Tchr. pub. schs. Mt. Vernon, O., 1911-12; asst. advt. mgr. F. & R. Lazarus & Co., Columbus, 1912-16; reporter Ohio State Journal and Cleveland Plain Dealer, 1916-20; member superintendent's staff Cleveland Public Schools in charge community relations, also editor School Topics, 1920-28; lecturer in pub. opinion and edn. Harvard, Ohio State U., Western Res. U., N.Y.U., Columbia, 1924-28; mem. adminstrv. staff and faculty Columbia U. Tchrs. Coll., 1928-48. Founder Inst. for Propaganda Analysis, 1937; several research studies on propaganda, community problems, race relations; mem. faculty several univs. and colls., from 1937; vis. prof. numerous univs., including N.Y. U., Pa. State U., Roosevelt U., So. Ill. U., 1963; ednl. cons. Am. Friends Service Commn., from 1950. Founder, Nat. Com. for Repeal McCarran Act; founder, member of the bd. trustees Am. United for Separation of Church and State, Emergency Civil Liberties Committee, Consumers Union. Mem. bd. Ch. of All Nations; member board Methodist Commn. for Social Action. Received award from Nat. Conf. Christians and Jews for Springfield Plan to deal with racial and religious prejudice, 1945. Served as the assistant to dir. Edn. Corps, U.S. Army, AEF, 1918-19. Mem. S.A.R., Am. Assn. U. Profs., Phi Beta Kappa, Sigma Xi. Republican. Author numerous books in fields sch. community relations, race prejudice and propaganda analysis from 1922, including Process of Persuasion; The Seven Common Propaganda Devices, and related essays; Publicity and the Public School (with Fred Charles). Home: New York, N.Y. †

MILLER, DEAN EDGAR, lawyer; b. Caldwell, Idaho, Sept. 26, 1922; s. Dean Wilson and Mary A. (Meek) M.; LL.B., U. Idaho, 1949; m. Josephine Ney, Aug. 20, 1945; children—Dean J., Nicholas G., Thomas F., Mary M., Patrick J. Admitted to Idaho bar, 1949; gen. practice law, Caldwell, 1949-83; partner firm Gigray, Miller, Downen & Weston, 1976-83. Active Democratic Party, including del. Nat. Conv., 1968. Served with U.S. Army, 1942-46; PTO. Recipient award of legal merit U. Idaho Coll. Law, 1978. Mem. Am. Bar Assn., Am. Trial Lawyers Assn., Idaho State Bar (pres. 1977). Roman Catholic. Club: Elks (pres. Idaho 1965). Contbr. articles to law revs. Home: Caldwell, Idaho. Died Nov. 4, 1983.

MILLER, DONALD WILLIAM, librarian; b. Cornwall, Ont., Can., July 19, 1933; s. William Laurence and Jessie Munro (MacDermid) M.; m. Patricia Marie Kirk, Mar. 27, 1965; children—Michael, Alison. B.A., U. Toronto, Ont., 1957; M.L.S., U. B.C., Can.), Vancouver, 1964. Library asst. Scarborough Public Library, 1961-62; head reference dept. Calgary (Alta.) Public Library, 1964-66; asst. dir. London (Ont.) Public Library, 1966-71; dir. Greater Victoria (B.C., Can.) Public Library, 1971-84. Pres. Art Gallery Greater Victoria, 1976-78. Mem. Can. Library Assn. (chmn. sect. adult services 1970-71), B.C. Library Assn. (pres. 1974-75), Instn. Victoria Librarians. Home: Victoria, B.C. Died Sept. 3, 1984.

MILLER, EDWIN LANG, mining exec.; b. Buffalo, Aug. 25, 1887; s. Edwin G. S. and Annie E. (Lang) M.; A.B., Georgetown U., 1910; m. Clara D. Mahony, Oct. 24, 1922; children—Edwin Lang, Donald Francis, Richard Marchal, Robert Jones, Gerard Mahony, Claire Marie. Pres. and dir. Wright-Hargreaves Mines, Ltd.; chairman of board and dir. Liberty Bank of Buffalo; vice chairman and trustee Buffalo and Ft. Erie Bridge Authority. Mem. council U. Buffalo; trustee Millard Fillmore Hosp., Father Baker's Our Lady of Victory Instns., Grosvenor Library, Buffalo Found., Cath. Charities of Buffalo. Mem. Buffalo C. of C. Clubs: Buffalo, Country (Buffalo); Cherry Hill, Saddle and Bridle, Saturn. †

MILLER, EMILY VAN DORN, librarian; b. Jackson, Miss., July 8, 1888; d. Thomas Marshall and Letitia (Dabney) M.; A.B. from Newcomb College, New Orleans, Louisiana, 1907; certificate N.Y. State Library Sch., 1911; m. J. Periam Danton, Nov. 29, 1933. Branch children's librarian Minneapolis Public Library, 1911-14; with Birmingham (Ala.) Public Library, 1914-20; hosp. librarian, U.S. Public Health Service, and U.S. Vets. Bur., 1920-23; with A.L.A. from 1923, editor The Booklist until 1927, gen. editor A.L.A. publs. from 1924. Pres. Ill. Library Assn., 1931-32. Mem. A.L.A., Am. Assn. Univ. Women, Chi Omega; official del. World Congress of Librarians, Rome, 1929, and Congrès Internat. de la lecture publique, Algiers, 1931. Democrat. Home: Chicago, Ill. †

MILLER, JOHN JOSE, judge; b. Savannah, Ga., July 28, 1932; s. Fred and Minnie (Edmond) M.; children—Duncan, Heather, Robin Hope. A.B., Talladega Coll., 1954; LL.B. (W.H.C. Brown fellow), Howard U., 1958; postgrad. (Walter Perry Johnson grad. research fellow in law), U. Calif., Berkeley, 1958-59. Bar: Calif. bar 1961. Practiced in Berkeley, San Francisco, 1961-78; mem. Calif. Legislature, 1967-78, minority leader, 1970-71, chmn. judiciary com., 1974-78; assoc. justice Calif. Ct. Appeals, 1st Appellate Dist., San Francisco, 1978-85; mem. Jud. Council Calif., 1974-78. Assoc. editor: Howard Law Jour, 1957-58. Pres. Berkeley Bd. Edn., 1966. Recipient Man of Year award Ch. by Side of Rd., Berkeley, 1965; Pub. Ofcl. of Year award Los Angeles Trial Lawyers Assn., 1975; Outstanding Service award Contra Costa Trial Lawyers Assn., 1976; Legislator of Year award Calif. Trial Lawyers Assn., 1976. Mem. Am. Judicature Soc., Am., Nat. bar assns., Alpha Phi Alpha. Democrat. Episcopalian. Club: U. Calif. Men's Faculty (Berkeley). Home: Berkeley, Calif. Died Feb. 16, 1985.

MILLER, JOHN ROBINSON, JR., communications exec.; b. La Grange, Ill., Jan. 19, 1914; s. John Robinson and Helen Dora (Smythe) M.; student Goldey Bus. Coll., Wilmington, Del., 1933-34; m. Helen Elizabeth Fulton, June 14, 1935; children—Dale Dunlap, John Robinson III, Mark Fulton. With Hearst Mags., Inc., N.Y.C., 1934-82, successively clk. circulation dept., agy. mgr., trade mgr., subscription sales dir., asst. treas., asst. gen. mgr., 1934-55, v.p., circulation dir., asst. gen. mgr., 1955-62, v.p., gen. mgr., 1962-67, exec. v.p., gen. mgr., 1967-73, also dir.; v.p. Internat. Circulation Co., N.Y.C., 1945-50; asst. treas. Hearst Corp., 1952-55, exec. v.p., 1973-74, pres., chief exec. officer, 1975-79, vice-chmn., 1979-82; v.p., asst. treas., dir. Periodical Pubs. Service Bur., Inc., Sandusky, Ohio, 1953-55, pres., dir., 1963-70, chmn. bd., 1970-72; v.p., dir. Popular Mechanics Co., 1958-59, Science Digest Co., 1958-59, Good Housekeeping, Inc.; dir., chmn. Nat. Mag. Co., London, Eng.; mem. adv. bd. Mfrs. Hanover Trust Co.; dir. Southwest Forest Industries, Am. Home Products. Dir., vice chmn., sec. Audit Bur. Circulations, 1958-74, chmn. bd. central registry, 1957-58, dir., 1958; dir. Nat. Better Bus. Bur., 1961-70, chmn. bd., 1966-68; bd. dirs. ABBI, 1968-70; dir. Council of Better Bus. Burs., 1970-72. Trustee St. Paul's Sch., Garden City, Hearst Found., William Randolph Hearst Found. Recipient Human Relations award Anti-Defamation League, 1972; Lee C. Williams Pub. award for distinguished industry and community service, 1975; Henry T. Zwirner award Assn. 2d Class Mail Publs., 1976; Humanitarian award United Cerebral Palsy, 1978. Mem. Am. Arbitration Assn. Episcopalian. Clubs: Metropolitan (N.Y.C.); Cherry Valley Golf (Garden City). Home: Garden City, N.Y. Died Jan. 5, 1982.

MILLER, KENNETH DEXTER, clergyman; b. Roselle, N.J., Apr. 27, 1887; s. Charles Dexter and Julia (Hope) M.; A.B., Princeton, 1908; grad. study in law, Columbia, 1908-09; B.D., Union Theol. Sem., 1912; D.D., U. of Prague, 1931; m. Ethel Anderson Prince, Apr. 27, 1920; children—Kenneth Dexter, Elizabeth Prince. Ordained Presbyterian ministry, 1912; immigrant fellow, Presbyn. Bd. Home Missions, 1912-13; dir. Jan Hus Ch. and Neighborhood House, N.Y. City, 1913-17; in charge Y.M.C.A., Czecho-Slovak Army, Russian Siberia, 1917-19; in charge immigrant work, Presbyn. Bd. Home Missions, 1919-21; dir. Jan Hus Ch. and Neighborhood House, 1921-23; sec. Presbyn. Bd. Nat. Missions, 1923-26, Federal Council of Chs., 1926-28; pastor Madison, N.J., 1928-36; exec. sec. Presbytery of Detroit, 1936-39; pres. New York City Mission Society from 1939. Club: Century. Author: Czecho-Slovaks in Am., 1920; Peasant Pioneers, 1926; We Who Are Americans, 1943. Home: New York, N.Y. †

MILLER, MARIE TASTEVIN, educator; b. Montmorency, France, Apr. 26, 1888; d. Auguste and Mathilde (Letellier) Tastevin; Agrégée des lettres, 1916; m. John Richardson Miller, July 31, 1928; 1 dau., Madeleine Marie. Came to U.S., 1918. Lycée de jeunes filles, Niort. 1916-18; with Stephens Coll., Columbia, Mo., 1918-22; asst. andx asso. prof. Vassar Coll., Poughkeepsie, N.Y., 1922-26, prof. from 1930, chmn. dept. French from 1950; with Lycée de jeunes filles, St. German-en-Laye, 1926-27, Lycée Victor Hugo, Paris. 1927-30, Lycée du Cours de Vincennes, Paris, 1938-39. Officer d'Académie. Mem. Modern Lang. Assn. Author: Les héroïnes de Corneille, 1924: also articles in French periodicals and reviews. Home: Poughkeepsie, N.Y. †

MILLER, RALPH JAMES, banker; b. Pitts., Mar. 20, 1890; s. James and Ellen (Hanna) M.; student U. Pitts.; m. Florence Lindstrom, Feb. 28, 1920; children—David L., Elise (Mrs. M. Schnure). With Peoples First Nat. Bank & Trust Co., Pitts., from 1946, exec. v.p., sec. Asst. treas. Community Chest, Pa. Economy League, Allegheny Conf. on Community Development. Home: Pittsburgh, PA. †

MILLER, SAMUEL MARTIN, clergyman, educator; b. Lowell, Mass., Aug. 26, 1890; s. Anders Peter and Julia Eleanor (Linderot) M.; A.B., Upsala Coll., 1910, D.D., 1926; B.D., Augustana Theol. Sem., Rock Island, Ill., 1913; m. Helene Forsberg, Jan. 8, 1914; children—Bernice Helene, Mary Grace (dec.), Grace Constance, Samuel Andreas, Faith Evangeline. Ordained ministry Luth. Ch., 1913; pastor Trinity Lutheran Ch., Moline, Ill., 1913-16, Messiah Luth. Ch., Minneapolis, Minn., 1916-19; dean Luth. Bible Inst., Minneapolis, Minn., 1919-31 and 1935-45; pastor First Lutheran Church, Jamestown, New York, 1931-35; executive director Immanuel Deaconess Institute, Omaha, Nebraska, 1946-48; pastor of Ebenezer Lutheran Church, Pierson, Florida, 1949-57; evangelist in Dept. of Evangelism of Augustana Lutheran Ch. from 1953. Author: Life in His Name, 1928; Love That Lasts, 1929; Better Life, 1930; Christ and His Cross, 1931; Have Faith in God, 1952; The World of Truth, 1952; also Bible studies in Acts, John, Matthew and Luke, Revelation, Pentateuch and Joshua; words and music —Jesus Only and Other Songs of Salvation,— 1936. Co-author of —The Word of Prophecy,— 1937. Home: DeBary, Fla. †

MILLER, VICTOR JOSEPH, mayor; b. Joplin, Jasper Co., Mo., Dec. 6, 1888; s. Julius C. and Ida Jane (Miller) M.; grad. high sch., Joplin, 1900; student, U. of Mo., 1907-08; LL.B., Washington U.; 1911; m. Mabel Katherine Cooney, of St. Louis, Mo., July 3, 1918. Admitted to Mo. bar, 1911, and began practice at St. Louis; mem. firm, Case & Miller from 1918; Republican candidate for gov. of Mo., 1924; served as lt. F.A., O.T.S., World War, 1918. Mayor of St. Louis, 2 terms, 1925-29, 1929-33; pres. Bd. Police Commrs., St. Louis. Mem. Am. Mo. State and St. Louis bar assns., St. Louis Chamber Commerce, S.A.R., Am. Legion, Mil. Order World War. Episcopalian. Mason (32 deg., K.T.K.C.C.H., Shriner). Clubs: Mo. Athletic, Optimist, Industrial, Advertising, Midland Valley Golf, Glen Echo Country, North Shore Country, Oasis Country. Home: St. Louis, Mo. Deceased.

MILLER, WARD (AMOS), business exec.; b. Saline, Mich., Aug. 22, 1887; s. Amos Jason and Sarah Elizabeth (Rozelle) M.; grad. high sch.; student Univ. Sch. of Music; U. of Mich., 1906-09; m. Elizabeth Blythe Bickel, Dec. 19, 1918 (died Apr. 19, 1919); 1 dau., Elizabeth Blythe (Mrs. John Aircy, Jr.); m. 2d, Mrs. Helen Wood Dempster, June 20, 1928 (died May 23, 1933); m. 3d, Joyce Colby, June 30, 1934. Dir. and v.p. Vanadium Corp. of Am.; dir. W. J. Gilmore Drug Co.; trustee and dir. Bronx Savings Bank, mem. exec. and real estate committees. Served as capt. U.S. Army Ordnance, World War I; mem. War Prodn. Bd. adv. com. on various ferro alloys, World War II. Pres., dir. Peruvian Am. Assn.; councillor U.S. Chamber of Commerce; mem. Inter-Am. Panel of Arbitration; mem. Fed. Grand Jury Assn., Pan-Am. Soc. of U.S.; mem. men's com. Am. Museum Natural History; mem. Boy Scouts of Am., Greater N.Y. Council at large, exec. bd. 1943-45. Mem. U.S. Senior's Golf Assn. Mem. Am. Iron and Steel Inst., Ry. Business Assn., Acad. Polit. Sci., Am. Geographical Soc., Newcomen Soc. of England, St. Andrews Soc. of N.Y. Republican. Presbyn. Clubs: Economic, Union League, Cloud (New York); Blind Brook Golf; Seigniory (Quebec, Can.); Siwanoy Country (Bronxville, N.Y.); Duquesne (Pittsburgh); Chicago (Chicago); Mohawk (Schenectady, N.Y.). Home: Bronxville, N.Y. †

MILLER, WARREN DRAKE, architect; b. Terre Haute, Ind., Aug. 24, 1887; B.Arch., U. Pa., 1911; m. Martha Jane Moore, 1916; children—Micha Jane Voght. Draftsman, Martin C. Miller, Bullalo, summers 1909-11; with Johnson, Miller & Miller, 1913-23, Miller & Yeager, 1923-46, Miller, Yeager, & Vrydagh, 1946, Miller & Vrydagh, 1946-55, Miller, Vrydagh, & Miller, 1955-61, Miller-Miller & Assos. 1961-70, past sr. partner; prin. arch. works include various bldgs. Ind. State Tchrs. Coll., U.S. P.O., Ct. House, Hulman Municipal Terminal Bldg., Union Hosp., Terre Haute. Chmn., Terre Haute chpt. A.R.C., 1948-50; mem. Planning and Zoning Commn. Terre Haute, 1944-61; pres. Nat. Council Archtl. Registration Bds., 1947-58; member Nat. Arch. Accrediting Bd., 1951-57. Registered architect, Ill., Ind., Ohio; licensed engr. Ind. Fellow A.I.A. (pres. Ind. chpt. 1926-30). Mason (K.T. Shriner). Club: Aero (chmn. 1949), Country (pres. 1953-54). Home: Terre Haute, IN. †

MILLER, WILLIAM CHRISTIAN, investment banker; b. N.Y.C., Oct. 7, 1905; s. William Christian and Virginia (Temple) M.; m. Caroline Burdett Mowry, Dec. 1, 1933; children—Carolyn (Mrs. Robert B. Knutson), William Christian, Sarah Kip. B.S., Rutgers U., 1926, LL.D., 1966. With Nat. City Co., 1926-29, Cassatt & Co., 1929-34; treas. Rustless Iron Co., 1934-35; with W.E. Hutton & Co., N.Y.C., 1936-74, partner, 1945-74; with Reynolds Securities Inc., N.Y.C., 1975-78, Thomson

McKinnon Securities Inc., N.Y.C., 1978-83; dir. Consol. Refining Co. Trustee Rutgers Research and Edn. Found.; trustee Rutgers U. Mem. Newcomen Soc., Pilgrims. Presbyn. Clubs: Recess (N.Y.C.); Englewood Field (N.J.), Englewood (N.J., ; Nantucket (Mass.) Yacht. Home: Englewood, N.J. Dec. July 4, 1983.

MILLIGAN, BURTON ALVIERE, ret. educator; b. Toledo, Oct. 19, 1903; s. Alviere and Grace Austin (Hand) M.; B.S., Northwestern U., 1926, M.A., 1930, Ph.D., 1939; m. Margaret Galland (dec. 1961); m. 2d Getty Krieg Murphy, June 12, 1963. Faculty, Southwestern Coll., Winfield, Kan., 1928-29, U. Mo., 1930-32, U. Fla., 1936-38; mem. faculty U. Ill., Urbana, 1939-72, prof. English, 1955-72, emeritus. Served with USNR, 1942-43. Mem. Modern Lang. Assn., Renaissance Soc. Am., Malone Soc., Modern Humanities Research Assn., Medieval Acad. Am., Am. Assn. U. Profs. Club: University (Chgo.). Editor: Three Renaissance Classics, 1953; John Heywood's Works, 1956. Chmn. editorial bd. Ill. Studies in Lang. and Lit., 1962-71. Contbr. numerous articles to profl. jours. Home: Urbana, Ill. Died Oct. 26, 1982.

MILLIGAN, LUCY RICHARDSON (MRS. HAROLD V. MILLIGAN), organization executive; b. San Luis Valley, Colo., July 22, 1888; d. William M. and Anna (Steese) Richardson; educated public and private schs.; m. Harold Vincent Milligan, 1912; children—Vincent, Robert Criswell. Past pres. Nat. Council Women of the U.S., Inc.; v.p. Internat. Council of Women; dir. of volunteer recruitment and training, Am. Cancer Soc. Inc.; pres. Golden Rule Found. Co-author: The Club Member's Handbook. Home: New York, N.Y. †

MILLIGAN, W(INFRED) O(LIVER), foundation executive, chemist; b. Coulterville, Ill., Nov. 5, 1908; s. John Winfred and Millie Mae (McMillan) M. A.B., Ill. Coll., Jacksonville, 1930, Sc.D., 1946; M.A., Rice Inst., 1932, Ph.D., 1934; D.Sc. (hon.), Tex. Christian U., 1960; LL.D. (hon.), Baylor U., 1979; D.Sc., Tex. Tech. U., 1980. Research chemist Harshaw Chem. Co., Cleve., 1934; prof. chemistry Rice U., Houston, 1934-63; dir. research Robert A. Welch Found., Houston, 1955-82; Distinguished Research prof. chemistry Baylor U., 1965-84; cons. Houdry Process Corp., 1936-45, Humble Oil & Refining Co., 1945-62, Oak Ridge Nat. Lab., 1950—; Chmn. Nat. Colloid Symposium, 1952-59; chmn. com. on application x-ray and electron diffraction Nat. Acad. Sci.-NRC, 1938-41, mem. panel on permanent magnet materials, from 1952, mem. panel on clay mineralogy, from 1953; mem. Tex. Adv. Com. Atomic Energy, from 1955; investigator OSRD, 1943-45. Assoc. editor: Jour. Phys. Chemistry, 1952; editorial bd., 1952-58; Contbr. papers to tech. lit. Pres. Tex. Christian U. Research Found., 1963-65. Recipient award of merit U. Tex., Arlington, 1975; Texana award Tex. Women's U., 1981. Fellow Am. Inst. Chemists (honor scroll S.W. chpt. 1969), Am. Phys. Soc.; mem. Am. Crystallographic Assn., Am. Chem. Soc. (dir. 1961-66, chmn. nat. def. com., chmn. com. future nat. meetings, chmn. com. awards and recognitions, S.W. regional award 1956, southeastern Tex. sect. award 1971), Faraday Soc., S.W. Sci. Forum (pres. 1977-79), Phi Beta Kappa, Sigma Xi, Phi Lambda Upsilon, Alpha Chi Sigma. Address: Houston, Tex. Died Feb. 17, 1984.

MILLIKEN, CHARLES M., army officer; b. Bridgewater, Me., Aug. 4, 1888; s. Elmer E. and Bertha M. (Lawrence) M.; B.S., U.S. Mil. Acad., 1914; grad. Command and Gen. Staff Sch., 1931, Army War Coll., 1937; m. Francis Painter, Sept. 19, 1916; children—Morton E., William Seth, Jane Frances. Commissioned 2d lt., Infantry, U.S. Army, June 12, 1914, and advanced through the grades to brig. general, Nov. 1941, maj. gen., 1944; served with A.E.F., Apr. 1917-June 1918; comdr. 302d Field Signal Batn., 77th Div.; exec. officer, Office of Chief Signal Officer, 3d Army, and signal officer of Base 5, Brest; comdg. gen. Central Signal Corps Replacement Training Center, Camp Crowder, Mo.; post comdr. Camp Crowder, June 1945-Apr. 1946, Camp Polk, La., April-June 1946; comdg. gen., Training Center, Fort Dix, N.J., from July 1946. Decorated Victory Medal, Legion of Merit with oak leaf cluster, Oisne-Aisne, Meuse-Argonne, Toul Sector and Army of Occupation medals. Mason. Home: Fort Dix, N.J. †

MILLIKEN, JOHN BARNES, lawyer; b. Lewisville, Tex., Dec. 10, 1893; s. William Dickerson and Margaret (Young) M.; m. Maybelle Michael, 1951; children by previous marriage—Mollie, William Dickerson. A.B., Southwestern U., Georgetown, Tex., 1914; studied law, U. of Tex. Bar: Tex. bar 1916. Began practice, Phoenix; asst. dir. U.S. Vets. Bur., Washington, 1919-22; asst. counsel U.S. Shipping Bd., 1922-23; asst. solicitor U.S. Bur. Internal Revenue, 1923-26; mem. U.S. Tax Ct., 1926-29; founder, partner firm Parker, Milliken, Clark & O'Hara, Los Angeles, 1931-81. Capt., judge adv. gen. O.R.C. Mem. Am. Bar Assn. (mem. tax council), Kappa Alpha. Methodist. Club: Masons (32 deg.). Home: Pasadena, Calif. Died May 2, 1981.

MILLIKEN, MAHLON G(EORGE), business exec.; b. New Hamburg, N.Y., May 15, 1890; s. George Burhans and Mary Alice (Black) M.; B.S., Rutgers U., 1913; m. Harriet Faye Fuller, Mar. 11, 1914; children—Howard Mahlon, Deane, Margaret Alice. Resident engr. with James B. Harding, cons. engr., N.Y. City, 1913-15; civil engr., Hercules Powder Co., 1915-23, project engr., 1923-24; operating supervisor, 1924-28, plant mgr., 1928-34, dept. mgr., 1934-45. vice pres. from 1945, dir. from 1936. Life trustee Rutgers Univ.; chmn. adv. com., Rutgers Research Council. Dir. Group Hosp. Service, Inc.; Y.M.C.A. Mem. Delta Kappa Epsilon, Tau Beta Pi. Republican. Presbyterian. Club: Chemist (New York). Inventor process for continuous viscosity reduction of nitrocellulose, 1931. Home: Wilmington, Del. †

MILLIKEN, WILLIAM MATHEWSON, art museum dir.; b. Stamford, Conn., Sept. 28, 1889; s. Thomas Kennedy and Mary Spedding (Mathewson) M.; prep. edn., King Sch., Stamford, and Lawrenceville (N.J.) Sch.; A.B., Princeton, 1911, Master Fine Arts, 1942; L.H.D., Western Reserve U., 1942, Ohio State U., 1959, Bowling Green State University, 1963; Dr. Fine Arts, Yale University, 1946, Oberlin Coll., 1955, Kenyon Coll., 1958. Asst. dept. decorative arts, Metropolitan Museum of Art, N.Y. City, 1913, asst. curator of dept., 1913-17; curator of decorative arts Cleve. Mus. Art, 1919-58, curator of paintings, 1925-30, dir. of museum, 1930-58, dir. emeritus, 1958—; regents prof. University of California at Berkeley, 1963. Organizer Exhbn. Masterpieces of Art, Seattle World's Fair, 1962, wrote catalogue. Served as 2d lt. U.S. Army, 1917-18, in comd. 282d Air Squadron, Millington, Tenn., and Duxford, Eng. Awarded Commander's Cross Hungarian Order of Merit; Order Cavalierato of the Crown of Italy; New Sweden Tercentenary Medal; Officer Chevalier of Legion of Honor (France); commander of Civil Order of Alfonso X el Sabio (Spain). Mem. Am. Com. for Restoration of Italian Monuments, Inc. Pres. Assn. of Art Mus. Dirs., 1946-49. Member bd. trustees Am. Fedn. Arts, 1929-62 (hon. vice president), Karamu House, Cleveland Art Association; secretary board of trustees Cleveland Museum Art, 1930-58; mem. adv. com. Am. Art Research Council; Cleve. Inst. Music, Cleve. Sch. Art; chmn. adv. council, Nat. Ceramics Exhbn.; mem. cons. com., "Phoebus". V.p. Am. Assn. of Museums, 1949-53, pres., 1953-57; member adv. council Am. Christian Palestine Com., Renaissance Soc. Am., 1954; mem. council Mediaeval Acad. Am., 1952-55; mem. bd. dirs. Am. Friends Versailles, 1953; mem. U.S. nat. commn. UNESCO, 1953-57; chairman nat. com. 1953-57, v.p. Internat. Council Mus., 1956-58, mem. art and applied Arts com., chmn. com. on edn. Paris meeting, 1948, honorary chairman internat. com. edn. work, 1950; collaborator, Arte Veneta; mem. comite d'honneur des "Melanges Leo van Puyvelde"; mem. editorial adv. com., American Art Annual; mem. cons. com. Art Quarterly. Fellow Royal Soc. Arts London, Am. Acad. Arts and Scis.; mem. American Committee Renaissance Studies, Am. Institute of Decorators (hon.). Democrat. Presbyn. Clubs: Century Assn. (N.Y.C.); Mid-Day, Union, Rowfant (Cleveland). Contbr. to Bulletin Cleveland Museum of Art, The Arts, Am. Mag. of Art, Gazette des Beaux Arts, Art in America, etc. Specialist in medieval art. Home: Wade Park Manor, Cleve.†

MILLS, BARRISS, translator, poet; b. Cleve., Jan. 26, 1912; s. Charles Wendell and Emma (Barriss) M.; m. Iola Jones, Aug. 7, 1937; children: John, Russell, William Barriss, Robert. A.B., Dartmouth, 1934; M.A., U. Chgo., 1936; Ph.D., U. Wis., 1942. Instr. English Iowa State Coll., Ames, 1937-40, asst. prof., 1944-46, asso. prof., 1946-47; instr. English Mich. State Coll., 1942-44; asso. prof., chmn. dept. English U. Denver, 1947-48, prof., chmn. dept., 1948-50; prof. English Purdue, Lafayette, Ind., 1950-73, now prof. emeritus, head dept., 1950-62. Author: (with Huntress, Orlovich, Walker) Minimum Essentials of Good Writing, 1952; poems The Black and White Geometry, 1955, Parvenus and Ancestors, 1959; verse trans. The Idylls of Theokritos, 1963; poems Occasions and Silences, 1964, Aftermath, 1964, The Carmina of Catullus: A Verse Translation, 1965, Letter to Felix, 1968, Epigrams from Martial: A Verse Translation, 1969, Domestic Fables: Selected Poems, 1971, (with George Mills) Broken Present, 1972, (with Lazarus, Stefanile, Woodford) A Suit of Four, 1973, The Soldier and the Lady: Poems of Archilochos and Sappho, 1975, (with others) Indiana Indiana, 1975; Poems Roughened Roundnesses, 1976; poems The Unheroic Muse: Essays on Five Classical Poets, 1978, The Eclogues of Virgil: A Verse Translation, 1980, Poems from the Greek Anthology, 1981; contbr. articles and poems to lit. jours. Home: Nashville IN.

MILLS, PAUL SWINTON, former association executive; b. Clinton, Ind., Feb. 1, 1914; s. Benjamin and Rosamond (Swinton) M.; B.S., Ind. State Tchrs. Coll., 1935; Ed.M., Harvard, 1942; student Ind. U. Grad. Sch. Bus. and Econs., 1948-49; m. Carolyn Sprague, June 12, 1943; children—Richard Paul, Janet Lee, Marsha Jo, Nancy Sue. Tchr., Fayette Twp. High Sch., New Goshen, Ind., 1936-42; instr. U.S. Naval Tng. Sch., Ind. U., 1942-43; asst. prof. accounting and ins. Mich. State U., East Lansing, 1946-49; supr. Great-West Life Assurance Co., Winnipeg, Can., 1949-52, br. mgr., 1952-56, mgr. advanced tng., 1956-57; exec. v.p., mng. dir. Am. Soc. C.L.U.'s, 1957-79. Served to lt. (j.g.) USNR, 1943-46. C.L.U. Recipient Distinguished Alumni award Ind. State U., Terre Haute, 1976. Mem. Am. Soc. C.L.U.'s. Mason. Contbg. author: Life and Health Insurance Handbook, 1959. Home: Drexel Hill, Pa. Died Apr. 21, 1982; interred Roselawn Cemetary, Terre Haute, Ind.

MILLS, WILSON WADDINGHAM, lawyer; b. Las Vegas, N.M., Sept. 9, 1888; s. William Joseph and Alice (Waddingham) M.; Ph.B., Yale, 1910; J.D., U. of Mich., 1913; m. Elizabeth Avery, Sept. 18, 1915 (divorced 1934); children—William Joseph (killed in action by Japanese), David Newell; m. 2d, Hazel Pingree Depew, 1935. Began practice, 1913, at Detroit, in office of Campbell, Bulkley & Leydard; admitted as general partner of firm, 1919, later member Bulkley, Ledyard, Mills & Dickinson; withdrew from partnership, March 1, 1931 to become chairman board Peoples Wayne County Bank, consolidated January 1, 1932, with First National Bank, under title of First Wayne Nat. Bank, of which was chairman of the board; resumed practice of law, 1934; dir. Bob-Lo Excursion Co., Mich. Bakeries, Inc., Floridagold Citrus Corp, Frederick Stearns & Co.; became chmn. Mich. Adv. Com. of Reconstruction Finance Corp., Feb. 1932; dir. Detroit Br., Federal Reserve Bank of Chicago, 1932-33. Dir. Detroit Citizens League. Mem. U.S.A. Regional Loyalty Bd. Republican. Episcopalian. Clubs: Detroit, Detroit Country Metamora, Bloomfield Open Hunt, Grosse Point. Home: Grosse Point, Mich. †

MINER, WORTHINGTON C. (TONY MINER), theatre and TV exec.; b. Buffalo, Nov. 13, 1900; s. Worthington Cogswell and Margaret (Willard) M.; m. Frances Fuller, Mar. 30, 1929; children—Peter, Margaret Miner Rawson, Mary Elizabeth. Grad., Yale U., 1922; postgrad., Cambridge U., Eng., 1922-24. Assoc. with legitimate stage, 1924-39. Asst. to: Guthrie McClintic prodns. including Saturday's Children; dir.: Guthrie McClintin prodns. including Both Your Houses (Pulitzer prize), Father Malachy's Miracle, On Your Toes, Bury the Dead, Excursion; mem. exec. bd. Guthrie McClintic prodns. including, Theatre Guild, 1937-41, author, dir., RKO Pictures, summers 1933, 34; asso. with TV, 1939; creator, producer: Studio One; producer: Mr. I. Magination; with, NBC-TV, 1952—; exec. producer: Play of the Week; producer: The Pawnbroker; (Emmy awards 1949, 50, also Sylvania, Peabody awards 1950, 51). Served with U.S. Army, 1918-19. Recipient Look awards, 1950-51. Mem. Am. Acad. Dramatic Arts (chmn. bd.), Phi Beta Kappa. Home: New York, N.Y. Dec. Dec. 11, 1982.

MINGENBACK, EUGENE CARL, ins. co. exec.; b. Greensburg, Kans., Apr. 8, 1888; s. C. F. and Julia J. (Miller) M.; student St. Edwards Coll., Austin, Tex.; m. Mary J. Aske, 1916; 1 dau., Julia Luisa (Mrs. William W. Shanks). With Farmers Alliance Mut. Ins. Co., from 1960, now chmn. bd., also general manager; Alliance Mut. Casualty Co. and Alliance Life Ins. Co., McPherson, Kans., from 1900, sec., gen. mgr., from 1929, pres., from 1929; pres. State Investment Co., McPherson, from 1945. Mem. Kan. C. of C. (past pres.). Elk, Rotarian. †

MINK, LOUIS OTTO, JR., educator; b. Ada, Ohio, Sept. 3, 1921; s. Louis Otto and Helen (Arndt) M.; m. Helen Louise Patterson, June 24, 1944; children—Louis Otto III, Sarah Patterson, Stephen Dorrance. B.A., Hiram (Ohio) Coll., 1942; M.A., Yale U., 1948, Ph.D., 1952; M.A. (hon.), Wesleyan U., Middletown, Conn., 1965. Instr. Yale, 1950-52; mem. faculty Wesleyan U., 1952-83, prof. philosophy, 1965-83, Kenan prof. humanities, 1979-83; dir. Center for Humanities, 1981-82; vis. prof. Carleton Coll., Northfield, Minn., 1963, Yale U., 1977; Kent fellow Nat. Council Religion Higher Edn. (now Soc. for Values in Higher Edn.), 1948, bd. dirs., 1953-56, 73-83, v.p., 1974-83. Author: Mind, History and Dialectic: The Philosophy of R.G. Collingwood, 1969, A Finnegans Wake Gazetteer, 1978; Contbr. articles to profl. jours.; Mng. editor: Rev. of Metaphysics, 1950-52; asso. editor: History and Theory, 1965—. Served with AUS, 1942-46, PTO. Mem. Am. Philos. Assn., AAUP, ACLU. Congregationalist. Home: Middletown, Conn. Dec. Jan. 19, 1983.

MINNICH, JOHN HARVEY, civil engineer; b. Landisville, Pa., Feb. 6, 1905; s. Harvey Wissler and Lizzie Johnstin (Bossler) M.; m. Charlotte La Bombard, Jan. 2, 1928. B.S., Dartmouth, 1928; C.E., Thayer Sch. Engring., 1929. Registered profl. engr., N.H., Vt., Mass. Insp., resident engr., design engr. N.H. Hwy. Dept., Concord, 1929-33; constrn. engr., supervising engr., acting bridge engr., 1935-37; constrn. engr. Kittredge Bridge Co., Concord, 1933-34; constrn. supt. Davison Constrn. Co., Manchester, N.H., 1934-35; resident engr. Pub. Works Adminstrn., Portsmouth, N.H., 1938-40; constrn. foreman USN Yard Portsmouth, 1940; office engr. power plant constrn. Stone & Webster Engring Corp., Boston, 1940-42; asst. prof. civil engring. Thayer Sch. Engring., 1942-45, prof., 1945-54; cons. civil engr., pvt. practice from 1944; asso. engr., mem. A.T. Granger Assos. Hanover, N.H., 1944-52; cons. structural engr. Anderson-Nichols & Co., Boston, from 1951, dir. engring. 1954-56; cons. structural engr. Am. Bridge Co., Pitts. 1955-56, Metcalf & Eddy, Boston, 1955-56, Dartmouth Coll., Hanover, from 1959, Fleck & Lewis (Architects) Hanover, from 1959, Pier Luigi Nervi, Rome, 1961-63 mem. Bd. Registration Profl. Engrs., N.H., 1945-52 Mem. ASCE, Am. Concrete Inst., Am. Soc. Engring Edn., Dartmouth Soc. Engrs. Address: Port Orange, Fla

MINOR, CLAUDE DRYDEN, ins. exec.; b. nr. Danville Ky., Jan. 15, 1888; s. G. Logan and Nancy L. (Johnson M.; student Elmwood Acad., Perryville, Ky., 1903-07 LL.B., Hamilton Coll. Law, Chicago, 1916; m. Len Hooe, Jan. 22, 1911 (dec. June 1952); m. 2d Marth Hannah, April 29, 1953; one son, Minor R. Admitted t Ky. bar, 1914; practiced law, Danville, 1914-24; mgr. sp service dept. Liverpool, London & Globe Ins. Co Chicago and N.Y. City, 1924-31, sec. spl. service dep Royal-Liverpool group N.Y. City, 1931-35, dir. edn 1935-42, dir. personnel, 1942-43; pres. Va. Fire & Marin

Ins. Co., Richmond, 1943-53; practicing law, mem. Denny, Valentine and Davenport; dir., mem. exec. com. Excelsior Ins. Co., Syracuse, N.Y., from 1943; mem. faculty, eve. sch. bus. adminstrn. U. Richmond from 1945; admitted to Va. bar, 1951. Mem. com. on ins. Legislative Council of Va., 1947-52; spl. lecturer bus. adminstrn., U. Va., 1952. Mem. Virginia Governing Committee, 1943-53; mem. Va. and Richmond C's of C. Mem. S.R., N.Y. So. Soc. Clubs: Country (Virginia); Commonwealth (Richmond); The Kentuckians (N.Y. City).†

MINOR, HAROLD BRONK, former ambassador; b. Holton, Kan., Feb. 1, 1902; grad. Holton High Sch. B.S. in Fgn. Service, Georgetown U., 1927; married to Helen W.; children—Alan, Marjorie, Robert. Clerk, Am. consulate, Tampico, 1927, vice consul, 1929, Cati, 1930, Rio de Janeiro, 1931; consul, Rio de Janeiro, 1935, Jerusalem, 1936; consul and 2d sec., Teheran, 1940; detailed to Dept. of State, 1943; chief Div. of Middle Eastern and Indian Affairs, 1946; assigned counselor of Am. embassy, Athens, 1947, with rank of minister, 1949; D.D. and M.P. to Lebanon, 1951, A.E. and P. to Lebanon, 1952-53; apptd. Govt. Relations Officer; Arabian Am. Oil Co., 1955-57. Bd. dirs. Am. Colony Chartflex Assn. of Jerusalem, Jordan; pres. Am. Friends of Middle East, Inc.; Near East Found.; pres. Am. Middle East Relief, Inc.; Welfare of Blind, Inc. Died Jan. 26, 1984.

MINTON, HUGH CHAPMAN, army officer; b. Smithfield, Va., Aug. 2, 1890; s. Junius Harvey and Sue Ada (Chapman) M.; B.S., Va. Polytech. Inst., 1911; grad. Field Arty. Sch., 1919. Ordnance Sch. Technology, 1921, Army Industrial Coll., 1934; m. Helen Tawney, July 19, 1918; 1 son, Hugh Chapman, Jr. Began as civil engr., 1911; commd. 2d lt. Va. Nat. Guard, 1916; commd. 2d lt., U.S. Army, 1917, and advanced through the grades to brig. gen. (temp.) Jan. 31, 1942; served as capt. and major, World War I; exec. officer to Chief of Ordnance Dept., U.S. Army, July 1938-June 1942; dist. chief, Pittsburgh Ordnance Dist., June 1942-Nov. 1942; director, Production Div., Headquarters, Army Service Forces, Nov. 1942-Aug. 1945, dep. dir. materiel, since Sept. 1945. Awarded Victory medal, Mexican Border medal. Mem. Newcomen Soc., Army Ordnance Assn., Am. Legion, Mil. Order World War. Mason (32 deg, Shriner). Home: Washington, D.C. †

MINTZ, BERNARD, univ. adminstr.; b. N.Y.C., July 30, 1914; s. Louis and Sadie (Robinson) M.; m. Bess Odesser, Mar. 22, 1936; children—Steven William, Nancy Ann; m. Frances Weisman, Oct. 1, 1970. B.S. in Social Sci, City Coll. N.Y., 1934; M.A., Columbia, 1938; student, N.Y. U., 1951-53. Asst. to pres. Ever Ready Label Corp., Belleville, N.J., 1944-46; instr., lectr. eve. and grad. divs. Bernard M. Baruch Sch. Bus. and Pub. Adminstrn., City Coll. N.Y., 1943-64, asst. bus. mgr. coll., 1953-64; asst. univ. dean bus. affairs City U. N.Y., 1965-66, univ. prof., vice chancellor bus. affairs, 1966-72, mgmt. cons., 1951-64; exec. v.p. Bernard M. Baruch Coll., City U. N.Y., 1972-76, acting pres., 1976-77; exec. asst. to pres. William Paterson Coll. of N.J., 1977-84. Author: Living with Collective Bargaining, 1979; contbr. articles to profl. jours. Mem. Eastern Assn. Coll. and Univ. Bus. Officers. Home: New York, N.Y. Died Nov. 1, 1984.

MIRO, JOAN, Spanish artist; b. Barcelona, Spain, Apr. 20, 1893; student art sch., Barcelona; studied with Dali; D.A. (hon.), Harvard Univ., 1968; married, 1 dau., Dolores. First exhibition, Barcelona, 1918, Paris, 1921; exhibited Valentine Galleries, N.Y.C., 1931; works include The Farm, Dog Barking at the Moon, Mrs. Mills in 1740 Costume, Still-Life with an Old Shoe. Died Dec. 25, 1983.

MITCHELL, BERNARD A., manufacturing company executive; b. Chgo., Dec. 12, 1912; s. Charles and Fan (Silver) M.; B.B.A., Northwestern U., 1936; m. Marjorie Iglow, Jan. 14, 1940; children—Lee Hartley, Victoria Carla. With Fulton Industries, Inc., Atlanta, after 1955, pres., chmn. exec. com., after 1956; pres. Precision Castings Co., Cleve., after 1958; founder Jovan, Inc.; dir. Continental Gin Co., Prattville, Ala.; inventor, producer first flourescent desk lamp, 1935; devel., producer inovations comml. and indsl. flourscent lighting, 1936-40, first hermetic type window air conditioner, 1945. Bd. dirs. Jewish Vocational Service, Chgo., 1952-56; mem. Bd. Jewish Edn., Chgo., 1950-54. With WPB, World War II, also govt. adv. coms. Home: Chicago, Ill. Died Dec. 5, 1983.

MITCHELL, CLARENCE M., JR., lawyer; b. Balt., Mar. 8, 1911; s. Clarence M. and Elsie (Davis) M.; m. Juanita Elizabeth Jackson, Sept. 7, 1938; children: Clarence M. III, Keiffer J., Michael B., George D. A.B., Lincoln U., Chester County, Pa., 1932; LL.B., U. Md.; H.H.D. (hon.), U. Md., 1979; postgrad., U. Minn., Atlanta U.; LL.D. (hon.), Morgan State Coll., Balt., Georgetown U., 1981, John Carroll U., 1981, Western Md. Coll., Lincoln U., 1965, Howard U., 1976, Boston U., 1979; D.C.L. (hon.), Temple U., 1975; H.H.D. (hon.), Western Md. Coll., 1977. Bar: Md. bar. Newspaper reporter; various govt. posts including Fair Employment Com., 1943, War Manpower Commn., WPB; labor sec. NAACP, 1945-50; dir. Washington bur., 1950-78, ret., 1978, cons., 1978-84; individual practice law, Balt., 1978-84; chmn. Leadership Conf. Civil Rights. Mem. Pres. Truman's Com. to Employ Physically Handicapped; U.S. rep. 7th spl. session, 30th gen. assembly UN, 1975—. Recipient Spingarn medal NAACP, 1969, Am. Medal of Freedom, 1980. Methodist. Home: Baltimore, Md. Dec. Mar. 18, 1984.

MITCHELL, DEAN HILLS, pres. Northern Indiana Public Service Co.; b. Erie, Pa., Dec. 1, 1894; s. Frank and Bertha (Hills) M.; student Chicago U., 3 yrs.; Northwestern U., 1 1/2 yrs.; m. Doris Wainwright, June 26, 1920. Freight and bill clerk, Western Electric Co., June 20, 1916-Dec. 31, 1916; asst. storekeeper, Gary Tin Mill, Jan. 1, 1917-24; auditor Calumet Gas & Electric Co., 1924-25. Auditor Northern Ind. Public Service Co., 1925-26, comptroller, 1926-33, v.p. and comptroller, 1933-34, v.p. and gen. mgr. 1934-38, pres., 1938-61, dir., 1933-61, chairman chief executive officer, 1961-78; president dir., Shore Line Shops, Inc.; dir. Gary Nat. Bank, Ind. State C. of C. (past pres.); mem. Am. Gas Assn. (past pres.), Indiana Electrical Assn. (past pres.), Ind. Gas Assn. (dir.). Mem. American Legion. Clubs: Chicago, Woodmar Country, Rotary, Columbia. Home: Hammond, Ind. Died Nov. 13, 1984.

MITCHELL, DEREK FENTON, oil co. exec.; b. Orford, Eng., Sept. 10, 1918; s. William Charles and Catherine Mary (Cunningham) M.; B.A. with honors, Cambridge U., 1940; m. Gertrude Irene Pfingst, July 10, 1946; children—Susan Joan, Betsy Anne. With Brit. Petroleum Group, from 1946, pres. BP N.Am., Ltd., N.Y.C., 1961-63, gen. mgr. Central Planning dept., London, 1963-66, dir. BP Trading, 1963; pres. BP Can., 1966-77, chmn., chief exec. officer, 1977-82; dir. Canadian Internat. Paper Co. Ltd., Served with Brit. Royal Naval Res., 1939-46. Mem. Brit. Can. Trade Assn. (mem. council), Brit.-N.Am. Com., Quebec Council of Industry. Anglican. Clubs: St. James's, St.-Denis, Mt. Royal, Mt. Bruno Golf and Country; Royal and Ancient Golf, Walton Health Golf (Gt. Britain). Home: Montreal, Que., Canada. Died 1982.

MITCHELL, ELMER DAYTON, prof. phys. edn.; b. Negaunee, Mich., Sept. 6, 1889; s. Samuel Sidney and Nellie (Morse) M.; A.B., U. of Mich., 1912, A.M., 1919, Ph.D., 1938; grad. study U. of Wis., 1913; m. Beulah Elizabeth Dillingham, July 10, 1913; children—Ann Elizabeth, Robert Dillingham. Teacher and athletic dir. Grand Rapids Union High Sch., 1912-15; athletic dir. and asst. prof. phys. edn., Mich. State Normal Coll., 1915-17; mem. varsity athletic coaching staff, U. of Mich., 1917-19, dir. intramural athletics since 1919, asst. prof. phys. edn., 1921-26, asso. prof., 1926-38, prof. from 1938. Consultant on phys. edn., Nat. Congress Parents and Teachers, 1935; spl. consultant edn. policies commn., Nat. Edn. Assn., 1936; mem. advisory com. on training of leaders in recreation, U.S. Office of Education, 1941; mem. Joint Army and Navy Com. on Welfare and Recreation, 1941. Lt. comdr. U.S.N.R., 1943, comdr., 1945; officer in charge of physical training, 8th Naval Dist., New Orleans, La. Fellow Am. Acad. Physical Edn. (president), Am. Physical Education Association (hon.); member Middle West Society Phys. Edn. (ex.-sec.), Intramural Dirs. Assn. (ex-pres. Western Conf.), Am. Assn. for Health, Physical Education and Recreation (executive secretary), College Physical Edn. Assn. (pres.), Nat. Collegiate Athletic Assn., Phi Delta Kappa, Alpha Kappa Delta, Sigma Delta Psi, Phi Epsilon Kappa, Phi Kappa Sigma. Conglist. Clubs: "M" Club, Ann Arbor Golf, Exchange (ex-pres.); Univ. of Mich. Author: (with E. J. Mather) Basketball, 1922; (with W. P. Bowen) Theory of Organized Play and Practice of Organized Play, 1923; Intramural Athletics, 1925; (with B. S. Mason) Theory of Play, 1934; Social Games for Recreation, 1935; Active Games and Contests, 1935; Sports for Recreation, 1936; Intramural Sports, 1939; Sports Officiating, 1949; A World History of Physical Education. Editor: Journal of Health and Physical Education, 1930-43, Research Quarterly. Contbr. articles to educational journals. Inventor game of speedball, 1921. Received Medal of Merit from Czecho-Slovakian Govt. for work as author and editor, 1939; Luther Gulick award for distinguished service. Home: Ann Arbor, Mich. †

MITCHELL, JOHN ALLEN, civil engr., mfg. exec.; b. Clearfield, Pa., Feb. 21, 1888; s. James and Grace Bell (Row) M.; B.S. in Civil Engring., U. Pa., 1912; m. Edith V. Stull, Oct. 31, 1917; children—Edith S., John Allen, Jean R. With Belmont Iron Works, Phila., from 1912, dir., from 1927, chmn. bd. from 1954; dir. Oliver B. Cannon & Sons, Incorporated; adv. com. Sovereign Investors, Inc. Exec. com. Phila. council Boy Scouts Am. Trustee Beaver Coll. Home: Haverford, Pa. †

MITCHELL, JOHN B., mfg. exec.; b. Scenery Hill, Pa., May 8, 1888; student U. W.Va., 1908-13; m. Mattie Ethel Kraft, 1914; children—Adelaide (Mrs. James P. Hughes), John B. Began Career as expeditor of the mechanical department of Jones & Laughlin Steel Corp., Aliquippa Works, 1915, annealer tin plate dept., 1915-16, draftsman engring., dept., 1916-17, asst. combustion engr., 1917-18, chief mech. engr. blooming mill dept., 1918-20, asst. gen. master mechanic, 1920-25, supt. 14" rolling mill, 1925-34, spl. rep. management, 1934-37, supt. blooming, billet bar mills, 14" rolling mill, 1937, supt. rolling mills Pitts. Works, 1938-46, asst. to v.p. charge mfg. operations, 1946, gen. mgr. charge operations, 1946, v.p. charge operations, 1947-52, dir. from 1947, exec. v.p. charge prodn., 1952, spl. cons. to pres. 1953-56; steel cons., Swindell-Dressler Corporation. Member American Iron and Steel Inst., Assn. Iron and Steel Engrs., Am. Ordnance Assn., Pitts. C. of C. Clubs: Duquesne; Oakmont Country; Aliquippa Golf. Home: Pittsburgh, PA. †

MITCHELL, JOHN EDWARD, machinery mfg. co. exec.; b. Lemont, Ill., Apr. 30, 1926; s. John Martialis and Laura Elizabeth (Wold) M.; student Chgo. campuses U. Ill., Northwestern U.; m. Lois Ann Bush, May 6, 1950; children—John Eric, Gary Alan, Gayle Ann, Lauren Marie. Indsl. engr. Johnson & Johnson Surg. Dressings Co., Chgo., 1943-44, 46-48; sales engr. Hyster Co., Chgo., 1948-49, dist. sales mgr., N.Y.C., 1949-51; gen. mgr. Field Machinery Co., Cambridge, Mass., 1951-57; gen. mgr. N.Y.C. br. Clark Equipment Co., gen. sales mgr., dir. sales, group dir. marketing mobile products, 1957-65, also v.p. subsidiary Clark Rental Corp.; v.p. indsl. and constrn. machinery Massey-Ferguson Ltd., Toronto, Ont., Can., 1965-66, group v.p. indsl. and constrn. machinery, 1966-72, exec. v.p. Americas, from 1972, also dir.; pres. Massey-Ferguson Inc., 1969-78, chmn., dir. Iowa-Des Moines Nat. Bank. Mem. Greater Des Moines Com. Bd. dirs. Iowa Coll. Found. Served with USNR, 1944-46. Mem. NAM, Farm and Indsl. Equipment Inst. (dir., mem. exec. com.). Clubs: Masons, Shriners, Wakonda (Des Moines). Died 1982.

MITCHELL, JOHN JAMES, rancher; b. Chgo., Apr. 28, 1897; s. John James and Mary Louise (Jewell) M.; student U. Sch. of Chgo., The Hill Sch., Pottstown, Pa., 1911-15; A.B., Yale, 1919; m. Lolita S. Armour, June 18, 1921; children—John J., Lolita S.; m. 2d Olga Eugenia Varchavsky, Dec. 21, 1942; 1 son, James Jay. Clk. Ill. Merchants Trust Co. (later Continental Ill. Nat. Bank & Trust Co.), Chgo., 1920, asst. to v.p., 1927-31; v.p., treas. Universal Oil Products Co., 1931-42; rancher nr. Santa Ynez, Cal.; dir. United Airlines, Inc. Clubs: Chicago, Rotary (Chgo.); Bohemian (San Francisco); Los Rancheros Visitadores, Santa Barbara, California. Home: Santa Ynez, Calif. Died Apr. 7, 1985.

MITCHELL, L. C., educator; born Lewistown, Mo., Oct. 22, 1890; s. John and Ida May (Crim) M.; B.F.A., U. Mo., 1927, A.M., 1929; student art schs. of Columbia, Harvard and Ohio State univs.; m. Marian Emmons, Aug. 17, 1929; children—John, James, Asst. instr., U. Mo., 1928; dept. head, William Woods Sch., Fulton, Mo., 1929-30; asst. prof., U. of S.D., 1930-35; prof. of painting Ohio U., Athens, from 1935, dir., sch. painting and allied arts, 1936-55, prof., from 1955; profl. landscape painter, from 1925. Served as corpl., 351st Inf., A.E.F., 1918-19. Home: Athens, Ohio. †

MITCHELL, MORRIS BOCKÉE, lawyer; b. Louisville, Ky., Aug. 21, 1890; s. Morris Miller and Elizabeth I. (Dwinnell) M.; A.B., U. of Wis., 1912; LL.B., Harvard, 1915; m. May Adams Lincoln, July 20, 1926; children—Morris Bockée, Lincoln Adams. Admitted to Minn. state bar, 1915; practiced Minneapolis, Minn., since 1915; partner Rockwood and Mitchell, 1920-35, Cronin, Mitchell & Shadduck, 1936-45, Cronin, Mitchell & Spooner, 1946-64, Mitchell & Meshbesher, from 1964; counsel for Fed. Ct. receiver, W. B. Foshay Company, 1929-35, receiver, from 1935. Mem. judicial council State of Minn., 1939-57. Served as sergt. maj., 1st F.A., Minn. Nat. Guard, 1916, on Mexican Border; ensign, U.S.N.R., 1918. Vice pres. and dir. Minneapolis Family Welfare Assn., 1935-45, 1946-48; Mpls. Family and Childrens Service, 1946-48. Dir., pres. Mpls. Athenaeum, 1953-54. Fellow American Bar Foundation; member of American Bar Association (chmn. sect. on bar orgn. activities, 1936; mem. bd. govs. 1941-44 (chmn. com. on jud. selection, tenure, compensation, 1948-55), Minn. (pres. 1931-32), Hennepin Co. bar Assns., Am. Law Institute, American Judicature Society, Sigma Chi. Republican. Episcopalian. Club: Minneapolis. Home: Minneapolis, Minn. †

MITCHELL, MOWATT MERRILL, commercial attaché; b. San Francisco, Calif., Sept. 18, 1887; s. John Samuel and Florence Standish (Mowatt) M.; A.B., Stanford, 1910;; m. Simone De Bruyn, of Brussels, Belgium, Aug. 30, 1927. In hotel business, Los Angeles, Calif., 1910-17; mem. mission to South Russia, Am. Relief Administration, May-Aug. 1919, chief of operations in Jugo-Slavia, Aug.-Dec. 1919, asst. dir. European operations, London, 1920-23; trade commnr., Am. Embassy, London, 1923; asst. commercial attaché, London, 1924, acting commercial attaché, 1925; commercial attaché, Brussels, Belgium, 1926-28, Am. Embassy, Rome, Italy, from Feb. 1928. Served as pilot, later lt., Air Service, U.S.A., May 1917-Sept. 1919. Tech. adviser to Am. delegation to Internat. Chamber Commerce, Brussels, 1925, Stockholm, 1927, and to Geneva Econ. Conf., 1927; official Am. del. to Internat. Copyright Conv., Rome, 1928, World Motor Conf., Rome, 1928, 15th Congress Permanent Internat. Assn. Navigation Congresses, Venice, 1931. Dir. Library for Am. Studies, Rome. Mem. Zeta Psi.†

MITCHELL, WILLIAM PAUL, automotive company executive; b. Calgary, Alta., Can., Sept. 27, 1929. B.Comm., U. Toronto, 1951; M.B.A., U. Western Ont., 1952; C.A., Inst. Chartered Accts., Calgary, 1956. Chartered acct. Clarkson Gordon & Co., 1952-56; cons. specialist Price Waterhouse & Co., Montreal; chief fin. officer Ford N.Z./Ford South Africa, 1962-63; asst. controller fin. analysis Ford Motor Co. of Can., Ltd., 1963-69, asst. treas., 1969-70, v.p. fin., treas., 1970-84, exec. v.p., 1981-84, dir., 1971-84, Ford Glass Ltd., 1971-84; mem. Bd. Trade Met. Toronto. Mem. Can. Econ.

Policy Com.; Mem. Can.-U.S. com. Council Fin. Execs. Club: Mississauga Golf and Country. *

MITCHELL, WYLIE WHITFIELD, city ofcl., engring., soc. ofcl.; b. Lithonia, Ga., Oct. 18, 1912; s. Henry Whitfield and Sarah Celia (Smith) M.; m. Iva Jean Roberts, June 12, 1937; children—Wylene (Mrs. Robert Lamar Whiting), Cheryl, Beverly (Mrs. Victor Jordan Bowers). Grad. pub. high sch. Registered profl. engr., Ga. Self employed, 1940-46; gen. supt. Whitehead Plumbing Co., Atlanta, 1946-50; chief plumbing insp. City of Atlanta, from 1950; cons. plumbing and air conditioning engr.; plumbing-heating code cons.; instr. code enforcements apprenticeship tng. programs U. Ga. Mem. Nat. Hosp. Standards Com., from 1969; mem. Ga. Examining Bd. Plumbers, from 1970. Recipient Phoenix award City of Atlanta, 1964, Georgian award Ga. Plumbing Inspectors, 1967. Mem. Am. Soc. San. Engrs. (internat. pres. 1972-74, Henry B. Davis award 1970), Bldg. Ofcls. Am. Internat. (chmn. plumbing code from 1968, Walker S. Lee award 1973, exec. com. 1974), Ga. Plumbing Inspectors Assn. (founder 1964, pres. 1964-66, dir. from 1966). Club: Mason. Home: Snellville, GA.

MITMAN, CARL WEAVER, mining engr.; b. Newburg, Pa., Apr. 27, 1889; s. Stewart Unangst and Sarah Anna (Weaver) M.; A.B., Lehigh U., 1909, E.M., 1911; post. grad. Princeton U., 1912-13; m. Doris Rodgers Dawson, Oct. 7, 1916 (died July 23, 1936); children—Doris Rodgers (Mrs. Thomas H. Darling), Lois Gray (Mrs. Jas. B. Newman III); m. 2d, Mrs. Margaret S. Brown, July 26, 1937; step-children—Betty Thompson Brown (Mrs. L.D. Thomas), John A. S. Brown III, Lucien Tillyer Brown. Instr. geol., Lehigh University, 1911; assistant prof. mineralogy, Princeton U., 1912-13; engr. N.J. Zinc Co., Palmerton, Pa., 1913-14; aid in mineral tech., U.S. Nat. Museum, Washington, D.C., 1914-15, asst. curator, 1915-17, curator mech. tech., 1919-21, curator mineral and mech. tech., 1921-32, head curator dept. engring. and industries, 1932-47, assistant to the sec., Smithsonian Inst., since 1947; orgn. and adminstrn. of National Air Museum, established Aug. 1946 as new Smithsonian Bureau chairman Smithsonian Institute. War Committee, 1942-45; quarry technologist Bureau Pub. Rds., 1917-19. Fellow A.A.A.S.; mem. Horological Inst. Am. (life), Newcomen Society (London), Theta Delta Chi. Episcopalian. Mason. Lion (asso). Author or editor and compiler several publs. relating to field. Home: Washington, D.C. †

MITRANY, DAVID, author, educator; b. Bucharest, Rumania, Jan. 1, 1888; Ph.D., D.Sc., London Sch. Econs. and Polit. Sci.; m. Ena Limebeer, June 9, 1923. Editorial staff Manchester Guardian, 1919-22; asst. European editor Carnegie Endowment's "Economic and Social History of the World War"; former lectr. politics U. London; vis. prof. govt. Harvard, 1931-33; Dodge lectr. Yale, 1932; permanent mem. Inst. for Advanced Study, Princeton, adviser on internat. affairs to Lever Bros. Fellow Royal Econ. Soc.; mem. Brit. coordinating com. for Internat. Study, Brit. del. to Internat. Conf. for Sci. Study Internat. Relations, Author several books; Marx Against the Peasant, 1951; William Neilson, professor, Smith, 1957. Home: Oxford, Eng. †

MITTEN, ARTHUR ALLAN, transportation; b. Attica, Ind., July 29, 1888; s. Thomas Eugene and Kitty (Warner) M.; prep. edn., St. John's Mil. Acad., Delafield, Wis., St. Paul's Sch., Concord, N.H., King's Sch., Stamford, Conn.; student Sheffield Scientific Sch. (Yale), and Med Sch., Yale.; M.D., U. of Buffalo; m. Gertrude H. Lemon, Dec. 27, 1911. Chmn. indsl. relations com. Philadelphia Transportation Co. Served as captain Medical Corps, commanding ambulance co., World War; wounded and captured by enemy, Aug. 4, 1918, and held prisoner till end of war. Trustee Temple U. Mem. Phi Rho Sigma. Republican. Episcopalian. Home: Philadelphia, Pa. †

MITZ, MILTON A., govt. ofcl.; b. Milw., May 24, 1921; s. Joseph and Sara (Kochmann) M.; m. Virginia Iren Rattin, Apr. 12, 1946; children—Owen David, Andrew, Jonathan, Daniel. B.S., U. Wis., 1944, M.S., 1945; Ph.D., U. Pitts., 1949. With Ciba Pharm. Products Inc., Summit, N.J., 1945-46; chief biochemistry sect. Central Research Labs., Armour & Co., Chgo., 1949-59; with Melpar, Inc., 1959-67, mgr. biomed. engring., 1965-67; with NASA, from 1968; program scientist NASA (Mariner, Jupiter/-Saturn 1977 program), from 1970; with Office Space Sci., Washington; cons. Nat. Artificial Heart Program, 1967-70; enzyme engring. program NSF, from 1970. Author. Mem. Am. Chem. Soc., Am. Soc. Biol. Chemistry, AAAS, Internat. Soc. Study Origin Life. Patentee in field. Home: Chevy Chase, MD. *

MIZEN, FREDERIC, portrait painter; b. Chgo., Jan. 29, 1888; s. George Frederic and Orinda (Kimball) M.; student J. Francis Smith Acad. Art, 1904-06, Art Inst. Chgo., 1907-19; studied with Walter Ufer, Taos, N.M., 1935; m. May Bendelow, Mar. 16, 1912; 1 son, Frederic Douglas. Comml. artist, 1906-39, painter portraits from 1939, also Western subjects; owner, dir. Frederic Mizen Acad. Art, Chgo., 1936-43; one man shows O'Brien Gallery, Phoenix, Taos (N.M.) Gallery, 1954-56, Tex. Fedn. Women's Clubs, 1960; commns. from Chgo. Galleries, 1936-52, also indsl., pvt. owners; chmn. art Baylor U., 1952-60. Mem. Chgo. Art Inst. Home: Waco, Tex. †

MOCK, VERNON PRICE, army officer; b. Ark., Sept. 19, 1912; B.S., U.S. Mil. Acad., 1935; grad. Cav. Sch., 1940, 41, Command Gen. Staff Sch., 1943, Armed Forces Staff Coll., 1949, Nat. War Coll., 1955; m. Jane Schumacher; children—Phillip, Christopher. Enlisted U.S. Army, 1929, commd. 2d lt., 1935, advanced through grades to lt. gen., 1965; dep. comdg. gen. 8th U.S. Army, 1966-71; active USO, Chgo. Decorated Legion of Merit, Commendation ribbon, D.S.M. Home: Chicago, Ill. Died May 8, 1983.

MODEL, LISETTE, photographer, educator; b. Vienna, Austria, Nov. 10, 1906; came to U.S., 1938, naturalized, 1944; d. Victor Hyppolite and Felicie Amelie (Picus) Seyberg; m. Evsa Model, Sept. 16, 1936. Student, Schwarzwald Schule, Vienna, 1914-18; pvt. studies with, Arnold Schoenberg, 1914-18; D.F.A. (hon.), N.Y. New Sch. Social Research, 1981. Photographer Harper's Bazaar, N.Y.C., 1941-53; tchr. New Sch. Social Research, N.Y.C., 1951-83; guest lectr. throughout, U.S. and Europe, 1950—. One-woman shows, Mus. Modern Art, N.Y.C., 1940, 43, 44, 46, 49, 51, 52, 53, 55, 57, 58, 60, 62, Photo League, N.Y.C., 1941, Art Inst. Chgo., 1943, Calif. Palace Legion of Honor, San Francisco, 1946, Limelight Gallery, N.Y.C., 1954, Nat. Gallery Can., Ottawa, 1967, Smithsonian Instn., Washington, 1969, Carl Siembab Gallery, Boston, Focus Gallery, San Francisco, 1975, Sander Gallery, Washington, 1976, Bucks County Community Coll., Newtown, Pa., 1977, Galerie Zabriskie, Paris, 1977, Yale Sch. Art, 1977, Vision Gallery, Boston, 1979, Port Washington (N.Y.) Public Library, 1979, Galerie Fiolet, Amsterdam, 1980, Galerie Viviane Esders, Paris, 1981, retrospective exhbn., Mus. New Orleans, 1981, group shows include, Mus. Modern Art, 1940, 43, 55, Limelight Gallery, 1954, Nat. Gallery Can., 1967, San Francisco Mus. Art, 1975, Photographers Gallery, London, 1977, Tiroler Landesmuseum Ferdinandeum, Innsbruck, Austria, 1979, Internat. Center Photography, N.Y.C., 1980; represented in permanent collections, Mus. Modern Art, Internat. Mus. Photography, George Eastman House, Rochester, N.Y., Smithsonian Instn., New Orleans Mus. Art, others; books Lisette Model; portfolio, 1976, Twelve Photographs, 1977, Lisette Model: An Aperture Monograph, 1979; photographs in books The Family of Man, 1955, Photography in the Twentieth Century, 1967, The Snapshot, 1974, Helen Gee and the Limelight: A Pioneering Photography Gallery of the Fifties, 1977, Concerning Photography, 1977, A Book of Photographs from the Collection of Sam Wagstaff, 1978, Darkroom 2, 1978, Instantanes, 1980, Photography of the Fifties: An American Perspective, 1980; numerous articles. Recipient Caps award N.Y. State, 1967; Guggenheim fellow, 1965; named Honored Photographer Arles Festival of Arts, 1976. Home: New York, N.Y. Dec. Mar. 29, 1983.

MOHORTER, WILLARD LEE, editor; b. Kiamensi, Del., Oct. 4, 1888; s. James Henry and Kate Walton (Davis) M.; student U. of Colo., Washington U.; A.B., Hiram (O.) Coll., 1910; m. Georgia May Grant, June 21, 1914. Office editor New England Messenger, Boston, 1901-03; asst. editor Christian Evangelist, St. Louis, 1910-17; asso. editor Christian Standard, Cincinnati, 1917-22, editor in chief, 1922-29; editor "What's on the Air?"; sec. Standard Pub. Co.; retired as gen mgr., editorial counsellor, 1958. Minister Disciples of Christ. Amateur Conchologists field trip to great barrier reef, 1954-55, Maurtius and Madagascar, Winter, 1956-57. Member American Assn. for Advancement of Sci., Am., Hawaiian, Australian, Malacological Unions. Mason. Home: Mt. Healthy, OH. †

MOHUN, C(ECIL) PEABODY, stock broker; b. Brussells, Belgium, Mar. 27, 1904; s. Richard Dorsey Lorraine and Harriette Louise (Barry) M.; m. Constance Greer McLane, Apr. 30, 1929; 1 dau., Patricia Barry (Mrs. Gerard W. Smith). Grad., Kent (Conn.) Sch., 1923. With Stern Lauer Co., N.Y.C., from 1928; asst. to partners, 1928-36, partner, 1936-79; spl. partner Lief Werle & Co., from 1979; Mem. N.Y. Stock Exchange, gov., 1955-59. Mem. Selective Service bd., N.Y.C., 1942-45; Chmn. emeritus bd. mgrs. William Sloane House, YMCA. Decorated Office Order of Leopold II Belgium). Episcopalian. Clubs: Union (N.Y.C.), Church (N.Y.C.). Home: New York, N.Y. Deceased.

MOLENAAR, HARRY, livestock association executive, farmer; b. Renville, Minn., June 18, 1924; s. Harry and Ivel A. (Clough) M.; m. Harriet Gadney, Fed. 3, 1951; children: Mary Beth, James Harry. Student, pub. schs., Minn. Pres. Roseland Farmers Shipping Assn., Minn., 1964-82; 1st vice chmn. bd. dirs. Central Livestock Assn., South St. Paul, 1974-70, chmn., 1979-82; mem. adv. council Future Farmers Am.; mem., adult leader 4-H Club. Asst. lay leader Renville United Methodist Ch., Minn., steward, trustee, chmn. stewardship and fin. coms. Mem. Farm Bur., Kandiyohi County Pork Producers Assn. (charter mem., dir.). Home: Renville, Minn. Died Aug. 3, 1982.*

MOLINA, EDGAR ROBERT, cons.; b. N.Y.C., Feb. 24, 1917; s. Frank John and Amalia (Meza) M.; m. Marie Dell Honeycutt, Sept. 18, 1944; children—Robert Stephen, Richard Ward. Student, NYU, 1934-36. Pres. Commodity Service Corp., N.Y.C., 1950-57; with Ford Motor Co., 1957-82; mng. dir. Ford Motor Co. (Ford Mex.), Mexico City, 1959-65; dir. Ford Motor Co. (Latin Am. Group), 1965-68, corporate v.p., 1968; v.p. sales Ford Motor Co. (Ford Europe), London, 1968-70; v.p. Ford Motor Co. (Latin Am./Asia Group), Dearborn, Mich., 1970-72, Ford Motor Co. (Latin Am. Group), Dearborn and Mexico City, 1973-79, cons., 1979-82; dir. ADELA Investment Co. (S.A.). Served to maj. U.S. Army, World War II. Decorated officer Orden Nacional do Cruzeiro do Sul Brazil; Argentine Mil. medal; Orden Francisco de Miranda Venezuela). Mem. Nat. Fgn. Trade Council (dir.), Council of the Ams. (trustee), Nat. Planning Assn. (dir.). Clubs: Bloomfield Hills Country (Detroit), Detroit (Detroit), Renaissance (Detroit); Dallas (Dallas), Bent Tree Country (Dallas); Chapultepec Golf (Mex.), Industriales (Mex.), Bankers (Mex.). Home: Mexico City, Mex. Died May 28, 1982.

MOLLISON, CLARENCE LONGMAN, lawyer; b. West View, Ohio, May 31, 1906; s. Alexander D. and Maria (Knight) M.; student Cleve. Coll. of Western Res. U., 1924-26; LL.B., Cleve.-Marshall Law Sch., Cleve. State U., 1930, LL.M., 1932, J.D., 1969; m. Ethel Denman, Dec. 24, 1930 (div.); 1 dau., Marlene Joyce (Mrs. David Alan Baker); m. 2d, Charlotte Yorke, Dec. 9, 1969. Admitted to Ohio bar, 1930; mem. Payer, Bleiweiss, Crow & Mollison, 1931-51; asst. law dir. City of Cleve., 1945-51; mem. Hauxhurst, Sharp, Mollison & Gallagher, Cleve., 1951-81. Mem. Am., Ohio, Cleve., Cuyahoga County bar assns., Internat. Assn. Ins. Counsel, Maritime Law Assn. U.S., Am. Coll. Trial Lawyers (state chmn.), Citizens League Cleve. Democrat. Baptist. Mason (32 deg., Shriner), Lion (past pres.). Clubs: Shrine Luncheon. Author articles in field. Home: Concord Township, Ohio. Died Jan. 1, 1981.

MOLTER, BENNETT ARTHUR, author; b. Chicago, Ill., May 23, 1890; ed. pvt. and pub. schs.; m. Mona de Broca, Apr. 2, 1919. Traveled extensively throughout the world, also serving as newspaper corr.; vol. Foreign Legion, French Army, 1916; trans. to aviation branch; pilot-aviator Escadrille No. 102 (Lafayette Flying Corps); trans. to air service, U.S.A., and commd. 1st lt., later capt. Author: Knights of the Air, 1918. Contbr. articles to New York Tribune Syndicate. Address: Lake Charles, La. †

MONAGHAN, HUGH JOSEPH, II, lawyer; b. Balt., Sept. 21, 1919; s. Patrick Joseph and Florence Virginia (Kennedy) M.; m. Charlotte Webner Main, Mar. 16, 1962; children—Florence K.W., Hugh Joseph, III. A.B., Loyola Coll., Balt., 1943; LL.B., Georgetown U., 1946. Bar: D.C. bar 1946, Md. bar 1947. Mem. legal staff Am. Oil Co., Balt., 1947-50; practice law, Balt., 1950-84; mem. firm Monaghan & Main, from 1962; judge Balt. Traffic Ct., 1954-55; part-time instr. Mt. Vernon Sch. Law, Balt., 1956-70, Loyola Coll. Bus. Sch., 1972. Mem. Am., Md., Balt. bar assns., Am. Judicature Soc., Md. Trial Counsels Assn., Balt. Estate Planning Council (program chmn. 1976-77), Georgetown U. Alumni Assn. (pres. Md.). Democrat. Roman Catholic. Clubs: Balt. Country (Balt.), Maryland (Balt.). Home: Baltimore, Md. Died July 8, 1984; buried N Cathedral Cemetery, Baltimore.

MONROE, ROBERT A(NSLEY), civil and hydraulic engr.; b. Willow Ranch, Cal., May 13, 1889; s. Joseph James and Fannie Cornelia (Ansley) M.; B.S. in Civil Engring., U. of Calif., 1912; m. Muriel Estelle Burnham, Aug. 20, 1919; children—Ruth Agnes (Mrs. Leland R. Ferrell), Robert Rawson. Civil and hydraulic engring. designer Pacific Gas & Electric Co., San Francisco, 1912-17 and 1919-20; with F. H. Tibbetts, San Francisco, 1920; F. G. Baum, San Francisco; 1920; asst. chief civil engr. Pacific Gas & Electric Co., 1920-29; hydroelectric project investigations and overhead conductor vibration studies Aluminum Co. of America, Pittsburgh, 1929-33; sr. engr. U.S. Bureau of Reclamation, Denver, 1933-37; with Tenn. Valley Authority, Knoxville, from 1937, successively as asst. chief water control planning engr., asst. chief engr., and chief design engr. Served as 1st lt. and capt. engrs. 4th Div., 4th Engrs., A.E.F., 1917-19. Mem. Am. Soc. C.E., Phi Beta Kappa, Sigma Xi, Tau Beta Phi. Club: Cherokee Country (Knoxville). Author articles in tech. assn. publs. Home: Knoxville, Tenn. †

MONTGOMERY, EDWARD, army officer; b. Omaha, Neb., Dec. 6, 1889; s. Eugene and Julia (Smith) M.; student Mass. Inst. Tech., 1908-11; grad. Command and Gen. Staff Sch., 1924, Army War Coll., 1931; m. Bess Pratt, Jan. 4, 1934. Commd. 2d lt. C.A.C., U.S. Army, Jan. 1912; transferred to Chem. Warfare Service as major, 1926, advanced through the grades to brig. gen., Sept. 1943; served in Philippines; returned to U.S. during World War I, served as instr. in F.A. Sch.; served with Army of Occupation; with Dept. of Army Gen. Staff, Sup. Ge., Log. Div., chem. warfare adv. to comdg. gen. and staff, Air Forces, ret. 1950; with Chem. Constrn. Corp., N.Y. City. Decorated Distinguished Service Medal, Legion of Merit, World War II. Mem. Delta Tau Delta. Clubs: Army-Navy, Army Navy Country (Washington). Home: Mamaroneck, N.Y. †

MONTGOMERY, GEORGE, agrl. economist; b. Sabetha, Kan., June 5, 1902; s. George West and Anna Grace (Culverhouse) M.; B.S., Kan. State Coll., 1925, M.S., 1927; Ph.D., U. Minn., 1954; student U. Chgo., U. Wis., Harvard; m. Florence Olsen, June 12, 1938; children—George Edward, Frances Cheryl. Instr. home study dept. Kan. Extension Service, 1925-28, marketing specialist, 1928-30; asst. prof. agrl. econs. Kan. State U., 1930-38, asso. prof. 1938-42, prof., 1942-72, head dept. econs. and sociology, 1947-60; head feed sect. OPA, 1943; cons.

United States Department of Agriculture, business firms; Kansas State T.C.M. India chief of party, 1958-62. Mem. of American and Western farm econ. assns., Am. Econ. Assn., Soc. Farm Mgrs. and Rural Appraisers, Soil Conservation Soc., Phi Kappa Phi, Alpha Zeta. Gamma Sigma Delta. Methodist. Mason, Kiwanian. Home: Manhattan, Kans. Died Oct. 26, 1984.

MONTGOMERY, JEFF, petroleum company executive; b. Winfield, Tex., Jan. 11, 1920; s. Jefferson Franklin and Bertha (Hofmann) M.; m. Leonora Ryan, July 1, 1944; children—Franklin Jefferson, Bethany Rebecca, Catherine Melinda, John Noland Ryan. B.S. in Petroleum Engring, Tex. A. and M. Coll., 1941; postgrad., Harvard Grad. Sch. Bus., Adminstrn., 1941-42; LL.B., George Washington U., 1948. Bar: Tex. bar 1948; Registered profl. engr., Tex. And practiced in, Midland; with firm Klapproth, Hamilton & Montgomery, 1948-50; mgr. Tex. Crude Oil Co., Fort Worth, 1950-53; v.p., dir. Murmanill Corp., Dallas, 1954-56; pres., dir. Kirby Industries, Inc., Houston, 1956-73, chmn. bd., 1973-76, Kirby Exploration Co., 1976—; dir. Cullen Center Bank & Trust. Editor: Tex. A&M Engr, 1941, George Washington Law Rev, 1948. Trustee Meadville Theol. Sch., 1978-81, St. Thomas U., 1972-78; bd. dirs. Planned Parenthood of Houston, 1967-73. Served to maj. USAAF, 1942-46. Mem. Am. Inst. Mining, Metall. and Petroleum Engrs., Am. Assn. Petroleum Geologists (asso.), Tex. Mid-Continent Oil and Gas Assn. (dir.), Nat. Petroleum Council, Ind. Petroleum Assn. Am. (dir. 1971-73), Natural Gas Supply Assn. (chmn. 1979-80), Am. Petroleum Inst., AIM, Am. Bar Assn., State Bar Tex., Houston C. of C., Tex. Mgrs. Assn., Order of Coif, Phi Delta Phi, Tau Beta Pi. Unitarian. Clubs: Ramada (Houston); Galveston (Tex.) Bay Cruising Assn. Home: Houston, Tex. Dec. Nov. 20, 1982.

MONTGOMERY, JOSEPH WEBSTER, JR., coop. exec.; b. Richmond, Va., Jan. 12, 1916; s. Joseph Webster and Lenora Montgomery; student Randolph Macon Coll., 1934-35, Va. Mechanics Inst., 1938-44, U. Richmond, 1943; m. Frances Ferrell Lloyd, Mar. 23, 1940; 1 son, Joseph Webster, III. With So. States Coop., Inc., Richmond, 1941-82, asst. treas., credit mgr., 1963-77, v.p., treas., 1977-82. C.P.A., Va. Mem. Am. Inst. C.P.A.'s, Fin. Execs. Inst., Va. Soc. C.P.A.'s, River Road Citizens Assn. Republican. Baptist. Clubs: Kiwanis, Dove. Home: Richmond, Va. Died June 5, 1982.*

MONTGOMERY, JOSEPH WEST, business exec.; b. Lake Providence, La., Mar. 31, 1887; s. Thomas Farrar and Emily Terrell (Ransdell) M.; A.B., Georgetown University, 1909; LL.B., Tulane University, 1912; married Antoinette Ray, April 17, 1918 (deceased May 1, 1953); children—Joseph W., George R. Admitted to La. Bar, June 1912; pvt. practice of law, New Orleans, La., 1912-21; asst. U.S. atty., Eastern dist. of La., hdqrs. New Orleans, La., 1913-17, U.S. atty., 1917-19; sec. Cuyamel Fruit Co., New Orleans, La., 1921-30; exec. United Fruit Co., New Orleans, 1930-38, mgr. Southern domestic div., 1938-42, v.p., 1948-58, dir., 1942-62, cons.; dir. Whitney Nat. Bank New Orleans, New Orleans Cold Storage & Warehouse. Mem. local SSS, World War II. Bd. adminstrs. Tulane. Mem. City Civil Service Commn., Bd. of Trade, Assn. of Commerce, U.S. C. of C., Order of Coif. Roman Catholic. Clubs: Boston, Louisiana, New Orleans Country, International House (New Orleans); Metropolitan (Washington, D.C.); Avoca Duck (Morgan City, La.). Home: New Orleans, LA. †

MONTGOMERY, ROBERT, actor; b. Beacon, N.Y., May 21, 1904; s. Henry and Mary Weed (Barney); m. Elizabeth Allen, Apr. 14, 1928 (div.); m. Elisabeth Grant, Dec. 9, 1950. Ed., Pawling (N.Y.) Sch. dir. MM Co. communications; cons. to John D. Rockefeller, 1965-69; Spl. cons. to Pres. U.S., 1952-60; pres. Lincoln Center Repertory Theater, 1969-70; Spl. cons. to Pres. Eisenhower, 1952-60; Trustee Motion Picture Players Welfare Fund, Nat. Citizens Com. for Broadcasting; mem. Outward Bound, Hurricane Island, Maine. Author: Open Letter From A Television Viewer, 1968; Stage career began N.Y.C. in The Mask and the Face; played in stock cos., Balt., Rochester, N.Y., Stamford, Conn., Providence, Dennis, Mass.; appeared in: film debut in So This Is College; Their Own Desire, Letty Lynton, The Man in Possession, Lovers Courageous, Private Lives, Fugitive Lovers, Riptide, Three Live Ghosts, Untamed; also appeared in: film debut in Earl of Chicago; appeared in: Sins of the Children, Big House, Divorcee, War Nurse, Strangers May Kiss, Shipmates, When Ladies Meet, Night Flight, Another Language, Hideout, Forsaking All Others, Vanessa, No More Ladies, Night Must Fall, Live, Love and Learn, Ever Since Eve, First Hundred Years, Yellowjack, Rage in Heaven, Here Comes Mr. Jordan, Mr. and Mrs. Smith, June Bridge; actor, dir.: film debut in Eye Witness; Lady in the Lake, Ride the Pink Horse; dir.: Broadway prodns. Calculated Risk, The Desparate Hours; dir., producer: film The Gallant Hours; producer: TV series Robert Montgomery Presents, 1950-57; commentator: radio program Robert Montgomery Speaking, 1955-57; exec. producer radio program, Cagney-Montgomery Prodns., Inc. Bd. dirs. Nat. Information Bur., Med. and Surg. Relief Com.; bd. dirs. Lincoln Center for the Performing Arts; asso. Woods Hole Oceanographic Instn.; bd. advs. Murrow Center. Commd. lt. USNR, 1938; advanced through grades to capt. 1952; served with Am. Field Service 1940, France; asst. naval attache 1941, London; duty 1942-46, PTO, ETO; capt. Res. (ret.). Fellow Pierpont Morgan Library; mem. Legal Aid Soc. (dir.), Actors Equity Assn., A.F.T.R.A., Dirs. Guild Am. (dir.), Screen Actors Guild (past pres.). Clubs: Players, Century, Racquet and Tennis, Brook, N.Y. Yacht, Grolier, North Haven Casino. Address: Canaan, Conn. Dec. Sept. 27, 1981.

MONTGOMERY, ROBERT HUMPHREY, lawyer; b. Oxford, O., Mar. 16, 1889; s. George Samuel and Mary (Bishop) M.; student Wahpeton (N.D.) Pub. Schs.; A.B., U. N.D., 1909; LL.B., Harvard, 1912; LL.D., Tufts U., 1952; m. Mary Murray, Feb. 20, 1917; children—Mary (Mrs. Hollis B. Chenery), Anne (Mrs. George P. Flannery), Robert Humphrey, Jr., Samuel (dec.). Admitted to Mass. bar, 1912, and from in gen. practice, Boston; mem. firm Powers and Hall, from 1916; dir. clk. and gen. counsel Am. Woolen Co. 1932-54; dir. gen. counsel N.E. Telephone & Telegraph Co., 1944-54; dir. F.S. Payne Co. Trustee, treas. Theodore E. Parker Found. Fellow Am. Soc. Genealogists; mem. Am., Mass., Middlesex and Boston bar assns. Soc. Cincinnati, Mass. Sons of Revolution, Soc. Colonial Wars, N.E. Hist. and Gen. Soc., Charitable Irish Soc. Bostonian Soc., Phi Beta Kappa, Phi Delta Theta. Clubs: Union (Boston); Century Association (New York City), Harvard Faculty (Cambridge); Cambridge; Country (Brookline). Author: Sacc-Vanzetti: The Murder and the Myth, 1960. Home: West Cambridge, MA.†

MONTGOMERY OF ALAMEIN, 1ST VISCOUNT OF HINDHEAD (FIELD MARSHAL BERNARD LAW MONTGOMERY), b. Nov. 17, 1887; s. Rt. Rev. H. H. Montgomery; m. Elizabeth Carver (died 1937); 1 son, David. Commdr.-in-chief Brit. Occupation Forces in Germany, 1945-46; chief Imperial Gen. Staff, 1946-48; chmn. Western Europe Comdrs.-in-chief Com. 1948-51; dep. supreme allied comdr. Europe, 1951-58. Decorated Knight of the Garter, Knight Grand Cross of Bath, Companion Distinguished Service Order. Author: The Memoirs of Field-Marshall Montgomery, 1958 The Path to Leadership, 1961. Home: Hampshire, Eng. †

MONTROLL, ELLIOTT WATERS, educator, scientist; b. Pitts., May 4, 1916; s. Adolph Baer and Esther (Israel) M.; m. Shirley Abrams, Mar. 7, 1943; children—Wendy, Brenda, Nicholas, Heidi, Mark, John, Toby, Andrew, Kim, Charles. B.S., U. Pitts., 1937, Ph.D., 1940. Sterling research fellow Yale U., 1940-41; research fellow Cornell U., 1941-42; instr. physics Princeton, 1942-43; head math, group Kellex Corp., 1943-46; asst., then asso. prof. U. Pitts, 1946-48; head physics br. Office Naval Research, 1948-50, phys. sci. dir., 1952-54; research prof. U. Md., 1950-59; gen. sci. dir. IBM Corp. Research Center, Yorktown Heights, N.Y., 1960-63; v.p. research Inst. Def. Analysis, Washington, 1963-66; Albert Einstein prof. physics U. Rochester, 1966-81; also dir. Inst. Fundamental Studies; prof. Inst. Phys. Sci. and Tech., U. Md., 1981-83; chmn. Commn. on Sociotech. Systems, NRC, Washington, 1980-83; Lorentz prof. U. Leiden, Netherlands, 1961, 68. Editor: Jour. Math. Physics, 1960-70. Recipient Lanchester prize Ops. Research Soc., 1959; Guggenheim fellow, 1958; Fulbright fellow, 1959. Mem. Nat. Acad. Scis., Am. Acad. Arts and Scis., Phi Beta Kappa, Sigma Xi. Club: Cosmos (Washington). Home: Chevy Chase, Md. Died Dec. 4, 1983.

MOODY, CLARENCE L(EMUEL), geologist; b. Compton, Calif., Oct. 26, 1888; s. Davis J. and Emma S. (Bowser) M.; A.B., U. of Calif., 1916; m. Hazel Alice Drummond, Dec. 31, 1916; children—Marjorie (wife of Dr. William H. Moorhead), John Drummond, Robert Austin. Petroleum geologist, Ohio Oil Co., Findlay, O., since 1918, division geologist, Shreveport, La., from 1921. Mem. Am. Assn. Petroleum Geologists (v.p., 1937, editor, 1947-49, pres., 1950-51), Geol. Soc. Am., Am. Geophys. Union, Soc. Ecol. Paleontologists and Mineralogists, A.A.A.S., Am. Petroleum Inst., Sigma Xi. Mason. Club: Petroleum (Shreveport). Home: Shreveport, La. †

MOODY, ROBERT EARLE, educator, librarian; b. S. Worthington, Mass., Mar. 30, 1901; s. George Reed and Sarah (Fallows) M.; A.B., Boston U., 1922, A.M., 1923; Ph.D., Yale U., 1933; LL.D. (hon.), Emerson Coll., 1961; m. Eleanor N. Wragg, Aug. 4, 1935; children—David Wright, Stephen Clark. Instr. history U. Mich., 1925-26, Boston U., 1926-30, asst. prof., 1930-35, prof. history, 1935-66, prof. history emeritus, 1966-83, chmn. dept., 1960-66, dir. univ. libraries, 1951-60. Fellow Am. Acad. Arts and Scis.; mem. Am. Antiquarian Soc., Am. Hist. Assn., Maine (hon.), Mass. hist. socs., Colonial Soc. Mass., Phi Beta Kappa, Phi Alpha Theta. Contbr. hist. articles to jours., reviews. Editor: Province and Court Records of Maine, vol. III, 1947, vol. VI, 1975; The Saltonstall Papers, 2 vols., 1972, 74; Bostonia, 1933-35. Home: Boston, Mass. Died Apr. 4, 1983.†

MOON, WILLIAM DEADERICK, lawyer; b. Jonesboro, Tenn., Nov. 9, 1887; s. John Austin and Adeline McDowell (Deaderick) M.; student Baylor U. Sch., 1901-05, U. Tenn., 1905-06; LL.B. U. Chattanooga, 1908; m. Elise L. Chapin, Apr. 28, 1917; children—Mildred (Mrs. William L. Montague), Adeline (Mrs. John R. Hersey), William Deaderick. Admitted to Tenn. bar, from 1908, practiced in Chattanooga; member Moon, Harris & Dineen; director Hamilton National Bank. Hamilton National Association; v.p., dir. Title Guaranty & Trust Co., Chattanooga. Trustee of the Frye Inst. Served from 1st lt. to capt. inf. U.S. Army, 1917-18. Mem. Am. Tenn., Chattanooga bar assns. Clubs: Mountain City, Signal Mountain Golf and Country (Chattanooga). †

MOORE, BRUCE, sculptor; b. Bern, Kans., Aug. 5, 1905; s. Elmer Bowdle and Edna Browning (Wooten) M.; student Pa. Acad. Fine Arts, 1921-25; vis. sculptor Am. Acad. in Rome, 1937-39; m. Alice Hügli, Apr. 2, 1931. Works in plaster, stone, bronze, clay, terra cotta; portrait busts, figures, animals, medals, drawing; Guggenheim fellow, 1929-31; tchr. modeling, history of sculpture U. Wichita, 1927-28; tchr. cast drawing N.Y. Sch. Applied Design for Women, 1941-42; dir. Rinehart Sch. Sculpture, Md. Inst., Balt., 1942-43. Work represented in pub., pvt. collections; works include sculpture for Nat. Meml. of Pacific, Honolulu, 2 heroic tigers Princeton, 1970, Hooker Meml. Doors, Grace Cathedral, San Francisco, 1965, King Doors, 1970, Fountain Group for Wichita Art Assn., heroic statue Gen. Billy Mitchell, D.C. Space Mus.; designer Samuel F.B. Morse medal NAD. Served with AUS, 1943-46. Recipient numerous prizes and awards; Widener gold medal Pa. Acad. Fine Arts, 1929. Fellow Am. Numis. Soc. (awarded J. Saltus Medal, 1952); mem. NAD, Nat. Inst. Arts and Letters, Nat. Sculpture Soc., Wichita Artists Guild. Address: Washington, D.C. Died Jan. 24, 1980.

MOORE, CHARLES HENKEL, retired research association executive, consultant; b. New Market, Va., Oct. 25, 1915; s. Charles Henkel and Meta (Burke) M.; m. Elsie W. Davis, 1939 (div. 1962); children—Sandra Lee, C. Donald; m. Virginia Barber, Sept. 16, 1962; 1 child, Carla Elizabeth. B.S., U. Va., 1936, M.S., 1937; Ph.D., Cornell U., 1940. Instr. Cornell U., 1937-40; chief petrographer Carborundum Co., Niagara Falls, N.Y., 1940-43; asst. prof. mineralogy Pa. State U., 1943-45; with Nat. Lead Co., 1945-51, tech. dir., Cin., 1951; mgr. metals and rectifier divs. P.R. Mallory & Co., Indpls., 1951-55, exec. dir. corp. research and devel., 1956-60; tech. dir. Internat. Copper Research Assn., N.Y.C., 1960-63, exec. v.p., 1963-76, pres., 1976-80, Moore Tech. Cons., 1980-83; founder Titania Gem Industry, 1949; vis. prof. Rutgers U., 1946-49. Author. Fellow AAAS, N.Y. Acad. Sci.; mem. AIME, Newcomen Soc. N. Am., Mining Club, Keramos, Sigma Xi, Phi Kappa Phi. Clubs: Ardsley Country (Ardsley-on-Hudson, N.Y.); Ardsley (N.Y.); Country and Curling. Patentee in field. Home: Dobbs Ferry, N.Y. Dec. Oct. 16, 1983.

MOORE, DALE GRANT, broadcasting exec.; b. Sheldon, N.D., Aug. 7, 1928; s. Grant S. and Edla (Johnson) M.; m. Shirley Mae Rice, Sept. 9, 1949; children—Douglas Gene, Richard Darrell, Dalynne Ruth, David Grant, Dale Dwight, Dawn. Student, Mont. State Coll., 1946-48; B.A., U. Denver, 1951; postgrad., Harvard U. Bus. Sch., 1960. Mgr. Sta.-KRAI, Craig, Colo., 1951-53; asst. gen. mgr. Community Network, Montrose, Delta, Craig, Colo., 1953-55, v.p., gen. mgr., Montrose, Delta, Craig, Monte Vista and Denver, 1955, Columbine Network, Denver, 1955-56; pres., gen. mgr. Penn Engring. Co., Bozeman, Mont., 1956-63; pres. KCAP Broadcasters, Inc., Helena, Mont., from 1958, Sta. KGVO, Missoula, Mont., from 1959, Sta. KCFW-TV, Kalispell, Mont., 1968-79, KTVM-TV, Butte, Mont., 1970-79, Sta. KMVT-TV, Twin Falls, Idaho, from 1970, Sta. KGVO-TV, Missoula, 1964-79, Sta. KCOY-TV, Santa Maria, Calif., 1968-71, Sta. KTFI, Twin Falls, 1968-73, Sta. KSEI, Pocatello, Idaho, from 1973, Little Beaver Creek Ranches, Inc., Missoula, 1971-81, Florence Motor Inn, Missoula, 1972-73, Sta. KCAP-FM, Helena, from 1975, KIDO-AM, Boise, Idaho, 1976-79, Sta. WAPA-TV, San Juan, P.R., from 1976; chmn., chief exec. officer WJBF-TV, Augusta, Ga., from 1980, WTVM-TV, Columbus, Ga., from 1980; owner, operator Dale G. Moore Stas., Missoula; v.p. Silver Dollar Network, 1959-64; dir. First Nat. Bank of Missoula, Mountain States TV Network; mem. State Industry Advisory Council, 1961-68, Missoula Facts Com., 1961-66; vice chmn. Mont. Govs.' Commn. on Postsecondary Edn., 1973-75, Mont. Internat. Trade Commn., from 1974, also dir. Mem. Mont. Broadcasters Assn. (pres. 1961-62), Missoula C. of C. (pres. 1966), Nat. Assn. Broadcasters (chmn. secondary market TV com. 1969-72, chmn. future of TV com. 1970-72). Clubs: Lions (Bozeman) (pres. local club 1957-58, dist. zone chmn. 1958), Execs. (Bozeman) (pres. 1958); Rotary (dir. Missoula club). Home: Ketchum, ID.

MOORE, FRANKLIN HARKNESS, banker; b. St. Clair, Mich., Sept. 1, 1907; s. Franklin and Martha Jane (Harkness) M.; m. Alice D. Wolfs, June 6, 1931; children—Franklin Harkness, Margaret Moore Roll, Susan Moore Ferris, David C. Grad., Phillips Acad., Andover, Mass., 1926; B.A., U. Mich., 1930; diploma, Grad. Sch. Banking, U. Wis., 1949. With Comml. and Savs. Bank St. Clair County, St. Clair, 1934-82; pres., 1953-72, chmn. bd., 1953-82, dir., 1942-82, pres. Algonac Savs. Bank, Mich., 1948-70, chmn. bd., dir., 1947-82; v.p. Diamond Crystal Salt Co., St. Clair, 1953-71, dir., 1953-82, chmn. bd., 1978-82; dir. Detroit br. Fed. Res. Bank Chgo., 1960-66. Chmn. trustees St. Clair County Community Coll., 1968-71; trustee St. Clair Bldg. Authority, 1977-82; pres. Mental Health Assn. in Mich., 1972-73; bd. dirs. Nat. Mental Health Assn., 1976-80. Served to capt. C.E. AUS, 1942-45. Mem. Am. Bankers Assn. (exec. council 1960-63), Mich. Bankers Assn. (pres. 1958-59), Econ. Club Detroit, Beta Theta Pi. Clubs: St. Clair Rotary, Port Huron Golf, Masons. Home: Saint Clair, Mich. Dec. Apr. 25, 1982.

MOORE, HARRY T., author, educator; b. Oakland, Cal., Aug. 2, 1908; s. Harry T. and Kathryn Winifred (Moore) M.; m. Winifred Sheehan, Mar. 21, 1934; children—Brian, Sharon; m. Beatrice Reynolds Walker, Oct. 12, 1946. Ph.B., U. Chgo., 1934; M.A., Northwestern U., 1942; Ph.D., Boston U., 1951. Instr. English Ill. Inst. Tech., 1940-41, Northwestern U., 1941-42; lectr. pub. relations Air U., 1946-47; assoc. prof. Babson Coll., 1947-57, chmn. dept., 1952-57; prof. English So. Ill. U., 1957-60, research prof., 1960-62, 63-79, research prof. emeritus, 1979-81; prof. U. Colo., 1962-63; Guggenheim fellow, 1958, 60, vis. prof. various univs. Author: The Novels of John Steinbeck, 1939, Life and Works of D. H. Lawrence, 1951, The Intelligent Heart, 1955, Poste Restante, 1956, E.M. Forster, 1965, (with Warren Roberts) D. H. Lawrence and His World, 1965, 20th Century French Literature, 2 vols, 1966, Twentieth Century German Literature, 1967, Age of the Modern, 1971, The Priest of Love, 1974, Henry James and His World, 1974, (with Albert Parry) 20th Century Russian Literature, 1974; Editor: (with Albert Parry) D. H. Lawrence's Letters to Bertrand Russell, 1948, D. H. Lawrence's Essays on Sex, Literature and Censorship, 1953, The Achievement of D. H. Lawrence, (with Frederick J. Hoffman), 1953, Lewis Mumford's The Human Prospect, (with Karl W. Deutsch), 1955, Letters of Rainer Maria Rilke, 1960, A D.H. Lawrence Miscellany, 1959, Collected Letters of D.H. Lawrence, 1962, The World of Lawrence Durrell, 1962, Contemporary American Novelists, 1964, Elizabethan Age, 1965, (with Warren Roberts) Phoenix II: Uncollected, Unpublished and other Prose Works by D.H. Lawrence, 1968, (with Ian S. MacNiven) Literary Lifelines: The Richard Aldington-Lawrence Durrell Correspondence, 1981, (with Robert S. Partlow) D.H. Lawrence: The Man Who Lived, 1981, (with Dale B. Montague) Frieda Lawrence and Her Circle, 1981, (with Ian S. MacNiven) The Correspondence of Ezra Pound, 1982; editor: (with Ian S. MacNiven) Crosscurrents/Modern Critiques, 1962-80; co-editor (with Ian S. MacNiven), 1980—; Contbr. (with Ian S. MacNiven) articles to popular, profl. jours.; A judge (with Ian S. MacNiven) Nat. Book awards, 1963. Served as maj. USAAF, World War II; lt. col. USAF Res., to 1981. Decorated Army Commendation medal. Fellow Royal Soc. Lit.; mem. Modern Lang. Assn., College English Assn. (nat. v.p. 1959-61, nat. pres. 1961), Am. P.E.N., Soc. Advancement Mgmt., Sigma Chi. Club: Cliff Dwellers (Chgo.). Home: Carterville, Ill. Dec.

MOORE, HUDSON, JR., Realtor; b. Atlanta, May 10, 1906; s. Hudson and Tochie (Davis) M.; m. Alice Evans, Dec. 30, 1930 (dec. May 5, 1979); children—Hudson III, Barbara Moore Rumsey, Walter Scott Cheesman; m. Mary Jeannette Johnson, Nov. 7, 1979. B.S. in Elec. Engring, U. Colo., 1927; Rhodes scholar, Oxford U., Eng., 1927-28. Engr. Pub. Service Co. of Colo., 1929-34; pres. Walter S. Cheesman Realty Co., Denver, 1934-76, vice chmn., 1976-78, chmn., 1978-80; pres. Republic Bldg. Corp., 1936-76, chmn., 1976-77; v.p. Evans Investment Co., 1939-76, Alice Foster Cheesman Realty Co., 1939-76; dir., mem. exec. com. Mountain States Tel. & Tel. Co.; Vice chmn. Downtown Denver Master Plan Com.; chmn. Denver Planning Bd., 1964-70. Bd. dirs., mem. exec. com. Denver Area Council Boy Scouts Am.; bd. dirs., past pres. Downtown Denver Improvement Assn.; trustee Boettcher Found.; trustee, past pres. Denver Mus. Natural History; life trustee Denver Botanic Gardens Found.; past mem., pres. Denver Bd. Water Commrs. Comdr. USNR; ret. Mem. Am. Soc. Real Estate Counselors. Clubs: Denver Country, Denver Athletic, University, Hiwan Golf. Home: Denver, Colo.

MOORE, LEONARD PAGE, judge; b. Evanston, Ill., July 2, 1898; m. Patricia Brown, Mar. 8, 1927; children—Leonard B., Sarah Lee (Mrs. John R. Hallberg), Margot (Mrs. Alan L. Greener), Dion W. A.B., Amherst Coll., 1919, LL.D., 1959; LL.B., Columbia U., 1922; LL.D., Bklyn. Law Sch., 1957. Bar: N.Y. bar 1923. Mem. firm. Chadbourne, Parke, Whiteside, Wolff & Brophy, N.Y.C., 1929-53; U.S. atty. Eastern Dist., N.Y., 1953-57; judge 2d Circuit Court U.S. Appeals, 1957-71, sr. circuit judge, from 1971. Mem. Am., Fed. bar assns., Fed. Bar Assn. of N.Y., N.J. and Conn., Assn. Bar City N.Y. Clubs: Century, University. Address: New London, Conn.

MOORE, MILLER, banker; b. Kansas City, Mo., July 26, 1905; s. William Gilbert and Alibel Caroline (Miller) M.; B.S., U. Pa., 1928; m. Kathryn Van Nest Law, Jan. 6, 1933; children—Marilyn Law (Mrs. Orren Bradley), Marcia (Mrs. Robert Bowen), Mary (Mrs. Donald C. Fawcett, Jr.). Joined with Comml. Nat. Bank of New York, N.Y.C., 1928, v.p., 1944-51; v.p. since merger into Bankers Trust Co., 1951; dir., mem. exec. com. Nat. Reinsurance Corp.; trustee Am. Youth Hostels, Inc.; dir., chmn. finance com. Pouch Terminal, Inc. Clubs: India House; Madison Square Garden; Montclair (N.J.) Golf; University (N.Y.C.); Pennsylvania of Suburban N.J. (Montclair); Pine Valley Golf (Clementon, N.J.); Eastward Ho! County (Chatham, Mass.); Elgin (Scotland) Golf. Home: Highland Beach, Fla. Died June 30, 1982.

MOORE, RODERICK DUNN, investment banker; b. High Point, N.C., June 24, 1903; s. Dr. John Langhorne and Annie (Dunn) M.; B.S., U. Va., 1927; m. Virginia Underwood Tabb, Oct. 6, 1932; children—West Tabb, Elizabeth Armistead. Registered rep. Scott & Stringfellow, Richmond, Va., 1927-42; v.p. C. F. Cassell & Co., Charlottesville, Va., 1945-47; limited mem. Branch, Cabell & Co., Richmond, 1947-82. Pres. Richmond Stock Exchange, 1955-57. Chmn. adv. bd. Assn. Preservation Va. Antiquities. Bd. mgrs. Riverside Hosp., Newport News, Va. Served with USNR, World War II. Mem. Investment Bankers Assn. (past gov.), Va. Hist. Soc., Soc. Colonial Wars (registrar). Episcopalian. Clubs: Country of Va., Commonwealth (Richmond). Home: Richmond, Va. Died 1982.

MOORE, STANFORD, biochemist; b. Chgo., Sept. 4, 1913; s. John Howard and Ruth (Fowler) M. B.A., Vanderbilt U., 1935; Ph.D., U. Wis., 1938, D.Sc., 1974; M.D. (hon.), U. Brussels, 1954; Dr. honoris causa, U. Paris, 1964. U. Wis. Alumni Research Found. fellow, 1935-39; asst. Rockefeller Inst. Med. Research, 1939-42, assoc., 1942-49, assoc. mem., 1949-52, mem., prof., 1952-82; tech. aide OSRD, Nat. Def. Research Com., 1942-45; vis. prof. (Franqui chair) U. Brussels, 1950-51; vis. investigator U. Cambridge, Eng., 1951; chmn. panel on proteins, com. on growth NRC, 1947-49; sec. commn. on proteins (Internat. Union Pure and Applied Chemistry), 1953-57. Author tech. articles on chemistry of proteins, carbohydrates.; Mem. editorial bd.: Jour. Biol. Chemistry, 1950-60. Trustee Vanderbilt U., 1974-82. Co-recipient Nobel prize in chemistry, 1972, Linderstrom-Lang medal Copenhagen, 1972. Mem. Am. Chem. Soc. (co-recipient chromatography award 1963, Richards medal 1972), Am. Soc. Biol. Chemists (pres. 1966-67), Brit., Belgian biochem. socs., Harvey Soc., AAAS, Nat. Acad. Scis., Am. Acad. Arts and Scis., Belgian Royal Acad. Medicine (hon.), Fedn. Am. Socs. Exptl. Biology (pres. 1970-71), Phi Beta Kappa, Sigma Xi. Home: New York, N.Y. Dec. Aug. 23, 1982.

MOOREHEAD, ALAN, writer; b. Melbourne, Australia, July 22, 1910; s. Richard and Louise (Edgerton) M.; student Scotch Coll., Melbourne, 1915-26; A.B., Melbourne Univ., 1931; m. Lucy Milner, Oct. 29, 1939; children—John, Caroline, Richard. War and fgn. corr. London (Eng.) Daily Express, 1937-46; contbr. New Yorker, Sat. Eve. Post, Holiday, Life, other mags. Author: Mediterranean Front, 1942; Don't Blame the Generals, 1943; The End in Africa, 1944; Eclipse, 1945; Montgomery, 1947; The Rage of the Vulture, 1949; The Villa Diana, 1951; The Traitors, 1952; Run Jungle, publ. 1953; Summer Night, 1954; Gallipoli, 1956; The Russian Revolution, 1958; No Room in the Ark, 1959; Winston Churchill, 1960; The White Nile, 1961; The Blue Nile, 1962; Cooper's Creek, 1963; The Fatal Impact, 1966. Decorated comdr. Order of British Empire; recipient London Sunday Times award for lit., 1956; Duff Cooper award, 1956; award Royal Soc. Lit., 1965. Mentioned in war dispatches, 1945. Clubs: Garrick; London. Address: London, England. Died Sept. 29, 1983.

MOOS, MALCOLM CHARLES, univ. adminstr., author; b. St. Paul, Apr. 19, 1916; s. Charles John and Katherine Isabelle (Grant) M.; A.B., U. Minn., 1937, M.A., 1938; Ph.D., U. Calif., 1942; LL.D., Ohio No. U., 1960, U. N.D., 1968, Georgetown U., 1968, Johns Hopkins U., 1969, U. Notre Dame, 1973, U. Md., 1974; Litt.D., Coll. St. Thomas, 1970; m. Margaret Tracy Gager, June 29, 1945; children—Malcolm, Katherine, Grant, Ann, Margaret. Teaching fellow U. Minn., 1938; research asst. League Minn. Municipalities, 1938-39; teaching fellow U. Calif., 1939-41; research asst. U. Ala., 1941-42; asst. prof. polit. sci. U. Wyo., 1942; asst. prof. polit. sci. Johns Hopkins U., 1942-46, asso. prof., 1946-52, prof., 1952-61, 63; pres. U. Minn., 1967-74; pres. Fund for the Republic, Inc., 1974-75; pres. Center for Study of Democratic Instns., Santa Barbara, Calif., 1974-75; dir. Carnegie Study on New Directions for the Univ., U. Md., 1979-80; cons. White House Office, 1957-58; adminstrv. asst. to the Pres., 1958-60, spl. asst., 1960-61; adviser pub. affairs to Messrs. Rockefeller, 1961-63; mem. President's Commn. Campaign Costs, 1961-62; vis. prof. U. Mich., 1955, Columbia U., 1963-65; asso. editor Balt. Eve. Sun, 1945-48; dir. policy planning Ford Found., 1964-66, dir. Office Govt. and Law, 1966-67. Mem. Balt. City Jail Commn., 1953-55, Prisoner's Aid Soc., 1952-58; cons. Md. Commn. Orgn. State Govt., 1952-54; dir. research Com. Govt. and Higher Edn., 1957-60; mem. Commn. Presdl. Scholars, Brit.-N.Am. Com., Pres.'s Task Force Priorities in Higher Edn.; mem. adv. council Pioneer Found., also President's Assn. Governing Bds. Univs. and Colls., 1968-71; vice chmn. fed. relations com. Nat. Assn. State Univs. and Land-Grant Colls., 1970-72, mem. com. urban problems, 1970-82; nat. adv. panel project computer data banks Nat. Acad. Sci., past mem. Nat. Book Award Com.; past chmn. Midwest Univs. Consortium Internat. Activities, 1969-74. Chmn. Republican Central Com., Balt., 1954-58. Bd. dirs. Govtl. Affairs Inst., Upper Midwest Research and Devel. Council, Overseas Devel. Council; trustee Citizens Research Found., Inst. for Future, Pub. Adminstrn. Service, Ednl. Testing Service; exec. council Minn. Hist. Soc., 1968-71; adv. council Brookings Instn.; chmn. higher edn. adv. com. on wages and prices Am. Council on Edn., 1968-70; chmn. commn. plans and objectives for higher edn., 1968-70; trustee Carnegie Found. for Advancement Teaching, 1969-77, mem. exec. com., 1971-73. Mem. Am. Polit. Sci. Assn., Polit. Economy Club, Phi Beta Kappa. Club: Century Assn. (N.Y.C.). Author: State Penal Administration in Alabama, 1942; Politics, Presidents and Coattails, 1952; A Grammar of American Politics (with Wilfred E. Binkley), 1949; State and Local Government (with Wilfred E. Binkley), 1952; Presidential Nominating Politics in 1952 (with Paul T. David), 1954; Power Through Purpose: The Bases of American Foreign Policy (with Thomas I. Cook), 1954; The Republicans: A History of the Party, 1956; (with Francis Rourke) The Campus and the State, 1959; (with Stephen Hess) Hats in the Ring, 1960; Dwight D. Eisenhower, 1964. Died Jan. 28, 1982.

MORAN, JAMES D., building material company executive; b. Jamaica, N.Y., Feb. 12, 1922; s. James D. and Alice (Carroll) M.; m. Monica Scherzinger, Nov. 5, 1947; children—Christine Carroll, James D. III, Rory Michael, Brian Eugene, Mark Andrew, Monica Harkin. B.A., U. Notre Dame, 1942; LL.B., Columbia U., 1948. Bar: N.Y. bar 1948, Calif. bar 1955. Asso. firm Hodges, Reavis, Pantaleoni & Downey, N.Y.C., 1948-50; with Flintkote Co., N.Y.C., 1950-83, asst. to pres., 1961-62, gen. v.p., 1962-63; v.p., gen. mgr. Flintkote Co. (Flintkote div.), 1963-65, v.p. bldg. products group, 1965-67, exec. v.p., 1967-71, pres., chief exec. officer, 1971-75, chmn., chief exec. officer, 1976-83, also dir.; dir. Larchmont Fed. Savs. & Loan Assn., Frontier Airlines, Kidde, Inc., Genstar Corp., Warnaco Inc.; mem. N.Y. adv. bd. Liberty Mut. Ins. Co. Served to 1st lt. USMCR, 1942-46. Home: Greenwich, Conn. Dec. July 22, 1983.

MORBY, EDWIN SETH, educator; b. San Francisco, Apr. 18, 1909; s. Seth and Elsa (Linder) M.; m. Elizabeth Priestley, June 20, 1935; 1 son, John Edwin. A.B., U. Calif. at Berkeley, 1931, M.A., 1933, Ph.D., 1936; student, Centro de Estudios Históricos, Madrid, Spain, 1934-35. Mem. faculty U. Calif. at Berkeley, 1931-85, prof. Spanish, 1954-85, chmn. dept. Spanish and Portuguese, 1961-64. Author articles, essays, book revs.; Editor: (Lope de Vega) La Dorotea, 1958, 68, 80, Arcadia, 1975. Served with OSS, 1942-45. Guggenheim fellow, 1950-51, 65. Mem. Modern Lang. Assn., Hispanic Soc. Am., Phi Beta Kappa. Home: Berkeley, Calif. Died Apr. 30, 1985; buried Dutch Flat, Placer County, Calif.

MORE, LENA GAY, Repub. Nat. committeewoman; b. Ballinger, Rumels Co., Tex., 1888; d. David Portus and Mary V. Gay; student, St. Mary's Hall Episcopal Sch., San Antonio, Tex.; m. Charles Hinton More, Nov. 12, 1907 (died 1918); children—Mary Gay (Mrs. James A. Maxwell, Jr.), Elizabeth Frances (Mrs. Alfred Bramer), Dorothy (Mrs. Walter W. Wilcox). Business career began upon death of husband in 1918; elected to Rep. National Com.; mem. for Texas, 1932-36, re-elected 1940, again for terms, 1944-48, 1948-52; del. at large Rep. Nat. Conv., 1932, 36, 40, 44. Mem. bd. dirs., Brownsville C. of C.; state bd. dirs., Texas Bus. and Professional Women. Mem. Brownsville Bus. and Professional Women (past pres.). Clubs: Cameron Co. Rep. Womens; Houston Rep. Women's. Home: Austin, Tex. †

MORE, WILLIAM GIBB, banker; b. Edinburgh, Scot., June 19, 1887; s. George and Isabella B. (Gibb) M.; student George Watson's Coll., 1894-1902, Edinburgh U., 1905-07; m. Dorothy Helen Phillips, July 14, 1913; children—Eric G., Ian G., Dorothy Willo (Mrs. John L. Mills.) Solicitor, Scotland, 1908, Ont., Can., 1913; sec. Imperial Bank of Can., 1916-22, supt. brs., 1922-37, asst. gen. mgr., 1937-44, gen. mgr., 1944-45, v.p., dir., 1945-48, pres., 1948-50, dep. chmn., from 1950. Home: Toronto, Ont., Canada. †

MOREHOUSE, NYE F., lawyer; b. Fremont, Neb., April 3, 1880; s. Benjamin Franklin and Lena Leota (Thurston) M.; Culver Mil. Acad., Culver, Ind., 1905-06; LL.B., Univ. of Nebraska, 1907-11; m. Mecla Stout, Dec. 8, 1917; children—Harriet (Mrs. Newton), Nye F. Dep. Co. atty., Dodge Co., Fremont, Neb., 1911-12; home office atty., Nat. Fidelity and Casualty Co., Omaha, Neb., 1912-15; special counsel for State Insurance Bd. and in gen. practice of law, Omaha, Neb., 1915-17; gen. atty., Chicago and North Western R.R. Co., 1919-25, asst. gen. solicitor, 1925-42; asst. gen. counsel, 1942-45, gen. solicitor, 1945-47, v.p., gen. counsel 1947-53, sr. v.p. from 1953. Dir., vice pres. and gen. counsel, mem. exec. com., Sioux City Bridge Co.; dir. and vice pres., gen. counsel, Western Town Lot Co. and Pioneer Town Site Co.; dir. and gen. counsel, Superior Coal Co.; v.p. and gen. counsel, C., St. P., M. and Omaha Ry. Co., from 1947. Served in U.S.A. as capt. and maj. inf., 1917-19; mem. O.R.C. maj., inf., 1919-29; lt. col., I.G., 1930-32; lt. col. inf., 1932-35. Mem. Am., Chicago, and Ill. Bar Assns., Assn. of Interstate Commerce and Industry, Sigma Chi (exec. com. 1922-29, 1933-40), Phi Delta Phi, Am. Legion. Conglist. Club: Union League. Home: Winnetka, Ill. †

MORELAND, CHARLES F(RED), prof. botany; born Homer, La., Aug. 6, 1888; s. William White and Edmond Dexter (Bugg) M.; student Washington and Lee U., 1907-08; B.S., La. State U., 1914, M.S., 1917; Ph.D., Cornell U., 1933; student U. of Chicago, summers 1921, 23, 26, Ohio State U. 1931; m. Hilda Martinez, July 17, 1918; children—William L., Mary Lee. Instr. in botany La. State U., 1919-20, asst. prof., 1920-25, asso. prof., 1925-33, prof. botany from 1933; on leave of absence as lab. asst., fellowship in botany, Cornell U., 1928-29. Made spl. investigation on morning glory plants of La. as host plants for sweet potato weevils, Bureau of Entomology, U.S. Dept. Agr., 1917-18. Mem. A.A.A.S., Bot. Soc. of Am., Am. Assn. Plant Physiologists, Phi Kappa Phi, Alpha Zeta. Democrat. Methodist. Clubs: Faculty, Science (La. State U.). Home: Baton Rouge, La. †

MOREY, GEORGE W(ASHINGTON), chemist; b. Minneapolis, Minn., Jan. 9, 1888; s. George Washington and Celia (Murphy) M.; B.S., U. of Minn., 1909; hon. ScD., Alfred Univ., 1939; m. Lillian Dame, Sept. 10, 1910; 1 dau., Jane Bell. Asst. in chemistry, U. of Minn., 1907-09; asst. chemist, U.S. Bur. Standards, 1909-12, phys. chemist Geophys. Lab. Carnegie Instn., Wash., 1912-57, acting dir., 1953-54; physical chemist United States Geological Survey. Cons. expert. Internat. Critical Tables (glass). Mfr. optical glass, War Industries Bd., 1917-18; gen. mgr. Spencer Lens Co., optical glass plant, 1918-20, Parkersburg Division, Corning Glass Works, 1942-43. Member section 161 (optical instruments) National Defense Research Committee, 1944-46. Baker lecturer, Cornell U., 1932; vis. prof. U. Cal. at Los Angeles, 1956. Recipient Hillebrand prize Chem. Soc. Washington, 1927; Potts medal, Franklin Institute, 1959. Fellow of the Geol. Society of America, Am. Ceramic Soc. (chmn. glass division, 1931-32); hon. fellow Soc. Glass Technology (England); member American Chemical Society, Washington Chem. Soc. (treas. 1926-28; pres. 1928), Alpha Chi Sigma. Received Arthur L. Day award, Geol. Soc. of Am., 1948. Mason. Club: Cosmos.†

MORGAN, BYRON, writer; b. Carthage, Mo., Oct. 24, 1889; s. Byron and Blanche (Sweatman) M.; ed. pub. schs., Carthage; m. Gladys Ruth McIntosh, of Brazil, Ind., Aug. 31, 1912; children—Dorothy, Byron, Douglas. Contbr. series of motor racing stories in Saturday Evening Post. Author: The Roaring Road, 1920; also many photoplay stories, including Rookies; The Fair Co-Ed; The Smart Set; Thunder; Speedway; Five Star Final; The Band Plays On; Hell in the Heavens; It's in the Air. Home Beverly Hills, Calif. †

MORGAN, CHARLES HILL, fine arts educator; b. Worcester, Mass., Sept. 19, 1902; s. Paul Beagary and Lessie (Maynard) M.; m. Janet Barton, Sept. 14, 1928; children: Audrey (Mrs. Carlton D. Leaf), George Barton, Prudence Gilbert (Mrs. Edward C. Eppich). A.B., Harvard, 1924, A.M., 1926, Ph.D., 1928; postgrad., Am. Sch. Classical Studies, Athens, Greece, 1928-29; L.H.D., U. Vt., 1960, Amherst Coll., 1972; Litt.D., Trinity Coll., 1965. Asst. and tutor Harvard, 1924-27; John Harvard fellow, 1926; lectr. in archeology Bryn Mawr (Pa.) Coll., 1929-30; asst. prof. fine arts Amherst (Mass.) Coll., 1930-34, asso. prof., 1934-38, Mead prof. fine arts, 1938-68, prof. emeritus, lectr., from 1968; vis. prof. Am. Sch. Classical Studies, 1933-34, asst. dir., 1935-36, dir., 1936-38; dir. Mead Art Bldg., 1949-68; vis. prof., head dept. arts Trinity Coll., 1964-66. Author: Corinth Vol. XI Byzantine Pottery, 1943, Life oF Michelangelo, 1960, George Bellows, Painter of America, 1965, The Development of the Amherst College Art Collection, 1972, The Drawings of George Bellows, 1973; Contbr. archeol. jours. Trustee Arch. Inst. Am.; mem. mng. com. Am. Sch. Classical Studies at Athens, chmn., 1950-60; trustee Am. Farm Sch., Salonika, Am. Sch. Classical Studies, Am. Internat. Coll., Amherst Acad. Commd. 1st lt., combat intelligence AAC, May 1942; served overseas with 9th Air Force and 1st Allied Airborne Army 3 years; col., Decorated Legion of Merit, Croix de Guerre (Belgium), comdr. Royal Order of Phoenix (Greece). Mem. Archeol. Inst. Am., Greek Archeol. Soc., Delta Kappa Epsilon. Clubs: Harvard (Boston); Century (N.Y.C.); Worcester (Mass.). Home: Amherst, Mass.

MORGAN, HENRY STURGIS, banker; b. London, Eng., Oct. 24, 1900; s. John Pierpont and Jane Norton (Grew) M.; prep. edn., Groton (Mass.) Sch.; A.B., Harvard, 1923; m. Catherine Adams, June 25, 1923; children—Henry Sturgis, Charles Francis, Miles, John Adams, Peter Angus. Began with J. P. Morgan & Co., 1923, partner, 1928-35; treas. Morgan Stanley & Co., Inc., 1935-41, partner Morgan Stanley & Co.; director Connecticut Gen. Life Insurance Company, Gen. Electric Co., Aetna Ins. Co. President Pierpont Morgan Library; trustee Morgan Meml. Park, Carnegie Institution of Washington, Metropolitan Mus. of Art. On active duty as comdr., U.S.N.R., 1941-45. Episcopalian. Clubs: Harvard, New York Yacht, Links, Brook, Century, City Midday, Pinnacle (N.Y. City); Royal Thames Yacht (London); Pacific-Union, Bohemian (San Francisco, Cal.); Chicago; Seawanhaka-Corinthian Yacht (Oyster Bay, L.I.); Metropolitan (Washington); White's (London); Somerset (Boston); Royal Yacht Squadron (Cowes, Eng.). Home: Northport, N.Y. Died Feb. 7, 1982.

MORGAN, SIDNEY, govt. official; b. Rosemont, Pa., May 7, 1890; s. Sidney George and Jean (Gould) M.; student George Washington Univ., 1921; 24; grad. Army Engr. Sch., 1924, Command and Gen. Staff Coll., 1941; m. Ethel Creager, Apr. 9, 1917. Credit mgr., Pa. and Med. Steel Cos. 1913-16; campaign dir., A.R.C., 1916-17; staff mem., U.S. Bur. of Efficiency, 1922-28; secretary U.S. Tariff Commn., 1930-50 (with absence for mil. service), U.S. rep., Sesquicentennial Exposition, Phila., Pa., 1926-27; U.S. rep. and mil. aide, Ibero-Am. Exposition, Seville, Spain, 1929-30. Served as 1st lt., U.S. Nat. Army, 1917-19; advanced from lt. to maj., Corps of Engrs., D.C.N.G., 1920-40; asst. chief of staff G-2, 29th Div., U.S. Army, 1941; lt. col. Mil. Intelligence Service, War Dept., 1942-43; U.S. Military Attache to Allied govts. in exile Norway, Holland, Belgium, Czechoslovakia, Poland), London, 1943-46; col. Mil. Intelligence Reserve, 1946-50; transferred to Honorary Reserve, U.S. Army, 1950. Decorated Comdr., Order of White Lion of Czechoslovakia; Comdr., Order of Polonia Restituta (Poland); Chevalier, Order of Orange Nassau with swords (Netherlands); Companion, Order of Mil. Merit, 1st class (Czechoslovakia). Awarded Bronze Star, U.S. Army commendations. Mem. U.S. Mil. Intelligence Assn. (pres.), U.S. Reserve Officers' Assn. (pres., D.C. dept., 1947-48; nat. councillor), U.S. Inf. Assn., Mil. Order of World Wars, Inst. of World Economics, Am. Mil. Inst. Presbyterian. Clubs: Cosmos, Army and Navy (Washington), Fed. Home: Washington, D.C. †

MORLEY, FELIX MUSKETT, writer, educator; b. Haverford, Pa., Jan. 6, 1894; s. Frank and Lilian Janet (Bird) M.; m. Isabel Middleton, Dec. 8, 1917; children—Lorna Janet, Christina Bird (Mrs. Richard L. Borden), Anthony Jefferson, Felix Woodbridge (dec.). A.B., Haverford Coll., 1915; Rhodes scholar, New Coll., Oxford (Eng.) U., 1919-21, A.B., 1921; Hutchinson research fellow, London Sch. Econs. and Polit. Sci., 1921-22; Guggenheim fellow polit. sci., 1928-30; Ph.D., Brookings Instn., 1936; D.Litt., George Washington U., 1940, Lebanon Valley Coll., 1952, Towson State U., 1979; LL.D., Hamilton Coll., 1941, U. Pa., 1941, Bethany Coll., 1951, Western Md. Coll., 1964. Reporter Phila. Pub. Ledger, 1916-17; with Washington bur. U.P.I., 1917, Phila. N.Am., 1919; spl. service Dept. Labor, 1917-18; editorial staff Balt. Sun, 1922-29, corr. in, Far East, 1925-26, Geneva, 1928-29; lectr. current polit. problems St. John's Coll., Annapolis, Md., 1924-25; dir. Geneva office League of Nations Assn. U.S., 1929-31; mem. staff Brookings Instn., 1931-33; editor Washington Post, 1933-40; pres. Haverford Coll., 1940-45; pres., editor Human Events, Inc., 1945-50; Washington corr. Barron's Weekly, 1950-54; cons. War Manpower Commn., 1942-45; adv. com. A.S.T.P.; mem. Human Relations Commn., Anne Arundel County, Md., 1966-68; Mem. adv. bd. Anne Arundel Community Coll.; bd. dirs. Washington Coll., Chestertown, Md. Author: Unemployment Relief in Great Britain, 1924 (Hart, Schaffner and Marx prize essay), Our Far Eastern Assignment, 1926, The Society of Nations, 1932, The Power in the People, 1949, repub., 1972, The Foreign Policy of the United States, 1951, Gumption Island, 1956, Freedom and Federalism, 1959, reprinted, 1981, The Message, 1968, For the Record, 1979; Contbr.: articles on polit., social and econ. issues to mags. and profl. jours., editorial sect. Nation's Bus, 1946-70. Trustee Presidential Library Assn.; trustee Herbert Clark Hoover Meml. Found.; Ambulance work with Brit. Army in Flanders, 1915-16. Recipient Pulitzer prize editorial writing, 1936, William Volker Distinguished Service award, 1961; Outstanding Alumnus award Friends Sch., Balt., 1977; Cutler Meml. lectr. U. Rochester, 1941. Fellow Royal Econ. Soc. (Gt. Brit.); mem. Mont Pelerin Soc. (charter), Phi Beta Kappa. Episcopalian (vestryman 1968-70). Club: Gibson Island. Home: Gibson Island, Md. Dec. Mar. 13, 1982.

MORLEY, GRACE MCCANN, art museum dir.; b. Berkeley, Calif., Nov. 3, 1900; d. Frederick W(alter) and Louise M. (Haley) McCann; A.B., U. of Calif., Berkeley, 1923, M.A., 1924; doctorat, U. of Paris, France, 1926; student U. of Grenoble, France, summers 1924, 25, Harvard, summer 1929; LL.D., Mills Coll., 1937, University of California at Los Angeles, 1958; A.F.D., Cal. College of Arts and Crafts, 1956; Dr. of Humane Letters, Smith College, 1957; married S. G. Morley, June 1933 (divorced 1936). Instr. French, later instr. French and art, Goucher Coll., Baltimore, 1927-30; curator Cincinnati Art Museum, 1930-33; dir. San Francisco Museum of Art, 1935-58, dir. on leave, 1958-61; asst. director Guggenheim Museums, 1959; dir. Nat. Mus., New Delhi, India, 1959-66; chmn. Central Adv. Bd. Mus., India, from 1960; dir. commemorative exhbn., U. Cal. at Berkeley, 1960; dir. Div. of Edn., Fine Arts Bldg., Golden Gate Internat. Expn., San Francisco, Feb.-Nov. 1939; mem. com. on art and collector South and Central American contemporary painting sections, and dir. Pacific House, Golden Gate Internat. Expn., 1940. Consultant on contemporary Latin American art, Com. on Art, Office of U.S. Coordinator of Inter-Am. Affairs, 1941-43; counselor for museums, International Secretariat, UNESCO, Paris, France, 1946-47, head museums div., 1947-49, cons., museums and hist. monument div., 1951; mem. U.S. Nat. Commn. for UNESCO, 1951-55; asst. dir. Guggenheim Mus., N.Y.C., 1959. Mem. selection com. paintings, Brussel's World Fair, 1958; dir. American, Virginia Museum quadrennial, 1958; member advisory committee on art Division of Cultural Relations, United States Department of State, 1941-45; consultant, Latin American exhibitions. Archives, Hispanic Foundation, Library of Congress, 1943; member U.S. Navy Civilian Adv. Com., 1946; mem. editorial adv. bd. Arts and Architecture; editorial board Museum. Decorated Chevalier Legion d'Honneur, 1949. Mem. College Art Asso., Am. Fedn. Arts (trustee), Internat. Council Mus. (exec. com. 1952, Am. Com. 1951-60), American Assn. of Museums (mem. council 1939-59), Western Assn. Art Museum Dirs. (pres. 1937-41), Am. Association Art Museum Directors (pres. 1954-56, 61), Western Museums Conference (council 1939-46; pres. 1946-47), Phi Beta Kappa. Clubs: Century (San Francisco, California); Women's Faculty (Berkeley, Cal.). Author: Le Sentiment de la Nature en France dans la Première Moitié du Dix-Septième Siècle, 1926; Carl Morris, 1960; also author articles in Cin. Art Mus. Bull., San Francisco Mus. Art Quarterly, art periodicals, catalogues, etc. Died Jan. 8, 1985.

MORNINGSTAR, JOSEPH, corp-exec.; b. N.Y.C., July 11, 1890; s. Joseph and Judith Salsedo (Peixotto) M.; A.B., Wesleyan U., Middletown, Conn., 1911; LL.B., Harvard, 1914; m. Lauretta Wood, June 14, 1923; children—Thomas Wood, Anne Wood (Mrs. Harry Huberth, Jr.). Admitted to N.Y. bar, 1914; with Office Dist. Atty. N.Y. County; with firm Birmingham, Montgomery & Beecher, N.Y.C.; pres. Morningstar-Paisley, Inc., and predecessor, N.Y.C., 1916-62, chmn. bd., from 1962. Trustee Wesleyan U., 1950-53. Served with U.S. Army, 1917-18. Mem. Delta Kappa Epsilon. Clubs: Harvard (N.Y.C.); Westchester Country. Home: Greenwich, Conn. †

MOROSS, JEROME, composer; b. Bklyn., Aug. 1, 1913; student Juilliard Grad. Sch., 1931-32; B.S. in Music Edn., N.Y.U., 1932; m. Hazel Abrams, Aug. 28, 1939; 1 dau., Susanna. Guggenheim fellow, 1947, 49. Composer: Paeans, 1931; Biguine, 1934; Parade, 1935; Frankie and Johnny, 1937; A Tall Story for Orchestra, 1938; Sussanna and the Elders, 1940; Symphony, 1942; Willie the Weeper, 1945; The Eccentricities of Davy Crockett, 1945; Riding Hood Revisited, 1946; The Golden Apple, 1950; The Last Judgement, 1953; Gentlemen, Be Seated, 1955, also Guns and Castinets, Paul Bunyon, An American Pattern; (film scores) The Big Country, 1958, The Cardinal, 1963, The War Lord, 1965. Died July 25, 1983.

MORRELL, JACQUE CYRUS, scientist, inventor; b. Savannah, Ga., Jan. 18, 1893; s. Jospeh and Rae (Cornwall) M.; B.Sc., Cooper Inst., 1915; M.A., Columbia, 1918, Ph.D., 1921; m. Mildred Newmarke, Sept. 8, 1920; children—Doris (Mrs. Henry B. Leader), Lois, Roger. Lectr., demonstrator, instr. dept. chemistry Columbia, 1914-20; instr. Sch. Journalism, 1919-20; asso. dir. research Universal Oil Products Co., Chgo., 1921-42; adjunct prof. petroleum engring. and catalysis Ill. Inst. Tech., 1938-39; v.p., gen. mgr. Bowman Gum Co. and affiliate Research Group Air Mills, Inc., 1945-47; research program planning U.S. Govt., 1949-57; dir., owner Research Products Labs., 1957-85; dir. Atomic Pioneers, asso. Basic Sci. Found., N.Y. Pres. bd. edn., Oak Park, Ill., 1933-38. Served as col. AUS, World War II; col. Spl. Intelligence Unit, USAF, 1948. Decorated Legion of Merit; recipient Pioneer award N.A.M. Registered patent atty.; profl. engr., Pa. Fellow A.A.A.S., Am. Inst. Chemists; mem. Am. Chem. Soc. (chmn. petroleum div., counsellor 1937-38; chmn., dir., trustee Chgo. sect. 1937-38), Am. Inst. Chem. Engrs., Soc. Am. Mil. Engrs., Res. Officers Assn., Retired Officers Assn., Am. Ordance Assn., Sigma Xi, Phi Lambda Upsilon. Clubs: Army and Navy, Inquirendo (pres. 1959-60), Torch (Washington); Naval Officers (Bethesda, Md.). Author: (with Berkman & Egloff) Catalysis Organic and Inorganic, 1940. Contbr. articles sci., tech. jours. Holder numerous patents high-octane motor and aviation fuels, prodn. butadiene for mfr. synthetic rubber, processes for conversion and refining hydrocarbons from petroleum and coal, for prodn. and utilization protective coatings, absorbents, asphalt and resin emulsions, basic patent on alkylation process for prodn. iso-octanes used in aviation, high-octane fuels. Home: Chevy Chase, Md. Died Mar. 20, 1985.

MORRIS, DANIEL LEIGH, lawyer; b. Washington, D.C., May 28, 1890; s. Finis Daniel and Helen Virginia (Moore) M.; LL.B., George Washington U., 1916; m. Elsie B. Ernst, Nov. 20, 1912; children—Barbara Virginia (Mrs. B. V. Dirst), Daniel Leigh, Jr.; m. 2d Marguerite R. Sears, Sept. 1, 1942. Admitted to D.C. bar, 1916; trade mark, patent and anti-trust lawyer, Washington, 1916-21, N.Y. City from 1921; spl. asst. to Atty. Gen. of U.S., 1919-25. Mem. Am. Bar Assn., N.Y. Co. Lawyers Assn., Am., N.Y. patent law assns., Am. Ordance Assn. Club: Advertising of N.Y. Home: Massapequa, N.Y. †

MORRIS, DELYTE WESLEY, ret. univ. pres.; b. Xenia, Ill., Apr. 11, 1907; s. Charles Cue and Lillie Mae (Brown) M.; B.A., Park Coll., 1928, D.H.L., 1960; M.A., U. Maine, 1934; Ph.D., U. Ia., 1936; D.Litt., Lincoln Coll., 1967; LL.D., McKendree Coll., 1967, James Milliken U., 1969; L.H.D., So. Ill. U., 1973; m. Dorothy Arnold Mayo, Dec. 18, 1930; children—Peter Craig, Michael Alan. Tchr. high sch., Sulphur, Okla., 1928-30; instr. pub. speaking, dir. forensic activities U. Maine, 1930-36; chmn. speech dept. Jr. Coll., Kansas City, Mo., 1936-38; chmn. speech dept., dir. spl. edn. clinics Ind. State Tchrs. Coll., Terre Haute, 1938-46; prof. speech, dir. speech and hearing clinic Ohio State U., 1946-48; pres. So. Ill. U., 1948-70, pres. emeritus, 1970-82, chmn. bd. Regional Indsl. Devel. Corp., from 1969; exec. dir. Nat. Council on Educating Disadvantaged, from 1971; cons. NIH. Dir. Gen. Tel. Co. Ill. Mem. Nat. council Boy Scouts Am.; treas. Am. Speech and Hearing Found., 1972; mem. nat. adv. neurol. diseases and stroke council NIH, 1972. Trustee Ill. Lincoln Acad. Recipient Mérito Universitàrio Gold medal Universida de Fed. de Santa Maria, Brazil. Mem. Wabash Valley Interstate Commn., Am. Speech and Hearing Assn. (pres. 1949, sec.-treas. 1941-48), Nat., Ill. edn. assns., Speech Assn. Am., Am., Ill. assns. sch. adminstrs., Bd. Natural Resources, Illinois Hist. Soc., Am. Forestry Assn. (dir.), Alpha Phi Omega, Sigma Pi Sigma. Methodist. Mason (33 deg.), Elk, Lion. Contbr. articles to profl. jours. Home: Gilbertsville, Ky. Died Apr. 10, 1982.

MORRIS, EDWARD KARRICK, univ. exec.; b. N.Y.C., Jan. 25, 1897; s. Henry Lincoln and Lucy (Karrick) M.; grad. Berkshire Sch., Sheffield, Mass., 1914; student Williams Coll., 1918; LL.D., Southeastern U., 1956; D.Pub. Service, George Washington U., 1973; m. Teresa

James, May 1, 1924. Faculty, Berkshire Sch., 1919-21; founder, 1925, pres., chmn. bd. Fed. Storage Co., Washington, 1925-63; chmn. bd. Victory Van Corp., 1945-63; chmn. bd. Security Storage Co., Washington, 1963-66, dir., 1966-81; mem. exec. com. Washington Gas Light Co., 1949-67; now adv. dir. Riggs Nat. Bank. Pres. Met. Washington Bd. Trade, 1959-60; trustee Fed. City Council, Washington Better Bus. Bur. Chmn. exec. com. Episcopal Home for Children, Washington, 1947; pres. Boys Club Greater Washington, 1949-51, Nat. Capital Area Found., 1960-62; founder, pres. United Givers Fund Nat. Capital Area, 1956-58; gen. campaign chmn. Community Chest Fedn. Washington, 1955; trustee, chmn. bd. George Washington U.; trustee Berkshire Sch., St. Albans Sch., Kiwanis Found., D.C. chpt. ARC, Washington Cathedral; dir. Boys Clubs Am.; treas. Consortium of Univs. Served with A.C., U.S. Navy, 1918. Recipient Brotherhood award NCCJ, 1957; Boss Year Award, Junior C. of C., 1961; first J. Edgar Hoover award, 1963, Silver Keystone award Boys Clubs Am., 1972; Service to Mankind award Sertoma Internat., 1978. Mem. Washington Execs. Assn. (pres. 1940-41), Sigma Phi, Omicron Delta Kappa. Mason, Kiwanian (pres. Washington 1952-53). Clubs: Metropolitan (Washington); Chevy Chase (Md.). Home: Washington, D.C. Died Nov. 20, 1981.

MORRIS, JAMES HAINES, design co. exec., former naval officer; b. Dayton, Ohio, Feb. 24, 1926; s. and Charlotte Mary (Haines) M.; m. Billie Coletti, Apr. 29, 1972; 1 dau., Jami Gascon. B.S. with honors, U.S. Mcht. Marine Acad., 1948. Deck officer Lykes Bros. Steamship Co., 1948-50; time study engr. Dayton Tire and Rubber Co., Ohio, 1950-51; advt. salesman L. M. Berry Co., 1954-55; commd. lt. (j.g.) U.S. Navy, 1951, advanced through grades to rear adm., 1976; mem. staff (Comdr. Task Force 95), 1951; comdr. (Naval Air Force, Pacific Fleet), 1952-53; (8th Naval Dist. Hdqrs.), New Orleans, 1963-65, (Amphibious Group 3), Pacific, 1969-70, (Amphibious Group 4), Atlantic, 1961-62; served at sea on torpedo boat, Korean waters, 1951, (destroyers Laffey), 1951, (Maddox), 1951 and; (Wiltsie), 1951, (heavy cruiser), Los Angeles, 1955-58, (dock landing ship Alamo), 1966-67, (Hermitage), 1959-61; comdg. officer dock landing ship (Comstock), 1967-69; comdg. officer combat stores ship (San Jose), 1970-72; dir. human resource mgmt. div. (Bur. Naval Personnel), Washington, 1972-73; spl. asst. for spl. projects to (Chief Naval Ops.), Washington, 1973-74; served as comdg. officer assault ship (Tarawa), 1974-76; comdr. (Amphibious Group 1, Hdqrs.), Okinawa, Japan, 1976-78; dep. comdr. (Naval Surface Force, U.S. Pacific Fleet), San Diego, 1978-80, ret., 1980; v.p. Coletti Design, Dayton, Ohio, 1981-83; Mem. adv. council Project Concern Internat. Decorated Legion of Merit with 2 gold stars and combat V, Bronze Star with 2 gold stars and combat V, Meritorious Service medal with 2 gold stars, Navy Commendation medal with combat V; recipient Disting. Grad. award U.S. Mcht. Marine Acad., 1977. Club: Rotary. Developed Navy human goals plan in 1973 as head human resource mgmt. br. Bur. Naval Personnel. Home: Dayton, OH. Died Mar. 26, 1983; interred Woodlawn Cemetery, Dayton, Ohio.

MORRIS, KELSO BRONSON, educator; b. Beaumont, Tex., Feb. 6, 1909; s. Isaiah H. and Frances (Kelso) M.; m. Marlene Isabella Cook, Apr. 29, 1961; children—Gregory Alfred, Karen Denise, Lisa Frances; 1 son by previous marriage, Kenneth Bruce. B.S., Wiley Coll., 1930; M.S., Cornell U., 1937, Ph.D., 1940. Instr. chemistry and math. Wiley Coll., 1930-36, prof. chemistry, 1936-46; mem. faculty Howard U., Washington, from 1946, prof. chemistry, from 1961, head dept., 1965-69; prof., chem. sect. head Air Force Inst. Tech., Wright-Patterson AFB, Ohio, 1959-61; vis. lectr. Atlanta U., summers 1946, 49, 51, NSF Sci. Inst., N.C. Coll. at Durham, summers 1957-59, U.N.C.F. Disting. Lecture, Series, 1974-78. Author: articles and monographs, including Togetherness: On a Scale From One to Ten. Recipient Disting. Alumni Achievement award Wiley Coll., 1972, Hall of Fame award, 1979. Fellow AAAS, Tex. Acad. Sci., Washington Acad. Sci. (Distinguished Teaching award 1968, sec. 1977-78), Am. Inst. Chemists (gen. chmn. annual meeting 1974); mem. Am. Chem. Soc., Nat. Assn. Research Sci. Teaching, D.C. Inst. Chemists (pres. 1974-79, Honor Scroll award 1979), Sigma Xi, Alpha Phi Alpha, Beta Kappa Chi. Unitarian. Club: Cosmos (Washington). Home: Washington, DC.

MORRIS, LAVAL SIDNEY, landscape architect; b. Salt Lake City, Dec. 3, 1899; s. Koran Lemuel and Louise (Bissigger) M.; m. Rachel Bankhead, June 3, 1925; children—John Koran, Wilford Byron, Tula Kristin. B.S., Utah State U., 1923; M.S. (fellow 1923), Mich. State U., 1925; M.L.A. (scholar 1931, 32), Harvard U., 1933. Prof. landscape architecture Brigham Young U., 1933-37; landscape engr. Utah Hwy. Commn., 1933-39; prof., head dept. landscape architecture and environ. planning Utah State U., 1939-65; cons. dust and erosion control, land mgmt. plans Army Dugway Proving Grounds, 1955-61; cons. grounds treatment Army 9th Service Command; cons. ground plans for mil. hosps.; Chmn. Planning Commn., Provo, Utah, 1933-37. Wood sculpture represented in permanent collection, Utah State U., also pvt. collections.; Author: The Gardens of Eden and Man; Contbr. articles to mags. Served to capt. C.E. U.S. Army, 1942-45, PTO; lt. col. Res. Named Outstanding Landscape Architect Asso. Landscape Architects Utah, 1961. Fellow Am. Soc. Landscape Architects, Am. Civic and Planning Assn., AAUP, Fedn. Utah Artists. Club: Harvard. Home: Providence, UT.

MORRISON, DONAL MACLACHLAN, newspaper columnist; b. San Antonio, Apr. 7, 1922; s. William Gamble Boyd and Belle Maxey (Robards) M.; m. Betty Carney, Dec. 20, 1947; children—Donal (dec.), Deborah, David, Andrew, Jeremy. A.B., Columbia Coll., 1950; M.S., Columbia U., 1951. Copy editor, picture editor, reporter Mpls. Tribune, 1951-61; daily columnist, critic arts, theater and entertainment Mpls. Star, from 1961. Author: (with Jerome Liebman) The Face of Minneapolis, 1968. Served with USAAF, 1942-46. Mem. Newspaper Guild, Am. Theater Critics Assn. Democrat. Home: Minneapolis, Minn.

MORRISON, ESTELLE O., Rep. Nat. committeewoman; b. Oshkosh, Wis., July 17, 1889; d. Samuel Henry and Sarah (Abrams) Owens; attended Eveleth (Minn.) High School, 1903-07; m. Howard Schofield Morrison, Mar. 29, 1907; children—Annabel Owens (Mrs. Loker Chittenden), William Howard, Helen Margaret (Mrs. Walter Spiegel), Ruth Louann (Mrs. John A. Unverferth), Mary Lee, Samuel James. Began career as Republican in 1924; precinct chmn. county chmn., dist. chmn. then elected mem. Nat. com. of Wis., 1944; vol. nurse's aide and Gray Lady, Wausau Memorial Hosp. Mem. White Shrine of Jerusalem (past high priestess), Am. Legion Auxillary (past pres.), Parent Teachers Assn. (past treas.). Address: Albany, Oreg. †

MORRISON, FRED WILSON, lawyer; b. Pioneer Mills, N.C., Oct. 29, 1890; s. Columbus Howard and Palmyra (Pharr) M.; A.B., A.M., U. N.C., 1913; Ph.D., Columbia, 1925; LL.D., Centre Coll. of Ky., 1957; m. Emma Neal McQueen, Oct. 22, 1938; 1 dau., Myra Neal. Prin. City High Sch., New Bern, N.C., 1913-14; supt. schs., Chapel Hill, N.C., 1914-23; asso. prof. edn. N.C. Coll. for Women, 1924-26; asst. exec. sec. N.C. State Ednl. Commn., 1926-27; exec. sec. N.C. Tax Commn., 1927-33; state dir. relief for N.C., 1932-33; admitted to N.C. bar, 1933, U.S. Ct. Appeals for D.C., 1934, U.S. Supreme Ct., 1943; pvt. practice of law, from 1933; mem. Gardner, Morrison, Sheriff & Beddow, Washington, from 1937. Dir. O. Max Gardner Found., Inc., from 1948. Served as 1st lt. F.A., U.S. Army, 1918. Mem. Bar Assn. D.C., Am., N.C. bar assns., U. N.C. Alumni Assn., N.Y. Southern Soc., N.C. State Bar, Am. Judicature Soc., Phi Beta Kappa, Phi Delta Kappa. Democrat. Club: University (Washington). Home: Washington, D.C. †

MORRISON, JAMES CARLETON, investment banker; b. East Orange, N.J., Nov. 26, 1905; s. William H. and Jennie (Nourse) M.; m. Anita Cheney, June 1931; 1 son, James Carleton; m. Mary Stedman, Sept. 18, 1943; children: Douglas C., Bruce H. Student, Mercersburg (Pa.) Acad., 1921-23; B.S., Cornell-Lehigh U., 1928. Salesman Brown Bros. & Co., N.Y.C., 1928-31; Salesman First Boston Corp., 1931-42, asst. v.p., 1942-45, v.p., 1945-61, sr. v.p., mem. exec. com., 1961-70, dir., 1955-72; pres. Richter Farm Assos. Inc., 1972-84. Mem. bd. Deafness Research Found. Mem. U.S. Sr. Golf Assn., Theta Delta Chi, Omicron Delta Kappa. Clubs: Baltusrol Golf (N.Y.), Cornell (N.Y.); Short Hills (N.J.); Gulf Stream Golf (Fla.); St. Andrew's Bath and Tennis (Delray Beach, Fla.). Home: Delray Beach, Fla. Died Oct. 4, 1984.

MORRISSEY, WILLIAM JOSEPH, army officer; b. Philadelphia, Pa., Feb. 3, 1888; s. Michael and Mary (McMahon) M.; B.S., U.S. Mil. Acad., 1912; grad. Command and Gen. Staff Sch., 1925; m. Charlotte Farris, Nov. 4, 1921. Commd. 2d. lt., U.S. Army, 1912, advancing through the grades to brig. gen., 1944; served as bn. comdr. and regtl. exec. officer 36th Div., during World War I; prof. mil. science and tactics, Syracuse (N.Y.) U., 1920-24; Gen. Staff Corps, 1935-37; dep. asst. chief of staff, G-4, War Dept. Gen. Staff, 1942-46; assigned to staff of comdg. general Am. Ground Forces in Pacific; retired as brig. gen., U.S. Army, Oct. 31, 1947. Decorated Silver Star, Legion of Merit, Bronze Star, Purple Heart, Asiatic-Pacific Theater, European-African Theater, Am. Defense and American Theater medals, Victory medals World War I and II (U.S.), Hon. Comdr. Order British Empire, Croix de Guerre (France). Mem. Assn. U.S. Army. Clubs: Commonwealth Cal.; Army and Navy (Washington); Press (San Francisco). Address: San Francisco, Calif. †

MORROW, ANDREW GLENN, surgeon; b. Indpls., Nov. 3, 1922; s. Henry Birt and Doras Belle (Gordon) M.; m. Phyllis Ruth Perry, June 2, 1945; children—Elizabeth Ruth, Andrew Glenn, Katherine Gordon. A.B., Wabash Coll., 1943; M.D., Johns Hopkins U., 1946. Surg. resident Johns Hopkins U. Hosp., 1946-52; sr. registrar thoracic surgery Gen. Infirmary, Leeds, Eng., 1952-53; asso., then instr. surgery Johns Hopkins U. Med. Sch., 1947-52, asst. prof., 1954-60, assoc. prof. surgery, 1960-82, chief clinic surgery Nat. Heart Inst., Bethesda, Md., 1953-82; mem. surgery study sect. NIH; med. dir. USPHS. Editorial bd.: Jour. Cardiovascular Surgery. Fellow A.C.S.; mem. Soc. Clin. Surgery, N.Y. Heart Assn., AMA, Soc. Vascular Surgery (pres. 1971-72), Am. Assn. Thoracic Surgery, Halsted Soc., Internat. Cardiovascular Soc. (pres. 1969-70), Am. Heart Assn., Am. Fedn. Clin. Research, Soc. Univ. Surgeons, Soc. Thoracic Surgeons Gt. Britain and Ireland, Am. Surg. Assn. Home: Rockville, Md. Dec. Aug. 12, 1982.

MORSE, GARIAN, electronic mfg. co. exec.; b. Marblehead, Mass., May 13, 1912; s. William H. and Edna May (Stillman) M.; B.S., Tufts Coll., 1934; m. Priscilla Slee, May 29, 1937; children—Priscilla Donovan (Mrs. John L. Donovan), Elizabeth (Mrs. Richard Hargraves), Garlan, Frank B. With Sylvania Electric Products, Inc., N.Y.C., 1936-71, sr. v.p., 1967-69, exec. v.p., 1969, pres. 1969-71, also dir.; dir. Gen. Telephone & Electronic Internat., Inc., Gen. Telephone & Electronics Labs., Inc., Wilbur B. Driver Co. Bd. dirs. Mass. Bay United Fund, 1967-68. Jr. Achievement; dir. of labor Mil. Govt. group working with British, French and Russians to reach uniform labor policy for all occupied Germany; on inactive mil. status since 1945. Decorated three bronze stars, Mediterranean and European theaters of operation, Legion of Merit, Mem. bd. dirs. Pub. Health Research Inst. of City of N.Y.; former mem. Somerville (N.J.) Bd. of Edn. Mem. Am. and N.J. bar assns., Am. Arbitration Assn., Phi Epsilon Pi. Clubs: Elihu Root Law (Harvard); Harvard (New York); Cosmos, Metropolitan (Washington). Home: Marblehead, Mass. Died May 26, 1985.

MORSE, GERRY ELDEN, mgmt. cons.; b. Worcester, Mass., July 2, 1908; s. John S. and Grace M. (Elden) M.; m. Martha P. Levis, Oct. 11, 1940 (dec. 1967); 1 dau., Gillian Lucy. B.S., Mass. Inst. Tech., 1930; M.B.A., Harvard, 1932. Airship mechanic Goodyear Zeppelin Corp., Akron, Ohio, summers 1929-32; tabulating clerk Pepperell Mfg. Co., Boston, 1933; from cost accountant to dir. employee relations Sylvania Electric Products, Inc., Salem, Mass. and N.Y.C., 1933-51; v.p. employee relations Honeywell, Inc., 1951-73; pres. Council Community Hosps., Mpls., 1973-76; prin. GE Morse/Staff Cons. Services, Lakewood, Colo., from 1973; mem. faculty div. mgmt. edn. Grad. Sch. Bus. Adminstrn., U. Mich., from 1976; research asso. U. Minn.; Mem. Nat. Labor Mgmt. Panel, 1963-66; adv. council to Commr. Employment Security Minn., 1963-73; mem. Minn. Bd. Human Rights, 1968-71. Trustee Career Clinic Mature Women, Mpls., 1964-69, exec. com., 1968-69; bd. dirs. Mpls. Employers' Vol. Plans Progress Assn., 1966-70, Asso. Industries Mpls., 1953-71, St. Barnabas Hosp., 1956-70, Greater Mpls. Safety Council, 1966-71, Council House Sr. Citizens, Mpls., 1956-58, Minn. Hosp. Service Assn. (Blue Cross), 1958-73, Minn. Safety Council, 1971-73, Twin City Hosp. Assn., 1961-72; bd. dirs., exec. com. Met. Med. Center, Mpls., 1970-72; personnel com. YMCA, 1963-70; mem. indsl. relations council U. Pa., 1960-72; mem. Columbia U. Seminar Labor, 1949-76; pres. Forest Glen Homeowners Assn., Lakewood, from 1979. Mem. Nat. Soc. Profl. Engrs. (bd. advisers 1958-70), Am. Mgmt. Assn. (personnel planning council, v.p. 1958-59). Republican. Congregationalist (deacon, moderator 1957, chmn. bd. trustees 1974-75, 80-81). Home: Lakewood, Colo.

MORSE, HERMANN NELSON, clergyman; b. Ludington, Mich., Sept. 29, 1887; s. Hermann Nelson and Sarah (Smith) M.; A.B., Alma (Mich.) Coll., 1908, D.D., 1927; diploma Union Theol. Sem., 1911; student Columbia U., 1908-12; LL.D., Waynesburg College, Pennsylvania, 1948; Litt.D., Beaver Coll., 1952; D.D., Yale U., 1953; ;m. Florence Vorpe 1913; children—Sarah Frances, Warren Wilson. Ordained Presbyn. ministry, 1911; spl. investigator for Presbyn. Bd. Home Missions, 1912-13; sec. Bennington County (Vt.) Improvement Assn., 1913-14; asso. dir. country ch. work, Presbyn. Bd. Home Missions, 1914-18, dir. research and publicity, 1918-23; recording sec. and dir. budget and research, Presbyn. Bd. Nat. Missions, 1923-49, adminstrv. sec., 1930-49, gen. sec., exec. v.p., 1949-59, now gen. sec. emeritus and general consultant, also chmn. Inst. Strategic Studies, 1964-66; vis. prof. Princeton Theol. Seminary, 1960-61, cons. in field edn., 1961-62, dir. continuing edn., 1962-64; past vice pres. Nat. Council Chs.; chmn. div. home missions 1950-52; moderator Presbyn. U.S.A. Gen. Assembly, 1952; dir. surveys, Home Missions Council (interdenom.), 1928-30; chmn. staff Intersem. Commn. for Tng. for Rural Ministry, 1931-50; Home Missions Council of N.A., 1945-47 (pres.). Lectr. rural sociology and ch. work. Pres. bd. trustees Barber-Scotia Coll., Concord, N.C. Mem. Chi Alpha fraternity. Democrat. Presbyterian. Author: The Country Church in Industrial Zones, 1922; The Town and Country Church in the United States (with E. de S. Brunner); The Social Survey in Town and Country Areas; The Every Community Survey of New Hampshire; The Every Community Survey of Maine; Toward a Christian America, 1935; These Moving Times, 1945; Again Pioneers, 1949; (book) From Frontier to Frontier, 1952; also miscellaneous pamphlets and repts. Editor of Home Lands (bi-monthly country ch. mag.), 1918- 24, also of Home Missions Today and Tomorrow. Home: New York, N.Y. †

MORSELL, H(ERNDON) TUDOR, federal official; b. Cambridge, Mass., Aug. 2, 1890; s. Herndon and Elizabeth (Burton) M.; B.S., Wesleyan U., Middletown, Conn., 1914; m. Marian Edella Preston, June 12, 1917; children—Mary-Tudor, Suzanne, Bonnie Burton. Mfrs. rep., Washington, D.C., 1915-18; real estate business, Washington, D.C., 1919-23; realtor (own firm), 1923-30; land purchasing officer Nat. Capital Park and Planning Commn., 1930-34; chief of land acquisition housing div., Pub. Works Adminstrn., 1934-38; dir. land div. U.S. Housing Authority, 1938-42; dir. land div. Fed. Pub. Housing Authority, since Feb. 1942; chmn. sub-com. of appraisals and purchase, of Central Housing Com.; consultant for Dist. of Columbia Airport Commn. and other govt. depts. on real estate; mem. site selection com.

for the Defense Housing Projects. Served as 2d lt. field arty., U.S. Army, 1918; apptd. aide to Gov. of Ky. (Ky. col.), 1934. Mem. Inst. Real Estate Appraisers, Nat. Assn. Real Estate Bds., Wesleyan Alumni Assn. (past pres.), Am. Legion, Alpha Delta Phi. Democrat. Episcopalian. Mason. Clubs: Gridiron, Chevy Chase, Alpha Delta Phi Alumni Assn. (Washington, D.C.). Home: Chevy Chase, Md. †

MORTON, THRUSTON BALLARD, former U.S. senator; b. Louisville, Aug. 19, 1907; s. David Cummings and Mary Harris (Ballard) M.; m. Belle Clay Lyons, Apr. 18, 1931; children—Thruston Ballard, Clay Lyons. Student, Woodberry Forest Sch., Orange, Va., 1922-25; A.B., Yale U., 1929. Held various positions with Ballard & Ballard, Louisville, since 1929; former chmn. bd.; mem. 80th to 82d Congresses, 3d Ky. Dist.; asst. sec. state for Congl. Relations, Dept. State, Washington, 1953-56; U.S. senator from, Ky., 1957-68; vice chmn. Liberty Nat. Bank & Trust Co., Louisville, 1968-82. Chmn. Republican Nat. Com., 1959-61; Trustee Frontier Nursing Service, Lincoln Inst. of Ky. Served as lt. comdr. USNR, 1941-45. Member Alpha Delta Phi, Order of Cincinnati. Republican. Episcopalian. Home: Louisville, Ky. Dec. Aug. 14, 1982.

MORTON, WALTER ALBERT, econ. cons., ret. educator; b. Cleve., Mar. 25, 1899; s. Louis and Wilhelmina (Reich) M.; B.A. and M.A., U. Mich., 1924, (Robert Brookings grad. sch. fellow, 1924, 25); Ph.D., U. Wis., 1927; student U. Chgo. and London Sch. Econs. (fellow social sci. research council), 1934-35; m. Rosalie Amlie, Aug. 12, 1929; children—Jane, Steve. Instr., U. Wis., 1925-27, asst. prof. econs., 1927-31, asso. prof., 1931-37, prof. econs., 1937-69, prof. emeritus, 1969-82; vis. prof. econs. Haynes Found. Lectureship, Pomona Coll., 1960-61; vis. prof. econs. U. Mo., 1964-65, Ill. State U., 1969-71; mem. tariff research com. U. Wis., 1929-32; cons. econ. policy com. Am. Bankers Assn., 1963-66. Trustee Wis. State Investment Bd., 1963-69. Mem. C. of C. U.S. (transp. and communication com.), Am., Midwest (pres. 1953-54) econs. assns., Delta Sigma Pi. Author: British Finance 1930-40, 1943. Editor: Agricultural Tariffs Series, 1929-35 (with John R. Commons and Benjamin H. Hibbard); Trade Unionism Full Employment and Inflation, 1950; Rate of Return and the Value of Money in Public Utilities, 1952; Housing Taxation, 1955; Federal Reserve Policy, 1957; also articles on tariffs and tariff theory, money, banking, taxation, unemployment insurance, fair rate of return for pub. utilities in popular and profl. jours. Researcher in monetary and banking theory, pub. utilities. Home: Madison, Wis. Died Sept. 21, 1982.

MORTON, WILLIAM W(ILSON), prof. philosophy and religion; b. Oxford, N.C., June 22, 1890; s. Joseph William and Mary Tazewell (Wilson) M.; A.B., Davidson Coll., 1909, D.D., 1933; B.D., Union Theol. Sem., 1913, student U. of Glasgow, 1914-15; m. Frances Wilson Campbell, June 25, 1930; 1 dau., Francis Wilson. Ordained to ministry of Presbyn. Ch., 1913; asso. pastor First Presbyn. Ch., Wilmington, N.C., 1919-24; asst. prof. Bible, Washington and Lee U., Lexington, Va., 1925-28, prof. philosophy and religion from 1928. Served as capt., chaplain 322nd inf., U.S. Army, 1917-19. Mem. Nat. Assn. Bibl. Instrs., Southern Society of Philosophy of Religion, S.R. Sons of the Confederacy, Phi Beta Kappa. Democrat. Presbyterian. Home: Lexington, Va. †

MOSBY, HENRY SACKETT, wild life management educator; b. Lynchburg, Va., Oct. 28, 1913; s. Alexander West and Jane Leyburn (Sackett) M.; m. Virginia Anderson Brown, July 12, 1941; children: Henry Sackett, Virginia Anderson, Walter Brown. B.S., Hampden Sydney Coll., 1935; B.S.F., M.F., U. Mich., 1937, Ph.D., 1941. Field biologist Va. Commn. Game and Inland Fisheries, 1939-42, acting supt., 1942-43; editor Va. Wildlife, 1942-43; dir. Wildlife Research Sta., Va. Poly. Inst., 1947-48; unit leader Va. Coop. Wildlife Research Unit, U.S. Fish and Wildlife Service, 1948-55; prof. wildlife mgmt. Va. Poly. Inst., 1955-77, prof. emeritus, 1977-84., head dept. fisheries and wildlife, 1973-77, chmn. agrl. faculty, 1964; Mem. panel preprofl. tng. agrl. scis. Commn. Undergrad. Edn. Biol. Scis., 1964—; mem. Va. Resources Use Edn. Council, 1952-84, instr., 1964-84. Author: (with C. O. Handley) The Wild Turkey in Virginia: Its Status, Life History and Management, 1943; Editor, contbr.: Wildlife Investigational Techniques, 2d edit, 1963. Mem. council Blue Ridge council Boy Scouts Am., 1955-84. Served with USAAF, 1943-46. Recipient Silver Beaver award, 1962, Meritorious Service award U.S. Fish and Wildlife Service, 1955; Wine award outstanding tchr. Va. Poly. Inst., 1963. Mem. Wildlife Soc. (hon. mem.; charter, v.p. 1961, pres. 1964-65, editor Wildlife Soc. News 1948-55, Wildlife Techniques publs. 1958-64, award outstanding wildlife publ. 1943, Leopold award 1978), Soc. Am. Foresters, Wildlife Disease Assn., Wilson Ornithol. Club, Va. Ornithol. Soc., Sigma Xi, Phi Kappa Phi, Chi Phi, Omicron Delta Kappa, Phi Sigma. Presbyn. (elder). Home: Blacksburg, Va. Died Aug. 12, 1984.

MOSES, ROBERT, pub. ofcl.; b. New Haven, Dec. 18, 1888; s. Emanuel and Bella Moses; B.A., Yale U., 1909, A.M. (hon.), 1936, LL.D., 1952; B.A. with honors in jurisprudence, Oxford U., 1911, M.A., 1913; Ph.D. in Polit. Sci., Columbia U., 1914, LL.D., 1952; LL.D., Syracuse U., 1936, Union Coll., 1938, Bates Coll., 1945, Princeton U., 1947, Hofstra Coll., 1948, Harvard U., 1953, L.I. U., 1954, Pratt Inst., 1955, N.Y. Law Sch., 1961, Coll. Charleston, 1969; L.H.D., Colgate U., 1954, Fordham U., 1959; D.E., N.Y.U., 1950, U. Mich., 1953, Manhattan Coll., 1954, Poly. Inst. Bklyn., 1956, U. Buffalo, 1959, St. John's U., 1959; D.F.A., Niagara U., 1961; Dr. Pub. Adminstrn., U. R.I., 1964; Litt.D., Mercy Coll., 1975; hon. fellow Wadham Coll., 1960; m. Mary Louise Sims, Aug. 28, 1915; children—Barbara (Mrs. Richard J. Olds), Jane Moses Collins; m. 2d, Mary A. Grady, Oct. 3, 1966. Municipal investigator, N.Y.C., 1913; chief staff N.Y. State Reconstrn. Commn., 1919-21; pres. L.I. State Park Commn., also chmn. State Council Parks, 1924-63; sec. state, N.Y., 1927-28; chmn. Jones Beach State Pkwy. and Bethpage Park authorities, 1933-63; N.Y.C. park commr. (consolidating city park and pkwy. system), 1934-60; apptd. mem. Triborough Bridge Authority, 1934, chmn., 1936; sole mem. Henry Hudson and Marine Pkwy. authorities, 1934-38; sole mem. N.Y.C. Pkwy. Authority (absorbed Henry Hudson and Marine Pkwy. authorities), 1938; mem. N.Y.C. Planning Commn., 1942-60; chief exec. officer N.Y.C. Tunnel Authority, 1945-46; chmn. consol. Triborough Bridge and N.Y.C. Tunnel Authority, 1946-68, now cons.; N.Y.C. constrn. coordinator, 1946-60; mem. L.I.R.R. Commn., 1950; chmn. Power Authority, State of N.Y., 1954-63; pres. N.Y. World's Fair 1964-65 Corp., 1960-67; cons. state and mcpl. planning affairs throughout U.S. and in Brazil, 1942-81; sec. Temporary State Commn. Protection and Preservation Atlantic Shore Front, 1962; cons. to chmn. Met. Transp. Authority, 1968-81; mem. N.Y. State Commn. to Commemorate 200th Anniversary Am. Revolution, State N.Y., 1974-81, spl. adviser to N.Y. Gov. on housing, 1974-75; mem. Com. People Public TV, 1977-81; lectr. many large univs. in U.S., 1939-81. Council mem.-at-large Greater N.Y. Boy Scouts Am., advisory mem. Suffolk council; life mem. N.Y. Bldg. Congress; mem. council Fordham U., 1967; hon. chmn. Prospect Park Centennial, 1966; mem. N.Y. State Commn. for Bicentennial Am. Revolution and Creation State N.Y. Republican candidate Gov. State N.Y., 1934. Trustee Hofstra Coll., 1944-69; trustee Miner Inst., Chazy, N.Y., 1971-78, hon., 1978-81; dir. emeritus Lincoln Center Performing Arts, 1969. Recipient numerous awards and medals from various instns., including Silver Beaver award Boy Scouts Am., 1954, Silver Buffalo award, 1964; Distinguished Achievement medal Holland Soc., 1954, Lord and Taylor award, 1955; hon. citizen Sao Paulo, Brazil, 1954; Metropolitan Amateur Athletic Union First gold medal for service, 1954; George Washington Honor medal Freedoms Found., 1955; Gov. L.I. award, 1955; named New Yorker of Year, N.Y. Daily News, 1956; named Constrn. Industry Man of Yr., 1967; 50 Yrs. of Park Service award N.Y. State Council Parks and Recreation, 1974, numerous subsequent awards, medals and honors for accomplishments in pub. service; Robert Moses Plaza at Fordham dedicated in his honor, 1970; Distinguished Service award Council Am. Artist Socs., 1972; Man of Year award L.I. Advt. Club, 1973; award Outstanding Leadership during Bicentennial Era, 1977, others. Fellow Nat. Sculpture Soc. (hon., Continuing Service to Sculpture award 1972), Benjamin Franklin fellow Royal Soc. Arts; mem. Am. Pub. Works Assn. (hon. mem.; chmn.), Public Works Hist. Soc. (hon.), Am. Soc. Landscape Architects (hon.), ASCE (hon.), Inst. Municipal Engring. (hon.), Phi Beta Kappa. Clubs: Players, Lotos (N.Y.C.); Lyford Cay (Nassau, Bahamas); Southward Ho (Bayshore, N.Y.). Author: Public Works: A Dangerous Trade, 1970. Contbr. articles on parks, housing, recreation to mags. and jours. Home: New York, N.Y. Died July 29, 1981.

MOSHER, CHARLES ADAMS, former Congressman; b. Sandwich, Ill., May 7, 1906; s. Edward Castle and Jessie (Adams) M.; m. Harriet Johnson, Oct. 5, 1929; children—Frederic A., Mary Jane. A.B. cum laude, Oberlin (Ohio) Coll., 1928; grad. student, Columbia, U. Chgo., 1928; LL.D., Ohio State U., 1976; L.H.D., Kent State U., 1976. Advt. salesman Aurora (Ill.) Beacon-News, 1929-38; advt. mgr. Janesville (Wis.) Daily Gazette, 1938-40; editor, pub. Oberlin News-Tribune, 1940-61; pres. Oberlin Printing Co., 1940-61; editor Oberlin Coll. Alumni mag., 1942-48; mem. 87th-94th Congresses from 13th Dist. Ohio; exec. dir. Com. Sci. and Tech. U.S. Ho. of Reps., 1977-79; adj. prof. George Washington U., 1977-80; public programs mgr. AAAS, 1979; fellow Woodrow Wilson Internat. Center for Scholars, Washington, 1979-80; Dir. Oberlin Improvement and Devel. Corp., 1964-73; vice chmn. Ohio Sch. Survey Commn., 1954-55; Ohio del. White House Conf. Edn., 1955; mem. Ohio Legislative Service Commn., 1955-59; adv. mem. Fed. Commn. Marine Sci., Engring. and Resources, 1967-69; mem. Office Tech. Assessment Bd., 1973-77, vice chmn., 1973-75; nat. advisory council NSF, Office Coastal Zone Mgmt.; nat. rev. panel Sea Grant Coll. Program; mem. Nat. Commn. on Research, 1979-80, Commn. on the Humanities, 1979-80, Com. on Basic Research in the Social Scis., Nat. Acad. Scis., 1980-82. Columnist for: Ohio/Washington News, 1977-78. Past pres. Oberlin Community Chest.; Vice chmn. Oberlin City Council, 1945-51; del. Republican Nat. Conv., 1948; mem. Ohio Senate, 27th-29th Dist., 1951-61, chmn. edn. com., 1953-57; Trustee Oberlin Coll., 1964-70, 73-79; bd. dirs. Common Cause, Marine Tech. Soc. Mem. Buckeye Press Assn. (past pres.), Oberlin C. of C. (past pres.), Am. Oceanic Orgn. (chmn. bd. 1973-75), ACLU, NAACP, Sigma Delta Chi. Congregationalist. Clubs: Cosmos, Rotary (past pres. Oberlin). Home: Washington, D.C. Died Nov. 16, 1984.

MOSIER, MAURICE LEE, association executive; b. Pittsburg, Kans., June 20, 1925; s. John Lee and Nellie Velma (Ledenham) M.; m. Irene Ballock, Jan. 22, 1946; children—John T., Patti L., Michael C., Stacy Anne. B.S., Northwestern U., 1945, Kans. State Coll., 1949; student, La. State U., 1956. Cert. Profl. Mgr. Personnel mgr. Kans. Ordnance Plant, Parsons, 1951-55; personnel mgr. Kaiser Aluminum & Chem. Corp., Chalmette, La., 1955-56, mgr. indsl. relations, Baton Rouge, La., 1958-64, Spokane, Wash., 1964-68; corp. dir. labor relations Kaiser Engrs., 1968-71; dir. indsl. relations Litton Shipbuilding, Pasagoula, Miss., 1971-72; pres. Nat. Constructors Assn., Washington, 1972-82. Mem. Constrn. Industry Stabilization Com., 1973-74; mem. President's Adv. Com. on Constrn., 1974-76. Trustee Piping Industry Tng. Trust. Served with USNR, 1943-46. Mem. Am. Council Constrn. Edn. (trustee), Am. Soc. Assn. Execs., Washington Assn. Assn. Execs., Am. Legion, VFW. Republican. Methodist. Clubs: Internat. of Washington, Capitol Hill, Presidents. Home: Arnold, Md. Dec. July 1, 1982.

MOSS, CHARLES MALCOLM, lawyer, ins. exec.; b. Sullivan, Ind., Apr. 18, 1905; s. Thomas Woodson and Beulah (Farley) M.; m. Annabel DeVore MacLeod, Feb. 24, 1932 (div. 1953); 1 dau., Annabel Elizabeth Cutter; m. Kathryn Muriel Holland, Dec. 24, 1954; children—Carol Ann (stepdaughter), Kathryn Gail. B.A., Vanderbilt U., 1927; J.D., U. Chgo., 1930. Bar: Ill. bar 1933, Calif. bar 1947. Profl. baseball pitcher Am. Assn. team, Louisville, 1927-29, Nat. League team Chgo. Cubs, 1930, Mpls. Am. Assn. team, 1930, Los Angeles Pacific Coast League team, 1931-32; asso. Wolf, Shaughnessy & Davis (law firm), Chgo., 1931-34; with Prudential Ins. Co. Am., 1934-64; counsel Mid America home office, Chgo., 1954-64, asso. gen. solicitor, 1961-64; gen. counsel Am. Life Conv., 1964-73; v.p., gen. counsel Am. Life Ins. Assn., 1973; of counsel Schiff, Hardin & Waite, Chgo., from 1973. Served from lt. to lt. comdr. USNR, 1942-46. Named Ky. col. Mem. Assn. Life Ins. Counsel, Am. Bar Assn. (chmn. Am. Bar Center facilities spl. com. 1963-67, chmn. life ins. law com. of ins., negligence and compensation sect. 1966-67, chmn. lawyer placement info. spl. com. 1968-72, mem. corp. law depts. com. corp. banking and bus. law sect. 1962-73, editor newsletter 1962-65, mem. spl. com. on assn. facilities 1974-76), Ill. Bar Assn. (bd. govs. 1962-67, chmn. ins. program com. 1964-65, past vice chmn. sect. ins. law, past chmn. corp. law depts. section, past mem. council sect. real estate law), Chgo. Bar Assn. (chmn. corp. law depts. com. 1962-64, past mem. profl. fees Com.); Fellows Am. Bar Found., Phi Beta Kappa, Sigma Alpha Epsilon, Phi Delta Phi, Omicron Delta Gamma. Methodist (past ofcl. bd., past lay leader). Clubs: Vanderbilt U. Alumni Assn. (pres. 1965-66), Chgo. Vanderbilt Alumni (past pres.), So. Calif. Vanderbilt Alumni (past pres.); Marshwood Country (Savannah, Ga.). Home: Savannah, GA.

MOSS, WASHINGTON IRVING, insurance; b. Waterproof, La., Jan. 27, 1888; s. Hartwig and Rosa (Rose) M.; ed. pub. schs.; m. Louise Kahn, of Montgomery, Ala., Feb. 6, 1912; children—Hartwig, Polly, W. Irving. Began with Hartwig Moss Ins. Agency, New Orleans, La., 1908; pres. Hartwig Moss Ins. Agency, Ltd., Midwest Cold Storage & Ice Corpn. Democrat. Jewish religion. Club: Bankers (New York). Home: New Orleans, La. †

MOSSE, BASKETT PERSHING, educator; b. Henderson, Ky., Sept. 9, 1917; s. Herbert and Lucille (Sandefur) M.; m. Mae Sipes, Jan. 30, 1942; children—Nancy Evelyn, Richard Baskett. B.A., U. Tulsa, 1941; M.S. in Journalism, Northwestern U., 1943. Reporter Tulsa Daily World, 1934-41; news editor, NBC, Chgo., 1941-46; prof. journalism Northwestern U., from 1946. Exec. sec. Am. Council Edn. Journalism, 1957-83. Mem. Sigma Delta Chi, Pi Kappa Alpha. Home: Deerfield, Ill. Dec. June 17, 1983.

MOTE, DON CARLOS, entomologist, educator; b. Greenville, O., Jan. 13, 1887; s. Irwin and Katherine (Felton) M.; B.S., Ohio State U., 1911, M.S., 1912, Ph.D., 1928; m. Josephine Mower, June 1914; 1 son, Richard H. Parasitologist O. Agrl. Exptl. Sta., 1912-19; Ariz. State entomologist, 1919-23; asso. entomologist Ore. State Coll., Corvallis, 1923-24, prof., head dept. entomologist in charge Agrl. Exptl. Sta., from 1924; entomologist F.A.O. U.N., 1952-53; agrl. supervisor, U.S. Bur. Census, Dept. Commerce; cons. Miller Products Co. Fellow A.A.A.S.; mem. Entomol. Soc. of Am., Sigma Xi, Phi Kappa Phi. Author bulls., circulars, articles. Home: Corvallis, Ore. †

MOTLEY, ARTHUR HARRISON, publisher; b. Mpls., Aug. 22, 1900; s. Leonard F. and Edith A. (Groff) M.; A.B., U. Minn., 1922; student Columbia, 1925-26; m. Helene Bishop, Sept. 22, 1928; children—Yvonne, Marcia. Instr. English, Hamline U., St. Paul, 1922; exec. sec. Zeta Psi, 1923-24; sales mgr. Smith Brothers, 1927; joined Crowell-Collier Pub. Co., N.Y.C., 1928, salesman, 1928-34, mgr. Detroit office, 1935-37, Western mgr., 1938-39, exec. asst. to pres., 1940, v.p., dir., 1941, pub. Am. mag., 1942-46; pres. Parade Publ., Inc., former pub. Parade, 1946-70, chmn. bd., 1970-78; dir. Sequoia Ins. Co., Starch/Inra/Hooper. Pres. U.S. C. of C., 1960-61, chmn., 1961-62, chmn. exec. com., 1962-63; mem. Advt. Adv. Com.; past chmn. Nat. Distbn. Council, Dept. Commerce. Past nat. pres. Zeta Psi Frat. N.A.; trustee Zeta Psi Ednl. Found.; chmn. bd. U. Minn. Found., 1968-71. Served with U.S. Army, 1918. Mem. Phi Beta Kappa. Republican. Clubs: Metropolitan, Sky (N.Y.C.); Tavern (Chgo.); Adcraft, (Detroit); Larchmont Yacht;

Racquet, Com. of 25 (Palm Springs, Calif.); Thunderbird Country (Rancho Mirage, Calif.). Home: Palm Springs, Calif. Died May 30, 1984.

MOULTON, ELTON JAMES, prof. mathematics; b. Le Roy, Mich., Aug. 4, 1887; s. Belah G. and Mary C. (Smith) M.; Albion (Mich.) Coll., 1903-05, Univ. of Chicago, 1905-08, B.S., 1907; M.A., Univ. of Wis., 1910; Harvard, 1910-11; fellow Univ. of Chicago, 1911-12, Ph.D., 1913; m. Edna Frances McCormack, June 18, 1911; children—James E., Helen Lois, Ralph E., Harold B. Instr. mathematics, Univ. of Wis., 1909-10, Harvard, 1910-11; instr. mathematics, 1912-13, asst. prof., 1913-17, asso. prof., 1917-21, prof. from 1921, asst. dean, 1930-31, Northwestern Univ., aslo dean of Grad. Sch., 1931-33; chairman of department, 1935-42; director of applied mathematics group for NDRC at Columbia, 1943-44, at Northwestern, 1944. Fellow A.A.A.S., mem. Council, 1943-44; mem. Am. Math. Soc., Am. Astron. Soc., Math. Assn. America (vice pres. 1937-38), Assn. Am. Univ. Profs., Phi Beta Kappa, Sigma Xi, Gamma Alpha. Republican. Methodist. Author of five mathematics books and numerous papers. Editor-in-chief, Am. Math. Monthly, 1937-41. Home: Glenview, Ill. †

MOWITZ, ROBERT JAMES, educator; b. Tonawanda, N.Y., Feb. 14, 1920; s. Benjamin Joseph and Mae Alice (Linton) M.; m. Clara E. MacDonald, Mar. 29, 1942; children—Eric, Carol Mowitz Wahls. A.B., Syracuse U., 1941, Ph.D., 1948. Mem. faculty Wayne State U., Detroit, 1948-64, prof. polit. sci., 1959-64; dir. Inst. Pub. Adminstrn., prof. pub. adminstrn. Pa. State U., University Park, from 1964; cons. Office Sec. Def., 1961-69, Office Adminstrn. Gov. Pa., 1968-70, Exec. Office Gov. Mich., 1971-73, Office Program Planning and Fiscal Mgmt., gov. Wash., 1973-74, Office Budget Sec., gov. Pa., from 1970, Mich. Dept. Mental Health, from 1977. Author: (with Schuler and Mayer) Medical Public Relations, 1952, (with Wright) Profile of a Metropolis, 1962, The Design and Implementation of Pennsylvania's Planning, Programming, Budgeting System, 1970, The Design of Public Decision Systems, 1979; contbr. to: (with Wright) Current Practice in Program Budgeting (Novick), 1973. Chmn. Mental Health Inquiry Bd. Mich., 1959-60, Gov.'s Task Force on Mental Health, 1960; mem. Gov.'s Commn. for Modern State Govt. Pa., 1967-69; mem. research adv. bd. Com. for Econ. Devel., 1974-79. Mem. Am. Soc. Pub. Adminstrn., Am. Polit. Sci. Assn., AAUP. Home: State College, PA.

MOWRER, ORVAL HOBART, educator, psychologist; b. Unionville, Mo., Jan. 23, 1907; s. John A. and Sallie (Todd) M.; m. Willie Mae Cook, Sept. 9, 1931; children—Linda, Kathryn, Todd. A.B., U. Mo., 1929; Ph.D., Johns Hopkins, 1932; NRC fellow, Northwestern U., 1932-33, Princeton, 1933-34; Sterling fellow, Yale, 1934-36. Diplomate: Am. Bd. Examiners Profl. Psychology. Instr. psychology, mem. research staff Inst. Human Relations, Yale, 1936-40; asst. prof. edn. Harvard, 1940-43, asso. prof., 1943-48; research prof. psychology U. Ill. at Urbana, 1948-75, prof. emeritus, from 1975; spl. cons. USPHS. Author: (with Dollard, et al) Frustration and Aggression, 1939, Learning Theory and Personality Dynamics, 1950, Psychotherapy Theory and Research, 1953, Learning Theory and Behavior, 1960, Learning Theory and the Symbolic Processes, 1960, The Crisis in Psychiatry and Religion, 1961, The New Group Therapy, 1964, Morality and Mental Health, 1967, (with others) Conscience, Contract and Social Reality, 1972, Integrity Groups: The Loss and Recovery of Community, 1974, The History of Psychology in Autobiography, 1974, Psychology of Language and Learning, 1980; Editor: (with others) Patterns of Modern Living, 3 vols, 1950, Harvard Ednl. Rev, 1945-48. Served as clin. psychologist OSS, 1944-45. Recipient Certificate of Merit U. Mo., 1956; Distinguish Contributions award Ill. Psychol. Assn., 1975. Fellow Am. Psychol. Assn. (pres. 1954, dir., pres. personality, social psychology, clin. and abnormal psychology div. 1953, Distinguished Contributions award div. 12 1975); mem. Am. Acad. Psychotherapists, AAUP, Am. Psychol. Found. (pres. 1959-60), Sigma Xi. Vol. 97 of Education devoted to his writings, 1976. Home: Urbana, Ill.

MOWRY, GEORGE EDWIN, historian; b. Washington, Sept. 5, 1909; s. James Reilly and Ibby Katherine (Green) M.; m. Katherine Mowry, Dec. 1, 1983. A.B., Miami U., 1933; M.A., U. Wis., 1934, Ph.D., 1938. Instr. U. Wis. Extension, 1937; instr. U. N.C., 1938-39, asst. prof., 1942-44; May Treat Morrison prof. Am. history Mills Coll., 1944-47; prof. Am. history State U. Iowa, 1947-50; prof. Am. history U. Calif. at Los Angeles, 1950-67, dean div. social scis., 1959-67, chmn. dept. history, 1955-56, 58-67; Kenan prof. Am. history U. N.C., 1967-84; Harmsworth prof. Oxford (Eng.) U., 1960-61; summer teaching U. Wis., U. Calif., Western Res. U., Columbia, also U. Strassbourg, 1950-51, U. Rennes, 1951, Hebrew U. Jerusalem, 1953-54, U. Marseilles, Nice, 1958. Author: Theodore Roosevelt and the Progressive Movement, 1946, California Progressivism 1900-20, 1951, The Era of Theodore Roosevelt, 1958 (Commonwealth Club award 1959); Co-author: American Society and the Changing World, 1942, Short History of American Democracy, 1955, The Federal Union, 1962, The American Nation, 1963, The Urban Nation, 1965, A History of American Democracy, 1966, Another Look at the Twentieth Century South, 1973; Contbr.: War As a Social Institution, 1941, gen. periodicals.; Editorial bd.: Miss. Valley Hist. Rev, 1949. Served as policy analyst for Army Q.M. Corps and WPB, 1942-44. Mem. AAUP, Am., Miss. Valley hist. Socs., Orgn. Am. Historians (pres. 1965), Sigma Alpha Epsilon. Address: Chapel Hill, N.C. Died May 12, 1984.

MUELLER, KATE HEVNER, educator; b. Derry, Pa., Nov. 1, 1898; d. Rev. Winnbert D. and Joie (McNaughton) Hevner; A.B., Wilson Coll., Sc.D., 1953; A.M., Columbia, 1923; Ph.D. (fellow), U. Chgo., 1928; L.H.D., Mills Coll., 1963; m. John H. Mueller, Sept. 3, 1935. Instr. in psychology Wilson Coll., 1923-26; asst. prof. psychology U. Minn., 1928-35; dean of women Ind. U., 1938-48, ednl. adviser, 1948-49, asso. prof. edn., 1949-52, prof. edn., 1953-69, prof. emeritus, 1969-84; vis. prof. Pa. State Coll., summer 1949, U. Oreg., 1958, U. N.C. Woman's Coll., 1959; specialist women's affairs High Commr. for Germany, Dept. State, summer 1951, in research Carnegie Found., U. Oreg., summers 1931, 1932; dir. Rockefeller Orch. Research Project, 1967-70; pres. Ind. State Deans, 1943-44. Diplomate in counseling Am. Bd. Examiners in Profl. Psychology. Fellow Am. Psychol. Assn. (pres. div. 10, 1951-52); mem. AAUW, Nat. Soc. Arts and Letters, Nat. Assn. Deans of Women (editor jour. 1959-69, chmn. univ. sect. 1943-45), Am. Coll. Personnel Assn., Aesthetics Soc., Music Tchrs. Nat. Assn., Ind. Assn. Clin. Psychology (v.p. 1946-48), Mortar Board, Sigma Xi, Phi Beta Kappa. Author: An Outline of Psychology, 1934; Appreciation of Music and Tests for Appreciation, 1935; Trends in Musical Taste (with John H. Mueller), 1941; Counseling for Mental Health, 1947; Women's Problems and Education, 1953; Educating Women for a Changing World (Delta Kappa Gamma award), 1954; Student Personnel Work in Higher Education, 1960; Twenty-Seven Major American Symphony Orchestras: A History and Analysis of Their Repertoires, 1842-1970, 1973, 74. Contbr. research papers to psychol. and personnel jours. Home: Bloomington, Ind. Died Aug. 10, 1984.

MUENCH, GEORGE ARTHUR, educator; b. Chgo., Mar. 9, 1919; s. Frank Anthony and Bertha (May) M.; A.B., Denison U., 1942; M.A., Ohio State U., 1943, Ph.D., 1945; m. Eleanor Raine, June 12, 1943; children—George Arthur, Margaret, John, Joseph. Sch. psychologist U. Sch., Columbus, Ohio, 1943-44, instr. psychology Ohio State U., 1944-45; clin. psychologist Bur. Juvenile Research, 1944-45; asst. prof. U. Louisville, 1945-47, asso. prof., 1947-49; chief clin. psychologist Adult and Child Guidance Clinic Santa Clara County, Calif., 1949-54; prof. psychology San Jose State U., 1949-80, past dir. Counseling Center, dir. Psychol. Studies Inst., 1975-80; vis. staff dept. psychiatry Santa Clara County Hosp., 1956-80. Mem. Ky. Bd. Examiners for Licensing Psychologists, 1948-49. Bd. dirs. Santa Clara County Mental Health Soc.; chmn. bd. trustees Los Gatos Union Elementary Sch. Dist., 1957; trustee Ming Quong Home; trustee Santa Clara County Sch. Bd., 1963-80, v.p., 1966-67, pres., 1967-69, 74-75; exec. com. Calif. Sch. Bd. Assn., 1965-67, bd. dirs., 1967-69, bd. dels., 1967-73; mem. Calif. County Bds. Edn., 1966-80, pres., 1967-68. VA grantee for work with war orphans and vets.; Mar Ad grantee for shipbldg. industry study. Diplomate Am. Bd. Examiners in Profl. Psychology. Mem. Am. Acad. Psychotherapists, Am. Psychol. Assn., Soc. Protective Techniques, Assn. Humanistic Psychology, Western, Calif. psychol. assns., AAUP, Phi Delta Kappa. Co-author or contbr. 6 books on clin. psychology, also articles in field, monographs. Home: Los Gatos, Calif. Died May 29, 1980.

MUETTERTIES, EARL LEONARD, chemist, educator; b. Elgin, Ill., June 23, 1927; s. Earl Conrad and Muriel Guinevere (Carpenter) M.; m. JoAnn Mary Wood, Mar. 3, 1956; children: Eric Joseph, Mark Conrad, Gretchen Ann, Maria Christine, Martha Alane, Kurt Andrew. B.S. with highest distinction, Northwestern U., 1949; A.M., Harvard U., 1951, Ph.D., 1952. Research chemist central research dept. E.I. du Pont de Nemours & Co., Wilmington, Del., 1952-57, research supr., 1957-65, asso. dir. research, 1965-73; prof. chemistry Cornell U., 1973-78, U. Calif.-Berkeley, 1978-84; adj. prof. U. Pa., 1969-73; asso. mem. Monell Chem. Sense Center, 1969-74. Author: (with W.H. Knoth) Polyhedral Boranes, 1969, (with J.P. Jesson) Chemist's Guide, 1969; editor-in-chief: (with J.P. Jesson) Inorganic Syntheses, vol. X, 1967; editor: (with J.P. Jesson) Chemistry of Boron and Its Compounds, 1967, Transition Metal Hydrides, vol. I of Chemistry of Hydrogen and Its Compounds, 1971, Boron Hydride Chemistry, 1975. Recipient John C. Bailar medal U. Ill., 1976. Fellow Royal Chem. Soc. (hon.); Mem. Nat. Acad. Scis., Am. Acad. Arts and Scis., Am. Chem. Soc. (Tex. Instruments Co. award in inorganic chemistry 1965, Mallinckrodt, Inc., award for disting. service 1979), Am. Phys. Soc., Chem. Soc. London, AAAS. Home: Oakland, Calif. Dec. Jan. 12, 1984.

MUHLENBERG, FREDERICK A(UGUSTUS), congressman; b. Reading, Pa., Sept. 25, 1887; s. William F. and Augusta Muhlenberg; B.S., Gettysburg Coll., Gettysburg, Pa., 1908, M.S., 1913; B.S. in Architecture, Univ. of Pa., 1912; Sc.D. (hon.) Muhlenberg Coll., Allentown, Pa., 1941; m. Elizabeth Young, Nov. 10, 1917; children—Elizabeth, Caroline, Frederica, David. In ind. practice of architecture, 1920-35; sr. member firm Muhlenberg, Yerkes, and Muhlenberg, Reading, Pa., from 1935; mem. 80th Congress (1947-49), 13th Dist., Pa. Mem. State Bd. Examiners, 1938-40; Reading councilman, 1934-38. Served as capt. 314th inf., W.W.I.; col. corps. of engrs., World War II; inf. reserve officer, 1922-40. Decorated Distinguished Service Cross, Purple Heart with Palm, Legion d'Honneur, Croix de Guerre, Legion of Merit, officially commended by chief of engrs. for work with Petroleum Adminstrn. for War. Served as chmn. Berks County Relief Bd., 1936, Assn. Schuylkill River Municipalities (engring. head), Fellow Am. Inst. Architects; mem. Social Welfare League (past mem. bd. 1922-35), Am. Red Cross (mem. bd. Berks County chapter, chmn. 1937), Salvation Army (past mem. adv. bd.), P.T.A. (pres. Foos Grade Sch., 1936-37), Am. Legion (life mem. Gregg post, comdr. 1924), Vets. Fgn. Wars, Reserve Officer's Assn., Inf. Assn., Soc. Am. Mil. Engrs. (comdr. Cincinnati chapter, 1945), Phi Delta Theta. Republican (former county chmn.). Lutheran. Club: Torch. Home: Wernersville, Pa.†

MULATIER, LÉON FRÉDÉRIC, United Nations ofcl.; b. Eurre, France, May 26, 1887; s. (Hippolyte) Frédéric and Nathalie (Savert) M.; B.S., College of Montélimar, 1905; student Nat. Higher Sch. Postal Service, Telegraphy and Telephony, 1920-22; m. Francoise Henriette Germaine Lavielle, Oct. 14, 1912; children—Jeannette (Mrs. Charles Debray), Gilles. Rédacteur Ministry of Post Telegraphs Telephones, France, 1923, dep. chief bur., 1924, chief bureau, 1933, dep. dir., 1934; dir. Telegraph and Radio-communications Services of France, 1935; asst. sec. gen. Internat. Telecommunications Union, U.N., 1940-50, sec. gen. from 1950; dep. dir. Postal, Telephone, Telegraph and Radio Services, Upper Silesia, 1920; lectures, translated from German, Nat. Higher Sch. Postal, Telegraph and Telephone Service, Paris, 1926-40. Chief French delegation Telegraphic Consultative Com., Warsaw, Poland, 1936, Consultative Com. for Radiocommunications, Bucharest, Romania, 1937, Telecommunications Conference, Cairo, Egypt, 1938, Radio Broadcasting Conf., Montreux, Switzerland, 1946; participated in confs. at Moscow, U.S.S.R., 1946. Comité Consultatif International Téléphonique, London, 1945, Montreux, 1946, sec. gen., Brussels, 1948, Telephone and Telegraph Conf., Paris, 1949, Atlantic City Plenipotentiary Conf., 1947, UNESCO, 1946, High frequency Broadcasting Conf., Florence and Rapallo, Italy, 1950; administrative extraordinary Radio Conference Geneva, 1951; sec. gen. Internat. Plenipotentiary Telecommunications Conference in Buenos Aires, 1952. Decorated Comdr. Legion of Honor (France); Grand Officer, Crown of Italy; Grand Officer Nat. Order of St. Sava (Yugoslavia); Grand Officer ordre national du Nicham Iftikar, Tunisie, Comdr. of White Lion (Czéchoslovakia); Commander of Order of St. Charles (Monaco). Home: Géneve, Switzerland. †

MULHEARN, JOHN ROBERT, utility company executive; b. Jersey City, Apr. 16, 1924; s. John Joseph and Estelle Marie (Holton) M.; B.E.E., Manhattan Coll., 1948; M.S., Stevens Inst. Tech., 1951; m. Regina Marie Robinson, Oct. 23, 1948; children—Mrs. Wesley von Schack, John Robert, Patrick Francis, Michael John, Regina Mary. With N.Y. Telephone Co., 1948-58, 59-61, 63-73, 76—, exec. v.p. corp. devel., 1971-73, pres., chief exec. officer, N.Y.C., 1976-79; staff asst. adminstrn. dept. AT&T, 1958-59, v.p., dir. corp. policy seminar, 1973-75, v.p. adminstrn. dept., 1975-76; gen. comml. mgr. Minn. area Northwestern Bell Telephone Co., 1961, v.p., gen. mgr. Iowa area, 1961-63; dir. incorporator Am. Republic Life Ins. Co. of N.Y.; dir. Allegheny Airlines, Inc., Fed. Res. Bank of N.Y., Carrier Corp., Municipal Art Soc., Econ. Devel. Council. Chmn. bd. trustees Manhattan Coll.; mem. exec. bd. ARC in Greater N.Y.C.; chmn. I Love A Clean N.Y., Inc.; gen. campaign chmn. United Fund Greater N.Y.; N.Y. State chmn. 1980 U.S. Olympic Com.; mem. cardinal's com. for edn. Archdiocese N.Y. Served with USN, 1942-46, PTO. Named First Eminent Engr., Tau Beta Pi, 1966; recipient award for accomplishment in bus. Manhattan Coll. Alumni Soc., 1972, Outstanding Exec. award Manhattan Coll. Sch. Bus., 1977. Mem. Newcomen Soc. North Am., N.Y. C. of C. and Industry, Navy League of U.S. (N.Y. council). Clubs: Econ. of N.Y., Scarsdale (N.Y.) Golf, Manhattan Coll. Spiked Shoe. Home: Bronxville, N.Y. Died Sept. 7, 1979.

MULLANEY, PAUL LYNCH, investment banker, association executive; b. Chgo., Dec. 9, 1900; s. Thomas F. and Theresa (Lynch) M.; m. Virginia Reiss, Nov. 3, 1931; children—Roger Paul, Paula (Mrs. Donald E. Murray). Student, Loyola Acad., 1914-18, Armour Inst. Tech., 1919-21; B.S., Northwestern U., 1929. Salesman bond dept. Merchants Loan & Trust Co., 1921-23, Ill. Mchts. Trust Co., 1924-29, Continental Ill. Co., 1929-33, Lawrence Stern & Co., 1933-38; chmn. bd. Mullaney, Wells & Co. (investment banking), from 1938; dir. C. Reiss Coal Co.; Dir., mem. bd. advisers Catholic Charities Archdiocese of Chgo., pres., 1961-64; bd. dirs. Comprehensive Health Planning Inc.; chmn. exec. com. health div. Welfare Council Met. Chgo., 1953-56, bd. dirs., 1956-67; bd. dirs. Community Fund Chgo., 1954-68. Chmn. Winnetka Caucus Com., 1951; trustee Village Winnetka, 1959-63; Trustee Barat Coll., 1965-70; vis. com. U. Chgo. Sch. Social Service Adminstrn., 1955; adv. council U. Notre Dame Coll. Arts and Letters; mem. citizens bd. Loyola U., Chgo., U. Chgo., 1972-84; hon trustee Gilmour Acad., Gates Mills, Ohio; trustee emeritus St. Francis Hosp., Evanston, Ill. Decorated knight of St Gregory the Great by Pope Pius XII, 1957. Mem. Investment Bankers Assn. Am. (gov., chmn. state legislation com. 1953-56), Travelers Aid Soc. Chgo. (hon. dir., pres. 1954-57), Travelers Aid Assn. Am. (hon. dir., pres. 1964-68), Chgo. Hearing Soc. (pres. 1949-53). Clubs Little-La Salle Street, Mid-America (mem. bd.; treas 1964-68), The Commercial, Chicago Athletic Association

Attic (v.p., bd. dirs. 1969-84), Bond (pres. 1953), Municipal Bond, Exmoor Country. Home: Winnetka, Ill. Died Feb. 27, 1985.

MULLEN, JOHN FRANCIS, banker; b. Omaha, Neb., Feb. 4, 1888; s. Patrick M. and Theresa B. (Donnelly) M.; student Creighton U., 1903-09, Hastings Coll. of Law, 1920; m. Beatrice M. Behrends, June 25, 1915; children—Bernhard B., Beatrice M., Virginia M. (Mrs. John B. Durney). In newspaper work, 1909-11, banking, 1915-19; in practice of law, 1920-21; again in banking from 1921; pres. and dir. B. M. Behrends Bank since 1936; B. M. Behrends Co. from 1936; treas. and dir. Central Properties, Inc. Roman Catholic. Elk, K.C. Club: Olympic (San Francisco). Home: Juneau, Alaska. †

MULLERGREN, ARTHUR L., bus. exec.; b. Helena, Ark., Apr. 15, 1890; s. Louis P. and Rosa (Marshall) M.; student pub. schs.; m. Christine Freeman, Nov. 27, 1912. Chief engr. Jefferson City (Mo.) Light & Power Co., 1908; asst. elec. engr., Ford, Bacon & Davis, New York, 1909; mgr. Poteau (Okla.) Light & Ice Co., 1910-11; cons. engr., 1912-14; cons. engr. and mem. Benham Engring. Co., Oklahoma City, and Benham & Mullergren, Kansas City, Mo., 1914-20; cons. engr. Kansas City, from 1920; pres. Am. Service Co., Kansas City, 1945-51, Western Power, Light & Telephone Co., successor, Western Light & Telephone Co., 1934-49, chmn. bd., from 1949, dir. City Nat. Bank & Trust Co. (Kansas City). Capt. Constrn. Div., U.S.A. in charge of light, heat and power, Camp Funston, Kansas, 1918-19. Mem. 16th Circuit Judical Commn. of Mo. Mem. American Inst. of Electrical Engrs., Am. Soc. M.E., Am. Soc. C.E., Kansas City C. of C., American Gas Assn. Mason (Shriner, Jester). Clubs: Rotary, Kansas City, Mission Hills Country (Kansas City, Mo.); Bankers (N.Y.C.); Saddle and Sirloin. Engineers (Kansas City, Mo.). †

MULLIGAN, HENRY A., govt. official; b. Newburg, W.Va., Oct. 5, 1887; s. Thomas and Anna (Moran) M.; student Del. State U., 1904-05; night student Coll. City of N.Y., 1917-22; unmarried. Asst. engr. B.&O. R.R. Co., 1906-09, liquidator U.S. Customs, New York, 1909-20; auditor Federal Reserve Bank of N.Y., 1920-22; auditor, later chief auditor War Finance Corp., 1922-27; examiner, later chief, Div. of Examinations, Fed. Farm Loan Bur., 1927-32; treas. Reconstrn. Finance Corp., 1932-47, dir. since July 1941; formerly dir. Fed. Nat. Mortgage Association; trustee and treas. Export-Import Bank of Washington, 1936-45; dir. Defense Plant Corp., Rubber Res. Co., Defense Supplies Corp., Metals Res. Co., and Disaster Loan Corp., 1941-45; dir. Rubber Development Corp., R.F.C. Mortgage Co., and War Damage Corp., 1941-47. Served as sergt., 306th Inf.; U.S. Army, A.E.F., 1917-29. Democrat. Club: University (Washington). Home: Washington, D.C.†

MUMFORD, L. QUINCY, former librarian of Congress; b. Ayden, N.C., Dec. 11, 1903; s. Jacob Edward and Emma Luvenia (Stocks); m. Permelia C. Stevens, Oct. 4, 1930 (dec. 1961); 1 child, Kathryn (Mrs. Lawrence Deane); m. Betsy Perrin Fox, Nov. 28, 1969. A.B magna cum laude, Duke, 1925, A.M., 1928, Litt.D. (hon.), 1957; B.S., Columbia, 1929; Litt.D. (hon.), Bethany Coll., 1954, Rutgers U., 1956, Belmont Abbey Coll., 1963; LL.D. (hon.), Union Coll., 1955, Bucknell U., 1956, U. Notre Dame, 1964, U. Pitts., 1964, U. Mich., 1970; H.H.D. (hon.), Kings Coll., 1970. Staff Duke Library, 1922-28, acting chief reference and circulation, 1927-28; student asst. Columbia Library, 1928-29; staff N.Y. Pub. Library, 1929-45, exec. asst. and coordinator, gen. services divs., 1943-45; asst. dir. Cleve. Pub. Library, 1945-50, dir., 1950-54; lectr., cons. sch. library sci. Western Res. U., 1946-54; dir. processing dept. Library of Congress, 1940-41, librarian of Congress, 1954-74; Chmn. ex officio Permanent Com. for the Oliver Wendell Holmes Devise, 1954-74; adv. commn. publ. Papers of George Washington; mem. ex officio, bd. regents Nat. Library of Medicine, until 1974; mem. ex officio Sci. Information Council, 1965-74, Fed. Council on Arts and Humanities, until 1974, Nat. Commn. Libraries and Information Sci.; mem. ex officio bd. trustees John F. Kennedy Center for the Performing Arts, until 1974; mem. sponsors com. Papers of Woodrow Wilson. Contbr. to library periodicals. Mem. bd. advisers Dumbarton Oaks Research Library and Collection; mem. Lincoln Sesquicentennial Commn., 1958-60; chmn. Fed. Library Com.; mem. Pres.'s Com. on Libraries, 1966-68; ex offico mem. bd. Historic Am. Buildings Survey, Nat. Park Service, 1954-74; mem. Nat. Book Com.; corr. mem. UNESCO Internat. Adv. Com. on Bibliography; mem. adv. bd. Cafritz Found.; mem. nat. adv. com. Am. Antiquarian Soc., Brit. Museum Soc., U.S. Com. for Am. Library in Paris; sec. ex officio, mem. Library of Congress Trust Fund Bd., 1954-74; hon. trustee U.S. Capitol Hill Hist. Soc.; trustee Woodrow Wilson Internat. Center for Scholars; hon. fellow Harry S. Truman Library Inst. Benjamin Franklin fellow Royal Soc. Encouragement Arts, Mfrs. and Commerce; mem. ALA (pres. 1954-55), Ohio Library Assn. (pres. 1947-48), Manuscript Soc. (bd. dirs., pres. 1968-70), Nat. Trust Historic Preservation, Mass. Hist. Soc. (corr.), Carolina Charter Corp., Omicron Delta Kappa, Beta Phi Mu, Phi Beta Kappa. Clubs: Cosmos (Washington); Explorers (N.Y.C.). Home: Washington, D.C. Dec. Aug. 15, 1982.

MUMMERT, ARDEN JOHN, automotive engr.; b. St. Louis, May 4, 1889; s. Louis Harry and Rosalie (Laurie) M.; B.S. in Mech. Engring., Purdue U., 1912; m. Nellie Fowler, May 3, 1916; 1 dau., Dorothy Ann (Mrs. John Beatty Biggs). Automotive engr. Cole Motor Car Co., 1912-14; engr. McQuay Norris Mfg. Co., 1914-50, pres., chmn., 1950-59, chmn., from 1959. Adviser to chief of ordnance, U.S. Army, World War II, Korean War. Served as lt. Flying Corps, USN, World War I. Mem. Soc. Automotive Engrs., Am. Ordnance Assn., Nat. Security Indsl. Assn., Automotive Safety Found., Nat. Assn. Mfrs., Asso. Industries of Mo. Mason. Home: St. Louis, MO. †

MUNRO, HARRY CLYDE, religious edn.; b. Cheboygan County, Mich., Apr. 1, 1890; s. Erastus and Anna Lucinda (Finn) M.; A.B., Hiram (O.) Coll., 1916; U. of Wash., 1919; A.M., Spokane (Wash.) U., 1922; University of Oklahoma, 1923-24; M.R.E., Transylvania Univ., 1925; married Vera Fern Segur, June 16, 1912 (died Mar. 23, 1949); children—Anna Laura, Frances Virginia, Rosalind, Harrison Segur. Ordained ministry Disciples of Christ Ch., 1916; missionary in Alaska for Am. Christian Missionary Soc., 1916-18; pastor First Christian Ch., Tacoma, Wash., 1918-19; prof. philosophy and religious edn., Spokane U., 1919-23; prof. religious edn., U. of Okla., 1923-24; editor of young people's lit., Christian Bd. of Publ., St. Louis, Mo., 1924-29; dir. leadership training, United Christian Missionary Soc., 1926-29; dir. adult work and field adminstrn., Internat. Council Religious Edn., 1930-38. dir. adult work and extension 1938-44; dir. Nat. Christian Teaching Mission, 1945-48; prof. religious edn., Brite Coll. of the Bible, Sem. of Tex. Christian U., Fort Worth, Tex., from 1948. Convention manager, 1929-30. International Conv. Religious Edn., Toronto, Can., June 1930. Author: Manual for the Vacation Church School, 1923; Jesus the Master and His Companions, 1923; Handbook for the Weekday Church School (with Hazel A. Lewis), 1924; Noble Lives and North American Leaders, 1924; The Life of Christ (with Vera S. Munro), 1924; The Christian Life (with Carl R. Swift), 1924; The World a Field for Christian Service (with Vera S. Munro), 1924; Agencies for the Religious Education of Adolescents, 1925; How to Increase Your Sunday School, 1928; The Church as a School, 1920; The Director of Religious Education, 1930; The Pastor and Religious Education, 1930; Christian Education in Your Church, 1933; The Effective Adult Class, 1933; Be Glad You're a Protestant, 1948; Contbr. many religious publs. Organizer, editor 3 yrs., Bethany Church School Guide (monthly). Home: Fort Worth, Tex. †

MUNSON, JOSEPH JONES, sugar mfr.; b. Jackson, La., Mar. 20, 1889; s. Albert Galletin and May Adele (Lemon) M.; B.S., La. State U., 1914, M.E., 1928; m. Emma Lea Harvey, May 3, 1918; 1 dau., Genevieve (Mrs. Morrell F. Trimble). With S. Puerto Rico Sugar Co., 1916-19; asst. engr., then chief engr. Western div. Cuba Cane Sugar Corp., 1919-24; prof. mech. engring. La. State U., 1924-25, prof. sugar engring., 1925-27; formerly with South Coast Corp., Houma, La., from 1927, v.p., gen. mgr., 1937-43, pres., 1943-65, former chmn.; co-owner, dir. Terrebonne Lumber & Supply Co., Houma, from 1937, v.p., exec. com., dir. State Agrl. Credit Corp., New Orleans, from 1939; dir. Citizens Nat. Bank & Trust Co., Houma, La., Celotex Corp. Mem. bd. dirs. Louisiana Sugar Exchange, New Orleans. Mem. Am. Sugar Cane League U.S., Am. Soc. Sugar Cane Technologists, Theta Xi. Club: Boston (New Orleans). Inventor can harvester, cane loader, mill journal bearings, crystallizer, hydraulic accumulator, vacuum pan, continuous centrifuge, sugar cane cleaner, clarifier, syrup process, mill roll grooving, turnplate for sugar cane mills, sugar cane gathering system. Home: Houma, LA. †

MUNSTER, JOE HENRY, JR., educator; b. Austin, Tex., July 28, 1912; s. Joe Henry and Ione (Reed) M.; m. Zola Lay Splawn, Nov. 4, 1942. A.B., U. Tex., 1933, M.A., 1933, LL.B., 1936; S.J.D., Northwestern U., 1952. Bar: Tex. bar 1936. Practice in, Austin, 1936-41; commd. lt. (j.g.) USN, 1941, advanced through grades to capt., 1954; dist. legal officer (15th Naval Dist.), 1947-49, (13th Naval Dist.), 1955-57; gen. insp. (Office Judge Adv. Gen.), 1952-55; comdg. officer (U.S. Naval Justice Sch.), 1957-60; asst. judge adv. gen., 1960-61; spl. counsel to (sec. Navy), 1961; ret., 1961; prof. law Western Res. U., 1961-66; asst. dean, Harrison prof. law Hastings Coll. Law, U. Calif., San Francisco, 1966-67, asso. dean, Harrison prof. law, 1967-71, prof., 1971-80, prof. emeritus, 1980-82. Author: (with Larkin) Military Evidence, 1959, 2d edit., 1978; co-author: (with Larkin) The Military in American Society; contbr. (with Larkin) articles to profl. publs. Mem. Fed., Tex., San Francisco bar assns., AAUP, Chancellors, Assn. Am. Law Schs. (chmn. com. on pre-legal edn. and admission to law sch. 1972, chmn. sect. 1973-74, sec. sect. 1975, Hastings Coll. Law rep. 1972-77, sec. sect. local govt. law 1978), Order of Coif (sec. Hastings chpt. 1966-81), Phi Beta Kappa, Beta Theta Pi, Phi Alpha Delta. Democrat. Episcopalian. Home: McLean, Va. Died Feb. 2, 1982.

MURDOCK, GEORGE PETER, educator, anthropologist; b. Meriden, Conn., May 11, 1897; s. George Bronson and Harriet (Graves) M.; A.B., Yale, 1919, Ph.D., 1925; postgrad. Harvard Law Sch., 1919-20; m. Carmen Emily Swanson, Sept. 4, 1925; 1 son, Robert Douglas. Instr. sociology U. Md., 1925-27; asst. prof. sociology Yale, 1928-34, asso. prof. ethnology, 1934-39, prof. anthropology, 1939-60; Andrew Mellon prof. social anthropology U. Pitts., 1960-85; field work among Indians, B.C., summer 1932, Ore., summers 1934, 35, Truk, 1947. Chmn. div. behavioral scis. NRC, 1964-66. Served as 2d lt. F.A., U.S. Army, 1918; lt. comdr. USNR, 1943-45, comdr. 1945-53. Viking Fund medallist, 1949; Herbert E. Gregory medallist, 1966; Thomas H. Huxley medallist, 1971. Fellow Am. Acad. Arts and Scis., Am. Sociol. Soc., Am. Anthrop. Assn. (pres. 1955); mem. Am. Ethnol. Soc. (pres. 1952-53), Soc. for Applied Anthropology (pres. 1974), Nat. Acad. Scis., Sigma Xi, Beta Theta Pi. Clubs: Cosmos (Washington); Century (N.Y.C.); University (Pitts.). Author: Our Primitive Contemporaries, 1934; Outline of Cultural Materials, 1938; Ethnographic Bibliography of North America, 1941; Social Structure, 1949; Outline of South American Cultures, 1951; Africa, 1959; Culture and Society, 1965. Editor: The Evolution of Culture (Julius Lippert), 1931; Studies in the Science of Society, 1937; Ethnology: An International Journal of Cultural and Social Anthropology, from 1962. Home: Pittsburgh, Pa. Died Mar. 29, 1985.

MURDOCK, JAMES OLIVER, lawyer, prof.; b Wichita, Kan., June 23, 1893; s. Willard Dolman and Sarah Jane (Blunt) M.; ed. University Sch., Mexico City, Mexico, 1900-05; Ph.B., Chicago U., 1918; George Washington U. Law Sch., 1921-22; Acad. Internat. Law (The Hague), 1923; LL.B., Harvard, 1924; m. Elizabeth Overton Lea, Dec. 2, 1922; children—James Oliver, Jr., Overton Lea. Admitted to N.Y. bar, 1925, and Dist. of Columbia, 1937; practiced with Cadwalader, Wickersham, and Taft, N.Y. City, 1924-25; private practice in Washington, D.C., since 1937; lecturer and professor, George Washington Univ. Law School, 1930-58; asst. U.S. atty., Southern District N.Y., 1923-27; asst. legal adviser, State Dept. 1927-38. Sec. Am. delegation Internat. Conf. Am. States on Concillation and Arbitration, Washington, 1928-29; counsel for U.S. and Canada, 1929-32; counsel for U.S., U.S.-Sweden Arbitration, 1932. Mem. Inter-Am. Juridical Committee, 1959, 61. First lieut. and capt. Field Arty., A.E.F., 1917-21. Awarded Order of the Purple Heart; Commander of the Order of Cespedes (Cuba). Member American Bar Association (section Internat. and Comparative Law, (chmn., 1936-37), Am. Soc. Internat. Law (sec., 1943-44), Inter-American Bar Assn., (council, and executive committee 1941-44), Dist. Columbia Bar Assn., Am. Law Inst., Inter-American Acad. of Comparative and Internat. Law, Havana, Cuba (member Curatorium), Phi Delta Phi, Phi Gamma Delta, Order of Coif. Episcopalian. Club: Harvard (Washington). Mason, Scottish Rite. Contbr. articles to internat. law and relations. Home: Washington, D.C. Died Dec. 20, 1981.

MURFEE, LATIMER, lawyer; b. Haskell, Tex., Sept. 5, 1901; s. James Edward and Emily (Griffin) M.; m. Kathryn Price, Jan. 1, 1925. LL.B., Samford U., 1921. Bar: Tex. bar 1925. Practiced law, Dallas, 1925-28, Houston, 1928—; Dir. Houston First Am. Savs. Assn., Post Oak Bank, Houston; owner Letter M Ranches. Mem., life trustee, past pres. bd. Inst. Religion, Tex. Med. Center, Houston; trustee Lon Morris Coll., S. Tex. Coll. Law, Retina Research Found., Meth. Hosp., Houston (life), Bell Home for Aged Women, Houston Mus. Natural Sci.; past chmn., now chmn. emeritus St. Paul's Meth. Found., Houston. Life fellow Am., Tex. bar founds.; mem. Houston Livestock Show and Rodeo (life), ABA, Houston Bar Assn. (pres. 1961-62), State Bar Tex. (dir. 1968-69), Am. Judicature Soc. (dir. 1975-77), Tex.-Gulf Coast Hist. Assn. (life), Houston Law Found. (life), Internat. Brangus Breeders Assn. (past dir., past v.p.), Tex. Brangus Breeders Assn. (past dir., past pres.), Am. Angus Assn. (life), Tex. and S.W. Cattle Raisers Assn., S.A.R. (past pres.). Methodist (trustee 1956-77, past pres., past. chmn. and life mem. adminstrv. bd.). Clubs: Mason (Houston) (32 deg., Scottish Rite, York, K.T., Shriner), Kiwanian (Houston) (past pres., past pres. Found.), Petroleum (Houston), Houston (Houston) (dir. 1964-67), Coronado (Houston), River Oaks Country (Houston). Home: Houston, Tex.

MURPHEY, BRADFORD, ret. psychiatrist; b. Kansas City, Mo., May 23, 1891; s. James Jay and Mary Alice (Hayes) M.; m. Margaret Winifred Griffin, Nov. 9, 1921; children—Bradford Griffin, Murray Griffin. A.B., U. Nebr., 1918, M.D., 1920; D.Sc. (hon.), Colo. Coll., 1939. Diplomate: Am. Bd. Psychiatry and Neurology. Intern Kings County Hosp., Brooklyn, 1920-21; asst. physician Elgin (Ill.) State Hosp., 1921-22, Chicago (Ill.) State Hosp., 1922-23; sr. physician N.J. State Hosp., Morris Plains, 1923-25; Rockefeller Found. fellow in extra-mural psychiatry with postgrad. work psychiatry at Boston Psychopathic Hosp. and Judge Baker Found., Boston, in neurology at Neurol. Inst., N.Y.C., in pediatrics at Children's Hosp., Boston, 1925-26; chief cons. psychiatrist New Eng. Home for Little Wanderers, Boston, 1926-27; dir. Bemis-Taylor Found. Child Guidance Clinic, Colorado Springs, Colo., 1927-38, Children's Service Center Child Guidance Clinic, Wilkes-Barre, Pa., 1938-40, practice medicine specializing in psychiatry, Denver, from 1940; vis. psychiatrist or cons. hosps., sanitaria, schs., homes, Denver; asso. clin. prof. psychiatry U. Colo. Coll. of Medicine, from 1940, emeritus. Mem. exec. coms., officer pub. confs. and meetings on med. problems. Mem. nat., state and local med. assns. and spl. med. orgns., has served as officer of several. Episcopalian. Clubs: Denver Clinical- Pathological, Denver City, Denver Country, Mile High, Mt. Vernon Country, Round Table, Cactus, Rotary. Home: Denver, Colo.

MURPHY, CHARLES FRANCIS, architect; b. Jersey City, Feb. 9, 1890; s. John and Catharine (McCarthy) M.; m. Josephine Loretta Christiani, June 30, 1926; children: Charles Francis, Robert Lawrence. Student, Northwestern U. Hon. chmn. Murphy/Jahn Assos., Architects. Work includes McCormick Place exhbn. hall, First Nat. Bank, State of Ill. Ctr., O'Hare Internat. Airport, IBM Bldg., all Chgo., FBI Hdqrs, Washington. Past pres., organizer Graham Found. for Advanced Studies in Fine Arts. Fellow AIA; mem. Western Soc. Engrs. Clubs: Chicago, Tavern, Chicago Yacht, Commercial. Home: Chicago, Ill. Died May 22, 1985.

MURPHY, CHARLES FRANCIS, JR., architect; b. Chgo., Dec. 17, 1928; s. Charles F. and Josephine (Christiani) M., children—Elita, Charles III, Marisa Alexandra, Luke Lawson. B.Arch., U. Notre Dame, 1951. Chmn. Murphy/Jahn, Inc., Chgo. Maj. archtl. works include Xerox Ctr.; Maj. archtl. works include: O'Hare Internat. Airport, First Nat. Bank, Chgo. Civic Ctr., State of Ill. Ctr., all Chgo. Mem. Graham Found. for Advanced Studies in Fine Arts, Chgo.; trustee Field Mus. Chgo. Fellow AIA. Clubs: Chicago, Saddle and Cycle, Economic, Tavern, Racquet (all Chgo.). Died.

MURPHY, CHARLES S., lawyer; b. Wallace, N.C., Aug. 20, 1909; s. William and Kate (Westbrook) M.; m. Kate Chestney Graham, Dec. 24, 1931; children: Courtenay (Mrs. Whitney Slater), Westbrook, Elizabeth. A.B., Duke U., 1931, LL.B., 1934, LL.D., 1967. Bar: N.C. 1934, Supreme Ct. 1944, D.C. 1947. With office of legislative counsel U.S. Senate, 1934-46; adminstr. asst. to Pres. U.S., 1947-50, spl. counsel, 1950-53; mem. firm Morison, Murphy, Clapp & Abrams, 1953-61; counsel to Democratic Nat. Adv. Council, 1957-60; undersec. agr., Washington, 1960-65; chmn. CAB, 1965-68; counselor to Pres. U.S., 1968-69; mem. Morison, Murphy, Abrams & Haddock, 1969-79; of counsel firm Baker & Hostetler, Washington, 1979-83. Mem. Brookings Adv. Com. Presdl. Transition, 1960. Trustee Duke U., to 1981; bd. visitors Duke Sch. of Law, 1973-83; pres. Harry S. Truman Library Inst.; gen. counsel Harry S. Truman Scholarship Found. Recipient Disting. Citizen citation Creighton U., 1967. Mem. Am., D.C., N.C., Fed. bar assns., Order Coif, Delta Sigma Phi, Pi Gamma Mu, Omicron Delta Kappa. Democrat. Methodist. Clubs: Nat. Democratic (Washington) (pres. 1956-58), Internat. (Washington), Metropolitan (Washington). Home: Annapolis, Md. Dec. Aug. 28, 1983.

MURPHY, EDWARD FRANCIS, editor; b. Tarrytown, N.Y., Jan. 27, 1914; s. James Francis and Mary Jane M.; m. Patricia Clare Flynn, Nov. 3, 1945; children—Maura Clare, Constance Patricia, Brian James, Dennis Edward. Student, Columbia U., 1939-40, Fordham U., 1944-45, Nat. Acad. Design, 1937-38, Art Students League, 1952-54. Bond order clk. Smith-Barney & Co., 1932-39; vocalist-musician radio with Tex. Ritter and others, 1939-40; editor-writer Holyoke Pub. Co., 1940-42; free lance writer, 1943-44, 53-55; editor Macfadden Publs., N.Y.C., 1944-45, Harle Publs., 1946-50, Ziff-Davis Publs., 1950-52, Kable News Co., 1952-53; sr. editor, exec. editor Hearst Corp., Sports Afield mag., Fishing and Hunting Annuals, N.Y.C., 1955-79. Editor: Sports Afield Almanac, 1979-85; Contbr. articles and short stories to mags.; Composer: Pride of My Heart, 1942. Served with AUS, 1942-43. Mem. Outdoor Writers Assn. Am., Inc., Cath. War Vets. Clubs: Racquet Internat. (Miami Beach, Fla.); Whitestone (S.C.); Cap D'Antibes (France). Home: Whitestone, N.Y. Died Jan. 16, 1985; buried Sleepy Hollow Cemetery, Tarrytown, N.Y.†

MURPHY, JOHN HARRY, physician; b. Omaha, Sept. 10, 1889; s. James and Anna (Westropp) M.; A.B., Creighton U., 1910, A.M., 1913, M.D., 1915; grad. Army Med. Sch., 1918; postgrad. N.Y. PostGrad. Hosp. and Med. Sch., 1920; m. Irene A. Langdon, Mar. 4, 1919. Intern, St. Vincents Hosp., Portland, Ore., 1915-16; intern St. Louis Children's Hosp., 1916, resident, 1916-17; with dept. pediatrics Creighton U. Med. Sch., 1920-61, successively instr., became prof., 1946, clin. prof. emeritus, 1964-71, prof. emeritus, from 1971, head dept. pediatrics, 1946-61; med. dir. Meyer Children's Therapy Center, 1961-67; pres. med. staff Children's Meml. Hosp., 1951, 60-61. Trustee Neb. Soc. Crippled Children. Served as lt. M.C., U.S. Army, 1918-20; maj. M.C. Res., 1939. Diplomate Am. Bd. Pediatrics, Pan.-Am. Med. Assn. Fellow A.M.A., Am. Acad. Pediatrics (state chmn., life, del. Internat. Polio Congress 1954, Internat. Pediatric Congress 1956), A.C.P.; mem. Am. Thoracic Soc., M.W. (pres. 1950-51), Neb. (pres. 1936) pediatric socs., Omaha MidWest Clin. Soc. (pres. 1951-52), Neb. Tb Assn. (pres. 1940-44, 47-51), Nat. Found. for Infantile Paralysis, World Med. Assn., N.Y. Acad. Medicine, Alpha Omega Alpha, Phi Rho Sigma. Club: Omaha. Contbr. articles to med. jours. Home: Omaha, NE. †

MURPHY, JOHN JOSEPH, univ. adminstr.; b. N.Y.C., Oct. 22, 1929; s. John Joseph and Sarah Mary (Hanlon) M.; B.A., St. Joseph's Sem. and Coll., 1951; J.D., St. John's U., 1956; m. Ann Maureen Vaughn, July 12, 1958; children—Thomas James, John Joseph (dec.), Paul Andrew. Admitted to N.Y. bar, 1956; asso. atty. firm Goodwin, Savage, Clare & Whitehead, N.Y.C., 1956-61; asst. dean, asst. prof. St. John's U. Sch. of Law, Jamaica, N.Y., 1961-63, asso. prof., 1963-66, prof., 1966-80, dean, 1970-80. Spl. counsel Bd. of Edn., N.Y.C., 1965-68; appellate disciplinary hearing examiner, appellate div., State of N.Y., 1972-80; examiner of attys. City of N.Y., 1966-69; insp. of law schs. for accreditation, Am. Bar Assn., 1967-80. Spl. counsel Joint Legis. Com. on Transportation, 1974-80; mem. com. on ct. adminstrn. appellate div., 1973-74; mem. Pub. Employment Relations Bd., North Hempstead, N.Y., 1968-80; reporter speedy trial planning com. Fed. Eastern Dist. N.Y., 1975-80; mem. adv. council N.Y. Housing Cts., 1976-80; mem. med., moral and ethics bd. N.Y. Archdiocese, 1976-80. Founding mem., bd. dirs. Bedford-Stuyvesant Legal Services Corp.; v.p., trustee Indsl. Home for the Blind; permanent arbitrator N.Y.C. Bd. Edn. and Union Custodial Engrs.; mem. Cardinal's Task Force on Health, N.Y. Archdiocese; chmn. N.Y. State Security and Privacy Commn., 1977-80. Mem. Am. (sec. legal edn. 1965-80), N.Y. State (sect. family law 1970-80) bar assns., Am. Law Inst. Roman Catholic. Contbr. articles to profl. jours. Home: Manhasset, N.Y. Died Sept. 23, 1980.

MURPHY, RICHARD ERNEST, educator, geographer; b. Hibbing, Minn., Sept. 21, 1920; s. John Philip and Ethel (Robinson) M.; m. Esther Zuleika Bailey, June 11, 1949; children—Richard Taggart, Alexander Bailey, Caroline Kendall. B. A., St. Lawrence U., 1943; M.A., George Washington U., 1952; Ph.D., Clark U., 1957. Cartographic aide U.S. Army Map Service, 1946-48; head reference sect. map div. Library of Congress, Washington, 1949-54; fellow, asst. Clark U. Grad. Sch. Geography, Worcester, Mass., 1954-55; from asst. prof. to asso. prof. geography George Washington U., Washington, 1955-59; from asso. prof. to prof. U. Wyo., 1959-63; vis. prof. U. Hawaii, 1963-64; prof., chmn. dept. geography U. N.Mex., Albuquerque, from 1965; Cons. George Washington logistics research project U.S. Army, 1955-56; tech. application center U. N.Mex., from 1968. Contbr articles to profl. jours. Served with AUS, World War II. NSF sci. faculty fellow Inst. Geography, U. Paris, 1964-65; Fulbright sr. lectr. Tohoku U., Sendai, Japan, 1968-69; Fulbright sr. lectr. U. of the Saarland, Saarbrücken, West Germany, 1975-76. Mem. Assn. Am. Geographers., Beta Theta Pi. Unitarian. Club: Twenty One (U. N.Mex.). Developer system for classification, mapping of world landforms. Home: Albuquerque, NM.

MURPHY, WILLIAM A., mgmt. cons.; b. Havensville, Kans., Sept 9, 1903; s. G. Sherman and Harriet (Murphy) M.; m. Monte L. Russell, Aug. 14, 1927. B.S., U. Kans., 1928, M.B.A., 1930. Tchr., prin. high sch., Kans., 1923-30; successively instr., asst. prof., asso. prof. bus. adminstrn. Southwestern Coll., Winfield, Kans., 1930-33, Kans. State Coll., Manhattan, 1933-36, U. Utah, 1948-49; statistician, spl. investigator Kan. Commn. Labor and Industry, part-time 1931-36; Kans. statis. coordinator, 1936-37; dir. (Div. Unemployment Compensation), State Kans., 1937-39; regional dir. U.S. R.R. Retirement Bd., 8th Region, Kansas City, Mo., 6 months 1939, 2d Region, N.Y.C., 1939-40; dir. Bur. Employment and Claims, Washington, 1940-42; chief bus. services br. W.P.B., Washington, 1942-43, dir. div. adminstrv. services, 1943-44; mgmt. cons. Griffenhagen & Assos., 1944-45; regional dir.-at-large Office Surplus Property, Dept. Commerce, July-Nov. 1945; cons. Hecht Co., 1946-48, Otto Buehner Co., 1948, Kiplinger Washington Agy., 1945, 46, 48, 49-50; acting exec. officer Def. Prodn. Adminstrn. and Nat. Prodn. Authority, Washington, 1950-51, asst. adminstr., 1951-53; cons. UN Internat. Children's Emergency Fund, 1953; spl. asst. to asst. postmaster gen., 1953-54; dir. Fed. Unemployment Ins. Programs, U.S. Dept. Labor, 1954-62, Fed. Unemployment Ins. Programs and Tng. Allowances, Dept. Labor, 1962-65. Author govt. reports, articles on mgmt.; Editor: Kans. Labor and Indsl. Bull, 1931-37. Recipient Outstanding Achievement citation in savs. bond program U.S. Dept. Treasury, 1943, also; Distinguished Service citations, 1942, 44; Merit award Nat. chpt. ARC, 1944, 52; Red Feather award Community Chest Fedn., 1952, 53; Distinguished Service award Dept. Labor, 1959; citation Notable Career Service Sec. of Labor, 1965; William A. Murphy scholarship fund established at Southwestern Coll. by former students. Mem. Wichita Art Assn., Pi Gamma Mu, Alpha Tau Omega (past pres. Wichita alumni), Alpha Kappa Psi. Presbyterian. Clubs: Chancellors of U. Kans. (charter), The Wichita, Univ., Knife and Fork, Farm and Ranch, Masons. Home: Wichita, Kans.

MURRAY, EDWIN P., stock broker, estate trustee; b. Hanalei, Kauai, T.H., Nov. 23, 1887; s. Edward and Mary (Werner) M.; ed. Kamehameha schs., Honolulu, T.H.; m. Lucy Perry, July 11, 1918; children—Edmund Stiles, Emily Leilani (Mrs. Baker). Bookkeeper, Mcabe, Hamilton & Renny Co., 1910-23; purchasing agt., cashier, accountant, Kamehameha Schs., 1923-31; auditor, City and County of Honolulu, 1932-40; trustee Bernice Pauahi Bishop, estate, apptd. by Chief Justice of Territorial Supreme Ct., since 1940; pres. E. P. Murray & Co., Ltd., stocks, bonds, gen. ins. agt., real estate since 1940. Trustee Charles R. Bishop Trust, Bernice Pauahi Bishop Museum. Conglist. Club: Hawaiian Civic Honolulu (pres. 1940). Home: Kailua, Oahu, Hawaii. †

MURRAY, GEORGE FRANCIS, TV producer-dir.; b. N.Y.C., Aug. 28, 1929; s. George Francis and Margaret R. (Myers) M.; grad. Power Meml. Acad. Boys, N.Y.C., 1948; m. Jeanne Anne Carey, Feb. 27, 1954; children—Noreen, George, Gregory, Carolyn. Began career as film editor for the NBC News, 1950-51, 54-56; junior writer Huntley-Brinkley Report, NBC News, 1956-58, program dir., 1958-62; asso. producer, prin. dir. NBC News election coverage, 1962, also Huntley-Brinkley Report; asso. producer, dir. documentaries NBC News, 1958-64, producer, prin. dir. convention and election coverage, 1964; producer Viet Nam Weekly Review, 1966-74; producer spl. events unit CBS-TV, N.Y.C., 1974-84, including 1976 nat. polit. convs., prodns. include The Many Faces of Spain, 1961, Finland Hostage Country, 1961, The Throne of Peter, 1963. Served with AUS, 1951-53; Korea. Recipient Robert E. Sherwood award (The American Stranger) Ford Found., 1959; co-recipient George Polk award fgn. TV reporting (Argentine Crisis Parts I and II), 1958, Emmy award (Huntley Brinkley Report), 1958, 59, 60, 63. Mem. Dirs. Guild Am., Writers Guild Am. Died Dec. 8, 1984.

MURRAY, HALSTEAD GRAEME, physician; b. Woodstock, Ont., Can., Dec. 20, 1890; s. William Graeme and Jessie Matilda (MacKay) M.; brought to U.S., 1895, naturalized by parent, 1906; student Albert Coll., Belleville, Ont., 1906-09; M.B., Queens U., 1915, M.D. C.M., 1919; m. Bessie Marie Harter, Dec. 15, 1917; 1 son, Halstead G. Intern Lying-in Hosp., N.Y. City, 1918; indsl. phys. Dennison Mfg. Co., Framingham, Mass., from 1919. Mem. courtesy staff Framingham Union Hosp. Fellow A.M.A., Industrial Medical Association; member Mass. Medical Soc., Am. Red Cross (chmn. local chpt. 1938-44), New England Conf. Indsl. Physicians (chmn. 1922-23). Episcopalian (sr. warden, 1944-49). Mason. Served as capt., M.C., Royal Army, 1915-17; England, France, Salonika (Greece). Contbr. articles to med. jours. Home: Framingham, Mass. †

MURRAY, JAMES NIGEL, JR., educator; b. Chgo., Feb. 11, 1925; s. James Nigel and Grace (Hoskins) M.; student Purdue U., 1943-44; A.B., U. Ill., 1947, Ph.D., 1953; M.A., Fletcher Sch. Law and Diplomacy, 1948; m. Patricia Jean Gilliam, Sept. 8, 1951; children—James Nigel III, Bruce, Kenneth. Instr., Northwestern U., Evanston, Ill., 1951-54; faculty U. Iowa, Iowa City, 1954-85, prof. polit sci., 1966-85, chmn. dept., 1965-68, dir. Center for Internat. Studies, 1968-85. Fulbright lectr. U. Istanbul (Turkey), 1964-65, vis. prof., 1970-71. Mem. Iowa Gov.'s Com. on Strengthening UN, 1969-70. Served with USNR, 1943-46. Mem. Am., Midwest polit. sci. assns., Internat. Studies Assn. Author: United Nations Trusteeship System, 1957. Contbr. chpts. on fgn. and mil. policy Functions of American Government (Burns, Peltason), Home: Iowa City, Iowa. Died Jan. 23, 1985.

MURRAY, J(OSEPH) HARTLEY, lawyer; b. Colorado Springs, Colo., Dec. 2, 1911; s. Joseph Patrick and Anna Mae (Hartley) M.; m. Constance Postlethwaite Carpenter, Jan. 23, 1948; children—Gilbert Carpenter (dec.), Peter W. B.A. magna cum laude, Colo. Coll., 1933; J.D., Colo. U., 1936. Bar: Colo. bar 1936. Partner firm Murray, Baker & Wendelken, Colorado Springs, from 1938; mem. U.S. prosecution staff Nurnberg Trials, 1945-46. Trustee Penrose Hosp., Colorado Springs, 1972-78; mem. Colorado Springs Sch. Dist. 11 Bd. Edn., 1949-55, pres., 1953-55. Served with JAGC U.S. Army, 1942-46. Decorated Bronze Star. Fellow Am. Coll. Trial Lawyers, Am. Coll. Probate Counsel, Am. Bar Found.; mem. Colo. Bar Assn. (pres. 1971-72), Order of Coif. Home: Colorado Springs, Colo.

MURRAY, PAULI, clergywoman; b. Balt., Nov. 20, 1910; d. William Henry and Agnes Georgianna (Fitzgerald) M. A.B., Hunter Coll., 1933; LL.B. cum laude, Howard U., 1944; LL.M. (Julius Rosenwald fellow), U. Calif., Berkeley, 1945; J.S.D. (grad. fellow, fellow Ford Found.), Yale U., 1965; M.Div. cum laude, Gen. Theol. Sem., N.Y.C., 1976; LL.D. (hon.), Stonehill Coll., 1967, Dartmouth Coll., 1976, Cedar Crest Coll., 1979; D.Sc. (hon.), Lowell Tech. Inst., 1973; D.Hum. (hon.), U. Fla., 1978; D.H.L. (hon.), Radcliffe Coll., 1978, Bryant Coll., 1980; D.D. (hon.), Yale U., 1979, Va. Theol. Sem., 1980. Bar: Calif. 1945, N.Y. 1948, U.S. Supreme Ct. 1960. Asso. Paul, Weiss, Rifkind, Wharton & Garrison, N.Y.C., 1956-60; sr. lectr. Ghana Law Sch., Accra, 1960-61; cons. EEOC, Washington, 1966-67; v.p. Benedict Coll., Columbia, S.C., 1967-68, also prof. polit. sci.; prof. Am. studies Brandeis U., 1968-73, Louis Stulberg prof. law and politics, 1972-73; lectr. Boston U. Sch. Law, 1972; ordained priest Episcopal Ch., 1977; priest-in-charge Ch. of the Holy Nativity, Balt., 1982; mem. adv. council Martin Luther King, Jr. Inst. Non-Violent Social Change, 1971-85, Ford Found. Study Law and Justice, 1972-75; dep. atty. gen., Calif., 1946; atty. commn. law and social action Am. Jewish Congress, 1946-47; cons. World Council Chs., 1968; Adv. council NOW, 1970-85, Schlesinger Library, Radcliffe Coll., 1969-73, Nat. Coalition Research Women's Edn. and Devel., 1971-73, OEO, 1967-68; mem. Gov. Mass. Council Security and Privacy, 1972-73, Joint Commn. Ordained and Lic. Ministries, P.E. Ch., U.S.A., 1969-70, Commn. Women in Today's World, Ch. Women United, 1968-70; mem. com. civil and polit. rights Presdl. Commn. Status Women, 1962-63; dir. Beacon Press, 1968-69, NOW Legal Def. and Edn. Fund, 1970-73, ACLU, 1965-73. Author: Dark Testament and Other Poems, 1970, The Constitution and Government of Ghana, 1961, Proud Shoes, 2d edit, 1978, States Laws on Race and Color, 1951, supplement, 1955; also articles. Recipient Whitney M. Young, Jr. award NEA, 1972; Eleanor Roosevelt award Profl. Women's Caucus, 1971; Homecoming award Howard U., 1971; Alumni award disting. postgrad. achievement law and public service, 1970; award Exemplary Christian Ministry, Boston Theol. Inst., 1970; award Nat. Inst. Women of Color, 1982;

named Woman of Year, Mademoiselle mag., 1947, Woman of Year, Nat. Council Negro Women, 1946. Mem. Hunter Coll. Alumni Assn. (named to Hall of Fame 1973, Outstanding Profl. Achievement award 1974), Nat. Bar Assn., ABA (vice chmn. com. women's rights 1971-73), N.Y. County Bar Assn., Nat. Assn. Women Lawyers, NAACP (life), Nat. Council Negro Women. Address: Pittsburgh, Pa. Died July 8, 1985.

MURRAY, W. J., JR., corporation executive; b. Columbia, South Carolina, Feb. 20, 1888; s. William J. and Mary (Connor) M.; B.S., S.C., Mil. Coll. (The Citadel); m. Minnie Blalock, Apr. 5, 1911. Sec. Murray Drug Co., 1911; v.p., 1916; pres., 1928; v.p. McKesson & Robbins, Inc., N.Y. City, 1929; sec. and v.p. McKesson & Robbins 1932-36, first v.p. 1936-41, pres., 1941, now mem. bd. dirs.; pres. Murray Real Estate Co. from 1928, Murhartom Co., 1928; bd. dirs. General Foods Corp., Owens Corning Fiberglas Corp., Murray Real Estate Co., Murhartom Company; trust com. Chase Manhattan Bank, N.Y.C. Mem. bus. adv. council Dept. of Commerce; trustee Committee for Economic Devel. Mem. bd. trustees Converse College. Clubs: Union, Forest Lake Country, Columbia, Pinnacle, Links. Home: Columbia, S.C. †

MURRAY, WILLIAM ARTHUR, educator, engr.; b. Helena, Mont., July 18, 1889; s. Daniel H. and May (McKay) M.; B.S., U. Ida., 1914; E.E., Mont. State Coll., 1927; M.S., U. Mich., 1933; m. Irene A. Watson, Mar. 20, 1921; children—Barbara Jean (Mrs. John K. Steckel), Janice Anne (Mrs. T. S. Temple). Electrician Fed. Mining & Smelting Co., Mullan Ida., 1914-15; test and radio research Gen. Electric Co., 1915-18; electrician Bunker Hill & Sullivan Mining & Smelt Co., Kellogg, Ida., 1919; instr. elec. engring. U. Ida., 1919-23; asst. prof. elec. engring. Mont. State Coll., 1923-29; asso. prof. elec. engring. Mich. State Coll., 1929-36; prof., head dept. elec. engring. Va. Poly. Inst., from 1936. Served with U.S. Army, 1918. Fellow Am. Inst. E.E.; mem. Am. Soc. Engring. Edn., Nat. Soc. Profl. Engrs., Va. Acad. Sci. Home: Blacksburg, Va. †

MUSSELMAN, THOMAS EDGAR, educator, biologist; b. Quincy, Ill., Apr. 28, 1887; s. De Lafayette and Mary Malissa (McDavitt) M.; A.B., U. of Ill., 1910, A.M., 1913; Master Accountant, Gem City Bus. Coll., Quincy, 1911; Sc.D., from Carthage (Ill.) Coll., 1934; m. Mary Locke Scripps, Oct. 18, 1916; children—Mary Margaret, Virginia. Vice president Gem City Bus. Coll.; researcher in ornithology from 1906; sec. Inland Bird Banding Assn., 1925, councillor from 1926; dir. nature study, Appalachian Boys' and Girls' Camp Assn.; lecturer on nature, Carthage Coll. and Chaddock Sch. for Boys, Quincy; Ill. State lecturer, Audubon Soc. (also dir. 1935); dir. Wild Life Sch., McGregor, Ia.; pres. Private Schools Dept., Nat. Commercial Teachers Fedn., 1935; commr. Boy Scouts, Quincy, 1926-28. Mem. A.A.A.S., American Ornithological Union, Wilson Ornithol. Club, Inland Bird Banding Assn. (Hornaday award for outstanding conservation, 1951), Kappa Delta Pi (founder), Phi Gamma Delta. Republican. Methodist. Mason. Author: History of the Birds of Illinois, 1923; Business English and Letter Writing, 1914-15; One Grand Year in Nature, 1936; Genuine Business Letters, 1937. Contbr. to Nature Magazine, Country Life in America, Flower Grower, etc. Home: Quincy, Ill. †

MUSSER, ELISE FURER, b. Neuchatel, Switzerland, Dec. 7, 1887; d. Jean Rodolphe and Marie (Bernhard) Furer; ed. in schs. of Switzerland, France and Germany and U. of Utah, Columbia and U. of Mexico; m. Burton W. Musser, Dec. 22, 1911; 1 son, Bernard Furer. Came to U.S., 1907, naturalized, 1911. Active in social welfare work from 1917. Democratic National Committeewoman, 1932-36. Mem. Utah State Senate, 1933-37; member Board of Regents of Utah State Agrl. Coll., 1925-33; mem. Utah Unemployment Com., 1930-34. One of 14 women selected to make suggestions to Dem. Nat. platform, 1936. Apptd. by President as del. to Peace Conf., Buenos Aires, Dec. 1936; selected by Peace Mandate Com. to head Flying Caravan to Latin Am. countries and visited 18 republics in interest of ratification of Buenos Aires treaties; U.S. del. to Internat. Conf. of Am. States at Lima, Peru, 1938 (v.p. com.). Mem. nat. bd. Y.W.C.A.; pres. British War Relief Soc. of Utah; pres. Utah Council Pan-Am. Affairs. Lecturer on world peace; spent 1 yr. in Europe studying post-war social conditions. Speaks French, German, Spanish, Italian. Home: Salt Lake City, Utah. †

MYERS, ABRAM FERN, lawyer, economist; b. Fairfield, Ia., July 27, 1889; s. Capt. Abram and Sarah Ellen (Gibbs) M.; LL.B., Georgetown U.; m. Mary G. Connor, 1929. Admitted to D.C. bar, 1912, and began practice at Washington; attorney in office of solicitor general of U.S., 1919-20; special asst. to atty. gen. of U.S., 1920-26; had charge of dissolution proceedings against the Reading Co., Lehigh Valley R.R. Co., Ward Food Products Corp., etc., under anti-trust laws; apptd. by President Coolidge mem. of Fed. Trade Commn., 1926, chmn., 1928-29; chmn. bd. and gen. counsel Allied States Assn. of Motion Picture Exhibitors from Jan. 1929, also counsel for numerous trade assns.; special asst. to atty. gen. N.D. in litigation involving constitutionality of legislation regulating the operation of theatres, 1938-39; gen. counsel Nat. Lime Assn. and Metal Window Inst. Republican. Episcopalian. Contbr. articles on legal and economic subjects. Clubs: Metropolitan, Gibson Island. Home: Washington, D.C. and (summer) Gibson Island, Md. †

MYERS, ALONZO H(ARRISON), orthopedic surgeon; b. nr. Wilkesboro, N.C., Apr. 14, 1888; s. John Ivey and Louisa Cornelia (Church) M.; Wake Forest Coll., 1906, 07; M.D., N.C. Med. Coll., Charlotte, N.C., 1911; M.D., New York Univ. and Bellevue Hosp. Med. Coll., 1916; attended orthopedic clinics, Paris and London, 1921; m. Eleanor Grace Gurney, Dec. 17, 1923; children—Eleanor (Cole), Alonzo Harrison. Interne German Hosp., Brooklyn, N.Y., 1911-12, Riverside Hosp., N.Y. City, 1912, N.Y. Orthopedic Hosp., 1912-15; practiced orthopaedics at Charlotte 1919-48; mem. staff Good Samaritan, Presbyterian, Mercy and Charlotte Memorial hosps.; past cons. orthopedic surgeon State Insane Hosp.; condr. orthopedic clinics N.C. State Board of Health, Crippled Children's Div., Charlotte and Wilmington; orthopedic consultant U.S. Vets. Bur. and U.S. Employees Compensation Commn. Served as maj. Med. Corps, U.S. Army, World War; spent 34 mos. in France, at Ris Oranges with Am. Red Cross 9 months prior to U.S. entrance into War, with A.E.F. at Alsace Lorraine, Chateau Thierry, and as orthopedic surgeon at base hosps.; inducted, July 1917, at A.R. Mil. Hosp. No. 2, Paris. Fellow Am. Coll. Surgeons; mem. A.M.A., N.C. Med. Soc., Southern Med. Assn., Am. Acad. Orthopedic Surgery, N.C. Acad. of Orthopaedic Surgery (honorary mem.), Am. Legion, Officers World War, Forty and Eight, Omega Upsilon Phi, Phi Beta Pi, and many others. Awarded Medaille d'Honneur (France). Democrat. Presbyterian. Mason (32 deg., Shriner). Elk. Clubs: Rotary, Charlotte Country, Executives. Contbr. on orthopedic surgery. Home: Ft. Lauderdale, Fla. †

MYERS, HERBERT LOWE, lawyer; b. Indpls., Oct. 28, 1921; s. Samuel Monroe and Lettie Elizabeth (Lowe) M.; m. Sara Jane Capehart, Sept. 13, 1951. A.B., Butler U., 1947; J.D., Ind. U., 1951; LL.M., Harvard U., 1959. Bar: Ind. 1951, U.S. Supreme Ct. 1972. Asso. firm Ice, Miller, Donadio & Ryan, Indpls., 1951-53; partner firm Fulmer & Myers, Indpls., 1953-58; asso. prof. law Drake U., Des Moines, 1959-62; prof., 1962-65, Temple U., Phila., 1965-84. Served with AUS, 1943-46. Christian R. and Mary F. Lindback Found. Disting. Teaching award, 1978. Mem. ABA. Republican. Unitarian. Home: Jenkintown, Pa. Died Dec. 18, 1984.

MYERS, HIRAM EARL, clergyman, educator; b. nr. Wadesboro, Anson County, N.C., July 29, 1889; s. George Franklin and Nora Florence (Braswell) M.; A.B., Trinity Coll. (now Duke), 1915; S.T.B., Boston U., 1920, S.T.M., 1926; D.D., Elon Coll., 1950; m. Rose Mae Warren, Oct. 12, 1926; 1 dau., Martha Rose (Mrs. Norris O. Anderson, Jr.). Ordained to ministry of Meth. Epis. Ch. S., 1918; pastor successively Graham (N.C.), Manchester (N.H.), Salisbury (N.C.), Elizabeth City, Duke Memorial Ch., Durham, until 1925; prof. of Biblical literature, Duke Univ., from 1926, chmn. dept. of religion, 1934-36, chmn. dept. of religion and dir. of undergraduate studies, 1937-57. Member Southeastern Jurisdictional Conf. of the Meth. Ch., 1940; del. rep. N.C. Meth. Conf. at 7th Ecumenical Conf. Mem. Nat. Assn. Bibl. Instrs., Am. Assn. Univ. Profs., Soc. of Bibl. Lit. and Exegesis, Tau Kappa Alpha, Phi Beta Kappa, Phi Kappa Sigma; asso. mem. Am. Schs. of Oriental Research. Home: Durham, N.C. †

MYERS, HORWOOD PRETTYMAN, clergyman, educator; b. Bridgewater, Va., Oct. 25, 1887; s. William R. and Cora A. (Jacobs) M.; prep. edn., Bridgewater Coll., Manassas (Va.) High Sch. and Front Royal Acad. till 1906; A.B. and A.M., Randolph-Macon Coll., Ashland, Va., 1911; m. Maude M. Wynn, July 16, 1913; children—John Wynn, Horwood P., William T., Robert M. Ordained M.E. ministry, 1910; pastor Courtland, Va., 1911-14, Onancock, 1914-17, Emporia, 1918-20, Charlottesville, 1920-24 (built $300,000 ch.); pres. Blackstone Coll. from 1924. Religious work at Camp Lee, Va., World War. Trustee Ferrum (Va.) Training Sch. Mason. Clubs: Kiwanis, Rotary. Frequent speaker on Christian education. Home: Blackstone, Va. †

MYERS, JOE CRAWFORD, manufacturing company executive; b. Indpls., Mar. 16, 1918; s. Talmadge F. and Esther L. (Crawford) M.; student Purdue U., 1937-38; m. Margaret Cavender, Dec. 27, 1941; children—Craig J., Ann (Mrs. Bryan D. Gilbert). Exptl. lab. technician Continental Optical Co., Indpls., 1939-40; with Link-Belt Co., 1945-67, plant engr. bearing plant, 1962-67; mgr. plant engring. Link-Belt Bearing div. FMC Corp., Indpls., 1967-73, facilities mgr., bearing div., 1973-85. Indsl. dir. Electric League. Indsl. mem. health com. Planning Council Central Ind. Environmental Health Com. Served with USNR, World War II. Mem. Am. Inst. Plant Engrs. (past mem. exec. com., internat. officer), Water Pollution Control Fedn., Indpls. C. of C. Elk. Home: Indianapolis, Ind. Dec. Jan. 11, 1985. Interned Washington Park, North Indianapolis, Ind.

MYERS, OREL JACOB, lawyer, chem. co. exec.; b. Ft. Recovery, O., Mar. 22, 1887; s. John W. and Christina Braden (Rantz) M.; LL.B., U. Mich., 1910; m. Inez Wykoff Zay, Sept. 27, 1916; 1 dau., Elizabeth Jeanette. Admitted to Ohio bar, 1910, Mich. bar, 1910, Fla. bar, 1929; mem. firm Myers & Myers, Celina, Ohio, 1910-47; pros. atty., Darke County, Ohio, 1922-25; receiver Palm Beach Bank & Trust Co., West Palm Beach, Fla., 1926-28; pvt. practice law, Dayton, from 1929. Vice pres. Reichhold Chemicals, Inc., White Plains, N.Y. Active Community Chest, Boy Scouts Am. Bd. dirs. Dayton Goodwill Industries, Am. Social Hygiene Assn. N.Y.C., Social Hygiene Assn. Dayton and Montgomery County, Nat. Family Life Found.; trustee Met. Health Council Dayton. Served with U.S. Army, 1917-19. Mem. Ohio Soc. N.Y. Methodist. Mason. Clubs: Kiwanis; Discussion; Executive; Lawyers; University of Michigan. Home: Dayton, OH. †

NABERS, CHARLES HADDON, clergyman; b. Laurens, S.C., Nov. 13, 1889; s; Alexander and Martha (Haddon) N.; prep. edn., high sch., Anderson, S.C.; A.B., Erskine Coll., 1909, D.D., 1928; grad. Erskine Theol. Sem., 1913; grad. student Bibl. Sem., New York, 1920, U. of Chicago, 1933; Litt.D., Presbyn. Coll., 1937; m. Minnie Whitesides, Oct. 20, 1914; 1 dau., Dorothy (Mrs. W. Kirk Allen, Jr.). Teacher mission sch., Cairo, Egypt, 1909-11; ordained ministry Presbyterian Ch. in U.S., 1913; pastor successively Prosperity, S.C., Tuscaloosa, Ala., Carrollton, Ala., and First Church, Camden, Ark., until 1923, First Church, Pensacola, Florida, 1923-30, First Church, High Point, N.C., 1930-32, First Ch., Greenville, S.C., 1932-54; broadcaster Morning Devotions, Radio Station WFBC 1936-54; interim pastor Presbyterian Churches, from 1954; studied and traveled in Europe, 6 times to 1949, chaplain, lecturer Mediterranean cruisers, 1925, 34, 37, 38, 39, 1948-51. South American Cruise, 1941, 48, 52; Holland Am. Line, 1953-57; Protestant Chaplain Rotterdam Round-the-World Cruise, 1961. Y.M.C.A. work, home camps during World War I. Moderator, Synod of N.C., 1949. Mason (K.T.), K.P. Clubs: Rotary (past president 4 Rotary clubs: Camden, Arkansas; Pensacola, Florida, High Point, North Carolina, Greenville, S.C.; district governor, 190th dist., Rotary Internat., 1948-49), Thirty-nine. Author: The Monuments of the Nile, 1914; Viewpoints, 1926; Crucial Chapters in My Father's Book, 1927; The New Testament Correspondence, 1928; When Rotary Hosts Trek Eastward, 1928; The Southern Presbyterian Pulpit, 1928; Youth Choosing, 1930; Gladness in Christian Living, 1931; Mediterranean Memories, 1934; Hear My Voice, O God, in Prayer, 1940; Upon Thee, O Lord, I Daily Call, 1944; My Morning Meditations, 1945; Mediterranean Meditations, 1949; Nieuw Amsterdam Meditations, 1954. Contbr. Greenville News; editor Homiletic Dept. The Expositor, 1930-32; asso. editor Expositor and Homiletic Review from 1935; on book reviewing staff, Presbyterian Com. Publication, Richmond, Virginia, Interpretation, Richmond. Home: Greenville, S.C. †

NAETER, ALBRECHT, elec. engr., educator; b. New Baden, Tex., Mar. 21, 1894; s. Albrecht and Marie (Hiltpold) N.; B.S. in E.E., U. Tex., 1917; student Westinghouse Grad. Student Course, 1918-19; M.S., Cornell, 1923; m. Ruby A. Wheaton, June 30, 1924; children—Carol A. (Mrs. Edwin H. Estrem), Audrey J. (Mrs. Bernard A. Stunkard, Jr.). Instr. elec. engring. Cornell U., 1919-23; gen. tester Consol. Edison Co., summers 1920-23, 25; asso. prof. U. N.C., 1923-24; charge dynamo lab. Pratt Inst., 1924-25; asso. prof. Mich. State U., 1925-29; with relay dept. Detroit Edison Co., summers 1926-29; prof., head Sch. Elec. Engring., Okla. A. and M. Coll. (name now changed to Oklahoma State University), 1929-60, prof., head Sch. Elec. Engring. emeritus, 1960-76. Served with aviation sect., Signal Corps, U.S. Army, World War I. Member Am. Inst. E.E. (chmn. Okla. City sect. 1934-35; recipient citation 1953), Am. Soc. Engring. Edn. (life; chmn. elec. engring. div. 1936-37), Okla. Soc. Profl. Engrs., Am. Legion, Eta Kappa Nu (nat. pres. 1959-61), Tau Beta Pi, Sigma Tau, Acacia. Presbyn. (past deacon). Mason. Home: Stillwater, Okla. Died Dec. 30, 1976; buried Fairlawn Cemetery, Stillwater, Okla.†

NAETZKER, LOUIS, banker; b. Dunkirk, N.Y., Mar. 19, 1891; s. Oscar Raimund and Amelia (Polinski) N.; m. Agnes O'Malley, May 29, 1920. Student, George Washington U., 1914-15; B.C.S. (Bus. fellow), NYU Sch. Finance, 1915-17. Clk. of ct. First Municipal Ct. of Dunkirk, 1910-14; Bur. of Corps. and Bur. Fgn. and Domestic Commerce Dept. of Commerce, Washington, 1914-15; comml. agt. Bur. Fgn. and Domestic Commerce, N.Y., 1915-16; research dept. Am. Internat. Corp. N.Y., 1916-20; with Nat. City Bank of N.Y., 1920-55, formerly v.p.; v.p., dir. Banque National de la Republique d'Haiti, 1929-35; dir. United Porto Rican Sugar Co., 1932-34; trustee, mem. exec. com., chmn. bd. Eastern Sugar Asso. P.R., 1946-58; dir., exec. com. Nat. Paper & Type Co., N.Y.C., 1942-52; dir. U. S. Life Ins. Co., 1954-62. Former mem. Cuban and Mexican coms. Nat. Fgn. Trade Council, Inter-Am. Comml. Arbitration Commn. Served as 2d lt. AEF, 1917-19. Mem. Pan Am. Soc. (past dir.), Haitian Am. Assn. (past dir.), Theta Delta Chi, Delta Mu Delta. Lutheran. Home: Cocoa Beach, Fla. Died May 26, 1983; buried Dunkirk, N.Y.

NAFE, JOHN PAUL, coll. prof.; b. Valley, Neb., June 2, 1888; s. John and Martha (Whitney) N.; A.B., U. of Colo., 1911; Ph.D., Cornell, 1924; Guggenheim fellow, 1930, U. of Berlin; m. Marie Bernard, Apr. 28, 1917. Instr. Cornell U., 1922-24; asst. prof., Clark U., 1924-26; asso. prof., 1926-28, professor, 1928-31; prof. psychology and head of department, Washington University; since 1931, on leave of absence; director. Project SOS-11, applied psychology panel, Office of Scientific Research and Development, 1944-45. Fellow A.A.A.S., American Psychological Association; mem. Society of Exptl. Psychologists, Southern Soc. for Philosophy and Psychology (pres. 1941). Midwestern Psychol. Assn., Sigma Xi, Phi Delta Kappa, Phi Alpha Delta, Phi Gamma Delta. Club: Town and Gown. Co-author: Handbook Experimental Psychology. On bd. editors Jour. of Psychology since 1935. Jour. of Gen. Psychology since 1928, Am. Jour. of Psychology, 1924-40. Contbr. psychol. jours. Home: St. Louis, Mo. †

NAGLER, BENEDICT, physician; b. Czerwowitz, Austria, Mar. 14, 1900; came to U.S., 1935, naturalized, 1941; s. Samuel Oswald and Charlotte Josephine (Schorr) N.; m. Hilde Laub, Oct. 20, 1927; children—Ralph Lewis, Eva (Mrs. Barron M. Hirsch). M.D., U. Hamburg, 1925. Diplomate: Am. Bd. Psychiatry and Neurology (asso. examiner 1953-66). Intern, resident neurology, psychiatry, internal medicine, Hamburg, Berlin, 1924-31, practice medicine specializing in psychiatry and neurology, Berlin, 1931-33, Tunis, North Africa, 1934, Newark, 1935-43; chief neurology-psychiatry service VA Hosp., Richmond, Va., 1946-53; chief neurology div. Psychiatry and Neurology Service VA, Washington, 1953-57; supt. Lynchburg Tng. Sch. and Hosp., 1957-73, pvt. practice, Lynchburg, 1973-81; asst. prof. psychiatry and neurology Med. Coll. Va., 1946-67; asso. prof. clin. neurology Georgetown U., 1953-57, professorial lectr., 1957-67; lectr. dept. neurology and psychiatry U. Va., 1957-67; staff psychiatrist Central Va. Mental Health Services, Lynchburg, 1973-80; cons. Nat. Inst. Neurol. Diseases and Stroke. Translator: from German to English Cerebral Function in Infancy and Childhood, 1963; also numerous other publs.; Cons. editor: Am. Jour. Mental Deficiency, 1961-71; mem. editorial bd.: Staff Am. Psychiat. Assn. Publ, 1964-67. Bd. dirs. Devel. Council Sweet Briar (Va.) Coll.; trustee Woodrow Wilson Rehab. Found. Served to maj. M.C. AUS, 1943-46. Recipient Nat. Brotherhood award Lynchburg chpt. Nat. Conf. Christians and Jews, 1970; cited by Pres.'s Com. on Employment of Handicapped, 1963. Fellow Am. Psychiat. Assn. (life; del. 1968-71, Gold Achievement award 1962), Am. Epilepsy Soc. (life; past councillor), So. Psychiat. Assn. (life), Am. Acad. Neurology (life; past councillor, past chmn. com. on problems mental retardation), Am. Assn. on Mental Deficiency (past councillor, past chmn. com. internat. activities, past chmn. Mid-Eastern region); mem. AMA (life), Va. Med. Soc. (life), Lynchburg Acad. Medicine, Va. Neuropsychiat. Soc. (life; past chmn. com. mental retardation), L'Alliance Francaise de Lynchburg (past dir.), Mil. Order World Wars (past comdr. Lynchburg chpt.), So. Electroencephalographic Soc. (life past pres.), Fedn. Am. Scientists, Assn. For Research Nervous and Mental Diseases, Va. Neurol. Soc. (Distinguished mem.), Am. Assn. Med. Supts. of Pub. Mental Hosps. (past councillor), Am. Acad. Mental Retardation (past pres.), Am. Med. EEG Soc. (asso. editor Clin. Electroencephalography from 1968), Internat. Assn. Sci. Study Mental Deficiency (past councillor, past chmn. finance com.). Home: Lynchburg, VA.

NAKARAI, TOYOZO WADA, religious studies educator; b. Kyoto, Japan, May 16, 1898; came to U.S., 1923, naturalized, 1953; s. Tosui and Wakae (Harada) N.; m. Frances Aileen Yorn, June 22, 1933; children—Charles Frederick Toyozo, Frederick Leroy. A.B., Kokugakuin U., Tokyo, 1920, Butler U., 1924; A.M., Butler U., 1925; Ph.D. (fellow Sch. Religion), U. Mich., 1930; Ph.D. also post-doctorate studies; postgrad., Nippon U., Tokyo, U. Chgo., Hebrew Union Coll., N.Y. U. Instr. Tokyo Fourth High Sch., Sei Gakuin Mission Sch., Matsumiya Lang. Sch., Tokyo, 192O-23; instr. Coll. of Missions, Indpls., 1923-25, Butler U. and Christian Theol. Sem., Indpls., 1927-28, asst. prof., 1928-29, asso. prof., 1929-31, prof., head dept. Semitics, 1931-65, prof. emeritus, from 1965; prof. Emmanuel Sch. of Religion, 1965-71, Disting. prof. O.T., 1971-83, head dept. O.T., 1965-83, ret., 1983, sr. prof., from 1983, chmn. curriculum com., 1965-77; Professorial appointee Am. Sch. Oriental Research, Jerusalem, 1947-48, hon. asso., 1962-63; alumni lectr. Ky. Christian Coll., 1956; T.H. Johnson Meml. lectr. Manhattan Bible Coll., 1957; lectr. Sch. Ministry, Milligan Coll., 1957, 66; vis. prof. Tainan Theol. Coll., Formosa, 1963; faculty lectr. Christian Theol. Sem., 1964; Inter-sem. lectr. Ashland Theol. Sem., 1974; lectr. Westwood Christian Found. Consortium, 1976. Author: A Study of the Kokinshu, 1931, Biblical Hebrew, 1951, rev. edit., 1976, (with others) To Do and To Teach, 1953, Sin Tosa Nikki, 1962, An Elder's Public Prayers, 1968, revised enlarged edit., 1979, Essays on New Testament Christianity, 1978, The Dead Sea Scrolls and Biblical Faith, 1979; Editor: Iggeret, 1974-77; Editorial com.: Hebrew Abstracts, 1954-75, Jour. Hebrew Studies, from 1976. Mem. Gov.'s Abraham Lincoln Commn. to Orient, 1960. Recipient Baxter Found. award; medal and scroll Internat. Order B'rith Abraham; J.I. Holcomb prize Butler U.; citation and scroll Histadrut Ivrit; Honored Minister Christian Ch.; citation of scholarship and merit Nat. Assn. Profs. Hebrew; Ch. Statesman of Day N.Am. Christian Conv. Mem. AAUP, Am. Oriental Soc., Am. Sch. Oriental Research (chmn. cast investigation com. 1941-42), Am. Acad. Religion, Soc. Sci. Study Religion, Soc. Bibl. Lit. (v.p. Midwest br. 1949-51, pres. 1951-52), Nat. Assn. Profs. Hebrew (pres. 1956-58, 1st ann. teaching award), Israel Exploration Soc., Israel Soc. Bibl. Research, Nippon Kyuyaku Gakkai, Eta Beta Rho, Phi Kappa Phi, Theta Phi. Home: Elizabethton, Tenn.

NARTEN, HELENE NORTH (MRS. C. CARL NARTEN), civic, philanthropic and social worker; b. Cleveland, OH., Aug. 2, 1888; d. Paul and Marguerite Beaugrand (Castle) North; A.B., Vassar Coll., 1910; student U. of Berlin, 1910-11; m. C. Carl Narten, May 9, 1914; children—David C. (dec.), Marguerite (dec.), Peter B., Philip C. de Joncaire. Asst. instr., dept. of economics, Vassar Coll., 1911-12. Mem. bd. of edn., Shaker Heights, OH., 1926-34. Trustee Vassar Coll., 1937-45. Mem. exec. com. Cuyahoga County unit Am. Cancer Soc. from 1946. Formerly pres. Goodrich Social Settlement, Cleveland Day Nursery Assn., Cleveland Child Health Assn.; mem. bd. of management Beechbrook Children'a Center; mem. bd. dirs. Maternal Health Assn., Children's Bureau, Cleveland Citizens' League and other similar orgns. West side consultant. Garden Center of Greater Cleveland from 1945. Mem. Phi Beta Kappa. Home: Cleveland, Ohio. †

NASH, MELL ACHILLES, coll. pres.; b. Tryon, Hardin County, Tex., July 20, 1890; s. Newton Achilles and Nancy Susan (Moody) N.; grad. Central State Teachers Coll., Okla., 1910; A.B., U. of Okla., 1919, M.A.; studied U. of Mich.; LL.D., Okla. Bapt. University, 1923; m. Mae Clarke, Aug. 6, 1916; children—Norman Clarke, Mary Jane, Don Rodman, Carl Griffin (dec.), David Acton. Successively teacher rural schs., high sch. prin. and supt. schs. until 1919; chief high sch. insp., Okla., 1919-20; state supt. pub. instrn., Okla., 1923-27, reëlected for 2d term, 1926; resigned Apr. 1927, to become pres. Okla. Coll. for Women. Editor Okla. Teacher, 1920-23. Pres. State Bd. of Edn., Okla.; mem. State Bd. Coördinator nation for Colleges of Okla. Mem. Okla. N.G., 1908. Mem. N.E.A., Okla. Edn. Assn., Phi Delta Kappa, Phi Gamma Delta, Phi Beta Kappa. Democrat. Baptist. Mason (32 deg., Shriner). Chancellor Okla. System Higher Edn. Home: Edmond, Okla. †

NASH, THOMAS PALMER, JR., educator; b. Elizabeth City, N.C., June 15, 1890; s. Thomas Palmer and Mattie (Forbes) N.; A.B., U. of N.C., 1910, A.M., 1911; Ph.D., Cornell U. (Med. Coll.), 1922; m. Edith Lyle Peatross, Mar. 1, 1919; children—Thomas Palmer, Peggy (Mrs. Bernard A. Rolfes). Instr. in chemistry, U. of Tenn. Coll. of Medicine, 1915-17, acting prof., 1917-19; instr. in chemistry, Cornell Med. Coll., 1919-22; prof. of chemistry, U. of Tenn. Colls. of Medicine and Dentistry, Schs. of Pharmacy and Nursing from 1922, chief of div. of chemistry and physiology, 1928-42, chemistry and pharmacology, 1942-45, chemistry, 1922-55, dean sch. of biol. scis. from 1928; consultant to Memphis Gen. Hosp. (John Gaston Hosp.), 1922. Sergt., Ordnance Dept., U.S. Army, 1918-19. Recipient Southern Chemist award, 1958. Member American Chemical Soc. (chmn. local sect., 1941-42), Am. Soc. of Biol. Chemists, Fedn. of Am. Socs. for Exptl. Biology, Memphis and Shelby Co. med. soc., Phi Beta Kappa, Sigma Xi, Alpha Omega Alpha, Phi Delta Chi. Asso. editor: Memphis Med. Jour. 1935. Contbr. papers on ammonia metabolism, intermediary carbohydrate metabolism, antienzymes, mechanism of phlorhizin diabetes in profl. jours. Home: Memphis, Tenn. †

NATHAN, HELMUTH MAX, physician; b. Hamburg, Ger., Oct. 26, 1901; s. Neumann and Regina (Seligmann) N.; came to U.S., 1936, naturalized, 1943; B.S., Freiburg U. (Ger.), 1922; M.D., Hamburg U., 1925; m. Irene Nelson, Jan. 17, 1926; 1 dau., Ruth Nathan Norden. Asst. staff U. Freiburg, 1927, Allgemeine Krankenhaus, Hamburg-St. George, 1928-33; asso. Jewish Hosp., Hamburg, 1933-36; cancer research fellow Beth Israel Hosp., N.Y.C., 1936-54; practice medicine, specializing in surgery, N.Y.C., 1937; cons. surgeon Bronx Municipal Hosp. Centre, N.Y.C., 1954-73, cons. surgeon, 1973-79; cons. surgeon Albert Einstein Coll. Hosp. and Montefiore Hosp. Center, N.Y.C., 1973-79; mem. faculty Albert Einstein Coll., N.Y.C., 1954-79, prof. surgery, 1960-69, emeritus prof. surgery and anatomy, 1969-79, prof., chmn. dept. history of medicine, 1973-79; prof. surgery Hamburg U., 1950-70, emeritus, 1970-79; attending staff Beth Israel Hosp.; lectr. Mt. Sinai Med. Sch., 1973; sr. cons. surgeon N.Y. Med. Soc. and Compensation Bd.; art work represented in permanent collections of museums and univs. Bd. dirs. Leo Baeck Inst., N.Y.C., Self Help, N.Y.C.; trustee Bronx Mus. Art, 1975. Decorated German Officers Cross of Merit 1st class; recipient Deneke medal U. Hamburg, 1932, Salomon Heine medal, 1936; Spl. Scroll, Albert Einstein Coll. Medicine, 1965, Spl. diploma as outstanding mem. faculty, 1973; also numerous prizes for paintings, graphics, glass windows, sculptures. Mem. AMA (life), N.Y. County (life), Virchow (past pres.) med. socs., N.Y. Physicians Assn. (past pres.), Pirquet Soc., Internat. Coll. Surgeons, Am. Coll. Cardiology, Am. Coll. Gastroenterology, Am. Soc. Facial Plastic Surgery (life), N.Y. Soc. Med. Illustrators (hon.), Deutschegesellschaft fur Chirurgie (life), Nordwestdeutsche Gesellschaft fur Chirurgie (life), N.Y. Acad. Medicine (life), Acad. Sci. (life), Acad. Gastroenterology (life), Am. Soc. Abdominal Surgeons, Am. Assn. Mil. Surgeons, N.Y. Physicians and Surgeons, Am. Physicians Art Assn. (pres. 1972-73), Soc. Med. Geriatrics, Am. Assn. Anatomists, Am. Assn. History of Medicine. Author: (with Samuel Standard) Should the Patient Know the Truth? 1954; contbr. articles to profl. jours., publs. in field of art and medicine. Developed theory of septic focus of circumscribed circulatory systems; 1st clin. case of encephalitis in bacterial endocarditis and total parotectomy with preservation of facial nerve. Home: New York, N.Y. Died July 15, 1979.

NATHAN, ROBERT, author; b. N.Y.C., Jan. 2, 1894; s. Harold and Sarah (Gruntal) N.; ed. pvt. schs., U.S., Switzerland, also Harvard; m. Dorothy Michaels, 1915 (div. 1922); 1 dau., Joan Frederick; m. 2d, Nancy Wilson, 1930 (div. 1936); m. 3d, Lucy Lee Hall Skelding, 1936 (div. 1939); m. 4th, Janet McMillen Bingham, 1940 (div.); m. 5th, Clara May Blum Burns, 1951; m. 6th, Shirley Kneeland White, 1955 (dec. 1969); m. 7th, Anna Lee (Joan Boniface Winnifrith), 1970. Lectr., N.Y. U. Sch. Journalism, 1924-25; mem. adv. council writers War Bd.; chancellor Acad. Am. Poets. Hon. fellow Acad. Am. Poets; charter mem. P.E.N. (pres.); mem. Nat. Inst. Arts and Letters (v.p.). A.S.C.A.P., Dramatists Guild, Screenwriters Guild, Acad. Motion Picture Arts and Scis. Clubs: Town Hall, Fencers, Coffee House, Woods Hole Yacht. Editorial bd. Huntington Hartford Found. Author: Peter Kindred, 1919; Autumn, 1921; Youth Grows Old, 1922; The Puppet Master, 1923; Jonah, 1925; The Fiddler in Barly, 1926; The Woodcutter's House, 1927; The Bishops Wife, 1928; A Cedar Box, 1929; There is Another Heaven, 1929; The Orchid, 1931; One More Spring, 1933; Road of Ages, 1935; Selected Poems, 1935; Music at Evening (play), 1935; Winter in April, 1937; The Barley Field, 1938; Journey of Tapiola, 1938; Portrait of Jennie. 1940; A Winter Tide, 1940; They Went on Together, 1941; Tapiola's Regiment, 1941; The Seagull Cry, 1942; Journal for Josephine, 1943; But Gently Day, 1943; Morning in Iowa, 1944; The Darkening Meadows (poetry), 1944; Mr. Whittle and the Morning Star, 1947; A Family Piece (play) 1947; Long After Summer, 1948; River Journey, 1949; Messer Marco Polo (dramatization); The Innocent Eve, 1951; Jezebel's Husband (play), 1941; The Sleeping Beauty (play), 1950; Susan and the Stranger (play), 1954; Sir Henry, 1955; The Rancho of the Little Loves, 1956; So Love Returns, 1958; The Snowflake and the Starfish, 1959; The Weans, 1960; The Color of Evening, 1960; The Wilderness Stone, 1961; A Star in the Wind, 1962; The Married Man (poems), 1962; The Devil with Love, 1963; The Fair, 1964; The Mallot Diaries, 1965; Juliet in Mantua (play), 1966; Stonecliff, 1967; Tappy, 1968; Mia, 1970; The Elixir, 1971; The Summer Meadows, 1973; Evening Song (poems), 1973; The Megas Factor, 1975. Composer violin sonata, also songs. Illustrator of Tina Mina Tales. Home: Hollywood, Calif. Died. May 25, 1985.

NATHANSON, NATHANIEL L(OUIS), law educator; b. New Haven, Dec. 21, 1908; s. Samuel Jacob and Lillian (Dante) N.; A.B., Yale, 1929, LL.B., 1932; S.J.D., Harvard, 1933, Rosenwald Fellow, 1932-33; m. Leah Smirnow, June 22, 1941. Admitted to Mass. bar, 1933, U.S. Supreme Ct. bar, 1942, Ill. bar, 1946; law clk., U.S. Circuit Judge Julian W. Mack, 1933-34, U.S. Supreme Ct. Justice Louis D. Brandeis, 1934-35; atty. SEC, 1935-36; asst. prof. law, Northwestern U., 1936-41, asso. prof., 1941-45, prof., 1945-66, Vose professor of law, 1966-77, prof. emeritus, 1977-83; asso. gen. counsel Office Price Administration, Washington, 1942-45; vis. prof. law, Stanford, 1948, Rutgers U., 1954; Fulbright prof. U. Tokyo, 1954-55; vis. research scholar Carnegie Endowment for Internat. Peace, 1964-65; vis. lectr. Internat. Christian University, Tokyo, Japan, 1965; associate firm Sonneschein, Berkson Lautmann Levinson & Morse, 1949; cons. Indian Law Inst., New Delhi, 1958; mem. Pub. Utility Laws Commn. Ill., 1951; vis. research scholar Carnegie Endowment Internat. Peace, 1964-65. Council, Adminstrv. Conf. U.S., 1961-62. Exec. com. Anti-Defamation League, Chgo., 1950-56; vice chmn. Illinois div. American Civil Liberties Union. Member American, Chicago bar associations, Am. Assn. Univ. Professors, Order of the Coif. Jewish religion. Co-author: Federal Regulation of Transportation, 1953; Administrative Law: Cases and Materials, 1961. Editor-in-chief, Yale Law Jour., 1931-32. Contbr. articles to legal jours. Home: Wilmette, Ill. Died Nov. 8, 1983.

NATVIG, PAUL, surgeon, educator; b. Prairie Farm, Wis., Jan. 15, 1920; s. Gerhard Alfred and Clara Emily (Knutson) N.; m. Anne Kirk Campbell, Mar. 2, 1957; children—Mary, Caroline, Elizabeth. B.A., St. Olaf Coll., 1942; D.D.S., Loyola U., Chgo., 1945; M.D., Marquette U., 1949. Intern Nat. Naval Med. Center, Bethesda, Md., 1949-50; resident gen. surgery Milw. County Gen. Hosp., Milw., 1950-52; plastic surgery St. Joseph Mercy Hosp., Ann Arbor, Mich., 1955-57, practice medicine specializing in plastic surgery, Milw., 1957-82; mem. staffs Luth. Hosp., Milw., Columbia Hosp., Milw., St. Mary's Hosp., Milw., Milw. County Gen. Hosp., Froedtert Meml. Luth. Hosp., Milw., VA Hosp., Wood, Wis.; asso. prof. plastic and reconstructive surgery Med. Coll. Wis., Milw., from 1957. Author: (with Reed Dingman) Surgery of Facial Fractures, 1964, Jacques Joseph, Surgical Sculptor, 1981. Served with USNR, 1949-50, 53-55. Fellow A.C.S., Am. Assn. Plastic Surgeons. Club: University (Milw.). Home: Milwaukee, Wis. Died Nov. 13, 1982.

NAVA, JULIAN, diplomat; b. Los Angeles, June 19, 1927; s. Julian and Refugio and (Flores) N.; m. Patricia Lucas, June 30, 1962; children—Carmen and Katie (twins), Paul. B.A., Pomona Coll., Los Angeles, 1951; M.A., Harvard U., 1952, Ph.D., 1955. Prof. Latin Am. history and affairs U.S. Cultural Center, Caracas, Venezuela, 1953-54; instr. U. P.R., 1955-57; mem. faculty Calif. State U., Northridge, 1957-79, prof. history, 1970-79, spl. asst. to pres., 1980; mem. faculty U. de Valladolid, Spain, 1962-63, Centro de Estudios Universitarios Colombo-Americano, Bogota, 1964-65; A.E. and P. to, Mexico, from 1980; chmn. McGraw-Hill Nat. Broadcasting Adv. Council Public Service Programs, 1974-79; pres. Pacific Coast Council Latin Am. Studies, 1966; past mem. bd. Plaza de la Raza, Hispanic Urban Center. Author: Mexican Americans: Past, Present and Future, 1969, The Mexican American in American History, 1970, Viva la

Raza: Readings on Mexican Americans, 1970, Nineteenth Century Emigration to Venezuela, 1960, A History of Mexican Americans, 1976, California: Five Centuries of Cultural Contrasts, 1979, also articles. Past mem. adv. com. Mexican-Am. Legal Def. and Edn. Fund; past mem. adv. com. Bilingual Children's TV.; Mem. Los Angeles Bd. Edn., 1967-80, pres., 1971, 75. Address: Mexico, Mexico.

NAY, GEORGE, church exec.; b. Budapest, Hungary, Jan. 19, 1890; s. Rudolph and Gisella (Straus) N.; M.S., Tech. U. Budapest, 1912; m. Mary Lee Gough, May 12, 1926. Came to U.S., 1912, naturalized, 1920. Structural engr. until 1927; Christian Sci. practitioner, 1927-52; mem. Bd. Lectureship, 1952-57; asso. editor Christian Sci. Herald, 1957-72; pres. First Ch. of Christ, Scientist, Boston, 1972-73; lectr. in N.Am., Europe and Asia. Home: Boston, MA †

NAYLOR, CHARLES EDWARD, engring. corp. exec.; b. Palestine, Tex., Oct. 15, 1890; s. Charles H. and Elizabeth (Parker) N.; ed. pub. schs. of Palestine; m. Marie Baker Armstrong, Jan. 14, 1924 (dec. Aug. 1953); children—Roger Armstrong, Bette (Mrs. Howard Park); m. 2d, Julia Williams Bertner, July 15, 1955. Passenger dept. M.P. R.R. and S.P. R.R., 1912-17; with C. E. Naylor R.R. Supplies, 1919-24; founder, pres. Maintenance Engring. Corp., from 1924; founder Coastal Engring. Corp., Erie Mfg. Corp., 1937; mem. bd. dirs. South Main State Bank, Gulfgate State Bank, City Nat. Bank. Dir. of the Material Petroleum Adminstrn., District 3, 1942-44; chmn. Harris Co. Red Cross, 1945; pres. of Houston United Fund, 1951-52. Served in 1st O.T.C., Ft. Logan H. Root, 1917-19. Mem. C. of C. (pres. Houston 1946-47), Newcomen Soc. Clubs: Tejas, Ramada, Eagle Lake, Houston Country. Home: Houston, Tex. †

NAYLOR, EUGENE RUDOLPH, educator; born Friendship, Tenn., June 16, 1889; s. William James and Maggie Azilee (Rudolph) N.; prep. edn. high sch., Covington, Tenn. and Ky. Western Jr. Coll., Loneoak; A.B., Emory and Henry Coll., 1910, D.D., 1936; A.M., Vanderbilt, 1912, B.D., 1914; Ph.D., Northwestern U., 1924; m. Bessie Estella Orr, July 8, 1912 (died Mar. 22, 1930); children—Catherine, Ralph; m. 2d, Angie Orgain Nichols, Aug. 22, 1931; 1 son, William Rudolph. Pres. Columbia Coll., Milton, Ore., 1914-17; pres. Woman's Coll., Jackson, Tenn., 1917-20; dean of Logan Coll., Russellville, Ky., 1920-22; prof. edn. and religious edn., Ky. Wesleyan Coll., Winchester, 1922-24; prof. religious edn., Emory and Henry Coll., 1924-28; pres., Logan Coll., 1928-30; pres., Athens (Ala.) Coll., 1930-49; head dept. psychology Emory & Henry Coll., Emory, Va., from 1949. Mem. Kappa Phi Kappa, Pi Gamma Mu, Pi Delta Kappa. Democrat. Methodist. Author: Introduction to Religious Education. Home: Emory, Va. †

NEAL, GEORGE ALFRED, public utilites; b. Osceola, Mo., Dec. 16, 1888; s. George Alfred and Lily Bell (High) N.; B.S., U. of Kan., 1910; Doctor of Science Morningside College; married Millie Johanne Eiler, Mar. 14, 1914; children—Tom, Alf., Mary, Nancy. Chairman of bd. Iowa Pub. Service Company; dir. First Federal Building and Loan Assn. of Sioux City, Live Stock Nat. Bank of Sioux City. Republican. Mason. Club: Rotary (Sioux City). †

NEAL, JULIAN SPENCER, ins. co. exec.; b. Spray, N.C., July 15, 1909; s. Lonnie Stedman and Minnie (Gilley) N.; student Duke, 1931; m. Harriet Kitterman, Oct. 21, 1937; children—Judith Mellinger, William S. With Fidelity and Deposit Co. Md., Balt., 1931-79, v.p., Chgo., 1952-59, mem. exec. staff, Balt., 1959-62, exec. v.p., 1962-64, pres., 1964-74, chmn. bd., 1974-79, dir., 1962-79; dir., mem. exec. com. Comml. Credit Co.; adv. dir. Md. Nat. Bank, Balt.; dir., mem. exec. com. Balt. Gas & Electric Co., Savs. Bank Balt. Pres., Surety Underwriters Assn. Chgo., from 1941. Trustee Goucher Coll. Mem. Surety Assn. Am. (exec. com.), Lambda Chi Alpha, Lambda Phi Gamma. Mason (K.T., Shriner). Clubs: Center, Country Maryland (Balt.). Home: Baltimore, Md. Died Oct. 5, 1980.

NEAL, M(ARCUS) PINSON, pathologist; b. Heflin, Ala., Sept. 23, 1887; s. William Alexander (M.D.) and Ella Jane (Pinson) N.; student U. of Ala., 1904-07; M.D., Univ. Coll. of Medicine, Richmond, Va., 1912; diplomate Am. Bd. Pathology; m. Mathilde Frances Evers, Apr. 25, 1917; 1 son, M. Pinson. Instr. in clin. pathology, Univ. Coll. of Medicine, 1912-13; asst. Von Ruck Research Labs. and Winyah Sanatorium Labs., 1913-16; asst. bacteriologist Chicago Bd. of Health, 1916; instr. in pathology, Northwestern U., 1916-20; asso., 1920; asst. prof. pathology and bacteriology, U. of Ia. Schs. of Medicine and Dentistry, 1920-22; prof. pathology, U. Mo. Sch. Medicine, 1922-58, emeritus, from 1958; acting dean Sch. of Medicine Sept. 1951-June 1953; dir. Univ. Hosps. Labs. U. Mo., 1930-50, chmn. dept. of pathology, bacteriology and preventive med., 1936-46; pathologist Boone Co. Hosp., 1922-57; cons. pathologist to Mo. State eleemosynary instns., 1922-57; coroner Boone County, Mo., 1955-58; vis. professor of pathology, University of Tennessee College of Medicine, summers 1932, 34; visiting dir. Memphis Gen. Hosp. Labs., summers 1932-34; consulting physician University of Mo., from 1953. Served successively as 1st lt., capt. and maj. M.C., U.S. Army, with A.E.F., 1917-19; maj. M.R.C., 1919-29. Cited for meritorious services with troops, A.E.F., France, 1918. Fellow College of American Pathologists, member Chicago Pathological Society, Boone County Med. Soc. (pres. 1928), Mo. State Med. Soc. (chmn. council 1937-38; speaker house of dels., 1940), A.M.A. Southern Med. Assn. (sec. sect. on pathology 1930; vice chmn. 1931, chmn. 1932, councillor from Mo. 1932-37; chmn. council 1936; chmn. sect. on med. education and hospital training, 1939; president 1942; trustee 1943-48), American Society Clinical Pathologists, Mississippi Valley Med. Society (trustee, v.p. 1937, pres. 1939; recipient Distinguished Service Award 1940), Am. Soc. for Control of Cancer, Mo. Acad. Sci. (chmn. med. sect., 1939), Internat. Acad. Pathology, Mo. Soc. Pathologists (pres. 1949), Mo. Heart Assn., Mo. State Tchrs. Assn., Am. Assn. U. Profs., Sigma Xi, Alpha Omega Alpha, Omega Upsilon Phi. Democrat. Presbyn. Mason (32 deg.). Contbr. many articles to med. jours. Home: Columbia, Mo. †

NEARING, SCOTT, sociologist; b. Morris Run, Pa., Aug. 6, 1883; s. Louis and Minnie (Zabriskie) N.; m. Nellie Marguerite Seeds, June 20, 1908; m. Helen Knothe, 1947. Student, U. Pa. Law Sch., 1901-02; B.S., U. Pa., 1905, Ph.D., 1909; B.Oratory, Temple U., 1904; D.Hum., Clark U., 1974. Sec. Pa. Child Labor Com., 1905-07; instr. econs. U. Pa., 1906-14, asst. prof., 1914-15, prof. emeritus econs., 1973-83; instr. econs. Swarthmore Coll., 1908-13; prof. social sci., dean Coll. Arts and Sci., Toledo U., 1915-17; lectr. Rand Sch. Social Sci., N.Y.C., 1916; chmn. People's Council Am., 1917-18; now chmn. Social Sci. Inst. Author or co-author numerous books, from 1908; (with Helen K. Nearing) The Maple Sugar Book, 1950, Living the Good Life, 1954, USA Today, 1955, Socialists Around The World, 1958, The Brave New World, 1958, Economics for the Power Age, 1952, Man's Search For the Good Life, 1954, Freedom: Promise and Menace, 1961, Socialism in Practice, 1962, The Conscience of a Radical, 1965; autobiography The Making of a Radical, 1972; (with Helen K. Nearing) Civilization and Beyond, 1975, The Sun-Heated Greenhouse, 1977, Continuing the Good Life, 1979. Address: Harborside, Maine. Died Aug. 24, 1983.

NEEDY, JOHN ALFRED, coll. prof.; b. Louisville, Ky., Aug. 28, 1889; s. John Albert and Sarah Louise (Shriner) N.; B.S. in M.E., U. of Ky., 1911; M.S. in M.E., Purdue U., 1922; student Ohio State U., 1929; m. Stella Rowe Payne, June 22, 1915; children—John Alfred, Robert Shriner. Draftsman Mengel Box Co., 1911-13; elec. engr. Kosmosdale Portland Cement Co., 1913-14; teacher manual training, Witherspoon Coll., 1914-16; prof. mech. engring., Ohio Northern U., 1916-20; asst. prof. Purdue U., 1922-26; dean of engring., Ohio Northern U., 1926-44; dir. tech. and engring. edn., Evansville Coll. (Evansville, Ind.), 1944-48; asso. prof. M.E., Ala. Polytechnic Institute, 1948-49, prof. from 1949. Dir. Auburn chapter American Red Cross. Coordinator Civil Aeronautics Adminstrn. War Training Service; institutional rep., engring. science and management war training, U.S. Office of Edn., 1941-44. Registered professional engr. and surveyor, State of Ohio. Mem. Am. Soc. Mech. Engrs., Am. Soc. for Engring. Edn., Professional Engrs., Northwestern Ohio County Engrs. Assn., Am. Assn. Univ. Profs., Pi Tau Sigma (hon.), Pi Tau Chi (hon.), Pi Kappa Phi, Delta Sigma Phi, Tau Beta Pi, Nu Theta Kappa, Phi Zeta. Republican. Methodist. Club: Kiwanis. Home: Auburn, Ala. †

NEEL, ALICE, artist; b. Merion Square, Pa., Jan. 28, 1900; d. George Washington and Alice Concross (Hartley) N.; m. Carlos Enriquez, June 1, 1925 (div.); children: Santillana (dec.), Isabella Lillian, Richard, Hartley. Diploma, Phila. Sch. Design (now Moore Coll. Art), 1925. Artist, 1920; participant Easel Project, WPA, 1933-43; lectr. U. Pa. Grad. Sch., 1971-72; vis. artist Bloomsbury State Coll., Pa., 1972; lectr. Skowhegan Sch. Painting and Sculpture, 1972. One-woman shows include, Contemporary Arts Gallery, 1938, Reed Coll., 1962, Graham Gallery, 1963, 66, 68, 70, 74, 76, 77, 78, 80, Dartmouth Coll., Fordham U., 1965, Bowling Green U., Ohio, 1972, Whitney Museum Am. Art, N.Y.C., 1974, Portland Ctr. Visual Arts, Oreg., 1975, Ga. Mus. Art, Athens, 1975, Smith Coll., Northampton, Mass., 1975, Choate Sch., Wallingford, Conn., 1976, U. Wis.-Oshkosh, 1977, Lehigh U., Bethlehem, Pa., 1977, Ft. Lauderdale Mus., Fla., 1977, Queens Coll. Library, N.Y., 1977, Wichita Mus., Kans., 1977, Skidmore Coll., Saratoga Springs, N.Y., 1978, SUNY-Plattsburg, 1978, Middendorf Ln. gallery, Washington, 1979, Akron Art Inst., Ohio, 1979, Williams Coll., Williamstown, Mass., 1979, U. Brideport, Conn., 1979, Sara Inst., N.Y.C., 1980, Boston U. Art Gallery, 1980, Nat. Acad. Scis., Washington, 1981, group shows include, Boyer Gallery, Phila., 1933, Hartford Athenaeum, 1964, U. Nebr., 1964, Am. Acad. Arts and Letters, 1969, Studio Mus. Harlem, 1969, Internat. Biennale, Tokyo, 1975, Fendrick Gallery, Washington, 1976, Wildenstein Gallery, N.Y.C., 1976, Phila. Mus. Fine Arts, 1976, Los Angeles County Mus., 1976-77, Whitney Mus. Am. Art, N.Y.C., 1977, Princeton U., N.J., 1977, WPA show Grey Gallery, N.Y.C., 1978, Harold Reed Gallery, N.Y.C., 1980, Hirshhorn Mus. and Sculputure Garden, Washington, 1982, Whitney Mus. Am. Art, N.Y.C., 1982, Dayton Art Inst., Ohio, 1982-83; represented permanent collections, Mus. Modern Art, N.Y.C., Met. Mus., N.Y.C., Whitney Mus. Am. Art, N.Y.C., Balt. Mus., Hirshhorn Mus. and Sculpture Garden, Washington, Princeton U. Mus., N.J., Oberlin Coll., Ohio, Everson Mus., Syracuse, N.Y., Yale U., Dartmouth Coll., other permanent collections. Recipient award Longview Found, 1962; recipient award Am. Acad. and Inst. Arts and Letters, 1969, Nat. Endowment for Arts, 1976, Benjamin Altman Figure prize, NAD, 1971. Mem. Nat. Inst. Arts and Letters. Home: New York, N.Y. Died Oct. 13, 1984.*

NEEL, LOUIS BOYD, orch. condr.; b. London, Eng., July 19, 1905; s. Louis Anthony and Ruby (Le Couteur) N. Student, Royal Naval Coll., Dartmouth, Eng., 1919-22; M.A., U. Cambridge, Eng., 1926; L.R.C.P., St. George's Hosp., London, 1930, M.R.C.S., 1930, R.A.M. (hon.), 1965; Mus.D. (hon.), U. Toronto, 1979. Practice medicine, London, 1930-35; staff St. George's Hosp., 1930-31; formed Boyd Neel Orch., London, 1933; now condr.; condr. Sadlers Wells Opera, 1945-46, D'Oyly Carte Opera Co., 1948-49; dean Royal Conservatory Music, Toronto, Ont., Can., 1953-71, condr. orchs. world-wide, 1972—. Decorated comdr. Brit. Empire, 1953; Order Can., 1973. Club: York (Toronto). Pioneer in revival of music of baroque period. Address: York Club 135 St George St Toronto ON M5R 2L8 Canada

NEFF, EMERY B., surgeon; b. Kansas City, Mo., Aug. 23, 1890; s. Emery I. and Ada J. (Bowers) N.; M.D., U. Ill., 1913; m. Ruth M. Heath, Nov. 27, 1917 (dec. 1948); children—William H. (dec.), Richmond C. Chief surgeon Deere & Co., Moline, Ill., 1926-47, med. consultant from 1947. Served as maj., M.C., U.S. Army, 1916-23; col., M.C., AUS, 1942-45. Diplomate Am. Bd. Pub. Health in occupational medicine. Fellow Indsl. Medicine Assn., A.C.S.; mem. A.M.A., Ill. State, Rock Island County med. socs. Elk, Mason (32 deg. Shriner).†

NEFF, ROBERT EMERY, hospital adminstr.; b. Eaton, Ind., Apr. 24, 1887; s. David Mitchell and Mary Alice (Brandt) N.; A.B., Ind. U., 1911; LL.D., Iowa State Coll.; m. Emma Ruth Clark, June 14, 1916; children—Robert Jennings, Richard Brandt. Asst. to bursar, Ind. U., 1911-13, dir. social service dept., 1921-24; administrator Ind. U. Hosps., Indianapolis, 1913-28; supt. Indianapolis City Dispensary, 1918-21; administrator State U. of Ia. Hosps., 1928-45; supt. Methodist Hospital, Indianapolis, since 1945. Pres. Ind. Hosp. Assn., 1925-26, Indianapolis Council of Social Agencies, 1926-28, Am. Assn. Social Workers (Indianapolis chapter), 1925-28, Children's Hosp. Assn. of America, 1925-28, University Hosp. Execs. Council, 1932-34; vice-pres. Ind. State Health Council, 1921-27; mem. Joint Purchasing Com., Ind., 1925-28; mem. exec. com. Ind. Com. for Mental Hygiene, 1927-28. Lecturer on hosp. adminstrn. State Teachers Coll., Greeley, Colo., summers 1931, 32. Del. Nat. Health Conf., Washington, D.C., 1938. Mem. 7th Service Command Procurement and Assignment Service, 1942-44. Hospital rep., advisory council, Iowa Emergency Med. Service for Civilian Defense, 1942-45. Member Iowa Survey Commission on Hospital Care; Deputy Recruitment Officer, U.S.P.H. Service Nursing Edn. Charter fel. Am. Coll. of Hosp. Administrators (president 1934-35; ex-vice-pres., mem. com. on relationship between adminstr. and governing bd.); member Iowa Hosp. Assn. (pres. 1929-31; trustee 1929-45), Am. Hosp. Assn. (v.p. 1932-33; member council on Association Development; president 1937-38; mem. com. on cost study of nursing service and nursing education, 1937-39, mem. com. on state and local welfare legislation), National Society for Crippled Children (trustee 1936-44), Association Instl. Heads and Trustees (life), Nat. Assn. Meth. Hosps. and Homes (ex-chmn. hosp. sect.), Am. Protestant Hosp. Assn. (mem. exec. com.); mem. bd. trustees Indiana Hosp. Assn., since 1946; mem. bd. dirs. Mutual Hosp. Ins., Inc., (Blue Cross); del.-at-large. Am. Hospital Assn., 1945-47; dir. Ind. Pub. Health Assn. Member Indiana State Adv. Com. Hospital and Health Center Plan; Phi Delta Theta. Presbyterian. Mason. Club: Rotary. Member editorial bd. The Modern Hospital. Contbr. scientific articles to hosp. jours. Home: Indianapolis, Ind. †

NEFF, WALLACE, architect; b. La Mirada, Calif., Jan. 28, 1895; s. Edwin D. and Nancy (McNally) N.; grad. Mass. Inst. Tech., 1918; m. Louise UpdeGraff, June 21, 1923; children—Phyllis, Wallace, Arthur. Individual practice architecture, Hollywood, Calif. Served with U.S. Army, Recipient Gold medal King of Egypt for airform house. Fellow AIA. Roman Catholic. Author: Architecture of Southern California, 1964. Pioneer Airform House (Bubble House), 1938. Important works include residences of Mary Pickford and Douglas Fairbanks, Herbert Hoover, King C. Gillette, Prince Rainier, Joan Bennett, Charles Thorne, Cary Grant, Amelia Gali-Curci, Robert M. Hutchins, Groucho Marx, Howard Hughes. Home: Pasedena, Calif. Died June 8, 1982.

NEFF, WANDA FRAIKEN (MRS. EMERY NEFF), writer; b. Minneapolis, Minn., May 6, 1889; d. Henry J. and Florence Belle (Manseau) Fraiken; A.B., U. of Minn., 1909; A.M., Columbia, 1917, Ph.D., 1929; grad. study Bedford Coll., U. of London, 1922; m. Emery Neff (asso. prof. English Columbia U.), 1925. Teacher of English, 1909-27, at Univs. of Colo. and Minn., Vassar Coll. and Columbia U. Author: We Sing Diana, 1928; Lone Voyagers, 1929; Victorian Working Women, 1929; also novels published under a pseudonym from 1932. Home: Westmoreland, N.H. †

NEIMAN, WALTER, broadcasting executive; b. Hartford, Conn., Jan. 12, 1926; s. Raymond and Anna Belle (Nachman) N.; m. Muriel Gelber, Oct. 26, 1958; children—Peter Samuel, Raymond Lawrence. A.B., Brown U., 1949. Gen. mgr. Sta. WDEM, Providence, 1949-51; program dir. Sta. WGSM, Huntington, N.Y., 1951-53;

program dir., v.p. ops. Sta. WQXR, N.Y.C., 1953-68, v.p., gen. mgr., pres., 1968-83. Dep. mayor Village of Ardsley, N.Y., 1974—; bd. dirs. Richard Tucker Music Found.; radio project Center for Public Resources, Brown U. Associated Alumni. Served with AUS, 1944-46. Mem. Concert Music Broadcast Assn., N.Y. Market Radio Broadcasters Assn. (past dir.), Internat. Radio and Television Soc. Democrat. Jewish. Home: Ardsley, N.Y. Died Mar. 29, 1983.

NELSON, BERNARD ANDREW, educator; b. Chgo., Jan. 10, 1910; s. Jacob Andrew and Anny (Swahn) N.; m. Ellen Lytle, Sept. 12, 1936. B.S., Wheaton Coll., 1931; M.S., Northwestern U., 1938, Ph.D., 1942. Indsl. chemist, Chgo., 1931-35; instr. Maine Twp. Jr. Coll., Des Plaines, Ill., 1938-42; asst. prof. Baylor U., 1942-43; asst. prof. Wheaton (Ill.) Coll., 1943-48, asso. prof., 1948-55, prof., 1955-78, prof. emeritus, from 1978, chmn. dept. chemistry, 1969-76; prof. sci. No. Bapt. Theol. Coll., 1949-55; Cons. chemist, from 1942; lectr. summer insts. for chemistry tchrs. NSF, from 1962; cons. All-India Conf. on Tests and Evaluations Chemistry, Jadavpur U., Calcutta, summer 1970. Recipient Service to Alma Mater and Sci. award Wheaton Coll. Alumni Assn., 1970; Tchr. of Year award Wheaton Coll., 1975. Fellow A.A.A.S., Am. Inst. Chemists; mem. Am. Chem. Soc. (vice chmn. exams. com. div. chem. edn.), N.Y. Acad. Sci., Nat. Sci. Tchrs. Assn., Am. Assn. U. Profs., Sigma Xi. Research in heterocyclic compounds-dioxane, chromanones, pyrazolines. Home: Wheaton, Ill.

NELSON, GEORGE CARL EDWARD, librarian; b. N.Y.C., Aug. 3, 1900; s. Charles and Christina (Gustafson) N.; B.S., Coll. City N.Y., 1925, M.S., 1926; Ph.D., Columbia, 1931; librarian certificate McGill U., 1932; m. Lillian Gleissner, July 5, 1935; m. Mary Baronowski, Feb. 18, 1966; m. Jane Gallagher, June 1, 1979. Asst., N.Y. Pub. Library, 1917; library asst. Coll. City N.Y., 1921-25, instr. biol. sci., 1925-31, asst. librarian. 1928, asso. librarian. 1934-52; prof., librarian Fairleigh Dickinson U., 1952-61, dir. Grad. Sch. 1954-55, dir. library, 1954, dean libraries, 1958-60; dir. Instituto de Arte y Literature de Cuernavaca, from 1961, Centro Para Retirados Cuahnauac, A.C., from 1966. Mem. AAUP, Am. Philatelic Soc., Am. Topical Assn., Phi Delta Kappa, Omega Epsilon Phi (past nat. pres.). Republican. Conglist. Author: Introductory Biological Sciences in Liberal Arts College, 1931; Omega Epsilon Directory, 1932; Thomas Jefferson's Garden Book; Go Native in Mexico, 1958; Guide to Selected Research Tools and Source Materials for Graduate Students, 1958; Retire on $65 a Week in Mexico, 1967; Live It Up on $65 a Week in Sunny Mexico, 1968; Mexico A-Z, An Encyclopedic Dictionary of Mexico, 1974. Contbr. library, sci. jours. Home: Oconomowoc, Wis., also Cuernavaca, Mexico. Dec. Feb. 20, 1982. Interned Cuernavaca, Mexico.

NELSON, JOHN A(LBERT), coll. dean; b. Cottage Hill, Ia., Nov. 2, 1890; s. John Henry and Mary Otilda Nelson; B.S., Ia. State Coll., 1922, M.S., 1923, Ph.D., 1932; m. Lillian M. Baker, Aug. 14, 1923; 1 son, John Howard. Mem. faculty Mont. State Coll. from 1922, prof. and head, dept. dairy industry from 1929, dean grad. div., from 1948. Served with inf., U.S. Army, World War I. Mem. Sigma Xi, Alpha Zeta, Gamma Sigma Delta, Phi Kappa Phi, Alpha Gamma Rho. Author: Judging Dairy Products (with G. M. Trout), 1934, 48, 51. Author tech. and semi tech. articles and bulls. on dairy bacteriology and dairy products. Home: Bozeman, Mont. †

NELSON, KATHERINE GREACEN, geology educator; b. Sierra Madre, Calif., Dec. 9, 1913; m. Frank H. Nelson. A.B., Vassar Coll., 1934; Ph.D. in Geology, Rutgers U., 1938. Asst. (in geology); Rutgers U., 1936-38; instr. geology and geography Milw.-Downer Coll., 1938-43, asst. prof., 1946-48, prof., 1948-54; sr. paleontologist Shell Oil Co., 1943-44; asst. prof. geography Wis. State Coll., 1955-56; asst. prof. geology U. Wis.-Milw., 1956-64, assoc. prof., 1964-66, prof., from 1966, chmn. dept., 1961-62. Mem. AAAS, Paleontol. Soc., Geol. Soc. Am., Am. Assn. Petroleum Geologists, Nat. Assn. Geology Tchrs. (sec.-treas. 1942-50, Neil Miner award 1978). Office: Milwaukee, Wis. Died Dec. 28, 1982.

NELSON, MARTIN A., justice; b. Hesper, Ia., Feb. 21, 1889; s. Andrew A. and Bertha (Jacobson) N.; LL.B., St. Paul Coll. Law, 1916; m. Merle Henifin, Nov. 23, 1920; children—Arthur Martin, Enid Marie. Admitted to Minn. bar, 1916, practiced in St. Paul, 1916-19, Austin, 1919-44; served on dist. bench, 10th Jud. Dist., Minn., 1944-53; asso. justice Supreme Ct. of Minn., from 1953. Congl. Del. to Nat. Rep. Conv., Kansas City, Mo., 1928, del. at-large for Minn., 1932; vice chmn. Minn. Rep. Com., 1932; Rep. nominee for Gov. Minn., 1934, 36. Formerly trustee and pres., St. Olaf Hosp. Served as aviator, World War I. Registered pharmacists, Minn. Mem. Am. Bar Assn., Am. Legion, 40 and 8, Delta Theta Phi. Lutheran, Elk, Mason. Home: Saint Paul, MN †

NELSON, MILES A., state ofcl.; b. Ithaca, Mich., Oct. 22, 1890; s. Wilbur and Mary (Hamilton) N.; student Ferris Inst., Big Rapids, Mich., 1910-11; m. Elizabeth Otterbein, May 15, 1920; 1 dau., Mary Louise. Dealer farm products as M. A. Nelson, Ithaca, Mich., 1919-35; marketing specialist, Mich. Dept. Agr., 1935-37, chief Bur. Marketing and Enforcement from 1939. Served with U.S. Army, 1917-19. Mem. Nat. Assn. Marketing Ofcls., Nat. Conf. Weights and Measures. Mich. Assn. Weights and Measures Ofcls. Home: Ithaca, Mich. †

NELSON, P. MABEL, home economist, prof.; b. Brookston, Ind., Nov. 9, 1887; d. Robert Jackson and Rebecca Pheriba (Benjamin) Nelson; diploma Santa Barbara (Calif.) State Normal Sch. of Manual Arts and Home Economics, 1912; B.S., Univ. of Calif. at Berkeley, 1915, A.M. cum laude, 1916; Ph.D., Yale (Currier Fellow, 1919-20), 1923; unmarried. Teacher, La Paloma Sch., Riverside Co., Calif., 1907-09; teacher home economics in city schs., Riverside, Calif., 1912-14; instr., home economics, Santa Barbara State Normal Sch. of Manual Arts and Home Economics, 1916-19; asst. physiol. chemistry, Yale, 1920-23; instr. home economics, Univ. of Calif. summer session, 1922; asso. prof. foods and nutrition dept., Ia. State Coll., Ames, 1923-24, acting head, 1925, head dept. foods and nutrition, 1926-44, dean div. of home economics from 1944. Chmn. Ia. State Nutrition Com., 1941-44; chmn. N. Central States Cooperative project studying the nutritional status of coll. women, 1935-47; adviser, div. of home-making and nutrition, Am. Home Dept., Ia. Fedn. Women's Clubs from 1942. Mem. Am. Chem. Soc., Am. Home Economics Assn., Am. Inst. Nutrition, Am. Dietetic Assn., Land Grant Coll. Assn., Alpha Nu, Omicron Nu, Phi Upsilon Omicron, Iota Sigma Pi, Sigma Delta Epsilon, Mortar Board. Republican. Author: Food Preparation, Principles and Procedures (with Elizabeth Sutherland), 1947. Contbr. articles on nutrition topics to various food and nutrition pubs. Home: Ames, Iowa. †

NELSON, RICHARD DOUGLAS, insurance company executive; b. N.Y.C., Feb. 23, 1906; s. George F. and Clara E. (Feindell) N.; M.E., Stevens Inst. Tech., 1927; m. Helen Stratford, Apr. 18, 1932; children—Helen Stratford (Mrs. Paul Bosland), Susan Lockwood (Mrs. William Marshall). Vice pres. Equitable Securities Corp., N.Y.C., 1937-52; v.p., treas. Colonial Life Ins. Co. Am., 1952-58, executive v.p., treas., 1958-59, exec. v.p., sec., 1959-62, pres., 1962-70, also dir.; dir. Motor Finance Co., Suburban Trust Co. Westfield, N.J. Fidelity Union Trust Co., Fed. Ins. Co., Vigilant Ins. Co. Chmn. finance com. N.J. Council Econ. Edn., 1955-56, mem. finance and exec. com., 1956-59, bd. dirs., 1957-59; chmn. Millburn-Short Hills chpt. A.R.C., 1956; exec. v.p. United Cerebral Palsy Essex County, 1958. Mem. adv. com. St. Barnabas Med. Center, Livingston, N.J., 1958-84; pres. trustees Beard Sch., Orange, N.J., 1958-59. Mem. Am. Life Conv. (chmn. investment problems com. 1956-58), Life Ins. Assn. Am., Life Insurers Conf. (exec. com. 1964-67), Soc. War 1812 (pres. N.J. 1946-47). Society Colonial Wars (gov. N.J. 1964-66), Pilgrims U.S., Delta Tau Delta. Clubs: Short Hills; Downtown Assn. (N.Y.C.). Home: Short Hills, N.J. Died Aug. 26, 1984.

NELSON, VICTOR EMANUEL, cons. chemist; b. Eau Claire, Wis., Jan. 21, 1888; s. Peter and Christina (Johnson) N.; B.S., U. of Wis., 1912, M.S., 1914; m. Katherine Diantha Johnson, June 16, 1917 (dec.). Asst. in chemistry, U. of Wis. 1912-13, instr. 1914-17; asso. in chemistry, Johns Hopkins, 1917-19; asst. professor chemistry, Iowa State College, 1919-20, associate prof. 1920-23, prof., 1923-44. Fellow A.A.A.S.; mem. Am. Chem. Soc., Soc. Biol. Chemists, Soc. Exptl. Biology and Medicine, Sigma Xi, Phi Kappa Phi, Phi Lambda Upsilon, Gamma Sigma Delta, Alpha Chi Sigma fraternities. Contributor to Journal of Biological Chemistry, Am. Journal Physiology, Jour. Am. Chem. Soc. Engaged in chem. research.†

NELSON, WILLIAM CLARENCE, clergyman; b. Chgo., Mar. 12, 1906; A.B., Lakeland Coll., 1931, D.D., 1954: B.D., Mission House Sem., 1935; S.T.M., Oberlin Grad. Sch, Theology, 1943; m. Lotta Hegnauer, July 5, 1935; children—William Leonard, Donald Robert. Ordained to ministry Evang. and Reformed Ch., 1935; minister St. John's Evang. and Ref. Ch., Glenmont, Ohio, 1935-37, Immanuel Evang. and Ref. Ch., Indpls., 1937-44, Trinity United Ch. of Christ, Akron, Ohio, 1943-68, Eastern Ohio Assn. United Ch. of Christ, 1968-71. Mem. long-range planning com. United Ch. Christ, mem. racial justice now com., 1963-65; mem. prudential com. Am. Bd. Commrs. Fgn. Missions; mem. World Service Commn., 1945-47; mem. Bd. Internat. Missions, 1948-61, pres. bd., 1959; pres. Bd. for World Ministries, 1961-67. Dir. Ministers Life and Casualty Union, 1962-81. Trustee Lakeland Coll., 1950-59. Recipient award Freedom Found., 1958, 59. Mem. United World Federalists, Internat. Torch. Mason, Kiwanian. Author hymns; New hymnal editor United Ch. Christ. Home: Cuyahoga Falls, Ohio. Died Oct. 16, 1981.

NELSON, WILLIAM LINTON, mutual fund executive; b. Phila., Jan. 20, 1900; s. William Robert and Ella Blanche (Johnson) N.; m. Grace Mehorter Solly, Feb. 8, 1934. Grad., U. Pa., 1926; LL.D. (hon.), Washington and Jefferson Coll., 1975. Employee Fidelity Phila. Trust Co., 1922-29; officer, dir. Investment Corp. of Phila., 1929-41; organizer Delaware Fund, Inc., 1938, dir., 1938-84, pres., 1942, 46-71, chmn. bd., 1963-77; mng. partner investment firm of Delaware Co., Phila., 1946-83; chmn. bd. Decatur Income Fund, 1963-77, Delta Trend Fund, 1967-71, Delchester Bond Fund, 1970-77; chmn. bd. DMC Tax-Free Income Trust-Pa., 1976-77, trustee, 1977-84; chmn. bd. Del. Mgmt. Co., 1952-57, 63-84, Del. Treasury Res., 1983-84; dir. Delaware Cash Res., 1978-84; dir. Del. Investment Advisers, 1972-76, chmn. bd., 1972-75; dir. operations Office Fgn. Liquidation, State Dept., 1945-46; dir. Decature Income Fund, Delta Trend Fund, Delchester Bond Fund, DMC Tax-Free Money Fund. Trustee Valley Forge Mil. Acad. and Jr. Coll. Served in World War I, World War II; advanced to rear adm. USNR. Decorated Legion Merit, Bronze Star, Commendation ribbon. Mem. Investment Co. Inst. (gov. 1958-63, 65-67, 69-72), Securities Industry Assn., Def. Orientation Conf. Assn., Naval Res. Assn., Navy League U.S., Nat. Assn. Security Dealers. Republican. Presbyn. Clubs: Racquet (Phila.), Philadelphia Country (Phila.), Union League (Phila.), Undine Barge (Phila.); Analysts (N.Y.C.). Mem. U.S. Nat. Championship Quadruple Sculls, 1921, Doubles Crew, 1924-26; winner Canadian Assn. Single Rowing Championship, 1926. Home: Gladwyne, Pa. Died Feb. 1984.

NEPRUD, CARL, govt. official, consultant Far Eastern Affairs; b. Coon Valley, Wis., Dec. 24, 1889; s. Carl N(elson) and Anna Karina (Bothne) N.; A.B., Univ. of Wis., 1912, A.M., 1927; student Am. Univ. (fellowship in internat. law and lecturer on world politics) Washington, D.C., 1927-28; student Chinese Lang. Sch., Mukden (Manchuria), 1914-15; m. Josephine Ladner Hutchison, June 28, 1923; children—Anne Caroline, Margaret Gordon, Elizabeth Bothne. Mem. U.S. Geol. Survey Party, Western Wyo., 1911-13; with customs service of Chinese Govt., 1914-47; asst. to commr. at Shanghai, 1914, Yochow, 1915, Chungking, 1915-18, Shanghai, 1918-23, Harbin Dist., N. Manchuria, 1923-26; appraising commr. Shanghai and mem. Tariff Bd. of Enquiry and Appeal, 1929-33; commr. of customs, Peiping and vice pres. of Customs Coll., 1934-35; commr. Pakhoi dist., S. China, 1935-36; tariff sec. of Inspectorate of Customs and mem. Tariff Bd., 1938-39, commr. on spl. duty with Minister of Finance, Chungking, 1939-45, exec. commr. of customs, Shanghai, 1945-46, also in charge of Wharf and Warehouse Control Office (set up for supervising ex-Japanese wharf properties and for checking and disposing of ex-enemy goods in all Shanghai warehouses on behalf of Chinese Govt's. Alien Property Adminstrn.); tech. consultant with Chinese del., Bretton Woods Monetary and Financial Conf., 1944; consultant United States War and Navy Depts., 1944-45; hon. advisor U.N.R.R.A. Office Supplies, Washington, D.C., 1944-45, China office, 1946; lecturer extension service U.S. Dept. Agr., 1943, extension service Univ. of Wis., 1943, 46, vis. prof. Calif. Colls. in China Foundation, 1947; apptd. to E.C.A. Mission to Austria, Oct. 1951. On mission with mems. Peiping Polit. Council to Inner Mongolia, 1935; mem. spl. financial com. to devise measures for safeguarding China's fgn. exchange, 1938; with Minister of Communications on inspection tour of Burma Rd. and on visit to Siam, Indo-China, May 1939; studied factors relating to possible direct air service between China and India on visit northeastern India (Upper Assam), spring 1941; mem. commn. to study problems along Burma Rd., summer 1941; spl. duty in Washington, 1940-41. Caught in Hongkong on Japan's attack, served with Am. Volunteer Unit handling transportation for Colony's Med. Dept., repatriated on 1st Gripsholm. Far Eastern Trade consultant, Boston Conf. on Distribn. Clubs: American University (pres. 1932), American Rowing (Shanghai); Rotary, Peiping, Peiping Golf (Peiping); Peking, Columbia Country, Hungjao Golf. Home: Coon Valley, Wis. †

NESS, ORDEAN GERHARD, speech communications educator; b. Buxton, N.D., Oct. 4, 1921; s. Ole Thomas and Gerda (Johnson) N. B.A. with highest honors, U. N.D., 1942; M.A., U. Wis., 1947, Ph.D. (fellow), 1953. Instr. Syracuse U., 1947-49; cons., personnel policies officer Office of Sec. of Army, 1950-52; asst. prof. Pa. State U., 1953-55; asst. prof. U. Wis., Madison, 1955-59, assoc. prof., 1959-61, prof. communication arts, 1961-82, assoc. chmn. dept. speech, 1961-70, assoc. dir. articulated instrnl. media program, 1964-66, prof. theatre and drama, 1973-80, chmn. dept., 1973-75, chmn. dept. communication arts, 1975-80, prof. dept. comparative lit., 1978-80, chmn. faculty div. humanities, 1976-77; mem. U. Wis. System Adv. Task Force on Telecommunications; free-lance stage, TV and radio actor-dir.; patron Madison Civic Repertory Theatre, Madison Community Access Center; acad. program cons. Author: (with A.T. Weaver) The Fundamentals and Forms of Speech, 1957, 63, An Introduction to Public Speaking, 1961; Deptl. editor: (with A.T. Weaver) Speech Tchr, 1955-63; Contbr. (with A.T. Weaver) articles to profl. jours. Served to 1st lt. U.S. Army, 1942-46; capt. 1950-52. Mem. Speech Communication Assn., Nat. Collegiate Players, Nat. Assn. Ednl. Broadcasters, Broadcasting Edn. Assn., AAUP, Am. Council for Arts, Am. Film Inst., Central States Speech Assn., Wis. Hist. Soc., Wis. Acad. Scis., Letters and Arts, Am., Wis. theatre assns., Wis. Communication Assn. (A.T. Weaver Outstanding Communication Tchr. award 1981), Consortium for Arts, Wis. Council for Arts, U. Wis., U. N.D. alumni assns., Bascom Hill Soc., Nature Conservancy, Center for Study of Dem. Instns., Friends of Channel 21, Wis. Public Radio Assn., Wis. Assn. for Alcohol and Other Drug Abuse, Phi Beta Kappa, Delta Sigma Rho, Blue Key, Phi Eta Sigma, Phi Beta (hon. patron). Home: Madison, Wis. Died July 7, 1982.

NETTELS, CURTIS PUTNAM, educator, historian; b. Topeka, Aug. 25, 1898; s. Charles Henry and Nannie Nesmith (Curtis) N.; m. Elsie Patterson, Dec. 21, 1923; 1 dau., Elsa. Asst. A.B., U. Kans., 1921; A.M., U. Wis., 1922, Ph.D., 1925. Instr. history U. Wis., 1921-22, univ. fellow, 1922-23, Pres. Adams fellow, 1923-24, instr. history, 1924-26, asst. prof., 1926-31, asso. prof., 1931-33, prof., 1933-44, chmn. dept., 1939-40; prof. Am. history

Cornell U., 1944-66, prof. emeritus, from 1966; lectr. Harvard U., 1937-38, Columbia U., 1938, Johns Hopkins U., 1941. Author: The Money Supply of the American Colonies, 1973, The Roots of American Civilization, 1963, George Washington and American Independence; hist. book club selection, 1977, The Emergence of a National Economy, 1775-1815, 1977; contbr. to numerous anthologies.; Editorial bd.: A History of American Economic Life (8 vols.), 1945-62, Jour. Econ. History, 1941-46, Am. Hist. Rev, 1943-49, William and Mary Quarterly, 1943-46, Presidential Studies Quarterly, from 1977; Contbr. to hist jours. Guggenheim Meml. Found. fellow, 1928; Social Sci. Research Council grantee, 1933. Mem. Am. Hist. Assn. (nominating com. 1939-40, chmn. program com. 1941), Miss. Valley Hist. Assn., Colonial Soc. Mass., Mass. Hist. Soc., Phi Beta Kappa, Beta Theta Pi. Unitarian.

NETZER, DONALD LEO, educator; b. Lena, Wis., Oct. 18, 1914; s. Henry Nathan and Julia Mary (Niquette) N.; Ph.B., U. Wis., 1942; M.A., U. Ill., 1946, Ph.D., 1952; m. Bernadette Brazeau, Sept. 10, 1949; children—Donald, Henry, John, Mary, Philip, Julia. Mem. faculty Atlanta div. U. Ga., 1951-55, St. Cloud State Coll., 1956-63; asso. prof. geography Wis. State U., Oshkosh, 1963-80. Active Twin Lakes council Boy Scouts Am., 1963-71. Named Wis. Conservation Educator of Yr., Nat. Wildlife Fedn., 1976. Mem. Nat. Council Geog. Edn., Assn. Am. Geographers, Sigma Xi. K.C. Clubs: Optimist, Conservation (Oshkosh). Home: Oshkosh, Wis. Died Sept. 2, 1980; interred Oshkosh, Wis.

NEUBERGER, KATHERINE (MRS. HARRY H. NEUBERBER), civic worker; b. N.Y.C., Apr. 30, 1907; d. Samuel and Elsie (Wallach) Kridel; m. Harry H. Neuberger, Mar. 7, 1929; children—Susan (Mrs. Donald M. Wilson), Joan (Mrs. Henry M. Woodhouse). B.A., Barnard Coll., 1927; postgrad., Columbia, 1932-33; LL.D. (hon.), Montclair State Coll., 1972, Monmouth Coll., 1973, Fairleigh Dickinson U., 1979; D.H.L. (hon.), Jersey City State Coll., 1978, Rutgers U., 1979. Mem., v.p. bd. mgrs. N.J. Reformatory for Women, 1940-57; mem. N.J. Law Enforcement Council, 1952-57, chmn., 1954-57; mem. bd. Monmouth County Orgn. Social Service, 1937-59, Family Service Soc. Monmouth County, 1959—; chmn. Home Service Corps, Monmouth County chpt. A.R.C., 1940-46; mem. bd. Assn. Aid Crippled Children, 1949-77; mem. N.J. Bd. Higher Edn., from 1970, vice chmn., 1972-75, chmn., 1975-78. Pres. N.J. Fedn. Republican Women, 1957-61; mem. exec. bd. Nat. Fedn., 1959-61; mem. Rep. Nat. Com. for N.J., 1961-76; Trustee Monclair State Coll., 1967-70, Fairleigh Dickinson U., 1973-74; warden Christ Episcopal Ch., Middletown, N.J., 1975-81. Mem. AAUW. Episcopalian. Clubs: Cosmopolitan (N.Y.C.); Navesink Country (N.J.); Woods Hole Golf (Mass.), Quissett Yacht (Mass.). Home: Lincroft, N.J. Died Oct. 15, 1982.

NEUDOERFER, JOHN L., steel exec.; b. Portsmouth, O., May 22, 1887; ed. pub. schs., Ohio; m. Mary Varner, Sept.10, 1919; children—Jane, Katherine. With Wheeling (W.Va.) Steel Corp., 1907-61, pres., 1950-58, chairman of the board, 1958-61; past president and director Wheeling Corrugating Co., from 1946, chmn.; v.p., dir. Consumers Mining Co.; dir. Ackerman Mfg. Company, Harmar Coal Company, Security Trust Co., Butler Bros., Consumers Ore Co., Douglas Mining Co., Hanna Ore Mining Co., Iron Ore Co. of Can., Mesaba Cliffs Mining Co. Clubs: Union (Cleve.); Duquesne (Pitts.); Ft. Henry, Wheeling Country (Wheeling, W. Va.). Home: Wheeling, W. Va. †

NEUMAN, LESTER, pathologist; b. Washington, D.C., Oct. 24, 1888; s. Isaac and Ella (Oppenheimer) N.; B.S., Georgetown U., 1915; M.D., 1913; grad. study U. of Vienna; m. Janet Nusbaum, Feb. 22, 1918; children—Robert Ballin, Alice. Began practice at Washington, 1915, specializing in clin. pathology and internal medicine; consultant in pathology Emergency Hosp., Glenn Dale Sanitarium, Doctor's Hospital; formerly asso. prof. of pathology, Med. Sch., Georgetown U. Served as 1st lt. Med. Corps, U.S. Army, World War I. Diplomate Am. Bd. Pathology. Fellow Am. Coll. Phys., A.M.A.; founding fellow Coll. Am. Pathologists emeritus; member Am. Soc. for Study Neoplastic Diseases, Am. Soc. Clin. Pathologists. Hebrew religion. Club: Woodmont Country. Home: Washington, D.C. †

NEUMANN, ALFRED ROBERT, univ. chancellor; b. Frankfurt am Main, Germany, Jan. 26, 1921; came to U.S., 1937, naturalized, 1943; s. Bernhard and Jenny (Heidenheimer) N.; m. Selma Smith, Sept. 5, 1944; children—Bernard Stephen, Carolyn Joyce. A.B., Marshall Coll., 1940; M.A., U. Ky., 1941; A.M., Harvard U., 1948; Ph.D., U. Mich., 1951; LL.D., Marshall U., 1964. Tchr. Latin and French, condr. orch. Beall High Sch., Frostburg, Md., 1941-42; instr. German and French Tulane U., 1946; teaching fellow German Harvard, 1946-48; instr. German U. Mich., 1948-52; asst. prof. U. Houston, 1953-56, assoc. prof. German, 1956-61, prof., from 1961, asst. to v.p. acad. affairs, 1956, asst. to pres., 1957-59; dean U. Houston (Coll. Arts and Scis.), 1958-72; chancellor U. Houston (U. Houston/Clear Lake City), from 1972, then chancellor emeritus; mem. Commn. Leadership Tng. Am. Council Edn., 1976-78, Commn. on Acad. Affairs, 1980-81; mem. nat. adv. council Council on Learning; presented coll. courses in German KUHT-TV, Houston, 1954-55; program annotator Houston Symphony Orch., 1958-75, chmn. search com. for mus. dir., 1978; program annotator Houston Grand Opera Assn.; cons. on accreditation SACS.; Examiner Coll. Entrance Exam. Bd., 1962-65. Mem. editorial bd.: Forum mag, 1956-59. Bibliographer: Literature and Other Arts Sect, M.L.A. Compiler: Literature and the Other Arts: A Select Bibliography, 1952-58, New York Pub. Library, 1959. Assoc. TV editor: German Quar. Contbr. numerous articles to learned and popular jours. Pres. Houston Jewish Family Service, 1969-70, So. Humanities Conf., 1969-70; vice chmn. Houston Municipal Art Commn., 1972. Decorated Order Merit 1st class, Comdr.'s Cross W. Ger.). Mem. Houston Contemporary Music Soc. (pres. 1962-63), Am. Council Learned Socs. (scholar 1952-53, past regional asso.), Houston Grand Opera Assn. (dir. 1956-67), Houston Friends of Music (pres.), Modern Lang. Assn. (chmn. commn. on trends in edn. 1968-71), Houston Council Fgn. Lang. Tchrs. (pres. 1967-68), Am. Assn. State Colls. and Univs. (chmn. com. internat. programs, chmn. com. upper-level instns.), Am. Assn. Tchrs. German, Stillwater Conf. Acad. Deans (chmn. 1965), South Central Modern Lang. Assn. (pres. 1965-66), Conf. Acad. Deans So. States (chmn. 1966-67), Clear Lake C. of C. (dir.). Club: Rotarian. Home: Seabrook, Tex. Died May 23, 1983.

NEVINS, ALLAN, educator, author; b. Camp Point, Ill., May 20, 1890; s. Joseph Allan and Emma (Stahl) N.; A.B., U. of Ill., 1912, A.M., 1913; Litt. D., Union, 1935, Dartmouth, 1936; LL.D., Washington and Lee Univ., 1935, Miami U., 1937; Litt.D., Oxford, 1965; Litt.D., Trinity Coll., 1948, University of Illinois 1953, Lincoln Coll., Gettysburg College, Lehigh University, Grinnell College, Columbia, 1960, Loyola U., 1961, U. of So. Cal., U. Cal., 1963, Oxford U., 1965; L.H.D., Ill. Coll., 1953; LL.D., Dartmouth College, 1958, Occidental Coll., 1967, L.I. University, 1968; married Mary Fleming Richardson, daughter of Anna Steese Richardson, December 30, 1916; children—Anne Elizabeth, Meredith. Instructor English, U. of Ill., 1912-13; editorial writer New York Evening Post, 1913-23; editorial writer the Nation, 1913-18; lit. editor New York Sun, 1924-25; editorial staff New York World, 1925-27; prof. American history, Cornell U., 1927-28; asso. in history, Columbia, and mem. editorial staff New York World, 1928-31; prof. Am. history, Columbia, 1931-58, senior research associate at the Huntington Library, San Marino, California, from 1958; Sir George Watson chair of American history, literature, and instns. in Great Britain, 1934-35; visiting prof. Calif. Inst. Tech., 1937-38; visiting scholar Huntington Library, 1937; Harmsworth prof., Oxford U., 1940-41, 64-65; spl. rep. Office War Information in Australia and New Zealand, 1943-44; chief public affairs officer, Am. embassy, London; 1945-46; visiting prof. Hebrew U. of Jerusalem, 1952. Trustee Woodrow Wilson Internat. Center for Scholars, at the Smithsonian Institution, from 1969. Member of American Hist. Assn. (past pres.), Am. Acad. Arts and Letters (pres. 1966-68), Council on Foreign Relations; hon. fellow New York State Hist. Assn.; corr. member Mass. Hist. Soc.; past pres. Soc. of Am. Historians; member N.Y. Hist. Soc. Presbyn. Clubs: Lotos, Century, (N.Y.C.); National Press (Washington); Atheneum (London). Author or co-author, from 1914; latest publs.: The Emergence of Lincoln, 2 vols., 1952; Statesmanship of the Civil War, 1953; Study in Power, 1953; Ford: the times, the man, the company (with Frank E. Hill), 1954, 2d vol., 1957, 3d vol., 1963; The War for the Union, 2 volumes, 1959, 2 vols., 1961; Herbert H. Lehman and His Era, 1963. Editor books, from 1927; latest: Diary of George Templeton Strong. Pub. in 1952; Leatherstocking Saga (James Fenimore Cooper), 1954; James Truslow Adams: Historian of the American Dream, 1968. Gen. editor of Am. Polit. Leaders series; Yale Press Chronicles of America, new series, D.C. Heath Colleges and University History series. Recipient Pulitzer prize for biography, 1932, 1937. Scribner Centenary prize and Bancroft prize, 1947, Gold Medal for history and biography Nat. Inst. Arts and Letters, 1957; Gold medal, N.Y. Hist. Soc., 1958, Commonwealth Club of Cal., 1960, Rice U., 1962; Golden Plate award Am. Acad. Achievement, 1966; Alexander Hamilton award, Columbia U., 1968. Address: San Marino, Cal. †

NEW, JOHN GABRIEL, educator; b. N.Y.C., Jan. 16, 1927; s. Gabriel B. and Margaret (Warshauer) N.; m. Helen Elizabeth Sharp, Dec. 22, 1950; children—Lois Ann, Nancy Alice, Kenneth Edward, Christopher John. B.S., Cornell U., 1950, M.S., 1951, Ph.D., 1956. High sch. biology tchr., 1951-53; mem. faculty State U. N.Y. at Oneonta, from 1956, prof. vertebrate ecology, from 1960. Author papers in field. Chmn. Oneonta Environ. Adv. Bd., active numerous local, state and nat. environ. orgns. Mem. AAAS, Am. Inst. Biol. Sci., Am. Ornithologists Union, Am. Soc. Ichthydogists and Herpetologists, Am. Soc. Mammalogists, Wildlife Soc., Sierra Club, Sigma Xi. Home: Oneonta, NY.

NEWBY, LEE C(LINTON), educator; b. Holyoke, Colo., Aug. 8, 1890; s. William J. and Clara (Glover) N.; B.S., U. of Calif., 1910, M.S., 1911; student U. of Geneva, Switzerland, 1915-16; traveled and studied in France, Italy, Germany, Mexico, Spain, 1927, 29, 31, 38; m. Olga W. Foyle, Aug. 26, 1918; 1 son, William Robert. Teacher math. and German, Gilroy (Calif.) High Sch., 1911; prin. Denair High Sch., 1912-14; supervisor modern langs., Univ. High Sch., Oakland, 1917; head modern lang. dept., San Jose (Calif.) State Coll. from 1923; exchange prof., U. of Hawaii, 1940-41. Mem. Spanish Honor Soc., Sigma Delta Phi. Home: Los Gatos, Calif. †

NEWCOMB, MACDONALD GRAY, retired exec.; b. Hilton, N.Y., Apr. 5, 1889; s. Z. Wm. J. and Addie (Judd) N.; A.B., U. Rochester, 1911; m. Carrie Fraser, Dec. 27, 1911; children—Jean Fraser (dec.), Eloise (Mrs. Robert T. Ley). Prin. Greigsville (N.Y.) High Sch., 1911-14; cashier State Bank Hilton, 1914-24, pres., 1924-29; v.p. Fed. Land Bank Springfield, 1929-44, pres. 1944-47; former fiscal agt. for 12 Fed. Land Banks and 12 Fed. Intermediate Credit Banks, serving the 48 states, P.R., Alaska, and Hawaii, retiring as fiscal agent, Jan. 1955; pres. Hilton Milling and Warehouse Co., Inc., 1924-65; trustee Springfield Five Cents Savs. Bank 1942-49. Trustee Am. Internat. Coll., 1944-50, Wesson Meml. Hosp., 1946-49; bd. dirs. Springfield A.R.C., 1945-47. Mem. U. Rochester Alumni Assn. (v.p. 1947, pres. 1948), Newcomen Soc., Delta Upsilon. Republican. Baptist. Club: University (Rochester). Home: Rochester, NY. †

NEWCOMER, FRANCIS KOSIER, army officer; born Bryon, Ill., Sept. 14, 1889; s. Henry Clay and Rebecca (Kosier) N.; B.S., U.S. Mil. Acad., 1913; grad. U.S. Engr. Sch., Washington, D.C., 1916, Command and Gen. Staff Sch., 1935, Army War Coll., 1940; m. Mary Brunot Roberts, June 17, 1914; children—Rebecca, Francis K., Thomas Roberts. Commd. 2d lt., Corps of Engrs., U.S. Army, 1913, advancing through the grades to brig. gen., 1944; asst. comdt. Engr. Sch., A.E.F., France, 1918-19; asso. prof. mathematics U.S. Mil. Acad., 1919-24; U.S. Dist. engr., Charleston, S.C., 1924-25; U.S. dist. engr. and Corps Area engr., Boston, Mass., 1926-27; instr. U.S. Engr. Sch., Fort Belvoir, Va., 1927-28; asst. chief engr. Fed. Power Commn., 1928-31; in charge contract and finance sect. Office Chief of Engrs., U.S. Army, 1935-39; asst. to pres. Miss. River Commn., 1940-41; engr., 3rd U.S. Army, 1942; chief engr. China-Burma-India Theatre of Operations, 1943-44; engr. of maintenance, Panama Canal, and 2d vice pres. Panama Canal R.R. Co., 1944-48, gov. Panama Canal, pres. Panama R.R. Co. from 1948. Decorated Distinguished Service Cross, Victory, Army of Occupation in Germany, Asiatic and Am. Theatre medals. Mem. Soc. Am. Mil. Engrs. Club: Army-Navy Country (Washington). Home: Balboa Heights, Canal Zone.†

NEWELL, FRANK S., publisher; b. Leadville, Colo., July 19, 1887; s. Ira E. and Jennie (Cone) N.; ed. pub. schs. Maysville, Ky.; m. Josie Killpatrick, June 14, 1909 (dec.); children—Helen (Mrs. Arlyn O. Wagner), Frances (Mrs. Horace Mackey); m. 2d, Margaret Montgomery, Nov. 16, 1952. Circulation dir., Toledo (O.) Blade, 1926-43, bus. mgr., 1940-44, v.p., 1940-44, mem. bd. dirs., 1930-44; pub. State Jour., Frankfort, Ky., 1944-50; general mgr. Perry Pub. Co., Frankfort, 1944-50. Past mem. bd. dirs. Audit Bur. of Circulations. Chmn. State of Ky. Save the Children Assn., Army Bd., Frankfort. Mem. Internat. Circulation Mgrs. Assn. (pres. 1935), Safety Council (pres. 1938-44), Salvation Army Bd. (pres. 1940-44), Toledo, O. Presbyterian. Clubs: Automobile (Toledo) (pres. 1943-44); Country (Frankfort, Ky.). Mason (Scottish Rite). Home: Versailles, Ky. †

NEWELL, HOMER EDWARD, physicist, mathematician; b. Holyoke, Mass., Mar. 11, 1915; s. Homer Edward and Annie Abigail (Davis) N.; A.B., Harvard, 1936, postgrad. 1936-37; Ph.D., U. Wis. 1940; D.Sc., Central Methodist Coll., 1963; m. Janice May Hurd, Feb. 12, 1938; children—Judith Deborah, Sue Ellen, Jennifer Dianne, Andrew David. Grad. asst. math. U. Wis., 1937-40; from instr. to asst. prof. math. U. Md., 1940-44; with Naval Research Lab., 1944-58, successively theoretical physicist, mathematician, sect. head, br. head, br. head Rocket-Sonde Research Br., acting supt. atmosphere and astrophysics div., sci. program coordinator for Project Vanguard; asst. dir. space scis. NASA, 1958-60, dep. dir. space flight programs, 1960-61, dir. Office Space Scis., 1961-63, asso. adminstr. for space sci. and applications, 1963-67, asso. adminstr., 1967-74; free-lance writer; rep., tchr.-lectr. U. Md., 1952-55; lectr. Nat. Park Coll., 1962. Mem. com. magnetosphere Internat. Union Radio Sci.; bd. advisers Missile, Space and Range Pioneers, Inc. Recipient Pendray award Am. Rocket Soc., 1958; Space Flight award Am. Astronaut Soc., 1960; Civil Servant of Yr. award Amvets, 1961; Career Service award Nat. Civil Service League, 1965; President's award for distinguished federal civilian service, 1965; Distinguished Service award NASA, 1967. Fellow A.A.A.S., Am. Inst. Aeros. and Astronautics, Am. Geophys. Union (v.p. 1968-70, pres. 1970-72); mem. Internat. Acad. Astronautics, Internat. Astronautical Fedn., Phi Beta Kappa, Sigma Xi, Sigma Pi Sigma. Author books, including: High Altitude Rocket Research, 1953; Vector Analysis, 1955; Space Book for Young People, 1958; Guide to Rockets, Missiles, and Satellites, 1958; Sounding Rockets, 1959; Window in the Sky, 1959; Express to the Stars, 1961; also articles for trade mags., reviews. Editorial bd. Space Sci. Revs. Home: Washington, D.C. Died July 18, 1983

NEWINS, H(AROLD) S(TEPHENSON), univ. prof.; b. Patchogue, N.Y., Nov. 30, 1887; s. Hiram DeWitt and Geraldine (Stephenson) N.; Ph.B., Lafayette Coll., 1909; M.F., Yale, 1911; m. Ella Helene Schmidt, June 23, 1915; children—Grace R. (Mrs. Ben O. Franklin), Harold Stephenson. Student aid, reconnaissance party, U.S. Forest Service, Aspen, Colo., summer, 1910, forest guard and asst. forest ranger, Albany, Ore., summers 1911-14; instr., prof. forestry, Ore. Agr. Coll., 1911-22; dry kiln engr., N.W. Blower Kiln Co., Seattle, Wash., summer, 1920; dry kiln salesman, Cutler Desk Co., Buffalo, N.Y., 1922-24; prof. wood utilization, Pa. State Coll., 1924-29; dir., Yale Forestry Sch. summer camp, Milford, Pa., 1926; state forester, W.Va., 1929-31; asso. prof. forestry, Mich. State Coll., 1931-35; prof. and dir., Sch. of Forestry, Univ. of Fla., from 1935; coordinating field ofcl., Mich. Emergency Conservation Work, 1933; airplane engr., Bur. Aircraft Prodn. and U.S. Air Service, 1918-19. Fellow A.A.A.S.; mem. Soc. Am. Foresters (chmn. memorial com. 1937-38, S.E. sect. 1937-38; sec.-treas. S.E. sect. 1946), Forest Products Research Soc. (sec.-treas. Fla., Ala., Ga. sect.), Am. Forestry Assn., Fla. Forest and Park Assn. (sec.-treas., 1942-46), Fla. Acad. of Sci., Am. Wood Preservers Assn., So. Shade Tree Conf. (sec.-treas. 1937-47, pres. 1947-48), Am. Assn. Univ. Profs., Nat. Shade Tree Conference, Florida Edn. Assn., Fla. Audubon Soc. (pres. 1947-49), Xi Sigma Pi, Phi Gamma Delta, Phi Sigma. Presbyterian. Mason. Clubs: Rotary International, Athenaeum. Home: Gainesville, Fla. Deceased.

NEWLIN, ALBERT CHAUNCEY, lawyer; b. Cin., Aug. 8, 1905; s. Edgar Christian and Elizabeth (Berwanger) N.; m. Janet Bethell, Oct. 19, 1929 (dec.); children—George Christian, John Bethell, Carl Albert; m. Mary Carson Bass Gibson, Aug. 23, 1976. A.B., Centre Coll., Danville, Ky., 1925, LL.D., 1958; LL.B., Columbia U., 1928; D.Sc., Fla. Inst. Tech., Melbourne. Bar: N.Y. bar 1928. Since practiced in, N.Y.C.; with White & Case, 1928-77, mem. firm, 1937-77, ret., 1977; dir. Tolten Corp., N.Y.C. Mem. bd. edn., Scarsdale, N.Y., 1947-52, pres., 1949-50; Pres., dir. Marshall H. and Nellie Alworth Meml. Fund, Duluth, Minn.; v.p., dir. Jessie Smith Noyes Found., Inc., Henry L. and Grace Doherty Charitable Found., N.Y.C.; bd. dirs. Met. Opera Assn., Guild Hall, East Hampton, N.Y.; trustee Solomon R. Guggenheim Found., N.Y.C.; former chmn. bd., trustee Centre Coll. Mem. Am., N.Y. State bar assns., Assn. Bar City N.Y., N.Y. County Lawyers Assn., Phi Beta Kappa, Sigma Chi, Omicron Delta Kappa. Republican. Episcopalian. Clubs: University (N.Y.C.), Down Town Assn. (N.Y.C.); Maidstone (East Hampton). Home: New York, N.Y. Died Sept. 3, 1983.

NEWLOVE, GEORGE HILLIS, accounting educator; b. Crystal, N.D., Dec. 16, 1893; s. Samuel and Vangie (Hillis) N.; Ph.B., Hamline Univ., St. Paul, 1914; A.M., U. of Minn., 1915; Ph.D., U. of Ill., 1918; C.P.A., State of N.C., 1918; State of Ill., 1919; m. Merle Marie White, Sept. 22, 1918 (divorced 1934); 1 son, Burt Hillis; m. 2d, Frances Beulah Williams, June 30, 1937. Instr. accounting Univ. of Ill., 1916-18; dean Washington (D.C.) School of Accountancy, 1919-23; sr. auditor income tax unit U.S. Department of Treasury, 1921-25; asso. prof. accounting, Johns Hopkins, 1923-28; prof. accounting, U. of Tex., since 1928. Served as lt. (j.g.) U.S. Navy Res. Force, 1918-19, World War I. Member National Association of Accountants, American Accounting Association (president 1933), Beta Alpha Psi (hon.), Beta Gamma Sigma (hon. member). Mem. Methodist Ch. Author: Income and Profit Taxes (with W.Clabaugh), 1920; Cost Accounts (3d edit.), 1923; Specialized Accounting (with L. A. Pratt), 1925; Consolidated Balance Sheets, 1926; Cost Accounting (2d edit.), 1928; C.P.A. Accounting (4th edit.), 1935; Elementary Accounting (with L. C. Haynes and J. A. White), 2d edit., 1941; Intermediate Accounting (with C. A. Smith and J. A. White), 1939, 2d edit. 1948; Consolidated Statements, 1948; Elementary Cost Accounting (with S. P. Garner), 1941, 2d edit. 1949; Accounting for Reorganizations, Bankruptcies, Fiduciaries, and Partnerships (with S. P. Garner), 1950; Accounting for Corporate Capital and Income (with S. P. Garner), 1951; Advanced Accounting Problems (with S. P. Garner), Book I, 1951, Book II, 1950; Advanced Cost Accounting, 1951; Process Costs: Actual Estimated and Standard, 1958. Contbr. to tech. jours. Home: Austin, Tex. Died Oct. 2, 1984.

NEWMAN, ALLEN THURMAN, dentistry; b. Hebron, Nebraska, March 18, 1888; s. A. Harry and Hulda (Binger) N.; Sc.B., U. of Neb., 1912; M.Sc., U. of Minn., 1916, D.D.S., 1921; m. Marie Louise Tuscany, June 1916 (died August 1935); m. 2d, Paula Elizabeth Youngs, January 1939; 1 dau., Paula Louise. Superintendent Dental College, Univ. of Minn., 1921-23; dean Dental Coll., U. of Denver, 1923-29; dean Dental Coll., New York U., 1929-44; private practice oral surgery from 1944. Capt. inf., U.S. Army, 26 mos. World War I; consultant to War Manpower Commn., World War II. Mem. Am. Assn. Dental Schools (pres. 1943-44), Pan Am. Odontological Assn. (pres. 1944-46), Alpha Tau Omega, Alpha Chi Sigma, Omicron Kappa Upsilon. Presbyterian. Club: Explorer's. Home: Larchmont, N.Y. †

NEWMAN, FLOYD ROY, oil co. exec.; b. Casnovia, Mich., Nov. 25, 1890; s. John C. and Hattie A. (Boehm) N.; A.B., Cornell, 1912; m. Helen A. Anderson, Mar. 17, 1949; children—Elizabeth N. (Mrs. Charles M. Wilds), John Ames. Asst. mgr. lubricating oil dept. at Shanghai, Standard Oil Co. of N.Y., 1912-16; asst. sales mgr. Am. Petroleum Products Co., Cleveland, 1916-17, fuel oil sales mgr., 1919-25; co-founder and sec.-treas. Allied Oil Co., Inc., Cleveland, 1925-48, co. merged with Ashland Oil & Refining Co., Inc., 1948, became dir., 1948; dir. Frazier Trucking Co., Cleveland. Trustee Cornell U. from 1951. Served as 1st lt. Shanghai Vol. Corps, 1914-16; 1st lt., Ordnance Corps, U.S. Army, 1917-18; 1st lt., Quartermaster Corps, 1918-19; Served with A.E.F. and the Army of Occupation. Mem. Am. Petroleum Inst., Phi Kappa Tau. Nuclear physics lab. Cornell U., Ithaca, N.Y., namd Floyd Newman Lab. of Nuclear Studies, 1949; member Cornell U. Council since 1950. Home: Medina, OH. †

NEWMAN, ROBERT BRADFORD, acoustical consulting company director, architecture educator; b. Unkung, Kwangtung, China, Nov. 5, 1917; s. Henry Ware and Ethel Marian (Smith) N. (parents Am. citizens); m. Mary Louise Herod, Oct. 18, 1941 (div. 1954); m. Mary Patricia Shaw, June 4, 1955; children: Catherine, Henry, Bradford. B.A., U. Tex., 1938, M.A., 1939; M. Arch., M.I.T., 1949; Sc.D. (hon.), Lawrence Coll., 1963. Partner Bolt Beranek & Newman, Cambridge, Mass., 1949-53, v.p., 1953-82, cons., from 1982; asso. prof. architecture M.I.T., 1949-76, adj. prof., from 1976; vis. lectr. acoustics Harvard U., 1955-71, prof. architecture tech., from 1971, acoustics designer auditoriums and concert halls in, U.S., Can., P.R., Venezuela, Australia, Philippines, Singapore. Contbr. to: Time Saver Standards. Bd. dirs. DeCordova Mus., Lincoln, Mass., 1968-78, pres., 1971-74. Recipient Franklin Inst. Brown medal, 1966. Fellow Acoustical Soc. Am. Episcopalian. Home: Lincoln, Mass.

NEWTON, BERT PERSING, corp. exec.; b. Erie County, O., July 1, 1889; s. William Henry and Catherine (Saunders) N.; C.P.A., Dist. of Columbia and State of Ohio; m. Edna Roe, Nov. 3, 1914. With Cleveland Southwestern & Columbus Ry. Co., 1907-16; accountant B. F. Goodrich Co., 1916-18, Ernst & Ernst, Cleveland, and Washington, 1918-21; mgr. tax dept. Gulf Oil Corp., 1921-24; asst. to pres. Standard Steel Car Co., 1924-28, v.p., comptroller, 1928-30; v.p. Pullman-Standard Car Mfg. Co., 1930-31; v.p. Gulf Refining Co., 1932-49, dir., 1939-49; v.p. Gulf Oil Corp., 1935-47, Standard Car Finance Corp. from 1931; dir. United Petroleum Securities Corp., Belgian Gulf Oil Co.-S.A., Antwerp, Crediervereeniging voor den Handel in Petroleumproducten N.V., Rotterdam, Holland, Danish American Gulf Oil Co. A/S, Copenhagen, Denmark, Kuwait Oil Co. Ltd. (London), Lubricating & Fuel Oils Ltd. (London), Gulf Oil Company A/B (Helsingfors, Finland), Svenska Gulf Oil Company A/B, Stockholm, Sweden, Sociedad Anonima Espanola de Lubriticantes (Barcelona, Spain), Nederlandsche Gulf Olie Maatschappij N.V. (Rotterdam, Holland), N.V. Olie Handelsvereeniging (Oil Trading Assn., Rotterdam, Holland); dir. Companhia Brasileira de Petrolco "Gulf," Rio de Janeiro, Brazil, 1945. Received Order Leopold I, conferred by Leopold III, King of Belgians, 1936, Comendador, Order of Cruzeiro do Sul by Pres. Enrico Gaspar Dutra of Brazilian Republic, 1946; recipient Order of Lion of Finland, grade of comdr., 1946. Republican. Presbyterian. Clubs: Duquesne (Pittsburgh); Bankers of America (New York). Home: Norwalk, Ohio. †

NEWTON, ROBERT, dir. research; b. Montreal, Can., Feb. 7, 1889; s. John and Elizabeth (Brown) N.; B.S.A., McGill U., Montreal, 1912; M.S., U. of Minn., 1921, Ph.D., 1923; D.Sc., U. of Alberta, 1933; student Cambridge U., 1919; LL.D., U. of Saskatchewan, 1948, U. of Alberta, 1950; Sc.D., Cambridge, 1948, Univ. of Manitoba, 1948; m. Emma Florence Read, July 31, 1914. Dist. Agriculturist, MacDonald Coll., Quebec, 1912-13; chief asst. dominion cerealist, 1913-14; dir. agrl. instrn. for New Brunswick, 1914-15; asst. prof. field husbandry, U. of Alberta, 1919-22, prof. plant biochem., 1922-24, head dept. of field crops, 1924-32; acting dir. div. of biology and agr., Nat. Research Council of Can., 1928-32, dir., 1932-40; dean Coll. of Agr., U. of Alberta, 1940-41; acting president University of Alberta, 1941-42, president 1942-50, director of research council from 1950. Trustee National Gallery of Canada. Served as captain, F.A., C.E.F., 1915-19. Awarded Mil. Cross 1917. Fellow Royal Soc. Can., A.A.A.S., Agr. Inst. Can., Canadian Geog. Soc.; mem. Nat. Research Council of Canada, Canadian Inst. Internat. Affairs, Sigma Xi, Phi Lambda Upsilon, Gamma Sigma Delta, Gamma Alpha, Alpha Zeta. Home: Edmonton, Canada. †

NEYMAN, JERZY, statistician; b. Bendery, Russia, Apr. 16, 1894; s. Czeslaw and Kazimiera (Lutoslawska) N.; ed. U. Kharkov (Russia), 1912-16; Ph.D., U. Warsaw (Poland), 1923, D.Sc. (hon.), 1974; postdoctoral study U. London, 1925-26, U. Paris, 1926-27; D.Sc. (hon.), U. Chgo., 1959, Indian Statis. Inst., 1974; LL.D. (hon.), U. Calif., Berkeley, 1963; Ph.D. (hon.), U. Stockholm, 1964; m. Olga Solodovnikova, May 4, 1920; 1 son, Michael John. Came to U.S., 1938. Lectr., Inst. Technology, Kharkov, 1917-21; statistician Inst. Agr., Bydgoszcz, Poland, 1921-23; lectr. Coll. Agr., Warsaw, 1923-24, U. Warsaw, 1928-34; spl. lectr. Univ. Coll., London, 1934-35, reader in statistics, 1935-38; spl. lectr. U. Paris, 1936, U. London, U. Paris, Universite Libre de Bruxelles, U. Warsaw, U. Amsterdam, U. Cambridge, U. Coll. London, U. Stockholm, U. Uppsala, 1950; prof. math. U. Calif., Berkeley, 1938-55, dir. Statis. Lab., 1938-81, prof., dir. statis. lab. emeritus, later recalled to active status; statis. expert U.S. Mission to observe Greek elections, 1946; del. Internat. Statis. Conf., 1947, Internat. Congress Philosophy of Sci., Paris, 1949. Recipient Nat. Sci. medal, 1968. Fellow Royal Statis. Soc., London Math. Soc. (hon.); mem. U.S. Nat., Polish, Royal Swedish acads. scis., Inst. Math. Statistics (pres. 1949), London Math. Soc. Am., French, Polish (hon.) math. socs., Am. Statis. Assn. (v.p. 1947), Inst. Statistics, Biometric Soc., AAAS, Internat. Statis. Inst. (hon. pres. 1972-81), Royal Soc. (fgn.). Author publs. on math. statistics and applications to astronomy, public health, weather modification; editor: Heritage of Copernicus: Theories More Pleasing to the Mind, 1974. Home: Berkeley, Calif. Died Aug. 5, 1981.

NIBECKER, A(LFRED) S(ANFORD), JR., architect; b. Spokane, Wash., June 4, 1890; s. A. S. and Sarah (Yandell) N.; spl. student architecture Mass. Inst. Tech., 1916; m. Mabel E. Everett, June 12, 1917; children—Alfred, Corinne (Mrs. William H. Banker), Robert, Evelyn. Practice of architecture, Los Angeles; architect Los Angeles City Schs., 1926-55, bus. mgr., 1936-55 practice as cons. architect, from 1955. Mem. adv. bd. Div. Architecture, State Cal., mem. archtl. commn. Claremont Colleges. Fellow A.I.A.; hon. mem. Structural Engr. Assn. Cal., Secondary Sch. Adminstrs. Cal. Home: South Pasadena, Cal. †

NICHOLL, DON, TV producer, writer; b. Sunderland, Eng., Aug. 9; s. James Girvan and Evelyn Pyet (Hopper) N.; came to U.S., 1969; ed. in Eng.; m. Gee Dore. Newspaper reporter, 1946; press relations officer J. Arthur Rank Orgn., 1952-55; music columnist London Daily Mail, also music trade papers, 1955-65; script writer, disc jockey BBC Sound Radio, 1964-68; writer feature movies and TV series, Eng., 1956-58; TV producer, writer, U.S., from 1968; TV series include All in The Family, The Jeffersons, The Dumplings, Three's Company. Served with Brit. Army, World War II. Recipient various commendations, nominations. Mem. Writers Guild Am. Author: Record Roundabout, 1955; (libretto) Xmas Carol, 1963; (films) Golden Disc, 1957, Emergency, 1959. Home: Los Angeles, Calif. Died July 5, 1980.

NICHOLS, BEVERLEY, author; b. Bristol, Eng., 1900; s. John and Pauline (Shalders) N.; B.A., Oxford U., 1921. Club: Garrick (London). Author: Prelude, 1920; Patchwork, 1921; Self, 1922; Twenty-Five, 1926; Crazy Pavements, 1927; Are They the Same at Home, 1927; The Star-Spangled Manner, 1928; Women and Children Last, 1931; Evensong, 1932; Down the Garden Path, 1932; For Adults Only, 1932; Failures, 1933; Cry Havoc, 1933; A Thatched Roof, 1933; A Village in a Valley, 1934; The Fool Hath Said, 1936; No Place Like Home, 1936; Revue, 1938; Green Grows the City, 1939; Men Do Not Weep, 1941. Plays: The Stag, 1929; Cochran's 1930 Revue; Avalanche, 1931; Evensong (with Edward Knoblock), 1932; When the Crash Comes, 1933; Dr. Mesmer, 1935; Floodlight, 1937; Song On The Wind, 1948; Shadow of The Vine, 1949. Additional books: Men Do Not Weep, 1942; Verdict on India, 1944; The Tree that Sat Down, 1945; The Stream that Stood Still, 1948; All I Could Never Be, 1949; Uncle Samson, 1950; Mountain of Magic, 1950; Merry Hall, 1951; A Pilgrims Progress, 1952; Laughter on the Stairs, 1953; No Man's Street, 1954; The Moonflower, 1955; Death to Slow Music, 1956; Sunlight on the Lawn, 1956; The Rich Die Hard, 1957; The Sweet and Twenties, 1958; Murder by Request, 1960; The Cats ABC, 1960; The Cats XYZ, 1962; Garden Open Today, 1963; Forth Favourite Flowers, 1964; Powers That Be, 1965; A Case of Human Bondage, 1966; The Art of Flower Arrangement, 1967; Garden Open Tomorrow, 1968. Died 1983.

NICHOLS, FLOYD BRUCE, b. Buffalo, Kan., Sept. 15, 1890; s. Hiram Armstrong and Lucinda (Milliron) N.; B.S. in Agronomy and Journalism, Kan. State Agrl. Coll., 1912; m. Nell Beaubien, June 21, 1917; 1 dau., Mary Elizabeth. Agrl. editor Fruit Grower and Farmer, St. Joseph, Mo., 1912-13; field editor The Capper Farm Press, Topeka, Kan., 1913-16, asso. editor, 1916-18, mng. editor, 1919-32; sec. Rep. Agricultural Committee, Washington, D.C., Nov. 1939-July 1940 (orgn. consisted of 42 Republican Congressmen from 22 states; the Hon. Clifford R. Hope of Kansas, chairman; committee conducted hearings at various points over the nation, from Salt Lake City to Charlotte, N.C., and made a study of the national farm problem). Non-commd. officer A.E.F., in France and Germany, 1918-19. Republican. Presbyterian. Address: Topeka, Kan. †

NICHOLS, FREDERICK ADAMS, newspaper exec.; b. Chgo., June 14, 1907; s. Frederick Adams and Eva (Beebe) N.; student U. Ill., 1925-28; m. Helen Glos, Mar. 3, 1928; 1 dau., Joan (Mrs. John E. Friedlund). With Chgo. Tribune, 1928-77, asst. classified advt. mgr., 1943-52, asst. advt. mgr., 1952-55, asst. to pub., 1955-60, asst. sec. Tribune Co., 1956-60, asst. to pres., 1960-67, exec. v.p., 1967-72, pres., 1972-74; chmn. bd. Gore Newspapers Co.,

Ft. Lauderdale, Fla., 1963-74, Sentinel Star Co., Orlando, Fla., 1965-74. Mem. U. Ill. Found.; mem. citizens bd. U. Chgo. Trustee Ill. Children's Home and Aid Soc., Robert R. McCormick Charitable Trust, Robert R. McCormick Found., Cantigny Trust; bd. dirs. Chgo. council Navy League, Northwestern Meml. Hosp., Western Golf Assn. Presbyn. Clubs: Indian Hill (Winnetka); University, Commercial, Chicago, Tavern, Commonwealth, Economic (Chgo.); Knollwood (Lake Forest, Ill.); Lake Zurich (Ill.) Golf; Old Elm; Bohemian (San Francisco). Home: Winnetka, Ill. Died Dec. 3, 1983.

NICHOLS, JEANNETTE PADDOCK, educator; b. Rochelle, Ill.; d. Hosea Cornish Savery and Janette (Styles) Paddock; A.B., LL.D. (hon.), Knox Coll.; A.M., Ph.D., Columbia; m. Roy F. Nichols, 1920. Instr. history extension div. Columbia, 1919-21; acting prof. Wesleyan Coll., Macon, Ga., 1922-23; asso. prof. U. Pa., 1957-61, chmn. Econ. History Group, 1961-63, collector Recollections, 1969-82; assembled source material for biography of N.W. Aldrich, 1922-25; vis. lectr. U. Birmingham (Eng.), 1948; Fulbright lectr., India, also Japan, 1962. Cons. U.S. Treasury Dept., 1945; condr. sessions internat. econ. relations at triennial confs. of Internat. Fedn. U. Women, Toronto, 1947, Zurich, 1950, London, Eng., 1953. Fellow Am. Philos. Soc.; mem. Middle States Council Social Studies (pres. 1943-44), Am. Hist. Assn. (chmn. com. govt. publs. 1941-53), Soc. Am. Studies (pres. 1956-57), Miss. Valley Hist. Assn. (council 1950-53; editorial bd. 1953-56), A.A.U.W. (V.J. Hill fellow 1944), League of Women Voters, Phi Beta Kappa, Gamma Assn. Pa. (pres. 1947-48), Pi Gamma Mu, Phi Alpha Theta. Author: History of Alaska, 1924; Industrial History of N.J. (sect. of Kull's History of N.J.), 1920; James Styles of Kingston, N.Y. and George Stuart of Schoolcraft, Mich., 1936; (with Roy F. Nichols) Growth of American Democracy, 1939, The Republic of the United States, 1942, A Short History of American Democracy, 1943; Twentieth Century United States, 1943. Editor: Democracy in the Middle West (with James G. Randall), 1941; History in the High School and Social Studies in the Elementary School (with M. Wolf and A. C. Bining), 1944. Contbr. to Dictionary Am. Biography, scholarly jours. Home: Philadelphia, Pa. Died June 22, 1982.

NICHOLSON, BEN, artist; b. Denham, Bucks, Eng., Apr. 10, 1894; s. William and Mabel (Pryde) N. (recipient 1st prize Carnegie Internat. Exhbn. 1952, Ulissi prize Internat. Jury Venice Biennale 1954, Governor of Tokyo prize 3d Internat. Exhbn., Tokyo, Japan 1955, grand priz 4th Internat., Lugano 1956, U.S. 1st Guggenheim Internat. award 1956, 1st prize for painting IV Biennial Sao Paulo, Brazil 1957, Rembrandt prize Johann Wolfgang van Goethe Found. 1974); Subject of monographs: Ben Nicholson: Paintings, Reliefs, Drawings 1911-48 (by Sir Herbert Read) vol. 1, 1947-55, vol. 2, Penguin Modern Painters (by Sir John Summerson), 1948, The Meaning of His Art (by J.P. Hodin), 1957, BN 'Peintures' (by Sir Herbert Read), 1962, monograph, 1969, Drawings, Paintings and Reliefs, 1911-68 (by John Russell), Studio Internat., London, 1969 (edited by M. de Saumarez), Ben Nicholson: Fifty Years of His Art, 1978; One-man exhbns. include, Lefevre, London, 1930, 32, 35, 37, 39, 45, 47, 48, 50, 52, 54, Stedilijk Mus., Amsterdam, 1954, Palais des Beaux Arts, Brussels, 1955, Gimpel Fils, London, 1955, 57, 59, 60, 63, 73, Kunsthalle, Bern, Switzerland, 1961, Tate Gallery, London, 1955, 69, Emmerich Gallery, N.Y.C., 1961, 65, 74, 75, Marlborough Gallery, London, 1963, 68, Waddington Galleries, London, 1976, 79, 80, retrospective exhbns., Albright-Knox Gallery, Buffalo, 1978, Hirshhorn Mus., 1978, Bklyn. Mus., 1979; exhibited other galleries, U.S., Can., Europe, S. Am., group exhbns., Musee Nat. d'Art Moderne, Paris, 1946, Venice Biennale, 1954, Mus. Modern Art, N.Y.C., 1956, Nat. Gallery, Washington, 1970, Tate Gallery, 1977, works pub. collections in, Eng., U.S., Can., Switzerland, Argentina, Australia, Italy, Belgium, Brazil, Japan. Decorated Order of Merit Eng. Address: New York, N.Y. Died 1982.

NICHOLSON, DONALD W., congressman; b. Wareham, Mass., Aug. 11, 1888; s. Angus and Annie (McLeod) N.; ed. pub. schs. of Wareham; m. Ethel Patten, Oct. 17, 1921; children—Malcolm McLeod, Mary Patten. Owner fish market, Wareham, 1908-09; engaged in polit. work, from 1920; selectman, assessor, pub. welfare, Wareham, 1921-26; rep. from Plymouth Dist., Mass. Legislature, 1925-26, senator, 1927-47, pres. senate, 1947; mem. 80th to 85th Congresses, 9th Mass. Dist. Served as sgt., 302d Inf., U.S. Army, 1917-20; prisoner of war escort, Co. 236, France. Mem. Am. Legion, Vets. Fgn. Wars. Elk, Odd Fellow; mem. Grange. Home: Wareham, Mass. †

NICHOLSON, P. J., clergyman; b. Beaver Cove, Nova Scotia, Sept. 8, 1887; s. George and Catherine (Johnston) N.; ed. St. Joseph's High Sch., N. Sydney; B.A., St. Francis Xavier U., 1909; A.M., Johns Hopkins, 1911, Ph.D., 1913; student Grand Seminary, Montreal, St. Augustine's Seminary, Toronto, LL.D., Univ. of New Brunswick, Univ. Alberta, U. Ottawa, St. Mary's U., Aberdeen U.; D.Sc., Laval University, Saint Francis Xavier. Ordained priest, June 29, 1916. Professor physics, St. Francis Xavier, 1912-13, 1946-54; registrar 1924-36; dean of studies, 1936-44, pres., 1944-54, emeritus, 1954, now pastor St. Joseph's parish, Sydney, N.S. Vicar gen. Diocese of Antigonish, from 1950. Sec. of the central adv. com. on edn. in the Atlantic Provinces, 1941-45, chmn., 1945-47; pres. Nat. Conf. of Canadian Universities, 1950-51. Elevated to rank of Domestic Prelate, 1945, Protonotary Apostolic, 1955. Fellow Am. Assn. for Advancement of Sci.; mem. Am. Physical Society, Am. Assn. Physics Teachers, Gamma Alpha, Phi Beta Kappa, K.C. Editor: Scottish Gaelic column in Antigonish weekly newspaper, 1919-44. Address: Sydney, Nova Scotia. †

NICKERSON, JOHN WINSLOW, management cons.; b. Boston, May 7, 1887; s. Winslow and Ella Frances (Robbins) N.; B.S., Mass. Inst. Tech., 1909; m. Alice Robinson, Aug. 30, 1913; children—Eleanor, Barbara (Mrs. Charles Gilbert). In charge indsl. engring. Cheney Bros., 1914-42, indsl. relations, 1936-42, dir. research, 1932-42, supt. in charge line and staff function, 1940-42; dir. management cons. div. W.P.B., 1942-45; management engr. Bigelow Kent Willard Co., 1945-49; cons. management engr. from 1949; chmn. adv. group European productivity, Mutual Security Agy. from 1951. Mem. A.S.M.E., Soc. Advancement Management (recipient indsl. incentive award 1950), Am. Arbitration Assn. (nat. panel). Home: West Hartford, Conn. †

NICOLL, ALFRED HARRIS, business exec.; b. San Francisco, Calif., July 30, 1889; s. Benjamin W. and Helena (Harris) N.; ed. in pub. schs. of San Francisco; m. Gladys Hazelrigg, June 1, 1913; 1 son, Dr. Gordon A. Began career as sales record clerk with Western Electric Co., San Francisco, (predecessor Graybar Electric Co.), 1910-11, salesman, 1912-17, sales manager (Salt Lake City), 1912-20, telephone specialist, appliance sales manager (San Francisco), 1922-24; district sales manager, 1925-31, district manager Northern California and Utah, 1932-38, assistant to president, New York City, 1939, vice president, 1940-41, president, 1942, chmn. bd., 1952. Past president San Francisco Electric Development League; past Pacific Coast pres. Nat. Elec. Wholesalers Assn.; formerly dir. Employers Council, San Francisco. Protestant. Mason. Clubs: Union League, Los Angeles Country, Newcomen of England, Rotary of N.Y. Home: Los Angeles, Calif. †

NIEDERMAIR, JOHN CHARLES, naval architect; b. Union Hill, N.J., Nov. 2, 1893; s. John and Katherine (Riess) N.; grad. as marine engr. and naval architect Webb Inst. Naval Architecture, 1918; m. Ethel Victoria May Irwin, Apr. 2, 1923 (dec. 1973); children—William I., Marion E. (Mrs. R.A. Williams), Patricia E. (Mrs. G. E. Long), John C., Mary Ann (Mrs. M. Mallinoff), George Edward, Richard Michael, Frank Robert. Ship draftsman, also supr. N.Y. Navy Yard, 1917-29; assisted salvage ops. submarines S-51, 1926, S-4, 1928; spl. work on watertight integrity and ship stability, 1925-60; with preliminary design br. Bur. Ships (constrn. and repair), Navy Dept., 1929-58, tech. dir., sr. civilian naval architect, 1939-58, cons. naval architect, 1958-74; cons. naval architect numerous engring. cos., 1929-74; designer LST, other type ships, World War II; design and research postwar types including basic designs aircraft carrier Forrestal and Enterprise, nuclear propelled submarines Nautilus and Skate, guided missile ships and Polaris submarine. Mem. tech. and research panels Nat. Acad. Scis., 1959-63. Recipient Distinguished Civilian Service medal Navy Dept., 1945; named one of 10 most outstanding persons in fed. service Nat. Civil Service League, 1956; recipient David W. Taylor gold medal Soc. Naval Architects and Marine Engrs. 1958; Gibbs Bros. Gold medal Nat. Acad. Scis., 1976; William S. Owen award Webb Inst. Naval Architecture, 1967. Fellow, hon. mem. Soc. Naval Architects and Marine Engrs. (chmn. Chesapeake sect. 1946-47); mem. Am. Soc. Naval Engrs. (past mem. council, Harold E. Saunders award 1978), U.S. Naval Inst., Assn. Scientists and Engrs. U.S. Navy Dept. (hon.; past pres.). Address: Stone Harbor, N.J. Died Mar. 6, 1982.

NIEMI, TAISTO JOHN, librarian; b. Aurora, Minn., Dec. 3, 1914; s. John and Edla (Kauppi) N.; m. Catherine Bruflat, June 23, 1948; children—Marylee, Nancy, John, Paula, David. A.A., Va. Jr. Coll., 1936; B.S., U. Minn., 1946; A.M., U. Mich., 1951, Ph.D., 1960. Tchr. adult edn., Aurora, 1938-41; library asst. Western Mich. U., 1947-53; librarian No. Mich. U., 1953-60, N.Y. State U. Coll., Buffalo, 1960-63; library dir. Le Moyne Coll., Syracuse, N.Y., from 1963; Second v.p. Mich. Library Assn., 1956-60; extension lectr. library sci. U. Mich., 1958-60, N.Y. State U. Coll., Geneseo, 1960-63. Contbr. articles to profl. jours. Served with AUS, 1942-45, PTO. Mem. Cath., N.Y. library assns., Spl. Libraries Assn., N.E.A., Central N.Y. Library Resources Council. Democrat. Roman Catholic. Home: Syracuse, NY.

NIEZER, LOUIS FOX, lawyer; b. Ft. Wayne, Ind., Sept. 10, 1907; s. Charles M. and Rose M. (Fox) N.; m. Rosemary Callahan, Apr. 21, 1937; children—Mary F., Louise, John, Charles, Elizabeth, James, Margaret. A.B., U. Notre Dame, 1929; LL.B., Ind. U., 1937; LL.D., St. Francis Coll., 1965. Bar: Ind. 1936. Practice law, Ft. Wayne, 1936-56; dir. Tokheim Corp., Ft. Wayne, 1936-83, treas., 1941-44, gen. counsel, 1944-57, vice chmn. bd., 1947-60, pres., 1957-66, chmn. bd., 1960-72, practice law, Ft. Wayne, 1972-83; dir. Ft. Wayne Nat. Bank. Mem. Am. Bar Assn., Ind. Bar Assn., Allen County Bar Assn. Clubs: K.C, Elks. Home: Ft. Wayne, Ind. Died Feb. 17, 1983.

NILES, FREDERICK ADOLPH, communications company executive; b. Milw., Sept. 12, 1918; s. Frederick William and Louise (DeTuncq) N.; m. Marye Evelyn Yates, June 29, 1963; children: Stephanie, Deborah, Victoria, Regina, Frederick A. B.A., U. Wis., 1941. Organizer film div. Kling Enterprises, Chgo., 1948-55; founder, 1955; pres. Fred A. Niles Communications Centers, Inc. (visuals communications and mktg.), Chgo.; bd. dirs. World Bus. Council, from 1975, pres., 1980-81; dir. Means Corp.; bd. dirs. Chgo. Film Festival; speaker in field. Bd. dirs. Jr. Achievement Chgo., Salvation Army Chgo., Shakespeare Globe Centre, Inc. Served to capt. AUS, World War II. Recipient Emmy award, 1959, Spl. award Jr. Achievement, 1977, Spl. award U.S. Indsl. Film Council, 1980, Gold Hugo award Chgo. Internat. Film Festival, 1980; named Man of Year City of Hope, 1974. Mem. Chgo. Pres.'s Orgn. (pres. 1976), Nat. Acad. TV and Radio, Arts and Scis., AFTRA, Screen Actors Guild, Internat. Film Producers Assn., Soc. Motion Picture and TV Engrs., Chief Execs. Forum, Screen Dirs. Guild, Actors Equity. Republican. Clubs: Friars, Variety. Home: Glenview, Ill.

NILES, JOHN JACOB, composer, folklore collector, folk singer; b. Louisville, Apr. 28, 1892; s. John Thomas and Lula Sarah (Reisch) N.; student U. Lyon, 1919, Cin. Conservatory Music, 1920-22, Mus.D. (hon.), 1949; D.F.A. (hon.), Transylvania U., 1968; Litt.D. (hon.), Episcopal Theol. Sem. in Ky., 1970, U. Ky., 1973; H.H.D. (hon.), U. Louisville, 1971; m. Rena Lipetz, Mar, 21, 1936; children—Thomas Michael Tolliver, John Edward. Concerts Am. folk music, maj. cities U.S., Eng. Holland, France, Germany, Scandinavian countries, 1927-78. Served to 1st lt. A.C., U.S. Army, 1917-19. Recipient nat. citation Fedn. Music Clubs, 1967. Mem. Am. Folklore Soc., Am. Dialect Soc., ASCAP. Episcopalian. Maj. compositions include Lamentation, Mary the Rose, Rhapsody for the Merry Month of May; best known songs include I Wonder As I Wander, Go 'Way from My Window, Black is the Color of My True Love's Hair, Venezuela, others; rec. artist for Tradition Everest Records, Folkways and RCA-Victor Records. Author: Singing Soldiers, 1927; Songs My Mother Never Taught Me, 1929; One Man's War, 1929; The Ballad Book of John Jacob Niles, 1961; Folk Ballads for Young Actors, 1962; Folk Carols for Young Actors, 1962; (poetry collection) Brickdust and Buttermilk, 1977. Home: Lexington, Ky. Died Mar. 1, 1980.

NISSEN, HARRY, physical educator; b. Oslo, Norway, Sept. 7, 1890 (father citizen of U.S.); s. Hartvig and Helené (Peterson) N.; grad. Mechanic Arts High Sch., Boston, 1910; B.S., Mass. State Coll., 1914; student Harvard Summer Sch. of Physical Education, 1911, 24; grad. study, Mass. State Coll. and Boston Univ., Harvard Graduate School of Education, 1927; diploma Posse Normal Sch. of Physical Edn., Boston, 1923; m. Jane Churchill, of Garden City, Kan., May 6, 1916; children—Harriet Jane, Helen Ann, Ruth Churchill, Priscilla Evelyn. Pres. and chmn. bd. Posse-Nissen School of Physical Edn., 1924-35. Mem. Am. Physical Edn. Assn., Mass. State Society Phys. Edn. (pres. 1934), Friends of Medical Progress, N.E.A. Bd. of Supts., Camp Directors Assn., Pi Gamma Mu, Alpha Sigma Phi. Universalist. Mason; mem. Order of De Molay (advisory council and camp dir.). Club: Hancock Church Men's. Home: Hillsboro, N.H. †

NISWONGER, C. ROLLIN, educator; b. Pitsburg, Ohio, Mar. 24, 1907; s. Clifford O. and Edith Rose (Vance) N.; S.B., Miami U., Oxford, Ohio, 1929, LL.D., 1973; S.M., U. Ill., 1931; Ph.D., Ohio State U., 1950; m. Sue Janes, Aug. 22, 1938; children—Cynthia Sue, Thomas Rollin. Asst. instr. accounting U. Ill. 1929-31; instr. accounting Wash. State U., 1931-35; asst. prof. accounting Miami U., 1935-41, asso. prof., 1941-47, prof., 1947-72, emeritus, 1972-80, head dept., 1947-66, asst. dean Sch. Bus. Adminstrn., 1940-56, acting dean, 1954-55, dir. summer session, 1946-48; cons. Office of U.S. Comptroller Gen., 1955-58; accounting exec. OPA, 1943. Served as lt. Supply Corps, USNR, cost inspection service, 1944-46. C.P.A., Washington, Ohio. Mem. Am. Inst. of C.P.A.'s, Financial Execs. Inst., Am. Accounting Assn. (pres. 1958), Ohio Soc. C.P.A.'s, Phi Beta Kappa, Beta Gamma Sigma, Sigma Chi, Beta Alpha Psi (nat. pres. 1962-63), Delta Sigma Pi (Delta Sig of Year 1978), Omicron Delta Kappa. Co-author: Federal Tax Accounting, ann. edits., 1940-46; Income Tax Procedure, ann. edits., 1947-67; Accounting Principles, 6th thru 12th edits., 1953-77. Contbr. to jours. Home: Oxford, Ohio. Died Feb. 28, 1980.

NIVEN, DAVID, actor; b. Kirriemuir, Scotland, Mar. 1, 1910; s. William Graham and Lady (Comyn Platt) N.; m. Primula Rollo (div. dec. 1946); 2 sons; m. Hjordis Tersmeden. Student, Sandhurst Coll. Successively lumberman, newspaper writer, laundry messenger, rep. London wine firm in, U.S. (N.Y. Film Critics award for best actor of year in Separate Tables 1958, Academy award for Separate Tables 1958, N.Y. Critics award 1960); Author: Rounding the Rugged Rocks, 1951, The Moon's A Balloon, 1971, Bring on the Empty Horses, 1975; motion picture debut, 1935; pictures include Murder by Death, 1975, Without Regret, Rose Marie, Dodsworth, Beloved Enemy, Charge of the Light Brigade, Dinner At The Ritz, Four Men and A Prayer, Three Blind Mice, Dawn Patrol,

Death on the Nile, Bluebeard's Eighth Wife, Wuthering Heights, Raffles, Eternally Yours, Kiss in the Dark, Toast of New Orleans, Soldiers Three, Lady Says No, The Moon is Blue, Candleshoe, Escape to Athena, 1978, Love Lottery, Tonight's the Night, Happy Go Lovely, Around the World in 80 Days, Separate Tables, Please Don't Eat the Daisies, Ask Any Girl, Happy Anniversary, Guns of Navarone, A Man Called Intrepid, 1979, Best of Enemies, 55 Days at Peking, The Pink Panther, Bedtime Story, Lady L, Where the Spies Are, Eye of the Devil, Casino Royale, Rough Cut, 1979, The Sea Wolves, 1980, Whose Little Girl Are You? , others; formed pictures include, Four Star TV, 1952; host, actor: TV David Niven Show, 1959-64; star: TV show The Rogues, 1964-65. Served Highland Light Infantry, Malta; gunnery instr. revolutionists in Cuba; served from 2d lt. to col. Brit. Army, 1939-45. Recipient Legion of Merit. Address: Los Angeles, Calif. Died July 29, 1983.

NIX, ABIT, lawyer; b. Jackson County, Ga., July 3, 1888; s. John Morgan and Dora (Bennett) N.; A.B., U. of Ga., 1910, LL.B., 1912; grad. study U. of Chicago and Harvard, 1912-13; LL.D., Atlanta Law Sch., 1938, Howard Coll., 1938; m. Eunice Little, Dec. 23, 1913 (dec.); children—Mary E. (Mrs. John Roy Hollingsworth), Barbara (Mrs. S. R. Kilgore). Associate professor law and secretary University of Georgia Law School, 1913-18; admitted to Georgia bar, 1912; referee in bankruptcy Athens Div., Northern Dist. of Ga., 1917-18; mem. law firm Erwin, Erwin & Nix from 1918; dir. Citizens & Southern Nat. Bank, Progressive Life Ins. Co., New Georgian Hotel Company, Southeasten Rubber Manufacturing Company, Incorporated, Climax Hosiery Mill, Athens Securities Co. Spl. lecturer U. of Ga. Law Sch. Dist. gov. Rotary Internat., 39th Dist., 1928-29, dir. 1931-32; chmn. conv. com., Cleveland Convention, 1939. Delegate to Dem. Nat. Conv., Chicago, 1940, pres. elector, 1940, 48. Regent U. of Ga. System; trustee Georgia Masonic Home. Fellow American College of Trial Lawyers; member Athens, Ga. and Am. bar Assns., Sigma Chi, Phi Beta Kappa, Sigma Delta Pi, Delta Theta Phi. Democrat. Baptist. Mason (Grand Master in Ga. 1935-36). Clubs: Rotary, Country (Athens). Contbr. to Rotarian Mag. and Christian Index. †

NIXON, ELLIOTT B., naval officer; b. New York, N.Y., Oct. 26, 1889; s. Theodore Totten and Harriet Isabela (Bodley) N.; B.S., U. S. Naval Acad., Annapolis, Md., 1911; student U. S. Naval War Coll., Newport, R.I., 1933-36; m. Ann Nicholls Wildman, Jan. 25, 1918; 1 son, Elliott B. Commd. ensign, U.S. Navy, 1911, advanced through grades to commodore. Decorated Mexican ribbon, 1914, World War I Star, Yangtze Campaign ribbon, Pre-Pearl Harbor ribbon, Atlantic and Pacific Area ribbons. Clubs: Yacht (New York); Army and Navy, Army-Navy Country (Washington). Home: New York, N.Y. †

NOBLE, GUY LEE, orgn. dir.; b. State Center, Ia., Feb. 24, 1888; s. Hubert Sedgwick and Clara (Brouhard) N.; B.S., Ia. State Coll., 1914, Master of Agr., 1933; m. Adah Belle Smith, Jan. 15, 1912; children—Constance Alberta (Mrs. Howard Noble), Newell Hamilton. Supervisor, by-products mfg., Armour & Co., 1914-18, pub. relations, 1918-21; one of founders and dir. Nat. Com. on Boys and Girls Club Work (service orgn. to 4-H Clubs) from 1921; founder and managing dir. "Nat. 4-H News" mag. for 4-H leaders; one of founders and dir. projects Rural Youth Foundation; vice president for farms, National Safety Council, 1945-56. Awarded nat. citation for outstanding service of 4-H Clubs, 1941, Ia. State Coll. Alumni Merit award, 1949; Silver Buffalo, Boy Scouts Am. Mem. Chgo. Assn. Commerce and Industry, Gamma Sigma Delta. Ind. Rep. Conglist. Mason. Clubs: Saddle and Sirloin, Chicago Farmers. Home: Lowell, Ind. †

NOEL-BAKER, PHILIP J., educator, M.P.; born Nov. 1889; s. J. Allen Baker; student Bootham Sch., York, also Haverford Coll., Pa.; M.A., King's Coll.; m. Irene Noel, 1915 (dec. 1956); 1 son. Pres. Cambridge Union Soc., 1914; vice prin. Ruskin Coll., Oxford, 1914; Sir Ernest Cassel prof. internat. relations U. London, 1924-29; mem. Parliament, Coventry, 1929-31, Derby, 1936-50, South Derby, 1950-70; parliamentary pvt. sec. to sec. state for fgn. affairs, 1929-31; parliamentary sec. Ministry of War Transport, 1942-45; minister of state, 1945-46; sec. state for air, 1946-47; sec. state for Commonwealth relations, 1947-50; minister fuel and power, 1950-51; Dodge lectr. Yale, 1934. Mem. Brit. delegation 10th Assembly, League of Nations, 1929-30; prin. asst. to president Disarmament Conference at Geneva, 1932-34; chmn. fgn. affairs group Parliamentary Labour Party, 1964. President International Council Sport and Physical Education, 1962. Served with ambulance unit Brit. Armed Forces, 1914-18. Decorated Mons Star, Silver Medal for Mil. Valor (Italy), 1917, Crocedi Guerra, 1918; recipient Howland prize for distinguished work in govt. Yale, 1934; Nobel Peace prize, 1959; created life peer, 1977. Author: The League of Nations at Work, 1924; The Juridicial Status of the British Dominions in International Law, 1929; The Private Manufacture of Armaments, 1936; The Arms Race: A Programme for World Disarmament, 1958. Capt. British Olympic Track Team, 1924. Address: London, England. Died Oct. 8, 1982.

NOLAN, JAMES PARKER, investment banker; b. Washington, July 12, 1897; s. Walter and Mary (Parker) N.; m. Ellen DuBose Ravenel Peelle, Nov. 15, 1928 (div. dec); children—James Paker, Stanton Peelle, Gaillard Ravenel; m. Florence Wetherill Walker, Dec. 9, 1978. Student, Georgetown Law Sch., 1917. With U.S. Dept. State, 1919-24, Nat. City Co., 1924-32; formed Folger, Nolan & Co., 1932; pres., treas. Folger, from Nolan-W.B. Hibbs & Co., Inc., Washington, 1953; pres., treas., dir. Folger, Nolan, Fleming & Co., Inc., from 1962; Washington Stock Exchange, 1944-45; bd. govs. N.Y. Stock Exchange, 1958-61; allied mem.; assoc. mem. Am. Stock Exchange; dir. Balt. & O. R.R. Co. Trustee Chestnut Lodge, Hosp., Bethesda, Md.; bd. dirs. Washington Inst. Fgn. Affairs. Served as lt. Tank Corps AEF, 1918-19. Decorated Knight Malta. Mem. Nat. Assn. Security Dealers (mem. bd. 1943-46), Assn. Stock Exchange Firms (bd. 1948-54), Investment Bankers Assn., Am., Delta Theta Phi. Republican. Roman Catholic. Clubs: The Brook (N.Y.C.); Bond (Washington), Metropolitan (Washington), Alfalfa (Washington); Chevy Chase Country. Home: Washington, D.C. Died Dec. 14, 1981.

NOLAN, JOHN LESTER, librarian; b. Concord, N.H., Apr. 14, 1909; s. Edmund P. and Grace (Heilbrun) N.; B.S. cum laude, Harvard, 1931; B.S. in L.S., Columbia, 1938; m. Dallas Fraser, June 20, 1935; children—David Fraser, Barbara Dallas. Librarian, Adams House Library, Harvard, 1931-34; sect. head, sr. reference librarian N.Y. Pub. Library, 1935-40; with Library of Congress, 1940-69, asst. dir. reference dept., 1954-58, asso. dir. reference dept., 1958-68, dir. reference dept., 1968-69, hon. cons., 1969-80; prof. library studies U. Hawaii, 1969-70; library cons., 1970-80; dir. library services in U.K. for USIS, 1952-54. Mem. Am., D.C., Brit. library assns. Clubs: Cosmos, Harvard (Washington). Editor: Library of Congress Quar. Jour. Current Acquisitions, 1945-51. Contbr. articles to profl. jours. Home: Kensington, Md. Dec. Oct. 10, 1980.

NOLAN, JOHN THOMAS, JR., advt. agy. exec.; b. Cin., Mar. 21, 1918; s. John Thomas and Laura Mary (McJoynt) N. A.B., U. Cin., 1940, M.A., 1942; postgrad., Xavier U., U.S. Marine Corps Command and Staff Coll., U.S. Naval War Coll., Air War Coll., Indsl. War Coll., Army War Coll. Pub. relations dir. Gruen Watch Co., Cin., 1944-46; pres. Nolan, Keelor & Stites Inc. (advt. agy.), Cin., 1947-79, chmn. bd., from 1979; pres. Campion Investment Co. Inc., Cin., from 1959. Chmn. men's com. Cin. Symphony Orch., 1965; bd. dirs. Cin. Mus. Festival Assn., from 1962, pres., 1961-64; trustee Pub. Library Cin. and Hamilton County, from 1951, pres., from 1965; past pres. Queen City Assn., 1949; bd. govs. St. Xavier High Sch., 1962-68; pres. Fenwick Club, 1963-65; chmn. council on camp study United Fund, 1962; chmn. basin area study com. Community Health and Welfare Council, 1964; Mem. pres.'s adv. council Xavier U., Cin., from 1973; mem. adv. council Navy Affairs, from 1959; hon. trustee Cin. Ballet Co., from 1964; bd. dirs. Bur. Govtl. Research; brotherhood chmn. NCCJ, 1980. Recipient Meritorious Public Service citation Sec. of Navy, 1957, Founder's award Xavier U., 1979; named man of year Cin. Marine Corps League, 1965. Mem. Cin. Council Navy League (pres. 1962-68), Def. Orientation Conf. Assn. (dir. from 1970), Cin. Indsl. Advertisers Assn. (Man of Distinction award 1975), Cin. Advertisers Club, Hist. and Philos. Soc. Ohio (life), Men. of Milford Retreat League (dir. 1960-62). Republican. Roman Catholic. Clubs: University, Queen City. Home: Cincinnati, OH.

NOLAN, WILLIAM LEO, business exec.; b. New Castle, Pa., Sept. 4, 1887; s. Edward and Bridget (Curran); student pub. schs.; widower; 1 son, William Leo. With McCrory Stores Corp., 1908-18; with McLellan Stores Co. from 1918, now dir. and chmn. bd. Clubs: Crescent Athletic (Huntington, N.Y.); New York Athletic, Union League (N.Y. City). Home: New York, N.Y. †

NOLL, ANTHONY F(RANCIS), JR., insurance company executive; b. Buffalo, June 24, 1922; s. Anthony F. N.; (married); children: Anthony Francis, Wendy. Student, Brown U., 1940-44; B.A., Boston U., 1947. Group mgr. John Hancock Mut. Life, St. Louis, 1945-49, N.Y.C., 1949-50; with N.Y. Life Ins. Co., 1951-84, v.p. group field mktg. ops., N.Y.C., 1970-78, v.p. home office staff ops., 1978-79, v.p. regular group underwriting, group mktg. services, 1979-84, v.p. group field mktg. orgn. and group mktg. services, 1982-84. Served to lt. USAAF, 1942-45, NATOUSA, ETO. Mem. Life Ins. Mktg. Research Assn. (group mktg. com. 1975-81). Episcopalian. Died June 4, 1984.

NORDBYE, GUNNAR HANS, judge; b. Urskog, Norway, Feb. 4, 1888; s. Halvor and Anna C. (Aarnes) N.; brought to U.S., 1888; LL.B., U. of Minn., 1912, LL.D., 1959; m. Eleanor Pfeiffer, June 26, 1915; children—Rodger Lincoln, Richard Arthur. In practice of law at Minneapolis, Minn., 1912-22; judge of Municipal Court, Minneapolis, 1922-25; judge Dist. Court, 4th Minn. Jud. Dist., 1925-31; judge U.S. Dist. Court, Dist. of Minn., from 1931. Recipient Centennial award, Northwestern U., 1951. Mem. Delta Theta Pi. Republican. Conglist. Mason (grand master of Minn. 1939, 33 deg.). Home: Minneapolis, Minn. †

NORMAN, ARTHUR GEOFFREY, biochemist, univ. adminstr.; b. Birmingham, Eng., Nov. 26, 1905; came to U.S., 1930, naturalized, 1946; s. Arthur and Charlotte (Mant) N.; m. Marian Foote, Sept. 5, 1933; children—Anthony Westcott, Stephen Trevor. B.Sc., U. Birmingham, 1925, Ph.D., 1928; M.S. (Rockefeller fellow), U. Wis., 1932; D.Sc., U. London, 1933. Research asso. U. Wis., 1932; biochemist Rothamsted Exptl. Sta., Harpenden, Eng., 1933-37; prof. soils Iowa State U.; research prof. Iowa Agrl. Exptl. Sta., 1937-46; biochemist and div. chief Chem. Corps. Biol. Labs., Frederick, Md., 1946-52; prof. botany U. Mich., Ann Arbor, 1952—, v.p. for research, 1964-72; dir. Bot. Gardens, 1955-66, Inst. for Environ. Quality, 1972-76; Adviser to pres. Nat. Acad. Scis., 1963-64; chmn. div. biology and agr. NRC, 1965-69; trustee Inst. Def. Analysis, 1968-77, Univ. Research Assos., 1969-74, chmn., 1973-74; trustee Biol. Sci. Info. Service, 1972-77, pres., 1976-77. Author: The Biochemistry of Cellulose, 1937; Editor: Advances in Agronomy (vols. 1 to XX), 1949-68, Agronomy Monographs (Vols. 1 to VI), 1948-56; Contbr. profl. papers to tech. jours. Fellow Am. Soc. Agronomy (pres. 1956-57), Royal Soc. Chemistry, Am. Acad. Microbiology, AAAS; mem. Biochem. Soc., Soil Sci. Soc. Am., Am. Soc. Microbiology, Am. Soc. Plant Physiologists, Sigma Xi, Phi Kappa Phi. Home: Ann Arbor MI.

NORRIS, LESTER J., bus. exec.; b. Elgin, Ill., Nov. 26, 1900; s. Carroll William and Gertrude (Flinn) N.; m. Dellora F. Angell, Mar. 28, 1923; children—Lavern G. (Mrs. George Gaynor), Lester J. (dec.), Joann D. (Mrs. James Collins), Robert, John (dec.). Grad., St. Charles High Sch., Chgo. Acad. Fine Arts. Chmn. bd. dirs. State Bank of St. Charles; dir., mem. exec. com. Texaco, Inc., 1933-73; Pres. Norbak Corp., Naples, Fla.; v.p. Collier County Cons. Comml. artist, cartoonist, 1921-25. Bd. dirs. St. Charles Charities; life trustee Northwestern U.; trustee Delnor Hosp., Henry Rockwell Baker Community Center; exec. pres. Key Island, Inc.; bd. dirs. Miami Heart Inst., Inc.; chmn. Nat. Victory Garden Inst., 1942-47. Mem. Nat. Audubon Soc., Ill. Wildlife Fedn. Methodist. Clubs: The Union League, The Dunham Woods Riding, St. Charles Country, National Press; Hole-in-the-Wall Golf (Naples, Fla.), Naples Yacht (Naples, Fla.). Home: Saint Charles IL.

NORTH, ELEANOR BERYL, educator, author; b. Mercer, Pa., July 6, 1898; d. Jacob Z. and Lois (Caldwell) North; B.A., Pa. State U., 1923, M.A., 1925; postgrad. Cambridge (Eng.) U., 1929, 30-32, Oxford (Eng.) U., 1934-36, Brit. Mus., 1936, 39, 49, (Philosophy scholar) Harvard, 1942-43. Asst. prof. English lit. Juniata Coll., 1925-28; prof. Youngstown (Ohio) U., 1929-37, Md. State Coll., 1941-49; prof. Shakespeare and world lit. Berry Coll., Mt. Berry, Ga., 1951-63. Lectr. to lit., ednl., ch. orgns.; judge poetry contests, London, Eng., Sidney, Australia, 1971-72; lit. cons. Internat. Poetry Soc., 1974. Lit. research grant, 1963-67, 70-71, 72, 73, 75; medal Academia Internat. Rome, 1968. Fellow Internat. Poets Acad. (founder), Internat. Biog. Assn.; mem. Royal Order Bookfellows, Modern Lang. Assn., Poetry League Am. (adv. council), Shakespeare Found., AAUP, Poetry Guild, Internat. Poetry Soc. (lit. cons.), Am. Classical Assn., Wagner Music Assn., Art League, Am. Philos. Assn., Nat. Council Tchrs. English, Authors' League, Internat. Acad. Poets, Centro Studi e Scambi Accademia Internat. (hon. v.p. 1973), Am. Poets Fellowship Soc., Writers Guild Gt. Britain, AAUW, Delta Kappa Gamma, Sigma Tau Delta (founder poetry contest 1972). Author: Reading and Personnel Guidance, 1942; (poetry) Star Dust, 1930; Fall 'o Dew, 1936; Grace Notes, 1952 (included in internat. poetry archive Manchester (Eng.) Library; My Heart Sings, 1969; High Tide, 1973; Bright Star, 1975; (poetry) Sunrise, 1979; also articles. Address: State College, Pa. Died Apr. 11, 1982; interred Pine Hall Cemetery, State College, Pa.

NORTH, JAMES WEIR, lawyer; b. Bklyn., Nov. 16, 1923; s. Nelson Luther and Sarah Evelyn (Weir) N.; m. Lois Emily Gunthel, Aug. 23, 1947; children—James Weir, Nancy Anne Leff, Cynthia Lois Marowski. Student, Princeton, 1941-43; A.B., Columbia, 1947, LL.B., 1949; grad. Advanced Mgmt. Program, Harvard Bus. Sch., 1962. Bar: N.Y. bar 1950. With Home Title Guaranty Co., Garden City, N.Y., 1949-51; with trust dept. Chase Manhattan Bank, N.Y.C., 1951-77, exec. v.p. trust dept., 1971-77; mem. firm Payne, Wood & Littlejohn, Glen Cove, N.Y., from 1977; mem. Nat. Market Adv. Bd., 1975-78. Mem. Glen Cove (N.Y.) Bd. Edn., 1957-61; pres. 961; mem. bd. edn. North Shore Central Sch. Dist. 1, 1965-68, pres., 1968; trustee N.Y. State Tchrs. Retirement System, 1974-77; bd. dirs. Community Hosp. at Glen Cove, from 1978, St. Christopher's Home, from 1978. Served with AUS, 1943-45. Mem. N.Y. State Bankers Assn. (pres. trust div. 1971-72), Am. Bankers Assn. (pres. trust div. 1976-77). Clubs: Princeton (N.Y.C.); Sea Cliff Yacht. Home: Sea Cliff, NY.

NORTH, ROY MOSES, assn. exec., born Meriwether Co., Ga., July 2, 1889; s. Richard Milner and Dolly (Bridges) N.; student Brantley Inst., Senoia, Ga., Emory Coll. (now Emory U.), Atlanta, Ga.; m. Mona Lewis, Aug. 15, 1923; children—Romona Ruth, Janis Elizabeth. Ry. mail clerk Nashville and Atlanta Ry. post office, 1909-15; post office insp., St. Louis and Chicago, 1915-33; dep. 3d asst. postmaster gen., 1933-49; appointed postmaster, Washington, 1949-58; legislative rep. Nat. Assn. Postmasters, from 1958; pres. post office dept. Mutual Benefit Assn. (insurance.). Hon. mem. Am. Air Mail Soc.; mem. Omicron Delta Kappa. Democrat. Methodist (steward Mt. Vernon Ch., Washington, D.C.). †

NORTHRUP, LORRY ROBBINS, born in Iola, Kan., Mar. 29, 1890; s. Frank A. and Alice Maude (Robbins) N.; Ph.B., U. Chgo., 1912; m. Charlotte Smith, Nov. 7, 1914; 1 dau., Alice (Mrs. H. E. Stanard). Merchandising bur. Chgo. Tribune, 1913-15; sales research Crowell Pub. Co., 1915-18; dir. research Erwin Wasey, Ruthrauff & Ryan, Inc., Chgo., 1918-40, gen. mgr. Chgo. office, 1940-57, exec. v.p., 1957-64. Publicity dir. Community Fund, 1939, A.R.C., 1949, 60. Recipient Arthor Olaf Andersen gold medal musical composition, Am. Conservatory Music, Chgo., 1923. Mem. Alpha Delta Phi. Clubs: Chicago, Tavern (Chgo.). Home: Newtown Square, Pa. †

NORTON, CLARENCE CLIFFORD, educator; b. Benton, Miss., July 2, 1896; s. Rev. Henry L. and May (Bogan) N.; B.S., Millsaps Coll., Jackson, Miss., 1919; M.A., Emory U., 1920; Ph.D., U.N.C., 1927; LL.D., Wofford Coll., 1953; m. Mable Binning, Aug. 22, 1922; children—Dorothy Alice, Howard Binning. Dean, prof. social sci. Lon Morris Coll., 1920-23; teaching fellow and instr. history, U. N.C., 1923-25; prof. polit. sci. and sociology Wofford Coll., 1925-47, 53-58, John M. Reeves prof. sociology, 1958-62, emeritus, 1962-81, chmn. dept., 1958-62, prof. sociology, 1947-53, dean coll., 1942-49, 52-53, dir. Summer Sch., 1942-53, dean adminstrn., 1949-52, acting pres., 1951-52; vis. prof. Am. govt. Wake Forest Coll., 1927. Del. World Meth. Conf., London, Eng., 1966. Mem. S.C. State Planning Bd. 1939-45, S.C. Council Tchr. Edn.; trustee Lake Junaluska Assembly, 1940-48, 52-56; past pres. Spartanburg Community Chest. Pres. Spartanburg Council Social Workers, 1936. Mem. Phi Beta Kappa, Sigma Upsilon, Alpha Psi Delta, Pi Kappa Alpha, Blue Key. Mason, Rotarian (gov. internat. 1958-59). Author: The Democratic Party in Ante-Bellum North Carolina; 1930; Enriching Family Life, 1945, rev. edit., 1962; The Art of Caricature, 1951; A Cartoon Commentary on Church Folks, 1967; Little Church Folks in Cartoons, 1969. Contbr. to various periodicals. Creator of Church Folks, syndicated cartoon. Home: Winter Park, Fla. Died Nov. 12, 1981; interred Mills River Cemetery, Hendersonville, N.C.

NORTON, KARL B., food consultant; born Adams, N.Y., Dec. 27, 1890; s. Horace Hiram and Cornelia (Grant) N.; student Syracuse (N.Y.) U., 1912; m. Marguerite Ann Wade, Sept. 22, 1917 (dec.); 1 son, Karl B. (Capt.); married 2d, Charlotte Kressler Law, 1950. Chemist, J. Hungerford Smith Co., Rochester, N.Y., 1912-14, Zinsser & Co., Hastings-on-Hudson, N.Y., 1914-15; Nat. Aniline and Chem. Co., Brooklyn, N.Y., 1916-17; chemist, Solvay Process Co., Syracuse, N.Y., 1916-17; asst. to chief chemist Semet-Solvay Co., 1920-21; operating chemist, Nat. Aniline and Chem. Co., Brooklyn, N.Y., 1917-20, Buffalo, N.Y., 1921-23; asst. supt., J. Hungerford Smith Co., Rochester, N.Y., 1923-30; research chemist and production manager fruits and vegetables, Frosted Foods Sales Corporation, New York, 1930-44; production manager frozen fruits and vegetables, Standard Brands, Inc., New York, 1944; food cons. from 1948. Mem. Phi Kappa Psi. Mason (Rising Sun Lodge No. 234, Adams, N.Y.; Watertown (N.Y.) Commandery, Shriner). Clubs: University; Patterson Golf (Fairfield, Conn.). Address: Westport, Conn. †

NORTON, MARGARET ALLTUCKER (MRS. JOHN KELLEY NORTON), educator; b. Sacramento, Calif., Nov. 3, 1888; d. Henry and Susan (Compton) Alltucker; Litt.B., Univ. of Calif., 1914, A.M., 1919, Ph.D., 1922; M. Dr. John Kelley Norton, Aug. 23, 1929; adopted children—John David, Margaret Adrienne. Began as teacher country school, Sacramento County, California, 1908-10; supervisor of mathematics, University High School, Oakland, Calif., 1914-16; head of depts. science and mathematics, Nordhoff Union High Sch., Ojai, Calif., 1916-18; teacher of mathematics, Berkeley, Calif., 1918-21; sch. counselor, Berkeley, 1921-23; asst. dir. research div., Nat. Edn. Assn., 1923-29, asso. dir., 1929-32; teacher, summers, Brigham Young U., 1926, Columbia, 1926, 32, U. of Calif., 1927-29; visiting asso. prof. of edn., U. of Chicago, summer, 1938. Mem. N.E.A., N.Y. City League of Women Voters (edn. chmn., 1948-49), Am. Association University Women (national chmn. Com. on Membership and Maintaining Standards, 1939-41), Phi Beta Kappa. Mem. The Riverside Ch. Editor year books Dept. of Superintendence, 1923-32; contbr. ednl. periodicals. Lecturer on ednl. topics. Co-author: Foundations of Curriculum Building, 1936; Wealth, Children and Education, 1937. Home: New York, N.Y. †

NORTON, PAUL T(HORNLEY), JR., industrial engr.; b. Elizabeth, N.J., Apr. 11, 1889; s. Paul Thornley and Carrie (Bain) N.; B.S., in Elec. Engring., U. of Wis., 1917, C.E., 1931; m. Eleanor Halsey, Sept. 6, 1919; children—Carolyn Darrach (Mrs. J. S. Brushwood), John Halsey, Frederic Thornley. Coal mine surveyor, 1906-13; division engineer United Coal Corp., Pittsburgh, 1917; sales engr. and manager Case Crane & Engineering Company, Columbus, Ohio, 1919, chief engr., 1920-23; v.p. Case Crane & Kilbourne Jacobs Co., Columbus, 1923-26, 1943-51; instr., asst. prof. mechanics dept., Univ. of Wis., 1927-29; profl indl. engring. Va. Poly. Inst., 1929-48; dir. industrial service, 1937-48, on leave from Feb. to Oct. 1943, to serve as chief, industrial processes and products branch, Office of Prodn. Research and Development, War Production Board, Washington; lectr. in indsl. engring. Stanford U., 1952-54, U. Fla., 1954-55; lectr. and writer in spl. field, depreciation. Served as 2d lt. Air Service, U.S. Army, 1917-19. Mem. A.S.M.E., Am. Management

Assn., Society Promotion of Engineering Edn. (council 1934-37), Tau Beta Pi, Sigma Xi, and Phi Kappa Phi fraternities. Episcopalian. Clubs: University (Blacksburg); Memorial Union (U. of Wis.); Cosmos (Washington). Author: Depreciation (with E. L. Grant), 1949; numerous articles on depreciation and related subjects. Home: St. Petersburg, Fla. †

NORWEB, R(AYMOND) HENRY, diplomat; b. Nottingham, Eng. (of Am. parents), May 31, 1894; s. Henry and Jeanne (Palmer) N.; A.B. cum laude, Harvard, 1916; m. Emery May Holden, Oct. 18, 1917; children—Raymond Henry, Jeanne Katherine, Albert Holden. Career U.S. diplomatic officer for 35 years, with world-wide service including ambassadorships in S.A., Europe; specialist in internat. communications, co-author N.Am. Broadcasting Treaty, 1936; negotiated Allied use bases in Azores, 1944. Pres., trustees Ohio Episcopal Diocese; honorary fellow Smithsonian; president of John Huntington Fund for Education. Member various international numismatic societies. Clubs: Harvard, Brook, India House, River, University (N.Y.C.); Union, Chagrin Valley Hunt, Kirtland Country (Cleve.); Metropolitan, Chevy Chase (Washington, D.C.); Home: Cleveland, Ohio. Died Oct. 1, 1983.

NOTESTEIN, FRANK WALLACE, demographer; b. Alma., Mich., Aug. 16, 1902; s. Frank Newton and Mary Elizabeth (Wallace) N.; m. Daphne Limbach, Oct. 8, 1927. Student, Alma (Mich.) Coll., 1919-20, LL.D., 1964; B.S., Wooster, Coll., 1923, LL.D., 1946; Ph.D., Cornell, 1927; D.Sc., Northwestern U., Evanston, Ill., 1953, Princeton, 1963, U. Mich., 1967. Instr. econs. Cornell U., 1926-27; fellow Social Science Research Council, 1927-28; research assoc. Milbank Meml. Fund, 1928-29, mem. tech. staff, 1929-36; lectr. charge Office Population Research, Princeton, 1936-41, dir., 1941-59, prof. demography, 1945-59, vis. sr. research demographer, from 1959; vis. lectr. Woodrow Wilson Sch., 1969-71; pres. Population Council, N.Y.C., 1959-68, then pres. emeritus; cons.-dir. population div. dept. social affairs UN, 1946-48; mem. UN adv. com. Experts on World Population Plan of Action; mem. Nat. Commn. Obervance World Population Year, 1974. Co-author: Controlled Fertility, 1940: The Future Population of Europe and the Soviet Union, 1944; Co-editor: Population Index, 1936-57; cons. editor, 1958-63. Fellow Am. Acad. Arts and Scis.; mem. Council on Fgn. Relations, AAAS, Am. Philos. Soc., Am. Sociol. Soc., Am. Statis. Assn., Population Assn. Am., Internat. Statis. Inst., Internat. Union for Sci. Studies Population, Phi Beta Kappa, Sigma Xi. Clubs: Princeton (N.Y.); Nassau (Princeton). Home: Newton, Pa. Died Feb. 19, 1983.

NOTTE, JOHN ANTHONY, JR., former governor R.I.; born Providence, May 3, 1909; s. John Anthony and Eva Theresa (Rondina) N.; A.B., Providence Coll., 1931; student Cornell U., 1931-32; LL.B., Boston U., 1935; m. Marie Joan Huerth, Sept. 19, 1934; children—John Anthony III, Joyce Ann. Admitted to R.I. bar, 1935; practice of law, 1936-83; sec. U.S. Senator Green, 1947-56; sec. state, R.I., 1957-58, lt. gov., 1958-61, gov., 1961-63. Lt. USN, 1943-45. Mem. Young Democrats R.I. (pres. 1949), Vets. Fgn. Wars (state dept. comdr. 1949-50), Am. Bar Assn., Alpha Phi Delta. Democrat. Elk. Club: Metacomet (R.I.) Golf. Home: North Providence, R.I. Died Mar. 6, 1983.

NOVACK, BEN, hotel exec.; b. N.Y.C., Feb. 24, 1907; s. Hyman and Sadie (Cohen) N.; student N.Y.U., 1924-26; 1 son, Ben Hadwyn. Operator Monroe Towers, Cornell, Atlantis, Sans Souci hotels, Miami Beach, Fla., 1940-52; pres. Hotel Fontainebleau, Miami Beach, from 1954, mng. dir., 1954-64, chmn. bd., owner 1964-77. Mem. Miami Beach Hotel Assn. (past pres.). Republican. Home: Miami Beach, Fla. Died Apr. 5, 1985.

NOVAK, ARTHUR FRANCIS, food science educator, executive; b. Balt., Oct. 25, 1916; s. Frank C. and Anna Barbara (Hulka) N.; B.S., U. Md., 1937; M.S., U. Ala., 1939; Ph.D., Purdue U., 1947; postgrad. Johns Hopkins U., 1939-40, U. Louisville, 1941-42, U. So. Calif., 1951-53; m. Mary Frances Miller, May 15, 1947; children—Martha Neal, Katrina Marie, Stephen Francis. Supr. fermentation Seagram-Calvert, Louisville, 1940-47; prof. bacteriology and chemistry U. Fla., Gainesville, 1947-51; dir. research Nutrilite Products, Inc., Buena Park, Calif., 1951-54; prof., head dept. food sci. and tech., prof. marine sci. La. State U., Baton Rouge, from 1954; pres. Internat. Tech. Consultants, 1978-79; v.p. for sci. and tech. Singleton Packing Corp., Tampa, Fla., 1979; cons. foods and drugs, 1947—; cons. to state and fed. agys., 1949—; Ford Found. adviser oceanography, food sci. to Brazil, 1968-69; prof. physiology U. Sao Paulo (Brazil) Faculty Medicine; adviser to India food programs, 1976; adviser to Venezuela, 1977; tech. dir. Internat. Shrimp Council, 1967—. Mem. Internat. Tech. Assistance Com., 1960—. Bd. dirs. Boys Clubs So. Calif., pres., 1952-54. Fellow Am. Inst. Chemists; mem. AAAS, Gulf Coast Inst. Food Technologists (pres. 1964-65, Man of Year award 1976), Am. Pharm. Assn., Am. Nuclear Soc., Oyster Inst. N.Am., Nat. Fisheries Inst., Nat. Shell Fisheries Assn., Am. Soc. Microbiology, Am. Chem. Soc., Marine Tech. Soc., Shrimp Assn. Ams., Shrimp Breeders and Processors Am. (tech. dir.), So. Assn. Food and Drug Ofcls., Council Am. Bioanalysts, ASHRAE, Inst. Food Technologists (chmn. constn. and by-laws, food quality control coms.), Rho Chi, Gamma Sigma Epsilon, Phi Kappa Phi, Gamma

Sigma Delta, Pi Tau Sigma, Lambda Tau, Phi Kappa, Omicron Delta Kappa. Author: Microbiology of Shellfish, 1962, Fundamentals of Food Science, Fish Proteins, 1977. Contbr. articles to profl. jours. Patentee in field. Home: Baton Rouge, La. Died July 29, 1979.

NOVILLE, GEORGE OTTILIE, aeronautical engr.; b. Cleveland, O., Apr. 24, 1890; s. Otto John and Rose Marie (Curran) N.; grad. Central High Sch., Cleveland, 1908; student U.S. Navy Tech. Sch., 1906-08; also Columbia; m. Sigrid Erica Matson of N.Y. City, Sept. 8, 1925. Lt. Aviation Corps, U.S.N., 1906-22; on French and Italian fronts, World War; lt. comdr. U.S.N.R.F.; engr. with Vacuum Oil Co., 1922-25, Standard Oil Co. from 1925. Third in comd. Byrd North Pole Flight, May 9, 1926; asst. pilot with Comdr. Byrd on trans-Atlantic flight, monoplane "America," 1927. Awarded Distinguished Flying Cross (U.S.); Medal of Valor (N.Y.); Croce di Guerra (Italy); also Belgian flying decoration. Mem. Professional Pilots' Assn., Nat. Aeronautical Assn. Clubs: Union League, Old Colony, Family.†

NOWLAN, ALDEN, author; b. near Windsor, N.S., Can., Jan. 25, 1933; s. Freeman and Grace (Reese) N.; m. Claudine Orser, Aug. 27, 1963; 1 son, John. Litt.D. (hon.), U. N.B., 1971; LL.D., Dalhousie U., 1976. News editor Telegraph-Jour., St. John, N.B., Can., 1963-68. Writer-in-residence, U. N.B., Fredericton, from 1968; Author: The Rose and the Puritan, 1958, A Darkness in the Earth, 1959, Under the Ice, 1961, Wind in a Rocky Country, 1961, The Things Which Are, 1962, Bread, Wine and Salt, 1967, Miracle at Indian River, 1968, The Mysterious Naked Man, 1969, Playing the Jesus Game, 1970, Between Tears and Laughter, 1971, Various Persons Named Kevin O'Brien, 1973, I'm A Stranger Here Myself, 1974, Campobello: The Outer Island, 1975, Smoked Glass, 1977, Double Exposure, 1978; (with Walter Learning) plays The Man Who Became God, 1974, The Dollar Woman, 1977, The Incredible Murder of Cardinal Tosca, 1978. Recipient Gov. Gen.'s award for poetry, 1968, medal for poetry Can. Authors Assn., 1978, Queen's Silver Jubilee medal, 1978; Can. Council fellow, 1961, 67; Guggenheim fellow, 1968. Mem. Writers Union of Can. Home: Fredericton, N.B., Can. Died June 27, 1983.

NUGENT, WILLIAM A., mfg. exec.; b. Mattoon, Ill., 1889. Exec. v.p. Thor Power Tool Co. unitl 1960, dir. Home: Chgo., Ill. †

NUSBAUM, JESSE LOGAN, archaeologist; b. Greeley, Colo., Sept. 3, 1887; s. Edward Moore and Agnes Strickland (Moodie) N.; B.Pd., Colo. Teachers Coll., 1907; studied U. of Colo., George Washington U.; D.Sc., Colorado State College of Education, 1946; mar. Aileen Baehrens, Sept. 21, 1920 (divorced 1939); married 2d, Rosemary L. Rife, December 11, 1947. Member archaeol. expdn. to Mesa Verde, Colo., 1906; instr. manual arts and science, N.M. Normal U., Las Vegas, 1907-09; from many yrs. photographer, explorer, excavator and repairer of ruins of Cliff Dwellers in Southwest, also mem. or dir. expdns. to Utah, Mexico, Yucatan, Guatemala, etc.; apptd. supt. Mesa Verde Nat. Park, June 3, 1921; apptd. archaeologist, Nat. Park Service, and designated archaeologist of Dept. of Interior, July 9, 1927. Granted leave of absence for 1 yr. to inaugurate and organize Laboratory of Anthropology, at Santa Fe, N.M., and elected dir. of the Lab., Dec. 31, 1930; resigned as supt. Mesa Verde Nat. Park, Mar. 16, 1931, and was redesignated as cons. archaeologist Dept. of Interior and Nat. Park Service; resigned as dir. Lab. of Anthropology, Dec. 31, 1935; supt. Mesa Verde Nat. Park, Jan. 1, 1936-July 31, 1939; apptd. senior archaeologist, National Park Service for Regions II, III, IV and later transferred to Region III, Santa Fe; supt. and senior archeologist Mesa Verde National Park, Apr. 1942-Mar. 1946; transferred to Santa Fe, N.M., as senior archeologist. National Park Service, also consulting archeologist, Dept. of Interior. With Pioneer and Engineer Unit, A.E.F., France, 1917-18. Trustee Laboratory of Anthropology, 1927-38; mem. advisory bd. from 1927. Mem. State Park Commn. on N.M., 1933-36; mem. Council Am. Assn. of Museums, 1932-38; vice chmn. bd. of regents, Mus. of N.M., 1932-35; trustee Indian Arts Fund from 1927; mem. com. Old Santa Fe Assn., from 1946; member mng. board School Amercian Research from 1947. Apptd. by Sec. of State as mem. U.S. Internat. (U.S. and Mexico) Park and Forest Commn. Honorary life member Mus. of N.M.; hon. mem. at large Pi Gamma Mu, fellow A.A.A.S. (chmn. social sciences, southwestern div., 1932-33; v.p. 1935-36); mem. Am. Anthropol. Assn., Soc. of Am. Archaeology, Am. Planning & Civic Assn. Republican. Episcopalian. Mason (32 deg.). Author: (with others) Basket Maker Cave in Kane County, Utah, 1923; Basket Maker Cave in Mesa Verde National Park, Colo., 1949. Address: Santa Fe, N.M. †

NUSSBAUM, MURRAY, physician; b. Bklyn., May 19, 1927; s. Jacob and Ida (Witkoff) N.; m. Sue-Carol Ludacer, Apr. 3, 1954; children—Jonathan David, Robert Alan. B.S., U. Vt., 1949, M.D., 1952. Diplomate: Am. Bd. Internal Medicine. Intern New Eng. Med. Center, Boston, 1952-53; resident Boston City Hosp., 1953-54; asst. in medicine Tufts U. Med. Sch., Boston, 1955-56; instr. in medicine Seton Hall Coll. Medicine, Jersey City, 1957-59; asst. prof. medicine Coll. Medicine and Dentistry, N.J. Med. Sch., Newark, 1959-66, asso. prof., 1966-70, prof. medicine, from 1970; dir. hematology div. N.J. Med. Sch. Author: Understanding Hematology, 1973; contbr. research articles to jours. Served with AUS, 1945-47. USPHS research fellow in hematology, 1954-55. Fellow A.C.P.; Internat. Soc. Hematology; mem. Am. Soc. Hematology, Am. Heart Assn. (council on Thrombosis). Democrat. Jewish. Home: Wayne, NJ.

NUTLY, WILLIAM B., judge; b. 1888; B.A., Bowdoin Coll.; student law U. Me. Admitted to Me. bar, 1917; asso. justice Supreme Ct. of Me.†

NYE, FRANK WILSON, author; b. Hudson, Wis., June 6, 1887; s. Edgar Wilson and Clara Frances (Smith) N.; father known as "Bill Nye"; ed. pvt. schs. in N.C., Washington and Berlin; grad. high sch., Ithaca, N.Y., 1903; m. Helen Radcliffe Mountfortt, Aug. 18, 1909; children—Edgar Wilson, Lorraine Mountfortt. Adv. mgr. Craftsman Mag., 1908-09; mgr. New York office, adv. dept. Butterick Pub. Co., 1910-13; adv. mgr. Today's Mag., 1914-17; pres. Churchill-Hall Adv. Agency, 1917-18; adv. mgr. Hearst's Mag., 1918-19; investment business, 1919-21; pres. Outdoor Adv. Agency of America from 1921; pres. Ivan B. Nordhem Co. Republican. Mason, Moose. Clubs: Lotos, Advertising, St. Andrew's Golf, St. George's Golf. Author: Bill Nye-His Own Life Story, 1926. Home: Spuyten Duyvil, N.Y. †

NYHOLM, JENS, univ. librarian; b. Hjörring, Denmark, July 24, 1900; s. Johannes and Ellen Marie (Bartsch) N.; came to U.S. 1927, naturalized, 1937; Ph.B., U. Copenhagen, 1920; certificate Danish State Library Sch., 1923; B.S., Columbia, 1928; M.A., George Washington U., 1934; m. Amy Wood, July 26, 1941. Asst., Pub. Library, Copenhagen, 1919-21; asst. librarian Nordjyske Landsbibliotek, Aalborg, Denmark, 1923-27; asst. library of Congress, Washington, D.C., also corr. Danish newspapers, 1928-37; head catalog dept. library U. Calif. at Los Angeles, 1938-39; asst. librarian U. Calif. at Berkeley, 1939-44; univ. librarian Northwestern U., 1944-68; bibilog. cons. U. Calif. Library, Santa Barbara, from 1969. Dir. Midwest Inter-Library Corp. (name now Center for Research Libraries), 1949-65, chmn., 1955-56. Fellow Am.-Scandinavian Found., 1927-28. Mem. ALA, Friends of U. Calif. Library Santa Barbara (chmn. 1971-76), Bibliog. Soc. Am., Soc. Advancement Scandinavian Study, Rebild Nat. Park Soc. Clubs: University (Evanston, Ill.); Caxton (pres. 1966-67 (Chgo.); Grolier (N.Y.C.). Author: Portal til Amerika, 1953; Amerikanske Stemmer, 1968. Editorial staff Libri, Internat. Library Rev., Scandinavian Studies, 1945-57. Contbr. to lit., profl. jours. Home: Santa Barbara, Calif. Died Jan. 27, 1983.

OAKLAND, SIMON, actor; b. N.Y.C., 1922. Student, Am. Theatre Wing. Former profl. violinist; various Broadway appearance; motion pictures include: I Want to Live, 1958, Who Was That Lady? , 1960, The Rise and Fall of Legs Diamond, 1960, Psycho, 1960, Murder, Inc, 1960, West Side Story, 1961, Follow That Dream, 1962, Third of a Man, Wall of Noise, 1963, The Satan Bug, 1965, The Plainsman, 1966, The Sand Pebbles, 1966, Tony Rome, 1967, Chubasco, 1968, Scandalous John, 1971, Chato's Land, 1972, Emperor of the North, 1973, Happy Mother's Day...Love, George, 1973; appeared: in TV series Toma, 1973-74, The Night Stalker, 1974-75, Baa Baa Black Sheep, 1976-77, Black Sheep Squadron, 1977-78. Served in mil., World War II. Address: New York, N.Y. Died Aug. 29, 1983.*

OATES, JAMES FRANKLIN, JR., lawyer; b. Evanston, Ill., Nov. 11, 1899; s. James Franklin and Henrietta (Jennings) O.; m. Rosalind Wright, June 19, 1925; children—Rosalind (Mrs. Cabell Arnold Pearse), James Franklin III. Grad., Phillips Exeter Acad., 1917; B.A., Princeton, 1921; J.D., Northwestern U., 1924; LL.D., Ill. Coll., 1952, Lake Forest Coll., 1958, George Williams Coll., 1959, Hampden-Sydney Coll., 1962, Centre Coll., 1967, Butler U., 1968, Willamette U., 1966, Hamline U., 1966; L.H.D., Neb. Wesleyan U., 1965; D.C.S., Pace Coll., 1965; Litt.D., Presbyn. Coll., 1968. Bar: Ill. bar 1924. Asso. firm Cutting, Moore & Sidley, Chgo.; Assoc. firm Cutting, Moore & Sidley (and successor, Sidley, Austin, Burgess & Harper), Chgo., 1924-48, partner, 1931-48; counsel Sidley & Austin, from 1970; legal adviser Chgo. Ordnance Dist., 1942; chief purchase policy Office Chief of Ordnance, Washington, 1942-44; chmn. chief exec. officer, dir. Peoples Gas Light & Coke Co., Chgo., 1948-57; chmn. bd., chief exec. officer, dir. Equitable Life Assurance Soc. U.S., N.Y.C., 1957-69; Mem. N.Y. State Commn. on Quality, Cost and Financing Elementary and Secondary Edn.; nat. chmn. Jobs for Vets. Charter emeritus trustee, former chmn. exec. com. bd. trustees Princeton; trustee Northwestern U. (life), George Williams Coll. (hon.), Chgo. Mus. Sci. and Industry (hon.), Chgo. Northwestern Meml. Hosp. Served as 2d lt., inf. U.S. Army, 1918-19. Recipient Key Man award Ave. of Ams. Assn., 1962, Gold Medal award Gen. Insurance Brokers Assn., 1964, Gold Medal of Merit award Wharton Sch. alumni assn., 1965, John Phillips award Phillips Exeter Acad., 1966. Mem. ABA, Chgo. Bar Assn. (past pres.). Republican. Presbyterian (past elder). Clubs: Links (N.Y.C.), Anglers (N.Y.C.), Princeton (N.Y.C.); Chicago (Chgo), Law (Chgo), Commercial (Chgo) (past pres.), Mid-Day (Chgo) Onwentsia (Lake Forest), Old Elm (Lake Forest); University Cottage (Princeton, N.J.), Nassau (Princeton, N.J.). Home: Lake Forest, Ill. Died Oct. 21, 1982.

OATES, WARREN, actor; b. Depoy, Ky., July 5, 1928. Student, U. Louisville. Film appearances include Up Periscope, 1959, The Rise and Fall of Legs Diamond, 1960, Ride the High Country, 1962, Mail Order Bride, 1964, Major Dundee, 1965, Welcome to Hard Times, 1967, In the Heat of the Night, 1967, The Wild Bunch, 1969, The Hired Hand, 1971, Dillinger, 1973, Badlands, 1974, 92 in the Shade, 1975, The Brinks Job, 1978, Stripes, 1981; TV appearances Baby Comes Home, And Baby Makes Six, True Grit, My Old Man. Home: Los Angeles, Calif. Died April 3, 1982.*

OBERNAUER, HAROLD, lawyer; b. Pittsburgh, Pa., Jan. 3, 1887; s. Herman and Bertha (Dinch) O.; A.B., Yale, 1910; LL.B., U. of Pittsburgh Law Sch., 1913; unmarried, Admitted to Pa. bar, 1913; also admitted to Supreme and Superior courts of Pa. and all Federal courts. Served as chmn. legal advisory bd. Dist. No. 2, Pittsburgh, during World War I; chmn. Selective Service Appeal Bd. A. Area 9, Pa., 1940-46. Vice chmn. bd. law examiners, Allegheny County, 1935-43. Mem. Y.M. and W.H.A. of Pittsburgh (director 1929-35 and 1939-42). Mem. Hebrew Free Loan Assn. (dir. 1934-37); mem. Fedn. Jewish Philanthropies of Pittsburgh (dir. 1933-36); trustee Irene Kaufmann Settlement, Pittsburgh, since 1941. Mem. Pittsburgh Council on Intercultural Education. Mem. Better Traffic Com. City of Pittsburgh, 1939-41. Mem. Am. Bar Assn. (com. pub. relations, 1937-40), Pennsylvania State Bar Association (regional director 6th Zone, 1941-42, chmn. com. on public relations, 1937-45), Allegheny County Bar Assn. (pres. 1938-40; trustee since 1942), Univ. of Pittsburgh Alumni Assn. (pres. 1935-36), U. of Pittsburgh Law Sch. Alumni Assn. (organizer and dir.), Boy Scouts of America (vice-pres. Allegheny County, 1917-23), Pittsburgh Charter Plan (exec. com.), Pittsburgh Defense Council (law enforcement com.), Home, Farm and Property Owners' Assn. of Allegheny County (v.p., dir., 1945-47), Bellefield Educational Trust (trustee), Omicron Delta Kappa. Jewish religion. Mason (past master; dist. dep. grand master from 1926), Elk (past exalted ruler). K.P., I.O.O.F. Clubs: Yale of Pittsburgh, Pittsburgh Athletic; Pennsylvania Soc. of New York, N.Y. †

OBERWINDER, JOHN FERDINAND, advt. exec.; b. St. Louis, Mo., Oct. 26, 1888; s. Jacob and Mary Louise (Kessler) O.; student pub. schs. of St. Louis, Mo.; m. Swann Gower Matthews, Oct. 28, 1911; 1 son, John Ferdinand. Apprentice Lesan Advt. Co., St. Louis, 1904; advt. rep. N.Y. Times, St. Louis Globe-Democrat. Phila. North American; Chicago br. mgr. Lewis Pub. Co.; pres. and dir. D'Arcy Advt. Co., St. Louis; pres. Publicidad D'Arcy, S.A., Mexico City; dir. Plaza Bank of St. Louis. Served as maj. A.E.F., World War I; Adm. Rationing Bd. St. Louis, World War II. Life dir. St. Louis Tuberculosis Soc.; dir. Advertising council. Mem. Am. Assn. of Advt. Agencies, Nat. C. of C., N.Y. C. of C., St. Louis Chamber of Commerce, Military Order of World War (life mem.). Clubs: Racquet, Noonday, Advertising (St. Louis, Mo.); Army and Navy (Washington, D.C.); Union (Cleveland). Home: St. Louis, Mo. †

O'BRIEN, DANIEL J., hotel exec.; b. Cork, Ireland, Jan. 8, 1888; s. Matthew D. and Johannah (Leahy) O'B.; came to U.S., 1909, naturalized, 1918; student Christian Coll., (Ireland), N.Y.U., Nat. U., Washington; Certified Pub. Accountant, Ky., 1925; m. Barbara Willis, July 11, 1914; m. 2d, Ethel M. Miller, 1953. Began hotel career at Belmont Hotel, N.Y. City, 1909; pres. co. operating Mayflower (Washington) and other hotels, 1925-31; pres., mng. dir. Commodore Perry Co., Toledo, operating Hotels Commodore Perry, Secor and Willard, 1934-56. Member bd. St. Vincent's Hosp. Decorated Order Crown of Italy. Mem. Am. Hotel Assn. (pres. 1950-51), Am. Inst. Accounting. Clubs: Rotary (past pres.), Toledo, Inverness, Tavern, Alfalfa, Friendly Sons of St. Patrick. Author: Hotel Administration and Control (with C. B. Couchman), 1927. Home: Santa Barbara, Cal. †

O'BRIEN, EDMOND, actor; b. N.Y.C., Sept. 10, 1915; s. James Alfred and Agnes (Baldwin) O'B.; student pub. schs, N.Y.C.; student Neighborhood Play House, Studio of the Theatre; m. Olga San Juan, Sept. 26, 1948; children—Bridget, Maria. Appeared numerous Broadway prodns., including the John Gielgud Hamlet as Prince Hal in Henry IV, as Mercutio in Romeo and Juliet, also Moss Hart prodn. Winged Victory; motion pictures include Barefoot Contessa, Julius Caesar, 711 Ocean Drive, White Heat, D.O.A., Up Periscope, The Rack, The Last Voyage, Third Voice, The Longest Day, Sylvia, Seven Days in May, The Great Imposter, The Man Who Shot Liberty Valance, Birdman of Alcatraz, Fantastic Voyage, 1966, The Viscount, 1967, The Love God?, 1969, The Wild Bunch, To Commit a Murder, 1970, They Only Kill Their Masters, 99 and 44/100ths % Dead, 1974; star weekly TV series Sam Benedict, 1962. Served with USAAF, World War II. Recipient Look mag. award, 1955; Fgn. Correspondents award, 1955; Acad. award for Barefoot Contessa, 1954; Exhibitor Laurel awards, 1956, 57. Mem. Screen Actors Guild. Screen Dirs. Guild, A.F.R.T.A. Died May 9, 1985.*

O'BRIEN, JOHN J., railway exec.; b. Brooklyn, N.Y., Nov. 4, 1888; s. John T. and Margaret (Monohan) O'B.; student St. John's; m. 2d, Gladys Comerford, Oct. 18, 1935; children—Patricia Anne, Emmett Timothy; children by previous marriage—Cecilia, John J., Jere E. (dec.), Maureen. With Coverdale & Colpitts from 1913, mgr. from 1920; asst. sec. Pierce Oil Corp., 1925-30, v.p., sec. and treas., 1930-1940; v.p., dir. and sec. Mpls. & St. Louis

Ry. Co., 1943-54; trustee West Caddo Oil Syndicate, 1922-54. Mem. Friends of McGill U., Inc. Pres. Am. Basketball League, Inc., 1928-53. K.C. Elk. Clubs: Catholic of Brooklyn (pres.); Rockville (L.I., N.Y.) Country Broad Street (N.Y.C.). Home: Rockville Centre, L.I., N.Y. †

O'BRIEN, LEO WILLIAM, congressman; b. Buffalo, Sept. 21, 1900; B.A., Niagara U., 1922; m. Mabel Jean; children—Robert, Mary. Newspaperman from 1922, also radio and TV commentator. Mem. Albany (N.Y.) Port Dist. Commn., 1935-52; elected rep. 30th N.Y. Dist., 82d Congress, Apr. 1952, to fill vacancy created by death of William T. Byrne; mem. 83d-85th Congresses, 30th N.Y. District. Democrat. Home: Albany, N.Y. Died May 4, 1982.

O'BRIEN, MAXWELL A., army officer, lawyer; b. Chgo., Nov. 21, 1890; LL.B., U. Ia., 1914; m. Virginia Slade, Nov. 24, 1915; children—Maxwell S., Samuel G., Mary Alice. Mem. law firm Parrish, Guthrie, Colflesh & O'Brien, Des Moines, Ia.; 1st asst. atty. gen. of Iowa, 1924-28; counsel for Iowa State Highway Commn., 1929-32; became comdg. officer, 113th Cav., April, 1936; asst. comdr., 4th Motorized Div., Camp Gordon Johnson, Fla., Jan. 1941-Nov. 1943; comdg. gen., U.S. troops, overseas; brig. gen. (inactive) retired with rank of major general. Former mem. bd. Bur. Municipal Research. Decorated Legion of Merit, 1945. Mason (Shriner). Clubs: Des Moines. Home: Des Moines, Ia. †

O'BRIEN, RAY J., lawyer; b. Mare Island, Calif., Nov. 2, 1889; s. John and Katherine (Hayes) O'B.; LL.B., Hastings Coll. of Law, 1913; m. Ruth Louise True, Oct., 1923; 1 son, Ray Joseph. Admitted to Calif. bar, 1913; associated in practice with Justice E. C. Peters, Hawaii, 1913-17; private practice in Honolulu, 1919-22; apptd. judge, circuit court, 1st Judicial Court, T.H., 1922-25; judge Territorial Tax Appeal Court and mem. territorial bar examiners, T.H., 1925-41; judge circuit ct., 3d Judicial Court, T.H., 1943-45; U.S. atty. for Hawaii from 1945. Served with 91st Div., A.E.F., U.S.A., 1917-19; judge advocate, Hawaiian Territorial Guard, 1941-42, comdr. (lt. col.), 1942-43. Mem. Phi Alpha Delta. Clubs: Oahu Country, Outrigger Canoe (Honolulu). Home: Honolulu, Hi. †

O'BRIEN, THOMAS STANLEY, III, lawyer; b. Albany, N.Y., May 28, 1916; s. Thomas Stanley and Marguerite Mary (Boyle) O'B.; m. Constance Ann Cole, Sept. 29, 1951; 1 dau., Ann Cole O'Brien Hamlin. A.B. Holy Cross Coll., 1937; LL.B., Harvard, 1942. Bar: N.Y. State bar 1942, S.C. bar 1978. Trust clk. First Trust Co., Albany, N.Y., 1937-38; asso. atty. Cravath Swaine & Moore, N.Y.C., 1942-48; atty., asst. sec. Air Reduction Co., Inc., 1948-51, sec., 1951-65; also sec. Air Reduction Co., Inc. (subs.); gen. counsel Union Camp Corp., 1965-76. Mem. Internat., Am., N.Y. State, S.C., Hilton Head bar assns., Am. Soc. Corp. Secs. Roman Catholic. Hilton Head Island SC.

OCHSNER, ALTON, surgeon; b. Kimball, S.D., May 4, 1896; s. Edward Phillip and Clara (Shontz) O.; A.B., U. S.D., 1918, D.Sc., 1936; M.D., Washington U., 1920; LL.D., Tulane U., 1966; Dr. h.c., U. Athens, Greece; m. Isabel Kathryn Lockwood, Sept. 13, 1923 (dec.); children—Alton, John Lockwood, Mims Gage, Isabel; m. 2d, Jane Kellogg Sturdy, Feb. 12, 1970. Intern, Barnes Hosp., St. Louis, 1920-21; Augustana Hosp. Chgo., 1921-22; exchange surg. asst. Kantons Hosp., Zurich, Switzerland, 1922-23, Staedtisches Krankenhaus, Frankfurt am Main, 1923-24; visited European and Am. clinics, 1924-25; instr. surgery Northwestern U. Med. Sch., 1925-26; asst. prof. surgery U. Wis. Med. Sch., 1926-27; prof. surgery, chmn. dept. Tulane U. Med. Sch., 1927-56, William Henderson prof. surgery, 1938-56, prof. clin. surgery, 1956-61, prof. emeritus, 1961-81, cons. in gen. surgery Ochsner Clinic, Found. Hosp.; hon. staff Touro Infirmary; cons. surgeon Charity Hosp.; cons. thoracic surgery USPHS Hosp., VA Hosp., New Orleans. Dir. Fawley Enterprises Inc., Nat. Airlines, Inc., Fla. Nat. Banks Fla. Pres., Alton Ochsner Med. Found., 1942-70. Decorated Order Vasco Nunez de Balboa (Panama); Orden al Merito (Ecuador); Cruz El Roy Alfaro de Fundacion Internacional El Roy Alfaro (Panama); Orden Rodolfo Robles (Guatemala), Ordenal Merito (Spain); recipient Times-Picayune Loving Cup as New Orleans' outstanding citizen; Distinguished Service award A.M.A.; named Distinguished Salesman-at-Large of New Orleans; Thomas F. Cunningham award Internat. House New Orleans. Fellow A.C.S. (regent, past pres.), Am., So. (past pres.) surg. assns., Royal Coll. Surgeons Ireland (hon.), Royal Coll. Surgeons Eng. (hon.); mem. Internat. Soc. Surgery (past pres.), AMA, Am. Assn. Thoracic Surgery (past pres., hon.), Soc. Vascular Surgery (past pres.), Internat. Surg. Soc. Clin. Surgery, Southeastern (past pres.), So. (past pres.) surg. assns., Orleans Parish Med. Soc., Am. Cancer Soc. (dir.), Pan-Pacific Surg. Assn. (pres. 1963), So., La. med. assns., Am. Acad. Orthopedic Surgeons (hon.), Academie Royale de Medecine de Belgique (fgn. hon.), numerous fgn. sci. assns. (hon.), Phi Beta Kappa, Sigma Xi, Nu Sigma Nu, Alpha Omega Alpha, Omicron Delta Kappa, Phi Delta Theta. Clubs: Boston, New Orleans Country. Author: Smoking and Cancer, 1954; Smoking and Health, 1959; Smoking and Your Life, 1964; Smoking: Your Choice Between Life and Death, 1970. Writer: sect. on intestines Nelson's Loose Leaf Surgery, 1928; sect. on diseases of veins Lewis'

System of Surgery; sect. on thoracic surgery and mediastinum Brennemann's Pediatrics; Monograph on Varicose Veins. Past chief editor Internat. Surg. Digest; past editor surg. sect. Cyclopedia of Medicine, Surgery and Specialties; past asst. editor Surgery of the Emergency; editor emeritus Surgery; asso. editor Lewis Practice of Surgery. Home: New Orleans, La. Died Sept. 24, 1981.

O'CONNELL, JOHN JAMES, III, publishing co. exec.; b. Bklyn., Feb. 17, 1921; s. John James and Hazel (Hines) O'C.; m. Carmel K. O'Reilly, May 15, 1944; children—Christine, John J. IV, Carmel, William Egan. A.B., Manhattan Coll., 1941. With Office of Prodn., Washington, 1941; staff Cosmopolitan Mag., N.Y.C., 1946-59, editor-in-chief, 1951-59, American Weekly, 1959-63; dir. editorial enterprises N.Y. Jour.-Am., 1963; exec. editor This Week mag., 1963-65, editor, 1965-68; dir. publs. Famous Schs., Inc., Westport, 1968-72; exec. asst. to William Randolph Hearst, Jr., Hearst Corp., N.Y.C., 1972-73; exec. editor Hearst Newspapers, 1973-82; dir. Hearst Headline Service, 1973-82. Served as lt. USNR, 1942-46, PTO. Decorated Bronze Star. Clubs: N.Y. Athletic (N.Y.C.), Dutch Treat (N.Y.C.); National Press, Overseas Press. Home: Stamford, Conn. Died Sept. 2, 1982.

O'CONNOR, CHARLES JEROME, mfg. exec.; b. Indpls., Feb. 22, 1889; s. Timothy Joseph and Mary (O'Connell) O'C.; student pub. schs.; m. Marie Burke, Dec. 28, 1914; children—Maurice F., Donald E., Mary Alice (Mrs. A. O. Baker). With O'Brien Varnish Co., 1913-20, Eastman Kodak Co., 1920-27; treas. Reichhold Chemicals, Inc., 1927-32, exec. v.p., 1932-41. president, 1941-57, chairman of the board, from 1957; director Japan Reichhold Chemicals, Inc., Reichhold Chemicals (Can.) Ltd., Reichhold Chemicals, Inc. (Australia) Proprietary, Ltd., Mardon Co. Mem. Nat. Security Indsl. Assn. (vice chmn. bd.), Nat. Paint Varnish and Lacquer Assn. (exec. com.), Chemists Club. Clubs: New York Athletic; Detroit Athletic; Chicago Athletic; Bohemian (San Francisco); Bloomfield Hills (Mich.) Country. Home: Birmingham, Mich. †

O'CONNOR, JOHN, JR., fine arts; b. Pittsburgh, Pa., Mar. 3, 1887; s. John and Ella (Lawler) O'C.; A.B., U. of Pittsburgh, 1910, A.M., 1913; m. Eleanor Jahn, 1911 (dec.); children—John, Dorothy. Resident dir. of work for boys, Irene Kaufmann Settlement, 1910-11; asst. on economic survey of Pittsburgh, 1911-12; economist, smoke investigation, Mellon Inst. Indsl. Research, 1912-13, sr. fellow, 1913-14; asst. dir., Mellon Inst., 1914-18; chief of credits div., Office Dir. of Finance of Army, 1918-19; dir. Sch. of Social Work, Duquesne U., 1919-20; bus. mgr., dept. fine arts Carnegie Inst., 1920-35, asst. dir., 1935-49, acting dir., 1941-45, asso. dir. from 1949. Democrat. Roman Catholic. Home: Pittsburgh, Pa. †

O'CONNOR, RODERIC LADEW, former govt. ofcl.; b. N.Y.C., Aug. 10, 1921; s. James William and Dorothy Ladew (Williams) O'C.; student St. Paul's Sch., 1935-40; B.A., Yale, 1943, LL.D., 1947; m. Ingrid Ellgar, Dec. 21, 1954; children—Michael, Christina. Admitted N.Y. State bar, 1947; asso. atty. firm Rathbone, Perry, Kelley & Drye (now Kelley, Drye, Newhall & Maginnes), N.Y.C., 1947-49, 49-50; legislative asst. U.S. Senator John Foster Dulles, 1949; atty. fed. govt., 1950-52; spl. asst. to sec. state, 1953-55; dep. asst. sec. state for Congl. relations, 1955-57; adminstr. with rank of asst. sec. Bur. of Security and Consular Affairs, Dept. State, 1957-58; mem. U.S. delegation Ministerial Sessions N. Atlantic Council, 1953, 54, meeting of fgn. ministers, Berlin, 1954, 10th Inter-Am. Conf., Caracas, 1954, Southeast Asia Def. Pact, Manila, 1954, Geneva Conf., 1954, Nine-Power Meeting, London, 1954, to Heads of Govt. Four-Power Meeting, Geneva, 1955, Fgn. Ministers Meeting, Geneva, 1955; chmn. U.S. sect. Caribbean Commn., 1956-60; U.S. rep. Council Inter-govtl. Com. on European Migration, Geneva, 1957; v.p., dir. Ciba Corp., 1959-62, v.p., sec., dir. 1962-69; asst. adminstr. AID, Dept. State, 1969-73; pres. Citizens Budget Commn., from 1973. Chmn., Civic Affairs Forum, from 1975. Mem. N.J. Republican Finance Com., 1965-69. Bd. dirs. Cooper Union. Served to 1st lt., navigator 15th Air Force, USAAF, 1943-45. Decorated comdr. Order Orange Nassau (Netherlands); recipient Superior Honor award Dept. of State, 1973. Clubs: 60 East, Yale (N.Y.C.); Somerset Hills Country; Essex Hunt. Died Oct. 24, 1982.

O'CONNOR, WILLIAM JEROME, business exec.; b. Barnesville, Minn., Apr. 4, 1888; s. William Cornelius and Alice (Butler) O'C.; student Gonzaga Coll., 1906; m. Mary Dick, Oct. 1910; children—William Jerome and Elizabeth (twins); m. 2d Grizzelle Lamb, 1929. Chemist Am. Smelting & Refining Co., Garfield, Utah, 1910-16, metallurgist, ore buyer, asst. mgr. later gen. mgr. Utah dept., 1917-48; broker J.A. Hogle, Salt Lake City, 1916-17; pres. Garfield Chem. Co., Independent Coal & Coke Co.; dir. First Security Bank; v.p. Western Rock Bit Co. (all Salt Lake City). Pres. Salt Lake Winter Sports Assn. Mem. C. of C., Am. Inst. Mining Engrs., Am. Metall. Soc., Community Chest, Symphony Orchestra. Mason (Shriner). Clubs: Alta, Salt Lake Country, Bear River Duck, Flat Rock Fishing. (Salt Lake City). Home: Salt Lake City, Utah. †

ODGERS, MERLE MIDDLETON, univ. pres.; b. Phila., Apr. 21, 1900; s. David and Elizabeth (Ramsay) O.; A.B., U. Pa., 1922, A.M., 1924, Ph.D., 1928, Litt.D., 1948; L.H.D., Temple U., 1938; LL.D., Ursinus Coll., 1943, Lafayette Coll., 1958, Bucknell U., 1964; m. Frances Bartram Bunting, June 28, 1927; children—Eleanor Bunting (Mrs. J.P. Laver, Jr.), John Bartram. Instr. Latin. U. Pa., 1922-28, asst. prof., 1928-36, prof., 1936, asst. dir. admissions, 1926-33, dean Coll. Liberal Arts for Women, 1933-36; pres. Girard Coll., Phila., 1936-54; pres. Bucknell U., 1954-64, emeritus, 1964-83. Dir. Geisinger Med. Center, 1962. Decorated Chevalier French Legion of Honor, 1947. Trustee Temple U., 1938-41; trustee Free Library of Phila., 1943-54, dir. 1948-54; dir. Sordoni Found., 1955-64, Western Saving Fund Soc., Phila., United War Chest (Phila., 1942-45), Presser Found., 1934-47, Phila. Vets. Adv. Center, 1944-48, Phila. Navy League Council; former trustee U. Pa.; mem. bd. visitors Air U., Maxwell AFB, Ala., 1960-63; former chmn. Phila. Com., Greek War Relief Assn. Chmn., Phila. Mayor's Scholarship Com.; formerly v.p. France Forever (Phila.); former chmn. Phila. Five County Dist. Commn. for Econ. Devel. Mem. Gen. Alumni Soc. U. Pa. (pres. 1943-45). Am. Legion, Classical Assn. Atlantic States, Am. Philol. Assn., Am. Assn. U. Profs., Linguistic Soc. Am., Phila. Art Alliance, N.E.A., L'Assn. Guillaume Budé (Paris). Numismatic and Antiquarian Soc. Phila., Phi Beta Kappa, Pi Kappa Alpha, Phi Delta Kappa, Pi Mu Epsilon, Eta Sigma Phi, Omicron Delta Kappa. Mason. Presbyn. Clubs: Rittenhouse (Phila.); St. Andrews Soc. (pres. 1943-45); Faculty; The University (N.Y.C.). Author: Latin Parens, 1929; Fifteen Hundred Looking On, 1943; Brothers of Girard, 1944; Alexander Dallas Bache, 1947. Co-author: Four Talks of Bibliophiles, 1958. Died Sept. 6, 1983.

ODISHAW, HUGH, university dean; b. N. Battleford, Can., Oct. 13, 1916; came to U.S., 1922, naturalized, 1941; s. Abraham and Miriam (Davajan) O.; m. Marian Lee Scates, 1958. A.B., Northwestern U., 1939, M.A., 1941; student, Princeton, 1939-40; B.S., Ill. Inst. Tech., 1944; Sc.D., Carleton Coll., 1958. Instr. Ill. Inst. Tech., 1941-44; with Westinghouse Electric Corp., 1944-45, 45-46; staff OSRD, 1945; asst. to dir. Nat. Bur. Standards, 1946-54; exec. dir. U.S. nat. com. IGY, 1954-65; dir. IGY World Data Center A., 1954-72; exec. sec., div. phys. scis. Nat. Acad. Scis., 1966-72; dean Coll. Earth Scis., U. Ariz., Tucson, 1972-84. Author, editor: (with L. V. Berkner) Science in Space, 1961; Editor: (with E.U. Condon) The Handbook of Physics, 1958; Author sci. articles. Fellow Am. Geophys. Union; mem. Am. Phys. Soc., AAAS, Phi Beta Kappa. Presbyn. Home: Tucson, Ariz. Died Mar. 4, 1984.

OEHLERT, BENJAMIN HILBORN, JR., business consultant, author; b. Phila., Sept. 13, 1909; s. Benjamin H. and Sarah (Landis) O.; m. Alice Greene, Mar. 27, 1937; children: Benjamin Hilborn, Alice Ann. B.S., U. Pa., 1930, J.D., 1933. Bar: Pa. bar 1933. Gen. law practice, Phila., 1933-35; atty. Mexican claims div. State Dept., Washington, 1935-38; asst. counsel Coca Cola Co., 1938-42, asst. to pres., v.p., 1942-48, v.p., 1953-65, sr. v.p., dir., 1965-67, U.S. ambassador to, Pakistan, 1967-69; pres. Minute Maid Co., 1961-65; v.p., dir. W.R. Grace & Co., N.Y.C., 1948-53. Author: Eminent Domain in Pennsylvania. Mem. Fed., Am., Pa., Phila. bar assns., Order of Coif, Phi Delta Phi, Theta Xi. Clubs: Capital City (Atlanta), Piedmont Driving (Atlanta); University (N.Y.C.); Everglades (Palm Beach), Bath and Tennis (Palm Beach), Four Arts (Palm Beach), Beach (Palm Beach). Home: Palm Beach, Fla. Died June 1, 1985.

OFFNER, ALFRED J(OHN), consulting engr.; b. Budapest, Hungary, June 24, 1888; s. John and Olga (Halavats) O.; brought to U.S., 1892, naturalized through parents; B.S., Cooper Union, New York, N.Y., 1910, M.E., 1913; m. Agnes L. Anderson. Draftsman and engr. Konrad Meier, New York, 1904-13; engr. Henry C. Meyer, Jr., New York, 1913-18; consulting engineer for heating, ventilating and air conditioning, New York, N.Y., from 1918. Mem. bd. govs. New York Bldg., Congress, 1946-47. Mem. Am. Soc. Heating and Ventilating Engrs. (nat. pres. 1946, pres. New York chapter, 1930-31), mem. New York Assn. of Cons. Engrs. (pres. 1936). Mem. Internat. Jury, 1947 Turkish Parliament and Govt. Bldg. mech. equipment plan world wide competition. Home: Beechhurst, N.Y. †

OGBURN, DOROTHY STEVENS, writer; b. Atlanta, June 8, 1890; d. George Webb and Abby Latham (Bean) Stevens; student pub. schs., Atlanta; m. Charlton Ogburn, June 8, 1910 (dec. Feb. 1962); children—Charlton, Dorothy Stevens (dec.). Lectr. on Shakespeare's works. Author: Ra-ta-plan—!, 1930; Death on the Mountain, 1931; The Will and the Deed, 1935; (with husband) This Star of England, 1952; The Renaissance Man of England, 1955; (with Charlton Ogburn, Jr.), Shakespeare: The Man Behind the Name, 1962. Home: New York, N.Y. †

OGDEN, FLOYD P., telephone official; b. Sherman, Ky., Sept. 7, 1887; s. Thomas M. and Sarah E. (Burton) O.; B.S., U. of Kan., 1911; m. Greta M. Curry, Nov. 4, 1922. Engr. Mo. & Kan. Telephone & Telegraph Co., Kansas City, Mo., 1911-12, dist. traffic chief, Topeka, Kan., 1912-14; dist. traffic supt., Mt. States Telephone & Telegraph Co., Butte, 1914-16, div. traffic supt., Helena, Mont., 1916-20, Salt Lake, Utah, 1920-22, gen. traffic mgr., Denver, Colo., 1922-29, vice pres. and dir., 1929-43, pres. and dir. since 1943. Mem. Am. Inst. E.E., Sigma Xi. Methodist. Clubs: University, Cherry Hills Country. Home: Denver, Colo. †

OGDEN, HARRY FORD, lawyer, ins. exec.; b. Baltimore, Dec. 9, 1887; s. William J. and Annie J. (Ford) O.; LL.B., U. Md., 1910; m. Mildred Byrd, Sept. 12, 1916 (dec.); children—Elizabeth Ogden Cooper, Jane Ogden Hamilton, Nancy B.; m. 2d Martha Speicher, Mar. 1, 1947. Admitted to Md. bar, 1910; practicing lawyer, Baltimore, 1910-17; adjuster Md. Motor Car Ins. Co., Baltimore, 1918, v.p., 1926-28; v.p. Fidelity & Guaranty Ins. Corp., Baltimore, 1928-40, pres., dir., from 1940; dir., mem. exec. com. U.S. Fidelity & Guaranty Co., Monumental Life Ins. Co.; dir. Union Trust Co. of Md., Factory Ins. Assn., Gen. Adjustment Bur. Chmn. A.R.C.; mem. adv. council Md. Civil Def. Dir. Baltimore Assn. Commerce. Mem. Md. Hist. Soc. Mem. Protestant Episcopal Ch. Clubs: Maryland, Merchants, Wine & Food Society, Maryland Yacht (Baltimore); Drug & Chemical (N.Y. City); Annapolis Yacht (Annapolis, Md.). Home: Baltimore, MD. †

OGDEN, SQUIRE REDMON, lawyer; b. Winchester, Ky., Sept. 9, 1898; s. William Baldwin and Margaret (Redmon) O.; m. Jean Hollingsworth Stewart, June 2, 1934; children—Stewart, William Baldwin, John Carter. A.B., Georgetown (Ky.) Coll., 1920, LL.D., 1957; LL.B., Harvard, 1923. Bar: Ky. bar 1922. Practiced law as asso. Bruce, Bullitt, Gordon & Laurent, 1923-26; partner firm Gordon, Laurent & Ogden, 1926-30, Gordon, Laurent, Ogden & Galphin, 1930-40, Ogden Galphin, Tarrant & Street, Louisville, 1940-1948, Ogden, Galphin & Abell, 1948-58, Ogden, Robertson & Marshall, 1958-84; gen. counsel Ky. Utilities Co., dir., mem. exec. com., 1952-77; gen. counsel Commonwealth Life Ins. Co., 1953-78, also dir., mem. exec. com., 1952-71; Tchr. Jefferson Sch. of Law, 1928-30. Former mem. exec. com. Louisville ARC, 1950-68; former trustee Georgetown (Ky.) Coll., 1940-43; bd. govs. J.B. Speed Art Mus.; trustee Louisville Country Day Sch., 1950-57; nat. chmn. Harvard Law Sch. Fund, 1963-65; mem. vis. com. Harvard Law Sch., 1963-70. Served as 2d lt. U.S. Army, 1918. Fellow Am. Bar Found.; mem. Assn. Life Ins. Counsel, Harvard Alumni Assn. (bd. dirs. 1954-55), English Speaking Union (pres. Ky. br. 1958), Newcomen Soc., ABA, Ky. Bar Assn., Louisville Bar Assn. (pres. 1953), Am. Law Inst., Harvard Law Sch. Assn. (exec. com. 1961-64), Filson Club, Kappa Alpha. So. Baptist. Clubs: Pendennis (Louisville), River Valley (Louisville), Louisville Country (Louisville), Wynn-Stay (Louisville). Home: Louisville, Ky. Died Sept. 18, 1984.

O'GORMAN, HELEN FOWLER, sculptor, painter, author; b. Superior, Wis., Aug. 29, 1904; d. Homer T. and Fannie Elizabeth (Alger) Fowler; m. Henry Coe Lanpher, Dec. 13, 1926 (div. 1939); 1 dau., Florence May (Mrs. Peter D. Ellis); m. Juan O'Gorman, Aug. 7, 1940; 1 dau., Maria Elena (Mrs. Bruce Wilson). Student, Bradford Jr. Coll., 1922; B.F.A., U. Wash., 1925; postgrad., Chouinard Sch. Art, 1930-31; student of, Alexander Archipenko, 1931-37. Bd. dirs. Botanical Gardens Universidad Nacional Autonoma de Mexico; mem. bd. examiners, lectrs., jurors and critics Inst. Allende, Guanajuato, Mexico. Exhibited sculpture in group shows, Los Angeles Mus., 1935, 36, 47th Annual Exhbn. Am. Painting and Sculpture, Art Inst. Chgo., 1936, 37, 38, N.Y. World's Fair, 1939, 40; exhibited paintings, Salon de Pintura, Mexico City, 1943, one-man show, Museo Nacional de Artes Plasticas, Palacio de Bellas Artes, Mexico, 1953; Author: illustrator Mexican Flowering Trees and Plants, 1961, Plantas y Flores de Mexico, 1963; designer jacket cover: for book Las Caetaceas de México (Helia Bravo Hollis); contbr.: articles to various publs. The News, Mexico City, 1953-56. Recipient Order of the Delta Gamma Rose, 1975. Mem. Sociedad Botanica de Mexico, Sociedad Mexicana de Cactologia, Asociacion Mexicana de Orquidelogia, Mexico City Garden Club (hon.). Address: San Antonio, Tex. Died Nov. 7, 1984.

O'GORMAN, JAMES MICHAEL, educator; b. Oswego, N.Y., May 12, 1888; s. Michael and B. Elizabeth (McGrath) O'G; B.S., Columbia, 1909, A.M., 1910; grad. study, same, 1911-12, and summers 1913-16, bachelors' diploma in elementary supervision; grad. study, Syracuse U., 1915; Sc.D., De Paul U., 1928; m. Josephine Newell, Sept. 12, 1920; children—James Newell, Mrs. Alfred Saisselin, John Sherman, Margaret. Headmaster elementary dept. Newman Sch., Hackensack, N.J., 1908; asst. dept ednl. psychology, Teachers Coll. (Columbia), 1911-12; asso. prof. psychology, Miami U., 1912-14; lecturer and instr. dept. of edn., U. of Ill., 1916-19; dir. edn. and head dept. of psychology, Mont. State Coll., 1919-21; prof. secondary edn., U. of Ida., 1921-23; head dept. edn. and acting dean, Grad. Sch., Marquette U., Milwaukee, 1923-24; head dept. edn. same, 1924-28; asso. prof. edn., Hunter Coll., from 1928, chmn. dept. of psychology and philosophy, from 1939. Lecturer summers, Syracuse U., 1915, U. of Mont., 1921, Notre Dame, 1923, Catholic Summer Sch. of America, Cliff Haven, N.Y., 1927, 28, 31, 39, 40. Mem. exec. bd. of Nat. Com. of Catholics for Human Rights; N.E.A. Am. Assn. Univ. Profs., Phi Delta Kappa, Kappa Delta Pi, Phi Eta. Elk. Club: Elks. Pub. lecturer. Contbr. to ednl. jours. Home: Flushing, N.Y. Deceased.

O'GORMAN, JUAN, architect, artist; b. Coyoacan, D.F., Mexico, July 6, 1905; s. Cecil Crawford and Encarnación (O'Gorman) O'G.; m. Helen Fowler, Aug. 7, 1940; 1 dau., María Elena (Mrs. Bruce Wilson). Architect deg., Nat. U. Mexico, 1926. With C. Obregon Santacillia and J. Villagran (architects), 1926-29; pvt. practice architecture, 1929-32; prof. sch. engring. Politechnical Inst., Mexico City, from 1932; head dept. architecture Secretariat of Pub. Edn., 1932-35. Author booklets and mag. articles on art and architecutre.; Works include murals for Patzcuaro (Mich.) Library; frescoes Castle Chapultepec; fresco Banco Internacional S.A, Center Social Studies Unidad Independencia, all Mexico City; mosaic, Hotel Pasada de la Mision, Taxco, Guerrero, Mexico, Santiago, Chile, mosaics for the, Library of the U. City of Mexico, Secretariat Pub. Works and Communications bldgs., mosaics for, Conv. Center Bldg., Hemisfair, San Antonio, one-man show easel paintings, Palace of Fine Arts, Mexico City, 1950, paintings in permanent exhbn., Modern Mus. Art, N.Y.C., Palace of Fine Arts, Mexico City. Recipient Elias Sourasky prize, 1967; Nat. Prize for Arts, 1972. Mem. Acad. Arts Mexico, Council of Superior Edn. and Sci. Investigation, Mexican Soc. Architects. Address: Mexico City, Mex.

OGURA, JOSEPH H., medical educator; b. San Francisco, May 25, 1915; s. Kikuji and Agnes (Akita) O.; m. Ruth Miyamoto, July 15, 1942; children—Susan, John, Peter. B.A., U. Calif. at Berkeley, 1937; M.D., U. Calif. at San Francisco, 1941. Diplomate: Am. Bd. Otolaryngology (bd. dirs.). Instr. U. Calif. at San Francisco Med. Sch., 1942, U. Cin. Med. Sch., 1942-45; resident otolaryngology Washington U. Sch. Medicine, St. Louis, 1945-48, mem. faculty, from 1948, prof. otolaryngology, from 1960, Lindburg prof., head dept., from 1966; mem. council Nat. Inst. Neurol. Diseases and Stroke, 1968—; mem. nat. cancer adv. bd. Nat. Cancer Inst. Contbr. articles to profl. jours.; author chpts. in books. Recipient Semon award, 1977. Fellow A.C.S. (mem. coll. program com., adv. council for otorhinolaryngology); mem. Triological Soc. (editor jour. from 1968, v.p. middle sect. 1970, pres. from 1976), Am. Laryngol. Assn. (Newcomb award 1967, Casselberry award 1968, Modern Medicine award 1971, pres. 1974, de Roaldes award 1979), Am. Soc. Head and Neck Surgery (pres. 1963-65), Soc. Head and Neck Surgeons, James Ewing Soc., Am. Acad. Ophthalmology and Otolaryngology (v.p.), Am. Coll. Chest Physicians, AMA, Am. Soc. Univ. Otolaryngologists, Am. Otolaryngol. Assn. (pres. 1975), Am. Acad. Facial Plastic and Reconstructive Surgery, Collegium Oto-Rhino-Larynologicum Amicitiae Sacrum, Am. Broncho-Esophologic Assn., AAUP, Am. Soc. Ophthal. and Otolargy Allergists, Soc. Acad. Chmn. in Otolaryngology (pres.). Home: Saint Louis, Mo. Died Apr. 14, 1983.

O'HARA, THOMAS WILLIAM, lawyer, govt. ofcl.; b. Pueblo, Colo., Oct. 19, 1890; s. Edward Joseph and Charlotte Mary (Harter) O'H.; LL.B., U. Colo., 1923; LL.M., Cath. U. Am., 1941; m. Mary Moynihan, Dec. 30, 1915. Admitted to Supreme Ct. U.S., 1936, Colo. bar, 1923, Wyo. bar, 1924, U.S. Ct. Claims, 1936, D.C. bar, 1939; tchr., prin., supt. dist. grade schs., Cook Co., Ill., 1909-15; lectr. law aviation and radio, law sch. Cath. U. Am., 1942-48; law practice, Wheatland and Rawlins, Wyo., 1923-33; city atty., Rawlins, 1926-28, 31-33; atty. Dept. Interior, N.R.A., Dept. Justice, 1933-49; spl. asst. to Atty. Gen., 1944-49; chmn. U.S. Motor Carrier Claims Commn. 1949-52. Served as sergeant, Co. F. 108th Ammunition Train, 33 Div. U.S. Army, World War I. Mem. Fed., Who. bar assns., Am. Legion (dept. comdr., Wyo., 1932), Alpha Sigma Phi, Delta Theta Phi. Home: Kansas City, Mo. †

OKADA, KENZO, painter; b. Sept. 28, 1902; came to U.S., 1950, naturalized, 1952; s. Kazo and Yasu O.; m. Kimi Kasono, May 10, 1931. Exhibited in one-man shows including, Betty Parsons Gallery, 12 shows, 1953-78, Corcoran Gallery, Washington, 1955, Sao Paolo (Brazil) Biennial, 1955, Venice (Italy) Biennial, 1958 (award), Albright-Knox Art Gallery, Buffalo, 1965, Phillip Collection, Washington, 1979; represented in permanent collections including, Met. Mus. Art, N.Y.C., Mus. Modern Art, N.Y.C., Art Inst. Chgo., Guggenheim Mus., N.Y.C., Whitney Mus. Am. Art, N.Y.C., Albright-Knox Art Gallery, Phillips Gallery, Washington, Internat. Mus. Modern Art, Tokyo and Kyoto, Japan, works include: Mural for, Hilton Hotel, Tokyo, Award Poster, N.Y. Council of the Arts, 1969; Subject of profl. articles. Recipient 1st prize Columbia (S.C.) Biennial, 1957, Mainichi Art award, 1966, Marjorie Peabody Waite award AAAL, 1977; recipient other awards and grants from Nikakai, 1936, other awards and grants from Showa Shorie, 1938, other awards and grants from Yomiuri Press, 1947, other awards and grants from Art Inst. Chgo., 1954, 57, other awards and grants from Carnegie Internat., 1955, other awards and grants from UNESCO, 1958, other awards and grants from Ford Found., 1960, other awards and grants from Dunn Internat., 1963. Home: New York, N.Y. Died Aug. 1982.

OKIN, FRANKLIN JAY, ins. co. exec.; b. N.Y.C., May 8, 1932; s. Steven Irving and Helen Margaret (Johantgen) O.; A.B., Princeton U., 1957; LL.B. cum laude, Yale U., 1962; m. Janet L. Atkinson, Jan. 8, 1966; children—Steven, Laura. Admitted to D.C. bar, 1962, Conn. bar, 1967; with firm Covington & Burling, Washington, 1962-66; with Travelers Corp., Hartford, Conn., 1966-81, sec., 1974-81, asso. gen. counsel, 1975-81; dir. Travelers Corp. Asia Ltd.; lectr. bus. adminstrn. U. Conn., Sec. 1969. Condr.'s council Hartford Symphony, 1972-74. Served with USAAF, 1951-55. Mem. Am. Soc. Corporate Secs. (dir.), Am., Conn., Fed., Hartford County bar assns., Assn. Life Ins. Counsel, Am. Council Life Ins., Order of Coif. Clubs: Hartford; Princeton (N.Y.C.). Home: West Hartford, Conn. Died Jan. 31, 1981.

OLAN, LEVI ARTHUR, clergyman, univ. regent; b. Cherkassy, Russia, Mar. 22, 1903; came to U.S., 1906, naturalized, 1912; s. Max and Bessie (Leshinsky) O.; m. Sarita Messer, June 9, 1931; children—Elizabeth Olan Hirsch, Frances, David. Student, U. Rochester, 1921-23; B.A., U. Cin., 1925; Rabbi, Hebrew Union Coll., 1929, D.D., 1953; L.H.D. (hon.), Austin Coll., 1967, So. Methodist U., Dallas. Rabbi, 1929; rabbi Temple Emanuel, Worcester, Mass., 1929-49, Dallas, from 1949; lectr. Perkins Sch. Theology, So. Meth. U., Dallas, from 1952, Leo Baeck Coll., London, Eng.; adj. prof. U. Tex., Arlington, from 1971; vis. lectr. Tex. Christian U., from 1976. Pres. Jewish Family Service, 1932-40; v.p. Worcester chpt. ARC, 1939-45; Mem. bd. regents U. Tex. Mem. Central Conf. Am. Rabbis (pres. 1967-69), Dallas UN Assn. (pres. 1960). Home: Dallas, Tex. Died Oct. 17, 1984; buried Emanu-El Cemetery, Dallas.

OLD, ARCHIE J., JR., airforce officer; b. Farmersville, Tex., Aug. 1, 1906; s. Archie J. and Ruby (Willis) O.; student Trinity U., Waxahachie, Tex., 1923-25; C.E., Texas U., Austin, Tex., 1927; m. Annis Allday, January 3, 1933; 1 dau., Frances Adeline (Mrs. Richard Allyn Vaill). Civil engineer, Texas Highway Department, 1927-31, 1935-36; owner and operator of retail automobile agency, Atlanta, Tex., 1936-39. Pres. Atlanta (Tex.) Chamber of Commerce, 2 yrs., Atlanta Rotary Club, 2 yrs. Flying cadet and lt., U.S. Army Air Corps, 1931-35; officer U.S. Army Air Force since 1939, now lt. gen.; group comdr. of a pioneer group assigned to operate from England; comd. force that bombed Schweinfurt, Germany, Oct. 14, 1943; comd. force making pioneer shuttle raid to Russia (England to Russia to Italy to England), June 1944. Following end of war, commanded Air Transport Command in southwest Pacific. Comdr. east Pacific wing of Air Transport Command; comdg. gen. Atlantic Div., Mil. Air Transport Service, 1948-50; comdg. gen. 8th Air Force, Carswell, Tex., 1950; comdg. gen. 7th Air Div., Eng., 1951; comdg. gen. 5th Air Div., Robat, French Morocco, 1951-53; dir. operations, Hdqrs. Strategic Air Command, Offutt Air Force Base, Omaha, Neb., 1953-55; comdg. gen. 15th air force, March AFB, Cal., 1955—; air comdr., pilot pioneer B-52 jet non-stop flight around world in 45 hrs. and 19 minutes, 1957; now v.p., mem. bd. dirs. Golden West Airlines, Inc., Long Beach, Cal. Decorated D. S.C., Silver Star with cluster. Distinguished Flying Cross with 3 clusters, Air Medal with 7 clusters, Battle Citation with three clusters, Purple Heart, Legion of Merit with cluster (United States); Croix De Guerre with Palm (Belgian); DFC (British); Order of Souvorov (Russian); Croix de Guerre (France). Mason. Became member Caterpillar Club when forced to make jump from disabled plane, 1934; air comdr. and pilot first non-stop around-the-world flight, of three B-52s, 1957. Died Mar. 24, 1984.

OLDENBERG, OTTO, prof. physics; b. Schöneberg, Germany, Nov. 2, 1888; came to U.S., 1929, naturalized citizen, 1936; student Heidelberg and Göttingen univs., 1908-13; Ph.D, Göttingen U., 1913; student Munich U., 1920-22. Privatdocent Göttingen U., 1923-26, asst. prof., 1926-29; lecturer Harvard U., 1929; prof. physics, Harvard U., from 1930. Mem. Acad. Arts and Sciences. Home: Cambridge, Mass. †

OLDFATHER, CHARLES HENRY, prof. ancient history; b. Tabriz, Persia, June 13, 1887; s. Jeremiah and Felicia Narcissa (Rice) O.; brought by parents to U.S., 1890; grad. Hanover (Ind.) Coll. Acad., 1902; A.B., Hanover Coll., 1906; LL.D. from same coll., 1933; grad. McCormick Theological Seminary, 1911; grad. study, U. of Munich, 1911-12; Ph.D., U. of Wis., 1922; m. Margaret Kinsey McLelland, Sept. 7, 1914; children—Ellanor Newton, Margaret Rebekah, Charles Henry. Instr., Syrian Protestant Coll., Beirut, 1912-14; prof. classics, Hanover Coll., 1914-16; prof. Greek and ancient history, Wabash Coll., Crawfordsville, Ind., 1916-26; prof. ancient history, U. of Neb., from 1926, chairman dept., 1929-46, dean Coll. of Arts and Sciences since 1932. Mem. Pub. Library Commn., Ind., 1922-25; pres. Ind. Library Trustees Assn., 1923-25; mem. commn. on higher edn. of N. Central Assn. of Colleges and Secondary Schools, 1933-41. Member Am. Historical Assn., Am. Philological Assn., American Association University Professors, Classical Assn. Middle West, Phi Delta Theta, Phi Beta Kappa. Presbyterian. Author: The Greek Literary Papyri from Greco-Roman Egypt, 1922; Pufendorf's De Jure Nature et Gentium, 1934, Translation of Diodorus of Sicily, Vols. I-V, Loeb Classical Library. Home: Lincoln, Nebr. †

O'LEARY, ARTHUR ALOYSIUS, univ. pres.; b. Washington, D.C., Sept. 27, 1887; s. Timothy A. and Mary (Sheehan) O'L.; prep. edn., Gonzaga High Sch. (Washington, D.C.) and St. Andrew-on-Hudson; A.B., Woodstock (Md.) Coll., 1910, M.A., 1911, Ph.D., 1920; D.D., Georgetown U., 1935; LL.D., Boston Coll., 1936; Ph.D., Gregorian U., Rome, 1938; LL.D., Fordham, 1939. Joined Soc. of Jesus, 1903; ordained priest Roman Catholic Ch., 1919; prof. classical lit., Canisius High Sch., Buffalo, 1911-12; prof. philosophy, Georgetown U., 1912-16, librarian, 1920-35, prof. ethics, 1923-35, pres. July 1935-42; spiritual dir. Georgetown Prep. Sch., 1943-47; pastor Holy Trinity Ch., 1947. Mem. Catholic Library Assn., Jesuit Philos. Assn. Mem. K.C. (4th degree). Address: Washington, D.C. †

O'LEARY, DANIEL HUGH, retired university administrator; b. Boston, Feb. 6, 1907; s. James Joseph and Bridget Josephine (McVann) O'L.; m. Marguerite F. Moriarty, Sept. 17, 1938; children—Nancy (Mrs. William Melia), James, Daniel, Ellen (Mrs. William Coughlin), Robert, Deborah (Mrs. William Chauncey Bryant). A.B., Boston Coll., 1927; M.A., Ph.D., 1936; postgrad., Harvard, summers 1930, 32, 33, U. Cambridge, summer 1931, U. Rome, 1938-39. Tchr. Ashland (Mass.) High Sch., 1928-31, South Boston High Sch., Boston, 1931-46; instr. Boston Coll. Grad. Sch., 1936-37, Hyannis (Mass.) State Tchrs. Coll., summers 1937-50; head dept. Roxbury Girls High Sch., Boston, 1946-50; prin. Roxbury Evening Schs., Boston, 1946-50; head history dept. Boston Tchrs. Coll., 1949-50; pres. Lowell (Mass.) State Coll., 1950-74; chancellor U. Lowell, Mass., 1975-77, chancellor emeritus, 1977-83; Chmn. Mass. Bd. Ednl. Assistance, 1956-65; ednl. cons. to Venezuela U.S. State Dept., 1963; ednl. cons. to Israel Am. Assn. Colls. Tchr. Edn., 1965. Trustee Moses Parker Greeley Fund, 1951-72, Lowell City Library, 1962-74, Mass. Community Colls., 1968-72, New Eng. Coll. Optometry, 1977-83. Recipient Honors award Internat. Assn. Univ. Pres., 1975; O'Leary Library at Lowell State Coll. named in his honor, 1974. Home: Lowell, Mass. Died May 24, 1983.

OLEVSKY, JULIAN, concert violinist; b. Berlin, Germany, May 7, 1926; came to U.S., 1947, naturalized, 1951; s. Seigmund and Augustina (Schachmeister) O.; m. Estela Kersenbaum, Jan. 29, 1966; 1 dau., Diane; children by previous marriage—Roxane, Ronald. Pupil of, Alexander Petschnikoff. resident artist U. Mass., 1967-85. Rec. artist for, Westminster Records.; World Wide concert violin tours, 1936-85. Home: Amherst, Mass. Died May 25, 1985.

OLIN, JOHN MERRILL, chem. corp. exec.; b. Alton, Ill., Nov. 10, 1892; s. Franklin W. and Mary M. (Moulton) O.; m. Evelyn B. Niedringhaus, May 11, 1940. Grad., Cascadilla Sch., Ithaca, N.Y., 1909; B.S. in Chemistry, Cornell U., 1913. With Olin Corp. (and predecessor cos.), from 1913, hon. chmn., dir. Trustee emeritus Cornell U.; fellow of the bd. Johns Hopkins U.; life trustee Washington U. Corp.; hon. trustee Am. Mus. Natural History. Home: St Louis, Mo. Died Sept. 8, 1982.

OLIVER, ANDREW, lawyer; b. Morristown, N.J., Mar. 14, 1906; s. William H. P. and Lydia (Seabury) O.; A.B., Harvard U., 1928, LL.B., 1931; Dr. Canon Law, Gen. Theol. Sem., 1970; m. Ruth Blake, Feb. 21, 1936; children—Andrew, Daniel, Ruth Field. Admitted to N.Y. bar, 1934; practice in N.Y.C., 1934-70; mem. firm Alexander & Green, 1944-70. Chancellor Episcopal Diocese N.Y., 1961-71, mem. council Inst. Early Am. History and Culture, 1967-70; commn. Nat. Portrait Gallery, 1968-81. Pres. Am. Friends Plantin Moretus Mus., Charlotte Palmer Philips Found., 1961-72, Essex Inst., Salem, Mass., 1973-75; trustee Gen. Theol. Sem., 1948-68, P.E. Soc. Promoting Religion and Learning, 1942-68, N.Y. Soc. Library, 1965-70, Boston Athenaeum, 1971-81. Fellow Soc. Antiquaries, London; mem. Am. Antiquarian Soc., N.Y. (1st v.p.), Mass. hist. socs., Walpole Soc., Colonial Soc. Mass. (v.p. from 1973). Clubs: Century Assn. (N.Y.C.); Tavern (Boston). Author: Faces of a Family, 1960; Portraits of John and Abigail Adams, 1967; Portraits of John Quincy Adams and His Wife, 1970. Editor: The Journal of Samuel Curwen, 1972; The Portraits of John Marshall, 1977; Auguste Edouart's Silhouettes of Eminent Americans, 1977. Home: Boston, Mass. Died Oct. 20, 1981.

OLIVER, JAMES ARTHUR, zoologist; b. Caruthersville, Mo., Jan. 1, 1914; s. Arthur L. and Mary E. (Roberts) O.; student U. Tex., 1932-34; A.B., U. Mich., 1936, A.M., 1937, Ph.D. (Univ. fellow 1938-40, Hinsdale scholar 1940-41), 1941; Sc.D., Southampton Coll., L.I. U., 1975; m. Elizabeth Kimball, May 3, 1941; children—Patricia A., Dexter K.; m. 2d, Ruth H. Norton, Dec. 22, 1967. Instr. No. Mich. Coll. Edn., 1941-42; asst. curator Am. Museum Natural History, N.Y.C., 1942-47, asso. curator, 1947-48; asst. prof. zoology U. Fla., 1948-51; curator reptiles N.Y. Zool. Soc., 1951-59, asst. dir. Zool. Park, 1958, dir., 1958-59, dir. emeritus, 1977-81; research asso. Am. Mus. Natural History, 1948-59, dir., 1959-69, coordinator sci. and environment programs, 1969-70, dir. emeritus, 1973-81; dir. N.Y. Aquarium, 1970-76. Adv. com. Mianus River Gorge Conservation Commn.; bd. dirs. Caribbean Conservation Corp.; steering com. Biol. Sci. Curriculum Study, 1962-66, exec. com., 1964-66; com. mus. resources N.Y. Commr. Edn., 1961- 64; organizing com. 16th Internat. Congress Zoologists, 1963; mem. Am. Commn. Internat. Wildlife Protection; trustee, treas., pres. Biol. Scis. Information Services, 1964-72. Served with USNR, 1943-46. Recipient Outstanding Achievement award U. Mich., 1963. Fellow Royal Soc. Arts (London), N.Y. Zool. Soc., Rochester Mus. Assn.; mem. Am. Soc. Ichthyologists and Herpetologists (bd. govs., editorial bd.), Herpetologists League, AAAS, Am. Assn. Museums (chmn. environment com. 1969-70, mem. council 1967-75, mem. accreditation commn. 1971-76), Mus. Council N.Y.C., Palisades Nature Assn. (dir.), N.Y. State Assn. Museums (council, v.p. 1964), Internat. Council Museums (exec. com.), Assn. Dirs. Systematic Collections, Dirs. Sci. Museums and Cultural Instns. N.Y.C., N.Y. Hist. Soc. (asso., Pintard fellow), Bklyn. Arts and

Culture Council (trustee). Clubs: Century Assn. Author: The Natural History of North American Amphibians and Reptiles, 1955; Snakes in Fact and Fiction, 1958; Prevention and Treatment of Snake Bite, 1952; also sci. papers. Address: Bronx, N.Y. Died Dec. 2, 1981.

OLIVER, JOHN WILLIAM, prof. history; b. nr. Jackson, Mo., Apr. 12, 1887; s. Lucius Clay and Mary Louise (Alexander) O.; B.Pd., Mo. State Teachers Coll., Cape Girardeau, Mo., 1906; A.B. and B.S. in Edn., U. of Mo., 1911, A.M., 1912; Ph.D., U. of Wis., 1915; m. Helen McClure, June 2, 1928; children—John William, Robert McClure. Scholarship in American history, U. of Wis., 1913-14, fellowship, 1914-15; research asst. Indiana State Library and History Commissions, 1915-16, Wis. State Hist. Soc., 1917-18; dir. Ind. Hist. Commn., 1919-23; prof. history and head of dept., U. of Pittsburgh from 1923. Enlisted as pvt. F.A., Central O.T.S., Camp Taylor, Ky., Aug. 5, 1918; 2d lt. and instr. F.A., Nov. 4-Dec. 15, 1918. Mem. Am. Hist. Assn., History of Science Society, Am. Polit. Science Assn., Miss. Valley Hist. Assn., Ind. Hist. Society, Western Pa. Hist. Soc., Acad. Science and Art (Pittsburgh), Am. Geog. Soc., Newcomen Soc., Phi Beta Kappa, Phi Delta Kappa, Delta Sigma Rho; fellow A.A.A.S. Presbyterian. Clubs: Authors, Junta, University, Faculty. Author: Civil War Military Pension (1861-65), 1917; Indiana Gold Star Honor Roll, 1921; Marshal Ferdinand L. Foch, 1922. Home: Pittsburgh, Pa. †

OLIVER, LUNSFORD ERRETT, army officer; b. Nemaha Neb., March 17, 1889; s. Thomas Jefferson and Mary Lorinda (Evans) O.; student Neb. State Normal Sch., 1901-04, Coiner U., Bethany, Neb., 1907-08; B.S., U.S. Mil. Acad., 1913; grad. Engr., Sch., 1916, Command and Gen. Staff Sch., 1928, Army War Coll., 1938; m. Janet Putnam, May 28, 1921; children—Thomas Kilbury, Mary Putnam, Rachel Louise. Commd. 2d lt., Corps of Engrs., June 12, 1913, and advanced through the grades to maj. gen.; 1948; engr. Armored Force, Ft. Knox, Ky., 1940-41; commdg. 5th Armored Div., March 2, 1943; Western front, 1944. Mem. Soc. of Am. Mil. Engrs. Address: Williamsburg, Mass. †

OLMSTED, CLARENCE EDWARD, oil exec.; b. Santa Paula, Calif., Sept. 4, 1890; s. Frank Cruison and Clara Alma (McCray) O.; student civil engring., Stanford U., 1910-11, Columbia U., 1911-15; civil engr., Columbia, N.Y. City; m. Helen N. Rogers, May 21, 1925; 1 dau., Louise. Engr. Litchfield Constrn. Co., N.Y. City, 1915-17, Standard Oil of Calif., 1917-18; served in Corps of Engrs., U.S. Army, 1918; engr. The Texas Co. (Del.), 1919-21, supt. Del. River Terminal, 1921-23, asst. supt. Lockport Works, 1923; mgr. refining and transportation, Calif. Petroleum Corp., Los Angeles, 1923-27, v.p. and dir., 1927-29; v.p., gen. mgr. The Texas Co. (Calif.), Los Angeles, 1929-34, pres., gen. mgr., 1934-38; v.p. The Texas Co. (Del.), N.Y. City, 1938-50, also dir., 1940-50. Republican. Clubs: Bohemian, California, Los Angeles Country. †

OLSEN, ARDEN BEAL, educator; b. Ephraim, Utah, Aug. 23, 1898; s. Ole M. and Mary Matilda (Beal) O.; student Snow Normal Coll., 1916-17; B.S., U. Utah, 1926, M.S., 1929; Ph.D., U. Cal., 1936; m. Laura Pearl Cowley, Sept. 3, 1919 (dec. Apr. 1938); children—Maralyn M. (Mrs. Russell M. Hess), Leon A.; m. 2d, Clara Grace Gillespie, June 1, 1939 (dec. Sept. 1957); m. 3d, Gertrude Prince, Sept. 7, 1958. Tchr., Murray (Utah) High Sch., 1920-25; instr. social sci. U. Utah, 1925-31; head teaching asst. econ. history U. Cal at Berkeley, 1931-35; asso. prof. econ. Utah State U. Agr. and Applied Sci., 1935-36; head dept. commerce Ariz. State College, 1936-42; professor of economics and marketing University of Denver, 1942-84, associate dean Graduate College, 1942-63. Assistant supt. Ephraim Canning Corp., summers 1921-23; research Zion's Coop. Merc. Instn., Salt Lake City, 1934. Supr. Berkeley Recreation Dept., 1935; vice chmn. OPA, Ariz., 1941-42; pub. mem. utilities div. War Labor Bd., Denver, 1943-45. Served with U.S. Army, 1917-18. Mem. Am. Econ. Assn., Am. Marketing Assn., Colo. Schoolmasters, Colo. Edn. Assn., Phi Kappa Phi, Omicron Delta Gamma, Beta Gamma Sigma, Pi Omega Pi, Alpha Kappa Psi, Delta Pi Epsilon. Mem. Ch. of Jesus Christ of Latterday Saints. Home: Denver, Colo. Died Jan. 15, 1984.

OLSON, GIDEON CARL EMIL, clergyman; b. Jungskola, Sweden, Jan. 27, 1887; s. Magnus and Johanna Mathilda (Johanson) O.; brought to U.S. 1895, naturalized, 1898; A.B., Augustana Coll., Rock Island, Ill., 1910; B.D., Augustana Theol. Sem., 1913; A.M., U. of Tex., 1917; S.T.M., Western Theol. Sem., Pittsburgh, 1927; student U. of Pittsburgh, 1926, Bibl. Seminary of New York, 1930-35; D.D., Hartwick Theological Seminary, New York, 1937; m. Anna Theresia Olson, June 25, 1913; children—Anna Linnea (wife of Rev. Hilding Kron), Evelyn Johanna (wife of Mr. Paul Simonson), Myrtle Marie, Vincent Carl Samuel, Eunice Josephine, Lois Eleanore. Ordained to ministry of Luth. Augustana Synod, June 15, 1913; pastor Gethsemane Ch., Austin, Tex., 1913-18, Bethany Ch., Woodhull, Ill., 1918-22, Tabor Ch., McKeesport, Pa., 1922-29, Bethlehem Ch., Brooklyn, N.Y., May 1929-44; Immanuel Luth., Detroit Mich. since Aug. 1944; prof. English Bible, Hartwich Theol. Sem. of New York. Vice-pres. N.Y. Conf., Luth. Augustana Synod; pres. Immigrant and Seamen's Home. New York; mem. bd. dirs. Harwick Luth. Sem. of New York, Swedish Hosp., Brooklyn. Apptd. mem. Mayor's Reception Com. of City of New York for Swedish Crown Prince, 1938. Republican. Contbr. to Luth. World Almanac, 1937, Light and Strength Calendar (Luth. annual), 1940. Contbr. to Luth. Companion. Home: Detroit, Mich. †

OLSON, GUS, university regent; b. Paso Robles, Cal., Dec. 2, 1888; s. Andrew G. and Ellen (Mattson) O.; grad. U. Cal., 1911; m. Mabel Lawlor, Aug. 9, 1913; children—Gus Olson, M. Elizabeth (Mrs. John F. Cleeves), Norman Andrew, Robert Lawlor, Sally (Mrs. Walter Peters), Jean Elin (Mrs. Robert E. McDonald, III). Engr. reclamation and land development Sacramento Valley, Cal., 1912-41; mgr. Holland Land Co., from 1918. Pres. bd. trustees Reclamation Dist. 999; bd. regents U. Cal., from 1951. Mem. Inst. Internat. Edn. (San Francisco bd.), Farm Bur. Fedn. (past state exec. com., past co. pres.), San Francisco C. of C., Cal. Central Valley Flood Control Assn. (exec. com.). Mason. Clubs: Rotary (pres. 1941-42), Sutter (Sacramento); Old Capitol (Monterey, Cal.). Home: Clarksburg, Cal. †

OLSON, ROBERT S., finance co. exec.; b. Columbus Junction, Ia., Jan. 10, 1913; s. Sylvan L. and Nelle E. (Edmondson) O.; student Antioch Coll., 1931-32; B.A., U. Mich., 1935; m. Mary Jane Hineman, Sept. 28, 1940; children—Lee R., Richard S., Thomas F., William M. Vice pres. Universal CIT Credit Corp., N.Y.C., 1936-56; v.p. Gen. Acceptance Corp., Allentown, Pa., 1956-59; chief exec. officer Ford Motor Credit Co., Dearborn, Mich., from 1959; chief exec. officer Am. Rd. Ins. Co., Ford Leasing Devel. Co., Ford Motor Credit Co. of Can., Ltd., Ford Motor Credit Co. Internat., Ford Life Ins. Co., Vista Ins. Co., Am. Rd. Services Co., Ford Consumer Credit Co., Ford Life Ins. Co., Am. Rd. Equity Corp. Trustee, mem. finance and exec. coms. Rehab. Inst., Detroit. Served with USNR, 1942-46. Mem. Detroit Advt. Assn. Clubs: Detroit Athletic, Detroit Press, Automotive Old Timers (Detroit); Orchard Lake (Mich.) Country; Ponte Vedra (Fla.). Home: Paradise Valley, Ariz. Died Aug. 9, 1982.

OLSON, SIGURD FERDINAND, biologist, author; b. Chgo., Apr. 4, 1889; s. Lawrence J. and Ida May (Cedarholm) O.; student Northland Coll., 1916-18; B.S., U. Wis., 1920, postgrad., 1922-23; M.S., U. Ill., 1931; L.H.D. (hon.), Hamline U.; D.Sc. (hon.), Northland Coll., 1961, Macalester Coll., 1963, Carleton Coll., 1965, U. Wis., 1972; m. Elizabeth Dorothy Uhrenholdt, Aug. 8, 1921; children—Sigurd T., Robert K. Head biology dept. Ely (Minn.) Jr. Coll., 1922-35, dean., 1935-46; zoology dept. Am. Army U., Shrivenham, Eng., 1945; I and E. Div., U.S. Army, Germany, France, Italy, Austria, 1946; ecologist Izaak Walton League Am.; cons., free-lance writer, lect., sci. researcher; cons. to sec. interior, dir. Nat. Park Service, 1962-82, Quetico-Superior Com.; adv. bd. on nat. parks, monuments, historic sites Sec. Interior, 1960-65; cons. Time-Life Books, Nat. Geog. Books, Readers Digest, Kodansha-Internat./U.S.A. Ltd., Japan. Served in U.S. Army, 1918. Recipient Journalism award Pi Delta Epsilon, 1959, Faculty award U. Wis. at Green Bay, Silver Antelope award Boy Scouts Am., 1963; named to Hall of Fame and recipient Founder award Izaak Walton League Am., 1963; H.M. Albright medal Am. Scenic and Hist. Preservation Soc., 1963; Dimock award ACA, 1969; Distinguished Service award Upper Mississippi Basin Commn., 1975. Fellow Assn. Interpretive Naturalists; mem. AAAS, Nat. Parks Assn. (pres. 1955-60), Ecol. Soc. Am.; Nature Conservancy, Wilderness Soc. Council (exec. com., pres. 1968-71). Mason. Clubs: Cosmos (Washington); Sierra (recipient John Muir award 1967); Explorers. Author: The Singing Wilderness, 1956; Listening Point, 1958; The Lonely Land, 1961; Runes of the North, 1963; The Hidden Forest, 1969; Open Horizons, 1969; Wilderness Days, 1972; Reflections, 1976. Died Jan. 13, 1982.

O'MALLEY, EDWARD VALENTINE, lumber co. exec.; b. Parnell, Mo., Feb. 23, 1905; s. Edward Lawrence and Mary Bernardine (Stephen) O'M.; student Harvard, 1928; m. Virginia Ann Mets, June 4, 1927 (dec. Nov. 1961); children—Edward Valentine, Ann (Mrs. John W. Knowlton); m. 2d, Marguerite M. Downing, April 22, 1963. Sec. O'Malley Lumber Co., Phoenix, 1929-47, pres., 1947-70, chmn. bd., 1970-76, chmn. emeritus, 1976-82; dir. 1st Nat. Bank Ariz., Phoenix, Phelps Dodge Corp., Ariz. Pub. Service Co. Trustee St. Luke's Hosp., Phoenix; bd. dirs. Am. Grad. Sch. Internat. Mgmt., Phoenix, St. Joseph's Hosp., Phoenix. Recipient Merit award U. Ariz., 1960. Clubs: Arizona, Phoenix Country, Paradise Country, Valley Field Riding and Polo. Home: Phoenix, Ariz. Died May 24, 1982.

O'MALLEY, MART J., judge; b. Pittston, Pa., Sept. 17, 1890; s. Michael Thomas and Mary Jane (Durkin) O'M.; student St. Thomas Coll., Scranton, Pa., 1910-12; LL.B., Valparaiso U., 1915; m. Cecile I. Phipps, March 7, 1916; children—Norman Joseph, John Richard. Admitted to Ind bar, 1915; county atty., Huntington, Ind., 1930-32; mem. bd of works and city atty. Huntington, Ind., 1939-43; judge Supreme Court of Ind., from Jan. 4, 1943. Mem. County and State bar assns. Elk. Club: Huntington Kiwanis. Home: Indianapolis, Ind. †

O'MELVENY, JOHN, lawyer; b. Los Angeles, Dec. 1, 1894; s. Henry William and Marie Antoinette (Schilling) O'M.; m. Alice Nilson, Sept. 16, 1967; children: Joan (Mrs. Mills), Patrick. A.B., U. Calif., 1918; J.D., Harvard U., 1922. Bar: Calif. 1922. Asso. atty. firm O'Melveny, Millikin, Tuller & Macneil, 1922-23, partner, 1923-36; sr. partner successor firm O'Melveny & Myers, Los Angeles, 1939-75, of counsel, from 1976; dir. Security-Pacific Nat. Bank of, Los Angeles, 1940-72. Life mem. adv. bd. Salvation Army; trustee, mem. exec. com. Calif. Inst. Tech., 1940-68, hon. life trustee, from 1968; chmn. budget and rev. com., dir., mem. exec. com. Los Angeles War Chest, 1942-46; hon. dir. Metabolic Found.; mem. adv. bd. Barlow Hosp. Guild., Los Angeles. Served as ensign USNRF, 1918-19. Mem. Am., Calif., Los Angeles bar assns., Phi Beta Kappa, Psi Upsilon. Republican. Clubs: California (Los Angeles), Sunset (Los Angeles); Bohemian (San Francisco). Home: Los Angeles, Calif.

O'MELVENY, STUART, business exec.; b. Santa Monica, Calif., Mar. 2, 1888; s. Henry William and Marie Antoinette (Schilling) O'M.; B.L., U. of Calif., 1910; student Harvard, 1911-12; m. Isabel Watson, June 6, 1914; 1 dau., Anne. Admitted to Calif. bar, 1911; associated in practice of law, successively with O'Melveny, Stevens and Milliken; O'Melveny, Milliken and Tuller; O'Melveny, Millikin, Tuller and MacNeil, 1911-23; first vice pres. Title Insurance and Trust Co., Los Angeles, 1923-35, pres., 1935-52, chmn. bd., 1952-55, director, from 1955; dir. State Mutual Saving and Loan Assn., Southern Cal. Gas Co.; chmn. bd. Del Amo Estate Co.; dir. Van Nuys Investment Co.; past president California Inst. Assos. Served as 1st lieut., Air Corp, U.S. Army, 1917-18. Regent University of California, 1937-40. Trustee Rancho Santa Ana Botanic Gaden, Havey Mudd College. Member of Pi Upsilon, Phi Beta Kappa, Phi Delta Phi. Clubs: Calif., Sunset, Athletic (Los Angeles); Bohemian (San Francisco); Annandale Golf (Pasadena); Bolsa Chica Gun (Huntington Beach); Automobile of Southern Calif. (dir.). Home: San Marino, Calif. †

O'NEIL, JAMES FRANCIS, magazine pub.; b. Manchester, N.H., June 13, 1898; s. Joseph H. and Mary (Dalton) O'N.; M.A., U. N.H., 1948; LL.D., St. Anselm's Coll., 1948; m. Edythe Reid Graf, Sept. 7, 1925; children—Kenneth G., J. Russell. Chief police Manchester, 1937-50; dir. aero. N.H., 1938-40, dir. civil def., 1940-44; pub. Am. Legion mag., N.Y.C., 1950-78; dir. N.H. Pub. Service Co. Mem. President's Amnesty Bd., 1946-47; spl. asst. to sec. navy, 1945-46; mem. Golf Course & Stadium Authority, Manchester, 1929-37; mem. adv. com. MacArthur Meml. Found., 1967-81; chmn. bd. dirs. Manchester Airport. Served to lt., inf., U.S. Army, 1916-19; AEF. Decorated Legion Honor, Croix de Guerre with palm (France); Navy Certificate Merit. Mem. Am. Legion (nat. comdr. 1947-48), Newcomen Soc. Republican. Catholic. Club: Dutch Treat (N.Y.C.). Home: Forest Hills, N.Y. Died July 28, 1981.

O'NEIL, WILLIAM J., mfg. exec.; b. Monona, Ia., Nov. 6, 1888; s. Michael and Mary (O'Leary) O'N.; student pub. schs. of Monona; m. Evelyn Washburn, 1908; 1 son, John Loren; married 2d, Isabel Weir, 1923 (died 1946); married 3d, Eileen McAndrews, 1952. Circulation Manager Waterloo (Iowa) Tribune, 1909, advertising manager, 1914, business mgr., 1919-26; U.S. and Canadian distbr. Field Mfg. Co., Chicago, 1926-34; sales mgr. Chicago br. Iron Fireman Mfg. Co., Cleveland 1934, mgr., 1939-51, became chmn. bd., chief exec. officer, 1951, now a vice pres. Home: Lakewood, OH. †

O'NEILL, RICHARD WINSLOW, housing exec.; b. Madison, Wis., Sept. 5, 1925; s. James Milton and Edith (Winslow) O'N.; student Hotchkiss Sch., 1941-43; B.S., Yale, 1950; student Oxford (Eng.) U., 1949; m. Barbara Powell, Jan. 3, 1953 (div. Feb. 1966); children—Richard Winslow, Susan Powell, Jennifer Anne, Julia Kay; m. 2d, Patricia Betz, Nov. 21, 1969. Constrn. supt. Bing & Bing, N.Y.C., 1950-53; asst. editor Engring. News-Record, McGraw-Hill Pub. Co., N.Y.C., 1953-55, asso. editor House & Home, 1955-64, chief editor, 1964-70; pres. Housing Adv. Council, Ltd., 1971-80. Mem. Citizens Housing and Planning Council N.Y., 1967-74, Nat. Commn. on Urban Problems, 1967-68. Served with inf. AUS, 1943-46; ETO, PTO. Independent. Author: High Steel, Hard Rock and Deep Water, 1965: The Unhandyman's Guide to Home Repair, 1966; The Dynamics of the New Housing Industry, 1970; Homebuyer's Guide to the '80s, 1980. Home: Lakeville, Conn. Died Nov. 24, 1980.

O'NEILL, WILLIAM JAMES, leasing transportation company executive; b. Cleve., Sept. 21, 1906; s. Hugh and Louise (Berchtold) O'N.; m. Dorothy Kundtz, May 28, 1932; children: William, Dorothy (Mrs. John Donahey), Kathleen (Mrs. William France), Molly (Mrs. George Sweeney), Timothy. A.B. magna cum laude, Notre Dame U., 1928. Operating mgr. Superior Transfer Co., CCC Hwy., Motor Express Inc., 1928-30; chief operating officer over-the-road carrier subs. U.S. Truck Lines, Inc., 1930-37; founder pres., chief exec. officer owner Niagara Motor Express, 1938-59; founder chmn. bd., chief exec. officer Lease Plan Internat. Corp., N.Y.C., 1959-61; founder, chmn. bd., chief exec. officer pres. Transp. Finance Corp., from 1954; pres., chief exec. officer Leaseway, Ltd., Can., 1959-75; founder, pres., chmn. bd., chief exec. officer Leaseway Transp. Corp., 1961-75; founder, chmn. bd., chief exec. officer Leaseway Intercontinental (LEASECO) S.A.), Zug, Switzerland, 1962-72; founder seven fin. leasing cos., Europe, Mex., Can.; dir. N.J. Zinc Co. Partner N.Y. Yankees; dir. Am. Life Inc.; Pres., trustee O'Neill Bros. Found.; trustee W.J. and D.K.

O'Neill Sr. Fund; 1st lay pres. Gilmour Acad., Gates Mills, Ohio. Mem. Newcomen Soc. N.A. Clubs: Pepper Pike (Pepper Pike, Ohio), Country (Pepper Pike, Ohio); Metropolitan (N.Y.C.); Hunting Valley Polo (Gates Mills, Ohio) (capt.), Chagrin Valley Hunt (Gates Mills, Ohio) (mem. polo team 1959); Union (Cleve.); Delray Beach ((Fla.); The Little Club of Delray Beach. Home: Delray Beach, Fla.

ONG, DAVID GRAHAM, corpn. pres.; b. Columbus, Ind., Aug. 3, 1888; s. Lewis Kinsey and Anna Jane (Graham) O.; ed. high sch., Columbus; m. Mary Elsie Wilson, June 12, 1911; 1 son, Graham Wilson. Successively mgr. with E.M.F. Co., Regal Motor Car Co., Metzger Motor Car Co., all in Detroit, Mich., 1908-13; successively with Wheeler & Schebler, Empire Automobile Co., Robert H. Hassler, Inc., Indianapolis, 1913-17; exec. with Gillespie Corpn., 1921-23, Servel Corpn. of N.Y., 1924-25; with U.S. Leather Co., 1925-35, pres., 1929-35; pres. and dir. U.S. Air Conditioning Corpn. Served as 1st lt., later capt. Air Service, 1919-24. Republican. Presbyn. Mason (K.T., Shriner). Clubs: Bankers, Union League (New York); Wykagyl Country; Columbia (Indianapolis). Home: New Rochelle, N.Y. †

OOST, STEWART IRVIN, educator; b. Grand Rapids, Mich., May 20, 1921; s. Jacob John and Bessie (Stewart) O.; A.B., U. Chgo., 1941, M.A., 1947, Ph.D. 1950; student Yale, 1943-44. Tchr., Starr Commonwealth for Boys, Albion, Mich., 1941-42; from instr. to asso. prof. history So. Methodist U., 1948-59; mem. faculty U. Chgo., 1959-81, prof. ancient history, 1965-81. Served with AUS, 1942-46. Ford fellow, Italy, 1955-56. Mem. Am. Hist. Assn., Am. Philol. Assn., Phi Beta Kappa (past pres. Gamma of Tex.). Republican. Methodist. Author: Roman Policy in Epirus and Acarnania in the Age of the Roman Conquest of Greece, 1954; Galla Placidia Augusta; A Biographical Essay, 1968; also articles. Mem. editorial bd. Classical philology, 1959-81, editor in chief, 1978-81. Home: Chicago, Ill. Died June 11, 1981.

OPPEN, GEORGE, author; b. New Rochelle, N.Y., Apr. 24, 1908; s. George A. and Elsie (Rothfeld) O.; m. Mary Colby, Aug. 11, 1928; 1 dau., Linda (Mrs. Alexander Mourelatos). Ed. pub. schs., Calif. Mem. Objectivist Press Coop., 1934-36; pub. To, Toulon, France, 1930-33. Author: Discrete Series, 1934, The Materials, 1962, This in Which, 1965, Of Being Numerous, 1968 (Pulitzer prize 1969), Seascape: Needle's Eye, 1973, Collected Poems, 1929-1975, 1975, 1976, Primitive, 1978. Served with inf. AUS, 1943-45. Decorated Purple Heart, Combat Inf. award; recipient award Acad. and Inst. Arts and Letters, 1980. Home: San Francisco, Calif. Died July 7, 1984.

OPPENHEIMER, FRANK FRIEDMAN, educator; b. N.Y.C., Aug. 14, 1912; s. Julius and Ella (Friedman) O.; B.S., Johns Hopkins, 1933; postgrad. Cavendish Lab., Cambridge, Eng., 1935; Ph.D., Cal. Inst. Tech., 1939; m. Jacquenette Yvonne Quann, Oct. 5, 1936; children—Judith, Michael. Research asso. Stanford, 1939-41, U. Cal. at Berkeley, 1941-47; asst. prof. physics U. Minn., 1947-49; rancher, Colo., 1949-59; prof. physics U. Colo., 1959-85; on leave as dir. Palace of Arts and Sci., San Francisco, 1969. Fellow Am. Phys. Soc.; mem. Phi Beta Kappa. Co-discoverer heavy nuclei component of cosmic rays. Home: Sausalito, Calif. Died Feb. 4, 1985.

OPPENHEIMER, JULIUS JOHN, educator; b. St. Joseph, Mo., Feb. 4, 1890; s. Sigmund and Dora C. (Willie) O.; Pd.B., Central Missouri State College, 1909; B.S. in Education, University of Mo., 1915, A.M., 1916; Ph.D., Columbia, 1923; m. Florence Hull Greer, Jan. 4, 1918; dau., Jean Britton. Principal of high school, Windsor, Missouri, 1909-11; superintendent schs., Lathrop, 1911-15; instr. in edn., U. of Mo., 1915-17, 1919; dean of faculty, Stephens Coll., 1920-30, asst. dir. research, 1923-30; dean Coll. Arts and Scis., U. of Louisville (Ky.), from 1930, head dept. edn., from 1930; tchr., summer sessions, U. Mo., 1923-24, 30, O. State U., 1925-29, 32, U. Ida. 1935, 37, 39, U. Minn., 1940, 41, 1946-50, 53-55; dir. Workshop in Higher Edn., University Chicago, 1945, University Minn., 1955. Specialist in higher edn. Dept. of State, office U.S. High Commr. for Germany, 1950-52; mem. Nat. Selection Commn. for Germany, 1953-54. Cons. Higher Edn. Commns. Gen. Edn., North Central Assn.; chmn. conf. Academic Deans of Southern States, 1936; exec. com. Nat. Conf. Academic Deans 1955-61; mem. State Bd. Higher Edn. Rockefeller Grant to Germany, 1955. Mem. German Soc. Am. Studies (honorary), Ky. State Teachers Assn., N.E.A., Soc. for Curriculum Study, Conf. on Pub. Instns. of Southern States (sec. 1942), Ky. Assn. Colls. and Secondary Schs. (past mem. commn. instns. higher learning; com. on research in higher edn.), Am. Ednl. Research Assn., Southern Assn. Colleges and Secondary Schools (com. on teacher edn.), Phi Kappa Phi, Phi Delta Kappa, Alpha Pi Zeta, Omicron Delta Kappa. Democrat. Presbyterian. Clubs: Louisville Torch (pres.). Conversation, Filson. Author: Visiting Teacher Movement in the United States, 1924. Author (with Paustian): Problems of Modern Society, 1938. Home: Louisville, Ky. †

OPPENHEIMER, REUBEN, judge; b. Balt., Oct. 24, 1897; s. Leon H. and Flora (Oppenheimer) Schwab; m. Selma C. Levy, June 26, 1922; children—Martin J., Joan F. (Mrs. Stanley Weiss). A.B., Johns Hopkins, 1917; LL.B. cum laude, Harvard, 1920. Bar: Md. bar 1921. Partner firm Emory, Beeuwkes, Skeen & Oppenheimer (and successors), Balt., 1922-55; assoc. judge Supreme Bench Balt. City, 1955-65, Ct. Appeals, Md., 1964-67; lectr. U. Md. Law Sch., 1947-55; Pub. mem., co-chmn. appeals and review coms. WLB, 1943-45; chief atty. Md. office OPA, 1942-43; chmn. com. reorgn. Peoples Ct. Balt. City, 1938; chmn. com. additional tax revenue, Balt., 1945; chmn. bd. Md. Dept. Correction, 1947-51; mem. U.S. del. Internat. Penal and Penitentiary Congress, The Hague, 1950, Com. Adminstrv. Orgn. Md., 1951-53, Com. Jud. Adminstrn., 1953-55; chmn. Com. Amendments Balt. City Charter, 1969-71, Md. Bd. Ethics, 1969-79. Contbr. articles to profl. jours. Mem. exec. bd. Am. Jewish Com., from 1946; pres. Balt. Jewish Council, 1940-41, Jewish Welfare Fund Balt., 1942; Trustee Sheppard and Enoch Pratt Hosp., 1963-75. Served with USNRF, World War I. Named to Md. Jewish Hall of Fame, 1980. Mem. Bar Assn. Balt. City (pres. 1952-53), ABA, Md. Bar Assn. (pres. 1955-56), Harvard Law Sch. Assn. Md. (pres. 1955-56), Phi Beta Kappa, Order Coif, Omicron Delta Kappa. Home: Baltimore, Md. Died July 10, 1982.

OPPENHEIMER, RUSSELL HENRY, physician; b. Fremont, O., Jan. 26, 1888; s. A. E. and Elizabeth (Pauli) O.; A.B., Ohio State U., 1911; M.D., U. of Mich., 1917. Served in Med. Corps, U.S. Army, 1918-19; resident physician Emory U. div., Grady Hosp., 1921-23, resident physician and pathologist, 1923-24; supt. Emory U. Hosp., 1924-37, med. dir., 1937-44; dean Emory U. Sch. of Med., 1925-45, also prof. medicine, 1930-42, prof. clin. medicine, 1942-54. Fellow Am. Coll. Physicians, Am. Bd. Internal Medicine; mem. A.M.A., Ga. State and Fulton County med. socs., Southern Interurban Clin. Club, Am. Coll. Hosp. Adminstrs., Phi Rho Sigma. Democrat. Episcopalian. Club: Atlanta Athletic. Home: Jacksonville, Fla. †

ORDWAY, A(LONZO) B(ENTON), steel exec.; b. Union, Ia., Aug. 3, 1887; s. George B. and Ellen M. (Bowers) O.; B.S., U. Wis., 1909; m. Wilma Robbins, Dec. 27, 1913; children—Edward R., Barbara E. With Henry J. Kaiser from 1912, v.p., dir. Kaiser Steel Corp. since 1944, Kaiser Services from 1948; v.p., dir. Henry J. Kaiser Co. (Oakland), Kaiser Industries Corp., Kaiser Jeep Corp. Trustee Kaiser Found. Home: Piedmont, Calif. †

ORELL, BERNARD LEO, forest products co. exec.; b. Portland, Oreg., Jan. 26, 1914; s. Leo J. and Lucy (LaMere) O.; m. Helen M. Kirchoff, June 24, 1941; children—Terrence M., Mary Kay. B.S. in Forestry, Oreg. State Coll., 1939, M.F., B.S. in Edn., 1941; D.Bus. Adminstrn. (hon.), Dakota Wesleyan U. Recreation officer Mt. Hood Nat. Forest, 1935-40; tng. officer Oreg. Dept. Forestry, 1941-47; asst. prof. forestry U. Wash. Sch. Forestry, 1947-49; state forester div. forestry, Wash., 1949-53; v.p. Weyerhaeuser Sales Co., 1953-58; v.p. Weyerhaeuser Co., 1958-79, spl. asst. to pres., 1979-83; mem. adv. bd. Seattle-1st Nat. Bank, Tacoma; dir. Gt. Northwest Fed. Savs. & Loan Assn.; Mem. natural resources com. Pres.'s Commn. on Intergovtl. Relations, 1955-56; mem. Pres.'s Outdoor Recreation Resources Rev. Commn., 1959-64; dir. forest products div. Dept. Commerce, 1954; Trustee Weyerhaeuser Co. Found., Am. Forest Inst.; bd. dirs. King County (Seattle) United Way; bd. dirs., mem. exec. com., chmn. devel. com. Consol. Hosps. Served to 1st lt. AUS, 1942-46. Fellow Soc. Am. Foresters (past v.p., pres.), Forest History Soc. (past pres., trustee, chmn. finance com.); mem. NAM (past dir., exec. com., regional v.p.), Forest Industries Council (past chmn.), Am. Pulpwood Assn. (past dir., past mem. exec. com.), Nat. Recreation Assn. (past dir.), Am. Forest Products Industries (pres. 1964-67), Am. Hort. Soc. (past dir.), Assn. Washington Bus. (past chmn.), Kappa Delta Rho, Xi Sigma Pi, Phi Sigma, Alpha Phi Omega. Clubs: Tacoma Country and Golf, Tacoma. Home: Tacoma, Wash. Died May 5, 1983.

ORFF, CARL, composer; b. Muenchen, Germany, July 13, 1895; s. Heinrich and Paula (Koestler) O.; student Acad. of Music, Muenchen; Ph.D. (hon.), U. Tombingen, 1955; 1 dau., Godela. Dir. Orff-Inst. at Academy Mozarteum Salzburg/Austria; composer concert and choir works; compositions for theatre including Carmina Burana, 1936, Der Mond (The Moon), 1938, Die Kluge (The Wise Woman), 1942, Catulli Carmina, 1943, Die Bernauerin, 1945, Antigonae, 1948, Astutuli, 1952. Trionfo di Afrodite, 1953, also composer of Comoedia de Christi Resurrectione, 1935, Oedipus the Tyrant, also music for Shakespeare's Midsummer Night's Dream; Ludus de nsio Infante mirificus, 1960, Prometheus, 1968. Mem. Pour le Merit for Arts and Sci., Bavarian Acad. Arts, Accademia de Santa Ceoilia Roma. Author: Orff-Schulwork, Music for Children (5 vols.). Home: St. Georgen, Germany. Died Mar. 1, 1982.

ORKIN, SAUL, college president; b. N.Y.C., Sept. 4, 1923; s. Aaron and Minnie O.; m. Maria Lydia Astorga, Nov. 21, 1953; children—Philip, Neil. B.A., Rutgers U., 1949; M.A., U. Mich., 1951; Ph.D., Columbia U., 1971. Instr. Highland Manor Jr. Coll., 1949-50; teaching fellow U. Mich., 1951-53; instr. Union Coll., Cranford, N.J., 1955-58, asst. prof. polit. sci., 1959-64, assoc. prof., 1965-67, chmn. dept. social scis., 1959-67, dir. admission, 1961-65, pres., 1974-83; dean Somerset County Coll., 1967-74; chmn. N.J. Consortium on Community Coll., 1975-80. Del. N.J. Constl. Conv. on Reapportionment, 1966; mem. Plainfield (N.J.) Charter Study Com., 1967. Served with AC U.S. Army, 1943-46. Mem. Phi Beta Kappa. Home: Somerville, N.J. Died Oct. 7, 1983.

ORMANDY, EUGENE, music dir.; b. Budapest, Hungary, Nov. 18, 1899; came to U.S., 1921, naturalized, 1927; s. Benjamin and Rosalie O.; m. Steffy Goldner, 1922 (dec.); m. Margaret Frances Hitsch, May 15, 1950. Youngest pupil at 5 1/2, Royal State Acad. of Music, B.A. at 14 1/2, state diploma for art of violin playing, state diploma as prof.; student, U. of Budapest, 1917-20; Mus.D., Hamline U., St. Paul, 1934, U. Pa., 1937, Phila. Acad. Music, 1939, Curtis Inst. Music, 1946; LL.D., Temple U., 1949; L.H.D., Lehigh U., 1953, C.W. Post Coll., 1965, Hahnemann Med. Coll. and Hosp., 1979; Mus.D. (hon.), U. Mich., 1952; Dr. honoris causa, Clarke U., 1956, Miami U., Oxford, Ohio, 1959, Rutgers U., 1960, L.I. U., 1965; Litt.D., Lafayette Coll., 1966; Mus.D., Villanova U., Peabody Inst., Renssalaer Poly. Inst., 1968, U. Ill., 1969, Jefferson Coll., 1974, Moravian Coll., 1976. Substituted for Toscanini as condr. Phila. Orch.; condr. Mpls. Symphony Orch., 1931-36; condr., music dir. Phila. Orch., 1936-80, condr. laureate, 1980-85. Decorated comdr. French Legion Honor, Order of Danebrog Denmark, Order of Lion Finland; Order Merit Juan Pablo Duarte Dominican Republic; knight Order of White Rose of Finland; commandatore of merit Italian Republic; hon. knight comdr. Order Brit. Empire; recipient citation Distinguished Service in music Boston U., 1957; Honor Cross for Arts and Sci. Austria, 1966; Golden medallion Vienna Philharmonic, 1967; Presdl. Medal Freedom, 1970; 1st award for excellence Pa. Council on Arts, 1970; Phila. award, 1970; Nat. Recognition award Freedoms Found., 1970; Gov.'s Com. 100,000 Pennsylvanians award for excellence in performing arts, 1968; Gallantry award Easter Seal Soc., 1971; Alice M. Ditson Condrs. award, 1977; Broadcast Pioneer award, 1979; Gold Baton award Am. Symphony Orch. League, 1979; Medal of Freedom award City of Phila., 1980. Mem. Am. Philos. Soc., Musical Fund Soc. Phila. (hon. life). Boy music prodigy at age 3 1/2; toured Hungary as child prodigy, later toured Central Europe; apptd. head of master classes State Conservatorium of Music, Budapest, at age 20 Died Mar. 12, 1985.

ORNBURN, IRA M., b. Moberly, Mo., Nov. 28, 1889; s. Cyrus P. and Sallie (Sims) O.; ed. pub. and pvt. schs., Moberly; m. Anna Gaffney, July 10, 1914; 1 son, Paul R. Identified with Cigar Makers Union for many yrs.; became pres. Cigar Makers Internat. Union of America, 1927; sec. Union Label Trades Dept., A.F. of L.; mem. Tariff Commn., 1931-33. Democrat. Baptist. Mason, Elk, Moose. Contbr. on labor topics. Home: New Haven, Conn. †

O'RORKE, EDWARD ARTHUR, pub. co. exec.; b. N.Y.C., Jan. 7, 1907; s. Michael and Mary (O'Rorke) O'R.; A.B., Holy Cross Coll., 1929, D.Litt. (hon.), 1976; J.D., Yale, 1932; postgrad. Harvard, 1937; m. Louise McEwan, Nov. 9, 1937. Admitted to N.Y. bar, 1933; personnel mgr. R.H. Macy & Co., N.Y.C., 1932-41; prodn. mgr. Uarco, Inc., Chgo., 1941-48; v.p., gen. mgr. Manifold Bus. Forms, Chgo., 1948-51; operating v.p. R.H. Donnelley Corp., N.Y.C., 1951-62, sr. v.p., 1962-67, exec. v.p., 1967-72, also dir.; chmn. bd. Asso. Bus. Publs., N.Y.C.; pres. Brewster/Carver, Inc.; v.p. Econ. Devel. Council N.Y.C., 1972-78; counsel firm Bradey & Tarpey, N.Y.C., 1978-82; dir. Lejacq Publs. Chmn. pres.'s council, asso. trustee, chmn. devel. com. Holy Cross Coll.; trustee Daytop Found., Regis High Sch., N.Y.C. Served to lt. comdr. USNR, 1943-46. Mem. N.Y. Bar Assn., N.Y. State C. of C. and Industry (pres. 1977-78). Clubs: University (N.Y.C.); Am. Yacht (Rye, N.Y.); Siwanoy Country (Bronxville, N.Y.). Home: Bronxville, N.Y. Died Dec. 6, 1982; buried Bronxville Cemetery, N.Y.

O'ROURKE, GEORGE MARTIN, railroad ofcl.; b. Chgo., Feb. 22, 1889; s. James Martin and Anna Theresa (Crotty) O'R.; student eve. sch. Armour Inst. Tech., 1906-13; m. Margaret Josephine Moore, June 10, 1909; children—Alice Moor, Anne Marie. With I.C. R.R., from 1905, successively engring. apprentice, chainman, rodman, instrumentman, masonry insp., resident engr., chief draftsman, asst. engr., supervisor of track, roadmaster, div. engr., dist. engr., asst. engr. maintenance of way, from 1929. Survey of railroads Western Germany for ECA, 1950; survey N.Y. Rapid Transit System, 1951; Mem. Am. Soc. C.E., Am. Ry. Engring. Assn. (pres. 1955-56), Roadmasters and Maintenance of Way Assn. Am. Republican. Roman Catholic. K.C. Clubs: Maintenance of Way, South Shore Country (Chgo.). Home: Chicago, IL. †

O'ROURKE, JOHN THOMAS, newspaper editor; b. Phila., Pa., Sept. 28, 1900; s. John Aloysius and Catharine (Kelly) O'R.; ed. Calvert Hall Coll. (Baltimore), St. John's Coll. (Washington, D.C.), Columbia, George Washington U.; m. Hilary Dabney, 1933. Mem. editorial staff Washington Daily News from 1928, editor from 1939. Decorated Order al Merito, Republic of Chile; also the Maria Moors Cabot citation, 1957; Inter-Am. Press Association, Tom Wallace award, 1960. Mem. Theta Delta Chi, Inter-American Press Assn. (president, 1957-58). Clubs: Press, Cosmos. Home: Washington, D.C. Died Dec. 7, 1983.

ORR, MILTON LEE, educator; b. Union Springs, Ala., Dec. 10, 1888; s. Dr. John Milton and Mattie (Lee) O.; B.S., U. of Ala., 1910; A.M., Peabody Coll., 1927, Ph.D., 1930; m. Annie Laurie Harris, Apr. 8, 1914; children—

Milton Lee, Marie Harris, John William, Annie Laurie. Teacher Ala. pub. schs., 1910-12; asst. prin. Geneva County (Ala.) High Sch., 1912-14; prin. Clarke County High Sch., 1914-18, Escambia County High Sch., 1918-22; with Ala. Coll., Montevallo, since 1922, as supt. training school, 1922-28, dir. teacher training, 1928-36, head of edn. dept. and dir. extension from 1936, asst. dir. summer school, 1935-37, dir. from 1937, acting dean, 1952, director grad. div., from 1954, dean, from 1957. Chairman reviewing com. and mem. steering com., Ala. Curriculum Program. Mem. N.E.A., Sch. Adminstrs. of Ala., Ala., Edn. Assn., Am. Assn. School Adminstrs., Am. Childhood Edn., Am. Education Fellowship (mem. nat. advisory bd., 1936-38; mem. advisory com. S.E. Sect.), Ala. Com. on Vocational Edn., Ala. Com. on Resource Use Edn., Ala. div. higher edn. of Ala. Edn. Assn. (past pres.), Phi Delta Kappa, Kappa Delta Pi, Sigma Nu. Baptist. Clubs: Rotary (Montevallo). Mason and Shriner. Author: State Supported Colleges for Women, 1930. Editor of Survey Workbooks for Community Analysis, 1937. Contbr. to Ala. Edn. Survey, 1944. Home: Montevallo, Ala.†

ORR, NEWELL HAMILTON, business exec.; b. Holiday's Cove, W.Va., Oct. 26, 1887; s. Joseph Reed and Mary Elizabeth (Hamilton) O.; student Carnegie Inst. Tech., 1905-09; m. Edith E. Gress, Mar. 4, 1914; children—Edith (Mrs. J. W. Borden), Lucinda (Mrs. Edmund H. Brown), Newell H., Jr. Timekeeper Am. Bridge Co., Pittsburgh, 1910-12, engr., 1912-14, asst. mgr. erection, 1914-26, salesman, Jones & Laughlin Steel Corp., Pittsburgh, 1926-27, mgr. sales of jr. beam dept., 1927-33; product mgr. Am. Iron and Steel Inst., N.Y. City, 1933-35, vice pres. in charge sales for corp. and all subsidiaries, Colo. Fuel & Iron Corp., Denver, 1935-50; Mutual Security Agency adviser in Germany from 1952. Member American Ordnance Association (director Rocky Mtn. post), Am. Mil. Engrs., St. Louis Ordnance Dist. (mem. adv. bd.), Denver C. of C. (dir.) Republican. Presbyterian. Clubs: Denver, Denver Country, Cherry Hills Country (Denver). Mem. Am. Soc. Civil Engrs., Am. Iron and Steel Inst., Colo. Soc. Civil Engrs. Home: Haddam, Conn. †

ORR, STANLEY LUTZ, lawyer, jurist; b. Kingston, O., Aug. 5, 1890; s. Weden Kelley and Elizabeth (Lutz) O.; A.B., Western Reserve Univ., 1912, LL.B., 1914; m. Katherine Elizabeth Murray, May 8, 1920; children—Mary (Mrs. Edwin M. Boynton), Stanley Lutz, Parker, David. Admitted to Ohio bar, 1914, and practiced since in Cleveland; asso. with Thompson, Hine and Flory, 1914-24; mem. firm of Gott, Bloomfield and Orr, 1926-34, Bloomfield, Orr and Vickery, 1934-38, Bloomfield and Orr, 1938-48; mem. faculty, Cleveland Law Sch., teaching law of bailments and law of municipal corps., 1933-43. Municipal lawyer as mem. firm of Bloomfield, Orr and Vickery; municipal judge, 1924-25; judge, Ct. of Common Pleas, 1941-48; solicitor for city of Euclid, 1926-38, village of Cuyahoga Heights, 1930-32, village of Valley View, 1930-38. Vice pres., Bd. of Park Commrs., Cleveland Park Bd.; mem. bd. of govs., A.R.C., also chapter chmn. and exec. bd. mem., Cleveland Red Cross; mem. Cleveland Council of Boy Scouts of Am. Vice chmn., bd. of trustees, Cleveland Law Sch., 1938-48. Served with U.S. Cavalry; Mexican Border campaign, 1915-17, A.E.F., France, 1917-19. Awarded World War I Victory medal, Mexican Border campaign ribbon; decorated with Silver Beaver award by Nat. Council, Boy Scouts of Am. Mem. Cleveland Bar Assn. (pres.), Cleveland Citizens League (pres.), C. of C., S.A.R., Beta Theta Pi, Delta Sigma Rho, Phi Delta Phi, Republican. Methodist. Mason (32 deg.). Clubs: Rotary, Mid-Day, Athletic (Cleveland). Home: Euclid, Ohio. Died Mar. 1, 1948.

ORTMAN, FRED BENSON, business exec.; b. New Salem, O., Jan. 5, 1888; s. Benson Clark and Mary Ellen (Hill) O.; B.S., in Ceramic Engring., Ohio State U., 1911; m. Josephine Quigg, Aug. 5, 1933; children—Robert Ashbrook, Florence Marie. Asst. gen. mgr. New York Archtl. Terra Cotta Co., Long Island City, 1911-18; chief ceramic engr. Northwestern Terra Cotta Co., Chicago, 1918-21; v.p. Tropico Potteries, Inc., Los Angeles, 1921-23; exec. v.p. Gladding, McBean & Co., Los Angeles, 1923-38, pres. 1938-55, chmn. bd. dirs., 1955-56; director of Security 1st Nat. Bank, Los Angeles. Past director Los Angeles National Association of Manufacturers. Republican. Methodist. Clubs: California, Los Angeles Country (Los Angeles); Pacific Union (San Francisco). Home: San Francisco. †

OSBORN, CHASE SALMON, JR., newspaperman; b. South Bend, Ind., Jan. 31, 1888; s. Chase Salmon and Lillian (Jones) O.; ed. U. of Mich., 1907-11; m. Marjorie Stanton, July 31, 1912 (died Aug. 4, 1926); children—Marjorie Stanton, Florence Salmon, Chase S. III; m. 2d, Mrs. Dorothy Manson Hulme, Apr. 21, 1932. Began as printer's devil and newsboy, Evening News, Sault Ste. Marie, Mich., 1900; reporter Saginaw (Mich.) Courier-Herald, 1905-12, Grand Rapids (Mich.) News, 1912-13; editor Sault Ste. Marie News, 1913-15, Fresno (Calif.) Herald, 1915-20, Fresno Republican, 1920 until sold, 1932. Mem. Delta Kappa Epsilon, Sigma Delta Chi. Republican. Episcopalian. Clubs: University, Sequoia, Sunnyside Country. Home: Fresno, Calif.†

OSBORN, FREDERICK, corp. exec.; b. New York, N.Y., Mar. 21, 1889; s. William Church and Alice C. H. (Dodge) O.; A.B., Princeton, 1910; post grad. study, Trinity Coll., Cambridge, England, 1911-12; LL.D., Washington and Lee University, 1943, Washington and Jefferson College, 1947; Sc.D., Norwich University, 1942; Litt.D., New York U., 1945; m. Margaret L. Schieffelin, Jan. 10, 1914; children—Frederick, Margaret Louisa, John Jay, Alice Dodge, Virginia Sturges, Cynthia. Began in business management, 1912; treas. and v.p. in charge of traffic, Detroit, Toledo and Ironton R.R., Detroit, 1914-17, pres., 1920-21; partner and spl. partner G.M.P. Murphy & Co., bankers, N.Y. City 1921-38; dir. Schieffelin & Co.; apptd. chmn. President's Advisory Com. on Selective Service, Oct. 1940; chmn. Joint Army and Navy Com. on Welfare and Recreation, Mar. 1941; apptd. to temporary rank of brig. gen. heading morale branch of army, 1941; promoted maj. gen. (temp.), 1943; dir. information and edn. div., AUS; resigned from army, 1945. Apptd. dep. representative U.S. on UN Atomic Energy Commission, 1947-50; trustee of The Population Council. Trustee Carnegie Corp. of N.Y., The Frick Collection, Princeton, Milbank Fund; member of the board of commrs. Palisades Interstate Park Com. Fellow A.A.A.S.; dir. Population Assn. of Am., Am. Eugenics Soc., mem. Phi Beta Kappa. Democrat. Presbyn. Clubs: Century, Princeton University (N.Y.C.); Highlands Country (Garrison, N.Y.); Colonial (Princeton, N.J.); Cosmos (Washington, D.C.). Author: (with F. Lorimer) Dynamics of Population, 1934. Editor: Heredity and Environment (by G. C. Schwesinger), 1933; Preface to Eugenics, 1940; Population, an International Dilemma, 1958. Contbr. articles on population. Home: New York, N.Y. †

OSBORNE, HENRY PLANT, lawyer; b. Jacksonville, Fla., June 21, 1888; s. Francis Ritchie and Sallie (Roberts) O.; A.B., Univ. of N.C., 1909; LL.B., Univ. of Fla., 1911; married Nancy M. Cooper, Mar. 1, 1916; children—Nancy Montgomery (Mrs. William W. Bennett), Elizabeth Ann, Sally Roberts (Mrs. Richard J. Barrett), Henry Plant, Jr. Admitted Jacksonville (Fla.) bar, 1911, and since in practice at Jacksonville; mem. Osborne, Copp & Markham from 1939. Served as 2d lt., Aviation Section, U.S. Army, during World War I. Chmn. State Bd. of Law Examiners of Florida. Director St. Luke's Hospital Association (former pres.), Evergreen Cemetery Association (pres.), Jacksonville Public Library, Jacksonville Humane Soc. (chmn.); chmn. Nat. Conf. Bar Examiners. Mem. Am. Palestine Com. (Jacksonville), Southern Council on Internat. Relations, Am., Fla. and Jacksonville bar assns., Am. Law Inst., Nat. Panel of Arbitrators Am. Arbitration Assn., Phi Beta Kappa, Sigma Alpha Epsilon. Democrat. Episcopalian. Clubs: Florida Yacht, Timuquana Country (Jacksonville). Home: Jacksonville, Fla. †

OSBORNE, JOHN, writer; b. Corinth, Miss., Mar. 15, 1907; s. John F. and Norma (Curry) O.; student Southwestern U., Memphis, 1925-26, U. Colo., 1926-27; m. Gertrude McCullough, May 9, 1942: 1 son, John F. Newspaper reporter Comml. Appeal, A.P., Memphis, 1927-31; pub. relations TVA, NRA, 1933-35; with Newsweek, 1936-38; writer, editor, fgn. corr. Time, Inc., 1938-61; free lance, 1961-68; asso. sr. editor New Republic, 1968-81. Clubs: Federal City, Cosmos (Washington). Author: Britain: A Country of Character, 1961: The Old South, 1965; The Nixon Watch, ann. 1970-75; White House Watch: The Ford Years, 1977. Address: Washington, D.C. Died May 2, 1981; interred Oakland Cemetery, Sag Harbor, N.Y.

OSIAS, CAMILO, Philippine commr.; b. Balaoan, La Union, P.I., Mar. 23, 1889; s. Manuel and Gregoria (Olaviano) O.; grad. Western Ill. State Normal Sch., Macomb, 1908; B.S., Columbia U., 1910; diploma in ednl. administration, Teachers Coll. (Columbia); LL.D., Otterbein Coll., 1929; m. Ildefonsa Cuaresma, of Bacnotan, La Union, 1914; children—Camilo, Salvador (dec.), Victor, Rebecca, Apolinario (dec.), Benjamin, Felicidad Rosita. First Filipino supt. of schs., P.I., 1915-17; professorial lecturer, U. of Philippines, 1919-21; pres. Nat. Univ., Manila, P.I., 1921-29. Mem. Philippine Senate, 1925-29; resident commr. from Philippines, Washington, D.C., from 1929, 2d term 1932-35. Trustee Union Theol. Sem. Mem. Philippine Edn. Assn. (1st pres.), Nat. Civic League (1st pres.), Philippine Amateur Athletic Federation (1st v.p.; sec-treas.), Far Eastern Students Alliance (promotion com.), Philippine Anti-Leprosy Soc. (trustee), Annual Students Conf. (chmn.), N.E.A., Pi Gamma Mu. Mason. Author: Philippines Under the Spanish Regime, 1917; Philippine Lesson Plan Book, 1917; Philippine Readers, Books V, VI, VII, 1919-20, Books III, IV, 1922, Book II, 1924, Book I, 1927; Rizal and Education, 1921; Barrio Life and Barrio Education, 1921; Stories and Games, 1926; Our Education and Dynamic Filipinism, 1927; Teachers Reading Manual, 1929; Ti Filipinas Ditoy Lubong, 1931. Co-author: Philippine Number Primer, 1923; Philippine Arithmetics, 1923, 25; Teachers' Manual for Teaching Arithmetic, 1925; Evangelical Christianity in the Philippines, 1931; The Philippine Charter of Liberty, 1933. Awarded Columbia U. Distinction Medal, 1929. Home: Balaoan, La Union, P.I. †

OSSORIO, MIGUEL JOSÉ, business exec.; b. Manila, P.I., Oct. 1, 1889; s. Miguel and Emilla (Lapuente) O.; student St. Edmund's Coll., Ware, Hertfordshire. Eng., 1902-04, Christian Brothers' Coll., Gibralter, 1904-06; m. Paz Yangco, Feb. 26, 1910; children—Miguel N., Luis C., Jose M., Alfonso A., Frederic E., Robert U. Business apprentice Hongkong and Shanghai Bank, Manila, P.I., 1907-08; with firm Castle Bros., Wolf and Sons (later Pacific Commerical Co.), Manila, 1908-10; in inter-island shipping and sugar bus. for self from 1910; organizer and pres., N. Negros Sugar Company, Incorporated, from 1917, Victorias Milling Company, Incorporated. Roman Catholic. Clubs: Down Town Assn., Union League, Downtown Athletic (New York); Manila Golf, Manila Polo, Manila Yacht, Army and Navy (Manila); Baguio (P.I.) Country. Home: Greenwich, Conn. †

OSTROM, CHARLES DOUGLAS YELVERTON, army officer; b. Alturas, Calif., Apr. 26, 1890; s. Charles M. and Ivy D. (Hager) O.; B.S., U. of Calif., 1912; grad. Coast Arty. Sch., Battery Officers Course, 1921, Advanced Course, 1930, Command and Gen. Staff Sch., 1934, Army War Coll., 1939; m. Margaret B. Ross, Sept. 22, 1917; children—Charles D. Y., Thomas R. Began as civil engr., 1912. Enlisted as private Calif. Nat. Guard, Jan. 20, 1910, advancing to capt., 1915; commd. 2d lt., Coast Arty. Corps, U.S. Army, Nov. 1916, and advanced through the grades to brig. gen., 1942; served as major, Coast Arty., World War I; Gen. Staff Corps, 1937-38. Awarded Legion of Merit, Aug. 1943. Mem. Sons Am. Revolution, Scabbard and Blade. Club: Army and Navy, Washington, D.C. Address: Washington, D.C.†

OTT, EDWARD STANLEY, army officer; b. Mt. Herman, La., Dec. 30, 1893; m. Elbert Weston and Martha (Loggett) O.; student U. of Ill., 1913-14; A.B., La. State U., 1917; grad. F.A. Sch., 1925, Command and Gen. Staff Sch., 1935, Army War Coll., 1938; m. Denise Marie Koch, Dec. 24, 1919; children—Edward Stanley, David Ewing. Commd. 2d lt., F.A., U.S. Army, Aug. 15, 1917, and advanced through the grades to brigadier general, June 24, 1942; instr. service schs., 1925-37; on War Dept. Gen. Staff, Washington, D.C., 1939-42. Army Ground Force Staff, 1942; arty. comdr., 91st Inf. Div. June 1, 1942-Sept. 15, 1943; comdr. SV Corps Arty., Sept. 15, 1943-45; assigned to Ground G-3 sect., Oct. 1945; retired for physical disability, 1947. Decorated Legion of Merit, Silver Star, D.S.M., Purple Heart with oak leaf cluster, Bronze Star Medal with oak leaf cluster (U.S.), Chevalier, Legion of Honor, Croix de Guerre with Palm (France), Distinguished Service Order (Gt. Britain). Member Omicron Delta Kappa, Lamdba Chi Alpha, Phi Kappa Phi, Sigma Delta Chi, Mu Sigma Rho. Seabbard and blade. Mason. Died Nov. 1, 1982.

OTT, LOUIS JOHN, ret. elec. equipment co. mfg. exec.; b. Mansfield, Ohio, Oct. 14, 1905; s. Louis A. and Rose J. (Menninger) O.; m. Helen Keating, Oct. 8, 1930; children—Margery Keating, Lisbeth Simpson (Mrs. David L. Clever). Grad., Univ. Sch., Cleve., 1923; A.B., Amherst Coll., 1927. With Ohio Brass Co., Mansfield, 1927-74, factory trainee, staff advt. dept., advt. mgr., mgr. priorities div., gen. sales mgr., 1927-53, v.p. sales, 1953-63, dir., from 1961, exec. v.p., 1963-67, pres., 1967-74; pres., chief exec. officer Mansfield Sanitary, Inc., Perrysville, Ohio, 1974-75; v.p. Shaw & Ott Drugs, Inc., Mansfield, 1976-79; gen. mgr. Lumbermen's Mut. Ins. Co., Mansfield, 1979-80; chmn. bd. Mansfield Graphics, Inc.; cons. Mansfield Typewriter Co., from 1980; dir. Lumbermen's Mut. Ins. Co., 1st Nat. Bank Mansfield.; Instr. mktg. North Central Tech. Coll., 1974. Pres. Johnny Appleseed area council Boy Scouts Am., 1961-64; mem. Richland County Planning Commn.; trustee Mansfield Gen. Hosp., pres., 1959-64; trustee, chmn. adminstrv. bd. Kingwood Center. Mem. Nat. Elec. Mfrs. Assn. (bd. govs. 1963-74), Am. Mining Congress (pres. mfrs. div. 1969-70), Delta Upsilon. Clubs: Rotary (pres. Mansfield 1955-56), Elks, Woodland, Westbrook Country, Mansfield U. Home: Mansfield, OH.

OTT, PERCY WRIGHT, coll. prof.; b. Mt. Hermon, La., Sept. 24, 1889; s. Elbert Weston and Martha (Leggett) O.; student Soulé Coll., New Orleans, 1906-07; B.S., Engring., U. of Ill., 1917; M.S., Ohio State U., 1929; student U. of Toulouse (while in army), 1919; m. Rose Ellen Bickham, Aug. 27, 1917; children—Mary Ellen, James Bickham, Carolyn Rose. Teacher La. Pub. Schs., 1911-13; analyst, Ill. State Water Survey, 1916; instr., mechanics, Ohio State U., 1919-20, asst. prof., 1921-28, asso. prof., 1928-32, prof. since 1932, dept. chmn. from 1935; engring. consultant work for Ill. State Bd. Pub. Health, Ohio State Highway Dept., Carl B. Harrop, Inc., Buckeye Steel Castings Co., Fuller-Lehigh Co., Ranco, Incorporated, Naval Ordnance Testing Station, Inyokern. Served as 2d lt., Engrs., to capt., adj. 603d, 1917-19. Won preliminary, final, spl. honors, U. of Ill. Mem. Am. Soc. C.E., Soc. Promotion Engring. Edn., Theta Tau, Tau Beta Pi (ex-pres. nat. council), Sigma Xi. Clubs: Ohio State Faculty, Saturday, Torch (Columbus). Home: Columbus, Ohio. †

OTTO, WALTER E., ins. exec.; b. Detroit, Feb. 24, 1889; s. Rudolph and Anna (Ewald) O.; m. Gertrude P. Valliere, Jan. 9, 1915; 1 son, Rudrick R. Actuary and dep. commr. of ins., State of Mich., 1907-18; sec.-treas. Michigan Mutual Liability Company, Detroit, 1918-36, president 1936-58, became chmn., 1959, now dir. Mem. Detroit C. of C., Traffic Safety Assn. of Detroit (dir.), Newcomen Soc. N. Am., Casualty Actuarial Soc. Am. Clubs: Detroit, Detroit Athletic, Adcraft, Economic, Aero of Michigan. Home: Detroit, Mich. †

OULLIBER, JOHN ANDREW, lawyer, banker; b. New Orleans, Feb. 24, 1911; s. John Andrew and Anna (Wirth) O.; J.D., Loyola U. at New Orleans, 1932; grad. Rutgers U. Grad. Sch. Banking, 1939; m. Gloria Yenni, Aug. 8,

1936 (dec. Nov. 2, 1979); children—Sandra Adele, Judith Ann. Profl. baseball player, New Orleans, Cleve., 1931-34; admitted to La. bar, 1933; atty. RFC, New Orleans, 1934; with 1st Nat. Bank of Commerce, New Orleans, 1935-73, exec. v.p., 1951-58, pres., 1958-69, chmn. bd., 1969-73, also dir.; vice-chmn. bd. Nat. Bank Commerce, Jefferson Parish; past dir., treas. Oulliber Coffee Co., Inc., New Orleans; dir. Consol. Cos., Inc., New Orleans, Sta. WWL-AM-FM-TV, New Orleans, Pan Am. Life Ins. Co., New Orleans; former v.p., dir. 1st Commerce Corp., 1st Commerce Real Estate Corp., New Orleans; of counsel Jones, Walker, Waechter, Poitevent, Carrere and Denegre, New Orleans, 1973—. Pres. New Orleans Clearing House Assn., 1964-65, La. Bankers Assn., 1971-72; mem. govt. borrowing adv. com. Am. Bankers Assn. to sec. of treas. U.S., 1971-73; pres., bd. dirs. Bus. and Indsl. Devel. Corp. La., 1972-73; mem. adv. com. La. Law Inst. Mem. adv. bd. Hotel Dieu Hosp., New Orleans, St. Vincent Infants Home, New Orleans; bd. dirs. Council for Better La., Pub. Affairs Research Council, Boys Clubs Greater New Orleans; mem. president's council Loyola U., New Orleans, chmn. corp. bd. dirs., 1975-78; past bd. dirs., organizer Met. Crime Commn., New Orleans; mem. career advancement com. Tulane U.; past treas., bd. dirs. Internat. House, New Orleans; former mem. budget com., vice chmn. speakers com. United Way of New Orleans Area; past chmn. adv. bd. Mt. Carmel Acad., New Orleans, Dominican Coll., New Orleans; past mem. adv. bd. Ursuline Acad., New Orleans; past chmn. budget com. task force Archdiocese of New Orleans. Mem. La., New Orleans bar assns., C. of C. Greater New Orleans (past dir.), Blue Key, Beta Gamma Sigma. Clubs: New Orleans Country, Pickwick. Home: New Orleans, La. Died Dec. 26, 1980.

OURSLER, WILLIAM CHARLES, (WILL OURSLER) author; b. Balt., July 12, 1913; s. Charles Fulton and Rose (Karger) O.; m. Adelaide Burr, May 20, 1939; 1 son, William Fulton. Student, Art Student's League, 1927, Collegiate Sch., 1933, Grand Central Sch. Art; A.B. cum laude, Harvard U., 1937. Reporter Boston newspapers, 1937-39, asst. editor detective mags., N.Y.C., 1940-41, Pacific war corr. for mag. syndicate, 1943-45, author, lectr., radio commentator. Author: The Trial of Vincent Doon, 1941, Folio on Florence White, 1942, Departure Delayed, 1947, (with Fulton Oursler) Father Flanagan of Boys Town, 1949, (under pseudonym Gale Gallagher) I Found Him Dead, 1947, (with Laurence Dwight Smith) Narcotics: America's Peril, 1952, (with E.C. May) The Prudential, 1950, Murder Memo, 1950, N.Y., N.Y, 1954, The Boy Scout Story, 1955, The Healing Power of Faith, 1957, From Ox Carts to Jets, 1959, The Road to Faith, 1960, (with H.J. Anslinger) The Murderers, 1961, Family Story, 1963, The Atheist, 1965, Marijuana-The Facts-The Truth, 1968, Religion: Out or Way Out, 1968, Protestant Power and the Coming Revolution, 1971, (with D. Kahn) My Life with Edgar Cayce, 1970, (with J. Klimo) Hemingway and Jake, 1972; Editor: Light in the Jungle, 1959, Explore Your Psychic World, 1970, (with H.N. Banerjee) Lives Unlimited: Reincarnation East and West, 1974; anthology As Tough as They Come, 1951; (pseudonym Gale Gallagher) Chord in Crimson, 1947, (pseud. Nick Marino) One Way Street, 1952; Contbr. articles, fiction to various mags., periodicals.; Established: Will Oursler Manuscript Collection at, Syracuse U. Recipient commendation for meritorious service as war corr. from Gen. Douglas MacArthur, commendation for service as Pacific war corr. from Forrestal. Mem. P.E.N., Sigma Delta Chi. Episcopalian. Clubs: Players (N.Y.C.), Overseas Press (N.Y.C.) (past sec., treas., v.p., pres.), Dutch Treat (N.Y.C.), Baker Street Irregulars (N.Y.C.); Overseas Yacht, Deadline. Address: New York, N.Y. Died Jan. 7, 1985.

OUTERBRIDGE, SIR LEONARD CECIL, business executive; born Asheville, No. Carolina, May 6, 1888; s. Sir Joseph and Maria Harvey (Tucker) O.; student Bishop Field Coll., St. John's, 1900; Marlborough Coll., Eng., 1901; B.A., U. of Toronto, 1911, LL.B., 1915, LL.D. (honorary), 1950; LL.D. from the University of Laval, 1952; Barrister-at-Law Osgoode Hall Law School, 1914; m. Dorothy Winnifred Strathy, Jan. 23, 1915; 1 dau., Nancy Diana (Mrs. Herbert Howard Winter). Pres., dir. Harvey & Co., Ltd., St. John's, Newfoundland, since 1920. Hon. pvt. sec. to gov. and comdr. in chief, Newfoundland, 1930-44, dir. civil defense, 1942-46, lt. gov. Province of Newfoundland 1950-57. Served as major C.E.F., 1914-18. Hon. col. Royal Newfoundland Regt., 1950. Awarded Distinguished Service Order, 1918; decorated Companion Order British Empire, 1926; created Knight Bachelor, 1946; Knight of Grace, Order of St. John of Jerusalem. Chmn. Newfoundland Com. arranging exhibits at British Empire Exhbn., 1924-25. Hon. life mem. British Red Cross Soc. Address: St. John's, Newfoundland, Can. †

OUTLAW, ROBERT SIDNEY, lawyer; b. New Orleans, Dec. 16, 1889; s. Phau Rivers and Mildred Genevieve (Dalton) O.; LL.B., Tulane U., 1911; m. Lucie Rivers McKeithen, Feb. 1, 1915. Admitted to La. bar, 1911, Ill. bar, 1917, practiced law, New Orleans, 1911-14; joined A., T. & S.F. Ry., 1914, commerce atty., 1922-33, gen. atty., 1933-47, gen. solicitor from Jan. 1948. Chmn. Western Conf., Railway Counsel, 1956-58. Mem. Am., Illinois State, Chicago bar assns., Assn. Practitioners Before I.C.C. Clubs: Union League, Traffic, South Shore Country. Home: Chgo. 15. †

OVEREND, JOHN, educator, chemist; b. Keighley, Eng., Oct. 3, 1928; came to U.S., 1955, naturalized, 1975; s. Arthur and Clara (Ramsden) O.; m. Betty Jane Greengross, Dec. 6, 1954 (div.); children: Susan Overend Koehler, Joanna, Christopher; m. Charlotte Lezzette Helgeson, Dec. 8, 1973. B.A., St. John Baptist Coll., Oxford (Eng.) U., 1952, D.Phil., 1955, D.Sc., 1978. Research fellow U. Minn., 1955-58; research chemist Dow Chem. Co., 1958-60; mem. faculty U. Minn., 1960-84, prof. chemistry, 1967-84, chmn. dept. chemistry, 1979-80; vis. staff mem. Los Alamos Sci. Lab., 1974-84. Assoc. editor: Jour. Chem. Physics, 1979-84; contbr. articles to profl. jours. Mem. region X com. Woodrow Wilson Fellowship Found., 1968-70. Served with Brit. Army, 1947-49. Recipient Casberd prize St. John Bapt. Coll., 1951, Coblentz Meml. prize Coblentz Soc., 1963, Lippincott medal, 1983; Guggenheim fellow, 1967-68. Fellow Japan Soc. for Promotion Sci.; Mem. Am. Chem. Soc., Am. Phys. Soc., Optical Soc. Am. Research on vibrational spectroscopy, molecular dynamics, optical activity, lasers, surface chemistry and catalysis Home: Minneapolis, Minn. Died Nov. 26, 1984.

OVERSTREET, NOAH WEBSTER, architect, engr.; b. Eastabuchie, Miss., July 4, 1888; s. Harvey Hazzard and Bettie (Floore) O.; B.S. in Mech. Engring., Miss. State Coll., 1908; B.S. in Archtl. Engring., U. Ill., 1910; m. Mabel Kinnear, Sept. 18, 1912; children—Noah Webster, Robert K., Patricia Ann (wife of Rev. Harold T. Kitchings). Practice architecture and engring., Jackson, from 1917, partner Overstreet & Spencer, 1912-14, N.W. Overstreet, 1914-31; Overstreet & Town, 1931-38, N.W. Overstreet & Assos., 1938-56, Overstreet, Ware & Ware, 1956-68; dir. Plaza Investment Co., Downtowner Hotel, Flowood Corp. Staff state govs. Fellow A.I.A.; mem. C. of C., Kappa Alpha, Newcomen Soc. Baptist (deacon). Club: Rotary. Home: Jackson, CA. †

OWEN, C(LIFFORD) E(UGENE), corp. exec.; b. Pontotoc, Miss., Feb. 24, 1890; s. Ben and Frances (Ginn) O.; student bus. coll.; m. Lonie M. Limerick, Dec. 25, 1912; children—Holt E., Clem B. Founder 1920, and since pres. East Texas Auto Supply Co., Tyler; founder 1947, and pres. Owentown Industrial Center (Tex.); chmn. bd. Lonestar Steel Co., Lonestar, Tex., Western Foundries, Tyler. Home: Tyler, Tex. †

OWEN, ERNEST L., publisher; b. Marion, O., Oct. 8, 1888; s. William T. and Sarah Ann O.; grad. Ohio Northern U., 1908; m. Bonnie Marie Pinyerd, Oct. 6, 1920; 1 dau., Jean Ruth (Mrs. Phillip Potter, Jr.). Former pres., pub. Syracuse Post-Standard; dir. Onondega County Savings Bank, WSYR Radio Projects. Dir. Syracuse Gen. Hosp., Syracuse Boys' Club, Syracuse Community Chest. Mem. N.Am. Newspaper Alliance of N.Y., Asso. Press, Salvation Army (vice-chmn. bd.). Republican. Presbyterian. Clubs: Century, Rotary (Syracuse). Home: Skaneateles, N.Y. †

OWEN, GEORGE E., university dean; b. St. Louis, Jan. 7, 1922; s. George E. and Ruth (Spradling) O.; m. Deha R. Gursey, Oct. 3, 1959. B.S., Washington U., St. Louis, 1943, M.A., 1948, Ph.D., 1950; student, U.S. Naval Postgrad. Sch., 1946. Mem. faculty U. Pitts., 1950-51; mem. faculty Johns Hopkins U., from 1951, prof. physics, from 1959, chmn. dept. physics, from 1968, dean arts and scis., 1972-78, dean Homewood faculty, 1978-83, Univ. prof., from 1983; established math. tng. program high sch. tchrs. under auspices Esso Edn. Found., 1958-60. Author: Fundamentals of Scientific Mathematics, 1961, Introduction to Electromagnetic Theory, 1964, Fundamentals of Electronics, Vols. I, II, III, 1967, Universe of the Mind, 1971, also numerous articles.; Illustrator mags., books. Served to lt. USNR, 1943-46. Fellow Am. Phys. Soc. Spl. research nuclear physics Spl. research nuclear physics. Home: Baltimore, MD.

OWEN, GUY, JR., author, educator; b. Clarkton, N.C., Feb. 24, 1925; s. Guy and Ethel (Elkins) O.; m. Dorothy Meadows Jennings, Apr. 6, 1952; children—William James, John Leslie. A.B., U. N.C., 1947, A.M., 1949, Ph.D., 1955. Mem. faculty dept. English Stetson U., DeLand, Fla., 1955-62, prof., 1960-62; assoc. prof. English, N.C. State U., Raleigh, 1962-66, prof., 1966-81; mem. N.C. State U. (Grad. Faculty), 1966-81. Author: fiction Season of Fear, 1960, The Ballad of the Flim-Flam Man, 1965, Journey for Joedel, 1970, The Flim-Flam Man and the Apprentice Grifter, 1972; Editor: (with M.C. Williams) fiction Contemporary Southern Poetry, 1980. Served with AUS, 1943-45. Recipient award for lit. N.C., 1971, Disting. prof. award N.C. State U., 1970-82. Mem. AAUP, MLA, South Atlantic MLA, Popular Culture Assn., Thomas Wolfe Soc. Democrat. Mem. United Ch. of Christ. Home: Raleigh, N.C. Died July 23, 1981.

OWEN, RALPH, credit card company executive; b. Hartsville, Tenn., Oct. 3, 1905; s. Richard Carter and Annie Clary (Bell) O.; grad. Vanderbilt U., 1928; m. Lulu Hampton, May 28, 1929; children—Ralph, Melinda Hampton. With First Nat. Co., 1928-30; assisted orgn. Equitable Securities Corp. (merged with Am. Express 1968), 1930, dir., 1930-70, pres., 1950-70; chmn. Am. Express; dir. Nashville Gas Co., R.C. Owen Co., Tenn. Natural Gas Lines, Inc. Mem. bd. trust Vanderbilt U.; trustee Montgomery Bell Acad. Mem. Sigma Alpha Epsilon. Clubs: Belle Meade Country, Cumberland (Nashville); Farmington Country (Charlottesville, Va.); Links (N.Y.C.); Internat. House (New Orleans). Home: Nashville, Tenn. Died Nov. 4, 1983.

OWENS, ALEXANDER MITCHELL, army officer; b. Anne Arundel County, Md., Jan. 21, 1887; son of Cyrus Whitefield and Eliza Providence (Brashears) O.; married Katherine Conez, July 6, 1908; children—Susan Elizabeth (Mrs. William Menoher), Annabelle Eliza (Mrs. D.E. Breakefield), Alexandria (Mrs. Malcolm Hoover), Alexander Mitchell. Enlisted in United States Army, 1906; commd. 1st lt., Cav. Res., 1917; commd. capt., Q.M.C., 1920, and advanced through the grades to brig. gen., 1944; quartermaster, 8th Div. and 1st Army Corps, 1940-41; dir., storage and distribution division, O.Q.M.G., 1944; retired, 1946. Decorated D.S.M. Address: Avon Park, Fla. †

OWENS, (JAMES) HAMILTON, editor; born Baltimore, Md., Aug. 8, 1888; s. Gwinn Fardon and Arabella Pierpoint (Smith) O.; student Baltimore City Coll.; A.B., Johns Hopkins, 1909, LL.D., 1950; Litt.D., University of Miami, 1950; m. Olga von Hartz, March 6, 1913; children—James Hamilton, Lydia Gwinn, Gwinn F., II, Olga, Lloyd. Began as reporter Baltimore News, 1909-13; with N.Y. Press, 1913, dramatic critic, 1914-15; with Guaranty Trust Co. of New York, 1920-22, asst. mgr. London office, 1921-22; became editor Batimore Evening Sun, 1922; editor The Sun, 1938-43, editor-in-chief The Sunpapers 1943-56; trustee Evergreen Found., 1956. Sec. N.Y. Com. Nat. Defense, 1917; mng. editor Fgn. Press Bur., Com. on Pub. Information, 1918. Mem. Am. Soc. Newspaper Editors. A.I.A. (hon. Balt. chpt.). Delta Phi. Democrat. Club: 14 W. Hamilton St.; Elkridge (Balt.); Century Assn. (N.Y.C.). Contbr. to Ency. Britannica, 14th edit. Author: Baltimore on the Chesapeake, 1941. Home: Baltimore, Md. †

OWENS, WILLIAM BROWNLEE, lawyer, educator; born Steubenville, Ohio, Mar. 14, 1887; s. William Steele and Elmira (McCaughy) O.; LL.B., Stanford, 1915; m. Marie McClurg, Aug. 4, 1915; children—Robert Verner, William McClurg, Nancy Marie (Mrs. Robert E. Wade). Admitted to Calif. bar, 1915, practiced law, Los Angeles, 1916-17; mem. law dept. U.S. Food Adminstrn., Washington, 1917-18, head license div., 1917-18; trust dept. Title Ins. & Trust Co., Los Angeles, 1918-20; instr. Stanford Law Sch., 1915-16, asso. prof., 1920-23, prof. law, 1923-52; prof. law U. Cal. Hastings Coll. Law, from 1953. Faculty athletic rep. Pacific Coast Athletic Conf., 1924-41, pres., 1928-33; hearing commr. for Nat. Production Authority, 1950-51. Mem. Calif. Code Commn., 1930-40, 1943-50. Mem. State Bar Cal., Nat. Collegiate Athletic Assn. (pres. 1938-40), Delta Chi, Phi Alpha Delta, Order of Coif. Author: Forms and Suggestions for California Practice, 1928. Home: Stanford, Calif. †

OWTHWAITE, ROBERT MORRELL, business exec.; b. Bradford, Eng., Apr. 19, 1888; s. Robert and Mary Hannah (Morrell) O.; went to Canada, 1911, to U.S., 1912, naturalized, 1927; student Woodhouse Grove Sch., Yorkshire, Eng., Bradford Tech. Coll.; m. 2d, Eva Miller Payne, Feb. 11, 1941; children—William W. Payne, Jr., Margaret Eva (Mrs. Delton Bennett, Jr.). With John Morrell Co. (hdqrs. Ottumwa, Ia.), at Phila., 1912, mgr. at Topeka, 1931, 50, dir. from 1938, v.p., 1944-50, State chmn. Selective Service Bd. Appeal from 1941. Served with 1st Canadian Tank Battalion World War I. Mem. Nat. Assn. Mfrs. (dir.), Am. Social Hygiene Assn. (dir.), A.R.C. (county dir.), Community Chest (pres. 1943-44), Am. Legion. Episcopalian. Mason (Shriner). Clubs: Kansas City, Saddle and Sirloin, (Kansas City); Topeka C. of C., Helianthus, Rotary, Soc. Sons of St. George. Home: Topeka, Kans. †

PABST, GEORGE HENRY, JR., R.R. exec.; b. N.Y. City, Apr. 14, 1888; s. George Henry and Minnie (Weckman) P.; student Central High Sch., Phila.; Evening Sch. of Accounts and Finance, U. of Pa.; m. Alyce E. Riley, Nov. 10, 1914. With Pa. R.R. since 1906; clk. accounting dept., 1906-09, in office of 2d v.p., 1909-17, chief clerk, spl. asst., pres., later vice pres. in charge of accounting, 1917-25, analyst, treasury department, 1925-26, assistant treasurer, 1926-29, treas., 1929-38, treas. and asst. vice pres., 1938-40, v.p. in charge finance and corporate relations, 1940-46, v.p. in charge of finance since 1946, dir. from Sept. 1943; also officer and director numerous subsidiary and affiliated companies of Pennsylvania Railroad system; director Norfolk & Western Ry. Co., First Nat. Bank, Phila., Fire Assn. of Phila., Reliance Ins. Company of Philadelphia. Gurantee Company of N. America (Philadelphia branch). Clubs: Philadelphia Cricket, The Midday, Racquet (Philadelphia); Bankers (N.Y. City). Home: Philadelphia, Pa. †

PACHECO, ANTONIO, optometrist; b. San Juan, P.R., Dec. 10, 1923; s. Sixto and Marta (Lafont) P.; O.D., Pa. State Coll. Optometry, 1951; m. Marta Ortiz, Dec. 30, 1947; children—Marta, Maria, Antonio, Rosa. Pvt. practice optometry, Santurce, P.R., from 1951. Pres., Bd. Examiners of Optometrists P.R., 1965-67; optometric cons. Div. Mother and Child Dept. Health, 1960-61; bd. dirs. P.R. Found. for Med. Care, 1981-83, U.S.A. Fed. Profl. Standards Rev. Orgn., 1981-83. Served with AUS, 1943-46. Fellow Am. Acad. Optometry; mem. Coll. Optometrists of P.R. (hon. life, pres. 1967-68), Am. Optometric Assn., Am. Acad. Optometry (pres. P.R. chpt. 1971), Am. Legion (post comdr. 1960-63), Optometric Hist. Soc. U.S.A., Ateneo Puertorriqueno, Armed

Forces Optometric Soc., Internat. Platform Assn., Phi Theta Epsilon. Elk. Club: Casino de Puerto Rico. Author: Visual Defects and Optometric Manpower in Puerto Rico, 1971; Legal and Historical Development of the Boards of Examiners of Optometrists of Puerto Rico 1898-1970; Optometrists in Who's Who in America, 1975; Summary of Optometric Literature of Puerto Rico, 1975; The 221 Legal Optometric Years of the Three Consecutive Generations of Optometrists in the Pacheco Optometric Family, 1909-1976. Address: Santurce, P.R. Died Nov. 15, 1983.†

PADELFORD, NORMAN J., political science educator; s. Frank W. and Grace (Ilsley) P.; m. Helen Proctor; children: Grace Anne, Carolyn, Margaret. Ph.B., Denison U., 1925, LL.D., 1947; A.M., Harvard U., 1928, Ph.D., 1929. Asst. prof. govt. Colgate U., 1929-33, prof., head dept. govt., 1933-36; prof. internat. law Fletcher Sch. of Law and Diplomacy (Tufts-Harvard), 1936-44; prof. polit. sci. Mass. Inst. Tech., from 1945; cons. Dept. State, 1942-46, 48-49. Author: Peace in the Balkans, 1935, International Law and Diplomacy of the Spanish Civil War, 1939, The Panama Canal in Peace and War, 1942, International Relations, Fundamentals and Problems, 1950, (with G. A. Lincoln) International Politics, 1954, Politics in UN Elections, 1959, (with G.A. Lincoln) The Dynamics of International Politics, 1967, 75; co-author: (with G.A. Lincoln) Africa and World Order, 1963, (with L. M. Goodrich) United Nations in the Balance, 1965, Public Policy for the Seas, 1970, New Dimensions in U.S. Marine Policy, 1972, (with S.R. Gibbs) Maritime Commerce and the Future of the Panama Canal, 1975, Between Classroom and Government, 1980; Mem. bd. editors: (with S.R. Gibbs) Internat. Orgn. Jour, from 1947, chmn. (with S.R. Gibbs), 1959-68. Mem. U.S. del. Dumbarton Oaks Conf. on Internat. Organizations, 1944; sec. Com. of Jurists to revise Statute of Permanent Court of Internat. Justice, Washington, 1945; exec. officer Commn. Jud. Orgn., San Francisco UN Conf. Internat. Orgn. and Security, 1945; adviser to sec. of state at Council Fgn. Ministers, London, 1945; mem. U.S. delegation European Inland Transp. Conf., 1945, Presdl. Task Force on Oceanography, 1969-70; Trustee Denison U., 1954-82. Fellow Am. Acad. Arts and Scis.; mem. Am. Soc. Internat. Law, Am. Polit. Sci. Assn., Marine Tech. Soc., Phi Beta Kappa, Tau Kappa Alpha. Congregationalist. Home: Claremont, Calif. Died July 13, 1982.

PADGETT, FREDERICK WARDE, petroleum chemist, engr.; b. Ft. Scott, Kan., Oct. 10, 1888; s. Willard W. and Laura A. (Wood) P.; B.S., U. of Pittsburgh, 1912, M.S., 1913; m. Helen Elizabeth Patterson, Dec. 29, 1913; children—Edward Duncan, John Willard, Laura Elizabeth, Mary Jane. With Mellon Inst., Pittsburgh, 1912-17, as researcher in petroleum and natural gas; asso. prof. chemistry, in charge petroleum technology, U. of Okla., 1917-25, prof. petroleum engring. from spring of 1925; with Sun Oil Co., Marcus Hook, Pa., 1933-36; dir. wax tech. department, Moore & Munger, from 1936. Mem. Phi Kappa Psi, Alpha Chi Sigma, Sigma Gamma Epsilon, Sigma Xi. United Presbyterian. Author: (with W. A. Hamor) the Technical Examination of Petroleum, Petroleum Products and Natural Gas, 1921; also tech. articles on petroleum and petroleum waxes. Home: Short Hills, N.J. †

PAGE, HARLAN ORVILLE (PAT), dir. athletics; b. Chicago, Mar. 20, 1887; s. Harlan Elias and Carrie May (Powell) P.; grad. Lewis Inst., Chicago, 1906; S.B., U. of Chicago, 1910; m. Louise Marie Speed, of Chicago, June 14, 1911; children—Harlan Orville, John Douglas. Mgr. Oriental baseball tours, Japan, China, P.I., 1910-15; coach maj. sports, U. of Chicago, 1910-20; dir. athletics and coach, Butler U., 1920-25; athletic coach, Ind. U., 1925-30, U. of Chicago, 1930-33; dir. athletics Montezuma Sch. for Boys, Los Gatos, Calif., from 1933. Mem. Am. Football Coaches Assn., Owl and Serpent, Delta Tau Delta. Republican. Episcopalian. Contbr. articles on scientific game analysis, Athletic Jour., Cosmopolitan Newspapers. Home: Chicago, Ill. †

PAIGE, SATCHEL, (LEROY ROBERT PAIGE) former baseball player; b. Mobile, Ala., July 7, 1906; m. La Homa Brown, Aug. 18, 1942; 3 children. Played in Negro leagues, 1925-47; played with maj. league teams Cleve. Indians, 1948-49, St. Louis Browns, 1951-53, Kansas City Athletics, 1965; coach Atlanta Braves, 1968; v.p., goodwill ambassador Springfield (Ill.) Redbirds, Am. Assn. Author: (with David Lipman) Maybe I'll Pitch Forever, 1962. Named to Am. League All-Star Team, 1952, 53; elected to Baseball Hall of Fame, 1971. Address: Springfield, Ill. Died June 8, 1982.*

PAINTON, JOSEPH FREDERICK, physician; b. Buffalo, Nov. 9, 1903; s. Joseph Grant and Frederica (Sames) P.; B.S., M.D., U. Buffalo, 1927; postgraduate internal medicine, Harvard, Boston, 1930; m. Mae Alberta Tabor, Aug. 26, 1933 (dec. 1962); 1 son, Joseph Frederick; m. 2d, Lucille Hirshman, June 29, 1963. Intern, Edward J. Meyer Meml. Hosp., Buffalo, 1927-28, resident in medicine, 1928-32, chief resident medicine, asst. med. supt., 1932-36, attending physician, 1940-82; faculty U. Buffalo Med. Sch., 1930-82, asso. clin. prof. medicine, 1947-74, emeritus, 1974-82; cons. VA Hosp.; attending physician, Millard Fillmore Hosp., Buffalo, 1940-82, chmn. dept. medicine, 1946-69. Mem. Mental Hygiene Commn., 1956-57; mem. council U. Buffalo, from 1949. Served from maj. to lt. col., M.C., USAAF, 1942-46. Diplomate Am. Bd. Internal Medicine. Fellow A.C.P.; mem. Buffalo Acad. Medicine (pres.), Am. Diabetic Assn., Western N.Y. Soc. Internal Medicine (pres.), Buffalo Alumni Assn. (pres. 1950-51), Erie County Med. Soc., Phi Chi. Club: Saturn (Buffalo). Home: Snyder, N.Y. Died Oct. 8, 1982.

PAKINGTON, HUMPHREY, author; b. London, Eng., Sept. 8, 1888; s. Herbert Perrott Murray (3d Baron Hampton) and Evelyn (Baker) P.; student Royal Naval Coll., Greenwich, Eng., 1908-09, Architectural Assn. Sch., London, 1919-24; m. Grace Spicer, 1913; children—Hilary (Mrs. David John Vaughan Bevan), Anne, Auriol Mary Grace, Richard Humphrey Russell. Enlisted in Royal Navy, 1903; participated in Battle of Folkland Islands, World War I, retired, 1919; practiced architecture, 1924-39; rejoined Royal Navy, 1939, served on staff of comdr. in chief Western Approaches. Decoratd Order of British Empire (mil. div.), 1942. Awarded Holloway scholarship, Architectural Assn. Fellow Royal Inst. British Architects. Mem. Left Wing Party. Author: English Villages and Hamlets, 1934; How the World Builds, 1932; (following pub. in U.S. and Eng.) Four in Family, 1930; The Roving Eye, 1933; The Eligible Bachelor, 1936; Family Album, 1939; Our Aunt Auda, 1942; Aston Kings, 1945; Young William Washbourne, 1949. Occasional contbr. to Punch. Home: Worcester, Eng.†

PALM, MAX J(OHN), JR., mfg. exec.; b. Cincinnati, June 25, 1887; s. Max J. and Rose (Bast) P.; student St. Joseph Coll. and Xavier U.; m. Grace Gates, June 30, 1915; children—Max J. III, Patricia (Mrs. Robert E. Sammis). With The Palm Bros. Decalcomania Co., Cincinnati, from 1906, chairman and president of company, from 1937. Clubs: Queen City, Recess (Cincinnati); Bay Head (N.J.) Yacht. Home: Cincinnati, OH. †

PALMER, CYRUS M., congressman; b. Pottsville, Pa., Feb. 12, 1887; s. Frank C. and Anna M. (Sheetz) P.; grad. high sch., Pottsville; student U. of Pa., 1907-08; m. Agnes M. Applegate, May 11, 1916; children—Anna Margaret, Jane Gray. Admitted to Pa. bar, 1911, and began practice at Pottsville; mem. Pa. Ho. of Rep. 3 terms, 1915-19; dist. atty., Schuylkill County, 1920-27; mem. 70th Congress (1927-29), 13th Pa. Dist. Republican. Lutheran. Home: Pottsville, Pa. †

PALMER, ELY ELIOT, foreign service officer; b. Providence, Nov. 29, 1887; s. George Frederick and Martha Josephine (Hunt) P.; B.A., Brown U., 1908; U. Paris, 1908-09; M.Dip., George Washington U., 1910; m. Eno Ham, June 19, 1913; 1 son, George Eliot. Assigned duty Dept. of State, Washington, Dec. 1910; with Am. Embassy, Mexico City, 1911-12; vice and dep. consul gen., Paris, 1913-15; with Dept. of State, 1915-16; consul, Madrid, Spain, 1916-21, Bucharest, Rumania, 1921-26; consul gen., Bucharest, 1926-29, Vancouver, B.C., 1929-33, Jerusalem, Palestine, 1933-35; counselor of legation and consul gen. at Ottawa, 1935-38; consul gen., Beirut, Syria, 1938-41, Sydney, Australia, 1941-44; became minister to Afghanistan, Oct. 1944, ambassador, 1948. Mem. Zeta Psi. Baptist. Home: Providence, R.I. †

PALMER, JOHN ALFRED, English language educator; b. Spokane, Wash., May 22, 1926; s. Cary Alfred and Blanche Leota (Trussell) P.; m. Jean Evelyn Steinbeck, June 20, 1957 (div. 1971). B.A., U. Wash., 1950; M.A., Cornell U., 1952, Ph.D., 1962. Instr. English Cornell U., 1957-62; from asst. prof., to prof. English Calif. State U. at Los Angeles, 1962-82, chmn. dept. English, 1967-69, dean Sch. Letters and Sci., 1969-70, v.p. acad. affairs, 1970-80. Author: Joseph Conrad's Fiction, 1968, Twentieth Century Interpretations of Nigger of the Narcissus, 1969. Served with USN, 1943-46. Mem. AAUP, Modern Lang. Assn. Democrat. Home: Los Angeles. Died July 2, 1982.

PALMER, JOHN ROY, naval officer; b. Ethlyn, Mo., Mar. 30, 1889; grad. U.S. Naval Acad., 1913. Commd. ensign, U.S. Navy, and advanced through the grades to commodore, 1945; served in U.S.S. Aylwin, based Queenstown, Ireland, 1918, U.S.S. Evans, 1918-20; served in U.S.S. Farragut, as exec. officer U.S.S. Somers, and as comdr. U.S.S. Moody, 1920-21; comd. U.S.S. Utah, 1940-41; production officer, Navy Yard, Washington, D.C., 1941-44; became comdr. transport squadron, Sept. 1944. Decorated Victory Medal with destroyer clasp, Am. Defense Service Medal with fleet clasp, Mexican Service and Asiatic-Pacific Area Campaign medals. Home: Newburg, Md.†

PALMER, LESTER JOERG, physician; b. Peabody, Kan., Oct. 15, 1890; s. Philip C. and Catherine (Joerg) P.; student U. of Wash., 1909-10; M.D., Northwestern U., 1914; m. Mercedes Blackledge, Feb. 13, 1918; 1 son, James Joerg. Intern, Cook Co. Hosp., Chicago, 1914-16; resident internal medicine St. Luke's Hosp., Chicago, 1916-17; pvt. practice medicine, Seattle, specializing in endocrinology and diabetes from 1917; clin. prof. medicine, med. sch. U. of Wash. from 1945; chief staff Virginia Mason Hosp. from 1945 (pres. bd. trustees from 1944), chief medicine Mason Clinic, 1944-54. Pres. Diabetic Trust Fund from 1938, Diabetes Teaching and Research Foundation; vice president of Virginia Mason Foundation. Captain, U.S. Medical R.C.; active duty, 1917-19. Diplomate Am. Bd. Internal Medicine, 1937. Fellow A.C.P., A.M.A., Am. Diabetes Assn. (pres. 1950-51, mem. council 1943-54); member Washington Diabetic Association (president), North Pacific Soc. Internal Medicine (pres. 1948), Assn. for Clin. Research, Alpha Omega Alpha, Alpha Kappa Kappa (past pres.). Roman Catholic. Home: Bellevue, Wash. †

PALMER, MARY BELL, librarian; b. Anniston, Ala., Nov. 22, 1889; d. Edward Bell and Alice Linda (Booher) P.; grad. high sch., Columbus, Ga.; grad. Library Sch., Carnegie Library, Atlanta, Ga., 1909. Organizer, and librarian Carnegie Library, Americus, Ga., 1909-10; librarian Carnegie Library, Charlotte, N.C., 1910-18; in War Camp Community Service, Charlotte, summer 1918; instr. Library Sch., Carnegie Library, Atlanta, 1918-19; sec. and dir. N.C. Library Commn. from Aug. 1919. Mem. A.L.A., N.C. Library Assn. (sec., 1910-15, pres., 1915-17), N.C. Lit. and Hist. Assn. Baptist. Clubs: Woman's Carolina Country. Address: Raleigh, N.C. †

PALMER, WALTER THOMAS, engr.; born Caywood, Ohio, Dec. 7, 1889; s. John Pemberton and Lucetta (Athey) P.; student Carnegie Inst. Tech., 1912; Ohio State U., 1911; New York U., 1936-39; Columbia, 1940-41; m. Justine Marie d'Ihingoue, Oct. 5, 1916; m. 2d, Katherine Phyllis Chaplin, Jan. 14, 1927; 1 dau., Jean (Mrs. John H. O'Keefe. Engr. railroad location, constrn. and maintenance C.R.I. & P. Ry., Little Rock, Ark., 1907-10; reinforced concrete designer Witherow Steel Co., Boston, 1913-15; New England mgr. Witherow Steel Co., Boston, 1916-18; asst. to pres. Lever Bros. Co., Cambridge, Mass., 1918-21; sec. Lever Transportation Co., Cambridge, 1918-21; gen. sales mgr. Russell mfg. Co., Middletown, Conn., 1921-33; dir. of budget, Seagram Distillers Corp. and affiliated cos., N.Y. City, 1936-42; vice pres. profit control, Schenley Distillers Corp. and subsequently Schenley Industries, Inc., New York, 1942-48; exec. v.p. Schenley Distillers, Inc., from 1949, dir. from 1949; v.p. Schenley Industries, Inc., from Jan. 1949; dir. Canadian Schenley, Ltd. Quebec Distillers, Ltd. Mem. U.S. Power Squadron, rank of celestial navigator, since 1933. Mem. Amateur Astronomers Assn., Guild of Former Pipe Organ Pumpers, Alpha Sigma Phi. Unitarian. Clubs: Middletown (Conn.) Yacht; Union League (New York). Home: Middle Haddam, Conn. †

PANNKOKE, OTTO HERMAN, clergyman; b. Hameln, Germany, July 12, 1887; s. Adolph (M.D.) and Minna (Wrede) P.; brought to U.S., 1897; B.A., Concordia Coll., Milwaukee, Wis., 1905; grad. Concordia Sem., St. Louis, 1908; post-grad. work, Columbia, 1912-16; B.D., Union Theological Seminary, New York, 1915; studied University of Chicago, 1932-33; D.D., Lenoir Coll., Hickory, N.C., 1920; m. Clara M. Dallmann, of Milwaukee, Wis., Nov. 10, 1915; children—Dorothy Minna, Paul Adolph. Ordained Luth. ministry, 1908; pastor Hebron, N.D., 1908-09, Rugby, Ill., 1909-11, Brooklyn, N.Y., 1911-17; prof. economics and sec. Concordia Sch. of Commerce and Accountancy, N.Y. City, 1914-16; sec. New York Reformation Quadricentenary Com., 1916-17; in charge campaign of edn., Nat. Luth. Commn. for Soldiers' and Sailors' Welfare, 1918-19, of Nat. Luth. Council Reconstruction Campaign, 1919, of Luth. Forward Movement for World Service, 1919; dir. many ednl. and financial campaigns within Lutheran Ch.; exec. sec. Lutheran Bureau, 1917-21; dir. Lutheran Seminar, U. of Chicago, 1933, U. of Minn., 1935. Mem. Am. Church History Soc. (exec. com., chmn. endowment fund. com.). Address: Quitman, Ga.†

PAPISH, JACOB, chemistry; b. Pinsk, Poland, Aug. 4, 1887; s. Samuel and Blume (Resnick) P.; came to U.S., 1905; B.S., Valparaiso (Ind.) U., 1910; A.M., Ind. U., 1917; Ph.D., Cornell U., 1921; m. Helen Hughes, Sept. 2, 1913; children—Philip George, Dorothy Lou. Prof. analytical chemistry, Valparaiso U., 1910-14; instr. in chemistry, Ind. U., 1916-18, Purdue U., 1918-19, same, Cornell U., 1919-25, asst. prof. chem. spectroscopy, 1925-29, prof. from 1929. Mem. Am. Chem. Soc. Research in spectroscopy, geochemistry and chemistry of rare elements and trace elements. Home: Cincinnatus, N.Y. †

PAPSDORF, HERMAN L., banker; b. N.Y.C., Mar. 29, 1887; s. Oswald and Marie Louise (Fischer) P.; student Rutgers U., 1943-45; m. Anna J. Buerkel, Sept. 8, 1917; children—Robert, Priscilla (Mrs. George Kraus). With Am. Express Co., 1902-16, Hannevig & Son, 1916-21; with Papsdorf Travel Bur., 1921-41; pres. Hamburg Savs. Bank, 1941-57, chairman of the board, from 1957. President of Wyckoff Heights Hospital Soc. Mem. Queensboro C. of C., Grand Jurors Assn. Clubs: Montauk (Bklyn.); Kiwanis (Ridgewood, N.Y.). Home: Glendale, N.Y. †

PARDUE, AUSTIN, bishop; b. Chgo., Aug. 9, 1899; s. Harry Austin and Jane (Landers) P.; student Hobart Coll., 1918-20, D.D., 1940; LL.D., U. Pitts., 1944; student Nashotah (Wis.) House, 1920-22; student General Theol. Sem., N.Y.C., 1922-25, S.T.D., 1945; S.T.D., Seabury Western Theol. Sem., 1941; D.D. (hon.), Duquesne U., 1968; m. Dorothy Klotz, Sept. 4, 1926; children—Peter Austin, Nancy. Nat. sec. Episcopal Young People's Movement, 1922-25; rector Lawrence Hall for Boys and mem. city mission staff Diocese of Chgo., 1925-27; rector St. James Ch., Hibbing, Minn., 1926-29, St. Thomas Ch., Sioux City, Ia., 1929-31; rector Gethsemane Church, Mpls., 1931-38; dean St. Paul's Cathedral, Buffalo, 1932-44; consecrated bishop of Pittsburgh, Jan. 25, 1944; chmn. field dept. Diocese of Minn., 1932; mem. Standing Com. of Diocese, 1933; mem. Diocesan Council, also Examining Chaplains, 1933; pres. Third province of Episcopal Church, 1968-81. State chaplain Minn. Am.

Legion, 1927. Chmn. Civic Clothing Drive, 1935. Dep. Gen. Conv. Episcopal Church, 1928, 35. Founder Soc. for Promotion of Industrial Mission. Recipient Citation for Service, U.S. Air Force, 1956. Mason. Elk. Author: Bold to Say, 1940; Your Morale and How to Build It, 1943; He Lives, 1946; Prayer Works, 1949; Create and Make New, 1952; Korean Adventure, 1953; A Right Judgment in all Things, 1954; The Single Eye, 1957; The Eucharist and You, 1964. Clubs: Buffalo, Maidstone (Easthampton, L.I.); Pitts. Athletic Assn., Duquesne (Pitts.); Rolling Rock (Ligonier, Pa.). Editor Handbook on Young People's Work, 1924. Breast stroke champion Western Amateur Athletic Union, 1919. Home: Pittsburgh, Pa. Died Apr. 28, 1981.

PARK, JOHN CALLAWAY, coll. dean; b. Dunksburg, Mo., Aug. 12, 1888; s. William and Oda (Fisher) P.; student Warrensburg (Mo.) Normal Sch., William Jewell Coll.; B.S., U. Ariz., 1926; M.S., Ia. State Coll., 1930; m. Marjorie A. Nelson, July 7, 1922; 1 son, John Nelson. Tchr., adminstr. pub. schs., Mo., 1910-17; supt. Chautauquas, summers 1914-17; asst. gen. mgr., supt. constrn., K.T. Oil Corp., Wichita, Kan., 1920-21; prof. civil engrng. U. Ariz., from 1926, dean Coll. Engring., from 1951; also consulting engineer; mem. Highway Research Bd. Served as capt. inf., U.S. Army, World War I; research and development design br. Engring. Bd., World War II. Decorated Order Purple Heart. Mem. Am. Society Civil Engineers, Am. Soc. Engring. Edn., American Society Profl. Engrs., Newcomen Society, Tau Beta Pi, Phi Kappa Phi, Theta Tau. Conglist. Kiwanian. Contbr. articles profl. jours. Home: Tucson, AZ. †

PARK, PHILIP MULVENA, mfg. exec.; b. Alpena, Mich., Mar. 23, 1910; s. Charles Thomas and Mae (Mulvena) P.; m. E. Maxine Bradley, June 20, 1935; children—James, Patricia, Susan. A.B., Olivet Coll., 1932. With Besser Co., Alpena, Mich., from 1933, beginning as mechanic, successively sales exec., personnel dir., export mgr., 1937-55, v.p., 1946-65, pres., from 1965, chmn. bd., chief exec. officer, from 1977; dir. Mich. Mut. Ins. Co., Detroit. Bd. dirs. No. Mich. Development Council; chmn. Alpena chpt. A.R.C.; organizer United Fund; fund chmn. Boy Scouts.; Bd. dirs. Alpena Pub. Schs.; trustee Olivet Coll. Served as lt. USNR, World War II. Mem. Mich. Mfrs. Assn. (dir.), Nat. Assn. Concrete Masonry (dir.), Nat. Bus. Aircraft Assn., Mich. C. of C. (dir.). Clubs: Mason, Elk, Rotarian (dist. gov.). Home: Alpena, Mich.

PARKER, ALBERT, lawyer; b. N.Y.C., Sept. 6, 1897; s. Jacob and Flora (Blumberg) P.; m. Jeannette Fox, Apr. 1933; children: Ruth (Mrs. Joseph S. Brody), Dorothy (Mrs. Arthur M. Greenbaum), Albert. Student, Columbia U., 1919, N.Y. Law Sch., 1921; LL.D. (hon.), Yeshiva U., 1964, N.Y. Law Sch., 1983; Ph.D. (hon.), Bar-Ilan U., 1972. Bar: N.Y. bar 1921. Practiced in N.Y.C., 1921-83; sr. mem. firm Parker, Chapin Flattau & Klimpl, 1934-83; dir. Bond industries, Comml. Alliance Corp.; dir., mem. exec. com. Belding Heminway Co. Inc.; hon. dir. Bank Leumi Trust Co., N.Y. Hon. nat. chmn., mem. nat. exec. com. United Jewish Appeal, also; hon. chmn. bd. govs. United Jewish Appeal Greater N.Y.; mem. adv. council Sch. Internat. Affairs; chmn. council govs., mem. bd. overseers Albert Einstein Coll. Medicine of Yeshiva U.; trustee Bar-Ilan U. Served with U.S. Army, 1918. Recipient Alumni medal Columbia U., 1975; Chmn.'s medal United Jewish Appeal, 1969; Joseph M. Proskauer award; fellow Brandeis U., 1967; also medal, 1979. Mem. Assn. Bar City N.Y., N.Y. State Bar Assn., N.Y. County Lawyers Assn. Clubs: Palm Beach (Fla.); Country; Harmonie (N.Y.C.), Princeton (N.Y.C.). Home: New York, N.Y. Died Nov. 20, 1983.

PARKER, EDWIN P., JR., army officer; b. Wytheville, Va., July 27, 1891; s. Edwin Pearson and Mary Lillington (Hardin) P.; student George Washington U., 1909-11; m. Hannah Matthews, February 3, 1915; children—Henry Stoddert, Edwin Parson, III, Nicholson, Somerville. Commd. 2d lt. F.A., U.S. Army, Mar. 3, 1913; promoted through grades to maj. gen., A.U.S., June 1942; now comdg. XXIII Corps in Germany. Mem. Delta Tau Delta. Episcopalian. Home: Washington, D.C. Died June 7, 1983.

PARKER, GEORGE M., JR., army officer; born Sac City, Ia., Apr. 17, 1889; grad. Command and Gen. Staff Sch., Ft. Leavenworth, 1923, Army War Coll., 1925; distinguished grad. Command and Gen. Staff Sch.; m. Dorothy Cooper, May 16, 1914. Commd. 2d lt., inf., U.S. Army, 1910, and advanced through grades to brig. gen. (temp.), 1941. major gen. (temp.), 1941. With 21st Inf., Philippines, 1910-12; served in Mex. Border campaign and Canal Zone; assigned to Philippine Dept., 1941; comd. So. Luzon Force, Bataan Defense Force and II Philippine Corps on Bataan during defense of the Philippines, 1941-42; prisoner of war of Japanese govt., 1942-45; for phys. disability incurred in combat, 1946. Decorated D.S.M. Home: Portland, Ore. †

PARKER, LOUIS ALEXANDER, clergyman; b. Goliad, Tex., June 29, 1887; s. Louis Alexander and Anna Belle (Burriss) P.; student Gen. Theol. Sem., 1914-16, U. of Chicago, 1917, Nat. Biblical Sem. (New York), 1928; B.S., New York U., 1929, A.M., 1932; m. Mrs. Mary Stalknecht Andersen, June 29, 1932; children—Mary Lou, Judith Ann (dec.). Ordained deacon, Protestant Episcopal Church, 1916, priest, 1921; pastor St. Ambrose Ch., Chicago Heights, Ill., 1917-18, Trinity Parish, Victoria, Tex., 1919-21, St. Agnes Chapel, Trinity Parish, N.Y. City, 1924-26, St. Simon's Parish, Brooklyn, N.Y., 1928-34, St. Andrew's Ch., Nogales, Ariz., 1935-38; rector —Old— St. John's Parish, Kingsville, Baltimore County, Md., 1938-45 (Baltimore County oldest parish, dating from 1680); resigned May 1945, to take up war work; appointed staff officer, U.S.O., Richmond, Va., in charge of religious and educational activities. Rector of All Saints Parish, San Benito, Texas till 1951; rector —Old Saint Anna's Church since 1951. Served as private 416th Railway Battalion, Signal Corps, U.S. Army, 1918, sgt. and unofficial bn. chaplain, 1918-19; with A.E.F.; acting chaplain 107th N.Y. Inf., Peekskill, N.Y., 1924. Asso. with Near East Relief Commn. operating in southern Russia, 1921-23; in charge relief work Princess Islands, Sea Marmora, 1921-23. Decorated Cross of Knight of Order George I (Greek); recipient letters of commendation by ecumenical patriarch Meletios IV for assisting Greek refugees. Del. to Gen. Conv. Protestant Episcopal Ch., 1910. Mem. Am. Legion, Vets. 7th N.Y. N.G., Kappa Phi Kappa, Alpha Omicron. Mason. Home: New Orleans, La. †

PARKER, NORMAN SALLEE, patent lawyer; b. Chgo., Oct. 23, 1890; s. Francis Warner and Alma Theresa (Chapman) P.; student Williams Coll., 1907-09; A.B., U. Chgo., 1910, Ph.D., 1916; A.M., Harvard, 1912; m. Nathalie Roberts, May 16, 1916; children—Norman Sallee, Marjorie Troy, Robert Warner, Francis (dec.), John Temple; m. 2d, Marion Stuart Scott, July 20, 1940. Admitted to Ill. bar, 1922, practiced in Chgo., mem. firm Parker, Carter & Markey and predecessor firm, 1921-69; Mem. Kappa Sigma. Republican. Baptist. Clubs: Univ., The Tavern (Chgo.); Cosmos (Washington). Home: Evanston, IL. †

PARKER, ROY HARTFORD, army chaplain; b. Hickory, Mo., May 15, 1890; s. Frank and Lizzie (Maxey) P.; grad. William Jewell Acad., Liberty, Mo.; A.B., William Jewell Coll., 1917, D.D., 1942; m. Brazilia Ginsburg, Aug. 1, 1918; 1 dau., Carlene Louise. Ordained to Bapt. ministry, 1912; pastor 1st Ch., Tipton, Mo., 1916-18. With U.S. Army since 1918; served at Camp Funston, Kan., 1918-19; various assignments, 1919-39; div. chaplain 1st cav. div., Ft. Bliss, Tex., 1939-40; dir. chaplain 2d Armored Div., Ft. Benning, Ga., 1940-42, 5th Army Corps, North Ireland and England, 1942-43; N. African Theatre chaplain, 1943-44; office chief of chaplains, Washington, 1944-48; theater chaplain gen. hdqrs. Far East Comd., 1948-49; chief of chaplains, Dept. of Army, since 1949. Received Legion of Merit, Army Commendation, European-African-Middle East Service and Am. Defense ribbons, Am. Theatre, World Wars I and II medals. Mem. Lambda Chi Alpha. Home: Washington, D.C. †

PARKHURST, CHARLES CHANDLER, educator, author, indsl. communications cons.; b. Somerville, Mass., Dec. 19, 1904; s. Charles Erwin and Helen Augusta (Chandler) P.; B.B.A., Boston U. Coll. of Bus. Adminstrn., 1926, A.M., 1930; D.Sc. in Bus Adminstrn., Piedmont Coll., 1964; Litt.D. (hon.), Olivet (Mich.) Coll., 1966; m. Lillian Andrews, June 1935. With Ford Motor Co., 1926, Chrysler Motor Car sales div., 1928; dir. English, Catherine Gibbs Sch., 1929-30; instr. English, Everett High Sch., 1930-37; chmn. All-University English Dept., 1949-51; instr. English, Boston U. Coll. of Bus. Adminstrn., 1931-35, asst. prof., 1935-42, asso. prof. 1943-69, prof., head English dept. Boston U. Coll. of Practical Arts and Letters, 1944, prof. English and Bus. Communications Coll. Bus. Adminstrn., 1956-69; indsl. communications cons., lectr., from 1970; lectr. Am. Inst. Banking; dir. English, Bentley Sch. of Accounting and Finance, 1937-48; lit. counsellor and corr. cons. for banks, ins. cos., bus. and indsl. plants; dir. edn. programs for bus. and indsl. orgns. Dir. Ware and Post-War Tng. Inst., Boston U. Coll. Bus. Adminstrn. Mem. Winchester Finance Com.; mem. Park Commn., Winchester, Mass.; pres. Hedding (N.H.) Chatauqua Assn.; trustee Hedding Camp Meeting Assn. Fellow Am. Bus. Writing Assn. (past pres.); mem. Nat. Office Mgr. Assn., AAUP, NEA, Nat. Council English Tchrs., Modern Lang. Assn., Eastern Comml. Tchrs. Assn., Newcomen Soc. of Eng., U.S. Power Squadron, USCG Aux., Francis Scott Key Meml. Assn., Lambda Chi Alpha. Methodist. Clubs: Internat. Rotary (hon.), Boston Authors, Boston University Faculty. Republican. Author: (with Grove) English Elements and Principles; (with Roy Davis) Business Writing Theory and Practice; Modern Business English; English for Business rev. 1964; Practical Problems in English for Business, rev. 1958; Using Words Effectively (vols A. and B.), rev. 1958; A Direct Approach to Writing; Business English for College, 1957; Modern Business Communication for Better Human Relations, 1942, rev. edits., 1949, 55, 61, 66, 76; Case Studies in Business Communication, 1960; Modern Executive's Guide to Effective Communication, 1962; also articles ednl., bus. mags. Editor: Say What You See. Home: Winchester, Mass. Died Apr. 15, 1976.

PARKINSON, BELVIDERA ASHLEIGH DRY, b. Albemarle, N.C., Sept. 4, 1887; d. G. Martin and Laura Belvidera Dodge (Myers) Dry; A.B., Flora Macdonald Coll., Red Springs, N.C., 1906; B.S., George Peabody Coll. for Teachers, Nashville, Tenn., 1919; A.M., U. of S.C., 1918, Ph.D., 1927; spl. student Columbia and Harvard Univs.; m. Burney Lynch Parkinson, June 30, 1914; Teacher in pub. schs. of North Carolina and South Carolina. 1906-14. Chicora Coll., Furman U. and adult night schs., 1914-27; dir. research Ala. Ednl. Assn., 1930-32. Mem. readers council The Am. Scholar. Del. Womans Centennial Congress, N.Y. City, 1940, Rural-Urban Conf., Washington, D.C., 1939, White House Conf., 1944. Mem. bd. trustees Stillman Inst., Tuscaloosa, Ala. Parliamentarian, Miss. Fedn. Womens Clubs. Chmn. United China Relief for Lowndes County, Miss. Mem. Am. Assn. Univ. Women (2d nat. v.p.), D.A.R., Am. Legion Auxiliary, Colonial Dames, Nat. Assn. Parliamentarians, Mortar Board, Phi Beta Kappa, Alpha Delta Pi, Delta Kappa Gamma, Presbyterian. Contbr. articles to numerous ednl. and assn. mags. Lecturer in southern states. Home: Columbus, Miss. †

PARKINSON, GEORGE AMBROSE, educator; b. Columbus, Ohio, Jan. 22, 1899; s. Daniel Homer and Cynthia Catherine (English) P.; m. Mildred Jane Smith, June 17, 1920 (dec.); children—Virginia Jane, George (dec.), Daniel Smith; m. Myrtle Ann Volger, June 20, 1975. 2B.S., Ohio State U., 1922, M.A., 1923; Ph.D., U. Wis., 1929. Prin. Parkinson High Sch., Zanesville, Ohio, 1916-17, Ripley High Sch., Greenwich, Ohio, 1917-18; instr. math. Worthington (Ohio) High Sch., 1921-23; instr. engring. math. U. Wis., 1923-27; mem. faculty (Milw. extension div.), 1927- 56, div. dir., prof., 1945-56; vice provost, prof. U. Wis., 1956-58; dir. Milw. Tech. Coll., 1958-68, dir. emeritus, from 1968; dir. NROS, Milw., 1949-59; adv. com. USCG Acad., 1955-63, chmn., 1960-62; Mem. Res. Forces Policy Bd. Office Sec. Def., 1949-56; mem. Wis. Gov.'s Adv. Com. CD, 1951-56; dep. dir. Milw. CD Adminstrn., 1948-62, dir., 1962-63; Chmn. Milw. Social Devel. Commn., 1962-65; chmn. program devel. com., dir. Milw. Met. YMCA, 1950-69; dir. Milw. Council Adult Learning; mem. Gov.'s Adv. Com. Title I, Higher Edn. Act of 1965, from 1966; Trustee, v.p. Midwestern Ednl. TV, Inc.; mem. policy bd. Gt. Plains Nat. Instrnl. TV Library, from 1962; cons. vocat. and tech. edn. HEW, 1969, GAO Evaluation Manpower Programs, from 1969. Author: Brief Introduction to Analytic Geometry, 1938; co-author: Mathematics and Society, 1939, also papers and articles on vocational, tech., adult edn. and civil def. Bd. overseers Rutgers U. Found. Served with USN, 1940-45; comdg. officer Escort Div. 48, Atlantic Fleet 1944-45; vice adm. ret. Decorated Legion of Merit, D.S.M. with Gold Star, Naval Res. medal, Armed Forces Res. medal; Engr. of the Yr.; Milw. Soc. Engrs., 1955; Citizenship gold medal; S.A.R.; State award Merit Wis. Restaurant Assn., 1967; Disting. Service award Milw. Council Adult Learning, 1967; Headliner award Milw. Press Club, 1968; Wisdom award of Honor, 1970. Mem. Am. Tech. Edn. Assn. (trustee 1962-75), Am. Math. Soc., Am. Math. Assn. (chmn. Wis. sect. 1935-36), Nat. Assn. Adult Edn., Assn. U. Evening Colls. (nat. pres. 1956), Wis. Vocat. Dirs. Assn. (pres. 1965-66), Am. Bus. Conf., S.A.R. (pres. Wis. 1955, nat. v.p. gen. 1957), Res. Officers Assn. U.S. (nat. chmn. naval affairs com.; pres. Wis. Dept.), Navy League U.S. (chmn., dir. Milw. council), N.J. C. of C. (dir.), Alpha Kappa Psi, Sigma Xi, Phi Delta Kappa, Gamma Alpha, Pi Mu Epsilon, Phi Eta Sigma., Acacia. Presbyn. Clubs: Mason. (Milw.), University (Milw.), Milwaukee Press (Milw.); Army and Navy (Washington); University (Madison, Wis.) (life). Home: Oostburg, Wis.

PARKINSON, ROY HARVEY, physician; b. Ashland, Ore., Mar. 13, 1890; s. George M. and Priscilla (Wise) P.; M.D., Stanford U. Med. Sch., 1912; m. Velva Helke, 1923; 1 dau., Ardeen Eleanor, Asst. in ear, nose and throat, Stanford Med. Sch., 1912-14; asst. in Eye Clinic, U. of Calif., Med. Sch., 1914-17; gen. practice. San Francisco, 1912-15; practice limited to eye, ear, nose and throat from 1915; chief of eye, ear, nose and throat dept. and chief of staff St. Joseph's Hospital, 1936-46. Served as 1st lt. U.S. Amry Med. Corps., 1917; chief eye dept. Base Hosp. No. 9, Chateauroux, France, also of Officers' Hosp., A.E.F., Paris; disch. as capt. Med. Corps, 1919. Fellow Am. Coll. Surgeons; mem. Am. and Calif. med. assns., San Francisco County Med. Soc., Pacific Coast Oto-Ophtalmol. Soc., Calif. Acad. Sci., Am. Hist., Assn., Calif. Hist. Soc. Club: Commonweath (chairman of the African problems section 1956). Mason. Author: Eye, Ear, Nose and Throat Manual for Nurses, 1925; Tonsil and Allied Problems, 1951. Home: Berkeley, Cal. †

PARKS, GEORGE SUTTON, educator; b. Tacoma, Jan. 7, 1894; s. Clarence Milton (M.D.) and Emma (Sutton) P.; B.S., U. of Wash., 1915, M.S., 1916; Ph.D., U. of Calif., 1919; m. Anne Scott Ireland, June 18, 1927; children—Lydia Anne (Mrs. Norman Wintemute), George Sutton. Asst. in chemistry, U. of Calif., 1916-18; instr. in chemistry, Calif. Inst. Tech., 1919-20; instr. in chemistry Stanford, 1920-25, asst. prof., 1925-30, asso. prof., 1930-37, prof. chemistry since 1937, acting exec. head dept., 1931-32, 1942-46, exec. head 1951-59, acting dean grad. study, 1950-51. Guggenheim fellow thermochemical studies, 1932. Dir. Am. Petroleum Inst. project 29, 1927-31. Mem. Am. Chem. Soc. (pres. Calif. sect., 1928), A.A.A.S., Am. Assn. Univ. Profs. (pres. Stanford chpt., 1949-50), Phi Beta Kappa, Sigma Xi, Phi Lambda Upsilon, Alpha Chi Sigma. Republican. Conglist. Author: The Free Energies of Some Organic Compounds (with H. M. Huffman), Am. Chem. Soc. Monograph 60, 1932. Asso. editor Journal of Physical Chemistry, 1938-42. Contbr. articles in chem. jours. Home: Stanford, Calif. †

PARKS, LEWIS SMITH, naval officer; born Bayport, L.I., N.Y., Apr. 13, 1902; s. John Emory and Minerva Alida (Smith) P.; B.S., U.S. Naval Acad., 1925; postgraduate marine engineering, U.S. Naval Acad., 1932-34; m. Zelda Ruth Leech, Dec. 31, 1927; 1 dau., Zelda Louis (wife of Lt. Comdr. Fred T. Berry, Jr.). Commd. ensign USN June 1925, and advanced through grades to rear adm., 1952; served in battleships and destroyers, 1925-29; entered submarine service, June 1929; combat submarine capt., submarine div. comdr., submarine wolf pack comdr., submarine squadron comdr., task group comdr., 1941-45; exec. aide to asst. secretary Navy, 1947, under secretary Navy, 1948-49, commanding U.S.S. Manchester (cruiser), 1950-51, comdr. Task Force 72 (engaged in protection of Formosa; apptd. deputy chief of Information, 1951, chief of Information, Navy Department, 1952-54; comdr. U.S. Naval Base, Norfolk, Va., 1954-55; Joint Staff UN Command and Far East Command Tokyo, 1955-57; comdr. Battleship Div. 2, 1957-60; ret., 1960. Awarded Navy Cross (3 awards), Legion of Merit with Combat V (2 awards), Commendation ribbon with Combat V (2 awards), Presdl. Unit citation, Korean Presdl. Unit Citation with oak leaf cluster, 2d Nicaraguan campaign medal, Yangtze service medal, American Defense service medal with fleet clasp, Asiatic-Pacific with 4 engagement stars, Am. Campaign medal, Navy occupation service medal with Asia Clasp, World War II victory medal, China Service medal, Nat. Def. Service medal, Korean Service medal with 5 engagement stars, UN Service medal. Home: Fall Church, Va. Died Apr. 27, 1982.

PARLIN, CHARLES COOLIDGE, lawyer; b. Wausau, Wis., July 22, 1898; s. Charles Coolidge and Daisy (Blackwood) P.; B.S., U. Pa., 1919; LL.B., Harvard, 1922; m. Miriam Boyd, Oct. 11, 1924 (dec. Oct. 1972); m. Kaye Chiange, Feb. 1976; children—Charles Coolidge, II, Camilla, Blackwood Boyd. Admitted to N.Y. State bar, 1923, since practiced in N.Y.C.; sr. partner Shearman & Sterling, N.Y.C., 1945-64; dir. Compania, Ontario, S.A., Potash Import & Chem. Corp., Guerlain, Inc. Trustee Am. U., Bethune-Cookman Coll., Drew U. Served at Pvt. 1st class, U.S. Army, World War I. Mem. Alpha Chi Rho. Methodist (pres. World Council Chs. 1961-68, lay rep. Nat. Council Chs., pres. World Meth. Council 1970-71). Mason. Home: Englewood, N.J. Died Nov. 15, 1981.

PARLOW, KATHLEEN, violinist; b. Calgary, Alberta, Can., Sept., 1890; was taken to Calif. by parents at age of 5 yrs.; first appeared on stage in San Francisco, at age of 6; went to London, 1905, and played with London Symphony Orchestra, and before Queen Alexandra; studied with Leopold von Auer, St. Petersburg, 1907; played at Internat. Music Festival, Ostende, 1907; toured in Germany, Scandinavia, Holland and British Isles; returned to U.S., 1910; made 16 appearances with the Boston Symphony Orchestra, season of 1911-12; later in Europe; returned to U.S., 1929.†

PARMENTER, CLARENCE EDWARD, educator; b. Kingman, Kan., Feb. 23, 1888; s. Perlin Horace and Sarah (Reed) P.; Ph.B., U. Chgo., 1911, Ph.D., 1921. Acting prof. modern langs., Hillsdale (Mich.) Coll., 1910; with U. Chgo., from 1911, successively fellow in Romance langs., 1911-14, instr., 1914-18, asst. prof., 1918-22, asso. prof., 1922-30, prof. Romance phonetics from 1930, acting chmn., 1941-43, chmn. 1943-49, emeritus, from 1953. Fellow A.A.A.S., Internat. Soc. Exptl. Phonetics (sec.); mem. Linguistic Soc. Am. (com. on publs.), Internat. Phonetic Assn. (mem. council; v.p.), Modern Lang. Assn. Am. (v.p. 1954), Accoustical Soc. Am., Nat. Assn. Tchr. of Speech, Am. Assn. Tchrs. Spanish, Inst. Hispanic Studies, Am. Assn. Tchrs. Italian, English-Speaking Union, Chgo. Council Fgn. Relations, Soc. Romance Lang. Tchrs. Chgo. and Vicinity (past pres.), Phi Beta Kappa (past pres. chpt.), Sigma Alpha Epsilon; corr. mem. Institut de Phonetique of U. of Paris. Clubs: Quadrangle, Quadrangle Players (Chgo.). Author: Beginners Spanish, 1918; A Spanish Reader, 1919; A Handbook of French Phonetics (in collaboration), 1920. Contbr. to Am. and fgn. periodicals. Home: Chicago, IL. †

PARRA PEREZ, CARACCIOLO, Venezuelan foreign minister; b. Mérida, Venezuela, Mar. 19, 1888, s. Ramon Parra Picón and Juana Pérez; student, Coll. of The Sacred Heart of Jesus, Mérida; Dr. Jurisprudence and Political Science, Univ. of Mérida, 1909; graduate work, Faculty of Law, Univ. of Paris, Public School of Political Sciences, Paris; m. María Luisa Osío Santana; 1 son, 1 daughter. Became Venezuelan attaché, Paris, 1913, sec. of legation, 1915-19, counselor, 1919; chargé d'affaires, Switzerland, 1919-26; special plenipotentiary to Swiss Federal Council, 1924-26; minister of public instruction, Peru, 1936; minister plenipotentiary to England, 1936-37; to Switzerland, 1937-40 and to Spain, 1939-40; recently appointed fgn. minister of Venezuela; rep. Venezuela at the Rio Conf. for Am. Fgn. Ministers. Mem. Caracas, Bogotá, Havana, Buenos Aires, and Montevideo, hist. socs. Awarded Grand Official, Order of the Liberator of Venezuela; Knight, Sovereign Mil. Order of Malta; Grand Cross, Order of the Crown of Italy; Grand Cross, Order of Merit of Cuba; Grand Official, Order of St. Maurice and St. Lazarus of Italy; Grand Official, Order of Boyacá of Colombia; Officer, Legion of Honor of France; Comdr., Order of Leopold of Belgium; of the Orders of the White Eagle and of St. Sava of Yugoslavia, of the Order of Merit (Chile); Medal of Public Instruction (Venezuela). Roman Catholic. Author: (in Spanish and French) of 7 books on politics and history, contbr. to periodicals.†

PARRY, FLORENCE FISHER, columnist; b. Brookville, Pa., July 5, 1887; d. Jacob Livengood and Carrie Ella (Wilson) Fisher; prep. edn., Mrs. Smallwood's Select School, Washington, D.C., 1900-05; student at the Wheatcroft Dramatic School, New York City, 1906-07; studied journalism, New York University; married David William Parry, June 8, 1915 (died 1922); children—Captain David Fisher, Mrs. Donald C. Heide. On stage as leading woman with Alla Nazimova, Walker Whiteside, Otis Skinner and others, 1907-15; actively identified with photography 1923-50, was proprietor of the Parry Studio, Pittsburgh; began writing for Pittsburgh newspapers, 1925, drama critic, daily columnist Pittsburgh Press, —I Dare Say,— until retirement, 1950; lectr., free-lance writer, broadcaster. Member League of American Pen Women, D.A.R., Dickens Fellowship, Drama League, Historical Society, Chamber of Commerce, Congress of Clubs. Republican. Baptist. Clubs: Woman's City, Woman's Press, Civic, Monday Luncheon. Home: Beverly Hills, Calif. †

PARRY, JOHN HORACE, historian, educater; b. Handsworth, Eng., Apr. 26, 1914; came to U.S., 1965; s. Walter Austin and Ethel (Piddock) P.; m. Joyce Carter, Mar. 18, 1939; children—Michael, Joanna, Katherine, Elizabeth. M.A., Ph.D., Clare Coll., Cambridge U., 1938; student, Harvard U., 1936-37. Fellow Clare Coll., 1938-49, univ. lectr. history, 1945-49; prof. modern history Univ. Coll. West Indies, 1949-55; vis. prof. history Harvard, 1955-56; prin. Univ. Coll., Ibadan, Nigeria, 1956-60, Swansea, Wales, 1960-65; vice-chancellor U. Wales, 1963-65; Gardiner prof. oceanic history and affairs Harvard U., 1965-82. Author: the Spanish Theory of Empire, 1940, The Audiencia of New Galicia, 1949, Europe and a Wider World, 1949, The Sale of Public Office in the Spanish Indies, 1953, A Short History of the West Indies, 1956, The Age of Reconnaissance, 1963, The Spanish Seaborne Empire, 1965, Trade and Dominion, 1971, The Discovery of the Sea, 1974, The Discovery of South America, 1979, also articles. Served with Royal Brit. Navy, 1940-45. Decorated Order Brit. Empire, 1942; companion Order St. Michael and St. George, 1960; comdr. Order of Alfonso X, Spain). Fellow Royal Hist. Soc., Am. Acad. Arts and Scis.; mem. Am. Philos. Soc. Clubs: Oxford and Cambridge (London), Athenaeum (London); Harvard (N.Y.C.); Odd Volumes (Boston). Home: Cambridge, Mass. Died Aug. 25, 1982.

PARSONS, BETTY PIERSON, artist, art dealer; b. N.Y.C., Jan. 31, 1900; d. J. Fred and Suzanne (Miles) Pierson; m. Schuyler Livingston Parsons, May 8, 1919. 1pvt. study sculpture and painting. Dir. Cornelius Sullivan Gallery, 1936-39, Wakefield Gallery, 1939-43, Mortimer Brandt Contemporary Gallery, 1943-46, Betty Parsons Gallery, N.Y.C., from 1946. Works exhibited in, Paris, 1932, Calif., 1934, throughout U.S., one-woman shows, Midtown Galleries, Miami Mus. Art, New Arts Gallery, Atlanta, Bennington Coll., Gallery Seven, Boston, Grand Central Modern, N.Y.C., White Chapel Gallery, London, Eng., Studio Gallery, Washington, Sachs Gallery, N.Y.C., Drew U., Benson Gallery, Bridgehampton, L.I., N.Y., David Hendriks Gallery, Dublin, Ireland, Kornblee Gallery, N.Y.C., USIA Traveling Exhbn., 1977, Louise Himelfarb Gallery, Watermill, L.I., 1977, 79, R.I. Sch. Design Mus., Providence, 1977, Barnard Coll., N.Y.C., 1977, Heath Gallery, Atlanta, 1978, 79, Kornblee Gallery, N.Y.C., 1978, 79, Truman Gallery, N.Y.C., 1978, Jeff Parsons Gallery, Shelter Island, N.Y., 1979, Hoshour Gallery, Albuquerque, 1979, Summit (N.J.) Art Center, 1979, Fairweather Hardin Gallery, Chgo., 1979, Barbara Fiedler Gallery, Washington, 1980, Nigel Greenwood Inc., London, 1980, Am. Center, Paris, 1980, Newspace, Los Angeles, 1980, others; exhibited, Finch Coll., Montclair Mus., Cranbrook Acad. Art, Mich., Brooks Meml. Art Gallery, Tenn. (Recipient Creative Arts award Brandeis U. 1980, N.Y.C. Mayor's award for arts and culture 1981). Home: New York, N.Y. Died July 23, 1982.

PARSONS, GEOFFREY, JR., corp. exec.; b. N.Y.C., July 3, 1908; s. Geoffrey and Carle (Taylor) P.; student Ecole de Soisy-Sous-Etioles, France, 1922-23, Phillips Exeter Acad., 1923-26, Harvard, 1927-31; m. Brenda Tweed, Sept. 12, 1933 (div. 1939); 1 son, Geoffrey; m. 2d, Dorothy Blackman Tartiere, June 6, 1945. Reporter Boston Globe, 1931-36; midwestern corr. New York Herald Tribune (hdqrs. Chicago), 1937-41, war corr., London, 1941, chief of London Bur., 1943-44, editor European edit. New York Herald Tribune, 1944-50; became chief of press and pub. relations NATO 1950, dir. information, 1954-57; v.p. for Europe, Northrop Internat., 1957-65; v.p. and European rep., 1965; European rep., 1977-81; dir. Société d'Etudes et de Prefabrican, France. Decorated comdr. French Legion of Honor. Mem. Assn. U.S. Aerospace Industries in Europe (pres. 1962-63), Anglo-Am. Press Assn. (Paris). Clubs: American of Paris; Century (N.Y.C.). Contbr. articles to Saturday Evening Post, Reader's Digest, others. Home: Paris, France. Died Sept. 17, 1981.

PARSONS, HARRIET OETTINGER, film producer, writer, realtor asso.; b. Burlington, Iowa; d. John Dement and Louella Rose (Oettinger) P.; m. King Kennedy, Sept. 28, 1939 (div. 1946). Grad., Horace Mann Sch. Girls, 1924; B.A., Wellesley Coll., 1928. Mem. scenario staff Metro-Goldwyn-Mayer Studios, Hollywood, 1928; columnist, staff interviewer, asso. editor Photoplay mag., 1929, staff writer, 1930, free lance writer fan mags., 1930-33; condr. column Liberty mag.; columnist, feature writer Hearst's Universal Service (later merged with Internat. News Service), 1931-43; producer Screen Snapshots, Columbia Pictures, 1933-40; mem. motion picture staff Los Angeles Examiner, 1935-43; weekly radio program Hollywood Highlights, NBC, 1938; editor column Hollywood in Review, Woman's Day, 1938-40; lectr. U. So. Calif., 1952; Dir., mem. entertainment com. Hollywood Canteen; realtor-asso. Lawrence Block Co., from 1964. Producer: Meet the Stars, Republic Studios, 1940-43, Joan of Ozark, 1942; writer, producer R-K-O Radio Pictures, 1943-55, including Enchanted Cottage, 1945, Night Song, 1947, I Remember Mama, 1948, Never a Dull Moment, 1950, Clash by Night, 1952, Susan Slept Here, 1954; co-producer: Broadway play The Rape of the Belt, 1960; producer Broadway play, 20th Century Fox TV, 1956-57. Mem. Acad. Motion Picture Arts and Sci., Wellesley Alumnae Assn., Producers Guild Am., Beverly Hills Realty Bd., Zeta Alpha. Republican. Club: Hollywood Women's Press. Home: Beverly Hills, Calif.

PARSONS, RICHARD TORRENCE, coll. pres.; b. Lock Haven, Pa., July 11, 1909; s. Irvin Torrence and Louise (Schreffler) P.; B.S., Pa. State Teachers Coll., 1931; Ed.M., Pa. State Univ., 1935, Ed.D., 1940; student U. of So. Calif., 1938; m. Janet Beman, Aug. 23, 1937; children—Torrence Douglas, Richard Lance. Teacher high sch., Pt. Marion, Fayette City (Pa.), 1931-35; instr. Lock Haven State Coll., supervisor lab. sch., 1935-38, dean of men, 1938-42, pres., 1942-83. Served as coordinator U.S. Navy V-5 program, Lock Haven State College, 1942-45. Mem. Gov.'s Priorities Commn., 1969. Mem. Pa. Assn. Colls. and Univs. (pres. 1968-69, member exec. com.), Phi Delta Kappa. Presbyn. Club: Rotary (pres. 1947; dist. gov. 1953). Author: Study of Backgrounds and Vocatnl. Interests of 1000 Students Attending State Teacher Colleges in Pennsylvania, 1940. Home: Lock Haven, Pa. Died Oct. 4, 1983.

PARTHEMOS, GEORGE STEVEN, political science educator; b. Charleston, S.C., Dec. 4, 1921; s. Steven and Katina (Arros) P.; m. Georgia Kachavos, July 10, 1947; children: Steven George, Pota Elaine. A.B., Erskine Coll., 1947; M.A., U. S.C., 1949; Ph.D., U. N.C., 1953. Instr. polit. sci. U. Ga., 1953-55, asst. prof., 1955-58, assoc. prof., 1958-63, prof. polit. sci., 1963-84, head dept. polit. sci., 1961-65, v.p. instrn., 1964-71, Alumni Found. disting. prof., 1971-84; mem. editorial bd. U. Ga. Press, 1977-80; Mem. Ga. Sci. and Tech. Commn., 1969-73. Author: Political Perspectives, 1961, (with Thomas R. Dye and Lee S. Green) American Government: Theory, Structure and Process, 2d edit, 1972, American Government: Policies and Function, 1967, Governing the American Democracy, 1980; editor, contbr.: Higher Education in a World of Conflict, 1962; Contbr. articles to profl. jours. Bd. dirs. St. Mary's Hosp., Athens, Ga., So. Consortium for Internat. Edn.; mem. Ga. Constnl. Revision Com., 1979. Served with USNR, 1943-46. Recipient U. Ga. Alumni Distinguished Faculty Service award, 1974, Outstanding Faculty award, 1979; Golden Key Nat. Honor Soc.; Rockefeller Found. fellow, 1958-59. Fellow Royal Soc. Arts; mem. Am. Polit. Sci. Assn., So. Polit. Sci. Assn. (v.p. 1968), Am. Acad. Social and Polit. Sci., U. Ga. Alumni Soc. (dir.), Phi Beta Kappa, Phi Kappa Phi, Kappa Delta Pi, Pi Sigma Alpha, Omicron Delta Kappa. Home: Athens, Ga. Died Dec. 25, 1984.

PARTRIDGE, (ERNEST) JOHN, b. Bristol, Eng., July 18, 1908; s. William Henry and Alice Mary P.; m. Madeline Fabian, 1934 (dec. 1944); 1 son, 1 dau.; m. Joan Johnson, 1949. Ed., Queen Elizabeth's Hosp., Bristol; hon. LL.D., Bristol U., 1972; hon. D.Sc., Cranfield Inst. Tech., 1974. Joined Imperial Group, Ltd., 1923, asst. sec., 1944-46, sec., 1946-57, dir., 1949-75, dep. chmn., 1960-64, chmn., 1964-75; pres. Confedn. Brit. Industry, 1970-72, v.p., 1972-76, chmn. CBI Edn. Found., 1976-81; mem. Tobacco Adv. Com., 1945-58, Cheque Endorsement Com., 1955-56, Nat. Econ. Devel. Council, 1967-75, Brit. Nat. Export Council, 1968-71, Internat. Adv. Bd. Chem. Bank U.S.A., 1972-78, Internat. Adv. Bd. Amax, Inc. U.S.A., from 1980. Pres. Found. for Mgmt. Edn., from 1972, Nat. Council Social Service, 1973-80, Clifton Coll.; bd. govs. Badminton Sch., Nat. Inst. Econ. and Social Research; chmn. United World Coll. of Atlantic, from 1979. Decorated knight comdr.; Order of Brit. Empire. Fellow Brit. Inst. Mgmt.; mem. Council of Industry for Mgmt. Edn. (chmn. 1967-71), Soc. Bus. Economists (v.p. 1976—). Address: Haslemere Surrey, England.

PARTRIDGE, JOHN FRANCIS, lawyer, corp. exec.; b. Chatham, Va., May 29, 1914; s. Horace E. and Mary (Johnson) P.; B.S. in Bus. Adminstrn., U. Fla., 1936; C.P.A., U. Ill., 1939; J.D., Chgo.-Kent Coll. Law, 1947; grad. Exec. Program Bus. Adminstrn., Columbia, 1956; m. Evelyn Weeks, Dec. 28, 1949; children—Lawrence Scott, Jacquelyn Mary. Accountant, Oldham & Gouwens, Chgo., summer 1936; investment analyst Welsh & Green, Inc., Chgo., 1937- 38; with Welsh, Davis & Co., Chgo., 1939-51, exec. v.p., 1948-51; admitted to Ill. bar, 1947; with AMSTED Industries Inc., Chgo., from 1951, sec., counsel, 1959-73; practice law, Chgo., from 1973. Instr. accounting U. Iowa, 1936-37; asst. prof. law Chgo.-Kent Coll. Law, 1947. Treas. local troop Boy Scouts Am., 1962-65; mem. com. to investigate pub. transp. for handicapped Welfare Council Met. Chgo., 1966; chmn. caucus in Wilmette, Ill. for Cook County Sch. Dist., 39, 1962. Bd. dirs., sec. Rehab. Inst. Chgo., from 1961. Mem. Am., Ill. (sec. corp. law dept. 1967-68, vice chmn. 1968-69, chmn.

1969-70), Chgo. bar assns., Am. Soc. Corp. Secretaries (sec. Chgo. regional group 1965-67, v.p. 1967-68, pres. 1969-70, chmn. mem. relations com. from 1965, mem. adv. com. 1965-68, v.p., dir. nat. from 1970). Presbyn. (elder 1960-62, trustee sec. bd. 1966-67, pres. 1968). Home: Skokie, Ill. Died July 2, 1980.

PARTRIDGE, ROI, etcher; b. Centralia, Ter. of Wash., Oct. 14, 1888; s. Archibald E. and Florence (George) P.; m. Imogen Cunningham, Feb. 11, 1915 (dec. June 1976) (div. 1934); children: Gryffyd, Rondal and Padraic (twins); m. Marion Lyman, June 27, 1935 (dec. Aug. 1940); m. May Ellen Fisher, July 29, 1941. Ed., N.A.D., N.Y.C., also in Europe. Instr. dept. art Mills Coll., 1920-22, prof., 1922-48; academician in graphic arts N.A.D., from 1949. Exhibited widely; represented in permanent collections, Art Inst. Chgo., Worcester (Mass.) Mus., Toronto Art Gallery, Library of Congress, Los Angeles Mus. Sci. and Art, Oakland (Calif.) Mus., Walker Art Gallery, Liverpool, Eng., Met. Mus. Art, Achenbach Collection at Palace of Legion of Honor, San Francisco, Acad. Arts, Honolulu, Wells Coll., Aurora, N.Y., Carnegie Inst., Nat. Fine Arts Collection, Washington, Bklyn. Mus., Mus. Modern Art. Recipient Syndam Silver medal N.A.D., 1910; Logan medal Art Inst. Chgo., 1921; Bijar prize Bklyn. Soc. Etchers, 1921; O'Melveney prize Print Makers Calif., 1922; BUMA prize, 1925; Los Angeles Gold medal, 1928; Gold medal San Diego, 1969. Fellow NAD. Pantheist. Home: Walnut Creek, Calif. Died Jan. 25, 1984.

PASCHALL, NATHANIEL, business exec.; b. Seattle, June 11, 1912; s. Nathaniel and Bertha Cranston (Potter) P.; student U. Wash., 1932, Boeing Sch. Aeronautics, Oakland, Calif., 1934-35; m. Mary Katherine Price, Feb. 18, 1947; children—Nathaniel Price, Boeing C. Co-pilot United Airlines, Oakland, 1936-38; with Douglas Aircraft Co., Inc., Santa Monica, 1939-59, v.p., 1945-59, dir., 1951-61; chmn. bd. dirs. Fidelity Northwest, Seattle; chmn. Paschall Internat. Corp.; chmn. Bank of Montreal (Calif.), 1972-79. Clubs: Calif. (Los Angeles); Pacific Union (San Francisco); Annandale Golf (Pasadena, Calif.); Wings (N.Y.); Seattle Yacht; Mt. Royal (Montreal); Birnam Wood Golf (Montecito, Calif.). Home: Pasadena, Calif. Died Jan. 22, 1979.

PASSMORE, ERIC WILLIAM, lawyer, manufacturer; b. Milw., July 7, 1893; s. William and Miriam (Bloodgood) P.; student St. Johns Mil. Acad., ex 1911, U. Wis., 1911-14; LL.B., Marquette U., 1916; m. Gertrude Cole, Apr. 24, 1937. Admitted to Wis. bar, 1916; practice corporate, ins., tax, estate and trust law, Milw., 1916-56; sr. assoc. Bloodgood & Passmore; exec. v.p. Simplicity Mfg. Co., Inc., Port Washington, Wis., 1937-67, cons., counsel, from 1967. Trustee Columbia Hosp., Milw. Served with USNRF, 1917-18. Mem. Am., Wis., Milw. bar assns., Sigma Nu. Clubs: University, Milwaukee Country, Milwaukee Athletic; Tavern (Chgo); Links (N.Y.C.). Home: Milwaukee, Wis. Died Nov. 6, 1979.

PASTA, JOHN ROBERT, govt. ofcl., physicist; b. N.Y.C., Oct. 22, 1918; s. William James and Janet (Williams) P.; B.S., Coll. City N.Y., 1946; Ph.D., NYU, 1951; m. Betty Ann Bentzen, May 2, 1943; children—Diane, David. Research fellow Brookhaven Nat. Lab., 1948-51; staff mem. Los Alamos Sci. Lab., 1951-56; head math. program, div. research AEC, 1956-61; prof. physics and computer sci. U. Ill., 1961-70, head dept. computer sci., 1964-70; vis. scientist C.E.R.N., Geneva, Switzerland, 1967-68; head office computing activities NSF, 1970-74, dir. div. computer research, 1974-75, dir. div. math. and computer scis., 1975-81. Liaison rep. div. math. sci. NRC, 1958-61, 70-81; cons. to govt. and industry, 1961-70; adj. prof., engring. and applied sci. George Washington U., 1973-76. Mem. math. and computer sci. research adv. com. AEC, 1961-70, chmn., 1965-67; chmn. internat. relations com. Am. Fedn. Information Processing Socs., 1965-66; Am. del. Internat. Fedn. Information Processing, 1965-66; trustee Interuniv. Communications Council, 1965-68; mem. computer sci. adv. com. Stanford, 1969-72; phys. scis. com. Ill. Bd. Higher Edn., 1969-70. Served to capt. USAAF, 1942-45. Decorated Bronze Star. Mem. Am. Phys. Soc., Am. Math. Assn., Philos. Soc. Washington. Contbr. profl. jours. and books. Assoc. editor Jour. Computational Physics, 1966-74. Home: Washington, D.C. Died June 5, 1981.

PASTORIZA, ANDRÉS, diplomat; b. Santiago de los Caballeros, Dominican Republic, Apr. 24, 1887; s. Tomas and Teresa (Valverde) P.; student Peekskill (N.Y.) Mil. Acad., 1901-04; grad. Peirce Sch. of Business Adminstrn., Philadelphia, Pa., 1905; m. Matilde Esapillat, 1911; children—Andrés, Tomas Agusto, Maria Matilde. Engaged in commercial and industrial enterprises; held cabinet portfolio Pub. Works and Communications, 1924-30; sec. agr. and labor, 1935; E.E. and M.P. from Dominican Republic to Washington from 1935. Was pres. Aldermanic Council, Santiago. Hon. vice-pres. Dominican Chamber of Commerce of U.S.; mem. U.S. Chamber of Commerce. Mem. Supreme Council 33 deg. of Dominican Republic; mem. Junta Colombina, Nat. Council Edn.; ex-pres. Chamber Commerce, Industry and Agr., Santiago, also Santo Domingo. Former venerable master Nuevo Mundo Lodge. Clubs: Metropolitan, Chevy Chase, National Press, Cosmos, University (Washington); Bankers' (New York). Home: Washington, D.C.†

PATCH, HOWARD ROLLIN, prof. English; b. Lake Linden, Mich., Aug. 7, 1889; s. Maurice Byron and Emily Isabella (White) P.; A.B., Hobart, Geneva, N.Y., 1910; A.M., Harvard, 1912, Ph.D., 1915; hon. Litt.D., Hobart, 1924; m. Helen Louise Kennedy, Aug. 12, 1916; children—Howard Rollin, Robert Kennedy, Priscilla Emily, Mary Helen, John Harvard fellow, Harvard, 1912-15, also asst. in English, 1912-13; instr. in English, Harvard and Radcliffe Coll., 1915-16; lecturer in English philology, Bryn Mawr, 1916-17, asso. 1917-19; asst. prof. English, Smith Coll., 1919-20, asso. prof., 1920-24, prof. from 1924, chmn. dept. of English, 1925-26, 1937-38, 1948-51; vis. prof., Harvard, summer 1925, second half-year, 1931. Fellow American Acad. of Arts and Sciences; Fellow Medieval Academy of Am.; mem. Modern Language Association of Am., Modern Humanities Research Assn. (Eng.), Dante Soc. (Cambridge, Mass.), Soc. for Study of Medieval Langs. and Lit. (Eng.), Phi Beta Kappa, Kappa Alpha. Catholic. Author: The Goddess Fortuna in Medieval Literature, 1927; The Tradition of Boethius, 1935; On Rereading Chaucer, 1939; The Cupid on the Stairs, a Romance in Rococo, 1942, The Other World, According to Descriptions in Medieval Literature, 1950. Editor: (with Pres. W.A. Neilson), Selections from Chaucer, 1921; (with others) Smith College Studies in Modern Languages. Contbr. to philol. jours. Home: Northampton, Mass. †

PATE, JOHN RALSTON, govt. ofcl., orgn. exec.; b. Scranton, S.C., Aug. 27, 1906; s. Charles H. and Nell (Singletary) P.; m. Alice Drew Chenoweth, Feb. 12, 1942; 1 son, John Ralston. A.B. in Edn; A.M., U. S.C., 1927; B.S., M.D., Duke U., 1933; J.D., U. Louisville, 1945; M.P.H., Johns Hopkins U., 1948; certificate hosp. adminstrn., U. Rochester, 1933. Bar: U.S. Supreme Ct. bar 1969. Instr. in English U. S.C., 1926-27; tchr. English Charleston (S.C.) High Sch., 1927-29; intern Strong Meml. Hosp., Rochester, N.Y.; mem. faculty George Washington U. Sch. Medicine, 1933-38; now asso. prof. community medicine and internat. health Georgetown U.; staff Ky. Dept. Health, 1938-47; with D.C. Dept. Pub. Health, from 1948, dir. bur. disease control, 1953-64, chief bur. communicable disease control, from 1964. Author articles, chpts. books. Mem. Civitan Internat., from 1955; gov. Chesapeake dist., 1961-62, v.p. zone 3, 1962-64, internat. pres.-elect, 1964-65, pres., 1965-66; nat. council Boy Scouts Am.; bd. visitors Freedoms Found. at Valley Forge; mem. Pres.'s Com. for Handicapped, mem., Gov. of Va. Com. for the Handicapped Employment; bd. dirs. Social Hygiene Soc. D.C.; adv. bd. Partridge Schs. and Rehab. Center, Gainesville, Va. Recipient 1st Albernon Sydney Sullivan medallion U. S.C., 1927; citation for service LWV D.C., 1952; scroll of honor Omega Psi Phi, 1957; named Mr. Civitan Chesapeake dist., 1962. Fellow Am. Pub. Health Assn., Am. Coll. Legal Medicine, Royal Soc. Health; charter mem. Am. Assn. Pub. Health Physicians, Am. Venereal Disease Assn., Omicron Delta Kappa; mem. AMA, Am. Assn. Pub. Health Physicians, Assn. Tchrs. Preventive Medicine, Royal Soc. Medicine Gt. Britain, Am. Assn. History of Medicine, D.C. Med. Soc., Clin. Club Washington, Ky. Bar Assn., Am. Geriatric Soc., World Med. Assn., Acad. Medicine, SAR, Phi Beta Pi, Alpha Tau Omega. Democrat. Episcopalian (vestryman). Clubs: Masons (32 deg.), Shriners. Home: Arlington, VA.

PATE, MARTHA B. LUCAS, (MRS. MAURICE PATE) educator; b. Louisville, Nov. 27, 1912; d. Robert H. and Gertrude (Lasch) Lucas; m. Maurice Pate, Oct. 1961 (dec. 1965). Student, Vassar Coll., 1931-32; A.B., Goucher Coll., Balt., 1933, LL.D., 1946; M.A., George Washington U., 1935; Ph.D., U. London, 1940; LL.D., Ala. Coll., 1946, Atlanta U., 1972; L.H.D., U. Louisville, 1950, Smith Coll., 1971. Assoc. prof. philosophy and religion, dean of students U. Richmond, Va., 1941-44; assoc. dean Radcliffe Coll., 1944-46; pres., prof. philosophy of religion Sweet Briar Coll., Va., 1946-50, Lyman lectr. in philosophy of religion, 1956; exec. dir. office of univ. and coll. relations Inst. Internat. Edn., 1961-62; chmn. Coll. and Sch. div. United Negro Coll. Fund, 1962-83, bd. dirs., 1967—; chmn. Dana Fellowship com., 1970-83; bd. dirs. Fgn. Policy Assn., 1963-83; also mem. gen. ops. exec. com., nominating com., program com.; bd. dirs. Rec. for the Blind, 1962-76, chmn. planning and devel. com., 1963-83, v.p., 1967-83; chmn. Nat. Scholastic awards, 1968-83; Mem. nat. selections com. for Fulbright Scholarships, 1948-50; U.S. del. UNESCO Prep. Conf. of U. Reps., Utrecht, Holland, 1948; 4th Gen. Conf. UNESCO, Paris, 1949; mem. Adv. Council for Jr. Year in France, 1947-50; mem. bd. dirs. Assn. Am. Colls., 1949-50; v.p. So. U. Conf. and chmn. com. on improvement of instruction, 1949-50; 2d vice chmn. Am. Council on Edn., 1949-50; mem. adv. council on health careers United Hosp. Fund; adv. council Columbia U. Sch. Social Work, 1967-83, chmn. nominations com., 1970-83; mem. U.S. Nat. Adv. Commn. on Internat. Edn. and Cultural Affairs, 1970-73, Nat. Com. on U.S.-China Relations, 1971-83; pub. mem. selection panel for fgn. service officers USIA, 1973; mem. commn. accrediting Assn. Theol. Schs. U.S. and Can., 1978—. Author: (with others) Religious Faith and World Culture, 1951; Lectr. on (with others) edn., philosophy and world affairs. Bd. dirs. N.Y. Met. com. UNICEF, 1972-83, incorporator nat. com., 1975-83; bd. regents Georgetown U., 1974-75, bd. dirs., 1975-83, vice chmn. bd. dirs., 1979-83; also bd. rep. to Med. Center; trustee N.Y. Med. Coll., 1967-83, chmn. ednl. policies com., 1974-83, chmn. academic and student affairs com., 1975-83; trustee Fund for Peace, 1967-83, chmn. nominations com., mem. exec. com., postdoctoral fellowship com., audit com.; trustee N.Y. Sch. Psychiatry, 1971-83, chmn. com. goals and acad. programs; trustee Fund for Theol. Edn., Inc., 1969-78; bd. dirs. Westchester Med. Center Found., 1969-83, YWCA, Richmond, Va.; trustee L.I. U., 1969-83, chmn. acad. policies com., 1970-83, student affairs com., audit com.; trustee Pierce Coll., Athens, Greece, 1962-69, chmn. acad. affairs com., 1962-69, hon. trustee, 1969-83; alumnae trustee Goucher Coll., 1968-71; chmn. univs. and colls. com. bd. dirs. Ralph Bunch Meml. Project, 1976-83; trustee St. Stephen's Sch. in Rome, 1977-83, mem. nominations com., 1978-83; mem. commn. on accreditation Assn. Theol. Schs. U.S. and Can., 1978-83; bd. advs. Inst. for Study World Politics, 1977-83; bd. advs. Center for Def. Info., 1979-83, mem. fin. planning com.; bd. advs. Global Perspectives in Edn., 1978-83. Decorated chevalier French Legion of Honor; recipient George Washington U. Alumni Citation, 1947; UN Internat. Women's Yr. award UN Secretariat and Sweet Briar Coll., 1975; Patrick Healy award Georgetown U. Alumni Assn., 1981; others. Fellow Soc. Values in Higher Edn. (dir. 1976-83); mem. Am. Philos. Assn., Nat. Inst. Social Scis., Council on Religion and Internat. Affairs (dir. 1968-77, chmn. 60th anniversary com. 1970-74), Acad. Religion and Mental Health, Acad. Polit. Sci., New Dramatists Soc. (dir. chmn. com. on univ. projects), Phi Beta Kappa (Bicentennial fellow 1976, asso. 1977). Episcopalian. Clubs: Faculty (New Haven); Vassar (N.Y.C.), Cosmopolitan (N.Y.C.). Home: West Redding, Conn. Died Apr. 27, 1983.

PATINO, ANTENOR R., tin exec.; b. Oruro, Bolivia, Oct. 12, 1894; s. Simon I. and Albina (Rodriquez) Patino; m. Princess Maria Cristina de Bourbon, Apr. 8, 1931; children—Maria-Cristina, Isabel (dec.); married 2d, Countess Beatriz di Borasenda, 1960. Chmn., dir. Patino Mining Corporation; president, director of Consol. Tin Smelters, Ltd., London. Gen. Tin Investments, Ltd., Gen. Metal Securities, Ltd. (all London); dir. British Tin Investment Corp., Ltd., London, British Am. Tin Mines, Ltd., Tahiland Tin Mines, Ltd., Tin Industrial Finance & Underwriting, Ltd. Address: Paris, France. Died Feb. 2, 1982.

PATON, WILLIAM ANDREW, economist, acountant; b. Calumet, Mich., July 19, 1889; s. Andrew and Mary (Nowlin) P.; Mich. State Normal College, 1907-08, 1911-12; A.B., University of Michigan, 1915, A.M., 1916, Ph.D., 1917; Litt.D., Lehigh University, 1944; m. Mary K. Sleator, July 9, 1914; children—William Andrew, Margaret Louise, Robert Warner (deceased). Instr. in economics, University of Mich., 1915-16, U. of Minn., 1916-17; asst. prof. Univ. of Michigan, 1917-19, asso. prof., 1919-21, prof. since 1921, Edwin F. Gay university professor of accounting since 1947; visiting teacher Univ. of California, 1921, 1937-38, Univ. of Chicago, 1924; Dickinson lecturer, Harvard Grad. Sch. Bus. Adminstrn., 1940. C.P.A., Mich. With Bur. of Research and Statistics, War Trade Bd., 1918; with Income Tax Unit, Bur. Internal Revenue, 1919. Fellow American Academy of Arts and Sciences; member Am. Econ. Assn., Am. Accounting Assn. (pres. 1922; dir. of research 1936-39), Mich. Assn. of C.P.As., Am. Inst. of Accountants, Phi Beta Kappa, Phi Kappa Phi, Beta Gamma Sigma. Author or co-author books relating to field; latest publs. include: Shirtsleeve Economics, 1952; Asset Accounting, 1952; (with W. A. Paton, Jr.) Corporation Accounts and Statements, 1955; (with R. L. Diyon) Essentials of Accounting, 1958. Editor Accounting Rev., 1926-28; editor, prin. contbr. Accountants Handbook, 1932, 43. Home: Ann Arbor, Mich. †

PATRICELLI, LEONARD JOSEPH, broadcasting company executive; b. New Haven, Mar. 1, 1907; s. Liberato Leonard and Palma (Lombardi) P.; B.A., Wesleyan U., Middletown, Conn., 1929; m. Lydia Erdman, Sept. 6, 1930 (dec. Nov. 1972); children—Joan (Mrs. Garvin Bawden), Robert; m. 2d, Isabel Scoville Peterson, Aug. 11, 1973. With Broadcast-Plaza, Inc., Hartford, Conn., from 1929, exec. v.p., 1966-67, pres., from 1967; pres. 1080 Corp. (sta. WTIC-AM-FM), from 1974, chmn. bd., from 1978. Conn. chmn. P.R. Flood Relief Campaign, 1971; chmn. Bellevue Square Boys Club. Bd. dirs. Hartford Symphony Orch., Conn. Opera Assn., Conn. Citizens for Jud. Reform; trustee Hartford Rehab. Center, Conn. Cancer Soc.; bd. corporators Mt. Sinai, Hartford, St. Francis hosps., Inst. Living. Recipient Americanism award Conn. Valley council B'nai B'rith; Outstanding Citizen award VFW; James McConaughy award Wesleyan U., 1971; award editorial excellence Radio and TV News Dirs. Assn., 1970; Presdl. commendation for efforts to combat drug abuse, 1970; Civic awards Greater Hartford Bd. Realtors, Hartford Better Bus. Bur., 1973, Christopher Columbus Soc., 1977. Mem. Nat. Assn. Broadcaster (tv bd. dirs.), Broadcast Pioneers Am. and Broadcasters Found. (nat. bd. dirs., pres.), Conn. Broadcasters Assn. (pres. 1969-70), U.S. Broadcasters Com. for UN, Greater Hartford C. of C. (past v.p., dir., exec. com.). Clubs: Rotary, Hartford, Hartford Golf, Hartford Wesleyan Alumni; Stuart Yacht and Country (Fla.). Editor: Wesleyan U. Songbook, 1953. Home: West Hartford, Conn. Died Jan. 25, 1982.

PATRICK, WALTER ALBERT, prof. chemistry; b. Syracuse, N.Y., Jan. 6, 1888; s. Walter A. and Mary (Manning) P.; B.S., Syracuse U., 1910, D.Sc., 1935; Ph.D., U. of Göttingen, 1914; m. Millicent Gertrude Leech, June 15, 1915; children—Virginia Mary, Patricia, Shirley. Asst.

in chemistry, Mass. Inst. Tech., 1910-12, Univ. Coll., London, 1914-15; instr. in phys. chemistry, Mass. Inst. Tech., 1915-16, Syracuse U., 1916-17; asso. Johns Hopkins, 1917-24, prof. chemistry from 1924; cons. chemist, Davison Chem. Corp. Mem. Am. Chem. Soc., Chem. Soc. (Eng.), Sigma Xi, Kappa Sigma, Phi Beta Kappa. Club: Baltimore Country. Inventor of silica gel; made researches on adsorption, surface energy and colloidal phenomena. Home: Mt. Washington, Md.

PATTBERG, EMIL JOSEPH, JR., investment banker; b. Jersey City, Feb. 10, 1910; s. Emil Joseph and Charlotte (Garrick) P.; grad. Randolph Macon Acad., 1926; m. Dorothy Egan, Jan. 14, 1939; children—Philip Robert, Linda Ann. Joined First Boston Corp., 1929, chmn. bd., pres., until 1976, dir.; cons., dir. First Boston Inc., dir. First Boston Europe, Pitney Bowes, Inc., Colonial Income Fund, Inc., Colonial Fund, Inc., Colonial Growth Shares Inc., Colonial Convertible & Sr. Securities Inc., Colonial Option Income Fund. Bd. govs. Fed. Hall Meml. Assos., N.Y.C. Served with 28th Inf. Div., AUS, 1944-45, ETO. Mem. Securities Industry Assn. Clubs: Bond, Links, Wall Street (N.Y.C.); Ridgewood (N.J.) Country; Blind Brook Golf (Port Chester, N.Y.); Mountain Lake. Home: Lake Wales, Fla. Died June 23, 1982.

PATTERSON, HERBERT, educator; b. Chilmark, Mass., Feb. 17, 1887; s. Rev. John Nelson and Etta Mary (Briant) P.; B.A., Wesleyan U., Conn., 1908, M.A., 1911; M.A., Yale, 1911, Ph.D., 1913; special student U. of Calif. and U. of Southern Calif., 1936-37; m. Susie Victoria Hartford, Sept. 9, 1913 (died July 8, 1921); children—Ruth Hartford (Mrs. Elmo Wolfe), John Herbert, Marion Esther (dec.); m. 2d, Mary Lillian Schenk, Aug. 9, 1922 (died Dec. 25, 1928); children—Nancy Jane (Mrs. Ralph Denham), Emily (Mrs. Lawrence V. Wilson), Esther Mary (Mrs. John T. Ward); m 3d, Florence Dora Schertz, July 26, 1930. High school teacher, Kingston, Pa., 1908-09, Mt. Hermon, Mass., 1909-10; fellowship student Yale U., 1911-13; professor of education and director of Summer School, 1913-19, dean College, Liberal Arts, Dakota Wesleyan U., 1919, dean Sch. of Edn. and dir. Summer Sch., Okla. Agrl. and Mech. Coll., 1919-37, dean of adminstrn. since 1937. Condr. joint inst. for teachers (11 counties), Mitchell, S.D., summers 1914-19. Mem. exec. council Southern Assn. of Teacher Training Instns., 1924-26; mem. Okla. Ednl. Survey Com., in charge of Washington County Survey, 1922; mem. Okla. State High Sch. Reorganization Com., 1927-28. Life mem. N.E.A. (consultant ednl. policies commn.), Okla. Edn. Assn. (life mem. pres. sect. coll. teachers edn. 1927); Am. Assn. Sch. Adminstrs. (life mem.); fellow and life mem., A.A.A.S.; fellow Okla. Acad. of Science (exec. council, 1925-33; sec. 1927-31, pres. 1931-32); mem. Okla. State Com. for Inspecting Junior Colleges, 1928-35; Oklahoma Assn. of Sch. Administrators, Am. Philos. Assn., Am. Assn. U. Profs., Nat. Soc. for Study Edn. (life mem.) Nat. Soc. Coll. Tchrs. of Edn., Phi Beta Kappa, Phi Kappa Phi, Kappa Delta Pi, Kappa Kappa Psi, Phi Delta Kappa, Pi Gamma Mu. Presbyterian (elder). Mason. Club: Lions (pres. 1932-33). Author: Thirty Contests in Spelling, 1920; Ethics of Achievement, 1927; How to Teach Thrift, 1927; also numerous articles in ednl. jours. Lecturer on ednl. topics. Home: Stillwater, Okla. †

PATTERSON, HERBERT PARSONS, consultant, former banker; b. N.Y.C., Sept. 3, 1925; s. Morehead and Elsie Clews (Parsons) P.; m. Louise S. Oakey, July 30, 1949 (dec. 1968); m. Patricia Shephard, Apr. 30, 1970 (div. 1979). B.S., Yale, 1948. With Chase Manhattan Bank, N.Y.C., 1949-85, asst. mgr., 1952, asst. treas., 1955, asst. v.p., 1956-59, v.p., 1959-62, sr. v.p., 1962-65; exec. v.p. Chase Manhattan Bank (U.S. dept.), 1965-67; exec. v.p. Chase Manhattan Bank (internat. dept.), 1967-69, pres., 1969-72; cons. Marshalsea Assos., Inc., N.Y.C., 1973-77; pres. Stonover Co., 1977-85; dir. Am. Machine & Foundry Co., Ryder System, Inc. Hon. trustee Brookings Instn. Mem. Tau Beta Pi, Chi Psi. Clubs: Links (N.Y.C.), Nat. Golf Links America (N.Y.C.), Racquet and Tennis (N.Y.C.); Bathing Corp. of Southampton, Brook, Shinnecock Hills Golf. Home: New York, N.Y. Died Jan. 29, 1985.

PATTERSON, LAFAYETTE, b. Clay Co., Ala., Aug. 23, 1888; s. Delona and Mary Green (Sorrell) P.; grad. Jacksonville (Ala.) State Normal Sch., 1922; A.B., Birmingham-Southern Coll., 1924; A.M., Stanford, 1927; m. Nannie Mann, of Daviston, Ala., Sept. 8, 1914; children—Geraldine LaFayette, Arline, Delona, Miriam. Engaged in farming until 1919; prin. jr. high sch., Randolph and Elmore counties, Ala., and in wholesale produce business, 1920-21; supt. sch. at Oakman, Ala., 1922-23; supt. schs., Tallapoosa County, Ala., 1924-26; mem. 70th, 71st and 72d Congresses (1927-33), 5th Ala. Dist.; field rep. Agrl. Adjustment Adminstrn., 1933-36, prin. administrative officer and gen. contact rep. from 1936. Democrat. Methodist. Mason, K.P. Home: Gadsden, AL. †

PATTERSON, ROBERT ALEXANDER, physicist; b. Engfield, Conn., July 12, 1890; s. Thomas Henry and Laura Belle (Dewey) P.; B.A., Yale, 1911, M.A., 1912, Ph.D., 1915; m. Edna Allen Sammis, May 29, 1920; 1 son, Allen Dewey. Inst. physics, Sheffield Scientific Sch. (Yale), 1912-14, Yale Coll., 1914-17 and 1919; asst. prof. physics, Yale, 1920-22; nat. research fellow. Harvard, 1919-20; prof. physics, Rensselaer Polytechnic Institute, from 1922, head department of physics, 1940-46; asst. dir. Brookhaven National Laboratory from 1946; staff mem. Radiation Laboratory Mass. Inst. Technology and technical consultant Bureau of Ordinance, Navy Department, 1942-45; lecturer Harvard University. summers 1925-32. Director Windham Plantations, Ltd. Student 1st Plattsburgh O.T.C.; commd. capt. F.A., Aug. 15, 1917; assigned to staff, School of Fire for F.A., Fort Sill, Okla., Jan. 1918; maj. F.A., July 1918; hon. discharged, Dec. 1918. Fellow Am. Physical Soc., A.A.A.S.; member Phi Beta Kappa, Sigma Xi, Beta Theta Chi, Gamma Alpha; hon. mem. Rensselaer Soc. Engrs. Clubs: Old Inlet; Bellport Bay Yacht; Yale (N.Y.C.). Home: L.I., N.Y. †

PATTON, JAMES GEORGE, agrl. leader; b. Bazar, Kans., Nov. 8, 1902; s. Ernest Everett and Jane Alice (Gross) P.; LL.D., Western State Coll. Colo., 1942, U. Colo., 1966; m. Velma A. Fouse, June 17, 1925 (dec. Sept. 1979); children—Marjorie Jane, James George (dec.), George Everett (dec.), Robert Lyle; m. 2d, Nathalie E. Panek, Nov. 8, 1972. Athletic dir., instr. phys. edn., Colo. and Nev., 1921-26; asst. business mgr. Western State Coll. Colo., 1927-29; organizer coop. ins. Colo. Farmers Union, 1932-34, exec. sec., 1934-37, pres., 1938-41; dir. Nat. Farmers Union, 1937-40, pres., 1940-66, ret.; pres. James G. Patton & Assos., Tucson, 1966-69; pres. United World Federalists, 1967-69; spl. cons. sec. agr., Pa., 1971-75; dir. ret. mems. dept. AFL-CIO, 1976-85. Formerly mem. Nat. Adv. Com. of Nat. Youth Adminstrn.; mem. Econ. Stblzn. Bd., 1942-43; mem. Nat. Labor Mgmt. Policy Commn.; former mem. adv. bd. War Moblizn. and Reconversion Bd.; rep. Carnegie Endownment for Internat. Peace, Am. Conf. of Assns. Commerce and Prodn., Montevideo, 1941; U.S. del. 2d Inter-Am. Conf. on Agrl., Mexico, 1942; U.S. adviser Inter-Am. Conf. on War and Peace, Mexico, 1945; U.S. cons. U.N. Conf. on Internat. Order, San Francisco, 1945; U.S. adv. to FAO convs., Quebec, 1945, Copenhagen, 1946, Geneva, 1947, Washington, 1948, Rome, 1949; del. Internat. Fedn. Agrl. Producers, 1946-85; mem. exec. com. Internat. Fedn. Agrl. Producers, 1950, v.p., 1955-58, pres., 1958-61; mem. Nat. Adv. Bd. Moblzn., 1951; pres. Freedom From Hunger Found. U.S.A., 1962-63, mem. exec. com., 1973-75; cons., observer World Food Conf., Rome, 1974. Home: Menlo Park, Calif. Died Feb. 17, 1985.

PATTON, JAMES WILLIAM, JR., lawyer; b. Columbus, Ga., July 6, 1914; s. JamesWilliam and Gertrude (Berry) P.; m. Marjorie Phinizy, Aug. 2, 1941; children—Jean Patton Parker, J. William, III, Peter E. LL.B., U. Ala., 1937. Bar: Ala. 1937. Assoc. firm Eyster & Eyster, Decatur, Ala., 1937-42; mem. firm Stone, Patton & Kierce (and predecessors), Bessemer, Ala., 1946-85. Past pres. Bessemer Salvation Army Adv. Bd.; past chmn. bd. dirs. Bessemer chpt. ARC; trustee Bessemer Meml. Hosp., 1964-73. Served with USAAF, 1942-46. Mem. Bessemer, Ala., Am. bar assns., Am. Judicature Soc., Bessemer C. of C. (pres. 1955-56). Democrat. Episcopalian. Clubs: Woodward Golf and Country, The Club; Lions (Bessemer) (pres. local club 1962-63). Home: Bessemer, Ala. Died Jan. 8, 1985.

PATTON, MARGUERITE COURTRIGHT (MRS. JAMES B. PATTON), orgn. exec.; b. Circleville, O., Feb. 5, 1889; d. Judge Samuel Wilson and Jennie Rosalthea (Martin) Courtright; H.H.D. (hon.), Lincoln Memorial U., 1952; Dr. Humane Letters (hon.), Am. Internat. College; m. James B. Patton, July 4, 1911; children—James Courtright, Robert Miller. Mem. D.A.R. since 1910, 2d vice regent Columbus chpt., 1925-28, 1st vice regent, 1928-30, regent, 1930, state librarian, 1937-41, state vice regent, chmn. nat. defense, 1941-44, state regent, 1944-47, 1st v.p. gen., nat. soc., 1947-50, national pres. gen., 1950-53, honorary president general for life, also national chairman of national def. com., 1953-56. Dir. Freedoms Found. Served on Franklin (O.) County Council Def., World War II; mem. Columbus Speakers' Bur. for all bond drives; assisted in work U.S.O. Recipient citation A.R.C., 1945; Ky. Col.; adm. Neb. Navy; Ark. Traveler. Mem. Ohio State Archaeol. and Hist. Soc., Franklin County Hist. Soc., Daus. Founders and Patriots, Daus. Colonial Wars, Daus. Am. Colonists, Huguenot Soc., Sons and Daus. Pilgrims, U.S. Daus. 1812, Nat. Soc. Arts and Letters, Nat. League Am. Pen Women. Republican. Presbyn. Home: Columbus, Ohio. †

PAUCK, WILHELM, educator; b. Laasphe, Westphalia, Germany, Jan. 31, 1901; s. Wilhelm and Maria (Hofmann) P.; grad. Real Gymnasium, Berlin-Steglitz, 1920; Lic. Theology, U. Berlin, 1925; Dr.Theology, h.c., U. Giessen, 1933; Litt.D., Upsala Coll., 1964, Thiel Coll., 1967; D.D., Gustavus Adolphus Coll., 1967, U. Edinburgh (Scotland), 1968; m. Olga C. Gumbel-Dietz, May 1, 1928 (dec. 1963); m. 2d, Marion Hausner, Nov. 21, 1964. Came to U.S., 1925, naturalized, 1937. Prof. ch. history Chgo. Theol. Sem., 1926-39; prof. hist. theology U. Chgo., 1939-53, prof. history, 1945-53; prof. ch. history Union Theol. Sem., 1953-60, Charles A. Briggs Grad. prof. ch. history, 1960-67; Distinguished prof. ch. history Vanderbilt U., Nashville, 1967-72, Stanford, 1972-81. Exchange prof. U. Frankfurt (Germany), 1948-49. Mem. United Ch. of Christ. Fellow Am. Acad. Arts and Scis.; mem. Am. Soc. Ch. History (pres. 1936), Am. Theol. Soc. (pres. 1962-63). Author: Das Reich Gottes auf Erden, 1928; Karl Barth-Prophet of a New Christianity?, 1931; The Heritage of the Reformation, 1951, rev. edit., 1961; Luther's Lectures on Romans, 1961; Harnack and Troeltsch, Two Historical Theologians, 1968; Melanchthon and Bucer, 1969. Co-author: The Church against the World, 1935; Religion and Politics, 1946; The Ministry in Historical Perspective, 1956; (with Marion Pauck) The Life of Paul Tillich, 1976. Contbr. to Environmental Factors in Christian History, 1939; Religion and the Present Crisis, 1942; also theol. and hist. jours. Home: Palo Alto, Calif. Died Sept. 4, 1981.

PAUL, WINSTON, business exec.; b. N.Y.C., Oct. 31, 1887; s. Alexander and Nellie E. (Winston) P.; grad. Newark Acad.; A.B., Columbia Coll., 1909; LL.D., Springfield Coll., 1965. Chairman bd. Gen. Aniline & Film Corp. 1953-55, chmn. finance com., 1955-61; chairman of the Lake Placid Company. Pres. N.J. Com. for Constl. Revision, 1944-48; del. Constl. Conv. for N.J., 1947; mem. N.J. State Investment Council. Treas. N.Y.C. Y.M.C.A., 1950-53; mem. bd. dirs. Nat. Civil Service League; member of the Columbia College Council, chmn., 1954-56; trustee Springfield (Massachusetts) College. Delegate Republican National Convention, 1952. Clubs: Union League, Lake Placid, Montclair Golf; Valley (Santa Barbara, Cal.). Home: Montclair, N.J. †

PAULEY, EDWIN WENDELL, oil corp. exec.; b. Indpls., Jan. 7, 1903; s. Elbert L and Ellen (Van Petten) P.; student Occidental Coll., 1919-20; B.S., U. Calif., 1922, LL.D., 1956; Litt.D., Santa Clara U., 1960; LL.D., Pepperdine Coll., 1956; m. Barbara Jean McHenry, Oct. 23, 1937; children—Edwin Wendell, Susan Jean, Stephen McHenry, Robert Van Petten. Founder Petrol Corp.; independent oil producer; real estate developer; chmn. bd. Pauley Petroleum Inc.; dir. Western Air Lines, Inc. Spl. rep. of gov. Cal. on Natural Resource Com., 1939, Interstate Oil and Compact Commn., 1940; petroleum coordinator for war in Europe on petroleum lend-lease supplies for Russia and Eng., 1941; U.S. rep. Reparations Commn., with rank of ambassador, 1945-47; adviser to sec. of state on reparations, 1947-48; spl. asst. to sec. of army 1947. Regent U. Calif., 1939-81, chmn. bd., 1956-81, chmn. regents, 1960-81. Past sec., treas. Dem. Com.; Dem. nat. committeeman of Calif., 1944-48. Pres. Ind. Petroleum Assn., 1934-38. Home: Beverly Hills, Calif. Died July 28, 1981.

PAULL, JOHN R., lawyer, govt. official; b. Taunton, Mass., Oct. 11, 1890; s. Edward Curtis and Jennie (Monks) P.; B.A., Yale, 1912; Harvard Law Sch., class of 1916; m. Grace Warner; children—John, Richard; m. 2d. Catherine Dungan. Admitted to bars of Mass., 1917, N.Y., 1920; practiced law in N.Y. City, 1920-43; former chmn. War Contracts Bd., Maritime Commn. Price Adjustment Bd., Washington; comptroller maritime adminstrn. Dept. of Commerce, chief Bur. Finance, 1951; pvt. law practice from 1951. Served Overseas in Judge Advocate General's Dept., 26th and 42d divs., A.E.F., World War I. Republican. Home: Washington, D.C. †

PAXSON, C(HARLES) EDWARD, lawyer; b. Camden, N.J., July 19, 1887; s. Charles G. and Margaret V. (Wurts) P.; B.S., U. of Pa., 1908; LL.B., 1911; m. Mabel D. Schussler Sept. 16, 1914; children—H. T. Kent, Charlotte Sophia, Charles G. II. Admitted to N.Y. bar, 1912, and began practice at N.Y. City; mem. editorial staff Edward Thompson Law Pub. Co., 1913-17; asst. gen. counsel Pa. Power & Light Co., Allentown, Pa., 1918-23; in practice at Bethlehem, Pa., mem. Taylor, Paxson & Fisher, 1923-24; gen. solicitor Met. Edison Co. and Reading (Pa.) Transit Co., 1924-27; gen. counsel W. S. Barstow & Co. (pub. utility holding and management) and subsidiaries, 1927-29; mem. Travis & Paxson later Travis, Brownback & Paxson, N.Y. City, 1929-40. Mem. Am. Bar Assn., N.Y. State Bar Assn., Sigma Phi Epsilon, Order of Coif. Republican. Episcopalian. Clubs: Downtown Athletic, U. of Pa. Club of N.Y. City. Home: Mamaroneck, N.Y. †

PAYNE, M. LEE, banker; b. Norfolk, Va., Aug. 13, 1925; s. Robert Lee and Mary Elizabeth (Harmon) P.; m. Eunice Wortham Jenkins, July 19, 1952; children—Meriwether, John Benson, Ruth Jenkins. Grad., Woodberry Forest Sch., 1943; B.S., U. Va., 1945; M.B.A., U. Pa., 1949. Investment analyst J.P. Morgan & Co., Inc., N.Y.C., 1949-51; with Seaboard Citizens Nat. Bank (now United Va. Bank), Norfolk, 1952-84, exec. v.p., dir., 1963-67, pres., dir., 1967-74, chmn., dir., 1974-84; pres., dir. Maritime Terminals, Inc.; pres. Norfolk-Portsmouth Clearing House Assn., 1971-72. Mem. Va. Commn. Outdoor Recreation, 1972-74, chmn., 1974-80; commr. Norfolk Area Med. Center Authority, 1969-75; mem. Commn. to Consider Matters Relating to Wetlands of State, 1974; bd. dirs. Tidewater Health Found., 1962-67, pres., 1962-67; bd. dirs. Norfolk Municipal Bond Commn., 1967-76; pres. Norfolk Symphony and Choral Assn., 1964, bd. dirs., 1959-66; bd. dirs. Norfolk United Communities Fund, 1959—, v.p., 1968-70, pres., 1971; bd. visitors Old Dominion U., 1978-84, rector, 1982-84; trustee Chesapeake Bay Found.; trustee, mem. exec. com. Va. Wesleyan Coll., 1969-84; trustee Norfolk Acad., 1968-82, Va. Mus. Fine Arts, 1977-82 Hermitage Found.; trustee, pres. Lincoln-Lane Found.; bd. dirs., v.p. Va. Coll. Fund, 1970-74; bd. dirs. Greater Norfolk Corp., 1977—, pres., 1977-80; regional v.p. Nat. Mcpl. League, 1978-80; bd. mgrs. U. Va. Alumni Assn. Served with the USNR, 1943-46. Mem. Norfolk C. of C. (dir. 1964-77, pres. 1975). Presbyn. Clubs: Norfolk Yacht and Country (Norfolk), Harbor (Norfolk), Virginia (Norfolk); Folly Creek (Accomac, Va.). Home: Norfolk, Va. Deceased.

PAYNE, ROBERT, educator, author; b. Saltash, Cornwall, Eng., Dec. 4, 1911; s. Stephen and Mireille Antoinette (Dorey) P.; student St. Paul's Sch., London, 1927-28, Diocesan Coll., Rondebosch, Cape Province, S. Africa, 1929-30, U. Capetown, 1931-32, U. Liverpool, 1933-36, The Sorbonne, Paris, France, 1938. Came to U.S., 1946. Shipwright apprentice, Cammel, Laird's shipyard, Liverpool, Eng., 1932-33; insp. taxes Guildford, 1937; shipwright Singapore Naval Base, 1939-41, armament officer, 1941; with British Ministry Information, Chungking, 1941-42; London Times corr. at Changsha, 1942; prof. English, lectr. naval architecture Southwest Asso. U. nr. Kunming, 1942-46; prof. Ala. Coll., Montevallo, 1949-54. Author (under pseudonym Valentin Tikhonov) The Mountains and the Stars, 1938; Forever China, 1945; Torrents of Spring, 1946; Sun Yat-Sen, 1946; David and Anna, 1947; The Rose Tree (poems), 1947; A Bear Coughs at the North Pole (novel), 1947; The Revolt of Asia, 1947; The White Pony (anthology of Chinese Poetry), 1947; China Awake, 1947; Report on America, 1949; Zero, the Story of Terrorism, 1950; Mao Tse-tung, Ruler of Red China, 1950; The Young Emperor (novel) 1950; The Fathers of the Western Church, 1951; Red Lion Inn, 1951; The Marshall Story, 1951; The Blue Negro, 1951; Red Storm over Asia, 1951; libretto for opera "Open the Gates" produced by Blackfriars Theatre, N.Y.C., 1951: The Great God Pan (study of Charlie Chaplin), 1952, Journey to Persia, 1952; Blood Royal, 1952; The Chieftain, 1953; Alexander the God, 1954; Brave Harvest, 1955; Lovers in the Sun, 1955; The Roaring Boys, 1955; A House in Peking, 1956; The Holy Fire, 1957; The Gold of Troy, 1958; The Canal Builders, 1959; The Holy Sword, 1959; The Shepherd, 1959; The White Rajahs of Sarawak, 1960; The Splendor of Greece; Hubris, 1960; Dostoyevsky; A Human Portrait, 1961; The Three Worlds of Boris Pasternak, 1961; Mao Tse-tung, Portrait of a Revolutionary, 1962; The Civil War in Spain, 1962; The Roman Triumph, 1962; Lost Treasures of the Mediterranean, 1962; The Image of Chekhov, 1963; The Splendor of Israel, 1963; Sun, Stones and Science, 1963; Ancient Greece, 1964; The Life and Death of Lenin, 1964; The Lord Jesus, 1964; The Isles of Greece, 1965; The Rise and Fall of Stalin, 1965; The Christian Centuries, 1966; The Horizon Book of Ancient Rome, 1966. Home: New York, N.Y. Died Feb. 11, 1983.

PAYNTER, RICHARD HENRY, consultant psychologist; b. Brooklyn, Mar. 27, 1890; s. Richard Henry and Catherine (Seebach) P.; A.B., Columbia, 1912, M.A., 1913, Ph.D., 1917; m. Susette Annan Johnson, Sept. 28, 1927. Psychologist legal dept. Coca Cola Co., 1915-16; asst. editorial work, Am. Mem. of Science, 1916; asst. in psychology, Columbia, 1914-17; psychologist various hosps., N.Y. City, 1920-23; chief psychologist Child Guidance Clinic No. 1, Nat. Com. Mental Hygiene, 1923-27; research psychologist Phila. Gen. Hosp., 1927-28; prof. psychology, Long Island U., 1928-44; chmn. div. of psychology and edn., 1933-44; visiting prof. psychology, Columbia U. Extension, 1934-37; summers Columbia, 1932, 44; senior personnel technician, Personnel Research Section, AGO, 1944-48; chief psychologist, mental hygiene service, New York Regional Office, Vets. Administration, since 1948. Chairman advisory com. of psychologists Board of Edn., N.Y. City, 1936-38; also cons. psychologist. Supervisor Manhattan Beach Day Camp, 1939. Psychol. examiner, U.S. Army, 1917-19; chmn. com. psychol. service in nat. defense, Metropolitan N.Y. Assn. Applied Psychology, 1940-42. Mem. A.A.A.S., Am. Psychol. Assn., Am. Assn. Applied Psychologists (v.p.; chmn. joint com. clinical, consulting and ednl. sects. and tech. com. 1937-38). Nat. Com. for Mental Hygiene, Am. Assn. Univ. Profs. Orthopsychiatric Assn., Assn. Cons. Psychologists (pres. 1932), N.Y. State Assn. Applied Psychologists, Am. Legion (past comdr. local post), Phi Sigma Kappa. Congregationalist. Mason (32 deg.). Author: A Psychological Study of Trademark Infringement, 1920; Educational Achievement of Problem Children (with Phyllis Blanchard), 1929. Co-op. editor Educational Abstracts, 1935-40; member editorial board Jour. of Consulting Psychology, 1937-42. Contbr. to psychol. jours. Home: Brooklyn, N.Y. †

PAYONZECK, JOHN AUGUST, bank executive; b. Cambridge, Mass., Oct. 7, 1936; s. Otto August and Margaret Agnes (Miskella) P.; m. Patricia Bunting, July 15, 1961; children—Susan, Jill, Steven. B.B.A., Boston Coll., 1958; student, Harvard U., 1979. Sr. v.p. adminstrn., corp. banking group Div. V, Security Pacific Nat. Bank, Los Angeles. Home: San Marino, Calif. Died Apr. 30, 1983.

PAYSON, CHARLES SHIPMAN, mfg. exec.; b. Portland, Maine, Oct. 16, 1898; s. Herbert and Sally Carroll (Brown) P.; grad. Yale, 1921; LL.B., Harvard, 1924; m. Joan Whitney, July 5, 1924 (dec. Oct. 4, 1975); children—Daniel Carroll (killed World War II), Sandra, Payne Payson Middleton, Lorinda Payson de Roulet, John Whitney; m. 2d, Virginia Kraft, Dec. 28, 1977. Past dir. Automation Industries, Inc., Armco Steel, Vitro Corp. Am. Home: Foreside, Maine. Died May 5, 1985.

PEABODY, MALCOLM ENDICOTT, clergyman; b. Danvers, Mass., June 12, 1888; s. Endicott and Fannie (Peabody) P.; ed. Groton Sch., 1900-07; Harvard, 1907-10 (A.B.); Trinity Coll., Cambridge, Eng., 1910-11; Episcopal Theol. Sch., Cambridge, Mass., 1913-16 (B.D.); D.D., Hamilton Coll., 1939; D.D., Hobart Coll., 1942; S.T.D., Syracuse U., 1943; m. Mary Elizabeth Parkman, June 19, 1916; children—Mary Endicott (Mrs. Ronald Tree), Endicott, George Lee, Samuel Parkman, Malcolm Endicott. Master, Boys School, Baguio Philippine Islands, 1911-13; ordained deacon P.E. Ch., June 10, 1916, priest, May 3, 1917; curate Grace Ch., Lawrence, Mass., 1916-17, 1919-20; rector, same, 1920-25; rector St. Paul's Ch., Chestnut Hill, Pa., 1925-38; bishop coadjutor, Diocese of Central N.Y., 1938-42, bishop from 1942. Pres. Synod of II Province P.E. Church, 1948. Member bd. of overseers of Harvard College, from 1955. Served as chaplain, Am. Red Cross, with Base Hosp. 5, 1917-18; chaplain, 102d Field Arty., 26th Div., U.S. Army, with A.E.F., 1918-19. Member National Council P.E. Ch., 1938-48; chmn. dept. religious liberty Nat. Council Chs. of Christ in Am., from 1952. †

PEABODY, W. RUSSELL, investment counsellor; b. Cambridge, Mass., Aug. 12, 1916; s. Charles Codman and Margaret (Davidson) P.; grad. St. Mark's Sch., 1935; A.B., Harvard, 1939; m. Phyllis Randolph, Apr. 1, 1944; children—Phyllis Cary, Gail Codman. Gen. partner Scudder Stevens & Clark, Boston; v.p., treas. dir. Scudder Funds Distbrs., Inc.; pres. Scudder Stevens & Clark Common Stock Fund Inc., treas., dir. Scudder Spl. Fund Inc. Served to lt. comdr. USNR, World War II. Home: Dedham, Mass. Died.*

PEACOCK, JAMES CRAIG, lawyer; b. Philadelphia, Pa., Feb. 29, 1888; s. Rev. John (D.D.) and Annie (Craig) P.; A.B., Central High Sch., Philadelphia, 1905; A.B., Princeton, 1909; LL.B., U. of Pa., 1912; m. Dorothy Hunt, Nov. 19, 1918; 1 son, John Hunt. Admitted to bar, Phila., 1912; mem. staff legislative drafting research fund of Columbia U., 1913-17, and took part in drafting much important federal and state legislation; examiner accounts in office of commr. of accounts, N.Y. City, 1915; successively sec. Excess Profits Advisors, Tax Reviewers, and of the Advisory Tax Bd., U.S. Treasury Dept., Washington, D.C., 1917-19; mgr. Washington office of Ernst & Ernst (accountants), 1919-20; sec. tax com. Nat. Industrial Conf. Bd., 1920; counsel for legislative com. Am. Inst. Accountants, 1921-22, for Nat. Council Am. Cotton Mfrs., 1920-27, also in practice of law in D.C., 1919-34; dir. Shipping Bd. Bur. of U.S. Dept. Commerce, 1934-36; pres. U.S. Shipping Bd. Merchant Fleet Corp., 1934-36; dir. Am. Bur. Shipping, 1934-36; spl. counsel U.S. Maritime Commn., 1936-37; resumed pvt. practice, 1937. Counsel Nat. Patent Planning Commn. and tech. aide Office of Scientific Research and Development, 1942; lecturer on taxation Washington College of Law, 1938-44, pres., 1945-48, trustee, 1943-54; trustee Am. U., from 1949; corporator Presbyn. Ministers Fund, from 1950. Mem. Fed., Am. bar assns., Bar Assn. D.C., Am. Law Inst. Presbyterian (trustee 1927-54). Clubs: Chevy Chase, National Press, (Washington); Lake Placid Club (Essex County, N.Y.); Cottage (Princeton); Propeller of U.S. (hon. mem.). Author: Notes on Legislative Drafting, 1961. Contbr. to Journal of Am. Bar Assn., Jour. of Am. Judicature Soc. and The Practical Lawyer. Home: Chevy Chase, Md. †

PEACOCK, STERLING ELDEN, advt. exec.; b. Phila., Oct. 12, 1888; s. Nathan R. and Anna (Laire) P.; student pub. schs., Phila., N.Y.C.; m. Lucille Gibson, Feb. 12, 1912; children—Mary Madaline, Donald Gibson, Barbara Sterling. Asst. to v.p. Street Railways Advertising Co., N.Y.C., 1910-12, sales rep, 1912-13, br. mgr., 1913-14; sales mgr. food div. Am. Linseed Corp., N.Y.C., 1914-18; mng. dir. Thomas J. Lipton Co. of Can., 1918-20; N.Y.C. rep. N.W. Ayer & Son, Inc., Phila., 1920-24, br. mgr., San Francisco, 1924-28, resident partner, Chgo., from 1928, v.p., from 1929. Mem. adv. bd. Ill. Childrens Hospital-School. Member Chgo. Better Bus. Bureau (dir.), Chicago Commons Association (dir.), Chgo. Crime Commn. Republican. Presbyn. Clubs: Union League, Chicago, Chicago Federated Advertising (Chgo.); Westmoreland Country (Wilmette, Ill). Home: Chicago, Ill. †

PEARCE, ROBERT E., banker; b. Bellefontaine, O., Aug. 18, 1889; s. Harry and Emma (Colton) P.; B.C.S., New York U., 1915; m. Margaret Clark, Nov. 1, 1916; 1 dau., Alice (Mrs. John J. Rox). Asso. with Nat. City Bank of N.Y. from 1915, sub-mgr. branches in Antwerp and Brussels, Belgium, 1919-21, mgr., Antwerp, 1921-23, mgr. Bussels, 1923-31, mng. dir. Paris, France, 1931-41, v.p., 1942, in London and Paris, 1943-46, v.p. and dep. mgr., head office overseas div. from 1946. Decorated; Order of the Crown (Belgium); Legion of Honor, Order of Merit, Commercial Class (France), Mem. Am. C. of C. in France. Republican. Methodist. Clubs: American, Travellers (Paris). Home: N.Y. City. †

PEARDON, THOMAS PRESTON, coll. prof.; b. Charlottetown, Prince Edward Island, Can., Oct. 24, 1899; s. Thomas Edwards and Christine Marjorie (Rose) P.; A.B., U. B.C., 1921; A.M., Clark U., 1922; student Cornell U., 1922-23; Ph.D., Columbia, 1933; m. Celeste Comegys, June 4, 1926; 1 son, Thomas P. Fellow in history Clark U., 1921-22; reader in English history Cornell U., 1922-23; instr. history Barnard Coll., Columbia, 1923-30, instr. govt., 1931-35, asst. prof. govt., 1935-42, asso. prof., 1942-45, prof. 1945-66, associate dean of the faculty, 1950-53, dean 1953-59, William Bayard Cutting fellow, Columbia, 1929-30, mem. Am. Hist. Assn., Am. Polit. Sci. Assn., Canadian Hist. Assn. Club: Century (N.Y.C.). Author: The Transition in English Historical Writing 1760-1830, 1933. Mng. editor Polit. Sci. Quarterly, 1958-63. Home: New York, N.Y.; also Bridgewater, Conn. Died May 6, 1985.

PEARKES, GEORGE RANDOLPH, Canadian govt. ofcl.; b. Watford, Eng., Feb. 26, 1888; s. George and Louise (Blair) P.; student Berkhamsted Sch., Eng.; grad. Brit. Army Staff Coll., 1919, Imperial Defence Coll., 1937; LL.D., U. B.C.; m. Constance Blytha, Sept. 25, 1925; 1 son, John Andre. Came to Can., 1906. Served with Royal Northwest Mounted Police in Yukon, then pvt. Canadian Mounted Rifles, Victoria, B.C., 1915; commd. acting lt. CEF, 1916, advanced through grades to major general Canadian Army, 1940; officer Princess Patricia's Canadian Light Inf.; staff various hdqrs., dir. mil. tng. and staff duties Army Hdqrs., 1935; comdg. officer 2d Canadian Inf. Brigade, 1939, 1st Div., 1940; gen. officer comdg. Pacific Command, 1942-45; minister nat. def., mem. Privy Council, 1957-60; lieutenant governor of B.C., Can., from 1960. Decorated Victoria Cross, 1917, Mons Star, Companion Order of Bath, Distinguished Service Order, Mil. Cross; Croix de Guerre (France); Officer Legion of Merit (U.S.). Progressive Conservative. Mem. Church of Eng. Club: Union (Victoria). Address: Victoria, B.C., Can. †

PEARNE, JOHN FREDERICK, lawyer; b. Los Angeles, June 13, 1912; s. Irving V. and Anna (Kwis) P.; B.S. in Mech. Engring., Calif. Inst. Tech., 1934; J.D., George Washington U., 1940; m. Jean C. Macklin, Dec. 3, 1938; children—Sally Ann, John C., Dennis H. Engr., Babcock & Wilcox Co., 1934-35; spl. agt. Pacific Nat. Fire Ins. Co., Los Angeles, 1935-36; admitted to D.C. bar, 1941, Ohio bar, 1955; examiner U.S. Patent Office, Washington, 1936-42; patent counsel Sherwin-Williams Co., Cleve., 1942-44, 46-48; practiced in Cleve., from 1949; sr. partner firm Pearne, Gordon, Sessions, McCoy & Granger, from 1964. Served to lt. USNR, 1944-46. Mem. Am., Ohio bar assns., Am., Cleve (pres. 1967-68) patent law assns. Home: Fripp Island, S.C. Died Sept. 6, 1981.

PEARSON, DONALD WILLIAM, telephone co. exec.; b. Rochester, N.Y., Mar. 1, 1924; s. Frank William and Marian Ann (Luckman) P.; m. Edna David, Feb. 1, 1947; children—Donna Pearson Werner, Michael, Mark, Steven. B.S. in Bus. Adminstrn, U. Rochester, 1951. With Rochester Telephone Corp., N.Y., from 1953, dept. head computer ops., 1965-67, controller, 1967-70, v.p. adminstrn., 1970-75, v.p. fin., treas., sec., from 1975; dir. Central Trust Co. Mem. exec. bd. Otetiana council Boy Scouts Am.; past bd. dirs. Assn. for Blind of Rochester and Monroe County, N.Y.; mem. Com. to Re-evaluate County Govt., 1969-72. Served with USMC, 1942-46. Decorated Purple Heart. Mem. U.S. Ind. Telephone Assn. (investor relations com.), Nat. Assn. Accountants (past dir.), Fin. Execs. Inst., Rochester Soc. Security Analysts, Am. Soc. Corporate Secs., Better Bus. Bur. Rochester and Monroe County (dir., past chmn. bd.), Rochester C. of C. Republican. Lutheran. Club: City Midday (N.Y.C.). Home: Fairport, NY.

PEARSON, FRANK ASHMORE, prof. agrl. economics; b. Topeka, Kan., Dec. 31, 1887; s. Elmer Grant and Annie Victor (Ogden) P.; U. of Ill., 1912-20; Harvard, 1921; B.S.A., Cornell U., 1912, Ph.D., 1922; m. Amelia P. Feldkamp, Aug. 4, 1915; children—Raymond, Frank Ashmore, III. Asst., first asst. and asso. in dairy husbandry, later asst. chief of dairy husbandry, U. Ill., 1912-20; instr. in farm mgmt. Cornell, 1920-22, asst. prof., 1922-23, prof., 1923-60, emeritus. Republican. Presbyn. Author: Wholesale Prices for 135 Years, 1932. Author or co-author numerous books relating to field since 1924; latest publ.: Prices of Dairy Products and Other Livestock Products (with E. E. Vial), 1946. Home: Ithaca, N.Y. †

PEARSON, JOHN WALTER, research adminstr.; b. Concord, N.H., Nov. 7, 1888; s. Edward Nathan and Addie Maria (Sargent) P.; A.B., Dartmouth Coll., 1911, M.A., 1940; m. Margaret Withey, July 3, 1917; 1 son, Edward Withey. Investment banking, 1912-33; dir. N. H. Foundation, 1934-36; New England dir. U.S. Social Security Bd., 1936-40; exec. dir. Dartmouth Eye Institute, 1940-46; mng. trustee Hanover Inst., 1946-49; exec. dir. Inst. for Asso. Research, Princeton, N.J., 1949-54; staff asso. U.S. Senator Flanders (Vt.), from 1953. Trustee U. of N.H., 1928-36, N.H. Hist. Soc., 1928-38; mem. N.H. Recess Tax Commn., 1927-30; mem. bd. dirs. N.H. Citizens Council for Gen. Welfare. Served as ensign, U.S. N.R.F., 1917-19. Conglist. Author: Death and Taxes (Atlantic Monthly) 1949. Editor: Internat. Public Opinion Poll Digest, 1953-54. Home: Hanover, N.H. †

PEARSON, MADISON, army officer; b. Dadeville, Ala., Jan. 12, 1890; commd. 2d lt. Inf., May 1917, and advanced through the grades to brig. gen., Dec. 1942; with 2d Armored Div., Ft. Knox, Ky., 1940-41, then transferred to hdqrs., Armored Force; assigned to Office of the Adjt. Gen., Washington, D.C., June-Nov. 1941; became mem. of Adjt. Gen's. Bd., Nov. 1941; dep. dir. Administrative Services, Services of Supply, Washington, D.C., June 1942; comdg. gen., Pine Camp, N.Y., Sept. 1943, Fort Dix, N.J., Feb. 1944. Awarded Distinguished Service Medal, Purple Heart, Silver Star citation, and Montenegrin Order of Prince Danile 1st (Commander 2d Class), World War I.†

PECHSTEIN, LOUIS AUGUSTUS, psychologist, educator; b. Clinton, Mo., Oct. 30, 1888; s. Otto Augustus and Elizabeth Dorothy (Banta) P.; Ped.B., State Normal Sch., Warrensburg, Mo., 1908; B.S., U. of Mo., 1912; Ph.D., U. of Chicago, 1916; m. Chloe Harlan, May 30, 1909; children—Elizabeth Dorothy, Louis Augustus, Richard Fuller. Asst. prof. psychology and edn., 1916-19, prof. and head of dept., 1919-22. U. of Rochester, also dir. div. of extension teaching and summer sch.; prof. and dean, Coll. of Edn., U. of Cincinnati, from 1922, dir. summer school, 1925-47, dean emeritus from 1947; educational consultant Cincinnati Board Education from 1937. Member National Committee on Education and Defense, 1940; chairman Cincinnati Civilian Defense Council, 1942; administrative director of war programs, University of Cincinnati, 1942. Commissioned 1st lieutenant Sanitary Corps, United States Army, Mar. 10, 1918; capt. Nov. 10, 1918; successively instr. Sch. Mil. Psychology, Camp Greenleaf, Ga., chief psychol. examiner Gen. Hosp., Ft. McPherson, Ga., chief of ednl. service, Gen. Hosp., II, Cape May, N.J., and Gen. Hosp. 10, Parker Hill, Boston; hon. disch. Feb. 22, 1919. Fellow A.A.A.S. (v.p.; chmn. sect. Q, 1924); mem. N.E.A. (pres. city training sch. sect. 1924), Am. Psychology Assn., Coll. Teachers of Edn., (in charge 20th Year Book; pres. 1939, 40), Nat. Council of Edn. (pres. 1937-44), Nations Schools (adv. com.), Assn. Municipal Teachers Colleges (president 1939-40), vice-president, American Council on Education, 1942-43; Phi Delta Kappa, Sigma Chi, Kappa Delta Pi, Sigma Xi, Sigma Delta Epsilon. Author: Whole vs. Part Methods in Motor Learning, 1917; (with A. L. McGregor) Psychology of the Junior High School Pupil, 1924; (with Francis Jenkins) Psychology of the Kindergarten-Primary Child, 1927; also numerous articles and reviews on psychol. and ednl. topics. Home: Cincinnati. †

PECK, ALEXANDER WELLS, business exec.; b. N.Y.C., Oct. 20, 1888; s. George Farmer and Mary Wells (Ferguson) P.; LL.B., Yale, 1911; m. Catherine R. Root, June 30, 1937; children—Alexander Wells, George Terhune. With Peck & Peck, N.Y.C., from 1905, pres., 1927-55, chmn. bd., 1955-70. Mem. bd. N.Y. Tb and Health Assn.; mem. bd. mgrs. Am. Soc. Prevention Cruelty to Animals, N.Y.C. Clubs: Yale, Anglers (N.Y.C.); University (Chgo.); Sanctum, Marshepang Forest (Litchfield). Home: New York, NY. †

PECK, FRANKLIN BRUCE, SR., physician; b. Remington, Ind., Sept. 26, 1898; s. Frank L. and May (Tedford) P.; m. Lisbeth C. Roeder, Sept. 18, 1924; children—Franklin Bruce, Elizabeth L. (Mrs. Harry Carlson). A.B. in Physiology, Ind. U., 1920; M.D., Jefferson Med. Coll., Phila., 1923. Asst. in physiology Ind. U., 1919-20; resident physician Jefferson Med. Coll., 1923-25; clin. asst. diabetes clinic Grace Hosp., Detroit, 1927-30, assoc. physician, 1930-32, physician in charge, 1932-35; staff Lilly Research Labs., Indpls., 1936-40, assoc. dir. med. div., 1940-46, dir., 1946-52, dir. med. research coop., 1953-58, dir. clin. research internat., 1958-61, spl. adviser diabetes dept., clin. research div., 1961-71; assoc. medicine Ind. U. Sch. Med., 1943-49, asst. prof., 1949-51, assoc. prof., from 1951; physician Indpls. Gen. Hosp., 1942-50, cons. medicine, 1950-65, pres. staff, 1951; cons. White County Meml. Hosp., 1961-65. Contbr. articles relating to diabetes, new insulin modifications to prof. jours. Organizing mem. Internat. Diabetes Fedn., Brussels, 1949, Am. Diabetes Assn.; del., Dusseldorf, 1958; hon. pres. Indpls. Diabetes Assn. Served with U.S. Army, 1918. Recipient Davis prize Jefferson Med. Coll., 1923; named Academician of Honor Acad. Medicine and Surgery Panama, 1957, Banting medal, 1961. Fellow ACP; mem. Am. Diabetes Assn. (mng. editor jour. 1942-52, chmn. sci. publs. com., sec. 1955-58, pres. 1960-61), AMA; hon. mem. numerous fgn. med. socs., diabetes assns. Home: Indianapolis, Ind. Died Sept. 22, 1982.

PECK, GIRVAN, lawyer; b. N.Y.C., Nov. 30, 1923; s. Laurence Freeman and Clara Temple (Boardman) P.; m. Nancy Mailliard, Jan. 5, 1966; children: Natalie, Laurence F., Christie B., Sheila, Alexander M. B.A., Yale U., 1946, LL.B., 1949. Bar: N.Y. 1950, Calif. 1952. Assoc. firm Debevoise Plimpton & McLean, N.Y.C., 1949-50; asst. counsel Bank of Am., San Francisco, 1952-54; assoc. firm Morrison Foerster Holloway Clinton & Clark, San Francisco, 1954-60; ptnr. firm Morrison & Foerster, San Francisco, 1961-83. Author: Writing Persuasive Briefs, 1984. Bd. dirs. Katherine Branson Sch., 1963-68, Youth Law Center, 1974-84, San Francisco Bail Project, 1978-80, San Francisco Neighborhood Legal Assistance Found., 1983-84. Served as navigator USAAF, 1943-45. Mem. Am. Bar Assn., Bar Assn. San Francisco (dir. 1972-73), Am. Law Inst., Phi Delta Phi. Republican. Club: Lagunitas Country (Ross, Calif.). Home: San Francisco, Calif. Died May 16, 1984.

PECK, LEROY EUGENE, newspaper publisher; b. Rugby, N.D., May 16, 1922; s. LeRoy Ellsworth and Elvira (Sostrom) P.; m. Margaret Elizabeth MacFadyen, June 29, 1946; children—John Christopher, Elizabeth Ann, David Harroun, James MacFadyen. B.A. in Journalism, U. Wyo., 1944. Track coach, dir. athletic pub. U. Wyo., 1946-49; co-pub. Riverton (Wyo.) Ranger, from 1949, Kemmerer (Wyo.) Gazette, 1962—, Powell (Wyo.) Tribune, from 1964, Lovell (Wyo.) Chronicle, from 1971, Thermopolis Ind. Record, from 1978, Star Valley Ind., from 1978, Basin Republican-Rustler, from 1979; v.p., dir. Morning Star Dairy, Inc., Riverton, 1953-72, Allied Nuclear Corp., 1957-68, Western Standard Corp., 1958-68, pres., from 1968. Exec. dir. Wyo. Dept. Econ. Planning and Devel., 1967-70; a founder Wyo. Mining Assn., 1956; founder Wyo. Sugar Council, 1963; chmn. com. which started Wyo. Indsl. Devel. Corp., Riverton Indsl. Com., 1955-67; chmn. natural resources council Fedn. Rocky Mountain States, 1966-77; Republican primary candidate for Congress, 1966, for Gov., 1974; mem. Wyo. Ho. of Reps., 1970-74, Wyo. Senate, from 1977; Chmn. bd. dirs. Wyo. Blue Cross, 1967-73; trustee U. Wyo., 1953-65. Served to capt., inf. AUS, 1943-46. Decorated Bronze Star, Silver Star; Croix de Guerre France).; Recipient Distinguished Service award Wyo. Kiwanis, 1965; Indsl. Leadership award Wyo. Assn. Realtors, 1967. Mem. Wyo. Press Assn. (pres. 1956), Sigma Delta Chi, Alpha Tau Omega. Methodist. Club: Mason. Home: Riverton, Wyo.

PECK, RALPH E., chem. engr.; b. Herbert, Saskatchewan, Can., Dec. 8, 1910; s. Percy Robert and Hattie Gertrude (Lightizer) P.; B.S. in Chem. E. with distinction, U. Minn., 1932, Ph.D., 1936; m. Joyce Elizabeth Mullen, Aug. 27, 1936; children—Keith A., Bruce G., Gail A. Instr. chem. engring. Drexel Inst., 1936-39; instr. chem. engring. Ill. Inst. Tech 1939-41, asst. prof., 1941-45, asso. prof., 1945-50, prof. chem. engring., 1950-82, chmn. dept., 1953-68. Dir. Auburn Highland YMCA. Mem. Am. Inst. Chem. Engrs., Am. Soc. Engring. Edn., Am. Assn. U. Profs., Am. Chem. Soc., Sigma Xi, Tau Beta Pi, Phi Lambda Upsilon, Alpha Chi Sigma. Contbr. articles profl. publs. Home: Chicago, Ill. Died Nov. 6, 1982.

PECK, RAYMOND ELLIOTT, educator; b. Hamilton, Mo. May 3, 1904; s. Frank Sherrard and Olive (Newton) P.; A.B., Park Coll., Parkville, Mo., 1926; A.M., U. Mo., 1928, Ph.D., 1932; m. Vaona Olive Hedrick, Oct. 13, 1929. Asst. geologist Mo. Hwy. Commn., 1929-30; faculty geology U. Mo., 1930-71, prof., 1947-71, prof. emeritus, 1971-84, chmn. dept. geology, 1950-59, asso. dean grad. sch., asst. to pres. for research, 1961-63, dean research adminstrn., 1963-65, v.p. research, 1965-69; spl. asst. to chancellor U. Mo., St. Louis, 1969-70. Prof. geology Am. Shrinvenham U., Eng., 1945; geologist U.S. Geol. Survey; geologist Shell Oil Co., summers 1956-58. Mem. Gov.'s Sci. Adv. Com., 1962-71. Served from 1st lt. to maj. USAAF Tng. Command. 1942-46. Fulbright award U. Paris, 1950-51. Fellow Geol. Soc. Am. (councilor 1963-66), Paleontol. Soc. Am.; mem. Am. Inst. Profl. Geologists, Soc. Econ. Paleontologists and Mineralogists (sec.-treas. 1958-59), Assn. Mo. Geologists (pres. 1957), Sigma Xi. Methodist. Contbr. articles to publs. Co-editor Jour. Paleontology, 1969-74. Home: Columbia, Mo. Died Nov. 3, 1984

PECK, SEYMOUR, newspaper editor; b. N.Y.C., Aug. 23, 1917; s. Louis and Henrietta (Kazurer) P.; m. Susan Lustig, June 6, 1958; children—Patricia, Louis, Nora, Amelia. B.A., CCNY, 1948. Reporter, critic The Newspaper PM, N.Y.C., 1942-48; film critic, arts editor The Daily Compass, N.Y.C., 1949-52; assoc. editor N.Y. Times Book Rev., N.Y.C., 1952-85. Mem. nominating com. Antoinette Perry Awards. Home: Hastings on Hudson, N.Y. Died Jan. 1, 1985.

PECKINPAH, DAVID SAMUEL, (SAM PECKINPAH) motion picture dir.; b. Fresno, Calif., Feb. 21, 1925; s. David Edward and Fern (Chruch) P.; m. Cecilia M. Selland, July 17, 1947 (div. Mar. 1962); children—Sharon, Kristen, Melissa, Matthew. B.A., Fresno State Coll., 1947; M.A., U. So. Calif., 1949. Author, dir.: TV series Rifleman, 1960; author, producer, dir.: TV series Westerner, 1958; also: TV series Klondike; dir.: TV series Deadly Companions, 1961, Ride the High Country, 1962 (Belgian Best Film award), Ballad of Cable Hogue, 1970 (Madrid Best Film award), Junior Bonner, 1972, The Getaway, 1972, Pat Garrett and Billy the Kid, 1973, Convoy, 1978; co-author, dir.: TV series Major Dundee, 1965, The Wild Bunch, 1969, Straw Dogs, 1971; author, dir.: TV series Bring Me the Head of Alfredo Garcia, 1974, The Killer Elite, 1975, Cross of Iron, 1977. Served with USMCR, 1943-46. Mem. Dirs. Guild Am., Writers Guild Am., Acad. Motion Picture Arts and Scis. Home: San Angel, Mexico. Died Dec. 28, 1984.

PEELE, TALMAGE LEE, physician; b. Goldsboro, N.C., Aug. 16, 1908; s. Ichabod and Nora (Spence) P.; A.B., Duke U., 1929; postgrad. Sch. Medicine, Vanderbilt U., 1929-31; M.D., Duke U., 1934. Intern Duke U. Hosp., 1934-35, resident in medicine, 1935-36; resident in neurology Bellevue Hosp., 1936-37; research fellow Johns Hopkins Hosp., 1937-38; asso. anatomy U. Rochester, 1938-39; practice medicine specializing in neurology, 1947-81; faculty Duke U., Durham, N.C., 1939-81, asso. prof. neurology, 1963-73, prof. neurology, 1973-81, asst. prof. pediatrics, 1958—, lectr. psychology, 1958-81; vis. prof. neuroanatomy Northwestern U., 1945; lectr. neurology U. N.C., 1947-50; vis. asst. prof., 1955. Recipient Golden Apple award Duke U. Sch. Medicine Students and Alumni, 1965, Distinguished Tchr. award, 1975. Mem. AMA, Am. Acad. Neurology, Med. Soc. N.C., Cajal Club, Duke Med. Alumni Assn. (sec. 1947-67), Phi Beta Kappa, Alpha Omega Alpha. Methodist. Author: Neuroanatomic Basis for Clinical Neurology, 3d edit., 1977. Contbr. articles to profl. jours. Home: Durham, N.C. Died Sept. 11, 1981.

PEERCE, JAN, tenor; b. N.Y.C.; children: Larry, Joyce, Susan. Hon. doctorates, N.Y. Coll. Music, Yeshiva U. Studied violin and played in orchs., debut as tenor with, NBC Symphony under Toscanini; appeared on: Radio City Music Hall broadcasts; leading roles in Italian operas, Met., San Francisco opera cos; Broadway debut Fiddler on the Roof, 1971; summer tours, 1972—, Rothschilds, 1971-74; concertizes extensively in summer tours, U.S., Can., Europe, Mexico, C.Am., Australia, S.Am., Israel, Eng., Austria, Germany, under auspices, Dept. State on tour in, Russia (voted favorite male singer in poll of critics), participated, Osaka (Japan) Festival, concert tour, Alaska, S. Africa, Australia; recitals, soloist with, Philharmonic orchs. in, Sweden, Norway, West Germany, Holland, Israel, 1972, golden anniversary recital, Carnegie Hall, 1980; starred in 4 motion pictures; operatic debut, Vienna Opera, State Opera Munich, 1970, European and Israel festivals of opera and concerts, 1968, recs. for, RCA Victor, Westminster, Vanguard, United Artists; appears on: TV shows Mike Douglas, PBS Over Easy; spl. shows over all networks.; Biography: Bluebird of Happiness, 1976. Recipient Tarbut medal, Mt. Scopus award, Handel medallion City of N.Y. Died Dec. 15, 1984.

PEERS, WILLIAM RAYMOND, army officer; b. Stuart, Ia., June 14, 1914; s. Harry D. and Milfred (Stigers) P.; student U. Cal. at Los Angeles, 1933-37; grad. Army War Coll., 1953; m. Barbara Browne, Oct. 7, 1939; children—Barbara Anne, Christina; m. 2d, Rose Mary Rau, Jan. 1, 1953. Commd. 2d lt., U.S. Army, 1938, advanced through grades to lt. gen., 1968; operations officer OSS, Burma, 1942, 43, comdr. Detachment 101 1944-45, dep. dir. China Theater, 1945; intelligence instr. Command and Gen. Staff Coll., Fort Leavenworth 1946-49; dir. CIA tng., 1950-51; assigned intelligence Dept. Army overseas, 1951-52; mem. Army Gen. Staff for Operations, 1953-56, Hdqrs. U.S. Forces Europe, 1956-57; comdr. 1st Battle Group, 5th Inf. in Germany, 1957-59; exec. sec. Weapons Systems Evaluation Group, Washington, 1959-61; head liaison group, joint strategic targets, planning staff Joint Chiefs Staff, 1962-63; asst. div. comdr. 4th Inf. Div., Fort Lewis, Wash., 1963-64; asst. dep. chief staff mil. operations for spl. operations, spl. asst. to chief staff spl. warfare activities, also sr. Army rep. Inter-Am. Def. Bd., 1964-66; spl. asst. for counter insurgency and spl. activities Joint Chiefs Staff, 1966-67; comdg. gen. 4th Inf. Div., U.S. Army, Vietnam, 1967-68; dep. comdg. gen. I Field Force, Nha Trang, Vietnam, 1968-69; chief Office Res. Components, Hdqrs., Dept. Army, Washington, 1969-84. Decorated D.S.M. with 2 oak leaf clusters, Silver Star, Legion of Merit with 2 oak leaf clusters, D.F.C., Bronze Star with cluster, Air Medal with 17 clusters, Presdl. Distinguished Unit citation, Chinese Order of Cloud and Banner, Vietnamese Nat. Order Fifth Class, Vietnamese Gallantry Cross with Palm, Korean Order Mil. Merit, Chung Mu and Eulgi. Mem. Assn. U.S. Army, Blue Key, Sigma Pi (pres. chpt. 1936-37). Author: (with Brelis) Behind the Burma Road, 1963. Contbr. to mil. publs. Home: Ft. Myer, Va. Died Apr. 6, 1984.

PEIXOTTO, EUSTACE M., army officer; b. San Francisco, Calif., July 29, 1887; s. Raphael and Myrtilla Jessica (Davis) P.; B.L., U. of Calif., 1908; m. Catharine Augusta Dishman, Oct. 3, 1925; children—James M., Roland E., Ernest D. Amateur sports writer San Francisco Examiner, 1908-10; athletic dir., sec. Pub. Schs. Athletic League of San Francisco, 1910-17; sec. Recreation League of San Francisco, 1919-20. Served as 2d and 1st lieut., inf., U.S. Army, 1917-18, appointed 1st lieut. inf., regular army, 1920, advanced through grades to brig. gen., 1947, served in adjutant gen.'s dept. from 1941, as asst. chief and chief. recruiting service, 1941-42, chief inspection and investigation, dir. of control div., Asst. to the adjutant gen. for mgt., 1943-47; for physical disability, 1948. Decorated Legion of Merit. Mem. Phi Beta Kappa. Author: Ten Boys' Farces, 1916. Address: Washington, D.C. †

PELGRIFT, DELANCEY, lawyer; b. Brooklyn, Nov. 29, 1889; s. Samuel L. and Kate (Brown) P.; student Poly. Prep. Sch., Bklyn., 1902-06, Dickinson Coll., 1906-09; LL.M., St. Lawrence U., 1912; m. Anne MacKinnon, Feb. 2, 1921; children—Robert Y., Nancy F. (Mrs. Bradford M. Cogswell). Admitted to N.Y. bar, 1913, Conn. bar, 1915; trial and appellate counsel Md. Casualty Co., Hartford, Conn., 1920-34; partner firm Pelgrift, Dodd & Stoughton, Hartford. Served as petty officer in U.S.N.R.F., World War I. Fellow Am. Coll. Trial Lawyers; mem. Assn. Bar City N.Y., Am. Conn. State bar assns., Internat. Assn. Ins. Counsel, S.A.R., Sigma Alpha Epsilon, Phi Delta Phi. Conglist. Mason. Clubs: University, City, Avon Country. Home: West Hartford, Conn. †

PELKOFER, JOHN, labor union ofcl.; b. Milwaukee, July 16, 1887; s. John and Anna (Felzen) P.; student pub. and parochial schs. of Milwaukee; m. Clara Mading, May 19, 1909; 1 dau., Dolores (Mrs. Antony Krolski). Successively blacksmith helper, apprentice, blacksmith, hammersmith, C., M., St. P. & P. R.R., 1902-16; elected gen. chmn. system council 10, Internat. Brotherhood of Blacksmiths, Drop Forgers and Helpers, 1916, apptd. internat. rep., 1929, gen. v.p., 1932, gen. pres. from 1946; mem. exec. council Ry. Employees Dept., A.F. of L. from 1946, 4th v.p., Metal Trades Dept. from 1950. Mem. Ry. Labor Execs. Assn., C.O.F. No. Woodman, Eagle. Editor of Anvil Chorus (publ. blacksmiths orgn.) since 1948. Home: Milwaukee, Wis. †

PELL, HAMILTON, partner Pell & Co.; b. New York, N.Y., Mar. 22, 1888; s. George Hamilton and Alice Josephine (Bates) P.; ed. Cutler Sch.; m. Emma Johnson Steele, Mar. 11, 1935. Began with the McVickar Trust Co., 1902; with R. G. Whittemore & Co.; later partner Whittemore, Pell & Co.; partner Hamilton Pell & Co.; partner Baker, Carruthers & Pell, 1915-21; partner Carruthers, Pell & Co., 1921; partner Sloane, Pell & Co., 1922-24; v.p. W. A. Harriman & Co., Inc., 1924-30; v.p.

G. E. Barrett & Co., Inc., 1930-32; partner Schatzkin, Pell & Co., 1933; partner Pell & Co., N.Y. City, from 1934; chmn. bd., mem. of exec. com. Compo Shoe Machinery Corp.; chmn. bd. and exec. comm. U.S. Vitamin Co., Acony Corp. (v.p. and dir.); dir. Directory of Directors, Profl. Labs., Inc. (chmn. board), Fidel Assn. N.Y., Inc. (chmn. bd.), Pell, Ltd. (president), Certainteed Products Corp., Ambrook Industries, Wood Newspaper Corp. Clubs: Seminole Golf, The Recess, St. Nicholas, St. Nicholas Soc., Everglades, Bath and Tennis, Sewanee, Atlantic Beach. Home: Palm Beach, Fla. †

PELLA, GIUSEPPE, fgn. minister of Italy; b. Valdengo, Piedmont, Italy, Apr. 18, 1902; s. Luigi and Vigllelma (Bona) P.; ed. U. Turin; m. Ines Cardolle, 1935; 1 dau., Wanda. Formerly prof. banking U. Turin; traveled throughout Europe as wool salesman and cons., connected with textile mfg., later became banker; resigned all bus. directorships upon entering govt. work, 1946; rep. of Christian Democrat Party to Constituent Assembly, 1946; under-sec. finance (cabinet of Alcide de Gasperf), 1946, minister of finance, 1947, treasury minister, 1952; minister of the budget, 1948-53; premier fgn. minister and minister of budget, 1953-57; pres. assembly European Steel and Coal Community, 1957; also gov. Internat. Monetary Fund; vice premier minister for fgn. affairs, 1957-58. Minister fgn. affairs, 1958-60, minister of budget, from 1960. Died May 31, 1981.

PELLETIER, WILFRID, symphony condr.; b. Montreal, Que., Can., June 20, 1896; s. Elzear and Zelire P.; m. Rose Bampton, May 24, 1937; children—Camille, Francois. Began study of piano at age 7; won Province of Quebec prize for European study, 1914; in Paris studied piano with, Isidore Philipp, 1915; harmony with, Rousseau; composition with, Widor; opera tradition with, Bellaigue; Mus.D. (hon.), U. Montreal, 1936, U. Ottawa, Laval U., U. Alta., N.Y. Coll. Music; H.H.D., Hobart Coll. With Met. Opera Assn., N.Y.C., 1917-50. Beginning asst. condr. French and Italian repertoire; condr., Ravinia Opera Co., Chgo., 1920, San Francisco Opera Co., for 10 years, N.Y. Philharmonic Childrens Concerts, 1953-56, orchs. on several radio programs; dir.: Met. Opera Auditions of the Air, 12 yrs; founder, dir., Conservatoire de Musique et Art Dramatic, Montreal, 1942-61; dir. musique: Ministere des Affaires Cultureles, Quebec, P.Q., 1961-69; dir., L'Orchestre Symphonique de Quebec.; Author: memoirs Une Symphonie inachevée, 1973. Decorated Companion of Can. Govt. Can.; Legion d'Honneur France; Comdr. St. Michael and St. George Eng.; Christian Den Tiendes Friheds Meds Denmark). Home: New York, N.Y. Died Apr. 9, 1982.

PELTZ, MARY ELLIS, archivist; b. N.Y.C., May 4, 1896; d. Leonard E. and Edith (Bell) Opdycke; student Chapin Sch., 1906-11, Spence Sch., 1911-15; A.B., Barnard Coll., 1920; m. John DeWitt Peltz, June 6, 1924; children—John DeWitt, Henry S., Mary Ellis Nevius. Employed as asst. music critic N.Y. Evening Sun, 1920-24; pres. Jr. League City of N.Y., 1928-30, arts and interest dir. Assn. Jr. Leagues Am., 1930-32; publs. dir. Met. Opera Guild, 1935-57; founder, editor Opera News, 1936-57; archivist Met. Opera Assn., after 1957, v.p. Bar Harbor (Maine) Hist. Soc. Bd. dirs. Mt. Desert Island Hosp., Jesup Meml. Library, Bar Harbor. Mem. Jr. League of N.Y.C. Club: Colony (N.Y.C.). Author: American Poems, The Plowshare, 1934; The Metropolitan Opera Guide (with Robert Lawrence), 1939; Spotlight on the Stars, 1943; Your Metropolitan Opera, 1945; Behind the Gold Curtain, 1950, Accents on Opera (with Boris Goldovsky), 1953; The Magic of the Opera, published in 1960, others. Editor: Opera Lover's Companion, 1948; Introduction to Opera, 1956. Died Oct. 24, 1981.

PEMBERTON, JOHN DE JARNETTE, surgeon; b. Wadesboro, N.C., May 3, 1887; s. John de Jarnette and Emma Marshall (Lilly) P.; A.B., U. of N.C., 1907, LL.D., 1932; M.D., U. of Pa., 1911; M.S. in surgery, U. of Minn., 1918; m. Anna T. Hogeland, June 4, 1918; children—John de Jarnette, Albert Hogeland, Henry Walter, Robert Gray, Elizabeth Anne. Intern Episcopal Hosp., Phila., 1911-13; intern Mayo Clinic, Rochester, Minn., 1913-14, asst. in surgery, 1914-18, surgeon since 1918; also prof. surgery, Mayo Foundation Grad. Sch., U. of Minn., from 1936. First lt. Med. R.C., World War. Fellow Am. Coll. Surgeons; mem. A.M.A., Am. Surg. Assn., Soc. Clin. Surgery, Southern Surg. Assn., Minn. State Med. Assn., Am. Assn. for Study of Goiter (pres. 1941-42), Southern Minn. Med. Assn., Internat. Soc. of Surgery, Am. Bd. of Surgery, Alpha Tau Omega, Nu Sigma Nu, Alpha Omega Alpha, Sigma Xi. Democrat. Episcopalian. Clubs: University, Country. Contbr. on gen. surgery and surgery of thyroid gland. Home: Rochester, Minn. †

PENDER, THOMAS MILLISON, clergyman; b. Lebanon, Ill., Feb. 11, 1888; s. Rev. Jacob Thomas and Martha E. (Hanner) P.; A.B., U. of Pittsburgh, 1910, D.D., 1929; B.D., Drew U., 1927; A.M., Columbia, 1918; Ph.D., Webster U., 1935; m. Jessie Florence Jarrett, June 17, 1913 (dec.); 1 dau., Mary Elizabeth. Ordained ministry M.E. Ch., 1910; pastor Mt. Lebanon and Walton chs., Pittsburgh, 1910-14, S. Orange, N.J., 1914-25, Englewood, N.J., 1925-30, Trenton, N.J., 1930-34, St. James Ch., Chicago, 1934-45; pastor First Ch., Waukegan, Ill., from July, 1945. Trustee Methodist Deaconess Bd., Chicago Deaconess Soc., M.E. Home for Aged, Ocean Grove, N.J., 1920-28; member Board of Education, Newark, 1915-30; mem. Newark and New Jersey conferences. Methodist Ch., 1914-34; del. to First North Central Jurisdictional Conf. of Math. Ch., 1930. Pres. of the Cathedral of the Air. Awarded first prize Intercollegiate Oratorical Contest, U. of Pittsburgh, 1910. Mem. Am. Acad. Polit. and Social Science, Acad. Polit. Science, Internat. Soc. Theta Phi. Mason (33 deg.), Rotarian. Home: Waukegan, Ill. †

PENDERGRASS, WEBSTER, ednl. adminstr.; b. Byrdstown, Tenn., Jan. 7, 1914; s. Andrew Pleasant and Maudie Mae (Bowden) P.; m. Mildred Knox Carter, June 20, 1937; 1 dau., Betty June. B.S., U. Tenn., 1936, M.S., 1947; D.P.A., Harvard, 1954. Asst. county agt., Wilson County, Tenn., 1936-37, Dickson County, 1937-39, asst. county agt., Henry County, 1940-42, county agt., 1942-44; instr. agronomy U. Tenn. Coll. Agr., 1946-47; agronomist, leader agronomy extension Agrl. Extension Service, 1947-57, dean agr., 1957-68; vice chancellor Inst. Agr., 1968-70, v.p. for agr., 1970-79, v.p. emeritus, 1979-83; Bd. dirs., v.p. internat. Fertilizer Devel. Center, 1974-80. Served from ensign to lt. USNR, 1944-46. Recipient Distinguished Service award for extension specialists Tenn. County Agts. Assn.; Man of Month award So. Seedman; Progressive Farmer Man of Year Tenn. Agr. award, 1964; citation for outstanding service to 4-H; named Hon. State Farmer Future Farmers Am. Mem. Tenn. Farm Bur. Fedn. (dir. 1957-79), Tenn. Livestock Producers (dir. 1957-74), Tenn. Edn. Assn., Assn. So. Agr. Workers (pres. 1963-64), U. Tenn. Nat. Alumni Assn. (council, pres. agrl. sec. 1959), Alpha Zeta, Phi Delta Kappa (pres. 1935-36), Phi Kappa Phi, Epsilon Sigma Phi, Gamma Sigma Delta, Omicron Delta Kappa, Phi Zeta. Mem. Christian Ch. (elder). Clubs: Block and Bridle, Rotary (pres. 1969-70, dist. gov. 1975-76). Home: Knoxville, Tenn. Died Apr. 1, 1983; buried Highland Meml. Cemetery, Knoxville.

PENGILLY, JOSEPH HILL, business exec.; born Minneapolis, June 3, 1888; s. James Lory and Abbie (Sparhawk) P.; E.E., U. of Minn., 1911; m. Edythe F. Fulton, Mar. 16, 1934. In engring. dept. Southern Calif. Edison Co., 1912-17; v.p. and treas. Square D, Inc., and predecessor cos., 1919-33; vice pres. Square D Co., Inc., 1933-36, when dissolved, v.p. and dir., Square D Co., from 1936; dir. Norris Thermador Corp., Elec. Products Corp. Col. Corps of Engrs. Res. (Ret.), Legion of Merit, World War II. Mem. Pacific Coast Elec. Assn. (past pres.), Cal. Mfrs. Assn. (dir.), Mchts. and Mfrs. Assn. Mason (Shriner). Clubs: Jonathan, Wilshire Country (Los Angeles). Home: Los Angeles, Calif. †

PENICK, SYDNOR BARKSDALE, JR., pharm. co. exec.; b. Bristol, Va., Sept. 7, 1905; s. Sydnor Barksdale and Margaret Henry (Dabney) P.; grad. Montclair Acad. 1921; A.B., Princeton, 1925; m. Mary Louise Schieren, Feb. 11, 1928; children—Sydnor Barksdale, Mary (Mrs. T.R. Burgin); m. 2d, Elizabeth Van Wie, Jan. 22, 1944; children—Douglas, Frank, Jeannette Elizabeth Penick Young, Margaret Lucy. With S.B. Penick & Co. (became div. Corn Products Co. (now CPC Internat., Inc., 1968), N.Y.C., 1925-83, v.p., dir., 1936-42, pres., 1942-60, chmn., 1960-70, hon. chmn., 1970-83, also dir., mem. exec. com. CPC Internat., Inc.; dir. Am. Nat. Bank & Trust (N.J.). Charter trustee Princeton U., 1952-76, trustee emeritus, 1976-83; trustee Montclair YMCA; bd. dirs., chmn. bd. Am. Found. Pharm. Edn.; pres. Montclair Art Mus. Mem. Pharm. Mfrs. Assn. (dir., chmn. 1963-64), N.Y. Bd. Trade (chmn. drug and chem. sect. 1942), Phi Beta Kappa. Clubs: Drug and Chemical (pres. 1947), University, River, Princeton (N.Y.C.); Montclair (N.J.) Golf; Chicago; Mill Reef. Home: Montclair, N.J. Died Oct. 19, 1983.

PENN, RAYMOND J., educator; b. Morris, Minn., May 25, 1911; s. John H. and Irene (Knight) P.; B.E., State Tchrs. Coll., River Falls, Wis., 1932; Ph.D., U. Wis., 1941; m. Evelyn Volla, July 30, 1937; children—David William, John Martin, James Raymond, Mary Jean. Research assistant fellow at the University of Wisconsin, Madison, 1933-35; asst. prof., asso. prof. agrl. econ. S.D. State Coll., 1935-40; asst. regional research supervisor div. land econs., bur. agrl. econs. Dept. Agr., Lincoln, Neb., 1940-42, regional research supervisor, Albuquerque, N.M., also Milw., 1942-46; prof. econs. U. Wis. 1946-82, chmn. department, 1948-55, also director Latin America Land Tenure Research Center, 1962-65, chairman advisory committee. Served USNR, 1943-46. Mem. Am. (v.p. 1957-58), Western, Canadian farm econ. assns., Am. Assn. U. Profs., Am. Econ. Assn., Phi Kappa Phi, Alpha Zeta, Delta Theta Sigma. Home: Madison, Wis. Died May 4, 1982.

PENNEY, JAMES, artist; b. St. Joseph, Mo., Sept. 6, 1910; s. John Rice and Laura Davis (Freel) P.; m. Frances Avery, 1941 (div. 1950); 1 son, James Avery; m. Rachel Seymour Bonner, May 30, 1953. B.F.A., U. Kans., 1931; student, Art Student's League, N.Y.C., 1931-34. prof. art Hamilton Coll., N.Y., 1948-55, 56-74, Margaret Bundy Scott prof. art, 1974-76, emeritus, 1976-82; guest instr. Calif. Coll. Arts and Crafts, 1960; tchr. art Munson-Williams-Proctor Inst., 1948-55, 79-81, also; Vassar Coll. Bennington Coll., Hunter Coll., U. Kans. One-man shows, Hudson D. Walker Gallery, N.Y.C., 1939, Kraushaar Galleries, N.Y.C., 1950, 54, 57, 61, 65, 69, 74, retrospective show, Munson-Williams-Proctor Inst., Utica, N.Y., 1955, 77-82, Utica Coll., 1972; exhibited in group shows, Corcoran Gallery, Met. Mus. Art, Art Inst. Chgo., U. Ill. annuals, U. Neb., Whitney Mus. Bklyn. Mus., Carnegie Inst., St. Louis Mus., others; represented in over 40 pub. and mus. permanent collections including, Springfield (Mass.) Mus., New Britain Inst., Kans. State U., Nelson Atkins Mus., Kansas City, Des Moines Art Center., Murdock Collection, Wichita, Lehigh U., Fort Worth Art Center, Joslyn Mus., Omaha, 1967, and others; executed murals, Hamilton Coll., Flushing High Sch., N.Y.C., post offices, Union and Palmyra, Mo.; in vestibule State Capitol Bldg, Lincoln, Nebr., 1963. Recipient Kansas City Art Inst. medal, 1931; Paintings of the Year award Pepsi-Cola Co., 1948; Allbright Gallery award for graphics, 1953; purchase Hassam Fund, 1953; Audubon Artists award, 1967, 77, 78. Mem. Art Student's League N.Y.C. (life), Audubon Artists, Century Assn., Nat. Soc. Mural Painters, Am. Fedn. Art, N.A.D. Address: Clinton, N.Y. Died Aug. 1, 1982.

PENNIMAN, ABBOTT LAWRENCE, JR., engring. exec.; b. nr. Bel Air, Md., Feb. 12, 1892; s. Abbott Lawrence and Frances Risteau Owings (Griffith) P.; student Bel Air Acad., 1905-07, Balt. Poly. Inst., 1907-10; m. Ethel M. Warrington, Oct. 6, 1917 (dec. Feb. 1962). With Balt. Gas & Electric Co., 1911-60, supt. power prodn., 1913-37, gen. supt. elec. ops., 1937-59, v.p., 1950-60; engring. cons., 1960-82. Trustee Ch. Home and Hosp. Mem. Md. Radiation Control Adv. Bd., 1960—, Water Pollution Control Commn. Md., 1951-61, Md. State Bd. Health, 1943-61; mem., past chmn. Md. State Bd. Boiler Rules, from 1939; mem. Commn. for Hist. and Archtl. Preservation, 1969-76; dir. Hosp. Cost Analysis Service, Inc., 1960-66; trustee Commn. Govtl. Efficiency and Economy, Inc. (Md.), 1960-63. Recipient Karl T. Compton Modern Pioneer award, 1940; George Westinghouse gold medal, 1965. Registered profl. engr., Md., N.J., Del., N.Y. Fellow ASCE, IEEE; mem. ASME (hon.; nat. dir. 1947-51), Engring. Soc. Balt. (hon.), Nat. Soc. Profl. Engrs., Md. Hist. Soc. (chmn. bd. trustees Athenaeum 1965-73), A.A.A.S., Navy League, Naval Inst., Am. Ordnance Assn., Edison Elec. Inst. (1923-60), Newcomen Soc., Md. Acad. Scis., Braintree Hist. Soc. (hon.), Tau Beta Pi. Clubs: Univ. (hon.), Md. (Balt.). Home: Baltimore, Md. Died July 19, 1982.

PENNINGTON, WELDON JERRY, newspaper executive; b. Tacoma, Mar. 1, 1919; s. Bert Archie and Marguerite Lucille (Heraty) P.; m. Dorothy Grace Kinney, Oct. 6, 1945; children: Susan Diane Merry, Scott Brian, Sally Jane Ringman, Steven Kinney. B.A., U. Wash., 1941. Staff accountant Allen R. Smart & Co. (C.P.A.s), Seattle, 1941-42; spl. agt. FBI, 1942-46; supervising accountant Touche Ross & Co. (C.P.A.s), Seattle, 1946-51; with Seattle Times, from 1951, pres., dir., 1967-82, pres., pub., chief exec. officer, dir., from 1982; pres., dir. Walla Walla (Wash.) Union-Bull., 1971-85, Times Communications Co., 1971, Blethen Corp.; dir. Rainier Nat. Bank, Seattle, Rainier Bancorp., Paccar, Inc.; dir., chmn. fin. com. Safeco Corp.; dir. Westin Hotels, Allied Daily Newspapers., pres., 1982-85. Pres. Seattle King County Community Chest, 1959-60, Seattle King County United Good Neighbor Fund, 1962-63, Downtown Seattle Devel. Assn., 1971-72, Virginia Mason Med. Found., 1980, Corp. Council Arts, 1980; Trustee Seattle Goodwill Industries; bd. dirs. Virginia Mason Hosp.; chmn. Council for Corp. Responsibility, 1982-83; trustee, pres. Seattle Found.; Chmn. adv. bd. U. Wash. Grad. Sch. Bus., 1980-81; treas. Fifth Avenue Theatre Assn., 1981, pres., 1982-83. Named Seattle's First Citizen of 1977 Seattle-King County Bd. Realtors. Mem. Am. Inst. C.P.A.s (Elijah Watts Sells award 1941), Wash. Soc. C.P.A.s (pres. 1951-52), Assn. Former Spl. Agts. FBI, Seattle C. of C. (pres. 1964-65), Sigma Delta Chi, Beta Alpha Psi. Clubs: Rotarian (pres. Seattle 1966-67), Seattle Golf (trustee 1974-77), Rainier (pres. 1968-69), Wash. Athletic, University; Desert Island Country (Palm Springs); Useless Bay Golf and Country. Home: Seattle, Wash. Died Mar. 17, 1985.

PENROD, ESTEL BURDELL, educator; b. North Manchester, Ind., Aug. 20, 1890; s. Guilford and Lu Ella (Flohr) P.; B.S. in mech. engring., Purdue, 1915, M.S., 1920; M.M.E., Cornell, 1923; D.Sc. (honorary), Hillsdale College, 1956; married to Martha Meighan, June 22, 1933; 1 dau., Ruth Evelyn. Prof. physics Mt. Union Coll., Alliance, O., 1916-18; instr. Purdue U., 1919-20, West Res. U., 1920-22; asso. prof. physics Hillsdale (Mich.) Coll., 1924-34, prof., head dept., 1934-42; research engr. Armour Research Found., Chgo., 1942-46; prof., head dept. mech. engring. U. Ky., 1946-60; visting professor of mechanical engineering Univ. Ill., 1960-62; group leader U. Ky. contract team U. Indonesia, Bandung, 1956-57, U. Ill., 1960-64. Recipient award Southeastern sect. Am. Society Engring. Edn. for outstanding research contbn., 1957. Profl. engr. Ky., Ill. Fellow A.A.A.S.; mem. Am. Soc. Heating, Refrigerating and Air Conditioning Engineers, American Society M.E., Newcomen Soc. Eng., Ky. Acad. Sci. (pres. 1950-51), Ky. Soc. Profl. Engrs., Sigma Xi, Pi Tau Sigma, Tau Beta Pi, Sigma Pi Sigma, Triangle. Baptist. Mason (Shriner). Author articles profl. jours. Home: Urbana, Ill. †

PERCEFULL, SABIN CUBBAGE, coll. pres.; b. Leitchfield, Ky., Feb. 20, 1889; s. Isaac Andrew and Ive (Cubbage) P.; A.B., Baylor Univ., 1912; A.M., Brown Univ., 1913; student Univ. of Ia., 1938-39, Univ. of Tex., 1939-40; m. Pearl Ellen Crawford, Aug. 6, 1919; children—Sabin Crawford (M.D.), Emily Ellen (Mrs. William C. Goodin). Teacher of sci. Lawton (Okla.) High School, 1913-15; head dept. physics, Northwestern Normal

School, Alva, Okla., 1915-18, prof. social sci. and dean of adminstrn., 1919-38; pres. Northeastern Okla. Jr. Coll., Miami, 1939-42; pres. Northwestern State Coll., Alva, from 1942. Served in U.S. Army, 1918-19. Mem. Am. Econ. Assn., Am. Acad. Polit. and Social Sci., Okla. Edn. Assn. (pres. 1926-27), N.E.A., Alva Chamber of Commerce (dir.), Am. Legion (comdr. 1943-44), Kappa Delta Pi. Democrat. Methodist. Mason. Club: Rotary (past pres. Alva and Miami clubs). Home: Alva, Okla. †

PEREA, CLIFFORD HARVEY, educator; b. Albuquerque, N.M., July 6, 1889; s. Jose Ynez and Susan (Gates) P.; A.B., Tusculum (Tenn.) Coll., 1910; student McCormick Theol. Sem., Chicago, 1910-13, Univ. Ill., summer 1924, Univ. Chicago, summer 1925; A.M., Wash. State Coll. (fellowship student 1925-26), 1926; m. Della Stevenson, Oct. 22, 1913; children—Helen and Laura, twins. Pastor Presbyn. Ch., Falmouth, Ky., 1913-15, Ponca, Neb., 1915-18; prof. of Spanish, Univ. of Dubuque, 1918-21, Trinity Univ., San Antonio, Tex., 1921-25, prof. and asst. registrar, 1926-34, prof. and registrar from 1934. Mem. bd. dirs. House of Neighborly Service. Mem. Am. Assn. Univ. Profs., Am. Assn. Collegiate Registrars, Tex. Assn. Coll. Registrars. Democrat. Author: Manual for Spanish Clubs (with Nelle Robinson), 1923. Editor: Curso Para Principiantes (Spanish grammar), 1931. Home: San Antonio, Tex. †

PERINI, FLORA, mezzo-soprano; b. Rome, Italy, Nov. 20, 1887; d. Carlo and Clemen (Romoli) P.; grad. liceo Musicale Santa Cecilia, Rome; m. Amelto Pollastri, Apr. 15, 1912. Déebut at La Scala, Milan, in "Cristoforo Colombo," under Toscanini; joined Metropolitan Opera Co., 1915; principal rôles in "Aida," "Trovatore," "Butterfly," "Norma," "Salome," etc. Home: Milan, Italy. †

PERKINS, DEXTER, educator; b. Boston, Mass., June 20, 1889; s. Herbert William and Cora (Farmer) P.; prep. edn., Boston Latin Sch. and Sanford Sch., Redding Ridge, Conn.; A.B., Harvard, 1909, Ph.D., 1914, Litt.D., 1953; LL.D., Union Coll., 1951; LL.D., U. Rochester, 1955, Tulane, 1963, Pittsburgh U., 1963; m. Wilma Lord, May 4, 1918; children—Bradford, Dexter. Instr. U. Cin., 1914-15; instr. and asst. prof. history, U. Rochester, 1915-22, prof. history, 1922-60, emeritus, head dept., 1925-54; John L. Senior prof. Am. civilization Cornell U., 1954-59, prof. emeritus, 1959-84, prof. Sch. Internat. Studies, New Delhi, 1961; Melton prof. history U. Pitts., 1962-63; Campbell prof. Wells Coll., 1963, 64; prof. U. of Colorado, 1968; chmn. council of Harvard Found. Advanced Study and Research, 1951-56; lectr. Commonwealth Fund at U. Coll., London, 1937; city historian of Rochester, New York, 1936-48. Official historian for Overseas Branch of OWI at UN Conf., San Francisco. First prof. of Am. history and institutions, Cambridge, England, 1945-46. Lecturer at the Nat. War Coll., from 1946; Prof. Univ. of Upsala, spring, 1949. Pres. Salzburg (Austria) Seminar Am. Studies, 1950-61; moderator Unitarian Chs. of U.S., Can., 1952-53. Served as 1st lt., later capt., infantry, U.S. Army, 1918; attached to hist. sect., G.H.Q., Chaumont, France, Oct. 1918-Feb. 1919; work connected with Peace Conf., Feb.-June, 1919. Mem. Am. Hist. Assn. (sec. 1928-39, president 1956), Am. Assn. of U. Profs., Phi Beta Kappa Fraternity. Author: The Monroe Doctrine, 1823-26, 1927; The Monroe Doctrine, 1826-67, 1933; John Quincy Adams as Secretary of State; The Monroe Doctrine, 1867-1907, 1938; Hands Off: The History of the Monroe Doctrine, 1941; America and Two Wars, 1944; The U.S. and the Caribbean, 1947; The Evolution of American Foreign Policy, 1948; The American Approach to Foreign Policy, 1952; Charles Evans Hughes and American Democratic Statesmanship, 1956; The American Way, 1957; The New Age of Franklin Roosevelt, 1932-45, 1957; Foreign Policy and The American Spirit, 1957; The United States and Latin America; American Quest for Peace; (with G.C. Van Deusen): The United States, 2 Vols., 1962, The American Democracy, Its Rise to Power, 1964; The Yield of the Years, 1969. Contbr. periodicals. Home: Rochester, N.Y. Died May 12, 1984.

PERKINS, JOHN ALANSON, polit. scientist; b. Owosso, Mich., June 29, 1914; s. Glenn Earl and Clara Myrtle (Reed) P.; A.B., U. Mich., 1938, A.M., 1939, Ph.D., 1941; LL.D. (hon.), U. S.C., 1960, U. Pa., 1963, U. Del., 1968; L.H.D., Waynesburg Coll., 1968, Wilkes Coll., 1969; m. Margaret R. Hiscock, Sept. 3, 1937; children—John James, Margaret Carey. Sec. to senator Arthur H. Vandenberg of Mich., 1936-37; teaching fellow dept. polit. sci. U. Mich., Ann Arbor, 1939-41, instr., 1941-43, asst. prof. polit. sci., 1945-46, prof., 1949-50, asst. provost, 1949-50, sec. Inst. for Pub. Adminstrn., 1945-46; budget dir. State of Mich., 1946-48, controller, 1948-49; pres. U. of Del., 1950-67; undersec. of HEW, 1957-58; pres. Dun & Bradstreet, 1967-68, chmn. bd., 1968-69; pres. and chief exec. officer Wilmington (Del.) Med. Center, 1969-70; prof. pub. mgmt. Northwestern U., Evanston, Ill., 1971-72, also dir. studies in adminstrn. of pub. affairs; prof. polit. sci. U. Calif., Berkeley, 1972-77, prof. emeritus, 1977-82, v.p. of adminstrn., 1972-77, v.p. emeritus, 1977-82; dir. Wilmington Trust Co., 1969-70, Bank of Del., 1966-67, Diamond State Telephone Co., 1962-67, Atlas Chem. Industries, 1963-67, Dun & Bradstreet, 1967-71. Mem. UNESCO exec. bd., 1953-55; chmn. HEW Commn. on Commd. Corps. of USPHS, 1971; trustee Ednl. Testing Service, 1971-75, Alfred P. Sloan Found., Calif. Coll. of Arts and Crafts. Recipient Distinguished Service award Ann Arbor Jr. C. of C., 1946, Order of Merit of the Italian Republic, 1959, Distinguished Alumni award U. Mich., 1967. Mem. Am. Polit. Sci. Assn. (v.p. 1960-61), Nat. Acad. of Pub. Adminstrn., Am. Soc. of Pub. Adminstrn., Wilmington Soc. Fine Arts, Assn. State Univs. and Land Grant Colls. (pres. 1960-61), Univ. Art Mus. Clubs: Faculty (Berkeley); Wilmington. Author: Role of Governor of Michigan in Enactment of Appropriations, 1943; (with Robeson Bailey) Harry Fletcher Brown, 1960; Plain Talk from a Campus, 1959; contbr. articles in field to profl. jours.; editor-in-chief Pub. Adminstrn. Rev., 1961-63. Died Apr. 6, 1982.

PERKINS, KENNETH, author; b. of Am. parents, Kodai Kanal, India, May 16, 1890; s. James C. and Charlotte Jane (Taylor) P.; prep. edn., Lowell high Sch., San Francisco, Calif.; B.L., U. of Calif., 1914, M.A., 1915; m. Grace Bemis, Dec. 25, 1919; 1 dau., Charlotte Joan. Instr. English, Pomona Coll., Claremont, Calif., 1916-18. Served as 2d lt. Field Arty., U.S. Army, Camp Taylor, Ky., and Ft. Sill Sch. of Fire, Aug. 28-Dec. 24, 1918. Republican. Presbyterian. Author books, scenarios, plays; co-author: Song of India, 1948; Louisiana Lady (prod. in N.Y. City), 1948; author: Hawk Larabee series (radio). Mem. Dramatists Guild, also Screenwriters Guild (both of Authors League of Am.). Home: Los Angeles, Calif. †

PERKINS, ROBERT M., army officer; b. Norfolk Va., September 26, 1887; s. Robert Sheild and Cornelia (Vaughan) P.; ed. pvt. schs., 1899-1905, Coll. William and Mary, 1905-08; B.S., U.S. Mil. Acad., 1913; student Coast Arty. Sch., 1926-27, Command and Gen. Staff Sch., 1927-28, Army War Coll., 1934-35; m. Miriam Paschall, Aug. 22, 1936. Commd. 2d lt., 1913; promoted through grades to brig. gen. (temp.), Mar. 1942; served overseas in World War, in Canal Zone, Phillipines, Hawaii; comdg. 53d C.A.C. Brigade since 1942. Awarded Victory (World War) and Pacific-Asiatic medals. Mem. Kappa Alpha. Clubs: Army and Navy (Washington, D.C. and Manila, P.I.).†

PERLOFF, HARVEY STEPHEN, univ. dean; b. 1915; ed. U. Pa., London Sch. Econs.; Ph.D., Harvard Economist, Fed. Res. Bd., 1941-43; cons. Govt. P.R., 1946-47, 50-51; prof. social sci. U. Chgo., 1947-55, head planning sch., 1951-55; cons. President's Water Resources Policy Commn., 1950, TVA, 1953-54; mem. UN Mission to Turkey, Israel, 1954; dir. program regional and urban studies Resources for Future, Inc., 1955-61, 65-68; dean Sch. Architecture and Urban Planning, U. Calif. at Los Angeles, 1968-83. Mem. Com. of Nine, Alliance for Progress, 1961-64; cons. Dept. State, Econ. Devel. Adminstrn., Dept. Commerce, Dept. Housing and Urban Devel., 1962-68; mem. environmental studies bd. Nat. Acad. Scis.; mem. task force Cal. Tomorrow Plan. Mem. bd. Washington Center for Met. Studies. Fellow Am. Acad. Arts and Scis. (commn. on year 2000); mem. Am. Econs. Assn., Regional Sci. Assn., Am. Soc. Planning Ofcls., Am. Soc. Pub. Adminstrn., Phi Beta Kappa, Pi Gamma Mu. Author or co-author: State and Local Finance in the National Economy, 1944; Puerto Rico's Economic Future, 1950; Education for Planning-City, State and Regional, 1957; Regions, Resources and Economic Growth, 1960; Planning and the Urban Community, 1960; How a Region Grows, 1963; Regional Economic Integration in the Development of Latin America, 1964; Design of a Worldwide Study of Regional Development, 1966; Issues in Urban Economics 1968; Alliance for Progress: A Social Invention in the Making, 1969; Quality of the Urban Environment, 1969; The Future of the U.S. Government, 1971. Home: Los Angeles, Calif. Died July 30, 1983.*

PERNICONE, JOSEPH MARIA, bishop; b. Regalbuto, Italy, Nov. 4, 1903; s. Salvatore and Petronilla (Taverna) P.; B.A., St. Joseph's Sem., Dunwoodie, Yonkers, N.Y., 1926; J.C.D., Cath. U., 1932. Ordained priest Roman Cath. Ch., 1926; asst. Our Lady Mt. Carmel, Yonkers, 1928-32; pastor Our Lady Mt. Carmel. Poughkeepsie, 1932-44, Our Lady Mt. Carmel, Bronx, 1944-66, Holy Trinity Ch., Poughkeepsie, N.Y., 1966-78; papal chamberlain, 1945, domestic prelate, 1952; aux. bishop, N.Y.C., 1954. Address: Bronx, N.Y. Died Feb. 11, 1985.

PERRY, CLAIR WILLARD, author; b. Waupaca, Wis., Apr. 13, 1887; s. Rev. Willard Jerome and Lillah Belle (Lombard) P.; grad. high sch., Weyauwega, 1907; student Lawrence Coll., Appleton, Wis., 1911; editor "The Laurentian," 1910-11; m. E. Christine Shankland, July 27, 1912; children—Ruth Audrey, Clair Leonard, Robert Willard, Loydann, Paul Arthur. Joined Springfield (Mass.) Union, 1911; Berkshire Hills rep. same, 1912; rep. in Berkshires of Boston and New York papers, 1912-23; began contributing fiction to mags., 1919; began writing articles for Saturday Evening Post, 1941, Esquire, Colliers, 1944; news editor radio station WNAW, N. Adams, from 1950. Publicity director Pittsfield Community Fund, 1924-31. President Massachusetts Division Izaak Walton League of America, 1930-31; sec. "Wild Acres," Walton Sanctuary, Inc. Spl. rep. Mil. Intelligence Div. Gen. Staff, U.S. Army, 1st Corps Area, 1921-23. Mem. Authors' Guild, Nat. Speleological Soc., Outdoor Writers Assn. Am. Author or co-author several books; latest publ.: Underground Empire, 1947; contbr. mags. Ednl. instructor emergency conservation work, Mt. Greylock State Park, 1934-35; supervisor in Berkshire Hills, Federal Writers' Project, 1935-37; exec sec. region 1, Mass. Commn. for Pub. Safety, 1942. Home: North Adams, Mass. †

PERRY, ELEANOR BAYER, author; m. Frank Perry. Author play Third Best Sport; screen plays David and Lisa, 1963, Ladybug, Ladybug, 1964, Last Summer, 1969, The Swimmer, 1968, Trilogy, 1968, Diary of a Mad Housewife, 1970, The Lady in the Car, 1970, (with Truman Capote) A Christmas Memory, 1966, The Man Who Loved Cat Dancing, 1973; author: Blue Pages, 1978. Address: Los Angeles, Calif. Dec. Mar. 14, 1981.*

PERRY, JOSEPH EARL, lawyer, former banker; b. Shelburne Falls, Mass., Dec. 30, 1884; s. Joseph Charles and Miriam Holbrook (Packard) P.; m. Bessie Luella Stanford, June 24, 1911 (dec. Oct. 1968); children—Miriam Elizabeth Perry Bell, Joseph Earl, Walter Stanford; m. Florence S. Kuhn, May 24, 1969. A.B., Williams Coll., 1906; J.D., Harvard U., 1909; B.B.A., Boston U., 1922. Bar: Mass. bar 1908. Practiced law, Boston, from 1909; income tax assessor Mass. State, 1917-19; mem. Mass. Ho. of Reps., 1925-30; chmn. com. on taxation and on constl. law, vice chmn. recess com. on taxation; commr. banks State of Mass., 1940-44; pres. Newton Savs. Bank, 1944-59; chmn. Mass. Bd. Bank Inc., 1940-44; sometime mem. faculty Boston U., Northeastern U., Grad. Sch. Banking, Rutgers U. Author: The Masonic Way of Life, 1968, also many articles and brochures on law, banking and masonry. Mem. Belmont Sch. Com., 1919-22; pres. Mass., R.I. State assns. YMCA, 1936-37; mem. budget com. Newton Community Chest, 1944; incorporator New Eng. Deaconess Hosp.; bd. dirs. Nat. Thrift Assn.; nat. bd. field advisers Fed. Small Bus. Adminstrn.; Pres. Nat. Assn. Suprs. State Banks, 1943; mem. council Harvard Law Sch. Assn., 1942-44; trustee Boston U., 1946-64, hon. trustee, from 1964, mem. exec. com., 1953-64, treas., 1954-57; trustee DeMolay Found., Mass., Internat. Coll., Beirut; trustee, pres. Masonic Edn. and Charity Trust. Mem. Mass. Savs. Bank Life Ins. Council (pres. 1949-50), Am. Bankers Assn. (pres. savs. and mortgage div. 1951-52, mem. exec. council 1951-52), Newton Bankers Assn. (pres. 1951-52), Boston Execs. Assn. (charter), Phi Beta Kappa Assn. Greater Boston (past sec.), Beta Gamma Sigma (hon.). Methodist (chmn. bd. trustees, hon. chmn. 50th anniversary com.). Clubs: Mason (33 deg., grand master Mass. 1938-40, dir. grand lodge Mass., only Western Hemisphere Mason to have official part in Duke of Kent installation as Eng. Grand Master by King George VI, London 1939), Rotarian (past pres.). Home: Shelburne Falls, Mass.

PERRY, JOSEPH SAMUEL, judge; b. Carbon Hill, Ala., Nov. 30, 1896; s. Barnabas Jackson and Mary (Brown) P.; m. Nelle Brookman, June 9, 1928; children—John Thomas, Maribeth Ann. A.B., U. Ala., 1923; M.A., U. Chgo., 1925, J.D., 1927. Bar: Ill. bar 1927. Coal miner, farmer, tchr. country schs., Brilliant, Ala., 1910-17, tchr. high sch., Mobile, 1923-24, Riverside (Ill.)-Brookfield High Sch., 1926-28; with Legal Aid Bur. United Charities, Chgo., summer 1928; asso. Cannon & Poague, 1928-29, Dunbar & Rich, 1929-33; master in chancery DuPage County, Wheaton, Ill., 1933-37; also pvt. law practice; mem. Ill. Gen. Assembly 41st Senatorial Dist., 1937-43; mem. Perry & Elliott, Wheaton, 1943-51; pub. adminstr. DuPage County, 1949-51, U.S. dist. judge, 1951-83; Chmn. DuPage County Democratic Central Com., 1934-42. Served as q.m. U.S. Navy, landing force duties, 1918, N. Russia; Served as q.m. U.S. Navy, landing force duties, 1919, Near East service; Served as q.m. Ill. Militia, 1942-44. Mem. Am., Ill., DuPage County bar assns., V.F.W., Am. Legion (judge adv. DuPage County), 40 et 8, Phi Beta Kappa. Episcopalian. Club: Mason (32 deg., Shriner). Home: Glen Ellyn, Ill. Died Feb. 18, 1984.

PERRY, RUFUS PATTERSON, cons.; b. Brunswick, Ga., June 4, 1903; s. Harry P. and Nannie Alice (Williams) P.; m. Thelma Davis, Nov. 30, 1945; children—Margaret Maribeth, Dorothy Patricia. B.A., Johnson C. Smith U., 1925, LL.D., 1956; M.S., U. Iowa, 1927, Ph.D., 1939. Chmn. natural sci. dept., prof., head dept. chemistry Prairie View (Tex.) A. and M. Coll., 1927-43, dir. div. arts and scis., 1939-43; adminstrv. dean, prof. chemistry, v.p. Langston U., 1943-57; pres. Johnson C. Smith U., 1957-69; cons., from 1969; pres. Perry Drug & Chem. Co., Oklahoma City, from 1947; sec.-treas. 1725 T St. Co-op. Assn., from 1973. Contbr. articles to profl. jours. Mem. exec. com. Council Protestant Colls. and Univs., 1963-68; v.p. Presbyn. Coll. Union, 1965, pres., 1966; 1st v.p. N.C. Council Ch. Related Colls., 1965-66; mem. adv. council N.C. Commn. Higher Edn. Facilities.; Bd. dirs. United Arts Council, So. Fellowship Fund; mem. bd. nat. missions U.P. Ch. U.S.A., 1964-70; del. World Presbyn. Alliance, Frankfurt, Germany, 1964. Fellow Am. Inst. Chemists, AAAS, Okla. Acad. Sci.; mem. N.C. Acad. Sci., Am. Chem. Soc., Nat. Inst. Sci., Sigma Xi, Alpha Phi Alpha, Sigma Pi Phi. Democrat. Club: Mason (32 deg.). Address: Washington, DC.

PERSHALL, EDWARD ESTES, business exec.; born East St. Louis, Ill., Aug. 17, 1887; s. Samuel Estes and Catherine (Weber) P.; student U. of Ill. Sch. Chemistry, 1910; m. Leita Horton, June 7, 1911 (died 1921); 1 dau., Dorothy (Mrs. Henry Belz); married 2d, Ethel Sultlan, Feb. 2, 1925. Chmn. bd. T. J. Moss Tie Co., 1936; dir. Boatmen's Bank in St. Louis; dir. Laclede Gas Light Co., The Pullman Co. (Chicago). Exec. and adv. bd. St. Louis Council, Boy Scouts of America. Commissioner of the Bi-State Development Agy., Mo. Ill. Metropolitan District, 1957-59; 1st chmn. bd. trustees Village of Hazelwood, Mo. Mem., past pres. Ry. Tie Association Mem. Defense Savings Staff U.S. Treasury, 1941. Past treas. Mo.

Democratic State Com., St. Louis County Dem. Finance Com. Adv. council Maryville College of Sacred Heart. Member The Burns Club, Newcomen Soc., Alpha Delta Phi. Methodist. Mason (Shriner). Clubs: Bellerive Country, Missouri Athletic, Noonday, Racquet, University (St. Louis); Indian Creek Country (Miami Beach, Fla.). Breeder thoroughbred horses. Home: Hazelwood, Mo. †

PESQUERA, HERNAN G., fed. dist. judge; b. San Juan, P.R., May 25, 1924; s. Angel M. and Ines F. (Guillermety) P.; m. Sonia Marty, Aug. 22, 1951; children—Sonia Pesquera Small, Maria M., Hernan G., Isabel. B.A., U. P.R., 1944; LL.D., Cornell U., 1948. Partner firm Geigel, Silva & Pesquera, San Juan, 1952-72; chmn. P.R. Racing Commn., 1971-72; judge U.S. Dist. Ct. for P.R., 1972-82, chief judge. Decorated Meritorious Service medal. Mem. Am., P.R., Fed. bar assns., Am. Judicature Soc., Am. Trial Lawyers Assn., Am. Legion, Mil. Order World Wars, Nu Sigma Beta. Roman Catholic. Club: Elks. Home: Santurce, P.R. Died Sept. 8, 1982; interred San Juan, P.R.

PETERSON, ABE RUDOLPH, lawyer; b. Chicago, Jan. 5, 1888; s. Heland and Anna C. P.; student Northwestern, 1905-07; LL.B., Kent Coll. Law, 1910; m. Elizabeth Kane, June 30, 1928; children—Elizabeth Ann, Thomas Kane, Jane Clair. Admitted to Ill. bar, 1910, practiced in Chgo.; sr. mem. Peterson, Lowry, Rall, Barber & Ross and predecessor, specializing in corporate, probate and insurance law; trustee Union League Found. for Boys Clubs. Past pres. Chgo. Lighthouse of Blind, New Trier Twp. High Sch.; trustee Chgo. Kent Coll. Law. Served as maj. inf. AEF, U.S. Army, World War I. Fellow Am. Coll. Trial Lawyers, Am. Bar Found.; mem. Am., Ill., Chgo. bar assns., Assn. Bar City N.Y., Soc. Trial Lawyers (past pres.), Internat. Assn. Ins. Counsel, Northwestern Univ. Assos., Am. Legion (past comdr.), Delta Theta Phi (past chancellor), Alpha Delta Phi. Republican. Mason. Clubs: Union League (past pres.), Law, Executives, Ind. Society, Attic (Chgo.); Glen View (Ill.) Golf: Kenilworth. Home: Kenilworth, IL. †

PETERSON, BEN, lawyer; b. Boise, Idaho, Sept. 23, 1910; s. Joseph H. and Eva T. (Rogers) P.; m. Louise Lauck, June 1, 1940; children—Linda, Ben, Keith. Student, Utah State Coll., 1931-33; LL.B., U. Utah, 1936. Bar: Idaho bar 1936, also U.S. Supreme Ct 1936. Practice in, Pocatello, 1936-57, city atty., 1948-57, U.S. atty., Boise, 1957-60; mem. firm Baum & Peterson, Pocatello, from 1959. Mem. Am. Bar Assn., Idaho State Bar, Sigma Chi. Club: Elk. Elk. Home: Pocatello, ID.

PETERSON, (FREDERICK) VAL(DEMAR) (ERASTUS), former ambassador, educator; b. Oakland, Nebr., July 18, 1903; s. Henry C. and Hermanda (Swanberg) P.; A.B., Wayne State Coll., 1927; M.A., U. Nebr., 1931, grad. student, 1931-33; LL.D., Midland Coll., 1949, Fairleigh Dickinson U., 1952, Stetson U., 1954, Muhlenberg Coll., 1955; D.Litt., Tex. Lutheran U., 1961; m. Elizabeth Pleak, June 6, 1929. Tchr. pub. sch., athletic coach, Nebr., 1925-30; instr. U. Nebr., 1930-33; supt. schs., Elgin, Nebr., 1933-39; pub., Elgin Rev., 1936-46; campaign mgr. for U.S. senator from Nebr., Aug. 1939-Nov. 1940; sec. to Gov. Dwight Griswold of Nebr., 1941-42; gov. of Nebr., 1947-53; adminstrv. asst. to the pres., 1953; former mem. Nat. Security Council; adminstr. Fed. Civil Def. Adminstrn., 1953-57; U.S. ambassador to Denmark, 1957-61, to Finland, 1969-73; distinguished prof. polit. sci. and pub. affairs Wayne (Neb.) State Coll., 1973-83. Chmn. Mo. River States Com., 1948-53; mem. Mo. Basin Intern-Agency Com., 1947-53; chmn. Nat. Govs.' Conf., 1952; mem. Commn. Intergovernmental Relations, 1953-55; mem. Def. Moblzn. Bd.; U.S. del. NATO Civil Def. Com.; sr. adviser NATO Emergency Planning. Commn., 1956-57. Vice chmn. bd. J. M. McDonald Co., Hastings, Nebr., 1961-66; v.p., adminstr. J. M. McDonald Found., Inc., 1961-65; chmn. bd. Life Investors Nebr., 1962-69; dir. Investors Growth Industries, Inc., Omaha, chmn. bd., 1969; dir. Investors Life Ins., 1961-68; dir. 1st Nat. Bank, Hastings, 1963-69, hon. dir. pub. relations Mary Lanning Meml. Hosp., Hastings, Nebr., 1967-68; trustee vice chmn. bd. People-to-People, Inc., 1969-70, chmn., from 1976; bd. regents U. Nebr., 1963-65, pres., 1965; pres. Wayne State Found, Wayne, from 1961. Nebr. del. at-large Republican Nat. Conv., 1960, 64, 68, 72, 76; resources coordinator for Congressman Charles Thone of Neb., 1973-74. Served to lt. col. U.S. Army, 1942-46; CBI. Decorated Bronze Star; grand cross Dannebrog (Denmark); recipient certificate of appreciation Fed. Civil Defense Corps Can., 1953, citation for work in disaster relief A.R.C., 1956, Exceptional Service award Dept. Air Force, award of merit U.S. Civil Defense Council, 1957, certificate of tribute Nat. Assn. State and Territorial Civil Defense Dirs., 1957, Internat. Service award Kearney (Nebr.) State Coll., 1969, Distinguished Pub. Service award, Wayne State Coll., 1960, award for distinguished service Native Sons and Daus. of Neb., 1971, Americanism award China Burma India Vets. Assn., 1973, Distinguished Alumnus award Am. Assn. State Colls. Univs., 1976; named Nebr. Builder U. Nebr., 1975. Mem. Am. Legion, V.F.W., Air Force Assn., Innocents Soc. U. Nebr. (hon.). Republican. Lutheran. Mason (32 deg., Shriner, Jester). Clubs: Omaha; Nat. Press, Omaha Press (hon.), Western Foreign (hon.); University (Lincoln). Died Oct. 16, 1983.

PETERSON, HARRY HERBERT, judge; b. St. Paul, Minn., Apr. 12, 1890; s. Swan Alfred and Mathilda Christina (Gustafson) P.; LL.B., cum laude, U. of Minn., 1912; m. Mabel V. Norquist, June 28, 1916; children—Harriet Mae, Donald E. In practice, St. Paul, 1912-15, 1922-23, 1927-33; asst. county atty. Ramsey County, Minn., 1915-22, county atty., 1923-27; elected atty. gen. of Minn., 1932, 34 and 36; apptd. asso. justice Supreme Ct. of Minn., Nov. 28, 1936, taking office Dec. 15, 1936; elected associate justice for 6 yr. term November 1938, re-elected, Nov. 1944, resigned as justice Supreme Ct. of Minn., 1950; drafted Minnesota Mortgage Moratorium law and successfully defended it through the courts, 290 United States 318; counsel before United States Supreme Court in case of taxation by state of cattle in stockyards, case of prison made goods, Great Lakes water level case. Minnesota chain banks case; before Minnesota State Supreme Court in state income tax case and homestead preferential tax case; before the United States District Court in truck strike case and others; counsel for state in telephone rate reduction case resulting in reducing telephone rates in St. Paul $700,000 per year. D.F.L. candidate for gov. of Minn. Home: St. Paul, Minn. †

PETERSON, JOHN EDWIN, hosp. adminstr.; b. Ottumwa, Iowa, Aug. 11, 1918; s. Harry E. and Lorene A. (Johnson) P.; B.B.A. with distinction, U. Minn., 1948; M.B.A., U. Chgo., 1951; m. Margaret L. Youngdahl, June 5, 1948; children—Todd, Janis, Catherine. Adminstrv. resident Highland-Alameda County Hosp., Oakland, Calif., 1949-50, adminstrv. asst., 1950-51, asst. supt., 1951-53; asst. adminstr. Alta Bates Hosp., Berkeley, Calif., 1953-54, adminstr., 1954-67; exec. v.p., adminstr. Eisenhower Med. Center, Palm Desert, Calif., 1967-68; exec. v.p., dir. Valley Hosp., Ridgewood, N.J., 1968-81; preceptor course in hosp. adminstrn. U. Calif., Berkeley. Served with USNR, 1942-46. Mem. Am. Hosp. Assn., N.J. Hosp. Assn., Am. Coll. Hosp. Adminstrs., Nat. Council Community Hosps., Am. Public Health Assn., N.J. Public Health Assn., Am. Health Planning Assn., Am. Assn. Hosp. Planning. Home: Ringwood, N.J. Died Mar. 28, 1981.

PETERSON, JOHN G., grain corp. ofcl.; b. Netherlands, W.I., Dec. 21, 1890; s. William S. and Helena (Every) P.; Ph.B., Brown U., 1917, A.M., 1944; m. Gladys Akin Yanke, Sept. 8, 1924; children—Elizabeth, John G. Trainee Nat. City Bank of N.Y., 1917-18, various positions 1919-22; with Chase Nat. Bank of N.Y., 1922-33, various capacities, 2d v.p., 1930-33; with Cargill, Inc. and various predecessor and subsidiary cos., from 1933, became chief financial officer, chmn. bd. dirs., chmn. finance com., mem. exec. and audit coms., ret. as chmn. bd., 1956; chmn. bd. Tradax Internacional S.A., Tradax Geneve, Geneva, Switzerland, Tradax Eng., Ltd., London Tradax Japan, Tokyo, Tradax Can., Montreal, Tradax, Inc., N.Y.C.; v.p. Cargil Neb. Co., Cargill Grain Co., Ltd.; chmn. Cargill Internacional, S.A., Kerrgill Co., Ltd.; dir. Car-Lin, Inc., Kerr Gifford & Co., Inc., Cal., Nutrena Mills, Inc., Minn. River Co., Western Co., Cargill Grain Co. Ltd., Cargill Manitoba Co., Ltd. Trustee Brown U., 1947-54, The Blake School, Hopkins, Minn., 1949-56. Mem. Phi Beta Kappa, Sigma Xi, Kappa Sigma. Republican. Episcopalian. Clubs: Bankers (N.Y.C.); Minneapolis, Minikahda, Brown University of the Twin Cities (pres. from 1951). Home: Wayzata, Minn. †

PETERSON, MILO JAMES, educator; b. Waconia, Minn., Sept. 6, 1910; s. Selby E. and Marie (Carlson) P.; B.S., U. Minn., 1934; M.S. Agr., Cornell U., 1937, Ph.D., 1940; m. Maxine Moore, Aug. 27, 1938; children—Milo, Karen, Stuart, Lyning. Agr. instr., Bertha, Minn., 1934-36; research asst. Cornell U., 1936-39; agr. economist Clemson (S.C.) Coll., 1939-43, U.S. Dept. Agr., 1943-46; asst. prof. agrl. edn. U. Minn., 1946-47, asso. prof., 1947-48, prof., from 1948, head dept., 1948-70; supt. edn. Minn. State Fair, 1948-70; internat. cons. in field; Fulbright research scholar, Japan, 1956; lectr. Internat. Center Agrl. Edn. Zurich, 1960; vis. prof. colls. and univs., from 1950. Hon. life mem. Nat. Vocational Agr. Instrs. Assn.; life mem. Am. Vocational Assn., (pres. 1961-62; Outstanding Service awards 1965); mem. Am. Assn. Tchr. Educators in Agr., Minn. Hist. Soc., Minn. Vocational Assn., Future Farmers Am. (trustee Minn. Found.), Internat. House Japan (Tokyo), Minn. Citizens Com. Pub. Edn. (past chmn.), Gamma Sigma Delta, Phi Delta Kappa, Phi Kappa Phi, Alpha Tau Alpha, Alpha Zeta, Farm House. Republican. Conglist. Mason. Co-author: Getting Started in Farming; The Three R's Plus. Editor The Visitor. Author articles in field. Home: Saint Paul, Minn. Died Oct. 8, 1981.

PETRIGRUE, WINFRED KING, lawyer; b. Hannibal, N.Y., July 22, 1889; s. Samuel D. and Orrie Luella (Kenney) P.; B.S., Wesleyan U., 1913; LL.B., N.Y. Law Sch., 1916; m. Ethel Hulburd Martin, May 4, 1918; children—Rae (Mrs. John C. Glidden), Shirley (Mrs. Peter K. Clough). Partner Breed, Abbott & Morgan, N.Y.C. Trustee emeritus Wesleyan U. Served as capt., 311th Inf., U.S. Army, World War I. Mem. Am., N.Y. State bar assns., Assn. Bar City N.Y., N.Y. County Lawyers Assn., Psi Upsilon. Clubs: University (N.Y.C.); Englewood, Knickerbocker Country (Englewood). Home: Englewood, N.J. †

PETRILLO, JAMES C., union official; married; 2 sons, 1 dau. Former pres. Chgo. Fedn. of Musicians, Am. Fedn. Musicians, past chmn. civil rights dept. past v.p. A.F.L. Home: Chicago, Ill. Died Oct. 23, 1984.

PETRY, LOREN C(LIFFORD), prof. botany; b. New Paris, O., Sept. 22, 1887; s. Francis Marion and Armina E. (Petry) P.; B.S., Earlham Coll., Richmond, Ind., 1907; B.S., Haverford (Pa.) Coll., 1908; M.S., University Chicago, 1911, Ph.D., 1913; D.Sc. (honorary), Earlham Coll., 1966; married Nellie von Runkle, June 12, 1915; children—Ruth M., Loren von Runkle. Instr. in botany, Syracuse U., 1914-16, asst. prof., 1916-19, asso. prof., 1919 to 1924; acting asst. prof. botany, Cornell U. (on leave from Syracuse U.), 1922-24; prof. botany, Syracuse U., 1924-25, also dir. summer session, 1919-25; prof. botany, Cornell U., 1925-55, emeritus, 1955, dir. summer session 1935-44, dir. vets. edn., 1944-48; vis. prof. botany, chmn. div. natural scis. Hofstra Coll., 1956-57; vis. prof. botany Univ. of Mo., 1955-56; vis. biologist to colls. Am. Inst. Biol. Sci., 1956-64; botanist Cape Cod Mus. Natural History, from 1960; vis. prof. botany Wellesley (Mass.) Coll., 1966-67. Fellow A.A.A.S.; member Bot. Soc. Am. (vice pres. 1937; chmn. paleo-bot. sect. 1938), Phi Beta Kappa, Phi Kappa Phi, Sigma Xi, Gamma Alpha. Quaker. Home: Yarmouth Port, Mass. †

PETTY, BEN(JAMIN) H(ARRISON), univ. prof.; born Hayes County, Neb., Oct. 12, 1888; s. Charles E. and Martha (Phillips) P.; B.S. in Civil Engring., Purdue U., 1913; m. Leah Ruark Holmes, June 12, 1913 (died May 17, 1945); 1 son, Joe Holmes; married 2d Elma L. Cosby, July 29, 1951. With Morgan Engring. Company, Miami Conservancy Dist., Dayton, O., 1913-20; instr. highway engring. Purdue U., 1920-22, asst. prof., 1922-28, asso. prof., 1928-32, prof., from 1933; in charge annual Purdue Road Sch. from 1924; summer highway extension work among Ind. state, county and city road officials from 1921. Mem. Highway Research Bd. Served as capt., later maj., Corps of Engrs., U.S. Army, 1942-45. Mem. Am. Soc. C.E., Am. Road Builders Assn. (mem. bd. dirs.), Am. Soc. Engineering Edn., Soc. Mil. Engrs., Soc. Profl. Engrs., Ind. Soc. of Chicago, Iron Key, Tau Beta Pi, Chi Epsilon, Sigma Delta Chi. Methodist. Editor, articles in profl. jours. Home: West Lafayette, Ind. †

PEW, GEORGE THOMPSON, investments co. exec.; b. Phila., Mar. 30, 1917; s. J. Howard and Helen (Thompson) P.; m. Constance Delk Clarke, May 4, 1940; children—George Thompson, Margaret Clarke (Mrs. William H. Moorhouse, Jr.). Grad., M.I.T., 1939. With Sun Oil Co., 1939-50; chmn. Aero Design & Engring. Co., 1950-57, pres., chmn., 1957-59, pres., 1958-61, George T. Pew Enterprises, from 1961; chmn. Par Truck Leasing, Inc., 1961-73, Joe Hodge Transp., Inc., 1963-71. Mem. Am. Inst. Aeros., Am. Ordnance Assn., Sportsman Pilot Assn., Quiet Birdmen, Nat. Pilots Assn. Clubs: Merion Cricket (Haverford, Pa.); Merion Golf (Ardmore, Pa.); Bay Head (N.J.) Yacht; Racquet (Phila.), Corinthian Yacht (Phila.), Philadelphia Aviation Country (Phila.) (past pres.), Union League (Phila.); Key Largo Anglers (Fla.). Home: Haverford, PA.

PEYSER, HERBERT F., music critic; b. N.Y. City, Aug. 6, 1889; s. John and Hannah (Hecht) P.; A.B., Columbia, 1909; studied in France and Germany; unmarried. Chief music critic of Musical America, New York, 1909-21; music critic Musical Observer 3 yrs.; critical work, New York Evening Post 4 yrs.; associated with Henry T. Finck in critical work on Evening Post; asso. music critic New York Telegram from 1924; program annotator Symphony Soc. of New York, 1926-28. Served 6 mos. in F.A., U.S.A., World War. Home: New York, N.Y. †

PFAELZER, MORRIS, lawyer; b. Phila., Apr. 12, 1913; s. Frank A. and Elsie (Levy) P.; grad. Mercersberg Acad., 1931; A.B., Harvard, 1935; LL.B., U. Pa., 1938; m. Marjorie Lesser, Apr. 12, 1938 (div. 1959); children—Fay (Mrs. Jon Abrams), Betty (Mrs. Michael Rauch); m. 2d, Mariana Richardson, Oct. 14, 1961. Admitted to Calif. bar, 1946, Pa. bar, 1939; practice in Los Angeles, 1946-80; partner Kadison, Pfaelzer, Woodard, Quinn & Rossi, 1967—. Lectr. law U. So. Calif., 1960-64. Pres., Los Angeles County Bar Found., 1972-74. Pres., trustee Resthaven Psychiat. Hosp., 1961-69; bd. councilors U. So. Calif. Law Center, 1971-80, chmn., 1976-80. Served with USNR, 1942-45. Fellow Am. Bar Found.; mem. Am., Los Angeles County, Pa., Phila. bar assns., Calif. State Bar. Home: Los Angeles, Calif. Died Nov. 16, 1980.

PFANN, WILLIAM GARDNER, scientist; b. N.Y.C., Oct. 25, 1917; s. John G. and Anna F. (Liedtke) P.; m. Mary L. Gronewold, May 31, 1946; children—Jean L., Susan D., Anna V. B.Chem.Engring., Cooper Union, N.Y.C., 1940. Lab. asst. Bell Telephone Labs., Murray Hill, N.J., 1935-43, staff scientist, 1943-59, dept. head research, 1959-74, cons., 1975-82; vis. scientist dept. metallurgy Cambridge (Eng.) U., 1962. Author: Zone Melting, 2d edit, 1966. Recipient Clamer medal Franklin Inst., 1957; Moisson medal Sch. Chemistry U. Paris, 1962; 1st award for Creative Invention Am. Chem. Soc., 1968; award for excellence Carborundum Co., 1972; award in Solid State Sci. and Tech., Electrochem. Soc., 1973; Profl. Progress award Am. Inst. Chem. Engrs., 1960. Fellow AIME (Mathewson medal 1955), Am. Soc. Metals (Sauveur achievement award 1958); mem. Nat. Acad. Scis., Am. Phys. Soc. (award for New Materials 1976). Patentee in field. Address: Murray Hill, N.J. Died Oct. 1982.

PHELPS, ASHTON, publisher; b. New Orleans, Dec. 30, 1913; s. Esmond and Harriott K. (Barnwell) P.; m. Jane C. George, Nov. 21, 1939 (dec.); 1 son, Ashton. A.B., Tulane U., 1935, LL.B., 1937; postgrad., U. Mich. Law

Sch., summer 1936. Bar: La. bar 1937. Practiced in, New Orleans; mem. firm Phelps, Dunbar, Marks, Claverie & Sims, 1946-67; chmn. bd. Times-Picayune Pub. Corp., New Orleans, from 1967, also dir. Mem. bd. Christian edn. Presbyn. Ch. U.S., 1958-61, also mem. com. wills and bequests.; Pres. New Orleans Community Health Assn., 1945-49, Howard Meml. Library Assn., from 1950; chmn. adv. bd. Female Orphan Soc., New Orleans, 1946-59; bd. visitors Tulane U., 1953-55, v.p. bd. administrs., 1955-72, adv. administr., from 1972; Active New Orleans chpt. ARC, 1954-60, Oschner Found. Hosp.; mem. Bd. of Liquidation City Debt, 1962-74, New Orleans Sewerage and Water Bd., 1964-67. Served from ensign to lt. USNR, 1942-45. Mem. ABA (spl. com. antitrust sect. on revision rules FTC), La. Bar Assn., New Orleans Bar Assn., Assn. Bar City N.Y., Am. Law Inst., Am. Newspaper Pubs. Assn. (dir. 1972-79, trustee found. 1978-79, chmn. press/-bar com.), Order of Coif, Phi Beta Kappa, Delta Tau Delta, Phi Delta Phi, Omicron Delta Kappa. Presbyn. (elder, trustee). Clubs: Boston (New Orleans), La. (New Orleans). Home: New Orleans, LA.

PHELPS, JOSEPH BARNWELL, lawyer; b. New Orleans, July 25, 1916; s. Esmond and Harriott Kinloch (Barnwell) P.; m. Euphemie Labatut Tobin, Mar. 26, 1942; 1 son, Esmond II. Grad., Woodberry Forest Sch., 1934; B.A., Tulane U., 1938, LL.B., 1940. Bar: La. bar 1940. Practiced in, New Orleans; partner firm Phelps, Dunbar, Marks, Claverie & Sims (and predecessor), from 1951. Chmn. spl. donors div. New Orleans Heart Fund drive, 1963-64; capt. Tulane U. Forward Fund drive, 1965; adviser Christian Women's Exchange, New Orleans, from 1965. Served to maj. F.A. AUS, 1941-46. Decorated Bronze Star. Mem. Am., La. bar assns., Phi Delta Phi, Delta Tau Delta. Clubs: Boston (New Orleans), Louisiana (New Orleans), Stratford (New Orleans), New Orleans Country (New Orleans). Home: New Orleans, LA.

PHELPS, RICHARD K., lawyer; b. in Vernon County, Missouri, Dec. 21, 1890; s. Joseph Clark and Mary Kathleen (Cavan) P.; student, summers, Southwest State Teachers Coll., Springfield, Mo., 1911-16; A.B., U. of Mo., 1917; m. Margaret Palmer, Feb. 10, 1916; children—Margaret Palmer (Mrs. Stacy Allen Haines), Mary Janet (Mrs. Albert Charles Bean), Richard Kimbrough, Jr. High Sch. prin., Mountain Grove, Mo., 1912-14, Neosho, Mo., 1914-17, Clinton, Mo., 1917-22; prof., Bus. Law, State Teachers Coll., Springfield, Mo., 1922-23; admitted to Mo. bar, 1924, began practice at Nevada, Mo.; pros. atty., Vernon County, 1927-29; mem. Mo. Gen. Assembly, 1933-34; asst. U.S. Atty. for Western Mo. Dist., 1934-41, first asst., 1939-43; acting U.S. Attorney, 1940-41; now member firm Gage, Hillix, Shrader & Phelps, Kansas City, Missouri. Member board of directors First National Television Corporation, Kansas City. Admitted to practice in U.S. Supreme Court, 1942. Mem. Am. Bar Assn., Kansas City and Mo. State bar assns., Lawyer's Assn. of Kansas City, Mo. Democrat. Episcopalian. Club: University (Kansas City, Mo.). †

PHELPS, RICHARDSON, pres. Round-Robin Libraries, Inc.; b. Minneapolis, Minn., Jan. 6, 1887; s. Edmund Joseph and Louise Ann (Richardson) P.; B.A., Yale, 1910; m. Anne Foley, of St. Paul, Minn., Feb. 8, 1916; children—Anne Foley, Richardson, Craig. Asst. sales mgr. Pillsbury Flour Mills Co., Minneapolis, 1910-14; pres. Phelps and Co., 1914-32, Round-Robin Libraries, Inc., from 1932. Served as 2d lt. Air Forces, A.E.F., World War. Trustee Minneapolis Soc. of Fine Arts; dir. Minneapolis Orchestral Assn. Mem. Alpha Delta Phi. Home: Minneapolis, Minn. †

PHILIPS, AURELIUS EDWIN, pres. Wisconsin Mineral Springs Co., Inc.; b. Sanford, Fla., Sept. 21, 1890; s. Aurelius Jackson and Agnes (Dunham) P.; A.B., U. of Tenn., 1911; LL.B., U. of Fla., 1912; m. Isabel Patton, Dec. 11, 1913; 1 dau., Susan Patton (Mrs. John Arthur Spruill, Jr.). Admitted to Fla. State bar, 1912; employee Welch Grape Juice Co., Westfield, N.Y., 1907-27, gen. sales mgr., vice pres. and dir., 1918-27; dir. merchandising Johnson & Johnson, New Brunswick, N.J., 1928-29; sales engr. and mgr. cereal dept. H. J. Heinz Co., Pittsburgh, Pa., 1930; dir. mechandising Candy Brands, Inc., Brooklyn, N.Y. and Boston, Mass., 1931-32; v.p., gen. mgr. dir. and chief exec. officer Tea Garden Products Co., San Francisco, Calif., 1933-40; pres. and dir. White Rock Corporation (formerly White Rock Mineral Springs Co.), N.Y. City and Waukesha, Wis., 1941-45; v.p. Internat. Plastic Corp., Morristown, N.J., 1946; pres. Wis. Mineral Springs Co., Inc., N.Y. City, from 1945. Pres. Asso. Grocery Mfrs. of Am., 1926-27; mem. Kappa Alpha, Phi Kappa Phi (founder U. of Fla. chapter, 1912). Club: Union League. Home: Stroudsburg, Pa. †

PHILIPS, FREDERICK STANLEY, pharmacologist; b. Mt. Vernon, N.Y., Sept. 25, 1916; s. Alfred I. and Rose R. (Rehberger) P.; m. Lisa Tallal, Aug. 18, 1968; children: Sally Burr, Susan Jane, John Frederick. B.A., Columbia U., 1936; Ph.D., U. Rochester, N.Y., 1940. Theresa Sessel fellow Osborn Zool. Lab., Yale U., 1940-41, NRC fellow, 1941-42, research assoc., 1942-43; research fellow M.I.T., 1946-47; mem. staff Sloan-Kettering Inst. Cancer Research, N.Y.C., from 1946, mem., from 1956; mem. faculty Cornell U. Med. Sch., 1946-51, asst. prof. pharmacology, 1948-51; mem. faculty Sloan-Kettering div. Cornell U. Grad. Sch. Med. Scis., from 1951, prof. pharmacology, from 1957, assoc. dir. div., 1969-74; head lab. pharmacology Sloan-Kettering Inst., 1967—; vis. investigator Chester Beatty Research Inst., London, 1965-66; mem. and/or cons. coms. NRC, Nat. Cancer Inst., NIH, USPHS, Nat. Acad. Scis. Served to capt. AUS, 1943-46. Fellow AAAS; mem. Soc. Exptl. Biology and Medicine (chmn. N.Y. chpt. 1962-65), Am. Assn. Cancer Research (sec.-treas. 1977-82, pres.-elect 1983), Am. Soc. Pharmacology and Exptl. Therapeutics, Harvey Soc., N.Y. Soc. Med. Research (pres. 1951-52). Home: New York, NY.

PHILIPS, JOSEPH LEON, army officer; b. nr. Valley Forge, Pa., June 15, 1890; s. William Edgar and Hannah Ann (Rapp) P.; B.S., Wash. State Coll., 1914; m. Ella Myrtle Tindall, July 19, 1918 (died 1949); 1 daughter, Margaret Leona (wife of Maj. Mason H. Morse, U.S.M.C.); m. 2d Marguerite N. Lee, Jan. 10, 1950. Commd. 2d lt., Cavalry, U.S. Army, 1916, and advanced through the grades to brig. Gen., 1942; A.E.F., France, 1917-1919; assigned procurement and planning work Office of Under Secretary of War, 1940-42; chief of priorities, Army and Navy Munitions Bd.; Gen. Staff Corps, Washington, D.C.; office chief of transportation, War Dept., Mar.-May 1943; European Theater of Operations, May 1943-May 1944, and Dec. 1944-Sept. 1945; retired for physical disability incident to mil. service, 1946. Decorated Legion of Merit with oak leaf cluster, Bronze Star Medal (U.S.), Chevalier Legion of Honor, Croix de Guerre with palm (France). Mem. Mil. Order World Wars, Am. Legion, Disabled Am. Vets., S.A.R., Phi Delta Theta. Mason. Home: La Jolla, Calif. †

PHILLIPS, JOHN CHARLES, oil company executive, lawyer; b. Metcalfe, Ont., Can., 1921. Student, U. Toronto (Ont.), 1940, Osgoode Hall Law Sch., 1949. Bar: Called to Ont. bar 1949. With Gulf Can. Ltd., Toronto, 1956-85, asst. gen. counsel, 1960-64, gen. counsel, 1964-71, v.p., sec., gen. counsel, 1971-76, sr. v.p., 1976-77, exec. v.p., 1977-79, chmn., 1979-85, also dir.; dir. Bank of Nova Scotia, Can. Life Assurance Co. *

PHILLIPS, JOHN MILTON, clergyman; b. Jacksonville, Ill., Dec. 27, 1889; s. Rev. Wm. Sandusky and Mary Caroline (Wood) P.; grad. high sch., Jacksonville, 1908; A.B., Ill. Coll., 1912; S.T.B., Boston U. of Theology, 1915; studied philosophy, Harvard Grad. Sch.; D.D., Ill. Coll., 1929, Northland Coll., 1930; m. Eleanore Elizabeth Sinclair, Oct. 3, 1917; children—Jean Wood (dec.), Charlotte Sinclair, John Milton. Licensed M.E. ministry, 1910; pastor Lynnville (Mt. Zion) Circuit, 1910-12; asst. pastor Central Congl. Ch., Jamaica Plain, Mass., 1912-14; ordained M.E. ministry, 1914; pastor Park Av. Congl. Ch., Arlington Heights, 1915-20; teacher Babson Inst., Wellesley Hills, 1920-21; pastor Central Congl. Ch., Lynn, 1922-23, Franklin St. Ch., Manchester, N.H., 1923-27; ordained Congl. ministry, 1924; pastor First Congl. Ch., Akron, O., 1927-30, Centre Congl. Ch., Hartford, Conn., 1930-38, First Central Ch., Omaha Neb., 1938-45; also head dept. of religion, U. of Omaha; pastor Pilgrim Ch., Duluth. Director Atlanta Theological Seminary; mem. bd. Chicago Theol. Sem.; mem. exec. com., Gen. Council Congregational and Christian Churches. Author: "The Peace Primer." Home: Duluth, Minn. †

PHILLIPS, MARJORIE, art gallery dir., painter; b. Bourbon, Ind., Oct. 25, 1894; d. Charles Ernest and Alice (Beal) Acker; student Classical Sch. for Girls, N.Y.C., Miss Fuller's Sch., Ossining, N.Y., Art Students League, N.Y.C.; m. Duncan Phillips, Oct. 8, 1921 (dec.); children—Mary Marjorie, Laughlin. Asso. dir. Phillips Gallery, Washington, from 1925; director Phillips Collection, Washington. Paintings exhbt. at Century of Progress, N.Y. World's Fair, Golden Gate Exposition, Mus. Modern Art, Am. Exhdn. in Paris, Art Inst. Chgo., Pa. Acad., Carnegie Inst., Whitney Mus., Mus. Legion of Honour; retrospective exhibition at Edward Root Art Center; rep. permanent collections of Whitney Mus., Boston Mus. Fine Arts, Yale Mus., Phillips Gallery, Corcoran Gallery Art, pvt. collections; one man shows include Kraushaars, Durand Ruel, Bignou, Durlacher Bros.; painting included in loan exhbn. to Tate Gallery, London, 1946. Hon. trustee Washington Gallery Modern Art. Recipient award of merit Pa. Mus. Sch. of Art, 1959. Clubs: Sulgrave (Washington); City Tavern, Cosmopolitan (N.Y.C.). Home: Washington, D.C. Died June 19, 1985.†

PHILLIPS, THOMAS GUTHRIE, biol. chemist; b. West Derby, Vt., Nov. 18, 1887; s. Jeremiah and Altie Fowler (Wright) P.; B.S., Ohio State U., 1912, M.S., 1913; Ph.D., U. of Chicago, 1918; m. Genevieve Kirkbride, Dec. 26, 1921. Instr. agr., chemistry, Ohio State U., 1912-15, asst. prof., 1915-23, prof. 1923-25; prof. agr. and biol. chemistry and chemist, Agrl. Expt. Sta., U. of N.H., from 1925. Mem. A.A.A.S., Am. Chem. Soc., Bot. Soc. America, Am. Soc. Plant Physiologists, Sigma Xi, Phi Kappa Phi, Phi Lambda Upsilon, Gamma Alpha, Alpha Zeta. Congregationalist. Author: Fundamentals of Organic and Biological Chemistry, 1923; also numerous bulletins, articles, etc. Address: Durham, N.H. †

PHILLIPS, WALLACE BENJAMIN, naval officer; b. Greensboro, N.C., Nov. 29, 1888; grad. U.S. Naval Acad., 1911. Entered U.S. Navy, 1907, and advanced through the grades to commodore, 1943; served in U.S. ships Louisiana, Terry, Cassin, and Nebraska, 1911-17; exec. and comdg. officer, U.S.S. Manley (operating from Queenstown, Ireland), 1917-18; comd. U.S.S. Parker (based Plymouth, Eng., and employed in interception of German submarines returning to Germany from Mediterranean), 1918-19; comd. U.S.S. Laub, 1919; engr. officer U.S.S. Rhode Island, 1919-20; com. Barnett, 1941-42; comd. division transports, amphibious force, Atlantic Fleet, 1942-43, becoming comdr. transports, with additional duty as comdr. of a transport div., Jan. 1943; later assigned a command in Pacific. Decorated Legion of Merit, Victory Medal with destroyer clasp, Am. Defense Service Medal with fleet clasp, Am. Area Campaign, European-African-Middle-Eastern Area Campaign and Asiatic-Pacific Area Campaign medals. Home: Oceanside, N.Y. †

PHILPOTT, CHARLES HUGHES, educator; b. Monroe County, Mo., Dec. 22, 1888; s. Charles Burwell and Elizabeth (Hughes) P.; A.B., Univ. of Mo., 1914, A.M., 1915, Ph.D., 1927; m. Evodia Gentry, Aug. 25, 1915; children—Charles Gentry, Jane. Supervisor univ. schs., Columbia, Mo., 1913-15; prof. biol. scis., Kansas City (Mo.) Jr. Coll., 1915-23; prof. biology, Harris Teachers Coll., St. Louis, Mo., 1923-43, dean of men, 1939-43, prin., 1943-47, director edn., in charge curriculum research and development, from 1947. Education advisor for Dept. of State in Germany, 1949-50. Fellow A.A.A.S.; member of Botanical Soc. of Am., Am. Soc. Zoologists, Sigma Xi, Phi Delta Kappa. Club: Kiwanis. Contbr. articles in field of protozoology and med. zoology to sci. jours. Home: St. Louis, Mo. †

PHIPPS, JOHN H., (BEN PHIPPS) television exec.; b. London, Nov. 3, 1904; s. John Shafer and Marguerita (Grace) P.; m. Elinor Klapp, June 26, 1928; children—John Eugene, Colin. Ph.B., Yale U., 1928. Salesman Ingersoll Rand Co., Boston, N.Y.C., 1929-31; v.p. Dugas Fire Extinguisher Co., N.Y.C., 1931-32; engaged in gen. bus. under name Westbury Corp., N.Y., Fla., 1932-42; owner John J. Phipps Radio Stas., throughout S.E.; including WTVS, Marianna, Fla., 1943—, WCTV, WKTG, Thomasville, Ga., WPTV, Palm Beach, Fla; pres. John H. Phipps Agy. (ins.), 1936—; chmn. bd. South Eastern Shares, Inc.; dir. Bessemer Truste Co., Ingersoll-Rand Co., W.R. Grace & Co. Pres. Carribean Conservation Corp.; mem. region 3 adv. bd. OCDM.; Patron Am. Mus. Natural History; mem. Fla. State U. Found. Bd. Served as col. USAAF, 1942-45, ETO; Served as col. USAAF, 1943-45, ETO. Decorated Bronze Star medal.; Named chevalier d'Agr., 1971. Mem. N.Y. Zool. Soc. (trustee), Am. Internat. Charolais Assn. (standards com.), Am. Charbray Breeders Assn. (dir.), Am. Legion. Democrat. Clubs: Pinnacle, Meadow Brook. Office: Tallahassee FL

PICKENS, SLIM, (LOUIS BERT LINDLEY, JR) actor; b. Kingsberg, Calif., June 1919. Ed. public schs., Hanford, Calif. Numerous appearances including: Beyond the Poseidon Adventure, 1949, Boy Oklahoma, Last Command, One-Eyed Jacks, Dr. Strangelove, Major Dundee, Rough Night in Jericho, The Cowboys, Pat Garret and Billy the Kid, Blazing Saddles, The Sweet Creek County War, Rancho Deluxe, White Line Fever, Mr. Billion, The Apple Dumpling Gang, The White Buffalo, The Swarm, Honeysuckle Rose, Tom Horn; regular on: TV series The Legend of Custer, The Outlaws; numerous other appearances including: Name of the Game, Wagon Train, Wide Country, Bonanza, Gunsmoke, Alias Smith and Jones, Men from Shiloh, The Mary Tyler Moore Show, Partridge Family, Hawaii Five-O, World of Disney, Baretta, McMillan and Wife, Mannix, Ironside; also TV film appearances. Home: Los Angeles, Calif. Died Dec. 8, 1983.

PICKERING, HAROLD GREGG, lawyer; b. Lake Mills, Ia., July 14, 1888; s. William Exum and Frank Rebecca (Gregg) P.; student U. Mich., 1907-08; LL.B., U. Wis., 1912; grad. U.S. Sch. Mil. Aeronautics, 1918; m. Susan Mildred Shipp, July 2, 1914. Admitted to Wis. bar, 1912, N.Y. bar, 1925; practicing lawyer, Superior, Wis., 1913-25; counsel Western Assn. Rolled Steel Mfrs. and 32 states in prosecution basing point case against U.S. Steel Corp. before Fed. Trade Commn., 1920-24; partner, specializing in trial work Rushmore, Bisbee & Stern (now Mudge, Stern, Williams & Tucker), N.Y. City, from 1925. Dir. Meth. Hosp., Brooklyn. Served as 2 lt., A.C. Res., 1918-27. Mem. Am. and N.Y. State bar assns., Assn. Bar City of N.Y., N.Y. Co. Lawyers Assn., Am. Judicature Soc., Legal Aid Soc., Am. Legion. Elk, Mason. Clubs: Union League, Grolier, Anglers, Downtown Athletic (N.Y. City). Author: Trout Fishing In Secret, 1931; Dog Days on Trout Waters, 1933; Angling of the Test, 1936; Neighbors Have My Ducks, 1937; Merry Xmas, Mr. Williams, 1940. Home: Greenwich, Conn. †

PICKERING, NELSON WINSLOW, corp. officer; b. Cambridge, Mass., Apr. 7, 1887; s. Joseph Winslow and Carolyn Belle (Langdon) P.; student Roxbury (Mass.) Latin Sch., 1898-1904; B.S., U.S. Naval Acad., 1908; LL.D. (hon.), Arnold College, New Haven, Conn., 1942; m. Amy H. Drury, Oct. 31, 1912; children—Nancy, Cynthia, Natalie. Officer U.S. Navy, 1904-19; resigned at lt. comdr. to join Farrel Foundry & Machine Co., Ansonia, Conn., and served as mgr. roll dept., 1926-30; pres. Farrel-Birmingham Co., Inc., 1930-43; exec. vice pres. Republic Industries, Inc., from 1946. Derby Gas & Electric Co., Ansonia Nat. Bank, Ansonia Water Co., Atwood Machine Co., Washington Trust Co. (Westerly, R.I.). Mem. Bd. of Apportionment, City of Ansonia. Served in World War I as lt. comdr. U.S. Navy; capt. U.S.

Naval Res. from 1919; comdg. officer 5th Batt. and Conn. Naval Militia; naval aide to Gov. John H. Trumbull, 6 years; naval aide to Gov. Raymond E. Baldwin. Called to active duty, U.S. Navy, Jan. 1943, rank of capt. Awarded Legion of Merit, for services in E.T.O. Pres. Nat. Metal Trades Assn.; v.p. N.A.M. Republican. Unitarian. Mason. Clubs: N.Y. Yacht (N.Y.); Army and Navy (Washington, D.C.); Graduate (New Haven); Misquamicut Golf, Watch Hill Yacht (Watch Hill, R.I.); Race Brook Country (Orange). Home: Westerly, R.I. †

PICKETT, HARRY KLEINBECK, marine corps officer; b. S.C., Jan. 9, 1888; commd. 2d lt., marine corps, Mar. 1913, and advanced through the grades to maj. gen., July 1945; Served both World Wars. Hon. mem. Order of the British Empire; twice awarded Legion of Merit Medal (U.S.).†

PICKRAL, GEORGE MONROE, educator; b. Gretna, Va., Jan. 2, 1922; s. George Monroe and Elizabeth (Gay) P.; m. Edna Moore McCormick, Mar. 10, 1945; children—James C., Robert M., Thomas M., Janet G., Elizabeth A. B.S., Va. Mil. Inst., 1943; M.A., Miami U., Oxford, O., 1950; Ph.D., U. Cin., 1953. Faculty Va. Mil. Inst., 1946-49, 53—, prof. chemistry, 1960—. Active local Boy Scouts Am., Little League Baseball. Served to 1st lt. USMCR, 1943-46. Mem. Am. Chem. Soc. (chmn. Va. Blue Ridge sect. 1971), Va. Acad. Scis., Sigma Xi, Phi Lambda Upsilon, Kappa Alpha. Club: Kiwanian. Home: Lexington VA.

PIDGEON, WALTER, actor; b. East St. John, N.B. Can., Sept. 23, 1898; m. Edna Pickles (dec.); 1 dau; m. 2d, Ruth Walker. Appeared with repertory groups, Boston; on tour with Elsie Janis troupe, 1925; stage plays include No More Ladies, Something Gay, The Night of January 16, There's Wisdom in Women; appeared Broadway comedy, The Happiest Millionaire, 1957, Broadway play, Take Me Along, 1959; numerous motion pictures, lastest being Big Brown Eyes, 1936, Girl Overboard, As Good As Married, Saratoga, 1937, Too Hot to Handle, Shopworn Angel, Girl of the Golden West, Listen Darling, 1938, Society Lawyer, Stronger than Desire, 1939, Nick Carter, It's a Date, 1940, How Green Was My Valley, Design for Scandal, 1941, Mrs. Miniver, White Cargo, 1942, Madame Curie, 1943, Week-end at the Waldorf, 1945, Holiday in Mexico, If Winter Comes, Command Decision, 1948, Executive Suite, 1954, The Rack, 1956, Advise and Consent, 1962, Warning Shot, Funny Girl, Skyjacked, 1972, also The Neptune Factor, Harry in Your Pocket. Served with Canadian Army, World War I. Home: Los Angeles, Calif. Died Sept. 25, 1984.

PIEPER, CHARLES JOHN, prof. education; b. Avilla, Ind., May 30, 1887; s. William and Rosina (Vogeding) P.; A.B., Wabash Coll., Crawfordsville, Ind., 1910; A.M., Columbia, 1926; m. Josephine Haley, 1929 (dec.); 1 son, Peter Joseph; m 2d, Clare E. Gerry, Nov. 17, 1938. Teacher chemistry, Shortridge High Sch., Indianapolis, 1910-13; teacher chemistry and gen. science, U. of Chicago High Sch., 1913-15; head dept. of science, U. of Minn. High Sch., 1915-16; head dept. of science U. of Chicago High Sch. and part time instr. in edn., U. of Chicago Sch. of Edn., 1916-18, 1919-26; asst. prof. edn., New York U., 1928-30, asso. prof., 1930-32, prof. from 1932. In Signal Corps and Chem. Warfare Service, U.S. Army, Apr. 1918-Dec. 1918, World War. Fellow A.A-.A.S.; mem. N.E.A., Phi Delta Kappa. Author: Everyday Problems in Science, 1925, rev. edit., 1932; (with W. L. Beauchamp and O. D. Frank) Everyday Problems in Biology, 1932. Home: New Rochelle, N.Y.

PIERCE, CHARLES CURRY, investment banker; b. Colorado City, Tex., Dec. 14, 1904; s. Charles Albert and Jessie (Curry) P.; m. Melverne Rawson, Mar. 28, 1932; children—Charles Curry, Marian Susan. Student, Wayland Coll., 1922-24; B.B.A., U. Mo., 1927. Securities dept. Merc. Nat. Bank, 1927-33; organizer Rauscher, Pierce & Co. (investment bankers), Dallas, 1933, v.p., 1933-64, pres., 1964-69, chmn., from 1969; dir. Henry Miller Real Estate Trust.; Past vice chmn. Midwest Stock Exchange. Sec. Tex. Scottish Rite Hosp. for Crippled Children; former trustee Wayland Coll. Mem. Investment Bankers Assn. (bd. govs., mem. legis. com., chmn. legis. com. Tex., v.p. 1964), Nat. Assn. Securities Dealers (past dist. chmn), Assn. Stock Exchange Firms (bd. govs.), Delta Sigma Pi. Methodist. Clubs: Mason (Dallas) (33 deg.), Dallas (Dallas), Dallas Country (Dallas); Petroleum. Home: Dallas, Tex.

PIERCE, JAMES HARVEY, mining engr.; b. Frackville, Pa., Sept. 26, 1887; s. Edward and Annette (Garaway) P.; E.M., Lehigh, 1910; Eng.D., 1946; m. Sara R. Hicks, Sept. 23, 1915 (dec. 1957). Mining engineer Lehigh Valley Coal Company, June-November 1910; division engineer Consolidation Coal Company, 1910-11; mining engineer Madeira Hill & Co., 1911-12; same, Paint Creek Collieries Co., 1912-13, gen. supt., 1913-15; same, East Bear Ridge Colliery Co., 1915-19; v.p. and gen. mgr. Thorne Neale & Co., 1919-27; v.p. and dir. Stuart, James & Cooke, Inc., engineers, 1927-32; president James H. Pierce & Co., engineers from 1932, changed to "Pierce Management," Feb. 1937, chmn.; supervisor numerous mining projects and surveys in Far East and the Balkans for ICA; dir. Internat. Ednl. Publishing Co.; Internat. Schs. Co. of Latin Am., Internat. Correspondence Schools, Ltd., Coaldale Mining Co., Inc. (pres.), Scranton, Sprague & Henwood Inc., Scranton, Internat. Text Book Co., Internat. Corr. Schs., Internat. Corr. Schs., Canadian Ltd., Sprague & Henwood, Inc., Registered professional engr. N.Y. Pa. Adviser to adminstr. on anthracite and bituminous coal under NRA; mem. Anthracite Industry Office Price Adminstration. Mining engring. consultant to Chinese Government. Panel and Solid Fuels Advisory War Council. Mem. Am. Inst. Mining and Metall. Engineers, Am. Mining Congress, Mining and Metall. Soc. of Am., The Pa. Soc. Republican. Mason (32 deg.). Club: Cranton; Mining (N.Y.C.); Blooming Grove Hunting and Fishing (Hawley, Pa.). Contbr. to Coal Age. †

PIERCE, MAURICE CAMPBELL, foreign service officer; b. Brodhead, Wis., Dec. 30, 1887; s. George Morris and Carolyn S. (Thompson) P.; prep. edn., high sch., Madison, Wis., and Hillside (Wis.) Home Sch.; student U. of Ill. 1 yr.; A.B., U. of Wis., 1913; unmarried. Began as vice consul, Barmen, Prussia, 1914; clk. at Consulate Gen., Zürich, Switzerland, 1915; clk. (temp.) Dept. of State, 1917; apptd. consul, Sept. 14, 1917; at Helsingborg, Sweden, 1917, Malmo, Sweden, 1918, Archangel, 1918, Murmansk, 1919, Christiania, 1919, Malmo, 1920, London, 1921-24. Bergen, Norway, 1924-29, Stuttgart, Germany, 1930, St. John, N.B., Can., from 1931. Unitarian. Address: Washington, D.C. Deceased.

PIERRE, EDWARD DIENHART, architect; b. Ft. Wayne, Ind., May 22, 1890; s. Joseph M. and Adelaide Barbara (Dienhart) P.; student Valparaiso U., 1913; B.S. in architecture, Armour Inst., 1915; m. Louise Strassner, June 30, 1926; 1 dau., Mary Dienhart (Mrs. Robert W. Hendrickson). Began career with J.M.E. Riedel, architect, 1905-12, Albert Kahn, 1915-17; pvt. practice from 1920. Author Cross Roads Parking Plan, Am. Legion Peace Symbol Found., Indpls. Christmas Com., Juvenile Aid Div.; adv. bd. Juvenile Ct., Child Guidance Clinic; v.p. Off St. Parking Commission, Indpls. member Indiana Sesquicentennial Commn. Fellow A.I.A.; mem. Ind. Soc. A.I.A. (chmn. civic design com.; pres. Indpls. sect.), C. of C., K.C. Author: Labeled Homes; Long Ranger. Home: Indianapolis, IN. †

PIERSON, LOUISE RANDALL, author; b. Quincy, Mass., May 18, 1890; d. John Chase and Henrietta Louise (Pickering) Randall; B.S., Simmons Coll., 1910; m. Rodney Dean, Dec. 23, 1911; children—Barbara, John vam Benschoten, Rodney, Jr., Louise Randall; m. Harold C. Pierson, July 31, 1924; 1 son, Frank Romer. Began career as stenographer. Unitarian. Author: Roughly Speaking, 1943.†

PIERSON, WILLIAM WHATLEY, JR., univ. dean; b. Brundidge, Ala., Nov. 30, 1890; s. William Whatley and Minto (Anglin) P.; Ph.B., State Normal Coll., Troy, Ala., 1908; A.B., U. of Ala., 1910, A.M., 1911; A.M., Columbia, 1912, Ph.D., 1916. Litt.D. Boston University, 1943; LL.D., Washington and Lee University, 1949; married Mary Bynum Holmes, 1945. Asst. in hist., Columbia, 1914-15; with Univ. of N.C. from 1915 as instructor hist., asst. prof., 1917-18, asso. prof., 1918-20, prof. history and govt. from 1920; Kenan traveling prof. (S.Am., Spain, France), 1924-25, acting dean of Grad. Sch., 1929-30, dean 1930-57, head department of polit. science, 1935-42, acting chancellor of Woman's College, 1956-57, 60-61, Kenan prof. polit. sci., 1959; acting director Board of Higher Education of North Carolina, 1960; secretary Assn. of American Universities, 1943-48; research associate in Venezuela, of Carnegie Instn., Washington, 1928. Research asso. Carnegie Endowment, 1940, survey state institutions of higher learning of Kans., 1941-42. Vice pres. So. U. Conf., 1951-52, president, 1953. Mem. bd. editors Hispanic Am. Hist. Rev.; editor, Inter-American Historical Series. Member American Hist. Assn., Am. Political Science Assn., N.C. State Lit. and Hist. Assn., Phi Beta Kappa, Sigma Alpha Epsilon; corr. mem. Hispanic Soc. America, Acad. Nac. de la Hist. de Venezuela. Acad. Nac. de Der. y Cien Soc., de Argentina. Rotarian. Democrat. Author: Texas V. White (a study in legal history), 1916; American Ideals (with N. Foerster), 1917; Hispanic American History—A Syllabus, 1926; Studies in Hispanic American History, 1927; The Diary of Bartlett Yancey Malone, pub. 1961; The Governments of Latin America (with F. G. Gil), 1956. Contbr. on hist. subjects. Home: Chapel Hill, N.C. †

PIKE, JOHN D., bldg. contractor; b. Rochester, N.Y., 1885; s. John B. and Nellie (Virgives) P.; student Rochester Inst. Tech.; m. Agnes Johnston, Aug. 4, 1909; children—Virginia Thoma (Mrs. Jackson), Sally (Mrs. Philip Farnham). Chmn. bd. John B. Pike & Son, Inc., Rochester, Central Trust Co., Rochester, Bd. dirs. Genesee Hosp., Reynolds Library. Home: Rochester, NY. †

PILLSBURY, DONALD MARION, physician; b. Omaha, Nebr., Dec. 29, 1902; s. Marion Albert and Amanda (Johnson) P.; student Creighton U., Omaha, 1919-20; A.M., U. Nebr., 1925, M.D., 1926; grad. tng. in dermatology and syphilology, U. Pa., 1928-33; m. Charlotte Forsman Denny, Sept. 3, 1929 (dec. 1970); children—Katherine Esmond, Donald Marion, David Chamberlain; m. 2d, Susan Peebles Cooper, Feb. 26, 1972. Intern U. Nebr. Hosp., 1926-28; engaged in research in bacteriology and chemistry of skin; pvt. practice, Phila., 1933-80; prof. dermatology and syphilology U. Pa. Med. Sch., 1945-80, chmn. dept. dermatology, 1945-65, prof. Grad. Sch. Medicine, 1946-80; cons. to surgeon gen. U.S. Army, 1946-80. Cons. dermatology to com. on medicine NRC, 1940-42, chmn. sub. com. dermatology, 1951-80. Served with AUS, 1942-45. Decorated Legion of Merit, Bronze star (U.S.); Bronze medal of honor Health Service France. Mem. Internat. Congress Dermatology (pres. 1958-62), Am. Dermatol. Assn., Coll. Physicians Phila., AMA, Soc. Investigative Dermatology, Soc. U.S. Med. Consultants in World War II (treas.), Assn. Am. Physicians, Am. Acad. Dermatology, Sigma Xi, Alpha Omega Alpha, Phi Rho Sigma. Independent Republican. Presbyn. Sr. author: Manual of Dermatology (prepared for Armed Forces), 1942; author: A Manual of Dermatology, 1971; co-author: Dermatology, 1956, A Manual of Cutaneous Medicine, 1961, Dermatology, 1975. Home: Rosemont, Pa. Died Oct. 9, 1980.

PILLSBURY, PHILIP WINSTON, food company executive; b. Mpls., Apr. 16, 1903; s. Charles Stinson and Nelle Pendleton (Winston) P.; m. Eleanor Bellows, July 5, 1934; children: Philip Winston, Henry Adams; m. Corinne Griffith, Nov. 7, 1977. A.B., Yale U., 1924; LL.D., Grinnell Coll., 1948. Began with The Pillsbury Co., 1924, dir., 1928-84, treas., 1940, pres., dir., 1940-52, chmn. bd., 1952-65, chmn. finance, exec. coms., 1965-70, hon. chmn., 1970-74, chmn. emeritus, 1974-84; dir. Sargent Mining Co.; Past mem. Chgo. Bd. Trade, Nat. Com. for Immigration Reform, Com. for Nat. Trade Policy; former mem. adv. com. Export-Import Bank of Washington, 1962-64; former mem. adv. com. bus. programs The Brookings Instn., Washington. Mem. adv. council Jr. Achievement of Mpls., 1956-64; mem. adv. council Indsl. Relations Center, U. Minn., 1945-71, Inst. Agr., U. Minn., 1950-62; former mem. Child Welfare League Am., Council on Social Work Edn.; Trustee Food Law Inst., Mpls. Found.; mem. exec. com. Yale Alumni Bd., bd. chmn., 1960-62; bd. dirs. Family and Children's Service, Mpls., 1939-60, pres., 1952-53, hon. French consul, 1960-79. Decorated officer Legion of Honor, France). Mem. Minn. Orchestral Assn. (past trustee, pres. 1956-58, dir.), Mpls. Soc. Fine Arts (former trustee), Met. Opera Assn., Jamestown Soc., Newcomen Soc., Soc. of the Cincinnati, Nat. Audubon Soc. (dir. 1968-74). Clubs: Racquet (Chgo.); Woodhill (Wayzata, Minn.); Minneapolis (Mpls.), Skylight (Mpls.). Home: Wayzata, Minn. Died June 14, 1984.

PINO, RALPH HARRISON, opthalmologist; b. Maple Rapids, Mich., July 4, 1888; s. Sander Pliny and Julia Anna (West) P.; student Ferris Inst., Big Rapids, Mich., 1908-11; M.D., U. of Ill. Coll. of Medicine, 1916; D.Sc. (honorary), Ferris Institute, 1958; m. Maude Erma Waite, Dec. 24, 1919 (div.), children—Eleanore A. (dec.), David Waite (dec.), Daniel Willis; m. 2d, Grace Marie Clark, Apr. 23, 1954. Interne, Harper Hospital, Detroit, 1916-18, actg. supt., 1918; asso. J. M. Robb, eye, ear, nose and throat, 1918-29; in individual practice of ophthalmology, from 1929; senior surgeon div. of ophthalmology, Harper Hosp.; surgeon Receiving Hosp. Originator, past chmn. Continuation Sch. of Med. of Wayne County. Chmn. Commn. on Health Care, Mich. State Med. Society. Fellow American College Surgeons, American Med. Assn., American Acad. Ophthalmology; mem. Am. Pub. Health Assn., Mich. State Med. Soc., Wayne County Med. Soc., Detroit Ophthal. Soc. Office: Detroit, Mich. †

PIPER, HOWARD, aviation cons.; b. Bradord, Pa., Nov. 3, 1917; s. William T. and Marie (Vandewater) P.; B.S., Harvard, 1939; m. Helen Wann, Dec. 29, 1939; children—David, Patricia, Howard. With Piper Aircraft Corp., 1939-73, v.p., 1950-73, also dir.; cons. Beech Aircraft Corp., 1973-76; gen. aviation cons., 1976-81; dir. aviation mgmt. program Wichita State U., 1978-81. Treas., Lock Haven (Pa.) Hosp., 1965-73. Served with USNR, 1942-45. Home: Wichita, Kans. Died June 16, 1981.

PIPPEN, RODGER HAMILL, sports editor; b. Baltimore, Feb. 21, 1888; s. Charles Edward and Roberta Olivia (Hamill) P.; grad. Baltimore City Coll., 1906; m. Nell Savage Wilkinson, Sept. 25, 1908. With Baltimore News, Post and Sunday American, from 1906, sports editor and columnist, from 1912; advt. writer for Tin Decorating Co., Howard W. French Co., also 10 other Baltimore business concerns, 1910-30. Received commendation for humanitarian service to dogs and horses (only such award given a citizen by a state body), Md. Ho. of Dels., 1944. Republican. Baptist. Club: Bolling Road Golf (Cantonville, Md.). Sr. golf champion of Md., 1944. Home: Baltimore, MD. †

PIRNIE, ALEXANDER, congressman; b. Pulaski, N.Y., Apr. 16, 1903; s. Roscoe C. and Mary R. (Price) P.; grad. Pulaski Acad.; A.B., Cornell U., 1924, J.D., 1926; m. Mildred Silvernail, July 7, 1938; children—Bruce R., Douglas J. Admitted to N.Y. bar, 1926; pres. Duofold, Inc.; mem. 86th to 87th Congresses, 34th Congl. Dist. N.Y., 88th to 93d Congresses, 32d Dist. N.Y. Past pres. Utica Community Chest. Past chmn. bd. mgrs. Faxton Hosp.; v.p. Utica Found. Served from 2d lt. inf. to col. Judge Adv. Gen. Corps, U.S. Army, 1942-46. Decorated Bronze Star, Legion of Merit. Mem. Am. Legion. Republican. Presbyterian. Club: Masons (33 deg.). Home: Utica, N.Y. Died June 12, 1982.

PITT, CARL ALLEN, educator; b. Three Forks, Mont., Sept. 6, 1911; s. John Marshall and Clara Rebecca (Biggs) P.; m. Olive Marguerite MacGillivray, June 29, 1935 (dec. Feb. 1963). B.A., Intermountain Union Coll., 1933; M.A., Wash. State Coll., 1946; summer postgrad., U. Iowa, 1947, U. Mich., 1949; Ph.D., Purdue U., 1952. Salesman Nat. Biscuit Co., Butte, Mont., 1933-40; dir. forensics

Highline High Sch., Seattle, 1942-46; dir. resources discussion U. Wash., 1946-48; faculty speech U. Ill., Chgo., 1950-73, prof., 1967-73, ret.; Lectr. on communication problems to coll. and civic groups. Editor: Chgo. Circle Studies, 1964-68; Past mem. editorial staff: Central States Speech Jour; contbr. articles to profl. jours. Air Age fellow, 1946. Mem. Speech Communication Assn. Am., Central States Speech Assn., Western Speech Communication Assn., Am. Forensic Assn., Internat. Communication Assn., Am. Assn. for Higher Edn., Am. Inst. Parliamentarians, Phi Delta Kappa, Pi Kappa Delta. Club: Mason (Shriner). Home: Seattle, WA.

PITTERMAN, BRUNE, Austrian govt. ofcl.; b. Vienna, Austria, Sept. 3, 1905; Ph.D. cum laude, Vienna U., 1928, student Faculty of Law, 1929-30, LL.D., 1938; married, 1 dau. Tchr. classical edn. Vocational Sch. Mech. and Elec. Engring., Vienna; sec. Chamber of Labour, Klagenfurt, 1929-34, staff ednl. and library affairs div., then. mem. social policy dept.; sec. to head dept. social welfare and adminstrn. Provisional Govt. Austrian Republic, 1945, sec.-gen. Vienna Chamber Labour, 1945; parliamentary dep. Nat. Assembly, from 1945; 1st sec., acting chmn. parliamentary party Socialist Nat. Assembly and Diet Deputies, 1948; exec. floor leader Socialist Parliamentary Party; chmn. Austrian Socialist Party, 1957-67; leader of the Socialist opposition and chmn. Socialist Parliamentary party, from 1966; in charge of the Dept. for Nationalized Industries within Fed. Chancellory (sect. 4), 1959-64; pres. Socialist Internat., from 1964; mem. Council European Consultative Assembly, from 1967. Active promotion unification of Europe; mem. polit, affairs com. Strasbourg and Council Europe's Consultative Assembly, 1952-57, dep. chmn., 1957. Address: Vienna, Austria. Died Sept 19, 1983.

PIZA, SAMUEL EMILIO, former Costa Rican consul gen., mcht.; b. San Jose, Costa Rica, Oct. 30, 1888; s. Benjamin E. and Emilia (Chamorro) P.; came to U.S., 1906-09, and 1917; naturalized, 1947, grad. Phillips Acad., Andover, Mass., 1909; m. Marie Calderon, Dec. 6, 1943. Junior clk., Ranco de Costa Rica, San Jose, 1911-12; consul gen., Nicaragua, Costa Rica, 1912-17; sec. in charge Costa Rican Legation. Washington, 1917-19; credit dept., fgn. trade, etc., Nat. City Bank of N.Y., 1919-22; pres. En Route Service, Inc., (travel orgn.), New York, 1924-31; dir. Artistic Prodns. (concert organ.); consul gen. Costa Rica to U.S. and posessions, 1944-48; head export-import business, N.Y. City, from 1948. Costa Rican del. del., 5th Internat. Congress of Chambers of Congress, Boston, 1912, to Pan-Am. Coffee Bur., 1942-48. Republican. Roman Catholic. †

PLACE, EDWIN BRAY, educator; b. La Harpe, Ill., Aug. 20, 1891; s. John and Anna (Bray) P.; A.B., U. Colo., 1913, A.M., 1916, Litt.D. (hon.), 1955; Ph.D., Harvard U., 1919; postgrad. research, Paris, Madrid, Rome, 1920, 25-26; m. Lula May Streamer, Aug. 5, 1914 (dec. Nov. 1956); children—Charles E., Dorothy-Lou (Mrs. J. D. Whicker), William O.; m. 2d, Marian Fredine, June 7, 1957. Instr., U. Colo., 1916-18, asst. prof. Romance langs., 1919-21, asso. prof., 1921-24, prof., 1924-35, head dept., 1931-35; instr. French, Harvard, 1918-19; prof. Romance langs. Northwestern U., 1935-56, emeritus, 1956-80, chmn. dept., 1935-45. Vis. prof. Spanish, U. Pa., 1934; vis. lectr. Spanish, U. Calif. at Berkeley, 1956-58, vis. prof., 1966-68; vis. prof. Romance langs. U. Chgo., 1963-64. Mem. Am. Assn. Tchrs. Spanish (pres. 1937), Mediaeval Acad. Am. (councillor 1942-45), MLA (exec. council 1946-47), Am. Assn. Tchrs. French (v.p. 1939-40), Am. Assn. Tchrs. Italian (councillor 1939), Phi Beta Kappa, Sigma Chi, Phi Sigma Iota (nat. pres. 1940-46); mem. Hispanic Soc. Am. Named Officier d'Academie (France). Author: María de Zayas, 1923; (with C.C. Ayer) Un viaje por España, 1924; Manuel elemental de novelística española, 1926; (with N.B. Adams) Lecturas modernas, 1939; (with A. Torres-Rioseco) Contemporary Spanish Grammar, 1943; contbg. author: A Critical Bibliography of Old French Literature, 1947. Editor: Así se escribe la historia, 1926; La casa del placer honesto, 1927, 68; Madame Corentine, 1927; Don Gonzalo González de la Gonzalera, 1931; Gilles de Chyn, 1941; Processo de cartas, 1950; Amadís de Gaula, 1959, 62, 65, 68. 69. Translator: (with H.C. Behm) Translation of Amadís de Gaula, Books I and II, 1974, III and IV, 1975. Contbr. Am., fgn. jours., encys. Home: Oakland, Calif. Died Feb. 27, 1980; buried Green Mountain Cemetery, Boulder, Colo.

PLANT, MARCUS LEO, emeritus legal educator; b. New London, Wis., Nov. 10, 1911; s. George Henry and Margaret (McGinty) P.; m. Geraldine Hefter, Dec. 27, 1944; children: Margaret, Elizabeth, Mark, Nancy. B.A., Lawrence Coll., 1932, M.A., 1934; J.D., U. Mich., 1938. Bar: Wis. 1939, N.Y. 1946, Mich. 1949. Pvt. practice Miller, Mack & Fairchild, Milw., 1938-44, Cahill, Gordon, Zachry & Reindel, N.Y.C., 1944-46; prof. law U. Mich., Ann Arbor, 1946-82, prof. law emeritus, 1982-84. Author: Cases on the Law of Torts, 1953, (with Burke Shartel) The Law of Medical Practice, 1959, (with Wex S. Malone) Cases and Materials on Workmen's Compensation, 1962, (with Wex S. Malone and Joseph W. Little) Cases and Materials on the Employment Relation, 1974, Cases and Materials on Workers' Compensation and Employment Rights, 1980; also (with Wex S. Malone and Joseph W. Little) various articles law jours. Rep. U. Mich. in Intercollegiate Conf. Faculty Reps., 1955-79, sec., 1956-79; mem. U.S. Olympic Com., 1969-72. Mem. Nat. Collegiate Athletic Assn. (pres. 1967-69), Order of Coif, Tau Kappa Alpha, Delta Tau Delta. Home: Ann Arbor, Mich. Died July 15, 1984.

PLATT, JOSEPH SWAN, lawyer; b. Columbus, Ohio, Jan. 8, 1902; s. Rutherford Hayes and Maryette (Smith) P.; grad. Hotchkiss Sch., 1920; B.A., Yale, 1924; LL.B. cum laude, Harvard, 1927; m. Margaret Hubbell Day, Feb. 24, 1930; children—Emily (Mrs. Roy L. Hilburn), Robert Day, William Rutherford, David Day, Elizabeth Swan (Mrs. Charles R. Carmalt). Admitted to Ohio bar, 1927, since practiced in Columbus; partner firm Porter, Wright, Morris and Arthur and predecessor firms, 1946-81; with AAA, 1933-34, Bd. Econ. Warfare, 1943; chief criminal and compromise sects. tax div. Dept. Justice, 1944-46; lectr., adj. prof. Coll. Law, Ohio State U., 1946-73. Mem. commr.'s adv. com. IRS, 1953-55; conferee estate and gift tax project Brookings Instn. Fellow Am., Ohio bar founds.; mem. Am., Ohio, Columbus bar assns., Am. Law Inst., Phi Beta Kappa, Order of Coif, Alpha Delta Phi, Phi Delta Phi. Contbr. articles to profl. jours. Home: Columbus, Ohio. Died May 8, 1981.

PLATT, WILLIAM, architect; b. N.Y.C., Feb. 6, 1897; s. Charles Adams and Eleanor (Hardy) P.; m. Margaret Littell, June 3, 1922; children—Eleanor, Clarissa, Charles Adams. A.B., Harvard, 1919; B.Arch., Columbia, 1923. Began as architect in, 1924, pvt. practice, 1928-33; mem. firm Charles A. Platt, William and Geoffrey Platt, 1933, William & Geoffrey Platt, 1934-72, Platt, Wyckoff & Coles, 1972-84; cons. architect Vanderbilt U., 1957-69. Recent works include bldgs. for Chapel at Am. Mil. Cemetery, Suresnes, France, Nat. Acad. Sch. Fine Arts, N.Y.C., Gen. MacArthur Meml; faculty housing, Princeton, N.J., N.Y. Bot. Garden, Garden Center Greater Cleve, Bennett Coll. Arts Center, Norfolk Mus. Arts and Scis. Hon. pres. Saint Gaudens Mus.; trustee emeritus Am. Acad. in Rome. Comdg. ensign, naval aviation World War I; lt. comdr. USNR, 1942; comdr. 1945. Recipient 1st prize internat. competition, Replanning Central Bus. Dist. City of Stockholm, 1933. Fellow AIA, Archtl. League. Club: Century Assn. (N.Y.C.). Home: Cornish, N.H. Died Apr. 30, 1984.

PLATTS, RALPH H., ins. exec.; b. Port Sanilac, Mich., Jan. 17, 1890; s. Henry c. and Barbara Ann (Matheson) P.; ed. pub. schs. of Mich.; grad. Ferris Inst., 1911; m. May E. MacPherson, Oct. 18, 1913; children—Ralph H., Jr., Irene M. (Mrs. Robert B. Kelly). Began as school teacher for two years; from engaged in the insurance business; pres. Standard Accident Ins. Co. and its affiliates, also dir., Detroit, from 1937; dir. Michigan Fire & Marine Ins. Co. Mason. Clubs: The Detroit, Detroit Athletic, Detroit Golf (Detroit); Bankers (N.Y. City). Home: Royal Oak, Mich. †

PLAXTON, CHARLES PERCY, judge; b. Barrie, Ont., Can., Dec. 21, 1889; s. Charles Wilson and Harriet Ann (Train) P.; barrister and solicitor, Osgoode Hall, Toronto, 1915; m. Gabrielle, Faribault, Feb. 15, 1919; children—Harriet Jane (Mrs. T. J. Bowie), Carol Beverley (Mrs. Norman Plant), Charles Gordon, Gabrielle, Iola, George Train, Anne Kathryn, James Lawrence Percy, Dawn. Newspaper reporter, Barrie Examiner, 1906-09; Toronto Mail and Empire, 1909-12; sr. advisory counsel, dept. justice, Ottawa, 1915-40; justice Supreme Court of Ontario, Dec. 13, 1940-Jan. 1, 1946; member Plaxton & Company. Legal adviser to Canadian ministers of justice at Imperial conferences preparing and approving draft Statute of Westminister, 1929-30; prepared argument for Canada in Labrador Boundary dispute with Newfoundland, 1921-26; King's Counsel, Government of Quebec, 1927; presented constitutional cases before Supreme Court, Can. and Eng. Privy Council's Judicial Com., 1927-40. Clubs: University (Toronto and Ottaswa.) Author: Dominion Income Tax Law, 1921 (3 edits.); Canadian Income Tax Law, 1939; Canadian Const. Law Cases (1929-39), 1940. †

PLENZKE, OSWALD H(ENRY), educator; b. Newburg, Wis., Sept. 16, 1888; s. William and Rosa (Schmidt) P.; grad. State Normal Sch., Oshkosh, Wis., 1911; A.B., Lawrence Coll., Appleton, Wis., 1914; A.M. U. of Wis., 1924; m. Edith Kirchner, Aug. 4, 1915; 1 dau., Ruth Louise. Teacher rural schools, Wis., 1907-09; prin. Menasha (Wis.) High Sch., 1914-16; prin. Lincoln Sch., Madison, Wis., 1916-18; supt. city schools, Menasha, Wis., 1918-26; asst. state supt. pub. instrn., Wis., 1926-34; exec. sec. Wis. Edn. Assn. and editor Wis. Jour. Edn. from 1934. Mem. N.E.A., Wis. Edn. Assn. (pres. 1933), Phi Delta Kappa, Phi Sigma Sigma. Mason (32 deg.). Club: Madison Cine 8 (pres.). Author of ednl. monographs. Home: Madison, Wis. †

PLETSCH, GEORGE BURGESS, lawyer; b. Tonica, Ill., June 24, 1921; s. Ernest Phillip and Grace (Burgess) P.; m. Joan E. Hammerschmidt, Feb. 16, 1946; children: George William, James Burgess. A.B., U. Chgo., 1942, J.D. 1944; LL.D., Ill. Inst. Tech. Bar: Ill. 1943, D.C. 1977, U.S. Supreme Ct 1958. Assoc. Pam, Hurd & Reichmann (now Schiff Hardin & Waite), Chgo., 1943-51, partner, 1952-84; dir. Groman Corp., Gen. Employment Enterprises, Inc., Hamler Industries, Inc., Head, Inc., Planning Decisions Group, Inc., Inca Plastics, Inc., Michael-Leonard, Inc., Porcelain Products Co., Pub. Communications Inc., Tonica State Bank., Tonica Bancorp, Inc., Farmers State Bank of Lostant. Trustee Millikin U., chmn., 1975-78; trustee, exec. com., sec. Ill. Inst. Tech.; trustee, bd. govs., sec., gen. counsel IIT Research Inst.; bd. overseers Chgo.-Kent Coll. Law; bd. dirs. Grover Hermann Found. Mem. Internat., Am., Fed. Energy, Ill., Chgo. bar assns., Law Club Chgo., Legal Club Chgo. Clubs: Mid-Am. (Chgo.), Union League (Chgo.), Metropolitan (Chgo.), Econ. (Chgo.). Home: Park Ridge, Ill. Died Apr. 24, 1984.

PLIMPTON, FRANCIS T. P., lawyer, diplomat; b. N.Y.C., Dec. 7, 1900; s. George Arthur and Frances Taylor (Pearsons) P.; m. Pauline Ames, June 4, 1926; children—George Ames, Francis T.P., Jr., Oakes Ames, Sarah Gay. A.B. magna cum laude, Amherst Coll., 1922, L.H.D. (hon.), 1973; J.D., Harvard U., 1925; LL.D. (hon.), Colby Coll., 1960, Lake Forest Coll., 1964, NYU, 1970, Yale U., 1972, Vt. Law Sch., 1979; L.H.D. (hon.), Pratt Inst., 1967, Adelphi U., 1972. Bar: N.Y. 1926. Assoc. firm Root, Clark, Buckner & Ballantine, N.Y.C., 1925-32, in charge Paris office, 1930-31; gen. solicitor RFC, Washington, 1932-33; partner firm Debevoise & Plimpton (and predecessors), N.Y.C., 1933-61, from 65; ambassador, dep. U.S. rep. UN, 1961-65; mem. U.S. dels. 15th-19th gen. Assemblies; mem. adv. com. internat. orgns. Dept. State, 1965-69; 1st v.p., mem. adminstrv. tribunal UN, 1966-80. Author mag. articles; contbg. author: As We Knew Adlai, 1965. Trustee U.S. Trust Co., N.Y.C., 1936-80; trustee Bowery Savs. Bank, 1948-75, Tchrs. Ins. and Annuity Assn., 1946-68, Stock and Coll. Retirement Equity Fund, 1949-75; pres. Tchrs. Ins. and Annuity Assn., 1951-75; Chmn. N.Y.C. Bd. Ethics, Mayor's N.Y.C. Com. Disting. Guests; trustee Phillips Exeter Acad., 1935-65, pres. or chmn. bd., 1956-65; trustee emeritus Amherst Coll., Bernard Coll., Union Theol. Sem., Athens (Greece) Coll., Lingnan (China) U., Met. Mus. Art; bd. overseers Harvard U., 1963-69; trustee N.Y. Lawyers Public Interest, French Inst.-Fedn. French Alliances, Am.-Italy Soc., UN Assn. U.S.; hon. trustee St. Luke's-Roosevelt Hosp., N.Y.C.; bd. dirs. Adlai Stevenson Inst. Internat. Affairs, 1965-76, Philharm. Soc. N.Y. Decorated chevalier Legion of Honor, France; comdr. Order of Merit, Italy; Order Law, Culture and Peace Mex.; asso. knight Order St. John Jerusalem; recipient Disting. Public Service award New Eng. Soc. N.Y., 1963, Disting. Public Service award Fed. Bar Council, 1964, Disting. Public Service award St. Nicholas Soc., 1974, Disting. Public Service award Inst. Man and Sci., 1975; Bronze medal City of N.Y., 1975; Gold medal N.Y. Bar Assn., 1977; Gold medal Assn. Bar City N.Y., 1980; medal of distinction Barnard Coll., 1979; Justice award Legal Aid Soc., 1981. Fellow Am. Acad. Arts and Scis., Am. Bar Found.; Benjamin Franklin fellow Royal Soc. Arts; mem. ABA (ho. of dels.), N.Y. State Bar Assn., Assn. Bar City of N.Y. (pres. 1968-70), Internat. Bar Assn., Inter-Am. Bar Assn., Union Internat. des Avocats (hon. v.p.), Am. Law Inst., Am. Soc. Internat. Law, Internat. Law Sch., Fgn. Policy Assn. (dir. 1935-49), Council Fgn. Relations, Washington Inst. Fgn. Affairs, Acad. Polit. Sci., Pilgrims, Soc. Mayflower Descs., Colonial Soc. Mass., Phi Beta Kappa, Delta Kappa Epsilon, Delta Sigma Rho. Presbyterian. Clubs: Union (N.Y.C.), Century (N.Y.C.), Brook (N.Y.C.), River (N.Y.C.), Grolier (N.Y.C.), Down Town (N.Y.C.), Coffee House (N.Y.C.), Economic (N.Y.C.); Piping Rock (L.I.), Cold Spring Harbor Beach (L.I.); Metropolitan (Washington); Ausable (Adirondacks); Mill Reef (Antigua, W.I.). Home: Huntington, N.Y. Died July 30, 1983.

PLOUGH, ABE, pharm. mfr.; b. Tupelo, Miss., Dec. 27, 1891; s. Mose and Julia (Isaacs) P.; ed. pub. schs. of Memphis; children—Jocelyn (Mrs. Rudner), Harriet Sternberger (Mrs. Solmson). Founded Plough, Inc., mfrs. pharmaceuticals with St. Joseph, Mexsana and Pentro labels, Memphis, 1908, pres. and dir. Dir. William R. Moore Sch. Tech. Mem. C. of C., Zool. Soc. Clubs: Ridgeway Country, Home: Hotel Peabody, Memphis. Home: Memphis, Tenn. Died Sept. 14, 1984.

PLOWMAN, LAURENCE CARRINGTON, real estate and indsl. devel. co. exec.; b. Berkeley, Calif., Aug. 13, 1906; s. George Taylor and Maude (Bell) P.; student Wentworth Inst., 1925-27; m. Mabel Christie, June 23, 1930; 1 dau., Anne Christie. Indsl., gen. real estate exec., Boston, also Portland, Maine, 1933-45; pres. Industries, Inc., Portland, 1945-52; propr. Laurence C. Plowman Co., Portland, 1950-52; v.p. Textron Inc., Providence, 1952-58; pres. Hawiian Textron, Inc., 1957-59; exec. v.p. R.I. Devel. Co., 1953-57; exec. v.p., regional mgr. Arthur Rubloff & Co. of Calif., 1972-76. Adv. Greater Portland Pub. Devel. Commn., 1945-52; mem. Gov.'s Adv. Com. Indsl. Devel., N.H., 1949-57; chmn. planning bd., City of Portland, 1951-52; commr. Greater Portland Regional Planning Bd., 1956-58. Mgr. Nashua (N.H.) Found., 1948-52. Home: Portland, Maine. Died June 24, 1983; buried Brooklawn Cemetery, Portland, Maine.

PLUMER, PAUL SOUTHWORTH, newspaper editor; b. Union, Maine, Sept. 12, 1907; s. Herbert Hall and Alice Linda (Southworth) P.; grad. Mount Hermon Prep. Sch., 1925; A.B., Conn. Wesleyan U., 1929; m. Claire E. Miller, Aug. 25, 1935; children—Paul, Stephen Hall, Timothy Carl. Mem. staff Kenebec Jour., Augusta, Maine, 1931-72, editor 1949-72, also asst. gen. mgr., 1950-56, editor, gen. mgr., 1956-72; v.p. Guy Gannett Pub. Co., 1959-72. Pres., Kennebec Valley Community Chest, 1960; vice chmn. Maine. State Mus. Com., 1966-72. Mem. New Eng. Asso., Press News Execs. Assn. (pres. 1958), Maine Daily Newspaper Pubs. Assn. (pres. 1965-66), Augusta Area C. of C. (pres. 1959), Sigma Nu. Methodist.

Rotarian. Home: Damariscotta, Maine. Died Jan. 24, 1982.

POCOCK, PHILIP F., archbishop; b. St. Thomas, Ont., Can., July 2, 1906; s. Stephen Bernard and Sarah-May (McCarthy) P. Student, Assumption Coll., 1922-23; A.B., U. Western Ont., 1926; grad., St. Peter's Sem., 1930; postgrad., Cath. U. Am., 1931-32; J.C.D., Angelicum, Rome, 1934. Ordained priest Roman Catholic Ch., 1930; prof. moral theology and canon law St. Peter's Sem., 1934-44, consecrated bishop, 1944, installed as bishop of, Saskatoon, Sask., Can., 1944; named apostolic adminstr. Archdiocese of Winnipeg, 1951, titular archbishop Apro and coadjutor archbishop of, Winnipeg, 1951, succeeded to See, 1952; titular archbishop of Isauropoli and coadjutor archbishop of, Toronto, 1961, succeeded to See, 1971, resigned, 1978. Address: Brampton, Ont., Canada. Died Sept. 6, 1984.

POGUE, JOSEPH EZEKIEL, petroleum consultant; b. Raleigh, N.C., June 6, 1887; s. Joseph Ezekiel and Henrietta (Kramer) P.; A.B., U. of N.C., 1906, M.S., 1907; Ph.D., Yale, 1909; spl. student U. of Heidelberg, 1911; m. Grace Needham, Apr. 17, 1919. Asst. curator div. mineralogy and petrology, Smithsonian Instn., 1909-13; asso. geologist, U.S. Geol. Survey, 1913-14; asso. prof. geology and mineralogy, Northwestern U., 1914-17; mineral technologist, div. of mineral technology, Smithsonian Instn., 1917-18; asst. dir. bur. oil conservation, U.S. Fuel Adminstrn., 1918; mgr. dept. econ. research, Sinclair Consol. Oil Corp., 1919-20; consulting engr., 1921-36; v.p. Chase Nat. Bank, 1936-49; petroleum consultant; director Gulf Oil Corporation. Acting chmn., petroleum econ. com. Federal Oil Conservation Bd., 1930; mem. mineral adv. com. to Army and Navy Munitions Bd., 1939; spl. asst. to chmn. Petroleum Industry War Council, 1942; member of the National Petroleum Council from 1946. Mem. Nat. Oil Policy Com., Petroleum Industry War Council, Fellow Geol. Society of America, American Statistical Association; member American Society M.E., Am. Inst. Mining and Metall. Engrs., Am. Econ. Association, American Association Petroleum Geologists, Soc. Automotive Engineers, American Petroleum Institute, Phi Beta Kappa, Sigma Xi, Alpha Tau Omega. Clubs: University, Yale, Duquesne, St. George's, Mountain Lake. Author: Prices of Petroleum and Its Products During the War, 1919; The Economics of Petroleum, 1921; The Economic Structure of the American Petroleum Industry, 1936; Economics of the Petroleum Industry, 1939; Oil and National Policy, 1948; Oil in Venezuela, 1949; Oil in Canada, 1949; Oil in Brazil, 1951; Future Growth and Financial Requirements of the World Petroleum Industry, 1956. Co-author: The Energy Resources of the United States, 1919; America's Power Resources, 1921; Capital Formation in the Petroleum Industry, 1952. Wrote brochure "The Turquoise." Contbr. numerous articles on tech. and econ. topics. Home: New York, N.Y.†

POHL, JOHN FLORIAN, orthopedic surgeon; b. Saint Cloud, Minn., Aug. 25, 1903; s. Francis William and Mary Ellen (Heartz) P.; B.S., U. Minn., 1926, M.B., 1928, M.D., 1929; student Carleton Coll., Northfield, Minn., 1922-23, Harvard, 1934-35, U. Manchester (Eng.), 1935-36; m. Alice Elizabeth Croze, June 16, 1941; children—Mary Ellen, Peter Jon, John Martin DeLand. Interne, City Hosp., St. Louis, 1928-29; pediatrician's asst., Mpls., 1929-31; house surgeon, Childrens Hosp., Boston, 1931-34, neuro-surg. asst., 1936-37; house surgeon, Mass. Gen. Hosp., Boston, 1934-35; orthopedic surgeon, Mpls., 1937-82; med. supr. Elizabeth Kenny Inst., 1940-48; clin. asst. prof. orthopedic surgery U. Minn., 1937-48; orthopedic surgeon Michael Dowling Sch. for Crippled Children, Mpls.; attending orthopedic surgeon Mpls. Gen., Abbott, Northwestern, Maternity and Asbury hosps. (all Mpls.), Glen Lake Sanatorium for Tuberculosis; orthopedic cons. Mpls. Bd. Edn. Served as lt. comdr. USNR, 1942-43. Traveling fellow WHO, Europe, 1951. Mem. Hennepin County, Minn. State med. socs., Mpls. Acad. Medicine, Acad. Orthopedic Surgeons, Theta Chi, Nu Sigma Nu. Club: Harvard. Author: The Kenny Concept of Infantile Paralysis and Its Treatment, 1943; Cerebral Palsy, 1950. Contbr. articles to med. jours. Home: Minneapolis, Minn. Died Mar. 5, 1982.

POLITZ, ALFRED, consumer and indsl. researcher; s. Alfred and Martha (Arlt) P.; student exptl. psychology, doctorate in Physics, U. Berlin; m. Martha Bruszat, Mar. 28, 1939. Founder, Alfred Politz Research Orgn., N.Y.C., 1943, dir. incorporation, 1947, pres. Alfred Politz Research, Inc., 1947-64, chmn. bd., 1964-67; lectr. Columbia, Yale, N.Y. U. Recipient leadership award for devel. sci. standards, mktg. research techniques Am. Mktg. Assn., 1946, for devel. econs., sci. sampling procedures, 1947; ann. award for creativeness Media-Scope mag., 1960, ann. award for creative media research, 1963; named to Mktg. Hall of Fame, 1953, Transit Advt. Hall of Fame, 1977. Mem. World Assn. Pub. Opinion Research, Market Research Council (life). Contbr. articles to profl. and sci. publs. Home: Odessa, Fla. Died Nov. 8, 1982.

POLLACK, JACK HARRISON, author; born Philadelphia, Pa.; s. Louis and Rebecca (Glick) P.; B.A., University of Pennsylvania, 1936; spl. studies Utrecht (Holland) U.; 1961-63; children—Susan Deborah. Magazine, newspaper advertising and public relations work, New York City and Phila., 1936-41; press liaison officer alien registration Dept. Justice 1941-42; information specialist Office Civilian Def., 1943; investigator, pub. relations adviser, subcom. war moblzn. Senate Mil. Affairs Com., 1943-44; spl. asst. to dept. chmn. and exec. dir. War Manpower Commn., 1945; investigator Senate Small Bus. Com., 1945; Washington editor This Month mag., 1946; contbr. pub. service articles leading nat. mags., 1946-84; lectr. mag. writing N.Y.U., parapsychology at various European universities. Recipient 1st prize Edn. Writers Assn., 1949. Nat. Community Chest award for articles, 1956, National School Bell award, 1965. Member of Soc. Mag. Writers (pres. 1957). Clubs: Nat. Press (Washington); Overseas Press (N.Y.C.). Author: A Psychology Outline, 1938; Croiset the Clairvoyant, 1964. Contbr. to many books. Home: New York, N.Y. Died Sept. 30, 1984.

POLLARD, HERMAN MARVIN, physician, educator; b. Lamar, Colo., 1906; 1 son, William Lee. M.D., U. Mich., 1931, M.S., 1938. Diplomate: Am. Bd. Internal Medicine. Intern U. Mich. Hosp., Ann Arbor, 1931-33, instr. internal medicine, 1933-38, asst. prof., 1938-45, assoc. prof., 1945-51, prof., from 1951, then prof. emeritus; cons. in gastroenterology VA Hosp., Ann Arbor, 1953. Fellow A.C.P. (pres. 1968-69); mem. AMA, Central Soc. Clin. Research, Am. Fedn. Clin. Research, Am. Gastroenterology Soc., Am. Cancer Soc. (pres. 1970—), Am. Gastroent. Assn. (pres. 1959), World Orgn. Gastroenterology (pres. 1970—), Am. Assn. for Cancer Research. Home: Ann Arbor, Mich. Died July 14, 1982.

POLLARD, VIOLET MCDOUGALL (MRS. JOHN GARLAND POLLARD), Dem. nat. committeewoman; b. Maxville, Ont., Can., July 17, 1889; d. Peter and Ellen (Robertson) McDougall; ed. pub. sch. and high sch., Ont., Can., and Cornwall (Ont.) Normal Sch.; student Regina (Saskatchewan) Coll., 1912-13, George Washington U., Washington, D.C., 1935-37; m. John Garland Pollard, July 31, 1933. Came to U.S., 1917, naturalized, 1934; teacher pub. schs., Ontario, Can., graded schs., Saskatchewan, Can., 1910-12; sec. in law office, 1913-17; exec. sec. to 4 successive governors of Va., 1918, and 1919-33; sec. to asst. adminstr. U.S. Housing Adminstrn., 1938-40; mem. Virginia Museum Fine Arts, asso. dir. until 1956. Mem. Dem. Nat. Com., from 1940, Dem. Woman's Club, Young Dem. Club of Richmond. Past v.p. Historic Richmond Found. Member board Richmond Symphony Orchestra. Mem. of the Academy Polit. Science, League of Women Voters, Federated Arts of Richmond (bd. mem.), English Speaking Union (bd. mem. Richmond br.), Va. Hist. Soc., Kappa Beta Pi. Presbyn. Clubs: Colony (bd. mem.), Womans (pres. 1961-63), Country of Virginia (Richmond). Home: Richmond, Va. †

POLLOCK, CARL ARTHUR, mfg. co. exec.; b. Kitchener, Ont., Can., 1903; s. Arthur B. P.; B.A.Sc., U. Toronto (Ont., Can.); B.Sc., Magdalen Coll., Oxford U. (Eng.); m. Helen Chestnut; children—Barbara, John. Hon. chmn. Electrohome, Ltd., Kitchener, 1976-79; dir. Central Ont. TV, Ltd., Burns Foods, Ltd., Dominion Life Ins. Co. Bd. govs. Ont. Research Found., chancellor U. Waterloo. Decorated Officer of Order of Canada. Mem. Can. Mfrs. Assn. (life mem.; pres. 1962-63), Elec. and Electronics Mfrs. Assn. Can. (past pres.). Clubs: Univ. (Toronto); Mount Royal (Montreal). Home: Kitchener, Ont., Canada. Died 1979.

POLLOCK, EDWIN A., Marine Corps officer; b. Augusta, Ga., Mar. 21, 1899; s. Edwin Barnet and Wilhelmina (Harben) P.; B.S., The Citadel, 1921, D. Mil. Sci., 1956; LL.D., Pennsylvania Military College, 1959; married Mary Essie Morgan, July 25, 1922; children—Edwin A., Martha Jane (Mrs. Edward J. Appel). Commd. 2d lt. USMC, 1921, advanced through grades to lt. gen.; served to various posts U.S. and Latin Am., 1921-42; comdr. 2d Bn., 1st Marine Post, 1942, exec. officer, 1942-43, asst. chief of staff, 1943-44; staff instr. Army-Navy Staff Coll., 1944; operations officer 4th Marine Div., 1944-45; comdg. officer Basic Sch., also exec. officer Marine Corps. Schs., chief of staff Marine Barracks, 1945-48; mil. sec. to Comdt. Marine Corps, 1948-49; dir. div. plans and policies Marine Hdqrs., 1949-51; comdg. gen. 2d Div., Camp Lejeune, N.C., 1951-52; comdr. 1st Div., Korea, 1952-53; dir. Marine Corps Ednl. Centr, 1953-54; comdr. Marine Corps Recruit Depot, Parris Island, S.C., 1954-56; comdt. Marine Corps Schs., Quantica, Va., 1956; comdg. gen., Fleet Marine Force, Pacific, 1956-57, Atlantic, 1957-82, Decorated Navy Cross, Army Distinguished Service Medal, Legion of Merit, B.S.M. (U.S.); Order Mil. Merit of Taiguk (Korea). Mason. Died Nov. 5, 1982.

POLLOCK, WILLIAM, ret. labor union exec.; b. Phila., Nov. 12, 1899; s. Louis and Agnes (Garner) P.; ed. high sch.; m. Anna M. Keene, Feb. 3, 1919; children—William F., Kenneth W. Textile weaver, 1920-30; local union ofcl., Phila., 1931-37; mgr. Phila. joint bd. Textile Works Union Am., 1937-39, gen. sec.-treas., 1939-53, exec. v.p., 1953-56, gen. pres., 1956-72; exec. com. indsl. union dept., AFL-CIO, 1956-72, gen. bd., 1956-68, exec. council, 1967-73, ret., 1973; exec. com. Internat. Fedn. Textile, Garment and Leather Workers Fedn.; treas. Inter-Am. Textile and Garment Workers Federation, 1967-70. Labor rep. for Pa., NRA, 1933-35; mem. Phila. Labor Bd., 1933-35, Fed. Textile Commn., World War II; del. Inter-Am. Conf. Free Trade Unions, Mexico City, 1951. Co-chmn. nat. labor div. March of Dimes. Author: Textiles: A National Crisis, 1956; No Rights at All, 1957; An Industry That's Sick, 1958. Died Mar. 10, 1982.

POMERANTZ, ABRAHAM L(OUIS), lawyer; b. Bklyn., Mar. 22, 1903; s. Louis and Lena (Betz) P.; m. Phyllis Cohen, Jan. 10, 1926; children—Dan, Charlotte. LL.B. cum laude, Bklyn. Law Sch., 1924. Bar: N.Y. 1924. Practiced law, N.Y.C., from 1924; founding mem. firm Pomerantz, Levy, Haudek & Block, 1940; instr. law Bklyn. Law Sch., 1925; lectr. Columbia U., U. Pa., Harvard U. Law Sch., Yale U. Law Sch., Northwestern U. Law Sch., U. London; dep. chief counsel in prosecution of Nazi War Criminals Nuremburg Trials, 1946; Mem. adv. com. rules of practice and procedure U.S. Supreme Ct.; mem. com. on qualifications to practice before U.S. cts. 2d Circuit Jud. Council of 2d Circuit; mem. Anglo-Am. Exchange, 1973. Participants seminars Am. Bar Assn., Am. Law Inst., Practicing Law Inst., N.Y. Law Jour. Home: New York, N.Y. Died Nov. 20, 1982.

POMEROY, CLEVE H., business exec.; b. Cleveland, O., Mar. 1, 1890; s. George H. and Clare (Lockwood) P.; A.B., Western Reserve Univ., 1912; m. Mary Day Ely, April 11, 1917, (died July 18, 1946); 1 son, Cleve H.; m. 2d, Elisabeth Stevens Shumann, June 12, 1948. With Investment Securities, Cleveland, 1912-20; credit mgr. Nat. & Steel Castings Co., 1920-26, asst. treas., 1926-35, treas., 1935-36, secretary, treas., 1936-38, dir., 1938, v.p. 1944-46, pres., 1946-58, chmn., from 1958; dir. Interlake Iron Corp., Norman's Kill Farm Diary Co., Nat. City Bank of Cleve. Mem. governing bd. Nat. Indsl. Conf. Bd., adv. com. Case Inst. Tech. Mem. bd. trustees Western Res. U., Cleve.; mem. Met. Park Commn. Mem. C. of C. (chmn.), Transportation Assn. Am. (dir.), Malleable Founders Soc. (dir.), Steel Founders Soc. (dir.), Ry. Progress Inst. (governing bd.), Newcomen Soc. Eng. (Am. br.). Republican. Clubs: Rowfant, University, University, Union (Cleve.); Chicago, Cleve. Country. Home: Cleveland, OH. †

POMEROY, JOSEPH GEORGE (GILBERT), naval officer; born San Francisco, Feb. 12, 1889; s. George Gilbert and Elizabeth (Grant) P.; student Plant Sch. of Elec. Engring., Seattle, 1913; Naval Sch. Engring. U. of Washington, 1918-19; m. Marie Johanna Doyle, June 1, 1919 (died 1921); 1 son, George E.; m. 2d, Frances Josephine Thompson, June 2, 1929; children—Mary E., Corbin T., David G. Helper W. A. Linton, Boatbldg., Seattle, 1908-11, engineer, gas and electric, 1911-12; asst. Municipal Light & Power Co., 1912-14, inside constructor, 1914-16, engr. of tests, 1916-19, 1919-20. Entered U.S. Navy, rank of E.M. to Ensign, Aug. 1918, and served to May 1919; reentered Navy, June 1920, commd. ensign, 1920, and advanced through grades to capt., 1944, retird Jan. 1947 with rank of rear admiral. Awarded Legion of Merit for action during Invasion of Sicily, 1943. Mem. Am. Inst. E.E., 1915-1940. Republican. Mem. Episcopal Ch. Home: Redlands, Calif. †

POND, CALVIN PARKER, supermarket chain public affairs exec.; b. Mpls., Nov. 6, 1924; s. Clarence Parker and Marie (Zweifel) P.; m. Elizabeth Jeanne Holden, Aug. 26, 1950; children—Shaun, Deborah, Berek Martin. Student, U. Wis., 1946, Grinnell Coll., 1946-48, Mich. State U., 1947; B.A., U. Minn., 1948; M.A., U. Denver, 1950. With San Antonio Express & News, 1950-51, Statewide Drive-In Theatres, 1951-52; mgr. C. of C., McCook, Nebr., 1952-53; exec. dir. Assn. Retailers, Omaha, 1953-54, Denver Retail Merchants Assn., 1954-60; v.p. Calamac Corp., 1956-58; formerly public relations dir. Denver div. Safeway Stores, Inc., mem. nat. public relations staff, Oakland, Calif., 1965-83, v.p., 1970-83; Mem. Gov.'s Ednl. Adv. Com., 1957-58; mem. exec. com. UN Com. in, Colo., 1955-58; mem. Gov.'s Econ. Devel. Council. Chmn. commerce com. Denver Centennial Commemoration Authority, 1958-59; mem. Denver Tb Soc.; bd. dirs. Second Harvest, Phoenix, Internat. Host Com., Oakland, Citizens Mission, Highlander Boys, Highlander Boys Sponsors; exec. com. Mile High United Fund; bd. trustees Colo. Women's Coll., Denver. Served to 1st lt. U.S. Army, 1950-59. Decorated Bronze Star, Purple Heart; Chevalier de l'Ordre du Merite Commercial et Industriel France, 1962. Mem. Colo. C. of C. (dir.), Am. Retail Assn. Execs., Pub. Relations Soc. Am. (past pres. Colo.), Calif. Retailers Assn. (dir.), Oakland C. of C. Clubs: Univ. (Washington); Sequoyah Country (Oakland). Address: Oakland, Calif. Died July 6, 1983.

POND, GEORGE AUGUSTUS, agrl. economist; born Shakopee, Minn., Aug. 10, 1889; s. Elnathan Judson and Minnie (Markus) P.; grad. Minn. Sch. of Agr., St. Paul, 1913; B.S., U. of Minn., 1918, M.S., 1921; Ph.D., Cornell, 1927; m. Martha Crow, June 11, 1921; children—Judson Samuel, Norman Eggleston. Farmer near Shakopee, Minn., 1907-11; instr. farm management, Minn. Sch. Agr., 1917-18; asst. prof. farm management, U. of Minn., 1919-24, asso. prof., 1924-40, prof. agrl. econ. from 1940; cooperative agt., div. farm management and costs, Bur. Agr. Econ., U.S. Dept. Agr., 1920-26, collaborator from 1928. Commd. 2d lt., Q.M.C., U.S. Army, 1918; overseas 1918-19. Mem. Internat. Conf. Agrl. Econs., Am. Farm Econ. Assn. (v.p. 1940), Am. Soc. Farm Mgrs. and Rural Appraisers (v.p. 1948), N. Central Regional Land Tenure Committee, 1938-48, N. Central Farm Management Research Com., 1947-51, Am. Assn. Univ. Profs., Minn. Farm Mgrs. Assn. (sec. treas. from 1931-50, pres. 1951), Minn. Acad. Sci., Alpha Zeta, Gamma Sigma Delta, Soc. Sigma Xi. Conglist. Author: Modern Farm Management (with Andrew Boss), 1947; agrl. expt. sta. bulls., tech. and extension bulls. Home: St. Paul, Minn. †

PONDER, AMOS LEE, judge; b. Ft. Jesup, La., Mar. 26, 1887; s. Amos Lee and Anita (Barbee) P.; ed. Mt. Lebanon (La.) Coll., 1902-06; Draughon's Bus. Coll., Shreveport, 1907; Tulane U., 1909-10; LL.B., La. State U., 1912; m. Amanda McMichael. Sept. 3, 1913; children—Julia Holden, Amos Lee, George McMichael, John David. Admittted to La. bar, 1912; jr. mem. Ponder and Ponder, attys., Amite, La., 1912-24; dist. atty., 21st Jud. Dist., 1924-30; dist. judge, 21st Jud. Dist., 1930-37; asso. justice, La. Supreme Court from 1937. Mem. La. Bar Assn. Baptist. Democrat. Home: New Orleans, La. †

PONSELLE, ROSA MELBA, dramatic soprano; b. Meriden, Conn.; d. Benjamin and Madalena (Conte) P.; ed. pub. schs., Meriden, and under pvt. tutors, N.Y.C.; m. Carie A. Jackson, Dec. 13, 1936. Joined Met. Opera Co., Nov. 1918; tchr. coach, artistic dir. Balt. Civic Opera Co.; was the first Am. to make debut in leading role with Caruso. Roman Catholic. Died May 25, 1981.*

POOLE, JAMES PLUMMER, coll. prof.; b. Gloucester, Mass., May 6, 1889; s. Samuel Gamage and Helen (Marr) P.; B.S., U. of Maine, 1912; A.M., Harvard, 1918; Ph.D., 1921, A.M., Dartmouth Coll., 1927; m. Mary Leona Glenn, Sept. 9, 1913; children—Margery Graham (Mrs. Richard Taylor), Barbara Hopkins (Mrs. Harvey P. Hall), Lois Janet (Mrs. Edward F. Mischler). Instructor in Botany, Washburn College, Topeka, Kansas, 1912-13; assistant in botany, Kansas State College, Manhattan, Kansas, 1913-16; Austin teaching fellow, Harvard University, 1916-18; asst. prof. botany, U. of Wyoming, 1918-20; instr. in evolution, Dartmouth Coll., 1922-23, asst. prof., 1923-27, prof., 1927-36, prof. in botany since 1936. Fellow A.A.A.S.; mem. New England Bot. Club, Phi Beta Kappa, Gamma Alpha, Alpha Tau Omega, Contbg. author: Marvels and Mysteries of Science, 1941. Home: Hanover, N.H. †

POPE, JOHN ALEXANDER, sinologist, museum dir.; b. Detroit, Aug. 4, 1906; s. Gustavus Debrille and Mary Theresa (Soper) P.; grad. Phillips Exeter Acad., 1921-25; A.B., Yale, 1930; M.A., Harvard, 1940, Ph.D., 1955; D.Litt., Middlebury Coll., 1972; m. Helen Rees Hebbard, Jan. 31, 1931; children—John Alexander, Sara Merchant (Mrs. Richard T. Cooper) m. 2d, Annemarie Henle, Dec. 10, 1947. Trainee, Chase Nat. bank, N.Y.C., 1930-32; exec. sec. People's Museum Assn., Detroit Inst. Arts, 1932-34; lectr. Chinese art Columbia, 1941-43; asso. research Freer Gallery Art, Washington, 1943-46, asst. dir., 1946-62, dir., 1962-71; research prof. Oriental art U. Mich., 1962-71; adviser in Oriental art Va. Mus. Fine Arts, 1972-82. Chmn. Am. selection com. for exhbn., Chinese Art Treasures, sent by Govt. Republic China, 1960; chmn. com. grants research on Asia, Am. Council Learned Socs., 1960-66. Mem. com. to visit dept. East Asian langs. and civilizations Harvard Bd. Overseers, 1957-62, 69-75. Recipient Hills Gold medal Oriental Ceramic Soc., 1971; decorated comdr. Royal Order No. Star (Sweden). Served as capt. USMCR, 1945-46. Mem. Am. Oriental Soc. (chmn. Louise Wallace Hackney scholarship com. 1962-71), Assn. Asian Studies, Oriental Ceramic Soc. (London, Eng.). Home: Washington, D.C. Died Sept. 18, 1982.

POPE, MAURICE ARTHUR, lt. gen. Canadian army; b. Riviere du Loup, P.Q., Aug. 29, 1889; s. Sir Joseph and Henriette (Taschereau) P.; B.Sc. in Civil Engring, McGill U., 1911; m. Comtesse Simonne du Monceau de Bergendal, Belgium, Sept. 2, 1920; children—John Joseph, William Henry, Simonne Emilie, Thomas M. du Monceau. In engring. dept. Canadian Pacific Ry., Montreal, 1911-15; Canadian Expeditionary Force, France, Belgium, 1915-19; Canadian Battlefields Memorials Commn., France, Belgium, 1920-21; Staff College, Camberley, 1924-25; War Office, 1931-33; Imperial Defense Coll., 1936; dir. military operations, Ottawa, 1939; brigadier, General Staff, Canadian Military Hdqr., London, 1940-41, vice-chief Gen. Staff, Ottawa, 1941; chmn. Canadian Joint Staff Mission, Washington, D.C., 1942-44; Military Staff Officer to Prime Minister, Sept. 1944; mil. advisor United Nations Conf., 1945; Canadian del. to Paris Conf. on Reparations, 1945; head Canadian Mil. Mission to Berlin, 1946-50; ambassador of Canada to Belgium from 1950; rank of lt. gen. from 1945. Home: Ottawa, Ont., Canada. †

POPHAM, ARTHUR C., lawyer; b. Hardin County, Ky., June 28, 1887; s. Virgil and Clara (Beauchamp) P.; LL.B., U. Louisville, 1907; m. Ethel Cobb Estes, Nov. 25, 1909 (dec.); children—Arthur C., Jeanne Estes (Mrs. Edward M. Roddington, Jr.). Admitted to Ky. bar, 1907, Mo. bar, 1915; practice in Kansas City, Mo., from 1915; sr. mem. firm Popham, Popham, Conway, Sweeney & Fremont, specializing in trial law, from 1915. Mem. Am., Mo., Kansas City bar assns., Am. Judicature Soc. Home: Kansas City, MO. †

POPPEN, HENRY ALBERT, clergyman, missionary, educator; b. Prairie View, Kan., Sept. 29, 1889; s. Albert and Henrietta (Walcott) P.; stud. Northwestern Classical Acad., 1906-10; A.B., Hope Coll., 1914, D.D., 1941; grad study Western Theol. Sem., 1914-17; Th.M., Princeton, 1925; m. Dorothy Catharine Trompen, June 18, 1918; children—Kenneth John, Anna Ruth, Albert Walcott. Ordained to ministry Ref. Ch. in Am., 1917; missionary, China, 1918-51; co-founder Mission Lugyen, Fukien, China, 1918-29; dir. Internat. Relief Com., Kulangsu, 1938-40; prin. Tung Wen Inst. Amoy, 1938-40; exec. sec. Amoy City Y.M.C.A., 1938-40; Changchow Fukien China resident bd. adv. Talmage Coll., 1946-51; prof. N.T. South Fukien Theol. Sem., 1946-51; mem. Kulangsu Municipal Council Internat. Settlement, Amoy; interned by Japanese, 1941-43; repatriated U.S.S. Gripsholm, 1943; deported from China by order of People's Ct., Mar. 1951; pioneer in newspaper Evangelism, Amoy, 1933-40; dir. S. Fukien Religious Tract and Bible Soc., 1934-40. Pres. Synod of Ref. Ch. in Am., 1952-53; dir. South Fukien Religious Tract Soc. (Kulangsu, Amoy), 1933-40. Rep. Kulangsu Municipal Council, drawing up Kulangsu Agreement with Imperial Japanese Govt. reps. to guaranty Internat. Status of Interant. Settlement during Sino-Japanese war, May 1940. Trustee Fukien Christian U., Fuchow, China, Hope Hosp., Kulangsu, Changchow Union Hosp., 1946-51. Translator: (into Chinese) Facts and Mysteries of the Christian Faith (Albertus Pieters). Address: New York, N.Y. †

PORCAYO URIBE, JUVENAL, bishop; b. Buenavista de Cuellar, Mex., May 3, 1917; s. Faustino Porcayo Rodriguez and Maria (Uribe) Velazco. Ed., Sem. of Chilapa, 1932-37, Montezuma Sem., 1937-41. Ordained priest Roman Catholic Ch., asst. pastor in, Ajuchitlan, Iguala and Taxco, pastor in, Pilcaya, also Acapulco, diocesan economist; now bishop of, Tapachula, Chiapas, Mex. Home: Tapachula Chiapas, Mexico.

PORTER, KATHERINE HARRIET, educator; b. Lansing, Mich., Mar. 16, 1888; d. Edward Charles and Stella (Randall) Porter; student Lake Erie Coll., 1906-07; A.B., Mount Holyoke Coll., 1910; A.M., U. of Chicago, 1914; Ph.D.,Cornell, 1930. Instr. in English, Lake Erie Coll., 1910-13; prof. of English, Alfred Coll., 1914-19; mem. faculty, Flora Stone Mather Coll., Western Reserve U., Cleveland, from 1919, prof. of English from 1949, asst. dean, 1928-32, 1944-45. Mem. Am. Assn. Univ. Profs., Modern Lang. Assn., Nat. Council Teachers of English, Phi Kappa Phi. Presbyn. Author: Style of Leaflet, 1934; Theme-Craft (with Margaret Waterman), 1950. Home: Cleveland, Ohio. †

PORTER, RALPH E., medical director, U.S. Public Health Service; b. Scottsboro, Ala., Jan. 1, 1890; s. Daniel L. and Martha Elizabeth (Moore) P.; M.D., Univ. Ala., 1916; m. Edna Armistead Lewis, Oct. 16, 1917. Scientific asst., 1917-18; commd. asst. surgeon, U.S. Public Health Service, 1918, surgeon, 1926, diplomatic mission to British Isles, 1925-28; senior surgeon from 1938; med. officer in charge U.S. Marine Hosp., Norfolk, Va. Fellow Am. Coll. Physicians.†

PORTER, VERNE HARDIN, editor, writer; b. Abilene, Tex., Dec. 2, 1889; s. Henry Alexander and Margaret (Moran) P.; ed. pub. schs., Everett, Wash.; m. A'Lillyan de Froza Morrow-Stanfield, of Echo, Ore., Dec. 31, 1910; m. 2d, Eileen Christie, Sept. 1925. Entered newspaper work at 16; city editor Duluth Star and St. Paul News, 1907; editor Washington Democrat, 1908; telegraph editor Portland (Oregon) Journal, 1911-13; city editor Salt Lake Herald-Republican and editor of Telegram, 1913-14; asso. editor The Red Book Magazine, The Blue Book Magazine, The Green Book Magazine, 1914-16; editor-in-chief Salt Lake Telegram, 1917; editor Cosmopolitan Mag., and asso. editor-in-chief Internat. Mag. Co.; became editor-in-chief Internat. Film Service Co. (Cosmopolitan Productions), 1918, was editor-in-chief Tower Publications; also publisher Smart Set mag., 1926; editor in chief Famous Players-Lasky (Paramount Pictures) Corpn., 1927; vice president, sec. and editor in chief Trade Publications, Inc.; editor Universal Pictures Corpn. Writer scenarios for Triangle Film Co.; western mgr. Paralta Productions, Inc., 1917; pres. Verne Porter, Inc., cons. editors. Co-Author: (serials) The Life Story of Maude Adams and Her Mother, 1914; George M. Cohan's Own Story, 1915; The Perfect Forty-six, 1917. Contbr. more than 100 short stories. Office: New York, N.Y.†

POSES, JACK I., perfume company executive; b. Russia, Dec. 28, 1899; s. Moses and Selma (Rivin) P.; came to U.S., 1911, naturalized, 1928; B.C.S., N.Y. U., 1923, M.B.A., 1924; L.L.D., Brandeis U., 1968; D.H.L., CUNY, 1976; m. Lillian L. Shapiro, Aug. 27, 1930; 1 dau., Barbara Joan (Mrs. Ernest Kafka). Pres. Jack I. Poses Assocs.; pres. Zanadu Mfg. Corp. N.Y.C., from 1932, Condon Products Corp., N.Y.C., from 1952. Vice chmn. Bd. Higher Edn. N.Y.C., 1963-74; mem. Citizens Adv. Com. FDA, 1962; chmn. industry drives United Jewish Appeal, from 1943. Trustee, treas. N.Y. Studio Sch. Drawing, Painting and Sculpture; trustee Brandeis U., also chmn. investment com., mem. edn. and budget coms., chmn. constrn. fund City U. N.Y., chmn. Council Fine Arts and founder Poses Inst. Fine Arts at univ.; bd. dirs. Fragrance Found.; bd. govs. Joint Def. Appeal; founder Einstein Med. Sch.; mem., contbr. to Detroit Inst. Art, Mus. Modern Art, Guggenheim Mus., Whitney Mus.; life fellow, contbr. Met. Mus. Art; established scholarships and/or fellowships at Harvard, Yale Law Sch., Radcliffe Coll., Bryn Mawr Coll., Brandeis U.; mem. N.Y.C. Bd. Correction, 1978, Dormitory Authority, 1979. Decorated chevalier Legion of Honor (France); recipient Madden award NYU, 1970; Pres.'s medal CUNY grad. div., 1970. Mem. Toilet Goods Mfrs. Assn. (v.p., dir.), Perfume Importers Assn., Quill Soc. Clubs: Harmony (N.Y.C.); Birchwood Country (past pres.) (Westport, Conn.). Home: New York, N.Y. Died Apr. 1, 1982.

POSEY, ADDISON CECIL, ins. co. exec.; b. Oakland, Cal., Aug. 2, 1890; A.B., U. Santa Clara, 1911. Resident mgr. met. dept. Hartford Accident & Indemnity Co., San Francisco, 1926-34, asst. mgr. Pacific Coast dept., 1934-39, v.p., supr. bonding bus., charge contract bond dept., 1939-46, v.p. charge Pacific dept., from 1946; asst. mgr. Pacific Coast dept. Hartford Fire Ins. Co., 1934-39, Pacific Coast mgr. Hartford Fire Ins. Co. and affiliates, from 1946. Mem. Soc. Cin. (State of Va.). Club: Stock Exchange (San Francisco). Home: San Francisco, Calif. †

POTTER, DAVID MAGLE, aero. and mech. engr.; b. Union, N.J., Apr. 10, 1905; s. David Magle and Rowena (Teas) P.; B.S., U. Mich., 1931; grad. student Rutgers U.; m. Edith Birch, Aug. 30, 1939; children—David Magle, Isabelle Elaine. Pres. Potter Engring. Co., Pottermeter Co., Potter Aero. Corp., Potter Pacific. Recipient Longstreth medal Franklin Institute, 1959. Member of the Royal Geographical Society, Instrument Society of America, Soaring Soc. Am. Club: Explorers (dir. 1954-56). Arctic exploration on U. Mich. expdn., 1928, others; discovered Sunderstrum Fiord Airfield, Greenland. Inventor flowmeter (turbine-type) for use in aero., astronautics, process industries. Home: Martinsville, N.J. Died Sept. 29, 1984.

POTTER, ERNEST W., banker; b. nr. Davison, Mich., Mar. 1, 1889; s. William E. and Justina E. Potter; student pub. schs.; m. A. Mae Davison, Nov. 3, 1910; children—E. Davison, H. Edson, James W. Bank messenger Nat. Bank of Flint, 1908; bank clk. Citizens Comml. & Savings Bank, 1910. successively asst. cashier, cashier, dir., v.p., cashier, exec. v.p., pres., from 1953; dir. Mich. Life Ins. Co., Fed. Res. Bank of Chgo. Mem. Bd. Edn. (past pres., treas.). Treas. Flint Coll. and Cultural Development. Active Boy Scouts. Republican. Presbyn. Mason, Elk. Clubs: Rotary, Flint Golf, Flint City, Scenic Golf. †

POTTER, LARS SELLSTEDT, museum trustee; b. Buffalo, June 21, 1888; s. Frank H. and Eva (Sellstedt) P.; B.A., Williams Coll., 1910; m. Janet Crawford, July 17, 1943; 1 son by previous marriage, Lars Sellstedt. Purchasing agt. Larkin Co., Buffalo, 1910-15; with O'Brian Potter & Co., Buffalo, 1915-40, Buffalo Found., 1940; dep. adminstr. Treasury Dept., 1940-45; sec. Blue Cross Western N.Y., 1948-58. Treas. Albright Knox Art Gallery, Buffalo, from 1923, bd. dirs., from 1921; hon. trustee Studio Arena Theatre, Buffalo, bd. dirs. Blind Assn. Buffalo, from 1946, pres., 1957-59; trustee Williams Coll., 1937-42; pres. Nichols Sch., Buffalo, 1939-49, Studio Theatre Sch., Buffalo, 1927-52; bd. dirs. Main St. Assn., Buffalo, 1957-60; treas. Allentown Assn., Buffalo, 1961-65, bd. dirs., from 1961. Served with Am. Field Service, 1917; as 1st lt. USAAS, 1917-18. Decorated Croix de Guerre (France). Mem. Bldg. Owners and Mgrs. Assn. (hon.), Kappa Alpha (trustee). Clubs: Williams (N.Y.C.); Midday, Canoe (Buffalo) Northshire Yacht (Bertie Bay, Can.). Address: Buffalo, N.Y. †

POTTS, JOSEPH MCKEAN, II, manufacturing company executive; b. Pottstown, Pa., Sept. 3, 1918; s. Lemuel Eastburn and Sara P. (Root) P.; B.A., Princeton, 1941; m. Helen Cashwell Bolling, July 22, 1949; children—Joseph McKean III, Thomas Bolling. With Bonney Forge & Tool Works, Allentown, Pa., 1949-65, pres., 1959-65; pres. Miller Mfg. Co., Detroit, 1965—; pres. Bonney Forge & Foundry, Inc., Allentown, 1965-69, chmn., 1969-74; pres. Bonney Group and v.p. Gulf and Western Mfg. Co., Allentown, 1972-74; pres. Taylor-Bonney Internat. and v.p. G & W Energy Products Group, 1974-77; v.p., gen. mgr. splty. products div. G & W Energy Products Group, 1977-80; chmn. Bonney Forge Internat. Ltd., Irvine, Scotland; dir. TF de Mexico, S.A., Mexico City, Metalmeg, S.A., Caracas, Venezuela, Bonney Forge Italia, Albano, Italy, Tubacex Taylor Accesorios, S.A., Llodio, Spain, John M. Henderson & Co. (Holdings) Ltd., London, 1974-77. Trustee, Hill Sch., Pottstown Pa. and Allentown YMCA, 1979-80. Served to maj. AUS, 1941-46. Mem. Allentown-Lehigh County C. of C. (bd. govs. 1964-69), Newcomen Soc., Pa. Soc. Republican. Presbyn. Mason. Clubs: Livingston, Lehigh Country, Lehigh Valley (Allentown); Mid Ocean (Bermuda); Country of N.C.; Princeton (N.Y.C.). Home: Allentown, Pa. Dec. Apr. 22, 1980. Interned Zion Cemetery, Pottstown, Pa.

POULSON, NORRIS, mayor Los Angeles; b. Baker Co., Ore., July 23, 1895; s. Peter Schonshoe and Jennie Elizabeth (Rainey) P.; student, Ore. Agrl. Coll., 1914-15, Southwestern Univ., Los Angeles, 1923-25; m. Erna June Loennig, Dec. 25, 1916; children—Erna Bea, Patricia, Norrisa. Farmes, 1916-23; licensed, C.P.A., 1933. mem. Calif. Legislature, 1938-42; mem. 78th to 83d Congresses, 13th, 24th Dists. Cal., resigned from Congress, 1955; elected mayor of Los Angeles, 1953. Mem. Am. Inst. Accts., Los Angeles and Cal. State Soc., Nat. Inst. C.P.A., Sigma Alpha Epsilon. Republican. Mason (Scottish Rite). Club: Lions. Home: Los Angeles, Calif. Died Sept. 25, 1982.

POULTERER, HENRY E., railway official; b. Portland, Ore., Jan. 3, 1888; s. William Henry and Ellen Louisa (Kent) P.; grad. high sch., 1906; married; 1 dau., Nancy Elizabeth (Mrs. Francis L. Smith); m. 2d, Angie Hitchock, Nov. 16, 1923. Office boy U.P. R.R., 1906, rate clerk, chief clerk, unitl 1912, freight traffic agt., 1912-16, traveling freight agt. 1918-20, chief clerk, Omaha, Neb., 1920-25, gen. agt. Kansas City, Mo., 1925-27 asst. gen. freight agt.

Omaha Neb., 1927-31; asst. freight traffic, mgr. and freight traffic mgr. W.P. R.R. Co., San Francisco, 1931-41, v.p. in charge traffic from Dec. 1941. Clubs: Transporation, The Family (San Francisco, Calif.); Union League (Chicago, Ill.). Home: Millbrae, Calif. †

POWELL, ANNIE MARION, educator; b. Columbia, Va., Mar. 14, 1887; d. John J. A. and Annie S. (Jones) P.; Hollins Coll., 1905-06; A.B., Sweet Briar Coll., 1910; A.M., Columbia, 1913; advanced work same, 1918. Instr. English, Sweet Briar Coll., 1910-14; mem. faculty, State Normal Sch., Farmville, Va., 1914-16; mem. English faculty, Savannah High Sch., 1916-18; prin. Chatham Episcopal Inst., 1920-25; dean of women and prof. English William and Mary Coll., from 1925. Episcopalian. Address: Williamsburg, Va. †

POWELL, ELEANOR TORREY, dancer, actress; b. Springfield, Mass., Nov. 21, 1912; d. Clarence Gardner and Blanch Helen (Torrey) Powell; ed. elementary schools and junior high school, Springfield; unmarried. Began as specialty dancer, 1925; dancer (in musical comedies) "Co-optimists," 1927, "Follow Through," 1928-29, "Fine and Dandy," 1929-31; appeared in Ziegfeld's "Ha-Cha" and "George White's Scandals," 1932; entered motion pictures, 1934; in "George White's Scandals," 1934, "Broadway Melody of 1936," "Born to Dance," "Broadway Melody of 1938," "Rosalie," "Honolulu," "Broadway Melody of 1940"; played in musical comedy "Home Abroad," New York stage, 1936. Named "Queen of Taps" by Dancing Masters Assn., 1929. Home: Beverly Hills, Calif. Died Feb. 11, 1982.

POWELL, RICHARD ROY BELDEN, prof. law; b. Rochester, N.Y., Oct. 11, 1890; s. Harry Teed and Carrie Louise (Brown) P.; A.B., University of Rochester, 1911; A.M., Columbia University, 1912, LL.B., 1914, LL.D., honoris causa, 1954; m. Anne Marie Klein, May 13, 1914; children—Margaret Ruth, Richard Gordon; m. 3d, Alice Thompson, Aug. 5, 1957. Admitted to New York bar, 1914, and practiced at Rochester until 1921; assistant professor law, Columbia, 1921-23, asso. prof., 1923-24, prof. from 1924, Dwight prof. law, 1931-59, emeritus Dwight professor law, from 1959; vis. prof. law University of Michigan, New York University, 1960, Harvard Univ., 1961, U. Cal. at Berkeley, 1962, Hastings College of Law, San Francisco, 1963-66. Reporter property, American Law Inst., 1929-47; research consultant N.J. Commn. on Consolidation of Statutes, 1929-30, N.Y. Law Revision Commn., 1935-47. Decorated Legion of Honor, 1955 (France). Mem. Assn. Bar City of N.Y., Am. Law Inst., Phi Beta Kappa, Delta Sigma Rho, Delta Theta Phi. Dem. Conglist. Author: Cases on Law of Agency, 1924; Tiffany on Agency, 1924; Cases and Materials on Trusts and Estates, 1932; Possessory Estates, 1933 and 1943; Future Interests, 1937; Trusts, 1940; Law of Property, 1942; Law of Land, 1949-58; Cases on Trusts and Wills, 1960; Cases on Future Interests, 1961. Contr. to Columbia Law Review, etc. Home: Hillsborough, Calif. †

POWELL, ROBERT NICHOLAS, ins. co. exec.; b. Detroit, June 14, 1928; s. Nicholas Miles and Helen (Davis) P.; B.B.A., U. Mich., 1951, M.A., 1952; m. Patricia Tashjian, Apr. 18, 1953; children—Pamela Rose, Laura Jean, Lucy Anne. With Calif.-Western State Life Ins. Co., Sacramento, 1952-69, asst. actuary, 1957-59, asso. actuary, 1959-61, actuary, 2d v.p., 1961-62, v.p., actuary, 1962-79, chief actuary, 1969-79; pres. West Coast Life Ins. Co. and Gulf Atlantic Ins. Co., San Francisco, 1979-80. v.p. Nationwide Corp., from 1969. Nat. Service, Inc., from 1969. Served with AUS, 1946-47. Fellow Soc. Actuaries; mem. Tri-State Actuarial Club. Home: Moraga, Calif. Dec. Oct. 28, 1980.

POWELL, WILLIAM, actor; b. Pittsburgh, Pa., July 29, 1892; s. Horatio Warren and Nettie Manila (Brady) P.; grad. Central High Sch., Kansas City, Mo., 1911; student Am. Acad. Dramatic Art, N.Y. City, 1912; m. Eileen Wilson, Apr. 15, 1915 (divorced); 1 son, Wm. D.; m. 2d, Carole Lombard, June 26, 1931 (divorced); m. 3d, Diana Lewis, Jan. 5, 1940. Began on stage, 1912, played in "The Ne'er Do Well," "Within the Law," "The King," "Going Up," "Spanish Love," etc.; starred in motion pictures; appeared in the following: "Sherlock Holmes," "When Knighthood Was in Flower," "The Bright Shawl," "Romola," "Beau Geste," "Street of Case," "Canary Murder Case," "The Road to Singapore," "High Pressure," "Manhattan Melodrama," "The Thin Man," "Evelyn Prentice," "Star of Midnight," "Rendezvous," "Reckless," "The Great Ziegfeld," "After the Thin Man," "The Baroness and the Butler," "Another Thin Man," "I Love You Again," "Love Crazy," "The Shadow of the Thin Man," "Crossroads," "The Heavenly Body," and others. Clubs: Bel-Air Country, Hollywood Athletic, Palm Springs Racquet; The Lambs (New York). Died Mar. 3, 1984.

POWERS, DAVID NEELY, corp. exec.; b. Butler, Ala., Oct. 21, 1890; s. Joseph Neely and Ada (Gavin) P.; B.S., U. Miss., 1917; LL.B., Millsaps Coll., 1914; m. Katharine Crane Robson, Mar. 21, 1939. Pres., gen. mgr. Colson Corp., Elyria, O., from 1935; dir. Colonial Trust Co., N.Y. City, Samuel D. Moore Co., Mantua, O. Mem. Phi Delta Theta. Elk. Mason (Shriner). Clubs: Union, University, Pepper Pike, Rowfant (Cleveland); Elyria Country, Portage Country (Akron, O.); Sedgefield Country (Greensboro, N.C.) Home: Oberlin, Ohio. †

POYNTZ, ARTHUR ROSS, ins. co. dir.; b. Toronto, Ont. Can., Apr. 8, 1909; s. Arthur and Lula Heath (Deadman) P.; student Upper Can. Coll.; B.A., U. Toronto, 1929; m. Katherine Jean Wood, Oct. 14, 1933; children—Judith, Ross, Katherine. With Imperial Life Assurance Co. of Can., from 1931, dir., mng. dir., 1950-53, pres., 1953-67, chmn. bd., chief exec. officer, 1967-77; dir. Investors Group, Consumers Gas Co., Imperial Life Assurance Co., Home Oil Co. Mem. Canadian Econ. Policy Com. Fellow Canadian Inst. Actuaries; mem. Inst. Life Ins. (dir. 1961-62), Canadian Life Ins. Assn. (pres. 1959-60), Life Ins. Assn. Am. (dir.), Phi Gamma Delta. Mem. United Ch. Rotarian. Clubs: Granite; Rosedale Golf; York. Home: Toronto, Ont., Canada. Died Apr. 28, 1982.

PRADO, JORGE, ambassador; b. Lima, Peru, May 13, 1889; s. Mariano I. and Medeleine (Ugarteche) P.; student Jesuit Colls. in Lima, Paris, London, 1896-1903; student Univ. of Lima, 1904-08; Mil. Sch., Lima, 1908-10; m. Grace Adelaide Flinders, Dec. 20, 1934. Lt. cav., 1910; editor El Diario, 1912-15; editor La Epoca of Lima, 1915-17; elected mem. Congress of Peru, 1917, 1919; leader of opposition, 1920; minister of the Interior and prime minister, 1933-34; candidate for presidency of Republic, 1936; ambassador to Brazil, 1938-44; to Great Britain, 1944-46, to United States 1946-47. Democratic Liberal. Clubs: National, Jockey, Polo and Golf (Lima); Jockey (Rio de Janeiro); Automovil (Paris); St. James (London). Author: Democratic Ideals, 1914; Political Articles, 1919; Parliamentary Speeches, 1925; Political Speeches, 1934. Home: Lima, Peru. †

PRAGER, ARTHUR, utilities exec.; b. Trinidad, Colo., Sept. 13, 1890; s. Phillip and Fannie (Michels) P.; grad. high sch.; m. Gertrude Conway, Dec. 27, 1923. Accountant, Trinidad Electric Transit Ry. & Gas Co., 1907; treas. Deming (N.M.) Ice & Electric Co., 1911; treas. Albuquerque Gas & Electric Co., 1911-14; gen. mgr., 1919-35, gen. mgr., pres., 1935-47; treas. Springfield (Mo.) Gas & Electric Co., 1914-17; pres. Pub. Service Co. N.M., Albuquerque, 1947-55, chmn. bd., from 1955, chmn. exec. com., from 1966, v.p., dir. Pubco Petroleum, Inc.; dir. Fed. Light & Traction Co., Stonewall Electric Co. Pres. Rocky Mountain Electric League. Recipient Govt. citation for work with scrap drive, 1943. Mem. Southwestern Golf Assn. Mason. Clubs: Elks, Rotary, Albuquerque Country (pres. emeritus). Home: Albuquerque, NM. †

PRAGER, SIGFRID, conductor; b. Berlin, Germany, June 12, 1889; s. Philip Johannes and Minna (Scholz) P.; Ph.D., U. of Halle, Germany; studied composition with Max Bruch, Royal Conservatory, piano with Eugene Francis Charles D'Albert and Ferrucio Benvenuto D'Albert (Berlin); m. Franziska Ruettinger, Aug. 28, 1925. Came to U.S., 1925, naturalized, 1930. Condr. of opera, Germany and Italy, 1910-18, South America, Argentina, 1919-24; condr. Yorkville Theatre, N.Y. City, 1925-26; condr. Civic Symphony Orchestra and Chorus, Madison, Wis., since 1926; also condr. Chicago Bach Chorus, Chicago, Ill., 1929-32, Wis. Symphony Orchestra, Milwaukee, Wis., 1936-40; lecturer Stanford U., summer, 1935, U. of Wis., summer, 1938. Composer: Sicania, symphonic poem for orchestra, given in Catania, Italy, 1912; Suite on Negro Spirituals, for orchestra, given in Madison, Wis., 1928, Milwaukee, 1927, 1929, Chicago, 1932; also 11 songs for voice and piano on Italian and Spanish poems. Home: Madison, Wis. †

PRATT, JULIUS WILLIAM, college prof.; b. Piedmont, S.D., Feb. 25, 1888; s. William McLain and Sophia Penfield (Rand) P.; A.B., Davidson (N.C.) Coll., 1908; M.A., U. of Chicago, 1914, Ph.D., 1924; m. Louisa Williamson, June 7, 1919; children—William Winston, Walden Penfield. Adj. prof. English, Ga. Sch. of Tech., 1908-09; with Cedartown (Ga.) Cotton & Export Co., 1909-12, sec. and asst. treas., 1910-12; instr. in English, N.C. State Coll., 1913-15, asst. prof., 1915-16; instr. in English and history, U.S. Naval Acad., 1916-20, asst. prof., 1920-24; asst. prof. history, Rutgers U., 1924-26; prof. history from 1926; head of dept., U. of Buffalo, 1926-48; dean, Grad. Sch. of Arts and Sciences, 1946-53; lecturer summers U. of Tex., Duke U., Harvard U. and U. of Chicago, U. of Md., summer 1948; visiting prof. Harvard, spring, 1949; Albert Shaw lecturer in Am. diplomatic history, Johns Hopkins, 1936; administrative sec. Council on Fgn. Relations, N.Y. City, 1943-44. Mem. Am. Hist. Association, Mississippi Valley Hist. Assn., Buffalo Hist. Soc., Foreign Policy Assn., Phi Beta Kappa. Author: Expansionists of 1812, 1925; also biographies of James Monroe and Robert Lansing in American Secretaries of State and Their Diplomacy, 1927, 29; expansionists of 1898, 1936; America's Colonial Experiment, 1950; also contributor to Dictionary of American Biography, also hist. articles and reviews. Home: Williamsville, N.Y. †

PRATT, MERRILL EDWARD, mfr.; b. Prattville, Ala., Oct. 15, 1889; s. Daniel and Ellen (Sims) P.; B.S., U. of Ala., 1910; S.B., Mass. Inst. Tech., 1916; m. Florence Marks, Sept. 4, 1912; children—Ellen (Mrs. Earl McGowin), Daniel. Entire bus. career with Continental Gin Co., Birmingham, from 1916, v.p., 1934-38, president, 1938-58, director from 1938, chmn. and pres. Served as second lieutenant, C.A., World War I. Mem. Am. Ordnance Association, Birmingham Alumni Association of Massachusetts Institute Technology. Clubs: Country (past president), Mountain Brook, Rotary (pres., 1950-51) (Birmingham). Home: Birmingham, Ala. †

PREBLE, ROBERT CURTIS, reference book pub. exec., ret.; b. Chgo., Aug. 3, 1897; s. Andrew Curtis and Jessie Janet (Work) P.; B.S., U. Ill., 1921; student Chicago Kent Coll. Law, 1923-25; m. Dorothy K. Seidel, 1918 (div. 1934); children—Robert C., William W., Patte Ann; m. 2d, Madge Jean Collar, Mar. 24, 1939 (dec. December 1952); m. 3d, Beatrice Dousett, 1963. Was vice president of the Midland Press, Chicago, 1921-25, W. F. Quarrie & Co., Chicago, 1925-36; exec. v.p., Quarrie Corp., Chicago, 1937-45; v.p., Field Enterprises Inc., Chicago, 1945-49; exec. v.p., Encyclopaedia Britannica, Inc., Chicago, 1949-50, pres., treas., dir., 1950-59; pres., treas., dir. Ency. Brit. of Can., 1950-59. Served as pilot, 2d lt., U.S. Army, World War I. Mem. Chi Psi, Phi Delta Phi. Clubs: Chicago Press, Chicago, Lake Shore, Tavern. Pub: World Language Dictionary. Home: Chicago, Ill. Died Nov. 26, 1983

PRENTICE, DONALD BISHOP, ret. engr., educator; b. Hartford, Conn., Apr. 27, 1889; s. Charles Hills and Kate Bacon (Bishop) P.; Ph.B. in Mech. Engring., Sheffield Sci. Sch. (Yale), 1910; M.E., Yale, 1914; M.A. in Edn., Lafayette Coll., 1927, Sc.D., 1936; LL.D., Wabash Coll., 1932; Eng. D., Rose Poly. Inst., 1948; m. Mary Louise Farnham, June 20, 1912 (dec. Aug. 1961); children—Katherine Farnham (Mrs. Vincent G.C. Best), Mary Osborne (Mrs. Warren K. Colby), Barbara (Mrs. Henry S. Broad); m. 2d, Carrie S. Curl, Apr. 7, 1964. With Britten Co., Hartford, 1910-12; asst. instr. mech. engring. Yale, 1912-14, instr., 1914-17; asst. prof. mech. engring. Lafayette Coll., 1917; prof., head dept., 1918-31, chmn. engring., 1921-31, dean, 1924-31, acting pres., 1926-27; pres. Rose Poly. Inst., 1931-48, bd. mgrs., 1931. Dir. Mchts. Nat. Bank of Terre Haute, 1941-48. Life trustee Lafayette Coll.; mem. univ. council Yale, 1951-58, chmn. com. on engring. sch. Dir. Camp Lafayette for vocational tng. for drafted soldiers, May-Dec. 1918; reg. adviser for Ind. Engring. Def. Tng., 1940-45; sec. Indiana Assn. Church Related and Ind. Colls., 1940-46, v.p., 1946-47, pres., 1947-48; mem. Engrs. Council for Profl. Devel., chmn. com. on engring. schs., 1941-47; spl. asst., USN, 1942-43; cons. U.S. Maritime Service, 1944-45; mem. nat. adv. com. USCG Acad., 1953-60, chmn., 1958-59. Del. World Engring. Congress, Tokyo, 1929. Registered profl. engr., Ind. Fellow A.A.A.S., Am. Soc. M.E., N.Y. Acad. Sci.; asso. fellow Calhoun Coll., Yale; mem. Am. Acad. Polit. and Social Scis., Acad. Polit. Sci., Am. Assn. U. Profs., Am. Soc. for Engring. Edn. (council 1927-30, 1941-46, v.p. 1939-40, pres. 1940-41), Sci. Research Soc. Am. (dir. 1948-69), Sigma Xi (nat. treas. 1949-64, pres. elect 1958-59), Phi Kappa Epsilon, Tau Beta Pi, Kappa Phi Kappa, Kappa Delta Rho, Alpha Phi Omega, Blue Key. Republican. Conglist. Clubs: Graduates, Faculty (New Haven); Bucks Harbor (Me.) Yacht. Author sect. on mech. engring. Am. Year Book, 1935-39; also articles in Engring. Edn., Mech. Engring., School and Society, etc. Home: Southbury, Conn. †

PRENTIS, MORTON MACNUTT, banker; b. St. Louis, Mo., Jan. 2, 1887; s. Henning W. and Mary Morton (MacNutt) P.; A.B., U. of Mo., 1906; m. Frances C. Lusk, Nov. 19, 1921; children—Morton M., Garnett M. Began with 3d Nat. Bank, St. Louis, 1899; various positions with Nat. Bank of Commerce, Norfolk, Va., 1906-14; nat. bank examiner, Va., 1915-18; mng. dir. Federal Reserve Bank, Baltmore, 1918-22; v.p., later pres. Merchants Nat. Bank, Baltimore, 1922-28; pres. First Nat. Bank, Baltimore, from 1928; dir. U.S. Fidelity & Guaranty Co., Savings Bank of Baltimore, Md. Life Ins. Co., Monumental Life Ins. Co. of Baltimore, Md., Federal Reserve Bank of Baltimore, 1931-39; State fiscal agent of Md., 1924-35; dir. Baltimore Assn. of Commerce; mem. Reconstruction Finance Corp. Advisory Com. from 1931; member Banking Board of the State of Maryland; trustee Community Fund of Baltimore, Harriet Lane Home (Johns Hopkins Hosp.), Goucher Coll., Episcopal Cathedral. Mem. Acad. Polit. Science, Newcomen Society of England, Sigma Alpha Epsilon, Theta Nu Epsilon. Democrat. Episcopalian. Clubs: Maryland, Elkridge Kennels, Merchants, L'Hirondelle. Home: Baltimore, Md. †

PRESCOTT, WILLIAM GOODWIN, lawyer; b. Colorado Springs, Colo., Sept. 24, 1906; s. William Chester and Pearl Eva (Cummings) P.; student Westminster Coll. and Law Sch. (later merged with U. Denver), 1926-27, LL.B., 1930; m. Frances Jeanne Dutton, Mar. 2, 1931 (dec. May 1974); m. 2d, Mona B. Henne, Aug. 31, 1974 (dec. June 1976); m. 3d, Bonnie Helen Ellis, Jan. 1, 1977 (dec. Dec. 1977); m. 4th, Royallene L. Kanan, Feb. 10, 1978. With Gt. Western Sugar Co., Denver, 1925, Nat. Cash Register Co., Denver, 1926; sales record clk. E.I. duPont de Nemours & Co., Inc., Denver, 1926-27; clk. Justice Charles C. Butler, Supreme Ct. of Colo., 1927-31; admitted to Colo. bar, 1930; atty. Denver & Rio Grande Western R.R. Co., Denver, 1931-55, asst. gen. atty., 1955-56, corp. sec., 1956-71, dir., 1961; sec., treas., dir. Northwestern Terminal R.R. Co., 1956-69; dir. Rio Grande Land Co., 1956-71; practice law, 1971-81. Mem. Colo., Denver bar assns., Am. Soc. Corp. Secs. (asso.). Mason. Home: Denver, Colo. Died Apr. 1, 1981; inurned Chapel of Memories, Crown Hill Cemetary, Denver, Colo.

PRESENT, RICHARD DAVID, educator, physicist; b. N.Y.C., Feb. 5, 1913; s. David and Blanche (Wertheimer) P.; m. Thelma Cohen, July 31, 1943; children: Irene Naomi, Constance Sarah. B.S., CCNY, 1931; M.A., Harvard U., 1932, Ph.D., 1935. Instr. physics Purdue U., Lafayette, Ind., 1935-40; research assoc. Harvard U.,

1940-41; asst. prof. physics N.Y.U., 1941-43; mem. div. war research Manhattan Project, Columbia, 1943-46; assoc. prof. physics U. Tenn., 1946-48, prof. physics, 1948-69, Disting. prof., from 1969; Cons. Clinton Nat. Labs., 1946-48; NSF vis. scientist, 1958-71. Author: Kinetic Theory of Gases, 1958; Contbr. articles to profl. jours. Fellow Inst. Internat. Edn., Paris, 1937-38; NSF Vis. Scientist Program, 1958; NSF grantee, 1963, 65. Fellow Am. Phys. Soc. (chmn. S.E. sect. 1964-65); mem. AAUP (chpt. pres. 1957-58, 63-64), Phi Beta Kappa, Sigma Xi. Research nuclear theory, molecular structure, statis. mechanics. Home: Knoxville, Tenn. Died July 2, 1983.

PRESSEY, SIDNEY LEAVITT, psychologist; b. Brooklyn, N.Y., Dec. 28, 1888; s. Edwin Sidney and Orie Belle (Little) P.; student, U. of Minn., 1908-09, A.B., Williams Coll., 1912, A.M., Harvard, 1915, Ph.D., 1917; m. Luella Winifred Cole, 1918 (divorced 1932); m. 2d, Alice Margaret Donnelly, 1934. Interne and asst. psychologist, Boston Psychopathic Hosp., 1915-17; research asso., Ind. Univ., 1917-21; asst. prof., Ohio State U., 1921-26, prof., from 1926; visiting prof., summers, U. of Utah, Teachers Coll., Columbia Univ., U. of Hawaii. Colo. State Coll., U. of So. Calif., U. Brit. Columbia. Expert cons. A.G.O. War Dept. 1943. Research for Navy on training aids, 1946-49. Fellow A.A.A.S. (v.p. sect. 1, 1946), fellow Ohio Acad. Sci. (v.p. and chmn. sect. psychol. 1949), Am. Psychol. Assn. (pres. div. on aging, 1946, on teaching, 1948), mem. Ohio Psychol. Assn. (pres. 1951), Am. Assn. Applied Psychol. (mem. council, chmn. ednl. psychol. 1941-42), Gerontol. Soc., Am. Educational Research Association, National Society College Teachers of Edn., N.E.A., Soc. for Psychol. Study of Social Issues, Am. Assn. Univ. Profs., Midwestern Psychol. Assn. (pres. 1943), Phi Beta Kappa, Sigma Xi, Phi Delta Kappa. Author: Introduction to the Use of Standard Tests, 1922; Mental Abnormality and Defiency (with L. C. Pressey), 1926; Research Adventures in University Teaching, 1927 (editor); Psychology and the New Education, 1933 (revised edit., with F. P. Robinson, 1944); Casebook of Research in Educational Psychology (with J. E. Janney), 1937; Life: a Psychological Survey (with J. E. Janney and R. G. Kuhlen), 1939; Educational Acceleration: Appraisals and Basic Problems, 1949. Home: Columbus, Ohio. †

PRIAULX, C(ECIL) NICHOLAS, b. Guernsey Channel Islands, Eng., Sept. 2, 1889; s. Nicholas William and Ellen (Roper) P.; student pub. schs. Eng.; m. Gabrielle Ledoux, July 8, 1916 (dec. Sept. 19, 1937); children—John, Jacqueline, Robert; m. 2d, Agnes FitzGerald, 1939. Came to U.S., 1910, naturalized, 1918. Vice pres. Am. Broadcasting Co., Inc., from 1943, treas. form 1944, also dir. C.P.A., N.Y., 1932. Mem. N.Y. State Soc. C.P.A.'s, Am. Inst. Accts. Club: Hudson River Country (Yonkers). Home: Yonkers, N.Y. †

PRICE, BYRON, newspaperman; b. Topeka, Ind., Mar. 25, 1891; s. John and Emaline (Barnes) P.; A.B., Wabash Coll., 1912; m. Priscilla Alden, Apr. 3, 1920. In newspaper work, Crawfordsville and Indianapolis, 1909-12; reporter and editor United Press Assn., Chicago and Omaha, May-Dec. 1912; with Associated Press from Dec. 1912, news editor, Washington bur., 1922-27, chief of same bur., 1927-37; exec. news editor Associated Press from 1937. Apptd. news censor by President Roosevelt, Dec. 1941. Served at 1st lt., later capt. inf., U.S. Army, 1917-19. Mem. Am. Legion, Phi Beta Kappa, Phi Delta Theta, Tau Kappa Alpha, Pi Delta Epsilon. Methodist. Clubs: Nat. Press, Gridiron (v.p. 1937; pres. 1938), Overseas Writers, Washington Golf and Country (Washington, D.C.); Scarsdale Golf. Home: New York, N.Y. Died Aug. 6, 1981.

PRICE, DEREK DE SOLLA, educator, science historian; b. London, Eng., Jan. 22, 1922; s. Philip and Fanny Marie (de Solla) P.; m. Ellen Hjorth, Oct. 30, 1947; children—Linda Marie, Jeffrey Phillip, Mark de Solla. B.S., U. London, 1942, Ph.D. in Physics, 1946; Ph.D. in History of Sci, Cambridge (Eng.) U., 1954; M.A., Yale, 1960. Lab. asst., research asst., lectr. war research S.W. Essex Tech. Coll. U. London, 1938-46; Commonwealth Fund fellow math. physics Princeton, 1946-47; lectr. applied math. U. Malaya, Singapore, 1947-50; cons. history physics, astronomy Smithsonian Inst., Washington, 1957; Donaldson fellow Inst. Advanced Study, Princeton, 1958-59; prof., Avalon prof. history sci. Yale U., 1960-83, chmn. dept. history sci. and medicine, 1960-64, 74-77; cons. NSF.; chmn. UNESCO Working Group Sci. Policy, 1967-70; pres. Internat. Commn. for Science Policy Studies, 1971-75. Author: The Equatorie of the Planetis, 1955, (with Needham and Wang) Heavenly Clockwork, 1959, Science since Babylon, 1961, enlarged edit., 1975, Little Science, Big Science, 1963, Gears From the Greeks, 1974; Editor: (with I. Spiegel-Rösing) Science, Technology and Society—A Cross-Disciplinary Perspective, 1977. Recipient Leonardo da Vinci medal Soc. History Tech., 1976; recipient J.D. Bernal award Soc. Social Studies of Sci., 1983; hon. research assoc. Smithsonian Instn.; Guggenheim fellow, 1969. Mem. Internat. Acad. History Sci., Soc. History Tech., History Sci. Soc., Soc. Social Studies Sci. (founding council mem.), Royal Swedish Acad. Sci. (fgn.), Sigma Xi. Home: New Haven, Conn. Died Sept. 2, 1983.

PRICE, GWILYM ALEXANDER, born in Canonsburg, Pa., June 20, 1895; s. John L. and Margaret Ann (Thomas) P.; LL.B., University of Pitsburgh, 1917; m. Marion Roberts, Mar. 9, 1921; children—Gwilym Alexander, Jr., Alfred Roberts, Richard Martin. Admitted to Pa. bar, 1917, practiced in Pittsburgh, 1919-20; asst. trust ofcr., Pittsburgh Trust Co., 1920-22; practiced law, 1922-23, trust officer, Peoples Savings & Trust Co., 1923-30, v.p. Peoples-Pitts. Trust Company (now Pittsburgh National Bank), 1930-40, v.p. in charge trusts, 1937-40, pres. and dir., 1940-43; v.p. Westinghouse Elec. & Mfg. Co., Pittsburgh, 1943-46, dir., from 1945, name changed to Westinghouse Electric Corp., 1945, pres., dir., 1946-55, chmn. bd., pres. and chief executive officer, 1955-58, chmn. bd., chief exec. officer, 1958-59, chairman of the board, 1959-64; member board of directors Mellon Nat. Bank & Trust Co., Eastman Kodak Co., Waynesburg & Washington R.R. Co., Great Atlantic & Pacific Tea Co. Trustee YMCA Pitts., Carnegie Inst.; chmn. bd. trustees emeritus U. Pitts.; board directors Radio Free Europe Fund. Recipient John Fritz gold medal Am. Soc. C.E., Am. Inst. E.E., Am. Soc. M.E. and Am. Institute of Mining, Metallergical and Petroleum Engrs., 1959. Captain, 302 Heavy Tank Batn. U.S. Army, World War I. Rep. 12th Legislative Dist., Allegheny County, Pa. Legislature, 1923-24. Member Allegheny Co. Bar Assn. Republican. Methodist. Clubs: Duquesne, University, Law, Rolling Rock (Pitts.); Pike Run Country; Links (N.Y.C.). Home: Carnegie, Pa. Died June 1, 1985.

PRICE, JAMES HARDY, JR., judge; b. Greenville, S.C., Oct. 3, 1914; s. James Hardy and Alyce Louise (Baker) P.; m. Alice Celeste Rogers, May 29, 1944; children—James Hardy, Lisa Bruce. B.A., Furman U., 1936; LL.B., U. S.C., 1939; grad., Nat. Coll. State Judiciary, 1971. Bar: S.C. bar 1939. Practiced in, Greenville, 1939-41, 45-61, county judge Greenville county, 1961-72, state circuit judge, from 1976; Lectr. seminars Greenville Tech. Edn. Center, 1969-70, 72; del. from S.C. to jud. sect. Am. Bar Assn., 1970-76; Mem. Jud. Reform Com., 1970-72; mem. Regional Com. Law Enforcement Assistance Program, chmn., 1973; chmn. S.C. Jud. Discipline and Standards Commn., from 1976; mem. State Task Force on Cts. (Omnibus Crime Commn.), 1968-70. Served with USNR, 1941-45. Recipient Outstanding Jud. Service award Assn. Trial Lawyers Am. and S.C. Trial Lawyers Assn., 1972; award of pub. safety Appalachin Council Govts. Mem. Am., S.C. bar assns., Greenville Lawyers Club (pres. 1960), Theta Chi (pres. 1936). Baptist (tchr. Bible class 1955). Clubs: Rotarian, Elk, Poinsett. Poinsett. Home: Greenville, SC.

PRICE, MARGARET EVANS, illustrator, author; b. Chicago, Ill., Mar. 20, 1888; d. Evan Rees and Elizabeth (Sutherland) Evans; grad. Mass. Normal Art Sch., 1908; pupil of Decamp and Major; m. Irving L. Price, 1908; children—Harriet Elizabeth, William, David Sutherland. Writer of books and serials; illustrator; also painter of portraits and murals, Murals in Aurora (N.Y.) Theatre. Author: (also illustrator) A Child's Book of Myths, 1924; Enchantment Tales of Children, 1926; Legends of The Seven Seas, 1929; The Windy Shore, 1930; (also illustrator) Monkey-Do, 1934, and Mota and the Monkey Tree, 1935; Down Comes the Wilderness (also illustrator), 1937, Night Must End, 1938, (French translation, Les Bebes Sont A Novs, 1948); Animals Marooned (also illustrator), 1943. Illustrator: The Real Story Book, 1927; Once Upon a Time, 1922; also numerous booklets. Home: East Aurora, N.Y.; (winter) "Fernwall by Saint Annes's," Southampton, Bermuda. †

PRICE, NELSON ALLEN, coll. adminstr.; b. Grangeville, N.Y., Feb. 22, 1889; s. Isaac G. and Estella A. (Langley) P.; A.B., Syracuse U., 1912; S.T.B., Boston U., 1915; B.D., Harvard, 1916; D.D. (hon.), Morningside College, 1945; m. Charlotte King, July 7, 1925; children—Charlotte Frances, Orsemus Nelson, Helen Gertrude, Margaret Esther. Ordained to Meth. ministry, 1915, commd. missionary, 1916, and served as missionary to Chinese, at Rangoon, Burma, 1916-23; pastor, Harvey, Dickinson and Valley City, N.D., 1923-29, Rockwell City, Ia., 1929-35; dist. supt., 1935-37; pastor Whitfield Ch., Sioux City, Ia., 1937-42, Algona, 1942-46; v.p. Morningside Coll. from 1946. Mem. Northwest Ia. Conf. Meth. Ch. Mason (K.T.; past grand chaplain Royal Arch Masons of Ia.). Club: Sioux City Auto. Home: Sioux City, Iowa. †

PRICHARD, WALTER, univ. prof., editor; b. Edinburg, Ind., June 5, 1887; s. Ira Lutrell and Sarah Jane (Jenkins) P.; A.B., Indiana U., 1914, M.A., 1915; grad. student summer 1915, session 1915-16, summer 1916; grad. student U. of Ill., 1916-17; student University of Chicago; married Mary Ellen Welborn, September 7, 1927; children—Sarah Belle, Nancy Ellen. Grade school teacher, Indiana, 1906-08, high sch. prin., 1908-12, 1913-14; grad. fellow in history Ind. U., 1914-15, tutor and grad. asst. in history, 1915-16, grad. asst. polit. sci., summer 1916; acting prof. history U. of N.M., 1917-18, Southwestern U., Georgetown, Tex., 1918-19; prof. and dept. head history La. State U., 1919-46, dean of men, 1927-30, Francois Xavier Martin prof. La. history from 1946; research asst. in history Ill. Hist. Survey, 1916-17; grad. asst. history U. of Chicago, summer 1919. Made hon. fellow Kan. State Hist. Soc., 1927; Officer d'Academie avee les Palmes, French Govt., 1938. Fellow Am. Geog. Soc.; mem. Am. Hist. Assn., Miss. Valley Hist. Assn. (mem. exec. council 1935-38), Southern Hist. Assn., La. Hist. Soc. (mem. exec. council from 1934), Am. Assn. Univ. Profs., A.A.A.S., Phi Kappa Phi, Pi Gamma Mu. Mason. Democrat. Club: Faculty (La. State U.). Mem. adv. council Atlas of Am. History, 1943. Editor: La. Hist. Quar. from 1934, La. Social Studies Maps, 1946; contbr. numerous articles and book reviews to hist. jours. and encys. Home: Baton Rouge, La. †

PRIESTLEY, JOHN BOYNTON, author: b. Bradford, Eng., Sept. 13, 1894; M.A., Trinity Hall, Cambridge; hon. LL.D. Author: (fiction), Adam in Moonshine, 1927; Benighted, 1927; Farthing Hall (with Hugh Walpole), 1929; The Good Companions, 1929; Angel Pavement, 1930; The Town Major of Miraucourt, 1930; Faraway, 1932; I'll Tell You Everything (with Gerald Bullett), 1933; Wonder Hero, 1933; Albert Goes Through, 1933; They Walk in the City, 1936; Let the People Sing, 1939; Black-out in Gretley, 1942; Daylight on Saturday, 1943; (plays), The Good Companions (with Edward Knoblock), 1931; Dangerous Corner, 1932; The Roundabout, 1933; Laburnum Grove, 1934; Eden End, 1934; Cornelius, 1935; Bees in the Boat Deck, 1936; Time and the Conways, 1937; I Have Been Here Before, 1937; When We Are Married, 1938; Music at Night, 1938; Johnson Over Jordan, 1939; The Long Mirror, 1940; Goodnight Children, 1941; They Came to a City, 1943; (miscellanous), Brief Diversions, 1922; Papers from Lilliput, 1922; I For One, 1923; Figures in Modern Literature, 1924; The English Comic Characters, 1925; Meredith, 1926; Talking, 1926; Peacock, 1927; Open House, 1927; English Humor, 1928; Apes and Angels, 1928; The Balconinny, 1929; English Journey, 1934; Midnight on the Desert, 1937; Rain Upon Godshill, 1939; Postscripts, 1940; Out of the People, 1941; Three Men in New Suits, 1945; Bright Day, 1946; (plays) Desert Highway, 1944; How Are They at Home?, An Inspector Calls, Ever Since Paradise, 1946; Arts Under Socialism, Jenny Villiers, Theatre Outlook, (play), The Linden Tree, 1947; (play) Home is Tomorrow, 1948; (play) Summer Day Dream, Delight, (libretto of opera) The Olympians, 1949; Festival, 1951; Last Holiday, 1952; Dragon's Mouth (with J. Hawkes), 1952; The Other Place, 1953; The Magicians, 1954; Low Notes on a High Level, 1954; (plays) Take the Fool Away, Mr. Kettle and Mrs. Moon, 1955; (with J. Hawkes) Journey Down a Rainbow, 1955; (play) The Glass Cage, 1957; The Art of the Dramatist, 1957; Literature and Western Man, 1960; Saturn Over the Water, The Thirty-first of June, 1961. Club: Saville (London). Address: Stratford on Avon, Warwickshire, Eng. Died Aug. 14, 1984.

PRINCE, GEORGE W(ASHINGTON), JR., lawyer; b. Galesburg, Ill., Oct. 9, 1887; s. George Washington and Lillie Cornelia (Ferris) P.; A.B., Knox Coll., 1908; student George Washington U., 1906-07; LL.B., Harvard, 1911; m. Alice Kingsbury Lewis, May 13, 1913; children—Mary, Charles L. Admitted to Ill. bar, 1911, Cal. bar, 1913; practice of law, Los Angeles, from 1913; mem. Overton, Lyman, and Prince; secretary Earle C. Anthony, Incorporated. Dir. Fifield Manors; trustee Honnold Library Soc., Claremont, California. Trustee of Knox College. Served as private F.A. United States Army, World War I. Mem. Am., Los Angeles bar assns., State Bar Cal., Phi Delta Theta. Republican. Conglist. Clubs: University, Bel-Air Country (Los Angeles); Bel-Air Bay (Pacific Palisades, Cal.). Home: Los Angeles, Calif. †

PRINCE, HENRY FERRIS, lawyer; b. Galesburg, Ill., Dec. 3, 1889; s. George W. and Lillie C. (Ferris) P.; B.S., Knox Coll., 1911; LL.B., Harvard, 1914; m. Marie A. Smith, May 1, 1915. Admitted to Cal. bar, 1914; counsel of Gibson, Dunn & Crutcher, Los Angeles, from 1927. Served with U.S. Army, World War I. Mem. Am., Cal., Los Angeles bar assns. Clubs: California, Los Angeles Country, University, Stock Exchange (Los Angeles). Home: Los Angeles, Calif. †

PRIOR, FRANK O., ret. oil exec.; b. Escondido, Calif., Aug. 25, 1895; s. William Wilson and Letitia (Wistar) P.; B.A., Stanford; m. Brennis Gardner, Apr. 15, 1923; children—Frank O., Thomas G.; m. 2d, Mrs. Elsie B. Bohannon, Aug. 25, 1951. Gen. supt. Dixie Oil Co., 1928-29, vice pres., 1929, pres., 1930; dir. and pres. Stanolind Oil & Gas Co., 1930; dir., v.p. prodn. pipe lines crude purchasing, Standard Oil Company of Indiana, 1945-51, executive vice president, 1951-55, president 1955-58, chairman bd., chief exec. officer, 1958-60; chmn. bd. Stanolind Oil & Gas Co., Stanolind Pipe Line Co., Stanolind Oil Purchasing Co., 1945-47; dir. First Nat. Bank (Palm Beach, Fla.), Am. Petroleum Inst. (hon. dir.), Am. Inst. Elec. Engrs., Mid-Continent Oil and Gas Assn., Transportation Assn. of Am. (dir.), Am. Inst. Mining Metall. and Petroleum Engrs., Transp. Assn. Am. (dir., chmn. bd.). Clubs: Chicago, Racquet, Commerical, Tavern (Chgo.); Everglades (Palm Beach, Fla.); The Links (N.Y.C.); Rolling Rock (Ligonier, Pa.); Bohemian, Pacific-Union (San Francisco). Home: Palm Beach, Fla. Died Jan. 18, 1984.

PRITCHARD, HARRY TURNBULL, pub. utilities exec.; b. New Britain, Conn., Jan. 23, 1887; s. Henry W. and Lillian J. (Turnbull) P.; Ph.B., Yale, 1908. With Lockport plant San. Dist. Chgo., 1908-10, asst. supt., 1910-11, supt. 1911-13, supt. constrn., Chgo., 1913-16; pres. River Falls Power Co., 1916-17, Carlsbad Light & Power Co., 1917-18; gen. supt. Ind. Power Co., Vincennes, 1919-20, v.p., gen. mgr., 1920-24; v.p. Eastern N.J. Power Co., Asbury Park, 1924-25; v.p. charge Eastern operations Utilities Power & Light Corp., N.Y.C., 1925-30, v.p. charge operations, Chgo., 1930-37; pres., chmn. bd. Indpls. Power & Light Co., 1934-57, chmn. bd., from 1957, also dir.; dir. C.C.C. & St.L. Ry., Lake Erie &

Eastern R.R., Am. Fletcher Nat. Bank & Trust Co. Trustee Marion County Health and Hosp. Corp.; dir. Hosp. Devel. Assn., Indpls. United Fund, Ind. Symphony Soc.; v.p., dir. Park Fletcher Indsl. Park; hon. chmn. Starlight Musicals, Inc.; adv. com. Ind. Central Coll.; mem. adv. bd. Indpls. sci. and Engring. Found., Inc. Mem. Edison Electric Inst. (past dir.), Indpls. Better Bus. Bur. (past dir.), Ind. Electric Assn. (dir., past pres.), C. of C. (dir., past pres.), Aplha Sigma Phi. Mason. Clubs: Hundred (dir.), Indianapolis Athletic, Columbia, Woodstock, Rotary (Indpls.); Yale of Indiana (past pres.); Contemporary. Home: Indianapolis, Ind. †

PRITCHARD, JOHN MCCLARY, petroleum exec.; b. London, Ont., Can., July 22, 1887; s. A. W. and Clara (McClary) P.; student Wesley Coll., Winnipeg; m. Una Lytell (dec.); children—John, Una Elizabeth; m. 2d, Adeline Hoover. Began career with Canadian Bank of Commerce. Winnipeg; mgr. for Province of Alberta, Winnipeg Oil Co.; mgr. for Eastern Can., Brit.-Am. Oil Co., Ltd.; organized Tidioute Refining Co. of Can., 1923 (later merged with McColl-Frontenac Oil Co., Ltd.; chmn. McColl-Frontenac Oil Co., Ltd.; chmn. Brandram-Henderson, Ltd.; pres. Canadian Montana Pipeline Company, Canadian Montana Gas Company; director of Canada Iron Foundries. Ltd., Commonwealth Internat. Corp., Ltd., Crown Trust Co., Beverage Fund of Can., Ltd., Royal-Southwestern Oil Corp., Resources of Can. Investment Fund, Ltd. Pres. nat. council YMCA of Can.; pres. Montreal Shriner's Hosp. Found.; gov. Children's Meml. Hosp., Montreal Shriners Hosp. for Crippled Children, Montreal Gen. Hosp.; corporator Springfield (Mass.) Coll. Mem. United Church of Can. (mem. bd. colls. and secondary schs.; exec. com. dept. pensions). Mason. Clubs: Seignory; Mount Royal (Montreal); Rideau (Ottawa); National, York (Toronto); Manitoba (Winnipeg); Beaconsfield Golf; Laval-sur-le-Lac Golf; Mount Bruno Golf; Royal Montreal Golf. Home: Westmount, Que., Can. †

PRITCHARD, WALTER HERBERT, physician, educator; b. Hancock, N.Y., Apr. 14, 1910; s. Edson Jay and Mertie (Cady) P.; m. Marian Louise Moore, Aug. 12, 1939; children—Walter Herbert, Lawrence, Diana, Marian, Timothy, Caroline. A.B., Hamilton Coll., Clinton, N.Y., 1932; M.D., Harvard, 1936. Intern. Univ. Hosps., Cleve., 1936-38, resident, fellow medicine, 1938-40; faculty Case Western Res. U. Sch. Medicine, from 1947, prof. medicine, 1960-65, Argyl J. Beams prof. medicine, from 1965, dir. div. cardiology, 1956-76; asso. dir. medicine Case Western Res. U. Sch. Medicine (Univ. Hosps.), from 1960, acting dir. dept. of medicine, 1970-71, chief of staff, 1971-78. Contbr. articles on cardiovascular diseases to profl. jours. Mem. Olympic Track Team, 1932; Trustee Hamilton Coll., Clinton, N.Y., 1973-77. Mem. Assn. Am. Physicians, Am. Soc. Clin. Investigation, Central Soc. Clin. Research, AMA, Am. Heart Assn. (chmn., council on clin. cardiology 1970-72), A.C.P., Soc. Exptl. Biology and Medicine, Assn. Univ. Cardiologists (pres. 1973), Sigma Xi. Home: Cleveland Heights, OH.

PRITIKIN, NATHAN, nutritionist; b. Chgo., Aug. 29, 1915; s. Jacob I. and Esther (Levitt) P.; m. Ilene Robbins; children: Jack, Janet, Robert, Ralph, Kenneth. Student, U. Chgo., 1933-35; DsC. (hon.), Kirksville Coll. Osteo. Medicine (Mo.), 1982. Self-employed inventor, Chgo. area, 1935-57, Santa Barbara (Calif.) area, 1957-76; with patents in chemistry, physics and electronics; dir. Pritikin Longevity Center, Santa Monica, Calif., 1976-85; chmn. Pritikin Research Found., 1976-85. Author: The Pritikin Permanent Weight-Loss Manual, 1981, The Pritikin Program, 1983; co-author: Live Longer Now, 1974, The Pritikin Program for Diet and Exercise, 1979. Home: Santa Barbara, Calif. Died Feb. 21, 1985.

PRITZKER, JACK NICHOLAS, lawyer; b. Chgo., Jan. 6, 1904; s. Nicholas J. and Annie (Cohen) P.; A.B., U. Mich., 1926; J.D., Northwestern U., 1927; m. Rhoda R. Goldberg, Jan. 9, 1944; 1 son, Nicholas J. Admitted to Ill. bar, 1927, since practiced in Chgo.; partner firm Pritzker & Pritzker. Dir. Hyatt Internat. Corp. Hon. dir. Jewish Children's Bur. Chgo. Served to lt. comdr. USNR, 1942-45. Mem. Ill., Chgo. bar assns. Clubs: Arts Mid-Day, Standard (Chgo.); University (Sarasota, Fla.). Home: Chicago, Ill. Dec.

PROBASCO, ABBIE, educator; b. Virgil, S.D., Sept. 24, 1890; d. Joseph Lincoln and Edna Elva (Spencer) P.; grad. high sch., Arlington, Ia., 1908; B.A. Upper Ia. U., Fayette, 1915; studied U. of Nanking (China) Lang. Sch., 1920-22; studied Garrett Bibl. Inst. and Northwestern U., 1925-27, M.A., 1927. Teacher rural sch., Fayette Co., Ia., 1908-10; teacher high sch., Lime Springs, 1912-13; prin. high sch., Arlington, 1915-17; same, Wessington Springs, S.D., 1917-18, 1919-20; head of Conf. Acad., Nanking, China, 1922-25; exec. sec. Gooding (Ida.) Coll., 1927-28; prin. Jennings Sem., Aurora, Ill., from 1928. Student Army Training Sch. for Nurses, Camp Dodge, Ia., 1918-19, World War. Mem. Am. Assn. Univ. Women, O.E.S. Methodist.†

PROCTOR, EDWARD OTIS, lawyer; b. Portland, Me., Feb. 14, 1887; b. Edward E. and Grace (Otis) P.; A.B., Yale, 1909; LL.B., Harvard, 1912; m. Fernande Girod, Sept. 30, 1918; children—Madeleine (Woodward), Jacqueline (de Brun), Edward O. Admitted to Mass. bar, 1912, gen. practice at Boston from 1912; asso. with Sherman L. Whipple, 1912-30; mem. firm Withington, Cross, Proctor & Park, 1930-40, Dever & Proctor, 1940-41 and 1947-49; asst. atty. gen. Commonwealth of Mass., 1937-40; state atty. O.P.A., 1941; regional atty., W.P.B., 1942-44; asso. with Ropes, Gray, Best, Coolidge & Rugg, 1944-47; mem. firm Dever and Proctor, from 1949. Served at 1st lt., inf., U.S. Army, A.E.F., Chaumont, France, 1917-19. Mem. Mass. Judicial Council from 1952; member Am., Mass. (president 1944-47) and Boston bar assns., Beta Theta Pi. Democrat. Episcopalian. Elk. Clubs: Elihu, Union, Yale. Home: Newton Centre, Mass. †

PROEHL, OTTO LUDWIG, clergyman, educator; b. Castleton, Ill., Apr. 12, 1887; s. Carl and Angie (Schwartz) P.; A.B., Wartburg Coll., Clinton, Ia., 1907; grad. Wartburg Theol. Sem., Dubuque, Ia., 1910; post-grad. work, U. of Rostock, Germany, 1910-11, U. of Leipzig, 1911-12, U. of Chicago, 1935-38; studied summers, U. of Wis. and Columbia U.; m. Caroline Reinhard, Apr. 16, 1914; children—Carl William, Paul Otto, Elsa Carolina, Louise Mathilda. Ordained ministry Lutheran Ch., 1912; pastor Trinity Ch., Woods Run, Pittsburgh, Pa., 1912-16, First Evang. Luth. Ch., Galveston, Tex., 1916-19; pres. Wartburg Coll., 1919-35; pastor Zion Evang. Luth. Ch., Philo, Ill. Address: Philo, Ill. †

PRUNTY, MERLE CHARLES, educator; b. St. Joseph, Mo., Mar. 2, 1917; s. Merle Charles and Emma Mae (Holliday) P.; m. Eugenia Wyatt, June 3, 1939; children—Mary Merle, Eugene Wyatt, Florence Holliday. B.S., U. Mo., 1939, A.B., 1940, A.M., 1940; Ph.D., Clark U., 1944. Grad. asst. U. Mo., 1939-40; grad fellow Clark U., 1940-42; asst. prof. geography Miss. State Coll., 1942-43, asso. prof. (on leave), 1943-46; prof., head dept. geography and geology U. Ga., 1946-61, prof., head dept. geography, 1961-70, Alumni Found. distinguished prof., from 1969, acting v.p. acad. affairs, 1977, sr. faculty adviser to pres., 1977-79; asst. to chancellor U. System of Ga., 1951; vis. prof. Northwestern U., 1954; cons. geographer Atlantic Steel Co., 1958-60, Tara Plantation, Inc., 1959-62, Jefferson Mills, Inc., 1962-63, U.S. Office Edn., 1965-67; vis. lectr. Oglethorpe U., 1956, Antioch Coll., 1959, Miss. State U., 1965, U. Utah, 1965, Western Mich. U., 1966, U. Wis., 1968, Clark U., 1967, Duke U., 1967, U. Fla., 1968, U. Tenn., 1969, 78, U. S.C., 1970, 78, Auburn U., 1971, U. Ky., 1972, U. So. Miss., 1973, 75, U. Minn., La. State U., 1975, U. N.C., 1976, U. N.C.-Charlotte, 1977, Valdosta State Coll., 1977, Eastern Carolina U., 1981, Fla. State U., 1981, others.; Mem. adv. bd. USAF Air U. Library, 1950-56, vice chmn., 1951, chmn., 1952; Middle Am. com. Sect. Geography and Geology, NRC, 1948-50. Author: The Central Gulf South, 1960, Festschrift: Clarence F. Jones, Northwestern University Studies in Geography, No. 6, 1962; Editorial bd.: U. Ga. Press, 1969-73, Southeastern Geographer, 1971-80, Ga. Rev, 1974-77, Annals, Assn. Am. Geographers, from 1980, cons. editor, Macmillan Co., from 1968, Coronet Films, 1972-73, Ency. Brit. Ednl. Corp., 1978; Contbr. articles to profl. jours., several textbooks. Cons. to Ednl. Testing Service, 1964-69; cons. Pres.'s Com. Equal Employment Opportunity, 1961-64; U.S. nat. del. 20th Internat. Geog. Congress, London, 1964; co-chmn. 5th Nat. Conf. Fire Ecology, Tall Timbers Found., 1965. Served as lt. USNR, 1943-46. Guggenheim Found. fellow, 1957-58; Michael Found. Research fellow, 1961-62; recipient citation meritorious research contbns. Assn. Am. Geographers, 1963, field research award, 1953. Mem. Am. Geog. Soc., Assn. Am. Geographers (chmn. membership and credentials com. 1953-54, chmn. adv. com. to Air Force ROTC 1954, chmn. honors and awards com. 1959-60, exec. com. 1953-55, 67-69, nat. program com. 1958, chmn. research grants com. 1962-63, S.E. div. mem. exec. com. 1947-69, pres. 1953-55, hon. life mem.), Nat. Council Geog. Edn. (dir. 1966-69), Am. Geophys. Union, Ga. Acad., Sci. (chmn. earth scis. div. 1949-50), Tenn. Acad. Sci., Internat. Geog. Union, Phi Kappa Phi, Alpha Kappa Delta, Sigma Nu. Democrat. Home: Athens, GA.

PRYALE, HARRY MORGAN, rubber company exec.; b. Pittsburgh, July 14, 1890; s. John and Margaret (Morgan) P.; student Staunton Mil. Acad.; m. Jeanne Elaine Walker, Dec. 4, 1912. Gen. constrn. bus., 1912-30; joined Baldwin Rubber Co., Pontiac, Mich., 1931, dir. from 1927; dir. Paymaster Gold Mine, Community Nat. Bank, Pontiac. Clubs: Bloomfield Hills (Mich.) Country; Old (St. Clair Flats, Mich.); Key Largo Anglers (Homestead, Fla.). Home: Bloomfield Hills, Mich. †

PUCKETT, HUGH WILEY, univ. prof.; b. Birmingham, Ala., June 21, 1887; s. Erastus Peru and Susan (Henry) P.; A.B., Birmingham-Southern College, Birmingham, Ala., 1905, M.A., Tulane University, New Orleans, La., 1907, M.A., Harvard, 1913, Ph.D., U. of Munich, Germany, 1914; m. Mary Clifford Dimmitt, Sept. 12, 1912; children—Mary Elizabeth, Hugh Wiley. Instr. in German U. of Ill., 1915-16; lecturer in German Columbia Univ., 1916-22, asst. prof., 1922-31, asso. professor, 1931-45, prof. from 1945; traveling fellow from Harvard, 1912-13; lecturer Volkshochschule, Berlin, 1927. Methodist. Democrat. Author: Elementargeister in the Middle High German Epic, 1916; Germany's Women Go Forward, 1930. Editor of numerous German texts. Contributor of articles to The Survey, Saturday Review of Literature, Sch. and Soc. Home: Leonia, N.J. †

PUIGCASAURANC, JOSE MANUEL, diplomat; b. Ciudad del Carmen, Campeche, Mexico, Jan. 21, 1888; s. Jose Puig and Carmen (Casauranc) Puig C.; M.D., U. of Mexico, 1917; m. Maria Elena Reyes Spindola, Mar. 26, 1926. Elected mem. Mexican Congress, 1912 and 1922, and to Senate, 1924; sec. pub. edn., 1924-28 and 1930-31; sec. of commerce, industry and labor, 1928-29; head, Dept. of Federal Dist., 1929-30; pres. Commn. for Reorganization of Pub. Administration, 1931; apptd. ambassador to U.S., Oct. 17, 1931. Mem. Nat. Acad. Medicine (Mexico), Hispanic Med. Assn. (Cadiz, Spain), Officer Legion of Honor (France). Author various works, prose and poetry. Address: Washington, D.C. Deceased.

PULLIAS, ATHENS CLAY, coll. pres.; b. Castalian Springs, Tenn., Dec. 3, 1910; s. John G. and Margaret (Leath) P.; student David Lipscomb Coll., 1928-29; A.B., Cumberland U., 1931, LL.B., 1932, LL.D., 1959; B.D., Vanderbilt U., 1934; J.D., Cumberland Sch. Law, Samford U., 1969; ednl. travel, Europe and Middle East, 1959; m. Mary Frances Newby, May 16, 1931; 1 son, Athens Clay. Ordained to ministry Ch. of Christ, 1926; minister, Bridgeport, Ala., 1931-34, Charlotte Av. Ch., Nashville, 1934-46; tchr. sociology David Lipscomb Coll., Nashville, 1934-36, head Bible dept., 1937-46, exec. asst., 1937-41, v.p., 1941-46, pres. 1946-85, dir. Lipscomb expansion program 1944-85; sec., treas. Lipscomb Coll. Found. Dir. Fed. Home Loan Bank Cin. Pres. Tenn. Ind. Colls. Fund. Chmn. Tenn. Tax Study Commn., 1966-67. Bd. dirs. Nashville Symphony Assn., Cumberland, Coll., Lebanon, Tenn.; trustee United Givers Fund. Mem. Am., Nashville bar assns., N.E.A., Tenn. Edn. Assn., Nashville C. of C. Democrat. Rotarina. Club: Freola. Home: Nashville, Tenn. Died Mar. 25, 1985.

PURSE, JAMES NATHANIEL, business executive; b. Detroit, Aug. 19, 1923; s. Gilbert R. and Eleanor F. (Leitert) P.; m. Rolonde M. L. Redon, Aug. 24, 1946; children—John R., Charles R. Student, Mich. Coll. Mining and Tech., 1943; B.S. in Metall. Engring, U. Wis., 1947. With Gt. Lakes Steel Co., Detroit, 1947-55; with Hanna Mining Co., Cleve., 1955-79, mgr. fgn. sales, then v.p. sales, 1960-69, exec. v.p., 1969-74, pres., chief exec. officer, dir., 1974-78, vice chmn., 1978-79, also dir.; dir. B.F. Goodrich Co., Lubrizol Corp. Mem. exec. bd. Greater Cleve. council Boy Scouts Am., from 1975; bd. dirs. Greater Cleve. Growth Assn., 1971-76, 78-82. Served with USNR, 1942-46. Mem. Am. Iron Ore Assn. (dir. 1970-79, chmn. bd. dirs. 1975-77), Am. Iron and Steel Inst. (dir. 1975-79), Am. Mining Congress (dir. 1977-79). Clubs: Union (Cleve.), Hudson Country (Cleve.), Pepper Pike (Cleve.); Imperial Golf (Naples, Fla.). Home: Hudson, Ohio. Died June 3, 1982.

PURVIS, HUGH FRANK, ret. accountant; b. Moultrie, Ga., Feb. 7, 1904; s. Elias Frank and Eva (Dodd) P.; student Pace Inst., 1922, Eastman Coll., Poughkeepsie, N.Y., 1924; m. Rachel Elizabeth Bowen, Oct. 12, 1963; children by previous marriage—Lorraine (Mrs. John E. Morris), Constance (Mrs. William F. Field); stepchildren—Joan T. Qratton, Barbara (Mrs. Eugene Patterson). Partner firm Pentland, Purvis, Keller & Co., C.P.A.'s, Miami, Fla., 1933-61; partner, charge Fla. offices Haskins & Sells, C.P.A.'s, Miami, 1961-69. Past pres. Miami Jr. C. of C., Dade County Com. 21. C.P.A., 1929. Mem. Am., Fla. (past pres.) inst. C.P.A.'s Beta Alpha Psi. (hon.). Clubs: Miami; Riveria Country (Coral Gables). Home: Coral Gables, Fla. Died Aug. 30, 1983; interred Woodlawn Cemetery, Miami, Fla.

PUTNAM, NINA WILCOX (MRS. CHRISTIAN ELIOT), author; b. New Haven, Conn., Nov. 28, 1888; d. Marrion and Eleanor (Sanchez) Wilcox; ed. at home by governess; m. Robert Faulkner Putnam, of New York, Oct. 5, 1907 (died 1918); 1 son, John Francis; m. 2d, R.J. Sanderson, of New Haven, Conn., Nov. 4, 1919; m. 3d, Arthur James Ogle, September 12, 1931 (divorced); m. 4th Christian Eliot, July 16, 1933. Has written and published stories and verse, since age of 11. Mem. Authors' League America, Poetry Soc. America. Author: In Search of Arcady, 1912; The Impossible Boy, 1913; The Little Missioner, 1914; Orthodoxy, 1915; Adam's Garden, 1916; When the Highbrow Joined the Outfit, 1917; Esmeralda, 1918; Sunny Bunny, 1918; Winkle Twinkle and Lollypops, 1918; Believe You Me, 1919; It Pays to Smile, 1920; West Broadway, 1921; Laughter, Ltd., 1922; Say It with Bricks, 1923; Easy, 1924; The Bear Who Went to War, 1928; The Making of an American Humorist, 1929; Laughing Through, 1930; Paris Love, 1931. Contbr. to mags., also N. Am. Newspaper Alliance. Home: Delray Beach, Fla.†

PUTNAM, REX, state supt. pub. instrn.; b. Buffalo Gap, S.D., June 7, 1890; s. Jay Samuel and Rebecca Charlotte (Sutton) P.; grad. State Normal, Spearfish, S.D., 1913; A.B., U. of Ore., 1915, A.M., 1929; student U. of Calif., summer 1930, U. of Ore., 1931; LL.D., Lewis and Clark Coll., 1945, U. of Portland, 1948; m. Elinor Gertrude Snow, June 20, 1919; children—Roger Ky, Rex Paul (lt. U.S. Army Air Corps, killed overseas, Apr. 15, 1942). Teacher, Springfield, Ore., 1915-16, Salem, Ore., 1916-18; teacher of science, high sch., Tacoma, Wash., 1918-23; supt. of schs., Redmond, Ore., 1923-32, Albany, Ore., 1932-37; state supt. pub. instrn. State of Ore. from 1937; exec. officer State Board of Education. Mem. State Apprenticeship Commn., mem. Ore. State Textbook and Curriculum Commn. Mem. O.T.C., 1918. Mem. U.S. Office Edn. (adv. com. for vocational edn. 1947-49). Mem. N.E.A., Ore. State Teachers Assn., Nat. Assn. Chief State Sch. Officers (pres. 1946), Ore. High Sch. Prin's. Assn. (pres. 1932), Dept. of Superintendence, Supts. of Dists. of the First Class (pres. 1935), Am. Legion, Grange, Phi Delta Kappa, Kappa Delta Pi. Democrat. Mason, Elk. Contributor to Oregon Education Jour. Home: Salem, Ore. †

PYATT, EDWIN EUGENE, environmental engineer, educator; b. Bloomington, Ill., May 13, 1929; s. Edwin Hulett Pyatt and Florence Irene (DeVore) P.; m. Carol Jean Collar, Feb. 25, 1961; 1 son, Dale Hulett. B.S., Calif. Inst. Tech., 1951; M.S., U. Calif., Berkeley, 1953; Dr.Eng., Johns Hopkins U., 1959. Research engr. Pomeroy & Assocs., Pasadena, Calif., 1955-56; asst. prof. Northwestern U., Evanston, Ill., 1959-62; sr. research engr. Travelers Research Center, Hartford, Conn., 1962-65; mem. faculty dept. environ. engring. U. Fla., Gainesville, 1965-81, prof., chmn. dept., 1970-81; cons. World Bank, Asian Devel. Bank, Occidental Chem. Co. Contbr. articles to profl. jours. Mem. Fla. Resource Recovery Council, 1974-79; founding dir. Gainesville YMCA, 1967-69. Served with USAF, 1953-55. Mem. ASCE, Water Pollution Control Fedn., Am. Water Works Assn., Am. Public Health Assn., Am. Soc. Engring. Edn., AAAS, Am. Water Resources Assn., Fla. Engring. Soc., Blue Key, Sigma Xi, Omicron Delta Kappa, Tau Beta Pi, Chi Epsilon, Sigma Tau, Phi Kappa Phi, Epsilon Lambda Chi, Kappa Sigma. Home: Gainesville, Fla.

PYLE, JOHN FREEMAN, coll. dean; b. Ind., Nov. 24, 1890; s. William Henry and Mary Elizabeth (Stapleton) P.; Ind. State Teachers Coll., Terre Haute, 1910-15; Ph.B., U. of Chicago, 1917, M.A., 1918, Ph.D., 1925; m. Lola Muril Webber, 1920; 1 son, John Carroll. Prof. polit. science and economics, Mo. State Teachers Coll., Kirksville, 1918-20; asst. in economics, Sch. of Commerce and Administration, U. of Chicago, 1920-21, instr. in business administration, 1921-25; also lecturer in economics, Sch. of Commerce, Northwestern U., 1923-25; prof. economics and marketing and dean of Robert A. Johnston Coll. Business Adminstrn., Marquette U., 1925-42, also head dept. of economics; dean, Coll. of Bus. and Pub. Adminstrn., U. of Md., since 1942; acting dean Coll. Arts and Sciences, University of Maryland, Dec. 1943-July 1949. Cons. Md. Commn. on Postwar Development and Reconstruction, 1943-46; mem. nat. bd. field advisors Small Bus. Adminstrn., 1954-61; mem. American Management Association, American Economic Assn., Delta Nu Alpha, Delta Sigma Pi, Phi Kappa Phi, Beta Alpha Psi, Pi Sigma Alpha, Pi Gamma Mu, Beta Gamma Sigma, Acacia; hon. mem. Milw. Sales Mgrs. Assn.; charter mem. Am. Marketing Assn. Mason. Methodist. Club: Rotary. Author: Marketing Principles—Organization and Policies, 1931, rev. edit., 1936; Marketing Management, 1942. Contbr. to tech. publs. Home: Hyattsville, Md. †

PYLES, THOMAS, philologist; b. Frederick, Md., June 5, 1905; s. Joseph Thomas and Charlotte (Bowers) P.; B.A., U. Md., 1926, M.A., 1927; Ph.D., Johns Hopkins, 1938; m. Bessie Alice Yort, Dec. 21, 1929; 1 son, Thomas. With dept. English, U. Md., 1927-44; instr. English, Johns Hopkins, 1938-44; prof. English, U. Okla., 1944-48; prof. English, U. Fla., 1948-66, prof. emeritus, 1972-82; prof. English and linguistics Northwestern U., 1966-71, prof. emeritus, 1971—1971-82; guest prof. English philology U. Göttingen (Germany), 1956-57; vis. prof. N.Y. U., summer 1965, Northwestern U., 1965-66. Mem. editorial adv. bd. Funk and Wagnalls Standard Dictionary, 1963; mem. internat. editorial adv. com. World Book Dictionary, 1963, 76; editorial adv. com. Thorndike-Barnhart Coll. Dictionary, from 1965. Mem. Am. Dialect Soc. (sec. 1952-56, v.p. 1958-60, pres. 1960-62), Linguistic Soc. Am., Modern Lang. Assn., Modern Humanities Research Assn., Am. Name Soc. (bd. mgrs. 1960-63), Internat. Assn. U. Profs. English, Phi Beta Kappa. Episcopalian. Author: Words and Ways of American English, 1952; The Origins and Development of the English Language, 3d rev. edit., 1980; The English Language: A Brief History, 1968; (with John Algeo) English: An Introduction to Language, 1970; Thomas Pyles: Selected Essays on English Usage (edited by John Algeo), 1979; also articles, revs.; editorial adv. bd. Dictionary Am. Regional English; adviser to editors Ency. Brit., 1968-76; editorial adv. com. Am. Speech, 1966-67, 70-71; editor: (with S.V. Larkey) An Herbal, 1941; Home: Gainesville, Fla. Died May 25, 1980.

QUEEN, STUART ALFRED, sociologist; b. Fredonia, Kan., Feb. 26, 1890; s. Charles Nicholas and Nettie Angelina (Swigart) Q.; A.B., Pomona Coll., Calif., 1910; A.M., U. of Chicago, 1913; Ph.D., 1919; m. Alice Hamilton, Apr. 29, 1918; 1 son, Stuart A.; m. 2d, Charlotte Dexter Barr, June 4, 1927; 1 dau., Margaret Ellen. Exec. sec. Calif. State Bd. Charities and Corrections, 1913-17; dir. Tex. Sch. Civics and Philanthropy, at Houston, Tex., 1917-18; instr. sociology, U. of Ill., 1919; asso. prof. social technology, Goucher Coll., Baltimore, Md., 1919-20; dir. ednl. service Potomac div. Am. Red Cross, 1919-20; prof. social economy and dir. Sch. of Social Work, Simmons Coll., Boston, 1920-22; prof. sociology, U. of Kan., 1922-30; associate secretary Detroit Community Union and Community Fund, 1930-32; prof. sociology, Washington University from 1932; acting librarian, 1943-45; dean, College of Liberal Arts, 1946-49. Served as pvt., United States Army, Apr.-Nov. 1918. Member American Sociological Society (pres. 1941), Nat. Conf. of Social Work, Am. Assn. Social Workers, Missouri Assn. for Social Welfare (president 1952-53), Alpha Kappa Lambda, Phi Beta Kappa, Omicron Delta Kappa, Artus. Author or co-author books relating to field. Home: St. Louis, Mo. †

QUINN, JOHN ROBERTSON, ex-nat. comdr. Am. Legion; b. Porterville, Calif., July 17, 1889; s. Harry and Katie (Robertson) Q.; A.B., U. of Calif., 1912; m. Maude Verne Bristol, of Bakersfield, Calif., June 16, 1917; children—Robert, Jane, Charlotte Ann. Grew up on father's cattle ranch in Calif.; grad. 2d O.T.C., Presidio, and commd. capt. Nov. 15, 1917; assigned as comdr. Battery F, 348th F.A.; served through Meuse-Argonne offensive and with Army of Occupation, Germany; hon. discharged, Apr. 1919, Victory medal. Dept. comdr. Calif. Am. Legion, 1921-22; nat. comdr. Am. Legion, 1923-24. Chmn. Calif. Vets.' Welfare Bd., 1925-30; mem. Governor's Council and dir. Dept. of Mil. and Vet. Affairs; dir. Mil. and Vet's. Affairs, State of Calif. Vice president Seaboard National Bank, Los Angeles. Mem. Bd. of Supervisors, Los Angeles County; assessor Los Angeles County from 1938; pres. bd. trustees Delano Union High Sch.; del. to Rep. Nat. Conv., Kansas City, 1928. Mason. Elk. Home: Los Angeles, Calif. †

QUINN, THOMAS HOWARD, banker; b. N.Y.C., Aug. 4, 1902; s. Thomas Charles and Frances (Quinn) Q.; m. Adele G. Pearl, Aug. 28, 1948. Ed. law, N.Y. U., 1927. Chmn. Inter-County Title Guaranty & Mortgage Co., N.Y.C., 1937-70; pres. US LIFE Title Ins. Co., N.Y.C., 1970-77; regional chmn. Key Bank, Albany, N.Y., from 1948; chmn. First Gen. Resources Co., N.Y.C., from 1962; pres. Pilgrim Devel. Corp., Plymouth, Conn., from 1974, Crystal River Devel. Corp., Fla., from 1975; chmn. Fiduciary Ins. Co. Am., N.Y.C., from 1977. Trustee Columbia Meml. Hosp., Hudson, N.Y., 1970-84; bd. dirs. N.Y.C. Pub. Devel. Corp., 1973-84, Cath. Community Welfare Assn., Columbia and Greene counties, N.Y.; pres. Caldwell B. Esselstyn Found., Hudson, Olana Hist. Site, Hudson. Mem. N.Y. State Land Title Assn. (pres. 1937-38, 53-54), Columbia County Coaching Soc. (pres.). Clubs: Old Chatham (N.Y.); Hunt (dir.); N.Y. Athletic (N.Y.C.), Met. (N.Y.C.); Columbia County dir. (Gt. Neck, N.Y.), Park Electro Chem. Co. (Gt. Neck, N.Y.); Westside Fed. Savs. and Loan (N.Y.C.); regional dir, County Trust & Valley Bank of L.I. (Bank of N.Y.). Home: New York, N.Y. Died Feb. 20, 1984.

QUIRK, CHARLES JOAQUIN, clergyman; b. New Orleans, La., Feb. 1, 1889; s. Henry Clay and Marie Louise (Shaw) Q.; ed. in pub. schs., U.S. and Belgium; A.B., Georgetown U., 1914; grad. student Columbia U. and Louvain U.; M.A., St. Louis (Mo.) U., 1937; unmarried. Mem. Society of Jesus. Ordained priest Roman Cath. Ch., 1922; chmn. English dept. Spring Hill (Ala.) Coll., 1926-37; prof. English, Loyola U., New Orleans, from 1937; dir. student poetry soc., Pegasus, from 1937. Mem. Poetry Soc. of Am., Modern Lang. Assn., English Inst., New Orleans Shakespeare Soc., Gallery of Living Catholic Authors, Nat. Literary Orgn., Mark Twain Internat. Soc., (hon.) Poetry Soc. of Ala., Eugene Field Assn., (charter mem. Pi chapter) Delta Epsilon Sigma. Democrat. Author: (poetry) Sails on the Horizon, 1926; Interlude, 1929; Candles in the Wind, 1931; Gesture Before Farewell, 1934; Full Circle, 1936; A Harvest of the Years, 1949. Address: New Orleans, La. †

QUO, TAI-CHI, Chinese diplomat; b. Kwang-tsi, China, 1888; ed. privately and at Wuchang; student Easthampton (Mass.) High Sch., and Willeston Sem., Mass., 1905-08; B.S. in Polit Science, U. of Pa., 1911. Sec. to Gen. Li Yuan-hung (vice pres., later pres., Republic of China), 1912-17; counselor, Waichiaopu, 1916-17; became sec. to Pres. Sun Yat-sen, following creation of constitutional govt. at Canton, 1917; mem. spl. commn. to U.S., 1918; tech. del. Paris Peace Conf., 1919; counselor to Dr. Sun Yat-sen, and chief of publicity bureau, President's Office, 1921-22; chief of polit. dept. Kwantung Provincial Govt., 1922; vice minister foreign affairs, Canton, 1923-24; pres. Nat. Wuchang Commercial Univ., 1925-26; commr. foreign affairs, and acting minister Foreign Office, 1927-28; mem. Legislative Yuan, 1928-30; mem. Fgn. Relations Commn., also polit. vice minister fgn. affairs, 1932; chief del. Shanghai armistice negotiations for cessation of hostilities and withdrawal of Japanese troops, 1932; minister to Great Britain, 1935, became first Chinese ambassador to Great Britain, 1935; apptd. fgn. minister of China by Central Exec. Com. of Kuomintang, 1941; chmn. fgn. affairs com. Supreme Nat. Defense Council, 1942-45; rep. on Security Council, U.N., also chmn. of council 1st New York meeting. Del. to 13th and 14th assemblies and spl. assembly of League of Nations, 1932, 1933, first del. to 15th Assembly, League of Nations, 1934; del. to Disarmament Conf., World Econ. Conf. and Monetary Conf., 1933. Address: Rio de Janeiro, Brazil. †

QUON, JIMMIE EARL, civil engr.; b. Canton, China, Apr. 13, 1934; s. Lester and Sau (Tse) Q.; came to U.S., 1939; B.S. in Civil Engring. with highest honors, U. Calif., Berkeley, 1955; M.S. in San. Engring. (NSF grad. fellow), 1956, Ph.D., 1961; m. Helen Tang, Aug. 4, 1956; children—Michael J., Mary A. Successively teaching asst., asso. in public health, grad. research engr. U. Calif., Berkeley, 1955-60; san. chemist Oro Loma San. Dist., San Lorenzo, Calif., 1956-58; mem. faculty Northwestern U., 1960-81, prof. civil engring., 1967-81, chmn. dept., 1976-81; cons. to govt. and industry. Recipient Legge award Am. Indsl. Hygiene Assn., 1960; diplomate Am. Acad. Environ. Engrs.; registered profl. engr., Ill. Fellow ASCE (Huber research prize 1968); mem. Air Pollution Control Assn., Water Pollution Control Fedn., Phi Beta Kappa, Sigma Xi, Tau Beta Pi, Chi Epsilon, Delta Omega. Author papers in field. Home: Wilmette, Ill. Died Apr. 13, 1981; buried Phoenix, Ariz.

RABINER, SAUL FREDERICK, educator, physician; b. Bklyn., Aug. 11, 1926; s. Abraham M. and Ella (Feldman) R.; B.S., Tulane U., 1949; M.D., State U. N.Y. at Bklyn., 1952; m. Marion Evans, Apr. 2, 1949; children—Mark, Elizabeth, David. Intern Maimonides Hosp., Bklyn., 1952, resident 1953; resident Montefiore Hosp., Bronx, 1956; attending dept. medicine VA Research Hosp., Chgo., 1960-68; asso. medicine Northwestern U. Med. Sch., 1960-65, asst. prof. medicine, 1960-69; asso. prof. medicine Pritzker Med. Sch., U. Chgo., 1970-71; asso. dir. clin. hematology Michael Reese Hosp., Chgo., 1962-63, dir., 1964-71; asso. prof. medicine U. Oreg. Med. Sch., 1971-74, prof. medicine, 1974-79; chief of medicine Good Samaritan Hosp. and Med. Center, 1971-79. Served with USAAF, 1943-45. Home: Portland, Oreg. Died Dec. 31, 1979.

RABINOWITZ, MURRAY, internist, biochemist; b. N.Y.C., Dec. 24, 1927; married, 1966. B.S., NYU, 1947, M.D., 1950. Intern Beth Israel Hosp., N.Y.C., 1950-51; asst. resident in medicine Montefiore Hosp., 1951-52; asst. in medicine Harvard U. Med. Sch., Cambridge, Mass., 1952-54; asst. resident Mass. Gen. Hosp., Boston, 1954-55; vis. investigator Rockefeller Inst., 1957-58; dir. cardiopulmonary lab. U. Chgo., 1958-66, form asst. prof. to prof., 1958-73, Louis Block prof. medicine and biochemistry, 1973-85; mem. staff Franklin McLean Research Inst., Pritzker Sch. Medicine, 1958-85. USPHS research fellow Peter Ben Brigham Hosp. Boston, 1952-54; research fellow Harvard Med. Sch., 1952-54; NSF fellow, 1956-57; USPHS research fellow in biochemistry U. Wis., 1955-56. Mem. Am. Heart Assn., Am. Fedn. Clin. Research, Assn. Am. Physicians, Am. Soc. Clin. Investigators, Am. Soc. Biol. Chemists. Died Aug. 1985.

RACKEMANN, FRANCIS MINOT, physician; b. Milton, Mass., June 4, 1887; s. Felix and Julia (Minot) R.; A.B., Harvard, 1909, M.D., 1912; m. Dorothy Mandell, Apr. 28, 1917; children—Dorothy, Francis M., Elizabeth, William M. Research fellow in medicine, Presbyterian Hosp., 1914-16; resident in medicine, Mass. Gen. Hosp., 1916-17; asst. in medicine, Harvard Med. Sch., 1916-25, instr., 1925-35, lecturer in medicine, from 1935; physician Mass. Gen. Hosp., 1918-48, now consultant. First lt., Med. Corps, U.S. Army, 1918-19; dist. Med. Officer for Civilian Defense, 1942-45; civ. expert consultant to the Surgeon Gen. from 1946. Chmn. bd. trustees Boston State Hosp.; sec. Harvard Med. Sch. Dormitory Fund, 1923-27. Mem. Am. and Mass. med. assns., Assn. American Physicians, Am. Society Clinic Investigation, American Assn. Study of Allergy (pres. 1925), American Academy Allergy, American Academy Arts and Sciences, Harvey Society, American Society Study of Asthma and Allied Conditions (pres. 1917), Am. Clin. and Climatol. Assn. (sec. 1933-41, pres. 1948), Harvard Med. Sch. Alumni Assn. (sec. and treas. 1923-27, pres. 1929); Clubs: Harvard, Union Boat (Boston); Country (Brookline); Harvard (New York). Author: Clinical Allergy; Asthma and Hay Fever, 1931. Home: Boston, Mass. †

RADIN, ABRAHAM, textile exec.; b. Lithuania, Jan. 5, 1890; s. Joseph and Rachael (Edelstein) R.; m. Anna Lazarow, June 19, 1921; children—Mildred (Mrs. Howard B. Leeds), Miriam, Saul H. Pres. Pacific Undergarment Co., N.Y.C., Richard Borden Industries, Inc., N.Y.C., Saltex Trading Corp., Winrad Realty Corp., Giant Food Properties, Inc., Washington; dir. Windsor Industries, Inc. Trustee Sinai Temple, Mt. Vernon. Home: Mt. Vernon, N.Y. †

RADITZ, LAZAR, artist; b. Dvinsk, Russia, Apr. 15, 1987; s. Sholom Mendel and Mary (Denenberg) R.; came to U.S., 1903; student Pa. Acad. Fine Arts, 1903-09; Boston Sch. of Art, 1909-10; 2d Toppen prize, 1906, traveling European scholarship, 1907, 08, 1st Toppen prize (for best picture painted in school), 1909; m. Henrietta Herman, pianist, July 25, 1910; children—Violetta Constance, Albert Herman. Awarded bronze medal, San Francisco Corp., 1915, 2d Hallgarten prize, Nat. Acad. Design, New York, 1919. Specializes in painting of portraits. Instructor The Graphic Sketch Club, Phila. One man portrait shows at Art Club. Phila., 1913, McClees Galleries, 1934 and 1935. Fellow Pa. Acad. Fine Arts; mem. Art Alliance, Phila. Studio: Philadelphia, Pa. †

RAFFERTY, MAX, educator; b. New Orleans, May 7, 1917; s. Maxwell L. and DeEtta (Cox) R.; m. Frances Longman, June 4, 1944; children—Kathleen, Dennis, Eileen. B.A., UCLA, 1938, M.A., 1949; Ed.D., U. So. Calif., 1955. Tchr. Trona (Calif.) Sch. Dist., 1940-48; prin. Big Bear High Sch., Big Bear Lake, Calif., 1948-51; dist. supt. schs. Saticoy (Calif.) Sch. Dist., 1951-55, Needles (Calif.) Sch. Dist., 1955-61, La Canada (Calif.) Sch. Dist., 1961-62; supt. pub. instrn., State of Calif., 1963-71; dean Sch. Edn., Troy (Ala.) State U., 1971-81, disting. prof. edn., 1981-82. Author: Suffer, Little Children, 1962, Practices and Trends in School Administration, 1961, What They are Doing to Your Children, 1964, Max Rafferty on Education, 1968, Classroom Countdown, 1970, A Handbook of Educational Administration, 1975. Mem. Am. Assn. Sch. Adminstrs. (Shankland Meml.

Research award 1955), Calif. Assn. Sch. Adminstrs., NEA, Calif. Tchrs. Assn. Clubs: Lion, Rotarian. Home: Troy, Ala. Dec. June 13, 1982.

RAGSDALE, A(RTHUR) C(HESTER), educator; born Aurora, Mo., Oct. 28, 1890; s. Henry Eleazar and Idella (Money) R.; B.S., U. of Mo., 1912; M.S., U. of Wis., 1925; Doctor of Science, Culver-Stockton College, 1956; m. Clara Allen Gebhardt, Oct. 23, 1918; children—Ruth Reading, Elizabeth Woodson (Mrs. Donald R. Fretz), Jean Jordan (Mrs. Buford H. Burch). Dairyman Brook Hill Farm, Genesee Depot, Wis., 1912; dairy supt. Bennett Ranch, Kimball, Neb., 1912-13; instr. animal husbandry, N.J. Coll. Agr., 1913-15; instr. dairy husbandry, U. of W.Va., 1915-16; extension asst. prof. dairy husbandry, U. of Mo., 1916-19, prof. and chmn. dept. 1919-61. U.S. del. 13th Internat. Dairy Congress, Hague, 1953. Mem. Am. Dairy Sci. Assn. (pres. 1944-45), A.A.A.S., Am. Soc. Animal Prodn., Am. Pub. Health Assn., Am. Assn. Milk and Food Sanitarians, Dairy Industries Council of Mo. (exec. sec. since 1926), Am. Assn. U. Profs., Mo. State Teachers Assn., U.S. Livestock San. Assn., Alpha Zeta, Alpha Gamma Rho, Gamma Sigma Delta. Mem. Disciples of Christ Ch. (state chmn. Unified Promotion, 1950-53; mem. nat. laymen's adv. commn. from 1945; national president Men's Work, 1948-50). Mason. Club: Rotary. Author: Dairy Laboratory Manual and Outline, 1958. Home: Columbia, Mo. †

RAMMELKAMP, CHARLES HENRY, JR., physician, educator; b. Jacksonville, Ill., May 24, 1911; s. Charles Henry and Jeanette (Capps) R.; A.B., Ill. Coll., Jacksonville, 1933, D.Sc., 1958; M.D., U. Chgo., 1937; D.Sc., Northwestern U., 1975; m. Helen Chisholm, Dec. 20, 1941; children—Charles Henry, Colin Chisholm, Anne Capps. Asst. medicine Washington U., 1939; research fellow medicine Harvard, 1939-40; instr. medicine Boston U., 1940-46; asst. prof. medicine and preventive medicine Case Western Res. U., 1946-47, asso. prof. preventive medicine, 1947-60, prof. medicine, 1950-81, prof. preventive medicine, 1960-81; dir. research Cleve. City Hosp., 1950-81; dir. medicine Cleve. Met. Gen. Hosp., 1958-81. Cons. sec. of war, mem. Commn. on Acute Respiratory Diseases, Ft. Bragg, N.C., 1943-46; dir. streptococcal disease lab. Francis E. Warren AFB, Wyo., 1949-55; dir. Com. Streptcoccal Disease 1955-57; dir. Commn. on Streptococcal and Staphylococcal Diseases, 1959-67. Recipient Lasker award, 1954, Am. Heart Assn. Research Achievement award, 1961, James Bruce Meml. award, 1963. Mem. Am. Epidemiol. Soc. (v.p. 1964-65), Central Soc. Clin. Research (pres. 1961-62), Am. Heart Assn. (v.p. 1960-63), Am. Soc. Clin. Investigation (v.p. 1956), Am. Fedn. Clin. Research, (pres. 1951), Infectious Disease Soc. Am. (pres. 1966-67), Am. Assn. Physicians, A.C.P. (gov. 1969-72, regent 1972-77), Armed Forces Epidemiol. Bd., Inst. Medicine Nat. Acad. Scis. Contbr. articles profl. periodicals. Home: Cleveland Heights, Ohio. Died Dec. 5, 1981.

RAMSDELL, WILLETT FORREST, prof. forest land management; b. Topeka, Kan., Dec. 1, 1890; s. Jacob Thomas and Mary Frances (Forrest) R.; B.S., U. of Mich., 1912, M.S.F., 1914; War Dept. Sch. Mil. Govt., Charlotteville, Va., 1943; m. Lucile Caroline Hyde, Mar. 9, 1920; children—Frances Willett, Forrest Hyde, Forest asst., U.S. Forest Service, U.S. Dept. Agr., 1914-17, dep. forest supervisor, 1917-20, forest supervisor, 1920-24, asst. chief of forest management, N. Pacific Region, 1924-29, asst. regional forester, N. Central Region, 1929-30; George Willis Pack professor of forest land managment, School of Forestry, Unviersity of Michigan, from 1930; dir. Land Utilization Research Program from 1936 and in charge, Chas. S. Osborn Preserve from 1933. Served as sergt., 2d and 1st lt., 10th Engrs., Forestry, 1917-19, with A.E.F. 22 months, World War I. Major. Specialist Reserves, 1943; dir. mil. govt. instrn., U. of Mich., 1943-44; dir. U. of Mich. Civil Affairs Training Sch. Far Eastern Area, 1944-45. Dir. Mich. Rural Rehabilitation Corp.; mem. State Land Use Planning Com.; sec. Mich. Forest Industries Information Com. Mem. Soc. Am. Foresters (senior mem.), Mich. Acad. Science, A.A.A.S., Sigma Xi. Mem. Les Voyageurs. Home: Ann Arbor, Mich. †

RAMSEY, PAUL HUBERT, naval officer; b. Springfield, O., Feb. 2, 1905; s. Murray and Mary Elizabeth (Sultzbaugh) R.; student Ohio State U., 1922-23; B.S., U.S. Naval Acad., 1927; m. Isabelle Turton, Apr. 2, 1929; children—William Edward, James Burnley. Commd. ensign, USN, 1927, advanced through grades to vice adm., 1964, dir. air warfare div. Office Chief Naval Operations, Washington, 1953-55; staff SHAPE, 1955-57, comdr. Carrier Div. One, 1957-58, chief staff U.S. Pacific Fleet, 1958-61, comdr. Naval Air Test Center, Patuxent River, Md., 1961-64; comdr. Naval Air Force, U.S. Atlantic Fleet, Norfolk, Va., 1964-66; dep. chief naval operations (air) Navy Dept., Washington, 1966; aerospace cons. Sperry Rand Corp., Gyrodyne Co. Am. Decorated Navy Cross, Legion of Merit (U.S.). Order of British Empire. Mem. Naval Order U.S., Legion of Valor. Helicopter Soc. Am., Kappa Sigma Nu. Kiwanian. Home: Washington, D.C. Died Feb. 15, 1982.

RAND, AUSTIN LOOMER, zoologist; b. Kennville, N.S., Can., Dec. 16, 1905; s. Stanley Bayard and Carrie (Forsythe) R.; B.Sc., Acadia U., 1927; Ph.D., Cornell U., 1931; D.Sc., Acadia U., 1961; m. Rheua Medden, Aug. 15, 1931; children—Austin Stanley, William Medden. With Am. Mus. of Natural History, 1929-42, research asso., 1937-41; with Nat. Mus. of Can., 1942-47, acting chief div. of biology, 1945-47; curator of birds Field Mus. of Natural History, 1947-54, chief curator zoology, 1955-70; research asso. Archbold Biol. Sta., 1971-82; exploration and research in Philippines, also in Madagascar, Dutch New Guinea, Papula, N.Am., C.Am.; mem. adv. bd. Archbold Expdns., past v.p.; ornithol. editor Canadian Field Naturalist, 1942-47. Fellow Am. Ornithologists Union (pres. 1962-64), mem. Am. Soc. Mammologists. Author: Distribution and Habits of Madagascar Birds, 1936; New Guinea Expedition (with R. Archbold), 1939; Mammals of Yukon, Canada, 1945; Mammals of Eastern Rockies and Western Plains of Canada; Development and Enemy Recognition of the Curvebilled Thrasher, 1941; Stray Feathers; American Water and Game Birds, 1956; A Midwestern Almanac; Ornithology, An Introduction, 1967; (with E. Thomas Gilliard) Handbook of New Guinea Birds, 1967. Contbr. articles to jours. Home: Lake Placid, Fla. Died Nov. 6, 1982.

RAND, AYN, writer, lectr.; b. St. Petersburg (now Leningrad), Russia, 1905; came to U.S., 1926, naturalized, 1931; m. Frank O'Connor, 1929. Grad., U. Leningrad, 1924; D.H.L. (hon.), Lewis and Clark Coll., 1963. Vis. lectr. Yale U., 1960, Princeton U., 1960, Columbia U., 1960, 62, U. Wis., 1961, Johns Hopkins U., 1961; Ford Hall Forum, Boston, from 1961, Harvard U., 1962, Mass. Inst. Tech., 1962, U.S. Mil. Acad. at West Point, 1974, other univs. Screen writer, 1932-34, 44-49; Author: play, revived as Penthouse Legend 1973 Night of January 16th, 1935, We the Living, 1936, Anthem, 1938, The Unconquered; play, 1940, The Fountainhead; also screenplay, 1943, Atlas Shrugged, 1957, For the New Intellectual, 1961, The Virtue of Selfishness, 1965, Capitalism; The Unknown Ideal, 1966, Introduction to Objectivist Epistemology, 1967, The Romantic Manifesto: A Philosophy of Literature, 1969, The New Left: The Anti-Industrial Revolution, 1971; Editor: The Objectivist, 1962-71, The Ayn Rand Letter, 1971-76. Home: New York, N.Y. Died Mar. 6, 1982.

RAND, ELBRIDGE DEXTER, consular service; b. Burlington, Ia., July 7, 1887; s. Charles Wellington and Lilian Cora (Higgins) R.; prep. edn., Montclair (N.J.) Mil. Acad., 1903-06; student Harvard, 1907-08; m. Lucy Gage, of Downey, Calif., 1910; children—Frances, Caroline. Served at 1st lt., later capt., inf., U.S.A., 1917-19; served as tech. asst. Intelligence Sect. Peace Commn., Paris, and asst. mil. attaché, Brussels, 1919; drafting officer Dept. of State, Washington, D.C., 1919-21; 3d sec. of embassy, assigned to Dept. of State, 1921-23; sec. diplomatic agency, Tangier, Morocco, 1923-25; pres. Internat. Sanitary Council, Morocco, 1924; 2d sec. of Embassy, Paris, 1925-26, Madrid, 1926-27; 1st sec. of Embassy, assigned to Dept. of State, 1927-28; consul, Geneva, from 1928. Served as tech. asst. Am. delegation to 2d and 3d sessions of spl. com. apptd. to draft a convention on pvt. manufacture and publicity of mfr. of arms, ammunition and implements of war (League of Nations), meeting at Geneva, Aug. 1928; sec. to Am. delegation to Diplomatic Conf. on Economic Statistics, Geneva, Nov.-Dec. 1928; adviser at meeting of tech. experts concerning manufacture of arms, etc., Geneva, to examine Belgian proposal, 1929; alternate Am. del. to Conf. on Counterfeiting of Currency, Geneva, Apr. 1929; retired from foreign service, Dec. 31, 1929. Home: Santa Barbara, Calif. †

RANNELLS, WILL, artist; b. Caldwell, Ohio, July 21, 1892; s. James Falls and Sarah (Allison) R. Ed., Art Acad. of Cin., 1913-16. Instr. in fine arts Ohio State U., 1926-32, asso. prof., 1932-64, asso. prof. emeritus, from 1964. Magazine and book illustrator specializing in dog portrature, from 1916; Contbr. of: cover designs and illustrations to Outing, etc; Illustrator: cover designs and illustrations to Dog Stars, 1916; collaborator and illustrator: cover designs and illustrations to Waif, The Story of Spe, 1937; illustrator: cover designs and illustrations to Animals Baby Knows, 1938, Jack, Jock and Funny, 1938, Farmyard Play Book, 1940, Timmy, 1941, Just a Mutt, 1947, Animal Play Book, 1947; illustrator and author: cover designs and illustrations to Animal Picture Story Book, 1938; illustrator: ann. Buckeye Union Dog Calendar. Pres. Columbus Humane Soc., 1936-39. Recipient awards Am. Humane Assn., 1972, awards Capital Area Humane Soc., 1974, awards Humane Soc. U.S., 1976, awards Pilot Dogs, 1977. Mem. The Artists' Guild, Ohio Water Color Soc., Am. Water Color Soc. Club: Faculty. Faculty. Address: Columbus, OH.

RAOUL, WILLIAM P(ERRIN), union official; b. Atlanta, Oct. 22, 1890; s. Frederick Alexander and Josephine Matilda (Pelfrey) R.; student Ga. Sch. of Tech., 1910-13. Joined Atlanta Local No. 41, Internat. Alliance of Theatrical Stage Employees and Moving Picture Machine Operators of U.S. and Can., 1910; charter mem. Atlanta Local 225 (pres.), 1911; internat. rep., 1918-41, asst. internat. pres., 1941-45, gen. sec. and treas. from 1945. Labor rep. and sec. Northern Ga. Draft Bd. of Appeals, World War I. Mem. Ga. Indsl. Com., 1920-22. Mem. Atlanta Bd. Examiners of Moving Picture Machine Operators, 1909-12; v.p. Ga. State Fedn. of Labor, 1918-20, pres., 1920-21. Democrat. Episcopalian. Mason (32 deg., Shriner). Club: Variety (charter mem.), Atlanta.†

RAPHAELSON, SAMSON, author; b. N.Y.C., Mar. 30, 1896; s. Ralph and Anna (Marks) R.; m. Dorothy Wegman, Dec. 24, 1927; children—Joel, Naomi. A.B., U. Ill., 1917; D.H.L., Columbia U., 1981. Reporter City News Service, 1917-18; with Chgo. advt. agys., 1918-20; instr. English U. Ill., 1920-21, vis. prof. creative writing, 1948; adj. prof. drama and film divs. Columbia U., from 1976. Short story writer, from 1915, playwright, from 1925, screen writer, from 1929, dir., from 1933, contbg. writer: films and TV Am. Film and Film Comment, from 1975; Author: The Human Nature of Playwriting, 1949; plays Jazz Singer, 1925, The Store, 1926, Young Love, 1928, The Magnificent Heel, 1930, The Wooden Slipper, 1933, Accent on Youth, 1935, Skylark, 1939, Jason, 1942, The Perfect Marriage, 1944, Hilda Crane, 1950, The Peanut Bag, 1967, Two Acts in October, 1974; screen plays The Crazy Americans; author: screen plays That Lady in Ermine, Green Dolphin Street, Heaven Can Wait, Suspicion, The Shop Around the Corner, Trouble in Paradise, The Smiling Lieutenant, Broken Lullaby, One Hour With You, Angel; Author others; radio play General Armchair (in book Free World Theatre), 1944; Contbr.: fiction to New Yorker; others.; Dir.: plays The Perfect Marriage; Stories included in Martha Foley's Best American Stories, 1947 and in Editor's Choice, 1948, Sat. Eve. Post Best Stories, 1957; other collections; entered photog. field, 1951. Mem. Dramatists' Guild, Screen Writers' Guild (Laurel award 1977), Authors' Guild. Home: New York, N.Y. Died July 1, 1983.

RAPKIN, JOSEPH E., lawyer; b. Phila., Apr. 17, 1907; s. David and Sophie (Lubotsky) R.; m. Beatrice Goldman, Dec. 30; children—Marjorie Rapkin Freed, Carolyn Rapkin Ausman. B.A., U. Wis.; LL.B., Harvard U. Bar: Wis. bar. Partner firm Foley & Lardner, Milw.; pres., dir. Froedtert-Mayfair, Inc.; dir. Republic Airlines, Inc., Apollo Fund, Inc., Jack Winter, Inc., Realist, Inc. Bd. dirs. Greater Milw. Com., Milw. Assn. Commerce, Milw. Symphony Orch.; chmn. bd. dirs. Mt. Sinai Med. Center, Inc., Milw.; trustee Kurtis R. Froedtert Luth. Hosp. Trust. Mem. Am. Bar Assn., State Wis. Bar Assn., County Bar Ass, Bar City N.Y. Jewish. Clubs: Univ. (Milw.), Brynwood Country (Milw.), Milw. (Milw.), Athletic (Milw.); Tamarisk County (Palm Springs, Calif.). Home: Milwaukee, Wis.

RARIG, HOWARD R., univ. adminstr., musicologist, conductor; b. Au Sable Forks, N.Y., Nov. 27, 1915; s. Howard R. and Isadora M. (Corneal) R.; student Temple U., 1941-42; B.Mus. cum laude, Ithaca (N.Y.) Coll., 1949, M.Mus., 1952; postgrad. Cornell U., 1951; Ph.D., U. Mich., 1958; m. Jean Clark Evans, June 1, 1946; children—Jonathan, Kim, Jan Ingrid. Asst. prof. Ithaca Coll., 1950-53; instr. U. Mich., Ann Arbor, 1954-58; asso. prof. Grinnell (Iowa) Coll., 1958-65, chmn. div. fine arts, 1961-64; prof. Eastern Mich. U., 1965-71, also head dept. music; prof. U. So. Calif., Los Angeles, 1971-79, dir. Sch. Music, 1971-79, asso. dean Sch. Performing Arts, 1971-79. Bd. dirs. Ford Found. Contemporary Music Project, Midwest region, 1966-70, project head Eastern Mich. U., 1966-70. Danforth Found. Research grantee, 1963, Grinnell Coll. grantee, 1964, Contemporary Music Project grantee, 1970; Tanglewood Scholar Berkshire (Mass.) Music Center, 1964; recipient Composition award Kappa Gamma Psi, 1950. Mem. Calif. Music Execs. Assn. (past pres.), Coll. Music Soc., AAUP, Music Educators Nat. Conf., Nat. Assn. Composers U.S.A., Am. Musicol. Soc., Nat. Assn. Schs. Music (regional Midwest dir. 1970-72, mem. commn. grad. studies 1970-76, 77—77-79), U. So. Calif. Sch. Music Alumni Assn. (pres. 1976-79), Skull and Dagger, Music Library Assn., Pi Kappa Lambda (pres. Eta chpt.), Phi Mu Alpha. Author: The 2d String Quartet of Charles Ives, 1952; The Instrumental Sonatas of Antonio Vivaldi, 1958. Conductor contemporary music ensembles, music for theater and dance, Chinese opera, collegium musicum and various choral, brass and orchestral ensembles. Composer songs, piano works, chamber music. Home: Los Angeles, Calif. Died Nov. 14, 1979; interred Forest Lawn Cemetery, Hollywood Hills, Calif.

RASCHE, WILLIAM FRANK, vocational educator; b. Milwaukee, Wis., June 6, 1888; s. William A. and Gertrude (Haessler) R.; B.S., Stout Inst., Menomie, Wis., 1925; A.M., Univ. of Chicago, 1927, Ph.D., 1936; m. Alice Amelia Geilfuss, Sept. 1, 1909; children—Esther Alice (Mrs. William H. Hollis), William (dec. World War II), Robert Edgar. Teacher and prin. rural and village schs., 1907-16; dir. Cudahy (Wis.) Vocational Sch., 1916-22; teacher trainer Milwaukee (Wis.) Vocational Sch., 1922-25; prof. vocational edn., Univ. of Pittsburgh, 1928; personnel dir. Gen. Motors Truck Corp., Pontiac, Mich., 1928-30; asst. dir. and prin. Milwaukee Vocational and Adult Schs., 1930-40, dir. and prin. since 1940. Served as consultant job skills training program of civilian training br., indsl. personnel div., Army Service Forces, 1944-45. Made vocational edn. surveys Chicago Continuation Schs., 1925, Strayer Survey of New York City Schs., 1943, Sch. of Mech. Industries, Tuskegee Inst., 1944. Chmn. tech. com. on classification and compensation of pub. employes of Five Units of Govt. of Metropolitan Milwaukee Area, 1942-45; chmn. tech. com. on classification and compensation of case workers, Community Fund, 1947; sec. Metropolitan War Memorial, Inc.; mem. Urban League (bd. dirs.); Town Hall (pres. 1945-47); Christian Center (pres. 1944-47), Civic Alliance (pres. 1942-43), Round Table (pres. 1940). Chmn. Metro. Youth Commn., Milwaukee Co., from Oct. 1948. Mem. Am. Vocational Assn. (life), N.E.A., Nat. Assn. Secondary Prins., Nat. Council for Social Studies, Wis. Edn. Assn., Wis. Assn. Secondary Sch. Prins., Vocational and Adult Edn. Assn.,

Indsl. Relations Assn., Engrs. Soc., Phi Delta Kappa. Conglist. Home: Milwaukee, WI. †

RASCHKE, KENNETH EDWARD, educator; b. Watertown, S.D., Oct. 7, 1918; s. Edward and Anna Marie (Jacobsen) R.; B.A. cum laude, Augustana Coll., 1941; LL.B., summa cum laude, U. S.D., 1948, J.D. summa cum laude, 1969; LL.D., Jamestown Coll., 1972; m. Avis Ione Bekke, Mar. 7, 1943; children—Kenneth Edward, Beverly Raschke Nielson, Steven. Instr. govt., psychology Worthington (Minn.) High Sch., 1941-42; coordinator instrn. USAAF Tech. Schs., 1942-43; spl. cons. S.D. Natural Resources Commn., 1949-52; admitted to S.D. bar, 1948; prof. bus. law U. S.D., 1948-56, exec. asst. to pres., 1956-64; prof. law U. Fla., 1950; commr. high edn. N.D. Bd. Higher Edn., Bismarck, 1964-78; asst. to pres, prof. bus. law N.D. State U., Fargo, 1978-84. Chmn., State Bd. Indian Scholarships, 1964-78; mem. State Licensure Bd. for Nursing Home Adminstrs., 1969-84, Gov.'s Com. on Safety, 1965-78; exec. officer Higher Edn. Facilities Commn., 1964-78; mem. State Planning Adv. Council, 1971-78, Health Manpower Com., 1969-78, State Health Planning Council, 1969-78, State Alcohol Commn., 1964-71, State Ednl. TV Council, 1969-78, State Library Commn., 1964-71; mem. adv. com. on higher edn. Midwest Council State Govts., 1964; v.p. Mo. Valley council Boy Scouts Am., 1967-70, advancement chmn., 1971-84. Bd. dirs. United Fund, Bismarck, Dakota Hosp., Vermillion, S.D. Served with USAAF, 1943-46. Mem. S.D. Bar Assn., Higher Edn. Exec. Officers Assn., North Central Assn. Colls. and Univs., Order of Coif, Phi Delta Phi, Delta Sigma Pi, Beta Gamma Sigma. Lutheran (pres. ch. council 1972). Clubs: Masons, Shriners, Lions, Elks. Home: Fargo, N.D. Died Dec. 18, 1984; interred Fargo, N.D.

RASH, JESSE KEOGH, educator; b. New Providence, Ia., Oct. 5, 1906; s. Junius D. and Matilda J. (Chance) R.; A.B., William Penn Coll., 1928; M.A., YMCA Grad. Sch., 1933; Dr. Health and Safety, Ind. U., 1949; M.P.H., U. Cal. at Berkeley, 1957; m. Mary F. Wood, Aug. 21, 1938 (dec.); children—Marjorie F. (Mrs. James R. Miller), William E.; m. 2d, Mary S. Fulwider, Aug. 25, 1962. Instr., Normal Sch., Berea Coll., 1928-31, Ia. State Tng. Sch. for Boys, 1933-34; phys. dir. Burlington (Ia.) YMCA, 1934-35; instr., coach William Penn Coll., 1935-37; athletic dir., coach Pikeville Coll., 1937-42; prof. health and phys. edn. bus. mgr. Wilmington Coll., 1942-47, health educator Ind. Dept. Pub. Welfare, 1948-49; prof. Ind. U., Bloomington, 1949-81, chmn. dept. health and safety, 1952-72, co-dir. Sch. and Community Health Workshop, 1950-56; co-dir. Sch. Health Workshop, U. Cal. at Berkeley, 1957. Past pres. Ky. Jr. Coll. Athletic Conf.; pres. Ind. Council Family Relations, 1960-62; mem. Ind. Health Council from 1952. pres., 1960-61; mem. Ind. Gov.'s Commn. Children and Youth, 1952-56, Ind. Farm Safety Council, 1952-57. Bd. dirs. Monroe County Anti-Tb Assn., 1948-57. Recipient William A. Howe award Am. Sch. Health Assn., 1969; Nat. Honor award Eta Sigma Gamma, 1974. Fellow Am. Sch. Health Assn. (pres. 1961-62), Am. Coll. Health Assn., Am. Pub. Health Assn.; mem. Pub. Health Nursing Assn. (dir. 1952, pres. 1970-73), Am., Ind. (past v.p.) assns. health phys. edn. and recreation, Adult Edn. Assn., Ind. Coll. Health Assn., Royal Soc. Health, Internat. Union Health Edn. of Pub., Phi Delta Kappa, Phi Epsilon Kappa, Delta Omega. Mem. Soc. of Friends. Club: Lions (pres. 1960-61). Author: The Health Education Curriculum. Contbr. articles to profl. jours. Home: Bloomington, Ind. Died Nov. 5, 1981.

RASKIN, JUDITH, soprano; b. N.Y.C., June 21, 1928; d. Harry A. and Lillian (Mendelson) R. B.A., Smith Coll., 1949, M.A. (hon.), 1963; D.Music (hon.), Ithaca Coll., 1979. Mem. voice faculty Manhattan Sch., Mannes Coll. Music, N.Y.C.; instr. voice 92d St YMCA master class for opera singers; panelist Nat. Opera Inst., 1978—, chief judge, 1978; chmn. opera panel, co-chmn. music panel Nat. Endowment Arts, 1972-76, co-chmn. chamber music panel, 1979, chmn. solo recital artist program, 1980-81; mem. task force for young artists program and regional auditions Met. Opera, 1981. Debut in: NBC-TV opera Dialogues of the Carmelites, 1957; debut, N.Y.C. Opera in, Cosi Fan Tutte, 1959, Met. Opera Co. in, Nozze di Figaro, 1962; recital debut in N.Y.C. as Ford Found. winner, 1964, appearances with symphony orchs. in, Cleve., Phila, N.Y.C., European debut, Glyndebourne, Eng., 1963, Lieder recital, N.Y. Town Hall, 1965; rec. artist, Columbia, London, Decca, RCA Victor, C.R.I. records. Trustee Martha Baird Rockefeller Fund for Music, 1976-82, Beth Israel Hosp., 1976-84; mem. adv. bd. Concert Artists Guild, 1983. Home: New York, N.Y. Died Dec. 21, 1984.

RASMUSSEN, CARL CHRISTIAN, clergyman; b. Troy, N.Y., Sept. 21, 1890; s. Hans and Bertha Marie (Andersen) R.; Hartwick Sem., N.Y., 1907-09; A.B., Gettysburg (Pa.) Coll., 1912, D.D., 1928; Gettysburg Theol. Sem., 1912-15; A.M., Columbia, 1923; U. of Pa., 1925-26; U. of Copenhagen, 1940; m. Alma Irene Sieber, June 28, 1916; children—Mary Elizabeth, (wife of Dr. Charles Robert Shelton III), Carl Christian. Ordained ministry United Lutheran Church in America, 1915; pastor Zion Luth. Ch., Newville, Pa., 1915-19, Trinity Luth. Ch., Altoona, Pa., 1919-22, Zion Luth. Ch., Greensburg, Pa., 1922-23, Messiah Luth. Ch., Harrisburg, 1923-30, Luther Pl. Memorial Luth. Ch., Washington, D.C., 1930-40; prof. systematic theology Luth. Theol. Sem. Gettysburg, Pa., from 1940. Director Christian education, Pa. State Sabbath Sch. Assn., 1925-26; pres. East Pa. Synod of United Lutheran Ch., 1929-30, Md. Synod United Lutheran Ch., 1937-39; speaker Nat. Preaching Mission, 1936-37, Nat. Christian Mission, 1940-41, Mem. Am. Theol. Soc. Mason. Author: What About Scandinavia?, 1948. Translator of Nygren's Commentary on Romans (from the Swedish), 1949; This is the Church (from Swedish), 1952. Contributor to vol., Am. Lutheran Preaching, 1928, and Epistle Messages, 1934; The Message and Method of the New Envangelism, 1937; also religious journals. Home: Gettysburg, Pa. †

RASMUSSEN, PHIPPS LOUIS, advt. exec.; b. San Francisco, June 12, 1912; s. Louis and Lillian (Phipps) R.; m. Shirley Frick, Aug. 22, 1939; children—Sherryl Frick (now Mrs. William Hosie), and Mark Phipps. B.S., St. Mary's Coll., Moraga, Calif., 1935. With McCann-Erickson, Inc., from 1939, v.p., from 1954; gen. mgr. McCann-Erickson, Inc. (San Francisco office), 1956-58, exec. v.p. and Western regional mgr., 1958-62; exec. v.p. McCann-Erickson (Corp.) Internat., 1959-63, pres., 1964-66; dir. various foreign subsidiaries; sr. cons. Interpublic, Inc., N.Y.C., from 1966; cons. fgn. service div. U.S. Dept. Agr. Served as lt. commdr. USNR., World War II; mem. U.S. Joint Purchasing Bd., New Zealand, Australia. Mem. Am. Assn. Advt. Agencies (gov. No. Calif. council), Am. Legion (mem. nat. security council 1947), Am. Marketing Assn., San Francisco Mus. Art, C. of C. Clubs: San Francisco Stock Exchange, San Francisco Advertising, Commonwealth, Press and Union League, Orinda Country; American (Switzerland). Home: Sutter Creek, CA.

RASSMAN, EMIL CHARLES, lawyer; b. Indpls., July 27, 1919; s. Fred Wolf and Helen (Leming) R.; m. Annie de Montel, Jan. 31, 1943; children—Laura Helen (Mrs. Edward E. Bates, Jr.), James Neal. B.A., Washington and Lee U., 1941; LL.B., U. Tex., 1947; LL.D., Baylor U., 1977. Bar: Tex. bar 1947, U.S. Supreme Ct 1951. Mem. firm Rassman, Gunter & Boldrick, Midland, Tex.; Dir. Comml. Bank & Trust Co., Midland.; Mem. Tex. Jud. Council, 1958-61. Campaign chmn., pres. Midland County United Fund, 1956-57; chmn. Midland County chpt. A.R.C., 1971-73; Trustee Midland Ind. Sch. Dist., 1958-61; bd. regents Tex. State Univ. System, 1961-79, chmn. bd., 1967-69; chmn. bd. executors Permian Basin Petroleum Mus., Library and Hall of Fame, 1973-78. Served to capt. AUS, 1941-46. Fellow Am. Coll. Trial Lawyers, Am., Tex. bar founds., Internat. Acad. Trial Lawyers, Am. Coll. Probate Counsel; mem. Internat. Assn. Ins. Counsel, Fedn. Ins. Counsel, Midland County Bar Assn. (pres. 1960), State Bar Tex. (dir. 1972-75, chmn. bd. 1974-75), West Tex. C. of C. (pres. 1973-74), Tex. State C. of C. (pres. 1973-74), Philos. Soc. Tex., Phi Delta Phi, Delta Tau Delta. Episcopalian. Club: Mason. Address: Rockport, Tex. Died Dec. 3, 1983; interred Rockport, Tex.

RAUSCH, JAMES STEVEN, clergyman; b. Albany, Minn., Sept. 4, 1928; s. James and Anna (Ohmann) R.; student Crosier Sem., 1946-49, Sacred Heart Sem., 1950-52; S.T.B., St. John's Sem., 1956; M.Ed., St. Thomas Coll., St. Paul., 1961; Ph.D. cum laude, Gregorian U., Rome, 1969, also L.H.D.; LL.D. (hon.), St. John's U., 1977; Ordained priest Roman Catholic Ch., 1956; asst. pastor St. Mary's Cathedral, St. Cloud, Minn., 1956-57; instr. govt. and econs. Cathedral High Sch., St. Cloud, 1957-67; instr. econs. St. Thomas Coll., 1965-69; spl. lectr. Clergy Conf. Econ. Edn., U. Minn. Center Contination Studies, 1966-67; aux. bishop Diocese St. Cloud, 1973-77; bishop of Phoenix, 1977-81. Chmn. Bishops' Com. on Farm Labor, 1977-81; nat. adv. council St. John's U., Collegeville, Minn. Recipient Pax Christi award St. John's U. (Minn.), 1978. Editor: Family of Nations, 1970; contbr. articles to profl. jours. Home: Phoenix, Ariz. Died May 18, 1981.

RAUSCHNING, HERMANN, author, former German official; b. 1887; ed. Prussian cadet schooling and studies; Ph.D., Potsdam, Lichterfelde, Munich and Berlin univs. Served in German Army, World War: joined German National Socialist (Nazi) Party; became pres. Danzig Senat, 1932 and head Fgn. and Commerce Depts., 1933-34; had confs. with Marshal Pilsudski (pres. of Poland); left Nazi Party and became a Liberal Conservative, supporting constitutionalism, 1935. Came to United States; became citizen, 1948. Author: The Revolution of Nihilism, 1939; The Voice of Destruction, 1940; Conservative Revolution, 1941; Makers of Destruction, 1942; Redemption of Democracy, 1943; Time of Delirium, 1946; Germany between West and East, 1950; The Responsibility of Power, 1952. Address: Portland, Ore. †

RAVIN, ARNOLD WARREN, geneticist, educator; b. N.Y.C., Aug. 15, 1921; s. Max and Rae (Levinson) R.; B.S., Coll. City N.Y., 1942; M.A., Columbia, 1948, Ph.D., 1951; m. Sophie Brody, June 11, 1956; children—Sonia, Andrea. Postdoctoral fellow Laboratoire de genetique, U. Paris (France), 1951-53; mem. faculty U. Rochester, 1952-68, prof. biology, 1962-68, chmn. dept., 1957-60, asso. dean Coll. Arts and Sci., 1960-61, dean, 1961-63; prof. biology U. Chgo., 1968-81, master collegiate div. biology, asso. dean div. biol. scis., 1968-73, chmn. com. on conceptual founds. of sci., 1973-77, Addie Clark Harding prof. biology, 1976-81, dir. Morris Fishbein Center for Study History Sci. and Medicine, 1978-81; mem. genetics tng. com. NIH, 1967-70; mem. com. biology Coll. Entrance Exam. Bd., 1956-60; mem. biology com. coll. proficiency exams. N.Y. State Edn. Dept., 1964-66; vis. prof. genetics of U. Calif. at Berkeley, 1963; Sigma Xi Bicentennial lectr., 1974-76; mem. Nat. Humanities Faculty, 1972-81. Trustee Bergey's Manual Trust, 1961, Am. Type Culture Collection, 1967-72. Recipient Edward Peck Curtis award for excellence in undergrad. teaching, 1966. Predoctoral fellow Nat. Cancer Inst., USPHS, 1949-50, post-doctoral fellow, 1951-53, spl. research fellow, 1960-61; NSF Faculty fellow, 1975. Served to 1st lt. USAAF, 1942-46. Fellow AAAS; mem. Genetics Soc. Am., Soc. Gen. Microbiology (Great Britain), Am. Soc. Microbiology, Am. Soc. Cell Biology, Am. Soc. Naturalists, Philosophy of Sci. Assn., History of Sci. Assn., AAUP, Sigma Xi. Author: Evolution of Genetics, 1965. Mem. editorial bd. Am. Naturalist, 1968-70; co-editor Genetic Orgn., 1969. Contbr. numerous articles to profl. jours. Home: Chicago, Ill. Died Feb. 28, 1981.

RAVIOLO, VICTOR GINO, consulting engineer; b. N.Y.C., June 20, 1914; s. John B. and Armida (Petrini) R.; m. Janet Holcomb, 1932 (div. 1946); children: Judith Ann (Mrs. A.D. Ericsson), Caren Jane and John Bruce (twins), Victor Gino; m. Eleanor Loretta Schettler, Oct. 21, 1954. Student, Wayne U., 1933-36. Design engr. Chrysler Corp., 1932-36, Packard Motor, 1936-37; chief engr. Van Ranst Co., Detroit, 1937-40; project engr. Ford Motor Co., 1940-42, head engine research, 1945-50, chief engr. engines, 1950-54; dir. Lincoln-Mercury Engring. Office, 1954-55; dir. Advanced Product Study and Engring. Research Office, 1955-56, exec. dir. engring. staff, 1957-61; dir. Ford Motor Co., Ltd., 1961-63; cons. engr., Detroit, from 1963; group v.p. Am. Motors., Detroit, 1966-68, mgmt. cons., from 1968; Instr. Edison Inst. Tech., Dearborn, Mich., 1941; head power plant research Consol. Vultee Aircraft Corp., 1942-45; dir., v.p. Great Lakes Airmotive, Inc., Willow Run, from 1958. Fellow Inst. Mech. Engrs. (U.K.); Mem. Soc. Automotive Engrs. (dir.), Coordinating Research Council (dir.), Instrument Soc. Am. (pres. Detroit 1948), Soc. Exptl. Stress Analysis, A.A.A.S., Mich. Aero. and Space Assn., Engring. Soc. Detroit, Am. Ordnance Assn., Assn. U.S. Army, Air Force Assn., Aircraft Owners and Pilots Assn., Amateur Yacht Research Soc., Detroit Mus. Art Founders Soc., N.Y. Acad. Sci., Sigma Xi, Tau Beta Pi. Clubs: Detroit Athletic, Detroit Yacht; Ford Yacht (Mich.) (dir. 1947-49), Grosse Ile (Mich.), Grosse Pointe (Mich.); Yacht. Home: Stuart, Fla.

RAWLS, FLETCHER HOOKS, foodstuffs expert; b. Deer Park, Ala., Apr. 5, 1890; s. James Benjamin and Ruth Morrison (Ray) R.; ed. St. Stephens (Ala.) Jr. Coll., 1906-08; m. Iris L. Crumpler, Feb. 11, 1917; children—Estelle R. Bishopp, Fletcher Hooks, Iris Rawls. Engaged in banana and tropical food shipping, United Fruit Co., Costa Rica, 1908-15; mfr. of sugar in Cuba, 1915-18; raw sugar specialist for U.S. Sugar Equalization Bd., N.Y. City, 1918; studied prodn. of sugar and demand for sugar and other food products in Scandinavia and Russia, 1919; became connected with Gilmer's, Inc., at Winston-Salem, N.C., 1920, establishing chain of dept. stores in Southeast; entered wholesale baking business, 1922, later associating with Liberty Baking Corp., with plants throughout the country; with brother purchased Crystal Candy Co. of Winston-Salem, 1927; chief of Foodstuff Div. of U.S. Dept. of Commerce, 1934-37, promoting export trade; asst. dir. in charge indsl. divs. and district offices, Bureau of Foreign and Domestic Commerce, 1937-40; chief, Merchandise Unit, Bur. of Foreign and Domestic Commerce, 1940-43; indsl. trade consultant, Washington, D.C., from 1943. Cited for meritorious service during World War I. Democrat. Methodist. Mason (32 deg.). Home: Kensington, Md. †

RAWLS, JOSEPH LEONARD, JR., food co. exec.; b. Rocky Mount, N.C., June 14, 1931; s. Joseph Leonard and Lallah (Mizzel) R.; m. Nancy Lee Williams, Dec. 21, 1951; children—Vivian Rawls Tefft, Joseph Leonard III. Student, U. N.C., 1949-51; B.C.S., Benjamin Franklin U., 1953; postgrad., U. E. Carolina, 1953-54. C.P.A., N.C. Partner Luper & Rawls (C.P.A.'s), 1958-61; pres., chmn. Hardee's Food Systems, Inc., Rocky Mount, 1961-75, chmn. bd., 1975-80; pres. Canton Sta., Ltd., Rocky Mount, from 1975; dir. Planter's Nat. Bank & Trust Co., Rocky Mount. Bd. dirs. U. N.C. Med. Found., from 1970; campaign chmn., pres. United Fund, 1977-78; trustee N.C. Wesleyan Coll.; bd. dirs. U. N.C. Bus. Found. Served with AUS, 1954-56. Recipient Golden Plate award as Foodservice Operator of Year Nat. Restaurant Assn. and Internat. Mfrs. Assn., 1972. Mem. Am. Inst. C.P.A.'s, Am. Mgmt. Assn., Young President's Orgn., Phi Gamma Delta. Republican. Episcopalian (vestryman, sr. warden). Clubs: Rotary, Order of Tar Heel 100. Home: Rocky Mount, NC.

RAWLS, NANCY VIVIAN, ambassador; b. Fla., Jan. 24, 1926; A.B., Shorter Coll., 1947. Joined U.S. Fgn. Service, 1947; clk., Washington, 1947-48, Vienna, 1948-49; assigned Washington, 1949-50. profl. and adminstrv. intern. 1950; clk., Frankfurt on Main, Germany, 1950; consular officer, Hamburg, Germany, 1950-54, Montreal, Can., 1954-58; fgn. affairs officer, Washington, 1958-60; econ. officer, Hamburg, 1960-63; supervisory comml. officer, Monrovia, Liberia, 1966-67; econ. and comml. officer, Nairobi, Kenya, 1967-70; detailed to Nat. War Coll., Washington, 1970; dir. policy planning staff Bur. African Affairs. Dept. State, Washington, 1971-74; ambassador to

Togo, 1974-76; alt. del. UN, 1976-79; ambassador to Ivory Coast, 1979-83. Died Apr. 10, 1985.

RAWN, A. M., civil engr.; b. Dayton, Ohio, Nov. 2, 1888; s. Abel M. and Susan Emma (Leet) R.; ed. public school, Toledo, O.; m. Edna Louise Robinson, June 8, 1920. Engr., U.S. Reclamation Service, Yakima, Boise, Salt River, King Hill and Columbia Basin project, 1912-17 and 1918-24; asst. chief engr. Los Angeles County Sanitation Dists., 1924-41, chief engr. and gen. mgr. from 1941. Served as pvt., advancing to 1st lt., U.S. Army, 1917-18; with 319th and 605th Engrs. regts., A.E.F. Cons. engr. to construction quartermaster, U.S. Army, on sewerage and refuse disposal for major cantonments, 1941. Ex-officio dir. sewerage and sanitation branch, governmental div., W.P.B., 1943, 44, 45; mem. Fed. Water Pollution Control Adv. Bd., Cal. State Water Pollution Control Bd. Pres. Los Angeles Engineering Council Founder's Socs., 1940, Nat. Fedn. Sewage Works Assns., 1944. Mem. Am. Soc. C.E. (director 1942-44, vice president 1952-53), Society of Am. Mil. Engrs., Calif. Sewage Works Assn. (pres. 1935), Am. Water Works Assn. (life), Ariz. Sewage and Water Works Assn., Tau Beta Pi. Awarded James Laurie prize, Am. Soc. C.E., 1940. Republican. Baptist. Home: Los Angeles, Calif. †

RAY, HOYT EVERETT, lawyer; b. Brideport, Mo., June 30, 1889; s. Samuel Grant and Viola (Hawke) R.; A.B., Cornell U., 1913; J.D., Stanford, 1915; m. Alice Olmstead, Feb. 18, 1920; 1 dau., Eleanor Everetta; m. 2d, Marion Boone Maclear, June 17, 1933. Practiced law in Idaho, 1916-46; U. S. Atty. for Dist. of Idaho, 1925-33. Republican. Mason (Scottish Rite 32 deg., Shriner). Author of The Robed Umpire, This Shall Not Pass, Crime and Prohibition. Address: San Diego, Calif. †

RAY, ROBERT FREDERICK, educator, dean; b. Davenport, Iowa, Mar. 29, 1922; s. William R. and Margaret (Ehlers) R.; m. Dorothy Frances Klein, Oct. 19, 1947; children—Jennifer Louise, Amelia Jo. B.A., Coe Coll., 1944; M.A., State U. Iowa, 1945, Ph.D., 1947; student, U. Mex., summer 1943. Sr. research analyst N.Y. State Div. Budget, Albany, 1947-49; research cons. Thomas E. Dewey, 1946, 47-49; assoc. prof., dir. Inst. Pub. Affairs, State U. Iowa, Iowa City, 1949-54; prof., dir. Inst. Pub. Affairs, 1954-61, prof., dean div. spl. services, 1961-63, prof., dean div. extension and univ. services, 1963-76, dean div. continuing edn., 1976-82; dir. Iowa Center for Edn. in Politics, 1954-63, chmn. bd. dirs., 1963-69; Dir. Iowa City Bldg. & Loan Assn.; Mem. Midwest Regional adv. com. on Higher Edn. of Council of State Govts., 1962-75; mem. Iowa Ednl. Television Bd., chmn., 1967-75; mem. U.S. Nat. Commn. for UNESCO, 1971-77; chmn. council on extension Nat. Assn. State Univs. and Land Grant Colls., 1974-75, mem. senate and exec. com., 1975-78; bd. dirs. Council on Postsecondary Accreditation, 1977-82. Assoc. editor: Quar. Jour. of Speech, 1947-49. Bd. dirs. Iowa City Community Chest, 1955-58, chmn., 1958; bd. dirs. United Fund of Iowa, 1955-56; pres. Iowa Council for Community Improvement, 1956-58; bd. dirs. Nat. Football Found. and Hall of Fame, 1963-65; bd. govs. Quad-Cities Grad. Study Center, from 1969, chmn. council mem. instns., from 1975; mem. adv. council Iowa chpt. Am. Phys. Therapy Assn., 1960-63; chmn. Iowa Bd. for Pub. Programs in Humanities, 1971-76; trustee Coe Coll., 1980-82. Recipient Disting. Alumnus award Coe Coll., 1979; Robert F. Ray disting. scholar athlete scholarship established in his honor U. Iowa, 1981. Mem. Nat. Collegiate Athletic Assn. (v.p. 1959-63, pres. 1963-65, exec. com. 1965-71), North Central Assn. Colls. and Secondary Schs. (examiner-cons. 1961-82, exec. bd. commn. on instns. of higher edn. 1971-82, chmn. 1977-82, pres. 1981-82), Am., Iowa adult edn. assns., Iowa City C. of C. (dir. 1957-60, 63-65, v.p. 1964), Nat. U. Continuing Edn. Assn. (treas. 1967-68, pres. 1970-71), Nat. Adv. Council on Extension and Continuing Edn. (chmn. 1970-72, 74-75), Intercollegiate Conf. Faculty Reps. (faculty rep. 1955—), Phi Beta Kappa, Omicron Delta Kappa, Phi Kappa Phi, Delta Sigma Rho, Pi Kappa Delta, Phi Gamma Mu. Presbyterian (elder). Clubs: Rotary, Outing, Triangle, The Club. Home: Iowa City, Iowa. Died Sept. 1, 1982.

RAY, ROYAL HENDERSON, educator; b. Scottsburg, Ind., July 27, 1905; s. John William and Eva Jane (Henderson) R.; m. Esther Shirk, June 13, 1937 (dec. 1971); 1 son, John Shirk; m. Rita Gilleylen, Aug. 13, 1972. A.B., DePauw U., 1927; A.M., U. Wis., 1935; Ph.D., Columbia, 1950. Various positions to bus. mgr. Kokomo (Ind.) Dispatch, 1922-30; advt. rep. St. Petersburg (Fla.) Times, 1930-31; instr. Ohio U., 1931-37; instr. advt. and journalism, 1940-41; chmn. advt. dept. Syracuse U., 1945-52; prof., chmn. advt. and pub. relations Fla. State U., 1952-75, prof. emeritus, from 1975. Author: American Daily Newspaper Industry, 1951. Active Leon County United Fund, 1961-70; dir. pub. relations Suwanee River area Boy Scouts Am., 1962-65. Served with USAAF, 1942-45; Served with USAF Res., 1945-65; lt. col. ret. Faculty fellow Assn. Am. R.R.'s, 1965; fellow Fla. Power Corp., 1966. Fellow Am. Acad. Advt. (nat. pres. 1962-63); mem. Pub. Relations Soc. Am., Advt. Fedn. Am. (nat. v.p. 1957-58), Beta Gamma Sigma, Sigma Delta Chi, Delta Upsilon. Club: Capitol City Country (Tallahassee). Home: Tallahassee, Fla.

RAYFIEL, LEO F., judge; b. New York, N.Y., Mar. 22, 1888; s. Hyman and Anna (Rich) R.; ed. public schools and high schools, Brooklyn, N.Y.; student New York U., 1906-08; m. Flora Marks, June 25, 1916; children—Robert D., David, Howard. Admitted to New York bar, and practiced in New York City; U.S. district judge for East District of N.Y. Mem. Brooklyn Bar Assn. Address: Brooklyn, N.Y. †

READ, ALBERT CUSHING, naval officer; b. Lyme, N.H., Mar. 29, 1887; s. Joseph Brown and Mary Elizabeth (Barker) R.; grad. U.S. Naval Acad., 1906 (in class of 1907); m. Bess Anderson Burdine, Jan. 30, 1918; children—Albert Cushing, Bess Burdine. Ensign, Sept. 16, 1908; lt., j.g., Sept. 16, 1911; lt., July 1, 1913; lieutenant commander, Aug. 31, 1917; commander, Sept. 23, 1919. Detailed to naval aviation, July 8, 1915; during World War, comdg. officer Naval Air Sta., Bayshore, New York, Miami, Fla., and in Aviation Sect. Navy Dept. until detailed for projected flight across the Atlantic; in charge N C-4 seaplane, in trip from Rockaway, N.Y., to Plymouth, Eng., via Azores, Portugal and Spain, in 57 hours and 16 minutes flying time, May 1919; this was the first flight in aircraft across the Atlantic Ocean. Mem. Naval History Soc., Reade Soc. Decorated D.S.M. (U.S.); Comenda de Torre d'Espada (Portugal); British Royal Air Force Cross. Baptist. Clubs: Army and Navy (Washington, D.C.); New York Yacht, Seawanhaka Yacht; Chevy Chase (Md.). Address: Washington, D.C. †

READ, JAMES MORGAN, educational consultant; b. Camden, N.J., Aug. 22, 1908; s. James Morgan and Lucia Vail (Foulks) R.; m. Henrietta Morton, Dec. 21, 1940 (dec. 1976); children: Austine Read Wood, James Morgan, Edward Morton; m.2d Theresa Kline Dintenfass, 1977. A.B., Dickinson Coll., 1929, LL.D., 1962; Dr.Phil., U. Marburg, (Germany), 1932; Ph.D., U. Chgo., 1940; D.Human Reconstrn., Wilmington Coll., 1973. Assoc. prof. history U. Louisville, 1935-43; civilian pub. service, 1943-45; assoc. sec. Friends Com. on Nat. Legislation, 1945-47; sec. fgn. service sect. Am. Friends Service Com., 1947-49; chief div. edn. and cultural relations Office U.S. High Commr. for Germany, 1950-51; UN dep. high commr. for refugees, 1951-60; pres. Wilmington Coll., 1960-69; v.p. for program mgmt. Charles F. Kettering Found., 1969-74, cons., 1975-85. Author: Atrocity Propaganda1914-1919, 1941, Magna Carta for Refugees, 1951, The Responsibility of a Quaker College to Train for World Leadership, 1960, The United Nations and Refugees—Changing Concepts, 1962. Mem. Phi Beta Kappa, Tau Kappa Alpha. Quaker. Home: New York, N.Y. Died Feb. 11, 1985.

READ, LEONARD EDWARD, organization executive; b. Hubbardston, Mich., Sept. 26, 1898; s. Orville Baker and Ada Melvina (Sturgis) R.; m. Gladys Emily Cobb, July 15, 1920; children: Leonard Edward, James Baker. Student, Hubbardston High Sch., 1913-16; grad., Ferris Inst., Big Rapids, Mich., 1917; Litt.D., Grove City Coll.; D.Sc., Univesidad Francisco Marroquin. Pres. Ann Arbor Produce Co., 1919-25; sec. Burlingame (Calif.) C. of C., 1927; mgr. Palo Alto (Calif.) C. of C., 1928; asst. mgr. western div. U.S. C. of C., 1929-32, mgr., 1932-39; gen. mgr. Los Angeles C. of C., 1939-45; dir. and mgr. Western Conf. Comml. and Trade Execs., Stanford U., 1929-40; dir. Nat. Assn. Comml. Orgn. Secs., 1942-44; exec. v.p. Nat. Indsl. Conf. Bd., N.Y., 1945-46; pres. Found. for Econ. Edn., N.Y., 1946-83. Author: Romance of Reality, 1937, Pattern for Revolt, 1945, Students of Liberty, 1950, Outlook for Freedom, 1951, Government-An Ideal Concept, 1954, Why Not Try Freedom, 1958, Elements of Libertarian Leadership, 1962, Anything That's Peaceful, 1964, The Free Market and Its Enemy, 1965, Deeper Than You Think, 1967, Accent on the Right, 1968, Let Freedom Reign, 1969, Talking to Myself, 1970, Then Truth Will Out, 1971, To Free or Freeze, 1972, Who's Listening, 1973, Having My Way, 1974, Castles in the Air, 1975, The Love of Liberty, 1975, Comes the Dawn, 1976, Awake for Freedom's Sake, 1977, Vision, 1978, Liberty: Legacy of Truth, 1978, The Freedom Freeway, 1979, Seeds of Progress, 1980, Thoughts Rule the World, 1981, How Do We Know? , 1981, The Path of Duty, 1982; contbr. to trade and comml. periodicals. Served in Air Service U.S. Army, with A.E.F., 1917-19. Mem. Am. Econ. Assn. Republican. Conglist. Clubs: Canadian (N.Y.); St. Andrew Golf. Survivor of torpedoed Tuscania. Home: Irvington, N.Y. Died May 14, 1983.

READ, OLIVER MIDDLETON, naval officer; b. Hobonny Plantation, S.C., Jan. 12, 1889; s. Oliver Middleton and Mary Louise (Gregory) R.; student Virginia Mil. Inst., 1905-06; B.S., U.S. Naval Acad., Annapolis, Md., 1911; m. Constance Sears, Dec. 18, 1918; children—Mary Louise, Oliver Middleton, III. Commd. ensign. U.S. Navy, 1911, promoted through grades to rear adm.; served in various types of ships, U.S. Navy, at Vera Cruz, Mexico, 1914, submarine service, World War, 1917-18, in Chinese waters and at Shanghai, 1932; became first U.S. naval ataché and U.S. Naval ataché for air, U.S. Legation, Ottawa, Can., Aug. 1940; on duty as staff comdr. in chief, U.S. Fleet until Mar. 1942, on sea duty, 1942-46; deputy commander of the Atlantic Reserve Fleet from 1946; promoted rear adm., Oct. 1942. Awarded Navy Cross for submarine service during World War; Mexican Service medal, Victory medal (with one star), Yangtze Service medal, Legion of Merit, gold star in lieu of second Legion of Merit, Combat Distinguishing Device (for actual combat with the enemy for which first Legion of Merit was awarded), Am. Defense Service Medal, Asiatic-Pacific Area Campaign Medal, Am. Area Campaign Medal, European-African-Middle Eastern Area Campaign Medal, Victory Medal (World War II), Cruzeiro do Sul (Order of Southern Cross—Brazil), War Service medal, Diploma, and Citation (Brazil), Comdr. of British Empire. Mem. Soc. of Cincinnati in State of S.C., Hero of Washington chapter of Heroes of 76. Mason (K.T.), Sojourners. Episcopalian. Club: Soc. of the Cincinnati in State of S.C. Home: Yemassee, S.C. †

READ, WILLIAM MERRITT, educator; b. Dupont, Ind., June 24, 1901; s. Parley Garfield and Ella Josephine (Smith) R.; m. Arletta Otis, Dec. 19, 1924 (dec. 1947); children—Virginia (Mrs. Stephen Dunthorne), William Merritt; m. Betty Jorgensen DeLacy, Apr. 30, 1948; children—Elaine Marie, James Garfield. B.A. (Rector scholar), DePauw U., 1923; M.A. (Pendleton fellow), U. Mich., 1924, Ph.D., 1927. Instr. Western Res. U., 1926-27; mem. faculty U. Wash., Seattle, 1927-84; dir. U. Wash. Press, 1943-63, prof. classical langs., 1945—. Author: Michigan Manuscript 18 of the Gospels, 1943, A Guide to Hans H. Oerberg, Lingua Latina Secundum Naturae Rationem Explicata, vol. 1, 1971, vol. II, 1973, A Manual for Teachers of Hans H. Oerberg, Lingua Latina Secundum Naturae Rationem Explicata, vols. I and II, 1973. Mem. Am. Philol. Assn., Classical Assn. Pacific N.W. (sec.-treas. 1972-75), Archeol. Inst. Am., Pacific N.W. Conf. Fgn. Langs., Wash. Assn. Fgn. Lang. Tchrs. (First Pro Lingua award 1973), Phi Beta Kappa. Democrat. Methodist. Home: Auburn, Wash. Died Apr. 20, 1984.

READING, ARTHUR KENNETH, lawyer; b. Williamsport, Pa., Mar. 9, 1887; s. Oscar and Anna C. (Wennermark) R.; LL.B., Harvard, 1912; m. Edith S. Davis, May 1, 1915; 1 son, Arthur K. Admitted to Mass. bar, 1912, and began practice at Boston; rep. Gen. Court of Mass., 1919-22 inclusive; dist. atty., Northern Dist. of Mass., 1923-27 inclusive; atty. gen. of Mass., term 1927, 28. Mem. Am., Mass. State and Suffolk County bar assns. Republican. Mason, Odd Fellow. Club: University. Home: Cambridge, Mass. †

REAM, LOUIS MARSHALL, govt. official; b. Chicago, Ill., July 7, 1887; s. Norman Bruce and Caroline (Putnam) R.; student Harvard Sch., Chicago, 1893-1902, Lawrenceville (N.J.) Sch., 1903-04, Princeton Univ., 1904-08; m. Mary Weaver, June 7, 1918 (divorced 1925); children—Mary Louise, Louis Marshall; m. 2d, Marion Mason, 1929. Spl. asst. to pres. in field of fgn. sales, U.S. Steel Corp., 1919-22; vice pres., gen. mgr. Phillips Wire Co., Pawtucket, R.I., 1923-38; asst. to Gen. William J. Donovan, Office of Strategic Services, Washington, D.C., 1942-45; adminstr. of adminstrn. management, Am. Nat. Red Cross, Washington, D.C., from Mar. 1, 1946. Trustee R.I. State Coll., R.I. Coll. Edn., 1939-46. Served as lt. (s.g.) in aviation constrn., U.S. Navy, World War I. Republican. Episcopalian. Clubs: Hope, University (Providence, R.I.); 1925 F Street (Washington, D.C.). Address: Clayville, R.I. †

REBADOW, RICHARD F., airport adminstr.; b. Buffalo, Feb. 13, 1923; s. Norman C. and Mary Carberry R.; m. Laurie Reigstead; children—Norman, Richard, Mark. Student, Canisius Coll., 1946-48, SUNY, Buffalo Sch. Law, 1949-50. Gen. mgr. airports Greater Buffalo Internat. Airport, Niagara Frontier Transp. Authority, from 1969. Served with USAF, 1943-46. Mem. Am. Assn. Airline Execs. (dir. 1971-73, N.E. chpt. pres. 1970-71), Airport Operators Council, N.Y. Airport Mgrs. Assn. Club: KC. Office: Buffalo, NY.

REBMANN, GODFREY RUHLAND, JR., lawyer; b. Phila., Feb. 6, 1898; s. Godfrey R. and Pauline (Cooper) R.; m. Mary H. Bull, Jan. 3, 1925 (dec. Apr. 1961); children—Ann (Mrs. M. Daniel Daudon), Beverly Mary (Mrs. William J. Bingham); m. Mary H. VanDoren, Nov. 27, 1970. M.E., Cornell, 1919; LL.B., U. Pa., 1922. Bar: Pa. bar 1922. Practiced in, Phila.; former partner, counsel firm Obermayer, Rebmann, Maxwell & Hippel; asst. gen. counsel Lend Lease Adminstrn., 1942, asst. adminstr., 1942-43. Former chmn., dir. Big Brother Assn., Phila.; former dir., now hon. dir. Big Bros./Big Sisters Am., Inc.; former dir., sec. Phila. Orch. Assn. and Acad. Music Phila., Inc.; emeritus dir. Phila. Orch. Assn., pres. community fund, Phila., 1941-42, chmn. war finance com., Pa., 1943-45; pres. Health and Welfare Council, Phila., 1950-53; asso. trustee U. Pa., until, 1971; emeritus mem. council Cornell U., presdl. counsellor, from 1971; mem., past chmn. bd. govs. Eastern div. Pa. Economy League; past mem. exec. com. bd. dirs. Phila. United Fund. Mem. Am. Law Inst., Am., Pa., Phila. bar assns. Clubs: Philadelphia, Union League, Merion Cricket. Home: Gladwyne, PA.

REDFERN, FRANK JAMES, banker, hospital administrator; b. Jersey City, July 1, 1910; s. John Joseph and Margaret Agatha (Barry) R.; grad. St. Peter's Prep. Sch., 1932; m. Gene Marie Crosby, Nov. 16, 1935; children—Peter J., James F. With Peter F. Redfern & Sons Co., constrn., Jersey City, 1932-65, pres., 1941-65; v.p., dir. Fifth Ward Savs. Bank Jersey City, 1948-66; chmn. bd., pres. Peoples Nat. Bank Sussex County (N.J.), 1964-70; sr. v.p. N.J. Bank, 1970-80; pres. Barn Hill Convalescent Center, Newton, N.J., 1972-80. Mem. Sparta (N.J.) Indsl. Commn., 1965-80. Clubs: Lake Mohawk Country (pres. 1971-72), Lake Mohawk Golf (Sparta); Carteret (Jersey City); PGA Golf (Palm Beach, Fla.). Home: Sparta, N.J. Dec. Jan. 8, 1980.

REDFIELD, ALFRED GUILLOU, phys. biochemist, educator; b. Boston, Mar. 11, 1929; s. Alfred Clarence and Martha (Putnam) R.; B.A., Harvard, 1950; Ph.D., U. Ill., 1953; m. Sarah Cossum, July 15, 1970; children—Rebecca, Samuel Duthie, Wendy. Fellow Harvard, 1953-55; prof. physics IBM Watson Lab. Columbia, 1955-70; research asso. biochemistry U. Calif. at Berkeley, 1970-72; prof. physics and biochemistry Rosensteil Center, Brandeis U., 1972—. Mem. Nat. Acad. Scis. Home: Woods Hole, Mass. Died Mar. 17, 1983.

REDGRAVE, MICHAEL SCUDAMORE, actor; b. Bristol, Eng., Mar. 20, 1908; s. Roy and Margaret (Scudamore) R.; student Clifton Coll., 1922-26; B.A., Magdalene Coll., Cambridge U., 1927, M.A., 1950; Litt.D. (honorary), Bristol University, 1966; m. Rachel Kempson, July 18, 1935; children—Vanessa, Corin William, Lynn Rachel. Actor Liverpool Repertory, 1934-36, Old Vic, 1936-37, John Gielgud's Co., 1937-38, Michel St. Denis Co., 1938-39; played roles in Beggar's Opera, Thunder Rock, A Month in the Country (dir. N.Y.C. 1956), Uncle Harry, Jacobowsky and the Colonel, Macbeth (N.Y.C., London), Hamlet (Old Vic), 1950, Country Girl, 1952, as Richard II, Hotspur, Prospero, Shylock, King Lear and Antony at Stratford-on-Avon, 1951-53, Tiger at the Gates (London, N.Y.C.), 1955-56; Sleeping Prince (N.Y.C.), 1956, Hamlet, Benedict (Stratford-on-Avon, Leningrad, Moscow), 1958; actor The Tiger and the Horse, 1960, The Complaisant Lover, 1961, Out of Bounds, 1962; toured in Holland, Belgium, Paris, 1954; appeared Chichester Festival, 1962-63; mem. Nat. Theatre Co., 1963-64; films include: Lady Vanishes, Thunder Rock, Dead of Night, Importance of Being Earnest (Eng.), Mourning Becomes Electra (Hollywood), The Dam Busters, The Happy Road, 1956, The Quiet American, Law and Disorder, 1957, Mr. Dickens of London, 1967, David Copperfield, 1968, Oh What A Lovely War, 1969, Battle of Britain, 1969, Connecting Rooms, 1969, Goodbye Mr. Chips, 1969, others; Rockefeller lectr. Bristol U., 1952-53; Theodore Spencer lectr. Harvard, 1956. Decorated Comdr. Order Brit. Empire, 1952; Comdr. Dannebrog (Denmark), 1955; recipient Elsinore Hamlet medal, 1950. Created Knight, 1959. Author: The Actor's Ways and Means, 1953; Mask or Face, 1958; The Mountebank's Tale (novel), 1959; The Aspern Papers (play), 1959. Home: London, England. Died Mar. 21, 1985.

REDMOND, ROLAND LIVINGSTON, lawyer; b. Tivoli, N.Y., Sept. 13, 1892; s. Geraldyn and Estelle (Livingston) R.; A.B., Harvard, 1915; LL.B., Columbia, 1917; m. Sara Delano, June 5, 1915 (div.); children—Sylvie R. Griffiths, Sheila R. Perkins, Joan R. Read, Cynthia R. Mead; m. 2d, Lydia Bodrero, Dec. 2, 1957. Admitted to N.Y. bar, 1919, began practice at N.Y.C. with Carter, Ledyard and Milburn, mem. firm 1925-55, counsel to firm, 1956-82. Pres. Met. Museum Art, 1947-64, also trustee emeritus; trustee emeritus Pierpont Morgan Library, N.Y. Pub. Library, Am. Geog. Soc. Served as 1st lt. F.A., U.S. Army, 1917-19, AEF in France. Decorated Order Orange-Nassau (Netherlands); Legion of Honor (France); comdr. Order of Dannebrog (Denmark). Mem. Am., N.Y. State bar assns., Assn. Bar City N.Y. Roman Catholic. Clubs: Recess, Links, Harvard (N.Y.). Died Apr. 20, 1982.

REED, CARROLL EDWARD, foreign language educator; b. Portland, Oreg., Nov. 21, 1914; s. Edward R. and Cora (Schienle) R.; m. Elizabeth Eshom, Dec. 26, 1938; children—John, Carolyn, Robin Dale, Janet, Paul, Carl, Michelle. B.A., U. Wash., 1936, M.A., 1937; Ph.D., Brown U., 1941. Mem. faculty U. Wash., 1946-66, prof., 1959-66; asst. in German Brown U., 1938-41, instr., 1941-42; cryptanalyst War Dept., 1942-46; asst. prof. U. Ga., 1946; prof., chmn. dept. German and Russian U. Calif., Riverside, 1966-69; prof. U. Mass., 1969-82, head dept. German, 1971-76; lectr. Columbia, 1950. Author: Linguistic Atlas of Pennsylvania German, 1954, Dialects of American English, 2d edit, 1977. Editor: The Learning of Language, 1971. Contbr. articles to profl. jours. Fulbright research scholar Germany, 1953-54. Mem. Modern Lang. Assn., Am. Dialect Soc., Linguistic Soc. Am., Pa. German Soc., Am. Assn. Tchrs. German, Can. Linguistic Assn., Phi Beta Kappa. Home: Amherst, Mass. Died May 7, 1985.

REED, ERNEST, botanist; b. Chicago, Ill., Mar. 8, 1890; s. Robert and Mary Anne (Watford) R.; A.B., U. of Mich., 1917, M.S., 1919, Ph.D., 1922; m. Alice H. Shaw, Sept. 11, 1919; 1 dau., Mary Alice. Geneticist in Bur. of Plant Industry, U.S. Dept. of Agr., 1920-22; asst. prof. of botany, Syracuse U., 1922-25, asso. prof., 1925-28, prof. from 1928; dir. Syracuse U. Summer Sch., 1927-52; assistant dean Grad. Sch. 1929-42, chmn. Mus. of Natural Sci., 1932-56, chmn. dept. of plant sciences, 1935-56; dir. Microbiological & Biochemical Research Center, Syracuse University Research Institute, from 1956. Botanist on sci. expdn. to Venezuela, 1930; botanist and dir. of expdn. to Gaspé Peninsula, 1933; geneticist on sci. expdn. to Venezuela, 1937. Served as sergeant major 339th Inf., U.S. Army, World War I. Coordinator for the Armed Forces, Syracuse U., 1942-52; dir. of training Civ. Defense, Onondaga Co., 1941-42. Dir. Veterans Ednl. Program Syracuse U., March, 1944-52. Member American Genetical Society, Sigma Xi, Gamma Alpha, Phi Kappa Phi, Phi Beta Kappa. Methodist. Contbr. articles to Bot. Gazette, Jours. Plant Physiology, Current History Mag., Newspapers Syndicate Supplements; also to newspapers. Home: Syracuse, N.Y. †

REED, FRANK OTHEMAN, clergyman, ednl. adminstr.; b. Auburn, N.Y., June 8, 1906; s. Harry Lathrop and Elsie Maynard (Otheman) R.; B.A., Yale, 1927; B.Th., Auburn Theol. Sem., 1932; M.Litt., Mansfield Coll., Oxford (Eng.) U., 1934; m. Grace Lovering Hosic, Sept. 1, 1932; children—David Hosic, Nancy Truesdale (Mrs. William P. Kellett), Margaret Otheman (Mrs. J. Lawrence Dunlap). Tchr. secondary sch. Hampton (Va.) Inst., 1927-29; ordained to ministry Presbyn. Ch., 1932; pastor in Trumansburg, N.Y., 1935-43, Ossining, N.Y., 1943-58; asso. prof. practical theology Auburn Theol. Sem. in assn. Union Theol. Sem., N.Y.C., 1958-71, adminstrv. dir. Auburn program, 1958-64, sec.-treas. Auburn Sem., 1964-71, dir. summer courses Union Theol. Sem., 1961-64; spl. asst. to pres. Eisenhower Coll., Seneca Falls, N.Y., 1971-72. Trustee, Presbytery Westchester (N.Y.), 1946-55, stated clk., 1957-60, moderator, 1954; stated clk. Presbytery Hudson River, 1961; asst. stated clk. Synod N.Y., 1959-64, stated clk., 1964-74; trustee Synod of N.E., 1974-75; moderator Presbytery Geneva, 1937; pres. Tompkins County Ministerial Assn., 1937. Pres. Ossining Council Social Agys., 1947; chaplain Ossining Police Dept., 1952-58; mem. Intersem. Commn. Tng. Rural Ministry, pres., 1962-64; municipal agt. for aging, Salisbury, Conn., 1973-83. Bd. mgrs. Nat. Temperance Soc. and Publ. House, 1967-83. Mem. Northeastern Assn. for Ch. and Soc. (pres. 1969-71), Hymn Soc. Am. (exec. com. 1971-76), Phi Beta Kappa. Rotarian. Address: Salisbury, Conn. Died Feb. 14, 1983; interred Salisbury, Conn.

REED, HAROLD LYLE, prof. economics; b. Dunlap, Ia., June 29, 1888; s. Marcellus A. and Olive (Harroff) R.; A.B., Oberlin, 1911; Ph.D., Cornell, 1914; m. Henrietta Koch, Sept. 5, 1917; children—Kenneth Owen (dec.), Doris Elizabeth, Roger Allan (dec.). Instr. economics, Cornell, 1914-15; instr. finance, N.Y.U., 1915-16; asst. prof. economics, Cornell, 1916-19, N.Y.U., 1919-20; prof. banking and finance, Washington U., 1920-23; prof. economics Cornell U., 1923-54, emeritus, 1954. Conducted banking investigation for U.S. C. of C. Washington, 1926-27; chmn. bd. First Nat. Bank, Ithaca, N.Y., 1937-56, dir.; dir. First Nat. Safe Deposit Co. Member New York State Banking Board, 1934-44. Member American Econ. Assn. (member executive com. 1924-27). Served as private and corpl., United States Army, World War. Author: Development of Federal Reserve Policy, 1922; Principles of Corporation Finance, 1925; Federal Reserve Policy, 1921-30, 1930; The Commodity Dollar, 1934; Money, Currency and Banking, 1942. Contbr. numerous articles in economic periodicals. Home: Ithaca, N.Y. †

REED, JAMES A., electric steel company executive; b. Burgettstown, Pa., 1927. Grad., Washington and Jefferson Coll., 1951. Pres., chief exec. officer, dir. Union Steel Electric Corp., Carnegie, Pa. Home: Carnegie, Pa. Died 1982.*

REED, MARK, playwright; b. Chelmsford, Mass., Jan. 14, 1890; s. Arthur Emerson and Carrie Estelle (White) R.; B.S., Dartmouth, 1912; Mass. Inst. Tech., 1910-11, Harvard Grad. Sch., 1913-15; m. Virginia Belding, of New York. Archtl. draftsman, 1910; circulation mgr., Woman's Jour., Boston, 1915; co-dir. Prairie Playhouse, Galesburg, Ill., 1916-17; wrote short stories, 1923-29. Sergeant 40th Engrs., camouflage sect., A.E.F., World War I, Member Dramatists Guild America, Phi Beta Kappa. Club: Harvard (N.Y. City). Author: She Would and She Did; Let's Get Rich; Petticoat Fever; Yes, My Darling Daughter; and other plays. Home: Boothbay Harbor, Maine. †

REED, ROBERT FINDLEY, chemist; b. Bellefontaine, O., Dec. 30, 1890; s. Robert Gill and Mattie Jane (Findley) R.; student Ohio Mechanics Inst., Cincinnati, 1905-09; Chem.E., U. of Cincinnati, 1914; m. Martha Charlotte Johnson, May 24, 1915; children—Robert Johnson, Janet Emily, Martha Carol. Analyst, research chemist, plant and research supervisor, asst. supt., supt., Ault and Wiborg Co., Cincinnati, 1914-19; adviser, later dir. lake div. tech. lab., E. I. du Pont de Nemours & Co., Wilmington, Del., 1919-25; research dir. Lithographic tech. Foundation, 1925-47, research cons., from 1947; lithographic cons., Armour Research Foundn. from Feb. 1946. Mem. Am. Chem. Soc., Am. Inst. Chem. Engrs., Tech. Assn. Pulp and Paper Industry, A.A.A.S., Soc. of Rheology, Sigma Xi, Alpha Chi Sigma, Tau Beta Pi. Presbyn. Author numerous research and tech. bulls. on lithography. Home: Deerfield, Ill. †

REED-HILL, ELLIS, coast guard officer; b. Belleville, Mich., Aug. 8, 1889; s. George Earing and Georgie Anna (Ellis) H.; B.S. U. of Mich., 1912; the grades to rear admiral, 1946; teacher; engring., Coast Guard Acad., 3 yrs.; engr. in chief, U.S. Coast Guard, from Aug. 1946. Served as pub. relations officer, World War II. Mem. bd. dirs. Navy Mut. Aid; mem. bd. control, U.S. Naval Inst.; pres. Coast Guard Welfare. Awarded Legion of Merit. Mem. Am. Soc. Naval Engrs., Soc. Colonial Wars, S.A.R. Clubs: National Press, Variety. Retired. Home: Summerville, S.C. †

REEDY, JOHN LOUIS, publisher; b. Newport, Ky., Oct. 16, 1925; s. Albert William and Margaret R. (Moser) R. A.B., Notre Dame U., 1948; postgrad., Holy Cross Coll., Washington, 1948-52; postgrad. journalism, Marquette U., Milw., 1953. Joined Congregation Holy Cross, Roman Catholic Ch., 1943, ordained priest, 1952; sec. Priests of Holy Cross, Ind. Province; exec. editor Ave Maria Press, Notre Dame, Ind., 1953-54, editor-pub., 1954-70, pub., from 1970, syndicated columnist. Co-author: The Perplexed Catholic: A Guide Through Confusion, 1966. Pres. bd. dirs. Urban League South Bend and St. Joseph County, Ind., 1974-76; Bd. dirs. Kings Coll., Wilkes-Barre, Pa., from 1981. Recipient award outstanding contbn. Cath. journalism Cath. Press Assn., 1966. Home: Notre Dame, Ind.

REEDY, THOMAS ALBERT, fgn. corr.; b. Reading, Pa., Sept. 10, 1910; s. William J. and Elizabeth M. (Geiser) R.; m. Ruth H. Springer; children—Richards T., Michael O. News reporter Reading Eagle-Times, 1929-35; with Asso. Press, 1936-73, assigned Harrisburg (Pa.), Phila., Washington, Berlin (Germany), 1946-56, chief of bur., Stockholm, Sweden, 1956-58; chief Scandinavian Services, 1958-60, corr. based in London, 1960-65, 66-72, Vietnam, 1965-66, Seattle, 1972-73. Home: London, England. Died Dec. 15, 1981.

REESE, ALGERNON BEVERLY, ophthalmologist; b. Charlotte, N.C., July 28, 1896; s. Algernon Beverly and Mary Cannon (Wadsworth) R.; m. Joan Leeds, Sept. 26, 1942; children—Algernon Beverly, III, Rigdon Leeds, Jonathan Wadsworth. B.S., Davidson Coll., 1917; D.Sc. (hon.), 1946; M.D., Harvard, 1921; student, U. Vienna, 1925-26; M.D. (hon.), U. Melbourne, 1952; LL.D., Duke, 1957. Externe Allgemeines Krankenhaus, Vienna, 1921, 1925-26; resident Mass. Eye and Ear Infirmary, Boston, 1924; Roosevelt Hosp., N.Y.C., 1921-23, N.Y. Eye and Ear Infirmary, 1923-27; chief eye clinic Cornell U. Med. Coll., N.Y.C., 1929-31; chief eye clinic N.Y. Eye and Ear Infirmary, 1929-31, pathologist, 1925-31; former attending ophthalmologist Vanderbilt Clinic, N.Y.C.; attending surgeon, pathologist Inst. Ophthalmology of Presbyn. Hosp.; cons. ophthalmologist, pathologist Eye Inst., N.Y.C.; cons. ophthalmologist to hosps. in N.Y. met. area. Roosevelt Hosp., Flushing Hosp., St. Clare's Hosp., Stamford (Conn.) Hosp., Southampton (L.I.) Hosp., Greenwich (Conn.) Hosp. Assn., St. Luke's Hosp., Manhattan Eye, Ear and Throat Hosp., N.Y. Eye and Ear Infirmary, Lenox Hill Hosp.; clin. prof. ophthalmology, emeritus Coll. Phys. and Surgs., Columbia; former mem. com. on ophthalmology Div. of Med. Sci., NRC.; DeSchweinitz lectr., 1946, Proctor lectr., 1949, Jackson lectr., 1954, Bedell lectr., 1955; Gifford lectr., 1955, Snell lectr., 1956; Snell lectr. Schoenberg lectr., 1959, Montgomery (Royal Coll. Surgeons, Dublin) lectr., 1962; Pres., dir. Ophthalmic Publishing Co.; cons. to, Surgeon Gen. U.S. Army; mem. bd. sci. counselors Nat. Inst. Neurol. Diseases and Blindness, HEW.; Bd. dirs. Nat. Soc. for Prevention Blindness. Author: Tumors of the Eye, 1951, 62, 76, Tumors of Eye and Adnexa (Fascicle 38, Armed Forces Inst. Pathology), 1956; contbr.: med. jours. and The Treatment of Cancer and Allied Diseases; Mem. editorial bd.: med. jours. and Am. Jour. Ophthalmology. Adv. panel Research to Prevent Blindness. Received Hon. Key Am. Acad. Ophthalmology, 1955; Merit citation Davidson Coll., 1948; Lucian Howe medal Am. Ophthalmol. Soc., 1950; Howe prize in ophthalmology U. Buffalo, 1956; Lucien Howe medal eye sect. AMA, 1961; also Herman Knapp medal, 1972; Bowman medal Ophthal. Soc. U.K., 1971; Vail medal Internat. Soc. Eye Surgeons, 1971; Trustees award Research to Prevent Blindness, 1973. Fellow A.C.S., AMA (chmn. eye sect. 1956-57), Am. Ophthalmol. Soc. (pres. 1960), Am. Acad. Ophthalmology and Otolaryngology (pres. 1954-55), Assn. Research in Ophthalmology (Proctor medal 1958), N.Y. Acad. Med. (chmn. eye sect. 1939), N.Y. State and County Med. Soc. (chmn. eye sect. 1937), N.Y. Ophthalmol. Soc. (pres. 1949), Gonin Soc., Phi Beta Kappa (hon.), Kappa Alpha (So.), Omicron Delta Kappa, Phi Beta Pi; hon. mem. Greek, Cuban, Mexican, Australian, Chilean, Panamanian, French, New Zealand ophthal. socs. Clubs: Bedford Golf and Tennis, Pilgrims. Home: Bedford Hills, N.Y. Died Oct. 19, 1981.

REESE, THOMAS WHELAN, educator, exptl. psychologist; b. Balt., Dec. 13, 1908; s. Philip Reigart and Helen (Whelan) R.; B.A., Cambridge U., 1931, M.A., 1944; Ph.D., Columbia, 1942; Fulbright fellow U. Ankara, Turkey, 1951-52; m. Ellen Hayward Pulford, Dec. 17, 1949. Instr., Columbia, 1940-42; faculty Mt. Holyoke Coll., 1945-85, asst. to asso. prof., 1945-50, prof., 1950-85, chmn. dept. psychol. edn., 1954-68. Bd. dirs. Hampshire Interlibrary Center, 1963-66. Served with O.W.I., London, 1943, OSS, London, 1944-45. Spl. NIH Research fellow Sub-Dept. Animal Behaviour dept. zoology U. Cambridge (Eng.), 1966-67. Fellow Am., Mass. psychol. assns., A.A.A.S., N.Y. Acad. Sci.; mem. New Eng., Eastern psychol. assns., Psychonomic Soc., Sigma Xi. Contbr. articles profl. jours. Home: Granby, Mass. Died Apr. 21, 1985.

REEVES, NORMAN PENNINGTON, retail chain exec.; b. Knightstown, Ind., Nov. 23, 1912; s. Norman Wilmont Chesterfield and Mabell (Pennington) R.; B.S. in Pharmacy, Butler U., Indpls., 1936, LL.D. (hon.), 1979; m. Evelyn Fort, Mar. 16, 1935; children—Delinda Reeves Caldwell, John Douglas. With Hook Drugs, Inc., Indpls., from 1945, v.p. ops., 1959-72, pres., from 1972, chmn. bd., chief exec. officer, from 1978, also dir.; dir. 1st Nat. Bank, Knightstown, Salt Creek Realty Corp.; past mem. Ind.

Bd. Pharmacy. Mem. Ind. State Police Bd.; bd. dirs., past pres. Crossroads Rehab. Center, Indpls.; bd. dirs., exec. com. United Way Greater Indpls.; mem. finance com. Community Hosp., Indpls.; mem. dean's adv. council Krannert Grad. Sch. Indsl. Adminstrn., Purdue U., 1974-75; past mem. Knightstown Pub. Sch. Bd. Mem. Nat. Assn. Chain Drug Stores (dir.), Ind. Retail Council (dir., exec. com.), Greater Indpls. Progress Com., Amateur Trap Shooting Assn. Clubs: Downtown Kiwanis, Columbia, Shriners, Masons, K.P. Home: Knightstown, Ind. Died Feb., 1981.

REEVES, ROSSER, author, advertising executive; b. Danville, Va., Sept. 10, 1910; s. Thomas R. and Mary Scott (Watkins) R.; m. Elizabeth Lovejoy Street, Dec. 2, 1934; children: Rosser Scott, Abbot Street, Elizabeth Lovejoy. Student, U. Va., 1928-30. Newspaper reporter Richmond Times-Dispatch, 1929; advt. mgr. Morris Plan Bank Va., 1930-33; copywriter N.Y.C. advt. agys., 1934-38; copy chief Blackett-Sample-Hummert, N.Y.C., 1938-39; with Ted Bates & Co., Inc. (and predecessor firms), N.Y.C., 1940-66, v.p., copy chief, 1942-48, partner, head creative dept., 1949-55, chmn. exec. com., 1953, vice chmn. bd., 1955, chmn. bd., 1955-66; pres. The Tiderock Corp., N.Y.C., 1967-69; ltd. partner Oppenheimer & Co., 1966-67, Bacon, Stevenson & Reeves, 1968-70; chmn. bd. Daniel Starch Inc., N.Y.C., 1968-70, Rosser Reeves Inc. (advt.), N.Y.C., 1976-80. Author: Reality in Advertising, 1961, The 99 Critical Shots in Pool, 1977, Popo, 1980, also poems, short stories. Dep. chmn. industry and labor Pres. Truman's Citizens Food Com., 1948; originator, dir. Eisenhower TV spot campaign, 1952; mem. FOA Marketing Commn. to West Germany, 1953; Chmn. bd. Am. Chess Found., 1958-74; trustee Randolph-Macon Woman's Coll., 1956-70; trustee nat. bd. St. Johns Coll., Annapolis, Md., Santa Fe, N.M. Named hon. fellow Smithsonian Instn.; named Copywriter's Hall of Fame, 1964. Clubs: Racquet and Tennis (N.Y.C.), N.Y. Yacht (N.Y.C.), Doubles (N.Y.C.), Dutch Treat (N.Y.C.), Manhattan Chess (N.Y.C.) (pres. 1971-72), Players (N.Y.C.). Home: Chapel Hill, N.C. Died Jan. 24, 1984.

REH, CARL WILLIAM, civil engineer; b. Chgo., Nov. 4, 1917; s. Paul Pius and Anna (Klausegger) R.; m. Regina Vanden Bosch, Dec. 27, 1941 (dec.); children—Carl Michael, Katherine Reh DeLisle, Elizabeth Reh Elliott, James C., Thomas A. B.S. in Civil Engring, Ill. Inst. Tech., 1939. Diplomate: Am. Acad. Environ. Engrs.; Registered profl. engr., D.C., Ill., 6 other states. With Ill. Dept. Pub. Health, 1941; civil engr. Bur. Yards and Docks, U.S. Navy, 1942-45; with Greeley and Hansen (engrs.), Chgo., from 1945, partner, 1957-83; mem. engring. adv. bd. Met. Sanitary Dist. Greater Chgo., 1960-62; engring. adv. bd. Ill. Inst. Tech., 1972-83; mem. water engring. conf. com. U. Ill., 1972-83; mem. U. Ill. NSF Project Steering Com., 1976, State of Ill. Adv. Bd. for Water Supply Operator Cert., 1980-83. Trustee Village of Lincolnshire, Ill., 1977-81. Fellow ASCE, Am. Cons. Engrs. Council; mem. Nat. Soc. Profl. Engrs., Am. Water Works Assn., Water Pollution Control Fedn. Roman Catholic. Clubs: Tower (Chgo.), Union League (Chgo.). Home: Lincolnshire, Ill. Died July 1983.

REHNER, HERBERT ADRIAN, writer, educator; b. Vincennes, Ind., Dec. 14, 1926; s. Herbert O. and Anna-Blanche (Chapman) R. A.B., Ind. State U.; M.A., Ind. State U., 1948; LUD, Royal Acad. Dramatic Art, U. London, 1949; student, Acad. Arts and Design in, Mex., Litt.D., 1960; Litt.D., Brantridge Forest Sch., Eng., 1967. Tchr. Ind. State U., 1947-48; lectr. Royal Acad. Dramatic Art, 1949-50; head theatre dept. Wilson br. Chgo. City Coll., 1950-68, head speech dept., 1959-68, chmn. and prof. speech and drama, from 1968; producer, dir. Shawnee Summer Theatre, Greene County, 1960; pres. Ind. Acad. Dramatic Art, 1953-56. Producer, dir.: profl. tour of You Can't Take It With You for, Dept. Def., Europe, 1959; programs over, radio sta. WBOW and WIHI, 1964-68; summer producer, White Barn Profl. Theater, Terre Haute, Ind., cultural rep., Internat. Theater Inst., Chgo., 1955, dir., All City Chicago Drama Festival, 1957, Shakespeare on TV, 1961, 69; producer: Guys and Dolls, Chgo., 1960, Westward the River; hist. drama, 1967; mgr. theatre tour to, S. Pacific, Dept. Def., 1971; dir TV variety hour, Seoul, Korea, 1971; prod., Profl. Performing Equity Co., Drama Guild, Chgo., 1972-75, mng. producer, Sta. WKKC, Chgo., from 1978; producer: profl. world premiere of Sinbad, 1979; designer Profl. theatre, Bloomfield, Ind., 1979; Contracted to develop 5 curricula, also design performing arts center for new univ., Iran, 1973; Author: Sons of the Prairie, 1950, Pastime of Eternity, 1948, The Dramatic Use of Oral Interpretation and Choral Speaking, 1951, The Constant Heritage, 1952, Out of this Land, 1954, Practical Public Speaking, 1957, Communication Through Speaking, 1959, rev., 1961, 62, 65, 68, 77, 78, Speaking in Public, 1961, Activities in Living and Speaking, 1965, rev., 67, 73; nat. editor: Cue mag, 1962-64. Recipient Fulbright grant to study in Eng. and Europe; James Yard award for human relations NCCJ, 1960; named Chgo. Tchr. of Yr., 1965; Kate Moremont travel grantee, 1965. Mem. Speech Assn. Am., Sadlers Wells-Old Vic. Assn., Soc. Midland Authors, ANTA (Chgo. bd. 1960-61), Theta Chi, Theta Alpha Phi (nat. pres. 1974-76, nat. council from 1977), Blue Key. Club: Players (N.Y.C.) (hon.). Home: Owensburg, Ind.

REICHELDERFER, FRANCIS WILTON, meteorologist; b. Harlan, Ind., Aug. 6, 1895; s. Francis Allen and Mae Olive (Carrington) R.; B.S., Northwestern U., 1917, D.Sc. (hon.), 1939; postgrad. Geophys. Inst., Bergen, Norway, 1931; m. Beatrice Coralyn Hoyle, June 19, 1920; 1 son, Bruce Allen. Chemist, Calumet Co., Chgo., 1917-18; enlisted U.S. Navy, 1918, commd. ensign, 1918, advanced through grades to comdr., 1938, ret., 1939; dir. U.S. Weather Bur., 1939-63, cons. atmospheric scis., 1963-77; pres. World Meteorol. Orgn. UN, 1951-55. Fellow AAAS; mem. Nat. Acad. Scis., Am. Meteorol. Soc. (pres. 1939-40), Am. Inst. Aeronautics and Astronautics (past pres. Washington chpt.), Am. Geophys. Union, Royal Meteorol. Soc. (London). Methodist. Clubs: Cosmos (Washington); Rotary. Contbr. to numerous publs. in field. Home: Washington, D.C. Died Jan. 25, 1983.

REICHER, LOUIS JOSEPH, bishop; b. Piqua, O., June 14, 1890; s. Jacob and Marie (Krebsbach) R.; student St. Jerome's Coll., Kitchener, Can., 1911; St. Mary's Sem., Cincinnati, 1911-12; St. Mary's U., LaPorte, Tex., 1918; LL.D., St. Edward's U., Austin, Tex., 1944. Ordained priest Roman Catholic Ch., St. Mary's Cathedral, Galveston, Tex., Dec. 6, 1918; chancellor Galveston diocese, 1918-48; vicar for religious and adminstrv. council, 1918-48; founded and built St. Christopher's parish, Houston, 1923-41; apptd. Domestic Prelate, Mar. 2, 1935. Protonotary Apostolic, July 9, 1940; consecrated bishop of Austin, (Tex.), Apr. 14, 1948. Address: Austin, Tex. Died Feb. 23, 1984.

REID, EDWIN KITCHEN, lawyer; b. Albany, Ga., Nov. 16, 1912; s. William Adolphus and Carrie Ida (Kitchen) R.; m. Betty Ann Thombs, Sept. 3, 1943; children—Kathy, Linda (dec.), Edwin. A.B., Syracuse U., 1936; J.D., Duke, 1939. Bar: N.Y. bar 1941, D.C. bar 1970. Asso. Barry, Wainwright, Thatcher & Symmers, N.Y.C., 1939-43; Asso. Dow & Symmers, N.Y.C., 1943-44, partner, 1946-52, Zock, Petrie, Sheneman & Reid, N.Y.C., 1952-72, Zock, Petrie, Reid, Curtin & Byrnes, 1972-75, Zock, Patrie, Reid & Curtin, 1975-79, of council, from 1980; asst. legal rep. U.S. War Shipping Adminstrn., U.K., N. Ireland, Europe, 1944-46; sometime spl. master U.S. Dist. Ct. for So. Dist. N.Y.; lectr. law and medicine Law Sci. Inst., Crested Butte, Colo., 1960; Chmn. adv. council for law enforcement, Bergen County, 1955-57; mem. Juvenile Conf. Commn., Demarest, Bergen County, N.J., 1966, chmn., 1967. Councilman Boro of Demarest, 1954-57; mayor Boro Demarest, 1961-64; chmn. 13th Assembly Dist. N.J., N. Valley, Passiac Valley Republican Fedn., 1967-68. Mem. Bar Assn. City N.Y., Assn. Trial Lawyers Am., N.Y. State Trial Lawyers Assn., Fed. Bar Assn., Am. Maritime Law Assn., Def. Assn. N.Y., Am. Arbitration Assn. (arbitrator), Phi Beta Kappa, Delta Kappa Epsilon. Clubs: Pinehurst (N.C.) Country; Whitehall (N.Y.C.). Home: Pinehurst, NC.

REID, FRANK A., lawyer; b. Oriskany, Va., Mar. 7, 1887; s. Benjamin W. and Hariet P. (Lemon) R.; student Daleville (Va.) Coll., 1902-04; A.B. Roanoke Coll., Salem, Va, 1908, LL.D., 1957; Rhodes scholar, Oxford, Eng., B.A., 1911, M.A., 1919; J.D., U. of Mich., 1913; Asst. in U. of Mich., Law Sch., 1913; admitted to Mich. bar, 1913, Ill. bar, 1914, N.Y. bar, 1917; began practice at Chicago; with Knapp & Campbell, 1913-16; moved to N.Y. City, 1916; with Simpson, Thatcher & Bartlett, 1916-21; atty. Elec. Bond & Share Co., 1921-26, gen. atty., 1926-31, v.p., 1931-35; now mem. law firm Reid & Priest. Dir. Fed. Prison Industries. Incorporated, 1953-59. Trustee of Roanoke College. Served as pvt. United States Army, 1918-19. Recipient of Roanoke Coll. Alumni citation. Mem. Am., N.Y.C., N.Y. State bar assns., Order of Coif. Gamma Eta Gamma. Republican. Presbyn. Mason. Clubs: Boca Raton, University. Home: Pompano Beach, Fla. †

REID, JAMES SIMS, physician, inventor, mfg. exec.; b. Yazoo City, Miss., Nov. 22, 1894; s. William H. and Sallie (Luse) R.; student (mech. engring.) Miss. Agrl. and Mech. Coll. (Starkville, Miss.), bus. coll. Atlanta, U. Tenn.; M.D., U. Louisville, 1916; m. Felice Crowl, Aug. 16, 1924; children—James Sims, George McKay, Margaret C. With Bd. of Health, Cleve., 2 yrs.; formed Easy-on-Cap (for automobiles) Co., 1921, serving as pres. until 1928; founded Standard Products Co., mfrs. rubber window channel and weatherstrips, plastic interior and exterior trim, other automotive products, with plants in U.S., Can., Europe, S.Am., later chmn. bd. and chief exec. officer, now chmn. bd. Served with U.S. Army, World War I; disch. with rank of capt.; cooperated in development and improvement of M-1 carbine, World War II. Mason. Clubs: Union, Tavern, Detroit Athletic. Inventor products and appliances pioneering in fields served by cos. he established. Home: Hudson, Ohio. Died Nov. 29, 1981.

REID, JOHN EDWARD, lawyer, forensic cons.; b. Chgo., Aug. 16, 1910; s. Thomas and Margaret (Hanley) R.; m. Margaret McCarthy, July 26, 1941. Student, Loyola U., Chgo., 1930-31; J.D., DePaul U., 1936. Began testing subjects with polygraph Chgo. Police Sci. Crime Detection Lab., 1940; revised questioning technique in lie detector tests, 1947; established John E. Reid & Assos. Lab for Lie Detection, Chgo., 1947; founder Reid Coll. for Detection of Deception; devised Reid Report and Reid Survey (psychol. questionnaires to determine job applicant and employee honesty.); Mem. Chgo. Crime Commn. Author: (with Fred. E. Inbau) The Polygraph (Lie Detector) Technique; also articles on lie detection, criminal interrogation. Fellow Am. Acad. Forensic Scis.; mem. Am. Polygraph Assn. (dir.), Ill. Polygraph Soc., Am. Acad. Polygraph Examiners (past pres.), Internat. Assn. Arson Investigators, Spl. Agts. Assn. (past pres.). Inventor polygraph for detection false rises in blood pressure, 1944. Home: Park Ridge, Ill. Died Jan. 11, 1982.

REID, PAUL APPERSON, ret. coll. pres.; b. Vade Mecum Springs, N.C., Aug. 10, 1902; s. William Henry and Margaret (Apperson) R.; A.B., U. N.C., 1929, M.A., 1938; Litt.D., High Point Coll., 1956; m. Magdalene Fulk, Dec. 20, 1924 (dec. Mar. 1955); m. 2d, Nettie Dockery Haywood, Nov. 10, 1956. Elementary sch. tchr., prin., Pilot Mountain, N.C., 1923-27; bus. mgr., asst. supt. schs., Roanoke Rapids, N.C., 1929-35, prin. jr.-sr. high schs., 1935-38; prin. Needham Broughton High Sch., Raleigh, N.C., 1938-41; supt. pub. schs., Elizabeth City, N.C., 1941-44; controller N.C. Bd. Edn., 1944-49; pres. Western Carolina U., Cullowhee, N.C. 1949-56, 57-68, pres. emeritus; served as asst. dir. higher edn., N.C., 1956-57, N.C. rep. edn. adv. com. Appalachian Regional Commn. Mem. N.C. Hist. Sites Commn.; mem. Jackson County-Sylva Planning Bd.; exec. com. Raleigh-Wake County Community Chest. Mem. N.E.A., Am. Assn. Sch. Adminstrs., N.C. Hist. and Lit. Soc., N.C. Edn. Assn. (pres. Western dist. higher edn. div., past pres. N.E. dist.), N.C. City High Sch. Prins. Assn. (past pres.), Western N.C. Schoolmasters Club, Western N.C. Assn. Communities (dir., past pres.), N.C. Children's Home Soc. (dir.), N.C. League Crippled Children (dir.), Wake County Tb Assn. (dir.). Methodist (steward). Clubs: Raleigh Kiwanis (past pres.); Sylva Rotary (past pres.) Author book on N.C. history, also mag. articles and other publs. Home: Pilot Mountain, N.C. Died June 1982.

REIFF, ROBERT FRANK, artist, educator; b. Rochester, N.Y., Jan. 23, 1918; s. Charles and Mabel (Doel) R.; m. Helen Hayslette, Nov. 26, 1955. B.A., U. Rochester, 1938; M.A., Columbia U., 1950, Ph.D., 1961. Mem. faculty Muhlenberg Coll., 1947-49, Oberlin Coll., 1950-54, U. Chgo., 1954-55, St. Cloud (Minn.) State Coll., 1955-58; Mem. faculty Middlebury Coll., from 1958, now prof. art. Exhibited in shows at, Finger Lakes Meml. Art Gallery, Rochester, 1961, 62, Yaddo, Saratoga Springs, N.Y., 1961, Pittsfield (Mass.) Mus., 1961, Fleming Mus., Burlington, Vt., 1962, Albright Art Gallery, Buffalo, Walker Art Center, Mpls., Allen Meml. Art Mus., Oberlin, Ohio, U. Va. Gallery, Johnson Art Gallery, Middlebury, Vt., Springfield (Mass.) Mus.; Author: Renoir, 1968, Indian Miniatures: The Rajput Painters, 1959 (reprinted as part of Oriental Miniatures, 1965). Served with USAAF, 1942-46. Belgian-Am. Found. scholar, 1952; Yaddo Found. scholar, 1961. Mem. Coll. Art Assn. Home: Middlebury, VT.

REILY, WILLIAM BOATNER, JR., coffee co. exec.; b. Morehouse Parish, La., Dec. 31, 1887; s. William Boatner and Estelle (Weaks) R.; student Tulane U., 1904-07; m. Elaine Pujo, Feb. 10, 1915; 1 son, William Boatner III. With Reily-Taylor Co., New Orleans, 1907-1916; organizer Standard Coffee Co., New Orleans, 1916; exec. v.p. Wm. B. Reily & Co., Inc., New Orleans, 1924-42, pres., 1942-68, chmn. bd., from 1968; executor Killarney Plantation, Collinston, La., from 1940. Founder, guarantor Tulane U. Sch. Bus. Adminstrn., 1914. Founder mem. Bur. Govtl. Research New Orleans; founder dir. Pub. Affairs Research Council La.; founder mem. La. Civil Service. Served to ensign USNRF, 1917-21. Mem. S.A.R., Sigma Alpha Epsilon. Clubs: Boston, Louisiana, Round Table (New Orleans); Little Lake (Lafitte, La.). Home: New Orleans, LA. †

REIMERS, CARL, advt. exec.; b. Louisville, July 18, 1890; s. Edward G. and Ida (Stuber) R.; student pub. schs.; m. Peg Holloway, Oct. 16, 1920. Gen. sales mgr. Charles H. Banfield & Co., Toronto, Can., 1920-22; account exec. Dorrance Sullivan & Co., N.Y., 1922-25; mem. plan bd. Charles W. Hoyt Co., N.Y.; pres. Carl Reimers Co., Inc., advt. agy., N.Y.C., 1925-55; sr. v.p. Bozell & Jacobs, Inc., N.Y.C., 1955-59; executive vice president Michale Newmark Agy., N.Y.C., from 1959. Served USN, 1917-20. Mem. Beaux Arts Inst. Design, Archtl. League N.Y. Republican. Episcopalian. Home: Port Washington, N.Y. †

REINARTZ, EUGEN GOTTFRIED, army officer; b. East Liverpool, O., Dec. 27, 1889; s. John Gottfried and Sarah Julia (Eppling) R.; M.D., Medico-Chirurgical Coll., Phila., Pa., 1916, Flight Surgeon, Sch. Aviation Med., Mitchel Field, Long Island, N.Y., 1920; grad. Med. Field Service Sch., Adv. Course, Carlisle Barracks, Pa., 1935; m. Jeannette Frances Park, June 18, 1918. Commd. 1st lt., Med. Corps, 1917, and advanced through the grades to brig. gen., 1942; comdt., Sch. Aviation Med., Randolph Field, Tex., 1941-46. Practice of psychiatry, consultant in aviation medicine, San Francisco, from 1946-48; chief med. officer and chief psychiatrist, Dept. of Corrections, State of Calif., assigned to Med. Security Prison, Soledad, July 1948. Recieved John Jeffries Award, Inst. Aero. Sciences, 1944, Legion of Merit. Fellow Am. Coll. Physicians, 1929, Aero Med. Assn. of U.S., 1942 (pres. 1944); hon. mem. Inst. Aero Sciences, Airlines Med. Dirs. Assn.; mem. Am. Med. Soc., Phi Beta Pi; hon. mem. Am. Psychiatric Assn. Mason. Address: Soledad, Calif. †

REINARTZ, LEO F., business exec.; b. East Liverpool O., Aug. 8, 1888; s. John Gottfried and Sarah Julia (Eppling) R.; B.S., Carnegie Inst. Tech., 1909; M.E., 1923; D.Sc., Capital University, 1959; married Mathilda Sophia Zix, September 12, 1916; children—Mathilda M. (Mrs. T.

E. Graham, III), Leo F. (killed in action at Leyte), Helen Marie (Mrs. G. T. Duffin, Jr.). Chemist Am. Rolling Mill Co., Middletown, O., 1909-13, asst. supt. central works open hearth dept., 1913-15, asst. supt. east works and central works open hearth dept. 1915-16; supt., 1916-23, asst. gen. supt., 1923-30, works mgr. East Works, 1930-38, div. mgr. Middletown and Hamilton plants, 1938-50; v.p. charge spl. operating developments Armco Steel Corp., 1951-55, consultant, from 1956; pres. Princess Dorothy Coal Co.; v.p., dir. Middletown Fed. Savs. & Loan Association, 1957; dir. Hosp. Care Corp., Southwestern O. Mem. metall. adv. bd. Nat. Acad. Sci., Washington. Chairman bd. regents, Capital Univ., (sec. 9 yrs.). Dir. Middletown Y.M.C.A., 1915-30, pres. 1927-29, honorary life member, from 1945. Trustee of the Butler County Childrens Home, Middletown Hosp. Assn., 1933-46, treas. 10 yrs.; treas. Middletown Indsl. Council. Recipient Alumni Award of Merit, Carnegie Institute Technology, Ben J. Fairless award, Am. Inst. Mining Engineers. Member Middletown Safety Council (hon. life; 1st pres.), Joint Engring. Societies (chmn. John Fritz award com.), Am. Inst. Mining, Metallurical and Petroleum Engrs., (chmn. Nat. Open Hearth Conf., mem. exec. com. 1926-46, hon. mem. Nat. Conf.), American Institute Mining and Metall. Engrs. (pres. 1954-56, dir. 1955), Bituminous Coal Operators Association (director), Soc. Polit. Sci. Am. Iron and Steel Inst. (regional award, 1952), Am. Management Assn., Am. Ordnance Assn., Mil. Engrs., Am. Navy League, Middletown Civic Assn., Jr. (hon. life), Middletown C.'s of C., Middleton Art Assn. (trustee), Tau Beta Phi. Republican. Lutheran. Clubs: Brown's Run Country, Hamilton Business Men's. Presented papers before Am. and Brit. Iron and Steel Insts. Home: Middletown, O. †

REINECK, WALTER S., foreign service officer; b. Gibsonburg, O., Dec. 11, 1887; A.B., St. Joseph's Coll., Rennselaer, Ind., 1912; student U. of Innsbruck, Austria, 1912-14; married. Clerk, Am. embassy, Vienna, 1914; in charge Am. archives in Spanish embassy, Vienna, 1917; with Am. mission, Vienna, 1919; at Budapest, 1920; became vice consul, Budapest, 1921; consul, Martinique, 1925-29, Antwerp, 1929-31; sec. in diplomatic service, 1937; consul, Vancouver, 1937-42, Calgary (temporary), 1938; consul, Regina, since 1912. Home: Washington, D.C.†

REINHARDT, SIEGFRIED GERHARD, artist; b. Germany, July 31, 1925; came to U.S., 1928, naturalized, 1936; s. Otto Fredrick and Minni (Kukat) R.; m. Hariet Fleming Reinhardt, Apr. 25, 1948. A.B. in English Lit, Washington U., St. Louis, 1950; L.H.D. (hon.), London Inst., 1970, Occidental U., 1974, Concordia Sem. in Exile, 1977. Tchr. painting Washington U., 1955-70. Designed, executed stained glass windows with, Emil Frei, Inc., Kirkwood, Mo., 1949-84; artist-in-residence So. Ill. U., Carbondale, 1950-54, 68-69, artist-in-residence St. Louis Community Coll. at Meramec, 1971-84; exhibited in one-man shows at Midtown Galleries, N.Y.C.; represented in permanent collections at, Whitney Mus., N.Y.C., St. Louis City Art Mus., Mo. Hist. Soc., Smithsonian Instn., Vatican Mus.; executed murals at, Concordia Sr. Coll., Ft. Wayne, Ind., Jefferson Nat. Expansion Meml. Mus., New City Bank, St. Louis, Internat. Lithographers and Photo-engravers Union Bldg., St. Louis, City Hall, Nevada, Mo., U. Mo., Rolla, Fabick Tractor Co., Fenton, Mo., Meramec Community Coll., St. Louis, City of Kirkwood; important works include The Man of Sorrows, 1955, Crucifixion, 1961; commd. to create: 11 lithographs for Ency. Brit.'s Propaedia, 1973. Served with AUS, 1944-46. Recipient Washington U. Alumni citation, 1969; named One of Nineteen Outstanding Young Artists Life mag., 1950. Mem. Assn. Profl. Artists, St. Louis Artists Guild, Mo., St. Louis chambers commerce. Lutheran. Home: Kirkwood, Mo. Died Oct. 24, 1984.

REINICKE, FREDERICK GEORGE, naval officer; b. Tripoli, Ia., Apr. 8, 1888; s. Rev. Joseph and Katherine (Forler) R.; grad. U.S. Naval Acad., 1910; m. Nan Chadwick, Aug. 22, 1921; children—Ann Chadwick, Frederick Rogers. Commd. ensign, U.S. Navy, 1912, and advanced through the grades to commodore, 1943; served in U.S.S. Va., 1910-13, U.S.S. Galveston, 1913-16; comd. U.S.S. Aylevin in Eng. Channel and North Sea; gunnery officer U.S.S. Miss., 1921-24; condr. U.S.S. Osborne and U.S.S. Paulding, 1926-29, U.S.S. Tulsa, 1932-35; exec. officer U.S.S. Tenn., 1937-38; served ashore, instr. U.S.-N.A. 1919-21, Training Sta., Newport, 1924-26; grad. mgr. athletics, U.S.N.A., 1929-31; sr. course Naval War Coll., 1931-32; in charge pub. relations, office Naval Operations, Navy Dept., 1935-37; naval director, Port of New York, 1939-45; commissioner, Marine and Aviation City of New York and mem. N.Y. Air Authority, 1946-47; advisor to the government of Thailand, 1950-51. President, Am. Asiatic Assn.; hon. mem. Maritime Assn. Decorated Navy Cross, Second Nicaraguan Campaign, Yangtze Service, Victory and Defense medals, Legion of Merit medal, Commander Order of the British Empire; Order of Orange and Nassau with Swords (Netherlands). Clubs: New York Yacht, Tuxedo, Leash. Home: New York, N.Y. †

REISENBERG, NADIA, pianist; b. Russia; student of Leonid Nikolaieff, Alexander Lambert, Josef Hofmann. U.S. debut, 1923; consecutive performances all 27 Mozart piano concerti; two sets of engagements single season N.Y. Philharmonic Orch.; recording artist for Westminster Records. Address: New York, N.Y. Died June 10, 1983.*

REISTRUP, JEANNE MOSS, interior designer; b. Glasgow, Mo., Aug. 11, 1905; d. Samuel and Jennie (Easley) Moss; m. James Reistrup, July 23, 1931 (dec. Apr. 1973); children—Paul H., John V. Student, U. Ill., 1923-27; study in, Europe, 1931. Head bur. interior decorating Davidson Bros., Sioux City, Iowa, 1928-31; owner firm Jeanne Moss Reistrup, from 1933; tchr. interior decorating YWCA, Catholic U.; lectr. in field. Author articles in field. Chmn. bd. Reistrup Arts Assn. Recipient Woman of Achievement award Sioux City, 1946. Fellow Am. Inst. Designers (nat. by-laws com., nominating com., chmn. nat. conf. 1953, chmn. exhibit Nat. Housing Center 1959, chmn. bd. govs., corr. sec. D.C. chpt. from 1971), Am. Soc. Interior Designers (life mem.; chmn. by-laws and ethics com. Potomac chpt.); mem. Nat. Symphony Orch. Women's Com., YWCA, P.E.O., Delta Zeta. Clubs: Fortnightly (past pres.), Morningside Coll. Faculty Women's (past pres.). Home: Washington, DC.

REITELL, CHARLES, economist; b. Steelton, Pa., Apr. 7, 1887; s. Samuel E. and Mary Elizabeth (Strayer) R.; B.S., Wharton Sch. Finance and Commerce (U. of Pa.), 1910, Ph.D., 1917; m. Jane Myer, June 7, 1916; 1 dau., Elisabeth. Prof. economics, Elmira (N.Y.) Coll., 1910-13; instr. economics, U. of Pa., 1913-16; prof. commerce, Lawrence Coll., Appleton, Wis., 1916-17; economist Nat. Bur. Standards, 1917-18; staff accountant War Dept., 1918-19; prof. accounting and head of dept., U. of Pittsburgh, 1919-31; dir. Greater Pa. Council, 1931-33; chief accountant A.A.A., U.S. Dept. Agr., 1933; partner Stevenson, Jordan & Harrison, Inc., management engrs.; lecturer in accounting, Columbia U. Dir. accounts and dep. sec. Commonwealth of Pa., 1922-23; mem. Bd. of Fish Commrs., 1923-31. Mem. Nat. Association Cost Accountants. Clubs: University (Pittsburgh, Pa.); Cosmos (Washington, D.C.); University (Montreal, Can.). Author several books relative to field; latest publ.: Cost Accounting, 1948.†

REITER, GEORGE H., cement exec.; b. Cincinnati, June 1, 1888; s. George and Clara Belle (McGowan) R.; C.E., U. Cin., 1910; m. LaCigale Ferris, Apr. 24, 1915; 1 son, James H. (dec.). Engr. Universal Portland Cement Co., Chgo., 1912-15; mgr. Ill. Paving Brick Mfrs. Assn., 1915-20; sec., pres. Springfield Paving Brick Co. of Ill., 1920-28; sec., treas. Poston Springfield Brick Co., 1928-30; mgr. Cement Inst., Chgo., 1930, mgr., sec., gen. mgr. Chgo. and Washington, 1933-37; sales mgr. Mo. Portland Cement Co., St. L., 1931-33; v.p. Universal Atlas Cement Co. (div. U.S. Steel), N.Y.C., 1937-51, exec. v.p. from 1951. Clubs: Chicago, Tavern (Chgo.); Union League, Uptown (N.Y.C.). Home: New York, N.Y. †

REITER, WALTER ANDERSON, ins. exec.; b. East Orange, N.J., Jan. 12, 1888; s. Charles Grant and Priscilla (Anderson) R.; A.B., Cornell, 1910, M.D., 1913; m. Elsie M. Agens, Mar. 5, 1915; children—Hulbert A., Charles G., Walter A. Intern S.I. Hosp., 1913-15, practiced medicine Summit, N.J., 1915-22, staff Overlook Hosp., 1915-25, city physician, 1916-22; assistant medical director, Mutual Benefit Life Insurance Company, Newark, 1922-28, medical director, 1928-46, vice president and med. director, 1946-49, administrative v.p. from 1949; dir. U.S. Savs. Bank, Newark. Served as 1st lt., Med. Corps, U.S. Army, Gen. Hosp. 6, Fort McPherson, Ga., 1917-19. Mem. Assn. Life Ins. Med. Dirs., A.M.A., N.J. State Mem. Soc., Newark C. of C., Alpha Omega Alpha. Clubs: University, Cornell (N.Y. City); Essex, Downtown (Newark); Canoe Brook Country (Summit, N.J.); Baltusrol Golf (Springfield, N.J.). Home: Chatham, N.J. †

REITHERMAN, WOLFGANG, animated motion picture producer; b. Munich, Bavaria, June 26, 1909; s. Philipp and Rosina Marie (Kuhner) R.; came to U.S., 1911, naturalized, 1919; student Pasadena Jr. Coll., 1927-28, Chouinard Art Sch., 1930-31; m. Janie Marie McMillan, Nov. 26, 1946; children—Richard Wolfgang, Robert King, Bruce Philip. Animator Walt Disney Studios, 1932-37, dir. animator, 1937-41, dir., producer, 1948-85. Served as pilot USAAF, 1941-45. Decorated D.F.C., Air medal with oak leaf cluster. Mem. Am. Acad. Motion Picture Arts and Scis. Home: Burbank, Calif. Dec. May 22, 1985.

REMBOLT, RAYMOND RALPH, pediatrician, hosp. adminstr., educator; b. Grand Island, Nebr., May 8, 1911; s. William Gustav and Lillian Elizabeth (Hershey) R.; A.B., U. Nebr., 1933, M.D., 1937; m. Mae Ione Street, Sept. 9, 1938; children—David, Diana, Richard. Extern, Evang. Covenant Hosp., Omaha, 1936-37; pediatric intern U. Minn. Hosps., Mpls., 1937-38; pvt. practice pediatrics Lincoln (Nebr.) Clinic, 1938-42, Lincoln Children's Clinic, 1947-48; resident dept. pediatrics State U. Iowa, 1946-47, successively asst. prof. pediatrics, asso. prof. pediatrics, 1948-52, prof. pediatrics, 1952-77, dir. U. Hosp. Sch., 1952-77, dir. State Services for Crippled Children, U. Iowa, 1948-52, dir. Birth Defects Center, 1966-70. Pres. Iowa Soc. Crippled Children and Adults, Inc., 1956-57; profl. adv. council Nat. Soc. Crippled Children and Adults, 1962-76; mem. nat. profl. services program com. Nat. United Cerebral Palsy Assns., 1966-72; mem. nat. adv. council div. developmental disabilities HEW, 1972-73, chmn. subcom. on univ. affiliated facilities, 1972-73, cons. to subcom., 1973. Served from lt. to lt. comdr., USNR, 1942-46. Fellow Am. Acad. Pediatrics (Ia. chmn. 1958-60), Am. Acad. Neurology, Am. Acad. Cerebral Palsy (sec. treas. 1956-58, pres. 1960), Internat. Cerebral Palsy Soc. (spl. mem.). Methodist. Clubs: Optimist Internat. (boy's work dir. 9th dist., 1956-57, gov. 9th dist. 1957-58, dir. Internat., 1958-59, v.p. Internat. 1958-59, pres. Internat. 1961-62, chmn. leadership Tng. com. 1967-70, chmn. achievement com. 1970-72), Masons, Shriners. Home: North Liberty, Iowa. Died Jan. 19, 1983.

REMENSNYDER, JOHN PAUL, business exec.; b. N.Y. City, Nov. 11, 1897; s. John L. and Emelia (Schmitz) R.; student univ. extension courses; m. Katherine Goodrich, May 17, 1922; children—Doris Brown, John Paul. Vice chmn. bd., dir. Heyden Newport Chem. Corp.; dir. Nuodex Products Co., Am. Plastics Corp. Mem. Am. Chem. Soc., Am. Inst. Chems., Soc. Chem. Industry. Reformed Ch. Clubs: Union League Drug and Chemical, Chemists, Pine Valley Golf. Home: Saugerties, N.Y. Died Sept. 30, 1981.

REMINGTON, JOHN WARNER, lawyer; b. Rochester, N.Y., Jan. 10, 1897; s. Harvey Foote and Agnes (Brodie) R.; A.B., U. Rochester, 1917, LL.D., 1960; LL.B., Harvard, 1921; student Rutgers U. Stonier Grad. Sch. Banking, 1937; m. Margaret Alcock, June 17, 1922; children—Edith R. (Mrs. Richard R. Haig), John L., Martha R. (Mrs. John A. King). Admitted to N.Y. bar, 1921; pvt. practice law, Rochester, 1921-30; asst. U.S. atty. Western dist. N.Y., 1924-25; with Lincoln Rochester Trust Co., 1930-79, exec. v.p., 1950-54, pres., 1954-61, chmn., 1961-62; partner Nixon, Hargrave, Devans & Doyle, 1963-73; counsel Remington, Gifford, Williams & Frey, Rochester, 1974-79; dir. Lincoln Nat. Life Ins. Co. N.Y., Superba Cravats, Inc., Alling & Cory Co., Hotel Waldorf-Astoria Corp., Gannett Newspaper Found., Rochester Investors, Inc.; chmn. adv. bd. Lincoln First Bank of Rochester. Pres. bd. Rochester Hosp. Fund. Served as lt. (j.g.) USN, 1917-19. Mem. Am., N.Y. bar assns., Am. Bankers Assn. (pres. 1959-60), U. Rochester Alumni Assn. (pres. 1947-48), Beta Gamma Sigma, Alpha Delta Phi. Clubs: Genesee Valley, Country (Rochester). Home: Rochester, N.Y. Died Aug. 23, 1979.

REMSEN, CHARLES CORNELL, JR., lawyer, indsl. property cons.; b. Newark, Dec. 3, 1908; s. Charles Cornell and Edna (Fisk) R.; E.E., Cornell U., Ithaca, N.Y., 1930; LL.B., George Washington U., 1934; m. Elizabeth Havens Atwood, July 1, 1933; children—Elizabeth Havens Remsen Fetz, Charles Cornell III, Derek Minor. Admitted to D.C. bar, 1934, N.Y. bar, 1941; examiner U.S. Patent Office, 1931-36; partner firm Dicke & Remsen, N.Y.C., 1936-46; with ITT, N.Y.C., 1942-75, asst. v.p., 1960-74, gen. patent counsel, 1961-73; v.p., dir. ITT Farnsworth Research Corp., 1960-75; v.p. Internat. Standard Electric Corp., 1961-74, ITT Industries, Europe Inc., 1964-75; partner firm Bierman & Bierman, N.Y.C., 1976-84. Mem. N.Y. Patent Law Assn., Electronics Industry Assn., Am. Belgian Assn. (dir. 1948-49), Nat. Fgn. Trade Council, Assn. Corporate Patent Counsel (sec.-treas. 1967-69), Internat. (U.S. patent com.), U.S. (patent adv. com.) chambers commerce, Pacific Indsl. Property Assn. (gov. 1973-84, pres. 1974), Alpha Tau Omega, Eta Kappa Nu. Episcopalian. Clubs: Cornell (N.Y.C.); Cosmos (Washington). Home: New Vernon, N.J. Died June 14, 1984; interred Basking Ridge, N.J.

RENAULT, MARY (LIT. PSEUDONYM FOR MARY CHALLANS), writer; b. London, Eng., Apr. 9, 1905; d. Frank and Mary Challans; M.A., St. Hugh's Coll., Oxford, Eng. Nurse, Radcliffe Infirmary, Oxford, 1933-45. Author: Promise of Love, 1938; Kind are Her Answers, 1940; The Middle Mist, 1942; Return to Night, 1945; North Face, 1948; The Charioteer, 1953; The Last of the Wine, 1956; The King Must Die, 1958; The Bull from the Sea, 1962; The Mask of Apollo, 1966; Fire from Heaven, 1969. Fellow Royal Soc. Lit. (Eng.). Mem. Progressive Party of South Africa. Home: Cape Town, South Africa. Died Dec. 13, 1983.

RENEKER, ROBERT WILLIAM, diversified industry executive; b. Chgo., Aug. 4, 1912; s. William Turner and Mary Ethel (Gilmour) R.; Ph.B., U. Chgo., 1933; spl. course Harvard, 1954; m. Eva Elizabeth Congdon, Mar. 2, 1935; children—William Carl, David Lee. With purchasing dept. Swift & Co., Chgo., 1934-44, asst. office of v.p. charge purchasing, 1944-46, tech. product sales, 1946-50, asst. in office of pres., 1950-55, 1955-64, pres., 1964-73, chief exec. officer, 1967-73, also dir.; pres., chief exec. officer Esmark, Inc., 1973, chmn., chief exec. officer, 1973-77; dir. Continental Ill. Bank, Gen. Dynamics Co., Chgo. Tribune, Trans Union Co., Jewel Cos., Inc., U.S. Gypsum Co., Lawter Chem., Inc., Morton Norwich. Nat. bd. dirs. Boy Scouts Am.; bd. dirs. Mus. Sci. and Industry; chmn. bd. trustees U. Chgo. Mem. United Ch. Clubs: Chicago, Commercial, Economics, Mid-Am., Chgo. Sunday Evening. Home: Chicago, Ill. Died Apr. 27, 1981.

RENWICK, WILLIAM WALTER, government official; b. Marengo, Ill., Dec. 5, 1889; s. William Henry and Isana (Hance) R.; student Beloit (Wis.) Coll., 1 yr.; B.A., Columbia, 1911; m. Mildred Virginia Boller, Nov. 30, 1912; 1 child, Mildred Virginia (dec.). With R. R. Donnelley & Sons, Chicago, 1911-12; with Nat. Cash Register Co., at Dayton, O., and in S. America and Argentina, 1912-18; connected with Nat. City Co., New

York, 1918-23; fiscal representative Republic of El Salvador, having control of customs, since 1923; mem. Kemmerer Commn. for reorganization of finances of Republic of Chile, 1925; head of commn. for reorganization of budget, accounting and banking legislation of Republic of El Salvador, 1925-26; consultant to Republic of Guatemala on customs legislation, 1927; mem. Kemmerer Commn. for Reorganization of Finances, Republic of Colombia, 1930; mem. El Salvador Commn. for Orgn. Nat. Mortgage Bank, 1931, Powell Commn. for formation of El Salvador Reserve Bank, 1934; pres. Com. of Economic Coordination in charge of Priorities and Price Control, El Salvador, from 1941. Dir. Social Betterment corp. since 1943. Mem. Beta Theta Pi, Delta Sigma Rho. Baptist.†

RESA, ALEXANDER JOHN, ex-congressman; b. Chicago, Ill., Aug. 4, 1887; s. William Frederick and Agnes (Bodden) R.; student St. Joseph's Coll., Kirkwood, Mo., 1904-08; LL.B., John Marshall Law Sch., Chicago, 1911; married Irene Mary Deegan, September 24, 1945. Law clerk, 1909-11; admitted to Illinois bar, 1911; engaged in pvt. practice of law, 1911-37; head appeals div. Law Dept. City of Chicago, 1937-40, head pub. improvements div., 1940-44; mem. faculty, John Marshall Law Sch., 1918-42. Mem. 79th Congress (1945-47), 9th Ill. Dist. Democrat. Club: Law (Chicago). Author: Essentials of Practical Logic. Home: Evanston, Ill. †

RETTGER, BENEDICT VINCENT, rector; b. St. Mary's, Pa., Apr. 3, 1889; s. Charles and Mary (Bender) R.; B.A., Belmont Abbey Coll., Belmont, N.C., 1910; M.A., Villanova (Pa.) Coll., 1925. Ordained priest R.C. Ch., 1914; served as priest and teacher, 1914-27; headmaster Benedictine High Sch., Richmond, Va., 1927-29; rector Belmont Abbey Coll. from 1932, also dir. Kiwanian (v.p., dir.). Home: Belmont, N.C. †

REULING, JAMES R., physician; b. Muscatine, Ia., June 1, 1889; s. J. Risley and Olive (Ewing) R.; student Phillips Exeter Acad., 1908-10; M.D., Jefferson Med. Coll., 1914; post grad., U. of Pa., 1920-21; m. Roberta Buttles, Aug. 5, 1933. Interne French Hosp., San Francisco, 1914-15; sr. house phys., City and County Tuberculosis Hosp., San Francisco, 1915-16, chief resident, 1916-17; clin. prof. med. N.Y. Med. Coll. from 1946; dir. medicine Queens Gen. Hosp., Jamaica, N.Y., 1945-53, now cons. physician; cons. phys. Flushing Hospital, Triboro Hosp., Rockaway Beach and Long Beach hospitals; pvt. practice medicine, Bayside, 1921-55; v.p., dir. Bayside Nat. Bank, 1938-53. Member medicial adv. com. national A.R.C. Served as lt. M.C., USN, 1915. Fellow Am. College Physicians; mem. Nat. Tb Assn. (pres. 1947-48), Am. Trudeau Soc., A.M.A. (past trustee, past speaker Ho. Dels.), N.Y. State Med. Soc. (past treas.), Queens County Med. Soc. (past pres. and chmn. bd. trustees), N.Y. Acad. Med. Am. Legion, Mason. Home: Windermere, Fla. †

REXROTH, KENNETH, author, critic, painter; b. South Bend, Ind., Dec. 22, 1905; s. Charles Marion and Delia (Reed) R.; m. Andree Dutcher, 1927 (dec. 1940); m. Marie Kass, 1940 (div. 1948); m. Marthe Whitcomb, 1949 (div. 1961); children—Mary, Katharine; m. Carol Tinker, 1974. Student pub. schs.; studied, New Sch., Art Students' League, Art Inst. Chgo. San Francisco corr. The Nation, 1953-68; columnist San Francisco Examiner, 1960-68; co-founder San Francisco Poetry Center; spl. lectr. U. Calif. at Santa Barbara. Exhibited one-man shows, Los Angeles, Santa Monica, Calif., N.Y.C., Chgo., Paris, San Francisco; creative writer prose and poetry.; (Eunice Tietjens award Poetry mag., Shelly Meml. award Poetry Soc. Am., William Carlos Williams award), 1975 (others); Author: In What Hour, 1940, The Phoenix and the Tortoise, 1944, The Signature of All Things, 1949, The Art of Worldly Wisdom, 1949, The Dragon and the Unicorn, 1952, 100 Poems From the Japanese, 1954, 100 Poems from the Chinese, 1956, 30 Spanish Poems, 1956, Thou Shalt Not Kill; poems In Defense of the Earth, 1956, 100 Poems From the Greek and Latin, 1959, The Bird in the Bush; essays, 1959, Assays, 1962, The Homestead Called Damascus, 1962, Natural Numbers; poems, 1965, An Autobiographical Novel, 1966, Complete Collected Shorter Poems, 1966, Beyond the Mountains; plays, 1966, Classics Revisited, 1968, Collected Longer Poems, 1968, Love and The Turning Year: 100 More Poems from the Chinese, 1969, Poems of Pierre Reverdy, transl, 1969, The Alternative Society essays, 1970, With Eye and Ear; essays, 1970, American Poetry in the 20th Century, 1971, Sky Sea Birds Trees Earth House Beasts Flowers, 1971, The Elastic Retort, 1973, New Poems, 1974, Communalism From Its Origins to the 20th Century; history, 1975, others.; Contbr. poems, articles to various mags.; Translator: 100 French poems, 1971, (with Ling Chung) The Orchid Boat: The Women Poets of China, 1973, 100 More Poems from the Japanese, 1976, (with Ikuko Atsumi) The Silver Swan, 1977, On Flower Wreath Hill, 1977, The Poems of Marichiko, transl, 1977, Selected Poems of Shiraishi Kazuko, transl, 1977, The Morning Star, 1979, (with Ling Chung) The Complete Poems of Li Ch'ing Chao, 1979. Recipient Commonwealth Club medal; Longview award; Chapelbrook award; Nat. Acad. award; Guggenheim fellow, 1948-49; Amy Lowell fellow, 1958; Fulbright sr. fellow in Japan, 1974-75; Nat. Endowment Arts grantee, 1977. Home: Santa Barbara, Calif. Died June 7, 1982.

REYNOLDS, CHARLES AUGUSTUS, investments; b. Brooklyn, N.Y., April 7, 1887; s. George William and Mary Frances (Peverelly) R.; student Boys High Sch., Brooklyn, 1903-07; m. Imogene R. Kelly, of Brooklyn, June 23, 1914; children—Charles Augustus, Regina Frances. With S.B. Chapin & Co., 1907-13, Colgate, Parker & Co., 1913-20, W. A. Harriman & Co., 1920-23; v.p. Blair & Co., Inc., 1923-30; exec. v.p. Gen. Outdoor Advertising Co., 1930-32; with Brooklyn Daily Eagle, 1932, chmn. bd. trustees and business mgr., 1932-34; with F. S. Moseley & Co. from 1935. Clubs: Union League (New York), Ox Ridge Hunt (Darien, Conn.). Home: Darien, Conn. †

REYNOLDS, CHARLES NATHAN, educator; b. Harper, Kan., Jan. 12, 1889; s. Nathan D. and Elleanor (Arthur) R.; A.B., U. of Ore., 1913, A.M., 1923; Ph.D., Stanford, 1927; m. Sarah Angeline Shaver, June 25, 1915; children—Carl Nathan, Donald Kelly. Instr. sociology U. of Ore., 1923-25, acting prof. sociology summer sessions, 1927, 1929-33; instr. economics Stanford, 1925-27, also. prof. sociology, 1929-34, prof. sociology, 1935-49, prof. sociology and anthropology from 1949; prof. economics and head dept. U. of Hawaii, 1927-28; vis. prof. sociology U. of Mich., summer 1935. Sr. social sci. analyst U.S. Br. Agrl. Economics, W.L.B., 1944-45. Mem. Am. and Pacific (pres. 1936) sociol. socs., Am. Acad. Polit. and Social Sci., Am. Assn. U. Profs., Phi Beta Kappa, Phi Alpha Delta, Phi Delta Kappa, Delta Tau Delta. Author chpt. VIII of Symposium, Social Problems and Social Processes (editor Emory S. Bogardus), 1932; also articles in profl. jours. Home: Stanford, Calif. †

REYNOLDS, EARLE HAY, banker; b. Hastings, Neb., May 13, 1887; s. George McClelland and Elizabeth (Hay) R.; Ph.B., Sheffield Scientific Sch. (Yale), 1909; m. Mary Scudder, of St. Louis, Mo., Jan. 20, 1915. Began with South Side State Bank, Chicago, 1909; with Peoples Trust & Savings Bank of Chicago, 1910-32, pres. 1913-32. Republican. Presbyn. Home: Chicago, Ill. †

REYNOLDS, EDWARD STORRS, pathologist; b. Orange, N.J., Dec. 3, 1928; s. Edward Storrs and Jean MacBean (Hadden) R.; m. Elizabeth Ann Gilliatt, June 22, 1950; children—Jean Elizabeth, Peter Morgan, William Storrs, Margaret Alice. B.A., Williams Coll., 1950; M.D., Washington U., St. Louis, 1954. Intern Peter Bent Brigham Hosp., 1954-55, chief resident in pathology, 1955-56, asst. in pathology, 1961-63, assoc., 1963-70, sr. asso., 1970-76; postdoctoral research fellow Peter Bent Brigham Hosp. and Harvard U., 1956-59; instr. Harvard U. Med. Sch., 1962-65, asst. prof. pathology, 1965-71, assoc. prof., 1971-76; prof., chmn. dept. pathology U. Tex Med. Br., Galveston, 1976-83; mem. bd. sci. counselors Nat. Inst. Environ. Health Sci. Contbr. numerous articles on chem. mechanisms of cellular injury, renal transplantation and other topics in field to profl. jours. Scoutmaster Minuteman council Boy Scouts Am., 1965-74. Served with M.C. U.S. Army, 1959-61. Recipient Research Career Devel. award NIH, 1966-76; NRC-Nat. Acad. Sci. nat. research fellow, 1957-59. Mem. Am. Assn. Pathologists, Am. Soc. Pharmacology and Exptl. Therapeutics, Soc. Toxicology, Biophys. Soc., Am. Soc. Cell Biology, AAAS, Tex. Med. Assn., Tex. Soc. Pathologists. Unitarian. Home: Galveston, Tex. Died Nov. 12, 1983.

REYNOLDS, EDWIN LOUIS, lawyer; b. Chevy Chase, Md., Apr. 13, 1901; s. Edwin Clark and Julia Vincenze (Solyom) R.; m. June Cooper, Oct. 26, 1929; 1 dau., Dorothy Holly. C.E., Lehigh U., 1922; LL.B., George Washington U., 1927. Bar: D.C. bar 1928, of, U.S. Ct. of Appeals bar 1928, of, Dist. Ct. of D.C 1928, of, U.S. Ct. of Custom and Patent Appeals 1928, of. Asst. examiner U.S. Patent Office, 1922-29, prin. examiner, 1939-40, law examiner, 1940-49, solicitor, 1949-55; chief tech. adviser U.S. Ct. Customs and Patent Appeals, 1955-61; first asst. commr. patents, 1961-69; mem. firm Newton Hopkins and Ormsby, Atlanta; asso. prof. patent law Georgetown U., 1950-61. Mem. Order of Coif. Home: Greenville, SC.

REYNOLDS, FRANK, news correspondent; b. East Chicago, Ind., Nov. 29, 1923; s. Frank James and Helen (Duffy) R.; m. Henrietta Mary Harpster, Aug. 23, 1947; children—Dean, James, John, Robert, Thomas. Student, Ind. U., Wabash Coll. With sta. WJOB, Hammond, Ind., 1947-50, WBKB-TV, Chgo., 1950, WBBM-CBS, Chgo., 1951-63; corr. ABC, Chgo., 1963-65, Washington corr., 1965-78; chief anchorman World News Tonight, ABC, 1978-83; Lectr. Council Fgn. Relations. TV documentaries Latin Am, VietNam, Africa, Middle East. Served with AUS, 1943-45, ETO. Recipient George Foster Peabody award, 1969. Mem. Chgo. Council Fgn. Relations. Club: Nat. Press (Washington). Address: New York, N.Y. Died July 20, 1983.

REYNOLDS, HENRY GRADY, lawyer; b. near Montevallo, Ala., Jan. 11, 1889; s. Lewis Henry and Dora (Marshall) R.; student Marion (Ala.) Mil. Inst., 1906-07; LL.B., U. of Ala., 1912; m. Estella Morgan, Sept. 10, 1914; children—Grady (U.S. A.A.F.; killed in action over France, Dec. 31, 1943), Morgan. Admitted to Ala. bar, 1912. Practiced at Clanton until 1924; U.S. dist. atty. Middle Dist. of Ala., 1924-31; mem. Reynolds & Reynolds, Clanton, from July 1, 1931. County treas. Chilton County, Ala., 1918-21. Chmn. Rep. Exec. Com., 4th Congl. Dist., Ala., 1920-24. Mem. Am. and Ala. State bar assns., Bar Assn. 19th Judicial Circuit of Ala., 1938-39 (pres.), Sigma Alpha Epsilon. Republican. Presbyterian. Mason (Shriner), Woodman of the World. Club: Exchange Luncheon. Home: Clanton, Ala. †

REYNOLDS, HEWITT, educator; b. Cumberland, Md., July 4, 1888; s. De Warren Hewitt and Sally Ann (White) R.; grad. Allegany County Acad., Cumberland, Md., 1905; A.B., Princeton, 1909, A.M., 1912; grad. study Harvard Law Sch., 1910-11; m. Annie Else Breuer, of Buffalo, N.Y., Sept. 6, 1922; children—John, Anton H. Teacher public schools, 1910-11, pvt. schools, Washington, D.C., 1911-13, Columbus, O., 1913-14, Samarcand, N.C., 1914-18; asso. headmaster, Marienfeld Sch., Samarcand, 1916-18; with Deane Sch., Santa Barbara, Calif., from 1919, headmaster from 1920, also sec. and treas. Attended R.O.T.C., Camp Zachary Taylor, Louisville, Ky., 1918. Republican. Episcopalian. Clubs: Princeton Charter, Valley Club of Montecito. Home: Santa Barbara, Calif. †

REYNOLDS, JOHN TODD, educator, surgeon; b. Dwight, Ill., Sept. 26, 1909; s. Peter J. and Mary (Todd) R.; B.S., U. Ill., 1930, M.S., M.D., 1932, grad. tng. pathology, 1932. Intern Cook County Hosp., Chgo., 1933-34; resident surgery U. Ill. Research and Ednl. Hosp., 1935-38; emeritus prof. surgery U. Ill. Coll. Medicine, 1977-81, Rush Med. Coll., 1979-81; attending surgeon Presbyn-St. Luke's Hosp., Chgo., 1952, Research and Ednl. Hosp., 1952-81. Diplomate Am. Bd. Surgery. Mem. Soc. Univ. Surgeons, Am., Western, Pan-Pacific surg. assns., Central, Chgo., Internat. surg. socs., Kansas City Anatomical Soc. (hon.), Inst. Medicine Chgo., A.C.S., So. Mich. Acad. Medicine (hon.), Am., Chgo. heart assns., Miss. Valley, Chgo., Ill. med. socs., Pan-Am. med. assns., Soc. Surgery Alimentary Tract, Warren H. Cole Soc., Cardiovascular Surgeons Club. Clubs: Tavern, University (Chgo.). Author papers in field. Home: Chicago, Ill. Died Jan. 24, 1981.

REYNOLDS, JULIAN LOUIS, business exec.; b. Winston-Salem, N.C., May 3, 1910; s. Richard S. and Julia Louise (Parham) R.; student Wharton Sch. of Finance, U. Pa., 1928-29, Duke, 1929-30; LL.D., U. Ark., 1956; m. Glenn Parkinson, Jan. 25, 1941; children—Glenn Parkinson (Mrs. Martin). With Reynolds Metals Co., Richmond, Va., 1931-83, now exec. v.p., dir.; mgr. export div., 1934-39, mgr. seal and label div., 1939-40, v.p. and gen. sales mgr., 1940-48, v.p. in charge operations, 1948-56, exec. v.p., 1956-59, dir., 1936-83; chmn., chief exec. officer Reynolds Internat., Inc., 1959-83; v.p. Eskimo Pie Corp., 1942-53, pres., 1953-83, also dir. Presbyterian. Clubs: Commonwealth, Country of Va. (Richmond); Athletic (N.Y.C.). Home: Richmond, Va. Died Nov. 18, 1983.*

REYNOLDS, SAMUEL ROBERT MEANS, anatomist, physiologist; b. Swarthmore, Pa., Dec. 9, 1903; s. Walter Doty and Elizabeth Brown (Means) R.; A.B., Swarthmore Coll., 1927, M.A., 1928, D.Sc. (hon.), 1950; Ph.D., U. Pa., 1931; Dr. honoris causa, U. Catolica de Chile, 1950; Prof. honoris causa, Fac. Med. Montevideo; L.H.D., Loyola U., Chgo., 1969; m. Mary Elizabeth Curtis, Aug. 18, 1931; children—Nancy Tupper, Harriet Jeffers (Mrs. Fred C. Clark). NRC fellow Johns Hopkins Med. Sch. and dept. embryology Carnegie Inst. of Washington, Balt., 1931-32; Guggenheim fellow U. Rochester Sch. Medicine and Dentistry, 1937-38, Oxford U., Eng., 1950-51; Commonwealth Fund fellow, Central and S. Am., 1965; instr. physiology Western Res. U., Cleve., 1932-33; instr. to asso. prof. physiology L.I. Coll. Medicine, 1933-41; physiologist dept. embryology Carnegie Inst., 1941-55, acting dir. dept. embryology, 1952-53; prof., chmn. dept. anatomy U. Ill. Coll. Medicine, 1956-69, prof. emeritus, 1969-82. Lectr. obstetrics Johns Hopkins, 1941-56; vis. prof. Montevideo, 1950, 55, 65, 67, Recife, 1955; vis. prof. obstetrics and gynecology U. Calif. at Los Angeles, 1965; Holmes lectr. Univ. Coll., London, 1951, also U.S., Can., Belgium, France; cons. developmental biol. tng. com. USPHS, 1958-61; cons. heart research com. NIH, 1959-60; chmn. Microcirculatory Soc., Inc., 1957-58. Served as aviation physiologist, maj. A.C., U.S. Army, 1942-45. Fellow AAAS, N.Y. Acad. Sci., Am. Gynecol. Soc. (hon.), Am. Coll. Obstetrics and Gynecology (hon. asso. fellow); mem. Am. Physiol. Soc., Am. Assn. Anatomists (2d v.p. 1962-64), Soc. Exptl. Biol. Medicine (mem. council 1955-56), Harvey Soc. N.Y., Am. Soc. Naturalists, Mil. Order World Wars, Soc. Mayflower Descs., Phi Beta Kappa Assos., Phi Sigma Kappa, Sigma Xi, Phi Beta Kappa; hon. mem. numerous U.S. and fgn. biol., gynecol. socs. Author: Physiology of Uterus and Clinical Correlations, 1939, rev. edits., 1949, 65; Physiological Bases of Obstetrics and Gynecology, 1952; Clinical Measurement of Uterine Forces, 1954; also many other publs. in physiology, anatomy, obstetrics, gynecology, and related fields. Home: Doylestown, Pa. Died Sept. 25, 1982.

REYNOLDS, WILLIAM G., metal co. exec.; b. Bristol, Tenn., 1913 Formerly v.p., now exec. v.p research and devel. Reynolds Metals Co.; also dir., mem. exec. com.; pres., dir. Reynolds Internat.; dir. Reynolds Alloys Co., U.S. Foil Co., Caribbean S.S. Co., Eskimo Equipment Co., Reynolds Jamaica Mines, Reynolds Internat. of Can., Ltd., Reynolds Sales Co., Reynolds Corp., Reynolds Mining Corp., Eskimo Pie Co., Richmond Radiator Co., Reynolds Aluminum Co. Recipient ·Advancement of Research medal Am. Soc. for Metals, 1965. Home: Richmond, VA. *

RHAME, FRANK PHIPPS, business exec.; b. Bellmore, N.Y., Oct. 12, 1887; s. William and Mary Elizabeth

(Foote) R.; M.E., Cornell, 1909; m. E. May S. Davis, Oct. 12, 1911; children—William Thomas, Sophie May (Mrs. John E. Mitchell, Jr.). Mech. engr. Pa. R.R., 1909-16; engring. examiner Municipal Civil Service Commn., New York, N.Y., 1916-18; sales engr. Lunkenheimer Co., Cincinnati, O., 1919-40, vice pres., sales engring., 1940-44, asst. gen. mgr., 1944, 1st vice pres. and gen. mgr., 1944-45, pres. and gen. mgr. from 1945, dir. from 1944. Dir. Central Trust Co., Cincinnati. Trustee Christ Hosp., Cincinnati. Served as 1st lt., capt., major ordnance dept., U.S. Army, 1918-19. Mem. Am. Soc. Mech. Engrs., Soc. Advancement Management, Engrs. Soc. of Cincinnati, Sigma Alpha Epsilon. Republican. Conglist. Clubs: Cornell (New York); Cornell of Southern Ohio, University, Queen City, Rotary (Cincinnati); Wyoming (O.) Golf. Home: Cincinnati, Ohio. †

RHEINSTEIN, ALFRED, constrn. co. exec.; b. Wilmington, N.C., Mar. 19, 1889; s. Frederick and Adele (Dannenbaum) R.; C.E., Princeton, 1911; m. Katherine Sproehnle, Aug. 10, 1926; children—Frederic Robert, Katherine. Inspector H. H. Oddie, Inc., N.Y.C., 1911-14, gen. supt., 1913-14; pres. Rheinstein Constrn. Co., Inc., N.Y.C., 1914-37, from 39; chmn. Precast Bldg. Sections, Inc., from 1945. Chmn. N.Y. City Housing Authority, 1937-39; commr. dept. housing and bldgs., N.Y.C., 1939-39; dir. housing, N.Y.C., 1939; mem. facility review com., WPB, 1942-43; dir. Regional Plan Assn., Union Settlement, from 1940; trustee of Citizns Budget Committee. Trustee Mt. Sinai Hosp. Served as 1st lt., U.S. Army, 1918. Mem. West Side Assn. Commerce (dir.), Bldg. Contractors and Mason Builders Assn. (past pres.), Am. Soc. C.E., Archtl. League N.Y.C. Clubs: Engineers, Princeton, Century Country, Grolier, Century Association (N.Y.C.). Home: New York, NY. †

RHODEN, ELMER CARL, theatre exec.; b. Lemars, Iowa, May 15, 1893; s. Charles A. and Ellen J. (Johnson) R.; m. Hazel M. Schiller, May 5, 1920; children—Elmer Carl, Clark S.; m. Esther Burger Geyer, Apr. 6, 1971. Student, Omaha U., Nebr. U. With Gen. Film Co., Omaha, 1912-20; organized Midwest Film Distributors, 1920, mgr., until 1927; organized Midwest Theatre Co., 1927, pres., until 1929; div. mgr. Fox Midwest Theatres, Inc., 1929-54; pres. Nat. Theatres, Inc., 1954-58, chmn. bd., 1958-59, Commonwealth Theatres, Inc.; also dir.; pres. Rhoden Investment Co.; dir. City Nat. Bank & Trust Co.; owner ranches in, Calif., Mo. Bd. dirs. St. Luke's Hosp., Kansas City, Mo., Dinner Playhouse, Inc. Served as flying cadet U.S. Army, World War I. Recipient Look Film Achievement award, 1956. Mem. Phi Sigma Kappa. Episcopalian. Clubs: River (Kansas City, Mo.), Saddle and Sirloin (Kansas City, Mo.), Kansas City Country (Kansas City, Mo.); Rancheros Visitadores (Santa Barbara, Calif.); Palm Beach (Palm Beach, Fla.), Everglades (Palm Beach, Fla.); Bath and Tennis. Home: Kansas City, Mo. Died July 14, 1981.

RICE, DONALD BLAIR, president Kiwanis International; b. Ashland, Ore., Jan. 6, 1890; s. David Lyle and Ella (Dunn) R.; A.B., Univ. of Ore., 1914; m. Hazel Morine Tooze, Dec. 11, 1917. Business mgr. Oakland (Calif.) Bd. of Edn. Participated in Community Chest, ARC, Chamber of Commerce, Salvation Army, activities. Pres. Kiwanis Internat., 1943. Served as 1st lt. 63d Inf., U.S. Army, World War I. Mem. Beta Theta Pi, Sigma Delta Chi, Am. Legion. Mason (Shriner), Elks. Republican. Presbyterian. Clubs: Oakland Forum, Claremount Country. Home: Oakland, Calif. †

RICE, FRANCIS OWEN, prof. of chemistry; b. Liverpool, Eng., May 20, 1890; s. James and Mary (Bryne) R.; B.Sc., Liverpool (Eng.) Univ., 1914, M.Sc., 1912, D.Sc., 1916; m. Katherine Kempner, May 23, 1930; children—Monica Ellen, Cecilia Joan. Came to U.S., 1919. Instr. in chemistry, New York U., 1919-20, asst. prof., 1920-24; asso. in chemistry, Johns Hopkins U., 1924-26, asso. prof., 1926-38; prof. and head of chemistry dept., Catholic U., Washington, D.C., 1938-59; research prof. Georgetown University, 1959, professor, chairman of the chemistry department, 1959-62; prin. research scientist radiation lab. chemistry dept. U. Notre Dame, South Bend, Ind., from 1962. Recipient Mendel Medal, 1935. Author: Mechanism of Organic Reactions, 1928; Aliphatic Free Radicals, 1935; Structure of Matter (with Edward Teller), 1949. Home: South Bend, Ind. †

RICE, JOHN STANLEY, U.S. ambassador; b. Arendtsville, Pennsylvania, January 28, 1899; son of Leighton H. and Florence Jane (Hartman) R.; B.S., Gettysburg College, Gettysburg, Pa., 1921; married to Luene Rogers, Nov. 10, 1934; 1 dau., Ellen Frances. Pres. Rice Trew & Rice Co., Biglerville, Pa., 1929-58; dir. Gettysburg Nat. Bank, State Container Co. State senator Pa., 1932-40, pres. pro tempore; mem. Pa. Liquor Control Bd., 1955-56; sec. of property and supplies Pa. Gov.'s Cabinet, 1956-57, secretary of the commonwealth, 1958-61; ambassador to the Netherlands, The Hague, from 1961. Chairman of trustees Gettysburg Coll. Dem. nominee gov. Pa., 1946. Chairman Democratic State Central Com., 1959-61. Served as col. USAAF, 1942-45. Decorated Legion of Merit. Mem. Am. Legion, Vets. Fgn. Wars, Phi Gamma Delta, Phi Beta Kappa. Lutheran. Elk, Mason. Club: Lions (Gettysburg) Home: Gettysburg, Pa. Died Aug. 2, 1985.

RICE, RAYMOND MAIN, physician; b. Bancroft, Nebr., Dec. 28, 1901; s. Eugene Taylor and Fannie (Dalton) R.; m. Charlotte Zurmuehlen, Sept. 1, 1931 (dec. 1973); children—Raymond Dalton and Ronald Bennett (twins); m. Adele Fehsenfeld, Dec. 15, 1973. Student, Coll. of Idaho, 1919-21; B.S., U. Nebr., 1924, M.D., 1929; LL.D. (hon.), Butler U., 1978. Intern Cleve. Municipal Hosp., 1929-30; practice of medicine, Council Bluffs, Iowa, 1930-36; instr. medicine U. Nebr. Coll. Medicine, 1930-36; with Eli Lilly & Co., Indpls., 1936-66, successively dir. med. div. research labs., asso. exec. dir. research, exec. dir. med. research, 1936-60, v.p. med. affiars, 1960-64, group v.p. sci. and medicine, 1964-66; v.p. Pharm. Mfrs. Assn. Found., 1966-73; asso. medicine Ind. U. Sch. Medicine, 1943-50, asst. prof. medicine, from 1950; cons. physician Marion County Gen. Hosp. Trustee Butler U., Community Hosp. of Indpls.; bd. govs. James Whitcomb Riley Found. Mem. AMA, Am. Rheumatism Assn., Am. Fedn. Clin. Research, AAAS, N.Y. Acad. Scis., Ind. Med. Assn., Marion County Med. Soc., Phi Rho Sigma. Episcopalian. Clubs: Columbia (Indpls.), Crooked Stick Golf (Indpls.), Meridian Hills Country (Indpls.); Imperial Golf (Naples, Fla.), Royal Poinciana Country (Naples, Fla.). Address: Indianapolis, Ind.

RICE, VICTOR ARTHUR, educator; b. Cleveland, O., May 4, 1890; s. Arthur and Frances (Mayo) R.; B.S., N.C. State Coll., 1916; M.Agr., Mass. State Coll., 1923; D.Agr., N.C. State Coll., 1946; m. Laura H. Bussells, June 23, 1921; children—Zipporah Frances, Mary Virginia. Teacher and administrator, Mass. State Coll. from 1916, prof. animal husbandry from 1919, dean sch. agrl., 1930-50. Member Alpha Zeta, Phi Kappa Phi, Kappa Alpha. Episcopalian. Author: Breeding and Improvement of Farm Animals. Home: Amherst, Mass. †

RICH, HENRY ARNOLD, director selective service for Utah; b. Ogden, Utah, Feb. 28, 1888; s. Fred Carmel and Emma (Arnold) R.; student U. of Utah, 1911-12; LL.B., Georgetown U., Washington, D.C., 1914, grad. study, 1914-15; m. Mary Elizabeth Summerhays, Oct. 1, 1913; children—Mary (Mrs. Edward B. Myers), Marjorie (Mrs. Chester C. Smith), Henry Arnold, Jeanne Summerhays. Admitted to bar, Dist. of Columbia, 1914, Supreme Court of Utah, 1915, Supreme Court of U.S., 1920; engaged in practice of law, Salt Lake City, Utah, 1915-40; sec.-treas. and dir., Utah Motor Park, Inc., dir. Utah Candy Co., Bullion Mining Co.; in active mil. service from 1940. Served with Utah Nat. Guard, 1903-05 and 1917-19; capt., Judge Adv. Gen.'s Dept., Utah N.G., 1927-28, major, 1928-40; with U.S. Army from 1940, assigned to administer Selective Service Law in State of Utah, acting state dir., 1940-42, dir. from 1942; promoted lt. col., 1942, col., Dec. 1942. Mem. Utah State Bar Assn., Gamma Eta Gamma. Club: Country (Salt Lake City). Home: Salt Lake City, Utah. †

RICHARD, AUGUSTE, civic worker; b. New York, N.Y., Jan. 28, 1890; s. Edwin A. and Alice B. (Moore) R.; ed. Pomfret (Conn.) Sch.; A.B., Harvard, 1912; m. Hetty Lawrence Hemenway, Aug. 21, 1917 (dec. Dec. 1961); children—Harriet Lawrence (Mrs. J. Crosbie Dawson), Elvine (Mrs. E.R. Rankine), Mark, Ian Bruce; m. 2d, Rita Conway Clark, Oct. 7, 1970. Began as an apprentice in the mfg. dept. and salesman, John H. Meyer & Co., 1912 (except for war service, 1917-19) until 1920; with Lawrence & Co. as dept. head and jr. partner, 1921-26; treas., dir. Ipswich Mills, 1927-28; v.p. The Spool Cotton Co., 1929, pres., dir., 1931-39; v.p., dir. Pacific Mills, 1940-42; dir. Bank of the Manhattan Co., resigned all positions to become chmn. Army and Navy Munitions Bd., Washington, 1942; partner F. Eberstadt & Co., investment bankers, 1944-54; pres., dir. 1060 Fifth Avenue Corp., mem. bd. dirs. Eberstadt Fund, Inc., also Chemical Fund, Inc. Pres., dir. Five Towns Community Chest, Cedarhurst, N.Y., 1939, dir., 1935-40; former v.p. and dir. Am. Mgmt. Assn., Mchts. Assn. N.Y.; dir. Manhattan Eye, Ear and Throat Hosp., from 1922, chmn., 1958-70; dir. Fountain House, from 1948, chmn., 1955-61; dir. Muscular Dystrophy Assns. Am., Manfred Sakel Found. Episcopalian. Republican. Clubs: Union, Harvard, Downtown Assn. (N.Y.C.); Maidstone; Connetquot River. Home: New York City, NY. †

RICHARDS, ALVIN, lawyer; b. Orlinda, Tenn., Aug. 11, 1890; s. John Marion and Martha Ellen (Samuel) R.; student Union U., Jackson, Tenn., 1905-06; m. Gertrude Giddings, May 6, 1914; children—Martha Adele (Mrs. J. H. Cullinan), John Giddings, Gertrude Virginia. Admitted to Okla. bar, 1911 and from practiced in Okla.; asst. div. atty. Pure Oil Co., Tulsa, 1918-24, div. atty. since 1924. Mem. Am. Bar Assn. (bd. govs. 1948-51), Mid-Continent Oil and Gas Assn., Kappa Sigma, Phi Delta Phi. Club: Tulsa. Home: Tulsa, Okla. †

RICHARDS, FRANK SELLS, lawyer; b. Salt Lake City, Nov. 30, 1890; s. Frank D. and Anna (Sells) R.; student pvt. schs., N.Y. and N.J.; student law, Columbia; m. Madeleine Cummings, Dec. 12, 1914 (dec.); 1 son, Joseph Tanner; m. 2d Natalie Van Order, August 5, 1949; one daughter, Natalie Virginia. Admitted to the bar of Utah, 1912, Calif., 1924; atty. Richards & Richards, Salt Lake City, 1920-24, Chapman, Trefethen, Richards & Chapman, Oakland, Calif., 1929-33, McCarthy, Richards & Carlson, Oakland, 1933-38, Donahue, Richards and Hamlin, 1938-47, Donahue, Richards, Rowell & Gallagher, 1947-60, Donahue, Richards & Gallagher, from 1960; general counsel Key System Transit Lines, from 1945, Hydraulic Dredging Co., Ltd.; general counsel, mem. of board of directors Lucky Stores, Inc., from 1949; asst. co. atty., Salt Lake Co., Utah, 1915-17; dist. atty. third judicial dist., Utah, 1917-20; atty. Oakland Soc. for Prevention Cruelty to Animals. Dir. Eastbay chpt. Nat. Safety Council, Am. Cancer Soc. (Cal. div.), Crippled Children's Soc. Alameda County, v.p., dir. Cerebral Palsy Found. of Alameda County. Mem. adv. bd. Coll. Holy Names. Mem. C. of C. (dir.), Am., Cal., Alameda County bar assns., Cal. Hist. Soc. Mason (32 deg.), Elk. Club: Claremont Country. Home: Piedmont, Calif. †

RICHARDS, HAROLD MARSHALL SYLVESTER, clergyman; b. Davis City, Ia., Aug. 28, 1894; s. Halbert Marshall Jenkin and Bertie Captolia (Sylvester) R.; grad. Campion Colo.) Acad.; A.B., Washington (D.C.) Missionary Coll., 1919; D.D., Andrews University, 1960; married to Mabel Eastman, April 14, 1920; children—Virginia Dale Elizabeth (Mrs. Walter Cason), Harold Marshall Sylvester, Kenneth Eastman Halbert, Justus Alfred Norman. Evangelist with father, 1911-13, Colo., Pa., 1913-15, Va., Md., summers 1916-19; ordained to ministry Adventist Ch., 1918; pastor, Ottawa, also Montreal, Can., 1919-26; tabernacle evangelist, Cal., 1926-38; daily radio program Tabernacle of the Air, So. Cal., 1930-37; speaker, dir. radio program Voice of Prophecy, Pacific Coast, 1937-42, Coast to Coast, 1942-69, networks other countries, 1953-85; mem. conf. com. Seventh Day Adventist Ch., Ont., Que., Central Cal., mem. gen. conf. radio and TV bd., mem. gen. conf. com., Washington, from 1953. Author: Revival Sermons, 1947; Radio Sermons, 1952; Indispensable Man, 1955; Promises of God, 1955; What Jesus Said, 1957; Feed My Sheep, 1958, also booklets on travels and religious subjects. Died Apr. 24, 1985.

RICHARDS, JOHN NOBLE, architect; b. Warren, Ohio, Apr. 23, 1904; s. Charles J. and Carrie May (Noble) R.; m. Norma Hayes, Apr. 12, 1938. B.Arch., U. Pa., 1931; D.Arts, Bowling Green State U., 1977. Registered architect, Ohio, Mich., Ind., W.Va., N.J., Mo., Pa. With Bellman, Gillett & Richards (architects and engrs.), Toledo, 1922-62, sr. partner, 1951-62, Richards, Bauer & Moorhead, 1962-76; univ. architect U. Toledo, Defiance Coll., Heidelberg Coll.; dir., chmn. bldg. com. Otis Avery Browning Masonic Meml. Complex.; Past pres. Art Interests, Inc.; past dir. Peoples Savs. Assn. Mayor of Ottawa Hills, 1965-71. Exhibited watercolors, Toledo, Phila., Kent State U., Bowling Green, Tiffin, Van Wert, Ohio; works include Student Union Bldg. and Mershon Auditorium, Ohio State U., MacGruder Meml. Hosp, Port Clinton, Ohio, Ritter Planetarium U. Toledo, Lebanon Correctional Instn, Med. Coll. Ohio, Toledo, Riverside Hosp, Toledo. Chmn. bd. Downtown Toledo Assos., Toledo Townscapes, from 1975; chmn. Toledo Arts Commn., 1965-71, spl. award, 1980; mem. Gov.'s Com. for Handicapped; adv. com. Ohio Arts Commn., 5th dist. Gen. Services Adminstrn.; float judge Tournament Roses Parade, 1975; past bd. dirs. Toledo Symphony Orch. Assn., Village Players, Toledo Conv. Bur.; adv. bd. Sch. Fine Arts U. Cin.; Life trustee YMCA; trustee Bowling Green State U. Found.; mem. president's council Bowling Green State U., 1978; mem. Pres.'s Council Toledo Mus. Art. Recipient Stewardson traveling scholarship to France, Italy, Germany, Eng.; Cret medal; Archtl. Soc. medal U. Pa.; Gold medal Architects Soc. Ohio, 1971; Paul Harris fellow Rotary Internat., 1979. Fellow AIA (dir. 1949-52, 1st v.p. 1956-58, pres. 1958-60, chancellor Coll. of Fellows 1968-70); hon. fellow Royal Inst. Canadian Architects, Philippine Inst. Architects; mem. Royal Inst. Brit. Architects, NAD (asso.), Mex. Soc. Architects, Nat. Sculpture Soc. (affiliate profl. mem.), Toledo Area C. of C. (pres. 1962, chmn. bd. 1964), Newcomen Soc., Archtl. League N.Y., Northwest Ohio Water Color Soc., Toledo Zool. Soc. (trustee), NAD (asso.), Tau Sigma Delta, Alpha Rho Chi, Phi Kappa Phi (hon.), Scarab. Episcopalian. Clubs: Mason (Toledo) (33 deg., Shriner, Jester), Rotarian. (Toledo), The Toledo (Toledo) (past pres.), Tile (Toledo) (pres.), Inverness Golf (Toledo). Home: Toledo, Ohio. Deceased.

RICHARDS, RICHARD KOHN, physician, educator; b. Lodz, Poland, June 16, 1904; came to U.S., 1935, naturalized, 1941; s. Stanley K. and Johann (Nachmann) R.; m. Erika Nord, Apr. 14, 1946; 1 dau., Evelyn Jean. Student, U. Hamburg, 1923-28, 29-30, M.D., 1931; student, U. Berlin, 1928-29. Intern St. George Hosp., Hamburg, Germany, 1930-31; asst. pharmacology U. Hamburg, 1930-33, asso. in medicine, 1934-35; research fellow Michael Reese Hosp., Chgo., 1935-36; research pharmacologists Abbott Labs., Chgo., 1936-57, dir. exptl. therapy, 1957-63, research adviser, 1963-66, limited pvt. practice, 1945-66; mem. med. faculty Northwestern U. Med. Sch., Chgo., 1945-72, prof. pharmacology, 1959-72; prof. pharmacology emeritus U. Hamburg, 1963-83; med. cons. St. Francis Hosp., Evanston, Ill., 1959-66; cons. prof. anesthesiology, medicine and pharmacology Stanford Med. Sch., 1967-83; cons. Palo Alto (Calif.) VA Hosp., 1966-83; cons. to research and govt. instns., univs. and hosps. Contbg. author: Therapeutics in Internal Medicine, 1952, Chemical Modulation of Brain Functions, 1973, also numerous articles.; Editor, contbr.: Clinical Pharmacology, 1968; editorial bd.: Rational Drug Therapy; bd. Archives: Internat. Pharmacodynamie. Recipient Research medal Internat. Coll. Anesthetists, 1938. Fellow A.C.P.; mem. Am. Pharmacol. Soc., Am. Physiol. Soc., AMA, Am. Soc. Anesthetists, Am. Soc. Clin. Pharmacology. Research in hypnotics, local anesthetics, exptl. and clin. toxicology and therapy, side effects of drugs, convulsive and anticonvulsive drug action Research in hypnotics, local anesthetics, exptl. and clin. toxicology and therapy, side effects of drugs, convulsive and anticonvulsive drug action. Home: Los Altos, Calif. Died Jan. 30, 1983.

RICHARDS, ROY, corp. exec.; b. Carrollton, Ga., Apr. 11, 1912; s. Thomas Wiley and Ida (Stovall) R.; B.S. in Mech. Engring., Ga. Inst. Tech., 1935; m. Alice Coyner Huffard, Jan. 25, 1958; children—Roy, James Case, Nancy Hufford, Lee Wiley, Elizabeth Kemper, Robin Anne, Laura Hudson. Propr. Richards & Assos., Inc., and predecessor, Carrollton, 1936-39, pres., 1935-85; pres. Roy Richards Realty Corp., Carrollton, 1950-85, Southwire Realty Co., Carrollton, 1950-85, Nat.- Southwire Aluminum Co., Hawesville, Ky., 1968-85, Richards Motor Co., Villa Rica, Ga., 1946-85, Southwire Internat. Corp., San Juan, P.R., 1952-85; chmn. bd. Peoples Bank, Carrollton, Southwire Co., Carrollton; dir. First Nat. Bank Atlanta, First Nat. Holding Corp., Atlanta, Ranchers Exploration & Devel. Corp., Albuquerque, Munford Inc., Atlanta. Bd. dirs. Carroll City-County Hosp. Authority, Carrollton, Tanner Meml. Hosp. Served to capt. AUS, 1942-45. Mem. Nat. Soc. Profl. Engrs. Episcopalian. Home: Carrollton, Ga. Died June 2, 1985.

RICHARDSON, ARTHUR BERRY, mfg. exec.; b. Rockland, Me., Mar. 20, 1889; s. Charles R. and Frances (Barlow) R.; U. Me., 1911, LL.D. (hon.), 1956; m. Annah Parkman Butler, May 27, 1914; children—Albert B., Frederick F., Charles A., Margaret A. Banking, 1910-14; joined Chesebrough Mfg. Co., Consol., mfrs. petroleum products, N.Y.C., fgn. service in Russia, China, Eng., 1914-36, asst. v.p., 1930-37, dir., from 1933, v.p. head officer, N.Y.C., 1937-44, pres., from 1944; chmn. bd. Chesebrough-Pond's Inc., 1955-61; bd. dirs. Civil Air Transport, Inc. Mem. bd. dirs. United Hospital Fund New York. Trustee Lenox Hill Hospital, N.Y.C. Republican. Protestant. Clubs: Royal Automobile (London, Eng.); Union, University (N.Y.C.). Home: New York City, NY. †

RICHARDSON, EDGAR PRESTON, b. Glens Falls, N.Y., Dec. 2, 1902; s. George Lynde and Grace (Belcher) R.; m. Constance Coleman, Sept. 15, 1931. A.B. summa cum laude, Williams Coll., 1925, D.H.L., 1947; student of painting, Pa. Acad. of Fine Arts, 1925-28; Dr. of Arts (hon.), Wayne U., 1951; Litt.D., Union Coll., 1957; Litt.D. U. Laval, 1955; D.H.L., U. Del., 1963; A.F.D., U. of Pa., 1966. Edn. sec. Detroit Inst. of Arts, 1930-33, asst. dir., 1933-45, dir., 1945-62, H. F. du Pont Winterhur Mus., 1962-66; Trustee Archives of Am. Art, 1954-74, H. F. du Pont Winterthur Mus., 1955-76, Library Co. Phila.; pres. Pa. Acad. of Fine Arts, 1968-70, Smithsonian Arts Commn., 1962-71, Nat. Portrait Gallery Commn., 1965-80. Author: Way of Western Art, 1939, American Romantic Painting, 1944, Washington Allston, A Study of the Romantic Artist in America, 1948, 67, Painting in America, 1956, rev. edit., 1966, A Short History of Painting in America, 1963, American Art, An Exhibition from the Collection of Mr. and Mrs. John D. Rockefeller 3d, 1976; Editor: The Art Quar, 1938-67; Editorial bd.: Magazine of Art, 1944-53, Art in America, 1953, Pa. Mag. History and Art, 1973-85; Editorial cons. Am. Art Jour, 1969-85. Decorated chevalier Legion of Honor France; chevalier Order of Leopold Belgium; Smithson medal Smithsonian Instn.; Disting. Service medal Am. Assn. Museums.; Benjamin Franklin fellow Royal Soc. Arts. Mem. Am. Philos. Soc., Hist. Soc. Pa. (v.p. 1975), Am. Antiquarian Soc., Colonial Soc. Mass. (corr.), Franklin Inn, Century Assn., Phi Beta Kappa. Home: Philadelphia, Pa. Died Mar. 27, 1985.

RICHARDSON, JOHN HAMILTON, aircraft company executive; b. Auburn, N.Y., July 30, 1922; s. John and Marion E. (Kuhn) R.; m. Dorothy Parmer, Dec. 4, 1944 (div. Nov. 1956); m. Barbara Nott, Dec. 1, 1956 (div. July 1966); m. Barbara Manning, July 20, 1966. Student, Princeton, 1941-43, U. W.Va., 1946, UCLA, 1950, MIT, 1959. With Hughes Aircraft Co., Culver City, Calif., 1948-83, v.p. mktg., 1960-61, v.p., asst. aerospace group exec., 1961-65, v.p. aerospace group, 1965-67, sr. v.p., 1967-69, sr. v.p. ops., 1969-76, sr. v.p., asst. gen. mgr., 1976-77, exec. v.p., 1977-78, pres., 1978-83. Served to 1st lt. USAAF, World War II. Decorated Air medal. Clubs: Los Angeles Country; Burning Tree (Bethesda, Md.); Balboa (Mazatlan, Mexico); Eldorado Country (Palm Desert, Calif.). Home: Los Angeles, Calif. Died Mar. 27, 1983.

RICHARDSON, LAWRENCE, railroad exec.; b. Shelbyville, Ky., July 11, 1889; s. Charles Cleves and Eliza Cordelia (Jones) R.; student U. Ill., 1908-09; M.E., Cornell, 1910; m. Dorothy Fox, June 4, 1917; children—Dorothy, Lawrence, Walker Scott. With Pa. R.R., 1907-17; staff U.S. R.R. Adminstrn., 1918-20; with Am. Steel Foundries, 1920-23, Whiting Corp., 1923-25, United Engrs. & Constructors, 1925-26; asst. to chmn. bd. B.&M. R.R., 1926-27, chief mech. officer, 1927-33, mech. asst. to v.p., 1933-47; asst. gen. mgr. N.Y. Susquehanna & Western R.R., 1947-50; advisor r.r. operation, Iran, 1949; pres., dir. Rutland R.R. from 1952; tech. advisor railroads, U.N., Yugoslavia, 1952. Mem. Am. delegation Allied Commn. on Reparations, Moscow, 1945. Served as ensign Aviation Corps, U.S.N., 1917-18. Mem. A.S.M.E. Episcopalian. Mason (Shriner). Clubs: Army-Navy (Washington); N.Y. Railroad, New England Railroad, Cornell (N.Y.C.); New England Transit. Home: Cambridge, Mass. †

RICHARDSON, RALPH DAVID, actor; born Cheltenham, Eng., 1902; s. Arthur and Lydia (Russell) R.; ed. Xaverian Coll., Brighton, Eng.; m. Muriel Hewitt, 1924 (died 1942); m. Meriel Forbes-Robertson, 1944; 1 son. Debut on stage, Brighton, 1921; toured in Shakespeare repertory, 1921-25; 1st London appearance, Haymarket Theatre, in Yellow Sands, 1925; played at Old Vic, 1930-32; first film appearance in The Ghoul, 1933; played Mercutio in Romeo and Juliet, in U.S., 1936; motion pictures include: Things to Come, Bulldog Drumond, Anna Karenina, The Heiress, Home at Seven, Sound Barrier, The Holly and the Ivy, Richard III, Our Man from Havana, 1950, Exodus, 1960; play The Last Joke, 1960; played in Cyrano de Bergerac, insp. in An Inspector Calls; played in Macbeth, Volpone, The Tempest, Shakespeare Festival Season, Stratford-on-Avon, 1952, The White Carnation, A Day by the Sea, Timon of Athens at Old Vic., 1956, Smiley, 1956, Waltz of the Torreordores, 1957, Flowering Cherry, 1958; A Novel Affair (film), 1956; Long Days Journey Into Night (film), 1961; School for Scandal (play), 1962; Woman of Straw (film), 1963; Six Characters in Search of an Author, 1963; Merchant of Venice, 1964; A Midsummer Night's Dream, 1964; Carving a Statue, 1964; Dr. Zhivago (film), 1965; Gordon of Khartoum (film), 1965; The Wrong Box (film), 1965; You Never Can Tell (play), 1965; The Rivals (play), 1966; toured in U.S., 1956, toured in South America in 1964. Created Knight, 1947. Clubs: Athenaeum, Beefsteak, Saville, Green Room. Address: London, England. Died Oct. 10, 1983.

RICHARDSON, WILLIAM ALAN, editor, pub., fin. exec.; b. Johannesburg, S. Africa, Oct. 9, 1907 (parents Am. citizens); s. Elliott Verne and Adelaide (Palmer) R.; student Harvard, 1927-30; m. Doris Ira Railing, Dec. 30, 1965; children by previous marriage—Nancy, Craig. Partner Richardson & Putnam, investment counsel, N.Y.C., 1932-33; editor Med. Econs., 1933-57; lectr. med. econs. L.I.U. Coll. Medicine, 1947-48, Yale U. Med. Sch., 1955; v.p. Soc. Bus. Mag. Editors, 1958; speaker, author, 1940-80; editor-in-chief Med. Econs., Hosp. Physician, also RN, 1957-69; v.p. Med. Econs. Book Div., Inc., 1960-69; dir. Heritage Fund, Inc., 1968- 69; pres., chmn. bd. Med. Econs., Inc., 1959-68; cons. Med. Econs., Inc., 1969-73; chmn. bd. Richardson & Roebuck, Inc., asset mgmt., Greenwich, Conn., 1970-71; pres. Richardson & Co., Vero Beach, Fla., 1971-80. Asso. mem. Conn. Med. Soc., Soc. Profl. Bus. Cons. Clubs: N.Y. Yacht (N.Y.C.); Watch Hill (R.I.) Yacht. Author: A Study of Britain's National Health Service, 1949. Editor: Personal Money Management for Physicians, 1969. Home: Vero Beach, Fla. Died Sept. 17, 1980.

RICHMOND, CARLETON RUBIRA, textile exec.; b. Boston, Feb. 13, 1887; s. Joshua Bailey and Josefa (Rubira) R.; A.B., Harvard, 1909; m. Helen Thomas Cooke, Sept. 28, 1912; children—Carleton R., Helen (Mrs. R. W. Ladd), Jean (Mrs. H. S. Stone), Joshua B. With Wellington Sears Co. from 1909, treasurer from 1932, chmn. bd., 1949-51; assistant treas., treas. Equinox Mill, Anderson, S.C., 1914-42, Anchor Duck Mill, Rome, Ga., 1928-42; treas., dir. Chattahoochee Valley Ry. Co., West Point, Ga., 1930-34, West Point Mfg. Co., 1930-64, pres., 1948-50, chmn. bd., 1950-51; treas., dir. Dixie Cotton Mills, LaGrange, Ga., 1930-49, treas. Columbus (Georgia) Manufacturing Company, 1947-49, director, 1947-51; director of Boston Mfrs. Mutual Fire Insurance Company, Macallen Co., Mutual Boiler Insurance Company of Boston, Inc., also Immanco, Inc. Chairman of Boston Regional Renegotiation Bd., 1952-53. Pres., trustee Boston Athenaeum; pres. Moses Pierce Williams House Assn.; past chairman John Carter Brown Library Assos. Served from 1st lt. to maj., U.S. Army, 1917-18. Mem. Am. Antiquarian Soc. (pres. 1963-65), Walpole Soc. (chmn. 1963-65), Society Mayflower Descendants, Colonial Society (treasurer from 1954), Bostonian Society, Massachusetts Historical Society, Little Compton (R.I.) Historical Society (president 1956-59), The Bibliog. Soc., Phi Beta Kappa. Clubs: The Country (Brookline); Union, Harvard, Odd Volumes (Boston); Grolier (N.Y.C.). Home: Milton, Mass. †

RICHMOND, LLOYD HEMINGWAY, personnel administrator; b. Flint, Mich., Apr. 11, 1909; s. Byron L. and Daisy S. (Hemingway) R.; student Flint Jr. Coll., 1927-29; LL.B., Washington and Lee U., 1932; m. Jane Elizabeth Roberts, Nov. 24, 1934; children—Lloyd Roberts, Gretchen Louise, Todd McDowell. Admitted to Mich. bar, 1932; spl. agt. in charge and adminstrv. asst. to dir. FBI, 1934-41; asst. personnel mgr. Marshall Field & Co., Chgo., 1944-47, mgr. employee relations, 1947-53, personnel mgr., 1953-55, v.p. personnel div., 1955-77. Mem. bd. dirs. Chgo. Crime Commn., Jr. Achievement Chgo. Mem. Alpha Chi Rho. Clubs: Kenilworth; Michigan Shores (Wilmette, Ill.); Exmoor Country (Highland Park, Ill). Home: Wilmette, Ill. Died Jan. 15, 1983.

RICHTER, RICHARD SCOTT, lawyer; b. Topeka, Aug. 3, 1894; s. William Henry and Ida May (Scott) R.; A.B., Washburn Coll., 1916; LL.B., Harvard, 1920; m. Kathryn Harford, Feb. 21, 1931; 1 son, William H. Admitted to Mo. bar, 1920, practiced in Kansas City; partner Lathrop, Koontz, Righter, Clagett, Parker & Norquist, Kansas City, 1928-82. Mem. Mo. Constl. Conv., 1943, 44. Mem. County Charter Commn., 1948. Mem. C. of C. (v.p., dir. 1953-54), Lawyers Assn. Kansas City (pres. 1948), Am., Mo., Kansas City bar assns. Clubs: University (pres. 1970); Kansas City Country. Home: Kansas City, Mo. Died Apr. 22, 1982.

RICKER, CHARLES HERBERT, clergyman; b. Providence, R.I., Sept. 10, 1890; s. Herbert Lawrence and Ida Frances (Bundy) R.; A.B., Brown U., 1913; S.T.B., Episcopal Theol. Sch., Cambridge, Mass., 1916; grad. study Gen. Theol. Sem., New York; m. Florence Ethel Smith, Apr. 29, 1919. Deacon, 1916, priest, 1917, P.E. Ch.; curate Grace Ch., Providence, R.I., 1916-17, St. George's Ch., N.Y. City, 1917-19; rector Christ Ch., Manhasset, L.I., New York, 1919-46; special Epsicopal missionary work from 1946; mem. faculty Gen. Theol. Sem. Dept. of Religious Edn.; chmn. Bd. of Religious Edn., Diocese of L.I.; chmn. Provincial Commn. of Religious Edn.; dean of Provincial Summer Sch.; dep. to Provincial Synod of N.Y. and N.J. from 1927; asst. sec. Provincial Synod, 1932-38, sec. from 1938; mem. Diocesan Council, 1930-32, and 1935-38; mem. Nat. Commn. on Coll. Work, chmn. Provincial Com. on Coll. Work; mem. Nat. Commn. on Youth; mem. L.I. Clerical League, Beta Theta Pi Fraternity, Clericus and The 22. Republican. Mason. Clubs: Hamilton, Crescent, North Hempstead Country. Home: Washington Depot, Conn. †

RIDDLE, CARL BROWN, clergyman, editor; b. Moore Co., N.C., Dec. 23, 1888; s. Kenneth Mack and Drucilla (Johnson) R.; Ph.B., Elon Coll., N.C., 1916; m. Susie Blanche Teague, Nov. 7, 1916. Worked way through high schs. and coll.; ordained ministry Christian Ch., 1914; editor The Christian Sun (official organ Southern Christian Conv.), 1916-22. Pres. Burlington Printing Co. Democrat. Club: Kiwanis. Author: College Men Without Money, 1914; (brochure) Trailing the Truth, 1914; (brochure) Thirty-Six, 1915. Home: Burlington, N.C. †

RIDDLE, JESSE HALE, economist; b. nr. Chatham, Va., Oct. 20, 1888; s. Nathan and Ida Matilda (Watson) R.; A.B., Davis and Elkins Coll., 1912; A.M., Princeton, 1915; m. Mary Lila Sinknet, Mar. 8, 1920; 1 dau., Rosamonde. Instr. economics, Dartmouth Coll., 1918-19; statistician, Fed. Res. Bank of New York, 1919-21; chief, div. of research and statistics, U.S. Treasury Dept., 1921-25; statistician and econ. adviser to gen. agent for reparations, Berlin, 1926-28; tech. expert at Young Conf. on Reparations and Allied Debts, Paris, 1929; exec. sec. and dir. of research, Fed. Res. System Com. Branch, Group and Chain Banking, 1930-33; economist for commn. on banking law and practice, Assn. of Res. City Bankers, 1933-35; econ. adviser, Bankers Trust Co., New York, 1934-45, vice pres. from 1945. Mem. Acad. of Polit. Science, Am. Econ. Assn., Am. Statis. Assn. Author: British and American Plans for International Currency Stabilization, 1944. Contbr. of articles to professional journals. Home: New York, N.Y. †

RIDDLE, JOHN INGLE, coll. pres.; b. Huntsville, Ala., June 27, 1890; s. James Matthew and Anna (Bradford) R.; student, Butler Training Sch., Huntsville, Ala., 1908-11; A.B., U. of Ala., 1912-16; M.A., Teachers Coll., Columbia U., 1926, Ph.D., 1937; m. Vera Esslinger, May 29, 1918. Teacher in rural schs., Madison County, Ala., 1911-12; instr., Blount County High Sch., Oneonta, Ala., 1916-17; prin., Cullman County High Sch., Ala., 1917-18; edn. dir., Camp Sheridan, Ala., 1918-19; prin. Etowah County High Sch., Attala, Ala., 1919-25; supt. city schs., Tuskagee, Ala., 1925-28; state supervisor of secondary edn., Montgomery, Ala., 1928-35; prof. edn. and dir. home study, Alabama Coll., Montevallo, 1935-43; pres. of Judson Coll. from 1943. Mem. Ala. Course of Study Com., Ala. Rural Sch. Survey Com., Ala. Assn. of Secondary Sch. Prins. (past pres.), Southern Association of Colls. for Women (past pres.), Southern Assn. of Baptist Colls. (past president), So. Bapt. Conv. (edn. commn. 1945-51), Pi Gamma Mu, Phi Delta Kappa, Mason. Woodmen. Baptist. Author: The Six Year Rural High School, 1937; contbr. to various mags. of religious edn., and spl. lecturer at summer assemblies. Address: Marion, Ala. †

RIDDLEBERGER, JAMES W., ambassador; born Washington, D.C., September 21, 1904; son Frank B. and Anne (Williams) R.; A.B., Randolph-Macon Coll., Ashland, Va., 1924; A.M., Georgetown U., 1926; student Am. Univ., 1926-27; m. Amelie Johanna Otken, Mar. 20, 1931; children—Christopher, Antonia, Peter. Asst. prof. internat. relations, Georgetown U., 1926-29; special expert, U.S. Tariff Comm., 1927-29; appt. for service officer and vice-consul of career, 1929-30; vice-consul at Geneva, 1930-35, consul 1935-36; 3d sec. of Am. Embassy, Berlin, 1936-37, 2d sec., 1937-41; with Dept. of State, Washington, D.C., 1941-42; chmn. com. on neutral trade, Bd. Econ. Warfare, 1942; 2d sec. of Am. Embassy, London, 1942-43, 1st sec., 1943-44; chief div. central European affairs, Dept. of State, Washington, D.C., 1944-47; counselor of embassy, chief polit. sect., Am. Mil. Govt., Berlin, Germany, 1947-50, acting political adviser to commander-in-chief U.S. Forces, Germany, 1949; polit. adviser to U.S. High Commr., Germany, 1949-50, E.C.A., Paris, 1950; apptd. career minister, 1950; dir. bureau of German affairs, state dept., 1952-53; ambassador to Yugoslavia, 1953-58; ambassador to Greece, 1958—. Dir. ICA, 1959—. Home: Woodstock, Va. Died Oct. 17, 1982.

RIDOUT, GODFREY, composer, educator; b. Toronto, Ont., Can., May 6, 1918; s. Douglas Kay and Amy Phyllis (Bird) R.; m. Freda Mary Antrobus, Aug. 5, 1944; children: Naomi (Mrs. Terrence Thomas), Victoria (Mrs. Terrence Kett), Michael. Student, Upper Can. Coll.,

Toronto, 1932-36, Toronto Conservatory of Music, 1937-39; grad. composition, U. Toronto, 1939-40; LL.D., Queen's U., Kingston, Ont., 1967. Mem. teaching staff Toronto Conservatory Music, 1940—; spl. lectr. music U. Toronto, 1948-61, asst. prof., 1961-65, asso. prof., 1965-71, prof., 1971-83, prof. emeritus, 1983-84. Composer, condr. scores, Nat. Film Bd., Ottawa, 1940-43, CBC, Toronto, 1941-85; prin. compositions Ballade for viola, string orch., 1938, Two Etudes for String Orch., 1946, Esther, dramatic symphony for soli, choir, orch., 1952, Cantiones Mysticae, Soprano and orch., 1953, The Dance, choir and orch., 1960, Pange Lingua, choir and orch., 1961, Fall Fair, orch., 1961, Cantiones Mysticae No. 2, soprano and orch., 1962, Cantiones Mysticae No. 3, baritone choir and orch., 1973, Jubilee, orch., 1973, Concerto Grosso, string orch. and piano, 1974, George III, His Lament, orch., 1976, The Lost Child, opera for TV, 1976, Concerto Grosso No. 2, brass quintet and orch., Ballade No. 2 for viola and string orch., 1980, No Mean City-Scenes for Childhood for orch., 1983; Comml. arranger, 1945-50; Compositions have been performed frequently in, N.Am., Europe, 1939-85. Recipient Centennial medal Govt. Can., 1967. Fellow Royal Canadian Coll. Organists (hon.); mem. Composers, Authors, Pubs. Assn. Can. (dir. 1966-73). Home: Toronto, Ont., Can. *

RIEFKOHL, FREDERIC LUIS, naval officer; b. Maunabo, Puerto Rico, Feb. 27, 1889; s. Luis and Julia (Jamieson) R. (brought to U.S., 1899); ed. Arroyo, Puerto Rico, St. Croix, Virgin Islands, Concord and Andover, Mass.; B.S., U.S. Naval Acad. (1st midshipman apptd. from Puerto Rico), 1911; grad. Naval War Col., 1934; m. Mary Scott Ferguson, 1916 (divorced 1926); m. 2d, Louisa Gibson Riley, Apr. 7, 1928. Commd. ensign U.S. Navy, 1912, and advanced through grades to rear adm., 1947; comdg. officer, U.S.S. Vincennes, Guadalcanal campaign, 1942; various duties at sea and shore stations during naval career; ret. from active service, Jan. 1, 1947. Awarded Navy Cross, World War I, Purple Heart, World War II. Mesito Naval 1st class (Mexico). Mem. U.S. Naval Inst. Episcopalian. Clubs: Army Navy (Washington); Yacht (New York City).†

RIEGER, ERNEST W., steel exec.; b. Erie, Pa., Dec. 25, 1889; s. William and Anna B. (Baumgardner) R.; student U. Chicago, 1907-09; M.E., Carnegie Tech., 1912; m. Elizabeth L. Williams, Mar. 23, 1915; children—James C., Robert E., William F. With Weirton (W. Va.) Steel Co. since 1915, v.p. charge engring. from 1936. Mem. Am. Iron and Steel Inst. Presbyn. Mason, Elk. Home: Bloomingdale, Ohio. †

RIGBY, HARRY, theatrical producer; b. Pitts., Feb. 21, 1925; s. Howard and Anne Halpin (Neely) R. Student, Haverford Sch., U. N.C. Co-producer play Make a Wish, John Murray Anderson's Almanac, Half A Sixpence, Hallelujah Baby, No, No, Nanette, Irene, Knock, Knock, I Love My Wife, Gorey Stories; co-producer, co-conceiver play Sugar Babies, 1979; adaptor musical comedy play Irene. Home: New York, N.Y. Died Jan. 17, 1985.

RIGG, HORACE ABRAM, JR., educator; b. Phila., Apr. 22, 1909; s. Horace Abram and Maud (Wynkoop) R.; A.M., Harvard, 1932; guest fellow Trinity Coll., Cambridge U., Eng., 1932, 33; student Ludwig-Maximillians Universitaet, Munich, Germany, 1932-33; student in Oriental studies U. Pa., 1934-35; Ph.D., Harvard, 1937, univ. fellow in philosophy, 1931-32, traveling univ. fellow in history, 1932-33; m. Ruth Bowman Lyman, Nov. 24, 1934; children—Alexandra (Mrs. John N. Samaras), Diana, Jonathan Lyman, Margaret R. Stewart, Peter Whitney (dec.). Asso. prof. history of religion Case Western Res. U., 1937-44; prof. history of religion, 1944-47, Severance prof. history of religion, 1947-65; chmn. dept. Bibl. lit. and history religion, 1937-58; research Harvard U., 1948-49, prehistoric cave research, France, 1956; prehistoric Bushmen studies So. Rhodesia, 1959, 61, 62; research asso. Carl Mackley Houses, Fed. Housing Project No. 1, Phila., 1933-34; co-ordinating editor history of religion, Ency. Americana, 1946-47. Spl. advisor Selective Service Bd. No. 41, Cleve., 1941-43; fgn. service Middle East sect. OSS, 1943-44. Mem. Archaeol. Inst. Am., Cleve. Soc. (past sec.-treas. and pres.), Am. Oriental Soc., Am. Soc. Ch. Hist., Am. Geog. Soc., Am. Soc. Bibl. Lit. and Exegesis, Cleve. Chamber Music Soc., Internat. Soc. African Culture (trustee). Editor, contbr. Bibl. dictionaries. Contbr. papers, monographs, and revs. to jours., ency. Home: Union, Maine. Died Dec. 25, 1978.

RIGGLEMAN, LEONARD, college pres.; b. Blue Spring, W.Va., Apr. 16, 1894; s. Samuel Creed and Harriet (Hamrick) R.; A.B., Morris Harvey Coll., Charleston, West Virginia, 1922; A.M., Southern Meth. Univ. 1924; D.D., Kentucky Wesleyan Coll., Winchester, Ky., 1933; LL.D., Davis and Elkins College, 1944, W.Va. Wesleyan Coll., 1944, Ohio State University, 1958, West Virginia University, 1962; m. Pauline Steele, Aug. 16, 1922; one daughter Roberta. Ordained to ministry of M.E. Ch. South, 1924; pastor Milton, W.Va., and part time instr. in history, Morris Harvey Coll., 1924-28; rural life specialist with agrl. extension div., W.Va. U., 1928-30; vice-pres. and head dept. religious edn., Morris Harvey Coll., 1930-31; pres. Morris Harvey Coll. 1931-83. Mem. board of trustees, Morris Harvey Coll.; dir. Y.M.C.A., Charleston. Mem. Kanawha Co. Pub. Library Bd.; pres State Ministers Conf. State W.Va.; mem. Gen. Bd. of Christian Edn. and pres. College sect. Ednl. Council, Bd. of Christian Edn., M.E. Ch., South, 1938; mem. W.Va. Farm Tenant Rehabilitation Com.; president Charleston Area Chs. 1948; president Assn. of Church-Related Colleges of West Virginia, 1941; member of Committee on Support of Churches in Spiritual Aims of Kiwanis Internat., 1941-44, 55-56; Gen. Conf. M.E. Ch., South, 1934 and 1938; mem. Northeastern Jurisdictional Conf., Meth. Ch., 1948-52, Gen. Conf. Meth. Ch., 1944, 56. Mem. West Virginia Chamber of Commerce (dir.), Theta Phi, Tau Kappa Alpha. Clubs: Kiwanis (pres. Huntington Club; dist. gov. W.Va. Dist., Charleston), Anvil, Executives. Author: (monograph) Significance of Rural Life in the South, 1934. Home: Charleston, W.Va. Died May 18, 1983.

RIGHTER, JAMES HASLAM, newspaper publisher; b. Phila., Sept. 1, 1916; s. James A. M. and Marie E. (Haslam) R.; divorced 1973; children—Edward B., Kate B.; m. Catherine M. Oehler, May 31, 1975. Student, U.S. Naval Acad., 1935-37, Drexel U., 1938-41. Sales engr. indsl. sales dept. Phila. Electric Co., 1939-41; with Buffalo Evening News, 1946-71, asst. bus. mgr., 1949-50, asst. treas., dir., 1950-56, pub., v.p., treas., dir., 1956-71; asst. treas. radio sta. WBEN, Inc., 1953-57, asst. sec., treas., dir., 1957-64, treas., sec., dir., 1964-71; mem. exec. com., dir. First Empire State Corp., Buffalo, Mfrs. & Traders Trust Co., Buffalo. Past chmn. adv. council Sch. Journalism, Syracuse U.; past pres. Buffalo Main St. Assn.; mem. bd. advisers Children's Hosp. Buffalo; past chmn. bd. trustees Villa Maria Coll., Buffalo; past chmn., life mem. council Buffalo Philharm. Orch. Soc.; trustee Forest Lawn Cemetery; hon. bd. dirs. Advt. Council N.Y.C.; bd. dirs., pres. Buffalo Naval and Servicemen's Park. Served from ensign to lt. comdr. USNR, 1942-46. Mem. N.Y. State Pubs. Assn. (past pres.), Navy League U.S. (past pres.), Niagara Frontier Council. Episcopalian. Clubs: Saturn (Buffalo), Buffalo Yacht (Buffalo) (hon.), Buffalo Country (Buffalo); Coral Beach (Bermuda). Home: West Amherst, N.Y. Died June 9, 1984.

RIGLEY, HAROLD TOWNSEND, union ofcl.; b. N.Y.C., July 2, 1913; s. William F. and Anna M. (Townsend) R.; m. Catherine C. Knoud, Aug. 26, 1946; children—Harold T., John, Robert. Student pub. schs., N.Y.C. Bus. rep. Consol. Edison Co., N.Y.C., 1930-55; nat. rep. Utility Workers Union Am., AFL-CIO, 1955-58; sec.-treas. Local Union, N.Y.C., 1958-62, pres., 1962-71, nat. pres., Washington, from 1971; mem. exec. bd. AFL-CIO. Mem. Pres.'s Com. Employment Handicapped, 1957-77; mem. exec. bd. Greater N.Y. council Boy Scouts Am., from 1970. Mem. Am. Arbitration Assn. (dir.). Democrat. Roman Catholic. Club: N.Y. Turner. Home: Jamesburg, N.Y. Deceased.

RINEY, ARTHUR HERBERT, petroleum co. exec.; b. Dodge City, Kan., Oct. 20, 1888; s. John T. and Mary Ann (McCarty) R.; B.S., U. of Kan., 1911; m. Margaret E. Lyons, Dec. 4, 1923; children—Joanne, Jeanne, Janet. Civil engr., Am. Lead & Zinc Co., Kansas City, Mo., 1911, with Brooks & Jacoby, 1911; draftsman and jr. engr., U.S. Engr. Office, 1911-17, engr. spl. reports and investigations, 1919; supt. constrn. Phillips Petroleum Co., Bartlesville, Okla., 1919-22, chief engr., 1922-38, v.p. in charge gen. engring. and constrn. from 1938. Served as capt. 28th Engineers A.E.F., 1917-19. Mem. Am. Soc. C.E., Am. Petroleum Inst., Okla. Soc. Profl. Engrs., Okla. C. of C., Am. Legion. Republican. Presbyn. Club: Hillcrest Country. Home: Bartlesville, Okla. †

RINGWOOD, GWEN PHARIS, author; b. Anatone, Wash., Aug. 13, 1910; m. John Brian Ringwood, 1939; children—Stephen Michael, Susan Frances Leslie, Carol Blaine, Patrick Brian. B.A., U. Alta., 1934; M.A., U. N.C., 1939; D.F.A., U. Victoria, 1981; LL.D., U. Lethbridge, 1982. Sec. to Elizabeth Sterling Haynes, dept. extension U. Alta., 1935. Author: plays Carolina Playmakers, Chapel Hill, N.C., 1937-38; Author: novel Younger Brother, 1950, Pascal, 1972; plays Still Stands the House, 1938, Dark Harvest, 1945, The Courting of Marie Jenvrin, 1951, Lament for Harmonica, 1960, Chris Axelson, 1939, The Jack and the Joker, 1945, The Drowning of Wasyl Nemitchuk, 1946, The Rainmaker, 1945, Widger, 1950, Stampede, 1946, The Deep Has Many Voices, 1966, The Stranger, 1970; librettos Look Behind You Neighbour, 1961, The Road Runs North, 1968; plays The Lodge, 1975, A Remembrance of Miracles, 1977, Stage Voices, 1978, Transitions I, 1978, The Collected Plays of Gwen Pharis Ringwood, 1982; numerous radio and TV plays for, CBC; contbr.: Best One Act Plays of 1939, 1940, American Folk Plays, 1939, International Folk Plays, 1949, Canadian Short Stories, 1952, Cavalcade of the North, 1958, Canada on Stage, 1960, Stories From Across Canada, 1966, Puerto Ricans Read in English, 1971, Sign Posts, 1974, Canadian Theatre Review, 1975, Ten Short Canadian Plays, 1975, The Magic Carpets of Antonio Angelini, 1979, The Sleeping Beauty and the Golden Goose, 1979, Mirage, 1979, Pasque Flower in Canada's Lost Plays, 1979, Kid's Plays, 1980, Can. Drama, fall 1979, fall 1980, Inquiry Into Literature, 1980; subject of: book Gwen Pharis Ringwood (Geraldine Anthony), 1981. Recipient Canadian drama award; Ottawa Little Theatre Workshop ann. Canadian playwriting competition prize for Lament for Harmonica, 1958. Mem. Canadian Theatre Centre., Can. Assn. Theatre History (hon.). Home: B.C., Can. Died May 24, 1984.

RIPLEY, GEORGE SHERMAN, boy scout executive; b. Hartford, Conn., Oct. 5, 1889; s. Clinton Beach and Clara Belle (Terry) R.; ed. high sch., New Haven, Conn., 2 yrs.; m. Lisla Buckland, Oct. 30, 1913. Draftsman, Factory Ins. Assn., 1907-13; engring. draftsman State Highway Dept., Conn., 1913-15; exec. sec. Boy Scouts of America, Hartford, from 1915. Sergt., 1st class, and sect. chief, Signal Corps, Conn. N.G., 3 yrs. Republican. Conglist. Club: Rotary. Sec. Poetry Club of Hartford. Author: Games for Boys, 1920; (pamphlets) Games for Boy Scouts, 1919; Mimetic Setting-up Exercises, 1919. Home: Hartford, Conn. †

RISH, LON M., business exec.; b. Canoe Ridge, Pa., July 6, 1889; s. John R. and Crissie (Tyger) R.; ed. pub. schs., Gipsy and Arcadia, Pa.; m. Minnie Houston Witt, Aug. 8, 1915; children—June (Mrs. Harman Woodward), Anne (Mrs. Robert J. Coakley). With coal co. store, Iselin, Pa., 1905-08; store mgr. Keystone (W. Va.) Coal and Coke Co., 1908-24; organized Clark Stores, Inc., 1920-28; co. merged with Bluefield Supply Co., 1928, pres. from 1931, also pres. 4 subsidiary cos., Clark Stores, Inc., Rish Equipment Co., Dixie Appliance Co., Counts Automotive Supply Co.; an organizer and sec. Elkhorn Valley Grocery Co., Keystone; dir. 1st Nat. Bank of Keystone, Flat Top Nat. Bank of Bluefield, Citizens Underwriters Agency. Mem. bd. deacons Coll. Av. Bapt. Ch., Bluefield. Mem. Bluefield C. of C. (past pres.), W.Va. State C. of C. (dir.) Republican. Baptist. Mason. Club: Bluefield Country (past pres.). Home: Bluefield, W.Va. †

RISHELL, CLIFFORD E., city ofcl.; b. Glenwood, Ia., Oct. 10, 1890; s. David and Catherine (Provost) R.; ed. pub. schs., Ia.; m. Marjorie Gray, Nov. 25, 1915; children—Robert C., Audrey (Mrs. Philip King). Painting and decorating contractor from 1923. Mem. council, City of Oakland, Calif., from 1947, mayor, 1949-53. Decorated: Order of Christopher Colon, Dominican Republic, 1951. Mem. U.S. Conf. Mayors, Am. Municipal Assn., Am. War Dads, Painting and Decorating Contractors Am., Am. Legion, League Calif. Cities, C. of C., Bay Area Council, Traveler's Aid Soc., Am. Fedn. Labor, Moose. Clubs: Athenian-Nile, Athens Athletic, Businessmen's Garden (Oakland). Home: Oakland, Calif. †

RISHER, JAMES FRANKLIN, ednl. adminstr.; b. Hampton, S.C., Nov. 26, 1889; s. Julius and Susie (Youmans) R.; B.Sc., The Citadel, 1911, LL.D., 1968; LL.D., Atlanta Sch. Law; m. Ella Ida McTeer, 1915 (dec.); children—James Franklin, Sarah Helen; m. 2d, Emma Jane Varn, Apr. 14, 1926; children—William Rhett, Lanning Parsons, Mary, Eugene Varn. Teacher pub. schs., Colleton County, S.C., 1911-12; supt. high school Smoaks, S.C., 1913-14, 1917-21, Ehrhardt, S.C., 1922-24; with Carlisle Sch., Bamberg, S.C., 1924-58, instr. until 1928; headmaster, 1928-58; pres. Carlisle Mil. Sch., Bambarg, also Camden (S.C.) Mil. Acad., from 1958. Mem. Bd. Edn. Colleton County, 1917-21. Served at 1st lt. Co. K. 3d S.C. Inf., N.G., 1912-15. Mason (grand master S.C.). Democrat. Methodist. K.P. Inventor submarine escaping apparatus. Home: Bamberg, SC. †

RISTINE, CHARLES SCOTT, broker; b. Bryn Mawr, Pa., Feb. 11, 1887; s. George Carpenter and Susannah (Shank) R.; B.S., Haverford Coll., 1910; m. Dorothy Stockton Haines, Jan. 17, 1925; 1 dau., Dorothy (Mrs. Alfred K. Althouse, Jr.). Partner F. P. Ristine & Co., brokers, Phila., from 1925; dir. S. S. White Dental Mfg. Co. Trustee Bapt. Home, Phila. Served as 1st lt., 23d Inf., U.S. Army, 1917-19; AEF. Decorated Purple Heart, Silver Star, Croix de Guerre. Mem. Mil. Order Fgn. Wars, Pa. Hist. Soc., Acad. Natural Sci. Clubs: Union League, Midday, Haverford (Phila.). Home: Wayne, Pa. †

RITTER, GEORGE WILLIAM, lawyer; b. Vermillion, Ohio, June 30, 1886; s. John and Louise (Hauth) R.; student Cleve. Law Sch., 1903-06; LL.B., Baldwin U., Berea, Ohio, 1906; LL.D., Baldwin-Wallace Coll., 1946, U. Toledo; m. Mary Fowler, June 30, 1911. Admitted to Ohio bar, 1907, since practiced in Ohio; dir. law City of Toledo, 1928-29; v.p., gen. counsel Overland Corp., Toledo, from 1936. partner law firm Ritter, Boesel, Robinson & Marsh. Trustee Toledo Hosp., Toledo Mus. Art, Baldwin-Wallace Coll. Mem. Toledo, Ohio, Lucas County, Am., Cleve., Toledo bar assns., Assn. Bar City of N.Y. Republican. Conglist. Clubs: Toledo, Inverness, Country (Toledo); Big Creek Hunting and Fishing (Can.); Bath, Surf, Indian Creek Country, Com. 100 (Fla.); Castalia Trout; La Gorce Country. Home: Ottawa Hills, Ohio. Deceased.

RITTS, LEONARD CHASE, oil exec.; b. Albany, N.Y., Aug. 5, 1889; s. John V. and Irene C. (Blakslee) R.; A.B., Haverford (Pa.) Coll., 1912; m. Gladys Clark, June 28, 1917; children—Marcia C., Leonard Chase, Clerk Butler County Nat. Bank, Butler, Pa., 1912-14; asst. to nat. bank examiner, Pittsburgh District, 1914-15; cashier, Lyndora Nat. Bank, Lyndora, Pa., 1915-19; v.p. and treas. Okla. Natural Gas Co., Tulsa, Okla., 1920-28; v.p. and treas. Devonian Oil Co., Tulsa, 1925-41, pres., dir., 1941-48; dir. Nat. Bank of Tulsa, Okla, Natural Gas Co. Served in U.S. Navy, 1918. Democrat. Mason (32 deg., K.T., Shriner). Clubs: Tulsa, Southern Hills Country (Tulsa). †

RIVERA, TOMÁS, university administrator; b. Crystal City, Tex., Dec. 22, 1935; s. Florencio and Josefa (Henandez) R.; m. Concepción Garza, Nov. 27, 1978; children: Ileana Imelda, Irasema, Florencio Javier. A.A. in English, SW Tex. Jr. Coll., 1956, B.S. in Edn, 1958, M.Ed., 1964; student, NDEA Spanish Inst., 1962, 63; M.A. in Spanish Lit, U. Okla., 1969, Ph.D. in Romance Langs. and Lit, 1969. Migrant worker, until 1957, tchr.

public secondary schs., Tex., 1957-65; instr. and chmn. dept. fgn. langs. SW Tex. Jr. Coll., 1965-66; teaching asst. dept. modern langs. U. Okla., 1966-68, instr., dir. lang. labs., 1968-69, asst. dir. Spanish studies program in, Madrid, summer 1969; asso. prof. Spanish Sam Houston State U., Tex., 1969-71; prof. Spanish lit., dir. div. fgn. langs., lit. and linguistics U. Tex.-San Antonio, 1971-73, prof. Spanish, assoc. dean Coll. Multidisciplinary Studies, 1973-76, v.p. for adminstrn., 1976-78; exec. v.p., acting v.p. acad. affairs U. Tex.-El Paso, 1978-79; chancellor U. Calif.-Riverside, 1979-84; lit. judge, speaker, cons. in field; mem. exec. com. Nat. Council Chicanos in Higher Edn., 1976-84, v.p., 1978, now chmn.; mem. task force on Hispanic arts Nat. Endowment Arts, 1977-79; trustee Carnegie Found. Advancement of Teaching, 1976-80, 80-84; mem. bd. fgn. scholarships Dept. State, 1978-80; mem. adv. com. Allied Health Professions, coordinating bd. state univ. and coll. system, Tex., 1979; bd. dirs. Hubert H. Humphrey Inst. Public Affairs, U. Minn., 1979, Tex. Commn. on Humanities, 1979, Nat. Center Higher Edn. Mgmt. Systems, 1979, Pres.'s Nat. Commn. Agenda for the 80's.; trustee Ednl. Testing Service. Author: books, the most recent being Always and Other Poems, 1973; (with others) A Public Trust, 1979; contbr. articles, fiction to profl. publs.; subject of profl. publs. Bd. dirs. Inman Christian Center, San Antonio, 1972-77, Commn. for Mexican-Am. Affairs, Archdiocese of San Antonio, 1972-77, Am. Issues Forum, San Antonio, 1975-76, Assn. Advancement Mexican Ams., Houston, 1977-79. Recipient Premio Quinto Sol., 1970-71; Project Milestone Recognition award Assn. Supervision and Curriculum Devel., 1977; Danforth Found. asso., 1971. Mem. Am. Assn. Higher Edn. (trustee), Am. Council on Edn. (trustee), Sigma Delta Pi (pres. U. Okla. chpt. 1968). Democrat. Roman Catholic. Clubs: Kiwanis (hon.), Sembradores de Amistad (hon.; Sembrador of Yr. 1974), Con Safo Artists San Antonio (hon.). Home: Riverside, Calif. Died May 16, 1984.

RIVERS, EURITH DICKINSON, JR., broadcasting executive; b. Mineral Springs, Ark., May 12, 1915; s. Eurith Dickinson and Margaret Lucile (Lashley) R.; m. Marie Georgine Bie, May 3, 1952; children: Eurith Dickinson, III, Rex B., Maria Kells, Lucile, Georgia. Ed., Ga. State U., Woodrow Wilson Law Sch. Bar: Ga. 1932. Asst. atty. gen., State of Ga.; legal dir. Ga. Welfare Dept., Atlanta; chief judge Ga. Indsl. Commn., Atlanta; then chmn. bd.; chmn. bd. Stars, Nat., N.Y.C., Stars, Inc., Miami Beach, Fla., WGOV, Inc., Valdosta, Ga., WEDR, Inc., Miami, Fla., Seminole Broadcasting Co., Fla., KWAM Inc., Memphis, WGUN, Inc., Atlanta, WEAS, Inc., Savannah, Ga., Sounds of Service, Inc., Suncoast Broadcasting Corp., Deesown Corp., Fla.; dir. Farmer's and Merchant's Bank, Lakeland, Ga. Served with USNR, World War II. Mem. Ga., Fla., Tenn., Ark. assns. broadcasters, Ga., Am. bar assns., Am. Judicature Soc. Clubs: La Gorce Country (Miami Beach), Rod and Reel (Miami Beach), Bankers (Miami Beach), Racquet (Miami Beach), Coral Reef Yacht (Miami Beach), Com. of loo (Miami Beach); Silver Springs Shores Country, Valdosta (Ga.) Country, Masons, Shriners. Home: Ocala, Fla.

RIVES, RICHARD TAYLOR, judge; b. Montgomery, Ala., Jan. 15, 1895; s. William Henry and Alice Bloodworth (Taylor) R.; m. Jessie Hall Dougherty, July 23, 1918 (dec. Nov. 23, 1973); children—Richard Taylor (dec.), Callie Dougherty Smith; m. Martha Blake Frazer, June 18, 1976. Student, Tulane U., 1911-12; studied law in office of, Hill, Hill, Whiting and Stern, Montgomery; LL.D., U. Notre Dame, 1966, Samford U., 1975. Bar: Ala. bar 1914. Gen. practice, Montgomery; judge Fifth Circuit, U.S. Ct. Appeals, 1951-59, chief judge, 1959-60, judge, 1960-66, sr. U.S. circuit judge, 1966-82. Del. Democratic Conv., Chgo., 1940. Served in N.G., 1916-17, Mexican Border; as 1st lt. Signal Corps. AEF, 1917-19. Mem. Montgomery Bar Assn. (former pres.), Ala. Bar Assn. (pres. 1939), ABA, Am.. Legion, Order of Coif (hon.). Presbtyerian. Club: Mason. Home: Montgomery, Ala. Died Oct. 27, 1982.

ROADRUCK, ROY KENNETH, university pres.; b. Morocco, Ind., May 28, 1890; s. Daniel Wesley and Maria Jane (Brown) R.; A.B., U. of Mich., 1914; studies in religious edn. in 20 training schs.; m. Sara Lenore Archibald, of Morocco, Ind., Sept. 8, 1917; children—Thomas Archibald, Robert Neal, Harriet Jane, Donna Gay. Religious educational work for Disciples of Christ in Western Ky., 1913-15; asso. supt. Ky. Christian Bible Sch. Assn., Louisville, Ky., 1915-17; northwest regional supt., Bible Sch. Work, at Spokane, Wash., 1917-20; with Am. Christian Missionary Soc., later merged into United Christian Missionary Soc., 1920-22; editor "Front Rank," St. Louis, 1922-28; asso. sec. Div. of Religious Edn. for U.S. and Can., under United Christian Missionary Soc., 1923-24; pres. Spokane U. from Sept. 1924. First pres. Inland Empire Council of Christian Edn.; dir. Bd. of Edn. of Disciples of Christ. Democrat. Woodman. Rotarian.†

ROARK, GEORGE JAMES, city manager; b. Denton, Tex., Dec. 13, 1889; s. Charles Hembry and Joann (Pinckley) R.; specialized in coll. work in law, civil engring. and economics; m. Maud Clark, of Royse City, Tex., Apr. 9, 1914; children—George James, John Clark (dec.). Formerly gen. mgr. Phoenix Furniture Co., Beaumont; v.p. Tex. Cold Storage Co., San Antonio. City mgr. (first) Beaumont, 1920-24; directed 1st Community Chest Campaign for Beaumont; reorganized financial affairs of Beaumont; built $100,000 S. Tex. State Fair plant in 2 mos., 1922; developed park and playground system for Beaumont; first city mgr. Pensacola, Fla., 1931-48; city mgr. Augusta, Ga., 1948, Meridian, Miss. from 1949; organized and dir. salvage and war drives, Civil Defense for Pensacola, 1941-43. Treas., and mem. bd. war camp recreation for soldiers at mil. camp, San Antonio, World War I; capt. Allied Mil. Govt., U.S. Army, 1943; gov. and civil affairs officer, Allied Control Commn. in Italy, 1943-45; returned Pensacola 1945, resumed city management; organized Liberty Bond sales. San Antonio, etc. Mem. Fla. City Mgrs. Assn. (pres.), Fla. League of Municipalities (vice-pres.), Internat. City Mgrs. Assn. (vice-pres.). Democrat. Methodist. Mason (32 deg.). Clubs: Rotary, Country (Pensacola). Home: Meridian, Miss. †

ROBARTS, JOHN PARMENTER, lawyer, former prime minister Ont.; b. Banff, Alta., Can., Jan. 11, 1917; s. Herbert and Florence May (Stacpoole) R.; B.A. in Bus. Adminstrn. with honors, U. Western Ont., 1939, also hon. LL.D.; LL.D., U. Toronto, Queen's U., U. Ottawa, Laurentian U., U. St. Dunstan's, P.E.I., McMaster U., McGill U., U. Waterloo, Waterloo Luth. U.; D.C.L., U.N.B.; m. Norah McCormick, July 6, 1944; children—Robin Hollis, Timothy Parmenter. Called to Ont. bar, 1947, created Queen's counsel, 1954; counsel law firm Robarts, Betts, McLennan & Flinn, London, Ont.; partner firm Stikeman, Elliott, Robarts & Bowman, Toronto, Ont.; mem. Provincial Parliament, 1951-71, minister without portfolio, 1958-59, minister of edn., 1959-62; prime minister Ont., 1961-71; mem. Queen's Privy Council For Can., from 1967. Chmn. bd., dir. Reed Shaw Stenhouse; sec., dir. Heitman Canadian Realty Investors; dir. Abitibi Paper Co. Ltd., Bell Canada, Canadian Imperial Bank Commerce, Commonwealth Holiday Inns Can. Ltd., Met. Life, Power Corp. Can. Ltd., Reed Shaw Osler Ltd. Chancellor U. Western Ont., 1972-82. Mem. London City Council, 1951. Bd. dirs. Inst. Research Pub. Policy. Served with Royal Canadian Navy, 1940-45. Decorated companion Order of Can. Knight of grace Order St. John Jerusalem; mentioned in dispatches. Mem. Delta Upsilon. Progressive Conservative. Anglican. Clubs: Kiwanis, London Hunt, London, Albany. Home: London, Ont., Canada. Died Oct. 18, 1982.

ROBBINS, MARTY, (MARTIN DAVID ROBINSON) musician; b. Glendale, Ariz., Sept. 26, 1925; s. Jack Joe and Emma (Heckle) R.; m. Marizona Baldwin, Sept. 27, 1945; children—Ronny, Janet. Grad. high sch. Mem. Grand Ole Opry, Nashville, 1954-82; artist CBS Records, 1952-72, MCA Records, 1972-74, Columbia Records, 1975-82; pres. Marioposa Music, 1960-82, Maricopa Music, 1960-82, Maricana Music, 1960-82, Charger Records, 1970-82, all Nashville; operator cattle farm, Franklin, Tenn., 1965-82, also auto racer. Composer over 500 songs; starred in 8 movies; star syndicated TV show Marty Robbins' Spotlight, from 1977. (Recipient gold records, platinum records, Gold Guitars, ASCAP awards, BMI awards, Grammy awards, Gold Trustees' medal for outstanding contbn. to Western heritage through music Nat. Cowboy Hall of Fame 1979, 2 Music City News Cover awards 1980. Composer: A White Sport Coat, 1955, El Paso, 1956, Devil Woman, 1962, You Gave Me a Mountain, 1966, Don't Worry, 1960, My Woman, My Woman, My Wife, 1970; Author: novel Small Man, 1966. Mem. Nat. Assn. Stock Car Racing, Am. Fedn. Musicians, Country Music Assn., Acad. Country and Western Music Assn., AFTRA, Screen Guild. Home: Brentwood, Tenn. Died Dec. 8, 1982.

ROBERTS, A(SHBEL) SELLEW, educator; b. North Chili, N.Y., June 26, 1888; s. Benson Howard and Emma Jane (Sellew) R.; student A.M. Chesborough Sem., North Chili, 1893-1905, Knox Coll., 1905-06; A.B., Cornell, 1910; M.A., U. Chgo., 1914; Ph.D., Harvard, 1922; m. Ruth N. Hofmann, Aug. 25, 1914. Asst. history dept. Cornell, 1910-11; with Swift & Co., Chgo., 1911-13; instr. history Boise (Ida.) High Sch., 1914-19, Simmons Coll., Boston, 1920-21; instr. U. Ill. Urbana, 1921-24, asso. in history, 1924-26; asst. prof., 1926-27; prof. history, head dept. Kent State U. from 1927; Mem. Am. Hist. Assn., Ohio Acad. History (pres. 1938), Portage Co. Hist. Soc. (trustee), Delta Upsilon (trustee). Presbyn. Club: Wranglers (pres. 1936). Editor: Selected Readings in American History (with T. C. Pease), 1928. Contbr. articles hist. jours. Home: Kent, OH. †

ROBERTS, EVERETT DAVID, judge; b. Buena Vista County, Ia., Aug. 17, 1890; s. John J. and Catherine (Jones) R.; student U. of Minn., 1912-14; LL.B., U. of S.D., 1918; m. Bonnie Martin, Nov. 1, 1924 (dec.); 1 son, William. Admitted to S.D. bar, 1918; in practice at Chamberlain, 1918-19; asst. atty. gen., S.D., 1920-30; judge Supreme Court of S.D. from 1930. Pres. State Hist. Soc., 1943-44. Mem. Am. Bar Assn., S.D. Bar Assn., Phi Delta Phi, Lambda Chi Alpha, Tau Kappa Alpha. Republican. Presbyn. Mason. Address: Pierre, S.D. †

ROBERTS, GEORGE, lawyer; b. Bklyn., July 3, 1884; s. George H. and Maria (Pettit) R.; B.A., Yale, 1905; LL.B. cum laude, Harvard, 1908; m. Grace Lee Middleton, Apr. 27, 1918; children—Constance (Mrs. Robert L. Hoguet, Jr.), Rosamond G. (Mrs. Donald Arthur, Jr.). Admitted to N.Y. bar, 1908, since practiced in N.Y.C.; mem. firm Winthrop & Stimson, 1912-14; partner Winthrop, Stimson, Putnam & Roberts, from 1914. Special consultant to Committee on Organization of Exec. Br. Govt., from 1954; spl. com. on Fed. Loyalty Security Program; mem. working group Pres. com on Transport Policy and Orgn.; spl. counsel R.F.C., 1932-33; adv. bd. Sec. of War's Bd. on Non-Appropriated Funds, 1945-46. Chmn. trustees Army Relief Soc.; trustee, chmn. bd. Roosevelt Hosp., N.Y.C., 1956. Fellow American Bar Assn.; member Am. Law Inst., Assn. Bar City N.Y. (mem. exec. com. 1933-37, v.p. 1941-43, chmn. com. bill of rights 1942-46), Am. (chmn. spl. com. retirement benefits 1951-56), N.Y. State bar assns., Council Foreign Relations. Clubs: University, Downtown, Century Assn., Links, River (N.Y.C.); Maidstone (Easthampton, N.Y.); Chevy Chase (Washington). Home: New York, N.Y. †

ROBERTS, HOWARD RADCLYFFE, museum dir., biologist; b. Villanova, Pa., Mar. 26, 1906; s. Howard Radclyffe and Eleanor Page (Butcher) R.; student St. Paul's Sch., Concord, N.H., 1919-25; B.S., Princeton U., 1929; Ph.D., U. Pa., 1941; m. Enid Hazel Warden, Aug. 23, 1933; children—Pauline Stella, Radclyffe Burnand, Eleanor Page. Instr. in zoology U. Pa., 1935-41; research asso. in entomology Acad. Natural Sci., Phila., 1936-46, dir., chief exec. officer, 1947-72, research fellow dept. entomology, from 1971. Served with San. Corps, M.C., U.S. Army, 1942-45; capt. malaria survey unit, New Guinea and Philippine campaigns. Trustee Acad. Natural Scis. Phila., Fairmount Park Art Assn.; bd. mgrs., sec. Wistar Inst. Anatomy and Biology; pres. Children's Seashore House at Atlantic City, 1956-65, treas. 1970-75. Mem. AAAS, Entomol. Soc. Am., Sigma Xi. Traveler and mem. expdns. to S. Am., Near East and Orient. Home: Villanova, Pa. Deceased.

ROBERTS, JOSEPH BENJAMIN, lawyer; b. Riceville, Tenn., Feb. 7, 1889; s. Christopher C. and Rella (Bishop) R.; student U. Chattanooga, 1913-14, U. Va. Law Sch., 1916-17; LL.B., U. Tenn., 1920; m. Robertine De Costa, June 12, 1923 (dec. June 1944); 1 dau., Robertine R. (Mrs. Jack N. Sokohl); m. 2d, Adeline P. Patterson, Aug. 24, 1949. Admitted to Tenn. bar, 1920, since practiced in Chattanooga; mem. firm Roberts, Weill, Ellis, Weems & Copeland, from 1920. Served to 1st lt., inf., U.S. Army, 1917-19. Mem. Am., Tenn. (life), Chattanooga (pres. 1938-39) bar assns., Am. Coll. Trial Lawyers; life mem. Fed. Judges 6th Jud. Conf. Presbyn. (elder). Club: Civitan (pres. 1949-50), Lookout Mountain, Fairyland (Chattanooga). Home: Lookout Mountain, TN. †

ROBERTS, JOSEPH KENT, geology; b. Saltville, Va., July 11, 1889; s. Henry Sinon and Alice Mary (Crenshaw) R.; B.A., Emory and Henry Coll., Emory, Va., 1910; M.A., Johns Hopkins, 1915, Ph.D., 1922; unmarried. Prof. geology and biology, Emory and Henry Coll., 1916-20; asst. prof. geology, Vanderbilt, 1922-24, asso. prof., 1924-26; prof. geology, U. of Va., from 1926, pres. and visitors' research prize, 1929; asst. geol. survey, Va., 1920-23, 27, 31, 40, 41, Tenn., summers, 1924, 25, Ky., 1926, 29, 44; Mt. Lake Va., Biol. Station, summers, 1938, 1942. U.S.N.R.F., 1918-22. Fellow A.A.A.S. Geological Soc. Am., Paleontol. Soc. Am., Geol. Soc. Washington, Virginia Acad. Science; mem. American Assn. Univ. Prof., Seismol. Soc. of America (Eastern Division), S.A.R. (president Virginia Soc. S.A.R., 1944-45), Shenandoah Nat. Hist. Assn., Va. Hist. Soc., Gamma Alpha, Sigma Xi (sec. Virginia chapter 1928-31, 35-47, pres. 1932-33), Raven Soc. of U. Va., Geochemical Soc., Sigma Gamma Epsilon. Episcopalian. Mason (Scottish Rite). Democrat. Writer reports on Virginia Triassic, Cretaceous and Tertiary of Upper Gulf Embayment of Tenn. and Ky., Virginia Tertiary, and various short articles on Virginia geology; Catalogue of Topographic and Geologic Maps of Va.; Annotated Bibliography of Virginia Geology; Laboratory Manual for Gen. Geology, 3d edit. Home: Charlottesville, Va. †

ROBERTS, WILLIAM PAYNE, church missionary; b. Summerdean, Va., Feb. 21, 1888; s. John Emil and Nannie Bryce (Smith) R.; B.A., Yale, 1909; B.D., Episcopal Theological School, Cambridge, Mass., 1914; D.D., Philadelphia Divinity School, 1945; m. Dorothy Mills, Oct. 2, 1918; children—Edith, Helen Mills, William Payne, John Carlton, Bruce Adams. Ordained Missionary in China, Protestant Episcopal Ch., 1914; teacher of New Testament, St. John's U., Shanghai, China, 1914-18, 1920-23; pastor, St. Paul's Ch., Nanking, China, 1923-37; bishop of the Missionary Dist. of Shanghai of the Am. Ch. Mission in China (Protestant Episcopal), 1937-50; vicar House of Prayer, Phila., from 1951. Address: Philadelphia, Pa. †

ROBERTSON, ARCHIBALD GERARD, lawyer; b. Staunton, Va., Oct. 6, 1889; s. Alexander Farish and Margaret Briscoe (Stuart) R.; student Woodberry Forest Sch., Orange, Va., 1904-08; LL.B., U. of Va., 1914; m. Frances Margaret Spencer, Apr. 21, 1923; children—Frances Durbin (Mrs. J. A. Gill), Margaret Briscoe (Mrs. S. G. Christian, Jr.), Pauline Spencer (Mrs. J. R. Newell, Jr.). Admitted N.C. bar, 1914, practiced in Charlotte, 1914-17; admitted to Va. bar 1917; atty. for War Dept. Bd. of Contract Adjustment, Washington, 1919-20; in pvt. practice law, Richmond, since 1921, under own name, 1921-22, 1923-32, with Hunton, Williams, Gay, Powell and Gibson and predecessor firm, from 1932, partner from 1937; asst. city atty., Richmond, 1922-23; counsel, mem. bd. dirs. St. Luke's Hosp. Corp., 1945-65, pres., 1949-65; counsel McGuire Clinic, 1945-65; v.p., counsel, dir. Children's Home Soc. Va., 1938-58; gen. counsel, dir. Va. Transit Co., Portsmouth Transit Co., 1958-59. Basic-Witz Furniture Industries, Inc., 1959-66.

Bd. overseers, bd. dirs. Sweet Briar Coll., 1941-60, pres. 1949-55. Mem. R.O.T.C. 1917; commd. 2d lt. Res. Corps, U.S. Army, Aug. 1917, overseas duty 1917-19; wounded in action with 9th U.S. Inf. at St. Michael, France, Sept. 12, 1918. Awarded D.S.C., Purple Heart (U.S.), Croix de Guerre (France). Mem. Am., Va., Richmond bar assns., Virginia Historical Soc. (mem. exec. com.), Soc. Cincinnati, Delta Psi. Episcopalian (chancellor Diocese of Va. 1943-58). Home: Richmond, VA. †

ROBERTSON, FRANK CHESTER, writer; b. Moscow, Ida., Jan. 12, 1890; s. William Hugh and Mary (Matthews) R.; ed. common schs.; m. Winnie Bowman, July 11, 1919 (dec.); children—Nellie (dec.), Glen E., Victor H. (dec.). Began as laborer, hered sheep, worked with cattle; located homestead of 320 acres, in 1914, and followed farming until 1922; contbr. about 1000 stories and articles to mags. Silver Spur award Western Writers of America, 1953. Mem. League Utah Writers (hon. pres.), Western Writers America (bd. dirs. from 1958, pres. from 1959), Author numerous books since 1925; latest publs.: Longhorns of Hate, 1949; Wrangler on the Prod, 1950; A Ram in the Thicket (autobiography), 1950; Hangman of the Humbug, 1951; Sadie on a Cloud, 1952; Where Desert Blizzards Blow, 1952; Sagebrush Sorrel, 1953; Cruel Winds of Winter, 1954; Horn Silver, 1955; Squatters Rights, 1956; Lawman's Pay, 1957; Disaster Valley, 1957; Rawhide, 1961; Cariboo, 1962; Hoofbeats of Destiny, a history of the Pony Express, 1959; A Man Called Paladin, 1964; Fort Hall-Gateway to Oregon, 1963; Bull Valley Bible, 1965; Valley of Frightened Men, 1967; Fort Hall-Gateway to the Oregon Country, 1963; Day the Colonel Wept, published in 1968; co-author: Soapy Smith, 1961; Boom Towns of the Great Basin, 1962; novelized television shows, including Rawhide and Wanted: Dead or Alive, 1960. Author newspaper column, The Chopping Block. Home: Visalia, Cal. †

ROBERTSON, HUGH, corp. exec.; b. Glasgow, Scotland, Feb. 12, 1887; s. James and Marjorie (Cowie) R.; educated in public schools and business coll., Chicago; m. Mable Irene Brunt, Feb. 12, 1912; children—Hugh, John (dec.), Marjorie (Mrs. Ezra Woodbury). Bank clk., 1902-07; paymaster Acme Harvesting Machine Co., harvesting machinery, 1907-09; auditor Peerless Motor Car Co., Chgo., 1910-13; sec. and mgr. National Motor Sales Company, 1913-24; with the Zenith Radio Corp., mfrs. radio apparatus from 1924, treas., 1926-52, exec. v.p., 1934-58, pres., 1958-59, chairman, chief exec. officer, 1959-65, dir., from 1929, hon. chairman, special consultant, from 1965; president, dir. Zenith Radio Corp. Cal., Zenith Radio Corp. Can., Ltd.; pres. Zenith Radio Research Corp. of Menlo Park, Cal., Wincharger Corp., Sioux City, Central Electronics, Inc.; dir. Zenith Sales Corp., Chgo., Rauland Corp., Zenith Radio Distributing Corp., Zenith Hearing Aid Sales Corp., Chgo. Home: Lake Forest, Ill. †

ROBERTSON, RODERICK FRANCIS, educator; b. Vancouver, C., Can., Sept. 9, 1920; s. Andrew Christie and Helen (Cameron) R.; m. Grace Theresa Girvin, Dec. 27, 1958; 1 son, Roderick. B.A., U. B.C., 1944, M.A., 1946; Ph.D., McGill U., 1955. Lectr. U. B.C., Vancouver, 1946-47; lectr. McGill U., Montreal, 1948-50, asst. prof., part-time, 1955-60, asso. prof., 1960-65, prof. chemistry, from 1972, asso. chmn. dept. chemistry, from 1974; officer-in-charge Ultracentrifuge Project, McGill U./Dept. Vets. Affairs of Can., 1953-60. Contbr. articles to profl. jours. Mem. Chem. Inst. Can., Sigma Xi. Home: Beaconsfield PQ, Canada.

ROBINSON, EMERY IRVING, physician; b. Brunswick, Ga., Feb. 16, 1889; s. Edward Theopolius and Julia Mary (Clark) R.; ed. Selden Inst., 1900-11; M.D., Meharry, 1919; m. Florence Elizabeth Cosby, Mar. 17, 1922. Engaged in practice of medicine, Los Angeles, Calif., from 1934. Mem. tech. adv. com. Los Angeles County-wide Hosp. Survey from 1946. Pres. Nat. Med. Assn. 1945-46. Author of address, Negro Physicians' Contribution to the History of Medicine in America, presented before Barlow Soc. of History of Medicine, 1946. †

ROBINSON, HARRY MAXIMILIAN, JR., physician; b. nr. Balt., Dec. 13, 1909; s. Harry and Verna (Wilson) R.; B.S., U. Md., 1931, M.D., 1935; m. Maurice Hardin, July 3, 1937 (dec. Dec. 1964); children—E. Ann, Harry Maximillian III; m. 2d, Elizabeth Shema Rehm, June 6, 1965. Intern U. Md. Hosp., 1935-36, asst. resident physician, 1936-37, pres. staff, 1959-60; fellow in medicine Johns Hopkins Hosp., 1937-40; prof. head dermatology div. U. Md., 1953-80; pvt. practice, Balt.; chief dermatologist St. Agnes Hosp., 1947-80, South Balt., 1948-80; dermatologist Md. penal insts. Med. examiner Balt. Boy Scouts Am., 1955-60; cons. Balt. VA hosps., chmn. physicians com. Balt. United Appeal; chmn. adv. com. FDA, 1963-71; mem., spl. cons. com., 1968-80; mem. Gov. (Md.) Com. Community Health, 1963-70. Served to lt. col. AUS, 1942-45. Recipient Clarke Finnerad award Am. Dermatol. Found., 1977. Mem. Am. Acad. Dermatology (dir. 1957-60; Gold medal for research 1970, Clark Finnerud award 1976), So. (councilor 1956-61, chmn. dermatology sect. 1977-78), Am. (mem. com. evaluation of phys. impairment 1965-80) med. assns., Balt. City Med. Soc. (v.p. 1960-61, pres. 1962-63), Am. Dermatologic Assn. (v.p. 1975-76), Med. and Chirurg. Faculty Md. (council 1963-80), U. Md. Alumni Assn. (pres. 1958-60). Presbyterian (elder). Author textbook in field, profl. publs. Mem. editorial bd. Cutis, 1975-80, Current Prescribing, 1975-80. Home: Baltimore, Md. Died July 18, 1980.

ROBINSON, J. FRENCH, gas utility exec.; b. Elizabeth, W. Va., Dec. 13, 1890; s. Jefferson Dent and Mamie (Jacobs) R.; B.S. in Civil Engring., W.Va. U., 1915, M.S. in Sci., 1918, Ph.D., 1951; Ph.D., University of Pittsburgh, 1918; m. Ethel Gertrude Broad; 1 son, James D. With B.&O. R.R., 1914-20, State Pa., 1920-21, Standard Oil Co. N.J., 1921-43, Consol. Natural Gas Co., 1943-55; chmn. bd. Fla. Gas Co., from 1955. Mem. Am. Gas Assn. (pres. 1944-45; Charles A. Monroe award 1945). Home: Fort Pierce, Fla. †

ROBINSON, JOSEPH, development engineer; b. Dayton, Wash., July 24, 1889; s. William Henry and Cynthia Anne (Smith) R.; student pub. schs., spl. courses in engring. law and bus. adminstrn.; m. Carolyn Mae Oliver, July 1907 (dec.); children—Barbara, Joseph Vincent, Madeleine Oliver. Macy Bradley, Elizabeth Joan (dec.); m. 2d, Nelly Valerie. Savage, Sept. 1930. Rodel cattle range in early teens; dep. sheriff in Ore. at 17; served in Ore. State Militia (expert marksman), 1907; began career as blacksmith; became pattern maker, foundryman, machinist, draftsman, designer; established own engring. office 1909; admitted to practice patent law, 1914; recipient of many patents; invented Robinson automatic connector (ry. coupling device); pres. Robinson Connector Co., Joseph Robinson, Inc., apptd. head engr. indsl. processes and products, Office Prodn. Research and Development. War Prodn. Bd., Feb. 1943; mem. adv. com. on precision castings War Metall. Com. of Nat. Research Council; supervisor, U.S.N. precision casting research in Japan aiding industrial recovery, from 1950. Made technol. survey, Germany, for Joint Chiefs Staff, U.S. Army, 1945; cited for patriotic service by War Dept., 1946, 51; engring. mem., chmn. Deconcentration Rev. Bd., Japan, 1948-49; made indsl. survey Formosa for Mutual Security Agy., U.S. Govt., 1952; apptd. member joint arbitration committee under Japan-American Trade Arbitration Agreement, 1956. Mem. Am. Soc. M.E., Am. Inst. of Mining and Metall. and Petroleum Engrs., Internat. Law Soc. Tokyo, Fgn. Corrs. Club Japan, A.A.A.S., Fed. Grand Jury Assn.; honorary life member Pacific Geographical Soc.; Am. Pioneer Trails Assn. (hon. life mem. and dir.), Am. C. of C. in Japan, Am.-Japan Soc. Clubs: American (Tokyo); Explorers (active mem.), Bankers (N.Y.); Authors (Los Angeles). Author: In the Lion's Den, 1937; also tech. articles; published The Problem of Meighen Island by Vilbialmur Stefansson, 1939. Home: New York, N.Y. †

ROBINSON, JULIA BOWMAN, mathematics educator; b. St. Louis, Dec. 8, 1919; d. Ralph Bowers and Helen (Hall) Bowman; m. Raphael Mitchel Robinson, Dec. 22, 1941. A.B., U. Calif.-Berkeley, 1940, M.A., 1941, Ph.D., 1948. Jr. mathematician RAND Corp., Santa Monica, Calif., 1949-50; lectr. math. U. Calif.-Berkeley, 1960, 63-64, 66, 69-70, 75, prof., 1976-85. MacArthur fellow. Mem. Am. Math. Soc. (pres. 1983-84), Assn. Symbolic Logic, AAAS, Nat. Acad. Sci., Council Sci. Soc. Pres. (chmn. 1985). Democrat. Home: Berkeley, Calif. Died July 30, 1985.

ROBINSON, MARY TURLAY, artist; b. South Attleboro, Mass., Sept. 7, 1888; d. Gilman Parker (M.D.) and Esther Mells (Turlay) Robinson; A.B., Vassar Coll., 1910; student Art Students League N.Y., 1919-22; diploma Am. Sch. Fine Arts, Fontainebleau, France, 1924. Liaison officer Am. Sch. Fine Arts, Fontainebleau, France, 1928-32; dir. Argent Galleries, N.Y.C., 1933-35; research early Am. portraits for Frick Art Reference Library, 1933-34; lectr. on art, from 1930; laymen's courses in creative seeing, from 1936; grant from Specialist div. Internat. Edn. Service, State Dept. for lectures on Am. art in Switzerland, Belgium, France, Algeria and Yugoslavia, 1954. Exhibited painting Salon d'Automne, Soc. Independents, Paris, 1925; one-man shows at Anderson Galleries, N.Y.C., 1930 and Binet Gallery, N.Y.C., 1950. Work in Cooper Union Mus. and pvt. collections. Decorated Officer of French Acad., 1933; received Lucille Douglass award, Am. Women's Assn., 1937. Alternate representative Vassar Alumnae Council, 1940-46, alternate life representative, from 1965. Chmn. Fine Arts Com. Am. Woman's Assn., 1934-38; mem. Art Students League (life mem.; 2d v.p. 1921-23), Nantucket Hist. Soc. (member council 1938-42), Vassar Alumnae Assn., French Soc. Fresco Painters (hon.), Am. Fedn. Arts, Artists Equity Assn. (dir. New York, 1953-54), Nantucket Art Assn. (exec. com. 1958-61), Museum of Modern Art of New York, Hort. Soc. N.Y. (lectr. 1964). Home: New York, N.Y. †

ROBINSON, MAURICE RICHARD, publisher; b. Wilkinsburg, Pa., Dec. 24, 1895; s. Richard Bradley and Rachel S.C. (Calderwood) R.; m. Florence Liddell, June 2, 1934; children—Richard, Susan, Barbara, Florence, William. A.B., Dartmouth, 1920, L.H.D. (hon.), 1980. Founded Western Pa. Scholastic, 1920, Western Pa. Scholastic (title changed to Scholastic), 1922; Founded Scholastic Mags., Inc., pubs. 27 elementary and secondary sch. classroom periodicals, pubs., distbrs. books, recs., filmstrips to schools, pres., pub., 1922-63, chmn. bd., chief exec. officer, 1963-75, chmn. bd., from 1975. Served to 2d lt. U.S. Army, 1917-19. Recipient Pa. award for excellence in edn., 1969; Henry Johnson Fisher award, 1970. Mem. Assn. Am. Pubs. (pres. 1962-63), Delta Tau Delta. United Presbyn. Clubs: Cosmos (Washington); Apawamis (Rye, N.Y.); University (N.Y.C.). Home: Pelham, N.Y. Died Feb. 7, 1982.

ROBINSON, MAURICE RICHARD, JR., pub. co. exec.; b. Pitts., May 15, 1937; s. Maurice Richard and Florence (Liddell) R.; B.A. magna cum laude, Harvard, 1959; postgrad. St. Catharines Coll., Cambridge U., 1959-60; m. Katherine Woodroofe, May 17, 1968. Tchr. English, Evanston Twp. (Ill.) High Sch., 1960-62; asst. editor Lit. Cavalcade, Scholastic Mags., Inc., N.Y.C., 1962-63, editor Scholastic lit. units, 1963-64, editor Scope mag., 1964-67, editorial dir. English, 1967-71, pub. sch. div., 1971-74, pres., chief exec. officer, 1974-82; chmn. bd. Advanced Typographic Systems. Mem. Tchrs. Coll. Alumni Council; adv. council Sch. Journalism Syracuse U., 1971-73. Mem. Assn. Am. Pubs. (exec. com. sch. div.). Clubs: University; Harvard (N.Y.C.); Quogue Field. Home: New York, N.Y. Died 1982.

ROBINSON, WILLARD HASKELL, JR., college pres.; b. Brooklyn, N.Y., Sept. 6, 1889; s. Willard Haskell Robinson and Ella Raymond (Moore) R.; A.B., U. of Chicago, 1909, Ph.D., 1915; B.D., McCormick Theol. Sem., 1913; study and travel in Palestine, France and Germany, 1913-15; student Am. Sch. of Archaeology, Jerusalem, 1913-14; unmarried. Prof. Bible and classics, Blackburn Coll., Carlinville, Ill., 1915-18; acting prof. N.T. interpretation, San Francisco Theol. Sem., 1918-19; prof. Bible and classics, Whitworth Coll., Spokane, Wash., 1919-21, pres. from June 1921. Mem. Archaeol. Soc. America (Spokane br.), Classical Soc. (pres.), Research Club of Spokane, Phi Beta Kappa. Presbyn. Home: Spokane, Wash. †

ROBITSCHER, JONAS, psychiatrist, educator; b. N.Y.C., Oct. 28, 1920; s. Jonas and Elsa (Eisinger) R.; A.B., Brown U., 1942; J.D., George Washington U., 1948, M.D., 1955; m. Jean Begeman, June 1, 1950; children—Jan, Christine, John. Intern, George Washington U., 1955-56; psychiat. resident Inst. Pa. Hosp., Phila., 1956-59; psychoanalytic tng. Inst. Phila. Assn. Psychoanalysis, 1970; practice medicine, specializing in psychiatry, psychoanalysis and forensic psychiatry, Phila., 1959-63, Bryn Mawr, Pa., 1963-72; lectr. law and psychiatry Villanova U. Law Sch., 1965-72; asst. prof. clin. psychiatry U. Pa. Sch. Medicine, 1968-72; Henry Luce prof. law and behavioral scis. Emory U., Atlanta, 1972-81. Program dir. social-legal uses of forensic psychiatry NIMH, 1970-72, prin. investigator dangerousness in psychiat. commitment study, 1974-81. Fellow Am. Coll. Legal Medicine, Inst. Soc., Ethics and Life Scis., Am. Psychiat. Assn. (commn. on jud. action 1974-81, Isaac Ray award); mem. Am. Bar Assn. (commn. on mentally disabled 1973-81), Am. Acad. Psychiatry and the Law (councillor), Phi Beta Kappa, Alpha Omega Alpha. Author: Pursuit of Agreement: Psychiatry and the Law, 1966; Powers of Psychiatry, 1980. Editor: Eugenic Sterilization, 1973. Home: Atlanta, Ga. Died Mar. 25, 1981.

ROBITZEK, EDWARD HEINRICH, physician; b. N.Y.C., Dec. 12, 1912; s. Arthur Harrison and Kate (Heinrich) R.; A.B., Colgate U., 1934; M.D., Columbia, 1938; m. Katherine Robertson, Nov. 9, 1940 (dec. Feb. 1945); children—Arthur Scott, John Edward; m. 2d, Christine Baldwin, June 4, 1952. Rotating intern Fordham Hosp., N.Y.C., 1938-40; med. resident Sea View Hosp., S.I., 1941-42, x-ray resident, 1942-43; chief med. resident, 1943-44, pathologist, 1944-46; dir. med. Sea View Hosp., 1954-61; dir. med. services Sea View Hosp. & Home, 1961-73; attending in medicine Sailors Snug Harbor, 1960-76; pathologist Richmond Meml. Hosp., 1944-46, now cons. staff; pvt. practice as lung specialist S.I., 1946-75; hon. cons. staff S.I. Hosp.; attending physician in medicine South Beach Psychiat. Hosp., 1974-75; cons. staff USPHS Hosp., S.I., 1967-84; hon. cons. staff St. Vincent Hosp. Recipient Albert and Mary Lasker award Am. Pub. Health Assn., 1955. Diplomate Am. Bd. Internal Medicine. Fellow A.C.P., Am. Coll. Chest Physicians; mem. Am. Thoracic Soc., Lambda Chi Alpha. Contbr. articles to med. jours. With asso. conducted pioneer trials of various derivatives of the hydrazides of isonicotinic acid in treatment of human tuberculosis, resulting in devel. of isoniazid. Home: Berlin, Md. Died Feb. 20, 1984.

ROBSON, DAME FLORA, actress; b. South Shields, Durham, Eng., Mar. 28, 1902; d. David Mather and Eliza (McKenzie) Robson; student Royal Acad. Dramatic Art, 1919-21; D.Litt., Durham U., 1958, also U. Wales. Appeared in numerous plays in West End theatres, 1924-55, then in House by the Lake, 1956, Ghosts, 1958, The Aspern Papers, 1959-61, The Corn is Green, 1961-62, Close Quarters, 1963; U.S. appearances include Ladies in Retirement, 1939-40, Elizabeth of England, 1941, The Damask Cheek, 1942, Macbeth, 1947, Black Chiffon, 1951; appeared in numerous motion pictures including Fire Over England, 1937, Wuthering Heights, 1939, The Sea Hawk, 1940, Bahama Passage, 1941, Saratoga Trunk, 1943, Great Day, 1944-45, 55 Days at Peking, Murder at the Gallop, Guns of Batasi, Seven Women, Young Cassidy, Eye of the Devil, The Shuttered Room, Cry in the Wind; appeared in play Justice Is a Woman. Decorated Order White Lion, Order White Rose (Finland); created dame Brit. Empire, 1960. Home: Brighton, Sussex, England. Died July 7, 1984.

ROBSON, JULIUS WILLIAM, pres. Standard Varnish Works; b. N.Y. City, Feb. 4, 1889; s. William and Yereth

(Frank) Rosenberg; ed. Horace Mann Sch., N.Y. City, and Phillips Exeter Acad., Exeter, N.H.; m. Myrtle Margaret Guggenheim, Oct. 8, 1913; children—William, Gerald, Robert Kenneth. Mgr. Internat. Varnish Co., Toronto, Can., 1913-15; gen. mgr. Standard Varnish Works, N.Y. City, 1916-24, pres. from 1924; dir. R.I.W. Damp Resisting Paint Co., Inc. Club: Chemists. Home: White Plains, N.Y. †

ROCHOW, W(ILLIAM) F(RED), refractory co. exec.; b. Columbia, Pa., Jan. 11, 1889; s. Charles R. and Emma Louise (Harm) R.; B.S., Pa. State Coll., 1912; m. Lillian Mary Simpkins, Sept. 1, 1944. Chem. engr. research Harbison-Walker Refractories Co., Pittsburgh, 1912, asst. gen. sales mgr. asst. to pres., 1947, v.p. 1949-54; asst. to pres. on research and development, from 1954. Fellow American Ceramic Soc.; mem. Engrs. Soc. Western Pa., Am. Inst. Mining, Metall. and Petroleum Engrs. Author: Modern Refractory Practice (with J.S. McDowell), 1950; numerous tech. papers. Home: Pittsburgh, Pa. †

ROCK, JOHN, physician; b. Marlborough, Mass., Mar. 24, 1890; s. Frank Sylvester and Ann Jane (Murphy) R.; B.S., Harvard, 1915, M.D., 1918, LL.D., 1966; Sc.D., Amherst Coll., 1965; m. Anna Thorndike, Jan. 3, 1925 (dec.1961); children—Rachel Sherman, John, Ann Jane, Martha, Ellen. Intern, Mass. Gen. Hosp., 1919, resident in urology, 1920, hon. surgeon; house surgeon Free Hosp. for Women, 1920, dir. Fertility and Endocrine Clinic, 1926-56, cons. gynecologist, 1956-84; dir. Rock Reproductive Clinic, Inc., 1956-71; resident Boston Lying-In Hosp., 1920; practiced in Boston, 1921-84; mem. cons. staff obstetrics and gynecology Faulkner Hosp.; clin. prof. gynecology Harvard, 1947-56, emeritus, 1956-84. Recipient Lasker award Planned Parenthood Fedn. Am., Margaret Sanger award, 1976; Ortho award Am. Gynecol. Soc., Am. Soc. for Study Sterility; Oliver Bird medal. Died Dec. 4, 1984.

ROCK, JOSEPH ALOYSIUS, univ. adminstr.; b. Phila., July 28, 1915; s. Michael J., Jr. and Helen Marie (Doyle) R. A.B., Georgetown U., 1938, M.A., 1941, Ph.D., 1957; Ph.L., Woodstock (Md.) Coll., 1939; S.T.L., Boston Coll., 1946; L.H.D., U. Scranton, 1981. Joined Soc. of Jesus, 1932; ordained priest Roman Catholic Ch., 1945; mem. faculty Georgetown U., 1940-42, 50-57, dir. student personnel, 1951-57; mem. faculty U. Scranton, 1946-47, from 59; dean U. Scranton (Evening Coll.), 1957-61; dean U. Scranton (Grad. Sch.), 1957-66, acad. v.p., 1966-75, v.p. emeritus, prof. history, from 1975; Formerly mem. pres.'s bd. Caldwell (N.J.) Coll. for Women. Trustee Coll. Misericordia; bd. dirs. Allied Services Handicapped; vice chmn. bd. trustees U. Scranton, 1965-70, sec. corp., 1970-72. Mem. Nat. Assn. Student Personnel Adminstrs. (exec. com. 1954-55, 56-57), Jesuit Assn. Student Personnel Adminstrs. (pres. 1952-54), Eastern Assn. Deans and Advisers Men, Jesuit Ednl. Assn. (commn. grad. schs.), Nat. Cath. Ednl. Assn., C. of C. (dir.), Am. Hist. Assn., Alpha Sigma Nu, Pi Gamma Mu, Phi Alpha Theta, Phi Delta Kappa. Address: Scranton, PA.

ROCKEFELLER, GODFREY STILLMAN, textile printing co. exec.; b. N.Y.C., May 1, 1899; B.A., Yale U., 1921; m. Halen Gratz; children—Godfrey A., Marion Rockefeller Stone, Audrey Rockefeller Blair, Lucy Rockefeller Stewart, Peter R. Faculty, Yale-in-China, 1921-22; with indsl. dept. Nat. Comml. Bank & Trust Co., Albany, N.Y., 1925-28; ltd. partner Clark Dodge & Co., 1929-40; dir., v.p., pres., chmn. bd. Cranston Print Works Co., N.Y.C., 1930-83; with indsl. div. Marshall Plan Hdqrs., Paris, 1946; dir. Freeport Minerals Co., Istel Fund, Inc. Served as 2d lt. U.S. Army, 1918; to lt. col. USAAF, 1943-45. Home: Greenwich, Conn. Died Feb. 23, 1983.

ROCKEFELLER, W.C., cons. engr.; b. Ogden, Utah, Apr. 2, 1910; s. William V. and Julia (Tullis) R.; m. Verna Margaret Rood, July 17, 1937; children—Alan Frank, Gail Frances. B.S., Cal. Inst. Tech., 1932, M.S., 1934. Instr. Cal. Inst. Tech., 1932-37; cons. aero. engr., 1934-38; chief of aerodynamics Vultee Aircraft, Inc., 1938-42; asst. chief engr. Avion, Inc., 1942-44; gen. mgr. Alvin R. Adams & Assos., 1944-48; dir., exec. asst. to chmn. bd. Consol. Vultee Aircraft Corp., 1947-53; v.p., dir. Airfleets Inc., 1949-56, San Diego Corp., 1952-56, Nut-Shel Co., 1952-56, Hidden Splendor Mining Co., 1954-58; v.p. Atlas Corp., 1954-58; v.p., dir. MVT Industries, Inc., 1960-64; v.p. Sonico, Inc., 1964-69; pres. Via Computer, Inc., 1969-82; asso. Calif. Inst. Tech., 1975-82. Contbr. articles to various engring. publs. Recipient Lawrence B. Sperry award Inst. Aero. Scis., 1936. Fellow Inst. Aero. Scis.; mem. Planning Execs. Inst. Home: Del Mar, Calif. Died May 23, 1982.

ROCKWELL, CHARLES BRISTED, mfr.; b. Cranston, R.I., Oct. 15, 1889; s. Charles Bristed and Martha Briggs (Skerry) R.; grad. Hill Sch., 1907; C.E., Princeton, 1912; m. Eleanor Benson, Oct. 29, 1913; children—Charles Bristed, Henry Benson, Paul Standish, Martha and Eleanor (twins). Pres. Millbury Spinning Co., 1914-20, Nassau Mfg. Co., 1917-18; v.p., treas. Collins & Aikman, mfrs. pile fabrics, Bristol, R.I., 1927-44; pres., treas. Allendale Co., Centerdale, R.I., from 1944; dir. R.I. Hosp. Trust Co., Blackstone Mut. Fire Ins. Co., Fireman's Mut. Fire Ins. Co., Wallace & Tucker Lumber Co., Crown Worsted Mills. Del. Internat. Wool Conf., Paris, France, 1928; mem. S.A. tour of NRC, 1941; chief wool br. WPB, Washington, 1943-44. Pres. Bristol Dist. Nurses Assn.; treas. Bristol YMCA, Rectory Sch., Pomfret. Republican. Unitarian. Clubs: New York Yacht, Bristol Yacht, Cruising of Am. Home: Bristol, R.I. †

ROCKWELL, LEO LAWRENCE, univ. prof.; b. New Albany, Pa., Aug. 20, 1888; s. John and Eugenie (Tracy) R.; A.B., Bucknell U., 1907; Litt. D., 1954; A.M., Harvard, 1908; Ottendorfer fellow, New York U.; student Univ. Munich and Heidelberg, 1912-13, Ph.D., N.Y. Univ., 1924; m. Vera Cober, Sept. 15, 1913; children—Frances Eugenie (Mrs. Warren Dentler), Carol Elizabeth (Mrs. James M. Sullivan), Marguerite Ely (Mrs. E. R. Weihing). Instructor in German, Bucknell University, 1908-11, New York University, 1914-15, summer, 1916; instructor German, Bucknell Univ., 1915-17, asst. prof., 1917-19, prof. German, 1919-36; asso. prof., English, asst. ed. Early Modern English Dictionary, U. of Mich., summers, 1934-38; prof. English lit., dir. Sch. Langs. and Letters, Colgate U., 1936-46, dir. Div. of Arts and Letters from 1946; prof. English and dir. English House, U. of Mich., summers 1941-43, and 1943-44, 1944-45; visiting professor of English, National Univ. of Chile, 1945, University of Guadalajara, Mexico, 1947, Queens Coll., Charlotte, N.C., 1957-58, Fla. So. Coll., 1958-62. Mem. Modern Lang. Assn. Am., Linguistic Soc. Am., Nat. Council Tchrs. English. South Atlantic Modern Lang. Assn., Phi Beta Kappa. Club: Hamilton. Contbr. profl. jours. Home: Lakeland, Fla. †

ROCKWELL, PAUL AYRES, writer; b. Marion County, S.C., Feb. 3, 1889; s. James Chester and Loula (Ayers) R.; student Wake Forest (N.C.) Coll., 1907-08, Washington and Lee U., 1908-10; m. Jeanne Leygues, Dec. 2, 1916; (divorced 1923); 1 dau., Francoise Jeanne Anne Loula (Mrs. V. Jordan Brown); m. 2d, Prue Durant Smith, Jan. 30, 1926; children—Kiffin Yates, II, William James Kenneth, Reporter Atlanta (Ga.) Constitution, 1912-14; mem. Paris staff Chicago Daily News, 1915-19; free lance feature writer for Am., French and English newspapers and mags. from 1919. Entered French Fgn. Legion, 1914; transferred to Grand Headquarters French Army, 1917, as official war corr., served until 1919; capt. French aviation regiment during Riff War, Morocco, 1925; reserve officer French Fgn. Legion; capt., French Army Gen. Staff, 1940; maj. U.S. Air Corps, June 1942, lt. col., Mar. 1943, serving abroad Sept. 1942 to June, 1946; col., May 1946. Decorated Bronze Star (United States); Officer Legion of Honor, Croix de Guerre, 1914, 1918, 1939, 1945, and Colonial War (France), Poz de Marruecos (Spain). Secretary Foundation du Memorial de l'Escadrille Lafayette, Paris, President United States Chapter, Trench and Air Association of American Volunteers in French Army, 1914-18, 1931-38, and from 1940. Member Sociétédes Etudes Historiques (France), American Legion (hon.), Order of the Stars and Bars, N.C. Soc. of the Cincinnati (president), N.C. Hist. Association (v.p. 1936), Soc. of Colonial Wars, S.A.R., Soc. of War 1812, Sons of Confederate Vets. (asst. historian), Sigma Phi Epsilon, Theta Nu Epsilon. Episcopalian, Clubs: Cercle Interallie, Cercle Milltaire, Aero Automobile, University (Paris); Civitan (Asheville, N.C.), Biltmore Forest Country (N.C.). Author: American Fighters in the Foreign Legion, 1914-18, 1930; Three Centuries of the Rockwell Family in America, 1630-1930, 1930. Edited War Letters of Kiffin Yates Rockwell, 1925; co-author of books pub. in France and England. Home: Asheville, N.C. †

ROCKWELL, WILLARD FREDERICK, JR., mfg. exec.; b. Boston, Mar. 3, 1914; s. Willard Frederick and Clara (Thayer) R.; B.S., Pa. State U., 1935, I.E., 1955; LL.D. (hon.), Grove City Coll., Lambuth Coll.; D. Eng. (hon.), Tufts U., Carnegie-Mellon U., Washington and Jefferson Coll.; m. Constance Templeton, July 16, 1942; children—Patricia Lynne R. Boorn, Willard Frederick lll, Steven Kent, George Peter, Russell Alden. Cost accountant Pitts. Equitable Meter Co., 1935-36, mgr. engring., 1937-39, v.p., controller, 1939-43, v.p., gen. mgr., 1945-47; asst. to controller Timken-Detroit Axle Co., Detroit, 1936-37; pres. Rockwell Mfg. Co., Pitts., 1947-64, vice chmn. bd., chief exec. officer, 1964-71, chmn. bd., 1971-73, also dir.; pres. Rockwell-Standard Corp., 1963-67, dir., 1942-67; chmn. bd., chief exec. officer N. Am. Rockwell Corp., 1967-73; chmn. bd. Rockwell Internat. 1973-79, chmn. exec. com., dir., from 1979; dir. The El Paso Co., Mellon Bank N.A., Mellon Nat. Corp., Lone Star Industries, Inc., Planning Research Corp., Magic Chef, Inc., Pitts. Athletic Co., Inc. (Pitts. Pirates), El Paso Products Co. Trustee U.S. council Internat. C. of C.; mem. Greater Pitts. Airport Adv. Bd.; trustee Am. Enterprise Inst. for Pub. Policy Research, Aerospace Edn. Found.; chmn. exec. com. Tax Found., Inc.; trustee U. So. Calif., Grove City (Pa.) Coll., Point Park Coll., Carnegie Mus. Natural History; bd. dirs. World Affairs Council Pitts.; chmn. bd. govs. Ford's Theatre, Washington. Served to capt., ordnance, AUS, World War II. Registered profl. engr., Pa., Calif. Fellow Royal Soc. Arts; mem. Natural Gas and Petroleum Assn. Can., Am. Petroleum Inst., Engrs. Soc. Western Pa., Gas Appliance Mfrs. Assn. (pres. 1956, dir.), Smithsonian Assos., Am. Soc. M.E., Am. Inst. Indsl. Engrs., Mil. Order World Wars, Pitts. Athletic Assn., Pa. C. of C. (past pres., dir.), Pitts. C. of C. (past v.p. dir.), Am. Ordnance Assn., Am. Water Works Assn., Pa. Soc., Soc. Automotive Engrs., S.A.R., Conf. Bd., Omicron Delta Kappa, Kappa Sigma, Delta Sigma Pi. Clubs: Duquesne, University, Longue Vue (Pitts.); University (N.Y.C.); Rolling Rock (Ligonier, Pa.); Bath, Indian Creek (Miami Beach); Chicago; Detroit Athletic; California (Los Angeles); Cat Cay (Bahamas); Laurel Valley Golf (Ligonier, Pa.). Address: Pittsburgh, Pa. Deceased.

RODERICK, DORRANCE DOUGLAS, newspaper publisher; b. Brooklyn, Iowa, Dec. 24, 1900; s. Taliesin Evan and Mary (Dorrance) R.; A.B., U. Okla., 1922; m. Olga Burnett, Aug. 14, 1922; children—Frances Rozelle, Dorrance Douglas. Reporter, Tulsa World, 1918; asst. editor AP, Oklahoma City, 1922; with advt. dept. Wichita (Kans.) Eagle, 1923; advt. and bus. mgr. Lubbock (Tex.) Jour., 1924-25, pub., 1926-29; pub. Lubbock Avalanche, 1926-29, El Paso Herald and Times, 1929-31, El Paso Times, 1931-75; ret., 1975; pres. El Paso Times, Inc. Newspaper Printing Corp., Newspaper Realty Corp., Sta. KROD-TV-AM, 1940-60; chmn. bd. Times Enterprises, Inc.; dir., mem. exec. com. El Paso Nat. Bank; dir. Trans Tex. Bancorp. Mem. Tex. Good Neighbor Commn., 1943-57, chmn., 1943; pres. Roderick Found., Inc.; bd. dirs. El Paso Mus. Art, United Fund, Radford Sch. for Girls, Armed Services YMCA; trustee Phi Gamma Ednl. Found; bd. dirs. U. Tex. El Paso Pres.'s Assos., Providence Meml. Hosp., Tex. Daily Press League. Served to maj. AUS, 1943-45. Recipient Human Relations award NCCJ, 1967; Citizen of Year award Bd. Realtors, 1971. Mem. El Paso Indsl. Bd. (dir.), El Paso Symphony Assn. (pres. 1923-63, chmn. bd. 1963-81), El Paso Hist. Soc. (trustee), VFW, Phi Gamma Delta, Sigma Delta Chi, Phi Mu Alpha, Phi Alpha Tau. Episcopalian (vestryman). Clubs: Masons (33 deg.), Shriners (potentate 1938), Jesters, Cabiri, Internat., Ormsbee (pres. 1934-36), Kiwanis (gov. S.W. dist. 1935), Knife and Fork (pres. 1938-39), Coronado Country, El Paso, Pioneer. Home: El Paso, Tex. Died Mar. 28, 1981.

RODGERS, ROBERT C., army officer; b. Mar. 17, 1887; B.S., U.S. Mil. Acad., 1908. Commd. 2d lt. cavalry, Feb. 14, 1908; promoted through grades to col., Dec. 1, 1936; temporary rank of brig. gen. since Oct. 1, 1940; apptd. comdt. Cav. Sch., Fort Riley, 1940.†

RODGERS, WILLIAM WOODSON, lawyer; b. Moberly, Mo., July 2, 1907; s. William and Elizabeth (Harris) R.; A.B., U. Mo., 1929; B.S., U. Okla., 1930, LL.B., 1933; m. Marguerite Louise Gurley, Mar. 9, 1935; children—William Woodson, James R. Admitted to Okla. bar, 1933; practice in Oklahoma City, 1933-37, Blackwell, from 1937; partner firm Rodgers, Rodgers & Boyd, from 1938. Chmn. bd. Security Bank & Trust Co., Blackwell, from 1970. Pres., Blackwell Council Youth; bd. regents No. Okla. Coll., Tonkawa; past regent Okla. Baptist U.; past mayor Blackwell. Mem. Am., Okla., Kay County bar assns., Am. Judicature Soc., Blackwell C. of C., Phi Beta Kappa, Phi Delta Phi. Baptist. Rotarian (past pres. Blackwell). Home: Blackwell, Okla. Died Dec. 12, 1979.

RODICK, BURLEIGH CUSHING, educator; b. Freeport, Me., June 12, 1889; eleventh in direct lineal descent from John Alden of the Mayflower; s. James and Lucy (Cushing) R.; A.B. Bowdoin Coll., 1912; A.M. (univ. scholar), Harvard, 1914; Ph.D., Columbia, 1928. Instr. English, Ill. State Normal Sch., 1915-16; master in history Lawrenceville (N.J.) Sch., 1918-19; prof. and head dept. history and polit. sci., Allegheny Coll., 1919-20; research, N.Y.C., from 1920; dept. history and govt., Hunter Coll. extension, 1920-42; lectr. history, govt. Bklyn. Coll. evening sessions, 1931-35, asst. prof. polit. sci., 1938-59, dep. chmn., 1946-50, grad. sch., 1958-59; head dept. history and social sci. Wagner Coll., S.I., 1933-38; organized first history seminar for graduates at Hunter; apptd. Penfield traveling fellow in internat. law and diplomacy by U. of Pa. for 1924-25; lectr. in history and psychology Bklyn. Tchrs. Assn., 1927-32; lectr. Fgn. Policy Assn.; air raid def. lectr. N.Y. City Police Dept., 1942; del. Pan.-Am. Comml. Congress, N.Y.C., 1927; mem. adv. com. on sociology, Bklyn. Inst. Arts and Scis., 1939. Decorated Knight of Malta-Hereditary Knight of Justice (non-Catholic mem., mem. supreme council under sec. of state from 1968). Fellow Am. Geog. Soc.; mem. Am. Platform Assn., Am. Assn. of U. Profs., A.A.A.S., Soc. of Mayflower Descs. in N.Y. (N.Y. del. to triennial congress 1954-66), N.Y. Soc. Order of Founders and Patriots of Am. (council, historian), Soc. Colonial Wars in the State of N.Y., S.A.R. (mgr. N.Y., 1965, historian 1966, v.p. 1972-73, nat. good citizenship award 1965, bd. mgrs. 1973), Kappa Sigma. Club: Univerity. Author: The Doctrine of Necessity in International Law, 1928; My Own New England Tales of Vanishing Types (fiction), 1929; American Constitutional Custom: A Forgotten Factor in the Founding, 1953; Appomatox: The Last Campaign, 1965. Contbr. mag. articles, book revs., etc. Home: New York, NY. †

RODMAN, CHARLES GILBERT, business exec.; b. Owego, N.Y., May 1, 1921; s. Lawrence L. and Lorena (Root) R.; m. Jane E. McCarthy, June 12, 1946; children—Lawrence L., Sarah J., Andrew C., John W. B.S. in Econs, Wharton Sch. of U. Pa., 1943; LL.B., Harvard, 1949. Bar: Admitted N.Y. bar 1949. With firm Sullivan & Cromwell, N.Y.C., 1949-52; with Grand Union Co., 1952-76, exec. asst. to pres., 1957-60, v.p. operations, 1960-65, exec. v.p., 1965-66, pres., 1966-74, chmn. bd., 1974-76, also chief exec. officer, dir.; trustee Estate of W.T. Grant Co., Bankrupt, from 1976; dir. United Jersey Banks, Hackensack, N.J.; dir. N.J. Bell Telephone Co., Nat. Assn. Food Chains, 1970-76. Mem. planning bd. Village of Ridgewood, N.J., 1965-67; Trustee Valley Hosp., Ridgewood, N.J.; bd. fellows Fairleigh Dickinson U., 1966-69. Home: Ridgewood, NJ.

RODNICK, DAVID, anthropologist, educator; b. New Haven, May 10, 1908; s. Louis David and Bryna (Kaplan) R.; B.S., N.Y. U., 1931; M.A., Yale U., 1933; Ph.D., U. Pa., 1936; m. Elizabeth Wright Amis, Mar. 24, 1945; 1 dau., Amie Bowman. Asst. dir. Inst. Internat. Social Research, Princeton, N.J., 1955-59; chmn., prof. div. social scis. Inter Am. U., P.R., 1959-61; prof. sociology and anthropology Iowa Wesleyan Coll., 1961-63; sr. sociologist Ops. Research, Inc., Washington, 1963-65; prof. sociology and anthropology Tex. Technol. U., Lubbock, 1965-75; vis. prof. U. Hamburg (W. Ger.), 1975-77, cons., 1977-80; cons. Columbia U. Project in Contemporary Cultures, 1947-51. Social Sci. Research Council grantee; Fulbright Sr. Research prof. in Norway and Germany. Fellow Am. Sociol. Assn., Am. Anthrop. Assn., Soc. Applied Anthropology, AAAS; mem. Soc. Internat. Devel., Soc. History of Tech., Am. Acad. Polit. and Social Sci., Internat. Studies Assn. Author: The Fort Belknap Assiniboine, 1938, reprinted, 1978; Postwar Germans, 1948; The Norwegians, 1955; An Introduction to Man and His Development, 1966; The Strangled Democracy, 1970; Essays on an America in Transition, 1972; Man's Quest For Autonomy, 1974; A Portrait of Two German Cities: Lübeck and Hamburg, 1979; contbr. articles to profl. jours. Home: Lubbock, Tex. Died Oct. 9, 1980.

ROE, JERROLD MELVIN, investments executive; b. Industry, Ill., May 29, 1933; s. William Sampson and Lena (Flinn) R.; m. Marilyn Matacia, Jan. 17, 1959; children—Michael, Emily, Timothy, Kathleen, Daniel, Jennifer. B.A. in Commerce, U. Notre Dame, 1955; postgrad., Loyola U. Law Sch., Chgo., 1958-58, Georgetown Grad. Law Sch., 1959. Mgr. accounting operations Md. div. Litton Industries, 1958-60; assoc. Robert Heller Assocs., Cleve., 1960-64; v.p. planning Greatamerica Corp.; also exec. v.p. First Western Bank, Los Angeles, 1964-68; chmn. bd. Minn. Nat. Life Ins. Co., 1968; pres. G.S.I. Inc., Chgo., 1973-82. Served to lt. (j.g.) USNR, 1955-57. Clubs: California (Los Angeles); Union League (Chgo.); Butler National Golf (Oak Brook); La Jolla Country (Rancho Mirage, Calif.), Springs Country (Rancho Mirage, Calif.). Home: La Jolla, Calif. Died May 2, 1982.

ROEDER, RALPH LECLERCQ, writer; b. N.Y. City, Apr. 7, 1890; s. George and Ida (Leclercq) R.; student Columbia, 1906; A.B., Harvard, 1911; m. Fania Mindell, Dec. 3, 1929. Mem. Authors League. Author: Savanarola, 1930; The Man of the Renaissance, 1933; Catherine De Medici and The Lost Revolution, 1937; Juarez and His Mexico, 1947. Home: Mexico City, Mexico. †

ROESCH, WILLIAM ROBERT, steel company executive; b. Large, Pa., May 20, 1925; s. William V. and Edith M. R.; m. Jane Holt. B.S. in Engring. and Bus. Adminstrn, U. Pitts., 1960; grad. advanced mgmt. program, Harvard U., 1966. With Jones & Laughlin Steel Corp., Pitts., 1946-74, pres., 1970-71, chmn. bd., chief exec. officer, 1971-74; pres., chief exec. officer Kaiser Industries, Oakland, Calif., 1974, vice chmn. bd., chief exec. officer, 1974-77; exec. v.p. steel and domestic raw materials U.S. Steel Corp., Pitts., 1978-79, pres., 1979-83; dir. Hilton Hotels Corp., Rockwell Internat. Mem. Am. Iron and Steel Inst. Address: Pittsburgh, Pa. Died Dec. 2, 1983.

ROETZEL, CLETUS G., lawyer; b. Suffield, O., July 24, 1889; s. John T. and Mary Jane, (Schuck) R.; grad. Buchtel Acad., 1908; student Buchtel Coll. (now U. Akron), 1908-09; pvt. study law; LL.D., University of Akron, 1952; married Clara Ester Moore, May 12, 1931. Admitted to Ohio bar, 1912. Practiced in Akron; member Wise, Roetzel, Maxon, Kelly & Andress; pros. atty. Summit Co., 1917-21. Trustee Community Chest Akron, Akron Art Inst.; mem. C. of C. Dir. U. Akron, 1927-52, chmn., 1943-52. Served with F.A., U.S. Army, World War I; commissioned 2d lieutenant, O.R.C., 1918. Decorated Knight Order of St. Gregory the Great by Pope Pius XII, 1949. Mem. Am., Ohio and Akron (past pres.) bar assns., Akron Law Library Assn., Cath. Service League (trustee, past pres.), Am. Legion, Izaak Walton League, Phi Delta Theta. Roman Catholic. K.C. Clubs: Congress Lake Country, Akron City (past pres.), Portage Country. Home: Akron, Ohio. †

ROGERS, BRYON GILES, former congressman; b. Greenville, Tex., Aug. 1, 1900; s. Peter and Minnie M. (Gentry) R.; LL.B., U. Denver, 1925; m. Helen Pauline Kepler, July 11, 1933; children—Shirley Ann, Byron Giles. Admitted to Colo. bar, 1925, and began practice in Las Animas; mem. Colo. Legislature, 1931; speaker House of Rep., 1933; county atty., Bent County, Colo., 1933; on legal staff A.A.A. and NRA Washington, 1933; asst. U.S. atty. Colo., 1934-36; atty. gen. for Colo., 1936-41; mem. 82d-89th, 91st Congresses, 1st Colo. Dist. Pub. Mem. Nat. War Labor Board, 9th region. Past chmn. Denver County Democratic Com. Served with U.S. Army, 1918. Mem. Am. Legion. Democrat. Baptist. Mason (Shriner), Odd Fellow, Elk, Lion. Home: Denver, Colo. Died Dec. 31, 1983.

ROGERS, IRVING EMERSON, newspaper publisher; b. Lawrence, Mass., Aug. 20, 1902; s. Alexander H. and Ethel Lynn (Emerson) R.; m. Martha Buttrick, June 16, 1928; children—Irving Emerson, Alexander H. II. Student, Phillips Andover Acad., 1921, Dartmouth, 1925. Reporter with Lawrence Eagle- Tribune, 1923, pub., pres. treas., from 1942; treas. Consol. Lawrence Eagle-Tribune Trust, both Lawrence; pub., treas. Andover Townsman, Methuen News; gen. mgr. Radio Sta. WLAW, Lawrence, 1937-53; pres., treas. Hildreth & Rogers Co., 1942-53. Chmn. bd. Bon Secours-Lawrence Gen. Joint Hosp. Corp.; chmn. bd. Lawrence Boys Club; chmn. bd. trustees Bon Secours Hosp.; trustee Rogers Family Found. Mem. N.E. Daily Newspaper Assn.

ROGERS, JOHN LENZIE, Interstate Commerce Commission; b. Knoxville, Tenn., June 27, 1889; s. Leon Osmond and Mary Elizabeth (Longbottom) R.; grad. high sch., Knoxville, 1905; student U. of Tenn., 1913-15, George Washington U., 1917-18, Nat. U. Law Sch., 1922-25; m. Rady Ester Ogle, Sept. 6, 1914; children—Leon William, John Lenzie. With Interstate Commerce Commn. from 1917; as mech. engr., 1917-25, spl. examiner, 1925-33, exec. asst. to federal coördinator of transportation, 1933-35, dir. Bur. of Motor Carriers, 1933-35; mem. Interstate Commerce Commn. from 1937; chmn. Interstate Commerce Commn., 1945; dir. motor transport, Office of Defense Transportation 1942-43, asst. dir. Office of Defense Transportation from 1943. Methodist. Admitted to Tenn. bar, 1925, U.S. Supreme Ct., 1935. Home: Washington, D.C. †

ROGERS, JOSEPH PATRICK, lawyer; b. Syracuse, N.Y., Sept. 3, 1906; s. Joseph P. and Mary (Ryan) R.; LL.B., Cornell U., 1928; m. Helen Montgomery, Aug. 17, 1935; children—Joseph Patrick, John Otto, Jane (Mrs. Robert J. Corcoran). Admitted to N.Y. bar, 1929, since practiced in Syracuse; partner firm Hiscock, Lee, Rogers, Henley & Barclay, 1948-81. Dir., sec. Columbian Rope Co.; dir. Excelsior Ins. Co. N.Y., Vega Industries, Inc.; dir., sec. Newton Line Co., Syracuse Cold Storage Co. Mem. Am., N.Y. State, Onondaga County bar assns., Am. Judicature Soc., Syracuse C. of C. Clubs: Cornell (dir.), University, Century (Syracuse); Skaneateles Country. Home: Syracuse, N.Y. Died June 5, 1981.

ROGERS, WILLARD BENJAMIN, hotel executive, insurance, advertising; b. Manchester, Connecticut, October 28, 1888; s. Alexander and Sarah (Sinnamon) Rogers; educated high sch., South Manchester, Connecticut; m. Ruth McCue, of Hartford, Conn., Mar. 15, 1911; 1 son, Kermit. Nat. pres. Fraternal Benefit League, New Haven, Conn., 1919-24; nat. rep. Am. Ins. Union, Columbus, O., 1924-26; gen. mgr., later also sec. and treas. Fuller Battery Co. since 1924; gen. mgr. and treas. Rogers Land Co. since 1926; dir. and in charge advertising Hotel Bond Co., since 1927; pres. and gen. mgr. The Bond Hotels; owner Rogers Ins. Agency. Mem. Conn. div. New England Council since 1929. Mem. Conn. House of Rep., 1917-21; selectman, Manchester, 1914-24, police commr., Manchester, since 1924. Chmn. Conn. State Publicity Commn., Connecticut Div. of New York World's Fair; Hartford Conv. and Publicity Bureau; mem. All-New England Recreational Development Com.; dir. Hartford Govtl. Research Bur.; dir. Conn. Hotel Assn.; mem. Hotel Greeters of America, U.S. Chamber of Commerce; dir. Conn. Chamber Commerce, Hartford Chamber Commerce. Republican. Episcopalian. Mason. Clubs: Manchester City, Lions, Hartford Advertising, Hartford Automobile (dir.). Home: South Manchester, Conn. †

ROGERSON, JAMES RUSSELL, lawyer, corp. exec.; b. Kiantone, N.Y., Oct. 1, 1892; s. David M. and Alberta M. (Campbell) R.; m. Eleanor E. Olson, Dec. 22, 1917; children—Adele (Mrs. Lyman C. Wynne), Rita (Mrs. Burton N. Lowe). LL.B., Syracuse U., 1914. Bar: N.Y. bar 1917. Since practiced in, Jamestown, corp. counsel, 1929-30; chmn. bd. Art Metal, Inc., 1963-68; pres. Phelps Can Co., 1966-82; dir., exec. com. Mid Continent Telephone Corp., 1968-76, Jamestown Telephone Corp., 1946-76. Del. Republican Nat. Conv., 1948. Served with U.S. Army, 1917-19; Served with AEF in, France. Fellow Am. Coll. Trial Lawyers; mem. Am., N.Y. State, Jamestown bar assns. Presbyn. Home: Jamestown, N.Y. Died May 3, 1982.

ROHLICH, GERARD ADDISON, civil and environmental engineer, educator; b. Bklyn., July 8, 1910; s. Henry Otto and Margaret Loretta (Burns) R.; m. Mary Elizabeth Murphy, Sept. 8, 1941; children: Mary Ellen, Gerard A., Thomas Henry, Karl Otto, Catherine Ann, Henry James, Virginia Jean, John Harold, Richard Joseph, James William. B.C.E., Cooper Union, 1934, U. Wis., 1936; M.C.E., U. Wis., 1937, Ph.D. in Civil Engring, 1940. Diplomate: Am. Acad. Environ Engrs. Instr. civil engring. Carnegie Inst. Tech., Pitts., 1937-39; asst. prof. civil engring. Pa. State Coll., State College, 1941-43, assoc. prof., 1945-46; sr. san. engr., office chief of engrs. Dept. War, Washington, 1943-44; chief project engr. Esna Corp., Union, N.J., 1944-45; prof. civil engring. U. Wis., Madison, 1946-72, assoc. dean grad. sch., 1963-65, dir. Water Resources Center, 1963-71, dir. Inst. Environ. Studies, 1967-70; C.W. Cook prof. environ. engring., prof. pub. affairs U. Tex., Austin, 1972-83; vis. prof. U. Calif., Berkeley, 1963, U. Helsinki, Finland, 1970; Walker-Ames prof. U. Wash., Seattle, 1972; mem. adv. bd. on hazardous wastes Office of Tech. Assessment, U.S. Congress; cons. WHO; commr. Madison Water Utility, 1961-70; mem. bd. Wis. Dept. Natural Resources, 1966-72. Contbr. articles in field to profl. jours. and books. Recipient Benjamin Smith Reynolds award Excellence Teaching Engring. U. Wis., 1962; named Wis. Water Man of Year Am. Water Works Assn., 1969; recipient hon. citation Cooper Union, 1971, Gordon Maskew Fair medal Water Pollution Control Fedn., 1980. Fellow ASCE (Karl Emil Hilgard Hydraulics award 1972); mem. Nat. Acad. Engring. Democrat. Roman Catholic. Home: Austin, Tex. Died Sept. 16, 1983.

ROHR, JOHN T., banker; b. Toledo, O., July 2, 1889; s. Samuel and Helen A. (Turner) R.; grad. Toledo High Sch., 1906; m. Clara I. Klauser, Sept. 20, 1911. With 2d Nat. Bank, Toledo and its successor Toledo Trust Co. since 1906, began as bank messenger, pres., 1936-59, chmn. bd., from 1959; mem. bd. dirs. De Vilbiss Co., Toledo Scale Corp., Bostwick-Baun Co., Toledo Plate & Window Glass Co., Bunting Brass & Bronze Co., Jennison-Wright Corp., Owens-Illinois Glass Company, Mather Spring Company and the Toledo Edison Company, O. Episcopalian. Mason. Clubs: Toledo, Toledo Country, Toledo Yacht, Inverness (Toledo). †

ROLL, LYLE CHARLES, grocery mfg. exec.; b. Easton, Ill., Sept. 13, 1907; s. Sidney R. and Margaret (Hurley) R.; student Ill. Wesleyan U.; Ph.D. in Law (hon.), Mich. State U.; m. Martha Angela Barrett (dec.); m. 2d, Marguerite Swallen. With Kellogg Co., 1927-84, sales mgr. Kellogg Co. of Can., 1947-49, asst. to pres. Kellogg Co., 1949-52, v.p., 1952, exec. v.p., 1953-57, pres., gen. mgr., 1957-68, chmn., chief exec., 1963-73, vice-chmn. bd., chmn. exec. com., 1973-79, chmn. emeritus, dir., mem. exec. com., 1979-84; dir. Consumers Power Co., J.M. Smuckers Co., Bankers Life Co. Trustee W.K. Kellogg Found., Ill. Wesleyan U. Home: Battle Creek, Mich. Died Sept. 4, 1984.

ROMANACH, MARIO JOSE, architect; b. Havana, Cuba, Dec. 2, 1917; came to U.S., 1965; s. Mario Jose and Estela (Paniagua) R.; Architect's Degree, U. Havana, 1945; M.A. (hon.), U. Pa., 1971; m. Josefa E. Romanach, Dec. 14, 1944; children—Maria Cristina, Josefina. With Bosch/Romanach Architects, 1945-54; prin. Mario Romanach Architect, 1954-76; exec. dir. Havana Met. Planning Office, 1954-59; dir. design, asso. Kelly & Gruzen, N.Y.C., 1962-64; partner Romanach Partnership, Phila., 1976-84; asso. prof. architecture Cornell U., 1960-62; prof. U. Pa., 1962-84; vis. critic, master class Grad. Sch. Design, Harvard U., 1959-60. Recipient Gold medal Colegio National de Arquitectos, Havana, 1947, 55; Progressive Architecture award, 1966, 67; Bard award, 1968. Fellow AIA; mem. Nat. Acad. Design, Pa. Soc. Architects, Phila. Art Alliance, Archtl. League (founding). Archtl. works include: Chatham Towers, N.Y.C., 1966, Residence Luis Vega, Caracas, Venezuela, U. Pa. Student Housing, 1970, Power Plant and Adminstrn. Bldg. CADAFE, Punta Moron, Venezuela, 1977, Residence D. Alger, Pottersville, N.J., 1978. Contbr. articles to Arts and Architecture, Architectural Forum, Progressive Architecture, Arquitectura, Album de Cuba. Home: Philadelphia, Pa. Died Mar. 8, 1984.

ROMANO, UMBERTO, artist, educator; b. Italy, Feb. 26, 1906; came to U.S., 1914, naturalized, 1926; s. Andrea and Raffaela (Cerrate) R.; m. Clorinda Corcia, June 12, 1941; 1 son, Umberto Roberto, Jr. Student, N.A.D., 1922-26; Tiffany Found. fellow, 1926; research study of old masters technique, Am. Acad. in Rome, 1926-27. Founder Romano Sch. Art (Gallery on the Moors), East Gloucester, Mass., 1933; founder Romano Winter Sch. Art, N.Y.C., 1941; head Worcester Art Mus. Sch., 1934-40; dir. Castle Hill Found.; Artists Equity Academician, Abbey Found.; bd. dirs. chmn. sch. com. N.A.D., 1st v.p., 1967. Illustrator: Great Men, 1979; illustrations for Dante's Divine Comedy, 1946; originals exhibited in museum, U.S., 1947-49, Europe, 1956-67, numerous one-man exhbns., 1928-82; works include portrait of Mrs. Sara Delano Roosevelt in Roosevelt Library, Hyde Park, N.Y., Three Centuries of New England History; mural in, Springfield (Mass.) P.O.; portrait of Gov. Foster Furcolo in Mass. State House, Boston; represented permanent collections, Fogg Art Mus., Worcester Art Mus., Springfield Mus. Fine Arts, Addison Gallery, Andover, R.I. Sch. Design, Smith Coll. Mus., Tel Aviv Mus., Pa. Acad. Fine Arts, San Diego Mus., Nat. Acad., Whitney Mus., N.Y., Corcoran Art Gallery, Washington, Cin. Mus., Smithsonian Instn., Brandeis U., U. Maine, Fairleigh Dickinson U., White Mus. at Cornell U., So. Ill. U., Ohio U., Syracuse (N.Y.) U., Nat. Collection Fine Arts, Washington U. Miami, Phoenix Mus., Birmingham (Ala.) Mus., Evansville (Ill.) Mus., Norfolk (Va.) Mus., Chrysler Mus., others, also numerous collections in the, U.S., Eng., France and, Italy; executed mosaic mural, New City and Municipal Cts. Bldg., N.Y.C., 1959-60 (Recipient awards including Peabody prize, Chgo. Art Inst., Pulitzer prize, Crowninshield award, Stockbridge, Mass., Tiffany Foundation medal, Atheneum prize, Conn. Academy, 1st prize and portrait prize, Springfield Art League, Lewis prize N. Shore Arts Assn., Suydam Silver Medal, Carnegie award Nat. Acad. 1951, Saltus Gold medal of Honor, Nat. Acad. N.Y. 1959, gold medal 1961, Allied Artist medal of honor 1961, Lillian Cotton prize 1963, 1st prize Rockport Art Assn. 1964, Grumbacher purchase award Audubon Artists 1967, Century Club medals 1967, 68). Mem. Internat. Assn. of Fine Arts (v.p. 1965), Nat. Soc. Mural Painters (v.p.), Allied Artists Am. (Emily Lowe prize 1962, 73), Audubon Artists (pres. 1971), Provincetown Art Assn. (v.p. 1963, dir.). Club: Century (N.Y.C.). (N.Y.C.). Home: New York, N.Y. Died Sept. 27, 1982.

ROMBERG, PAUL F(REDERICK), univ. pres.; b. Nebr., Dec. 31, 1921; s. Alexander and Catherine (Hiebenthal) R.; m. Rose Mayer, Apr. 23, 1944; children—Catherine, Rose Marie. Ph.D. in Botany, U. Nebr., 1954. Asso.

prof. botany Wabash Coll., 1952-56, Iowa State U., 1956-62; prof. biology, v.p. acad. affairs Chico State Coll., 1962-67; founding pres. Calif. State Coll. at Bakersfield, 1967-73; pres. San Francisco State U., 1973-83; Mem. nat. adv. council on health professions edn. Dept. Health, Edn. and Welfare; mem. Nat. Commn. Future State Colls. and Univs.; cons. NSF. Past pres. YMCA; chmn. San Francisco Consortium, 1973; mem. Fromm Inst. for Life-Long Learning. Recipient Weber-Ernst Bot. award. Mem. A.A.A.S., Am. Assn. State Colls. and Univs. (task force on allied health professions), Am. Coll. Health Assn., Am. Inst. Biol. Scis., San Francisco C. of C., Bakersfield C. of C. (dir.), Nat. Assn. Biology Tchrs., Blue Key, Sigma Xi, Phi Kappa Phi. Clubs: Commonwealth (San Francisco), University (San Francisco). Home: San Francisco, Calif. Died Apr. 6, 1985.*

ROME, MORTON PHILLIPS, elec. co. exec., lawyer; b. Phila., Apr. 2, 1913; s. John J. and Etta (Phillips) R.; B.A., U. Pa., 1933, LL.B., 1936; m. Marjorie Taussig, June 20, 1942; children—Mary T., Sally P., Thomas M. Admitted to Pa. bar, 1936; with firm Sundheim, Folz & Sundheim, Phila., 1936-42; partner firm Sundheim, Folz, Kamsler & Goodis, Phila., 1946-51; v.p. contracts Emerson Radio & Phonograph Corp., N.Y.C., 1951-60, dir., 1966, v.p., sec., 1962-66; pres., dir. Emertron, Inc.. Jersey City and Washington, 1960-62; sec., counsel Nat. Union Electric Corp., Greenwich, Conn., from 1966; sec. Onward Mfg. Co., Ltd., Kitchener, Ont., Can., from 1973. Served to capt. U.S. Army, 1942-46. Decorated Commendation ribbon. Mem. Am., Pa., Phila. bar assns., Order of Coif. Clubs: Philmont Country; Princeton (N.Y.C.). Address: Wyncote, Pa. Deceased.

ROMNEY, ROXEY STOWELL, Dem. Nat. Committeewomen Utah; b. Salt Lake City, Apr. 13, 1889; d. Brigham and Rhoda (Bybee) Stowell; student Brigham Young U., 1912-13, Dixie Coll., 1943-44; grad. Riverside Library Sch., 1923; m. Erastus Snow Romney, Aug. 31, 1910; children—Elwood Snow, Roxey (Mrs. Albert Davis), Wanda (Mrs. C. C. Gardner), Myles Waldo. Librarian, Washington Co., Utah, 1923-51; library project dir. Works Progress Adminstrn., 1935-36. Mem. Washington Co. Cancer Control Commn., 1938-44; chmn. Washington Co. A.R.C., 1944-45. Dir. Nat. Youth Adminstrn., Washington Co. project, 1937-38; city commr. St. George, Utah, 1937-39; v. chmn. Washington Co., Dem. Com., 1935-48; Utah committeewoman Dem. Nat. Com., 1948-52. Mem. bd. regents U. Utah, 1947-51. Mem. Am. Polit. Sci. Assn., Utah Library Assn. (pres. 1938-39, exec. com. 1938-51). Mem. Latter Day Saints Ch. Clubs: Literary, Utah Federated, Athena, Reynolds, St. George, Business and Professional Women (Salt Lake City). Home: Salt Lake City, Utah. †

RONEY, JAY LOUIS, social worker; b. Chester, S.D., Feb. 12, 1913; s. Ray W. and Caroline (Krumm) R.; A.B., Augustana Coll., Sioux Falls, S.D., 1936; M.A., Western Res. U., 1938; m. Jean M. Tollefson, July 15, 1937; children—Susan, Linda, Jennifer. Social caseworker Inst. Family Service (now Family Service Assn.), Cleve., 1938-40; chief of pub. assistance S.D. Dept. Social Security (now Dept. Pub. Welfare), Pierre, 1940-42, dir. dept., 1947-50; exec. sec. Luth. Welfare Soc. Minn., Mpls., 1942-47; regional child welfare rep., children's bur. Social Security Adminstrn., Dept. Health, Edn. and Welfare, Kansas City, Mo., 1950-54, dir. Bur. Pub. Assistance, Washington, 1954-59; dir. Pub. Welfare Project Aging, Am. Pub. Welfare Assn., Chgo., 1959-68; dir. community relations staff Office External Affairs, Social Security Adminstrn., Balt., 1968-78; ret., 1978. Recipient Centennial award Augustana Coll., 1960; certificate honor Western Res. U. Alumni, 1966. Mem. Council Social Work Edn., Am. Pub. Welfare Assn., Nat. Assn. Social Workers. Lutheran. Home: Columbia, Md. Died Dec. 25, 1982.

ROOP, JAMES CLAWSON, airline exec.; b. Upland, Pa., Oct. 3, 1888; s. Albert A. and Mary (Clawson) R.; grad. Blight School, Phila., Pa., 1905; B.S. in E.E., U. of Pa., 1909; m. Rebecca Haigh, Mar. 7, 1929. Instr. in elec. engring., U. of Pa., 1909-10; with Phila. and West Chester Traction Co., 1910-15; cons. work under Prof. G. F. Sever, N.Y. City, 1915-16; in charge constrn. and testing work, J. G. White Management Corp., 1916-17, gen. supervision and spl. reporting on pub. utilities, 1919-21; with Bur. of Budget, Washington, D.C., June 1921-June 1922, asst. dir., Jan.-June 1922; with Woods Bros. Constrn. Co., Lincoln, Neb., 1922-25; pres. Monomarks, Inc., May 1925-Oct. 1926; with Dawes Bros., Inc., Chicago, 1926-29; mem. Dominican Econ. Commn., Apr.-July 1929; dir. U.S. budget, Aug. 1929-Mar. 1933; with Pan-Am. Airways, Inc., 1935-49; consultant to chmn. munitions bd., 1949, retired. Vice president and treas. Pan-Am. Airways Corp. and its principal subsidiaries. Served as captain, major and lt. col. Engr. Corps, U.S. Army, World War I; in Engr. Supply Office, Sept.-Dec. 1917, Office of Gen. Purchasing Agt., A.E.F., Dec. 1917-Sept. 1919; mem. staff Mil. Bd. of Allied Supply, July-Nov. 1918; served as col., brig. gen. U.S. Army, 1942; gen. purchasing agt. U.S. Army Forces in Australia and U.S. Mem. of Allied Supply Council in Australia. Decorated D.S.M. (U.S.); Legion of Honor (France); Order Crown of Italy. Republican. Episcopalian. Clubs: Army and Navy (Washington); University (New York). Home: New Canaan, Conn. Deceased.

ROOSEVELT, NICHOLAS, author; b. New York, N.Y., June 12, 1893; s. J. West and Laura (d'Oremieulx) R.; A.B., Harvard, 1914; m. Tirzah Maris Gates, June 5, 1936. Attaché Am. Embassy, Paris, France, 1914-16; sec. mission to Spain, Am. Internat. Corp., 1916-17; editorial writer, New York Tribune, 1921-23; spl. corr. Vienna (Austria) Neue Freie Presse, Le Temps (Paris), De Haagsche Post of Holland, since 1921; editorial writer and spl. corr. New York Times, 1923-30; vice-gov. Philippine Islands, July-Sept. 1930; U.S. minister to Hungary, 1930-33; mem. editorial staff N.Y. Herald-Trib. from 1933; dep. dir. Office of War Information, Dec. 1942-Sept. 1943; asst. to pub. N.Y. Times, from Feb. 1944. Served as capt. 322d Inf., U.S. Army, 1917-19; attached to Am. Com. to Negotiate Peace, 1919. Republican. Clubs: Century; Metropolitan (Washington). Author: The Philippines, a Treasure and a Problem, 1926; The Restless Pacific, 1928; America and England?, 1930; The Townsend Plan, 1936; A New Birth of Freedom, 1938. Home: L.I., N.Y. Died Feb. 16, 1982.

ROOT, WAVERLEY LEWIS, author; b. Providence, Apr. 15, 1903; s. Francis Solomon and Florence (Lewis) R.; B.A., Tufts Coll., 1924; m. Colette Debenais, Apr. 9, 1959; 1 dau. by previous marriage, Diane Lane. Corr., Chgo. Tribune, Paris, London, Rome, 1927-30, news editor, Paris edit., 1930-34; Paris corr. Politiken, Copenhagen, Denmark, 1932-40, U.P., 1934-38, Time mag., 1938, MBS, 1938-40, Chgo. Times, 1939-40; editor World Behind Headlines, N.Y. Daily Mirror, 1941-42; syndicated columnist Press Alliance, N.Y.C., 1941-44; radio news analyst Sta. WINS, N.Y.C., WAAT, Newark, 1941-42; ghost writer Opera Mundi, Paris, 1950-52; editor Fodor's Modern Guides, The Hague, 1952-55; Paris corr. Washington Post, 1958-67; Paris editor Holiday mag., 1968-71. Mem. exec. com. Franco-Am. Club, N.Y.C., 1940-43. Decorated officer Legion of Honor (France). Mem. Anglo-Am. Press Assn. Paris (pres. 1967). Club: Overseas Press (v.p.) (N.Y.C.). Author: The Truth About Wagner, 1929; Secret History of the War, 1945; Casablanca to Katyn, 1946; Winter Sports in Europe, 1956; The Food of France, 1958; (with Richard D. Rochemont) Contemporary French Cooking, 1962; The Cooking of Italy, 1968; Paris Dining Guide, 1969; The Food of Italy, 1971; (with Richard de Rochemont) Eating in America: A History, 1976. Home: Paris, France. Died Oct. 31, 1982.

ROPER, JOHN LONSDALE, II, ship building, conversion and repair co. exec.; b. Norfolk, Va., Sept. 18, 1902; s. George Wisham and Isabelle Place (Hayward) R.; m. Sarah Engle Dryfoos, Apr. 7, 1926; children—John Lonsdale III, George Wisham II, Isabel Roper Yates. Student, Princeton U., 1920-21. With Norfolk Shipbuilding & Drydock Corp., from 1925, pres., gen. mgr., 1956-68, pres., chief exec. officer, 1968-73, chmn. bd., from 1973; officer, dir. John L. Roper Estate, Inc., Lonsdale Bldg. Corp. Trustee, mem. distbn. com. Norfolk Found.; pres. Norfolk United Fund, then gen. chmn., dir. emeritus; bd. dirs. Urban Coalition of Norfolk. Recipient Disting. Service medal Cosmopolitan Club of Norfolk, 1969. Mem. Hampton Rds. Maritime Assn., Inc. (pres., life dir., Disting. Service award 1973), Am. Bur. Shipping, Am. Inst. Mgmt. (pres.'s council, 1st Marquis award), Soc. Naval Architects and Marine Engrs., Propeller Club U.S. Episcopalian. Clubs: Capitol Hill (Washington); Commonwealth (Richmond, Va.); Whitehall (N.Y.C.), Princeton (N.Y.C.); Va. (Norfolk) (pres.), Norfolk Yacht and Country (Norfolk) (dir.); Princess Anne Country (Virginia Beach, Va.). Home: Norfolk, Va. Deceased.

RORK, GLEN V., utilities exec.; b. Reedsburg, Wis., Dec. 26, 1887; s. Willard Wilcox and Mary (Bishop) R.; student Ripon (Wis.) Col., 1908; m. Eleanor Angeline Weidman, Sept. 28, 1911; children—Whitman, Allen, Kathryn. Sales clerk, Reedsburg, 1902-06; mechanic, later electrician and foreman, Northwestern Improvement Co., 1908-14; supt. Greenwood (Wis.) Municipal Light & Power System, 1914-19; dist. mgr. Wis.-Minn. Light & Power Co., Blair, Wis., and Owen, Wis., 1919-28; div. mgr. No. States Power Co., Eau Clire, Wis., 1928-32, v.p., 1932-38, pres. from 1938; pres. Eau Claire Dells Improvement Co. from 1938; pres. Chippewa Flambeau Improvement Co. Conglist. Office: Eau Claire, Wis. †

ROSALES, JULIO RAS, cardinal; b. Calbayog, Samar, P.I., Sept. 18, 1906; s. Basilio Cinco and Agueda Sison (Ras) R.; grad. Colegio-Seminario de San Vicente de Paul, Calbayog; LL.D. (hon.), U. San Carlos, 1962; L.H.D. (hon.), La Salle Coll., 1966. Ordained priest Roman Catholic Ch., 1929; dir. Tacloban Catholic Institute (now Divine Word University), 1930-41, pastor, 1943-45; bishop of Tagbilaran, Bohol, P.I., 1945-50; archbishop Met. Cebu (P.I.), 1950—; named cardinal, 1969. Decorated knight of Corpus Christi, Toledo, Spain, Grand Cross of Ramond de Penfort, Spain. Mem. Cultura Hispanica (hon.), K.C. (4 deg.). Address: Cebu City, Philippines. Died June 2, 1983.

ROSE, ALVIN EMANUEL, pub. housing ofcl.; b. Chgo., Dec. 13, 1903; s. Emanuel Joseph and Winona (Pruitt) R.; student James Millikin U., 1923-25; A.B., U. Ill., 1927; m. Anita B. Bartlesmeyer, Sept. 13, 1929; children—Alan, Peter. Newspaperman, 1927-37; city editor Chgo. Times, 1935-37; pub. welfare worker, 1937-57, commr. welfare City of Chgo., 1946-57; exec. dir. Chgo. Housing Authority, 1957-67. Mem. Welfare Council Met. Chgo. Served as lt. comdr., air combat intelligence, USNR, 1942-45. Recipient Good Am. award Com. 100, 1964. Mem. Am. Pub. Welfare Assn., Ill. Welfare Assn., Nat. Assn. Housing and Redevelopment Ofcls., Beta Theta Pi, Lambda Alpha. Clubs: Chicago Press; Columbia Yacht; City (Chgo.). Author: The Restless Corpse, 1950, other mystery novels, short stories. Home: Oceanside, Calif. Died May 28, 1983.

ROSE, EARL GRIFFITH, coast guard officer; b. Lithopolis, Ohio, 1888; s. Calvin U. and Sallie Elizabeth (Griffith) R.; student Ohio State U., 1907-10, Coast Guard Acad., 1910-13; m. Dorothy Reeder, June 21, 1921; 1 daughter, Marilyn Eleanor. Commd. ensign, U.S. Coast Guard, 1913, advancing through the grades to rear admiral, 1945; comd. U.S.S. Rambler in European waters during World War I; comd. Coast Guard destroyer squadron in Cuban waters, 1933; comd. U.S.C.G. Cutter Tampa in rescue of crew from burning steamship Morro Castle (off coast of New Jersey), 1934; comd. Greenland Patrol, U.S. Atlantic Fleet, 1943-45; comdg. Task Force 24, 1945-46. Chief, Office of Operations, U.S. Coast Guard Headquarters, Washington, D.C., 1946-49. Decorated Navy Cross and Legion of Merit (U.S.), Chevalier of Legion of Honor (France). Home: Alexandria, Va. Died Oct. 20, 1982.

ROSE, EDWARD C., army officer; b. Colo., Dec. 12, 1890; B.S., U.S. Mil. Acad., 1912; grad. Inf. Sch., 1927, Command and Gen. Staff Sch., 1928, Army War Coll., 1933. Commd. 2d lt., Inf., 1912, and advanced through the grades to brig. gen., 1943.†

ROSE, IVAN MURRAY, clergyman; b. Hebron, N.S., Canada, Dec. 29, 1888; s. Edson A. and Bessie J. R.; A.B., Acadia Univ. (N.S.), 1911, M.A. 1915, D.D., 1929; student Rochester Theological Seminary, 1915-18; married Mildred B. Rose, September 3, 1912 (died March 8, 1947); children—Robert B., Murray L.; married Margaret M. Rose, July 5, 1949. Came to U.S., 1915, naturalized, 1925. Ordained Bapt. ministry, 1912; successively minister in N.S., 1912-15, at Malone, N.Y., 1918-22, Rome, N.Y., 1922-25, First Bapt. Ch., Phila., Pa., from 1925. Republican. Club: Union League. Home: Brynwood Apts., Wynnewood, Pa. Address: Philadelphia, Pa. Deceased.

ROSE, LEONARD, cellist; b. Washington, July 27, 1918; s. Harry and Jennie (Frenkel) R.; m. Minnie Knopow, Dec. 1, 1938 (dec. June 1964); children: Barbara Jean, Arthur Ira; m. Xenia Petschek, Jan. 29, 1965. Grad., Curtis Inst. Music, Phila., 1938. Mem. faculty Juilliard Sch. Music, N.Y.C., 1947—, Curtis Inst. Music, 1951-62; vis. instrumentalist Eastern Music Festival, Greensboro, N.C., 1980. Asst. 1st cellist, NBC Symphony, 1st cellist, Cleve. Orch., 1939-43, debut, N.Y. Philharmonic, 1943; first cellist, 1944-51; soloist recitals, Town Hall, N.Y.C., also orchs. including, Boston Symphony, Phila. Orch., Chgo. Symphony, St. Louis Symphony, San Francisco Orch., London Symphony; also orchs., Paris, soloist, The Hague, ann. tours, U.S., Can., Europe, rec. for, Columbia Masterworks; mem. Istomin, Stern, Rose trio; Editor numerous compositions, Internat. Music, N.Y.C. Home: Croton-on-Hudson, N.Y. Died Nov. 16, 1984.*

ROSE, R(OBERT) S(ELDEN), coll. prof.; b. Geneva N.Y., Feb. 12, 1887; s. Oswald John Cammann and Edith Ayrault; ed. Groton Sch., 1900-04; Hobart Coll., 1904-05; B.A., Yale, 1909, M.A., 1927; Ph.D., U. of Calif., 1915; m. Annette Blake Moran, Apr. 26, 1919; children—Gertrude Vander Poel, Anne Fitzhugh, Edith Ayrault, Virginia, Robert Selden. Instr., St. Paul's Sch., 1909; studied in Madrid, Paris, 1912-14; instr., U. of Calif., 1914-17; instr., Yale U., 1919-23, asst. prof., 1923-25, asso. prof., 1925-27, prof. from 1927. Fellow Calhoun Coll. Served with Army Signal Corps, 1917-19. Chmn. Yale Athletic Assn., 1930-32. Mem. Modern Lang. Assn. America, Sigma Phi, Psi Upsilon, Scroll and Key. Clubs: Mary's Assn. (bd. govs.), Graduates Club (pres., 1938-40). Episcopalian. Democrat. Author: Wine Making for the Amateur, 1930. Editor: El Buscon, 1927; El Passagero, 1914; Letters of Diego de Mendoza, 1936. Home: New Haven, Conn. †

ROSEMOND, ALICE, coll. prof.; b. Cambridge, O., July 30, 1890; d. Fred Leslie and Ella (Grimes) Rosemond; A.B., Randolph-Macon Woman's College, 1912; Certificate of Proficiency, Centro de Estudios Historicos, Madrid, Spain, summer 1918; A.M., Ohio State (scholarship, 1921), 1923, grad. work, 1926-28; student U. of Calif., summer 1935; Columbia, summer 1940; Fla. Southern Coll. Summer School, Guatemala, 1946. Teacher, Mary J. Platt Sch. for Mexican Girls, Tucson, Ariz., 1912-15; teacher of English Colegio Internacional, Barcelona, Spain, 1916-19; teacher Spanish, Niles (O.) High Sch., 1920-31; instr. Denison U., Granville, O., 1921, asst. prof. Spanish, 1925; head Spanish dept. Henderson (Ark.) Coll., 1925-26; asst. to dean of women, Ohio State U., 1926-29; dean of women and prof. modern langs., Marietta (O.) Coll., 1929-46, prof. modern langs. 1946-53. Mem. Am. Assn. Univ. Women (pres. Marietta br. 1931-35, vice pres. state assn. and state membership chmn., 1933-35, sec. Marietta br., 1929-31, 1937-39), Am. Assn. Univ. Profs., Am. Assn. Teachers Spanish, Am. Red Cross (flood relief worker, Mar. 1945-Apr. 1948), Ohio Assn. Deans of Women (hon. mem.; v.p. 1930-32, state com. chmn., 1932-34, Nat. Assn. Deans of Women (active mem., 1928-46), Marietta County Concert Assn., Marietta Pub. Library Assn., 1949, Delta Kappa Gamma (state founder, 1938; pres., 1939-43, v.p. state orgn., 1938-40, state com. chmn., 1940-42, state research chmn.,

1944-46). Mem. state research com., Delta Kappa Gamma. Methodist. Clubs: Reading, Music, Executive. Home: Columbus, Ohio. †

ROSEN, MARTIN M., investment banker; b. Cin., Aug. 7, 1919; s. Samuel and Sarah (Fradkin) R.; m. Judith Frank Jacobs, Mar. 27, 1949; children: Andrea, Henry Samuel, Yereth, Irene Rochelle, Marshall Aaron, Jania Joy. A.B. with high honors, U. Cin., 1940; M.A., U. Minn., 1947. Economist, U.S. Treasury Dept., 1941-42; dep. chief finance div. U.S. Element, Allied Commn. Austria, 1945-46; with IBRD, 1946-61, dir. dept. ops. Far East, 1957-61; dir. ops. Far East, Internat. Devel. Assn., 1960-61; exec. v.p. Internat. Finance Corp., 1961-69; pres. First Washington Securities Corp., 1969-72, chmn., 1972-84; pres. Model, Roland & Co. Inc., 1972-73, co-chmn., 1973-74; vice chmn. Shields Model Roland, 1974-77; dir. Atlantic Bank of N.Y., LogEtronics, Inc., Internat. Horizons, Inc., TAIR A.G., City Nat. Bank, Internat. Developers Inc., City Nat. Bank Corp., Miami; dir. Calif. Commerce Bank, Los Angeles; mem. internat. adv. bd. Am. Security & Trust.; lectr. internat. econs. Am. U., 1947; dep. chief finance br. Office Spl. Rep. in Europe, ECA, 1948. Contbr. articles to profl. jours. Served with AUS, 1942-46. Decorated govts. Colombia, Japan, Mauritania, Senegal. Mem. Am. Econ. Assn., Fgn. Policy Assn. (gov.), Royal Econ. Soc. Clubs: International (Washington); Wall Street (N.Y.C.), Lotos (N.Y.C.). Home: Alexandria, Va. Died Nov. 23, 1984.

ROSENBERG, A. H., b. Chicago, May 7, 1889; founder Universal Match Corp., St. Louis, 1926, pres. from 1951. Home: Clayton, Mo. †

ROSENBERG, LOUIS COMRAD, artist; b. Portland, Ore., May 6, 1890; s. Charles and Hannah (Wikstrand) R.; spl. student Mass. Inst. Tech., 1912-14, traveling fellow, 1920-22; Royal Coll. of Art, London, 1925-26; m. Marie Louise Allen, June 24, 1919. Archtl. draftsman, 1906; prof. architecture U. Ore., 1915-20; archtl. illustrator, 1922-25; chief designer of architect Kifk-Colcam-Voss & Souder, N.Y.C., from 1948. Represented in collections large museums and galleries in U.S., abroad. Recipient awards, prizes. Served with Camouflage Corps, 40th Engrs., A.E.F., U.S. Army, 1917-19. Nat. academician, 1936. Fellow Royal Soc. Painter-Etchers and Engravers, Royal Soc. Arts (London); mem. Soc. Am. Etchers, Gravers, Lithographers and Wood Cutters, Palm Beach Art League, A.I.A., New Eng. Print Assn., Audubon Artists, Am. Vet. Soc. Artists. Republican. Lutheran. Author: Davanzati Palace, 1922; Cottages, Farm Houses and Other Minor Buildings in England, 1923; Harvard (in Am. U. series), 1934. Home: Lake Oswego, OR. †

ROSENBERGER, HOMER TOPE, historian, personnel tng. cons.; b. Lansdale, Pa., Mar. 23, 1908; s. Daniel Hendricks and Jennie Kulp Markley R.; m. Gertrude Pauline Richards, July 14, 1934 (dec. June 1975); children—Arley Jane (Mrs. Harry C. Furminger), Lucretia Hazel (Mrs. Patrick R. Myers); m. Jean Hershey Richards, Apr. 12, 1977. Grad., Albright Coll., 1929, LL.D., 1955; M.A., Cornell U., Ithaca, N.Y., 1930, Ph.D., 1932. High sch. hist. tchr., Tidioute, Pa., 1930-31; prof. history and govt. Susquehanna U., summer 1933; adult night sch. instr., Lock Haven, Pa., 1933-35; ednl. research and adminstrn. U.S. Office Edn., 1935-42; supr. tng. Bur. Prisons, U.S. Dept. Justice, 1942-57; chief of tng. Bur. Pub. Rds., U.S. Dept. Commerce, 1957-65; cons. U.S. Post Office Dept., 1969, Pa. Dept. Hwys., 1965-78; mem. safety council U.S. Civilian Conservation Corps, 1938-42; chmn. U.S. Tng. Officers Conf., 1949-50, 55-57, mem. steering com., 1947-67, citation, 1957; mem. Pa. Com. Correctional Staff Tng., 1955-57; cons. on personnel mgmt. to United Hosps., Newark, N.J., 1960-69; mem. adv. com. on counseling, testing and programmed learning Grad. Sch., U.S. Dept. Agr., 1965-66, adviser on devel. adminstrv. competence govt. employees, Nigeria, Africa, 1963-64; Bd. dirs. Bur. Rehab., Nat. Capital Area, 1951-79, pres., 1958-61, mem. exec. com., 1967-71, citation, 1968, 79, mem. personnel com., from 1975; co-chmn. Bur. Rehab., Nat. Capital Area (50th Anniversary com.), 1980; mem. Pa. Bd. Pvt. Corr. Schs., 1957-73, chmn., 1972-73. Author: Testing Occupational Training and Experience, 1948, What Should We Expect of Education? , 1956, Manuals for Executives, 1956, 58, Recommendations Concerning the Use of Case Material in the Institute of Administration, Ibadan, Nigeria, 1964, Techniques for Getting Things Done, 7th edit, 1964, Letters from Africa, 1965, The Pennsylvania Germans, 1891-1965, 1966, Harriet Lane, 1967, Adventures and Philosophy of a Pennsylvania Dutchman, 1971; trilogy Horizons of the Humanities Man and Modern Society: Philosophical Essays, 1972, Grassroots Philosophy for the Modern Mind, 1976, Vignettes of Philosophy: Thirty-Five Vital Subjects, 1977, Mountain Folks: Fragments of Central Pennsylvania Lore, 1974, The Philadelphia and Erie Railroad: It's Place in American Economic History, 1975, The Enigma: How Shall History Be Written? , 1979; also hist. articles, visual edn. and vocational guidance materials, employee tng. courses and occupational tests, many govtl. monographs and reports.; Contbg. editor: Pa. History, 1943-75; mem. editorial bd., from 1975, Social Studies for Tchrs. and Adminstrs, 1949-59, Pa. Heritage, 1974-80; Collector of material on history of Pa. and Pa. Germans. Organizer, moderator Rose Hill Seminars, from 1963; proposed, promoted William Penn Meml., Harrisburg, Pa., 1943-46; incorporator Franklin County (Pa.) Heritage, Inc., v.p., 1968-74, dir., from 1968; mem. Pa. adv. bd. rev. Nat. Register Historic Places, 1969-80; mem. Pa. Hist. and Mus. Commn., 1972-80; bd. dirs., mem. grants com. Hist. Found. Pa.; mem. Pa. State Hist. Preservation Bd., from 1980. Mem. Pa. Fedn. Hist. Socs. (exec. com. 1969-75, chmn. awards com. 1970-74), Pa. Prison Soc. (exec. com. 1949-66, chmn. awards com. 1952-64), Kittochtinny Hist. Soc. (v.p., dir. 1969-80, pres., dir. from 1980), Howard League Penal Reform, London, Pa. Hist. Assn. (mem. council from 1945, chmn. of publs. com. 1946-48, 51-67, pres. 1967-69), Columbia Hist. Soc. (Washington) (pres. 1968-76, bd. mgrs. from 1953, chmn. exec. com. 1963-68, chmn. com. on nominations 1980), Pa. Hist. Junto (Washington) (founder, past pres., past program chmn., mem. exec. com., citations 1957, 67), Am. Peace Soc. (dir. from 1960, mem. exec. com. 1961-64, chmn. com. on pub. of monographs 1962-64), Pa. German Soc. (pres. 1957-69, dir. from 1949, chmn. nominating com. from 1976), Am. Correctional Assn., Phi Delta Kappa, Phi Alpha Theta, Pi Gamma Mu, Alpha Pi Omega. Mem. United Methodist Ch. Club: Cosmos (Washington) (history com. 1960-65, from 70, awards com. 1977-80, bd. mgmt. from 1980), Home: Washington, DC.

ROSENHAUPT, HANS, educator; b. Frankfurt-on-Main, Germany, Feb. 24, 1911; came to U.S., 1935, naturalized, 1940; s. Heinrich and Marie (Freudenthal) R.; m. Maureen Church, Dec. 15, 1945; 1 dau., Elise. Student univs., Frankfurt, Berlin, Munich, 1928-33; Ph.D., U. Berne, 1935; LL.D., Colo. Coll., 1963, Valparaiso U., 1963, U. Chattanooga, 1965, Franklin Coll., 1969; Litt.D., Centenary Coll., 1975, Lincoln U., 1983; Dr.Phil., Johann Wolfgang Goethe U., 1979. Tchr. German and French Oak Park Jr. Coll., 1935-37, Knox Coll., 1937-38, Colo. Coll., 1938-42, 46-47; lectr. Rotary Internat., 1947-48; asso. dir. admissions Columbia U., 1948-58; nat. dir. Woodrow Wilson Nat. Fellowship Found., 1958-69, pres., 1969-85; research asso. com. on future of univ. Columbia U., 1956-57; mem. adv. council German dept. Princeton U. Author: Isolation in Modern German Literature, 1939, How to Wage Peace, 1949, The True Deceivers, 1954, Graduate Students Experience at Columbia, 1940-56, 1958; contbr. to: American Education Today, 1963, Macmillan Ency. Edn, 1973. Bd. dirs. Nat. Med. Fellowships, Inc. Served from pvt. to capt., M.I. AUS, 1942-46. Clubs: Century (Princeton), Nassau (Princeton). Home: Princeton, N.J. Died Apr. 18, 1985.

ROSENSTEIN-RODAN, PAUL N, educator; b. Cracow, Poland, Apr. 19, 1902; s. Maximilian and Anna (Schragen) R.-R.; Dr. rer. pol., U. Vienna; m. Margaret T. Rosenstein-Rodan, Dec. 30, 1939; 1 son, Gary N. Asst. U. Vienna, 1926-29; spl. lectr. dept. polit. economy Univ. Coll., U. London, 1931-36, reader, sr. prof., 1936-47, head dept. polit. economy, 1939-47; asst. dir. econs. dept., head econ. adv. staff Internat. Bank for Reconstrn. and Devel., Washington, 1947-53; sr. staff mem. Center for Internat. Studies, Mass. Inst. Tech., Cambridge, 1953-70, vis. prof. econs., 1953-59, prof., 1959-70; prof. U. Tex. at Austin, 1970; prof. econs., former dir. Ctr. for Latin-Am. Devel., Boston U. Mem. panel experts Alliance for Progress, 1961-66; cons. FAO, UN, Rome, Italy, UN Econ. Commn. for Latin Am., Santiago, Chile, Asia and Far East, Bangkok, UN Bur. Econ. Affairs, N.Y.C. Recipient Commendatore dell'Ordine al Merito Republic of Italy, 1958, Comendador de la Orden del Libertador Republic of Venezuela, 1967, Accademia Tiberina, Rome, 1967; grand officer Order Merit Chilean Republic, 1970. Fellow Am. Acad. Arts and Scis., Inst. Social Studies. Editor: Library of Econs. Contbr. articles to profl. jours. Died Apr. 28, 1985.

ROSENTHAL, ARTHUR, univ. prof.; b. Fuerth, Bavaria, Feb. 24, 1887; s. Otto and Jette (Heilbronner); Ph.D., U. of Munich, 1909; grad. student, U. of Göttingen, 1911-12. Came to U.S., 1940, naturalized, 1945. Asst. Technische Hochschule, Munich, 1909-11; privatdozent, U. of Munich, 1912-20, asst. prof. math., 1920-22; asso. prof. applied math., U. of Heidelberg, 1922-30, prof. math., dir. math. inst., 1930-35, dean of science, 1932-33, prof. emeritus, from 1935; research fellow, lecturer, U. of Mich., 1940-41; lecturer U. of N.M., 1942, asst. prof. math., 1943-46, asso. prof., 1946-47; prof. math. Purdue U. from 1947. Fellow A.A.A.S.; mem. Am. Math. Soc., Math Assn. Am., Am. Assn. U. Profs., Heidelberg Akademie d. Wiss., Phi Kappa Phi, Sigma Xi, Kappa Mu Epsilon. Author: (with L. Zoretti, P. Montel, M. Fréchet) Neure Untersuchungen über Funrtionen reeller Veränderlichen, 1924; (with H. Hahn) Set Functions, 1948. Contbr. articles to math. jours. Home: West Lafayette, Ind. †

ROSENTHAL, BENJAMIN STANLEY, congressman; b. N.Y.C., June 8, 1923; s. Joseph and Ceil (Fischer) R.; m. Lila Moskowitz, Dec. 23, 1950; children—Debra, Edward. Student, L.I.U., Coll. City N.Y.; LL.B., Bklyn. Law Sch., 1949; LL.M., N.Y.U., 1952. Bar: N.Y. bar 1949. Practiced in, N.Y.C.; elected to 87th Congress in spl. election, 1962; mem. 88th-97th Congresses from 8th Dist. N.Y.; mem. fgn. affairs com., mem. govt. ops. com., chmn. commerce, consumer and monetary affairs subcom.; mem. consumer task force Democratic Study Group; dep. house whip; mem. Mems. Congress for Peace Through Law.; Participant Anglo-Am. Parliamentary Conf.; congl. del. 34th UN Gen. Assembly, 1979. Served with AUS, 1943-46. Mem. Am., N.Y. State, Queens County bar assns. Democrat-Liberal. Home: Elmhurst, NY.

ROSEWALL, O. W., univ. prof.; b. Algona, Ia., Mar. 12, 1889; s. Charles and Marie (Jacobson) R.; A.B., State U. Ia., 1913, M.S., La. State U., 1916; Ph.D., Ia. State Coll., 1928; m. Elizabeth Bertram, Sept. 13, 1919; 1 son, Robert O. Instr. zoology and entomology, La. State U., 1913-17; asst. prof. entomol., 1917-20, asso. prof., 1920-24, prof. entomol. from 1924, chairman dept. zool. and entomology, 1951-56; summers; assistant in entomol. Lakeside Lab., Ia., 1912; field asst., U.S. Bur. Entomol., 1913; asst. U.S. Bur. Fisheries, 1914. Mem. La. Pest Control Commn. from 1942. Mem. A.A.A.S., Am. Assn. Econ. Entomol., Entomol. Soc. Am., Cotton State Entomol., La. Acad. Sci., National Pest Control Association (honorary), Southern Pest Control Operators Confs. (director), Sigma Xi, Phi Kappa Phi, Alpha Zeta, Alpha Gamma Rho. Methodist. Mason. Home: Baton Rouge. †

ROSS, DAVID PRESTON, JR., publishing co. exec.; b. St. Louis, Feb. 21, 1908; s. David Preston and Irene (Robinson) R.; student Art Inst. Chgo., 1930-31, 37, U. Kans., 1933-34; m. VerLita Laurett Dodsen, Jan. 3, 1935; children—Jacquelyn Jane, Danelle Lita. Free lance comml. artist, Chgo., 1938-40; exhibit dir. Art Project, WPA, Chgo., 1940-42; draftsman Map Office, U.S. Army, Chgo., 1943-45; dir. Community Art Center, Chgo., 1946-50; advt. layout artist N.Y. Age newspaper, N.Y.C., 1950-52; asst. dir. promotion Chgo. Daily Defender Newspaper, 1953-58; exec. asst. dir. Emancipation Centennial Authority, Chgo., 1959-63; pres. and founder Afro-Am. Pub. Co., Inc., Chgo., 1963-84; cons. Singer-Soc. Visual Edn., 1965-84. Pres. South Side Community Art Center, Chgo., 1953-55. Recipient Best Pub. Service Radio Program award Freedom Found., 1963. Mem. Assn. Study Afro-Am. Life and History, African Assn. Black Studies, Hyde Park-Kenwood Conf., Art Inst. Chgo., Kappa Alpha Psi. Editor: Great Negroes, Past and Present, 1963. Died Feb. 2, 1984.

ROSS, GEORGE MURRAY, millng co. exec.; b. Alden, Kan., Dec. 20, 1887; s. George Brinton and Lydia (Stout) R.; grad. Salt City Bus. Coll., 1905; m. Ella Hervey Jeter, Dec. 15, 1909; children—Fleming (dec.), Genevieve. Engaged in retail lumber and implements, 1907, flour milling, 1907-10, 13-16; mgr. lumber yard, 1910-13; pres. Ross Feed Co., Wichita, 1916-18, White Water Flour Mills Co., Whitewater and Ottawa, Kan., 1918-36, Am. Flour Corp., Newton, Kan., 1936-59, Ross Industries, Inc., Newton, 1959-67; dir. Kan. State Bank, Ottawa, Kan. State Bank, Newton. Trustee Baker U., Baldwin, Kan., from 1944, Methodist Youthville, Newton, from 1951; bd. mgrs. Axtell Christian Hosp., Newton, from 1952. Mason, Rotarian (past dist. gov.). Home: Newton, Kan. †

ROSS, GRIFF TERRY, medical school dean, physician; b. Mt. Enterprise, Tex., 1920. M.D., U. Tex., 1945; Ph.D. in Medicine, U. Minn., 1961. Diplomate: Am. Bd. Internal Medicine. Intern John Sealy Hosp., Galveston, Tex., 1945-46; fellow in medicine U. Minn.-Mayo Found., 1955-60; research asso. in path. anatomy Mayo Clinic, Rochester, Minn., 1960; gen. practice medicine, Mt. Enterprise, 1946-53; chief reprodn. research br., clin. dir. Nat. Inst. Child Health and Human Devel., NIH, Bethesda, Md., 1975-76; dep. dir. Clin. Center, NIH, 1976-81; assoc. dean clin. affairs U. Tex. Med. Sch., Houston, 1981-85, also assoc. dean patient services. Served with M.C., USAF, 1953-55. Died July 1, 1985.

ROSS, SILAS EARL, b. Truckee Meadows, Washoe County, Nev., Feb. 11, 1887; s. Orrin Charles and Ellen Frances (McCormack) R.; B.S., 1909, LL.D., 1946, U. of Nev.; grad. study, University of Wisconsin, 1914; married Emily Coffin, June 11, 1913 (deceased, Jan., 1958); children—Emily Ross Baxter, Silas Earl, M.D.; m. 2d, Mervylle Payne, Apr. 24, 1960; 1 stepdau.—Evelyn P. Sherman. Asst. prof. of chemistry at University of Nevada, 1909-14; also chemist State Dept. Foods, Drugs and Soils, summers; life ins. agt. at Reno, 1914-15; pres. and mgr. Ross-Burke Co., funeral service, Reno, Nev., from 1915. Chmn. Nev. State Rep. Central Com., 1922-24; mem. city council, Reno, 1919-27; mayor pro tem. Reno, 1923-27. Regent U. Nev. (chmn.), 1932-57. Mem. Nat. Selected Morticians (pres. 2 terms). Conf. Funeral Service Examining Bds. of U.S. (past pres.), Nat. Funeral Dirs.; sec.-treas. Nev. State Bd. Embalmers (past pres.), Nev. Funeral Service Assn. (ex-pres.), Reno C. of C., Alumni Assn. U. Nev. (ex-pres.), Sigma Alpha Epsilon, Phi Kappa Phi. Listed on U. of Nev. Alumni Honor Service Roll. Republican. Episcopalian. Mason (33 deg., Sovereign Grand Inspector Gen. of state of Nev.; Knight Templer Shriner—Past Potentate; Knight of Constantine, Past Sovereign; Past Grand Master of Nev.). Elk, K.P. mem. O.E.S. (Past Grand Patron of Nev.). Clubs: Rotary (charter mem.), Alumni Club of Sigma Alpha Epsilon; Athletic (U. of Nev.). Author: A Directory of Nevada Medical Practioners Past and Present. Home: Reno, Nev. †

ROSS, STANLEY ROBERT, educator; born N.Y.C., Aug. 8, 1921; s. Max George and Ethel (Aks) R.; A.B., Queens Coll., 1942; M.A., Columbia, 1943, Ph.D., 1951; m. Leonore Jacobson, Oct. 7, 1945; children—Steven David, Alicia Ellen, Janet Irene. Instr. history Queens Coll., 1946-48, Bklyn. Coll., spring 1948; from instr. to prof. history U. Neb., 1948-62; prof. history, chmn. dept. State N.Y. at Stony Brook, 1962-66, acting dean Coll. Arts and Scis., 1963-66, dean, 1966-68; prof. history, dir. Inst. Latin Am. Studies, U. Tex., Austin, from 1968;

summer tchr. City Coll. N.Y., 1946, Columbia, 1960, U. Colo., 1962. Chmn., Conf. on Latin Am. History, 1968; U.S. nat. mem. commn. on history Pan American Inst. of Geography and History, from 1969. Vice chmn. Suffolk Co. (N.Y.) Com. to Study Sch. Redistricting, 1965; chmn. Three Village Council Edn., 1966-67. Served to 1st lt. USAAF, 1943-46. Queens Coll. scholar, 1942; Schiff fellow Columbia, 1947-48; Travel grantee State Dept., summer, 1947-48; Doherty Found. fellow, 1952-53; Faculty Summer grantee U. Neb., 1955; Rockefeller Found. research grantee, 1958-59, 61, 68-69; Summer fellow U. Neb., 1961. Mem. Conf. Latin Am. History (chmn. Bolton Prize com. 1965), Am. Hist. Assn., Assn. Am. Historians, Latin Am. Studies Assn. (chmn. com. govt. relations), Am. Assn. U. Profs. Author: Francisco I. Madero, Apostle of Mexican Democracy, 1955; co-author, co-editor: Historia Documental de México, 2 vols., 1964. Editor: Is the Mexican Revolution Dead?, 1965; Fuentes de la Historia Contemporáneas de México: Periódicos y Revistas, 2 vols., 1966-67. Adv. editor, The Americas, from 1956; contbr. editor The Handbook of Latin American Studies, from 1960; mem. editorial bd. Hispanic Am. Hist. Rev., 1900-66. Home: Austin, Tex. Died Feb. 10, 1985.

ROSSHEIM, IRVING DAVID, stock broker; b. New York, N.Y., Sept. 26, 1887; s. David and Carrie (Simon) R.; B.A., Central High Sch., Phila., Pa., 1905; B.S. in Econ., Wharton Sch., U. of Pa., 1908, LL.B., Law Sch., 1911; m. Ellen Viola Baer, June 1, 1912; children—Richard Irving, Robert Jules. Mem. faculty of Wharton Sch., U. of Pa., 1908-18; admitted to Pa. bar, 1911, and practiced in Phila., 1911-19, asso. firm Wolf, Bloch, Schorr; auditor Stanley Co. of America, 1919-24, treas., 1924-28, pres., 1928-29; pres. First Nat. Pictures, Inc., 1928-29; dir. Warner Bros. Pictures, Inc., 1928-29; gen. partner Newburger, Loeb & Co., Phila., stock brokers, from 1930. Mem. Zeta Beta Tau. Clubs: Lawyers (Phila.); Philmont (Pa.) Country (treas.). Co-author: First Year Bookkeeping and Accounting, 1912. Home: Rydal, Pa. †

ROST, OTTO FREDRICK, author, editor; b. Hamburg, Germany, Feb. 5, 1889; s. Carl Louis and Margaret Ann (Fitchen) R.; student Claudius Gymnasium; m. Julie H. Aveling, Nov. 26, 1943. Came to U.S., 1906, naturalized, 1914. Pres. Chelsea Motor Car Co., Newark, 1914-16, Newark Electric Co., 1916-28, Utica Electric Appliance Co., 1922-26, Trenton Electric Co., 1923-28; dir. distbn. surveys McGraw-Hill Pub. Co., 1928-29; chief marketing editor Business Week, 1929-36; chief editor Radio Retailing, 1936-39; chief editor, pub. Elec. Wholesaling, 1940-51; v.p. Appleton Electric Co., Chgo. from 1951. Recipient James H. McGraw award and medal, 1927. Mem. Am. Marketing Assn., Nat. Assn. Mfrs., Boston Conf. Distbn. (adv. bd. 1930-51), Nat. Elec. Wholesalers Assn. (chmn. 1924-26). Club: Sales Execs. (N.Y.C.). Author: Constructive Salesmanship, 1927; Distribution Today, 1935; Going into Business, 1945. Contbr. articles marketing, selling, bus. econs. trade publs. Lectr. extension courses Harvard, N.Y.U., Ohio State U. etc. Home: Monmouth County, N.J. †

ROSZAK, THEODORE, sculptor; b. Posen, Poland, May 1, 1907; s. Kasper and Praxeda (Swierczynska) R.; came to U.S., 1909, naturalized, 1921; student Art Inst. Chgo., 1922-25, 26-29, N.A.D., N.Y.C., 1925-26, Columbia, 1925-26; m. Florence Sapir, Oct. 24, 1931; 1 dau., Sara Jane. Faculty, Art Inst. Chgo., 1927-29, Sarah Lawrence Coll., Bronxville, N.Y., 1941-56, Columbia, 1970-73; one man exhbn. Venice Bienalle, Italy, 1960, Pierre Matisse Gallery, 1961, Whitney Mus., 1932-66, Century Assn., N.Y.C., 1971, Harold Ernest Galleries, Boston, 1972, Pierre Matisse Gallery, N.Y.C., 1974, Arts Club Chgo., 1975, Fairweather Hardin, Chgo., 1975-81; exhibited maj. museums in U.S., Darmstadt and Kassel (Germany), Vienna, Madrid, Paris, London, Antwerp, Brussels, Stockholm, Milan, Zurich, Whitney Mus. Am. Art, 1929-56, World's Fair in Brussels, 1958, retrospective exhbn., N.Y.C., Walker Art Center, Mpls.; permanent collections Whitney Mus. Art, Mus. Modern Art, Norton Mus. Art, Fla., Mus. Modern Art, Saō Paulo, Brazil, U. Ill., Urbana, U. Ariz., Iowa State U., Tate Gallery, Yale U. Art Gallery, John Barnes Found., N.Y.C., Cleve. Mus. Fine Arts, Solomon Guggenheim Mus., N.Y.C., Art Inst. Chgo., others. Mem. adv. bd. cultural presentations program State Dept., 1960-66; commr. fine arts N.Y.C., 1964-70; mem. Pres.' Fine Arts Commn., 1963-67. Recipient silver medal Posen Expn., 1930; Eisendrath award, 1934, Frank G. Logan medal and award Art Inst. Chgo., 1947-51; purchase award Mus. Modern Art, Saō Paulo, Brazil, 1951, U. Ill., 1953; George E. Widener Gold medal Pa. Acad. Fine Arts, 1956; Ford Found. study grantee, 1959. Fellow Nat. Inst. Arts and Letters. Address: New York, N.Y. Died Sept. 3, 1981.

ROTH, ROBERT, journalist; b. N.Y.C., Nov. 11, 1901; s. Abraham Lincoln and Sophie (Hafer) R.; m. Katherine Lennehan, July 22, 1928 (dec. July 1958); m. Edith R. Brill, Oct. 16, 1959. Student, Amherst Coll., 1919-21. Reporter various newspapers, 1925-33; editor Mt. Vernon (N.Y.) Daily Argus, 1934-42; reporter Phila. Record, 1943-44, Washington corr., 1945-47; reporter, spl. writer Phila. Bull., 1947-49, chief Washington corr., from 1954. Mem. Sigma Delta Chi. Clubs: Nat. Press (Washington), Cosmos (Washington), Gridiron (Washington). Home: Washington, DC.

ROTH, STANLEY, chain store executive; b. Chgo., Sept. 19, 1898; s. Henry and Lucy (Duschner) R.; m. Elsie Erman, Aug. 19, 1920; children—Stanley, Robert Merle. Ph.B., U. Chgo., 1918. Engaged in personnel, mdsg. and operations research Retail Research Assn., 1919-21; personnel and mdse. mgr. L. S. Ayres & Co., Indpls., 1921-28; v.p., gen. mgr. Gimbel Bros., Milw., 1928- 33; v.p., mng. dir. The Golden Rule, St. Paul, 1934-37; v.p., gen. mdse. mgr. D.A. Schulte, Inc., N.Y.C., 1937-47; exec. v.p. Darling Stores Corp., N.Y.C., 1947-59, pres., dir., 1960-64; pres. dir. Grayson-Robinson Store, Inc., N.Y.C., 1960-64; vice chmn., dir. A.S. Beck Shoe Corp., 1961-64; pres. Apparel Buying Assos., N.Y.C., 1964-83, chmn., 1966-83. Trustee Jewish Home and Hosp. for Aged, N.Y.C. Served as 1st lt. U.S. Army, 1918. Mem. Phi Beta Kappa. Established Roth Program Retailing Research, Harvard Grad. Sch. Bus., Roth Program Cardiovascular Research, N.Y. U. Grad. Sch. Medicine. Home: New York, N.Y. Dec. Sept. 11, 1983.

ROTHERMICH, NORMAN OLIVER, physician; b. St. Louis, Oct. 9, 1912; s. Anton P. and Gertrude E. (Shaw) R.; m. Margaret M. Bene, Sept. 6, 1935; children: F. Donald, Patricia Ann, Nancy Shaw, Linda Mary. B.S., St. Louis U., 1934, M.D., 1936. Diplomate: Am. Bd. Internal Medicine. Intern St. Louis City Hosp., 1936-37; resident in medicine Robert Koch Hosp.; resident in pathology Ohio State U., Columbus, 1939, mem. faculty dept. medicine, 1940-85, clin. prof., 1960-85, practice medicine specializing in internal medicine, Columbus, 1946-85; chief div. rheumatology Mt. Carmel Med. Center; mem. med. adv. council Merck, Sharp & Dohme Internat.; cons. Council on Drugs AMA; med. dir. Columbus Med. Center Research Found.; mem. arthritis adv. com. FDA, 1969-72; mem. Ohio State Med. Bd., 1978. Contbr. articles to med. jours. Co-founder, dir. Central Ohio Arthritis Found.; founder, 1st pres. Ohio Rheumatism Soc. Served to maj. AUS, 1942-46. Recipient Disting. Service award Nat. Arthritis Found., 1974. Fellow ACP; mem. Columbus Acad. Medicine (pres. 1957), AMA, Am. Rheumatism Assn., Am. Soc. Clin. Pharmacology and Therapeutics, Nat. Soc. Clin. Rheumatologists, Peruvian Rheumatism Soc. (hon.), Yugoslavian Rheumatism Soc. (hon., Japanese Rheumatism Soc., hon.). Clubs: Scioto Country, Muirfield Village Golf. Home: Columbus, Ohio. Died Mar. 5, 1985.

ROTHROCK, E(DGAR) P(AUL), geologist; b. Garrettsville, O., Aug. 26, 1889; s. Edgar Sylvanus and Mary Ellen (Moore) R.; A.B., Oberlin Coll., 1912, A.M., 1914; Ph.D., U. of Chicago, 1922; m. Grace Rhoda Foster, Sept. 15, 1917; children—David Paul, Donald Foster. Field geologist for state surveys and comml. oil producers, 1914-22; asst. prof. geology University of South Dakota, Vermillion, S.D., 1922-26, professor 1926-57; state geologist, 1926-57, cons. Served as officer candidate, Field Arty. Replacement Troops, U.S. Army, 1918. Fellow A.A.A.S., Geol. Soc. of Am.; mem. Am. Assn. Petroleum Geologists. Republican. Conglist. Author numerous articles on S.D. geology Home: Vermillion, S.D. †

ROTTSCHAEFER, HENRY, educator; b. Stedum, Groningen, Holland, Sept. 9, 1888; s. William Dirk and Grietje (Schuitema) R.; brought to U.S., 1893; A.B., Hope Coll., Holland, Mich., 1909; J.D., U. of Mich., 1915; S.J.D., Harvard, 1916; m. Helen Grow, May 18, 1918; children—William Frederick, Judith Fairgrieve. High sch. prin., 1909-11; instr. economics, U. of Mich., 1912-15; admitted to Mich. bar, 1915, N.Y., 1919. Minn., 1932, federal courts, 1937; counsel Thompson & Black, N.Y. City, 1916-17, 1919-22; tax consultant, N.Y. City, 1919-22; prof. law U. Minn., 1922-57; ret.; acting prof. law, summers, Stanford U., 1927, U. of Mich., 1930, U. of Chicago, 1930. Cornell Law Sch., 1931, U. of N.C., 1932, 1934, U. of Colo., 1936; adviser to Minn. Ho. of Rep. on tax matters, 1933, 35, 37; mem. governor's spl. com. bd. Minn. tax problems, 1932; asso. mem. Advisory Board for Registrants, 1943; special mediation rep. National War Labor Board; pub. mem. panel Nat. War Labor Bd., Region VI. Served as capt. Motor Transport Corps, U.S. Army, 1917-18. Decorated: Officer, Order of Orange-Nassau, 1946. Mem. Am. Bar Assn. (com. on improving procedure for the levy and collection of local and municipal taxes, 1937-39; com. on state taxes of Section on Taxation, 1940-42), Minn. State Bar Assn., Am. Law Sch. Assn. (exec. com. 1933). Editor-in-chief, Minnesota Law Review, 1942-48; mem. Netherlands University League of North America, Order of Coif, Phi Delta Phi. Republican. Author: Selective Cases on Law of Taxation, 1929; Cases on Constitutional Law, 1932; Supplements to Cases on Constitutional Law, 1936, 37; Handbook of American Constitutional Law, 1939; Revision of Black's Cases on Constitutional Law, 1939; Cases and Materials on Constitutional Law, 1948; The Constitution and Socio-Economic Change; 1948. Contbr. to legal publs. Home: Minneapolis, Minn. †

ROUND, LESTER A(NGELL), pub. health official; b. Foster, R.I., Nov. 5, 1888; s. John Angell and Roena Frances (Yeaw) R.; A.B., Brown U., 1910, A.M., 1911, Ph.D., 1914; m. Mildred M. Gay, Feb. 18, 1915; 1 son, Charles Brayton. Biologist and bacteriologist to Commrs. of Shellfisheries, R.I., 1910-14; bacteriologist U.S. Bur. of Chemistry, Washington, D.C., 1914-18; bacteriologist and pathologist State Bd. Health, R.I., 1918-29, dir., 1929-35, chief lab. div., 1935-36; sec. Bd. of Milk Control, R.I., 1933-35 and from 1939; prof. bacteriology, R.I. Coll. of Pharmacy and Allied Sciences, 1927-41, prof. pharmodynamics, 1936-41. Director R.I. State Department of Health, 1939-41; registrar of vital statistics, R.I., 1929-35 and 1939-41; cons. in vital statistics, R.I. State Dept. of Health, 1941-42; on leave for duration from 1942; asst. pathologist, R.I. Hosp., Providence, R.I.; pathologist to State Med. Examiner from 1950. Fellow A.A.A.S., Am. Public Health Assn.; member Kappa Sigma, Sigma Xi; hon. mem. Providence Med. Soc. Methodist. Mason. Home: Providence, R.I. †

ROUNDS, DAVID, actor, writer; b. Bronxville, N.Y., Oct. 9, 1930; s. Harry M. and Beatrice T. (Beveridge) R. B.A., Denison U., 1952. Actor: Broadway plays, including Foxy, 1965; Child's Play, 1970 (Theatre World award), The Rothschilds, 1971, The Last of Mrs. Lincoln, 1973, Romeo and Juliet, 1977, Morning's at Seven (Tony award), Broadway plays, including, 1980 (Drama Desk award); off-Broadway plays include You Never Can Tell, 1958, The Real Inspector Hound, 1972, Enter a Free Man, 1974; repertory seasons include, Center Stage Balt., 1966, 67, Theatre of the Living Arts, Phila., 1969, Am. Shakespeare Theatre, 1973, 74, Phila. Drama Guild, 1978, 79, Hartford Stage Co., 1979; films include Child's Play, 1971; King of the Gypsies, 1979, So Fine, 1981; TV includes Love of Life, 1962-65; Beacon Hill, 1975, Mary Hartman, 1976, Alice, 1983; author: (with Madeleine Edmondson) From Mary Noble to Mary Hartman: The Complete Soap Opera Book, 1976. Served to lt. (j.g.) USNR, 1953-56. Home: Kingston, N.Y. Died Dec. 9, 1983.

ROURA-PARELLA, JUAN, educator; b. Tortella, Spain, June 29, 1897; s. José Roura Bergés and Margarita Parella Güell; grad. Escuela Superior Magisterio, Madrid, 1923; student Institut Rosseau, Geneva, Switzerland, summer 1927, Instituto Orientacion Profesional, Madrid, 1929, U. Berlin, Germany, 1930-32; Ph.D. summa cum laude, U. Barcelona, 1937; M.A., Wesleyan U., Middletown, Conn., 1952; m. Teresa Ramon Llígé, Aug. 21, 1939. Came to U.S., 1945. Psychologist, head bur. vocational guidance Escuela Superior Trabajo Las Palmas, Spain, 1929; prof. pedagogy, co-dir. seminar aesthetic edn. U. Barcelona, 1933-39; prof. ethics, sociology Escola Normal Catalunya, 1933-39; prof. philosophy edn. Internat. U. Santander, 1934; mem. El Colegio de México, 1939-45; prof. psychology U. México, 1939-45; vis. prof. psychology U. Guadalajara, 1939, San Luis, 1940, Guanajuato, 1941, Morelia, 1941; lectr. Pendle Hill, Pa., 1946; lectr. romance langs., psychology Wesleyan U., Middletown, 1946- 52, prof. humanities and romance langs. since 1952; chmn. internat. seminar internat. understanding, Caracas, 1948; prof. philosophy U. Havana, 1950, Guggenheim fellow, 1954, philosophy of Wilhelm Dilthey. Mem. Mex. Soc. Sociology, Instituto Filosoffa México, Phi Beta Kappa. Club: Apostles. Contbr. articles profl. publs. Home: Middletown, Conn. Died Dec. 26, 1983.

ROUSE, W. R., lawyer; b. Galena, Ill., June 11, 1890; s. William A. and Susan B. (Gardner) R.; grad. sch. law Creighton U., 1923; m. Louise Yates, 1917 (dec. Sept. 26, 1935); children—Anne T. (Mrs. Reynolds C. Seitz), Dr. James W., William A.; m. 2d Marcella A. Eckermann, 1940; children—Timothy John, Susan, Walter. Joined engring. dept. U.P.R.R., 1911, contract dept., 1918, various positions law dept., 1918-42, asst. western gen. counsel, 1942-51, western gen. counsel, 1951-59, v.p., 1955-59, exec. dir. Found., from 1959. Admitted to Neb. bar, 1923. Mem. Am., Neb. State, Omaha bar assns. Clubs: Union League (Chgo.); Omaha Country. Home: Omaha, Nebr. †

ROUTH, JOHN SYLVESTER, business exec.; b. N.Y.C., Oct. 31, 1888; s. John S. and Margaret T. (Phelan) R.; student pub. schs., N.Y.C.; m. M. Isabel Rodriguez, Feb. 16, 1915; children—Ethel Marie (Mrs. Andres G. Carrillo), Carlos Joaquin, John Sylvester. Shipper wholesale, retail coal from 1914; pres. Routh Coal Corp., from 1940, chmn. bd. Routh Coal Export Corp., from 1952, v.p. Pittston Co., from 1951; dir. Am. Coal Shipping, Inc., A. II. Bull Steamship Co. Mem. Coal Exporters Assn. U.S. (pres. 1948-52). Clubs: River (N.Y.C.), Havana Country. Home: N.Y.C. †

ROWE, ALFRED S(TANLEY), jewelers, horologist; b. Frankfort, Ind., Dec. 24, 1888; s. John Albany and Mary Ann (Noton) R.; student pub. schs. Bedford, Ind.; m. Pauline M. Kercheval, Oct. 12, 1915; 1 dau., Julian Jean (Mrs. D.C. Rhodes), Apprentice horology, 1905-11; retail jeweler, Sheridan, Ind., 1911-17, Indpls., from 1917. Pres. Ind. State Bd. Examiners in Watch Repairing from 1939. Certified master watchmaker, Horological Inst. Am. Mem. Ind. Jewelers Assn. (past pres.), Horological Inst. Am. (past pres.). Mason. Home: Indianapolis, Ind. †

ROWE, JAMES HENRY, JR., lawyer; b. Butte, Mont., June 1, 1909; s. James Henry and Josephine (Sullivan) R.; m. Elizabeth Holmes Ulman, Sept. 6, 1937; children—Elizabeth (Mrs. Douglas Costle), Clarissa (Mrs. Stephen Batzell), James III. A.B., Harvard, 1931, LL.B., 1934. Engaged as attorney with the Nat. Emergency Council, 1934; sec. to Oliver Wendell Holmes, asso justice Supreme Ct. of U.S., 1934-35; atty. RFC, 1935 Dept. Labor, 1935-36; power div. Pub. Works Ad minstrn., 1936, SEC, 1937; staff Dem. Nat. Com., 193[illegible] campaign; asst. to James Roosevelt (sec. to Pres.), 1938 adminstrv. asst. to Pres. of U.S., 1939-41; asst. atty. gen dept. of Justice, 1941-43; tech. adviser Internat. Mil Tribunal, Nuernburg, 1945-46, pvt. law practice, fro[illegible]

1946; Dir. Comml. Credit Co.; Cons. Bur. of Budget, 1947; mem. First Hoover Commn., 1948-49; pub. mem. Fgn. Service Selection Bd., State Dept., 1948; chmn. commn. to reorganize govt. P.R., 1949; chmn. adv. com. on personnel Sec. State, 1950; counsel Senate Majority Policy com. U.S. Senate, 1956; commr. Franklin Roosevelt Meml. Commn., 1956, Roosevelt-Campobello Internat. Park Commn., 1967; mem. Conf. on Pub. Service, 1960-63; chmn. U.S.-P.R. Commn. on Status, 1964-67; mem. panel on study Presidency for the 80's, Acad. Public Adminstrn., 1980; mem. task force on study Presidency and the Press, U. Va., 1980. Trustee, former chmn. 20th Century Fund; bd. overseer Harvard, 1965-71; bd. visitors Air U., 1964-67; adv. council Sch. Advanced Internat. Studies, Johns Hopkins. Served as lt. USNR, 1943-45, PTO. Decorated two Presdl. citations, Navy Commendation ribbon, battle stars (8). Democrat. Roman Catholic. Home: Washington, D.C. Died June 17, 1984.

ROWE, STANLEY M., SR., business exec.; b. Cin., June 2, 1890; s. Casper Hartman and Fanny (Saman) R.; grad. Asheville Sch., 1908; grad. Yale, 1912; m. Dorothy Snowden, Nov. 9, 1915; children—Stanley M., Snowden. Sec. The Cincinnati Rubber Mfg. Co., Norwood, O., 1912-17; past pres. Shepard Warner Elevator Co. Cin., chmn. bd., from 1956; pres. Cin. Metal Crafts, chmn. bd.; dir. Howard Paper Mills, Inc., Dayton. The Kroger Co. Cincinnati Equitable Fire Ins. Co. Served in U.S. Ordnance Dept., 1917-19. Dir. Emery Meml., Spring Grove Cemetery Assn., trustee Diocese Southern O. Republican. Episcopalian. Clubs: Camargo, Queen City, Commercial, Cincinnati Yale. Home: Cincinnati, Ohio. †

ROWE, WALLACE PRESCOTT, physician, virologist; b. Balt., Feb. 20, 1926; s. George Davis and Mary Wallace (Buck) R.; m. Marjorie Louise Power, May 29, 1948 (div. 1981); children—Wallace Prescott, Wendy; m. Paula Mahr Pither, 1981. Student, Coll. William and Mary, 1943-44; M.D., Johns Hopkins, 1948. Intern N.C. Bapt. Hosp., Winston-Salem, 1948-49; virologist Naval Med. Research Inst., Bethesda, Md., 1949-52; commd. sr. asst. surg. USPHS, 1952, advanced through grades to med. dir., 1961; virologist NIH, Bethesda, Md., 1952-83; instr. Howard U., Washington, 1960-74. Vice chmn. Frederick County (Md.) Human Relations Council, 1968-70. Served with USNR; Served with 1945, 49-52. Recipient Eli Lilly award, 1960; Langer-Teplitz award, 1965; Rockefeller Pub. Service award, 1972; G.H.A. Clowes award, 1973; Ricketts award, 1974; Selman Waksman award in microbiology Nat. Acad. Scis., 1976; Virus Cancer Program award, 1976; Paul Ehrlich-Ludwig Darmstaedter Preis W. Ger., 1979; Alfred P. Sloan Jr. award Gen. Motors Cancer Research Found., 1981; Harvey lectr., 1976. Mem. Nat. Acad. Scis. Address: Bethesda, Md. Died July 4, 1983.

ROWLAND, THOMAS MIFFLIN, college administrator; b. Phila., Oct. 13, 1924; s. Thomas Mifflin and Gladys Berrell (Cummings) R.; B.S., Temple U., 1948; LL.D. (hon.), Phila. Coll. Osteo. Medicine, 1973. Asst. registrar Phila. Coll. Osteo. Medicine, 1950-52, registrar, dir. admissions, 1952-59, adminstrv. asst. to pres., 1959-65, v.p. for adminstrv. affairs, 1965-73, exec. v.p., 1973-74, pres., 1974-84, asst. prof. profl. econs., 1960-75, prof., chmn. dept. community health, 1972-84. Chmn. profl. adv. com. Phila. chpt. ARC; 1st vice chmn. Republican City Com., Phila., 1972; del. Rep. Nat. Convs., 1968, 72, 76; mem. Phila. Dist. Atty's. Com. on Alcoholism and Drug Addiction; mem. adv. council Salvation Army Men's Social Service. Served with USAAF, 1943-46; ETO. Recipient Lindback Found. award for Distinguished Teaching, 1973, certificate of merit North City Congress Police Community Relations Program, 1965, Achievement award Lambda Omicron Gamma, 1973, Distinguished Achievement award Golden Slipper Club, 1975, State of Israel award, 1976, Distinguished Guest award Pa. Osteo. Med. Assn., 1977, 1st Distinguished Service award Philadelphia County Osteo. Soc., 1977, Alumni award N.E. High Sch., 1977. Mem. Am. Osteo. Assn. (Andrew Taylor Still Meml. lectr. 1976), Am. Osteo. Hosp. Assn., Temple U., N.E. High Sch. alumni assns., Assn. Schs. Allied Health Professions, Am. Pub. Health Assn., Am. Assn. Colls. Osteo. Medicine, Assn. Am. Med. Colls., Am. Legion, Welsh Soc. (pres. 1966-68), Phila. Hot Stove Leaguers, Sigma Sigma Phi, Phi Sigma Gamma (hon. mem. Zeta chpt.). Republican. Baptist. Clubs: Union League of Phila., Bala Golf, Pa. Soc., Masons. Office: Philadelphia, Pa. Dec. Jan. 11, 1984.

ROY, GABRIELLE, (MRS. MARCEL CARBOTTE) writer; b. St. Boniface, Man., Can.; d. Leon and Melina (Landry) R.; m. Marcel Carbotte, Aug. 30, 1947. Student, Institut Collegial St. Joseph, Winnipeg, Man., Normal Sch. Tchr. pub. schs. St. Boniface. Freelance writer for Canadian papers and mags., Montreal, 1939-83; (Can. award for best short story of 1979); Author: novels The Tin Flute, 1947, Where Nests the Water Hen, 1951, The Cashier, Street of Riches, The Hidden Mountain, The Road Past Altamont, 1966, Windflower, 1970, Enchanted Summer, 1976, Garden in the Wind, 1977, Children of My Heart, 1978, Cliptail, a Tale for Children, 1979 (awarded prize for best children's book Can. Council). Recipient Prixfemina, 1947; Gov. Gen. award; Prix Duvernay; Medaille de L'Academie Francaise; prix David, 1971; Molson award, 1977; 3 Gov.-Gen. awards; companion Order of Can. Mem. Royal Soc. Can. Address: Quebec, Que., Can. Died July 13, 1983.

ROY, ROSS, advertising agency executive; b. Kingston, Ont., Can., July 22, 1898; came to U.S., 1900, naturalized, 1928; s. Dr. Emile and Josephine (Pronovost) R.; m. Mary Agnes Hillemeyer, June 28, 1927; children—Robert Regis, Arlene Marie, Jon; m. Celia Christiansen Wormer, June 30, 1960; children—Rex Regis, Ross Regis Roy, Jr.; stepchildren—Chris, Sally, Sigrid. Student pub. schs., Wis.; hon. doctorate of econ. edn., Wayne U., 1981. Automobile salesman O'Connell Motor Co., Janesville, Wis., 1919-26; founder Ross Roy, Inc., Detroit, N.Y.C., Windsor, Ont., Can., pres., 1926-60; chmn. bd., exec. officer Ross-B.S.F. & D., Inc. (name changed to Ross-Roy, Inc. 1962), 1960-83. Mem. exec. bd. Detroit area council Boy Scouts Am., 1946; nat. bd. dirs. Jr. Achievement, Inc., chmn. bd., dir. S.E. Mich. area; past pres. Mich Soc. Mental Health; v.p. and dir. United Found. Met. Detroit; bd. directors Boys' Clubs Met. Detroit; past pres. Greater Detroit Bd. of Commerce; dir. Detroit Inst. Econ. Edn.; lay trustee U. Detroit; dir. Mich. Colls. Found. Recipient honor medal Freedoms Found., 1951, Silver Beaver award Boy Scouts Am., 1956, George Washington Honor medal, 1962. Republican. Clubs: Economic, Adcraft, Detroit Athletic, Detroit Boat, Grosse Pointe Yacht, Detroit Country, Grosse Pointe Hunt, Otsego Ski. Home: Grosse Pointe Shores, Mich. Died Aug. 16, 1983.

ROYCE, RALPH, army officer; b. June 28, 1890; B.S., U.S. Mil. Acad., 1914. Commd. 2d. lt. inf., June 12, 1914; promoted through grades to lt. col., Dec. 1, 1935; temporary rank of brig. gen., Apr. 1941, major gen., June 1942; asst. mil. attaché Am. Embassy, London, 1941; comd. Southeast Air Corps Training Center, Maxwell Field, Ala., Sept. 1942-Apr. 1943; comd. 1st Air Force, Mitchel Field, N.Y., Apr.-Sept., 1943; apptd. comdr. U.S. Forces in Middle East, Sept. 1943.†

ROYSTER, FRANK SHEPPARD, JR., mfr. fertilizers; b. Tarboro, N.C., Oct. 30, 1887; s. Frank Sheppard and Mary (Stamps) R.; student Princeton, 1913; m. Selby Leeds Rowland, July 3, 1937 (dec. July 1958); 1 dau., Frances Sheppard. From clk. to v.p. and dir. F. S. Royster Guano Co., Norfolk, Va., chmn. bd. Dir. United Community Fund, Norfolk. Norfolk Gen. Hosp., Gen. Hosp. of Virginia Beach, Va.; trustee Norfolk Academy, Norfolk, Virginia. Served as ensign, Air Corps, U.S. Navy World War I. Presbyn. (elder). Clubs: Princeton (N.Y.C.); Maryland. Green Spring Valley Hunt (Balt.); Norfolk Yacht and Country, Virginia (Norfolk); Colonial (Princeton, N.J.); Princess Anne Country (Virginia Beach, Va.). Home: Virginia Beach, Va. †

RUBEN, SAMUEL A., physician; b. 1889; M.D., U. Pa., 1911. Mem. gynecological staff Washington (Pa.) Hosp.; inventor pacemaker for heart attack victims, also dry electrolyte condenser, rectifier tube and flexible wire with ceramic insulation. Named Inventor of Year, Patent, Trademark and Copyright Inst., George Washington U., 1965. Diplomate Am. Bd. Obstetrics and Gynecology. Fellow A.C.S.; mem. A.M.A., Am. Assn. Obstetricians and Gynecologists. Address: Washington, PA. †

RUBIN, EDWARD PERRY, investment counsel; b. Payne, Ohio, Mar. 27, 1903; s. Henry E. and Blanche (Reader) R.; A.B., Heidelberg Coll., 1925, LL.D. (hon.), 1968; post grad. Harvard, 1926; m. Mary Allene Myers, Nov. 27, 1930; 1 son, Edward P. Pres., dir. Selected Am. Shares, Inc., 1942-70; pres. Selected Investments Co., 1943-55, chmn. bd., 1955-68; chmn. bd. Selected Spl. Shares, Inc., 1968-70; adviser, dir. Security Suprs., investment counsel, 1969-70, partner, pres. predecessor orgns.; a prin. organizer Selected Am. Shares, Selected Cumulative Shares, Selected Income Shares, Selected Am. Shares, Inc., Selected Spl. Shares, Inc. Adv. gov. Midwest Stock Exchange, 1956-59. Trustee Heidelberg Coll., 1954-80, mem. fin. and investment com. 1958-80, chmn., 1958, 64-66, 70-73, 76-80, chmn. planning com., 1967; trustee Library Internat. Relations, 1960-77. Mem. Investment Co. Inst. (bd. govs. 1949-52, 58-61, 63-67, 68-70, chmn. tax com. 1958-60, 67-70, chmn. instl. studies com. 1963-66), Fin. Writers Assn. Chgo. (pres. 1965-66), Investment Analysts Soc. Chgo., Am. Rose Soc. Episcopalian. Clubs: Bond, Attic, Economic, Heidelberg, Harvard, Execs. (Chgo.); Internat.; 71; Rotary. Writer, lectr. fin. subjects. Home: Winnetka, Ill. Died Nov. 12, 1980.

RUBIN, MORRIS HAROLD, author; b. N.Y.C., Aug. 7, 1911; s. Jacob and Leah (Abrahamson) R.; B.A., U. Wis., 1934; m. Mary Barbara Sheridan, Sept. 12, 1936. With Portland (Me.) Evening Express, 1929-34, Boston Globe, 1929-34, N.Y. Times, 1935-38, N.Y. Herald Tribune, 1939, Time Mag., 1935-38, Milw. Jour., 1933-35, Wis. State Jour., Madison, 1934-38; editor The Progressive Mag., Madison, 1940-73, pres., pub., 1973-76; editorial cons., free-lance writer, 1976-80; trustee, dir. Madison Capital Times; dir. Madison Newspapers, Inc.; aide to Gov. Philip F. LaFollette and Sen. Robert M. LaFollette, Jr., Madison, 1938-40. Founder, Wis. Civil Liberties Union, 1941, pres., 1941-47; v.p. ACLU, 1947. Recipient Sidney Hillman Found. award for outstanding journalism in domestic field for spl. issue on Senator Joseph R. McCarthy, 1954; George Polk Meml. award for distinguished fgn. reporting for spl. issue on Latin Am., 1962. Mem. Madison Newspaper Guild (founder). Editor: McCarthy—The Documented Record, 1954; The Crisis of Survival, 1970. Home: Madison, Wis. Dec. Aug. 8, 1980.

RUBINOW, SYDNEY GODFREY, agricultural economist, publicist; b. Lodz, Russia, Mar. 16, 1887; s. George Max and Mary R.; brought to U.S., 1892; B.S. in Agr., Cornell U., 1909; M.S., U. of Wis., 1914; post-graduate student, U. of Minn., 1925; m. Ruth Fisher, June 10, 1913; children—Sydney G., Hugh Fisher. Asst. dir. agrl. extension, N.C., 1916-20; assisted in organizing in interest of marketing the Am. Cotton Assn., Tex. Farm Bur., Okla. Cotton Growers' Exchange, Red River Valley Sweet Clover Growers' Exchange; organized Maine and Minn. Potato Growers' exchanges; cons. organizer N.D. Potato Growers' Exchange; gen. mgr. Minn. Potato Growers' Exchange, 1924-25. Lecturer, Am. Inst. of Coöperation, U. of Pa., 1925; spl. publicist Upper Mississippi Barge Line Co., 1925-26; mgr. farm development dept. Minneapolis Tribune, 1925-27. Mem. Nat. Council Defense, N.C., World War; also agrl. adviser. Mem. Nat. Council Farmers' Coöperative Marketing Assns. Republican. Author of numerous bulletins, monographs and articles on coöp. marketing and agricultural organization. Home: Kalispell, Mont. †

RUBINSTEIN, ARTUR, pianist; b. Lodz, Poland, Jan. 28, 1887; s. Ignace and Felicia (Heyman) R.; m. Aniela Mlynarski, July 27, 1932; children—Eva, Paul, Alina-Anna, John-Arthur. Student at Warsaw and Berlin Acad. of Music; studied under Joachim, the violinist, Berlin; studied piano with Rozycki and Barth; Hon. degree in music, Northwestern U., 1949. (recipient gold medal Royal Philharmonic Soc. London, Grammy awards for best classical album, 1976, for best classical performance, 1959, 63, 65, 72, 76, 77, for best chamber music 1974-76); Author: autobiography Vol. I, My Young Years, 1973, Vol. II, My Many Years, 1979; tours throughout, Europe, S. Am. Australia, South and North Africa, China, Japan, Java, Philippine Islands, and many other parts of the world, among many other records has recorded entire work of Chopin. Decorated comdr. Legion of Honor France; officer Order of Santiago Portugal; Cross of Alfonso XII Spain; comdr. of the Crown and officer Order of Leopold I Belgium; Polonia Restituta Poland; comdr. Chilean Republic; U.S. medal of Freedom; comdr. Order Orange Nassau Holland. Mem. French Académie des Beaux-Arts de l'Instut de France, Acad. Music of Brazil (hon.), Accademia Santa Cecilia (Rome) (hon.). First concert at 6 in Warsaw; debut with Berlin Symphony Orch. at 13; made first U.S. tour, 1906 (debut with Phila. Orch). Office: New York, NY

RUCKER, TINSLEY WHITE, IV, cons.; b. Warrenton, Ga., Dec. 26, 1909; s. Tinsley White, III and Elon (Cason) R.; m. Lorol Bowron Rediker, Apr. 7, 1966; stepchildren—John Michael, Diana (Mrs. Slaughter); 1 dau. by previous marriage, Barbara (Mrs. Seaton). Grad., Episcopal Acad., 1927; B.S., Mass. Inst. Tech., 1931. Prodn. mgr. G.W. Smith Woodworking Co., 1931-34; engr. Factory Ins. Assn., 1934-37; plant mgr. Mengel Co., 1937-41; v.p. Gen. Plywood Corp., 1941-49; pres., dir. Dixon-Powdermaker Furniture Co., Jacksonville, 1949-79; dir. Rucker Industries, from 1966, cons. Dir., past pres. Asso. Industries Fla. Mem. NAM (past dir.), Nat. Assn. Furniture Mfrs. (dir., past pres.), Jacksonville C. of C. (past v.p.), SAR, SCV, Gen. Soc. Colonial Wars, Huguenot Soc. of S.C., Descs. Colonial Clergy, Nat. Huguenot Soc., Jamestowne Soc., Order Stars and Bars, English Speaking Union Jacksonville (pres.), Sigma Nu. Episcopalian (past sr. warden). Clubs: River and Timuquana Country (Jacksonville), Rotary (Jacksonville); Mountain Brook (Birmingham); Masons, Shriners. Home: Jacksonville, Fla. Died Mar. 20, 1983.

RUDE, ARTHUR H., mfg. exec.; b. Rice Lake, Wis., Mar. 29, 1890; s. Hans A. and Martha Rude; grad. high sch.; m. Edith Selly, Dec. 1, 1941. Engaged in retail and wholesale tire bus., 1913-40, lumber and sawmill bus., 1940-44; exec. v.p. Aerojet Gen. Corp., 1945-61, chmn.; dir. General Tire & Rubber Co. (Akron, O.). Home: Arcadia, Calif. †

RUDESILL, CECIL LOGAN, physician; b. Johnsonville, Ill., Jan. 24, 1887; s. Tobias and Eliza Jane (Porter) R.; B.S., Valporaiso (Ind.) U., 1909; B.S., Ind. U., 1916, M.D., 1918, M.D. cum laude, 1919; m. Florence Eleanor Harry, July 2, 1921; children—Helen Gwyneth, Robert Louis. Teacher grade sch., Wayne County, Ill., 1905-06; high sch. instr., Goodland, Ind., 1909-11; high sch. prin., Kentland, Ind., 1911-12; supt. and high sch. instr., Morocco, Ind., 1912-14; interne Robert W. Long Hosp., Indianapolis, Ind., 1918-19; practice of internal medicine, Indianapolis, from 1919; faculty sch. of medicine Indiana University, 1919-57, clin. prof. medicine, 1941-57, professor emeritus, from 1957; collaborated in experimental clinical use and testing unitage strength of various lots of insulin, Eli Lilly & Co., Indianapolis, Ind., 1922-23. Diplomate Am. Bd. Internal Medicine. Fellow Am. Coll.

Physicians; mem. Indianapolis Med. Soc., Ind. State Med. Assn., A.M.A., Am. Diabetes Assn., Nu Sigma Nu, Alpha Omega Alpha. Author articles to med. jours. Home: Indianapolis, Ind. †

RUDIN, JACOB PHILIP, clergyman; b. Malden, Mass., Sept. 5, 1902; s. Louis and Dora (Vendrofsky) R.; B.A. cum laude, Harvard, 1924; M.H.L., Jewish Inst. Religion, 1928, D.D., 1948; m. Elsie Katz, June 29, 1926 (dec. Dec. 1958); children—Stephen Isaac, Priscilla Sarah; m. 2d, Janet Weiland Solinger, June 21, 1960 (div. Mar. 1961); m. 3d, Lili Tairstein Canfield, Feb. 1, 1962. Asst. rabbi Stephen S. Wise Free Synagogue, N.Y.C., also asst. to pres. Jewish Inst. Religion, N.Y.C., 1928; rabbi Temple Beth-El, Great Neck, N.Y., 1930-71, rabbi emeritus, 1971-82; founder Great Neck Zionist Dist. Mem. exec. com. Nassau County Mental Health Assn.; adv. com. bd. edn. Great Neck; mem. div. religious activities Nat. Jewish Welfare Bd. Bd. dirs. Indsl. Home for Blind; bd. govs. Union Am. Hebrew Congregations, Hebrew Union Coll., Jewish Inst. Religion. Served as lt. comdr., Chaplains Corps, USNR, 1942-45; Jewish chaplain U.S. Merchant Marine Acad. Recipient award for leadership in intercreedal relations NCCJ. Mem. Central Conf. Am. Rabbis (past pres.), Jewish Inst. Religion Alumni Assn. (past pres.), Alumni Assn. Hebrew Union Coll. (past pres.), N.Y. Met. Assn. Reform Rabbis (past pres., treas.), N.Y. Bd. Rabbis (exec. bd.), Great Neck Ministers' Assn., Synagogue Council Am. (pres.), L.I. Zionist Region (past exec. bd.). Author: So You Like Puzzles, 1934; A Children's Hagada, 1936; (collected sermons) Very Truly Yours, 1971. Editor, contbr. Jewish Inst. Quar.; editorial bd. CCAR Jour.; adv. bd. Book of Jewish Thoughts, 1944. Contbr. sermons, related articles to periodicals. Home: Great Neck, N.Y. Died Sept. 10, 1982.

RUITENBEEK, HENDRIK M., psychoanalyst; b. Leyden, Holland, Feb. 26, 1928; came to U.S., 1955, naturalized, 1962; s. Johannes and Marie (de la Court) R. B.A., U. Leyden, 1948, Ph.D., 1952, LL.D., 1955; tng. in psychoanalysis, Holland and U.S. Tchr. existential psychoanalysis N.Y. U., 1963-83, pvt. practice psychoanalysis, N.Y.C., 1960-83. Author: The Individual and the Crowd: A Study of Identity in America, 2d edit, 1965, Freud and America, 1966, The Male Myth, 1967, The New Group Therapies, 1970, The New Sexuality, 1974, Psychotherapy, 1976, The Women in Freud's Life, 1981, (in Dutch) The Rise and Origin of the Dutch Labour Party, 1955; Editor: (in Dutch) Psychoanalysis and Existential Philosophy, 1962, Psychoanalysis and Social Science, 1962, Problem of Homosexuality in Modern Society, 1963, The Dilemma of Organizational Society, 1963, Varieties of Classic Social Theory, 1963, Varieties of Modern Social Theory, 1963, Psychoanalysis and Contemporary American Culture, 1964, Psychoanalysis and Literature, 1964, Varieties of Personality Theory, 1965, The Literary Imagination, 1965, The Creative Imagination, 1965, Heirs to Freud, 1966, Psychoanalysis and Female Sexuality, 1966, Psychoanalysis and Male Sexuality, 1966, The Psychotherapy of Perversions, 1967, Homosexuality and Creative Genius, 1968, Death: Interpretations, 1969, Group Therapy Today, 1969, Sexuality and Identity, 1971, Going Crazy: The Radical Theory of R.D. Laing, 1972, The Analytical Situation: How Patient and Therapist Communicate, 1973, Homosexuality, 1973, Freud As We Knew Him, 1973. Fellow Am. Inst. Psychotherapy and Psychoanalysis (supr., mem. faculty, mem. exec. com.); mem. Am. Acad. Psychotherapists, Am. Group Psychotherapy Assn., Am. Otoanalytic Assn., Assn. Applied Psychoanalysis, Am. Psychol. Assn. Address: New York, N.Y. Died May 25, 1983.

RUNALS, CLARENCE RIDER, lawyer; b. Arcade, N.Y., Mar. 27, 1893; s. Leonard Earl and Nellie Gray (Rider) R.; m. Edith Ruth Landsheft, Dec. 17, 1919; children—John E., Jane Elizabeth (Mrs. William Mentz Crandall, Jr.), Ruth (Mrs. William Stewart). LL.B., U. Buffalo, 1915; LL.D., Niagara U., 1957. Bar: N.Y. bar 1916. Counsel to firm Runals, Broderick & Shoemaker (and predecessors), Niagara Falls, N.Y., from 1951; mem. hon. adv. bd. Marine Midland Bank. Del. N.Y. State Constl. Conv., 1938; commr. Niagara Frontier State Park, 1955-57; Past pres. Community Chest, Niagara Falls; adv. bd. Salvation Army, Niagara Falls. Recipient citation for meritorious achievement U. Buffalo, 1956. Fellow Am. Coll. Trial Lawyers; mem. N.Y. State Bar Assn. (pres. 1957-58), Am. Bar Assn. (ho. of dels. 1957-62), Niagara County Bar Assn. (past pres.), Niagara Falls Bar Assn. (past pres.), Niagara Falls (N.Y.) C. of C. (past pres.), NCCJ (past Protestant co-chmn. Niagara Falls chpt.). Clubs: Rotary (Niagara Falls) (past pres.), Niagara Falls Country (Niagara Falls) (past pres.), Niagara (Niagara Falls) (past pres.). Home: Niagara Falls, NY.

RUNES, DAGOBERT DAVID, publishing co. exec.; b. Zastavna, Austria-Hungary, Jan. 6, 1902; came to U.S., 1926, naturalized, 1936; s. Isadore and Adele (Sussman) R.; m. Mary Theresa Gronich, Oct. 18, 1936 (dec.); children—Regeen Lenore, Richard Norton; m. Rose Morse, Apr. 13, 1978. Ph.D., U. Vienna, Austria, 1924. Lectr., free lance writer, 1936-31; dir. Inst. Advanced Edn., N.Y.C., 1931-34; editor Modern Thinker, N.Y.C., 1923-36, Current Digest, N.Y.C., 1936-40; editor-in-chief Philos. Library N.Y., N.Y.C., from 1940; bd. dirs., from 1940. Author: Der Wahre Jesus, 1927, Jordan Lieder, 1948, Letters to My Son, 1949, Spinoza Dictionary, 1951, Of God, the Devil and the Jews, 1952, The Soviet Impact on Society, 1953, Letters to My Daughter, 1954, On the Nature of Man, 1956, A Book of Contemplation, 1957, Dictionary of Judaism, 1958, Letters to My God, 1958, Pictorial History of Philosophy, 1959, Dictionary of Thought, 2d edit, 1965, The Art of Thinking, 1961, Letters to My Teacher, 1961, Lost Legends of Israel, 1961, Despotism: A Pictorial History of Tyranny, 1963, The Disinherited and the Law, 1964, Crosscuts Through History, 1965, The Jew and the Cross, 1965, Treasury of Thought, 1967, The War Against the Jews, 1968, Philosophy for Everyman, 1968, Handbook of Reason, 1972, Let My People Live, 1974, also articles. Group comdr. Red Cross Mil. Legion, 1918, Vienna. Mem. Vienna Acad. Soc. Platonica (pres. 1924), Am. Soc. Aesthetics. Jewish. Home: New York, N.Y.

RUNNSTROM, JOHN AXEL MAURITZ, biologist; b. Stockholm, Sweden, June 17, 1888; s. Mauritz Leonard and Augusta (Björklund) R.; Ph.D., U. Stockholm, 1914; M.D. (hon.), Karolinska Inst., 1940; m. Astri Wintzell, Nov. 3, 1917; children—Vera (Mrs. Lembitu Reio), Elsa (Mrs. Aake Krantz). Asst. prof. exptl. biology, Wenner-Gren Inst., 1914-21, asso. prof., 1921-32; prof., 1932-55, dir. inst., 1939-55; supr. Kristineberg Zool. Sta., Sweden, 1954-58; vis. prof. dept. zoology U. Pa., 1950-51. Mem. Swedish Med. Research Council, 1948-55. Mem. Swedish Acad. Scis.; fgn. mem. Accademia dei Lincei Rome, Am. Philos. Soc., Am. Acad. Arts and Scis., others. Author tech. papers concerning developmental physiology, contbr. sci. publs. Bd. editors Exptl. Cell Research. Home: Stockholm, Sweden. †

RUSHTON, JOHN HENRY, chem. engr.; b. New London, Pa., Nov. 25, 1905; s. Edward Wester and Daisy Rich (Garber) R.; B.S. in Chem. Engring., U. Pa., 1926, M.S., 1929, Ph.D., 1933; m. Ellott May McLellon, Dec. 9, 1933 (dec. 1978); 1 son, Edward Wester, II (dec.); m. 2d Harriet K. Zimmer Scott, 1978. Chem. engr. Royal Electrotype Co., 1926-28; instr. Drexel Inst., 1928, asst. prof. chem. engring., 1929-35; asst. prof. U. Mich., 1935-37; prof., head dept. chem. engring. U. Va., 1937-46, Ill. Inst. Tech., 1946-55; prof. Purdue U., 1955-71, prof. emeritus, 1971-85; cons. chem. engring. to petroleum, chem., equipment and mineral cos., 1935-85; sec., head office sci. research and devel. U.S. Army, 1942-46; cons., mem. rev. com. Oak Ridge Nat. Labs., 1941-65. Recipient Widsom Soc. award, 1970. Fellow Am. Inst. Chem. Engrs. (Walker award 1952, Founders award 1962, Van Antwerpen award 1979, pres. 1957, treas. 1958-62, adminstr. Design Inst. for Multiphase Processing 1972-85); mem. Am. Chem. Soc. (chmn. div. industry and engring. chemistry 1960, citation 1961), Am. Soc. Engring. Edn. Republican. Presbyterian. Clubs: Chemists (N.Y.C.); Univ. (Chgo.); Masons. Author: Oxygen Research, 1942; Process Equipment Design, 1945; contbr. numerous articles in field of mixing, process design cryogenics to profl. jours. Home: Lafayette, Ind. Died June 16, 1985; buried Abington, Pa.

RUSK, WILLIAM SENER, educator; b. Balt., Sept. 29, 1892; s. George Glanville and Mary Elizabeth (Yeisley) R.; A.B., Princeton U., 1915; A.M., Johns Hopkins U., 1924, Ph.D., 1933; student Am. Acad. in Rome, summer 1925, Ecole du Louvre, Paris, summer 1928, Harvard U., summers 1930-31; m. Evelyn T. Carroll, Aug. 31, 1932. Master Greek and Latin, Boys' Latin Sch., Balt., 1915-18; master English, Gilman Country Sch., Balt., 1918-19; instr. Wells Coll., 1921-25, prof. fine arts, 1928-58, prof. emeritus, 1958-84, vis. prof. fine arts, 1961-65; asst. prof. modern art Dartmouth Coll., 1925-28; lectr. fine arts Columbia U., summers 1924, 26, 27, U. Calif. at Los Angeles, summer 1939; vis. prof. fine arts Cornell U., 1959; vis. prof. art U. Richmond, 1965-66; tour dir. Am. Inst. Ednl. Travel, summer 1937. Chmn. Middle Atlantic States Art Conf., 1941-42. Mem. AAUP, Am. Inst. Archaeology, Coll. Art Assn., Am. Soc. Aesthetics, Phi Beta Kappa, Phi Beta Kappa Assos. (Bicentennial fellow). Democrat. Roman Catholic. Clubs: Cloister Inn (Princeton); Princeton (N.Y.C.). Author: Art in Baltimore—Monuments and Memorials, 1924; William Henry Rinehart, Sculptor, 1939; William Thornton, Benjamin H. Latrobe, and Thomas U. Walter and The Classical Influence in Their Work, 1939; Art in its Environment, 1969. Editor: Methods of Teaching the Fine Arts, 1935. Contbg. editor Dictionary of the Arts; contbr. sketches to Thieme-Becker Allgemeines Kûnstlerlexikon, Dictionary of American Biography, others; also articles and reviews. Home: Aurora, N.Y. Dec. Jan. 24, 1984.

RUSSELL, HENRY EASTIN, naval architect and consulting engr.; b. New Bern, N.C., July 5, 1889; s. William Trent and Jane (Ellis) R.; student Staten Island Acad., New Brighton, N.Y., B.Sc., U.S. Naval Acad., 1910, M.Sc., Mass. Inst. of Tech., 1915; m. Agnes O'Connor, Jan. 31, 1914; children—Henry E., Bernard Daves. Served as midshipman and ensign on U.S.S. Vermont; New York Navy Yard in charge of all hull repair and dry-docking, 1915-20; Philadelphia Navy Yard production supt., 1921-25; supt., new design, Bur. of Construction and Repair, Navy Dept., 1925-27; head of dept. math., U.S. Naval Acad., 1927-31; prof. of naval construction, Mass. Inst. of Tech., 1931-43; sec., The Am. Maritime Council, 1942; pres. and gen. mgr., Cramp Shipbuilding Co., 1943-48. Director Shipbuilders Council of America, 1943-46; Vice Pres. Navy Indsl. Assn. 1944-46. Appointed assistant naval constructor, United States Navy, 1913, and promoted to commander, 1920, retired from active service, 1936. Mem. Soc. of Naval Architects and Marine Engrs., Newcomen Soc. England, Naval Order U.S., U.S. Naval Inst. Clubs: Army-Navy Country (Washington); Wyantenuck Country (Gt. Barrington, Mass.); M.I.T. Alumni Assn. Author: Riveting and Arc Welding. Co-editor: Principles of Naval Architecture. Home: Sheffield, Mass. †

RUSSELL, SAMUEL MORRIS, congressman; b. Stephenville, Tex., Aug. 9, 1889; s. S.N. and Clara May (Chastain) R.; attended John Tapleton Coll., Stephenville; m. Lorena Senter, Apr. 26, 1922; children—Laverne, Mary Louise. Taught sch., 1913-18; admitted to Tex. bar, 1919; county atty., Erath County, 1920-24; dist. atty., 29th Judicial Dist., Tex., 1924-28, dist. judge, 1928-40; mem. 77th to 79th Congresses (1941-47), 17th Tex. Dist. Mem. Tex. Chamber of Commerce, Lions Club. Democrat. Baptist. Mem. Odd Fellows, Woodmen of the World. Home: Stephenville, Tex.†

RUSSELL, THOMAS DAMERON, textile manufacturer; b. Alexander City, Ala., Oct. 12, 1903; s. Benjamin and Roberta (McDonald) R.; m. Julia Walker, Mar. 7, 1929; children—Nancy, Julia, Ann. A.B., U. Ala., 1925, LL.D., 1970. With Russell Mills, Inc. (name changed to Russell Corp.), Alexander City, 1925-82, successively purchasing agt., v.p., pres., 1945-68, chmn., 1968-82; pres. Alexander City Mfg. Co. (name changed to Alexander City Bldg. Supply Co.), from 1945. Hon. chmn. First Nat. Bank, Alexander City, past dir., Montgomery; past dir. Ala. Bankshares, Birmingham.; Past mem. Ala. State Docks Commn.; hon. mem. bd. dirs. George Washington Carver Found.; life trustee Samford U., Tuskegee Inst., U. Ala.; trustee So. Research Inst., Birmingham; bd. dirs. Nat. Found., Ala. Safety Council, Julia and Thomas D. Russell Ambulatory Center U. Ala., Birmingham, Ala. Assn. Ind. Colls. named to Ala. Hall of Fame. Mem. NAM (past dir.), Ala. Cotton Mfrs. Assn. (past pres.), Nat. Knitwear Mfrs. Assn. (dir.), Am. Textile Mfrs. Assn. (dir.), Newcomen Soc., Ala. Acad. Honor, Chi Phi, Beta Gamma Sigma, Omicron Delta Kappa. Club: Lions. Biology bldg. at Stamford U., Birmingham, also library at Alexander City Jr. Coll. named in his honor, also Thomas D. Russell Dormitory Tuskegee (Ala.) Inst. Home: Alexander City, Ala. Died Dec., 1982.

RUST, EDWARD BARRY, insurance company executive; b. Bloomington, Ill., Sept. 5, 1918; s. Adlai H. and Florence Fifer (Barry) R.; m. Harriett B. Fuller, Aug. 7, 1940; children: Florence M., Harriett H., Edward B. A.B. cum laude in Econs, Stanford U., 1940. Asst. sec. State Farm Mut. Automobile Ins. Co., 1941, dir. br. offices, 1946-51, v.p., 1951-58, pres., 1958-85, also chief exec. officer, dir., exec. com.; pres., dir. State Farm Fire & Casualty Co., State Farm Life & Accident Assurance Co., State Farm Gen. Ins. Co., State Farm Annuity and Ins. Co., State Farm Lloyd's of Tex. Inc.; pres. State Farm County Mut. Ins. Co. of Tex.; dir. Gen. Telephone Co. Ill. Trustee Ill. Wesleyan U.; bd. dirs. Ill. State U. Found. Served as lt. USNR, 1943-46. Mem. U.S. C. of C. (dir., pres. 1972-73), Phi Beta Kappa. Home: Bloomington, Ill. Died Aug. 18, 1985.*

RUTHENBURG, LOUIS, industrial consultant; b. Louisville, Mar. 20, 1888; s. R. and Minnie D. (Brittingham) R.; student Purdue, 1905-07; hon. M.E., U. of Detroit, 1929; Dr. Engring. (hon.), Purdue University, 1947; honorary Dr. Humanities, Evansville Coll., 1951; m. Katherine B. Singleton, Oct. 6, 1914; children—Louis Coalter, James Neill, Katherine Bates. Mgr. E. C. Walker Mfg. Co., Louisville, Ky., 1907-09; engring. work, London, Eng., 1909-10; chief engr. and supt. electric vehicle div. Ky. Wagon Works, Louisville, 1910-12; asst. chief engr., later chief insp. and gen. supt., Dayton (O.) Engring. Labs., 1912-22; mgr. Yellow Sleeve Valve Engine Co., Moline, Ill., 1922-27; v.p. and asst. gen. mgr. Gen. Motors Truck Co., Pontiac, Mich., 1927-29; pres. Copeland Products, Inc., Mt. Clemens, Mich., 1929-32; pres. Servel, Inc., Evansville, Ind., 1934-49, chmn. bd. 1949-59; dir. St. Louis Fed. Res. Bank, 1945-56. Recipient three awards Freedoms Foundation. Chmn. for Ind., Com. for Econ. Development, 1943-46. Pres. Gas Appliance Mfrs. Assn., 1950. Mem. bd. trustees, Purdue U., 1942-45; dir. com., boys and girls club work, 4-H Clubs, 1942-49. Mem. Ind. State C. of C. (dir. from 1940; pres. 1941-42), Evansville C. of C. Clubs: Country, Petroleum (Evansville, Ind.). Home: Evansville, Ind. †

RUTHERFORD, JAMES J., holding company executive; b. Syracuse, N.Y., Aug. 18, 1929; s. Edward Cooper and Alma Louise (Finster) R.; m. Marilyn Jean Zitzow, June 11, 1955; children—James J., David Mark, Dwight Steven. B.S. in Bus. Adminstrn, Syracuse U., 1962. With

Crouse-Hinds Co., Syracuse, 1947-66, mgr. acctg., 1955-57, controller-mgr. Mexican plant, 1959-60, chief fin. officer, 1962-64, v.p., 1964-66; chief exec. officer Financial Execs. Inst., N.Y.C., 1966-69, mgr. dir., 1966-67, sec., 1967-69; exec. v.p. Giffen Industries, Inc., Miami, Fla., 1970-71; v.p. Blount, Inc., Montgomery, Ala., 1971-77, chief fin. officer and treas., 1971-74, group exec. officer, 1974-77; pres., chief exec. officer Rutherford & Assocs. Inc., Montgomery, 1977-82; dir. Pa. Engring. Corp., 1977-82, Birdsboro Corp., Pa., 1978—. Chmn. adminstrv. bd. Dalraida United Meth. Ch., 1979—. Mem. Soc. for Advancement Mgmt. (Profl. Mgmt. award 1979, 1st pres. Montgomery area chpt. 1976-77, internat. pres.), Am. Mgmt. Assn., Nat. Assn. Accts. (pres. Syracuse chpt. 1963-64, nat. v.p. 1966-67), Newcomen Soc., Montgomery Mus. of Fine Arts, Beta Alpha Psi. Republican. Methodist. Clubs: Montgomery Country, Capital City, Masons, Shriners. Home: Montgomery, Ala. Died Apr. 23, 1982.

RUTHRUFF, CLIFFORD NEIL, wholesale grocery executive; b. Seattle, May 24, 1933; s. Neil Alvin and Katheryn Marie (Adnersen) R.; June 12, 1957; children: Jill, Brian, Kim, Eric. Grad., U. Wash., 1960. With Assoc. Grocers, Inc., Seattle, from 1967, exec. v.p. fin. and adminstrn., 1982. Served with USAF, 1950-54. Mem. Wash. Soc. C.P.A.'s, Fin. Execs. Inst. Republican. Lutheran. Home: Seattle, WA.

RUTLEY, FREDERICK GEORGE, engr., constrn. exec.; b. Toronto, Can., Sept. 28, 1890; s. William F. and F. A. (Oldershaw) R.; B.A. Sc., Toronto U., 1912. Resident engr. Calgary Power Co., 1912-13; with Foundation Co. of Can., Ltd., Montreal, Can., from 1914, successively resident engr. supt., purchasing agt., sec. and purchasing agt., asst. to gen. mgr., sec. asst. gen. mgr., v.p. and dir., v.p., gen. mgr., dir., 1914-52, pres., gen. mgr., 1952-55, pres., 1955-58, chmn. bd., from 1958; chmn., dir. Found. of Can. Engring. Corp. Ltd.; dir. Constrn. Equipment Co. Ltd.; mem. adv. council Export Credits Ins. Corp., Ottawa. Montreal regional dir. Dollar Sterling Trade Council; mem. Canadian Trade Mission to United Kingdom, 1957. Served as capt. Canadian Overseas Force, 1915-18. Mem. Corp. Profl. Engrs. of Que. Mem. Canadian Constrn. Assn. (past pres.), Montreal Builders Exchange (past. pres.), Engineering Institute of Canada (life member), Delta Kappa Epsilon. Clubs: Rideau (Ottawa); St. James, United Services, Mt. Royal (Montreal); Forest and Stream. Home: South Lancaster, Ont., Can. †

RUTTENBERG, JOSEPH, motion picture photographer; b. Russia, July 4, 1889; came to U.S., 1893, naturalized, 1910; s. Frank D. and Miriam (Gelfl) R.; m. Rose Wilson, Mar. 25, 1917; 1 dau., Virginia Ruttenberg Silver. Ed. pub. schs. News photographer Boston American, 1907-12; dir. photography Fox Films, N.Y.C., 1915-22, Paramount Pictures, N.Y.C., 1928-31; dir. photography M.G.M. Studios, Los Angeles, from 1935. Cinematographer: The Great Waltz (Acad. award 1938), Waterloo Bridge, Gaslight, Mrs. Miniver, (Acad. award 1942), Random Harvest, The Great Caruso, Madam Curie, Julius Caesar, Brigadoon, Dr. Jekyl and Mr. Hyde, Somebody Up There Likes Me, (Acad. award 1956), Gigi, (Acad. award 1958), numerous others. Fellow Soc. Motion Picture and TV Engrs.; mem. Am. Soc. Cinematographers, Acad. Motion Picture Arts and Scis. Home: Beverly Hills, Calif. Died May 1, 1983; buried Hillside Meml. Park, Los Angeles.

RYAN, ALLAN A., business exec.; b. N.Y.C., July 4, 1903; s. Allan A. and Sarah (Tack) R.; student Canterbury Sch., New Milford, Conn., 1914-20; A.B., Yale, 1924; m. Janet Newbold, Feb. 6, 1929; children—Nancy Anne, Allan A.; m. 2d, Eleanor Barry, Jan. 19, 1937; m. 3d, Priscilla St. George, Aug. 5, 1941; 1 dau., Katherine Delano; m. 4th, Grace M. Amory, Dec. 13, 1950. Mem. N.Y. Curb Exchange, 1924-28, N.Y. Stock Exchange, 1930-32; dir. Royal Typewriter Co., Inc., 1932-54, chmn. bd., 1945-54; chmn. bd., dir. Royal McBee Corp. (merged with Litton Industries 1965), 1954-65; chmn. bd., dir. Kaysam Corp., Inc. (formerly Molded Latex Products, Inc.), 1941-81. Mem. N.Y. State Senate from 28th Dist., 1938-42. Served to maj. AUS, 1943-45. Mem. Elihu, Alpha Delta Phi. Roman Catholic. Clubs: Racquet and Tennis (N.Y.C.); Seminole (Palm Beach, Fla.); Creek (Locust Valley, N.Y.); The Honourable Co. Edinburgh Golfers (Gullane, Scotland). Home: Palm Beach, Fla. Died Oct. 13, 1981.

RYAN, JOHN DALE, air force officer; b. Cherokee, Ia., Dec. 10, 1915; s. Edward Thomas and Mabel Catherine (Dubel) R.; student Cherokee Jr. Coll., 1932-34; B.S., U.S. Mil. Acad., 1938; grad. AC Flying Sch., 1939; LL.D., Creighton U., Omaha, 1966; LL.D. (hon.), Akron (Ohio) U., 1967; m. Jo Carolyn Guidera, Aug. 26, 1939; children—Michael E., Patricia Jo. Commd. 2d lt. U.S. Army, 1938, advanced through grades to gen. USAF, 1964; various assignments AC Tng. Command, 1939-43; overseas service, Italy, 1944-45; comdr. 810th Air Div., SAC, Biggs AFB, El Paso, 1951-53, 19th Air Div., SAC, Carswell AFB, Tex., 1953-56; dir. materiel, Hdqrs. SAC, Offutt AFB, Neb., 1956-60; comdr. 16th AF, SAC, Spain, 1960-61; comdr. 2d Air Force, SAC, Barksdale AFB, La., 1961-63; insp. gen. USAF, Washington. 1963-64; vice comdr. in chief SAC, Offutt AFB, 1964, comdr. in chief, 1964-67; comdr. in chief Pacific Air Force, Hickman AFB, Hawaii, 1967-68; vice chief staff USAF, Washington, 1968-69, chief of staff USAF, 1969-73. Decorated D.S.M. with 2 oak leaf clusters, Silver Star with cluster, Legion Merit, D.F.C., with cluster, Air medal with 5 clusters, Purple Heart (U.S.); Order Cloud and Banner (China); comdr. Nat. Order Vietnam, Gallantry Cross (Vietnam); Nat. Security Merit 1st Class (Korea); comdr. Légion d'Honneur, Croix de Guerre with Palm (France); grand ofcl. Order Aero. Merit (Brazil); Mil. Star Armed Forces (Chile). Died Oct. 27, 1983.

RYAN, MICHAEL ALLAN, automotive co. exec.; b. Pontiac, Mich., Aug. 2, 1935; s. Willard James and Lorraine Jane (Steinhelper) R.; m. Mary Pamela Scolaro, Aug. 27, 1955; children—Michael, Timothy, Terrance, Christina. B.B.A., Gen. Motors Inst., 1959; M.A., U. Detroit, 1964. Systems and procedures analyst Gen. Motors Corp., Detroit, 1954-60; fin. program mgr. Vickers, Inc. div. Sperry Rand Co., Troy, Mich., 1960-64; sr. internat. budget coordinator Ford Motor Co., Dearborn, Mich., 1964-68; div. controller Carborundum Co., Niagara Falls, N.Y., 1968-70, group controller abrasive systems, 1970-71, corporate controller, 1971-76; v.p.-fin. Volkswagen Mfgr. Corp. Am., Warren, Mich., 1976-81; pres. subs. VW Credit Inc., Troy, Mich., from 1981. Home: Bloomfield Hills, Mich.

RYAN, OSWALD, lawyer; born at Anderson, Indiana, April 11, 1888; son of William Antony and Agnes (Fitzgerald) R.; student Butler Coll., Indianapolis, Ind., 1907-09; A.B., Harvard U., 1911; student Harvard Law School, 1911-13; LL.D., Salem Coll. (W.Va.), 1947, Marietta Coll., 1948; LL.D. (honorary), Butler University, 1960; married Rebecca B. Noland, July 1, 1918; children—Noland Haynes, Rachel Leonora (Mrs. W. J. Montgomery). Asst. in history and government, Harvard University and Radcliffe College, 1911-12; began practice of law in Anderson, Ind., 1913; elected state's atty., 50th Ind. Judicial Dist., 1916, resigned 1918 to enlist in Nat. Army; city atty. of Anderson, Ind., 1925-29; states atty. 50th Ind. Judicial Dist., 1929-31; gen. counsel Fed. Power Commn., 1932-38; mem. U.S. Civil Aeros. Bd., 1938-55, chmn., 1952-53; pvt. law practice, from 1955; chmn. Fed. Interdepartmental Com. Mechanic Tng. for Aircraft Industry, 1939; chmn. U.S. Commission of Permanent Am. Aeronautical Commn., 1944; mem. U.S. Air Mission to Spain, 1944; chmn. fed. investigation of multiple taxation of aviation by states, 1944-45. Mem. U.S. delegation for negotiation of aviation agreement with Can., N.Y., 1945; with United Kingdom at Bermuda, 1946; with Mexico (Chmn. U.S. Delegation), Mexico City, 1946; with Argentine Republic, at Washington, 1946; with Canada, 1946, Washington and Ottawa; with the Netherlands, Washington, 1946; vice chairman U.S. del. at negotiations for multiple air treaty, Geneva, Switzerland, 1947; U.S. rep. air policy negotiations with United Kingdom, London, Aug. 1949; chmn. bilateral negotiations U.S. and Spain, 1954. Mem. spl. U.S. mission in 1923 to confer with the heads of European govts. with respect to immigration policy. Mem. Ind. Bar Assn., Am. Legion (national executive com.), Phi Delta Theta, Tau Kappa Alpha (a founder), Phi Beta Kappa, Phi Delta Phi, Sigma Alpha Tau. Republican. Clubs: Harvard of Indiana, Columbia (Indianapolis). Author: Municipal Freedom, 1915; The Challenge of the Prophets, 1929. Contbr. to Harper's Am. Polit. Science Rev., Pub. Utilities Fortnightly, Jour. of Air Law and Commerce; Popular Science Monthly, etc. Awarded Baldwin nat. prize for essay on govt., 1910. Home: Washington, D.C. †

RYAN, THOMAS JEFFERSON, ex-congressman; b. N.Y. City, June 17, 1890; s. John L. and Mary Belle (Tracy) R.; B.S., Fordham U., 1908, LL.B., 1911; m. Gertrude B. Keleher, July 19, 1923. Admitted to N.Y. bar, 1912, and practiced at N.Y. City. Mem. 67th Congress (1921-23), 15th N.Y. Dist. Democrat. Grad. 2d R.O.T.C., Plattsburg; with Air Service in France, 1918-19; cited for gallantry in action; decorated Croix de Guerre with palm (French). Mem. N.Y. Co. Lawyers' Assn., Am. Legion, Vets. of Fgn. Wars, K.C. Clubs: N.Y. Athletic, Nat. Democratic, Catholic (New York); Congressional (Washington). Home: New York, N.Y. †

RYAN, WILLIAM FRANCIS, mech. engr.; b. Woodbury, Conn., May 18, 1889; s. William and Mary Agnes (Skelly) R.; A.B., Harvard, 1911, M.M.E., 1913; D.Sc. (hon.), Catholic Univ. of America, 1954; married Mary Josephine Donaher, October 16, 1918 (deceased August 6, 1951); children—Mary Josephine (Mrs. Leo R. Landrey), John Donaher. Assistant engineer Interborough Rapid Transit Co., New York, N.Y., 1913-15, superintendent of construction, 1915-17; chief power engr. Wright Martin Aircraft Corp., New Brunswick, N.J., 1917-19; mech. engr. Harry M. Hope Engring. Corp., Boston, Mass., 1919-24, The Solvay Process Co., Syracuse, N.Y., 1924-29, Stone & Webster Engring. Corp., Boston, Mass., 1929-48, engring. mgr., 1948-50, v.p., 1950-57, dir., 1952-57; pvt. practice as cons. engineering, from 1957. Recipient N.E. Award, 1954. Fellow Am. Soc. M.E. (pres. 1956-57), Royal Soc. Arts London; mem. Nat. (v.p.), Mass. (past pres.) socs. profl. engrs., Boston Society of Civil Engrs., U.S. Naval Inst., Mediaeval Acad. Am., Harvard Engring. Soc., International Electrochem. Commn. (mem. adv. com.), Am. Numismatic Soc., Boston Alumni Sodality. Dem. Roman Catholic. Knights of Columbus. Clubs: Harvard Varsity; Harvard (N.Y.); Demi Tasse (Boston). Address: West Newton, Mass. †

RYAN, WILLIAM RUSSELL, naval officer; b. Apr. 7, 1890; entered U.S. Navy, 1921, and advanced through the grades to commodore, 1945.†

RYDER, LOREN LINCOLN, motion picture, TV exec.; b. Pasadena, Calif., Mar. 9, 1900; s. Fred L. and Lillie (Duncan) R.; B.A., U. Calif. at Berkeley, 1924; m. Isabel Snyder, Aug. 8, 1923; children—Claire Isabel (Mrs. Sherrod C. Swift), Joyce Marrian (Mrs. Judson Vandevere). Research engr. Telephone Co., 1924-25; radio importer Sherman-Clay & Co., San Francisco, 1926-28; sound dir. Paramount Pictures, 1929-45, chief engr., 1945-56; pres. Ryder Sound Services, Inc., Hollywood, Calif., 1948-74, Los Angeles, 1974-85, Ryder Magnetic Sales Corp., Hollywood, 1954-85, Sound Mart, Hollywood, 1967-85; v.p., gen. mgr. Nagra Magnetic Recorders, Inc., N.Y.C., 1967-85. Served with NDRC, 1945-47. Recipient Motion Picture Acad. awards, 1938, 42, 50, 53. Registered profl. engr., Calif. Fellow Soc. Motion Picture and TV Engrs. (pres. 1947-48); mem. Acad. Motion Picture Arts and Scis. (former mem. sound com.), Nat. Acad. TV Arts and Scis. (sec. 1961-63), Acad. Polit. Sci., Acad. TV Arts and Scis., Audio Engring. Soc., Am. Soc. Cinematographers (asso.), Hollywood C. of C., Tau Kappa Epsilon. Home: Sherman Oaks, Calif. Died May 28, 1985.

RYSKIND, MORRIE, author, columnist; b. N.Y.C., Oct. 20, 1895; s. Abraham and Ida (Ettelson) R.; m. Mary House, Dec. 19, 1929; children—Ruth, Allan House. B.Litt., Columbia U., 1917. Reporter N.Y. World, 1917; contbr. Nat. Rev., 1955-85; columnist Los Angeles Times Syndicate, 1960-65, Washington Star Syndicate, 1965-78, Human Events, 1978-85. Author: several sketches for musical Garrick Gaieties, 1925; (with George S. Kaufman) plays Coconuts, 1925, Animal Crackers, 1928, Strike Up the Band, 1930, Of Thee I Sing, 1932 (Pulitzer prize), Let 'Em Eat Cake, 1933; alone Louisiana Purchase, 1940; screenplays include Coconuts, 1929, Animal Crackers, 1930, A Night at the Opera, 1935, My Man Godfrey, 1936, Stage Door, 1937, Room Service, 1938, Man About Town, 1939, Penny Serenade, 1941, Claudia, 1943, Where Do We Go from Here? , 1943, It's in the Bag, 1945; verse Unaccustomed As I Am, 1921, Diary of an Ex-President, 1932. Republican. Jewish. Home: Beverly Hills, Calif. Died Aug. 24, 1985.

SABES, HAROLD, publisher; b. Mpls., Aug. 17, 1912; s. Abraham and Eva (Haskvitz) S.; m. Jessie Winnick, Oct. 11, 1936; children—Earl Martin, Franklin Ellis. B.A., U. Minn., 1932; postgrad., Tulane U., 1943, Northwestern U., 1965-66. Sales and mgmt. positions Brown & Bigelow, Mpls., 1941-51; nat. sales mgr. Esquire, Inc., Chgo., 1951-54; pub. Exec. Rev., also owner Harold Sabes & Assos., Chgo., 1954-84; sec., treas. Alert Office Services, Inc., Chgo., 1970-84. Mem. Ill. Mfrs. Assn., Indsl. Advertisers Assn., Am. Diabetic Assn., Chgo. Lung Assn. Jewish. Clubs: Masons, Shrine (sec.). Home: Scottsdale, Ariz. Died May 31, 1984.

SABIN, PAULINE MORTON (MRS. DWIGHT F. DAVIS), b. Chicago, Ill., Apr. 23, 1887; d. Paul and Charlotte (Goodridge) Morton; educated private schs. and abroad; m. Charles Hamilton Sabin, of N.Y. City, Dec. 28, 1916; m. 2d, Dwight F. Davis, May 8, 1936. Elected member Republican Com. of Suffolk Co., N.Y., 1919; made mem. Rep. State Exec. Com., N.Y., 1920; pres. Women's Nat. Rep. Club, 1921; del. Rep. Nat. Conv., Cleveland, O., 1924; mem. Rep. Nat. Com., term 1924-28; resigned, 1929, to organize Women's Organization for Nat. Prohibition Reform, of which was made nat. chmn., organization disbanded Dec. 1933. Apptd. by Pres. Coolidge mem. Lexington-Concord Sesquicentennial Commn., 1925. Episcopalian. Clubs: Colony, Woman's City. Recipient of Am. Woman's Assn. award "for eminent attainment," 1934. Home: Southampton, L.I.

SACHAR, EDWARD JOEL, psychiatrist; b. St. Louis, June 23, 1933; s. Abram Leon and Thelma (Horwitz) S. A.B., Harvard U., 1952; M.D., U. Pa., 1956, Intern Beth Israel Hosp., Boston, 1956-57. Resident Mass. Mental Health Center, Boston, 1957-59; asso. in psychiatry Harvard Med. Sch., Boston, 1964-66; asso. prof. psychiatry Albert Einstein Coll. Medicine, Bronx, N.Y., 1966-72, prof. psychiatry, 1972-76, chmn. dept., 1975-76; prof., chmn. dept. psychiatry Columbia U. Coll. Physicians and Surgeons, N.Y.C., from 1976; dir. N.Y. State Psychiat. Inst., from 1976; chmn. program-projects rev. com.

NIMH, 1975-77. Author: Topics in Psychoendocrinology, 1975, Hormones, Behavior and Psychopathology, 1976; Mem. editorial bd.: Psychoneuroendocrinology; Contbr. articles to profl. jours. Served to capt. M.C. U.S. Army, 1959-61. Recipient Anna-Monika Found. prize for research in depression, 1975; USPHS NIMH grantee, from 1963. Mem. Am. Psychosomatic Soc. (sec. treas. 1976), Am. Psychopathol. Assn. (council 1976), Assn. for Research in Nervous and Mental Diseases (trustee from 1975), Am. Psychiat. Assn. (council on research from 1976), Psychiat. Research Soc. (pres. 1975), Am. Coll. Neuropsychopharmacology. Home: New York, NY.

SACK, A. ALBERT, JR., investment banker; b. Providence, R.I., June 25, 1887; s. A. Albert and Alice R. (Davis) S.; prep. edn., Phillips Exeter Acad., Exeter, N.H.; student Acadia U., Wolfville, N.S., Can.; m. Marion Grant, June 29, 1927. Asst. treas. and sec. Lymansville (R.I.) Co., worsted mfrs., 1914-23, later pres.; pres., treas. Providence Oil Co., 1923-25; pres., treas. Sack & Co. from 1926. Clubs: Wannamoisett Country; New York Yacht. Home: Providence, R.I. †

SACKLER, HOWARD, playwright; b. N.Y.C., 1929; m. Greta Lynn Lungren, 1963; two children. B.A., Bklyn. Coll., 1950. Dir., Caedmon Records, N.Y.C., 1953-68, plays produced in, London, San Francisco, Boston and, Washington; dir.: TV spl. Shakespeare, Soul of an Age, 1964; movies, TV.; (Pulitzer prize 1969, Drama Critics Circle award 1969, Tony award 1969); Author: The Great White Hope (Pulitzer prize 1969), The Pastime of Monsieur Robert, Uriel Acosta, Mr. Welk and Jersey Jim, The Yellow Loves, A Few Inquiries, The Nine O'Clock Mail; also TV Semmelweiss, 1977; screenplays include Desert Padre, 1950, Killer's Kiss, 1952, Fear and Desire, 1953, A Midsummer Night's Dream, 1961, Bugsy, 1973, Jaws II, 1976, Gray Lady Down, 1978. Grantee Rockefeller Found., 1953; Grantee Littauer Found., 1954; recipient Maxwell Anderson award, 1954, Sergei award, 1959. Home: Ibiza, Spain. Died Oct. 14, 1982.*

SADLER, GEORGE MARION, airlines executive; b. Clarksville, Tenn., Feb. 7, 1911; s. George Marion and Emma Lester (Townsend) S.; m. Joy Whitson, Apr. 2, 1936 (dec. Feb. 1974); children—George Marion (dec.), M. Whitson; m. Marguerite Bush, Aug. 23, 1976. A.B., Duke U., 1932, M.A., 1933. Tchr. Tenn. secondary schs., 1933-41; with Am. Airlines, Inc., 1941—, gen. mgr., 1959-64, pres., 1964-67, vice chmn. bd. dirs., N.Y.C., 1969-83. Dir. Nat. Council on Alcoholism. Served to sgt. USAAF, 1943-45. Mem. Am. Numismatic Soc. (mem. council). Home: Tucson, Ariz. Died Sept. 11, 1983.

SAFRAN, HYMAN, printing company executive; b. Detroit, Feb. 9, 1913; s. Elias and Freida (Mendelson) S.; m. Leah Yoffee, July 25, 1937; children: Sharon Elaine, Frederick David, Kenneth Jay, James Allan. Student, Wayne U., 1929-32. Pres. Safran Printing Co., Detroit, 1932-76; chmn. bd., chief exec. officer Stecher-Traung-Schmidt Corp., Detroit, from 1976. Pres. Jewish Welfare Fedn., 1964-69, Congregation Shaarey Zedek, 1958-60. Served to lt. USN, 1944-46. Recipient Marshall award Jewish Theol. Sem., 1960; Butzel award Jewish Welfare Fedn., 1970. Mem. Jewish War Vets (post comdr.). Clubs: Knollwood Country (West Bloomfield, Mich.); Boca Rio Country (Boca Raton, Fla.). Home: Bloomfield Hills, Mich. Died Dec. 1983.

SAHAKIAN, MABEL MARIE LEWIS, (MRS. WILLIAM S. SAHAKIAN) clergywoman, author, educator; b. West Newton, Pa., Mar. 2, 1921; d. Paul Tyson and Blanch Theresa (d'Happart) Lewis; m. William S. Sahakian, Mar. 27, 1945; children—James William, Richard Lewis, Barbara Jacquelyn, Paula Leslie. Student, W.Va. U., 1939-40; A.B., Gordon Coll., 1944; M.Div. (Hester Ann Beebe fellow 1947), Boston U., 1947, postgrad., 1947-49; D.Sc., Curry Coll., 1957. Ordained to ministry Conglist. Ch., United Ch. of Christ, 1953; asso. pastor Riverdale Congl. Ch., Dedham, Mass., 1953-55, pastor, 1967-68, from 78; asso. pastor First Congl. Ch., Chelsea, Mass., 1956-58, Ch. of Christ, Bedford, Mass., 1958-60; lectr. philosophy, speech Northeastern U., Boston, 1960-77, sr. lectr., 1970-77, mem. counseling service, 1963-77; interim minister East Congl. Ch., Milton, Mass., 1966-67, South Congl. Ch., Braintree, Mass., 1968-69, 1st Congl. Ch., Norwood, Mass., 1972-73. Author: (with William S. Sahakian) Realms of Philosophy, 1965, 3d edit., 1981, Ideas of the Great Philosophers, 1966, Rousseau as Educator, 1974, John Locke, 1975, Plato, 1977. Chmn. drive Am. Cancer Soc., Dedham, 1964-65. Mem. Am. Philos. Assn., D.A.R. (regent 1964-67), Mass. Children Am. Revolution (sr. state chaplain 1967-69), Met. Boston Ministerial Assn., Boston Authors Club, Boston Bus. and Profl. Women, Alpha Phi. Home: Wellesley, Mass.

ST. JOHN, JAMES H(AMILTON), coll. dean; born Muscatine, Ia., Nov. 21, 1890; s. James Hamilton and Agnes Louise (Hatch) St. J.; A.B., Grinnell (Ia.) Coll., 1912; Ph.D., State U. of Ia., 1927; Rhodes Scholar. Oxford U., Eng., 1914-17; m. Naomi Elizabeth Wylie, Apr. 27, 1918 (divorced 1941); m. 2d, Martha Barbara Trossen, 1941; 1 dau., Barbara Wylie (Mrs. Richard Bruce Canright). Teacher, Grinnell Coll., 1913-14, 1935-36; teacher, Tech. High Sch., Indianapolis, 1913-14; asst. cashier Am. Nat. Bank, Arlington, Ia., 1919-25; asst. prof. history Miami U., 1927-37, asso. prof., 1937-43, prof., 1943-47, asst. dean, Coll. of Arts and Science, and prof. from 1947, upperclass adviser from 1930; summer teacher State U. of Ia., 1928, Humboldt State Coll., Arcata, Calif., 1935, 37, N.Y. State Coll. for Teachers, Albany, 1936, 1938-42. Teacher marine navigation, Navy V-12, Miami U., 1943-45. Fellow, history, State University of Iowa, 1925-27. Member Phi Beta Kappa. Conglist. Author: Edmund Dummer and His West India Packets, 1941. Home: Oxford, OH. †

SAKURAI, JUN JOHN, educator, physicist; b. Tokyo, Japan, Jan. 31, 1933; came to U.S., 1949; s. Yasuemon and Shizue (Ito) S.; m. Noriko Tsunefuji, June 10, 1961; children—Ken, George. A.B., Harvard U., 1955; Ph.D., Cornell U., 1958. Asst. prof. U. Chgo., 1958-62, assoc. prof., 1962-64, prof., 1964-70; prof. physics UCLA, 1970-82; cons. Argonne Nat. Lab., 1960-69, Nat. Accelerator Lab., 1967-70. Author: Invariance Principles and Elementary Particles, 1964, Advanced Quantum Mechanics, 1967, Currents and Mesons, 1968; editor: Zeitschrift für Physik, 1979-81; contbr. articles to profl. jours. Alfred P. Sloan fellow, 1962-66; John S. Guggenheim fellow, 1975-76; recipient Alexander von Humboldt Sr. U.S. Scientist award, 1981-82. Fellow Am. Phys. Soc. Home: Los Angeles, Calif. Died Oct. 1982.

SALATHE, ALBERT, chemistry; b. in New York, N.Y., Nov. 1, 1887; s. Mathias and Augusta (Baker) S.; A.B., Colgate U., Hamilton, N.Y., 1910, A.M., 1912; Ph.D., U. of Chicago, 1922; grad. study, Columbia, 1911, 12, 15, Union Coll., Schenectady, N.Y., 1916-18; m. Sophia Christine Erka, of Edmeston, N.Y., June 28, 1917 (died Feb. 24, 1936). Athletic dir. and teacher mathematics and German, Ashtabula (O.) High Sch., 1910-11; lab. instr. inorganic chemistry, Columbia, 1911-12; instr. chemistry, Union Coll., 1912-19, actg. head of dept., 1914-15, also employed during that period and subsequently by Gen. Electric Co., Aluminum Co. of America and other corpns.; fellow and asst. in chemistry, U. of Chicago, 1919-20; prof. chemistry, Albany (N.Y.) Coll. Pharmacy, 1920-21; prof. physics and geology, Ia. Wesleyan Coll., Mt. Pleasant, 1922; prof. chemistry and geology, Sweet Briar (Va.) Coll., 1922-24; head of science dept., Centenary Coll. of La., Shreveport, 1924-27; head of dept. chem. engring., Syracuse (N.Y.) U., 1927-37; travelling research coordinator Brown Co. since 1937; v.p. and sec. Organic Products Corpn., Schenectady, 1916-18. Fellow A.A.A.S.; mem. Am. Inst. Chem. Engrs., Am. Inst. Chemists, Am. Philatelic Soc., Am. Chem. Soc. (sec. and treas. Eastern N.Y. sect. 1916-18, v.p. 1920-21, pres. Northern La. sect. 1924-25, councillor 1925-26), Phi Beta Kappa, Sigma Xi, Alpha Chi Sigma, Pi Kappa Delta, Phi Delta Theta (pres. N.Y.Z. from 1930). Clubs: Faculty (dir.), Technology. Contbr. chem. articles. Home: L.I., N.Y. †

SALINGER, HERMAN, educator, writer; b. St. Louis, Dec. 23, 1905; s. Isadore and Florence (Treichlinger) S.; A.B., Princeton, 1927; M.A., Stanford, 1929; postgrad. U. Berlin, 1929-30, U. Cologne, 1930-31; Ph.D., Yale, 1937; postgrad. U. Wis., summers 1951-53; m. Marion G. Casting, Nov. 29, 1941; children—Jill Hudson (Mrs. F. Duane Lamkin), Wendy Lang, Jennifer Wilson. Grad. asst. German, Stanford, 1927-29; instr. Princeton, 1932-35, U. Wis., 1937-42; asst. prof., acting chmn. fgn. langs. U. Kansas City, 1946-47; asso. prof., chmn. modern fgn. langs. dept. Grinnell Coll., 1947-50, prof. German, 1950-55; prof. Germanic langs. and lit. Duke, 1955-75, chmn., 1955-70, chmn. undergrad. program in comparative lit., 1972-75, prof. comparative lit., 1974-75; vis. lectr. comparative lit. U. Wis., 1954, 1957. Served from 2d lt. to capt. USAAF, 1942-46. Recipient Badge of Honor Poetry prize, 1942, Roanoke-Chowan (N.C.) Poetry award, 1963. Fellow Alex von Humboldt Found., 1930-31, 71. Mem. Modern Lang. Assn. Am., Internat. Arthur Schnitzler Research Assn. (sec.-treas. 1961-72), Am. Assn. Tchrs. German, S. Atlantic Modern Lang. Assn., Am. Comparative Lit. Assn., Phi Beta Kappa. Episcopalian. Mason. Compiler and editor: An Index to the Poems of Rainer Maria Rilke, 1942. Translator and editor: Twentieth Century German Verse: a Selection, 1952. Translator: Heinrich Heine: Germany: A Winter's Tale, 1944; Rudolf Hagelstange: Ballad of the Buried Life, 1962. Author: Angel of Our Thirst: Poems, 1950; A Sigh is the Sword: Poems, 1963. Co-editor: The Creative Vision, 1960; Studies in Arthur Schnitzler, 1963; Ernst Elster's Prinzipien der Litteraturwissenschaft, 1972. Translator, editor: Karl Krolow, Poems Against Death, 1969. Home: Durham, N.C. Died Jan. 22, 1983.

SALISBURY, HAROLD PRESTON, lawyer; b. Coventry, R.I., July 1, 1890; s. Everett E. and Laura E. (Pearce) S.; A.B., Brown U., 1912; LL.B., Harvard, 1915; m. Marguerite W. Shackford, Dec. 15, 1917; children—Preston Shackford, Everett Wilson. Admitted to R.I. bar, 1916; asso. Green, Hinckley & Allen, Providence 1916-23; partner Hinckley, Allen, Salisbury & Parsons from 1923; sec. Distbrs. Finance Co., Indsl. Paper & Cordage Co., Indsl. Papers, Inc., Speidel Corp.; dir. H.W. Clark Biscuit Co., Desitin Chem. Co., Howard & Lewis Motor Sales, Inc., John D. Lewis, Inc., Seekonk Lace Co., R.I. Lace Works, Inc. Served as 1st lt. 302d Inf., also G-4 1st Army, World War I. Mem. Am. and R.I. State bar assns., Am. Law Inst. Clubs: Brown, Turks Head (Providence). Home: Exeter, R.I. †

SALLES, GEORGE ADOLPHE, curator; b. Sevres, France, Sept. 22, 1889; s. Adolphe and Claire (Eiffel) S.; student Sorbonne, Faculty of Law, Paris. Curator national museums, director Louvre. Served as capt., French Army, 1914-18, 39-44. Decorated Legion of Honor, Mil. Cross (France). Mem. Internat. Assn. Mus. Curators. Author: Aesthetic Study; Facts About Life in a Large Museum. Author articles on art, aesthetic history. Home: Paris, France. †

SALMON, PAUL BLAIR, association executive; b. Charleston, Mo., Jan. 10, 1919; s. Joseph Oscar and Miriam Rebecca (Crow) S.; m. Doris Beryl McKenzie, June 6, 1941; children: Julie Salmon Bretz, Thomas Blair, Timothy Mark, Terrell Paul, Sally Salmon Nichols. A.B., Whittier Coll., Calif., 1941; M.S. Edn. in Sch. Adminstrn., U. So. Calif., 1949, Ed.D., 1957. Elem. sch. tchr. East Whittier Sch. Dist., 1941-42; marine electrician leadman, concrete shop constructors National City, Calif., 1942-44; elem. tchr. Los Nietos Sch. Dist., Calif., 1946-47; supt. schs. Bloomfield Sch. Dist., Artesia, Calif., 1947-55; supt. schs Covina Sch. Dist., Calif., 1955-60; supt. Covina Valley Unified Sch. Dist., 1960-67, Pasadena Unified Sch. Dist., Calif., 1967-68; supts. schs. Sacramento Unified Sch. Dist., 1968-71; exec. dir. Am. Assn. Sch. Adminstrs., Arlington, Va., 1971-85; vis. prof. ednl. adminstrn. Calif. State U.-Long Beach, 1950-55, Calif. State U.-Los Angeles, 1963; adj. prof. sch. adminstrn. Claremont Grad. Sch., 1970-71. Served with USNR, 1944-46. Mem. Am. Assn. Sch. Adminstrs., Va. Assn. Sch. Execs., NEA (life), Phi Delta Kappa. Methodist. Lodge: Masons. Home: Vienna, Va. Died Aug. 2, 1985.

SALSBURY, NATE, writer; b. Newburgh, N.Y., Apr. 27, 1888; s. Nate and Rachel (Samuels) S.; A.B., Columbia, 1909, LL.B., 1911; m. May Schloss, of N.Y. City, Aug. 2, 1919. Practiced law, 1912-17; column conductor Chicago Evening Post, 1917-19; adv. business, 1919-20; free lance writer. Republican. Clubs: White Paper, Forty Club of Chicago (hon.). Author: Our Cat, 1934. Contbr. prose and verse to Saturday Evening Post, Harper's Mag., etc. Home: Caldwell, N.J. †

SALTONSTALL, RICHARD, investment banker; b. Chestnut Hill, Mass., July 23, 1897; s. Richard Middlecott and Eleanor (Brooks) S.; A.B., Harvard, 1920, student bus. sch., 1921; m. Mary Bowditch Rogers, June 18, 1921; children—Mary Bowditch Pease (dec.), Richard, Sally Brooks. With Brookline Trust Co., 1921-22, Merchants Nat. Bank, Boston, 1922-23, Tucker, Anthony & Co., Boston, 1924-25; partner State Street Research & Mgmt. Co., Boston, from 1924; v.p., dir. State Street Investment Co.; dir. Ins. Co. of North America, State St. Bank and Trust Company (Boston), Electric Bond and Share Co., Fed. Street Fund. Treas. Judge Baker Guidance Center; trustee Perkins Sch. for Blind, Mass. Soc. for Promoting Agr. (pres.). Served from seaman to ensign USNRF, 1917-18. Home: Sherborn, Mass. Died May 4, 1982.

SALTZSTEIN, HARRY C., surgeon; b. Washingtrn, D.C., Nov. 11, 1890; s. A. L. and Fannie (Cohen) S.; Ph.B., Sheffield Sci. Sch., Yale, 1910; M.D., Johns Hopkins U. Med. Sch., 1914; unmarried. Intern Mt. Sinai Hosp., New York, N.Y., 1914-17; surg. asst., Dr. Max Ballin, Detroit, 1920-22; pvt. practice gen. surgery, Detroit, from 1922; attending surgeon Harper Hosp.; chief surgeon Sinai Hospital, Detroit. Served as lieut., later captain, Base Hosp. No. 3, A.E.F., 1917-19. Fellow Am. Coll. Surgeons; mem. Wayne County Med. Soc., Am. Med. Assn., Detroit Acad. Surgery, Am. Bd. Surgery. Democrat. Jewish religion. Clubs: Great Lakes, Franklin Hills Country (Detroit). Contbr. articles to surg. jours. Home: Detroit, Mich. †

SAMPSON, HERBERT MARTIN, JR., diversified energy company executive; b. Greeley, Nebr., July 23, 1925; s. Herbert Martin and Florence Marie (Harrahill) S.; m. Adelene V. Coad, Aug. 27, 1949; children: Herbert Martin, III, Steven J., Richard M., Mark C., Laura M., Nancy M. B.S. in Bus. Adminstrn. cum laude, U. Notre Dame, 1950. With InterNorth, Inc., Omaha, 1951-82, sr. v.p., chief devel. officer, 1980-82; dir. Am. Nat. Bank, Omaha. Mem. adv. council Coll. Bus. Adminstrn., U. Notre Dame; mem. president's council Creighton U., Omaha; bd. dirs. Father Flanagan's Boys' Home, Boys Town, Nebr. Served with USAAF, World War II. Mem. Ind. Natural Gas Assn., Am. Gas Assn., Mfg. Chemists Assn., Soc. Chem. Industry, Assn. Corp. Growth, Chemists Club N.Y.C. Roman Catholic. Club: Omaha Country. Home: Elkhorn, Nebr. Died 1983.

SAND, PAUL MEINRAD, justice N.D. Supreme Court; b. Balta, N.D., Oct. 21, 1914; s. Paul and Clara A. (Vetsch) S.; m. Gloria L. Gray, Jan. 15, 1952; 1 dau., Sheila. LL.B., U. N.D., Grand Forks, 1941, J.D., 1969. Bar: N.D. 1941, U.S. Supreme Ct 1961. Asst. atty. gen. State of N.D., 1949-63, 1st asst. atty. gen., 1963-75; justice N.D. Supreme Ct., Bismarck, 1975-84. Served from pvt. to lt. col. U.S. Army, 1941-47. Mem. Am., N.D. bar assns., Am. Judicature Soc., Order of Coif, Am. Legion, Phi Alpha Delta. Roman Catholic. Clubs: Lions, Elks. Home: Bismarck, N.D. Died Dec. 27, 1984.

SANDEFUR, RAY HAROLD, univ. dean; b. Nowata, Okla., Jan. 4, 1915; s. Thomas Blaine and Ella Lillian (Greenlee) S.; A.B., B.S. in Edn., Emporia (Kans.) State Coll., 1936; M.A., U. Colo., 1941; Ph.D., U. Iowa, 1950;

m. Arlene Joyce Roberts, Sept. 2, 1936; children—Robin Ray, Renee Suzanne. Tchr., Kans. schs., 1936-43; asst. prof. speech Emporia State Coll., 1946-47, U. Iowa, 1947-50; prof. speech U. Akron, 1950-84, head dept., 1950-68, chmn. humanities div., 1957-67, supr. radio-TV broadcasting services, 1962-67, dean Coll. of Fine and Applied Arts, 1967-84. Chmn. ednl. div. Akron United Fund, 1964-67; rep. to Am. Assn. Colls. Tchrs. Edn., from 1964; mem. radio-TV com. Akron Council Chs.; mem. Akron Sesquicentennial Com. Trustee, Ohio Chamber Ballet. Served to lt. (j.g.) USNR, 1943-46. Mem. Speech Assn. Am., Central States Speech Assn., Assn. Coll. and U. Concert Mgrs., Ohio Arts Council, Akron Area Council for Arts, Internat. Council Fine Arts Deans, Performing Arts Hall Assn., Pi Kappa Delta, Delta Sigma Rho, Omicron Delta Kappa, Phi Kappa Tau. Baptist. Author: (with J.T. Auston) Guidelines to Effective Speaking, 1965, rev. edit., 1966; also articles in field. Home: Akron, Ohio. Died Aug. 24, 1984.

SANDELL, ERNEST BIRGER, analytical chemist, educator; b. Mpls., Feb. 20, 1906; s. John August and Esther (Magnusson) S. B.S., U. Minn., 1928, M.S., 1929, Ph.D. (DuPont fellow 1931-32), 1932. Instr. div. analytical chemistry sch. chemistry U. Minn., 1932-37, asst. prof., 1937-43, asso. prof., 1943-46, prof., from 1946; vis. prof. Cairo U., 1960. Author: Textbook of Quantitative Inorganic Analysis, 1936, Colorimetric Determination of Traces of Metals, 3d rev. edit. 1959, (with H. Onishi) Photometric Determination of Traces of Metals, Part I, 4th rev. edit, 1978; editorial cons. (with H. Onishi), Elsevier Pub. Co., Holland, Interscience, N.Y.C., others. Fellow Am. Mineral. Soc., Geol. Soc. Am., AAAS; mem. Am. Chem. Soc., Minn. Acad. Sci., Geochem. Soc., Royal Chem. Soc. Gt. Britain (hon.), Sigma Xi, Phi Lambda Upsilon. Home: Minneapolis, Minn.

SANDERS, J(ESSE) T(HOMAS), economist; b. Duncanville, Tex., Feb. 26, 1889; s. William Nathaniel and Martha Elizabeth (Garner) S.; A.B., Okla. U., 1915; A.M., George Peabody Coll., 1917; Ph.D., U. of Wis., 1925; m. Margaret Boylin, July 26, 1917; children—Mildred Virginia (Mrs. Donald Goldthorpe), Thomas Gerald, Martha Elizabeth (Mrs. Byrd Keating Dozier). Head rural edn. Ala. State Normal Sch., Moundville, 1916-17, head dept. rural edn. La. State Normal Coll., 1918; asso. agrl. economist U.S. Dept. of Agr., hdqrs. Washington, 1919-24; prof. agrl. economics and head dept. agrl. economics, Okla. A. and M. Coll., 1925-36; asst. regional dir., region 8, resettlement adminstrn., U.S. Dept. of Agr., hdqrs. Dallas, 1936-39; sr. agrl. economist Bur. Agrl. Economics, 1939-42; prin. econ. farm mach. br. War Food Adminstrn., 1942-44; chief analysis br. agrl. rehabilitation div. U.N.R.R.A., 1944-47; cons. land classification for Burmese Govt., 1951; legislative counsel The Nat. Grange, 1947-54; agrl. consultant CARE, Inc., 1954-56; agrl. economist Department of Agriculture, Washington, 1957-60; economic consultant, from 1960. Special economic investigator and adv. to Okla. Corp. Commn. on ry. rate cases, 1925-30; spl. econ. investigator for U.S. Dept. of Agr. and State Dept. in evaluation of smelter damage in internat. dispute between Canada and U.S., 1930-38; in charge spl. research project on world wheat and cotton situation, under dir. Met. Life Ins. Co., 1931-32. Mem. Am. Farm Econ. Association, United World Federalists, U.N. Assn. Former mem. nat. UNESCO Commn. representing the Nat. Grange. Independent Democrat. Methodist. Home: College Park, Md. †

SANDERSON, JOSEPH MONTEITH, educator; b. Maitland, Hants Co., N.S., July 1, 1888; s. Frederick Currie and Nancy Ellen (Monteith) S.; brought to U.S., 1897; grad. Boston Latin Sch., 1907; A.B., Harvard, 1911; m. Marjorie Gordon Taylor, June 20, 1916. Teacher Cedarcroft Sch., Kennett Sq., Pa., 1911-12. Milton (Mass.) Acad., 1912-13, Volkmann Sch., Boston, 1913-17, William Penn Charter Sch., Phila., 1917-19; prin. Monson Acad. from 1919; dir. Camp Wampanoag (summer camp for boys), Buzzard's Bay, Cape Cod, Mass., 1921. Mem. High School Masters' Club of Mass., Headmasters' Club of Western Mass., Conn. Valley Harvard Club. Republican. Conglist. Singer and dir. of choruses. Home: Monson, Mass. †

SANDIDGE, ROY PRESTON, U.S. Pub. Health Service; b. Lynchburgh, Va., Mar. 26, 1889; s. William Lee and Lula Jane (Cox) S.; M.D., U. of Va., 1914; m. Jane Perley Gleason, Mar. 8, 1917; 1 son, Roy Preston. Intern Ellis Island, 1914-15; commd. asst. surgeon U.S. P.H.S., 1917, passed asst. surgeon, 1921, surgeon, 1925, sr. surgeon, 1937, asst. surgeon gen. Chief Hosp. Div., June 1940; med. officer in charge U.S. Marine Hosp., Boston (Brighton), Mass., from Apr. 1, 1942. Fellow A.M.A.; mem. Assn. Mil. Surgeons, Founders and Patriots of America. Club: Columbia Country Club: Columbia Country.†

SANDS, LESTER BURTON, univ. chancellor; b. Bklyn., June 10, 1905; s. George and Musette (Bruton) S.; A.B., Stanford U., 1929, M.A., 1933, Ed.D., 1939; m. Carol Brown; children—Anne Musette, Margaret Claire. Vice prin. Haight Sch., Alameda, Calif., 1931-35; coordinator curriculum prin. Palo Alto (Calif.) schs., 1936-40; asso. prof. edn. DePauw U., Greencastle, Ind., 1940-44, coordinator U.S. Naval Flight Sch., 1942-44; dean, chmn. dept. edn. N.Mex. Highlands U., Las Vegas, 1944-46; vis. prof. U. Alaska, Fairbanks, 1973; prof. edn. U. Calif., Santa Barbara, 1946-72; chancellor Laurence U., Santa Barbara, 1974-81; Fulbright prof., Peru, 1960-61; cons. in field; cons. AID, Guatemala, 1966, UNESCO, Costa Rica, 1967, U.S. Office Edn., P.R., 1968. Mem. NEA, Philosophy Edn. Assn., History Edn. Soc., Phi Delta Kappa. Club: Rotary. Author: Introduction to Teaching High School, 1949; American Public School Administration, 1952; Audio-Visual Procedures, 1956; History of Education Chart, 1938-81. Home: Ventura, Calif. Died May 13, 1981.

SANDS, ROBERT KENNETH, lawyer; b. Worcester, Mass., Aug. 25, 1926; s. John M. and Edith C. (Hammarlund) S. B.A. cum laude with distinction in Polit. Sci, Ohio State U., 1949; J.D., Yale, 1952. Bar: Tex. bar 1952. Since practiced in, Dallas; pres. firm Sands & Tyler (and predecessors), from 1973. Contbr. articles to legal publs. Bd. dirs. Yale Law Sch. Fund, 1974-80; mem. exec. com. Yale Law Sch. Assn., 1977-80; trustee Timberlawn Psychiat. Research Found., 1974—. Served with USNR, 1944-46. Mem. Am., Dallas bar assns., State Bar Tex., Yale Law Sch. Assn. Dallas (pres. 1966—), Confrerie des Chevaliers du Tastevin, Phi Beta Kappa. Clubs: Dallas (Dallas), Inwood Racquet (Dallas). Home: Dallas, Tex.

SANROMA, JESUS MARIA, pianist; b. Carolina, P.R., Nov. 7, 1902; s. José Maria and Maria Torra (de la Riva) S.; m. Mercedes Pasarell, Aug. 15, 1934; children—Marisol, Amelia, Mercedes, Natalia. Grad., New Eng. Conservatory Music, 1920; student of, Szumowska, Boston, Cortot, Paris, Schnabel, Berlin; Mus.D. (hon.), Boston Coll., 1949; A.F.D. (hon.), U. P.R., 1950; Mus. D., U. Miami, 1955, New England Conservatory, 1963, World U. of P.R., 1972, Conservatory of Music of P.R., 1972; D.H.L., Catholic U. of Ponce P.R., 1969, St. Peter's Coll., Jersey City, 1973. mem. faculty New Eng. Conservatory of Music, 1930-40; vis. prof. music U. P.R., summers, 1932-36; now head piano faculty Conservatory Music P.R. Victor Red Seal rec. artist, numerous others.; Recital debut, Boston, 1924, orch. debut with, Boston Symphony, 1926, recitals in, London, Paris, Vienna, Berlin, Madrid, Barcelona, also, throughout U.S. and Can.; played at, 1st Pan. Am. Chamber Music Festival, Mexico City, Library of Congress Festival, Casal's Festival, P.R., also festivals at, Pittsfield, Worcester, Berkshire, Mex., Central and S. Am. tour, summer 1945. Named Equitem Commendatorem Ordinis Sancti Silvestri Papae by Pope Paul VI, 1977. Mem. Acad. Arts and Scis. P.R., Kappa Gamma Psi; hon. mem. Atenco Puertorriqueno. Roman Catholic. Clubs: Lion, Rotarian. Home: Guaynabo, P.R. Died Oct. 12, 1984.

SANTELLI, T(HOMAS) ROBERT, mfg. co. exec.; b. Pitts., Jan. 20, 1923; s. Joseph Lester and Goldie (Craig) S.; B.S., Westminster Coll., New Wilmington, Pa., 1944; M.S., Purdue U., 1946, Ph.D., 1948; m. A. Irene Treat, June 30, 1945; children—Thomas R., James Craig. Research chemist Gen. Tire & Rubber Co., Akron, Ohio, 1948-49; research asso. Purdue U., 1949-50; sr. research chemist Plaskon div. Allied Chem. Co., Toledo, 1950-54; with Owens-Ill., Inc., 1954-81, tech. dir. forest products div., 1965-73, v.p. new product and process devel., Toledo, 1973-74, v.p., dir. research and devel., 1974-78; dir. Pantek, Inc., Mid-Am. Solar Energy Complex, Sunmaster Corp., Andover Controls Corp., Electro Oxide Corp.; mem. operating com. Nat. Petro Chem. Corp., 1976-81, also dir.; v.p., gen. mgr. Energy Products and Ventures Group, 1978-81. Div. chmn. Toledo United Way, 1976-78. Fellow AAAS; mem. Am. Chem. Soc. (counsellor), Soc. Plastics Industry, Plastics Inst. Am. (chmn. trustees), Fourdrinier Kraft Bd. Inst., Indsl. Research Inst. (co. rep.), Sigma Xi, Phi Beta Upsilon. Club: Toledo. Patentee silicone compositions for surface treatment glass fibers, plastic blowing processes, foamed plastic articles, plastic container design. Home: Sylvania, Ohio. Died Apr. 18, 1981.

SAPERSTON, ALFRED MORTON, lawyer; b. Buffalo, Apr. 7, 1898; s. Willard W. and Julia (Wilson) S.; LL.B., Cornell U., 1919; m. Josephine Lee, Nov. 24, 1924; children—Frances J. (Mrs. Lee P. Klingenstein), Lee R. Admitted to N.Y. bar, 1920, since practiced in Buffalo; with firm Saperston, Day & Radler and predecessors, from 1919, partner, 1921-83. Dir. emeritus Brockway Glass Co., Inc. (Pa.), The John W. Cowper Co., Inc. Mem. N.Y. Com. Child Care, 1946-49; past pres., past mem. exec. com. Research and Planning Council; N.Y. rep. White House Conf. on Child Care, 1960; mem. exec. com. Buffalo chpt. NCCJ, from 1954, chmn. Brotherhood Week, 1957, chmn. award dinner, 1968; nat. chmn. Cornell Fund, 1962, 66, 67; mem. nat. council Jewish Joint Distbn. Com., Am. Jewish Com. Former mem. bd. trustees, past pres. United Jewish Fedn.; past trustee Buffalo Ednl. TV Corp., mem. adv. com.; bd. dirs. United Fund of Buffalo and Erie County, Erie County chpt. Arthritis and Rheumatism Found.; hon. past dir., past pres. Childrens Aid, Soc. Prevention Cruelty to Children; trustee Cornell U., 1962-72, mem. exec. com., 1964-72, presdl. councilor, trustee emeritus, 1972-83; emeritus mem. council Cornell Law Sch. Recipient Brotherhood Week award NCCJ, 1967, Nat. Brotherhood award, 1969. Mem. Am. N.Y. State, Erie County bar assns., Cornell Law Sch. Assn. (past pres., past exec. com.), Cornell Alumni Assn. (past dir.), Marine Corps League (past nat. judge adv.), Buffalo C. of C. (past dir., past exec. com.), Buffalo City Planning Assn. (past v.p., past dir.), Cornell Men's Clubs of U.S. (past pres., past exec. com.), Am. Legion. Clubs: Buffalo, Westwood Country (past pres., dir.), Advertising (past pres., past dir.), Lawyers, Marshall, Cornell (past pres.) (Buffalo); Cornell (N.Y.C.); Mid-Day. Home: Buffalo, N.Y. Died Mar. 28, 1983.

SARGEANT, HOWLAND H., internat. radio consultant, foundation executive; b. New Bedford, Mass., July 13, 1911; s. M. Motley and Grace E. (Howl) S.; m. Dorothy Psathas; children: Kimon, Paul. A.B. summa cum laude, Dartmouth Coll., 1932; A.B. honours sch, Oxford (Eng.) U., 1934, A.M., 1938, B. Litt. (Rhodes scholar), 1940. With Fed. Home Loan Bank Bd., 1935-40; editor Fed. Home Loan Bank Rev., 1937-40; exec. sec. NSF of Nat. Acad. Scis., 1940-47; chief div. patent adminstrn. Office Alien Property Custodian, 1942-47; chmn. Tech. Indsl. Intelligence Com., U.S. Joint Chiefs of Staff, 1944-46, dep. asst. sec. of state for pub. affairs, 1947-51, asst. sec. pub. affairs, 1952-53; cons. State Dept. and Ford Found., 1953-54; pres., trustee Radio Liberty Com., Inc., 1954-75; dir. RFE/RL, Inc., 1976-77, Commonwealth Fund's Harkness Fellowships, from 1980; Pres. Magnesium Devel. Corp., 1945-50. Author: The Representation of the United States Abroad, 1965, Soviet Propaganda, 1972; contbr. article to profl. jour. Pres. UNESCO Gen. Conf., Paris, 1951; chmn. U.S. delegations 5th-7th confs.; Pres. Dartmouth Alumni Council, 1968-69; mem. advisory com. Dartmouth Inst., 1972-80, Grad. Sch. Corporate and Polit. Communication Fairfield U., from 1968; mem. Panel Ideas and Polit. Communication in Soviet Union, from 1976; Trustee Freedom House; mem. bd. Internat. Broadcasting, 1974-75. Recipient certificate of appreciation U.S. Army, Superior Service award State Dept., Dartmouth Alumni award. Mem. Assn. Am. Rhodes Scholars, Internat. Radio and TV Execs., Soc. Internat. Broadcasters (chmn. adv. bd. from 1982), Council Fgn. Relations, Am. Fgn. Service Assn., Phi Beta Kappa, Sphinx, Kappa Kappa Kappa. Clubs: West Side Tennis (Forest Hills, N.Y.); Dartmouth College (N.Y.C.), Century Assn. (N.Y.C.). Home: New York, N.Y.

SASLOW, DANIEL L., dental supply and equipment co. exec.; b. Chgo., Oct. 28, 1926; s. Joseph J. and Olga E. S.; m. Fay Finke, Nov. 23, 1949; 1 dau., Lynn Dani. B.S. in Bus. Adminstrn., Northwestern U., 1948. Salesman Nobilium Products Co., 1948-51; founder, pres. D.L. Saslow Co., Chgo., 1951-83. Served with U.S. Army, 1944-45. Mem. Dental Dealers Am. (pres. 1980-81). Home: Chicago, Ill. Died Dec. 1983.

SATTERFIELD, JOHN CREIGHTON, lawyer; b. Port Gibson, Miss., July 25, 1904; s. Milling Marion and Laura Stevenson (Drake) S.; A.B., Millsaps Coll., 1926; J.D., U. Miss., 1929; LL.D., Mont. State U., 1961, Dalhousie U., 1962; S.J.D., Suffolk U., 1962; m. Ruth Quin, Nov. 13, 1933 (dec.); children—John Creighton, Ellen Drake; m. 2d, Mary Virignia Fly, Sept. 5, 1943; 1 dau., Mary Laura (Mrs. H. Mickey Graham). Admitted to Miss. bar, 1929, since practiced in Jackson; with firm Alexander & Alexander, 1929-35; mem. firm Alexander & Satterfield 1935-43, sr. partner firm Satterfield, Shell, Williams & Buford, 1943-75, Satterfield, Allred & Colbert, 1976-81. Mem. Miss. Ho. of Reps., 1928-32, chmn. constn. com., sec. judiciary and ways and means coms., co-author Stansel Hwy. Act. Dir. Hinds County chpt. ARC; state dir. YMCA. Recipient Distinguished Mississippian award U. Miss., 1966. Fellow Am. Bar Found.; mem. Nat. Conf. Commrs. Uniform State Laws, Am. Bar Assn. (gov. 1956-59, pres. 1961-62), Miss. Bar (pres. 1955- 56, past v.p.), Am. Judicature Soc. (dir.), Am. Coll. Probate Counsel (regent 1967-81), Scribes, Phi Delta Phi, Beta Theta Pi, Omicron Delta Kappa, Sigma Epsilon. Democrat. Methodist (del. Gen. Conf. 1952, 60, 64, 66, 68, 70, 72, 76, jurisdictional conf., 1952, 56, 60, 64, 66, 68, 70, 72, 76). Clubs: Masons, Shriners. Contbr. articles to legal publs. Home: Jackson, Miss. Died May 5, 1981.

SAVAGE, HENRY HAROLD, clergyman; b. Blair, Neb., July 23, 1887; s. Hubbard and Lucy Ellen Savage; A.B., Denver U., 1909, A.M., 1910; student Moody Bible Inst., 1911; D.D., Georgetown Coll., 1931; m. Bessie E. Jenson, Dec. 25, 1912; children—Robert C., James A., Helen V. (Mrs. Broach). Ordained to ministry, Bapt. Ch., 1916; pastor, Barron, Wis., also River Falls, Almond, Baraboo, 1911-24, First Bapt. Ch., Pontiac, Mich., from 1924; dir. Maranatha Bible Conf., Muskegon, Mich., from 1936. Mem. church div. Nat. Council Def. Mem. Nat. Assn. Evangs. (past pres., sec.-at-large), Conservative Bapt. Fgn. Missions Soc. (past pres.). Author: Facts, 1930; Steps, 1932; Realities, 1934; Days, 1936; And Peter, 1954; Finalities, 1959; also articles. Home: Pontiac, Mich. †

SAVITCH, JESSICA, television news correspondent; b. Kennett Square, Pa.; m. Donald Rollie Payne, Mar. 1981. B.S., Ithaca Coll., 1968. Researcher Sta. WCBS-Newsradio, N.Y.C., 1969-70; with Sta. KHOU-TV, Houston, 1970-72; gen. assignment reporter, anchor Sta. KYW-TV, Phila., 1972-73, weekend anchor, 1973-74; co-anchor Eyewitness News, 1976-77; corr. NBC News, N.Y.C., 1977-83; anchor NBC Nightly News, Saturday/Sunday edit., also anchor nightly updates, polit. corr. Recipient Clarion award for documentary, 1974; Broadcast Media Conf. award Woman in Communications award, 1977. Address: New York, N.Y. Died Oct. 24, 1983.

SAWYER, HAROLD MOORE, business exec.; b. Waverly, N.Y., Apr. 15, 1890; s. Fred A. and Mary Stone (Moore) S.; M.E., Cornell U., 1911; m. Regina Lutz, Nov. 18, 1914; 1 son, Harold M. Began as asst. power engr.

Scranton (Pa.) Electric Co., 1911-12; power engr., Wheeling (W.Va.) Electric Co., 1912-19, gen. sales mgr., 1919-20; with Am. Gas & Electric Co. from 1920, first as asst. gen. contract agent, 1920-24, gen. contract agent, 1924-28, and vice pres. from 1928; v.p., dir. Am. Gas & Electric Service Corp.; also vice pres., dir. all Am. Gas & Electric Co. operating subsidiaries. Mem. Sales Execs. Conf. chmn., 1945-46. Mem. S.A.R., N.Y. Geneal. and Biog. Soc., Am. Inst. Elec. Engrs., Am. Geog. Soc., Newcomen Soc. (Am. br.), Edison Electric Inst., Assn. Edison Illuminating Com. (pres. 1938-40). Dir. and mem. exec. com. Tioga Hist. Soc. (dir.). Trustee Packer Hosp. Mason. Clubs: Railroad and Machinery, Cornell (N.Y. City); Shepard Hills Country. Home: Jackson Heights, N.Y. †

SAWYER, LUKE E., business exec.; b. Malden, Mass., Sept. 22, 1887; s. Henry Thomas and Martha Caroline (Sawyer) S.; S.B., Mass. Inst. Tech., 1910; LL.D., Geneva Coll., 1951; m. Helen Melissa Foxall, Nov. 8, 1921; 1 son, John. Mech. engr. Babcock & Wilcox Co. from 1911, gen. supt. from 1938, v.p. from 1948, dir. tubular products div. from 1948; pres., dir. Providence Hosp., Beaver Falls, from 1948; dir. Farmers Nat. Bank, Beaver Falls, Mfrs. Light & Heat Co., Pitts. Mason (32 deg., Shriner). Clubs: Cloud (N.Y.C.); Duquesne (Pitts.). Home: Beaver Falls, Pa. †

SAXER, EDWIN LOUIS, educator; b. New Glarus, Wis., Dec. 4, 1915; s. John Ulrich and Mary (Mueller) S.; B.S., U. Wis., 1939; M.S., U. Mich., 1947; m. Martha Joyce Evans, Aug. 9, 1947; children—Kathlyn, Jon, Timothy, Marybeth, Randall. Engr., Babcock & Wilcox Co., Barberton, O., 1939-42; prof., chmn. civil engring. dept. U. Toledo, O., form 1946, dir. research on concrete Research Found., from 1953; cons. engr. Dir. Trulay Corp. Served to 1st lt. USAAF, 1942-45; ETO. Mem. Am. Assn. U. Profs., Am. Concrete Inst., Am. Soc. Testing Materials. Club: Southern Michigan Sportsmans (pres.) (Temperance, Mich.). Home: Toledo, OH. Died June 27, 1984.

SCAMMELL, WILLIAM KIRK, U.S. coast guard officer; b. Washington, D.C., Dec. 3, 1889; s. Henry William and Ina L. (Rice) S.; grad., McKinley High Sch., Washington, 1908, U.S. Coast Guard Acad., 1911; m. Mary Meares, Nov. 6, 1912; children—Mary Elizabeth (Mrs. Ernest Allen), William Kirk. Commd. ensign, U.S. Coast Guard, 1911, and advanced through grades to rear adm., 1945; served in various Coast Guard vessels and at shore stations, 1911-48; comdr. 12th Coast Guard dist. with collateral duty as comdr. Western Area. Awarded Victory medal, World War I; Legion of Merit and Bronze Star, World War II. Republican. Episcopalian. Clubs: Bohemian, Propeller, Commonwealth (all San Francisco). Home: San Francisco, Calif. †

SCANLON, GERARD THOMAS, radiologist; b. Norwich, N.Y., Nov. 4, 1928; s. Thomas S. and Irene S.; m. Barbara Brown, June 20, 1953; children—Timothy J., Kelly M. B.S., Muhlenberg Coll., 1951; M.D., SUNY Med. Coll., 1959. Intern U. Utah, Salt Lake City, 1959-60; resident SUNY, Syracuse, 1960-63; instr. Med. Sch., Yale U., New Haven, 1963-65, asst. prof., 1965-68; asso. prof. Med. Coll. Wis., Milw., 1968-72, prof. radiology, from 1972, also chief diagnostic radiology. Contbr. sci. articles to profl. publs., chpts. to books. Served with U.S. Army, 1952-54. Mem. AMA, Radiol. Soc. N. Am., Assn. Univ. Radiologists (pres. 1979). Home: Brookfield, Wis. Died June 10, 1982.

SCARFF, JOHN HENRY, architect; b. Baltimore, Md., Oct. 23, 1887, s. Charles Reid and Margaret (White) S.; B.S., Mass. Inst. Tech., 1910, M.S., 1911; student Am. Acad. in Rome, 1913-14; unmarried. Mem. firm Wyatt & Nolting, Baltimore, Md., from 1919. Served as 1st lt., motor transport corps, U.S. Army, 1917-19. First pres., Citizens Planning and Housing Association of Baltimore; member board trustees Baltimore Museum of Art; member Council Maryland Historical Society; lecturer History architecture, Maryland Institute Art and Design; first pres. board trustees, Baltimore Municipal Museum. Fellow Am. Inst. Architects. Club: Sixteen West Hamilton St. (Baltimore). Home: Hyde. R.D., Md. †

SCARPITTA, SALVATORE CARTAINO, sculptor; b. Palermo, Italy, Feb. 28, 1887; s. Gaetano and Maria (Scarpitta) Cartaino; grad. Royal Italian Acad. Came to U.S., 1910. Exhibited Nat. Acad. Design, New York; Pa. Acad. Fine Arts; Art Inst. Chicago; Milwaukee Art Inst.; San Diego Mus.; Palace of Legion of Honor, San Francisco, etc. Hon. mention, Art Inst. Chicago, Architectural League America; winner 1st prize San Diego Fine Arts Soc., 1926; works on exhbn. Santa Fe Mus.; San Diego Mus.; Palace of Legion of Honor; sculptural works in Ch. of St. John, Los Angeles; portal of Ch. of the Sacred Blood, Los Angeles; "Rosewall" (horse), in bronze, for owner, Irving H. Hellman, Los Angeles; (portraits) Chancellor David Starr Jordan; Dr. Edgar Lee Hewett, archaeologist; Sergei Rachmaninoff, composer; Samuel O. Buckner, of Milwaukee; Milton A. McRae, of San Diego; Miss Elen Scripps, La Jolla, Calif.; Dr. and Mrs. Jarvas Barlow, Sierra Madre, Calif.; Mussolini for New Forum in Rome (awarded P. F. O'Rourke prize by Fine Arts Gallery, San Diego); Harold F. McCormick; life size statue of Marlene Dietrich for Paramount picture, "Song of Songs"; sculpture work, new County Gen. Hosp., Los Angeles; fountain sculptures for George I. Cochran, Los Angeles; sculptural work on Los Angeles Stock Exchange Bldg. (awarded prize of Southern Calif. br. A.I.A.), 1931; mausoleum for Mrs. Charles Boldt of Santa Barbara, 1931; sculptural work for State Mut. Building & Loan Assn. of Los Angeles (also prize of Southern Calif. br. A.I.A.). Decorated by Cuba, also Order Shon Skoo by Japan. Mem. Architectural League of New York, Nat. Sculpture Soc., Sculptors Guild of Southern Calif. (pres.); hon. mem. San Diego Mus., Milwaukee Art Inst. Address: Los Angeles. †

SCHAEFER, EDWIN M(ARTIN), congressman; b. Belleville, Ill., May 14, 1887; s. Martin W. and Louise (Weigle) S.; prep. edn., Western Mil. Acad., Alton, Ill.; student U. of Ill., 1905-07; B.S., Washington U., 1910; m. Lorene Catherine Kohl, Sept. 19, 1914; children—Edwin M., Martin W. Chmn. engr. with Morris & Co., East St. Louis, Ill., 1913-16; asst. gen. supt. Morris & Co., packers, 1916-18, asst. to chmn. bd., 1918-19, gen. supt. plants, 1919-28; dir. Western Brewery Co. County treas. St. Clair County, Ill., 1930-32; mem. 73d to 77th Congresses (1933-43), 22d Ill. Dist. Chmn. St. Clair County Dem. Com., 1928-34. Presbyterian. Elk. Home: Belleville, Ill. †

SCHAEFER, GEORGE JOSEPH, motion pictures; b. Brooklyn, N.Y., Nov. 5, 1888; s. Jacob and Anna (Gruber) S.; student Heffiey Inst., Brooklyn, 1907-09; m. Mary Agnes Tonry, Nov. 1912; children—George J., Gerard J., Isabel. Connected with automobile mfg. business, 1909-14; sec. to L. J. Selznick, 1914-16; asst. sales mgr., later dist. mgr., World Film Co., 1916-20; joined Paramount-Famous-Lasky Corp., 1921, dist. mgr., New England, 1922-26; divisional sales mgr. Paramount Publix Corp., 1926-32; gen. sales mgr. Paramount Pictures Distributing Corp., 1932-33; apptd. v.p. and gen. mgr. Paramount Pictures Corp., 1933, later gen. mgr., dir. and mem. finance and exec. coms. Paramount Productions; pres. RKO-Radio Pictures, B. K. Keith Corp., Keith-Albee-Orpheum Corp. Catholic. Clubs: New York Athletic; Winged Foot Golf, Orienta Beach (Mamaroneck, N.Y.). Home: Larchmont, N.Y. †

SCHAEFER, PAUL A., banker; b. St. Louis, Sept. 23, 1888; s. Henry and Martha (Erck) S.; ed. pub. schs., also Alexander Hamilton Inst.; m. Eleanor Tuegel, Sept. 7, 1911; children—P. James, Eleanor Ruth (Mrs. Fleming), Ralph H., Irma Mae (Mrs. Milster). With Central Mo. Trust Co., Jefferson City, from 1903, treas., 1918-55, vice chmn., from 1955, also dir., v.p., dir. Mut. Savs. & Loan Assn., Jefferson City, from 1932. Treas. Jefferson City Pub. Library, Lincoln U., Jefferson City; chmn. quota and admissions com. Jefferson City United Community Fund. Mem. Mo., Cole County (past sec.) bankers assns., Jefferson City C. of C. Kiwanian (pres. Jefferson City 1921, treas. from 1922, chmn. child welfare com.; recipient Civic award 1953). Lutheran (treas.). Home: Jefferson City, Mo. †

SCHAEFER, RUDOLPH J., ret. brewery exec.; b. Larchmont, N.Y., July 9, 1900; s. Rudolph Jay and Frederica Vilette (Beck) S.; ed. Carpenter Sch., New Rochelle High Sch. and Princeton Prep. Sch.; B.S., Princeton, 1924; m. Lucia Moran, Sept. 30, 1924 (dec.); children—Edmee (Mrs. William Combs), Lucy Katherine (Mrs. Peer T. Pedersen), Rudolph Jay III, William M.; m. 2d, Janet Udall, Feb. 1, 1968. Became v.p., dir. F. & M. Schaefer Brewing Co., 1923, v.p., treas., 1926, pres., 1927-69, chmn. bd., 1950-69, dir.; trustee emeritus Mystic Seaport, Inc. Hon. dir. U.S. Brewers Assn.; gov. New Rochelle Hosp. Med. Center. Clubs: Cruising Club of America; N.Y. Athletic, N.Y. Yacht, Princeton, Princeton (N.Y.C.); Winged Foot Golf; Larchmont (N.Y.) Yacht; Royal Bermuda Yacht. Home: Mamaroneck, N.Y. Died Sept. 2, 1982.

SCHAEFFER, FRANCIS AUGUST, clergyman, author, found. adminstr.; b. Phila., Jan. 30, 1912; s. Francis August and Bessie W. (Williamson) S.; m. Edith Rachel Seville, July 6, 1935; children—Janet Priscilla, Susan Jane, Deborah Ann, Francis August. A.B. magna cum laude, Hampden-Sydney Coll., 1935; B.D., Faith Theol. Sem., Phila., 1938; LL.D., Gordon Coll., Wenham, Mass., 1971. Ordained to ministry Ref. Presbyn. Ch. (Evang. Synod), 1938; pastor chs. in, Pa. and Mo., 1938-48; pres. L'Abri Fellowship Found., Huemoz, Switzerland, from 1955. Author: 21 books, including Art and The Bible, 1973, (with Mrs. Schaeffer) Everybody Can Know, 1973, No Little People, 1974, Two Contents, Two Realities, 1974, Joshua and The Flow of Biblical History, 1975, No Final Conflict, 1975, How Should We Then Live? , 1976, (with C. Everett Koop) Whatever Happened to the Human Race? , 1979, A Christian Manifesto, 1981; narrator: (with C. Everett Koop) documentary films Whatever Happened to the Human Race? . Mem. Phi Beta Kappa. Home: Rochester, Minn. Died May 15, 1984.

SCHAEFFER, OLIVER ADAM, educator; b. Fleetwood, Pa., Feb. 20, 1919; s. Charles Boyd and Mary Kaufman (Heffner) S.; m. Alice Viola Long, Oct. 21, 1944; children—Mary, Oliver, Nancy, George, Clare, Alice. B.S., Pa. State U., 1941; M.S., U. Mich., 1942; Ph.D., Harvard, 1946. Analytical chemist TVA, Wilson Dam, Ala., 1942-44; postdoctoral research asso. Harvard, 1946-47; asso. chemist Brookhaven Nat. Lab., Upton, N.Y., 1947-60, sr. chemist, 1960-65; prof. earth and space scis. State U. N.Y., Stony Brook, 1965-81, chmn. dept., 1965-71; vis. scientist Max-Planck-Institut für Kernphysik, Heidelberg, Germany, 1961-62, 71-72, 74-81; vis. prof. U. Heidelberg, Germany, 1971-72, 74-81. Editor: Potassium Argon Dating, 1966; asso. editor: Jour. Geophys. Research, 1965-67, Modern Geology, 1970-81. Trustee U. Space Research Assn., 1969-78. Recipient Boris Pregel prize N.Y. Acad. Scis., 1954; research grantee NASA, 1967-81; research grantee NSF, 1979-81; research grantee AEC, 1965-75. Mem. AAAS, Am. Geophys. Union, Meteoritical Soc., Am. Chem. Soc., Am. Astron. Soc., N.Y. Acad. Scis., Auswärtiges mitgleid der Max-Planck-Gesellschaft zur Forderung der Wissenschaften. Research on cosmochemistry, ages of lunar rocks and meteorites, history of cosmic rays, marine chemistry. Home: Setauket, N.Y. Died Nov. 11, 1981.

SCHALL, FREDERICK MUELLER, sugar executive; b. N.Y. City, June 26, 1889; s. Frederick Mueller and Mary Teresa (Muller) S.; student schs. of Eng. and Germany; m. Margaret Elizabeth Muller, Aug. 5, 1914. Ptnr., Mueller, Schall & Co. (later William Schall & Co.), N.Y. City, 1914-29; dir., treas. S. Porto Rico Sugar Co., N.Y. City, since 1926, sec. since 1935, v.p. since 1950; trustee Central Savs. Bank, from 1929. Clubs: Knickerbocker, Lunch, Ox Ridge Hunt. Home: New York, N.Y. †

SCHARPER, PHILIP JENKINS, editor; b. Balt., Sept. 15, 1919; s. William Albert and Marie Louise (Griffin) S.; A.B., Georgetown U., 1943, Ph.L., 1944, M.A. in Edn., 1945; M.A. in English, Fordham U., 1947; Litt.D., Loyola Coll., 1966, Mt. Mary Coll., 1966, St. Joseph's Coll., 1975; m. Sarah J. Moormann, June 11, 1949; children—Grail, Philip, Katherine, Alice, David, Bede. Instr. English, Xavier U., Cin., 1948-50; asst. prof. English Fordham U., 1950-55; asso. editor The Commonweal, 1956-57; editor-in-chief Sheed & Ward, Inc., N.Y.C., 1957-70, v.p., 1962-70; editor-in-chief Orbis Books, Maryknoll, N.Y., 1970-85. Adviser Nat. Fedn. Catholic Coll. Students Program on Pluralism, 1960-61; del. Nat. Conf. Race and Religion, 1962. Bd. dirs. Manhattan region Nat. Conf. Christians and Jews, Nat. Com. Support Pub. Schs.; nat. adv. com. Cath. Council Civil Liberties. Trustee John XXIII Inst., St. Xavier Coll., Chgo. Recipient Xavier award Xavier U., 1961, Kelley award Loyola High Sch., Balt., 1963; Edith Stein award, N.Y.; recipient fellowship for visit to Israel, Jewish Theol. Sem. Mem. Religious Edn. Assn. U.S. and Can. (pres. 1963-64; chmn. 1964-70), Am. Benedictine Acad. Author: Meet the American Catholic, 1969; also TV scripts. Editor: American Catholics: A Protestant-Jewish View, 1959; Torah and Gospel, 1966; The Radical Bible, 1972; The Patriot's Bible, 1975. Contbg. author: Catholics and Vietnam, 1968. Home: Stamford, Conn. Died May 5, 1985.

SCHAUM, WILLIAM HENRY, sugar co. exec.; b. Wooster, O., Mar. 23, 1899; s. Henry and Olivia Jane (Lynn) S.; student Western Res. U., 1917-18; B.S. in Civil Engring., Ohio No. U., 1923; m. Elizabeth Howell, June 24, 1926; children—Pauline (Mrs. C. Eric Elmquist), Amy (Mrs. Richard R. Owen). Civil engr. constrn. Ward Line Warehouses & Docks, Havana, Cuba, 1923; civil engr. Florida Sugar Mill, then agrl. supt., asst. mgr., mgr., 1923-52; v.p., gen. mgr. subsidiary cos. Punta Alegre Sugar Corp., 1952-57, pres., 1958-62, dir., from 1958; chmn., dir. Punta Alegre Commodities Corporation; president and director of Baragua Sugar Estates, Florida Indsl. Corp. of N.Y., Baragua Indsl. Corp. of N.Y., Macareno Indsl. Corp. of N.Y. (all Cuba). Served with Heavy Tank Corps, U.S. Army, 1918-19. Mem. Internat. Soc. Sugar Cane Tech., Cuban Soc. Sugar Tech., Am. Legion, Am. C. of C. of Cuba, Santa Gertrudis Breeders Internat., Instituto Cultural Cubano, Sigma Pi. Episcopalian. Clubs: Marco Polo (N.Y.C.); Rotary, American, (Havana). Home: Panama City, Fla.

SCHEIBE, FRED KARL, educator, author, artist; b. Kiel, Germany, Dec. 2, 1911; s. Karl Johannes and Anna Katharine (Kreutzfeldt) S.; m. Rosalie Robertson, June 9, 1956 (div. July 1964); m. Margaret Stucki, June 25, 1966; children—Sean, Wilfred; stepchildren—Hans, Ann. Student, CCNY, 1932-34, Fordham U., 1934-35, Bklyn. Law Sch., 1935-36; L.I. U., Bklyn. Law Sch., 1936-37; B.A., Clark U., 1938; postgrad., Boston U., 1938-39; M.A., U. Pa., 1941; postgrad, U. Wis., 1942; Ph.D., U. Cin., 1954. Tchr. high sch., 1945-46; faculty Sampson Coll., 1946-47; asso. prof. German Western Coll. for Women, 1947-51; tchr. English Universidad Nacional de Mexico, 1952; Taft teaching fellow U. Cin., 1952-54; lectr. German Bklyn. Coll., spring 1955; prof. modern langs. Alderson-Broaddus Coll., 1955-57; head German dept. Thiel Coll., 1957-61; prof., chmn. dept. modern and ancient langs., asso. editor rev. Emory and Henry Coll., 1961-64; prof. modern langs., editor rev. Hartwick Coll., Oneonta, N.Y., 1964-71; chmn. dept. fgn. langs. Shelton Coll., Cape Canaveral, Fla., 1971-74; curator Stucki-Scheibe Mus. and Gallery, Tallahassee, 1978-80, Art Sch. and Mus. Gallery, 1980-82; v.p. acad. affairs Freedom U., Fla. Author: Dem Licht Entgegen, 1941, Wiskonsin Erlebnis, 1942, Isle of Tears, 1942, Life and Poetry, 1942, Lost Souls, 1944, Rubinrot, 1944, Reflections, 1948, All, Erde und Mensch, 1950, Union of Fools, 1953, Walther von der Vogelweide-Troubadour of the Middle Ages, 1968; Lit. editor: Christian Educator; executed murals for, Langenheim Meml. Library, water tank, Abingdon, Va.; exhibited paintings, Stuttgart, Germany, 1963. Served with AUS, 1942-44. Recipient Gold medal Associazione di Cultura Letteraria e Scientifica Genoa, Italy, 1949; named knight Sovereign Order St. John Jerusalem. Mem. Modern Lang. Assn. Am., U. Profs. for Acad. Order, Am. Assn.

Tchrs. German, Archaeol. Inst. Am., W.Va. Hist. Soc., South Atlantic Modern Lang. Assn., Sigma Iota, Delta Phi Alpha. Clubs: Rotarian, Mason (32 deg., Shriner). Home: Rogers, Ark. Died Feb. 5, 1982.

SCHERER, WILLIAM FRANKLIN, physician, microbiologist; b. Buffalo, Aug. 2, 1925; s. William F. and Helen (Seymour) S.; M.D., U. Rochester, 1947; m. Janice Spicer, Aug. 10, 1946; children—Judith, John, Robert. Intern internal medicine Barnes Hosp., St. Louis, 1947-48; intern pathology Strong Meml. Hosp., Rochester, 1948-49; asst. resident internal medicine Vanderbilt U. Hosp., 1949-50; from instr. to prof. microbiology U. Minn., 1950-62; prof. microbiology Cornell U. Med. Coll., N.Y.C. from 1962, chmn. dept., from 1962; dir. com. viral infection Armed Forced Epidemiology Bd., 1965-72; chmn. bd. sci. counsellors Nat. Inst. Allergy and Infectious Disease, 1966-68. Recipient Theobald Smith award AAAS, 1959; NRC fellow, 1950-51; Markle scholar, 1953-55, 57-60. Mem. Soc. Exptl. Biology, Soc. Tropical Medicine, Assn. Bacteriologists and Pathologists, Assn. Immunologists, Am. Acad. Microbiology, Epidemiological Soc., Soc. Cell Biology, Soc. Microbiology, Infectious Disease Soc. Discoverer of poliovirus growth in HeLa human cancer cells. Home: Bronxville, N.Y. Died May 12, 1982.

SCHERMERHORN, LYMAN GIBBS, univ. prof.; b. Malden, Mass., June 28, 1887; s. James V. and Mary Gates (Brigham) S.; student Friends Sch., Providence, 1901-02, R.I. State Coll. Prep. Sch., 1902-03, R.I. State Coll., 1904-05; B.S., Mass. Agr. Coll., 1910; A.M., Columbia, 1932; m. Lillian Edna Tolman, Aug. 4, 1910; 1 son, Lyman Gibbs. Instr. horticulture, Mont. State Coll., 1910-12, asst. prof., 1912-14; instr. vegetable gardening, Rutgers U., 1914-16, asst. prof., 1916-25, prof. from 1925, olericulturist Expt. Sta., from 1918. Mem. planning com. Borough of Highland Park. Mem. A.A.A.S., Am. Soc. for Hort. Sci., N.J. State Hort. Soc., Sigma Xi, Alpha Zeta. Mason. Club: Rotary. Home: Highland Park, N.J. †

SCHETTINO, C. THOMAS, state justice; b. Newark, Sept. 9, 1907; s. Joseph and Maria A. (Capasso) S.; B.Letters, Rutgers University, 1930, LL.D., 1961; LL.B., Columbia University, 1933; Dr. Jud. Sci., N.Y.U., 1939; m. Thesera M. Lorenzo, Sept. 9, 1936 (dec. 1969); children—Anne M., Jean E. Admitted to N.J. bar, 1934; atty. law dept. Port of N.Y. Authority, 1936-41; instr. bus. law Univ. Coll., Rutgers U., 1941-42; exec. clk., then sec. to Gov. Edison of N.J., 1942-44; asst. to pres. Thomas A. Edison, Inc., 1944-47, also mem. firm Budd, Larner & Schettino, Newark; spl. judge Ct. Errors and Appeals, N.J., 1947-48; judge Superior Ct. N.J., 1948-59; asso. justice Supreme Ct. N.J., 1959-72. Mem. Am., N.J., Essex County bar assns., Edison Pioneers. Rutgers U., Columbia Law Sch. alumni assns., Tau Kappa Epsilon. Democrat. Club: Varsity (Rutgers U.). Home: Summit, N.J. Died, Mar. 21, 1983.

SCHEUCH, WILLIAM ALLEN, metals company executive; b. Brooklyn, July 15, 1889; s. Louis Albert and Alina Lucienne (Guerringue) S.; E.M., Columbia, 1912, grad. study, 1915-17; m. Marjorie Lucilla Tuller, July 8, 1919; 1 child, Richard. With Western Electric Co., Inc., labs. of Bell System, N.Y. and Hawthorne works, Chicago, 1916 and subsidiary Nassau Smelting & Refining Co., Inc., S.I., N.Y., since 1931, pres. from 1946. Trustee S.I. Savs. Bank; mem. adv. com. S.I. Nat. Bank & Trust Co. Served as capt., U.S. Army, World War I. Mem. Am. Inst. Mining and Metall. Engrs., Mining and Metall. Soc. Am., Brit. Inst. Metals, Acad. Polit. Sci., S.I. C. of C., Sigma Xi, Tau Beta Pi. Club: Richmond County Country. Home: Staten Island, N.Y. †

SCHEUER, SIDNEY HENRY, internat. trade exec.; b. N.Y.C., July 17, 1893; s. Henry and Sarah (Schiff) S.; m. Linda Ullman, Nov. 18, 1920; children—Robert, Thomas, James. Sr. partner Scheuer & Co., N.Y.C., from 1930; chmn. bd. Scheuer Mgmt. Corp., holding co.; Scheuer Internat. Trading and Scheuer & Co., Inc.; econ. fin. cons. to industry and social instns.; speaker, discussion leader seminars on internat. relations and East-West trade Johns Hopkins, Columbia, N.Y.U., Am. Mgmt. Assn., 1960, 65-66; Exec. dir. Fgn. Econ. Adminstrn., 1942-45; exec. v.p. U.S. Comml. Corp., R.F.C., 1944-45; mem. U.S. delegation to Inter-Am. Conf. on Problems War and Peace, Mexico City, 1945; founder Nat. Com. For Effective Congress, 1948, chmn., from 1955; chmn. Textile Mission to Occupied Germany, 1947; mem. Econ. Mission to, Japan, Korea, 1948; del. White House Conf. on Export Expansion, 1963. Bd. govs. Ethical Culture Schs., N.Y. Served to capt. Q.M.C. U.S. Army, World War I. Mem. Ethical Culture Soc. N.Y. (trustee, past pres.), Internat. Humanist and Ethical Union (treas.). Home: Pound Ridge, NY.

SCHICK, GEORGE, former opera and symphony condr.; b. Prague, Czechoslovakia, Apr. 5, 1908; s. Vilem and Hedwiga (Polákova), S.; ed. State Conservatory Music, Prague; m. Leonora Meyer, Sept. 19, 1940; 1 son, William Bernard. Came to U.S., 1930, naturalized, 1944. Condr., Prague Opera House, 1927-38, Opera House, Covent Garden, London, 1939, New Opera Co., also N.Y. Opera Guild, Miami (Fla.) Summer Opera, Cin. Summer Opera, and festivals in Newark, Chgo., Los Angeles, Mpls. and San Francisco, 1940-48; music dir. Montreal Symphony Orch., 1948-50; asso. condr. Chgo. Symphony Orch., and music dir. Chgo. Civic Orchestra, 1950-56; music coordinator TV opera dept. NBC, N.Y.C., 1956-58; former condr. Metropolitan Opera Assn.; head of music dept. U. of B.C., Vancouver, Canada; orch. condr. in concert, opera, radio, TV and ballet; concert pianist appearing in Europe, U.S. and Can.; vis. prof. Ill. Wesleyan U., Colo. Coll. Music dir. short wave broadcasts to Czechoslovakian div. O.W.I., World War II. Pres. Manhattan Sch. Music, 1969-76. Served with USNR, World War II. Mem. Am. Fedn. Musicians. Home: New York, N.Y. Died Mar. 7, 1985.

SCHIFFLER, ANDREW C(HARLES), ex-congressman; b. Wheeling, W.Va., August 10, 1889; s. Andrew and Emma C.; student public schools, West Virginia; m. Emma Muldrew; children—Virginia A., Robert A. Studied law and admitted to West Virginia bar, 1913, and engaged in general practice of law, Wheeling, 1913-39; served as prosecuting atty. Ohio County, W.Va., 1925-33; referee in bankruptcy northern dist. W.Va., 1918-22; mem. 76th and 78th Congresses (1939-41 and 1943-45), 1st District of West Virginia. Served various government units during World War. Chairman Ohio County Republican Committee 2 yrs. Mem. W.Va. Bar Assn., Ohio County Bar Assn. Republican. Presbyterian. Mason, Odd Fellow, K.P., Elk. Club: Fort Henry (Wheeling). Address: Wheeling, W.Va. †

SCHILT, JAN, astronomer; b. Gouda; Holland, Feb. 3, 1894; s. Arie Johannes and Marrigje Klazina (de Jong) S.; student U. of Utrecht, 1912-16; Ph.D., U. of Groningen, 1924; m. Jo Timmer, Feb. 6, 1925; 1 dau., Joan. Came to U.S., 1925. Asst. Leiden Obs., 1922; fellow Internat. Edn. Bd., Mt. Wilson Obs., 1925; asst. Yale Obs., 1926, asst. prof. researches on proper motions and photometry, 1929; head dept. and asso. prof. astronomy, Columbia, 1931-37; Rutherfurd prof. astronomy from 1937; dir. Rutherfurd Obs. of Columbia U. from 1936. Inventor Schilt photometer. Awarded gold medal. Bachiene Inst., prize essay with Dr. J. H. Oort. Mem. A.A.A.S., Internat. Astron. Union, Am. Astron. Soc., Nedrelandsche Astronomen Club: Sigma Xi. Contbr. various astron. jours. Home: Leona, N.J. Died Jan. 10, 1982.

SCHILTGES, WILLIAM BYNUM, banker; b. Indpls., Dec. 3, 1890; s. John Peter and Antoinette (Feld) S.; m. Mary Thoburn, Apr. 18, 1917; children—John William, Nora (Mrs. Karl C. Kohlstaedt). With Fletcher Trust Co., 1912-55, pres., 1948-55; became vice chmn., then chmn. exec. com. Am. Fletcher Nat. Bank & Trust Co. (merger Fletcher Trust Co. and Am. Nat. Bank), 1955, chmn. trust com. Address: Indpls. †

SCHINE, LEONARD ALBERT, lawyer; b. Bridgeport, Conn., Jan. 20, 1917; m. Lois V. Gildersleeve, Dec. 20, 1951; children—Leslie, Daniel, Lindsay, Lauren, Edward. B.S., U. Vt., 1938; J.D., U. Conn., 1941. Bar: names of bars and dates of admission) Conn. bar 1942, U.S. Dist. Ct. bar 1950, U.S. Tax Ct. bar 1952, U.S. Supreme Ct. bar 1955, U.S. Circuit Ct. bar 1965. Sr. partner firm Schine, Julianelle, Karp & Bozelko (P.C.), Westport, Conn., from 1947; gen. counsel Natural Sci. for Youth Found.; gen. counsel, dir., mem. exec. com., univ. sec. Sacred Heart U.; dir. State Nat. Bank of Conn. Asso. Bd.; dir., gen. counsel All State Venture Capital Corp. Presdl. commr. Nat. Commn. Air Quality; founder, bd. dirs. Aspetuck Land Trust Inc., Westport, Conn.; trustee, chmn. fin. com. Fairfield (Conn.) Country Day Sch.; trustee YMCA, Westport; Conn. del. Regional Plan Assn. Served with U.S. Army, 1944-45, ETO. Mem. Am. Judicature Soc., Am. Bar Assn., Conn. Bar Assn. (chmn. legal aid 1952-53, mem. exec. com. antitrust sect. from 1965), Am. Trial Lawyers Assn. (past gov.). Clubs: Patterson-Fairfield County, Landmark. Home: Westport, Conn.

SCHIRICK, HARRY E., supreme ct. justice; born Ruby, N.Y., June 15, 1890; s. Eustace and Katherine (Wagner) S.; student Kingston Acad., 1906-10; LL.B., Cornell, 1914; unmarried. Professional baseball player St. Louis Browns, 1914; admitted to N.Y. State bar, 1915, practiced under own name in Kingston, 1915-35; judge Kingston City Ct., 1916-24; justice of supreme ct., State of N.Y., from 1935. Mem. N.Y. State and Ulster County bar assns. Democrat (chmn. Ulster County com., 1924-34). Mason. Elk. †

SCHLAIKJER, JES (WILHELM), artist; b. N.Y.C., Sept. 22, 1897; s. Erich and Clara (Ryser) S.; ed. Ecole des Beaux Arts, Lyons, France, also Art Inst. Chgo.; studied with Forsberg, Cornwell, Dunn and Henri; m. Gladys de Groot, Sept. 14, 1922; children—Jes Erich, Helen Jean. Works represented in permanent collections Ranger Collection, U.S. Naval Acad., War Dept., Nat. Hdqrs. ARC, Army Med. Center, Dept. State (all Washington), Nelson Gallery, Kansas City, Mo., also other pub. bldgs. and pvt. collections. Recipient 1st Hallgarten prize N.A.D., 1926, 1st Altman prize, 1928, Ranger fund, 1928, 2d Hallgarten prize, 1932. N.A. Mem. Nat. Acad., Grand Central Art Gallery, Artists Guild, Am. Legion, First Div. Soc. Lutheran. Club: Armor and Arms. Contbr. illustrations to Woman's Home Companion, Am. Mag., Collier's, Red Book Mag., Am. Legion Monthly, others. Important works include inspiration series Army posters, World War II. Home: Washington, D.C. Died Aug. 18, 1982; cremated.

SCHLECHTEN, ALBERT WILBUR, metallurgist; b. Bozeman, Mont., Nov. 28, 1914; s. Albert and Clara (Schmidt) S.; B.S., Mont. Sch. of Mines, 1937; D.Sc., Mass. Inst. Tech., 1940; m. Eleanor L. Rodgers, Aug. 23, 1941; children—Mark, Carol, Jean, Eric, Brian. Asst. prof. metallurgy U. Minn., 1940-42; asst. research engr. Anaconda Copper Mining Co. (Mont.), 1941; asso. prof. mining engring. Oreg. State Coll., 1942-44; metallurgist U.S. Bur. Mines (devel. ductile zirconium metal), Albany, Oreg., 1944-46; prof. and chmn. dept. metall. engring. Mo. Sch. Mines and Metallurgy, Rolla, prof., head dept. metall. engring. Colo. Sch. Mines, Golden, 1963-68, dir. inst. for extractive metallugy, 1964-84, v.p. for acad. affairs, 1968-71, Alcoa prof. metallurgy, 1971-75; cons. metallurgist, 1964-84. Fulbright lectr., Australia, 1966. Mem. Am. Inst. M.E. (bd. dirs.), Am. Soc. Metals, ASEE Am. Foundrymen's Soc., Sigma Xi, Sigma Phi Epsilon, Theta Tau. Episcopalian. Contbr. articles to tech. jours. Departmental editor Ency. Brit. Home: Golden, Colo. Dec. Feb. 16, 1984.

SCHLEGEL, RICHARD, physicist, educator; b. Davenport, Iowa, Aug. 29, 1913; s. Richard and Mayme (Hansen) S.; m. Frances Stanley McKee, June 26, 1946; children—Thomas H., Catherine M. A.B., U. Chgo., 1935; M.A., U. Iowa, 1936; postgrad., U. Colo., 1940-41; Ph.D., U. Ill., 1943. Lectr. Mus. Sci. and Industry, Chgo., 1938-40; asso. physicist Metall. Lab., U. Chgo., 1941-43; instr. physics Princeton, 1945-48; faculty Mich. State U., East Lansing, 1948-82, prof. physics, 1957-82, acting head dept. physics, 1955-56; vis. prof. U. Calif., Berkeley, summer 1959; Vis. assoc. Cavendish Lab., Cambridge, Eng., 1954-55, 68-69, 75-76; affiliate History and Philosophy of Sci. Group, Cambridge, Eng., 1961-62, 81-82. Author: Time and the Physical World, 1961, Completeness in Science, 1967, Inquiry Into Science, 1971, Superposition and Interaction, 1980. Fellow Am. Phys. Soc. Research on Lorentz transformations and quantum theory, cosmology, cultural and religious implications of modern physics, limits of sci. Home: East Lansing, Mich. Died May 30, 1982.

SCHLESINGER, LEE HAROLD, physician, univ. ofcl.; b. Pitts., May 9, 1905; s. Maurice and Rose (Braun) S.; B.S., U. Pitts., 1927; M.D., N.Y. U., 1931; m. Gertrude Mary Coggins, Nov. 15, 1935; children—Mary Ann (Mrs. John C. Cram), Patricia. Intern, resident U. Pitts. Hosps., 1931-34; pvt. practice, Pitts., 1933-38; asst. chief medicine Hines (Ill.) VA Hosp., 1938-42; clin. dir. Newington (Conn.) VA Hosp., 1946, White River (Vt.) VA Hosp., 1946-52; dir. VA Hosp., Clarksburg, W.Va., 1952-53, VA Hosp., Westside, Chgo., 1953-58; area med. dir. VA, Columbus, Ohio and Washington, 1958-63; dir. VA Hosp., Hines, 1963-73, ret. Vis. lectr. hosp. adminstrn. U. Chgo., 1964-68; asst. prof. medicine Stritch Sch. Medicine, Loyola U., 1966-79, emeritus, 1979-81, asso. dean, 1971-78. Mem. coordinating com. Loyola Med. Center, 1963-73; mem. Adv. Council for Comprehensive State Health Planning, 1970-73. Mem. Western Suburban Planning Council, 1964-73. Served to col. M.C., USAAF. Decorated Purple Heart, Bronze Star. Fellow Am. Coll. Hosp. Adminstrs.; fellow Inst. Medicine Chgo.; mem. Chgo. Heart Assn., Am. Legion, VFW, DAV. Home: Oak Brook, Ill. Died Oct. 21, 1981.

SCHLINK, THEODORE A., utilities exec.; b. Peoria, Ill., 1890; s. Frederick and Pauline (Dilzer) S.; student parochial schs. Peoria; LL.D., Bradley University, Peoria, Ill., 1958; married Margery J. Thurlow, June 22, 1927; children—Theodore Aloysius, Roger Frederick, Margery Josephine. Messenger Peoria Gas & Electric Co., 1904; treas., later sec. Central Ill. Light Co., 1911-39, v.p., sec., 1939-44, v.p., comptroller, 1944, dir. since 1923, pres. gen. mgr., 1951-56, dir. chmn. bd., from 1956; pres., dir. Travelers Savs. and Loan Assn., from 1957; v.p., treas., dir., Nitrose Co.; dir. Comml. Nat. Bank, Peoria, Ill. Home: Peoria. †

SCHMID, WILLIAM ERNEST, business exec.; b. Washington, D.C., June 4, 1890; s. Ernest and Perdita (Alschuh) S.; student high sch. and commercial coll.; married Dee Magee, 1949. Associated with Julius Garfinckel & Co., 1912, in capacities of credit mgr., gen. mgr. and pres. of successor, Julius Garfinckel & Company, Inc., 1939-43, and 1947-50, chmn. board, 1943-47 and from 1950; co-executor and co-trustee, Estate of Julius Garfinckel; dir. Brooks Brothers, A. De Pinna Co., both New York City, The Riggs Nat. Bank, Washington. Mem. Nat. Retail Dry Goods Assn., Merchants and Mfrs. Assn.; Washington Bd. of Trade, Inst. of Banking, Columbia Hist. Society. Methodist. Home: Washington, D.C. †

SCHMIDT, PAUL FELIX, scientific consultant; b. Narva, Estonia, Aug. 20, 1916; came to U.S., 1952, naturalized, 1957; s. Paul Rhoderich and Olga Peraskeva (Kuznetsov) S.; m. Eva Luise Kohn, Oct. 14, 1944; children—E. Regine Schmidt Magacs, A. Irene. B.S., Inst. Tech., Tallinn, Estonia, 1938; M.S., U. Königsberg, Germany, 1945; Ph.D., U. Heidelberg, West Germany, 1951. Chemist Leimen Cement Works, Baden, Germany, 1945-48; research assoc. Temple U., Phila., 1952-54; sect. mgr. research div. Philco Corp., Phila., 1954-59; sect. mgr. research labs. Westinghouse Electric Corp., Pitts., 1959-64; mem. tech. staff Bell Telephone Labs., Inc., Allentown, Pa., from 1964, later ret., cons. impurity problems in silicon device mfg. Author: Schachmeister denken, 1949. Served with German Air Force, 1940-45. Recipient 1st prizes in internat. chess tournaments Tallinn, 1935; recipient 1st prizes in internat. chess tournaments Pärnu, Estonia, 1937, 1st prizes in internat. chess tournaments Cracow, Poland, 1941. Mem. Electrochem.

Soc., Am. Phys. Soc., IEEE, Am. Chem. Soc., various chess clubs. Research and publs. on anodic oxidation of semiconductors, radiation effects in insulators, mechanism of electrolytic rectification, neutron activation analysis Research and publs. on anodic oxidation of semiconductors, radiation effects in insulators, mechanism of electrolytic rectification, neutron activation analysis Home: Allentown, Pa. Deceased.

SCHMIDT, REGINALD M., business exec.; b. N.Y.C., Aug. 6, 1888; s. Carl G. A. and Jennie Elizabeth (Mayher) S.; student Betts Acad., Stamford, Conn., 1903-05; m. Mae C. Kennedy, June 12, 1915. With Libbey & Struthers, 1906-11, Estabrook & Co., 1911-26; mgr. municipal dept. R. M. Schmidt & Co., 1926-29; partner Emanuel & Co., 1929-32; with Blyth & Co., Inc. from 1932, mgr. municipal dept., 1932-40, has been vice president, from 1940. Clubs: West Side Tennis (Forest Hills); Stock Exchange Luncheon, Municipal Bond (past pres.), Bond (N.Y.C.) Home: Forest Hills, N.Y. †

SCHMULOWITZ, NAT, lawyer; b. New York, N.Y., Mar. 29, 1889; s. Solomon and Minna (Rosen) S.; B.S., U. of Calif., 1910; student Hastings Coll. of Law, San Francisco, 1910-12; unmarried. Admitted to Calif, bar, 1911, practiced in San Francisco; admitted to practice in Sup. Ct. of U.S., 1916; member of the firm of Gavin, McNab, Schmulowitz, Wyman & Sommer from 1928. Mem. Am. Bar Assn., State Bar of Calif., Bar Assn. of San Francisco, and various civic orgns. Mem. Library Commn. of San Francisco (pres. 1944-45), Art Commn. of San Francisco, Fedn. of Jewish Charities (pres. 1944-46); chmn. Speakers Bur., San Francisco Civilian War Council; co-chairman, San Francisco Round Table, National Conference Christians and Jews, 1944-46; mem. bd. dirs. Maimonides Health Center for chronic sick. Republican. Mason, B'nai B'rith. Clubs: Commonwealth, Press, Concordia Argonaut, Roxburghe. Contributor to magazines on legal subjects. Home: Saratoga, Calif. †

SCHNACKE, FRANCIS DEAN, lawyer; b. Clay Center, Kan., Dec. 2, 1889; s. L.C. and Winifred (Davis) S.; A.B., U. Kan., 1911, A.M., 1912; LL.B., Columbia, 1914; m. Mary Reding, Dec. 27, 1918 (dec. 1942); children—Arthur W., Helen Dean, Winifred K.; m. 2d, Mildred H. Barney, Mar. 28, 1946; one step-son, Kay H. Barney. Admitted to N.Y. bar, 1915, Ohio bar, 1922; with firm Joline, Larkin & Rathbone, N.Y.C., 1915-19; atty. U.S. Air Service, 1919-25; lectr. comml. law Antioch Coll., Yellow Spring, O., 1922-23; sr. partner firm Smith & Schnacke, and predecessors, Dayton, from 1926. Dir. Consol. Aircraft Corp., 1928-42, v.p., 1940-42; dir. Maxon Constrn. Co. Trustee Dayton Art Inst., 1953-61. Served from pvt. to capt. with air service, U.S. Army, 1917-19. Mem. Am., Ohio, Dayton (past pres.) bar assns. Republican. Clubs: Lawyers, Engineers, Moraine Country (Dayton). Home: Dayton, OH. †

SCHNADIG, EDGAR L., business educator; b. N.Y.C., Apr. 16, 1892; s. Louis and Theresa (Perlbach) S.; M.B.A., U. Chgo., 1950; m. Nell J. Fackson, Sept. 15, 1915; children—Edgar, Alicerose. Collector, asst. bookkeeper, salesmen Schwartzchild & Sulzberger, packers, 1909-10; chemist, master mechanic, factory costs, purchasing agent, asst. to mfg. mgr., personnel mgr., Barrett Co., 1910-17; with Chgo. Mail Order Co. (now Alden's Inc.), 1917-46, supt., 1917-22, advt. mgr., 1922-25, asst. merchandise mgr., 1925-27, asst. to pres., 1927, v.p. sales, 1928-30, exec. v.p., 1930-39, pres., 1939-46, chmn. bd., 1946-48; pres. Boston Store, Chgo., 1946-48; dean Retailing Inst. of Chgo., 1948-49; prof. marketing Loyola U., 1950-51; prof. bus. U. Notre Dame, 1952-59; pres. Edgar L. Schnadig and Asso., Rovick & Stryke Shoe Co., Chgo. Asst. to dir. softgoods OPS, 1951; dir. Chgo. Patriotic Found., 1952. Pres. We The People, 1968. Home: Chicago, Ill. Died Nov. 29, 1984.

SCHNEEBELI, HERMAN T., congressman; b. Lancaster, Pa., July 7, 1907; s. Alfred and Barbara (Schneider) s.; grad. Mercersburg (Pa.) Acad., 1926; A.B., Dartmouth, 1930, M.C.S., Amos Tuck Sch. Dartmouth. 1931; m. Mary Louise Meyer, Sept. 21, 1939; children—Marta, Susan. Commn. distbr. Gulf Oil Corp., Williamsport, Pa., 1939-82; automobile dealer, Williamsport, 1948-82; mem. 86th-94th congresses, from 17th Pa. Dist. Pres. United Fund Williamsport, 1952, YWCA, Williamsport, 1959-60; bd. mgrs., Williamsport Hosp., 1958. Served to capt. AUS, World War II. Mem. Am. Legion. Republican. Episcopalian (vestry). Elk, Kiwanian. Home: Williamsport, Pa. Died May 6, 1982.

SCHNEIDER, ALAN, theatre director, educator; Prof. drama U. Calif., San Diego, 1979-84. Dir.: Waiting for Godot, 1956, Endgame, 1958, Happy Days, 1961, Albee's Who's Afraid of Virginia Woolf?, 1962, Tiny Alice, 1964, Beckett's Play, 1964; dir.: Albee's A Delicate Balance, 1966, Anderson's You Know I Can't Hear You When the Water's Running, 1967, Pinter's Dumbwaiter and The Collection, 1962, The Birthday Party, 1967, Albee's Box and Quotations from Chairman Mao Tse-Tung, 1968, Anderson's I Never Sang For My Father, 1968, Inquest, 1970, Edward Bond's Saved, 1970, Michael Weller's Moonchildren, 1971, Gunter Grass' Uptight, 1972, E.A. Whitehead's Foursome, 1972, Beckett's Not I, 1972, Elie Wiesel's The Madness of God, 1974, Preston Jones' The Last Meeting of the Knights of the White Magnolia, 1975, Texas Trilogy, 1976, Beckett's That Time, Footfalls, 1976, Weller's Loose Ends, 1979, Beckett's Rockaby and Ohio Impromptu, 1981, Beckett's Catastrophe, 2nd What Where, 1983, Theater Center, Juilliard Sch., 1976-79, (Recipient Antoinette Perry (Tony) award 1962, Off-Broadway (Obie) award 1962). Home: East Hampton, N.Y. Died May 3, 1984.

SCHNEIDER, HEINRICH, educator, author; b. Offenbach Main, Germany, Apr. 30, 1889; s. Heinrich Christian and Lina Katharine (Robn) S.; student U. of Tuebingen, 1908-09, Univ. of Leipzig, 1909-10; Ph.D., Univ. Giessen, 1911, Examen pro facultate docendi, 1912; A.M. (hon.), Harvard, 1948; m. Alice Agnes Hackhausen, July 6, 1921; children—Marianne Alice (Mrs. John E. Weigel), Burkhard Heinrich. Came to U.S., 1936, naturalized, 1943. Asst. librarian Univ. Giessen, 1914-20, asso. librarian, 1920-21, instr. history, 1920-21; vice dir. and research librarian, State Library, Wolfenbuettel, 1921-23, dir. and head librarian, 1923-26; vice dir. State Libraries of State of Luebeck; lecturer Univ. Extension Luebeck, 1926-33; prof. German and head modern lang. dept. Am. Coll. in Sofia, 1933-36; asst. prof. German Wheaton Coll., Norton, Mass., 1936-37; instr. German, Cornell, 1937-38, asst. prof, German, 1938-42, asso. prof. German literature, 1942-48; vis. lecturer on German lit., Harvard, 1947, prof. German from 1948. Dismissed from office by the Hitler regime because of his strong opposition to Nazism and went immediately into polit. exile, 1933. Fellow American Academy of Arts and Sciences; member Modern Lang. Assn. of Am., Am. Assn. Teachers of German, Delta Phi Alpha. Clubs: Research of Cornell. Author: Joachim Morsius und sein Kreis, 1929; Klaus Groth und Emanuel Geibel, 1930; Quest for Mysteries, 1947;' Lessing, 1951, and others. Contbr. numerous articles on history of German lit. to profl. jours. Collector rare books and autographs. Home: Belmont, Mass. †

SCHNEIDER, HERBERT WALLACE, philosopher; b. Berea, O., Mar. 16, 1892; s. Frederick William and Marie (Severinghaus) S.; Coll. City of New York, 1911-12; B.A., Columbia, 1915, Ph.D., 1917; L.H. D., Union Coll., 1947; L.H.D., Baldwin Wallace Coll., 1960, Colo. Coll., 1968; LL.D., Claremont Grad. Sch., 1962; m. Carol Catherine Smith, Dec. 29, 1921; m. 2d, Grenafore Westphal, 1942; children—Edward W., Frederick, Robert. With Columbia U. as instr. in philosophy, 1918, asst. professor, 1924-28, prof. religion, 1929-57, prof. emeritus, 1957-84, prof. philosophy, 1942; acting-dean Claremont Grad. Sch., 1960-61; Distinguished Service prof. Colorado Coll., 1958-59; fellow Rockefeller Research, 1926-27. Mem. staff Blaisdell Institute, Claremont, Cal. 1959-63. Head div. internat. cultural cooperation Dept. Cultural Activities, UNESCO, Paris, 1953-56. Served as private United States Army, 1918-19. Mem. Am. Philos. Assn., Church History Soc.; fellow Am. Acad. Arts and Scis. Club: Century Assn. Author or co-author books relating to field; latest publ.: A History of American Philosophy, 1946; Religion in Twentieth Century America, 1952; Three Dimensions of Public Morality, 1956; Morals for Mankind, 1960; Ways of Being, 1962. Home: Claremont, Calif. Died Oct. 15, 1984.

SCHNEIDER, RALPH FREDERICK, physician; b. N.Y.C., Feb. 28, 1910; s. William and Wilhelmina (Arrenberg) S.; B.S, Hobart Coll., 1931; M.D., U. Rochester, 1935; m. Edith Weed, June 10, 1938; children—Ralph Weed, Susan Scott. Intern Bellevue Hosp., N.Y.C., 1935-37; resident in medicine N.Y. Postgrad. Hosp., 1937-38; pvt. practice of medicine, N.Y.C., 1938-43; asst. med. dir. overseas sect. Exxon Corp., Talara, Peru, 1946-48, N.Y.C., 1948-54, med. dir., 1954-74, ret. Trustee Teagle Found., World Health Found. Served as lt. comdr. M.C., USNR, 1943-46; PTO. Diplomate Am. Bd. Internal Medicine, Am. Bd. Preventive Medicine in Occupational Medicine. Fellow A.C.P., N.Y. Acad. Scis.; mem. AMA, Med. Soc. County of Nassau, Indsl. Med. Assn., Am., N.Y. heart assns., Soc. Alumni Bellevue Hosp. Episcopalian. Club: Lake Placid (pres. 1971-73) (N.Y.). Home: Garden City, N.Y. Died June 21, 1981.

SCHNEIDER, WILLIAM HENRY, trucking executive; b. Tiltonville, O., May 3, 1889; s. John and Wilmena (Kuckuck) S.; student pub. schs.; m. Hazel Stilwell, children—Hazel Hardesty, William Henry. Vice pres., dir. Tol. Trust Co., 1933-41; treas., comptroller Willys-Overland Motors, Inc., 1941-43; with Mack Trucks, Inc., N.Y.C., since 1943, asst. comptroller 1943-50, v.p.-comptroller from 1950, v.p. finance from 1953, also dir. Presbyterian. Home: New York, N.Y. †

SCHNITZER, GERMAINE ALICE, pianist; b. Paris, France, May 28, 1888; d. Henri and Ernestine (Kluck) S.; ed. Conservatoire National, Paris; 1st prize in harmony at same school, at age of 10, and 1st prize for piano, at 14; nat. prize offered by Emperor of Austria, at Meister Schule, Vienna, 1904; m. Dr. Leo Buerger, of New York, May 5, 1913; children—Gerald Henry, George, Yvonne Sarah Bernhardt. Served as soloist with Berlin Philharmonic Orchestra, Vienna Philharmonic, Paris Concerts du Conservatoire, Leipzig Gewandhaus Orchestra, Dresden Conzerte der Königl. Hofkapelle, London Philharmonic, Warsaw Philharmonic and with chief orchestras in Hamburg, Mönchen, Brussels; also of Holland, France and all large cities of Germany; in America, soloist with Boston Symphony Orchestra, New York Philharmonic, New York Symphony Orchestra, Chicago Thomas Orchestra, and leading orchestras of U.S. and Can. Decorated by Queen Elizabeth of Roumania (Carmen Sylva). Mem. New York Beethoven Assn.; hon. mem. Mu Phi Epsilon. Catholic. Address: New York, N.Y. †

SCHOECH, WILLIAM ALTON, management consultant and naval officer; born at Blakesburg, Ia., October 17, 1904; son of Joseph and Adeth (Hudgens) S.; B.S., U.S. Naval Acad., 1928; M.S., Cal. Inst. Tech., 1938; graduate Nat. War College, 1951; Sc.D. (hon.), Adelphi U., 1963; m. Barbara Bennie, Dec. 14, 1930; children—Barbara (Mrs. Blake Baumstark), William W., Joseph A. Commd. ensign USN, 1928, advanced through grades to vice adm., 1961; naval aviator, 1930-65; staff comdr. Aircraft 7th Fleet, 1942-44; comdr. aircraft carriers U.S.S. Sable, 1945, U.S.S. Sicily, 1951, U.S.S. Ticonderoga, 1954; comdr. Asiatic wing Naval Air Transport Service, 1946-47; dir. plans div. Bur. Aero. Navy Dept., 1947-50; asst. chief staff operations Naval Air Force Pacific, 1952; dir. current air plans div. Office Chief Naval Operations, 1953-54; asst. chief for research and development Bur. Aero., 1955-57, dep. chief Bur., 1957-58; comdr. Carrier Div. 3, 1958-59; dep. chief Bur. Naval Weapons, 1959-61; comdr. 7th Fleet, 1961-62; dep. chief naval operations for air, 1962-63; chief naval material, 1963-65, retired, 1965; mgmt. cons., 1965—. Decorated Legion of Merit, D.S.M. and gold star; Service medals (China and Korea). Club: Army-Navy Country (Arlington, Va.). Home: Escondido, Calif. Died Jan. 26, 1982.

SCHOEN, MAX, educator; b. Austria, Feb. 11, 1888; s. Elias and Rose (Rosenberg) S.; A.B.; Coll. of City of N.Y., 1911; Ph.D., U. of Ia., 1921; m. Rose Jacobs, Jan. 1, 1912; 1 dau., Lillian Ruth. Came to America, 1900, naturalized, 1918. Instr. high sch., Chattanooga, Tenn., 1912-14, East Tenn. State Normal Sch., 1914-20, U. of Ia., 1920-21; with Carnegie Inst. Tech. from 1921, prof. and head dept. of edn. and psychology, 1925, emeritus, Editor: The Effects of Music, 1927; The Enjoyment of the Arts, 1944; Author: The Beautiful in Music, 1928; Human Nature, 1930; Art and Beauty, 1932; The Psychology of Music, 1940; The Understanding of Music, 1945; Human Nature in the Making, 1945; co-author, Understanding the World, 1947; co-editor, Music and Medicine, 1948. Home Thetford, Vt. †

SCHOENBERGER, H(AROLD) W(ILLIAM), university prof.; b. Northampton, Pa., Feb. 3, 1889; s. George Franklin and Ida (Lerch) S.; A.B., Muhlenberg Coll., 1909; A.M., U. of Pa., 1915, Ph.D., 1924; m. Gladys Pickrell, Aug. 28, 1916. Instr. English, Pa. State Coll., 1913-18, asst. prof. English, 1921-22; Y.M.C.A. sec., Camp Gordon, 1918, N.Y. Office, 1919-20; asst. prof. English, U. of Pittsburgh, 1924-29, prof. English from 1929. Mem. Modern Lang. Assn. Author: American Adaptations of French Plays on the New York and Philadelphia Stages, 1790-1833. Editor: the Sentinel and Other Plays by Richard Penn Smith in America's Lost Plays Series (with R. H. Ware), 1941. Contbr. to Dictionary of Am. Biography. Home: Pittsburgh, Pa. †

SCHOENEMAN, GEORGE J., U.S. govt. official; b. Newport, R.I., Mar. 4, 1889; s. Charles and Catherine (Shea) S.; student pub. schs., Newport, R.I.; m. Lorena Rouse; children—Ruth (Mrs. Chas. W. Adams), Bettymae (Mrs. Robert M. Moore). Began in Post Office Dept., 1911; sec. to mem. Fed. Reserve Bd., 1919-20; in charge Collectors' Personnel, Internal Revenue Bur., 1920-24; asst. dep. commr., Accounts and Collections Unit, Internal Revenue Bur., 1924-29; dep. commr., 1929-44; asst. commr. Internal Revenue, 1944-45; administrative asst. to President Truman, May 1945-Sept. 1945; special executive asst. to President Truman, Sept. 1945-June 1947; commr. of Internal Revenue from July 1, 1947. Home: Chevy Chase, Md. †

SCHONLAND, HERBERT EMERY, naval officer (ret.); b. Portland, Me., Sept. 7, 1900; s. Richard Robert and Helene (Geisler) S.; student Severna Preparatory School, Severna Park, Md.; B.S., U.S. Naval Acad., 1925; student Mass. Inst. Tech., 1925, U.S. Naval Torpedo Sch., 1929; m. Claire Mills, Nov. 29, 1932; children—Dianne Morgan, Rodney Carl. Commd. ensign U.S. Navy, 1925, and advanced through grades to rear adm., 1947; served in U.S.S. Utah, 1925, U.S.S. Lawrence, 1926-29, U.S.S. Camden, 1930, U.S.S. Bushnell, 1931; shore duty at Naval Torpedo Sta., Newport, R.I., 1931-33; in U.S.S. Milwaukee, 1934, U.S.S. Argonne, 1935-37; at Naval Training Sta., Newport, 1937-39; in U.S.S. San Francisco, 1939-42, exec. officer, 1943; at Damage Control Sch., San Francisco, 1944; chief staff officer, U.S. Naval Training and Distbn. Center, Treasure Island, Calif., 1945-46; ret. from active service, Jan. 1, 1947; asst. prof. mathematics, Univ. of Santa Clara from 1947. Awarded Congl. Medal of Honor, Presidential unit citation, Asiatic-Pacific ribbon with 9 stars, Am. Defense medal with fleet clasp, Am. Theatre ribbon. Mem. Congl. Medal of Honor Soc., Army Navy Legion of Valor. Roman Catholic. Club: San Francisco Press (hon. mem.). Home: New London, Conn. Died Nov. 13, 1984.

SCHOONMAKER, GEORGE NELSON, engring. exec.; b. Toledo, O., Sept. 9, 1888; s. Wm. Henry Schoonmaker and Mary Ellen (Shaughnessy) S.; stu. Toledo Univ., 1914-18, Univ. of Wis., 1922-23; m. Anna Marie Schoonmaker, June 27, 1914; children—George Nelson, James William, Marilyn June (Mrs. Nolan A. Ryan), Lois Carol. In engring. dept. City of Toledo, 1906-14; engr. water dept., 1914-26, commr. of water, 1920-22, mem. Water Supply Commn., 1925-26; sanitary engr., H. P. Jones & Co., 1926-30, 1932-34; commr. of engring., 1930-32; dir. pub. service, 1934-37; chief engr., div. of water, 1937-39; city mgr. of Toledo, O., 1939-49; sr. mem. Jones & Henry sanitary engring., Toledo. Mem. adv. com. Ohio Water Supply Bd. Mem. Am. Soc. Civil Engrs., Am. Waterworks Assn., Am. Pub. Works Assn. Mason, Elk. Rotarian. †

SCHOW, ROBERT ALWIN, army officer; b. Hoboken, N.J., Oct. 19, 1898; s. William Robert and Marie M. (Briggs) S.; B.S., U.S. Mil. Acad., 1918; m. Tiny Wait, Nov. 9, 1929; children—Bobbie Ann (Mrs. Jack Mangham), Robert Alwyn. Commd. 2d lt., U.S. Army, 1918, advanced through grades to maj. gen., 1954; mem. Am. Battle Monuments Commn., Paris, France, 1928-34; asst. mil. attache and mil. attache to France, 1939-44; asst. chief of staff G-2 15th U.S. Army, 1945-46; asst. dir. Central Intelligence Agy., Washington, 1949-51; asst. chief of staff intelligence SHAPE, Paris, France, 51-54; dep. asst. chief of staff G-2, Dept. of Army Washington, 1954-56; assistant chief staff, Intelligence, Dept. of the Army, 1956-58; with RCA. Decorated Legion of Merit, Army Commendation Ribbon with metal pendant and oak leaf cluster, American Defense Service Medal; Distinguished Service medal; also the Army of Occupation Medal with clasp (Germany) Legion of Honor, Croix de Guerre with palm, Medal of Resistance (France); War Cross (Czechoslovakia) Order of Leopold, Croix de Guerre with Palm (Belgium); Comdr. Mil. Order of Ayacucho (Peru); Knight Grand Cross of Most Nobil Order of Crown of Thailand; Medal Mil. Merit 1st Class (Portugal); Grand Cross Order Mil. Merit with white badge (Spain). Mem. Assn. Grads. U.S. Mil. Acad. Clubs: Army and Navy (Washington); Army, Navy and Marine Corps Country (Arlington, Va.). Home: Falmouth, Va.

SCHRAMM, JAMES SIEGMUND, business exec; b. Burlington, Iowa, Feb. 4, 1904; s. Frank Edgar and Carrie Ash (Higgason) S.; student Amherst Coll., 1923-24, L.H.D., 1961; LL.D., Coe Coll., 1954; D.F.A., Grinell Coll., 1972; m. Dorothy Daniell, Sept. 26, 1931; children—Sieglinde Schramm Martin, Kristina Schramm Doughty. Joined J. S. Schramm Co., Burlington, 1924, exec. v.p., 1946-62; dir. Burlington Bank & Trust Co. Republican fin. chmn. Iowa, 1950-51, state chmn., mem. Rep. Nat. Com. Iowa, 1952-54; trustee Parsons Coll., Fairfield, Iowa, 1953-58; exec. v.p. Com. for Nat. Trade Policy, 1952-53; mem. U.S. Trade Mission to Japan, 1959, France, 1960; mem. bd. com. Internat. Trade Orgn., 1950-51; pres. Am. Fedn. Arts, 1956-58, trustee, exec. com.; past pres., trustee, chmn. acquisition and exhbn. com. Des Moines Art Center; chmn. Amherst Coll. adv. com. on contemporary art; mem. adv. council Iowa Econ. Studies Council; bd. mem. Iowa Mental Health Soc., 1950-52; chmn. Iowa Arts Council, 1966-68; mem. adv. com. John F. Kennedy Center Co. Performing Arts; trustee Chgo. Mus. Contemporary Art, 1967-70; hon. chmn. Amherst Coll. Friends Art; assisted in re-orgn. U.S. Office Civilian Def., 1942; mem. SBA adv. council, 1954-56. Served as lt. col., AUS, 1942-45; assisted in establishing controlled materials plan Army Service Forces. Recipient Legion of Merit; Distinguished Service award U. Iowa, 1971. Benjamin Franklin fellow Royall Soc. Arts; mem. Nat. Retail Mchts. Assn., Nat. Planning Assn. (nat. council, bus. com. 1955), Alpha Delta Phi. Presbyterian (elder). Clubs: Collectors Am., Des Moines; Century Assn. (N.Y.C.). Home: Burlington, Iowa. Died Aug. 23, 1980.

SCHREIBER, GEORGE ARTHUR, utility co. exec.; b. Ellwood City, Pa., June 1, 1919; s. George Leroy and Christene (McGinley) S; student U. N.Mex., 1936-38; A.B. in Econs., U. Notre Dame, 1941; m. Mary Taylor Cook, Apr. 16, 1944; children—Peter F., George Arthur, Mary T. With Pub. Service Co. of N.Mex., 1949—, pres., 1966-75, chmn. bd., 1975-82; dir. Pub. Service Co. N.Mex. Served as lt. comdr. USNR, 1942-46. Mem. Albuquerque C. of C. (dir. 1954-60), Sigma Chi. Club: Albuquerque Country. Home: Albuquerque, N.Mex. Died Nov. 1982.

SCHROEDER, JOSEPH JEROME, banking edn.; b. Chicago, Ill., May 10, 1889; s. Carl Stephen and Frances Catherine (Cornelisen) S.; grad. Am. Inst. of Banking, 1915; m. Frances Walker Noyes, Feb. 10, 1923; 1 son, Joseph Jerome. Clerk Nat. Bank of the Republic, Chicago, 1906-17; exec. sec. Chicago chapter, Am. Inst. of Banking 1920-57; editor The Bank Man 1921-57. Served as sergeant U.S. Army 149th F.A., Rainbow Div., 1917-19; capt. F.A. Reserve, 1920-40. Sec. Banking Research Fund. Sec. Chicago and Cook County Bankers Assn. 1920-21; sec. Assn. Reserve City Bankers from 1925; Republican. Club: Westmoreland Country (Wilmette, Illinois). Author: Elements of Banking, 1928; Bank Administration, 1938. Home: Wilmette, Ill. †

SCHROEPFER, GEORGE JOHN, educator, civil engr.; b. St. Paul, Sept. 7, 1906; s. Joseph J. and Katherine (Dippel) S.; B.S. in Civil Engring., U. Minn., 1928, M.S., 1930, C.E., 1932; m. Catherine R. Callahan, Sept. 5, 1931; children—George John, Mary Catherine. From asst. engr. to chief engr. Mpls.-St. Paul San. Dist., 1928-45; mem. faculty U. Minn., from 1945, prof. san. engring., 1945-72; cons. in field, from 1940. Recipient awards in field for research and distinguished service. Mem. Water Pollution Control Fedn. (pres. 1943, hon., Gordon M. Fair award 1976, William J. Orchard medal 1977), Am. Water Works Assn. (life mem., past chmn. N. Central sect.), ASCE (hon. life), Am. Acad. Environmental Engrs., Assn. Environmental Engring. Profs., Nat. Acad. Engring., Internat. Assn. San. Engrs. (hon.), Sigma Xi, Tau Beta Pi, Chi Epsilon. Contbr. articles to profl. jours. Home: Minneapolis, Minn. Died Mar. 11, 1984.†

SCHROY, LEE D., ex-mayor; b. Greenford, O., Sept. 10, 1887; s. William Henry and Millie P. (Stahl) S.; student grade and high schs., Salem, O.; m. Agnes Bess Williams, July 4, 1911; children—Richard William, Robert Lee, Betty Mae (Mrs. Thomas Morrison). Began as shoe clk., Akron, O., 1909; was in furniture and equipment business; organized own firm of L.D. Schroy Co., Akron, 1916, now pres. reorganized and inc. as Commercial Office Furniture Co., 1924, as Commercial Office Supply Co., 1928. Elected mayor of Akron, 1935, reelected, 1937, 39. Republican. Methodist. Lodges: Masons (32 deg. Shriner, Grotto), Eagle, Moose, Elk. Clubs: German-American, Liedertafel, Akron City, Akron Auto, Craftsman Recreation (Arkon). Home: Akron, Ohio. †

SCHUIRMANN, ROSCOE ERNEST, naval officer; b. Dec. 17, 1890; entered U.S. Navy, 1908, and advanced through the grades to rear adm., 1942. Address: Washington, D.C. †

SCHULTE, EDWARD J., architect; b. Cincinnati, O., Apr. 27, 1890; s. John and Mary Louise (Otto) S.; prep. edn., high sch., Norwood, O.; student Cincinnati Art Acad.; m. Louise E. Franke, Oct. 10, 1912; 1 dau., Dorothy Louise. Began as draftsman with Werner & Adkins, Cincinnati, 1908; in practice as architect from 1912; mem. Crowe and Schulte, 1921-34; practicing independently from Oct. 1934. Works include cathedrals and other church buildings in various parts of the U.S. Awarded Sach's prize, Cincinnati Fine Arts Institute "for outstanding achievement in architecture," 1930. Mem. Inst. Architects, Cincinnati Literary Club, Cincinnati Art Club, MacDowell Soc., Medievalists. Home: Cincinnati, Ohio. †

SCHULTE, PAUL CLARENCE, archbishop; b. Fredericktown, Mo., Mar. 18, 1890; s. Frederick and Anna (Priggel) S.; A.M., St. Francis Solanus Coll., Quincy, Ill., 1912; student Kenrick Theol. Sem., St. Louis, Mo., 1912-15. Ordained priest R.C. Ch., 1915; asst. pastor The Old Cathedral, St. Louis, 1915-22, adminstr., 1922-29, pastor, 1929-37; became bishop Diocese of Leavenworth in Kan., 1937; archbishop of Indianapolis from 1946. Wrote The Catholic Heritage of St. Louis, 1934. Home: Indianapolis, Ind. Died Feb. 17, 1984.

SCHULTZ, EDWIN WILLIAM, pathologist; b. Lomira, Wis., Dec. 12, 1887; s. Herman Carl and Clara Cornelia (Brown) S.; B.S.A., Winona (Ind.) Coll. of Agr., 1913; A.B., U. of Mich., 1914; M.D., Johns Hopkins, 1917; spl. student Sch. of Hygiene and Pub. Health, Johns Hopkins, 1919; fellow in pathology, Mayo Foundation, 1922; Guggenheim memorial fellow for research abroad, 1925-26; m. Anna Francel Roberts, June 17, 1914; children—Edwin Willam, Robert Brown. Junior field dir. Internat. Health Bd., 1917; with Dept. Bacteriology and Exptl. Pathology, Stanford U. from 1919, prof. and exec. head of dept., 1926-53, emeritus, also prof. bacteriology and pathology, Coll. Phys. and Surg., School of Dentistry, San Francisco, 1930-46; dir. Palo Alto (Calif.) Hosp. and Public Health Laboratory, 1921-37; consultant in bacteriology to Calif. State Bd. of Health, 1939-50; consultant to Sec. of War on epidemic diseases, 1941-46. Mem. bd. trustees, Am. Bd. Pathology, 1946-52; asso. examiner bacteriology Nat. Bd. Med. Examiners, 1952-53. Spl. Research Fellow, Nat. Insts. of Health, Bethesda, Md., 1950-51, spl. cons. from 1952. Served as 1st lieutenant, later captain Med. Corps, A.U.S., major A.R.C., 1917-19; chief mobile lab., 33d Div. pathologist Base Hosp. No. 42, A.E.F., 1917-18; chief of lab., Am. Red Cross Mil. Hosp. No. 9, Paris; bacteriologist. Commn. to Germany and chief Bur. of Med. Research, Am. Red Cross. Commn. to Poland, 1918-19; maj. Med. corps, A.U.S., 1924-39. U.S. del. 2d Internat. Cong. for Microbiology, London, 1936. Fellow A.A.A.S., Am. Pub. Health Assn., Coll. Am. Pathologists, Am. Soc. Clin. Pathol.; mem. Soc. Am. Bacteriologists, Am. Assn. Pathologists and Bacteriologists, Am. Assn. Immunologists, Soc. Exptl. Biol. and Medicine, American Society Exptl. Pathology, Electron Microscope Society of America, Calif. Acad. Medicine, Calif. Acad. Scis., Am. Assn. U. Profs., Washington Soc. Pathologists, Sigma Xi, Alpha Omega Alpha, Phi Beta Pi. Club: Commonwealth of Cal. Mem. advisory editorial board American Journal Clin. Pathology, 1947-53. Contributor on pathology, bacteriology and filtrable viruses. Home: Stanford, Calif. †

SCHULZE, J(OHN) WILLIAM, manufacturing executive; b. Newark, Sept. 21, 1890; s. C.F. William and Marie (Hermann) S.; B.C.S., N.Y.U., 1910; Dr. Bus. Adminstrn., Portland U., 1959; m. Mary Belle Whitmore, May 20, 1945. Pres., gen. mgr. Alfred Vester Sons, Providence, 1920-33; sec. Nat. Assn. Textile Products, N.Y., 1933-34; with Mengel Co., Louisville, 1935-36; dir. planning, dir. banking N.Y. World's Fair, 1936-40; exec. asst. to pres. Mergenthaler Linotype Co., Bklyn., 1940-42; v.p., comptroller New Eng. Shipbldg. Co., South Portland Me., 1943-45; also plant comptroller Todd Shipyards Corp., San Pedro, Cal., 1944-45; v.p. Bath Iron Works Corp., 1945-55, v.p., treas. 1947-55, chmn. exec. com., from 1955; v.p., dir. Todd Atlantic Shipyards Corp., 1948-58; v.p., treas. Pa. Crusher Co., Phila., 1947-54, pres., from 1956; pres., treas. Dixie-Machinery Mfg. Co., St. Louis, 1950-55; dir. Development Credit Corp. of Me., Sheepscot River Atlantic Salmon Assn. Dir. YMCA. Trustee Portland University, England Higher Education Foundation. Mem. Asso. Industries Maine (president, 1955-56). National Office Mgmt. Association (honorary life). National Association Accountants; Navy League U.S., Soc. Advancement Management. Soc. Naval Architects and Marine Engrs., Pine-Tree Soc. Crippled Children and Adults. Delta Sigma Pi. Mason. Clubs: Propeller of U.S., Cumberland (Portland, Me.); Bath (Me.) Country (dir. chmn. exec. bd.). Author: American Office, 1914; Office Administration, 1916. Home: Wiscasset, Mass. †

SCHUTT, WALTER TURVIN, orgn. exec.; b. Milwaukee, Oct. 18, 1887; s. Hermann G. and Isabelle (Smith) S.; student pub. schs., of Milwaukee; m. Gertrude H. Lutz, Sept. 8, 1914; children—John Casper, Richard Turvin. With No. Ind. Gas & Electric Co., 1908-10; spl. sales Milwaukee Electric Light & Traction Co., 1910-11; sales mgr. and asst. to gen. mgr. Central Ind. Gas Co., 1911-13; dir. sales Columbus Gas & Fuel, 1913-15; dir. sales promotion and asst. to gen. mgr. St. Clair Co. Gas & Electric, 1915-17; gen. ins., gen. auditing co., promotion and orgn. builders supply co., Miami, Fla., 1918-45; dist. mgr. Equitable Life Assurance Soc., also gen. agt. Penn Mut. Life Ins. Co., 1941-45, ret. 1945; former v.p., dir. Meteor Transport and Trading Co. Mem. Pan Am. League from 1947, exec. v.p., 1947, pres. internat. orgn. from 1947. Civilian advisor Miami Navy Procurement Office, also organizer and chmn. V-D Com. working with mil. force, Southeastern Fla., World War II. Awarded 3 certificates of recognition for civilian work (U.S.N.); Citation for orgn. and direction fund drive for Ambato earthquake victims (Quito Ecuador). Mem. Navy League U.S. (past pres.), Fla. Navy League (past sec. treas.), Fla. State Underwriters Assn., Miami Life Underwriters Assn. (organizer; past dir.), Elk. Clubs: Missouri Athletic (St. Louis); Delaware Country, LaGorce Country, Kiwanis (past dir.), Town (Miami). Home: Miami, Fla. †

SCHWARTZ, ABRAHAM, educator; b. N.Y.C., June 13, 1916; s. Nathan and Lena (Swoff) S.; B.S.S., Coll. City N.Y., 1936; M.S., Mass. Inst. Tech., 1937, Ph.D., 1939; m. Sylvia Paymer, June 16, 1940; children—Ina Barbara (Mrs. Lewis Heafitz), Susan Doris (Mrs. Lewis Steinberg), Margery Helen (Mrs. Gerald Goldman). Research asst. Inst. Advanced Study, Princeton, 1939-41; instr., then asst. prof. Pa. State U., 1941-48; mem. faculty Coll. City N.Y., 1948-84, prof. math., 1966-84, chmn. dept., 1964-66, dean Sch. Gen. Studies, 1966-70, provost, 1970-71. Bd. mgrs. N.J. YMCA, 1959-84, pres., 1972-84. Mem. Math. Assn. Am. (bd. govs. 1966-69), Am. Math. Soc., Phi Beta Kappa, Sigma Xi. Author: Analytic Geometry and Calculus, 3d edit., 1974. Home: Englewood, N.J. Died Feb. 4, 1984.

SCHWARTZ, ARTHUR, composer; b. Brooklyn, N.Y., Nov. 25, 1900; s. Solomon S. and Dora (Grossman) S.; B.A., New York U., 1920, J.D., 1924; M.A., Columbia U., 1921; m. Katherine Carrington, July 7, 1934 (dec.); one son, Jonathan; married 2d, Mary O'Hagon Scott, 1954. Teacher of English lit., N.Y. high schs., 1921-24; admitted to N.Y. bar, 1924, and in practice in N.Y. City, 1924-28; writing music professionally since 1928. Mem. Am. Soc. of Composers, Authors and Pubs., Nat. Assn. Am. Composers and Conductors. Authors League of America (treas.), Dramatists Guild (mem. council), Phi Beta Kappa, Pi Lambda Phi. Composer music for stage shows since 1929; latest: Inside U.S.A., 1948; A Tree Grows in Brooklyn, 1951; By the Beautiful Sea, 1954; also for motion pictures, 1936-84; latest: Dangerous When Wet, 1952; Band Wagon, 1953; You're Never Too Young, 1954; wrote score for radio mus. comedy in serial form, The Gibson Family, 1934-35. Produced motion pictures: Cover Girl, 1944; Night and Day, 1945; produced N.Y. stage musical, Inside U.S.A., 1948; produced play, Hilda Crane, 1950, Jennie, 1963; produced spl. CBS-TV shows, 1955-57; composer mus. The Gay Life, 1961. Address: New York, N.Y. Died Sept. 4, 1984.

SCHWARZ, GERHART STEVEN, radiologist, educator; b. Vienna, Austria, June 19, 1912; came to U.S., 1939, naturalized, 1944; s. Gottwald and Charlotte (Hiller) S.; m. Gertrude Aschner, Aug. 22, 1942; children: Doris Audrey, Marion Janet, Richard Michael. Student, Vienna Inst. Tech., 1931-32, U. Vienna Med. Sch., 1932-38; M.D., U. Basle, Switzerland, 1939. Intern Michael Reese Hosp., Chgo., 1939-41; resident radiology U. Chgo. Clinics, 1942-44; instr. roentgenology U. Chgo., 1945-46; dir. radiology Clifton Springs (N.Y.) Sanitarium and Clinic, 1946-50; asst. attending radiology Columbia-Presbyn. Med. Center, N.Y.C., 1950-60; dir. radiology Squier Urol. Clinic, 1960-64; chief radiol. service Bird S. Coler Hosp., N.Y.C., 1964-70; dir. radiology N.Y. Eye and Ear Infirmary, from 1971; vis. physician Met. Hosp., from 1964; attending Flower Hosp., from 1964; cons. Prospect Hosp., from 1964; asst. prof. Columbia Coll. Phys. and Surg., 1952-64; prof. radiology N.Y. Med. Coll., 1964-70, clin. prof., from 1971; vis. assoc. dept. history medicine Albert Einstein Coll. Medicine.; Vice chmn. subcom. U.S. Standards Inst., 1967-73, mem., from 1974. Author: Unit-Step Radiography, 1961, (with Golthamer) Radiographic Atlas of The Human Skull, 1965, (with Powsner) Alphabetical Index of Roentgendiagnoses and Procedures, 1966; Editor-in-chief: (with Powsner) Procs. Virchow-Pirquet Med. Soc. from 1976. Recipient Siemens prize elecromed. research Siemens-Reiniger-Veifa Werke,

1936; Col. Martin award for Teaching, 1974. Fellow N.Y. Acad. Medicine, Am. Coll. Radiology; mem. N.Y. Acad. Scis., N.Y. Acad. Medicine (past chmn. sect. history medicine), AMA, Am. Roentgen Ray Soc. (Merritt award 1968), Radiol. Soc. N.Am., Interam. Coll. Radiology, Pirquet Soc. Clin. Medicine (past pres.), Virchow-Pirquet Med. Soc. (pres. 1978—). Patentee in field. Home: New Rochelle, N.Y.

SCHWENNING, GUSTAV THEODOR, univ. prof.; b. Russia, Nov. 24, 1888; s. Rev. Karl and Rosa (Süss) S.; brought to U.S., 1892, naturalized 1912; grad. German-Am. Acad., Rochester, N.Y., 1913; B.H., Springfield Coll., 1920; A.M., Clark U., 1921, Ph.D., 1925; m. Carrie May Heath, July 22, 1915 (deceased); married 2d Emily Golding, Dec. 23, 1950. Assistant secretary Inst. Branch, Y.M.C.A., New York, 1913-16; bus. sec. Bronx Br., Y.M.C.A., N.Y., 1916-17; camp gen. sec., Army Y.M.C.A., Camps Stuart and Morrison, Va., 1917-18; prof. of economics and dir. industrial relations course, Springfield Coll., 1921-26; interim instr. in labor management, Northeastern U., Springfield, Mass., 1924-25; nat. industrial sec., Y.M.C.A. in China, 1925-26; asso. prof. business adminstrn., U. of N.C., 1926-32, prof. 1932-59; visiting lecturer at various universities, from 1959; organizer and director Student Branch of Taylor Soc., U. of N.C., 1928-32; time study engr. Western Electric Co., Kearney, N.J., summer 1930; prof. N.C. Coll. for Women, summer 1931; research in indsl. relations in Europe, summer and fall 1932; prof. of industrial management, Ohio State U., summer 1941; on leave to serve as principal specialist in management education for Engring., Science, and Management War Training, U.S. Office of Edn., 1941-45; head Bus. Adminstrn. Br., Shrivenham Am. U., Eng., 1945-46. Mem. Am. Econ. Assn., American Inst. Mgmt., So. Econ. Assn. (1st vice pres. 1947, pres. 1948), Soc. Advancement of Management, Am. Arbitration Assn., Acad. of Management, Kappa Delta Pi, Delta Sigma Pi, Beta Gamma Sigma. Co-author: The Science of Production Organization, 1938 (Portuguese trans.). Editor and co-author: Management Problems, 1930. Mng. editor of The Southern Economic Journal, 1936-42 and 1946-61. Contbr. to Am. Econ. Rev., Am. Federationist, Monthly Labor Rev., Social Forces, etc., also law reviews. Special research on dismissal legislation and compensation. Home: Chapel Hill, N.C. †

SCOBIE, JAMES RALSTON, educator; b. Valparaiso, Chile, June 16, 1929 (parents Am. citizens); s. Jordan Ralston and Freda Otela (Johnson) S.; A.B., Princeton U., 1950; M.A., Harvard U., 1951, Ph.D., 1954; m. Patricia Pearson Beauchamp, Nov. 1, 1957 (dec. 1965); children—William Ralston, Clare Beauchamp; m. 2d, Ingrid Ellen Winther, June 14, 1967; children—Kirsten Winther, Bruce Robert. Instr. history U. Calif. at Berkeley, 1957-59, asst. prof., 1959-62, 63-64; vis. scholar Columbia U., 1962-63; asso. prof. Ind. U., Bloomington, 1964-65, prof. history, 1965-77, dir. Latin Am. studies, 1965-68, chmn. dept. history, 1970-74; prof. history U. Calif. at San Diego, 1977-81. Mem. Inst. for Advanced Studies, 1974-75. U.S. nat. rep. History Commn., Pan Am. Inst. Geography and History, 1973-78; Latin Am. adv. com. Council Internat. Exchange of Scholars, 1976-79. Served to 1st lt. AUS, 1954-57. Doherty fellow, 1952-53, OAS fellow, 1959-60, Social Sci. Research Council fellow, 1959-60, 68-69, Rockefeller Found. vis. scholar Columbia, 1962-63; Guggenheim fellow, 1967-68; research grantee Nat. Endowment for Humanities, 1974-76. Mem. Am. Hist. Assn. (mem. Beveridge prize com. 1973-75), Latin Am. Studies Assn., Conf. Latin Am. History (chmn. 1977-78), Phi Beta Kappa. Author: Correspondencia Mitre-Elizalde, 1960; Argentina: A City and a Nation, 1964, 2d edit., 1971; La lucha por la consolidacion de la nacionalidad argentina, 1852-1862, 1964; Three Years in California: William Perkins' Journal of Life at Sonora, 1849-1852, 1964; Revolution on the Pampas: A Social History of Argentine Wheat, 1860-1910, 1964; Buenos Aires: Plaza to Suburb, 1870-1910, 1974. Contbg. and adv. editor Handbook of Latin American Studies, 1966-81; adv. editor Latin American Research Rev., 1967-69, 79-81; bd. editors Hispanic Am. Hist. Rev., 1966-72, 77-81. Address: La Jolla, Calif.

SCOGGIN, WILLIAM ALLEN, gynecologist; b. Norfolk, Va., Feb. 12, 1926; s. Arthur Owen and Jessie Bolling (Eggleston) S.; m. Celestine Townes Wellman, June 15, 1980; children—James, John, William, David. B.A., U. Va., 1949, M.D., 1953. Diplomate: Am. Bd. Ob-Gyn. Intern Ohio State U. Hosp., 1953-54; resident in Ob-Gyn U. Va. Hosp., 1956-59, fellow in biochemistry dept. cancer research, 1960-61, NIH postdoctoral fellow, 1962-63; instr. dept. Ob-Gyn U. Va., 1960-62, asst. prof., 1962-64; asso. prof. Western Res. U., 1964-66; asst. dir. dept. Ob-Gyn Cleve. Met. Gen. Hosp., 1964-65, acting dir., 1965-66; prof., chmn. dept. Ob-Gyn Med. Coll. Ga., Augusta, from 1966; cons. VA Hosp., Augusta, Med. Center Central Ga., Macon, Meml. Hosp., Savannah, Ga., Greenville (S.C.) Gen. Hosp., U.S. Army Specialized Treatment Center, Fort Gordon, Ga.; examiner Am. Bd. Ob-Gyn; counterpart dept. chmn. dept. Ob-Gyn U. Saigon, 1969-74. Contbr. articles to med. jours. Served with USNR, 1944-46; Served with U.S. Army, 1946-48. Recipient Found. prize S. Atlantic Assn. Obstetricians and Gynecologists, 1964. Mem. AAAS, Am. Assn. Obstetricians and Gynecologists, Am. Coll. Obstetricians and Gynecologists, AMA, Ga. State Ob-Gyn Soc., Med. Assn. Ga., Richmond County Med. Soc., Soc. Gynecologic Investigation, Soc. Obstet. Anesthesiologists and Perinatologists, S. Atlantic Assn. Obstetricians and Gynecologists, So. Med. Assn., So. Perinatal Assn., Royal Soc. Medicine, Southeastern Ob-Gyn Soc., Sigma Xi. Home: Augusta, Ga. Deceased.

SCOTFORD, JOHN RYLAND, clergyman, author; b. Chicago, Ill., Sept. 7, 1888; s. Louis Kossuth and Martha Williams (Proctor) S.; A.B., Dartmouth, 1911; Union Theological Seminary, 1910-12; D.D., Elon College, 1942; m. Mable Matteson, August 12, 1912; children—Ruth, John Ryland, David Matteson. Ordained Congregational ministry, 1912; successively pastor Kingfisher, Oklahoma, Junius Heights Church, Dallas, Texas, First Church, Waukegan, Ill., Glenville Ch., Cleveland, O., until 1927; traveled in S.A., 1928; speaking and writing principally about S.A., 1928-31; editorial sec. Congl. Mission Boards, 1931-42; editor Advance, 1943-50; ch. bldg. cons. from 1950. Pres. N.A. Conf. Ch. Architecture, 1947-52. Club: Quill. Author: Mating Ministers and Churches, 1930; Spanning a Continent, 1939; Together We Build America, 1943, The Church Beautiful, 1946; Church Union, Why Not?, 1948; Within These Borders, 1953; When You Build Your Church, 1955. Home: Mt. Vernon, N.Y. †

SCOTT, ANNIE VELLNA, physician; b. Guilford Co., N.C., June 28, 1889; d. Levi Calvin and Nancy Jane (Roach) Scott; B.S., N.C. Coll. for Women, 1914; M.D., Woman's Med. Coll. Pa., 1918. Intern Lying-in Hosp., N.Y. City, 1918, Bellevue Hosp. Children's Med., 1918-19; commd. fgn. missionary Presbyn. Ch. in U.S.A., 1920; pediatrician Woman's Med. Coll., North China, 1920-24; pediatrician in charge Cheeloo Med. Coll. and Hosp., Tsinan, Shantung, China, 1924-39, prof. pediatrics, chief pediatrics service, 1939-51; observer Harriet Lane Hosp., 1925-26, Babies Hosp., N.Y. City, 1932-33, asst. attending pediatrician Vanderbilt Clinic, 1942-46; instr. Coll. Phys. and Surg., Columbia, 1942-46, vis. prof. pediatrics, 1951-52. Recipient Elizabeth Blackwell Citation for distinguished achievement in fgn. med. missions, 1952. Diplomate Am. Bd. Pediatrics. Mem. American Academy of Pediatrics, Chinese Med. Assn., Chinese Pediatric Association. Presbyterian. Author: Care and Feeding of Infants and Children (Chinese) 1934.†

SCOTT, ARTHUR FERDINAND, chemist, educator; b. Coytesville, N.J., Aug. 14, 1898; s. George John and Carrie (Kerwien) S.; B.S., Colby Coll., 1919, D.Sc. (hon.), 1964; A.M., Harvard, 1921, Ph.D., 1924; student U. Munich, 1922-23; D.Sc. (hon.), Reed Coll., 1973; m. Vera Prásilova, Mar. 19, 1925; children—Kytja (Mrs. John Kemph), Nadia Scott Autrey, Dascha S. Nicholl. Asst. prof. chemistry Reed Coll., Portland, Oreg., 1923-26, prof. chemistry, 1937-82, past chmn. dept., past acting pres. coll.; instr. in analytical chemistry Rice Inst., Houston, 1926-37; past dir. Reed Reactor Project; past head spl. projects sci. edn. NSF, Washington, 1962-64. Past chmn. Oreg. Nuclear Devel. Coordinating Com.; past acting pres. Oreg. Grad. Center. Bd. dirs. Learning Resource Center. Served in O.T.C., Plattsburg, N.Y., summer 1918; assigned S.A.T.C., for duration World War I. Recipient award Mfg. Chemists Assn., 1957; Am. Chem. Soc. Petroleum Research Fund study grantee, 1958; Sci. Apparatus Mfrs. award Am. Chem. Soc., 1960; citation Oreg. Acad. Sci., 1962. Mem. Am. Chem. Soc. (ex-councillor), Phi Beta Kappa, Sigma Xi. Editor: Survey of Progress in Chemistry, Vol. 1, 1963, Vol. 2, 1964, Vol. 3, 1966, Vol. 4, 1968, Vol. 5, 1970, Vol. 6, 1973, Vol. 7, 1976, Vol. 8, 1977; contbr. papers to chem. jours. Home: Portland, Oreg. Died Jan. 8, 1982.

SCOTT, CHARLES E., coll. pres.; b. Elmo, Mo., Jan. 15, 1889; s. Edgar Charles and Arminta D. (Puntenney) S.; student, U. of Mo., 1910; B.A., State Teachers Coll., Greeley, Colo., 1921, M.A., 1922; student, George Peabody Coll. for Teachers, Nashville, Tenn., 1936; m. Hazel E. Morcom, Apr. 6, 1912; children—Marjorie (Mrs. O. Bjarne Eidem), Charles M., Virginia P. (Mrs. D. B. Benzie), Stanley R. Teacher of rural schools, of Missouri and Colorado, 1909-12; principal Severance, Colorado, 1913-16; superintendent Dist. No. 12, Pueblo, Colo., 1916-18, Timmath, Colo., 1918-21; instr. in edn., Psychology, State Normal Sch., Dickinson, N.D., 1922-27; dir. training State Teachers Coll., Minot, N.D., 1927-39; pres. State Teachers College, Dickinson, N.D., from 1939. Consultant E.&C.R. Branch, OMG, Germany, 1949. Pres. C. of C. 1945; deputy state chmn. Com. for Econ. Development. Congregationalist. Member North Dakota Higher Education Association (pres., 1935-38), N.D. Edn. Assn. (pres., 1939-40), Am. Assn. Sch. Adminstrs., Am. Assn. Teachers Colleges, Assn. of Commerce, Kappa Delta Pi, Phi Sigma Pi. Mason. Clubs: Rotary (past president of clubs at Dickinson and Minot). Author: Ednl. Supervision, 1924; Purposeful Teaching-Learning Activities, Teacher's Handbook, 1940. Contbr. to ednl. jours. †

SCOTT, CHARLES RAY, federal judge; b. Adel, Iowa, Jan. 13, 1904; s. Walter E. and Elma (Harrington) S.; m. Exie Smith, June 17, 1933 (dec. Nov. 1942); children—Barbara Exie Scott Majure, William, Charlene Scott Edwards; m. Grace Kathryn Stephens, Mar. 21, 1947. J.D., Valparaiso U., 1924. Bar: Ind. bar 1925, Fla. bar 1926. Asso. and partner Fleming, Hamilton, Diver & Jones, and Fleming, Jones, Scott & Botts, 1926-55; sr. mem. Fleming, Scott & Botts, 1955-57, Scott & Cox, 1957-60; circuit judge 4th Jud. Circuit, 1960-66; U.S. dist. judge Middle Dist. Fla., 1966-76, sr. judge, 1976-83; mem. Fla. Bd. Law Examiners, 1954-55; mem. bd. govs. Fla. bar, 1958-61. Fellow Am. Coll. Trial Lawyers; mem. SAR. Presbyterian (elder). Clubs: Masons, Shriners, Jesters, San Jose Country; Nat. Lawyers (Washington); River, Ponte Vedra. Home: Jacksonville, Fla. Died May 12, 1983.

SCOTT, FRANK, (FRANCIS REGINALD SCOTT) legal educator, poet; b. Quebec, Que, Can., Aug. 1, 1899; s. Frederick George and Amy S.; m. Marian Mildred Dale, 1928; 1 son. B.A., Bishop's Coll., 1919, Magdalen Coll., Oxford U., 1922; B.Litt, Magdalen Coll., Oxford U., 1934; B.C.L., McGill U., 1927. Bar: Que. 1927. Practices law, 1927; mem. faculty McGill Faculty Law, Montreal, Que., Can., 1928—, dean faculty, 1961-64; vis. prof. Toronto U., 1953, Mich. State U., 1957, French Can. Studies Program, McGill U., 1967-71, Dalhousie U., 1969-71; co-founder and past pres. League for Social Reconstrn.; mem. Royal Commn. on Bilingualism and Biculturalism, 1963-71; del. to Brit. Commonwealth Labour Parties Cons., London, 1944, Toronto, 1947; adviser to Govt. of Sask. at Constnl. Confs., 1950, 60; UN tech. assistance resident rep. to Burma, 1952; counsel civil liberties cases Supreme Ct. of Can., 1956-64. Co-editor: McGill Fortnightly Rev., 1925-27, Can. Mercury, 1928, Can. Forum, 1936-39, Preview, 1942-45, No. Rev., 1945-47; collections of poems include Overture, 1945,, The Eye of the Needle, 1957, (transl.) Poems of Garneau and Hebert, 1962, Signature, 1964, Selected Poems, 1966, Trouvailles, 1967, The Dance is One, 1973, (transl.) Poems French Canada, 1977 (Can. award for Poetry 1982), The Collected Poems, 1981 (Gov. Gen.'s award for poetry 1981); editor: (with A.J.M. Smith) New Provinces: poem of several authors, 1936, The Blasted Pine: An Anthology of Satire, Irreverent and Disrespectful Verse, 1957, The Blasted Pine: An Anthkology of Satire, Irreverent and Disrespectful Verse, rev. edit., 1967; co-author: Social Planning for Canada, 1935, Canda Today, Her National Interests and National Policy, 1938, Democracy Needs Socialism, 1938, Make This Your Canada, 1943, Canada after the War, 1943; author: Civil Liberties and Canadian Federalism, 1959, Quebec States Her Case, 1964, Essays on the Constitution: aspects of Canadian law and politics, 1977 (Gov.'s Gen.'s award for non-fiction 1978). Recipient numerous hon. degrees; recipient Guarantor's prize for Poetry Chgo., 1944, Lorne Pierce medal Royla Soc. Can., 1964, Molson award Can. Council, 1967; Guggenhiem fellow, 1940. Fellow Brit. Acad. (corr.); mem. Am. Acad. Arts and Sci. (hon.). Clubs: McGill Faculty, University, International; PEN (Montreal). Home: Montreal, Que., Canada. Died Jan. 30, 1985.

SCOTT, JAMES RALPH, M.D.; b. Walton, N.Y., Apr. 21, 1888; s. Thomas H. and Jane (Ormiston) S.; A.B., Yale Coll., 1916; M.D., Coll. of Physicians and Surgeons, New York, N.Y., 1918. Practiced, Kerhonkson, N.Y., 1919-23, N.Y. City since 1923; asst. attending physician, St. Luke's Hospital, 1926-30, asso. attending physician, 1930-42 attending physician, 1942-48, consulting physician, from 1948; secretary medical board, 1939-44; instructor clinical pathology College Phys. and Surg., 1923-25; chmn. com. on diabetes, N.Y. World's Fair, 1939. First lt., Med. Officers Res. Corps, U.S. Army, World War I; lt. col. attached to Evacuation Hosp. 2, 1940-42. Diplomate Am. Bd. Internal Medicine. Fellow Am. Coll. Physicians, N.Y. Acad. Med. (sec. 1940-42), Am. Diabetes Assn. (founder, trustee 1941-44); mem. A.M.A., N.Y. Diabetes Assn. (pres. 1936-42, dir.), Hosp. Grads. Club, Phi Beta Kappa, Sigma Xi. Republican. Club: Century Association (N.Y.C.). Author: Diabetes, 1936. Home: Patterson, N.Y. †

SCOTT, JEROME HAYES, banker; b. Kensington, Kans., Oct. 26, 1922; s. Jerome Hawthorne and Edith Weeks (Hayes) S.; m. Elizabeth Ess, Apr. 22, 1950; children—Deborah, Jerome, Elizabeth, Barbara, Robert. B.S. in Econs, U. Pa., 1943. Automotive dealer, Kansas City, Mo., 1947-67; pres. Jerry Scott, Inc., Kansas City, Mo., Scott Leasing Co., Kansas City, Mo., 1957-67; pres. United Mo. Bank of Kansas City, from 1971, now vice chmn.; sec., dir. United Mo. Bancshares, Inc., Kansas City, from 1969. Treas. bd. govs. Kansas City Art Inst.; past pres. Kansas City area council Boy Scouts of Am., 1971-72; dir. Kansas City Mayor's Corps of Progress.; Bd. dirs. Kansas City Mus. History and Sci., Heart of Am. United Way, Heart of Am. council Boy Scouts Am.; treas. bd. govs. Am. Royal Assn.; bd. govs. Friends of Art. Served with USNR. Mem. C. of C. of Greater Kansas City (treas., dir.). Clubs: River (Kansas City, Mo.), Kansas City Country (Kansas City, Mo.), Kansas City (Kansas City, Mo.), Saddle and Sirloin (Kansas City, Mo.). Address: Kansas City, MO. *

SCOTT, JOHN VIRGIL, banker; b. Mason, Ky., Dec. 22, 1888; s. Charles and Annie (Finegan) S.; ed. in pub., private, bus. schs.; m. Louise Thomson, April, 1914; 1 son, John Virgil (dec.). Dir. of The Second Nat. Bank of Houston; pres. Halo Co., Inc.; v.p. J. Weingarten & Co., Houston Royalty Co., Houston; dir. Gulf, Colo. & Santa Fe Ry. Co. Democrat. Presbyterian. Clubs: Houston, Texas, Bayou, Houston Country. Home: Houston, Tex. Deceased.

SCOTT, K. FRANCES, coll. professor; b. Vincennes, Ind., Apr. 16, 1890; d. Thomas Smith and Lucy Kate (Shaw) Scott; Ph.B., Coll. of Wooster, Wooster, O., 1912; M.D., Rush Med. Coll., Chicago, 1919; unmarried. Asst. physician Smith Coll., 1919-25, asso. prof. of hygiene from 1927; summer conf. physician and lecturer, Nat. Bd. Y.W.C.A., N.Y. City, 1918-28, 1933-36. Asso. dir. salvage div. Mass. Com. of Pub. Safety, Region II, 1942-45; mem. bd. dirs. Nat. Safety Council from 1949; mem. adv. com. women in services, Dept. Defense from 1951; mem. U.S. commission for UNESCO, 1949-52. Awarded certificate of appreciation for 1st Aid Work, Am. Nat. Red Cross, 1944; citation Mass. salvage com., 1942-45; war finance award, U.S. Treasury, 1945. Mem. Am. Assn. Univ. Profs., Phi Beta Kappa, Delta Delta Delta, Alpha Epsilon Iota. Republican. Club: Business and Professional Women's (pres. Hampshire County club, 1938-41; pres. Mass. Fedn., 1942-44; 1st v.p. Nat. Fedn., 1946, pres., 1948-50). Author: A College Course in Hygiene, 1939. Home: Northampton, Mass. †

SCOTT, N(ATHAN) STONE, surgeon; Oberlin College, 1885-87; M.D., Western Reserve U., 1889; hon. A.M., Oberlin, 1895; married; children—Flora Lucee, William Justus Merle, Olive Ray. Prof. principles of surgery, and dean, Cleveland Coll. Phys. and Surg.; consulting surgeon, Cleveland Gen., and St. John's Hosps. Mem. A.M.A., Ohio State Med. Soc., Cleveland Med. Soc., Am. Assn. Gynecologists and Obstetricians. Home: Cleveland, OH. †

SCOTT, THEODORE P., business exec.; born Phila., Jan. 18, 1887; s. Wallace and Susan (Root) S.; student Penn. Charter Sch., Phila., 1898-1906; Peirce Sch. of Bus. Adminstrn., Phila.; m. Ida Irish, Oct. 18, 1910. Bank clerk Fourth Street Nat. Bank, Phila., 1906-13; with the Lehigh Coal and Navigation Co., Phila., from 1913, vice pres., from 1942; dir. Tradesmens Nat. Bank & Trust Co., Allentown Terminal R.R. Co., Blue Ridge Real Estate Co., Monroe Water Supply Co., Nesquehoning Valley R. R. Co., Panther Valley Water Co., Split Rock Lodge, Inc., Summit Hill Water Co., Tresckow R.R. Co., Wilkes-Barre, and Scranton Ry. Co., Lehigh Service Company. President Lycoming House; trustee Hahnemann Medical Coll. and Hosp. of Phila. Clubs: Aronimink Golf, Midday. Home: Bala-Cynwyd, Pa. †

SCOTT, WALTER TANDY, educator; b. Haskell, Tex., Dec. 12, 1912; s. Samuel Walter and Fanny Elizabeth (Tandy) S.; B.A., Rice U., 1933, M.A., 1935, Ph.D., 1938; m. Nora Evelyn Broome, June 12, 1943; children—Noral (Mrs. Craig Welty Walker), Elizabeth (Mrs. William Joseph Beran), Sarah (Mrs. George Loren Goina). Carter fellow Rice U., 1936-38; instr. Northwestern U., 1938, 40-41, asst. prof., 1946-50, asso. prof., 1950-61; instr. Ill. Inst. Tech., 1939, U. Mich., 1939-40; prof. math. Ariz. State U., Tempe, 1961-78; with Ballistic Research Lab., Aberdeen, 1941; instr. Army U. Center, Biarritz, France, 1945; cons. Lawrence Radiation Lab., Livermore, Cal., 1958. Served to maj. AUS, 1941-46. Fellow A.A.A.S.; mem. Am. Math Soc., Math Assn. Am., Soc. for Indsl. and Applied Math., Ariz. Acad. Sci. Sigma Xi. Republican. Methodist. Contbr. articles to profl. jours. Home: Paradise Valley, Ariz. Died May 24, 1984.

SCOVILLE, HERBERT, JR., author, disarmament consultant; b. N.Y.C., Mar. 16, 1915; s. Herbert and Orlena (Zabriskie) S.; m. Ann Curtiss, June 26, 1937; children: Anthony Church, Thomas Welch, Nicholas Zabriskie, Mary Curtiss. B.S., Yale, 1937; Ph.D., U. Rochester, 1942; postgrad, U. Cambridge, Eng., 1937-39. Sr. scientist Los Alamos contract AEC, Washington, 1946-48; tech. dir. armed forces spl. weapons project Dept. Def., Washington, 1948-55; dep. dir. sci. and tech. CIA, Washington, 1955-63; asst. dir. sci. and tech. ACDA, Washington, 1963-69; dir. arms control program Carnegie Endowment for Internat. Peace, Washington, 1969-71; mem. adv. com. nuclear safeguards AEC, 1970-72, ACDA, 1969-73; pres. Arms Control Assn.; Chmn. U.S. del. NATO Disarmament Experts Meetings, 1966-68; mem. sci. adv. bd. Air Force, 1955-62; Pres.'s Sci. adv. com. cons., 1957-63. Author: (with R. Osborn) Missile Madness, 1970; contbr. (with R. Osborn) articles to profl. jours., mags. and newspapers; chpts. to books MX: Prescription for Disaster. Bd. dirs. Pub. Welfare Found., Washington, 1971, Council for a Livable World. Mem. AAAS (council), Union Concerned Scientists (dir.), Sigma Xi. Clubs: Century (N.Y.C.); Cosmos (Washington). Home: McLean, Va. Died July 30, 1985.

SCRIMENTI, ADOLPH ROBERT, architect; b. Bklyn., Jan. 21, 1913; s. Matthew and Maria (DiPolito) S.; m. Rachel R. Rush, Dec. 6, 1945; children—Janet R., Michael B. Diploma, Pratt Inst. Sch. Arch., 1934; postgrad., Beaux Arts Inst. Design-Atelier-Fletcher-Moore, 1934-37. Designer, asst. to architect H. Hurwit, N.Y.C., 1934-39; asso. architect Office Chief of Engrs., U.S. Dept. War, Washington, 1939-42; partner J.C. Van Nuys & Assos., 1945-57, Tectonic Assos., 1950-54; both Somerville, N.J.; sr. partner Scrimenti, Swackhamer & Perantoni, Somerville, 1957-73, Scrimenti, Shive, Spinelli and Perantoni, Somerville, from 1973; Mem. N.J. Comm. to Make Bldgs. Useable to Physically Handicapped, 1960-64; mem. N.J. Bd. Architects on Licensing, 1965-72, pres, 1969-71; mem. com. arch. Commn. to Study Arts in N.J., 1964-67; mem., chmn. Parking Authority, 1957-61, Improvement Commn., 1960-66; both Somerville; chmn. adv. council N.J. Sch. Architecture, N.J. Inst. Tech., 1975-81. Prin. works include Hillsborough (N.J.) Sch, 1951, Hanover Park (N.J.) Regional High Sch, 1957, Meditation Chapel, Trenton State Coll., 1962, Lab. Sch. and Child Study Clinic, Newark State Coll., 1966, Fine Arts-Theatre Arts bldg, 1971, Somerset County Coll, 1976. Served with C.E. AUS, 1942-45, ETO. Decorated Bronze Star; recipient Architect of the Year Bronze plaque

State of N.J., 1970, Citizen of the Year Bronze plaque N.J. Jewish Community Centers, 1968, Architect of Year Bronze Plaque award N.J. Subcontractors Assn., 1974, also various archtl. awards. Fellow A.I.A. (treas. N.J. chpt. 1957-58, v.p. 1959-60, pres. 1961-62, nat. and regional dir. 1974-78); mem. Nat. Inst. Archtl. Edn. (trustee 1972-78), Am. Assn. Sch. Adminstrs., N.J. Soc. Architects, Central N.J. Soc. Architects (pres. 1957-58), Water Pollution Fedn. Club: Pratt Architectural (Bklyn.). Home: Somerville, N.J.

SCURFIELD, RALPH THOMAS, builder, developer, energy company executive; b. Broadview, Sask., Can., Jan. 7, 1928; s. Ralph and Anne Marie (Parsons) S.; m. Sonia Onishenko, July 24, 1954; children: Ralph D., Susan J., Katheryn L., Serge M., Allan P., John W. B.Sc., U. Man., 1948; grad., Advaced Mgmt. Program, Harvard U., 1976. Tchr. Winnipeg, Man., Can.; with Nu-West Group Ltd. (builders and developers, and predecessors), Calgary, Alta., pres., 1957-85; dir. Carma Ltd., MICC Investments and Mortgage Ins. Co. Can., Alta. Gas Chems. Ltd.; mem. faculty mgmt. adv. bd. U. Calgary; bd. govs. Banff Centre Continuing Edn. Mem. Housing and Urban Devel. Assn. Can. (past pres.). Mem. United Ch. Can. Clubs: Ranchmen's, Calgary Winter, Calgary Petroleum, Silver Springs Golf and Country. Home: Calgary, Alta., Can. Died Jan. 18, 1985. *

SEAL, LEO W., banker; born Bay Saint Louis, Miss., Oct. 25, 1888; s. William Riley and Virginia (Favre) S.; B.S. in Civil Engring., Miss. State Univ. (formerly Miss. A. and M.), 1911; m. Rebecca Baxter, July 13, 1918; children—Leo W., Virginia Elizabeth. Engaged in civil engring. and banking from 1919; dir. Southern Company, Mississippi Power Co., Gulfport, from 1931. Mem. Am. Legion, Vets. Fgn. Wars, C. of C.; past pres. Miss. Bankers Assn., Ind. Banks Assn., Newcomen Soc. Ind. Democrat. Mason, Rotarian. Club: Boston (Boston); Capitol City (Jackson, Mississippi). Home: Bay Saint Louis. †

SEARCH, FREDERICK PRESTON, composer; b. Pueblo, Colo., July 22, 1889; s. Preston Willis and Margaret (Fitzgerald) S.; ed. schs. in U.S., Switzerland and Germany, also New England Conservatory and Cincinnati Coll. of Music; grad. Royal Conservatory, Leipzig, also post-grad. course there; studied cello with Braschawanoff (Weimar), Adamowski (Boston), Mattioll (Milan), Rogovoy (Cincinnati), Klengel (Leipzig); harmony and composition with Gustav Schreck, orchestration with Richard Hofman; m. Opal Piontkowski Heron, Feb. 27, 1923. Has appeared in recitals in leading cities of U.S. and Europe; mem. Gewandhans Orchestra, Leipzig, 1910-11; first cellist, Am. Symphony Orchestra, Chicago, 1915-16; mus. dir. Forest Theatre Summer Festivals and Western Drama Original Plays, Carmel-by-the-Sea, Calif., 1914, 15, 16, 18, 19. Enlisted 1st musician U.S.N.R.F.; called to service Feb. 15, 1918; apptd. condr. Mare Island orchestra; trans. to regular navy, Sept. 25, bandmaster Mare Island Naval Training Sta. Band of 74 musicians; discharged Mar. 1919. Solo cellist, Philharmonic Chamber Music Soc., Honolulu, H.T., 1919-20. Composer of Festival Overture, played at San Francisco Expn., 1915; Sixth String Quartet in D Minor (first performance in August 1932, at Carmel-by-the-Sea) and Cello Concerto in A Minor (first performance in August 1933, at Carmel-by-the-Sea); Romantic Symphony in D Major, Second Symphony in G Minor, Third Symphony, Fourth Symphony in B Flat Minor, Fifth Symphony in G Minor (first place in California Federation of Music Clubs, 1941), String Quartet in E Minor (first performance by the San Francisco String Quartet, Jan. 1942), Symphonic Poem and Suite Fantastique, Exhilaration Overture (first performance by Federal Symphony Orchestra of San Francisco under Ernst Bacon, 1936), The Dream of McKorkle, for symphony orchestra, quartets, and sextets; Teresita, Sweet Dreams, Amara, Valse D'Amour, for alto saxophone, with orchestra accompaniment; Aria, Minuet, Berceuse, Tangiers, Under the Cypress Trees, Rhapsodie Fantastique, Romanze, Oriental Dance, solos for cello or violin, songs; sextet in F Minor for 2 violins, 2 violas and 2 cellos, winning number in 1934 competition of Society for Publication of American Music, etc. Dir. orchestra, Hotel Del Monte, Del Monte, Calif., 1920-32; supervisor of orchestra, band and chorus, Monterey County High Sch., 1927-29; concert tour of U.S., 1932 and 1934. Composed The Bridge Builders for soloists, chorus and symphony orchestra in celebration of completion of Golden Gate Bridge, first performance, the composer conducting, San Francisco, 1938; Romantic Overture in G Minor for symphonic band. Awarded hon. mention, contest conducted by National Composers Congress, Colorado Springs, 1945. President Musical Arts Club of Monterey, 1933; mem. San Francisco Sinfonietta Orchestra; bandmaster Federal Symphonic Band of San Francisco, 1936-40; supervisor Works Progress Adminstrn. Project for Composers and Arrangers, 1936-40; conductor of San Francisco-International Band, 1939. Mem. Am. Composers Alliance, Nat. Assn. for Am. Composers and Conductors, Soc. for Publication of Am. Music. Home: Monterey, Calif. †

SEARER, R. FLOYD, lawyer; b. Kokomo, Ind., Feb. 26, 1905; s. Clarence A. and Alice (Herr) S.; m. Marguerite Westphal, Sept. 5, 1932; children—Russell F. (dec.), Susan M. A.B., U. Notre Dame, 1928, J.D., 1930. Bar: Ind. bar 1930. Mem. legal dept. Assocs. Investment Co.,

South Bend, Ind., 1931-32; v.p., trust officer First Bank & Trust Co., South Bend, 1932-47; partner firm May, Searer, Oberfell & Helling, South Bend, 1948-82. Past pres. St. Joseph County Bd. Aviation Commrs., local Community Fund, March of Dimes, Crippled Children's Soc. Mem. ABA, Ind. Bar Assn., St. Joseph County Bar Assn. (past pres.). Club: Mason (33 deg.). Home: South Bend, Ind. Died Oct. 22, 1982.

SEARS, ARTHUR, JR., electric co. exec.; b. Pitts., July 1, 1928; s. James Arthur and Matilda (Hardy) S.; m. Bettie Jean Virgis, Sept. 21, 1957 (div. Oct. 1977); children— Norma Jean, Arthur III, Galana, Jory, Ryan. Student, U. Wis., 1951; B.A., U. Pitts., 1954. Reporter Norfolk (Va.) Jour. and Guide, 1954-57; reporter Cleve. Call and Post, 1957-58, Cin. dist. mgr.-editor, 1958-59; asso. editor Jet mag., 1959-64; N.Y. editor Jet mag., asso. editor Ebony mag., 1964-66; asso. dir. pub. relations dept. Nat. Urban League, N.Y.C., 1966-67; staff reporter Wall St. Jour. (N.Y. Bur.), 1967-69; cons. bus. environment studies dept. Gen. Electric Co., N.Y.C., 1969-72, cons. corporate ednl. communications, Fairfield, Conn., 1972-76; mgr. pub. affairs Internat. Trading Support Operation, N.Y.C., from 1976; summer lectr. journalism Plainfield (N.J.) High Sch., 1970, Middlesex (N.J.) Coll., 1971, Rutgers U., 1972. Contbr.: chpt. to Malcolm X: A Man and His Times, 1968. Mem. Mayor's Adv. Com. on Econ. Devel., Plainfield, 1970-72, Webelo Cub Scout leader, 1969-72; Bd. dirs. Plainfield Library Bd., 1970-72, Plainfield Area United Fund, 1971-73. Served with C.E. AUS, 1950-52. Recipient Meyer Berger award for journalism Grad. Sch. Journalism, Columbia, 1970. Mem. Alpha Phi Alpha. Baptist. Home: New York, N.Y. Deceased.

SEARS, BARNABAS FRANCIS, lawyer; b. Webster, S.D., Nov. 13, 1902; student St. Thomas Coll., St. Paul; LL.B., Georgetown U., 1926, LL.D., 1971; LL.D., John Marshall Law Sch., 1971, William Mitchell Coll. Law, 1972. Admitted to Ill. bar, 1926; practice in Chgo., 1942-85; now partner Boodell, Sears, Giambalvo, Sugrue & Crowley. Named Chicagoan of Year, Chgo. Jr. C. of C., 1971. Mem. Am. (ho. dels. 1952-75, chmn. 1968-70, standing com. on fed. judiciary 1959-68), Ill. (past mem. council, chmn. sect. on jud. compensation, selection and tenure 1962-85, pres. 1957-58), Kane County, Aurora, Chgo. bar assns., Soc. Trial Lawyers of Chgo., Am. Law Inst., Am. Judicature Soc., Am. Coll. Trial Lawyers (bd. regents 1961-65, pres. 1970-71; award Courageous Advocacy 1975), Internat. Acad. Trial Lawyers. Clubs: Chgo. Athletic Assn. Home: Chicago, Ill. Died Jan. 1, 1985.

SEATH, JOHN, communications co. exec.; b. Edinburgh, Scotland, Oct. 25, 1914; s. John and Elizabeth A. (Sutherland) S.; came to U.S., 1915, naturalized, 1918; B.B.A. cum laude, Coll. City N.Y., 1948; m. Rose A. Featherstone, June 17, 1939; children—John, Ellaine A. Mgr., Milton M. Bernard, C.P.A., N.Y.C., 1946-55; tax mgr. Gen. Dynamics Corp., N.Y.C., 1955-59, Budd Co., Phila., 1959-61; asst. v.p., dir. taxes ITT, 1961-64, v.p., 1964-73, dir. taxes, 1964-79, sr. v.p., 1973-79. Served with AUS, 1943-46. C.P.A., N.Y. Mem. Am. Inst. C.P.A.'s, Tax Execs. Inst., Fin. Execs. Inst. (tax com.), Tax Found., Tax Inst., NAM (tax com.), Nat. Fgn. Trade Council (tax com.), Internat. Fiscal Assn., Machinery and Allied Products Assn. (tax com.). Republican. Presbyterian. Clubs: Knickerbocker Country (Tenafly, N.J.); Englewood. Home: Englewood, N.J. Died Feb. 15, 1979.

SEAY, EDWARD WARD, coll. pres.; b. Rockvale, Tenn., Nov. 20, 1910; s. Harvey Weakly and Mary Elizabeth (Peeler) S.; B.S., George Peabody Coll. Tchrs., 1934, M.A., 1935; postgrad. Scarritt Coll. for Christian Workers; Pd.D., W. Va. Wesleyan Coll., 1951; LL.D., Tenn. Wesleyan Coll., 1958, Centenary Coll., 1976; m. Helen Harriet Welch, Apr. 12, 1941; 1 son, Robert Edward. Tchr. English, Elba (Ala.) High Sch., 1935-36; asso. headmaster, master English, Morgan Sch. for Boys, Tenn., 1936-37; dean instrn. Pfeiffer (N.C.) Jr. Coll., 1937-39; pres. Wood Jr. Coll., Miss., 1939-43; dir. admissions, asso. prof. econs. Knox Coll., Ill., 1943-48; pres. Centenary Coll. Women, Hackettstown, N.J., 1948-76; ret., 1976. Former v.p. N.J. Coll. Fund Assn.; past bd. dirs. N.J. Assn. Colls. and Univs.; past pres. Nat. Assn. Schs. and Colls. Methodist Ch. Past mem. Univ. Senate of the Methodist Ch. Past trustee Morristown Preparatory Sch., Santiago (Chile) Coll., Alumnae Adv. Centre, Inc. (former). Mem. Am. Acad. Polit. and Social Sci., Am. Econ. Assn., N.E.A., Middle States Assn. Colls. and Secondary Schs. (former comr. instns. higher edn.), Nat. Commn. on Accrediting, N.J. Scholarship Commn., N.J. Jr. Coll. Assn., Phi Theta Kappa, Pi Gamma Mu, Phi Delta Kappa. Methodist. Clubs: Rotary; University. Contbr. articles to profl. jours. Home: Sarasota, Fla. Died Mar. 8, 1984.

SEBALD, JOSEPH FRANCIS, heat transfer equipment co. exec.; b. Pitts., May 24, 1906; s. Joseph Henry and Cornelia Margarette (Biedermann) S.; m. Dorothy Elizabeth Davis, Nov. 23, 1932. B.S. in Mech. Engring., Va. Poly. Inst. and State U., 1928; M.S., Stevens Inst. Tech., 1953, postgrad., 1953-56. With Worthington Corp., Harrison, N.J., 1928-70, chief engr., 1955-62, sr. cons. engr., 1962-70; organizer Heat Power Products Corp., Bloomfield, N.J., 1966, pres., 1966-81, cons. engr., 1966-81; instr. mech. engring. Rutgers U., 1941-46. Fellow ASME (John C. Vaaler Top Honors award 1968, Engring. Leadership award Met. sect. 1968, Codes and Standards medal 1979, v.p. 1968-71); mem. Soc. Naval

Architects and Marine Engrs. (life), Nat. Soc. Profl. Engrs., Essex County Soc. Profl. Engrs., Montclair Soc. Engrs., Tau Beta Pi (life). Republican. Clubs: Highland Lakes (N.J.) Country, Engrs. Patentee in field of mech. engring. Home: Bloomfield, NJ.

SEBELIUS, KEITH GEORGE, former congressman; b. Almena, Kans., Sept. 10, 1916; s. Carl Elstrom and Minnie (Peak) S.; m. Bette A. Roberts, Mar. 5, 1949; children—Keith Gary, Ralph Douglas. A.B., Ft. Hays (Kans.) State U., 1941; J.D., George Washington U., 1939. Bar: Kans., D.C., U.S. Supreme Ct. bars. With Bur. Printing and Engraving, 1936-40; jr. examiner ICC, 1940-41; spl. agt. investigation div. CSC, 1941, practiced in Norton, Kans., from 1946, atty., Norton County, 1947-53, mayor, Almena, 1949-51, city atty., 1953-69, councilman, 1947-49; mem. Kans. Senate from 38th Dist., 1962-68, 91st-96th congresses 1st Dist. Kans. Pres. Norton County Fair Bd., 1957; mem. adv. bd. Nat. Park System, 1981-82; Chmn. Kans. Republican Vets. Club, 1968-70. Served from pvt. to maj. AUS, 1941-45, 51-52. Mem. Ft. Hays State U. Alumni Assn. (pres. 1954), Am. Legion (comdr. Kans. 1955-56), Norton C. of C. (pres. 1958-59), Farm Bur. Methodist. Clubs: Lion (pres. Norton 1953), Mason (33 deg.), Odd Fellow. Home: Norton, Kans. Died Sept. 5, 1982.

SEEL, GEORGE AUGUSTUS, newspaper editor; b. Warm Springs, Ark., Nov. 22, 1888; s. George A. and Ella S. (Kibler) S.; grad. Corpus Christi (Tex.) High Sch., 1906; m. Sarah E. Vann, Sept. 30, 1911. Reporter Corpus Christi Caller, 1909-11; free lance writer, 1911-13; telegraph editor Galveston Tribune, 1913-23, city editor, 1928-38; editor, 1935-45; asso. editor Houston Post, 1946-52. Elk, Episcopalian. Home: Houston, Tex. †

SEEMAN, ERNEST, b. Durham, N.C., Nov. 18, 1887; s. Henry E. and Bettie (Albright) S.; ed. pub. sch.; m. Julia Henry, of Durham, Dec. 29, 1919; 1 son, William Henry. Entered printing business with father, 1903; picture originator, Life Pub. Co., N.Y. City, 1915-18; pres. Seeman Printing Co., Durham, 1917-23; organizer, 1925, mgr. Duke Univ. Press. Served as seaman U.S.N., Mediterranean Service, 1918-19. Contbr. to The Birds of North Carolina, 1916; also contbr. to scientific jours. Creator of newspaper syndicate feature "The Date Tree," 1924. Mem. Nat. Vocational Guidance Assn., Nat. Advisory Council on Radio in Edn., Progressive Edn. Assn., N.J. Criminol. Assn., N.C. Archaeol. Soc. Asst. to Samuel Langley in experiments on flight of vultures, 1902; collaborator with Harlow Shapley on light rays and energy of insects; research in vocational guidance with Thomas A. Edison and L. Rice, 1930-31; made studies of gifted children for N.C. Fed. of Women's Clubs, 1931, studies of abnormal children at Camp Sequoyah, 1932; with Robert Savdek, research in handwriting of twins; consultant in personality; Am. editor Character and Personality. Home: Durham, N.C. †

SEENER, RALPH BERGER, hosp. administrator; b. Bangor, Pa., May 16, 1890; s. Thomas Harrison and Emma Cecelia (Hartzell) S.; Ph.B., Lafayette Coll., Easton, Pa., 1912; M.D., Johns Hopkins, 1916; unmarried. Interne and resident phys., St. Luke's Hosp., Chicago, 1916-18; med. supt. James Wheeler Memorial Hosp., Chicago, 1918-22; asst. supt. Burlington Hospital, Milwaukee, 1922-30; acting supt., 1930-32; dir. Albert Merritt Billings Hosp., U. of Chicago, 1932-34; supt. Peking (China) Union Med. Coll. Hosp., 1934-38; physician supt. Jefferson Hosp., Chicago, Sept. 1, 1939. Home: Chicago. †

SEGAL, MARTIN, economist, educator; b. Warsaw, Poland, Feb. 5, 1921; came to U.S., 1940, naturalized, 1943; s. Jacob and Sarah (Rabinowicz) S.; m. Ruth Berkowicz, June 26, 1945; children—Naomi, Jonathan. B.A., Queens Coll., 1948; M.A., Harvard, 1950, Ph.D., 1953. Instr. Harvard, 1953-56; economist N.Y. Met. Region Study, N.Y.C., 1956-57; asst. prof. Williams Coll., Williamstown, Mass., 1957-58; prof. econs. Dartmouth, 1958-82; sr. economist Council Econ. Advisers, Washington, 1965-66; Ofcl. econ. br. ILO, Geneva, Switzerland, 1968-69; cons. Senate Subcom. on Antitrust, 1955, U.S. Dept. Commerce, 1963-64, A.I.D., 1971-72. Author: Wages in the Metropolis, 1960, The Rise of the United Association, 1970, Government Pay Policies in Ceylon, 1971; Contbr. articles to profl. jours. Served with AUS, 1942-46. Named Alumnus of Year Queens Coll., 1962. Mem. Am. Econ. Assn., Indsl. Relations Research Assn., Phi Beta Kappa (hon.). Home: Hanover, N.H. Died Jan. 1982.

SEGAR, LOUIS HAROLD, physician; born Indianapolis, Apr. 4, 1890; s. Elias Linse and Frances (Kiser) S.; A.B., Ind. U., 1910. M.D., 1912; m. Beatrice, Felsenthal, Apr. 4, 1922; children—Dr. William Elias, Geoffrey, Carol-Frances, Interne Ind. Meth. Episcopal Hosp., 1913; N.Y. City Hosp., 1913-14; Children's Hosp., Boston, 1914; practice of medicine, Indianapolis, from 1915, specializing in pediatrics from 1915. Clin. prof. pediatrics, Ind. U., from 1915. Served as lt., U.S.N.R., 1917-19. Mem. Ind. Pediatric Soc. (pres. 1937), A.M.A., Am. Acad. Pediatrics, B'nai B'rith. Jewish Reformed. Mason. Club: Indianapolis Literary. Home: Indianapolis, Ind. †

SEGHERS, ANNA, author; b. Mainz, Rhine, Germany, Nov. 19, 1900; d. J. and H. (Fuld) Reiling; Ph.D., U. of Heidelberg, 1923; student Mus. for Oriental Art, Rein, U. of Rein, Germany; m. Dr. Radvanyi, 1925; children—Peter, Ruth. Author: Revolt of the Fisherman, 1923; On the Way to the American Embassy (burned by Hitler); The Price on His Head (published in Amsterdam); The Fellow Travellers (burned by Hitler); The Rescue (published in Amsterdam); The Way Through February (published in Paris); The Seventh Cross, 1942; Transit, 1944; Home: Mexico, D.F. Died June 2, 1983.*

SEHRT, EDWARD HENRY, philologist; b. Baltimore, Md., Mar. 3, 1888; s. Henry and Caroline (Becker) S.; A.B., Johns Hopkins, 1911, grad. study, 1911-13, Ph.D., 1915; grad. study, U. of Leipzig, 1913-14; m. Cecelia M. Schane, Sept. 8, 1915; 1 dau., Cecelia Schane (dec.). Instr. German U. of Delaware, 1915-16; lecturer in Germanic philology, Bryn Mawr, 1916-18; prof. of modern languages, Washington Coll., 1918-20; research fellow in Germanic philology, Johns Hopkins, 1920-22; prof. modern langs., Gettysburg Coll., 1922-26; prof. German, George Washington U., from 1926. Mem. Modern Lang. Assn. America, Linguistic Soc. America, Medieval Acad. America, Am. Philol. Assn., Goethe Soc., Verien fÜr niederdeutsche Sprachforschung, Phi Beta Kappa. Author: Zur Geschichte der Konjunktion "Und" im Westgermanischen, 1916; Vollständiges Wörterbuch zum Heliand und der altsächsischen Genesis, 1925. Contbr. to philol. jours. Editor: Studies in Honor of Professor Collitz (with Taylor Starck), 1930; Notkers des Deutschen Werke, Vol. I (with T. Starck), 1933. Voll. II (with same), 1935. Home: Washington, D.C. †

SEIBEL, CLIFFORD WINSLOW, corporate executive; b. Kansas City, Mo., Nov. 10, 1890; s. Dr. Richard M. and Lida (Kittle) S.; B.S., U. of Kan., 1913, M.S., 1915; Sc.D., Texas Tech., 1937; m. Ruth Bowdie, Dec. 22, 1915 (dec. Sept. 20, 1951); children—Richard M. II, Margaret Dorothea; m. Mrs. Thelma P. Pallette, Nov. 29, 1952. Instr. in chemistry, U. of Kan., 1913-17; chemist, Bur. of Mines since 1917; chief helium engr. Bureau of Mines, Dept. of Interior; supervised design and constrn. and operation 4 helium production plants for World War II; in charge all helium field work, Bureau of Mines; designed helium plants for Army and Navy; regional dir. region VI. Bur. of Mines, 1949-52, asst. dir., 1954-59, ret.; cons. Stearns-Roger Mfg. Co., after 1959. Dept. of Interior rep. Nat. Acad. Science, NRC. Recipient Dept. Interior award, 1954; Silver Beaver (Boy Scouts); Career Service Award, National Civil Service League, 1956; citation U. Kansas and Alumni Assn., 1959. Mem. Am. Inst. Mining and Metall. Engrs., AAAS, American Chem. Soc., Amarillo Boy Scout Council (past pres.), Alpha Chi Sigma, Sigma Xi. Presbyterian (elder). Lodges: Mason Shriner, K.T. Clubs: Cosmos (Washington, D.C.); Rotary. Office: Denver, Colo.†

SEIDLIN, OSKAR, b. Koenigshuette, Feb. 17, 1911; came to U.S., 1938, naturalized, 1942; s. Heinrich and Johanna (Seidler) Koplowitz. Student, univs. Freiburg, Berlin and Frankfurt/Main, 1929-33; Ph.D. summa cum laude, U. Basel, Switzerland, 1935; postgrad., U. Lausanne, Switzerland, 1935-38; D.H.L., U. Mich., 1969. Asst. prof. Smith Coll., 1939-46; mem. faculty Ohio State U., Columbus, 1946-72, prof. German lit., 1950-66, Regents prof., 1966-72; prof. German lit. Ind. U., Bloomington, 1972-74, Distinguished Service prof., 1974-79, emeritus, 1979-84; Vis. prof. German Summer Sch., Middlebury (Vt.) Coll., U. Wash., 1949; lectr. Am., Swiss and W. German univs., 1954-84; guest Fed. Republic Germany, 1956; Ford prof. in residence Free U. Berlin, 1959. Author: Essays in German and Comparative Literature, 2d edit, 1966, (with others) An Outline History of German Literature, Von Goethe zu Thomas Mann, 2d edit, 1969, Versuche ueber Eichendorff, 1965, 2d edit., 1978, Klassische und moderne Klassiker, 1972, Der Briefwechsel Arthur Schnitzler-Otto Brahm, 1975, Der Theaterkritiker Otto Brahm, 1978, Von erwachendem Bewusstein und vom Sündenfall, 1979; also numerous articles.; Co-editor: jour. Arcadia, 1966-73, German Quar, 1972-77, Mich. Germanic Studies, 1975—; Festschrift: Herkommen und Erneuerung, Essays für Oskar Seidlin, 1976. Served to 2d lt. AUS, 1942-46. Recipient Distinguished Teaching award Ohio State U., 1960, Eichendorff medal Eichendorff Mus., Wangen, 1961; Golden Goethe medal Goethe Inst., Munich, Germany, 1963; named Tchr. of Year Ohio State U., 1967; recipient prize for Germanic studies abroad German Acad. Lang. and Lit., 1968; Wisdom award of honor, 1970; Eichendorff medal Eichendorff Soc., Würzburg, 1974; Kulturpreis Nordrhein Westfalen, 1975; Georg-Dehio prize Kunstlergilde, 1983; Guggenheim fellow, 1963, 77. Mem. Akademie der Wissenschaften (Göttingen), Modern Lang. Assn. (1st v.p. 1965), Am. Assn. Tchrs. German, Internat. Humanities Research Assn., Internat. Germanisten Verband, Internat. Kleist Gesellschaft, Freies Deutsches Hochstift, Phi Beta Kappa (chpt. pres. 1965). Home: Bloomington, Ind. Died Dec. 11, 1984.

SEIFERT, ELIZABETH (MRS. JOHN GASPAROTTI), author; b. Washington, Mo., June 19, 1897; d. Richard C. and Anna (Sanford) Seifert; A.B., Washington U., St. Louis, Mo., 1918; m. John Gasparotti, Feb. 3, 1920; children—John Joseph, Richard Seifert, Paul Anthony, Anna Catharine. Writer since 1938. Mem. Authors League of America, American Association University Women, Beta Sigma Phi (hon. internat. member). Republican. Episcopalian. Mem. Sorosis Club (Moberly, Mo.). Author numerous books since 1938; latest publs.: Hospital Zone, 1948; The Bright Coin, 1949; Homecoming, 1950; The Story of Andrea Fields, 1950; Miss Doctor, 1951; A Doctor Takes a Wife, 1952; The Doctor Disagrees, 1953; Doctor at the Crossroads, 1954; Marriage for Three, 1954; A Call for Dr. Barton, 1956; Substitute Doctor, 1957; The Doctor's Husband, 1957; The New Doctor, Love Comes to the Doctor, 1958; Hometown Doctor, 1959; Doctor on Trial, 1959; When Doctors Marry, 1960; The Doctor's Bride, 1960; Dr. Jeremy's Wife, 1961; The Doctor Makes a Choice, 1961; The Honor of Dr. Shelton, 1962; The Doctor's Strange Secret, 1962; A Doctor Comes to Bayard, 1964; Doctor Samaritan, 1965; Pay the Doctor, 1966; Rival Doctors, 1967; Doctor with a Mission, 1967. Contbr. fiction to popular mags. Home: Moberly, Mo. Died June 17, 1983.*

SEILER, PAUL WALDO, corp. official; b. at Hudson, Ind., Aug. 15, 1888; s. Franklin Pierce and Mino (Andrews) S.; ed. Auburn (Ind.) High Sch.; m. Frances Dorris, Oct. 18, 1916; children—Paul Waldo, Robert Dorris, John Findley. Began as employee in machine shop W. H. Kiblinger Co., Auburn, Ind.; service mgr. W. H. McIntyre Co., Auburn, Ind., 1909; service mgr. Streator (Ill.) Motor Car Co., 1909-11, sales mgr., 1911; mgr. field service dept., Hudson Motor Car Co., Detroit, Mich., 1912; spl. rep. Ford Motor Co., Detroit, Mich., asst. mgr., Nashville, Tenn., 1915, mgr. San Antonio, Tex., 1916; asst. mgr. Airplane div., Fisher Body Corp., 1917; mgr. Ternstedt Mfg. Co., Detroit, Mich., 1918-21, pres. and gen. mgr. 1921-27; pres. and gen. mgr. Yellow Truck & Coach Mfg. Co., Pontiac, Mich., 1927-35; pres., gen. mgr. Gen. Motors Truck Corp., Pontiac, Mich., 1927-35; pres. Motor Tool Mfg. Co., Detroit, 1936-47; pres. Polaris Gold Mines, Ltd., Timmis, Ont., 1935-44; mfrs. rep. from 1948. Metal Cutting Tools & Mfg. Co., Detroit, 1942-44. Automobile Old Timers. Republican. Methodist. Mason (Shriner). Clubs: Detroit Athletic, Detroit, Economic, Bloomfield Hills Country, Recess, Question, Detroit Golf (Detroit); Lake Shore (Chicago). Home: Detroit. †

SELBY, PAUL OWEN, coll. dean; b. LaPlata, Mo., Jan. 20, 1890; s. Hiram and Ella (Clay) S.; student Northwestern U., 1915-16; B.S., 1st Dist. Normal Sch., 1918; A.M., U. Mo., 1926; Ph.D., University of Iowa, 1934; m. Louise A. Willard, 1918 (deceased 1964). Engaged as high school tchr., Bartlesville, Okla., 1910-11, Carthage, Mo., 1911-12; registrar 1st Dist. Normal Sch., Kirksville, Mo., 1912-18; prof. bus. edn. N.E. Mo. State Tchrs. College, Kirksville, 1919-54, dean instruction, 1954-60, dean of instruction emeritus, from 1960; visiting professor Fresno (Cal.) State College, 1950-51. Served with U.S. Army, 1918-19. Mem. Am. Legion, Pi Omega Pi (founder, 1st nat. pres.), Phi Delta Kappa, Kappa Delta Pi, Sigma Tau Gamma, Delta Pi Epsilon. Presbyn. Club: Kirksville Kiwanis (past pres.). Author: The Principles of Business Operation, 1936; The Teaching of Bookkeeping, 1946; Bits of Adair County History, 1960-62; Board of Regents of the State Teachers College, 1961; Biographies of Deceased Faculty Members, 1962; Coal Mining in Adair County, 1963; List of Mark Twain Books, 1964; The Violette Museum and the Violette-McClure Missouriana Collections, 1964; A Chronology of Adair County, 1964; Index to a Chronology, 1964; A Bibliography of Missouri County Histories and Atlases, 1966. Home: Kirksville, Mo. †

SELEY, JASON, sculptor; b. Newark, May 20, 1919; s. Simon M. and Leah (Kridel) S.; B.A., Cornell U., 1940; student Art Students League, 1943-45, Ecole des Beaux-Arts. Paris, 1949-50; m. Clara Kalnitsky, Feb. 27, 1942. One man exhbns. include Le Centre D'Art, Port-Au-Prince, Haiti, 1946, 48, 49, Am. Brit. Art Center, N.Y.C., 1947, 48, Asso. Am. Artists Gallery, N.Y.C., 1955, Barone Gallery, N.Y.C., 1960, Kornblee Gallery, N.Y.C., 1962, 64, White Mus., Cornell U., 1965; exhbt. group shows Mus. Modern Art, 1961, 62, 63, Guggenheim Mus., 1962, Whitney Mus., 1952, 53, 62, 64; rep. permanent collections Mus. Modern Art, Whitney Mus., Chase-Manhattan Bank, Nat. Gallery, Ottawa, Can., Art Gallery of Ont., Toronto, others; asso. prof. fine arts Hofstra U., Hempstead, N.Y., 1963-65; asso. prof., artists-in-residence Sch. Edn., N.Y. U., 1965-67; artist-in-residence Dartmouth, 1968; prof. art. chmn. dept. Coll. Architecture, Art and Planning, Cornell U., Ithaca, from 1968. Fulbright scholar, 1949-50. Mem. Coll. Art Assn., Sculptors Guild, New Sculpture Group, Am. Assn. U. Profs., Art Students League. Home: Ithaca, N.Y. Died June 23, 1983.

SELF, SIR HENRY, British govt. official; b. London, Eng., Jan. 18, 1890; s. S. A. T. and Mary Jane (Wills) S.; B.Sc., U. of London, 1911, B.Sc. in Mathematics, 1913, B.A. in Classics, 1929, B.D., 1932, B.D., in Philosophy, 1934; m. Rosalind Audry Otter, Aug. 22, 1918; 2 sons. Barrister at law, Lincoln's Inn (certificate of honour, 1922). British government official from 1907; served with Board of Trade, Post Office, Foreign Office, War Office and Local Govt. Bd.; with War Office and Ministry of Munitions, 1914-19; Air Ministry, 1919; prin. asst. sec., 1936; deputy undersecretary of state, 1937; served on special air mission to Middle East Africa in connection with British Empire Air Mail Scheme, 1935, on two air missions to U.S.A. and Can., 1938, in connection with placing aircraft orders for R.A.F.; head of Mission to U.S.A. and Can., 1940, from which emerged British Air Commn. in Washington, D.C.; dir.-gen. Brit. Air Commn., Washington, 1940-41; attached for spl. duties with Brit. Joint Staff Mission concurrently with establishment of Combined Chiefs of Staff Organization, Washington, Jan.-June 1942; permanent sec. to Brit. Ministry of Production, London, 1942-43; United Kingdom representative on Combined Production and Resources Bd., also United Kingdom mem. Combined Raw Materials Bd., Washington, D.C., 1943-45; permanent sec. British Ministry of Civil Aviation, 1946-47. Decorated Knight Companion of the Bath, Knight Order of British Empire, Knight Comdr. St. Michael and St. George. Club: Reform (London). Home: Brighton, Eng. †

SELF, VICTOR H(ARRISON), govt. official; b. Pilot Knob, Tenn., Apr. 8, 1889; s. Josiah Franklin and Francis Augusta (Wright) S.; A.B., Oakland Sem., Baileyton, Tenn., 1907; student U. of Tennessee, 1909; m. Willie Dell Kidwell, Dec. 11, 1911 (died 1948). Teacher in pub. schs., Tenn., 1907-11; employee U.S. Post Office, Dept., Washington, 1912-21 (assisted in installation central accounting system in post offices); asst. supervisor of collectors' offices. Bureau of Internal Revenue, 1921-23, head of office accounts and procedure div., 1923-29, asst. dep. commr., 1929-44 (organizer unit to administer taxing provisions of Social Security Act), dep. commr., accounts and collections unit, 1944-46, dep. commr. employment tax unit from 1946. Author: The Family of Josiah Franklin Self and Francis Augusta (Wright) Self, 1939. Home: Riverdale, Md. †

SELL, EDWARD SCOTT, teacher; b. Hoschton, Ga., Mar. 9, 1887; s. Howell Jackson and Julia (Anderson) S.; B.S.A., U. of Ga., and State Coll. of Agr., 1910. M.S. Agr., 1918; m. Nettie Whatley, Dec. 30, 1913; 1 son, Edward Scott. Prin. of schs., Blythe, Ga., 1910-11; head of dept. of agr., Ga. State Teachers Coll., 1911-31; prof. of geography, U. of Ga., from 1932. Meteorological observer, U.S. Weather Bureau. Editor of Home and Farmstead, 1913, 14, Faculty mem. U. of Ga. Summer School from 1915. Dir. Athens Fed. Savings and Loan Co. Dir. School Garden Assn. of America; mem. Bd. of Edn., City of Athens. Chmn. gasoline ration bd. for Clarke Co., 1942-43. Mem. Am. Meteorol. Soc., Am. Assn. Univ. Profs., Ga. Acad. Social Science, Methodist. Clubs: Cloverhurst Country, Peabody. Author: Agricultural Laboratory Manual-Soils, 1915; Methods of Instruction in Agriculture; History of the State Normal School, 1923; Physical Map of Georgia, 1935; Geography of Georgia. Co-author: (text book) The Story of Georgia. Home: Athens, Ga. †

SELLECK, CLYDE ANDREW, army officer; b. Brandon, Vt., July 29, 1888; s. Andrew and Jennie (Barbar) S.; student Norwich Univ., Vt., 1906; B.S., U.S. Mil. Acad., 1910; m. Gertrude Troth, Aug. 15, 1923; children—Mary Jane, Jo Anne, Clyde. Commd. 2d lt., 1910, and advanced through the grades to brig. gen., Dec. 18, 1941. Served with 21st F.A., France, Vosges front, 1918, later chief of staff 7th Army Corps Arty.; Nat. Guard instr., N.Y. City, 1921-25; Nat. Guard Bureau, Washington, 1927-31; assigned duty with Organized Reserves, 1939; served in Philippines through the Bataan Campaign, 1941-42; then prisoner of war of JapaneseGovt. Home: Alexandria, Va. †

SELLERS, CHARLES WILBUR, lawyer; b. Columbus, O., Feb. 12, 1888; s. Charles Lawrence and Flora (Price) S.; student Ashland Coll., 1905-06; B.A., Ohio Wesleyan U., 1910; LL.B., Western Res. U., 1913; m. Lucille Jardine, Aug. 18, 1921. Admitted to Ohio bar, 1913, practiced in Cleve.; mem. firm Thompson, Hine & Flory, from 1925. Served with Ohio N.G., Mexican Border Service, 1916-17; served to maj. U.S. Army, 1917-19. Mem. Am., Fed., Ohio, Cleve. bar assns., Phi Delta Phi, Beta Theta Pi. Mason. Clubs: City (past pres.), Mid Day, Union (Cleve.). Home: Cleveland, OH. †

SELLS, JOHN F(RANCIS), business exec.; b. Calcutta, India, 1889; s. John Henry and Edith (March) S.; Chartered Acct., U. Alberta, 1917; m. Isabelle Jones, 1915; children—John Arthur, Frances Isabelle (wife of Dr. R. A. Ryan). Came to U.S., 1920, naturalized, 1938. Admitted to bar, 1919; gen. office mgr. John Morrell & Co., 1940-43, controller from 1943, also dir. Mem. Ottumwa Hosp. Assn. (dir.). Inst. Chartered Accts. Can., Am. Inst. Accts. Republican. Episcopalian. Club: Ottumwa Country, Home: Ottumwa, Iowa. †

SELYE, HANS, physician; b. Vienna, Austria, Jan. 26, 1907; s. Hugo and Maria Felicitas (Langbank) S.; m. Louise Drevet, Oct. 5, 1978; children—Catherine Michel, Jean, Marie, André . Student, Coll. Benedictine Fathers, Komárom, Hungary, 1916-24; med. student, German U., Prague, 1924-25, 27-29, U. Paris, 1925-26, U. Rome, 1926-27; M.D., German U., Prague, 1929, Ph.D., 1931; D.Sc., McGill U., 1942; D.Sc. hon. degree, U. Windsor, 1955, Cath. U. Chile, 1956, Hahnemann Med. Coll. and Hosp., 1962, U. San Carlos, 1959, Nat. U. Argentina, 1950, U. Montevideo, 1956, Westfälische Wilhelms Universität, 1966, U. Cagliari, Italy, 1967, Karl-Franzens U., 1967, J.E. Purkyne U., Brno, 1969, U. Guelph, 1973, Laval U., 1975, Phila. Coll., 1975, Hebrew U. Jerusalem, 1977, U. Haifa, Toronto, 1978, U. Alta., 1978. Asst. in exptl. pathology, histology lab. German U., 1929-31; Rockefeller research fellow dept. biochem. hygiene Johns Hopkins U., 1931; research fellow dept. biochemistry McGill U., Montreal, Que., Can., 1932-33, lectr. biochemistry, 1933-34, asst. prof. biochemistry, 1934-37, asst prof. histology, 1937-41, asso. prof. histology, 1941-45; prof., dir. Inst. Exptl. Medicine and Surgery, U. Montreal, 1945-76, prof. emeritus, 1977-82; pres. Internat. Inst. of

Stress, 1976-82, Hans Selye Found., 1979; expert cons. to Surgeon Gen., U.S. Army, 1947-57. Author: several specialized med. books including Annual Reports on Stress, 1951-56, The Story of the Adaptation Syndrome, 1952, The Stress of Life, 1956, The Chemical Prevention of Cardiac Necroses, 1958, Calciphylaxis, 1962, From Dream to Discovery, 1964, The Mast Cells, 1965, Thrombohemorrhagic Phenomena, 1966, In Vivo, 1967, Anaphylactoid Edema, 1968, Experimental Cardiovascular Diseases, 1970, Hormones and Resistance, 1971, Stress Without Distress, 1974, Stress in Health and Disease, 1976, The Stress of Life, 2d edit, 1976, The Stress of My Life, 1977, 2d edit., 1979 (Can. Authors Assn. Lit. award), Selye's Guide to Stress Research, Vol. 1, 1979, Vol. 2, 1981; editor: (with others) several specialized med. books including Cancer, Stress and Death, 1979; editorial bd.: (with others) several specialized med. books including Ars Medici, Belgium, Experimentelle Chirurgie, Germany, Am. Jour. Clin. Hypnosis, Internat. Jour. Neuropsychiatry; others; author (with others) philosophy of altruistic egoism to cope with stress. Recipient Casgrain and Charbonneau prize, 1946; Gordon Wilson medal, 1948; Heberden medal, 1950; medal Academia Medico Fisica Fiorentina, 1950; Henderson Gold medal Am. Geriatrics Soc., 1964; medal Swedish Med. Soc., 1965; Canadian Centennial medal, 1967; companion Order of Can., 1968; gold medal Rudolf Virchow, 1970; commemorative plate Paul D. White symposium Am. Coll. Cardiology, 1971; Harry G. Armstrong lectr. Aerospace Med. Assn., 1972; Grieve Meml. lectr. Canadian Assn. Orthodontists, 1972; Starr medal Canadian Med. Assn., 1972; Prix de l'Oeuvre Scientifique Assn. medecins langue française Can., 1974; Distinguished Service award Am. Soc. Abdominal Surgeons, 1974; Killam prize, 1974; Kittay award, 1976; Order of Flag Hungary, 1977; Queen's Silver Jubilee medal Can., 1977; Achievement in Life award Ency. Brit., 1977; medal U. Calcutta, 1979; other honors and awards. Fellow Royal Soc. (Can.), N.Y. Acad. Scis., AAAS, Pan Am. Med. Assn. (N.Am. chmn. sect. endocrinology); hon. fellow Alpha Ency. (Montreal), Acad. Pharm. Scis., Société medicale polonaise; mem. Ohio Hungarian Soc., Hungarian Med. Soc. Am. (hon. pres.); hon. and corr. mem. fgn., nat., state and local profl. med. assns. and orgns., in both gen. and spl. fields. Home: Montreal, Que., Can. Died Oct. 23, 1982.

SEMPLE, FLORENCE EMMA, ex-mem. Rep. Nat. Com.; b. Exline, Ia., Sept. 7, 1888; d. Chas., Anna Jane (Huff) Fullerton; student pub. schs., Chickasha, Okla.; grad. Hill's Bus. U., Oklahoma City; married John Benjiman Ireton, Mar. 15, 1906 (dec. June 13, 1912); children—George Raymond (dec.); (adopted) Barbara (Mrs. Meek), Elizabeth (Mrs. Hayes); m. 2d, Carl Y. Semple, Apr. 17, 1938 (dec. Sept. 1959). Grain exporter, Oklahoma City, to 1918; lead, zinc, coal mining, Baxter Springs, Kan., from 1918; mgr. Semple Mining & Investment Co.; real estate, investments. Mem. bd. Baxter Springs Hosp.; chmn. Baxter Springs Youth Center. Precinct committeewoman; past mem. Rep. Nat. Com. Kan. Mem. endowment bd. Kan. State Coll. Mem. Nat. Fedn. Rep. Women, Kan. Rep. Women, Cherokee Co. Rep. Women, D.A.R., Kan. State, Baxter Springs C.'s of C., Dames of Court of Honor, Daus. of Am. Colonists. Presbyn. Clubs: Baxter Springs Women, Kansas Day (v.p. 1950). Home: Baxter Springs, Kan. †

SENDER, RAMON JOSÉ, educator, writer; b. Alcolea de Cinca, Spain, 1902; s. José and Andrea (Garcés) S.; Bachillerato, Inst. Zaragom, 1918; Licenciado en filosofia y letras U. Madrid, 1924; m. Amparo Barayon, Jan. 7, 1934 (died Oct. 11, 1936); children—Ramon, Andrea; m. 2d Florence Hall, August 12, 1943 (div. September 3, 1962). Came to the United States, naturalized, 1946. Journalist, editor El Sol, Madrid, Spain, 1924-31; Guggenheim fellow, 1942; then lectr., prof. Spanish lit. Amherst (Mass) Coll., U. Denver, U. N.M., 1947-63. Vis. prof. Ohio State U. summer 1951. U. Cal., Los Angeles, 1952, Univ. So. Cal., 1965; speaking tour of U.S. as rep. of Spanish Rep., 1938. Served as res. officer Spanish Inf., mission to Morocco, 1923-24; maj., gen. staff, Spanish Rep. Army, 1936-39. Decorated Medal of Morocco; Mil. Cross of Merit (Spain). Awarded Nat. prize of Lit. (Spain), 1935; Asso. Press Author of the Week, May 1948. Mem. Ateneo (mem. governing bd., sec. Ibeco-Am. sect.). Nat. Council Culture, Alliance Intebectuals for Def. Democracy (all Spain), Hispanic Soc. Am., Phi Sigma Iota, Author: Pro Patria, 1934; Seven Red Sundays, 1935; Mr. Witt among the Rebels, 1936; Counterattack in Spain, 1938; A Man's Place, 1940; Dark Wedding, 1943; Chronicle of Dawn, 1944; The King and the Queen, 1948; The Sphere, 1949; The Affable Hangman, 1954; Before Noon, 1957; Requiem for a Spanish Peasant, published in 1960; Exemplary Novels of Cibola, 1963; others translated into 16 langs. Contbr. popular and lit. mags., columnist Latin Am. newspapers. Address: San Diego, Calif. Died Jan. 17, 1982.

SERFASS, EARL JAMES, cons.; b. Allentown, Pa., Dec. 22, 1912; s. James M. and Ida Alice (Shafer) S.; B.S. in Chemistry, Lehigh U., 1933, M.S., 1935, Ph.D., 1938; m. Mabel Dowling, Sept. 5, 1935; children—Nancy Alice, Robert Earl, Richard Eric. Instr. analytical chemistry Lehigh U., Bethlehem, Pa., 1938-40, asst. prof., 1940-42, asso. prof., 1942-45, prof. 1946-59, curriculum dir. chemistry, 1950-52, head chemistry dept., 1952-59; pres. Serfass Corp.; v.p., research dir. Milton Roy Co., 1959-66, sr. v.p. 1966-68, pres., 1968-76, chmn. bd., chief exec. officer, 1974-78; pres. Sercon Corp., cons., 1978-82. Project dir.

Am. Electroplaters Soc.; cons. various indsl. firms; Fellow Instrument Soc. Am.; mem. Am. Chem. Soc., Am. Inst. Physics, Phi Beta Kappa, Sigma Xi, Tau Beta Pi. Contbr. numerous articles to profl. jours. Home: Largo, Fla. Died Nov. 24, 1982.

SERLIS, HARRY GEORGE, business executive; b. Kansas City, Feb. 22, 1912; s. Harry and Hattie (Weissenbach) S.; m. Kathryn Isreal, Dec. 14, 1935; children—Charles Harry, Barry Edward; m. Roberta Maleville; 1962. Student, U. Ill., 1928-29. Advt., investment banking, Midwest, 1932-34; asst. gen. sales mgr. Schenley Distillers, Inc., 1936-41; mng. dir. Schenley Import Corp., 1942; dir. sales, advt. CVA Co., 1943-51, chmn. bd., 1954-59, pres., chmn., 1955-58; pres., dir. Schenley Distillers, Inc., 1951-55; v.p., dir. Schenley Industries, Inc., 1952-59; founder Harry G. Serlis & Assocs. (mgmt. cons.-pub. relations), San Francisco, 1961-69; pres. Wine Inst., San Francisco, 1969-75; dir. Robert Mondavi Winery, Oakville, Calif. Decorated officier de l'Ordre National du Merit de France, Medaille d'Honneur du Comité Nationale des Vins de France; recipient gold insignia Club Oenologique. Mem. Calif. Agrl. Fgn. Trade Adv. Com., Pub. Relations Soc. Am., Am. Assn. Mgmt. Cons. Home: Palm Springs, Calif. Died Feb. 12, 1984.

SERT, JOSE LUIS, architect, city planner; b. Barcelona, Spain, July 1, 1902; came to U.S., 1939, naturalized, 1951; s. Francisco and Genara (Lopez) S.; m. Ramona Longás, Oct. 2, 1938; 1 dau., Maria. M.Arch., Escuela Superior de Arquitectura, Barcelona, 1929; M.A. (hon.), Harvard U.; Art.D., Harvard U., 1968; Litt.D., Boston Coll.; D.H.L., Boston U., 1970. Registered architect, N.Y., Mass., Fla., Colombia. S.Am. Worked with Le Corbusier, Pierre Jeanneret, Paris, 1929-30; pvt. practice architecture, Barcelona, 1929-38; co-founder, partner Town Planning Assocs., N.Y.C., 1941-59; partner Sert, Jackson & Gourley, 1958-64, Sert, Jackson & Assocs., from 1964; prof. city planning Yale U., 1944-45; dean, prof. architecture Harvard Grad. Sch. Design, 1953-69, prof. emeritus, 1969-83; Thomas Jefferson Meml. Found. prof. architecture U. Va., 1970-71; adv. council Princeton Sch. Architecture and Urban Planning, 1972-74; Chmn. com. for habitat bill of rights Iran Ministry Housing and Urban Planning, 1974—. (Recipient Thomas Jefferson medal in architecture U. Va. 1970); Author: Can Our Cities Survive?, 1947, (with Rogers, Tyrwhitt) The Heart of the City, 1952, The Shape of Our Cities, (with Jaqueline Tyrwhitt), 1957, (with James Johnson Sweeney) Antoni Gaudi, 1960; contbr. (with James Johnson Sweeney) articles to profl. publs.; archtl. projects include apt. houses, Barcelona, 1930-31, central dispensary, Dept. Health, Catalan Govt., 1934-35, Spanish Pavillion, Expn. Internationale des Arts et Techniques, (with Luis Lacasa), Paris, 1937; (with P.L. Wiener) master plan Cidade dos Motores, Rio de Janeiro, Brazil, Cali, Columbia; pilot plan for resort, Varadero, Cuba, 1954-55, U.S. embassy bldgs., Baghdad, Iraq, 1956, Holyoke Center, Married Students Dormitories, Undergrad. Sci. Center (all Harvard); design cons.: Univ. Centre Adminstrn. Bldg, all U. Guelph, Ont., George Sherman Union, Mugar Library, Schs. Law and Edn, Pappas Law Library, all Boston U.; Found. Maeght Mus, St. Paul de Vence, France; urban renewal plan for Central Bus. Dist, Worcester, Mass., Martin Luther King, Jr. Elementary Sch, Cambridge, resort community, Marseille, France, moderate rental housing, Brookline, Mass. Harvard planning devel. and design, from 1957, Roosevelt Island Devel, Riverview Devel. for N.Y. State Urban Devel. Corp, Joan Miro Center for Study Contemporary Art, Barcelona, student housing, M.I.T., housing complex, Barcelona, freeway, La Junquera, Spain. Fellow AIA (award 1977, Gold medal 1981), Royal Archtl. Inst. Can. (hon.), Royal Soc. Arts (London); mem. Nat. Inst. Arts and Letters, Internat. Congress Modern Architecture (pres. 1947-56), Royal Inst. Brit. Architects (hon.), Acad. Royal Belgium, Akademie der Kunste (Berlin), Soc. Architects Mex. (hon.), Inst. Urbanism Peru (hon.), Boston Soc. Architects, Am. Acad. Arts and Scis., Academie d'Architecture France (Gold medal 1975), Sociedad Colombiana de Arquitectos (hon.). Home: Cambridge, Mass. Died Mar. 15, 1983.

SESSIONS, ROGER HUNTINGTON, composer; b. Bklyn., Dec. 28, 1896; s. Archibald Lowery and Ruth Gregson (Huntington) S.; m. Barbara Foster, 1920; m. Elizabeth Franck, Nov. 26, 1936; children—John Porter, Elizabeth Phelps. A.B., Harvard U., 1915, Mus.D., 1964; Mus.B., Yale U., 1917; Mus.D., Wesleyan U., 1958, Rutgers U., 1962, New Eng. Conservatory, 1966, Amherst Coll., 1969, Williams Coll., 1971, Princeton U., 1972, Cleve. Inst. Music, 1975, Boston U., 1977; LL.D., Brandeis U., 1965; A.F.D., U. Pa., 1966; D.F.A., U. Calif. at Berkeley, 1967, Northwestern U., 1971; D.A., Rider Coll., 1978. Instr. music Smith Coll., 1919-21; tchr. theory Cleve. Inst. Music, 1921-25; resided in Florence, Rome, Berlin, 1925-33; instr. Boston U. Coll. Music, 1933-35; lectr. N.J. Coll. for Women, 1935-37; instr. Princeton U., 1935-37, asst. prof., 1937-40, asso. prof., 1940-45; prof. music U. Calif. at Berkeley, 1945; Fulbright scholar Academia Luigi Cherubini, Florence, Italy, 1951-52; William Shubael Conant prof. music Princeton, 1953-65; faculty Juilliard Sch. Music, N.Y.C., 1965-85; Ernest Bloch prof. music U. Calif., Berkeley, 1966-67; Charles Eliot Norton prof. Harvard U., 1968-69. Composer: Symphony No. 1, 1927, Sonata for Piano, 1930, Suite from The Black Maskers, 1923, Three Chorales for Organ, 1926, Concerto for Violin, 1935, String Quartet, Coolidge

Festival 1937, 1936, Chorale for Organ, 1938, Duo for Violin and Piano, 1942, Turn O Libertad (mixed chorus and piano, 4 hands), 1944, Sonata No. 2 for piano, 1946, Symphony No. 2, 1946, String Quartet No. 2, 1950-51; opera The Trial of Lucullus, 1947, Sonata for Violin, unaccompanied, 1953, Idyll of Theocritus, for soprano and orch, 1954, Mass in celebration of the 50th Anniversary of Kent School, 1955, Concerto for Piano and Orchestra, 1956, Symphony No. 3, 1957, No. 4, 1958, String Quintet, 1958, Divertimento for Orchestra, 1959-60, Montezuma, 1959-63, Psalm 140 for soprano and orch, 1963, Symphony Number 5, 1964, Sonata No. 3, 1965, Symphony No. 6, 1966, Six Pieces for Violoncello Solo, 1966, Symphony No. 7, 1967, Symphony No. 8, 1968; cantata When Lilacs Last in the Dooryard Bloom'd; soloists, chorus and orch., 1967-70, Rhapsody for Orch, 1970, Double Concerto for Violin, Violincello and Orch, 1970-71, Concertino for Chamber Orch, 1972, 3 Choruses on Bibl. Text with Small Orch, 1972, Five Pieces for Piano, 1974, Symphony No. 9, 1978 (Recipient Creative arts award Brandeis U. 1958, elected Ausserordentliches Mitglied, Akademie der Kunste, Berlin 1960, Gold medal Nat. Inst. Arts and Letters 1961, Academico Corr., Academia Nacional de Bellas Artes, Argentina 1965, medal Edward MacDowell Assn. 1968); Author: The Musical Experience of Composer, Performer and Listener, 1950, Harmonic Practice, 1950, Questions About Music, 1970, Roger Sessions on Music, 1979. Recipient spl. citation Pulitzer Prize Com., 1974; Pulitzer prize, 1982; John Simon Guggenheim fellow, 1926-28; Walter Damrosch fellow Am. Acad. in Rome, 1928-31; charter mem. Berkeley Fellows 1968. Mem. Am. Acad. Arts and Scis., Internat. Soc. Contemporary Music (hon.), Am. Acad. Arts and Letters, League of Composers, Internat. Soc. for Contemporary Music (co-chmn. U.S. sect.), Broadcast Music, Nat. Inst. Arts and Letters. Died Mar. 16, 1985.*

SETO, YEB JO, elec. engr., educator; b. China, July 31, 1930; came to U.S., 1951, naturalized, 1962; s. Jo Ting and Shee (Chang) S.; m. Jane Mei-Chun Wong, Feb. 14, 1958; children—Samuel K., Susanna L. B.S., U. Idaho, 1957; M.S., U. Wash., 1960; Ph.D., U. Tex., 1964. Research engr. Boeing Airplane Co., Renton, Wash., 1957-60; instr. U. Houston, 1960-61, asst. prof., 1964-66; instr. U. Tex., Austin, 1961-63; prof. elec. engring. Tulane U., New Orleans, from 1966, dir. electrosci. and biophysics research group, from 1969; pres., dir. Applied Research Corp., New Orleans, 1967-71, Sealong, Inc., New Orleans, 1971—. Contbr. sci. articles to profl. jours. Served with U.S. Army, 1953-55. NASA-Am. Soc. Engring. Edn. fellow, 1964, 65. Mem. IEEE, Profl. Group on Antenna Propagation (sect. chmn. from 1967), Sigma Xi, Tau Beta Pi, Eta Kappa Nu. Home: Metairie, LA.

SETTERBERG, CARL, artist; b. Las Animas, Colo., Aug. 16, 1897; s. Herman and Emma (Davidson) S. Student, Chgo. Acad. Fine Arts, 1917, Chgo. Art Inst., 1920-23, Grand Central Sch. Art, N.Y.C., 1939. Paintings exhibited, N.A.D., Am. Watercolor Soc., Audubon Artists, Allied Artists Am., Hudson Valley Artists, Knickerbocker Artists, Salmagundi Club, Nat. Arts Club, Swedish-Am. Club Chgo., Soc. Illustrators, Soc. Painters in Casein, Laguna Beach (Cal.) Art Assn., Birmingham (Ala.) Mus., Tweed Gallery, Duluth, Minn., Norton Gallery, West Palm Beach, Fla., Columbus (Ga.) Mus., Royal Watercolor Soc., London, also numerous travelling shows in U.S.; works represented in permanent exhbns. including, Air Force Acad., Colorado Springs, Columbus (Ga.) Mus., McChord AFB, Washington, DeBeers Collections, N.Y. Met. Mus., N.Y.C., also pvt. collections. (Recipient Adolph and Clara Obrig-prize N.A.D. 1956, Ranger purchase prize 1958; 1958, citation world-wide operational art program USAF 1956, medal Am. Artist mag. 1961, prize and medal Swedish-Am. Art Exbhn. 1959, Emily G. Clindinst prize Salmagundi Club 1951, Sterling Silver Medal award Nat. Arts Club 1972). Served as capt. AUS, 1942-43, 58. Mem. Am. Watercolor Soc. (Lena Newcastle Meml. award 1958, William Church Osborne award 1969, U.S.A. Watercolor award 1967), Nat. Acad. Design, Hudson Valley Art Assn. (Caroline Arcier prize 1953, Jane Peterson award 1970), Audubon Artists, Allied Artists Am. (1st prize 1966, Annonymous award 1970), Soc. Illustrators (life), N.A.D., Soc. Painters in Casein, Knickerbocker Artists.*

SETTLE, PEVERIL OZROE, lawyer; b. Stephenville, Tex., Feb. 14, 1889; s. Robert H. and Tennie A (Oxford) S.; student U. Tex., 1909-12, law sch., 1912-14; m. Helen M. Hetzler, Sept. 15, 1917; children—Peveril Ozroe, Jr., Robert Daniel. Admitted to Tex. bar, 1914; mem. Kennerly, Williams, Lee & Hill, and predecessor firm, Houston, 1917-26; asso. legal dept. Gulf Prodn. Co., Gulf Refining Co., Gulf Pipe Line Co., 1926-29; head legal dept. Gulf Oil Corp., Ft. Worth 1929-45. sec., asso. gen. counsel corp. and domestic subsidiaries, Pitts., 1945-55; became mem. firm Settle & Settle, Fort Worth, 1955, mem. Garrett, Settle & Callaway, Ft. Worth. Served with F.A., U.S. Army, 1918; capt. Res. Mem. Am., Ft. Worth bar assns., State Bar Tex. Clubs: Ft. Worth, River Crest Country (Fort Worth); Duquesne, University (Pitts.). Home: Ft. Worth, TX. †

SEULKE, KARL JOHN, animal husbandman; b. Seymour, Ind., Feb. 15, 1890; s. August H. and Marie J. (Heins) S.; B.S.A., Purdue, 1913; M.S., Pa. State Coll., 1914; Ph.D., Cornell, 1916; m. Mayme Dee Kahle, of Brazil, Ind., Aug. 24, 1913; children—Robert John (dec.), Donald Karl, Randall Louis. Instr. animal husbandry, 1914-16, asst. prof., 1916-19, prof., 1919-20, Cornell U.; extension rep. Am. Aberdeen-Angus Breeders' Assn., 1921, 22; pres., gen. mgr. Jefferson Farms, Inc., from 1922; spl. rep. Purina Mills, St. Louis, Mo., 1928. Mem. Am. Soc. Promotion of Agr., Alpha Gamma Rho, Theta Alpha, Hoof and Horn Club. Methodist. Mason. Author: The Curing of Meat and Meat Products on the Farm, 1915; The Beef Breeding Herd in New York State, 1918; Beef Breeding in New England. Home: Albany, N.Y. †

SEWARD, MERRITT ELMER, business exec.; b. Kansas City, Mo., July 29, 1888; s. John M. and Lyda (Hayes) S.; student pub. schs.; m. Helene Moriarty, July 5, 1924; 1 dau., Peggy Marie. With F. W. Woolworth Co., from 1908, store mgr., 1913-19, supt. 1920-24, mdse. mgr., 1924-33, gen. supervisor, restaurant operations from 1934, dir. from 1950. Served with U.S. Army, 1918-19. Mem. Nat. (dir.), N.Y. State (dir.) restaurant assns. Home: Larchmont, N.Y. †

SEWELL, FRANK ASA, banker; b. Lavonia, Ga., Apr. 18, 1889; s. John Russell Parker and Nobia (Chandler) S.; student Hargrove Coll., 1902-03, Hendrix Coll., 1906-07; H.H.D., Oklahoma City U., 1958; m. Leila Yates, May 17, 1910; children—Patience (Mrs. Trimble B. Latting), Frank A. Various positions First Nat. Bank, Texhoma, Okla., 1906-09, later asst. cashier, cashier, v.p., pres., 1920; organizer, pres. First Nat. Bank, Clinton, Okla., 1936-57, chmn. bd., from 1958; pres. Liberty Nat. Bank & Trust Co., Oklahoma City, 1942-55; chmn. bd. Liberty Nat. Bank, 1955-59, hon. chmn. bd., from 1959; dir. Citizens Nat. Bank. Trustee, Oklahoma City U. Mem., Oklahoma City C. of C. (past v.p.). Democrat. Methodist. Mason (33) Rotarian. Clubs: Oklahoma City Golf and Country, Petroleum (Okla. City), Men's Dinner. Home: Oklahoma City, OK. †

SEXAUER, ELMER H., business exec.; b. Winona, Minn., July 31, 1888; s. George Phillip and Elisa (Ulrich) S.; B.S., S.D. State Coll., 1910; distinguished Service in Business Award. U.S.D.; D.Sc. (honorary), S.D. State University, 1963; married Cecile Irene Welch, June 28, 1916; children—Dorothy Jean (Mrs. Hal Chase), Robert Sargeant. Entered grain business with father, firm of The Sexauer Co., Brookings, S.D., 1911, became secretary-treasurer, 1915, president, 1943-62, chmn. also engaged in livestock and grain farming operations. Served with military police, 1918. Past pres. Grain and Feed Dealers Nat. Assn., Am. Seed Trade Assn., Greater South Dakota Assn. Dir., vice pres. and chmn. agrl. com. U.S. Chamber of Commerce. Chmn. State Rep. delegation Nat. Conv., 1936. Mem. Minneapolis Grain Exchange. Mason (Shriner). Clubs: Minneapolis, Rotary. Home: Brookings, S.D. †

SEYDOUX, ROGER, govt. ofcl.; b. Paris, France, Mar. 28, 1908; s. Jacques and Mathilde (de Clausonne) S.; Free Sch. Polit. Scis., Paris; m. Jacqueline Doll, 1944; children—Eric, Pierre. Asst. to financial attache of French Embassy in London, 1931-32; asst. dir. to resident gen. of France in Morocco, 1934-35; sec.-gen., later dir. Sch. Polit. Scis., 1936-43; head cabinet of Mr. Leon Blum (Minister of Fgn. Affairs), months, 1946-47; counselor of Embassy in charge of Consulate Gen. of France in N.Y. City, since Nov. 1950; mem. exec. bd. UNESCO since Dec. 1948 (del. to gen. confs., 1945-50, asst. sec.-gen. French del., 1945-49); sec. French del., Montreaux Conf., 1935; asst. sec.-gen. United Nations Conf., San Francisco, 1945. Clubs: Cercle de L'Union (Paris); Knickerbocker (N.Y. City). Home: New York, N.Y. Died July 3, 1985.

SEYMOUR, DAN, advertising agency executive; b. N.Y.C., June 28, 1914; A.B., Amherst Coll., 1935; m. Louise Scharff, Apr. 6, 1935; children—Nancy Louise (Mrs. Robert Morgan), Judith Ann (Mrs. John W. Fowler), Stephen Dana, Kathie Joan (Mrs. Eric Stevens). Radio-TV announcer, emcee and producer, 1935-53; v.p. radio-TV dir. Young & Rebicam, 1945-55; v.p., radio-TV dir. J. Walter Thompson Co., N.Y.C., 1955-63, sr. v.p., 1961-63, pres., chief exec. officer, 1963-72, chmn. bd. chief exec. officer from 1972, then chmn. exec. com. Mem. nat. task force Pres.'s Council on Youth Opportunity; nat. communications coordinator summer youth programs Pres.'s Council on Youth Opportunity; mem. Ad Hoc Adv. Group on Presdl. Vote for P.R.; mem. Eisenhower Exchange Fellowships' Finance Com., 1968. Pres.'s Com. on Health Edn., 1972, Pub. Adv. Com. on Trade Policy, 1968; mem. steering com. N.Y. Urban Coalition Jobs. Bd. dirs. United Fund Greater N.Y., UN Internat. Sch., Gen. Leisure, Inc., Istel Fund; bd. dirs. mem. exec. com. Boys Clubs Am.; mem. exec. com., trustee Council of Americas. Mem. Am. Assn. Advt. Agys. (mem. operations com., dir.-at-large). Internat. Radio and TV Soc. Address: New York, N.Y.

SEYMOUR, EDWARD PALMER, publishing executive; b. N.Y.C., June 18, 1888; s. James Sherwood and Martha Steever (Palmer) S.; B.A., Yale, 1910; m. Alice Barhyt Hovey, Sept. 25, 1915; children—Edward H., Hovey, Roger S. With Crowall-Collier Pub. Co., N.Y.C., from 1910; gen. advt. sales mgr., v.p., dir., from 1950. Treas., dir. Advt. Research Found. Pres. bd. trustees Greenwich (Conn.) Pub. Library. Clubs: University (N.Y.C. and Chgo.); Field, Indian Harbor Yacht (Greenwich). Home: Greenwich, Conn. †

SEYMOUR, FORREST W., former editor; b. Arlington, S.D., July 10, 1905; s. Arthur Hallock and Floral Margaret (Wilson) S.; A.B., Drake U., 1928, L.L.D., 1952; Litt.D., Parsons Coll., 1947, Grinnell Coll., 1949; m. Pearl Bernice Yeager, Nov. 9, 1927; children—Arthur Hallock, Peter Butler, Susanna Lee, Constance Brinn. Reporter, Des Moines Tribune, 1923; copyreader, telegraph editor, asst. city editor Des Moines Register, 1924-27; state editor Des Moines Register & Tribune, 1927-29, editorial writer, 1929-43, asso. editor, 1943-46, editor editorial pages, 1946-53; asso. editor Worcester Telegram & Gazette, 1953-55, editor, 1955-70. Bd. mgrs. Am. Variable Annuity Life Assurance Co., Worcester, Mass. Pres. Cape Cod (Mass.) Symphony Orch. Assn., 1974-76. Recipient Stephen A. Chadwick Editorial Appreciation award Am. Legion, 1942; Pulitzer prize for distinguished editorial writing, 1942. Mem. Am. Antiquarian Soc., Phi Beta Kappa. Sigma Delta Chi. Home: South Dennis, Mass. Died Oct. 3, 1983.

SEYMOUR, JAMES OWENS, lawyer; b. Columbus, Ohio, Aug. 23, 1904; s. Augustus T. and Evelyn (Owens) S.; A.B., Princeton, 1926; LL.B., Harvard, 1929; m. Jane H. Farrar, Mar. 30, 1940; 1 dau., Antoinette F. Admitted to Ohio bar, 1929, practiced in Columbus; mem. firm Vorys, Sater, Seymour & Pease, from 1936; dir. Credit Life Ins. Co., Springfield. Mem. Am., Ohio, Columbus bar assns. Home: Columbus, Ohio. Deceased.

SEYMOUR, WHITNEY NORTH, JR., lawyer; b. Huntington, W.Va., July 7, 1923; s. Whitney North and Lola (Vickers) S.; m. Catryna Ten Eyck, Nov. 16, 1951; children—Tryntje, Gabriel. A.B. magna cum laude, Princeton, 1947; LL.B., Yale, 1950; LL.D. (hon.), N.Y. Law Sch., 1972. Bar: N.Y. bar 1950. Assoc. firm Simpson Thacher & Bartlett, N.Y.C., 1950-53, 56-59, partner, 1961-70, 73-83, asst. U.S. atty., 1953-56; chief counsel N.Y. State Commn. Govtl. Operations, N.Y.C., 1959-60, Spl. Unit N.Y. State Commn. Investigation, 1960-61; mem. N.Y. Senate, 1966-68; U.S. atty. So. Dist. N.Y., 1970-73; Chmn. legal adv. com. Pres.'s Council on Environmental Quality, 1970-73; v.p. Art Commn., N.Y.C., 1975-77; pres. Municipal Art Soc., 1965, Park Assn. N.Y., 1962-64. Author: The Young Die Quietly: The Narcotics Problem in America, 1972, Why Justice Fails, 1973, United States Attorney, 1975, For the People: Fighting for Public Libraries, 1979; Editor: Small Urban Spaces, 1969; contbr.: articles to Redbook; legal periodicals, others. Past bd. dirs. N.Y. Pub. Library; bd. dirs. Natural Resources Def. Council, Council for Pub. Interest Law, South St. Seaport Mus., Com. for Modern Cts., Urban Libraries Council; past bd. dirs. N.Y. Bot. Garden, Citizens Housing and Planning Council, Citizens for Clean Air, Boys Brotherhood Republic, Edward MacDowell Assn.; organizer, sec. Nat. Citizens Emergency Com. to Save Our Pub. Libraries, 1976-80; sec. Nat. citizens for Public Libraries, 1980-83; chmn. exec. com. Citizens Action on Crime, 1980—. Served from pvt. to capt. AUS, 1943-46. Recipient Thelma K. Moore award N.Y. Pub. Library, 1977; Environ. Award Natural Resources Def. Council, 1972. Fellow Am. Bar Found.; mem. N.Y. State Bar Assn. (pres. 1974-75, ho. of dels.), ABA (chmn. centennial com. 1972-75), Am. Coll. Trial Lawyers, Am. Judicature Soc. (dir. 1973-76), Fed. Bar Council (Emory Buchner award 1977, pres. 1980-83), Assn. Bar City N.Y. (exec. com. 1960-64, chmn. spl. com. on criminal justice 1976-80), N.Y. County Lawyers Assn. (dir. 1968-71), N.Y. Bar Found. (v.p., dir.), Authors Guild. Republican. Episcopalian. Clubs: India House (N.Y.C.), Century (N.Y.C.), Players (N.Y.C.). Home: New York, N.Y. Died May 21, 1983.

SHADLE, CHARLES STRICKLEN, army officer; b. Altoona, Pa., Nov. 1, 1888; s. I. Thomas and Ina A. (Fenton) S.; student U.S. Army Inf. Sch., Chemical Warfare Sch., Indsl. Coll.; m. Martha Grace McCall, Sept. 23, 1920; children—Charles M., Robert F. Entered U.S. Army as pvt., 1917, and advanced through the grades to brig. gen., 1944; chief chem. officer A.F. Hdqrs., England, France, Italy, 1942-45; comdg. gen. Rocky Mt. Arsenal, 1946-47; Decorated: D.S.C., Legion of Merit, Commendation Ribbon; Comdr. Brit. Empire (England); Grand Officer Order Italy; Croix de Guerre (France). Address: Denver. †

SHAILER, FRANK ALTON, insurance exec.; b. Haddam, Conn., Mar. 18, 1888; s. Rollo Leroy and Hancy (Hills) S.; B.A., Wesleyan U., Middletown, Conn., 1909; m. Elizabeth Katherine Gannon, Nov. 11, 1913. Actuarial dept. Travelers Ins. Co., Hartford, Conn. and Met. Life Ins. Co., N.Y. City, 1909-12; mng. dir. and actuary Insular Life Assurance Co., Manila, P.I., 1912-17; asst. actuary Lincoln Nat. Life Ins. Co., Ft. Wayne, Ind., 1917-20; actuarial dept. Equitable Life Assurance Soc. of U.S., N.Y. City, 1920-29, asst. actuary, 1929-33, auditor, 1933-35, vice president, 1935-50, executive vice president, 1950-52. Fellow Soc. Actuaries; mem. Phi Beta Kappa, Delta Tau Delta. Republican. Home: New York, N.Y. †

SHANDS, HARLEY CECIL, psychiatrist; b. Jackson, Miss., Sept. 10, 1916; s. Harley Roseborough and Bessie Webb (Nugent) S.; m. Janet Hoffman, Mar. 25, 1943; children—Kathryn, Betsy, Paul. B.S., Tulane U., 1936, M.D., 1939; M.S. in Medicine, U. Minn., 1945. Fellow medicine Mayo Clinic, 1941-45; research fellow psychiatry Mass. Gen. Hosp., Boston, 1945-48; asso. prof. psychiatry U. N.C. Med. Sch., 1953-61; prof. State U. N.Y. Med. Sch., Bklyn., 1961-66; dir. psychiatry St. Luke's-Roosevelt Hosp. Center, N.Y.C., from 1980; clin. prof. psychiatry Columbia Coll. Phys. and Surg., from 1966; impartial specialist Workmen's Compensation Bd. N.Y. State. Author: Thinking & Psychotherapy, 1960, Semiotic Approaches to Psychiatry, 1970, The War with Words, 1971, Language and Psychiatry, 1973, Speech as Instruction, 1977. Commonwealth Fund fellow London, 1958-59. Fellow Am. Psychiat. Assn.; mem. Group Advancement Psychiatry (pres.-elect), Semiotic Soc. Am. Club: Cosmos (Washington). Home: New York, NY.

SHANDS, WILLIAM AUGUSTINE, advt. exec.; b. Bronson, Fla., July 21, 1889; s. Thomas Walter and Coris Annie (Parker) S.; LL.D. (hon.) U. Fla., 1960; m. Catherine London Hawkins, June 12, 1912; 1 dau., Elizabeth (Mrs. Sam T. Dell, Jr.). Became v.p. Shands & Baker, Inc., Jacksonville, Fla., 1935, now chmn. bd.; (Fla. Rock Products, Inc., Brooksville, All Fla. Sand Co., Inc., Jacksonville, Consolidated into Shands & Baker, Inc.); advisor Fla. Power & Light Co., Inc. Mem. nat. council Episcopalian Ch., 1952-58. Mem. Fla. Senate, 1940-58, pres. Senate, 1957-58. Democrat. Home: Gainesville, FL. †

SHANE, CHARLES DONALD, astronomer; b. Auburn, Calif., Sept. 6, 1895; s. Charles Nelson and Annette (Futhey) S.; A.B., U. Calif., 1915, Lick Obs. fellow, 1916-17, 19-20, Ph.D., 1920, LL.D., 1965; m. Ethel L. Haskett, Dec. 24, 1917 (dec. Jan. 1919); 1 son, Charles Nelson; m. 2d, Mary Lea Heger, Dec. 29, 1920; 1 son, William Whitney. Instr. nav. U.S. Shipping Bd. 1917-19; instr. math., astronomy U. Calif., 1920-24, asst. prof. astronomy, 1924-29, asso. prof., 1929-35, prof., 1935-45, chmn. astronomy dept., Berkeley, 1941-42, asst. dir. Radiation Lab., Manhattan Project, 1942-44, asst. dir. in charge personnel Los Alamos Lab., 1944-45, dir. Lick Obs., 1945-58, astronomer, 1958-63. Pres., Assn. Univs. for Research in Astronomy, 1958-62; chmn. U.S. nat. com. for astronomy Internat. Astron. Union, 1966-68. Mem. Astron. Soc. Pacific (pres. 1940), Am. Philos. Soc., Nat. Acad. Scis., Royal Astron. Soc. (asso.), Sigma Xi, Phi Beta Kappa. Republican. Club: Faculty (Berkeley). Contbr. papers to profl. lit. Home: Santa Cruz, Calif.

SHANK, WILLIAM CAPEN, coal exec.; b. St. Louis, Mar. 1, 1889; s. William Daniel and Mary Alexander (Degnan) S.; student Cornell, 1907-09, U. of Kan., 1909-10; Ph.B., Yale, 1911; m. Mariee Stephens, June 3, 1916. With Crowe Coal Co., Kansas City, Mo., from 1911, mem. engring. dept., 1911-13, pres., general manager and director, 1935-55; consultant Peabody Coal Company, from 1955, director First National Bank Kansas City, Inter-State Cattle Loan & Oil Co., Stauffer Publs., Inc., Hotel President, Inc., Wabash R.R. Co. (mem. exec. com.), Ann Arbor R.R. Co. (mem. exec. com.), N.J., Ind. & Ill. R.R. Co. Mem. adv. bd. Salvation Army Trustee St. Luke's Hosp., Kansas City Art Inst. Mem. Consol. Underwriters (mem. adv. com.). Rep. Episcopalian (vestryman). Clubs: Kansas City, Kansas City Country, River, University (Kansas City); Chicago (Chicago); Racquet (St. Louis); Yale (N.Y. City). Home: Kansas City. †

SHANKLAND, ROBERT SHERWOOD, physicist; b. Willoughby, Ohio, Jan. 11, 1908; s. Frank North and Margaret Jane (Wedlock) S.; m. Hilda C. Kinnison, June 20, 1931 (dec. 1970); children—Ruth (Mrs. William Fielder), Dorothy (Mrs. John Eisenhour), Ava (Mrs. Thomas Prebys), Lois (Mrs. Ronald McIntyre), Sherwood John; m. Eleanor Newlin Griffiths, 1971. B.S., Case Inst. Tech., 1929, M.S., 1933; Ph.D., U. Chgo., 1935. Physicist Nat. Bur. Standards, Washington, 1929-30; faculty physics dept. Case Inst. Tech., 1930; on leave at U. Chgo., 1934-36, Ambrose Swasey prof. physics, 1941-82, head physics dept., 1939-58; on leave to Columbia, 1942-45; Physicist Naval Ordnance Lab., Washington, 1941; dir. Unnderwater Sound Reference, Labs. OSRD, N.Y.C., 1942-46; physics cons. Standard Oil Co., Ohio, 1947-82; physicist Radiation Lab., U. Calif., summers 1946, 49, AEC Materials Testing Reactor, Ida., summers 1955-58, 61-69; cons. Philips Petroleum Co., 1957-82; cons. in archtl. acoustics. Chmn. hydrophone adv. com. USN, 1942-46; Mem. council of participating instns. Argonne Nat. Lab., 1946-82, mem. exec. council, 1951-54. Author: Atomic and Nuclear Physics, 1955, 60; Editor: Sonar Calibration Methods, 1946, Sonar Calibrations, 1946, Collected Papers of Arthur H. Compton, 1973; Asso. editor: Review of Scientific Instruments, 1949-52, Am. Jour. Physics; Contbr. articles to sci. publs. Pres. bd. trustees Andrews Sch. for Girls, Willoughby, Ohio; bd. dirs. Asso. Midwest Univs., 1958-82, past v.p., pres., 1960-61. Recipient Presdl. certificate of Merit, 1948. Fellow Am. Phys. Soc. (pres. Ohio sect. 1947-48), Acoustical Soc. Am. (exec. council 1944-47), A.A.A.S.; mem. Am. Inst. Physics (chmn. com. on student orgn. 1958-82, mem. governing bd. 1966-69), Am. Standards Assn. (chmn. underwater sound com. 1946-49), Optical Soc. Am., Franklin Inst., Clev. Physics Soc. (pres. 1948-49), Am. Assn. Physics Tchrs. (exec. council 1963-66), Sigma Xi, Sigma Pi Sigma, Tau Beta Pi, Theta Tau, Sigma Alpha Epsilon. Home: Cleveland, Ohio. Died Mar. 5, 1982.

SHANNON, PHILIP FRANCIS, business exec.; b. Lexington, Ky., Nov. 12, 1887; s. Martin and Elizabeth (Maguire) S.; B.S. in C.E., Univ. of Ky., 1907; m. Janet Menzies, Dec. 8, 1917; children—Philip Francis, Janet M., James M. Railroad engr., M.P. R.R., 4 yrs.; refinery constrn., Indian Refining Co., 2 yrs.; petroleum prodn. engr. and field supt., Continental Oil Co., 6 yrs.; head petroleum engring. dept. Colo. Sch. of Mines, 1924-28; with Tropical Oil Co., Colombia, S.A., 1928-44, mgr. prodn. operations, 1933-44; pres. Royalite Oil Co., Can., 1944-46; mgr. producing operations in western Can., Imperial Oil, Ltd., 1944-46; exec. asst. producing dept. Standard Oil Co., N.J., from April 1946. Served with 307th Engrs., 82d Div., A.E.F., U.S. Army during World War I. Mem. Am. Inst. of Mining and Metall. Engrs., Colombian Petroleum Inst. Democrat. Roman Catholic. †

SHAPLEIGH, A. WESSEL, business exec.; b. St. Louis, Mo., August 22, 1890; s. Alfred Lee and Mina (Wessel) S.; A.B., Yale, 1911; m. Lois McKinney, Apr. 21, 1917; children—A. Wessel, Alfred Lee, Warren McKinney, Mary Suzanne. With Merchants Laclede Bank, St. Louis, 1911-12; with George H. Burr & Co., commercial paper brokers and bankers, St. Louis, 1912-13; with Shapleigh Hdw. Co., St. Louis, 1913-56, pres., 1942-48, chmn., 1948-56; chairman Mound City Paint & Color Company to 1956; president of Longblock Realty Company, to 1956; trustee of the Shapleigh Investment Company; sec., treas. Washington Land & Mining Co.; dir. Boatmans Nat. Bank of St. Louis, Laclede Gas Light Co., Ann Arbor R.R. Co. (exec. com.), Wabash R.R. Co. (mem. finance com.), Mo. Portland Cement Co., New Jersey, Illinois & Indiana Railroad, Scruggs-Vandervoort-Barney Dry Goods Co.; former dir. Fed. Res. Bank of St. Louis. Trustee, Bellefontaine Cemetery Assn., Govtl. Research Inst., Jefferson Nat. Expansion Meml. Assn., Fordyce Lane Assn. (treas.), Mo. Botanical Garden. Mem. corp. Wash. U., St. Louis; former trustee, St. Louis Country Day Sch.; pres. St. Louis Light Arty. Armory Assn. Mem. Appellate Commn. of Mo., 1941-46. Mem. St. Louis and St. Louis Co. Cs. of C., Soc. Colonial Wars State of Mo., S.R., New England Historic Geneal. Soc., Newcomen Soc., Nat. Hardware Assn., Yale U. Alumni Assn. Republican. Presbyterian. Clubs: St. Louis Country, Noonday, Stack. Home: Clayton, Mo. †

SHAPLEY, JOHN, educator, author; b. near Jasper, Mo., Aug. 7, 1890; s. Willis Harlow and Sarah (Stowell) S.; A.B., U. of Mo., 1912; fellow, Princeton, 1912-13, A.M., 1913, Procter fellow, 1914-15; fellow Am. Acad. at Rome, 1913-14; Ph.D., U. of Vienna, 1914; m. Fern Helen Rusk, Sept. 19, 1981; children—Dora, Ellen. Instr. in art Brown U., 1915-19, asst. prof., 1919-24; asso. prof., Washington Square Coll., New York U., 1924-26, prof., New York U., 1926-29, U. of Chicago, 1929-39, Sch. for Asiatic Studies from 1939; visiting prof. U. of Chicago, 1920, Harvard, 1921, U. of Mo., 1927, London, 1933-35, Johns Hopkins, 1939-42; prof. art and archaeology Catholic U. from 1952. Trustee Bur. University Travel. Member College Art Association, Byzanthine Inst., Asia Inst. (dir. studies, from 1953), Archaeol. Inst. Am., Am. Association Museums, Phi Beta Kappa. Translator: Form Problems of the Gothic, 1918. Contbr. to Ency. Britannica, Dictionary of Religion Co-author: Comparisons in Art, published 1957. and Ethics, Am. Jour. Archaeology, etc.†

SHARP, DALE E(LBERT), banker; b. Topeka, Kan., Oct. 3, 1903; s. Elbert Clay and Anna (Ballagh) S.; A.B., Washburn Coll., 1924; M.B.A., New York Univ., 1928; m. Elizabeth McLellan Estes, Nov. 22, 1941; children—Nancy Jane, Cornella Dale. Credit department, National Bank of Commerce, N.Y. City, 1924-28; buying dept., John Nickerson & Co., 1928-30; instr. econ., Bucknell U., 1930-31. Finance, N.Y. Univ., 1928-30; vice pres. Guaranty Trust Co. of New York 1931-57, pres., from 1957; dir. Standard Accident Ins. Co., Planet Ins. Co. Trustee and treas. Spence Sch., Inc., N.Y. City, from 1943; trustee Turtle Bay Music Sch. since 1949. Mem. Commerce and Industry Assn., Academy Political Sci., N.Y. Democrat. Presbyterian. Clubs: River, Skating (N.Y. City); Seawanhaka Corinthian Yacht (Oyster Bay, N.Y.); The Detroit; Attic (Chicago). Mem. Kappa Sigma. Home: New York, N.Y. Died Sept. 6, 1984.

SHARP, EDWARD PRESTON, criminologist, educator, lectr.; b. Avalon, Pitts., June 28, 1904; s. Archie Kerr and Agnes (Preston) S.; A.B., Geneva Coll, Beaver Falls, Pa., 1926, L.H.D., 1966; A.M., U. Pitts., 1930, Ph.D., 1933; m. Catharine Irene Simons, Aug. 14, 1931; children—Katharine Williams, Judith Cawthorne Sharp Nadeau. Supervising prin. Hickory Twp. (Pa.) Schs., 1926-28, Blawnox (Pa.) Schs., 1928-30, Westmont Upper Yoder Schs., Johnstown, Pa., 1930-34; supr. rehab. Eastern State Penitentiary, Phila., 1934-42; supt. Pa. Tng. Schs., Morganza, 1942-45; dir. Bur. Community Work, Pa. Dept. Welfare, Harrisburg, 1945-48; chief div. tng. schs. Md. Dept. Pub. Welfare, Balt., 1948, 1952; dir. Md. Commn. for Youth, 1950-52; exec. dir. Youth Study Center, Phila., 1952-65; lectr. psychology, sociology U. Balt., 1950-52; lectr. Temple U., Phila., exec. dir. Am. Correctional Assn., 1965-74; prof. Va. Commonwealth U., Richmond, 1974-77; cons. Va. Dept. Corrections, from 1974, Ariz. Dept. Corrections, 1977, Fla. Dept. Offender Rehab., from 1977; chmn. Adv. Com. on Naval Corrections, 1970-71; mem. spl. civilian com. Study U.S. Army Confinement System, 1969; sec., treas. Joint Commn. Correctional Manpower and Tng., 1966-70; mem. task force on correction Md. Gov.'s Commn. on Law Enforcement and Adminstrn. Justice, 1968; mem. Adv. Com. Fed. Probation, from 1965; cons. U.S. Bur. Prisons, from 1965; nat. corr. to UN in field social def., 1965-74; mem. nat. follow up com. Midcentury White House Conf. on Children and Youth, 1951; mem. exec. bd. Nat. council Boy Scouts Am.; adv. bd. Inst. Criminal Justice and Criminology, U. Md., from 1972. Recipient Pa. Prison Soc. award; August Vollmer award Am. Soc. Criminology, 1973; E.R. Case award Am. Correctional Assn., 1974; Others award Salvation Army, 1974; Distinguished Pub. Service award Dept. Navy, 1974. Mem. Am. Correctional Assn. (pres. 1956), Am. Jail Assn., Acad. Assn. Social Workers, Nat. Conf. Juvenile Agys. and Tng. Schs. (past pres.), Am. Soc. Criminology, Nat. Conf. Social Work, Nat. Conf. Crime and Delinquency, Phi Delta Kappa, Lambda Chi Alpha. Presbyterian (moderator Phila. presbytery 1963, 64). Club: Rotary. Mem. editorial com. U.S. atty. gen's Study of Release Procedures, 1939; asso. editor Am. Jour. Correction, 1965—. Home: Cape Coral, Fla. Died Apr. 15, 1982; buried Philadelphia, Pa.

SHARP, HAROLD HARRIS, business exec.; b. Newton, Mass., Oct. 11, 1888; s. Arthur Page and May Louise (Harris) S.; B.A., Boston U., 1909; B.S., Mass. Inst. Tech., 1912; m. Rose Mary Jenkins, Jan. 15, 1915; children—Barbara, Lucille, Pamela, Thomas. In mining dept. of Mexican subsidiaries of A.S.&R. Co., 10 yrs., supt. Veta Grande Unit, same; asst. gen. mgr. El Potosi Mining Co., Chihuahua, Mex., 1929-36; v.p. Howe Sound Co., N.Y. City, 1936-43, pres. from 1943, also dir. and mem. exec. com. Mem. Theta Delta Chi. Republican. Clubs: Winged Foot Golf (Mamaroneck, N.Y.); Vancouver (Vancouver, B.C.). Home: Larchmont, N.Y. †

SHARP, LESTER WHYLAND, prof. botany; b. Saratoga Springs, N.Y., Apr. 21, 1887; s. Lester Allen and Emma (Whyland) S.; prep. edn., high sch., Alma, Mich.; B.S., Alma Coll., 1908; studied Johns Hopkins, 1908-10; Ph.D., U. of Chicago, 1912; studied U. of Louvain, 1912-13; D.Sc., Alma (Mich.) Coll., 1930; U. of Louvain, 1947; m. Mabel Gunther, Dec. 28, 1915; 1 son, Lester Gunther. Instr. in botany, Cornell U., 1914, asst. prof., 1915-17, prof., 1917-47, emeritus from 1947. Mem. A.A.A.S., Bot. Soc. Am. (pres. 1930), Am. Soc. Naturalists, Gamma Alpha, Phi Beta Kappa, Phi Kappa Phi. Author: An Introduction to Cytology, 1921; Fundamentals of Cytology, 1943; also tech. papers on cytology and morphology. Home: Nueoo, Calif. †

SHARP, MORRIS LOUIS, psychiatrist; b. St. Louis, Aug. 2, 1908; s. Henry and Rebecca (Boxerman) S.; M.D., Tufts U., 1932; m. Ida Reiser, Aug. 12, 1945; 1 dau., Harriet R. Rotating intern St. Mary's Hosp., East St. Louis, Ill, 1932-33; resident contagious diseases Belleville (N.J.) Hosp., 1933; mem. staff Foxboro (Mass.) State Hosp., 1934-52, asst. supt., dir. psychiatry, 1946-52; asst. to commr. Mass. Dept. Mental Health, 1952-53; supt. Westboro (Mass.) State Hosp., 1953-72, also hosp. area program dir.; pvt. practice psychiatry East Falmouth, Mass., 1972-79, Served to maj. M.C., AUS, 1942-46; MTO. Recipient Cutting Gold award for medicine and religion, 1972. Diplomate Am. Bd. Psychiatry and Neurology. Life fellow Am. Psychiat. Assn.; mem. New Eng. Soc. Psychiatry (life), A.M.A., Mass., Barnstable County, med. socs. Contbr. articles to profl. jours. Died Nov. 8, 1982.

SHARPE, DORES ROBINSON, ch. ofcl.; b. Pembroke, N.B., Can., Jan. 23, 1886; s. Charles Frederick and Frances (Robinson) S.; m. Harriet Maude Holdsworth, Sept. 8, 1914 (dec. 1917); children—Margaret Louise, Roger Holdsworth and Harriett Frances (twins); m. Ruth Leila Mitchell, Feb. 25, 1920 (dec. 1972). A.B., U. N.B., 1908, A.M., 1910, LL.D., 1943; B.D. (scholar, fellow), Rochester Theol. Sem., 1911; postgrad., U. Chgo., 1911-12; D.D., Hillsdale (Mich.) Coll., 1930; LL.D., Ark. Bapt. Coll., 1931; L.H.D., Wilberforce U., 1951. Ordained to Bapt. ministry, 1908, pastor in, Edmonton and Calgary, Alta., also, Moose Jaw, Sask.; gen. sec. Sunday Sch. Assn. Sask., 1917-19; dir. Forward Movement for Protestant chs. in Sask., 1919; gen. supt. Bapt. chs. in, Sask., 1917-25; exec. sec. Cleve. Bapt. Assn., 1925-53, exec. sec. emeritus, 1953—; Rauschenbusch lectr. Colgate-Rochester Sem., 1946; cons. Grad. Theol. Union, Berkeley, Calif.; Lectr., writer, dir. instnl. finance, organizer. Author: book Rise and Place of American City, 1959, Call to Christian Action: The Triumph of Religious Liberty, Of One Blood, The Golden Fountain; also other pageants Biography of Walter Rauschenbush. Former mem. Council of Finance and Promotion and Council of World Evangelization, No. Bapt. Conv.; past chmn. Com. on City Missions, Com. on Ch. and City of Ch. Fedn., Com. on Pub. Edn. and Service; mem. speakers bur. Community Chest; founder, dir. Cleve. Sunday Evening Hour; founder ann. Theol. Conf. Roger Williams Fellowship and Div. Sch. U. Chgo., also Dores Robinson Sharpe lectureship.; Past mem. Calif. Democratic State Central Com.; Dem. candidate Assembly, 47th dist., Calif.; mem. exec. com. Los Angeles County Dem. Central Com.; foreman Grand Jury Cuyahoga, Cleve., which uncovered corruption in mental hosps.; Former dir. Bapt. Home No. Ohio., Northwestern Bapt. Hosp. Assns.; trustee Grad. Theol. Union; trustee emeritus Colgate-Rochester Div. Sch.; past trustee Rio Grande Coll.; past vice chmn. Cleve. Community Relations Commn.; hon. pres. Consumers League of Ohio; founder, past pres. Ohio Mental Hygiene Assn.; exec. com. Community Relations Bd., N.A.A.C.P.; former chmn. State Hosps. Betterment Com; founder, pres. Ch. Civic League; chmn. Interaward, Nat. Com. Mental Hygiene, 1946; v.p. Rauschenbusch Fellowship; past chmn. com. Internat. Justice and Peace, Pasadena Council Chs. Recipient Albert Lasker award). Mem. Pi Gamma Mu. Clubs: Mason. (Can.), Professional (Can.), Alpine (Can.). Home: Pasadena CA

SHARPLES, PHILIP T., industrialist; b. West Chester, Pa., Aug. 12, 1889; s. Philip M. and Helen Edwards (Brinton) S.; A.B., Swarthmore Coll., 1910; m. Edith W. Walz, June 16, 1917; children—Philip Price, Wynne. Organized Sharples Corporation, 1915; president 1915-48, chairman bd., 1948-62; pres. Sharples Oil Co., 1946-53, chmn. bd., 1953-64; member board of dirs. Lehigh Valley Railroad Company. Vice chairman of the board Swarthmore College; president bd. Good Samaritan Hosp. (Palm Beach, Florida); regional executive committee of Boy Scouts of America. Mem. bd. trustees Eisenhower Exchange Fellowships. Mem. Sigma Xi. Home: Haverford, Pa. †

SHAVITCH, VLADIMIR, symphony conductor; b. Russia, July 20, 1888; s. Morris and Olga (Urman) S.; brought by parents to U.S., 1890; ed. pub. schs.; studied piano in Berlin under Leopold Godowsky and Ferruccio Busoni, composition under Hugo Kaun and Paul Yuon, 1902-12; m. Tina Lerner, Nov. 19, 1915; 1 dau., Dollina Francisca. Guest conductor various orchestras, among them the Berlin Philharmonic Orchestra, the Dresden Philharmonic, Paris Conservatoire, Montevideo Symphony Orchestra, etc. Apptd. condr. Syracuse Symphony Orchestra, 1925; condr. in chief Moscow State Opera from Mar. 1930; served as guest conductor London Symphony, Madrid Philharmonic, Moscow Philharmonic. Condr. Beethoven Festival, with chorus of 400, Syracuse U., 1927. Home: Syracuse, N.Y. †

SHAW, ALFRED O., educator; b. Camas, Utah, Aug. 9, 1907; s. Charles Holbrook and Emma (Obray) S.; B.S., U. of Ida., 1932, M.S., 1932; Ph.D., Pa. State, 1935; m. Thirza Althear Ottley, Aug. 28, 1929; children—Ottley Ann, Aletta. Instr. dairy husbandry, U. of Ida., 1935-39; asso. prof. dairy husbandry, Kan. State Coll., 1939-41; head dept. animal industry, N.C. State Coll., 1941-43; supt. Cable Dairy Products, Lexington, N.C., 1943-44; head dept. animal industry, U. of Me., 1944-47; became chmn. dept. dairy husbandry State Univ. of Wash., 1947-56, chairman department of dairy sci., 1947-54, 57-60; chief of ednl. party Foreign Operations Administration-State College of Washington mission to University Punjab and its affiliated colleges, 1954-56. Ofcl. U.S. del. Internat. Dairy Congress, Rome, 1956. Mem. American Dairy Scientific Association, Animal Science Assn., Wash. Purebred Dairy Cattle Association, Sigma Xi, Alpha Zeta, Phi Kappa Phi, Gamma Sigma Delta, Pi Kappa Alpha, Rho Epsilon, Lambda Rho Epsilon (charter mem.). Contbr. articles on dairy cattle, nutrition and biochemistry to publs. Home: Pullman, Wash. Died May 17, 1984.

SHAW, BRUNO, writer; b. N.Y.C., Mar. 17, 1905; s. David and Regina (Altman) S.; m. Regina Hyman, Oct. 13, 1928; (dec.); children—Anthony, Judith. Editor, Hankow (China) Herald, 1923-31; A.P. corr., China, 1925-29; asso. editor China Weekly Rev., 1924-27; gen. mgr. Trans-Pacific News Service, 1937-41; nat. dir. Am. Bur. for Med. Aid to China, exec. Far Eastern div. OWI 1942-43; radio commentaror WJZ, WQXR, 1943-44; writer, producer newsreel commentary films Embassy Theatres, 1944-45; radio commentator WNEW, 1944-54. Decorated Order of Jade (China); recipient Am. Freedoms Found. award, 1952. Elk. Clubs: Shanghai Tiffin; Overseas Press of America (v.p. club, pres. Corrs. Fund), Advertising (N.Y.C.). Editor, annotator Mao Tse-Tung's Selected Works, 1970; Selected Works of Mao Tse-tung Abridged, 1972; Illusion and Delusion About the Middle Kingdom, 1973. Contbr. to articles, mags., newspapers. Home: New York, N.Y. Died Oct. 2, 1984.

SHAW, WALTER RUSSELL, premier Prince Edward Island; b. St. Catherines, P.E.I., Dec. 20, 1888; s. Alexander Crawford and Isabell (Maynard) S.; student Prince of Wales Coll.; B.Sc., Truro Agr. Coll.; student U. Toronto, m. Margaret MacKenzie, June 1, 1921; children—Norma Catherine, Margaret Eileen, Walter Maynard. Agrl. rep. P.E.I. Govt., 1916-34, deputy minister of agriculture, 1934-59, premier, from 1959. Leader Conservative Party, from 1958. Rep. Atlantic provinces Internat. Farmers Fedn. in Europe, 1950. Served with 9th Siege Battery, Canadian Army, World War I. Decorated Order of the British Empire. Member P.E.I. Federation Agr. and Agrl. Council, Agrl. Sci. Soc. (pres.), Can. Hort. Council (pres.). Mem. United Ch. of Can. Mason. Home: St. Catherines, Prince Edward Island, Can. †

SHAW, WARREN CHOATE, coll. prof.; b. Lowell, Mass., Nov. 16, 1887; s. Ralph Henry and Mary Abbie (Choate) S.; A.B., Dartmouth, 1910, A.M., 1916; Ph.D. in history, U. of Ill., 1938; m. Helen Abbott Morey, June 23, 1913 (dec. 1930); 1 s., Roger Morey; m. 2d Nonna Dolodarenko, 1950. Instr. history and English, Lowell High Sch., 1910-11, instr. pub. speaking, 1911-14, asst. prof., 1914-20, Dartmouth; prof. of public speaking, Knox Coll., 1920-33; hist. research; part-time instr. in history, U. of Ill., 1936-38; prof. of history. Blackburn Coll. from 1939; spl. lectr. in history, U. of Munich, summer 1948. Mem. Am. Hist. Assn., Miss. Valley Hist. Assn., Ill. State Hist. Soc. Am. Legion, Delta Sigma Rho, Phi Kappa Phi, Kappa Kappa Kappa. Tau Kappa Epsilon, Rotary (Carlinville). Author: The Brief-Maker's Note Book, 1916; The Art of Debate, 1922; History of American Oratory, 1928. Home: Carlinville, IL. †

SHEAHAN, HENRY B(ESTON), author; b. Quincy, Mass., June 1, 1888; s. Joseph Maurice and Marie Louise (Maurice) S.; B.A., Harvard, 1909, M.A., 1911; studied U. of Lyons, France, 1911-12; unmarried. War service with French army, 1915-16; with U.S. Navy, 1918. Republican. Author: A Volunteer Poilu, 1916 (popular edition, 1917); Full Speed Ahead, 1919; The Firelight Fairy Book, 1919 (sch. and library edition, 1922, Roosevelt edition, 1923); The Starlight Wonder Book, 1923. Home: Quincy, Mass. †

SHEAR, MURRAY J(ACOB), biomedical scientist; b. Bklyn., Nov. 7, 1899; s. Victor J. and Henrietta (Robinson) S.; B.S. in Chemistry, City Coll. N.Y., 1920; M.A., Columbia, 1922, Ph.D. in Chemistry, 1925; m. Rose Roseman, Aug. 14, 1935; children—David Ben, Jonathan, Victor Henry. Chemist, Pease Labs., Inc., N.Y.C., 1922-23; asst. chemistry Columbia, 1923-25; research chemist, then adminstrv. officer pediatric research labs., Jewish Hosp., Bklyn., 1925-31; biochemist Office Cancer Investigation, USPHS, Harvard Med. Sch., 1931-39; biochemist Nat. Cancer Inst., NIH, Bethesda, Md., 1939-51, chief lab. chem. pharmacology, 1951-64, special adviser, after 1964. Instructor of pediatrics at Long Island College of Medicine, 1930-31; fellow Harvard Med. Sch., also Harvard U., 1931-39; cons. biochemistry Childrens Med. Center, Boston, 1948-61; chmn. bioassy panel, com. on growth NRC, 1946-48; chmn. bd. civil service examiners NIH, 1947-51; chmn. chemotherapy com. Internat. Union Against Cancer, 1954-62, chairman of the finance com., 1958-62, mem. U.S. nat. com., 1961-64; mem. research commn. International Union Against Cancer, 1962-64, sec.-gen., 1964-66. Pres. Bethesda-Chevy Chase Jewish Community Group, 1942. Served with S.A.T.C., 1918. Mem. Am. Assn. Cancer Research (pres. 1960-61), Soc. Exptl. Biology and Medicine, Am. Soc. Biol. Chemists, Am. Soc. Pharmacology and Exptl. Therapeutics, Washington Acad. Medicine, Royal Soc. Medicine, Soc. Italiana di Cancerologia. Clubs: Harvard (Boston); Cosmos (Washington). Spl. research mechanism deposition of bone salts, genesis tumors with chemicals, chemotherapy and immunology of cancer. Home: Bethesda, Md. Died Sept. 27, 1983.

SHEARER, ALLEN EVERETT, college president; b. Gaylesville, Ala., June 24, 1902; s. Allen V. and Eva (Carter) S.; A.B., Lincoln Meml. U., 1924; M.S., Mercer U., 1928; Ph.D., Peabody Coll., 1937; m. Mildred Pinkerton, May 24, 1926. Adminstrv. positions in pub. schs. of Ga., Fla., 1921-36; dir. curriculum labs., edn. instr. Peabody Coll., 1936-37; prof. edn. Ga. State Tchrs. Coll., Statesboro, 1937-38; dean Southeastern State Coll., Durant, Okla., 1938-52, pres., 1952-67, president emeritus, 1967-83; tchr. Grayson County Community Coll., 1967-82. Mem. N.E.A., Okla. Education Assn., Nat. Soc. Study Edn., Am. Assn. Sch. Adminstrs., Durant C. of C., Am. Legion, Kappa Delta Pi, Kappa Phi Kappa, Phi Delta Kappa, Phi Alpha Theta, Blue Key. Methodist. Mason, Lion. Home: Sherman, Tex. Died Dec. 17, 1983.

SHEARER, NORMA, actress; b. Montreal, Can., Aug. 10, 1902; d. Andrew and Edith Mary (Fisher) Shearer; ed. public schs. of Montreal; m. Irving G. Thalberg, 1928 (died 1936); children—Irving Thalberg, Katharine. Came to U.S., 1919, naturalized, 1931. Began as film actress in small parts, 1920; starred under Metro-Goldwyn-Mayer since 1926; best known films—"He Who Gets Slapped"; (talking pictures) "Trial of Mary Dugan"; "Last of Mrs. Cheyney"; "The Divorcee"; "Let Us Be Gay"; "Strangers May Kiss"; "Smiling Through"; "A Free Soul"; "Private Lives"; "The Barretts of Wimpole Street"; "Romeo and Juliet"; "Marie Antoinette"; "The Women"; "Idiot's Delight"; "Escape"; "We Were Dancing." Recipient of award of Acad. of Motion Picture Arts and Sciences for best performance in 1930. Home: Santa Monica, Calif. Dec. June 12, 1983.

SHEARER, P(HINEAS) S(TEVENS), coll. prof., born Melbourne, Ia., May 24, 1889; s. William Robert and Laura Edith (Andrews) S.; B.S., Ia. State Coll., 1912, M.S., 1928; m. Mary C. Kelly, Dec. 21, 1918; children—Robert William, Patricia (Mrs. J. L. Jenkins), Mary (Mrs. R. Staley). Instr. animal husbandry, Univ. of Nebr., 1912; asst. prof. animal husbandry, Ia. State Coll., Ames, Ia., 1913-14, asso. prof., 1914-19, prof., 1919-35, head, animal husbandry dept. and sect., 1935-54, professor from 1954. Trustee of Iowa State College Agricultural Foundation. Member of the Iowa Beef Producers Assn. (exec. com.), Ia. Horse and Mule Breeders Assn. (exec. com.), Am. Soc. Animal Prodn., Farm Bur., Alpha Zeta, Phi Kappa Phi, Gamma Sigma Delta, Theta Delta Chi. Clubs: Rotary, Golf and Country (both Ames). Contbr. bulletins and articles on livestock prodn. to coll. and assn. publs. Home: Ames, Ia. †

SHEARON, MARJORIE (MRS. WILLIAM SHEARON), palaeontology, statistics; b. Newark, N.J., Aug. 15, 1890; d. James Jay and Phebe Jane (Slater) O'Connell; student Ethical Culture Sch., New York, 1893-1908; A.B., Barnard Coll., 1911; A.M., Columbia, 1912, Ph.D., 1916; m. William Shearon, May 17, 1927. Curator palaeontology, Columbia, 1914-16; with Am. Mus. Nat. History, 1916-22; research asso., Research Bur., N.Y. State Dept. Social Welfare, 1933-34; assistant dir. division of statistics, Emergency Relief Bur., N.Y. City, 1934-36. Fellow A.A.A.S., Am. Geog. Soc., Palaeontol. Society America, Geological Society America; mem. Phi Beta Kappa, Sigma Xi. Won Walker first prize, Boston Soc. Natural History, 1914; Sarah Berliner research fellowship for women ($1,000), 1917, in world competition. Author: The Habitat of the Eurypterida, 1916; The Schrammen Collection of Cretaceous Siliceous Sponges, 1919; The Jurassic of Cuba, 1920-21; also numerous articles. Home: Springfield Gardens L.I., N.Y. †

SHEEHAN, JOSEPH GREEN, clin. psychologist, educator; b. Battle Creek, Mich., May 27, 1918; s. Leo Clark and Florence Belle (Green) S.; m. Vivian Mowat, Dec. 22, 1945; children—Marian Louise, Kathleen Erin, Joseph John; m. Margaret McMillan, June 4, 1966. B.S. in Chemistry, Western Mich. U., Kalamazoo, 1941, M.A. Speech Pathology, in 1946; Ph.D. in Psychology, U. Mich., 1950. Research chemist Gen. Foods Co., 1941-45; speech therapist U.S. Army Hosp., Ft. Custer, Mich., 1945-46; USPHS fellow, VA intern U. Mich., 1947-48; mem. faculty UCLA, from 1949, prof. psychology, from 1963; cons. clin. psychology VA, from 1950, Mental Hygiene Dept. Calif., from 1966; Commr. psychology exam. com. Calif. Bd. Med. Examiners. Author: Stuttering: Research and Therapy, 1970; co-author: Stuttering: A Second Symposium, 1975, Controversies About Stuttering Therapy, 1979; Editorial cons.: Jour. Speech and Hearing Research; pubs. bd.: Jour. Communication Disorders. Fellow Am. Psychol. Assn., Am. Speech and Hearing Assn. Democrat. Home: Santa Monica, Calif.

SHEEHAN, MURRAY, writer; b. Hamilton, Ohio, Dec. 15, 1887; s. David Este and Alfarata (Winder) S.; A.B., Miami U., 1908; studied at Sorbonne, Paris, 1908-09; A.M., Harvard U., 1917. Teacher successively at Miami U., U. of Wis. and U. of Ark., until 1925; supt. students, Royal Thai Legation, Washington, from 1930. Served in 6th Div., U.S. Army, 18 mos., 12 mos. in France. Mem. Beta Theta Pi, Phi Beta Kappa. Club: Harvard. Author: Half-Gods, 1928; Eden, 1929. Home: Arlington, Va.†

SHEFFY, L(ESTER) FIELDS, educator; b. Henrietta, Tex., Mar. 27, 1887; s. W.B. and Alice (Sherwood) S.; A.B., Southwestern U., 1911; M.A., U. Tex., 1914; Litt.D., Austin Coll., 1937; m. Carolyn Virginia Smith, July 26, 1911. Assisted orgn. Panhandle-Plains Hist. Soc., 1921; helped build Panhandle-Plains Mus., 1931-32; faculty mem. West Tex. State Coll. from 1918, prof. history from 1918. Fellow Tex. State Hist. Assn.; mem. Am. Hist. Assn., Panhandle-Plains Hist. Soc. (sec.). Author: The Life and Times of Timothy Dwight Hobart, 1855-1935, 1950; History of Texas (with Irma C. Barlow), 1954; also articles. Editor of Panhandle-Plains Historical Review, 1930-50. Home: Canyon, Tex. †

SHEHAN, LAWRENCE JOSEPH CARDINAL, b. Balt., Mar. 18, 1898; s. Thomas Patrick and Anastasia (Schofield) S. Student, St. Charles Coll., Balt., 1911-17; A.B., St. Mary Sem., Balt., 1919, A.M., 1920; S.T.D., N.Am. Coll., Rome, Italy, 1923. Ordained priest Roman Cath. Ch., 1922; asst. St. Patrick Ch., Washington, 1923-41, pastor, 1941-45, Saints Philip and James Ch., Balt., 1945, named titular bishop Lydda, aux. bishop, Balt. and Washington, 1945, aux. bishop, Balt., 1948, 1st bishop, Bridgeport, Conn., 1953, coadjutor archbishop, Balt., 1961, archbishop, 1961-74, elevated to cardinal, 1965; Consultor Post-Conciliar Commn. for Revision Code of Canon Law; pres. Permanent Commn. for Internat. Eucharistic Congresses, 1969-73; Papal legate 40th Internat. Eucharistic Congress, Melbourne, Australia, 1973. Home: Baltimore, Md. Died Aug. 26, 1984.

SHELBOURNE, ROY MAHLON, judge; b. Bardwell, Ky., Nov. 12, 1890; s. Moreau Thomas and Jenny Lind (Dennis) S.; ed. pub. schs., Bardwell; A.B., Union U., Jackson, Tenn., 1912; LL.B., Cumberland U., 1913; LL.D., Catherine Spalding Coll., Louisville, 1964; m. Edith Richardson, Oct. 8, 1914; children—Mahlon R., Jane, Nancy. Admitted to Ky. bar, 1913; practiced of law at Bardwell (with father) under firm name of Shelbourne & Shelbourne, until father's death, 1927; county atty. Carlisle County, 1918-26; pres. Bardwell Deposit Bank, 1926-36; partner in law firm Wheeler & Shelbourne, Paducah, Ky., 1936-46; U.S. dist. Judge Western Dist. Ky., 1946-64, sr. dist. judge. Mem. Ky. Highway Commn., 1930-32. Pres. Four Rivers council Boy Scouts Am., 1939-41; Silver Beaver Award. Mem. Ky. Bd. Bar Examiners, 1940-46. Mem. McCracken County Bar. Assn. (pres. 1941), Kappa Sigma. Democrat. Christian Ch. Rotarian (pres. Paducah chpt. 1938-39). Home: Louisville, KY. †

SHEPARD, CHARLES CARTER, physician; b. Ord, Nebr., Dec. 18, 1914; s. Charles Carter and Margaret Catherine (Ferguson) S.; m. Regina Elizabeth Schmidt, Nov. 22, 1939. Student, Stanford U., 1932-35; B.S., Northwestern U., 1936, M.S., 1938, M.D., 1941. Commd. med. officer USPHS, 1941; research in rickettial disease and biophys. technique NIH, Bethesda, Md., 1942-48, 49-51; guest mem. Biochemistry Inst. Uppsala U., Sweden, 1948-49; research in biophys. technique Rocky Mountain Lab., 1951-53; with Ctrs. for Disease Control, Atlanta, 1953-85, chief leprosy sect.; cons. WHO, others; adj. asso. prof. Emory U., U. N.C., Ga. State U. Contbr. articles in field of leprosy and rickettsial diseases to profl. jours. Recipient World Leprosy Day award, 1970, others. Fellow AAAS; mem. Am. Assn. Immunologists, Am. Acad. Microbiology, Am. Soc. Microbiology, Internat. Leprosy Soc., Soc. Exptl. Biol. Medicine. Home: Atlanta, Ga. Died Feb. 18, 1985; buried Ord, Nebr.

SHEPARD, FRANCIS PARKER, educator, geologist; b. Brookline, Mass., May 10, 1897; s. Thomas Hill and

Edna (Parker) S.; B.A., Harvard, 1919; Ph.D., U. Chgo., 1922; D.S.C. (hon.), Beloit Coll.; m. Elizabeth Buchner, June 12, 1920; children—Thomas Hill II, Anthony Lee. Began as instr. U. Ill., 1922, prof. geology, 1939-46; research asso. Scripps Instn. of Oceanography, La Jolla, Cal., 1942-45, prin. geologist. 1945-48, prof. submarine geology, 1948-85; marine geologist, working on Navy projects for U. Cal., Div. War Research, and Scripps Instn., 1942-85; dir. Am. Petroleum Inst. project on sediments No. Gulf of Mexico, 1951-58. Recipient Wollaston medal Geol. Soc. London. Mem. Geol. Soc. Am., Internat. Assn. Sedimentologists (pres. 1958-63, councilor, editor Sedimentology 1963). Soc. Econ. Paleontologists and Mineralogists (hon.), Sigma Xi. Gamma Alpha, Alpha Sigma Phi. Author: Submarine Topography off Cal. Coast. 1942; Submarine Geology, 3d edit., 1973; Earth Beneath the Sea, rev. edit., 1967. (with R.F. Dill) Submarine Canyons and other Sea Valleys, 1966; (with H.R. Wanles) Our Changing Coastlines, 1971. Editor: Recent Sediments Northwest Gulf of Mexico, 1960. Contbr. sci. articles to geol. jours. Home: La Jolla, Calif. Died Apr. 29, 1985.

SHEPARD, WARD, forester; b. Hicksville, Ohio, Mar. 14, 1887; s. Charles G. and Fannie Josephine (Huffman) S.; A.B., Harvard, 1910, M.F., 1913; m. Jean Frances Duer Key, Oct. 12, 1918; children—Ward, Charles, Francis Key. Forest ranger, forest supervisor and asst. chief of research, U.S. Forest Service, 1921-27; fellow Carl Schurz Memorial Foundation, Central Europe, 1932-33; econ. advisor to U.S. commr. of Indian affairs, 1933-36; dir. Harvard Forest and mem. faculty, Grad Sch. Pub. Adminstrn., Harvard, 1936-39; special adviser on forest policy, Bureau of Agrl. Economics, U.S. Dept. of Agr., 1939-40; advisor on natural resources development, Office of Indian Affairs, Washington, D.C., 1940-48. Member Society Am. Foresters. Author: Food or Famine; The Challenge of Erosion, 1945. Co-author (with Brinser) Our Use of the Land, 1939. Contbr. articles on forestry, conservation and public affairs to mags. Home: Vienna, Va.†

SHEPHARD, RONALD WILLIAM, educator; b. Portland, Oreg., Nov. 22, 1912; s. Robert E. and Jessie W. (Hunter) S.; m. Hilda May Maloy, Dec. 26, 1940; children—Jessie M., William H. A.B. in Math. and Econs, U. Calif. at Berkeley, 1935, Ph.D. in Math. and Statistics, 1940; D.Econ. Sci., U. Karlsruhe, W. Ger. Statis., cons. Bell Aircraft Corp., 1943-46; sr. economist RAND Corp., 1950-52; mgr. systems analysis dept. Sandia Corp., 1952-56; prof. engring. sci. U. Calif., Berkeley, 1957-80, prof. emeritus, from 1980, chmn. ops. research center, 1966-72, also chmn. indsl. engring. and ops. research dept., 1970-76, past chmn. indsl. engring. dept.; cons. ops. research OECD, Paris, France, 1959-60; dir. Market Research Corp. Am., 1961-66; cons. to industry, from 1950, internat. authority on math. econ. theory of prodn. and tech. Author: Cost and Production Functions, 1953, Theory of Cost and Production Functions, 1970, Indirect Production Functions, 1974, Dynamic Theory of Production Correspondences, 1980. Served as lt. (j.g.) USNR, World War II. Recipient Humboldt prize Alexander von Humboldt Found., Bonn, 1976; Berkeley citation U. Calif. Fellow Econometric Soc.; mem. Ops. Research Soc. Am. (past pres. Western sect.), Inst. Mgmt. Sci. (past chmn. No. Calif. sect.), Phi Beta Kappa, Sigma Xi. Home: Berkeley, Calif.

SHEPHERD, ROBERT ASHLAND, ret. lawyer; b. Huntsville, Tex., July 7, 1894; s. James L. and Julia (Josey) S.; m. Opal Powell, July 8, 1922; children—Robert Ashland, William Leftwich. Grad., Sam Houston State Tchrs. Coll., 1914; student, U. Tex., Austin, 1916-17. Bar: Tex. bar 1921. With James L. Shepherd, Cisco, Tex., 1921; With Vinson, Elkins, Weems & Searls, Houston, 1921, partner, 1929—, mng. partner, 1951-59; then partner Vinson, Elkins, Searls, Connally & Smith (name change), ret., 1971; Vice pres., dir. Duval Corp., 1947-70; sr. chmn. bd., dir. Heights State Bank, Houston. Trustee Lon Morris Coll., Tex. Med. Center, Meth. Hosp., Houston, Tex. Meth. Found. Served as 2d lt. F.A. and aviation U.S. Army, World War I. Mem. Am., Houston bar assns., State Bar Tex., S.A.R., Sons Republic of Tex. Democrat. Methodist (trustee). Club: Mason (Shriner, K.T.). Home: Houston TX

SHEPPARD, EUGENIA, newspaper columnist; grad. cum laude, Bryn Mawr Coll.; m. Walter Millis (dec.). Fashion writer Women's Wear Daily, N.Y.C., 1938-40; writer women's feature dept. N.Y. Herald Tribune, 1940-47, fashion editor, 1947-49; head women's staff, women's editor World Jour. Tribune (merger with Herald Tribune), 1949-56; writer syndicated column Inside Fashion, from 1956. Died Nov. 11, 1985.

SHERA, JESSE HAUK, librarian, educator; b. Oxford, Ohio, Dec. 8, 1903; s. Charles H. and Jessie (Hauk) S.; m. Helen M. Bickham, 1928; children—Mary Helen, Edgar Brookins. A.B., Miami U., Oxford, 1925; M.A., Yale, 1927; Ph.D., U. Chgo., 1944; LL.D., Ball State U., 1976. Asst. cataloger Miami U. Library, 1927-28; bibliographer Scripps Found. for Research in Population Problems, 1928-40; chief census library project Library of Congress, 1940-41; asst. chief, central information div. O.S.S., 1941-44; asst. dir. U. Chgo. Library, 1944-47; asst. prof. Grad. Library Sch., U. Chgo., 1947-51, asso. prof., 1951-52; dean sch. library sci. Western Res. U., Cleve., 1952-70, prof., dean emeritus, from 1972; Brazilian lectr. Inst. Bibliography and Documentation, 1957; vis. prof. Grad. Sch. Library Sci., U. Tex., Austin, 1970-71, U. Ariz., summer 1973, U. Ky., summer 1974, U. Minn., spring 1977; lectr. seminar on library edn. Liverpool (Eng.) Poly., 1974, U. P.R., 1979; Mem. Pres.'s Com. Employment of the Handicapped, 1969-80, Pres.'s Com. Library Research and Edn.; U.S. del. UNESCO Internat. Conf., Paris., 1950, Internat. Conf. on Bibliog. Classification, Dorking, Eng., 1957; bd. educators United Educators, Inc.; Dir. Center Documentation and Communication Research, Western Res. U., 1960-71. Author: Foundations of the Public Library, 1949, Bibliographic Organization, (with Margaret E. Egan), 1951, Historians, Books, and Libraries, 1953, The Classified Catalog, (with M.E. Egan), 1956, Libraries and the Organization of Knowledge, 1965, Documentation and the Organization of Knowledge, 1966, The Compleat Librarian, 1970, Sociological Foundations of Librarianship, 1971, Foundations of Education for Librarianship, 1972, Knowing Books and Men, 1973, Introduction to Library Science, 1976; Editor: American Documentation, 1953-60, Western Res. U. Press, 1954-59, Documentation in Action, 1956, Information Systems in Documentation, 1957, Information Resources: A Challenge to American Science and Industry, 1958, Toward a Theory of Librarianship (Conrad H. Rawski), 1973; Editorial bd.: Jour. Library History; asso. editor: Library Quar, 1947-52; adv. editor, 1952-55, Jour. Cataloging and Classification, 1947-57; editor-in-chief: Wiley-Interscience texts in Documentation and Library Science, 1958-81; editorial bd.: Library Sci, India; bd. editors: United Educators, 1961-74. Trustee Council Nat. Library Assns. Recipient Beta Phi Mu award, 1965; Melvil Dewey award ALA, 1968; Lippincott award, 1973; Disting. Service award Drexel U., 1971; award of merit Am. Soc. for Info. Sci., 1973; Scarecrow Press award ALA, 1974; Hilbert T. Ficken award Baldwin-Wallace Coll., 1976; Alumni award U. Chgo., 1977; Gold Medal Kaula Found., India; elected to Ohio Library Hall Fame, 1973. Mem. Spl. Libraries Assn. (hon. life), AAAS, Assn. Am. Library Schs. (pres. 1964-65), English-Speaking Union, ALA (hon. life mem., chmn. com. on bibliography 1950-52, council 1964-68), Ohio Library Assn. (hon. life mem., pres. 1963-64, Librarian of Year 1969), Chgo. Library Assn., Bibliog. Soc. Am., Miss. Valley Hist. Assn., Phi Beta Kappa, Beta Phi Mu (pres. 1970-71), Phi Alpha Theta. Clubs: Cliff Dwellers, Caxton, Rowfant. Home: Cleveland Heights, OH.

SHERAN, ROBERT JOSEPH, judge; b. Waseca, Minn., Jan. 2, 1916; s. Michael J. and Eleanor A. (Bowe) S.; m. Jean M. Brown, Feb. 3, 1940; children—Michael, Thomas, Kathleen, John, Daniel. B.A., Coll. St. Thomas, St. Paul, 1936; LL.B., U. Minn., 1939. Bar: Minn. bar 1939. Practice in, Glencoe, 1939-42, Mankato, 1945-63; spl. agt. FBI, 1942-45; asso. justice Supreme Ct., Minn., 1963-70, chief justice, 1973-81; mem. firm Lindquist & Vennum, Mpls., 1970-73; Mem. Minn. Bd. Law Examiners, 1956- 62, 70-73; mem. Minn. Bd. Tax Appeals, 1961-63; chmn. Gov.'s Commn. on Crime Prevention and Control, 1970-73. Mem. Minn. Ho. of Reps. from Blue Earth County, 1946-50; Trustee Coll. St. Thomas, 1964-73. Fellow Am. Coll. Trial Lawyers, Internat. Acad. Trial Lawyers, Am. Bar Found.; mem. Am. Law Inst., Am. Judicature Soc., Inst. Jud. Adminstrn., Conf. Chief Justices U.S. (chmn. 1980-81), U. Minn. Alumni Assn. (pres. 1979-80). Home: Saint Paul, Minn.

SHERIF, CAROLYN WOOD, psychologist; b. Loogootee, Ind., June 26, 1922; d. Lawrence Anselm and Bonny (Williams) Wood; m. Muzafer Sherif, Dec. 29, 1945; children—Sue, Joan, Ann. B.S., Purdue U., 1943; M.A., State U. Iowa, 1944; Ph.D. in Psychology, U. Tex., 1961. Asst. to research dir. Audience Research, Inc., Princeton, N.J., 1944-45; asst. Princeton, 1945-47; research, free-lance writer, Norman, Okla., 1949-58; research asso. Inst. Group Relations, U. Okla., Norman, 1959-65, asso. prof. sociology, 1963-65; cons. asst. prof. U. Okla. Med. Sch., 1963-65; vis. lectr. Pa. State U., 1962, asso. prof. psychology, 1965-66, asso. prof., 1966-69, prof, from 1970; vis. prof. psychology and sociology Cornell U., 1969-70; disting. vis. prof. Smith Coll., 1979; G. Stanley Hall lectr. on social psychology, 1981; nat. lectr. Sigma Xi, from 1981; cons. NSF; bd. cons. Smith Coll. projection women and social change, from 1980. Author: (with M. Sherif) Groups in Harmony and Tension, 1953, An Outline of Social Psychology, 1956, Problems of Youth, Transition to Adulthood in a Changing World, 1965, Attitude, Ego-Involvement and Change, 1967, Interdisciplinary Relationships in the Social Sciences, 1969, Social Psychology, 1969, (with M. Sherif, O.J. Harvey, B.J. White, W.R. Hood) Intergroup Conflict and Cooperation, 1961, (with M. Sherif and R. Nebergall) Attitude and Attitude Change, 1965, Instructor's Manual for Social Psychology, 1969, Orientation in Social Psychology, 1976; contbr. (with M. Sherif and R. Nebergall) numerous articles to profl. jours. Fellow Am. Psychol. Assn. (policy and planning bd. 1979—, pres. div. 35 1979-80); mem. Am. Sociol. Assn., AAUW, AAAS, Mortar Bd., Sigma Xi, Theta Alpha Phi, Alpha Lambda Delta, Pi Beta Phi. Home: State College, PA.

SHERIFF, ARTHUR NEUTRAL, educator; b. Chicago, Ill., Dec. 18, 1887; s. Arthur Grant and Harriet (Gulliver) S.; grad. Tuley High Sch., Chicago, 1909; A.B., Yale, 1913, A.M., 1915; m. Charlotte Wharton Gray, of N.Y. City, June 15, 1913. Mem. staff Chicago Examiner, 1905-09; teacher of English, Cheshire Acad. (formerly Roxbury Sch.), from 1917, dean, 1920-23, headmaster from 1923, trustee. Mem. Phi Beta Kappa, Beta Theta Pi, Berzelius. Conglist. Clubs: Yale (New York); Quinnipiack, Graduate (New Haven). Home: Cheshire, Conn. †

SHERIFF, FRED B., wool grower; b. Canyon Ferry, Mont., 1890; s. Court and Mary (Hooper) S.; B.S., U. of Wis., 1912; m. Berneice Sieben, June 2, 1915; 1 dau., Mrs. Jean Baucus. Engaged in ranching from 1920; now operator of one of largest sheep ranches in Mont., also engaged in aviation from 1928, and did all of own flying for about 10 yrs. Served on bd. dirs. Nat. Parks Airways, also Northwest Air Lines; as commr. of aeronautics for Mont. supervised spending of about $1,000,000 in establishing Mont. airport system, 1933-42; apptd. to bd. dirs. Regional Agrl. Credit Corp., Farm Credit Adminstrn., 1939. Home: Helena, Mont. †

SHERLOCK, PAUL, physician; b. N.Y.C., Oct. 7, 1928; s. Joseph and Estelle (Salzman) S.; m. Marcia Regina Rohr, Mar. 29, 1952; children: Diane, Susan, Nancy. B.S., Queens Coll., 1950; M.D., Cornell U., 1954. Diplomate: Am. Bd. Internal Medicine (assoc. mem. bd. govs. 1975-81,) mem. gastroenterology subsplty. bd. Intern Bellevue Hosp., N.Y.C., 1954-55; resident Bellevue Hosp.-Meml. Sloan-Kettering Cancer Center, 1957-60; trainee Nat. Cancer Inst., 1959-60; postdoctoral research fellow Am. Cancer Soc., 1960-62; head gastrointestinal physiology sect. Sloan Kettering Inst. for Cancer Research, N.Y.C., 1963-70, asso., 1963-78, mem., 1978-85; chief gastroenterology service Meml. Sloan-Kettering Cancer Center, 1970-78, assoc. chmn. dept. medicine, 1976-77, acting chmn., 1977-78, chmn., 1978-85, Practice medicine specializing in gastroenterology and internal medicine, N.Y.C., 1962-85; attending physician N.Y. Hosp.; prof. medicine Cornell U. Med. Coll., N.Y.C., 1975-85, vice chmn. dept. medicine, 1979-85; cons. med. staff North Shore U. Hosp., 1978-85; vis. physician Rockefeller U. Hosp., 1978-85; med. dir. Moore McCormack Lines, Inc., N.Y.C., 1967-83; mem. Nat. Commn. on Digestive Diseases, 1976-79; chmn. Nat. Digestive Diseases Adv. Bd., 1980-84; mem. exec. com. Am. Joint Com. on Cancer, 1980-84; chmn. gastrointestinal drugs adv. com. FDA, 1981-84. Asso. editor: Am. Jour. Digestive Diseases, 1973-77; mem. editorial bd., 1977-80; editorial staff: Gastroenterology, 1973-76; mem. editorial bd.: Cancer Center, 1979—, Oncology, 1981-85, Your Patient and Cancer, 1981-85; editorial dir.: oncology Lit. News, 1982-85; editor: Medilex Digest, 1981-85; editorial cons.: Biol. Abstracts; contbr. articles to profl. jours. Trustee Lenox Sch., N.Y.C., 1972-76; Alumni Assn. Queens Coll., Flushing, N.Y. Served to lt. comdr. USNR, 1955-57. Recipient Gold medal VII Internat. Congress Gastroenterology, 1968. Fellow A.C.P., Am. Coll. Gastroenterology, N.Y. Acad. Gastroenterology, N.Y. Acad. Scis.; mem. Am. Soc. Internal Medicine, AMA, Am. Fedn. Clin. Research, AAAS, Soc. Surg. Oncology (exec. council 1976-79), Am. Soc. Gastrointestinal Endoscopy (mem. governing bd. 1974-81, pres. 1978-79), Am. Soc. Clin. Oncology, Am. Gastroent. Assn. (chmn. council on cancer 1975-78, gov. bd. 1982-85), N.Y. Gastroent. Assn. (pres. 1973-74), Harvey Soc., Am. Cancer Soc. (chmn. nat. adv. commn. colon and rectal cancer), Am. Soc. Preventive Oncology, N.Y. Cancer Soc., Nat. Found. Ileitis and Colitis, Am. Assn. Study Liver Diseases, Internat. Assn. Study of Liver, N.Y. Soc. Gastrointestinal Endoscopy (council 1974-78), Fedn. Digestive Disease Socs. (chmn. council 1980-81), others. Home: New York, N.Y. Died May 6, 1985.

SHERLOCK, ROBERT HENRY, engr., educator; b. Lafayette, Ind., Feb. 23, 1887; s. Robert and Mary Ann (McPhillips) S.; B.S., Purdue, 1910; m. Mary Louise Egan, June, 1915. Engr. Am. Bridge Co., Toledo, Pitts., 1910-23; asst. prof. civil engring. U. Mich., 1923-26, asso. prof., 1926-33, prof., from 1933. Recipient Norman medal Am. Soc. C.E., 1954. Mem. Am. Soc. C.E. (chmn. com. on wind loading 1952, nat. dir. from 1956), Engring. Soc. Detroit, Am. Soc. M.E., Am. Concrete Inst., Am. Meteorol. Soc., Internat. Assn. Bridge and Structural Engring. (chmn. U.S. council 1936-42, chmn. U.S. delegation Berlin Congress 1936, internat. permanent com. 1940-48), Am. Soc. Engring. Edn., Sigma Xi, Tau Beta Pi, Phi Kappa Phi. Author: Storm Loading and Strength of Wood Pole Lines and a Study of Wind Gusts, 1936. Author tech. papers. Home: Ann Arbor, Mich. †

SHERMAN, BENJAMIN, vending co. exec.; b. N.Y.C., Aug. 11, 1889; s. Lewis and Anna (Gore) S.; student pub. schs.; m. Bessie Rosen. Propr. trucking co., 1909-25; propr. circuit of theatres, 1925-26; organized San. Automatic Candy Corp., 1926, name changed to ABC Consol. Corp., chmn. bd., from 1958. Dir., past pres. United Home for Aged Hebrews; v.p., dir. hom pres. Hebrew Nat. Orphan Home. Home: New York, NY. †

SHERMAN, CLARENCE EDGAR, librarian; b. Brooklyn, N.Y., Jan. 14, 1887; s. James Horze and Josephine Estelle (Hamer) S.; student Williston Acad., Easthampton, Mass., 1905-07; B.S., Trinity Coll., Hartford, Conn., 1911; study N.Y. State Library Sch., 1911-12; hon. M.A., Trinity Coll., 1941; L.H.D. (hon.), Brown University, 1952; Litt.D., University of Rhode Island, 1957; married Inez B. Copeland, October 8, 1913; children—Stuart Capen, Carolyn, Louise Copeland, Richard Dana. Asst. librarian, Amherst Coll. Library, 1912-17; librarian, Lynn (Mass.) Pub. Library, 1917-22; asst. librarian, Providence

(R.I.) Public Library, 1922-28, asso. librarian, 1928-30, librarian, 1930-57, emeritus, from 1957. Lectr., R.I. College Edn., 1923-25, Simmons Coll., Boston, Mass., 1928-39, 1943-52; mem. faculty, Columbia U., summers, 1937, 39, 40, 41; lecturer Pratt Institute, Brooklyn, N.Y., 1939-47. Trustee, Citizens Savings Bank. In Am. Library Assn. war service, 1918. Mem. bd. dirs., Victory Book Campaign, 1942-44. Mem. Sch. Com., Lynn, 1920-22. Chairman of R.I. special commn. to study comic books conditions, 1955-56; mem. state commission to study morality in youth, 1956-57. Trustee of R.I. School of Design, 1930-57; past pres., Providence Y.M.C.A.; member corporation Rhode Island Hospital, Roger Williams General Hospital; chairman R.I. Apprenticeship Council; bd. of fellows Trinity Coll., 1947-54. Mem. A.L.A. (2d v.p. 1942-43), R.I. Hist. Soc. R.I. Library Association, Massachusetts Library Association, Boston Society of Printers, Delta Kappa Epsilon. Conglist. Mason. Clubs: Art Club, Club of Odd Volumes, Players, Rotary. Author: with others) Current Problems in Public Library Finance, 1933: The Providence Public Library; An Experiment in Enlightenment, 1938; Current Issues in Library Administration (with others), 1939. Contbr. to library publs. †

SHERMAN, EDWARD DAVID, physician; b. Sydney, N.S., Can., Mar. 15, 1908; s. Frederick and Sara (Epstein) S.; 1938; 1 son, Neil; m. Anne Helen Doner, Feb. 22, 1955. M.D., C.M., McGill U., 1932. Intern Womans Gen. Hosp., Montreal, 1931-33; resident Mt. Sinai Hosp., N.Y.C., 1933-35, practice internal medicine, Sydney, N.S., 1935-46, N.Y.C., 1947- 55, Montreal, 1956-84; became asso. physician-in-chief Maimonides Hosp. and Home for Aged, Montreal, 1956; now hon. attending staff; dir. research Rehab. Inst., Montreal, 1962—; became asso. physician med. staff, also geriatric clinic Jewish Gen. Hosp., Montreal, 1956; now hon. attending staff; med. dir. Sheltered Workshop of Jewish Vocational Service, Montreal, 1959—; v.p. Inst. Gerontology, U. Montreal, 1962-65; lectr. geriatrics Sch. Rehab., 1958-84; mem. med. research com. and superior studies Faculty Medicine, 1973-84; Cons., sr. citizens' program Quebec div. Canadian Red Cross Soc. Contbr. articles in field.; Abstract editor: N.S. Med. Bull, 1942-46. Exec. com. Canadian Conf. on Aging, 1963-66; Canadian rep. White House Conf. on Aging, Washington, 1971; Bd. dirs. med. com. Herzl Dispensary, 1958—, Baron de Hirsch Inst., 1958-65. Served with Royal Canadian Army Med. Corps, 1943-44. Recipient Malford W. Thewlis award Am. Geriatrics Soc., 1965, Rabbi Harry J. Stern award Temple Emanu-El, Canadian Silver Jubilee medal, 1977. Fellow Royal Coll. Physicians Can., A.C.P., Internat. Coll. Angiology, Am. Geriatrics Soc. (dir. 1961-71, past pres., past chmn. bd.), Royal Soc. Medicine, Am. Coll. Preventive Medicine, Royal Soc. Arts; mem. Que. Med. Assn. (chmn com. aging 1963-77, dir.), Canadian Assn. Phys. Medicine and Rehab., Internat. Soc. Internal Medicine, Internat. Assn. Gerontology (council 1963-66, mem. history com. 1975), Gerontol. Soc., N.Y. Acad. Scis., Canadian Med. Assn. (chmn. com. on aging 1963-67, mem. gen. council), Am. Psychosomatic Soc., Canadian Geriatric Research Soc. (med. adv. bd.), Canadian Assn. Gerontology, St. James Lit. Soc., St. John Ambulance Assn. (hon. life), Sigma Xi, Pi Lambda Phi. Jewish. Club: Mason. Home: Montreal, Que., Canada. Died Sept. 5, 1984.

SHERMAN, JOHN HARVEY, economist, educator; b. Ash Grove, Va., Dec. 20, 1887; s. Franklin and Caroline Matilda Clapp (Alvord) S.; A.B., Cornell Univ.; LL.B., John Marshall Law Sch.; A.M. and Ph.D. in Economics, U. of Wis.; studied University of Pa., Georgetown U., U. of Minn.; Ed.D. Honoris Causa, U. Tampa, 1940; m. Mary Mosby Stephens, Sept. 13, 1914 (dec. 1951); children—Frances (Mrs. Edwin M. Bailey), John Harvey, Dora Frantz (Mrs. Richard Willoughby), Caroline Matilda Clapp Alvord; adopted John Henry Stephens III; m. 2d, Dorothy Gould Cannon, Feb. 22, 1962. Asst. Cornell University, 1910-11; statistician Harrison Boiler Works, Phila., 1911-13; cons. The Emerson Co., N.Y.C., 1913-14; supt. of markets, Dist. of Columbia, 1914-16; gen. manager Paramount Pictures Corporation, 1916-17; lecturer, economics and marketing, U. of Minn., 1919-20; gen. mgr. Wis. Specialties Co., 1920-22; prof. economics and commerce, U. of Chattanooga, 1922-25, dir. summer courses, 1923, 24, 25; D. K. Pearsons prof. of economics, and dean, Lake Forest U., 1925-28; exec. sec. Chicago Income Trust, 1930-34; practiced law, 1934-37; president University of Tampa, 1937-40. President Florida High School Music Festival Assn., 1937-40. Served as capt. Air Service in France, World War I; lt. col., col. Army of U.S., last mil. assignment, dir. of edn., U.S. Military Govt., Ryukyu Islands; retired devoting time to research and writing. Mem. Bar of Ill. Mem. Am. Econ. Assn., Am. Statis. Assn., Am. Sociol. Soc., Spanish War Vets., Am. Legion, Pi Gamma Mu. Democrat. Conglist. Mason. Author: Principles of Commercial Law; also numerous tech. articles in field econs. and social scis. Home: Berkeley, Cal. †

SHERR, IVENS, business exec.; b. Russia, Oct. 2, 1888; s. Abraham and Gladys S.; came to U.S., 1890, naturalized, 1915; m. Ethel Kurlan, Mar. 21, 1909 (dec. Aug. 1953); children—Abraham, Mrs. Milton Gluckman; m. 2d, Ellen Hill, Oct. 3, 1964; stepchildren—Fred Hill, Mrs. Dorrit Greene. With Sherr Bros., mfrs., 1908-30, Barnard Phillips, factors, 1914-33; pres., dir. Fownes Bros. & Co., Inc., N.Y.C., from 1936. Home: New York City, NY. †

SHERWOOD, ARTHUR MURRAY, lawyer; b. Portland, Oreg., Dec. 4, 1913; s. Arthur Murray and Evelyn (Wilson) S.; m. Marjorie F. Catron, Dec. 27, 1947; children—Philip T., Thomas C., Evelyn W. Grad., Milton Acad., 1932; B.S., Harvard U., 1936; J.D., Columbia, 1939. Bar: N.Y. bar 1940, N.J. bar 1972. Asso. atty. firm Shearman & Sterling, N.Y.C., 1939-41, 46-54; counsel law dept. Mobil Oil Corp., N.Y.C., 1954-55, asst. sec., 1955, sec., 1956-72; asso. atty. Smith, Stratton, Wise & Heher, Princeton, N.J., 1972-80; Bd. visitors Columbia U. Sch. Law, 1963-77, Woodrow Wilson vis. fellow, 1974-75. Served from pvt. to lt. col. U.S. Army, 1941-46; asst. chief staff G-1, 2d Inf. Div. 1944-45. Decorated Legion of Merit, Bronze Star; Croix de Guerre with palm France; Mil. Cross Czechoslovakia). Clubs: Fly (Cambridge, Mass.); Nassau (Princeton, N.J.). Home: Princeton, NJ.

SHERWOOD, SIDNEY, former UN adviser; b. Balt., May 10, 1901; s. Sidney and Mary A. (Beattie) S.; m. Olita Schlichten, May 28, 1927. Grad., Storm King Sch., Cornwall-on-Hudson, N.Y., 1919; A.B., Princeton U., 1923. With Bankers Trust Co., N.Y.C. and Phelps Dodge Corp., Bisbee, Ariz., 1923-32, Farm Credit Adminstrn., U.S. Treasury Dept., 1933-35; supr. alcohol tax unit, also co-ordinator Treasury enforcement agys., New Eng., 1933-40; asst. sec. adv. commn. Council of Nat. Def.; asst. liaison officer Office for Emergency Mgmt., Exec. Office of Pres.; dir. Nat. Policy Com.; exec. officer Div. of Industry Operations, WPB; Combined Prodn. and Resources Bd. and cons. on fgn. programs Office of War Moblzn., White House; spl. asst. to adminstr. Fgn. Econ. Adminstrn., 1940-45; sec. Export-Import Bank of Washington and chief of econ. survey missions to, Afghanistan, Saudi Arabia and Israel, 1945-59; econ. attache Am. embassy, New Delhi, India, representing Export-Import Bank, and loan adviser to U.S. AID Mission in India, 1959-64; Am. investment adviser Indian Investment Centre, and U.S. adviser The Central Bank of India, Ltd., cons. to Govt. of Ceylon, cons. to UNIDO, 1964-69; sr. financial adviser UN Devel. Program, 1969-72. Bd. govs. Middle East Inst. Mem. Washington Inst. Fgn. Affairs, Am. Soc. for Internat. Devel., Asia Soc. Club: Cosmos (Washington). Address: Cockeysville, MD.

SHEVELOVE, BURT, writer, theatrical dir.; b. Newark, Sept. 19, 1915; s. Jacob J. and Betty (Lessner) S.; A.B., Brown U., 1937; student drama Yale, 1937-39. Producer, dir., author numerous TV programs, 1950-82; dir., co-author Small Wonder, 1948; co-author A Funny Thing Happened on the Way to the Forum (Tony award 1962-63), 1962; co-author, co-producer The Wrong Box, 1966; dir. Hallelujah Baby, 1967; adaptor, dir. No, No, Nanette, 1971; dir. A Funny Thing Happened on the Way to the Forum (revival), 1973, Sondheim: A Musical Tribute, 1973, The Frogs, 1974, Rodgers and Hart, 1975. Served with Am. Field Service, World War II. Club: The Players (N.Y.C.). Died Apr. 8, 1982.*

SHEWMAKE, EDWIN FRANCIS, educator; b. Minto, N.D., Oct. 16, 1887; s. Edwin Francis and Nancy (Salter) S.; A.B., William and Mary Coll., 1908; A.M., Columbia, 1914; Ph.D., U. Va., 1920; m. Cornelia M. Switzer, Dec. 22, 1914; children—Elizabeth Warren (Mrs. G. K. Harrington), Edwin Francis, Charles Tiffin (dec.). Tchr. high schs., 1908-10; prin. Staunton (Va.) High Sch., 1910-15; head dept. English State Normal Sch., Fredericksburg, Va., 1915-16; asst. prof. English U. Va., 1917-19; professor English Davidson (North Carolina) College, 1919-53, professor emeritus, from 1953. Mem. Va. Assn. Colls. and Secondary Schs. (sec. 1912-13), S. Atlantic Modern Lang. Assn., Raven Soc., Phi Beta Kappa, Pi Kappa Alpha. Author: College English Composition (with C. L. Carmer), 1927; Working with Words, 1951. Contbr. Am. Speech, Modern Lang. Notes, Sch. and Soc., S. Atlantic Quarterly. Editor of U. Va. News Letter (with T. R. Snavely), 1919. Mem. bd. adv. editors Va. Jour. of Edn., 1918. Home: Davidson, N.C. †

SHIELDS, CORNELIUS, investment banker; b. St. Paul, Apr. 7, 1895; s. Cornelius and Theresa (McHugh) S.; student Polytechnic Prep. Sch., Bklyn., 1913; Loyola, Montreal, Can., 1910-11; m. Josephine Lupprian, Jan. 1, 1922; children—Aileen, Cornelius. Asso. Merrill Lynch & Co., 1920-23; partner Shields & Co., N.Y. City, 1923-74. Served as lt. USNR, 1917-19. Republican. Roman Catholic. Clubs: Larchmont (N.Y.) Yacht, New York Yacht. Royal Bermuda Yacht, Mid-Ocean, Winged Foot Golf, Down Town Assn., Blind Brook Golf, Shenorock Shore; Everglades and Seminole Golf (Fla.). Author: Cornelius Shields on Sailing. Home: Larchmont, N.Y. Died Oct. 15, 1981.

SHIELDS, CURRIN VANCE, educator; b. LaPorte, Ind., Feb. 18, 1918; s. Clarence Vance and Harriet (Swanson) S.; m. Phyllis Rae Greene, June 10, 1941 (div.); children—Currin Burk, Craig Vance, Malinda Rae, Colin Kent; m. Marjorie Miller Rowe, May 28, 1960. A.B., U. Nebr., 1941; Ph.M., U. Wis., 1943; Ph.D., Yale U., 1950. With advt. art dept. Chgo. Tribune, 1937-38; research asst. Legis. Council, Nebr., 1939-41; research asst. dept. polit. sci. U. Wis., 1941-43; asst. to dir. Civil Affairs Tng. Sch., 1943-44; asst. in instrn., Cowles fellow dept. polit. sci. Yale U., 1946-47, instr., 1948-50; asst., asso. prof. dept. polit. sci. UCLA, 1950-60; prof. govt. U. Ariz., from 1960, head govt. dept., 1960-69; dir. Inst. Govt. Research, 1963-72, dir. community services, from 1972; vis. lectr. Boston U., summer 1947, U. N.H., 1948, U. Wis., 1955; mem. adv. council Electric Power Research Inst., Palo Alto, Calif.; asso. Consumer Affairs Assos., Washington, Virginia Knauer & Assos. (consumer consultants), Washington; consumer affairs cons. AT&T, Pacific Telephone Co.; co-chmn. Ariz. Consumer/Mountain Bell Joint Panel.; Dir. Group Health of Ariz., 1975-78, Nat. Consumer Symposium, Inc., 1977—; cons. Legis. edn. program United Steelworkers Am., 1953-61; co-chmn. corp. seminar Fund for Republic, 1959-60; cons. Nat. Endowment for Humanities, 1969-75; pres. Ariz. Consumers Council, 1969-80; bd. mem. Consumer Fedn. Am., 1969-74, mem. exec. com., 1970-74, resolutions chmn., 1971-74, v.p., 1973-74; chmn. Nat. Conf. Consumer Orgns., 1974-77; mem. consumer adv. com. Fed. Energy Adminstrn., 1973-75, mem. constrn. adv. com., 1974-76; mem. Nat. Advt. Rev. Bd., 1975-79, President's Consumer Adv. Council; dir. Nat. Consumer Affairs Internship Program, from 1976. Host radio program: What's the Issue? , Sta. KFWB, Hollywood, 1953-55; Author: Democracy and Catholicism in America, 1958; Bd. editors: Western Polit. Quar; Contbr. numerous articles to profl. publs. Vice chmn. 22d Congressional Dist., Democratic Council Calif., 1953, 54, chmn., 1955; co.-chmn. polit. action com. Calif. Dem. Council, 1955-57; candidate for gov., z., 1968; chmn. 1970 Platform Com. Dem. Party Ariz.; Mem. exec. bd. Arizona Acad. Served as 2d lt. U.S. Army, 1944-46. Mem. Am. Polit. Sci. Assn. (chmn., com. on relations with regional assos.), Western Polit. Sci. Assn. (exec. bd., pres. 1971-72), Am. Soc. Pubilc Adminstrn., AAUP, UN Assn. Tucson (pres. 1964-67), Western Govs. Research Assn., Tucson Council Fgn. Relations, Am. Council on Consumer Interests, Am. Soc. Assn. Execs., Phi Beta Kappa, Pi Sigma Alpha (nat. council 1968-78). Episcopalian. Club: Univ. Faculty (U. Ariz.) (pres.). Home: Tucson, Ariz. Deceased.

SHIELDS, GERTRUDE M., writer; b. Indianapolis, Ind., Jan. 6, 1890; d. Elmer E. and Bertha (Applegate) S.; A.B., Ind. U., 1914; studied U. of Chicago, 1916, Columbia, 1925-26. Teacher of English, Anderson (Ind.) High Sch., 1914-17, Shortridge High Sch., Indianapolis, 1917-26; advertising copy writer with Homer McKee Co., Indianapolis, from Sept. 1926. Mem. Delta Gamma Sorority. Presbyn. Author: Caste Three, 1918. Contbr. short stories to Century, Collier's, College Humor, etc. Home: Indianapolis, Ind. †

SHIVERS, ALLAN, b. Lufkin, Tex., Oct. 5, 1907; s. Robert A. and Easter (Creasy) S.; m. Marialice Shary, Oct. 5, 1937; children: John, Allan, Marialice Sue, Brian McGee. B.A., U. Tex., 1931, LL.B., 1933. Mem. Tex. Senate from 4th dist., 1935-46, lt. gov., of Tex., 1947-49, gov., 1949-57; chmn. bd. Western Pipe Line, Inc., 1957-63; sr. chmn. bd. Interfirst Bank Austin, N.A. (formerly Austin Nat. Bank), farmer, lawyer and other bus. interests; dir. Tex. Good Roads Assn., Austin, Interfirst Corp., Dallas, Global Marine, Inc., Los Angeles, Citizens State Bank of Woodville, Houston; adv. dir. People's Nat. Bank of Spring Branch.; Past chmn. adv. bd. dirs. Export-Import Bank. Former U.S. chmn. bd. regents U. Tex. system. Mem. C. of C. U.S. (past pres.). Democrat. Baptist. Clubs: Masons (33 deg.); Shriners. Home: Austin, Tex. Died Jan. 14, 1985.

SHOEMAKER, FRANCIS HENRY, congressman; b. Renville Co., Minn., Apr. 25, 1889; s. Francis Michael and Regina Fredricka (Dreyer) S.; self ed.; m. Lydgia H. Schneider, Apr. 5, 1912 (divorced August 1934); 1 child, Frederic Warren. Began as farmer; later organizer Western Federation of Miners, Non-Partisan League, American Society of Equity, Farmers CoÖperative and Ednl. Union, and Equity CoÖperative Exchange; labor leader, Panama Canal, during construction; speaker and organizer Steel Strike, 1919; leader Packing House Strike, 1920, Railway Shopmen's Strike, 1922; editor and publisher People's Voice, Green Bay, Wisconsin, 1921-27, The Organized Farmer, Red Wing, Minn., since 1928. Mem. 73d Congress (1933-35), Minn. at large. Farm-Laborite. Home: Red Wing, Minn. †

SHOEMAKER, MYRL HOWARD, lieutenant governor Ohio; b. Chillicothe, Ohio, Apr. 14, 1913; s. Royal and Sadie (Mick) S.; m. Dorothy Ruth Cook, 1935; children: Ronald Jerome, Keith Alan, Myrl Howard Jr., Michael Cook, Kevin Lee, Deborah Lou, Kathy Ann, Brenda Susan. Student, Bliss Coll., 1930-32. Owner Twin Constrn. Co., to 1966; mem. Ohio State Ho. of Reps., 1958-83; lt. gov. State of Ohio, Columbus, 1983-85. Mem. Twin Sch. Dist. Sch., 1937-59; clk. Paint Valley Sch. Bd., 1958-60. Mem. Farmers Union, Farm Bur. Club: Paint Valley Foxhunters. Home: Columbus, Ohio. Died July 30, 1985.*

SHOOK, KAREL FRANCIS ANTONY, balletmaster, choreographer, author; b. Renton, Wash., Aug. 29, 1920; s. Walter Burnell and Ida Maria Teresa (Tack) S. Student, Cornish Sch. Allied Arts, Seattle, Sch. Am. Ballet. tchr. Katherine Dunham Sch., 1952-54, Studio Dance Arts, 1954-57, June Taylor Sch., 1957-59, Het Nationale Ballet, Amsterdam, Holland, 1959-68. Dancer, Ballet Russe de Monte Carlo, 1940-47, 49-52, N.Y.C. Ballet, 1949; co-dir. Dance Theatre Harlem, N.Y.C., 1968—; artistic adviser, Maris Battaglia's Am. Acad. Ballet, Tonawanda, N.Y.; choreographer: Souvenir, 1954, Jazz-Nocturne, 1959, Alceste, 1966, Le Corsaire, 1972, Don Quixote, 1974; author: Beyond The Mist, 1968, Elements of Classic Ballet Technique, 1978. Recipient Human Resources award N.Y.C. Housing Authority, 1976; Presdl. award for excellence The White House, 1980. Mem. Am. Guild Mus.

Artists. Roman Catholic. Home: Englewood, N.J. Died July 25, 1985.

SHORE, SIDNEY, educator; b. Phila., Sept. 13, 1921; s. Maurice William and Freda (Sillman) S.; B.S. in Civil Engring., U. Pa., 1943; M.S. in Civil Engring., Columbia, 1949; Ph.D., Harvard, 1960; m. Mildred Cohen, Dec. 21, 1946; children—Neal Adam, Monica Gail, Fred Eric. Research and test engr. Bur. Aeros., U.S. Navy, 1943-45; asst. prof. Princeton, 1946-52; mem. faculty U. Pa., 1952-81, prof. civil and urban engring., 1960-81, chmn., dept. civil and urban engring., 1973-78; dir. ops. analysis standby unit USAF, 1963-66; teaching fellow Harvard, 1950-51; vis. lectr. Swarthmore Coll., 1961; vis. prof. Royal Inst. Tech., Stockholm, Sweden, 1962-63; partner Structural Mechanics Assos. Served with USNR, 1945-46. Fulbright scholar, Sweden, 1962-63. Registered profl. engr., Pa. Fellow ASCE; mem. Am. Soc. Engring. Edn., Internat. Assn. Bridge and Structural Engring., Am. Acad. Mechanics, Soc. Exptl. Stress Analysis, Sigma Xi, Tau Beta Pi. Contbr. articles to profl. jours. Home: Narberth, Pa. Died May 9, 1981.

SHORES, LOUIS, univ. dean, author, editor; b. Buffalo, Sept. 14, 1904; s. Paul and Ernestine (Lutenberg) S.; A.B., U. Toledo, 1926; M.S., Coll. City N.Y., 1927; B.L.S., Columbia U., 1928; student U. Chgo., 1930-31; Ph.D., George Peabody Coll., 1934; D.H.L. (hon.), Dallas Bapt. Coll., 1970; m. Geraldine Urist, Nov. 19, 1931. Asst., Toledo Pub. Library, 1918-22, U. Toledo Library, 1924-26; reference asst. N.Y. Pub. Library, 1926-28; librarian, prof. library sci. Fisk U., 1928-33; librarian George Peabody Coll., Nashville, 1933-35, dir. Library Sch., 1933-46; asso. editor Collier's Ency., 1946-60, editor in chief, 1960-81; dean Library Sch., Fla. State U., 1946-67, prof. and dean emeritus, 1967-81; Fulbright research fellow U.K., 1951-52; spl. lectr. library sci. McGill U. 1930, U. Dayton, 1931, Colo. State Coll. Edn., 1936; vis. prof. U. So. Ill., 1968, U. Colo., 1969; vis. lectr. Dalhousie U., 1970; dir. Tex-Tec, 1967-68. Served from 1st lt. to maj. USAAF, 1942-46; maj. Res., 1946-53. Decorated Legion of Merit. Recipient Beta Phi Mu award, 1967; Mudge citation, 1967; cited as founder library-coll. movement Library-Coll. Assos., 1971; named charter mem. Pres.'s Club, Fla. State U., 1977. Mem. Assn. Coll. and Reference Librarians (dir.), ALA, NEA, Southeastern Library Assn. (pres. 1950-52), Phi Kappa Phi, Phi Delta Kappa, Kappa Delta Pi, Pi Gamma Mu. Author: Origins of the American College Library, 1638-1800, 1935; Bibliographies and Summaries in Education, 1936; Basic Reference Books, 1937, 2d edit., 1939; Highways in the Sky, 1947; Challenges to Librarianship, 1953; Basic Reference Sources, 1954; Instructional Materials, 1960; Mark Hopkins' Log and Other Essays, 1965: The Library-College, 1966; Around the Library World in 76 Days, 1967; Tex-Tec. 1968; Library-College USA, 1970; Looking Forward to 1999, 1972; Library Education, 1972; Audiovisual Librarianship, 1973; Reference as the Promotion of Free Inquiry, 1974; Quiet World, 1975; The Generic Book, 1977; Speculation: Concerns with Ultimates, 1977; Encyclopedia: A Commonplace Book, 1977; also articles in various library jours., also The Ednl. Forum, Sch. and Soc., N.Y. Herald-Tribune Books, Saturday Rev.; contbg. author: Best Methods of Study, 1938, Compton's Picture Ency.; editor Current Reference Books, Wilson Bull.; Current Reference Aids, Coll. and Research Libraries; Ann. Reference Check List Library Jour., 1954-58; Jour. Library History, 1965-68; contbg., adv. editor Learning Today. Home: Tallahassee, Fla. Died June 19, 1981.

SHORT, MAXWELL NAYLOR, mineralogist; b. Pembina, N.D., Mar. 21, 1889; s. Augustus and Eliza Jane (Naylor) S.; B.S., U. Calif., 1911; Ph.D., Harvard, 1923; unmarried. Mining engr., Mexico and Ariz., 1912-17; instr. Harvard, 1923-24, lecturer, 1927-28; jr. geologist, U.S. Geol. Survey, 1924-26, asst. geologist, 1926-30, asso. geologist from 1930; prof. of geology, U. of Ariz. from 1931. Fellow Mineral Soc. America (pres. 1939); mem. Geol. Soc. America (v.p. 1940), Soc. Econ. Geologists, Am. Inst. Mining and Metall. Engrs. Methodist. Author: Microscopic Determination of the Ore Minerals, 1940. Asso. editor of Am. Mineralogist. Contbr. to professional jours. Home: Tucson, Ariz. †

SHORT, ROBERT EARL, motor freight co. exec., hotel exec.; b. Mpls., July 20, 1917; s. Robert Lester and Frances (Niccum) S.; A.B., Coll. St. Thomas, 1940; postgrad. U. Minn. Law Sch., 1940-41, Harvard U., 1941-42, Fordham U. Law Sch., 1945-46; LL.B., Georgetown U., 1948; m. Marion McCann, Sept., 1947; children—Robert, Brian, Marianne, Kevin, Elizabeth, Carolyn, Colleen. Asst. U.S. Dist. Atty., 1948-50; pres. Mueller Transp. Co., from 1950 (name changed to Admiral Merchants Motor Freight), now chief exec. officer; pres., owner Leamington Hotel, Leamington Motor Inn, Francis Drake Hotel, Dyckman Hotel, Mpls., owner Washington Senators (later Tex. Rangers), Am. League, Los Angeles Lakers, Nat. Basketball Assn. Trustee Coll. St. Thomas, St. Paul; mem. bd. trustees St. Mary's Hosp., Mpls; mem. law sch. adv. council Notre Dame U.; candidate U.S. Senate, 1978; treas. Nat. Democratic Com., 1968; nat. treas. Humphrey-Muskie campaign, 1968; past mem. Council Twin Cities Area. Served to comdr. USN, 1941-47. Mem. Minn. Motor Transport Assn., Ill.-Minn. Motor Carriers Conf. (past pres.), Am. Trucking Assn., Am. Bar Assn., Minn. Bar Assn., Hennepin County Bar Assn. Roman Catholic. Clubs: Interlachen Country (Edina, Minn.), Mpls. Athletic, Minn. Home: Minneapolis, Minn. Died Nov. 20, 1982.

SHOUP, DAVID MONROE, marine corps officer; b. Battle Ground, Ind., Dec. 30, 1904; s. John Lamar and May (Layton) S.; A.B., De Pauw U., Greencastle, Ind., 1926; LL.D., Tufts U., DePauw U., Indiana University; m. Zola De Haven, Sept. 19, 1931; children—Carolyn E., Robert D. Commd. 2d lt., USMC, 1926, advanced through grades to general, 1960; served in USS Maryland, 1929-31; instr., marine corps sch., Quantico, Va., 2 yrs.; operations officer, 1st marine brigade, Iceland, 1941; command, 2nd bn., 6th Marine Regt., 1942, later asst. operations and tng. officer 2d Marine Div.; comd. forces ashore Tarawa, 1943; div. chief staff 2d div., 1944; logistics officer, div. plans and policies Marine Corps Hdqrs., Washington, 1944; comdg. officer Service Command, Fleet Marine Force, Pacific, 1947; div. chief staff 1st Marine Div., Camp Pendleton, Cal., 1949; comd. basic sch., Quantico, 1950-52; fiscal dir. Office Fiscal Dir., Washington, 1953-56; inspector general U.S. Marine Corps., 1956-58; commanding gen. 3d marine div., Okinawa, 1958-59; comdg. gen. recruit depot, Parris Island, 1959; chief staff USMC, 1959; commandant USMC, 1960-63, ret., 1963; dir. United Services Life Ins. Co. Mem. Nat. Adv. Commn. Selective Service. Decorated Congressional Medal of Honor, Purple Heart with oak leaf cluster, Legion of Merit with Combat V, D.S.M., Brit. Distinguished Service Order. Mem. Am. Legion, V.F.W., Delta Upsilon. Home: Arlington, Va. Died Jan. 13, 1983.

SHROYER, FREDERICK BENJAMIN, educator, author; b. Decatur, Ind., Oct. 28, 1916; s. Benjamin Franklin and Huldah (Mutschler) S.; m. Patricia Grace Connor, Jan. 13, 1949; 1 dau., Madeline Gwynn (Mrs. George J. Christophiades). Student, U. Mich., 1935-37; B.A., U. So. Calif., 1948, M.A., 1949, Ph.D., 1955. Mem. faculty Calif. State U. at Los Angeles, 1950-76, prof. English and Am. lit., 1959-75, emeritus, chmn. dept. lang. arts, 1951-53; vis. prof. U. So. Calif., 1958, vis. lect., 1961, Redlands U., 1965, Eastern Ky. U., 1966; Bingham prof. humanities U. Louisville, 1969-70; sr. prof.-lectr. Jesse Stuart Symposium, Jesse Stuart Found. (and affiliated univs.), 1980; founder, dir. Pacific Coast Writers Conf., 1953-55, novelist-in-residence, 1965, 66, 67; founder, dir. Idyllwild Writers Conf., 1956-57; literary editor, columnist Los Angeles Herald-Examiner, 1962-77; lit. cons., moderator, lectr. many TV programs. Author: novels Wall Against the Night, 1957, Quest for Truth, 1961, It Happened in Wayland, 1963, There None Embrace, 1966, Critical Essays in Science Fiction Literature, 1979, Science Fiction Writers, 1981; author, editor: (with H.E. Richardson) novels Muse of Fire, 1971; Editor: (with Paul A. Jorgensen) novels A College Treasury, 2d edit, 1967, The Informal Essay, 1961, The Art of Prose, 1965, (with Dorothy Parker) Short Story; A Thematic Anthology, 1965, (with Louis Gardemal) Types of Drama, 1969. Served to capt. USAAF, 1942-46. Named Alumnus of Distinction U. So. Calif., 1961; resident fellow Huntington Hartford Found., 1958, 65; recipient Sylvania award, 1959, Christopher award, 1965; outstanding prof. award Calif. State U. at Los Angeles, 1967; Disting. Achievement award Louisville Arts Assn., 1969; Cine Gold Eagle award, 1970; named Ky. col. Mem. Nat. Acad. TV Arts and Scis., Blue Key, Epsilon Phi, Phi Delta Kappa, Phi Kappa Phi. Clubs: Greater Los Angeles Press, Hollywood Authors (dir. from 1966, exec. v.p. 1967-77); Kent County Cricket (Canterbury, Eng.); Athenaeum (London); So. Calif. Cricket (Los Angeles); British United Services, Masons (32 degree). Home: Monterey Park, Calif. Died Aug. 24, 1983.

SHURCLIFF, SIDNEY NICHOLS, landscape architect; b. Boston, Mar. 24, 1906; s. Arthur Asahel and Margaret Homer (Nichols) S.; A.B. magna cum laude, Harvard U., 1927, student Sch. Landscape Architecture, 1927-28, 29-30; m. Katharine Noyes Balch, June 28, 1935; 1 foster son, James C. Heigham. Assisted Restoration of Williamsburg, Va., 1928-40; landscape architect, town planner, from 1930; partner Shurcliff and Merrill; prepared town plans for Dedham, Falmouth, Sherborn, Randolph, Marion, Mattapoisett, Needham, Mass.; adviser Boston Park Dept., Met. Dist. Commn. of Mass., from 1930, also colls., univs., instns.; prepared recreation plan for Taiwan, 1971. Mem. adv. com. Trustees of Reservations (Mass.), from 1963; mem., sec. Commonwealth of Mass. Art Commn., 1954-77. Served as lt. comdr. USNR, 1942-45. Fellow Am. Soc. Landscape Architects (v.p. 1952-54); mem. Am. Inst. Planners, Internat. Fedn. Landscape Architects (pres. 1958-62), N.A.D. (assoc.), Gore Place Soc. (gov.). Clubs; St. Botolph, Harvard Travellers, Veteran Motor Car of Am. (Boston); Country (Brookline, Mass.). Author: Jungle Islands, 1929; Upon Road Argilla, 1958; The Day it Rained Fish, 1977; Roughing It in Roughwood, 1979; contbr. to mags. Home: Ipswich, Mass. Died Jan. 1981.

SHURTLEFF, ROY LOTHROP, investment banker; b. Nevada City, Calif., Sept. 19, 1887; s. Samuel and Charlotte (Avery) S.; B.S., U. Calif., 1912; m. Hazle Lawton, Oct. 13, 1913 (dec. 1948); children—Lawton L., Eugene A., Nancy L. Miller; m. 2d Mabel Mitchell Dunn, Mar. 12, 1949. Salesman Louis Sloss & Co., 1912-14, Blyth & Co., Inc. (formerly Blyth Witter & Co.), 1914-18, sales mgr., 1918-19, v.p., dir., from 1949, now chmn. exec. com.; dir. Broadway Hale Stores, Inc., Del Monte Properties Co., Consol. Freightways, Inc. Clubs: Bohemian, San Francisco, Pacific Union. †

SHUTZE, PHILIP TRAMMEL, architect; b. Columbus, Ga., Aug. 18, 1890; s. Philip Trammell and Sarah Lee (Erwin) S.; B.S., Ga. Tech. Coll., 1912; B.S., Columbia U., 1913. Prin., Hentz Apler & Shutze, 1927-35; prin. Shutze & Armistead, Architects, 1935-50; prin. Philip T. Shutze, Architect, Atlanta, 1950-82. Served in World War I. Recipient Bronze medal for design Ga. chpt. AIA, 1976. Fellow AIA; mem. Hist. Soc. Atlanta (hon. trustee). Clubs: Capital City, Piedmont Driving. Home: Atlanta, Ga. Died Oct. 17, 1982.

SIBLEY, JOHN RUSSELL, dept. store exec.; b. Rochester, N.Y., Sept. 18, 1890; s. Rufus Adams and Elizabeth (Conkey) S.; grad. St. Georgse Sch., Newport, R.I., 1908; A.B., Harvard, 1912; m. Charlotte Chace, Apr. 23, 1921; children—Russell Adams, Carolyn Wolfe (Mrs. Andrew D. Wolfe), Susan (Mrs. Lincoln Kinnicott), Elizabeth (Mrs. Nathaniel Saltonstall). With Sibley, Lindsay & treasurer, director, 1926-57; owner of Sibley Farms, Spencer, Massachusetts; also director of Erie Dry Goods Company. Director Worcester Area council Boy Scouts Am. from 1942, pres., 1948-50; former trustee Rochester Community Chest, past mem. bd. Worcester Music Festival. Mem. Clubs: American Jersey Cattle (director), Genesse Valley (Rochester); Worcester, Tatunck Country (Worcester, Mass.). Home: Hilltop, Spencer. †

SIEBERT, FREDRICK SEATON, educational administrator; born at Tower, Minn., December 13, 1902; s. Frank Seaton and Sarah (Paine) S.; A.B., U. of Wis., 1923; J.D., U. of Ill., 1929; m. Eleanor Barkman, July 13, 1932; children—Mary Elise, Andrew W. Reporter Duluth Herald, 1923-24; worked on copy desk Chicago Herald-Examiner, 1924; instr. journalism, U. of Ill., 1929-37, prof., 1927-40; prof. journalism Northwestern University, 1940-41; director Sch. of Journalism and Communications of University of Illinois, 1941-57; director of Division of Mass Communications and School of Journalism at Mich. State U., 1957-60, dean College Communication Arts, 1960-66; admitted to Illinois Bar, 1929. Mem. editorial bd. Journalism Quarterly. Awarded Ill. Press Assn. medal, 1938. Legal counsel for the Inland Daily Press Association and the Mich. Press Assn. Mem. Am. Council Edn. for Journalism. Pres. Am. Assn. Schools and Department of Journalism, 1944. Member Association for Edn. in Journalism (pres. 1960). Sigma Delta Chi, Kappa Tau Alpha, Alpha Delta Sigma. Author: Copyreading, 1930; Rights and Privileges of the Press, 1934; Freedom of the Press in England, 1952; Copyrights, Clearance and Rights of Teachers in the New Educational Media, 1964; co-author: Four Theories of the Press, 1956. Home: Okemos, Mich. Died Mar. 5, 1982.

SIENKO, MICHELL J., chemist, educator; b. Bloomfield, N.J., May 15, 1923; s. Felix and Teofila (Kislova) S.; m. Carol Tanghe, Aug. 25, 1946 (dec. Aug. 9, 1983); 1 dau., Tanya. A.B., Cornell U., 1943; Ph.D., U. Calif.-Berkeley, 1946. Research assoc. Stanford U., 1946-47; instr. chemistry Cornell U., Ithaca, N.Y., 1947-50, asst. prof., 1950-53, assoc. prof., 1953-58, prof., 1958-83; Fulbright lectr. U. Toulouse, France, 1956-57; vis. prof. Am. Coll. in Paris, 1963-64; guest prof. U. Vienna, Austria, 1974-75, 82-83; vis. fellow Cambridge U., 1978-79. Author: (with Robert A. Plane) Chemistry, 5th edit., 1976, Experimental Chemistry, 6th edit., 1983, Physical Inorganic Chemistry, 1963, Stoichiometry and Structure, 1964, Equilibrium, 1964, Principles and Properties, 3d edit., 1979, Chemistry Problems, 2d edit., 1972; editor: (with Gerard Lepoutre) Solutions Metal-Ammoniac, 1964, (with Joseph Lagowski) Metal-Ammonia Colloque Weyl II, 1970, Jour. Solid State Chemistry. Recipient Sporn award Coll. Engring., Cornell U., 1963, Clark Disting. Teaching award Coll. Engring., Cornell U., 1982; Guggenheim fellow Grenoble, France, 1970-71. Mem. Am. Phys. Soc., Am. Chem. Soc. (Chem. Edn. award 1983), Phi Beta Kappa, Sigma Xi, Phi Kappa Phi. Home: Ithaca, N.Y. Died Dec. 4, 1983.

SIGNORI, EDRO ITALO, psychologist, educator; b. Calgary, Alta., Can., July 29, 1915; s. Giovanni Battista and Angela Teresa (Chicchiani) S.; m. Dolores Alba Scarpelli, Apr. 24, 1942; children—Dolores Anne and Donna Lea (twins). B.A., U. Alta., 1937; M.A., U. Toronto, 1938-41, Ph.D., 1947. With NRC Can., 1940-41; instr. U. Toronto, 1946-48; asst. prof. Queens U., 1948-49; asso. prof. U. B.C., Vancouver, 1949-59, prof., from 1959, acting head dept. psychology, 1961-65, 69-72, individual practice psychology, from 1949; Cons. to industry, from 1949; dir. research B.C. Commn. on Edn., 1958-61; coordinator and spl. cons. B.C. Govt. Community Care Services Soc., 1974-75. Co-author: Interpretive Psychology, 1957; Contbr. numerous articles to profl. jours. Served to F./lt. RCAF, 1942-46. Mem. B.C. Acad. Scis. (pres. 1957), Canadian Psychol. Assn. (dir. 1954-57), Am. Psychol. Assn., B.C. Psychol. Assn. (pres. 1952-53), Can. Assn. Gerontology. Home: Vancouver BC, Canada.

SIIPOLA, ELSA MARGAREETA, (MRS. HAROLD E. ISRAEL) educator; b. Fitchburg, Mass., Mar. 15, 1908; d. George William and Lydia (Tikka) S.; m. Harold E. Israel, July 24, 1939 (dec. Oct. 1961). B.A., Smith Coll., 1929, M.A. (Marjorie Hope Nicholson fellow), 1931; Ph.D. (Mary E. Ives fellow), Yale, 1939. Faculty Smith Coll., from 1929, asst., instr., asst. prof., asso. prof., 1929-54, prof. psychology, 1954-69, Harold E. Israel prof.

psychology, from 1969, chmn. dept., from 1956, sci. research dept. psychology, from 1933; vis. prof. psychology U. Calif., 1962-63. Contbr. numerous articles in field. Chmn. Mass. Adv. Com. on Service to Youth, from 1965. Mem. Am. Psychol. Assn., Phi Beta Kappa, Sigma Xi. Home: Northampton, Mass.

SILL, WEBSTER HARRISON, agriculturist; b. Bloomfield Township, Crawford County, Pa., Apr. 22, 1887; s. Lucien Elijah and Delanie Genet (Taylor) S.; student Edinboro State Normal, 1905-07, B.S., Pa. State Coll., 1911; m. Grace Elaine Clark, Dec. 24, 1910; children—Elaine Banning (Mrs. Sidney T. Davis), Webster Harrison, Maurice Lucien. With U.S. Dept. of Agrl. Bur. of Entomology, Washington, D.C., 1911-13; county agrl. agent, Brooke, Ohio, Hancock Counties, W.Va., 1913-19; mem. Bethany Coll. staff, 1913-19; supt. agrl. dept. Wheeling (W.Va.) Steel Corp., 1919-24; county agrl. agent, Parkersburg, Wood County, W.Va., Sept. 1925-48. Recipient Certificate of Distinguished Service, Nat. Assn. of Co. Agrl. Agents, 1941. Pres. Brooke County, W.Va., Bd. of Edn., 1920-21; pres. Brooke County, W.Va., Farm Bur., 1922-24; adviser to bd. dirs. Wood County Farm Bur., Farm Bur. Service Co., Inc., Ohio Valley Cooperative Assn., W.Va. Wool Pool, Toppins Grove Wool Pool, Producers Milk Assns., Agrl. Planning and Community Orgns. Mem. Parkersburg Community Chest, Red Cross (dir. civic orgns. funds campaign) Wellsburg and Parkersburg, W.Va., W.Va. County Agts. Assn. (pres.) Chamber of Commerce (agrl. com.), Pomona and Lincolnville, Pa. grange No. 958, Nat. Assn. County Agrl. Agts (mem. Agrl. Adjustment Assn. com., 1940, chmn. land use com., 1941-42, sec. 1943-45, pres. 1946, mem. exec. com. 1947), W.Va. Univ. Agrl. Extension Div., Dairy, Poultry and Seed improvement assns., Parkersburg Camp of Gideons (pres. 1946-47). Republican. Methodist (mem. bd. of stewards). Author (circulars) Grapes of Pennsylvania, 1911; Pruning, Gardening, 1914, Landscaping the Home Grounds, 1915; farm page, Parkersburg News, 1930-48; lecturer for various civic groups from 1928. Home: Parkersburg, W.Va. †

SILLCOX, LUISA MARIE, orgn. exec.; b. N.Y. City, Dec. 23, 1889; d. George and Anna (Ulmo) Sillcox; A.B., Columbia, 1911. Employee pub. firm Silver Burdett Co., 1911-15; exec. sec. Authors League of Am., N.Y. City, from 1915, also treas. Authors League Fund. Mem. Writers War Bd., 1941-46. Home: Hartford, Vt. †

SILLS, ARTHUR JACK, lawyer; b. Bklyn., Oct. 19, 1917; s. Herman Silverman and Ida (Rosenzweig) S.; m. Mina Minzer, May 7, 1947; 1 dau., Hedy Erna. B.A., Rutgers U., 1938; LL.B. (Kirkpatrick scholar 1938), Harvard, 1941; LL.D., Rutgers U., 1966, Newark State Coll. Bar: N.J. bar 1941. Pub. rate counsel, N.J., 1958-61, atty. gen., 1962-70; sr. partner Sills, Beck, Cummis, Radin & Tischman, 1971-83; Counselor-lectr. counselors course Rutgers U., 1953-55; Mem. Nat. Council Responsible Firearms Policy, Inc. Co-author: The Imbroglio of Constitutional Revision; contbr. to profl. publs. Formerly trustee WNDT-TV, Channel 13; formerly trustee N.J. Easter Seal Soc.; trustee Rabbinical Coll. Am.; past bd. dirs. J.F.K. Community Hosp., Edison, N.J.; past pres. Hillell Bldg. Corp., Rutgers U.; adv. bd. Fed. Bar Assn.; mem. internat. public affairs policy com. B'nai B'rith. Recipient Louis Brownlow Meml. prize for article in State Govts. publ., 1967, Pope Paul VI Humanitarian award, 1968. Mem. Internat. Platform Assn., Am. Bar Assn., N.J., Middlesex County bars, Am. Judicature Soc., Nat. Assn. Attys. Gen. (pres. 1969-70), Phi Beta Kappa. Democrat. Jewish. Home: Metuchen, N.J. Died 1983.

SILSBEE, FRANCIS D(RIGGS), physicist; b. Lawrence, Mass., July 8, 1889; s. Francis H(enry) Silsbee and Ellen (Hudson) S.; B.S., Mass. Inst. Tech., 1910, M.S., 1911; Ph.D., Harvard, 1915; m. Clara L. Gillis, July 22, 1921; children—Henry B., Frances G. (Mrs. H. T. Ames), Robert H. With Nat. Bur. Standards from 1911, lab. asst., chief electricity instrument sect., 1939-46, chief of the electricity and electronics division, from 1946. Fellow of the American Inst. E.E., Am. Phys. Soc., A.A.A.S.; mem. Washington Acad. Scis. (pres. 1950), Philos. Soc. Wash. (pres. 1936), Instrument Soc. Am. Club: Cosmos (Washington). Author articles on elec. sci. jours., trade mags. Home: Washington, DC. †

SILVER, CHARLES HOWARD, wool executive; born Dec. 5, 1888; s. Simon and Anna (Herschkowitz) S.; LL.D., Fordham U.; L.H.D., Yeshiva U.; D.Sc., St. Johns University; Doctor Pedagogy, Manhattan College, m. Hannah Burnstine, January 4, 1912; children—Evelyn Bernstein, Natalie Moscow, Robert L. Dir., v.p. Am. Woolen Co.; pres. Amun-Israeli Housing Corp., N.Y.C., after 1950; pub. interest dir. on bd. Fed. Home Loan Bank of N.Y. Adviser U.S. delegation UN Commn. on Human Rights, 1967; mem. Gov.'s Council on Rehab.; member national executive board Am. Jewish Committee; mem. Pres. Truman's Loyalty Commn., after 1951. Pres. N.Y.C. Bd. Edn., 1952-61; mem. Higher Bd. Edn.; bd. dirs. N.Y.C. Council on Economic Edn. Chmn. N.Y. drive for Infantile Paralysis, Salvation Army; pres. Beth Israel Med. Center, Joseph and Helen Yeamans Levy Found.; mem. Regional Export Expansion Council) dir. N.Y. World's Fair 1964-65 Corp.; pres. Internat. Synagogue, JFK International Airport; vice president Alfred E. Smith Meml. Found.; overseer Jewish Theol. Sem. Trustee Urban League, Yeshiva University; vice president, trustee Jewish Philanthropies, Grand St. Boys Association; member business research board Fordham Univ.; founder Albert Einstein Coll. Medicine. Recipient citatior Yeshiva U.; Star Italian Solidarity; Papal Knighthood St. Sylvester; medallion City N.Y. Mem. Fou Chaplains Brotherhood. Jewish religion (pres. congregation). Home: New York, N.Y. Died Aug. 24, 1984.

SILVERMAN, WILLIAM MAURICE, lawyer; b. Boston, Oct. 21, 1896; s. Isadore and Rebecca (Kudisch) S.; A.B. cum laude, Harvard, 1918, LL.B., 1920, spl. course Sch. Bus. Adminstrn., 1918; m. Edith Bronstein, June 28, 1928; children—Richard, Donald. Admitted to Mass. bar, 1920; practice law, Boston, 1920-81; exec. dir. Boston Coat and Suit Mfrs. Assn. 1942-45, exec. com. Nat. Coat and Suit Recovery Bd., 1943-65; dir., clk. Schaefer Brewing Co. of Mass., Inc.; dir. Valley North Sales Corp. Mem. Mass. Legislature, 1927, 28; commr. Interstate Compact Minimum Wage, 1940-43. Served to ensign USNRF, World War I. Mem. Comml. Law League Am. (gov. 1950-53, v.p. 1954-55, pres. 1955-56), Am., Mass., Norfolk County, Boston bar assns., Union Am. Hebrew Congregations (v.p. New Eng. region), C. of C., Met. Singers (past chmn.), Am. Law Inst., Sigma Alpha Mu (chmn. Boston alumni club, 1948-52). Jewish (v.p., hon. trustee temple). Mason (Shriner). Home: Brookline, Mass. Died Nov. 26, 1981.

SILVIUS, GEORGE HAROLD, educator; b. Virdi, Minn., Apr. 4, 1908; s. George A. and Mell (Goodwin) S.; B.S., Stout State Coll., Menomonie, Wis., 1930; M.A., Wayne State U., 1937; Ed.D., Pa. State U., 1946; m. Josephine O. Edinger, Aug. 29, 1931; 1 dau., Diana Faye (Mrs. Gerald B. Gits). Tchr. indsl. arts Detroit pub. schs., 1929-41, asst. supr. vocational edn., 1941-45, supr. vocational edn., 1945-46; faculty Wayne State U., 1941-81, prof. indsl. edn., 1946-81, chmn. dept., 1946-70; vis. prof. summers Kent State U., Bradley U., Man. Tech. Inst., Winnipeg, Ont., Pa. State U., Wash. State U. Mem. Nat. Assn. Indsl. Tchr. Educators (pres. 1947-48), Am. Vocational Assn. (v.p. 1963-66, mem. indsl. arts policy and planning com. from 1948, v.p. indsl. arts div. 1953-56, editor for indsl. arts of Jour. 1957-63), Indsl. Arts Conf. Miss. Valley, New Eng. Indsl. Arts Assn. (hon. life), Mich. Indsl. Edn. Soc. (hon. life), Am. Indsl. Arts Assn., Am. Tech. Edn. Assn., Epsilon Pi Tau (laureate mem.), Iota Lambda Sigma, Phi Delta Kappa, Mu Sigma Pi, Phi Alpha Delta. Author: Safe Work Practice in Sheet Metal, 1948; Teaching Successfully, 1953, rev. edit., 1967; Teaching Multiple Activities, 1956, rev. edit. pub. as Managing Multiple Activities, 1971; Safe Practices in Woodworking and Plastics, 2d edit., 1957, Organizing Course Materials 1961; The Student Planning Book, 4th edit., 1960. Home: Detroit, Mich. Died Aug. 13, 1981.

SIMMONS, DONALD MACLAREN, business exec.; b. N.Y. City, July 29, 1889; s. Edwin S. and Elizabeth MacLaren; A.B., Princeton, 1911. E.E., 1913, Eng. D., 1939; m. Rachel L. McKnight, Jan. 28, 1921; children—Donald M., Mary Elizabeth Davis. Research and development engr. Standard Underground Cable Co., 1913-27; after its merger into General Cable Corp., successively dir. high voltage transmission, chief elec. engr., chief engr., 1927-39, vice pres., dir. 1939-49. Mem. Insulated Power Cable Engrs. Assn. (past pres.), Am. Inst. Elec. Engrs. Republican. Presbyterian. Clubs: University (New York); Army and Navy (Washington); Electric (Los Angeles); Allegheney Country, Edgeworth (Sewickley, Pa.); Union Interalliée, Paris. †

SIMMONS, HAVEN YOCUM, lawyer; b. Chicago, Ill., May 26, 1888; s. Thomas Harvey and Luella (Yocum) S.; B.S., Coe Coll., Cedar Rapids, Ia., 1910; LL.B., Harvard, 1913; m. Mary Esther Ely, Oct. 4, 1916; children—Haven Ely, William Westerman, John Ashley. Admitted to Ia. bar, 1913, and practiced in Cedar Rapids; senior partner Simmons, Perrine, Albright, Ellwood & Neff; president and dir. Kilborn Photo Paper, Inc.; dir. Roosevelt Hotel Company, Laurance Press Co. Trustee, Oak Hill Cemetery Assn., Home for Aged Women. Mem. Am., Ia. State and Linn County bar assns. Republican. Methodist. Elk. Clubs: Cedar Rapids Country, Pickwick. Home: Cedar Rapids, Ia. †

SIMMONS, JOHN WILLIAM, mfg. co. exec.; b. Toledo, Aug. 12, 1919; s. Francis W. and Stella (Arnsman) S.; B.A., Williams Coll., 1941; grad. Advanced Mgmt. Program, Harvard, 1958; m. Paula Marie Johnston, Oct. 10, 1944; children—Lorraine (Mrs. John Tuohy), Carol, Paula (Mrs. Mark Butler), John William Jr. With Scott Paper Co., 1945-46; with Becton, Dickinson & Co., Rutherford, N.J., 1946-72, exec. v.p., chief ops. officer, dir., chmn. exec. com., mem. finance com., 1961-72; with Morton-Norwich Products, Inc., Chicago, 1972-81, pres., chief exec. officer, dir., chmn. exec. com., mem. fin. com., chmn. bd., 1976-81; chmn. bd., dir. Eaton Labs. P.R., Inc., Canadian Salt Co. Ltd.; vice chmn., dir. Rohm Pharma GmbH; dir. Noroma Produtos Quimicos Ltd. (Brazil), Williams (Hounslow) Ltd. (Eng.), Burlington Industries, Morton Bahamas Ltd.; adv. dir. Arkwright-Boston Ins. Co. Mem. Brazil-U.S. Bus. Council; governing mem. Orchestral Assn.; mem. citizens bd. U. Chgo.; trustee Am. Health Found., Rush-Presbyn.-St. Luke's Med. Center; bd. dirs. Lyric Opera of Chgo. Served to lt. USCGR, 1941-45. Named master knight Sovereign Mil. Order of Malta, 1962. Mem. Pharm. Mfrs. Assn. (dir.). Clubs: Arcola (N.J.) Country; Casino, Glen View, Mid-America, Chicago, Metropolitan, Commercial, The Plaza, Saddle and Cycle, Economic, Tower (Chgo.); Devon Yacht (East Hampton, N.Y.); Maidstone (L.I., N.Y.); Union League, Williams (N.Y.C.); Lyford Cay (Nassau, Bahamas). Home: Chicago, Ill. Died Apr. 1, 1981.

SIMON, WILLIAM JOHN, dental educator; b. Mpls., June 12, 1911; s. Jay Alois and Grace Julia (Funk) S.; m. Lela Belle Tarter, Feb. 26, 1933; children—Elizabeth Grace, Jay Daniel. A.B., U. Minn., 1935, D.D.S., 1936, M.S.D., 1940. Diplomate: Am. Bd. Oral Medicine. Dental intern U. Minn., Mpls., 1936-37, instr., 1937-39, asst. prof., 1939-41, asso. prof., 1941-43, prof., chmn. div. oral diagnosis, 1945-48, prof., chmn. div. operative dentistry, 1948-53; dean, prof. operative dentistry Coll. Dentistry, State U. Iowa, 1953-61; practice dentistry, Mpls., part time, 1936-43; dental dir. mem. nat. adv. council dental research USPHS, 1959-62, dir. clin. devel., 1962-70; prof. dentistry U. Louisville Sch. Dentistry, 1970-83; chmn. advisory com. health careers program Dakota County Vocat. Center, 1976-83. Author: Clinical Dental Assisting, 1973; Co-author: Clinical Operative Dentistry, 1948, Review of Dentistry, 1949; Contbr. articles to profl. jours. Trustee Rosemount United Methodist Ch. Served as 1st lt. Dental Corps U.S. Army, 1943-45. Fellow Am. Coll. Dentistry, Internat. Coll. Dentists; mem. Am. Dental Assn., Internat. Assn. Dental Research, Minn. Acad. Sci., Am. Acad. Oral Roentgenology, AAAS, Minn. Dental Found., Dakota County Hist. Soc. (dir. 1978-83), Nat. Sojourners, Heroes of 76 (past comdr.), Sigma Xi, Omicron Kappa Upsilon, Alpha Sigma Epsilon, Psi Omega. Methodist. Clubs: Mason, Rotarian. Home: Rosemount, Minn. Died Oct. 5, 1983.

SIMONS, JOSEPH H., educator; b. Chgo., May 10, 1897; s. David and Esther (Simons) S.; B.S. in chem. engring., U. Ill., 1919, M.S. in chemistry and mathematics, 1922; Ph.D., in chemistry and physics, U. Cal., 1923; m. Eleanor Mae Whittaker, Aug. 22, 1936; children—Dorothy E., Robert W. Research physicist Atmospheric Nitrogen Corp., Syracuse, N.Y., 1924; head dept. physics and chemistry U. P.R., 1925-26; asst. prof. Northwestern, 1926-32; prof. phys. chemistry, dir. fluorine labs. Pa. State Coll., 1934-50; coordinator fluorine research, research prof., prof. chemistry, chem. engring. U. Fla. since 1950; cons. dir. fluorine research and development Minn. Mining and Mfg. Co., 1944-65. Mem. Am. Chem. Soc., Am. Assn. U. Professors, American Assn. for the Advancement of Science, Am. Inst. Chem. Engrs., Sigma Xi, Alpha Chi Sigma, Phi Lambda Upsilon, Sigma Pi Sigma. Author: A Structure of Science, 1960. Editor: Fluorine Chemistry, 5 vols., 1950—. Home: Gainesville, Fla. Died Jan. 3, 1984.

SIMPSON, BETHEL W., army officer; b. Lansing, Mich., July 11, 1888; s. Lt. Col. Wendell Lee (U.S. Army) and Marian Ottlilie (Wood) S.; B.S., U.S. Mil. Acad., 1911; grad. Army Indsl. Coll., 1926, Command and Gen. Staff Sch., 1927; M.B.A., with high distinction, Harvard Grad Sch. of Business Adminstrn., 1936; m. Mary Laure Cecilia Byrne, Oct. 21, 1912; children—Charles Lee (lt. col., U.S. Army), May Byrne. Commd. 2d lt., U.S. Army, 1911, and advanced through the grades to brig. gen., Feb. 1, 1942; served with 3d F.A., 1911-16; detailed in Ordnance Dept., 1916; proof officer Sandy Hook Proving Ground, 1916-17; in charge planning and operation of inspection proving grounds of Ordnance Dept., World War I; chief engr. Rock Island Arsenal, Oct. 1919-Dec. 1920; ordnance officer, armament officer and mem. F.A. Bd., Ft. Sill, 1920-22; chief ammunition div., tech. staff, Office of Chief of Ordnance, 1922-26; assistant commandant, Ordnance Sch., 1927-34; chief military personnel and training and civilian personnel divs., Office Chief of Ordnance, 1936-41; comdg. Ordnance Replacement Training Center, Aberdeen Proving Ground, Md., 1941-42; comdg. Ordnance Training Center, Camp Santa Anita, Arcadia, Calif., 1943-44; ordnance officer Army Ground Forces, Washington, D.C., 1944-45; mem. Joint Prodn. Survey Com., Joint Chief of Staff, 1945; with rank of col., 1945; brig. gen., 1948. Mem. Army Ordnance Assn., Assn. of Grads. of U.S. Mil. Acad., Alumni Assn. Harvard Business Sch. Club: Army and Navy Country (Arlington, Va.). †

SIMPSON, DONALD JAMES, lawyer; b. Des Moines, Sept. 28, 1907; s. John Clarence and Ora E. (Barlow) S.; B.S., Northwestern U., 1929, E.E., 1930; LL.B., George Washington U., 1935; m. Genevieve Wheeler, July 6, 1931; children—John Douglas, Marcia Lynne. Elec. engr. Gen. Electric Co., 1930, with patent dept., 1931-36; admitted to D.C. bar, 1934, Ill. bar, 1939; practiced in Chgo., from 1936; asso. firm Hill, Gross, Simpson, VanSanten, Steadman, Chiara and Simpson, 1936-43, partner, from 1943. Mem. Chgo. Patent Law Assn. (past mem. bd. mgrs.), Am., Ill., Chgo. bar assns., Chgo. Mountaineering Club, Evanston Hist. Soc. (former trustee), Tau Beta Pi, Sigma Xi. Republican. Congregationalist. Clubs: Union League, Chicago Yacht, Adventurers, Metropolitan, Westmoreland Country; American Alpine; Alpine of Canada; Swiss Alpine; Chgo. Mountaineering (past pres.). Home: Evanston, Ill. Died Feb. 11, 1985; buried Meml. Park Cemetery, Evanston.

SIMPSON, JOHN ERNEST, clergyman, author; born Washington, Ia., Jan. 17, 1889; s. John Francis and Nancy Ellen (Ransom) S.; A.B., Monmouth (Ill.) Coll., 1915, D.D., 1931; student Pittsburgh Theol. Sem., 1917; LL.D. (honorary), Tarkio College, 1953; married Gail Cathcart White Aug. 9, 1917; children—Frances Ellen (Mrs.

Robert H. Block), John W. Ordained to ministry of United Presbyn. Church, 1917; pastor North Ch., Pittsburgh, 1916-32, North Park Ch., Buffalo, 1932-40, First Ch., Oak Park, Illinois, 1940-55. Evanshire Church, Skokie, Illinois, 1955-58; dir. ch. relations Monmouth (Ill.) Coll., 1958-61; dir. Capital Funds program Synod of Ill., 1961-65; pastor of visitation 1st Ch., San Fernando, Cal., 1965-66; minister stewardship Geneva Presbyn. Ch., Laguna Hills, Cal., 1966. Sec. bd. dirs. Homemaker and Related Services, Laguna Hills, Cal., from 1967. Vice moderator United Presbyn. Ch. of N. Am., 1950-51, moderator Illinois Synod. Vice pres. Laymen Tithing Found., Chgo. Recipient Distinguished Alumni award Monmouth Coll., 1961. Author: This Grace Also, 1933; He That Giveth, 1936; This World's Goods, 1939; Into My Storehouse, 1940; Faithful Also in Much, 1941; A Lad's Lunch, 1942; Stewardship and the World Mission, 1944; A School of Stewardship, 1946; Great Stewards of Bible, 1947; God the Supreme Steward, 1956; Stewardship Devotionals, 1960; numerous pamphlets and articles. Home: Laguna Hills, Calif. †

SIMPSON, JOHN MCLAREN, steel co. exec.; b. Chgo., July 27, 1908; s. James and Jessie (McLaren) S.; m. Nancy Townsend Heyser, Dec. 29, 1951; children—Susan Simpson; (by previous marriage)—Michael, Patricia. Student, U. Chgo., 1933. Pvt. sec., 1933-34; with A.M. Castle & Co., steel distbrs., Chgo., from 1934, asst. to pres., 1936-37, v.p., 1937-43, pres., 1944-61, chmn., 1961-77, chmn. exec. com., from 1977. Trustee Rush-Presbyn.-St. Luke's Med. Center, Chgo., Field Mus. Natural History. Republican. Clubs: Chicago (Chgo.), Shore Acres (Chgo.), Onwentsia (Chgo.), Tavern (Chgo.), Racquet (Chgo.). Home: Lake Forest, Ill. Died Oct. 31, 1983.

SIMPSON, MALCOLM DOUGLAS, banker; b. Riverdale-on-Hudson, N.Y., Dec. 31, 1884; s. William and Louise Parker (Vermeire) S.; Eastman Coll., 1900; B.C.S., N.Y.U., 1913; m. Annette Adelaide Hemphill, June 19, 1912. Staff J.P. Morgan & Co., 1909-49; instr. accounting sch. commerce, N.Y.U., 1913-19; treas., dir. Fieldston, Inc., from 1924; pres. Alderbrook, Inc., from 1934. Staff Am. Commn. to Negotiate Peace, Paris, 1919; staff German Loan Commn., 1922. trustee N.Y.U. from 1933; treas., dir. Masonic Found. Med. Research and Human Welfare. Mem. Alpha Kappa Psi (past v.p., mem. exec. com.), Phi Gamma Delta. Protestant Episcopalian. Mason (33). Clubs: Winged Foot Golf (Mamaroneck, N.Y.); New York University, Masonic, Church (New York City). Home: Riverdale-on-Hudson New York City, NY. †

SIMPSON, RICHARD CLAUDE, indsl. distbn. exec.; b. Los Angeles, Apr. 23, 1918; s. Claude Vernon and Evelyn (Bowers) S.; A.B., Stanford, 1940; M.B.A., Harvard, 1942; div.; children—Barbara (Mrs. Edwin A. Meserve, Jr.), Diane (Mrs. James Cunningham), Carol; m. 2d, Mary Alice Clark, Mar. 1971; stepchildren—Karin, Susan (Mrs. John Janneck), Michael and James Burnap, Anne Marie and Bruce Cordingly. Mdse. mgr. Rexall Drug & Chem. Co., Los Angeles, 1946-56; dir. marketing devel. Ducommun, Inc., Los Angeles, 1956-58, v.p., 1958-66, dir., 1960-80, gen. mgr., 1964-66, exec. v.p., 1966-73, pres., 1973-77, vice chmn., 1977-80; dir. 1st Am. Financial Corp., Mattel Inc., Calif. Fed. Savs. & Loan Assn. Bd. dirs. Los Angeles YMCA, 1964-80, Los Angeles C. of C. Served to lt. USNR, 1942-46. Mem. Los Angeles C. of C. (dir.), Phi Beta Kappa, Zeta Psi. Clubs: California; Los Angeles Country; Tuna (Avalon, Calif.); Newport Harbor Yacht (Newport, Calif.). Home: Beverly Hills, Calif. Died Nov. 22, 1980.

SIMPSON, SEYMOUR DAVID, food chain executive; b. N.Y.C., Dec. 31, 1923; s. Philip and Mae (Levy) S.; m. Diane Rosengarten, May 19, 1946; children—Tina Carol, Adrienne Lee, Ronald Allen. B.B.A., CCNY, 1942. With Garden Markets, Inc., N.Y.C., 1946-62; exec. v.p. Shopwell Inc. (formerly Daitch Crystal Dairies, Inc.), N.Y.C., 1962-80, chief adminstrv. officer, 1971-80, pres., chief operating officer, 1980-82, also dir. Food Industry chmn. United Jewish Appeal N.Y., 1964- 66. Served to 1st lt. USAAF, 1943-46, PTO. Mem. Nat. Assn. Food Chains (dir. 1966-69, 70-76), N.Y. State Food Mchts. Assn. (dir. 1971-82). Clubs: Mason. (White Plains, N.Y.), Elmwood Country (White Plains, N.Y.) (treas., bd. govs. 0963-69). Home: Harrison, N.Y. Died Dec. 1982.

SIMPSON, WILLIAM ARCHIBALD, constrn. exec.; b. Denver, Mar. 29, 1887; s. William and Anna F. (MacHardy) S.; student U. Colo., 1907-08, U. Ill., 1909-10; m. Georgia A. Clapp, Jan. 31, 1912; children—William A., David W. With William Simpson Constrn. Co., Los Angeles, from 1910, pres., dir., from 1917; dir., mem. exec. com. Pacific Mut. Life Ins. Co.; dir. Pacific Indemnity Co., Citizens Nat. Bank, both Los Angeles. Mem. Los Angeles C. of C. (pres. 1933), Alpha Tau Omega. Mason (Shriner). Clubs: California, Bel-Air Bay (Los Angeles). †

SIMPSON, WILLIAM H., army officer; b. Weatherford, Tex., May 19, 1888; s. Edward James and Elizabeth Amelia (Hood) S.; student Hughey and Turner Training Sch., Weatherford, Tex., 1903-05; B.S., U.S. Mil. Acad., 1909; grad. Inf. Sch., Fort Benning, Ga., 1924, Command and Gen. Staff Sch., 1925, Army War Coll., 1928; m. Ruth Webber Krakauer, Dec. 24, 1921; step-children—Syble Kight (Mrs. Robert H. Stevenson), Ralph Krakauer. Commd. 2d lt., Inf., U.S. Army, 1909; advanced through the grades to lt. gen., Sept. 1943; served in Phillippines, 1910-12, in Mexico, 1916; aide to Maj. Gen. Bell, Jr., 1917; asst. chief of staff for operations, and chief of staff, 33d Div., A.E.F., France, 1918-19; chief of staff, 6th Div., Camp Grant, Ill., 1919-21; Office, Chief of Inf., War Dept., Washington, D.C., 1921-23; in command of Fort Washington, Md., 1925-27; duty in War Dept. Gen. Staff, Washington, D.C., 1928-32; prof. mil. science and tactics, Pomona Coll., Claremont, Calif., 1932-36; instr. Army War Coll., Washington, D.C., 1936-40; comd. 9th Inf. regt., 2d Div., Fort Sam Houston, Tex., Aug.-Sept. 1940; asst. to div. comdr., 2d Div., Oct. 1940-Apr. 1941; comd. Camp Wolters, Tex., Apr.-Oct. 1941; comdg. 35th Inf. Div., Oct. 1941-Apr. 1942; comdg. 30th Inf. Div., May-Sept. 1942; comdg. XII Army Corps, Sept. 1, 1942-Sept. 28, 1943; comdg. Fourth Army, Sept. 28, 1943-May 4, 1944; comdg. Eighth Army, May 5, 1944-May 21, 1944; comdg. 9th Army, European Theatre, May 22, 1944-June 23, 1945, 2d Army, Sept. 27, 1945-Nov. 30, 1946; for physical disability, Nov. 30, 1946. Decorated D.S.M., Silver Star, Legion of Merit, Bronze Star Medal (U.S.), Croix de Guerre, Comdr. Legion of Honor (France), Knight of British Empire (Gt. Britain), Order of Kutuzov (Russia), Grand Comdr. Order of Orange-Nassau (Netherlands), Grand Officer Order of Leopold with palm, Croix de Guerre (Belgium). Clubs: Army and Navy, Army and Navy Country (Washington, D.C.). Address: Washington, D.C. †

SIMS, JOHN HALEY, (ZOOT SIMS) jazz saxophonist; b. Inglewood, Calif., Oct. 29, 1925; s. Peter and Kate (Haley) S.; m. Louise Choo, Nov. 17, 1970. Grad. high sch. Mem. N.Y. Jazz Repertory Co. Saxophonist, Benny Goodman, Woody Herman, Bobby Sherwood orchs., 1941-50, also with Stan Kenton, Benny Goodman, Gerry Mulligan, 1950-59, formed, Zoot Sims-Al Cohn Quintet, 1959, toured, Europe, U.S., with Norman Granz, with Jazz At The Philharmonic, 1966-67, Monterey Jazz Festival, 1971, 84, Newport Jazz Festival, 1972-77, 79-81, Montreux Festival, 1975, 77, Kool Jazz Festival, 1982-84, 1st White House Jazz Concert, Smithsonian Instn., 1978; composer: Red Door, 1949; Composer: Dark Cloud, 1956, Nirvana, 1974, Blues for Nat Cole, 1975, Bloos for Louise, 1976, Pomme Au Four, 1982, Fish Horn, 1981; numerous jazz recs. Served with USAAF, 1944-46. Recipient Grammy award, 1977, Grammy nomination (3), 1979, 81. Mem. ASCAP (Popular award 1976, 77, 78, 79, 80, 81, 82, 83), Defenders of Wildlife Soc., South St. Seaport. Democrat. Home: West Nyack, N.Y. Died Mar. 23, 1985.

SIMS, PORTER, judge; b. Bowling Green, Ky., Nov. 11, 1887; s. James Caswell and Jane Boyd (McLure) S.; student Virginia Mil. Inst., 1905-08, Univ. of Va., 1908; LL.B., U. of Mich., 1914. Mem. Sims, Rodes & Sims, Bowling Green, Ky., 1914-21, Sims & Sims, 1921-27; judge, 8th Judicial Dist. of Ky., 1928-38; apptd. commr. to Court of Appeals, 1938; elected judge of the Court of Appeals, 1942; became chief justice, 1947. Vice pres. Potter-Matlock Trust Co. In Paris office of asst. auditor, War Dept., 1918-19. Episcopalian. Mason, Elk. Club: Bowling Green Country. Home: Bowling Green, Ky. †

SINGER, CAROLINE, writer; b. Colfax, Wash., Apr. 6, 1888; d. Rev. Edwin James and Anna Cora (Neale) Singer; ed. private schs. and under private tutors; m. C(yrus) Le Roy Baldridge (artist), 1920. Newspaper work on The Bulletin, Daily News, Examiner and Call, San Francisco, 1909-18; free lance writer for mags. and newspapers. With War Dept., Washington, and Am. Red Cross in France, World War. Mem. Women's Internat. League for Peace and Freedom. Author: Turn to the East, 1926; White Africans and Black, 1929; Boomba Lives in Africa, 1935; Half the World is Isfahan, 1936; Ali Lives In Iran, 1937; Santa Claus Comes to America, 1942; "Race? What the Scientists Say."Home: New York, N.Y. †

SINGLETON, GORDON GRADY, educator; b. Bluffton, Ga., June 15, 1890; s. Patrick Henry and Anne (Hammack) S.; B.S., U. of Ga., 1919; student Cambridge U., England, 1919; A.M., Columbia, 1924, Ph.D., 1925; honorary D. Litt., from Baylor University, 1941; m. Hallie Jenkins, June 15, 1920. Sch. prin., Springvale, Ga., 1909-10, Cuthbert, Ga., 1910-11, Shellman, Ga., 1911-12; supt. of schs., Stapleton, Ga., 1914-17, Pavo, Ga., 1919-21, Cordele, Ga., 1921-23; dir. div. of information and statistics, Ga. State Dept. of Edn., 1925-35; prof. summer schs., U. of Ga., 1922, 34, Emory U., 1925-27, Peabody Coll., 1928; mem. sch. survey coms., Providence, R.I., 1924, Dekalb Co., Ga., 1927, Chatham County, 1932; dir. Georgia Normal and Agricultural College, Albany, Ga., 1930; Director of Survey of Georgia Baptist Colleges for Georgia Baptist Convention, 1935; prof. edn. and dir. summer quarter, Mercer U., 1934-37; pres. Mary Hardin-Baylor Coll., Belton, Tex., 1937-52; prof. higher edn. Baylor University from 1952. Served U.S. Army, A.E.F., 1917-19. Fellow A.A.A.S.; mem. Nat. Soc. Study of Edn., Am. Ednl. Research Assn., Nat. Soc. Coll. Teachers of Edn., N.E.A., Nat. Assn. Sch. Administrs., Am. Legion (comdr. Atlanta Post 1930-31), Forty and Eight (exec.-com. 1933), Phi Delta Kappa, Kappa Delta Pi, Kappa Phi Kappa, Pi Gamma Mu, Kappa Alpha. Baptist. Mason (Shriner). Clubs: Kiwanis (pres. Atlanta club 1931, gov. Ga. Dist. Kiwanis Internat. 1935, Legion of Honor). Author: State Responsibility for the Support of Education, 1925; The Government of Georgia, 1930. Contbr. ednl. jours. Home: Waco, Tex. †

SINGLETON, WILLARD RALPH, ret. educator, geneticist; b. Jacksonville, Mo., Apr. 24, 1900; s. John Thomas and Sarah Elizabeth (Polson) S.; B.S. (research fellow), Wash. State Coll., 1922, M.S., 1924; S.M., Harvard, 1926, Sc.D., 1930; m. Dorothy Amrine, Oct. 10, 1931; children—Willard Ralph, Mary (Mrs. Jon Tabor), Thomas Amrine, Margaret Elizabeth (Mrs. Edward Bonarek). Asst. supt. Harvard Botanic Garden, Soledad, Cienfuegos, Cuba, 1925-26; asst. zoology genetics Harvard, 1926-27; asst. geneticist Conn. Agr. Expt. Sta., New Haven, 1927-35, research asso., 1935-48; sr. geneticist Brookhaven Nat. Lab., Upton, L.I., 1948-55; Miller prof. biology U. Va., Charlottesville, 1965-70, prof. emeritus, 1970-82, dir. Blandy Exptl. Farm, U. Va., Charlottesville, 1955-65, helped install 1st Co. 60 source continuous radiation of growing plants to induce mutations; cons. Internat. Atomic Energy Agy., Vienna, 1964-65. Invitation speaker 7th Internat. Genetics Congress, Edinburgh, Scotland, 1939; chmn. Northeastern Corn Improvement Conf., 1948-49; cons. on atomic energy in South, So. Regional Edn. Bd., Atlanta, 1956-57; mem. food and agrl. study group Nat. Acad. Scis., 1957-60; tech. adviser U.S. delegation Geneva Conf. Peace Time Uses Atomic Energy, 1955; Fulbright awards com., 1955-59; NRC com. on plant breeding, 1957-63; Bio-Astronautics com., 1959-60; nuclear radiation and food agr. com., 1960-65; UN atomic energy adviser to Govt. Thailand, 1964-65; dir. Nat. Colonial Farm, Accokeek, Md., 1966-70. Served as pvt. S.A.T.C., 1918. Fellow A.A.A.S.; mem. Am. Genetic Assn. (v.p. 1967, pres. 1968-69), Genetics Soc. Am. (sec.-treas. 1950, sec. 1951-52, v.p. 1953, chmn. awards com. IX Internat. Genetics Congress, Bellagio, Italy, 1953), Am. Inst. Biol. Scis. (chmn. publs. com. 1952-53), Am. Soc. Agronomy, Am. Soc. Naturalists, Sigma Xi, Phi Sigma, Alpha Gamma Rho, Alpha Zeta, Phi Kappa Phi, Phi Delta Kappa. Democrat. Presbyn. Author: Foreword to Genetics in the 20th Century (L.C. Dunn), 1951; Elementary Genetics, 1962, 2d edit., 1967; also sci. papers. Editor Applications of Nuclear Radiation in Food and Agriculture, 1958. Home: Charlottesville, Va. Died July 28, 1982.

SINSABAUGH, ART, (ARTHUR REEDER) photographer, educator; b. Irvington, N.J., Oct. 31, 1924; s. Grant Regynold and Helyn Edna (Reeder) S.; children: Elisabeth Helyn, Katherine Anne. B.S., Inst. Design, Chgo., 1949; M.S., Ill. Inst. Tech., 1967. Jr. photographer War Dept., 1942-43; instr. Inst. Design, Ill. Inst. Technology, Chgo., 1949-52, instr., head eve. div. photography, 1951-59; faculty U. Ill., Champaign-Urbana, from 1959, prof. art, from 1969, head photography and cinematography program, 1959-77, head photography program, 1959-80; founder, co-dir. Visual Research Lab., 1974-78; vis. artist U. Oreg., Eugene, 1964, U. N.H., Durham, 1968, Williams Coll., Williamstown, Mass., 1973, Chgo. Art Inst., 1968; photog. surveys, City of Chgo. and City of Balt. Author: (with Anderson) 6 Mid-American Chants/11 Midwest Landscapes, 1964, American Landscapes (Portfolio), 1980, The Chicago Landscapes of Art Sinsabaugh, 1983; Art Sinsabaugh Archive established at, Ind. U. Art Mus., Bloomington, 1978. Served with USAAC, 1943-46. Guggenheim fellow, 1969; asso. Center for Advanced Studies U. Ill., 1972-73; grantee Ill. Arts Council, 1966; grantee Ill. Arts Council Graham Found., 1966; grantee Ill. Arts Council Nat. Endowment for Arts, 1976; Nettie Marie Jones fellow, 1983. Mem. Soc. for Photog. Edn. (founding mem.). Home: Champaign, Ill. Died 1983.

SIRAGUSA, CHARLES, ret. state ofcl.; b. N.Y.C., Oct. 28, 1913; s. John and Rosa (LoPresti) S.; B.S., N.Y.U. Sch. Edn., 1933; m. Louise McDowell, Jan. 7, 1938; children—John Charles, Charles William. With Immigration and Naturalization Service, 1935-39; with Bur. Narcotics, 1939-63, successively narcotic agt., dist. supr. Europe and Near East, field supr. enforcement, asst. dep. commr., asst. to commr., 1939-62, dep. commr., 1962-63, ret.; exec. dir. Ill. Crime Investigating Commn., 1963-76, ret.; mem. Chgo. Mayor's Riot Study Com., Cook County Jail Com.; vice chmn. central zone Law Enforcement Intelligence Units. Served with OSS, USNR, World War II; lt. comdr. Res. Decorated knight of Merit (Italy); recipient gold medal for exceptional civilian service U.S. Treasury Dept.; Colombo award Italian-Am. Man of Year award for 1960. Mem. Internat. Assn. Chiefs Police, U.S. Treasury Agts. Assn., World Peace Through Law (narcotics control expert), Ill. Assn. Police Chiefs, Am. Legion. Author: The Trail of the Poppy: Behind the Mask of the Mafia, 1966. Tech. adviser, actor motion picture Lucky Luciano, 1973. Home: Buffalo Grove, Ill. Died Apr. 15, 1982.

SISTO, JOSEPH ANTHONY, business exec.; b. Newark, Aug. 11, 1889; s. William and Filomena (Corbo) S.; student pub. schs. Orange; m. Katherine S. Williams, Jan. 1913 (dec.); m. 2d Gladys White, Aug. 11, 1926. Pres., dir. Costal Steel Corp.; chmn. bd., pres. Phoenix Steel Corp., Del., New Jersey; past chmn. bd. Phoenix Steel Corp., Phoenix Bridge Company, cons. Member American, British iron and steel insts., Am. Acad. Polit. and Social Sci., Assn. Iron and Steel Engrs. Clubs: Bankers of Am. (N.Y.C.); Essex County Country, Loan-taka Skeet. Home: South Orange, N.J. †

SITLINGTON, WILLIAM TICHENOR, newspaper editor; b. Kansas City, Mo., Dec. 8, 1890; s. William Scott and Hedwig (Boley) S.; ed. pub. schools and DePauw U.; m. Mayme Naylor, April 7, 1915 (now deceased); 1 son, William Joseph. Began as reporter Greencastle, 1912; editor Arkansas Democrat, Little Rock. Mem. Sigma

Delta Chi. Democrat. Methodist. Home: Little Rock, Ark. †

SKAGGS, MARION BARTON, chmn. bd. Safeway Stores; b. Aurora, Mo., Apr. 5, 1888; s. Samuel M. and Nance E. (Long) S.; ed. in grade and high school; m. Estella Iona Roselle, Oct. 28, 1907. Started in grocery business in Okla., 1907; opened first store in Safeway Chain in American Falls, Ida., 1915; chmn. bd. Safeway Stores. Home: Piedmont, Calif. †

SKELDON, PHILIP CASS, zool. park adminstr.; b. Toledo, Apr. 12, 1922; s. Frank L. and Helen M. (Halpin) S.; student DeSales Coll., Toledo, 1940-42; D.Pub. Service, U. Toledo, 1976; m. Bernadine G. Wambold, Oct. 12, 1946; children—Thomas, Claudia, Martin, Constance, Barry, Stephen, Kim, Peter, Jeffery, Monica, Philip. Zookeeper Toledo Zoo, 1950-51, bus. mgr., 1952, exec. dir., 1953-81. Served with USMCR, 1942-46. Decorated Purple Heart. Mem. Am. Assn. Zool. Parks and Aquariums (pres. 1958-59), Internat. Union Dirs. of Zool. Gardens. Home: Toledo, Ohio. Died.

SKOG, LUDWIG, cons. engr.; b. Bodo, Norway, Mar. 24, 1888; s. Peter and Elen (Pedersen) S.; M.E., Trondheim Poly. Inst., Norway, 1909; m. Agnes Mueller, Dec. 8, 1912; children—Marie Zuver, Ludwig, Reidar M. Came to U.S., 1909, naturalized, 1920. Draftsman, Inland Steel Co., Indiana Harbor, Ind., 1909-10; draftsman Sargent & Lundy, Chgo., 1910-19; chief mech. draftsman, 1919-24, mech. engr., 1924-31, chief mech. engr., 1931-32, chief mech. engr. and dir., 1932-38, v.p., chief engr., 1938-40, partner, chief engr., 1940-46, sr. partner, 1947-53; cons. engr., design and engr. power plants for elec. utilities, indsl. plants, municipalities, from 1954; dir. Ill. Power Co. Dir. Ill. Inst. Tech.; exec. com. Armour Research Found., Chgo. Fellow Am. Soc. M.E.; mem. Western Soc. Engrs. Clubs: Chicago, Michigan Shores (mem. bd. dirs.), Norwegian (all Chgo.). Home: Wilmette, Ill. †

SKOLSKY, SIDNEY, journalist, motion pictures producer; b. N.Y.C., May 2, 1905; s. Louis and (Mildred); m. Estelle Lorenz, Aug. 27, 1928; children—Nina, Steffi. Student, N.Y. U., 1925. Press agt., 1925-29, Broadway columnist, 1929-33, Hollywood columnist, from 1933. Writer: monthly column From A Stool at Schwabs, Photoplay mag.; producer: Columbia film The Jolson Story, 1946, The Eddie Cantor Story, 1953; TV spl., 1961; writer TV documentary, 1962, Hollywood, The Golden Years, 1970; Author Don't Get Me Wrong—I Love Hollywood, 1975. Home: Los Angeles, Calif. Died May 3, 1983.

SKYNNER, HENRY JOHN, librarian; b. Ft. William, Ont., Can., Nov. 10, 1930; s. Henry John and Susan Beatrice (Carter) S.; B.A., U. Man., Winnipeg, Can., 1951; L.Th., St. Johns Coll., Winnipeg, 1952; S.T.M., McGill U., Montreal, Que., 1956; B.L.S., U. Toronto (Ont., Can.), 1962. Ordained to ministry Anglican Ch., 1952; curate St. James Ch., Winnipeg, 1952-53, St. Johns Cathedral, Winnipeg, 1953-54, St. Matthias Ch., Montreal, 1954-56, St. John Evangelist Ch., Montreal, 1956-58; rector St. John Baptist Ch., Winnipeg, 1958-61; asst. prof. Near Eastern langs. St. Johns Coll., 1958-68, librarian, 1962-68; asso. dir. tech. services library U. Man., 1968-81. Recipient Inkster medal, 1957; Birks div. fellow, 1956-57; H.W. Wilson scholar, 1961-62. Mem. Canadian Assn. Coll. and Univ. Libraries (past pres.), Can. Library Assn., Man. Library Assn. Home: Winnipeg, M.B., Canada. Died Sept. 7, 1981; interred Winnipeg, M.B., Canada.

SLANE, CARL POWELL, newspaper pub.; b. Princeville, Ill., June 19, 1889; s. Oliver C. and Mina (Powell) S.; student Bradley U., Peoria, 1903-06; m. Frances Adele Pindell, June 3, 1914; 1 son, Henry Pindell. With Peoria (Ill.) Jour.-Transcript, Inc., from 1915, pres., treas. and pub.; pres. Peoria Newspapers, Inc., from 1943, chmn. The Peoria Jour. Star, Inc., from 1956; dir. Toledo, Peoria & Western R.R. Co., Comml. Nat. Bank of Peoria, Gt. Lakes Paper Co. Ltd., Toronto, Can. Trustee Bradley U. Served as ensign in Pay Corps. U.S. Navy, World War I. Mem. Sigma Delta Chi, Kappa Tau Alpha. Republican. Congl.-Presbyn. Mason (33). Clubs: Country, Creve Coeur; Chicago Athletic Assn.; Gulf Stream Bath and Tennis (Delray Beach, Fla.). Home: Peoria, IL. †

SLANTZ, FRED WILLIAM, college dean; b. Scranton, Pa., Feb. 18, 1890; s. John C. and Mary (Rice) S.; B.S. in Civil Engring., U. Pa., 1912, C.E., 1923; M.S., Princeton, 1934; m. May Davis, Sept. 19, 1919; children—Fred William, Elizabeth Mary, Robert D. Instr. math. and physics Asheville (N.C.) Prep. Sch., 1912-13; instr. graphics Lafayette Coll., 1913-15; field engr. valuation C.&C. R.R. for ICC, 1915-17; sr. instr. charge sch. for radio mechanics on airplanes, A. and M. Coll. Tex., 1919-21; asso. prof. graphics Lafayette Coll., 1921-24, prof., head dept., 1924-52, dir. James Lee Pardee Placement Bur., from 1927, dean engring., from 1952; cons. engr. on constrn. Lehigh Valley R.R., 1925-27; research engr. William Wharton Corp., 1927-30; with bridge engr. office Me. Hwy. Dept., 1930-32; research on stress analysis of manganese steel under George E. Beggs, Princeton, 1932-34. Served as capt., aviation, U.S. Army, 1917-17; AEF in France. Mem. Am. Assn. U. Profs., Middle Atlantic States Placement Officers Assn. (exec. bd., pres.), Am. Soc. C.E., Am. Soc. Engring. Edn., Lehigh Valley Engrs. Soc., Instrument Soc. Am., Tau Beta Pi, Theta Xi. Publ. editor-in-chief, publ. Soc. Promotion Engring. Edn., also Jour. Engring. Author articles in field. Home: Easton, Pa. †

SLAUGHTER, HARRISON T., lawyer; b. Leesburg, Ohio., Aug. 6, 1910; s. Thomas Terry and Mary (Polk) S.; m. Ruth Nations, Dec. 20, 1938; children—Mary Teresa, Harrison T. Student, Ohio U., 1928-32; LL.B., Nat. U., 1937. Bar: D.C. bar 1937. With USDA, Washington, 1933-34; clk. FCC, Washington, 1934-38, atty., 1938-43, practiced in, Washington, from 1943; sr. partner firm Pierson, Ball & Dowd, Washington, from 1946; Industry adviser U.S. del. 3d N.Am. Broadcasting Conf., Montreal, 1949, Washington, 1950; Industry adviser U.S.-Mexican Broadcasting Conf., Mexico City, 1954. Mem. Am. Bar Assn., Bar Assn. D.C., Fed. Communications Bar Assn., Lambda Chi Alpha. Methodist. Clubs: International (Washington), Congressional Country (Washington), Columbia Country (Washington), Counsellors (Washington). Home: Washington, DC.

SLAVIK, JURAJ, ex-ambassador Czechoslovakia; b. Jan. 28, 1890, Dobrá Niva, Czechoslovakia; s. Dr. Ján and Izabella (Maróthy) C.; student Ecole de Droit, Paris, 1910-11; College de France, 1911; JUDr., Budapest Univ., 1913; m. Gita B. Ruhmann, Jan. 7, 1929; children—Tatjana, Dusan, Juraj. For a short time practised law and took an active part in polit. life of Slovakia; sec. Slovak Nat. Council at Bratislava, 1918, later mem. Czechoslovak Nat. Assembly, Praha; apptd. head of County of Kosice, 1922; minister of Agr. and of Unification of Laws, 1926; mem. of Parliament, 1929-35; minister of Interior, 1929-32; M.P. and E.E. to Poland, 1936-39. Came to U.S. as lecturer, 1939. Mem. Czechoslovak Nat. Com., Paris, 1939; minister of Interior, 1940-45; minister of edn., 1940-45, in Czechoslovak Cabinet, London, Eng.; Czechoslovak minister of fgn. affairs, Praha, June 1945-June 1946; A.E. and M.P. of Czechoslovakia to Washington, D.C., 1946-48. Author: numerous essays, novels and poems.†

SLAVSON, SAMUEL RICHARD, group psychotherapy cons.; b. Russia, Dec. 25, 1890; s. Samuel and Fanny (Tarsy) S.; B.S., Cooper Union, N.Y.C., 1913; postgrad. Coll. City N.Y., Tchrs. Coll. Columbia; m. Cornelia Slavson, Dec. 1926; children—Robert Miles, Hertha Ann, Gerda Louise. Came to U.S. 1903, naturalized, 1913. Deptl. dir., curriculum cons. Walden Sch., 1918-27; ednl. cons. Pioneer Youth Am., N.Y.C., 1921-27; dir. research child psychology Malting House Sch., Cambridge, Eng., 1927-29; speaker Internat. Congress on Edn., Denmark, 1929; ednl. cons. group work Madison House, also YMHA, N.Y.C., 1931-34; dir. group psychotherapy Jewish Bd. Guardians, 1934-56; lectr., sch. edn. N.Y. U., 1935-41, Yeshiva U, 1950-53, summer sch. Springfield Coll., 1939, 40; cons. group psychotherapy Bridgeport (Conn.) Mental Hygiene Soc., 1945-48. Community Service Soc., N.Y.C., 1946-51. Jewish Child Guidance Clinic, Newark, 1947-51; youth consultation service, 1950-57. Hudson Guild Counselling Service, 1949-56, Childrens Village, 1956-63. Northshore Youth Consultation Service, 1959-63, Mental Health Consultation Center Bergen County, N.Y., 1963-65; cons. staff devel. Bklyn. State Hosp., 1964-68; lectr. U. N.Y. Med. Centre, 1965-81; chmn. commn. on group psychotherapy, speaker Internat. Congress Mental Health, Eng., 1948, 57, 68; co-pres. Internat. Congress Group Psychotherapy, Toronto, Ont., Can., 1954. Zurich, Switzerland, 1957. Cons. to com. on study Japanese problems World War II. Recipient Parents Mag. award, 1940, Adolph Meyer award in Mental Health, 1956; Wilfred C. Hulse award, 1964, Fellow Am. Orthopsychiat. Assn., Am. Acad. Psychotherapists, Am. Group Psychotherapy Assn. (pres. 1943-45, former chmn. com. research and adminstrn.); mem. Assn. Study Group Work (exec. bd. 1939-42), Nat. Conf. Social Work, Welfare Council N.Y.C. (exec. com. on street clubs), Am. Acad. Polit. and Social Sci., N.Y. Acad. Scis., N.E.A., Soc. Applied Anthropology, Inst. Social Psychiatry Eng., A.A.A.S., Group Psychotherapy Inst. (pres.). Author: Science in the New Education (with Robert K. Speer), 1934; Creative Group Education, 1937; Character Education in a Democracy, 1939; Introduction to Group Therapy 1942; Recreation and the Total Personality, 1946; The Practice of Group Therapy, 1947; Analytic Group Psychotherapy, 1950; Child Psychotherapy, 1952; Re-Educating the Delinquent, 1954; The Fields of Group Psychotherapy, 1956; Child-Centered Group Guidance of Parents, 1958; A Textbook in Analytic Group Psychotherapy, 1964; Reclaiming the Delinquent through Para-analytic Group Psychotherapy and the Inversion Technique, 1965; Because I Live Here, Vita-Erg Therapy with Regressed Psychotic Women, 1970, (with Mortimer Schiffer) Group Psychotherapies with Children, 1974. Contbr. articles, chpts. to ednl., psychiat. therapeutic publs. Asso. editor Psychiatric Dictionary, Vol. 2; founder, cons. editor Internat. Jour. of Group Psychotherapy. Home: New York, N.Y. Died Aug. 5, 1981.

SLEETH, CLARK KENDALL, physician, educator; b. Logansport, W.Va., Apr. 10, 1913; s. Waitman T. Willey and Pleasant (Kendall) S.; A.B., W.Va. U., 1933, B.S. in Medicine, 1935; M.D., U. Chgo., 1938; D.Sc., Davis-Elkins Coll., 1966; m. Nellie Juniata Strouss, May 23, 1936; children—Ann Alice, Mary Virginia, Jane Adella. Fellow physiology W.Va. U. Sch. Medicine, 1935-37; intern, then resident in medicine Henry Ford Hosp., Detroit, 1939-41; mem. faculty W.Va. U. Sch. Medicine, Morgantown, 1938-82, asso. prof. medicine, 1948-60, prof., 1961-82, prof. family medicine, 1973-82, asst. to dean, 1958-60, dean, 1961-70, acting chmn. dept. family medicine, 1973-74; physician W.Va. U. Health Service, 1941-60; attending physician Vincent Pallotti, Monongalia Gen. hosps., Morgantown, 1941-60; staff physician internal medicine W.Va. U. Hosp. and Clinics, 1960-82. Examiner for practical nurses W.Va. State Bd., 1957-63. Past pres. W.Va. div. Am. Cancer Soc.; mem. Monongalia County Bd. Edn., 1957-68. Served to capt. USAAF, 1942-46. Mem. Am., W.Va. (past 1st v.p.) med. assns., Am., W.Va. (past pres.) heart assns., Morgantown C. of C. (past v.p.), Phi Beta Kappa, Sigma Xi, Alpha Omega Alpha. Methodist. Mason, Rotarian. Contbr. articles on physiologic effects hypoxia to med. jours. Home: Morgantown, W.Va. Died Nov. 30, 1982.

SLETTO, RAYMOND FRANKLIN, educator, sociologist; b. Gibbon, Minn., July 20, 1906; s. Andrew E. and Olina M. (Bakke) S.; B.S., U. Minn., 1926, A.M., 1932, Ph.D., 1936; post doctoral study, Columbia, 1939, U. Chgo., 1940; m. Beatrice Jorgenson, Sept. 18, 1934; 1 dau., Sandra. High sch. prin., Appleton, Minn, 1927-30; instr. U. Minn., Mpls., 1930-36, asst. prof., 1937-39, asso. prof., 1940-47, coordinator research, gen. coll., 1934-36; Social Sci. Research Council post-doctoral fellow, 1939-40; prof. sociology Ohio State U. Columbus, 1947-76, prof. emeritus, 1976-83, chmn. sociology, anthropology dept., 1955-67; psychologist Bur. Agrl. Econs., USDA, 1941-42; dir. bur. sociol. research Mpls. Council Social Agys., 1937; research cons. USDA, USAF, other fed. agys. Mem. mental health tng. com. NIMH. Mem. AAAS, AAUP, Am. Acad. Polit. and Social Sci., Am. Psychol. Assn., Am. Sociol. Assn. (chmn. research com. 1949-52, mem. council and exec. com. 1956-59, chmn. nat. membership com. 1963-68, mem. nominating com. 1967-70), Ohio Valley (pres. 1952-53), Rural sociol. socs., Am. Statis. Assn., Nat. Council Family Relations, Sociol. Research Assn. (sec.-treas. 1954-55, pres. 1955-56), Beta Gamma Sigma, Alpha Kappa Delta (mem. exec. com. 1965-70). Mason. Author: (with E.A. Rundquist) Personality in the Depression 1936; Construction of Personality Scales by the Criterion of Internal Consistency, 1937. Contbr. articles to profl. publs. Home: Westerville, Ohio. Died May 9, 1983.

SLEZAK, JOHN, printing co. exec.; b. Stara Tura, Czechoslovakia, Apr. 18 1896 (came to U.S. 1916); s. Simon and Ann (Trokan) S.; B.S. in Mech. Engring., U. Wis., 1923; m. Dorothy Goodwill, Aug. 23, 1926; children—Nancy Jean, Doris Ann. Mech. engr. Western Electric Co., Chgo., 1923-30; pres. Turner Brass Works, Sycamore, Ill., 1930-53; chmn. bd. Kable Printing Co., Mt. Morris, Ill., 1947-72; pres., chmn. bd. Pheoll Mfg. Co., Chgo., 1948-53; asst. sec. of Army, 1953, under sec., 1953-55; dir. Hazeltine Corp., Clayton Mark Co., Roper Corp., Hazeltine Research, Inc., Western Pub. Co. Past chmn. res. forces policy bd. Dept. Def., Washington; past dir. Inst. Am. Strategy. Trustee Ill. Inst. Tech., from 1949, Found. for Econ. Edn., 1955-67, Am. Mus. Immigration, 1955-69. Served as col. AUS, 1943-46, chief Chgo. Ordnance Dist., 1944-46; cons. Army and Navy Munitions Bd., 1947. Decorated Legion of Merit with oak leaf cluster, Freedom medal. Mem. Am. Ordnance Assn. (dir.), Ill. Mfrs. Assn. (pres., chmn. bd. 1950-52), NAM (dir. 1952-53), Western Soc. Engrs., Ill. C. of C. (past dir.), Assn. U.S. Army (pres. 1955-57), Am. Legion. Clubs: Chicago, Commercial, Chicago Athletic (Chgo.). Lodge: Moose. Home: Sycamore, Ill. Died Apr. 14, 1984; interred Arlington Nat. Cemetery.

SLEZAK, WALTER, actor; b. Vienna, Austria, May 3, 1902; s. Leo and Elizabeth (Wertheim) S.; student Vienna U., 1920-21; m. Johanna Van Rijn, Oct. 10, 1943; children—Erica, Ingrid, Leo. Came to U.S., 1930, naturalized, 1935. Debut, U.S. stage, 1930; star of stage plays, Meet My Sister, Music in the Air, Fanny, Maywine, I Married an Angel, My Three Angels, The First Gentleman; appeared in Broadway play, The Gazebo, 1958-59; appeared in motion pictures as actor for RKO Studios, 1942-47; pictures include: Once Upon a Honeymoon, Cornered, Sinbad the Sailor, Bedtime for Bonzo, White Witch Doctor, People Will Talk, Riff Raff and others, most recent title being Emil and the Detectives. Recipient Antoinette Perry award, also N.Y. Drama Critics award, both for best male starring performance in a musical (Fanny), 1955. Author: When Does the Next Swan Leave, 1962. Address: Larchmont, N.Y. Died Apr. 22, 1983.

SLIFER, H. SEGER, frat. sec.; b. Greenfield, Ind., June 15, 1890; s. Harry Ottis and Elmira (White) S.; A.B., Wesleyan U., 1911; A.M., Univ. of Mich., 1912, J.D., 1915; m. Ruth E. Robinson. Mar. 20, 1928; children—H. Seger, Paula. Practice of law, Minneapolis, Minn., 1915-19, at Ann Arbor, Mich., from 1919. Editor of Chi Psi Frat. Catalogue, 1915 and 1929, and Centennial Catalogue and History, 1941; sec. and treas. Chi Psi from 1921. Mem. exec. com. Coll. Frat. Editors Assn., 1944. Organizer U. of Mich. Interfrat. Alumni Conf., 1932, sec.-treasurer from 1932. Secretary College Fraternity Secs. Assn., 1943, pres. 1944. Mem. Chi Psi. S.A.R. Democrat. Episcopalian. Vestryman and treas. St. Andrew's Episcopal Ch. Club: Detroit (Detroit). Home: Ann Arbor, Mich. †

SLITOR, RICHARD EATON, financial cons., economist; b. St. Paul, July 1, 1911; s. Ray Francis and Nelle (Eaton) S.; m. Louise Bean, Dec. 24, 1937; children—Prudence Van Zandt (Mrs. William M. Crozier, Jr.), Deborah S. Christiana, Nicholas W., Christopher W. Eaton. Student, U. Wis., 1928-30; S.B. magna cum laude, Harvard U., 1932, Ph.D., 940; M.A. (Carnegie Teaching fellow), Colgate U., 1934. Instr., tutor econs. Harvard, 1934-41, Radcliffe Coll., 1940-41; asso. prof., chmn. dept. econs. and bus. adminstrn. Mt. Union Coll., 1941-42; economist div. tax research Treasury Dept., 1942-49; asst. dir. tax adv. staff Sec. of Treasury, 1949-51, taxation specialist, 1951-53; fiscal economist, tax analysis staff U.S. Treasury, 1953-61, chief bus. taxation staff, asst. dir., office tax analysis, 1961-72; head Richard E. Slitor Assos., from 1972; Fed. exec. fellow Brookings Instn., 1963-64; vis. prof. econs. U. Mass., 1967-68; cons. Nat. Commn. on Urban Problems, 1967-68, Colombian Commission on Tax Reform, 1968, Com. for Econ. Devel., 1970-71, RAND Corp., 1972-74, Adv. Commn. Intergovtl. Relations, 1973-75, EPA, 1976-79, Council Environ. Quality, 1976-77, FRS, 77-78, NEA, 1980-82, others. Author articles and books on taxation. Mem. Am. Econ. Assn., Internat. Inst. Pub. Fin., Royal Econ. Soc., Nat. Tax Assn., Phi Beta Kappa, Chi Phi. Episcopalian. Club: Harvard (Washington). Address: Bethesda, MD.

SLOAN, JOHN EMMET, army officer; b. Greenville, S.C., Jan. 31, 1887; s. Thomas and Anna Lucia (Johnston) S.; B.S., U.S. Naval Acad., Annapolis, Md., 1910; student Field Artillery Sch., 1924-25, Command and Gen. Staff Sch., 1925-26, Army War Coll., 1931-32, Chem. Warfare Sch., 1932; m. Amy Eubanks, Feb. 21, 1919; 1 child, Lucia Marie. Commd. 2d lt., U.S. Army, 1911, advanced through ranks to maj. gen., 1942; served in Panama, 1914-17; comd. 30th F.A., World War; prof. mil. science and tactics, Texas A. and M. Coll., 1926-31; instr. Field Arty. Sch., 1917-18, Command and Gen. Staff Sch., 1932-36; service in Hawaii, 1936-38; prof. mil. science and tactics, Oregon State Coll., 1938-40; brig. gen., comdg. 8th Div. Artillery, Ft. Jackson, S.C., 1941, maj. gen. comdg. 88th Inf. Div. 1942 to 44, took part in Italian Campaign and capture of Rome. Decorated by U.S., France and Italy. Baptist. Address: Washington, D.C.†

SLOAN, MARTIN L(UTHER), electrical manufacturing company executive; b. Sioux City, Ia., May 18, 1887; s. Martin Luther and Ida (Hill) S.; E.E., Ames Coll., 1910; m. Jane M. Hunter, Aug. 15, 1911. Began with Gen. Electric Co., 1910, quality engr. Youngstown Lamp Works, 1912-14, employed in lamp mfg. dept., Cleveland, O., 1914-21, mgr. 1921-27, employed in adminstrn. dept. 1927-42, mgr. lamp dept. from 1942. Mem. Musical Arts Assn., bd. exec. com. Cleveland Symphony Orchestra. Mem. Tau Beta Pi. Republican. Presbyterian. Home: Shaker Heights, Ohio. †

SLOAN, RAYMOND PATON, ret. editor, publishing co. exec.; b. Bklyn., Dec. 12, 1893; s. Alfred Pritchard and Katharine (Mead) S.; student Bklyn. Prep. Inst., 1908-11; L.H.D., Colby Coll., 1946; LL.D., St. Lawrence U., 1954; D. Social Welfare, Women's Med. Coll. Pa., 1958; m. Mabel V. MacArthur, Nov. 20, 1916. Mem. editorial staff Automobile Topics, N.Y.C., 1920-33; editor The Modern Hospital, Chgo., 1933-53, pres., dir. The Modern Hosp. Pub. Co., Inc., 1953-58; v.p. Alfred P. Sloan Found., N.Y.C.; spl. lectr. Sch. Pub. Health, Columbia, 1945-66. Bd. dirs. Thayer Hosp., Waterville, Me.; trustee Community Hosp. at Glen Cove, N.Y., Colby Coll., Waterville; bd. mgrs. Meml. Center for Cancer and Allied Diseases, N.Y.C.; chmn. N.Y. City Hosp. Vis. Com. Recipient la Grande Medaille d'Argent de la-ville de Paris, 1961. Hon. fellow Am. Coll. Hosp. Adminstrs.; mem. Am. Hosp. Assn. (hon.). Clubs: Creek (Locust Valley, N.Y.); Metropolitan, Sky (N.Y.C.). Author: Hospital Color and Decoration, 1944; This Hospital Business of Ours, 1952; On A Shoestring and A Prayer, 1964; Today's Hospital, 1966; Not for Ourselves Alone: The Story of Norfolk General Hospital, 1969. Contbr. articles on hosp. and health topics to profl. and nat. publs. Home: New York, N.Y. Died Mar. 20, 1983.

SLOANE, ERIC, author, artist, meteorologist; b. N.Y.C., Feb. 27, 1910; s. George Francis and Marietta (O'Brien) S.; student Yale, 1929, N.Y. Sch. Fine and Applied Art, 1935; m. Myriam Heyne-Bailey. Artist, 1939-85; lecturer on cloudform and also weather phenomena, 1940-85; designer and builder of Hall of Atmosphere, Am. Mus. Natural History, 1949; dir. Weatherman of Am., 1950-85; executed murals Air and Space Mus., Washington, 1975; syndicated columnist It Makes You Think. Recipient Leadership award for writing Freedom Foundation Valley Forge, 1964. Mem. N.A.D. Clubs: Salmagundi, Wings, Dutch Treat (N.Y.C.). Author: Clouds, Air and Wind, 1941; Camouflage Simplified, 1942; Your Body in Flight, 1943; Skies and the Artist, 1951; Eric Sloane's Weather Book, 1952; American Barns and Covered Bridges, 1954; Our Vanishing Landscape, 1955; Almanac and Weather Forecaster, 1955; Book of Storms, 1956; American Yesterday, 1956; Eric Sloane's Americana, 1957; Seasons of American Past, 1958; Return to Taos, 1960; Look at the Sky, 1961; Diary of Early American Boy, 1962; ABCs of Early Americana, 1963; Folklore of American Weather, 1963; Museum of Early American Tools, 1964; Reverence for Wood, 1965; The Sound of Bells, 1966; An Age of Barns, 1966; The Cracker Barrel, 1967; Mr. Daniels and the Grange, 1967; Don't, 1969; The Second Barrel, 1969; I Remember America, 1971; Little Red Schoolhouse, 1972; The Do's and Don'ts of Early America, 1972; Spirit of '76, 1973; Recollections in Black and White, 1974; For Spacious Skies, 1975; Eric Sloan's I Remember America Calendar. Contbr. articles to Army, Navy manuals. Donor Eric Sloane Mus. Early Am. Tools, Kent, Conn. Home: Cornwall Bridge, Conn. Died Mar. 6, 1985.

SLONE, DENNIS, physician; b. Pretoria, S. Africa, Jan. 9, 1930; s. Simon and Jane (Gerber) S.; came to U.S., 1961, naturalized, 1967; M.B., B.Ch., U. Witwatersrand, Johannesburg, S.Africa, 1956; M.A. (fellow pediatric endocrinology), Harvard U., 1964; m. Annetta Roman Korsunski, Feb. 16, 1956; children—Gregory, Alan, Mark. Intern in medicine and surgery Johannesburg Gen. Hosp., 1956-57; resident in pediatrics Baragwanath Hosp., Johannesburg, 1957-58; asso. dir. clin. pharmacology unit Lemuel Shattuck Hosp., Boston, 1964-69; co-dir. Boston Collaborative Surveillance Program, Boston U. Med. Center, 1969-75, co-dir. drug epidemiology unit, 1975-82; asst. prof. medicine Tufts U. Med. Center, Boston, 1968-71; asso. prof. Boston U. Med. Sch., 1971-82. Mem. Am. Diabetes Assn., Am. Pub. Health Assn., Soc. Epidemiol. Research, Drug Info. Assn., Am. Acad. Pediatrics, Am. Soc. Clin. Pharmacology and Therapeutics, Lawson Wilkins Pediatric Endocrine Soc., Internat. Epidemiol. Assn. Jewish. Author: Birth Defects and Drugs in Pregnancy, 1977; also other books; contbr. articles to med. publs. Home: Lexington, Mass. Died May 1982.

SLOSSER, GAIUS JACKSON, clergyman, theol. sem. prof.; b. near Hoytville, O., June 2, 1887; s. James Elliott and Mary Elizabeth (Jackson) S.; ed. Ohio Northern U., summers 1903, 04; A.B., cum laude, Ohio Wesleyan U., 1912; S.T.B., Boston U. Sch. of Theology, 1915, S.T.M., 1921; grad. study Harvard U. Grad. Sch., 1915-16; Ph.D., King's Coll. U. of London, England, 1928; m. Marguerite Louise Holbrook, June 27, 1917 (died 1925); m. 2d, Esther Victoria Thurston, Apr. 14, 1927; children—Ruth Elouise (Mrs. William C. Gilkey), Gaius Jackson II. Ordained to ministry Methodist Episcopal Church, 1917; served pastorates in Lynnfield, Chicopee, Medford, Holyoke and Natick, Mass., 1917-25; prof. ecclesiastical history and history of doctrine, Western Theol. Sem., Pitts., 1928-56, prof. emeritus, from 1957; mem. faculty Johnson C. Smith U., Charlotte, N.C., from 1957. Chaplain, capt. Mass. N.G. 1917-18, 1919-23; chaplain, 1st lt. then capt., 212th Engrs. World War I; then Reserves, 1919-37. Exec. sec. Pub. Safety Com., City of Chicopee, 1917. Dir. and v.p. dept. history. Presbyn Church U.S.A., 1931-60. Fellow Royal Hist. Soc., London, Eng. Mem. Ohio Wesleyan Union, Delta Sigma Rho. Independent Republican. Mason, Odd Fellow. Del. from M.E. Ch. to First World Conf. on Faith and Order, Lausanne, Switzerland, 1927; asso. del. from Presbyterian Ch., U.S.A., to 2d Universal Conf. on Life and Work, Oxford, Eng., and del. from latter church to 2d World Conf. on Faith and Order, Edinburgh, Scotland, 1937. Mem. Am. Commn. of Fifteen Theologians which prepared study texts for the Edinburgh Conf. Admitted as an expert witness in church canon law and distinctions in numerous court cases, in Pa., New York and Conn., as between Greek and Eastern Rite churches and the Roman Catholic Church. Moderator Presbyn. Synod of Pennsylvania, 1946-47, pres. corp. of this synod and pres. bd. trustees, 1946-56. Author: History of the 212th Engineers, 1918; Christian Unity, Its Hist. and Challenge in All Communions and in All Lands, 1929; The Communion of Saints, 1937; History of the Westminster Assembly and Standards, 1943; They Seek a Country, American Presbyterianism, Some Aspects.†

SLOTKIN, HUGO, food products executive; b. Bklyn., June 12, 1912; s. Samuel and Fanny (Rivkin) S.; m. Babette Walsey, Sept. 1935; children: A. Donald, Mitchell, Curtis, Todd. Student, L.I. U., 1931. Joined Hygrade Food Products Corp., 1931, dir., 1934, asst. sec., 1935, v.p., asst. sec., 1936-49, pres., 1949-68, chmn. bd., 1956-69; owner Hy Meadow Farms, Holly, Mich., 1956—; pres. K & K Provisions Inc., Lake Worth, Fla., 1972-77; dir. Nathans Famous, N.Y.C., 1969-78; sr. v.p., dir. United Brands Co., 1977—; chmn. bd. John Morrell & Co., Chgo., 1977—; pres., chmn., mem. exec. com., dir. Chgo. Bd. Trade; vice chmn., mem. exec. com., dir. Am. Meat, Inst. Bd. dirs. Sinai Hosp., Detroit, United Found., Project Hope.; Mem. inedible animal fats adv. com. W.P.B., 1943. Mem. Eastern Meat Packers Assn. (past pres.). Clubs: Bankers of America; Lawyers (N.Y.C.); Franklin Hills Country (Franklin, Mich.); Standard (Chgo. and Detroit); Harmonie (N.Y.C.); Banyan Golf (Palm Beach, Fla.). Home: Palm Beach FL.

SMAIL, LLOYD LEROY, educator, author; b. Columbus, Kans., Sept. 23, 1888; s. Israel L. and Adda (Thomas) S.; A.B., U. of Wash., 1911, A.M., 1912; Ph.D., Columbia, 1913; m. Margaret Ethel Barton, Sept. 15, 1921; 1 dau., Helen Arlene. Instr., U. Wash., 1913-21, asst. prof. math. and astronomy, 1921-23; asst. prof. math. U. of Oreg., 1923-25; asso. Math. Assn. of Am., Sigma Xi, Phi Beta Kappa. Author: Elements of the Theory of Infinite Processes, 1923; History and Synopsis of the Theory of Summable Infinite Processes, 1925; Mathematics of Finance, 1925; Plane Trigonometry, 1926; College Algebra, 1931; Preparatory Business Mathematics, 1947; Calculus, 1949; Trigonometry, Plane and Spherical, 1952; Analytic Geometry and Calculus, 1953; Mathematics of Finance, 1953; also Math. portion of Van Nostrand's "Scientific Ency.", 1938, rev., 1947. Contbr. articles to various math. jours. Home: Honolulu, Hawaii.†

SMALL, ROBERT OREN, railway exec.; b. Deer Creek, Ill., Aug. 10, 1889; s. George H. and Margaret E. (Pinckard) S.; student pub. schs.; m. Minnie Mae Archibald, Jan. 4, 1913, (died Oct. 14, 1940); 1 dau., Margel Christine (wife Dr. Eugene Hildebrand); m. 2d Marie B. Helmstadter, Feb. 25, 1942. With C.&N.-W. Ry. from 1910. gen. agt., Indianapolis, 1920-24, Phila., 1924-29, gen. freight agt., Chicago, 1929-38, freight traffic mgr. 1938-41, traffic mgr., 1941-47; apptd. gen. freight traffic mgr. C.&N.-W. and C., St.P., M.&O. Ry. 1947-50, asst. v.p., 1950-52, v.p. charge rates and divs., 1952-54, vice president, traffic 1954-55 executive consultant, from 1955; director C.&N.W. Ry. Mem. Nat. Freight Traffic Assn., Chgo. Assn. Commerce. Republican. Presbyn. Mason (Shriner, 32 deg.). Clubs: Union League, Traffic, Western Ry. (Chgo.); Traffic (Milw.); Transportation (Peoria, Ill.)†

SMART, JAMES DICK, clergyman, educator; b. Alton, Ont., Can., Mar. 1, 1906; s. John George and Janet (Dick) S.; B.A., U. Toronto 1926, M.A., 1927, Ph.D., 1931; Lic. Theol., Knox Coll., Toronto, 1929, D.D., 1956; student univs. Marburg and Berlin (Germany), 1929-30; m. Christine McKillop, Sept. 24, 1931; children—Margaret Jean (Mrs. Robert J. Watson), Mary Eleanor, Janet Ann (Mrs. Paul Young). Ordained to ministry Presbyn. Ch. in Can., 1931; minister Ailsa Craig, Ont., 1931-34, Galt, Ont. 1934-41, Peterboro, Ont., 1941-44; editor-in-chief curriculum publs. Presbyn. Ch. U.S.A., 1944-50; minister Rosedale Presbyn. Ch., Toronto, 1950-57; lectr. Christian edn. and homiletics Knox Coll., 1951-57; Jesup Found. prof. Bib. interpretation Union Theol. Sem., N.Y.C., 1957-71; asso. minister Rosedale Presbyn. Ch., Toronto, 1970-74; Carnahan lectr., Buenos Aires, 1963; guest prof. Christian edn. Luth. Theol. Sem., Columbus, Ohio, spring 1977. Mem. Soc. Bibl. Lit. and Exegesis. Author: What a Man Can Believe, 1943; God Has Spoken, 1948; A Promise to Keep, 1948; The Recovery of Humanity, 1953; The Teaching Ministry of the Church, 1954; The Rebirth of Ministry, 1960; Servants of the Word, 1960; The Interpretation of Scripture, 1961; The Creed in Christian Teaching, 1962; The Old Testament in Dialogue with Modern Man, 1964; Revolutionary Theology in the Making (trans.), 1964; History and Theology in Second Isaiah, 1965; The Divided Mind of Modern Theology, Karl Barth and Rudolph Bultmann, 1908-33, 1967; The ABC's of Christian Faith, 1968; The Quiet Revolution, 1969; The Strange Silence of the Bible in the Church, 1970; Doorway to a New Age, A study of Paul's letter to the Romans, 1972; The Cultural Subversion of the Biblical Faith, 1977. Home: Islington, Ont., Canada. Died Jan. 23, 1982.

SMILEY, MALCOLM FINLAY, educator; b. Monmouth, Ill., Dec. 15, 1912; s. Robert Rennsalear and Annie Laurie (Kerr) S.; m. Dorothy Manning, Aug. 20, 1941. B.S., U. Chgo., 1934, M.S., 1935, Ph.D., 1937. Mem. Inst. Advanced Study, 1937-38; instr. Lehigh U., 1938-40, asst. prof., 1940-42, asso. prof., 1946; vis. instr. U. Chgo., 1939, vis. asst. prof., 1941; instr. U.S. Naval Postgrad. Sch., 1942-46; asso. prof. Northwestern U., 1946-48; prof. State U. Iowa, 1948-60; prof. U. Calif., Riverside, 1960-67, chmn. dept. math., 1962-63; prof. SUNY, Albany, from 1967, asso. dean div. scis. and math., 1972-73. Served from lt. (j.g.) to lt. comdr. USNR, 1942-46. Hon. research asso. in math. Harvard, 1975; Fellow Fund Advancement of Edn., 1954-55. Mem. Am. Math. Soc., Math. Assn. Am., Phi Beta Kappa, Sigma Xi. Home: Glenmont, NY.

SMITH, ADA BEATRICE QUEEN VICTORIA LOUISA VIRGINIA (BRICKTOP), performing artist; b. Alderson, W.Va., Aug. 14, 1894; d. Thomas Milton and Harriet Elizabeth (Thompson) Smith; D.Arts, Columbia, 1975; m. Peter Du Conge, Dec. 29, 1929. Dancer, singer throughout U.S.A., 1910-24; singer, dancer in Paris Clubs, 1924-26; owner, mgr., singer/hostess Chez Bricktop, Paris, 1926-39, Mexico City, 1944-49, Bricktops, Rome, Italy, 1949-62. Recipient scroll Du Sable Mus. African Am. History, Chgo., 1975. Home: New York, N.Y. Died Jan. 31, 1984.*

SMITH, ALAN KELLOGG, lawyer; b. Hartford, Conn., Aug. 17, 1888; s. Frank B. and S. Amelia (Kellogg) S.; A.B., Trinity Coll., Conn., 1911, LL.D., 1968; LL.B., Harvard, 1914; m. Gwendolyn Miles, July 31, 1939. Admitted to Conn. bar, 1914, and began practice at Hartford; mem. firm of Day, Berry & Howard, 1923-77; apptd. by Pres. Harding U.S. atty. Dist. of Conn., Feb. 12, 1923; dir. Montgomery Co., Loctite Corp. Mem. Am., Conn. State bar assns., Conn. Hist. Soc., Sigma Nu. Republican. Universalist. Mason. Clubs: University, Hartford, Twentieth Century. Home: West Hartford, Conn. Died Apr. 9, 1985.

SMITH, ALBERT DANIEL, army officer; b. Farley, Mo., Feb. 6, 1887; enlisted in U.S. Army, serving as pvt., corpl. and sergt., Co. E, 22d Inf., 1904-07; served as pvt. 1st class, corpl. and sergt., aviation section, Signal Corps, 1915-16; apptd. capt., Signal Res., 1917, and called to active duty, 1917; promoted major, 1917; hon. disch., 1920; commd. capt., Air Service, U.S. Army, 1920; retired for disability in line of duty, 1923; promoted major on ret. list, 1930; called to active duty, with rank of capt., 1940, and advanced through the grades to brig. gen., 1944; base operations officer and supervisor, Army Extension Sch., Albuquerque (N.M.) Air Base, 1940-42; comdr., Eastern Sector, Air Transport Command, North American Theater of Operations, 1942-43; became base comdr., North American Theater of Operations, 1943. Decorated Legion of Merit. Address: Washington, D.C.†

SMITH, ARTHUR D(OUGLAS) HOWDEN, author; b. New York, N.Y., Dec. 29, 1887; s. Charles Howden and Marie Eulalia (Ferrell) S.; self-ed.; m. Dorothy N(ieter) Doner. Reporter New York Evening Post, 1905-18; polit. and Washington corr., New York Globe, 1918-20; spl. corr. New York Evening Post, 1920-21; asst. counsel, State of N.Y., 1921. Author: Fighting The Turk in The Balkans, 1908; The Real Colonel House, 1918; Porto Bello Gold, 1924; A Manifest Destiny, 1926; Commodore Vanderbilt, 1927; John Jacob Astor, 1929; The Eagle's Shadow, 1931; Swain's Saga, 1931; Conqueror, 1933; Alan Breck Again, 1934; Men Who Run America, 1936; Old Fuss And Feathers, 1937; The Dead Go Overside, 1938; Mr. House Of Texas, 1940; also numerous other books. Address: Washington, D.C.†

SMITH, BLANCHE A(NNETTE), librarian; b. Monroe, Ia., Aug. 26, 1887; d. Otis Ezra and Annie Mabee (Slusser) Smith; A.B., Simpson Coll., Indianola, Ia., 1908; student Pratt Inst. Library Sch., Brooklyn, N.Y., 1921; instr. Collegio Methodista, Rome, Italy, 1910-11; unmarried. Teacher, Indianola (Ia.) High Sch., 1908-14, Loveland, Colo. High Sch., 1914-18; asst. librarian Fort Des Moines Hosp. Library, 1918, Omaha (Neb.) Pub. Library, 1918-20; reference librarian Des Moines Pub. Library, 1921-27; supervisor extension div. Pub. Library, Washington, 1927-29; librarian and instr., Cleveland Coll., 1929-32; instr., Western Reserve Univ., 1929-30, summer, 1931; asst. prof., Wis. Univ. and mem. Wis. Free Library Commn. staff, 1932-38; librarian Ia. State Traveling Library since 1938. Mem. A.L.A. (extension bd.), Ia. Library Assn. (exec. bd.), Am. Assn. Univ. Women, P.E.O., Delta Delta Delta, Delta Kappa Gamma. Republican. Methodist. Clubs: Des Moines Library, Professional Women's League. Editor Ia. Library Quarterly. Home: Indianola, Iowa. †

SMITH, CARLETON, art authority, foundation executive; b. Bement, Ill., Feb. 19, 1910; s. Roy Harte and Kathryn Cosette (Ravellon) S.; m. Anne Josephe Boireau, Feb. 19, 1957; children: Christophe C., Colombe A., Raphael. B.S., U. Ill., 1927; M.A., U. Md., 1928; student, U. Chgo., 1928-30, also London Sch. Econs.; research in, Brit. Mus., Bibliothèque Nationale, Preussische Staatsbibliothek, Hofbibliothek, Vienna and other European libraries; LL.D., Marietta Coll., 1952; A.F.D. (hon.), James Milliken U., 1956. Research staff Sch. Commerce and Bus. Adminstrn., U. Chgo., 1928; instr. econs. and fgn. trade DePaul U., 1928-30, asst. prof., 1930-34; music editor Esquire, 1934-42; critic and columnist Coronet, 1936-42; fin. adviser Rubber Devel. Corp. (Reconstruction Fin. Corp. subs.), 1942-43; asst. to pres. Celotex Corp., 1943-45; advisor pub. relations to various corps.; dir. Nat. Arts Found., from 1947, chmn. adv. com., from 1954, cons. public affairs Austrian Fgn. Ministry, 1962-68; chmn. adv. com. Internat. Communications Found., 1969-79; European corr. N.Y. Herald Tribune, summers 1932-37; visited composers Sibelius, Strauss, Shostakovich, Ravel, Elgar, Delius, deFalla, Vaughan Williams and others; radio commentator N.Y. Philharmonic-Symphony Stadium Concerts, 1938; guest speaker for Met. Opera, Phila. Orch., BBC; lectured at Art Inst., Chgo., Berkshire Symphonic Festival.; Curtis Inst. Music, Eastman Sch. Music, San Francisco Mus. Art, N.Y. Philharmonic-Symphony League, Chgo., Cleve., Cin., Mpls., St. Louis, and Kansas City symphonies; also at, Columbia, Princeton, Stanford univs., univs. of Ill., Ind., Minn., Tex., Bryn Mawr Coll., principal town halls and forums of U.S.; vis. lectr. Cambridge (Eng.) U.; Cons. to Nat. Found.; Mem. advisory com. Schola Cantorum of N.Y.; co-founder Ballet Theatre Found.; organizer, sec. to jury Getty Wildlife Conservation prize, 1974, Pritzker Architecture prize, 1978; chmn. Internat. Awards Found., 1979; cons. to sec. Smithsonian Instn., Washington, pres. Ind. U.; founder, dir. M.U.S.I.C. (Music from Univs. and State of Ind. Colls.); cons. on philanthropy to J. Paul Getty; cons. on philanthropy to Franz Cardinal König, Archbishop of Vienna, Jay Pritzker, H.M. King of Saudi Arabia, edn. ministers Orgn. Petroleum Exporting Countries, Norwegian Polar Inst., numerous Am. founds. Collected and recorded folk songs in, Finland, Lapland, USSR, Iran, Iraq, Afghanistan, Africa, Brazil, Chile, Mexico, Ecuador and Peru, interview, Hitler, Molotov, Trotsky, Mussolini, Shah of Iran and, presidents and leading statesmen of African and S.Am. republics; broadcasted via NBC short-wave from, many European and S.Am. capitals; gave (with Josef Hofmann and others) lecture recitals, remarks on music recorded and broadcast by, RCA-Victor; Author: trans. into French, German, Spanish, Russian, Chinese and Arabic The Search for Autograph Musical Manuscripts Lost During World War II; Contbr. to newspapers and mags. Knight Order of the White Rose conferred by Pres. of Finland, 1950; Order of Merit conferred by Pres. of Austria, 1960. Mem. Am. Acad. Polit. and Social Sci., Am. Econ. Assn., Council on Fgn. Relations, Phi Beta Kappa. Clubs: Arts (Chgo.), Attic (Chgo.); St. James's (London), Aetheneum (London); Racquet (N.Y.), Lotos (N.Y.). Home: Bement, Ill. Died May 28, 1984.

SMITH, CHARLES A., supermarket chain exec.; b. Loch Sheldrake, N.Y., 1889. Chmn., treas. Victory Markets, Inc., Norwich, N.Y.; chmn. Chenango Nat. Bank & Trust Co., Norwich; pres., dir. Dunco Realty and Equipment Corp.; dir. Tracy Baking Co., Inc. Home: Norwich, NY. †

SMITH, CHASE MCKENZIE, lawyer, ins. exec.; b. Plainfield, Ind., Jan. 14, 1892; s. Franklin M. and Alida (Allen) S.; student Lincoln Coll. Law, 1917; m. Hypatia Ross, 1919; 1 son, Chase McKenzie. Sec. ins. supt. Ill. Dept. Ins., Springfield, 1912-13, charge casualty and fire div., 1913-19; asso. Ekern & Myers Chgo., 1919-20; admitted to Ill. bar, 1920; asso. firm Smith, Rowe, Barker & Allan, Chgo., 1920-68; dir. Kemper Ins. Group, Chgo., Lumbermens Mut. Casualty Co., and affiliates, 1933-67; past chmn. Fire Com. Interstate Rating and Industry Com. Interstate Ins. Coop.; past chmn. legis. com., tax com., automobile com., legal com. Am. Mut. Ins. Alliance; fed. taxation com. NAM. Served as pvt. 308th F.A., 78th Div., U.S. Army, World War I; Industry Com. on War Damage Ins., and co-draftsman war damage ins. program, World War II. Mem. Am. (past chmn. ins. sect.), Ill., Chgo. bar assns., Internat. Assn. Ins. Counsel, U.S. C. of C. (dir. fed. taxation com.; chmn. ins. com., chmn. fgn. affairs com.), Chgo. Civic Fedn. (adv. bd.), Ins. Fedn. Ill. (exec. com.), Ins. Inst. Hwy. Safety (co-founder, gov.). Clubs: Lake Forest Golf (Wis.); Chicago; Exmoor Country; Met. (Washington); El Niguel Country (Laguna Niguel, Calif.). Home: Laguna Niguel, Calif. Died June 3, 1985.

SMITH, DAN THROOP, economist, educator, govt. ofcl.; b. Chgo., Nov. 20, 1907; s. Elbert Ellis and Olive (Cole) S.; m. Martha Louise Vaughan, June 15, 1935; children—Deborah Throop (Mrs. Charles M. Leighton), Louise Lord (Mrs. William Bowman), Dan Throop Smith. A.B., Stanford U., 1928; student, U. London, 1928-29; Ph.D., Harvard, 1934; D.Sc., Iowa Wesleyan Coll., 1962. Mem. faculty Harvard, from 1930, prof. finance, 1945-69, prof. emeritus, 1969-82; lectr. Stanford, 1968-73; sr. research fellow Hoover Instn., 1969-82; dir. AAF Statis. Sch.; spl. cons. to comdg. gen. U.S. Air Force, 1943-45; asst. to sec. Dept. Treasury, 1953-55, spl. asst. to sec., 1955-57, dep. to sec., 1957-59; dir. CML Group, Hon Industries.; Mem. Pres.' Task Force on Bus. Taxation, 1969-70; mem. Commn. on Internat. Trade and Investment, 1970-71; chmn. tax adv. com. Council on Environ. Quality, 1970-73. Author: Deficits and Depressions, 1936, Taxable and Business Income, (with J. Keith Butters), 1949, Effects of Taxation on Corporate Financial Policy, 1952, Federal Tax Reform; The Issues and a Program, 1961, Tax Factors in Business Decisions, 1968; Contbr. articles to profl. jours. Trustee Iowa Wesleyan Coll., 1962-76, life trustee, 1976—. Mem. Am. Econ. Assn., Am. Finance Assn., Tax Inst. Am. (pres. 1963), Nat. Tax Assn. (pres. 1967), Phi Beta Kappa. Republican. Unitarian. Clubs: Harvard (N.Y.C.); Cosmos (Washington). Home: Portola Valley, Calif. Died May 29, 1982.

SMITH, DELANCEY C., lawyer; b. Oakland, Calif., Apr. 11, 1888; s. Leigh Richmond and Harriette Louise (Corwine) S.; student Hastings Coll. of Law, 1908-10; Leland Stanford U., 1910-12; m. Ida Graff, Mar. 11, 1916; children—DeLancey Corwine, Barbara Leigh. Practiced at Oakland, 1912-20, San Francisco since 1920; asst. city atty., Oakland, 1916-18; dep. dist. atty. Alameda County, 1915; chmn. Fact Finding Bd., Alaska Canned Salmon Industry, 1938; atty. Pacific Bridge Co., Washington Properties Co.; Pacific Coast atty. for Newport News Shipbuilding and Dry Dock Co. Mem. Am. Bar Assn., Phi Delta Phi. Democrat. Clubs: University, Claremont Country. Home: Berkeley, Calif. †

SMITH, DICK, newspaper editor; b. Leavenworth, Kan., July 10, 1889; s. Thomas K. and Annie A. (Nugent) S.; ed. pub. schs. Kan. and Mo.; m. Marion Ware, of Kansas City, Mo., May 18, 1910; 1 son, Richard Ware. Began as errand boy with Swift & Co., Kansas City, Mo., 1905; office boy Kansas City Star, 1906, library file clerk, 1906-08, reporter, 1908-10; reporter, copy reader, asst. city editor, Kansas City Post, 1910-13, city editor, 1913-19, mng. editor, 1919-28; mng. editor Kansas City Journal-Post from 1928, also dir. and sec., 1931-36. Democrat. Clubs: Kansas City, Kansas City Athletic. Home: Kansas City, Mo. †

SMITH, EARL HAMILTON, writer; b. at Prescott, Arizona, Apr. 7, 1887; s. Eber Clark and Lilian Elton (Crossman) S.; student high school, Manila, P.I., 1905; LL.B., Nat. Univ. Law Sch., Washington, D.C., 1917, LL.M., 1920; courses, American Univ., 1921, and Columbia University, 1927-28; m. Olga Lucie Nicholson of Tacoma, Wash., Oct. 23, 1911; children—Pauline Elton, Lilian Nicholson, Earl Hamilton. City editor Manila Cablenews-American, 1909-12; editor Far Eastern Bur., New York, 1913; editor Bulletin, 2d Pan Am. Scientific Congress, 1915; in charge (with Rear Adm. Robert E. Peary) of Washington office, Aero Club America, 1916-17; editor Press Review (confidential), Gen. Staff, France, 1918; publicity dir. 2d Pan Am. Financial Conf., 1920; staff Washington Post, 1920-21; nat. exec. sec. of assn. which bought and preserved Belleau Wood as a permanent memorial; with N.Y. Commercial, 1923, N.Y. Times, 1924-27; now writer on business and finance. Served in A.E.F. as capt. q.m. and maj. inf.; maj. O.R.C. U.S.A., 1921. Fellow Am. Geog. Soc.; mem. Overseas Writers of Washington (charter mem.), Am. Legion, Vets. of Foreign Wars, Sigma Nu Phi. Mason (32 deg.). Democrat. Methodist. Clubs: Nat. Press (Washington, D.C.); Advertising (New York). Author: American Investment Trusts and Non-Trusts. Address: New York, N.Y. †

SMITH, EDGAR WILLIAM, rancher; b. Pendleton, Ore., June 8, 1888; s. Edgar Leslie and Elisabeth (Fish) S.; A.B., Cornell U., 1909; LL.D., U. Portland, 1948; Dr. Pub. Adminstrn., Lewis and Clark Coll., 1953; m. Irene Simington, Jan. 12, 1911; children—Edgar L., John W. Partner Edgar W. Smith & Sons, Lancaster, Wash., from 1946; agy. mgr. Equitable Life Assurance Soc. U.S., 1910-18; pres. Astoria Flouring Mills Co., 1919-29, Columbia Navigation Co., 1919-33, Pillsbury-Astoria Flour Mills, 1929-31; pres. Northwest Hospital Association (Blue Cross), 1952-64. Pres. Oregon Board Higher Edn., 1947-53; pacific Coast adv. bd. Inst. Internat. Edn., 1953-58; mem. President's evaluation com. Fgn. Aid Program, Belgium, Holland, 1953; chmn. governor's com. on higher edn. in Ore., 1956-59; mem. President's Com. on Edn. Beyond High Sch., 1956-58, Com. on Govt. and Higher Edn., 1957-59; civilian aide to the Sec. of the Army, 1954-62. Served as 2d lt. U.S. Army, World War I. Named Portland's first citizen, 1952, Ore. man of the year, 1952; admiral Astoria (Ore.) Regatta, 1953; Outstanding Civilian Service medal Dept. Army, 1962. Mem. U.S. (mem. agr. com. 1952-55), Portland (pres. 1950-54) chambers commerce. Am. Legion (nat. com. edn. and scholarships, 1953-56), Portland Freight Traffic Assn. (treas.), Transp. Assn. Am. (past gov.), Kappa Sigma. Republican. Presbyn. Clubs: Rotary (pres. 1957-58, dist. gov. 1960-61, 65-66), Multnomah Athletic, Arlington, University, Waverly Country. Home: Portland, Ore. †

SMITH, EDRIC BROOKS, engr. and adminstr.; b. Cambridge, Mass., June 9, 1887; s. George W. and Sarah (French) S.; S.B. in Mech. Engring., Lawrence Scientific Sch., Harvard Univ., 1908; Austin teaching fellow, Harvard Grad. Sch. Applied Science, 1908-09; married Laura Jewett Seaver, June 9, 1915 (deceased); children—Edric Brooks, Benjamin Seaver, Cornelius Latta, Prudence French (Mrs. John H. Griffin, Jr.). Engr., Dennison Mfg. Co., 1909-11; designing engr. B&M R.R., 1911-13; with Rockefeller Inst. Med. Research, 1913-55, asst. bus. mgr., 1913-20, bus. mgr., 1920-55, sec. corp., 1937-55, Mem. vis. com. Harvard Grad. Sch. Engring., 1940-46; past trustee, Halsted Sch., (pres. 1946-52), Hudson River Mus. (both Yonkers). Fellow A.A.A.S.; mem. Am. Soc. M.E., Harvard Engring. Soc. (pres. 1930-31). Presbyn. Clubs: Harvard (N.Y.C.); Appalachian Mountain, Harvard (Boston); Fortnightly Club for Study of Anthropology (Yonkers). Home: Belmont, Mass. †

SMITH, EDWARD BYRON, physician, educator; b. Petersburg, Ind., Apr. 24, 1912; s. Jacob Owen and Estella Merle (Richardson) S.; m. Edith Cash, Nov. 18, 1937; children: Michael Edward, Allen Richardson, Philip Allison. Student, Hanover Coll., 1930-31, D.Sc. (hon.), 1970; B.S., Ind. U.; M.D., Ind. U., 1938. Intern Cleve. City Hosp., 1938-39; resident pathology Charity Hosp., Cleve., 1939-40; instr. pathology Washington U., 1940-42, asst. prof., 1949-51; asso. pathology Presbyn. Hosp., also U. Pa., 1946-48; cons. pathology Valley Forge Army Hosp., 1946-48; asso. prof. pathology Baylor Med. Coll., 1948-49; prof. pathology Ind. U. Sch. Medicine, 1951-62, chmn. dept., 1952-62; chief hematologic pathology br. Armed Forces Inst. Pathology, Washington, 1962-65; clin. prof. pathology George Washington U. Sch. Medicine, 1962-65; prof. pathology U. Mich., Ann Arbor, 1965-68; pathologist Patterson-Coleman Labs., Tampa, Fla., from 1968; clinical prof. pathology U. South Fla., Tampa, from 1972; chief med. staff Citrus Meml. Hosp., from 1980; cons. Ind. U. Hosps., Indpls. Gen., Sunnyside, VA hosps., Surgeon Gen. U.S. Army, 1959-61; Mem. Adv. Bd. Med. Specialties, 1956-64; trustee Am. Bd. Pathology, 1955-67, sec., 1955-65, pres., 1965-66; mem. bd. sci. cons. Armed Forces Inst. Pathology, 1957-61; mem. Forensic Scis. Commn. Ind., 1959-62; dir. Marion County unit Am. Cancer Soc.; com. profl. edn. Marion County unit Am. Cancer Soc. (Ind. div.). Author: (with others) Principles of Human Pathology; Mem. editorial bd.: (with others) Directory Med. Specialists, 1956-67, Survey Pathology in Medicine and Surgery, 1964-70. Served from lt. to maj. AUS, 1942-46. Recipient Alumni Achievement award Hanover Coll., 1967. Mem. Internat. Acad. Pathology (council 1951-55, pres. 1956), Ind. Med. Assn. (chmn. commn. on conv. arrangements 1959), Ind. Soc. Pathologists, AMA, Citrus County Med. Soc. (pres.-elect 1982-83), Am. Assn. Pathologists and Bacteriologists, Am. Soc. Hematology, Electron Microscopy Soc. Am., Am. Soc. Exptl. Biology, Am. Soc. Clin. Pathologists, Coll. Am. Pathologists, N.Y. Acad. Scis., Phi Gamma Delta, Nu Sigma Nu, Alpha Omega Alpha. Home: Inverness, Fla.

SMITH, EDWARD J., business exec.; b. Ridgeway, Mich., Feb. 15, 1890; s. Harry and Mary (Anderson) S.; M.E., University Mich., 1915; D.Sc., Hartwick College, 1959; married Emma Koch, July 22, 1913. Supt. Marshall (Mich.) Furnace Co., 1915-17; foundry engr. and supt. Ingersoll-Rand Co., Painted Post, N.Y., 1917-33, gen. mgr., 1933-55; dir. Ingersoll-Rand Co., N.Y.C., from 1943, v.p., 1945-55, mfg. cons., from 1955; adv. com. Lincoln Rochester Trust Co. Mayor, Village Painted Post, 1929-35. Mem. exec. bd. Steuben area council Boy Scouts Am., from 1930. Dir. Corning Hosp.; mechanical engring. adv. com. Clarkson Coll. Mem. Sigma Xi. Republican. Episcopalian. Elk, Mason. Clubs: Elmira City; Canadian of N.Y.; Corning Country, Elmira Country, Sky Top. Home: Painted Post, N.Y. †

SMITH, ELWYN L., business exec.; b. Syracuse, N.Y., 1894; grad. Cornell U., 1917; m. Louise Edwards, 1919;

children—Elwyn L., Mrs. Charles E. Roberts, Jr., Wilbert L. II. With Smith-Corona, Inc., successively exec. v.p., 1945-51, pres., 1951-58; pres. Smith-Corona Marchant, Inc., 1958-60, chmn. exec. com., from 1960; dir. Ithaca Gun Co., Inc., Crucible Steel Co. of Am., Marine Midland Trust Co. of Central N.Y. Past mem. bd. regents State N.Y. Home: Syracuse, N.Y. †

SMITH, FRANCIS PALMER, architect; b. Cincinnati, O., Mar. 27, 1886; s. Henry Howard and Eva Belle (Kendall) S.; B.S. in Architecture, U. of Pa., 1907; m. Ella Sorin, June 15, 1910 (dec. 1930); children—Margaret Ella (Mrs. Henry Rauh Kingdon), Francis Palmer, Jr. (dec.), Robert, Henry Howard. Engaged in business as draughtsman, Cincinnati and Columbus, 1907-08; travel and study in Europe, 1909; prof. architecture, Georgia Sch. of Tech., Atlanta, 1909-22; mem. firm Pringle & Smith, Atlanta, 1922-34; pvt. practice, from 1934; partner firm Francis P. Smith & Henry H. Smith, arch.; designer 1st Nat. Bank, Wm. Oliver Bldg., Doctors Bldg., Rhodes Haverty Bldg., Whitehead Bldg., Cox Carlton Hotel (Atlanta), Lynch Bldg. (Jacksonville), Venetian Hotel (Miami), (Pringle & Smith). Druid Hills Presbyterian Ch., annex to Trust Co. of Ga. Bldg., Cathedral of St. Philip (Ayers & Godwin Assos.), Atlanta Comml. Bank & Trust Co., Ocala, Fla., Decatur branch First Nat. Bank, Atlanta, Ga., also numerous churches, residences, commercial works in the South and S.E. Awarded Brooke Silver medal, U. of Pa., Walter Cope Meml. Prize. Capt. Corps of Engrs., U.S. Army, 1942; asst. to dist. engr., Atlanta, exec. and engring. officer with Post Engr., Troop Supply officer, Post Engr., and Custodial officer, Camp Tyson, Tenn., major, 1946. Fellow A.I.A. (past pres. Ga. chapter), Stained Glass Assn. of Am. (asso. mem.), Sigma Xi, Phi Kappa Phi. Episcopalian. Translator and publisher of Viollet-le-Duc's Mediaeval Stained Glass. Home: Atlanta, GA.†

SMITH, FREDERICK REUBEN, banking, milling; b. Kimball, S.D., Jan. 22, 1888; s. Frank C. and Rose Anna (Wolf) S.; grad. high sch., Platte, S.D.; Ph.B., Dakota Wesleyan U., Mitchell, S.D., 1910; m. Grace Joy Cool, Jan. 21, 1918. Cashier Farmers State Bank, Platte, 1910-25; sec.-treas. Charles Mix County Milling Co. from 1910; partner Platte Grain Co. and L. C. Button Grain Co. from 1916. State supt. of banks, S.D., since 1925, reappointed, 1929, for term 1929-33; chmn. State Banking Bd.; pres. S.D. Securities Commn.; mem. State Bd. of Finance. Served as pvt. inf., U.S.A., 1918; 2d lt., O.R.C. Trustee Dakota Wesleyan U. Mem. Am. Legion. Republican. Methodist. Mason (32 degree, Shriner), Elk. Home: Platte, S.D. †

SMITH, GEOFFREY F. N., life ins. co. exec.; b. Box Hill, Eng., Mar. 11, 1926; s. Sydney A. and Phyllis I. (Elworthy) S.; came to U.S., 1963, naturalized, 1969; B.A., U. Toronto, 1946; m. Marguerite H. Scaife, Sept. 1954; children—G. Lawrence, Craig D., Gail B. Actuarial trainee, then supr. Can. Life Ins. Co., Toronto, 1947-53; successively asst. actuary, actuary, v.p. and actuary Sovereign Life Ins. Co., Winnipeg, Man., 1953-63; v.p., actuary Am. Mut. Life Ins. Co., Des Moines, 1963-67, pres., 1967-80, chief exec. officer, 1969-80. Chmn. capital fund drive Campfire Girls, 1978; exec. com. Jr. Achievement of Des Moines, 1975-80. Fellow Soc. Actuaries, Canadian Inst. Actuaries; mem. Am. Acad. Actuaries. Episcopalian. Clubs: Des Moines, Des Moines Golf and Country. Home: Des Moines, Iowa. Died Sept. 28, 1980.

SMITH, HALSEY, banker; b. South Orange, N.J., July 10, 1921; s. Albridge C. and Frances (Halsey) S.; grad. Lawrenceville Sch., 1940; A.B., Princeton, 1944; LL.D. (hon.), U. Maine, 1961; m. Margaret Haskell, Dec. 19, 1942; children-Margaret Coburn, Karen Woodbridge, Halsey, Ellen Barry. With N.Y. Trust Co., N.Y.C., 1946-51, asst. treas., 1950-51; v.p. Casco Bank & Trust Co., Portland, Maine, 1951-55, pres., 1955-69, chmn. bd., 1969-73, also dir.; dir. Center for Research and Advanced Study, U. Maine, 1972-77; pres., chief exec. officer, dir. N.E. Bankshare Assn., Lewiston, Maine, 1977-81; dir. Milliken Tomlinson Co., Portland, Hussey Mfg., North Berwick, Maine; mem. adv. bd. Bingham Assoc., 1975-81. Chmn., Commn. on Maine's Future, 1974-77; corporator Maine Med. Center; pres. Maine Cancer Research Found., 1977-81; trustee Westbrook Coll., Portland. Served with USMCR, 1942-46; PTO. Decorated Bronze Star; recipient Distinguished Service award Portland Kiwanis Club, 1968, Maine Bar Assn., 1978; Brotherhood award Temple Beth El, Portland, 1970. Mem. Maine (past treas.), Greater Portland (past dir., pres.) chambers commerce, Me. Bankers Assn. (past pres.). Republican. Conglist. Home: Freeport, Maine. Died Aug. 21, 1981.

SMITH, HENRY OLIVER, ins. co. exec.; b. Worcester, Mass., May 19, 1923; s. Philip S. and Marion W. (Strout) S.; A.B., Bowdoin Coll., 1947; LL.B., Boston U., 1950, J.D., 1970; m. Mary Dana Lane, Aug. 13, 1949; children—Henry Oliver, Dana Lane, Stoddard Lane. Admitted to Mass. bar, 1951, also U.S. Supreme Ct. bar; mem. firm Proctor & Howard, Worcester, 1950-53; v.p., gen counsel State Mut. Life Assurance Co. of Am., Worcester, 1953-82; pres., chmn. bd. SMA Mgmt. Corp.; exec. com. Life Ins. Assn. Mass.; counsel Worcester Mut. Fire Ins. Co. Served with USNR, 1943-46. Mem. Internat., Am., Worcester County bar assns., Assn. Life Ins. Counsel (exec. com.), Nat. Assn. Ins. Commrs. (chmn. adv. com.), Am. Counsel Life Ins. (chmn. subcom. state matters, chmn. com. all lines charters), Alpha Delta Phi. Clubs: Union (Boston); Worcester Country. Home: Shrewsbury, Mass. Died 1982.

SMITH, HERBERT BURLING, oil co. exec.; b. Eldorado, Kan., Feb. 21, 1889; s. John Fernandez and Mary Jane (Barker) S.; student Beaune U., France; m. Miriam Gertrude Wright, Dec. 17, 1922 (dec. Dec. 1944); children—Herbert Burling, Randel P., Sandra, John F.; m. 2d, Julia Elizabeth Francis, September 11, 1947; children—Sidney Davis, Julia Francis. Associate with the Gulf Oil Corporation, 1914-17; with Sinclair Oil & Gas Co., from 1919, v.p. charge oil exploration, 1932-53, pres., chief exec. officer, 1953-57, chairman of board, and chief exec. officer, 1958-59, cons., from 1961. Served with the United States Army, 1918-19. Mem. Tulsa C. of C., Tulsa Philharmonic, Am. Petroleum Inst., Rocky Mountain, Midcontinent oil and gas assns. Am. Republican. Methodist. Clubs: Southern Hills Country, Tulsa (Tulsa); International, Beau Nash (Chgo.). †

SMITH, HERBERT LIVINGSTON, III, architect; b. Norfolk, Va., Nov. 10, 1920; s. Herbert Livingston, Jr. and Alla Burtis (Ransom) S.; m. Martha Birdsong Macklin, Aug. 26, 1948; children—Herbert Livingston, Henry Garrett, William Macklin. B.Arch., U. Va., 1949. Registered architect, Va., N.C., S.C., Ga., Fla., Del., Md., Mich. Asst. naval architect Norfolk Navy Yard, also mech. div., Panama Canal, 1940-42; chmn. Oliver, Smith & Cooke (architects), Norfolk and Virginia Beach, Va., from 1950; v.p. M.M.M. Design Group; partner Oliver, Smith, Cooke & Lindner (architects), Richmond. Important works include Medium Security Instn, Brunswick County, Va., Southeastern Tng. Center for Mentally Retarded, Chesapeake, Va., Ch. Good Shepherd, Norfolk. Chmn. historic rev. bd. City of Virginia Beach, from 1968, Virginia Beach City Planning Com., 1954-58; past pres. Virginia Beach Research and Adv. Council. Fellow AIA (pres. Va. chpt. 1958-59, award merits Va. chpt. 1964); mem. Soc. Am. Mil. Engrs., U. Va. Alumni Assn., Pi Kappa Alpha. Episcopalian (vestry from 1980, sr. warden 1968-70). Clubs: Princess Anne Country, Farmington Country, Harbor, Va, Commonwealth. Home: Virginia Beach, VA.

SMITH, HOWARD GODWIN, educator; b. Bklyn., Apr. 9, 1910; s. Frederick Howard and Agnes J. (Godwin) S.; E.E., Cornell, 1930, M.E.E., 1931, Ph.D., 1937; m. Jane E. Blakeslee, Sept. 5, 1933; children—John Howard, Donald Arthur, Barbara Ruth. Mem. dept. physics Cornell U., 1931-34, Sch. Elec. Engring., 1934-82, prof., 1947-74, prof. emeritus, 1974-82, asst. to dir., 1949-52, dir. div. of basic studies coll. engring., 1961-71. Mem. I.E.E.E., Am. Soc. Engring. Edn., Sigma Xi, Tau Beta Pi, Eta Kappa Nu. Republican. Home: Ithaca, N.Y. Died Oct. 28, 1982.

SMITH, J. JOSEPH, U.S. judge; b. Waterbury, Conn., Jan. 25, 1904; s. James Emile and Margaret Loretta (Dunn) S.; m. Eleanor M. Murnane, Aug. 16, 1939; children—J. Joseph, Richard P., Mary Eleanor McCarthy, Mary Martha Murphy. A.B., Yale, 1925, LL.B., 1927; LL.D. (hon.), U. Hartford, 1979. Bar: Conn. bar 1927. Law practice at, Waterbury; research fellow Yale Sch. Law, 1927-28; mem. 74th to 77th Congresses (1935-41), 5th Conn. Dist.; apptd. U.S. dist. judge, Conn., 1941, U.S. circuit judge, 2d circuit, 1960; now sr. U.S. Circuit judge, 2d Circuit, Hartford, Conn. Mem. Am., Conn., Waterbury bar assns., Am. Judicature Soc., Phi Delta Phi. Catholic. Home: West Hartford, Conn.

SMITH, J. STANFORD, land resources management executive; b. Terre Haute, Ind., Jan. 4, 1915; s. William J. and Forrest Julia (Luther) S.; m. Elaine Showalter, Dec. 26, 1938; children—Barbara, Carol Smith Witherell, Stephen, Douglas. A.B., DePauw U., 1936, LL.D. (hon.), 1968; LL.D. (hon.), Rose-Hulman Inst. Tech., 1977. With Gen. Electric Co., N.Y.C., Schnectady and Hendersonville, N.C., 1936-73; vice chmn. bd. Internat. Paper Co., N.Y.C., 1973, chmn. bd., chief exec. officer, 1974-80; vis. prof. bus. policy, exec.-in-residence Cornell U. Grad. Sch. Bus., 1981-83; dir. Gen. Motors Corp., Eli Lilly Co., Am. Gas and Oil Investors; dir., mem. exec. and policy coms. U.S.-USSR Council; chmn. Internat. Task Force Bus. Roundtable, 1972-80; mem. (Bus. Council), 1974-83, Pres.'s Adv. Com. for Trade Negotiations, 1978. Chmn. bd. trustees DePauw U.; bd. dirs. Nat. Action Council for Minorities in Engring. Mem. NAM (dir.), Phi Beta Kappa, Phi Gamma Delta. Clubs: Greenwich (Conn.) Country; Sky (N.Y.C.); No. Lake George Yacht. Address: New York, N.Y. Died Jan. 6, 1983.

SMITH, JAMES GERALD, banker; b. Queens, N.Y., June 18, 1918; s. Harry G. and Margaret (Buck) S.; m. Dorothy Kollmer, Sept. 15,1946; children—Margaret, Madeline, Maureen, Marilyn, Valerie. Grad., Stonier Grad. Sch. Banking, 1953. With Franklin Nat. Bank, N.Y.C., from 1943, sr. v.p., 1965-69, exec. v.p., 1969-70, pres., from 1970, vice chmn., from 1972; sr. v.p. European-Am. Bank & Trust Co., from 1974, East N.Y. Savs. Bank, Bklyn., from 1978. Home: West Hempstead, N.Y. Died Nov. 3, 1983; buried Holy Rood, Westbury, N.Y.*

SMITH, JAMES HOPKINS, JR., former govt. ofcl.; b. N.Y.C., Dec. 15, 1909; s. James Hopkins and Pauline (Morton) S.; A.B., Harvard, 1931; LL.B., Columbia, 1935; m. Nancy Morgan, Oct. 9, 1937 (div. 1969); children—Charles Morgan, Sandra, Dinah; m. 2d, Diane Hartman; 1 dau., Joy. Vice pres. Pan Am. Airways, Inc., 1946-49; spl. asst. to sec. Navy, 1951-53, asst. sec. for air, 1953-56; dir. ICA, 1957-59; dir. South Tex. Devel. Co., Exec. Jet Aviation, Inc., Aspen Skiing Corp. Bd. dirs. Planned Parenthood Fedn.; trustee Fountain Valley Sch., Outward Bound Sch., Marble, Colo.; trustee, vice chmn. Aspen Inst. Served as comdr. USNR, 1942-45. Mem. Inst. Aero. Scis. Clubs: Metropolitan (Washington); Links (N.Y.C.); Denver (Colo.); Royal Aero (London). Home: Aspen, Colo. Died Nov. 24, 1982.

SMITH, JAMES MONROE, univ. pres.; b. Jackson Parish, La., Oct. 9, 1888; s. John Henry and Mary Adney (Sims) S.; Pd.B., Valparaiso U., 1913; B.A., La. State U., 1921; grad. work, U. of Chicago, summer 1922; M.A., Teachers Coll. (Columbia), 1925; Ph.D., Columbia, 1927; m. Thelma Ford, June 3, 1914; children—Marjorie Lee, James Monroe. Dean Coll. of Edn., Southwest La. Inst., 1920-30; pres. La. State U. from Nov. 17, 1930. Mem. Am. Acad. Polit. and Social Science, Phi Kappa Phi, Phi Delta Kappa, Phi Kappa Delta. Commendatore Order of the Crown of Italy; Knight Legion of Honor (France). Democrat. Baptist. Mason. Author: Training of High School Teachers in Louisiana 1927. Home: Baton Rouge, La. †

SMITH, JOSEPH HENRY, lawyer, educator; b. N.Y.C., Sept. 4, 1913; s. Adolph Q. and Agnes (Buchner) S.; m. Edith C. Stenberg, Jan. 5, 1946; 1 dau., Linda E. (Mrs. Donald G. Price, Jr.). A.B., Yale U., 1935; LL.B., Columbia U., 1938; student, Inst. Hist. Research U. London, 1938-39. Bar: N.Y. bar 1940. Research asst. Found. for Research in Legal History, Columbia Law Sch., 1938-42; pvt. practice, N.Y.C., 1946-61; prof. N.Y. Law Sch., 1951-61; prof. Columbia Law Sch., 1961-67, George Welwood Murray prof. legal history, 1967—; Chmn. Found. for Research in Legal History, 1961—; mem. adv. com. Am. Bar Found. Project in Legal History, 1966-77; chmn. com. for Littleton-Griswold Fund, Am. Hist. Assn., 1967-69, mem. com., 1973-81; mem. editorial adv. bd. Studies in Legal History, Harvard U. Press, 1970-76, U. N.C. Press, 1977—; spl. asst. to atty. gen. U.S., 1965; chmn. Seminar on 18th Century European Culture, 1977-79. Author: Appeals to the Privy Council from the American Plantations, 1950, Colonial Justice in Western Massachusetts: 1639-1702, 1961, Cases and Materials on the Development of Legal Institutions, 1965; editor: (with P.A. Crowl) Court Records of Prince Georges County, Maryland, 1696-1699, 1964; Co-editor: (with P.A. Crowl) Law Practice of Alexander Hamilton, 1974—. Served with USNR, 1942-45. Hon. fellow Am. Soc. for Legal History (treas. 1972-73, v.p. 1974-75, pres. 1976-77, dir. 1979—); mem. Assn. Am. Law Schs. (chmn. legal history sect. 1973), Selden Soc., Am. Bar Assn. Home: Floral Park N.Y.

SMITH, JOSEPH WILSON, lawyer; b. Phenix City, Ala., Feb. 12, 1917; s. Ernest Clifford and Essie (Baker) S.; m. Lenora West Coghlan, July 17, 1943; children-Sydney Bowen Smith Smith, Lenora West Smith Gregory, Joseph Wilson, Walter Clifford II. LL.B., U. Ala., 1941. Bar: Ala. bar 1941. Practice in, Phenix City, from 1946; partner firm Smith & Smith, 1946-79; sr. partner firm Smith & Smith (P.C.), from 1980; legal counsel Ala. C. of C., from 1969; Dir. Phenix-Girard Bank.; Mem. Ala. Edn. Commn., 1957-58, Phenix City Bd. Edn., 1950-60; chmn. Chattahoochee Valley Airport Commn., from 1969. Mem. Ala. Senate, 1954-58, 62-66, Ala. Ho. of Reps., 1958-62; del. Democratic Nat. Conv., 1956. Served with AUS, 1941-46. Named Young Man of Year Phenix City Jr. C. of C., 1947; Outstanding Legislator Ala. Press Assn., 1959. Mem. Am., Ala. bar assns., Am. Legion, Assn. U.S. Army, Omicron Delta Kappa, Phi Alpha Delta, Pi Kappa Alpha. Democrat. Methodist. Home: Phenix City, Ala.

SMITH, LAWRENCE BREESE, author; b. Plainfield, N.J., Feb. 19, 1889; s. William Palmer and Georgianna (Hoadley) S.; grad. Mr. Leal's Sch., Plainfield, N.J., 1907; B.L., Princeton University, 1911; m. Margaret Hayes Thorne, June 7, 1923. Employed by Breese & Smith, brokers, Internat. Motor Co. (now Mack Trucks, Inc.) and Locke & Co., auto body builders; interested in writing, game breeding, shooting, field trials and dogs. Commissioned U.S. Marine Corps with rank of 2d lt. (temp.), later 1st lt. and capt. (temp.), 10th Regt., Arty., World War I. Asso. ordnance engr., tech. writer, publications div., Raritan Arsenal, Metuchen, N.J., 1941 to 1946. Mem. St. Nicholas Soc. of New York, Colonial Club of Princeton U. Republican. Episcopalian. Club: Union (New York). Author: Better Trapshooting, 1931; American Game, Preserve Shooting, 1933; Modern Shotgun Shooting, 1935; The Sunlight Kid (verse), 1935; Modern Gun Dogs, 1936; Dude Ranches and Ponies, 1936; Shotgun Psychology, 1938; Fur or Feather, 1946. Illustrated with photographs Fishing a Trout Stream (by Eugene V. Connett), 1934. Contbr. articles on sport and outdoors, verse to mags., newspapers, etc.; also 2 chapters to Upland Game Bird Shooting in America, 1930. †

SMITH, LINN CHARLES, architect; b. Flint, Mich., Dec. 15, 1917; s. Charles Montgomery and Floy (LeFurgey) S.; m. Grace Walker, Sept. 10, 1938; children—Cece Marianne, Linn Charles, Kim Walker. B.S. in Architecture, U. Mich., 1942. With archtl. firms Lyndon and Smith, Detroit, 1942, Maynard Lyndon, Los Angeles, 1945, Eberle M. Smith Assos., Inc., Detroit, 1945- 54; pvt. practice, Birmingham, Mich., 1954-56; pres. firm Smith, Tarapata, MacMahon, Inc., Birmingham, 1956-59, Linn

Smith Assos., Inc., Birmingham, 1959-69, 74-76, Linn Smith, Demiene, Adams, Inc., 1969-74; v.p. architecture Ellis/Naeyaert/Genheimer Assos., Inc., Troy, Mich., from 1976. Prin. works include, high schs. in area. Mem. city plan bd., Birmingham, 1959-72, chmn., 1963, 68, mem. bldg. code bd. appeals, Birmingham, 1958-63, co-chmn. sch. adv. com., Detroit, 1957; mem. com. sch. bldg. Mich. Dept. Pub. Instrn., 1954; mem. Nat. Archtl. Accrediting Bd., 1963-69, pres., 1968-69; Chmn. architecture scholarship fund U. Mich., from 1958; bd. dirs. Birmingham Community House, 1973-76. Served to lt. (s.g.) USNR, 1942-45. George G. Booth travelling fellow in architecture U. Mich., 1947; recipient better sch. design award Sch. Exec. competition, 1957, 59, design awards Progressive Architecture, 1957, 58; Gold medal Detroit chpt. A.I.A., 1965; Outstanding Achievement award U. Mich., 1969; Gold medal Mich. Soc. Architects, 1969. Fellow A.I.A. (regional dir. 1959-62); mem. Mich. Soc. Architects (pres. 1953- 54, bd. dirs. 1950-56), Architects Soc. Ohio (hon.), Alpha Rho Chi. Home: Birmingham, Mich.

SMITH, LLOYD L., business exec.; b. Copley, O., Aug. 19, 1887; s. Benjamin E. and Ettie (Capron) C.; student Hammel Bus. Coll., Akron, O., 1906-07; m. Coila B. Cover, June 25, 1909 (dec. June 10, 1925); children—Jack C., Robert B.; m. 2d, Louise King Fritz, Sept. 29, 1928. Tire adjuster, B. F. Goodrich Co., Akron, O., 1908, asst. mgr., Kansas City, 1909-15, credit dept., Akron, O., 1915-17, gen. credit mgr., 1917-20, asst. treas., 1920-40, treas. from 1940; treas. American Anode Inc., The Akron Rubber Co., Lone Star Defense Corp.; assistant treasurer The B.F. Goodrich Rubber Company of Canada, Limited. Director Mayflower Hotel Company. Trustee Akron Chamber of Commerce, Childrens' Hosp. of Akron, Better Bus. Bur., United Community Chest Inc., Community Service Center, Inc.; Dir. Summit County chapter Am. Red Cross. Conglist. Clubs: Congress Lake (Hartville, O.), Portage Country, Akron City. Home: Akron, Ohio. †

SMITH, LOUISE PETTIBONE, teacher; b. Ogdensburg, N.Y., Oct. 4, 1887; d. Alonzo Albertus and Mary Louise (Pettibone) Smith; A.B., Bryn Mawr Coll., Ph.D., 1917. Teacher Wellesley Coll., from 1915; hon. lecturer, Hartford Theol. Sem., 1937-38; prof. Pierce Coll., Athens, Greece, 1945. Mem. Soc. Biblical Literature. Oriental Soc. Conglist. Home: Winchester Center, Conn. †

SMITH, MARION LOFTON, college president; b. Chambers County, Ala., Jan. 26, 1889; s. Benjamin Franklin and Henrietta Fredonia (Morris) S.; B.A., Kingswood Coll., at Kingswood, Ky., 1914, M.A., 1915; M.A., Emory U., Atlanta, Ga., 1921, B.D., 1921; Ph.D., Yale, 1929; m. Bertha Elizabeth Wallace, Aug. 11, 1907 (died 1935); children—Mary Jim (Mrs. Hiram Schuyler Hart), Evelyn Elizabeth (Mrs. H. C. Aldridge), Mildred Louise (Mrs. T. L. Shelton); married 2d, Mary Elizabeth Hanes, June 2, 1938. Assistant classical language department, Kingswood College, 1911-15; pastor Epworth Chapel, Huntsville, Alabama, 1915-17; assistant New Testament dept., Candler Sch. of Theology, Emory U., 1918-21, acting prof., 1920; head dept. religious edn., Woman's Coll., Montgomery, Ala., 1921-26; head dept. religious edn., Birmingham-Southern College, 1929-38; pres. of Millsaps College since 1938; pastor various Methodist chs., Ala. and Congl. chs., Conn.; lecturer ch. confs. N.C., Miss., Ark.; teacher Soochow U., China, 1935-36. Pres. Assn. Meth. Coll., 1945, pres. coll. section Miss. Edn. Assn., 1943-45; pres. bd. Edn. Southeastern Jurisdiction Methodist Ch., 1944-48. Mem. Omicron Delta Kappa, Kappa Alpha, Eta Sigma Phi, Phi Beta Kappa, Phi Beta Kappa Asso., Exec. Club (pres. Jackson, Miss., unit. 1941-42). Methodist. Mason, Rotarian. Contbr. to religious publs. Made trip around the world, 1935-36. Club: University (N.Y.) Home: Jackson, Miss. †

SMITH, MATTHEW JOSEPH, lawyer; b. Columbus, Ohio, Jan. 21, 1905; s. Edward John and Anna (Doyle) S.; B.A., Ohio State U., 1927, J.D., 1929; m. Mary L. Jahnke, Jan. 15, 1936; children—Kathleen (Mrs. Johnson), Edward, Margaret (Mrs. Hicks), Robert. Research asst. Yale, 1929-31, Johns Hopkins, 1931-32; admitted to Ohio bar, 1929, practiced, Columbus, 1932-34, New Philadelphia, 1934-75; mem. Smith, Renner, Hanhart, Miller & Kyler. Trustee Union Hosp. Assn., Dover, Ohio, 1958-76, v.p., 1971-72; trustee Ohio State Bar Asso. Found., 1962-66; past trustee, past pres. Tuscarawas Valley Comprehensive Mental Health Center; past trustee Ohio Legal Center Inst. Fellow Am. Coll. Trial Lawyers, Am. Bar Found., Ohio Bar Assn. Found., Am. Coll. Probate Counsel; mem. Am., Ohio (pres. 1960-61), Tuscarawas County (past pres.) bar assns., Internat. Assn. Ins. Counsel, Soc. Hosp. Attys., Am. Judicature Soc., U.S. 6th Circuit Jud. Conf. (life), Order of Coif, Delta Theta Lodges: Kiwanis, KC (life), Elks (life). Home: New Philadelphia, Ohio. Died Mar. 25, 1980.

SMITH, MILES WOODWARD, editor religious publs.; b. Cincinnati, O., Nov. 23, 1889; s. Henley Woodward and Sadie Beall (Miles) S.; A.B., William Jewell Coll., Liberty, Mo., 1911, A.M., 1912, D.D., 1935; B.D., Newton (Mass.) Theol. Instn., 1917, M.R.E., 1930; grad. student Boston U. Sch. Religious Edn. and Social Service, 1920-28 (various terms); m. Elisabeth B. Arnold, June 25, 1913; children—Dorothy Woodward, Hugh Arnold, Marjory Kemper, Robert Miles. Ordained Bapt. ministry, 1910; pastor 1st Ch., Tarkio, Mo., 1911-12, E. Sedalia Ch., Sedalia, Mo., 1912-14, Stratford St. Ch., W. Roxbury, Boston, 1917-22, Norwood, O., 1922-24; dir. religious edn. for Mass. Bapt. Conv. in cooperation Am. Bapt. Publ. Soc., Boston, 1924-30; dir. intermediate work and editor intermediate publs. Am. Bapt. Publ. Soc., Phila., 1930-33, editor-in-chief Dept. of S.S. Publs. of same, 1933-39, editor of adult publications from April, 1939. Y.M.C.A. worker at Camp Wentworth, Boston, 1917; asst. religious work dir. Greater Boston Dist., War Work Council, Y.M.C.A., Charlestown, Mass. 1918. Mem. Internat. Council Religious Edn. (Com. on Internat. Bible Lessons: uniform series and graded series; com. on Religious Edn. of Adults; Editors' Professional Advisory Section), curriculum com. of bd. of edn. and publication of Northern Baptist Conv. Member Heilikrinites, Lambda Chi Alplha. Author: Homeland of the Master, 1933; Light of the Nations, 1934; Way of Wisdom, 1935; Workers with God, 1946; On Whom The Spirit Came, 1948. Editor of "Adult Class," "Home," "Bible Lessons," and "Baptist Leader." Contbr. editorials and articles on methods in religious edn. Author of popular fiction under pen name, S. M. Woodward. Home: Philadelphia, Pa. †

SMITH, MORTIMER BREWSTER, author, assn. editor, exec.; b. Mt. Vernon, N.Y., Feb. 17, 1906; s. Mortimer Allen and Matilda (Wolfe) S.; m. Sylvea Shapleigh, June 11, 1932 (div. Nov. 1959); children—Patricia, Stephen, Olea, Shapleigh; m. Edna Burrows Crilley, Jan. 18, 1962. Ed. pub. schs. Formerly asst. to out-of-town dept. mgr. Johnson and Faulkner; co-founder Council for Basic Edn., Washington, 1956; editor Council for Basic Edn. Bull., 1957-74, exec. dir., 1960-74, bd. dirs., 1975-80; Del. White House Conf. on Edn., 1965, White House Conf. on Children, 1970; Spaulding lectr. Yale, 1966; Dana lectr. Psychiat. Inst. U. Md. Hosp., Balt., 1969; mem. adv. bd. Ency. Brit. Reading Achievement Center, Oak Brook, Ill., 1969-71. Author: Evangels of Reform, 1933, The Life of Ole Bull, 1944, And Madly Teach, 1949, William Jay Gaynor, Mayor of New York, 1951, The Diminished Mind, 1954, A Citizen's Manual for Public Schools, 1965; co-author: A Consumer's Guide to Educational Innovations, 1972, My School the City: A Memoir of New York in the Twenties, 1980; contbg. author: anthologies and textbooks including Essays on Educational Reform, 1970, Farewell to Schools, 1971, Teaching: A Course in Applied Psychology, 1971, Rhetoric in Thought and Writing, 1972, Controversies in Education, 1973, School: Pass at Your Own Risk, 1974; Contbr. numerous articles to profl. jours., popular mags., newspapers. Vice pres. Newtown (Conn.) Orchestral Soc., 1936-40; chmn. Rationing Bd., Newtown, 1942-45, Conn. Regional High Sch. Bd. Number 3, 1945-47; Trustee Booth Library, Newtown, 1940-50, chmn., 1950-60. Club: Nat. Press (Washington). Home: Scottsdale AZ.

SMITH, OSCAR, naval officer; b. Wilkes Barre, Pa., Jan. 8, 1887; s. Oscar and Anna (Tubbs) S.; B.S., U.S. Naval Acad., 1908; m. Louise Gautier, June 11, 1913; 1 dau., Betty Gautier. Midshipman, U.S. Navy, 1904; advanced through the grades to commodore, 1943; comd. spl. air task force, U.S. Fleet, 1943; commodore U.S.N. (temp.), chief of staff to comdr. in chief, U.S. Atlantic Fleet, Sept. 17, 1945. Home: Virginia Beach, Va. †

SMITH, PAUL, JR., lawyer; b. N.Y.C., Jan. 24, 1923; s. Paul and Barbara Frances (Cronin) S.; m. Patricia M. Larkin, Feb. 12, 1949; children—Monica Frances, Andrea Patricia, Christopher Paul. B.S., Fordham U., 1943; LL.B., Columbia U., 1946; J.S.D., N.Y. U., 1950. Bar: N.Y. bar 1946, N.J. bar 1952, Colo. bar 1974. Asso. firm Davis Polk & Wardwell, N.Y.C., 1946-50; counsel Socony-Vacuum Oil Co., N.Y.C., 1951-59; v.p. Mobil Petroleum Co., 1960-65; also dir.; exec. Mobil Oil Corp., N.Y.C., 1965-68, asst. gen. counsel internat., 1968-73; counsel Hamilton Bros. Oil Co., Denver, 1973-77, individual practice law, 1977—. Editor: Columbia Law Rev, 1945-46; mem. editorial adv. bd.: Internat. Lawyer, 1979-81. Served with U.S. Army, 1942-43. Mem. Am. Bar Assn, Am. Law Inst., Am. Soc. Internat. Law, Internat. Bar Assn., Union Internationale des Avocats, Assn. Bar City of N.Y., Colo. Bar Assn. Republican. Roman Catholic. Club: Univ. (Denver). Home: Denver CO.

SMITH, PAUL DAVIS, lawyer; b. Rochester, N.Y., May 2, 1916; s. Earle David and Mabel (Andrus) S.; m. Nancy Dudley Hanks, Oct. 17, 1942; children—Paul Davis, David Bradford. A.B., U. Rochester, 1937; LL.B., Columbia U., 1940. Bar: N.Y. bar 1940. Mem. firm Conboy, Hewitt, O'Brien & Boardman, N.Y.C., 1948-57; v.p., gen. counsel Philip Morris, Inc., 1958-71, also dir. Served from ensign to comdr. USNR, 1941-46. Mem. Phi Beta Kappa. Home: Short Hills, NJ.

SMITH, RALPH BOYD, restaurant co. exec.; b. Fredericksburg, O., Oct. 13, 1890; s. Boyd William and Susan Katherine (Skiles) S., ed. pub. schs., Ohio; m. Martha M. Johns, June 2, 1917; 1 son, R. Boyd. Pres. Ralph B. Smith Co., realtors, Toledo, 1919-30; exec. v.p. Grace E. Smith Co., food chain, Toledo, 1938-51, pres., from 1951, Pres. Toledo Conv. and Visitors Bur., 1946-47, Downtown Toledo Assos., 1958-59, 60-61. Served as inf. officer, U.S. Army, World War I. Mem. Nat. (bd. dirs. 1949-57, treas. 1958-59, pres. 1961-62), Ohio (pres. 1947-48), Toledo and Northwestern Ohio (pres. 1945) restaurant assns. †

SMITH, RAY M., business exec.; b. Geneva, N.Y., Apr. 20, 1888; s. Frank Benjamin and Mary (Mosher) S.; B.S., Colgate U., 1909; m. Jane Smith, Nov. 15, 1915. Vice pres. and dir. Union Tank Car Co., Chicago. Mem. Am. Soc. M.E. Presbyterian. Mason. Clubs: University (Chicago); Skokie Country (Glencoe, Ill.). Address: Chicago, Ill. †

SMITH, RAYMOND WILLIAM, librarian; b. Deposit, N.Y., Sept. 25, 1923; s. Henry William and Jean (Stinson) S.; B.A., Syracuse U., 1950, M.S. in L.S., 1951; m. Evelyn Lewis, Aug. 31, 1946; children—Robert L., Stephen W., Jerrold A. (dec.). Reference asst., br. librarian Schenectady County (N.Y.) Pub. Library, 1952-57; head librarian Eastern Shore Pub. Library, Accomac, Va., 1957-59, 60-61; head readers services State U. Coll. Edn. at New Paltz, N.Y., 1959-60; asst. dir. So. Tier Library System, Corning, N.Y., 1961-65; state librarian Library Commn. Del., 1965-66; asst. dir. Four County Library System, Binghamton, N.Y., 1967-77, dir., 1978—; del. N.Y. State Gov.'s Conf. on Libraries, 1978. Mem. Gov. of Delaware Com. Reading, 1965-66. Served to 1st lt. AUS, 1942-45, 51-52; ETO, Korea. Decorated Combat Infantrymen's badge with star. Mem. A.L.A., N.Y. State Library Assn. (chmn. bookmobile com. 1965, mem. membership com. 1967-75, v.p. 1976-77, pres. pub. libraries sect. 1977-78). Home: Binghamton, N.Y. Died Nov. 23, 1980.

SMITH, RED, (WALTER WELLESLEY) sports columnist; b. Green Bay, Wis., Sept. 25, 1905; s. Walter Philip and Ida Elizabeth (Richardson) S.; m. Catherine Cody, Feb. 11, 1933 (dec. 1967); m. Phyllis Warner Weiss, Nov. 2, 1968; children—Catherine W. Smith Halloran, Terence F. A.B., Notre Dame U., 1927, LL.D., 1968. Reporter Milw. Sentinel, 1927-28; copyeditor, sportswriter, rewrite man St. Louis Star, 1928-36; sportswriter, columnist Phila. Record, 1936-45; sports columnist N.Y. Herald Tribune, 1945-66, World-Jour.-Tribune, N.Y.C., 1966-67, Pubs. Newspaper Syndicate, 1967-71, N.Y. Times, 1971-82. Author books and mag. articles. Recipient numerous awards. Clubs: Players (N.Y.C.); Louis Norman Newsome Home: New Canaan, Conn. *

SMITH, ROBERT NELSON, chemist, educator; b. Long Beach, Calif., Sept. 25, 1916; s. Robert Nelson and Catherine (Davis) S.; m. Nancy Stahl, Sept. 10, 1938; children—Eric, Roger, Anne. B.A., Pomona Coll., 1938; M.S., Stanford, 1940, Ph.D. (Shell Oil Co. fellow 1940-41), 1942. Instr. chemistry Stanford, 1941-42, U. Mo. Sch. Mines and Metallurgy, 1942-44; asso. chemist Manhattan Project, U. Chgo., 1944; group leader Manhattan Project, E.I. duPont de Nemours & Co., Inc., 1944-45; mem. faculty Pomona Coll., 1945-82, prof. chemistry, 1956-82, Carnegie prof., 1959-69, Blanche and Frank Seaver prof., 1969-82, prof. emeritus, 1982-83; mem. adv. com. grants Research Corp., 1961-68. Author: Chemistry: A Quantitative Approach, 1969, (with W.C. Pierce) General Chemistry Workbook, 5th edit, 1980. Guggenheim fellow, 1951-52; Petroleum Research Fund fellow, 1958-59; recipient Wig Distinguished Prof. award Pomona Coll., 1959, 65, 82, award for college teaching Mfg. Chemists Assn., 1961; Research Corp. fellowship, 1965-66. Mem. Am. Chem. Soc. (chmn. San Gorgonio sec. 1958, exec. com. colloid div. 1957-62), Faraday Soc., Calif. Assn. Chemistry Tchrs. (chmn. So. sect. 1964-65), Phi Beta Kappa, Sigma Xi. Home: Mount Baldy, Calif. Died Dec. 23, 1983.

SMITH, ROY LEMON, clergyman; b. Nickerson, Kan., Jan. 28, 1887; s. John Newman and Mary (Lemon) S.; student Nickerson Coll., 1904-06; A.B., Southwestern Coll., Winfield, Kan., 1908; D.D., 1923, LL.D., 1941; D.D., Gammon Theol. Seminary, 1953; B.D., Garrett Bibl. Inst., 1915, D.D., 1941; A.M., Northwestern U., 1915; D.Litt., Upper Ia. U., 1927; S.T.D., U. of Southern Calif., 1936; D.D., Chapman Coll., 1937; LL.D., Sam Houston Coll., 1937; L.H.D., Fla. Southern Coll., 1941; Litt.D., Ohio Wesleyan U., 1941, Millsaps Coll. and Southern Meth. U., 1945; L.H.D., McMurry Coll., 1946; m. Mabel D. Conley, Apr. 6, 1908; children—Frank Elroy, Pauline Florence. Began preaching at Wellington, Kan., 1908; pastor successively Cimarron, Kan., St. Paul's Ch., Chicago, Simpson Meth. Ch., Minneapolis; pastor First Meth. Ch., Los Angeles, Calif.; editor Christian Advocate (official publ. Meth. Church), 1940-48, publishing agent Methodist Church, 1948-52. Was associate pastor Central Ch., Chicago, with Dr. Frank W. Gunsaulus, 1914-15; acting pastor People's Ch., St. Paul, Minn., 1915. Dept. editor Northwestern Christian Advocate, Chicago, 1916-22; feature writer Chicago Tribune Synd., 1923-41; free lance writer, 1912-40; editorial writer Mpls. Star, 1926-31; syndicate writer Nat. Council of Churches from 1947; grad. faculty U. of So. Calif., 1935-40; dir. Ministers Life and Casualty Union from 1923. Del. Methodist Gen. Conf., 1936, 40, 44. Mem. Meth. Uniting Conf., 1939, Methodist Ecumenical Conference, 1948, 52, Methodist Board of Temperance, 1940-44, Meth. Bd. Evangelism, from 1944; dir. Pacific Old People's Home, 1933-35; v.p. Los Angeles div. Vols. of America; chmn. missions com. Meth. Gen. Conf., 1940. Decorated Order of the Jade by Chinese Republic, 1940. Fellow Am. Geog. Soc. Mem. Foreign Policy Assn., Am. Council Pacific Affairs Inst., Am. Acad. Polit. and Social Science, Pi Kappa Delta, Pi Gamma Mu, Phi Chi Phi. Mason. Club: Internat. Lyceum Assn. Author numerous books relating to religion since 1920; latest publs.: Making a Go of Life, 1948; We Follow the Swallow, 1948; New Lights from Old Lamps, 1953. Spl. lectr. at univs. Named one of 10 most rep. Meth. ministers in America, 1935. Home: La Jolla, Calif. †

SMITH, RUSSELL HUNT, lawyer; b. Mt. Vernon, Mo., Feb. 9, 1922; s. Ivan Louis and Grace (Hunt) S.; m. Gloria Warren, Dec. 28, 1947; children—Cynthia Dianne, Windsor Hunt, Diana Marie. Student, S.W. Mo. State Coll., 1945-47; LL.B., U. Mich., 1950. Bar: Okla. bar 1951, 10th Circuit Ct. Appeals bar 1951, 7th Circuit 1962, Mo. bar 1950. Atty. Amerada Petroleum Corp., Tulsa, 1950-55; asst. U.S. atty. No. Dist. Okla., 1955-59, U.S. atty., 1960-61; atty. Cities Service Oil Co., Bartlesville, 1961-81, asst. gen. counsel. Served with AUS, 1940-45. Mem. Am., Okla. bar assns., Mo. Bar. Home: Tulsa, Okla. Died Dec. 6, 1981; buried Memorial Park, Tulsa.

SMITH, ST. CLAIR, judge; b. Rondell, Brown County, S.D., July 10, 1889; s. James William and Mary Martha (Caw) S.; student Northern Normal and Industrial Sch., Aberdeen, S.D., 1905-09; LL.B., George Washington U., 1912; student U. of Southern Calif., 1912-13; m. Catherine Fagg, May 21, 1920; children—Mary Elva, James Enlo. Admitted to S.D. bar, 1912; practiced at Aberdeen, 1913-37; apptd. judge of Supreme Court of S.D., Jan. 9, 1937, reelected present term expires 1965. Served with United States Army, World War. Mem. S.D. Bar Assn., Phi Delta Phi, Delta Tau Delta. Republican. Conglist. Mason. Home: Pierre, S.D. †

SMITH, SYLVESTER COMSTOCK, JR., lawyer; b. Phillipsburg, N.J., Aug. 27, 1894; s. Sylvester C. and Mary Elizabeth (Davis) S.; student Lafayette Coll., LL.D., 1951; LL.B., N.Y. Law Sch., 1918, LL.D., 1962; LL.D., Marietta Coll., 1962, Seton Hall U., 1963, Pace Coll., 1971; m. Thalia Graff, May 17, 1922 (dec. Mar. 1958); children—Page Elizabeth (Mrs. William S. Bigelow), Thalia Barbara (Mrs. Elbert E. Husted, III). Admitted to N.J. bar, 1917, practiced in Phillipsburg, 1917-38; mem. Smith & Smith; town atty. Phillipsburg, 1921-41; prosecutor pleas Warren County, N.J., 1912-38; gen. counsel Prudential Ins. Co. Am., 1948-63; counsel Carpenter, Bennett & Morrissey, Newark, 1963-81. Commr., N.J. Hwy. Authority, 1955-74, treas., 1955-65, chmn., 1965-70, treas. 1970-74; pres. Bur. Municipal Research, Newark, 1960-63; pres. N.Y. Law Sch., N.Y.C., 1964-75. Trustee Pace Coll., 1968-75. Served as seaman USN, 1918. Mem. Internat., Inter-Am., Am. (chmn. com. supreme ct. proposals 1937, bd. govs. 1940-43, chmn. sect. adminstrv. law 1946-47, chmn. ho. of dels. 1958-60, pres. 1962-63), N.J. State (pres. 1940-41), Warren County (pres. 1938), City N.Y. bar assns. Am. Judicature Soc., Am. Law Inst., Assn. Life Ins. Counsel (pres.), Chi Phi. Democrat. Episcopalian. Mason. Clubs: Essex (Newark); Harkers Hollow Golf, Bay Head Yacht, N.Y. Yacht; Cruising of America. Author: Modern Trends in Pleadinng and Trial Practice; The Supreme Court Fight; Improving Administration of Justice in Administration Process. Contbg. author: The Insurance Contract, 1954. Home: West Orange, N.J. Died Nov. 26, 1981.

SMITH, WALTER, newspaperman; b. Green Bay, Wis., Sept. 25, 1905; s. Walter Philip, (Ida Richardson) S.; A.B., U. of Notre Dame, 1927; m. Catherine Cody, Feb. 11, 1933; children—Catherine Wellesley, Terence Fitzgerald. Gen. news assignments, Milwaukee Sentinel, 1927-28; sports and news writer, St. Louis Star (now Star-Times), 1928-36; sports writer and columnist Philadelphia Record, 1936-45; sports columnist, N.Y. Herald Tribune from 1945. Home: Stamford, Conn. Died Jan. 15, 1982.

SMITH, WALTER F., publisher; b. Gardner, Ill., 1890; grad. Knox Coll., 1914. Former chmn. dir. Kingsport Press, Inc. (Tenn.), Press Mgmt., Inc.; sport Press, Inc. (Tenn.), Press Management, Inc.; v.p., dir. First Nat. Bank, Kingsport; dir. Southern Publishers, Inc. Home: Kingsport, TN. †

SMITH, WALTER IRVINE, coll. pres.; b. Thamesville, Ont., Can., Dec. 11, 1888; s. William Elgin and Rosamond (Wilde) S.; came to U.S., 1904; B.A., Union Coll., College View, Neb., 1911; student U. of Neb., 1913; M.A., Whitman Coll., Walla Walla, 1917; m. Mary Eva Livingston, Wash., Aug. 16, 1915; children—Hermas Irvine, Maurice Eugene, Louis Livingston. Began teaching in rural schools of Mich., 1907; with Walla Walla Coll., dept. of mathematics, 1912-17, pres. same coll. from 1917. Ordained Seventh Day Adventists ministry, 1920. Home: College Place, Wash. †

SMITHIES, ARTHUR, economist; b. Hobart, Tasmania, Australia, Dec. 12, 1907; s. John and Hilda (Stephenson) S.; LL.B., U. of Tasmania, 1929; B.A. (Rhodes scholar), Magdalen Coll., Oxford U., 1932; Ph.D. (Commonwealth Fund Fellow), Harvard U., 1934; m. Katharine Ripman, Feb. 22, 1935; children—Richard, Pamela, Juliet. Instr. economics U. of Mich., 1934-35, econ. Treasury Dept., Commonwealth of Australia, 1935-38, asst. and asso. prof. econ. U. of Mich., 1938-43; econ. and chief of econ br., U.S. Bur. Budget, 1943-48; dir. Fiscal and Trade Policy div. ECA, 1948-49; prof. econ. Harvard U. from 1949, chmn. dept. econs., 1950-55, Nathaniel Ropes prof. political economy, 1957-78, master of Kirkland House, 1965-74; Fulbright vis. prof., Oxford Univ., 1955-56, and Guggenheim fellow, 1955-56; vis. prof. Australian Nat. U., 1962-63; econ. adviser Office Def. Mblzn., 1951-52; cons. Hoover Commn., 1954; mem. research adv. Com. Econ. Devel., 1956-81. Fellow Econometric Soc. Author: The Budgetary Process in the United States, 1954. Editor Quar. Jours. Econs., Jour. Econ. Abstracts. Contbr. articles to sci. periodicals. Home: Cambridge, Mass. Died Sept. 9, 1981; buried Belmont Cemetery, Cambridge.

SMITHIES, ELSIE MAY, coll. dean; b. Phila., Pa., Jan. 18, 1888; d. John and Alice (Tattersall) Smithies; A.B., Lawrence Coll., Appleton, Wis., 1910; A.M., U. of Chicago, 1926; grad. student U. of Minn.; unmarried. Teacher Latin, Stevens Point, Wis., 1911-13, Wausau, Wis., 1913-15, U. of Minn., 1915-17; head of Latin dept., asst. prin., U. of Chicago High Sch., 1914-44; dean of women, Occidental Coll., Los Angeles, from 1944; summer sch. grad. course teacher U. of Chicago, Allegheny Coll., Mills Coll., Syracuse Univ., Occidental Coll. Organizer Smithies Ednl. Club, 1930. Mem. Am. Assn. Univ. Women, Nat. Assn. of Deans of Women (treas. 1933, pres. 1943-45), Ill. Deans of Women (treas. 1930), Calif. Deans of Women, Council of Guidance and Personnel Assn. (vice pres. 1945-46, pres. 1946-47), Phi Beta Kappa. Republican. Episcopalian. Club: Altrusa (international first vice president 1951-53). Author: (book) Case Studies of Normal Adolescent Girls, 1935; (chapter of book) Social Studies: Orientation 1937; contbr. articles to mags. and jours. Home: South Pasadena, Calif. †

SMYTH, CHARLES EDWARD, ednl. publisher; b. Milton, Mass., July 23, 1931; s. Ralston Blackburn and Eleanor Rogers (Greene) S.; B.A., Ohio Wesleyan U., 1953; M.Ed., Miami U., Oxford, Ohio, 1957; m. Patricia Ann Rhodes, July 4, 1953; children—Cynthia, William, Scott, Judith. Pub. sch. prin. Spring Valley (Ohio) Schs., 1955-57; guidance dir. Upper Arlington (Ohio) City Schs., 1957-60; staff asso. sci. Research Assos., Ohio, Mich., 1960-62; rep. Learning Materials Inc., Chgo., 1961-63; dir. devel. services Ency. Brit., Chgo., 1963-65; v.p. edn. div. Random House, Inc., N.Y.C., 1965-76; v.p. Baker & Taylor, 1976-77; exec. v.p. Macdonald/Raintree, Inc., pubs., Milw., from 1977; instr. Ohio State Guidance Inst., Columbus, Ohio, from 1959. Chmn. Citizens Com. Quality Edn., White Plains, N.Y., from 1972; mem. Com. Sch. Enrollment, White Plains, 1972-74. Served with USAF, 1953-55. Mem. Am. Assn. Publishers (chmn. research com. from 1973, mem. Great Cities Com. 1973-74), Phi Delta Kappa. Home: Wauwatosa, Wis. Deceased.

SNADER, DAVID L., civil engineering educator; b. Westminster, Md., July 8, 1887; s. Henry Maurer and Sarah Catherine (Zepp) S.; Arch. E., O. Northern U., 1913, C.E., 1914; M.S., 1918; A.M., Columbia U., 1926, Ph.D., 1937; m. Lelia Rogers, Sept. 2, 1919. Engaged in various capacities in constrn. operations, until 1914; in professional archtl. and engring. practice since 1914; prof. arch. and engring. Valparaiso U., 1914-17, Southwestern Presbyn. Univ., 1917-19; cons. archt. and engr. for State of S.D., prof. in charge dept. civil engring., S.D. State Coll., 1919-24; prof. civil (formerly structural) engineering, Stevens Institute Technology since 1924; for ten yrs. conducted research and investigation of condition of concrete structures in service throughout U.S.; cons. specialist on the microscopic science of concrete structures. In charge engring. courses in S.A.T.C. Fellow AAAS; mem. Am. Assn. Engrs., Am. Soc. Civil Engrs., Ind. Soc. Architects, Sigma Xi, Alpha Epsilon. Licensed professional engr. Democrat. Contbr. articles and bulletins, on condition concrete structures. Home: New York, N.Y. †

SNAPPER, ISIDORE, physician; b. Amsterdam, Holland, Jan. 5, 1889; s. David and Helena (Barends) S.; M.D., U. of Amsterdam, 1911; Ph.D., U. of Groningen, 1913; m. Henrietta Van Buuren, Dec. 1, 1911. Came to U.S., 1940, naturalized, 1947. Prof. medicine and gen. pathology, U. of Amsterdam, the Netherlands, 1919-38; prof. med. Peiping (China) Union Med. Coll., 1939-42; cons. Office of Surgeon Gen., U.S. War Dept., Washington, 1943-44; expert advisor Fgn. Econ. Administrn., Washington, 1943-45; physician and dir. Mt. Sinai Hosp., 1944-52; clin. prof. medicine, Columbia, 1944-52; cons. physician from 1952; dir. med. edn. Cook Co. Hosp. 1952-53, prof. of medicine Cook Co. Grad. Sch. 1952-53; prof. of medicine Chgo. Med. Sch. 1952-1953; member board trustees Hektoen Inst., 1952-59 member board dirs. medicine, med. edn. Beth-E Hosp., Brooklyn from 1953. Fellow N.Y. Acad. Medicine, Am. Coll. Physicians. Editor: Advances of Internal Medicine. Author: Chloorretentie by Koortsige Zickten, 1913; (with P. K. Pel and P. H. Enthoven) De ziekten van hart en bloedvaten, 1923; Zickten van het skelet, 1937; Maladies osseuses, 1938 (with A. W. M. Pompen) Pseudo-tuberculosis, 1938 (with A. A. Hymans Van den Bergh and C. D. de Langen) Leerboek der Inwendige Geneeskunde, 1941 Chinese Lessons to Western Medicine, 1941; Medical Aspects of Bone Diseases, 1943, 1949; Rare Manifestations of Metabolic Bone Disease, pub. 1952 Multiple Myeloma, 1953; Meditations on Medicine and Medical Education, published 1956; Netherlands East Indies and China, in Global Epidemiology by Simmons, Whayne, Anderson, Horack, 1944; Bone Diseases in Medical Practice, 1957; Bedside Medicine, 1960. Contbr. to professional jours. Home: New York, N.Y. †

SNELL, C(LARENCE) E(ASTLAKE), publisher; born Chgo., Apr. 26, 1897; s. William George and Margaret (McElroy) S; A.B., U. Ill., 1918; m. Ruth Arline Meloy, Feb. 11, 1928; children—Helen (Mrs. Peter Neumeyer), Natalie (Mrs. Robert Brymer), Jack Eastlake, Thomas Andrew. With Advance-Rumely Co., LaPorte, Ind., 1920-21; sales mgr. Hobart M. Cable Co., 1922-28; sales promotion mgr. F. E. Compton & Co., Chgo., 1928-36, v.p., 1937-51, president, 1952-63, director and consultant, 1963-66; director of Am. Textbook Publishers Institute, 1954-57. Pres. bd. edn., Glencoe Pub. Schs., 1944-50; Glencoe (Ill.) Park Dist. commr., after 1965. mem. Cook County Board of School Trustees, 1966- I. Member of Chi Phi. Clubs: Skokie Country (Glencoe); Chicago Athletic Association (Chicago). Home: Glencoe, Ill. Died Feb. 20, 1985.

SNELL, WALTER HENRY, educator; b. West Bridgewater, Mass., May 19, 1889; s. Alton Wesley and Clara Bartlett (Leach) S.; grad. Phillips Andover Acad.; A.B., Brown U., 1913, A.M., 1916; Ph.D., U. of Wis., 1920; m. Adelaide Elva Scott, Oct. 25, 1913; children—Walter Scott, George Valentine, Donald Francis. Played profl. baseball, 1913-16; agent and forest pathologist, Office of Forest Pathology, U.S.D.A., 1916-23; asst. prof. and asso. prof. botany, Brown U., 1920-42, Stephen T. Olney prof. natural history, 1942-59, professor emeritus of natural history, from 1959; asst. forest pathologist, N.Y. Conservation Dept., summers 1923-40. Chmn. Northeastern Forest Pest Com., 1949-54. Member A.A.A.S., Am. Phytopath. Soc., American Mycological Society, Bot. Soc. of America, Phi Beta Kappa, Sigma Xi. Republican. Author: Three Thousand Mycological Terms, 1936; (with E. A. Dick) A Glossary of Mycology, 1957. Contbr. 75 articles on forest pathology and mycology to jours. Home: Providence, RI. †

SNIDECOR, JOHN CLIFTON, educator; b. Washta, Iowa, Oct. 18, 1907; s. George E. and Jessie June (Ferrin) S.; m. Lois Eleanor Allison, Dec. 30, 1929; 1 son, John Carl. A.B., U. Calif., 1931; M.A., U. Iowa, 1937, Ph.D., 1940. Certified state psychologist, Calif. Instr. Antelope Valley Jr. Coll., Lancaster, Calif., 1932-33, dean, 1934-35; instr. U. Idaho, 1935-39; instr. Santa Barbara State Coll., 1940-41, asst. prof., 1941-43; asso. prof. speech U. Calif. at Santa Barbara, 1946-48, acting dean applied arts, 1948-50, acting provost, 1955-56, prof. speech, from 1948, dean applied arts, 1950-60. Contbr. articles profl. jours., books. Adv. bd. Santa Barbara County chpt. Am. Cancer Soc.; program com. Soc. Crippled Children and Adults. Served as lt. comdr. USNR, 1944-46. Fellow Am. Speech and Hearing Assn.; mem. Am. Psychol. Assn., Calif. Speech and Hearing Assn., Sigma Xi. Home: Santa Barbara, Calif.

SNOKE, HARRY CONWELL, lawyer, ch. ofcl.; b. Phila., July 29, 1905; s. Harry Albert and Bertha (Schultz) S.; A.B., U. Pa., 1927; LL.B., Temple U., 1931; LL.D., Baldwin Wallace Coll., 1961, Lycoming (Pa.) Coll., 1962; m. Alice Foster Hansen, Sept. 6, 1932. Admitted to Pa. bar, 1931, since practiced in Phila. Treas. nat. div. Meth. Ch., 1948-60, gen. sec., 1960-64, gen. treas. bd. missions, 1964-67; pres. Meth. Investment Fund, 1960-70; sec., treas. pension fund Eastern Pa. conf. United Meth. Ch., 1970-73; treas. div. home missions Nat. Council Chs., 1950-60. Bd. dirs. Goodwill Industries Am., 1948-80, pres., 1967-71, chmn. bd., 1971-74; treas., trustee William Duncan Trust, Metlakatla, Alaska; sec., trustee George A. Ruck Trust, Phila.; trustee Alaska Meth. U., Spartanburg Jr. Coll., Paine Coll. Mem. Am., Phila. bar assns. Club: Atlantic City Country. Home: Southampton, Pa. Died Aug. 26, 1980.

SNOOK, THOMAS E., architect and engr.; b. Brooklyn, New York, Oct. 7, 1888; s. Thomas E. and Anita Adele Snook; C.E., Columbia Univ., 1910; m. Virginia Dabney Wright, Aug. 15, 1917; 1 dau. Asst. engr., Jno. B. Snook Sons, architects and engrs., 1910-17, jr. mem. and chief engr., 1919-30, sr. mem. from 1930 (now Jno. B. Snook Sons-Victor C. Farrar). Represented the Brooklyn Chapter of The American Inst. of Architects in joint com. on city depts. giving advice on formation of New York City Building Code, 1920-28; surveyor and expert in court trials in cases of unsafe buildings for the City of New York, 1930-40. Served as capt., Corps of Engrs., U.S. Army, A.E.F., 1917-19. Mem. Am. Inst. of Architects (Brooklyn chap., past pres., 1925-27), New York State Soc. of Architects, Theta Xi. Home: New York, N.Y. †

SNYDER, ASA EDWARD, mgmt. cons., engr.; b. McGehee, Ark., May 17, 1923; s. Lucien Edward and Oliva (Richardson) S.; B.S. in Mech. Engring., Swarthmore Coll., 1951; M.S. in Mech. Engring., Princeton, 1952; m. Jean Elizabeth Mosher, Sept. 14, 1946; children—Kim S. Rice, Jon Richardson, Jared Mark, Adam Edward. Engr. Baldwin Locomotive Works, Eddystone, Pa., 1947-48; sr. project engr. Internat. Harvester Co., 1953-55; supr. advanced component design Gen. Electric Co., 1955-58; dir. research clearing div. U.S. Industries, Inc., 1958-60, exec. v.p. tech. center, Pompano Beach, Fla., 1960; v.p. research Pratt & Whitney Co., West Hartford, Conn., 1960-64; dir. tech. planning Colt Industries, 1964-69; founder, prin. Snyder Assos., mgmt. cons. and engrs., Essex, Conn., 1970-81. Instr. engring., evening div. Northeastern U., 1957-58. Pres., Middlesex council Boy Scouts Am. Served as lt. (j.g.) USNR, 1943-46. Mem. Internat. Assn. Exchange Tech. Students (chmn. 1962-70), ASME, Soc. Automotive Engrs., Soc. Internat. Devel., AAAS, Sigma Xi, Sigma Tau. Clubs: Princeton (N.Y.C.); Miles Creek Beach, Pettipaug Yacht; Old Saybrook Racquet. Home: East Essex, Conn. Died June 3, 1981.

SNYDER, DANIEL J., JR., federal judge; b. 1916; B.A., Wooster Coll.; LL.B., U. Pitts. Admitted to Pa. bar, 1941; judge U.S. Dist. Ct. Western Dist. Pa. Mem. Am. Bar Assn. Home: Pittsburgh, Pa. Died May 2, 1980.

SNYDER, HARRIS NOBLE, mineral aggregates co. exec.; b. Bloomville, O., May 13, 1889; s. Charles O. and Elizabeth (Seemuth) S.; grad. high sch.; m. Blanch Van Valkenburg, Nov. 25, 1914. Director Fed. Crushed Stone Corp., Buffalo, from 1929; pres., treas., Buffalo Slag Co., Incorporated, from 1913; dir. Am. Steamship Co., Bituminous Products, Inc., Buffalo Gravel Corp.; adv. com. Mfrs. & Traders Trust Co.; mem. adv. council Buffalo Savs. Bank. Trustee YMCA, Buffalo Community Chest; v.p., dir. Millard Fillmore Hosp., Buffalo. Mem. Nat. Slag Assn. (past pres.), Nat. Sand and Gravel Assn., C. of C. (past v.p.). Methodist. Home: Buffalo, N.Y. †

SOGNNAES, REIDAR FAUSKE, dentist, educator; b. Bergen, Norway, Nov. 6, 1911; came to U.S., 1938, naturalized, 1951; s. Johannes Olsen and Thora Gurine (Fauske) S.; m. Edel Marie Holand, June 29, 1939; children—Solveig Eleanor (Mrs. J. Barnes), Thor Heige, Reidun Kristine (Mrs. G. Racz), Anne Lise (Mrs. R. Spees). Examen Artium, Tanks Latin Gymnasium, Bergen, 1931; Examen Philosophicum, Oslo U., 1932; Examen Physicum, Leipzig U., 1932; Licensed Dental Surgeon summa cum laude, Norwegian Dental Sch. Oslo U., 1936; Ph.D., Rochester U.; Ph.D. (Carnegie Dental fellow), 1941; A.M. (hon.), Harvard, 1948, D.M.D., 1951; honorary doctorate, U. Oslo, Norway, 1961. Dental investigator Norwegian Sci. Expd. to Tristan da Cunha, 1937-38; intern Forsyth Dental Infirmary for Children, Boston, 1938-39, cons., 1949-60; asst. prof. dentistry Sch. Dental Medicine, Harvard, 1945-48, assoc. prof. dental medicine, 1948-52, assoc. dean and Charles A. Brackett prof. oral pathology, 1952-60; dean of dentistry U. Calif., 1960-69; prof. oral biology Sch. Dentistry, UCLA, 1960-81, prof. anatomy Sch. Medicine, 1963-81, dean emeritus, 1981-84; dental mem. Unitarian Service Co. Med. Mission to Greece and Italy, 1948; mem. nat. dental adv. council NIH; chmn. Gordon Conf. Bones and Teeth, 1956. Author: Oral Health Survey of Tristan da Cuba, 1954; Co-author: Tristan da Cunha—The Lonely Island, 1938, Greep's Histology, 1954, Fluoridation as a Public Health Measure, 1954, Mineral Metabolism—An Advanced Treatise, 1961, Radioistopes and Bone, 1962, Preventive Medicine for the Doctor in his Community, 1965; Co-editor, co-author: Fundamentals of Keratinization, 1962; Editor, co-author: Advances in Experimental Caries Research, 1955, Calcification in Biological Systems, 1960, Chemistry and Prevention of Dental Caries, 1962, Mechanisms of Hard Tissue Destruction, 1963, Ciba Conferences on Hard Tissues, 1972; Contbr. articles profl. jours. Served as dental officer Royal Norwegian Air Force, 1941-45, overseas and Can. Recipient Chgo. Dental Soc. award (with Dr. J.H. Shaw), 1952. Fellow Am. Acad. Arts and Scis., Am. Acad. Dental Sci.; mem. Am. Inst. Oral Biology (pres. 1964-70), Internat. Assn. of Dental Research (pres. 1957-58, Mineralization award 1965), AAAS (sec. sect. D 1959-62), Internat. Soc. Forensic Odonto-Stomatology (pres. 1975-78), Norwegian dental assns., Oslo Dental Soc. (hon. mem.), Danish Dental Soc. (corr. mem.), Stomatological Soc. Greece (hon.), Swedish Dental Assn. (hon.), Sigma Xi, Omicron Kappa Upsilon. Home: Thousand Oaks, Calif. Died Sept. 21, 1984.

SOKOL, ANTHONY EUGENE, educator; b. Vienna, Austria, Mar. 28, 1897; s. Anton and Klara (Kuban) S.; came to U.S., 1924, naturalized, 1934; student Austro-Hungarian Sch. for Naval Officers, 1915-16, Vienna Sch. Tech., 1918-19, U. Vienna, 1927-28; B.S., State Tchrs. Coll., Hattiesburg, Miss., 1928; A.M., Stanford U., 1930, Ph.D., 1932; m. Martha Hille, Oct. 8, 1927 (died Feb. 12, 1938); 1 son, Otto M.; m. 2d, Else Mueller, June 23, 1939. Officer, Royal Dutch Steamship Nav. Co., Netherlands East Indies, 1920-23; asso. prof. and head dept. fgn. langs. State Tchrs. Coll., Hattiesburg, 1928-29; prof. Germanic langs. Stanford U., 1934-48, prof. Asiatic and Slavic studies, 1949-57, asso. dir. Pacific-Asiatic and Russian program, 1945-57, prof. internat. security affairs, 1957-62, prof. emeritus, 1962-82; Fulbright prof. U. Vienna, 1957. Served as lt. Austro-Hungarian Navy, 1915-18. Decorated Austrian Cross Honor 1st class for sci. and art, 1975. Mem. AAUP, U.S. Naval Inst., Am. Mil. Inst., Far Eastern Assn. Author: Grosse Forscher and ihre Beitrage, 1938; Sea Power in the Nuclear Age, 1961; The Imperial and Royal Austro-Hungarian Navy, 1968; Seemacht Osterreich, 1972; contbr. articles on German lit. and civilation, on naval affairs and on Southeast Asia to profl. jours. Home: Palo Alto, Calif. Died Nov. 11, 1982.

SOKOL, HERMAN, b. Bloomfield, N.J., Oct. 14, 1916; s. Joseph and Rose (Mann) S.; m. Margaret Augusta McCormack, July 4, 1942. B.A., Montclair State Coll., 1937; M.S., U. Mich., 1940; Ph.D. in Organic Chemistry, N.Y. U., 1944. Research chemist Rubber Reserve Corp. (OSRD), 1942-44; research chemist, group leader, tech. supt. Heyden Chem. Corp., 1944-50, mgr. antibiotics research div., 1950-53; v.p. research and devel. Heyden Newport Chem. Corp., 1954-58, exec. v.p., dir., 1958-62; pres., dir. Am. Plastics Corp., N.Y.C., 1958-61; pres. Bristol Labs. Internat. Corp., 1963-67; v.p. Bristol-Myers Co., 1963-67, sr. v.p., 1967-76, pres., 1977-82, also dir.; trustee East River Savs. Bank., N.Y.C., 1971—; dir. Internat. Flavors & Fragrances, Inc., N.Y.C., GAF Corp., N.Y.C., 1980-83, Albany Internat. Corp. (N.Y.), 1981-83. Bd. dirs. Whitehead Inst. for Biomed. Research, Greenwich, Conn. Mem. Am. Chem. Soc., AAAS, N.Y. Acad. Scis., Pharm. Mfrs. Assn. (dir. 1975-82), Sigma Xi, Phi Lambda Upsilon. Home: New York, N.Y. Died June 21, 1985.

SOLARI, JOSEPH G., business exec.; b. Chgo., 1918; ed. Northwestern U. Pres., dir. Great Lakes Carbon Corp.; chmn. Gen. Refractories Co.; dir. Graphite India Ltd., India Carbon Ltd., Anglo Great Lakes Corp. Ltd., Great Eastern Indsl. Corp. Ltd., G.L.C. Bldg. Corp., Great Lakes Char Products Corp., Great Lakes Mid-Continent Corp., Great Lakes Properties Inc., Great Lakes Research Corp., Great Lakes Tech. Services Inc., Island Creek Coal Co., Japan Inc., Paolos Verdes Water Co., Rancho Ida, Inc., Great Lakes Carbon Internat. Ltd., Twentieth Century Trading Corp., Rancho Palos Verdes Corp., Jefferson Electric Co., Tech-Ohmn Electronics Inc. Home: Manhassett, N.Y. Died Mar. 27, 1984.

SOLBERG, CARL EDWARD, history educator; b. St. Paul, Apr. 4, 1940; s. Walter O. and Helen Mary (Worden) S. B.A., U. Minn., 1962; M.A., Stanford U., 1963, Ph.D., 1967. Asst. prof. history U. Wash., Seattle, 1968-71, asso. prof. history, 1971-78; prof. history Univ. Wash., 1978-85; vis. prof. Stanford Univ., Palo Alto, Calif., 1981. Author: Oil and Nationalism in Argentina: A History, 1979, Immigration and Nationalism: Argentina and Chile, 1890-1914, 1970; contbr. articles to profl. jours.; editorial bd. Bus. History Rev. Recipient Conf. Latin Am. History prize Am. Hist. Assn., 1972. Mem. Am. Hist. Assn., Latin Am. Studies Assn., Assn. Can. Studies in U.S., Conf. Latin Am. History. Democrat. Home: Seattle, Wash. Died.

SOLIS-COHEN, D. HAYS, lawyer; b. Phila., Aug. 21, 1887; s. Solomon and Emily Grace (Solis) Solis-C.; grad. William Penn Charter Sch., 1905; LL.B., U. Pa., 1910; LL.D., Jefferson Med. Coll., 1965; m. Erna Sultan, June 10, 1914; children—Helen (Mrs. Herbert Spigel), D. Hays. Admitted to Pa. bar, 1910, practiced in Phila.; partner firm Wolf, Block, Schorr Solis-Cohen, from 1924, sr. partner, from 1959. Dir. Bankers Securities Corp., Horn & Hardart Baking Co., Phila., George Allen Inc., Rosenau Bros. Inc., William Goldman Theatres. Treas., bd. govs. Dropsie Coll. Hebrew and Cognate Learning, 1926-43. Life trustee Jefferson Med. Coll., Fedn. Jewish Agencies Greater Phila., Philip and A.S.W. Rosenbach Museum and Found., Percival and Ethel Brown Foerderer Found., Joseph V. Horn Found., Lessing and Edith G. Rosenwald Found., Signey R. Rosenav Found. Mem. Am., Pa., Phila. (past bd. govs.) bar assns., Am. Judicature Soc., Lawyers Clubs Phila. (past bd. dirs.), S.R., Hist. Soc. Pa., Phila. Mus. Art, Acad. Fine Arts, Friends of Free Library Phila. Jewish religion (past pres. congregation). Home: West Jenkintown, PA. †

SOLOMON, HARRY C(AESAR), neuropsychiatrist; b. Hastings, Neb., Oct. 25, 1889; s. Jacob C. and Lena (Fist) S.; B.S., U. of Calif., 1910; M.D., Harvard, 1914; m. Maida Herman, June 27, 1916; children—Peter Herman, Joseph Herman, Babette, H. Eric. Began practice Boston, 1914; emeritus prof. psychiatry, Harvard Med. Sch.; spl. instr. clin. psychiatry, Simmons Coll. Sch. of Social Work; past med. dir., Boston Psychopathic Hosp; consultant in psychiatry and neurology, Beth Israel Hosp.; mem. bd. consultants Massachusetts General Hospital. Charitable Eye and Ear Infirmary, Faulkner Hosp.; consultant U.S. Vets. Hosp.; formerly mem. med. council, U.S. Vets. Adminstrn. Former mem. adv. com. Dept. Pub. Welfare of Commonwealth of Mass.; commissioner Mental Health Com. of Mass. Mem. subcoms. on neurology and personnel training Nat. Research Council; chief neuro-psychiatric examiner, U.S. Army Recruiting and Induction Sta., Boston. Mem. med. adv. bd., Selective Service; Selective Service Medal; spl. cons., Sec. of War; chmn. of Deans' Sub-com. on Neuropsychiatry, Vets. Adminstrn., Boston District. Served as 1st lieut. Medical Corps., U. S. Army, 1918-19. Fellow American Medical Association; member Am. Neurol. Assn. (pres. 1941), Boston Soc. Neurology and Psychiatry (pres. 1928-29), Am. Psychiatric Assn. (pres. 1957-58), N.E. Soc. Psychiatry (pres. 1938-39), Assn. Research in Nervous and Mental Diseases (pres. 1956), American Psychopathological Association (pres. 1958-59), Greater Boston Med. Soc. (ex-pres.), Sigma Xi, Phi Delta Epsilon. Clubs: University, Harvard. Author: Neurosyphilis (with Elmer E. Southard), 1918; Syphilis of the Innocent (with Maida H. Solomon), 1922. Editor, Manual of Military Neuropsychiatry (with P. I. Yakovlev); Neurosyphilis by Merritt, Adams and Solomon; Studies in Lobotomy (with Milton Greenblatt); Frontal Lobes and Schizophrenia (with Greenblatt). Home: Jamaica Plain, Mass. †

SOLOMON, HYDE, artist; b. N.Y.C., May 3, 1911; s. Samuel and Ida (Chasin) S. Student, Art Students League, Pratt Inst., Columbia U. artist-in-residence Princeton U., 1959-62. Represented in permanent collections, Whitney Mus., N.Y.C., Wadsworth Atheneum, Hartford, Conn., Helena Rubenstein Pavilion, Tel Aviv Mus., Palestine, Newark Mus., Walker Art Centre, Minn., Telfair Acad. Fine Arts, Savannah, Ga., Munson-Williams Proctor Mus., Utica, N.Y., U. Va. Mus., U. Calif., Mus. at Berkeley, Mus. of N.Mex., Santa Fe, Amarillo (Tex.) Area Arts Found., numerous corporate collections. (Recipient Purchase award Acad. Arts and Letters, k91970, Mark Rothko Found. grantee 1973, Grant Adolph and Esther Gottlieb Found. grantee 1978); One-man shows, Peridot Gallery, N.Y.C., 1954-55, 56, Poindexter Gallery, N.Y.C., 1957, 58, 60, 63, 65, 67, 69, 70, 73, 74, Princeton Art Mus., 1959, Gallery of Modern Art, Taos, N.Mex., 1974, Stables Gallery, Taos, 1978, Mus. Fine Arts, Santa Fe, N.Mex., 1979, Roswell (N.Mex.) Mus., 1979, group shows, Whitney Mus., Carnegie Internat., 1965, 67. Address: Succasunna NJ

SOLOMON, JOEL W., gen. services adminstr.; b. Chattanooga, Tenn., June 22, 1921; s. Abe and Ida (Borisky) S.; B.A. in Maths., Vanderbilt U., 1942; m. Rosalind Fox, June 13, 1953; children—Joel W., Linda Ilene. Mgr., Independent Theatres, Tenn./Ga., 1942-45, v.p., mgr., 1945-61; partner Independent Interprises, Inc. (comml. real estate devel. firm), Chattanooga, 1942-77, pres., 1961-71, sr. v.p. Atlen Realty & Devel. Corp. (subs.), 1971-77, also mem. bd. and corp. pres., chmn. Arlen Shopping Centers Co., Chattanooga, 1971-77, adminstr. GSA, 1977-79. Commr. and chmn. Chattanooga Housing Authority, 1952-65. Mem. Chattanooga Opera Assn. (bd. dirs. 1953-64), Tenn. Mental Health Assn. (pres., mem. bd. Chattanooga br. 1962-66, Internat. Council Shopping Centers, Chattanooga Jr. C. of C. (mem. bd. and v.p. 1948-54). Democrat. Jewish. Home: Nashville, Tenn. Died July 29, 1984.

SOMERS, GROVER THOMAS, educator; b. Bloxom, Va., May 26, 1888; s. William J. and Margaret Ann (Mears) S.; A.B., Coll. of william and Mary, 1907; A.M., Teachers Coll., Columbia, 1912, Ph.D., 1923; m. Celia McCall, Aug. 22, 1945. Prin., Chase City (Va.) High Sch., 1910-13; prin. of training sch., Jacksonville, Ala., 1913-15; prof. ednl. psychology Farmville (Va.) State Teachers Coll., 1915-19; ednl. cons. Pelman Inst., N.Y. City, 1920-22; prof. psychology and edn. measurements Bloomsburg (Pa.) State Teachers Coll., 1923-24, prof. ednl. psychology U. of Ky., 1924-25; asso. prof. ednl. psychology Ind. U., 1925-35; prof. edn. from 1935; mem. Va. Edn. Survey, 1918-19; asso. supervisor sec. of edn. State Dept. of Edn., Va., 1916-19. Mem. Mecklingburg Teachers Assn. (pres., 1912-13), Am. Council on Edn. (mem. collaboration group, div. on child development; teacher personnel com. on teacher edn.), N.E.A., Progressive Edn. Assn., Internat. Council for Exceptional Children, Nat. Soc. for Coll. Teachers of Edn., Tawse Soc., Phi Beta Kappa, Phi Delta Kappa, Kappa Delta Pi, Kappa Phi Kappa. Author: Pedagogical Prognosis, 1923; Students' Test Attitudes, 1926; (mimeograph) Workbook in Educational Psychology, 1934; (mimeograph) Workbook in Child Development, 1940 (poetry) Lovelicks of a Layman, 1928; Within My Castle Walls, 1942; Beyond The Garden Gate, 1949. Home: Bloomington, Ind. †

SONNEBORN, TRACY MORTON, scientist, educator; b. Balt., Oct. 19, 1905; s. Lee and Daisy (Bamberger) S.; B.A., Johns Hopkins, 1925, Ph.D., 1928, D.Sc (hon.), 1957; D.Sc. (hon.), Université de Genève, Northwestern U., 1975, Ind. U., 1978, U. Münster (W. Ger.), 1979; m. Ruth Meyers, June 6, 1929; children—Lee M., David R. Fellow, NRC, 1928-30; research asst. zoology Johns Hopkins U., 1930-31, research asso., 1931-33, asso., 1933-39; asso. prof. zoology Ind. U., 1939-43, prof., 1943-53, distinguished prof., 1953-76, distinguished prof. emeritus, 1976-81, acting chmn. div. biol. scis., 1963-64; vis. prof. U. Wash., Seattle, Battelle Research Center, 1971; vis. researcher U. Paris South, Orsay, France, Laboratoire de Génétique Moleculaire, Gif-sur-Yvette, France, 1973; vis. prof. zoology U. Geneva (Switzerland), 1979. Discoverer of mating types in ciliated protozoa, 1937, roles of genes, cytoplasm and environment, control cell heredity, 1943-81. Co-winner Newcomb-Cleveland prize for outstanding research paper AAAS, 1946; Kimber Genetics award Nat. Acad. Scis., 1959; Mendel medal Czechoslovakia Acad. Sci., 1965. Mem. Am. Soc. Naturalists (pres. 1949), Am. Soc. Zoologists (pres. 1956), Genetics Soc. Am. (pres. 1949), Soc. Study Evolution (v.p. 1958), Nat. Acad. Sci. (1946), Am. Philos. Soc. (Phila.), Am. Acad. Arts and Sci. (Boston), Am. Soc. Protozoologists (hon.), Royal Soc. London (fgn.), Am. Soc. Cell Biology, Am. Inst. Biol. Scis. (pres. 1960-61), Phi Beta Kappa (vis. scholar 1969, asso. lectr. 1975-81), Sigma Xi (nat. lectr. 1949, 68); hon. mem. Faculdad de Biologia y Ciencias Medicas, Universidad de Chile, Sociedad de Biologia de Santiago de Chile, Sociedad de Biologia de Concepcion (Chile), Sociedad Medica de Concepcion (Chile), French Soc. Protozoology (hon.), Genetics Soc. Japan (hon.). Editor: The Control of Human Heredity and Evolution, 1965; editorial bd. Jour. Morphology, 1946-49; Genetics, 1947-62; Jour. Exptl. Zoology, 1948-60; Physiol. Zoology, 1948-60; editorial com. Ann. Rev. Microbiology, 1954-58; contbr. articles to mags. and chpts. to books on genetics. Home: Bloomington, Ind. Died Jan. 26, 1981.

SOPWITH, SIR THOMAS OCTAVE MURDOCH, aero. engr.; b. 1888; m. Phillis Brodie Gordon; 1 son, Thomas Edward Brodie. Founder Sopwith Aviation Co., 1912; pres., dir. Hawker Siddeley Group Ltd. Created Knight Comdr. Order Brit. Empire. Hon. fellow Royal Aero. Soc. Home: Stockbridge Hants, England. †

SORENSEN, CHRISTIAN ABRAHAM, lawyer; b. Harrisburg, Neb., Mar. 24, 1890; s. Jens Christian and Annie (Madsen) S.; student Grand Island (Neb.) Coll., 1909-12; A.B., U. of Neb., 1913, LL.B., 1916; m. Annis Chaikin, July 9, 1921; children—Robert, Thomas, Theodore, Ruth, Philip. Admitted to Neb. bar, 1916; began practice at Lincoln. Exec. sec. Neb. Popular Govt. League, 1915-17; asst. dir. Neb. Legislative Reference Bur., 1916; sec. and atty. Neb. League of Municipalities, 1917; atty. Neb. Woman Suffrage Assn., 1917; campaign mgr. for Senator Norris, 1918, 24; atty. gen., Neb., 2 terms, 1929-33; author in 1933 of Senate File No. 310 under which Nebraska's public power districts and public power and irrigation districts are organized; chmn. of Campaign Com. for Neb. One-House Legislature, 1934; 1st pres. Neb. Assn. of Rural Pub. Power Dists., 1937. Mem. Am., Neb. State and Lincoln bar assns. Unitarian. Clubs: Open Forum, Laymen's. Home: Lincoln, Nebr. †

SORENSEN, CLARENCE WOODROW, coll. pres.; b. Loup City, Nebr., Apr. 6, 1907; s. James C. and Anna (Madsen) S.; Ph.D., U. Chgo., 1951; L.H.D., Wittenberg U., 1963, Marycrest Coll., 1970; m. Edna L. Schaus, Aug. 13, 1938. Dir. Pakistan edn. project, 1951-52; asst. prof. Ill. State U., 1949-52, asso. prof., 1952-56, prof. geography, 1956-59, dean Grad. Sch., 1959-62; pres. Augustana Coll., Rock Island, Ill., 1962-75. Bd. dirs. Found. Inter Confessional Research, France, Luth. Sch. Theology, Chgo., 1976-82. Recipient Distinguished Service award Quad-Cities Grad. Studies Center, Rock Island, Ill., 1975, Distinguished Community Service award Rock Island Rotary, 1975; named Man of Yr., Quad-Cities chpt. B'nai B'rith, 1975; decorated comdr. Order of North Star (Sweden). Fellow Royal Geol. Soc.; mem. Nat. Council Social Edn. (editorial bd. 1952-55), Phi Beta Kappa, Pi Kappa Delta, Gamma Theta Upsilon. Author: A World View, 1950; Ways of Our Land, 1954; (with H.H. Barrows, E.P. Parker) Our Big World, 1945, Old World Lands, 1948, The American Continents, 1947; co-author vols. published in Urdu: Neighbors in Asia, Europe and North America, The Southern Continents, Pakistan and the World, Regions and Resources, Economic Geography Physical Geography and Geology, 1952-54; also numerous articles, filmstrips in field. Home: Bloomington, Ill. Died Aug. 17, 1982.

SORENSEN, ROYAL MILNER, lawyer; b. Pasadena, Calif., Oct. 22, 1914; s. Royal Wasson and Grace (Milner) S.; B.A., Stanford, 1936; LL.B., U. So. Calif., 1939; m. Dorothy Louise Russell, Sept. 1, 1938; children—Eric Russell, Julia Margaret (Mrs. Lee Martin Serjak), Jane Anne (Mrs. Joseph Arnold Thibedeau). Admitted to Calif. bar, 1941; dep. city atty., Pasadena, 1941-43, 46-47; city atty. Santa Monica, Calif., 1947-52; partner firm Burke, Williams & Sorensen, Los Angeles, 1952-83; cons., spl. atty. municipalities. Mem. Santa Monica City Council, 1965-69. Served with USNR, 1943-45. Mem. State Bar Calif., Am., Los Angeles County bar assns., League Calif. Cities (dir. 1965-67). Club: Calif. Yacht. Home: Santa Monica, Calif. Died June 29, 1983.

SOTTILE, JAMES, financier; b. Charleston, S.C., Oct. 19, 1913; s. James and Louise (Mohlman) S.; m. Ethel Hooks, June 16, 1936; children: Linda (Mrs. Frank Hammond), James III (dec.), Suzanne (Mrs. Charles Guanci), Jeanne (Mrs. Harold Walsh III), John. Pres, dir. Canaveral Indian River Groves, Inc., 1962-70, Brevard Indian River Groves, Inc., 1963-68; pres., dir. Indian River Orange Groves, Inc., 1959-68, chmn. bd., 1968-73; pres., dir. Gulfstream Groves, Inc., 1962-65; pres. Lake Byrd Citrus Packing Co, 1960-81; pres., dir. Valencia Center, Inc.; dir., chmn. bd. Harlan Fuel Co., 1975-82, Goldfield Corp.; dir. No. Goldfield Investments, Ltd., U.S. Treasury Mining Co., Black Range Mining Corp., Detrital Valley Salt Corp., Fla. Transport Corp., Goldfield Consol. Mines Co., Mamba Engrng. Co., Inc., San Pedro Mining Corp.; pres., dir. Pan Am. Bank of Miami, 1956-58. Trustee U. Miami, 1956-66. Mem. Fla. C. of C. (dir.-at-large). Clubs: K.C. (Fla.), Elk. (Fla.), Country of Coral Gables (Fla.); Riviera Country (Coral Gables); Eau Gallie Yacht (Melbourne, Fla.); Rotary. Home: Coral Gables, Fla. Died June 10, 1983.

SOUERS, LOREN EATON, lawyer; b. Canton, Ohio, Jan. 29, 1916; s. Loren Edmunds and Ilka (Gaskell) S.; m. Mildred M. McCollum, June 21, 1941; children: Mary Sue (Mrs. J. James), Loren Eaton. A.B., Denison U., 1937; J.D., Western Res. U., 1940, postgrad., 1954-55. Bar: Ohio 1940, U.S. Supreme Ct 1960. Assoc. Black, McCuskey, Souers & Arbaugh, Canton, from 1940, partner, from 1946, chmn., from 1979; dir. Harter Bank and Trust Co., Ohio Bar Liability Ins. Co., Phoenix Mfg. Co., Joliet, Ill., Whitacre-Greer Fireproofing Co., Continental Steel Corp., Kokomo, Ind.; Cons. Ohio Supreme Ct. Continuing Com. Admissions, 1957-59; mem. Ohio Bd. Bar Examiners, 1959-64; citizens adv. com. to State Library System. Contbr. to legal publs.; lectr. on legal subjects. Pres. McKinley Area council Boy Scouts Am., 1954-57, mem. Nat. council, 1954-70; Mem. Canton City Council, 1948-49; del. Rep. Nat. Conv., 1948; Rep. city campaign mgr., 1951, 53; mem. Ohio Bd. Edn., 1956-60, v.p., 1958-60; mem. Canton City Bd. Edn., 1962-72, pres., 1965, 68, 71; mem. Canton Recreation Bd., 1964-72; trustee Canton Welfare Fedn., 1965-72; trustee Canton Area YMCA, from 1977, v.p., from 1981; mem. Canton Planning Commn., 1972-78; trustee Stark County Law Library Assn., 1945-76, pres., 1972-76; trustee Ohio Bar Found., Denison U., from 1967, Ohio Legal Center Inst.; mem. trust com. Hoover Found., from 1967, sec., from 1980; mem. vis. com. Case Western Res. U. Law Sch., 1968-77, from 81. Served to capt. inf. AUS, 1942-45, ETO. Decorated Fourragere Belgium; recipient research prize in econs. Denison U., 1937, Disting. Service award Canton Jr. C of C., 1950, Silver Beaver award Boy Scouts Am., 1957; Outstanding Alumnus award Case Western Res. U. Law Sch., 1981. Fellow Am. Bar found. (Ohio chmn. from 1984); mem. ABA, Ohio Bar Assn. (exec. com. 1976-79, pres. 1980-81), Am. Legion, Canton Jr. C. of C. (pres.), Canton C. of C. (v.p. 1959-60), Phi Delta Theta, Phi Delta Phi, Omicron Delta Kappa, Tau Kappa Alpha, Pi Delta Epsilon. Mem. DIsciples of Christ Ch. Clubs: Masons (32 deg.); The Canton (Canton), Oakwood Country (Canton), Brookside Country (Canton); Univ. (Columbus, Ohio). Home: Canton, OH.

SOULBURY, 1ST BARON (HERWALD RAMSBOTHAM), gov. gen. Ceylon; b. 1887; s. Herwald and Ethel Margaret (Bevan) R.; M.A., Univ. Coll., Oxford; LL.D., hon., U. of Ceylon; m. Doris Violet de Stein, 1911; 3 children; m. 2d, Anthea Margaret Wilton, 1949 (dec. 1950). Parliamentary sec. Bd. Edn., 1931-35, Ministry Agr. and Fisheries, 1935-36; minister of pensions, 1936-39; first commr. of works, 1939-40; pres. Bd. Edn., 1940-41; chmn. Assistance Bd., 1941-48, Ceylon Commn., 1944; gov. gen. Ceylon from 1949. Served with Brit. Army, World War I, 1914-18. Privy councilor. Created 1st Baron Soulbury, 1941. Decorated Order Brit. Empire, Mil. Cross. Address: Colombo, Ceylon. †

SOULE, GEORGE HENRY, JR., b. Stamford, Conn., June 11, 1887; s. George Henry and Ellen (Smyth) S.; A.B., Yale Univ., 1908; m. Flanders Dunbar, M.D. 1 dau., Marcia Winslow Dunbar-Soule. Began in employ of Frederick A. Stokes Co., publishers, New York, 1908, and became advertising mgr.; joined editorial staff The New Republic, Dec. 1914; Washington corr. same, Sept.-Dec. 1918; joined editorial staff N.Y. Evening Post, Jan. 1919; investigator for Inter-Church World Movement Commn. on Steel Strike, 1919; statistician for Nautical Gazette Jan.-Mar. 1921; editor, The New Republic, Jan. 1, 1924-Jan. 1, 1947; dir.-at-large Nat. Bur. Econ. Research, from 1922; prof. econ. Bennington Coll., until 1957, grant Fund for Advancement Edn., 1958-59; prof. econs. Colgate U., 1958, U. Tenn., 1961-62; Whitney Distinguished prof. Wash. Coll., 1958-59; tchr. Columbia, summers 1948-52; cons. 20th Century Fund, 1948-57. Dir. research Washington College for U.S. Small Bus. Adminstrn., vertical integration in agrl., 1959-60. Spl. adviser to sec. of interior on reclamation and rural development in South, 1927. Asso. fellow Trumbull Coll. of Yale. Enlisted in Coast Arty., May 10, 1918; corpl., July 1, 1918; detailed to study anti-submarine devices, at New London, Conn., Aug. 1918; trans. to C.A. Officers Training Sch., Ft. Monroe, Va., Sept. 1918; commd. 2d lt. C.A. Reserve, Nov. 1918, and put on inactive list. Fellow A.A.A.S.; member American Economic Assn., Am. Polit. Sci. Assn., Am. Psychosomatic Soc. Author or co-author books from 1920; latest publ.: Introduction to Economic Science, 1948; Economic Forces in American History, 1952; Ideas of the Great Economists, 1952; Men, Wages and Employment in the Modern U.S. Economy, 1954; Time for Living, 1955; American Economic History, 1957; Longer Life, 1958; The Shape of the Future, 1958; Economics, Measurements, Theories, Case Studies, 1961; Economics for Living, 1961; The New Science of Economics, 1964; Planning U.S.A., 1967. Home: South Kent, Conn. †

SOUPART, PIERRE, physician, educator; b. Morlanwelz, Belgium, Oct. 1, 1923; came to U.S., 1962, naturalized, 1969; s. Arthur and Angèle (Couteau) S.; m. Simone Haegeman, July 23, 1949; children—Evelyne, Antoinette, Pascale. M.D., Brussels U., 1949, Ph.D., 1959, hon. prof., 1975. Asst. prof. dept. biochemistry Brussels U. Sch. Medicine, 1950-56, asso. prof., 1956-62; head clin. labs. Clinic for Indsl. Accidents, Brussels, 1952-62; prof. biochemistry and human nutrition Province of Brabant Inst. Tech., Brussels, 1959-62; research asso. div. reproductive physiology, dept. Ob-Gyn Vanderbilt U. Sch. Medicine, Nashville, 1962-63, asst. prof. Ob-Gyn, 1963-66, asso. research prof., 1966—; sr. investigator Vanderbilt Center for Population Research and Studies in Reproductive Biology, 1969—, mem. univ. com. for protection of human subjects, 1973-76; vis. prof. Universidad Catolica de Chile and Universidad de Chile, Santiago, 1976, U. Calif., spring 1979; guest speaker numerous confs.; vis. prof. U. B.C., Vancouver, Can., 1979, Karolinska Inst., Stockholm, 1979, Monash U., Melbourne, Australia, 1979. Author: Aminoaciduria of Pregnancy, 1959; editorial bd.: Advances in Reproductive Biology, 1975—; contbr. articles to profl. jours. Served as med. officer Belgian Army, 1949-50. Francqui Found. fellow, 1948; advanced fellow, 1961; Vanderbilt U. Centennial fellow, 1974-75; grantee NSF; grantee March of Dimes, others. Mem. Soc. Study of Reprodn. (chmn. bylaws com. 1973-75), Société Belge de Biochimie, N.Y. Acad. Scis., Soc. Study of Fertility (U.K.), Am. Fertility Soc., Sociedad Latino Americana de Microscopia Electronica, Am. Soc. Andrology (charter), Soc. Cryobiology, Am. Assn. Tissue Banks, Internat. Embryotransfer Soc., Am. Assn. Gynecologic Laparascopists, Sigma Xi, Belgian Dietetic Assn. (hon.). Democrat. Club: Masons (Brussels). Pioneer in in vitro fertilization of human ovum.

SOUR, ROBERT BANDLER, musical company executive; b. N.Y.C., Oct 31, 1905; s. Bernard and Adele (Somborn) S.; ed. Princeton, 1925; m. Geraldine Scofield, Oct. 24, 1940; children—R. Thomas, Peter, Bonnie (Mrs. Arthur A. Anderson), Victoria Jean (Mrs. John R. Raben, Jr.). With S.W. Straus, real estate, 1925-29; free-lance song writer, 1929-31; mem. Am. Stock Exchange, 1931-37; asso. producer Fed. Theatre, 1937-39; with Broadcast Music, Inc., 1940-70, cons. to pres., vice chmn. bd., 1970-85; cons. adv. council dept. music Princeton; cons. Am. Guild Authors and Composers. Bd. dirs. Songwriters Hall Fame, also v.p.; bd. dirs. N.Y. Com. Young Audiences. Mem. Contemporary Music Soc. (dir.). Club: Century Assn., Princeton (N.Y.C.); Innis Arden (Old Greenwich, Conn.). Composer lyrics to Body and Soul, Practice Makes Perfect, Walking By the River, We Could Make Such Beautiful Music Together, I See a Million People. Home: Old Greenwich, Conn. Dec. Mar. 6, 1985.

SOUTHARD, CECIL D., wholesale company executive; b. Charleston, Ark., Feb. 8, 1890; s. Richard and Ella Ernestine (Hamilton) S.; student, U. Ark, 1907-08; m. Alice Pearl Clay, 1909; children—Cecil D., Mary Lou. Mercantile bus., Charleston, 1909-13; editor and pub. Dem. co. newspaper Franklin Co., Ark., 1913; retailer men's and boys' clothing, Ft. Smith, Ark., 1913-17; with Berry Dry Goods Co., 1917-31, v.p., gen. mgr., 1920-31; with Butler Bros., Chicago, since 1931, v.p., dir. distbr. stores, dir. sales and advt. 1937-47, gen. mgr. wholesale div., since 1947. Dir. Chicago Assn. Commerce. Democrat. Methodist. Clubs: Union League (Chicago); Westmoreland Country (Evanston). Home: Evanston, Ill. †

SOUTHERLAND, CLARENCE ANDREW, lawyer; b. Baltimore, Apr. 10, 1889; s. Clarence and Amey (Fairbank) S.; student Friends Sch., Wilmington, Del., 1895-1905, Princeton, 1905-07; LL.B., Georgetown U., 1913; LL.D., U. Del., 1956; married Katharine Virden, Jan. 11, 1923; children—Katharine Virden (Mrs. Stuart H. Johnson, Jr.), Clare Amey (Mrs. Charles B. Lenahan II). Admitted to Del. bar, 1914, practiced at Wilmington, 1914-51; atty. gen. State Del., 1925-29; chief justice Supreme Ct. Del., 1951-63; counsel Potter, Anderson & Corroon. Member of the Am., Del. State (pres. 1933-35), New Castle Co. and City of N.Y. bar assns. Republican. Clubs: Greenville Country; Wilmington. Home: Wilmington, Del. †

SOUTHGATE, HARVEY WILLIAM, newspaper editor; b. Rochester, N.Y., Oct. 2, 1890; s. Herbert John and Mary (Banham) S.; ed. pub. schs., Rochester; m. Mabel Roxanna Ross, Oct. 11, 1930; 1 dau., Virginia Putnam. Reporter, Rochester Post Express, 1909-11; drama editor Rochester Herald, 1911-25; editorial writer, columnist Rochester Democrat and Chronicle, 1927-53, music editor, 1953-49, author Sunday column Scanning the Scores, from 1953, monthly column on astronomy, from 1945. Recipient award for articles on Music Week, Nat. Fedn. Music Clubs, 1963. Mem. Music Critics Assn., Rochester Newspaper Guild. Kiwanian (pres. Rochester 1949). Home: Palmyra, NY. †

SOUTHWORTH, HERMAN MCDOWELL, agrl. economist; b. Binghamton, N.Y., Apr. 7, 1909; s. Herman Roy and Grace Marilla (Belknap) S.; A.B., Cornell U., 1930; postgrad. Iowa State Coll., 1938-41; D.Agr., Seoul Nat. U., 1973; m. Carol Louise Treyz, June 29, 1935; children—Edward Gordon, Thomas Roy, Harrison Treyz, Douglas Belknap. Research technician Consumer's Research, Inc., 1934-36, Consumers Union U.S., 1936-38; agrl. economist Bur. Agrl. Econs. and War Food Adminstrn., Dept. Agr., 1940-47; bus. economist Council Econ. Advisers, 1947-50; asst. to asso. chief Bur. Agrl. Econs., Dept. Agr., 1950-52, asst. to dep. adminstr. Agrl. Mktg. Service, 1953-57; prof. agrl. econs. Pa. State U., 1957-66; asso. Agrl. Devel. Council, Inc., N.Y.C., 1966-73; faculty Dept. Agr. Grad. Sch., 1945-57; tng. materials specialist Agrl. Devel. Council, Inc., 1964-65; mem. com. agrl. econs. Social Sci. Research Council, 1955-66, chmn., 1959-66; guest prof. agrl. econs. Seoul Nat. U., 1966-72. Recipient Rockefeller Pub. Service award, 1955. Mem. Phi Beta Kappa, Phi Kappa Phi. Author: Agricultural Marketing for Developing Countries, 1971; co-author: The School Lunch Program and Agricultural Surplus Disposal, 1941; Marketing Policies for Agriculture, 1960; editor: Farm Mechanization in East Asia, 1972; co-editor: Agricultural Development and Economic Growth, 1967; Experience in Farm Mechanization in S.E. Asia, 1974; Agricultural Growth in Japan, Taiwan, Korea, and the Phillipines, 1979. Home: State College, Pa. Died Apr. 28, 1984.

SOUTTER, WILLIAM HENRY, packing exec.; b. Chicago, Apr. 16, 1888; s. William and Sarah A. (Smith) S.; ed. pub. schs. of Chicago; student Northwestern U. Evening Schs.; m. Helen L. Smallwood, Oct. 11, 1919 (dec. Feb. 21, 1951). With Swift & Co., Chicago, from 1902, messenger, 1902, clerk, 1906-16, asst. sec., 1916-42, sec. from 1942. Home: Chicago, Ill. †

SOUZA, EDGAR MILTON, lawyer; b. Bklyn., Dec. 23, 1887; s. Frederick W. and Eugenia (Heineman) S.; LL.B., N.Y. Law Sch., 1909; m. Dorothy Eising, Mar. 3, 1941; Admitted to N.Y. bar, 1909, practiced in N.Y.C.; sr. mem. firm Lehman, Rohrlich, Solomon & Heffner and Predecessors. Pres., dir. Birmingham Devel. Co., New Birmingham Minerals Corp. Mem. Am., N.Y. State bar assns., Assn. Bar City N.Y., N.Y. County Lawyers Assn., Lawyers Club. N.Y.C. (hon.), Am. Arbitration Assn., Empire State Soc., S.A.R. Club: Fairview Country (past pres., bd. govs.). Home: Scarsdale, NY. †

SOVIAK, HARRY, artist; b. Lorain, Ohio, May 25, 1935; s. Steve and Tessie (Dukas) S. Student, Bowling Green State U., 1953-55; B.F.A., Cranbrook Acad. Art, 1957, M.F.A., 1959. Prof. painting Phila. Coll. Art, 1963—.

One-person shows, Feigen/Herbert Gallery, N.Y.C., 1964, Richard Feigen Gallery, Chgo., 1964, N.Y.C., 1967, 70, Marian Locks Gallery, Phila., 1970, 73, 76, 78, 81, Arthur Roger Gallery, New Orleans, 1980, 81, Orion Edits., N.Y.C., 1981, Pam Adler Gallery, N.Y.C., 1982, 83; exhibited in group shows, Albright-Knox Gallery, Buffalo, 1963, San Francisco Mus. Art, 1965, De Cordova Mus., Lincoln, Mass., Mus. Modern Art, N.Y.C., 1966, Finch Coll. Mus. Art, N.Y.C., 1967, Monmouth Mus., N.J., 1968, U. P.R., 1968, Sch. Visual Arts, N.Y.C., 1969, N.J. State Mus., 1970, Phila. Mus. Art, Whitney Mus., N.Y.C., Whitechapel Art Gallery, London, 1971, Squibb Gallery, Princeton, 1977, Iran-Am. Soc. Tehran, 1977, Goddard Riverside Center, N.Y.C., 1980, Webster Coll., St. Louis, 1981; represented in permanent collection, New Orleans Mus. Art, Millersville (Pa.) State Coll., Phila. Mus. Art, N.J. State Mus., Trenton, N.Y. U. Buenos Aireas Conv. fellow Haiti, W.I., 1958-59. Home: Brooklyn, N.Y. Deceased.

SOYER, ISAAC, artist; b. Russia, Apr. 23, 1907; s. Abraham and Bella (Schneyer) S.; came to U.S., 1914; naturalized, 1919; ed. Hebrew's Teachers Inst., 1923-27; Cooper Union Art Sch., 1920-24; Nat. Acad. Fine Arts, 1924-25; Ednl. Alliance Art Sch., 1925-28; studied in museums and art schs. of Paris and Madrid one year; m. Sofia Borkson, Aug. 19, 1928; 1 son, Avron. Artist from childhood; taught at the Ednl. Alliance Art Sch. and at the Am. Artists Sch., Buffalo Fine Arts Acad., 1941, U. of Buffalo, summer 1943; head own art sch., Buffalo until 1946; teacher, Sch. for Art Studies, 1946-58; art instr. Bkly. Mus. Art Sch., 1958-81; faculty New School for Social Research, Art Students League (both N.Y.C.). Exhibited at Golden Gate Exposition, San Francisco; Paris (France) Expn.; N.Y. World's Fair; Mus. Modern Art, Whitney Mus. of Art, N.Y. City; Corcoran Gallery, Washington, D.C.; Chicago Art Inst.; Milwaukee Art Inst.; Columbus Gallery Fine Arts; R.I. Sch. of Design; Richmond (Va.) Biennial; Pa. Acad. Fine Arts. One-man shows at Midtown Galleries, N.Y. City, 1936, 38; William Rockhill Nelson Gallery of Art; Art Inst., Buffalo, 1944. Two pictures, —Employment Agency— and —Girl Embroidering—, added to permanent collection of Whitney Mus. Am. Art, N.Y. City; represented in permanent collections at Bklyn. Mus., Dallas Mus., Brooks Meml. Gallery, Memphis, others; —Rebecca— (awarded 1st prize Western N.Y. Exhbn.) purchased by Albright Art Gallery Buffalo. Awarded prize for best winter landscape, Audubon Artists Exhbn., 1945. Mem. Am. Artists Congress, An Am. Group, Inc.; Patterson, Audubon Artists. Home: New York, N.Y. Died July 8, 1981.

SPAETH, RAYMOND JULIUS, banker; b. Salina, Kans., Nov. 13, 1907; s. Julius H. and Laura (Lavina) S.; m. Ruth Lee Rinkel, Sept. 3, 1931; children—Raymond Julius, Ruth Lee. A.B., Am. U., 1930; M.B.A., Harvard, 1932; D.H.L., Ill. Coll. Optometry, 1967. Asst. bus. mgr. and adminstrv. asst. to pres. Am. U., 1932-40; bus. mgr. Ill. Inst. Tech., Chgo., 1940-42, exec. sec., treas., bus. mgr., 1942-1950, v.p., treas., 1950-60, 64-70; treas. IIT Research Inst., Inst. Gas Tech., 1964-70; pres. Beverly Bank, Chgo., 1960-64; pres., dir. Lakeside Bank, Chgo., 1965-66, vice chmn., dir., from 1966; v.p., dir. First Security Bank, Cary, Ill., 1971-74; v.p., sec., treas. UARCO, 1963-64. Trustee Jane and Washington Smith Home; chmn. bd., dir. YMCA Hotel, Chgo.; past v.p. Cook County Sch. Nursing; mem. bd. St. Xavier Coll.; trustee, treas. Ill. Coll. Optometry, 1970-78; mem. South Side Planning Bd.; dir. Met. Planning and Housing Council, Am. Inst. Planners. Mem. Lambda Alpha, Sigma Kappa, Pi Gamma Mu. Republican. Methodist. Clubs: Econ. (Chgo.), Union League (Chgo.). Home: Hindsale, Ill.

SPAFFORD, EARLE, business exec.; b. Lennoxville, Quebec, Can., 1889. Pres. and dir. Imperial Tobacco Co. of Canada, Ltd. Address: Montreal, Can. †

SPAFFORD, IVOL, home economics; b. Footville, O., July 26, 1889; d. Edward A. and Cynthia A. (Hyneman) Spafford; B.Pd., Mich. State Teachers College, 1913, M.Ed. (honorary), 1942, B.S., Teachers College (Columbia University), 1918, M.A., 1926; Ph.D., Ohio State University, 1935. Teacher public schools of Ohio, 1907-08, 1909-10; teacher home economics, high school and adult program Columbia City, Ind., 1913-17; state supervisor home economics, Alabama, 1919-34; field agent (on leave) for Federal Board of Vocational Edn., 1927-28, also part time, head for dept. home economics, Ala. Coll., 1928-29; asso. prof. euthenics, U. of Minn., 1935-40, also asst. to dir. Gen Coll., in charge of curriculum. Mem. N.E.A., Progressive Edn. Assn. (mem. adv. bd. 1936-38), Am. Home Economics Assn., Am. Vocational Assn., Omicron Nu, Phi Upsilon Omicron, Pi Lambda Theta; chmn. Nat. Assn. of State Supervisors of Home Economics, 1931-33. Author of Fundamentals in Teaching Home Economics; A Functioning Program of Home Economics. Co-author and editor Building a Curriculum for General Education. Democrat. Baptist. Address: Rock Creek, OH. †

SPAFFORD, JOHN LESTER, trade assn. exec.; b. Springfield, Mo., Dec. 7, 1919; s. Lester K. and Genevieve L. (Frizzell) S.; m. Mary Ellen McKaig, May 5, 1945; children—Barbara Sue Spafford Barbles, John McKaig. B.S., Washington U., 1942. With Associated Credit Burs., Inc., Houston, from 1946, exec. v.p., 1958-69, pres., from 1969; also dir., mem. exec. com.; dir. Fannin Bank, Houston. Contbr. to credit publs., trade jours. Mem. Pres.'s Commn. on Personnel Interchange, 1972-73. Served with USAAF, 1942-46. Mem. U.S. C. of C. (chmn. assn. com. 1963-65, mem. com. on policy 1966-67, public affairs com. 1974-75), Am. Soc. Assn. Execs. (sr. v.p. 1968-69, pres. 1969-70), Am. Mgmt. Assn. (mem. pres.'s assn.), Sigma Nu. Roman Catholic. Clubs: Lakeside Country (Houston); Capitol Hill (Washington), Metropolitan (Washington). Address: Houston, Tex.

SPALDING, ISAAC, army officer; b. Denton, Tex., Dec. 18, 1887; s. Henry Moses and Eleanor (Lindsay) S.; B.S., U.S. Mil. Acad., 1912; grad. Mounted Service Sch., 1916, F.A. Sch., 1925, Command and Gen. Staff Sch., 1926. Army War Coll., 1931, Naval War Coll., 1932; m. Alice Trippet, Nov. 4, 1913; 1 child, Ansley Lues Spalding Hill. Commd. 2d lt., U.S. Army, 1912, and advanced through the grades to brig. gen., Jan. 1942; apptd. commdg. gen. 12th F.A. Brigade, Fort Bragg, June 1942. Address: Fort Bragg, N.C.†

SPALDING, PHILIP EDMUNDS, business exec.; b. Minneapolis, Minn., Nov. 5, 1889; s. A. Walter and Anna Mary (Talbot) S.; student Stanford, 1911-13; m. Alice T. Cooke, Mar. 18, 1917; children—Philip Edmunds, Charles Cooke. Building contractor, 1913-18; with Lewers & Cooke, Ltd., 1919-23; with C. Brewer & Co. from 1923, pres. and dir. from 1941; chmn. bd. dirs. Hawaiian Electric Co., Ltd.; dir. Bank of Hawaii, Mutual Telephone Co., Cooke Trust Co., Limited, Lewers & Company, Limited. Served as captain, asst. chief of staff Hawaiian Department, U.S. Army, 1918-19. Chmn. bd. regents U. of Hawaii; pres. Honolulu Acad. Arts. Clubs: Pacific, Waialae Golf, Oahu Country (Honolulu); Pacific Union (San Francisco). †

SPALDING, SIDNEY P., army officer; b. Lowell, Mass., Aug. 5, 1889; commd. 2d lt. Coast Arty. Corps, June 1912, and advanced through the grades to maj. gen., Aug. 1944; chief of the Small Arms Div., Mfg. Service, Office of the Chief of Ordnance, Washington, D.C., June 1936-July 1939; exec. officer, Springfield Arsenal, Springfield, Mass., 1939-40; on duty in the Office of the Asst. Secretary of War, from June 1940. Awarded the Meritorious Citation Certificate and the French Order of the Black Star, for services in World War I.†

SPANEL, ABRAM NATHANIEL, mfr., inventor; b. Odessa, Russia, May 15, 1901; s. Heyman and Hannah (Sarokskaya) S.; m. Margaret R. Spanel; children—Ann, David Louis. Ed., U. Rochester. For their manufacture formed Vacuumizer Mfg. Corp., 1926; served as pres., chmn. bd.; founded internat. Latex Corp., 1932 (became known as Internat. Playtex Corp., served as chmn. bd.; Chmn. bd. Spanel Found., Inc.; founder, chmn. bd. Playtex Park Research Inst.; founder, pres. Spanel Internat., Ltd., 1976-85; bd. assocs. Linus Pauling Inst. Sci. and Medicine. Author: others. Blackmailing Trapped Humans. Decorated grand officer Legion of Honor France; recipient Gold Medal of Honor Paris, 1957, 1st Lafayette Bicentenary medal Com. France-Amerique; decorated comdr. du Merite Postal; hon. citizen Vichy; hon. citizen Chavaniac-Lafayette; hon. citizen Istres; hon. citizen Cherbourg. St. Lo. Le Puy; hon. citizen Pessac and Antibes (all France)?; comdr. Ordre des Lettres et des Arts; grand cross Condor of the Andes. Mem. Cousteau Soc., Am. Soc. French Legion Honor (v.p., medal of Honor). Club: Mason (32 deg.). Inventor elec. appliances and pneumatic products. Home: Princeton, N.J. Died Mar. 30, 1985.

SPARLING, EDWARD JAMES, univ. pres. emeritus; b. Panoche, Calif., Nov. 22, 1896; s. Edward James and Gertrude (Smith) S.; A.B., Stanford U., 1921; A.M., Columbia U., 1925, Ph.D., 1933; LL.D., Lincoln U., 1947; D.H.L., Roosevelt U., 1967; m. Marion Bailey, Mar. 19, 1927, 1 dau., Mary Ann (Mrs. Joseph C. Dodd). Asst. gen. sec. Young Men's Christian Assn., Stanford U., 1921-24; teacher, Palo Alto Union High Sch., 1925-28; asst. dir. personnel Long Island U.; 1930-33; ednl. dir. Christodora House, N.Y.C., 1933-34; dean men, prof. psychology Hiram (Ohio) Coll., 1934-36; pres. Central YMCA Coll., Chgo., 1936-45; founder, pres. Roosevelt U., 1945-64, pres. emeritus, 1964-81. Chmn. Chgo. Citizens Commn. to study Disorders of Conv. Week, 1968-69. Mem. bd. edn. New Trier Twp. High Sch., 1964-71; trustee World U., San Juan, P.R., 1965-81. Instr., flight comdr., asst. officer in charge flying Carruthers Field, Fort Worth; 2d lt. Air Service, U.S. Army, 1918-19. Recipient Civil Rights Award Phila. Fellowship Commn., 1950. Bd. dirs. U.N. Assn. Greater Chgo., from 1950, pres., 1950-52; co-chmn. Chgo. div. Internat. Peace Acad., 1970-76. Mem. World Federalists Assn. (past pres. Chgo. region, mem. nat. council), Fedn. Ill. Colls. (sec. treas. 1941-48, pres. 1948-50, exec. com. 1950-52), Am. Civil Liberties Union (mem. nat. com. 1949-81, Am. Com. Africa (adv. bd. 1954-81), Toward Freedom (exec. bd. from 1953, pres. 1972-81), Phi Delta Kappa, Kappa Delta Pi, Alpha Delta Phi. Democrat. Conglist. Club: University (Chicago). Author: Do College Students Choose Vocations Wisely?, 1933; Civil Rights: Barometer of Democracy. Contbr. to Personnel Jour., John Dewey Yearbook. Home: Winnetka, Ill. Died Sept. 23, 1981.

SPATER, GEORGE ALEXANDER, airline co. exec.; b. Detroit, May 3, 1909; s. Alexander M. and Julia (Robinson) S.; A.B. U. Mich., 1930, J.D., 1933; m. Hope W. Clark, Aug. 12, 1936; children—Thomas, William, Mary, Alexander, Paul. Admitted to N.Y. bar, 1935, and practiced privately in N.Y.C. until 1958; partner Chadbourne, Wallace, Parke & Whiteside, 1942-58; exec. v.p., gen. counsel Am. Airlines, Inc., until 1968, president, chief executive officer, 1968-73, vice chairman. Consultant to Department Def., 1954-57. Board vistors U. Michigan Law Sch. Mem. Am. Bar Assn., Bar Assn. City N.Y. Clubs: Ardsley (N.Y.) Country; Lawyers (Ann Arbor, Mich.); Pinnacle, Cloud (N.Y.C.); Mid-Ocean (Bermuda). Home: Ardsley-on-Hudson, N.Y. Died June 14, 1984.

SPAULDING, EUGENE RISTINE, magazine pub.; b. Galion, O., Oct. 30, 1889; s. Clement David and Jane (Ristine) S.; grad. Germantown Acad., 1906; B.S., Haverford Coll., 1911; m. Elizabeth Shaw, Apr. 22, 1913; children—Robert Eugene, Barbara Lee. Bus. mgr. The Churchman, N.Y.C., 1917-20, dir., from 1918, also chmn. bd.; bus. mgr., Town and Country, 1920-25; gen. mgr. New Yorker mag. from 1925, v.p. from 1926. Dir. Electronic Control Corp., 1947-48. Mem. bd. adjustment Village Ridgewood, N.J., 1938-47. Dir. Nat. Publicity Council 1945-49; mem. finance com. Nat. Orgn. Pub. Health Nursing, 1943-48; dir. Fed. Union, Inc.; mem. council Atlantic Union Com. Mem. Research Inst. of Am., Am. Forestry Assn., Triangle Soc., Newcomen Soc. Eng. (N.Y.). Clubs: The Players, Advertising (N.Y.). Home: Saddle River, N.J. †

SPEAKS, CHARLES EDWARD, born Washington, District of Columbia, May 21, 1887; s. James Edward and Mary Jane (Cooper) S.; ed. pub. and pvt. schs.; m. Tatiana Tarassoff, M.D., June 1, 1921. Identified with automotive and tire industries from 1911; with Ford Agency, Washington, D.C., 1911-12; asso. with Firestone Tire & Rubber Co., in U.S., 1913, European mgr., 1919-26; v.p. and gen. mgr. Firestone Footwear Co., 1927-32, pres. and gen. mgr., 1932-36; pres. Fisk Rubber Corp., 1936-43. Mason (Shriner). Clubs: Army and Navy (Washington); Colony, Bankers, Longmeadow Country. Home: West Newton, Mass. †

SPEAR, RUSSELL BAILEY, banker; b. Somerville, Mass., Mar. 13, 1889; s. John Moore and Flora Cameron (Bailey) S.; student Somerville Latin School, 1903-06, Burdett Coll., 1906-07; C.P.A., Pace Inst. of Accounting, 1914; m. Marion Genevieve Harrington, Apr. 22, 1914 (dec.); children—Genevieve Rose (Mrs. Winton Stuart Bowie) (dec.), Philip H., Virginia Marion (Mrs. Charles Thomas McCarthy); m. 2d, Rose Harrington Fuoss, May 23, 1958. Bank messenger, clk., bond salesman, Estabrook & Company, 1907-14; assistant Federal Reserve agent of the Fed. Reserve Bank of Boston, 1914-19; v.p. Atlantic National Bank, Boston, 1919-32; pres. Atlantic Corp., Boston, 1927-32; asst. v.p. First Nat. Bank of Boston, 1931-33; treas., v.p. and dir. Depositors Trust Co., Augusta, Me., 1933-37, pres., from 1937, chmn. bd., from 1943; pres., dir. Depositors Trust Found. from 1954. Incorporator Agusta Savs. Bank and Kennebec Savs. Bank, C.P.A., Mass. Chmn. stockholders adv. com. Fed. Res. Bank, Boston, 1946-47. Pres. bd. trustees Augusta (Me.) Gen. Hosp., 1945-50. Mem. Am. (mem. exec. council, 1948-51) and Me. (pres. 1944-45) bankers assn., Newcomen Society of England, Soc. Mayflower Descs. Clubs: Ormond Beach (Fla.) Golf Assn.; Augusta Country. Home: Winthrop, Me. †

SPECK, JOHN KING, lawyer; b. Crawford, Tex., Aug. 4, 1904; s. James Malachi and Mary (King) S.; m. Lavon Evelyn Gildersleeve, July 14, 1929; children—James Stanley, Carolyn Kay Speck Schnorrenberg, Bonnie Jean Speck Schroer (dec.). Student, Okla. State U., 1921-22; B.S., U. Okla., 1928; LL.B., Oklahoma City U., 1941; D.Hum., Phillips U., 1979. Bar: Kans., Okla. bars 1939. Mdse. mgr. Central States Power & Light Co., Stillwater, Okla., 1928-31; commd. agt. Continental Oil Co., Stillwater, 1930-33; owner John K. Speck (accountant), Stillwater, 1931-35; auditor income tax div. Okla. Tax Commn., 1935-37; dir. income tax div. Kans. Tax Commn., 1937-40; practice in, Oklahoma City, 1940-83; sr. mem. Speck, Philbin, Fleig, Trudgeon & Lutz, Inc. (and predecessor cos.), 1955-83; instr. Oklahoma City U. Law Sch., 1940-41; Past pres. Oklahoma City Estate Planning Council, Oklahoma City Tax Lawyers Group. Contbr. articles to profl. jours.; lectr. legal and tax subjects various state and regional bar insts. Mem. exec. com. and trustee Okla. Med. Research Found.; life trustee, mem. exec. com., chmn. sem. council Phillips U.; trustee Okla. Christian Home Apts., Inc., Okla. Ind. Coll. Found.; founder, trustee, former pres. Okla. Halfway House, Speck Homes, Inc. Recipient Service to Mankind award Oklahoma City Sertoma Club, 1977. Mem. ABA, Okla. Bar Assn. (past chmn. probate and tax sects.), Oklahoma County Bar Assn., Okla. Inst. Taxation (founder, dir. past pres.), Oklahoma City C. of C., Okla. Poetry Soc., Oklahoma City Econ. Club, Christian Men's Fellowship (past pres. Okla., past mem. nat. adv. bd.). Republican. Mem. Christian Ch. (Disciples of Christ) (past moderator Okla. region; mem. gen. bd., bd. homeland ministries; elder). Clubs: Masons (Oklahoma City), Shriners (50 year medal) (Oklahoma City), Men's Dinner (Oklahoma City), Sooner Dinner (Oklahoma City), Economic (Oklahoma City), Petroleum (Oklahoma City), Lions (Oklahoma City) (past dir.), Fortune (Oklahoma City) (past pres.), Quail Creek Golf and Country (Oklahoma City), Twin Hills Golf and Country (Oklahoma City) (past treas., dir.). Home: Oklahoma City, Okla. Died Nov. 13, 1983; buried Rose Hill Cemetery, Oklahoma City.

SPEDDING, FRANK HAROLD, educator; b. Hamilton, Ont., Oct. 22, 1902; s. Howard Leslie and Mary Ann Elizabeth (Marshall) S.; B. Chem. E., U. Mich., 1921-25; M.S., Chem., 1925-26, D.Sc., 1949; Ph.D., Chem., U.Cal., 1926-29; LL.D., Drake U., 1946; D.Sc., Case Inst. Tech., 1956; m. Ethel Annie MacFarlane, June 21, 1931; 1 dau., Mary Ann Elizabeth. Teaching asst. analytical chemistry U. Mich., 1923-25; teaching fellow, 1925-26; teaching fellow chemistry U. Cal., 1926-29, instr. chemistry, 1929-30, Nat. Research fellow chemistry 1930-32, instr. chemistry, 1932-34; Guggenheim professorship abroad (England, Germany, Russia), 1934-35; George Fisher Baker asst. prof. Cornell U., 1935-37; asso. prof. phys. chemistry, head of phys. chemistry sect. Iowa State Coll., 1937-41, prof. phys. chemistry, from 1941, prof. physics, from 1950, prof. metallurgy, 1962, prof. emeritus chemistry, metallurgy and physics; also Distinguished prof. of sci. and humanities; dir. Inst. Atomic Research, Ia. State U., and Ames Lab. of AEC, 1948-68; prin. scientist Ames Lab., AEC, Ia. State Univ., from 1968. Organized and directed the chemistry div. of Plutonium Project at Chgo. for atomic bomb research, 1942-43; mem. bd. govs., Argonne Nat. Lab., Chgo., (Govt. atomic research lab.), 1946-48. Lt. (s.g.) USNR, 1937-51, hon. discharge, 1951. Recipient Langmuir award Am. Chem. Soc. award in pure chemistry for chemists under 31, 1933, Iowa medal, 1948; Jubilee Plaque, Phi Lambda Upsilon, 1949; W.H. Nichols medal, 1952; James Douglas gold medal Am. Inst. Mining Metall. and Petroleum Engrs., 1961; Distinguished Citizen award State of Ia., 1962; Atomic Energy Citation award for meritorious contributions to nation's atomic energy program, 1967; Midwest award Am. Chem. Soc., 1967; Clamer Gold medal Franklin Inst. Mem. Plutonium Project Council, 1942-46. Fellow Am. Phys. Soc., A.A.A.S.; mem. Nat. Acad. Scis., Austrian Chem. Soc. (hon.), Am. Chem. Soc., Faraday Soc., Soc. Applied Spectroscopy, Sigma Xi, Phi Kappa Phi, Phi Lambda Upsilon, Tau Beta Pi. Contbr. arts. to Physical Review, Jour. Am. Chem. Soc., Jour. Chem. Physics, etc. Home: Ames, Iowa. Died Dec. 15, 1984.

SPEER, EDGAR B., steel co. exec.; b. Pitts., July 28, 1916; s. Edgar B. and Gladys (Kelly) S.; m. Arlene R. Kline, Apr. 8, 1946; children—Edgar B. III, John Michael, Stephen Fox, Tony Scott. Student, U. Pa., Harvard Bus. Sch. With U.S. Steel Corp., 1938—; gen. supt. U.S. Steel Corp. (Fairless works), 1955-58, gen. mgr. steel ops., Pitts., 1958-79, exec. v.p. for prodn., 1967-69, pres., 1969-73, now chmn. bd.; dir. Am. Tel. & Tel. Co., Procter & Gamble Co. Trustee Widener Coll., Waynesburg Coll.; bd. overseers U. Pa. Mem. Am. Iron and Steel Engrs., Am. Iron and Steel Inst. (dir.), Internat. Iron and Steel Inst. (dir.), Bus. Council, Harvard Bus. Assn., Phi Gamma Delta. Home: Pittsburgh, Pa. Died May 18, 1984.

SPEERS, THOMAS GUTHRIE, clergyman; b. Atlantic Highlands, N.J., Aug. 27, 1890; s. James Milliken and Nellie (Carter) S.; A.B., Princeton, 1912, D.D., 1949; student Union Theol. Sem., 1912-16; D.D., Coll. Wooster, 1935; m. Elizabeth Thacher, May 27, 1926; children—Thomas Guthrie, Ellen Carter. Ordained ministry, Presbyn. Ch., 1916; asst., later asso. minister, Univ. Pl. Ch., New York, 1916-18; asso. minister First Ch., New York, 1920-28; minister Brown Memorial Ch., Baltimore, Md., from 1928. Pub. mem. War Labor Bd., Region 3, 1943-45. Served as 1st lt. and chaplain 102nd Inf. U.S. Army in France, World War I. Awarded D.S.C. (U.S.); Croix de Guerre with Palm (France). Trustee Princeton U., 1932-36, Goucher Coll., 1932-40, Union Memorial Hosp., Presbyterian Eye, Ear and Throat Hosp. (Baltimore), Lincoln University, 1947; mem. Presbyn. Bd. Nat. Missions; pres. Md.-Del. Council of Churches, 1939-42. Mem. Phi Beta Kappa. Home: Baltimore, Md. †

SPEIGHT, HAROLD EDWIN BALME, educator; b. Bradford, Eng., Apr. 21, 1887; s. Edwin and Charlotte (Hall) S.; M.A., U. of Aberdeen, 1909; studied Exeter Coll. (Oxford); D.D., Tufts College, 1925; A.M. (hon.) Dartmouth, 1927 (Phi Beta Kappa); m. Mabel Grant, 1911; children—Christine Ray Grant, Charlotte Frances. Asst. prof. logic and metaphysics, U. of Aberdeen, 1909-10; fellow Manchester Coll. (Oxford), 1910-12; served in the ministry, London, Victoria, B.C., Berkeley, Calif., Boston, Mass., 1912-27; prof. philosophy, Dartmouth, 1927-29, prof. biography and chmn. dept., 1929-33; dean of men, Swarthmore College, 1933-38, dean of Coll., 1938-40; exec. sec. com. on teacher edn., assn. of Coll. and Univ. of State of N.Y., 1940-42; dean Coll. of Letters and Science, St. Lawrence University, 1942-45, acting pres. 1944-45; dean of students Cornell University, 1945-56; dean of Elmira Coll., 1946-49. Trustee Bradford Jr. Coll. Chaplain A.U.S. overseas, 1918-19; mem. commn. investigating religious minorities in Transylvania, 1922. Mem. Am. Philos. Assn. Mem. Soc. of Friends. Author: Life and Writings of John Bunyan, 1928. Editor of Week Day Sermons in King's Chapel, 1925. Contbr. to Best Sermons, Book IV and to Boston Preachers. Editor Creative Lives (series of biographies). Literary editor Christian Leader, 1927-38. Home: Nahant, Mass. †

SPENCER, ROSCOE ROY, public health service educator; b. King William County, Va., July 28, 1888; s. Branch Worhsam and Emma Roy (Burke) S.; A.B., Richmond (Virginia) Coll., 1909, hon. D.Sc., 1943; M.D., Johns Hopkins, 1913; m. Mary Garland Grasty, Oct. 23, 1915; children—Nathaniel Roscoe, Mary Garland. In United States Public Health Service since 1913; now medical director; sanitary adviser to Navy Department, 1917-18; officer in charge bubonic plague suppressive measures, Pensacola, Fla., 1919-21; in charge investigations of Rocky Mountain spotted fever, 1922-29; adjunct prof. preventive medicine, George Washington U., 1932-39. Asst. chief Nat. Cancer Inst., 1938, chief, 1943-47. Mem. A.M.A., American Soc. Bacteriologists,Assn. Mil. Surgeons of U.S., Montana Health Officers Assn. (pres. 1928), S.A.R., Phi Chi, Phi Beta Kappa, Kappa Sigma Xi. Author: (with Dr. R. R. Parker) Rocky Mountain Spotted Fever, 1929. Discoverer of a preventive vaccine for Rocky Mountain spotted fever, and awarded gold medal for same, 1930, by American Medical Assn. Clement Cleveland Award for Cancer Health Education, 1943; hon. prof. Univ. of Guadalajara, Mexico. Editor of "The Health Officer," 1936-38. Home: Washington, D.C. †

SPENCER, WILLIAM MARVIN, transportation exec.; b. Erie, Pa., May 14, 1892; s. William and Mary Richards (DuPuy) S.; B.A., Hill Sch., Pottstown, Pa., 1911; B.A., Princeton, 1915; m. Gertrude White, July 19, 1924; children—Edson White, William Marvin, Suzanne. Asst. to sec. Hammermill Paper Co., Erie, Pa., 1915-21; pres. Erie Brass & Copper Co., Erie, Pa., 1921-23; pres. and dir. Spencer, Kamerer & Co., Erie, Pa., 1924-29; partner Jackson Bros., Boesel & Co., brokers, Chicago, 1930-34; pres. and dir. Burke Electric Co., Erie, Pa., 1934-35; pres. and dir. Inland Car Lines, Inc., Chicago, 1934-40; v.p. and dir. Perry, Spencer & Co., investment banking, Chicago, 1939-40; chmn. bd. of dirs. North American Car Corp., Chicago, 1941-59; dir. Fundamental Investors, Inc., Thiokol Chem. Corp., N.Am. Car Corp., La Salle Nat. Bank, Chgo. Served as lt., 165th Inf., A.E.F., 1918-19; major, Pa. Nat. Guard, 1920-25; lt. col. G-2, Ill. Nat. Guard, 1934-40; colonel (chief of staff) Ill. Reserve Militia, 1941-43. Decorated D.S.C. Trustee Chgo. Latin Sch. Found., Ill. Children's Home and Aid Society, Chgo. Boys Clubs; chmn. of Chicgo Plan Commission, 1951-56; trustee Northwestern University, The Orchestral Assn. of Chgo., Lyric Opera of Chgo. Republican. Presbyn. Clubs: Chicago, Saddle and Cycle, Racquet, Old Elm, Adventurers (Chicago); Country (Lake Geneva, Wis.); Princeton, The Brook, Explorers (N.Y.C.); Rolling Rock Country (Pitts.); Mill Reef (Antiqua). Home: Chicago, Ill. Died Oct. 17, 1984.

SPENCER, WILLIAM MICAJAH, JR., lawyer; b. Gallion, Ala., June 29, 1890; s. William Micajah and Bertha Gracey (Steele) S.; B.S., Marion Inst., 1908, U. Ala., 1910; LL.B., Harvard, 1913; m. Margaret Woodward Evins, June 23, 1915 (dec. June 1966); children—Margaret (Mrs. Edgar G. Givhan, Jr.), William Micajah III, Bertha (Mrs. Adrian Alton Ringland, Jr.). Admitted to Ala. bar, 1913, since practiced in Birmingham. Staff Birmingham Ordnance Dist., World War II, cons.; dir. Woodwar Iron Co. (Ala.), Robertson Banking Co., Black Warrior Electric Membership Corp. (Demopolis, Alabama), Owen-Richards Co., Inc., Metalplate & Coatings, Inc. (both Birmingham). Chmn. mus. bd. Birmingham Mus. Art; bd. regents Ala. Mus. Natural History; dir. Ala. State Fair Authority; trustee Children's Hosp. of Birmingham. Served to 1st lt. U.S. Army, World War I; retired as lt. col. O.R.C., 1935. Mem. Warrior-Tombigbee Development Assn. (dir.), Am. Ordnance Assn., Am., Ala., Birmingham bar assns., Newcomen Soc. N.Am., Delta Kappa Epsilon, Theta Nu. Epsilon. Episcopalian (registrar Ala. Diocese). Clubs: Country, Mountain Brook, Redstone, Downtown, The Club, Rotary (Birmingham). Home: Birmingham, AL. †

SPENDER, SIR PERCY CLAUDE, pres. Internat. Ct. of Justice; b. Sydney, Australia, Oct. 5, 1897; s. Frank Henry and Mary Hanson (Murray) S.; A.B., U. Sydney, 1918. LL.B., 1921; LL.D., U. of B.C., Hamilton Coll., 1952, U. Colo., 1953. Trinity Coll., 1955, Yale U., 1957, U. Cal., 1965, U. E. Philippines, 1966; D.C.L., Union U. (Schenectady, N.Y.), 1955; Litt.D., Springfield Coll., 1955; m. Jean Maud Henderson, Apr. 10, 1925 (dec. Mar. 1970); children—Peter Beaufort, John Michael. Admitted to bar of New South Wales, 1923, apptd. Kings Counsel, 1935. Clk. Sydney Town Hall, 1915; petty sessions office, Newtown, Sydney, 1916. Mem. Commonwealth Parliament, 1937-51; mem. Menzies cabinet; acting treas. of Commonwealth, 1939, treas., 1940, v.p. exec. council, 1940, Minister for Army, 1940-41, mem. War Cabinet, 1940-41, mem. War Council, 1940-45, chmn. Australian Mil. Bd., 1940-41, chmn. Australian Loan Council, 1939-40; Minister for External Affairs and External Terrs., 1949-51, ambassador to U.S., 1951-58; judge International Court of Justice, The Hague, Netherlands, 1958-67, pres. court, 1964-67. Australian gov. Internat. Bank and internat. Monetary Fund, 1952. Chmn. Australian delegation Conf. Brit. Commonwealth Fgn. Ministers, 1950; v.p. Gen. Assembly of U.N., 1950-51; chmn. Australian delegation to the UN, 1950, vice chmn., and the leader of delegations to the 7th-11th gen. assemblies; v.p. Japenese Pace Conference, 1951. Mem. gen. council Assicurazione Generali Italy. Hon. lt. col. A.A.L.C. Reserve, ret. Created Knight of Brit. Empire, 1952, Knight Comdr. of Royal Victorian Order; Knight Order of St. John of Jerusalem, 1959; awarded Coronation medal in Coronation Honours, 1937, 52. Member Council Australian Nat. U., 1949-51. Mem. bd. dirs., Fulbright Found. in Australia. Mem. U.S. Committee of Study and Training in Australia, 1950-51. Mem. Parliamentary Com. Privileges, Parliamentary Standing Committee on Broadcasting, 1947-49. Mem. Church of England. Mem. Royal Overseas League (pres. N.S.W. br.). Clubs: Elancra Country (Sydney, Australia); Athenaeum (Melbourne, Australia), Australisian Pioneers; Sydney. Author: Company Law and Practice, 1939; Foreign Policy-Next Phase, 1944; Exercises In Diplomacy, 1969. Home: Sydney, New South Wales, Australia. Died May 3, 1985.

SPENS, JOHN IVAN, chartered accountant; b. Glasgow, Scotland, Feb. 22, 1890; s. John Alexander and Sophie Nicol (Baird) S.; ed. Cargilfield, and Rugby; m. Gwendoline Helen Donaldson, 1915; 1 son, William Peter; m. 2d Frances May Lidiard Murdoch, (St. Admitted mem. Inst. Accountants and Actuaries, Glasgow, 1914; partner Brown, Fleming & Murray, London, 1919; accountant gen. Ministry of Supply, 1939-42; head indsl. div. Ministry of Prodn., 1942-43; adv., 1943-45; dir. Union Discount Co. of London Ltd., United Steel Cos. Ltd., and others; extraordinary dir. Scottish Amicable Life Assurance Soc. Served with 5th Batn., Cameronians, Scottish Rifles, 1914. Mem. Royal Co. Archers, King's Bodyguard for Scotland. Clubs: City of London, Carlton, Boodle's, Western (Glasgow); Royal and Ancient Golf (St. Andrews). Home: London, England. †

SPEYER, JOHN WALTER, corp. exec.; b. San Francisco, July 24, 1887; s. Walter William and Charlotte (Zeile) S.; U. Calif., 1908; m. Eleanor Landers, Mar. 9, 1914; 1 dau., Eleanor (Mrs. Allen K. Lane). With Alexander & Baldwin, Ltd., sugar and pineapple factors, San Francisco, from 1912, dir. from 1929, v.p. from 1938; dir. Alexander Properties Co., Bay & River Nav. Co., Calif. & Hawaiian Sugar Refining Corp., Ltd., Honolulu Oil Corp., Matson Nav. Co., Oceanic S.S. Co., Pacific Chem. & Fertilizer Co. Mem. Pineapple Growers Assn. of Hawaii (dir.). Clubs: Bohemian, Pacific Union (San Francisco); Burlingame (Calif.) Country.†

SPICER, EDWARD HOLLAND, anthropologist; b. Cheltenham, Pa., Nov. 29, 1906; s. Robert Barclay and Margaret Lucretia (Jones) S.; m. Rosamond Pendleton Brown, June 21, 1936; children—Robert Barclay, Margaret Pendleton, Lawson Alan. Student, U. Del., 1925-27, Johns Hopkins, 1927-28; B.A., U. Ariz., 1932, M.A., 1933; Ph.D., U. Chgo., 1939. Instr. anthropology Dillard U., New Orleans, 1938-39; instr. anthropology U. Ariz., Tucson, 1939-41, asso. prof., 1946-50, prof., 1950-78, prof. emeritus, from 1978; head, community analysis sect. War Relocation Authority, Washington, 1943-46; vis. prof. anthropology Cornell U., Ithaca, N.Y., 1947-50, U. Calif., Santa Barbara, 1958; dir. Pascua Yaqui Devel. Project OEO, Tucson, 1966-69; cons. Stanford Research Inst., 1954, U.S. Bur. Indian Affairs, 1967-69, Office Edn., 1967-70, Weatherhead Found., 1969-70; mem. Ariz. Commn. Civil Rights, 1961-62, Ariz. Commn. Indian Affairs, 1964-66. Author: Cycles of Conquest, 1962, A Short History of the Indians of the U.S, 1969, The Yaquis: A Cultural History, 1980; editor: Human Problems in Technological Change, 1952, Perspectives in American Indian Culture Change, 1961, Jour. Am. Anthrop. Assn, 1960-63. Recipient award Best Southwestern Book S.W. Library Assn., 1965; Guggenheim fellow, 1941-42, 55-56; NSF sr. postdoctoral fellow, 1963-64; Nat. Endowment Humanities sr. fellow, 1970-71. Fellow Am. Anthrop. Assn. (pres. 1974), AAAS, Soc. Applied Anthropology (Malinowski award 1976); mem. Am. Philos. Soc., Nat. Acad. Scis. Democrat. Home: Tucson, Ariz.

SPICER, ELMER DELANCY, corp. official; b. Wellsville, N.Y., Sept 14, 1888; s. Elmer Ellsworth and Etta Lucy (Gowdy) S.; M.E., Cornell U., 1910; m. Inez Gaylord Farnum, June 10, 1914; children—Elmer Farnum, Jean Gaylord. Shopwork Kerr Turbine Co., Wellsville, N.Y., summer, 1909, testman and draughtsman, 1909-11, chief draughtsman and chief engr., 1912-16; one of organizers, dir., sec. and treas. Moore Turbine Co., Wellsville, 1916-18; sales engr. and works mgr. Kerr Turbine Co., 1918-24; with General Electric Co., 1924, successively supt. dept. of radio and refrigeration, asst. mgr., mgr. Schenectady Works, and asst. to v.p. in charge mfg., v.p. in charge employee relations. Mem. Newcomen Soc., Sigma Phi Sigma. Republican. Presbyterian. Mason. Clubs: Mohawk, Mohawk Golf. †

SPICER, ROBERT THURSTON, physician; b. Ithaca, N.Y., Feb. 22, 1903; s. Clarence Winfred and Anna Olive (Burdick) S.; m. Marion Aldine Carter, Nov. 24, 1926 (dec. 1968); 1 dau., Aldine R.; m. Frances C. Cale, Nov. 16, 1968. A.B., Alfred U., 1925; M.D., Cornell U., 1929; D.Sc. (hon.), Alfred U., 1965. Diplomate: Am. Bd. Obstetrics and Gynecology. Intern Jackson Meml. Hosp., Miami, Fla., 1929-30, resident, 1930-31, practice of obstetrics and gynecology, Miami, 1931-53; dean, prof. obstetrics and gynecology U. Miami, 1953-54. Mem. Fla. Bd. of Med. Examiners, 1957-61; Trustee City Miami Pub. Libraries System, 1965-70, Fairchild Tropical Garden, 1958-81. Served from lt. comdr. to capt. M.C. USNR, 1942-46. Fellow A.C.S., Southeastern Surg. Congress; mem. Am. Coll. Obstetrics and Gynecol. (founder), Am. Soc. Study Sterility, Internat. Fertility Assn., South Atlantic Assn. Obstetricians and Gynecologists, Fla. Obstetric and Gynecologic Soc. (founder, past pres.), Miami Obstet. and Gynecol. Soc. (founder, past pres.), AMA, Fla. Med. Assn., Dade County Med. Assn. (past pres.), Miami-Dade County C. of C. (pres. 1957-58). Conglist. Clubs: Mason. (Miami), Rotary (Miami); Biscayne Bay Yacht. Home: Sanibel, Fla.

SPIEGEL, JACOB J., lawyer; b. Boston, Nov. 24, 1901; s. Israel and Mollie (Greenbaum) S.; LL.B., Boston U., 1922; J.S.D., Suffolk U., L.H.D., Mass. Coll. Optometry;

LL.D. Boston U.; J.D., Portia Law School; m. Peggy Schwarz, Aug. 26, 1941 (div.); 1 dau., Lynne Mara. Admitted to Mass. bar, 1923; pvt. practice, Boston, 1923-61; spl. justice Municipal Ct. Boston, 1939-60; legis. sec. to U.S. Senator Lodge, 1937; 1st asst. atty. gen. Mass., 1945-46; counsel Port of Boston Authority, 1948; justice Supreme Jud. Ct. Mass., 1961-72; chmn. Jud. Council Mass., 1976-84. Past dir., gen. counsel Mass. Health Research Inst. Mem. Mass., Am., Boston bar assns., Am. Law Inst. Home: Boston, Mass. Died Apr. 9, 1984.

SPIEGEL, SHALOM, educator; b. Unter Stanestie, Austria, Jan. 26, 1899; s. Simon and Regina (Schwitz) S.; Ph.D., U. Vienna, 1922; m. Rose Goldschmiedt, Sept. 10, 1922 (dec.); 1 dau., Raya (Mrs. Burton S. Drehen). Came to U.S., 1928, naturalized, 1936. Instr., Hebrew lit. Beth Sepher Reali, 1922-28; lectr. Tech. Inst. in Haifa, Palestine, 1925-28; prof. bibl. and postbibl. lit., librarian Jewish Inst. Religion, N.Y.C., 1929-43; William Prager prof. medieval Hebrew lit. Jewish Theol. Sem. Am., 1943-73. Chmn. nat. edn. adv. com. Hadassah, from 1956; sec. Alexander Kohut Meml. Found. Trustee I. Matz Found. Recipient La-Med prize, 1950. Fellow Am. Acad. Jewish Research (v.p.), Israel Acad. Hebrew Lang. Jerusalem (hon.); mem. Soc. Bibl. Lit., Am. Oriental Soc. Author: Hebrew Reborn, 1930; Ezekiel or Pseudo-Ezekiel, 1931; Noah, Daniel and Job, 1945; Me-Agadoth ha-Akedah, 1950; Amos versus Amaziah, 1958. Home: New York, N.Y. Died May 24, 1984.

SPIEGELMAN, SOL, biologist, educator; b. N.Y.C., Dec. 14, 1914; s. Max and; m. Helen Wahala; children—Willard, George, Marjorie. B.S., Coll. City N.Y., 1939; postgrad., Columbia, 1940-42; Ph.D., Washington U., St. Louis, 1944; D.Sc. (hon.), Rensselaer Poly. Inst., 1966, Northwestern U., 1966, St. Louis U., 1968, U. Chgo., 1970, U. Ill., 1975, N.Y. Med. Coll., 1975, City U. N.Y., 1976; LL.D., U. Glasgow, 1973; D. Philosophy, Hebrew U., Jerusalem, 1975; Ph.D. (hon.), Weizmann Inst. Sci., 1979. Lectr. physics Washington U., 1942-44, lectr. applied math., 1943-44; instr. bacteriology Washington U. (Sch. Medicine), 1945-46, asst. prof. bacteriology, 1946-48; USPHS spl. fellow U. Minn., 1948-49; prof. microbiology U. Ill., Urbana, 1949-69; mem. U. Ill. (Center Advanced Study), 1964-69; dir. Inst. Cancer Research, prof. human genetics and devel. Coll. Phys. and Surg., Columbia, 1969-83, Univ. prof., 1975, Univ. lectr., 1974; dir. Coll. Phys. and Surg., Columbia (Comprehensive Cancer Center), 1980-83; Mem. Nat. Cancer Adv. Bd., 1972-83; Marrs McLean lectr. Baylor Coll. Medicine, 1974; S. Steven Brodie Meml. lectr. Jewish Meml. Hosp., N.Y.C., 1974. Contbr. articles to profl. jours. Recipient Pasteur award Ill. Soc. for Microbiology, 1963; Alumni citation award Washington U., 1966; Bertner Found. award in cancer research, 1968; Townsend Harris medal Alumni Assn. City Coll. N.Y., 1972; Lila Gruber Meml. award Am. Acad. Dermatology, 1972; Papanicolaou award for cancer research, 1973; Albert Lasker Basic Med. Research award, 1974; numerous distinguished lectureships. Fellow Am. Acad. Arts and Scis.; mem. Nat. Acad. Scis., Am. Soc. Biol. Chemists, Am. Soc. for Microbiology, N.Y. Acad. Scis. (life), Soc. for Gen. Microbiology (Brit.), Soc. Gen. Physiologists, Internat. Assn. for Promotion Clin. and Exptl. Research in Medicine, Soc. Am. Naturalists, Genetics Soc. Am., German Acad. Sics. Leopoldina, Nat. Acad. Medicine Brazil (fgn.), Phi Beta Kappa, Sigma Xi, Phi Kappa Phi, Tau Pi Epsilon. Home: New York, N.Y. Died Jan. 21, 1983.

SPIERS, MARK HERBERT CARVER, schoolmaster; b. Wayne, Pa., Apr. 27, 1887; s. Isidore Henry Bowles and Jane Owen (Williams) S.; grad. William Penn Charter Sch., Phila., 1905; B.S., Haverford Coll., 1909; m. Faith Randall, Sept. 9, 1910. Teacher, William Penn Charter Sch., 1909-14; pres. and head master Spiers Junior Sch., Devon, Pa., from 1914; dir. Camp Mowana, Readfield, Me., 1911-17. Republican. Episcopalian. Home: Devon, Pa. †

SPIGENER, GLADDEN H(UNTT), mfg. exec.; b. nr. Columbia, S.C., Jan. 19, 1888; s. Maynard R. and Sallie F. (Sims) S.; student The Citadel, Charleston, S.C., 1908; m. Mary M. Condon, Dec. 1, 1921. With Edwin G. Seibels, mgr. So. Dept. Fire Ins. Cos. of N.Y., Columbia, 1907-14; spl. agt. Eastern seaboard N. Brit. & Merc. Ins. Co., 1914-19; with Cotton Fire & Marine Underwriters, N.Y.C., 1919-26; with Am. Snuff Co., Memphis, from 1926, chmn. bd. from 1949. Served as capt., U.S. Army, World War I. Mem. Assn. Citadel Men, S.A.R. Clubs: Memphis Country, Army and Navy (Memphis). Home: Memphis, Tenn. †

SPIKER, CLARENCE JEROME, foreign service officer; b. Washington, D.C., June 14, 1888; s. Titus Jerome and Lucy Ann (Quesenberry) S.; grad. Central High Sch., Washington, 1906; School of Political Science, George Washington Univ., 1912-14; m. Helen Francis Aldrich, Feb. 9, 1934; 1 child, Richard Jerome. Office of Engineer Commr., Washington, 1906-14; appointed student interpreter, Am. Legation, Peking, China, Apr. 4, 1914; vice consul, Shanghai, China, also interpreter, Am. Consulate Gen., 1916-17; Am. assessor, Internat. Mixed Court, Shanghai, 1917-19; named to exercise judicial authority and jurisdiction in Am. civil and criminal cases, Sept. 1918; v. consul in charge, Antung, Manchuria, 1919; v. consul and acting asst. Chinese sec., Peking, 1920-22; in charge consulate, Chungking, China, 1922-23, consul, 1923-24; consul at Swatow, China, Oct. 1924-Apr. 1926; assigned to Am. Consulate Gen., Shanghai, 1926-28; Am. commr., Sino-Am. Reparations Commn. to assess losses arising out of Nanking incident, Aug. 1928-Mar. 1929; consul at Nanking, 1928; appointed to diplomatic service; 2d sec. and Chinese sec., Am. Legation, Peiping, 1928-30, first sec., 1930-34; consul gen. at Canton, China, 1934-36, at Basel, Switzerland, 1936-39, Hankow, China, July 1939-Dec. 1941; Dept. of State, 1941-42; became consul gen., Melbourne, Australia, 1943; consul gen., Tsingtao, China, 1946-49; ret. 1949. Clubs: International (Tsingtao); Peking (Peiping). Address: Washington, D.C. †

SPIVEY, HERMAN EVERETT, English language educator; b. Hemingway, S.C., Aug. 10, 1907; s. James Greer and Julia LeHarp (Baxley) S.; A.B., U. N.C., 1928, A.M., 1929, Ph.D., 1936, LL.D., 1969; Litt.D., Maryville Coll., 1968; m. Havens Edna Taylor, Dec. 15, 1928; children—Herman E., H. Olin, Mark Allan, Margaret Katherine. Instr. U. N.C., 1928-30, 1933-36; instr. to prof. English, U. Fla., 1930-33, 1936-42, 1945-48; head dept. English, U. Ky., 1948-51, dean grad. sch., 1950-60; acad. v.p. U. Tenn., 1960-68; prof. English, U. Fla., Gainesville, from 1968. Fulbright lectr. in Italy, 1955, India, 1956; FOA cons. in Yugoslavia, 1954; Phi Beta Kappa vis. scholar, 1970-71. Bd. dirs. Oak Ridge Asso. Univs., Presbyn. Homes, Inc., Maryville Coll. Served as comdr. USNR with naval air duty in U.S. and South Pacific, 1942-45; VTB operations officer at Guadalcanal, 1943, Miami Naval Air Sta., 1944-45; now capt. USNR. Received Presidential Unit citation, 1943, Commendation Comdr. Air Solomons, 1943. Mem. Modern Lang. Assn. Am., So. Atlantic Modern Lang. Assn. (several offices), Bibliog. Soc. Am., Am. Assn. Land Grant Colls. and Univs. (chmn. council on grad. work 1957-58, sec. council on instrn. 1956-58, mem. exec. com. 1966-68), Tenn. Coll. Assn. (pres. 1965-66), So. Humanities Conf. (vice chmn. 1966—), Conf. So. Grad. Deans (sec. 1954-59), Ky. Council Tchrs. English (mem. exec. com.), Am. Studies Assn., Newcomen Soc. Eng., Phi Beta Kappa, Omicron Delta Kappa. Presbyterian (ruling elder). Kiwanian. Author: Essentials of Correctness in English (with A.C. Morris), 1932; Essays for Better Reading (with Wise, Congleton, Skaggs), 1941; The Meaning in Reading (with Wise, Congleton, Morris), 1943, rev. edit., 1947. Contbr. bibliographies, reviews, articles learned jours. Home: Saint Augustine, Fla. Died Feb. 12, 1981.

SPOERL, CLIFFORD A., banker; b. Bklyn., 1888. Pres., dir. First Nat. Bank of Jersey City. Home: Red Bank, N.J. †

SPRAGUE, LAURENCE M., lawyer; b. Vermontville, Mich., Nov. 27, 1890; A.B., U. Mich., 1914, J.D., 1916. Admitted to Mich. bar, 1961; partner firm Fischer, Sprague, Franklin & Ford, Detroit. Mem. Am., Detroit bar assns., State Bar Mich., Order of Coif. Home: Detroit, MI. †

SPRINCHORN, CARL, artist; b. Broby, Sweden, May 13, 1887; s. Claés and Johanna (Edmundson) S.; came to U.S., 1904; ed. New York Sch. of Art and Henri Sch. of Art, New York; Colarossi Acad., Paris, etc.; unmarried. Exhibited in London, Kensington Mus., Stockholm, Gothenburg, Internat. Armory Show, New York, 1912, San Francisco Expn., 1915; one man shows in galleries of N.Y. City and Chicago; Worcester Art Mus., 1922; etc. Mgr. Henri Sch. of Art; dir. New Gallery; instr., Art Students' League, Los Angeles. Mem. Modern Artists America, New Gallery Art Club. Represented in permanent collection of Brooklyn Mus. Address: New York, N.Y. †

SPROUT, HAROLD, author; b. Benzonia, Mich., Mar. 14, 1901; s. George Milton and Grace Emily (Hance) S.; A.B., A.M., Oberlin Coll., 1924; postgrad. U. Wis. Law Sch., 1924-25, Western Res. Law Sch., 1925-26; Ph.D. (Carnegie fellow), U. Wis., 1929; m. Margaret Ascenath Tuttle, Aug. 6, 1924; children—Donald Francis, Chastina Elisabeth. Asst. prof. govt. Miami U., Oxford, Ohio, 1926-27; asst. prof. polit. sci. Stanford, 1929-31; instr. politics Princeton, 1931-35, asst. prof., 1935-41, assoc. prof., 1941-45, prof., 1945-80, chmn. dept. politics, 1949-52, Henry Grier Bryant prof. geography and internat. relations in dept. politics, prof. emeritus, 1969-80, research assoc. Center Internat. Studies, 1969-80. Vis. prof. internat. relations Columbia, 1948-50, U. Denver, summer 1950; vis. lectr. U.S. Army War Coll., 1936-38, 71, U.S. Naval Acad., 1941, U.S. Mil. Acad., 1942, U.S. Nat. War Coll. 1946, U.S. Naval War Coll., 1953, 63, 70; vis. prof. polit. sci. U. Pa., summer 1938; vis. prof. Nuffield Coll., Oxford U., 1955, Rutgers U., 1970; cons. OWI, War Dept., 1943, Dept. State 1944, Navy, 1944-47. Mem. Am. Polit. Sci. Assn., AAAS, Internat. Studies Assn., Naval Hist. Found., Phi Beta Kappa, Congregationalist Author: (with Margaret Sprout) The Rise of American Naval Power, rev. edit., 1967, Toward a New Order of Sea Power, rev., 1943, Foundations of National Power 1946, rev. 1951, Man-Millieu Relationship Hypotheses in Context of International Politics, 1956, Foundations of International Politics, 1962, The Ecological Perspective on Human Affairs, with Special Reference to International Politics, 1965, An Ecological Paradigm for the Study of International Politics, 1968, Toward a Politics of the Planet Earth, 1971, Ecology and Politics in America, 1971; Multiple Vulnerabilities: The Context of Environmental Repair and Protection, 1974, The Context of Environmental Politics, 1978. Contbr. articles to profl. Jours. and encys. Home: Princeton, N.J. Dec. Dec. 12, 1980. Interred Princeton, N.J.

SPRUNT, DOUGLAS HAMILTON, pathologist; b. Wilmington, N.C., Aug. 2, 1900; s. William Hutcheson and Bettie Massie (Hamilton) S.; B.S., U. of Va., 1922; M.D., Yale, 1927, M.S., 1929; D.Sc., Southwestern at Memphis (Tenn.), 1967; m. Edith Charlescraft Lucas, Oct. 17, 1933; children—Alice Hamilton, Edith Lucas. Asst. Yale U. Sch. of Medicine, 1927-28, instr., 1928-29, Sterling research fellow, 1929-30; acting resident in pathology New Haven (Conn.) Hosp., 1927-28, resident in pathology, 1928-29; asst. Hosp. Rockefeller Inst. for Med. Research, 1930-32; asso. prof. pathology, Duke U. School of Medicine, 1932-44; prof. pathology, U. of Tenn. Coll. of Medicine, 1944-70; chief of lab. City of Memphis hosps., 1944-70; cons. to Sec. of War for epidemic diseases, World War II; cons. in medicine Oak Ridge Institute Nuclear Physics, Inc., 1945-55; mem. pathology sect. USPHS, 1949-53, mem. cancer control com. Nat. Cancer Inst., 1955-60; cons. to Chem. Corps, U.S. Army, 1955-65; mem. com. on growth NRC, 1947-50; v. chmn. of Internat. com. pathology, 1960-63; chairman American coordinating com. of International Intersociety Committee on Pathology. Chairman of second teaching institute, pathology, microbiology, immunology and genetics Am. Assn. Med. Colls., 1954; mem. Lederle Med. Faculty award com., 1954-68. Mem. bd. vis. Duke Med. Center. Fellow Am. Coll. Physicians, Coll. Am. Pathologists (bd. govs. 1948-51), Internat. Acad. Pathology (council 1947-53); mem. Am. Soc. Exptl. Pathology (pres. 1947-48, chmn. Parke-Davis award com. 1957-59), Am. Soc. Clin. Pathology, Am., So. (chmn. sect. on med. edn. and hosp. tng. 1945-46) med. assns., Memphis and Shelby County Med. Soc., Am. Assn. Pathologists and Bacteriologists (sec. 1961-62, pres. 1960), Association Immunologists, Soc. Exptl. Biology and Medicine, A.A.A.S., Tenn. Soc. Pathology (sec-treas. 1957-59), Internat. Platform Assn., Kappa Alpha (South), Nu Sigma Nu. Presbyn. Clubs: University (N.Y.C.); Memphis Country; Cosmos (Washington). Author of articles in sci. jours. on viruses, toxins, endocrines, antibiotics and gerontology. Home: Memphis, Tenn. Died Oct. 30, 1983.

SQUIRES, JAMES DUANE, judge, educator; b. Grand Forks, N.D., Nov. 9, 1904; s. Vernon Purinton and Ethel Claire (Wood) S.; m. Catherine Emily Tuttle, Sept. 5, 1928; children—Vernon Tuttle, James Wood. A.B., U. N.D., 1925, LL.D., 1958; A.M., U. Minn., 1927; Ph.D., Harvard, 1933. Tchr. Dickinson (N.D.) High Sch., 1925-26; grad. asst. U. Minn., 1926-27; prof. history State Tchrs. Coll., Mayville, N.D., 1927-31; faculty history Colby-Sawyer Coll., New London, N.H., chmn. dept. social studies, 1935-70, chmn. summer forum, 1942-47; Vis. lectr. several colls.; dist. judge Town of New London, 1959-70; hist. cons. Author numerous books, from 1935; later publs. include Mirror to America, 1952, Experiment in Cooperation, 1953, Community Witness, 1954, The Granite State: A History of New Hampshire, 1923-1955, 1956; and, The Story of New Hampshire, N.Y, 1964, New Hampshire: A, Students Guide to Localized History, 1966; Co-author: later publs. include Western Civilization, rev. edit, 1945; Editor several books, brochures; editorial com., N.H. Hist. Soc. Pres. New London Hosp.; active several community orgns. as USO, ARC; mem. regional adv. council Nat. Archives; mem. adv. com. N.H. Library Assn.; mem. N.H. Council for Humanities; pres. N.H. Council Chs. and Religious Edn., 1945-48, Boys Club New London; del. 2d Assembly World Council of Chs., Evanston, Ill., 1954; pres. N.H. YMCA, 1944-45, N.H. State Bapt. Conv., 1946-49; mem. Bd. Edn. and Publ. Am. Bapt. Conv., 1952-61; del. N.Am. conf. on Faith and Order, Oberlin, 1957; Mem. Citizens adv. com. U.S. Commn. on Govt. Security, 1957; chmn. N.H. Civil War Centennial Commn., 1958-81, N.H. Revolutionary War Bicentennial Commn., 1970-81; mem. Gov.'s Task Force on State Problems, 1970, Com. for a New Eng. Bibliography, Bicentennial Council 13 Original States.; N.H. del.-at-large Republican Nat. Conv., 1952, 56, 64; trustee Cathedral of Pines; vice chmn. bd. dirs. Am. Revolution Bicentennial Adminstrn.; mem. N.H. Preservation Rev. Bd., 1978; chmn. 200th Anniversary Planning Bd. for New London. Recipient George Washington Honor medal Freedoms Found., 1954; Granite State award U. N.H., 1970; 3d of a Century award New London Service Orgn., 1970; William M. Beall award, 1976; Charles H. Pettee medal U. N.H., 1976; ABC Disting. Service award, 1976; Robert Frost Contemporary Am. award for outstanding service to people of N.H., 1979. Mem. nat., state, local hist. socs., profl. socs., Am. Bapt. Hist. Soc. (pres. 1968-70). Baptist. Home: New London, N.H. Died Apr. 9, 1981.

STACK, JAMES KEANE, educator, orthopedic surgeon; b. Duluth, Minn., Nov. 10, 1904; s. James Keane and Mary C. (Larkin) S.; m. Mary Solon, Sept. 24, 1932; children—John and James (twins), Christopher. A.B., U. Notre Dame, 1926; M.D., Northwestern U., 1931. Diplomate: Nat. Bd. Med. Examiners, Am. Bd. Surgery, Am. Bd. Orthopedic Surgery. Intern St. Vicent's Hosp., N.Y.C., 1931-32; resident Bellevue Hosp., N.Y.C., 1932-33; practice orthopedic surgery, Chgo., 1933-83; clin. asst. surgery Med. Sch. Northwestern U., 1933-35, instr. surgery, 1935-36, asso. bone and joint surgery, 1936-46, asst. prof. bone and joint surgery, 1946-49, asso. prof., 1949-72, prof., 1972-83; attending surgeon orthopedics Cook County Hosp.; attending surgeon orthopedics, pres. med. staff Passavant Meml. Hosp.; chief surgeon C.

& N.W. R.R. Author: (with Paul B. Magnuson) Fractures, 1949; Editorial bd.: (with Paul B. Magnuson) Quar. Bull. Northwestern U. Med. Sch; Contbr. (with Paul B. Magnuson) sci. articles to profl. jours. Served to comdr. M.C. USNR, World War II. Fellow A.C.S. (vice chmn. bd. govs.); mem. A.M.A., Chgo. Surg. Soc., Central Surg. Assn., Chgo. Orthopedic Soc. (pres. 1973-74), Assn. R.R. Surgeons (recorder), Am. Assn. Surgery Trauma (pres. 1959-60), Assn. Am. R.R.'s, Am. Assn. R.R. Surgeons (chmn. exec. com.). Club: Lake Shore (Chgo.). Home: Chicago, Ill. Died June 8, 1983.

STAFFORD, PAUL TUTT, educator, mgmt. cons.; b. Liberty, Mo., Sept. 16, 1905; s. Thomas Polhill and Anna Gardner (Tutt) S.; m. Helen Elizabeth Thomson, Dec. 14, 1951; children—Paul T., Timothy A., Mark T., Todd L.; 1 dau. by former marriage, Lucile Stafford Proctor. A.B., U. Mo., 1926, A.M., 1930; Ph.D. (Procter fellow in politics), Princeton, 1933. Instr. polit. sci. Princeton, 1933-36, asst. prof., 1936-42, asso. prof., 1942-48; exec. dir. N.J. Civil Service Commn., Trenton, 1948-50; exec. sec. to gov. N.J., Trenton, 1951; asst. to dir. personnel and community relations Internat. Shoe Co., St. Louis, 1952-53; prin., dir. Ashton Dunn Assos., N.Y.C., 1955-59; founder, chmn. Paul Stafford Assos., Ltd. (Mgmt. Cons.), N.Y.C., Chgo. and Washington, from 1959. Author: (with W.S. Carpenter) State and Local Goverments in the United States, 1936, Government and the Needy: A Study of Public Assistance in New Jersey, 1941; Contbr. (with W.S. Carpenter) articles on polit. sci. and exec. recruiting to profl. jours. Served with Naval Intelligence USNR, 1942-46; comdr. USN; ret.). Mem. Beta Theta Pi. Republican. Presbyterian. Clubs: Apawamis (Rye, N.Y.); Coral Beach (Bermuda); Hillsboro (Pompano Beach, Fla.); Princeton (N.Y.C.). Home: Princeton, NJ.

STAFFORD, RUSSELL HENRY, clergyman; b. Wauwatosa, Wis., Apr. 4, 1890; s. Charles Mason and Jennie (Russell) S.; student U. of Calif.; B.A., U. of Minn., 1912; M.A., New York U., 1915; B.D., Drew Theol. Sem., 1915; D.D., Chicago Theol. Seminary, 1924, Colby College, Waterville, Maine, 1931; LL.D., Oglethorpe Univ., 1929; S.T.D., Columbia Univ., 1934; m. Lillian Mae Crist, Apr. 23, 1921; children—Anne, Thomas Russell. Asst. pastor Central Congl. Ch., Brooklyn, N.Y., 1912-15; ordained Congl. ministry, 1914; pastor Open Door Congl. Ch., Minneapolis, 1915-19; 1st Congl. Ch., Minneapolis, 1919-23, Pilgrim Congl. Ch., St. Louis, 1923-27; minister Old South Ch. in Boston, 1927-45; pres. Hartford Sem. Found., 1945-58; moderator International Congregational Council, from 1958. Served as 1st lt. chaplain U.S. Army, 1918; mem. O.R.C., 1919-24. Trustee Anatolia Coll., Ch. Peace Union, Pres. A.B.C.F.M., 1940-50. Fellow Am. Acad. Arts and Scis.; mem. Soc. Mayflower Descs., Soc. Colonial Wars, S.A.R., Soc. War 1812, Delta Upsilon. Clubs: Authors' (London); Harvard Faculty (Cambridge, Mass.); University (Hartford). Author: Finding God, 1923; Christian Humanism, 1928; Religion Meets the Modern Mind, 1934; A Religion for Democracy, 1938; We Would See Jesus, 1947. Mem. editorial bd. Religion in Life. Home: Columbia, Conn. †

STAIR, LOIS HARKRIDER, church ofcl.; b. Waukesha, Wis., June 22, 1923; d. Lester Dore and Lola (Brown) Harkrider; m. Ralph Martin Stair, Oct. 14, 1944; children—Ralph Martin, Stuart Randall. B.A., Smith Coll., 1944, L.H.D. (hon.), 1981; L.H.D., Carroll Coll., 1971, Keuka Coll., 1975; D.D., Dubuque C. Coll., 1971; Litt.D., Wilson Coll., 1972. Sec., v.p. Gen. Casting Corp. div. Grey Iron Foundry, Waukesha, 1960-73; moderator various levels Presbyterian Ch., 1966-81; for Synod Wis., 1969; for gen. assembly United Presbyn. Ch. U.S., 1971-81; Sec. bd. dirs. United Fund, Waukesha, 1960-61; sec. Equal Opportunities Commn., Waukesha, 1966-69; mem. bd. counselors Smith Coll., Higher Ednl. Aids Bd. State of Wis. Bd. dirs. Vis. Nurse Assn., Waukesha, 1962-64, Presbyn. Ministers' Fund, Fund for Theol. Edn.; trustee Carroll Coll., Waukesha, McCormick Theol. Sem., Univ. Lake Sch., Hartland, Wis., 1964-67. Recipient Civic award UNICO, Waukesha, 1968. Home: Deerfield Beach, Fla. Died July 13, 1981.

STALKER, GALE HAMILTON, ex-congressman; b. Long Eddy, N.Y., Nov. 7, 1889; s. David M. and Zelma E. (Braman) S.; pub. and high schs., business coll. and night schs.; m. Helen B. Rutledge, of Liberty, N.Y., June 5, 1912; children—Helen Lucile, Norma Gail. Engaged in lumber and banking business; mem. 68th to 73d Congresses (1923-35), 37th N.Y. Dist. Republican. Methodist. Home: Washington, D.C. †

STALLAND, KNUTE DOROTHEUS, lawyer, dean; b. St. Paul, Mar. 24, 1897; s. Martin C. and Hannah N. (Growe) S.; B.A., Luther Coll., 1918, LL.D., 1955; LL.B., William Mitchell Coll. Law, 1922; m. Katinka H. Preus, Sept. 4, 1920; children—Betty Louise, Knute P., Luther M. Admitted to Minn. bar, 1921, practiced in South St. Paul, 1922-32, St. Paul, 1932-42; asst. atty. gen., Minn., 1942-55; dean Sch. Law, Valparaiso U., from 1955. Mem. Am., Ind. bar assns., Am. Assn. Law Schs. Clubs: Rotary (Valparaiso); St. Paul Athletic. Home: Valparaiso, Ind.

STALLMAN, ROBERT WOOSTER, educator, author; b. Milw., Sept. 27, 1911; s. Paul Michael and Hazel (Wooster) S.; m. Virginia Blume, Aug. 21, 1939; children—William Wooster, Robert Wooster. A.B., U. Wis., 1933, A.M., 1939, Ph.D., 1942. Part-time instr. U. Wis., 1939-42; instr. R.I. State Coll., 1942-43, Yale, 1943-44, Katharine Gibbs Sch., Boston, 1944-46; asst. prof. English U. Kans., 1946-49; asso. prof. English U. Conn., 1949-53, prof., 1953-82; Bingham prof. U. Lousville (Ky.), 1966; asso. editor The Western Review, 1946-48; staff mem. Writers' Conf., Kans., summer 1948; lectr. U. Wis., summers 1946, 49, U. Minn., summer 1947; Ford Found. fellow, 1953-54; Fulbright lectr. Am. lit. U. Strasbourg, 1958-59, European univs.; vis. prof. Citizen's chair U. Hawaii, 1970; dir. U. Conn. Writers' Conf., 1950-55; fellow La Fondation Camargo, Cassis, France, 1974-75; lectr. French univs., 1977. Author: The Houses That James Built and Other Literary Studies, 1961, 77, Stephen Crane: A Biography, 1968, rev. edit., 1973, Stephen Crane: A Critical Bibliography, 1972, The Figurehead and Other Poems, 1978; Editor: Critiques and Essays in Criticism, 1920-48, 1949, The Critic's Notebook, 1950, 77, Stephen Crane: An Omnibus, 1952, 54, Stephen Crane: Stories and Tales, 1955, Seventeen American Poets, 1958, The Ambassadors, 1960, The Art of Joseph Conrad, 1960, 81, The Red Badge of Courage and Other Stories, 1960, Stephen Crane: Sullivan County Tales and Sketches, 1968, The Stephen Crane Reader, 1972; Co-editor: The Art of Modern Fiction, 1949, 56, The Creative Reader, 1954, rev., 1962, Stephen Crane: Letters, 1960, American Literature: Readings and Critiques, 1961, The War Dispatches of Stephen Crane, 1964, 77, The New York City Sketches of Stephen Crane, 1966, 77; Contbr. poems and essays, anthologies and jours.; contbr. to: Ency. Brit.; Stephen Crane, 1974; adv. editor: Studies in the Novel. Recipient U. Conn. Alumni Assn. Excellence award, 1968. Mem. Phi Beta Kappa. Address: Storrs, Conn. Died Oct. 13, 1982.

STAMBAUGH, JOHN WESLEY, Canadian senator; b. Melvin, Mich., July 1, 1888; s. Albert S. and Christine (Zimmerman) S.; student pub. schs. Mayville, and Wellsville, N.Y.; m. Amey Lake, Dec. 25, 1912; children—Lyall, Kenneth, Donald, Evelyn (Mrs. Charles Nolan), John. Homesteader nr. Bruce, Alberta, Can., 1905, farmer, 1905-11, 1914-49; operater machine agy. with R. J. Wilson, Bruce, 1928-35. Apptd. Canadian senator from Alberta Sept. 8, 1949. Trustee Rich Dist. 1912-20; mem. Bruce Sch. Bd., 1920-37; chmn. Holden Divisional Sch. Bd., 1937-49. Mem. Viking Hosp. Bd., 1935-49. Liberal (pres. Alberta assn. 1945-52; pres. North Edmonton assn., 1911, Bruce Constituency povincial assn., 1935-45, Camrose fed. assn. from 1940). Home: Bruce, Alberta, Can. †

STAMBAUGH, LYNN UPSHAW, lawyer; b. Abilene, Kan., July 4, 1890; s. Winfield Scott and Lina (Upshaw) S.; student Fargo (N.D.) Coll., 1909-10; LL.B., U. of N.D., 1913; m. Enid Erickson, Sept. 11, 1915. Admitted to N.D. bar, 1913; dep. clerk Dist. Court, Fargo, 1913-15; practiced law at Hazen, N.D. 1915-17, at Fargo, N.D., from 1919; mem. Cupler, Stambaugh & Tenneson; mem. board Export-Import Bank, from 1945, first v.p., vice chmn. bd., 1954-60, senior vice pres., 1960-62. Served with F.A. during World War; nat. comdr. Am. Legion, 1941-42. Mem. Fargo Chamber of Commerce (past pres.). Mem. Am. Bar Assn., N.D. Bar Assn., Cass County Bar Assn. (past pres.), Order of Coif, Sigma Chi, Phi Delta Phi. Republican. Episcopalian. Mason. †

STANFORD, ALFRED BOLLER, editor, publisher; b. East Orange, N.J., Feb. 12, 1900; s. Joseph Marsh and Mary Newbold (Boller) S.; grad. Neward (N.J.) Acad., 1917; B.A., Amherst, 1921; m. Dorothy Janet Taylor, Sept. 1922; children—John, Peter, Nicholas; m. 2d, Berenice Langton Ladd, Mar. 2, 1951. Served at sea as sailor, officer Mcht. Marine; ensign USNRF, resigned, 1920; commd. lt. comdr. USNR, Sept. 1942; comdr., 1943; ret. as capt., 1954; dir. Bur. Advt., Am. Newspaper Pubs. Assn., 1947-49; 2d v.p., advt. dir., dir. N.Y. Herald Tribune until 1951; past pres. Citizen Pub. Co., Milford, Conn., past pub. Milford Citizen; former editor, pub. Boats Mag. Past pres., dir. Quinnipiac council Boy Scouts Am., Milford United Fund. Mem. Marine Hist. Soc., Alpha Delta Phi. Clubs: Amhert Cruising of Am. Author several books; latest publs.: Pleasures of Sailing, 1942; Force Mulberry, 1951; Mission in Sparrow Bush Lane, 1966. Contbr. articles, short stories to mags. Home: Milford, Conn. Died Feb. 8, 1985.

STANFORD, JAMES EDWIN, editor and executive; born Mount Enterprise, Texas, April 2, 1887; son of John Madison and Sarah Cumile (Holleman) S.; educated University of Georgia, 1904-05; also summer courses Texas A. and M. College and business coll.; m. Drunetta Davis, Mar. 27, 1910; children—Alia Jane (Mrs. W. Vance Thompson), Evelyn Elizabeth (Mrs. R. M. Searcy, now dec.), John Edwin. Teacher pub. schools, Tex., 1908-11; county farm agent, Tex. Extension Service, 1911-20, dist. agt., 1920-26; asst. mgr. and agrl. dir. East Tex. Chamber of Commerce, 1926-29; field editor Southern Agriculturalist, 1929-33; state dir. rural rehabilitation, Tex., 1934-36; editor Southern Agriculturalist, 1936-43; exec. sec., Ky., Farm Bur. Fedn. from 1943. Democrat. Baptist. Mason. Also writes under name of Zeke Carsie. Home: Louisville, Ky. †

STANGEL, WENZEL LOUIS, dean emeritus, ins. co. exec.; b. Stangelville, Wis., Aug. 16, 1889; s. John Joseph and Anne (Seidenglanz) S.; B.S., Texas A. and M. Coll., 1915, LL.D., 1956; M.S., U. Mo., 1916; grad. study U. Wis.; m. Mary Ruth Canon, Dec. 29, 1920; children—Menon (Mrs. Hugh English), Ava (Mrs. Clifford B. Barr). Instr. animal husbandry Texas A. and M. Coll., 1916-18, asso. prof., 1918-20, prof., 1920-25; head dept. animal husbandry Tex. Technol. Coll., 1925-45; dean agr., 1945-58, dean agr. emeritus, from 1958; chmn. bd., dir. Nat. Farm Life Ins. Co., Agrl. Workers Mut. Auto Ins. Co. Mgr. livestock dept. Tex. Centennial Expns., 1935-36; gen. livetock supt. State Fair Tex., from 1946, hon. vice pres.; supt. steer dept. Southwestern Expn. and Fat Stock show, from 1951. Councilor Tex. A. and M. Coll. Research Found.; dir. Texas Technol. Coll. Found., Texas 4-H Youth Development Found. Named Man of Year in Tex. Agr., 1951; Top West Texan, 1956, Man of Yr. in agr. Tex. Agrl. Agts. Assns., 1963. Fellow Am. Soc. Animal Sci.; mem. Nat. Block and Bridle Club (pres. 1937-39), Am. Brahman Breeders Assn., Tex. Panhandle-Plains Dairy Assn. (pres. 1932-33), Tex. Holstein-Friesian Assn. (pres. 1943-44), Tex. Agrl. Workers Assn. (pres. 1945-46), Nat. Ret. Tchrs. Assn., Tex. Technol. Rodeo Assn. (hon.), Southwestern Ranchers Assn. (pres.). Phi Eta Sigma, Gamma Sigma Delta, Alpha Zeta. Baptist (deacon). Clubs: Country, Kiwanis (pres. 1940). Home: Lubbock, TX. †

STANKIEWICZ, RICHARD PETER, sculptor; b. Phila., Oct. 18, 1922; s. Anton and Rose (Pietrociewicz) S.; m. Patricia M. Doyle, Sept. 30, 1961 (div. Nov. 1978); children—Peter Alex, Anthony Leslie (adopted). Student pub. schs.; student, Hans Hofmann Sch., N. M.C., 1948-50, Atelier Fernand Leger, Paris, 1950, Ossip Zadkine, Paris, 1950-51. Co-organizer, officer Hansa Gallery, N.Y.C. (a co-operative gallery), 1952-58; Lectr. Amherst Coll., U. Miami, 1966; Ford Found. artist in residence Tampa Art Inst., 1965, Amherst Coll., 1970-71; prof. art State U., N.Y., 1967—; Salzman vis. artist Brandeis U., 1973. Sculpture exhibited in one-man shows, Hansa Gallery, 1952-58, Frumkin Gallery, Chgo., 1958, Stable Gallery, N.Y.C., 1959, 60, 65, Tampa (Fla.) Art Inst., 1965, Galerie Neufville, Paris Galerie Claude Bernard, Frank Watters Gallery, Sydney, Australia, 1969, Nat. Gallery of Victoria, Australia, 1969, Zabriskie Gallery, N.Y.C., 1971, 72, 73, Litchfield, Conn., 1973, two-man show, Robert Fraser Gallery, London, 1963, group shows, Hansa Gallery, Stable Gallery, Silvermine Guild, Riverside Mus., Smith Coll., Providence Art Club, Art Inst. Chgo., Watters Gallery, Nat. Gallery, Melbourne, Australia, Trend House Gallery, Tampa, Moderna Museet, Stockholm, Sweden, Mus. Modern Art, Belgrade, Yugoslavia, 1980, numerous others, biannual show, Pa. Acad. Fine Arts, Phila., 1954, also retrospectives; represented in collections, Mus. Modern Art., N.Y.C., Art Inst. Chgo., Whitney Mus. Am. Art, Guggenheim Mus., N.Y., Mus. Modern Art, George Pompidou Center of Culture and Arts, Paris, others. Mem. Nat. Council Arts and Humanities, Century Assn. Address: Huntington, Mass. Died March 27, 1983.

STANLEY, HELEN (MRS. LOUDON CHARLTON), opera singer; b. Cincinnati, O., Feb. 24, 1889; d. William Wilson and Clara Dodson (Wood) McGrew; studied music in Chicago, New York and Berlin, Germany; m. Loudon Charlton, of New York, Oct. 3, 1917; 1 dau., Cynthia Charlton. Appeared with Royal Opera, Würzburg, seasons 1911-12, Chicago-Phila. Opera Co., season, 1912-14, Montreal Opera Co., season 1914-15, Chicago Opera Co., season 1915-16, Ellis All-Star Opera Co., autumn, 1916, Civic Opera Co., Phila., 1923-26. Repertoire includes Mimi in "Bohème," Donna Elvira in "Don Giovanni," Desdemona in "Othello," Marguerite in "Faust," Salome in "Hérodiade," Sieglinde in "Die Walkure," Eva in "Meistersinger," Elizabeth in "Tannhauser," Elsa in "Lohengrin," Maliella in "Jewels of the Madonna," Fiora in "L'Amore di tre Re," etc. Address: New York, N.Y.†

STANLEY, PAUL ELWOOD, electrical engineer, educator; b. Huntington, Ind., Nov. 6, 1909; s. Noah E. and Bertha (Chalmers) S.; A.B., Manchester Coll., 1930; M.A., Ohio State U., 1933, Ph.D., 1937; m. Lucille Klutz, Nov. 27, 1930; children—Mary Louise Johnson, Carol Ann (Mrs. Paul Conrad), Barbara Jean (Mrs. Stephan Grenat). Mem. faculty Purdue U., 1943-83, interim head Sch. Aeros. and Astronautics Engring. Scis., 1963-65, prof., 1965-76, prof. emeritus, 1976-83, assoc. dir. Biomed. Engring. Center, 1973-76. Cons. numerous hosps. and indsl. firms. Assoc. fellow AIAA; mem. IEEE, Am. Soc. Engring. Edn., Assn. for Advancement Med. Instrumentation, Am. Hosp. Assn. Author: (with Joseph Liston) Creative Product Envolvement, 1940. Contbr. tech. papers to profl. lit. Home: West Lafayette, Ind. Dec. May 16, 1983. Interned Tippecanoe Gardens, West Lafayette, Ind.

STANSBURY, WILLIAM BROWN, lawyer, former mayor; b. Corydon, Ind., Mar. 18, 1923; s. James Bernard and Alliene (Brown) S.; m. Mary Ellen Stansbury; 1 dau., Patricia Ann Stansbury Beckman. B.A. in Econs, U. Louisville, 1947, J.D., 1950. Bar: Ky. 1950. Asst. sales mgr. Peerless Mfg. Co., Louisville, 1947-48, Stratton & Terstegge, Louisville, 1948-49; with firm Mapother, Morgan & Stansbury, Louisville, 1950-69; mem. Jefferson County Probate Commn., probate judge pro tem, 1968-76; sr. ptnr. firm Wood, Goldberg, Pedley, Stansbury, Louisville, 1969-77; mayor, City of Louisville, 1977-82; ptnr. Mobley, Zoeller & Celebreeze, 1982-85. Chmn. Louisville and Jefferson County Dem. Exec. Com., 1968-76; mem. City of Louisville Bd., Aldermen, 1973-77, pres., 1974. Served to capt. USAF, 1942-49. Decorated Air medal with cluster. Mem. Am. Bar Assn. (ho. of dels. 1971-77), Ky. Bar Assn. (ho. of dels. 1960-77), Louisville

Bar Assn. (pres. 1974), U.S. Conf. of Mayors, Nat. League of Cities, Ky. Mcpl. League. Roman Catholic. Home: Louisville, Ky. Died Apr. 4, 1985.

STANWOOD, HENRY CHAPMAN, dir. of Selective Service for Md.; b. Evanston, Ill., Oct. 4, 1890; s. Thaddeus Perkins and Louise (Brockway) S.; M.E., Cornell, 1913; m. Neel Zouck, Aug. 11, 1917 (dec.). Ins. underwriter, Baltimore, Md., 1913-16; ins. broker, Baltimore, 1919-40. Mem. Md. Nat. Guard, 1915-19 and from 1921. Served with U.S. Army, 1916-19, and 1940-50; ret. from army as col., 1950; dir. Selective Service for Md., 1940-47, and from 1948; dir. office Selective Service Records, 1947-48. Decorated Legion of Merit, Army Commendation Ribbon. Mem. Am. Legion, Veterans of Fgn. Wars, Military Order of Foreign Wars, 29th Division Association, Phi Kappa Psi. Awarded Legion of Merit. Home: Baltimore, Md. †

STARBIRD, ALFRED DODD, army officer; b. Ft. Sill, Okla., Apr. 28, 1912; s. George A. A. and Mary Ethel (Dodd) S.; B.S., U.S. Mil. Acad., 1933; C.E., Princeton, 1937; m. Evelyn Wallington, July 7, 1938; children—Edward A., Susan E., Catharine D. Commd. 2d lt. U.S. Army, advanced through grades to maj. gen.; various assignments, U.S., 1933-42; operations div. Gen. Staff, War Dept., 1942-44; comdr. engring. combat group, 1944-45; dep. chief staff Hawaii, also 2d atomic test series, 1946-50; engr. constrn. duty, 1951, 52-55; sec. hdqrs. SHAPE, 1952-53; dir. mil. application AEC, then dir. Def. Communications Agy.; mgr. Safeguard system. Decorated D.S.M., Legion of Merit, Bronze Star. Home: Alexandria, Va. Died July 29, 1983.

STARCK, TAYLOR, educator; b. Independence, Mo., Oct. 15, 1889; s. Christian and Conradine (Kaessmann) S.; A.B., Johns Hopkins, 1911, Ph.D., 1916; student, U. of Berlin, 1914-15, U. of Madrid, 1919-20; A.M. (hon.), Harvard, 1942; Ph.D. (hon.), U. of the Saarland, 1960; m. Gretchen Todd, Sept. 16, 1921 (dec.); 1 dau., Elizabeth Manby. Asst. German, Johns Hopkins, 1913-14; instr. Smith Coll., 1915-18; acting asst. prof., New York U., 1919; sec. and teacher, Ministry of Pub. Instrn., Madrid, Spain, 1919-20; instr. in German, Harvard, 1920-26, asst. prof., 1926-29, asso. prof., 1929-42, prof., 1942-52, chmn. dept. Germanic lang. and lit., 1927-32 and 1938-52, Kuno Francke prof. German art and culture, 1952-56, emeritus prof., from 1956; Fulbright vis. prof Germanic philology U. Leiden, 1956-57; vis. prof. Germanic philology U. Saarland, 1958-59, Harvard, 1959-60, Johns Hopkins, 1961; summer faculty N.Y. U., 1919, Columbia, 1920. Editor publs. Am. Acad. Arts and Scis., 1946-54. Served with AUS, 1918-19. Decorated knight Order of North Star (Sweden), 1955, Gold Goethe medal Goethe Inst., Munich, 1961; grand cross of merit Fed. Republic Germany, 1964. Fellow Mediaeval Acad. of Am., Am. Acad. of Arts and Scis.; mem. Modern Lang. Assn. Am. (pres. 1957), Am. Dialect Soc., Am. Folkslore Soc., Mediaeval Acad. of Am. (clk. from 1957), Linguistic Soc. Am., Soc. for Advancement of Scandinavian Studies, Deutsche Akademie der Sprache and Dichtung (corresponding mem.). Clubs: Harvard (New York); Faculty (Cambridge). Author: Der Alraun, 1917; Notker, des Deutschen Werke (5 vols. with E. H. Sehrt), 1935-55. Contbr. learned jours. Translator: The Inevitable War (F. Delaisi), 1915. Home: Cambridge, MA. †

STARK, JAMES ARTHUR, holding co. exec.; b. Chgo., June 2, 1933; s. Herbert O. and Florence M. (Bofinger) S.; m. Sarah Ann Spencer, June 9, 1956; children—Carolyn, James, Janet. B.S. in Bus, U. Colo., 1955. C.P.A. Mgr. Arthur Andersen & Co., Chgo., 1958-66; treas. Chicago Musical Instrument Co., Lincolnwood, Ill., 1966-73; exec. v.p. Western Pub. Co., Inc., Racine, Wis., 1973-80; pres. B.B. Walker Co., Asheboro, N.C., from 1980. Bd. dirs. Racine United Way, 1973-76, Racine County Area Found., 1977-80, St. Luke's Hosp., 1978-80. Served to lt., j.g. USN, 1955-57. Mem. Nat. Alliance Businessmen (dir., vice chmn. from 1975), Am. Inst. C.P.A.'s. Episcopalian. Clubs: Asheboro Country, Grandfather Golf, CCNC, Somerset, Chgo. Yacht. Home: Asheboro, NC.

STARRING, DAVID SWING, ret. bus. exec.; b. Calmar, Ia., Oct. 18, 1887; s. Mason Brayman and Helen Beth (Swing) S.; student Chgo. Latin Sch., 1895-1905; A.B., Harvard, 1909; m. Elizabeth Austin Miller, Oct. 9, 1919 (dec. Feb. 1960); 1 son, David Swing; stepchildren—Carolyn (Mrs. J. Edward Meyer, Jr.), Elizabeth (Mrs. Donald Fraser) (dec.); m. 2d, Ysabel M. Ingram, Oct. 6, 1962. Asso. Allerton, Green & King, bond brokerage, Chgo., 1909-14; mem. firm D.S. Starring & Co., investment brokers, Chgo., 1914-21; dir. Wheeler Indulated Wire Co., Bridgeport, Conn., 1921-43; sr. partner Starring & Co., Inc.; chmn. bd. Permian Oil & Gas. Home Utilities Co., Interstate Utilities, Sander Corp., mem. exec. and finance coms. Bridgeport Brass Co.; mem. exec. com., dir. Penick & Ford; ltd. partner Phelps, Fenn & Co.; former dir. Nat. Distillers and Chem. Corp.; Served as lt., aviation sect. Signal Corp. U.S. Army, 1917-19. Republican. Episcopalian. Clubs: Country of Fairfield (Conn.); Pequot Yacht of Southport (ex-commodore). Home: Greens Farms, CT. †

STARSHAK, ALPHONSE LEON, retail mcht.; b. Lemont, Ill., Apr. 7, 1887; s. John Francis and Anna Maria (Theis) S.; student U. Ill., 1907-08; m. Frances Foley Downes, Sept. 17, 1927. Pharmacist's apprentice, Chgo., 1902-07; registered pharmacist Seaman Drug Co., Livingston Mont., 1909-11; with Walgreen Co., Chgo., from 1912, beginning as personnel dir., successively mem. real estate dept., pub. relations, treas., 1912-34, v.p., from 1938, dir., from 1940. Mem. Am. Pharm. Assn., Ill. Fedn. Retail Assns. (dir.), Chgo. Retail Mchts. Assn. (trustee), Am. Legion, 40 and 8. Republican. Roman Catholic. Home: Chgo. †

STAUFFER, JOHN N(ISSLEY), coll. pres.; b. Palmyra, Pa., Mar. 29, 1907; s. Harry M. and Martha N. (Heisey) S.; B.S., Juniata Coll., 1936; M.A., U. Pa., 1942; D.Ed., Pa. State U., 1956; student Harvard, 1946-47. Ohio State U., 1949; LL.D., Juniata Coll., 1964; D.H.L., Wittenberg U. m. M. Louise Lee, Aug. 20, 1938; children—Thomas M., Nancy K., John L., Donald David. Tchr. math. Milton Hershey Sch., 1936-43; sr. psychologist Pa. Indsl. Sch., 1943-44; dir. counseling service Hartford (Conn.) YMCA, 1944-45; asst. dir. Vets. Guidance Center, Harvard, 1945-47, also lectl. ednl. guidance Grad. Sch. Edn., 1945-46, 47; mem. grad. faculty Pa. State U., summer 1953; dean students Wittenberg Univ., Springfield, O., 1947-57, asst. prof. psychology, 1947-53, asso. prof., 1953-57, professor psychology, 1957-68, dean, 1957-63, pres., 1963-68; president Juaniata College, Huntington, Pa., from 1968. Dir. Columbia Gas System. Mem. personnel services committee national board YMCA, 1955-68, chmn., 1967-68, chmn. recruiting com., 1956-62, representative So. Ohio nat. council, 1956-69, v.p., 1965-67, nat. bd., 1961; trustee, chmn. personnel com. Ohio-W.Va. area YMCA's 1954-60, pres., 1960-62; pres. Pub. Forum of Springfield, 1960-61. Community Welfare Council Springfield and Clark County, O., 1957; v.p. United Appeals Fund Springfield and Clark County, 1967-68; treas. Ohio Found. Ind. Colls., 1966-68; adv. com. Ohio Pvt. Colls. and Univs., 1965-68. Bd. dirs. Luth. Ednl. Conf. N. Am., 1967-68; member board of college education Lutheran Church in Am., 1968. Mem. Nat., Ohio (pres. 1954-55) assns. student personnel adminstrs., Ohio (dir., chmn. com. program edn. 1952-54), Clark County (president 1949-50) mental health associations, Assn. Ohio Coll. Presidents and Deans (president 1963-64), Alumni Assn. Juaniata Coll. (pres. 1958-59), Assn. Higher Edn., Am. Assn. U. Profs., N. Central Assn. of Colls. and Secondary Schools (member of commn. on colls. and univs. 1960-64), Ohio Coll. Assn. (exec. com. 1967-68). Blue Key, Kappa Phi Kappa, Psi Chi, Phi Eta Sigma, Phi Delta Kappa, Phi Gamma Delta. Lutheran. Rotarian. Author: Judgements of Liberal Arts College Teachers and Deans Regarding College Teacher Qualifications, 1956; also articles. Mem. editorial bd. Harvard Ednl. Rev., 1945-64. Died Sept. 28, 1983.

STAUFFER, OSCAR STANLEY, editor, publisher; b. Hope, Kans., Nov. 26, 1886; s. Solomon Engle and Elizabeth (Conrad) S.; m. Ethel Lucille Stone, Sept. 7, 1914 (dec. July 1964); children—Betty Stauffer Collinson, Stanley Howard, John Herbert; m. Cornelia Hardcastle, Conwell, July 15, 1965 (dec. July 1973). Student, U. Kans., 1908-10. Reporter Emporia Gazette, 1906-08, Kansas City Star, Mo., 1910-15; editor, owner Peabody Gazette, Kans., 1915-24; editor Arkansas City Traveler, Kans., 1924-40; editor, pub. Topeka State Jour. and Topeka Daily Capital; chmn. bd., exec. head Stauffer Publs.; pubs. Ark. City Daily Traveler, Pittsburg (Kans.) Morning Sun, Grand Island (Nebr.) Daily Ind., Beatrice (Nebr.) Daily Sun, Maryville (Mo.) Daily Forum, Shawnee (Okla.) News & Star, Nevada (Mo.) Daily Mail, York (Nebr.) News Times, Newton (Kans.) Kans., Independence (Mo.) Examiner, Capper's Weekly, Marshall (Mo.) Democrat News, Brookings (S.D.) Register, Glenwood Springs (Colo.) Post, Hillsdale (Mich.) Daily News, Hannibal (Mo.) Courier-Post; pres. KGFF Broadcasting Co., Shawnee., Okla., WIBW-TV, AM-FM, Topeka, KGNC AM-FM, Amarillo, Tex., KSOK Broadcasting Co., Arkansas City, KRNT-AM-FM, Des Moines; former v.p. A.P. Trustee Washburn U., Menninger Found.; Former chmn. Kan. Indsl. Devel. Commn., Kans. State Bd. Regents; past pres. Inland Daily Press Assn. Mem. Am. Soc. Newspaper Editors, Beta Theta Pi, Sigma Delta Chi. Republican. Presbyterian. Clubs: Topeka Country (Ariz.), Scottsdale (Ariz.); Villa Monterey, Rotary. Home: Topeka, Kans. Died 1982.

STAUFFER, S. WALTER, ex-congressman; b. Walkersville, Maryland, August 13, 1888; graduate Dickinson College Manufacture lime, crushed stone, 1916-36; president National Lime Association, 1936-46; v.p., dir., chmn. exec. com. York County (Pa.) Gas Co. 1946; partner Southern Farms, Walkersville, Md.; owner timberland in York County; dir. First Nat. Bank, York Water Co., J. E. Baker Co., Farmers Fire Ins. Co. (all York), Columbia Water Co. (Pa.). Member of 83d and 85th Congresses, 19th Dist. Pa. Trustee Dickinson Coll. Mem. Sigma Alpha Epsilon. Methodist. Address: York, Pa. †

STEAD, CHRISTINA ELLEN, author; b. Sydney, New South Wales, Australia, July 17, 1902; d. David George and Ellen (Butters) Stead; grad. Tchrs. College, Sydney University, 1922; m. William J. Blake (dec. February 1968). Began as demonstrator psychology Sydney Tchrs. Coll., tchr. city schs., 1922-24; bus. sec., Sydney, 1925-28; went to London, 1928, Paris, 1929; French and English sec. in Paris, 1929-35, came to U.S., 1935. Author: The Salzburg Tales, 1934; Letty Fox, 1946; A Little Tea, A Little Chat, 1948; The People with the Dogs, 1951; The Man Who Loved Children, 1965; Dark Places of the Heart, 1966; For Love Alone, 1966; The Puzzelheaded Girl, 1967; others Eng., Australia. Died Mar. 31, 1983.

STEARNS, RUSSELL BANGS, industrialist; b. Chgo., Feb. 9, 1894; s. Robert Bangs and Emma (Owens) S; B.A., U. Mich., 1916; m. Edna Dilley, June 14, 1918 (dec. Feb. 1950); 1 child, Virginia S. Gassel; m. Andree Beauchamp Ryan, June 5, 1958; stepchildren—Anthony H. Ryan, Thomas A. Ryan. Partner, Arthur Perry & Co., 1926-30, pres., 1930-38. Chmn. War Dept. Price Adjustment Bd., Washington, 1942; chmn. U.S. del. OEEC Conf., Paris. 1954. Mem. U. Mich. President's Club. Chmn. Mass. Republican Finance Com., 1944-46, regional vice chmn., 1946-48. Chmn. U.S. delegation OEEC Conf., Paris, 1954. Trustee, hon. vice chmn., mem. exec. com. Northeastern U.; trustee Civic Edn. Found., Tufts U., Boston Hosp. for Women, Trustees of Reservations, Milton; trustee, life mem. exec. com. Mus. Sci., Boston; bd. dirs. Boston Opera Assn.; bd. govs. Mass. Inst. Tech. Endicott House; life mem. Boston Episcopal Charitable Soc. Served as arty. officer U.S. Army, World War I. Mem. Squibnocket Assos. (life), Delta Kappa Epsilon. Clubs: Country (Brookline, Mass.); Down Town, (Boston); Hingham (Mass.) Yacht; Somerset (Boston); Edgartown (Mass.) Yacht; Mill Reef (Antigua, W.I.) Home: Dedham, Mass. Dec. Aug. 6, 1981.

STEED, TOM, congressman; b. nr. Rising Star, Tex., Mar. 2, 1904; m. Hazel Bennett, Feb. 26, 1923; children—Richard, Roger (dec.). Connected with Okla. daily newspapers, 20 yrs.; mng. editor Shawnee News & Star, 4 yrs. Mem. 81st to 96th Congresses, 4th Okla. Dist. Served from pvt. to 2d lt. A.A.A., AUS, 1942-44; with OWI, 1944-45; CBI. Democrat. Home: Shawnee, Okla. Dec. June 8, 1983.

STEEL, WILLIAM CARLTON, lawyer; b. Cincinnati, Iowa, Feb. 6, 1916; s. David and Myrtle (Stickler) S.; m. Margaret M. Gordon, 1940; 1 dau., Jane Steel Wilken. A.B., Grinnell Coll., 1938; LL.B., Harvard, 1941. Bar: N.Y. bar 1942, Fla. bar 1946. Practice in, Miami, from 1946; with Steel, Hector & Davis (and predecessor firms.). Served with AUS, 1943-46. Fellow Am. Coll. Trial Lawyers, Am. Bar Found.; mem. Internat. Bar Assn., ABA (ho. of dels. 1962-68), Inter-Am. Bar Assn., Dade County Bar Assn. (past pres.), Fla. Bar, Am. Soc. Internat. Law, Am. Judicature Soc., So. Fla. Interprofl. Council (past pres.). Lutheran. Clubs: Miami, Bankers. Home: Key Biscayne, Fla.

STEEN, THOMAS WILSON, psychologist; b. Wash., Ia., Apr. 12, 1887; s. Samuel Briton and Emma (Cooper) S.; A.B., Emmanuel Missionary College, Berrien Springs, Mich., 1910; M.S., Northwestern U., 1932; Ph.D., U. of Chicago, 1939; m. Margaret Mallory, Apr. 21, 1910; children—Rebecca Jane, Ramira. Began as teacher Fox River Acad., Sheridan, Ill., 1910; prin. Adelphian Acad., Holly, Mich., 1913-18; dir. College Adventista, São Paulo, Brazil, 1918-28; pres. Broadview Coll., La Grange, Ill., 1928-34, pres. Emmanuel Missionary Coll., Berrien Springs, Mich., 1934-37; dean Washington Missionary Coll., Takoma Park, D.C., 1939-40; dir. Colegio Adventista del, Argentina, 1940-44. Dir. Instituto Adventista del Uruguay, 1944-45; dir. Colegio Unión, Peru, 1945-46; pres. Madison Coll., Madison College, Tenn., 1946-48; chmn. div. edn. and psychology, So. Missionary Coll., 1948-55; psychologist Wash. Sanitarium, 1955-56, Miller Med. Clinic, Pomona, Cal., from 1956. Certified psychologist Cal. Mem. Am., Western, So. Cal. psychol. assns., Soc. Projective Techniques, Rorschach Inst. Seventh Day Adventist. Home: Loma Linda, Cal. †

STEERE, LORA WOODHEAD, sculptor; b. Los Angeles, Calif., May 13, 1888; d. Charles Burton and Ida Eugenia (Gard) Woodhead; B.Sc. Stanford U., 1911; M.A., George Washington U., 1927; studied art Schule Reiman, Berlin, 1912-13, Boston Museum Sch. of Art, 1914, Calif. Sch. of Fine Arts, 1918; m. Thomas I. Steere, Apr. 25, 1914; children—Florence Virginia (Mrs. James R. Russell), Charles Warren (deceased), John Edward, James Henry. Contributed statue for Belgium relief 1918. Works include statues and bronze and marble portrait busts of famous Americans. Mem. bd. trustees Idyllwild Arts Found. and donor of Lora Steere Sculpture Studio for the school. Prepared sci. illustrations for Smithsonian publs. on cephalods by Dr. Stillman Berry. Mem. Pi Beta Phi. Republican. Club: Entres Noris. Home: Hollywood, Calif. †

STEESE, EDWARD, architect; b. Scarsdale, N.Y., Oct. 2, 1902; s. Edwin Sturtevant and Maud (Heaton) S.; A.B. (Latin salutatorian), Princeton, 1924, M.F.A. in Architecture, 1927. Instr. art dept. Princeton, 1924-25; chief designer Carrere & Hastings, N.Y.C., 1927-30; partner Noyes & Steese, N.Y.C., 1930-33; pvt. practice, N.Y.C. and Scarsdale, 1933-81; landscape and portrait artist, working oils and charcoal. Mem. constrn. div. WPB, 1942-43; chmn. vol. services com. Artists For Victory, 1944-46; founder, chmn. com. hist. architecture Greater N.Y., Muncipal Art Soc., 1951-56, hon. mem., 1964. Mem. Soc. Archtl. Historians, Nat. Trust Hist. Preservation, Poetry Soc. Am., Poetry Soc. Eng., S.R., AIA (emeritus), Phi Beta Kappa. Clubs: Univ., Coffee House, Century Association (archivist N.Y.C. 1962-72); Metropolitan (Washington). Author: Storm in Harvest and Other Poems, 1923; Spring Night, 1927; Twelve Versicles, 1937; Ephemerae, 1951; First Snow, 1954. Editor: A Princeton Anthology 1925, 1925; Poems of Neilson Abeel, 1951. Compiler, editor: Index of Historic Architecture, 2 edits. Home: Scarsdale, N.Y. Died Aug. 8, 1981.

STEEVES, HARRISON ROSS, educator; b. N.Y.C., Apr. 8, 1881; s. John Francis and Imogene (Upson) S.; A.B., Columbia, 1903, A.M., 1904, Ph.D., 1913, Litt.D., 1972; m. Jessie Hurd, June 16, 1906 (div. 1947); children—Imogene Hurd, Harrison Ross; m. 2d, Edna R. Leake, Jan. 28, 1947. Asst. and instr. English, Columbia, 1905-13, asst. prof., 1913-19, assoc. prof., 1919-26; prof. English, 1926-49, then emeritus. Mem. Nat. Conf. on Uniform Entrance Requirements in English (chmn. 1925-31); pres. Coll. Conf. on English of Central Atlantic States, 1919- 20. Mem. Phi Beta Kappa, Theta Delta Chi. Author: Learned Societies and English Scholarship, 1913; The Teaching of Literature (with C.C. Fries, J.H. Hanford), 1926; Literary Aims and Art, 1927; Good Night, Sheriff (fiction), 1941; Before Jane Austen, 1965. Co-author: A College Program in Action 1946. Editor: Representative Essays in Modern Thought (with F.H. Ristine), 1913; Selected Poems of Wordsworth, 1922; Three Eighteenth Century Romances, 1931; Plays from the Modern Theatre, 1931; Anatole France's Penguin Island, 1933; (with Edna L. Steeves) Wild Sports in the Far West (Friedrich Gerstäcker), 1968. Translator: Maurice Donnay's Lovers, 1931. Contbr. articles on edn., lit. to newspapers, mags., scholarly publs. Home: Kingston, R.I. Dec. Aug. 1, 1981.

STEIN, EMANUEL, educator, labor arbitrator; b. N.Y.C., Oct. 9, 1908; s. Jacob and Yetta (Liebreich) S.; B.S., N.Y. U., 1928, A.M., 1930, Ph.D., 1933; m. Florence S. Gordon, Dec. 23, 1934; children—Barbara Judith, Kenneth Douglas. Teaching fellow econs. N.Y. U., 1930-31, instr., 1931-38, asst. prof., 1938-43, asso. prof., 1943-46, prof., 1946-74, head dept. econ., 1955-67, acting dir. Grad. Div. for Tng. in Pub. Service, 1942-46; acting chmn. dept. econs. Washington Sq. Coll., 1946-51, chmn., 1951-67; chmn. Social Sci. Group Grad. Sch. Arts and Science; exec. dir. N.Y. U. Inst. Labor and Social Security, 1948-62, prof. humanities and social sci., 1967-74, emeritus prof., 1974-85; lectr. in pub. adminstrn. and bus. adminstrn., 1974-85. Pub. mem. Regional War Labor Board II, 1942-45, N.Y. Regional W.S.B., 1951-52; mem. Panel Pub. Relations Employment Bd., N.Y. State, Office of Collective Bargaining, N.Y.C. Bd. overseers Jewish Theol. Sem. Am. Mem. Arbitration Assn. (mem. panel), N.Y. State Bd. Mediation, N.J. Bd. Mediation, Nat. Acad. Arbitrators, Fed., Mediation and Conciliation Service, Indsl. Relation Research Assn., Met. Econ. Assn. (pres. 1960-61), Phi Beta Kappa. Author books in field. Editor: (with Carl Raushenbush) Labor Cases and Materials, 1941. Editor Proceedings of N.Y. Univ. Annual Conf. on Labor, 1948-62; bd. editors Labor History. Home: Long Beach, N.Y. Died Jan. 26, 1985.

STEIN, JOSEPH SIGMUND, jeweler, perfumer; b. Chgo., Mar. 31, 1890; s. Sigmund and Bella (Adler) S.; student pub. schs., Chgo.; m. Rita Senger, Mar. 1, 1920; 1 son, Tom. Began as stockboy Rosenwald & Well, wholesale clothier; began jeweler's career, 1907; v.p. Stein & Ellbogen Co. from 1920; pres. Lucien Lelong, Inc. from 1928; Jewish religion. Home: Chicago, Ill. †

STEINBACH, HENRY BURR, ednl. adminstr., biologist; b. Dexter, Mich, Oct.7, 1905; s. Henry August and Mary (Laney) S.; m. Eleanor Parsons, June 9, 1934; children—Alan Burr, Mary Parsons, Joseph Henry, James Burr. A.B., U. Mich., 1928; A.M., Brown U., 1930; Ph.D., U. Pa., 1933. Demonstrator physiol. and bio-chemistry Brown U., Providence, 1928-30; instr. zoology U. Pa., 1930-33; instr. zoology U. Minn., Mpls., 1935-37, asst. prof., 1937-38, prof., 1947-57; asst. prof. zoology Columbia, N.Y.C., 1938-42; asso. prof. zoology Wash. U., 1942-46, prof., 1946-47; prof., chmn. dept. zoology U. Chgo., 1957-68; dean Grad. Sch. Woods Hole Oceanographic Inst., 1968-73; cons. MP&OM Program; sci. dir. Harbor Br. Found. Lab., 1973; pres. Oceanic Inst., Makapuu Point, Waimanalo, Hawaii, 1974-76, pres. emeritus, 1976-81; asst. dir. NSF, 1952-53; chmn. div. biology and agr. NRC, 1958-62; pres., dir. Marine Biol. Lab., 1966-70. Contbr. articles to profl. jours. NRC fellow U. Chgo. and U. Rochester med. schs., 1933-35; Guggenheim fellow, 1955-56. Fellow AAAS (dir. 1964-69); mem. Am. Soc. Zoologists (pres. 1957), Soc. Gen. Physiologists (pres. 1953), Am. Physiol. Soc., Sigma Xi. Clubs: Mason. (Washington), Cosmos (Washington). Home: Woods Hole, Mass. Died Dec. 21, 1981.

STEINBERG, MARTIN REMEZ, physician, hosp. adminstr.; b. Russia, June 5, 1904; came to U.S., 1907, naturalized, 1914; s. Harry and Rose (Remez) S.; m. Cecily J. Kaplan, June 30, 1931; children—Deborah, Howard. M.Med. Sci., U. Pa., 1931; M.D., Temple U., 1927. Diplomate: Am. Bd. Otolaryngology. Intern Mt. Sinai Hosp., Phila., 1928-29; resident Grad. Hosp. U. Pa., 1929-31; pvt. practice, Phila., 1929-42; asst. prof. U. Pa. Grad. Med. Sch., 1932-43; chmn. med. adv. bd. Sidney-Hillman Clinic, from 1953; dir. Mt. Sinai Hosp., N.Y.C., from 1948; prof., chmn. dept. adminstrv. medicine Mt. Sinai Sch. Medicine; also lectr. Sch. Pub. Health, Columbia.; Mem. N.Y. State Hosp. Rev. and Planning Council. Served to lt. col. M.C. AUS, 1942-46. Fellow Am. Acad. Otorhinolaryngology, N.Y. Acad. Medicine, Am. Coll. Hosp. Adminstrs.; mem. Greater N.Y. Hosp Assn. (bd. govs., past pres.), Hosp. Assn. N.Y. State (trustee pres.), Am. Hosp. Assn. (trustee). Home: Philadelphia, PA.

STELOFF, FRANCES, book dealer; b. Saratoga Springs, N.Y., Dec. 31, 1887; d. Simon and Tobe (Metzner) Steloff; student Phillips Brooks Sch., Roxbury, Mass., 1900-02; m. David Moss, June 19, 1923. With book dept. Loeser's Dept. Store, N.Y.C., 1907-08; with Brentano's N.Y.C., 1916-19, charge drama dept., 1917-19; founder, 1920, from propr. Gotham Book Mart, N.Y.C. Recipient Distinguished Service to Arts award Nat. Inst. Arts and Letters, 1965. Mem. James Joyce Soc. (treas.).

STEMPEL, JOHN EMMERT, journalist, ret. educator, b. Bloomington, Ind., May 6, 1903; s. Guido Hermann and Myrtle (Emmert) S.; A.B., Ind. U., 1923, postgrad. 1926-27; M.S. in Journalism, Columbia, 1928; m. Mary Roberts Farmer, Aug. 30, 1928 (dec. Dec. 1981); children—John Dallas, Thomas Ritter. Reporter on Bloomington Evening World, 1917-19; instr. journalism and director publicity Lafayette Coll., Easton, Pa., 1923-26; part time instr. in journalism, Ind. U., Bloomington, 1926-27, prof. journalism, chmn. dept., 1938-68, prof. emeritus, 1968-82; asso. editor Bloomington Star, 1926-27; news editor Columbia Univ. Alumni News, 1927-30; staff New York Sun, 1929-36; news and mng. editor Easton (Pa.) Express, 1936-38; ednl. adviser Def. Info. Sch., Ft. Benjamin Harrison, 1968-69. Past chmn. United Episcopal Charities Diocese Indpls.; past chmn. Ind. Conf. ARC. Named Newspaperman of Yr., Indpls. Press Club, 1968; recipient Distinguished Alumnus award Columbia Sch. Journalism, 1963, Elihu Stout Plaque for distinction in journalism, Vincennes U., 1970, Distinguished alumni award Ind. U., 1972; named to Ind. Journalism Hall Fame, 1970. Mem. Assn. Edn. Journalism, Internat. Typographical Union, Greater Bloomington C. of C. (exec. v.p. 1976, pres.'s award 1977), Phi Kappa Psi, Sigma Delta Chi (past nat. pres. Wells Meml. Key 1936), Mason. Democrat. Episcopalian. Clubs: Rotary (past dist. gov.); Indpls. Press; Univ. (Ind. U.). Author textbooks. Contbr. to journalism publs. Home: Bloomington, Ind. Died Jan. 21, 1982.

STENSETH, MARTINUS, air officer; b. Heiberg, Minn., June 11, 1890; commd. 1st lt. Air Service, Regular Army, July 1920, and advanced through the grades to brig. gen., Apr. 1943; became comdg. officer, 2d Observation Squadron, Nichols Field, Philippine Island, July 1934; comdg. officer, Air Corps Primary Flying Sch. Detachment, Randolph Field, Tex., Apr. 1936, and later commanded the 52d Sch. Squadron; became asst. mil. attaché to Latvia, Estonia, Lithuania, Norway, May 1940, returned to U.S. Sept. 1940; post administrative inspector, Moffett Field, Calif., 1940-41; became base comdg. officer, Air Corps Gunnery Sch., Las Vegas, Nev., May 1941-June 1943; organized and comd. 36th and 82d Flying Training Wings, June 1943-Apr. 1945; comd. American troops, Iceland, May-Dec. 1945; returned to U.S. Dec. 1945. Awarded Distinguished Service Cross, Silver Star, Legion of Merit.†

STEPHENS, WILLIAM EDWARDS, educator, physicist; b. St. Louis, May 29, 1912 s. Eugene and Marie P. (Gelwicks) S.; A.B., Washington U., 1932, M.S., 1934; Ph.D., Calif. Inst. Tech., 1938; m. Helen Elizabeth Burnite, Oct. 27, 1942; children—Richard Burnite, William Massie. Westinghouse Research fellow, East Pittsburgh, 1938-40; lectr. physics U. Pitts., 1938-39; instr. Stanford U., 1940-41; instr. U. Pa., Phila., 1941-42, asst. prof., 1942-46, assoc. prof., 1946-48, prof., 1948-80, chmn. dept. physics, 1955-56, 63-68, dean Coll. Arts and Scis., 1968-74. Vis. prof. U. Zurich, 1957, 69; sci. investigator NDRC, 1942-46; vis. fellow Australian Nat. U., 1974, Princeton U., 1975. Fellow Am. Phys. Soc.; mem. AAUP, AAAS, Am. Inst. Physics, Phi Beta Kappa, Sigma Xi. Author: (With G.P. Harnwell) Atomic Physics, 1955. Editor: Nuclear Fission and Atomic Energy, 1950. Home: Philadelphia, Pa. Dec. July 16, 1980. Interned King of Prussia, Pa.

STEPHENSON, FRANCIS MARION, newspaperman; b. Chicago Heights, Ill., Jan. 2, 1899; s. David Thomas and Alma (Carpenter) S.; student Northwestern U., 1915-16; A.B., DePauw U., 1919; m. Treva Monschien, July 2, 1938; 1 child, Nancy Jane; 1 step-dau., Marcia. On editorial staff Indianapolis Star, 1919-20, Washington Herald, 1920-22; with Washington bureau, Associated Press, 1922-36, chief Senate corr., 1928-32, White House corr., 1933-36; Chicago Daily Times, 1938-39; N.Y. Herald-Tribune, 1939-48; N.Y. Daily News, from 1948. Pres. White House corr., 1934, 56-57. Mem. Delta Upsilon, Sigma Delta Chi. Methodist. Club: Nat. Press. Home: Manassas, Va. Dec. Sept. 8, 1981.

STEPHENSON, ROY L., judge; b. Spirit Lake, Iowa, Mar. 14, 1917; (m); children—Betty Jean, Douglas Lane, Randall. A.B., State U. Iowa, 1938, J.D., 1940. Bar: Iowa bar 1940. Practiced in, Des Moines; mem. firm Fountain, Bridges, Lundy & Stephenson; U.S. atty. for So. Iowa, 1953-60, U.S. dist. judge, So. Iowa, 1960-71, chief judge, 1962-71; judge U.S. Court of Appeals (8th Circuit), from 1971. Chmn. Polk County Republican Central Com., 1951-53. Served to capt. AUS, 1941-46, ETO; brig. gen. ret. Iowa N.G. Decorated Silver Star, Bronze Star. Mem. Am., Iowa, Polk County bar assns., Order of Coif, Gamma Eta Gamma. Clubs: Masons, Shriners, Sertoma. Home: Des Moines, IA. *

STERLING, JOHN EWART WALLACE, university chancellor; b. Linwood, Ont., Can., Aug. 6, 1906; came to U.S.,, naturalized, 1947; s. William Sterling and Annie (Wallace) S.; m. Anna Marie Shaver, Aug. 7, 1930; children—William W., Susan Hardy (Mrs. Bernard Monjauze), Judith Robinson (Mrs. Frank Morse). B.A., U. Toronto, 1927; M.A., U. Alta., 1930; Ph.D., Stanford U., 1938; LL.D., Pomona Coll., Occidental Coll., 1949, U. San Francisco, U. Toronto, 1950, U. B.C., Northwestern U., U. Calif., 1958, U. Denver, Loyola U., McGill U., 1961, Columbia U., 1962, McMaster U., 1966, Harvard U., 1968, U. Alta., 1970; D.C.L., Durham U., England, 1953; Litt.D., U. Caen, France, 1957, U. So. Calif., 1960; L.H.D., St. Mary's Coll., 1962, Santa Clara U., 1963, Mills Coll., 1967, U. Utah, 1968. Lectr. history Regina (Sask., Can.) Coll., 1927-28; asst. in history, dir. phys. edn. U. Alta., 1928-30; mem. research staff Hoover War Library, Stanford U., 1932-37, instr. history, 1935-37; asst. prof. history Calif. Inst. Tech., 1937-40, asso. prof., 1940-42, prof. history, 1942-45, Edward S. Harkness prof. of history and govt., exec. com., 1945-48, chmn. faculty, 1944-46; news analyst CBS, 1942-48; dir. Huntington Library, 1948-49; pres. Stanford U., 1949-68, lifetime chancellor, 1968; past dir. Fireman's Fund Am. Ins. Cos., Kaiser Aluminum & Chem. Corp., Shell Oil Co., Tridair Industries, Dean Witter & Co.; Civilian faculty Nat. War Coll., 1947, bd. cons., 1948-52; bd. visitors U.S. Naval Acad., 1956-58, Tulane U., 1960-74; mem. nat. adv. council Health Research Facilities, HEW, 1956-57. Editor: (with H.H. Fisher, X.J. Eudin) Features and Figures of the Past (V.I. Gurko), 1939. Chmn. Commn. Presdl. Scholars, 1965-68; adv. bd. Office Naval Research, 1953-56; chmn Am. Revolution Bicentennial Commn., 1969-70; mem. Ford Internat. Fellowship Bd., 1960, Can.-Am. Com., 1957-74, Am. adv. com. Ditchley Found., Eng., 1962-76; mem. adv. com. fgn. relations U.S. Dept. State, 1965-68; bd. dirs. Council Fin. Aid to Edn., 1967-70; mem. Brit.-N.Am. Com., 1969-74. Decorated knight comdr. Order Brit. Empire, 1976; comdr.'s cross Order Merit Fed. Republic Germany; chevalier Legion d'Honneur France; 2d degree Imperial Order Rising Sun Japan; Grand Gold Badge of Honor for Merits Republic of Austria; Herbert Hoover medal Stanford Alumni Assn., 1964; Clark Kerr award U. Calif., Berkeley, 1969; Uncommon Man award Stanford Assos., 1978; fellow Social Sci. Research Council, 1939-40. Fellow Am. Geog. Soc.; mem. Council on Fgn. Relations, Western Coll. Assn. (pres. 1953), Am., Pacific Coast hist. assns., Assn. Am. Univs. (pres. 1962-64). Clubs: Commonwealth (Palo Alto, San Francisco, N.Y.C., Los Angeles), Bohemian (Palo Alto, San Francisco, N.Y.C., Los Angeles), California (Palo Alto, San Francisco, N.Y.C., Los Angeles), Burlingame Country (Palo Alto, San Francisco, N.Y.C., Los Angeles), Pacific-Union (Palo Alto, San Francisco, N.Y.C., Los Angeles), University (Palo Alto, San Francisco, N.Y.C., Los Angeles) (hon.). Home: Woodside, Calif. Died July 1, 1985.

STERLING, PHILIP, lawyer; b. Phila., 1887; A.B., LL.B., U. Pa. Admitted to Pa. bar, 1910; partner firm Mancill, Sterling, Magaziner & Seamans, Phila. Chmn. adv. com. children and youth Pa. Dept. Welfare, 1961. Mem. Pa. Legislature, 1918-34. Mem. Am., Pa., Phila. (bd. govs.) bar assns., Lawyers Club Phila. Address: Philadelphia, Pa. †

STERN, CURT, zoologist; b. Hamburg, Germany, Aug. 30, 1902; s. Barned S. and Anna (Liebrecht) S.; Ph.D., University of Berlin, Germany, 1923; D.Sc., MacGill, 1958; married Evelyn Sommerfield, Oct. 29, 1931; children—Hildegard, Holly Elisabeth, Barbara Ellen. Came to U.S., 1933, naturalized, 1939. Investigator, Kaiser Wilhelm Inst., 1923-33; fellow Internat. Zin. Bd., 1924-26; privatdozent, U. of Berlin, 1928-33; fellow Rockefeller Foundation, 1932-33; research associate in zoology, U. of Rochester, 1933-35, asst. prof., 1935-37, asso. prof., 1937-41, prof., chmn., dept. zoology, 1941-47; chmn. dir. biol. sciences 1941-47, prof. exptl. zoology; prof. zoology, U. Cal., Berkeley, 1947-81, prof. genetics, 1958-81; vis. prof. Western Res. U., 1932; vis. lectr. Columbia U., 1944. Mem. adv. com. biology and medicine AEC, 1950-55. Fellow A.A.A.S.; mem. Am. Genetic Soc. (pres. 1950), Am. Soc. Human Genetics (president, 1957), Am. Philos. Soc., Nat. Acad. Scis., American Academy of Arts and Sciences, Am. Soc. Zoologists, Am. Society Naturalists. Soc. Growth and Development, Sigma Xi. Author: Multiple Allelie, 1930; Faktorenkoppelung u. Faktorenaustausch, 1933; Principles of Human Genetics, 1949. Editor. Genetics, 1947-51. Mem. editorial bd. Advances in Genetics. Contbr. articles on genetics to sci. publs. Home: Orinda, Calif. Died Oct. 24, 1981.

STERN, MARTIN, advt. agy. exec.; b. Munich, Germany, Sept. 17, 1924; came to U.S., 1938, naturalized, 1943; s. Alfred and Elly (Lambert) S.; m. Charlotte Brown, July 1, 1950 (div. July 1971); children—Alan, Joni, Suzi. B.A., N.Y. U., 1948, M.B.A., 1951. Mgr. research dept. Biow Co., N.Y.C., 1949-56; dir. research J. Walter Thompson Co., N.Y.C., 1956-68; asst. to pres., sr. v.p., sales dir. Wells, Rich, Greene, Inc., N.Y.C., 1968-74, exec. v.p., dir. info. planning services, from 1974; instr. mktg. and advt. Queens Coll., from 1967. Served with AUS, 1943-46. Home: New York, N.Y. Deceased.

STERN, MAX, business exec; b. Fulda, Germany, Oct. 22, 1898; s. Emanuel and Caroline (Mainzer) S.; student Gymnasium; m. Ghity Amiel, 1950—; children—Stanley, Leonard, Gloria. Came to U.S., 1926, naturalized, 1934. Pres. Hartz Mountain Products Corp., N.Y.C., 1930-82; with Am. Bird Food Corp., Chgo., 1951, pres., 1953-82; pres. 34 Pet, Inc. Vice chmn. Yeshiva U.; v.p. Jewish Center, N.Y.C.; chmn. Manhattan Day Sch.; dir. Am. Fund Israel Instns., and several other charitable orgns.

Founder Stern Coll. for Women, N.Y.C. Home: New York, N.Y. Died May 20, 1982.

STERN, PHILIP VAN DOREN, author; b. Wyalusing, Pa., Sept. 10, 1900; s. I.U. and Ann (Van Doren) S.; m. Lillian Diamond, 1928; 1 dau., Marguerite Louise Robinson. Litt.B., Rutgers U., 1924, Litt.D., 1940; Litt.D., Lincoln (Ill.) Coll., 1958. Engaged in advt. work, 1924-33; connected with Alfred A. Knopf, Simon & Schuster, Pocket Books, Inc., 1933-54; gen. mgr. Edits. for Armed Services, 1943-45. Author: An Introduction to Typography, 1932, (with Herbert Asbury) The Breathless Moment, 1935, The Selected Works of Thomas DeQuincey, 1937, The Man Who Killed Lincoln, 1939, The Life and Writings of Abraham Lincoln, 1940, The Midnight Reader, 1942, The Drums of Morning, 1942, The Moonlight Traveler, 1943, The Greatest Gift, 1944, The Portable Library Poe, 1945, (with Bernard Smith) The Holiday Reader, 1947, Travelers in Time, 1947, Lola, 1949, Love is the One with Wings, 1951, Our Constitution, 953, A Pictorial History of the Automobile, 1953, The Assassination of President Lincoln and the Trial of the Conspirators, 1954, Tin Lizzie, the Story of the Fabulous Model T Ford, 1955, An End to Valor, the Last Days of the Civil War, 1958, Secret Missions of the Civil War, 1959, They Were There: The Civil War in Action as Seen by its Combat Artists, 1959, Prologue to Sumter, 1961, The Confederate Navy: a Pictorial History, 1962, Robert E. Lee, the Man and the Soldier, 1963, The Annotated Uncle Tom's Cabin, 1964, When The Guns Roared: World Aspects of the American Civil War, 1965, (with Lillian D. Stern) Beyond Paris: A Touring Guide to the French Provinces, 1967, Prehistoric Europe: from Stone Age Man to the Early Greeks, 1969, The Other Side of the Clock, 1969, The Annotated Walden, 1971, Henry David Thoreau, Writer and Rebel, 1972, Edgar Allan Poe, Visitor From The Night of Time, 1973, The Beginnings of Art, 1973, The Pocket Book of America, 1975; Contbr. (with Lillian D. Stern) articles to nat. mags. Guggenheim fellow for research, 1959-60. Address: Longboat Key, Fla. Died July 31, 1984.

STEUERMANN, CLARA, music librarian, archivist; b. Los Angeles, Feb. 10, 1922; d. Samuel and Sarah (Nathanson) Silvers; A.B., U. Calif., Los Angeles, 1943, M.A., 1944; M.L.S., Columbia U., 1964; piano studies with Jakob Gimpel and Edward Steuermann; m. Edward Steuermann, Nov. 11, 1949 (dec.); children—Rebecca, Rachel. Teaching asst. to Arnold Schoenberg, 1943-44: free lance music editor, N.Y.C., 1944-45; music editor Carl Fischer, Inc., 1945-47, Music Pubs. Holding Corp., N.Y.C., 1947-51; adminstrv. asst. Juilliard Sch. Music, Opera Theatre, 1951-56, New York Philharmonic Orch., 1965; asst. librarian Kingsborough Community Coll., Bklyn., summer 1965; cataloguer Juilliard Sch. Music Library, 1965-66; librarian Cleve. Inst. Music, 1966-75; archivist Arnold Schoenberg Inst., Los Angeles, 1975-82; co-dir. Music Library Inst., Kent State U., summer 1969, vis. prof. Sch. Library Sci., summer 1970; vis. instr. music dept. Claremont (Calif.) Grad. Sch., spring 1979; cons. State U. N.Y. Purchase Univ. Library, 1972-73, Curtis Inst. Music, Phila., 1973-74. Vice pres., bd. dirs. Cleve. Modern Dance Assn., 1969-74. MacDowell Colony fellow, summer 1973. Mem. Am. Fedn. Musicians (Local 802), Am. Musicol. Soc., Coll. Music Soc., Internat. Assn. Music Libraries, Music Library Assn. (chmn. Midwest Regional chpt. 1969-71, chmn. Music Librarians of Ohio 1971-72, chmn. MLA/NASM Joint Com. 1971-72, dir. 1972-74, pres. 1975-76, rep. Internat. Music Council, Toronto 1975, rep. Internat. Fedn. Library Assns. 1977, rep. Internat. Conf. on New Musical Notation, Belgium, 1974, chmn. Round Table for Music in Libraries, 1978-82), Soc. Am. Archivists, Internat. Soc. for Contemporary Music (dir. U.S. sect. 1960). Home: Los Angeles, Calif. Died Jan. 9, 1982.

STEVENS, ARCHIE MCDONALD, radio engr.; b. Glidden, Carroll Co., Ia., Sept. 22, 1887; s. Henry Mathew and Emma G. (Livingston) S.; A.B., Stanford, 1909; post-grad. work, Columbia; unmarried. Asst. engr. Federal Telegraph Co., Palo Alto, Calif., 1909-13, Universal Radio Syndicate, London, Eng., 1913-14; radio electrician Mare Island Navy Yard, 1915; inspection and constrn. San Diego and Pearl Harbor High Power Naval Radio stas.; expert radio aide at Cavite, 1917; trans. to Bur. Steam Engring., High Power Radio Div., 1918; consulting and research work, 1921-22; radio engr. and sec. Am. Radio News Corpn., 1922-24; with Internat. News Service from 1924. Lt. (s.g.) U.S.N.R.F., Mar. 1918; served at Bordeaux, France, as engr. and exec. officer Lafayette Radio Sta.; lt. comdr., May 1919. Decorated Officier de l'Instruction Publique (French), 1920. Asso. mem. Am. Inst. E.E.; mem. Am. Inst. Radio Engrs. Republican. Portestant. Club: Peninsula (Palo Alto). Author: Radio Simplified, 1922. Home: Palo Alto, Calif. †

STEVENS, ROBERT TEN BROECK, corporate executive; born Fanwood, N.J., July 31, 1899; s. John Peters and Edna (Ten Broeck) S.; grad. Phillips Andover, 1917; B.A., Yale, 1921; D.C.S., N.Y.U., 1950; L.H.D., Lafayette Coll., 1950; LL.D., Presbyn. Coll., 1938, Syracuse U., 1953. U. Kansas City, Mo., 1956; Dr. Textiles, Phila. Textile Inst., 1956; D.Sc., Norwich U., 1953; Dr. Textile Industries, Clemson Coll., 1951; Dr. Textile Sci., N.C. Coll., 1954; married Dorothy Goodwin Whitney, October 6, 1923; children—Robert Ten Broeck, Whitney, Joan Peters (dec.), William Gallon Thomas Estes. Entered employ of J. P. Stevens & Co., Inc., 1921, pres., 1929-42, chmn. bd., 1945-53, pres., 1955-83; chief exec. officer, chmn. exec. com., 1966-83; class B dir. Fed. Res. Bank of New York, 1934-42, Class C dir. and chmn., 1948-53; dir. General Electric Co., Morgan Guaranty Trust Co. New York; trustee Mut. Life Ins. Co. of N.Y.; Secretary of the Army, Dept. Defense, 1953-55. Served as 2d lt., F.A., World War I; col., Office of Q.M. Gen., World War II, Awarded Medal Legion of Merit, Distinguished Service Medal. Exceptional Civilian Service Medal. USAE Staff National Recovery Administration, 1933; head textile section, National Defense Advisory Commn., 1940; appointed district coordinator of defense contract service. Office Production Management for New York Area, Bd; attended Command and General Staff Sch., Ft. Leavenworth, Kan., 1941; assigned to Q.M. Corps, 1942, apptd. dep. dir. purchases, 1943-45. Mem. vis. com. Harvard Grad. Sch. Bus. Adminstrn. 1956-62; alumni fellow Yale Corporation, 1950-56. Member of the Business Council. Mem. Am. Textile Mfrs. Inst. Inc. (pres. 1963-64), Psi Upsilon. Wolf's Head Society. Clubs: Biltmore (North Carolina) Forest Country; Downtown Association, Links, Merchants, Union League, Yale (N.Y. City); 1925 F Street (Washington); Plainfield (N.J.) Country; Brook (N.Y.C.); Chevy Chase (Md.). Home: South Plainfield, N.J. Died Jan. 31, 1983.

STEVENS, SAMUEL STANCLIFT, lawyer; b. Indpls., Feb. 17, 1889; s. George G. and Julia M. (Stanclift) S.; grad. Phillips Acad., 1910; J.D., U. Cal., Hastings Coll. Law, 1913; m. Lois Voswinkel, Jan. 30, 1917; children—Samuel P., Mary (Mrs. Charles A. Wood, Jr.). Admitted to Cal. bar, 1913, practiced in San Francisco; asso. firm Heller, Ehrman, White & McAuliffe, 1913-22, mem. firm, from 1922. 2d lt. U.S. Army, World War I; AEF in France. Mem. San Francisco, Cal., Am. bar assns., Sigma Nu. Clubs: Bohemian, Cercle de L'Union, Family, Pacific-Union, Wine and Food Soc. (past chairman board governors) (San Francisco; California (Los Angeles); Chevaliers du Tastevin (Beverly Hills, Cal.). Home: Piedmont, CA. †

STEVENSON, EDNA BRADLEY, univ. prof.; b. Hebron, Neb., Feb. 8, 1887; d. Lewis Waller and Jane (Frederickson) Bradley; supervisor's certificate, Art Inst. of Chicago, 1907; student U. of Ill., summers 1904, 05, 06, Snow-Froelich Sch., 1921, student, Chautauqua, 1920; B.F.A. in Design, Oklahoma City U., 1929; student Bisttram Sch. of Art, Taos, N.M., 1932, 33, 34, Julien Acadamie, Paris, France, 1936, Florence, Italy, 1937, U. of Calif. at Los Angeles, 1949; m. James O. Stevenson, Mar. 18, 1909 (div. Oct. 1920); 1 dau., Dorothea Jane (wife of Richard Robbins Casady, M.D.). Head of art dept. Classen High Sch., Oklahoma City, 1920-43, Oklahoma City U. from 1943. Exhibited: Art Center, Y.M.-C.A., and Oklahoma City U., Oklahoma City; Harwood Gallery, Taos, N.M.; Santa Fe; Shawnee, Okla. Mem. Art League, Assn. Oklahoma Artists (past pres.), Coll. Art Assn., Western Arts, Delta Kappa Gamma, Kappa Pi, Nat. Honor Art Soc. Republican. Methodist. Clubs: Internat. Pilot; Art Renaissance (pres.). Home: Oklahoma City, Okla. †

STEVENSON, GEORGE HENRY, banking; b. Lincoln, Neb., Oct. 24, 1886; s. George Henry and Caroylin Bell (Blanchard) S.; ed. pub. schs.; m. Rachel Burbank, Sept. 12, 1911; children—George Henry, Eleanor, Elizabeth Ann. Began with First State Bank, Pleasant Dale, Neb., 1901, later with Stull Bros., bankers, Omaha, Neb.; mgr. Nat. Corn Expn., Columbus, O., 1910, Columbia, S.C., 1911; agrl. extension expert, U.S. Dept. Agr., 1915; pres. Federal Land Bank of Baltimore, Md., 1917-18; organizer, 1920, and since mgr. Md. Tobacco Growers' Assn.; with Federal Farm Loan Bur. and U.S. Treasury Dept., 1922-26; establishing system of rural credit banking for Govt. of Peru, 1927-28. Address: Lima, Peru. †

STEVENSON, HARVEY, architect; b. Croton-on-Hudson, N.Y., Nov. 29, 1894; A.B., Yale U., 1917; postgrad. France; m. Winifred K. Worcester; children—Eric, James. Pvt. archtl. practice, 1923-77; lectr. in humanities Stevens Inst. Tech. War effort including designer underground War Dept. Protected Command Post, Navy stas. and hdqrs., S. Atlantic; dir. mil. publs. Mediterranean. Trustee N.Y.C. Center Music and Drama. Served as 1st lt. F.A., A.E.F., World War I. Recipient various nat. prizes for design. Fellow AIA (pres. N.Y. chpt. 1941-42); mem. Fine Arts Fedn. (pres. 1950-53). Club: Century Assn. Designer East River Dr., Battery-Bklyn. Tunnel approaches, park sects., overpasses, also adminstrn. bldg. World's Fair, 1939. Home: Lyme, Conn. Died Sept. 19, 1984.

STEVENSON, JOHN, investment banker; b. Airdrie, Scotland, Apr. 10, 1905; s. Andrew Bonar and Agnes Cleland (Dalglish) S.; came to U.S. 1910, naturalized 1921; B.C.S., N.Y. U., 1928; m. Helen Espie, Oct. 9, 1934 (dec.); children—John E., Carol G.; m. Esther Anne Burke, Feb. 3, 1970. With N.Y. Stock Exchange, 1923-28, examiner stock list dept., 1927-28; lectr. N.Y. Inst. Finance, 1928-37; mgr. statis. dept. Kidder, Peabody & Co., N.Y.C., 1928-34; financial analyst Analytical Research Bur., Inc., N.Y.C., 1934-35; mgr. corporate finance dept. Salomon Bros. & Hutzler, N.Y.C., 1935-54, partner charge corporate finance dept., 1954-68; ltd. partner Salomon Bros., 1968-85; pub. Financial Analysts Jour., 1959-66. Recipient Madden Meml. award, 1964; named life mem. Nat. Trust for Scotland. Mem. Inst. Chartered Financial Analysts, N.Y. Soc. Security Analysts, N.Y. U. Finance Club, St. Andrews Soc., Albert Gallatin Assos. N.Y. U. (life), Beta Gamma Sigma, Delta Phi Epsilon. Conglist. Clubs: New York University, Downtown Athletic, University (N.Y.C.); Apawamis, Westchester Country (Rye, N.Y.). Home: Rye, N.Y. Dec. Apr. 28, 1985. Interned Valhalla, N.Y.

STEVENSON, JOSEPHINE REESE, univ. trustee; b. Chgo., Dec. 30, 1890; d. D. Joseph and Clara (Hopkins) Reese; student U. Ill.; B.S., U. Wis., 1913; m. John Alford Stevenson, Sept. 19, 1914; 1 son, John Reese. Mem. bd. Health and Welfare Council, 1953-56; bd. govs. Heart Assn. of Southeastern Pa., 1953-56; trustee Temple U., from 1950; mem. Commonwealth com. Reed Street Neighborhood House, Woman's Med. Coll. of Pa. Mem. Navy League (nat. dir. 1952-55), Soc. Colonial Dames Am., D.A.R., Alpha Phi. Clubs: Cosmopolitan, Acorn (Phila.). Home: Phila. †

STEVENSON, ROGER, ret. naval med. officer; b. Mansfield, Ark., June 2, 1918; s. Roger and Lula (Wills) S.; student Ark. State Tchrs. Coll., 1935-36, summer 1938, Hendrix Coll., 1936-38; B.S., U. Ark., 1940, M.D. (Buchanan award 1941), 1942; m. Patricia Ann Sullivan, Nov. 10, 1965; children by previous marriage—Roger, Nell Elizabeth, Karen Anne, Franklin Theodore. Intern, Santa Rosa Hosp., San Antonio, 1942-43; practice medicine specializing in gen. medicine and anesthesiology, Kerrville, Tex., 1946-52; preceptorship ophthalmology with Dr. K.W. Cosgrove, Little Rock, 1952-54; practice medicine specializing in ophthalmology, Kerrville, 1954-56; commd. lt. (j.g.) M.C., USN, 1942, advanced through grades to capt., 1960; chief eye, ear, nose and throat service U.S. Naval Hosp., Corpus Christi, Tex., 1956-60, U.S. Naval Hosp., Yokosuka, Japan, 1960-62; chief opthalmology service Naval Hosp., Chelsea, Mass., 1962-64, Naval Hosp., Bethesda, Md., 1964-68, dir. profl. div. Bur. Medicine and Surgery, Navy Dept., Washington, 1968-70; sr. med. officer U.S. Naval Acad., Annapolis, Md., 1970-74; adviser ophthalmology to surgeon gen. USN, 1964-74; dir. Dept. Def. med. exam. rev. bd. US Acad., Colo., 1974-78, ret., 1978. Mem. staff Peterson Meml. Hosp., Kerrville, 1949-56; clin. instr. ophthalmology U. Ark. Med. Sch., 1953-54. Decorated Commendation medal, 1945, 70; Meritorious Service medal, 1975; Joint Service medal, 1978. Diplomate Am. Bd. Ophthalmology. Fellow Soc. Eye Surgeons, Internat. Eye Found., A.C.S.; affiliate Royal Soc. Medicine; mem. Nat. Soc. Prevention Blindness, A.M.A. (vice chmn. sect. mil. medicine 1969-71, chmn. 1971-72), Am. Acad. Ophthalmology and Otolaryngology, Assn. Research Ophthalmology, Assn. Mil. Surgeons U.S., Soc. Mil. Ophthalmologists (pres. 1965-66), Res. Officers Assn., Am. Assn. Ophthalmology (contbr. material to corr. course), Phi Beta Pi. Roman Catholic. Contbr. articles to med. jours. Home: Portsmouth, R.I. Died May 6, 1981.

STEVENSON, RUSSELL ALGER, ret. dean sch. bus. adminstrn.; b. Muskegon, Mich., Oct. 31, 1890; s. Augustus Walter and Carlie (Gray) S.; B.A., Univ. of Mich., 1913, Ph.D., 1919; M.A., State U. of Ia., 1915; hon. LL.D., U. of Mich., 1941; m. Edna Kampenga, Jan. 1, 1914; children—Robert Edwin, Harold William. Instr. in economics, U. Of Mich., 1913-14; instr. in accounting, U. of Ia., 1914-16, asst. prof., 1916-17, asso. prof., 1917-19, prof., 1919-20; prof. accounting and head dept. of commerce, Coll. of Engring. and Commerce, U. of Cincinnati, 1920-26; dean Sch. of Business Administration, U. of Minn., 1926-44; dean Sch. Bus. Adminstrn. U. Mich., 1944-60, emeritus. Dir. Employment Stabilization Research Inst., 1931-44; consultant on bus. econ. Mich. Planning Commn., 1944-47; director Ann Arbor Bank, Lear, Incorporated. Member advisory panel, Committee to Study State Govt. Reorgn., Economic Progress Adv. Com.; pres. Mich. Council on Econ. Edn., from 1958; mem. pub. relations adv. com. Adv. Com. on Indsl. Expansion Research; adv. com. econ. progress Mich. Economic Development Commission. Member of the American Accounting Assn., American Assn. Collegiate Schs. of Bus. (past pres.), Am. Econ. Assn., Beta Gamma Sigma, Delta Sigma Pi, Beta Alpha Psi, Acacia, Phi Kappa Phi. Mason. Clubs: Economic of Detroit (member bd. dirs.); Newcomen Society. Author: Principles of Accounting (with William A. Paton), 1918; Problems and Exercises in Accounting (with same), 1918; Problems and Questions in Accounting (with R. Emmet Taylor), 1926; Accounting Principles, 1930; The Minnesota Unemployment Research Project, 1931. Advisory editor Accountant's Handbook, 1931. Editor: A Type Study of American Banking—Non-Metropolitan Banks in Minnesota, 1934; Balancing the Economic Controls (with Roland S. Vaile), 1935. Home: Ann Arbor, Mich. †

STEVENSON, WILLIAM EDWARDS, ambassador, lawyer, coll. pres.; b. Chgo., Oct. 25, 1900; s. J. Ross and Florence (Day) S.; A.B., Princeton, 1922; M.A. (Rhodes scholar), Balliol Coll. Oxford (Eng.) U., 1925; L.H.D., Case Inst. Tech., 1948, Alfred U., 1969; LL.D., Wooster Coll., 1948, Colo. Coll., 1950, Princeton, 1956, Fairleigh Dickinson U., 1956, Coe Coll., 1958; Oberlin Coll., 1960, San Carlos U., P.I., 1963; Litt.D., Rider Coll., 1974; m. Eleanor Bumstead, Jan. 9, 1926; children—Helen Day (Mrs. Robert B. Meyner), Priscilla (Mrs. Richard McM. Hunt). Admitted as barrister-at-law Inner Temple (Eng.). 1925; admitted to N.Y. bar, 1927; asst. U.S. atty. South Dist. N.Y., 1925-27; asso. with Davis, Polk, Wardwell, Gardiner & Reed, 1927, 29-31; founding partner Debevoise, Stevenson, Plimpton & Page, N.Y.C., 1931-46; pres.

Oberlin Coll., 1946-59; U.S. ambassador to Philippines, 1961-64; pres. Aspen Inst. Humanistic Studies, 1967-70. A.R.C. del. Gt. Britain, 1942, North Africa and Italy, 1942-44, vice chmn. bd. govs. nat. orgn., 1965-71; vice chmn. League Red Cross Socs. (Geneva), 1965-73; mem. Pres.'s Com. on Equality of Treatment and Opportunity in Armed Services, 1948-50; ednl. cons. Japan, India, Lebanon, Egypt for Dept. State, 1952-53; chmn. World Bank Econ. Devel. Commn., Tanganyika, 1959-60. Served with USMC, 1918. Decorated Bronze Star; U.S. AAU 440 yard champion, 1921, Brit. AAU champion, 1923; mem. Olympic Championship 1600 Meter Relay Team, 1924. Mem. Am. Acad. Arts and Scis., Phi Beta Kappa. Club: University (N.Y.C.). Address: Fort Myers, Fla. Died Apr. 2, 1985.

STEWARD, DONN HORATIO, artist, master printer; b. Moose Jaw, Sask., Can., Nov. 26, 1921; s. Roy Denver and Bessie Marie (Anderson) S. Student, Boone Jr. Coll., Iowa, 1939-40; B.A., U. Iowa, 1942, M.F.A., 1948; student (Fulbright scholar), Ecole des Beaux Arts, Paris, 1952-53. Instr. U. Iowa, 1948-54; asst. prof. Fla. State U, 1954-57; vis. lectr. Washington U., St. Louis, 1957-58; coordinator Douglas Aircraft, Calif., 1958-64; master printer Universal Ltd. Art Editions, N.Y.C., 1966-74; prin. Donn Steward, Master Printer and Pub., Halesite, N.Y., 1974—; printer-fellow Tamarind Lithography Workshop, Los Angeles, 1965-66; instr. Huntington Twp. (N.Y.) Art League, 1975—, Pratt Graphic Center, N.Y.C., 1981; vis. artist U. Iowa, summer, 1978. Master printer for first etchings, Jasper Johns, 1967-68, Lee Bonterou, 1968, Helen Frankenthaler, 1968—, Robert Motherwell, 1972, Marisol, Barnett Newman, Larry Rivers, Cy Twombley, 1968. Served to lt. (j.g.) USN, 1943-46. Home: Halesite, N.Y. Died May 27, 1985.

STEWART, CARLTON D., railway executive; b. Apollo, Pa., April 15, 1888; s. Charles L. and Jennie (Moore) S.; ed. Blairsville High Sch.; Pa. State Coll.; m. Ruth Pregitser, Feb. 27, 1914; children—Robert D., Carlton M. Machinist Westinghouse Air Brake Co., 1905-08, engring. dept., 1910, mech. expert Calif. office, San Francisco, 1913-17, dist. engr., 1917-25; v.p. and dir. Westinghouse Pacific Coast Brake Co., 1922-35; chief engr. Westinghouse Air Brake, Wilmerding, Pa., 1935-44, dir. engring., 1944, vice pres., 1945. Fellow Am. Soc. M.E.; mem. Soc. Automotive Engrs., Engrs. Soc. Western Pa., Air Brake Assn.; Newcomen Soc. Republican. Presbyterian. Clubs: Duquesne, Pittsburgh Railway, Pittsburgh Athletic, Long Vue Country. Contbr. tech. articles to ry. jours. Home: Pittsburgh, Pa. †

STEWART, DAVID WALLACE, lawyer; b. New Concord, O., Jan. 22, 1887; s. Wilson and Mary Ann (Wallace) S.; A.B., Geneva Coll., Pa., 1911; J.D., U. Chgo., 1917; m. Helen E. Struble, Sept. 15, 1920; 1 son, Robert Bruce. Admitted to Ia. bar, 1917, practice law, Sioux City from 1917; mem. Stewart, Hatfield & Klass. Apptd. U.S. senator, 1926 to fill vacancy, served to 1927. Trustee Sioux City YMCA, Sioux City Boy Scouts Am.; pres. trustees Morningside Coll. Served with USMC, World War. Mem. Am. Ia., Woodbury County bar assns., Sioux City C. of C. (pres. 1925-26), Am. Legion. Republican. Presbyn. Mason. Home: Sioux City, IA. †

STEWART, GEORGE FRANKLIN, educator; b. Mesa, Ariz., Feb. 22, 1908; s. Mahonri Alma and Anna (Metz) S.; m. Grace Sledge, June 19, 1933; children—Kent, Carol, Jane. B.S., U. Chgo., 1930; Ph.D., Cornell U., 1933. Research chemist Ocoma Food, Inc., Omaha, 1933-38; asso. prof. Iowa State Coll., 1938-42, prof., 1942-51; asso. dir. Agrl. Expt. Sta., 1948-51; chmn. dept. poultry husbandry U. Calif. at Davis, 1951-58; exec. editor Inst. Food Technologists, 1958-66, prof. food sci. and tech., 1959—, chmn. food sci., tech., 1959-64, dir. food protection and toxicology center, 1965-70, chmn. agr. toxicology and residue research lab., 1966-68, chmn. dept. environ. toxicology, 1968-70. Co-editor: also Monographs in Food Science and Technology. Advances in Food Research. Past pres. Internat. Union Food Sci. and Tech. Recipient Christie Research award.; Fulbright research scholar Australia, 1957. Fellow AAAS, Poultry Sci. Assn., Inst. Food Technologists (pres. 1967-68, Internat. and Appert awards), Inst. Food Sci. and Tech. (hon.; Eng.); mem. Am. Inst. Nutrition, Sigma Xi, Phi Kappa Phi. Home: Davis, Calif. Died Mar. 18, 1982.

STEWART, JAMES KISTLER, clergyman;' b. New Kensington, Pa., Aug. 19, 1888; s. Reid T. and Anna M. (Kistler) S.; A.B., Westminster Coll., 1912, D.D., 1937; B.D., Pittsburgh-Xenia Theol. Sem., 1919; m. Margaret M. Carnes, Aug. 21, 1917; children—James S., Peggy (Mrs. John E. Anderson), Mary Arden (Mrs. George B. Jackson), Beck (dec.), John R. Ordained to ministry United Presbyn. Ch., 1919; pastor Herron Hill U.P. Ch., Pitts., 1918-21, Second U.P. Ch., 1921-26, Beverly-Vista U.P. Ch., Beverly Hills, Cal., from 1927; instr. pub. speech Pittsburgh-Xenia Theol. Sem., 1917-26; moderator Cal. U.P. Synod, 1935-36; v. moderator U.P., Gen. Assembly, 1952-53. Mem. Denominational Bd. Adminstrn., com. on union U.P. Ch. Pres. Beverly Hills Library Bd. Club: Rotary. Home: Beverly Hills, Calif. †

STEWART, JARVIS ANTHONY, educator, artist; b. Maryville, Mo., Dec. 28, 1914; s. John Andrew and Ella Joanna (Pryor) S.; student St. Joseph (Mo.) Jr. Coll., 1933, Escuela de Bellas Artes, San Miguel, 1941; B.F.A., Phillips U., 1942; M.A., Ohio State U., 1947, Ph.D. 1951; m. Madge Ella Smith, Jan. 24, 1942; children—Deborah Susan, Peter Michael Anthony (dec.). Mural painter Am. Hotels Corps., 1939; instr. Phillips U., 1942; chmn. dept. fine arts Ohio Wesleyan U., Delaware, 1953-73, Packard prof. fine arts, 1953-81; exhbns. include Art USA, 1958, Momentum, 1951: one-man show Columbus (Ohio) Gallery, Bryson Gallery; represented permanent collections Columbus Gallery Fine Arts, Otterbein Coll. Recipient Welch Teaching award, 1974. Great Lakes Colls. Assn. research grantee. Mem. Am. Studies Assn., Okla., N.W. Mo. art assns., Columbus (pres. 1951), Enid Art League, Delta Phi Delta. Home: Delaware, Ohio. Dec. Apr. 23, 1981.

STEWART, JOHN GEORGE, congressman; b. Wilmington, Del., June 2, 1890; s. Hamilton and Marie (Schaefer) S.; student U. of Del., 1907-11; m. Helen Taber Ferry, of Boston, Oct. 7, 1911 (died Jan. 1, 1936); children—Frank Hamilton, Irene Taber. Mem. Del. State Athletic Commn., 1931-35, Temporary Emergency Relief Commn., Del., Jan. 1-Apr. 30, 1934; mem. 74th Congress (1935-37), Del. at large. Pres. Stewart & Donohue, Inc., landscape constructionists, Wilmington. Republican. Episcopalian. Mason. Clubs: Wilmington Kennel, Country (Wilmington); Concord Country (Concordville, Pa.). Home: Wilmington, Del. †

STEWART, MURRAY EDGAR, b. Brandon, Man., Can., Sept. 30, 1926; s. William Murray and Mary Elizabeth (Williams) S.; m. Muriel Allison Young, Dec. 28, 1949; children: Janet, Arden, Joan, Karen. B.Sc. cum laude, U. Alta., Can., 1947; M. Com., U. Toronto, Ont., Can., 1949. Engr. Northwestern Utilities, Ltd., Edmonton, Alta., 1949-56, gen. mgr., 1956-60, gen. mgr., v.p., 1960-65; pres., chief exec. officer, dir. Northwestern Utilities & Canadian Western Natural Gas Co., 1965-68, Gen. Waterworks Corp., 1968-70; sr. v.p. IU Internat. Corp., Phila., 1970-72; pres., chief exec. officer, dir. C. Brewer & Co. Ltd., Honolulu, 1972-75; exec. v.p. Alexander & Baldwin, Inc., Honolulu, 1975-78; exec. v.p., dir. Foothills Pipe Lines (Yukon) Ltd., Calgary, Alta., Can., from 1978. Clubs: Mayfair Golf and Country (Edmonton) (past pres.); Calgary Golf and Country (Calgary, Can.); Oahu Golf and Country (Honolulu), Waialae Country (Honolulu). Home: Calgary AB, Canada.

STEWART, ROBERT EDWIN, agricultural engineer, emeritus educator; b. Carthage, Mo., May 4, 1915; s. Harry Adrian and Mary Evaline (Bridges) S.; m. Bonnie Ruth Nance, July 3, 1942; 1 dau., Lillian Moore. B.S., U. Mo., 1948, M.S., 1950, Ph.D., 1953. Registered profl. engr., Mo., Tex. Instr., then prof. agrl. engring. U. Mo., 1948-61; prof. agrl. engring., chmn. dept. Ohio State U., 1961-68; Distinguished prof. agrl. engring. Tex. A. and M. U., 1968-80, emeritus, from 1980; Mem. agrl. bd. NRC-Nat. Acad. Scis., from 1962; chmn. Engrs. Joint Council Com. on Engring. Interactions with Biology and Medicine. Author: History of the American Society of Agricultural Engineers; Contbr. to: profl. jours. Ency. Britannica. Served with USAAF, 1941-45. Recipient award for distinguished service in engring. U. Mo., 1970. Fellow AAAS, Am. Soc. Agrl. Engrs. (pres. 1970-71, Cyrus Hall McCormick gold medal 1983); mem. Nat. Soc. Profl. Engrs., Nat. Acad. Engring., N.Y. Acad. Sci., Sigma Xi, Gamma Sigma Delta (award outstanding service to agr. 1959), Tau Beta Pi, Gamma Alpha, Alpha Epsilon. Episcopalian. Club: Briarcrest Country (Bryan, Tex.). Home: Bryan, Tex.

STICHNOTH, DEAN ROGER, lawyer, utilities executive; b. Benton County, Ind., Feb. 21, 1926; s. August and Lulu M. (Laudenslager) S.; m. Emilie Fredericks, Oct. 28, 1950; children: Frederick J., H. Jane, Timothy J., Todd J., James M., John A. B.S., State U. Iowa, 1948, J.D., 1950; postgrad., U. Mich., 1958. With Iowa-Ill. Gas and Electric Co., 1950-84, sec., asst. treas., 1960-63, sec., asst. to pres., 1963-69, sec., dir. staff services, 1969-71, v.p., sec., 1971-74, v.p. adminstrn., 1974-75, dir., 1974-84, pres., 1975-77, pres., chief exec. officer, 1977-84, chmn., 1979-84. Bd. dirs. Mercy Hosp., United Way of Rock Island and Scott Counties, 1973-74; trustee Marycrest Coll. Bd. Served with USAAF, 1944-46. Mem. Iowa, Scott County bar assns., Mo. Valley Electric Assn., Midwest Gas Assn. (dir.), Davenport, Bettendorf Chambers Commerce. Republican. Episcopalian. Clubs: Outing, Davenport, Rock Island Arsenal Golf. Died Mar. 28, 1984.*

STILL, CLYFFORD, artist; b. Grandin, N.D., Nov. 30, 1904; B.A., Spokane U., 1933; M.A., Wash. State Coll.; D.F.A., Md. Inst., Balt., 1967; D.F.A. (hon.), N.D. State U., 1972, San Francisco Art Inst., 1976. Mem. faculty Wash. State Coll., 1935-41, Richmond Profl. Inst. Coll. of William and Mary, 1943-45, Calif. Sch. Fine Arts, 1946-50, (originated) Subject of the Artist, N.Y.C., 1947-48, U. Pa., 1963, Hunter Coll., 1951, Bklyn. Coll., 1952; mem. Yaddo, 1934, 35; exhibited in one-man shows at San Francisco Mus. Art, 1943, Palace of Legion of Honor, San Francisco, 1947 Betty Parsons Gallery, N.Y., 1947, 50, 51, Metart Gallery, San Francisco, 1950, Art of This Century, N.Y.C., 1946, Albright Art Gallery Buffalo, 1959, U. Pa., 1963, Marlborough Gallery, N.Y., 1969, Met. Mus. Art, N.Y.C., 1979, others; exhibited in group shows 15 Americans, Mus. Modern Art, N.Y., 1952, The New Am. Painting, Europe, 1958-69, Documenta II, Kassel, 1959, others; represented in permanent collections Balt. Mus. Art, Albright-Knox Gallery, Buffalo, Kunsthalle Mus., Basel, Switzerland, Mus. Modern Art, N.Y.C., Whitney Mus. Art, N.Y.C., Tate Gallery, London, San Francisco Mus. Modern Art, numerous others. Mem. Am. Acad. Arts and Letters (Gold medal award of merit for painting 1972). Donor paintings to San Francisco Mus. Modern Art, 1975. Address: New Windsor, Md. Died June 23, 1980.

STILLA, PETER ANTHONY, newspaper editor; b. Cambridge, Mass., Mar. 27, 1928; s. Peter and Lena (Cutroni) S.; m. Rose Marie Tuttavilla, Feb. 21, 1951; children—Stephanie, Laura, Peter. With copy desk, then makeup editor Boston Record-Am., 1947-61; with Boston Globe, from 1961, asst. day editor, 1975-79, day editor, from 1979. Served with AUS, 1950-52. Home: Cambridge, Mass.

STILLWELL, MARGARET BINGHAM, bibliographer, writer; b. Providence, Jan. 26, 1887; d. Edward Augustus and Mary Elizabeth (Pindar-Bingham) S. Spl. student, R.I. Sch. Design, 1899-1905; A.B., Brown U., 1909, hon. A.M., 1925; Litt.D., U. R.I., 1952. Asst. John Carter Brown Library, Providence, 1909-14; cataloguer rare book div. N.Y. Pub. Library, 1914-17; curator, librarian Annmary Brown Meml., 1917-53; prof. emerita bibliography Brown U., 1954-84, Pres.'s fellow, 1951; hon. fellow Pierpont Morgan Library.; Lectr. Sch. Library Service Columbia, 1927-31. Author: The Influence of William Morris and the Kelmscott Press, 1912, The Heritage of the Modern Printer, 1916, Washington Eulogies, 1916, General Hawkins as He Revealed Himself to His Librarian, 1923, The Fasciculus Temporum, 1924, The Annmary Brown Memorial: A Descriptive Essay, 1925, Incunabula and Americana, 1450-1800, A Key to Bibliographical Study, 1931, Gutenberg and the Catholicon, 1936, The Seventeenth Century (in The Dolphin History of the Printed Book), 1938, The Annmary Brown Memorial, A Booklover's Shrine, 1940, Noah's Ark in Early Woodcuts and Modern Rhymes, 1942, Bibliographical Survey; 15th and 16th Century books in The Hunt Botanical Collection, 1958, The Awakening Interest in Science during the First Century of Printing, 1450-1550, 1970, The Beginning of the World of Books, 1450 to 1470, with a Synopsis of the Gutenberg Documents, 1972, Rhythm and Rhymes: The Songs of a Bookworm, 1977, Essays on the Heritage of the Renaissance from Homer to Gutenberg: The Growth of Knowledge and its Transmission through the First Printed Books, 1982; author and illustrator: While Benefit Street Was Young, 1943, The Pageant of Benefit Street Down Through the Years, 1945, Librarians Are Human: Memories In and Out of the Rare Book World, 1907-70, 1973; Editor, compiler: Incunabula in American Libraries, A Second Census, 1940. Mem. Colonial Dames Am., Bibliog. Soc. Am. (v.p. 1935-36, hon.), Providence Preservation Soc., R.I. Hist. Soc., Institut d'Etudes Europeennes et Mondiales (corr. mem.), R.I. Short Story Club (past pres.), Phi Beta Kappa (pres. Women's Sect. R.I. Alpha chpt. 1925-26). Episcopalian. Clubs: Review, Providence Art; Grolier (N.Y.) (hon.); Hroswitha (hon.). Home: Greenwich, R.I. Died Apr. 22, 1984.

STILLWELL, RICHARD, archeologist, educator; b. Niagara Falls, N.Y., Feb. 16, 1899; s. Lewis Buckley and Mary Elizabeth (Thurston) S.; A.B., Princeton, 1921, M.F.A., 1924; m. Agnes Newhall, Aug. 3, 1932 (dec.); children—Richard Newhall, Theodora; m. 2d, Celia Sachs Robinson, May 14, 1971. Spl. fellow architecture Am. Sch. Classical Studies, Athens, Greece, 1924-31, asst. dir., 1932, dir., 1932-35; instr. dept. art and archeology Princeton, 1926-29, asst. prof., 1929-38, asso. prof., 1938-54, prof., 1954-59, Howard Crosby Butler Meml. prof. history architecture, 1959-67, emeritus; mem. Inst. Advanced Study, 1936-42, dir. publs. com. excavation Antioch and vicinity, 1936-42. Served from lt. to lt. comdr. USNR, 1942-45. Fellow Royal Soc. Arts; mem. Archaeol. Inst. Am., Soc. Mayflower Descs., Soc. Colonial Wars, Order Founders and Patriots Am., Holland Soc. N.Y. Republican. Episcopalian. Clubs: Century Association (N.Y.C.); Nassau (Princeton). Author: Corinth III, Upper Peirene (with Blegen, Broneer), 1930; I, The Temple of Apollo (with Fowler, Robinson), 1932; The Peribolos of Apollo and Other Buildings (with Askew, Freeman), 1941; II The Theater, 1952; Kourion; The Theater, Procs. Am. Philos. Soc., vol. 105, 1961; The Chapel of Princeton University, 1971. Editor and co-author: Antioch-on-the-Orontes (2 vols.), 1938, 41; editor-in-chief Am. Jour. Archeology, 1953-73; editor Princeton Ency. Classical Sites, 1976. Contbr. articles to profl. publs. Home: Princeton, N.J. Died July 27, 1982.

STITT, EDWARD SONNY, saxophonist, orchestra leader; b. Boston, Feb. 2, 1924; s. Lonnie Wicks (stepfather) and Claudine Thibou; m. Pamela W. Gilmore, Dec. 19, 1960; children—Katea Denise, Jason Cesaré . Grad. high sch. tchr. harmony, mus. theory. (Jazz Poll winner, Outstanding Achievement in Field of Music, Artists and Models Creative Music award.), Toured Europe with, Jazz at Philharmonic; played with, Billy Eckstine Band, Miles Davis Quintet, Dizzy Gillespie Band, appeared, Hollywood Bowl; 2 world tours with, Giants of Jazz, 1970-72. Recipient All Am. award Esquire mag., All Star award Playboy mag.; Am. Legion award; awards Cook County Dept. Corrections; Ellington fellow Yale U., 1973. Home: Chillum, Md. Died July 1982.

STODDARD, ROBERT WARING, corporate executive; b. Trenton, N.J., Jan. 22, 1906; s. Harry Galpin and Janett (Waring) S.; Ph.B., Yale, 1928; postgrad. Harvard, 1929;

D.Eng. (hon.), Worcester Poly. Inst., 1952; LL.D., Assumption, 1959; D.Sc., Piedmont Coll., 1966; L.H.D., Central New Eng. Coll. Tech., 1974; m. Helen Esterbrook, Oct. 7, 1933; children—Judith (Mrs. B.A. King), Valerie (Mrs. S.B. Loring). Asst. works mgr. Wyman & Gordon Co., Worcester, Mass., 1936, works mgr., 1938, v.p., dir., 1941. exec. v.p., dir., 1951-55, pres., dir., 1955-67, chmn. bd., from 1967; chmn. bd. Worcester Telegram & Gazette, Inc.; dir. Internat. Paper Co., Worcester County Nat. Bank, 1st Nat Bank Boston, Raytheon Co., L.S. Starrett Co. Dir., past pres. Asso. Industries Mass.; trustee Worcester Poly. Inst.; bd. dirs., past pres. YMCA; trustee Hahnemann Hosp., Art Mus., Found. for Exptl. Biology, Natural History Soc. Mem. Am. Antiquarian Soc. (council Worcester). Clubs: University, Worcester, Worcester Country, Tatnuck Country (Worcester); Federal (Boston); Safari International (Los Angeles); Anglers (N.Y.C.); Algonquin (Boston); Chicago. Home: Worcester, Mass. Dec. Dec. 14, 1984.

STOKE, HAROLD WALTER, educator; b. Bosworth, Mo., May 11, 1903; s. Josiah Walter and Nettie Belle (Boyd) S.; A.B., Marion (Ind.) Coll., 1924; M.A., U. So. Cal., 1925; Ph.D., Johns Hopkins, 1930; LL.D., U. Me., 1946, Tulane, 1949, U. of N.M., 1950, U. N.H., 1951, m. Persis Warren, Aug. 18, 1928; 1 daughter, Marcia Phyllis. Asso. professor of history and political science. Berea College, 1926-28; assistant, associate, and prof. polit. science, U. of Neb., 1930-37; prin. supervisor of training in pub. adminstrn., Tenn. Valley Authority, also lecturer in polit. science, U. of Tenn., 1937-38; ednl. asso. Inst. of Local and State Govt., and visting asso. prof. polit. science, U. of Pa., 1938-39; dean of grad. sch., U. of Neb., 1939-40; asst. dean of grad. sch. and prof. polit. science, U. of Wis., 1940-43, acting dean, 1943-44; pres. U. of N.H., 1944-47; pres. Louisiana State University, 1947-51; dean grad. sch. U. Washington, 1951-55; dean grad. Sch. Arts and Sci., N.Y.U., 1955-58; pres. Am. Assn. Grad. Schools, 1955-56; sec.-treas. National Association State Universities, 1949-51. Mem. bd. dirs. Oak Ridge Inst. of Nuclear Studies, 1949-51; mem. adv. panel Nat. Citizens Commn. for Pub. Schs. Dir. civil affairs tng. program U. Wis., 1943-44; cons. on mil. tng. Office of Provost Marshal Gen., 1943-44. Chief of war records sect. and cons. Bur. of Budget, 1944. Mem. Am. Acad. Arts and Scis., Am. Polit. Sci. Association, Chi Phi. Author: The Foreign Relations of the Federal State, 1931; The Background of European Governments (with Norman L. Hill), 1935. Contbr. to jours. in polit. science and edn. Home: New York, N.Y. Died Apr. 6, 1982.

STOKES, COLIN, former tobacco company executive; b. Winston-Salem, N.C., Apr. 4, 1914; s. Henry Straughan and Eloise (Brown) S.; m. Mary Louise Siewers, Jan. 1, 1943; children: Louise Siewers (Mrs. Philip G. Kinken), Henry Straughan, Daniel Shober. Grad., McCallie Sch., Chattanooga, 1931; B.S., U. N.C., 1935. With R.J. Reynolds Tobacco Co., 1935-72, asst. to supt. mfg., 1947-53, asst. supt. mfg., 1953-56, supt. mfg., 1956-59, dir., 1957-84, v.p., 1959-61, exec. v.p., 1961-70, chmn. bd., 1970-72; pres. R.J. Reynolds Industries, Inc., 1972-73, chmn. bd. dirs., 1973-79, also dir.; dir. N.C. Nat. Bank, 1st Home Fed. Savs. & Loan Assn., NCNB Corp. Bd. dirs. YMCA, 1946-52; campaign chmn. United Fund Forsyth County, 1957, dir., 1957-59; trustee N.C. Bapt. Hosp., chmn. bd. trustees, 1961, 69, 70, chmn. finance com., 1959; chmn. Ind. Coll. Fund N.C., 1979-81; bd. dirs. William and Kate B. Reynolds Meml. Park, 1958-64, Child Guidance Clinic, 1959-61; trustee Salem Coll. and Acad., 1966-74; trustee Wake Forest U., 1971-75, 78-84, chmn., 1980-81. Served from pvt. to capt., inf. AUS, 1941-46. Mem. Winston-Salem C. of C. (dir. 1951-55, 68-70), Zeta Psi. Baptist (deacon, mem. finance com.). Club: Kiwanian (dir., pres. 1963). Home: Winston-Salem, N.C. Died Dec. 14, 1984.

STOKES, HOWARD GALE, advertising, motion pictures; b. Hermon, N.Y., June 30, 1888; s. Frank Adelbert and Carrie Adelaide (Gale) S.; A.B., Colgate, 1911, M.A., 1934; m. Ulga Ultima Muller, Apr. 18, 1914, deceased; m. 2d, Ida Jane Basett, December 3, 1932; children—Gale, Jane Austin. Advertising copywriter, 1911-12; copy manager N.Y. Telephone Co., 1912-19; production manager Prizma Color Pictures, 1919-20; editor Capitol Theater Colorland Review, 1920; v.p. Prizma, Inc., 1920-24; exec. asst. Am. Telegraph & Telephone Co., 1924-25; motion picture dir., 1925-29; development mgr. ednl. dept. Electrical Research Products, Inc., subsidiary of Western Electric Co., 1929-31; became dir. of Development Erpi Picture Consultants, Inc., 1931; advertising supervisor Am. Telephone & Telegraph Co., 1936-46, radio advt. mgr., 1946-48. Del. convention of Advertising Federation of America, Berlin, 1929; dir. Colgate Univ. Alumni Corp., 1935-38, president, 1940-44; nat. chmn. Colgate University Alumni Fund, 1935-38; trustee Colgate University, 1937-46, awarded alumni medal, 1945. Mem. Theta Nu Epsilon, Phi Gamma Delta, Phi Beta Kappa, Skull and Scroll. Republican. Protestant. Clubs: Advertising (New York); Rock Spring (W. Orange, N.J.). Author: (with F. L. Devereux) The Educational Talking Picture; scenario; —Golden Years of Progress— of motion picture shown by Advt. Fdn. Am. during Century of Progress Expn., Chicago; author, dir. or production mgr. more than 200 scientific industrial or ednl. motion pictures. Home: Hamilton, N.Y. †

STONE, CHARLES TURNER, physician; b. Caldwell, Tex., July 24, 1890; s. Wooten Meriwether and Emily Norris (Parkman) S.; A.B., Southwestern U., Georgetown, Tex., 1911; M.D., U. Tex., 1915; postgrad. Harvard Med. Sch., 1925-26, U. Berlin, Germany, 1926; m. Bertha Neubauer, Oct. 21, 1916; 1 child, Charles Turner, Jr. Instr. medicine U. Tex. Med. Br., 1915-18; adj. prof. clin. medicine U. Tex. 1918-23; assoc. prof. clin. medicine U. Tex. Med. Br., 1923-26, prof. medicine, 1926-60, emeritus, 1960-81; chmn. dept. internal medicine, 1926-58. Recipient Ashbel Smith Distinguished Alumnus award U. Tex. Med. Br. Diplomate Am. Bd. Internal Medicine. Fellow ACP (former mem. bd. regents); mem. Soc. Internal Medicine, Tex. Med. Assn, AMA (former mem. house dels., past chmn. sect. internal medicine, past mem. council med. edn. and hosps.), Endocrine Soc., Am. Thoracic Soc., Am. Heart Assn., AAAS, Am. Geriatrics Soc. (editorial bd.), Phi Delta Theta, Alpha Omega Alpha. Mason (32 deg., Shriner), Rotarian (past pres.). Clubs: Texas Internists; Port Bay. Contbr. articles on various phases of internal medicine to Am. med. jours. Home: Galveston, Tex. Dec. Mar. 31, 1981.

STONE, ELLERY WHEELER, former communications exec., naval officer; b. Oakland, Cal., Jan. 14, 1894; s. Edgar P. and Florence P. (Weeks) S.; student radio engring. U. Cal., 1913-14; m. Heidi Margareta Bertel, Mar. 17, 1963; children by former marriages—Elaine, Patricia, Sally Florence, Ellery (dec.), Marina. U.S. radio insp., 1914-17; commd. lt. (j.g.) USNR, 1917, advancing through grades to rear adm., 1944; dist. communications supt. 12th Naval Dist., 1917-19; pres. Fed. Telegraph Co., 1924-31; operating v.p., dir. Mackay Radio & Telegraph Co., 1931-37; v.p. All Am. Cables & Radio, Inc., 1937-38; v.p., dir., mem. exec. com. Postal Telegraph, Inc., Postal Telegraph-Cable Co.; became pres. Postal Telegraph, Inc., subsidiaries, 1942, pres., dir. Fed. Telephone & Radio Corp., Internat. Standard Elec. Corp., 1940-50; v.p. Internat. Tel.&Tel. Corp., 1947-69; pres., dir. Globe Wireless, Ltd., Am. Cable & Radio Corp., All Am. Cable & Radio, Inc., Comml. Cable Co., Mackay Radio & Tel. Co., 1950-58; chmn. bd. Am. Cable & Radio Corp., 1958-69; group v.p. U.S. Def. I.T.T., 1960-61; pres. I.T.T. Europe, Inc., 1961-65, vice chmn., 1965-69; dir. Fed. Electric Co., Internat. Electric Co., Internat. Standard Elec. Co., until 1969. Tech. cons. Def. Communications Bd., 1941. Served as naval chief of staff to Vice Adm. William Glassford, USN, Dakar, 1943; chief commr. Allied Control Commn., Italy, 1944-47. Decorated D.S.M. (USN, U.S. Army); knight comdr. Brit. Empire; grand cross St. Maurice and St. Lazarus (Italy); grand officer Crown of Italy; grand cross of San Marino; officer Legion of Honor (France); comdr. Order of Leopold II (Belgium); Cross of Merit, 1st Class with Crown, Sovereign Order of Knights of Malta; comdr. 1st grade Order of Isabel the Catholic (Spain). Fellow I.E.E.E., Royal Soc. Arts (Eng.); mem. U.S. Naval Inst., Soc. Colonial Wars, S.A.R., Naval Order of U.S., Soc. for French Am. Cultural Services and Ednl. Aid (trustee). Republican. Roman Catholic. Club: Army and Navy (Washington). Author: Elements of Radio Communication, 3d edit., 1926; also tech. articles to profl. publs. Home: Nutley, N.J. Died Sept. 18, 1981.

STONE, JAMES AUSTIN, lawyer; b. Lincoln, Va., Aug. 28, 1887; s. Isaac Scott and Thomasin Jane (Taylor) S.; A.B., Swarthmore Coll., 1910; LL.B., Nat. U., of Washington, D.C., 1915; m. Margaret L. Free, 1919; children—Margaret Taylor, Austin Craig, Cornelia, Robert Douglas. Asst. to patent lawyer, 1910-16; admitted to Dist. of Columbia bar, 1917, Bar Supreme Court U.S., 1923, mem. firm Stone, Boyden & Mack, Washington, D.C., patent law, from 1919. Served as 1st lt. Air Service, production section, U.S. Army, 1918-19. Pres. bd. trustees Sidwell Friends Sch., Dist. of Columbia, from 1936. Mem. Am. and Dist. of Columbia bar assns., Am. Patent Law Assn. (pres. 1934-35); pres. Nat. Council of Patent Law Assn., 1935; mem. Am. Chem. Soc., Delta Upsilon. Mem. Religious Soc. of Friends. Home: Washington, D.C. †

STONE, NORMAN H., corp. exec.; b. Chgo., Dec. 20, 1901; s. Joseph and Mary (Hefler) S.; student pub. schs.; m. Ida Finkelstein, Dec. 19, 1926; children—Alan, Ira, Judith. Salesman P. Lorillard Co., N.Y.C. and Chgo., 1922-25, Consumers Papers Co., Chgo., 1925-27; sr. partner J. H. Stone & Sons, 1926-45; inc. Stone Container Corp., 1945, pres., 1945-68, chmn. bd., 1945-72, also chief exec. officer; president Stone Found., S.C. Industries, Inc., Florence. Bd. dirs. Jewish Youth Service of B'nai B'rith. Mental Health Assn. Greater Chgo. Exec. bd. Nat. Conf. of Christians and Jews. Mem. Am. Paper Inst. (member of the board of dirs. paperboard group). Member Temple Sholom (hon. bd. S. Shore Temple). Clubs: Standard, Mid-Am. (Chgo.); Tamarisk Country, Racquet (Palm Springs, Fla.); Bryn Mawr Country. Home: Chicago, Ill. Died Mar. 16, 1985.

STONECIPHER, ALVIN HARRISON MORTON, educator; b. Corydon, Ind., Oct. 6, 1888; s. Levi Thomas and Margaret Ann (Patterson) S.; A.B., Vanderbilt U., 1913, A.M., 1914, Ph.D., 1917; grad. study, George Peabody Coll. for Teachers, 1916-17; m. Blanche Marie Ritchie, June 21, 1920; children—Verna Pauline, Virginia Irene, Evelyn Marie. Prof. classical langs., Ind. Central Coll., 1917-32; prof. Latin, Lebanon Valley Coll., 1932-47, and from 1950, prof. of Latin and Greek, 1947-50, dean coll., 1936-52, adv. dean, head dept. fgn. languages and prof. German; ordained ministry Ch. United Brethren in Christ, 1922. Mem. Classical Assn. of Atlantic States, Eastern Assn. Coll. Deans and Advisers of Men (pres. 1948-49), Pa. State Edn. Assn., Phi Beta Kappa. Democrat. Mem. Evangelical United Brethren Church. Clubs: Torch, Harrisburg Executives. Author: Gracco-Persian Names. Home: Annville, Pa. †

STONEY, THOMAS PORCHER, lawyer; b. Medway Plantation, Berkeley County, S.C., Dec. 16, 1889; s. Samuel Porcher and Eliza Chaplin (Croft) S.; prep. edn., Catawba Mil. Acad., Rock Hill, S.C., Porter Military Academy, Charleston, South Carolina, and U. of the South, Sewanee, Tenn.; LL.B., U. of S.C., 1911; m. Beverly DuBose, Oct. 7, 1915; children—Randell Croft, Theodore DuBose, Laurence O'Hear. Admitted to S.C. bar, 1911, and began practice with J. P. Kennedy Bryan, Charleston; mem. firm Stoney & Cordes, 1914-18; solicitor 9th Judicial Circuit, S.C., 1916-23; mayor of Charleston 2 terms, 1923-31; member of law firm Stoney and Crosland. Member of Preparedness for Peace Commission for South Carolina. Pres. Alumni Assn. Univ. of South Carolina, 1938-40. Member of Board of Trustees Univ. of South, Sewanee, Tenn. Trustee Porter Acad., Coll. of Charleston. Mem. Charleston (S.C.) Bar Assn. (pres. 1947-48), Am. Bar Assn. Mem. Huguenot Soc. S.C., St. Cecelia Soc., Alumni Assn. of U. of S.C. (pres. 1938-40), Alpha Tau Omega, Omicron Delta Kappa. Dem. Episcopalian. Mason (32 deg., Shriner), Elk, Moose, K.P., Tall Cedar of Lebanon. Club: Ashley Rifle. Home: Charleston, S.C. †

STOPHLET, DONALD VICTOR, university administrator; b. Oak Park, Ill., Nov. 12, 1918; s. Donald Stirling and Anne (Gilmer) S.; Ph.B., U. Wis., 1941, Ph.M., 1946. Mng. dir. Central City Opera Assn., Central City and Denver, 1948-52; sec. of coll., dir. devel. Rockford (Ill.) Coll., 1952-58; dir. devel. programs U. Pitts., 1958-59; v.p. for devel. Western Res. U., 1959-63; v.p. for devel. affairs Miami (Fla.), 1963-67; v.p. for devel. Fla. Inst. Tech., from 1967. Served as pilot USAAF, 1943-46. Mem. Am. Coll. Pub. Relations Assn., Am. Alumni Council, Nat. Collegiate Players, Alpha Delta Phi. Home: Melbourne Beach, Fla. Dec. Sept. 1980.

STORER, TRACY I(RWIN), educator; b. San Francisco, Aug. 17, 1889; s. Frank and Olietta May (McDowell) S.; B.S., U. Calif., 1912, M.S., 1913, Ph.D., 1925; m. Ruth Charlotte Risdon, June 16, 1917. Asst. and instr. zoology U. Calif., 1912-14, asst. curator birds and field naturalist Mus. Vertebrate Zoology, 1914-23, asst. prof. zoology, coll. agr., 1923-26, asso. prof., 1926-32, prof. and zoologist, from 1932; chmn. dept. zoology, U. Calif.-Davis, 1926-51. Served as 1st lt. San. Corps, A.U.S., 1917-19, capt. O.R.C., 1925-35. Fellow A.A.A.S., Calif. Acad. Sci.; mem. Cooper Ornithol. Club, Am. Ornithologists' Union, Am. Soc. Mammalogists (v.p. 1947-49, pres. 1949-51), Wilson Ornithol. Club, Am. Soc. Ichthyologists and Herpetologists, Ecol. Soc. Am. (asso. editor 1949-51), Wildlife Soc. (pres. 1948-49), Sigma Xi. Republican. Clubs: Faculty (Berkeley and Davis); Commonwealth of California; X, Sacramento. Author: Game Brids of California (with Joseph Grinnell and Harold C. Bryant), 1918; Animal Life in the Yosemite (with J. Grinnell), 1924; A Synopsis of the Amphibia of California, 1925; General Zoology, 1943, 1951; Laboratory Manual for General Zoology, 1944, 1951; Bibliography of Rodent Control (with M. P. Mann), 1946. Editor: Journal of Wildlife Management (quarterly), 1942-46. Contbr. articles on ecology and econ. relations of vertebrates in Western N.A. and other sci. data to mags. Home: Davis, Calif. †

STOREY, CHARLES MOORFIELD, lawyer; b. Brookline, Mass., Mar. 4, 1889; s. Moorfield and Anna Gertrude (Cutts) S.; grad. St. Mark's Sch.; A.B., Harvard, 1912, A.M., 1913, LL.B., 1915; m. Susan Jameson Sweetser, June 24, 1913; children— Charles M., Anderson (killed in action, Jan. 17, 1943), Susan Jameson (Mrs. Ronald T. Lyman, Jr.), Gertrude Cutts (Mrs. William M. Bancroft), James Moorfield. Admitted to Mass. bar, 1915; asst. atty., later atty. U.S. Dept. Justice, Washington, 1915-18; asst. commr. Commn. Relating to Prisoners of War, also attache commn. to negotiate peace, U.S. Commn. to Austria-Hungary, Budapest, 1918-19; partner Peabody, Brown Rowley & Storey, Boston, 1920-79; head atty. N.E. regional office WPB, 1942-43; compliance commr. N.E. region, 1943-44; appeal agt. Selective Service, 1941-47, 62-69; cons. (renegotiator) Boston Q.M. price adjustment dist. office U.S. War Dept., 1943-47; chmn. bd. trustees Park Sch. Corp., 1920-30; v.p. Winsor Sch., 1930-32; pres. Mass. Soc. Prevention Cruelty to Children, 1942-49; trustee Mt. Auburn Cemetery, 1932-79; mem. Boston Finance Commn., 1932-35; past chmn.; overseer Harvard, 1945-51. Mem. Am., Mass., Boston (mem. council 1935-36) bar assns., Harvard Alumni Assn. (dir. 1935-37, v.p. 1938), Mass. Hist. Soc., Mass. Soc. Cin. (sec. 1955-72), N.E. Hist. Geneal. Soc. (pres. 1961-63). Clubs: Tavern, Somerset. Home: Chestnut Hill, Mass. Died Mar. 19, 1980.

STORROW, JAMES J., JR., retired magazine publisher; b. Boston, May 7, 1917; s. James J. and Margaret (Rotch) S.; m. Patricia Blake, June 26, 1940 (dec. May 1962); children: Gerald B., Peter, James J. III, Margaret R.; m. Linda Eder Jamieson, Dec. 15, 1962. Grad., Milton (Mass.) Acad., 1936; B.S., Harvard U., 1940, postgrad., 1940-41. Dir. North Shore Players, Inc., Marblehead, Mass., 1939-41; office mgr., asst. treas. Baush Machine Tool Co., Springfield, Mass., 1941-43; treas. Brooks Green Co., Boston, 1946, Gen. Microfilm Co., Cambridge, Mass., after 1947, The Stamp Show, Inc., N.Y.C.,

1953-55, Trident Films, Inc., N.Y.C., from 1961; pres. Henry Thayer Co., Cambridge, 1947-53; pub. The Nation mag., N.Y.C., 1965-77; dir. Farrar, Straus & Giroux, Inc. Chmn. Joint Council on Fgn. Affairs, Boston, 1947; Mem. Brookline (Mass.) Democratic Town Com., 1958-61; Bd. dirs. Housing Assn. Met. Boston, 1948-53, Cath. Guild for All the Blind, Newton, Mass., The Med. Found.; trustee New Eng. Coll. Pharmacy, 1956-62; trustee, mem. exec. com. Fund for Peace. Served with USNR, 1943-45. Clubs: Century; Harvard (Boston and N.Y.C.); The Players. Home: New York, N.Y. Died Jan. 13, 1984.

STORY, AUSTIN PUTNAM, paper manufacturer; b. Chillicothe, Ohio, Dec. 19, 1890; s. Walter Sprague and Carrie (Denning) S.; B.A., Council U., 1913; m. Cordelia Wallace, Apr. 24, 1920; children—Austin Putnam, Jr., William Wallace. Chemist Mead Pulp & Paper Co., Chillicothe, 1914-15, salesman, 1915-17; treas. Chillicothe Paper Co., 1919-45, vice president, 1928-42, pres. and treas., 1942-45, president from 1945; director of the Mead Corporation. Served as captain, 332d Infantry, A.E.F., 1917-19. Mem. Sigma Alpha Epsilon. Republican. Episcopalian. Elk. Clubs: Cornell (N.Y. City); Rotary (Chillicothe). Home: Chillicothe, Ohio. †

STOUGH, HOWARD BROWN, educator; b. Lena, Ill., Oct. 29, 1887; s. John Howard and Edith Armida (Gipson) S.; A.B., Midland Coll., 1907; M.A., U. Kan., 1909; Ph.D., Harvard, 1925; m. Ruth Elizabeth Schwarz, June 21, 1928; 1 dau., Edith Catherine. High sch. tchr., 1909-11; various positions bus. offices, 1911-18; supt., high sch. tchr., 1919-23; asst. prof. U. Ida., 1925-27, asso. prof., 1927-30, prof., chmn. zoology, 1930-58, prof., chmn. emeritus, 1958; assistant professor biology Gonzaga University, Spokane, 1958-63, now professor of biology emeritus; research department of zoology U. Sydney, Australia, 1949-50. Served as sgt., A.S., World War I; capt. 375th Photo Wing Reconnaissance, USAAF, World War II. Mem. Sigma Xi, Alpha Epsilon Delta. Home: Moscow, Ida. †

STOUT, WESLEY WINANS, editor; b. Junction City, Kan., Jan. 26, 1890; s. Francis Wellington and Dora (Dougherty) S.; m. Mary Lee Starr, Sept. 15, 1923. Reporter and editor various newspapers in Kan., Mo., Tex., Calif., Wash., City of Mexico, New York and Okla., 1907-17 and 1921-22; asso. editor and writer Saturday Evening Post, 1922-36, editor in chief, 1937-42. Enlisted man U.S. Naval Air Force, World War, 1917-18; at sea for U.S. Shipping Bd., 1919-21.†

STOVALL, WILLIAM DAVISON, pathologist, bacteriologist; b. Longtown, Miss., Oct. 31, 1887; s. Joseph Pendleton and Lula (Davison) S.; B.S., Miss. Coll., 1907; M.D., Tulane U., 1911, post-grad. study to tropical medicine hygiene, 1913; m. Etta Bucholtz, Mar. 29, 1915; 1 child, William Davison. Intern, St. Vincent's Hosp., Birmingham, Ala., 1912-13, U.S. Marine Hosp., 1913; became state bacteriologist, Lab. of Hygiene, U. of Wis., 1914, now prof. emeritus hygiene, dir. of State Lab. of Hygiene, dir. course in clin. pathology; acting supt. U. Wisconsin Hosps., 1938-40; clin. pathologist Wis. Gen. Hosp.; consultant on desquamative cytology of cancer to National Cancer Institute, U.S. Pub. Health Service; former mem. staff and cons. pathologist St. Mary's Hosp. and Madison Gen. Hosp. Mem. State Bd. Public Welfare; chmn. Bd. Pub. Welfare, Mem. bd. dirs. Wis. div. Am. Cancer Soc.; former spl. cons. Nat. Cancer Inst. on Cancer Control; formerly mem. Nat. Adv. Com. on Med. Edn.; mem. subcom. on blood, nat. health resources com. ODM. Mem. Am. Pub. Health Assn., A.M.A. (house of dels.), Wis. (past pres., council award of honor, chmn. sect. med. history), Dane County, Univ. med. socs., Am. Soc. Clin. Pathol., Phi Delta Theta, Alpha Kappa Kappa, Sigma Xi. Republican. Club: Professional Men's Club. Author articles in field. Home: Madison, Wis. †

STOVER, ROSS HARRISON, clergyman; b. Mechanicsburg, O., Nov. 30, 1888; s. Peter Columbus and Hattie (Mahan) S.; B.A., Wittenberg Coll., Springfield, O., 1912; B.D., Hamma Div. Sch. (Wittenberg Coll.), 1915; D.D., Gettysburg (Pa.) Coll., 1923; LL.D., Temple Univ., 1939; S.T.D., Am. Theol. Sem., Wilmington, Del.; m. Emma Stanford, Dec. 21, 1910; 1 dau., Martha Corrine. Ordained Luth. ministry, 1915; pastor First Ch., Wapakoneta, O., 1915-19, Messiah Ch., Phila., from 1919. Camp singing master for Y.M.C.A., World War. Mem. Alpha Tau Omega. Club: Union League. Author: (booklets), On the Road to Heaven, 1927; Three Cheers, 1928; Why Am I Living, 1929; The Christian's Rainbow, 1931; What Do We Know About Life After Death?, 1940; How Shall I Say It, 1940. Contbr. to mags. Home: Philadelphia, Pa. †

STRANATHAN, J(AMES) D(OCKING), physicist, educator; b. Kansas City, Mo., Nov. 2, 1898; s. Samuel Woods and Bertha (Docking) S.; B.S., U. of Kan., 1921, M.S., 1924; Ph.D., U. of Chicago, 1928; m. Lena Pearl Monroe, Sept. 6, 1921; children—Ona Fern (Mrs. Eugene V. Nininger), Mary Maud. Mem. faculty U. of Kans. from 1921, prof. physics from 1934, chmn. dept. since 1941. Fellow Am. Phys. Soc., AAAS; mem. Am. Assn. Physics Tchrs., AAUP, Sigma Xi. Author: The Particles of Modern Physics, 1942; articles profl. jours. Home: Lawrence, Kans. Dec. May 22, 1981.

STRANDNESS, THEODORE BENSON, educator; b. St. Paul, Mar. 23, 1915; s. Theodore Andrew and Hilda Theresa (Benson) S.; B.A., Jamestown Coll., 1937; M.A., U. Minn., 1942; Ph.D., Mich. State U., 1951; m. Laura Thorleifson, Oct. 23, 1943; children—Jean Theresa, Linda Ellen, Patricia Lynn. Tchr. pub. schs., N.D., Minn., 1937-42; prof. English, Mich. State U., East Lansing, 1946—, chmn. dept. Am. thought and lang., 1962-67. Served to lt. (j.g.) USNR, 1942-45. Mem. AAUP, Coll. English Assn., Modern Lang. Assn. Nat. Council Tchrs. English, Am. Studies Assn. Author: The Experience of Writing, 1958; Curriculum Building in General Education, 1960; The American Identity, 1962; Language, Form and Idea, 1963; Samuel Sewell; A Puritan Portrait, 1967. Editor, U. Coll. Quar., 1955-61, 67-72. Home: East Lansing, Mich. Died Feb. 23, 1985.

STRASBERG, LEE, theatrical dir.; b. Budzanow, Austria, Nov. 17, 1901; s. Baruch Meyer and Ida (Diner) S.; student Boleslavsky-Ouspenskaya, Am. Laboratory Theatre; m. Nora Z. Orecaun (dec.); m. 2d, Paula Miller, Mar. 16, 1934 (dec.); children—Susan, John; m. 3d, Anna Mizrahi, Jan. 7, 1968; children—Adam Lee Baruch, David Lee Isaac. Came to U.S., 1909, naturalized, 1936. Made first appearance as dir., actor Chrystie Street Settlement House N.Y.C., 1925; began profl. career, 1925; actor Processional, Theatre Guild, also Garrick Gaieties I, 1925; stage mgr. Garrick Gaieties II, 1926; asst. stage mgr. to Alfred Lunt-Lynne Fontanne, The Guardsman; actor in Red Rust, Green Grow the Lilacs; founder Group Theatre, N.Y.C., 1930, dir., 1930-37, including House of Connelly, Night Over Taos, Success Story, Men in White (Pulitzer prize winner), Gold Eagle Guy, Johnny Johnson; director of All The Living, also Clash by Night, Fifth Column; co-producer Country Girl, 1950; director The Big Knife, 1949, Skipper Next to God, 1948; artistic dir. Actors' studio, N.Y.C., 1948—, Actors' Studio Theater, Inc., 1962-66; artistic dir. The Silent Partner, Felix; dir. The Three Sisters, 1964; film debut in The Godfather, Part II, 1974; other film: And Justice for All, 1979, Going in Style, 1979, The Cassandra Crossing, Boardwalk; TV movie The Last Tenant; lectr. Harvard U., Brown U., Yale, Brandeis U., Northwestern U. Established Lee Strasberg Inst. of Theatre, N.Y.C. and Los Angeles, 1969. Recipient Kelcey Allen award, N.Y.C., 1961; Centennial Gold medal award for excellence in dramatic arts Boston Coll., 1963. Author articles on the theatre. Contbr. Ency. Brit., Ency. Spettacolo, Ency. Funk and Wagnall, Ency. Americana. Address: New York, N.Y. Died Feb. 17, 1982.*

STRAW, H. THOMPSON, geographer; b. Antigo, Wis., Mar. 21, 1907; s. Harold Parker and Clara A. (Thompson) S.; m. Hilda Smith Jackson, Dec. 16, 1932. B.A., Hillsdale Coll., 1930; M.A., U. Mich., 1934, Ph.D., 1936. Teaching fellow geography U. Mich., 1934-36; asst. prof. geography Middle Tenn. State U., Murfreesboro, 1936-37, asso. prof. geography, 1937-39; prof. geography Western Mich. U., 1939-47; vis. prof. George Washington U., 1945, Mich. State U., 1946; chief Africa sect. topographic detachment G-2 Dept. of Army, Washington, 1947-50; geographer Reconnaissance Br. AFCIN Hdqrs. USAF, Washington, 1950-51, dep. for research and geography, 1951-55, dep. chief photog. intelligence utilization sect., 1955-57; chief photog. intelligence utilization sect. Hdqrs. USAF (Reconnaissance Br. AFCIN), 1957-59, ret., 1959, pvt. research and publs., 1959—; lectr. Strategic Intelligence Sch., Dept. Def., 1947-59; Air Force mem. U.S. Bd. on Geog. Names, 1950-58, chmn., 1954-58; Air Corps instr. maps and charts, 1943-44, chief cartographic sect. hist. br. G-2, 1944-45. Author: Battle Creek Michigan—A Study in Urban Geography, 1939; Contbr. articles to profl. mags. Town councilman, Hillsboro, Va., 1960-66. Grantee Social Research Council, 1940; Grantee NRC So. Studies Project, 1941; Recipient Cert. of Appreciation U.S. Govt., 1959. Fellow AAAS; mem. Am. Geog. Soc., Assn. Am. Geographers, Mich. Acad. Sci. Arts and Letters (chmn. geog. sect. 1942-43), Nat. Council Geography Edn. (chmn. calendar reform com. 1941-42), Sigma Xi, Chi Gamma Phi, Epsilon Delta Alpha. Episcopalian (past vestryman, treas.). Home: Fredericksburg VA

STREET, ELWOOD VICKERS, social worker; b. Cleveland, O., Nov. 23, 1890; s. Thomas Elwood and Josephine (Hanks) S.; A.B., Western Reserve U., 1912; A.M., U. of Louisville, 1921; m. Augusta Jewitt, Sept. 9, 1913; children—Catherine Earls (Mrs. C. William Chilman), Thomas Elwood, Sibyl Vickers (Mrs. Samuel C. Vanneman), Sarah Jewitt (Mrs. John F. Van Camp). In newspaper work with the editorial dept. Cleveland Leader, 1907-13; asst. dir. Cleveland Fedn. for Charity and Philanthropy, 1913-16; circulation mgr. The Survey, N.Y. City, 1916-17; dir. Welfare League, Louisville, Ky., 1917-21; dir. Community Council, St. Louis, 1921-28, also dir. Community Fund, 1922-28; dir. Community Chest, Washington, 1928-34; dir. of public welfare, Washington, 1934-39; dir. Richmond Community Fund and Community Council, 1939-43; dir. Community Chest and Council of Houston and Harris County, 1943-47; dir. Community Chest and Council, greater Bridgeport and Stratford, 1947-55; prof. social service Inst. Ch. Social Service. Hartford Sem. Found., 1956-59, dir. pub. information, from 1959. Member council on Social Work Education; 2d v.p., Conn. Prison Assn. Mem. Nat. Religious Publicity Council, Nat. Conf. Social Work, Nat. Assn. Social workers, Beta Theta Pi, Phi Beta Kappa. Congregationalist. Clubs: Torch (past pres. sec. Conn. Valley), Rotary, Connecticut Valley Camera. Author: Sympathy and System in Giving, 1921, Social Work Administration, 1931; The Public Welfare Administrator, 1939; A Handbook for Social Agency Administration, 1947. Contbr. mag. articles. Home: West Hartford, Conn. †

STRITZINGER, RAYMOND K(NEAS), pres. and dir. Continental Baking Co.; b. Norristown Pa., Dec. 15, 1888; s. Lewis G. and Sarah Ella (Kneas) S.; student high sch., Norristown, Lehigh U., Columbus Sch. of Baking Technology; m. Marion Harley Custer, June 18, 1913; children—Robert Lewis (dec.), Deborah Ann (Mrs. B. Wheeler Dyer, Jr.), Lee Marshall. With Continental Baking Co., N.Y. City, from Feb. 2, 1925, v.p. 1925-42, dir. of operations from Sept. 1934 to Dec. 1942, pres., 1942-51, chmn. bd. from 1950, now dir. Trustee Am. Bakers Found. Mem. Pa. Bakers Assn. (past pres.), Am. Bakers Assn. (gov., ex-pres.), Am. Inst. Baking (past chmn.), Fox Meadow Assn., Scarsdale, N.Y. (past pres.), American Society of Bakery Engrs., Nat. Rifle Assn., Eastern Small Bore Rifle Association (past president), United States Revolver Association, Pa. Soc., Phi Delta Theta. Mason (K.T., Shriner). Presbyterian. Republican. Clubs: Union League of N.Y., N.Y. Bakers (past pres.), Campfire Club of Am., Scarsdale Golf, Outers; Lehigh (New York) (past pres.); Saddle and Sirloin (Kansas City); Shenorock Shore. Home: Scarsdale, N.Y. †

STROMINGER, DONALD B., physician; b. N.Y.C., May 11, 1928; s. William and Esther (Rosenthal) S.; m. Marleah Sprague Hammond, Dec. 22, 1951; children—Linda R., Dale Hammond, Mark Randall. B.A., Yale U., 1948; postgrad., N.Y. Med. Coll., 1949-51; M.D., Washington U., St. Louis, 1953. Diplomate: Am. Bd. Pediatrics, Am. Bd. Allergy and Immunology. Intern St. Louis Children's Hosp., 1953-54, asst. resident, then chief resident in pediatrics, 1954-57; preceptor allergy Washington U. Clinics, 1960-65; med. dir. Children's Cons. Services, Inc., St. Louis; pediatrician St. Louis Maternity, McMillan hosps.; mem. staff Barnes Hosp.; mem. vis. staff St. Luke's, St. John's hosps.; mem. faculty Washington U. Med. Sch., from 1960, prof. pediatrics, from 1979; chmn. Cystic Fibrosis Nat. Center com. Cystic Fibrosis Found., Rockville, Md., 1973-75. Contbr. articles to med. jours. Pres. St. Louis Little Symphony, 1974-78. Served with USAF, 1956-60. Grantee Cystic Fibrosis Found., from 1964. Fellow Am. Acad. Pediatrics, Am. Coll. Chest Physicians (chmn. cardiopulmonary diseases of children from 1980), Am. Acad. Allergy, Am. Assn. Clin. Immunology and Allergy, Am. Coll. Allergy; mem. Am. Assn. Cert. Allergists, Am. Thoracic Soc. (sec. pediatric assembly 1970), Soc. Med. Cons.'s Armed Forces, N.Y. Acad. Scis., Pan Am. Med. Assn., Am. Lung Assn. (dir. Eastern Mo. chpt. from 1974), Am. Heart Assn. (council cardiopulmonary diseases), Alpha Omega Alpha. Club: Yale (treas. from 1975, gov. from 1969). Home: Saint Louis, MO.

STRONG, ALBERT L., banker; b. Broken Bow, Neb., June 16, 1888; s. James Decatur and Martha Amelia (Purdy) S.; ed. high sch. (Thayer, Kan.) and business coll. (Independence, Kan.); m. Neva Margaret Cromb, Nov. 3, 1928. Began as bank clerk, 1910; mgr. Reconstruction Finance Corp. and agent of all its subsidiaries in Kansas City Fed. Reserve Dist. Served as non-commd. officer, 12th Engrs. Railway Btn., 1917-19; with A.E.F., 1917-19. Decorated Victory Medal. Mason (Shriner). Club: Mission Hills Country (Kansas City, Mo.). Home: Kansas City, Mo. †

STRONG, OLIVER SMITH, neurologist; b. Red Bank, N.J., Dec. 30, 1864; s. Benjamin and Adeline Torrey (Schenck) S.; A.B., Princeton, 1886, A.M., 1888; Ph.D., Columbia, 1895. Asst. Lake Lab., Milwaukee, Wis., 1890-91; asst. in biology, Columbia, 1892-93, tutor in comparative neurology and asst. in normal histology, Coll. Physicians and Surgeons (Columbia), 1893-1904, instr. in histology, 1904-09, instr. in anatomy, 1909-17, asst. prof. neurology and instr. in histology, 1917-18, assoc. prof. neurology and neuro-histology, 1918-27, prof. neurology and neuro-histology, 1927-37; ret. In charge chem. room Marine Biol. Lab., 1904-30; consultant in neuroanatomy, Vanderbilt Clinic, Columbia. Asso. editor Jour. Comparative Neurology, 1896-37 (now hon. mem. editorial bd.), Neurol. Bull., 1918-21; editor Bull. of Neurol. Inst. of New York, 1930-32; mem. Marine Biol. Society Corp. Asso. fellow N.Y. Acad. of Medicine; mem. Am. Neurol. Assn. (hon.), Am. Assn. of Anatomists (hon.), Sigma Xi. Presbyterian. Club: Men's Faculty. Wrote one chap. in Bailey's Text Book of Histology, 7th edit., 1927; Lab. Course in Histology (with Adolph Elwyn), 1920; Human Neuroanatomy (with Adolph Elwyn), 1943; Cranial Nerves of Amphibia (Jour. of Morphology 1895, also Anatomischer Anzeiger 1889). Contbr. to Neurol Bull., Jour. Comparative Neurol. and Archives of Neurology and Psychiatry, also chap. in Starr's Atlas of Nerve Cells. Wrote one chap. in Bailey and Miller's Embryology, chapters in Bailey's Histology. Home: Litchfield, Conn.†

STRONG, ROBERT WILLIAM, army officer; b. Kingsville, O., Mar. 12, 1890; grad. U.S. Mil. Acad., 1915; commd. 2d lt. Cav., June 1915, and advanced through the grades to brig. gen., Feb. 1943; assigned for duty with the supply Div. War Dept. Gen Staff, Washington, D.C., Aug. 1936-July 1940, then to 7th Cav. Brigade, Ft. Knox, Ky.; transferred to 1st Armored Regiment, Ft. Knox, Ky., Nov. 1940; joined 3d Armored Regiment, Camp Beauregard, La. (33d Armored Regiment), May 1941; moved with his regiment to Camp Polk, La., June 1942; overseas assignment, July 1942; joined the Cav. Replacement Training Center, Ft. Riley, Kan., Feb. 1943.†

STRONG, TRACY, orgn. sec.; b. Mt. Vernon, O., Aug. 6, 1887; s. Dr. Sydney and Ruth Maria (Tracy) S.; A.B., Oberlin Coll., 1908, LL.D., 1943; m. Edith Adelaide Robbins, June 23, 1910; children—Robbins, Tracy, Ruth Adelaide (Mrs. Robert Harmon), Boys' work sec., Y.M.-C.A., Seattle, Wash., 1908-23; mem. boys' work staff, World's Alliance of Y.M.C.A.'s, hdqrs. Geneva, Switzerland, 1923-26, exec. boys' work, 1926-38, gen. sec., from 1938, also exec. dir. War Prisoners' Aid (organized by World's Alliance of Y.M.C.A.'s). Author: We Prisoners of War, 1941; Camping (pub. only in Chinese), 1934. Home Geneva, Switzerland. †

STROOCK, ALAN MAXWELL, lawyer; b. N.Y.C., Nov. 12, 1907; s. Solomon Marcuse and Hilda (Weil) S.; m. Katherine Wyler, June 12, 1931; children: Robert, Mariana Stroock Leighton, Daniel. A.B. magna cum laude, Harvard U., 1929; J.D.. cum laude, Yale U., 1934; LL.D., Jewish Theol. Sem. Am., 1961. Bar: N.Y. 1934. Law clk. Justice Benjamin N. Cardozo, U.S. Supreme Ct., 1934-36; assoc. Stroock & Stroock, N.Y.C., 1936-37; ptnr. Stroock & Stroock & Laven and predecessor, 1939-83, of counsel, 1984-85, asst. corp. counsel, City of N.Y., 1938. Trustee NYU, 1955-79, life trustee, 1979—; chmn. bd. Jewish Theol. Sem. Am., 1947-63, pres. of corp., 1963-75, chmn. exec. com., 1975-83, hon. chmn. bd., 1983-85; mem. com. visitors dept. history Harvard U., 1951-56, 58-64, 67-71, dept. philosophy, 1956-62; mem. overseers com. on univ. resources Harvard, dept. history, 1951-56, 58-64, 67-71, dept. philosophy, 1974-77; mem. U.S. Nat. Commn. UNESCO, 1965-67; trustee Horace Mann Sch. for Boys, 1946-59; v.p. Am. Jewish Com., 1948-51, 55-58, chmn. adminstrv. com., 1958; trustee at large Fedn. Jewish Philanthropies of N.Y., 1960-74, life trustee, 1974-85; chmn. bd. dirs. Am. Friends of the Alliance Israelite Universelle, Inc. Mem. N.Y. County Lawyers Assn., ABA, Assn. Bar City N.Y. (mem. grievance com. 1951-54, 60-63), Order of Coif, Phi Beta Kappa. Clubs: Regency Whist (N.Y.C.), Harmonie (N.Y.C.). Home: New York, N.Y. Died Mar. 29, 1985.

STRUDWICK, SHEPPERD, actor; b. Hillsborough, N.C., Sept. 22, 1907; s. Shepperd and Susan (Read) S.; m. Mary Loren Jeffrey Shannon, Dec. 23, 1976; 1 son by previous marriage, Shepperd. A.B., U. N.C., Chapel Hill, 1928. artist-in-residence U. Detroit., 1971-72. Appeared in: plays Morming's at Seven; appeared in: plays Both Your Houses, Biography, Who's Afraid of Virginia Woolf, As You Like It, Measure For Measure, Doctors Dilemma, Three Sisters, Ghosts, Galileo, The Price; Appeared in: films Cops and Robbers, The Red Pony, All The King's Men, A Place in the Sun, Kent State; (Actors Studio award 1980, Tony nomination 1981). Calif. state chmn. Am. Vets. Com., 1946. Served to lt. USNR, WW II, ETO. Recipient Disting. Alumnus award U. N.C., 1977. Mem. Actors Equity Assn., Screen Actors Guild, AFTRA. Democrat. Presbyterian. Club: Century Assn. Home: New York, NY.

STUART, JESSE HILTON, author; b. W-Hollow, nr. Riverton, Ky., Aug. 8, 1907; s. Mitchell and Martha (Hilton) S.; m. Naomi Deane Norris, Oct. 14, 1939; 1 child, Jessica Jane (Mrs. Julian Juergensmeyer). A.B., Lincoln Meml. U., Harrogate, Tenn., 1929, D.H.L. (hon.), 1950; student, Vanderbilt U., 1931-32, Peabody Coll.; D.Litt., U. Ky., 1944, Marietta (Ohio) Coll., 1952; LL.D., Baylor U., Ball State U.; D.Litt. (hon.), Morris Harvey Coll., 1959, Marshall U., 1962, No. Mich. U., 1964, Eastern Ky. State Coll., 1964, Morehead State U., 1974; Dr. Pedagogy (hon.), Murray State U., 1968, Pfeiffer Coll., 1969; Litt.D. (hon.), Berea Coll., 1966; L.H.D. Honoris Causa, U. Louisville, 1974. Tchr. Sch., lectr. Colls. and Univs., 1940-84, supt. city schs., Greenup, Ky., 1941-43; vis. lectr., prof. Am. U., Cairo, 1960-61; tchr. Grad. Coll. Edn., U. Nev., summer 1958; writer in residence Eastern Ky. U., 1965-69; dir. creative writing workshops Murray State U., summers 1969-72, 75-76; Specialist Dept. State, USIS, 1962-63; Am. rep. Asian Writers' Conf., 1962. Author short stories, poetry, articles.; Author: poems Man With a Bull-Tongue Plow, 1934, Head O' W-Hollow; stories, 1936, Beyond Dark Hills; autobiography, 1938, Trees of Heaven; novel, 1940, Men of the Mountains; stories, 1941, Taps for Private Tussie (Thomas Jefferson Southern Award $2500, Book-of-the-Month 1943), Mongrel Mettle (autobiography of a dog), 1944, Album of Destiny; poems, 1944, Foretaste of Glory; novel, 1946, Tales From the Plum Grove Hills; Stories, 1946, The Thread That Runs So True, 1949 (NEA selection as best book 1949), Hie to the Hunters, 1950, Clearing in the Sky, 1950, Kentucky Is My Land; poems, 1952, The Good Spirit of Laurel Ridge, 1953, The Beatinest Boy, 1953, A Penny's Worth of Character, 1954, Red Mule; juvenile, 1954, The Year of My Rebirth, 1956, Plowshare in Heaven; collection short stories, 1958, The Rightful Owner, 1960, God's Oddling, 1960, Andy Finds A Way, 1961, Hold April, 1962, A Jesse Stuart Reader, 1963, Save Every Lamb, 1964, Daughter of the Legend; novel, 1965, My Land Has A Voice, 1966, Ride with Huey the Engineer; Jr. book, 1966, Mr. Gallion's School, 1967, Come Gentle Spring; story collection, 1969, To Teach to Love, 1969, Old Ben, 1970, Come Back to the Farm; non-fiction, 1971, Come to My Tomorrow Land, 1971, Dawn of Remembered Spring, 1972, The Land Beyond The River; novel, 1973, Thirty-Two Votes Before Breakfast, 1974, My World, 1975, The World of Jesse Stuart: Selected Poems, 1975, The Seasons: Autobiography in Verse, 1976, Dandelion On The Acropolis, 1978, The Kingdom Within, 1979, Lost Sandstones and Lonely Skies Essays, 1979, If I Were Seventeen Again, 1980; Author of: short stories in anthologies Best Short Stories, O. Henry Meml. Collection; Co-editor: textbook Outlooks Through Literature; Contbr. to: others. Mem. group to revise Ky. State Constrn., chmn. health, welfare and edn. com.; bd. dirs. Ky. Heart Assn., state chmn., 1964. Served as apprentice seaman USN, 1944; commd. lt. (j.g.) 1944, 75, 76. Recipient Jeanette Sewal Davis Poetry prize, 1934; 5000 prize Acad. of Arts and Scis., 1941; 5000 prize Acad. Am. Poets, 1961; Guggenheim fellow for European travel, 1937. Mem. Poetry Soc. Am. Republican. Methodist. Home: Greenup, Ky. Died Feb. 17, 1984.

STUBNITZ, MAURICE, mfr. metal products and chemicals; b. Balt., Dec. 15, 1890; s. Hilliel and Ida (Bransky) S.; B.S. in Civil and Mech. Engring., Carnegie Inst. Tech., 1916; m. Dorothy Loretta Swartz, Apr. 3, 1926; 1 dau., Jean M. Mech. and sales engr., 1913-34; founder Stubnitz Greene Corporation, 1935, president, dir., 1935-61, chairman board, chief executive officer, 1961-65; cons., dir. of Hoover Ball & Bearing Co., Ann Arbor, Mich., from 1964; director of the Commercial Savs. Bank of Adrian. Past pres., life dir. of the Lenawee County United Fund; past pres. Asso. Charities. Served with 18th Inf., Pa. N.G., 1910-13. Mem. American Society Body Engineers (life member), Soc. Automotive Engrs., Engring. Soc. Detroit. Clubs: Adrian, Lenawee Country, (Adrian). Home: Manitou Beach, Mich. †

STUDEBAKER, JOHN WARD, educational publisher; b. McGregor, Ia., June 10, 1887; s. Thomas Henderson and Mary (Dorcas) S.; A.B., Leander Clark Coll., 1910; A.M., Columbia, 1917; LL.D., Drake U., 1934; LL.D., Muhlenberg Coll., 1938, U. of Md., 1945; honorary LL.D., Boston University, 1948; married Eleanor Regina Winberg, Dec. 25, 1907; one son, John Gordon. Earned way through college working as a union bricklayer; began as principal high sch. and coach of athletics, Guthrie Center, Ia., 1910, then prin. elementary and Junior high sch., Mason City, Ia., 1911-14; asst. supt. schs., Des Moines, 1914-20, supt. from 1920; apptd. U.S. commr. of edn., May 18, 1934, and accepted the office, on leave of absence from Ia. position; resigned the Des Moines superintendency, Feb. 1937; U.S. Commr. Edn. to 1948; vice-pres. and chmn. editorial bd., Scholastic magazines from July 1948. National dir. Junior Red Cross, Washington, D.C., during World War I. Widely known for successful administrative abilities and knowledge of instructional techniques; especially concerned in the welfare of handicapped children, in adult education, education by radio, conservation education, youth guidance, crime prevention and correction through education. Organized as a part of the public school system of Des Moines "the most comprehensive and carefully planned program of public forums ever inaugurated under public auspices"; as commr. of edn. he has promoted public forum demonstrations throughout U.S. Organized nat. defense training program in engring. colls. and vocational schs. and in rural areas, 1940-41, later converted to war training, for which Congress made further appropriations, 1942-43, 1943-44. Member N.E.A., Religious Education Association, etc. Methodist. Mason (Shriner), Rotarian. Author: Plain Talk, The American Way, and numerous text books; co-author supplementary reading book series entitled, Our Freedoms, also series self-teaching arithmetic books. Contbr. on edn. Address: New York, N.Y. †

STURC, ERNEST, economist; b. Bekescaba, Hungary, Jan. 12, 1915; s. Jindrich Jan and Regina (Atlas) S.; J.D., Comenius U., Bratislava, Czechoslovakia, 1938; postgrad. U. Chgo., 1939-42; m. Hilda Sirluck, Dec. 26, 1946; children—Marta Elizabeth, John Henry. Fgn. service officer of Czechoslovakia, 1939-46; dep. dir. Czechoslovakia Govt. Information Service, 1942-46; with IMF, 1946-80, dir. exchange and trade relations dept., 1965-80. Del. Czechoslovakia to Bretton Woods Conf. Internat. Monetary Coop., 1944, to San Francisco Conf. on UN, 1945. Mem. Am. Econ. Assn. Home: Washington, D.C. Died Oct. 27, 1980.

STURGEON, THEODORE HAMILTON, author; b. S.I., N.Y., Feb. 26, 1918; s. Edward and Christine (Dicker) Waldo; m. Helen Jayne Tannehill, July 22, 1976; children by previous marriage—Patricia (Mrs. Dana Shires), Cynthia (Mrs. J.W. Pegram), Robin, Tandy, Noel, Timothy, Andros. Author short stories, novels, 1938—; TV script writer for: others. Star Trek (Recipient Argosy award 1949, Internat. Fantasy award 1954, Nebula award 1970, Hugo award 1971); Author: Killdozer, 1944, The Dreaming Jewels, 1950, More Than Human, 1954, Some of Your Blood, 1961, The Joyous Invasions, 1965, Starshine, 1968, Caviar, 1968, E Pluribus Unicorn, 1970, Beyond, 1970, Sturgeon is Alive and Well, 1971, The Worlds of Theodore Sturgeon, 1972, More Than Human, 1972, Case and The Dreamer, 1974, The Synthetic Man, 1974, The Stars Are the Styx, 1979, The Golden Helix, 1979, Slow Sculpture, 1981; Book editor: Twilight Zone mag. Mem. Writer's Guild Am. W., Sci. Fiction Writers Am. Died May 8, 1985.

SUBLETTE, CLIFFORD MACCLELLAN, writer; b. Charleston, Ill., Aug. 16, 1887; s. James MacClellan and Kate (Heath) S.; grad. Shortridge High Sch., Indianapolis, Ind., 1906; student Art Inst. Chicago, 1907, Acad. Fine Arts (Chicago), 1908; m. Mary Shuler, of Indianapolis, Oct. 18, 1913; 1 dau., Mary Catherine (dec.). With traffic dept. N.Y.C.R.R., at Indianapolis, 1910; sec. Central Electric Traffic Assn., Indianapolis, 1911-14; newspaper writer, oil business, etc., until 1921; assisting in development of green vegetable growing in mountain dists. of Colo.; with Associated Press, Denver, 1927-29; has devoted attention to writing novels from 1929. Served at Central Machine Gun O.T.S., Camp Hancock, Augusta, Ga., Aug.-Dec. 1918. Author: The Scarlet Cockerel, 1925 (winner $2,000 Charles Boardman Hawes prize, offered by Atlantic Monthly); The Bright Face of Danger, 1926; The Golden Chimney, 1931; Greenhorn's Hunt, 1934.†

SUGGS, JOHN THOMAS, lawyer; b. Denison, Tex., Dec. 22, 1904; s. John Thomas and Ruby Edna (Bunch) S.; B.B.A., U. Tex., 1925, LL.B., 1927; m. Mary Hope Robinson, Jan. 31, 1929; children—Ann Lee, Mary Shelly. Admitted to Tex. bar, 1927; gen. practice of law, Dallas, 1927-38; State Dist. judge 1938-44; ret. pres., chmn. bd. T. &P. Ry.; dir. State Nat. Bank of Denison, First Nat. Bank of Van Alstyne, Tex.; practicing law; cattel raiser. Instr., So. Methodist U. Law Sch. Mem. initial bd. dirs. State Bar of Tex., 1940-41. Fellow Tex. Bar Found.; mem. Dallas Citizens Council, Am. Bar Assn., State Bar Tex., Sigma Alpha Epsilon. Democrat. Episcopalian. Mason. Clubs: City, Dallas Country (Dallas). Home: Dallas, Tex. Died Oct. 20, 1983.

SUITER, GRANT, clergyman; b. Black Bear, Idaho, Jan. 26, 1908; s. Elmer Marshall and Winifred Rosaland (Handson) S.; m. Edith Rettos, May 12, 1956. Ordained to ministry Oct. 10, 1926; dir. Watch Tower Bible and Tract Soc. Pa., from 1938, asst. sec.-treas., 1943-47, sec.-treas., 1947; dir. Watchtower Bible and Tract Soc. N.Y., from 1947, asst. sec.-treas., 1944-47, sec.- treas., 1947. Home: Brooklyn, N.Y. Died Nov. 22, 1983.

SULLIVAN, FRANCIS WILLIAM, author; b. at Evanston, Ill., Feb. 16, 1887; s. Arthur Nahum and Lizzie (White) S.; Ph.B., Lafayette Coll., Easton, Pa., 1908; M.A., Columbia, 1909; m. Beatrice Elwell Lawrence, Nov. 15, 1911. Mem. Theta Delta Chi. Episcopalian. Author: Children of Banishment, 1914; Alloy of Gold, 1915; Star of the North, 1916; The Godson of Jeannette Gontreau, 1917. Contbr. short stories to Ladies' Home Journal, Munsey's, Smart Set, etc. Home: Norwalk, Conn. †

SULLIVAN, JOHN JOSEPH, investment banker; b. Denver, Dec. 30, 1894; s. William and Catherine (Clear) S.; A.B., Regis, Coll., Denver, 1915, LL.D., 1940; m. Anne O'Neill, Aug. 7, 1940; 1 dau., Sheila Mary. Investment banker Boettcher & Co., 1915-27; with Bosworth, Sullivan & Co., Denver, and predecessor Sullivan & Co., 1927-81, former pres., chmn.; pres. The Fiducial Corp. Mem. bd. govs. N.Y. Stock Exchange, 1961-64. Dir. Denver Community Chest, from 1927, pres., 1940-42; treas. Cath. Charities Archdiocese of Denver, from 1930. Bd. dirs. Bonfils Theater, Central City Opera House Assn.; trustee Denver Found., Bonfils Found. Decorated Knight of St. Gregory the Great, Pope Pius XII; Knight of Malta. Mem. Assn. Stock Exchange Firms (past pres. bd. govs.), Nat. Assn. Securities Dealers (past chmn. bd. govs.), Investment Bankers Assn. (past gov.). Clubs: Denver, Denver Country, Rotary (past pres.), Mile High (Denver); Stock Exchange, Luncheon (N.Y.C.); Attic (Chgo.). Home: Denver, Colo. Died Nov. 2, 1981.

SULLIVAN, JOHN LAWRENCE, lawyer; b. Manchester, N.H., June 16, 1899; s. Patrick Henry and Ellen J. (Harrington) S.; m. Priscilla Manning, Dec. 28, 1932; children—Patricia, Charles Manning, Deborah. A.B., Dartmouth 1921; LL.D., Dartmouth 1921, 1949; LL.B., Harvard, 1924; LL.D., Duquesne U., 1948, U. N.H., 1949, Loyola U., 1949, U. Portland, Ore. Bar: N.H. bar 1923. And began practice in, Manchester, 1924; as mem. firm Sullivan & White; county solicitor Hillsborough Co., 1929-33; partner Sullivan & Sullivan, 1930, became sole owner, 1931; now sr. partner Sullivan & Wynot, Manchester, N.H.; also Sullivan & Beauregard, Washington; dir. emeritus Nat. Savs. & Trust Co.; Apptd. asst. to commr. of internal revenue, 1939; asst. sec. of treasury, 1940-44; asst. sec. Navy for Air, 1945; undersec. of navy, 1946-47, sec. of, 1947-49. Trustee Naval Hist. Found. Served with U.S. Navy, 1918. Mem. D.C., N.H. bar assns., Navy League of the U.S. (dir.), Am. Legion (comdr. N.H. Dept. 1937), Chi Phi, Delta Sigma Rho. Democrat. Roman Catholic. Clubs: K.C. (Boston), Clover (Boston); Burning Tree (Bethesda, Md.); Chevy Chase (Md.); Metropolitan (Washington). Home: Manchester, N.H. Died Aug. 8, 1982.

SULLIVAN, JOSEPH PETER, city ofcl.; b. Chgo., June 13, 1888; s. Patrick John and Marion Rachel (Cellow) S.; student Orr's Bus. Coll., 1905-07. With Graselli Chem. Co., subsidiary E. I. duPont de Nemours & Co., 1908-53, mgr. sales, Chgo., 1924-37, dist. mgr. Midwest, 1937-53; dir. Northwest Tire & Supply Co. Mem. bd. commrs. Chgo. Housing Authority, from 1953, chmn., from 1956. Trustee, gov. Glenwood Sch. for Boys. Mem. Chgo. Drug & Chem. Assn. (dir., past pres.), Chgo. Athletic Assn., Chgo. Perfumery Soap and Extract Assn. Roman Catholic. Club: Olympia Fields Country (past pres.). Home: Chicago, Ill. †

SULLIVAN, JOSEPH V., bishop; b. Kansas City, Mo., Aug. 15, 1919; s. John L. and Anastasia Agnes (Prosser)

S. S.T.D., Cath. U., 1949. Ordained priest Roman Cath. Ch., 1946, bishop of, Baton Rouge, from 1974; aux. bishop of, Kansas City-St. Joseph, Mo., titular bishop of, Tagamuta, 1967-74. Address: Baton Rouge, LA.

SULLIVAN, RICHARD HOWARD, foundation executive; b. Arcanum, Ohio, Nov. 1, 1917; s. Henry Lee and Margery (Penn) S.; m. Jean Elizabeth Fox, Dec. 20, 1941; children—Barbara Lee (Mrs. Lish Whitson), Mary Jean (Mrs. James J. Ragen, Jr.), Richard Penn. A.B., Harvard, 1939, A.M., 1940; LL.D., Pacific U., 1960; D.H.L., Hebrew Union Coll., 1962, Manhattan Coll., 1968; LL.D., Reed Coll., 1967, Coll. Notre Dame of Md., 1967, Lycoming Coll., 1968, Occidental Coll., 1968; H.H.D., Central Coll., 1967; Litt.D., Beaver Coll., 1967, Marietta Coll., 1968. Asst. dean Harvard, 1941-42; adminstrv. asst., coll. entrance exam. bd. Princeton, 1946, asst. dir., 1946-48; asst. treas. Ednl. Testing Service, 1948-49, exec. v.p., treas., 1949-56; pres. Reed Coll., Portland, Oreg., 1956-67, Assn. Am. Colls., 1967-69; mng. dir. Am. Book Pubs. Council, 1969-70; asst. to pres. Carnegie Corp. N.Y., 1970-76, treas., 1976-82, v.p. fin., 1980—. Sec. Carnegie Found. for Advancement Teaching, 1974-76, treas., 1976-80; Trustee, mem. finance com. Coll. Entrance Exam. Bd., 1961-66; mem. Nat. Sci. Bd., 1966-72; Mem. bd. edn. Princeton Twp., N.J., 1956; chmn. Oreg. Colls. Found., 1958; Trustee Oreg. Grad. Center Study and Research, 1963-66, Coll. Retirement Equities Fund, 1963-66, Com. Econ. Devel., 1964-70; trustee Found. Center, 1967-73, chmn., 1970-73; trustee, mem. investment com. Common Fund, 1968-81; bd. dirs. John and Mary R. Markle Found., 1965-71, Investor Responsibility Research Center, 1977-81. Served from ensign to lt. USNR, 1942-46. Mem. Phi Beta Kappa, Phi Beta Kappa Assos. Club: Harvard (N.J.). Home: Princeton, N.J. Died June 22, 1982.

SULLIVAN, RICHARD THOMAS, educator, author; b. Kenosha, Wis., Nov. 29, 1908; s. Thomas A. and Rose (Pitts) S.; A.B., U. Notre Dame, 1930; student Art Inst. Chgo., 1930-31; m. Mabel Constance Priddis, May 2, 1932; children—Jill Mary (Mrs. David Keiffer), Molly Ann. Free-lance writer, 1931-36; mem. faculty U. Notre Dame, 1936-76, prof. English, 1952-74, prof. emeritus, 1974. Recipient Lay Faculty award U. Notre Dame, 1946. Author: (novels) Summer After Summer, 1942, The Dark Continent, 1943, The World of Idella May, 1946, First Citizen, 1948, 311 Congress Court, 1953, The Three Kings, 1956; (short stories) The Fresh and Open Sky, 1950; (non-fiction) Notre Dame, 1951; also revs., plays. Home: South Bend, Ind. Died Sept. 13, 1981.

SULLIVAN, WILLIAM FRANCIS, assn. exec.; b. Nashua, N.H., Oct. 8, 1913; s. William Francis and Mary Elizabeth (Thomas) S.; student Phillips Exeter Acad., 1930-33; A.B., Harvard, 1938; LL.B., 1941; m. Helen B. Dolan, Feb. 27, 1943; children—Christine B., William, Mary. Admitted Mass. bar, 1941, and practiced with firm of Ropes, Gray, Best, Coolidge & Rugg, specializing in labor law practice, Boston, 1941-50; treas., pres. Nat. Assn. Cotton Mfrs. 1950-79; pres. No. Textile Assn., 1959-79. Mem. N.H., Boston bar assns. Roman Catholic. Home: Belmont, Mass. Died Apr. 12, 1979.

SULZBERGER, MARION BALDUR, physician, dermatologist; b. N.Y.C., Mar. 12, 1895; s. Ferdinand and Stella (Ullmann) S.; student Harvard, 1912-13; studied medicine, France, Switzerland, Germany, 1920-29; degree of basic med. sci., U. Geneva, Switzerland, 1921; M.D., U. Zurich, Switzerland, 1926; m. Edna F. Lowenstein, 1915; 1 dau., Margaret L. (Mrs. Francis Dobo); m. 2d, Kathryn Mullen Conway, Oct. 23, 1933; m. 3d, Roberta Zechiel Merrill, Sept. 1958. Miscellaneous activities, 1913-20; intern Kantonspital, Zurich, 1925-26; asst. dermatology and syphilis Dermatologic U. Clinic (Bruno Bloch, dir.), 1926-29; in U. Clinic (J. Jadasshon, dir.), Breslau, Germany, 1929; asst. clin. prof. dermatology and syphilology Columbia, 1935-46, asso. clin. prof., 1946-47; George Miller Mackee prof. dermatology and syphilology N.Y. U. Bellevue Med. Center; prof. emeritus N.Y. U. Sch. Medicine; chmn. dept. dermatology and syphilology Post-Grad. Med. Sch., N.Y. U., 1954-60, now prof. emeritus dermatology and syphilology; now clin. prof. dermatology U. Calif. at San Francisco; cons. dermatology and syphilology VA Hosp., Univ. Hosp., N.Y. U. Med. Center, Bellevue Hosp. Asso., dermatology. Montefiore Hosp., N.Y.C., 1931-46; cons. dermatology and syphilology, French Hosp., 1938; attending dermatologist and syphilologist, skin and cancer unit, N.Y. Post-Grad. Hosp., Columbia, 1938-46; dir. N.Y. Skin and Cancer Unit, N.Y. U. Hosp., 1949-60; research asso. Cornell U. Med. Coll., 1942, Spl. cons. USPHS, USN, several other orgns.; pres. Internat. League Dermatologic Socs., 1957-62; mem. gen. medicine study sect. NIH, USPHS, 1957-59; tech. dir. research U.S. Army Med. Research & Devel. Command, Office Surgeon Gen., 1961-64; tech. dir. research Letterman Gen. Hosp., San Francisco, 1964-68; past sci. adviser Letterman Gen. Hosp. and U.S. Army Med. Research Unit, Presidio. Pilot USNR, lt. (j.g.), 1917-19; lt. comdr. MC USNR 1940, comdr. 1943, capt. 1945. Decorated Legion of Merit (U.S.); comdr. Cross of Anjouan, Legion of Honor (France); recipient Meritorious Civilian Service medal Army Dept., 1970. Fellow N.Y. Acad. Medicine, Am. Acad. Allergy, Am. Acad. Dermatology and Syphilology, A.C.P.; mem. Am. Dermatol. Assn. (pres. 1959-60); mem. or hon. mem. fgn., nat. and state profl. socs. Editor: (with Dr. Fred Wise) Yearbook of Dermatology and Syphilology, 1931-42, sr. editor, 1943-55; editor numerous other tech. works. Author: Dermatologic Allergy; Dermatologic Therapy in General Practice (with Dr. Jack Wolf), 1940; Manual of Dermatology, 1942; (with others) Office Imunology 1947. Contbr. sci. articles to jours. Home: San Francisco, Calif. Died Nov. 24, 1983.

SUMMERS, LANE, lawyer; b. Beatrice, Neb., Mar. 21, 1889; s. Williamson Shaw and Helen (Lane) S.; student U. Chicago, 1909-10, U. Mich., 1907-09; LL.B., U. Wash., 1912; m. Hazel Thain, Nov. 20, 1909 (died 1932); children—Elizabeth (Mrs. Harold D. Mitchell), Thane (dec.), Helen Jane (1917), Elane (Mrs. Jerome Hellmuth), Jenness (Mrs. V. Chetwood Brewer, Jr.); m. 2d Lillian Churchill, Nov. 22, 1934. Admitted to Wash bar, 1912; dep. pros. atty., Seattle, 1914-18; practicing lawyer, specializing in maritime law, Seattle, from 1912; partner Summers, Howard & Le Gros. Chmn. com. to draft admiralty rules, apptd. by U.S. Dist. Ct., 1940-41; advisor to Japan Ship Owners Mut. Protection and Indemnity Assn., from 1948; president of the Japan Society of Seattle, 1954-55. Mem. Am. (adv. bd. jour. 1948-54), Wash. State and Seattle bar assns., Maritime Law Assn. U.S. (exec. com. 1935-36, v.p., 1949-51), Nat. Assn. Legal Aid Orgns. (v.p. 1940), Am. Judicature Soc., Social Welfare League (pres. 1924-27), Seattle C. of C., Municipal League Seattle, Propellor Club U.S., Assn. Average Adjusters U.S., Inter-American Bar Assn., Delta Tau Delta. Republican. Clubs: Rainier, Automobile, Young Men's Business (pres. 1919) (Seattle). Author surveys and articles in legal jours. Asso. editor of American Maritime Cases, 1926—. Home: Seattle, Wash. †

SUMMERS, OWEN, army officer; b. Portland, Ore., May 23, 1890; s. Gen. Owen Summers, Sr.; commd. 2d lt. Inf. Res., May 1917; capt. Inf. Regular Army, July 1, 1920, advancing through the grades to brig. gen., Sept. 1942; grad. Infantry School 1923, Command and General Staff School 1935, Army War College, 1939; dist. comdr. Civilian Conservation Corps, Ft. McPherson, Georgia, 1940; G-1 Trinidad Base Command, Port-of-Spain, Brit. West Indies, Apr. 1941; commanded 33rd U.S. Infantry, Trinidad Mobile Force and Fort Read, Trinidad, B.W.I., 1942-43; asst. div. comdr., 80th U.S. Inf. Div., third U.S. Army, 1943-45; comdg. gen., 12th Reinforcement Depot, 1945; comd. gen., U.S. Task Force, Norway, 1945; chief, Theater Visitors Bur., U.S. Forces, European Theater, 1945. Served with 91st Div., France and Belgium, World War I; awarded Silver Star. Served with 80th U.S. Inf. Div. in France, Belgium, Luxemburg and Germany, World War II, awarded Legion of Merit, Bronze Star, Purple Heart, Legion d'Honneur and Croix de Guerre with Palm, Commander of the British Empire, Order of St. Olaf, Knight Commander. Home: Oklahoma City, Okla. †

SUMRALL, FRANKLIN H., coll. prof.; b. Shubuta, Miss., Mar. 1, 1889; s. Rufus W. and Annie (Phillips) S.; A.B., Miss. Coll., 1916; A.M., U. of Chicago, 1927; student Univ. Liverpool, Eng., 1919, U. of Chicago, summers 1930, 33, 36, 41; m. Emma F. Cowsert, Aug. 9, 1922 (deceased); m. 2d, Mrs. Marcella Christianson Dunmire, June 30, 1949. Principal Stinson Sch., Meridian, Miss., 1909-10; prin. Obadiah High Sch., Meridian, 1912-14, Cascilla (Miss.) High Sch., 1916-18, 1919-20; head comml. dept. Little Rock (Ark.) High Sch., 1920-26; prof. commerce, Grove City (Pa.) Coll., 1927-47, prof. accounting from 1948; propr. Capital Duplicating Service, Jackson, Miss., 1947-48. Served in U.S. Army, 1918-19. Mem. Nat. Bus. Teachers Assn., N.E.A. (bus. sect.), C. of C. Democrat. Presbyn. Club: Rotary. Contbr. articles to business mags. Home: Grove City, Pa. †

SURREY, STANLEY STERLING, lawyer, educator; b. N.Y.C., Oct. 3, 1910; s. Samuel and Pauline (Sterling) S.; m. Dorothy Mooklar Walton, June 6, 1938; 1 son, Scott Stanley. B.S. magna cum laude, CCNY, 1929; LL.B., Columbia U., 1932. Bar: N.Y. 1933, Mass. 1951. Research asst. Columbia Law Sch., 1932-33; atty. Proskauer, Rose & Paskus, N.Y.C., 1933; with NRA, Washington, 1933-35, NLRB, Washington, 1935-37, U.S. Treasury Dept., Washington, 1937-44, 46-47; vis. prof. Calif. Sch. Law, Berkeley, summer 1940; vis. lectr. Columbia Law Sch., summer 1947; prof. law. U. Calif., Berkeley, 1947-50, prof. law, Harvard, 1950-61, Jeremiah Smith prof. law, 1958-61, 1969-81, Jeremiah Smith prof. law emeritus, 1981—, also dir. program for internat. taxation, 1953-61; chief reporter Am. Law Inst. income tax project, 1948-61, supr., 1975—; asst. sec. for tax policy Treasury Dept., 1961-69, cons., 1977-81; Mem. Am. Tax Mission to Japan, 1949, 50; spl. counsel U.S. House ways and means King subcom. on internal revenue adminstrn., 1951-52; cons. Treasury Dept., P.R., 1954; spl. adviser UN Expert Group on Tax Matters, 1969—; mem. permanent sci. com. IFA, 1969—. Author: (with others) casebooks in fed. taxation field Federal Income Taxation, Cases and Materials, 2 vols, 1972, 73, 82, Federal Wealth Transfer Taxation, Cases and Materials, 1977, 80, Pathways to Tax Reform, 1973; Contbr. (with others) articles to legal and sailing periodicals. Bd. overseers Florence Heller Sch. Brandeis U., Coll. of V.I.; trustee TIAA, 1972-78. Served as lt. (j.g.) USNR, 1944-46. Decorated Order Sacred Treasure Japan). Fellow Am. Acad. Arts. and Scis.; mem. Am. Bar Assn. (council taxation sect. 1958-60), Nat. Tax Assn. (pres. 1979-80), Phi Beta Kappa. Home: Cambridge MA

SURTEES, ROBERT LEE, motion picture photographer; b. Covington, Ky., Aug. 9, 1906; s. James Daniel and Besse Ranton (Sayers) S.; m. Maydell Powell, Sept. 17, 1930; children—Nancy Lee (Mrs. Walter Corby), Bruce, Linda, Thomas. Grad. high sch., Cin. With, EFA Studio, also UFA Studio, Berlin, Germany, 1928-30, with, Metro-Goldwyn-Mayer Studio, Culver City, Calif., 1942—; dir. photography motion picture prodns., 1941—(Recipient Look mag. award for King Solomon's Mines 1950, Fgn. Corr. award for King Solomon's Mines, 1950, for Quo Vadis, 1951, Academy award for King Solomon's Mines, 1951, Bad and the Beautiful, 1953, Ben Hur 1960, Acad. award nominations 1944, 50, 51, 52, 55, 59, 62, 67 (2), 71 (2), 73, 75, 76, 77, 78). Home: Carmel, Calif. Died Jan. 5, 1985.

SUSSMAN, SIDNEY X., accountant; b. N.Y.C., July 5, 1919; s. Jacob F. and Anna (Liebowitz) S.; m. Sylvia Blumenthal, Sept. 12, 1948 (dec. Sept. 1968); children—Diane, Philip, Gloria; m. Sally Bleim, Nov. 24, 1973. B.B.A., CCNY, 1941; J.D., U. Toledo, 1958. Bar: Ohio bar 1958; C.P.A., Ohio. With I.R. Miller & Co. (C.P.A.s), Toledo, 1948-70, partner, 1954-70, J. K. Lasser and Co., Toledo, 1970, Lublin, Sussman, Rosenberg & Damrautor, Toledo, 1970-84; tax lectr., 1960-84. Pres. Lucas County Assn. Retarded Children, 1962-63; chmn. budget and com. Ohio State Assn. Retarded Children, 1964-66, treas., 1966-68; vice-chmn. citizens adv. bd. N.W. Ohio Devel. Center, 1979. Served with AUS, 1942-45. Recipient cert. of service Ohio Assn. Retarded Children, 1966. Mem. Am. Inst. C.P.A.s, Ohio Soc. C.P.A.s. Home: Sylvania, Ohio. Died Dec. 1, 1984.

SUTCLIFFE, EMERSON GRANT, univ. prof.; b. Fall River, Mass., Oct. 2, 1890; s. George Lincoln and Sarah Alice (Taylor) S.; A.B., Harvard, 1911; A.M., U. of Ill., 1914, Ph.D., 1918; m. Hazel Mildred Chadderdon, June 22, 1918; children—Sarah (wife of Dr. William H. Todd), Grant Hopkins, Lecturer in English, Queens Univ., Kingston, Ont., 1911-12; asst. in English, U. of Ill., 1912-16, instr. in English, 1916-18, U. of Minn., 1919-20, asst. prof. in English, 1920-28; asso. prof. in English, Purdue U., 1928-32, prof. in English from 1932. Entered M.C., U.S. Army as pvt., 1918, disch. with rank of sergt. 1st class, 1919. Mem. Modern Lang. Assn. Author: Emerson's Theories of Literary Expression, 1923. Contbr. articles on Charles Reade to Proc. Modern Lang. Assn., Studies in Philology, The Trollopian. Home: West Lafayette, Ind. †

SUTHERLAND, WILLIAM ALEXANDER, JR, naval officer; b. Washington, Mar. 8, 1906; s. William Alexander and Minnie Wilson (Newberry) S.; student N.M. A. and M. Coll., 1922-23; B.S., U.S. Naval Acad., 1927; grad. Nat. War Coll., 1953; m. Maude Williams Perrin, Aug. 24, 1929 (dec. Apr. 1958); 1 son, William Perrin (USN); m. 2d, Dorothy Elizabeth Redwood Cooke, Oct. 31, 1959; stepchildren—Dorothy Dickson Cooke, Grace Redwood Cooke, Anne Sheppard Cooke. Commd. ensign U.S. Navy, 1927, advanced through grades to rear adm., 1955; served in surface commands, 1927-30; designated naval aviator, 1931; comdg. officer U.S.S. Altamaha, World War II; pub. information officer Naval Air Sta., Memphis, 1946-48; comdg. officer CIC Sch., Naval Air Sta., Glenview, Ill., 1948-49; chief staff Fleet Air Wings, U.S. Atlantic Fleet, 1949-50; aviation detail sect. Office Chief Naval Operations, 1950-52, dir. fgn. mil. assistance div., 1955-57; comdg. officer U.S.S. Bennington, 1953-54; chief staff, aide to staff Comdr. 2d Fleet, Atlantic, 1954-55; comdr. Fleet Air Wings Atlantic, 1957-59, Carrier Div. 2, 1959-60; comdr. Fleet Air Western Pacific, Fleet Air Japan, Naval Air Sta., Atsugi, Japan, 1960-62; dep. comdt. Nat. War Coll., Washington, 1962-83. Decorated Bronze Star medal, Navy Commendation ribbon, Navy Unit citation. Mason. Clubs: Army-Navy Country (Arlington, Va.); Princess Anne Country (Virginia Beach, Va.); Army-Navy (Washington). Home: Las Cruces, N.M. Died Aug. 31, 1983.

SUTPHIN, WILLIAM HALSTEAD, former congressman; b. Browntown, Middlesex County, N.J., Aug. 30, 1887; s. James Taylor and Charlotte (Brown) S.; ed. pub. schs., Matawan, N.J.; m. Catharine Bonner, Oct. 19, 1922; children—Susan, William Taylor. Mayor of Matawan, 1916-19 and 1922-28; mem. 72d to 77th Congresses (1931-43), 3d N.J. Dist. Served with 1st Squadron, N.J. Cav., Mexican Border, 1916; enlisted as pvt., U.S. Army, May 1917; discharged as capt., July 1919. Mem. Holland Soc., Sons of Am. Revolution. Democrat. Presbyterian. Home: Matawan, N.J.†

SUTTER, DONALD E(VANS), banker; b. Pass Christian, Miss., Sept. 26, 1911; s. John A. and Lillian (Evans) S.; m. Mary Elizabeth Sweatt; 1 son, Donald E. Edn. Sch. Banking of South, La. State U.; grad/ St. Bank Officer Seminar, Harvard U. With Hancock Bank, Gulfport, Miss., v.p., 1947-63, exec. v.p., 1963, later chmn. bd., dir. Served with USN, 1942-46. Mem. Gulfport C. of C. (past pres., dir.), Miss. Bankers Assn. (past group v.p.), Gulfport C. of C. (past pres.). Clubs: Gulfport Yacht (past commodore); Met. Dinner (dir.). Lodge: Rotary (past pres.). Died June 13, 1984.

SUTTON, GEORGE MIKSCH, ornithologist, bird artist; b. Bethany, Neb., May 16, 1898; s. Harry Trumbull and Lola Anna (Miksch) S. Student, Tex. Christian U., Ft. Worth, 1913-14; B.S., Bethany (W.Va.) Coll., 1923, Sc.D., 1952; Ph.D., Cornell U., 1932. Mem. staff Carnegie Mus., Pitts., 1919-25; Pa. state ornithologist, 1925-29; curator of birds Cornell U., Ithaca, N.Y., 1931-45; mem. of expdns.

for Carnegie Mus. to Labrador, 1920, 28, Carnegie Mus. to Labrador (to Hudson Bay), 1923, 26, solo expdn. to, Southampton Island, Hudson Bay, 1929-30, expdn. to Churchill, Hudson Bay, 1931, discovered eggs of Harris's sparrow); expdns. since 1930 to, Sask., So. states of U.S., (for ivory-billed woodpeckers), Western Okla., Rio Grande Valley, B.C., Hudson Bay, Mexico, Iceland, Victoria Island, Bathurst Island, Galápagos Islands; now George Lynn Cross research prof. zoology and curator of birds emeritus U. Okla.; Adviser to Arctic Inst. N.Am. Devoted much time to painting birds, furnishing: illustrations for Phillips, Monson, and Marshall's Birds of Arizona, H.H. Bailey's Birds of Florida, Allen's American Bird Biographies and Golden Plover and Other Birds, Burleigh's Georgia Birds, Pettingill's Guides to Bird Finding, Vale's Wings, Fur and Shot, Todd's Birds of Western Pa., Birds of Santa Marta, Colombia and Birds of Labrador Peninsula, Meyer de Schavensee's Birds of Colombia and Birds of South America, Van Tyne and Berger's Fundamentals of Orinthclogy, Burgess's Seashore Book, Roberts' Birds of Minnesota, bird sect. World Book Ency., Brandt's Arizona Birdlife; Author: Introduction to Birds of Pennsylvania, 1928, Exploration of Southampton Island, Hudson Bay, 1932, Eskimo Year, 1934, Birds in the Wilderness, 1936, Mexican Birds, 1951, Iceland Summer, 1961 (recipient John Burroughs medal 1962), Oklahoma Birds, 1967, High Arctic, 1971, At A Bend in a Mexican River, 1972, Mexican Bird Portraits, 1975, Fifty Common Birds of Oklahoma, 1977, To a Young Bird Artist, 1979; autobiography Bird Student, 1980; Contbg. editor: autobiography Audubon Mag. Ornithology; editor: autobiography Ency., Arctica. Hon. trustee Oglebay Inst., Wheeling, W.Va. Served to maj. USAAF, 1942-45. Decorated knight cross Icelandic Order Falcon. Mem. Am. Ornithologists Union, Wilson Ornithol. Soc. (past pres.), Cooper Ornithol. Soc., Okla. Zool. Soc. (dir.), Okla. Ornithol. Soc. (dir.), Biol. Soc. Washington, Cranbrook Inst. Sci., Southwestern Assn. Naturalists, Arctic Inst. N.Am., Am. Polar Soc., Am. Geog. Soc., Am. Falconers Assn., Phi Beta Kappa, Sigma Xi, Phi Kappa Phi, Beta Theta Pi. Home: Norman, Okla.

SWAIN, ANNA SPENCER CANADA, pres. Northern Baptist Convention; b. Versailles, O., March 18, 1889; d. Rev. Prentice A. and Adelaide (Spencer) Canada; student Oberlin Coll., 1907-09; A.B., Brown University, 1911, honorary A.M., 1945; Doctor Letters Humanity, Franklin College, 1958; married Prof. Leslie Earl Swain, June 27, 1911. President Rhode Island Baptist Woman's Mission Soc., 1925, 1931, R.I. br. Am. Assn. U. Women, 1935, 1942; pres. Woman's Am. Bapt. Fgn. Mission Soc., 1935, pres. 1942; del. Internat. Missionary Council, Madras, India, 1938; chmn. semi-contenary gift com. Pembroke Coll., Brown U., 1942; pres. Fgn. Missions Conf. N. America, 1946; pres. Northern Bapt. Conv., 1944-46; mem. exec. com. World Council of Churches 1948-54; member Commission of Churches on Internat. Affairs. Trustee Brown U., 1949; Newton Theol. Seminary, 1947. Del. World Council of Churches, Amsterdam, 1948, India, 1952, Evanston, Illinois, 1954; mem. central com. World Council of Churches. Republican. Author: My Book of Missionary Heroines, 1930; Pioneer Missionary Heroines in America, 1932; Youth Unafraid, 1935 (all published Baptist Bd. Edn.); Christ and the World Community (Friendship), 1939. Traveled to Europe, 1931, 1933, around the world, 1938. Honorary degree Doctor of Humane Letters Keuka College, 1944. Home: Craigville-on-Cape-Cod, Mass. †

SWAIN, O.E., food company executive; b. 1917; (married). Salesman Ozburn & Abstow Parts Co., 1937-39; with Kraftco Corp., 1939-82; salesman Kraft Foods div., 1939-45, dist. sales mgr., 1945-49, product sales mgr., 1949-51, asst. to div. gen. mgr., 1951-55, assoc. div. mgr., 1955-57, div. mgr., v.p., 1957; assoc. gen. mgr. Kraft Foods Ltd., Can., 1957-58, pres., gen. mgr., dir., 1958-68; pres. Kraft Foods Ltd. (Kraft Foods div.), 1968-82, corporate exec. v.p., 1968-82, chmn. retail food group, 1976-82, chmn. dairy group, 1979, also dir.; ptnr. Delta Aquaculture, Indianola, Miss. Home: Winnetka, Ill. Died Mar. 13, 1985.*

SWAIN, ROBERT LEE, editor, teacher; b. Redden, Del., Sept. 29, 1887; s. Rev. Charles Philip and Martha Hester (Messick) S.; Pharm. D., U. of Md., 1909, LL.B., 1932, D.Sc., 1958; Pharm. M., Phila. Coll. Pharmacy and Science, 1934; Pharm. D., Conn. Coll. of Pharmacy, New Haven, 1934; Sc.D., Washington College, New England Coll. Pharmacy, 1956; Chestertown, Md., 1935; LL.D., Temple U., 1944; Dr. Pharmacy Adminstrn., Ohio No. Univ., 1956; m. Esther Beach Sprecher, Oct. 3, 1911; children—Daniel B. (dec.), Robert Lee. Pharmacist, Sykesville, Maryland, 1909-28; member Maryland Board of Pharmacy, 1920-40 (secretary 1925-40); deputy food and drug commr. Md. Dept. of Health, 1922-39; professor pharmacy law, Temple U., 1933-39; professorial lecturer on contemporary pharmacy, George Washington University; vice president Topics Publishing Co.; pharm. consultant to surgeon gen. U.S. Army. Remington honor medalist, 1939; distinguished service pharmacy alumni medal, U. of Md., 1950; J. Leon Lascoff Memorial Award, 1950; Henry Hurd Rusby award, 1958. Trustee U.S. Pharmacopoeia since 1936, West Nottingham Acad. (Colora, Md.), Coll. Pharmacy, Columbia. Mem. Am. Council Pharm. Edn., from 1933; treas. Com. on Status of Pharmacy in Govt. Service; mem. exec. com. Am. Foundation for Pharm. Edn.; adv. mem. Nat. Pharm. Council, John W. Dargavel Found. Mem. Am. Pharm. Assn. (pres. 1934), Nat. pres. Assn. Bds. of Pharmacy (pres. 1938), World Med. Assn. (dir.). Am. Inst. History of Pharmacy (dir.), other profl. and tech. assns.; mem. Nat. Pharmaceutical Syllabus Committee from 1928, chmn. bd. trustees, U.S. Pharmacopoeial Conv., 1945-60; mem. The Pharmaceutical Survey (Am. Council on Edn.), 1946. Presbyn. Club: Pharmaceutical Advertisers. Editor of Md. Pharmacist, 1925-39; contbg. editor Drug Topics, 1933-39; editor-in-chief Drug Topics and Drug Trade News, from 1939. Home: Jackson Heights, L.I., N.Y. †

SWAN, HERBERT S., city planner, industrial consultant; b. Shickley, Neb., Jan. 8, 1888; s. A. and Emma (Johnson) S.; Ph.B., U. of Chicago, 191 grad. study Columbia, 1910-11; m. Alma Oswal Aug. 21, 1915; children—Hugo, Herbert S. Engag in industrial development city planning and zoning work since 1911; consultant to Nat. City Bank of New York, Inst. of Public Adminstrn., New York Title and Mortgage Stockholders Protective Com., Indsl. Commn. of Paterson, and to cities of Newark, Paterson, Plainfield, Hoboken, Atlantic City (N.J.), New York, Albany, Troy, Yonkers, White Plains (N.Y.), Hartford, Waterbury, Danbury, Bridgeport, Norwalk, Greenwich, Bristol, New London (Conn.), Harrisburg (Pa.), Durham, Charlotte (N.C.), and many others; consultant Mid-Hudson Port Survey Com., Committee on Nat. Resources, Greater Youngstown (Ohio) Area Foundation. Mem. North Jersey Transit Commn.; mem. Am. Inst. City Planning, Nat. Conf. on City Planning; mem. com. on city planning and zoning of Pres. Hoover's Conf. on Home Bldg. and Ownership. Author: The Housing Market in New York City; New York City's Debt and Future Capital Outlays; The Jacquard Industry; The Plain Goods Silk Industry; Labor Policies vs. Competitive Conditions in the Dyeing Industry. Author or co-author of numerous booklets and reports on indusl. development, zoning and planning of Am. cities. Contbr. to The Appraisal Journal, Technology Review, Nat. Municipal Rev., Am. City Jour. of Land and Pub. Utility Economics, Am. Architect, and other jours. Home: Chicago, Ill. †

SWANSON, DAVID VERNER, clergyman; b. Axtell, Neb., Oct. 13, 1890; s. Olof and Bengta (Eriksdotter) S.; student Luther Coll., Wahoo, Neb., 1907-10; A.B., Augustana Coll., Rock Island, Ill., 1913, B.D., Augustana Theol. Sem., 1916, S.T.M., 1926, D.D., 1940; graduate studies, University of Neb., 1923-24; married Edith H. Peterson, June 21, 1916 (died December 9, 1947); children—Ruth La Vern (Mrs. Philip A. Farley), Pauline (Mrs. Harry Johnson), Vernon, David, Alan; married Euphemia Peterson-Stewart, February 1, 1950. Pastor, Saron Lutheran Ch., Iron Mountain, Mich., 1916-19, First Lutheran, Lincoln, Neb., 1919-28, Zion Lutheran, Gowrie, Ia., 1928-46, Geneva Lutheran, Ill., 1946-57; instr. Luther Theol. Sem., Lincoln, Neb., 1927. Mem. bd. of dir. Home for Aged, Madrid, Ia., 1936-40; v.p. Ia. Conf., 1936-40, pres., 1940-46; mem. bd. of Christian edn. and literature, 1930-42; bd. of parish edn., 1942-46; mem. exec. com. and sec. Lutheran Augustana Synod, from 1945; mem. Commission on Lutheran Unity, from 1955; member board dirs. Augustana Theol. Sem., 1947-59, Home for Aged, Marinette, Wis., 1918-19. Luther Coll., Neb., 1922-26; chmn. Com. for Lutheran Students, U. of Neb., 1926; v.p. Neb. Conf., 1926-27; mem. bd. of trustees, Superior Conf., 1918-19. Lutheran. Author of religious articles. Home: Geneva, Ill. †

SWANSON, GLORIA, (GLORIA MAY JOSEPHINE SWANSON) actress; b. Chgo., Mar. 27, 1899; d. Joseph T. and Adelaide (Klanowski) S.; m. Wallace Beery, Feb. 1916 (div.); m. Herbert K. Somborn (div. 1923); 1 child, Gloria (Mrs. Wilfrid Augustin Daly); m. Marquis de la Falaise de la Coudray, 1925 (div. 1931); m. Michael Farmer, Aug. 16, 1931 (div.); 1 child, Michelle Bridget (Mrs. Robert Amon); m. William N. Davey, 1945 (div. 1948); 1 child, Joseph (adopted); m. William Dufty, 1975. Student pub. schs., Chgo. Introduced Gloria Swanson Fashions, 1952. Actress on screen, from 1913; began with, Essanay Studios, Chgo., later with, Mack Sennett Comedies, Calif., Triangle Prodns., C.B. DeMille, Famous Players, Lasky-Paramount; formed own co., Gloria Swanson Prodns., 1926; dissolved, 1932; starred in: motion pictures, including Sunset Boulevard, 1950, Airport 1975; motion pictures including Don't Change Your Husband, The Impossible Mrs. Bellew, Male and Female, Bluebeard's Eighth Wife, Zaza, Manhandled, Madame Sans-Gene, Sadie Thompson, Tonight or Never, Music in the Air, Father Takes a Wife; 1st picture to record her speaking and singing voice The Trespasser, 1929; stage appearances Reflected Glory, 1942, Let Us be Gay, 1943, A Goose for the Gander, 1945, Twentieth Century, 1950-51, Nina, 1951-52; star: stage appearances Gloria Swanson TV Show, 1948-49; narrator, actress TV series, 1953; appeared in: film Nero's Big Week-End (Italian), 1956; TV film Killer Bees, 1974; on tour Red Letter Day, 1959-60, Between Seasons, 1961-62, The Inkwell, 1962-63, Reprise, 1967; appeared on: Broadway and on tour in Butterflies are Free, 1970-72; Author: Swanson on Swanson, 1980. Commr. youth and phys. fitness, City of N.Y., 1975; mem. nutrition com. Dist. 9, N.Y.C. Schs., 1976; v.p. Rep. Sr. Citizens for Ronald Reagan-George Bush, N.Y. State, 1980. Recipient Neiman-Marcus Fashion award, 1955; award for contbn. to World Fedn. of UN Assn.'s Decade for Women, 1981. Died Apr. 4, 1983.

SWANSON, ROY PAUL, lawyer; b. Kansas City, Mo., Apr. 6, 1896; s. Charles and Christina (Nelson) S.; student Park Coll., 1915-17; LL.B., Mo. U., 1923; children—Charles L., Paula (Mrs. Charles E. Bloczynski). Admitted to Mo. bar, 1923, since practiced in Kansas City; sr. partner firm Swanson, Midgley, Gangwere, Thurlo & Clarke, 1956-85; dir. U.S. Supply Co.; mem. fed. ct. martial bd. Gt. Lakes Naval Tng. Center. Mem. bd. police commrs. Kansas City, Mo., 1960-64; pres. Naturalization Council Kansas City, Mo., 1958-59; mem. Jackson County Park Bd., Kansas City, Mo., 1953-55; gen. counsel Order DeMolay. Trustee Liberty Meml. Assn. Served as ensign U.S. Navy, 1917-18. Recipient Citation of Merit, U. Mo. Law Sch. Mem. Am., Kansas City bar assns., Mo. Bar (pres. 1962-63, award of merit), Lawyers Assn. Kansas City (pres. 1950-51), S. Central Bus. Assn. (past pres.), Phi Delta Phi, Kappa Alpha. Conglist. Mason (Shriner). Club: University. Home: Kansas City, Mo. Died May 25, 1985; buried Kansas City, Mo.

SWARR, DAVID WHITMYER, lawyer; b. Manheim, Pa., Sept. 10, 1887; s. John P. and Harriet (Whitmyer) S.; A.B., Albright Coll., 1911; LL.B., U. Neb., 1915; m. Ellen Cole, Mar. 11, 1921; 1 dau., Jean E. (Mrs. Robert K. Andersen). Admitted to Neb. bar, 1915, practiced in Omaha; mem. firm Swarr, May, Smith & Andersen. Dir. Washington Natural Gas Co., 1943-67; chmn. bd., 1959-64. Mem. Order of Coif. Unitarian. Rotarian. Drafted Neb. constl. right to work amendment, Neb. anti-mass picketing law. Home: Omaha, Nebr. †

SWART, CHARLES ROBBERTS, state pres. of South Africa; b. Winburg, South Africa, Dec. 5, 1894; s. Hermanus and Aletta (Robberts) S.; B.A., U. Orange Free State, 1912, LL.B., 1918, LL.D., 1955; grad. student Columbia University, 1921-22; LL.D., Rhodes Univ., Grahamstown, South Africa, 1962, Potchefstroom University, 1963; m. Nellie de Klerk, Dec. 2, 1924; children—Dalena, Herman, Mem. Union Parliament, 1923-59; minister of justice in cabinet, 1948-59, minister edn., arts and sci., 1949-51; dep. prime minister Union South Africa, 1954-59, acting prime minister, 1958, governor general, 1960-61, state pres. of South Africa, 1961-82. Advocate, Supreme Ct. of South Africa 1919-48. Chancellor U. Orange Free State, 1951-82. Hon. fellow Coll. Physicians, Surgeons and Gynecologists of South Africa, 1963. Author of historical works, writings in Afrikaans lang. Home: South Africa. Died July 16, 1982.

SWARTSWELTER, ERNEST E., industrialist; b. Youngstown, O., May 11, 1889; s. John and Christine (Maxwell) S.; student Youngstown pub. schs.; m. Marian Mathers; children—Ernest E., Anne (Mrs. John Marshall Warren). Indsl. banker, 1912-31; propr., gen. partner Soucy, Swartswelter & Co., investment bankers, 1933-40; pres., chmn. bd. Aetna-Standard Engring. Co., 1940-56, chmn. of bd. and chief executive officer, 1956; vice chairman board Blaw-Knox Company, Pitts.; dir. Buckeye Pontiac Co., Buick Youngstown Co., Century Food Markets Co., Youngstown, Trans-World Traders, Inc., Pitts. Clubs: Duquesne (Pitts.); Iroquois Boating and Fishing (Conneaut Lake, Pa.); Surf (Miami Beach); Union (Cleve.); Youngstown (O.). Home: Conneaut Lake, Pa. †

SWEETSER, ARTHUR, author; b. Boston, July 16, 1888; s. Moses Foster and Edith Ashton (Balch) S.; A.B., Harvard, 1911, A.M., 1912; LL.D., Rollins Coll., Winter Park, Fla., 1938; Litt.D., Muhlenberg Coll., 1939; m. Ruth Gregory, June 19, 1915; children—Harold Foster (dec.), Adelaide Vanderpoel, Arthur Balch and Susan Gold (twins), Alan. With Springfield (Mass.) Republican, 1912-13; war corr. in France and Belgium, early part of World War I; corr. Associated Press, Washington, D.C., assigned to Dept. of State, 1916-17; commd. capt. Aviation Section of Signal Corps, U.S.A., 1917. Asst. dir. press sect. of Am. Commn. to Negotiate Peace; mem. information sect. of League of Nations, Geneva, 1918-32, apptd. counselor, 1930, acting dir. during 1933; dir. without section, Jan. 1, 1934-May 15, 1942; dep. dir. O.W.I., Washington, May 1942-June 1946. Chmn. United Nations Information Board, 1942-46. Attached to U.S. dels., United Nations Conf. at Atlantic City, Montreal (U.N.R.R.A.), Bretton Woods, San Francisco, and General Assembly, London, 1946. Special Adv. Sec.-Gen. U.N., March 1946; dir. United Nations Washington Information Office, Sept. 1946; president Woodrow Wilson Foundation, 1943-45; chmn. Washington World Affairs Center, 1948-49. Member Phi Beta Kappa. Clubs: Century, Harvard (New York); Chevy Chase (Washington). Author: Roadside Glimpses of the Great War, 1916; The American Air Service, 1919; The League of Nations Starts, 1920; also various pamphlets and articles on the League. Home: Washington, D.C. †

SWEIGERT, WILLIAM T., U.S. judge; b. 1900. Admitted to bar, 1923; U.S. judge No. Dist. Cal. Home: San Francisco, Calif.

SWENSON, RINEHART JOHN, prof. govt.; b. Ellsworth, Ia., Nov. 22, 1887; s. Samuel and Rachel (Kirkhus) S.; A.B., U. of Minn., 1915, M.A., 1916; Ph.D., U. of Wis., 1918; m. Aagot Thomte, Dec. 24, 1917. Scholar in polit. science, U. of Minn., 1915-16; fellow in polit. science U. of Wis., 1916-17; teaching asst., same, 1917-18; instr. in govt. N.Y. Univ., 1919-21, asst. prof. in govt., 1921-26, asso. prof. of govt., 1926-28, prof. of govt. from 1928; chmn. dept. of govt., Washington Sq. Coll., N.Y. U., 1932-50, head dept. govt. grad. Sch. Arts and Scis., 1950-52. Pvt. U.S. Army, World War. Mem. American Polit. Science Association, National Council on Naturalization and Citizenship, and Phi Beta Kappa Fraternity.

Author: Public Regulation of the Rate of Wages, 1916; National Government and Business, 1924; Methods and Status of Scientific Research (with Walter Earl Spahr), 1930. Contbr. to Tomorrow in the Making, 1939. Co-editor (with Rufus D. Smith) of the Ronald Press Political Science Series. Contbr. to ednl. jours. Home: Manhasset, N.Y. †

SWERN, DANIEL, educator; b. N.Y.C., Jan. 21, 1916; s. Philip and Ida (Sternfield) S.; m. Ann Ruth Siegel, Aug. 14, 1938; children—Harriet Ellen (Mrs. Stuart Solomon), Dorothy Jane (Mrs. Jay Federman). B.S., Coll. City N.Y., 1935; M.A., Columbia, 1936; Ph.D., U. Md., 1940. Research chemist Eastern regional research lab. U.S. Dept. Agr., Phila., 1940-48, research supr., 1948-63; prof. chemistry, sr. research investigator Temple U., 1963—; adj. prof. Drexel Inst. Tech., 1954-63; cons. Armstrong Cork Co., Mobil Research and Devel. Corp. Author: Industrial Oil and Fat Products, 1964, 4th edit., 1981, Organic Peroxides, vol. I, 1970, Vol. II, 1971; Vol. III, 1972; Contbr. to profl. jours. Recipient Arthur S. Flemming award U.S. Jr. C. of C., 1955, Lipid Chemistry award Am. Oil Chemists Soc., 1968. Mem. Phila. Organic Chemists' Club (past chmn.), Am. Chem. Soc. (chmn. 1968), Am. Oil Chemists' Soc., AAAS, AAUP, Am. Assn. Cancer Research, Sigma Xi, Phi Beta Kappa. Patentee in field. Home: Philadelphia PA

SWIETLIK, F(RANCIS) X(AVIER), judge; born Milwaukee, Nov. 24, 1889; s. Joseph and Michalina (Novak) S.; A.B., Marquette U., 1910, A.M., 1911, LL.B., 1914; LL.D. (hon.) Creighton U., 1942; m. Marie J. Czerwinski, July 25, 1923. Admitted to Wis. bar, Sept. 1914, and practiced in Milwaukee under firm name of Swietlik and Burns, 1914-34; spl. asst. dist. atty. Milwaukee Co., 1923; dean Marquette Univ. Law Sch., 1933-53; circuit judge Milw. County 1953-59. National chmn. Am. Relief for Poland from 1939. Served as captain, F.A., United States Army, World War I. Mem. Am., Wis., Milwaukee bar assns., Am. Legion. Republican. Roman Catholic. K.C. Elk. Home: Milwaukee, Wis. †

SWIFT, EMERSON H(OWLAND), educator; b. East Orange, N.J., Jan. 21, 1889; s. Dr. Arthur L. and Lilias (Howland) S.; A.B., Williams Coll., 1912; A.M., Princeton, 1916, Ph.D., 1921; m. Anne Wallis Davis, June 14, 1923; children—Lilias (Mrs. D. W. Barton), Anne (Mrs. S. B. Tanner), Emerson Howlad, Isabel J. Instr. in classics, Williams Coll., 1916-17, Amherst Coll., 1919, U. of Mich., 1922-23; asst. prof. art, U. of Chicago, 1923-26, asso. prof. fine arts, Columbia, 1926-46, prof. since 1946, Mathews lectr., 1946-47, 1952. Williams fellow, Am. Sch. Classics, Athens, Greece, 1912-13; fellow Archaeol. Inst., Athens, 1913-15 (engaged in Am. excavations at Corinth); asso. fellow Am. Acad. Rome, 1915. Served as 2d lt., 1917-18. Mem. Archaeol. Inst. Am., Society of Architectural Historians, Mediaeval Acad. Am., Phi Delta Theta. Republican. Club: Men's Faculty, (Columbia U.). Author: Roman Portraits at Corinth, 1921; Arte, Civilizacion y Ambiente, 1937; Hagia Sophia, 1940; Roman Sources of Christian Art, 1951; contbr. and adviser Columbia Encyclopedia, 1950; contbr. articles to scientific jours. Home: Princeton, N.J. †

SWIFT, GEORGE HASTINGS, JR., salt company executive; b. Boston, Jan. 24, 1919; s. George Hastings and Lucile (Casey) S.; m. Byrd Worthington Littlefield, Jan. 24, 1942; children—Byrd G., Silvia L., George Hastings III, Ann Swift Robinson. Grad., Deerfield Acad., 1938; student, Harvard, 1938-39; grad., Advanced Mgmt. Program, 1953. With N.E.D.M. & W., Somerville, Mass., 1939-40; with Swift & Co., Chgo., 1940-42, 46-50, mgr., Evansville, Ind., 1950-52, asst. v.p., Chgo., 1952-58, v.p. beef, lamb, veal, hides and wool, 1958-60, v.p. assisting pres., coordinator future planning and comml. research, 1960-61, v.p. assisting pres. purchasing, transp., pub. relations, agr. relations, bus. research, printing, patents, 1965-68; also dir. all Swift & Co. ins. affiliates, until 1968; mng. partner Independent Salt Co., Kanopolis, Kans., 1969-82; owner, breeder thoroughbreds Augean Stable, Chgo., Quail Run Farm, Middleburg, Va.; hon. chmn. Park Travel Agy. Mem. Chgo. Crime Commn. Served from pvt. to capt. Q.M.C. AUS, 1942-46. Mem. S.A.R., Soc. Mayflower Descs., Soc. Colonial Wars State Ill., Order Founders and Patriots Am. Episcopalian. Clubs: Rotary, Harvard, Economic, Chicago, Mid-Day. Home: Chicago, Ill. Died Dec. 14, 1982.

SWIFT, GEORGE ROBINSON, former senator; b. Baldwin County, Ala., Dec. 19, 1887; s. Charles Augustus and Susie (Roberts) S.; ed. Univ. Mil. Sch., Mobile, Ala., 1902-06; U. of Ala., 1906-07; m. Margherita Ligon, Nov. 25, 1914; children—Margherita Ligon (Mrs. Carl E. Jones), Susan Roberts (Mrs. Geoffrey P. Norman), George Robinson. Engaged in lumber business since 1907, Ala. and Mississippi. Mem. Ala. House of Reps. from Escambia County, Ala., 1931-35, Ala. State Senate from dist. composed of counties of Baldwin, Escambia and Monroe, 1935-39; dir. State Highway, 1943-46; apptd. to U.S. Senate, June 15, 1946, to fill vacancy caused by death of John H. Bankhead until election of successor, Nov. 1946. Mem. Delta Kappa Epsilon. Mason. Home: Atmore, Ala.†

SWIGERT, JOHN LEONARD, JR., former astronaut, business exec.; b. Denver, Aug. 30, 1931; s. John Leonard and Virginia S. B.S. in Mech. Engring, U. Colo., 1953; M.S. in Aerospace Sci, Rensselaer Poly. Inst., 1965; M.B.A., U. Hartford, 1967; D.Sc. (hon.), Am. Internat. Coll., 1970, Western Mich. U., 1970; LL.D., Western State U., 1970. Former engring. test pilot N.Am. Aviation, Inc., Pratt and Whitney Co., 1957-65; astronaut NASA, 1966-73; mem. support crew for Apollo 7 mission, mem. Apollo 13 backup crew, later command module pilot, 1970; exec. dir. Com. on Sci. and Tech., U.S. Ho. of Reps., Washington, 1973-79; v.p. BDM Corp., Denver, 1979-81, Internat. Gold & Minerals, Ltd., 1981—. Recipient Presdl. Medal for Freedom, 1970, Disting. Service medal NASA, Disting. Alumnus award U. Colo., 1970, Gold medal City of N.Y., 1970, Gold medal City of Chgo., 1970, Medal for Valor City of Houston, 1970, Antonian gold medal, 1972, Citizenship medal SAR, 1979; VFW Citizen of Yr. award, 1979. Fellow Am. Astronautical Soc. (co-recipient Flight Achievement award 1970), Soc. Exptl. Test Pilots (asso.), Am. Inst. Aeros. and Astronautics (asso., Octave Chanute award 1966, Haley Astronautics award 1971); mem. Quiet Birdmen, Phi Gamma Delta, Pi Tau Sigma, Sigma Tau. Home: Denver CO

SWINDLER, WILLIAM FINLEY, emeritus legal educator, author; b. St. Louis, Oct. 24, 1913; s. Merton Clay and Pearl (Traller) S.; m. Benetta Rollins, Oct. 7, 1939 (dec. Apr. 23, 1978); children: Elizabeth Pearl Henrietta, William Rollins Clayton. A.B., B.S., Washington U., 1935; A.M., U. Mo., 1936; Ph.D., 1942; LL.B., U. Neb., 1958. Bar: Nebr., D.C., Va., U.S. Supreme Ct. bars. Reporter St. Louis Star-Times, 1933, editorial writer, 1936-38; spl. corr. St. Louis Post-Dispatch, 1938-40; instr. in journalism U. Mo., 1938-40; asst. prof. journalism U. Idaho, 1940-44, head dept. journalism, 1941-46, assoc. prof., 1944-45, prof., 1945-46; prof. journalism U. Nebr., 1946-58; dir. U. Nebr. (Sch. Journalism), 1946-56; spl. corr. Columbia Broadcasting System, 1952; prof. law and dir. devel. Coll. William and Mary, 1958-65, prof. law, 1965-74, John Marshall prof. law, 1974-79, emeritus, 1979-84; Disting. vis. prof. law Okla. U., 1974; prof. law Summer Sch. Law in Eng., Exeter, 1970, 73, 78. Author: A Bibliography of Law on Journalism, 1947, Problems of Law in Journalism, 1955, Common Law in America, 1959, Magna Carta: Legend and Legacy, 1965, Court and Constitution in the 20th Century: The Old Legality, 1889-1932, 1969, The New Legality, 1932-68, 1970, The Modern Interpretation, 1974, Magna Carta (for high schools), 1968, The Constitution and Chief Justice Marshall, 1978, The Fourth United States Circuit: A History, 1984, American Constitutional Principles, 1984; Editor: Justice in the States, 1971, Sources and Documents of U.S. Constitutions, 1972-79; series editor: Studies on Bicentennial of American Legal Education, 1984. Mem. Am. Soc. Legal History (dir. 1960-62, v.p. 1962-64), Am. Judicature Soc. (dir. 1972-75), Am. Bar Assn., Am. Law Inst., Hist. Soc. Mo. (life), Supreme Ct. Hist. Soc. (dir. publs.), Order of Coif, Phi Delta Phi, Sigma Delta Chi, Kappa Tau Alpha (nat. sec. 1948-50, nat. pres. 1950-52). Democrat. Episcopalian. Home: Williamsburg, Va. Deceased.

SWING, JOSEPH M., govt. ofcl.; b. Jersey City, Feb. 28, 1894; s. Joseph and Mary Ann (Snellgrove) S.; B.S., U.S. Mil. Acad., 1915; grad. F.A. Sch., 1926, Command and Gen. Staff Sch., 1927, Army War Coll., 1935; m. Josephine Mary March, June 8, 1918; children—Joseph March, Mary Ann. Commd. 2d lt., U.S. Army, 1915, and advanced through the grades to lt. gen., Feb. 1951; served on Punitive Expdn., Mexico, 1916; comd. Headquarters Battery, 8th F.A., Ft. Bliss, 1916; instr. 1st O.T.C., Ft. Meyer, Va., Apr.-May 1917; aide de camp to General March, Washington, D.C., 1917; adjutant and capt., 1st F.A. Brigade, France, Aug. 1917-Mar. 1918; War Dept. Gen. Staff, Washington, D.C., Mar. 1918; aide de camp to chief of staff, Apr. 1918-May 1919; comdg. 1st Batn., 11th F.A., Hawaii, 1920-25, 9th F.A. Batn., Ft. Des Moines, 1925-26; instr. F.A. Sch., Ft. Sill, 1927-31; Office Chief of F.A., Washington, D.C., 1931-34; exec. 6th F.A., Ft. Hoyle, Md., 1936-38; Gen. Staff, 2d Div., Ft. Sam Houston, 1938-40; comd. arty. 1st Cav. Div., Ft. Bliss, Tex., 1940-41; comdg. arty., 82d Inf. Div., Camp Claiborne, La., 1942; comdg. gen. 11th Air Force Div., Camp Mackell, N.C., Feb. 1942; comd. 11th Airborne Div. in retaking Manila, Feb. 1945, and in occupation of Japan, Aug. 1945; comdg. gen. 1st Corps, 1948; participated in New Guinea, Leyte and Luzon campaigns; commanding general Artillery Center and comdt. Artillery Sch., Fort Sill, Oklahoma, 1949-50; commandant Army War Coll., comdg. gen. Ft. Leavenworth 1950-51; commanding general of Sixth Army, 1951-54; retired from army, 1954; commissioner of immigration and naturalization Dept. of Justice, from 1954. Decorated D.S.C., D.S.M., L.M., Silver Star with 2 oak leaf clusters, B. S. M. with oak leaf cluster, A.M.; with oak leaf cluster, Mexican campaign medal; Victory medal with battle clasp; Legion of Honor. Clubs: Army and Navy, Army and Navy Country (Washington). Home: Washington, D.C. Died Dec. 9, 1984.

SWINNERTON, FRANK ARTHUR, author; b. Wood Green, Middlesex, Eng., Aug. 12, 1884; s. Charles and Rose (Cottam) S.; ed. Home and Colonial Sch., Kings X, 1890-92; Church Sch., Hornsey, 1894-95; m. Mary Dorothy Bennett, Mar. 15, 1924; children—Jane Christine, Olivia Mary. Began as office boy, 1899; clerk J. M. Dent & Co., pubs., 1901-07; reader Chatto & Windus, pubs., 1909-26; lit. critic London Evening News, 1928-31; prin. novel reader, Observer, London, 1937-42; John O'London in John O'London's Weekly, 1949-54. Member Reform Club (London). Author numerous books from 1909; A Month in Gordon Square, 1953; The Sumner Intrigue, 1955; Background with Chorus, 1956; The Woman from Sicily, 1958; The Grace Divorce, 1960; Death of A Highbrow, 1960. Home: Cranleigh, Surrey, Eng. Died Nov. 9, 1982.

SWINTON, STANLEY MITCHELL, journalist; b. Charlevoix, Mich., Sept. 1, 1919; s. Roy Stanley and Jane Ann (Mitchell) S.; m. Helen Meek, Feb. 16, 1955; children—Scott, Donald, Neil. A.B., U. Mich., 1940. Editor A.P., Detroit, 1940-41, corr., Philippines, Indonesia, Indochina, 1945-47, chief of bur., Southeast Asia, 1947-48, Middle East 1948-50, war corr., Korea, 1950-51, chief of bur., Italy, 1951-57; gen. news editor Asso. Press World Service, 1957-60, dir. world services div., 1960-64, asst. gen. mgr. and dir. world services, 1964-82, v.p., 1972-82; vice-chmn. AP, Ltd., 1964-82; Howard R. Marsh disting. vis. prof. U. Mich., 1980. Contbg. author: Heartbreak Ridge, 1951, The Stars and Stripes, 1961, How I Got That Story, 1967, Crisis in International News Policies and Prospects, 1981. Former pres., chmn. exec. center Corrs. Fund. Am. Served as sgt. AUS, 1941-45; combat corr. Stars and Stripes North Africa, Italy, France, Austria. Recipient Regents' Outstanding Achievement award U. Mich., 1966, Sesquicentennial award, 1967; award for Outstanding Contbn. to Journalism Ohio U., 1979. Mem. Council Fgn. Relations, Silurians, Phi Gamma Delta, Sigma Delta Chi, Michigamua. Episcopalian. Clubs: Edgewood (Tivoli, N.Y.); Dutch Treat, Century Assn. Home: New York, N.Y. Died Aug. 29, 1982.

SWORDS, RAYMOND JOSEPH, educational administrator, clergyman; b. Springfield, Mass., Feb. 9, 1918; s. Raymond L. and Josephine (Noonan) S. A.B., Coll. Holy Cross, 1938; M.A., Boston Coll., 1943; M.A. in Math, Harvard, 1947; S.T.L., Weston Coll., 1951; LL.D., Clark U., 1967, U. Mass., 1967; D.Sc., Lowell Inst. Tech., 1967, Worcester Poly. Inst., 1969; Litt.D., Suffolk U., 1969; L.H.D., Stonehill Coll., 1970. Ordained priest Roman Catholic Ch., 1950; instr. math. Coll. Holy Cross, Worcester, Mass., 1943-45, dir. admissions, 1953-55, chmn. dept. math., 1955-60, pres., 1960-70, Cranwell Sch., Lenox, Mass., 1972-76, Regis High Sch., N.Y.C., 1976-80, asst. to pres., 1980—. Address: New York, N.Y. Died Jan. 12, 1984.

SYKES, GERALD, author; ed. U. Cin., Columbia, Sorbonne, New Sch. for Social Research; m. Claire Metcalfe; 1 dau., Jenny. Former lectr. Salzburg Seminar, Smith, Amherst, Mt. Holyoke, Dartmouth colls., N.Y. U., univs. Algiers, Bologna, Hamburg, Bonn, Cologne, Erlangen, Athens, Zagreb, Ljubljana; pub. affairs officer Fgn. Service; lectr. Columbia, Princeton, Am. U. Beirut; prof. interdisciplinary studies. Author: The Hidden Remnant, The Nice American, The Center of the Stage, The Children of Light; The Cool Millennium, 1967; The Perennial Advantgarde, 1971; Foresights: Self-Evolution and Survival, 1975. Editor: Alienation: The Cultural Climate of Our Time. Contr. articles to publs. including The Nation, The Reporter, N.Y. Times, New Republic, Saturday Rev.; also chpts. in books. Home: Rye, N.Y. Died July 15, 1984.

SYKES, ROOSEVELT, singer, pianist; b. Helena, Ark., Jan. 31, 1906; s. Ed and Allia (Bragg) S.; ed. pub. schs.; m. Merce Dee Duckworth, Dec. 3, 1956. Profl. debut, St. Louis; recording artist for Okeh Records, 1929, later RCA, Paramount, Brunswick, Champion records during 1930s, Decca Records, 1935-40; formed blues combo, 1958; toured of night clubs throughtout U.S. and Europe; mgr. Tiki Recording Studios. Composer: (songs) Night is the Time, Driving Wheel, numerous others. Home: Gulfport, Miss. Died July 11, 1983.

SYNAN, JOSEPH ALEXANDER, SR., clergyman; b. Pocahontas, Va., Feb. 18, 1905; s. Thomas Sylvester and Maude (Sherratt) S.; m. Minnis Evelyn Perdue, Aug. 12, 1926; children: Evelyn Maurine, Maurice Edwin, Joseph Alexander, Harold Vinson, Hubert Vernon, Doris Jean, Ronald Kay. Student pub. and corr. schs., pvt. study; D.D. (hon.), Holmes Theol. Sem., 1958. Ordained to ministry Pentecostal Holiness Ch., 1926; pastor numerous chs., 1926-34; supt. E. Va. Conf. Pentecostal Holiness Ch., 1934-41, asst. gen. supt., 1941-45, gen. supt., 1945-69, sr. bishop, from 1950, chmn. gen. bd. adminstrn. and gen. conf., 1950-69, chmn. gen. bd. edn., 1945-53, chmn. bd. publs., 1966-69; Chmn. Pentecostal Fellowship of North Am., 1950-52, 63-65; mem. bd. adminstrn.; chmn. presidium Pentecostal World Conf., Jerusalem, Israel, 1961, mem. adv. com., 1967-70. Author: The Good Minister of Jesus Christ, 1951, Christian Life in Depth, 1964, The Shape of Things to Come, 1969, The Trinity or the Tri-personal Being of God, 1980; articles in religious publs. Trustee Holmes Theol. Sem., Greenville, S.C., Southwestern Bible Coll., Oklahoma City, 1946-69, Falcon (N.C.) Orphanage, 1943-69; trustee Emmanuel Coll., Franklin Springs, Ga., 1941-69; mem. adv. bd. Sch. Christian Ministries, from 1974, chmn., 1974-76. Mem. Nat. Assn. Evangs. (mem. bd. adminstrn. 20 years). Address: Hopewell, VA.

SYRETT, HAROLD COFFIN, coll. adminstr., editor; b. N.Y.C., Oct. 22, 1913; s. Frank H. and Dorothy (Provost) S.; A.B., Wesleyan U., 1935; M.A., Columbia, 1938, Ph.D., 1944; m. Patricia D. McCarthy, June 19, 1937; children—David, John, Matthew. Tchr. Harvey Sch.,

Hawthorne, N.Y., 1936-39; instr. history U. Maine, 1941; instr. history Columbia, N.Y.C., 1941-46, asst. prof., 1946-50, asso. prof., 1950-54, prof., 1954-61; exec. editor Alexander Hamilton Papers, from 1955; dir. grad. studies Queens Coll., Flushing, N.Y., 1961-62, dean faculty, 1962-65, acting pres., 1964; exec. dean grad. centers State U. N.Y., 1965-66, vice chancellor univ., 1967-68; pres. Bklyn. Coll., 1968-69; prof. history City U. N.Y., 1969-79; vis. prof. history Manhattan Sch. Music, 1946-48, Yeshiva U., 1954-55. Mem. Mass. Hist. Soc., Am., N.Y. (trustee) hist. assns., Orgn. Am. Historians, Phi Beta Kappa. Author: The City of Brooklyn, 1865-1898, 1944; (with others) A History of the American People, 1952; Andrew Jackson, 1953; Papers of Alexander Hamilton, 26 vols., 1961-79. Editor: The Gentleman and the Tiger (autobiography of George B. McClellan, Jr.), 1956; (with others) A Short History of New York State, 1957; American Historical Documents, 1960; contbr. articles to profl. jours. Home: Craryville, N.Y. Died July 29, 1984.

SZABO, GABOR, guitarist, sitarist, composer; b. Budapest, Hungary, Mar. 8, 1936; came to escaped to U.S., 1956. Former Hungarian freedom fighter. With Chico Hamilton's quintet, 1961-65, Gary McFarland combo, 1965, Charles Lloyd quartet, 1965-82; played at Monterey Festival, Newport Jazz Festival, 1970-73, Fillmore West with Jimmy Hendrix and Janis Joplin, command performance, London Palladium; gave Carnegie Hall concert, 1974; rec. artist: albums including Femme Fatale; produced record, Lena & Gabor; composer: score for Repulsion (Roman Polanski); wrote: score for Gypsy Queen (for Santana); wrote and recorded: score for Breezin.'. Named No. 1 New Star Down Beat Critics Poll, 1964. Died Feb. 16, 1982.*

SZEFTEL, MARC M., educator; b. Starokonstantinov, Russia, Feb. 10, 1902; s. Uriel and Anna (Kovner) S.; Certificate of maturity, Lublin, 1919; LL.M., U. Warsaw, 1925; LL.D., U. Brussels, 1934; Licentiate of Slavic Philology and History, 1939; grad. studies sociology Columbia, 1943-45; m. Catherine Bowne Crouse, June 18, 1949; children—Daniel Maynard Crouse (adopted), Tatiana Hunt, Marc Watson. Came to United States, 1942; naturalized, 1959. Public translator, Antwerp, 1930-40; lecturer in Polish and Russian, University of Brussels, 1936-39, asst. prof. Slavic history, 1939-40; prof. Russian history, Ecole Libre des Hautes Etudes, N.Y.C., 1942-45; prof. French history, 1945; acting asst. prof., asst. prof. and asso. prof. Russian and Slavic history, Cornell U., 1945-56, prof., 1956-61; prof. Russian mediaeval history U. Wash., from 1961; vis. prof. Bard Coll., spring 1945; vis. asso. prof. Columbia, Grad. Sch. and Russian Inst., spring 1950-51, fall 1952, 53; cons. Ford Found., spring 1954. Belgian Am. Ednl. Found. advanced fellow, 1943-45; sr. fellow Columbia U. Russian Institute, 1949-50, 52-53; Guggenheim Foundation fellow, 1959-60. Royal license to practice law in Belgium, 1938. Mem. Am. Hist. Assn. (pres. conf. Slavic studies 1962-63), Internat. Commission for the History Parliamentary Instns., Societe Jean Bodin Pour L'Etude Comparative de L'Histoire des Institutions, Institut de Sociologie Solvay, Groupe D'Etudes Sociologiques (1936-40); Polish Inst. Arts and Scis., Internat. Pour L'Histoire des Assemblées D'Etats (commission), Phi Beta Kappa, Author: Le Commentaire Historique au Slovo d'Igor, 1948; The Vseslav Epos (in memoirs of Am. Folklore Soc., Vol. 42) (with R. Yakobson), 1949; Editor: La Geste Du Prince Igor (with others), 1948. Contbr. articles and revs. in jours. of U.S. and abroad. Home: Seattle, Wash. Died May 31, 1985.

TABER, GLADYS, author; b. Colorado Springs, Colo., Apr. 12, 1899; d. Rufus Mather and Grace (Raybold) Bagg; B.A., Wellesley Coll., 1920; M.A., Lawrence Coll., 1921; student Columbia, 1931-33; m. Frank Albion Taber, Jr., June 10, 1922; 1 dau., Constance Ann. Tchr. English, Lawrence Coll., 1921, Randolph-Macon Women's Coll., 1925-26; profl. writer, 1932-80; tchr. profl. short story writing Columbia, N.Y.C., 1936-80; columnist Ladies Home Jour., 1937-58, asst. editor, 1946-58; columnist Family Circle, 1959-80, The Oracle, Orleans, Mass. Writer of plays, among them a one-act play which received Little Theater award in nat. contest, 1925. Mem. Authors League Am., Nat. P.E.N., Pen and Brush Club, Kappa Alpha Theta. Author numerous books, the latest being: Especially Father, 1949; Stillmeadow Seasons, 1950; Stillmeadow Kitchen, 1951; When Dogs Meet People, 1952; Flower Arranging for American Home, 1952; (with Barbara Webster) Stillmeadow to Sugarbridge, 1953; Stillmeadow Daybook; What Cooks at Stillmeadow, 1958; Mrs. Daffodil, 1958; Stillmeadow Sampler, 1959; Spring Harvest, 1959; Road to Stillmeadow, 1960; Another Path, 1963; Gladys Taber's Favorite Stillmeadow Recipes, 1965; Stillmeadow Calendar A Countrywoman's Journal, 1967; Especially Dogs-Especially at Stillmeadow, 1968; Flower Arranging, A Book to Begin On, 1969; Stillmeadow Album, 1969; Amber A Very Personal Cat, 1970; Reveries at Stillmeadow, 1970; (short stories) One Dozen and One; My Own Cape Cod, 1971; My Own Cookbook, 1972; Country Chronicle, 1974; Harvest of Yesterdays, 1976; The Best of Stillmeadow, 1976; Conversations with Amber, 1977. Contbr. to mags. in U.S., Eng., Sweden, Australia. Home: Orleans, Mass. Died Mar. 11, 1980.

TABER, JOHN STARR, banker; b. Chgo., Sept. 1, 1890; s. Frank M. and Lydia (Starr) T.; grad. Lawrenceville Sch., 1916; student Princeton, 1916-17; m. Katharine Clark, Mar. 8, 1919; children—Marcia (Mrs. Frederick B. MacKinnon), Ann (Mrs. Paul Richards), Starr (Mrs. Joseph E. Arleo). With Bradstreet Co., N.Y.C., 1923-33; company merged to become Dun & Bradstreet, Inc., v.p., treas., 1933-36; with Lawrence Warehouse Co., N.Y.C., 1937-43, Washington, 1943-44; v.p. Bankers Trust Co., N.Y.C., from 1945; dir. Ohio Edison Co. (Akron, O.), Taber Pump Co. (Buffalo), Dun & Bradstreet, Inc. (N.Y.C.), Sanborn Map Co., Inc., (Pelham, N.Y.), Milgo Electronic Corp. (Miami, Fla.). Served with Royal Flying Corps., Can., 1918. Home: Rye, N.Y. †

TABER, LOUISE EDDY, author; b. Oakland, Cal., Apr. 18, 1890; d. Isaiah West and Annie (Slocum) T.; ed. pub. schs. and under pvt. teachers. Christian Scientist. Author: The Flame, 1911. Contbr. short stories and articles on art. Home: San Francisco, Calif. †

TABOR, FREDERICK ALFRED MERLIN, educator; b. N.Y. City, Nov. 16, 1888; B.A., Cambridge U., Eng., 1912, M.A., 1914; m. T. Kathleen Kelly, May 23, 1923; children—Frederick Hebard, Niall Edward, Eithne Mary. Asst. master Santer's Sch., Milwaukee, Wis., 1913-15; founder, 1916, headmaster 1916-38, Aiken (S.C.) Prep. School for Boys; prin. Fermata Sch. for Girls, Aiken, from 1926. Served in Ambulance Corps of British, French, Italian and Am. armies as capt., World War. Awarded War Cross of Italy (twice), Volunteer's medal (France); Victory and Service medals (Great Britain); Cavalier Crown of Italy. Episcopalian. Clubs: Racquet and Tennis (New York); United Universities (London). Home: Aiken, S.C. †

TAFT, CHARLES PHELPS, lawyer; b. Cin., Sept. 20, 1897; s. William Howard and Helen (Herron) T.; m. Eleanor K. Chase, Oct. 6, 1917 (dec. 1961); children—Eleanor Kellogg Taft Hall, Sylvia Howard Taft Lotspeich, Seth Chase, Lucia (dec.), Cynthia Taft Morris, Rosalyn (dec.), Peter R. B.A., Yale U., 1918, LL.B., 1921; LL.D., U. Toledo, 1934, U. Rochester, Miami U., Ohio Wesleyan U., Yale U., 1952; D.C.L., Union Coll.; D.H.L., Hebrew Union Coll. Bar: Ohio bar 1922. Since practiced in, Cin.; pros. atty., Hamilton County, Ohio, 1927-28; mem. Cin. City Council, 1938-42, 48-51, 55-77; mayor of Cin., 1955-57. Author: City Management: The Cincinnati Experiment, 1933, You and I and Roosevelt, 1936, Why I Am for the Church, 1947, Democracy in Politics and Economics, 1950. Pres Fed. Council Chs. Christ Am., 1947-48, Friends World Council Chs.; dir. U.S. Community War Services, Fed. Security Agy., 1941-43, Wartime Econ. Affairs, Dept. State, 1944, Transport and Communications Policy, 1945; Republican candidate for gov. Ohio, 1952; trustee Twentieth Century Fund, Carnegie Instn., Washington, Com. Econ. Devel. Served to 1st lt. U.S. Army, 1917-18, AEF in France. Mem. Am., Ohio, Cin. bar assns., Beta Theta Pi, Phi Delta Phi. Republican. Episcopalian. Home and Office: Cincinnati, Ohio. Died June 24, 1983.

TAFT, FREDERICK LOVETT, educator and librarian; b. Cleve., Aug. 15, 1906; s. Frederick Lovett and Mary Alice (Arter) T.; m. Eleanor Dale Barnes, Dec. 30, 1931; children—Morgan Barnes, Eleanor Dale (Mrs. R. Bruce King, Jr.). B.A., Amherst Coll., 1928; Ph.D., Western Res. U., 1942. Engaged in bus., Cleve., 1928-33; part-time instr. English Adelbert Coll., Western Res. U., Cleve., 1935-38; instr. English Case Sch. Applied Sci., 1938-43; from asst. prof. to prof. English Case Inst. Tech., Cleve., 1946-67, dir. library, 1959-67; acting dir. libraries Case Western Res. U., 1967-68, asso. dir. libraries, 1968-71, emeritus, from 1971; Dir. Colton Chem. Co., Cleve., 1950-53. Editor: John Milton's Apology for Smectymnuus, 1953. Served to 1st lt. USAAF, 1943-46. Mem. Modern Lang. Assn., Internat. Assn. Technol. U. Libraries (sec. 1967-70), Am. Soc. Engring. Edn., Friends of Case Western Res. U. Library (sec. 1972—), Amherst Coll. Alumni Assn. (v.p. 1972-73), Phi Beta Kappa, Phi Kappa Psi. Home: Shaker Heights, OH.

TAFT, HORACE DWIGHT, educator, physicist; b. Cin., Apr. 2, 1925; s. Robert A. and Martha (Bowers) T.; m. Mary Jane Badger, Sept. 9, 1952; children—John Godfrey, Hugh Bancroft, Horace Dutton. B.A., Yale, 1950; M.S., U. Chgo., 1953, Ph.D., 1955. Faculty Yale, 1956-83, prof. physics, 1964-83; master Davenport Coll., 1966-71; dean Yale Coll., 1971-79. Chmn. bd. trustees Taft Sch., Watertown, Conn., 1975-80. Served with AUS, 1943-46. Mem. Am. Phys. Soc. Home: New Haven, Conn. Died Feb. 12, 1983.

TAGGART, JOSEPH HERMAN, consulting economist; b. Wakefield, Mass., Dec. 29, 1902; s. David and Josephine (Jess) T. Ph.B., Yale U., 1924; M.B.A., Harvard U., 1927; Ph.D., Columbia U., 1938; LL.D., L.I.U., 1964, U. Lagos, Fed. Republic Nigeria, 1968. Instr. Lehigh U., 1927-28; from asst. prof. to prof. econs. U. Kans., Lawrence, 1928-46; prof. finance Rutgers U., New Brunswick, N.J., 1947-52, prof. econs., 1952-56; prof. finance Grad. sch. Bus. Adminstrn., N.Y. U., 1956-71, asso. dean, 1956-59, dean, 1959-70, exec. dean schs. of bus, 1962-70, spl. cons. to pres. for univ. affairs, 1970-71, dean emeritus, prof. finance emeritus, 1971-84, econ. cons., 1971-84; cons. Hubbard Real Estate Investments.; Pub. gov. Am. Stock Exchange, 1966-72; economist, bus. cons. Dept. Commerce, 1941-42, chief of finance and tax research unit, 1945; econ. adviser commr. in Europe, also dir. planning Fgn. Liquidation Commn., Washington, 1945-46; econ. adviser chmn. munitions bd. Dept. Def., 1946-52; U.S. rep. Western Union Mil. Supply Bd., London, 1949-50; cons. Def. Prodn. Adminstrn., 1951-52; mem. U.S. delegation Internat. Conf. Am. States, Bogota, Colombia, 1948. Author: Federal Reserve Bank of Boston, 1938. Served to maj. AUS, 1942-45. Mem. Am. Econ. Assn., Am. Finance Assn., Am. Assn. U. Profs., Alpha Sigma Phi, Alpha Kappa Psi, Beta Gamm Sigma. Independent. Conglist. Home: New York, N.Y. Died Feb. 27, 1984, buried Lakeside Cemetery, Wakefield, N.Y.

TAISHOFF, SOL JOSEPH, publishing company executive; b. Minsk, Russia, Oct. 8, 1904; s. Joseph and Rose (Orderv) T.; m. Betty Tash, Mar. 6, 1927 (dec. Nov. 1977); children—Joanne Taishoff Cowan (dec. Dec. 1977), Lawrence Bruce. Ed. pub. schs., Washington. Copy boy Washington bur. AP, 1920-21, successively telegraph operator, mem. news staff, 1922-26; reporter U.S. Daily (now U.S. News and World Report), Washington, 1926-31; radio editor Consol. Press (pen name Robert Mack), 1927-34; mng. editor, co-founder Broadcasting Pub., Inc., 1931-82, editor, 1933-82; v.p., treas. Broadcasting mag., 1931-34, pres., editor, pub., 1944-71, chmn., editor, 1971-82; partner Jolar Assos.; Bd. dirs. Washington Journalism Center. Recipient Distinguished Service in Journalism award U. Mo., 1953, Distinguished Service award Nat. Assn. Broadcasters, 1966, Paul White Meml. award Radio-TV News Dirs. Assn., 1967, Spl. citation Internat. Radio and TV Soc., 1975, Disting. Communications medal So. Bapt. Conv. Radio-TV Commn., 1976; Peabody award U. Ga., 1980; Robert Eunson award AP Broadcasters, 1980; Am. Bus. Press award, 1981. Mem. IEEE (sr.), Broadcast Pioneers (past nat. pres.), Sigma Delta Chi (past nat. pres., journalism fellow 1964). Clubs: Nat. Press (Washington), Overseas Writers (Washington), Woodmont Country (Washington), Nat. Communications (Washington). Home: Washington, D.C. Died Aug. 15, 1982.

TALARICO, SAMUEL JOSEPH, labor union official; b. Chgo., Sept. 20, 1913; s. Joseph and Jennie (Astorino) T.; student U. Wis. Sch. for Workers, 1945-46, Roosevelt U. Labor Edn. Div., 1946-47, Trade Union Program, Harvard U., 1958-59; m. Rita F. De Traglia, June 12, 1937; children—Joseph C., Samuel Joseph, Louis C. Hog and cattle butcher Gold lMedal Packing Co., Utica, N.Y., 1930-33; steward, committeeman Packinghouse Local 13, Utica, 1933-36; internat. rep. Meat Cutters Union, Utica, 1940-53; pres. local 1, Utica, 1953-60; internat. v.p. Amalgamated lHeat Cutters Union, Utica, 1960-76, internat. sec.-treas. Amalgamated Meat Cutters Union, AFL-CIO, 1976-79; internat. sec.-treas. United Food and Comml. Workers Internat. Union, AFL-CIO, 1979-83; dir. Bank of Utica. Recipient Contemporary Ams. award Marist Coll., 1968; Israeli Labor award, 1973. Mem. NAACP (life). Democrat. Roman Catholic. Club: Ft. Schuyler Men's (Utica). Home: Utica, N.Y. Dec. May 17, 1983. Interned Calvery, Utica.

TALIAFERRO, MABEL, actress; b. New York, May 21, 1888; sister of Edith Taliaferro; m. Frederick W. Thompson. First appeared on stage at age of 2 1/2, later in "Blue Jeans," "Children of the Ghetto," "The Land of the Heart's Desire," etc.; played Lovey Mary, in "Mrs. Wiggs of the Cabbage Patch," 1903; visited Australia in "On the Quiet," 1906; scored success in "Price of Peace," "You Never Can Tell," "In the Bishop's Carriage," "Pippa Passes," Polly in "Polly of the Circus" (written for her), "Springtime," "Call of the Cricket," "Young Wisdom"; starred in "The New Henrietta," 1914-15. Star with Metro Pictures Corpn., 1915-17; returned to stage, 1917. Home: New York, N.Y. †

TANNENBAUM, SAMUEL WILLIAM, lawyer; b. N.Y.C., Mar. 3, 1890; s. Max and Lena (Falk) T.; m. Frieda M. Stone, June 4, 1922; children: Claire F. Ollstein, Ellen Shadick. A.B., Columbia U., 1910, M.A., 1912, LL.B., 1912. Bar: N.Y. 1912, also U.S. Supreme Ct 1912. Partner Johnson & Tannenbaum (merged with Washington firm Brylauski & Cleary), 1982; copyright counsel and cons. Metro-Goldwyn-Mayer, Lorimar Prodns., Warner Bros., Paramount, Universal, WNET-13, Fuji Telecasting Co., Japan, CBS, NBC, ABC, EMI, Dino DeLaurentis Corp., Dick Clark Prodns., other prin. motion picture, TV and radio broadcasting cos., radio and TV agys., Tams-Witmark Music Library; arbitrator under motion picture Fed. consent decree; panel expert UNESCO; lectr. on copyrights and unfair competition Yale U., Columbia U., N.Y. U., N.Y. Law Sch., Practising Law Inst. Author: Protection of Fictional Characters in the Entertainment and Literary Fields. Served as ensign U.S.N.R.F., World War I. Recipient Columbia Alumni medal, Dean's award of Merit Columbia Coll.; Certificate of Merit Practising Law Inst.; Harlan Fiske fellow Columbia Law Sch. Mem. Am. Bar Assn. (chmn. copyright div. 1961-62), Assn. Bar City N.Y. (com. on copyrights com. on round table confs., municipal cts., legal edn.), N.Y. County Lawyers Assn., N.Y. Patent Law Assn., Fed. Bar Assn. (trustee N. Y. N.J. and Conn., award of Merit 1959, copyright com.), Copyright Soc. U.S.A. (founder, pres., trustee), Copyright Luncheon Circle (founder). Club: Masons. Revision U.S. Copyright Law. Home: New York, N.Y.†

TAPPAN, ANNA HELEN, coll. prof.; b. Mt. Pleasant, Ia., Oct. 22, 1888; d. David Stanton and Anna (Grand-Girard) Tappan; A.B., Western Coll., Oxford, O., 1909; A.M., Cornell U., 1912, Ph.D., 1914; unmarried. Instr. mathematics, Western Coll., 1909-11; instr. mathematics, Ia. State Coll., 1914-17, asst. prof., 1917-21, asso. prof., 1921-25; prof. of mathematics, Western Coll., from 1925, dean of women, 1927-41, academic dean, 1941-44. Mem. A.A.A.S., Am. Math. Soc., Math. Assn. America, N.E.A., Am. Assn. Univ. Profs., Am. Assn. Univ. Women, Sigma Xi, Sigma Delta Epsilon, Pi Mu Epsilon. Republican. Presbyterian. Home: Oxford, Ohio. †

TARAS, ANTHONY F., educator; b. Dickson City, Pa., Nov. 13, 1927; s. Stanley and Mary (Zalewska) T.; B.A., U. Scranton, 1948; M.A., Kent State U., 1950; Ph.D., Fordham U., 1961; m. Eleanor M. Sostowski, Aug. 4, 1956; children—Robert, Raymond, Linda. Instr. modern langs. Ida. State U., 1950-52, asst. prof., chmn. dept. modern langs., 1952-58, asso. prof., chmn. dept., 1958-63, designer, dir. lang. labs., 1952-73; asso. prof., chmn. dept. modern langs. Ithaca (N.Y.) Coll., 1963-65, designer, dir. lang. lab., 1963-73, prof. modern langs., 1965-84, chmn. dept. modern langs., 1965-73, dir. Peace Corps Tng. session, 1966, designer lang lab. Eisenhower Coll., 1968. Author: (textbook) English and French Grammar I. Recipient Fulbright Summer Seminar grant Sorbonne, Paris, 1955. Mem. Modern Lang. Assn., Am. Assn. Tchrs. French (chpt. pres. 1972-74), Am. Council on Teaching Fgn. Langs., N.Y. State Fgn. Lang. Tchrs. Assn. Editorial cons. in French and Spanish for Ency. Brit. World Lang. Dictionary, 1955-56. Home: Ithaca, N.Y. Died Sept. 26, 1984; interred FinchHill Cemetery, Carbondale, Pa.

TARSKI, ALFRED, scientist, educator; b. Warsaw, Poland, Jan. 14, 1902; s. Ignacy and Rose (Prussak) T.; Ph.D., U. Warsaw, 1924; D.Sc. (hon.), Universad Catolica de Chile, 1975; m. Maria Josephine Witkowski, June 24, 1929; children—Jan Andrew, Eva Kristina Ehrenfeucht. Came to U.S., 1939, naturalized, 1945. Instr., Polish Pedagogical Inst., 1922-25; docent adjoint prof. U. Warsaw, 1925-39; prof. Zeromski Lycée, Warsaw, 1925-39; research asso. Harvard, 1939-41; mem. Inst. for Advanced Study, Princeton, N.J., 1941-42; lectr. U. Cal. at Berkeley, 1942-45, asso. prof., 1945-46, prof. math., 1946-68, research prof., 1958-60, prof., 1968-73. Vis. prof. Coll. City N.Y., 1940, Nat. U. Mexico, 1957, Universidad Catolica de Chile, 1974-75; Flint prof. philosophy, U. Cal., Los Angeles, 1967. Mem. Nat. Acad. Scis., Am. Math. Soc. (past council), Assn. Symbolic Logic (past pres.), Royal Netherland Acad. Scis. and Letters, Brit. Acad., Dutch Math. Soc. (hon.). Author: (with Z. Chwialkowski, W. Schayer) Geometrja (Polish), 1935; Introduction to Logic (Polish), 1936, (English translation), 1941; Pojecie prawdy w jezykach nauk dedukeyinych (Polish), 1933; (with B. Jonsson) Direct Decomposition of Finite Algebraic Systems, 1947; A Decision Method for Elementary Algebra and Geometry, 1948; Cardinal Algebras, 1949; (with A. Mostowski, R.M. Robinson) Undecidable Theories, 1953; Ordinal Algebras, 1956; Logic, Semantics, Metamathematics, 1956; The Axiomatic Method with Special Reference to Geometry and Physics (editor with L. Henkin, P. Suppes), 1959; Logic, Methodology and Philosophy of Science (editor with E. Nagel, P. Suppes), 1962; The Theory of Models (editor with J.W. Addison, L. Henkin), 1965; The Completeness of Elementary Algebra and Geometry, 1967; (with L. Henkin, J.D. Monk) Cylindrie Algebras, part I, 1971; La concepción semántica de la verdad y los fundamentos de la semántica, 1972. Hon. editor Jour. Algebra Universalis. Home: Berkeley, Calif. Died Oct. 26, 1983.

TATE, JAMES HUGH JOSEPH, former mayor of Philadelphia; b. 1910; m. Anne M. Daly; children—Frank X., Anne M. Ed., Strayer's Bus. Coll., Tucker Inst., St. Joseph's Coll., Labor Sch.; LL.B., Temple U., 1938; LL.B. hon. degrees, Villanova U., La Salle Coll., Drexel Inst., St. Joseph Coll. Mem. Pa. Legislature, 1940-46; mem. Phila. City Council, 1951-62, pres., 1955-62, mayor, Phila., 1962-72; mem. Delaware River Port Authority, 1956-63, chmn., 1962-63. Bd. dirs. Phila. Citizens Crime Commn.; pres. Nat. League Cities, 1967-68, U.S. Conf. Mayors, 1970-71; exec. and steering com. Nat. Urban Coalition, 1967-74; chmn. Pa. State Tax Equalization Bd., 1975-79; mem. Phila. Council for Labor and Industry, 1981; ret. Past vice chmn. Phila. Democratic City Com.; past mem. Pa. Dem. State Com.; treas. Atlantic County Dem. Com., 1980; chmn. Atlantic County Dem. Fin. Com.; mem. Southeastern Pa. Transp. Authority, 1972-75; del. Dem. Nat. Convs., 1960, 64, 68, 72, 74; sec. Longport Dem. Assn.; Bd. govs., chmn. transp. com. Internat. Eucharistic Congress for, 1975-76; former trustee, chmn. fin. com. Immaculata Coll.; mem. Villanova Econ. Devel. Council; bd. dirs., exec. com. Old Phila. Devel. Corp.; trustee Einstein Med. Center, Daroff div. Einstein Med. Center, WHYY-TV Public TV Sta.; adv. bd. St. Joseph's Hosp.; bd. dirs., exec. com., investments com. Temple U. Gen. Alumni; bd. dirs. South Jersey Diocesan Tuition Assistance Fund. Mem. Phila. and Atlantic City chpts. Serra Internat. (pres. Phila. 1974-75, chmn. internat. conv. 1975), Temple U. Law Alumni Assn., World Affairs Council Phila., Am. Acad. Polit. and Social Sci., Fed. Bar Assn., Friendly Sons of St. Patrick (past pres.), Navy League U.S., Navy League Phila., Capt. Laymen's Malvern Retreat League (asso.). Clubs: Temple U, Varsity and Downtown, Atlantic City Country, K.C. (4 deg., past grand Knight). Home: Longport, N.J. Died May 27, 1983.

TATE, JOE TOM, clergyman; b. Pulaski, Tenn., Oct. 7 1914; s. Tom T. and Hester (King) T.; m. Velma Evelyn Bowden, July 12, 1942; children—Margaret Lucille, Roxanna, Barry Joe. A.B. in English; B.Th., Aurora (Ill.) Coll., 1942. Ordained to ministry Advent Christian Ch., 1942; pres. Advent Christian Gen. Conf., from 1964. Deceased.*

TAUB, BEN, banker; b. 1890. With J.N. Taub & Sons, Houston, 1910, owner, from 1945; chmn. bd. MacGregor Park Nat. Bank; with Tex. Commerce Bank, 1951-82, chmn. bd., 1966-70, sr. chmn., 1970-82, also dir.; officer Gulf Bithulithic Co., Ace Vendors, Inc. Chmn. bd. Ben Taub Gen. Hosp. Died Sept. 9, 1982.

TAUBER, OSCAR ERNST, educator, physiologist; b. Decatur, Ill., May 23, 1908; s. Emil and Anna (Stephan) T.; student U. Ill., summers 1929-30; B.S., James Millikin U., 1930; M.S., Ia. State U., 1932, Ph.D., 1935; postgrad. Marine Biol. Lab., Woods Hole, Mass., summer 1934; m. Anne W. Hager, Aug. 22, 1940; children—Thomas Stephen. John Peter. Faculty, Ia. State U. Sci. and Tech., Ames, from 1935, prof. physiology, 1946-82, chmn. dept. zoology and entomology, 1962-73, Distinguished prof. Coll. Scis. and Humanities, 1969-82, chmn. gen. grad. studies program, 1965-82. Vis. prof. zoology U. Hawaii, summer 1962. Rockefeller fellow, 1932; grantee USPHS, 1957-64. Recipient award distinction James Millikin U., 1955; Alumni Recognition award Ia. State U., 1955. Mem. Am. Physiol. Soc., Soc. Exptl. Biology and Medicine, Am. Soc. Zoologists, Entomol. Soc. Am. (exec. com. 1951-54), A.A.A.S., Am. Inst. Biol. Scientists, Ia. Acad. Sci., Assn. Study Animal Behavior, Osborn Research Club (pres. Ia. 1963), Sigma Xi, Phi Kappa Phi, Gamma Sigma Delta, Tau Kappa Epsilon. Author: Laboratory Guide in Elementary Physiology, 1958; Elementary Physiology and Anatomy, rev. 3d, edit., 1972. Contbr. articles to profl. jours. Home: Ames, Iowa. Died Nov. 8, 1982.

TAUBES, FREDERICK, artist; b. Austria, Apr. 15, 1900; s. Louis and Fanny (Taëni) T.; ed. Acad. of Art, Munich, 1918-20, Bauhaus, Weimar, 1920-21; student Vienna, France, Italy, 1920-23; m. Lili Jacobsen, May 25, 1923; 1 son, Frank Alex. Came to U.S., 1930. Exhibited in most European art centers, also Palestine, included in all important art exhibits in U.S., 1930-81; over 100 one-man exhbns. in museums in U.S., 30 one-man exhbns. N.Y.C.; rep. Met. Mus., San Francisco Mus., Santa Barbara Mus. Art, San Diego Fine Arts Gallery, Bloomington (Ill.) Art Assn, collection of Mills Coll., (Calif.), U. Ill., M.H. De Young Mus, San Francisco, High Mus. Atlanta, William Rockhill Mus., Kansas City, Mo., Ency. Brit., IBM Corp. collections. Former Carnegie vis. prof. art, resident painter U. Ill.; vis. rof. U Hawaii, Mills Coll., U. Wis., Colo State U.; instr. Cooper Unon, N.Y.; head painting div. Corpus Christi (Tex.) Fine Arts Colony, Ruidoso (N.Mex.) Art Colony; art seminars, Palm Springs, Calif., San Antionio; lectr. Art Students League; guest lectr. various schs. art in Eng. Named hon. col. State of N.Mex., hon. adm. Leche State of La., hon. citizen of San Antonio, New Iberia, La., Charlotte, N.C. Fellow Royal Soc. Arts. Author: Technique of Oil Painting, 1941; You Don't Know What You Like, 1942; Studio Secrets, 1943; Oil Painting for the Beginner, 1944; The Amateur Painter's Handbook; The Painters Question and Answer Book; Anatomy of Genius; The Art and Technique of Oil Painting, 1948; Pictorial Composition and the Art of Drawing, 1949; Painting and Essays on Art, The Mastery of Oil Painting, The Quickest Way to Paint Well; Pictorial Anatomy of the Human Body; Dictionary of Artists Materials and Techniques; The Art and Technique of Portrait Painting; Pen and Ink Drawing; Restoration of Antiques; Technique Still Life Painting; others. Contbr. articles to The Illustrator, Mag. of Art, Pacific Art Rev., Groiler Ency; contbg. editor Ency. Brit., Am. Artist mag., 1943-62; columnist Am. editor Artist mag.; lectr., orginator Taubes Painting Media, Taubes Varnishes. Home: Haverstraw, N.Y. Died June 20, 1981.

TAURIELLO, ANTHONY F., congressman; born Buffalo, N.Y., Aug. 14, 1889; s. Sebastian and Lucia (Tita) T.; student law sch., Cumberland U., Lebanon, Tenn. Mem. bd. supervisors. Erie Co., N.Y., 1933-37; councilman Niagara Dist., Common Council, City of Buffalo, 1937-41, 1948; dep. city treas., 1942-45; mem. 81st Congress (1949-51), 43rd dist. N.Y. Mem. Elks, K.C., Moose, Eagles, Loyal Order of Columbus. Democrat. Catholic. Club: Basilius. Home: Buffalo, N.Y. †

TAYLOR, A. STARKE, cotton exec; b. Mason, Tenn., Feb. 19, 1890; s. William Lee and Betty (Claiborne) T.; student Memphis U. Sch., 1906-10; m. Veryl Lamb, Aug. 4, 1918; children—A. Starke, Veryl Evelyn, Miles Cary. With firm of Cohn & Ellett, cotton shippers, Memphis, 1912-16; participating partner, Calexico, Calif., and Dallas, Tex., Silvan Newburger & Son of New Orleans, 1916-18, M. Hohenberg & Co., Memphis, 1928-42; organized Starke Taylor & Son, Dallas, 1942, senior partner, president; dir. Mayor, Highland Park, Texas, 1946-48. Mem. Am. (past pres.), Dallas (past pres.) cotton shippers assns.; Dallas (past pres.) and N.Y. (past dir., mem. adv. com.) cotton exchanges; Tex. and Liverpool (asso. mem.) cotton assns. Democrat. Presbyn. Club: Dallas Country (past pres.). Home: Dallas. †

TAYLOR, ALVA PARK, prof. English; b. Girard, Kan., Sept. 27, 1887; s. Clarence Ewing and Lois Ella (Park) T.; prep. edn., high sch., Macomb, Ill.; student Park Coll., Parkville, Mo., 1905-06; A.B., Colorado Coll., Colorado Springs, Colo., 1910; A.M., U. of Chicago, 1919; m. Ruth Anna Cramer, June 20, 1913. Prof. English, Westminster Coll., Denver, Colo., 1911-14; instr. English, Kansas State Normal Sch., Emporia, Kan., 1914, Oklahoma Agrl. and Mech. Coll., 1915; teacher high sch., Colorado Springs, 1915-18; prof. English, New Mexico Coll. Agr. and Mech. Arts, from 1919, dean from 1924. Mem. Am. Assn. Teachers of Journalism, Assn. Land Grant Colls. Presbyn. Mason. Editor New Mexico School Rev., 1925, 26. Home: State College, N.M. †

TAYLOR, ARCHER, prof. German lit.; b. Phila., Pa., Aug. 1, 1890; s. Lowndes and Florence (York) T.; A.B., Swarthmore Coll., 1909; A.M., U. of Pa., 1910; Ph.D., Harvard, 1915; m. Alice Jones, Sept. 9, 1915 (died June 16, 1930); children—Margaret B., Richard L., Cynthia; m. 2d, Hasseltine Byrd, June 17, 1932; children—Mary Constance, Ann Byrd. Instr. in German, Penn. State College, 1910-12; instructor, assistant prof., asso. prof. German, Washington U., St. Louis, Mo., 1915-25; also editor Washington Univ. Studies, 1919-25; ehrensenator, U. of Giessen, Germany, 1925; prof. German lit., U. of Chicago, 1925-39, chmn. of dept. 1927-39; John Simon Guggenheim fellow, 1927, prof. medieval lit. and folklore, 1938-39; prof. German lit., U. of Calif., Berkeley, from 1939. Fellow of Newberry Library, 1945. Fellow Medieval Acad. Am., Am. Acad. Arts and Scis., Am. Philos. Soc.; mem. Modern Lang. Assn. (v.p. 1950, pres. 1951). Club Internacional de Folklore, Am. Folklore Soc. (pres. 1935-37), Phi Beta Kappa; hon. mem. Schweizerische Gesellschaft für Volkskunde, Finnish Lit. Soc. (Helsinki); Asociación folklórica Argentina (Buenos Aires), Kgl. Gustav Adolfs Akademi for folklivsforskning (Uppsala), Société Finno-ougrienne (Helsinki), Folklore of Ireland Soc. (Dublin), Sociedad Folklórica (Mexico City), Finnish Academy of Science (Helsinki), Norsk Videnskapsselskab (Oslo). Home: Berkeley, Calif. †

TAYLOR, BISMARCK H., railroad exec.; b. Winton, N.C., Jan. 8, 1890; s. Hilliary and Fannie C. (Harrell) T.; ed. pub. schs.; m. Mae Jacobs, of Winston-Salem, N.C., July 17, 1919. Clerk N.&W. Ry., 1903-11; city freight agent Old Bay Line, 1911-17; gen. agent and asst. gen. freight agent Gulf Coast Lines, 1920-24; with D.&R.G.W.R.R. Co., 1925-35, v.p., 1929-35; asst. v.p. C.,B.&Q. R.R. Co. from June, 1935. Served as lt., later capt., Q.M.C., U.S.A., 1917-19. Protestant. Clubs: Denver; Alta (Salt Lake City); Medinah, Union League (Chicago). Home: Chicago, Ill. †

TAYLOR, EDWARD HARRISON, herpetologist; b. Maysville, Mo., Apr. 23, 1889; s. George Washington and Loretta (Mills) T.; A.B., U. of Kan., 1912; M.S., 1920, Ph.D., 1927; m. Hazel Blanche Clark, Sept. 19, 1916; children—Jeanne Louise (dec.), Patricia Anne, Richard Clark. Asst., Province Agusan, Mindanao, P.I., 1912-14; supervisor, Bur. Edn., Negroes Occidental, P.I., 1914-16; chief, Fisheries, Bur. of Science, Manila, P.I., 1916-20; exploration in Sulu Archipelago Mindanao, Luzon, P.I., 1920-21; head dept. of zoölogy, U. of Philippines, 1922-23; exploration in Mindanao, Palawan and Luzon, P.I., 1923-24; teacher, Junior Coll., Kansas City, Mo., 1925-26; asst. prof. of zoölogy, U. of Kan., Lawrence, 1927-28, asso. prof., 1928-34, prof. from 1934; curator of hepetology and ichthyology, Museum of Natural History, U. of Kan. from 1946; explorations in Mexico, summers, 1932-40, Oaxaca, 1914; delegate to Pan Am. Congresses, Mexico City, 1935, Washington, D.C., 1940. Served as civilian with Am. and British army, CBI and SEAC Theatres, 1945, 1946. Decoration: Civilian Services Medal. Engaged in civilian relief work, typhus epidemic, Siberia, Russia, 1918-19. Mem. Am. Soc. Mammalogists, A.A.A.S., Am. Soc. Icthyologists and Herpetologists, Kan. Acad. Sci., Sigma Xi, Phi Sigma, Pi Gamma Mu, Pi Kappa Alpha. Club: University (Lawrence, Kansas). Author: Snakes of the Philippine Islands; Philippine Land Mammals; The Lizards of the Genus Eumeces; The Amphibians and Turtles of the Philippine Islands; The Lizards of the Philippine Islands; (with H. M. Smith) Annotated Checklist and Key to the Snakes of Mexico and Annotated Checklist and Key to the Amphibians of Mexico; and more than 100 other scientific articles and pamphlets on reptiles and amphibians. Editor, Kansas University Science Bulletin. Home: Lawrence, Kansas. †

TAYLOR, ELKANAH EAST, poet critic; b. Norfolk, Va., July 26, 1888; d. Wilmer Bailey and Mamie (Stroud) East; ed. Sweetbriar Coll., Lynchburg, Va., 1906-07, William and Mary Coll., 1919; m. E. Jordan Taylor, June 5, 1912; 1 child, Wilmer East. Contbr. verse and stories to mags. from childhood; founder, 1925, and since editor Will-o'-the-Wisp, mag. of verse. State chmn. of poetry, Va. Fedn. Women's Clubs; mem. Poetry Soc. America, Nat. League Am. Penwomen, Poetry Soc. Va., Am. Lit. Assn., Norfolk Soc. of Arts, Order of Bookfellows, Empire

Poetry League (London); hon. mem. Ala. State Poetry Soc., Springhill Coll. Poetry Soc. Democrat. Methodist. Clubs: Woman's (Norfolk, Va.); Driver Book Club. Author: Whisperings and Other Poems, 1919; Dust and Flame, 1923; Candles on the Sill, 1927; also (brochures); Pen-Points, A Wreath of Holly. Home: Driver, Va.†

TAYLOR, HENRY JUNIOR, ambassador, journalist, economist, author; b. Chgo., Sept. 2, 1902; s. Henry Noble and Eileen Louise (O'Hare) T.; m. Olivia Fay Kimbro, Mar. 2, 1928; 1 child, Henry Noble; m. Marion J.E. Richardson, July 3, 1970. Grad., U. Va., 1924; Litt.D., Marietta Coll., Troy State U.; L.H.D., U. Geneva, U. Laussane, U. Zurich, Switzerland. Adv. bd. Chem. Bank, N.Y.; dir. Waldorf-Astoria Hotel, N.Y.C., The Pittston Co.; chmn. bd. Silicone Paper Co. Am., Inc.; fgn. corr. for Scipps-Howard Newspaper Syndicate in, Finland, Germany, Eng., Sweden, Switzerland, France, Belgium, Spain, Portugal, Italy, Greece, Egypt, Palestine, Syria, Turkey, West, Central and North Africa, India, China and, the Philippines, and on assignment around the world through all theatres of war, in 1945, ambassador to Switzerland, 1957-61; del. Disarmament and Nuclear Control Conf., Geneva, 1958-60, Fgn. Minister's Conf., Geneva, 1959; attended Internat. Conf., Dumbarton Oaks, Quebec (2), Cairo, San Francisco, Berlin, Paris, London; also Summit Conf., Geneva. Author: It Must Be a Long War, 1939, Germany's Economy of Coercion, 1940, Time Runs Out, 1942, Men in Motion, 1943, Men and Power, 1946, An American Speaks His Mind, 1957, The Big Man; novel, 1964, Men and Moments, 1966; contbr.: book Deadline Delayed, 1947; author: chpt. on Africa in Book of Knowledge; Broadcast: Gen. Motors radio network program Your Land and Mine, 1945-56; columnist: Gen. Motors radio network program United Features Syndicate, 1961-81; contbr. to: Gen. Motors radio network program and econ. jours in, U.S., Eng., Switzerland, Sweden.; Reader's Digest, Sat. Eve. Post, Sat. Rev. of Lit., N.Y. Times Sunday Mag. Lifetime trustee U. Va. Endowment Fund; trustee emeritus Thomas Jefferson Meml. Assn., Monticello; bd. dirs., exec. com. Am.-Scottish Found., Gen. Douglas MacArthur Meml. Found.; trustee Carnegie Lifesaving Fund; bd. dirs. John Paul Jones Found., Herbert Hoover Presdl. Library, Com. to Unite Am.; mem. nat. alumni council Lawrenceville Sch. Recipient Alfred I. Dupont Radio award; war dept. citation for conspicuous service in a theatre of combat; gold medals (9) Freedom Found., Valley Forge; gold medal for pub. service ASME; Paul Revere Bowl for good citizenship SAR; Gen. Douglas MacArthur medal Mil. Order Fgn. Wars; Wallace award Am.-Scottish Found.; French Order of LaFayette; Finland Order of the Rose; Papal Medal Pope Pius XII; Hungarian Freedom medal UN Assn. for Oppressed Nations; Benjamin Franklin medal Poor Richard Club. Mem. Raven Scholastic Soc. (Edgar Allan Poe award (2), Soc., Cin., SAR, Mil. Order Fgn. Wars, Delta Kappa Epsilon (nat. council), Sigma Delta Chi, Colonial Lords of Manor, Loyal Legion. Republican. Clubs: River (N.Y.C.); Farmington Country (Charlottesville, Va.); Corviglia Ski (St. Moritz, Switzerland). Address: New York, N.Y. Died Feb. 24, 1984.

TAYLOR, HENRY LONGSTREET, physiologist, educator; b. St. Paul, Feb. 2, 1912; s. Henry Longstreet and Ethelberta (Geer) T.; m. Catherine Morton Elliott, Mar. 21, 1941; children—David H., James F., Geoffrey E. B.S., Harvard, 1935; postgrad., Med. Sch., 1935-37; Ph.D. in Physiology, U. Minn., 1942. Staff Lab. Physiol. Hygiene, U. Minn. Sch. Pub. Health, 1942-44, asst. prof., 1944-49, asso. prof., 1949-56, prof., 1956-83, acting dir., 1951-52, 63-64, field work in nutrition, phys. activity, coronary heart disease, Italy, 1955-70; cons. research com. Internat. Cardiol. Soc., 1963-65; chmn. steering com. Nat. Coop. Study Feasibility of Exercise in Trials of Prevention of Coronary Heart Disease, 1965-70; co-prin. investigator Mpls. unit Multiple Risk Factor Intervention Trial, 1972-77; mem. epidemiology com. Lipid Research Clinics. Author: (with others) The Biology of Human Starvation, 1950; monograph Coronary Heart Disease in Seven Countries, 1970; also numerous articles, sect. in handbook. Mem. Am. Heart Assn. (exec. com. council epidemiology 1964-65), Am. Physiol. Soc., Soc. Exptl. Biology and Medicine, Gerontol. Soc., Am. Statis. Soc., Am. Coll. Sports Medicine (Honor award 1980), Internat. Cardiol. Soc., Am. Pub. Health Assn. Home: Saint Paul, Minn. Died Nov. 10, 1983.

TAYLOR, HOWARD CANNING, JR., physician; born N.Y. City, Feb. 17, 1900; s. Howard Canning and Alice C. (Gibbs) T.; Ph.B., Yale Sheffield Scientific Sch., 1920; M.D., Columbia College Phys. and Surgs., 1924; Doctor of Science, New York University, 1955; m. Caroline Colgate, Sept. 8, 1923; children—Barbara (Mrs. Donald Schoen), Caroline Alice (Mrs. Lincoln Day), Howard C. III. Asso. prof. obstetrics-gynecology N.Y.U., 1935-39, 1940-43, prof., chmn. dept., 1943-46; attending gynecol. 1936-46, cons. gynecol., from 1946, Roosevelt Hosp., N.Y.C., attending gynecol. Memorial Hosp., 1943-46. Prof. gynecology, U. of Pa., 1939-40; prof. obstetrics-gynecol., chmn. dept., Columbia Coll. Phys. and Surgs., 1946-65; vis. gynecologist and obstetrician in charge Bellevue Hosp., 1943-46; director dept. obstetrics and gynecology Presbyterian Hospital, 1946-65; dir. gynecology Francis Delafield Hosp., 1949-65; dir. Internat. Inst. Study Human Reproduction, Columbia U., prof. emeritus obstetrics and gynecology. Honorary life time director American Cancer Society, Incorporated, president 1954-55. Diplomate Am. Board Obstetrics-Gynecology. Fellow A.C.S. (regent 1951-60); Am. Coll. Obstetricians and Gynecologists (president 1966-67), N.Y. Acad. of Medicine, N.Y. Acad. Sci., Royal College of Obstetricians and Gynecologists London (hon.); mem. Internat. Fedn. Gynecologists and Obstetricians (pres. 1961-64), A.M.A., American Assn. Obstetricians and Gynecologists, Am. Gynecol. Soc. (pres. 1957-58), Am. Radium Soc., American Assn. Cancer Research, N.Y. Obstet. Soc., N.Y. Gynecol. Soc. (pres. 1962-63), Am. Assn. Planned Parenthood Physicians (pres. 1967-69); hon. mem. Central Assn. Obstetricians and Gynecologists, S. Atlantic Soc. Obstetricians and Gynecologists; fgn. hon. mem. Obstet. and Gynec. Soc. Sweden, Sociedad Peruana de Obstetricia y Genecologia, Obstet. Soc. Edinburgh, Obstet. and Gynec. Soc. Jugoslavia, The German Gynecological Society, The Italian Obstetrical and Gynecological Society, Japanese Obstetrical and Gynecological Soc., The Obstetrical and Gynecological Society of Brazil, The Medical Society of Czechoslavakia. Clubs: Century, University, American Gynecological, Harvey Society, Fairfield Country. Contbr. articles to med. jours. Home: New York, N.Y. Died Feb. 1985.

TAYLOR, JOHN C., dir. agrl. extension service; b. Utica, Mont., Oct. 15, 1887; s. Lewellyn Burbank and Augusta Caroline Taylor; B.S., Mont. State Coll., 1912; m. Isabella Ewen Helen Shiell, Apr. 22, 1915; children—Janet Caroline, Helen Douglas, Agnes Eugenia, William Burbank. Began as dist. agrl. agent, 1914; county agrl. agent, Custer County, Mont., 1915-16, dist. agrl. supervisor, Feb.-June 1917, asst. county agent leader, 1917-20, acting county agent leader, 1921-22, county agent leader, 1923-24; dir. Extension Service, Mont. State Coll., Bozeman, 1924-45, dir. emeritus, 1946. Chmn. State Agrl. Planning Com., 1937-41; mem. Nat. Ext. Com. on organization and policy, 1937-40. Charter mem. and mem. Northern Great Plains Council, 1938-46. Mem. Phi Kappa Phi, Alpha Zeta, Epsilon Sigma Phi (given certificate of recognition), Sigma Chi, Lambda Gamma Delta. Mason. Clubs: Bozeman Kiwanis (pres., 1932) (mem. Kiwanis Internat. com. on agrl., 1932-33, chmn., 1934). Home: Bozeman, Mont. †

TAYLOR, JOHN WILLIAMS, artist; b. Balt., Oct. 12, 1897; s. John Williams and Maude (Butner) T.; m. Andree Ruellan, May 28, 1929. Studied with, S. McDonald Wright, J. Francis Smith, Los Angeles, 1920-23, Boardman Robinson, Art Student's League, N.Y.C., 1927-28; studies abroad, principally France, 1929-31. Instr. Art Students League N.Y. summer sch., Woodstock, N.Y., 1948, 50, 51, 54, Pa. State U., 1957; Mich State U., 1958; guest instr. John Herron Mus. Sch., Indpls., 1950, 54, 57, 60, U. Tulane, 1956, 58-59, U. Fla., 1960-62, U. Wash., 1963. Executed mural decoration, Richfield Springs (N.Y.) Post office, 1942, works exhbtd., Macbeth Galleries, 1938, 44, 50, Am. Acad. Arts and Letters, 1948, Milch Galleries, 1955, 63, exhbns. include annuals of, Carnegie Inst., Whitney Mus., Pa. Acad., U. Ill., Va. Mus. biennials, Nat. Acad. Design, Art Inst. Chgo., Am. Watercolor Soc., Bklyn. Mus. Internat., John Herron, Met., Balt., Montclair, Worcester and Toledo museums, others; rep. permanent collections, Met. Mus., Am. Acad. Arts and Letters, Currier Gallery Am. Art, John Herron Mus., Art Students League N.Y., N.A.D., Whitney Mus. Am. Art, Va. Mus., other museums, galleries, pvt. collections.; (recipient 1st prize 42d Watercolor annual Balt. Mus. 1939, prize for watercolor 33d Ann. Exhbn. Albany Mus. 1968). Guggenheim fellow, 1954; John Barton Payne medal and purchase award Va. Mus. Biennial, 1946; hon. mention Carnegie Inst.'s, Painting in the U.S., 1947; 1000 award Paintings of the Year, Nat. Acad. Galleries, 1948; citation and $1000 grant in arts Am. Acad. Arts and Letters, 1948; gold medal honor Am. Watercolor Soc., 1949. Mem. Woodstock Artists Assn. Nat. Academician. Address: Ulster County, NY.

TAYLOR, JOSHUA CHARLES, art historian, educator; b. Hillsboro, Oreg., Aug. 22, 1917; s. James Edmond and Anna L.M. (Scott) T. Student, Mus. Art Sch., Portland, Oreg., 1935-39; B.A., Reed Coll., 1939, M.A., 1946; M.F.A., Princeton, 1949, Ph.D., 1956. Tchr. theatre Reed Coll., 1939-41; tchr. history art Princeton U., 1948-49; faculty U. Chgo., 1949-74, chmn. 1st yr. program humanities in coll., 1954-58, William Rainey Harper prof. humanities, prof. history art, 1963-74; dir. Nat. Collection Fine Arts, Smithsonian Instn., 1970—; Lectr. in U.S., also on TV, 1953—; lectr. Inst. Interuniversitario, Argentina, 1962; spl. research 19th and 20th century painting and artistic theory, Italy, U.S.; Mem. adv. com. 20th Century art Art Inst. Chgo.; bd. dirs. Am. Fedn. Arts, Mus. Contemporary Art, Chgo.; faculty adv. com. Ency. Brit.; mem. adv. bd. Lillie P. Bliss Internat. Study Center, Mus. Modern Art; council Archives Am. Art. Designer for theatre, 1936-41, San Francisco Opera Ballet, 1936-37; Author: William Page, the American Titian, 1957, Learning to Look, 1957, Futurism, 1961, Graphic Works of Umberto Boccioni, 1961, Vedere prima di Credere, 1970, To See is to Think: Looking at American Art, 1975, also articles, revs. Served to maj., inf. AUS, 1941-46, ETO. Fellow Royal Soc. Arts; mem. Coll. Art Assn. Am. (dir.), Internat. Inst. Conservation Historic and Artistic Works, Assn. Art Mus. Dirs., Am. Assn. Museums, Phi Beta Kappa. Home: Washington DC.*

TAYLOR, PAUL SCHUSTER, economics; b. Sioux City, Iowa; June 9, 1895; s. Henry James and Rose Eugenia (Schuster) T.; B.A., U. Wis., 1917; M.A., U. Calif.-Berkeley, 1920, Ph.D., 1922, LL.D., (hon.), 1965; m. Katharine Page Whiteside, May 15, 1920; children—Katharine Page, Ross Whiteside, Margaret Agnes; m. 2d, Dorothea Lange, Dec. 6, 1935. With U. Calif., from 1922, prof. econs., 1939-62, chmn. dept., 1952-56; chmn. Inst. Internat. Studies, 1956-62, emeritus, 1962; research dir. Cal. Labor Fedn., 1970 Chief investigator research project Social Science Research Council of Mexican labor in U.S., 1927-29; cons. Pacific Coast of studies of crime and fgn. born Nat. Commn. Law Observance and Enforcement, 1930-31; field dir. div. rural rehab. Cal. Emergency Relief Adminstrn., 1935; regional labor adviser U.S. Resettlement Adminstrn., 1935-36; cons. economist Social Security Bd., 1936-41; pres. Cal. Rural Rehab. Corp., 1935-43; cons. economist Dept. Interior, 1943-52; cons. Pres. Migratory Labor Commn., 1950-51, ICA (now AID), 1955, 58, 61, 63, 66, 67, 68, UN, 1960, 62, 63, Ford Found., U. Alexandria (UAR), 1962, 63; adv. council Cal. Dept. Employment, 1935-42; mem. Govs. Commn. Reemployment, 1939, mem. Cal. Bd. Agr., 1940-44. Served to capt. USMC, 1917-19, with 2d Div., AEF Decorated Purple Heart; Guggenheim fellow, 1931. Mem. Am. Econ. Assn., Chi Phi, Phi Alpha Delta, Delta Sigma Pi, Delta Sigma Rho, Phi Beta Kappa; academico corresponsal Mexican Academia Nacional de Ciencias. Clubs: Faculty (U. Cal.); Cosmos (Washington). Author: Sailors Union of the Pacific, 1923; Mexican Labor in the United States, 2 vols., 1928-32; A Spanish-Mexican Peasant Community Arandas in Jalisco, Mexico, 1933; An American-Mexican Frontier, 1934; An American Exodus (with Dorothea Lange), rev. edit., 1969. Home: Berkeley, Calif. Dec. Mar. 13, 1984.

TAYLOR, WALTER PENN, biologist; b. Elkhorn, Wis., Oct. 31, 1888; s. Benton Ben and Helen R. (West) T.; Throop Poly. Inst., Pasadena, Calif., 1902-08, grad. academic dept., 1906; Stanford U., fall semester, 1908; B.S., U. of Calif., 1911, Ph.D., 1914; m. Mary E. Fairchild, Aug. 5, 1912; children—Theodore Walter, Harriet, Elizabeth Fairchild, Benton Chester. Asst. in biology, Throop Poly. Inst., 1906-08; asst. curator mammals, 1909-11, curator, 1911-16, Museum of Vertebrate Zoölogy, U. of Calif.; asst. biologist, U.S. Biol. Survey, Dept. of Agr. (combined with Bur. of Fisheries to form Fish and Wildlife Service in U.S. Dept. of Interior, July 1940), Washington, 1916-24, biologist, 1924-28, sr. biologist from 1928; prof. zoology, University of Arizona, 1932-36; in charge Tex. Coöperative Wild Life Research Unit., 1936-48; head dept. of wild game, A.&M. Coll. of Tex., 1937-1944; chief div. of wildlife research, Tex. Agrl. Expt. Station, 1937-47; prof. zoology Oklahoma A. and M. Coll. from 1948; leader Okla. Coop. Wildlife Research Unit, since 1948. Field work with higher vertebrates, Calif., Nev., Ariz., N.M., Tex. and Wash., since 1908; mem. U.S. Dept. Agr. Advisory Committee on Migratory Bird Protection, 1913-16; chmn. Committee on Texas Marine Resources, 1942-45; chmn. joint com. on Wildlife, Wildlife Soc.; and National Research Council, 1945. Author monographs and numerous shorter papers, chiefly in systematic mammalogy, ecology and game protection. Sec. Calif. Associated Societies for Conservation of Wild Life, 1912-16; pres. Ecol. Soc. of America, 1935; pres. Am. Soc. of Mammalogists, 1940-41; v.p. Nat. Fedn. Fed. Employees from 1928, pres. Wildlife Society, 1943-44, pres. Tex.-Acad. Sci., 1944-45.†

TAYLOR, WILLIAM JAMES, transportation company executive; b. Eddystone, Pa., July 29, 1926; s. William J. and Clara Ella (Harris) T.; m. Jane Currie, Oct. 18, 1958; children—Deborah Ann, Timothy J., Jeffrey Harris. A.B., Dickinson Coll., 1949; J.D., U. Pa., 1952. Bar: Pa. bar 1953, N.Y. bar 1961, also U.S. Supreme Ct 1961. Law clk. to chief justice Supreme Ct. Pa., 1952-53; mem. legal dept. Pa. R.R., 1953-61; mem. law dept. REA Express, 1961-62, gen. counsel, 1962-65, v.p., gen. counsel, 1965-66, exec. v.p., gen. counsel, 1966, pres., chief exec. officer, 1966-68, chmn., 1968-69; v.p. Ill. Central Gulf R.R., 1969-74; v.p. govtl. affairs I.C. Industries, 1969-74, v.p. legal affairs, 1974-76; pres., chief exec. officer Ill. Central Gulf R.R., 1976-83, also dir.; legis. counsel to trustees Penn Central R.R., 1971-74. Trustee Dickinson Coll. Served with USNR, 1944-46. Mem. Am. Bar Assn., Assn. ICC Practitioners, C. of C., Newcomen Soc. N.Am., Sigma Chi, Omicron Delta Kappa. Clubs: Congressional Country (Washington), Internat. (Washington); Chgo. (Chgo.), Econ. (Chgo.); Barrington Hills (Ill.). Home: Barrington Hills, Ill. Died Nov. 15, 1983.

TEAGUE, WILLARD CONWELL, editorial writer; b. Sweetwater, Tenn., Aug. 4, 1889; s. John Lawson and Mary Summers (Conwell) T.; grad. Branham and Hughes Sch., Spring Hill, Tenn., 1908; A.B., Vanderbilt U., 1912, grad. student, 1916-19; m. Georgia Fletcher Cole, Aug. 25, 1926; children—Lois Carolyn, John Webster, Willard Conwell. Teacher of Latin and English, Massey Sch., Pulaski, Tenn., 1912-16; teacher English and mathematics, Wallace Univ. Sch., Nashville, Tenn., 1916-19; exec. sec. Sigma Chi Fraternity and editor of magazine, 1919-20; reporter and editorial writer Nashville (Tenn.) Banner, 1921-33; editorial writer Nashville Tennessean, 1933-34; editorial writer and radio commentator Commercial Appeal from 1934. Dir. Vanderbilt Alumni Assn. Mem. Sigma Chi, Sigma Upsilon, Phi Beta Kappa.

Democrat. Methodist. Club: Kiwanis (Memphis). Contbr. to periodicals. Home: Memphis, Tenn. †

TEAL, JOHN JEROME, JR., educator, ecologist; b. N.Y.C., Feb. 7, 1921; s. John Jerome and Isabelle (O'Sullivan) T.; m. Penelope Holden, May 6, 1950 (div. 1971); children—Pamela N., Ptarmigan P., John A., Lansing H. B.S., Harvard U., 1944; M.A., Yale U., 1946. First sr. fellow McGill U. Arctic Inst. N. Am., 1951-52; traveling fellow Carnegie Corp., 1950-51; research asso. McGill U., 1951-52; fellow Ford Found., 1958; asso. prof. anthropology and geography U. Vt., 1958-59; prof. human ecology U. Alaska, 1964-77; numerous arctic expdns., 1946-82; pres. Inst. No. Agrl. Research, 1954-82. Author: Gift of Dominion; Contbr. articles to profl. jours., spl. TV programs on human ecology. Chmn. Fairbanks Sister City Com., 1965-66, Fairbanks PTA, 1966-67, Interior Alaska chpt. Am. Scandinavian Found., 1966-67. Served as pilot USAAF, World War II. Decorated D.F.C., Air medal (6).; Lithow Osborne Travelling fellow, 1966-67. Mem. AAAS, Am. Anthrop. Soc., Fedn. Am. Scientists, Am. Soc. Mammalogists, Norwegian Polar Soc., N.Y. Acad. Scis., Conn. Acad. Arts and Scis., Sigma Xi. Spl. research domestication of musk ox. Home: Bainbridge Island, Wash. Died Aug. 26, 1982.

TEDESCHE, SIDNEY S(AUL), rabbi; b. Elmwood Place, O., Apr. 9, 1890; s. Alexander and Jeannette (Greenfield) T.; grad. as rabbi, Hebrew Union Coll., Cincinnati, 1913; A.B., U. of Cincinnati, 1913; Ph.D., Yale, 1928; LL.B., U. of St. John's Law Sch., 1938; m. Irma Goldman, May 31, 1916; children—Tekla Jeanne Williams, Carol Irene Simon. Rabbi, Springfield, Illinois, 1913-16, Providence, Rhode Island, 1916-19, San Antonio, 1920-22, New Haven, Connecticut, 1922-28, Union Temple, Brooklyn, N.Y., since 1929. Dir. Brooklyn Pub. Library (chmn. book committee, mem. executive committee); dir. Jewish Publication Soc., Bd. of Publs., Jewish Cultural Foundation of New York U.; mem. bd. dirs. Central Conf. American Rabbis; member Am. Jewish Com. Member American Oriental Society, New York Association Reform Rabbis (past president), Soc. Bibl. Lit., Yale Sem. Club, Economic Club, N.Y. Historical Society, Phi Beta Kappa, Zeta Beta Tau, Pi Tau Pi, Yod Kaf Tav. Mason (Grand Chaplain). Club: Unity. Author: Critical Edition of I Esdras, 1928; also translations various publications, numerous scientific papers, including "Jewish Champions of Religious Liberalism," "Prayers of the Apocrypha." Contbr. articles in Universal Jewish Ency. Home: Brooklyn, N.Y. †

TEEGEN, OTTO JOHN, architect; b. Davenport, Iowa, Aug. 19, 1899; s. Otto and Laura (Boeck) T.; B.S. cum laude, Harvard, 1922, M.Arch., 1924, Julia Amory Appleton fellow, 1925; grad. study Am. Acad., Rome Italy, 1925, Atelier Umbdenstock-Tournon, Paris, 1926; m. Dorothy Schmidt, Oct. 6, 1934; 1 dau., Carola. Asst. to Joseph Urban, dir. color and lighting, Chgo. World's Fair, 1933; dir. color Gt. Lakes Expln., Cleve. 1936; coordinating architect Town of Tomorrow, N.Y. World's Fair, 1939; partner Scott & Teegen, N.Y.C., 1933-41; asso. mem. Voorhees, Walker, Foley & Smith, architects, 1945-49; univ. architect State U. N.Y., Albany, 1949-64; architectural cons., from 1964. Mem. visiting com., sch. architecture, Harvard, 1933-51, Princeton 1938-52, Mass. Inst. Tech., 1936-38; dir. architecture Nat. Inst. for Archtl. Edn., 1935-40, chmn. bd. trustees, 1940-55, dir., treas., 1955-59. Served as sgt. S.A.T.C., World War I.; lt. comdr., USNR, 1942-45. Fellow A.I.A.; mem. Nat. Inst. for Archtl. Edn., Phi Beta Kappa. Rep. Episcopalian. Clubs: Century Assn., Harvard (N.Y.C.). Contbr. profl. jours. Home: New York, N.Y. Died Apr. 8, 1983.

TEETOR, RALPH R., automotive engr.; b. Hagerstown, Ind., Aug. 17, 1890; s. John H. and Kate C. (Rowe) T.; B.S. in M.E., U. of Pa., 1912, M.E., 1930; m. Nellie Van Antwerp, Dec. 30, 1922; 1 dau., Marjorie. In charge of engring., Teetor-Hartley Motor Co., 1912-18; asst. to supt. N.Y. Ship Bldg. Corp., 1918-19; chief engr. Perfect Circle Co., 1919-38, v.p. since 1938; v.p. Union Trust Co. Pres. Hagerstown Sch. System, 1921-28. Mem. Nat. Council of Boy Scouts of America. President Society Automotive Engineers, 1936-37; member Am. Soc. M.E., Engring. Soc. of Detroit, Theta Tau, Tau Beta Pi. Republican. Mason (32 deg.). Clubs: Detroit Athletic (Detroit); University (Chicago); Columbia, Indianapolis Athletic (Indianapolis); Engineers (Dayton, O.). Home: Hagerstown, Ind. Died Feb. 15, 1982.

TEICHMAN, SABINA, artist; b. N.Y.C.; m. David A. Teichman; 1 dau., Wendy Teichman Levine. B.A., Columbia U., 1941, M.A., 1943. Author newspaper article.; One-woman shows, Salpeter Gallery, 1947, 49, 52, 54, A.C.A. Gallery, 1957, 60, 63, 69, Fairleigh Dickinson U., 1963, ACA Gallery, Rome, 1965, Orpheus Ascending Gallery, Stockbridge, Mass., 1972, N.Y. Cultural Center, N.Y.C., 1975, St. Mary's Coll. of Md., 1977, Shore Galleries, Boston, 1978, Tower Gallery, Southampton, N.Y., 1978, Phoenix Gallery, N.Y.C., 1979-82, North Truro Gallery, 1980-81, group shows include, Salpter Gallery, 1946-55, A.C.A. Gallery, from 1955, Whitney Mus., 1957, John Herron Mus., Butler Inst. Am. Art, U. Tex., Mint Mus., Ann. shows, Audubon Artists, N.Y.C., 1967-82, Silvermine Guild, New Canaan, Conn., 1970-78, U. Tex. Art Gallery, Austin, Phoenix Gallery, N.Y.C., paintings in permanent collections, Balt. Mus. Art, Bklyn. Mus., Carnegie Inst., Pitts., Butler Inst. Am. Art, Nat. Mus. Israel, San Francisco Mus. Art, Syracuse U. Mus., Whitney Mus. Am. Art, George Vincent Arthur Smith Mus., Springfield, Mass., U. Mass., Brandeis U., Tel-Aviv Mus., U. P.R. Mus., Living Arts Found. Collection, Vatican Mus., Norfolk Mus. Art, James A. Michener Found. Collection, Sheldon Swope Art Mus., Neuburger Mus., SUNY, Colby Coll. Mus., others, also pvt. collections. Mem. Artists Equity Assn., Provincetown Art Mus., Audubon Artists N.Y. Home: New York, NY.

TEMKIN, ASCHER MARK, symphony condr.; b. Chgo., Feb. 9, 1938; s. William and Ida (Schaeffer) T.; m. Penelope Carney, May 31, 1964; children—Nicole, Alexei. Mus.B. in Viola, Northwestern U., 1960; Mus.M. in Composition, Butler U., 1966. prof. music SUNY, Brockport, 1966-81, Rochester Inst. Tech., 1981-82; founder N.Y. Festival Advanced Condr.'s Tng. Program. First violinist, N.C. Symphony, 1958, prin violist, soloist, sect. coach, Kansas City (Mo.) Philharm., 1959-61, Buffalo Philharm, 1961-64, Indpls. Symphony Orch., 1964-66, music dir., Brockport (N.Y.) Symphony, 1966-79, Genesee (N.Y.) Symphony, 1969-72, N.Y. Festival, 1970-82, R.I.T. Philharmonia, 1981-82, asso. music dir., Bogotá (Colombia) Philharm., 1972-73, guest condr. orchs. in, S.Am., Mex., U.S., Asia and, Europe, (One of 6 Americans invited to participate in Mitropoulos Internat. Conducting Competition, Carnegie Hall 1970, guest of honor Internat. Tchaikovsky Music Competition, USSR 1978). Mem. Am. Symphony Orch. League (past dir.), Condrs. Guild. Home: Brockport, N.Y. Died Nov. 23, 1982.

TENENBAUM, JOSEPH, urologist, author; b. Sassow, Poland, May 22, 1887; s. Berish Bienstock and Rebeka (Tenenbaum) T.; student U. of Vienna, 1908-11; M.D., U. of Lwow, 1914; m. Otilia John, Sept. 21, 1914; children—Edward, Bertrand, Robert; m. 2d, Sheila Schwartz, Jan. 23, 1943. Came to United States, 1920, naturalized, 1926. Capt. M.C. Austrian Army, World War; del. Peace Conf., Paris, 1919. Attending urologist and surgeon, Goldwater Memorial Hosp., and Neurol Hosp., Welfare Island, N.Y., from 1925, then cons.; assoc. surgeon Beth Israel Hosp., N.Y.C., from 1930, now cons.; attending urologist Israel-Zion Hospital, Bklyn., from 1925, then cons.; instructor in urology, Columbia Coll., 1922-24. Chmn. med. bd., Workmen's Circle, frat. orgn. Awarded Golden Cross (Austria); Commander Cross Polonia Restituta. Diplomate Am. Bd. Urology. Fellow American College of Surgeons, N.Y. Acad. of Medicine, Am. Urol. Assn., N.Y. and Brooklyn urol. socs., Am. Academy Polit. and Social Sci.; mem. N.Y. County Med. Soc., Am. Med. Assn., New York State Med. Soc. (med. sec.), Am. Jewish Congress (chmn. executive com. 1929-36, vice pres. 1945); nat. chairman Joint Boycott Council; exec. chmn. Comm. for Inter-American Cooperation, also United Jewish War Effort; delegate Am. Jewish Conf., 1943; interim comm. mem. 1944; mem. World Jewish Congress (exec. comm.), Am. Hebrew-Speaking Med. Assn. (past pres.), Jewish Acad. Arts and Sciences. President Polish Physicians Alliance; national pres. American and World Fedn. Polish Jews; chmn. Joint Distbrs. Committee on Poland; mem. Am.-Jewish Physicians Committee (bd. dirs.); nat. v.p., pres. Manhattan region Zionist Orgn. America; hon chmn. Nat. Coordinating Committee for Admission War Refugees to U.S.A.; mem. Author's League of Am. Mason. Club: Jewish Writers. Author numerous books since 1917, latest: In Search of a Lost People—The Old and New Poland, 1948; Underground—The Story of a People 1952; Race and Reich, 1956. Address: New York, N.Y. †

TENER, ALEXANDER CAMPBELL, lawyer; b. Newcastle, Pa., Oct. 13, 1888; s. George E. and Annie F. (Fallbush) T.; grad. Hill Sch., 1908; A.B., Yale, 1912; LL.B., Harvard, 1915; m. Marion Clement, June 15, 1916 (dec. Oct. 1918); 1 son, George Evans II; m. 2d, Ethel D. Logan, Jan. 9, 1948. Admitted to Pa. bar, 1916, from practiced in Pitts.; asso. with brother, 1918-47; sr. mem. Tener, Van Kirk, Wolf & Moore, from 1952; judge orphans ct., Allegheny County, Pa., 1943-45. Dir. Phelps Dodge Corp., Fidelity Trust Co. Pitts. Mem. Pa. Bd. Law Examiners, from 1946. Chmn. Renegotiation Bd., U.S. Army Ordnance Office, Pitts., 1942-43. Corporator St. Andrews Hosp., Boothbay Harbor, Me. Clubs: University (N.Y.C.); Duquesne (Pitts.); Allegheny Country, Edgeworth (Sewickley, Pa.). Address: Sewickley, Pa. †

TEN HOOR, MARTEN, educator; b. Franeker Vriesland, Netherlands, Apr. 21, 1890; s. Foppe Marten and Elizabeth Petranella (Kok) ten H.; came to U.S., 1896; Calvin Junior College, 1909; A.B., University of Michigan, 1913, A.M., 1914, Ph.D., 1921; LL.D., Washington Coll., 1958, U. Ala., 1960; m. Marie Magdalen Schanz, Dec. 31, 1920. Pvt. sch. tchr., 1909-11; mem. faculty Washington Coll., U. Mich., U. Ill., Tulane U., 1914-44; prof. philosophy and dean, Coll. Arts and Sciences, U. Ala., 1944-60, dean emeritus, from 1960. Served as sergt. 1st class, U.S. Army Med. Corps, 1918-19. U.S. rep., exec. com. Internat. Conf. Philo. Socs., from 1948. Officer in the Order of Orange-Nassau (Netherlands) 1947. Chevalier de la Legion d'Honneur, 1952. Mem. several orgns. field of music; mem. Oak Ridge Institute of Nuclear Studies, from 1947, chmn., 1955-58, mem. of board of dirs.; from 1958. Fellow A.A.A.S.; mem. numerous, sometime officer several profl. orgns. and assns., including Phi Beta Kappa. Phi Beta Kappa Associates, Kappa Kappa Psi, Omicron Delta Kappa. Episcopalian. Clubs: Round Table, Boston (New Orleans); Michigan Union (Ann Arbor); University (Tuscaloosa). Author several books, latest: Education for Privacy, 1960; also articles, fiction and translations; contbr. to tech. and profl. jours. Home: Tuscaloosa, Ala.†

TENNANT, JOHN SELDEN, lawyer; b. Saginaw, Mich., Feb. 3, 1906; s. John S. and Sarah (Barnard) T.; A.B., U. Mich., 1928, J.D., 1931, research fellow, 1931-32; LL.D. Central Mich. U., 1967; m. Mary Kent-Miller, June 17, 1930; children—John Selden III, William K. admitted to N.Y. bar, 1933; asso. firm White & Case, N.Y.C., 1932-47, partner, 1948-76; gen. counsel U.S. Steel Corp., 1955-71. Pres., Internat. Legal Aid Assn., 1964-74. Mem. Am., N.Y. State, Internat., Inter-Am. bar assns., Assn. Bar City N.Y., N.Y. County Lawyers Assn., Order of Coif, Delta Theta Phi. Clubs: Downtown Assn., Links (N.Y.C.); Pine Valley Golf (Clementon, N.J.); Baltusrol Golf (Springfield, N.J.); Royal and Ancient Golf (St. Andrews, Scotland); Hon. Co. of Edinburgh (Scotland) Golfers; Royal St. George's Golf (Sandwich, Eng.). Home: Summit, N.J. Died July 30, 1983.

TENNEY, MERRILL CHAPIN, clergyman, educator; b. Chelsea, Mass., Apr.16, 1904; s. Wallace Fay and Lydia Smith (Goodwin) T.; m. Helen Margaret Jaderquist, Sept. 5, 1930; children—Robert Wallace, Philip Chapin. Diploma, Missionary Tng. Sch., Nyack, N.Y., 1924; Th.B., Gordon Coll. Theology and Missions, Boston, 1927, Litt.D. (hon.), 1974; A.M., Boston U., 1930; Ph.D., Harvard, 1944; D.D. (hon.), Gordon-Conwell Theol. Sem., 1980. Ordained to ministry Baptist Ch., 1928; pastor (Storrs Av. Ch.), Braintree, Mass., 1926-28; mem. faculty Gordon Coll., 1930-43, prof. N.T. and Greek, 1938-43; mem. faculty Wheaton (Ill) Coll., from 1943, prof. Bible and theology, from 1945; dean Wheaton (Ill) Coll. (Grad. Sch.), 1946-71; spring lectr. Goshen (Ind.) Coll., 1950; Mid. Winter lectures Western Conservative Bapt. Theol. Sem., 1951; Griffith Thomas lectr. Dallas Theol. Sem., 1962; lectr. Denver Bapt. Sem., 1964, Grace Theol. Sem., 1974; Past chmn. ednl. commn. Nat. Soc. Evangs. Author: Resurrection Realities, 1945, John: The Gospel of Belief, 1948, Galatians; The Charter of Christian Liberty, 1950, The Genius of the Gospels, 1951, The New Testament: A Survey, 1953, Philippians, 1956, Interpreting Revelation, 1957, Proclaiming the New Testament; The Reality of the Resurrection, 1963, New Testament Times, 1965, Roads a Christian Must Travel, 1979, Twelve Questions Jesus Asked, 1980; Editor: The Word for this Century, 1960, Pictorial Bible Dictionary, The Bible: The Living Word of Revelation, 1967, Pictorial Bible Ency, 1975, The Bible Almanac, 1980. Mem. Soc. Bibl. Research, Soc. Bibl. Lits. and Exegesis, Evang. Theol. Soc. (pres. 1950-51), Near East Archaeol. Soc., Phi Alpha Chi. Home: Wheaton, Ill. Died Mar. 18, 1985.

TENNEY, RAYMOND PARKER, consul; b. Tientsin, China, Sept. 13, 1887; s. Charles Daniel and Anne Runcie (Jerrel) T.; Oberlin and Ithaca high schs.; A.B., Harvard, 1909; unmarried. Apptd. student interpreter, 1909; v. and dep. consul gen. at Tientsin, 1911, Canton, 1912; asst. Chinese sec. to Legation at Peking, 1913; detailed to Shanghai and designated to exercise judicial authority and jurisdiction in civ. and criminal cases, 1919; assigned to Canton, 1922, Tsinan, 1923-24, Mukden, Mar. 1924-Feb. 1925; detailed to Dept. of State, Feb. 24, 1925. Address: Washington, D.C. †

TERMAN, EARLE LUTHER, educator; b. Mansfield, O., Apr. 14, 1889; s. George W. and Julia (Bush) T.; A.B., Ohio State U., 1912; A.M., Columbia, 1915; Ph.D., N.Y. Univ., 1930; m. Lucile Fitzgerald, of London, O., Aug. 14, 1916; children—Miriam Ruth, Maurice J. Supt. schs., Derby, Hilliards, Grand Rapids, O., 1912-16; head master Nanchang Acad., Nanchang Ki, China, 1916-20; asso. prof. edn. and sec. dept. of edn., Yenching Univ., Peiping, 1922-27; supt. schs. Monroeville, O., 1927-29; prof. edn., Defiance (O.) Coll., 1929-30; prof. edn. and actg. head dept. of edn., Swarthmore Coll., 1930-31; dir. Ulverston Sch., Swarthmore, from 1931. Dir. Nat. Ednl. Survey, China, 1923, under auspices Chinese Nat. Soc. for Advancement of Education. Member Progressive Edn. Assn., Academy Political Science. Protestant. Mason (32 deg., Shriner), Kiwanian. Author: The Efficiency of Elementary Schools in China (Chinese Nat. Survey report), 1924; New Basis for Curriculum Building, 1925; The Development of a National Educational Survey Technique, 1931. Contbr. ednl. jours. Home: Swarthmore, Pa. †

TERMAN, FREDERICK EMMONS, educator, electronics engr.; b. English, Ind., June 7, 1900; s. Lewis Madison and Anna Belle (Minton) T.; m. Sibyl Walcutt, Mar. 22, 1928 (dec. 1975); children—Frederick Walcutt, Terence Christopher, Lewis Madison. A.B. in Chem. Engring, Stanford U., 1920, E.E., 1922; Sc.D. in Elec. Engring, M.I.T., 1924; Sc.D. (hon.), Harvard U., 1945, U. B.C., 1950, Syracuse U., 1955, So. Meth. U., 1977; D.H.L. (hon.), J.F. Kennedy U., 1978. Instr. to prof. elec. engring. Stanford U., 1925-37, exec. head elec. engring. dept., 1937-45, dean engring., 1945-58, provost, 1955-65, v.p., 1959-65, emeritus, 1965—; pres. SMU Found. Sci. and Engring., 1965-74; cons. ednl. surveys, Calif., Colo., N.Y., Fla., Mass., Utah, others, 1965—; dir. Harvard Radio Research Lab., 1942-45; Mem. divs. 14 and 15 Nat. Def. Research Com., 1942-45; mem. spl. tech. adv. group and TAPEC com. Dept. of Def., 1953-56; research and devel.

adv. com. Signal Corps, 1954-62; mem. Bd. Fgn. Scholarships, Dept. State, 1960-65; adv. council Army Electronics Proving Ground, 1954-57; mem. Naval Res. Adv. Com., 1956-64, chmn., 1957-58; mem. Def. Sci. Bd., 1957-58; dir. emeritus Hewlett-Packard Co. Author several books, 1927—; (with J.M. Pettit) latest being Electronic Measurements, 1952, Electronic and Radio Engineering, 4th ed, 1955; Contbr. to tech. mags.; Cons. editor: Elec. and Electronic Engring. Series of, McGraw-Hill Book Co., Inc. Trustee Inst. Def. Analyses, 1956-73. Decorated by Brit. govt., 1946; U.S. Medal for Merit, 1948; Herbert Hoover medal Stanford Alumni Assn., 1969; U.S. Medal Sci., 1975; Uncommon Man award Stanford U., 1978; Order Civil Merit South Korea; Letter of Commendation Pres. Carter, 1978; Silver medal Assn. Old Crows, 1980. Fellow IEEE (pres. predecessor assn. 1941, medal of honor 1950, edn. medal 1956, founders award 1962), Nat. Acad. Sci. (chmn. engring. sect. 1953-55, mem. council 1956-59), Am. Soc. Engring. Edn. (hon. mem., v.p. 1949-51, Lamme medal 1964, named to Hall of Fame 1968), Audio Engring. Soc. (hon. mem.), Am. Philos. Soc., Nat. Acad. Engring. (founding mem.), Phi Beta Kappa, Sigma Xi (exec. bd. 1956-58, 67-70, 74-76, pres. 1975), Theta Xi, Tau Beta Pi, Eta Kappa Nu. Home: Stanford CA.

TERRY, CLYDE RAY, educator; b. Jackson Co., O., Jan. 19, 1889; s. John Collins and Sidney (Clark) T.; A.B., Ohio Wesleyan U., 1910; student Ohio State Univ.; A.M., University of Chicago, 1912; m. Elsa Hanauer, of Springfield, O., Sept. 25, 1913 (died March 23, 1921); children—Jack, Jim, Joe, Jay. Ordained to ministry of Methodist Church, 1913; pastor Delta Av. Ch., Cincinnati, O., 1913-14, Germantown, O., 1914-16; instr. Miami Mil. Inst., Germantown, 1916-17; chaplain 35th Div., U.S.A., in France, 1918-19; organized mil. sch. in Kan., 1919; moved school to Illinois, 1924; pres., Ill. Military School, Abingdon, 1924-36; supt. visual edn., Nat. Youth Adminstrn. Democrat. Mason (Shriner). Home: Chicago, Ill.†

TERRY, LUTHER LEONIDAS, physician, heart specialist, educator; b. Red Level, Ala., Sept. 15, 1911; s. James Edward and Lula M. (Durham) T.; m. Beryl Janet Reynolds, June 29, 1940; children: Janet Reynolds Kollock, Luther Leonidas, Michael D. B.S., Birmingham-So. Coll., 1931, D.Sc., 1961; M.D., Tulane U., 1935; D.Sc., Jefferson Med. Coll., 1962, Union Coll., 1964, Rose Poly. Inst., 1965, McGill U., 1966, U. Ala., 1966, St. Joseph's Coll., 1966; LL.D., U. Alaska, 1964, Calif. Coll. of Med., 1965; M.D. (hon.), Women's Med. Coll., Phila., 1964; D.Sc., U. R.I., 1964, Tulane U. Sch. Medicine, 1964; LL.D., Marquette U., 1968, Phila. Coll. Pharmacy and Sci., 1970. Diplomate: Am. Bd. Internal Medicine, Nat. Bd. Med. Examiners. Intern Hillman Hosp., Birmingham, Ala., 1935-36; asst. resident medicine Univ. Hosps., Cleve., 1936-37; resident medicine City Hosps., Cleve., 1937-38, asst. admitting officer, intern pathology, 1938-39; instr., research fellow medicine Washington U., St. Louis, 1939-40; instr. medicine and preventive medicine and pub. health U. Tex., Galveston, 1940-41, asst. prof., 1941-42, assoc. prof., 1942-46; instr. medicine Johns Hopkins Med. Sch., 1944-53, asst. prof., 1953-61; mem. staff USPHS Hosp., Balt., 1942-43, chief med. service, 1943-53; chief clinic, gen. medicine and exptl. therapeutics Nat. Heart Inst., Bethesda, Md., 1950-58, asst. dir., 1958-61; surgeon gen. USPHS, 1961-65; v.p. med. affairs U. Pa., Phila., 1965-71, prof. medicine, 1965-75, prof. community medicine, 1965-75, adj. prof., 1975-82, emeritus prof., 1982—; corp. v.p. for med. affairs ARA Services, Inc., Phila., 1980-83, med. cons., 1983—; Mem. cardiovascular study sect. NIH, 1950-55; chmn. med. bd. Clin. Center, 1953-55, mem., 1953-58; dir. residency tng. program Nat. Heart Inst., 1953-61, chmn. cardiovascular research tng. com., 1957-61; mem. med. div. Strategic Bombing Survey, Japan, 1945-46; com civilian health requirements USPHS, 1955-58, mem. adv. com. nutrition div. Indian health, 1957-61; chief U.S. del. WHO, 1961-65; mem. adv. bd. Leonard Wood Meml. Inst. Nutrition Scis., Columbia U.; Herman E. Hilleboe prize lectr. in pub. health N.Y. State Ann. Health Conf., 1965; mem. chmn. Nat. Interagy. Council on Smoking and Health, 1967-70; mem. facilities and resources com. Nat. Library Medicine; mem. adv. bd. Nat. Resuscitation Soc.; mem. adv. council Am. Mus. Health; mem. expert com. WHO, 1974. Mem.-at-large Nat. council Boy Scouts Am.; trustee Inst. for Advancement Med. Communication, Inst. Med. Research; pub. trustee Nutrition Found; vis. com. Sch. Hygiene and Pub. Health, Johns Hopkins, bd. dirs., trustee, bd. govs. many insts., orgns. Recipient George B. Glendening Meml. award washington Dental Soc., 1965, Distinguished Service medal USPHS, 1965. Fellow A.C.P. (past gov., hon. master 1973), Am. Coll. Cardiology (Robert D. Bruce award 1965), Am. Coll. Chest Physicians, Am. Coll. Hosp. Adminstrs., Am. Coll. Dentists, Phila. Coll. Physicians; mem. A.M.A. (past mem. ho. dels), Am. Heart Assn. (com. ethics), Am. Pub. Health Assn., Am. Found. Tropical Medicine (hon. dir., also hon. dir. Liberian Inst.), Assn. Am. Physicians, Am. Social Health Assn. (dir.), Nat. Tb Assn. (hon. v.p.), Am. Hosp. Assn. (hon.), Heart Assn. Southeastern Pa. (gov.), N.Y. Acad. Medicine, Nat. Soc. for Med. Research (dir.), Nat. Wildlife Fedn. (asso.), Royal Soc. Health (Gt. Britain), Pub. Health Service Clin. Soc. (past pres.), Pan Am. Med. Assn., Med. and Chirurgical Faculty Md. (hon.), Montgomery County (Md.) Med. Soc. (hon.), Ala. Acad. Honor, Omicron Delta Kappa, Pi Kappa Alpha (Distinguished Alumnus award Delta chpt. 1961, Distinguished Achievement award 1962). Home: Philadelphia PA.

TERRY, WALTER, dance critic; b. Bklyn., May 14, 1913; s. Walter Matthews and Frances Lindsay (Gray) T. A.B., U. N.C., 1935; A.F.D. (hon.), Ricker Coll., 1968. Dance critic Boston Herald, 1936-39; dance critic, editor N.Y. Herald Tribune, 1939-42, 45-66; editor World Jour. Tribune, 1966-67, Saturday Rev., 1967-72; with World Magazine, 1972-73, Saturday Rev./World mag., 1973-75, Saturday Rev., 1975-82; tchr. dance Adelphi Coll., 1942, Yale, 1975, So. Conn. State Coll., 1974-75. Lectr., condr. radio program on subject of dance, 1940; dancer: mus. comedy Rose Marie, Royal Opera House, Cairo, 1943; selected: dances and dancers for Ford TV Workshop's Excursion, 1953, Frontiers of Faith, 1955, Eye on New York, 1958; several appearances and selection of dances and dancers for, Camera 3, CBS-TV, 1953, 54; Author: Invitation to Dance, 1942, Star Performance, 1954, (with Paul Himmel) Ballet in Action, 1954, The Dance in America, 1956, rev., 1971, Ballet: A New Guide to the Liveliet Art, 1959, On Pointe, 1962, Isadora Duncan, 1964, The Ballet Companion, 1968, Miss Ruth: The More Living Life of Ruth St. Denis, 1969, Ballet: A Pictorial History, 1970, Careers for the '70's: Dance, 1971, Ballet Guide, 1976, Ted Shawn: Father of American Dance, 1976, I Was There, 1978, Great Male Dancers of the Ballet, 1978, The King's Ballet Master: A Biography of Denmark's August Bournonville, 1979, Alicia and the Ballet Nacional de Cuba, 1981; Contbr.: (with Paul Himmel) chpt. to Dance: A Basic Educational Technique, 1941; also articles dance publs.; Dance editor: (with Paul Himmel) Ency. Brit. Served with USAAF, 1942-45. Decorated knight Order of Dannebrog, Denmark; Egyptian-Am. U. fellowship. Mem. Newspaper Guild N.Y. Home: New Canaan, Conn. Died Oct. 5, 1982.

TEUFEL, WALTER CASPER, U.S. Pub. Health Service; b. Hazelton, Pa., Sept. 6, 1890; s. Severin and Lavina (Wasserman) T.; M.D., University of Pennsylvania, 1913; married Dorothy Belcher, September 2, 1930 (now deceased); children—Walter Casper, Severin; married 2d, Mrs. Mildred B. Grüner, Oct. 2, 1945; stepchildren—Lois M., (Helen) Jean, Arlene E. Commd. assistant surgeon U.S.P.H.S., 1915, passed asst. surgeon, 1919, surgeon, 1923, sr. surgeon, 1935, med. dir., 1941; served in various marine hosps.; became chief surgeon U.S. Marine Hosp., Seattle, Wash., 1933; later med. officer in charge U.S. Marine Hosp., Buffalo, N.Y., med. officer in charge U.S. Marine Hosp., Boston, Mass.; now med. officer in charge U.S. Public Health Service, Phila. Fellow Am. Coll. of Surgeons; mem. Founders Group, Am. Bd. of Surgery. Lutheran. Mason. Home: Philadelphia, Pa. †

THAYER, ROBERT HELYER, diplomat; b. Southboro, Mass., Sept. 22, 1901; s. William Greenough and Violet (Otis) T.; m. Virginia Pratt, Dec. 30, 1926; children: Robert Helyer, Sally Sears, Stephen Badger. Student, Amherst Coll., 1918-19; A.B., Harvard U., 1922, LL.B., 1926. Bar: N.Y. 1926. With Cadwalader, Wickersham & Taft, 1926-29, 47-49, asso. counsel pub. service law investigation, N.Y. State, 1929, asso. counsel fed. bankruptcy laws investigation, So. Dist. N.Y., 1929; with Donovan, Leisure, Newton & Lumbard, 1929-32, mem. firm., 1932-37, asst. dist. atty., N.Y. County, 1937-41, chief indictment br., 1938-41; asst. N.Y. State commr. housing, 1946; commr. against discrimination, N.Y. State, 1949-51; asst. U.S. ambassador to France, 1951-54; officer charge Western European affairs Ops. Coordination Bd., 1954-55; U.S. minister to, Rumania, 1955-58; asst. sec. Dept. State, 1958-61; asso. dir. gen. Am. Field Service Internat. Scholarships, 1961-65, dir. govt. relations, 1965-71; cons. to sec. of state, 1961-84; asst. to John Foster Dulles, UN Charter Conf., San Francisco, 1945. Candidate for Congress from Bklyn., 1946; bd. dirs. N.Y. Philharm. Soc., 1935-55; bd. mgrs. N.Y.C. Mission Soc., 1939-55; bd. dirs. Fgn. student Service Council, 1964-78, Washington Performing Arts Soc., 1967-72, Kennedy Center Prodns. Inc., Alliance Française, AFS Internat. Scholarships, 1967-78; trustee St. Mark's Sch., 1940-78, Nat. Trust Hist. Preservation, 1966-77, AFS Internat./Intercultural Programs; adv. council Sch. Advanced Internat. Studies Johns Hopkins; exec. com. Internat. Council on Monuments and Sites. Served from lt. comdr. to comdr. USNR, 1941-45. Decorated French Legion of Honor. Mem. N.Y. Bar Assn., Audubon Soc., Fgn. Policy Assn., Washington Inst. Fgn. Affairs, Council on Fgn. Relations, English Speaking Union. Clubs: Somerset (Boston); Harvard (N.Y.C.); Porcellian (Cambridge, Mass.); Met. (Washington); Travellers (Paris). Home: Washington, D.C. Died Jan. 20, 1984.

THAYER, SCOFIELD, editor; b. Worcester, Mass., Dec. 12, 1889; s. Edward Davis and Florence (Scofield) T.; grad. Milton (Mass.) Acad., 1908; A.B., A.M., Harvard, 1913; studied Magdalen Coll. (Oxford U.), Eng., 1913-15; unmarried. Asso. editor, The Dial, 1918, also contbr.; resigned Dec. 1918; returned to The Dial, Nov. 1919, as editor, also dir. Dial Pub. Co. and v.p. The Dial Press, pub. books, continuing until discontinuance of magazine, 1929. Clubs: Harvard, University, Coffee House (New York); Worcester (Worcester, Mass.). Editor: Living Art (folio of reproductions after paintings, drawings and engravings, and photographs of sculpture, by contemporary artists of America and Europe), 1924. Address: New York, N.Y. †

THEBAUD, LEO HEWLETT, naval officer; b. Madison, N.J., Feb. 15, 1890; s. Edward Vincent and Elizabeth Hewlett (Scudder) T.; student Berkeley Sch., N.Y., Hodder Sch., Stonyhurst Coll., England, Chestnut Hill (Pa.) Acad.; grad. U.S. Naval Acad., 1913; m. Eleanor Laurie McCawley, May 14, 1921; 1 dau., Diana Maris Elizabeth Laurie. Midshipman, 1909, commd. ensign, 1913, and advanced through the grades to rear adm., 1943; with occupation Vera Cruz, 1914, commanded U.S.S. Paul Jones, destroyer, World War I; American naval attaché, Paris, France; Naval Inspector General, Washington, D.C.; now commandant First Naval District, Boston, Mass. Awarded the Navy Cross; Commander of the Legion of Honor of France. Legion of Merit, Gold Star in lieu of 2nd Legion of Merit, Oak-Leaf Cluster in lieu of 3rd Legion of Merit, Gold Star in lieu of 4th Legion of Merit, British Commander of the Order of the British Empire. Clubs: Union, University (N.Y. City). Author: Naval Leadership, 1924.†

THEODOROVICH, JOHN VOLODYMYR, clergyman; b. Ukraine, Oct. 6, 1887; s. Volodymyr A. and Agapie (Chervinska) T.; student schs., Zhitomyr, Volynia, Theol. Sem., 1915; m. Julia Kornievich, May 24, 1914 (dec. Aug. 15, 1915); 1 dau., Valentina (Mrs. E.M. Prosen). Came to U.S., 1924, naturalized, 1929. Ordained priest, 1915; served with Army Red Cross, Russia, 1915-17; chaplain Ukrainian Army, 1918-19; ordained bishop, Diocese of Podolia, City of Vinnitza, 1921-23; archbishop Ukrainian Orthodox Ch. in U.S., from 1924, archbishop Ukrainian Greek Orthodox Ch. in Can., 1924-47; metropolitan of the Church, 1950, in jurisdiction affiliated churches, Brazil and Argentina. Address: Bala Cynwyd, Pa. †

THEORELL, AXEL HUGE TEODER, biochemist; b. Linköping, Sweden, July 6, 1903; s. Ture and Armida (Bill) T.; M.D., Caroline Inst., Stockholm, 1930; Dr. (hon.), U. Paris (Sorbonne), U. Brazil, U. Pa., U. Brüssel, U. Ky., U. Mich., Dr. (honorary), University of Louvain, Belgium; m. Margit Alenius, 1931; 3 sons. Lectr. physiol. chemistry Caroline Inst., Stockholm, 1930-32; asst. prof. med. chemistry U. Uppsala, 1932-36; with Prof. Otto Warburg, Kaiser Wilhelm Institut fÜr Zellphysiologie, Berlin-Dahlem, 1933-35; prof., dir. dept. biochemistry Nobel Med. Inst., 1937-70. Chairman Stockholm Symphony Soc.; chmn. board directors Wenner-Gren Society, Wenner-Gren Center Foundation, Stockholm. Recipient of Nobel prize in psysiology and medicine, 1955. Decorated comdr. Order No. Star; comdr. Royal Order St. Olaf (Norway); officer Cruzeiro do Sul (Brazil); comdr. Finland's Lion; comdr. Legion of Honor (France). Mem. Swedish Academy Sciences (president 1967-68), Swedish Academy Engineering Sciences, Royal Danish Academy Science and Letters, Norwegian Academy of Science, American Academy Arts and Sciences, l'Accademia Nazionale del XL of Rome, Swedish Soc. of Physicians and Surgeons (pres. 1957-58; hon. mem.), Swedish Soc. Med. Research, Swedish Chemists' Assn., Sci. Council Swedish Bd. Health, Swedish Acad. Music, Nat. Acad. Scis., Am. Philos. Soc., Polska Akademia Nauk Warszawa, Royal Soc. London, Bavarian Acad. Scis. (hon.), German Acad. Natural Scis. (hon.), A.C.P. (hon.). Home: Stockholm, Sweden. Died Aug. 15, 1982.

THIEL, LEO FRANCIS, college pres.; b. Alexandria, S.D., Nov. 16, 1888; s. Fred and Anna K. (Anderson) T.; A.B., Union Coll., College View, Neb., 1911; studied U. of Neb., 1912-15; U. of Chicago, summer, 1913; Whitman Coll., 1921-22; m. Myrtle Andrews, June 10, 1913; children—Dorothy Elaine, John Frederick, Francis Andrews. Pres. Union Coll. from June 1925, Seventh Day Adventist. Home: College View, Neb. †

THIELE, ALBERT E., foundation exec.; b. Bklyn., Oct. 1, 1892; s. Albert E. and Matilda (Foster) T.; m. Alice Irene Kelly, Sept. 26, 1918; 1 son, Roger Harvey. B.C.S., N.Y. U. With Guggenheim Bros., from 1909; partner; pres., dir. Elgerbar Corp. Bd. dirs. Corlette Glorney Found., Inc.; trustee Estate Solomon R. Guggenheim; life trustee N.Y. U.; trustee, chmn. exec. and finance coms. Solomon R. Guggenheim Found. Clubs: Maidstone (N.Y.C.), Blind Brook (N.Y.C.), N.Y. U. Finance (N.Y.C.); City Mid-day, Scarsdale Golf, Devon Yacht; Everglades (Palm Beach). Home: Scarsdale, NY.

THIMMESCH, NICHOLAS PALEN, columnist; b. Dubuque, Iowa, Nov. 13, 1927; s. Leo Nicholas and Victoria Maria (Glatzmaier) T.; B.A., Iowa State U., 1950, postgrad., 1955; m. Wynora Susan Plum, Apr. 17, 1953 (div. 1975); children—Nicholas Palen, Elizabeth, Martha, Peter, Michael. Reporter, Davenport (Iowa) Times, 1950-52, Des Moines Register, 1953-55; corr. Time Mag., 1955-67; Washington Bur. chief Newsday, 1967-69; syndicated columnist, Washington, 1969-85; contbg. editor New York mag., 1976-78; commentator Cable News Network, 1981. Mem. Nat. Commn. for Observance of World Population Year, 1974-75; nat. adv. council St. John's U., Minn. Served with U.S. Mcht. Marines, 1945-47. Fellow, Inst. of Politics, John F. Kennedy Sch. Govt., Harvard U., 1980-81. Mem. H.L. Mencken Soc. Roman Catholic. Author: (with William Johnson) Robert Kennedy at 40, 1965; The Bobby Kennedy Nobody Knows, 1966; Condition of Republicanism, 1968. Home: Chevy Chase, Md. Died July 11, 1985.

THOMAS, ADEEB ELIAS, dentist, educator; b. Lawrence, Mass., Sept. 16, 1923; s. Elias Ayoub and Edna

(Abraham) T.; grad. Boston Latin Sch., 1940; D.M.D., Tufts Coll., 1945; M.S., U. Ala., 1964; m. Frances Anne Pharo, Dec. 29, 1952; 1 son, Adeeb Elias Jr. Externship oral surgery Capt. John Andrews Hosp., Boston, 1943-45; pvt. practice dentistry, Scituate, Mass., 1947-52; instr. clin. dentistry Tufts Coll. Dental Sch., 1947-52; prof. dentistry, chmn. dept. operative dentistry and endodontics U. Ala. Sch. Dentistry, 1952-68; cons. endodontics VA Hosp., Tuskegee and Birmingham, Ala., Am. Dental Assn. Jour. Chmn., Teenagers March, Birmingham, 1970—1970; bd. St. Jude Children's Research Hosp., also mem. exec. mgmt. bd. Served with USNR, 1945-47. Diplomate Am. Bd. Endodontics; Fellow Am. Assn. Endodontists; mem. Am., Ala. dental assns., Am. Assn. Endodontists, Internat. Assn. for Dental Research, Sigma Xi, Omicron Kappa Upsilon. Roman Catholic. Contbr. articles to dental jours., also chpts. to dental textbooks. Research on efficacy of therapeutic dentifrices in preventing dental decay in children, cavity preparation design. Home: Birmingham, Ala. Died Dec. 8, 1982.

THOMAS, BERT LESTER, supermarket chain exec.; b. Malad, Idaho, Feb. 27, 1918; s. Henry E. and Pearl (Ward) T.; m. Barbara Palmer, Apr. 30, 1941; children—Bert L., Val, Scott. B.S. in Bus. Adminstrn, Utah State U., 1939, D. Bus. (hon.), 1977. Auditor Standard Stas., Los Angeles, 1939-41; with Winn-Dixie Stores, Inc., Jacksonville, Fla., 1946-82, v.p., 1952-65, pres., 1965-82, chmn. exec. com., 1976-82, also dir.; dir. Barnett Banks of Fla. Trustee Jacksonville U. Served to maj. Q.M.C. U.S. Army, 1941-46. Mem. Food Mktg. Inst. (vice chmn. pub. and legis. affairs). Mormon. Clubs: River (Jacksonville), San Jose Country (Jacksonville); Masons, Shriners, Jesters. Died Sept. 29, 1982.

THOMAS, CHARLES ALLEN, retired chemical company executive; b. Scott County, Ky., Feb. 15, 1900; s. Charles Allen and Frances (Carrick) T.; m. Margaret Stoddard Talbott, Sept. 25, 1926 (dec. Oct. 1975); children—Charles, Margaret (Mrs. James H. Davis), Frances (Mrs. T.R. Martin), Katharine (Mrs. Stephen E. O'Neil); m. Margaret Chandler Porter, Mar. 6, 1980; children—Charles, Margaret (Mrs. James A. Walsh), Frances (Mrs. T.R. Martin), Katharine (Mrs. Stephen E. O'Neil). A.B., Transylvania Coll., 1920, D.Sc., 1933; M.S., Mass. Inst. Tech., 1924; LL.D., Hobart Coll., 1950; D.Sc., Washington U., St. Louis, 1947, Kenyon Coll., 1952, Princeton, 1953, Ohio Wesleyan U., 1953, Brown U., 1956, Bklyn. Poly. Inst., 1957, U. Ala., 1958, St. Louis U., 1965, Simpson Coll., 1967; Engring., U. Mo., 1965; LL.D., Lehigh U., 1960, Westminster Coll., 1968. Research chemist Gen. Motors Research Corp., 1923-24, Ethyl Gasoline Corp., 1924-25; pres. Thomas & Hochwalt Labs., 1926-36; v.p., tech. dir., mem. exec. com. Monsanto Co., 1945, exec. v.p., 1947-51, pres., 1951-60, chmn. bd., 1960-65; dir. St. Louis Union Trust Co.; Dep. chief NDRC, 1942-43, sect. mem., 1943—; mem. Manhattan project, in charge Clinton Labs., Oak Ridge; mem. sci. panel U.S. Rep. to UN AEC; apptd. chmn. sci. manpower adv. com. NSRB, 1950; mem. sci. adv. com. ODM, 1951; cons. Nat. Security Council, 1953. Formerly chmn. bd. trustees Washington U.; mem. corp. Mass. Inst. Tech.; curator Transylvania U.; mem. adv. bd. St. Louis council Boy Scouts Am. Recipient Medal for Merit by Pres. Truman, 1946, Gold medal Am. Inst. Chemists, 1948, Mo. Honor award for Distinguished Service in Engring., 1952, Perkin medal Am. sect. Soc. Chem. Industry, 1953, Order of Leopold, 1962, Palladium medal Am. sect. Soc. de Chimic Industrielle, 1963; named Globe Democrat Man of Year award, 1966. Fellow A.A.A.S., Am. Acad. Arts and Scis.; mem. Nat. Acad. Engring., Am. Chem. Soc. (dir., mem. bd. editors 1937-38, pres. 1948, chmn. bd. dirs. 1950-53, recipient Priestley Medal 1955), Nat. Acad. Sci., Am. Philos. Soc., Am. Inst. Chem. Engrs., Am. Inst. Chemists, Chem. Soc. London, Soc. Chem. Industries, Phi Beta Kappa, Sigma Xi, Alpha Chi Sigma. Clubs: Chemists (N.Y.C., D.C.), Links (N.Y.C., D.C.); Cosmos (Washington); Log Cabin (St. Louis), St. Louis Country (St. Louis). Patentee in field.

THOMAS, CHARLES S., ex-sec. of navy; b. Independence, Mo., Sept. 28, 1897; s. Charles Rogers and Della (Rouse) T.; student U. Cal., 1915-16, Cornell, 1916-18; LL.D., Lehigh U.; LL.D., Villanova U.; LL.D., Bryant Coll.; LL.D. (honorary), Kansas City University; married Julia B. Hayward, Apr. 15, 1920; children—Hayward, Julia Louise, Charles Rogers, Comstock Archer. V.p. George H. Burr, Conrad & Broom, Inc., 1925-32; v.p. Foreman & Clark, Inc., Los Angeles, 1932-37, pres., dir., 1937-53; under sec. of Navy, Jan.-Aug. 1953; asst. sec. of def., for supply and logistics, 1953-54; secretary of navy, 1954-57; pres. Trans World Airlines, 1958-60, dir.; president The Irvine Co., Tostin, Cal., 1960-66; dir. Pacific Finance Corp. (Los Angeles); director Broadway-Hale Dept. Stores, Hilton Hotels Internat., Inc. Airport commr. (Los Angeles), 1945-50. Republican finance chmn., 1957-58. Mem. All Year Club. Spl. asst. to sec. of Navy, 1942-45. Awarded Presdl. Medal for Merit and Distinguished Civilian Service award for wartime service, Dept. Defense Distinguished Civilian Service award; Dept. Navy Distinguished Pub. Service award; Dept. Army Decoration Exceptional Civilian Service; Grand Cross Merit Naval (Brazil), (Spain); Order Merit Naval (Argentina). Member Psi Upsilon. Republican. Episcopalian. Clubs: Country, California (Los Angeles); Chevy Chase (Md.); Pinnacle, Links (N.Y.C.). Home: Newport Beach, Calif. Died Oct. 17, 1983.

THOMAS, CHRISTOPHER YANCEY, business exec.; b. Roanoke, Va., Jan. 5, 1900; s. Frank Watkins and Elizabeth (Carson) T.; m. Dorothea Louise Engel, June 12, 1922 (dec. Apr. 1977); children—Christopher Yancey, Dorothea Louise (Mrs. Joe B. Dickey, Jr.), Cora Elizabeth (Mrs. Paul R. Dring); m. Georgia Wilhelm Hall, Aug. 18, 1978. B.S., Purdue U., 1921, M.E., 1926; LL.B. (hon.), Baker U., 1966. Apprentice instr. A.T. & S.F. Ry., 1921-24; supr. apprentices K.C.S. Ry., 1925-29; mech. engr. Pittsburg & Midway Coal Mining Co., Kans., 1930-41, chmn. bd., 1964-65; gen. mgr. Mil. Chem. Works, Pittsburg, Kans., 1941-46; gen. mgr. Spencer Chem. Co., Kansas City, Mo., 1946-63, chmn., 1960-63, Thomas Mfg. Corp., Parkton, Md. Mayor, City of Mission Hills, 1959-63; mem. Kans. Senate from, Johnson County, 1969-73; Del. Republican Nat. Conv., 1964; presdl. elector, 1972; Trustee So. Meth. U., 1956-68; chmn. bd. trustees Baker U., Baldwin, Kans., 1956-64, 66-81; v.p. K.A. & H.F. Spencer Found., Kansas City, Mo. Mem. Kans. C. of C. (pres. 1965-66), Nat. Soc. Profl. Engrs., Am. Inst. Mining and Metall. Engrs., ASME, Kans. Engring. Soc., Sigma Delta Chi, Tau Beta Pi, Beta Theta Pi. Methodist. Clubs: Mason (Kansas City, Mo.) (Shriner), Univ. (Kansas City, Mo.), River (Kansas City, Mo.), Mission Hills Country (Kansas City, Mo.), Rotary (Kansas City, Mo.) (pres. 1963-64). Home: Shawnee Mission, Kans.

THOMAS, FAY M., hotel cons.; b. Creston, Iowa, July 9, 1890; s. Lincoln and Fannie Elizabeth (Brenanstal) T.; m. Willa Mae Adams, July 19, 1919; children—Clinton L., Jean-Faye, Mgr. Richmond (Va.) Cafeterias, Inc., 1920-22; gen. mgr. United Hotels Corp. Cafeterias, Toronto, Montreal, Can., 1922-25; mgr. Cavalier Hotel, Virginia Beach, Va., 1925-27; gen. mgr. Hotel Roanoke (Va.), 1927-29. Hotel Patrick Henry, 1929-32, Exchange Buffet Corp., N.Y. City, 1932-35; v.p. and gen. mgr. Hotel Carter, Cleveland, 1935-39; asst. to pres. Hotel New Yorker, N.Y.C., 1939-41; v.p., gen. mgr. Hotel Roosevelt; New Orleans, 1941-42, Hotel Book—Cadillac, Detroit, 1942-52; dir. Sheraton-Cadillac Hotel, Detroit, Key Biscayne Hotel and Villas, Miami, Jacksonville Coach Co., Jacksonville, Fla. Served with U.S. Army, World War I. Mem. Am. Legion, Mil. Order World Wars., Det. Hotel Assn., Det. Bd. Com. Mason. Clubs: Detroit Athletic, Detroit Players; The Old; Grosse Pointe Yacht; Wings (N.Y. City); Army and Navy (Washington). Home: Fort Lauderdale, Fla. Deceased.

THOMAS, GEORGE COMYNS, JR., past chmn. board Thomas & Betts Co.; b. Elizabeth, N.J., March 29, 1890; s. George Comyns and Miriam (Clark) T.; B.S. with honors, Princeton, 1911; m. Julia Stamm, Oct. 11, 1919; children—George Comyns, III, Julia Terrill, Alexandra Stamm (Mrs. Gordon Powers), Edward Drummond; m. 2d, Elizabeth Morgan Ellis, Aug. 15, 1966. Electrician's helper, later electrical engineer in the research br. engineering department of Western Electric, 1911-13; began as machine hand Standard Electric Fittings Co., Stamford, Conn., 1913, later firm combined forming Thomas & Betts Co., 1917, gen. mgr., 1928-30, v.p., 1930-40, became pres. and treas., 1940, chmn., 1955-65, mem. bd. dirs. and consultant. Served as capt. 315th Field Artillery, 80th div. U.S. Army, 1917-19; with A.E.F. 1 yr. Awarded James H. McGraw prize for constructive leadership by elec. industry 1938. Mem. bd. Vail Deane Sch. for Girls; mem. bd. Elizabeth Gen. Hospital. President National Electrical Manufacturers Assn., 1941-42; past member Nat. Indsl. Conference Bd., Com. for Econ. Development. Member of the board of trustees Point Pleasant Hospital. Member C. of C., New Jersey Soc. Colonial Wars. Episcopalian. Clubs: Gulf Stream Golf, Manasquan Golf, Bay Head Yacht; Ivy (Princeton); Electrical Manufacturers. Home: Bay Head, N.J. †

THOMAS, LOWELL, author, cinerama and TV producer, radio and TV commentator; b. Woodington, Ohio, Apr. 6, 1892; s. Harry George and Harriet (Wagner) T.; B.S., U. No. Ind., 1911; B.A., M.A., U. Denver, 1912; M.A., Princeton, 1916; Litt.D., Grove City Coll., 1933, St. Bonaventure, 1938, Franklin and Marshall Coll., 1942, Rider Coll., 1948, Ohio Wesleyan, 1949; LL.D., Albright Coll., 1934, Lafayette Coll., 1937, Washington and Jefferson Coll., 1942, Olivet Coll., 1950; L.H.D., Clark U., 1941, Boston U., 1943, Union Coll., 1944, U. Tampa, 1949; H.H.D., Temple U., 1942; D.L., Olivet Coll., 1950; m. Frances Ryan, Aug. 4, 1917 (dec. 1975); 1 son, Lowell; m. Marianna Mann, 1977. Reporter, editor various newspapers, Cripple Creek, reporter Chgo. Jour. until 1914; prof. oratory Chgo. Kent Coll. Law, 1912-14; instr. dept. English, Princeton, 1914-16; lectr. on Alaska, 1914-16; chief civilian mission sent to Europe by Pres. Wilson to prepare hist. record of World War I; news commentator, radio 1930-76, movie news reels, 1935, television 1940-81, producer-host High Adventure TV series, 1957-59; asso. editor Asia Mag., 1919-23. Recipient Chauncey M. Depew medal SAR, 1964; Nat. Assn. Broadcasters Distinguished Service award, 1968; named Personality of Year, Internat. Radio and TV Soc.; George Washington award Freedoms Found., 1978. Fellow Am. Geog. Soc., Royal Geog. Soc.; mem. Assn. Radio News Analysts, English Speaking Union (hon. life), Explorers Club, Kappa Sigma, Tau Kappa Alpha, Phi Delta Phi, Sigma Delta Chi, Alpha Epsilon. Mason. Clubs: Princeton, Dutch Treat, Overseas Press (N.Y.C.); St. Andrew's Golf, Bohemian (San Francisco). Author books latest being; These Men Shall Never Die, 1943; The Seven Wonders of the World, 1956; History As You Heard It, 1957; The Vital Spark; A Hundred and One Outstanding Lives, 1959; The Silent War in Tibet, 1959; Sir Hubert Wilkins, His World of Adventure, 1961; More Great True Adventures, 1963; Book of the High Mountains, 1964; Raiders of the Deep, 1964; Story of the St. Lawrence Seaway; With Lawrence in Arabia, 1971; (with Lowell Thomas, Jr.) Famous First Flights That Changed, 1969; (with Edward Jablonski) Doolittle: a Biography, 1976; (autobiography) Good Evening, Everybody: From Cripple Creek to Samarkand, 1976; (with Joy L. Sanderson) First Aid for Backpackers and Campers; So Long until Tomorrow, 1977; contbr. to periodicals. Home: Pawling, N.Y. Died Aug. 29, 1981.*

THOMAS, ORLANDO PENDLETON, oil exec.; b. Forney, Tex., June 14, 1914; s. William Pendleton and Lottye (Trail) T.; B.S., East Tex. State Coll., 1935; M.B.A., U. Tex., 1941; m. Alice Alexander, Sept. 30, 1939; children—William Pendleton II, Alexander Cole, James Trail. With Sinclair Oil Corp., N.Y.C., 1945-69, beginning as sr. accountant, successively asst. to asst. comptroller, asst. comptroller, v.p., 1945-69, beginning as sr. accountant, successively asst. to asst. comptroller, asst. comptroller, v.p., 1945-60, exec. v.p., 1960-64, pres., 1964-69; chmn. exec. com., dir. Atlantic Richfield Co., N.Y.C., 1969; vice chmn. bd., chief exec. officer B.F. Goodrich Co., Akron, Ohio, from 1971; trustee Mut. Life Ins. Co., N.Y.; dir. Kraftco Corp., Koppers Co., Inc., Bristol-Myers Co. Dir. Boys' Clubs Am. Served as lt. USNR, 1942- 45. Mem. Am. Petroleum Inst. (dir.). Clubs: University, Economic, Links (N.Y.C.); Blind Brook; Augusta (Ga.) Nat. Golf; Houston Country. Died Feb. 8, 1985.

THOMAS, RUSSELL BROWN, educator; b. Larned, Kan., Feb. 4, 1900; s. James N. and Jessie (Brown) T.; A.B., Eureka Coll., 1921; A.M., U. Chgo., 1927; Ph.D., 1942; m. Catherine Bassor, June 15, 1923. Tchr. high schs., Gibson City, Ill., 1921-22, Springfield, Ill., 1922-25, U. Chgo. Lab. Sch., 1925-35; instr. humanities The Coll., U. Chgo., 1936-42, asst. prof., 1942-45, asso. prof., 1945-51, prof., 1951-65, chmn. humanities staff, 1944-51, cons. Fund for Adult Edn., 1954-55. Trustee Eureka Coll., from 1953. Recipient Quantrell Award for excellence in undergrad. teaching, 1942. Mem. Modern Lang. Assn., Pi Kappa Delta, Delta Sigma Rho. Author: A New Approach to Poetry, 1930; Plays and the Theatre, 1937. Editor: Introduction to the Humanities, 1955. Mem. editorial bd. of Jour. Gen. Edn., from 1950. Contbr. profl. jours. Home: Chicago, Ill. Died Jan. 15, 1982.

THOMAS, WALTER IVAN, government official, educator, agronomist; b. Elwood, Nebr., Mar. 27, 1919; s. Percy E. and Ethel (Major) T.; m. Margaret Ann Thompson, Feb. 15, 1941; 1 dau., Linda Margaret. B.S., Iowa State U., 1949, M.S., 1953, Ph.D., 1955. Clk. Soil Conservation Service, Civilian Conservation Corps, Broken Bow, Nebr., 1937-39, U.S. Civil Service, Washington, 1940-41; grad. asst. Iowa State U., Ames, 1949-50, instr., then asst. prof., 1953-59; mem. faculty Pa. State U., University Park, 1959-79, prof. agronomy, 1963-79, head dept., 1964-69, chmn. div. plant scis., 1967-69; asso. dean for research Pa. State U. (Coll. Agr.), 1969-79; asso. dir. Pa. State U. (Agrl. Exptl. Sta.), 1969-79; adminstr. coop. State Research Service, U.S. Dept. Agr., 1979; Pres. Pinchot Consortium for Environ. Forestry Studies, 1976-78. Served with the USMCR, 1942-45, 50-52; col. Res. (ret.) 1966. Decorated Bronze Star with combat V, Navy Commendation medal. Fellow AAAS, Am. Soc. Agronomy, Soil Sci. Soc. Am.; mem. Am. Soc. Agronomy, Washington Acad. Scis., Sigma Xi, Alpha Zeta, Gamma Sigma Delta, Alpha Gamma Rho, Phi Mu Alpha. Presbyn. (elder). Home: State College, Pa. Died Oct. 13, 1979.

THOMAS, WILLIAM, JR., manufacturing company executive; b. Edgar, Nebr., Jan. 19, 1923; s. William L. and Marie I. (Culver) T.; m. Marjorie E. Harman, June 14, 1947; children—Randy L., Ronald, Deborah, Bruce, Patricia. Student, U. Nebr., 1940-41. Various mgmt. positions Montgomery Ward Co., 1946-48, Greeley Gas Co., 1948-52, Norge Sales Corp., Chgo., 1952-56, Chambers Corp., 1956-60; pres., chief exec. officer Preway, Inc., Wisconsin Rapids, Wis., 1975-82; dir. Wood County Nat. Bank. Bd. dirs. Riverview Hosp., 1977-78. Served with U.S. Army, 1941-46. Mem. Gas Appliance Mfg. Assn., Fireplace Inst. (past pres.). Republican. Clubs: Bulls Eye Country, Up River Gun, Rotary, Masons. Home: Wisconsin Rapids, Wis. Died Oct. 23, 1982.

THOMASON, ALAN MIMS, media cons.; b. Lynchburg, Va., Dec. 1, 1910; s. John Earl and Rachel Ellen (Mims) T.; student U. Tenn., 1927-31; m. Elizabeth Jane Pfeffer, Dec. 29, 1936; children—Ann Elizabeth, Paul Alan, Mary Mims. Reporter Knoxville (Tenn.) Sentinel, 1927-33; reporter Knoxville Jour., 1927-33, city editor, 1934; N.C.-Va. mgr. United Press, 1935; mng. editor Suffolk (Va.) News-Herald, 1935; reporter Detroit Times, 1935-36; with United Press Assn. (name changed to U.P.I., Inc.) 1936-74, mgr. central div. Chgo., 1943-52, v.p., 1952, gen. bus. mgr., dir., 1955-62, 1st v.p., 1958-62, pres., gen. mgr., dir., 1962-72, chmn. bd., dir., 1972-74, later cons. Mem. Delta Tau Delta, Sigma Delta Chi. Clubs: Dutch Treat, (N.Y.C.): Milbrook (Greenwich, Conn.); Nat. Press (Washington). Home: Greenwich, Conn. Died July 26, 1985.

THOMPSON, CLARK WALLACE, former congressman; b. La Crosse, Wis., Aug. 6, 1896; s. Clark Wallace and Jessie Marilla (Hyde) T.; student U. Oreg., 1915-17; m. Libbie Moody, Nov. 16, 1918; children—Libbie (Mrs. James Stansell) (dec.), Clark Wallace. Treas. Am. Nat. Ins. Co., Galveston, Tex., 1919-20; pres. Clark W. Thompson Co., 1920-32; sec.-treas. Cedar Lawn Co., 1927-34; pub. relations counsel Am. Nat. Ins. Co., allied Moody interests, 1936-47; dir. Washington operations Tenneco, Inc. Mem. 73d, 80th to 89th U.S. Congresses, 9th Tex. Dist.; now public affairs cons. Served with USMC, 1917-18; lt. col. Res.; organized and commanded 15th Bn. Marine Corps Res., on active duty, 1940-46; served with 2d Marine Div., and various units in Southwest Pacific area; grad. Naval War Coll.; dir. Marine Corps Res., ret. as col., 1946. Mem. Galveston C. of C. (past pres.), Am. Legion, VFW, Phi Delta Theta. Democrat. Episcopalian. Mason (32 deg., KCCH), Eagle, Red Man. Clubs: Georgetown, 1925 F St., Army and Navy (Washington); Arty. (Galveston). Home: Galveston, Tex. Deceased.

THOMPSON, FREDERICK ROECK, physician; b. Galveston, Tex., July 20, 1907; s. James Edwin and Eleanor Waters (Roeck) T.; student Upper Can. Coll., 1917-25; B.A., U. Tex., 1927, M.D., 1931; D.Sc., Columbia, 1938; m. Carolyn Laura Bryan, Oct. 7, 1936; children—Guy Bryan, Carolyn Carter (Mrs. Gary E. Morrison), Eleanor Cave (Mrs. Christopher C. Wragge). Surg. intern Roosevelt Hosp., N.Y.C., 1932-33, cons. orthopedic surgery; resident fellow N.Y. Orthopaedic Dispensary and Hosp., 1934-39; practice medicine, specializing in orthopaedic surgery, N.Y.C., 1939-83; dir., chief orthopedic surgery St. Luke's Hosp. Center, N.Y.C., 1961-72; clin. prof. N.Y. Polyclinic Hosp., 1946-72, Columbia; 1971; cons. Columbia Meml. Hosp., Elizabeth A. Horton Meml. Hosp., Drs. Hosp., N.Y.C., numerous others. Impartial med. panelist Supreme Ct. City N.Y., from 1962. Recipient Ashbel Smith Distinguished Alumni award U. Tex., 1973. Diplomate Am. Bd. Orthopedic Surgery. Mem. Am. Acad. Orthopaedic Surgeons (v.p. 1966-68, chmn. subcom. orthopaedic abstracts 1968-70), Bone and Joint Assn. (pres. 1961), A.M.A. (pres. 1955, sec. 1948-54), Ga., New Eng. orthopaedic socs., Am. Assn. Surgery Trauma, A.C.S., Am. Orthopedic Foot Soc., Can., Am. orthopedic assns., Hosp. Grads. Soc. N.Y., Med. Soc. County N.Y., N.Y. Acad. Medicine, N.Y. Clin. Soc., Orthopedic Research Soc., Riverside Practitioners N.Y., Hip Soc. (founder), Russell Hibbs Soc., Soc. Internat. Chirurgie Orthopaedic et Traumatica, Roosevelt Hosp., U. Tex. Med. Br. alumni assns., West Side Clin. Soc., Nat. Rifle Assn., Trout Unltd., Ducks Unltd., Phi Delta Theta, Phi Alpha Sigma, Alpha Omega Alpha. Clubs: Anglers; Brodhead Fly Fishers; Camp Fire; Camp Fire Rifle, University, River, St. Hubert Soc., Maidstone (N.Y.C.); Mashomach Fish and Game Preserve (L.I.). Contbr. numerous articles to profl. jours. Developed practical artificial metal hip for replacement arthroplasty. Home: New York, N.Y. Died Apr. 12, 1983.

THOMPSON, HOPE KEACHIE, lawyer; b. London, Can., Mar. 20, 1887; d. George Russell and Mary Hope (Keachie) T.; came to U.S., 1896; grad. St. Joseph's Convent, Toronto, Ont., Can., 1904; LL.B., Washington (D.C.) Coll. Law, 1913; studied internat. law, Columbia, 1916-17. Clk., Anderson & Anderson, attys., N.Y. City, 1907-11; clk., counselor's office, U.S. Dept. State, 1911-13, Am. and Brit. Claims Arbitral Tribunal, Washington, Ottawa, Can., London and Paris, 1913-14; asst. to Ambassador Page, London, Aug.-Oct. 1914; clk., Dept. State, Feb.-Sept. 1915; jr. asst. to counsel for Guatemala and Nicaragua, boundary mediations, 1918-21; admitted to D.C. bar, 1919, and to practice before Supreme Court of United States, 1922; joint secretary American and British Claims Arbitration Tribunal, Washington, Nov.-Dec. 1921; sec. for U.S., U.S.-Norway Arbitration Tribunal, The Hague and London, July-Oct. 1922; asso. counsel for Costa Rica, Costa Rica-Great Britain Arbitration, 1923; atty. U.S. Agency, Mixed Claims Commn., U.S. and Mexico, Apr. 1925-Feb. 1927; counsel, same, Feb.-Sept. 1927; professional advisor on internat. law for Phi Delta Delta from 1930; chmn. com. Woman's Bar Assn. of D.C. to study documents concerning Permanent Court of Internat. Justice of League of Nations. Mem. American Bar Assn., Am. Soc. Internat. Law, Women's Bar Assn. D.C., Am. Assn. Univ. Women, Phi Delta Delta; hon. mem. Brant County Bar Assn. Republican. Presbyn. Club: Brantford Golf. Address: New York, N.Y.†

THOMPSON, JAMES SCOTT, educator; b. Saskatoon, Sask., Can., July 31, 1919; s. Walter Palmer and Marjorie (Gordon) T.; m. Margaret Anne Wilson, Aug. 19, 1944; children—Gordon Moore, David Bruce. B.A., U. Sask., Saskatoon, 1940, M.A., 1941; M.D., U. Toronto, Ont., Can., 1945. Lectr. anatomy U. Western Ont., London, 1948-50, asst. prof., 1950; asso. prof. anatomy U. Alta., Edmonton, Can., 1950-55, prof., 1955-63, also asst. dean faculty medicine, 1959-62; prof. anatomy U. Toronto, from 1963, chmn. dept. anatomy, 1966-76. Author: (with M.W. Thompson) Genetics in Medicine, 1966, 73, 80, Core Textbook of Anatomy, 1977. Served with Royal Canadian Army M.C., 1943-46. Mem. Am. Assn. Anatomists, Can. Assn. Anatomists (pres. 1975-77), genetics socs. Can., Am., Am. Soc. Human Genetics, Alpha Omega Alpha. Home: Willowdale ON, Canada.

THOMPSON, JOHN B., army officer; b. Fort Davis, Tex., June 14, 1890; s. James K. and Mary (Swan) T.; B.S., U.S. Military Acad., 1914; grad. of Cav. Sch., Command and Gen. Staff Sch. and Army War Coll.; m. Nina Cameron, Nov. 3, 1917; children—Cameron, Jacqueline Cameron. Commd. 2d lt., 1914, and advanced through the grades to brig. gen., Feb. 1942. Served during World War I in the cavalry and infantry; served with armored troops World War II; comd. Combat Command B. 7th Armored Div., from Feb. 1942. Home: Staunton, Va. Deceased.

THOMPSON, PAUL DEAN, foreign service officer; b. Waitsburg, Wash., Apr. 26, 1888; s. John Given and Lydia (Reid) T.; student Cooper Coll., Sterling, Kan., 1903-05; A.B., U. of Neb., 1909; M.A., U. of Mich., 1910; student law sch. U. of Southern Calif., Los Angeles, 1915-16; m. Patricia Keppel-Reede, Oct. 1, 1931. Law Clerk, Los Angeles, 1912-13; govt. stenographer, Manila, P.I., 1914-15; law clerk and stenographer, County of Los Angeles, 1915-17; apptd. Am. vice consul, Valencia, Spain, Aug. 1917, then at Tampico, Corunna, Barcelona, Spain; resigned 1921; with dist. atty., Los Angeles County, 1923-24; re-apptd. Am. vice consul, Cherbourg, France, Aug. 1925; then successively at Tananarive, Madagascar, Paris, Plymouth (England), Ponta Delgada, Azores, Milan, Italy; vice consul, Hull, 1935, London 1939-40, Dublin, Ireland, 1941-47, Algiers, 1947-49, Montreal since 1949. Mem. S.A.R., Phi Beta Kappa. Home: Los Angeles, Calif. †

THOMPSON, PAUL LAMONT, coll. pres.; b. Boone County, Ind., Sept. 26, 1889; s. Luzerne and Lillian (Murphey) T.; A.B., Emmanuel Missionary Coll., Berrien Springs, Mich.; grad. study U. of Colo., U. of Neb.; B.D., Colgate-Rochester Div. Sch., 1932; LL.D., Franklin (Ind.) Coll., 1935; m. Ruth Frances Peel, 1915; children—Lamont Luzerne, Edward Peel. Prin. Southwestern Junior College, Keene, Texas; president Union College, Lincoln, Nebraska; pres. Shurtleff College, Alton, Ill., 1933-38; pres. Kalamazoo Coll., 1938-49. Trustee Colgate-Rochester Divinity School. Mem. S.A.R. Baptist. Rotarian. Contbr. to mags. Lecturer. Home: Kalamazoo, Mich. †

THOMPSON, RANDALL, musician, composer; b. N.Y.C., Apr. 21, 1899; s. Daniel Varney and Grace Brightman (Randall) T.; m. Margaret Quayle Whitney, Feb. 26, 1927; children: Varney, Edward Samuel Whitney, Rosemary, Randall. A.B., Harvard U., 1920, M.A., 1922; postgrad. (Walter Damrosch fellow in music composition), Am. Acad. in Rome, 1922-25; Mus.D., U. Rochester, 1933, U. Pa., 1969; studied composition under, Ernest Bloch, N.Y.C., 1920-21. Asst. prof. music, organist, choir dir. Wellesley Coll., 1927-29, apptd. lectr. music, 1936; lectr. music Harvard, 1929; Guggenheim fellow, 1929-31; dir. coll. music study, investigation Assn. Am. Colls., 1932-35; prof. music, dir. chorus U. Calif., Berkeley, 1937-39; dir. Curtis Inst. Music, 1939-41; prof. music, head dept. U. Va., 1941-45; prof. music Princeton, 1945-48; prof. music Harvard, 1948-65, now Walter Bigelow Rosen prof. music emeritus, chmn. dept., 1952-57; Dir. U.S. sect. Internat. Soc. for Contemporary Music, 1934-35; mem. exec. bd. League Composers, 1939-41, dir., 1945-48. Wrote: music for The Straw Hat, 1926, Grand Street Follies, 1926; guest condr., Dessoff Choirs, N.Y.C., 1931-32; condr.: Madrigal Choir and Suprs. Chorus, Juilliard Sch. Music, 1931-32; Composer symphonies, choral works, string quartets, opera and other forms of mus. works; composition include The Last Words of David, commd. by Boston Symphony Orch. for Voice of America film, Tanglewood, 1949, A Trip to Nahant, Fantasy-Rondo for Orch, commd. by Koussevitzky Found., 1954, Mass of the Holy Spirit, 1955, Ode to the Virginian Voyage, 1956, Requiem, commd. by U. Calif., 1958, Frostiana, commd. by 200th Anniversary of Amherst, Mass., 1959, The Nativity according to Saint Luke, commd. by Christ Ch., Cambridge, Mass., 1961; cantata A Feast of Praise, commd. by Stanford U. music dept., 1963; oratorio The Passion According to St. Luke, commd. by Handel and Haydn Soc., 1965, String Quartet No. 2, commd. by Harvard Mus. Assn., 1967, The Place of the Blest, commd. by St. Thomas Ch., N.Y.C., 1969; Author: oratorio College Music, 1935; Contbr. articles to mus. revs. Decorated Cavaliere Ufficiale al Merito della Repubblica Italy; recipient Elizabeth Sprague Coolidge medal, 1941; Ditson award, 1944. Mem. Nat. Inst. Arts and Letters, Am. Acad. Arts and Scis., ASCAP, Phi Beta Kappa. Clubs: Century (N.Y.C.); Somerset (Boston), Tavern (Boston). Home: Cambridge, Mass. Died July 9, 1984. *

THOMPSON, ROLLIN W., school adminstrn.; b. Brookfield, N.Y., May 27, 1887; s. Rollin John and Sarah Jane (Walton) T.; A.B., Colgate U., 1908; A.M., Teachers Coll., Columbia U., 1924; m. Janet Bonnyman, June 30, 1915; 1 dau., Janet Elizabeth. Teacher, Brown Sch. of Tutoring, New York, N.Y., 1908-09; prin. East Bloomfield (N.Y.) High Sch., 1909-10; head dept. Latin and Greek, Perkiomen Sch., Pennsburg, Pa., 1910-13; prin., Ellenville (N.Y.) High Sch., 1913-18, Deposit (N.Y.) High Sch., 1918-20, Whitesboro (N.Y.) High Sch., 1920-24, Roscoe Conkling Sch., Utica, N.Y., 1924-36, Thomas R. Proctor High Sch., Utica, N.Y., from 1936. Chmn. local Selective Service Bd., 428. Mem. Utica branch Fgn. Policy Assn. (chmn.), N.Y. State Elementary Prins. Assn. (past pres.), N.Y. State Teachers Assn., Phi Kappa Psi. Clubs: Colgate Alumni (past pres.), Torch (past pres.) (Utica). Supt. Sunday Sch. Tabernacle Baptist Ch., Utica, N.Y., 1944-46. Home: Utica, N.Y. †

THOMPSON, THOMAS WILLIAM, zoo executive; b. Toronto, Ont., Can., Oct. 15, 1913; s. Robert George and Cecelia Emily (House) T.; B.S.A., U. Toronto Ont. Agrl. Coll., 1936; m. Lois Beryl Noble, Oct. 23, 1937; children—Barry Noble, Thomas Bryce, Randolph Kent. Horticulturist, landscape designer Toronto Gen. Burying Grounds, 1936-44; dir. parks and recreation City of Port Arthur (Ont.), 1945-50; adv. parks and recreation facilities, community programs br. Ont. Dept. Edn., 1950-55; met. parks commr. Municipality of Met. Toronto, 1955-78; interim dir. Met. Toronto Zoo, 1976-78, gen. dir., 1978-85; bd. dirs. Royal Agrl. Winter Fair, 1962-78; mem. Provincial Parks Adv. Council; bd. dirs. Civic Garden Centre, 1970-78. Mem. senate U. Guelph (Ont.), 1974-77; bd. dirs. Sports Hall of Fame, Toronto, Hockey Hall of Fame, Toronto. Served with RCAF, 1941-42. Decorated Queen's Silver medal; recipient Centennial medal Ont. Agrl. Soc., 1977; Gold medal Garden Club Toronto, 1978. Mem. Can. Parks and Recreation Assn. (pres. 1965-66, award of merit 1968), Gardeners and Florists Assn. (pres. 1940-41), Toronto Soc. Architects, Ont. Landscape Architects Assn., Bruce Tr. Assn. (hon. pres.), Am. Assn. Zool. Parks and Aquariums. Anglican. Contbr. numerous articles to profl. jours., poetry to lit. jours. Home: Toronto, Ont., Can. Died Mar. 1, 1985.

THOMPSON, WILLIAM BENBOW, obstetrician; b. Monrovia, Ind., Dec. 26, 1890; s. Dr. Thomas Lindley and Mary B. (Hubbard) T.; A.B., U. So. Cal., 1912; M.S., U. Cal., 1914, M.D., 1916; m. Ruth Locke, June 12, 1916; children—Nancy Jane (Mrs. Alfred Seale, Jr.). William Benbow, III, Charles Edwarde Locke. Intern U. Cal. Hosp., 1916-17; house officer N.Y. Lying-In Hosp., 1919; grad. fellow obstetrics Johns Hopkins Hosp., 1920; asst. resident gynecology Sloane Maternity Hosp., N.Y.C., 1920, Henry Ford Hosp., Detroit, 1921-24, asst. obstetrician, 1922-24; practicing obstetrician, Los Angeles, 1925-59; asso. clin. prof., U. So. Cal., 1944-53; clin. prof. obstetrics U. Cal. at Los Angeles, 1953-61, emeritus clinical professor obstetrics, from 1961; emeritus staff Hollowood Presbyterian, Cedars of Lebanon hosps.; med. dir. Am. Inst. Family Relations; med. dir. Florence Crittenton Assn., 1939-57; consultant to the Cal. State Dept. Pub. Health. Served as 1st lieutenant M.C., U.S. Army, 1918-19. Diplomate Am. Bd. Obstetrics and Gynecology. Mem. Am. Medical Assn., Cal. Med. Assn., Am. Assn. Obstetricians and Gynecologists, Pacific Coast (president 1949), Los Angeles (pres. 1931-32) obstet. and gynec. socs. Am. College of Obstetricians and Gynecologists (founder mem.). Nat. Fedn. Obstetric-Gynecologic Socs. (president 1948), Los Angeles Acad. Medicine, Los Angeles Symposium Society (president 1939-40), Phi Beta Kappa, Sigma Xi, Alpha Omega Alpha, Nu Sigma Nu, Chi Phi. Author articles in med. publs. Address: Hollywood, Calif. †

THOMSON, ALFRED RAY, foreign service officer; b. Linden, Md., Jan. 16, 1889; s. Lewis Beecher (M.D.) and Anna Merryman (Ray) T.; grad. Central High School, Washington, D.C., 1907; studied political science, George Washington U., 1908-10; m. Marion Mary Moffat, Aug. 5, 1925; children—David Ray, Malcolm Stuart. With U.S. Weather Bureau, 1907-11; appointed consular asst., 1911; dep. consul gen. and later vice and dep. consul gen., at Berlin, Germany, 1912-14; vice-consul, Saloniki, 1914-15; Belgrade, 1915; Saloniki, 1915-16; detailed to Dept. of State, 1916; apptd. consul, 1917; at Consulate-Gen. Moscow and Irkutsk, 1917-20; successively consul at Charlottetown (Canada), Zagreb (Jugoslavia), and Copenhagen, until 1923, Madras, India, 1923-25, Bradford, Eng., 1925-29, Manchester, Eng., 1929-35; consul gen. Dresden, Germany, 1935-40; apptd. sec. in the Diplomatic Service, 1937; consul gen. Hamburg, Germany, Feb.-Dec. 1941, Glasgow, Scotland, 1941-42; retired from foreign service June 1, 1942. Mem. Order of Washington, Phi Sigma, Kappa, Pi Gamma Mu. Presbyterian. Home: Washington, D.C. Deceased.

THOMSON, BRUCE RANDOLPH, clergyman, coll. adminstr.; b. Harlan, Iowa, Feb. 13, 1922; s. Howard Peter and Myrtle (Knudsen) T.; m. Margaret Ellen Beasley, June 1, 1948; children—Susan Kay, Bruce Randolph. A.B., William Jewell Coll., 1949; B.D., So. Bapt. Theol. Sem., 1952, Th.M., 1953, M.A., U. Louisville, 1955; Ph.D., Fla. State U., 1959. Ordained to ministry Baptist Ch., 1951; prin. San Jacinto Pub. Sch., Vernon, Ind.; instr. U. Louisville, 1954-55, Fla. State U., 1955-57; asso. prof. Queens Coll., Charlotte, N.C., 1957-59; prof., head dept. sociology William Jewell Coll., Liberty, Mo., 1959-64, coll. dean, prof. sociology, 1964-83, v.p. academic affairs, dean of coll., 1973-76, v.p. adminstrn., 1976-78, exec. v.p., 1978-83; vis. prof. sociology Tex. Tech. U. at Lubbock, 1962 (summer). Mem. Family Life Council, Charlotte, 1957-59; adv. bd. Clay County Welfare Assn., Mo., 1960-63. Served with USNR, 1943-46; capt. Res. Mem. Am. Sociol. Soc., Nat. Council Family Relations, Pi Gamma Mu. Home: Liberty, Mo. Died 28, 1983; buried Liberty, Mo.

THOMSON, GEORGE CAMPBELL, banker; b. Tustin, Mich., Apr. 9, 1888; s. Archibald J. and Annabelle (Campbell) T.; LL.B., U. Mich., 1913; m. Dorothy Diggins, Jan. 4, 1914; children—Dorothy A. (Mrs. J. Boyd Pantlind). Evelyn (Mrs. Earle Watterworth). Admitted to Mich. bar, 1913; practice in Mich., 1913-17;

engaged in investment banking, 1919-27; v.p. Mich. Trust Co., Grand Rapids, 1927-33, pres., 1933-56; Mich. Trust Co. merged with Old Kent Bank, 1956; chmn. bd. Old Kent Bank and Mich. Trust Co., 1956-58, Old Kent Bank and Trust Co., from 1958; v.p., dir. Cadillac-Soo Lumber Co., 1950-56, Tensas-Delta Corp., Electric Sorting Machine Co., pres., dir. Cadillac Malleable Iron Co., 1950-58. Mem. Grand Rapids Bd. Edn., 1934-45, Grand Rapids Parking Authority, 1951-58. Bd. in control athletics U. Mich., 1944-51. Served with U.S. Army, 1917-19. Mem. Alpha Delta Phi. Mason. Clubs: Kent Country, Peninsular, University (Grand Rapids). Home: Grand Rapids, Mich. Deceased.

THOMSON, HARRY FREEMAN, engr.; b. Cincinnati, Oct. 6, 1887; s. Sydney H. and Celia M. (Udell) T.; B.S., Washington U., 1910; grad. study Mass. Inst. Tech., 1910-12; m. Marie St. Clair Davis, Oct. 23, 1919. Instr., sec. elec. engring. research Mass. Inst. Tech., 1910-14; successively asst. supt., sales mgr., v.p. Provident Chem. Works, St. L, 1914-17, 19-24; exec. asst. Fed. Phosphorus Co., Birmingham, Ala., 1924-27; v.p., later pres. Gen. Material Co., St. L. 1927-48; cons. engr., St. L., from 1948; pres. Madison (Ill.) Concrete, Inc., from 1952. Water cons. Nat. Resources Planning Bd., 1936-40. Served as lt., U.S. Navy, 1917-19; lt. comdr., (ret.), C.E.C., U.S.N.R. Registered civil engr., Mo. Mem. Am. Soc. C.E. (dir. 1944-47), Am. Concrete Inst. (pres. 1951; Wasson medalist 1951), Nat. Ready Mixed Concrete Association (dir. 1939-53, pres. 1933-35), St. Louis C. of C. (dir. 1942-46), Sigma Xi, Sigma Chi, Tau Beta Pi. Presbyterian. Clubs: Engineers (director 1934-36). Mo. Athletic, Circle (St. L.). Author articles tech. publs.; corr. Pit and Quarry from 1934. Asst. editor-in-chief; Am. Elec. Engring. Handbook, 1914. Home: Clayton, Mo. †

THOMSON, LEONARD KEENE, hotel mgr.; b. Watertown, Wis., Aug. 6, 1889; s. Thomas Leonard and Mary Louise (Keene) T.; m. Kathryn M. Longmire, May 8, 1920; children—Carol Jacqueline, Thomas Longmire. Office boy to cost accountant Johns Manville Co., Milwaukee, 1904-14, asst. accountant, Chicago. 1914-15, traveling auditor, N.Y. City, 1915-18, chief accountant, St. Louis, Mo., 1918-20, spl. rep. Northwestern Mutual Life Ins. Co., St. Louis, 1921-22; spl. rep. on construction loans Miss. Valley Trust Co., 1923-25; sec.-treas. Langford Constrn. Co., Miami, Fla., 1925-27, sec. and dir. from 1927; mng. dir. McAllister Hotel, Miami, 1927-45; mgr. Everglades Hotel, 1945-50, dr., 1951; asst. dir. Miami Internat. Airport from 1951; sec. and dir. Dallas Park Hotel, Miami, from 1927; dir. Langford & Ledbetter Ins. Co. Mayor, City of Miami, 1943-45; pres. Dade Co. (Fla.) Community Chest 1939. Mem. exec. council Boy Scouts of Am. of Dade Co., 1936-37; pres. Am. Legion Conv. Corp., Miami, 1934. Dir. for Fla. Southeastern Development Bd., 1933-35. Mem. Greater Miami Hotel Assn. (pres. 1931). Hotel Greeters of Am., Fla. and Cuba Greeters Assn., Hotel Men's Mutual Benefit Assn., Fla. State Hotel Assn., Greater Miami Airport Assn., C. of C. (pres. Fla. since 1946), Am. Hotel Assn. (v.p. 1938). Club: Kiwanis. Home: Miami, Fla. Deceased.

THON, ROBERT WILLIAM, JR., banker; b. Richmond, Va., Dec. 23, 1908; s. Robert William and Amanda (Kosslow) T.; m. Evelyn Ellen Singleton, Apr. 1, 1936; children: Robert William III, Susan Cecelia, Richard McMichael. Ph.D., Johns Hopkins, 1933. Asst. to pres. Savs. Bank of Balt., 1933-45, v.p., dir., 1945-59, pres., dir., 1959-75, chmn. bd., 1975-83, chmn. exec. com., from 1983; Mem. Banking Bd. of Md., Bank Relations Bd. of Md. Commr., Balt. Urban Renewal and Housing Agy., 1962-64. Chmn. Balt. Community Chest-Red Cross United Appeal, 1958. Mem. C. of C. of Met. Balt., Nat. Assn. Mut. Savs. Banks (exec. com. 1956-57), Asso. Mut. Savs. Banks Md. (pres. 1956-57). Clubs: Johns Hopkins, Merchants. Home: Baltimore, MD.

THORNING, JOSEPH FRANCIS, educator, author, lecturer; b. Milw., Apr. 25, 1896; s. Cully M. and Julia Theresa (Hallissey) T.; student Marquette Acad., 1910-14; A.B., Holy Cross Coll., 1918; A.M., St. Louis U., 1922; Ph.D., Cath. U., 1931; S.T.D., Gregorian U., 1932; D.D. h.c., Cath. U. Chile, 1944; Oxford U., Eng., Sorbonne, Paris; J.U.D. (hon.), U. Santo Domingo, 1954. Prof., Loyola U., Chgo., 1922-25; ordained priest Roman Cath. Ch., 1928; prof. sociology, acting dean Grad. Sch. Georgetown U., 1933-35; Washington corr. Am. (mag.), 1935-36; asso. editor internat. relations Thought, 1935-36; chmn. dept. sociology and social history Mt. St. Mary's Coll., Emmitsburg, Md., 1937-85; prof. Latin Am. history Marymount Coll.; spl. corr. Nat. Cath. Welfare Conf. News Service Europe, from 1937; spl. lectr. Nat. War Coll., 1956-57; Washington corr. Sign (mag.); commentator NBC, League of Nations sessions, 1931-32, Eucharistic Congress, Budapest, Hungary, 1938. Dir. First Inter-Am. Seminar in Latin Am., U. San Marcos, Lima, Peru, 1941; dir. Inter-Am. Seminar, U. Havana, Cuba, 1942 (apptd. judge of univ. seminar prize scholarship contest sponsored by Com. on Cultural Relations with Am. Republics); dir. Inter-Am. seminars U. Havana, Nat. U. Mexico, 1943. Bd. dirs. Am. Peace Soc., mem. editorial staff World Affairs (mag.). Vice chmn. univ. extension com. Inter-Am. Inst.; mem. Cuban-Am. Council on U. Studies, 1943; vis. prof. social history U. Havana, 1944. Mem. ofcl. U.S. delegations for presdl. inaugurations Central, S.Am. 1951, 56; spl. adviser U.S. senatorial delegation 10th Pan Am. Conf., Caracas, Venezuela, 1954. Fellow Am. Geog. Soc., Hist. and Geog. Inst. Brazil (hon.). Mem. panel lectrs. Office Coordinator Inter-Am. Affairs; awarded gold medal Pan-Am. Frat., St. John's U., N.Y.C., 1942; mem. U.S. Cath. Hist. Soc., Cath. Assn. for Internat. Peace, Internat. Mark Twain Soc. (trustee, dir.), Pi Gamma Mu, Mediaevalists (hon. Chgo.), Charles Carroll Forum. Decorated grand cross Order of Isabella the Cath., with rank of comdr.; 1945, Supreme officer, 1948, Mil. Order of Christ (Portugal), 1959; recipient honors, decorations from several C. Am. countries, elected asso. editor Americas (jour. inter-Am. cultural history), 1946; asso. editor, World Affairs. On all ofcl. celebrations Pan Am. Day on Capital Hill invited by U.S. Congress to offer invocation, 1944-85; gave series spl. lectures U. Md., Rollins Coll. Am. U., 1947. K.C. Author several books since 1935; contbr. to Dictionary of Theology (compiled at Oberlin Coll. 1945). By spl. decree of Pres. Jose Maria Velasco Ibarra (Ecuador), awarded Order of Merit, 1945; Nat. Order So. Cross, Brazil, 1956; Legion of Honor and Merit, Haiti; Order of Carlos Manuel de Císpedes, Cuba; Cross of Boyacá ,Colombia; Grand Cross Order of Alfonso El Sabio, Spain; Order of Vasco Nuñez de Balboa, Panama; Order of Quetzal, Guatemala; Nicaragua's grand cross Order of Ruben Dario, Order of Sun (Peru); Order Francisco de Miranda, Venezuela, 1972; Josí Maria Delgado, El Salvador, 1973; Gold cross Order of Don Quijote, Georgetown U. Hispanic Studies Frat. Clubs: Congressional Country, Metropolitan (Washington); Maryland (Balt.). Contbr. on fgn. affairs to Cath. jours., N.Y. Times, Washington Post. Elected to Gallery Living Am. Authors. Home: Frederick, MD. Died Mar. 8, 1985.

THORNLEY, EDWARD WILLIAM, business exec.; b. Connellsville, Pa., Sept. 24, 1887; s. William and Martha E. (Hodskin) T.; ed. pub. schs. Pittsburgh; m. Florence B. Falk, June 5, 1915; 1 son, William. With Baltimore & Ohio R.R. Co., Pittsburgh, 1903-16, stores apprentice, 1907-14, div. storekeeper, 1914-16, dist. storekeeper, 1916-18, asst. gen. storekeeper, Baltimore, 1918-20, with U.S. R.R. Adminstrn., Allegheny Region, Phila., as regional supervisor of stores; 1920-27, asst. gen. purchasing agent Baltimore & Ohio R.R. Co., Baltimore 1927; asst. dir. of purchases, Guggenheim Interests, N.Y. City, 1928-34; chief purchasing agent Am. Smelting & Refining Co., Kennecott Copper Corp., Anglo-Chilean Nitrate Corp., Yukon Gold Co., Fed. Mining & Smelting Co., Guggenheim Bros., Braden Copper Co., Compagnie Aramayo de Mines en Bolivie from 1934; v.p. purchases Am. Smelting & Refining Co., chief purchasing agt. Guggenheim Bros., Fed. Mining & Smelting Co., Compagnie Armayo de Mines en Bolivie; pres., dir. Asarco Mercantile Co., El Paso, Texas; dir. Mines Trading Company, Ltd., London; Eng., Revere Copper & Brass, Inc. Mason. Clubs: Bankers (N.Y. City); Ridgewood (N.J.) Country; Skytop, (Skytop, Pa.). Home: Ridgewood, N.J. †

THORNTON, CHARLES BATES, industrialist; b. Knox County, Tex., July 22, 1913; s. W.A. and Sara Alice (Bates) T.; B.C.S., Columbus U., 1937; LL.D., Tex. Tech U., 1957, U. So. Calif., Pepperdine U., 1971; D.C.S., George Washington U., 1964; m. Flora Laney, Apr. 19, 1937; children—Charles Bates, William Laney. Dir. planning Ford Motor Co., 1946-48; v.p., asst. gen. mgr. Hughes Aircraft Co., Culver City, Calif., v.p. Hughes Tool Co., 1948-53; pres. Litton Industries, Inc., 1953-61, chmn. bd., chief exec. officer, 1953-81; dir., mem. exec. com. Cyprus Mines Corp.; dir. Trans World Airlines, Inc., United Calif. Bank, Western Bancorp., MCA, Inc. Mem. Bus. Council; nat. execs. com. Nat. Council on Crime and Delinquency; mem. Emergency Com. for Am. Trade; co-vice chmn. U.S. Internat. Transp. Exposition Com., 1971-72; mem. internat. bus. advisory com. Sec. Commerce, 1971-73; chmn. Pres.'s Commn. on White House Fellows, 1971-73; vice chmn. United Crusade campaign, 1972-75, gen. chmn., 1976; mem. Stanford Bus. Sch. Adv. Council; mem. headmasters council Harvard Sch.; life trustee U. So. Calif.; bd. dirs. Greater Los Angeles Visitors and Conv. Bur., So. Calif. Visitors Council, Los Angeles World Affairs Council; nat. dir. Jr. Achievement. Served to col. USAAF, World War II; cons. to comdg. gen. AAF, 1946, to undersec. Dept. State, 1947. Decorated D.S.M., Legion of Merit, Commendation ribbon with two oak leaf clusters; recipient numerous awards including Merit award Albert Einstein Coll. Medicine, Yeshiva U., 1963; Horatio Alger award Am. Schs. and Colls. Assn.,, 1964; Western Electronic medal achievement Western Electronic Mfrs. Assn., 1965; Golden Plate award Am. Acad. Achievement, 1966; Nat. Industry Leader award B'nai B'rith, 1967; Outstanding Achievement in Bus. Mgmt. award U. So. Calif., 1967; Bus. Leadership award U. Mich., 1968; Big Bros. Community Service award Jewish Big Bros. Assn. Los Angeles County, 1975; Community Leadership award United Way, 1976; named Man of Year, Beverly Hills C. of C., 1964, Calif. Industrialist of Year, Calif. Mus. Sci. and Industry, 1964, Industrialist of Year, Soc. Indsl. Realtors, 1966, Exec. of Yr., UCLA, Exec. Program Assn., 1978. Mem. Calif. Inst. Assocs., U. So. Calif. Assocs., Music Center Opera Assn. (dir., exec. com. 1966-68), Beta Gamma Sigma (hon.), Sigma Alpha Epsilon (life). Clubs: Army and Navy (Washington); Beach (Santa Monica); Los Angeles Country, California, One Hundred (Los Angeles); Hollywood Turf (dir.); Tex. Tech U. Century. Office: Beverly Hills, Calif. Died Nov. 24, 1981.

THORNTON, ROBERT AMBROSE, educator; b. Houston, Mar. 6, 1902; s. Frank and Mary Jane (Sullivan) T.; m. Jessie Lea Bullock, June 4, 1925. B.S., Howard U., 1922; M.S., Ohio State U., 1925; postgrad. (Rockefeller fellow), U. Chgo., 1928-29; Ph.D., U. Minn., 1946; postgrad., Harvard U., summers 1949, 51; D.Sc. (hon.), U. San Francisco, 1979. Instr. physics, math. Shaw U., 1922-25; faculty physics, math. Talladega Coll., 1929-44; dir. basic studies, prof. physics U. P.R., 1944-47; asso. prof. phys. scis. U. Chgo., 1947-50; asso. prof. physics Brandeis U., 1950-53; dean Dillard U., 1953-55; dean basic coll. Fisk U., 1955-56; prof. physics San Francisco State Coll., 1956-63; dean San Francisco State Coll. (Sch. Natural Scis.), 1963-67, prof. physics, 1967-82, U. San Francisco, 1967-77; Disting. vis. prof. U. D.C., 1980-82; participant Einstein Project, 1977; Mem. Gov. Calif. TV Adv. Com., 1964-74; mem. accrediation com. Calif. Bd. Edn., 1965-74; mem. Statewide Liaison Com. for Natural Scis., 1965-69; mem. planning com. for program, leadership, structure, theme issues and total activities ann. meeting Assn. Higher Edn., 1954-56; mem. adv. panel for natural and phys. scis. Calif. Commn. Tchr. Preparation and Licensing, 1972-76; mem. sr. commn. Western Assn. Schs. and Colls. for Accrediting Sr. Colls. and Univs., 1972-75; mem. adv. com. Consortium Colls. and Univs. San Francisco, 1977-80; sr. commn. rep. on accrediting commn. Western Assn. Schs. and Colls. for Secondary Schs., 1973-75; mem. panels NSF. Co-author: Introduction to the Physical Sciences, 1937, Course in The Physical Sciences, 3 vols, 1949, Problems in Physics, 1949. Regent St. Ignatius Coll. Prep., 1972-78; mem. adv. bd. Schs. of Sacred Heart, 1972-79; lectr. Fromm Inst. Continuing Edn., 1976—; mem. Sr. Citizens Com. San Francisco, 1978-80; mem. engring. adv. bd. Calif. State U., San Francisco, 1969-78. Recipient Disting. Teaching award Calif. State Coll., 1968; Asso. Students Faculty award San Francisco State Coll., 1959; commendation Calif. Senate, 1978; Rockefeller fellow, 1935-36. Mem. Am. Physics Soc., N.A.A.C.P., Phi Delta Kappa, Phi Beta Sigma, Alpha Sigma Nu. Episcopalian. Home: Fairfax, Va. Died Mar. 7, 1982.

THORP, ROY LOVELADY, clergyman, educator; b. Weston, Mo., Dec. 6, 1890; s. Coriolanus and Maude (Lovelady) T.; A.B., Drake U., Ia., 1911, B.D., 1913; m. Dorothy Mae Close, Dec. 23, 1911; children—Gerald Roy, Merle Bernice (Mrs. George F. Hails). Began as instructor of Old Testament history, Drake U., 1911-13; ordained ministry Disciples of Christ, 1913; pastor Tarkio, Mo., 1913-16; pres. Mo. Christian Coll., 1916-22; pastor, Canton, Mo., 1922-29; instr. in religious edn., Culver Stockton Coll., 1923-29; pastor First Christian Ch., Hastings, Neb., 1929-34, First Christian Ch., Centralia, Ill., 1934-52; nat. dir. stewardship, Disciples of Christ, 1952-58; pastor First Christian Ch., Fullerton, Cal., from 1960. Pres. Ill. Christian Missionary Society, 1949-51; mem. exec. com. dept. stewardship Nat. Council of Chs. in U.S., 1952-58, also mem. life and work div., 1956-58. Author books, articles on Christian stewardship. Contbr. religious and ednl. subjects. Home: Ventura, Cal. †

THORPE, WILLIAM FREDERICK, educator; b. Dubuque, Ia., Nov. 21, 1890; s. John Ballard and Lucy Emma (Gerner) T.; grad. Lake View High Sch., Chicago; student Lewis Institute (Chicago), University of Illinois, Northwestern University; m. May Allport Thomas, 1924 (she died 1926). Founder, 1919, and pres. Thorpe Acad., Lake Forest, Ill.; pres. Camp Thorpe, Pelican Lake, Wis. Student O.T.S., Camp Gordon, Atlanta, Ga., 1918; mem. 58th Pioneers, Camp Wadsworth, Spartanburg, S.C.; designated as col., Thorpe Acad. Mem. Camp Directors of America, Pvt. Sch. Assn. Central States (dir.), Am. Bur. of Civics (pres.), Am. Legion, Phi Sigma Kappa. Republican. Christian Scientist. Mason (K.T., 32 deg., Shriner). Clubs: Kiwanis, Lake Forest Music; Collegiate, Hamilton, Phi Sigma Kappa (Chicago). Home: Lake Forest, Ill. †

THORSEN, CARL S., elec. engr.; b. Toledo, Ia., July 29, 1890; s. Samuel E. and Dorothy (Walker) T.; B.S. in E.E., Ia. State Coll., 1913, E.E., 1923; m. Selma White, June 24, 1932; children—Paul, Rosalind, Ann. With Western Electric Co., Chicago and New York, engring., research and transcontinental line experimentations, 1913-17; asst. purchasing agent Allied Machinery Corp., Feb.-Sept. 1917; with Internat. Western Electric Co., 1918-19; mng. dir. Nat. Electric Light Assn., 1926-32; cons. engr., Chicago, from 1932. Sec. St. Lawrence Commn. of U.S., 1924-26, Second Nat. Radio Conf., 1925. Commd. 1st lt., Signal Corps, U.S. Army, 1917, later capt.; served in U.S. and France. Mem. Am. Inst. Elec. Engrs., Edison Electric Inst., Nat. Assn. Mfrs., Tau Beta Pi, Delta Upsilon. Republican. Clubs: Union League. University, Recess (New York); University (Chicago). Address: Chicago. †

THRELKELD, ARCHIE LOYD, supt. schools; b. Lancaster, Mo., Mar. 4, 1889; s. James Mancel and Emily Evelyn (Hounsom) T.; B.Pd., Northeast Mo. State Teachers Coll., Kirksville, Mo., 1911; studied U. of Wis. and U. of Chicago; B.S. in Edn., U. of Mo., 1919; M.A., Columbia, 1923; LL.D. (honorary), University of Denver, 1930, Colorado College, 1935; Ed.D. (honorary), University of Colorado, 1932; m. Anna Rebecca Miller, June 11, 1913 (died Jan. 16, 1923); children—Aubrey Miller, Richard Allen, Ellen Hounsom; m. 2d, Mary Ethel Miller, Aug. 12, 1925, Teacher, high sch., Kirksville, 1909-11; supt. schs, Bunceton, Mo., 1911-12, Unionville, 1912-17, Chillicothe, 1917-21; asst. supt. schs., Denver, 1921-24, dep. supt., 1924-27, supt, 1927-37; supt. schs., Montclair, N.J., 1937-50; head div. sch. relations, citizenship edn. project Teachers Coll., Columbia, 1950-52; lectr, edn. grad. sch. edn. Harvard since 1952. Pres, Mo. State Tchrs. Assn., 1921; pres. Am. Assn. Sch. Adminstrs., 1936-37;

chmn. commn. character edn. yearbook of 1932, Am. Assn. Sch. Adminstrs. Nat. dir. High School Victory Corps, U.S. Office of Education, 1942-43; mem. bd. dirs. Teaching Film Custodians, Inc. Fellow A.A.A.S.; mem. N.E.A. (life), Am. Acad. Polit. and Social Sci., Horace Mann League, Nat. Soc. for study of Edn. Phi Delta Kappa, Kappa Delta Pi; hon. life mem. Am. Assn. Sch. Adminstrs., John Dewey Soc. Methodist. Clubs: Mile High, Cactus (Denver). Home: South Londonderry, Vt. Deceased.

THRESHER, BRAINERD ALDEN, educator; b. Dayton, O., May 17, 1896; s. Brainerd Bliss and Mary L. (Colby) T.; student Hotchkiss Sch., 1911-14; S.B., Mass. Inst. Tech., 1920; A.M., Harvard, 1928; m. Irene Kattwinkel, Nov. 29, 1923; children—Naomi (Mrs. Daniel Colyer) (dec.), Sonia (Mrs. Robert A. Weaver), Rosemary (Mrs. William F. Edson), B. Colby. In engineering and industrial management, Pennsylvania and Massachusetts, 1920-27; dept. econ., social science, Mass. Inst. Tech., since 1929, dir. admissions, 1936-61, prof. econ., 1945-61; consultant Office Scientific Research and Development, 1944-45. Mem. exec. com. Coll. Entrance Exam. Bd. 1952-54, vice chmn., 1955-58, chmn., 1958-60. Trustee Ednl. Testing Service, 1960-64, chmn. research com., bd. trustees, 1963-64; vice chmn. National Commission on Tests, from 1967; trustee Thayer Acad., 1959-63. Mem. Am. Econ. Assn., Am. Assn. U. Profs., Am. Soc. for Engring. Edn., Sigma Chi. Republican. Conglist. Co-author: Organization and Management of a Business Enterprise, 1935; The Economic Process, 1935. Author: College Admissicns and the Public Interest, 1966; also articles. Home: Cocoa Beach, Fla. Died Jan. 23, 1984.

THRIFT, CHARLES TINSLEY, JR., coll. chancellor; b. Kenbridge, Va., Apr. 11, 1911; s. Charles Tinsley and Nell (Webb) T.; m. Ruth King, June 30, 1934; children—Ruth Nell, Helen Sue, Mary King. A.B., Duke, 1930, A.M., 1932, R.D., 1933; Ph.D., U. Chgo.; Ph.D. (fellow in ch. history), 1936; D.D., Southwestern U., 1965; L.H.D., Bethune-Cookman Coll., 1976. Prof. religion, dir. religious life Southwestern U., Georgetown, Tex., 1936-39; prof. religion Fla. So. Coll., Lakeland, from 1940, v.p. of coll., 1946-57, acting pres., 1957, pres., 1957-76, chancellor, from 1976; Vis. prof. Northwestern U. Garrett Bibl. Inst., summer 1946, Emory U., summer 1949, 52, Perkins Sch. Theology, So. Meth. U., 1952; Mem. Meth. Gen. Conf., 1960, 64, Bd. Edn., from 1960; Certification com. So. Regional Edn., Fla., from 1949; Mem. Fla. Conf. Meth. Ch.; dean Fla. Pastors' (Meth.) Sch., 1945-60. Author: The Trail of the Florida Circuit Rider, 1944, Through Three Decades at Florida Southern College, 1955, A Study of Theological Education in The Methodist Church, 1956, Of Fact and Fancy at Florida Southern College, 1979; Contbr. to: The Florida Story, Fla. papers; Editor: Marshaling Florida's Resources, 1945; Contbr. articles to religious, ednl., hist. publs. Mem. Am. Soc. Church History, Southeastern Hist. Soc. (Meth.) (sec. 1944-48), Fla. Assn. Colls. and Univs. (exec. com. 1945-53, v.p. 1949-50, pres. 1950-51), Ind. Colls. and Univs. Fla. (chmn. 1974-76), Fla. Hist. Soc. (dir. 1944-46, v.p. 1952-54, pres. 1954-56), Fla. Acad. Scis., Phi Beta Kappa, Omicron Delta Kappa, Kappa Delta Pi, Pi Gamma Mu. Home: Lakeland, Fla.

THRUN, ROBERT, lawyer; b. Eagle River, Wis., July 1, 1913; s. Ferdinand Julius and Florence (Zwicker) T.; m. Roberta Read Lewis, June 22, 1937; children: Sally Grosvenor, Roberta Read, Robert Read. B.A., U. Wis., 1936; J.D., Harvard U., 1939. Bar: N.Y. 1940. Sec. Wis. R.R. Assn., 1934-36; since practiced in, N.Y.C.; mem. firm Reavis & McGrath, from 1946; atty. Village of Croton-on-Hudson, N.Y., 1959-60, 61-67; v.p., mem. bd., exec. com. U.S. com. for UNICEF, 1954-81, gen. counsel, 1954-82, hon. mem. bd., from 1981; counsel, sec. Ringling Bros.-Barnum & Bailey Combined Shows, Inc., 1952-67, dir., from 1971; gen. counsel Pulitzer Pub. Co., from 1971, dir., from 1977; v.p., dir. Sells-Floto, Inc., from 1974; dir., mem. exec. com. Nat. City Lines, Inc., 1978-80. Trustee, sec. Sotterley Mansion Found., Hollywood, Md., from 1962. Served with AUS, 1943-44; to lt. (j.g.) USNR, 1944-46. Decorated commendations from sec. navy, asst. sec. war. Mem. Am. Bar Assn., Assn. Bar City N.Y., Phi Beta Kappa, Phi Gamma Delta. Home: Croton-on-Hudson, NY.

THURBER, CLARENCE HOWE, univ. pres.; b. Guilford, Vt., Sept. 19, 1888; s. John Wilkins and Eva L. (Howe) T.; A.B., Colgate, 1912; A.M., Teachers Coll. (Columbia), 1921, Ph.D., 1922; m. Alice Helen Egbert, June 30, 1913; children—Alice Helen, Eleanor, Clarence. Instr. Phillips Acad., Andover, Mass., 1912-13; prof. of English and debate, Wabash Coll., 1913-15; prof. of English and debate, Purdue U., 1915-20; asso. prof. ednl. administration, Syracuse U., 1922-24; exec. sec. and dir. summer session; prof. of edn., U. of Buffalo, 1924-30; dean of faculty and dir. of ednl. progam. Colgate, 1930-33; pres. U. of Redlands, 1933-38. U.S. Treasury, 1943-45; Investment Banking after 1945. Lecturer Calif. State Dept. of Edn. 1939-42. Mem. Phi Beta Kappa, Phi Delta Kappa, Beta Theta Pi. Mason. Writer on ednl. administration and Latin Am. affairs. Home: Altadena, Calif. Deceased.

TIDYMAN, ERNEST, screenwriter, author, film producer; b. Cleve., Jan. 1, 1928; s. Benjamin and Catherine (Kascsak) T.; m. Susan Gould, Dec. 25, 1970 (div.); children—Adam, Nicholas; children by previous marriage—Benjamin, Nathaniel. Ed. pub. schs. Newspaper writer, editor Cleve. News, 1954-57, N.Y. Post, 1957-60; editor N.Y. Times, N.Y.C., 1960-66; mag. editor, writer Signature Mag., also others, N.Y.C., 1966; lectr. in field. Freelance screenwriter, author, 1969-84, (Recipient Acad. award 1971, Writers Guild award 1971, Mystery Writers Am. award 1971, for best screenplay The French Connection, N.A.A.C.P. Image award for motion picture Shaft 1971, Peabody award 1980, Gavel award for TV movie Dummy, Am. Bar Assn. 1980); Author: series Shaft, 1970-75, Absolute Zero, 1971, High Plains Drifter, 1973, Dummy, 1974, Line of Duty, 1974, Starstruck, 1975, Tablestakes, 1978; writer: screenplay The French Connection, 1971, Shaft, 1971, Shaft's Big Score, 1972, High Plains Drifter, 1973, Report to the Commissioner, 1975, Street People, 1975, A Force of One, 1979; teleplay To Kill a Cop, 1978, Power: An American Saga, 1980; writer and co-producer: teleplay Dummy, 1979, Guyana Tragedy, 1980, Alcatraz: The Whole Shocking Story, 1980. Served with AUS, 1945-46. Mem. Acad. Motion Picture Arts and Scis., Writers Guild Am. West, Acad. TV Arts and Scis., Am. Film Inst. Home: Los Angeles, Calif. Died July 14, 1984.

TIGERINO, J(OSÉ) ANTONIO, diplomat; b. Chinandega, Nicaragua, Dec. 4, 1889; s. Toribio and Maria Antonia (Vaca) T.; grad. Univ. of Leon and Univ. of Managua; LL.D., Supreme Court of Justice, Nicaragua, 1916; m. Maria Clotilde Vega, May 5, 1924. Apptd. judge Criminal Superior Court of Chinandega, 1912; apptd. same yr. sec. to exec. rep. for Western Depts. of Nicaragua and made col. Nat. Army; apptd. gov. and comdr. in chief of Army of Chinandega, after revolution of 1912; mem. Nat. Congress, 1913-15; asso. justice Court of Appeals for Western Div. 1917; consul gen. of Nicaragua, at Hamburg, Germany, 1918-20; again gov. and comdr. in chief; sec. and charge d'affaires Nicaraguan Legation to U.S. since 1924. Address: Washington, D.C. †

TILFORD, JOHN EMIL, railroad exec.; b. Atlanta, Ga., July 12, 1888; s. John H. and Mary E. (Kirchofer) T.; ed. pub. and private schs.; m. R. Cecil Jester, Sept. 1911; children—John E., Charles H., William A. Traffic officer, Atlanta, Birmingham & Atlantic R.R. (now A.C.L. R.R.) and L.&N. R.R., 1918-28; chmn. So. Freight Assn., 1928-37; asst. v.p. L. & N. R.R., 1937-45, v.p. traffic, 1945-47, exec. v.p., 1947-50, pres. and dir., 1950-59, chairman advisory com. board dirs., 1959-61; director Citizens Fidelity Bank and Trust Company, Louisville. Independent. Episcopalian. Clubs: Pendennis, Louisville Country (Louisville); Union League (N.Y.C.); Metropolitan (Washington). Home: Louisville, Ky. †

TILLMAN, LAWRENCE J., ins. exec.; b. Boston, Jan. 12, 1888; s. Edward J. and Elizabeth (MacManus) T.; student pub. schs. of Boston; m. Hazel M. King, Nov. 27, 1935. In fire and marine ins. bus. from 1909; U.S. mgr. Century Ins. Co., Ltd., of London and Edinburgh, Pacific Coast Fire Ins. Co. of Vancouver, B.C., from 1938. Mem. State of N.Y. C. of C., Ins. Execs. Assn. Club: Canadian (New York). Home: New York, N.Y. †

TILTON, CHARLES ELLIOTT, b. Tilton, N.H., May 6, 1887; s. Charles E. and E. Genieve (Eastman) T.; A.B., Harvard, 1908; student Mass. Inst. Tech., 1909-10; m. Glenna Webb, Oct. 5, 1910; children—Charles E., 3d, S. Webb, Glenna. Mem. N.H. Ho. of Rep., 1913-17; mem. N.H. Constitutional Conv., 1912 and 1930; mem. N.H. State Board of Pub. Welfare, 1913-15 and 1922-31 (chmn.); mem. bd. mgrs. N.H. Soldiers Home from 1920. Vice pres. and trustee Iona Savings Bank (Tilton); mem. bd. dirs. Citizens Nat. Bank (Tilton); dir. United Life & Accident Ins. Co. (Concord), N.H. Acceptance Corpn. (Concord). Dem. candidate for gov. of N.H., 1920. Served in U.S. Army, Sept. 1917-Jan. 1919. Chmn. N.H. State Advisory Board under Federal Emergency Adminstrn. of Pub. Works, 1934, also state dir. NRA and Nat. Emergency Council; asst. gen. mgr. Home Owners Loan Corpn., 1934-38; asst. gen. mgr. Federal Savings and Loan Ins. Corpn. from July, 1938. Democrat. Episcopalian. Clubs: University, Harvard (Boston). Mason (32 deg., K.T.). Home: Tilton, N.H. †

TILTON, ROLLIN LARRABEE, army officer; b. Chicago, Feb. 22, 1888; s. John Neal and Emily Wood (Larrabee) T.; student Cornell U., 1907-09, Coast Artillery Sch., Ft. Monroe, 1928-29, Command and Gen. Staff Sch., 1933-35, Army War Coll., 1937-38; m. Kathleen Glendower Cates, Apr. 25, 1914; children—Emily Neal (Mrs. Charles J. Ryan), Elizabeth LaMotte (Mrs. James Henry Seeley), Ann De Koven. Commd. 2d. lieutenant, Coast Artillery Corps, United States Army, 1909, advanced through ranks to brig. gen., 1940; served at various posts in U.S. and abroad, 1909-38, Mexican Border, 1916, in World War, 1917-19, in U.S. and A.E.F., France; in Panama, 1920-23; comd. harbor defenses, Pensacola, Fla., 1923-24; insp. gen. 4th Corps Area, 1924-28; instr. and sec., Coast Arty. Sch., 1929-33; comdr. harbor defenses, Boston, Mass., 1935-37; gen. staff corps, Panama Canal Dept., 1938-40; brig. gen. (temp.) comdg. 3d Coast Artillery Dist., and harbor defenses of Chesapeake Bay, Ft. Monroe, 1940-41; comd. Chesapeake Bay Sector, North Atlantic Coastal Frontier, Dec. 8, 1941 to Feb. 29, 1944; comd. Harbor Defenses of Chesapeake Bay, March 1, 1944 to June 15, 1946; inspector general, Army Ground Forces, 1946-48. Awarded Mexican Punitive Expedition Medal, Victory, American Defense, American Theater, Legion of Merit medals; Army Commendation Ribbon. Asso. U.S. Naval Inst. Home: Hampton, Va. †

TIMBERLAKE, CLARE HAYES, government official; b. Jackson, Mich., Oct. 29, 1907; s. Wilbur Bateman and Dorothy (Silsbee) T.; A.B., U. of Mich., 1929; student grad. sch. Harvard, 1929-30; M.A., George Washington University, 1963; m. Julia Frances Catherine Meehan, Sept. 6, 1945; children—Charles Bateman, William Lansdell, Frances Mildred, Katherine Dorothy, Mary Anne. Became fgn. service officer for the Department of State, December, 1930, vice consul, Toronto, 1931, Buenos Aires, 1932-35, Zurich, 1937-38, Vigo, Spain, 1938-40, Aden, 1940, consul, 1940-43, consul gen. Bombay, 1948-50; 3rd sec. legation, Montevideo, 1935-37; desk officer Nr. Eastern affairs Dept. of State, 1943-45, asst. chief African affairs, 1945-46, chief, 1946-47; counselor of Embassy and chief pub. affairs officer, New Delhi 1950-52; consul gen. Hamburg, 1952-55; counselor of embassy, Lima Peru, 1955-57; minister counselor of embassy, Buenos Aires, 1957, Bonn. 1958-60; ambassador to Congo, 1960-61; State Dept. adviser to comdr. Air U., Maxwell AFB, 1961; spl. asst. to under sec. of state for polit. affairs, 1962-63; chmn. Disarmament Adv. Staff, Arms Control and Disarmament Agy., 1963-64; permanent U.S. rep. to 18 Nation Disarmament Com., Geneva, 1964-66; fgn. affairs officer Bur. Inter-Am. Affairs, Office Asst. Sec., Dept. State, 1966-67; mem. bd. examiners Fgn. Service, Dept. State, from 1967. Mem. Fgn. Service Assn., Alpha Tau Omega. Club: International (Washington). Home: Fort Sumner, Md. Died Feb. 22, 1982.

TIMBRELL, HOWARD, newspaper editor; b. New Britain, Conn., Oct. 31, 1887; s. Thomas William and Elizabeth Anna (Turton) T.; grad. high sch., New Britain, 1906. Began as reporter, Hartford Times, Oct. 15, 1906; editor New Britain Record since 1923; v.p. Beaton & Corbin Mfg. Co., Southington, Conn.; sec. Empire Electric Co., Plainville, Conn. Pvt. at Camp Devens, Mass., World War; mem. Common Council, New Britain, 1921-22; mem. New Britain Public Amusement Commn., 1916-19; mem. Bd. of Pub. Works, from 1930. Member American Legion. Republican. Conglist. Mason (32 deg., Shriner), Elk. Home: New Britain, Conn. †

TINKER, MORT D., business exec.; b Maquoketa, Ia., May 10, 1889; s. Fred S. and Helen C. (Goodenow) T.; ed. pub. schs. of Ia.; m. Mabel Barclay, June 28, 1924. Began as salesman with the Frank B. Tinker Co. of Chicago, 1912-26; partner Tinker Bros., mfrs. agt. of glassware, 1926-36; pres. Tinker Glassware, Inc., 1936-42; owner Tinker Glassware from Jan. 1942. Served with U.S. Army as pvt., Co. D, 131st inf., 33rd div., Oct. 1917-July 1919. Mem. Glass-Pottery Assn. of Chicago (pres. 1944-45), Izaak Walton League of Am. (pres. Chicago chapter, 1944-46, v.p. Ill. div., 1945-46, nat. sec., 1946-48), Am. Legion. Protestant. Mason. Clubs: Lincoln Park Casting (vice pres. 1940-41), Campfire. 15th Floor Merchandisers of Merchandise Mart, Merchants and Mfrs. of Mdse. Mart, Elk. †

TINKLE, DONALD WARD, zoologist; b. Dallas, Dec. 3, 1930; s. Maurice Ward and Rubye Lucille (Still) T.; B.S., So. Meth. U., 1952; M.S., Tulane U., 1955, Ph.D., 1956; m. Marjorie Anne White, Feb. 24, 1951; children—Donna Lynn, Randall Troy, Steven Lance, Melanie Anne. Asst. prof. biology West Tex. State U., 1956-57; asst. prof. zoology Tex. Tech. U., 1957-60, asso. prof. zoology, 1960-63, prof. zoology, 1963-65; prof. zoology, curator amphibeans and reptiles U. Mich., 1965-80, dir. Mus. Zoology, 1975-80; Maytag prof. vertebrate ecology Ariz. State U., 1972. NSF fellow, 1955-56; Carnegie Found. fellow, 1954-55; Guggenheim fellow, 1979-80; Fellow AAAS, Herpetologists League; mem. Am. Soc. Naturalists, Ecol. Soc. Am. (Eminent Ecologist award 1980), Am. Soc. Ichthyologists and Herpetologists, Soc. for Study Evolution, Southwestern Assn. Naturalists, Sigma Xi. Author: The Life and Demography of the Side-blotched Lizard, 1967; editor: (with Carl Gans) Biology of the Reptilia on Ecology and Behavior, 1978; editor Southwestern Naturalist, 1958-63; asso. editor Evolution, 1966-71, Biology of Reptilia, 1969—. Home: Saline, Mich. Died Feb. 21, 1980.

TIPTON, STUART GUY, lawyer, airline exec.; b. Knightstown, Ind., Dec. 26, 1910; s. Guy Stuart and Bessie (Walters) T.; A.B., Wabash Coll., 1932; J.D., Northwestern U., 1935; m. Lorraine Arnold, May 15, 1937; children—Susan Arnold, Judith, Ann, Patience. Admitted to Ind. bar, 1935; atty., office gen. counsel Treasury Dept., Washington, 1935-38, CAA, Washington, 1938-40; asst. gen. counsel CAB, 1940-43; gen. counsel Air Transport Assn., 1944-55, pres., 1955-72, chmn., 1972-74; sr. v.p. fed. affairs Pan Am. World Airways, Washington, 1974-77, cons., 1977-81. Chmn. nat. bd. dirs. Ariz.-Sonora Desert Mus. Mem. D.C. Bar, Phi Beta Kappa, Sigma Chi. Clubs: Burning Tree, Congressional Country, Metropolitan. Home: Potomac, Md. Died Aug. 14, 1981.

TISDALE, W(ILLIAM) B(URLEIGH), plant pathologist; b. Georgiana, Ala., Sept. 13, 1890; s. William Riley and Josephine L. (Higdon) T.; B.S., Ala. Polytech. Inst., 1914; M.S., U. of Wis., 1917, Ph.D., 1920; m. Ruth Blakely King, June 28, 1922; children—Elizabeth Anne (Mrs. Franklin L. DeBusk), William Allan, Ellen, Jane. Instr. Miss State Coll., 1915-16, U. of Wis., 1917-18, 1919-22; asst. plant pathol. Fla. Agr. Expt. Sta., 1922-24, asso. plant pathol., 1924-27, plant pathol. in charge, 1927-29, plant pathol. and head dept., 1929-35, head botany dept. and plant pathol. dept. from 1935. Served in

U.S. Army 7 mos. 1918. Mem. A.A.A.S., Am. Phytopath Soc., Sigma Xi, Phi Sigma, Gamma Alpha, Phi Kappa Phi. Democrat. Methodist. Club: Rotary. Research in plant pathol., disease resistance in plants. Home: Gainesville, Fla. †

TISHMAN, DAVID, corp. exec.; b. N.Y.C., Apr. 22, 1889; s. Julius and Hilda (Karmel) T.; LL.B., N.Y.U., 1909, LL.M., 1910, LL.D. (hon.), 1960; m. Ann Valentine, Jan. 8, 1914; children—Robert V., Alan V., Virginia (Mrs. David L. Rand). Vice pres. Julius Tishman & Sons, Inc., 1912-28; pres. Tishman Realty & Constrn. Co., Inc., 1928-48; chmn., from 1948. Dir Citizens Housing and Planning Council of N.Y., Inc.; trustee Citizens Budget Commn. Dir. N.Y. chapter Am. Red Cross. Trustee N.Y. Univ., N.Y.U.-Bellevue Med. Center, N.Y.U. Law Center Found., Bennington Coll. Recipient meritorious service award N.Y.U., 1955. Mason (32). Clubs: New York University (dir.) (N.Y.C.); Sunningdale Country (Scarsdale, N.Y.). Home: New York, NY. †

TITTMANN, HAROLD HILGARD, JR., fgn. service ofcr., ret.; b. St. Louis, Jan. 8, 1893; s. Harold Hilgard and Emma Roe (Copelin) T.; student Taft School, Watertown, Conn., 1908-12; A.B., Yale U., 1916; m. Eleanor Dulaney Barclay, Feb. 21, 1928; children—Harold Hilgard, III, Barclay. Began as salesman Wagner Electric Co., St. Louis, 1916; sec. of Embassy, Paris, 1921-25, Rome, 1925-36; alternate del. 3d Internat. Conf. on Private Aerial Law, Rome, 1933; asst. chief Div. of European Affairs, Dept. of State, 1936-39; consul gen., Geneva, Switzerland, 1939-40; asst. to personal rep. of the President of U.S. to His Holiness the Pope, Rome, 1940; counselor of Embassy, Rome, 1940; asst. to personal rep. of President to His Holiness the Pope, Rome, 1941-46; ambassador extraordinary and plenipotentiary to Haiti, 1946, Peru, 1948-55; director of Intergovernmental Committee for European Migration, Geneva, 1955-58, ret. Served as first lt., pilot, United States Air Service, 1917-20, wounded in action. Awarded D.S.C., Order of the Purple Heart, Victory Medal, Croix de Guerre. Club: Metropolitan (Washington). Episcopalian. Home: Washington, D.C. Died Dec. 30, 1980.

TITUS, HAROLD, writer; b. Traverse City, Mich., Feb. 20, 1888; s. Dorr B. and F. Josephine (Smith) T.; studied U. of Mich., 1907-11, hon. M.A., 1931; m. Beth Benedict, Apr. 14, 1914; children—Elizabeth Louise, John Smith. Reporter, Detroit News, 1907-10; fruit grower, Grand Traverse County, Mich., from 1911. Mem. Michigan Conservation Commission, 1927-35, and 1937-49, chmn., 1945, 46. Enlisted in United States Army, August 17, 1917; ordnance sergeant 111th Ordnance Depot Company. Mem. Sigma Alpha Epsilon frat. Author: I Conquered, 1916; Bruce of the Circle A, 1918; The Last Straw, 1920; Timber, 1922; The Beloved Pawn, 1923; Spindrift, 1924; Below Zero, 1932; Code of the North, 1933; Flame in the Forest, 1933; The Man from Yonder, 1934; Black Feather, 1936. Contbr. to many mags. Conservation editor, Field & Stream (mag.). Home: Traverse City, Mich. †

TITUS, NORMAN EDWIN, psychiatrist; b. New York, N.Y., July 29, 1889; s. Edward C. and Fanny (Gibson) T.; Ph.B., Yale, 1910; M.D., Columbia, 1914; m. Helen A. de Witt, June 11, 1917; children—Josiah Hornblower de Witt, Norman Edwin, Nathalie Anita and William Downing. Practiced in N.Y. City, 1914-42, Former asso. in surgery, dir. physical therapy, Columbia Univ.; attending surgeon and dir. physical therapy, Vanderbilt Clinic and the Presbyterian Hosp., N.Y. City; consultant in physical therapy various hosps. and New York Police Dept.; ex-pres. Am. Congress of Physical Therapy, 1929-30. Served in U.S. Army, 1917-19, 1942-46. Col., med. res. (inactive). Fellow A.M.A.; mem. Phi Gamma Delta. Republican. Club: Rumson Country. Home: Downington, Pa. †

TOALSON, NATHAN AUGUSTUS, mfr. elec. equipment; b. Centralia, Mo., Jan. 25, 1911; s. Alex R. and Alice Lee (Hardin) T.; student U. Mo., 1929-30; m. Gara C. Williams, Oct. 5, 1941; children—Gara Ann, (Mrs. James S. Martin), Williams Nathan, Alice Bowman (Mrs. Robert K. Peiser). With A.B. Chance Co., Centralia, Mo., 1930—, exec. v.p., 1956-60, pres., 1960-72, chmn. bd., 1972-76; dir. A. B. Chance Co., Emerson Electric Co., 1975-80, Can. Dir. Asso. Industries Mo., Mo. Pub. Expenditures Survey, So. States Indsl. Council; pres., exec. com. Gt. Rivers council Boy Scouts Am. Pres. bd. trustees William Jewell Coll.; bd. mgrs. Mo. Bapt. Hosp., St. Louis; bd. dirs. Chance Found. Recipient Silver Beaver award Boy Scouts Am.; Paul Harris fellow Rotary Internat. Mem. Am. Inst. E.E. Baptist (deacon). Home: Centralia, Mo. Died May 21, 1985; interred Centralia, Mo.

TOBIN, FREDERICK M., packing co. ofcl.; b. Syracuse, N.Y., 1887. Chmn., sr. officer Tobin Packing Co., Inc. K.C. †

TODD, ALVA CRESS, educator, engr.; b. Ligonier, Ind., July 30, 1917; s. Frederick White and Bessie Pearl (Cress) T.; B.S. in Elec. Engring., Purdue U., 1947, M.S., 1949, Ph.D., 1957; m. Mary Elizabeth Schelle, Apr. 17, 1941; children—Richard Schelle, Carol Jean (Mrs. Everett A. Biegalski), Joanne Frances (Mrs. Louis E. Horton), Elizabeth Ann (Mrs. Scott R. Lowry). Broadcast engr. radio sta. WSBT, South Bend, Ind., 1936-40, radio sta. WBAA, Lafayette, Ind., 1940-42; elec. engr. U.S. Signal Corps., Washington, 1942; instr., research engr. Sch. Elec. Engring., Purdue U., 1947-53, asst. prof., 1953; dir. engring. Fournier Inst. Tech., Lemont, Ill., 1953-55; sr. engr. Farnsworth Electronics Co., Ft. Wayne, Ind., 1955-56; individual practice engring., Lafayette, 1956-57; research engr. Ill. Inst. Tech. Research Inst., 1957-60; mgr. active electronic warfare div. Hallicrafters Co., 1960-61; mem. faculty Ill. Inst. Tech., 1961-62, prof. elec. engring., 1962-67; founder, pres. Midwest Coll. Engring., 1967-81; sr. partner Todd Assos., Villa Park, Ill., 1961-81. Served to lt. USCGR, 1942-46. Registered profl. engr., Ind., Ill. Mem. IEEE (sr.), Armed Forces Communications and Electronics Assn., AAAS, Nat. Fire Protection Assn., Nat., Ill. socs. profl. engrs., Am. Soc. Engring. Edn., Soc. Broadcast Engrs., Sigma Xi, Tau Beta Pi, Eta Kappa Nu. Patentee in field. Home: Villa Park, Ill. Died Aug. 3, 1981.

TODD, CHARLES GILLETT, food company executive; b. Indpls., Feb. 28, 1914; s. John Picken and Laura (Gillett) T.; m. Genevieve Steiner, Dec. 11, 1939; children—John P., Suzanne (Mrs. Milton R. Dodge). A.B., Ind. U., 1935; LL.B., Chgo. Kent Coll. Law, 1940; student, Wabash Coll., 1931-33, DePaul U., 1940, Northwestern U., 1941-42. Bar: Ill. bar 1940, Calif. bar 1951. Atty., tax mgr. First Nat. Bank Chgo., 1936-41; tax mgr. Allen R. Smart Co., Chgo., 1941-44; with Carnation Co., 1944-50, 56-82, sec., asst. v.p., 1962-63, treas., 1963-69, v.p., 1965-67, mem. exec. com., chmn. finance com., dir., 1965-82, sr. v.p., 1967-73, exec. v.p., 1973-82; v.p. Gen. Milk Co., 1951-56. Bd. dirs. Carnation Found. Mem. State Bar Calif., Phi Delta Phi, Phi Delta Theta. Clubs: Wilshire Country (Los Angeles); Lomas Santa Fe Country (Solana Beach). Home: Encino, Calif. Died Aug. 24, 1982.

TODMAN, WILLIAM SELDEN, TV producer/program packager; b. N.Y.C., 1916; s. Frederick Simpson and Helena Diana (Orlowitz) T.; m. Frances Holmes Burson, 1950; children—Lisa Susan, William Selden. B.S., Johns Hopkins U., 1933; B.A., N.Y. U., 1941. Partner Goodson-Todman Prodns., N.Y.C., from 1946; pres. Goodson-Todman Prodns., Mid-Atlantic Newspapers, Central States Pub. Co., Inc.; v.p. Capitol City Pub. Co., Inc., Seattle Broadcasting Co., New Eng. Newspapers, Am. Tribune Pub., Inc.; v.p., dir. Acme Newspapers, Inc., New Eng. Newspapers, Inc., N.E. Pub., Inc., Pearless Publs., Inc., Shenandoah Valley Pub. Corp.; exec. v.p., pres., dir. Goodson-Todman Broadcasting Inc., Milford Pub., Inc., Riverdale Pub., Inc.; dir. Central StatesPub., Inc., Mid-Hudson Publs., Inc.; lectr. Queen's Coll., from 1947. Free-lance radio writer and producer, 1938-41, writer, producer, Sta. WABC, 1941-43, producer, agy. supr., Blow Co.; also writer, dir.: Connie Boswell Show for, Blue Network, 1943; writer, dir.: Anita Ellis Sings, 1944; writer: dramas Treasury Salute, 1945-46; developer/producer: TV programs numerous others; developer,producer: TV programs It's News to Me, What's My Line, The Name's the Same, I've Got a Secret, To Tell the Truth, Two for the Money, Beat the Clock, Judge for Yourself, The Price is Right, Play Your Hunch, Split Personality, Say When, One Happy Family, Don Rickles Show, Snap Judgement, He Said She Said, Password; Author: (with Mark Goodson) The Take All Home Quiz Book, 1949; contbr.: Television Advertising and Production Handbook, 1954. Chmn. radio-TV, stage artists and musicians div. United Jewish Appeal, 1954, 56; chmn. broadcasting industry campaign Fedn. Jewish Philanthropies, 1961-63; chmn. N.Y. Heart Fund. Mem. Phi Epsilon Pi. Address: Palm Beach, Fla. *

TODRANK, GUSTAVE HERMAN, educator; b. Huntingburg, Ind., Apr. 9, 1924; s. Christian William and Lillian Catherine (Ahrens) T.; m. Elizabeth Chalmers, June 25, 1949; children—Stephen Knight, Josephine. B.A., DePauw U., 1948; S.T.B., Boston U., 1951, Ph.D. (Boston U. Alumni fellow), 1956. Ordained to ministry United Ch. Christ, 1951; minister North Congl. Ch., Newton, Mass., 1951-56; mem. faculty Colby Coll., Waterville, Maine, 1956-82, prof. philosophy and religion, 1970-82. Author: The Secular Search for a New Christ, 1969, The Eden Connection, 1981, also articles, book revs. Served with USAAF, 1943-46. Mem. Am. Acad. Religion, Am. Soc. Christian Ethics, Am. Philos. Assn., Phi Beta Kappa. Home: Waterville, Maine. Dec. Sept. 8, 1982.

TOLES, ELSIE, state supt. edn.; b. Bisbee, Ariz., Sept. 19, 1888; d. George Edward and Elsie Jane (McGraw) T.; Pomona Coll., Calif. 1 yr.; grad. State Normal School, San Jose, Calif., 1908; studied U. of Mich. Began as teacher pub. schs., Bisbee, 1909; co. sch. supt., Cochise Co., 1917-20; state supt. edn., Ariz., term 1921-23 (first woman state official in Ariz.). Mem. N.E.A., Ariz. Ednl. Assn. Republican. Presbyn. Club: College (Phoenix). Home: Phoenix, Ariz. †

TOLSON, HILLORY ALFRED, conservationist, lawyer; b. nr. Laredo, Mo., Oct. 24, 1897; s. James William and Joaquin Miller (Anderson) T.; grad. Cedar Rapids (Iowa) Bus. Coll., 1918; A.B., George Washington U., 1924, A.M., 1927; J.D., Nat. U., 1930, LL.M., M.P.L., 1931; m. Catharine Ann Hough, May 31, 1926 (div.); children—Walter J., Robert H.; m. Charlotte May Nell, Aug. 2, 1941; 1 child, Pamela Lynn. With war plans div. War Dept., Washington, 1919-21, Panama Canal, Washington, 1921-31; spl. agt. FBI and atty. Nat. Park Service, Dept. Interior, 1932, asst. dir., 1933-39, regional dir. region 3, Santa Fe, 1939-40, chief of ops., 1940-43, asst. dir., 1943-63, cons., 1964-66; exec. dir. White House Hist. Assn., 1966-78. Served with USMC, World War I; lt. comdr. USNR, 1935-41. Chmn. Coronado Internat. Meml. Commn. to Mex., 1942. Mem. Internat. Park Commn., Mex.-U.S., and conservation com. Micronesia, Pacific Sci. Bd. Admitted to D.C. bar, 1930, U.S. Supreme Ct. bar, 1935. Awarded Delta Tau Delta Activity medal George Washington U., 1924; Cornelius Pugsley Conservation medal Am. Scenic and Historic Preservation Soc., 1949; named to Hall of Fame, 1959, recipient Alumni Achievement award George Washington U., 1962; Distinguished Service award Interior Dept., 1963. Mem. Am., Fed., D.C. bar assns., Westerners, Am. Legion, Save-the-Redwoods League, Thornton Soc., Interior Dept. Recreation Assn. (founder), George Washington U. Alumni Assn. (life), U.S. Supreme Ct. Hist. Assn., Sigma Nu, Pi Delta Epsilon. Mason. Clubs: Cosmos, Nat. Lawyers (Washington); Kenwood Country. Compiler: Laws Relating to the National Park Service, 1933, 63. Home: Bethesda, Md. Died Aug. 23, 1983; buried Arlington National Cemetery, Arlington, Va.

TOMITA, KOJIRO, museum curator; b. Kyoto, Japan, Mar. 7, 1890; s. Koshichi and Ran (Nakanishi) T.; grad. Kyoto Municipal Art Sch., 1906; m. Harriet E. Dickinson, Oct. 13, 1923. Came to U.S., 1906, naturalized 1953. Mem. staff Mus. Fine Arts, Boston, from 1908, asst. curator Chinese and Japanese art, 1916-31, curator Asiatic art, 1931-63, curator emeritus Asiatic art, from 1963; hon. curator Japanese ethnology Peabody Mus., Salem, Mass., from 1938. Decorated Order Sacred Treasures (Japan); recipient citation Boston U., 1959. Fellow Am. Acad. Arts and Scis.; mem. Am. Assn. Museums. Author: Portfolio of Chinese Paintings in the Museum of Fine Arts, Boston, Han to Sung, vol. I, 1933, 2d edit., 1938; Yuan to Ch'ing, vol. 11, 1961; also articles. Home: Jamaica Plain, MA. †

TOMLIN, DANIEL OTIS, real estate broker, developer, investor; b. Duster, Tex., Feb. 14, 1915; s. Daniel and Marie (Echols) T.; m. Erline Schuessler, June 4, 1938; children: Daniel Otis, Carolyn Orene (Mrs. Tomlin Hurst). B.S., So. Methodist U., 1935; postgrad., Harvard Grad. Sch. Bus. Adminstrn., 1935-37, Washington U., St. Louis, 1937-38. Accounting clk. Am. Zinc Co., St. Louis, 1937-40, chief accountant, Dumas, Tex., 1940-42, asst. mgr., 1942-46; treas., asst. gen. mgr. Briggs-Weaver Machinery Co., Dallas, 1946-53, dir., 1959-61; pres. Dearborn Stove Co., Dallas, 1953-56, Lone Star Boat Co., Plano, Tex., 1956-61; pres., dir. Acme Brick Co. (now Justin Industries), Ft. Worth, 1961-69; v.p., dir. Good & Assos., Inc., Dallas, 1970-72; now real estate broker, investor Tomlin Properties, Dallas.; Mem. adv. bd. U. Dallas, 1961-72, Pvt. Jr. Coll. Found., 1961-69; mem. adv. council U. Tex. at, Arlington, 1967-72; mem. com. of 125, Southwestern U., 1966-74; mem. Tex. Air Control Bd., 1968-69, Tex. Advisory Commn. on Tech. Services, 1966-69, Nat. Indsl. Conf. Bd., 1957-69. Trustee Tarrant County United Fund, 1964-69, v.p., 1968; trustee Harris Hosp., Ft. Worth, 1968-71, So. Meth. U., 1969-72, Tex. Christian U. Research Found., 1969-72; bd. dirs. C.C. Young Meml. Home, from 1981, vice chmn. bd., 1982-83; bd. dirs. Casa Manana Theatre, 1964-69, Ft. Worth Chamber Devel. Corp., 1965-69; mem. adminstrv. bd. Highland Park United Meth. Ch., from 1975. Mem. NAM (dir. 1967-69), Clay Products Assn. S.W. (pres. 1965-66), Tex. Assn. Bus. (pres. 1958, dir. from 1955), Soc. for Advancement Mgmt. (pres. Dallas chpt. 1955), Am. Mgmt. Assn. (gen. mgmt. council 1968-71), Structural Clay Products Inst. (dir. 1967-69, mem. exec. com. 1967-69), Boat Mfrs. Assn. Am. (pres. 1959-60), West Tex. C. of C. (v.p. 1965-66), Ft. Worth C. of C. (dir. 1962-69), Lambda Chi Alpha. Clubs: Northwood Country (Dallas), Lancers (Dallas), Chaparral (Dallas), Salesmanship (Dallas). Home: Dallas, Tex.

TOMLINSON, PAUL GREENE, author; b. New Brunswick, N.J., Feb. 8, 1888; s. Everett Titsworth and Ann (Greene) T.; A.B., Princeton University, 1909; LL.B., New York Law School, 1911; married Gabriella Prout, January 1917; children—Henry Prout, Ann (Mrs. S. C. Finnell). Editor McClure's Magazine, 1917-23, The Outlook, 1919-24, The Elks Magazine, 1923-31, Am. Legion Weekly, 1924, Harper's Mag., 1925-36; dir. and sec. Princeton University Press, 1918-38; Chief, Bur. of State Publicity N.J. Department Econ. Development. Editor N.J. Compass. Dir. Co. relations Lawrence Portland Cement Co. from 1948. Mem. Princeton Borough Council, 1923; sec. Princeton Hosp., 1924-33. Episcopalian. Clubs: Ivy (Princeton); Princeton (N.Y. City). Author numerous books. Home: Princeton, N.J. †

TOMLINSON, PRIDE, judge; b. Chreoka, Tenn., July 16, 1890; s. Jesse and Augusta (Pride) T.; A.B., U. of the South, 1914; LL.B., George Washington U., 1920; m. Frances Williams Craige, June 25, 1914; children—Pride, Frances Craige. Prin. and supt. Jones High Sch., Lynnville, Tenn., 1914-16; admitted to Tenn. State bar, 1920, and practiced under own name in Columbia, 1920-47; county atty. Maury County, 1921-47; asso. justice Supreme Ct. of Tenn. from 1947. Mem. and chmn. Code of Tenn. Commn., 1945-47. Mem. State Tenn. and Maury County bar assns., Kappa Alpha. Democrat. Episcopalian. Elk. Home: Columbia, Tenn. †

TOMLINSON, WILLIAM WEST, univ. adminstr.; b. Salem, Ohio, Nov. 28, 1893; s. Lindley and Miriam Belle (Lease) T.; A.B., Swarthmore Coll., 1917; L.H.D., Susquehanna U., 1954; LL.D., Gettysburg Coll., 1954, Phila.

Coll. Osteopathy, 1954, Phila. Textile Inst., 1959; m. Rebecca Kirkpatrick Scott, Mar. 6, 1923; children—Jane (Mrs. Jane Myhre), William, Rebecca (Mrs. William L. Lindblom). Exec., Scott Paper Co., Chester, Pa., 1922-37, dir., 1934-37; adminstrv. dir. William W. Tomlinson & Assos., ednl. pub. relations, Phila., 1937-42; sec. Temple U., 1942-44, v.p., 1944-81. Chmn. projects com., mem. exec. and edn. coms. Pres.' People-to-People program; spl. ednl. mission to Germany, 1955-56, 58. Chmn. Christmas Seal campaign, 1956-58; bd. mgrs. Armed Services YMCA, Phila., 1940—, chmn. bd., 1953-58; pres. YMCA Met. Phila., 1964-65; armed services com. nat. council YMCA, now mem. internat. com.; mem. nat. council USO, 1971-72; pres. Phila. Tb and Health Assn., 1959-64; mem. Mayor's Adv. Council on Tb; adv. bd. Am. Coll. Admissions Adv. Center; trustee Eastern Pa. Psychiat. Inst.; hon. trustee Phila. Coll. Textiles and Sci.; vice chmn. Phila. United Charities campaign, 1939; bd. mgrs. Swarthmore Coll., 1944-48; trustee Penn Center Acad., chmn. bd., 1969-73; hon. life trustee Temple U. Served as ensign USNRF, World War I. Recipient Freedoms Found. award, 1951, 65; Russell H. Conwell award Temple U., 1966; Layman of Year award Met. Phila. YMCA, 1968; Outstanding Career citation George Sch. Pa., 1970; Distinguished Service medal Huguenot Soc. Pa., 1974. Mem. Am. Acad. Polit. and Social Sci., Am. Scandinavian Found., Pa. Hist. Soc., World Affairs Council Phila., English Speaking Union, Acad. Polit. Sci., Franklin Inst., Newcomen Soc., Swarthmore Coll. Alumni Assn. (pres. 1935-37), Phi Beta Kappa, Delta Sigma Rho, Delta Upsilon, Pi Gamma Mu, Alpha Phi Omega. Presbyterian. Clubs: Rotary, Merion Cricket. Author: Time Out to Live, 1939; The Flickering Torch, 1942; There is No End, 1952. CBS Script This I Believe, 1952 on Voice of America to 97 countries. Contbr. to radio series, Search For Peace, 1958; nat. award winning series, Anatomy of Freedom, 1961-62. Home: Haverford, Pa. Died Mar. 28, 1981.

TOMPKINS, ELON FARNSWORTH, newspaperman; b. Scott Bar, Calif., Oct. 10, 1887; s. Henry James and Sarah (Davison) T.; Oakland (Calif.) High Sch., 1901-04; m. Pearl Lewis Scharege, Oct. 1931 (dec.); m. 2d, Mary F. McCarthy Couch, Feb., 1956. Began career as reporter on Calif. and New York City newspapers, 1909; with New York Jour.-American, New York City, from 1927, chief editorial writer from 1937. Recipient two Freedom Found. awards, 1949. Mem. Am. Acad. Polit. and Social Sci., Acad. of Polit. Sci. Roman Catholic. Home: Baldwin, L.I., N.Y. †

TOROK, JOHN WILLIAM CHARLES TOCH, bishop; b. Nagykanizsa, Hungary, Mar. 26, 1890; s. Adolphus Toch and Josephine (Fleischner) T.; B.A., Hungarian Royal State Coll., Budapest, 1908, D.C.L., 1914; studied Royal Theol. Acad., Eperjes; m. Mary Agnes Gorsuch, of Westminster, Md., July 11, 1925. Prof. canon law in Coll. of St. Athanasius, at Rome, Italy, 1914-16; chaplain (capt.) in Hungarian Army, 1916-19; sec. to Bishop of Eperjes, 1919-20; imprisoned in Hungary as "politically suspicious" but escaped from prison with assistance of Am. Military Mission; came to U.S. Dec. 1, 1920, naturalized citizen, 1926; asso. prof. of polit. science, St. Stephen Coll., Annandale, N.Y., 1921-22; archdeacon Hungarian (Greek Catholic) Orthodox Ch., Fond du Lac, Wis., 1922-24; missionary bishop from Nov. 1924; v.p. Chicago Evening Post, 1929-30. Republican. Clubs: City (New York); Union (Pittsburgh, Pa.); Baltimore Club, Maryland Club (Baltimore); University (Chicago). Home: Valencia, Pa. †

TORREY, OWEN CATES, ins. exec.; b. Pine Bluff, Ark., June 13, 1889; s. Walter Taylor and Emma Rebekah (Haynes) T.; A.B., Cornell, 1911; m. Emily Gertrude McChesney, Mar. 4, 1920; 2 sons, Owen, Thomas. With South Tex. Comml. Nat. Bank, Houston, 1911-12, F. Herrmann & Co., and successor firm O.G. Orr & Co., marine ins. underwriting, N.Y.C., 1912-17; joined Marine Office of Am., 1919, asst. gen. mgr., 1928-44, gen. mgr. from 1944; co-dir. Asso. Aviation Underwriters; v.p. U.S. Protection & Indemnity Agy., Inc.; pres. S.D. McComb & Co., Inc.; 1st v.p., dir. N.Y. Bd. Underwriters (all N.Y. C.). Served as 2d lt., Mil. Aeronautics, A.S., 1917-18. Mem. Am. Bur. Shipping (mem. bd. mgrs.), Am. Inst. Marine Underwriters (pres., dir.), Assn. Marine Underwriters of U.S., Alpha Tau Omega. Clubs: India House, University (N.Y.C.); American Yacht, Manursing Island (Rye, N.Y.). Home: New York, N.Y. †

TORS, IVAN, producer, dir.; b. Budapest, Hungary, June 12, 1916. Ed., U. Budapest, Fordham U. Pres. Ivan Tors Films; lectr. U. Calif. at, Irvine. Author plays in, Europe, Mimi, Keep Your Distance, Wind Without Rain; now, in U.S.; author: original story Below the Deadlines; collaborator: screen plays Watch the Birdie, Song of Love; author: screen plays In The Good Old Summertime, That Forsyth Woman; co-producer, collaborator: screen play Storm Over Tibet; producer, collaborator: screen plays The Magnetic Monster, The Glass Wall; producers: TV program A-Men; charge prodn.: motion pictures include 49th Man, Ziv Sci Fiction Theatre, Sea Hunt, Man and the Challenge, The Aquanauts, Ripcord, Story; producer: motion pictures include Texas Style, 1967, Riders to the Stars, Underwater Warrior, Flipper, Flipper's New Adventure, Clarence the Cross-Eyed Lion, Around the World Under the Sea, Birds Do It, Namu—The Killer Whale, Africa, Gentle Giant, 1967, Daring Game, 1968, Hello Down There, 1969, Island of the Lost, The Aquarians; story G.O.G; co-producer: story Battle Taxi; producer, dir.: story Zebra in the Kitchen, Rhino; exec. producer: TV shows Elephant Country, Flipper, Daktari, Gentle Ben, Cowboy in Africa, Primus; creator: 3 spls. animal mysteries Where the Lions Rule; producer, dir.: 3 spls. animal mysteries March of the Desert; exec. producer: theatrical feature Escape from Angola; dir.: Galyon and the Abductors; Author: My Life in the Wild. Bd. dirs. Vista Hill Found. Mem. Acad. Motion Picture Arts and Scis., Writers Guild, Dirs. Guild, Explorers Club. Address: Playa Del Rey, Calif. Died June 4, 1983.

TOSDAL, HARRY RUDOLPH, b. Estherville, Ia., Aug. 8, 1889; s. Henry Hendrickson and Anna Annette (Oleson) T.; S.B., St. Olaf Coll., Minn., 1909, hon. LL.D., 1940; studied univs. of Leipzig and Berlin; Ph.D., Harvard, 1915; m. Thora Helseth, July 15, 1925. Instr. economics Mass. Inst. Tech., 1915-16; assistant prof. economics, 1917-18, asso. prof., 1918-19, prof. and head of dept., 1919-20, Boston U.; lecturer on economics, Harvard, 1918-19; dir. student research, and asst. prof. marketing, Harvard Grad. Sch. of Business Administration, 1920-22, prof. marketing, 1922-42; professor of business administration from 1942. Faculty editor Harvard Business Review, 1922-39. Fellow Am. Acad. of Arts and Sciences; mem. Am. Econ. Assn., Am. Acad. Polit. and Social Science, National Fedn. Sales Execs., American Management Association, American Marketing Association, Phi Beta Kappa, Delta Mu Delta, Beta Gamma Sigma; pres. Boston Sales Managers Club, 1932-34; dir. Boston Chamber Commerce, 1938-41. Lutheran. Clubs: Faculty. Author: Problems in Sales Management, 1921, 4th rev. edit., 1939; New England Exporter, 1922; Problems in Export Sales Management, 1922; Principles of Personal Selling, 1925; Introduction to Sales Management, 1933, revised edit., 1950; contbr. to tech. jours. Home: Belmont, Mass. †

TOULOUKIAN, YERAM SARKIS, educator; b. Istanbul, Turkey, Dec. 28, 1920; s. Sarkis Hagop and Zaruhi (Feradian) T.; B.S., Robert Coll., 1939; M.S., Mass. Inst. Tech., 1941; Ph.D., Purdue U., 1946; m. Arsilva Istanbulian, Aug. 8, 1948; children—James Sarkis, Eileen Zabell. Came to U.S., 1939, naturalized, 1952. Dir., Center for Info. and Numerical Data Analysis and Synthesis. Distinguished Atkins prof. engring. Purdue U., 1944-81; vis. prof. thermodynamics Auburn U., 1963-81; cons. to maj. indsl. cos. and U.S. Govt. Dir. OEA, Inc., Des Plaines, Ill. Recipient Gold medal Associatione Termotecnica Italiana, Bologne, Italy, 1968. Registered profl. engr., Ind. Fellow ASME (meml. award heat transfer div.), Am. Inst. Aeros. and Astronautics (asso.). Co-author, editor Thermophysical Properties of Matter-TPRC Data Series, 13 vols., 1970-81. Mem. editorial adv. bd. jours. in field. Home: West Lafayette, Ind. Died June 12, 1981.

TOWLES, OLIVER, prof. French; b. University, Va., Dec. 31, 1887; s. William Beverley and Mary Ellen (Thomson) T.; A.B., U. of Va., 1906; Ph.D., Johns Hopkins U., 1912; m. Cécile Hélène Long, July 10, 1923; children—Marion Thomson Aubert, William Beverley, Eleanor Woodson. Asso. prof. French, U. of N.C., 1909-20, prof., 1920-25; prof. French, New York U., from 1925, also administrative chmn. dept. French, Washington Square Coll. mem. senate, New York U., 1938-41. Served as sergt. inf., later 2d lt. machine gun co., U.S. Army, Nov. 1917-Aug. 1919. Mem. Modern Lang. Assn. America, Linguistic Soc., Modern Humanities Research Assn., Alpha Delta Phi. Democrat. Author: Prepositional Phrases of Asseveration and Adjuration in Old and Middle French, 1920. Contbr. to scholarly journals. Address: New York, N.Y. †

TOWNER, EDWIN EARL, orchestra conductor, composer; b. Latah, Wash., Mar. 3, 1890; s. Thomas Alvin and Ida Jane (Pitt) T.; B.M., Coll. of Pacific, 1910; studied composition and conducting with George W. Chadwick, of Boston, and others; m. Grace Irene Kinney, of San Jose, Calif., Sept. 5, 1911; children—Edwin Earl, Phyllis Jean, Mildred Grace. Lecturer in music, San Jose State Coll., 1912-13; dir. music, Fresno pub. schs., 1913-24; director music San Jose State Teachers' Coll., 1924-26; pres. Calif. Coll. of Music, San Francisco, 1926-28; dir. Fresno Symphony Orchestra, 1916-24; instr. music various summer sessions, U. of Calif. Methodist. Author: Glee and Chorus Book for Male Voices, 1922. Composer songs, choruses, choir, orchestra and organ music, opera, pageant, etc.; mus. dir. and producer in radio from 1928. Home: Chicago, Ill. †

TOWNES, CLAYTON C., lawyer; b. Cleveland, O., Jan. 30, 1887; s. William C. and Kate (Hoyt) T.; LL.B., Western Reserve University, 1911; m. Grace Dix, February 22, 1916; children—Betsy, Jean, Rachel; m. 2d, Mrs. Robert Guyer, 1944. Admitted to Ohio bar, 1911, practiced at Cleveland. Mem. City Council, 1911-24, pres. 1920-24; mayor of Cleveland, 1924-25; del. Rep. Nat. Conv., 1920, 24. Pres. Ohio Mayors' Assn., 1924-25. Mem. Delta Tau Delta, Phi Alpha Delta. Clubs: Union, Bath and Tennis (Palm Beach, Fla.). Home: Palm Beach, Fla. †

TOWNSEND, CHARLES LOUIS, prof. English; b. Hamilton, Ont., Can., Nov. 6, 1887; s. Watton Gibbs and Isabella (Baillarge) T.; A.B., McGill U., 1909; A.M., Harvard, 1912, Ph.D., 1915; studied U. of Leipzig, Ohio State U., U. of Colo., Cornell, U. of Chicago, Oxford U.; m. Margaret Huxtable, Nov. 26, 1915; 1 dau., Audrey. Teacher in Can., 1909-10; instr. French and German, Trinity Coll., N.C., 1913; prof. modern langs., Washington Coll., Chester, Md., 1915-17; prof. same, Southwestern Presbyn. U., 1917, dir. War Issues Course, 1918, prof. English. Episcopalian. Author: The Cultural Method of Teaching French, 1920; The Foes of Shakespeare, 1924; Shakespeare and Woodrow Wilson; Problems on Nine Plays of Shakespeare; Shakespeare the Prophet; Four Paths for American Foreign Policy; What Are Aristophanes?; This Changing World. Translator various German and French works. Home: Memphis, Tenn. †

TOWNSEND, G(EORGE) MARSHALL, university press director; b. Mundo, S.D., Aug. 2, 1916; s. George Marshall and Freda E. (Gilkinson) T.; m. Ruth Helen Killam, July 29, 1951; children: Gregg Marshall, Jane Elizabeth. B.S., Iowa State U., 1941. Sales mgr., prodn. mgr. Iowa State U. Press, Ames, 1945-48, dir. book pub., 1948-63; asst. dir., bus. mgr. U. Chgo. Press, 1963-65; dir. U. Ariz. Press, Tucson, from 1965, mem. faculty Senate, 1976-82, univ. long-range planning com., 1978-80; Mem. Govt. Industry Adv. Bd., 1952. Pres. Iowa TB and Health Assn., 1956, mem. exec. com., 1950-56; hon. chmn. Iowa Christmas Seal, 1962; pres. Ames PTA Council, 1962-63; sec. Mary Greeley Hosp. Assn., 1953-56. Recipient Ames Community Service award, 1952; Service to Univ. and Community award Tucson Trade Bur., 1972. Mem. Assn. Am. Univ. Presses (exec. bd. 1951-52, nat. v.p. 1960-61, treas. 1963-64), Phi Kappa Phi, Sigma Delta Chi. Methodist. Club: Kiwanian (pres. Ames 1954, Tucson 1972). Home: Tucson, Ariz.

TOWNSEND, PAUL HENSON, bus. exec.; b. Clermont, N.J., Dec. 19, 1889; s. Eli and Frances (Dryburgh) T.; m. Clarissa Marie Davis, Sept. 3, 1920; children—Ann (Mrs. Rodney F. Wood), Paul H. Grad., Hotchkiss Sch., 1913; B.A. honoris causa, Yale, 1918. Tchr. grade schs., Cape May County, N.J., 1908-10, 13-14; clk. Huron Portland Cement Co., 1919, supt. plants, ships, 1920-39, gen. mgr., 1938-53, v.p., 1942- 53, dir., 1944-69, pres., 1953-59, chmn. bd., 1959-66; v.p., dir. Detroit Chem. Works, 1937-63; dir. Fed. Motor Truck Co., 1942-49, Nat. Gypsum Co., 1957-64. Dir. adv. com. Great Lakes Protective Assn., 1940-58, mem. exec. com., 1940-57. Served as capt. 315th F.A. U.S. Army, World War 1. Recipient Purple Heart. Mem. Lake Carriers Assn. (dir.), Detroit Bd. Commerce, Detroit Engring. Soc., N.J. Hist. Soc., Detroit Soc. Geneal. Research, Newcomen Soc., Alpha Delta Phi. Mem. Grosse Pointe Meml. Ch. Clubs: Propeller (Detroit), Detroit (Detroit), Univ. (Detroit); Hunters Creek. Home: Grosse Pointe, Mich. †

TRACY, BERRY BRYSON, art museum curator; b. Hampton, Iowa, Sept. 4, 1933; s. James Bendel and Muriel (Bryson) T. B.A., U. Iowa, 1955; student, Attingham Park (Eng.) Adult Coll., 1955. Hist. technician Ill. Dept. Conservation, Springfield, 1957-60; curator decorative arts Newark Mus., 1960-64; asst. curator Am. wing Met. Mus. Art, N.Y.C., 1964-65, asso. curator, 1965-68, curator, 1968-72, curator-in-charge, 1973-81; charge New Am. Wing, 1980-81, now decorative arts cons., Goshen, N.Y.; cons. restoration and furnishing Old Merchants House, N.Y.C., Bull Jackson House, Orange County, N.Y.; re-restoration Boscobel Restoration Inc., 1976-77; mem. spl. fine arts com. Dept. State, Washington, 1971-77, 77-81. Exhbns. and catalogues include Newark Mus, 1963, 19th Century America, Met. Mus. Art, 1970, Federal Furniture and Decorative Arts at Boscobel, 1981. Bd. dirs. Am. Friends of Attingham Inc. Served with USN, 1955-57. Mem. Mus. City N.Y., Nat. Trust Historic Preservation, Newark Mus. Assn. Episcopalian. Home: Goshen, N.Y. Died Oct. 10, 1984.

TRACY, OSGOOD VOSE, chemical company executive; b. Syracuse, N.Y., Oct. 27, 1902; s. James G. and Florida (Seay) T.; B.S., U.S. Naval Acad., 1924; Sc.D., Clarkson Coll. Tech., 1958; m. Pauline Crawford, Oct. 2, 1926; children—Sally (Mrs. Edmond G. Thomas), Mary M., Susan C. (Mrs. Timothy Mellon). Ensign, USN, 1924-25; with Solvay Process Co., 1926-30, Standard Oil Co. La., 1930-39; with Esso Standard Oil Co., N.Y.C., 1939-60, v.p., 1956-59, pres., 1959-60, dir., 1954-60; dir. Enjay Co., Inc., 1948-60, pres., 1953-58; exec. v.p., dir. W.R. Grace & Co., N.Y.C., 1960-67, dir. emeritus, cons., 1968-83; chmn., dir. RAC Corp., 1963-79; dir. Inexco Oil Co. Dir. chem. div. NPA, 1951-52. Trustee Clarkson Coll. Tech., 1958-67. Mem. Am. Chem. Soc., Mfg. Chemists Assn., Soc. Chem. Industry. Clubs: N.Y. Yacht (N.Y.C.); Metropolitan, Army and Navy (Washington); Morris County (N.J.) Golf. Home: Morristown, N.J. Dec. July 3, 1983.

TRACY, ROBERT M., ret. ins. co. exec.; b. Burlington, Vt., May 16, 1907; s. James E. and Mary R. (Long) T.; m. Helen Prouty, Oct. 9, 1937. B.S., U. Vt., 1930. Staff acct. Lybrand, Ross Bros. & Montgomery, N.Y.C., 1930-40; asst. to treas. Nat. Life Ins. Co., 1940-43, asst. treas., 1943, treas., 1944, treas., controller, 1958-59, v.p., controller, 1959-61, sr. v.p., controller, 1961-72; past dir. Nat. Life Ins. Investment Mgmt. Corp.; Past mem. fin. com., treas., dir., mem. exec. com. Asso. Industries Vt. Mem. budget com. United Fund, 1956-57; Trustee U. Vt.; past pres. trustees Aldrich Public Library; chmn. bd. trustees, past chmn. exec. com. Central Vt. Med. Center; treas. Vt. Ednl. and Health Bldgs. Fin. Agy.; past treas. Vt. Library Trustees' Assn.; bd. dirs. Vt. YMCA, Barre City Hosp.; bd. dirs., chmn., past v.p., sec.-treas. Vt. sect. New Eng. Council. Mem. A.I.M. (asso.), Controllers Inst. Am., Barre Brotherhood Assn. (past pres.), Am. Inst.

Accts., N.Y., Vt. socs. C.P.A.s, Inst. Internal Auditors, Am. Acctg. Assn., ALA, SAR. Baptist. Clubs: Mason (Shriner), Lake Mansfield Trout. Home: Barre VT.

TRAER, GLENN W., corp. official; b. Chicago, Ill., Apr. 9, 1889; s. Glenn Wood and Ida (Solberg) T.; Ph.B., Sheffield Scientific Sch. (Yale), 1909; m. Nadyne McNeill, Jan. 16, 1915 (divorced Sept. 1, 1939); children—Milton McNeill, Sylvia; m. 2d, Marjory Stewart Acklin, Jan. 19, 1941. Clerk in law office, 1909-11; asst. mgr. Traer Coal Co., 1911-14; salesman A. B. Leach & Co., 1914-17; mgr. branch office, Minneapolis, 1917-20; partner Lane, Piper & Jaffray, Inc., Minneapolis, 1920-28; chmn. exec. com., and dir. Greyhound Corp., 1928-Sept. 1944; chmn. exec. and finance coms., dir. Truax-Traer Coal Co. from 1928, Central Barge Co., 1938-52 (merged with Miss. Valley Barge Line Co., 1952). First lt., Coast Arty. Corps, World War I. Clubs: Tavern, Chicago, Racquet (Chgo.). Home: Chgo. †

TRAGER, FRANK NEWTON, political science educator; b. N.Y.C., Oct. 9, 1905; s. Benjamin and Eda (Schapiro) T.; m. Helen Gilbson, Oct. 9, 1936. B.S., NYU, 1927, A.M. (Butler fellow philosophy), 1928, Ph.D., 1951; grad. scholar philosophy, Johns Hopkins U., 1928-31. Instr. philosophy Johns Hopkins U., 1928-34; with Resettlement Adminstrn., 1935-36; nat. labor sec. Socialist Party of U.S., 1936-37; program dir. Am. Jewish Com., 1938-43; asst. to pres. NCCJ, 1945-46; program dir. Anti-Defamation League, 1946-51; dir. AID mission, Rangoon, Burma, 1951-53; adminstr., research prof. NYU, 1953-58, prof. internat. affairs, 1958-81; research prof. Navy Postgrad. Sch., 1981—; prof. Nat. War Coll., 1961-63; vis. prof. Yale, 1960-61; dir. studies Nat. Strategy Info. Center, 1966—; Cons. RAND Corp., Hudson Inst.; govt., industry and founds. Mem. adv. panel East Asian and Pacific Affairs, Dept. State, 1966-69; sec.-treas. Bur. Intercultural Edn., 1938-53; chmn. Am. Asian Ednl. Exchange. Editor, author: (with others) Burma, 3 vols., 1956, Burma: Japanese Military, Selected Documents, 1941-45, 1971, (with William Henderson) Communist China, 1949-69, A Twenty Year Appraisal, 1970; author: (with William Henderson) Building a Welfare State in Burma, rev. edit., 1958, (with others) Marxism in Southeast Asia, A Study of Four Countries, 1959, Furnivall of Burma: An Annotated Bibliography, 1963, Why Viet Nam? , 1968, Burma, From Kingdom to Republic, a Historical and Political Analysis, 1966, National Security and American Society: Theory, Process and Policy, 1973, (with William J. Koenig) Burmese Sit-Tans 1764-1862: Records of Rural Life and Administration, 1979; Editor: Annotated Bibliography of Burma, 1971, Japanese and Chinese Language Sources on Burma: An Annotated Bibliography, 1957, (with Klaus Knorr) Economics Issues and National Security, 1977, Oil, Divestiture and National Security, 1976; Contbr. articles and revs. to publs., chpts. to books.; Mem. editorial bd.: Asian Affairs, Asian Survey, Armed Forces and Society; chmn. editorial bd.: (with Klaus Knorr) Strategy Research Series. Bd. dirs., mem. editorial bd. Fgn. Policy Research Inst. Served with USAAF, 1943-45. Fellow Center Internat. Studies, Mass. Inst. Tech., 1953-54; Carnegie Research fellow Council Fgn. Relations, 1957-58. Mem. Am. Polit. Sci. Assn., Assn. Asian Studies (dir., acting treas.), Asia Soc. (exec. com. Burma council), Council Fgn. Relations, Royal Siam Soc., Burma Research Soc. Home: Carmel, Calif. Died Aug. 26, 1984.

TRAHER, WILLIAM HENRY, artist, mural painter; b. Rock Springs, Wyo., Apr. 6, 1908; s. Stephen John and Catherine Laura (Utzinger) T.; student Nat. Acad. Design, N.Y.C., 1930-33, Sch. Fine Arts, Yale, 1938-39; m. Frances Manette White, June 14, 1942; children—Anita, Elissa, Steven. Exhibited woodcuts State Hist. Mus., Denver, 1934-35; art dir. Philip H. Gray, Inc., advt., 1945-47; 1952; sr. staff artist Denver Mus. Natural History, completing over 26,000 square feet of super-real life size diarama backgrounds, 1954-76; other major works include Traher Wilderness murals Columbia Savs. & Loan Assn., Pueblo, Colo., 1967, Four Faces of the West paintings (7 X 10 feet each) Jefferson Nat. Expansion Meml., under the Arch, St. Louis, 1970. Bd. dirs. Floyd Wilson Wilderness Edn. Found., Denver Art Mus., 1960-62. Served with USAAF, 1942-46; PTO. Mem. Denver Artists Guild (hon. life, past pres.). Clubs: Jackson Color Camera, Denver Figure Skating (a founder, soloist). Home: Denver, Colo. Died Dec. 13, 1984; buried Buffalo Creek, Colo.

TRASK, OZELL MILLER, judge; b. Wakita, Okla., July 4, 1909; s. Ozell and Nina (Miller) T.; A.B., magna cum laude, Washburn Coll., 1931; LL.B., Harvard, 1934; m. Barbara Draper, Oct. 2, 1939 (dec. 1985); children—Deborah, Melinda. Admitted to Kan., Mo. bars, 1934, Ariz. bar, 1940; mem. firm Jennings, Strouss, Salmon & Trask, Phoenix; now judge U.S. Ct. Appeals, 9th Circuit, Phoenix. Bd. dirs. Am. Cancer Soc., dir., past pres. Ariz. div.; pres. bd. dirs. Phoenix YMCA; trustee Phoenix Art Mus. Mem Am., Ariz., Maricopa County bar assns., State Bar Ariz. (past chmn. com. examinations and admissions), Phoenix C. of C. (past pres., dir.), Phi Delta Theta Conglist, (chmn. cabinet). Clubs: Arizona (past pres., dir.), Paradise Valley Country. Home: Phoenix, Ariz. Died May 5, 1984.

TRAUBE, SHEPARD, theatrical producer and dir.; b. Malden, Mass., Feb. 27, 1907; s. William and Helen (Newhouse) T.; m. Mildred Gilbert, June 29, 1935; children—Victoria, Elizabeth. Student, U. Pa., 1925-26; B.S., N.Y. U., 1929. Producer, dir.: Precedent, 1931, No More Frontier, 1932, A Thousand Summers, 1933, Angel Street, 1941, revival, 1976, The Patriots, 1942, The Gioconda Smile, 1950, Time Out for Ginger, 1952, The Girl in Pink Tights, 1952, Holiday for Lovers, 1957, Monique, 1957, Children of the Wind, 1973; Author: Glory Road, 1935, So You Want To Go into the Theatre, 1936; Contbr. articles to profl. jours. Served to maj. U.S. Army, 1943-46. Voted Best Dir. N.Y. Drama Critics, 1942; recipient Sidney Howard prize for Winter Soldiers Playwrights Co., 1942. Mem. Soc. Stage Dirs. and Choreographers (past pres.), League N.Y. Theatres (gov. 1954-83), Dirs. Guild Am. Democrat. Club: Beverly Hills Tennis. Home: New York, N.Y. Died July 23, 1983.

TRAUTMAN, RAY L., educator, ret. army officer; b. Mowrystown, Ohio, July 22, 1907; s. George H. and Bertha (Parrot) T.; children—Eric Ray, Roger Scot. B.S., U. Ky., 1931, M.S., 1932; B.S. in L.S, Columbia U., 1940. Mgr. bookstore, Lexington, Ky., 1932, San Antonio, 1933-34; dist. ednl. adviser CCC, Fort Thomas, Ky., 1935-39; with Enoch Pratt Free Library, Balt., 1940; v.p., gen. mgr. Omnibook, Inc., N.Y.C., 1945-48; prof. library service Columbia U., 1948-76; cons. MBA Communications, Inc., N.Y.C., 1978-79; cons. instn. libraries, N.Y. State; cons. Job Corps, Office Econ. Opportunity, Nat. Accreditation Council for Agys.; Serving Blind, Corning Glass Works Found. on Libraries St. Thomas Aquinas Coll.; dir. Swinburne Press. Author: History of School Library Service Columbia University, 1954; co-author: Technical Dictionary of Librarianship (Spanish-English), Mexico, 1965, A Plan to Provide Library Services to People in N.Y. State Institutions, 1965, Standards for Reading Materials for Blind and Physically Handicapped, 1970; Cons. editor 20 books Individualized Reading series, McGraw-Hill, 1966. Trustee Yonkers Pub. Library, 1947-58, pres., 1953-54; adviser spl. services div. War Dept.; Bd. dirs. Wilderness Resources Center. Served as flying cadet U.S. Air Corps, 1933; 1st lt. to col. U.S. Army, 1940-46; war dept. observer 1944-45, ETO; comdg. officer Spl. Services Unit Tng. Center 1949-62, N.Y.C. Awarded Legion of Merit, Conspicuous Service Cross. Home: Columbia, SC.

TRAVER, LEWIS B(ENZON), book seller; b. Trenton, N.J., June 27, 1890; s. Clayton L. and Katherine (Benzon) T.; student Lawrenceville Prep. Sch., 1904-07, Carnegie Inst. Tech., 1908-11; m. Elizabeth B. Callear, Oct. 14, 1915; children—M. Callear, Virginia (Mrs. W. A. Haney). Book seller Traver's Book Store, Trenton, from 1922. Mem. Am. Booksellers Assn. (dir. 1929-36, 38-52, pres. 1936-37, chmn. bd. 1938-39, 1st v.p. 1952-54), Trenton (pres. 1940-42), N.J. hist. socs., Trenton C. of C., Sigma Nu. Mason (past master; Shriner). Club: Trenton Rotary (dir.). Home: Titusville, N.J. †

TRAVIS, MERLE ROBERT, country music singer, songwriter; b. Rosewood, Ky., Nov. 29, 1917; s. William Robert and Laura Etta (Latham) T.; children—Patricia, Chelene, Rebecka. Student public sch., Muhlenburg County, Ky. Debut with, Knox County Knockabouts, Sta. WGBF, Evansville, Ind., 1937-38, appeared with, Tennessee Tomcats, Sta. WGBF, 1938; appeared in road shows with, Clayton McMichen's Georgia Wildcats, 1939, Drifting Pioneers, 1939-42; on program Hometown Jamboree, Hollywood, Calif., 1944-50, Town Hall Party, Hollywood, 1953-59, Hollywood Barndance, CBS, 1945-47, Renfro Valley (Ky.) Barndance, 1938-39, Gene Autry's Melody Ranch, CBS Radio, Hollywood, 1954-58, Grand Ole Opry, Nashville, 1960's, also numerous other TV and radio appearances; master of ceremonies various shows; rec. artist: songs written include Sixteen Tons, 1945, Smoke, Smoke, Smoke, 1947, Bayou Baby, 1948, Sweet Temptation, 1949; others. Served with USMC, 1942-43. Named to Songwriters Hall of Fame, 1970; Named to Country Music Hall of Fame, Nashville, 1977; Named to Gibson Guitar Hall of Fame, 1979; recipient 7 Gold Records Capitol Records, 1945-68, 12 Broadcast Music, Inc. awards, 1947-69, Country Music Pioneer award, 1979. Mem. AFTRA, Screen Actors Guild, Musicians Union, Nashville Assn. Musicians, Nat. Acad. Rec. Arts and Scis. (Grammy award 1976), Country Music Assn., Writers Guild Am., Acad. Country Music. Designer solid body guitar, built first by Paul A. Bigsby. Died Oct. 20, 1983.*

TRAYNOR, ROGER JOHN, educator, former judge; b. Park City, Utah, Feb. 12, 1900; s. Felix and Elizabeth (O'Hagan) T.; A.B., U. Calif., 1923, J.D., 1927, Ph.D., 1927, LL.D., 1958; LL.D., U. Chgo., 1960, U. Utah, 1963, Boston Coll., 1968; m. Madeleine Lackmann, August 23, 1933; children—Michael, Joseph, Stephen (dec.). Instr. polit. sci. U. Calif.-Berkeley, 1926-29, prof. law, 1929-40; acting dean, 1939; dep. atty. gen. Calif., 1940; assoc. justice Supreme Ct. Calif., 1940-64, chief justice, 1964-70; prof. law U. Va., U. Colo., U. Utah, Hastings Coll. Law, San Francisco, from 1970; Goodhart prof. legal sci. Cambridge (Eng.) U., 1974-75. Chmn. Nat. News Council, 1973-74. Cons. expert U.S. Treasury Dept., 1937-40; cons. tax counsel State Bd. Equalization Calif., 1932-40; lectr. Inst. Am. Studies, Salzburg, summer, 1956. Mem. Am. Law Inst. (mem. council), Am. Acad. Arts and Scis., Phi Beta Kappa, Order of Coif. Home: Berkeley, Calif. Dec. May 14, 1983.

TRAYWICK, LELAND ELDRIDGE, business administration educator, university chancellor; b. Okmulgee, Okla., June 7, 1915; s. Nathaniel Eldridge and Hattie Estelle (Lel) T.; m. Harriet Juliet Nordhem, Sept. 12, 1942; children: Eric Leland, Harriet Ingeborg. A.A., Okmulgee Jr. Coll., 1934; B.A., U. Mo., 1936, M.A., 1939; Ph.D., U. Ill., 1942. Instr., research asst. Sloan Found. Consumer Edn., Stephens Coll., Columbia, Mo., 1937-39; lectr. econs. U. Ill., Urbana, 1946; asst. prof. Western Res. U., Cleve., 1946-47; asst. prof. Mich. State U., East Lansing, 1947-48, asso. prof., 1948-57, prof., 1957-60, asst. dean, 1957-60; pres. S.W. Mo. State Coll., Springfield, 1961-64, U. Omaha, 1965-67; chancellor, prof. bus. adminstrn., dir. Bur. Bus. Research, Coll. William and Mary, Williamsburg, Va., from 1967. Author: (with W. Adams) Readings in Economics, 1948, (with G. Soule) Economics, 1961, Business Ups and Downs, 1961; contbr. articles to profl. jours. Trustee Va. Council Econ. Edn., from 1969; cons. Busch Gardens, 1976-77, Kings Dominion, 1976-78; advisor to Mo. gov., 1961-64; mem. Mich. Gov.'s Council Econ. Advisers, 1954-60, mem. adv. bd. edn. to Nebr. gov., 1965-67, mem. adv. bd. to Va. govs., from 1975; bd. dirs. Joslyn Art Mus., 1965-67, Omaha chpt. NCCJ, 1966-67; mem. econ. adv. bd. Gov. Va., from 1975. Served to 1st lt., Ordnance Corps AUS, 1943-46. Decorated Army Commendation medal. Mem. Am. Econ. Assn., Am. Statis. Assn., Va. Acad. Sci., Order Artus, Phi Kappa Phi, Beta Gamma Sigma, Omicron Delta Kappa, Tau Kappa Alpha, Kappa Delta Pi, Pi Delta Kappa, Lambda Chi Alpha. Episcopalian. Club: Masons (32 deg.). Home: Williamsburg, VA.

TREBILCOCK, PAUL, portrait painter; b. Chgo., Feb. 13, 1902; s. William Paul and Adele Christine (Christensen) T.; grad. Oak Park and River Forest High Sch., 1920; student U. Ill., 1920-22, Art Inst. Chgo., 1922-24; m. Amaylia Chiarina Castaldo, Apr. 8, 1929; children—William Anthony, Adrienne Claire. Principal works: portraits of notable persons, including: President Franklin D. Roosevelt, Governor Albert A. Ritchie, Mrs. Reginald Vanderbilt, Viscountess Furness, Harold W. Dodds, Stephen Francis Voorhees, Charles H. Warren, Edward Shelton, Willard C. Rappleye, Charles Proctor Cooper, Dr. William G. MacCallum, Dr. Edwards A. Park, Dr. George E. Bennett, Dr. E.V. McCollum, David Kinley, George Eastman, Rush Rhees, Harvie Branscomb, Walter Dill Scott, Irving S. Cutter, George I. Haight, Oliver C. Carmichael, Francis Henry Taylor, Bishop Horace W. B. Donegan, Benjamin F. Fairless, Mrs. Benjamin F. Fairless, Wilfred S. Sykes, Cleo F. Craig, Walter S. Franklin, William B. Storey, Carle C. Conway, K. S. Adams, Harrison Jones, Charles Hayden, Lucius M. Boomer, George O. May, Harold H. Helm, Clarence C. Michalis, James E. Gowan, J. Hamilton Cheston, Edwin S.S. Sutherland, Alfred H. Cosden, C. Brewster Rhoads, others. Recipient Martin B. Cahn prize, 1925, William Randolph Hearst prize, 1926, Frank G. Logan medal and prize, 1928, William H. French gold medal, 1929, Municipal Art League Portrait prize, 1937 (all recieved at Chicago Art Inst.), first prize $1,000 Chicago Galleries Assn., 1926, 1st Hallgarten prize NAD, N.Y., 1931; Newport (R.I.) Art Assn. prize. Mem. NAD. Clubs: Arts, Tavern, Cliff Dwellers (Chgo.); Chelsea Arts (London); Century Assn. (N.Y.C.). Home: New York, N.Y. Died Apr. 8, 1981.

TRELOGAN, HARRY CHESTER, cons. agrl. economist and statistician; b. Versailles, Pa., Dec. 29, 1908; s. Charles Henry and Annie May (Dowie) T.; m. Ruth Grytbak, June 21, 1937; children—Robert Martin, Peter Dowie, Susan Lynn (dec.), Jeanne Karen (Ms. J.K. Trelogan-Nutter). B.S., W.Va. U., 1931; M.S., U. Minn., 1933, Ph.D., 1938. Mgr. Kanawha Valley Milk Producers Assn., 1931; instr. agrl. mktg. U. Minn., 1936-38; economist FCA, 1939-41, Dept. Agr., 1942; chief order adminstrn. div. dairy and poultry br. War Food Adminstrn., 1943-44; chief research and analysis div. dairy br. Dept. Agr., 1945-46; asst. adminstr. Dept. Agr. (Research and Mktg. Act), 1947-49, Dept. Agr. (Agrl. Research Adminstrn.), 1950-53; dir. mktg. research Agrl. Mktg. Service, 1954-59, asst. adminstr. agrl. mktg. service, 1960-61, adminstr. statis. reporting service, 1961-75; mem. faculty U.S. Dept. Agr. Grad. Sch., from 1948, mem. gen. adminstrv. bd., 1965-72, mem. soc. sci. com., 1956-76, chmn., 1972-76; cons. Nat. Agrl. Mktg. Workshop, 1949-56; U.S. del. 13th Internat. Dairy Congress, The Hague, 1952. Author: (with Warren C. Waite) Agricultural Market Prices, 1951; Contbr. (with Warren C. Waite) to textbooks, standard and year books. Recipient Outstanding Achievement award U. Minn., 1964; superior service award Dept. Agr., 1952; Distinguished Service award, 1960; Fed. Land Banks' 50th Anniversary Commemorative medal, 1967; Soc. Am. Florists Research/Edn. award, 1971; Distinguished Service plaque Nat. Assn. State Depts. Agr., 1975; others. Fellow Am. Agrl. Econs. Assn., Am. Statis. Assn., AAAS; mem. Am. Agrl. Econ. Assn. (pres. 1957-58), Am. Econ. Assn., Am. Dairy Sci. Assn., Agrl. Research Inst. (gov. bd. 1957-58), Internat. Assn. Agrl. Economists (hon. life), Internat. Statis. Inst., Alpha Zeta, Gamma Sigma Delta, Gamma Alpha, Alpha Gamma Rho (Outstanding Alumni award 1967). Clubs: Cosmos; Nat. Economists (Washington). Home: Arlington, Va. Died Feb. 8, 1985; buried National Memorial Park, Falls Church, Va.

TRIMMER, JOHN DEZENDORF, educator, physicist; b. Washington, Sept. 19, 1907; s. Daniel K. and Louise (Dezendorf) T.; A.B., Elizabethtown Coll., 1926, Sc.D.

(hon.), 1953; M.S. in Physics and Math., Pa. State U., 1933; Ph.D. in Physics, U. Mich., 1936; m. Mildred L. Ebersole, Dec. 31, 1930; children—Daniel Ross, Maud Alice. High sch. tchr., 1927-32; tchr., research aero. engring. dept. Mass. Inst. Tech., 1937-41, underwater sound research, 1941-43; engaged in electro-magnetic isotope separation, Oak Ridge, 1943-46; prof. physics U. Tenn., 1946-57, also cons. automatic control nuclear reactors and wind tunnels; prof. physics, head dept. U. Mass., 1957-63, prof. physics, 1963-66; prof., head dept. physics Washington Coll., 1966-73; spl. research in acoustics, instrumentation, cybernetics, physics ionized fluids. Fellow A.A.A.S.; mem. Am. Phys. Soc., Acoustical Soc. Am. Conglist. Author: Response of Physical Systems, 1950; also articles. Home: Millington, Md. Died Jan. 24, 1983.

TRIPLETT, WILLIAM HANSFORD, physician; b. Upper Glade, W.Va., Oct. 6, 1887; s. Hedgman Sinnett and Alice Blanche (Given) T.; M.D., Univ. of Md., 1911; m. Emma Arther, June 14, 1916. Interne Miners Hospital No. 2, McKendree, W.Va., 1911-12; gen. practice in Southern W.Va., 1912-17, Baltimore, Md., 1919-40; asst. in medicine Univ. of Md. Med. Sch., 1926-40, principles of medicine, Dental Sch., 1930-40; retired Apr. 27, 1945. Served in Reserve Corps, Med. Dept., U.S. Army, 1921-36; an organizer 104th med. regiment, Md. Nat. Guard. exec. officer, 1940-41; commanding officer Feb. 7, 1941; surgeon 29th inf. div., Feb. 1941-Mar, 1943; retired as col. med. corps, A.U.S., because of physical disability. Mem. Assn. Mil. Surgeons (4th vice pres.), local and nat. med. socs. Democrat. Presbyterian. Mason. Home: Baltimore, Md. Deceased.

TRIPPET, BYRON KIGHTLY, association executive; b. Princeton, Ind., Sept. 21, 1908; s. Sanford and Edith (Kightly) T.; B.A., Wabash Coll., 1930; postgrad. Geneva (Switzerland) Inst. Internat. Studies, 1930-31; B.A., Oxford (Eng.) U., 1934, M.A., 1939; LL.D., Ind. U., 1962; L.H.D., Wabash Coll., 1955, DePauw U., 1957, Valparaiso U., 1958; m. Dorothy Clark O'Neall, June 21, 1936 (div. July, 1967); 1 stepson, David C.; m. 2d, Lorenza Galdeano Turillas, Nov. 8, 1968. Mem. faculty and adminstrn., Wabash Coll., 1935-65, dean coll., prof. history, 1942-55, pres., 1955-65; v.p. U. Americas, Mexico City, 1965-66, cons., 1966-68, pres., 1973-75; pres. Independent Coll. Funds Am., N.Y.C., 1968-73; dir. Lilly Endowment Fund, 1973-82; dir. Princeton Telephone Co. Coll. examiner N. Central Assn. Colls. and Secondary Schs., 1948-54; mem. Rhodes Scholar Selection Com., Great Lakes dist., 1946-64; mem. exec. com., trustee United Student Aid Funds, Inc., 1968—; mem. coll. self study com. Ford Found., 1952-54. Chmn. bd. dirs. Independent Coll. Funds Am., Inc., 1963; bd. dirs. Tuition Exchange Inc., 1957-61, Research Corp., N.Y.C., 1959-62. Served to lt. comdr. USNR, 1942-46. Rhodes scholar, 1931-34. Mem. Am. Conf. Acad. Deans (chmn. 1955), Assn. Am. Colls. (chmn. commn. liberal edn. 1958-61), Am. Council Edn. (sec. 1962-63), Ind. Hist. Soc., Phi Beta Kappa (nat. lectr. panel 1955-60), Beta Theta Pi. Club: University (N.Y.C.). Home: Princeton, Ind. Died Aug. 4, 1982.

TROMBLY, ALBERT EDMUND, author; b. Chazy, Clinton County, N.Y., Aug. 21, 1888; s. Peter and Marie Camille (Roberge) T.; grad. State Normal Sch., Worcester, Mass., 1910; B.A., Harvard, 1913; M.A., U. of Pa., 1915; m. Mary Elizabeth O'Connor, Oct. 4, 1913 (died Jan. 10, 1937); children—Lawrence, Alberta, Jeanne (dec.); m. 2d, Thelma Woodhouse, June 4, 1938. Instr. Romance Langs., U. of Pa., 1913-18; adj. prof. same, U. of Tex., 1918-22; actg. prof. same, U. of Mo., 1922, prof. Romance langs., 1923-26, prof. French and Italian from 1926. Mem. Am. Assn. Univ. Profs. Author: (poems) Masque of American Drama, 1917; North of the Rio Grande, 1936; Santa Fe Santa Fe, 1941; Acorns and Apples, 1942; Grain of Sand, 1944 (prose) Rossetti the Poet, 1921; Vachel Lindsay Adventurer, 1929. Editor: The Rhymers, 1917. Home: Columbia, Mo. †

TROUPE, RALPH ANDERSON, educator; b. Darby, Pa., Apr. 21, 1916; s. Ralph S. and Janet (Anderson) T.; B.S., Drexel Inst. Tech., 1939; M.S., Va. Poly. Inst., 1940; Ph.D., U. Tex., 1949; m. Ada Giunta, Feb. 3, 1951; children—Janet A., Barbara J., Laurel A., Ralph S. Instr. Northeastern U., Boston, 1940-43, asso. prof., 1946-47, prof., 1954-84, chmn. chem. engring. dept., 1962-84; supr., prodn. engr. synthetic div. Gen. Tire & Rubber Co. Baytown, Tex., 1943-46; asst. prof. U. Tex., 1949; asso. prof. U. Louisville, 1949-50; tech. supt. Goodyear Synthetic Rubber Corp., Akron, O., 1950-54; lectr. in field, participant internat. seminars. Year-in-Industry prof. duPont, 1961-62; Fulbright lectr. Seville, Spain, 1967-68. Named Outstanding Grad., Drexel Inst. Tech., 1961. Fellow Am. Inst. Chem. Engrs. (chmn. research com. 1975, past local chmn., treas.), mem. Am. Chem. Soc., Nat. Assn. Corrosion Engrs., Sigma Xi, Tau Beta Pi, Phi Kappa Phi, Omega Chi Epsilon. Contbr. articles to profl. jours. Home: Wakefield, Mass. Died Aug. 8, 1984.

TROUTMAN, ROBERT BATTEY, lawyer; b. Rome, Ga., Nov. 26, 1890; s. Marcellus L. and Elizabeth (Battey) T.; A.B., U. Ga., 1911; LL.B., Columbia, 1914; m. Nellie Hood Ridley, Apr. 24, 1917; children—Robert B. Eleanor (Mrs. Thomas V. Bockman). Admitted to Ga. bar, 1914, since practiced in Atlanta; mem. firm King & Spalding, and predecessors firms, from 1914. Ga. chmn. Civil Def., 1942-43; mem. (region 4) War Labor Bd., 1943-45. Served as maj., inf., AUS, 1917-19. Fellow Am. Coll. Trial Lawyers; mem. Am. Judicature Soc. (dir.), Jud. Council of Ga., Am. (ho. dels.), Ga. (pres. 1947), Atlanta (pres. 1927) bar assns., Assn. Bar City of N.Y., Atlanta C. of C., Am. Law Inst., U. Ga. Alumni Assn. (trustee Alumni Found., past pres. assn.), Am. Legion, Mil. Order World Wars, Phi Delta Theta, Phi Delta Phi, Phi Beta Kappa. Democrat. Roman Catholic. Clubs: Capital City, Piedmont Driving, Lawyers, Rotary (Atlanta). Editor-in-chief Columbia Law Rev., 1913-14. Home: Atlanta, GA. †

TRUESWELL, RICHARD WILLIAM, educator, indsl. engr.; b. Newark, Oct. 12, 1929; s. Richard and Mary (Sudsbear) T.; m. Wilma Anita Morgan, June 27, 1953; children—Wilma Mary, Richard Douglas, William James, John Charles. M.E., Stevens Inst. Tech., 1952; M.S. in Indsl. Mgmt, 1958; Ph.D. in Indsl. Engring, Northwestern U., 1964. Registered profl. engr., Mass. Mfg. engr. Westinghouse Electric Corp., Pitts., Bath, N.Y., 1954-56; instr. Stevens Inst. Tech., Hoboken, N.J., 1957-58; instr. U. Mass., Amherst, 1958-59, asst. prof., 1959-63, asso. prof., 1963-65, chmn. indsl. engring., program, 1965-66, prof., head dept. indsl. engring., 1966-75, prof., from 1975; Joseph Lucas vis. prof. U. Birmingham, Eng., 1971-72; cons. Savage Arms Corp., So. Hadley Electric Light Dept., Pro-Phy-Lac-Tic Brush Co., Asso. Data Processing Co., Nonotuck Mfg. Co. Editor: Collection Mgmt. quar. jour; Contbr. articles to profl. jours. Served to 1st lt. USAF, 1952-54; col. Res. Mem. Am. Soc. Mech. Engrs., Am. Inst. Indsl. Engrs., Am. Soc. Engring. Edn., Operations Research Soc. Am., ALA, Inst. Mgmt. Scis., Am. Soc. for Information Scis., Sigma Xi, Alpha Pi Mu (nat. pres. 1970-72). Home: Hadley, Mass.

TRUFFAUT, FRANCOIS, motion picture dir.; b. Paris, France, Feb. 6, 1932; s. Rol and Janine (de Monferr) T.; m. Madeleine Morgenstern, Oct. 29, 1957 (div.); children—Laura, Eva. Reporter, motion picture critic Movie Jour. and Arts, 1954-58, dir. motion pictures, 1957—, producer, 1961-84. Prodns. include Les Mistons, 1958, Les 400 Coups, 1959, Tirez sur le Pianiste, 1960, L'Amour a 20 ans, 1962, Jules and Jim, 1961, La Peau Douce, 1963, Fahrenheit 451, 1966, La Mariée était en Noir, 1967, Baisers Voles, 1968, La Sirène du Mississippi, 1969, L'Enfant Sauvage, 1969, Domicile Conjugal, 1970, Les Deux Anglaises et le Continent, 1971, Une Belle Fille Comme Moi (Such a Gorgeous Kid Like Me), 1972, La Nuit Américaine, (Day for Night), 1972-73, L'Histoire d'Adèle H. (The Story of Adele H.), 1975, L'Argent de Poche (Small Change), 1975-76, L'Homme qui aimait les Femmes (The Man Who Loved Women), 1976-77, La Chambre Verte (The Green Room), 1977-78, L'Amour en Fuite (Love on the Run), 1978-79, Le Dernier Metro (The Last Metro), 1980, La Femme d'à coté (The Woman Next Door), 1981; appeared: in film Close Encounters of the Third Kind, 1977; dir., appeared in: in film The Green Room, 1979 (Recipient Cannes Film Festival prize for Les 400 Coups 1959, best dir. and best film award for Day for Night, N.Y. Film Critics 1973, Oscar award for best fgn. lang. film Am. Acad. Motion Picture Arts and Scis. 1974); Author: in film Le Cinema Selon Hitchcock, 1966, Les Aventures d'Antoine Doinel, 1970, La Nuit Americaine et le Journal de Fahrenheit, 1974, Les Films de Ma Vie, 1975, L'Argent de Poche, 1976, L'Homme qui aimait les Femmes, 1977. Home: France. Died Oct. 21, 1984.*

TRUMAN, BESS WALLACE (MRS. HARRY S. TRUMAN), wife of former president U.S.: b. Independence, Mo., Feb. 13, 1885; grad. high sch.; student Barstow Sch. for Girls, Kansas City, Mo.; m. Harry S. Truman, June 28, 1919 (dec. Dec. 26, 1972); 1 child, Mary Margaret (Mrs. E. Clifton Daniel, Jr.). Democrat. Episcopalian. Home: Independence, Mo. Dec. Oct. 18, 1982.

TRUMP, GUY WINSTON, assn. exec.; b. Churubusco, Ind., Mar. 30, 1918; s. Lewis Orl and Romalie (Hapner) T.; m. Virginia Lucille Stillwaugh, Nov. 22, 1941; children—Kristan, Virginia, Kathryn. B.B.A., Tulane U., 1947, M.B.A., 1948; Ph.D., State U. Iowa, 1951. Prof., chmn. dept. bus. Stephen F. Austin State Coll., Nacogdoches, Tex., 1950-52; prof., chmn. dept. bus. So. Ill. U., Carbondale, 1952-55; dean U.S. Mcht. Marine Acad., 1955-59, Emory U. Sch. Bus. Adminstrn., 1959-65; v.p. edn. Am. Inst. C.P.A.'s, N.Y.C., 1965-78, ret., 1978. Served with USNR, 1941-46. Mem. La. Soc. C.P.A.'s, Nat. Assn. Watch and Clock Collectors. Home: Decatur, Ga. Died Nov. 18, 1984.

TRUMP, JOHN GEORGE, engr.; b. N.Y.C., Aug. 21, 1907; s. Frederick and Elizabeth (Christ) T.; E.E., Poly. Inst. Bklyn., 1929; M.A., Columbia, 1931; D.Sc., Mass. Inst. Tech., 1933; m. Elora Gordon Sauerbrun, May 25, 1935; children—John Gordon, Christine Elora, Karen Elizabeth. Instr. elec. engring. Poly. Inst. Bklyn., 1929-31; research asso. Mass. Inst. Tech., 1933-36, asst. prof., 1936-41, asso. prof. elec. engring., 1941-52, prof. elec. engring., 1952-73; sec. microwave com. Nat. Def. Research Com., 1940-42; dir. Brit. Br. Radiation Lab., Gt. Malverne, Eng., 1944-45, asst. dir. Radiation Lab., 1945; chmn. bd. Electronized Chems. Corp., 1963-78, High Voltage Power Corp., 1967-72; dir., tech. dir. High Voltage Engring. Corp., 1947-85. Chmn. bd. trustees Lahey Clinic Found., 1974-85. Decorated King's medal (Eng.), 1946, Presdl. citation, 1946. Fellow Am. Phys. Soc., I.E.E.E. (Lamme medal 1961, Power-Life award 1973), Am. Acad. Arts and Sci., Am. Coll. Radiology (hon., Gold medal 1982, Nat. Medal of Sci. 1983), mem. New Eng. Roentgen Ray Soc., Nat. Acad. Engring., Am. Radium Soc. Contbr. sci. papers to profl. lit. Home: Winchester, Mass. Died Feb. 21, 1985.

TRUSLOW, JOHN BACCHUS, physician; b. Bklyn., Aug. 28, 1912; s. Walter and Josephine Stearns (Bacchus) T.; student Polytechnic Prep. Country Day Sch., Bklyn., 1925-30; A.B., Yale, 1934; M.D., Harvard, 1939; m. Georgia Anne Hight, Dec. 7, 1940; children—Sarah Anne, Robert Dickinson. Intern, Springfield (Mass.) Hosp., 1940-41; research in X-ray pelvimetry N.Y. Acad. Medicine, 1939; asst. dean grad. medicine Coll. Phys. and Surg. Columbia, 1946-51; dean Sch. Medicine, prof. adminstrv. medicine Med. Coll. Va., 1951-56, exec. dean dir., prof. adminstrv. medicine Med. Br., U. Tex. at Galveston, 1956-64; study dir. N.C. Med. Center Study Commn., 1964-65, Maine Legis. Research Com. Med. Sch. Feasibility Study, 1965-66; cons. med. edn. U. Del., 1966-69; adviser edn. and planning in health field, 1969-83; research dir. So. Maine Comprehensive Health Assn., 1970-76; staff cons. Maine Health Planning and Devel. Agy., 1976-83. Mem. Christian med. council Nat. Council Chs., 1966-72. Mem. adv. staff U.S. Senate, sub-com. on wartime health and edn. Com. on Edn. and Labor, 78th Congress, 1944-45. Served from lt. (j.g.) to comdr. USN, 1941-46; on spl. duty Office Surgeon Gen., 1943-46. Mem. adv. staff U.S. Senate, Fellow N.Y. Acad. Medicine, A.C.P.; mem. Royal Soc. Medicine London (affiliate), Nu Sigma Nu. Home: Biddeford, Maine. Died Mar. 11, 1983.

TRYON, HENRY HARRINGTON, forester; b. Rumford, R.I., June 7, 1888; s. James Seymour and Mary (Harrington) T.; student Milton (Mass.) Acad., 1906-08; A.B., Harvard, 1912, M.F., 1913; m. Margaret Ramsay, Dec. 28, 1915; children—Ramsay Harrington (dec.), Katharine, James Seymour. Began as forester, 1907; cruiser, New Eng., Can., 1910-15; mem. faculty, N.Y. State Forestry Coll., 1915-17; Air Service, U.S. Army, 1918; engr. with James W. Sewall, Washington, D.C., 1919-24; extension forester for S.C., 1924-27; dir. Black Rock Forest, N.Y., 1927-49. Mem. A.A.A.S., Soc. Am. Foresters, Internat. Inst. for Forest Research, Ecol. Soc., Soc. of Foresters in Great Brit., Royal Scottish Forestry Soc., Liberal Republican. Unitarian. Clubs: Harvard (Boston and N.Y.); Nat. Rifle Assn. Author, co-author or editor numerous bulls. and reports relating to field. Home: Cornwall-on-Hudson, N.Y. †

TSCHACBASOV, NAHUM, artist; b. Baku, Russia, Aug. 31, 1899; came to U.S., 1907; s. Stephen and Sophia (Tibel) T.; m. Esther Liss, 1919; children: David, Corinne; m. Esther Sorokin, 1929; 1 child, Sondra; m. Irene Zevon, Aug. 30, 1966. Student, Lewis Inst., Chgo., Armour Inst. Tech., Columbia. former instr. Am. Artists Sch., Art Students League; formerly operated Tschacbasov Sch. of Fine Arts; pres. Am. Archives of World Art, N.Y.C. Exhibited one-man shows, Galerie Zak, Paris, 1933, Gallery Secession, N.Y.C., 1934, A.C.A. Gallery, 1936, 38, 40, 42, Perls Galleries, 1944, 46-48, Arts and Crafts Club, New Orleans, 1945, Colorado Springs Fine Arts Center, 1946, U. Tex., 1946, James Vigeveno Gallery, Los Angeles, Jewish Mus., N.Y.C., 1955, San Francisco Mus., 1946, William Rockhill Nelson Gallery Art, John Heller Gallery, Waker Art Gallery, Delgado Mus., La Jolla (Calif.) Mus. Art, Columbus (Ga.) Mus. Arts and Crafts, Carnegie Pub. Library, Clarksdale, Miss., Pace U., N.Y.C., 1974, also numerous colls., Univ. Mus., 1951, 52, 53, 55; exhibited, France, Spain, Whitney Mus. Am. Art, Mus. Modern Art, Met. Mus. Art, Art Inst. Chgo., Carnegie Internat., Phila. Acad., Corcoran Gallery Art, St. Louis, San Francisco, Richmond museums fine arts, Berkshire Mus., Rochester Meml. Gallery, Riverside Mus., Ind. U., U. Ill., U. Iowa, Galerie Bonaparte, Salon de Tuilerie, Paris; represented in permanent collections, Met. Mus. Art, Whitney Mus. Am. Art, Dallas Mus., Pa. Acad., Butler Art Inst., Youngstown, Ohio, Jewish Mus., N.Y.C., Bklyn. Mus., Tel Aviv Mus., Israel, Pensacola (Fla.) Art Center, Wustom Mus. Fine Arts, Racine, Wis., Devereux Found., Phoenix and Devon, Pa., also numerous colls., univs., and pvt. collections, three paintings purchased by, State Dept.; Author: (autobiography) The Moon is My Uncle; (poetry) Machinery of Fright, 1982; Contbr. articles to art mags.; Pub. 2 portfolios of etchings, 1947; compiler, author, pub.: American Library Compendium and Index of World Art, 1961, An Illustrated Survey of Western Art. Served as seaman USN on U.S.S. Delaware, 1917-18, Scapa Flow. Awarded Pepsi-Cola prize, 1947. Address: New York, N.Y. Died Feb. 1984.

TSUTSUI, MINORU, chemist, educator; b. Wakayama City, Japan, Mar. 31, 1918; came to U.S., 1951, naturalized, 1960; s. Juntaro and Tazu (Hirata) T.; m. Ethel

Ashworth, Mar. 3, 1956; 1 son, William Minoru. B.A., Gifu (Japan) U., 1938; M.S., Tokyo (Japan) U. Lit. and Sci., 1941, Yale, 1953; Ph.D., Yale, 1954; D.Sc., Nagoya (Japan) U., 1960. Asst. prof. Tokyo U. Lit. and Sci., 1950-53; vis. research fellow Sloan-Kettering Inst., N.Y.C., 1954-56; research chemist Monsanto Chem. Co., 1957-60; research scientist N.Y. U., 1960-69, project dir., 1962-65, lectr. chemistry, 1964-65, asso. prof. dept. chemistry, 1965-69; prof. Tex. A. and M. U., College Station, from 1969; U.S.-USSR exchange scholar, 1967; Ford Found. cons. U. Delhi, India, 1977; invited scholar Japan Soc. Promotion Sci., 1978; cons. to industry, from 1963; hon. research prof. of Inst. of Chemistry Chinese Acad. Sci., 1980. Editor: (with E.I. Becker) Organometallic Reactions, 1965-76, Organometallic Syntheses and Reactions, from 1976, Characterization of Organometallic Compounds, from 1969; asso. editor: (with E.I. Becker) Jour. Coordination Chemistry, from 1970; Am. Chem. Soc. Monographs, from 1970; Contbr. (with E.I. Becker) articles to profl. jours. Mem. Am. Chem. Soc. (ad hoc com. on pub. relations 1972), N.Y. Acad. Scis. (v.p. 1965, chmn. chem. scis. sect. 1963, div. organometallic chemistry 1964, A. Cressy Morrison award 1960, pres. 1968), Japan-U.S. Chemists Assn. N.Y. (pres. 1967), chem. socs. Japan, London, West Germany, Am. Inst. Chemists, S.W. Catalysis Soc. (dir. 1972-74), S.W. Sci. Forum (exec. officer, dir. from 1976), Japan Soc., Tex. Acad. Scis., AAAS, Sigma Xi. Patentee in field. Home: Bryan, Tex.

TUBB, ERNEST DALE, singer, composer; b. nr. Crisp, Tex., Feb. 9, 1914; ed. Tex. pub. schs.; m. Olene Adams, June 3, 1949; children—Elaine Walker, Justin Wayne, Erlene Dale, Olene Gayle, Ernest Dale, Larry Dean, Karen Delene. With radio sta. KONO, San Antonio, 1933-35, radio sta. KGKL, San Angelo, Tex., 1936-40, radio sta. KGKO, Ft. Worth, 1941-42; with Grand Ole Opry radio sta. WSM, Nashville, 1943-84, own weekly show Ernest Tubb Midnight Jamboree; owner, operator Ernest Tubb Record Shop, Nashville; rec. artist Decca Records (now MCA Records), 1940—, numerous albums and songs including Rainbow at Midnight, Soldier's Last Letter, Letters Have No Arms, Mr. and Mrs. Used to Be, Sweet Thing, Let's Say Goodbye Like We Said Hello, Blue Christmas, It's Been So Long, Darling; composer songs including Walking the Floor Over You, Try Me One More Time; entertained troops in Korea, 1950, 51; performs in nightclubs. Named to Country Music Hall of Fame Country Music Assn., 1965. Home: Nashville, Tenn. Dec. Sept. 6, 1984.*

TUCHMAN, JOSEPH, architect; b. Akron, Ohio, Oct. 20, 1920; s. Samuel and Celia (Magilowitz) T.; m. Evelyn R. Siplow, Nov. 3, 1946; 1 dau., Janice Lyn. B.Arch., Carnegie Inst. Tech., 1942. Ptnr., Tuchman-Canute (architects), Akron, 1951-81. Pres. Internat. Inst., 1964-65. Served with AUS, 1943-45. Fellow AIA (pres. Eastern Ohio chpt. 1957-58, regional dir. 1967-70, mem. finance com. 1972, 73, resolutions com. 1972, treas. 1974-75); mem. Architects Soc. Ohio (pres. 1964-65), Akron C. of C. (chmn. betterment com. 1956). Club: Atwood Yacht. Home: Akron, Ohio. Dec. Feb. 20, 1981.

TUCK, JAMES LESLIE, physicist; b. Manchester, Eng., Jan. 9, 1910; s. James Henry and Selina Jane (Reece) T.; B.Sc., Victoria U., Manchester, 1932, M.Sc., 1936; Salter fellow Clarendon Lab., U. Oxford, 1936-39, M.A., 1949; m. Elsie Mary Harper, Aug. 11, 1937; children—Sarah Catherine Mary (Mrs. Donald F. Pasieka), Peter Humphrey James. Came to U.S., 1949, naturalized, 1955. Chief sci. adviser to Lord Cherwell, mem. personal staff Winston Churchill, 1939-44; mem. Brit. mission to Manhattan Project, Los Alamos, 1944-46; supr. Inst. Advanced Studies, Clarendon Lab., Oxford U., 1946-49; mem. staff theoretical div. Los Alamos Sci. Lab., 1950-55, asso. physics div. leader, also head controlled thermonuclear research, 1955-73; Walker-Ames distinguished prof. U. Wash., 1974-79; vis. prof. U. Waikeato, New Zealand, 1974; Regents' lectr. U. Calif. at La Jolla, 1975. Guggenheim fellow, Paris, Rome, 1962; decorated Order Brit. Empire. Fellow Am. Phys. Soc. Contbr. numerous papers to profl. lit. Home: Los Alamos, N.Mex. Died 1979.

TUCK, WILLIAM MUNFORD, lawyer, former governor and congressman; b. Halifax County, Va., Sept. 28, 1896; LL.B., Washington and Lee U., 1921, LL.D., 1949; LL.D., Hampden Sydney Coll., William and Mary Coll., 1946, Elon Coll., 1948; m. Eva Lovelace Dillard, Feb. 26, 1928 (dec.). Admitted to Va. bar, 1921, since practiced in South Boston, Va.; mem. Ho. of Dels. Va., 1924-32, Va. State Senate 1932-42; gov. Va., 1946-50; now sr. mem. Tuck, Bagwell, Dillard, Mapp & Nelson. Mem. 83d to 90th congresses, 5th Dist. Va. Served with USMC, World War I. Mem. Am., Va. State bar assns., Sigma Phi Epsilon, Phi Delta Phi. Ind.-Democrat. Mason (33 deg., Shriner). Club: Commonwealth (Richmond, Va.). Home: South Boston, Va. Dec. June 9, 1983,

TUCKER, WILLIAM ROSCOE, ex-mem. Rep. Nat. Com.; b. Dawsonville, Ga., July 2, 1888; s. William Jasper and Sarah Ann (McKee) T.; student N. Ga. Coll., Dahlonega, 1906-10; B.S., Ga. Inst. Tech., 1915; D.Sc. Golden State Univ., Los Angeles, 1957. Faculty dept. sci. Ga. Mil. Acad., 1916-20; admitted to Ga. bar, 1922; practice of law, Atlanta, 1926-30, Dawsonville, Ga., 1930-53; biol. research, 1908-34. Chmn. Rep. State Com., 1944-52, mem. Rep. Nat. Com., 1952-56. Chmn. Savs. Bond Com., Dawson Co., Ga., 1946-50. Govt. appeal agt. Dawson Co. Draft Bd., 1942-45. Mem. Emerson Chem. Soc. (past pres.). Presbyn. Home: Dawsonville, Ga. †

TULL, E. DON, indsl. mfg. exec.; b. Columbus, Ind., Aug. 28, 1906; s. Elmer and Ethel (Rockwell) T.; m. Joyce Skaggs; children (by previous marriage)—Kenneth Wayne, Frank David. With Cummins Engine Co., Inc., Columbus, from 1928, succesively various positions in shop, factory supt., supt. and asst. works mgr., mgr. mfg., v.p. personnel and plant, v.p., gen. mgr., 1928-55, exec. v.p., 1955-60, pres., 1960-69, vice chmn. exec. com., from 1969, also dir.; dir. Irwin Mgmt. Co., Columbus. Trustee Asso. Colls. Ind.; bd. dirs. Cummins Engine Found. Mem. Ind. C. of C. Baptist. Clubs: Kiwanian. (Scottsdale, Ariz.), Paradise Valley Country (Scottsdale, Ariz.). Home: Columbus, Ind.

TURNER, C(LARENCE) L(ESTER), zoölogist; b. Beaver O., May 19, 1890; s. Marion Bartlett and Ida May (Benner) T.; A.B., Ohio Wesleyan Univ., Delaware, 1912, A.M., 1914; Ph.D., U. of Wis., 1918; m. Irene Kissner, Sept. 3, 1919; children—Dorothy Jean, James Edmiston. Instr. in zoölogy, U. of Kan., 1914-15; instr. and asst. prof. zoölogy, Marquette U. Sch. of Medicine, Milwaukee, Wis., 1915-17; served in U.S. Navy, 1918; prof. zoölogy, Wooster Coll., Ohio, 1918-20, Beloit Coll., Wis., 1920-27; asso. prof. zoölogy, Northwestern University, 1927-30, professor zoölogy from 1930, chairman of department, 1936-1940. Investigator for Ohio State Div. of Fish and Game, 1918-21; biologist Wis. State Bd. of Health, 1924-26. Mem. A.A.A.S., Am. Soc. Zoölogists, Am. Assn. Anatomists, Am. Soc. Naturalists, O., Chgo. Acads. Sci. (mem. bd. govs.), Sigma Xi, Alpha Sigma Phi, Alpha Kappa Kappa. Republican. Meth. Contbr. to Science, Biol. Bull., Am. Naturalist, Biol. Abstracts, etc. Clubs: University (Evanston); Chaos (Chicago). Home: Evanston, Ill. †

TURNER, HOMER GRIFFIELD, geologist, chemist; b. Toronto, Can., Nov. 3, 1887; s. Berkley Griffield and Eleanor (Temple) T.; B.S., Syracuse U., 1912, M.S., 1914; student U. of Chicago, summer, 1913; m. Nina Ida Cornish, of Syracuse, N.Y., Nov. 28, 1916; children—J. Eleanor, Erma Norine, Byron Berkley. Came to U.S., 1981, naturalized, 1903. Instr. mineralogy, Syracuse, 1913-16, asst. prof., 1916-18; asst. prof. geology, Lehigh U., 1918-26 and 1927-29, acting head dept. geology, 1926-27; dir. research Anthracite Inst. from 1929; research engineer Anthracite Equipment Corporation. Mem. Nat. Coal Classification Com. Fellow A.A.A.S.; mem. Am. Chem. Soc., Am. Inst. Mining & Metall. Engrs., Am. Water Works Assn., Pa. Acad. Science, Pa. Waterworks Operators' Assn., Pa. Sewage Works Assn., Alpha Chi Sigma, Sigma Xi, Sigma Beta. Republican. Methodist. Clubs: University, Lehigh Valley Engineers, Center County Engrs. (State College, Pa.); Coal Research (U.S. and Eng.). Author of numerous publs. on fundamental properties of anthracite and new uses of anthracite. Discoverer of method for showing micro-structure of anthracite. Home: State College, Pa. †

TURNER, VICTOR WITTER, anthropology educator; b. Glasgow, Scotland, May 28, 1920; came to U.S., 1964; s. Norman and Violet (Witter) T.; m. Edith Lucy Brocklesby Davis, Jan. 30, 1943; children: Frederick, Robert, Irene Helen, Alexander Lewis Charles, Rory Peter Benedict. B.A. with honours, Univ. Coll., London, Eng., 1949; Ph.D., U. Manchester, Eng., 1955. Research officer Rhodes-Livingstone Inst., Lusaka, No. Rhodesia, 1950-54; Simon research fellow U. Manchester, 1955-57, from lectr. to sr. lectr., 1958-64; fellow Center Advanced Study Behavioral Scis., 1961-62; prof. anthropology Cornell U., 1964-68; prof. social thought, anthropology U. Chgo., 1968-83; chmn. social thought, 1976-77; William R. Kenan Jr. prof. anthropology U. Va., Charlottesville, 1977-83; vis. prof. Makeree Coll., Uganda, 1967, U. Minn., 1980, Smith Coll., 1982, Hebrew U., Jerusalem, 1983, Bar-Ilan U., 1983; Lewis Henry Morgan lectr., 1966; Am. lectr. history religions Am. Council Learned Socs., 1973-74, Inst. for Advanced Study, Princeton, 1975-76. Author: Schism and Continuity in an African Society, 1957, Chihamba The White Spirit, 1962, The Forest of Symbols, 1967, The Drums of Affliction, 1968, The Ritual Process, 1969, Dramas, Fields and Metaphors, 1974, Revelation and Divination in Ndembu Ritual, 1975, Image and Pilgrimage in Christian Culture, 1978, Process, Performance and Pilgrimage, 1979, From Ritual to Theater, 1982, Celebration, 1982; Editor: Profiles of Change: African Society and Colonial Rule, 1970; series Symbol, Myth, Ritual, 1972-83. Served with Brit. Army, 1941-46. Fellow Am. Soc. for Study Religions, Am. Acad. Arts and Scis., Royal Anthrop. Inst. (Rivers Meml. medal 1965), Am. Anthrop. Assn., Internat. African Inst., African Studies Assn., Soc. for Humanities. Club: Explorers. Home: Charlottesville, Va. Died Dec. 18, 1983.

TUSLER, WILBUR H(ENRY), architect; b. Miles City, Mont., Aug. 26, 1890; s. Henry and Melissa (Kinsey) T.; grad. St. John's Mil. Acad., 1909; student U. Minn., 1909-11; B.S., U. Pa., 1914; m. Ottilie Geisenheimer, 1916; children—Ottilie, Theodore, Stephen; married 2d, Margaret Gable, Aug. 31, 1931; 1 son, Wilbur Henry. Partner Magney & Tusler, Inc., Mpls., 1917-35, Magney, Tusler & Setter, after 1935; designed Foshay Tower, Mpls. Post Office, North Western Hosp., Deaconess Hosp., Heart Hosp. (all Mpls.) State chmn. Nature Conservancy Fellow A.L.A. (dir. 1949-52), mem. Am. Hosp. Assn., Zeta Psi. Clubs: Kiwanis, Minneapolis, Home: Minneapolis, Minn. Deceased.

TUTTLE, JOHN RAYMOND, ret. elec. mfg. exec.; b. Oneida, N.Y., Dec. 29, 1890; s. John F. and Nellie W. (Dyer) T.; B.A., Yale, 1913; M.E.E., Harvard, 1915; L.H.D., LeMoyne Coll., 1968; m. Louise Buckley, May 29, 1923; children—Forbes S., Sally L. (Mrs. Richard H. Merrick), John D., Richard P. Controller Brown-Lipe-Chapin div. Gen. Motors Corp., Syracuse, N.Y., 1918-33; with Crouse-Hinds Co., Syracuse, from 1933, successively controller, sec., v.p., treas. and dir., 1933-55, pres., 1955-58, 64-65, chmn. 1955-70; dir. Formerly officer Citizens Found., Syracuse, Blue Cross Hosp. Plan, N.Y. State Coll. Forestry, Mfrs. Assn.; pres. Community Found. of Syracuse. Mem. C. of C., Phi Beta Kappa, Sigma Xi, Zeta Psi. Clubs: Century, Gyro (Syracuse); Yale, Electric Manufacturers (N.Y.C.). Home: Syracuse, NY. †

TUVE, MERLE ANTONY, research physicist; b. Canton, S.D., June 27, 1901; s. Anthony G. and Ida Marie (Larsen) T.; prep. edn. Augustana Acad., Canton, 1915-18; B.S. in Elec. Engring., U. Minn., 1922, A.M., 1923; Ph.D., Johns Hopkins, 1926; D.Sc., Case, Kenyon, Williams, Johns Hopkins, U. Alaska; LL.D., Augustana Coll., Carleton; m. Winifred Gray Whitman (M.D.), Oct. 27, 1927; children—Trygve Whitman (dec. 1972), Lucy Winifred Tuve Comly. Teaching fellow U. Minn., 1922-23; instr. physics Princeton, 1923-24, Johns Hopkins, 1924-26; mem. staff dept. terrestrial magnetism Carnegie Inst. Washington, 1926-46, dir. 1946-66, distinguished service mem., from 1966; on leave, 1940-46, war work (proximity fuse, etc.); home sec. Nat. Acad. Scis., 1966-72. Chmn. Sect. T. OSRD, 1940-45; dir. Applied Physics Lab., Johns Hopkins (Navy) 1942-46; U.S. exec. com. Nat. Com of IGY, 1954-59; mem. Pres.'s Sci. Adv. Com.-Internat. Sci. Panel. Recipient AAAS prize (with L.R. Hafstad, O. Dahl) 1931; Presdl. Medal of Merit, 1946; Research Corp. Award 1947; comdr. Order of Brit. Empire, 1948; John Scott Award, 1948; Comstock Prize, Nat. Acad. Sci., 1949; Howard N. Potts medal Franklin Inst., 1950; Achievement medal U. Minn., 1950; Barnard medal Columbia, 1955, Medal Condor de Los Andes (Bolivia); Bowie medal Am. Geophys. Union, 1963; Cosmos Club award, 1963. Fellow Am. Phys. Soc., IEEE, AAAS, Am. Acad. Arts and Sci.; mem. Am. Philos. Soc., Nat. Acad. Scis. (chmn. NRC geophysics research bd. 1969-72), Philos. Soc. Washington, Washington Acad. Scis., Phi Beta Kappa, Sigma Xi, Tau Beta Pi, Gamma Alpha. Club: Cosmos. Contbr. to Phys. Rev., other sci. jours. on nuclear physics, geophysics and biophysics. Editor: Jour. Geophys. Research, 1949-58. Home: Chevy Chase, Md. Died May 20, 1982.

TWADDLE, HENRY LEWIS, army officer; b. Clarksfield, Ohio, June 2, 1888; s. Herbert Allen and Sadie Arabella (Campbell) T.; grad. Ossining (N.Y.) High Sch., 1905; E.E., Syracuse U., 1910; grad. Inf. Sch., 1920, Command and Gen. Staff Sch., 1923. Army War Coll., 1925, Field Arty. Sch., 1933. Chem. Warfare Sch., 1935; m. Sara Maud Udell, Aug. 17, 1917; children—Herbert Granger, Warren William. Elec. engr. Nat. Electric Lamp Assn., 1910-12; commd. 2d lt., U.S. Army, 1912; promoted through grades to major gen., 1942; served in Alaska, 1914-18; condr. most northern Army post, Fort Gibbon, Alaska, 1917-18: completed arrangements for acceptance of men drafted in Alaska, 1918; served in 153 Depot Brigade, Camp Dix, N.J. (comdr. training group of about 800 officers and 10,000 men). 1918; organized and conducted first convalescent center in U.S. (over 3,000 men wounded in France accepted and discharged), 1918-19; instr., Infantry Sch., 1921-22; instr. tactics. Command and Gen. Staff Sch., Ft. Leavenworth Kan., 1927-32; duty War Dept. Gen. Staff, 1926-27 and from 1938; revised War Dept. Mobilization Plan; drew up forces to be mobilized under Selective Service Law, 1940; comdr. 95th Inf., World War II; ret., 1948. Home: Washington, D.C. Deceased.

TWINING, NATHAN FARRAGUT, ret. air force officer, pub. co. exec.; b. Monroe, Wis., Oct. 11, 1897; s. Clarence Walter and Maize (Barber) T.; grad. U.S. Mil. Acad. 1919; student Inf. Sch., 1919-20. Air Corps Tactical Sch., 1935-36, Command and Gen. Staff Sch., 1936-37; rated command pilot; m. Maude McKeever, Mar. 9, 1932; children—Richard McKeever, Nathan Alexander, Olivia T. Hansell. Mem. Ore. N.G., 1916-17; comd. 2d lt. Inf., 1918; transferred to AC, 1924; promoted through grades to gen. USAF, 1950; chief of staff to comdg. gen. USAFISPA, 1942-43; comdg. gen. 13th AF, Solomon Islands, 1943, 15th AF, Italy, and Mediterranean Allied Strategic Air Forces, 1943, 20th AF, Pacific, 1945, Air Materiel Command, Wright Field, O., 1945-47; comdr. in chief Alaska, 1947-50; vice chief of staff AF, 1950-53, chief of staff, 1953-57; chmn. Joint Chiefs Staff 1957-60; vice chmn. bd. Holt, Rinehart & Winston, Inc., 1960-67; dir. United Tech. Labs., Inc. Decorated D.S.M. (Army, Navy), Legion of Merit with oak leaf cluster, D.F.C., Bronze Star medal, Air Medal with oak leaf cluster (U.S.); Croix de Guerre with 2 palms. Comdr. Legion of Honor (France); Medal of Merit with swords (Poland); Order of Sphinx (Greece), knight Brit. Empire, companion Brit.

Empire (Gt. Britain); Aviation Cross 1st class (Peru); Order of White Elephant (Thailand), Medal of Merit (Egypt); recipient James Forrestal Meml. award Nat. Security Indsl. Assn., 1961. Mem. Am. Security Council (nat. adv. bd.). Home: Hilton Head Island, S.C. Died Mar. 29, 1982.

TWORKOV, JACK, artist; b. Biala, Poland, 1900; came to U.S., 1913, naturalized, 1928; s. Hyman and Esther (Singer) T.; children—Hermine Ford Moskowitz, Helen. Student, Columbia, 1920-23, N.A.D., 1923-25, Art Students League, 1925-26; D.F.A., Md. Inst. Art, 1971; L.H.D., Columbia, 1972; D.F.A., R.I. Sch. Design. Tchr. Am. U., summers 1948-51, Black Mountain Coll., summer 1952, U. Ind., summers 1954, 55, U. Miss., fall 1954; formerly with Pratt Inst., Bklyn.; lectr. modern Am. painting; vis. artist Yale, 1962, chmn. dept. art, 1963-69; William Leffingwell prof. painting emeritus Sch. Art and Architecture, Yale; vis. prof. Cooper Union, 1970-71. Author articles in field.; One man shows, Egan Gallery, 1947, 49, 52, 54, Balt. Mus. Art, 1948, Miss. U., 1954, Stable Gallery, 1957, 59, Walker Art Center, 1957, Castelli Gallery, 1961, 63, Whitney Mus., 1971, Toledo Mus. Art, 1971, French & Co., 1971, Gertrude Kasle Gallery, Detroit, 1966, 69, 71, 73, Jaffe-Friede Gallery, Dartmouth Coll., Hanover, N.H., 1973, Harcus, Krakow, Rosen, Sonnabend Gallery, Boston, 1974, Portland Center for Visual Arts, 1974, Denver Mus., 1975, retropective exhbn., Whitney Mus. Am. Art, 1964, Guggenheim Mus., 1982, others; exhibited, N.Y. Soc. Anonyme, 1929, Dudensing Gallery, 1931-35, recent group shows include, Whitney Mus., Mus. Modern Art, Am. Vanguard Art of Paris, Pa. Acad. Art Ann., Calif. Palace Legion of Honor, Pitts. Internat. Carnegie Inst., Santa Barbara Mus., Corcoran Gallery, Va. Mus., Chgo. Arts Club, Mus. Modern Art New Am. Painting Show, Amsterdam, Basle, Berlin, Belgrade, London, Madrid, Paris, Rome, 1958-60, many others including, Documenta II exhbn. Mus. Fridericianum, Kassel, Germany, 1959; represented in permanent collections, Watkins Gallery, Am. U., Balt. Mus. Fine Arts, New Paltz State Tchrs. Coll., U. N.Y., Walker Art Center, Milw., San Francisco Mus., Portland Mus., Bklyn. Mus., Mus. Modern Art, Met. Mus. Art, Santa Barbara Mus., Cleve. Mus., Hartford Athaeneum, Albright-Knox Gallery, Buffalo, Rockefeller U., Yale U., Whitney Mus. Am. Art, Guggenheim Mus., Ciba Geigy collection, others. Recipient 1st William A. Clark award and; Corcoran Gold medal Corcoran Gallery Art, 1963; Painter of Year award Skowhegan Sch. Art, 1974; Guggenheim fellow, 1970. Mem. Am. Acad. and Inst. Arts and Letters. Home: New York, N.Y. Died Sept. 4, 1982.

TYLMAN, STANLEY DANIEL, dental educator; b. Chgo., May 15, 1893; s. Vincent and Frances (Dobbs) T.; student Notre Dame Prep. Sch., 1906-10, U. Notre Dame, 1910-13; D.D.S., Northwestern U., 1918, M.S., 1930; B.S., Ill. Inst. Tech., 1927; Doctor honoris causa, univs. of Brazil, Argentina, Venezuela, Bolivia; m. Isabelle Hannam, Nov. 21, 1964; children by previous marriage—Stanley George, Vincent Ritchey, Theodore Andrew. In practice dentistry, specializing in dental prosthodontics, 1918-82; tchr. Northwestern U. Dental Sch., 1918-20; prof. dentistry U. Ill. Coll. Dentistry, 1920-62, emeritus, 1962-82. Mem. U.S. Nat. Commn. UNESCO; mem. U.S. Mission to Japan, 1951. Past pres. Am. Acad. Plastics Research. Served with Dental Corps, U.S. Army, World War I. Recipient William John Gier ann. meritorious service award Am. Coll. Dentists, 1973. Fellow Am. Coll. Dentists; mem. Am. Dental Assn., Am. Equilibration Soc. (pres. 1964), Ill. Dental Assn., Chgo. Dental Soc. (pres. 1934), A.A.A.S., Sigma Xi, Omicron Kappa Upsilon, Psi Omega. Club: Rotary Chgo.). Author: Theory and Practice of Crown and Bridge Prosthesis, 1960; Synthetic Resins in Dentistry, 1945. Editor: Yearbook of Dentistry, 1943-66. Contbr. jours. Am. Dental Assn. Dental Edn., State Dental Socs. Del. of Am. Dental Assn., as clinician and lectr. to Argentina, Brazil, Uruguay, Chile, Peru, Colombia and Panama, 1942, Bolivia, Peru, Chile, Argentina, Brazil, P.R., 1947, 48, Eng., France, Germany, Switzerland, 1952, Portugal, Spain, Italy, 1953, Norway, Sweden, Denmark, Poland, 1957. Home: Lombard, Ill. Died Sept. 9, 1982.

TYNION, JAMES T., lawyer; b. Bklyn., Dec. 4, 1902; s. William and Mary (Huber) T.; m. Julia L. Egan, Aug. 8, 1922; children—James T., Donald W., Louisemary (Mrs. John McDonald). Grad, Pulcifer Bus. Inst., Bklyn., 1920; LL.B., St. John's U., 1931; LL.D., St. Michael's Coll., Winooski, Vt., 1958. Bar: N.Y. bar 1932. With O'Brien, Boardman, Harper & Fox, 1917; law clk., sec. Justice M.J. O'Brien, 1920-32; mem. firm Conboy, Hewitt, O'Brien & Broadman, N.Y.C., 1943-72, sr. partner, 1965-72, pvt. practice, N.Y.C., from 1972; Chmn. bd., sec., dir. Hamilton Press. Bd. dirs. St. Vincent's Hall, Bklyn.; v.p., dir. Marquis George MacDonald Found., from 1961. Named knight of Malta, 1943 (sec. Am. chpt. 1951-78, dep. master sec. from 1957, bd. founders), from 1950; knight grand cross Order Holy Sepulchre, 1951; bronze cross merit, 1954, (Eastern lt.-treas. 1951-78, sec.-treas., 1957-78, councilor), from 1951. Mem. Am. Irish Hist. Soc., Ancient Order Hibernians, Friendly Sons St. Patrick. Club: K.C. (4 deg.). Home: New York, NY.

UDY, STANLEY HART, lawyer; b. Bartonsville, Pa., Apr. 7, 1889; s. William Hart and Clara Jane (Slutter) U.; Ph.B., U. of Chicago, 1916, J.D., 1919; m. Hilda Huse, Sept. 10, 1927 (dec.); 1 son, Stanley Hart. Assistant secretary of Agency of U.S. in United States-Venezuela Arbitration, at The Hague, 1910; disbursing officer Commn. of Engrs., Costa Rica-Panama Boundary Arbitration, 1911-13; asst. prof. law, U. of Mo. Law Sch., 1920-21; asst. solicitor Dept. of State, 1921-22; asso. counsel for U.S. in U.S.-Norway Arbitration, May-Oct. 1922, also in Am.-British Claims Arbitration, 1922-25; asso. legal adviser to President, Plebiscitary Commn., Tacna-Arica Arbitration, 1926; counsel for U.S., General and Special Claims Commns., United States and Mexico, 1927-30; practiced in N.Y. City from Nov. 1930. Made special study of judicial system of State of Illinois, 1919-20, for Legislative Reference Bureau of Illinois, and wrote about half of bulletin on the judiciary, for use of delegates of Illinois Constl. Conv. Served as 1st lt. U.S. Army, on staff of Provost Marshal Gen. Crowder, Dec. 23, 1917-Jan. 31, 1919. Mem. Am. Bar Assn., Am. Soc. Internat. Law, Phi Sigma Kappa, Phi Delta Phi, Phi Beta Kappa, Order of the Coif. Republican. Mason (32 deg., Shriner). Clubs: University. Home: Orange, N.J. †

UELAND, ELSA, educator; b. Minneapolis, Minn., Mar. 10, 1888; d. Andreas and Clara (Hampson) U.; B.A., U. of Minn., 1909; New York Sch. of Philanthropy, 1909-10; M.A., Columbia, 1911. Resident worker, Richmond Hill Settlement, N.Y. City, 1909-11; investigator, Vocational Guidance Assn., 1911-12, Vocational Edn. Assn., 1912-14; teacher pub. schs., Gary, Ind., 1914-16; organizer and pres. Carson Coll. (a progressive sch. for orphan girls), Phila., from 1917; mem. teaching staff Cooperative Sch. for Student Teachers, N.Y. City, 1934-35; supervisor of schs., Tygart Valley Homestead, W.Va., for U.S. Resettlement Adminstrn., 1935-36. Mem. N.E.A., Progressive Edn. Assn., Am. Assn. Social Workers, Pa. Hort. Soc., Phi Beta Kappa, Alpha Phi. Unitarian. Home: Flourtown, Pa. †

ULAM, STANISLAW MARCIN, educator, scientist; b. Lwow, Poland, Apr. 13, 1909; s. Josef and Anna (Auerbach) U.; M.A., Polytech. Inst., Lwow, 1932, Dr. Sci., 1933; D.Sc. (hon.), U. N.Mex., 1967; m. Francoise Aron, Aug. 19, 1941; 1 dau., Claire Anne. Came to U.S., 1936, naturalized, 1943. Vis. mem. Inst. Advanced Studies, Princeton, 1936; fellow Harvard Soc. Fellows, 1936-39; lectr. math. Harvard, 1939-40; asst. prof. math. U. Wis., 1941-43; staff Los Alamos Sci. Lab., 1943-67, research adviser, 1958-67; prof. U. Colo., 1965-77; prof. U. So. Calif., 1945; vis. lectr. Harvard, 1951; vis. prof. Mass. Inst. Tech., 1956-57, U. Colo., fall 1961, U. Calif. at La Jolla, 1963; vis. grad. research prof. U. Fla., 1974-84. Cons. to Pres.'s Adv. Com. Recipient Polish Millenium award, 1966. Bd. govs. Weizman Inst. Sci., 1975-84. Mem. Math. Assn. Am., Am. Philos. Soc., Am. Math. Soc., Am. Phys. Soc., Am. Acad. Arts and Scis., Nat. Acad. Scis., A.A.A.S. (chmn. math. div. 1976-84). Author: A Collection of Mathematical Problems, 1960; Mathematics and Logic, 1967; Sets, Numbers, Universes, 1974; Adventures of a Mathematician, 1976. Contbr. articles profl. jours. Home: Santa Fe, N.Mex. Died May 13, 1984.

ULICH, ROBERT, prof. edn.; b. Riedermuehl bei Lam, Bavaria, Germany, Apr. 21, 1890; s. Robert and Helene (Schaarschmidt) U.; came to U.S., 1934; Humanistisches Gymnasium, 1900-09; student univs. of Freiburg, Neufchatel, Munich, Berlin, Leipzig, 1909-15, Ph.D., 1915; m. Elsa Braendstroem, Nov. 16, 1929; married 2d, Mary Ewen, December, 1948. Research fellow University of Leipzig, 1915-16; librarian, 1917-21; asst. counselor in the Saxon Ministry of Edn., 1921-23, counselor in charge of Saxon univs., 1923-33, hon. prof. philos. dept. Dresden Inst. Tech., 1928-33; prof. of edn., Harvard U. Grad. Sch. of Edn. from 1934. Mem. Am. Acad. Arts and Sciences, Medieval Acad. of Am., Phi Delta Kappa, Phi Beta Kappa. Author books relating to edn.; latest publ.: Crisis and Hope in American Education, 1951. Home: Cambridge, Mass. †

ULLMAN, MYRON E, lawyer; b. Youngstown, O., Dec. 12, 1889; s. Edward D. and Frederica (Seeger) U.; A.B., U. Chgo., 1912, J.D., 1914; m. Helen E. Seifert, June 7, 1916 (dec. Feb. 1961); 1 son, Myron E. Admitted to Ohio bar, 1914, practiced in Youngstown; mem. firm Manchester, Bennett, Powers & Ullman. Dir. Town House Motel, Inc., Elec. Equipment Co., Union Nat. Bank, Youngstown Bldg. Material & Fuel Co. (all Youngstown). Trustee, v.p. Mahoning County Vocational Sch. Mem. Am., Ohio, Mahoning County bar assns. Mason (32). Home: Canfield, OH. †

UNGER, SHERMAN EDWARD, lawyer, government official; b. Chgo., Oct. 9, 1927; s. Mel I. and Helen (Strong) U.; m. Polly Van Buren Taylor, Dec. 29, 1953 (div. Feb. 1972); children—Cathleen Estelle, Peter Van Buren; m. Nancy McBryde Turnbull, Aug. 20, 1976. B.A., Miami U., Oxford, Ohio, 1950; J.D., U. Cin., 1953. Bar: Ohio bar 1953, D.C. bar 1972. Partner firm Frost & Jacobs, Cin., 1956-69; gen. counsel Dept. Housing and Urban Devel., 1969-70; v.p. Am. Financial Corp., Cin., 1971-72; practice law, 1972-81; gen. counsel U.S. Dept. Commerce, 1981-83; mem. Nat. Fgn. Intelligence Council, 1981-83; Bd. dirs. Fed. Nat. Mortgage Assn., 1969-72; gen. counsel Govt. Nat. Mortgage Assn., 1969-70; mem. Adminstrv. Conf. U.S., 1969-71, 81-83; mem. nat. adv. com. for legal services program OEO, 1969-71; chmn. bd. Modern Talking Picture Service Inc., 1968-69, Modern Media, 1968-69; mem. Ohio Water and Sewer Commn., 1965-69, Nat. Adv. Council Econ. Opportunity, 1971-73. Bd. dirs. Shared Med. Services, 1973-81. Served to 1st lt. AUS, 1946-47; Served to 1st lt. USAF, 1953-56. Mem. Am., Ohio, Cin. bar assns., World Peace Through Law Center, Beta Theta Pi. Presbyterian. Clubs: Cincinnati Country (Cin.), Queen City (Cin.); Metropolitan (Washington); Racquet and Tennis (New York); Masons. Home: Cincinnati, Ohio. Died Dec. 3, 1983.

UNTEREINER, RAY EDWARD, lawyer, economist; b. Redlands, Cal., Apr. 25, 1808; s. Edward N. and Andrea L. (Nielson) U.; A.B., U. Redlands, 1920; A.M., Harvard, 1921, student Law Sch., 1921-23; J.D., Mayo Coll. Law, Chgo., 1925; Ph.D., Northwestern U., 1932; m. Edith L. Whitlock, June 27, 1925; children—Wayne, Donald E. Instr. econs. Harvard, 1921-23; prof. speech Huron (S.D.) Coll., 1923-24; mem. faculty Cal. Inst. Tech., 1925-68, prof. history and econs., 1943-68, prof. emeritus, 1968-83, dean freshmen, 1937-43; economist N.A.M., 1943-45; economics consultant, from 1945; admitted to California bar, 1926, and practiced in Los Angeles until 1931; cons. AEC, 1959-61. Dir. Beckman Instruments, Inc. Chmn. committee local tax reform Los Angeles County Citizens Com., 1940-41; mem. Pasadena Bd. Edn., 1951-54, pres., 1953-54; chmn. Pasadena Recreation Commn., 1951-53; mem. Cal. Pub. Utilities. Commn., 1954-59; chmn. com. nuclear energy Nat. Assn. R.R. and Utilities Commnrs., 1957-58. Mem. policy com. Republican Central Com. Los Angeles County. Mem. Am. Enterprise Forum (economist), Internat. Platform Assn., Conf. Bus. Economists, Am. Assn. U. Profs., Los Angeles, Pasadena chambers commerce. Author: The Tax Racket, 1933, also articles various publs. Home: Pasadena, Calif. Died July 7, 1983.

UPCHURCH, THERON ACRIEL, ins. co. exec.; b. Apex, N.C., Oct. 25, 1915; s. Malpheus Gilbert and Lessie Helen (Upchurch) U.; m. Mabel Stuart Weatherspoon, June 17, 1939; 1 child, Stuart (Mrs. William Thomas Buice, III). B.S., U. N.C., 1936. With Wachovia Bank & Trust Co., Raleigh, N.C., 1936-42; with Durham Life Ins. Co., Raleigh, 1942-83, asst. treas., 1945-50, dir., 1950-83, treas., 1951-56, v.p., treas., 1956-67, pres., chief exec. officer, chmn. exec. com., 1967-78, chmn. bd. dirs., 1976-83; chmn. bd., exec. com. Durham Life Broadcasting, Inc., Raleigh, 1972-83, Durham Corp., Raleigh, 1979-83; chmn. bd. State Capital Ins. Co., Raleigh, 1976-83. Served with AUS, 1943-46, 50-51. Mem. Raleigh C. of C. (past dir., treas.), Sigma Chi. Baptist. Clubs: Kiwanian. (Raleigh), Carolina Country (Raleigh). Home: Raleigh, N.C. Died Feb. 11, 1983.

UPTON, ELDON CLAGGETT, JR., ins. broker; b. New Orleans, May 14, 1911; s. Eldon Claggett and Emily Massie Burton (Lewis) U.; m. Winifred Leone Suydam, Nov. 9, 1939; children—Leone Suydam, Claggett Coldham. B.B.A., Tulane U., 1932. Agt., instr. Travelers Ins. Co., 1932-35; agt., mgr. Sun Life Assurance Co. of Can., 1935-43, br. mgr., 1943-48; gen. agt. Mut. Benefit Life Ins. Co. of Newark, 1948-55; mem. Fed. Maritime Bd., 1953-54. Past pres. Met. Crime Commn. New Orleans, Inc.; v.p. Eye Found. Am.; past pres. YMCA. Mem. Am. Soc. C.L.U.'s (past pres.), Nat. Assn. Life Underwriters, New Orleans Assn. Life Underwriters (past pres.), Soc. Colonial Wars, Life Mgrs. Assn. New Orleans (past pres.), Nat. Tulane Alumni Assn. (past pres.), Delta Kappa Epsilon, Omicron Delta Kappa. Clubs: Boston, Recess, Tulane Alumni T, Tulane Commerce Alumni, Southern Yacht, Lakeshore. Home: New Orleans, LA.

URDANETA ARBELAEZ, ROBERTO, govt. ofcl. Colombia; b. 1890. Formerly prof. internat., pub. and pvt. law, Nat. U. of Colombia; formerly ambassador to Peru and to Argentina; fgn. minister, 1931-35; now minister of war. Permanent rep. to Security Council, U.N., with rank of A.E. and P., 1948; chmn. delegation 3d Gen. Assembly, U.N., 1948, 5th Gen. Assembly, 1950. Address: Bogotá, Colombia. †

URQUHART, GEORGE ALEXANDER, judge, High Court of Justice (Ont.); b. Toronto, Mar. 19, 1888; s. Daniel and Mary Ellen (Spence) U., B.A., LL.B., U. of Toronto, 1908; student Osgoode Hall Law Sch. (gold medal in polit. science, 1908, sliver medal, 1911), 1908-11; m. Eileen Alma Taylor, June 1, 1916; children—Jane (Mrs. Bruce S. Russel), John Daniel. Began as barrister, May 1911; asst. corp. counsel, City of Toronto, 1911-12; mem. Bartlet, Bartlet, Urquhart & Barnes, Windsor, 1913-21; Crown atty., Windsor, 1921-25; mem. Urquhart & Urquhart, Toronto, 1925-38; judge High Court of Justice since Jan. 25, 1938. Adlerman city of Windsor, 1920-21. Enlisted 1916 and served in France with 2d Batn. C.M.G.C., 1918, World War I. Mem. Phi Delta Phi (past pres.). Clubs: Toronto Golf, Arts and Letters (Toronto). Mem. Anglican Ch. †

VACCARA, BEATRICE NEWMAN, economist, government official; b. N.Y.C., Sept. 20, 1922; d. Wilfred and Gussie (Tannenbaum) Newman; m. John Vaccara, June 15, 1944; 1 child, Richard John. B.A. cum laude, Bklyn. Coll., 1943; M.A. (Univ. scholar), Columbia U., 1944, postgrad., 1944-45; postgrad., Am. U., 1958. Research asso. Brookings Instn., 1954-59; asst. chief nat. econ div. Dept. Commerce, Washington, 1959-65, coordinator econ. growth studies, 1965-71, chief econ. growth div., 1971-73; asso. dir. Dept. Commerce (Bur. Econ. Analysis), 1973-77; dep. asst. sec. for econ. policy Dept. Treasury, Washington, 1977-79; dir. Bur. Indsl. Econs., Dept. Commerce, 1980-83. Author: Employment and Output in Protected Manufacturing Industries, 1960, (with Walter Salant) Import Liberalization and Employment, 1961, A Study of Fixed Capital Requirements of the U.S. Business Economy, 1971-80, 1975; editor: (with John Kendrick) New Developments in Productivity Measurement, 1980; contbr. (with John Kendrick) numerous articles to profl. jours. Mem. exec. com. Montgomery County LWV, 1959-65. Recipient Adam Smith award Bklyn. Coll., 1943; Silver award Dept. Commerce, 1965; Gold Medal award, 1974. Fellow Am. Statis. Assn. (chmn. fellowship com. 1975-76, dir. 1975-78, v.p. 1979); mem. Am. Econ. Assn., Nat. Economist Club (dir. 1973), Washington Statis. Soc. (pres. 1971-72), Conf. on Research in Income and Wealth (exec. com. 1972-74), Internat. Assn. Research in Income and Wealth, Caucus for Women in Stats. (pres. 1981). Home: Washington, D.C. Died Jan. 7, 1983.

VADAKIN, JAMES CHARLES, educator; b. Lima, Ohio, Mar. 8, 1924; s. James Charles and Grace (Miller) V.; B.A., Denison U., 1946; M.B.A., Harvard, 1947; Ph.D., Cornell U., 1952; m. Mary Ann Willoughby, Sept. 8, 1946; 1 son, Jeffrey J. Mem. faculty U. Miami (Fla.), 1947-81, prof. econs., 1957-81, chmn. dept., from 1961; coordinator Cuban Econ. Research Project, from 1961; arbitrator labor-mgmt., 1950-81; frequent speaker. Mem. panel arbitrators Fed. Mediation and Conciliation Service; mem. Fed. Service Impasses Panel; mem. Presdl. Emergency Bd. 177, 1970; mem. Fla. Council Econ. Edn. Served with USNR, 1942-46. First hon. mem. Personnel Assn. Miami, 1954. Mem. Nat. Acad. Arbitrators (bd. govs.), Am. Arbitration Assn., Am., So. econ. assns., Phi Kappa Phi, Omicron Delta Kappa, Lambda Chi Alpha. Club: Harvard (Miami). Author: Family Allowances, 1958; Children, Poverty and Family Allowance, 1968; also articles. Home: Coral Gables, Fla. Died Mar. 19, 1981.

VAIL, HERMAN LANSING, lawyer; b. Cleve., July 6, 1895; s. Harry L. and Sarah A. (Wickham) V.; A.B., Princeton, 1917; LL.B., Harvard, 1922; m. Delia B. White, June 29, 1922 (dec.); children—Herman Lansing, Thomas Van Husen; m. 2d, Mary Louise Frackelton Gleason, Feb. 11, 1965. Admitted Ohio bar, 1922, since practiced in Cleve.; ptnr. firm Vail, Steele, Howland & Olson, from 1931; former pres., dir. Holden Estates Co., Forest City Pub. Co., Art Gravure Corp. of Ohio; dir. Cleve. Trust Co., 1948-70, adv. dir., 1970-75; dir. Island Creek Coal Co., Occidental Petroleum Corp., 1968-79. Hon. trustee Western Res. Hist. Soc., Univ. Sch., Garden Center of Greater Cleve., No. Ohio Opera Assn., Cleve. Health Museum, St. Luke's Hosp., Hiram House; hon. trustee Cleve. Travelers Aid Soc., Friends of Cleve. Pub. Library; trustee, v.p. Horace Kelley Art Found., Norweb Found.; mem. Ohio Gen. Assembly, 1929-32. Served as 1st lt. 332d Inf., U.S. Army, 1917-19. Mem. Citizens League Cleve. (past pres.), Cleve. Council World Affairs (past pres.), Ohio, Cleve., Am. bar assns. Clubs: Country, Union. Home: Cleveland Heights, Ohio. Dec. Jan. 7, 1981.

VAILE, ROLAND SNOW, prof. economics; b. Ojai, Calif., Nov. 23, 1889; s. Charles Selden and Octavia (Barrows) V.; B.A., Pomona (Calif.) Coll., 1910; M.A., Harvard, 1922; m. Marjorie Maynard, Mar. 18, 1912; children—David Selden, Marjorie Glyde, Roland Barrows. Began as econ. entomologist, 1910; with Hort. Commn. of Ventura County, Calif., 1911-14; asst. prof. of orchard management, U. of Calif., 1914-23; mem. Am.-Persian Commn., 1918-19; asso. prof. economics, U. of Minn., 1923-27, prof. economics and marketing from 1927; consultant Nat. Resources Com. and Minn. State Planning Bd., 1934-36; chmn. Mayor's Housing Commn., Minneapolis, 1933-38; branch chief Division of Civilian Supply, WPB, 1942. Mem. Am. Statis. Assn. (v.p. 1935), Am. Econ. Assn., Am. Farm Econ. Assn., Am. Marketing Assn., Phi Beta Kappa, Alpha Kappa Psi. Conglist. Author or co-author books relating to field. Editor: Consumer Cooperatives, 1941; mng. editor, Journal of Marketing, 1937-38, editor-in-chief, 1939-40, research editor, 1941-42. Home: New Brighton, Minn. †

VALE, CLAIR FREMONT, surgeon; b. Ewington, O., July 31, 1887; s. Fremont Fordyce and Margaret Ella (Ewing) V.; prep. edn. Ewington Acad.; A.B., Washington and Tusculum Coll., Greenville, Tenn., 1909; student Princeton, 1909-12; M.D., U. of Pa., 1916; unmarried. Resident surgeon Receiving Hosp., Detroit, 1919-22; pvt. practice from 1922; instr. surgery, Wayne U. School of Medicine, 1920-27, asst. prof., 1927-36, clin. prof. from 1936; pres. Receiving Hosp., 1933; chief of surg. div. Florence Crittenton Hosp. from 1930, pres., 1932-36; surgeon Harper Hosp., Jennings Hosp.; emeritus surgeon Receiving Hosp.; visiting surgeon East Side Gen. Hosp. With Med. Corps, U.S. Army, 1918-19, adjt. base hosp., Camp Mills, Fellow Am. Coll. Surgeons, Am. Bd. of Surgery, A.M.A.; mem. Mich. State and Wayne County med. socs., Central Surg. Assn., Am. Diabetic Assn., Detroit Acad.-Surgery (pres. 1938-39), Detroit Acad. of Medicine, Am. Acad. of Polit. and So. Science, American Cancer Society, Nu Sigma Nu. Republican. Presbyterian (presbytery moderator 1958). Mason (32 deg., Shriner). Clubs: Detroit Medical, Detroit Athletic, Players, Economic, Orpheus; University (Winter Park). Home: Winter Park, Fla. †

VALENSTEIN, LAWRENCE, advt. exec.; b. N.Y.C., July 31, 1899; s. Morris and Fannie (Lewis) V.; student Townsend Harris Hall, N.Y.C., 1914-17; m. Alice Sternberg, May 10, 1934; children—Linda Starr, John Martin. Founder Grey Advt. Agy., N.Y.C., 1917, pres., treas., dir., 1917-55, chmn. bd., 1955-61, chmn. exec. com., 1961-67; founder chmn., 1968-82, also chmn. finance com., dir.; chmn. exec., com. dir. Grey Advt., Ltd., dir. Charles Hobson & Grey, Ltd., London, Eng., Grey Public Relations, N.Y., Dorland & Frev S.A., Paris, Brussels, Grey Advt. Ltd., Can., Milano & Grey, S.P.A., Milano, Grey-Daiko Advt., Tokyo, Pres. Lawrence Valenstein Fund; bd. dirs. Council for Arts, Westchester; trustee emeritus Hofstra U. Cons. WPB, World War II. Mem. Am. Assn. Advt. Agencies (past dir.), Am. Assn. World Health (v.p., dir.), Advt. Council (dir., mem. exec. com.). Clubs: Fairview Country, Greenwich Riding and Trails (Greenwich); Nippon, Circumnavigators, Harmonie (N.Y.C.). Author: Business Under The Recovery Art (with E.B. Weiss), 1934. Contbr. articles profl. publs. Home: Scarsdale, N.Y. Died Sept. 10, 1982.

VALENTE, MAURICE REMO, corporation executive; b. Racine, Wis., Nov. 25, 1928; s. Rocco B. and Rose (Guarascio) V.; m. Dolores Grant, Aug. 28, 1954; children: Candace, James, Steven. B.S., DePaul U., 1951, M.B.A., 1958. With ITT, 1967-79; dir. N.Am. staff, N.Y.C., 1967-69, v.p., group exec., Nutley, N.J., 1969-71, sr. v.p., dir. ops., N.Y.C., 1971; pres. ITT, Europe, Brussels, Belgium, 1974-78; exec. v.p. Office Chief Exec. Consumer Products and Services, N.Y.C., 1978-79; pres., chief operating officer RCA Corp., 1980-83; partner Wolsey & Co., 1981-83; chief exec. officer, chmn. CCI, 1982-83; prin. Maurice R. Valente & Assocs., Inc., 1983. Served with USMCR, 1950-52. Decorated Air medal with 2 gold stars; recipient Disting. Alumni award DePaul U. Mem. Work Factors Assos., Am. C. of C. in Brussels. Clubs: Upper Montclair Country, Elkview Country, N.Y. Athletic, Murray Hill Racquet. Home: New York, N.Y. Died Sept. 3, 1983.

VALLARINO, DON JOAQUIN JOSÉ, diplomat; b. Panama, Republic of Panama, Oct. 24, 1889; s. Joaquin and Hilda (Zachrisson) V.; ed. La Salle Sch., Panama, Townsend Harris Hall (High Sch.), N.Y. City, Franklin and Marshall Coll., Lancaster, Pa., 1907-09; M.D., U. of Pa., 1913; m. Isabel Espinosa, Feb. 9, 1920; children—Joaquin José II, Hilda Isabel. Interne Presbyterian Hosp., Philadelphia, Pa., 1913; resident surgeon Santa Tomas Hosp., Panama, 1915-20, roentgenologist, 1920-35; roentgenologist, The Herrick Clinic and Panama Hosp., 1920-45; sec. Fgn. Affairs, Panama, 1931; mem. Grand Electoral Jury, Panama, 1932-36; mem. bd. dirs. Nat. Brewery, Panama, 1939; pres. Panama Coca Cola Bottling Co. A.E. and P., Republic of Panama to the U.S. from 1945. Gov. from Panama to Internat. Bank for Reconstrn. and Development and to Internat. Monetary Fund; del. from Panama to World Health Orgn. Awarded El Merito, Ecuador; Vasco Nunez de Balboa, Panama. Mem. Med. Assn. of Panama (founder), (pres. 1932, re-elected 1939-40), Am. Med. Assn., Isthmian Canal Zone Med. Soc., Am. Coll. Surgeons, Am. Coll. Radiology, Am. Acad. Polit. and Social Sciences. Am. Soc. Internat. Law; mem. (hon.) Sociedad Argentina de Radiologia, Sociedad Colombiana de Radiologia, Sociedad Cubana de Radiologia, Chi Phi, Phi Rho Sigma. Clubs: Union, Golf (Panama) (charter mem.); Chevy Chase (Washington). Deceased.

VALPEY, FRANK RUSSELL, automotive parts mfr.; b. Detroit, Jan. 23, 1889; s. Henry Hodges and Janet Emily (Carr) K.; student Detroit U., Internat. Corr. Schs.; m. Ethel Ellen Sheridan, Feb. 5, 1916; children—Grant R. (U.S. Army), Robert G. (USAF). Factory rep. Willys-Overland Co., Toledo, 1914-25; asst. gen. sales mgr. Dodge Brothers, Detroit, 1925-28; v.p., dir. Graham Paige Motor Car Co., 1928-38; with Standard Products Co., Cleve., from 1940, sec., v.p., 1945-50, pres., from 1958, also dir. Past adviser for Ohio, Mich., Ky. Small Bus. Adminstrn. Mem. Am. Ordnance Assn., Soc. Automotive Engrs., Detroit Engring. Soc. Clubs: Detroit Athletic, Recess (Detroit); Oakland Hills Country (Birmingham, Mich.). Home: Pleasant Ridge, Mich. †

VAN BUREN, EVELYN, author; b. N.Y. City, Oct. 10, 1888; d. George Winter and Edna Adelaide (Wright) V.; ed. Am. pub. schs. and English private sch. Actress, appearing principally in Eng., 1907-1911. Author: Pippin, 1913; Zizi's Career, 1921. Home: Piermont, N.Y. †

VAN CAMPENHOUT, JACQUES LOUIS, obstetrician and gynecologist; b. Can., Apr. 2, 1933; s. Ernest and Marie Louise (Dewit) Van C.; m. Francoise Moreaux, June 18, 1960; children: Catherine, Isabelle, Eric. M.D., U. Louvain, Belgium, 1958. Practice medicine specializing in obstetrics and gynecology, Montreal, Que.; chief dept. obstetrics and gynecology Notre Dame Hosp., Montreal, 1972-81; asst. prof. U. Montreal, 1964-70, asso. prof., 1969-74, prof., 1974-81, chmn. dept., 1972-81. Contbr. articles to med. jours. Research fellow USPHS, 1962-63. Fellow Royal Coll. Surgeons (Can.), Am. Coll. Obstetricians and Gynecologists, Am., Gynecol. Soc.; mem. Assn. des Medecins de langue francaise du Can., Am., Canadian fertility socs., Soc. Obstetricians and Gynecologists Can., Soc. for Study Fertility (pres. elect), Assn. Profs. Obstetrics and Gynecology Am. (council), Assn. Profs. Obstetrics and Gynecology Can., Canadian Investigators in Reproduction, Internat. Fedn. Gynecologists and Obstetricians, Assn. Obstetricians and Gynecologists of Que., Fedn. internationale des Obstetriciens-gynecologues de langue francaise. Home: Saint Bruno, P.Q., Canada. Died Mar. 7, 1981; interred Saint Bruno, P.Q., Canada.

VANCE, MARSHALL MOUNTS, foreign service officer; b. Middletown, O., July 26, 1889; s. David Colville and Rebecca Isabel (Mounts) V.; student Ohio Wesleyan U., 1908-09; B.S. in economics, U. of Pa., 1912; post grad. work Yale, 1913-14; m. Ethel Irene Hatfield, July 27, 1921; children—Martha Marjorie, Marshall Dewitt. With Standard Oil Co. of New York, Dutch East Indies, 1914-16; with Detroit Bur. of Govt. Research, 1917-18; mgr. in India, Internat. Trade Developer Co., 1918-20; with foreign dept. Nat. Cash Register Co., 1920-21; apptd. foreign service officer, 1921; consul at Colombo, Ceylon, 1921-24, Windsor, Can., 1924, Fort William and Port Arthur, Can., 1924-28; assigned to Dept. of State, 1928; became consul at Windsor, Can., 1932; became consul at Lyons, France, 1941 (detained in Baden Baden, Germany); Dept. of State, 1944. Counselor of Mission and consul general, Berlin, 1946; Frankfort (Germany), 1948, retired, 1950. Mem. Sigma Phi Epsilon, Acacia. Mason. Home: Washington, D.C. †

VANDER PYL, MARY CHAMBERLAIN, naturalist, assn. ofcl.; b. Brockton, Mass., May 16, 1888; d. Fred W. and Mary E. (Brown) Chamberlain; ed. pub. schs., N.E.; m. John C. Vander Pyl., July 8, 1914. Confidential sec. to R. H. White, dept. store exec., Boston, 1910-16; dir., treas. R. J. Caldwell Co., textiles, 1916-26; dir., partner, treas. Wood-Vander Pyl Co., textile and rubber brokers, 1926-32; field asso. dept. tropical research N.Y. Zool. Soc., 1942-52; mem. N.Y. Zool. Soc. expdns. to Bermuda, 1929, 36, deep sea exploration, jungle life study, Venezuela 1941. Mem. Soc. Women Geographers, from 1944, 1st v.p., 1948-51, pres., 1957-60, co-founder fellowship fund, 1949, del. to 17th Internat. Congress Geog. Union, Washington, 1952; chmn. women's com. centennial celebration Am. Geog. Soc., 1952. Co-founder Hiram Halle Meml. Library, Pound Ridge, N.Y., 1950, v.p., 1950-56; bd. dirs. Westchester County (N.Y.) Soc. Prevention Cruelty to Children, from 1952. Hon. life mem. N.Y. Zool. Soc.; mem. N.Y. Acad. Sci., Am. Geog. Soc. Clubs: Women's City (charter) (Boston); Cosmopolitan (N.Y.C.). Author: (with Dr. William Beebe) Pacific Myctophidae, 1944. Address: Pound Ridge, N.Y. †

VANDER SLUIS, GEORGE JACOB, artist; b. Cleve., Dec. 18, 1915; s. Gerrit and Hilda (Koopman) Vander S.; m. Hildegarde Bristol, Oct. 24, 1948; children—Sylvia, Peter, Jeffrey. Diploma, Cleve. Inst. Art, 1939; student, Colorado Springs Fine Arts Center, 1940. Instr. Colorado Springs (Colo.) Fine Arts Center, 1940-42, 45-47; prof. painting Syracuse (N.Y.) U., from 1947; chmn. grad. div. Syracuse (N.Y.) U. (Coll. Visual and Performing Arts), 1970-77. One-man shows, Jacques Seligmann Gallery, N.Y.C., 1959, Royal Marks Gallery, N.Y.C., 1962, 63, 64, Krasner Gallery, N.Y.C., 1968, 69, 71; exhibited in group shows, Whitney Mus. Art, N.Y.C., 1954, Mpls. Inst. Art, 1957, U. Ill., 1961, White House, 1966, Mus. Contemporary Crafts, N.Y.C., 1968, Enviro-Vision N.Y. State Expo, Syracuse, 1972; represented in permanent collections, Everson Mus., Syracuse, Rochester (N.Y.) Meml. Art Gallery, Colorado Springs Fine Arts Center; painted mural, Rena Pierson Meml. Chapel, Syracuse U., 1981. Served with U.S. Army, 1942-45. Fulbright grantee, 1951-52; N.Y. State Council Arts grantee, 1966; Ford Found. grantee, 1978, 79. Home: Camillus, NY.

VANDERVEER, HAROLD C., army officer; b. Brooklyn, N.Y., Aug. 14, 1889; s. John Charles and Charlotte Grace (Baird) V.; grad. Field Arty. Sch., 1915, 1920, 1925. Command and Gen. Staff Sch., 1926, Army Indsl. Coll., 1934, Army War Coll., 1935; m. Margaret Hoyt Manning, Jan. 25, 1930. Served with U.S. Marine Corps, 1907-11; commd. 2d lt., F.A., U.S. Army, 1912, and advanced through the grades to brig. gen., Feb. 1942; served as maj. and lt. col., World War I; became arty. officer 9th Army Corps, Fort Lewis, Feb. 1941; assigned to 38th Inf. Div., Camp Shelby, Miss., Feb. 1942. Comd. Arty., 5th Inf. Div., in Iceland, United Kingdom, France and Germany after Sept. 1942. Deceased.

VAN DER ZEE, JAMES AUGUSTUS JOSEPH, photographer; b. Lenox, Mass., June 29, 1886; m. Kate Brown, 1906 (dec.); children—Rachael (dec.), Emil (dec.); m. Gaynella Greenlee, 1920 (dec.); m. Donna Mussenden, June 15, 1978. Student, Carlton Conservatory, N.Y.C., 1906. Dark room developer Gertz Dept. Store, Newark, 1907; opened Guarantee Photo Studio, N.Y.C., 1918; (name changed to GGG Photo Studio, 1932). 1st violinist, John Wanamaker Orch., resumed photog. career, 1980, photographer, Bill Cosby, Lou Rawls, Muhammed Ali, Romare Bearden, others; exhibited, Met. Mus. Art, jN.Y.C., 1969, other maj. museums; represented in permanent collections, Met. Mus. Art, other museums, also pvt. collections; publs. include Harlem On My Mind, 1969, rev. edit., 1979, The World of James Van Der Zee, 1969, James Van Der Zee, 1973, The Harlem Book of the Dead, 1978, James Van Der Zee: The Picture Takin' Man, 1979; video prodns. include Uncommon Images, 1975 (Recipient Pierre Toussaint award 1978). Living Legacy award Pres. U.S., 1979. Address: New York, N.Y. Died May 15, 1983.

VAN DEUSEN, JOHN GEORGE, educator, lectr.; b. Kipton, O., Apr. 21, 1890; s. George E. and Lydia (Durian) Van D.; A.B., Ohio State U., 1913, A.M., 1914; Ph.D., Columbia, 1928; student U. Chgo., summer 1916, Duke, 1923, Yale, 1924; m. Louise M. Brune, Dec. 12, 1917; children—Emma L., John G. Tchr. secondary schs., Ohio, 1914-25; head dept. history Libbey High Sch.,

Toledo, 1923-25; prof. history Columbia, 1925-28; asst. prof. history Hobart Coll., 1928-36, prof. Am. history, from 1936; prof. history U. Rochester, summers. Mem. Phi Beta Kappa, Delta Sigma Rho, Tau Kappa Alpha, Theta Delta Chi, Pi Gamma Mu (gov. N.Y. province). Republican. Presbyn. Mason. Author: The Loyalists in London, 1914; The Ante-Bellum Southern Commercial Conventions, 1927; Economic Basis of Disunion in South Carolina, 1928; The Black Man in White America, rev. edit., 1944; Brown Bomber: The Story of Joe Louis, 1940, also pamphlets. Contbr. Dictionary Am. Biography, Dictionary Am. History, Annals Am. Acad. Polit. and Social Scis., others. Home: Geneva, N.Y. †

VANDEVEER, WELZIE WELLINGTON, oil exec.; born Haubstadt, Ind., Feb. 16, 1887; s. Louis Bennett and Mary Ellen (Gwaltney) V.; student Southern Ill. U., 1908-10, LL.D., 1950; m. Wilda Ruth, March 7, 1919; children—James Wellington, Ruth Marie. Teacher country school, Edgewood and Dietrich, Ill., 1910-13; with Western Union Telegraph Co., 1913-16; sales and sales training Goodrich Tire & Rubber Co., 1916-21; with Am. Petroleum Co., 1921-25; co-founder Allied Oil Co., Inc., Cleveland, 1925, co. merged with Ashland Oil & Refining Co., 1948; dir. Ashland Oil & Refining Co., Am. Independent Oil Co., Am. Petroleum Inst., Toledo, Peoria & Western R.R. Dir. in charge Dist. II, Petroleum Adminstrn. for War, 1943-45. Mem. Nat. Petroleum Council. Pres. So. Ill. U. Alumni Assn. Mem. Indiana Soc. of Chicago. Mason (32 deg., Shriner). Clubs: Westwood Country (dir.); Union, Cleveland Advertising, Cleveland Petroleum. Author: (pamphlet) Mergeritis. Home: Rocky River, Ohio.

VAN DE WALL, WILLEM, educator; born Amsterdam, Holland, July 3, 1887; son of Marinus Emmarikus and Anna Wilhelmina (Welgel) van de W.; ed. Royal Conservatory, The Hague, 1902-06; Mus.Doc., Muhlenberg Coll., Allentown, Pa., 1925; m. Helene Trumm, 1909; children—Wasill, Roelof; m. 2d, Blanca F. Crooswyck, 1916; children—Bianca (Mrs. J. Walsh Stull), Wilhelmina Ruth (Mrs. Ken E. Pohlmann), married 3d, Clara Maria Liepmann, J.D., 1937. Came to United States, 1909, naturalized, 1918. Began career as harpist, concert and opera, in Europe, 1906-09; with Metropolitan Opera Co., 1910-16, N.Y. Symphony Orchestra, 1916-17, U.S. M.C. Band, 1917-19. Washington (D.C.) Opera Co., (choral dir.), 1919-20; pioneer in scientific use of music in social work; dir. Com. for Study of Music in Instns. since 1921; field rep. Bur. Mental Health, Pa. State Welfare Dept., 1923-32; lecturer on music in social and health work, Teachers College, Columbia, 1925-32 and 1936-37, visiting prof. of music edn., summer 1939; field rep. Am. Assn. for Adult Edn., 1936-37; prof. of music edn. and dir. community music study, University of Kentucky, 1937-40; dir. School of Music and professor music education. La. State U., 1940-43; research asso. Russell Sage Foundation after 1943; lecturer (on leave) New Sch. for Social Research, New York, since 1945; head adult edn. sect., edn. branch, I.A. and C. div., of Mil. Govt. (U.S.) for Germany, 1945-49; chief, community edn. br. Cultural Relations Div., Office Military Government (U.S.) for Germany, after 1949. Spl. mem. Nat. Fedn. of Music Clubs. Mem. Am. Assn. Adult Edn., Netherland-America Foundation, Music Edn. Nat. Conf.; Music Teachers Nat. Assn. Author: The Utilization of Music in Prisons and Mental Hospitals, 1924; Music in Institutions, 1936; The Music of the People, 1938; Music in Hospitals, 1946, also pamphlets (trans. into Dutch). Home: New York, N.Y. Deceased.

VAN DOREN, LLOYD, chem. consultant, patent atty.; b. Oldwick, N.J., Dec. 11, 1889; s. Benjamin and Emma Louise (Miller) Van D.; student Gettysburg Acad., 1903-05; B.S., Gettysburg (Pa.) Coll., 1909, M.S., 1913; Ph.D., Johns Hopkins Univ., 1912; m. Temperance A. Carpenter, Oct. 12, 1946; children—Cecil, Lloyd. Instr. chemistry, Lowell (Mass.) Textile Sch., 1912-13; asst. prof. Akron, 1913-14; prof. and head of chemistry dept. Earlham Coll., Richmond, Ind., 1914-19; chem. adviser Emery, Varney, Blair, & Hoguet, New York, 1919-20; cons. chemist and patent attorney, Chemical Foundation, Inc., New York, 1920-22; chem. consultant patents and patent causes, Mayer, Warfield and Watson, New York, 1922-29; mem. patent div. Allied Chem. and Dye Corp., N.Y., 1929-31; chem. cons. patents and patent causes, Watson, Leavenworth, Kelton and Taggart, N.Y.C., 1931-59. Trustee Gettysburg College, 1954-60. Member Board of Education, North Plainfield, New Jersey (1938-45), Common Council, 1944-48. Served as 1st lieutenant chemical warfare service, U.S.A., 1918, World War I. Fellow Am. Inst. of Chemists (v.p. 1923-29, chmn. N.Y. chapt. 1928, sec. 1945-59; honorary fellow), Arizona Academy of Science, A.A.A.S.; sr. mem. American Chemical Society; member Chemists Club of N.Y. (sec. 1945-59); New York Patent Law Association (life), also Phi Gamma Delta, Gamma Alpha, Phi Beta Kappa. Republican. Lutheran. Mason. Author of papers relating to chemical research and chemical patent causes published in Chemical Age (N.Y.); Jour. of the A.C.S.; Industrial and Chemical Engineering; Jour. of Chemical Education. Address: Tempe, Ariz.†

VAN DUSEN, FRANCIS LUND, U.S. circuit judge; b. Phila., May 16, 1912; s. Lewis H. and Muriel (Lund) Van D.; m. Rhe Brooke Meserole, June 11, 1942 (dec. Nov. 1976); children: Rhe Van D. Jain, Muriel Van D. Berkeley, Francis Lund, Clinton Meserole; m. Margaret Brooks Goodenough, Aug. 19, 1978. A.B., Princeton U., 1934; LL.B., Harvard U., 1937. Bar: Pa. 1938. Assoc. Dechert, Smith & Clark, 1937-41; with Barnes, Dechert, Price, Myers & Rhoads, 1945-55, ptnr., 1950-55; sr. atty. WPB, 1941-42; U.S. judge Eastern Dist. Pa., 1955-67, 3d U.S. circuit, from 1967; mem. Com. on Adminstrn. of Probation Systems, Jud. Conf. of U.S., 1963-72, chmn., 1971-72; mem. Com. on Adminstrn. of Criminal Law, 1969-71; Vice chmn. exec. com. Crime Prevention Assn. Served as lt. comdr. USNR, 1942-45. Decorated Bronze Star medal USN and USAAF. Mem. ABA, Fed. Bar Assn., Pa. Bar Assn. (exec. com. 1953-56), Phila. Bar Assn., Harvard Law Sch. Assn. Phila. (past pres.), World Affairs Council Phila., Am. Legion, Mil. Order Fgn. Wars, Navy League, Pa. Soc., S.A.R., Phi Beta Kappa. Clubs: Princeton (dir. 1947-52, 77-81, pres. 1978-79); Merion Cricket (Phila.), Lawyers (Phila.), Phila. (Phila.). Home: Wynnewood, PA.

VAN FOSSAN, ERNEST HARVEY, fed. judge; b. Lisbon, O., Sept. 6, 1888; s. William Harvey and Eva Sophia (Morris) Van F.; grad. New Lyme Inst., South New Lyme, O., 1904; A.B., Oberlin Coll., 1909; A.M. and LL.B., Columbia, 1913; m. Frances Brady, June 26, 1926 (dec. 1958). Mem. firm Billingsley, Moore & Van Fossan, Lisbon, 1913-17; made survey of efficiency and economy, Panama Canal Zone govt., 1919; counsel and mem. War Dept. Claims Bd., 1919-21; chief counsel and mem. War Credits Bd., 1920-23; sec. spl. Panama Canal Commn., 1921; asst. counsel U.S. Shipping Bd., 1921-24; dir. of claims, U.S. Shipping Bd., Feb.-Dec. 1923; mem. Gregg & Van Fossan, 1924-26; mem. U.S. Bd. of Tax Appeals, from 1926, the Tax Ct. of the U.S., 1942. Served U.S. Army, 1917-1919. Mem. Am., Ohio bar assns., Phi Kappa Psi, Delta Sigma Rho, Sons of Vets., Am. Legion. Republican. Presbyn. Mason. Club: National Press. Home: Lisbon, OH. †

VAN HOUTEN, LYMAN HENRY, pres. state teachers coll.; b. Bismarck, N.D., Mar. 10, 1888; s. William and Aria Gertrude (Van Helden) Van H.; grad. Pella (Iowa) High Sch., 1904; A.B., Central Coll., Pella, 1908; student U. of Chicago, summers, 1908, 09, 15; A.M., U. Iowa 1913; Ph.D., Columbia, 1932; m. Olive Blanche Henderson, June 4, 1916; children—Margaret, Olive Blanche. Supt. of schs., Ainsworth, Ia., 1908-09, Winfield, Ia., 1909-12; asst. in edn., U. of Ia., 1912-13; supt. of schs., Toledo, Ia., 1913-16; prof. of edn. State Teachers Coll., Cedar Falls, Ia., 1916-18, U. of Wyo., 1920-21; field sec. U.S. Chamber of Commerce, 1920; prof. of edn. and psychology, State Teachers Coll., Edinboro, Pa., 1921-40, pres., 1940-54; visiting professor psychology and education Westminster College, New Wilmington, Pa., after 1954; visiting lecturer Ohio U., summers 1939, 40. Mem. board of directors Pennsylvania Heart Assn. Served as captain Sanitary Corps, U.S. Army, psychol. service, 1916-18; ednl. reconstruction service in army hosps. Licensed pub. sch. psychologist in Pa. Vice pres. Erie (Pa.) Ednl. Television Corporation. Mem. N.E.A., Pa. State Edn. Assn., Pa. Assn. Clin. Psychologists, Am. Assn. Applied Psychologists, Am. Psych. Assn., Pa. Assn. for Edn. of Exceptional Children, Am. Legion, Grange, Phi Delta Kappa, Kappa Delta Pi. Republican. Presbyterian (elder). Mason (32 deg., Shriner). Club: Rotary (Edinboro-Cambridge Springs). Home: New Wilmington, Pa. Deceased.

VAN KLEECK, HAROLD L., banker; b. N.Y.C., 1888. Vice pres. Chase Nat. Bank, N.Y.C. Home: Brooklyn, N.Y. †

VAN METER, CRAIG, lawyer; b. Charleston, Ill., Aug. 25, 1895; s. John and Ina (Craig) Van M.; LL.B., U. Ill., 1917; m. Eliza Haynes, Apr. 7, 1921; 1 child, Alice. Admitted to Ill. bar, 1917; practiced in Mattoon, Ill., from 1919; ptnr. firm Craig & Craig, from 1923; asst. atty. gen. Ill. Inheritance Tax Div., 1932-33; judge 5th Jud. Circuit Ill., 1933-36; master-in-chancery Fed. Ct. Eastern Dist. Ill., 1951-65; mem. legal com. Interstate Oil Compact Commn., 1951-52. Mem. Mattoon Bd. Edn., 1925-31; appeal agt. Draft Bd. 2, Coles County, 1941-45. Del. Democratic Nat. Conv., 1932. Vice pres., bd. dirs. United Fund, 1963-64; former pres. bd. trustees Meml. Methodist Hosp.; mem. U. Ill. Found. Served as 2d lt. U.S. Army, 1917-19; AEF. Mem. Mattoon Assn. Commerce (past dir. indsl. com.), Am., Ill. (chmn. exec. com. mineral law 1955-56), 7th Fed. Circuit bar assns., Am. Coll. Probate Counsel, Am. Judicature Soc., Soc. Trial Lawyers, Am. Legion (past comdr.), Order of Coif, Phi Delta Phi, Phi Delta Theta. Episcopalian. Club: Mattoon Country. Home: Mattoon, Ill. Deceased.

VAN METRE, THOMAS EARLE, naval officer (ret.); b. Berkeley Co., W. Va., Aug. 24, 1887; s. Elijah Whitson and Mary Ann (Byers) V.; B.S., U.S. Naval Acad., 1909; grad. Naval War Coll., 1937; m. Anne Heap Gleaves, June 19, 1915 (dec. April 17, 1940); children—Evelina Gleaves (Mrs. Frank Thompson), Thomas Earle, Albert Gleaves; m. 2d, Jane Sites Geyer, June 8, 1945. Commd. ensign U.S. Navy, 1909, and advanced through grades to commodore, 1944; served in U.S.S. New Jersey and North Dakota, 1909-12, U.S.S. New York, 1914-15, U.S.S. Wilkes and Stribling, 1917-18; comdr. U.S.S. C 1 (submarine), 1911-13, U.S.S. Ellis, 1919-21; served at U.S. Naval Torpedo Sta., Newport, R.I., 1922-24; staff mem. light cruiser div., 1925-27; comdr. Pacific coast torpedo sta., Keyport, Wash., 1927-29, U.S.S. Dent, 1929-31, U.S.S. Concord, 1934-36; communications div., U.S. Navy Dept., 1937-38; comdr. destroyer squadrons, 1939-41; dep. insp. gen. of U.S. Navy, 1942-47. Awarded Legion of Merit, World War I and II medals, Mexican campaign medal, Am. Defense medal. Republican. Protestant. Episcopalian. Club: Army and Navy (Washington). Home: Martinsburg, W. Va. †

VAN NIEL, CORNELIS BERNARDUS, prof. microbiology; b. Haarlem, Netherlands, Nov. 4, 1897; s. Jan Hendrik and Geertien Gesiena (Hagen) van N.; Chem. E. Tech. Univ., Delft, Holland, 1922, D.Sc., 1928; D.Sc., Princeton U., 1946, Rutgers U., 1954; LL.D., University of California at Davis, 1968; m. Christina van Hemert, August 17, 1923; children—Ester, Ruth, Jan. Came to U.S., 1928. Asst. in microbiology, Tech. Univ., Delft, 1922-23, conservator, 1923-28; acting asso. prof. of microbiology, Stanford U. 1929-31, asso. prof., 1931-35, prof. from 1935, Herzstein professor of biology, 1946-63, Herzstein prof. biology emeritus, 1963-85; vis. prof. microbiology U. Cal., Santa Cruz, part time, 1964-68. Served in Dutch Army, 1917-19. Recipient Nat. Medal Sci., 1964. Emil Christian Hansen Medal, 1964, Rumford Medal, 1967, mem. Deutsche Akademie Der Naturforscher Leopoldina A.A.A.S., Am. Soc. Microbiol. (hon.), Am. Philos. Soc., Am. Acad. Arts and Scis., Sci. Gen. Microbiol. (Gt. Brit.), erlands Soc. Microbiology, Calif. Acad. Sci., Am. Microbiol. (hon. mem.), Am. Soc. Naturalists (hon.), Göttingen Akademie der Wissenschafted, Koninklyke Nederlandse Akademie van Wetenschappen. Author: The Propionic Acid Bacteria, 1928; The Microbe's Contbribution to Biology (with A.J. Klyver), 1956. Contbr. to sci. jours. Home: Carmel, Calif. Died Mar. 10, 1985.

VAN SLYKE, HELEN, novelist; b. Washington, July 9, 1919; d. Frederic Vogt and Lenore Vogt (Lyon); Journalist, Washington Evening Star, 1938-43, Glamour Mag., 1945-60; v.p. Norman, Craig & Kummel Advt. Agy., 1961-63; pres. Givenchy Perfumes, N.Y.C., 1963-68; v.p. Helena Rubinstein, Inc., N.Y.C., 1968-72; author: All Visitors Must Be Announced, 1972; The Heart Listens, 1974; The Mixed Blessing, 1975; Always Is Not Forever, 1977; The Best Place To Be, 1976; The Rich and the Righteous, 1971; Sisters and Strangers, 1978; A Necessary Woman, 1979; contbr. nat. mags. Recipient Today's Woman award, 1977. Mem. Fashion Group (internat. pres. 1966-67), AFTRA. Fgn. reprints of books in 16 langs. Home: Key Largo, Fla. Dec. July 3, 1979.

VAN TUYL, FRANCIS MAURICE, geologist; b. Denmark, Ia., Oct. 15, 1887; s. Howard M. and Dorothy (Graeber) Van T.; A.B., State U. of Ia., 1911, M.S., 1912; studied U. of Chicago, 1914-15; Ph.D., Columbia, 1915; m. Euphama Jane Green, May 5, 1920; children—Euphama Jane (Mrs. H. A. Rogers), Catrina Frances (Mrs. G. W. Hoffman). Asst. geology State U. Ia., 1911-12; fellow geology, Columbia University, 1912-13; asst. in paleontology, 1913-14; investigations on Mississippian faunas, for state geol. surveys of Ia., Ill. and Mo., 1914-15; instr. in geology, U. of Ill., 1915-17; served as geologist Iowa Geol. Survey (1912-17) and U. of Ill. Hudson Bay Exploring Expdn. (1916); with Colo. Sch. of Mines, from 1917, prof. geology and head of dept., 1919-53, professor emeritus, from 1953, consultant, from 1953; geologist Texas Co., 1919, 1922, geologist Midwest Refining Co., 1920; pres. Plains Exploration Company, 1930-41; consulting practice Brazil, 1945. Captain Engineers O.R.C., 1923-38. Mem. engineer Committee Interstate Oil Compact Commn., 1940-59, research and coordinating com., 1941-51; mem. Colo. oil and gas conservation commn., 1954-57. Mem. com. author's abstracts National Research Council, 1941-43. Fellow Geol. Soc. Am., Ia. Acad. Sci; hon. Mem. Am. Assn. Petroleum Geologists (mem. research com. 1940-46); mem. Ill. Acad. Science, Paleontol. Soc. America, Colo. Scientific Soc., Rocky Mt. Assn. Geologists (hon.), Sigma Xi, Phi Beta Kappa, Tau Beta Pi, Sigma Gamma Epsilon, Kappa Sigma, Scabbard and Blade. Rep. Author or co-author book relating to field; also sci. papers, articles and reports. Home: Golden, Colo. †

VAN VLIET, CORNELIUS, cellist; b. Rotterdam, Holland, Sept. 1, 1889; s. Teunis and Petronella Johanna (van Stight-Thans) Van V.; began at 6 to study violin and piano under father; studied cello with Prof. Oskar Eberle, Rotterdam, and Prof. J. Mossel, Amsterdam; m. Elsa Schmidt, Jan. 2, 1909. Appeared as soloist in larger cities of Holland, at 12; mem. Amsterdam Concertgebouw Orchestra at 15; became solo cellist of Philharmonic Orchestra, Leipzig, 1903, later with Philharmonic Orchestra, Prague, and the Kaim Orchestra, Munich; solo cellist Vienna Royal Opera House, 1908-11; came to U.S., 1912; has played with marked approval in leading musical centers; first cellist and soloist, New York Philharmonic Orchestra, 1919-29; has toured U.S. and Can. as soloist; first cellist Pittsburgh Symphony Orchestra, 1938-41; touring U.S. and Can. in recital and concert; founder New York Trio, and Van Vliet Trio; prof. music U. Colo., 1948-53; touring Mexico, Central and South Am. Mem. Beethoven Assn., Pro Musica. Club: The Bohemians. †

VAN VOLKENBURGH, ROBERT HEBER, army officer; b. Detroit, Mich., Feb. 5, 1890; s. Heber Smith and Ida Maria (Taylor) Van V.; B.S., U.S. Mil. Acad., 1913; M.S., Mass. Inst. Tech., 1920; grad. Coast Arty. Sch. (advanced course), 1927, Command and Gen. Staff Sch., 1928, Army War Coll., 1933, Naval War Coll., 1938; m. Jean Walker Robertson, June 12, 1913; children—Robert

Heber, Jeannette. Commd. 2d lt., Coast Arty. Corps., June 12, 1913; promoted through grades to brig. gen. (temp.), Sept. 30, 1941. Awarded Victory medal; La Estrella de Abdón Calderón. Methodist. Deceased.

VARCOE, FREDERICK PERCY, b. Toronto, Ont., Canada, Oct. 1, 1889; s. Frederick Richard and Charlotte V.; student Harbord Coll.; U. of Toronto; m. Helen Gregory Stewart, 1928. Deputy minister of justice; mem. Kings Counsel. Decorated Companion of St. Michael and St. George. Clubs: Rideau, University, Royal Ottawa Golf. †

VARRELMAN, FERDINAND ARMIN, biologist; b. St. Louis, Mo., June 6, 1888; s. Ferdinand Frederick and Whilemena (Bruné) V.; student U. of Mo., 1907-09, 1910-11; A.B., U. of Calif, 1915; A.M., Columbia, 1922; student Mo. Bot. Gardens, 1909-10, N.Y. Bot. Gardens, 1922-25, U. of Vienna, and Agrl. Inst., Vienna, 1935-36; m. Sallie Bell Kappes, June 15, 1926 (dec.); 1 son, F. Kappes; married 2d, Mary E. Osborn, Aug. 15, 1960. Began as florist, St. Louis, 1907; instr. of zoology and entomology, Pa. State Coll., 1911-13; asst. in entomology, U. of Calif., 1913-15; instr. in biology, New York U., 1922-25; biologist Nat. Research Council in marine investigations, 1922-25; prof. of biology, American University, 1925-37, DePaul University, Chicago, 1937-41, George Williams College, Chicago, 1941-43. Horticulturist (stationed in Central America) Foreign Econ. Administration Economic Warfare, 1943-45, Bur. Entomology and Plant Quarantine, 1945-47; prof. botany, Madison Coll., Harrisonberg, Va,; prof. emeritus botany, dir. arboretum, Miss. So. College. Apptd. by House Lib. Com., 74th Congress, to inspect European botanical gardens for purpose of establishing botanical garden in Washington, D.C., 1935-36. Awarded fellowship N.Y. Bot. Garden, 1929-30. Fellow A.A.A.S.; mem. Bot. Soc. America, Torrey Bot. Club, Am. Microscopical Soc., Entonol. Soc. America, Am. Genetic Assn., Calif. Acad. Sciences, N.Y. Acad. of Sciences, Am. Assn. Univ. Profs., Beta Beta Beta, Quaker. Author of govt. reports and contbr. to professional jours. Address: San Diego, Cal. †

VASS, GUY BOYD, merger and acquisition company executive; b. Galax, Va., Aug. 23, 1918; s. Dennis Shelby and Laura E. (Payne) V.; m. Katherine S. Pittenger, Dec. 10, 1938; children: Suzanne Kay, Dennis Boyd, Carol Lynn. Grad. bus. adminstrn., Jackson Bus. U., 1937; student, Mich. State U. With Hayes Industries Inc., Jackson, Mich., 1937-69, exec. v.p., 1955-59, pres., 1959-69, Thompson Industries, Inc. subsidiary ITT, Southfield, 1970-73, Cova Corp., Jackson, 1973-84; v.p. Am. Chain & Cable Co., Bridgeport, Conn., 1974-82; pres. Fifty Plus Five Corp., West Unity, Ohio, 1957-84, Plastigage Corp., Jackson, 1957-84, Denva Corp., 1982-84; exec. v.p. Hayes-Albion Corp.; dir. Macklin Co., Jackson, City Bank and Trust Co., Jackson. Past pres. dir. Jackson YMCA; trustee Hillsdale Coll. Mem. Am. Mgmt. Assn., Jackson C. of C. (dir.), Soc. Automotive Engrs., Indsl. Execs. Club (past pres., dir.), Mfrs. Assn. Jackson (past dir.). Presbyterian. Clubs: Masons, Jackson Country, Recess, Detroit Athletic. Home: Jackson, Mich. Died Oct. 9, 1984.

VAUGHAN, AGNES CARR, educator, author; b. Richland, N.J., Feb. 1, 1887; d. Alexander S. and Ida Elizabeth (Pettit) Vaughan; A.B., Galloway Coll., 1907; A.M., U. of Mich., 1910; Ph.D., 1917; student, Bryn Mawr Coll., 1915-18 (fellow in Greek, 1915-16); spl. student, Columbia U., Sorbonne, College de France, Paris, Am. Sch. of Classical Studies, Athens, Am. Acad., Rome; unmarried. Instr. classics, Hardin Coll., Mexico, Mo., 1911-15; asst. prof. Greek, Wells Coll., Aurora, N.Y., 1918-24; asso. prof. classics, Smith Coll., 1926-45, prof., 1945-52, fgn. student advisor, 1944-52. Mem. Am. Philol. Assn., Am. Archaeol. Assn., New Eng. Classical Assn., Am. Assn. of Univ. Profs., Am. Assn. of Univ. Women, Nat. Assn. Fgn. Student Advisers, Am. Sch. of Classical Studies, Athens (mng. com.). Author: (hist. fiction) Lucian Goes A-Voyaging; Within The Walls, 1935; Evenings in a Greek Bazaar; Akka, Dwarf of Syracuse; (anthropol. study) The Genesis of Human Offspring, 1945. Contbr. articles to various publs. Home: Northampton, Mass. †

VAUGHT, GEORGE WASHINGTON, b. Palestine, Tex., June 21, 1888; s. William Everett and Emmie Harrison (Cochran) V.; student Southwestern U., 1907-10; m. Clatie Harrell, July 10, 1916; children—Elaine V. Adams, George Harrell. Teacher, 1910-13; with First National Bank, Port Arthur, Texas, 1913-17; with Montgomery Ward & Co., 1917-40, treas., 1933-40, dir., 1936-40; v.p. B. F. Goodrich Co. 1940-51, dir. Methodist. Address: Medina, Tex. †

VEAZEY, GEORGE ROSS, lawyer; b. Balt., Apr. 19, 1890; s. Duncan and Annie (Knight) V.; A.B., Johns Hopkins, 1910, M.A., 1913; LL.B., U. Md., 1912; m. Grace Rogers Roberts, Oct. 21, 1922. Admitted to Md. bar, from 1912, practiced in Balt.; mem. firm Niles, Barton & Wilmer. Home: Baltimore, MD. †

VEGA, JUAN BAUTISTA, Maya chief (Tata); b. Isla Cozumel, Quintana Roo, Mexico, June 24, 1889; s. Gerada Arguelles Vega; m. Marie Cen; children—Petrouillo, Martiano, Kidnapped by Maya Indians of Territory Quintana Roos at age ten; adopted by Maya chief Florintino Cituk at age eleven; translator, sec. to chief in peace negotiations of War of the Castes (Mexican Govt. and Mayas); sec. of church with title sec. of the saint, 1918; custodian Maya holy book of ch. of Chumpon, Quintana Roo; mem. Tatoob (chief), 1919; commnd. by Maya Gen. Guadalope Tun to receive return of city No Cah Santa Cruz to automony, renamed Carrillo Puerto; offered generalship in Mexican army but evaded acceptance as incompatible with religious work; with deaths of other chief became Tata of these tribes; popularly called El Rey de los Maya (King of the Mayas), but calls himself sec. gen. †

VEHE, KARL LEROY, physician; b. Palatine, Ill., Oct. 19, 1888; s. John George and Caroline N. (Engelking) V.; M.D., Northwestern U. Med. Sch., 1915; m. Emily A. Mielke, June 12, 1911; children—Ruth Emily, Karl Leroy, Robert Richard. In practice of medicine at Chicago from 1915; prof. of anatomy, Northwestern U. Dental Sch.; also asso. in surgery Northwestern U. Med. School. Fellow A.M.A., Am. College of Surgeons. Home: Chicago, Ill. †

VELDE, GAIL PATRICK, TV producer; b. Birmingham, Ala., June 20; d. Lawrence C. and La Valle (Smith) Fitzpatrick; A.B. with honors, Howard Coll. (now Samford U.); m. John E. Velde, Jr., Sept. 28, 1974; children by previous marriage—Jennifer Stanley Jackson, Thomas Cornwell Jackson, Jr. Actress in motion pictures including My Man Godfrey, Stage Door, My Favorite Wife, Up in Mabel's Room, Claudia and David; propr. Gail Patrick's Enchanted Cottage, children's shop, Beverly Hills, Calif., 1945-54, Gail Patrick's Enchanted Weavers, Beverly Hills, 1950-51; exec. producer Perry Mason Show, Paisano Prodns., Hollywood, Calif., 1957-66; mng. partner Paisano Prodns., 1957-80, pres., 1966-80; exec. cons. The New Perry Mason, 1973-74. Treas., Los Angeles County chpt. Freedoms Found. at Valley Forge, 1967-68; 1st v.p. The Muses, Mus. Sci. and Industry, Los Angeles, 1967-68, 1st vice-chmn. bd. dirs., 1979-80; co-chmn. Mayor's Celebrity Com., Los Angeles, 1966-80; nat. hon. chmn. Christmas Seal Campaign, 1970, Am. Lung Assn.; chmn. bd. dirs. Am. Diabetes Assn., 1973-74, bd. dirs., 1972-76, mem. nat. adv. council, 1979-80, chmn. public affairs com., 1972-76, bd. dirs. So. Calif. affiliate, 1977-80; mem. Nat. Commn. on Digestive Diseases, 1977-79; mem. bd. councilors Brain Research Inst., U. Calif. at Los Angeles, 1978-80; mem. nat. arthritis, metabolism and digestive diseases adv. council NIH, 1972-76; mem. adv. council U. Mid Am., 1974-80; regent Immaculate Heart Coll., Los Angeles, 1968-73; bd. dirs. Film Industries, Workshop, 1966-68; bd. dirs., co-chmn. bd. trustees Center for Ulcer Research and Edn. Found., 1977-80; bd. dirs., mem. fin. com. YMCA Met. Los Angeles, 1974-80; trustee Columbia Coll., 1963-84; v.p. bd. dirs. Digestive Diseases Info. Center, 1978-84. Named Woman of Year, Los Angeles Times, 1961. Businesswomen of Year, Nat. Assn. Accountants, 1962; recipient Muses award, 1966; Justica award Nat. Assn. Women Lawyers, 1960. Mem. Acad. TV Arts and Scis. (nat. trustee, bd. govs. 1959-63, chpt. pres. 1960-62, nat. v.p. 1960-62), Am. Women for Internat. Understanding, Les Dames de Champagne (Los Angeles), Delta Zeta (v.p. found. 1961-62, dir. 1961-65), Zeta Phi Eta. Home: Hollywood, Calif. Died July 6, 1980.

VELTFORT, THEODORE ERNST, engr.; b. N.Y. City, Sept. 29, 1888; s. Ernst Herman Frederick and Rosa (Bleyer) V.; B.S., New York U., 1911, C.E., 1912; m. Elsie Baxter, 1945; children—Theodore Ernst, Mrs. Mary Jean Cox-Ameen, Richard G. Baxter, Robert C. Baxter, Brooke D. Baxter. With Stone & Webster Engring. Corp., successively as engr., exec. asst. and cons. on assignments in different locations throughout U.S., 1911-38; mng. dir. Copper and Brass Research Assn. until 1964; Copper and Brass Fabricators Council, 1964-71, cons., from 1971; chmn. adv. council on Fed. Reports 1950-52. Mem. bus. research council Bur. Labor statistics, U.S. Dept. Labor. Mem. Am. Trade Assn. Execs. (pres. 1948), Trade Assn. Execs. N.Y.C. (pres. 1947), Am. Soc. C.E. (life), Am. Arbitration Assn. (panel arbitrators), Am. Standards Assn. (past chmn. standards council), Inst. Orgn. Mgmt. (regent 1959-60), Soc. Bus. Adv. Professions (pres., dir.), Phi Beta Kappa, Phi Gamma Delta, Tau Beta Pi, Iota Alpha. Republican. Episcopalian. Clubs: Sales Executives, Engineers, Copper (past pres.). Home: Westport, CT. †

VERBRUGGE, FRANK, physics educator; b. Chandler, Minn., Dec. 22, 1913; s. James and Maria (Vander Vliet) V.; B.A., Calvin Coll., Grand Rapids, Mich., 1934; M.A., U. Mo., 1940, Ph.D., 1942; m. C. Helen Roelofs, Dec. 27, 1940; children—Anne Louise, Lois Marie, Robert Roelofs, Martha Helen. Instr. physics U. Mo., 1940-41; prof. N.E. Mo. State Tchrs. Coll., Kirksville, 1941-43; from asst. prof. to prof. physics Carleton Coll., 1943-56; mem. staff radiation lab. Mass. Inst. Tech., 1944-46; assoc. prof. physics U. Minn., 1956-59, prof., 1959—, assoc. dean Inst. Tech., 1959-68, dir. University Computer Services, 1968—. Mem. Commn. Coll. Physics, 1961-63; cons. higher edn. Latin Am., West Africa, Ford Found. Mem. Am. Assn. Physics Tchrs. (sec. 1956-61, pres. 1962-63), Am. Phys. Soc., AAAS, Sigma Xi. Home: Saint Paul, Minn. Died Jan. 15, 1985.

VERITY, CALVIN, bank exec.; b. Newport, Ky., Sept. 19, 1889; s. George Matthew and Jennie M. (Standish) V.; M.E., Cornell U., 1911; m. Elizabeth O'Brien, June 8, 1912; children—Elizabeth Jane (Mrs. John Blakey), Calvin, Jean Standish (Mrs. James Woodhull). Began in machine shop American Rolling Mill Company, Middletown, Ohio, 1904, successively pump tender, foreman boiler house, assistant superintendent of sheet mill, supervisor betterment dept. and asst. to gen. supt., became treas., 1921, asst. gen. mgr., 1926, v.p., 1930, dir. from 1926, mem. finance com. since 1927, exec. v.p. and gen. mgr., 1938, chmn. finance com., 1947; gen. consultant from 1948. Indsl. Advisor to Gen. MacArthur as dep. chief Econ. and Sci. Sect. of Supreme Comdr. of Allied Powers, 1949. Chmn. First Nat. Bank, Middletown; chmn., member board directors Business International, Cincinnati Gas & Electric Co. Mem. Ohio (v.p., dir.), Middletown (dir.) Chamber of Commerce, Sigma Alpha Epsilon. Clubs: Queen City (Cin.). Home: Middletown, OH. †

VERMEULEN, THEODORE, chemical engineer; b. Los Angeles, May 7, 1916; s. Aurele and M Scott (Douglas) V.; m. Mary Dorothy Cole, June 24, 1939; children: Raymond, Bruce. B.S., Calif. Inst. Tech., 1936, M.S., 1937; Ph.D., UCLA, 1942. Registered profl. engr., Calif. Research chem. engr. Union Oil Co., Wilmington, Calif., 1937-40, Shell Devel. Co., Emeryville, Calif., 1941-47; assoc. prof. chem. engring. U. Calif., Berkeley, 1947-51, prof., 1951-83, chmn. div. chem. engring., 1947-53, Miller research prof., 1960-61, faculty scientist Lawrence Berkeley Lab., 1947-83, dir. Water Tech. Center, 1980-83, Fulbright prof., Belgium, France, 1953-54; Guggenheim fellow, resident Cambridge (Eng.) U., 1963-64; vis. prof. Nat. U. Mexico, 1967, Syracuse U., 1971, U. Karlsruhe, 1974, South China Inst. Tech., 1981; Reilly lectr. U. Notre Dame, 1972; cons. in field; dir. Memorex Corp., 1963-81. Sect. editor: Chem. Engrs. Handbook, 1963-83; co-editor: Advances in Chem. Engring, 1964-81; contbr. articles to profl. jours. Fellow Am. Inst. Chem. Engrs. (William H. Walker award 1971); mem. Am. Chem. Soc. (nat. council 1975-77), Am. Inst. Aeros., Astronautics, Am. Meteorol. Soc., Am. Nuclear Soc., Combustion Inst., Catalysis Soc., Am. Water Works Assn., Water Supply Improvement Assn., Am. Soc. Engring. Edn., Sigma Xi, Tau Beta Pi, Alpha Chi Sigma. Clubs: Commonwealth (San Francisco); Faculty (Berkeley). Patentee in chem. processes, process principles; inventor Optel spelling. Home: Berkeley, Calif. Died Oct. 29, 1983.

VER WIEBE, WALTER AUGUST, prof. of geology; b. Schenectady, N.Y., Aug. 26, 1887; s. Ernest Christian and Mary Alice (Lock) Ver W.; A.B., Cornell U., 1911, Ph.D., 1917; m. Amy Williams, June 27, 1916; 1 dau., Eugenia Beatrice. Instr. in geology, Cornell U., 1911-13, Ohio State U., 1913-18; field geologist Sinclair Oil Co., 1918-20; chief geologist Mexican Sinclair Oil Co., 1920-23; instr. of geology, U. of Mich., 1923-27; head dept. of geology, U. of Wichita, from 1927. Fellow Geol. Soc., America; mem. Am. Assn. Petroleum Geologists (editor), Phi Beta Kappa, Sigma Xi, Delta Epsilon. Author: Oil Fields in the United States, 1930; Historical Geology, 1935; Science of Petroleum (with Dunstan and others), 1938. Compiler: Proceedings of 8th Annual Field Conf., 1934, 9th Conf., 1935. Contbr. articles to professional jours. Home: Wichita, Kans. *

VESIC, ALEKSANDAR SEDMAK, civil engr., educator; b. Resan-Bitolj, Yugoslavia, Aug. 8, 1924; came to U.S., 1958, naturalized, 1964; s. Bozidar P. and Teofanija (Jancic) V.; m. Milena Sedmak, May 5, 1946. B.C.E. with highest honor, U. Belgrade, 1950, C.E., 1952, D.Sc., 1956; postgrad., U. Manchester, Eng., 1957, M.I.T., 1959, U. Ghent, Belgium, 1957-58; Dr.h.c., U. Ghent, Belgium, 1980. Engring. aide Bur. Reclamation, Belgrade, 1942-44; instr. U. Belgrade, 1949-52; civil engr. large dam Drina I and Corps Engrs., Yugoslav Army, 1952-53; also cons. engr., Belgrade, 1952-56; lectr. U. Belgrade; also cons. Nat. Inst. Testing Materials, 1953-56; research engr. Nat. Geotech. Inst. Belgium, Ghent, 1956-58; asst. prof., then asso. prof. civil engring. Ga. Inst. Tech., 1958-64, also cons. engr., Atlanta; prof. civil engring. Duke, 1964-71, J.A. Jones prof., 1971-82, chmn. dept., 1968-74, dean engring., 1974-82; cons. engr., Durham, 1964-82; fellow Churchill Coll., Cambridge (Eng.) U., 1971-72; Chmn. com. theory pavement design Hwy. Research Bd., 1965-70; mem. adv. panel pavements, nat. coop. hwy. research program Nat. Acad. Scis., 1967-82; gen. reporter 3d Panam. Conf., Caracas, 1968, 5th Conf., Buenos Aires, 1975; v.p. main session 5th European Conf., Madrid, 1972. Author: Bearing Capacity of Shallow Foundations, 1971; also, papers.; Editor, contbr.: Bearing Capacity and Settlement of Foundations, 1967. Recipient prize scholastic achievement Nat. Com. Univs. Yugoslavia, 1949; 3d prize competition design Sava River bridge, 1953; Chi Epsilon award as outstanding prof. civil engring., 1967; Hwy. Research Bd. award for paper spl. merit NRC, 1969; Overseas fellow Churchill Coll., Cambridge (Eng.) U., 1970. Fellow ASCE (chmn. com. deep founds. 1968-74, Thomas A. Middlebrooks award 1974); mem. Internat. Soc. Soil Mechanics, Internat. Assn. Bridge and Structural Engrs., Am. Soc. Engring. Edn., AAAS, Duke U. Engring. Alumni Assn. (Disting. Service award 1981), Sigma Xi, Chi Epsilon (hon.), Tau Beta Pi (hon.); corr. mem. Venezuelan Soc. Soil Mech. Found Engring.; hon. mem. Colombian Geotech. Soc. Club: Cosmos (Washington). Home: Durham, N.C. Died May 3, 1982.

VESTAL, ALLAN DELKER, lawyer, educator; b. Indpls., Nov. 26, 1920; A.B., DePauw U., 1943; LL.B., Yale U., 1949. Admitted to Iowa bar, 1949; instr. law U. Iowa, Iowa City, 1949-50, asst. prof., 1950-53, asso. prof., 1953-57, prof., 1957-67, Murray prof., 1967-72, Carver prof., 1972-83; vis. prof. Tex. Tech. U., Lubbock, summer

1974, U. Tenn., Knoxville, 1975, U. N.C., Chapel Hill, 1976, U. So. Calif., 1977. Mem. Johnson County Regional Planning Commn., 1965-78; mem. Nat. Conf. Commrs. on Uniform State Laws, 1964-83. Mem. Order of Coif (v.p.). Author: Res Judicata/Preclusion, 1969, Iowa Practice, 1974, Iowa Land Use and Zoning Law, 79. Home: Iowa City, Iowa. Died May 5, 1983.

VESTAL, EDGAR FRED, plant pathologist; b. Ashland, Ore., Spet. 5, 1890; s. William H. and Anna A. (Bushnell) V.; B.S. in Horticulture, Ore. State Coll., 1916; M.S. in Botany and Plant Pathology, U. Wis., 1923; Ph.D., Ia. State U., 1932; m. Grace Trestrail, Aug. 26, 1925; 1 dau., Elizabeth Ann. Tchr. biology colls. in U.S., also Allahabad (India) Agrl. Inst.; emergency plant disease survey, Ia. and Ind., 1944-45; staff Ia. State Coll-Guatemala Tropical Research Center, 1948-50; research prof. Ia. State Coll., 1950-52; plant pathology adviser ICA, Dept. State, 1952-63, Agy. International Development, from 1963, assigned Korea. Served as 1st lt., inf., U.S. Army, World War I; AEF in France. Decorated Croix de Guerre with bronze star. Mem. Sigma Xi. Presbyn. Home: Ames, Ia. †

VIDOR, KING WALLIS, motion picture dir. and producer; b. Galveston, Tex., Feb. 8, 1895; s. Charles Shelton and Kate (Wallis) V.; m. Eleanor Boardman, Sept. 1926; children—Suzanne, Antonia, Belinda; (m. 3d), July 26, 1937. Ed. high sch., Galveston, and Peacock Mil. Acad., San Antonio. mem. cinema dept. U. So. Calif. Dir.: many motion pictures, including Solomon and Sheba, in 1959, The Big Parade, The Crowd, Hallelujah, Street Scene, The Citadel, Northwest Passage, H.M. Pulham, Esq., The Fountainhead, War and Peace; and others; Recipient (of the Christopher award 1957, and of the D. W. Griffith award 1957, Golden Thistle award Edinburgh Film Festival 1964, Outstanding Achievement award Dirs. Guild Am. 1957); Author: autobiography A Tree is a Tree, 1953, Guerra e Pace, 1956, King Vidor on Film-Making, 1972. Decorated Order of Merit Italian Gout., 1970. Mem. Acad. Motion Picture Arts and Scis. (recipient Oscar 1979). Club: Bel Air Country. Died Nov. 1, 1982.

VIERLING, BERNARD JULIUS, cons.; b. Bakersfield, Calif., Dec. 27, 1914; s. Bernard Julius and Elizabeth J. (Wilcox) V.; B.S. in Mech. Engring., Stanford U., 1936; m. Martha Jane Peairs, July 20, 1939; children—Lawrence Bernard, Bruce Wilcox, Karen Jane. Engr., Douglas Aircraft Co., 1936-39; chief engr., dir. engring. and maintenance Pa.-Central Airlines, 1939-47; pres. Aircraft Advisers, Inc., Washington, 1946-48, Aircraft Supply Corp., Washington, 1948-54, Helidusters, Inc., Washington, 1950-52; partner Aircraft Supply Co., Washington, 1954-62; dir. systems maintenance service FAA, 1962-65, dep. dir. supersonic transp. devel., 1965-71; dir. Morgantown program Urban Mass Transp. Adminstrn., Dept. Transp., 1971-73, spl. counselor to asso. adminstr. research and devel., 1973-74, dir. bus and rail research and devel., 1974-75, dir. bus. and paratransit tech. devel., 1975-79, cons., 1979-83. Recipient Nat. award for economy achievement Pres. Johnson, 1964; Sec.'s award Dept. Transp., 1973. Mem. Nat. Aero. Assn., Air Force Assn., Phi Gamma Delta. Clubs: Nat. Aviation (life; gov. 1954—, v.p. 1954-56, pres. 1956-58), Aero (Washington); Belle Haven Country (Alexandria). Home: Flint Hill, Va. Died Dec. 27, 1983; interred Flint Hill, Va.

VIETS, HENRY ROUSE, neurologist; b. Lynn, Mass., Mar. 7, 1890; s. Henry Rouse and Annie Rebecca (Tufts) V.; B.Sc., Dartmouth Coll., 1912; M.D., Harvard Med. Sch., 1916, Moseley travelling fellow, 1916-17 (Oxford University); unmarried. In practice neurol. since 1916; neurologist Mass. Gen. Hosp.; lecturer on neurology, Harvard Med. Sch.; lecturer on neurology and historical and cultural medicine U. of Texas, medical branch. Galveston; medical adviser to Nat. Broadcasting Co.; Mayo Meml. lectr. Dartmouth Med. Sch., 1959; cons. hist. collections Francis A. Countway Library Medicine. Lt. U.S. Army Med. Corps, 1917-19; maj. Med. Corps Reserve, 1920-30. Recipient citation for services, Myasthenia Gravis Found., 1959. Member advisory com., Nat. Foundation for Infantile Paralysis; sec. adv. bd. on Health Services. A.R.C.; chmn. med. adv. bd. National Muscular Dystrophy Research Found, Inc., Myasthenia Gravis Foundation, Incorporated. Diplomate Am. Bd. of Psychiatry and Neurology. Mem. A.M.A., Am. Neural Assn. (v.p. 1942-43), Medical Hist. Section, Swedish Medical Society, Editorial Board, New England Journal of Medicine, Mass. Hist. of Science Soc., A.A.A.S., Am. Assn. History of Medicine (pres. 1949-50), Mass. Historical Society. American Antiquarian Society, American Acad. Arts and Sciences, Colonial Soc. of Mass., Boston Med. Library (curator), Psi Upsilon. Mem. hist. sect. Nat. Research Council. Republican. Club: Harvard (Boston and N.Y.). Author: Brief History of Medicine in Mass., 1930; Medical History, Humanism and the Student of Medicine, pub. 1960; Thymectomy For Myasthenia Gravis (with R.S. Schwab), 1960; Myasthenia Gravis: The Second International Symposium Proceedings, 1961; (with Dr. Irving S. Cutter) A Short History of Midwifery, 1964. Contributor to scientific journals. Editor: A Brief Rule to Guide the Common People of New England, by Thomas Thacher, 1937; Neurology and Psychiatry in General Practice, 1950. Home: Brookline, Mass.†

VIGNESS, DAVID MARTELL, educator; b. La Feria, Tex., Oct. 12, 1922; s. Lewis Martell and Nina (Hegge) V.; B.A., U. Tex., 1943, M.A., 1948, Ph.D., 1951; m. Winifred Woods, Jan. 29, 1949; children—Margaret, Richard. Instr., U. Tex., 1951; prof. history, head dept. social scis. Schreiner Inst., Kerrville, Tex., 1951-55; mem. faculty Tex. Tech. Univ., 1955-79, prof. history, 1961-79, chmn. dept., 1961-78; Fulbright lectr. U. Chile, also Cath. U. Santiago, 1957-58; vis. prof. Pan Am. U., summer 1973, U. N.Mex., spring 1979. Cons. Peace Corps, 1965, 1966; participant Congress de Historia de Noreste de Mexico, 1971. Mem. Tex. Com. Humanities and Pub. Policy, 1971-78, vice chmn., 1976-77; mem. Nat. Endowment for the Humanities, also program cons. Trustee Austin Presbyn. Theol. Sem., 1973-79. Served with USNR, 1943-46; PTO. Recipient H. Bailey Carroll award S.W. Hist. Quar., 1972. Fellow Tex. Hist. Assn.; mem. Am. Hist. Assn., Southwestern Council Latin Am. Studies (pres. 1972-73), Latin Am. Studies Association, Western History Association, Conf. Latin American History, Southwestern Social Sci. Assn. (exec. council 1964-65), Phi Kappa Phi, Phi Alpha Theta, Pi Sigma Alpha, Sigma Delta Pi. Rotarian. Presbyterian. Author: The Revolutionary Decades, 1965; (with others) Estudios de Historia del Noreste de Mexico, 1972. Staff writer, contbr. Handbook of Texas History, 1951; asst. editor Documents of Texas History, 1963; editorial cons. Arizona and The West: A Quar. Jour. of History, 1977-79; mem. editorial adv. bd. N.Mex. Hist. Quar., 1978-79. Contbr. articles to profl. jours. Home: Lubbock, Tex. Died July 16, 1979.

VILJOEN, PHILIP RUDOLPH, diplomat; b. Transvaal Republic Feb. 28, 1889; s. A. C. and J. M. (Roos) V.; student South Africa, until 1907; student, M.R.C.V.S., London, 1908-12; Dr. Med. Vet., Berne, Switzerland, 1920; m. Gladys Margaret, Lyle, 1915; children—Renée (Mrs. H. J. Martin), Jeannette (Mrs. J. P. Kempster). Bacteriologist, Onderstepoort Veterinary Research Lab., Pretoria, S. Africa, 1913-8; prof. of vet. science, Transvaal Univ. Coll. (Univ. of Pretoria, Africa), 1918; asst. dir. Veterinary Services for Union of S. Africa, Pretoria, 1921-25, dept. dir. 1926-30; under-sec. of agr., 1930-33, sec. of Agr. and Forestry, 1933-July 1945; high commr. for Union of South Africa in Canada from July 1945. Served in S. African War with Boer Commandoes during 1901-02; with Allies, World War I. Awarded Mil. Cross. Chmn. Nat. Marketing Council, 1938-45; mem. Nat. Nutrition Council, 1940-45 (chmn. of agr. and econ. com.); chmn. Royal Commn., inquiring into cooperation and agriculture credit, 1934. Attended Empire Econ. Conf., Ottawa, 1932, Empire Scientific Conf., London, 1936, Imperial Conf., London, 1937; leader, Union Del. Quebec Food and Agr. Conf., 1945 (mem. exec. com. 1945-48), Copenhagen Food and Agr. Conf., 1946. Life mem. South African A.A.S., Royal Soc. of S. Africa, S. African Veterinary Med. Assn. Mem. Geog. Soc. of Can. Clubs: Pretoria, Pretoria Country; Rideau, Royal Golf (Ottawa). Home: Ottawa, Ont., Can. Deceased.

VILLARD, HENRY HILGARD, economist, ret. educator; b. N.Y. City, Jan. 18, 1911; s. Oswald Garrison and Julia Breckenridge (Sandford) V., A.B., Yale, 1932, Cambridge U., 1934, M.A., 1939; Ph.D., Columbia, 1941; m. Mary Caroline St. John, June 27, 1940; children—Henry Hilgard, Elizabeth St. John. Instr. bus. adminstrn. U. Minn., 1937-40; asst. prof. economics Amherst (Mass.) Coll., 1940-41; prof. economics Hofstra Coll., 1946-49; sr. economist div. research and statistics Treasury Dept., 1941; prin. economist div. civilian supply W.P.B., 1941-42; br. chief service trades br. O.P.A., 1942-43; economist N. Africa Econ. Bd., State Dept., 1943-44; analyst A.A.F. Evaluation Bd. for E.T.O., War Dept., 1944-45; economist div. research and statistics Fed. Res. Bd., 1945-46; professor, chmn. dept. econs. City Coll. N.Y., 1949-67, prof., 1967-75, on leave as dir. econ. devel. and adminstrn. program Ford Found., 1962-63. Bd. dirs. Planned Parenthood, N.Y.C.; trustee Joint Council Econ. Edn. Mem. Am. Econ. Assn., Royal Econ. Soc., Econometric Soc., Am. Assn. U. Profs., Am. Finance Assn. Clubs: Century Assn., N.Y. Yacht (N.Y.C.); Cosmos (Washington). Author: Deficit Spending and the National Income, 1941; Economic Development, 1959; Economic Performance, 1961. Editor: Jour. Econ. Edn. Home: New York, N.Y. Died Dec. 28, 1983.

VILSACK, CARL GREGORY, business exec.; b. Pittsburgh, Pa., Apr. 27, 1888; s. Leopold and Dorothy (Blank) V.; student Georgetown U., Washington, D.C., 1910; m. Alice Johnston, Jan. 20, 1913; children—Carl Gregory, William J., Mary Belle. Pres. Pittsburgh (Pa.) Brewing Co., Tech. Food Products Co., Vilsack-Martin Real Estate Co.; retired. Mem. Pittsburg C. of C., East Liberty C. of C. Clubs: Athletic, Long Vue Country, Field (Pittsburgh). †

VINCENT, BEVERLY M., congressman; b. Mar. 28, 1890; son of Gillis and Calvernia Vincent; student Western Teachers Coll., 1910-14, U. of Ky., 1914-16; studied law at U. of Ky.; m. Stella Smith, Feb. 20, 1916. Admitted to Ky. bar, 1916, and practiced in Brownsville; county judge Edmonson County, 1917-18; mem. State Senate, 1929-33; atty. gen. State of Ky., 1935-37; elected Mar. 27, 1937, to fill vacancy in 75th Congress (1937-39) 2d Ky. Dist.; re-elected 76th to 78th Congresses (1939-45), same dist.; v.p. Brownsville Deposit Bank; dir. Ten Brother Corp. Served in World War, 1918-19. Presidential elector, 1932. Mem. Am. Legion. Democrat. Baptist. Odd Fellow. Home: Brownsville, Ky. Deceased.

VINSON, FRED MOORE, JR., lawyer; b. Louisa, Ky., Apr. 3, 1925; s. Fred Moore and Roberta (Dixon) V.; m. Nell P. Morrison, Jan. 15, 1955; children—Fred Moore III, Carolyn. A.B., Washington and Lee U., 1948, LL.B., 1951, LL.D. (hon.), 1968. Bar: D.C. bar 1951. Partner firm Reasoner, Davis & Vinson, Washington, 1963-65, 69-82; asst. atty. gen. criminal div. Dept. Justice, 1965-69; dir. Lockheed Aircraft Corp., 1971-82; Chmn. com. law and legislation D.C. Bd. Trade, 1964-65; mem. Jud. Conf. D.C. Circuit, 1960-82, Adminstrv. Conf. U.S., 1963-65; gen. counsel Inaugural Com., 1961; chmn. com. admissions and grievances U.S. Ct. Appeals, D.C. Circuit, 1974-78; bd. govs. D.C. Bar, 1975-78; mem. bd. on profl. responsibility D.C. Ct. Appeals, 1979-82. Chmn. bd. trustees D.C. Pub. Defender Service, 1976-78. Served with USAAF, 1943-46. Mem. Am. Bar Assn. (ho. dels. 1971-74), Bar Assn. D.C. (pres. 1971-72), Phi Beta Kappa, Omicron Delta Kappa. Home: Washington, D.C. Died Nov. 21, 1982.

VIOSCA, RENÉ ADAMS, judge; born New Orleans, La., Nov. 14, 1890; s. Paul Percy and Wilhelmina (Bischoff) V.; A.B., Tulane U., 1910, LL.B., 1912; m. Gladys Marie Arnoult, Sept. 14, 1915; children—Gladys Marie, Shirley Mathilde, Dorothy Helen, Lysle Sylvia (dec.), Reneée Ann. Admitted to La. bar, 1912, in practice New Orleans until 1942; asst. city atty. New Orleans, 1920-23; mem. Sanders, Baldwin, Viosca and Haspel, 1921-33; atty. for La. Tax Commn., 1924-32; U.S. atty. Eastern Dist. of La., 1933-1941; prof. civil law, Tulane U. College of Law, from 1921; judge Civil District Court, Parish of Orleans, State of Louisiana, from April 9, 1942. Member Louisiana Constl. Conv., 1921. Dir. Bd. of Commrs. New Orleans City Park; mem. La. Supreme Court Committee on Bar Admissions, 1940-42; Board of advisory editors, Tulane Law Review; comm. of Juris. consults., Louisiana Law Institute. Mem. American and La. bar assns., New Orleans Bar Assn. (past pres.), Federal Bar Assn. (past pres. New Orleans Chapter), American Judicature Society, Order of the Coif (past pres. Tulane chapter), Phi Beta Kappa, Phi Alpha Delta. Democrat. Catholic. K.C., Elk. Home: New Orleans, La. †

VIVIAN, ROBERT EVANS, chem. engr.; b. Melvin, Ill., Apr. 20, 1893; s. Robert Lorenzo and Mary Blanche (Weatherby) V.; A.B., U. of Southern Calif., 1917, M.A., 1922; Ph.D., Columbia U., 1933; m. Belle Doyle, Aug. 15, 1919; children—Robert Edmund (dec.), Richard Weatherby, Lawrence Doyle. Head chemistry div. and petroleum tech. div., science dept., Kern County Union High Sch. and Jr. Coll., Bakersfield, Calif., 1918-28; chief, Kern County Assay Office, Bakersfield, 1918-28; asst. in process development, chem. engring. dept., Columbia U., 1929-38; electrochem. engr. in charge pilot plant operations, Internat. Agrl. Corp., 1930-31; research chemist and chem. engr., Gen. Chem. Co., New York, N.Y., 1931-35; dir. research Metals Disintegrating Co., Elizabeth, N.J., 1935-37; prof. and head dept. chem. engring. U. So. Cal., 1937-40, dean Sch. Engring., 1940-58; chmn. div. engring. Long Beach State Coll., 1958-64, dean emeritus, 1964-82; ednl. cons. Northrop Institute Tech., Inglewood, Cal., 1964-82, research associate, consultant on engineering to trustees of California State Colleges, 1961-62; cons. on indsl. research Dept. of Commerce, 1947. Chem. prodn. specialist Mutual Security Agency, Italy, 1952, tech. cons. Orient, 1953; coordinator lecture program on guided missiles for NATO, Paris, 1958. Institutional rep. Engring., Science, and Mgt. War Training, 1941-45. Del. Cal. Legislative Council Profl. Engrs., 1948-56, president 1951-52. Member American Institute of Chem. Engrs. (chmn. So. Cal. sect., 1945, 1956), Am. Chem. Soc. (chmn. S. Calif. Sect., 1943-44), Electrochemical Society, Amer. Soc. Engr. Educ. Phi Beta Kappa, Sigma Xi, Phi Kappa Phi, Phi Lamda Upsilon, Epsilon Chi, Tau Beta Pi, Alpha Chi Sigma. Methodist. Mason. Club: University. Home: Los Angeles, Calif. Died May 11, 1982.

VOEGELIN, ERIC (HERMAN WILHELM), educator; b. Cologne, Germany, Jan. 3, 1901; s. Otto and Elisabeth (Ruehl) V.; Dr. rer. pol., U. Vienna, 1922; postgrad. univs. Oxford, Berlin, Heidelberg, 1922-23, Rockefeller, Columbia, Harvard, U. Wis., Yale and Sorbonne; m. Lissy Onken, July 30, 1932. Came to U.S., 1938, naturalized 1944. Asst. in law faculty U. Vienna, 1923-24, 28-29, pvt. dozent, 1929, asso. prof. 1936; dismissed by Nazi govt.; instr. and tutor Harvard, 1938-39; instr. Bennington Coll., 1939; asst. prof. U. Ala., 1939-42; asso. prof. La. State U., 1942-46, prof. 1946, Boyd prof. 1952-68; prof. polit. sci. U. Munich, 1958; Henry Salvatori Distinguished scholar Hoover Instn. on War, Revolution and Peace, Stanford (Cal.). Mem. adminstrv. bd. Volkshochschule Wien Volksheim, 1936-38. Mem. Commn. Civil Service Examiners, Austria, 1936-38; sec. Austrian com. Internat. Studies Conf., 1936-38. Mem. Am. and So. polit. sci. assns. Lutheran. Author: Ueber die Form des amerikanischen Geistes, 1928; Rasse und Staat, 1933, Die Rassenidee in der Geistesgeschichte, 1933; Der Autoritaere Staat, 1936; Die Politischen Religionen, 1939; The New Science of Politics, 1952; Order and History I; Israel and Revelation, 1956; Order and History II; The World of the Polis, 1957; Order and History III; Plato and Aristotle, 1957; Anamnesis, 1966; Order and History IV; The Ecumenic Age, 1974; From Enlightenment to Revolution, 1975. Home: Stanford, Calif. Died Jan. 19, 1985.

VOGE, MARIETTA, educator; b. Yugoslavia, July 7, 1918; d. Bernard and Augusta (Meyer) Jirku; came to U.S., 1942; A.B., U. Calif. at Berkeley, 1944, M.A., 1946, Ph.D., 1950; m. Noel H. Voge, June 12, 1942; 1 son, Nicholas C. Mem. faculty Sch. Medicine U. Calif. at Los Angeles, 1952—, asso. prof.. infectious diseases, 1962-69, prof. dept. med. microbiology and immunology, 1969-84. Cons. Cal. Dept. Pub. Health. Recipient many fellowships and travel grants for research in tropical diseases and parasitology. Mem. Am. Soc. Tropical Medicine and Hygiene, (council, v.p.), Am. Soc. Parasitologists (council, pres.), Helminthological Soc. Wash., Brazilian Soc. Tropical Medicine, British Soc. Parasitology, Phi Beta Kappa, Sigma Xi. Co-author: Medical Parasitology, 1958; Experiments and Techniques in Parasitology, 1970. Contbr. to profl. jours. Home: Los Angeles, Calif. Died July 2, 1984.

VOGEL, CHARLES JOSEPH, judge; b. Star Lake Twp., Otter Tail County, Minn., Sept. 20, 1898; s. Philip Francis and Anna Marie (Jenson) V.; m. Fern Nesbitt. Ed., Huron (S.D.) Coll., 1917-18; LL.B., U. Minn., 1923. Bar: Minn bar 1923, N.D. bar 1924. Practiced at Minot in office of Lewis & Bach, U.S. referee in bankruptcy, 1924, practiced in Fargo, N.D., 1925-41; partner firm Vogel & Vogel, 1934-38, Thorp. Wattam & Vogel, 1938-41, U.S. dist. judge, N.D., 1941-54, U.S. circuit judge, 1954-65; chief judge U.S. Ct. Appeals, 8th Circuit, 1965-68; sr. judge U.S. Circuit Ct., 1968—. Democratic candidate for U.S. Senate, 1940. Served with U.S. Army, 1918-19. Episcopalian. Address: Fargo, N.D. Deceased.*

VOGEL, CYRIL J., bishop; student Duquesne U., St. Vincent's Sem., Latrobe, Pa. Ordained priest Roman Catholic Ch., 1931; bishop of Salina (Kans.), from 1965. Home: Salina, Kans. Deceased.

VOGEL, F. A., bank executive; b. St. Cloud, Minn., Feb. 6, 1888; s. Abram and Sarah (Taylor) V.; grad. Teachers Coll., St. Cloud, Minn.; m. Louella Larsen, Dec. 25, 1913; children—David, Robert, Frank, Jr., Paul, William. Teacher, 1909-16; banking, 1916-30; internal revenue collector, 1931-33; state tax commr., 1933; state highway commr., 1933-34; motor transportation dir., 1935-36; mgr. Bank of North Dakota, 1937-45; staff mem. U.S. Senate Civil Service Commn., Washington. Mem. State Legislature, 1921, 23, 25. Mem. Non Partisan League. Methodist. †

VOGEL, HERBERT DAVIS, civil engineer; b. Chelsea, Mich., Aug. 26, 1900; s. Lewis P. and Pearl M. (Davis) V.; m. Loreine Elliott, Dec. 23, 1925; children: Herbert D., Richard E. B.S., U.S. Mil. Acad., 1924; M.S. in Civil Engring, U. Calif., 1928; Dr.-Ing., Berlin Tech. U., 1929; C.E., U. Mich., 1933. Registered profl. engr., N.Y., Tex., Tenn., D.C. Commd. 2d lt. U.S. Army, 1924, advanced through grades to brig. gen.; founder, builder, dir. U.S. Army Engrs. Waterways Expt. Sta., Vicksburg, Miss., 1929-34, student Command and Gen. Staff Sch., 1934-36, with 3d Engrs., Hawaii, 1936-38, instr. Army Engrs. Sch., Ft. Belvoir, 1938-40, asst. to dist. engr., chief inspection div., Pitts., 1940-41, dist. engr., 1942-43, grad. Army-Navy Staff Coll., 1943, (with), S.W. Pacific Theatre Operations, 1944, chief of staff intermediate sect. (New Guinea), then base comdr. Base M, Philippines, 1944-45, with Army of Occupation, Yokohama, Japan, 1945, dist. engr. C.E., Buffalo, 1945-49; engr. maintenance Panama Canal, v.p., dir. Panama R.R. Co., 1949-50, lt. gov. C.Z. Govt., v.p. Panama Canal Co., 1950-52, div. engr. Southwestern div. C.E., 1952- 54; chmn. bd. TVA, 1954-62; engr. adviser World Bank, 1963-67, including Indus Basin project, 1964-67, resource devel. engring. cons., 1967-84; 1st occupant George W. Goethals chair mil. constrn. U.S. Army Engr. Sch., 1973-84; Dir. Internat. Gen. Industries, 1973-80, Planning and Devel. Collaborative, 1968-74; Mem. Beach Erosion Bd., 1946-49, Internat. Boundary Commn., 1946-49; mem. Miss. River Commn., 1952-54, Bd. Engrs. for Rivers and Harbors, 1952-54; chmn. Ark., White, Red Basin Inter-Agy. Com., 1952-54; mem. permanent internat. com. Permanent Internat. Assn. Navigation Congresses, 1957-64, hon. mem., 1967; mem. cons. panel Ludington pumped storage project, 1969-73; chmn. bd. consultants to Panama Canal, 1971-72; engring. cons. GAO, 1977; Mem. visitors com. Sch. Engring., Vanderbilt U., 1967-80; vice chmn. WHO/FAO UNEP Panel of Experts on Environ. Mgmt. for Vector Control, 1982-83. Writer numerous papers on hydraulic models and lab. procedures, 1930-40, articles and speeches on TVA, 1954-63, papers defining U.S. position on inland navigation. Decorated D.S.M., Legion of Merit, Philippine Liberation and Independence medals, knight Grand Cross Thailand, Colon Alfaro medal; recipient Distinguished Alumnus award U. Mich., 1953; Meritorious Service award for service to engring. profession Cons. Engrs. Council, 1967; Benjamin Franklin fellow Royal Soc. Arts. Fellow Am. Cons. Engrs. Council; mem. U.S. Com. Large Dams, Am. Power Conf., ASCE (hon., mem. nat. water policy com. 1971-74, chmn. 1974-76, mem. nat. energy policy com. 1976—, pres.'s award 1979), Soc. Am. Mil. Engrs. (hon., nat. dir. 1956-62, 66, treas. 1974-76), Nat. Acad. Engring., Nat. Soc. Profl. Engrs., Pub. Works Hist. Soc. (hon.), Order of Carabao. Episcopalian. Clubs: Army-Navy (Washington), Cosmos (Washington). Home: Washington, D.C. Died Aug. 26, 1984.

VOIGT, CHARLES OGDEN, corp. exec.; b. N.Y.C., Apr. 18, 1888; s. Maximillian G. and Elizabeth (Algea) V.; student pub. schs.; m. Grace Fisher, Sept. 24, 1914;

children—Charles Ogden, Shirley McCoy, Richard M., Janice E. (Mrs. Frank LaFetra). With De LaVergne Machine Co., N.Y.C., 1910-17; with Stearns Roger Corp., Denver, from 1917, v.p., gen. mgr., 1939-46, pres., gen. mgr., 1946-63, chmn. bd., from 1963; v.p., gen. mgr. Gen. Iron Works, Denver, 1929-39, pres., 1939-61, former chmn. bd., from 1961; dir. Denver Nat. Bank. Pres. Denver chpt. Nat. Safety Council; bd. mgrs. St. Lukes Hosp. Mem. Colo., Denver (life dir., past pres.) chambers commerce, N.A.M., Mfrs. Assn. Colo. Rotarian. Clubs: Denver, Mile High, Denver Country. Home: Denver, CO. †

VOLLMER, CLEMENT, b. Brooklyn, N.Y., Aug. 10, 1889; s. Philip and Mathilde Wilhelmine (Osann) V.; A.B., Heidelberg Coll., Tiffin, O., 1909; grad. study, U. of Berlin, Germany, 1914; Ph.D., U. of Pa., 1915; m. Maude Rosalind Hugo, June 24, 1924. Instr. Cornell U., 1915-16; instr. and asst. prof., U. of Pa., 1916-26; prof. Germanic lit. and philology, Duke U., from 1926, Mem. Modern Lang. Assn. America, Am. Assn. Univ. Profs., Alpha SIgma Phi, Phi Eta, Sigma Upsilon. Protestant. Clubs: Nat. Travel, Duke U. Faculty. Author: The American Novel in Germany, 1871-1913, 1918. Home: Durham, N.C. Deceased.

VON EULER, ULF SVANTE, physiologist; b. Stockholm, Sweden, Feb. 7, 1905; s. Hans and Astrid (Cleve) Von E.; m. Jane Sodenstierna, Apr. 12, 1930; children—Leo, Christopher, Ursula (Mrs. L. Sjöberg), Marie (Mrs. Anthony John); m. Dagmar Cronstedt, Aug. 20, 1958. M.D. Karolinska Inst., 1930; M.D. h.c. U. Dijon, 1963, U. Ghent, 1963, U. Tubingen, 1964, U. Rio de Janeiro, 1953, U. Buenos Aires, 1971, U. Edinburgh, 1971, U. Madrid, 1973, U. Manchester, Eng., 1973. Asst. prof. Karolinska Inst., Stockholm, 1930-39, prof. physiology, 1939-71; Mem. Nobel Com. for Medicine, 1953-60, chmn., 1958-60, gen. sec., 1961-65; pres. Nobel Found., 1966-75; v.p. Internat. Union Physiol. Sci., 1965-72. Author: Noradrenaline, 1956, (with R. Eliasson) Prostaglandins, 1968; also articles. Decorated comdr. Order North Star Sweden, Cruzeiro do Sul Brazil, Palmes academiques France, grand cross Al Mérito Civil Spain; recipient Gairdner award, 1961, Jahre award, 1965, Stouffer award, 1967, Nobel prize in physiol. medicine, 1970. Mem. Nat. Acad. Sci., Am. Acad. Arts and Scis. Am. Philos. Soc., Royal Soc., acads. sci. Sweden, Denmark, Belgium, Leopoldina of East Germany, U.S. Home: Stockholm, Sweden. Died Mar. 10, 1983.

VON GLAHN, WILLIAM CARSON, educator; b. Wilmington, N.C., May 26, 1889; s. William Carson and Katie (Bisset) Von G.; B.S., Davidson Coll., N.C., 1911; M.D., Johns Hopkins, 1915. Intern New Haven Hosp., 1915-17; instr. pathology Johns Hopkins, 1917-18, 1919-20, asst. resident pathologist Johns Hopkins Hosp., 1917-18; resident pathologist City Hosp., Balt., 1919-20; asso. pathology Coll. Phys. and Surg., Columbia, 1920-23, asst. prof., 1923-24, assoc. prof., 1925-41; asst. resident pathologist, resident pathologist Presbyn. Hosp., N.Y.C., 1920-22, asso. attending pathologist, 1922-41; prof. chmn. dept. pathology, coll. medicine N.Y.U., 1941-54, prof. emeritus, from 1954; dir. pathology Bellevue Hosp., N.Y.C., 1941-49, cons. pathologist, 1949-54; attending pathologist University Hosp., N.Y.C., 1949-54; prof. pathology, sch. medicine La. State U., 1954-57. Served as 1st lt. M.C., U.S. Army, 1918-19. Fellow N.Y. Acad. Medicine; mem. N.Y. Clin. Soc. (pres. 1941), Am. Assn. Pathologists and Bacteriologists, N.Y. Path. Soc. (v.p. 1928, pres. 1934), Internat. Acad. Pathology, Phi Beta Kappa. Contbr. articles med. periodicals. Home: Wilmington, N.C. †

VON SCHMIDT, HAROLD, painter, illustrator; b. Alameda, Cal., May 19, 1893; s. Edward Alexander and Isabel (Hill) von S.; student Cal. Coll. Arts and Crafts, Oakland, 1912-13, San Francisco Art Inst., 1915-18; pupil Worth Ryder, Maynard Dixon, Harvey Dunn; m. Edna Clost, Nov. 15 (div.); 1 dau., Joan (Mrs. Richard M. Brace); m. 2d, Forest Gilmore, Jan. 4, 1927; children—Peter Alexis, Eric Alexander. Illustrator books: Song of Songs, Oscar Well Letters and Papers. Death Comes for the Archbishop, December Night, Indian Gold, Queer Person, Homespun, also illustraator various popular magazines; paintings represented in collections State Capitol, Sacramento, U.S. Mil. Acad., USAF Acad., Hist. Soc. Montana, Helena, Baseball Mus., Cooperstown, N.Y., John Hancock Ins. Co., Boston, also pvt. collections; founder, faculty mem. Famous Artists Schs., Westport. Police commr., Westport; bd. finance, dir., trustee Pub. Library. Publicity dept. USN, World War I; artist-corr. USAAF, ETO, also King Features Syndicate, AFPAC, World War II. Mem. Soc. Illustrators (pres. 1938-41), Westport Artists (pres. 1950-51), Artists Guild of N.Y.C. (trustee). Club: Cedar Point yacht of Westport. Mem. Am. Olympic Rugby Football Team, Antwerp, Belgium, 1920. Home: Westport, Conn. Died June 3, 1982.

VOORHIS, HARRY MALCOLM, lawyer; b. E. Smithfield, Pa., Oct. 19, 1889; s. Wilson Fremont and Carrie (Cowell) V.; LL.B., Dickinson Sch. Law, Carlisle, Pa., 1914; m. Caroline McFarquhar, Apr. 11, 1917; children—Elinore (Mrs. Fred Land), Harry Malcolm II. Admitted to Fla. bar, 1920, also U.S. Supreme Ct.; practice in Orlando, from 1920; partner firm Maguire, Voorhis & Wells, from 1921. Dir. Winter Park Telephone Co. (Fla.); cons. dir. First Nat. Bank Orlando, Coll. Park Nat. Bank,

Orlando. Organizer, pres. Civic Music Assn., Orlando, 1933. Served with U.S. Army, World War I. mem. Am., Fla. bar assns. Episcopalian (sr. warden). Rotarian (pres. Orlando 1940), Mason (Shriner). Club: Orlando Country (pres. 1936). Home: Orlando, FL. †

VOORHIS, HORACE JERRY, former congressman, executive; b. Ottawa, Kans., Apr. 6, 1901; s. Charles Brown and Ella Ward (Smith) V.; A.B., Yale, 1923; M.A., Claremont Colls., 1928; LL.D. (hon.), St. Francis Xavier University, 1953, Claremont Grad. Sch., 1979; m. Alice Louise Livingston, Nov. 27, 1924; children—Alice Nell, Charles Brown, Jerry Livingston. Traveling rep. YMCA, Germany, 1923-24; worker Ford assembly plant, Charlotte, N.C., 1924-25; tchr. Allendale Farm Sch., Lake Villa, Ill., 1925-26; dir. Dray Cottage, Home for Boys, Laramie, Wyo., 1926- 27; headmaster and trustee Voorhis Sch. for Boys, 1928-38; spl. lectr. Pomona Coll., 1930-35; mem. 75th to 79th Congresses 12th Calif. Dist. Exec. dir. Cooperative League U.S., 1947-67, now cons., bd. dirs. Group Health Assn. Am., from 1947; chmn. The Co-op. Found., from 1967; Mem. Am. Country Life Assn., Pomona Valley Council Chs., Nat. Cath. Rural Life Conf., Adult Edn. Assn., Am. Pub. Health Assn., World Federalists, Phi Beta Kappa, Phi Delta Kappa. Democrat. Episcopalian. Author: Out of Debt, Out of Danger; Confessions of a Congressman; The Christian in Politics; American Cooperatives; Strange Case of Richard Milhous Nixon; Life and Times of Aurelius Lyman Voorhis; Confession of Faith. Home: Claremont, Calif. Dec. Sept. 11, 1982.

VORSTER, BALTHAZAR JOHANNES, prime minister of S. Africa; b. nr. Jamestown, S. Africa, Dec. 13, 1915; s. William Carel Vorster; LL.B., U. Stellenbosch, 1938, D. Phil., 1968; LL.D., U. Pretoria, 1968; married Martini Malan, Dec. 20, 1941; children—Elsa, Willem, Peter. Registrar to judge-pres. Cape Province, 1938-39; established law practice, Port Elizabeth, 1939; interned during World War II for anti-British-African sentiments; established law practice, Brakpan, 1944; practice of law, Johannesburg, 1945-58; mem. S. African Parliament for Nigel constituency in Transvaal, 1953-79; dep. prime minister for edn., arts and scis., also for social welfare and pensions, 1958-61; minister of justice, 1961-66, also of justice, police and prisons, 1966; prime minister S. Africa, 1966-79. Mem. Nationalist Party. Clubs: Zawalop, Randebosch. Died Sept. 10, 1983.

VOSE, CLEMENT ELLERY, political scientist, educator, archivist; b. Caribou, Maine, Mar. 18, 1923; s. Arthur G. and Florence (Murphy) V.; m. Doris Foran, 1947 (div. 1981); children—John S., Celia L. B.A., U. Maine, 1947; M.A., U. Wis., 1949, Ph.D., 1952; M.A., Wesleyan U., Middletown, Conn., 1961. Project mgr. French study tours on U.S. U. Wis. Indsl. Relations Center, Madison, 1951-52; instr. Beloit (Wis.) Coll., 1952-53; asst. prof. Western Res. U., Cleve., 1953-55; dir. Bur. for Research Municipal Govt.; asso. prof. govt. Bowdoin Coll., Brunswick, Maine, 1955-58; asso. prof. govt. Wesleyan U., Middletown, 1958-61, prof., 1961-85, chmn. dept. govt., 1961-67, 68-69, 72-73, 78-81, John E. Andrus prof. govt., 1965-85; dir. Collection on Legal Change, 1970-85; research dir. study constl. change 20th Century Fund, 1969-70; mem. Nat. Archives Adv. Council, 1971-83, chmn., 1977-78; sr. fellow Yale Law, Yale U., 1958-59; vis. prof., 1962-63, Columbia U., 1968-69, Princeton U., 1982-83; prin. investigator Civil Rights Law Manuscripts Microfilm Project, 1974-80. Author: Caucasians Only: The Supreme Court, the NAACP and the Restrictive Convenant Cases, 1959, Constitutional Change: Amendment Politics and Supreme Court Litigation since 1900, 1972, Guide to Library Sources in Political Science: American Government, 1975; Contbr. articles to profl. jours. Mem. Maine Gov.'s Com. on State Govt., 1956-58. Served with AUS, 1943-46, ETO. Decorated Purple Heart.; Soc. Sci. Research Council grantee, 1956-58; Rockefeller Found. research grantee, 1958-59; Nat. Endowment Humanities fellow, 1976-77; Project '87 grantee, 1981. Mem. Am. Polit. Sci. Assn. (exec. council 1977-78), New Eng. Polit. Sci. Assn. (exec. com. 1971-72, 76-79, pres. 1977-78), AAAS, Soc. Am. Archivists. Home: Middletown, Conn. Died Jan. 28, 1985.

VOTH, BEN, computer co. exec.; b. Enid, Okla., Apr. 21, 1899; s. John and Suzanne (Fast) V.; m. Yukola Gilbert, June 25, 1930; children—Suzanne (Mrs. Richard R. Dillenbeck), Janet (Mrs. Merrill Jerome Foote). Student, Phillips U., Enid, 1919-20, Ind. U., 1920-21, Columbia U., 1922-23; LL.D., Phillips U., 1959. Salesman Powers Paper Co., Springfield, Mass., 1923-27; real estate and ins., Tulsa, 1927-35; partner Frates Co., 1935-40, Voth & Wright (ins.), 1940-62; founder Standard Ins. Co. Tulsa, 1944, pres., 1944-60; v.p. Springfield Fire & Marine Ins. Co., 1960-61, Marsh & McLennan, Inc. (ins.), 1961-63; chmn. bd. Univ. Computing Co., Dallas, 1964-69, chmn. exec. com., 1969-72; chmn. bd., chief exec. officer Swift-Ohio Corp., from 1972. Author: A Piece of the Computer Pie, 1973. Pres. bd. trustees Hillcreast Med. Center, 1964-68, formerly trustee; pres. bd. govs. Tulsa Club, 1962; trustee Phillips U. Mem. Tulsa C. of C. Episcopalian. Club: Tulsa Southern Hills Country (Tulsa). Home: Tulsa, Okla.

VOYE, JOSEPH JAMES, accountant; b. Klamath Falls, Oreg., Dec. 3, 1919; s. Arthur James and Louise (Lee) V.; student Mass. Inst. Tech., 1938-39, Stanford, 1940-42, 47; B.B.A., Golden Gate Coll., 1950; m.

Elizabeth Patton Will, Nov. 22, 1943; children—Lee, Sally, Robert James, Anne. Mem. staff Farquhar & Heimbucher, C.P.A.'s, 1950-51; office mgr. Wunderlich Co., 1951-59; sec., controller Gordon H. Ball, Inc., Danville, Calif., 1960-70, bd. dirs., 1968-70; controller Heath Electric Co., Santa Clara, Calif., 1970-76, Western Traction Co., Hayward, Calif., 1976-80. Served to 1st lt. USMCR, 1942-45. C.P.A., Calif. Mem. Am. Inst. C.P.A.s, Delta Kappa Epsilon. Home: Alamo, Calif. Dec. July 31, 1980.

VROOMAN, VERNON A., univ. prof.; b. Middleburgh, N.Y., Jan. 22, 1889; s. Thompson B. and Lettie (Gernsey) V.; LL.B., Albany Law Sch., 1911, LL.M., 1912; A.B., U. of Nev., 1921; J.D., Stanford, 1923; m. Gertrude Anna Streeter, Feb. 23, 1918 (dec. 1922); children—Helen, Anna; m. Loretta Rudolph, June, 1926 (div. 1944); children—Frederica, David. Admitted to bar, N.Y., 1913, Dist. Ct. of U.S. No. dist. N.Y., 1916, Nev., 1919, Calif., 1924, Mo., 1925, Ia., 1931, Superior Ct. U.S., 1935, S.D., 1947. Asst. prof. St. Louis U., 1924, asso. prof., 1925; prof. Drake U. Law Sch., 1926-46; vis. prof., U. of Ore. Sch. of Law, 1945-46, prof. U. of S.D., from 1946. Served as capt., World War I, lt. col., World War II. Awarded Silver Star citation, Distinguished Service Cross Mem. Bd. of Bar Examiners of S.D. from 1947. Mem. Vermillion C. of C., Am. Bar Assn., Am. Assn. Univ. Profs., Nat. Sojourners, Heroes of '76, Am. Legion, Vets. Foreign Wars, Reserve Officers Assn. of U.S. (vice pres., dept. of Ia., 1936, pres., 1937, pres. 7th corps area council, 1938-39), Delta Theta Phi, Phi Kappa Phi. Democrat. Presbyterian. Author: Method of Instructing in the Use of Law Books, 1928; Sageflowers and Golden Poppies, 1930; The Amiable Cynic, 1932. Contbr. articles to law jours.; poetry to jours. and anthologies. Home: Vermillion, S.D. †

WADDELL, CHAUNCEY L., investment banker; b. Greenfield, O., Sept. 4, 1895; s. Edwin Jones and Minnie (Crothers) W.; A.B., Harvard, 1918; m. Catherine Hughes, June 10, 1922; children—Richard Hughes, Theodore Hughes. Reporter, Wall Street Journal. 1919-21. New York Tribune, 1921; investment banker and mfr., from 1921; dir. various indsl. public utility and ins. cos.; chmn. bd., dir. Waddell & Reed, Inc., N.Y.C.; chmn. United Investment Services, Ltd., United Funds Mgmt., Ltd.; pres. Waddell & Reed International, Ltd., United Funds Can. Internat., Ltd.; dir. United Funds, Inc., United Accumulative Fund, Ltd., N.A.A.C.P. Legal and Def. Fund, United Negro Coll. Fund; trustee Atlanta U., Spelman Coll. Served 2d lt., pilot, Am. Air Service, World War I. Home: New York, N.Y. Died July 4, 1984.

WADDELL, HAROLD NEWTON, fgn. service officer; b. Jefferson, Ga., Sept. 23, 1911; s. Charles Marion and Estelle (Hanson) W.; LL.B., Atlanta Law Sch., 1937; student George Washington U., 1948-51; m. Edith Ball, Dec. 17, 1947; children—Harold Newton, Susan Watson. Admitted to Ga. bar, 1937; clk. Southern Mfg. Co., Athens, Ga., 1929-31, VA, Atlanta, 1931-35, SEC, Atlanta, 1935-38; jr. atty. SEC, Atlanta, 1938; clk. Am. embassy, Moscow, 1938-42, 43-45, vice consul, 1945; clk., Cairo, Egypt, 1942-43; vice consul, adminstrv. asst., Brussels, Belgium, 1945-46, 46-47, London, 1946; adminstrv. analyst div. fgn. service adminstrn. Dept. of State, 1947-49, fgn. mgmt. specialist Office Exec. Dir., Bur. Far Eastern Affairs, 1949-51, adminstrv. mgmt. specialist, post mgmt. specialist, 1951-53, fgn. affairs officer and staff asst. Office Asst. Sec. Far Eastern Affairs, 1952-56; 1st sec., consul Am. embassy, Tokyo, 1956-59; assigned Dept. State, 1961—. Recipient Medal of Freedom, 1947. Mem. Assn. Corcoran Gallery of Art, Fairfax Hosp. Assn., Mus. Modern Art, Met. Mus. Art (assoc.). Methodist. Home: Arlington, Va. Deceased.

WADE, HAROLD HAMILTON, educator; b. Wrentham, Mass., Aug. 16, 1890; s. William Leonard and Anne (Snider) W.; A.B., Beloit Coll., 1914; student Harvard, 1924; m. Meta E. Bennett, Aug. 23, 1917; children—Virginia, Alan, Harold H., Anne, Miriam, Paul. Master in pub. speaking, Mercersburg Acad., 1914-18; master in speaking and English, Pawtucket High Sch., 1918-19; master in speaking, Worcester Acad., 1919-33, headmaster, 1933-43; retired, 1943. Author, lecturer. Mem. N.E. Assn. Secondary Schs., New Eng. Assn. of English Teachers, Delta Sigma Rho. Unitarian. Author: What to Say and How to Say It, 1927; Dozen a Day in Spelling, Punctuation and Grammar, 1929; Expressing Yourself, 1934. Home: Bustins Island, Maine. Deceased.

WADE, IRA OWEN, univ. prof.; b. Richmond, Va., Oct. 4, 1806; s. Martin David and Mary Elizabeth Frances (Lyle) W.; A.B., John Hopkins U., 1916; M.A., Columbia U., 1919; Ph.D., Princeton U., 1932; m. Mabel Winifred Hamilton, Aug. 8, 1925. Instr. John Marshall High Sch., Richmond, 1916-17, William and Mary Coll., Williamsburg, VA., 1917-18; head dept. of Romance langs., Marietta (O.) Coll., 1919-21; instr. in French, Princeton U., 1923-25; head dept. of Romance langs., U. of Western Ont., London, Can., 1925-27; asst. prof., Princeton U., 1927-31, asso. prof., 1931-40, prof. French from 1940, John N. Woodhull prof., 1951, chmn., 1946-58; dir. spl. program on European Civilization, 1958, vis. prof., U. Chgo., 1945, U. Pa., 1955; visiting lectr., Harvard, 1946, 47; vis. prof. French, Pa. State U., 1965; vis. prof. Harvard, 1966, Penn State U., 1966, U. Del., 1967, Fordham Univ., 1967-68, Princeton U., 1968. Mem. Com. Internat. Exchange of Persons, 1953-56. Served USNRF, 1918. Recipient French Legion of Honor, 1955. Held Jacobus fellowship, Princeton University, 1922-23. Mem. Modern Lang. Assn. of America, Am. Assn. Teachers of French, Am. Assn. Univ. Profs. Author: The Clandestine Organization and Diffusion of Philosophic Ideas in France from 1700 to 1750, 1938; Voltaire and Mme. du Châtelet, 1941; Studies in Voltaire, 1947; Micromégas, A Study in the Fusion of Myth, Art and Science, 1950; The Search for a New Voltaire, 1958 Voltaire and Candide, 1959. Editor lit. papers. Mem. Nassau Club. Home: Princeton, N.J. Died Mar. 7, 1983.

WADE, PRESTON ALLEN, surgeon; b. Helena, Mont., Mar. 22, 1901; s. John William and Claudia (Hillman) W.; A.B., Cornell U., 1922, M.D., 1925; m. Evangeline Schreiter, Aug. 4, 1934. Engaged in pvt. practice, 1927-68, 70; instr. Cornell U. Med. Coll., 1927-32, asst. prof., 1932-40, asso. prof., 1940-53, prof. clinical surgery, 1953—; assistant attending surgeon, 1927-40, associate attending surgeon, 1940-50, attending surgeon N.Y. Hosp., 1950—; chief combined fracture service N.Y. Hosp. and Hosp. Spl. Surgery, 1955—; cons. surgeon City Hosp., 1950—, Eliza A. Horton Meml. Hosp., Middletown, N.Y., 1950—, St. Francis Hosp., Poughkeepsie, N.Y., 1953—, Hasbrouck Heights (New Jersey) Hospital, Concord (New Hampshire) Hospital. Mem. bd. directors National Safety Council. Trustee Cornell University, 1950-55, 1958-59. Served from maj. to lt. col. M.C., AUS, 1942-45 chief surg. service 9th Gen. Hosp. Diplomate Am. Bd. Surgery. Fellow A. C.S. (chmn. bd. of regents 1964-67, president elect 1968). Internat. Soc. Surgery, Internat. Soc. Surgery of Orthopedics and Traumatology; member Am. Assn. Surgery of Trauma (bd. mgrs., recorder (pres. 1961), A.M.A., Am. Acad. Compensation Medicine, N.Y. Acad. Medicine (pres.), N.Y. Surg. Soc., Am. Geriatric Soc., N.Y. Acad. Scis., Am. Surgical Am. Orthopedic Assn. (hon.), Delta Phi, Alpha Omega Alpha, Nu Sigma Nu Society. Republican. Episcopalian. Clubs: University, Cornell, Century (New York City); Farmington Country (Charlottesville, Virginia); Piping Rock (Locust Valley, N.Y.). Author: Outline of the Treatment of Fractures (with E. F. Cave), 1959; co-author, editor; Surgical Treatment of Trauma, 1960. Co-editor Abdominal Surgery, 1946. Contbr. articles in surg. jours. Home: Concord, N.H. Died Aug. 17, 1982.

WADE-GERY, HENRY THEODORE, philosopher, author; b. Apr. 2, 1888; s. Arthur Staunton Wade-Gery; hon. fellow Wadham and New Colls., Oxford, U., fellow Merton Coll., 1953-58; Litt.D. (hon.). Dublin U.; m. Vivian Whitfield, 1928; 1 son. Asst. master Sherborne Sch., 1913-14; fellow Wadham Coll., Oxford, 1914-39; Sather lectr. U. Cal., 1938; Wykeham prof. ancient history Oxford U., 1939-53, prof. emeritus; mem. Inst. Advanced Study, Princeton, 1947-48, 56-58. Served with 19th Lancs, World War I. Corr. mem. German Archaeol. Inst. Author: (with C.M. Bowra) Pindar's Pythian Odes, 1928; (with B.D. Meritt, M.F. MacGregor) The Athenian Tribute Lists, vols. 1-4, 1939-53; The Poet of the Iliad, 1952; Essays in Greek History, 1958. Contbr. articles to profl. jours. Address: Upton, Berkshire, Eng. †

WADSWORTH, JAMES J., govt. ofcl.; b. Groveland, N.Y., June 12, 1905; s. James Wolcott, Jr., and Alice (Hay) W. student Fay Sch., St. Marks Sch., Southboro, Mass.; A.B., Yale, 1927; LL.D., Alfred U., 1937; LL.D., Bowdoin Coll., 1962, Wilmington Coll., 1964; m. Harty Griggs Tilton, June 16, 1927 (dec. Dec. 1965); 1 dau., Alice Tilton (Mrs. Trowbridge Strong); m. 2d, Mary Donaldson, May 22, 1967. Mem. assembly N.Y. State Legislature 1931-41; asst. mgr. indsl. relations Curtiss Wright Corp., Buffalo, 1941-45; dir. public service div. War Assets Adminstrn., 1945-46; dir. govt. affairs dept. Air Transport Assn. of Am., 1946-48; special asst. to adminstr. ECA, 1948-50, acting director Civil Defense Office, 1950; dep. adminstr. F.C.D.A., 1951; dep. U.S. rep. to UN, 1953-60; permanent United States representative, 1960-61; chmn. bd. trustees Freedom House, 1961; pres. Peace Research Inst., 1961-62; mem. FCC, 1965-69. Trustee People to People, U.S. Com. Dag Hammarskjold Found.; bd. dirs. U.S. Com. for UN, Meridian Found. Mem. UN Assn. U.S.A. (v.p. 1964), Council Fgn. Relations. Republican. Episcopalian. Clubs: Chevy Chase, International (pres. 1963) (Washington); Yale (N.Y.). Author: The Price of Peace; The Glass House. Home: Washington, D.C. Died Mar. 13, 1984.

WAGENET, R(USSELL) G(ORDON), govt. official; b. San Diego, Calif., Mar. 28, 1890; s. Henry William and Julia Magdalen (Scherz) W.; B.L., U. of Calif., 1914; m. Elizabeth Herroitt Morrison, Nov. 18, 1914 (dec.); children—Gordon Morrison, Margaret Herriott; m. 2d, Margaret Helen Lyman, Aug. 2, 1952. Dep., commn. on immigration and housing, Calif., 1914-17; asst. labor mgr. B. Kuppenheimer and Co., Chicago, 1919-20, New York Clothing Mfrs., 1920-21; labor mgr. Rochester Clothers' Exchange, 1921-26; exec. dir. N.Y. Bldg. Congress, 1926-34; regional dir. Nat. Labor Relations Bd., San Francisco, 1934-35; dir. Bur. Unemployment Compensation, Social Security Bd., 1935-40; dir. dept. employment, State of Calif., 1940-43; labor relations counsellor, Marinship Corp., Sausalito, Calif., 1943-46; re-apptd. dir. bur. of employment security, Social Security Adminstrn., 1946, asst. dir. in charge of unemployment ins. from July 1948. Conducted survey labor relations for U.S. Coal Commn., Pa., 1924; sec. N.Y. Slum Clearance Com., 1932-33; mediator U.S. Labor Com., shoe industry, Mass.; auto, N.J.; pipe, N.Y. City, 1933-34. Served U.S. Army, 1917-19. Grad. Army Gen. Staff Coll., Langres, France. Mem. Soc. for Advancement of Management. Home: Westmoreland Hills, Md. †

WAGNER, HERMAN BLOCK, educator; b. Balt., Dec. 25, 1923; s. Henry N. and Gertrude L. (Loane) W.; B.E., Johns Hopkins, 1944, M.A., 1946, Ph.D., 1948; m. Mary Louise Hagel, June 5, 1946; children—Joseph, Marita, Stephen, Mary Lou, Gertrude. Asst. prof. chemistry Loyola Coll. at Balt., 1949-50; research chemist E.I. duPont Co., Phila., 1950-55; asso. research prof. Rutgers U., 1955-57; dir. chem. research TCA Research Center, Princeton, 1957-61; prof. chemistry Drexel U., Phila., 1961-79; cons. Dow Chem. Co., TCA Research Center. Recipient research grants NSF, 1964-65, Dupont Co., 1962-64, Dow Chem. Co., 1963-77, Glycerin Research award for 1958. Mem. Am. Chem. Soc., A.A.A.S., Am. Inst. Chemists, Sigma Xi, Phi Lambda Upsilon. Patentee in field. Home: Perkasie, Pa. Died Oct. 16, 1979.

WAGNER, WALTER FREDERICK, JR., mag. editor; b. Yonkers, N.Y., Oct. 28, 1926; s. Walter F. and Georgia (Lawrence) W.; S.B., Mass. Inst. Tech., 1949, S.M., 1950; m. Barbara Jane Alden, Mar. 12, 1952; children—Jonathan, Jennifer Ann, Daniel, Margaret. Asso. editor Factory Mgmt. and Maintenance mag., 1950-57; asst. mng. editor House and Home mag., 1957-63; editor Popular Boating Mag., 1963-65; exec. editor Archtl. Record mag., 1965-68, editor, 1969-85. Served with USNR, 1945-46. Home: Weston, Conn. Died July 6, 1985.

WAGONER, JOHN LEONARD, editor; b. Claremore, Okla., July 16, 1927; s. Silvanus and Vivian (Nicholson) W. B.A. (McMahon fellow), U. Okla., 1951. Writer, editor Kansas City (Mo.) Star, 1953-60; various editorial positions Chgo. Tribune, 1961-84, sr. news editor, 1972-80, mem. editorial bd., 1980-84. Served with USNR, 1945-46. Mem. Phi Beta Kappa, Sigma Delta Chi, Kappa Tau Alpha. Clubs: Chgo. Headline, Chgo. Press. Home: Chicago, Ill. Died Apr. 28, 1984.

WAKELAND, HENRY H., govt. ofcl.; b. Rochester, Pa., Oct. 20, 1922; s. Ray Warren and Eva (Hice) W.; m. Barbara Wyatt Primm, May 19, 1962; children—Charles Warren, Eva Catherine. B.S. in Mech. Engring, Purdue U., 1943, M.S. in Mech. Engring, 1954; M.A. in Govt, N.Y. U., 1960. Registered profl. engr., Wis. Asst. devel. engr. Nash-Kelvinator Corp., 1947-52; engr. Engring. Expt. Sta., Purdue U., 1952-54; sr. engr. aero. equipment Sperry Gyroscope Co., 1954-61; interdivisional marketing coordinator gyro group Sperry Rand Corp., 1961-65; project dir. safety car program N.Y. Dept. Motor Vehicles, 1965-66; cons. Fairchild-Hiller Corp., 1966-67; dir. bur. surface transp. safety Nat. Transp. Safety Bd., Washington, 1967-76; dir. Bur. Plans and Programs, 1976-78, chief scientist, 1978-80, spl. asst., 1980-85; staff cons. joint legis. com. on vehicles and safety N.Y. State Legislature, 1961-67. Contbr. articles to profl. jours.; bd. editors: Jour. Safety Research. Chmn. N.Y. Legislative-Industry Adv. Com. on Tire Safety, 1964, N.Y. County Republican committeeman, 1956-63. Served to 1st lt. AUS, World War II. Recipient spl. commendation Am. Assn. Automotive Medicine, 1964; Edward J. Speno award Nat. Motor Vehicle Safety Adv. Council, 1976. Mem. Am. Polit. Sci. Assn., ASME, AIAA, System Safety Soc., Am. Assn. Automotive Medicine, Soc. Automotive Engrs. (mem. gov. bd. Milw. and Met. sects.). Presbyterian. Patentee in field. Home: Potomac, Md. Died Feb. 10, 1985; buried Myrtle Hill Cemetery, Tampa, Fla.

WALD, HASKELL PHILIP, government official; b. Worcester, Mass., Sept. 6, 1916; s. Joseph A. and Minnie (Bernstein) W.; A.B., Clark U., 1938; A.M., Harvard, 1942, Ph.D., 1950; m. Ruth Jacobs, July 2, 1939; children—Sharon Anne (Mrs. Ronald Krauss), Alan Maynard, Michael Ellis. Economist with various fed. agencies, 1938-53; research asso. Harvard Law Sch., 1953-55; economist Fed. Res. Bank N.Y., 1955-62; UN econ. cons., Korea, 1953; UN tech. assistance expert, Greece, 1958- 59; chief economist FPC, 1963-77, Fed. Energy Regulatory Commn., 1977-80; vis. prof. grad. faculty New Sch. Social Research, 1957-62. Littauer fellow, 1941-42, 49. Mem. Am. Econ. Assn., Phi Beta Kappa. Author: Taxation of Agricultural Land in Underdeveloped Economies, 1959. Home: Bethesda, Md. Dec. Nov. 21, 1981.

WALDEN, JOHN SAMUEL, JR., banker; b. Danville, Va., Apr. 22, 1888; s. John Samuel and Ida Virginia (Dickenson) W.; C.P.A., Va., 1918; m. Lula Richardson Sydnor, June 17, 1914; children—John Samuel III, Stuart Sydnor, Harriett Virginia (Mrs. Wm. Crawford French). With Virginia State Ins. Co., Richmond, Va., 1906-14; accountant, 1915-18; auditor Fed. Reserve Bank of Richmond (Va.), 1919-20, asst. to gov. 1921-23, controller, 1924-34, dep. gov. 1935; vice pres., 1936, 1st vice pres. from Oct. 1936. Democrat (state), Independent (nat.). Baptist.†

WALDRON, CARL WILLIAM, surgeon; b. Waubaushene, Ont., Can., Sept. 24, 1887; s. Charles Henry and Harriet Annie (Bowles) W.; M.B., U. of Toronto, 1911, M.D., 1911, D.D.S., 1913; Licentiate Dental Surgery, Royal Coll. Dental Surgeons, Toronto, 1913; m. Cora Berdina Fossen, Sept. 1, 1921; children—Charles Andrew, Robert Douglas, John Fossen. Naturalized Am. citizen, 1926. Interneships, Canada, 1911-12; interne, Johns Hopkins Hosp., 1913-15; in private practice as oral, maxillo facial, plastic and reconstructive surgeon, Minneapolis, Minn., from 1920; prof. oral and maxillo facial surgery, U. of Minnesota, from 1927, chmn. div. oral and maxillo facial surgery and hosp. dental service, 1924-47; civilian cons., oral and facial surgery, Office of Surgeon Gen.; mem. Nat. Faculty War Sessions; Consultant Plastic Surgery Veterans Admn. Hospital; Mem. Advisory Comm. Federal Hospital Council. Mem. med. advisory bd. Visiting Nurses Assn. of Community Health Service. Served as organizer and in charge Canadian Army Med. Service for Facial Injuries, 1916-20. Mentioned in dispatches for service World War I. Diplomate Am. Bd. Plastic Surgery, American Bd. Oral Surgery, Fellow Am. Coll. Surgeons; mem. Minn. and Am. Dental assns., Minn. State and Am. Med. assns.; American Soc. Maxillo Facial Surgeons, American Academy Oral Pathology; Minn. Acad. Opthalmology and Otolaryngology, Am. Assn. Plastic Surgeons, Am. Soc. Plastic and Reconstructive Surgery, Am. Soc. Oral Surgeons, Am. Coll. Dentists, Internat. Assn. for Dental Research; Nu Sigma Nu, Xi Psi Phi. Editor, Yearbook Publishing Co.; editor Jour. of Oral Surgery (Am. Dental Assn.), 1943-38. Author of chapter on oral tumor pathology, Bunting's Oral Pathology, 1929. Contbr. over 60 articles to professional jours. Home: Minneapolis, Minn. Deceased.

WALKER, DELOSS WINFIELD, editor and lectr.; b. Baldwin, Kan., July 5, 1890; s. James Winfield and Emma (Beck) W.; prep. edn., DePauw Acad.; A.B., DePauw U., Greencastle, Ind., 1912; L.H.D., Palmer Coll., 1966; m. Nell E. Williams (dec. 1964); 1 son, James. Invited to China as mem. faculty Chinese Govt. univs., Tientsin, 1913-15; directed athletic teams for Far-Eastern Olympic Games which were won by Chinese contestants in 1915; in charge New England sales of bituminous coal, 1916-17; gen. supt. Trojan Coal Mining Co., Clearfield, Pa., 1917-18; pres. Allied Mining Co., Inc.; treas. Woodland Coal Mining Co.; asso. editor Liberty Mag., New York, 1934-41. Co-founder Am. Ecconomic Found. from 1939. Sr. indsl. specialist War Prodn. Bd., 1942. Mem. bd. govs. Transportation Assn. Am., 1940-41. Student Officers Tng. Sch. (field artillery), Camp Zachary Taylor, Louisville, Ky., 1918; served as corpl. inf., and in field arty.; hon. disch., Jan. 1919. Co-founder Nat. Recovery Crusade, starting in N.Y. City, 1932, and mem. bd. dirs.; organized recovery com. in many cities, delivered addresses in many states. Former pres. Ind. Soc. of State of Wash.; organized DePauw Alumni Assn., Puget Sound. Wash. Mem. Beta Theta Pi. Mason. Elk; mem. Sciots. Winner of championship in U.S. of running high jump, 1913; Extensive contbr. on econ. subjects to trade mags. Home: Chicago, IL. †

WALKER, ESTELLENE PAXTON, librarian; b. Bristol, Va., Sept. 13, 1911; d. John Camp and Willie (Ropp) W. B.A., U. Tenn., 1933; B.L.S., Emory U., 1935; Litt.D., Presbyn. Coll., Clinton, S.C., 1975; H.H.D. (hon.), Lander Coll., Greenwood, S.C., 1979. Head county dept. Lawson McGhee Library, Knoxville, Tenn., 1935-41; post librarian, Ft. Jackson, S.C., 1941-45; materials supply librarian Army Spl. Services, ETO, 1945-46; dir. S.C. Library Bd., 1946-69; librarian S.C. State Library, Columbia, 1969-79; mem. adv. com. on library services program U.S. Office Edn., 1956-57; chmn. Southeastern States Co-op. Library Survey, 1972-76. Editor: S.C. Library Bull, 1946-56; contbr. articles to library, ednl. periodicals. Mem. S.C. Adv. Com. Adult Edn., S.C. Com. Welfare Children and Youth, S.C. Com. for Humanities, S.C. Child Devel. Council, S.C. Com. Primary Prevention in Mental Health; sec. Interdepartmental Council State Agys.; adv. mem. S.C. Confederate Centennial Commn.; del. White House Conf. Children and Youth, 1960. Mem. ALA (council 1952-56, adv. com. recruiting project 1962-84), S.C. Library Assn. (v.p. 1972-73, pres. 1973-75), Southeastern Library Assn. (chmn. county and regional library sect. 1940), Am. Assn. State Libraries (pres.), Caroliniana Soc., Phi Kappa Phi, Order Palmetto. Died May 15, 1984.

WALKER, EVERETT, newspaper editor; b. Bklyn., Aug. 18, 1906; s. Milton Everett and Elizabeth Ann (Bandholtz) W.; student Cooper Union, 1924; m. Frances Elizabeth Lander, Oct. 18, 1930; children—Shirley Ann, Carol Joan, Barbara Jean. Reporter, feature writer N.Y. Herald Tribune, 1924-37, Sunday sections editor, 1937-39, asst. to mng. editor, 1939-41, asst. mng. editor, 1941-44, sent to Paris to arrange republication European edit., 1944, war corr. 9th Army, Feb.-Mar. 1945, mng. editor, 1953-55, Sunday editor, 1955-61, asst. editor 1961-62, dir. N.Y. Herald Tribune div. Pubs. Newspaper Syndicate, 1963-66; mng. editor Washington Star Syndicate, 1967-68, Newsweek, N.Y.C., 1968-70; exec. editor Daily Mirror, 1971-72; cons. editor, asst. mgr. N.Y. Times Spl. Features, 1972-73; editorial cons. econs. dept. Citibank, NA, N.Y.C., 1973-78, cons., 1978-83. Trustee Hood Coll., 1955-61. Member of the Society of Siulrians, Overseas Press Club, Pi Delta Epsilon. Clubs: Essex County Country (West Orange, N.J.); Dutch Treat. Home: Bloomfield, N.J. Dec. Apr. 18, 1983. Interned Glendale Cemetery, Bloomfield, N.J.

WALKER, JACOB ALLEN, lawyer; b. Alexander City, Ala., Oct. 3, 1889; s. John Edward and Vara (Leslie) W.; B.S. with honor, Auburn U., 1908, M.S., 1909; Ph.B., U. Chgo., 1912, J.D. cum laude, 1913; m. Emma Lillian Pearson, June 15, 1911; 1 son, Jacob Allen. Instr. history Ala. Poly. Inst., 1909-11; admitted to Ala. Bar, 1913, practice of law, Alexander City, 1913-17, Opelika, from 1917; elected mem. Ho. of Reps., Ala., 1923-27, Senate, 1927-31; spl. asst. to U.S. Atty. Gen., 1941-46. Member of Alabama Commission for Judicial Reform, 1955-57. Member Institute of Judicial Adminstrn. Served as 2d lt. F.A., U.S. Army, 1918. Fellow American College of Trial Lawyers; member Am. Ala. State (pres. 1942-43) bar assns., Phi Delta Theta, Order of Coif. Methodist. Home: Opelika, AL. †

WALKER, JAMES FRENCH, educator; b. Flushing, O., Nov. 1, 1889; s. Abel and Hannah Letitia (French) W.; prep. edn., Friends Boarding Sch., Barnesville, O., 1905-06, Westtown (Pa.) Sch., 1906-08; B.S. in Agr., Ohio State U., 1914; grad. study Columbia, summer 1921, Harvard, summers 1925, 27; m. Alice Nicholson Bell, June 24, 1916; children—Robert Bell, Ruth Nicholson, Margaret Louise. Teacher of agr. and mgr. of orchard, Westtown Sch., 1914-24, acting prin., 1924-25, prin. from 1925. Sch. dir. Westtown Tp. from 1926. Quaker. Address; Westtown, Pa. †

WALKER, JOHN LUTHER, lawyer; b. Lynnwood, Va., Aug. 3, 1905; s. Luther V. and Sarah V. (Hopkins) W.; m. Katherine E. Crawford, Oct. 6, 1934; children—John Luther, Jane C. A.B., Roanoke Coll., 1925; LL.B., U. Va., 1928. Bar: Va. bar 1927, Fla. bar 1928, also to U.S. Supreme Ct. bar 1928. Practiced with Wideman & Wideman, West Palm Beach, Fla., 1928-30; asso. with Woods, Chitwood, Coxe & Rogers (now Woods, Rogers, Muse, Walker & Thornton), from 1930, mem., 1937-80, counsel for firm, from 1981; Lectr. ins. law U. Va. Law Sch., spring 1957; Mem. Va. Bd. Bar Examiners, from 1964. Chmn. Roanoke City-County Pub. Forum, 1943-44; trustee Elks Nat. Found., from 1962, vice chmn., acting chmn., 1966, chmn., 1966-81; bd. mgrs. U. Va. Alumni Assn., 1951-54. Fellow Am. Coll. Trial Lawyers, Am. Bar Found.; mem. U. Va. Law Sch. Alumni Assn. (pres. 1975-77), C. of C. (dir. 1950, 51), ABA, Va. Bar Assn. (life mem., pres. 1947-48), Roanoke Bar Assn. (pres. 1948-49), W. Va. Bar Assn. (hon.), Am. Judicature Soc. (dir. 1952-57), Am. Law Inst. (life mem.), Jud. Conf. 4th U.S. Circuit, Raven Soc., Order of Coif, Phi Beta Kappa, Phi Delta Phi, Tau Kappa Alpha. Democrat. Presbyn. Clubs: Elk. (Roanoke) (pres. Va. state assn. 1941-42, dist. dep. Va., West 1945-46, Grand Lodge judiciary com. 1947-50, mem. Grand Forum from 1950, chief justice 1954-55, grand exalted ruler 1955-56, mem. adv. com. from 1956, chmn. 1961-66, mem. nat. service commn. 1957-60, sec. 1960-74), Shenandoah (Roanoke), Kiwanis (Roanoke); Farmington Country (Charlottesville, Va.). Home: Roanoke, VA.

WALKER, JOHN O, corporation exec.; b. Lynchburg, Va., Aug. 6, 1887; s. David and Agatha Bernard (Taylor) W.; ed. public and prep. schools; m. Evlyn M. Denley, June 8, 1920; children—John Denley, Agatha Taylor. With Bd. of Trade and Retail Merchants Assn., Lynchburg, 1906-07; fire insurance, 1907-11; bank cashier, Moneta, Va., 1911-17; with Export and Import Co., N.Y. City, 1919-20; pub. adminstr. (city govt.). 1920-27; canning operation, 1927-28; municipal advisor and community manager, 1928-36; federal adminstr. from 1936, asst. adminstr. Farm Security Adminstrn. since 1941; dir. council on Intergovernmental Relations; became acting dir. Civil Govt. Div., E.C.A., Greece, 1948; gen. mgr. Bridgeport Mut. Managing Corp., 1954-56; gen. mgr. Greenbelt Veterans Housing Corp., 1957-59; consultant Webber Knapp, Greenbelt, from 1960. Served as 2d lt. to maj. 120th Inf., 30th Div., 1917-19; lt. col. Reserve to 1935. Mem. Am. Acad. Polit. and Social Sci. Home: Alexandria, Va. †

WALKER, LAURENCE ALBERT, university dean; b. Gillette, Wyo., Nov. 13, 1919; s. Marion A. and Ruth Elizabeth (Spielman) W.; B.A., U. Wyo., 1949, M.A., 1951; Ed.D. (Grad. fellow), U. Fla., 1964; m. Mathilda Martha Michalek, June, 1946; 1 son, David Laurence. Tchr., Campbell County (Wyo.) Rural Schs., 1937-42, Albin (Wyo.) Pub. Sch., 1942-43, Torrington (Wyo.) Pub. Schs., 1943-45; elementary prin. Jackson (Wyo.) Pub. Schs., 1945-49; tchr. lab. sch. U. Wyo., Laramie, 1949-53, dir. lab. sch., 1954-56, 59-60, coordinator extension classes, 1960-63, prof. elementary edn. and curriculum, after 1964, asst. dean, 1956-59, asso. dean, 1964-66, 67-70, acting dean, 1966-67, 70-71, dean, after 1971; cons. Lear Sigler Corp.; vis. lectr. U. No. Colo., U. Fla., Fla. Inst. Continuing Edn. Studies; sch. cons. or evaluator, S.D., Nebr., Nev., Colo., Fla., Tex., Ohio, Wyo., P.R. Pres., Albany County (Wyo.) Hist. Soc., 1975-79; mem. Laramie Parks Recreation Bd. Recipient Distinguished Service award Future Farmers Am.; Silver Beaver award Boy Scouts Am.; Luther Wesley Smith Edn. award Am. Bapt. Chs., 1978; Laramie Community Service award, 1978. Republican. Baptist. Author: School Camping, 1952; (with Dorris Sander) First Grade Entrance Requirements, 1951. Contbr. to edn. jours. and curriculum guides. Home: Laramie, Wyo. Dec. June 12, 1981.

WALKER, RAYMOND BRIDGHAM, clergyman; b. Denver, Sept. 5, 1888; s. Arthur M. and Linnie E. (Bridgham) W.; student Hamline U., St. Paul; D.D. (hon.), Yankton (S.D.) Coll., 1928; m. Ruth B. Schafer, July 24, 1912; 1 son, Raymond Richard. Ordained to ministry of Congl. Ch., 1912; pastor, Wibaux, Mont., 1912-16, Sidney, Mont., 1916-19, Sheridan, Wyo., 1919-22, First Church, Billings, 1922-29, First Church, Portland, Ore., from 1929. Served as Home Service Red Cross sec. and acting county agrl. agt., Sidney, World War I; pub. mem. 12th Regional War Labor Bd., World War II. Chmn. Ore. State Bd. of Labor Conciliation, 1939-45. Mem. exec. com., gen. council, Congl. Christian Chs. of U.S., mem. bd. dirs., council for social action, 1942-48, mem. prudential com., Am. Bd. of Commrs. for Fgn. Missions, 1933-39. Mem. bd. trustees Pacific U. Mem. S.A.R. Republican. Mason (32 deg.; grand chaplain, Grand Lodge of Ore., 1942, grand orator, 1944). Clubs: Kiwanis (Billings, president 1925-26), City of Portland (pres. 1940-41), Rotary (Portland). Staff corr. (Ore.) The Christian Century. Home: Portland, Oreg. †

WALKOWICZ, THADDEUS F., manufacturing company executive; b. Webster, Mass., Apr. 10, 1920; s. John and W.; m. Mary-Lucy McGrath; children—Christian Ann, Thaddeus Jan, Lucianne; stepchildren—Winston M. Smith, Chantal L. Smith. B.S., M.I.T., 1941, Sc.D., 1948; M.S., Calif. Inst. Tech., 1944. Commd. 2d lt. U.S. Air Force, 1941, advanced through grades to lt. col., resigned, 1952; chmn. Am. Fund Advisors, N.Y.C.; pres. Nat. Aviation and Tech. Corp., N.Y.C., 1983; gen. partner Advanced Tech. Ventures, N.Y.C.; dir. CCI Corp., Tulsa, Evans & Sutherland Computer Corp., Salt Lake City, Itek Corp., Lexington, Mass., Mitre Corp., Bedford, Mass., Quotron Systems, Inc., Los Angeles, Safetran Systems Corp., Louisville, Sci. Applications, Inc., La Jolla, Calif., Wackenhut Corp., Coral Gables, Fla. Bd. dirs. Hertz Found., Inst. Ednl. Affairs, Nat. Space Inst.; trustee Meml. Sloan-Kettering Cancer Inst.; mem. Space Applications bd. NRC; mem. Citizens Adv. Com. on Environ. Quality, 1970-72, cons., 1972-76; bd. visitors Def. Systems Mgmt., Dept. Def. Decorated Legion of Merit with oak leaf cluster. Mem. Council Fgn. Relations. Clubs: Maidstone, Met, Recess, River, Piping Rock, Beaver Dam. Home: New York, N.Y. Died Oct. 6, 1983.

WALLACE, ANTHONY EDWARD, utility executive; b. Stamford, Conn., Dec. 6, 1915; s. Anthony John and Ann (Bordus) W.; m. Helen Barton, Oct. 19, 1941; children: Richard Anthony, Anthony Edward. B.S., UCLA, 1941; postgrad. Harvard Sch. Bus. Adminstrn., 1942-43. Faculty Hillyer Coll., U. Hartford, Conn., 1946-52; asst. dir. research and planning div. Conn. Devel. Commn., 1943-52; with Conn. Light & Power Co., 1952-80, exec. v.p., 1964-68, pres., 1968-80, also dir.; trustee corp. Soc. for Savs., Hartford; exec. v.p., dir. N.E. Utilities Service Co., 1975-80, Holyoke Water Power Co., 1975-80; dir., exec. v.p. Hartford Electric Light Co., 1975-80; exec. v.p., dir. Western Mass. Electric Co., 1975-80; dir. Conn. Water Service, Inc., Conn. Mut. Life Ins. Co., Mohasco Corp. Chmn. Conn. Bd. Pesticide Control, 1964-68; mem. Citizens Commn. Conn. Gen. Assembly, Conn. Regional Med. Program; Conn. chmn. U.S. Savs. Bonds Vol. Com., 1975-76; mem. exec. com. Natural Resources Council Conn.; mem. nat. emergency com. Nat. Council Crime and Delinquency; mem. com. fed. finance Council State Chambers Commerce.; Mem. Conn. Ho. of Reps., 1956-62, speaker, 1961-62; Trustee, 1st vice chmn. Conn. Ednl. TV Corp., 1967-75; trustee Conn. Pub. Expenditure Council, 1969-75, Samuel I. Ward Tech. Coll., Sterling Opera House Found., 1972-75; corporator Mt. Sinai Hosp., Hartford, Inst. Living, New Britain Gen. Hosp.; nat. adv. council Bus.-Industry Polit. Action Com., U. Conn. Found., 1968-74, hon. life dir.; bd. dirs. Am. Sch. Deaf; mgmt. adv. com. Hartford Grad. Center, Rensselaer Poly. Inst. Conn.; mem. exec. com., co-chmn. regional bd. dirs. NCCJ. Mem. Conn. Electric and Gas Assn. (pres., chmn. exec. com. 1968-80), C. of C. U.S. (dir., v.p. 1968-75), Conn. C. of C. (pres. 1965-67, chmn. bd. 1967-68), Conn. Bus. and Industry Assn. (dir. 1966-68), New Eng. Gas Assn. (dir. 1968-72). Clubs: Shuttle Meadow Country; Economic (N.Y.C.); Hartford, Harvard Business School No. Conn. Home: Southington, Conn. Dec. June 1, 1984.

WALLACE, CARL S., business executive; b. Ontario, Wis., Sept. 27, 1918; s. David Wallace and Mae (McQueen) W.; m. Marian E. Jones, Feb. 22, 1941; children—Carl S., Mary Ann Green. Ph.B., U. Wis., 1943. Mgr. Wausau office Wis. Employment Service, 1951-53, Stevens Point (Wis.) Area C. of C., 1953-65; adminstry. asst. to U.S. rep. Melvin Laird, 1965-69; spl. asst. to sec. and dep. sec. def., 1969-72; asst. sec. manpower and res. affairs U.S. Army, 1973-74; corp. v.p. Purolator, Inc., 1974-82; mem. Bus. Govt. Relations Council. Served with AUS, 1943-45. Decorated Bronze Star (2); recipient medal for distinguished service Dept. of Def., 1973; Distinguished Civilian Service medal Dept. of Army, 1974. Mem. Am. Legion. Republican. Methodist. Clubs: Elk, Kiwanian. Home: Alexandria, Va. Dec. Sept. 23, 1982.

WALLACE, EARLE SESSIONS, headmaster; b. Clinton, Mass., July 29, 1887; s. Silas Ives and Lucy Maria (Sessions) W.; grad. Dean Acad., Franklin, Mass., 1906; B.S., Tufts Coll., 1910; grad. work U. of Calif. and U. of Southern Calif., 1927-33; m. Marion Wheeler Hartwell, of Clinton, Oct. 25, 1913; 1 dau., Janet Marsylvia. Insp. Mut. Fire Ins. Co., Boston, 1910-13; asst. supt. Pasadena Mil. Acad. and Calif. Prep. Sch., Pasadena, 1921-28; founder Boys' Mountaineering Camp in Calif.; instr. Pasadena high schs., 1928-35; headmaster Dean Acad., Franklin, Mass., from 1935; owner date garden from 1915; pioneer grower of commercial grapefruit on desert lands in Calif. Served as capt. Air Service, A.E.F., 1917-19; citations. Dir. Franklin Library Assn., Y.M.C.A. Mem. N.E.A., Calif. Teachers Assn., Assn. Colls. and Secondary Schs., Am. Legion, French Legion, Theta Delta Chi. Republican. Universalist. Clubs: Rotary (Franklin); Sierra of Calif. Home: Franklin, Mass. †

WALLACE, FRED CLUTE, army officer; b. McMinnville, Tenn., July 1, 1887; s. Percival Sumter and Mary Susan (Rains) W.; B.S., U.S. Mil. Acad., 1910; grad. Command and Gen. Staff Sch., 1931, Army War Coll., 1936; m. George Butler Magoun, Apr. 14, 1920; children—Fred Clute Jr. (killed in action, Normandy, July 19, 1944), George Magoun II. Commissioned 2d lt., F.A., 1910, advanced through ranks to maj. gen., 1942; served in 3d, 2d, 14th, 313th and 18th F.A.; dir. dept. gunnery and materiel, F.A. Basic Sch., 1919-22; chief, R.O.T.C. sect., Office Chief of F.A., 1922-24; mem. F.A. Bd., 1931-35; comdt. and comdr., R.O.T.C., Ala. Poly. Inst., 1936-39; exec. officer, Office Chief of F.A., 1939-40; div. artillery comdr., 4th Motorized Div. to Sept. 1941; comdg. 4th Motorized Div., Oct. 1941-June 1942; comdg. 5th Service Command, July, 1942-Sept. 1943. Comdg. Espiritu Santo Island Command, Oct. 1943-Nov. 1944; comdg. Army Garrison Forces, APO 331, Nov. 1944-45. Comdg. Okinawa Combined Base, Apr.-Sept. 1945; retired Apr. 30, 1946. Awarded Distinguished Service (with Oak Leaf Cluster), Legion of Merit, (Army), Legion of Merit (Navy). Mem. Omicron Delta Kappa, Scabbard and Blade, hon. mem. Auburn "A" Club. Clubs: Army and Navy (Washington). Address: Stony Point, Va. Deceased.†

WALLACE, GEORGE ROBERTS, fisheries executive; b. Morehead City, N.C., Oct. 13, 1906; s. Charles Slover and Nina (Webb) W.; A.B., Duke, 1927; m. Laura Abernathy Mace, Oct. 21, 1936; children—George Roberts (dec.), William Borden. Trustee emeritus Duke U. Mem. Lambda Chi Alpha. Republican. Episcopalian. Clubs: Masons, Shriners, Coral Bay, Dunes. Home: Morehead City, N.C. Dec. Apr. 11, 1985. Interned Bayview Cemetery, Morehead City.

WALLACE, JAMES BREVARD, organist, orchestra-choral director, educator; b. Westminster, S.C., July 17, 1915; s. Joseph Edward and Mary (Reynolds) W.; A.B., U. Miss., 1936; B.Mus., Westminster Choir Coll., Princeton, N.J., 1939, D.Fine Arts, 1967; Mus.M., U. Mich., 1947; D.Mus., Hillsdale (Mich.) Coll., 1961. Organist, choir dir. various chs. N.Y., Pa., Miss., Mich., 1937-60; tchr. music, Phila., 1937-39; concert organist U.S., Europe, 1939-46; dean music Belhaven Coll., Jackson, Miss., 1939-42; prof. music U. Mich., Ann Arbor, from 1949, assoc. dean Sch. Music, 1950-60, dean, 1960-70, Guest lectr., tchr. U.S. Army Chaplain's Sch., 1947-48; cons. music and fine arts. Trustee Nat. Music Camp and Interlochen Arts Acad. Co-chmn. Mich. Council Arts, 1961-70. Bd. dirs. United Fund Ann Arbor; trustee Westminster Choir Coll. Served with AUS, 1942-46. Mem. Nat. Assn. Schs. Music, Music Educators Nat. Conf., Bohemians Detroit, Nat. Music Execs. of State Univs., Pi Kappa Lambda, Phi Mu Alpha, Kappa Kappa Psi. Presbyterian. Rotarian. Co-author: (textbooks) Richard Wagner and the Music Drama, 1954; Masterpieces of Music Literature, 1958. Home: Ann Arbor, Mich. Died July 12, 1983; buried Lakewood Meml. Park, Jackson, Miss.

WALLACE, LEW, Dem. nat. committeeman; b. Furnas County, Neb., Mar. 27, 1889; s. Henry Malanthon and Margaret (Scott) W.; grad. Lexington (Neb.) High Sch., 1908; student U. of Nebraska, 1908 and 1910, Creighton U., Omaha, Neb., 1909; m. Pearl G. Hoch, Sept. 2, 1914; 1 dau., Shirley June Carnahan. Began as bookkeeper with plumbing company, 1910; agent Columbia Life and Trust Company, Portland, Ore., 1910-15; state agent American Life Ins. Co., Des Moines, Ia., 1915-21; gen. agent Canada Life Assurance Co., Portland, Ore., from 1921; state rep. 1935; Ore. state game commr., 1935-38; state senator from 1938; Dem. nominee for gov., 1942; became Democratic nat. committeeman for Ore., 1944. Presbyterian. Mason (Shriner), Elk (past exalted ruler), Eagle. Clubs: Progressive Business Men's, University, Life Underwriters, Multnomah Hunters and Anglers, Isaac Walton League. Home: Portland, Oreg. †

WALLACE, LILA ACHESON, publisher; b. Virden, Man., Can.; d. T. Davis and Mary E. (Huston) Acheson; m. DeWitt Wallace, Oct. 15, 1921. Student, Ward-Belmont Coll., Nashville, Tenn.; A.B., U. Oreg. Co-founder, past co-chmn. with husband Reader's Digest. Recipient medal freedom Pres. U.S., 1972. Presbyterian. Home: Mount Kisco, N.Y. Dec. May 8, 1984.

WALLACE, RAYMOND MCELWAIN, editor; b. Camanche, Ia., May 1, 1888; s. Dr. Walter S. and Mina (McElwain) W.; student Northwestern U., 1909-12; m. Bertha Schmidt, Apr. 5, 1913; 1 dau., Dorothy Margaret. Reporter City Press Assn., Chicago, 1912-13; advertising copy writer for Black Diamond, trade jour., Chicago, 1913-14; sales promotion, own agency, Chicago, 1915-18; sales promotion Woman's World Mag., 1918-20, asso. editor, 1921-32, complete charge of editorial, circulation and production depts. from 1933; v.p. and treas. Pubs. Circulation and Fulfillment Service, Inc., New York, Mem. Sigma Chi. Republican. Club: Seminole (Forest Hills, L.I.). Home: Forest Hills, N.Y. †

WALLACE, ROBERT GEORGE, business exec.; b. Chicago, Ill., Oct. 5, 1889; s. William and Margaret (Johnstone) W.; student Coll., 2 yrs.; m. Ethel Nelson, Aug. 12, 1911; 1 son, Robert George. Div. mgr. Nat. Fireproofing Co., 1918-20, vice pres., 1920-26; with Masonite Corp. from 1926, gen. sales mgr., 1926-35, vice pres. from 1935, also dir.; v.p. and dir. Masonite Co.; Ltd., of Canada. Mem. Chicago Assn. of Commerce, Ill. C. of C. Mason (Shriner). Clubs: Chicago Advertising, Union League, South Shore Country, Flossmoor Country, Executives. Home: Chicago, Ill. Deceased.

WALLENBERG, MARCUS, banker; b. Stockholm, Sweden, Oct. 5, 1899; s. M.L. and Amalia (Hagdahl) W.; ed. at U. of Commerce, Stockholm; m. Dorothy Helen Mackay, 1923; children—Marc, Peter, Ann-Mari; m. 2d, Marianne de Geer, 1936. Asst. v.p. Stockholms Enskilda Bank, 1925, v.p., 1927-46, pres., 1946-58, vice chmn. bd., 1958-69, chmn., 1969-76; chmn. SAAB Scania Aktiebolag, Linkoping, Sweden; Swedish chmn. Scandinavian Airlines System; chmn. Atlas Copco AB, Allmanna Svenska Electriska AB, Telefon AB, L.M. Ericsson, vice chmn. Stora Kopparbergs Berglags AB. Incentive AB, Kopperfors AB, Liberian Swedish-American Minerals Co., Swedish del. to trade negotiations with Gt. Britain, 1939-43, and U.S., 1943. Bd. dirs. Nobel Found., Knut and Alice Wallenberg Found. Mem. Internat. C. of C. (pres. 1965-67). Club: Royal Swedish Lawn Tennis (chmn.). Home: Osmo, Sweden. Died Sept. 13, 1982.

WALLENDER, ELMER FORREST, army officer; b. Arthur City, Tex., Dec. 21, 1889; s. James Arthur and Elizabeth (Sargent) W.; ed. Catholic and pub. schs., and Paris (Tex.) Bus. Coll.; grad. Motor Transport Sch., 1921, Inf. Sch., 1926, Army Indsl. Coll., 1940; m. Evelyn M. Torrance, Dec. 29, 1918; children—Lillian May (wife of Major John Fielding Longley), Elizabeth Ann (Mrs. James Luther Chamberlain, Jr.). Enlisted in United State Army, 1914, and advanced through the grades to brig. gen., 1944; served in Philippine Islands, 1915-17, China, 1917-19, Hawaiian Islands, 1932-35; comdg. San Antonio Gen. Depot, 1947. Decorated Legion of Merit. Mason. Club: Army and Navy (Washington). Address: Slingerlands, N.Y. †

WALLENDORF, PAUL E., business executive; b. 1909; B.S., Northwestern U., 1931; m. With Gen. Electric Co., 1931-74, v.p., treas., 1968-74; pres. Pvt. Export Funding Corp., N.Y.C., 1974-77. C.P.A., Ill. Home: New Canaan, Conn. Died Apr. 14, 1985.

WALLENSTEIN, ALFRED FRANZ, conductor; b. Chgo., Oct. 7, 1898; s. Franz Albrecht Von and Anna (Klinger) W.; m. Virginia Wilson, May 10, 1924. Ed. pub. schs.; hon. Mus.D., Wooster Coll., 1943, U. So. Calif., 1951, Redlands U. Calif., 1954, Peabody Inst., Balt., 1962. Head cello dept. Chgo. Mus. Coll., 1927-29. Began playing cello in pub. at age 9; made concert tours through, Europe, S.Am., N.Am.; solo cellist, Chgo. Symphony Orch., 1923-29, N.Y. Philharmonic Orch., 1929-36; Has made many transcriptions for cello.; Mus. dir., Radio Station WOR, 1935-45, condr., mus. dir., Los Angeles Philharmonic Orch., 1943-56, condr., Symphony of the Air, 1961-63, vis. condr., Juilliard Sch. Music, 1966-83. Head Ford Found. project for young Am. condrs., 1962-64. Decorated Legion of Honor France). Address: New York, N.Y. Dec. Feb. 8, 1983.

WALLER, ALFRED ERNEST, electrical engr.; b. White Plains, N.Y., Mar. 23, 1888; s. James Taylor and Sarah Louise (Fisher) W.; grad. high sch., White Plains, 1906; student in E.E., Cooper Union, N.Y.; spl. courses in mineralogy and radio frequency currents, Columbia; m. Berthe Helene MacMonnies, Sept. 19, 1917; children—Leonard, Marjorie, David; m. 2d, Carolyn Hobart Harris, March 8, 1941. Employed in underground department N.Y. Edison Co.; became connected with Ward Leonard Electric Co., 1909, production mgr., 1916, chief engr., 1918, dir., 1923-28; mng. dir. Nat. Elec. Mfrs. Assn., 1926-29; then employment mgr. of Met. Life Ins. Co. of New York. Member board of trustees and in charge of Public Works of Village of Bronxville, 1939-48, in charge Division of Public Works, same, 1939-48; mem. N.Y.C. Adv. Council on Business Education. Special mention for work on signal corps equipment, World War. Fellow American Institute E.E.; member New York State Society Professional Engineers, Society American Mil. Engrs., Electric Power Club (gov. 1922-26; pres. 1925-26), Westchester County Village Official Association, National Rifle Assn., Little Academy. Clubs: National Republican (N.Y.C.); American Yacht (Rye, New York). Republican. Episcopalian. Mason. Contbr. on tech. subjects to mags., also syndicated articles. Home: Bronxville, N.Y. Deceased.

WALLER, THOMAS SMALL, lawyer; b. Morganfield, Ky., Oct. 12, 1890; s. Benjamin Gibson and Pearl (Ray) W.; B.S., Vanderbilt U., 1912; LL.B., Yale, 1914; m. Olga Lucille Nunn, Apr. 7, 1915; 1 dau., Ida Ray (Mrs. Rolph H. Nagel). Admitted to Ky. bar, 1914; practice in Morganfield, 1914-29, Paducah, from 1929; Mem. Jud. Council Ky., 1950-54. Comdr. civilian def. Paducah, World War II. Mem. exec. com. Ky. Democratic Party, 1921-25. Mem. com. 100 Emory U., 1958-62; trustee Lake Junaluska, 1954-62, Paducah Jr. Coll., from 1932. Mem. Ky. Bar Assn. (pres. 1962-63), Ky. Shorthorn Assn. (pres. 1951-54), Phi Delta Phi. Author articles. Home: Paducah, Ky. †

WALLNER, WOODRUFF, former fgn. service officer; b. Chatham, N.J., Apr. 7, 1909; s. Louis Woodruff and Doris (Cole) W.; grad. Phillips (Andover) Acad., 1924-27; student Sorbonne U., Paris, 1929-30; A.B., Columbia Coll., m. Gertrude Monica Pickering, Sept. 25, 1944; children—Nicholas, Louise Ann. Fgn. service officer, 1935-70, vice consul, Naples, 1935, Barcelona, 1937, Vanencia, 1938; 3d sec. embassy, Paris, 1939, Vichy, 1940; interned by Germans, 1942-44; with div. Western European Affiars, Dept. of State, 1944-48, asst. chief. 1946, asso. chief, 1947, 1st sec., then counselor of Embassy, Paris, 1948-52; counselor embassy, Belgrade, 1952-54; polit. adviser to dep. comdr.-in-chief Europe, 1954-57, dep. chief of mission, minister Am. embassy, Rio de Janeiro, 1957-59; dep. asst. sec. of State for Internat. Orgn. Affairs, 1959-63; dep. comdt. NATO Def. Coll. Paris, 1964-66, Rome, 1967; dep. chief mission, minister Am. embassy, Paris, 1967-68; sr. fgn. service inspector, 1969-70. Mem. Delta Psi. Home: Holderness, N.H. Died Dec. 26, 1983.

WALSH, ELLARD A., pres. Nat. Guard Assn., b. Hull, P.Q., Can., Oct. 3, 1887; s. Edward and Mary Anne (Roach) W.; came to U.S., 1891; naturalized, 1896; student, U. of Minn., 1908-09, Sorbonne, Fr., 1918-19; m. Viola Herrick, July 9, 1917; 1 dau., Mary Patricia. Asst. adj. gen. State of Minn., 1919-25, adj. gen., 1925-46. Served as pvt. Co. F., 1st Minn. Inf., 1907-16, 2d lt., 135th Inf., 1916, 1st lt., 1918, capt. Inf. 1919, maj., Feb. 1920, lt. col., Sept. 1921, Col., Oct. 1924, brig. gen. July 1927, maj. gen., July 1940, comdg. 34th Div., July, 1940-Nov. 1941. Mem. Nat. Guard Assn. of U. S. (pres. from 1943), Adjutants Gen. Assn. of U. S. (pres. from 1943), Minn. Capitol Commn. (chmn.). Contbr. numerous articles and reports on mil. adminstrn. and mil. policy to mil. jours. Home: Minneapolis, Minn. †

WALSH, FRANCIS W., coll. pres.; b. Newport, R.I., June 8, 1889; s. William J. and Bridget J. (Martin) W.; A.B., Holy Cross Coll., Worcester, Mass, 1910, hon. A.M., 1923, LL.D., 1938; student St. Bernard's Sem., Rochester, N.Y., 1911-12, St. Joseph's Sem., Yonkers, N.Y., 1912-15. Ordained priest, Roman Cath. Ch., 1915; asst. priest Holy Innocent's Ch., New York, 1915-17, All Saints Ch., New York, 1917, Cathedral, Denver, 1921-26; pastor St. Vicent de Paul's Ch., Denver, 1926-32, Ch. of the Assumption, Peekskill, N.Y., 1932-39; dean Westchester County, N.Y., 1938-39; pres. New Rochelle (N.Y.) Coll. from 1938; pastor of New St. Gabriel's Parish, Riverdale Bronx, New York, N.Y., from Dec. 1939; dir. Ladycliff Coll., Highland Falls, N.Y.; dir. St. Joseph's Orphanage, Peekskill; dir. Cath. Guardian Soc.; mem. bd. consultors of Archdiocese of New York. Served as chaplain, 1st lt., 307th Inf., 1917-19; with A.E.F., 9 months; partially disabled by mustard gas, Sept. 1918. Address: New Rochelle, N.Y. †

WALSH, JAMES EDWARD, clergyman; b. Cumberland, Md., Apr. 30, 1891; s. William E. and Mary (Concannon) W.; A.B., Mt. St. Mary's Coll., Emmittsburg, Md., 1910, LL.D., 1937; student Maryknoll (N.Y.) Sem., 1912-15. Entered Cath. Fgn. Missions Soc. Am., Sept. 15, 1912; ordained priest Roman Cath. Ch., 1915; dir. Maryknoll Prep. Coll., Clarks Summit, Pa., 1916-18; assigned to mission in China, 1918; apptd. superior Maryknoll Mission China, 1919; consecrated titular bishop Sata and vicar apostolic of Kongmoon, China, May, 1927; Superior General Cath. Fgn. Mission Soc., Maryknoll, N.Y., 1936-46; gen. sec. Cath. Central Bur., Shanghai, China, 1948-58, imprisoned by Peoples Republic of China; with Maryknoll Fathers, 1971-81. Founder, Little Flower Sem., 1926, Native Congregation of Sisters of Immaculate Heart of Mary, 1927, both Kongmoon, South China. Author: Father McShane of Maryknoll, 1932, 2d edit. as The Man on Joss Stick Alley, 1947; Tales of Xavier, 1946; Maryknoll Spiritual Directory, 1947; Church's Worldwide Mission, 1948; The Young Ones, 1958. Contbr. to Field Afar mag. Address: Maryknoll, N.Y. Dec. July 29, 1981.

WALSH, MICHAEL PATRICK, coll. pres.; b. Boston, Feb. 28, 1912; s. Coleman and Bridget (McDonough). W.; A.B., Boston Coll., 1934, A.M., 1935; M.S., Fordham U., 1938, Ph.D., 1948; S.T.L., Weston Coll., 1942; LL.D., U. Mass., 1961. St. Anselm's Coll., 1963, Brandeis U., 1963, Loyola U., Chgo., 1967, Xavier U., 1968; D.Ed. Suffolk U., 1963; D.Sc., Villanova, 1961, Stonehill Coll., 1964; Litt.D., Coll. Holy Cross, 1962; L.H.D., North eastern U., 1962, Norwich University, 1967. Joined Society of Jesus, 1929, ordained as a priest Roman Cath. Ch., 1941; acting prin. Fairfield U. Prep., 1942; instr. biology Boston Coll., 1943-45, asso. prof., 1948-58, pres., 1958-69; pres. Fordham U., Bronx, N.Y., 1969-72. Mem. Pres.'s Commn. Presdl. Scholars, Northeastern Regional Com. Marshall Scholarships, Mass. Adv. Com. Racial Imbalance and Edn., Massachusetts Higher Edn. Facilities Commission; member of Boston Civic Progress Com., from 1958; chmn. ednl. div. United Fund, 1958; mem. commn. on legislation Assn. Am. Colls., 1958; mem. Mass. Edn. Commn., 1962-65. Board of trustees of John F. Kennedy Memorial Library. Recipient Freedom Foundation Award, 1960. Mem. A.A.A.S., American Assn. Zoologists, Bot. Soc. Am., Am. Micros. Soc., Genetics Soc. Am., Am. Assn. Jesuit Scientists (pres. 1951), Nat. Cath. Ednl. Assn. (pres. coll. and univ. dept. 1966-68), Sigma Xi, Alpha Sigma Nu, Alpha Kappa Psi (chmn. New Eng. unit 1962-68). Author publs. on cytology, genetics. Died Apr. 23, 1982.

WALTEMYER, WILLIAM CLAUDE, educator; b. Beckleysville, Md., Apr. 27, 1889; s. Joseph and Keziah

Jane (Royston) W.; A.B., Gettysburg Coll., 1908; B.D., Luth. Theol. Sem., 1911; M.A., Am. U., 1925, Ph.D., 1929; m. Mildred Butzler, Sept. 5, 1911; children—Miraim E., M. Ruth (Mrs. W. Edward McHale), Charlotte L. (Mrs. James M. Smith), William Claude, Grace V. (Mrs. George E. Stauffer), Jeanne F. (Mrs. Thomas J. Weber). Ordained to ministry Luth. Ch., 1911; pastor Landisville and Butler, Pa., 1911-16, Thurmont, Md., 1916-23, Washington, 1923-29; asso. prof. philosophy Gettysburg Coll., 1929-30, Amanda Rupert Strong prof. bibl. lit. and religion, from 1930. Served as 1st lt., 71st Arty., AEF, 1917-18, chaplain Boston Coast Defenses. Mem. Am. Assn. U. Profs., Nat. Assn. Bibl. Instrs., Am. Legion, Phi Beta Kappa. Mason Contbr. articles religious publs. Home: Gettysburg, Pa. †

WALTER, ADOLPH SCHINNER, mining engr.; b. Denver, Colo., May 7, 1889; s. Rudolph Jacob and Augustine Stephanie (Schinner) W.; student U. of Va., 1911-12; Engr. of Mines, Colo. Sch. of Mines, 1915; m. Mildred E. Maxwell, June 3, 1915; children—Phyllis Jane (Mrs. Albert Monroe Bosworth), Carolyn. Asst. engr. Florence Goldfield Mining and Milling Co., 1907; sampler, battery man, table man, and cyanide man, Nevada Goldfield Reduction Works, 1908; asst. engr. of constn., weighmaster, chemist, research engr. and asst. supt. Modern Smelting and Refining Co., 1909-11; cons. engr., Denver City Lode, Crystal, Colo., and Kittimack Mines Co., Eureka, Colo., summers, 1912-14; various positions Durango, Ark. Valley and Pueblo plants of Am. Smelting & Refining Co., 1915-21; cons. engr., Uinta Oil & Exploration Co., Uinta County, Utah, and Am. Electric Smelting & Refining Co., 1921-22; mine appraisal N.M., Coal amd Metal Mines, 1929-30; prof. chemistry and asst. prof. metallurgy, N.M. Sch. Mines, 1922-23; prof. mining and metallurgy, 1923-39, dean mining and metallurgy, 1939-44; mine appraisals Ordcit and Almagordo Bombing Ranges, 1948-49; city manager of Socorro, N.M. from 1948. Served as 1st lt., O.R.C. Engrs., 1925-35. With mine appraisals, real estate div., U.S. Army Engrs., War Dept., 1943-53. Mem. Am. Inst. Mining and Metall. Engrs. (com. on edn., metall. div.), N.M. Miners and Prospectors Assn. (pres. 1940; dir.), N.M. Soc. Engrs. (dir. and chmn. legislative com., 1942-43), El Paso Metals Sections, Am. Mining Congress (gov. for N.M.); mem. Mining and Metallurgical Soc. of Am.; Colo. Mining Assn., Sigma Nu. Consulting mining and metall. engrs., from 1944. Mason (33 deg., Shriner); grand master N.M., 1940-41. Contbr. to tech. papers. Address: Socorro, N.Mex. †

WALTERS, CHARLES, motion picture director; b. Pasadena, Calif., Nov. 17; 1 son, Joseph. Ed., U. So. Calif. Appeared in Fanchon & Marco stage shows, 1934, in dance team, Versailles Club, 1935; appeared in: stage shows including Du Barry Was a Lady, Musical Parade, Jubilee, The Show is On, Between the Devil, New Faces, I Married An Angel; choreographer: stage shows Let's Face It; dir.: dance sequences in movies including Ziegfeld Follies, Best Foot Forward, Du Barry Was A Lady, Meet Me In St. Louis, Abbott & Costello in Hollywood; motion pictures including The Unsinkable Molly Brown, Good News, Easter Parade, Lili, Dangerous When Wet, Torch Song, Easy to Love, Glass Slipper, Tender Trap, High Society; TV Shows Governor & J.J; motion pictures including Walk Don't Run, Barkleys of Broadway, Summer Stock, Three Guys Named Mike, Texas Carnival, Belle of New York, Don't Go Near the Water, Ask Any Girl, Two Loves, Please Don't East the Daisies, Jumbo; TV Shows Here's Lucy; 2 Lucille Ball spls. Home: Malibu, Calif. Dec. Aug. 13, 1982.

WALTERS, FREDERICK J(AMES), mgmt. cons.; b. N.Y.C., Feb. 18, 1906; s. Frederick J. and Laura Patricia (O'Connor) W.; m. Virginia Cross, Jan. 18, 1934; children—Rosa Lee (Sister Marie Virginia O.P.), Virginia (Mrs. R. M. Stormont), Frederick James (dec.), James Anthony. A.B., Princeton, 1927. With Gen. Motors Corp., 1927-45; mem. exec. staff Gen. Electric Co., 1945-46; v.p. Hotpoint, Inc., 1946-52, Packard Motor Car Co., 1952-53; pres. Fred Walters Oldsmobile, Atlanta, 1953-62; v.p. Boyden Assos., Inc., 1962-73; pres. Walters & Co. (mgmt. cons.), Atlanta, from 1973; dir. Flex-Comm Internat., Vital Products Co. Author: Handbook for District Representatives, 1939, A Summary of Veterans' Reemployment Rights, 1944. Roman Catholic. Clubs: Capital City (Atlanta), Rotary (Atlanta); Princeton. Home: Atlanta, GA.

WALTERS, WALTER HENRY, university dean; b. Troy, Ala., Dec. 19, 1917; s. Walter Henry and Julia (Coleman) W.; m. Geraldine Ross, Sept. 18, 1947; children—Ross Atwell, Ann Coleman, Kirk Madison. B.S., Troy State Coll., 1939; Ph.M., U. Wis., 1947; M.F.A., Western Res. U., 1949, Ph.D., 1950. Tchr. pub. schs., Ala., 1939-42; faculty U. Wis., 1946-48; faculty Pa. State U., 1950—, chmn. dept. theatre arts, 1954-66; producer Pa. State U. (Mateer Playhouse), 1958-62, Pa. State U. (Pa. State Festival Theatre), 1963-66; dean Pa. State U. (Coll. Arts and Architecture), from 1968, dir. univ. arts services, from 1973; cons. in field, 1955-82; mem. adv. council Am. Acad., Rome, 1968-82. Mem. Commonwealth Pa. Council on Arts, 1969-71; chmn. Theatre Adv. Panel Pa. Council Arts, 1972; chmn. fine arts commn. Nat. Assn. State Univs. and Land-Grant Colls., 1975-81, mem. internat. affairs com., 1979-82; bd. dirs. Am. Research Inst. for Arts, 1975-82, sec.-treas., 1975-79. Served with USNR, World War II. Fellow Am. Theatre Assn. (pres. Univ. and Coll. Theatre Assn. 1970-71, chmn. chief adminstrs. program 1978—), U.S. Inst. Theatre Tech. (bd. dirs. 1976-83, editor newsletter 1966-68, 1st v.p. 1970-71, pres. 1971-72); mem. Internat. Council Fine Arts Deans (chmn. 1974). Home: Ponte Vedra Beach, Fla. Dec. Dec. 28, 1982.

WALTERSDORF, MAURICE CLEVELAND, economist; b. Hanover, Pa., Feb. 15, 1888; s. John Franklin and Alverta Jane (Sterner) W.; grad. Shippensburg State Normal School (now Shippensburg State Coll.), 1911; Grad. Perkiomen Sch., 1914; A.B., Franklin and Marshall Coll., 1916; A.M., Princeton, 1922, Ph.D., 1925; L.H.D. (hon.), Washington and Jefferson Coll., 1956; m. Catherine Elizabeth Crapster, Sept. 13, 1924; 1 s., John Maurice. Tchr. pub. schs., Pa., 1908-09; prin. Glendola (N.J.) School, 1911-13; instructor Perkiomen School, 1913-14; instr. and asst. registrar Mercersburg Acad., 1916-21; instr. Hun Sch., Princeton, N.J., 1921-24; asst. prof. economics, Washington and Jefferson Coll., 1924-27, prof., head dept., 1927-56, prof. emeritus, from 1956, sec. faculty, 1928-56, chmn. athletic council, 1951-56, dean of bus. adminstrn. 1939-47; assisted State Budget Bureau in making survey of state and local taxation in Pa., 1934. Mem. Washington-Greene Counties Council, Boy Scouts of America, 1928-32; member Nat. Com. on Economic Guidance, Lions Internat, 1933; mem. Advisory Bd., Am. Economic Foundation, 1935; mem. Com. for Economic Stability, mem. Stable Money Assn.; mem. Citizens Conf. on Internat. Econ. Union; mem. Acad. of World Economics, mem. Am. Econ. Assn., public panel mem. and hearing officer, Regional War Labor Bd., Phila., 1943-46; training war plant personnel in indsl. relations during World War II; mem. Nat. Panel Arbitrators, Am. Arbitration Assn.; instnal. representative of Rhodes Scholarships, 1928-56; mem. N. Am. Com. China's Relief Fund; member American Association University Profs. (pres. local chap. 1944-46), Pi Gamma Mu, Lambda Chi Alpha; honorary member Eugene Field Society. Presbyterian. Clubs: Fortnightly, Lions, (formerly director, vice-president and pres.). Author: Regulation of Public Utilities in New Jersey, 1936. Contributor to Am. Economic Rev., Nat. Municipal Rev., Yale Law Jour., Social Science, Economic Jour. (Eng.), Bull. Nat. Tax Assn., Public Utilities Fortnightly, and other mags. Asso. editor New Century Book of Facts. Home: Washington, Pa. †

WALTON, LEO ANDREW, army officer; b. Salem, Ore., Oct. 7, 1890; grad. U.S. Mil. Acad.; commd. 2d lt. Cav., June 1915, and advanced through the grades to maj. gen., Oct. 1947; awarded Flying Wings, Rockwell Field, Aug. 1917; grad. Air Service Field Officer's Sch., 1921; Air Service Engring. Sch. and Aero Engring. Course, 1925, Command and Gen. Staff Sch., 1938; served in Philippine Islands, 1925-28; Asst. Commandant, Air Corps Primary Flying Sch., 1928; instr. Air Corps Tactical Sch., Maxwell Field. Ala., June 1938; comdg. officer, Air Corps Advanced Flying School, Stockton Field, Calif., 1940; assigned to Hdqrs. Western Flying Training Command, Feb. 1942. Designated chief of staff, 6th Air Force, Nov. 1944; chief of staff Caribbean Defense Command, 1945, assigned Air Inspector China Theater, July 1945; assumed Command 14th Air Force, May 1946; sec. Air Force Personnel Council. Awarded Legion of Merit, Bronze Star. Rated command pilot and combat observer.†

WALTON, SIR WILLIAM TURNER, composer; b. Oldham Lancs, Eng., Mar. 29, 1902; s. Charles Alexander and Louisa Maria (Turner) W.; m. Susana Gil Passo, Jan. 20, 1949. Student, Christ Ch. Cathedral Choir Sch., 1912, Christ Church Oxford, 1918-21; hon. student, Christ Church Oxford, 1950; Mus.D. (hon.), Durham, 1937, Oxford, 1940, Trinity Coll., Dublin, 1946, Manchester, 1953, Cambridge, 1955, London, Sussex, U. Ireland, Cork. Compositions include Piano Quartet, 1918, rev., 1974, Facade, 1923, Viola Concerto, 1929, Belshazzar's Feast, 1931, Symphony No. I, 1935, Coronation March Crown Imperial, 1937, Violin Concerto, 1939, String Quartet, 1947, Coronation Te Deum, 1953, Orb and Sceptre, 1953, Troilus and Cressida (opera), 1954, Cello Concerto, 1956, Partita, 1957, Anon in Love, 1960, Symphony Number II, 1960, Gloria, 1961, Variations on a Theme by Hindemith, 1963, The Twelve, 1965, The Bear, 1967, Capriccio Burlesco, 1968, Improvisations on an Impromptu of Benjamin Britten, 1970, Jubilate Deo, 1972, Sonata for String Orch, 1972, Cantico del Sole, 1974, Magnificat and Nunc Dimittis, 1974, Varii Capricci, 1976, Facade 2, 1978, The First Shoot, 1981; Films Richard III. Recipient gold medal Royal Philharmonic Soc., 1947; Worshipful Co. of Musicians, knight bachelor, 1951; Order of Merit, 1967. Fellow Royal Coll. Music, Royal Acad. Music (hon.); hon. mem. Swedish Acad. Music. Clubs: Athenaeum (London, Eng.), Garrick (London, Eng.). Home: London, England.

WANG, SHIH YI, educator; b. Peking, China, June 15, 1923; came to U.S., 1948, naturalized, 1962; s. Yen Chao and Li Hwa (Kung) W.; m. Chun Lien Chi, Aug. 17, 1947; children—Robert Tung-hsing, Ethylin Tung-ying. B.S., Nat. Peking U., 1944; Ph.D., U. Wash., 1952. Postdoctoral fellow Boston U., 1952-54; research fellow Harvard, 1954-55; asst. prof. Tufts U. Med. Sch., 1955-61; faculty Johns Hopkins, 1961-83, prof. biochemistry, 1966-83, prof., dir. div. radiation chemistry, 1976-78, prof., dir. environ. chemistry, dept. environ. health scis., 1977-83. Mem. Am. Chem. Soc., Chem. Soc. London, AAAS. Home: Phoenix, Md. Dec. Oct. 3, 1983.

WARBURG, SIEGMUND GEORGE, banker; b. Tuebingen, Germany, Sept. 30, 1902; s. George S. and Lucie (Kaulla) W.; grad. Gymnasium, Reutlingen, Germany, 1918; grad. Humanistic Sem., Urach, Germany 1920; m. Eva Maria Philipson, Nov. 8, 1926; children—George S., Anna Maria (Mrs. Dov Biegun). Tng. in Hamburg, London, Boston and N.Y.C., 1920-30; partner M. M. Warburg & Co., Hamburg, 1930-38; dir. New Trading Co. Ltd., London, 1938-46; dir. S. G. Warburg & Co. Ltd., London, 1946-69; partner Kuhn, Loeb & Co., N.Y.C., 1956-64. Created knight, 1966. Home: London, Eng. Died Oct. 18, 1982.

WARD, ALFRED GUSTAVE, naval officer; b. Mobile, Nov. 29, 1908; s. Ben Edward and Helen (Toulmin) W.; B.S., U.S. Naval Acad., 1932; M.S., Mass. Inst. Tech., 1940; m. Winona Vjereck, Mar. 10, 1937; children—Marion (Mrs. Toby G. Warson), Lesley Adele (Mrs. Thomas Winingder), Cynthia Lynn. Commissioned ensign in United State Navy, 1932, advanced through grades to admiral, 1965; assigned destroyers, cruisers, battleships, 1932-41; gunnery officer U.S.S. North Carolina, World War II; comdr. U.S. Task Force, Western Pacific, 1960; asst. chief naval operations for fleet operations, Navy Dept., 1960-61; comdr. Amphibious Force, Atlantic Fleet, 1961, comdr. Second Fleet, 1962-63, dep. chief naval operations for plans and policy, 1963, fleet operations and readiness, 1964; U.S. rep. to mil. com. and standing group NATO, 1965-68; headmaster Severn Sch., Md., from 1968. Decorated Bronze Star medal (2), D.S.M. (2), Legion of Merit. Mem. Sigma Xi. Club: N.Y. Yacht. Home: Theodore, Ala. Died Apr. 3, 1982.

WARD, BERNARD JAMES, lawyer, educator; b. New Orleans, Aug. 31, 1925; s. Albert James and Maude Marie (Bernard) W.; m. Elaine McMurray, Aug. 5, 1948; children—Bernard James, Margaret Eleanor. A.B., Loyola U., New Orleans, 1944, LL.B., 1949, LL.M., Yale U., 1954. Bar: La. bar 1949. Asst. prof. law U. Notre Dame, 1954-58, assoc. prof., 1958-62, prof., 1962-68, U. Tex., Austin, 1968-82, Thomas Watt Gregory prof. law, 1970-82; reporter to adv. com. on appellate and civil rules Jud. Conf. U.S., 1961-78, mem. com. on rules, 1978-82. Author: (with J.W. Moore) U.S. Courts of Appeals: Jurisdiction and Practice, 1970. Served to lt. (j.g.) USNR, 1944-46. Mem. La. Bar Assn., State Bar Tex., Am. Law Inst. Roman Catholic. Home: Austin, Tex. Died May 7, 1982.

WARD, C(HESTER) FRANKLIN, church official; b. Pawtucket, R.I., July 1, 1889; s. Fawcett Ephraim and May (Polsey) W.; grad. English High Sch., Boston, Mass., 1909; student Boston U. Law Sch.; grad. McCormick Theological Sem., 1918; D.D. from Albany (Oregon) College, 1928; m. Elizabeth Tracy Collins (A.B., Smith Coll. 1915), of Virginia, Ill., Aug. 25, 1917; 1 dau., Virginia Elizabeth. Ordained ministry Presbyn. Ch., 1918; dir. New Era Movement, 1919-20; exec. sec. Auburn (N.Y.) Theol. Sem., 1920-23; pastor Mount Kisco, N.Y., 1924-25; Pacific Coast Sec. Gen. Council of Gen. Assembly Presbyn. Ch. in U.S.A., 1925-29; promotional sec. Gen. Council and Chmn. Operating Com. in charge of all promotional programs of bds. and agencies of the Ch., 1929-34; sec. Gen. Council, 1931-32; dir. Allied Temperance Forces of Rochester (N.Y.), Family Welfare Soc., Political Action Com. for World Peace; exec. sec. Federation of Chs. of Rochester and Monroe Counties, 1935-37. Served as chaplain, U.S.N., 1918-19. Trustee Albany Coll. since 1932. Mem. Merchants Assn. of Westwood Village, Chi Alpha. Mason. Contbr. to religious publs. Clubs: Rotary, Ad Club, Oak Hill Country. Lectures on The Germany of Hitler, The Passion Play at Oberammergau, The Face of Paris. Home: Los Angeles, Calif. †

WARD, EDWARD ALEXANDER, osteopathic physician; b. Mt. Pleasant Twp., Ind., Nov. 27, 1890; s. John Alexander and Clara Jane (Jones) W.; D.O., Am. School of Osteopathy, 1913; married Edith Marie Field, September 14, 1918; children—Mildred Ann (Mrs. Ercell Carley), Janice Marie (Mrs. Wm. Ball). Gen. practice as osteopathic physician, Noblesville Indiana, 1913; Saginaw, Michigan, from 1914. Served as private, Med. Corps., U.S. Army, 1918. Chmn. 8th Dist. Rep. Congl. Com. of Mich., 1936-48. Secretary Mackinac Island State Park Commn., 1950-55. Received Scientific award of Sigma Sigma Phi, 1930; Distinguished Service award, Mich. Osteopathic Assn. of Physicians and Surgeons. 1931; Distinguished Service award, Am. Osteopathic Assn., 1952. Del. Nat. Health Conf., 1938, White House Conf. on Children, 1939-40, Pan-Am. Sci. Congress, 1940. Certified by Am. Coll. of Osteopathic Internists. 1950. Fellow Am. Coll. Osteopathic Internists; member American Osteopathic Assn. (pres. 1937-38), mem. council emergency med. services, member of council on federal health programs 1958-61), Nat. Maternal and Child Health Council, Sigma Sigma Phi (pres. Grand Chapter 1939-40). Republican. Methodist. Mason. Club: Caravan (Saginaw, Mich.). Contbr. to Jour. of Am. Osteopathic Assn., Osteopathic Mag. Home: Saginaw, Mich. †

WARD, ELMER L., apparel exec.; b. Boston, Mass., Feb. 25, 1898; s. Lawrence Stephen and Mary (O'Connell) W.; grad. Boston English High Sch., 1916; m. Alice G. Brown, Aug. 14, 1924; children—Elmer L., Lawrence W., William A., Robert B. Mem. firm Forte-Moran Co., Boston, 1921-24, Campbell-Ward Co., Boston, 1924-31; gen. mgr. Goodall Co., Sanford, Me., 1931-35, pres., 1935-44, pres. Goodall-Sanford, Inc. (merger Sanford Mills and Goodall

Worsted Co.), 1944-54; pres. Goodall Fabrics, Inc., 1944-54; pres. Palm Beach Co. (Goodall Co.), 1955-68, chmn. bd., chief exec. officer, 1968-82. Knight, Order Malta. Mem. Men's Fashion Assn. Am. (dir.). Republican. Roman Catholic. Clubs: Algonquin (Boston); New York Athletic (N.Y.C.); Seminole Golf, Everglades (Fla.). Won N.E. amateur golf championship, 1930. Home: Kennebunk Beach, Maine. Died 1982.

WARD, HOWARD LEON, periodontist, dental educator; b. N.Y.C., July 24, 1921; s. Edward M. and Min (Brenner) W.; m. Leona Auster, Aug. 8, 1946; children: Richard Lee, Kenneth Andrew. B.A., NYU, 1946, D.D.S., 1949, M.A. in Higher Edn, 1969; postgrad., Tufts U. Coll. Dentistry, 1950, Columbia, 1951. Diplomate: Am. Bd. Periodontology, Am. Bd. Oral Medicine. Practice periodontics, N.Y.C., 1951—; prof. dept. periodontia and oral medicine, chmn. dept. N.Y. U. Coll. Dentistry, 1970-72; prof., chmn. dept. preventive dentistry and community health Brookdale Dental Center of N.Y. U., dir. hosp. dentistry program, 1972—, head div. health service mgmt., 1977; dir. continuing dental edn. program N.Y. U. Coll. Dentistry, N.Y.C., asst. dean clin. affairs, 1978—, prof. periodontics, 1979—; attending dept. surgery N.Y. U. Med. Center; former head periodontics sect. L.I. Jewish Med. Center; former cons., lectr. periodontology U.S. Naval Hosp., St. Albans, L.I.; now cons. dentistry Goldwater Meml. Hosp-N.Y. U. Coll. Medicine; pvt. practice periodontics; cons. periodontics Nassau County Med. Center; Berkshire asso. in periodontia and oral medicine Tufts Coll. Dentistry; spl. cons. U.S. Dept. Pub. Health. Editor: texts Preventive Point of View (Thomas); Contbr. articles to profl. jours. Served with M.C. AUS, 1942. Recipient numerous awards, honors including S.C. Miller Meml. award oral medicine, Alumni Meritorious award N.Y. U.; Hirshfield award in periodontics; Harry Strusser award in public health; Achievement award N.Y. U. Coll. Dentistry. Fellow Am. Coll. Dentists (chmn. N.Y. sect.), Internat. Coll. Dentists, N.Y. Acad. Dentistry, AAAS, Am. Pub. Health Assn., N.Y. Acad. Scis., Am. Acad. Oral Medicine, Internat. Coll. Dentists; mem. Nassau County Dental Soc. (past pres.), 10th Dist. Dental Soc. (past pres.), L.I. Acad. Dentistry, Nassau-Suffolk Acad. Dentistry (past pres.), NE Soc. Periodontists (past pres.), Am. Assn. Dental Examiners, N.Y. State Bd. Dentistry, NE Regional Bd. Dental Examiners, N.Y. U. Alumni Assn. (past pres., dir. emeritus), Omicron Kappa Upsilon (past pres. Omega chpt.). Home: 150 Central Park S New York NY 10019 Office: NY U Dental Center of 345 E 24th St New York NY 10010 also 150 Central Park S New York NY 10019

WARD, LEE, lawyer, lecturer; b. Piggott, Ark., Dec. 13, 1906; s. Thomas Henry and Ida Elnora (Hughes) W.; student Washington U., St. Louis, 1927-29, Ark. Law Sch., 1935-38; m. Pearl Fulks, Oct. 13, 1929; 1 child, Carol Lee (Mrs. William D. Jenness III). With Shell Petroleum Corp., 1929-33; law clk. to atty. O.T. Ward, Rector, Ark., 1933-35; admitted to Ark. bar, 1938, U.S. Supreme Ct. bar, 1956; pvt. practice, Little Rock, 1938-42, Paragould, Ark., 1947-54, Jonesboro, Ark., 1961-71; trial judge 12th Chancery Dist. Ark., 1955-60. Pres., Abundant Life Inst. Bd. dirs. Ozark Creative Writers, Inc. Served with USNR, 1943-45. Mem. Am., Ark. bar assns., Am. Judicature Soc., Am. Legion (past dept. comdr.), Am. Acad. Polit. and Social Sci., Internat. Platform Assn. Democrat. Methodist (tchr. men's Bible class). Lion (past dist. gov.). Club: Sugar Creek Country. Author weekly newspaper column About Your U.S. Constitution and Supreme Court. Editor-pub. The Spoken Word Newsletter. Home: Piggott, Ark. Dec. May 20, 1981.

WARD, LYND KENDALL, graphic artist, illustrator; b. Chgo., June 26, 1905; s. Harry Frederick and Daisy (Kendall) W.; m. May Yonge McNeer, June 11, 1926; children: Nanda Weedon Ward Haynes, Robin Kendall Ward Savage. B.S., Columbia Tchrs. Coll., 1926; postgrad. Staatliche Akademic Fuer Graphische Kunst, Leipzig, Germany, 1926-27. Illustrator, 1927-85; dir. graphic arts div. Fed. Art Project, N.Y.C., 1937-39. Prints represented permanent collections, Library of Congress, Smithsonian Inst., Neward Mus., Met. Mus., Victoria and Albert Mus., others; author-illustrator: (novels in wood cuts) Gods' Man, 1929, Madman's Drum, others, 1930, Wild Pilgrimage, 1932, Prelude to a Million Years, 1933, Song Without Words, 1936, Vertigo, 1937, Story-teller Without Words—The Wood Engravings of Lynd Ward; Children's books The Biggest Bear, 1952; Children's book Nic of the Woods, 1965, The Silver Pont, 1973. Recipient Zella de Milhan prize, 1947; recipient award for wood engraving Library of Congress, 1948, award for wood engraving NAD, 1949, Caldecott medal, 1953, silver medal Ltd. Edits. Club, 1954, John Taylor Arms Meml. prize, 1962, Samuel F. B. Morse gold medal, 1966, Rutgers medal, 1969, U. So. Miss. Silver medal, 1973; co-recipient Regina medal Catholic Library Assn., 1975. Mem. NAD, Soc. Am. Graphic Artist (pres. 1953-59). Home: Reston, Va. Died June 28, 1985.

WARD, THEODORE JAMES, dramatist; b. Thibodeaux, La., Sept. 15, 1902; s. John Everett and Mary (Pierre) W.; extension student, U. Utah, 1930; Zona Gale scholar, U. Wis., 1931-33; m. Mary Sangighian, June 15, 1940; children—Elise Virginia, Laura Louise. Tchr. dramatics Lincoln Center, Chgo., 1937; exec. dir. Negro Playwrights Co., Harlem, 1940-83; founder S. Side Center Performing Arts, Chgo., 1960. Recipient award Nat. Theatre Conf., 1946-47, Theatre Guild, 1946; Guggenheim fellow, 1948. Author Plays; Sick & Tiahd. 1937; Big White Fog, 1938; Our Lan', 1947. Home: Chicago, Ill. Died May 8, 1983.

WARDEN, CLARENCE ARTHUR, JR., manufacturing company executive; b. Phila., Oct. 27, 1904; s. Clarence A. and Helen (Corning) W.; grad. Hill Sch., Pottstown, Pa., 1922; student Sheffield Sci. Sch., Yale, 1926; LL.D., Ursinus Coll.; m. Katharine B. Chase, Apr. 24, 1930 (dec. Jan. 1958); children—William G. III, Sally; m. Anna M. F. Thompson, Oct. 24, 1959. Student, Nat. City Co., N.Y.C., 1926; various office, sales positions Brown Bros. (later Brown Bros. Harriman & Co.), Phila., 1926-32; pres., dir. Superior Tube Co. and affiliated cos., 1948-67, chmn., after 1967; dir., mem. exec. com. Germantown Trust Co., 1936-47; dir. 1st Pa. Co., 1959-74, Peter A. Frasse & Co., Inc., N.Y.C., Williams & Co., Inc., UGI. Corp., 1947-77, Phila. Suburban Corp., 1969-75. Bd. dirs. Big Bros. Assn., Phila., 1939-45, Bryn Mawr (Pa.) Hosp., 1951-77, Ursinus Coll., 1957-76, Legal Aid Soc., 1953-76; chmn. bd. dirs. Del. Valley Hosp. Council, 1958-73; bd. dirs. Phila. Maritime Mus. Hon. fellow Am. Coll. Hosp. Adminstrs. Clubs: Sunnybrook Golf (Plymouth Meeting, Pa.); Yale, Racquet, Corinthian (Phila.); N.Y. Yacht; Merion Golf (Ardmore); Gulph Mills Golf; Cruising of America; New Bedford (Mass.) Yacht. Home: Haverford, Pa. Dec. Dec. 23, 1980.

WARDLAW, FRANK ANDREW, JR., mine exec.; b. Schroon Lake, N.Y., July 14, 1887; s. Frank Andrew and Media (Russell) W.; E.M., Columbia U., 1906-10; m. Lela Moore, June 16, 1914; children—Eleanor Miles (Mrs. Henry Jackson), Anne Moore (Mrs. Frank M. Hagan), Virginia (Mrs. C. D. Pearce III). Began as underground miner, 1910; chief engr. Utah Consol. Mining Co. Bingham Utah, 1912-16; mine foreman Braden Copper Co., Chile, S.A., 1917-18; supt. Vipont Silver Mining Co., 1919-23; supt. Utah Del. Mining Co., 1923-29; asst. gen. mgr. Inspiration Consolidated Copper Co., 1930-42; gen. mgr. Internat. Smelting & Refining Company from 1944; president Tooele Valley Railroad Company; director Walker Bank & Trust Co., Salt Lake City; pres. Mountain City Copper Co. and North Lily Mining Co. Mem. Soc. Am. Inst. Mining and Metall. Engrs. (nat. dir. 1940-45), Am. Red Cross (dir. for Utah), Delta Kappa Epsilon. Republican. Episcopalian. Clubs: Alta, Salt Lake Country (Salt Lake City). Home: Salt Lake City, Utah. †

WARNEKE, HEINZ, sculptor; b. Bremen, Germany, June 30, 1895; came to U.S., 1923, naturalized, 1930; s. Heinrich and Anna (Ritterhof) W.; m. Jessie Jay Gilroy Hall, Mar. 16, 1927. Student, Staatliche Kunstgewerbe Schule and Akademie, Berlin, 1912-15, 18-23. Head sculpture dept. Corcoran Sch. Art, ret. Represented by works in many large cities of U.S.; latest works include Nat. Collection Fine Arts, Washington, War Meml., Lyme, Conn., decorations Mellon Chapel of Washington Cathedral, also tympanum South Portal, entire decoration clerestory South Transcept; statues granite Elephant Group for, Phila. Zool. Garden, 1963; carved oak pulpit, interior decorations, Trinity Ch., Upperville, Va.; portrait Allen C. Dulles for C.I.A. bldg, Langley, Va., Wildcat statue, Pottstown (Pa.) High Sch. Complex, Nittany Lion statue, Pa. State U., Mountain Lion in bronze, Altoona, Pa.; unicorn statue Upperville garden Mrs. Paul Mellon; decorations of entire baptistry ceiling Washington Cathedral; portrait bust Judge John Bassett Moore, U. Va., Charlottesville, Pelican bronze, Norfolk (Va.) Mus., Immigrant, Samuels Meml, Phila., Railway Mail Clerk, Anteroom Postmaster Gen.'s Office, Washington; large stone panel Lewis and Clark Expdn, Dept. Interior Bldg., Washington, OurangUtang Thinking, Addison Gallery, Andover, Mass., Percheron Colts, U. Nebr., Omaha, Wild Boars and Hissing Geese, Art Inst. Chgo. Recipient numerous prizes, 1925—. Fellow Internat. Inst. Arts and Letters (life), Nat. Sculpture Soc., NAD; mem. New Eng. Sculptors So., Conn. Acad. Fine Arts, Associe de Salon des Tuileries, N.A. Home: East Haddam, Conn. Died Aug. 16, 1983.

WARNER, FRANCES LESTER (MRS. MAYO D. HERSEY), author, educator; b. Putnam, Conn., July 19, 1888; d. Edgar Morris and Jane Elizabeth (Carpenter) Warner; A.B., Mt. Holyoke Coll., 1911, Litt.D., 1937; m. Mayo Dyer Hersey, June 24, 1922. Asst. in English, Newton (Mass.) High Sch., 1911-12; head of English dept., Miss Mason's Sch., Tarrytown, N.Y., 1912-13; teacher of English, Newton High Sch., 1913-16, North High Sch., Worcester, Mass., 1916-17; instr. English composition, Mt. Holyoke Coll., 1917-19, asst. prof., 1919-20; asst. prof., Wellesley Coll., 1920-21; asst. to the editor Atlantic Monthly, 1921-22. Lecturer on English, Simmons Coll., 1942-46; head English dept., N.E. Conservatory Music, 1946-49. Member Phi Beta Kappa, Boston Authors Club, D.A.R. Conglist. Republican. Author or co-author of books from 1919; latest publ.: Inner Springs, 1942. Home: Monument Beach, Mass. †

WARNER, HAROLD JOHNSON, justice; b. Ft. Wayne, Ind., Nov. 6, 1890; s. Thomas C. and Katherine E. (Johnson) W.; A.B., U. Ore., 1913, LL.B., 1916; m. Aluta M. Larsen, Aug. 5, 1925; children—Mary Ellen, Thomas Larsen. Admitted to Ore. bar, 1916; asso. Raley & Raley, Pendleton, 1916-17, Raley, Raley & Steiwer, 1919-27; partner Raley, Raley & Warner, 1927-34, Henderson & Warner, 1934-37, Platt, Henderson, Warner, Cram & Dickinson, Portland, 1937-50; city atty. Pendleton, 1920-22; asso. justice Ore. Supreme Ct., from 1950, acting chief justice, 1952-54, chief justice, 1955-57. Rep. presidential elector, 1928. Served as 1st lt. aviation U.S. Army, World War I; maj. Judge Adv. Gen., World War II. Mem. Am., Ore. State Multnomah Co. (v.p. 1949), bar assns., Am. Legion (Ore. State comdr. 1933, nat. v. comdr. 1934), S.A.R. (pres. Ore. soc. 1949), Mil. Order World Wars, Phi Delta Phi, Beta Theta Pi. Episcopalian. Mason (32 deg.). Clubs: University, City (Portland). Home: Portland, Oreg. †

WARNER, SAM BASS, publisher; born Chicago, Ill., May 27, 1889; s. Murray and Gertrude (Bass) W.; A.B., Harvard U., 1912; LL.B., Harvard U. Law Sch., 1915; S.J.D., 1923; m. Helen Wilson, Apr. 26, 1916; children—Murray, Sam B., Jr. Employed as law clk. San Francisco, Calif., 1915-17; prof. law, U. of Ore., 1919-28, Syracuse U., 1928-29; asst. prof. of law, Harvard University, 1929-32, prof. law, 1932-45; register of copyrights, 1945-50; owner, pub. The Shore Line Times, The Clinton Recorder, from 1952; publisher, The Shore Line Shopper; Thayer teaching fellow Harvard University Law Sch., 1922-23, visiting prof. law, Northwestern U., summer, 1922-24, Columbia U., spring 1931. Served as aerial observer, 2d lieut. U.S. Amry, 1917-18. Dir. research Am. Inst. Criminal Law and Criminology, 1922-26; mem. staff Harvard Crime Survey, 1927-35; advisor to Nat. Commn. on law Observance and Enforcement, 1929-31; reporter for Interstate Commn. on Crime 1937-44; with Civil Service Commn., treas., Office of Strategic Services and War Prodn., 1942-45. Mem. American and Massachusetts bar associations. Republican. Mem. Episcopalian. Ch. Clubs: Rotary, Brotherhood of St. Andrews (Washington), Harvard (N.Y.). Author: Crime and Criminal Statistics in Boston, 1934; (with H. B. Cabot) Judges and Law Reform, 1936. Contbr. legal essays and articles to various jours. Home: Clapboard Hill. †

WARNOCK, JANE F., Rep. nat. committeewoman; b. Quinton, N.J., Aug. 10, 1888; d. Theodore and Laura (Wood) Birchneier; ed. public sch. and high sch., Quinton, N.J., business coll., Philadelphia, Pa.; m. William Warnock, Aug. 12, 1906 (died 1932). Financial clerk to husband, an employe of U.S. Dept. of Interior (later mgr. cattle co.), 1908-32; proprietor, insurance and real estate agency, Eagle Butte, S.D., from 1936. Republican nat. committeewoman for South Dakota since 1944. Sec., Eagle Butte Ind. Sch. Dist. Sch. Bd., Eagle Butte chapter Dewey County Red Cross. Mem. bd. dirs. Eagle Butte Congl. Ch. Mem. Business and Professional Womens Club, Kensington Fedn. Womens Clubs. Mem. Order Eastern Star. Home: Eagle Butte, S.D. †

WARREN, CURTIS E., professor; b. Barnes City, Ia., Aug. 26, 1887; s. Willis T. and Minnie A. (Browning) W.; A.B., U. of Southern Calif., 1915, Ed.D., 1936; m. Mary Evans Logan, July 3, 1915; children—Tully Evans, Carol Evans (Mrs. Eugene L. Burdick); m. 2d. Lelah Hulse Ollis, July 1, 1944. Principal high sch., Lancaster, Calif., 1918-24; dist. supt., high sch. and junior coll., Marysville, Calif., 1924-32; supt. schs., Burbank, Calif., 1932-34, Santa Barbara, Calif., 1934-42, San Francisco, 1943-47; instr. Santa Barbara State Coll., summer 1940, U. of Southern Calif., summer 1942, 47; cons. dept. information, O.P.A., Washington, 1942-43; vis. prof. U. of Ida, summer, 1948, U. of So. Calif., summer, 1947; ednl. consultant Bureau of Census. President Calif. Teachers Assn., N.S., 1930-31; mem. advisory staff, Calif. Jour. Elementary Edn., 1945; cons. United Nations Conf., San Francisco. Mem. Calif. State Bd. Edn., Phi Delta Kappa, Phi Alpha Delta. Mason. Club: Commonwealth (San Francisco). Author: (with Leiter and Lamoreaux) Living, the Basis of Learning, 1942. Home: Palo Alto, Calif. †

WARREN, FERDINAND E., painter, educator; b. Independence, Mo., Aug. 1, 1899. Recipient artist U. Ga., 1950-51; head dept. art Agnes Scott Coll., Decatur, Ga., 1951-69. Represented in collections Met. Mus., Bklyn. Mus., Rochester (N.Y.) Meml. Gallery, Butler Inst., Youngstown, O., High Mus., Atlanta, Currier Gallery, Manchester, N.H., NASA, Washington, Supreme Ct. D.C. Art Trust Collection, others. Recipient 2d Julius Hallgarten prize N.A.D., 1935, William Palmer Meml. prize, 1962; Opaque Water color prize S.E. Artists Exhbn., 1950; Water Color purchase award Butler Art Inst., 1954; Watercolor prize Assn. Ga. Artists, 1956. Nat. academician. Mem. Am. Watercolor Soc. (Osborn Water Color prize 1944), Ga. Artists Assn. (pres. 1956-57), Audubon Artists, other assns. Home: Decatur, Ga. Dec. Oct. 24, 1981.

WARREN, GEORGE LEWIS, govt. official; b. Wellesley, Mass., Mar. 13, 1890; s. David H. and Julia (Washington) W.; A.B., Harvard, 1910; m. Mary Gertrude Cunniff, Oct. 15, 1919; children—Mary Louise (Mrs. George Phillips Rogers), George Lewis, Helen Elizabeth (Mrs. Robert E. Langley). With Associated Charities of Boston, Massachusetts, 1908-16, Charity Orgn. Soc., 1916-19, Warner Bros. (both Bridgeport), 1919-28, Internat. Migration Service, 1928-38; U.S. Govt. expert, League of Nations Temporary Commn. on Assistance to Indigent Aliens, Geneva, 1933, 36, 38; adviser to U.S. Rep., Evian Conf. on Refugees, Evian, France, 1938; tech. expert, Conf. of Am. States members, Internat. Labor Orgn., Havana, 1939; tech. adviser, United States delegation to Anglo-Am. Conf. on Refugees, Bermuda, 1943; consultant Fgn. Economic Adminstrn., 1943; with President's Adv. Com. on Polit. Refugees, 1938-44; mem. U.S. del. to 2d, 3d, 4th and 5th Sessions Council of

UNRRA, Montreal, 1944, London, 1945, Atlantic City, 1946, Geneva, 1946; U.S. rep., 5th and 6th plenary meetings, Intergovernmental Com. on Refugees, Paris, 1945, London, 1946; U.S. rep., Spl. Com. on Refugees and Displaced Persons, U.N., London, Apr.-May 1946; adviser to U.S. rep., Economic and Social Council and Gen. Assembly, U.N., N.Y., 1946; adviser on refugees and displaced persons, Dept. of State, 1944; U.S. rep. to Preparatory Commn., International Refugee Organization, Lausanne, 1947, Geneva, 1948; U.S. Rep. Gen. Council and Exec. Com., Internat. Refugee Orgn., Geneva, 1948-52; adv. U.S. Dels. Gen. Assembly, U.N., Paris, 1948, N.Y., 1949, 50; U.S. rep. to Conf. on Migration, Brussels, 1951, Provisional Intergovtl. Com. on Movement of Migrants from Europe, Brussels, 1951, Geneva, Washington, 1952; U.S. representative Advisory Committee to UN High Commissioner for Refugees, Geneva, 1953; U.S. rep. and prin. advisor U.S. Rep. Intergovtl. Com. for European Migration, Geneva, 1953, 55-57, Venice, 1954. Export mem. permanent migration com., Internat. Labour Office, Montreal, Can. Received decorations in recognition of service to Czechoslovakian refugees, Czechoslovakia, 1940, Dominican Republic for services in establishing refugee colony in that country, 1941; Knight Comdr. Order St. Gregory the Gt. (Vatican). Clubs: Harvard (Boston); Cosmos (Washington, D.C.). Contbr. articles to tech. and professional publications. Home: Washington, D.C. Deceased.

WARREN, HAROLD COLLINS, clergyman; b. Lansdowne, Pa., Dec. 9, 1890; s. George W. (D.D.S.) and Helen (Collins) W.; A.B., Princeton, 1912; student New Coll., Edinburgh, Scotland, 1912-13; grad. McCormick Theol. Sem., 1915; m. Josephine Fox, of Norristown, Pa., Dec. 9, 1916; children—Rebecca Coleman, Helen. Ordained Presbyn. ministry, 1915; asst. pastor Ch. of the Covenant, Washington, D.C., 1915-16; pastor First Ch., Walla Walla, Wash., 1917-20, Trumbull Av. Ch., Detroit, Mich., 1920-31, South Shore Ch., Chicago, from 1931. Y.M.C.A. sec. with 29th Div. A.E.F., in France, 1918-19. Republican. Clubs: Dial Lodge, Princeton, Detroit Athletic. Author: With the Y.M.C.A. in France, or Souvenirs of a Secretary, 1919. Home: Chicago, Ill. Deceased.

WARREN, HENRY, song writer and composer; b. Bklyn., Dec. 24, 1893; s. Anthony and Rachel (Deluca) W.; ed. in pub. schs. Bklyn.; mus. ed. choir of Our Lady of Loretto, Bklyn.; m. Josephine Wensler, Dec. 19, 1917; 1 dau., Mrs. John Hacker. Began playing drums in brass bank carnival shows; asst. dir. Vitagraph Co., Bklyn.; first song pub., 1922; Billie Rose mus. reviews, Sweet and Low, 1930; Crazy Quilt, 1931; Ed Wynn's Laugh Parade, 1931; over 100 mus. motion pictures, including 42nd Street, All Gold Diggers. Down Argentine Way. Served in U.S.N., 1918. Recipient of Two Motion Picture Acad. Awards; Nat. Fedn. of Music Clubs Award. Roman Catholic. Club: Bel Air Country. Composer: Cheerful Little Earful; Would You Like to Take a Walk?. I Found a Million Dollar Baby in the 5 to 10 Store: You're My Everything: Shuffle Off to Buffalo: 42d Street: Lullaby of Broadway; Shadow Waltz; Chattanooga Choo-Choo; Serenade in Blue; I Had the Craziest Dream; You'll Never Know; I've Got a Gal in Kalamazoo; Maga Saki; Down Argentine Way; Don't Give Up the Ship (song, adopted by U.S. Navy Acad.); Song of the Marines (adopted by U.S. Marines); On the Atchison, Topeka and the Santa Fe (winner Acad. Award); Songs; Stanley Steamer, Afraid to Fall in Love, Spring Isn't Everything; New songs: I Wish I Knew, The More I See You, Zing a Little Zong, Dig for Your Dinner, That's Amore, Friendly Star, You Wonderful You, My One and Only Highland Fling, I Only Have Eyes for You, September in the Rain, There Will Never Be Another You, I'll String Along with You, An Affair to Remember, Tiny Scout, Tomorrow Land, You Make it Easy to be True, others. Pictures: Belle of New York, Summer Stock, Barkleys of Broadway, Just for You, The Caddy, Skirts Ahoy, An Affair to Remember, Artists and Models, Birds and the Bees. Home: Beverly Hills, Calif. Died Sept. 22, 1981.

WARREN, HERMON ELMO, r.r. exec.; b. Crockett Co., Tenn., Sept. 4, 1890; s. John Thomas and Ida L. (Jones) W.; student pub. schs. Jackson, Tenn.; m. Margaret Movius, June 15, 1915 (div. 1939); children—John Movius, Patricia, Hermon Elmo; m. 2d Agnes, R. Ousley, June 1942. Clerk, later supt. dining cars, transportation dept. Mobile & Ohio R.R., Jackson, Tenn. and Mobile, Ala., 1907-20; asst. gen. mgr. G., M.&N. R.R., Mobile, 1920, mgr. purchases and stores, 1921-40; dir. Gulf Transport Co., Mobile, from 1936; mgr. purchases and stores G., M.&O. R.R. (consolidation G., M.&N. and Mobile & Ohio R.R.), 1940-45, v.p. purchases and stores, from 1945, dir. from 1954. Clubs: Country, Lakewood, Athlestan (Mobile, Ala.). Home: Montrose, Ala. †

WARREN, JOHN RUSH, botany educator; b. Columbus, Ohio, July 20, 1919; s. John Rush and Martha (Jewell) W.; m. Ruth Spargo (div.); children: Penelope, John; m. Aida Martinez (div.); children—Juana, Ricardo, Felicity; m. Carolyn Cox. A.B., Marietta Coll., 1941; postgrad., Ohio U., 1941-42; M.S., Ohio State U., 1947, Ph.D., 1950. Asst. plant pathologist Ohio Agrl. Exptl. Sta., Columbus, 1942-44, 46; asst. prof. botany Duke, 1946-52; plant pathologist Midwest Research Inst., La Ceiba, Honduras, 1952; plant pathologist Standard Fruit Co., Honduras, 1953-55, dir. tropical research, 1955-59; assoc. prof. Tenn. Poly. Inst., 1960-61, prof., chmn. dept. biol. scis., 1961-64; prof. botany Marshall U., Huntington, W.Va., 1964-83; dean Marshall U. (Grad. Sch.), 1964-72; cons. environ. scis. br. AEC.; Fulbright lectr., chmn. dept. biology Nat. Autonomous U., Republic Honduras, 1968-69; Fulbright lectr. U. Guayaquil, Ecuador, 1980-81. Author sci. publs. on mycology, bacteriology, plant pathology, isotopes, antibiotics, archaeology. Served with AUS, 1944-46. Mem. Sigma Xi, Phi Delta Kappa. Club: Mason. Office: Huntington, W. Va. Dec. Dec. 17, 1983.

WARREN, LINGAN ALLEN, pres. Safeway Stores; b. Norfolk, County, Va., Aug. 28, 1889; s. John Jay and Sarah Elizabeth (Lynch) W.; ed. public schools; m. Sara Denham, Apr. 26, 1916; 1 dau., Mary Elizabeth . Began in newspaper office, 1905; with Lumber Trade Assn., Norfolk, Va., 1907-10, Trexler Lumber Co., successively at Norfolk, Va., Allentown, Jacksonville, Fla., 1910-12; operated his own timber brokerage business, 1914-24; organized and operated woodworking business, Jacksonville, Fla., 1928; new business exec. for Merrill, Lynch & Co., investment securities, New York, 1931; exec. Safeway Stores, Inc., Oakland, Calif., 1931-34, pres. from 1934. Clubs: Burlingame Country (Burlingame, Calif.); San Francisco Golf, Pacific-Union (San Francisco). Home: Hillsborough, Calif. †

WARREN, W. FRANK, supt. of schools; b. Prospect Hill, N.C., Apr. 26, 1887; s. F.R. and Eudora Ida (Satterfield) W.; A.B., Elon (N.C.) Coll., 1910; M.A., Univ. of North Carolina, 1911; graduate student Columbia University, Duke University; m. Anne Brown, July, 1927; children—Nancy Douglas, W. Frank. Principal, Reidsville (N.C.) High Sch., 1911-13, Greensboro (N.C.) High Sch., 1913-16, McMaster High Sch., Columbia, S.C., 1916-20, Greenville (S.C.) High Sch., 1920-26, Durham (N.C.) High Sch., 1926-33; supt., Durham (N.C.) city schs., from 1933; teacher Duke U. summer sch. and extension courses Winthrop Coll. Pres. dept. principals and high sch. teachers, N.C. Edn. Assn.; vice pres. dept. secondary sch. principals, Nat. Edn. Assn., 1930; pres. Durham Edn. Assn.; 2d vice pres. and mem. exec. com., Am. Assn. Sch. Administrs. Mem. Secondary Sch. Principals. Presbyn. Mason, K.P., Kiwanian. Home: Durham, N.C. Deceased.

WARTHEN, HARRY JUSTICE, JR., surgeon; b. Port Norfolk, Va., Sept. 30, 1901; s. Harry Justice and Marian (Sheppard) W.; m. Martha Winston Alsop, Sept. 1, 1938; children—Harry Justice III, Benjamin P.A., George A. II. M.D., U. Va., 1925. Diplomate: Am. Bd. Surgery, Am. Bd. Plastic Surgery. Intern St. Elizabeth's Hosp., Richmond, 1925-27; asst. resident, resident surgeon Johns Hopkins Hosp., 1927-32; research U. Freiburg, Germany, 1932-33; mem. staff Med. Coll. Va., 1933-65; staff Richmond Meml. Hosp., chief surgery, 1956-59, chief staff, 1961-63; attending, courtesy staff various Richmond hosps.; sr. surg. cons. McGuire VA Hosp., 1947-65; chief surg. cons. Commonwealth of Va., 1972-84; cons. Armed Forces, 1948—, mem. council cons., 1960-64; lectr. Civil War medicine. Mem. Richmond Bd. Health, 1950-60, chmn., 1955-60. Editor: Va. Med. Monthly, 1955-75; Contbr. editorials and articles to profl. and hist. jours. Chmn. Confederate Med. Exhibit, Richmond, 1961-65; chmn. Va. Med. BiCentennial Commn., 1976—; trustee Historic Richmond Found., 1962—; mem. Commn. Archtl. Rev., 1969-79, Monument Ave. Commn., 1969—. Served to lt. col. USAAF, World War II; flight surgeon, cons. to Air Surgeon. Recipient A.H. Robins Community Service award, 1978. Fellow Am., So. surg. assns.; mem. U. Va. Med. Alumni Assn. (pres. 1961), Richmond Surg. Soc. (pres. 1964-65), Richmond Acad. Medicine (pres. 1949-50), Soc. Va. Creepers, Soixant Plus, Va. Hist. Soc., Antiquarian Soc. Richmond, Mil. Order World Wars (comdr. Richmond chpt.), Raven Soc., Phi Beta Kappa, Sigma Xi, Alpha Omega Alpha, Delta Sigma Phi, Nu Sigma Nu. Presbyterian (elder). Clubs: Commonwealth, Westmoreland. Home: Richmond, Va. Died Mar. 1984.

WASHBURN, BRYANT, actor; b. Chicago, Ill., Apr. 28, 1889; s. Bryant and Metha Catherine (Johnson) W.; of Danish and British parentage; ed. Lake View High Sch., Chicago; m. Mabel Forrest Chidester, of Chicago, July 3, 1914 (divorced 1928); children—Bryant, Dwight Ludlow; m. 2d, Dahlia Pears, of Toronto, Can., Mar. 1929; 1 dau., Roberta Catherine. Began on stage, 1907; toured with George D. Fawcett; moving picture career since 1911; rôles include leading parts in "Till I Come Back to You," "The Skinner Dress Suit Series," "Why Smith Left Home," "It Pays to Advertise," "Too Much Johnson," "Six Best Cellars," "Mrs. Temple's Telegram," "The Sins of St. Anthony," "The Road to London," "Hungry Hearts," "Rupert of Hentzau," "The Meanest Man in the World," "The Common Law," "Temptation," "Mine to Keep," "The Love Trap," "Other Men's Daughters," "Try and Get It," "The Love Thrill," "Beware of Widows," "Breakfast at Sunrise," "Honeymoon Flats," "Skinner's Big Idea"; "What Price Innocence." Presbyn. Mason (32 deg., Shriner). Kiwanian. Home: Hollywood, Calif. †

WASSERMAN, JACK, educator, art historian; b. N.Y.C., Apr. 27, 1921; s. William and Pearl (Bajcz) W.; B.A., N.Y. U., 1949, M.A., 1953, Ph.D., 1961; m. Ambra Amati, July 6, 1952; children—Shara, Talya. Instr., N.Y. U., 1952-53, U. Conn., 1953-60; faculty Ind. U., 1960-62; faculty U. Wis. at Milw., 1962-75, prof., curator Art History Gallery, 1964-75, chmn. dept. art history, 1962-75; prof. art history Tyler Sch. Art, Temple U., Phila., 1975—, dean, 1975-77. Mem. Archaeol. Research Fund, N.Y. U. with excavation at Samothrace, Greece, 1949; cons. Choice and Cultura, 1967—; mem. ednl. adv. bd. Milw. Sch. Arts; mem. fgn. fellowship selection com. Samuel H. Kress Found., 1972-74. Served with USAAF, 1942-45. Recipient Fulbright award, 1952-53, Fels Fund award, 1959-60. Am. Philos. Soc. Research grantee, 1970; Am. Council Learned Socs. research grantee, 1971; Samuel H. Kress research grantee, 1975. Fellow Royal Soc. Arts; mem. Amici di Brera (hon.), Coll. Art Assn. (chmn. area com. to rescue Italian art 1963—, co-chmn. film com.), Soc. Archtl. Historians (dir., archtl. preservation com.). Author: Ottaviano Mascarino, 1966; Leonardo da Vinci, 1975. Contbr. numerous articles to profl. jours. Home: Glenside, Pa. also Rome, Italy. Dec. May 1980.

WATERBURY, LESTER ELBA, lawyer; b. LaGrange, Ill., May 17, 1895; s. Walton Cleveland and Luzora Venepha (Plass) W.; A.B., U. Mich., 1917, J.D., 1921; m. Jean Grosvenor Parker, Apr. 17, 1949; children—Walton Whitwell, Jonathan Ainsworth, Holly Arundel. Admitted to N.Y. bar, 1922; joined law dept. Am. Sugar Refining Co., 1921; with law dept. Gen. Foods, Corp. (then Postum Co., Inc.), 1927-56, asst. sec., 1928-49, gen. atty., 1943-49, gen. counsel, 1949-56, sec., 1949-55, v.p., 1951-60, dir., 1954-61; pres. Gen. Foods Fund, Inc., 1956-60. Mem. adv. council Marine Midland Bank N.Y., 1965-72. Trustee, Gardens Nursery School-Kindergarten, 1957-65, Collegiate Sch., 1961-63. Enlisted in Army (U.S.S.E.R.C.), 1917, overseas 1917-19; commd. 1st lt. U.S. AS, 1918, with 99th Aero Squadron, 1918-19. Mem. Assn. Gen. Counsel, Order of Coif, Phi Beta Kappa, Sigma Delta Chi, Delta Upsilon, Phi Delta Phi. Home: Hancock, N.H. Died Dec. 23, 1984.

WATERMAN, STERRY ROBINSON, judge; b. Taunton, Mass., June 12, 1901; s. Zeno Sterry and Sarah Wood (Robinson) W.; m. Frances Chadbourne Knight, May 13, 1932 (dec.); children—Robert Sterry, Thomas Chadbourne. A.B., Dartmouth Coll., 1922, LL.D., 1963; postgrad., Harvard U. Law Sch., 1922-23, George Washington U. Law Sch., 1923-26; LL.D., George Washington U. Law Sch., 1969; J.D., Vt. Law Sch., 1977; LL.D., U. Vt., 1973, N.Y. U., 1979. Bar: D.C. bar 1926, Vt. bar 1926, U.S. Supreme Ct. bar 1935. Practice law, St. Johnsbury, Vt., 1926-55; mem. firm Waterman & Downs, 1949-55; chmn., gen. counsel Vt. Unemployment Compensation Commn., 1937-41; mem. Vt. Uniform State Laws Commn., 1938-58; judge U.S. Ct. of Appeals, 2d Circuit, St. Johnsbury, 1955-70, sr. judge, 1970-84; Trustee St. Johnsbury Acad., 1956-84, pres., 1973-84; trustee, pres. Vt. Law Sch., 1974-84. Fellow Am. Bar Found.; mem. Am. Acad. Jud. Edn. (dir. 1971-75, 77-84, pres. 1977-78), Vt. Hist. Soc. (trustee, v.p. 1972-84), Am. Law Inst., Am. Judicature Soc. (past pres.), ABA, Fed. Bar Assn., Vt. Bar Assn. (past pres.), Caledonia County Bar Assn., Assn. Bar City N.Y., Nat. Conf. Commrs. Uniform State Laws, Nat. Lawyers Club, Inst. Jud. Adminstrn., Selden Soc., U.S. Supreme Ct. Hist. Soc. Republican. Congregationalist. Clubs: Century (N.Y.C.), Dartmouth (N.Y.C.); Rotary, Sphinx, Masons (33d degree), Elks. Home: Saint Johnsbury, Vt. Dec. Feb. 6, 1984.

WATERS, MUDDY, (MCKINLEY MORGANFIELD) singer, songwriter; b. Rolling Fork, Miss., Apr. 4, 1915. Moved to Chgo., 1943; since played various clubs there; first toured, Eng., 1958, first performed, Carnegie Hall, 1959, rec. artist, Chess Records, 1947-75, Blue Sky Records, 1977-83; recs. include The Best of Muddy Waters, 1958, Live at Newport, 1960, Folk Singers, 1964, Real Blues, 1966, They Call Me Muddy Waters, 1971 (Grammy award), London Sessions, 1972 (Grammy award), McKinley Morganfield a/k/a Muddy Waters, 1973, Muddy Waters Woodstock Album, 1975 (Grammy award), Hard Again, 1977 (Grammy and Rolling Stone Mag. Critics awards), I'm Ready, 1978 (Grammy award), Muddy "Mississippi" Waters Live, 1979 (Grammy award), King Bee, 1981; appeared: film The Last Waltz. Named to Ebony Black Music Hall of Fame, 1973; numerous other awards. Learned to play harmonica and guitar as child; discovered by folklorist Alan Lomax while working in cotton fields. Address: Western Springs, Ill. Dec. Apr. 30, 1983.

WATKINS, DAVID WAYNE, dir. extension service; b. Anderson County, S. C., Feb. 1, 1889; s. Thomas Elliot and Virginia (Smith) W.; B.S., Clemson Agrl. Coll., 1909; student Grad. Sch. of Agr., Mich. Agrl. Coll., summer, 1912; A.M., in economics, Harvard, 1929; m. Daisy Patton, June 24, 1915; children—David Wayne, Mary Virginia. Farm mgr. 1909-14; teacher agr., Ga., 1911-13; husbandman U.S. Dept. of Agr., 1914-18; asst. dir. of extension, Clemson, 1918-34, (on leave U.S. Dept. Agr. extension service, Washington, D.C., 1930, and asst. chief cotton div. A.A.A., 1934); dir. of extension service for S.C. since Dec., 1934; mem. bd. of dirs. Charlotte br. Fed. Reserve Bank of Richmond, 1939-45. Life mem. State Fair Soc. (mem. exec. com., 1934-48); chmn. State Nutrition Com., State Soil Conservation Com.; mem. Clemson Alumni Assn. (former pres., chmn. fund raising com.). Democrat. Baptist. Address: S.C. †

WATKINS, MARY FITCH, author; b. New Haven, Conn., Jan. 11, 1890; d. Rev. S. Halsted and Helen (Smith) W.; ed. pub. schs., Vt., and Miss Spence's Sch., N.Y. City. Sec. to Olive Fremstad, opera singer, 1911-18; ambulance driver with French Army, and engaged in civilian relief work, 1918-19. Republican. Protestant.

Author: First Aid to the Opera-Goer, 1924; Behind the Scenes at the Opera, 1925. Contbr. to mags. and newspapers. Home: New York, N.Y. †

WATSON, BARBARA M., lawyer; b. N.Y.C., Nov. 5; d. James S. and Violet (Lopez) W. A.B., Barnard Coll., 1943; LL.B., N.Y. Law Sch., 1962; LL.D., U. Md.; L.H.D., Mt. St. Mary Coll. Bar: N.Y. bar 1962. Atty. N.Y.C. Bd. Statutory Rev., 1962-63; atty. law dept. Office Corp. Counsel, N.Y.C., 1963-64; exec. dir. N.Y.C. Commn. to UN, 1964-66; spl. asst. to dep. undersec. state for adminstrn., 1966; dep. adminstr. Bur. Security and Consular Affairs, State Dept., 1966-67, acting adminstr., 1967-68, adminstr., 1968-74, asst. sec. state, 1977-80, ambassador to Malaysia, from 1980, with Van Klobery & Assocs., internat. cons. firm, Washington, until 1983; pvt. practice law, 1975-76; mem. ex-officio women's adv. bd. Office Econ. Opportunity. Bd. dirs. Wolf Trap Found. for Performing Arts, Mus. African Art, Washington, Greater Washington Ednl. Telecommunications Assn.; trustee Fed. Women's Award, Barnard Coll. Recipient Hadassah Myrtle Wreath Achievement award, 1968, Am. Caribbean Scholarship Fund Inc. award, 1969, Service award Women's Div. United Hias, 1970, Service award United Seamen, 1970, award of merit Internat. Aviation Club, Washington, 1971, Black Women's Distinguished Service award Nat. Council Negro Women, Inc., 1971, Woman of Year award Deliverance Evangelistic Center, Inc., 1971, certificate of Recognition Washington Urban League, 1971, Rev. Hirsch Masliansky award, 1972, Am. Immigration and Citizenship Conf. award, 1972, Jr. Citizens Corps Achievement award, 1972, Woman of Yr. award State Beauty Culturalist Assn., 1973, Luther I. Replogle award State Dept., 1974; decorated Nat. Order Ivory Coast Republic, 1973; Internat. Consular Acad. fellow, 1971. Mem. N.Y. County Lawyers Assn., Am. Bar Assn., Fed. Women's Bar Assn., Assn. Am. Fgn. Service Women, Internat. Women's Lawyers Assn., Urban League Guild, Fed. Women's Assn., Delta Sigma Theta (hon., Social Action award 1974). Clubs: Women's (N.Y.C.), Cosmopolitan (N.Y.C.); Internat. (Washington); Business and Professional Women's. Home: Washington, D.C. Died Feb. 17, 1983.

WATSON, C. HOYT, coll. pres.; b. Eudora, Kan., Dec. 12, 1888; s. Isaac Newton and Elizabeth Ann (Hagadorn) W.; A.B., U. of Kan., 1918, A.M., 1923; grad. study University of Chicago, 1919, U. of Wash., 1924-26; LL.D., Whitworth Coll., 1941; Litt. D., Greenville College, 1952; married Elsie Cora Waters, June 15, 1910; children—Warren Newton, Lyle Sherman, Lola Irene, Miriam Winifred. Was: teacher mathematics, Orleans (Nebraska) Seminary, 1910-11, 1912-14; prin. Central Acad. and Coll., McPherson, Kan., 1914-16; asst. prof. edn. and supervisor physical sciences in training sch., U. of Kan., 1918-23; head of science dept., Seattle Pacific Coll., 1923-25; asso. in edn., U. of Wash., 1925-26; pres. Seattle Pacific Coll., from 1926. Secretary exec. commn. Free Meth. Ch., from 1951. Fellow A.A.A.S.; mem. N.E.A. Nat. Soc. for Study Edn. Am. Assn. of Sch. Adminstrs. Phi Delta Kappa. Free Methodist. Rotarian. Author: De Shazer-The Doolittle Raider Who Turned Missionary, 1950. †

WATSON, CECIL JAMES, physician, educator; b. Mpls., May 31, 1901; s. James Alfred and Lucia (Coghlan) W.; B.S., U. Minn., 1923; M.B., 1924, M.D., 1926, M.S., 1925, Ph.D., 1928; student U. Mich. 1921-22; M.D. honoris causa, U. Mainz, 1961, U. Munich, 1972; m. Joyce Petterson, Sept. 10, 1925. Pathologist, dir. labs. Mpls. Gen. Hosp., 1926-28, pathologist, dir. labs. and engaged in practice internal medicine, N.W. Clinic, Minot, N.D., 1928-30; research and postgrad. chem. study Hans Fischer's Lab., Munich, Germany, 1930-32; NRC fellow, 1931-32; fellow in medicine, resident physician U. Minn., also Mpls. Gen. Hosp., 1932-33; instr. in medicine U. Minn., 1933-34, asst. prof. 1934-36, asso. prof., dir. div. internal medicine, 1936-40, prof. medicine, 1940-83, distinguished service prof., 1962-69, emeritus, 1969-83, chmn. dept. medicine, 1943-66, Regent's prof. medicine, 1968-69, emeritus, 1969-83; vis. prof. U. Chgo., 1943-45, Columbia, 1943-44; asso. dir. health div. Manhattan Project, 1943-45; dir. U. Minn. unit teaching and research internal medicine Northwestern Hosp., Mpls., 1966-72, sr. cons., from 1972. Former mem. adv. com. on metabolism and nutrition Surgeon Gen's Office, U.S. Army; former dir. commn. liver disease A.F. Epidemiological Bd.; former mem. council Nat. Inst. Arthritis and Metabolism Diseases; George R. Minot lectr. A.M.A., 1956; also John Phillips lectr. and medal A.C.P.; Tinsley Harrison lectr. U. Ala. med. Sch., 1969; Fogarty scholar and medal John P. Fogarty Internat. Center, NIH, 1972; Decorated Order of Merit (Republic of Chile); recipient James F. Bell award Minn. Med. Found.; Distinguished award Minn. chpt. Sigma Xi, 1970; Friedrich Müller lectr. and medal U. Munich, 1969; Gold headed cane award and lectr. U. Cal., San Francisco, 1967. Master A.C.P.; mem. A.M.A. (chmn. sect. practice of medicine, 1948-49), Am. Clin. and Climatol. Assn. (Gordon Wilson lectr. 1947; pres. 1966), Harvey Soc. (hon. lectr. 1948), Am. Soc. Clin. Investigation (past pres.), Assn. Am. Physicians (pres. 1960-61, Kober medal 1972), Nat. Acad. Scis., Am. Soc. Biol. Chemists, Soc. Exptl. Biology and Medicine, Central Soc. Clin. Research (past pres. and councillor), Minn. Path. Soc. (pres. 1942), Minn. Soc. Internal Medicine (pres. 1942-43), Sigma Xi, Delta Kappa Epsilon, Nu Sigma Nu. Home: Minneapolis, Minn. Died Apr. 11, 1983.

WATSON, DONALD STEVENSON, educator; b. Greenwood, C., Can., Oct. 28, 1909; came to the U.S., 1930, naturalized, 1938; s. James Livingstone and Roberta (Stevenson) W.; m. Liselotte Bunge, Oct. 4, 1935; children—Margot (Mrs. Thomas A. Zener), Wendy. B.A., U. B.C., 1930; Ph.D., U. Calif. at Berkeley, 1935. Teaching asst. U. B.C., 1929-30, U. Calif. at Berkeley, 1930-33; apptd. to faculty George Washington U., from 1935, prof. econs., from 1948, exec. head dept., 1945-51, 56-60, coordinator research project for USAF, 1951-52, instrn. program for USAF, 1954-56; cons. Operations Research Office, 1950-60, also govt. agys., trade assns., bus. firms; vis. prof. U. Hawaii, summer 1964; dir. research project for NASA, 1963-66. Author: Business and Government, 1960, Spanish edit., 1965, (with Burns and Neal) Modern Economics, 2d edit, 1953, (with Burns) Government Spending and Economic Expansion, 1940, Price Theory and Its Uses, 1963, (with Holman) evaluation of NASA's Patent Policies, 1966; also articles in profl. jours.; Editor: (with Holman) Price Theory in Action, 1965, 3d edit., 1973, (with Getz), 4th edit., 1981. Home: Port Angeles, Wash.

WATSON, JAMES S., JR., radiologist; b. Rochester, N.Y., Aug. 10, 1894; s. James Sibley and Emily (Sibley) W.; M.D., N.Y.U., 1921; grad. course radiology U. Rochester Sch. Medicine and Dentistry, 1942-45; m. Hildegarde Lasell, Oct. 16, 1916 (dec. Sept. 1976); children—Michael Lasell, Jeanne W. (Mrs. James Quackenbush); m. 2d, Nancy Love Prince, Dec. 8, 1977. Pres., Dial Pub. Co., N.Y.C., 1919-29; research asst. physiology N.Y.U., 1922-23; ind. film producer, 1927-40, films including Lot in Sodom, 1932, Highlights and Shadows, 1937; mem. part-time staff U. Rochester Sch. Medicine and Dentistry, from 1941, research prof. radiology, from 1958; cons. in medicine; charge x-ray motion picture devel. Mem. AMA, Sigma Xi. Club: Harvard (N.Y.C.). Home: Rochester, N.Y. Died Mar. 31, 1982.

WATSON, OSBORN STONE, foreign service officer; b. Decatur, Ga., Apr. 27, 1890; s. Charles and Ila Marion (Stone) W.; attended Georgia Inst. of Tech., Atlanta, 1907, Georgetown Foreign Service Sch., Washington, D.C., 1921-22; m. Margareta Cecilia Lyckholm, Nov. 5, 1937; 1 dau., Gertrude Margareta. Rep. U.S. Shipping Bd., 1919-21; spl. agt., Dept. of Commerce, 1921-22; trade commr., Canton, China, 1924-25, Peking, 1925-26; Bur. of Foreign and Domestic Commerce, 1927-28; asst. exec. officer, Internat. Civ. Aeronautics Conf., Washington, D.C., 1928-29; commercial attaché, Helsingfors, Finland, 1929; del. 5th Congress of Internat. Chamber of Commerce, Amsterdam, Holland, 1929; detailed to N.R.A., 1933-34; acting commercial attaché, Caracas, Venezuela, 1937; commercial attaché, Wellington, New Zealand, 1945. Served in O.T.C., 2d lt., 1st lt., arty., U.S. Army, 1917-19. Mem. Delta Phi Epsilon. Presbyn. Mason. Club: University (Washington, D.C.). Home: Blackshear, Ga. †

WATSON, ROBERT EARL, controls mfg. co. exec.; b. Cleve., Jan. 28, 1925; s. Earl and Alice Marie (Evans) W.; m. Eileen C. Fulton, Nov. 18, 1950; children—Susan Evans, William Earl, Richard Edward. B.Indsl. Engring., Ohio State U., 1949; postgrad., Harvard U. Sch. Bus., 1967. With Ranco Inc., 1949-81, v.p. mfg., then v.p. planning, 1970-74, exec. v.p. N. Am., Columbus, Ohio, 1974-77, exec. v.p. planning, 1977-81, dir., 1975-81; sr. v.p., plant mgr. Honda of Am., East Liberty, Ohio, 1981-84. Served with USN, 1943-46. Recipient Disting. Alumnus award Ohio State U., 1979. Mem. Nat. Elec. Mfrs. Assn. (exec. com. residential controls from 1977), Ohio Mfrs. Assn., Columbus Indsl. Assn. Club: Catawba Island. Home: Worthington, Ohio. Died Aug. 27, 1984; buried Walnut Grove Cemetery, Worthington.

WATSON, THOMAS GAYLORD, JR., advt. exec.; b. Hugo, Colo., Aug. 24, 1917; s. Thomas Gaylord and Sarah Menefee (Petersen) W.; A.B., Yale, 1940; student Law Sch., 1941; student Harvard Bus. Sch., 1942-45; m. Adele Morrison, Aug. 7, 1955 (dec.); children—Thomas Gaylord III, Elena; m. 2d, Lois Barnes Crittenden, Mar. 29, 1969; children—Barbara Crittenden, Philip L. Crittenden III. With Vick Chem. Co., Inc., N.Y.C., 1946-57, v.p., 1950-52; v.p. N.Y.C. office N.W. Ayer, 1952-59, v.p., mgr. Chgo. office, 1959-66, exec. v.p., regional mgr., dir. N.W. Ayer & Son, Inc., 1967-70; exec. cons. for communications Unimark Internat., from 1970. Vice chmn. Chgo. unit Am. Cancer Soc.; vice chmn. health rev. com. Community Fund; vice chmn. Ill. sequicentennial com. advance gifts sect. chmn. Met. Crusade Mercy; pres., dir. Fine Arts Quartette. Bd. dirs. United Charities. Served to lt. comdr. USNR, World War II; lt. comdr. Res. Clubs: Chicago, Arts, DuEham Woods Riding, Mid-America (Chgo.). Home: Geneva, Ill. Died Nov. 24, 1983.

WATTLEY, DONALD HUBERT, clergyman; b. Lansdowne, Pa., Oct. 21, 1894; s. John Berkeley and Emily Morgan (Pritchard) W.; A.B., Kenyon Coll., Gambier, O., 1917; student Western Theol. Sem., Chicago, 1921-23; B.D., Episcopal Theol. Sch., Cambridge, Mass., 1924; S.T.D., Seabury-Western Theol. Seminary, 1955; married Cornelia Hutton Laurans, June 21, 1924; children—James Cooper, Cornelia Bancker. Ordained to ministry Episcopal Ch., May 27, 1923; curate Emmanuel Ch., Cleveland, O., 1924-25; rector Grace Ch., New Orleans, 1925-46; asso. priest Trinity Ch., New Orleans, 1948-49; canon pastor Christ Ch. Cathedral, New Orleans, 1949-54; instnl. chaplain and canon missioner Diocese of La., from 1954. Pres. standing com., vice chmn. Bishop and Council, chmn. constitution and canons com., and examing chaplain, Diocese of La.; dep. Gen. Conv. Diocese La., 1937, 40, 43, 49, 52, 55, 61; mem. nat. council Episcopal Ch., from 1958, also mem. joint commission on approaches to unity. Served in USN, 1917-19; disch. as ensign. Mem. Psi Upsilon. Clubs: Boston, Round Table (New Orleans). †

WAUGH, ALBERT E(DMUND), university professor, author; born Amherst, Mass., Sept. 28, 1902; s. Frank Albert and (Mary) Alice (Vail) W.; B.S., Mass. Agricultural Coll., 1924; M.S., Conn. Agricultural Coll., 1926; student Columbia, 1925, U. of Chicago, 1931-32 and 1942-43; m. Edith Holbrook Stewart, June 26, 1926; children—John Stewart, Robert Edmund, Dan Holbrook. Instructor economics, Conn. Agricultural Coll., 1924-28, asst. prof., 1928-32, asso. prof., 1932-33; asso. prof. econ., Conn. State Coll., 1933-37, prof., 1937-39; prof. econ. U. of Conn. from 1939, dean, Coll. Arts and Sciences, 1945-50, provost from 1950; visiting professor of economics, University of Nebraska, summer 1935; visiting professor economic California Institute Technology, 1944; director Willimantic Trust Company. Vice chairman Connecticut Commn. to Revise the Election Laws, 1939-41; chmn. Conn. Postwar Planning Bd., 1943-45. Trustee Norwich State Hosp., 1944-50 (chmn. 1946-48); Joint Com. State Mental Hosps., 1945-47 (chmn. 1946-48); chmn. State Institutional Bldg. Commn., 1947-51; trustee Windham Community Hosp. (pres. 1948-50, 55); Moderator of Town Meeting, Mansfield, Conn. Fellow A.A.A.S.; member American Economic Association, American Statistical Association, Econometric Society, American Assn. U. Professors, Conn. Acad. Arts and Scis., Kappa Sigma; hon. mem. Stratford Minutemen. Republican. Conglist. Author: Elements of Statistical Method, 1938 (revised 1943, 52, translated into Portuguese, 1946); Statistical Tables and Problems, 1938 (revised 1944, 52); Principles of Economics, 1947. Genealogist of descendants of John Waugh (1687-1781). Died Mar. 6, 1985.

WAUGH, ALEX (ALEXANDER RABAN WAUGH), Brit. novelist; b. London, Eng., July 8, 1898; s. Arthur Waugh; student Sherborne Sch., also Royal Mill Coll., Sandhurst, Eng.; m. Joan Chirnside, 1932 (dec. 1969); children—Andrew, Veronica, Peter; m. 2d, Virginia Sorenson, 1969. Entered Brit. Army and assigned to Dorset Regt., 1917; served with BEF in France, 1971-18 (prisoner of war, 1918, and wrote a book on it); transferred to Res., 1919; rejoined Dorset Regt., 1939; with BEF, France, 1940; staff capt., 1940; MEF, 1941, PAIC, 1942-45; promoted maj., 1944; became lit. dir., Chapman & Hall, 1924; lectr. tour in U.S., 1931; traveled extensively; writer in residence Central State Coll., Edmond, Okla., 1966-67; fellow Boston U. Libraries, 1966. Author numerous books, from 1917; latest publs.; The Sugar Islands, 1949; The Lipton Story, 1950; Where the Clocks Strike Twice, 1951; Guy Renton, 1952; Island in the Sun, 1956; Merchants of Wine, 1957; Love and the Caribbean, 1959; In Praise of Wine, 1959; Fuel for the Flame, 1959; (short stories) My Place in the Bazaar, 1961; The Early Years of Alec Waugh, 1963; A Family of Islands, 1964; The Mule on the Minaret, 1965; My Brother Evelyn and Other Portraits, 1968; Wine and Spirits, 1968; A Spy in the Family, An Erotic Comedy, 1970; Bangkok, The Story of a City, 1971. Died Sept. 3, 1981.

WAUGH, RICHEY LAUGHLIN, surgeon; born Morden, Manitoba, Canada, January 4, 1888; son of James Church and Fanny (Laughlin) W.; brought to U.S., 1890, naturalized, 1909; Ph.C., U. of Washington, 1908, B.S., 1909; M.D., U. of Minn., 1915; m. Lyda Leamer, June 27, 1916; children—Dr. Richey L., Dr. Robert John Leamer, Dr. William H., Charles Ruggles, Druggist, 1909-11; intern King County Hosp., Seattle, Wash., 1915-16; commissioned assistant surgeon U.S. P.H.S., 1917, passed assistant surgeon, 1921, surgeon, 1925, senior surgeon, 1937, medical director, 1943, stationed Seattle, Washington, Portland Ore., Manila, P.I., and Ellis Island, New York; at the Am. Consulate, Cobh, Irish Free State, 1926-29; chief of surg. service, Marine Hospitals, San Francisco, 1929-35, New Orleans, 1935-39, Boston, 1939-49. Instructor orthopedic surgery, Tufts Medical School. Assigned to U.S. Coast Guard and U.S. Navy during World War. Fellow Am. College of Surgeons, Am. Assn. Surgery of Trauma; mem. A.M.A., Southern Med. Assn., Mass. Med. Soc., Boston Orthopedic Club, Am. Assn., Mil. Surgeons, Am. Acad. Orthopedic Surgery, Nu Sigma Nu. Mason (32 deg., Shriner). Contbr. to surg. jours. Home: Brookline, Mass. †

WAYNICK, CAPUS MILLER, ambassador; born at Rockingham County, N.C., Dec. 23, 1889; s. Joshua James N. and Anna (Moore) W.; student U. of N.C., 1907-09; m. Elizabeth McBee, June 19, 1915. Reporter Greensboro Daily Record, 1911-13, Charlotte Observer, 1913-14; editor Greensboro Daily Record, 1915-17, pub., 1920-22; editor High Point (N.C.) Enterprise. Mem. N.C. Ho. of Reps. 1931, Senate, 1933; state dir. Nat. Reemployment Service, 1933-34; chmn. N.C. State Highway and Pub. Works Commn., 1934-37; chmn. State Planning Bd., 1937; founder and dir. Health Edn. Inst. to 1949; chmn. N.C. Dem. Party, 1948. A.E. and P. to Nicaragua, 1950-51; ambassador to Colombia from 1951. Acting adminstr. Point 4 Program, 1950. Served as pvt., Inf., U.S. Army, 1918. Democrat. Presbyn.†

WAYS, MAX, mag. editor; b. Balt., Aug. 13, 1905; s. Max and Katherine (McDonnell) W.; student Loyola Coll.,

Balt., 1926, Litt.D., 1964; m. Dorothea Smith Olivier; children—Peter O., Brigid A.; m. 2d, Constance Anne St. Onge; 1 son, John St. Onge. Reporter, Balt. Sun, 1926-29, Balt. News, 1929-30; reporter, editorial writer Phila. Record, 1930-41; econ. intelligence analyst Bd. Econ. Warfare, 1942; chief enemy br. FEA, 1944-45; mem. joint intelligence staff Joint Chiefs Staff, 1943-45; writer Time mag., 1945, sr. editor fgn. news, 1946-51, nat. affairs, 1951-56; chief Time-Life London Bur., 1956-58; bd. editors Fortune mag., 1959-60, asst. mng. editor, 1960-64, asso. mng. editor, 1964-67, mem. bd. editors, 1967-76. Roman Cath. Author: Beyond Survival, 1959. Home: New York, N.Y. Died June 4, 1985; buried Gate of Heaven Cemetery, Hawthorne, N.Y.

WEARN, JOSEPH TRELOAR, physician; b. Charlotte, N.C., Feb. 15, 1893; s. Joseph Henry and Anne (Treloar) W.; B.S., Davidson (N.C.) Coll., 1913; M.D., Harvard University, 1917; D.Sc. (honorary), Davidson College, 1943, Oberlin College, 1951, U. Pa., 1962; LL.D., University N.C., 1961; married to Susan Channing Lyman, August 30, 1927; 1 dau., Susan Lyman. Resident staff Peter Bent Brigham Hosp., Boston, 1919-21; instr., dept. of Pharmacology, U. of Pa., 1921-23; asst. and asso. prof. medicine, Harvard, 1923-29; prof. medicine, Western Res. U., 1929-59, Hord prof. medicine emeritus, 1960-84, v.p. med. affairs, 1959-60, now consultant medical affairs, dir. medicine Lakeside Hosp., Cleve., 1929-56, dean sch. of medicine, 1945-59. Served as 1st lt. Med. Corps, U.S. Army, 1917-18; consultant to q.m. gen., U.S. Army, 1943-45; chief div. physiology, Com. Med. Research, Office Sci. Research and Development, 1944-46; chmn. sub-com. on blood substitutes, Nat. Research Council, 1944-46; consultant to surgeon gen., U.S. Army, 1943-49; consultant to sec. of War and mem. central bd., Army Epidemiol. Bd., 1946-49; mem. adv. com. on biology and medicine AEC, 1947-53, cons. div. biology and medicine, 1953-61; member Atomic Bomb Casualty Com., 1952-56; mem. adv. bd. of quartermaster research and development Nat. Acad. Sci. and NRC, 1952-59. Advisor to the American Board Internatl Medicine. Recipient Medal of Freedom, 1945. Mem. A.M.A., Am. Acad. Arts and Scis., Assn. Am. Physicians (pres. 1953), Am. Soc. Clin. Investigation, Am. Climatol. and Clin. Assn., Am. Physiol. Soc., Harvey Soc., Interurban Clin. Club, Phi Beta Kappa, Alpha Omega Alpha, Sigma Xi. Presbyn. Clubs: Century Assn. (N.Y.); Harvard, Tavern (Boston); Metropolitan (Washington); Union, Chagrin Valley Hunt (Cleveland). Contbr. papers in field. Home: Brooklin, Maine. Died Sept. 26, 1984.

WEARSTLER, EARL FORD, manufacturing executive; b. North Canton, Ohio, Mar. 1, 1924; s. Russell John and Goldie Marie (Young) W.; m. Catherine Nora Duren, Apr. 19, 1974; 1 child, Joyce Ann. Student, Northwestern U., 1942, Kent State U., 1946. With Diebold Inc. (various locations), 1947-84, v.p., gen. mgr., Canton, 1965-76, exec. v.p., 1977-81, pres. and chief operating officer, 1981-82, pres. and chief exec. officer, 1982-84, also dir.; dir. Diebold Can. Ltd., Union Metal Mfg. Co., Canton. Served with USN, 1942-46, ETO. Republican. Mem. United Ch. Clubs: Brookside Country, Congress Lake Country, Union of Cleve, Prestwick Country. Home: Canton, Ohio. Dec. Feb. 3, 1984.

WEATHERFORD, HARRISON MARK, lawyer; b. Albany, Ore., Dec. 23, 1925; s. Mark Vern and Emmaline (Kuhn) W.; student Ore. State U., 1943, 46-48, Willamette U., 1948-50; J.D., Northwestern, 1952; m. Lillian Irene Odberg, July 24, 1952; children—Mark Harrison, Alice Vaughn, Joyce Verne. Wheat rancher, Arlington, Ore., 1944, 46-52; admitted to Ore. bar, 1952, since practiced in Albany; partner Weatherford, Thompson, Horton, Brickey & Powers, and predecessor firm, 1953-79; wheat and cattle rancher, Arlington and Condon, 1966-79. Chmn. Benton County Sch. Dist. reorgn. com., 1957-62; mem. Gov.'s Conf. on Edn., 1958; mem. Albany Zoning Commn., 1960-62; mem. adv. com. Intermediate Edn. Dist. Commn. of Ore. Legislature, 1967-69; dir. Rock Creek Water Control Dist., 1974-79. Pres., sec., bd. dirs. Albany Boys Club; pres., trustee McDowell-Catt Found.; v.p., bd. dirs. Willamette Osteo. Hosp. Served with AUS, 1944-46: PTO. Named Gilliam County and Ore. Co-Conservation Farmer of Year, 1962. Mem. Ore., Linn County bar assns., Air Force Assn., Ore. Wheat, Cattlemens and Rye grass Growers Assn., Aircraft Owners and Pilots Assn., Am. Legion, Phi Delta Theta. Democrat. Presbyn. (deacon, elder). Elk. Home: Albany, Oreg. Died Apr. 25, 1979.

WEATHERHEAD, ARTHUR CLASON, architecture; b. Minneapolis, Minn., Oct. 9, 1888; s. Eugene Haskell and Hattie (Clason) W.; student Willamette U., Salem, Ore., 1908-11; A.B., U. of Southern Calif., 1912, A.M., 1914; studied Univ. of Ore., 1918-19; B.Arch., Univ. of Pa., 1925; Ph.D., Columbia U., 1941; m. Mabel Stewart, Dec. 24, 1913. Architectural draftsman, 1907; isntr. in art, U. of Southern Calif., 1914-18, asst. prof. art and architecture, 1919-24; prof. architecture and acting dean Sch. of Architecture, 1925-30, dean Coll. of Architecture (including fine arts depts.), 1930-45; industrial designer from 1945. Mem. Am. Inst. Architects, State Assn. Calif. Architects, Phi Beta Phi, Tau Sigma Delta, Alpha Rho Chi, Delta Phi Delta. Republican. Methodist. Contbr. to professional jours. Home: Los Angeles, Calif. †

WEAVER, FREDERIC NIXON, educator, engr., author; b. Boston, Sept. 21, 1889; s. George Edwin and Margaret Isabel (Nixon) W., B.S., Tufts U., 1913; student Columbia, 1916-17, Harvard, 1917, U. de Caen, France, 1918; m. Ruth Cornelia Johnson, Dec. 19, 1923; children—Arthur Sargent, Dorothy Ruth. Engr., 1913-15; tchr. Passaic (N.J.) High Sch., 1915-17; instr. civil engring. Tufts Coll., 1919-23, asst. prof., 1923-32, prof., from 1932, chmn. dept., from 1936; cons. engr. Mem. exec. com. Medford (Mass.) Salvation Army; chmn. Sch. of Nursing com. Lawrence Meml. Hosp. Served with AEF in France, 1917-19. Mem. Am. Soc. C.E. (past pres. Northeastern sect.), Boston Soc. Civil Engrs. (past pres.), Am. Soc. Engring. Edn. (past pres. Tufts chpt.), Am. Assn. U. Profs. (past pres. Tufts chpt.), Sigma Xi, Tau Beta Pi. Conglist. Author: The History of F Company, 101st Engineers (with Philip N. Sanborn), 1924; Applied Mechanics, 1930. Contbr. articles tech. jours. Home: Mass. †

WEAVER, JAMES R. N., army officer; b. Fremont, O., May 20, 1888; s. James Trumbull and Jennie (Boyer) W.; student Oberlin Coll., 1906-07; B.S., U.S. Mil. Acad., 1911 and commd. 2d lt.; m. Mary Conklin Pontius; children—Marian, James Rainier (lt. col. U.S. Army); advanced through the grades to brig. general, Dec. 1941; assumed command of 68th Armored Regt., Fort Benning, Ga., Aug. 3, 1940 and assigned to command 2d Armored Brigade Apr. 14, 1941; transferred to Philippine Dept., Oct. 1941; and participated in the defense of the Philippine Islands during Dec. 1941 and early months of 1942; on Bataan Peninsula when battlefield fell to Japanese, Apr. 9, prisoner of war of Japanese govt.; released Aug. 1945; brig. gen., 1948. Awarded D.S.M., S.S., D.S.C., B.S.M. Home: Menlo Park, Calif. †

WEAVER, WILLIAM GAULBERT, army officer; b. Louisville, Ky., Nov. 24, 1888; s. Charles Parsons and Anna Mary (Sewell) W.; B.S., U.S. Mil. Acad., 1912; grad. Inf. Sch., 1920, Command and Staff Sch., 1923; m. Dorothy Meyers, Jan. 11, 1930; 1 son, William Gaulbert, Jr. Commd. 2d lt. inf., June 1912 and advanced through the grades to major gen., Jan. 25, 1945; comd. 8th Machine Gun Btn., 3d div., World War I; became prof. mil. science and tactics, U. of Wis., July 1937; assigned to Inf. Replacement Center, Camp Roberts, Calif., comdg. 16th Inf. Training Group and 17th Infantry Training Regiment April-December 1941, then transferred to Fort Sam Houston, Tex. to command 38th Inf. Regt., 2d Inf. Div. to July 1942; assigned to 3d Detachment, 2d Army troops, Camp Gordon, Ga., overseas Sept. 1942; chief of staff and field dep. comdr. Supply Services, European Theater of Operations to July 1944; asst. div. comdr. 90th Inf. Div., July-Nov. 1944; comdr. 8th Inf. Div., Nov. 1944-Feb. 25, 1945; retired from active service as maj. gen., Feb. 1946. Decorations: (World War I) Distinguished Service Cross, Purple Heart (U.S.); Croix-de-Guerre with silver star (France); (World War II) Distinguished Service Cross, Distinguished Service Medal, Silver Star, Legion of Merit (2), Bronze Star (2), Purple Heart (2), Commendation Ribbon (U.S.); Distinguished Service Order (England); Chevalier Legion of Honor, Croix-de-Guerre with palm (2) (France). Mem. Army and Navy Legion of Valor U.S.A., Am. Legion, 2d, 3d, 8th and 90th Inf. Div. Assns. Mason. Author: Vanishing Vignettes. Address: San Antonio, Tex. †

WEBB, GEORGE ARTHUR, chem. engr.; b. Liverpool, Eng., July 7, 1910; s. George and Alice E. (Shields) W.; brought to U.S., 1920, naturalized, 1924; B.S. with highest honors, U. Pitts., 1934, Ph.D., 1941; grad. student Carnegie Inst. Tech., 1934-37; m. Sara R. Baumann, July 31, 1937; 1 dau., Barbara Jeanne. With Clairton By-Products Coke plant U.S. Steel Corp., 1934-37; indsl. fellow Mellon Inst., 1937-40, sr. fellow, 1941-43, dir. engring, 1956-57, dir. adminstrn., 1957-67, asso. dir., 1967-71; dir. sponsored research Carnegie-Mellon U., 1971-74, pres. Carnegie-Mellon Inst., 1974-75, emeritus, 1975-82; research engr. Firestone Tire & Rubber Co., 1940-41; with Koppers Co., Inc., 1943-56, successively research engr., mgr. engring sect., asst. mgr. devel. dept., asst. to v.p. research, exec. sec. new products com., mgr. planning dept., 1945-56. Registered profl. engr., Pa. Diplomate Am. Acad. Environ. Engrs. Fellow Am. Inst. Chem. Engrs. (chmn. Pitts. sect. 1949); mem. Am. Chem. Soc. (dir. Pitts. sect. 1956), ASME, AAAS, Am. Soc. Engring. Edn., Nat. Soc. Profl. Engrs., Engrs. Soc. Western Pa. (v.p. 1975, pres. 1976), Sigma Xi, Phi Lambda Upsilon, Tau Beta Pi, Sigma Tau. Clubs: Chemists (v.p. 1945), University (pres. 1971-72) (Pitts.). Holder 19 U.S. and fgn. patents in field of dehydrogenation, hydrolysis, halogenation, polymerization. Home: Pittsburgh, Pa. Died Jan. 10, 1982.

WEBB, HERSCHEL F., historian, educator; b. David City, Nebr., Oct. 31, 1924; s. Orie Lee and Olga Margarita (Gereke) W. B.A., U. Chgo., 1949; M.A., Columbia U., 1951, Ph.D., 1958. Mem. faculty Columbia U., N.Y.C., 1957-83, prof. Japanese history, 1974-83, chmn. dept. East Asian langs. and cultures, 1977-80. Author: (with Marleigh Ryan) Research in Japanese Sources: A Guide, 1965, An Introduction to Japan, 1955, The Japanese Imperial Institution in the Tokugawa Period, 1968. Served with USNR, 1943-46. Home: New York, N.Y. Dec. Jan. 8, 1983.

WEBB, JACK, radio, TV producer, writer, dir., actor; b. Santa Monica, Calif., Apr. 2, 1920; s. Samuel Chester and Margaret (Smith) W.; m. Julie Peck, July 1947 (dec. div); children—Stacy, Lisa; m. Dorothy Thompson, Jan. 1955 (div. 1957); m. Jackie Loughery, June, 1958 (div. 1964). Student pub. schs. owner releasing firm Mark VII, Ltd.; music pub. firms Mark VII Music, Pete Kelly Music. Starred: radio show Pat Novak for Hire, San Francisco, 1945, Johnny Modero Pier 23, 1947; created: radio show Dragnet, 1949; began TV show, 1951; producer-dir.: TV series Noah's Ark; created: radio show Pete Kelly's Blues, 1950, True Series, 1961; exec. charge TV prodn., Warner Studios, 1963; producer, dir., star: Dragnet, 1967-70; exec. producer, creater: Adam-12, 1968-71; exec. producer: The D.A, 1971, O'Hara, U.S. Treasury, 1971, Emergency, Mobile One, 1975; narrator: TV show Escape, 1973; exec. producer: TV show Sam, 1977, Project U.F.O, 1978-79, Little Mo, 1978; feature roles in: films Sunset Boulevard, The Men, Halls of Montezuma, He Walked by Night, You're in the Navy Now; producer, dir.: motion picture Archie, 1959; actor-dir.: motion picture Dragnet, 1954, 66, Pete Kelly's Blues, 1955, The D.I, 1957, All About Archie, 1960; Author: motion picture The Badge, 1958. Hon. chmn. United Cerebral Palsy Assn. Served with USAAF, World War II. Holder over 100 commendations of merit, award by radio TV critics.; named hon. sgt. USMC. Mem. Screen Actors Guild, Screen Dirs. Guild, Am. Soc. Cinematographers, Am. Fedn. Radio Actors. Address: Los Angeles, Calif.

WEBB, ROBERT, educational administrator; b. Knoxville, Tenn., Feb. 8, 1919; s. Daniel Clary and Julia Hannah (McCulley) W.; m. Julia Dossett, July 28, 1949; children: Julia Jennings, Susan Hunter. A.B., U. Tenn., 1941, M.S., 1947. Tchr. Webb Sch., Bell Buckle, Tenn., 1946-54, Webb Sch. of Calif., Claremont, 1954-55; founder, pres. Webb Sch. of Knoxville, 1955-84. Mem. Knox County Library Bd., 1961-64, chmn., 1964; Bd. dirs. Nat. Study Sch. Evaluation; trustee So. Assn. Colls. and Schs.; bd. dirs. Tenn. chpt. Nature Conservancy. Served to 1st lt. USAAF, 1942-46. Mem. Nat. Assn. Ind. Schs. (sec., dir.), Tenn. Assn. Ind. Schs. (pres. 1974), assns. ind. schs), Sigma Alpha Epsilon (pres. local chpt. 1941). Democrat. Presbyterian (elder). Home: Knoxville, Tenn. Died May 4, 1984.

WEBER, HAROLD CHRISTIAN, educator; b. Boston, Mar. 20, 1895; s. Christian and Ellen (Arnold) W.; m. Madeleine A. Duffy, Nov. 14, 1931 (dec. Apr. 1960); m. Marian F. Shaughness, Apr. 18, 1963. B.S., Mass. Inst. Tech., 1918; Sc.D., Eidgenossische Technische Hochschule, Zurich, Switzerland, 1935, Suffolk U., 1963. Cons. Walker, Lewis, McAdams & Knowland, Boston, 1919-20; prof. chem. engring. Mass. Inst. Tech., 1920-65, prof. emeritus, from 1965; cons. in oil, textiles, paper, mech. and electronic equipment, from 1925. Author: Thermodynamics for Chemical Engineers, 1939, 2d edit., 1958; also thermodynamics sect. in Marks' Mechanical Engineers Handbook, 1950. Tech. adviser Chem. Warfare Service, 1941-45; chief sci. adviser U.S. Army, 1958-66; mem. Army Sci. Adv. Panel, 1954-74. Served as 2d lt. Chem. Warfare Service U.S. Army, 1918-19. Recipient Presdl. certificate of merit for work in World War II, 1947, Chem. Corps certificate of merit, 1958, Army Meritorious Civilian Service award, 1959, Army Distinguished Service award, 1966. Fellow A.A.A.S., Am. Acad. Arts and Scis.; mem. Am. Inst. Chem. Engrs., Am. Chem. Soc., Sigma Xi, Tau Beta Pi. Roman Catholic. Patentee in field of electronics and petroleum. Home: Peoria, Ariz.

WEBSTER, GEORGE LEWIS, chemist; b. Maquoketa, Ia., Nov. 30, 1900; s. Charles Orange and Sarah Frances (McComb) W.; Ph.G., U. Ill., 1922; B.S., U. Mich., 1927, M.S., 1931, Ph.D., 1937; m. Anna Bee Haller, July 17, 1928. Mem. dept. chemistry Coll. Pharmacy, U. Ill. since 1922, asst., 1922-25, instr., 1925-26, asso., 1927-37, asst. prof., 1937-39, asso. prof., 1939-41, prof. chemistry, 1941-47, professor, head department, 1947-58, dean college pharmacy, 1958-69. Mem. Pharm. Syllabus Com., 1943-46, Com. Revision U.S. Pharmacopeia, 1950-60. Mem. A.A.A.S., Am. Chem. Soc., Am. Pharm. Assn., Assn. Vitamin Chemists (pres. 1952-53) Am. Assn. Colls. Pharmacy (pres. 1967-68), Sigma Xi, Phi Kappa Phi, Phi Lambda Upsilon, Rho Chi (nat. pres. 1948-50), Kappa Psi. Co-author: The Pharmaceutical Curriculum, 1952. Home: Wilmette, Ill. Died Nov. 18, 1984.

WEBSTER, LUTHER DENVER, JR., steel co. exec.; b. Lubbock, Tex., June 10, 1910; s. Luther Denver and Johncy (Hardin) W.; children—Lydia Hayes (Mrs. Frankie Dell Green), Rebel. Student, So. Meth. U., 1930-33. Sports editor, pub. relations dir. Dallas Dispatch, 1932-41; gen. mgr. Air Force Contract Flight Sch., 1941-44; exec. v.p. Red Arrow Freight Lines, Houston, 1944-47; owner Red Webster & Assos. (advt agy.), 1947-49; v.p. Lone Star Steel Co., Dallas, from 1950; v.p., dir. Marshall Broadcasting Corp. Author: I Saw Russia, 1958, The Red Whip. Mem. Tex. Commn. on Alcoholism. Mem. Am. Petroleum Inst., Am. Iron and Steel Inst. (pub. relations com.), Pub. Relations Soc. Am., Soc. Am. Indsl. Editors, Sigma Delta Chi. Democrat. Methodist. Club: Mason (Shriner). Home: Dallas, Tex.

WEBSTER, PAUL FRANCIS, songwriter; b. N.Y.C., Dec. 20, 1907; s. Myron Lawrence and Blanche Pauline (Stonehill) W.; m. Gloria Lenore Benguiat, June 10, 1937; children: Guy Michael, Roger Edmund. Student, Horace Mann Sch., also N.Y.U., 1924-27, Cornell U., summer 1925. Composer: songs Masquerade, 1932, Reflections in the Water, My Moonlight Madonna, 1933, Two Cigarettes in the Dark, 1934; co-author: scores for motion pictures The Sandpiper; Co-author: scores for motion pictures Giant, Friendly Persuasion, Rose Marie, Student Prince, Merry Widow, Calamity Jane, Great Caruso, The Alamo, Guns at Navarone, Tender Is the Night, Mutiny on the Bounty, Raintree County; co-author also others; songs for the stage musical Jump for Joy, 1940; songs for films and stage include The Shadow of Your Smile; Co-author: songs for films and stage include Love is a Many Splendored Thing, Somewhere, My Love, I'll Walk With God, Secret Love, I Got it Bad and That Ain't Good, Lamplighter's Serenade, Loveliest Night of the Year, The Green Leaves of Summer, A Certain Smile; co-author also collaborated with, Oscar Strauss and; Co-author: songs for films and stage include The Twelfth of Never, April Love; co-author also collaborated with, Rudolph Friml and, Hoagy Carmichael, Franz Lehar, Sammy Fain, Jerome Kern, others. (Recipient Best Song Award A.S.C.A.P. 1934, Acad. Award 1953, 55, 65, gold medal Photoplay mag. 1955, bronze plaque Down-Beat mag. 1955, Best Song 1956, Song Hit of the Year, Radio and TV Daily award 1956, Diploma di Onore Messina, Italy 1956, Limelight Film Critics award 1961, Grammy award 1965, Laurel award 1965, elected to Songwriter's Hall Fame 1972); Author: The Children's Music Box, 1945. Mem. A.S.C.A.P. (award of Merit 1966), Writers Guild Am. (hon. life), Songwriter's Protective Assn., Acad. Motion Picture Arts and Scis., Author's League, Dramatist's Guild. Home: Beverly Hills, Calif. Dec. Mar. 23, 1984.

WEBSTER, REGINALD NATHANIEL, manufacturing executive; b. Dublin, Ireland, Feb. 7, 1898; s. Nathaniel and Marguerite E. (Barnett) W.; m. Lillian A. McDonald, December 12, 1947; children—George A., Audrey J. Webster, John K. Webster. Associated with The National Park Bank, 1915; jr. partner Brown & Barlow, textiles, 1919-22; head own firm, taxation and finance, 1923-33; exec. v.p., dir. Fulton Sylphon Co., Knoxville, Tenn., Reynolds Metal Co., Richmond, Va., 1933-38; chairman Standard-Thomson Corp., Waltham, Mass., 1939—; dir. Smith & Wesson, Heli-Coil Corp., Fla. Land & Minerals Corp., Delray Indsl. Properties, Ltd. Clubs: Madison Square Garden, Pinnacle, River, Turf and Field (N.Y.C.); Rumson (N.J.) Country; Monmouth Beach, Seabright Beach (N.J.). Home: Palm Beach, Fla. Died Feb. 8, 1983.

WECHSBERG, JOSEPH, writer; b. Moravska-Ostrava, Aug. 29, 1907; came to U.S., 1938, naturalized, 1944; s. Siegfried and Hermine (Krieger) W.; m. Jo-Ann Novak, Mar. 24, 1934; 1 dau., Poppy. Student, Vienna State Acad. Music, 1925-30, Sorbonne, 1926-29; grad. summa cum laude, Prague U. Law Sch., 1930. Musician, lawyer, journalist in, Europe, free-lance writer, U.S., 1938—; writer New Yorker mag., 1943—, mem. staff, 1948—, fgn. corr., 1949—. Author: Looking for a Bluebird, 1945, Homecoming, 1946, Sweet and Sour, 1948, The Continental Touch, 1948, Blue Trout and Black Truffles, 1953, The Self-Betrayed, 1955, Avalanche, 71958, Red Plush and Black Velvet, 1961, Dining at the Pavillon, 1962, The Best Things in Life, 1964, Journey Through the Land of Eloquent Silence, 1964, The Merchant Bankers, 1966, Vienna, My Vienna, 1968, The Voices, 1969, The First Time Around, 1970, Prague, The Mystical City, 1971, The Opera, 1972, The Glory of the Violin, 1972, The Waltz Emperors, 1973, Verdi, 1974, Dream Towns of Europe, 1976, In Leningrad, 1977, Schubert, 1977, The Vienna I Knew, 1979, The Lost World of the Great Spas, 1979; Contbr. nat. mags. Served as lt. Czechoslovak Army, 1938; as tech. sgt. psychol. warfare div. AUS, World War II. Recipient lit. fellowship award Houghton Mifflin, 1944; ann. mag. award Sidney Hillman Found., 1953. Mem. Authors Guild. Office: New York, N.Y. Dec. Apr. 10, 1983.

WECHSLER, JAMES ARTHUR, journalist; b. N.Y.C., Oct. 31, 1915; s. Samuel and Anna (Weisberger) W.; m. Nancy Fraenkel, Oct. 5, 1934; children—Michael (dec.), Holly. A.B., Columbia U., 1935. Asst. editor Nation mag., 1938-40; labor editor, then Washington bur. chief PM newspaper, 1940-47; with N.Y. Post, 1947-83, editor editorial page, columnist, 1961-80, asso. editor, columnist, 1980—. Author: Revolt on the Campus, 1935; co-author: War Our Heritage, 1937, War Propaganda and the U.S, 1940, Labor Baron, 1944, Age of Suspicion, 1954, Reflections of an Angry Middle Aged Editor, 1960, In a Darkness, 1972. Served with AUS, 1945. Recipient Lasker award Fla. chpt. ACLU, 1968; Roosevelt award Americans for Democratic Action, 1962; Karl Menninger award Fortune Soc., 1978. Democrat. Jewish. Home: New York, N.Y. Dec. Sept. 11, 1983.

WEDD, STANLEY MUSGRAVE, banker; b. Kitchener, Ont., Can., Sept. 21, 1889; s. George Maynard and Mabel Alexandra (Goodman) W.; ed. pub. schs.; m. Gretchen van Nostrand, Oct. 8, 1913; children—Cornelia Laurence, Sylvia Henrietta, Andrew Allan. Joined The Can. Bank of Commerce as jr. officer, Walkerton, Ont., br., 1905, asst. inspector head office, Toronto, Ont., 1920-23, asst. mgr. br. Sherbrooke, P.Q., 1923-25, inspector head office, Toronto, Ont., 1925-28, chief inspector head office, 1928-37, asst. gen. mgr., 1937-42, gen. mgr. head office, Toronto, 1942-45, dir., 1944, v.p. and gen. manager, 1945-47, exec. v.p., 1947-48, pres., from 1948, chairman of the board of directors, 1952-56; chmn. bd., dir. Anglo-Scandinavian Investment Corp., dir. British Am. Assurance Co., Great Lakes Power Corp., Ltd., Internat. Bus. Machines Co., Ltd., Nat. Trust Co., Ltd., Western Assurance Co., and Investors Syndicate of Can., Ltd., McIntyre Porcupine Mines, Ltd., others. Anglican. Clubs: Royal Canadian Yacht, Toronto, York, Toronto Hunt. Home: Toronto, Ont., Can. Deceased.

WEDELL, HUGO THEODORE, judge; b. Hillsboro, Kan., Jan. 6, 1890; s. Franz E. and Katherine (Goertz) W.; student Kan. State Teachers Coll., Emporia, 1909-12; A.B., U. of Kan., 1915, LL.B., 1920; m. Hazel Houston, Sept. 2, 1917; 1 dau., Wilma Jeanne. Teacher rural sch., Marion County, Kan., 1910-11, Hill City High Sch., 1912-13; professional baseball player, 1913-17, part time with Phila. Nat. Club, and coached at Haskell Indian Sch., Lawrence, Kan.; admitted to Okla. bar, 1920, to Kan. bar, 1922; practiced in Nowata, Okla., 1920-22; partner, firm Jones & Wedell, Chanute, Kan., 1922-29, Wedell & Donaldson, 1933-35; county atty. Neosho County, Kan., 1927-31; prosecutor of Finney bond forgeries, 1933; mem. com. to revise Kan. Code of Criminal Procedure, 1934; apptd. asso. justice Supreme Court of Kan. to fill vacancy, July 1935, elected to Supreme Court, 1936, 42 and 48. Served as gen. dir. athletics, Camp Crane, Pa., 1917; later corpl. Med. Corps, 1918, World War. Cited by Kansas U. for distinguished service in the legal profession and to the University, 1950. President Kansas Univ. Alumni Assn., 1941; pres. Topeka Citizens Council and Forum, 1944. Mem. American Bar Association, Am. Legion (mem. Kan. state exec. com. 4 yrs.). Republican. Methodist. Mason. Rotarian. Home: Topeka, Kans. Deceased.

WEDGE, GEORGE ANSON, author and music educator; b. Danbury, Conn., Jan. 15, 1890; s. Anson Curtis and Cora Belle (McHan) W.; grad. in organ, Inst. of Musical Art, N.Y. City, 1910, piano, 1914, composition, 1915; honorary Litt.D., Ursinus College, Oct. 27, 1941. Unmarried. Organist M.E. Ch., Danbury, Conn., 1903-09, St. Stephen's Episcopal Ch., Ridgefield, Conn., 1909-11, Madison Av. M.E. Ch., N.Y. City, 1911-24; instr. Inst. of Musical Art, 1909, St. Agatha's Sch., N.Y. City, 1918-22, H. Witherspoon Studios, 1917-25; accompanist Musical Art Soc., 1913-18; instr. New York Univ., 1920-27, Settlement Music Sch., Phila., 1923; head of theory dept., Manhattan School of Music, 1923, Curtis Inst., Phila., 1924-26, Teachers Coll. (Columbia), 1925-26; head theory dept. Inst. of Musical Art of the Juilliard Sch. of Music, 1926-39, dir. 1937-39, dean, 1939-47. Director Summer Sch. from 1932; member Bohemians of New York. Episcopalian. Author: Eartraining and Sightsinging, 1921; Advanced Eartraining and Sightsinging, 1922; Keyboard Harmony, 1924; Applied Harmony, Book I, 1930, Book II, 1931; also (brochure) Rhythm in Music, 1927; The Gist of Music, 1936. Home: Fort Myers, Fla. †

WEEKS, LAWRENCE B., army officer; b. Fort Porter, Buffalo, N.Y., Oct. 16, 1888; s. Edwin B. (lt. U.S. Army) and Harriet A. (Ovenshine) W.; student Mass. Inst. Tech., 1907-08; B.S., U.S. Mil. Acad., 1913; grad. Coast Arty. Sch., 1928, Command and Gen. Staff Sch., 1930, Army War Coll., 1939; m. Rietta Brainard, Oct. 19, 1921; children—Henry Chambers, Mary Norvell, Margaret Lawrence. Commd. 2d lt., U.S. Army, Coast Arty. Corps, 1913, and advanced through the grades to brig. gen. (temp.), U.S. Army, Feb. 16, 1942; served as instr. 244th Coast Arty., N.Y. Nat. Guard, 1930-33; Nat. Guard Bureau, War Dept., 1933-37; comdg. officer Northern Dist., Civilian Conservation Corps, Pa., 1937-38; exec. officer 2d Coast Atty., Fort Monroe, Va., 1938; dir. dept. arty. and engring., Coast Arty. Sch., Fort Monroe, 1939-40; asst. comdt., Coast Arty. Sch., 1940-42, comdt. from Feb. 21, 1942; col. Coast Arty. Corp. Nov. 13, 1945; on duty in Nat. Guard Bur., Washington, D.C. from Nov. 1945. Awarded Victory medal, World War I; Order of Estrella Abdon Calderon (Ecuador). Clubs: Army and Navy, Army and Navy Country (Washington, D.C.); Rock Spring (West Orange, N.J.). Home: Washington, D.C. Deceased.

WEEKS, SOLAN WILLIAM, museum director; b. Detroit, Feb. 2, 1930; s. Otto William and Vera Wanda (Zeller) W.; m. Patricia Kathryn Dolby, May 28, 1954; children—Douglas William, Kathleen Marie, Cynthia Mae. B.A., Wayne State U., Detroit, 1953, M.Ed., 1960. Curator indsl. history Detroit Hist. Mus., 1955-60; now dir.; dir. Mich. Hist. Mus., Lansing, 1960-66; asst. to pres., assoc. dir. devel. Old Sturbridge (Mass.) Village, 1967-70; dir. hist. dept. City of Detroit; coordinating dir. Detroit Hist. Soc., from 1970; co-chmn. heritage com. Detroit Bicentennial Commn., 1974-76; treas. Detroit Adventure, 1973-84; mem. Detroit Historic Designation Adv. Bd.; trustee Detroit Ednl. TV Found. Mem. Hist. Soc. Mich. (v.p. 1974-76), Midwest Mus. Conf. (v.p. 1966, 71), Mich. Mus. Assn., Am. Assn. Mus., Am. Assn. State and Local History, Nat. Trust Hist. Preservation, Civil War Round Table, Univ. Cultural Center Assn. (treas. 1977, pres. 1984), Gt. Lakes Maritime Inst., Vet. Motor Car Club Am., Assn. Study Afro-Am. Life and History. Clubs: Rotary, Torch, Prismatic, Algonquin. Home: Detroit, Mich. Died Oct. 14, 1984.

WEIDENMILLER, CARL REED, steel product's mfr.; b. Worcester, Mass., Sept. 14, 1889; s. Frank Charles and Inez Francis (Reed) W.; B.S. in Elec. Engring., Worcester Poly. Inst., 1911; m. Inez Christine Goff, June 25, 1938. With Union Switch & Signal div., Westinghouse Air Brake Co., 1911-15; with Washburn Wire Co., from 1915, v.p., 1949-58, dir., mgr. N.Y. div., from 1949, pres., from 1958. Club: New York Athletic. Home: New York, N.Y. †

WEIDHOPF, J. S., business exec.; b. Bklyn., Dec. 21, 1889; s. Oscar and Rose (Seerman) W.; student pub. schs.; m. Louise Bartling, June 30, 1919. Salesman Alfred II. Smith Co., 1907-20; treas., pres. Guy T. Gibson, Inc., N.Y.C., 1921-39; pres. Parfums Ciro, Inc., from 1939. Acting mayor, trustee Saltaire, N.Y. Member Perfume Importers Assn. (treas.), Toilet Goods Assn., Fragrance Found. (1st pres.). Club: Saltaire (N.Y.) Yacht. Home: New York, N.Y. †

WEIDLEIN, EDWARD RAY, ret. chem. engr.; b. Augusta, Kan., July 14, 1887; s. Edward and Nettie (Lemon) W.; B.A., U. Kan., 1909, M.A., 1910; hon. Sc.D., Tufts Coll., 1924; LL.D., U. Pitts., 1930, Washington and Jefferson, 1947; Sc.D. (hon.), Rutgers U., 1937, Waynesburg (Pa.) Coll., 1939, U. Wichita, 1945, Southwestern Coll., 1952, Phila. Coll. Pharmacy and Sci., 1952, U. Miami, 1953; Eng.D., Rennselaer Poly. Inst., 1949; m. Hazel I. Butts, Apr. 24, 1915; children—Edward Ray, Robert Butts, John David. Indsl. fellow, research on camphor U. Kan., 1909-10, research on ductless glands, 1910-12; sr. fellow, Mellon Inst. Indsl. Research, Pitts., charge of investigations on metallurgy and hydrometallurgy of copper, also exptl. plant, Thompson, Nev., 1912-16; asst. dir. Inst. at Pittsburgh, July-Oct. 1916, asso. dir., 1916-21, actg. dir., 1918-19, dir. 1921-51; dir. Mellon Inst., v.p. bd. trustees, 1929-51, pres., 1951-56, chmn., 1951-55, ret., former trustee emeritus; tech. advisor Rubber Research Group, NSF, World War II; past mem. wartime and emergency bds. on materials. Pres. Regional Indsl. Devel. Corp. Fund Southwestern Pa.; exec. com. Pitts. Regional Planning Assn.; exec. com. Allegheny Conf. on Community Devel.; adv. com. Expn. Chem. Industries. Trustee Shadyside Acad. (Pitts.); mem. bd. dirs. Western Pa. Hosp. Mem. Guild Brackett Lecturers, Princeton. Served as chem. expert War Industries Bd., 1918-19. Mem. adv. bd. Salvation Army; mem. at large nat. council nat. council Boy Scouts Am. Fellow A.A.A.S., Am. Inst. Chemists, Royal Soc. Arts (London); mem. nat., state and local profl. and sci. assns. and orgns., past pres. or other officer of several, mem. coop. coms. Recipient awards, State of Pa., 1939; Soc. of Chem. Industry, 1935; Pitts. award for 1939; Jr. C. of C., 1941; U. of Kan., 1943; Naval Ordnance Devel. award, 1947; Priestley medal by Am. Chem. Soc., 1948; Richard Beatty Mellon award, air pollution control, 1956; William Proctor prize, A.A.A.S., 1961; Founder's award Am. Inst. Chem. Engrs., 1966; Edward R. Weiklein professorship in environmental engring. established in his honor, U. Pitts., 1967. Republican. Clubs: Chemists (N.Y., Pitts.); Pittsburgh Faculty, University, Pittsburgh, Authors' of Pittsburgh, Duquesne, Rolling Rock, Pittsburgh Golf, Co-author books and articles chiefly relating to indsl. research. Home: Rector, PA. †

WEIGER, ROBERT WILLIAM, physician; b. Grantwood, N.J., Nov. 23, 1927; s. Joseph Anthony and Helen Marie (Cochrane) W.; B.S., Northwestern U., 1951, M.D., 1955; m. Nadine Luxmore, Oct. 19, 1957; 1 child, Wendy Anne. Intern Passavant Meml. Hosp., Chgo., 1955-56; officer USPHS, 1956-85, med. dir., 1964; clin. assoc. Nat. Cancer Inst., 1956-58; med. clinic physician, Miami, Fla., 1958-59; resident internal medicine USPHS Hosp., Balt., 1959-62; asst. dir. Nat. Cancer Inst., NIH, 1962-65; chief Office of Pesticides USPHS, 1965-66; program coordinator pharmacology and toxicology programs Nat. Inst. of Gen. Medical Scis., Office of Dir., NIH, 1966-85; spl. asst. to dir. Nat. Insts. Health, 1964-85. Spl. research internal medicine, diabetes melitus, tumor proteins. Mem. AMA, Mil Surgeons Assn., Am. Diabetes Assn., Am. Cancer Soc., Am. Diabetes Assn., Am. Pub. Works Assn., Phi Rho Sigma (award 1954). Roman Cath. Author articles in field. Home: Wheaton, Md. Dec. Sept. 7, 1985.

WEIGLE, EDWIN F., war photographer; b. Chicago, Mar. 13, 1889; s. Adolph H. and Sophie H. W.; ed. public schs., Chicago; m. Mrs. Florence (Marshall) Johnson, May 4, 1920. Made motion pictures of American Marines at capture of Vera Cruz, Mexico, Apr. 21 and 22, 1914; spent 3 months with Belgian Army, 1914, returning to U.S. with first European war pictures; was at the front with German-Austrian armies two periods of 7 months and 6 months, respectively; commd. 1st lt. Officers' Reserve Signal Corps, July 1917; assigned to Photographic Div. of Signal Corps as one of 3 officers to organize the photographic div. of U.S. Army; capt., Signal Corps, May 6, 1919; served 10 mos. in France. Spent 3 months, 1920, making motion pictures of Irish revolution. Motion picture corr. Chicago Tribune. Author: My Experiences on Belgian Battlefields, 1914; On Four Battle Fronts with the German Army, 1915, 1916. Home: Deerfield, Ill. †

WEIL, FERDINAND THEOBALD, lawyer; b. Youngstown, O., Apr. 23, 1890; s. A. Leo and Cassie (Ritter) W.; student Shady Side Acad., 1908, Phillips Exeter Acad., 1909; Litt.B., Princeton, 1913; LL.B., U. Pitts., 1916; divorced; children—Andrew L. III, Richard A. (dec.). Admitted Pa. bar, 1916, also U.S. Supreme Ct.; practice in Pitts., from 1919; partner firm Weil, Vatz & Weil, from 1948. Mem. Pitts. Panel Bd. Arbitrators, N.Y. Stock Exchange. Life trustee Nat. Fedn. Temple Brotherhoods, Jewish Family and Children's Service Bur. Served as ensign USNRF, World War I. Mem. Allegheny County Bar Assn., Am. Counsel Assn., Am. Arbitration Assn. (nat. panel). Republican. Jewish religion. Clubs: Pittsburgh Athletic, Harvard-Yale-Princeton, Circus Saints and Sinners (sec. Humpty Tent), Pittsburgh Playhouse (a founder) (Pitts.); Westmoreland Country (Export, Pa.). Home: Pittsburgh, PA. †

WEILL, HAROLD, lawyer; b. N.Y.C., Apr. 30, 1908; s. Isaac and Fannie (Fogler) W.; m. Lisbeth Goldmann, June 29, 1934; children—Patricia Rosenthal, Judith (Mrs. Louis Levy), Victoria. Student, Columbia, 1927-31; LL.D. (hon.), Beaver Coll. Bar: N.Y. bar 1932, also D.C. bar 1932, U.S. Circuit Ct. of Appeals, Washington, D.C 1932, U.S. Supreme Ct 1932. Practice in, N.Y.C., 1932-81; ptnr. firm Leon, Weill & Mahony, 1932-81; dir., mem. exec. com. Helena Rubinstein, Inc., 1955-73; pres., dir. Brit. Controlled Oil Fields, Inc., 1959-70; treas., dir. World Vets. Fund, 1957-70; dir. London and N.Y. Investments (S.A.), Ansbacher & Co. Ltd., Dublin, Ireland. Chmn. bd. Childrens Blood Found.; bd. govs., chmn. sub-com. on obstetrics, gynecology and pediatrics, mem. subcoms. on finances, fund raising, investment com., ops. com. Soc. N.Y. Hosp.; bd. govs. Weizmann Inst. Sci.; pres., bd. dirs. Talisman Found., Helena Rubinstein Found.; trustee Palm Springs Desert Mus. Decorated Chevalier Order Legion of Honor, Ordre Nat. du Mérite France).; Harold Weill Children's Blood Found. clinic, N.Y. Hosp.-Cornell Med. Center named in his honor, 1975; hon. fellow Weizmann Inst. Sci., 1972; Harold Weill medal awarded annually in his honor N.Y. U. Sch. Law. Mem. Am., Fed. bar assns., N.Y. County Lawyers Assn., Am. Soc. Internat. Law. Clubs: Hillcrest Country (Calif.); City Athletic (N.Y.C.), Town Tennis Mem. (N.Y.C.). Home: New York, N.Y.

WEIN, SAMUEL, chemist, inventor; b. Lemberg, Austria, May 1, 1888; s. Moses and Sophie Rose (Boritz) W.; brought to U.S., 1896; student Columbia, 1913; m. Esther Burger, July 30, 1917. Formerly editor Perfumery Art; asso. editor Color Trade Jour. Discovered method of producing light aluminum alloy; method of recording sound by photography; method of producing plastic images in copper and other metals by photography; process of lithography in which copper plates are used; a new method of producing red glass; etc. Wrote: (brochures) Selenium Cells and How They Are Made; Modern Photographic Developers; Organic Photographic Developers; also many articles on chemistry and photo-physics. Home: New York, N.Y. †

WEINBERG, JACK, psychiatrist; b. Kiev, Russia, Jan. 18, 1910; came to U.S., 1924, naturalized, 1937; s. Morris M. and Gunia (Geichman) W.; m. Ruth S. Skidelsky, Aug. 14, 1935; 1 son, Daniel R. B.S., U. Ill., 1934, M.D., 1936. Diplomate: Am. Bd. Psychiatry and Neurology. Intern St. Elizabeth's Hosp., Chgo., 1926-27; resident in psychiatry U. Ill. Med. Sch. and Hosps., 1938-39, Chgo. Inst. Psychoanalysis, 1941-43; asso. dir. residency tng. program Michael Reese Hosp. and Med. Center, Chgo., 1946-50; practice medicine, specializing in psychiatry, Chgo., 1950-64; clin. dir. Ill. State Psychiat. Inst., 1964-75, dir., from 1975; adminstr. Ill. Mental Insts., from 1975; prof. psychiatry Abraham Lincoln Sch. Medicine, U. Ill., Chgo., 1962—, Rush Med. Coll., Chgo., from 1972; vis. prof. Gerontology Inst., U. So. Calif., from 1969; lectr. Indsl. Relations Center, U. Chgo., from 1955; sr. attending psychiatrist Psychosomatic and Psychiat. Inst., Michael Reese Hosp. and Med. Center, from 1955; Disting. sr. scholar Center for Study of Mental Health of the Aging, NIMH, 1978; cons. in field; mem. numerous coms. on aging and elderly. Contbr. chpts. to books, articles to med. jour. Bd. dir. Council Jewish Elderly, Chgo., from 1971, Jewish Family and Community Services, from 1969. Served to maj. M.C. USAF, 1943-46. Life fellow Am. Psychiat. Assn. (pres. 1977-78), Ill. Psychiat. Soc.; mem. Am. Gerontol. Soc. (Donald P. Kent award 71974), Am. Geriatric Soc. (Edward B. Allen award 1970), AMA, Group Advancement of Psychiatry (pres.-elect from 1979), AAAS. Jewish. Home: Glencoe, Ill.

WEINSTEIN, BORIS, organic chemist; b. New Orleans, Mar. 31, 1930; s. Israel and Norma Rebecca (Levy) W.; m. Barbara Joan LeVine, Aug. 16, 1953; children: William Stephen, Michael Simon. B.S., La. State U., 1951; M.S., Purdue U., 1953; Ph.D., Ohio State U., 1959; postgrad. (Univ. fellow), U. Calif., Berkeley, 1959-60. Chemist Stanford Research Inst., Menlo Park, Calif., 1960-61; lab. dir. chemistry Stanford U., 1961-67; asso. prof. chemistry U. Wash., 1967-74, prof., 1974—. Editor: Peptides: Chemistry and Biochemistry, 1970, Chemistry and Biochemistry of Amino Acids, Peptides, and Proteins, vols. 1-6, 1971—; editor: Organic Reactions, 1973—, sec., 1973—. Served to 1st lt. USAF, 1953-55. Mem. AAAS, AAUP, Am. Chem. Soc., Am. Inst. Chemists, Am. Soc. Neurochemistry, Chem. Soc., N.Y. Acad. Scis., Phytochem. Soc. N.Am. Home: Seattle, Wash. Dec. June 29, 1983.

WEINSTOCK, MAX E., clothing mfr.; b. Miawa, Poland, June 1, 1888; s. Harry and Gittel W.; brought to U.S., 1892; student pub. schs., Chgo.; m. Goldie Goodman, June 20, 1916; children—David R., Gertrude (Mrs. David E. Schoch). Messenger boy Am. Dist. Telegraph Co., Chgo.; errand boy, office boy, clk. S. Siegel & Bros., Chgo., 1904; co-founder Rothmoor Corp., Chgo., 1921, chmn., dir. Mem. Nat. Coat and Suit Industry Recovery Bd., 1935, also chmn. Trustee retirement fund Chgo. joint bd. Internat. Ladies Garment Workers Union. Mason. Clubs: Standard, Bryn Mawr (Chgo.). Home: Chicago, IL. †

WEINTRAUB, SIDNEY, educator; b. N.Y.C., Apr. 28, 1914; s. Aaron and Martha (Fisch) W.; student London Sch. Economics, 1938-39; Ph.D., N.Y.U., 1941; m. Sheila E. Tarlow, Aug. 25, 1940; children—Eliot Roy, Arthur Neil. Research staff inst. Internat. Finance, 1935-37; instr. St. John's U., Bklyn., 1939-41, prof. econs., 1948; economist U.S. Treasury Dept., 1942; vis. prof. grad. faculty New Sch. Social Research, 1950, 58, U. Minn., summer 1959; professor econs. U. Pa., 1950-83, chmn. adminstrn. com. gen. econs., 1959-61, 64-65, chmn. econs. dept., 1960-61. Faculty Research fellowship, Ford Found., 1956-57; cons. U.S. Forest Service, 1957-58; Nat. Council Applied Econ. Research, India, 1964, Fed. Power Commn., 1965-83, Fed. Communications Commn., 1966-83. Mem. American Econ. Association. Econometric Society, Royal Econ. Society, American Assn. U. Profs., Mark Twain Society, Beta Gamma Sigma. Author: Price Theory, 1949; Income and Employment Analysis, 1951; Theory of Income Distribution, 1958; Forest Service Appraisal and Price Policies, 1958; A General Theory of the Price Level Output, Income Distribution and Growth, 1959; Classical Keynesianism Monetary Theory, and the Price Level, 1960; Wage Theory and Policy, 1963; Intermediate Price Theory, 1964, Growth Without Inflation in India, 1965; A Kenyesian Theory of Employment Growth and Income Distribution, 1966. Contbr. profl. jours. Home: Drexel Hill, Pa. Died June 19, 1983.

WEIR, MILTON NELSON, banker; b. Johnson City, N.Y., Sept. 7, 1899; s. John Lewis and Lida Jane (Russell) W.; student Colgate U., 1918-19; m. Mildred Lydia Young, Oct. 29, 1921; children—Milton Nelson, John H., William M. Partner constrn. firm, homes and comml. structures, 1920-33, devel. West Side Airlines Terminal, N.Y.C.; organized N.Y. real estate dept. Gulf Oil Corp., 1933, various positions, 1933-48, asst. to v.p., 1945-48, pres. subsidiary corp., 1944-48; founder, chmn. Delray Beach Nat. Bank; pres., chmn., founder, dir. Boca Raton Nat. Bank; founder, dir. Fidelity Nat. Bank of Lauderdale; chmn. Security Exchange Bank, W. Palm Beach, Fla., Pompano Investers, Inc., South-Beach Devel. Co., Weir Mgmt. Co., Weir Realty Co., Weir & Sons of Fla., Inc., Weir-Plaza Co., Weir Enterprises, Inc.; chmn., dir. Castleton Industries, Inc.; dir. Ft. Lauderdale. Clubs: Metropolitan, Bankers, Wings (N.Y.C.); The Miami (Fla.). Died Oct. 17, 1981.

WEIR, WALTER C., Canadian provincial ofcl.; b. High Bluff, Man., Can., Jan. 7, 1929; s. James Dixon and Christina Maude (Cox-Smith) W.; student pub. schs., Portage la Prairie, Man.; m. Harriet Thompson, Nov. 3, 1951; children—Leslie, John, Pat, Cameron. Funeral dir. Minnedosa, Man., 1953-63; minister of municipal affairs Province of Man., 1961-62, acting minister pub. works, 1962, minister pub. works, 1962-63, minister hwys. and pub. works, 1965-67, premier, 1967-69, pres. of council, minister fed. provincial relations, 1967-69; leader Man. Progressive Conservative Party, 1967-85; Chmn. Town Planning Commn., Minnedosa, Minnedosa Dist. Hosp. Assn., 1954-56. Dep. mayor Minnedosa Town Council, 1958-59. Mem. Minnedosa C. of C., Canadian, Man. funeral dirs. assns. Elk, Odd Fellow. Club: Minnedosa, Kinsmen's. Home: Winnipeg, Manitoba, Canada. Died Apr. 17, 1985.

WEISS, MILTON, savings and loan association executive, lawyer; b. Bklyn., Feb. 7, 1913; s Jeremiah A. and Rose (Sayetta) W.; LL.B., U. Miami (Fla.), 1935; m. Cecile Alexander, June 8, 1941; children—Kay Esta (Mrs. Neil Harris), Alexa Sara (Mrs. William E. Shockett). Admitted to Fla. bar, 1935; ptnr. firm Meyer, Weiss, Rose Arkin, Sheppard & Shockett, P.A., and predecessor, Miami Beach, Fla., after 1937; pres. Miami Beach Fed. Savs. & Loan Assn. (name changed to Fin. Fed. Savs. and Loan Assn.), after 1964; dir. City Nat. Bank Miami Beach, 1949-57, City Nat. Bank Miami, 1950-57. An organizer Miami Beach Jr. C. of C., 1935; mem. Dade County Sch. Bd., 1940-53, chmn., 1947-49; campaign chmn. Dade County Combined Jewish Appeal, 1967; pres. Greater Miami Jewish Fedn., after 1969. Organizer, 1st pres., sustaining bd. fellow Mt. Sinai Hosp., Miami Beach, 1965, trustee 1968—; trustee Miami U., 1971—. Recipient Silver medallion award Nat. Conf. Christians and Jews; elected to Wisdom Hall Fame, 1970. Mem. Fla. State Bar., Dade County, Miami Beach bar assns., C. of C. Miami Beach (past bd. dirs.). Jewish religion. Kiwanian (past pres. Miami Beach), Elk (past exalted ruler Miami Beach), Mason; mem. B'nai B'rith. Author article. Home: Miami Beach, Fla. Dec. Dec. 27, 1981.

WEITZMAN, ELLIOT DAVID, neurologist; b. Newark, Feb. 4, 1929. B.A. cum laude, U. Iowa, 1950; M.D., U. Chgo., 1955. Intern Kings County Hosp., Bklyn., 1955-56; resident in neurology Presbyn. Hosp., N.Y.C., 1956-58; asst. in neurology Columbia U., 1958-59; assoc. in neurology Albert Einstein Coll. Medicine, N.Y.C., 1961-63, asst. prof. neurology, 1963-68, asso. prof., 1968-69, prof., 1969-83, chief dept. neurology Montefiore Hosp. and Med. Center, 1969-83; dir. Montefiore Hosp. and Med. Center (Sleep-Wake Disorders Center), 1976—; chmn. dept. neurology Montefiore div. Albert Einstein Coll. Medicine, 1971-83, prof. neurosci., 1974; vis. prof. neurology and psychiatry Stanford (Calif.) U. Sch. Medicine, 1974-75; Adv. bd. Am. Naval Com., 1975, Am. Naval Com. (Brain Info. Service), 1977-83. Editor: series Advances in Sleep Research; Editorial bd.: series Jour. Sleep, 1978—; Contbr. articles to med. jours., chpts. to books. Served with M.C. U.S. Army, 1959-61. USPHS grantee, 1961-81; NASA grantee, 1968; Office Naval Research grantee, 1976-77. Mem. Am. Neurol. Assn., Am. Assn. Univ. Profs. Neurology, Am. Acad. Neurology, Soc. Neurosci., AAAS, Assn. Research in Nervous and Mental Diseases, N.Y. Acad. Sci., Assn. Psychophysiol. Study of Sleep (exec. council 1964-69), N.Y. Neurol. Soc. (pres. 1972-73), Internat. Soc. Chronobiology, Nat. Found. Sudden Infant Death, Assn. Sleep Disorders Clinics (v.p. 1975-80), Pan Am. Med. Assn. (chmn. N.Am. sect. on neurology). Home: New Rochelle, N.Y. Dec. June 13, 1983.

WELCH, JAMES OVERMAN, food company executive; b. Hertford, N.C., Aug. 26, 1905; s. Robert H.W. and Lina (James) W.; student U. N.C., 1921-23; m. Vedna Bate, Oct. 1, 1926; children—James Overman, Deborah (Mrs. Eugene Johnson III). Pres. James O. Welch Co., 1927-63; v.p. Nat. Biscuit Co., pres. James O. Welch div., 1964-65; dir. Harvard Trust Co., H.A. Johnson Co., Nat. Biscuit Co., Felters Co.; trustee Cambridgeport Savs. Bank. Trustee Lesley Coll., Cambridge, Boston Mus. Sci. Clubs: Algonquin (Boston); Country (Brookline); Eastern Point Yacht (Gloucester, Mass.). Home: Delray Beach, Fla. Died Jan. 29, 1985.

WELCH, JOHN DAVID, cons. civil engr.; b. Madison, Wis., Dec. 13, 1924; s. John Douglas and Lillian M.A. (Gascoigne) W.; m. Jacqueline Watson, Dec. 6, 1975; children by former marriage—John David, Vicki Leigh, Jeffrey Dalton, Leslie Carolyn, James Daniel. B.S. in Civil Engring, U. Wis., 1947; M.S. in Engring, Princeton U., 1949. Licensed profl. engr., D.C., Md., N.J., N.Y., W.Va. Chief soils engr., cons. engr. Howard, Needles, Tammen & Bergendoff, N.Y.C., 1949-60; partner Welch & Malinofsky, Summit, N.J., 1960-67; pres. Eastern Exploration Corp., Summit, 1967-69; prin. Welch & Assos., Summit, 1967-69; partner Joseph S. Ward & Assos., Caldwell, N.J., 1969-72, partner-in-charge, Washington, 1973-76, mktg. devel. cons., pvt. practice geotech. engring., Rockville, Md., 1976-78; v.p. NFS/Nat. Soil Services Inc., Rockville, Md., 1978-79; dir. mktg. Johnson, McCordic & Thompson (P.A.), 1979-80; exec. v.p. McLeod Ferrara Ensign (Architects and Engrs.), from 1980. Contbr. articles on soil mechanics to profl. jours. Mem. Bernards Twp. (N.J.) Planning Bd., 1958-60; vestryman St. Marks Ch., Basking Ridge, N.J., 1962-65, mem. bldg. com., 1966-69; bd. dirs. Somerset Hills (N.J.) YMCA, 1964-70. Served as ensign USN, World War II. Fellow Am. Cons. Engrs. Council (dir. 1971-73); mem. ASCE, Internat. Soc. Soil Mechanics and Found. Engring., Soc. for Mktg. Profl. Services, Cons. Engrs. Council N.J. (pres. 1969-70), Cons. Engrs. Council Met. Washington, Sigma Xi. Home: Rockville, MD.

WELCH, ROBERT, publisher, orgn. exec.; b. Chowan County, N.C., Dec. 1, 1899; s. Robert H. W. and Lina (James) W.; m. Marian Lucile Probert, Dec. 2, 1922; children—Robert III, Hillard Walmer. A.B., U. N.C., 1916; student, U.S. Naval Acad., 1917-19, Harvard Law Sch., 1919-21. Engaged in candy mfg., 1922-56; pres. Robert Welch, Inc. (publishers), 1956-85; founder, pres. John Birch Soc., 1958-83; Mem. adv. com. candy mfg. bus. OPA, World War II. Author: The Road to Salesmanship, 1941, May God Forgive Us, 1952, The Life of John Birch, 1954, Blue Book of the John Birch Society, 1958, The Politician, 1963, The New Americanism, 1966, The Romance of Education, 1973; Editor: Am. Opinion, 1956—. Mem. Belmont (Mass.) Sch. Com., 1952-55; Candidate for Republican nomination for lt. gov. Mass., 1950. Recipient Candy Industry Man of Year award, 1947. Mem. Nat. Confectioners Assn. (dir. 1945- 49, v.p. 1946-47, chmn. Washington com. 1947-49), United Prison Assn. (dir. 1945-53, treas. 1949), N.A.M. (dir. 1951-57, exec. com. 1953-54, 57, chmn. ednl. adv. com. 1953-54, regional v.p. 1955-57). Clubs: Oakley Country (Boston), Harvard (Boston); Harvard (N.Y.C.); Union League (Chgo.). Home: Belmont, Mass. Died Jan. 6, 1985.

WELCH, VINCENT BOGAN, lawyer; b. Portland, Maine, Oct. 3, 1917; s. Arthur Deehan and Jane Agnes (Bogan) W.; m. Barbara Gross, Nov. 15, 1941. B.A., Bowdoin Coll., 1938, LL.D., 1975; J.D., Harvard, 1941. Bar: Maine bar 1941, D.C. bar 1946. Atty. FCC, Washington, 1941-42; sr. partner firm Welch & Morgan, Washington, 1946-77; partner Capital City Oil Co., Washington, 1949-84, Dulles Indsl. Center (real estate), Loudoun County, Va., 1969-77; chmn. bd. Conti-Urban TV Corp., San Jose, Calif., 1964-80, Warrangal Pty. Ltd. (real estate), Sydney, Australia, 1969—; chmn. bd., pres. Linda-Pont Corp. (restaurants), Washington, 1966-77; mng. partner Holomua Holdings (real estate), Maui, Hawaii, 1973-84, Te Awanui Holdings (real estate), Tauranga, N.Z., 1973-84, Rica Cosecha Holdings (real estate), Benidorm, Spain, 1974-84; v.p. Rich Hill Corp. (real estate), West Bath, Maine, 1973-76; chmn. bd., treas. Des Indes Corp. (internat. investments), Washington, 1975-76; mng. partner Pine Tree Holdings (real estate), Maine, 1975-84; owner J&P Advt. Agy., Portland, 1977-80, Welch Enterprises, Portland, 1977-84. Mem. NCCJ, 1955-72; v.p. Ravenwood Citizens Assn., Falls Church, Va., 1954; mem. Fairfax (Va.) Hosp. Assn., 1958-77, Muscular Dystrophy Assn., Washington, 1958-60, Legal Aid Bur., 1954-60; mem. campaign steering com. Portland Public Library, 1978, Portland Mus. Art, 1980-84; corporator, mem. devel. com., ann. fund com., trustee Maine Med. Center, Portland, 1978-84; Trustee Bowdoin Coll., Brunswick, Maine, 1972-80, North Yarmouth Acad., Yarmouth, Maine, 1980-84; bd. dirs. Washington Chpt. Epilepsy Found. Am., 1973-74.

Served to lt. (s.g.) USNR, 1942-45; lt. col. USAF Res.; ret. Fellow Am. Bar Found.; mem. Am. Legion, AMVETS (comdr. Washington 1948), Harvard Law Sch. Alumni Assn., ABA (ho. dels. 1955), D.C. Bar Assn., Fed. Communications Bar Assn. (pres. 1954), bar assns), Nat. Conf. Bar Presidents, Portland C. of C., Portland Com. on Fgn. Relations, Portland Soc. Art. Clubs: Cumberland (Portland, Me.); University (Washington). Home: Raymond, Maine. Died Dec. 3, 1984.

WELCH, WILLIAM, corp. ofcl.; b. Fine, N.Y., Sept. 22, 1887; s. William and Katie (McDonald) W.; student pub. schs., Watertown, N.Y.; m. Loretta Burns, Feb. 23, 1914. Sales rubber reclaiming div. Goodyear Tire & Rubber Co., Akron, O., 1916-23; organizer Akron Rubber Reclaiming Co., 1923, became Midwest Rubber Reclaiming Co., 1928, pres., 1928-52, now chmn.; dir. Security Nat. Bank, St. Louis, 1940-50. Mem. Rubber Reclaimers Assn. Am. (pres. 1946-47), Am. Chem. Soc. Clubs: Noonday, Missouri Athletic (St. Louis). †

WELCHER, AMY OGDEN, pres. United Council Church Women; b. Pleasantville, N.Y., Mar. 24, 1887; d. Manfred Philester and Fanny Falconer (Avery) W.; ed. Packer Collegiate Inst.; unmarried. Began career as com. mem. and club leader in church and Y.W.C.A., 1910; pres. Hartford, Conn., Y.W.C.A., 1922-25; mem. Am. Bd. Fgn. Missions deputation to India and Ceylon, 1925-26; pres. Council Congregational Women of Conn., 1928-31; chmn. Northfield (Mass.) Missionary Conf., 1935-37; member Prudential com., A.B.C.F.M., Boston, 1932-41; pres. United Council of Church Women, 1941-44; vice pres. United Council of Church Women, 1944-46. Trustee Fukien Christian U., Yenching U., United Bds. of Christian Colls. of China; mem. Archeol. Inst. America (life), Mus. Nat. Hist., (in perpetuity) Met. Mus. of Art, Soc. Mayflower Descendants in Conn. Conglist. Clubs: Town and Country (Hartford); Vergennes (Vt.) Country; National Arts (New York). Home: Hartford, Conn. †

WELKER, GEORGE ERNEST, natural gas engr.; b. Oil City, Pa., Oct. 24, 1888; s. George A. and Jennie R. (Ellsworth) W.; prep. edn., Mich. Mil. Acad., Orchard Lake; B.S., in C.E., Clarkson Coll. Tech., Potsdam, N.Y., 1909; B.S. in Mining Engring., Mich. Coll. Mines, 1910, E.M., 1910; m. Josephine Wilson Powell, July 14, 1917; children—George Wilson (dec.), Mary Joan. Civ. engr. and geologist, United Fuel Gas Co., Charleston, W.Va., 1910-12; chief engr. and geologist, Iroquois Natural Gas Corp., Buffalo, N.Y., 1912-17; with United Natural Gas Co. and affiliated companies, Oil City, Pa., from 1918, chief civil engr. and geologist, 1918-24; also cons. engr. for affiliated cos. from 1918; vice-pres. and cons. engr., United Natural Gas Co., Mars Co., 1924-27, president both companies; president Ridgway Natural Gas Co., St. Mary's Natural Gas Co., The Sylvania Corp., Smethport Natural Gas Co., Mercer County Gas Co.; dir. National Fuel Gas Co., 1927-50, engineering consultant, from 1950; natural gas consultant and asso. Management Counselors, Inc., N.Y.C. Director of Oil City Y.M.C.A. Member advisory com. (past chmn. and departmental v.p.) natural gas dept., Am. Gas Assn.; mem. Pa. Natural Gas Men's Assn. (twice pres.), Oil City Chamber Commerce (ex-councillor), Theta Tau, Tau Beta Pi, Omicron Pi Omicron. Republican. Presbyterian. Clubs: Rotary (past president), Wanango Country; Shorewood Country (Dunkirk, N.Y.). He has acted as consulting engineer in many proceedings before courts and regulatory commissions in U.S. and Can. Addresss: Oil City, Pa. †

WELLMAN, RITA (MRS. EDGAR F. LEO), author; b. Washington, D.C., Dec. 2, 1890; d. Walter and Laura (McCann) W.; father newspaper man, airman, and explorer; ed. pub. schs., Washington, D.C., and Pa. Acad. Fine Arts, Phila.; m. Edgar F. Leo, 1910; 1 dau., Meta Leo. Mem. Soc. Am. Dramatists and Composers. Author: The Gentile Wife (play), 1919; The Wings of Desire (novel), 1919; The House of Hate, 1924. Translator: My War Diary (Benito Mussolini), 1925; also six one-act plays. Home: New York, N.Y. †

WELLS, HARRY LUMM, former univ. ofcl.; b. Coshocton, O., June 23, 1889; s. Charles Howard and Fannie T. (Lumm) W.; B.S., Northwestern U., 1913, LL.D., 1960; LL.D., Lawrence Coll., 1949; D.Litt., Rockford Coll., 1958; m. Viola E. Shearer, Oct. 6, 1915; children—David Howard, Richard Grant, Virginia Ruth, Harry Shearer. Mfg. exec. B. Kuppenheimer & Co., clothing mfr., 1915-16; operating exec., Hart Schaffner & Marx, clothing mfrs., 1917-29, on leave 1917-18 as asst. and acting chief Uniform div. U.S. Army; v.p., gen. mgr. Bauer & Black div. Kendall Co., 1929-34; became bus. mgr. Northwestern U., 1934, v.p. bus. mgr., 1937, trustee, 1932-34; hon. chmn. John Evans Club, Northwestern U., from 1964. Trustee H. R. Kendall Estate; chmn. bd. Wells Badger Corp. Milw.; dir. Hart Schaffner & Marx, Washington Nat. Ins. Co. Former mem. Northeastern Ill. Met. Governmantal Services Commn.; mem. bd. Evanston (Ill.) Devel. Corp. Mem. Delta Sigma Rho, Alpha Delta Phi, Deru, Beta Gamma Sigma. Protestant. Club: University. Author: Higher Education is Serious Business. Home: Evanston, IL. †

WELLS, WESLEY RAYMOND, univ. prof.; b. Bakersfield, Vt., June 20, 1890; s. Lucian Lemuel and Katherine Elizabeth (Learned) W.; grad. Brigham Acad., Bakersfield, 1907; Ph.B., U. of Vt., 1913; A.M., Harvard, 1914, Ph.D., 1917; m. Flora Seraphine Monroe, June 24, 1922; 1 son, Roger Willis. Asst. in philosophy, Harvard, 1916-17; instr. in edn., Washington U., 1917-19; asst. prof. philosophy and psychology, Colby Coll., Waterville, Me., 1919-21; prof. philosophy and psychology, Lake Forest Coll., 1921-27, acting dean, 1922-25, dean, 1925-26; prof. of psychology, Syracuse University, 1927-56, professor emeritus, from 1956; lecturer on education, Trinity Coll. (now Duke U.), N.C., summer 1919; instr. in psychology, U. of Wyo., summer 1923. Fellow A.A.A.S., Am. Psychol. Assn.; mem. Soc. Clin. and Exptl. Hypnosis, British Soc. Med. Hypnotists (hon.), S.A.R., N.Y. State Psychol. Assn., Am. Philos. Assn., Am. Assn. University Professors, Phi Beta Kappa, Sigma Xi, Kappa Sigma. Author of numerous articles in psychol. and philos. jours. Home: Moravia, N.Y. †

WELLS, WILLIAM FIRTH, biologist, sanitarian; b. Boston, Mass., Aug. 25, 1887; s. Obadiah Firth and Helen Marian (Deeds) W.; grad. Phillips Exeter Acad., 1905; B.Sc. in Biology and Pub. Health, Mass. Inst. Tech., 1910; m. Mildred Washington Weeks, Apr. 9, 1917; 1 son, William Firth. With Mass. and Conn. State bds. of health, also pub. health labs. of N.D., and Washington, D.C., filtration plant, 1910-12; with U. of Ill., 1912-13, U.S. P.H.S., 1913-17; apptd. to U.S. Bur. Fisheries, 1917; biologist and sanitarian, N.Y. State Conservation Commn., 1919-29; leave of absence with North Atlantic Oyster Farms, 1927-29; instr. in sanitary science, Harvard, 1930-37; asst. prof. sanitary engring., U. of Pa. Med. Sch., 1937-39, asso. prof. research in air-borne infection from 1939; consultant to Veteran's Adminstrn. on air-borne infection. Enlisted in U.S. Army, 1917; commd. 1st lt. San. Corps, 79th Div., Camp Meade, Md.; capt., May 24, 1918, 301st Water Tank Train; served in France; hon. disch., Aug. 12, 1919; major San. Corps Res. to 1930. Episcopalian. Mason. Developed Chlorination method of purifying oysters; first to propagate oyster artificially, quahaug, soft clam, scallop and mussel from egg. Invented air centrifuge for bacteriol. air analysis; demonstrated air-borne infection by droplet nuclei as vehicles of respired contagion, and control of epidemic spread of contagion by increasing sanitary ventilation through means of radiant disinfection of air with ultra-violet light.†

WELSH, HARRY LAMBERT, physicist; b. Aurora, Ont., Can., Mar. 23, 1910; s. Israel and Harriet Maria (Collingwood) W.; B.A., U. Toronto (Ont.), 1930, M.A., 1931, Ph.D., 1936; postgrad. U. Goettingen (Germany), 1931-33; D.Sc. (hon.), U. Windsor, 1964, Meml. U., 1968; m. Marguerite Hazel Ostrander, June 13, 1942. Demonstrator, U. Toronto, 1936-42, asst. prof. physics, 1942-48, asso. prof., 1948-54, prof., 1954-78, prof. emeritus, 1978-84, chmn. research bd., 1971-73. Served to lt. comdr. Royal Can. Naval Vol. Res., 1943-45. Decorated officer Order Can. Fellow Royal Soc. Can. (Tory medal 1963), Royal Soc. London, Am. Phys. Soc., Optical Soc. Am. (Meggers medal 1974); mem. Can. Assn. Physicists (medal 1965, pres. 1973-74). Liberal. Contbr. articles on molecular spectroscopy, physics of high pressure gases, intermolecular forces and other topics to profl. publs. Home: Willowdale, Ont., Can. Died July 23, 1984.

WELT, MRS. JOSEPH M. (MILDRED GOLDSMITH WELT), orgn. executive; b. Ligonier, Ind., July 21, 1889; d. Abraham and Theresa (Straus) Goldsmith; ed. pub. schs. of Ligonier, Ind., Liggett Sch., Detroit, Mich.; m. Joseph M. Welt, June 24, 1913; children—Louis A., Josephine (Mrs. John A. Sills). Served as 1st pres. Detroit sect., Nat. Council Jewish Women, Inc., 1925-28, nat. vice pres., 1931-43, nat. pres. from 1943; 1st pres. League of Jewish Women's Orgns. 1926-28; vice pres. Jewish Community Center of Detroit, 1941-44, Visiting Nurse Assn. of Detroit, 1940-44; mem. bd. dirs. Jewish Welfare Fed. of Detroit; chmn. women's drive of Allied Jewish Campaign; chmn. tribute com. Detroit Community Fund (mem. other coms.); hon. pres. United Service for New Americans, hon. vice pres. Jewish Pub. Soc. of Am., hon. chmn. United Jewish Appeal; nat. dir. Am. Jewish Joint Distrbn. Com.; mem. bd. Nat. Jewish Welfare Fund; mem. bd. sponsors of Albert Einstein Foundation for Higher Learning; dir. Am. Cancer Soc.; trustee Nat. Conf. on Family Life. Home: Detroit, Mich. †

WELTNER, PHILIP, univ. pres.; b. N.Y. City, July 18, 1887; s. Rev. C. E. and Augusta (Ruprecht) W.; A.B., U. of Ga., 1907; LL.B., Columbia, 1910; LL.D., Oglethorpe U., Atlanta, Ga., 1933; m. Sally Cobb Hull, Sept. 3, 1913; children—Callender Hull, Philip, May Pope, Marion Augusta, Charles Longstreet. Admitted to Ga. bar, 1910. Pres. Oglethorpe University, 1944-53. Regent at large, Univ. System of Ga., 1932-33, chancellor, 1933-35. Regional atty. Office of Price Administration. Member Phi Delta Phi, Phi Beta Kappa. Democrat. Presbyterian. Mason. Home: Ga. Died Sept. 5, 1981.

WEN, CHIN YUNG, educator; b. Shintzu, Taiwan, Dec. 5, 1928; came to U.S., 1951; s. Chi and Yueh Eh (Yu) W.; m. Amy Kuo; children—Emily, Edward, Pauline. B.S., Nat. Taiwan U., 1951; M.S. in Chem. Engring, W.Va. U., 1954, Ph.D., 1956. Mem. faculty W.Va. U., Morgantown, 1954-82, prof. chem. engring., 1964-82, chmn. dept., 1969-81, Claude Worthington Benedum prof., 1980-82; Indsl. and govt. cons. and advisor. Author books and chpts. on coal conversion tech., fluidization, chem. reaction engring., pneumatic transport and reactor flow models.; Editor: series Energy Technology and Science, Addison-Wesley Pub. Co.; Contbr. articles to profl. jours. Grantee NSF; Grantee HEW; Grantee Dept. of Energy; Grantee EPA; Grantee NASA; Grantee others; ALCOA Found. awards, 1977-79. Fellow Am. Inst. Chem. Engrs.; mem. Am. Chem. Soc., Am. Soc. Engring. Edn., Chem. Engring. Soc. Japan, Chinese Inst. Chem. Engrs., Sigma Xi, Phi Lambda Upsilon, Omega Chi Epsilon. Home: Morgantown, W. Va. Dec. May 8, 1982.

WENDT, EDGAR FORSYTH, mfr., b. Buffalo, N.Y., Nov. 6, 1888; s. Henry W. and Edith M. (Forsyth) W.; M.E., Cornell U., 1911; m. Florence E. Brigham; children—Susanne B. (Mrs. George B. Kellogg), Phyllis E. (Mrs. Frederick S. Pierce). Factory and sales engineering Buffalo Forge Company, 1911-14; factory manager of the Buffalo Steam Pump Company, North Tonawanda, N.Y., 1914-17; sales mgr., sugar div., Buffalo Forge Co., 1917 to 1934, asst. to pres. and treas., 1924-29, pres., treas., dir. Buffalo Forge Co., 1929-59, dir., pres. Buffalo Pumps, Inc.; v.p., treas. Canadian Blower and Forge Co., Kitchener, Can.; vice pres. Aerofin Corp., Syracuse, New York. Trustee Joint Charity and Community Fund. Director Buffalo Philharmonic Society. Member American Society H. & V.E., M.E., Am. Soc. Naval Architects, Newcomen Soc. Clubs: Buffalo (N.Y.) Buffalo Country.†

WENDT, KURT FRANK, educator; b. Milw., Jan. 5, 1906; s. Frank J. and Maria (Wendt) W.; m. Adelaide Roma Jandre, Aug. 24, 1927; children—Jerome David, Richard Kurt, Franklin Jule. B.C.E., U. Wis., 1927, grad. student, 1927-29; D.Sc. (hon.), W. Va. Inst. Tech., 1964. Registered profl. engr. Instr. mechanics U. Wis., 1927-36, asst. prof., 1936-41, assoc. prof., 1941-46, prof., 1946-71, assoc. dir. engring. expt. sta., 1948-53; dean U. Wis. (Coll. Engring.), 1953-71, spl. asst. to chancellor, 1971-78; cons. U.S. Forest Products Lab., 1941-56, NSF, 1951-56, 59-61; exec. com. engring. and indsl. research NRC, 1961-63. Contbr. articles to profl. publs. Pres. Univ. Park Corp., 1967-82; bd. dirs. Wis. Tchrs. Retirement System, 1970-76; mem. Wis. Investment Bd., 1971-79; Mem. Nat. Transp. Research Bd.; chmn. Wis. Registration Bd. Architects and Profl. Engrs., 1953-71; bd. dirs. Midwest Univs. Consortium for Internat. Activities, 1969-75; chmn. Engineering Coll. Research Council, 1958-60; pres. Assn. NROTC Colls. and Univs., 1958-60; Pres. Madison United Community Chest, 1969-70. Recipient medal Soc. Am. Mil. Engrs., 1959; Engr. of Year award Engrs. Soc. Milw., 1962; Cons. Engrs. Council award outstanding contbrn. engring. profession field edn., 1964; Roy W. Crum award distinguished service Hwy. Research Bd., 1965; Distinguished Service award Wis. Utilities Assn., 1966; Golden Plate award Am. Acad. Achievement, 1966; Distinguished Service award U. Wis. Alumni Assn., 1971; Distinguished Service citation Coll. Engring., U. Wis., 1971; Benjamin S. Reynolds award excellence in teaching U. Wis., 1971; Wason research medal Am. Concrete Inst., 1976. Mem. Am. Soc. Testing Materials, Nat. Soc. Profl. Engrs. (nat. bd. ethical rev.), Wis. Soc. Profl. Engrs., Soc. Exptl. Stress Analysis, Am. Soc. Engring. Edn. (pres. 1963-64), Engrs. and Scientists Milw., Sigma Xi, Chi Epsilon, Phi Eta Sigma, Tau Beta Pi, Phi Kappa Phi, Triangle. Methodist. Clubs: Rotary, University. Kurt F. Wendt Library at U. Wis. named in his honor, 1976. Home: Madison, Wis. Died June 9, 1982.

WENNERSTRUM, CHARLES F., judge; b. Cambridge, Ill., Oct. 11, 1889; s. Charles F. and Anna Mathilda (Vinstrand) W.; A.B., Drake U., 1912, LL.B., Coll. of Law, 1914; m. Helen F. Rogers, Feb. 14, 1925; children—Roger F., Scott T., Joann H. Admitted to Ia. bar, 1914, in practice Adel, Ia., 1914-15, Chariton, Ia., 1915-30; county atty., Lucas County, Ia., 1917-22; dist. judge, Ia., 2d Judicial Dist., 1930-40; justice, Supreme Court of Ia. from Jan. 1, 1941. Served as 2d lt., U.S. Army, 1918; presiding judge hostage case, Nurnberg War Trials Trustee, Drake U. Mem. Am. Bar Assn., Ia. State Bar Assn., Am. Law Inst., Am. Legion (past post comdr.), Sigma Alpha Epsilon, Delta Theta Phi, Order of Coif. Republican. Presbyterian. Club: Rotary (Chariton). Home: Chariton, Ia. †

WENTWORTH, RALPH STRAFFORD, naval officer; b. Brockton, Mass., Dec. 18, 1890; s. Frank Willis and Linnie Glee (Garney) W.; B.S., U.S. Naval Acad., 1912, student post grad. sch., 1928-29; grad. Naval War Coll., 1938; m. Gladys Davison Kaull, Sept. 12, 1914; children—Barbara Kaull (wife of lt. comdr. Charles H. Morrison, Jr.), Ralph Strafford, William. Commd. ensign, U.S. Navy, 1912, advancing through the grades to commodore, 1943; served in U.S. ships Michigan, Florida, New Jersey, Petrel, Delaware, Arkansas, Henshaw, Texas, Decatur, Hull, Nashville; also served at U.S. Naval Acad. U.S. Naval War Coll. and R.O.T.C. Harvard Coll. Participated in Mex. Border Campaign, 1914, and in World War I and World War II. Decorated Legion of Merit. Methodist. Mason, Sojourner, Hero of '76. Home: Brockton, Mass. Deceased.

WENTZELL, CECIL RODNEY, business supplies co. exec., exec.; b. Bethel, Maine, Aug. 10, 1921; s. Stanley H. and Millie (Baker) W.; m. June Elise Little, June 20, 1940; children—Melinda, Stephen. Grad., Bentley Coll., 1947. With Gen. Electric Co., 1947-74; treas. gen. Electric Tech. Services Co., Inc., N.Y.C., 1962-72, mgr. Latin Am. fin. planning and analysis, 1972-74; treas. Nashua Corp., N.H., 1974—. Served with U.S. Army, 1942-45. Republican. Episcopalian.

WERKER, HENRY FREDERICK, judge; b. Glendale, N.Y., Apr. 16, 1920; s. August Henry and Celia (Michel) W.; m. Virginia Jane Pearson, July 27, 1941; children: Virginia Jane, Henry Frederick. B.A., N.Y. U., 1941, J.D., 1946. Bar: N.Y. 1946, U.S. Dist. Ct. (so. dist.) N.Y 1947, U.S. Tax Ct. 1950. Assoc. Abberley Kooiman & Amon, N.Y.C., 1946-51, ptnr., 1957-58, pvt. practice law, Greenville, N.Y., 1958-69; ptnr. Fray, Bagley & Chadderdon, Catskill, N.Y., 1961-69, social services atty., asst. county atty., Greene County, N.Y., 1967-69, judge Greene County, Surrogate and Family Ct. judge, 1969-74; U.S. Dist. judge So. Dist. of N.Y., N.Y.C., 1974-83; past dir. Nat. Bank Coxsackie, Greenville-Norton Hill Lumber, Inc., Stiefel Labs., Inc. Chmn. Greenville Town Republican Com., 1964-68; mem. exec. com. Green County Republicans, 1964-68; pres. Greenville Sch. Bd., 1959-60. Served with USNR, 1942-46, asst. naval attaché, London. Fellow Am. Bar Found., N.Y. Bar Found.; mem. Am., N.Y. State, Greene County bar assns., Am. Judicature Soc., Assn Bar of City of N.Y. Lodge: Rotary (Greenville pres.). Home: Pelham, N.Y. Dec. May 10, 1984.

WERTHAM, FREDRIC, psychiatrist, neurologist; b. Germany, 1895; student Kings Coll., London, Eng., Univs. of Munich and Erlangen, Germany; M.D. Wurzburg, Germany, 1921; post-grad. study, London, Vienna, Paris. Asst. in psychiatry, psychiatric clinic, Univ. of Munich, 1921; chief resident psychiatrist and asst. in charge out-patient dept., Johns Hopkins Hosp., later asso. in psychiatry Johns Hopkins Hosp. and Med. Sch. 1922-29; fellow NRC, Washington, 1930-31; sr. psychiatrist Dept. of Hosps. N.Y.C., from 1932; asst. prof. clin. psychiatry New York U. and physician-in-charge, psychiat. clinic Court of Gen. Sessions, N.Y.C., 1932; sr. psychiatrist Bellevue Hosp., N.Y.C., 1933-35; dir. mental hygiene clinic Bellevue Hosp., 1936-39; dir. mental hygiene clinic Queens Gen. Hosp., 1939-52; cons. psychiatrist Queens Med. Center, N.Y.C. Dept. of Hosps., from 1952; dir. Lafargue Clinic, Harlem; dir. Quaker Emergency Service Readjustment Center. Recipient Emil A. Gutheil award, 1968; Sigmund Freud award, 1971. Fellow A.M.A., Am. Acad. Neurology. A.A.A.S., N.Y. Acad. Medicine, NRC; mem. Am. Neurol. Assn., Am. Psychiat. Assn., Am. Assn. Neuropathologists, Assn. for Research in Nervous and Mental Diseases, N.Y. County Med. Soc., Assn. for Advancement Psychotherapy (pres. 1943-51). Author: The Brain as an Organ, 1935; Dark Legend: A Study in Murder, 1941; The World Within, 1948; The Show of Violence, 1949; Dark Legend, 1949; Seduction of the Innocent, 1954; The Circle of Guilt, 1956; A Sign for Cain. An Exploration of Human Violence, 1966; 1969; The World of Fanzines: A Special Form of Communication, 1973 (Chgo. Book Clinic award 1974); various papers and monographs on psychiatry, neurology, neuropathology, psychoanalysis and criminology. Died Nov. 25, 1981.

WERTIME, THEODORE ALLEN, govt. ofcl.; b. Chambersburg, Pa., Aug. 31, 1919; s. Rudolf and Flora (Montgomery) W.; B.A., Haverford Coll., 1939; M.A., Am. U., 1941; John Martin Vincent fellow, Johns Hopkins, 1942; m. Bernice O. Schultz, June 20, 1940; children—John T., Richard A., Steven F., Charles M. With FEA, 1942-44; research specialist Far East, State Dept., 1946-55; dep. dir. Office Research and Analysis, USIA, 1955-61; cultural attache Am. embassy, Tehran, Iran, 1961-63; editor Forum, Voice of Am., 1963-69; cultural attache Am. embassy, Athens, Greece, 1969-73; dep. dir. Info. Center Service, USIA, 1973, program officer energy, food and population, 1974-75; research asso. Smithsonian Instn., 1965-82, leader 5 Smithsonian expdns., 3 Nat. Geog. expdns. to Middle and Far East in search early pyrotechnology, 1966-76; vis. scientist U. Pa., U. Minn., Duluth. Served with AUS, 1944-46. Social Sci. Research Council grantee, 1947-48. Mem. A.A.A.S., Soc. History Tech., Middle East Studies Assn., N.Y. Acad. Scis., Am. Polit. Sci. Assn., Pi Gamma Mu. Author: The Coming of the Age of Steel, 1962; (with others) North Korea: Case Study of A Soviet Satellite, 1962; also articles, contbns. in books. Home: Arlington, Va. Died Apr. 8, 1982.

WESCOTT, THURMAN CARY, engr., business exec.; b. Patten, Maine, Feb. 27, 1887; s. Charles Warren and Cora (Leslie) W.; student Patten Acad., 1904; Ricker Classical Inst., Houlton, Me., 1905; B.S., 1909, E.D. 1951, U. Maine; m. Daisy Holt Haywood; Apr. 15, 1944; children—Emily Benbury (Mrs. Wade H. Anderson. Jr.), Charlotte Leslie (Mrs. William T. Coulbourn). With N.Y.C. and Erie R.R., N.Y., 1909-11; resident engr. power systems and hydroelectric development, Electric Bond & Share Co., N.C., Tex., Ore., and Idaho, 1911-14, design engr., N.Y. office, 1914-16, engr. in charge of investigations of hydroelectric power sites in N.C. and S.C., 1916-18, resident engr. and constrn. mgr. on public utility constrn., N.C. and Pa., 1918-24; constrn. mgr., N.Y. office, 1924-31, engring. mgr., 1931-33; pres. and dir. Phoenix Engring. Corp., 1933-38; engineering manager, vice pres., dir. Ebasco Services, Inc., (subsidiary of Electric Bond & Share Co., 1938-45, pres., dir., 1945-54, past vice chmn. bd., from 1954; dir. Electric Bond & Share Co., 1948-55. Licensed profl. engineer, New York; registered engr., Nat. Bur. Engring., Registration. Mem. Kappa Sigma. Conglist. Clubs: Manhasset Bay Yacht, North Hempstead, Country (Port Washington). Home: Port Washington, N.Y. Deceased.

WEST, JESSAMYN, novelist; b. Ind., 1902; m. H.M. McPherson. Student, Whittier Coll., U. Calif.; also studied in, Eng.; hon. doctorates, Whittier Coll., Mills Coll., Ind. U., Swarthmore Coll., Western Coll. for Women, U. Ind., Terre Haute, Juniata Coll., Wilmington Coll. Tchr. at writers confs. Bread Loaf, U. Notre Dame, U. Wash., Ind. U., U. Utah, Stanford, U. Colo., U. Ky.; former writer in residence Wellesley Coll., Mill Coll., Whittier Coll., U. Calif., Irvine. Writer: movie scripts Stolen Hours, Big Country; Author: movie scripts Mirror for the Sky, 1948, The Witch Diggers, The Friendly Persuasion (wrote screenplay for motion picture), 1956, Love, Death and the Ladies Drill Team, 1955, Love Is Not What You Think, 1958, South of the Angels, 1960, The Quaker Reader, 1961, A Matter of Time, 1966, Leafy River, 1967, Except for Me and Thee, 1969, Crimson Ramblers of the World, Farewell, 1970, Hide and Seek, 1973, The Secret Look, 1974, Massacre at Fall Creek, 1975, The Woman Said Yes, 1976, The Life I Really Lived, 1979, Double Discovery, 1981; Contbr. to: mags., including New Yorker. Trustee Whittier Coll.; Mem. bd. Foster Parents Plan. Mem. Am. Civil Liberties Union, N.A.A.C.P. Mem. Soc. of Freinds. Home: Napa, Calif. Dec. Feb. 22, 1984.

WEST, REBECCA (CICILY ISABEL FAIRFIELD), novelist; b. Edinburgh, Scotland, Dec. 21, 1892; d. Charles and Isabella Campbell (MacKenzie) Fairfield; grad. George Watson's Ladies Coll., Edinburgh; m. Henry Maxwell Andrews, Nov. 1, 1930. Began as reviewer, Freewomen, 1911; joined staff of Clarion as political writer, 1912. Author: Henry James, 1916; The Return of the Soldier, 1918; The Judge, 1922; The Strange Necessity, 1928; Harriet Hume, 1929; St. Augustine, 1930; D. H. Lawrence, an Elegy, 1930; Ending in Earnest, 1932; The Rake's Progress, 1934; The Harsh Voice, 1935; The Thinking Reed, 1936; Black Lamb and Grey Falcon, 1941; The Meaning of Treason, 1947; A Train of Powder, 1955; The Fountain Overflows, 1957; The Court and the Castle, 1957; The New Meaning of Treason, published in 1964; The Birds Fall Down, 1966. Named comdr. Order Brit. Empire, chevalier Legion Honor 1957, dame comdr. Brit. Empire, 1959; recipient A. C. Benson silver medal, 1966. Mem. Am. Acad. Arts. and Scis., Royal Soc. Lit. Address: Bucks, England. Died Mar. 15, 1983.

WEST, ROBERT NIAS, lawyer; b. Newtonville, Mass., Sept. 13, 1898; s. Robert F. and Maude (Nias) W.; A.B., Columbia, 1920, LL.B., 1923; m. Mary F. Sime, Nov. 18, 1927; children—Ruth (Mrs. Amory Houghton, Jr.), Judith (Mrs. David F. Sheldon), Maude (Mrs. John Bigelow). Admitted to N.Y. State bar, 1924, since practiced in N.Y.C.; mem. firm of Shearman & Sterling, and predecessors, after 1957; dir. Seaboard Oil Corp., Granitevaile Co. Mem. Am., N.Y. State bar assns., Assn. Bar City N.Y., Delta Kappa Epsilon, Phi Delta Phi. Protestant Episcopalian. Clubs: University, Down Town Assn. (N.Y.C.); Bedford (N.Y.) Golf and Tennis. Home: Katonah, N.Y. Dec. Apr. 25, 1983.

WESTBROOK, JAMES SEYMOUR, investments; b. Ogdensburg, N.Y., Dec. 15, 1889; s. James George and Jenny (Foote) W.; ed. public school; B.A., Williams Coll., 1910; post-grad. Kent Sch. Law, Columbia U.; m. Beatrice Davenport, June 17, 1918; 1 son, James Seymour; 1 stepson, Daniel Davenport. Began with Western Union Telegraph Co., 1910; an organizer, Morris Plan Bank, 1915; with Nat. City Bank, New York, N.Y., 1919-21; asst. sec. Foreign Trade Banking Corp., 1921-24; partner, McEldowney & Co., investment banking, Bridgeport, Conn., 1924-31; prin. in firm James S. Westbrook, Bridgeport, Conn., from 1931. Served as lt., U.S. Navy, during World War I. Sec. Nat. Small Business Men's Assn. from 1938. Home: Bridgeport, Conn. †

WESTBY, GERALD HOLINBECK, geologist; b. Stoughton, Wis., Aug. 4, 1898; s. Julius A. and Harriet (Holinbeck) W.; m. Elaine Carlson, June 5, 1927 (div. Feb. 1942); children—Joan C. (Mrs. John A. Weaver III) (dec.), Dorothy J. (Mrs. Jonathan Westby Campaigne); m. Kathleen Patton, Feb. 2, 1944; children—Kathleen Harriet, Gerald Holinbeck, John Trygve. Ph.B. in Geology, U. Chgo., 1920; student, Stanford, 1924, Colo. Sch. Mines, 1926-27; D.Sc. (hon.), U. Tulsa, 1964; LL.D., Okla. Christian Coll., 1973. Tchr. geology U. Mont., summer 1920; resident geologist in Algeria for S. Pearson & Son, London, Eng., 1920-24; field geologist Empire Oil & Refining Co., 1924-26, chief geophysicist, 1927-33; with Seismograph Service Corp., Tulsa, 1933-70, pres., 1935-67, chmn. bd., chief exec. officer, 1967-68, then hon. chmn. dir.; pres., dir. subsidiaries; dir. Brookside State Bank, 1st Nat. Bank & Trust Co., both Tulsa. Bd. dirs. Internat. Petroleum Exposition, from 1938 chmn. exposition Hall of Sci., 1953; chmn. bd. Tulsa Psychiatric Found.; bd. govs. Am. Citizenship Center, 1972—; Comdr. N.E. Okla. Group, CAP, 1941-45; Chmn. bd. of trustees U. Tulsa, 1966-69. Served to 2d lt. U.S. Army, World War I. Recipient award for leadership in civic, social and religious activities U. Chgo. Alumni Assn., 1950. Mem. Am. Assn. Petroleum Geologists, Soc. Exploration Geophysicists (founding com., past officer, hon.), Geophys. Soc. Tulsa (hon. life), Am. Geophys. Union, European Assn. Exploration Geophysicists, Tulsa C. of C. (dir., past pres.), Fgn. Policy Assn., Tulsa (founder), Tulsa Com. Fgn. Relations (charter), Alliance Francaise Tulsa. Clubs: N.Y. Yacht, Cherokee Yacht, So. Hills Country, Tulsa, Tulsa Press (Headliner mem.). Home: Tulsa, Okla. Dec. May 9, 1983.

WESTCOTT, RALPH MERRILL, water quality engr.; b. Redlands, Calif., Jan. 7, 1906; s. Clyde Merrill and Effie Rachel (Blodgett) W.; m. Elizabeth Campbell, June 26, 1926; children—Marilyn Westcott McIntyre, Mila Westcott Moyse. Student, U. Calif., Los Angeles, 1923-24, 37-39. Registered profl. engr., Calif. Owner, operator printing bus., Los Angeles, 1926-32, date grower, Coachella Valley, Calif., 1925-47; owner, operator Water Treating Service Co., Los Angeles, 1939-49; cons. engr. Pomeroy & Westcott, Los Angeles, 1949-51; pres. Holladay & Westcott, Los Angeles, 1952-64, cons. water quality, waste disposal, 1964-73, corrosion specialist, Fallbrook, Calif., from 1973; mem. com. on water problems Rainbow Mcpl. Water Dist., Fallbrook, from 1975. Contbr. numerous articles to trade, tech. jours. Recipient Engr. of Yr. award Cons. Engrs. Assn. Wash., 1960, Actual Specifying Engr. Mag. award, 1965. Fellow ASHRAE (life, Distinguished Service award 1968), Am. Cons. Engrs. Council (life, founding mem. 1956, pres. 1959-60); mem. Cons. Engrs. Assn. Calif. (pres. 1956-57), Am. Water Works Assn. (life mem.), Nat. Assn. Corrosion Engrs. (life, cert. corrosion specialist, chmn. tech. practices com. T-7K non-chem. water treating devices). Clubs: Fallbrook Golf and Country, Men's (pres. 1976). Home: Fallbrook, Calif.

WESTERMANN, HORACE CLIFFORD, sculptor; b. Los Angeles, Dec. 11, 1922; s. Horace Clifford and Forita Lynd (Bloom) W.; student Art Inst. Chgo., 1947-53; m. Joanna May Beall, Aug. 31, 1959. Exhibited in one-man shows Corcoran Gallery, Los Angeles, 1974, Assan Frumkin Gallery, 1974, Moore Coll., Phila., 1972, retrospective at Los Angeles County Mus., 1968, Mus. Contemporary Art, Chgo., 1968; exhibited in group shows Made in Chgo. group show Smithsonian Inst., 1974, Guggenheim Mus., N.Y.C., 1970, Carnegie Mus., 1971, Mus. Modern Art, N.Y.C., 1960, Whitney Mus., 1976, Venice Biennale, 1976, others; retrospective exhbn. Whitney Mus. Am. Art, New Orleans Mus. Art, Des Moines Mus. Art, Seattle Mus. Art, San Francisco Mus. Modern Art, 1978; represented in pvt. collections. Served with USMC, 1942-46, 50-52. Recipient Nat. Arts Council award, 1967, Sao Paulo Biennal award, 1972. Mem. Artists Equity Assn. Home: Brookfield Center, Conn. Dec. Nov. 3, 1981.

WESTON, WILLIAM HENRY, JR., educator; b. N.Y.C., Jan. 24, 1890; s. William Henry and Frances (Pope) W.; A.B., Dartmouth, 1911; A.M., Harvard, 1912, Ph.D., 1915; m. Lora Standish, June 5, 1916 (div. Oct. 1934); m. 2d, Doris Walker, Dec. 26, 1935; children—Seth Walker, Sabrina Broomfield. Instr. biology Western Res. U., 1915-17; path. insp., Federal Hort. Bd., U.S. Dept. Agr., Washington, 1917; pathologist, cereal investigations, Dept. Agr., detailed to Guam, P.I., 1917-21; asst. prof. botany, Harvard, 1921-27, asso. prof., 1927, prof., 1928; chmn. dept., 1927-32; made survey cane disease losses in Cuba for Tropical Plant Research Found., 1924; on leave of absence from Harvard as agrl. adviser to Cuba Sugar Club, 1925; investigator of fungi, Panama, 1928-29; cons., Puerto Rico, 1935, Office of Q.M. Gen., 1944-47; tech. dir. Nat. Defense Research Com. and Nat. Acad. of Sci. contract work for Q.M.C. on fungi concerned in deterioration of materiel, 1944-46. Ropes Meml. lectr.; Salem, 1923, 26, Lowell lectr., Boston, 1927; Johns Hopkins lectr., on mycology, 1937; staff lectr. U. Mich., 1942; Darwin Anniversary Address, Mich. State U., 1942; vis. prof. botany La. State Univ., 1942; mem. staff Marine Biol. Lab., Woods Hole, Mass., 1915, 16, 22-26. Mem. Harvard Cancer Commn., 1926-32. Trustee Boston Soc. Natural History, from 1935. Fellow A.A.A.S., Am. Acad. Arts and Scis.; mem. Bot. Soc. America, Am. Phytopathol. Soc., Am. Mycol. Soc. (pres. 1932), New Eng. Bot. Club (pres. 1931-33), Boston Bacteriology Club, Gamma Alpha, Sigma Xi. Vice pres. mycol. sect. 6th Internat. Bot. Congress, Amsterdam, 1935. Corr. mem. 3d Internat. Microbiol. Congress, N.Y., 1939; contbr. Hydrobiol. Symposium, Madison, 1940. Republican. Clubs: Harvard Travellers (past pres.), Thursdan Evening. Contbr. to sci. publs. Home: Winchester, Mass. †

WESTOVER, HARRY CLAY, judge; b. Williamstown, Ky., May 19, 1894; s. John Homer and Anna R. (Musselman) W.; m. Helen E. Equen, Oct. 3, 1919; children—Harry, Dorothy. Ed., U. Ariz., 1919. Mem. Calif. State Senate; judge U.S. Dist. Ct. of So. Calif., Los Angeles, then sr. judge. Served with U.S. Army. Democrat. Methodist. Office: Laguna Hills, Calif. Dec. Apr. 14, 1983.*

WEYERBACHER, RALPH DOWNS, naval architect; b. Boonville, Ind., July 12, 1888; s. William Frederick and Mary (Downs) W.; student Ind. U., 1904-05; B.S., U.S. Naval Acad., 1909; M.S., Mass. Inst. Tech., 1914; m. Margot Kallenbach, Sept. 7, 1921. Served in U.S. Navy to 1937, advancing to comdr.; cons. engr., 1937-40; v.p., gen. mgr. and dir. Cramp Shipbuilding Co., Phila., 1940-42. Fellow Am. Inst. Architects, Soc. Naval Architects; mem. Sigam Chi. Club: Union League (Phila.). Home: Boonville, Ind. †

WEYERHAEUSER, VIVIAN O'GARA (MRS. FREDERICK K. WEYERHAEUSER), welfare; b. Chicago, Oct. 10, 1900; d. Thomas J. and Mae V. (Brady) O'Gara; ed. pvtly. and Convent of St. Mary-of-the-Woods, Vigo County, Ind.; m. Frederick King Weyerhaeuser, Mar. 22, 1923; children—Marianna O'Gara (dec.), Frederick King (dec.), Vivian O'Gara (Mrs. Frank Nicholas Piasecki), Lynn O'Gara (Mrs. Stanley R. Day). Active in Junior League, Chicago, prior to 1923; head of

Women Willkie Workers, headquarters New York, 1940; member nat. com. on volunteer services A.R.C., 1941-43; dir., vice chmn., chmn. vol. spl. services, chmn. pub. relations, St. Paul chpt. A.R.C., 1941-43; trustee Community and War Relief Chest, 1942-46; trustee budget com. Community Chest and Council, 1944-49; mem. Atlantic Union Council to 54; dir. Inter-Club Council St. Paul, 1949-52; chmn. Women's Inst. St. Paul, 1945-46; Minn. co-chmn. nat. council Womens Nat. Rep. Orgn., 1948-52; exec. com. Rep. state central com., 1948-52; chmn. pub. relations Minn. Fed. Women's Rep. Clubs, 1949-51; nat. dir. spl. orgn. Citizens for Eisenhower-Nixon, 1952; founder Women's Orgn. of Minn. Hist. Soc., 1949 (recipient Award of Merit, Am. Assn. State and Local History), Mem. exec. council, v.p. Minn. Hist. Soc., 1951-58; dir. St. Paul Civic Opera Assn., from 1954, Twin Cities Opera Festival, 1954; co-chmn. Upper Midwest Met. Regional Auditions, from 1953; vice chmn. nat. council Met. Opera Assn., 1954, past pres. nat. council; hon. pres. 1962-83; mem. Met opera Bd., from 1954; dir. Orchestral Assn. Mpls., 1944-55, dir. Seattle Symphony, 1954-56; dir. women's affairs div. Am. Forest Products Industries, Inc., 1966-68; mem. Women's bd. Lyric Opera of Chgo., from 1966; chmn. exec. com. Minn. Centennial Women's Div., 1956-57, mem. hon. council, 1956; exec. com. Minn. Centennial Arts Com., 1956-57; bd. dirs. Vancouver Festival Soc., 1959; mem. adv. com. Minn. Young Ams. For Freedom, 1966. Home: Saint Paul, Minn. Died June 6, 1983.

WHALEY, W(ILLIAM) GORDON, university dean; b. N.Y.C., Jan. 16, 1914; s. Frank H. and Mae (Manson) W.; B.S., Mass. State Coll., 1936; Ph.D., Columbia, 1939; m. Clare Youngren, 1938; 1 dau., Patricia Anne. Lectr. Barnard Coll. Columbia, 1939-40; instr. Columbia, 1940-43; asso. agronomist to sr. geneticist, bur. plant industry, soils and agrl. engring. U.S.D.A., 1943-46, cons. geneticist agrl. research administration, 1946-48; asso. prof. botany U. Tex., 1946-48, chmn. dept., 1948-62, prof., 1948-82, dir. plant research inst., 1948-63, dir. cell research inst., 1964-82, asso. dean grad. sch., 1955-57, dean, after 1957; vis. prof. Rockefeller Univ. 1964. Chmn. adv. com. for sci. edn. NSF, 1966-84. Fellow A.A.A.S.; mem. Internat., Am. socs. cell biology, Am. Soc. Plant Physiologists, Soc. Developmental Biology, Nat. Assn. Land-Grant Colls. and State Univs. (chmn. commn. on grad. edn.). Bot. Soc. Am., Torrey Bot. Club, Sigma Xi. Club: Cosmos. Author: Biology for Everyone, 1948; Principles of Biology, 1954, rev., 1957, 64; also articles. Editor: Grad. Jour.; Jour. of Proc., Assn. Grad. Schs. Editorial bd. jour. Ultrastructure Research. Home: Austin, Tex. Died Dec. 15, 1982.

WHARTON, CYRUS RICHARD, lawyer; b. m. Gibsonville, N.C., Jan. 30, 1890; s. Cyrus A. and Anna B. (Donnell) W.; A.B., U. N.C., 1912, LL.B., 1915; m. Lessie Norma Lindsey, Dec. 27, 1917; children—Richard Lindsey, Jane (Mrs. Robert A. Darnell). Admitted to N.C. bar, 1915; gen. practice law, Greensboro, from 1916, mem. firm Wharton, Ivey & Wharton; former gen. counsel vice pres., director, exec. com. Pilot Life Ins. Co., special counsel. Chmn. bd. trustees Palmer Meml. Inst., Sedalia, N.C., from 1942. Mem. Am. (state del. ho. dels. 1947-53, chmn. standing com. jud. selection, tenure and compensation 1953-57), N.C. bar assns., Am. Life Conv. (legal sect.), Assn. Life Ins. Counsel, Am. Judicature Soc. Home: Greensboro, N.C. †

WHATLEY, BROWN LEE, mortgage banker, realtor; b. Ashland, Ala., Mar. 19, 1900; s. Madison Hayne and Ola (Northen) W.; m. Marion Harlan, June 4, 1924; children—Brown L., Marion H. Whatley Law. Student, Riverside Mil. Acad., 1917-19, Chgo. Art Inst., 1919-20, Art Students League N.Y., 1920-21, U. Ga., 1922-23. Mgr. Western Ga. Fair Assn., La Grange, 1919-20; advt. mgr. Southeastern Fair, Atlanta, 1920-21, Fla. State Fair, Jacksonville, 1922-23, Believers in Jacksonville, 1923-24; advt. mgr. Telfair Stockton & Co., Jacksonville, 1925-27, mgr. sales, 1927-29, exec. v.p., 1929-37; pres. Whatley, Davin & Co., St. Nicholas Park Co., San Marco Pl. Co., Southside Properties Inc., 1937-46; all Jacksonville; pres. Stockton, Whatley, Davin & Co., Jacksonville, 1946-60, chmn. bd., mem. exec. com., 1960-80, chmn. emeritus, 1980-82; pres., mem. exec. com. Arvida Corp., Miami, 1961-72, chmn. bd., mem. exec. com., 1972-77, chmn. emeritus, 1977-82; dir. Gen. Am. Oil Co. of Tex., 1964-80, emeritus, 1980-82; pres. Arvida Realty Sales Inc., Miami, 1961-72, chmn., 1972-77; vice chmn., dir. Am. Nat. Bank of Jacksonville, 1945-51; dir. Fla. Nat. Bank of Jacksonville, 1951-62, Fla. Nat. Bank of Miami, 1962-82, Fla. Nat. Banks of Fla., 1981-82. Mem. Duval County (Fla.) Bd. Pub. Instruction, 1933-45; mem. com. govt. expenditures U.S. C. of C., 1958-62; mem. Jacksonville Com. One Hundred, 1961-82, Nat. Bd. Fed. City Council, Washington, 1964-80; trustee Bapt. Meml. Hosp., Jacksonville, Fla., Grand Central Art Galleries of N.Y.C., Met. Mus. and Art Center Miami. Mem. Jacksonville Bd. Realtors (pres. 1943), Jacksonville C. of C. (dir.), Fla. State C. of C., Mortgage Bankers Assn. Am. (pres. 1952-53, life mem. bd. govs.), Mortgage Bankers Legion (life), Sigma Chi (life). Democrat. Baptist (deacon). Clubs: Masons, K.T, Shriners, Rotary; Fla. Yacht (Jacksonville), San Jose Country (Jacksonville), River (Jacksonville), Univ. (Jacksonville), Ponte Vedra (Jacksonville); Bankers (Miami), Miami (Miami); Indian Creek Country (Miami Beach), Indian Creek Village (Miami Beach), La Gorce Country (Miami Beach); Boca Raton (Fla.); Hotel and Club; Longboat Key Golf (Sarasota, Fla.). Home: Miami Beach, Fla. Dec. 1982.

WHATMORE, MARVIN CLEMENT, broadcasting executive; b. Albia, Iowa, June 22, 1908; s. John and Nora (Evans) W.; m. Lois Reynolds, Mar. 3, 1934; children: Sharon Lee, Sue Ann, James Marvin, Linda Reynolds. A.B., Drake U., 1932, L.H.D., 1966; postgrad., State U. Iowa, 1931-32; Litt.D., St. Bonaventure U., 1964. Asst. auditor Iowa-Des Moines Nat. Bank & Trust Co., 1932-35; accountant Des Moines Register & Tribune Co., 1936; office mgr. Look, Inc., N.Y.C., 1937, asst. treas., 1940, treas., 1941; mem. bd. dirs., bus. mgr. Look mag., 1943; mem. bd. dirs., bus. mgr. Look, Inc. (became Cowles Mags., Inc., 1943), mem. bd. dirs., 1943, v.p., 1949-64, pres., 1964-77, chief exec. officer, 1969-77, chmn. bd., chief exec. officer, 1977-84, (co. name changed to Cowles Mag. & Broadcasting, Inc., 1961, to Cowles Communications, Inc. 1965). Trustee, mem. exec. com. Atlantic Center for Arts, 1979-85. Recipient Disting. Service award Drake U., 1958. Clubs: Mission Valley Golf and Country (N.Y.C.); University (N.Y.C.); University (Sarasota), Field (Sarasota), Sanderling (Sarasota); Country of Sapphire Valley (NC). Home: Sarasota, Fla. Died Apr. 9, 1985.

WHEELER, ALEXANDER, lawyer; b. Andover, Mass., Aug. 10, 1889; s. Henry and Ellen (Hayward) W.; A.B., Harvard, 1911, LL.B., 1913; m. Agnes Hoppin Grew, June 16, 1921; children—Alexander, James Grew, Agnes. Admitted to Mass. bar, 1913, practiced in Boston; partner firm Hutchins & Wheeler, from 1915. Past dir. Boston Safe Deposit and Trust Co. U.S. commnr. at Boston for Dist. Mass., 1915-24; chmn. Boston Finance Commn., 1934-36. Vice pres. Childrens Hosp. Med. Center, 1945-66, trustee, from 1934; mem. com. Permanent Charity Fund, 1941-66, pres., 1955-66. Served to maj., cav., U.S. Army, 1917-19. Mem. Am., Mass., Boston bar assns. Clubs: Cruising of Am., Harvard, Union (Boston); Essex County (Manchester). Home: Manchester, Mass. †

WHEELER, JOSEPH LEWIS, librarian; b. Dorchester, Mass., Mar. 16, 1884; s. Rev. George Stevens and Mary Jane (Draffin) Wheeler; Ph.B., Brown U., 1906, M.A., 1907; B.L.S., N.Y. State Library Sch., 1909, M.L.S., 1925; Litt.D., U. of Maryland, 1934, Brown U., 1936; m. Mabel Archibald, Oct. 20, 1910; children—John Archibald, Joseph Towne (killed in action, 1944), Robert Reid, Mary Bethel. Asst. Providence Pub. Library and Brown U. Library, 1902-07; asst. librarian Pub. Library, Washington, D.C., 1909-11; librarian Jacksonville (Fla.) Pub. Library, 1911-12; asst. librarian Los Angeles Pub. Library, 1912-15; librarian Youngstown (O.) Pub. Library, 1915-26; librarian Enoch Pratt Library, Baltimore, 1926-45, retired. Vis. prof. adminstrn. Columbia Library Sch., 1949-50. Surveyor and cons. over 170 adminstrv. and bldg. projects, from 1924; Enoch Pratt Library Auditorium designated, 1963. Recipient Joseph W. Lippincott award A.L.A., 1961. Pres. Ohio Library Assn., 1921; mem. A.L.A. (hon. life; Drexel Library Sch. Alumni award 1966; past v.p.; exec. bd., 1929-33; bd. of edn. for librarianship, 1931-36), N.E.A., Am. Sociol. Soc., Am. Hist. Assn., Nat. Council Social Studies, N.A.A.C.P., The Hugeuenot Soc. mem. Md. Hist. Soc.; fellow A.A.A.S (council), Am. Soc. Pub. Adminstrn., Spl. Lang. Assn., Colonial Wars. Unitarian. Rotarian. Author: The Library and the Community, 1924; (with others) My Maryland (textbook), 1934; (with A.M. Githens) The American Public Library Building, 1941; Progress and Problems in Education for Librarianship (Carnegie Corp.); 1946; Location of Pub. Library Buildings, 1956; Project for 6,000 Small Libraries, 1958; (with Herbert Goldhor) Practical Administration of Public Libraries, 1962; Small Library Buildings, 1963; Reconsideration of Public Library Location, 1967; Current Trends in Public Library Buildings, 1967. Mount Independence-Hubbardton 1776 Military Road, 1968. Address: Benson, VT. †

WHEELER, RAYMOND MILNER, physician, educator; b. Farmville, N.C., Sept. 30, 1919; s. George Raymond and Sallie Kate (Collins) W.; certificate in medicine, U. N.C., 1941; M.D., Washington U., St. Louis, 1943; m. Mary Lou Browning, June, 1942 (div. 1956); children—Linda Lou, Margaret Browning, David Stewart; m. Julie Buckner Carr, June 6, 1958. Intern Barnes Hosp., St. Louis, 1943-44; asst. resident medicine N.C. Baptist Hosp., Winston-Salem, N.C., 1946-48; pvt. practice internal medicine, Charlotte, N.C., from 1948; chmn. dept. medicine Charlotte Meml. Hosp., 1961-63; clin. assoc. prof. medicine U. N.C. Med. Sch., 1966-70. Mem. Field Found. commn. physicians who studied hunger in Miss., 1967; mem. Citizens Bd. Inquiry into Hunger in U.S., 1968, into Brookside Strike, 1974; cons. prodn. film Hunger in America, 1968. Mem. N.C. Council Human Relations, from 1956, pres., 1957-61; mem. So. Regional Council, from 1956, chmn. exec. com., 1964-69, pres., 1969-74. Chmn. bd. dirs. Children's Found., 1973-74; chmn. exec. com. Nat. Sharecroppers' Fund, 1976-78, pres., from 1978; chmn. exec. com. N.C. Hunger Coalition, 1975-77, pres., 1977-79; bd. dirs. Voter Edn. Project, 1970-75, Southerners for Econ. Justice, from 1977. Served to capt. M.C., AUS, 1944-46. Decorated Silver Star, Purple Heart; recipient Disting. Service award U. N.C. Med. Sch., 1969; Frank Porter Graham award N.C. Civil Liberties Union, 1979. Diplomate Am. Bd. Internal Medicine. Fellow A.C.P.; mem. Am. Pub. Health Assn., Mecklenberg County Med. Soc. Democrat. Unitarian. Author articles. Home: Charlotte, N.C. Died Feb. 17, 1982.

WHEELER, ROGER MILTON, corporate executive; b. Boston, Feb. 27, 1926; s. Sidney S. and Florence W. (Kendall) W.; m. Patricia Jane Wilson, Sept. 6, 1946; children—Roger Milton, Pamela, David, Lawrence, Mark. Student, Mass. Inst. Tech., 1943-44, Notre Dame U., 1944-45; B.S., Rice U., 1945-46. Engr. Gulf Oil Co., 1946-47, Standard Oil Co., Ohio, 1947-48; pres. Standard Magnesium & Chem. Co., 1949-64; gen. mgr. magnesium projects Kaiser Aluminum & Chem. Co., 1964-65; chmn. bd. Telex Corp., Tulsa, 1965-81; chmn. bd. Phoenix Resources Inc., 1973-81; Cert. Appliance Distbrs., 1975-81; pres. Am. Magnesium Co., 1968-81. Author papers in field. Served with USNR, 1943-46. Mem. Magnesium Assn. (pres.), Young Pres. Orgn. Home: Tulsa, Okla. Dec. May 27, 1981.

WHELAN, BERNARD LEONARD, aircraft exec.; b. Cin., Nov. 19, 1890; s. Thomas and Mary Ellen (Leonard) W.; student St. Mary's Coll., Dayton, O., 1908-12; m. Blanche Van Buskirk, Sept. 16, 1919; 1 dau., Mary Anne. Aviator, Dayton Wright Airplane Co. 1918-24; gen. mgr. Sikorsky Aircraft, div. United Aircraft Corp., from 1943; v.p. United Aircraft Corp., East Hartford, from 1954. Mem. Inst. Aero. Scis. Clubs: Wings, Early Birds. Home: Fairfield, Conn. †

WHELAN, EDWARD J., univ. pres.; b. San Francisco, Calif., Sept. 20, 1887; s. James J. and Mary A. (Kelly) W.; A.B., U. of Santa Clara (Calif.), 1910; A.M., Gonzaga U., Spokane, Wash., 1913; S.T.D., Coll. of Burgos (Spain), 1923; LL.D., Fordham U., 1930. Ordained priest Roman Catholic Ch., 1921; pres. Loyola U., Los Angeles, Calif., 1942-49; Superior Manresa Retreat House, Azusa, Calif., from 1949. Home: Azusa, Calif. †

WHERRY, ROBERT JAMES, psychologist; b. Middletown, Ohio, May 16, 1904; s. Bertrand Shields and Mary Almar (Badger) W.; B.S., Ohio State U., 1925, A.M., 1927, Ph.D., 1929; m. Carrie Mae Blair, Dec. 23, 1929; children—Carrie Jean and Gloria Mae (twins), Robert James, John Richard. Tchr. history and economics Salem (Ohio) High Sch., 1924-25; grad. asst. psychology Ohio State U., 1927-29, prof. psychology (statistics and indsl.), 1948-81, chmn., 1960-70; prof. psychology and econs. Cumberland U., Lebanan, Tenn., 1929-37; asst. prof. psychology U. N.C., 1937-39, asso. prof., 1939-44, prof., 1944-48. Lectr. on rating scales in industry Western Res. U., 1948, 49, Okla. A. and M. Coll., 1949. Mem. Richardson, Bellow, Henry & Co., Inc., personnel consultants, N.Y.C., 1946-54; cons. Am. Tel. & Tel Co., Gen. Motors Corp. Resident dir. research Aerial Free Gunnery Sch., U.S. Navy, Jacksonville, Fla., 1942; chief, statis. sect., personnel research br. Office of Sec. of War, Washington, 1944; asst. chief for research, personnel research sect. Adj. Gen.'s Office, Dept. Army, 1944-47, expert, 1947-51; expert USAF, 1951-54. Mem. Am. Psychol. Assn. (fellow in indsl. psychology, in evaluation and measurement), Psychometric Soc., Sigma Xi. Presbyterian. Mem. editorial bd. Personnel Psychology, 1947. Inventor Wherry-Doolittle and Wherry-Gaylod test selection methods, 1931, 46; Wherry-Winer Item Factor Method, 1952; Hierachical Factor Analysis without Rotation, 1959. Home: Columbus, Ohio. Died Dec. 13, 1981.

WHETTEN, NATHAN LASELLE, sociologist, dean; b. Colonia Garcia, Chihuahua, Mexico, July 20, 1900 (Am. parentage); s. John Thomas and Agnes Belzora (Savage) W.; A.B., Brigham Young U., Provo, Utah, 1926, M.A., 1928; Ph.D., Harvard, 1932; student U. of Minn., 1929-30; m. Theora Lucile Johnson, Sept. 2, 1926; children—Nathan Rey, John Theodore. Instr. Spanish and sociology, Brigham Young Univ., 1926-29; instr. sociology, U. of Minn., 1929-30; asst. and tutor in sociology, Harvard, 1931-32; asst. prof., U. of Conn., 1932-35, asso. prof., 1935-38; prof., from 1938; dean Grad. Sch. since 1940, head of dept. of rural sociology, 1946-56, sociol. research in W. Can. for Canadian Pioneer Problems Com., summer, 1930; vis. prof. Yale, 1950-51; state Supr. rural research, Fed. Emergency Relief Adminstrn. Conn., 1933-36; sr. agrl. economist & leader, Div. Farm Population and Rural Welfare, U.S. Dept. Agr. Berkeley, Calif., 1939; rural sociologist of the American Embassy in Mexico, 1942-45; research C.A., 1945; Guggenheim fellow. Guatemala, 1952-53. Member of the United States delegation to Third Inter-Am. Conf. on Agr., Caracas, Venezuela, July 1945; consultant Pa. Am. Union, 1948-56, president Conn. Council Higher Edn., 1960-61; mem. exec. com. Council Grad. Schs. U.S., 1962-65; visited E. African univs. for African-Am. Inst., 1968. Fellow Social Science Research Council, Harvard, 1930-31; book review editor, Rural Sociology, 1940-42, translation editor, 1943-48, editor, 1952-54. Fellow American Sociological Association; member American (exec. com. 1949-52), Rural (president 1953-54), Eastern (pres. 1950-51), sociol. socs., Con. Acad. Arts and Scis., New England Conf. on Grad. Edn. (president 1949-50, 56-57), Nat. Planning Assn. (mem. nat. council, 1954). Sociedad Mexicana de Geografia y Estadistica. Sociol. Research Association, Population Association of America, Institut Internat. de Sociologie, Association for Latin-American Studies, Phi Beta Kappa, Phi Kappa Phi, Gamma Sigma Delta. Author: Studies of Suburbanization in Connecticut, 1936-39; Rural Families on Relief (with C. C. Zimmerman), 1938; Rural Mexico, 1948; Guatemala: The Land and the People, 1961; also research bulls. on rural sociology of Conn.; articles for profl. jours. Home: Storrs, Conn. Died June 25, 1984.

WHIPPLE, LAWRENCE ALOYSIUS, federal judge; b. N.Y.C., July 26, 1910; s. Earle and Mary E. (Flynn) W.; m. Virginia C. Golden, Apr. 20, 1940; children—Donald, Lawrence, Nancy, Virginia, John. B.S., Columbia, 1933; LL.B., John Marshall Law Sch., 1939. Bar: N.J. bar 1941. Acting magistrate, Jersey City, 1949-51; law enforcement dir. OPS, 1950; spl. asst. to U.S. atty. Justice Dept., 1951; exec. dir. Jersey City Housing Authority, 1953; dir. pub. safety, Jersey City, 1953-57; county counsel Judson County, 1958-62; prosecutor Hudson County, 1958-63; judge Superior Ct. of N.J., 1963-67; judge U.S. Dist. Ct., Dist. of N.J., Newark, 1967-78, sr. judge, 1978-83. Mem. Fed. Bar Assn., N.J. Bar Assn., Hudson County Bar Assn. (pres. 1957), N.Y. Lawyers Assn., Am. Judicature Soc., Catholic Lawyers Guild, Nat. Assn. Pros. Attys., State Prosecutors Assn. N.J. Office: Newark, N.J. Dec. June 8, 1983.*

WHIPPLE, SIDNEY BEAUMONT, editor; b. Lowell, Mass., Mar. 16, 1888; s. S. Foster and Abigail (Brydon) W.; grad. high sch., Lowell; student Dartmouth Coll., 1906-07; m. Hazel Seeley, Apr. 24, 1916; 1 dau., Victoria Smith. Newspaper corr., London, Eng., 1910-13; mng. editor Syracuse Journal, 1916-20; mem. editorial bd. Scripps-Howard Newspaper Alliance, 1921-22; editor Denver (Colo.) Express, 1922-26; editor South Bend (Ind.) News-Times since 1926; lecturer on journalistic ethics, U. of Notre Dame, from 1926; contbg. editor Eagle Mag. Mem. Sigma Delta Chi. Conglist. Clubs: Rotary, Round Table, Knife and Fork. Home: South Bend, Ind. †

WHITAMORE, CHARLES ERIC, British consul-general; b. Madras, India, Nov. 17, 1890; s. Thomas Henry and Martha (Roberts) W.; ed. Tonbridge Sch. (Eng.), 1904-09, France 1909-10, Germany, 1910-12; m. Virginia Cook, Oct. 5, 1921; 1 son, John Anthony. Entered Brit. consular service, China, 1912, serving at Peking, Shanghai, Hankow, 1912-21; vice-consul Shanghai, Canton, 1923-34; consul Canton, Tsinan, Hankow, Swatow, 1934-39; acting consul-gen. Hankow, Mukden, 1938-41; interned by Japanese, 1941-42; consul-gen. Kweilin, Chungking, Tientsin, 1944-47, Boston from 1947. Awarded Officer of Brit. Empire, 1941. Clubs: Royal Automobile (London), Tavern, Somerset (Boston), Essex Co. (Manchester, Mass.), various (China). Home: Boston, Mass. †

WHITBY, G. STAFFORD, chemist; born Hull, Eng., May 26, 1887; s. Stafford Beeston and Harriet (Smith) W.; A.R.C.S., Royal Coll. of Science, London, Eng., 1906, B.S., 1907, instr., 1907-10; M.S., McGill U., Montreal, Can., 1918, Ph.D., 1920, D.Sc., 1939; LL.D., Mount Allison University, Canada, 1932; Sc.D., Akron University, 1958; m. Wynne Atkinson, May 12, 1915 (dec.); children—Oliver Wynford, Phillipa. Chemist on rubber plantations, E. Indies, 1910-17; prof. organic chemistry McGill U., 1917-29; dir. div. chem., Nat. Research Council, Can., 1929-39; dir. Chem. Research Lab., Teddington, Eng., 1939-42; prof. rubber chem., dir. rubber research, U. of Akron, 1942-54; chmn. Canadian Synthetic Rubber Tech. Adv. Com., 1942-44. Awarded Officer d'Academie, 1928; Colwyn Gold Medal, Instn. Rubber Industry, 1928; Charles Goodyear Medal, Am. Chem. Soc., 1954. Mem. Canadian Inst. of Chem. (pres. 1927), Canadian Chem. Assn. (pres. 1928). Club: University (Akron). Author: Plantation Rubber and the Testing of Rubber, 1920. Editor: Rubber Section, Internat. Critical Tables, 1926; asso. editor: Jour. Am. Chem. Soc., 1934-39; joint editor: Sci. Progress in the Field of Rubber and Synthetic Elastomers, 1946; mem. editorial bd. series of monographs on High Polymers. Editor: Synthetic Rubber, 1954. Address: Akron, Ohio. †

WHITCHURCH, IRL GOLDWIN, educator, prof. of religion; b. Marissa, Ill., Sept. 7, 1889; s. Joseph Clinton and Caroline Sophia (Hachmeister) W.; A.B., Northwestern, 1916, A.M. (grad. scholarship), 1917; B.D., Garrett Biblical Inst. (travelling fellowship), 1919; Ph.D., Cornell (fellow in the Sage Sch. of Philosophy), 1921; m. Anna Dean Kellman, Aug. 2, 1917; 1 son, Charles Goldwin; m. 2d, Dorothy Emmons Kremser-Stoddard, May 14, 1947. Student pastorates in Okla., Ill., and New York, 1912-21; ordained to ministry of Methodist Ch., Sept., 1912; instr. Garrett Biblical Inst., 1921-23, registrar and asst. prof. of theology, 1923-27, asso. prof. of ethics and philosophy of religion, 1927-32, prof., 1932-45; dean grad. sch. of religion and prof. of philos. theology, Univ. of Southern Calif., 1945-47; interim pastorates Decatur and Peoria, Ill., and Iowa City, Ia., 1927-32; lecturer in schs. for ministerial training of Methodist Ch. and philos., theol., civic and cultural clubs from 1921; pastor Old South Congl. Ch., Farmington, Me., from 1953. Chmn. A.R.C. Co. Fund drive, 1952. Mem. Am. Philos. Assn., Am. Theol. Soc. (past pres., sec.-treas. midwest branch, 1942-45), Pi Epsilon Theta, Phi Chi Phi, Internat. Soc. of Theta Phi. Clubs: University, Twenty. Author books, including: Quality in Religious Faith, 1953; also chpts. in books, relating to field. Lectr. Home: Kingfield, Maine.

WHITCOMB, JAMES LANMON, educator, clergyman; b. Keene, N.H., Oct. 1, 1889; s. Frank Herbert and Grace (Nims) W.; prep. edn., high sch., Keene, and Trinity Sch., N.Y. City; St. Stephens Coll., Annandale, N.Y., 1914; spl. student Gen. Theol. Sem., 1925-28; m. Josephine Hale, Jan. 12, 1918; children—David William, Francis Hale, Priscilla. Served as dir. Lake Delaware Boys' Camp and Club, N.Y. City (sociol. and ednl. instn.), 1912-30; curate Trinity Ch., Ossining, N.Y., 1927-28; ordained priest P.E. Ch., 1928; curate Ch. of St. Edward the Martyr, N.Y. City, 1928-30; rector-headmaster and pres. bd. trustees Hoosac Sch. for Boys, 1930-41; rector St. Barnabas Ch., Troy, N.Y., 1941-45, also president bd. trustees. Trustee Bard Coll., 1939-41. Mem. bd. dirs. Church Mission of Help, Albany, N.Y., and N.Y. Ch. Mission of Help. Examining chaplain Diocese of Albany, 1933-45, rural dean of Troy, 1943-45, mem. bd. missions, 1943-45, diocesan council, 1944-45. Chaplain Rock Point Conf., Diocese of Vt., 1940-47, rector, Grace Church, from 1945. Dean, Valley Forge Conf. for Young People, 1938-45, Bd. of Religious Edn. Diocese of N.Y. from 1946. Mem. Kappa Gamma Chi. Home: Hastings-on-Hudson, N.Y. †

WHITCOMB, LOUIS GORMAN, lawyer; b. Taunton, Mass., July 30, 1903; s. Louis Anceland Mary Elizabeth (Gorman) W.; LL.B., Suffolk Law Sch., Boston, 1929; J.D. (hon.), Suffolk U., 1955; m. Alice Elizabeth Stiles, Aug. 24, 1946; children—Priscilla, Susan. Admitted to Vt. bar, 1929, since practiced in Springfield, 1929; justice of peace, 1932-53; judge Windsor Municipal Ct., 1947-48; exec. clk. Gov. E. W. Gibson, 1947; spl. counsel Vt. Pub. Service Commn., 1949; U.S. atty. Dist. of Vt., 1953-61; sr. mem. Whitcomb, Clark, & Moeser, 1961—. Trustee Claremont Savs. Bank (N.H.). Commr. Springfield Housing Authority. Trustee Springfield Town Library, 1951-75. Served to lt. comdr. aviation br. USNR, 1943-45. Mem. Municipal Judge's Assn. (pres. 1947-48), Am., Vt. (pres. 1966-67), Windsor County bar assns., Am. Legion. Elk. Home: Springfield, Vt. Died Oct. 20, 1984.

WHITE, ARTHUR ARNIM, army officer; born Coatsburg, Ill., Oct. 21, 1889; s. J. Alvan and L. Jane (Poling) W.; B.S., U.S. Mil. Acad., 1915; grad. F.A. Sch. battery comdrs. course, 1920, advanced course, 1927. Command and Gen. Staff Sch., 1928; m. Therese Sterling Bain, Sept. 15, 1917; 1 son, Arthur B. Commd. 2d lt., U.S. Army, 1915, and advanced through grades to maj. gen., 1944, brig. gen., 1947; served with field arty., World War I; asst. chief of staff, G-3 and G-4, VIII Corps, 1940-42; G-4 and chief of staff XIV Corps on Guadalcanal, 1942-43; chief of staff IV Corps, 1943-44; chief of staff Seventh Army in invasion South France and throughout campaigns in Europe, 1944-45; comd. 75th Inf. Div., June-Oct. 1945, 71st Inf. Div., German Occupation. Decorated D.S.M. with oak leaf cluster, Legion of Merit with oak leaf cluster, Army Commendation ribbon with oak leaf cluster (U.S.), Officer Legion of Honor, Croix de Guerre with palm (France). Deceased.

WHITE, ARTHUR KENT, clergyman, educator; b. Denver, Mar. 15, 1889; s. Kent and Mollie Alma (Bridwell) W.; A.B., Columbia, 1915; A.M., Princeton, 1921; D.D., Alma White Coll., 1927; m. Kathleen Merrill Staats, Sept. 6, 1915 (dec. Apr. 1973); children—Arlene (Mrs. Jerry Lawrence), Horace M., Constance (Mrs. David Brown), Pauline (Mrs. Robert Dallenbach); m. 2d, Bertha H. Hollander, July 5, 1974. Ordained to ministry Pillar of Fire Ch., 1910, bishop, 1932; national pres., gen. supt. Pillar of Fire Ch., also various offices in connection with publs. of ch.; pres. emeritus Alma White Coll. and Prep. Sch., Zarephath, N.J.; dir. Belleview Jr. Coll., Denver; lectr. stas. WAKW, Cin., WAWZ, Zarephath, KPOF, Denver. Mem. Am. Guild Organists, S.A.R. Republican. Author: Your Home Your College, 1922; (with Ray Bridwell White) A Toppling Idol—Evolution, 1933; The Boys Made Good, 1936; Some White Family History, 1948; Protestant Ideals, 1951; Your Alabaster Box and Other Sermons, 1961; Crusading Christian Women, 1963; also brochures. Home: Zarephath, N.J. Died Sept. 14, 1981.

WHITE, BARBARA MCCLURE, education and international affairs consultant; b. Evanston, Ill., July 23, 1920; d. Earl A. and Helen M. (Johnston) W. A.B., Mt. Holyoke Coll., 1941, LL.D. (hon.), 1972; M.A., Harvard U., 1962. Researcher Ency. Brit., 1941-42; policy asst. OWI, 1942-43, field rep. in, Cairo and Rome, 1944-46; regional specialist State Dept., 1946-47; program sec. internat. affairs, nat. staff LWV, 1947-51; asst. information officer USIS, Rome, 1951-56, pub. affairs officer, Turin, Italy, 1956-58; fgn. affairs officer USIA, Washington, 1958-61; pub. affairs officer Am. embassy, Santiago, Chile; also chmn. Fulbright Commn., Santiago, 1962-65; spl. asst. to dir. USIA, Washington, 1965, 72, asso. dir. policy and research, 1966-70, dep. dir. policy and plans, 1970-71, career minister for info., 1971-76; pres. Mills Coll., Oakland, Calif., 1976-80, edn. and internat. affairs cons., 1981-84; ambassador, alt. U.S. rep. for spl. polit. affairs U.S. Mission to UN, N.Y.C., 1973-76; alt. U.S. rep. to 6th and 7th spl. sessions and 29th and 30th sessions UN Gen. Assembly, 1973-76; U.S. rep. 16th session Econ. Commn. for Latin Am., 1975; alt. U.S. rep. to Internat. Women's Year Conf., 1975; bd. dirs. Am. Council on Edn., 1977-80; Mem. Am. Council for UN U.; mem. internat. adv. panel East-West Center, Edward R. Murrow Center, Fletcher Sch. Law and Diplomacy. Recipient Career Service award Nat. Civil Service League, 1967; Rockefeller Pub. Service award, 1972. Mem. Council on Fgn. Relations, Phi Beta Kappa. Home: Washington, D.C. Died Dec. 30, 1984.

WHITE, CHARLES SAFFORD, distillery exec.; b. Burlington, Vt., Apr. 20, 1903; s. Charles E. and Alice (Roberts) W.; student U. Wis., 1923-26; m. Nan Womelsdorf, Feb. 9, 1939 (dec. Dec. 1962); m. 2d, Sally Shadwick, June 25, 1965. Salesman, U.S. Gypsum Co., Boston, 1927-30; traffic mgr. Am. Airlines, St. Louis, Chgo., 1930-34; v.p. Fleischmann Distilling Corp., N.Y.C., 1945-55, pres., 1956-65, chmn. bd., 1965-67. Served to col. USAAF, 1941-45. Mem. Am. Legion, Air Force Assn., Delta Tau Delta, Skull and Crescent, Haresfoot. Episcopalian. Clubs: Boca Raton, Golden Harbour Yacht. Home: Boca Raton, Fla. Died June 18, 1984.

WHITE, GEORGE WILLARD, geologist; b. North Lawrence, Ohio, July 8, 1903; s. William Sherman and Ora Octavia (Battin) W.; B.A., Otterbein Coll., 1921, Sc.D., 1949; M.A., Ohio State U., 1925, Ph.D., 1933; D.Sc. U. N.H., 1955, Bowling Green (Ohio) State U., 1963; m. Mildred Mae Kissner, Dec. 22, 1928. Instr. geology U. Tenn., 1925-26; from instr. to prof. geology, head dept. U. N.H., 1926-41, acting dean Grad. Sch., 1940; prof. geology, Ohio State U., 1941-47 (part time 1946-47); state geologist of Ohio, 1946-47; prof. geology, dept. head U. Ill., 1947-65, research prof., 1965-71, emeritus, 1971—; Gurley lectr. Cornell U., 1955; geologist Geol. Survey Ohio, N.H. Hwy. Dept., N.H. Fish & Game Dept., N.H. Plan. Commn., summers, 1925-45, U.S. Geol. Survey, 1944-46, 49-67; vice-chmn. Ohio Water Resources Bd., 1946-47; cons. Ohio Div. Geol. Survey, 1972-85. Fellow Geol. Soc. (chmn. geomorphology group 1957-59, council 1963-66). A.A.A.S. (sec. geol. sect. 1944-48, v.p. 1951), Ohio Acad. Sci. (v.p. 1944-46; hon.); mem. Am. Inst. Mining Engrs. (chmn. Ohio Valley sect. 1946-47), Internat. Com. History Geol. Scis. (v.p. for N.Am. 1967-75), N.H. Acad. Sci. (sec.-treas. 1930-38, pres. 1939-40), U.S. Com. for History of Geology (chmn. 1974-75), Am. Assn. Petroleum Geologists, Boston Geol. Soc. (pres. 1940-41), Sigma Xi, Phi Kappa Phi, Sigma Gamma Epsilon. Conglist. Mason. Editor: Contributions to History of Geology. Contbr. geol. and scientific jours. Home: Champaign, Ill. Died Feb. 20, 1985; interred Mt. Hope Mausoleum, Champaign, Ill.

WHITE, HARVEY ELLIOTT, educator, physicist; b. Parkersburg, W.Va., Jan. 28, 1902; s. Elliott Adam and Elizabeth (Wile) W.; A.B., Occidental Coll., 1925, also Sc.D. (hon.); Ph.D., Cornell U., 1929; m. Adeline Dally, Aug. 10, 1928; children—Donald H., Jerald P., Vernita L. Teaching asst. Cornell U., 1925-26, instr., 1926-29; internat. research fellow Physikalische Techneische Reischsanstalt, Berlin, Germany, 1929-30; asst. prof. U. Calif., 1930-36, asso. prof., 1936-42, prof. 1942-69. prof. emeritus, 1969-82; planner, 1st dir. Lawrence Hall Sci., 1960-69; tchr. nationwide NBC-TV broadcast physics course for high sch. tchrs., 1958, Civilian AEC; with OSRD, 1942-45, Guggenheim Fellow, Hawaii, 1948; recipient War Dept. citation, 1947; Thomas Alva Edison TV award, Peabody TV award, Parents mag. medal, Sylvania award, Hans Christian Oersted award Am. Assn. Physics Tchrs., 1968, others. Fellow Am. Phys. Soc.; mem. Optical Soc. Am., Phi Beta Kappa, Sigma Xi, Phi Kappa Phi. Club: Bohemian. Author: Introduction to Atomic Spectra, 1934; Fundamentals of Optics, 4 edits., 1937; Classical and Modern Physics, 1940; Modern College Physics, 6 edits., 1948; Descriptive College Physics, 1955; Atomic and Nuclear Physics, 1964; Introduction to College Physics, 1969; others. Author and lectr. for 1st complete introductory physics course to be put on color film. Home: Berkeley, Calif. Died Nov. 18, 1982.

WHITE, HORACE GLENN, book publisher; b. Trumbull, Conn., Nov. 21, 1887; s. William John and Emma Teresa (Berman) W.; A.B., Wesleyan U., 1909; m. Edith Mason Stuart Baum, July 2, 1910; one son, Horace G., Jr.; married 2d, Ruthanne Frame, February 22, 1946. Corr. Am. Book Co., 1909-11; dir. coll. dept., P. Blakiston's Son & Co., Phila., Pa., 1911-12, sales mgr., 1912-29, gen. mgr., 1929-37, exec. vice pres., 1937-39; pres. The Blakiston Co. from 1939; consultant Doubleday and Co. (Blakiston Co. merged as subsidiary, 1944). Trustee Wesleyan U. Mem. several sci. socs. Ind. Republican. Protestant. Clubs: Aronimink Golf, Penn Athletic (Phila.). Home: Edgemont Township, Pa. †

WHITE, JOHN JAMIESON, JR., architect; b. Calgary, Alta., Can.; s. John Jamieson and Mary Martha (Walters) W.; m. Leonore Ruth Snyder; children—Nancy, Alexandra (dec.), John Jamieson III, Alison. B.Arch., U. Mich.; grad., Naval War Coll., 1962. Prin. in archtl. and engring. firms Mackenzie Bogert & White, N.Y.C., 1950-54, White Noakes & Neubauer, Washington, 1954-57, John Jamieson White & Assos., Washington, 1957-59, White & Mariani, Washington, 1959-61, White-Greer Assos., Paris, from 1961; archtl. cons. surgeon gen. USAF; chief architect Howard Research Corp.; archtl. adviser Republic Vietnam, 1967-72, Republic Indonesia, 1972-74. Prin. works include Naval Air and Communications Complex, Port Lyautey, Morocco, 1950-54, Children's Hosp, San Jose, Costa Rica, 1955, Northwest, Northeast and Braniff air terminal facilities, Kennedy Internat. Airport, 1960-61, Orly Hilton Hotel, Paris, 1965. Served to comdr. USN, 1940-47; capt. ret. 1969. Decorated Navy Commendation medal; Public Works medal 1st class Republic Vietnam). Mem. AIA (dir. pub. and profl. relations 1947-50, v.p. Washington Met. chpt. 1943, life), ASCE, Société des Ingenieurs Civils de France. Republican. Clubs: Univ. (N.Y.C.); Army and Navy (Washington), Internat. (Washington). Home: Chevy Chase, MD.

WHITE, KATHARINE ELKUS, U.S. diplomat; b. N.Y.C., Nov. 25, 1906; d. Abram Isaac and Gertrude

(Mess) Elkus; A.B., Vassar College, 1928; LL.D. (honorary), Douglass Coll., Rutgers, 1967; m. Arthur J. White, Oct. 3, 1929; children—Lawrence, Frances (Mrs. John H. Cohen, Jr.). Mayor, Red Bank, N.J., 1950-56; chmn. N.J. Hwy. Authority, 1955-64; acting treas. N.J., 1961; U.S. ambassador to Denmark, 1964-68. Mem. Annual Assay Coin Commn., 1937, 50; chmn. adv. council President's Com. Traffic Safety, 1963-64. Chmn. Monmouth County (N.J.) Heart Fund drive, 1951, Monmouth County United Negro Coll. Fund drive, 1956. Mem. N.J. Democratic Com. for Monmouth County, 1940-64; vice chmn. N.J. Dem. Com., 1954-64; del.-at-large Dem. Nat. Conv., 1956, 60; candidate for U.S. Ho. of Reps., 1960. Trustee Red Bank Community YMCA, Monmouth County Orgn. Social Service, Monmouth County Welfare Council; pres. bd. mgrs. N.J. State Hosp., Marlboro, 1955-64. Mem. Alumnae Assn. Vassar Coll. (treas. 1949-52), Am. Assn. U. Women (treas. 1950-53), Internat. Fedn. Univ. Women (asst. hon. treas. 1959-64), Gen. Fedn. Women's Clubs, Bus. and Profl. Women's Assn. Club: Soroptimists. Home: Red Bank, N.J. Died Apr. 24, 1985.

WHITE, LUCIUS READ, JR., architect; b. Balt., July 20, 1887; s. Lucius Read and Cora Virginia (Boarman) W.; grad. Balt. City Coll., 1905; B.S., U. Pa., 1909; m. Roberta Duncan, June 5, 1912; children—Mildred D., Edward C. Instr. U. Pa., 1909-10; chief draftsman Otto G. Simonson, 1912-17, asso. draftsman, 1917-21, partner, 1922-23; partner Lucius R. White, Jr., Balt., 1923-56, Edward C. White, 1947-56, Lucius White, Edward White & Associates, from 1956; pres., dir. Govanston Bldg. Assn., Inc., 1925-52, Midstate Fed. Savings & Loan Assn., from 1952. Mem. city bldg. code com., Balt., 1937-42, city fire protection code, 1943-45, planning com., from 1945; mem. Bd. Archtl. Review, Md., 1948-56, City of Balt., from 1952; mem. adv. com. bldg. code State Md., 1950-51. Fellow A.I.A. (pres. Balt. 1941-42); mem. Bldg. Congress of Balt. (pres. 1930-31), Md. Hist. Soc. (gov. from 1948). Universalist-Unitarian (chmn. bd. 1919-34). Mason (Shriner). Clubs: Baltimore Country, Kiwanis, Engineers, University. Home: Balt., Md. †

WHITE, RAYMOND BAIRD, lumber mfr.; b. Grandin, Mo., Mar. 18, 1889; s. John Barber and Emma (Siggins) W.; student U. of Wis., 1909-12; A.B., Cornell U., 1913; m. Helen Carroll, June 7, 1924; children—John Barber (deceased), William Nicholas (deceased). Began in retail lumber business at Newark, O., 1915; asst., later mgr. Exchange Sawmills Sales Co., 1920-22, pres. and gen. mgr., from 1922; pres. Forest Lumber Co. (del.), Yoncalla Lumber Co. (Ore.), Western Timber & Land Co.; president, director of the La Central Oil & Gas Co., La. Sawmill Co., Louisiana Central Minerals Co.; sec., dir. La. Long Leaf Lumber Co. Dir. So. Pine Assn. Served with Bureau of Aircraft, A.U.S., 1918. Member Sons of the Revolution, Delta Upsilon. Republican. Conglist. Clubs: Kansas City, University, Kansas City Country, River (Kansas City, Mo.); Newport Harbor Yacht (Newport Beach, Calif.); St. Francis Yacht, Bohemian (San Francisco); California (Los Angeles). Home: Mission, Kan. †

WHITE, ROBERT JAMES, professor law, priest; b. Concord, Mass., Sept. 12, 1893; s. Patrick J. and Mary E. (Dowd) W.; A.B., Harvard, 1915, LL.B., 1920; S.T.B., Catholic U. Am., 1929, J.C.D., 1934; LL.D. (hon.), St. John's U., 1961; Dr. Canon and Civil Law, Nasson Coll., 1963. Practice law in Boston, 1920-27; asst. dist. atty. Middlesex County, Mass.; ordained priest Roman Cath. Ch., 1931; prof. comparative civil and canon law, criminal law and legal ethics Sch. of Law, Cath. U. Am., from 1931, dean Sch. Law, 1937-48; cons. Dept. Def.; lectr. service schs. Chmn. Gov. Mass. Adv. Com. on Penal Instns.; mem. Mass. Com. to Revise Criminal Law; mem. Mass. Commn. Firearms Control and Prisoner Parole. Served to lt. U.S. Navy, World War I; lt. comdr., chaplain and sr. chaplain, USNR; fleet chaplain, VIII Fleet; retired as rear adm., 1947. Decorated Bronze Star. Mem. Am. Bar Assn., N.Y. Cath. Lawyers Guild, Am. Legion (past nat. chaplain), Fed. Interalliee des Anciennes Combattants (v.p.), Assn. Former Nat. and State Chaplains Am. Legion (pres.), Chaplains' Assn. Army and Navy U.S. (pres.), Clubs: Harvard (Boston and Washington). Author: The Legal Effects of Ante-Nuptial Promises in Mixed Marriages, 1932; The Lawyer and His Profession; Confession and the Law; A Study of Five Hundred Naval Prisoners and Naval Justices; Mobilization, Morale and Combat Success in the U.S. Navy; Has the Uniform Code of Military Justice Improved Courts-Martial; The Universal Code of Military Justice, 1951-61; Promise and Performance. Contbr. revs. Home: Old Orchard, Maine. Died Dec. 3, 1984.

WHITE, THOMAS P(ATRICK), state judge; b. Los Angeles, Sept. 27, 1888; s. Peter and Catherine (Clark) W.; student parochial schs., Los Angeles; LL.B., U. So. Cal., 1911; LL.D., Loyola U., Los Angeles, 1925; m. Helen Hickson, Feb. 3, 1915 (dec. Aug. 1935). Clk. A.T. & S.F. Ry., Los Angeles, 1905-08; admitted to Cal. bar, 1911; judge Los Angeles City Police Ct., 1913-19; practice of law, Los Angeles, 1919-31; judge Superior Ct., Los Angeles Co., 1931-37; justice Dist. Ct. Appeals, 2d Appelate Div. of Cal., 1937-49, presiding justice, 1949; now asso. justice Supreme Ct. of Cal. Mem. Am. Bar Assn., Native Sons Golden West, Phi Delta Phi, Delta Chi, Sigma Delta Kappa. Republican. Roman Catholic. K.C., Elk. †

WHITE, WILLIAM BEW, lawyer; b. Albany, N.Y., 1888; son of John Jay and Charlotte Eliza (Bew) W.; LL.B., Cornell U., 1909; m. Mary Lee Drennen. Nov. 10, 1914; children—Marjorie (wife of Dr. James L. Tullis), William Bew, Mary Alice (Mrs. John W. Sample, Jr.). Admitted to N.Y. bar, 1909, Ala. bar, 1913, asso. Davies, Auerbach & Cornell, N.Y.C., 1909-13, Tillman, Bradley & Morrow, Birmingham, 1913-16; jr. mem. 1916-25, senior member firm of White, Bradley, Arant, All & Rose, 1925-63, counsel to successor firm Bradley, Arant, Rose & White. Member board directors Birmingham Trust Nat. Bank. Mem. Am., Alabama, Birmingham bar assns., Phi Delta Phi, Sigma Alpha Epsilon. Republican. Episcopalian. Clubs: Birmingham Country, Downtown. Home: Birmingham, Ala. †

WHITE, WILLIAM HENRY, shipbldg. co. exec.; b. Plymouth, Eng., July 12, 1922; s. George Hilliard and Hannah (Bath) W.; m. Catherine Jean McNally, Jan. 12, 1946; children—Peter William, Edward George. Diploma, Royal Naval Tech. Coll., Bermuda. With Brit. Admiralty, 1935-45, mem. tech. mission to, Ottawa, Ont., Can., 1944-45; ship draughtsman Davie Shipbldg. Ltd., Lauzon, Que., Can., 1945-48, chief hull and elec. draughtsman, 1948-51, asst. naval architect, 1951-52, naval architect, 1952-55, asst. to gen. mgr., 1955-59, tech. mgr., 1959-60, sr. v.p., 1976-79, pres., 1979-82; gen. mgr. Bermuda Marine Services, 1960-62; mgr. ops. Hall Corp. Ltd., Montreal, Que., 1962-65; v.p., gen. mgr. St. John Shipbldg. & Dry Dock Co. Ltd., N.B., Can., 1965-69; gen. mgr. marine Industries Ltd., Sorel, Que., 1970-74, v.p. shipbldg., 1974-76; dir. Soconav Limitée, D.A.C. Group Ltd. Fellow Royal Inst. Naval Architects; mem. Can. Shipbldg. and Ship Repairing Assn. (dir., past pres.), Soc. Naval Architects and Marine Engrs., Am. Bur. Shipping, Bur. Veritas Internat. Com. Clubs: Laurentian (Ottawa); Masons (past dist. dep. grand master Que.). Home: Quebec, Que., Can. Died Apr. 17, 1982.

WHITE, WILLIAM R(OBERT), army officer; b. Portsmouth, Va., Jan. 14, 1887; s. William Norman and Dorah (Walton) W.; student Portsmouth Bus. Coll., 1906; Dowd's Prep. Sch., Washington, 1911-12; Q.M.C. Sch., 1924-25; Command and Gen. Staff Sch., 1927-28, Army War Coll., 1932-33; m. Mabel Wheeler, May 2, 1914. Commd., 1912; promoted through grades to col., 1941; brig. gen. (temp.), 1942; dir. food control T.H. from Jan. 1941. Decorations; Mexican War, World War (2 stars); Legion of Merit, Clubs: Army and Navy, Pacific (Honolulu). Deceased.

WHITEHEAD, FRANK, marine corps officer; b. Camden, N.J., Jan. 4, 1888; s. Joseph and Annie (Jarvis) W.; m. Eleanor V. Ashcom. Entered U.S., Marine Corps, 1908, and advanced through the grades to brig. gen., 1944; retired, 1944. Decorated Navy Cross, Purple Heart (twice), Distinguished Service Cross (U.S.), Croix de Guerre (France). Home: Washington, D.C. Deceased.

WHITEHEAD, THOMAS HILLYER, university dean; b. Maysville, Ga., Sept. 5, 1904; s. Asa Hillyer and Clara (Comer) W.; B.S., U. Ga., 1925; M.A., Columbia, 1928, Ph.D., 1930; m. Dorothy Lou Simms, Dec. 19, 1931; children—Thomas H., John S. Mem. faculty U. Ga., Athens, from 1930; prof. chemistry, 1946-51, from 1952, coordinator instructional instns. Grad. Sch., 1960-68, dean, 1968-72. With Chem. Warfare Service, 1942-46, Army Chem. Center, 1951-52; cons. AEC, after 1952, Wright-Patterson AFB, 1964-68. Decorated Legion of Merit; recipient Distinguished Alumnus award U. Ga., 1973. Fellow Ga. Acad. Sci.; mem. Am. Chem. Soc., AAAS, Sigma Xi, Phi Kappa Phi, Phi Lambda Upsilon. Author: Theory of Elementary Chemical Analysis, 1950. Home: Athens, Ga. Dec. Feb. 13, 1982.

WHITELAW, JORDAN M., TV and radio producer; b. N.Y.C., Oct. 15, 1920; s. Louis and Dora (Schatzberg) W. Grad., Phillips Acad., Andover, Mass., 1938; A.B., Harvard U., 1942, M.A. in Am. History, 1948; postgrad., Sch. Arts and Sci., 1948-51; D.Music (hon.), New Eng. Conservatory of Music, 1981. Music producer, Sta.-WGBH-FM, Boston, 1951-62; music mgr., producer Boston Symphony Orch. broadcasts, 1953-62, music mgr. and producer, Sta.-WGBH-TV, 1957-62; broadcast producer, Boston Symphony Orch., 1970, free-lance TV producer, primarily for, Sta.WGBH-FM and its; series Evening at Symphony, from 1970; producer Boston Symphony Orch. broadcasts and syndicated tapes, Sta.-WCRB, Waltham, Mass., from 1971; Author: organ transcription Bach Prelude to Cantata 156, 1966. Served with OSS, 1944-46, ETO. Home: Boston, Mass.

WHITELEY, GEORGE HENRY, mgr. exec.; b. Phila., Jan. 31, 1888; s. George H. and Isa (Osborne) W.; student Princeton, 1910; m. Purdon Smith, Jan. 28, 1914; children—Virginia (Mrs. Henry M. Thornton), George Henry III, Morgan S., Purdon (Mrs. William S. Frey). With Dentsply Internat. (formerly Dentists Supply Co.), York, Pa., chmn. bd.; dir. The Amalgamated Dental Co., Ltd., London, England. Pres. Martin Library Assn., York; trustee YMCA, YWCA, Hist. Soc., Colonial Restoration Assn. (all York). Mem. York Mfrs. Assn. (dir.), York C. of C. Presbyn. Clubs: York Country, Lafayette (York). Home: York, PA. †

WHITENACK, CAROLYN IRENE, educator, librarian; b. Harrodsburg, Ky., Apr. 20, 1916; d. John Hughes and Grace (Chilton) Whitenack; A.B., U. Ky., 1948; M.S., U. Ill., 1956. Tchr., Ky. pub. schs., 1934-47; instr. library sci., librarian U. Ky., 1947-50; head cataloger Louisville pub. schs., 1950-53; dir. div. sch. libraries, teaching materials Ind. Dept. Edn., 1953-56; asst. prof. library sci. and audiovisual edn. Purdue U., 1956-60, asso. prof., 1960-67, prof., chmn. media scis., 1967-79; ret., 1979. Mem. NEA-ALA joint com., 1955—, chmn., 1957-58; del. World Confedn. Orgn. Teaching Profession, Stockholm, 1962, Vancouver, 1967, Dublin, 1968, Singapore, 1974; ALA del. Internat. Fedn. Library Assns., Switzerland, 1962, Moscow, 1970; AID cons. Middle East Tech. U., Ankara, Turkey, 1972. Mem. Ednl. Media Council (sec. 1959—), ALA (library edn. div., resources and tech. services div., 2 v.p. 1960-61, councilor 1955-60, chmn. appointment com. 1959, nominating com. 1959-60; Beta Phi Mu award 1976), NEA (and depts.), Am. Assn. Sch. Librarians (joint com. A.A.S.L.-A.C.R.L.-D.A.V.I., chmn. 1959—, pres. 1968), Ind. Sch. Librarians Assn. (pres.), Hoosier Student Librarian Assn., Ind. Library Assn., Ind. Assn. Ednl. Communication and Tech., Assn. Ind. Media Educators, Ind. Assn. Supervision and Curriculum Devel., Ednl. Media Council, Am. Assn. U. Profs., Kappa Delta Pi, Beta Pi Mu. Contbr. articles profl. jours. Home: Harrodsburg, Ky. Dec. Jan. 13, 1984. Interned Harrodsburg, Ky.

WHITFIELD, ALLEN, lawyer; b. Ruthven, Iowa, Jan. 26, 1904; s. Rev. George and Sarah (Allen) W.; m. Irma Cowan, Aug. 18, 1927; children—Lura Mae (Mrs. M.K. Johnson), Harley Allen. Student, U. Nebr., 1920-21; B.S., Iowa State U., 1924; LL.B., Harvard, 1927; grad. study, Drake U., 1928; D.H.L. (hon.), Morningside Coll., 1978. Bar: Fla. and Iowa bars 1928, D.C. bar 1961. Practice in, Des Moines, from 1928; partner firm Whitfield, Musgrave, Selvy, Kelly & Eddy.; Pres. Des Moines Joint Stock Land Bank, 1936-40; dir. Internat. Bank, Valley Nat. Bank, Fin. Security Group, Inc. Chmn. Vets. Meml. Auditorium Commn., 1946-57; mem. commn. chaplains and related ministries United Methodist Ch., 1968-74, mem. bd. publ., 1956-68; hon. trustee Morningside Coll., Simpson Coll.; bd. govs. Iowa State U. Found.; trustee U.S. Jaycees Found.; bd. dirs. Greater Des Moines Community Found. Served to lt. col., internat. div. War Dept. AUS, 1942-45. Decorated Legion of Merit. Mem. U.S. Jr. C. of C. (pres. 1935-36), Iowa Jr. C. of C. (pres. 1934), Greater Des Moines C. of C. (pres. 1949), U.S. C. of C. (dir. 1963-69, 72-78, treas. 1969-72), Am., Iowa, Polk County bar assns., Internat. Assn. Ins. Counsel, Fedn. Ins. Counsel, Am. Legion, V.F.W., Amvets, Iowa State U. Alumni Assn. (pres. 1942), Kappa Sigma, Sigma Delta Chi, Delta Sigma Rho. Methodist (lay leader Iowa-Des Moines conf., 1951-55). Club: Mason. Home: Des Moines, IA.

WHITFIELD, ROBERT JOSEPH, banker; b. Oxford, Miss., July 26, 1889; s. Albert Hall and Isadore (Buffalo) W.; student U. Miss., 1907-09, Johns Hopkins, 1909-10, U. Tex. Law Sch., 1916-17; m. Clinton Brooks, Aug. 23, 1930; 1 son, C. Brooks. Prin. various high schs., 1910-16; v.p. Fed. Commerce Trust Co., St. Louis, 1921-27, Chase Securities Corp.-Chase Nat. Bank, 1927-54; pres. Machine Product Co., Inc., Aberdeen, Miss., from 1955; dir. Am. Erika Corp., N.Y. Herald Tribune, Inc. Served as capt., inf., U.S. Army, 1916-18. Mem. Kappa Alpha, Phi Delta Phi. Episcopalian. CLubs: Rotary, Greenville Golf and Country. Home: Greenville, Miss. †

WHITING, PHINEAS WESCOTT, geneticist; b. Lowell, Mass., Oct. 28, 1887; s. Henry Fairfax and Louise Hazeltine (Wescott) W.; student Dartmouth Coll., 1907-09; A.B., Harvard, 1911, M.S., 1912; student Bussey Inst., Forest Hills, Mass., 1912-14; Ph.D., U. of Pa., 1916; m. Anna Rachel Young, June 29, 1918. Harrison research fellow, U. of Pa., 1916-18; prof. biology Franklin and Marshall Coll., Lancaster, Pa., 1918-20; asso. prof. biology St. Stephen's Coll., Annandale-on-Hudson, 1920-21; research asso. prof. in eugenics Ia. Child Welfare Research Sta., Iowa City, Ia., 1921-24; prof. biology and head dept. U. of Me., 1924-27; research investigator in problems of sex Nat. Research Council, Bussey Instn., Harvard, 1927; asso. prof. zoology U. of Pittsburgh, 1928-31, prof., 1931-33; asso. prof. zoology U. of Pa., 1935-46, prof. from 1946. Mem. corp. Marine Biol. Lab., Woods Hole, Mass. Fellow A.A.A.S.; mem. Am. Genetic Assn., Am. Soc. Zoölogists, Am. Society Naturalists, Sigma Xi, Sigma Phi Epsilon. Author of about 100 research papers; specialist in investigation in parthenogenesis and sex-determination in Hymenoptera. Home: Secane, Pa. †

WHITINGER, RALPH JUDSON, accountant; b. Muncie, Ind., Oct. 5, 1908; s. James F. and Emma (Young) W.; m. Geraldine E. Geis, Aug. 1, 1952. B.S., Ball State U., 1929, LL.D., 1969. Practice pub. accounting, Muncie, 1930-82; sr. ptnr. R.J. Whitinger & Co., 1943-82; dir. Mchts. Nat. Bank Muncie, Maxon Corp., N.G. Gilbert Corp., Muncie Power Products, Inc. Pres. United Fund Delaware County, Ind., 1956; trustee Muncie YMCA; bd. dirs. N.G. Gilbert Found., Margaret Ball Petty Found.; pres. bd. dirs. Ball State U. Found., from 1952. Recipient Silver Beaver award Boy Scouts Am., 1947; Disting. Service award Muncie Jr. C. of C., 1954; Distinguished Alumni award Ball State U., 1960; Horatio Alger award Boys Club, 1970; named Ky. col. Mem. Am. Inst. C.P.A.s, Am. Acctg. Assn., Ind. Assn. C.P.A.s (pres. 1948-49), Newcomen Soc., Muncie C. of C. (pres. 1961), Theta Chi. Republican. Presbyterian. Clubs: Columbia (Indpls.); Muncie (Muncie), Delaware Country (Muncie). Home: Muncie, Ind. Dec. May 25, 1982.

WHITLEY, WYATT CARR, educator; b. Salma, N.C., Oct. 17, 1900; s. John Berry and Nancy (Greene) W.; B.S. in Chemistry, Wake Forest Coll., 1928; M.S. in Chemistry, Ga. Inst. Tech., 1933; Ph.D. in Chemistry, U. Wis., 1939; m. Lora Magdeline Dills, Dec. 26, 1934; children—John Bryan, Margaret, Nancy Lucinda. Instr. chemistry George Washington U., 1929; cons. Puritan Chem. Co., Atlanta, 1942-46, Internat. Minerals and Chem. Corp., Atlanta, 1945; faculty Ga. Inst. Tech., from 1929, prof. chemistry, from 1944, chief chem. scis. div., engring. expt. sta., 1956-61, asso. dir. engring. expt. sta., 1962-63, dir. engring. expt. sta., 1963-68, dir. emeritus, 1968-82; research participant Oak Ridge Nat. Lab., summers 1951-54; spl. research inorganic and analytical chemistry, radiochemistry, instrumental methods analysis. Mem. Am. Chem. Soc., Ga. Acad. Sci., Ga. Tech. Research Club, Ga. Tech. Athletic Assn. (dir. 1946-58), Sigma Xi, Golden Bough, Alpha Chi Sigma, Phi Lambda Upsilon, Gamma Sigma Epsilon. Democrat. Baptist (deacon). Club: Optimist Internat. (gov. Ga. dist.). Author: (with John L. Daniel) Theory of Analysis, 1939. Home: Atlanta, Ga. Died Nov. 5, 1982.

WHITLOCK, ALBERT NEWTON, lawyer; b. Richmond, Ky., Sept. 1, 1887; s. James V. and Alice F. (Baker) W.; B.A., U. of Ky., 1906, M.A., 1908; LL.B., Harvard Univ., 1911; LL.D., University Mont., 1953; m. Charlotte Reed Thurston, Aug. 29, 1912 (dec. May 1959). Prin. Caldwell High Sch., Richmond, Ky., 1906; instr. dept. of English, U. of Ky., 1906-08; admitted to Ky. bar, 1909; asst. prof. law, 1911-12, prof., 1912-35, acting dean, 1913-15, dean, 1915-19, U. of Mont.; mem. Murphy & Whitlock, Missoula, Mont., 1917-1940; general attorney C.,M.St.P.&P. R.R. Co., Seattle, Wash., 1935-39; counsel trustees, same r.r., Chgo., 1939-45, v.p., gen. counsel, 1945-51. Member of State Board Law Examiners, Mont., 1917-33. Mem. Am., Ky., Ill., Mont., Wash. bar assns., Am. Newcomen Soc., Sigma Chi. Democrat. Mem. Christian (Disciples) Ch. Clubs: Rainier (Seattle); Filson. Home: Lexington, Ky. †

WHITMER, JOSEPH RUTLEDGE, coll. pres.; b. Bremen, Ky., Mar. 18, 1890; s. John T. and Nannie J. W.; grad. Western Ky. State Normal Sch., 1920 (pres. of class); B.S., University of Ky., 1922; A.B. Western Ky. State Normal and Teachers Coll., 1924; grad. work, Peabody Coll., 1925; hon. M.S., Iowa State College, 1929; m. Beulah Wiggins, June 21, 1914; children—Theresa Elizabeth, Carolyn. Began teaching in common schs. at 17, later in graded and high schs., and high sch. prin. 2 yrs.; mem. faculty, Western State Normal Sch., 1922-23; pres. Bethel Coll., McKenzie, Tenn., 1923-27; mem. Floating University, world cruise, 1926-27; now mem. faculty Western State Normal and Teachers Coll. Y.M.C.A. work, Camp Zachary Taylor, World War. Mem. Phi Kappa Phi. Republican. Cumberland Presbyn. Mason. Home: Bowling Green, Ky. †

WHITNER, ROBERT LEE, educator; b. Seattle, Dec. 30, 1917; s. Walter Bronson and Norine (O'Hara) W.; B.A. in Edn., Central Wash. Coll. Edn., 1941; M.A., Wash. State Coll., 1948; Ph.D., U. Minn., 1958; m. Lola Alice Mitchell, Aug. 25, 1940; children—Karen, Stephen, Christine (Mrs. David Scheafer). Faculty, Whitman Coll., Walla Walla, Wash., 1951-82, prof. history, 1964-68, dean of students, 1964-67, William Kirkman prof. history, 1968-82. Bd. curators Wash. State Hist. Soc., from 1962, v.p., 1968. Served with AUS, 1943-46. Mem. Am. Hist. Assn., Orgn. Am. Historians, Western History Assn., Assn. Am. U. Profs. Home: Walla Walla, Wash. Died Nov. 23, 1982.

WHITNEY, GEORGE KIRKPATRICK, investment consultant; b. Concord, Mass., Nov. 9, 1907; s. Charles Hayden and Caroline (Patrick) W.; A.B., Harvard U., 1929, M.B.A., 1931; m. Donita Stahl, 1936 (dec.); children—Robert Hayden, Sarah Minot, Faith Thomas Newcomb; m. Una Rogers King, Sept. 6, 1951. With trust investment div., trust dept. First Nat. Bank Chgo., 1931-34; investment dept. Conn. Bank & Trust Co., 1934-43; investment research dept. Mass. Investors Trust, 1943-47, trustee, 1947-70; dir., mem. investment mgmt. com. Mass. Investors Growth Stock Fund, Inc., 1945-70, v.p., 1963-70; gov. Investment Co. Inst., 1960-63, mem. exec. com., 1960-62; sr. v.p., dir. Mass. Financial Services, 1969-70, cons., 1970-77, ltd. partner, from 1977. Bd. dirs. Big Bros. Assn., Boston; corporator Emerson Hosp., Concord; chmn. Harvard Bus. Sch. Fund, 1963-66; mem. Harvard Overseers Com. to Visit Bus. Sch., 1968-74; bd. dirs. Harvard Bus. Sch. Assocs., 1971-74, 75-79; mem. adminstrv. bd. Adams Papers. Mem. Mass. Hist. Soc. (v.p., fin. com.), Harvard Bus. Sch. Assn. (exec. council 1966-73, pres. 1967-68; Distinguished Service award 1969), Asso. Harvard Alumni (dir. 1968-70), World Affairs Council Boston (dir., exec. com.), Nat. Trust Historic Preservation (life), Transp. Assn. Am. (dir. from 1947, chmn. 1968-70, hon. chmn. 1970-74, chmn. bd. govs. 1976-77, Seley award 1974), Nat. Assn. Investment Cos. (pres. 1960-61), Am. Hist. Assn. (life), Soc. Preservation of New Eng. Antiquities, Soc. Colonial Wars, New Eng. Historic Geneal. Soc., Bostonian Soc. (life), Am. Forestry Assn. (life), New Eng. Forestry Found. (founder). Republican. Episcopalian. Clubs: Econ., Union (Boston); Harvard (N.Y.C.); Country (Brookline, Mass.); Concord Country; Ekwanok Country (Manchester, Vt.); Harvard Varsity, Speakers' (Cambridge, Mass.); Met. (Washington); Mid-Ocean (Bermuda). Home: Concord, Mass. Died Dec. 30, 1979.

WHITNEY, JOHN HAY, publisher; b. Ellsworth, Maine, Aug. 17, 1904; s. Payne and Helen (Hay) W.; m. Betsey Cushing Roosevelt, Mar. 1, 1942; children—Sara Wilford, Kate. Student, Oxford (Eng.) U., 1926-27, Yale U., 1922-26; L.H.D., Kenyon Coll.; LL.D., Colgate U., Brown U., 1958, Exeter U., 1959, Colby Coll., Columbia U.; M.A. (hon.), Yale U. Sr. ptnr. J.H. Whitney & Co., N.Y.C.; chmn. Whitney Communications; U.S. ambassador to Gt. Britain, 1956-61; pub. N.Y. Herald-Tribune (and subs.'s), 1957-61, pres., pub., 1961, editor-in-chief, pub., 1961-66; dir., mem. editorial com. World Jour. Tribune, Inc., 1966-67; chmn. Internat. Herald Tribune, Paris; ptnr. Whitcom Investment Co.; John Hay Whitney prof. humanities Yale U., 1977; past dir. Dun & Bradstreet, Inc. Chmn. John Hay Whitney Found.; former mem. N.Y. State Youth Commn., also, Pres.'s Com. on Edn. Beyond High Sch.; apptd. spl. adviser and cons. on pub. affairs Dept. State; grad. mem. Bus. Council; past mem. Corp. Pub. Broadcasting, N.Y. Banking Bd.; mem. Commn. Fgn. Econ. Policy, 1954, Policy Com. on Personnel, 1954; past mem. Saratoga Springs Commn.; trustee emeritus Saratoga Performing Arts Center; hon. mem. bd. govs. N.Y. Hosp.; hon. trustee Mus. Modern Art; trustee N.Y. Racing Assn., 1955-81; former trustee Nat. Gallery Art (v.p.); co-chmn. emeritus bd. trustees North Shore Hosp.; fellow Yale Corp., 1955-70, sr. fellow, 1970-73; bd. dirs. Ednl. Broadcasting Corp., 1969-70. Served as col. USAAF, World War II. Recipient Yale medal award, 1954; Tuition Plan award, 1954; Hundred Year Assn. gold medal; Albert Einstein Commerative award; Benjamin Franklin medal Eng.; Elijah Parish Lovejoy award Colby Coll.; decorated Legion of Merit, Bronze Star; chevalier French Légion d'Honneur; chevalier La Grande médaille de Vermeil, Paris; knight St. John of Jerusalem; comdr. Order Brit. Empire. Mem. Pilgrims U.S. (hon. v.p.), English-Speaking Union (chmn. nat. bd. 1961-63), Scroll and Key. Clubs: Jockey (N.Y.C.), Augusta Nat. Golf (N.Y.C.), N.Y. Yacht (N.Y.C.), Racquet and Tennis (N.Y.C.), Scroll and Key (N.Y.C.). Home: Manhasset, N.Y. Dec. Feb. 8, 1982.

WHITNEY, SIMON NEWCOMB, educator; b. N.Y.C., Apr. 5, 1903; s. Edward Baldwin and Josepha (Newcomb) W.; grad. Taft Sch., 1919; student Deep Springs (Calif.) Jr. Coll., 1919-21; B.A., Yale, 1924, Ph.D., 1931; German-Am. exchange student Bonn U., 1925-26; m. Eunice Gilbert McIntosh, Aug. 23, 1941; children—Eunice Elizabeth, Simon Newcomb, Roger Sherman, Walter McIntosh. Instr. econs. Yale, 1926-28; economist antitrust div. Dept. Justice, 1928-29; asst. to economist Chase Nat. Bank of N.Y., 1931-34; sr. economist research and planning div. Nat. Recovery Adminstrn., 1934-36; staff div. research and statistics, bd. govs. Fed. Res. System, 1936; asso. Lionel D. Edie & Co., investment counsellors, N.Y.C., 1936-40; economist O'Ryan Financial Commn. to Japan, 1940; prin. economist Office Export Control and Bd. Econ. Warfare, 1941-42; pres. Telluride Assn., endowed ednl. found., Ithaca, N.Y., 1930-31, dean, 1942-48, dir. Deep Springs (Calif.) Jr. Coll., 1942-48; cons. ECA, 1948; asso. prof. econs. Coll. Arts and Sci., N.Y.U., 1948-49, prof., 1949-54, lectr., 1954-55; v.p. Econometric Inst., 1949; asso. economist Twentieth Century Fund, N.Y.C., 1949-54, dir. research, 1954-55; dir. Bur. Econs., FTC, 1956-61; prof. econs. Rutgers U., 1961-67, N.Y.U., 1967-71; adj. prof. econs. Baruch Coll., City U. N.Y., 1971-72, vis. prof., 1972-73; adj. prof. econs. Iona Coll., 1971-72, vis. prof., 1973. Mem. Royal Econ. Soc., Am. Econ. Assn., Phi Beta Kappa. Author: Trade Associations and Industrial Control: A Critique of the NRA, 1934; Antitrust Policies: American Experience in Twenty Industries, 1958; Principles of Macroeconomics, 1973; Principles of Microeconomics, 1973; Economic Principles, 2 vols., 1975. Home: Scarsdale, N.Y. Died Jan. 14, 1982.

WHITTAKER, DOUGLAS ARTHUR, business exec.; b. Morrisburg, Ont., June 21, 1889; s. Charles Theodore and Mary (Colquhoun) Whittaker; ed. Morrisburg Collegiate Inst.; m. Gertrude Isobel Ballantyne, June 2, 1920. Began as a junior with the Sherwin-Williams Co. of Canada, Ltd., Montreal, in Oct., 1905, pres. and mng. dir.; pres. Can. Paint Co., Ltd., Winnipeg Paint & Glass Company, Limited, Canada, Carter White Lead Company of Canada, Limited, Lowe Brothers Company, Limited, Martin-Seour Company, Limited, Sherwin-Williams Company of Canada, Ltd. Pres. Quebec Division, Canadian Credit Men's Trust Assn., 1925-26, and Dominion pres., 1930. Pres. Montreal Board of Trade, 1943-44. Fellow Chartered Institute of Secretaries, Credit Institute (Canada). Clubs: Mount Stephen, Kanawaki Golf, Caledonia Curling, Massawippi Country, St. James's. Home: North Hatley, Que. †

WHITTEMORE, ARTHUR AUSTIN, concert pianist; b. Vermillion, S.D., Oct. 23, 1916; s. Arthur Henry and Helen (Austin) W. B.F.A., U. S.D., 1935, Mus. D. (hon.), 1965; Mus.M., U. Rochester, 1937. founder Bravo mag. serious music cons. SESAC, 1978—. Co-founder, Whit/Lo Singers, nat. tour, 1967; appearing on TV show Personal Touch of Whittemore and Lowe; Piano debut with Jack Lowe, N.Y. Town Hall, 1940, recitals throughout, Am., Can., and Europe, engagments with major symphonies including Boston, N.Y., Phila., Chgo., San Francisco, and St. Louis; premier performance of contemporary works, Vaughan Williams, Morton Gould, Poulenc, Krenek and, others, recording pianist with, Mitropoulos, Stokowski and, others; regular guest: TV Today-Garroway Show, NBC; Recs. for, RCA Victor, Capitol, Angel. Served with USNR, 1942-46. Recipient citations U.S. Treasury Dept., citations U. Rochester. Mem. Delta Tau Delta. Club: Lotos. Home: Quogue, N.Y. Died Oct. 23, 1984.

WHITTEMORE, MANUEL, lawyer; b. Dover, N.H., July 27, 1890; s. Arthur Gilman and Caroline (Rundlett) W.; A.B., Dartmouth, 1912; LL.B., N.Y.U., 1915; m. Elizabeth Odlin, Aug. 14, 1915 (died Dec. 28, 1926); children—Mary W. McEvoy, Margaret W. Mirick, Elizabeth W. Getty, Aaron; m. 2d Helen P. Barber, June 27, 1928. Admitted to N.Y. bar, 1915, U.S. Supreme Ct., 1922; asso. and mem. Emery, Varney, Whittemore & Dix, N.Y. City, specializing in patent and trade mark law, from 1915; spl. asst. to Atty. Gen. U.S., 1920-25; patent and trade mark counsel numerous large corps. and mfg. industries. Trustee Village of Scarsdale, N.Y., 1935-37, mayor, 1937-39, police justice from 1951; chmn. Westchester Co. War Council, 1940-45. Recipient Scarsdale Bowl, 1948. Mem. Am. Bar Assn., Am. and N.Y. patent laws assns., Dartmouth Alumni Assn., Beta Theta Pi, Phi Delta Phi. Clubs: Golf, Town (past pres.), Greenacres Association (past pres.) (Scarsdale); Appalachian Mountain. Home: Scarsdale, N.Y. Deceased.

WHITTEN, GUY RAYMOND, educator; b. Frankin, Me., June 5, 1890; s. George Googins and Jennie May (Huckins) W.; ed. Coburn Classical Inst. and Colby Coll.; m. Edith Pierce Priest, of East Bassalboro, Me., June 30, 1920. With Coburn Classical Inst. from 1919, treas. from 1927, acting prin., 1929-30, prin. from 1930. First lt. Field Arty. O.R.C. Mem. Delta Upsilon, Upsilon Beta. Mason Mem. Friends Soc. Kiwanian. Home: Waterville, Me. †

WHITTIER, WARREN FAXON, agriculturist; b. Boston, Mass., Mar. 6, 1887; s. Frank Weston and Maria Davenport (Faxon) Whitcher (direct descendant in 9th generation of Thomas Whittier; adopted original family name 1910 by permission Mass. court); grad. Milton (Mass.) Acad., 1905; A.B., Harvard, 1909, student Sch. Bus. Administrn., 1909, Grad. Sch. Applied Sci., 1913-15; Mass. State Coll. Agr., 1913-15; m. Lucy Lee Collins, Apr. 18, 1911; children—Blair Lee, Jean (Mrs. Richard A. Mahler); m. 2d, Katharine Cushing Boshart, May 8, 1920; 1 son, Frank Weston. Engaged in raising citrus fruit, San Bernardino, Calif., 1910-13; dairy farmer, Minn., 1915-17; commission agt. for improved livestock, 1919-25; dairy cattle breeder and agrl. consultant, Chester Springs, Pa., from 1925; pres. Taunton River Co., Boston; dir. Fed. Res. Bank of Phila. from 1940, dep. chmn., 1941, acting chmn., 1942-46, chmn., 1949-52. Enlisted U.S. Army, 1917, F.A.; commd. 2d lt., June 1918; hon. disch. June 1919. Chmn. N.Y. Met. Milk Marketing Conf., 1937, 38. Mem. Pa. Guernsey Breeders' Assn. (dir. from 1931, sec.-treas. 1933, 34, v.p., 1944-46), Pa. Dairymen's Assn. (vice pres. 1933, pres. 1934-38), Pa. State Council of Farm Organizations (vice pres. 1936-38), Pa. State Com. for Agrl. Adjustment Adminstrn. (vice chmn. 1936, chmn. 1937-38), Am. Acad. of Polit. and Social Sci., Quaker City Farmers, Pa. Guernsey Breeders' Assn., Friends of the Land, Pa. Soc. of New York. Republican. Presbyterian. Clubs: Brookside Country (Pottstown, Pa.); Union League (Phila.). Home: Chester Springs, Pa. †

WHITWORTH, JOHN BURTON, utility exec.; b. Piedmont, W.Va., Oct. 23, 1888; s. Edwin Walter and Laura Virginia (Burton) W.; ed. pub. schs. and Bliss Elec. Sch. (Washington); m. Alice Crooks, Sept. 10, 1914; children—John Burton, Elizabeth, Laura Virginia. Supt. of distribution Schuylkill div., Pa. Power & Light Co., 1911-12; mgr. Lykens Valley Light & Power Co., 1913-23; v.p. Gen. Utilities & Operating Co., 1918-35; gen. mgr. Peoples (Miami Beach) Gas Co., 1931-32; pres. Compania Electria De Santo Domingo, 1930-32; pres. Am. States Pub. Service Co., 1932-36; chmn. bd. and pres. Am. State Utilities Corp., 1936-42; pres. Citizens Gas Co. and Sussex Gas Co., 1939-49; pres. Frozen Food Lockers, Inc., 1943-50; pres. Kent Packing Co., Inc., from 1948; pres. and dir. Kent County Savings Bank from 1950; director First National Bank, Chestertown, Md., 1944-48. Republican. Episcopalian. Club: Chester River Yacht and Country. Address: Chestertown, Md. †

WIBBERLEY, LEONARD PATRICK O'CONNOR, author; b. Dublin, Ireland, Apr. 9, 1915; s. Thomas and Sinaid (O'Connor) W.; m. Katherine Hazel Holton, Apr. 10, 1948; children—Kevin, Patricia Wibberley Sheehey, Christopher, Arabella Wibberley Van Hoven, Cormac. Student, Cardinal Vaughan's Sch., London, 1925-30. Reporter London Sunday Dispatch, 1931-32, London Sunday Express, 1932-34, London Daily Mirror, 1935-36; editor Trinidad Evening News, B.W.I., 1936; oilfield worker, Trinidad, 1936-43; cable editor AP, 1943-44; chief N.Y. bur. London Evening News, 1944-46; editorial writer Los Angeles Times, 1950-54. Author: The Mouse that Roared, 1955, Last Stand of Father Felix, 1974, Meeting with a Great Beast, 1973, 1776 and All That, 1975, One in Four, 1976, Homeward to Ithaka, 1978, The Good-Natured Man—A Portrait of Oliver Goldsmith, 1979, The Mouse That Saved the West, 1981; over 90 other books, also 6 plays; contbr.: numerous short stories to Sat. Evening Post; articles to Los Angeles Times; weekly columnist: The Wibberley Papers syndicated by, San Francisco Chronicle,; profl. publs. Served with Trinidad Arty. Vols., 1938-41. Mem. Authors Guild, Dramatists Guild. Home: Hermosa, Calif. Dec. Nov. 22, 1983.

WICK, WARNER ARMS, educator; b. Youngstown, Ohio, May 19, 1911; s. James Lippincott and Clare

(Dryer) W.; B.A., Williams Coll., 1932; B.A., Oxford (Eng.) U., 1934; Ph.D., U. Chgo., 1941; m. Mary Elisabeth Wills, Sept. 12, 1936; children—James Lippincott, Laura Bardsley, John Dryer. Instr. philosophy Central YMCA Coll., Chgo., 1936-37, asst. prof., 1937-43; vis. asst. prof. Dartmouth Coll., 1941-42; asst. supt. Falcon Bronze Co., Youngstown, 1943-44, asst. gen. mgr. prodn., 1944-46, dir., 1946-53; asst. prof. philosophy U. Chgo., 1946-52, asso. prof., 1952-58, prof., from 1958, William Rainey Harper prof. humanities, from 1974, dean of students div. humanities, 1950-53, asso. dean coll., chmn. council advanced gen. studies, 1959-63, dean students, 1962-67, master humanities collegiate div., asso. dean div. humanities, 1971-74; vis. research fellow Princeton U., 1956-57. Bd. dirs. Internat. House Assn., 1937-41; bd. govs. Internat. House, Chgo., 1962-75, vice chmn., 1972-74; trustee Art inst. Chgo., from 1966, vice chmn. com. on sch., 1967-75, chmn., from 1975, trustee Beloit Coll., from 1960; bd. dirs. George M. Pullman Ednl. Found., from 1965, sec., from 1972. Mem. Am. Philos. Assn. (exec. com. Western div. 1957-60), Metaphys. Soc. Am., Phi Beta Kappa. Author: Metaphysics and the New Logic, 1942; co-editor Ethics, 1967-73, editor, from 1974. Home: Chicago, Ill. Died May 28, 1985.

WICKSTROM, JACK KENNETH, b. Omaha, Aug. 7, 1913; s. Albin E. and Agnes B. (Nelson) W.; m. Mary Elizabeth Wilson, Sept. 14, 1940; children: Cynthia (Mrs. Richard E. Wright), Merrilee (Mrs. Frederick S. Kullman), Charles Wilson. M.D., U. Nebr., 1939, D.Sc. (hon.), 1979. Diplomate: Am. Bd. Orthopedic Surgery. Med. tng. Charity Hosp., New Orleans, 1939-42; fellow U. Nebr., 1944; fellow Tulane U., 1944-46, instr., 1946-48, asst. prof., 1948-51, asso. prof., 1951-55, prof., 1955-61, Lee C. Schlesinger prof., 1961-79, prof. emeritus, 1979-84; cons. in field. Asso. editor: Jour. Bone and Joint Surgery, 1957-63, Jour. Trauma, 1964, Bull. Am. Acad. Orthopedic Surgeons, 1960-71. Bd. dirs. La. chpt. Arthritis and Rheumatism Found., Muscular Dystrophy Found. Served with USN, 1942-44. Decorated 2 Purple Hearts, Presdl. citation; recipient Surgeons award Nat. Safety Council, 1975. Mem. A.M.A., Assn. Bone and Joint Surgeons, Am. Orthopedic Assn. Clubs: Alpine, Round Table, Lamplighter. Home: New Orleans, La. Died June 17, 1984.

WIDNALL, WILLIAM BECK, former congressman, lawyer; b. Hackensack, N.J., Mar. 17, 1906; s. William Jr., and Edith Alvilda (Beck) W.; Ph.B., Brown U., 1926; LL.B., N.J. Law Sch. (now Rutgers), 1931; m. Marjorie Soule, Oct. 24, 1933; children—Barbara (Mrs. James A. Williams), William Soule. Admitted to N.J. bar, 1932, practiced in Hackensack; chmn. Nat. Commn. on Electronic Funds Transfer, Washington. Mem. N.J. Assembly, 1946-51; mem. 81st to 93d Congresses, 7th N.J. Dist. Mem. Bergen County Bar Assn., Phi Delta Theta, Delta Theta Phi. Republican. Episcopalian. Home: Saddle River Borough, N.J. Died Dec. 28, 1983.

WIEDHOPF, J. S., business exec.; b. Bklyn., Dec. 21, 1889; s. Oscar and Rose (Seerman) W.; student pub. schs.; m. Louise Bartling, June 30, 1919. Salesman Alfred H. Smith Co., 1907-20; treas., pres. Guy T. Gibson, Inc., N.Y.C., 1921-39; pres. Parfums Ciro, Inc., 1939-54; chmn. bd. Roure-DuPont, Inc., from 1955. Acting mayor, trustee Saltaire, N.Y., 1948-54, police commr., 1954-60. Mem. Perfume Importers Assn. (treas.). Toilet Goods Assn. (dir. 1959-60), Fragrance Found. (1st pres.), Saltaire Assos. (pres. 1955-59, dir. 1960). Club: Saltaire (N.Y.) Yacht. †

WIEGAND, WILLIAM BRYAN, research exec.; born Conestogo, Ontario, Can., Feb. 17, 1889; s. John and Melvina (Stauffer) W.; B.A., U. of Toronto, chemistry, 1912; M.A. physics, 1913; m. Janet Lee, June 17, 1925; children—John, Pamela, Philip, Jeffrey, Frederick. Technical supt., Dominion Rubber Co., Montreal, 1914-18; gen. mgr. Ames Holden McCready, Montreal, 1919-23; mng. dir. Ames Holden Tire Co., 1923-25; dir. research, Binney & Smith Co., N.Y. City, 1925-35; dir. research, Columbian Carbon Co., N.Y. City, since 1936; vice president, 1948-51; now research consultant; member bd. directors Peerless Carbon Black Co. since 1948. Fellow Canadian Inst. of Chemists, 1920; fellow Instn. of the Rubber Industry London, from 1925; fellow Am. Inst. Chemists, 1935; mem. Am. Inst. Chem. Engrs., from 1937, exec. com. Soc. Chem. Industry, 1941-47; chmn. Am. Chem. Soc. Rubber Div., 1923. chmn. N.Y. Rubber Group, Am. Chem. Soc., 1929, Synthetic Rubber Advisory Com., Nat. Research Council, Ottawa, from 1942, Research Bd., Office of Rubber Dir. Washington, 1943-44. Episcopalian. Author: The C.G.S. Arctic in Hudson Strait; Fort Churchill and Port Nelson, 1913; The Awakening East, 1934; Motivation in Research, 1946; Attitude and Education, 1948; also 62 papers on colloidal carbon and rubber technology. Patents on same. Home: Old Greenwich, Conn. †

WIESEN, DAVID STANLEY, educator; b. N.Y.C., May 27, 1936; s. Seymour and Mae (Halperin) W.; m. Ellen Cohen, June 23, 1963; children—Rachel Melanie, Seth Robert, Seymour Jonathan. A.B., Harvard, 1957, Ph.D., 1961. Instr. classics Cornell U., 1961-63; asst. prof. Swarthmore (Pa.) Coll., 1963-66; prof. classics Brandeis U., 1966-75, U. So. Calif., 1975-82. Author: St. Jerome as a Satirist, 1964, St. Augustine, City of God, Books 8-11, 1968; contribution of: Antiquity to American Racial Thought, 1976, Ancient History in Early American Education. Fellow Nat. Endowment Humanities, 1970-71. Home: Rancho Palos Verdes, Calif. Dec. Aug. 16, 1982.

WIGGINS, DOSSIE MARION, banker; b. Crowley, La., Dec. 9, 1895; s. Robert Bruce and Ruth A. (Jordan) Wiggins; B.A., Hardin Simmons U., 1919, LL.D., 1943; M.A., Yale, 1926, Ph.D., 1930; LL.D., Tex. Tech. U., 1952; m. Winnie Lee Kinard, May 7, 1918. Dean, Hardin Simmons U., 1926-35; pres. U. Tex., El Paso, 1935-48; pres. Tex. Tech. U., 1948-52; v.p. Citizens Nat. Bank of Lubbock (Tex.), 1952-54, exec. v.p., 1954-59, pres. 1959-61, chmn. exec. com., 1961-63, dir., 1952-78; v.p., pres. Junell-Wiggins Broadcasting Corps., West, Tex., from 1960; dir. Tex. Commerce Bank, Lubbock. Mem. coordinating bd. Tex. Coll. and U. Systems, 1965-69. Bd. dirs. Tex. Tech. U. Found.; trustee Hardin-Simmons U. Recipient Distinguished Alumni award Hardin-Simmons U. Mem. Lubbock C. of C. (pres. 1963-64), West Tex. C. of C. (dir. 1960-66), Philos. Soc. Tex., Phi Delta Kappa, Phi Delta Theta. Democrat. Baptist. Mason. Home: Lubbock, Tex. Died Sept. 2, 1978.

WIGHT, OLIVER WESLEY, software systems co. exec.; b. Bridgeport, Conn., Feb. 21, 1930; s. Charles Winthrop and Roberta (Shipman) W.; m. Joan Marilyn Obey, Oct. 19, 1974; children from previous marriage—Donna, Margaret, Roberta. B.A., New Eng. Coll., 1952. Inventory mgr. Raybestos, Bridgeport, Conn., 1952-61; prodn. control cons. Stanley Works, New Britain, Conn., 1961-65; mfg. industries edn. mgr. IBM Corp., White Plains, N.Y., 1965-68; pres. Oliver Wight, Inc. (Mfg. Software Systems), Newbury, N.H.; chmn. bd. Oliver Wight Edn. Assos., Oliver Wight Video Prodns. Author: The Executive's New Computer, 1972, Production and Inventory Management in the Computer Age, 1974; co-author: Production and Inventory Control, 1967. Mem. chmn.'s com. U.S. Senatorial Bus. Adv. Bd. Mem. Am. Prodn. and Inventory Control Soc. (v.p. edn. and research 1965). Home: Newbury, NH.

WILCE, JOHN WOODWORTH, physician, phys. edn.; b. Rochester, N.Y., May 12, 1888; s. John and Rosetta Marcy Maria (Woodworth) W.; B.A., U. of Wis., 1910; studied summers U. of Chicago, U. of Wis., M.D., Ohio State U., 1919; post grad., int. med., N.Y. Post Grad. Med. Sch., 1929; cardiology, Nat. Hosp. Dis. Heart, London, 1929; Harvard, 1933; m. Minerva Willard Conner, Aug. 2, 1920; children—John W., James M., Mary R., Dorothy Alden. Became teacher of history and dir. athletics, La Crosse (Wis.) High Sch., 1910-11; asst. prof. physical edn., U. of Wis., 1911-13, prof. physical edn. and head football coach, Ohio State U., 1913-28. Mem. med. staff Univ. and Grant Hosps.; dir. Univ. Health Service, prof. clinical medicine from 1934, Ohio State Univ. Mem. Med. R.T.C. at Ohio State Univ., Jan.-Dec. 1918. Co-organizer and sec.-treas. Am. Football Coaches Assn., 1921-27, v.p., 1928, hon. life mem., 1929. Med. contribution Nat. Phys. Fitness Movement, 1944; continuing research and med. jour. publn. of the Heart and Athletics from 1929; fellow Am. Coll. Physicians; mem. Am. Heart Assn., Am. Student Health Assn., Ohio Student Health Assn. (pres. 1944-46), Am. and Ohio State med. assns., Columbus Acad. Med., Central Ohio Council of Boy Scouts (mem. at large Nat. Council), Delta Kappa Epsilon, Phi Rho Sigma, Republican. Mason (33 deg., Shriner). Clubs: Rotary (pres. 1928), Lions (hon.), Faculty, Young Business Men's. Author: Football, 1923. Co-author: How to Enjoy Football, 1923. Home: Columbus, Ohio. †

WILCOX, FRANCIS ORLANDO, educator, government official; b. Columbus Junction, Iowa, Apr. 9, 1908; s. Francis Oliver and Verna (Gray) W.; m. Genevieve C. Byrnes, July 23, 1933 (dec. Aug. 1946); 1 dau., Carol Lenore; m. Virginia Summerlin Sullivan, Aug. 8, 1968; 1 son, Francis Oliver Wilcox. A.B., U. Iowa, 1930, A.M., 1931, Ph.D., 1933; Dr. ès sciences politiques, U. Geneva, 1935; grad., Inst. Internat. Studies, Geneva; grad. (fellow 1934-35), 1933-35; fellow, Hague Acad. Internat. Law, 1937; LL.D., U. Louisville, 1960, Hamline U., 1960, Dakota Wesleyan U., 1961; Litt.D., Simpson Coll., 1964. Teaching asst. polit. sci. U. Iowa, 1931-33; fellow Carnegie Endowment Internat. Peace, 1933-34; asst. prof. polit. sci. U. Louisville, 1935-37, asso. prof., 1937-39, chmn. div. social scis., 1939-42; vis. prof. U. Mich., summer 1941; fellow Gen. Edn. Bd., U. Chgo., 1940; cons. Am. Council Edn., 1941-43; with Office Coordinator Inter-Am. Affairs, Washington, 1942; asso. chief Div. Inter-Am. Activities in U.S.; chief program services sect. Office Civilian Def., 1943; internat. orgn. analyst Bur. of Budget, 1943-44; head internat. relations analyst Library of Congress, 1945-47; chief of staff U.S. Senate Fgn. Relations Com., 1947-55; asst. sec. state, 1955-61; dean Sch. Advanced Internat. Studies, Johns Hopkins, 1961-73; exec. dir. Commn. on Orgn. of Govt. for Conduct of Fgn. Policy, 1973-75; dir.-gen. Atlantic Council of U.S., 1975-84, vice-chmn., 1984-85; lectr. internat. orgn. George Washington U., 1945-46; lectr. internat. orgn. and fgn. relations, Sch. Advanced Internat. Studies, Washington, 1946-52; Dir. Dreyfus Corp.; Mem. U.S. del. to UN Conf., San Francisco, 1945, 1st Gen. Assembly UN, London, 1946, 3d Gen. Assembly, Paris, 1948, Japanese Peace Conf., San Francisco, 1951; and subsequent annual meetings of UN Gen. Assembly; U.S. del. World Health Assembly, Geneva, 1956, Mpls., 1958; U.S. del. ILO Conf., Geneva, 1957, 58; mem. President's Commn. on UN, 1971-85. Author or co-author books relating to field, also U.S. govt. reports, articles in tech. jours. Served as 2d lt. O.R.C., 1930-35; lt. (j.g.) USNR, 1944-45. Mem. Am. Soc. Internat. Law (exec. com. 1946-49, 51-54), Am. Polit. Sci. Assn. (exec. council 1948-50, bd. editors Am. Polit. Sci. Rev. 1952-56, v.p. 1957-58, chmn. com. undergrad. instrn. 1946-48, pres. Washington br. 1946-47), Atlantic Council (bd. dirs.), Council Fgn. Relations, Phi Beta Kappa, Phi Kappa Phi, Omicron Delta Kappa, Sigma Chi. Home: Washington, D.C. Died Feb. 20, 1985.

WILCOX, JOHN, univ. prof.; b. Warsaw, Ind., June 5, 1887; s. Melvin Alfred and Mary Rebecca (Cook) W.; A.B., Ind. Univ., 1911; A.M., U. of Wis., 1924; Ph.D., U. of Mich., 1931; student U. of Dijon, France, 1919; m. Myra Arlen, 1912 (divorced 1924); m. 2d, Nettie E. Krantz, June 23, 1925; adopted twins, Robert and Janet. Teacher public schs., Kosciusko County, Ind., 1905-09; supt. schs., Buffalo, Wyo., 1911-12; newspaper reporter and editor, Buffalo, Sheridan, Cheyenne, and Laramie, 1912-14; teacher of English, Lewis and Clark High Sch., Spokane, Wash., 1914-17; instr. in English, Wayne U., 1921, asst. prof. English, 1927-33, asso. prof., 1933-43, prof. of English from 1943. Served as lt., Coast Artillery and Air Service, 1917-19; with A.E.F., 1918-19. Mem. Am. Assn. Univ. Profs., Shakespeare Assn. of Am., Modern Lang. Assn. of Am., Mich. Acad. Sci., Arts and Letters, Alpha Tau Omega. Author: The Relation of Moliere to Restoration Comedy, 1938. Contbr. research articles and revs. to philol. and ednl. jours. in England and U.S. Home: Highland Park, Mich.

WILDER, ALEC, composer; b. Rochester, N.Y., Feb. 16, 1907; s. George and Lillian (Chew) W. Student, Lawrenceville (N.J.) Sch., St. Paul's Sch., Concord, N.H.; music edn., Eastman Sch. Music, Rochester, N.Y.; studied counterpoint with, Herbert Inch, Edward Royce. Traveled, Europe, resided in, Italy, returned, U.S., 1925; songs used Thumbs Up, Three's A Crowd; composer: songs used It's So Peaceful in the Country, All the King's Horses, Soft as Spring; writer arrangements various singers, including, Bing Crosby, Frank Sinatra, Perry Como, others; composer original music for records; music Juke Box; ballet performed by, Am. Ballet Co. in, S.A.; began writing chamber music in, 1950s, selections performed by, Alec Wilder Octet for Columbia Records; composer: music for film The Sand Castle, 1961; formed woodwind group, The Wilder Winds, 1971; host weekly show on Nat. Public Radio honoring great Am. Songwriters, from 1976; Author: American Popular Song: The Great Innovators, 1900-1950. Address: New York, NY. *

WILDER, RAYMOND LOUIS, science historiographer, mathematician, educator; b. Palmer, Mass., Nov. 3, 1896; s. John Louis and Mary Jane (Shanley) W.; Ph.B., Brown U., 1920, M.S., 1921, D.Sc. (hon.), 1958; Ph.D., U. Tex., 1923; D.Sc. (hon.), Bucknell U., 1955; m. Una Maude Greene, Jan. 1, 1921; children—Mary Jane Wilder Jessop, Sally May Wilder Watkins, Betty Ann Wilder Dillingham, David Elliott. Instr. in math. Brown U., Providence, 1920-21, U. Tex., Austin, 1921-24; asst. prof. math. Ohio State U., Columbus, 1924-26; asst. prof. math. U. Mich., Ann Arbor, 1926-29, assoc. prof., 1929-35, prof., 1935-47, research prof., 1947-67, emeritus prof., 1967-82; lectr. math. U. Calif., Santa Barbara, 1970-71, research assoc., 1971-82; vis. research prof. Fla. State U., Tallahassee, 1961-62; mem. staff Inst. Advanced Study, Princeton U., 1933-34; Henry Russel lectr. U. Mich., 1958-59; Josiah Willard Gibbs lectr. Am. Math. Soc., 1969. Served as ensign USN, 1917-19. Guggenheim Meml. Found. fellow, 1940-41; Office Naval Research grantee, 1949-50; NSF grantee; Air Force Office Sci. Research grantee. Mem. Nat. Acad. Scis., Am. Math. Soc. (pres. 1955-56), Math. Assn. Am. (pres. 1965-66, Distinguished Service Math. award 1973), AAAS (v.p. 1948), Assn. Symbolic Logic; fellow Am. Anthropol. Assn. Author: (with W.L. Ayres) Lectures in Topology, 1941; Topology of Manifolds, 1949; Introduction to the Foundations of Mathematics, 1952, rev. edit., 1965; Evolution of Mathematical Concepts, 1968; contbr. articles to profl. jours. Home: Santa Barbara, Calif. Died July 7, 1982.

WILDHACK, WILLIAM AUGUST, physicist; b. Breckenridge, Colo., Sept. 24, 1908; s. Louis Amandus and Lizzie Frances (Smith) W.; B.S., U. Colo., 1931, M.S., 1932, postgrad., 1932-34; grad. George Washington U., 1936-39; m. Martha Elizabeth Parks, Nov. 26, 1931; children—William August, Michael David. Physicist, Nat. Bur. Standards 1935-69, chief, missile instrument sect., 1948-50, chief Office Basic Instrumentation, 1950-60, spl. asst. to dir., 1960-61, asso. dir. 1961-65, asso. dir. Inst. Basic Standards, 1965-69; tech. cons., 1969-85. Chmn. com. sci. equipment NRC, 1947-52; panel aircraft equipment Research and Devel. Bd., 1949-53; cons. sci. equipment for Europe, ECA, 1950; chief U.S. Metrology Delegation to Russia, 1963. Bd. dirs. Nat. Conf. Standards Labs. William A. Wildhack award established by Nat. Conf. Standards Labs., 1970. Fellow Instrument Soc. Am. (hon. mem. 1968, pres. 1954); mem. Am. Assn. Physics Tchrs., Am. Phys. Soc., Inst. Aero. Scis., AAAS, Fedn. Am. Scientists, Washington Acad. Scis., Sigma Xi, Tau Beta Pi, Sigma Pi Sigma. Club: Cosmos (Washington). Inventions, sci. publs. in field. Address: Arlington, Va. Dec. July 9, 1985.

WILEY, SAMUEL HAMILTON, foreign service officer; b. of Am. parentage, London, Eng., June 19, 1888; s. William Murdoch and Marion Easton (Paterson) W.; student N.C. State Coll., Raleigh, 1904-05, U. of N.C., 1905-07, LL.B., 1912; m. Nancy Rhoda Hay, Jan. 15,

1912; children—Walter William, Patrick Hamilton, Marion Errol Hay. Admitted to N.C. bar, 1912; in practice at Salisbury, 1912-14; consul Ascuncion, Paraguay, 1914-16, St. Pierre-Miquelon, 1916-19, Oporto, Portugal, 1918-25, Vigo, Spain, 1925, Cherbourg, France, 1925-31, Naples, Italy, 1931-33, Havre, France, 1933-40; consul gen., Lisbon, Portugal, 1940-42, Algiers, Algeria, from 1942. Mem. Sigma Nu. Democrat. Presbyn. Rotarian. Deceased.

WILGUS, A(LVA) CURTIS, educator; b. Platteville, Wis., Apr. 2, 1897; s. James Alva and Flavia Alberta (McGurer) W.; grad. State Tchrs. Coll., Platteville, 1916; A.B., U. Wis., 1920, A.M., 1921, Ph.D., 1925; m. Karna Steelquist; 1 son, Robert. High sch. tchr., 1916-18; teaching fellow history U. Calif., 1921-22; asst. instr. history U. Wis., 1922-24; asso. prof. history U. S.C., 1924-30; chmn. Hispanic-Am. history George Washington U., 1930-51; acting dean Columbian Coll., 1932-34; dir. Center Inter-Am. Studies, 1932-36; tchr. summer schs., Maine, Mo., Ohio, S.C., George Washington, Am. U., Coll. City N.Y., Northwestern U., Oreg.; vis. prof. U. Fla., 1950-51, dir. Sch. Intern-Am. Studies, 1951-63, dir. Caribbean Confs., 1950-67, prof. history, 1951-67; vice chancellor Internat. Inst. Ams., San Juan, P.R. and Miami, 1967-69; vis. prof. inter-Am. studies Inter-Am. U. P.R., 1971-72, 73-74; lectr. schs. colls., univs. of U.S. Mem. Cuban-Am. Council Univ. Studies, U. Havana, 1943; nat. council Am. Documentation Inst., 1938, nat. council Inst. Internat. Edn., 1971, nat. adv. com. Portuguese Double Centenary Celebration, 1939; Latin-Am. expert U.S. Office Edn., 1942; program officer, dir. edn. and tchr. aids Office Coordinator Inter-Am. Affairs, 1943-44; mem. Bd. Fgn. Scholarships, 1963-65; sec.-gen. Inter-Am. Acad., 1966-70; chmn. bd. dirs. Latin Am. Book Programs, Inc., N.Y.C.; del. 5 Pan-Am. Confs. Served with U.S. Army, 1918. Decorated Medalla de Honor de la Insturcción Pblica, Venezuela; knight grand cross Mil. Order of St. Brigida of Sweden, 1953; Cervantes medal Hispanic Inst. Fla., 1954; Bi-Centennial medal Columbia U., 1954; chevalier et compagnon Honnarie Croix de Lorrainne, 1954. Mem. Am. Hist. Assn., AAUP, Quivira Soc., Soc. Advancement Edn. (charter), Inter-Am. Bibliog. and Library Assn. (charter mem., pres. 1935—), Inter-Am. Forum (organizer, 1st pres.), Instituto de las Españas (council), Am. Peace Soc. (nat. adv. council, bd. dirs., exec. com., editor), Assn. Latin Am. Studies (pres. 1961), Good Neighbor Forum (nat. adviser), Pan-Am. Found. (dir.), Com. Library Coop. with Latin Am. Econ. Inst. (charter, bd. dirs.), Pan Am. League (council), Instituto de Estudios Económicos e Sociales of Mexico, Soc. History Discoveries, Delta Phi Epsilon, Omicron Delta Kappa, Pi Gamma Mu; corr. mem. Hispanic Soc. Am., also 7 societies in Latin Am. Mason. Club: University (Washington). Author, co-author, compiler and editor many books on Latin America, including text books and syllabi; edited books include vols. on the Caribbean, 1956-67; (with Raul de'Eca) Latin American History, 1964; editor Historical Dictionary of Latin America, 23 vols., 1967—; author Historical Atlas of Latin America, 1967; Latin America, 1492-1942, 1973; Latin America in the Nineteenth Century: A Selected Bibliography of Books of Travel and Description Published in English, 1973; The Historiography of Latin America, 1500-1800, 1975; Latin America, Spain and Portugal. A Selected and Annotated Bibliographical Guide to Books Published in the U.S., 1954-74, 1977; founder, 1959, chmn. editorial bd. Jour. Inter-Am. Studies; editorial adv. bd. Luso-Brazilian Rev., 1965; editor Praeger Scholarly Reprints, 8 vols., 1969. Contbr. chpts. various books; author many articles, monographs, bibliographies in jours., articles to encys.; book reviews. Home: North Miami Beach, Fla. Died Jan. 27, 1981.

WILHELM, ROSS JOHNSTON, writer, bus. cons.; b. Arlington, N.J., Jan. 24, 1920; s. Roy Pierre and Annie (Ross) W.; m. Rowena May, Jan. 4, 1944; 1 son, Peter Bradbury. B.B.A., Western Res. U., 1947, M.B.A., 1948; Ph.D., U. Mich., 1963; LL.D. (hon.), Eastern Mich. U., 1977. Mgr., cons. in bus. and govt.; prof. bus. econs. Grad. Sch. Bus., U. Mich., Ann Arbor, 1950-51, 1954-82, chmn. bus. econs. dept., 1979-82; writer, narrator Business Rev., weekly radio program, 1960-81; dir. Perry Drug Stores, Inc., Plymouth, Mich., Rospatch Corp., Grand Rapids, Mich., Earhart Condominium, Ann Arbor, 1975-77. Co-author, narrator: TV series Everybody's Business, The Challenge of Change, 1965; commentator, WXYZ-TV, ABC, Detroit, 1969, 70; weekly radio program The Business Roundtable, MBS, 1975-76; columnist: weekly radio program Motor Age; Author numerous books and, articles; weekly newspaper column Inside Business, 1974-77. Bd. advs. Adrian (Mich.) Coll., from 1980. Served to 1st lt. U.S. Army, 1942-46. Recipient Disting. Faculty Service award U. Mich., 1964; Janus award Mortgage Bankers Assn., 1973. Mem. Am. Econ. Assn., Am. Mktg. Assn., Mont Pelerin Soc., Sigma Zeta. Home: Ann Arbor, Mich.

WILKINS, GEORGE THOMAS, ret. educator; b. Anna, Ill., Jan. 16, 1905; s. B. Frank and Nellie Mae (Hileman) W.; m. Mary Alice Treece, July 4, 1926; 1 son, George Thomas. B.Ed., So. Ill. Normal, 1937; A.M., U. Ill., 1940; LL.D. (hon.), McKendree Coll., 1959. Tchr. pub. schs., Anna, 1923-24, tchr., coach pub. sch., Cobden, Ill., 1924-29, prin., coach high sch., Wolf Lake, Ill., 1929-37, supt. pub. schs., 1937-39, Thebes, Ill., 1939-43, Madison, Ill., 1943-47; vis. prof. edn. Shurtleff Coll., Alton, Ill., 1948-56; county supt. schs., Madison County, Ill., 1947-59; ednl. cons., asso. prof. McKendree Coll., Lebanon, Ill., 1956-58; asso. prof. Monticello Coll., Godfrey, Ill., 1955-58; supt. pub. instrn., Ill., 1959-63; asso. prof. edn. So. Ill. U., 1963-69, prof. ednl. adminstrn., 1969-71, prof. emeritus, from 1973; Vice pres. Nathan Hale Life Ins.; dir. Nathan Hale Investment Corp., Vernon Fire and Casualty Ins. Co., Vernon Investment Corp., Colonial Bank of Granite City, Ill. Co-author: School Building Construction, 1967; author: The School Law, 1968; Editor: S.W. Div. Bull, Ill. Edn. Assn., 1944-48. Mem. bd. So. Ill. U. Found.; mem. Ill. Council on Community Schs., Ill. Sch. Problems Commn., 1959-73; Past pres. Cahokia Mound council Boy Scouts Am.; Pres. city planning commn., Madison, Ill.; Dir. YMCA, Granite City, Ill. Recipient Silver Beaver award Boy Scouts; Community Leader of America award, 1968; spl. recognition award Belleville Area Coll., 1978; Mentor Graham award.; George T. Wilkins Jr. High Sch., Oak Lawn, Ill. named for him. Mem. Ill. Edn. Assn. (past pres. Marquette div.), N.E.A., Ill. Ofcls. Assn., Am., Ill. assns. sch. adminstrs., Madison County Adminstrs. Conf. (past pres.), Central States Chief Sch. Officers (pres.), U. Ill. Alumni Assn. (life mem.), So. Ill. U. Alumni Assn. (life mem., pres.), Ill. Assn. County Supts. Schs., Tri-City C. of C. (past chmn. edn. com.), Ill. C. of C., Silver Century Club Found., No. Ill. Round Table Assn., Kappa Phi Kappa, Phi Delta Kappa (past pres. Gateway East chpt.). Democrat. Presbyn. (elder). Clubs: Mason (Shriner), mem. Order Easter Star, Rotary (past pres., past dist. gov.), Tri-City Shrine. Home: Granite City, Ill.

WILKINS, ROY, organization executive, human rights advocate; b. St. Louis, Aug. 30, 1901; s. William D. and Mayfield (Edmondson) W.; A.B., U. Minn., 1923; hon. degreee Lincoln U., 1958, Morgan State Coll., 1963, Central State Coll., 1962, Manhattanville Coll. Sacred Heart, 1964, Oakland U., 1965. Manhattan Coll., 1965, Iona Coll., 1965, Howard U., 1965, Swarthmore Coll., 1965, Notre Dame U., 1965, Middlebury Coll., 1965, Atlanta U., 1965, Fordham U., 1966, Tuskegee Inst., 1966, Oberlin Coll., 1967, Bucknell U., 1968, St. Francis Coll., 1968, C.W. Post Coll., 1968, U. Calif., 1968, Columbia, 1969, St. Peters Coll., 1969, Hebrew Union Coll., 1971, Yeshiva U., 1972, Va. Sem., 1973, Springfield Coll., 1973, Boston U., 1968, Drake U., 1975, Fisk U., 1975, St. John's U., 1975, Temple U., 1977, Villanova, 1977, Niagra U., 1976, Ind. State U., 1977, others; m. Aminda Badeau, Sept. 15, 1929. Mng. editor Kansas City Call, 1923-31; asst. sec. NAACP, 1931-49, acting sec., 1949-50, adminstr., 1950, exec. sec., 1955-64, exec. dir., 1965-77, editor Crisis mag., monthly ofcl. NAACP organ, 1934-49. Pres. Leadership Conf. Civil Rights, 1969; chmn. Am. del. Internat. Conf. Human Rights, Teheran, 1968. Recipient Spingarn medal NAACP, 1964; Freedom award Freedom House, 1967; Theodore Roosevelt Distinguished Service medal. 1968; Presidential Medal Freedom, 1969; Zale award, 1973; Joseph Prize for Human Rights. Hon. fellow Hebrew U., Jerusalem, 1972. Home: Jamaica, N.Y. Died Aug. 4, 1981.*

WILKINSON, JAMES RICHARD, architect; b. Washington, Ga., Mar. 21, 1907; s. Thomas Gregg and Mary Agnes (Ezell) W.; B.S. in Architecture, Auburn U., 1928; m. Kathleen Shearer Asher, Mar. 9, 1940; children—James R., Clay Thomas, Thomas Perry. Practiced architecture with various firms, 1928-36; asso. Burge & Stevens, Architects, Atlanta, 1936-45; ptnr. Stevens & Wilkinson, Architects, Engrs., Planners, Inc., Atlanta, 1945-68, pres., 1968-72, chmn. bd., 1972-77, chmn. fin. com., 1977-80; profl. advisor Archtl. Sch. Auburn U.; works include: Daniel Bldg., Greenville, S.C., Continuing Edn. Center U. Ga., Athens, Ga. Bapt. Hosp., Atlanta, Sears, Roebuck & Co. stores in SE, Rich's, Inc. stores, Law Sch. Emory U., Atlanta, Hartsfield Internat. Airport, Central Library, Tower Pl., Atlanta, Citgo Hdqrs., Tulsa. Served to 1st lt., constrn. officer USMCR, 1944-45; PTO. Fellow AIA (recipient regional and nat. awards); mem. Phi Delta Theta. Presbyterian. Clubs: Capital City, Piedmont Driving. Home: Atlanta, Ga. Dec. July 24, 1980.

WILLCUTTS, MORTON D., naval med. officer; b. Carthage, Ind., Mar. 10, 1889; s. William Henry and Emma (Galloway) W.; B.S., Ind. U., M.D., 1916; student Naval Med. Sch., 1919-20; m. Marie Barbara Collins, June 5, 1929; children—Morton Douglas, David Harrison, Diane Marie, Ann Elizabeth. Commd. lt. (j.g.), U.S. Navy, 1917, and advanced through grades to vice adm., formerly chief of surgery, Canacoa Naval Hosp., Newport Naval Hosp., U.S.S. Relief (hosp. ship), Great Lakes Naval Hosp. and Washington (D.C.) Naval Hosp.; comdg. officer, San Diego (Calif.) Naval Hosp.; fleet med. officer, staff comdr. Fifth Fleet; comdr. Nat. Naval Med. Center, Bethesda, Md.; medical director San Quentin State Prison. Holds United States Navy, Chinese and Haitian awards. Diplomate and a founder Am. Bd. Surgery. Fellow Am. Coll. Surgeons. Mem. Washington (D.C.) Acad. of Surgery, Phi Beta Pi. Elk. Home: Belvedere, Cal. †

WILLET, HENRY LEE, stained glass artist; b. Pitts., Dec. 7, 1899; s. William and Anne (Lee) W.; m. Muriel Crosby, Oct. 22, 1927; children: E. Crosby, Ann (Mrs. John M. Kellogg, Jr.), Zoe (Mrs. William C. Cotton). Student, Princeton, 1918-20, Wharton Sch. of U. Pa., 1920-21; study and research in, Europe, 1924-27; Art D. (hon.), Lafayette Coll., 1951; L.H.D. (hon.), Geneva Coll., 1966, Ursinus Coll., 1967; D.F.A. (hon.), St. Lawrence U., 1972, Smith Coll. (Class of 24), U.S. Mil. Acad. (Class of 1944). chmn. bd. Willet Stained Glass Studios. Creator of stained glass, from 1920; Represented by windows in, Washington Cathedral, Cadet Chapel, U.S. Mil. Acad., many others in chs., chapels throughout, U.S., 50 States, 13 fgn. countries, latest, Covenant Presbyn. Ch., Charlotte, N.C., St. Thomas Episcopalian Ch., N.Y.C., 1973, Princeton U. Chapel, Cathedral of St. John the Divine, N.Y.C., all glass, Nat. Presbyn. Ch., Washington, also in St. Mary's Roman Cath. Cathedral, San Francisco, 6 Bays Grace Cathedral, San Francisco, St. Mark's Cathedral, Mpls., sculpture and glass facade, Ch. Center at UN, 1963, 5400 glass panels, Hall of Sci., N.Y. World's Fair, 1964, Mormon Temple, Washington, 1973, St. Anselm Ch., Tokyo, Japan, Coral Ridge Presbyn. Ch., Ft. Lauderdale, Pres. Garfield and Pres. Lyndon B. Johnson meml. windows, Nat. Christian Ch., Washington., Exhibited leading art galleries; lectr. art and craft of stained glass. Pres. bd. commrs. Upper Dublin Twp., 1946-59; dir. bd. Christian edn. Presbyn. Ch. U.S.A., 1948-60, mem. spl. com. arts, from 1968, commr. to Gen. Assembly, 1936, 43; pres. 22 Found., Princeton U. Recipient Craft award Archtl. League N.Y., 1956; citation Religious Heritage Am., 1971; Brown meda Franklin Inst., 1972. Fellow Stained Glass Assn. Am. (pres. 1942-44); Benjamin Franklin fellow Royal Soc. Arts (London); fellow Am. Soc. Ch. Arch.; mem. AIA (hon.), Guild Religious Architecture (dir., Conover award 1963), Archtl. League N.Y., Fairmont Park Art Assn., Phila. Art Alliance (dir., medal achievement 1952), Pa. Mus. Art, Pa. Acad. Fine Arts., Am. Fedn. Art, T Square (Phila.), Woodmere Art Gallery Phila. (hon.), Smithsonian Instn. Presbyn. Club: Union League (Phila.). Home: Wyndmoor, PA.

WILLIAMS, ALBERT LYNN, corp. exec.; b. Berwick, Pa., May, 1911; s. William F. and Mabel (Lynn) W.; student Beckley Coll., 1928-30; m. Ruth Bloom, Sept. 19, 1931 (dec. Nov. 1964); children—Albert Lynn, Gail B.; m. 2d Katherine Y. Carson, 1966. Accountant, Commonwealth Pa., Harrisburg, 1930-36; student sales rep. IBM Corp., N.Y.C., 1936, sales rep., 1937, controller, 1942, treas., 1947, v.p., treas., 1948, dir., 1951-82, exec. v.p., 1954-61, pres., 1961-66, chmn. exec. com. bd. dirs., 1966-71, chmn. finance com. of bd. dirs., 1971-82; dir. Mobil Corp., Citibank, Eli Lilly and Co. Chmn. President's Commn. Internat. Trade and Investment Policy, 1970-71. Clubs: Siwanoy Country (Bronxville, N.Y.); Links (N.Y.C.); Country of Fla., Ocean of Fla.; Gulf Stream Golf, Gulf Stream Bath and Tennis, Delray Beach (Fla.) Yacht. Died Dec. 30, 1982.

WILLIAMS, BEN T., chief justice Supreme Ct. Okla.; b. 1911. LL.B., U. Okla. Bar: Okla. bar 1933. Practiced in, Pauls Valley; chief justice Supreme Ct. Okla. Office: Oklahoma City, Okla. *

WILLIAMS, BIRKETT LIVERS, born at Hot Springs, Arkansas, February 5, 1890; son of Arthur Upton and Elizabeth (Birkett) W.; B.A., Ouachita College, Arkadelphia, Arkansas, 1910; student University of Va. Law Sch., 1911-12; m. Edna Campbell, Sept. 12, 1917; children—1st lieutenant William Birkett (pilot 57th Fighter Group, killed in action, Lybia, 1943), Shirley Jane (Mrs. Hugh R. Gibson). In cattle business, 1912-15; in retail automobile and automobile finance business, Cleveland, Ohio, from 1920; pres. Birkett L. Williams Co., Manark Securities, Inc. Dir. Public Safety, City of Cleveland from 1952. Apptd. regional adminstr. for W.Va., Ky., Ind., Mich. and Ohio, Office of Price Adminstrn., Jan. 1942; resigned Oct. 1945. Past pres. Cleveland Asso. Charities; past dir. Nat. Automobile Dealers Assn.; dir., past pres. Cleveland Automotive Trade Assn.; chmn. Greater Cleveland Red Cross; chmn. bd. Better Bus. Bureau of Cleveland; mem. exec. council Boy Scouts of America (Cleveland chapter); mem. Beta Theta Pi, Phi Delta Phi. Presbyterian. Mason (Shriner). Clubs: Cleveland Rotary (past pres.), University, Mayfield Country, Union (Cleveland). Home: Cleveland, Ohio. †

WILLIAMS, CARRINGTON, surgeon; b. Richmond, Va., June 21, 1889; s. Walter Armistead and Alice Marshall (Taylor) W.; B.A., U. of Va., 1910, M.D., 1913; m. Fanny Braxton Miller, Nov. 25, 1916; children—Carrington, Mason Miller, Armistead Marshall. Instr. in anatomy, U. of Va., 1912-13; house surgeon St. Luke's Hosp., New York, 1913-15, St. Mary's Hosp., 1915; attending surg. Stuart Circle Hosp. and Hosp. Div. Med. Coll. of Va., Richmond, from Jan. 1, 1916; prof. of clin. surgery, Med. Coll. of Va.; director of the Bank of Va., Williams & Reed, Inc., Stuart Circle Hosp. Corp. Member dean's committee McGuire V.A. Hospital. Served as captain Medical Corps, United States Army, 1917-19. Chmn. Richmond Chapter, Am. Red. Cross, 1943-45. Mem. Richmond Academy Medicine, Medical Society of Virginia (pres. 1955), A.M.A. (mem. House of Dels. 1939), Southern Soc. Clin. Surgeons, Southern Surg. Assn. (pres. 1955), Am. Surgical Association, Southern Medical Association, A.M.A. (ho. of delegates), Eastern Surgical Society, Soc. of the Cincinnati (Va.) (v.p. 1957-58), English Speaking Union, Delta Psi, Phi Beta Kappa, Alpha Omega Alpha. Democrat. Episcopalian. Member Country Club of Virginia (Richmond) and Commonwealth Club. Contbr. numerous articles to med. and surg. jours. Home: Richmond, Va. †

WILLIAMS, CLARKE, science administrator, nuclear engineer, physicist; b. N.Y.C., May 4, 1902; s. William Robert and Flora (Nabersberg) W.; m. Lindsay Clement Field, June 30, 1927 (div. Apr. 1933); 1 son, David Field

Williams South; m. Margaret Stevens Button, Aug. 12, 1933; children—Evan Thomas, Thomas Button Williams. A.B., Williams Coll., 1922, Sc.D. (hon.), 1964; B.C.E., Mass. Inst. Tech., 1924; Ph.D. in Physics, Columbia U., 1935. Rodman Duke Price Power Co., 1924-25; asst. engr. N.Y. Central R.R., 1925-26; asst. physics Columbia U., 1926-30; research, devel. gaseous diffusion project Columbia U. (Div. War Research), 1941-46; tutor, instr., asst. prof. physics Coll. City N.Y., 1930-49; sr. physicist Brookhaven Nat. Lab., 1946-83, chmn. nuclear engring. dept., 1952-62, dep. dir., 1962-67, dep. dir. emeritus, 1967-83; research adminstr. Marine Resources Council, L.I. Regional Planning Bd., Hauppauge, N.Y., from 1967; mem. N.Y. State Atomic Energy Adv. Com., 1956-59, 66; chmn. 1960 Nuclear Congress; mem. atomic safety and licensing bd. panel AEC, 1966-74; tech. adviser, paper coordinator 2d Internat. Conf. Peaceful Uses Atomic Energy, 1958; adviser U.S. del. 3d Geneva Conf., 1964. Mem. exec. council Suffolk County council Boy Scouts Am., 1966-76; mem. Brookhaven Town Indsl. Commn., 1962-83; bd. dirs. Skills Unltd., 1962-83, v.p., 1968, pres., 1971-78; bd. dirs. Suffolk County Community Council, v.p., 1968-70; trustee United Fund L.I.; trustee emeritus Williams Coll. Fellow Am. Nuclear Soc. (dir. 1957-60, pres. 1963), AAAS; mem. Am. Phys. Soc., N.Y. Acad. Sci., Fedn. Am. Scientists, U.S. Power Squadron, Phi Beta Kappa, Epsilon Chi, Sigma Psi. Club: Williams (N.Y.C.). Home: Bellport, N.Y. Dec. Mar. 15, 1983.

WILLIAMS, CRATIS DEARL, university dean; b. Blaine, Ky., Apr. 5, 1911; s. Curtis and Mona (Whitt) W.; m. Sylvia Graham, Aug. 7, 1937 (div. dec. Dec. 1942); m. Elizabeth Lingerfelt, July 31, 1949; children—Sophie, David Cratis. B.A., U. Ky., 1933, M.A., 1937; Ph.D., N.Y.U., 1961. Tchr. rural schs., Eastern Ky., 1929-33; tchr. English, prin. Blaine (Ky.) High Sch., 1933-38; prin. Louisa (Ky.) High Sch., 1938-41; instr. Apprentice Sch. of Internat. Nickel Co., Huntington, W.Va., 1942; critic tchr., asst. prin., guidance dir. Appalachian Demonstration High Sch., Boone, N.C., 1942-46; asst. prof. English and speech Appalachian State U., Boone, 1946-49, prof. English, 1952-85; dean Appalachian State U. (Grad. Sch.), 1958-74, acting vice chancellor, 1974, acting chancellor, 1975; part-time instr. English Washington Sq. Coll., 1949-50. Author: Mountain Speech, 1960, Southern Mountaineer in Fact and Fiction, 1975; Contbr. articles to ednl. jours. Recipient Founders Day award N.Y.U., 1962, O. Max Gardner award, 1973, Brown Hudson award, 1975, So. Found. fellow, 1954. Mem. Modern Lang. Assn., Am. Folklore Soc., N.C. Folklore Soc. (past pres.), Appalachian Consortium (dir.), So. hist. assns., N.C. Hist. Soc., Western N.C. Hist. Assn. Club: Mason. Address: Boone, N.C. Died May 11, 1985.

WILLIAMS, E. VIRGINIA, artistic director, choreographer; b. Melrose, Mass.; d. Charles F. and Mary Virginia (Evitts) W.; m. Herbert Hobbs; 1 child. Trained in, N.Y.C.; also student piano, drama and art 6 hon. doctorates in the arts. Profl. dancer in concert cos. and opera ballet; tchr. ballet, choreographer, dir., New Eng. Civic Ballet Co., 1958-62, founder, artistic dir., Boston Ballet, 1962-84. Adv. council, Jacob's Pillow Dance Festival, artistic adviser, Lyric Opera of Chgo. Ballet, 1971-73. Disting. Woman of Yr. award Boston chpt. Sigma Alpha Iota; regional citation NE Theater Conf.; named An Outstanding Woman of Mass. Internat. Women's Yr., 1975; recipient Dance Mag. award, 1976. Mem. Dance Teacher's Club Boston (past pres., hon. citation). Home: Malden, Mass. Dec. May 8, 1984.

WILLIAMS, EDWARD FRANCIS, textile exec.; born Franklin, Mass., June 22, 1888; s. Patrick Francis and Annie May (Barrows) W.; ed. pub. schs. of Mass.; Colby Coll., 1910; Dr. of Commercial Sci., Merrimack Coll., 1956; LL.D., Boston College, 1956; m. Margaret Elizabeth Shay, Oct 16, 1918 (died 1949); m. 2d, Louise Maguire Hennessy, May 14, 1956; 1 son, Daniel Hennessy. Worked as designer American Woolen Company, North Vassalboro, Me., 1911-13; supt., designer Raritan (N.J.) Woolen Mills, 1913-15; gen. supt. Middlesex Mills, Lowell, Mass., 1915-18; gen. mgr. Hillsboro (N.H.) Woolen Mills, 1918-20; pres. Springfield (Mass.) Metal Stamping Co., 1922-25, W.G. Fisher & Co., N.Y. City, 1930-37; gen. mgr. Warren (Mass.) Woolen Assos., 1920-37; mgr. Am. Woolen Co., Inc., Assabet Mill, Maynard, Mass., from 1937; v.p., dir. Sandorval Oil & Gas Co.; pres. Boston Terminal Co.; dir. Found. Co. N.Y.C., Palmer (Mass.) Nat. Bank, N.E. Transportation. Co., N.Y., N.H. & H. R.R. Co. (member executive com.), Roper (N.C.) Lumber Co., Guaranty Trust Co. (Waltham, Mass.). Dir. McGinnis Indsl. Center, Norfolk, Va. Trustee New Eng. Home for Little Wanderers. Mem. adv. bd. Boston Coll. Sch. Bus. Adminstrn.; regent Boston Coll. Decorated Knight of St. Gregory, Knight of Holy Sepulchre of Jerusalem. Knight of Malta. Clubs: Algonquin, Downtown, Beacon Society, Hatherly Country, Scituate Harbor Yacht. Home: Newton, Mass. †

WILLIAMS, FERD ELTON, physicist, educator; b. Erie, Pa., June 9, 1920; s. Earl V. and Osa M. (Riddle) W.; m. Anne Lindberg, Nov. 25, 1948; children: Karen, Gareth, Geoffrey, Kevin, Quentin. B.S., U. Pitts., 1942; M.A., Princeton U., 1945, Ph.D., 1946. Research engr. RCA, 1942-46; asst. prof. chemistry U. N.C., 1946-49; mgr. light generation research Gen. Electric Research Lab., 1949-61; H. Fletcher Brown prof. physics U. Del., Newark, 1962-84, chmn. dept., 1961-77; vis. prof. univs., Liège, Nijmegen and Paris, 1975-76, U., Tokyo, 1978, U. Paris, 1981, 84, Tech. U. Berlin, 1980, 81; prin. investigator basic luminescence program sponsored by Army Research Office, 1962-84; indsl. and govt. cons. solid-state and chem. physics. Mem. adv. com. solid state Oak Ridge Nat. Lab., 1963-67; chmn. Com. for Internat. Confs. on Luminescence., 1970-84. Editor-in-chief: Jour. Luminescence, 1970-84; Contbr. articles to profl. jours. Named Outstanding Educator of Year, 1974; recipient Humboldt prize Fed. Republic Germany, 1981. Fellow Am. Phys. Soc., AAAS; mem. Am. Chem. Soc., Optical Soc. Am., AAUP (pres. Del. chpt. 1968-69), Am. Inst. Physics (regional councilor Del. 1964-84), Am. Assn. Physics Tchrs. (pres. Chesapeake sect. 1966-67), Sigma Xi. Patentee in field Home: Newark, Del. Died June 19, 1984.

WILLIAMS, FRANK D, lawyer; b. Crete, Neb., Dec. 21, 1890; J.D., U. Neb., 1914. Admitted to Neb. bar, 1914; now mem. firm Cline, Williams, Wright, Johnson, Oldfather & Thompson, Lincoln, Neb. Dir. 1st Nat. Bank & Trust Co. Lincoln, from 1967, mem. State Bd. Bar Exam., 1933-42. Mem. Am., Neb., Lincoln bar assns., Order of Coif.†

WILLIAMS, FRANK HENRY, banker; b. Menands, N.Y., Sept. 23, 1887; s. Adam J. and Lizzie (Reuter) W.; ed. pub. schs.; m. Elizabeth Clark, Oct. 9, 1912; 1 son, Harold C. Began as clerk Nat. Commercial Bank & Trust Co., Albany, New York, 1903; teller City Savings Bank of Albany (City and County Savings Bank), 1905-12, asst. treas., 1912-17, sec.-treas., 1917-26, vice-pres., 1926-29, pres., 1929-48, pres. City Safe Deposit Co. from 1929. Meth. Mason. Clubs: Fort Orange, Aurania, Albany Country. †

WILLIAMS, FRANK STARR, foreign service officer; b. Fannin, Miss., Oct. 11, 1888; s. William Mathew and Mattie (Starr) W.; B.S., Millsaps Coll., Jackson, Miss., 1910; m. Mabel Macher, June 22, 1914; 1 son, Frank Starr; married 2d, Adele S. Born, November 17, 1937 (died January 20, 1944); married 3d, Fannie A. Williamson, Dec. 12, 1945. Instructor chemistry and agriculture, Canton (China) Christian College, 1911-14; member faculty Soochow (China) University, 1914-18; with Am. Trading Co., Shanghai, China, 1918-22, A. W. Olsen Co., Tientsin, China, 1922-27; in service U.S. Dept. Commerce from 1927, commercial rep. at Shanghai, 1928-30, Bangkok, Siam, 1930-31, Singapore, 1931-33; attaché Am. Embassy, Tokyo, Japan, 1933-Dec. 8, 1941; Evacuated to U.S.A. Aug. 1942; in State Dept., Washington, D.C., Sept. 1942-June, 1945; retired, June 30, 1945. Mem. Pi Kappa Alpha. Methodist. Mason (32 deg., Shriner). Clubs: Burning Tree Golf, Metropolitan (Washington, D.C.). Address: Vicksburg, Miss. Deceased.

WILLIAMS, HOWARD DAVID, advt. exec.; b. Lee, Mass., June 21, 1889; s. Henry David and Mary Agnes (Pease) W.; B.S., Mass. Inst. Tech., 1907-11; m. Margaret B. Clark, 1914; children—David Benton, Anne Sinclair; m. 2d, Katherine A. Lawson, Nov. 16, 1944. Engr. San. Dist., Chgo., 1911; successively with James McCreery & Co., N.Y.C., Stewart Dry Goods Co., Louisville, Nat. Cash Register Co., Dayton, O. v.p. in charge fgn. bus,; exec. v.p., sec., partner, gen. mgr. Erwin, Wasey & Co., advt. agency, until 1947, pres., gen. mgr. 1947-56, chmn. bd. 1956; chmn. finance com. Erwin, Wasey, Ruthrauf & Ryan (merger of Erwin Wasey & Co. and Ruthrauf & Ryan), N.Y.C., from 1957, also dir.; founding chmn. Erwin Wasey, Inc.; dir. Wilshire Terrace Corp., Early Cal. Foods Co., DeMille Found., Brown Derby Restaurants, Thomas Deegan Co., N.Y.C. Mem. devel. com. Mass. Inst. Tech. Corp. Trustee, Pitzer Coll., now chmn. trustees. Served with CAC, W W I. Mem. Am. Assn. Advt. Agys., Advt. Research Found. (dir.). Republican. Presbyn. Mason (32). Clubs: Cloud, University, St. Nicholas N.Y.C.); Sleepy Hollow Country (Scarborough, N.Y.); Los Angeles Country; Preston Mountains (Kent Conn.); Seignory (Montebello, Que., Can.), Cat Cay (B.W.I.); American (London, Eng.). Home: Los Angeles, CA. †

WILLIAMS, J. HAROLD, lawyer; b. Waterbury, Conn., Dec. 23, 1893; s. John Ellis and Geneva Louise (Porter) W.; m. Martha Schultz, June 5, 1926 (div. 1943); children—Marcia, John H. A.B., Yale, 1917, LL.B., 1920. Bar: Conn. bar 1920. Since practiced in, Hartford; sr. mem. firm Gross, Hyde & Williams.; Former dir. Heublein, Inc. Mem. City Plan Commn., Hartford, 1947-56; pres. Ch. Council Found.; hon. mem. bd. dirs. Am. Heart Assn. Greater Hartford, Inc., Ch. Homes, Inc.; trustee Hartford Sem. Found. Served with U.S. Army, World War I. Mem. Am., Conn., Hartford County bar assns., Am. Judicature Soc., Christian Activities Council (life). Conglist. Club: Mason.

WILLIAMS, JACK KENNY, med. center adminstr.; b. Galax, Va., Apr. 5, 1920; s. Floyd Winfield and Mary Josephine (Vass) W.; m. Emma Margaret Pierce, June 10, 1943; children—Katherine Winfield, Mary Kenny. B.A., Emory and Henry Coll., 1940; M.A., Emory U., 1947, Ph.D., 1953; summer student, U. Va., 1948, U. Ky., 1949. High sch. tchr., Va., 1940-42; mem. faculty Clemson (S.C.) U., 1947-66; dean Clemson (S.C.) U. (Grad. Sch.), 1957-60, dean univ., 1960-66, v.p. acad. affairs, 1963-66, commr. coordinating bd. Tex. Colls. and Univs., 1966-68; v.p. U. Tenn. System, Knoxville, 1968-70; chancellor U. Tenn. Med. Sch., 1969-70; pres. Tex. A. and M. U. and Univ. System, College Station, 1970-77, chancellor, 1977-79; exec. v.p. Tex. Med. Center, Houston, from 1980; mem. Coll. Entrance Exam. Bd., 1974-76; dir. Frozen Food Express, Inc., Anderson-Clayton Co., Diamond Shamrock Co., Campbell-Taggert Co., Gifford-Hill Co. Author: Vogues in Villiany, 1958, Dueling in the Old South, 1980; Contbr. articles to profl. jours. Bd. dirs. Nat. Merit Scholarship Corp.; Mem. Sam Houston Council Boy Scouts Am., U.S. nat. com. World Energy Conf., 1976-77; chmn. Tex. Natural Fibers and Food Protein Commn., 1978; Mem. civilian adv. com. U.S. Army Command and Gen. Staff Coll., 1966-70. Served as officer USMCR, 1942-46. Mem. So. Assn. Colls. and Schs. (chmn. commn. colls. 1968-76, bd. dirs.), Assn. Tex. Colls. and Univs. (pres. 1978-79), USMCR Officers Assn., Phi Beta Kappa, Phi Kappa Phi. Methodist. Home: Houston, Tex.

WILLIAMS, JAMES PATRICK, mathematician, educator; b. Highland Park, Mich., Jan. 15, 1938; s. John Leo and Mary Theresa (Dalton) W.; m. Patricia Jo Williams, June 25, 1960; children—Megan, Matthew, Michael, Christopher. Grad., U. Detroit, 1959; postgrad., U. Mich., 1959-60, 62-65. Engr. Sperry Gyroscope Co., 1960-62; grad. research asst. U. Mich., 1963-65; mem. faculty Ind. U., Bloomington, 1966-83, prof. math., 1977-83. Mem. Am. Math. Soc., Math. Assn. Am. Democrat. Roman Catholic. Home: Bloomington, Ind. Dec. May 1, 1983.

WILLIAMS, JOHN BELL, lawyer, former gov. Miss.; b. Raymond, Miss., Dec. 4, 1918; s. Graves Kelly and Maude Elizabeth (Bedwell) W.; student Hinds Jr. Coll., Raymond, Miss., 1934-36, Univ. of Miss., 1938; LL.B., Jackson (Miss.) Sch. of Law, 1940; m. Elizabeth Ann Wells, Oct. 12, 1944; children—Marcia Elizabeth, John Bell, Kelly Wells. Admitted to Miss. bar, Apr. 1940; practiced in Raymond, 1940-46; pros. atty. Hinds County, Miss., May 1944-46; mem. 80th to 82d congresses 7th Miss. Dist., 82d to 87th congresses 4th Miss. Dist., mem. 88th to 90th congresses 3d Dist. Miss.; gov. State of Miss., 1968-72. Served with USAAF, 1941-44. Mem. Miss. State Bar Assn., Am. Legion, VFW, DAV. Democrat. Baptist. Mason (32 deg.). Home: Brandon, Miss. Died Mar. 26, 1983.

WILLIAMS, JOHN DAVID, indsl. mfg. exec.; b. Utica, N.Y., May 13, 1904; s. Ishmael and Elizabeth (Jones) W.; Indsl. Mech. Engr., Pratt Inst., 1926; m. Ernestine St. Auburn, June 18, 1926 (dec. Apr. 1947); 1 son, Frederick R.; m. 2d, Helen Wilder, Mar. 21, 1951. Prodn. engr., chief indsl. engr. Savage Arms Corp., Utica, N.Y., 1926-30; prodn. mgr., asst. mgr., then mgr., gen. mgr., dir. W.C. Lipe, Inc., Syracuse, N.Y., 1930-42; v.p., gen. mgr., dir. Lipe-Rollway Corp., Syracuse, 1942-58, pres., chief exec. officer, 1968-70, chmn. bd., chief exec. officer, 1970-73, also dir.; v.p., gen. mgr. Rollway Bearing Co., Inc., Syracuse, 1953-58, pres., chief exec. officer, 1968-70, chmn. bd., chief exec. officer, 1970-73, also past dir.; v.p., chmn. bd. First Fed. Savs. & Loan Assn.; hon. trustee N.Y. Bank for Savs.; dir. First Trust & Deposit Co., Syracuse Supply Co., First Comml. Banks Inc. Past mem. bd. dirs., past v.p. Met. Devel. Assn.; past pres., trustee Everson Mus. Art; trustee Oakwood Cemetery; former bd. dirs. United Way Syracuse and Onondaga County, Syracuse Symphony Orch. Recipient Community Service award Rotary Club Syracuse, 1958, Outstanding Bus. Exec. award Syracuse Herald-Jour., 1961, Distinguished Service award Greater Syracuse C. of C., 1968, medal for service Everson Mus., 1973; named Man of Year, Syracuse Herald Jour., 1968; named to Pillars of Thrift Soc. of Savs. Assn. League N.Y. State, 1976. Mem. Syracuse C. of C. (past dir.), Anti-Friction Bearing Mfrs. Assn. (past dir.), Mfrs. Assn. Syracuse (past dir., past pres., chmn. bd.), Syracuse Council of Chs. (past dir.), NAM (past dir.), Soc. Automotive Engrs., Citizens Found. Presbyn. Mason (32 deg.), Clubs: Century (gov. 1967-72, pres. 1971-72), Onondaga Golf and Country (Syracuse). Died June 21, 1981.

WILLIAMS, JOHN DAVIS, univ. ofcl.; b. Newport, Ky., Dec. 25, 1902; s. Victor Oldham and Lucy (Davis) W.; A.B., U. of Ky., 1926, M.A., 1930; Ed.D., Columbia U., 1940; LL.D., W.Va. Wesleyan, 1946, U. Ky., 1950; married Ruth Margaret Link, June 14, 1924; 1 dau., Ruth Harter. Began teaching in elementary sch. Southgate, 1923-25; supt. of schs., Crab Orchard, 1926-28, Falmouth, 1928-29; prin. Jr.-Sr. High Sch., Danville, 1929-34; supt. Tenn. Valley Authority Schs., Norris, Tenn., 1934-35; dir. U. High Sch. and asso. prof. edn., U. of Ky., 1935-36; dir. Univ. Elementary and High Sch. and prof. edn., U. of Ky., 1936-42; pres. Marshall Coll., 1942-46, chancellor, U. Miss., 1946-83. Past pres. S.E. Conf.; past chmn. Armed Forces Edn. Program Com.; vice pres. So. Regional Edn. Board, chmn. Ednl. Planning and Policies Adv. Committee; past pres. State Universities Association; past pres. Nat. Assn. State Univs.; elector N.Y. Hall of Fame. Mem. N.E.A., Am. Assn. U. Profs., Am. Council Edn. (past mem. exec. com.; com. relationships higher edn. on federal govt.; chmn. membership com.), Phi Kappa Pi, and the Omicron Delta Kappa, Phi Delta Kappa, Kappa Delta Pi, Phi Sigma Kappa, Delta Pi Epsilon. Club: Rotary (Oxford, Miss.). Home: University, Miss. Died May 29, 1983.

WILLIAMS, JOSEPH CAMPBELL, banker; b. Springfield, Mo., May 23, 1888; s. John W. and Juliette (Vinton) W.; student Drury Coll., Springfield, Mo., 1907-09; m. Nona Herrick, Oct. 31, 1918; children—Marie (Mrs. Albert I. Decker), Joseph C., Robert S., Juliette (Mrs. Robert Beeler). Pres., dir. Commerce Trust Co., Kansas

City, 1949-56; chmn. Nat. Bank North Kansas City (Mo.), from 1946, dir. Price Candy Co. Past pres. Kansas City Crime Commn. Trustee Drury Coll. Mem. Mo. Bankers Assn. (past pres.), Kansas City (past pres.), Mo. (dir.) chambers commerce, Assn. Res. City Bankers, Kappa Alpha. Clubs: Kansas City, Saddle and Sirloin, Seven-Eleven. Home: Kansas City, MO. †

WILLIAMS, KARL C., lawyer; b. Egan, Ill., Oct. 2, 1902; s. Aaron Otis and Alma (Glynn) W.; m. Mary E. Commons, May 10, 1934; children—Judith Glynn Callender, Meredith Ogilby. A.B., Dartmouth, 1923; LL.B., Harvard, 1926; LL.D. (hon.), Rockford Coll., 1959, Coll. Gt. Falls, 1966. Bar: Mass. 1926, Ill. 1927. Asst. states atty., Winnebago County, Ill., 1927-32, master in chancery, 1940-42, spl. asst. atty. gen. Ill., 1943-49; mem. law firm Williams, McCarthy, Kinley, Rudy & Picha (and predecessor firm.). Trustee Rockford Coll., from 1939, chmn., 1949-70. Fellow Am. Bar Found. (chmn. fellows 1969-70, treas. 1972-75), Am. Coll. Trial Lawyers; mem. Bar Assn. 7th Fed. Circuit (dir. 1967-76, 78—), ABA (ho. of dels. 1949-51, 54-56, 60-77, bd. govs. 1968-72, treas. 1972-75, chmn. com. jurisprudence and law reform 1958-59, 62, chmn. com. clients security fund 1961-68, chmn. com. on scope and correlation 1963-64, chmn. consortium on legal services and the pub. 1975-76), Ill. Bar Assn. (bd. govs. 1944-51, pres. 1954-55), Winnebago County Bar Assn. (pres. 1954-55), Am. Judicature Soc. (dir. 1953-56), Nat. Conf. of Bar. Pres. (mem. exec. council 1954-, chmn. 1958-59), Ill. Soc. Trial Lawyers. Republican. Methodist. Clubs: Rotarian. (Chgo.), Union League (Chgo.), University (Chgo.); Country (Rockford), University (Rockford). Home: Rockford, Ill. Dec. Feb. 21, 1984.

WILLIAMS, LYNN ALFRED, JR., univ. vice pres.; b. Evanston, Ill., Jan. 6, 1909; s. Lynn A., and Helen (Harvey) W.; A.B., Yale, 1929; LL.B., Harvard, 1932; student Mass. Inst. Tech., 1932-33; m. Dora DuPont, Sept. 12, 1932; children—Eve, Anne, Lynn A. III, Dora, Susan. Engaged practice law, 1933; vice pres. in charge of heater div., Stewart-Warner Corp., Chicago, 1942-47; pres. Great Books Foundation since 1947; also vice pres. U. of Chicago in charge development, from 1948. Home: Winnetka, Ill. Died Apr. 21, 1985.

WILLIAMS, RALPH CHESTER, pub. health service; b. Uchee, Russell County, Ala., July 24, 1888; s. Arthur R. and Susan K. (Tatum) W.; B.S., Ala. Poly. Inst., Auburn, 1907; M.D., U. of Ala., 1910; m. Annie W. Perry, Feb. 26, 1913; 1 son, Ralph Chester. Pvt. practice, Ala., 1910-13; field dir. sanitation, Ala. State Health Dept., 1913-17; entered U.S.P.H.S. March 1917; epidemic duty New Orleans and Tampico, Mex., in connection with outbreak of bubonic plague; asst. personnel officer P.H.S., 1923-27; in charge div. of sanitary reports and statistics and editor Pub. Health Repts., 1927-36. Chief Med. Officer Farm Security Adminstrn., June 1936-42; dist. dir. P.H.S. Dist. No. 1 (10 eastern states), 1942-44; asst. surgeon gen., chief, Bur. Med. Services, 1944-51, director division of hospital services, Ga. Dept. Pub. Health, 1951-59, coordinator of research, from 1959; instructor hospital administration Georgia State College Bus. Adminstrn., Atlanta, from 1952. Pres. Profl. Interfrat. Conf., 1930-31. rep. U.S., 6th, 10th, 11th Internat. Congress Mil. Medicine and Pharmacy, The Hague, 1931, Basle, 1947, Mexico City, 1949. Member Association of Military Surgeons of U.S. (pres.), S.A.R., Theta Kappa Psi (national president, nat. editor), Tau Kappa Epsilon (nat. pres.). Democrat. Baptist. Club: Cosmos (Washington, D.C.). Author: The United States Public Health Service, 1798-1950, 1951; sr. author: Nursing Home Management, pub. 1959. Contbr. pub. health subjects. Compiler of Health Almanac for 1919 and 1920, also of Miners Safety and Health Almanac for 1920, 21 and 22. Home: Atlanta, Ga. †

WILLIAMS, SAMUEL BAKER, born in Orinoke, Norton County, Kan., Aug. 2, 1889; s. James Walter and Margaret (McCulloch) W.; Litt.B., Princeton, 1912. E.E., 1914; m. Katherine Abbott, June 22, 1928; children—Anne, Jean. Asst. editor, Electrical World, 1914-22; mng. editor and editor. Elec. Record, 1922-24; editor, The Electragist, 1924-28, Elec. Contracting, 1928-36; mng. editor, Elec. World, 1936-37, editor, 1937-46; mgr. of public relations, Sylvania Electric Products, Inc. after 1949. Mem. Am. Nat. Com., Internat. Commn. on Illumination; mem. Tech. Socs. Council of N.Y. Past pres. Illuminating Engring Soc. (trustee research fund). Mem. Am. Inst. E.E. Club: Engineers (New York). Author: Cutting Central Station Costs, 1920. Home: East Orange, N.J. Deceased.

WILLIAMS, TENNESSEE THOMAS LANIER, playwright; b. Columbus, Miss., Mar. 26, 1911; s. Cornelius and Edwina (Dakin) W. Student U. Mo., 1931-33, Washington U., St. Louis, 1936-37; A.B., U. Iowa, 1938; hon. L.H.D., H.H.D. Author: plays Battle of Angels, 1940, The Glass Menagerie, 1944 (N.Y. Drama Critics Circle award), You Touched Me, 1946, A Streetcar Named Desire (Pultizer prize), 1947 (Drama Critics Circle award), Summer and Smoke, 1948, Rose Tattoo, 1950, Roman Spring of Mrs. Stone, 1950, Camino Real, 1953, Cat on a Hot Tin Roof (N.Y. Drama Critics Circle award), 1954 (Pulitzer prize for drama), Orpheus Descending, 1957, Garden District, 1958, Sweet Bird of Youth, 1959, Period of Adjustment, 1950, The Night of the Iguana (Drama Critics award), 1962 (Tony award), The Milk Train Doesn't Stop Here Anymore, 1963, Slapstick Tragedy, 1966, In the Bar of Tokyo Hotel and Other Plays, 1969, Small Craft Warnings, 1973, Outcry, 1974, Red Devil Battery Sign, 1976, This is an Entertainment, 1976, Vieux Carre, 1977, A Lovely Sunday for Creve Coeur, 1979, Clothes for a Summer Hotel, 1980, Kirche, Hutchen, und Kinder, 1980, A House Not Meant to Stand, 1981, Something Cloudy-Something Clear, 1981; others; screenplays Suddenly Last Summer, 1959, The Fugitive Kind; book 27 Wagonsfull of Cotton, 1946; short play collection Dragon Country, 1970; short story collections Eight Mortal Ladies Possessed, One Arm, Hard Candy, The Knightly Quest; novel Memoirs, 1975, Noise and the World of Reason; TV play Imagine Tomorrow, 1970; poems In the Winter of Cities, 1956, Androgyne, Mon Amour; essays Where I Live, 1979 (Recipient Brandeis U. Creative Arts medal in theater 1965, Rockefeller fellow 1940). Nat. Inst. Arts and Letters grantee, 1943; Gold medal for drama, 1969; Theatre Hall of Fame, 1979; Kennedy Honors award, 1979; Medal of Freedom Pres. Carter, 1980. Mem. Alpha Tau Omega. Address: New York, N.Y. Dec. Feb. 24, 1983.

WILLIAMS, WALKER ALONZO, automobile company executive; b. Wellington, Mo., June 8, 1901; s. Henry A. and Helen (Walker) W.; student U. Ill., 1922-23, Kansas City Sch. Law, evenings 1921, Kansas City Jr. Coll., evenings 1921; m. Evelyn Forrester, Sept. 25, 1926; children—Walker Forrester, John Haviland. With traffic dept. Armour Grain Co., Kansas City, Mo., 1920-22; with accounting dept. Am. Can Co., Kansas City, Mo., 1924-25; various positions up to wholesale mgr. Ford Motor Co., Kansas City, Mo., 1925-34, asst. br. mgr., Omaha, 1934-39, Kansas City, Mo., 1939-41, br. mgr., Salt Lake City, 1941-42, 44-45, Somerville, Mass., 1945-46, Ford sales mgr., Dearborn, Mich., 1946-48, gen. sales mgr. Ford div., 1948-50, v.p. sales and advt. for co., 1950-56, v.p., also vice chmn. dealer policy bd. for co., 1956- 58, v.p., asst. gen. mgr. Lincoln-Mercury div., 1958-61, ret., 1961; bus. mgr. Kalunite Inc., Salt Lake City, 1942-44. Charter mem. Detroit Symphony Orch.; mem. Detroit Grand Opera Assn.; gen. chmn., bd. dirs. United Found. Detroit, 1958; chmn. Crusade for Freedom, State Mich., 1951-52; past bd. dirs. Automobile Safety Found., Washington; founder mem. Soc. Performing Arts, Boca Raton, Fla. Past mem. Rapid Transit Commn., Detroit. Mem. Automotive Old Timers (life), DeMolay Legion of Honor, Fla. Atlantic Music Guild, Opera Soc. Ft. Lauderdale, English Speaking Union, Founders Soc. of Detroit Inst. Arts, Phi Gamma Delta. Clubs: Detroit Athletic; Boca Raton (Fla.), Boca Raton Hotel and Club, Royal Palm Yacht and Country; Vermilion Fairways Golf (Cook, Minn.). Home: Boca Raton, Fla. Died Feb. 14, 1981.

WILLIAMS, WARNER, sculptor, painter; b. Henderson, Ky., Apr. 23, 1903; s. Warner and Harriet (Burst) W.; m. Jean Aber, 1948; children—Carroll, Earle, David, Sylvia. Student, Berea Coll., 1921-23, Butler U., 1924, Herron Art Inst., 1925-27, Chgo. Art Inst., 1929-31; B.F.A., U. Chgo., 1930. Free-lance sculptor, Chgo., 1929-40, artist-in-residence, Culver Ednl. Found., 1940-69; prin. works include Arthure Schmitt relief, U. Chgo., Hippocrates portrait and oath, U. Mich., Maimonides meml. tablet, U. Ill. Sch. Pharmacy, U. S.D. Sch. Pharmacy, Beth-El Hosp., Bklyn., Stephen Foster meml, U. Pitts., busts and bas-reliefs, Culver Ednl. Found., St. Vincent DePaul medallion, DePaul U., Chgo., Roland F. McGuigan medal for Evans scholarships, Northwestern U., John F. Kennedy medallion, Cath. Schs., Westchester, Ill., Franklin Mint, Pres.'s medal, St. Louis U., John Wayne medal, Bronze, Inc., Colman music award medal, U. Wis., archbishop meml., Nat. Polish Cath. Ch., Chgo., Dr. Bucher medal, Am. Geophysical Soc., Ernst Abbe medal, N.Y. Microscopical Soc., Ind. Sesquicentennial medal, 1966, Indpls. Speedway medal 50th Anniversary, Mozart medal, Am. Symphony Orch., 50th Anniversary medallion, Culver Military Acad., Bicentennial medal, Ind. Numismatic Assn. (Recipient numerous art prizes including: City of Chgo. prize 1931, Buckingham prize 1934, Studebaker prize 1935, Hickox prize 1935, North Shore Artists prize 1937, Lucy Ball prize 1938, Daus. of Ind. prize 1939, Mcpl. Art league prize 1941, Spaulding prize 1942). Address: Culver, Ind.

WILLIAMSON, EDWARD, educator; b. Bluffton, Ind., Jan. 16, 1908; s. Dwight and Mary (Warner) W.; A.B., Wabash Coll., 1925; LL.B., Harvard, 1930, Ph.D., 1948. Asso. Nutter, McClennen & Fish, Boston, 1930-35, mem. firm, 1935-42; staff Lend-Lease Adminstrn., North Africa, 1942-45; asst. prof. Johns Hopkins, 1948-52, asso. prof., head dept., 1952-53; Fulbright research fellow, Italy, 1950-51; prof., head Italian dept. Columbia, 1953-56; professor, head dept. Romance, Wesleyan, 1956-74; fellow coop. program in humanities Duke U., 1964. Guggenheim fellow, 1959-60. Mem. Accademia Arcadia (Rome), Modern Lang. Assn., Medieval Acad., Am. Assn. Tchrs. Italian, Am. Assn. Tchrs. French, Beta Theta Pi. Clubs: Tudor and Stuart (Balt.); Columbia Faculty (N.Y.C.). Asso. editor of Romanic Review, from 1953. Home: Higganum, Conn. Died June 24, 1984.

WILLIAMSON, MAC Q., lawyer; b. Nebraska City, Neb., Oct. 13, 1889; s. Thomas Jefferson and Susan Elizabeth (MacQuiddy) W.; student U. of Okla., 1909-10; m. Beulah Conner Bowman, Nov. 14, 1920; 1 dau., Eleanor Jane (Mrs. James T. Blanton, Jr.). Admitted to Okla. bar, 1913, and in practice at Pauls Valley from 1913; city atty. Pauls Valley, 1914-17; atty. for Garvin County 2 terms, 1920-22 and 1922-24; mem. Okla. State Senate 2 terms, 1924-28 and 1928-32; atty. gen. Okla., 1935-43, resigned 1943, reelected 1946, 50, 54, 58. Served as lt. U.S. Army, World War I; capt. Inf. Reserve; commd. major in U.S. Army Sept. 1943; served overseas, rank of lt. col., World War II. Member of Oklahoma Hall of Fame. Mem. Am. and Okla. State bar assns. Democrat. Mason. Rotarian. Home: Oklahoma City, Okla. †

WILLIAMSON, ROBERT CROZIER, univ. prof. and physicist; born Havana, Ill., Nov. 2, 1887; s. William Henry and Dora Sophia (Tripp) W.; Ph.D., U. Wis., 1923; m. Maude Miller, 1920 (deceased); m. 2d, Muriel Coghill, April 9, 1942; children—Anne (Mrs. Raymond G. Herb), Robert M., Louis (dec.). Successively instr., asst. prof., associate prof. physics, U. of Wis., 1919-30; prof., head dept. physics, U. of Fla., 1930-58; prof. physics, Univ. Mandalay, Burma, Ford Foundation, University of Florida Program, from 1958. Member of the A.A.A.S., Am. Phys. Soc., Am. Phys. Teachers Assn., Fla. Acad. Sci., Am. Assn. Univ. Profs., Phi Beta Kappa, Sigma Xi, Gamma Alpha. Home: Gainesville, Fla. †

WILLIAMSON, WILLIAM RULON, actuary; b. Wales, N.Y., July 1, 1889; s. Rev. Harvey Raymond and Mary Matilda (Smith) W.; student Griffith Inst., Springville, N.Y., 1902-05; A.B., Wesleyan U., Middletown, Conn., 1909, A.M., 1910; m. Carolee Churchill, June 26, 1917; children—William Rulon, Addison Heaton. Actuarial clk., Travelers Ins. Co., 1910-16, asst. actuary life dept., 1916-36; actuarial consultant Com. on Econ. Scurity, Oct.-Dec., 1934; actuarial consultant Social Security Bd., 1936-47; senior actuarial consultant Wyatt Company, actuaries, 1943-54, president 1947-48; research actuary, from 1955; actuarial consultant Costa Rica, Guatemala on social security and insurance, 1947, Blue Shield and Blue Cross Commissions, 1949; cons. actuary, from 1915; lecturer on social security and group ins.; actuarial consultant for U.S. to Internat. Labor Office, 1937-40; Guggenheim fellowship, 1951-52. Tech. witness Sen-Finance Com.; mem. Merrill Center Conferee (Amherst). Del. U.S. Govt. 11th Internat. Congress Actuaries, Paris, 1936. Fellow Soc. Actuaries, Casualty Actuarial Soc., Am. Geog. Soc., A.A.A.S.; mem. Am. Statis. Assn., Am. Acad. Polit. and Social Sci., Acad. Polit. Sci., Am. Econ. Assn., Population Assn. Am., Phi Beta Kappa, Sigma Chi. Independent Republican. Episcopalian (vestryman). Clubs: Middle Atlantic Actuarial; Appalachian Mountain (Boston); Potomac Appalachian Trail (councilor), Cosmos (Washington). Author: Social vs. Personal Budgeting or Feudalism vs. Freedom. Contbr. tech. periodicals. Author: Employee Insurance Plans, 1948. Address: Washington, D.C. †

WILLIS, FRANCES ELIZABETH, foreign service officer; b. Metropolis, Ill., May 20, 1899; d. John Gilbert and Belle Whitfield (James) Willis; A.B., Stanford, 1920. Ph.D., 1923; student Universite Libre de Bruxelles, 1920-21. Instr. history, Goucher Coll., 1923-24; instr., asst. prof. polit. sci., Vassar, 1924-27. Internat. Grenfell Assn., Labrador, 1926; fgn. service officer, unclassified, vice consul of career, 1927; vice consul. Valparaiso, Chile, 1928-31, Santiago, 1931; sec. in diplomatic service, Dec. 17, 1931. 3d sec., Stockholm, Brussels, Luxembourg, 1931-37; 2d sec. Brussels and Luxembourg, 1937-40; 2d sec. and consul Madrid, 1940-43, 1st sec. 1943-44; office of the sec. dept. of State, 1944; office of under-sec., 1944-46, div. of western European affairs, 1946-47; 1st sec. and consul, London from 1947; later consul of legation, Helsinki, Finland. Mem. Phi Beta Kappa. Died July 20, 1983.

WILLKIE, EDITH (MRS. WENDELL WILLKIE), civic worker; b. Nashville, Aug. 6, 1890; d. Phil and Cora (Smith) Wilk; student U. Ind.; m. Wendell Willkie, Jan. 14, 1918 (dec.); 1 son, Philip H. Mem. Am. Battle Monuments Commn., Washington, from 1953; dir. Barter Theater, Abingdon, Va. Mem. N.Y. Library Council; trustee N.Y. Infirmary, Skidmore Coll., Salvation Army of N.Y.C.; mem. nat bd. U.S.O.; dir. Girls Club of N.Y. Mem. Nat. Conf. Christians and Jews, Nat. Inst. Social Scis. Home: New York, NY. †

WILLS, BERNARD O., naval officer; b. Walla Walla, Wash., Aug. 22, 1887; s. William Henry and Clara (Oviatt) W.; grad. U.S. Naval Acad., 1906-10; m. Ethel Lee Hanscom, Aug. 11, 1942. Resigned from U.S. Navy in 1926; joined U.S.N.R. and called to active duty in 1940, advanced to commodore. Home: San Francisco, Calif. Deceased.

WILLSON, FRED E., advt. exec.; b. Kansas City, Mo., Oct. 22, 1917; s. Fred E. and Hazel Inez (Tarter) W.; m. Pat Mary Draper, July 12, 1946; children—Michael, Haley, Jill, Laurie, Peter, Mark. B.S., U. Ill., 1940. Writer, salesman Sta. WDWS, Champaign, Ill., 1940-42; program dir. Sta. WIND, Chgo., 1942-45; account exec. Ivan Hill, Inc., Chgo., 1945-50; art and prodn. mgr. Cunningham & Walsh, Chgo., 1950-51, account exec., 1951-55, account supr., 1955-64, mgmt. supr., 1964-70, sr. v.p., gen. mgr., 1970-81, also dir. Bd. dirs. Kidney Found., Ill., 1976-81; mem. End Stage Renal Disease Network 15. Episcopalian. Club: Lake Shore. Home: Hinsdale, Ill. Dec. 1983.

WILMOT, SYDNEY, civil engr., editor; b. Providence, R.I., Dec. 8, 1887; s. David and Henrietta (Flaxman) W.; B.S. in C.E., Brown U., 1909; A.M., Columbia U., 1913; student special courses, Harvard U., 1921-22; m. Alice Mary Barr, Apr. 26, 1913; children—David Barr, Robert

Stanley. Civil engineer U.S. Office of Pub. Roads, 1909-11; draftsman Panama Canal, 1911; civil engr. Highway Dept., Brooklyn, N.Y., 1912-13, Pub. Service Commn. of N.Y., 1913-16, Turner Construction Co., N.Y. City, 1916-18; asst. prof. Brown U., 1918-23; successively tech. editor, mgr. publs. and mgr. tech. publs. Am. Soc. Civil Engineers, 1923-52, publications consultant from 1953. Director of Foreign Mission Realty Corporation; dir. Jennie Clarkson Home for Children, Valhalla, N.Y. (pres. 1941-48). Mem. bd. mgrs. Am. Bapt. Foreign Missionary Soc., 1935-47; mem. Am. Soc. C.E., Brown Engring. Assn. (pres. 1927, 1946). Sigma Xi, Chi Epsilon. Baptist. Author and editor of various tech. articles. Home: Tuckahoe, N.Y. †

WILSON, CAROLYN ANNE, newspaper corr. and lecturer; b. Beverly, Mass., July 28, 1889; d. Joseph Austin and Anne (Embery) W.; B.A., Wellesley, 1910; studied U. of Berlin, 1910-11, Sorbonne, Paris, 1912. With Chicago Tribune, 1913-19, war corr., 1914-Feb. 1919, hdqrs. Paris; spl. work in Eng., Italy, Germany and Holland, 1920-22, in Far East for 10 industrial magazines, India, Philippines, China, etc. Lecturer on questions of the Pacific. Address: Chicago, Ill. †

WILSON, CARROLL LOUIS, engring. adminstr.; b. Rochester, N.Y., Sept. 21, 1910; s. Louis William and Edna (Carroll) W.; m. Mary Bischoff, Apr. 1, 1937; children—Paul, Diana (Mrs. Paul B. Hoven, Jr.), Rosemary, Barbara. B.S., MIT, 1932; Sc.D. (hon.), Williams Coll., 1947; Eng. D. (hon.), Worcester Polytech. Inst., 1976. Asst. to pres. MIT, 1932-36, adviser to v.p. and dean engring., 1936-37; with Research Corp. of N.Y., 1937-40; exec. asst. to dir. OSRD, 1940-46; sec. to bd. of cons. to State Dept. for preparation report on plan for internat. control atomic energy, 1946; v.p. Nat. Research Corp. of Boston, 1946-47; gen. mgr. U.S. AEC, 1947-51; with Climax Molybdenum Co., 1951-54; pres. Climax Uranium Co., 1951-54; v.p., gen. mgr. Metals & Controls Corp., Attleboro, Mass., 1954-56, pres., gen. mgr., 1956-58; dir. Millipore Corp., Hitchener Mfg. Corp., IPI Income & Price Index Fund; prof. MIT, from 1959, Mitsui Prof. emeritus problems contemporary tech., from 1974; dir. workshop Alternative Energy Strategies, from 1974; dir. World Coal Study, from 1977; Mem. Rockefeller Bros. Fund panel on internat. security, 1957-58; governing bd. Internat. Centre Insect Physiology and Ecology, Nairobi, 1969-74; Dir. study on critical global environ. problems, 1970, man's impact on climate, 1971; trustee Woods Hole Oceanographic Instn.; dir. MIT fellows in Africa, 1960-67. Hon. dir. R.I. Hosp., R.I. Hosp. Trust Co.; trustee World Peace Found. of Boston, Internat. Fedn. Inst. Advanced Study, Stockholm; U.S. mem. com. sci. research OECD, 1961-70; mem. adv. com. on application sci. and tech. to devel. ECOSOC UN, 1964-70; sr. adviser UN Conf. on Human Environ.; mem. Trilateral Commn., Commn. on Critical Choices for Ams.; mem. energy prize selection com. Krupp Found., Essen, W. Ger. Decorated Officer Order Brit. Empire. Mem. AIME, Council Fgn. Relations (dir., Elihu Root lectr. 1973), Am. Acad. Arts and Scis., Royal Swedish Acad. Engring. Scis., Pilgrim Soc. Am., UN Assn. (dir.). Clubs: Century Association (N.Y.C.); Cosmos (Washington); of Rome. Home: Seekonk, Mass.

WILSON, CHARLES H., congressman; b. Magna, Utah, Feb. 15, 1917; s. Charles H. and Janet Chalmers (Hunter) W.; ed. pub. schs., m. Betty Gibbel, Mar. 23, 1947 (dec. July 5, 1974); children—Stephen C., Donald H., Kenneth A., William J.; m. Hyun Ju Chang. With Security First Nat. Bank; propr. Charles H. Wilson Ins. Agy., Los Angeles, from 1945; mem. Calif. Assembly, 1954-62, chmn. com. on revenue and taxation; mem. 88th-96th Congresses, 31st Calif. Dist., mem. coms. on armed services, post office, civil service. Served with AUS, 1942-45. Mem. Am. Legion. Democrat. Clubs: Masons, Shriners, Elks, Kiwanis. Home: Tantallon, Md. Died July 21, 1984.*

WILSON, CHARLES WILLIAM, lawyer; b. Walls, La., Feb. 22, 1910; s. Charles William and Elizabeth (Slaughter) W.; B.A., La. State U., 1931, J.D., 1933; m. Claire Prince, Jan. 2, 1933; children—Linda (Mrs. Thomas P. Landry), Claire (Mrs. Harold I. Bahlinger), Rebecca, Mary Scott (Mrs. L. J. Fergesen), Charles William III, Alonzo Prince, Alexander Jerome. Admitted to La. bar, 1933, since practiced in Baton Rouge; mem. firm Watson, Blanche, Wilson, & Posner and predecessor firms, 1940-82. Dir. State Nat. Life Ins. Co., Air Waves, Inc., Baton Rouge Motor Lodge Corp. Trustee, v.p. Womans Hosp. Found. Fellow Am. Coll. Trial Lawyers; mem. Am., La. (dir. 1966-67). Baton Rouge (pres. 1956), Internat., Fed., Inter-Am. bar assns., Internat. Assn. Ins. Counsel, Def. Research Inst., Ins. Club New Orleans, Nat. Rifle Assn., Amateur Trap Shooting Assn., Nat. Skeet Shooting Assn., Baton Rouge Assembly, Baton Rouge C. of C., Phi Delta Phi, Sigma Chi. Democrat. Roman Catholic. Kiwanian. Clubs: Serra, Baton Rouge Country, City, Camelot (Baton Rouge). Home: Baton Rouge, La. Died 1982.

WILSON, CHRISTOPHER WILLIAM, lawyer; b. Bklyn., Apr. 27, 1910; s. Christopher W. and Marion A. (Smith); m. Margaret Ella Pettengill, June 5, 1948; children—Anthony P., Nancy F., Priscilla P. (Mrs. Wells), Christopher William, III. A.B., Cornell U., 1931; LL.B., Harvard U., 1934; LL.D., Blackburn Coll., 1967. Bar: N.Y. bar 1934, Ill. bar 1951. With firm White & Case, N.Y.C. and Paris, 1934-51; atty. First Nat. Bank Chgo., 1952-56, v.p., gen. counsel, 1956-62, sr. vice pres., gen. counsel, 1962-63, exec. v.p., 1963-67, exec. v.p., cashier, 1967-70, exec. v.p., gen. counsel, 1970-72; counsel Hopkins & Sutter (and predecessor firm), Chgo., 1972-83; dir. Scott, Foresman & Co. Bd. dirs. Children's Meml. Hosp.; advisory trustee Blackburn Coll.; life trustee U. Chgo. Served as lt. USNR, 1944-46. Mem. Am., Ill. Chgo. bar assns., Delta Upsilon. Clubs: Mid-Day (Chgo.), Chicago (Chgo.), Commonwealth (Chgo.), Commercial (Chgo.); Indian Hill (Winnetka, Ill.); Old Elm (Fort Sheridan, Ill.); Mission Valley (Laurel, Fla.). Home: Winnetka, Ill. Dec. Aug. 12, 1983.

WILSON, DELLA F(ORD), univ. prof.; b. Hartsell, Ala., Mar. 31, 1888; d. William Paca and Isora (Morison) Wilson; B.S., James Millikin U., 1910; M.A., Teachers Coll., Columbia, 1927; grad. student Peoples U., St. Louis, 1911. Applied Arts Summer Sch., Chicago, 1912, Alfred (N.Y.) U., summer 1918. Teacher, James Millikin, summer session 1910; teacher elementary schs., Decatur, Ill., 1910-11, high sch., 1911-13; teacher James Millikin U., 1913-15; with art edn. dept. U. of Wis. from 1915, prof. Mem. Nat. League Am. Pen Women, Nat. Com. on Art Edn., N. E. A., Wis. Edn. Assn., (life) Wis. Memorial Union, Madison Art Assn., Civic Music Assn., So. Wis. Teachers Assn., Delta Phi Delta, Phi Delta Gamma, Sigma Lambda. Democrat. Presbyterian. Author: Primary Industrial Art, 1927. Director research in Wis. clays U. of Wis., 1937. Home: Madison, Wis. †

WILSON, DON, actor-announcer; b. Lincoln, Neb., Sept. 1900; s. Lincoln and Louise (Hatch) W.; grad. high sch., Denver; student U. of Colo., 2 years; married Lois Corbet, June 22, 1950. Salesman, 1921-27; radio work from 1927, at San Francisco, 1927, Los Angeles, 1928; chief announcer, KFI, KECA, 1929-33; sports announcer Nat. Broadcasting Co., N.Y. City, 1933-34; announcer on Jack Benny program from 1934; also appeared on television. Selected as most popular radio announcer 17 times, from 1935. Mem. Sigma Chi (Significant Sig.). Republican. Presbyn. Club: Civitan (Denver). Died Apr. 26, 1982.

WILSON, ELMER DEE, geophysical company executive; b. Joplin, Mo., July 23, 1921; s. John Elmer and Verda Bess (Douse) W.; m. Betty Jean McGhee, Dec. 6, 1944; children—Paula Jo, Dee Anne. Student, Tex. A&M U., Tulsa U. With Seismograph Service Corp., Tulsa, 1946-81, treas., then fin. v.p., 1961, pres., 1966, chief exec. officer, 1969-81, also chmn. bd. Chmn. Tulsa Met. Crime Commn., 1971-73; trustee Tulsa Psychiat. Center; coordinating chmn. Energy Advocates. Served with USAAF, 1942-45. Decorated D.F.C., Air medal with 4 oak leaf clusters. Mem. Tulsa C. of C., Soc. Exploration Geophysicists, Inst. Internal Auditors., Fin. Execs. Inst., Nat. Assn. Accountants. Republican. Clubs: Cedar Ridge Country, Tulsa, Petroleum, Summit, Elks. Home: Tulsa, Okla. Died Mar. 11, 1981.

WILSON, EVAN M(ORRIS), ret. fgn. service officer; b. Rosemont, Pa., Jan. 20, 1910; s. Charles and Elizabeth Cutter (Morris) W.; grad. Montgomery Sch., Wynnewood, Pa., 1926; A.B., Haverford Coll., 1931; B.A., Oxford U., 1934; student Geneva Sch. of Internat. Studies, summers 1932, 33; m. Leila Whitney Fosburgh, Sept. 7, 1935; children—Leila F., Martha L. Clk., Home Owners Loan Corp., 1935; research for Pan Am. Union, 1937; apptd. fgn. service officer Dept. State, 1937; vice consul, Guadalajara, Mexico, 1937-38; assigned Dept. State, 1938; vice consul, later 3d sec., Cairo, Egypt, 1938-41; 3d sec., vice consul, Mexico City, 1942-43; assigned Dept. State, 1943-47; Am. sec., Anglo-Am. Com. of Inquiry (Palestine), 1945-46; asst. chief div. Nr. Eastern affairs, 1946-47; 2d sec., vice consul, later 1st sec., consul, Tehran, Iran, 1947-49; student Nat. War Coll., Aug. 1949-50; consul gen., Calcutta, India, 1950-53; 1st sec., London, 1953-57; assigned to Dept. State, Washington, 1957-61; counselor of embassy, Beirut, Lebanon, 1961-64; Am. consul gen., Jerusalem, from 1964, with personal rank of minister, 1966; ret., 1967; bd. dirs. Middle East Inst., chmn. Am. Near East Refugee Aid. Mem. U.S. del. 1st, 2d Suez Canal Confs., London, 1956. Clubs: Metropolitan (Washington); Chevy Chase (Md.); North Woods (Minerva, N.Y.). Author: Jerusalem, Key to Peace, 1970. Contbr. numerous articles on Middle East to profl. publs. Home: Washington, D.C. Died Mar. 13, 1984.

WILSON, FLORENCE K(ISSICK), nursing educator; b. Tonica, Ill., Nov. 5, 1889; d. William and Araminta (Kissick) W.; A.B., U. of Mich., 1913; diploma, City Hosp. Sch. of Nursing, New York City, 1920; A.M., Western Reserve U., 1930; student, Vassar Training Camp for Nurses, 1918. Med. supervisor, Western Reserve U., 1923-29; asst. to grading com. on Nursing Schs., 1929-30; med. supervisor, U. of Neb. Sch. of Nursing, 1932-34, N.Y. Hosp. Sch. of Nursing, 1934-37; supt. of nurses, Memorial Hosp., Syracuse, N.Y., 1937-45; asst. prof. nursing edn., Syracuse U., 1943-45; dean, Duke U. Sch. of Nursing, also prof. nursing edn., from 1946. Mem. N.Y. State Nursing Council for war service, 1942-46. Mem. Am. Nurses Assn., Nat. League Nursing Edn., Nat. Orgn. Pub. Health Nursing, N.Y. State League Nursing Edn. (pres.), N.C. State League Nursing Edn. (pres.), Conglist. Author: Ward Study Units in Medical Nursing, 1930. Home: Brecksville, Ohio. †

WILSON, FRANK WILEY, U.S. judge; b. Knoxville, Tenn., June 21, 1917; s. Frank Caldwell and Mary Elizabeth (Wiley) W.; m. Helen Elizabeth Warwick, Apr. 6, 1942; children—Frank Carl, William Randall. B.A., U. Tenn., 1939, LL.B., 1941. Bar: Tenn. bar 1941. With firm Poore, Kramer & Cox, Knoxville, 1941-42, Wilson & Joyce, Oak Ridge, 1946-61, county atty., Anderson County, 1948-50, city atty., Norris, 1950-61; U.S. dist. judge Eastern Dist. Tenn., Chattanooga, 1961-82, chief judge, 1969-82; Vice pres., dir. Bank of Oak Ridge, 1953-61. Trustee Siskin Meml. Found., Democratic candidate for Congress, 1950. Served with USAAF, 1942-46. Mem. Am. Bar Assn., Am. Judicature Soc., Am. Legion (past post comdr.), Order of Coif, Scabbard and Blade, Phi Kappa Phi, Phi Delta Kappa. Club: Rotarian (past pres. Oak Ridge). Home: Signal Mountain, Tenn. Dec. Sept. 29, 1982.

WILSON, HARRIS WARD, educator; b. Frederick, Okla., Sept. 8, 1919; s. John Benjamin and Anna (Harris) W.; children—Golder North, John Robert. A.B., U. Mo., 1941; A.M., U. Chgo., 1947; Ph.D. in English, U. Ill., 1953. Instr. Auburn U., 1947-49; instr. U. Ill., Urbana, 1953-55, asst. prof., 1955-57, asso. prof., 1957-60, prof. English, from 1960. Author: Correspondence H.G. Wells-Arnold Bennett, 1960, University Handbook of English, 1960, University Readings, 1962; Editor: The Wealth of Mr. Waddy (H.G. Wells); Contbr. articles to publs. Served to capt. AUS, 1941-46. Decorated Air medal; Guggenheim fellow, 1960-61. Mem. Modern Lang. Assn., Nat. Council Tchrs. English, Am. Assn. U. Profs. Home: Urbana, Ill.

WILSON, JAMES HERBERT, prof. French; b. Bethel, Vt., Oct. 10, 1889; s. James Jay and Mary (McCoy) W.; grad. Whitcomb High Sch., Bethel, 1906; B.A., Trinity Coll. (Oxford U.), Eng., 1917 (first class in French honors); Ph.D., U. of Wis., 1921; M.A., Oxford, 1922. With Oxford U. Training Corps, Apr.-July 1917; served as 2d lt. A Battery, 5th F.A., U.S.A., A.E.F., Aug. 20, 1917-Jan. 9, 1918; 1st lt., Jan. 9, 1918-Sept. 10, 1919; participated in battles of Cantigny and Château Thierry. Instr. French, U. of Wis., 1919-22; prof. French, St. Stephen's Coll. (Columbia U.), Annandale-on-Hudson, N.Y., from 1922; same, Northwestern U., summer 1925, 30; dir. School of Foreign Travel, 1929, 31. Mem. Modern Language Assn. America, Phi Beta Kappa, Delta Psi. Episcopalian. Author: Victor Hugo, the Novelist, 1925. Editor: Hugo's Notre Dame de Paris, 1926; Hugo's Les Travailleurs de la Mer, 1929. Home: Bethel, Vt. †

WILSON, JOAN, TV producer; d. John Harlan and Esther (Stanton) W.; m. Jeremy Brett, Nov. 22, 1977; children: Caleb, Rebekah. Student, Grinnell Coll.; B.A., U. Wis.; D.F.A. (hon.), Salem (Mass.) State Coll., 1979, Grinnell Coll., 1980. charter mem. com. Harvard Theatre Collection. Producer, Sta. WGBH-TV, Boston, 1967-85; producer: nat. series Mystery!, 1980-85, Classic Theatre: The Humanities in Drama, 1975-76, Masterpiece Theatre, 1973-85, Piccadilly Circus, 1976-77; weekly series Elliot Norton Revs, 1971-74; nat. spl. Growing Up Female, 1974; local spl. To Be Irish in Boston, 1974; local series Kitchen Sync, 1973; asso. producer nat. spl.: local series Godspell Goes to Plimoth Plantation for Thanksgiving with Henry Steele Commager, 1972; nat. series on art Eye to Eye, 1971; asso. project dir., producer, actress nat. radio series: nat. series on art The WGBH Radio Drama Development Project, 1967-69; (Recipient (as series producer for Masterpiece Theatre) 9 Emmy awards, Christopher award, Peabody award, Edgar award.). Mem. AFTRA, Nat. Acad. TV Arts and Scis., Am. Film Inst., NOW. Unitarian-Universalist. Home: Marblehead, Ma. Died July 4, 1985.

WILSON, PHILIP DANFORTH, mining engr.; b. Chicago, Ill., Feb. 22, 1888; s. William Rowley and Nettie Louise (Danforth) W.; B.S., Princeton, 1909; E.M., Sch. of Mines (Columbia), 1911; m. Virginia Greenway Albert, January 8, 1915; children—Danforth, Virginia Greenway; m. 2d, Cornelia Reid, Sept. 16, 1940; children—Margaret Deil, Edith Reid. Connected with the Phelps Dodge Corp., Douglas, Ariz., later with Transvaal Copper Mining Co., Sonora, Mexico, and the Shattuck Ariz. Copper Co., Bisbee, Ariz., 1911-13; geologist and chief geologist Calumet & Ariz. Mining Co., Warren, Ariz., 1914-24; mining engr. and geologist with Am. Metal Company, Ltd., in S. America, S. Africa, Europe, Cuba, Mexico and N.Y. City, and gen. mgr. subsidiaries in Chile and S. Africa, 1925-33; v.p. Pardners Mines Corp., 1934-42; on War Prodn. Bd., chief prod., dir. Aluminum and Magnesium Div., vice chmn. for metals and minerals, 1941-45; cons. mining engr., Lehman Bros. and Lehman Corp., 1946-51. Mem. Mining and Metall. Society America, Am. Inst. Mining and Metall. Engrs., Soc. Economic Geologists Council on Foreign Relations, Tau Beta Pi, Sigma Psi, Delta Kappa Epsilon, Phi Beta Kappa. Republican. Episcopalian. Clubs: University, Mining, Downtown Assn. (N.Y.C.); Baltusrol, Short Hills (N.J.). Home: Short Hills, N.J. †

WILSON, REX HAMILTON, physician; b. Hendrysburg, Ohio, Aug. 22, 1909; s. Harvey Hoyt and Margaret Maude (Hamilton) W.; A.B., Ohio Wesleyan. 1931; M.D.; Ohio State U. 1935; m. Maribel McDaniel, Apr. 11, 1936 (dec. July 1972); 1 son, Peter McDaniel. Intern Presbyn. Hosp., Chgo., 1935-36, resident in medicine, 1936-38; pvt. practice internal medicine, Akron, Ohio, 1938-42; cons. medicine Goodyear Tire & Rubber Co., 1938-42; med. dir. B.F. Goodrich Co., 1946-74; dir., med. dir., v.p. Summit Nat. Life Ins. Co.; utilization appeal com., hon. staff medicine Akron City Hosp.; staff Children's St. Thomas hosps., Akron; mem. hon. med. Staff Akron Gen. Hosp.; past asst. dir. health Summit County. Speaker 11th Internat. Congress Indsl. Medicine, Naples. 1954. Former v.p., trustee, mem. exec. com. United Found. of Akron, Inc.; mem. adv. com. Arthritis and Rheumatism Found. Akron; founder, trustee, past pres. Rehab. Center, Summit County; Mem. Summit-Portage City Comprehensive Health Planning Agy.; med. com. Chlorine Inst.; mem. Com. Workmen's Compensation Ohio State Med.; mem. com. environmental health Ohio Comprehensive Health Planning Adv. Council; mem. Summit-Portage Red Cross Health and Med. Com. Troop counselor Boy Scouts Am.; past chmn. health com., rubber sect., mem. exec. and adv. coms. Nat. Safety Council; mem. Pres. Com. on Safety. Served as maj. M.C., AUS, 1942-46. Diplomate Am. Bd. Internal Medicine, Am. Bd. Preventive Medicine (founders group occupational medicine). Fellow Am. Coll. Preventive Medicine A.M.A., A.C.P., Am. Acad. Occupational Medicine, Assn. Mil. Surgeons U.S., Indsl. Med. Assn. (dir. 1955-57), Royal Soc. Health; mem. Indsl. Med. Assn., World Med. Assn., Internat. Congress Indsl. Medicine (past pres. Pitts.), Akron Internat. Med. Soc. (past pres.), Nat. Med. Dirs. Forum (emeritus), Aerospace Med. Assn., Pan Am. Med. Assn., Am. Rheumatism Assn., Am. Med. Writers Assn., Nat. Air Pollution Control Assn., Nat. Rehab. Assn., Am. Assn. Phys. and Surgs., Am. Assn. Ins. Med. Dirs., Med. Round Table, Ramazzini, Ohio (ex-chmn. sect. indsl. medicine; chmn. com. environmental and pub. health), Summit County (chmn. hosp. laision com.) med. socs., Rubber Mfrs. Assn. (chmn. environmental health com.), Am. Soc. Internal Medicine, Phi Rho Sigma, Alpha Tau Omega. Methodist. Mason (32), Rotarian. Club: Portgage Country. Recipient citation excellence med. author-ship, American Association Industrial Physicians and Surgeons, 1948. Asso. editor Industrial Medicine and Surgery, Jour. Occupational Medicine, (column) Tips to Better Health. Contbr. articles to profl. jours. Speaker before med. orgns. Home: Akron, Ohio. Died Feb. 24, 1981.

WILSON, ROBERT DOUGLAS, constrn. co. exec.; b. Holly, Colo., Jan. 3, 1920; s. John Albert and Nelly Grace (Simpson) W.; m. Mary Harrell, Nov. 5, 1948; children—Rebecca Sue, Marsha Ann. B.C.E., Colo. State U., 1947. With Peter Kiewit Sons Co., Omaha, from 1947, gen. supt., 1951-60, asst. to pres., 1961-63, v.p., 1964-65, exec. v.p. ops., 1965-69, pres., from 1969; dir. No. Natural Gas Co., Guarantee Mut. Co. Bd. dirs. Boys Town; mem. exec. bd. Mid-Am. council Boy Scouts Am., from 1974. Served with U.S. Army, 1942-46. Decorated Bronze Star, Silver Star; Croix de Guerre France; named Man of Year Boy Scouts Am. Mem. ASCE. Republican. Presbyterian. Clubs: Moles, Beavers, Masons, Omaha Country, De Anza Desert Country. Home: Omaha, Neb. *

WILSON, ROBERT JAMES, airline executive; b. Grand Rapids, Mich., June 15, 1902; s. James Alexander and Annie E. (McAlpine) W.; m. Alice Beckham, May 29, 1935 (div. Aug. 1955); m. Marilyn Jones, Dec. 26, 1956 (div. dec. 1958); m. Helen Gillespie, Aug. 22, 1959. A.B., U. Mich., 1925, LL.B., 1929. Bar: Bar Mich. 1929. Ptnr. Warner, Norcross & Judd, Grand Rapids, 1936-42; v.p. Capital Airlines, Inc., Washington, 1942-61; also dir.; mem. firm Patterson, Belknap & Webb, from 1963; chmn. bd. Airlines Nat. Service Co.; pres. Zantop Air Transport, Inc., from 1966, also dir.; pres., dir. Universal Airlines, Inc., 1966-67, chmn. bd., from 1967; pres., dir. Universal Aircraft Service; dir. Airlines Personnel Relations Conference, Airlines Terminal Corp., Airlines Nat. Terminal Service Co., Inc. City commissioner of, East Grand Rapids, Mich., 1936-42; chmn. Indsl. Adv. com., Loudoun County, Va. Recipient Presdl. commendation, 1972, Presdl. citation, 1976, 78. Mem. Am., Mich. State bar assns., Nat. Alliance Businessmen (exec. v.p., sec.-treas. 1969-78), Sigma Phi, Phi Delta Phi. Episcopalian (sr. warden from 1972). Home: Leesburg, Va. Dec. Feb. 25, 1983.

WILSON, STEVEN BAYARD, mfg. exec.; b. Washington, Dec. 12, 1890; s. William Alexander and Nellie (Herbert) W.; student Coll. Engring. U. Mich., 1911-13, George Washington U., 1914-16; m. Mary Sullivan, Apr., 1921 (dec. Dec. 1925); children—Steven Bayard, Charles Alexander; m. 2d, Laurel Mae Poulson, Sept. 25, 1943. Salesman in automotive industry, 1921-28; organized Fleming Mfg. Co., Providence, name changed to Fram Corp., 1940, 1929, v.p. sales, 1929-32, became pres., 1932, chmn., 1942-66, chmn. exec. com., from 1966; chmn. Mason Can Co., East Providence, R.I., Vokar Corp., Dexter, Mich., Warner Lewis Co., Tulsa, Fram Can., Ltd., Stratford, Ontario. Del. to Republican Nat. Conv., 1944, 48, 52; treas. R.I. Rep. State Central Com., 1947-48; acting nat. committeeman, 1952; mem. Nat. Rep. Finance Com., 1947-48. Trustee Robert A. Taft Meml. Found. Served from lt. to capt., inf., U.S. Army, 1917-21; from maj. to lt. col., inf., AUS, 1942-43. Mem. N.A.M., Motor and Equipment Mfrs. Assn., Navy League (nat. dir.), Defense Orientation Conference Assn. (dir.), Phi Gamma Delta. Mason (32, Shriner). Home: Barrington, R.I. †

WILSON, WILLIAM JOHN, transp. co. exec.; b. Idaho Falls, Idaho, Nov. 28, 1912; s. John J. and Anna (Metzner) W.; student bus. coll., Salt Lake City, 1932-33; m. Janet Nicholes, Jan. 30, 1938; children—Gail (Mrs. Ron L. Kvartfordt), Norma (Mrs. William Pieper), William Alan. Engaged in sales, 1933-35; with Garrett Freightliners, from 1935, exec. v.p., 1957-67, pres., 1967-79; dir. Idaho Bank & Trust Co., Pocatello. Trustee Machinist Health and Welfare Fund Machinists. Mem. Trucking Employers (bd. dirs.), Pocatello C. of C. (bd. dirs.). Kiwanian. Home: Pocatello, Idaho. Died Mar. 18, 1979.

WILTSHIRE, WILLIAM ERNEST, life ins. exec.; b. Richmond, Va., Aug. 1, 1890; s. James McKnight and Bettie (Ratcliffe) W.; ed. pub. schs. and bus. coll.; m. Essie Watkins (dec.); children—William Ernest, Richard Watkins. Chmn. bd. Home Beneficial Life Ins. Co., Richmond, Va., from 1907, also dir. Home: Richmond, Va. †

WILZBACH, CARL ALBERT, physician; b. Martinsville, Ind., June 18, 1889; s. Robert and Margarett (Vance) W.; B.S., U. of Cincinnati, 1918, M.D., 1922; m. Ida Elizabeth Walter, May 20, 1914; 1 dau., Ruth Elizabeth. Dir. physical edn., Y.M.C.A., Cin., 1912-17, dir. of dept., 1917-23; exec. dir. all work, Central Y.M.C.A., Cin. 1923-28; engaged in social hygiene and public health ed. from 1928; was nationally known as radio commentator on health. Commissioner of health for Cincinnati from 1938. Consultant to U.S. Public Health Service. Active in civic organizations. Fellow Am. Med. Assn.; mem. Am. Pub. Health Assn. (past pres. health edn. sect.), Ohio State and Hamilton County med. socs. (chmn. both pub. relations coms.), Alumni Assn. U. of Cincinnati Coll. of Medicine Assn. (past Pres.). Mason. Club: Kiwanis (past pres.) (Cincinnati). Home: Cincinnati, Ohio. Deceased.

WIMMER, GUY HALBERT, clergyman, college president; b. Smith County, Kans., Dec. 8, 1890; s. Lester Dee and Sarah Alice (Hutto) W.; B.A., Ottawa (Kan.) U., 1923, D.D., 1938; student Northern Bapt. Theol. Sem., Chicago, 1930-31; student Div. Sch., U. of Chicago, summers, 1931-37; m. Edna Marie Bailey, Oct. 29, 1913; children—Ruth Aileen, Flora Marie, Gaye Lee. Ordained Bapt. minister, 1911; pastor, Ellsworth, Kan., 1923-24. Hutchinson, 1924-29, Chicago, Ill., 1930-37; exec. sec. Ill. Bapt. State Conv., 1937-39; pastor Forest Park Baptist Ch., Chicago, from 1945. Pres. Ill. Bapt. State Convention; chmn. Dept. Life and Extension, Ch. Fedn. of Greater Chicago. Author: (pamphlet) Can a College be Christian. Club: Rotary (Alton); T. (Chicago). Home: Chicago, Ill. Deceased.

WINCHELL, CONSTANCE M(ABEL), librarian; b. Northampton, Mass., Nov. 2, 1896; d. Joseph E. and Inez Bliss) W.; A.B., U. Mich., 1918; M.S., Columbia, 1930. Librarian, Central High Sch., Duluth, Minn., 1918-19; asst. lighthouse div. Merchant Marine Service, N.Y.C., 1920; reviser, cataloging dept. U. Mich. Library, 1920-21, reference asst., 1921-23; head cataloger Am. Library, Paris, France, 1924-25; reference asst. Columbia U. Libraries, 1925-33, asst. reference librarian, 1933-41, reference librarian, 1941-62. Mem. A.L.A., Assn. Coll. and Reference Libraries, N.Y. Library Assn., Kappa Alpha Theta. Author: Locating Books for Interlibrary Loan, 1930; Guide to Reference Books, 1951, others. Home: New York, N.Y. Died May 23, 1983.

WINDES, DUDLEY W., judge; b. 1888; Certificate in law, Ind. U.; children—Honor G., Dudley W., John A. Admitted to the bar, 1915; presently asso. justice Supreme Ct of Ariz. Home: Phoenix. †

WINDLE, WILLIAM FREDERICK, educator; b. Huntington, Ind., Oct. 10, 1898; s. William C. and Georgia (Kimball) W.; m. Ella Grace Howell, June 14, 1923; children—Mary (Mrs. R.A. Skyer), William. B.S., Denison U., 1921, D.Sc. (hon.), 1947; postgrad., U. Mich., 1923, U. Chgo., 1924, U. Wis., 1925; M.S., Northwestern U. Med. Sch., 1923, Ph.D., 1926. Asst. in anatomy Northwestern U. Med. Sch., 1922, instr., 1923-26, asst. prof., 1926-29, asso. prof., 1929-35, prof. microscopic anatomy, 1935-42; prof. neurology, dir, Inst. Neurology, 1942-46; prof. anatomy, dir. dept. U. Wash. Med. Sch., Seattle, 1946-47; prof. anatomy, chmn. dept. U. Pa., 1947-51, research prof., 1951; sci. dir. Baxter Labs., Inc., Morton Grove, Ill., 1951-53; chief lab. neuroanat. scis. Nat. Inst. Neurol. Diseases and Blindness, NIH, 1953-60, asst. dir., 1960-61, chief lab. perinatal physiology, San Juan, P.R., 1960-64; research prof. rehab. medicine, also dir. research Inst. Rehab. Medicine, N.Y. U. Med. Center, N.Y.C., 1964-71, emeritus, 1971-85; research prof. Denison U., Granville, Ohio, 1971—; Vis. instr. U. Colo. Med. Sch., 1926; lab. guest physiology Cambridge U., 1935-36; Commonwealth prof, Louisville, 1944; professorial lectr. Emory U., 1948; miembro honorario facultad de medicina U. Chile, 1961-85; prof. ad-honorem U. P.R., 1962—; vis. prof. U. Cal. at Los Angeles, 1970, 72, 74, 76; Robert Zeit Meml. lectr. Northwestern U., 1963, Ranson Meml. lectr., 1964; Distinguished Scientist lectr. Tulane U., 1970; guest lectr. Orbeli Inst. Physiology, Yerevan, USSR, 1974. Author: Physiology of the Fetus, 1940, Textbook of Histology, 1949, 5th edit., 1976, Asphyxia Neonatorium, 1950, Fetal Physiology, 1971, Clarence Luther Herrick, 1979, Spinal Cord and its Reaction to Traumatic Injury, 1980; Editor: NINDB Symposia in Neuranatomical Sciences, 1954-64; founder: Experimental Neurology, 1959; editor, 1959-75, chmn. editorial bd., 1975-85. Trustee, v.p. Biol. Stain Commn., 1943-46; Mem. research adv. bd. United Cerebral Palsy Assn.; mem. Human Embryology and Devel. Study Sect., div. research grants NIH, 1954-60, mem. anat. scis. tng. com., 1958-60; mem. sci. adv. com. Div. Research Facilities and Resources, NIH, 1964-67; chmn. sci. adv. com. Nat. Paraplegic Found., 1970-74. Served as pvt. U.S. Army, World War I. Recipient War-Navy award, 1948; Max Weinstein award United Cerebral Palsy, 1957; Albert Lasker Med. Sci. award, 1968; William Thomson Wakeman award, 1972; Paralyzed Vets. Am. award, 1972; Henry Gray award, 1977. Fellow AAAS; mem. Am. Acad. Neurology, Assn. for Research Nervous and Mental Diseases (award 1971), Soc. Exptl. Biology and Medicine (chmn. Ill. sect. 1945-46), Am. Neurol. Assn., Phila. Neurol. Assn., Chgo. Neurol. Assn., Seattle Neurol. Assn. (pres. 1950-51), Nat. Acad. Medicine Buenos Aires (corr.), Harvey Soc. (hon.), Am. Assn. Anatomists (exec. com. 1957-61, 1st v.p. 1966-67), Am. Physiol. Soc., Soc. Obstetrics and Gynecology Chile (hon.), Soc. Pediatrics Brazil (hon.), Alpha Kappa Kappa, Sigma Chi, Sigma Xi. Club: Cosmos (Washington). Home: Granville, Ohio. Died Feb. 20, 1985.

WINE, RUSSELL BRUCE, lawyer; b. Broadway, Va., June 8, 1889; s. B.F. and Laura (Bruce) W.; student Washington and Lee U., 1910-12; m. Ruth Wiley, June 23, 1926. Admitted to Va. bar, 1912, Tex. bar, 1913; pvt. practice, San Antonio, 1913-25, 33-55; asst. U.S. atty., 1925-33; U.S. atty. Western Dist. Tex., 1955. Mem. Am., Tex., San Antonio bar assns. †

WINFIELD, WILLIAM HOOD, chem. co. exec.; b. Clarksburg, W.Va., Oct. 10, 1907; s. John Buckner and Frances (McKee) W.; m. Alice M. Turner, Apr. 15, 1939; children—Mary, Frances, William, Alice. A.B., W.Va. U., 1930; M.B.A., Harvard, 1934. Asst. to gen. mgr. TVA, 1934-37; dir. indsl. research Weyerhaeuser Co., 1937-43; cons. McKinsey & Co., 1946-48; dir. marketing research Monsanto Chem. Co., 1948-55; pres. Allied Chem. Internat. Corp., from 1955. Served to commdr. USNR, 1943-46. Home: Riverside, Conn.

WING, HERBERT, JR., educator; b. Minneapolis, Dec. 8, 1889; s. Herbert and Elizabeth D. (Potter) W.; A.B. magna cum laude, Harvard, 1909; M.A., U. Wis., 1911, Ph.D., 1915; grad. study Am. Sch. Classical Studies, Athens, Greece, 1913-14; m. Helen Leonard Gilman, June 10, 1916; 1 son, Herbert Gilman. Tchr., Wilmington (Mass.) High Sch., 1909-10; asso. prof. history U. Mich., summer 1917; asso. prof. Greek Dickinson Coll., Carlisle, Pa., 1915-20, prof., 1920-40, prof. history from 1940; active Pa. State debating activities, 1916-43. Mem. Am. Hist. Assn., Soc. Promotion Hellenic Studies, Am. Assn. U. Profs., Debating Assn. Pa. Colls. (past pres.), Phi Beta Kappa, Omicron Delta Kappa, Tau Kappa Alpha. Republican. Methodist. Mason (K.T.). Author articles and book reviews hist. jours. Home: Carlisle, Pa. †

WINGATE, HENRY SMITH, business exec.; b. Talas, Turkey, Oct. 8, 1905; s. Henry Knowles and Jane Caroline (Smith) W.; m. Ardis Adeline Swenson, Sept. 11, 1929; children—Henry Knowles, William Peter. B.A., Carleton Coll., 1927, L.H.D., 1973; J.D., U. Mich., 1929; LL.D., U. Man., 1957, Marshall U., York U., 1967, Laurentian U., 1968, Colby Coll., 1970. Bar: N.Y. bar 1931. Asso. Sullivan & Cromwell, N.Y.C., 1929-35; asst. sec. Internat. Nickel Co. of Can., Ltd., 1935-39, sec., 1939-52, dir., 1952-75, v.p., 1949-54, pres., 1954-60, chmn. bd., chmn. exec. com., 1960-72, chmn. adv. com. dir., 1972-75, mem. adv. com., from 1978; former dir. Am. Standard, Inc., U.S. Steel Corp., J.P. Morgan & Co., Morgan Guaranty Trust Co., Bank of Montreal; trustee Seamen's Bank for Savs., N.Y.; mem. adv. council Morgan Guaranty Trust Co. N.Y. Hon. mem. Bus. Council Washington; mem. council Found. for Child Devel.; mem. Can.-Am. com. sponsored by Nat. Planning Assn. and C.D. Howe Research Inst. Can.; bd. dirs. People's Symphony Concerts, Societe De Chimie Industrielle, Paris; v.p., bd. dirs. Am. Friends Can. Com.; sr. mem. Conf. Bd. N.Y.C. Recipient Sesquicentennial award U. Mich., 1967. Mem. Canadian Inst. Mining and Metallurgy, Mining and Metall. Soc. Am., Council Fgn. Relations, Pilgrims U.S., Canadian Soc. N.Y., Order of Coif, Delta Sigma Rho. Clubs: Lloyd Harbor Bath, Huntington Country; Union (N.Y.C.), Univ. (N.Y.C.), Recess (N.Y.C.). Home: New York, NY.

WINKLER, ELMER LOUIS, petroleum company executive; b. Wichita, Kans., Sept. 12, 1930; s. Louis Emil and Clara (Roeder) W.; m. Norma Jean Lenhart, Nov. 10, 1966; children—Michael, Philip, Eric, Holly. B.S., Swarthmore Coll., 1952. Engr. Westinghouse Elec. Corp., Balt., 1952-54; controller, asst. to treas. Rock Island Refining Corp., Indpls., 1956-62, asst. to pres., 1962-66, v.p., 1966-70, pres., dir., 1970-82; pres. Progressive Oil Co. Inc., Ft. Wayne, Ind., 1963-76, Hartley Oil Co., Muncie, Ind., 1962-72; dir. Am. Fletcher Nat. Bank, Indpls., Am. Fletcher Corp., Indpls., Stan West Corp., Qietlite Internat., Ltd. Served with AUS, 1954-56. Mem. Nat. Petroleum Refiners Assn. (dir.), ASME. Club: Kiwanian. Home: Indianapolis, Ind. Dec. Nov. 23, 1982.

WINNE, HARRY ALONZO, elec. engr.; b. Cherry Valley, N.Y., Oct. 27, 1888; s. Frank and Cora Dell (Finehout) W.; E.E., Syracuse U., 1910, D.Sc., 1947; D.Eng., Rensselaer Polytechnic Inst., 1947, Newark College of Engineering, 1949; married Dorothy Louise Hodges, February 11, 1918; children—Barbara Jean, David Hollister. With Gen. Electric Co. from 1910, beginning as student engr., with power and mining engring. dept., 1916-30, head steel mill sect., industrial dept., 1930-36, mgr. steel mill and mining sales, 1936-37, asst. to v.p. in charge of engring., 1937-41, v.p. in charge design engring. apparatus dept. 1941-45, v.p. in charge engring. policy from 1945; dir. Internat. General Electric Company, Inc. Mem. sci. adv. com. Nat. Security Resources Board. Trustee Rensselaer Polytech. Inst., Syracuse U., Green Mt. Jr. Coll. Fellow Am. Inst. Elec. Engrs., Am. Soc. Mech. Engrs.; member Navy League, Army Ordnance Assn., Newcomen Soc., American Soc. for Engring. Edn., N.Y. State Soc. Professional Engrs. Unitarian. Mason. Clubs: Edison, Mohawk, Mohawk Golf (Schenectady). Home: Rexford, N.Y. †

WINNER, LILY, writer, editor, playwright; b. Mar. 27, 1890; d. Louis and Rebecca (Kelny) Wynner; educated Washington U. and U. of Chicago; m. Louis Weitzenkorn (divorced); 1 son, William Wynner. Began as reporter Buffalo Times, 1910; with St. Louis Post Dispatch, 1910-11; spl. writer for Buffalo Times, St. Louis Post Dispatch and Chicago Tribune, 1911-14; editor on staffs of Ainslee's, Live Stories, etc., 1916-19. Mem. Mo. Writers' Guild, Authors' League America, Civic Club (New York). Author: The Tomorrow Man (4-act drama), also short stories, photo plays and spl. articles. Address: New York, N.Y. †

WINOGRAND, GARRY, photographer; b. N.Y.C., Jan. 14, 1928; s. Abraham and Bertha (Gross) W.; m. Eileen Adele Hale, Nov. 12, 1972; children—Laurie, Ethan, Melissa. Student Columbia U., CCNY, New Sch. Social Research. Books include Public Relations. Served with USAAF, 1945-47. Guggenheim fellow, 1964, 69, 78; NEA fellow, 1977. Jewish. Home: Los Angeles, Calif. Dec. Mar. 19, 1984.

WINSTON, RICHARD, writer, translator; b. N.Y.C., July 21, 1917; s. Robert and Etta Winston; B.A., Bklyn. Coll., 1939; m. Clara Brussel Sept. 12, 1941; children—Krishna, Justina. Books include: Charlemagne: From the Hammer to the Cross, 1954; Thomas Becket, 1967; (with Clara Winston) Notre-Dame de Paris 1971, Daily Life in the Middle Ages, 1975; translator: (with Clara Winston) The Demons (Heimito von Doderer), 1961, Memories, Dreams, Reflections (C.G. Jung), 1963, A Part of Myself (Carl Zuckmayer), 1967, The Glass Bead Game (Hermann Hesse), 1969, Inside the Third Reich: Memoirs (Albert Speer), 1970, The Letters of Thomas Mann, 1971, The Inward Turn of Narrative (Erich Kahler), 1973, Letters to Family, Friends and Editors (Franz Kafka), 1977, Winterspelt (Alfred Andersch), 1978, numerous others; reviewer N.Y. Herald Tribune Book Week, 1955-63; adviser in field. Trustee pub. funds Town of Halifax (Vt.), 1975-79. Guggenheim fellow, 1971-72; recipient Alexander Gode medal Am. Translators Assn., 1966; PEN Transl. prize, 1971; Nat. Book award, 1978. Mem. PEN, Am. Translators Assn. Home: Brattleboro, Vt. Dec. Dec. 22, 1979.

WINTER, GEORGE, engineer, educator; b. Vienna, Austria, Apr. 1, 1907; came to U.S., 1938, naturalized, 1943; s. Morris and Hedwig (Fleischer) W.; m. Anne Singer, July 4, 1931; 1 son, Peter Michael. Dipl. Ing., Technische Hochschule, Munich, 1930; Ph.D., Cornell U., 1940; student, Technische Hochschule, Stuttgart, 1927-28; Dr. Ing. (hon.), Technische U. Munich, 1969. Structural designer, Vienna, 1930-32, fgn. cons., Sverdlovsc, USSR, 1932-38; charge structural design large indsl. plants, and part-time lectr. Mining Inst. and Indsl. Inst., 1932-38; mem. faculty dept. structural engring. Cornell U., 1938-75, as research investigator, instr., asst. prof., assoc. prof., prof., 1948-63, Class of 1912 prof. engring., 1963-75, emeritus, 1975-82, chmn. dept. structural engring., 1948-70; dir. research cold-formed steel structures Cornell U. (for Am. Iron and Steel Inst.), 1939-75, dir. other research projects at univ. sponsored by industry and govt.; Vis. prof. Calif. Inst. Tech., 1950, U. Calif. at Berkeley, 1969; vis. lectr. U. Liege, Belgium, 1957; vis. scholar U. Cambridge, 1956-57; cons. to Am. Iron and Steel Inst., others. Author: (with A.H. Nilson) Design of Concrete Structures, 9th edit, 1979; Contributed numerous research papers on structural mechanics, steel and concrete structures profl. periodicals U.S., abroad; contbr. Structural Engring. Handbook. Recipient Moisseiff award, 1948, J.J. Croes medal, 1961; both ASCE; Wason Research medal, 1965; Turner medal, 1972; Kelly award, 1979; all Am. Concrete Inst.; Guggenheim Meml. fellow. Mem. Am. Acad. Arts and Scis., Nat. Acad. Engring., Structural Stability Research Council (chmn. 1974-78), Am. Concrete Inst. (hon. mem.; mem. com. bldg. code), ASCE (hon. mem.; mem. several tech. coms.), Internat. Assn. Bridge and Structural Engring. (mem. permanent com., chmn. com. on stabilty of joint com. on tall bldgs.), Archaeol. Inst. Am., Sigma Xi, Tau Beta Pi, Chi Epsilon. Home: Ithaca, N.Y. Died Nov. 2, 1982.

WINTERNITZ, EMANUEL, museum curator, educator, musicologist, art historian; b. Vienna, Austria, Aug. 4, 1898; s. Dr. Paul and Gisela (Steingraber) W.; grad. humanist, Gymnasium Vienna, 1916; LL.D., U. Vienna, 1922. Came to U.S., 1938, naturalized, 1943. Seminar in philosophy with Ernst Cassirer, also lectr. philosophy of law U. Hamburg, 1922; lectr. philosophy and aesthetics Volkshochschule Vienna, 1922-25; legal tng. in civil cts. and law offices, 1923-29; admitted to Vienna bar, 1929, corp. lawyer, 1929-38; lectr. Fogg Mus., Cambridge, Mass., also numerous U.S. univs. and museums, 1938-41; peripatetic prof. Assn. Am. Colls., 1941; joined Met. Mus. of Art, 1942, curator mus. collections, 1949-73, curator emeritus, 1973-83; reorganizing Crosby-Brown Collection of mus. instruments; lectr. Columbia, 1947-48; prof. music, sch. music Yale, 1949-60; vis. prof. history of music Rutgers U., 1961-65; vis. prof. music State U. N.Y., Binghampton, 1966-68, City U., N.Y., 1968. John Simon Guggenheim fellow for research, 1946, Am. Council Learned Socs. fellow, 1962, Bollingen Found. fellow, 1964. Recipient Cross of Honor 1st class for sci. and art (Austria). Mem. Am. Musicol. Soc. (chmn. N.Y. chpt. 1960), Internat. Council Museums (pres. internat. com. museums and collections musical instruments 1965), Osterreichische Gesellschaft für Musikwissenschaft (hon.), Raccolta Vinciana. Author: Musical Autographs from Monteverdi to Hindemith, 1955; Keyboard instruments in the Metropolitan Museum of Art, 1961; Musical Instruments of the Western World, 1966, Gaudenzio Ferrari, His School and the Early History of the Violin, 1966; Musical Instruments and Their Symbolism in Western Art, 1967; contbg. author: The Unknown Leonardo, 1974. Contbr. to Rendiconti della Pontificia Accademia Romana di Archeologia, 1952, also articles to profl. publs. Home: New York, N.Y. Died Aug. 18, 1983.

WINTERS, DENNY, artist; b. Grand Rapids, Mich., 1909; d. James Henry Sonke and Eva May (Taylor) Sonke; m. Herman Joseph Cherry, Sept. 20, 1940; m. Lew Dietz, 1951. Student, Chgo. Acad. Fine Arts, Chgo. Art Inst. Tchr. Camden (Maine) Extension. Illustrator: Wilderness River (Lew Dietz); Work exhibited, Mus. Modern Art, Carnegie Mus., Pa. Acad. Fine Arts, Chgo. Art Inst., San Francisco (Calif.) Mus., Nat. Acad. show, 1968, Nat. Acad. Art, 1970-72, one-man shows, Los Angeles Mus., San Francisco Mus., Mortimer Levitt Gallery, N.Y.C., Wiscasset (Maine) Mus., 1961, Rehn Art Gallery, N.Y.C., 1953, 57, 63, 72, 76, U. Maine, 1959, 65, 78, C. of C. Northeast Harbor, Maine, 1960, 62, Phila. Art Alliance, 1964, Bowdoin Coll., 1968, Grand Rapids (Mich.) Art Mus., 1972, Kalamazoo Inst. Fine Arts, 1972, Talent Tree Gallery, Augusta, Maine, Bates Coll., Lewiston, Maine, 1975, U.S. Ct. House, Phila., 1976, Unity (Maine) Coll., 1976, Barridoff Gallery, Portland, Maine, 1978, Payson Mus., Westbrook Coll., Portland, 1978, Camden (Maine) Gallery, 1980, Maine Coast Artists Gallery, Rockport., traveled, painted in, France, Italy, 1949. Mem. Maine Visual Arts Com. for Arts and Humanities Commn. Recipient first prize for prints San Francisco Mus., 1941, 1st prize for oils Denver Mus., 1940; Purchase prize Butler Inst. Am. Art, 1964; Skowhegan Art award, 1973; Henry Ward Baxter purchase award NAD, 1979; Guggenheim fellow, 1948. Mem. Me. Coast Artists (exhibitor 1951-85), Maine Hist. Soc. Address: Rockport, Maine. Died Mar. 4, 1985.

WINTERS, MATTHEW, pediatrician; b. Wadesville, Ind., May 15, 1890; s. Matthew and Ellen Eve (Owen) W.; A.B., Indiana U., 1915, A.M., 1917; M.D., Rush Med. Coll., 1921; m. Ninetta G. Illingworth, Feb. 16, 1918; children—Jane, Barbara, Matthew. Interne Cook County Hosp., Chicago, 18 mos., 1921-23, Children's Memorial Hosp., Chicago, 1 yr., 1923-24; in private practice of pediatrics, Indianapolis, from 1924; prof. pediatrics, Indiana U. Sch. of Medicine, from 1932. Served as capt. Co. A, 356th Inf., 89th Div., 1916-17; now maj. Reserves. Fellow Am. Acad. Pediatrics; licentiate Am. Bd. Pediatrics; mem. Sigma Xi, Alpha Omega Alpha, Phi Kappa Psi, Nu Sigma Nu. Republican. Presbyterian. Mason. Clubs: Service, Meridian Hills Country. Contbr. to med. jours. Home: Indianapolis, Ind. †

WIRTHLIN, MADELINE BITNER (MRS. JOSEPH L. WIRTHLIN), civic and polit. worker, educator; b. Holladay, Utah; d. Brenaman Barr and Martina (Halseth) Bitner; student U. Utah Normal, 1914; m. Joseph Leopold Wirthlin, Sept. 14, 1916 (dec.); children—Joseph B., Judith B. (Mrs. Thomas O. Parker), Gwendolyn (Mrs. Philip F. Cannon), Richard B., David B. Tchr. church orgns., from 1910; tchr. Granite and Salt Lake City pub. schs., 1914-16; dir. Wirthlins, Inc. Comdr. Utah Cancer Soc., 1945-47; historian women's Legislative Council, 1946; mem. Murray City Library Bd., 1958-69. Mem. Utah Bd. Edn., 1952-59, mem. com. for study edn. of deaf children, 1956, v.p. Utah Guide Dogs for Blind, Inc., 1960-63, Utah Council for Gifted, 1961; mem. Utah textbook and curriculum commn., 1961-64. Pres. Salt Lake Women's Republican Club, 1945-46, Utah Fedn. Women's Rep. Clubs, 1951-53; del. Rep. state conv., 1952, mem. platform com., 1952, 54, 56; del. Rep. nat. conv., 1952, mem. platform com., 1952; chmn. Rep. women's Kitchen Kabinet of Utah, 1954-56; mem. Rep. Nat. Com. for Utah, 1964-68. Clubs: Contemporary Readers, Authors (pres. 1948-49). Home: Salt Lake City, Utah. Died Mar. 18, 1980.

WIRTZ, ARTHUR MICHAEL, business executive; b. Chgo., Jan. 23, 1901; s. Frederick C. and Leona (Miller) W.; m. Virginia Wadsworth, Mar. 1, 1926; children—Cynthia, William, Arthur Michael, Elizabeth V. B.A., U. Mich., 1922. Founder, chmn., chief exec. officer Wirtz Corp. (realtors), Chgo.; founder, chmn., chief exec. officer Consol. Enterprises, Inc., Chgo., also an officer, dir. controlled and affiliated cos.; chmn., chief exec. officer Chgo. Milw. Corp.; chmn. Griggs-Cooper & Co., Inc., St. Paul, Rathjen, San Francisco; chmn. 1st Nat. Bank of South Miami, Fla., Chgo. Stadium Corp., Chgo. Blackhawk Hockey Team, Inc.; founder, chmn. bd., chief exec. officer Wirtz Prodns. Inc. (internat. ice shows); chmn. Standard Theatres, Inc., Milw.; dir. Longhorn Liquors, Inc., Arlington, Tex. Mem. bd. Met. Fair and Expn. Authority; operators McCormick Pl. Chgo.; trustee, pres. Chgo. Urban Transp. Dist. Mem. Hockey Hall of Fame; recipient Man of Year award Chgo. Boys' Clubs, 1977. Clubs: Knollwood Country; Racquet (Chgo.), Chgo. Athletic (Chgo.), Saddle and Cycle (Chgo.), Tavern (Chgo.), Chgo. Yacht (Chgo.). Home: Chicago, Ill. Dec. June 21, 1983.

WIRTZ, CABLE AMBROSE, lawyer; b. Honolulu, May 9, 1910; s. Ambrose J. and Mary Emma (Meyer) W.; A.B., Santa Clara U., 1932; LL.B., Harvard U., 1935, J.D., 1970; m. Margaret Virginia Hughes, June 17, 1937; children—Richard Paul, Sheila Marie. Admitted to Hawaii bar, 1935; with firm Smith, Wild, Beebe & Cades, Honolulu, 1935-39; dep. city and county atty., Honolulu, 1939-42, city and county atty., 1942-44; judge Circuit Ct. 2d Jud. Circuit, 1944-51, 56-59; dist. magistrate Hana, Maui, 1954-56; assoc. justice Supreme Ct. of Hawaii, 1959-67; pvt. practice law, Wailuku, Maui, 1951-56, 68-79, Honolulu, 1968-73; mem. firm Wooddell Mukai, Wirtz Ichiki & Whitfield, 1968-73; of counsel to Mukai, Ichiki, Raffeto & MacMillan, 1974-79. Mem. Territorial Commn. on Children and Youth, 1949-54, Maui Commn. on Children and Youth, 1949-54, Territorial Loyalty Bd., 1951-57, Hawaii Aero. Commn., 1953-56; chmn. Maui Cath. Bd. Edn., 1968-69; arbitrator labor disputes. Del. Constl. Conv., 1950. Bd. dirs. Ka Lima O'Maui (Rehab. Center). Mem. Am. Judicature Soc., Inst. Jud. Adminstrn., Am., Hawaii, Maui County (pres. 1970-71, bd. ethics) bar assns., Maui C. of C. (dir. 1971-74), Harvard Law Sch. Assn., Santa Clara Alumni Assn., Maui County Fair and Racing Assn., Maui Hist. Soc., Polynesian Voyaging Soc., Hawaiian Ry. Soc. Clubs: Harvard (Hawaii); Maui Rotary. Home: Wailuku, Hawaii. Died Dec. 29, 1980.

WISE, JAMES ARNOLD, paper mfr.; b. Kalamazoo, Mich., Jan. 20, 1905; s. Charles Augustus and Margaret (Moore) W.; B.S. magna cum laude, Yale, 1926; m. Mary Janet Robertson, Apr. 9, 1932; children—Anne, Alfred James, Mary. Engring. dept., prodn. asst. Bryant Paper Co., 1926-30; with Kalamazoo Paper Co., 1930-84, successively asst. gen. supt., gen. supt., v.p. charge prodn., exec. v.p. and gen. mgr., 1930-53, pres. and gen. mgr., 1953-84, dir., 1942-84. Mem. Am. Pulp and Paper Mill Supts. Assn., Tech. Assn. Pulp and Paper Industry. Presbyn. Home: Bronx, N.Y. Died Jan. 7, 1984.

WISE, JAMES DECAMP, business exec.; b. Greencastle, Ind., Oct. 7, 1898; s. William Henry and Florence (Line) W.; student Leland Stanford U., 1916-19, A.B., Columbia Coll., 1921, LL.B., Columbia Law Sch., 1925; m. Katherine Ulrich, June 19, 1930; children—Henry Ulrich, Joanna DeCamp. Admitted to N.Y. bar, 1925, and since practiced in that state; asso. with firm Cotton & Franklin, N.Y. City, 1925-33, partner in that firm and its successors, Wright, Gordon, Zachry & Parlin, 1933-45; spl. counsel for R.F.C., 1940; spl. asst. to undersec. of navy, 1940-41; pres. Bigelow-Sanford Carpet Co., Inc., N.Y.C., 1944-56, chmn., 1956-61, now dir.; dir. Fed. Res. Bank of New York, 1959-64, dep. chmn., 1961-64; trustee Consol. Edison Co. of N.Y., Inc.; chmn. bd. trustees Bank Street Coll. Edn.; trustee Nat. Indsl. Conf. Bd., 1948-63. Mem. Am. Mgmt. Assn., Assn. Bar City N.Y., Phi Beta Kappa, Phi Delta Phi. Editor Columbia Law Rev., 1924. Home: Frenchtown, N.J. Died Jan. 7, 1984.

WISEHART, MARION KARL, writer; b. Nov. 12, 1880; s. William Edmund and Ida May (Carey) W.; Ph.B. Hamilton Coll., Clinton, N.Y., 1911, Ph.M., 1914; m. Mary Theresa Patterson, July 8, 1913. Reporter, Washington corr. and polit. writer, Evening Sun, New York, 1911-18; European corr. Leslie's Weekly, 1918-19; editorial and contributing staff Am. Magazine, 1920-31 (reader and critic of fiction 4 yrs.); European corr. Am. Mag. and the Mentor, 1920-30; lecturer in charge "Writer's Workshop" of evening session Coll. City of New York, 1932, specializing in principles of narrative psychology and their application in the short story, novel and magazine article. Made survey for New York League of Women Voters, with reference to bipartisan conditions in the N.Y. legislature; social and industrial surveys for inter-ch. World Movement, in connection with steel strike of 1919; survey for Cleveland Foundation, of effect of newspapers on the administration of criminal justice in Cleveland, 1921. Mem. Authors' League America, English-Speaking Union, Chi Psi. Republican. Clubs: Nat. Arts, Town Hall, Chi Psi (New York). Author: The Kiss (novel), 1928; Marvels of Science, 1928; also numerous stories and articles in mags. Home: New York, N.Y. †

WISEHART, ROY PARKER, educator; b. in Grant County, Ind., Mar. 17, 1887; s. Nimrod and Laura Estella (Davenport) W.; A.B., Ind. U., 1910; grad. study, U. of Wis., summer 1912, U. of Bordeaux, France, Mar.-June 1919; A.M., Columbia, 1926; m. Frederica Gustin, of Anderson, Ind., Aug. 30, 1916; children—James Archibald, Marcia Ruth, Paul Frederick. Teacher dist. sch., Fall Creek Twp., Madison Co., Ind., 1909-12; teacher, high sch., Carthage, Ind., 1912-13, Morristown, 1913-14; prin. high sch., Pendleton, 1915-17; prin. high sch., Union City, 1919, supt., 1919-27; apptd. state supt. pub. instrn., Ind., 1927, and elected, 1928, to same office for term 1929-31. Served as 1st class pvt. Hdqs. Co., 129th Inf., 33d Div., U.S.A., overseas, 1918-19. Dir. Ind. State Coll. for Teachers, Terre Haute, and Ball State Teachers Coll., Muncie, Ind. Mem. N.E.A. and Dept. of Superintendence same, Ind. State Teachers Assn. Republican. Methodist. Mason (Shriner). Home: Indianapolis, Ind. †

WISELY, WILLIAM HOMER, civil engr.; b. Coulterville, Ill., Oct. 20, 1906; s. William B. and Helena (Burkhardt) W.; B.S. in Civil Engring., U. Ill., 1928, C.E., 1941; D.Engring. (hon.), Norwich U., 1967; m. Hazel A. Steinberg, June 25, 1930; children—Janet Lee, Nancy Ann. Engring. asst. Ill. State Water Survey, 1926-28; asst. san. engr., div. san. engring. Ill. Dept. Pub. Health, 1928-40; engr., mgr. Urbana-champaign (Ill.) San. Dist., 1940-44; exec. sec., editor Water Pollution Control Fedn., 1941-54; exec. dir. Am. Soc. C.E., 1955-72, emeritus, 1972-82; vis. prof. U. Fla., 1972-82. Ill. commr. Ohio River Valley Water San. Commn., 1952-54; mem. N.Y. State Pub. Health Council, 1958-72; adv. council N.Y. State Health Planning Commn., 1970-72. Dir. United Engring. Trustees, Inc., 1960-72, World Fedn. Engring. Orgns., 1967-72, Pan Am. Fedn. Engring. Socs., 1966-72. Diplomate Am. Acad. Environ. Engrs. Fellow ASCE (hon.); mem. Water Pollution Control Fedn. (hon.), Nat. Ill. (hon.) socs. profl. engrs., Central States Water Pollution Control Assn. (hon.), Chi Epsilon (hon.). Author: The American Civil Engineer 1852-1974. Author handbook and articles tech. jours. Home: Gainesville, Fla. Died Nov. 16, 1982.

WISEMAN, MARK HUNTINGTON, author, educator; b. Springfield, O., June 15, 1889; s. Henry Clay and Mary Emma (Cummings) W.; Ph.B., Kenyon Coll., 1910; M.A., Harvard, 1911; m. Gwendolyn Robbins Lowe, 1916 (dec. 1923); children—Parker Cummings, Mary Gwen (Mrs. Donald Armstrong); m. 2d, Evelyn Sayre, 1925; children—Ann Sayre (Mrs. Peter Denzer), John Sayre; m. 3d, Eleanor Carter Wood, 1935; 1 son, Carter Sterling. Reporter, spl. writer N.Y. Morning World, 1911-13; editor Richmond County Advance, Staten Is., 1913-15; asst. promotion mgr., then mgr. Collier's Weekly, 1916-19; copywriter, creative partner Blackman Co., advt., N.Y.C., 1919-32; advt. dir. Hudson Motor Car Co., Detroit, 1932-34; founder, dir. Lab. for Advt. Analysis, N.Y.C., 1938-41; v.p. L. M. Clark Co., N.Y.C., 1939-41; account exec. Young & Rubicam, N.Y.C., 1941-45; dir. Mark Wiseman's Advt. Sch., N.Y.C., 1945-53; creative cons. advertisers and agencies, from 1950; mem. guiding faculty Famous Writers Sch., Westport, Conn., from 1959. Formerly trustee of American Child Labor Com. Served as 1st lt., San. Corps, U.S. Army, 1917-18. Mem. Authors League Am., Am. Humanist Assn., Am. Legion (past post comdr.), Phi Beta Kappa, Alpha Delta Phi. Club: Harvard (N.Y.C.). Author: Before You Sign the Advertising Check, 1938; The Anatomy of Advertising, 1941; Advertising—What it is, What it does, How it Works, 1950; (with Daniel Starch and staff) How Magazine Readership Can Help You Create More Effective Advertising, 1954; The New Anatomy of Advertising, 1959, also articles. Home: Westport, Conn. †

WISLAR, GEORGE GARSED, ins. co. exec.; b. Bucks County, Pa., Jan. 24, 1901; s. George Brouse and Mary Benton (Garsed) W.; m. Marian B. Wakefield, Dec. 8, 1923; children—Edwin Wakefield, George Rowland. Student, Drexel Inst. With Raymond Concrete Pile Co., 1919-20, John W. Ferguson Co., 1920-23; with N.J. Mfrs. Ins. Co., 1923-84, pres., 1957-66, ret. Mem. S.R. Republican. Episcopalian. Club: Bedens Brook. Address: Lambertville, N.J. Died Apr. 20, 1984; buried Harbourton, N.J.

WITHEY, ROBERT ARTHUR, state ofcl.; b. Long Branch, N.J., Dec. 21, 1929; s. Clarence Waldo and Mary Josephine (White) W.; m. Maria Ann Foderaro, Aug. 16, 1952; children—Robert J., Kimberly S., Theodore P. B.A., Rutgers U., 1952, M.A., 1957, postgrad., 1957-59. Tchr., counselor, coach, adminstr. pub. schs., Metuchen, N.J., 1952-59; cons. N.J. Dept. Edn., 1959-60, asst. dir., 1960-70, chief, 1970-72; dep. commr. Vt. Dept. Edn., Montpelier, 1972, commr., 1972-81. Author transparencies. Mem. Vt. Gov.'s Cabinet, Vt.-1202 Commn., Bicentennial Commn., Tchr. Retirement Commn., Ednl. TV Commn.; exec. sec. N.J. Assn. High Sch. Councils, 1961-68; mem. steering com. Ednl. Commn. of States. Mem. Nat., Vt. edn. assns., New Eng., Vt. supts. assns., Am. Assn. Sch. Adminstrs., Vt. Sch. Dirs. Assn. Clubs: Rotarian, Exchange. Home: Montpelier, VT.

WITT, SYLVESTER J., r.r. exec.; b. Cin., Nov. 14, 1889; s. Frank J. and Elizabeth (Weigand) W.; ed. pub. schs. Bellevue, Ky.; m. Marguerite Murphy, June 24, 1914; children—Sylvester F., Sarah Jane (Mrs. John Kelley), Ralph F. With Balt. & O. Southwestern Ry., B.&O. R.R., Cin., 1905-11; chief clk. in traffic dept. to traffic mgr. Akron, Canton & Youngstown R.R., Akron, O., 1911-35; with N.Y., C.& St.L. R.R., from 1935, successively freight traffic mgr. rates, asst. v.p. rates, asst. v.p. sales, v.p. traffic, 1954-59; v.p., dir. Lorain & W.Va., Ry.; dir. Detroit & Toledo Shore Line R.R. Vice chmn. transportation adv. council John Carroll University, Cleveland, Ohio. Member Newcomen Society. Roman Catholic. Clubs: Cleveland Athletic, Traffic (Cleve.), (director), Nat. Soc. Remedial Teaching (director). Nat. Soc. Study Edn. (dir.), N.E.A., International Council Improvement Reading Instrn. (pres. 1954), Am. Assn. Gifted Children (v.p.). Sigma Nu. Phi†

WITTER, WILLIAM MAURER, investment banker; b. San Francisco, Feb. 18, 1923; s. Jean Carter and Catharine (Maurer) W.; m. Christene Allen, Aug. 20, 1953. B.A., U. Calif.-Berkeley, 1947. Partner Dean Witter Reynolds Orgn. (formerly Dean Witter & Co.), 1949-54; mng. partner Dean Witter Reynolds Orgn. (Midwest div.), Chgo., 1953-68; exec. v.p., dir. Dean Witter & Co., Inc., 1968-69, pres., 1969-70, chmn., chief exec. officer, 1970-80, hon. chmn., dir., 1980-84; Gov. Midwest Stock Exchange, 1964-67, chmn., 1968-69; chmn. Chgo. Assn. Stock Exchange Firms, 1963-64. Trustee Ill. Children's Home and Aid Soc. Mem. Investment Bankers Am. (chmn. central states group 1966-67, gov. 1967-69), Nat. Assn. Security Dealers (gov. 1969), San Francisco C. of C. (pres. 1974, chmn. bd. dirs. 1975). Clubs: Pacific Union (San Francisco), Bohemian (San Francisco). Home: San Francisco, Calif. Died July 17, 1984.

WITTERS, HARRY WELLINGTON, lawyer; b. St. Albans, Vt., Mar. 18, 1889; s. Wellington Barton and Mary Curtis (Soule) W.; LL.B., U. Mich., 1911; m. Grace Ila Barney, Mar. 28, 1914; children—Virginia A. (Mrs. J. R. Merrill), Betty Lou (Mrs. J. G. Barry), Chester Wellington, Barbara Rae (Mrs. M. G. MacDonald). Admitted to Vt. bar, 1911, practiced in St. Johnsbury, Vt. from 1911. Mem. Gen. Assembly, Vt., 1919; state counsel Alien Property Custodian, 1918-20, R.F.C., 1933-35; state dir. Nat. Recovery Adminstrn., 1933, Nat. Youth Adminstrn., 1935-36; adminstr. Vt. Emergency Relief, 1934-38, State W.P.A., 1935-38; spl. asst. to atty. gen., 1948-53. Dem. candidate for Congress, 1920, 28, for U.S. senator, 1934, 44. Mem. Am., Vermont bar assns. Elk. Club: St. Johnsbury Country. Home: Johnsbury, Vt. †

WITTLAKE, JESSE CLARKE, ins. co. exec.; b. McCook, Nebr., Sept. 15, 1910; s. Charles and Effie Maude (McCain) W.; student Rutgers U., 1929-30; B.S., U. Nebr., 1935; M.S., U. Iowa, 1936; m. Jamie Jewell Lewis, Aug. 20, 1935; 1 dau., Linda. With Bus. Men's Assurance Co., Kansas City, Mo., from 1936, asst. actuary, 1946-47, asst. to pres., 1947-56, v.p. adminstrn., 1956-64, exec. v.p., 1964-71, exec. v.p., chief adminstr. officer, 1971-73, pres., 1973-77, ret., also dir. Vice pres., bd. dirs. United Campaign; bd. dirs. Kansas City Mus., United Community Services, Greater Kansas City Sports Commn., Civic Council; chmn. corp. div. United Way Campaign; bd. dirs. Community Service Broadcasting of Mid-Am., Inc. Served to maj. AUS, 1942-46. Mem. Casualty Actuarial Soc., Am. Acad. Actuaries, Am. Legion, Pi Mu Epsilon, Beta Gamma Sigma. Presbyterian. Clubs: Kansas City; Mission Hills. Home: Leawood, Kans. Died Oct. 11, 1980.

WODEHOUSE, ROGER PHILIP, allergist; born Toronto, Ontario, Canada, Dec. 9, 1889; s. Thomas Frederick and Laura Emily (Briant) W.; student St. Albans Cathedral Sch., 1901-03, Upper Can. Coll., 1903-07; A.B., U. of Toronto, 1913; A.M., Harvard, 1916; Ph.D., Columbia, 1927; m. Helene A. Roux, June 1916; m. 2d, Ellys Butler, Dec. 25, 1941; children—Armine, Anne, Edmund, Dora, Roger. Came to the United States, 1930, naturalized, 1942. Asst. to Dr. J. L. Goodale (Boston) as protein chem., 1915-16; research chemist and botanist in hayfever and asthma, Peter Bent Brigham Hosp., Boston, 1916-17; dir. Hayfever Lab., Arlington Chem. Co., Yonkers, N.Y., 1914-44; director research in allergy, Lederle Labs., Pearl River., to 1957. Served to 2d lt., Royal Air Force, World War I. Fellow A.A.A.S.; mem. Torrey Bot. Club (editor 1938-40); Botanical Society of America, National Research Council, Com. on Aerobiology; corr. mem. Inst. Ecutoriano de Ciencias; hon. mem. Collar with the gold medal, Institute de Coimbre; asso. fellow Am. Coll. of Allergists. Clubs: Wanosca Boat of Oscawana Lake, New York (past pres.). Author: Pollen Grains, Their Structure, Identification and Significance in Science and Medicine, 1935; Hayfever Plants, 1945; and various papers on morphology of pollen grains, aerobiology, and hay fever in relation to soil conservation. Home: South Burlington, Vt. †

WOLF, RICHARD CHARLES, educator, ch. historian; b. Dayton, Ohio, Aug. 2, 1912; s. Norman Samuel and M. Estella (Tawney) W.; A.B., Gettysburg (Pa.) Coll., 1934; B.D., Luth. Theol. Sem., Gettysburg, 1937; postgrad. Oberlin Coll. Grad. Sch. Theology, 1937-41; Ph.D., Yale Div. Sch., 1947; m. Marjorie Edith Gongwer, Nov. 25, 1944; 1 son, Norman Tracy. Ordained to ministry Luth. Ch., 1937; pastor, Plymouth, Ohio, 1937-41; from teaching fellow to asst. prof. ch. history and adminstrv. asst. to pres. Luth. Theol. Sem., 1942-49; lectr. history Gettysburg Coll., 1943-45; asst. prof. Am. ch. history Yale Div. Sch., 1949-52; from asso. prof. to prof. Oberlin Coll. Grad. Sch. Theology, 1952-66; Charles Grandison Finney prof. ch. history Vanderbilt U. Div. Sch., 1966-78, emeritus, 1978-84; pastor emeritus First Luth. Ch., Nashville, 1978-84. Mem. bd. theol. edn. Luth. Ch. Am., 1964-70. Pres., Oberlin chpt. Am. Field Service, 1964-65; mem. Oberlin Health and Welfare Commn., 1963-66, Oberlin Fair Housing Com., 1962-63. Mem. Am. Hist. Assn., Am. Soc. Ch. History, Luth. Hist. Conf., Am. Acad. Polit. and Social Sci., Am. Soc. Reformation Research, Miss. Valley Hist. Soc., Phi Beta Kappa, Phi Alpha Theta, Tau Kappa Alpha, Phi Sigma Iota. Author: History of First Lutheran Church, Plymouth, Ohio, 1940; Our Protestant Heritage, 1956; The Americanization of the German Lutherans, 1683-1829, 1964; Lutherans in North America, 1965; Documents of Lutheran Unity, 2d edit., 1978. Editor: American Church, Facet Books hist. series. Contbr. articles to profl. jours. Home: Nashville, Tenn. Died Oct. 1, 1984.

WOLFE, CLIFFORD HENRY, mktg. cons.; b. Kasota, Minn., Mar. 25, 1904; s. Jacob Albert and Caroline Marie (Gilbertson) W.; B.S., Iowa State U., 1927; m. Nell Mabel Taylor, Feb. 25, 1933; children—Jon T., Linda (Mrs. Rodger A. Salman). Marketing exec. Ralston Purina Co., St. Louis, 1927-32; sales promotion mgr. Swift & Co., Chgo., 1932-40; advt. and sales promotion mgr. Pabst Brewing Co., Chgo., 1940-42; account exec., v.p. Biow Co., advt. agy., N.Y.C., 1942-49; sr. v.p. Dancer-Fitzgerald-Sample, Inc., advt. agy., N.Y.C., 1949-72; mktg. cons. Wolfe Assos., Inc., Larchmont, N.Y., 1972-85. Bd. govs. New Rochelle Hosp. and Med. Center, 1956-85, pres., 1968-71; bd. govs. Iowa State U. Found., 1958-85; bd. dirs. Asso. Vis. Nurses Service Westchester, 1976-85, pres., 1979. Mem. Cardinal Key, Sigma Delta Chi, Alpha Zeta. Presbyterian. Clubs: Larchmont Yacht, Royal Norwegian Yacht, Saratoga Reading Rooms. Address: Larchmont, N.Y. Died Apr. 16, 1985; buried Larchmont, N.Y.

WOLFE, JAMES, bass and baritone singer; b. Riga, Latvia, Apr. 27, 1890; s. Alexander and Zara (Eydus) W.; ed. high sch. and Technicological Inst., Riga, until 1909; m. Lilian Lauferty, Oct. 15, 1924. Came to U.S., 1920, naturalized, 1925. Began as a dancer, 1897, and continued with Breslau opera cos. until 1910; singer from 1910; appeared in various cities in Switzerland, later in Berlin, Paris and London, Chicago, St. Louis, Cleveland, Mexico, etc.; with Metropolitan Opera Co., New York, from 1923; also with Los Angeles and Cincinnati zoölogical gardens opera cos. Mem. Beethoven Assn. Clubs: Lambs; Masquers (Hollywood). Address: New York, N.Y. †

WOLFE, ROBERT HUSTON, publisher; b. Columbus, O., Nov. 7, 1899; s. Harry Preston and Maude Earhart (Fowler) W.; ed. Culver Mil. Acad., Columbus Acad.; two children—William Culver and Michael Lambert Wolfe. Mem. bd. trustees, publisher Dispatch Printing Co., 1935-81, now also chmn. bd.; dir. WBNS Radio Corp., Wolfe Wear-U-Well Shoe Corp. Served in U.S. Navy, World War I. Mem. Am. Legion. Republican. Presbyn. Mason. Clubs: Athletic, Columbus Country, University, Siegniory, Scioto Country; Over Sea Press. Home: Columbus, Ohio. Died Oct. 31, 1981.

WOLFF, BRUCE WALTER, advertising agency and management training executive; b. Berlin, Germany, Mar. 30, 1927; came to U.S., 1946, naturalized, 1950; s. Felix and Margaret (Wolitzer) W.; m. Anne Irmgard Lieb, Sept. 15, 1948 (div. 1979); children: Nina Joan, Eric Roger, Amy Margaret; m. Layne Richards Littlepage, Mar. 29, 1980 (div. 1981); m. Renate Wolff, July 19, 1983. Student, CCNY, 1947-51, Hunter Coll., 1980-81. Market research analyst Netherlands C. of C., N.Y.C., 1947-50; internat. sales corr. Hygrade Food Products Corp., Newark, 1950-52; asst. to pres. Cosmos Chem. Corp., N.Y.C., 1953-57; group v.p., mem. exec. com. Frohlich/Intercon Internat., Inc., N.Y.C., 1957-72; chmn. bd. Lavey/Wolff/Swift, Inc., N.Y.C., 1972-82; pres. Group for Advanced Mgmt. Tng., Inc., N.Y.C., 1981-85; pres. Strategic Planning Group Hall Decker McKibbin, Inc., N.Y.C. and Los Angeles, 1983-85. Pres. Riverdale-Yonkers Ethical Culture Soc., 1967-69. Mem. Assn. for Advancement Med. Instrumentation, Am. Med. Writers Assn., Biomed. Mktg. Assn. (bd. dirs., past pres.), Am. Assn. Counseling and Devel. Home: Big Sur, Calif.

WOLFOWITZ, JACOB, mathematician, educator; b. Warsaw, Poland, Mar. 19, 1910; s. Samuel and Helen (Pearlman) W.; B.S., Coll. City N.Y., 1931; M.A., Columbia, 1933; Ph.D., N.Y. U., 1942; m. Lillian Dundes, Mar. 3, 1934; children—Laura M. (Mrs. Tsvi Sachs), Paul D. Asso. dir. statis. research group Columbia, 1942-45, assoc. prof., 1946-49, prof., 1949-51; asso. prof. math. stats. U. N.C., 1945-46; disting. prof. math. Cornell U., Ithaca, N.Y., 1951-70, U. Ill. at Urbana, 1970-78; prof. math. U. South Fla., Tampa, 1978-81; vis. prof. U. Calif. at Los Angeles, 1952-53, U. Ill., 1953, Israel Inst. Tech., Haifa, 1957-58, U. Paris, 1967, U. Heidelberg (Germany), 1969; mem. Nat. Acad. Scis. Fellow Am. Acad. Arts and Scis., Inst. Math. Stats. (past pres., Rietz lectr., Wald lectr.), Econometric Soc.; mem. Am. Math. Soc., IEEE (Shannon lectr. 1979), Internat. Statis. Inst. Author monographs on sci. subjects. Asso. editor Annals Math. Stats., 1953-57, Jour. Statis. Planning and Inference, Jour. Combinatorics, Info. and Systems Scis., Am. Jour. Math. and Mgmt. Scis. Contbr. articles to profl. jours. Office: Tampa, Fla. Dec. July 16, 1981.

WOLFSON, IRVING S., insurance company executive; married; 2 children. Exec. v.p., dir. Phoenix Mut. Life Ins. Co.; pres., dir. Phoenix-Chase Series Fund; pres. Income and Capital Shares, Inc., Chase Convertible Fund of Boston, Inc.; v.p., dir. Phoenix Gen. Ins. Co., Phoenix Life Ins. Co.; dir. Phoenix Equity Planning Corp., Phoenix Investment Counsel of Boston, Inc.; mem. bus. and econ. adv. bd. Conn. Bank & Trust Co. Fellow Soc. Actuaries; mem. Phi Beta Kappa. Address: Hartford, Conn. Dec. 1982.

WOLFSON, MILTON A., corp. exec.; b. Chgo. 1889. Sr. v.p. Maremont Corp. †

WOLFSON, MITCHELL, television broadcasting, cable television bottling, vending company executive; b. Key West, Fla., Sept. 13, 1900; s. Louis and Rose (Gruner) W.; m. Frances Louise Cohen, Jan. 27, 1926 (dec.); children—Louis (dec.), Frances Wolfson Cary, Mitchell. Student, Columbia U., 1918; LL.D. (hon.), U. Miami, Fla., 1955. Founder, 1925, then pres., chmn. bd. Wometco Enterprises, Inc., Miami; chmn. bd. Fin. Fed. Savs. and Loan

Assn., Miami Beach, from 1958. Trustee Miami-Dade Community Coll., 1957-80, chmn., 1968-78; chmn. Miami Off-Street Parking Authority, from 1961; trustee Mt. Sinai Med. Center, Miami Beach; adv. trustee Fla. House, Washington; mem. Miami Beach City Council, 1939-43, mayor of Miami Beach, 1943. Served to lt. col. AUS, World War II. Decorated Bronze Star; Croix de Guerre France; recipient Walt Disney Humanitarian award Nat. Assn. Theatre Owners, 1972, Alfred I. DuPont award in broadcasting journalism Columbia U., 1972, Leonard L. Abess Human Relations award Anti-Defamation League, B'nai B'rith, 1975, Humanitarian award Miami Heart Inst., 1976, Gov.'s award Miami chpt. Nat. Acad. TV Arts and Scis., 1978; Mitchell Wolfson Pier Park dedicated by City of Miami Beach, 1977. Mem. Nat. Assn. Theatre Owners (exec. bd.). Clubs: Shriners, Elks, Rotary. Home: Miami Beach, Fla. Dec. Jan. 28, 1983.

WOLFSON, ROSINA MARGUERITE, welfare worker; b. New Orleans, La., April 12, 1887; d. Joseph N. and Esther (Dinkelspiel) W.; ed. Am. pub. schs. and private schs. in Europe; unmarried. Worker for Belgian Relief, Hoover Com., London, Eng., 1914-16; with Am. Red Cross, France and Siberia, 1917-19, in Philippine Islands during World War II. Vol. speaker for Republican Nat. Com., 1920, 26, 29, 32; speaker in U.S.A. and Philippine Islands from 1920. Mem. Rep. Nat. Com. for Philippine Islands, 1924-47. Mem. Nat. Council Women's Nat. Rep. Club of New York, 1938-47. Has held roving commns. from various orgns. Home: Manila, Philippine Islands. †

WOLL, JOSEPH ALBERT, lawyer; b. Chgo., Feb. 16, 1904; s. Matthew and Irene (Kerwin) W.; m. Genevieve Carey, May 15, 1930; children—Mary Cynthia Geddes, Phyllis Irene (Mrs. Paul Stokes, Jr.), David Carey. J.D., U. Ill., 1927. Bar: Ill. bar 1927. Chgo.'s asst. state's atty. for, Cook County, 1930-34; trial work and preparation briefs before Ill. Supreme Ct., in charge preparation all indictments, 1932-34, apptd. spl. asst. to atty. gen., U.S., 1934; head comml. frauds sect. U.S. Dept. Justice, 1939-40; apptd. U.S. atty. No. Dist. Ill. (by Pres. Roosevelt), 1940-47, individual pvt. practice, 1947-84. Gen. counsel AFL-CIO, Internat. Union Operating Engrs.; labor orgns. Com. on Polit. Edn. Div.; mem. exec. com. Union Labor Life Ins. Co., now chmn. bd. Former mem. exec. com., chmn. adv. com. Fed. Bus. Assn. Chgo. area. commr.; mem. exec. bd. Chgo. council Boy Scouts Am., 1942-47; mem. Nat. council; mem. exec. com., bd. dirs. Soldiers and Sailors Service Council Ill., 1941-45; past bd. dirs. Cath. Charities D.C., Cath. Youth Orgn., Washington, D.C. Tb Assn.; bd. dirs. Nat. Legal Aid and Defender Assn.; bd. dirs., treas. Nat. Conf. on Citizenship; mem. Pres.' Conf. on Adminstrv. Procedure, Pres.' White House Conf. to Fulfill These Rights; bd. dirs. Nat. Council on Crime and Delinquency; trustee Supreme Ct. Hist. Soc. Recipient Prime Minister's medal State of Israel, 1980. Mem. Am., D.C., Md., Fed. bar assns., Am. Arbitration Assn. (dir. N.Y.C.), Am. Judicature Soc., Selden Soc., John Carroll Soc., Friendly Sons St. Patrick, Phi Kappa, Phi Alpha Delta. Roman Catholic. Club: University. Home: Potomac, Md. Dec. June 19, 1984.

WOLLENBERG, ALBERT CHARLES, fed. judge; b. San Francisco, June 13, 1900; s. Charles M. and Romilda (Judell) W.; m. Velma Bercovich, Sept. 5, 1925; children—Jean (Mrs. M.J. Waldman), Albert Charles. A.B., U. Calif. at Berkeley, 1922, J.D., 1924. Bar: Calif. bar 1925. Gen. practice law, San Francisco, 1925-28, 34-47; asst. U.S. atty. No. Dist. Calif., 1928-34; judge Superior Ct., City and County of San Francisco, 1947-58, U.S. Dist. Ct. No. Dist. Calif., 1958-81; pres. Conf. Calif. Judges, 1956-57; mem. Jud. Council Calif., 1957-81; Mem. Calif. Legislature from 21st Dist., 1939-47. Served with USN, 1918. Jewish (past pres. temple). Club: Masons. Home: San Francisco, Calif. Died Apr. 19, 1981.*

WOOD, FRANKLIN SECOR, lawyer; b. Hopewell Center, N.Y., Aug. 3, 1901; s. Albert Frank and Elizabeth (Ketcham) W.; m. Kate Visscher, Dec. 28, 1931; children—Franklin Secor, Harmin Visscher, Mary Visscher. A.B., Cornell U., 1923, LL.B., 1925. Bar: N.Y. bar 1925. With firm Cotton & Franklin, N.Y.C., 1925-29, Prosser, Anderson & Marx, Honolulu, 1930, Robb, Clark & Bennitt, N.Y.C., 1933-34; pvt. practice, N.Y.C., 1934-45; mem. firm Hawkins, Delafield & Wood, 1945-70, counsel, 1971-74. Mem. council Cornell U. Mem. Assn. Bar City N.Y., Am., N.Y. State bar assns., Phi Delta Phi. Clubs: University (N.Y.C.); Siwanoy Country; Wadawanuck Yacht (Stonington, Conn.). Home: Bronxville, NY.

WOOD, JAMES PLAYSTED, author; b. N.Y.C., Dec. 11, 1905; s. William Thomas and Olive Padbury (Hicks) W.; m. E.S. Elizabeth Craig, Aug. 14, 1943. A.B., Columbia, 1927, M.A., 1932. Editorial library N.Y. Tribune, 1922-24; advt. copywriter McGraw-Hill Book Co., N.Y.C., 1927-29; tchr. English Dalton (Mass.) High Sch., 1929-30, duPont Manual High Sch., Louisville, 1930-37, Tabor Acad., summer 1936; instr. English Amherst, 1937-42, asst. prof., 1942-46; with Curtis Pub. Co., Phila, 1946-66. Author: The Presence of Everett Marsh, 1937, Magazines in the United States, 1949, Selling Forces, 1953, German edit. 1955, The Beckoning Hill, 1954, An Elephant in the Family, 1957, The Story of Advertising, 1958, Of Lasting Interest, 1958, Advertising and the Soul's Belly, 1960, The Queen's Most Honorable Pirate, 1961, The Elephant in the Barn, 1961, A Hound, A Bay Horse, and a Turtle Dove, 1963, Trust Thyself, 1964, The Life and Words of John F. Kennedy, 1964, The Lantern Bearer, 1965, Very Wild Animal Stories, 1965, Elephant on Ice, 1965, The Snark Was a Boojum, 1966, What's the Market? , 1966, When I was Jersey, 1967, Alaska, The Great Land, 1967, Spunkwater, Spunkwater, 1968, Mr. Jonathan Edwards, 1968, I Told You So, 1969, The Mammoth Parade, 1969, Scotland Yard, 1970, The Unpardonable Sin, 1970, This Little Pig, 1971, The Curtis Magazines, 1971, Emily Elizabeth Dickinson, 1972; Poetry Is, 1972, The Great Glut, 1973, Kentucky Time, 1977, Chase Scene, 1979; also others.; Editor: American Literature of, 1847, 1947, American Literature of 1848, 1948; text editor, contbr. to: Marketing Research Practice, 1950; Contbg. editor: Limited Editions Club, 1974-76. Served from 2d lt. to maj. USAAF, 1943-46. Home: Springfield, Mass.

WOOD, LYNN HARPER, coll. pres.; b. Lamar, Barton Co., Mo., Aug. 1, 1887; s. Alphous Hamilton and Nelia (Griggs) W.; B.S., in Arch. Engring., U. of Mich., 1909, post-grad. study, same univ., 2 summers; m. Maude Guilford, Sept. 6, 1911. Instr. in mathematics, Washington (D.C.) Foreign Mission Sem., 1909-12; prof. science, Union Coll., College View, Neb., 1912-14; prin. Southern Training Sch., Graysville, Tenn., 1914-15; sec. edn., Nashville, Tenn., 1915-18; pres. Southern Jr. Coll., Dottowah, Tenn., 1918-22; pres. Australasian Missionary Coll., Cooranborg, N.S. Wales, Australia, 1922-28; pres. Stanborough Coll., Watford, Herts, Eng., 1928-30; pres. Emmanual Missionary Coll., Berrien Springs, Mich., since 1930, also sec. of bd. Mem. Lake Union Conf. Com., Seventh Day Adventist Ch. Mem. Mich. State Coll. Presidents Assn. Home: Berrien Springs, Mich.†

WOOD, NATALIE (NATASHA GURDIN), actress; b. San Francisco, 1938; d. Nicholas and Marci (Kuleff) Gurdin; m. Robert Wagner, 1957 (div. 1962); m. Richard Gregson, May 31, 1969 (div.); 1 child, m. Robert Wagner, July 16, 1972; 1 Courtney. First motion picture performance at age 4 in Happy Land, 1943; appeared in Tomorrow is Forever, 1946; other motion pictures include: The Bride Wore Boots, 1946, Miracle on 34th St., 1947, No Sad Songs for Me, 1950, Our Very Own, 1950, The Star, 1953, Rebel Without a Cause, 1955, The Searchers, Burning Hills, Girl He Left Behind, 1956, Marjorie Morningstar, 1957, Kings Go Forth, 1958, Cash McCall, 1959, All the Fine Young Cannibals, 1960, West Side Story, 1961, Splendor in the Grass, 1961, Gypsy, 1963, Sex and the Single Girl, 1964, The Great Race, 1965, Inside Daisy Clover, 1966, Penelope, 1966, Love with the Proper Stranger, 1964, This Property is Condemned, 1966, Bob and Carol and Ted and Alice, 1969, Peeper, 1975, Meteor, 1979; appeared on TV in Cat on a Hot Tin Roof, From Here to Eternity. Address: Los Angeles, Calif. Dec. Nov. 30, 1981.*

WOOD, WILLIAM PLATT, educator; b. Ypsilanti, Mich., May 26, 1888; s. Maurice Granville and Margaret Sophia (Platt) W.; B.Pd., Mich. State Normal Coll., 1909; A.B., U. of Mich., 1912. B. Chem. Eng., 1914, M.S.E., 1916; m. Antoinette Willey, Apr. 6, 1917; children—William Maurice, Helen Margaret. Instr. of sci. and mathematics, Stafford (Kan.) High Sch., 1909-10; instr. and asst. prof. chemistry, Mich. State Coll., 1914-17; supervisor of materials, U.S. Bur. Aircraft Constrn., Detroit, 1917-19; mem. faculty U. of Mich. from 1919, prof. of Metall. engring. from 1931; consultant in field of metall. engring. Mem. Am. Soc. for Metals, Am. Foundrymen's Soc., Am. Soc. Engring. Edn., Research Club, Sigma Xi, Theta Xi, Alpha Chi Sigma, Phi Lambda Upsilon. Presbyn. Club: Exchange. Author: Pyrometry (with J. M. Cork), 1st ed., 1927; Unit Operations (with G. G. Brown et al), 1950. Home: Ann Arbor, Mich. †

WOODALL, WILLIAM CLEMENTS, JR., broadcasting company executive; b. Columbus, Ga., Oct. 2, 1916; s. William C. and Virginia Ethel (McGehee) W.; A.B., U. Ga., 1940; m. Margaret Anne Swindle, June 29, 1940; children—Dorothy, Orson, Hardy. Founder, mgr., owner Sta. WDWD, Dawson, Ga., 1948-84; owner, mgr. Sta. WGRA, Cairo, Ga., 1950-84, Sta. WFPM, Fort Valley, Ga., 1952-84, Sta. WIMO, Winder, Ga., 1954-84, Sta. WGSW, Greenwood, S.C., 1955-84, Sta. WBBK, Blakeley, Ga., 1956-84, Sta. WDSR, Lake City, Fla., 1968-84, WTLD-FM, Lake City, 1968-84, WMEN, Tallahassee, Fla., 1971-84, Sta. WPFA, Pensacola, Fla., 1971-84, Sta. WWNS, Statesboro, Ga., 1975-84, Sta. WMCD, Statesboro, 1975-84; dir. Bank of Terrell, Dawson; chmn. Ga. Radio Inst., U. Ga., Athens, 1955. Served with USN, 1942-45. Mem. Nat., Ga. (award 1955) assns. broadcasters, Nat. Radio Broadcasters Assn. Republican. Methodist. Club: Rotary. Home: Dawson, Ga. Dec. Oct. 27, 1984. Interned Dawson, Ga.

WOODARD, LAWRENCE BAKER, investment banker; b. Mpls., Aug. 20, 1890; s. Francis R. and Helen (Nichols) W.; A.B., Williams Coll., 1913; m. Cora Stevenson, Jan. 3, 1931 (dec.); 1 dau., Nancy S.; m. 2d, Marian M. Ervin, Jan. 26, 1968. Mgr. bond dept. Northwestern Trust Co., 1915-28; partner Harold E. Wood & Co., St. Paul, 1928-31; dir. Woodard-Elwood & Co. Mpls., 1933-59, chmn. bd., from 1947. Mem. Midwest Stock Exchange. Mem. Nat. Assn. Securities Dealers (past gov., past vice chmn.), Investment Bankers Assn. Am. (past gov.). Clubs: Minneapolis; Woodhill Country; Twin City Bond (past pres.). Home: Wayzata, MN. †

WOODBERRY, JOHN HENRY, army officer; born Johnsonville, S.C., Feb. 22, 1889; s. Watcoat G. and Rosa Belle (Eaddy) W.; ed. Clemson Coll., S.C., 1906-07; The Citadel, S.C., 1907-10; B.S., U.S. Mil. Acad., 1914; grad. Army Industrial Coll., 1928, Command and Gen. Staff Sch., 1930, Army War Coll., 1935; m. Maarguerite Flint, Sept. 12, 1914; children—Marguerite Wightman (Mrs. Nathan B. Chenault, Jr.), Marilyn Eaddy (Mrs. Pierpont F. Brown, Jr.). Commd. 2d lt., cavalry. U.S. Army, 1914, detailed to Ordnance Dept., and trans. to F.A., 1916, trans. to Ord. Dept., 1920; advanced to lt. col. (temp.), 1918, brig. gen. (temp.), 1945; holds numerous patents on munitions of war, notably artillery fuze devices for control of detonating waves used in practically all U.S.A. high explosive ammunition; served in War Dept. Gen. Staff, 1934-39; chief ordnance officer, Supply Services, Hdqrs., S.W. Pacific Area, 1944-45; ordnance officer, Army Service Command, Japan Army of Occupation, 1945; later pres. Sunray Awning Shutter Corp. Awarded Legion of Merit. Mem. Army Ordnance Assn. Mason. Author of papers on reaction of high explosives in heavy containers and control and directive influence of detonating waves, etc. Home: San Antonio, Tex. Deceased.

WOODBRIDGE, FREDERICK WELLS, educator; b. Topeka, Kan., May 10, 1889; s. George Brayton and Adelia May (Sharpe) W.; student Whitworth Coll., 1909-12; M.B.A., U. Wash., 1923; m. Florence Davis, Feb. 13, 1915; m. 2d Beatrice Dunn, Mar. 25, 1934; children—David, Helen Adelia. Mgr., partner Automobile Freight Lines, 1914-15; asst. r.r., bldg. contractor, 1915-17; teaching asst., asso. U. Wash., 1921-23. instr. summer session, 1932; instr. summer session U. Cal. at Los Angeles, 1923, Berkeley, 1929; adjunct prof. U. Tex., 1924-27; asso. prof. Lehigh U., 1927-28; prof. accounting and head department University of So. Cal., 1928-54, chmn. div. bus. and social sci. Long Beach State Coll., 1956-58, chairman of the division of business, from 1958. Served with United States Army, 1917-19; charge auditor hosp. funds, A.E.F. Mem. Disabled Vets. (state adj., Wash., 1921, state comdr. 1922), Am. Accounting Assn. (v.p. 1936-38), Nat. Assn. Cost Accountants (past pres. Los Angeles), Phi Kappa Phi, Beta Alpha Psi (pres. grand council 1943), Artus, Beta Gamma Sigma. Club: University (Los Angeles). Author: Elements of Accounting 1925; A System of Accounting Procedures for Livestock Ranches, 1930; Fundamentals 1947; Manufacturing and Cost, 1947; Accounts Proprietorship-Analysis, 1948, others. Contbr. articles profl. publs. Home: San Pedro, Cal. †

WOODMAN, ROY HARPER, corporate executive, management consultant; b. Winnipeg, Man., Can., June 4, 1922; s. Alonzo Edwin and Flora McIntosh (Harper) W.; B.A., U. B.C., 1949, B.Comm., 1950; M.B.A., Harvard 1952; m. Marcia M. Carmichael, June 14, 1947 (div. June 1974); m. Irene Bolshakov, Sept. 1974; children—Roderick Earl, Cameron Roy, Neil Elliot, Kimberly Paige. With John Labatt Ltd., London, Ont., 1952-62, v.p., regional gen. mgr., pres., 1959-62; pres. Lucky Lager Breweries, San Francisco, 1963-65; cons. to industry, U.S., Can., 1966-81; exec. v.p., treas. Saga Adminstrv. Corp., Menlo Park, Calif., 1967-73; exec. v.p., dir. Video Logic Corp., 1974-75, pres., dir., chief exec. officer, 1976-81; pres., dir., chief exec. officer Internat. Video Corp., 1977-79; chmn. Internat. Video, 1978-81. Bd. dirs. La Salle Gen. Hosp. Served with RCAF, 1941-45. Club: St. James's (Montreal). Home: Los Altos, Calif. Dec. July 22, 1981.

WOODRING, MAXIE NAVE, educator; b. Nashville, Tenn., Jan. 25, 1888; d. William Thomas and Ellen (Tucker) W.; grad. Peabody Model Sch., Nashville, 1903; grad. Peabody Normal Sch., 1905; B.S. and A.M., George Peabody Coll., 1918; Rockefeller Foundation scholarship, Columbia, 1923-24; Ph.D., 1925; attended summer schs., Peabody Normal Sch., 1908, George Peabody Coll., 1914, 18, 20, U. of Colo., 1913, U. of Calif., 1922, Teachers Coll., Columbia, 1919, 21, 23, 24. Teacher of Latin, high sch., Chickasha, Okla., 1906-07; teacher of grades, Peabody College Demonstration Sch., 1907-08, high sch. English, 1908-11; prof. Latin and German, Okla. State Coll. for Women, Chickasha, 1911-17, prof. secondary edn. and dir. coll. high sch., 1918-23; instr. in secondary edn., Teachers Coll., Columbia, 1924-25, asso. in secondary edn., 1925-26, asst. prof. edn., 1926-28, asso. prof., 1928-35, prof. of edn. from 1935. Mem. N.E.A. Assn. Coll. Teachers Edn., A.A.U.W., AAUP, Assn. Supervisors and Curriculum Dirs., Delta Theta Beta, Kappa Delta Pi. Democrat. Methodist. Author or co-author books relating to field; contbr. to ednl. mags. Home: New York, N.Y. Deceased.

WOODRUFF, ROBERT WINSHIP, mfg.; b. Columbus, Ga., Dec. 6, 1889; s. Ernest and Emily (Winship) W.; ed. Ga. Mil. Acad. and Emory U.; m. Nell Hodgson, Oct. 17, 1912. Former chmn. of bd. The Coca-Cola Co., ret., 1955, dir.; dir. So. Ry. Company, Trust Company of Ga., Metropolitan Life Insurance Company; mem. directors adv. council Morgan Guaranty Trust Co. N.Y. Trustee Berry Schs., Mt. Berry, Ga., Tuskegee Inst., Nat. Safety Council, Ga. Warm Springs Found., Nat. Found., Nat. Fund for Med. Edn. Home: Atlanta, Ga. Died Mar. 7, 1985.

WOODS, GEORGE DAVID, banker; b. Boston, Mass., July 27, 1901; s. John and Laura A. (Rhodes) W.; student Am. Inst. Banking, 1920-23; LL.D., U. Notre Dame, 1963, Allegheny Coll., 1963, Bowdoin Coll., 1964, Harvard U., 1956, Columbia 1966; L.H.D., Lafayette Coll., 1964, Kenyon Coll., 1968; m. Louise Taraldson, Apr. 29,

1935. With firm Harris Forbes & Co., N.Y.C., 1918-34; with First Boston Corp., 1934-62, chmn. bd., 1952-62; dir. various corps., 1931-62; pres., chmn. internat. Bank of Reconstrn. and Devel. (World Bank), also Internat. Devel. Assn. Washington, 1963-68; chmn. bd., pres. Internat. Finance Corp. 1963-68; dir. Spruce Falls Power and Paper Co., Ltd., First Boston Corp., Kaiser Industries Corp., N.Y. Times Chmn., N.Y. State Urban Devel. Corp., from 1968; internat. Exec. Service Corps, from 1968. Chmn., Trustee Henry J. Kaiser Family Found.; mem. of the bd. Notre Dame U.; mem. bd. dirs. Lincoln Center for Performing Arts, Inc., Kaiser Found. Hosps.; chmn. bd. Repertory Theater of Lincoln Center, Inc.; trustee Rockefeller Found., N.Y. Found., John Fitzgerald Kennedy Library, Inc. Served from maj. to col., Gen. Staff Corps., U.S. Army, 1942-45. Clubs: Recess, Racquet and Tennis, Pinnacle, Players, Links (N.Y.C.); Duquesne, Rolling Rock (Pitts.): Federal City, F Street (Washington). Home: New York, N.Y. Died Aug. 20, 1982.

WOODS, MARK WINTON, biologist, educator; b. Takoma Park, D.C., Oct. 15, 1908; s. Albert Frederick and Bertha Gerneaux (Davis) W.; B.S., U. Md., 1931, M.S., 1933, Ph.D., 1936; m. Vera Lorraine Klein, Dec. 23, 1933; children—Judith Patricia, Mark Alvin. From instr. plant pathology to assoc. prof. U. Md., 1936-47; biologist Nat. Cancer Inst., 1947-73, ret., 1973, spl. research metabolism cancer, hereditary properties mitochondria, cell responses to plant viruses. Served with USNR, 1942-45. Fellow AAAS; mem. Phytopathol. Soc. Am., Am. Assn. Cancer Research, Am. Soc. Biol. Chemists, Washington, N.Y. acads. scis., Sigma Xi, Phi Kappa Phi, Alpha Zeta, Alpha Tau Omega. Presbyterian (elder). Home: Sun City, Ariz. Died Mar. 4, 1983.

WOODS, WILLIAM JOHNSON, glass sand corp. executive; b. Lewistown, Pa., Dec. 11, 1888; s. Joseph Milliken and Sarah E. (Johnson) W.; A.B., Princeton, 1911; m. Myrtle E. Sebrell, Nov. 1914; children—Margaret Sebrell, William J., Jr., Ann Witherspoon. Asso. with Pa. Glass Sand Corp., Lewistown, Pa. continuously from 1911, successively laborer, asst. foreman, foreman, salesman, asst. gen. mgr., gen. mgr., president, 1927-65, chairman of the board, from 1965; president Pennsylvania Pulverizing Company, Pioneer Silica Products Co., Tavern Rock Sand Company. Mem. Tiger Inn Club, Princeton. Republican. Presbyterian. Clubs: Union League (Phila); Duquesne (Pitts.); Fifth Avenue (N.Y.C.). Home: Lewistown, Pa. †

WOODWARD, FRED WILLIAM, publisher; b. Dubuque, Ia., Mar. 26, 1888; s. Charles L. and Anna (Weirmiller) W.; ed. pub. schs., Dubuque; m. Elsie M. Mueller, May 17, 1910; 1 son, Frederick R. With Telegraph Herald, Dubuque, from 1899, office boy, 1899, circulation mgr., 1909-15, bus. mgr. and sec., 1915-22, pres. from 1922, chmn. bd. dirs., from 1922; licensee radio sta. KDTH, Dubuque, from 1941, also radio sta. KFMD, radio sta. WGEZ, Beloit, Wis. Named Ky. col. Presbyn. Mason, Elk. Club: Dubuque Golf. Home: Dubuque, IA. †

WOODWARD, HARPER, lawyer; b. Rochester, N.Y., Nov. 26, 1909; s. Roland B. and Anne (Murray) W.; m. Ruth Keller, Aug. 1, 1942 (dec. July 1966); m. Edith M. Laird, Mar. 18, 1967; children—Bruce A., Belinda B. (Mrs. Glen R. Kendall), Edwin C. Laird III, Bonnie B. (Mrs. Stephane Y. Christen). Grad., St. Paul's Sch., Concord, N.H., 1927; A.B., Harvard, 1931, LL.B., 1934. Bar: N.Y. bar 1936. Sec. to pres. Harvard U., 1934-35; mem. firm Barry, Wainwright, Thacher & Symmers, 1935-37, Woodward & Woodward, 1937-38, Spence, Windels, Walser, Hotchkiss & Angell, 1938-42, Spence, Hotchkiss, Parker & Duryee, 1946; asso. Laurance S. Rockefeller, N.Y.C., 1946-66; asso. Rockefeller Family & Assos., 1966-76, cons., 1976-81; dir., mem. exec. com. Eastern Air Lines; dir. Rockresorts, Inc., Caneel Bay Plantation, Wayfarer Ketch Corp. Trustee Meml. Sloan-Kettering Cancer Center. Served with USAAF, 1942-45. Mem. Harvard Law Sch. Assn. Clubs: Wings (N.Y.C.); Essex Yacht, Old Lyme Country.

WOOLLETT, G(UY) H(AINES), educator; b. Minneapolis, July 14, 1888; s. George Purdy and Anna Grace (Haines) W.; B.S., U. of Minn., 1910, M.S., 1916, Ph.D., 1918; m. Eva Victoria Stade, Sept. 1, 1919; 1 son, Albert Haines. Mem. dept. physiol. chemistry Med. Sch., U. of Miss., from 1916, chmn. admissions from 1936. Fellow A.A.A.S.; mem. Am. Chem. Soc., Miss. Acad. Sci., Sigma Xi. Home: Biloxi, Miss. †

WOOLLEY, CLARENCE NELSON, lawyer; b. Cumberland, R.I., Sept. 13, 1887; s. Thomas Edward and Mary Jane (Ball) W.; LL.B., Boston U., 1908; studied Brown U. and Child's Business Coll.; m. Ruth Inman Searll, Nov. 18, 1919. Practiced in Pawtucket, R.I., from 1910. Mem. Am. and R.I. bar assns., Phi Delta Phi, Sigma Alpha Epsilon. Mem. Conf. Commrs. Uniform State Laws, 1909-15 (sec., 1913-15). Mem. 1st Co. Coast Arty., R.I.N.G., 1908. Republican. †

WOOLLEY, KNIGHT, comml. banker; b. Bklyn., May 1, 1895; s. Ulysses Grant and Helen Eaton (Knight) W.; grad. Phillips Acad., Andover, Mass., 1913; A.B., Yale, 1917; m. Sarah Currier, Aug. 7, 1934 (dec. 1954); m. 2d, Marjorie Fleming, Apr. 16, 1957. With Guaranty Trust Co., 1919-20, Am. Exchange Nat. Bank, 1920-27; partner Harriman Brothers & Co., 1927-31; partner Brown Brothers, Harriman & Co., 1931-82; dir. So. Ry. Co. Trustee Boys Club N.Y., Southampton Hosp. Served to maj. F.A., 78th Div., U.S. Army, 1917-19; AEF. Mem. Council Fgn. Relations. Clubs: Links, Racquet and Tennis, India House, Knickerbocker, River (N.Y.C.); Nat. Golf Links (Southampton); Maidstone (East Hampton). Republican. Presbyn. Home: New York, N.Y. Died Jan. 18, 1984.

WOOSTER, CARL GOULD, farmer; b. Union Hill, N.Y., May 20, 1889; s. Fred M. and Elia J. (Snow) W.; B.S.A., Cornell, 1912; m. Stella M. Kircher, July 23, 1913; 1 dau., Thelma M. (Mrs. Louis J. Van Alstyne). Pres., prin. Wooster Fruit Farms Inc., Union Hill, N.Y. Chmn. N.Y. State Agrl. Adjustment Com., 1938-40; asst. dir. N.E. div. A.A.A., 1941-42; chief marketing div. fruit and vegetable br. War Food Adminstrn., 1942-44; dir. Buffalo br. Fed. Res. Bd. N.Y. from 1946, chmn. from 1951. Mem. bd. edn. Webster (N.Y.) High Sch.; mem. Webster Twp. Bd. Mem. N.Y. State Holstein Assn. (pres., 1935-42), Holstein Friesian Assn. Am. (pres. 1947; dir., chmn. exec. com. from 1949), Pure-bred Dairy Cattle Assn. Am. (pres. 1947), N.Y. State Fedn. 4H Clubs (pres. 1938-39), N.Y. State Cherry Growers Assn. (dir.), Western N.Y. State Apple Growers Assn. (dir.), N.Y. State Hort. Soc. (pres. 1947; dir.). Home: Union Hill, N.Y. †

WORK, RICHARD NICHOLAS, educator; b. Ithaca, N.Y., Aug. 7, 1921; s. Paul and Helen Grace (Nicholas) W.; m. Catherine Verwoert, July 17, 1948; children—Barbara Jane, Douglas Richard, Sarah Grace. Student, Oberlin Coll., 1938-39; B.A., Cornell, 1942, M.S. (John C. McMullen scholar), 1944, Ph.D., 1949. Physicist Nat. Bur. Standards, Washington, 1949-51; research asso. Princeton, 1951-56; asst. prof. Pa. State U., 1956-61, asso. prof., 1961-65; prof. physics Ariz. State U., Tempe, from 1965; asst. dean Ariz. State U. (Coll. Liberal Arts), 1965-68, asso. dean, 1969-73, chmn. dept. physics, 1977-81; Cons. White Sands Missile Range, 1953-65, Sandia Corp., Albuquerque, 1964-68, Acushnet Co., New Bedford, Mass., from 1973. Contbr. to: Dielectric Properties of Polymers (F.E. Karasz), 1972; also, articles to profl. jours. Mem. State College (Pa.) Housing Code Commn., 1964-65, Bldg. Code Commn., 1964-65, Bldg. Bd. Appeals, 1964-65. NSF research grantee, 1965-74, from 81. Fellow Am. Phys. Soc., AAAS; mem. Am. Assn. Physics Tchrs., Sigma Xi. Research on polymer physics and dielectric theory and measurements. Home: Tempe, Ariz.

WORMSER, RENÉ ALBERT, lawyer, author, lectr. estate planning, internat. law, taxes, pub. affairs; b. Santa Barbara, Cal., July 17, 1896; s. David and Angeline Louise (Boeseke) W.; B.S., Columbia, 1917, LL.B., 1920; LL.D., Valparaiso U., 1964, U. Miami, 1976; m. Ella Madge Ward, Aug. 7, 1945; children—Angela Boeseke, Elissa Ward. Admitted to N.Y. State bar, 1920, and practiced as asso. Hornblower, Miller, Garrison & Potter, 1920-22, Bate, Boyd, & Swinnerton, 1923; individual practice, 1924-30; partner Wormser & Kemp, 1930-35, Wormser, Morris & Kemp, 1935-37, Folger, Rockwood, Wormser & Kemp, 1937-39, Delaney, Myles & Wormser, 1939-40, Haggerty, Myles & Wormser, 1941-50, Myles, Wormser & Koch 1950-60, Wormser, Koch, Kiely and Alessandroni, 1960-71, Wormser, Kiely, Alessandroni & McCann, 1972-77; firm Wormser, Kiely, Alessandroni, Hyde & McCann, from 1978; lectr. estate planning N.Y. U., 1948-55; mem. faculty and planning com. N.Y. U. Fed. Tax Inst., 1945-55; vis. adj. prof. Law Sch., U. Miami, 1973—. Gen. counsel Ho. of Reps. Spl. Com. to Investigate Tax Exempt Founds., 1953-54; chmn. advanced estate planning panels Practising Law Inst., 1956-68; chmn. adv. com. Miami U. Estate Planning Inst., 1967-81; mem. advisory com. on tax-exempt orgns. Commr. Internal Revenue. Served with USN, World War I. Mem. Am., N.Y. State bar assns., Assn. Bar City N.Y., Delta Upsilon. Clubs: Belle Haven (Greenwich); Union League (N.Y.C.). Author: Your Will and What Not to do about It, 1937; Personal Estate Planning in a Changing World, 1942; Collection of International War Damage Claims, 1944; The Theory and Practice of Estate Planning, 1944; The Law, 1949; Family Estate Planning, 1953; The Myth of the Good and Bad Nations, 1954; Foundations, Their Power and Influence, 1958; Wormser's Guide to Estate Planning, 1958; The Planning and Administration of Estates, 1961; The Story of the Law, 1962; Wills That Made History, 1974; Conservatively Speaking, 1979; also articles in periodicals. Home: Greenwich, Conn. Died July 14, 1981.

WORNHAM, THOMAS ANDREWS, marine corps officer; b. Rensselaer, N.Y., Dec. 12, 1903; s. Thomas Gregg and Emily Caroline (Dennis) W.; B.S., U.S. Naval Acad., 1926; m. Laura Amelia Van Allen, June 3, 1926; 1 son, Thomas Van Allen. Commd. 2d lt., USMC, 1926, advanced through grades to lt. gen., 1959; comd. 27th Marines, 5th Marine div. at Iwo Jima, 1945, 1st Marines, 1st Marine Div., Korea, 1951; asst. chief of staff G-3 Marine Corps Hdqrs., Washington, 1952-55; comdg. gen. 3rd Marine Div., Japan, 1955-56, Marine Corps Recruit Depot, San Diego, Cal., 1956-59; comdg. gen. fleet marine force (Pacific) 1959-62. Decorated Navy Cross, Legion of Merit, Bronze Star, Commendation Ribbon. Club: Army-Navy. Home: San Diego, Calif. Died Dec. 17, 1984.

WORTMAN, STERLING, scientist; b. Quinlan, Okla., Apr. 3, 1923; s. Leo Sterling and Gladys (Richwine) W.; m. Ruth Eleanor Bolstad, June 17, 1949; children—Linda Susan, Steven Sterling, Mark Jeffry, David Eric. B.S., Okla. State U., 1943; M.S., U. Minn., 1948, Ph.D., 1950. Geneticist charge corn breeding Rockefeller Found., 1950-54, dir. agrl. scis., 1966-70, v.p., from 1970, acting pres., 1979-80, cons. to pres., from 1980; pres. Internat. Agrl. Devel. Service, 1975-79; asst. field dir. Internat. Rice Research Inst., 1960-64; head dept. plant breeding Pineapple Research Inst., Hawaii, 1955-59, dir., 1964-65; dir. Campbell Soup Co.; Mem. agrl. bd. Nat. Acad. Scis.-NRC, 1967-71; chmn. Plant Studies Delegation to Peoples Republic of China, Nat. Acad. Scis., 1974, mem. bd. on sci. and tech. in internat. devel., 1974, mem. com. on scholarly communication with Peoples Republic of China, 1974-76; mem. steering com. Pres.'s Food and Nutrition Study, 1975-77; mem. advisory com. sci., tech. and devel. Exec. Office of Pres.; Coromandel lectr., India, 1977; Trustee Agronomic Sci. Found., 1967-69; bd. dirs. Agribus. Council, 1967-73, v.p., 1967-69; bd. dirs. Internat. Center Maize and Wheat Improvement, Mex., from 1966, vice chmn. bd., 1968-74; bd. dirs. Boyce Thompson Inst. at Cornell, from 1980; mem. adv. com. Monell Chem. Senses Center, from 1980; mem. biol. and med. scis. advisory com. NSF, 1970-72, mem. research advisory com., 1972-74; mem. nat. plant genetic resources com. Dept. Agr., from 1977; trustee Internat. Rice Research Inst., Philippines, 1970, Internat. Inst. Tropical Agr., Nigeria, 1970; mem. vis. com. dept. nutrition Mass. Inst. Tech., 1971-74; vis. prof. Cornell U., 1980-81. Author: To Feed This World, 1979. Served to capt., inf. AUS, 1943-45, PTO. Decorated Medal of Merit Philippines; recipient Outstanding Achievement award U. Minn., 1975, Joseph C. Wilson award for achievement in internat. affairs, 1975; Disting. Alumnus award Okla. State U., 1978; named to Hall of Fame, 1980. Fellow AAAS; mem. Crop Sci. Soc., Am. Soc. Agronomy (Internat. Agronomy award 1975), Am. Inst. Biol. Scis., Am. Acad. Arts and Scis., Sigma Xi. Home: Greenwich, Conn.

WRATHER, JOHN DEVERAUX, JR., oil producer, motion picture producer, financier; b. Amarillo, Tex., May 24, 1918; s. John D. and Mazie (Cogdell) W.; m. Bonita Granville, Feb. 5, 1947; children—Molly, Jack, Linda, Christopher. A.B., U. Tex., 1939. Ind. oil producer, Tex., Ind., Ill.; pres. Evansville (Ind.) Refining Co., 1938-40, Overton Refining Co., Amarillo Producers & Refiners Corp., Dallas, 1940-49, Jack Wrather Pictures, Inc., 1947-49, Freedom Prodns., Inc., 1949-84, Western States Investment Corp., Dallas, 1949-84, Wrather Television Prodns., Inc., 1951-84, Wrather-Alvarez Broadcasting, Inc., The Lone Ranger, Inc., Lassie, Inc., Disney-land Hotel, Anaheim, Calif., R.M.S. Queen Mary and Howard Hughes' Flying Boat Spruce Goose, L'Horizon Hotel, Palm Springs, Calif.; owner KFMB, KERO and; KEMB-TV, San Diego, KOTY-TV, Tulsa; part owner WNEW, N.Y.C.; pres. Sgt. Preston of the Yukon, Inc.; chmn. bd. Muzak, Inc., Ind. Television Corp. and Television Programs of Am. Inc., Stephens Marine, Inc.; pres. Balboa Bay Club, Inc., Kona Kai, Inc.; pres., chmn. bd. Wrather Corp.; dir. TelePrompTer Corp., Continental Airlines, Transcontinent. Television Corp., Jerold Elec. Corp., Capitol Records, Inc.; Bd. dirs. Community Television of So. Calif.; Am. Found. Religion and Psychiatry, Corp. for Pub. Broadcasting. Motion pictures produced include The Guilty, 1946, High Tide, Perilous Water, 1947, Strike It Rich, 1948, Guilty of Treason, 1949, The Lone Ranger and The Lost City of Gold, 1958, The Magic of Lassie, 1978, The Legend of the Lone Ranger, 1981, others. Mem. devel. bd. U. Tex., vice chmn. chancellor's council; mem. advisory council Ariz. Heart Inst.; bd. counselors for performing arts U. So. Calif.; Commr. Los Angeles County-Hollywood Mus.; mem. adv. bd. Los Angeles Rams. Served to major USMC Res., 1942-53. Mem. Ind. Petroleum Assn. of Am., Internat. Radio and Television Soc., Acad. Motion Pictures Arts and Scis., Nat. Petroleum Council. Clubs: Dallas Athletic, Dallas Petroleum; Cat Cay Yacht (Bahamas); Players (N.Y.), Hemisphere (N.Y.), Skeeters (N.Y.); Marks (London), Bucks (London), White Elephant (London), Harry's Bar (London). Home: Los Angeles, Calif. Died Nov. 12, 1984.

WRIGHT, DONALD RICHARD, state chief justice; b. Orange County, Calif., Feb. 2, 1907; s. David L. and Lillie (Andrew) W.; A.B. cum laude, Stanford U., 1929; LL.B., Harvard, 1932; grad. Command and Gen. Staff Coll.; LL.D., U. Pacific, 1971; LL.M., U. So. Calif., 1973; m. Margaret McLellan. Admitted to Calif. bar, 1932; pvt. practice, Pasadena, Calif., 1932-53; judge Pasadena Municipal Ct., 1953-60, Los Angeles County Superior Ct., 1960-68, 2d Dist., Ct. Appeals, Los Angeles, 1968-70; chief justice Calif. Supreme Ct., 1970-77. Charter incorporator Pasadena Legal Aid Soc., 1949; chmn. Calif. Water Rights Commn., after 1977; Pres. bd. dirs. Hastings Sch. Law, U. Calif., San Francisco; bd. visitors Stanford Law Sch.; bd. dirs. Ralph M. Parsons Found.; bd. councilors U. So. Calif. Law Center; trustee Pathfinder Mines Corp. Served to lt. col. USAAF, World War II. Mem. Order of Coif. Home: Pasadena, Calif. Dec. Mar. 21, 1985.

WRIGHT, GEORGE CALEB, architect; b. Libertyville, Ill., Apr. 25, 1889; s. Caleb Frank and Emma Jane (Price) W.; student U. Ill., 1908-12; m. Helen May Moss, Oct. 13, 1913; children—William Caleb, Jane. With George G. Nimmons, Chgo., 1913-23, Herbert Foltz, Indpls., 1923-25, Pierre & Wright, 1925-45, Wright, Porteous & Associates, Inc. Pres. Met. Planning Commn. of Marion County, Ind.; mem. of bd. Community Service Council, Ind. Community Resources Assn.; bldg. commr. Indpls.; mem. Ind. Constrn. Project study Com. Fellow Am. Inst.

of Architects (past pres. Ind. chpt.); mem. Constrn. League Indpls. (pres., dir.), Indpls. C. of C., Art Assn. Indpls., Ind. Econ. Council (chmn.), Ind. Adminstrv. Bldg. Council, Constrn. Specification Inst. Club: Columbia (Indpls.). Home: Indianapolis, IN. †

WRIGHT, LAFAYETTE HART, legal educator; b. Chickasha, Okla., Dec. 3, 1917; s. L.C. and Jessie (Hart) W.; m. Phyllis Jeanne Blanchard, June 4, 1938; children: Robin Blanchard, Jana Hart. A.B., U. Okla., 1938, LL.B., 1941; LL.M., U. Mich., 1942. Bar: Okla. 1941, Mich. bar 1952. Mem. faculty U. Mich., 1947-83, prof. law, 1953-83, Paul G. Kauper prof. law, 1979-83; vis. assoc. prof. Stanford U., 1953; cons. IRS, 1956-60, 67-68, mem. adv. group, 1960-61; vis. disting. prof. law U. Okla., 1976. Author: Tax Affairs of Individuals, 1957, Tax Affairs of Corporations, 1962, Needed Changes in Internal Revenue Service Conflict Resolution. Procedures, 1970; Co-author: Comparative Conflict Resolution Procedures in Taxation, 1968, American Enterprise in the European Common Market: A Legal Profile, 1960, Federal Tax Liens, 1967. Bd. dirs. Ann Arbor Family Service, 1954, Ann Arbor chpt. Americans for Democratic Action, 1968; mem. adv. bd. Internat. Bur. Fiscal Documentation, Amsterdam, from 1970; mem. legal policy activities bd. Taxation with Representation Fund, Washington, from 1975. Served to maj. F.A. AUS, 1942-46, ETO. Decorated Bronze Star; recipient award for meritorious civilian service Treasury Dept., 1958, Disting. Faculty award U. Mich., 1968. Mem. ABA, Order of Coif, Phi Beta Kappa, Phi Delta Theta. Democrat. Home: Ann Arbor, Mich. Dec. Apr. 12, 1983.

WRIGHT, LEROY AUGUSTUS, lawyer; b. San Diego, Apr. 12, 1914; s. Lester A. and Georgie S. (Hardy) W.; m. Mary L. Lindley, June 20, 1940; children—Shelley Wright Bassman, Bruce M., Marcy, Jean. A.B., Stanford U., 1936, LL.B., 1939. Bar: Calif. bar 1939. Practiced in, San Diego; partner firm Glenn, Wright, Jacobs & Schell, from 1952; dir., exec. com. Imperial Corp. Am. Fellow Am. Bar Found.; mem. ABA, Calif. Bar Assn., San Diego Bar Assn. (pres. 1951), Am. Law Inst. (life). Club: San Diego Yacht. Home: San Diego, Calif.

WRIGHT, LOUIS BOOKER, historian, library director; b. Greenwood County, S.C., March 1, 1899; s. Thomas Fleming and Lena (Booker) W.; m. Frances Marion Black, June 10, 1925; 1 son, Louis Christopher. A.B., Wofford Coll., Spartanburg, S.C., 1920; A.M., U. N.C., 1924, Ph.D., 1926, L.H.D., 1950; Litt.D., Wofford Coll., 1941, Mills Coll., 1947, Princeton U., 1948, Amherst Coll., 1948, Occidental Coll., 1949, Bucknell U., 1951, Franklin and Marshall Coll., 1957, Colby Coll., 1959, U. B.C., 1960, U. Birmingham, Eng., 1964, U. Leicester, Eng., 1965; LL.D., Tulane U., 1950, George Washington U., 1958, U. Chattanooga, 1959, U. Akron, 1961, St. Andrews U., Scotland, 1961, Washington and Lee U., 1964, Mercer U., 1965, Winthrop Coll., 1980; L.H.D., Northwestern U., 1948, Yale U., 1954, Rockford Coll., 1956, Coe Coll., 1959, Georgetown U., 1961, Calif. State Coll., Fullerton, 1966, U. Calif. at Los Angeles, 1967, Brown U., 1968, U. S.C., 1972, Lander Coll., 1974. Mem. faculties U. N.C., Johns Hopkins U., Emory U., Calif. Inst. Tech., U. Calif. at Los Angeles, U. Wash., U. Minn., Pomona Coll., Ind. U., 1926-48; Guggenheim research fellow in, Eng. and Italy, 1928-30; mem. research staff Huntington Library, 1932-48; dir. Folger Shakespeare Library, Washington, 1948-68; cons. Xerox-Univ. Microfilms, 1968-71; cons. in history Nat. Geog. Soc., from 1971; Mem. adv. bd. John Simon Guggenheim Meml. Found., 1942-71, chmn. bd., 1950-71; vice chmn. dirs. Council Library Resources, Inc., from 1956. Author: many books on hist. subjects, latest Shakespeare for Everyman, 1964, Dream of Prosperity in Colonial America, 1965, Everyday Life in Colonial America, 1967, Everyday Life on the American Frontier, 1968, Gold, Glory and the Gospel, 1970, (with Elaine W. Fowler) Everyday Life in New Nation, 1972, Barefoot in Arcadia: Memories of a More Innocent Era, 1973, Tradition and the Founding Fathers, 1975, South Carolina: A Bicentennial History, 1976, Of Books and Men, 1976; Editor alone or with others: numerous items on Am. and English history, including William Byrd of Virginia, The London Diary, 1712-1721, 1958, The Folger Library General Reader's Shakespeare Series, (with Virginia LaMar), 1957-68, The Prose Works of William Byrd of Westover, 1966, (with Elaine W. Fowler) English Colonization of North America, 1968, West and By North: North America Seen Through the Eyes of Its Seafaring Discoverers, 1971, The Moving Frontier, 1972, The John Henry County Map of Virginia 1770, 1977; editorial bd.: numerous items on Am. and English history, including History Book Club; contbr. articles to profl. jours. Life trustee Shakespeare Birthplace Trust, Stratford-upon-Avon, from 1964; trustee Nat. Geog. Soc., 1964-74, Winterthur Mus.; bd. dirs. Harry S. Truman Library Inst. for Nat. and Internat. Affairs, from 1956; bd. visitors Tulane U., from 1965, chmn., 1972-74. Served in U.S. Army, World War I. Decorated officer Order Brit. Empire; recipient Benjamin Franklin medal Royal Soc. Arts, 1969. Fellow Royal Soc. Lit., Royal Soc. Arts, Royal Hist. Soc.; mem. Am. Hist. Assn. (exec. sec. 1964-65), Mass. Hist. Soc., Am. Philos. Soc. (v.p. 1974-78), Am. Antiquarian Soc., Am. Acad. Arts and Scis., Modern Humanities Research Assn., Am. Assn. Learned Socs. (dir. 1971-77), Phi Beta Kappa (senator, Distinguished Service award 1976), several other profl. assns. Clubs: Tudor and Stuart (Johns Hopkins); Cosmos (Washington) (Ann. Award for distinction in letters 1973); Century (N.Y.C.). Home: Chevy Chase, MD.

WRIGHT, OLGIVANNA LLOYD, educational administrator; b. Cetinje, Montenegro, Yugoslavia; came to U.S., 1924, naturalized, 1933; d. Iovan and Militza (Milianova) Lazovich; m. Frank Lloyd Wright, Aug. 25, 1926 (dec. 1959); children: Svetlana Wright Peters (dec.), Iovanna Lloyd. Attended sch., Belgrade, Russia, Turkey, France. Co-founder (with Frank Lloyd Wright) Taliesin Fellowship, 1932; v.p. Frank Lloyd Wright Found., 1941-59, pres., 1959-85, Frank Lloyd Wright Sch. Architecture, 1959-85; pres., cons., adv. Taliesin Associated Architects, 1959-85; lectr. in art, philosophy; newspaper columnist. Interior and color coordinator numerous Frank Lloyd Wright bldgs. and Taliesin Associated Architects bldgs., 1959—; Author: The Struggle Within, 1955, Our House, 1959, The Shining Brow, 1960, Roots of Life, 1963, Frank Lloyd Wright, His Life, His Work, His Words, 1966; composer numerous works for chamber orch., including sonatas, trios, quartets; orchestral music for Taliesin Festivals of Music and Dance. Mem. Nat. Fedn. Press Women; hon. mem. Am. Soc. Interior Designers, Nat. League Am. Pen Women, Women In Communication. Home: Scottsdale, Ariz. Died Mar. 1, 1985.

WRIGHT, S. EARL, lawyer; b. nr. Richmond, Va., Sept. 5, 1904; s. William Samuel and Ruth Rosena (Gregory) W.; m. Doris E. Miller, Dec. 18, 1931 (dec. 1970); children—Stephen E., Clifford B.; m. Pauline Reynolds, 1972. Student, U. So. Calif., 1932. Bar: Calif. bar 1931. Practiced in, Los Angeles; mem. firm Wright & Wright (and predecessor firms), from 1931; Dir. Zane Grey, Inc., Zane Grey Prodns., San Gabriel Valley Newspapers, Inc. Mem. Met. Los Angeles adv. bd. Salvation Army. Mem. State Bar of Calif., Am., Los Angeles bar assns. Home: Bonsall, Calif.

WRIGLEY, JOHN EVELETH, historian; b. Phila., Sept. 7, 1919; s. Edmund J. and Mary (Suder) W.; m. Ruth L. Ditchey, June 12, 1970; children—Frank Ditchey, Robert Ditchey, Ruth Brill, Edith Burkey. A.B., St. Charles Sem., 1942, M.A., 1952; M.A., U. Pa., 1952, Ph.D., 1965. Mem. faculty Villanova U., 1951-53, La Salle Coll., 1965-70, St. Charles Sem., 1967-68, Chestnut Hill Coll., 1968-69; mem. faculty U. N.C., Charlotte, from 1970, asso. prof. medieval history, 1970-74, prof., from 1974. Contbr. articles to profl. jours. Fulbright fellow India, 1968; Am. Philos. Soc. grantee. Mem. Mediaeval Acad. Am., Am. Hist. Soc., Am. Cath. Hist. Soc. Democrat. Roman Catholic. Home: Charlotte, NC.

WUERTHNER, JULIUS JONOTHAN, lawyer; b. Manchester, Mich., May 18, 1890; s. John and Caroline (Yeutter) W.; LL.B., U. Mich., 1912; m. Clista Edith Pierce, July 28, 1920; children—John Pierce, Julius Jonothan, Benjamin James, Willis Keith. Admitted to Mich. bar, 1912, Mont., 1913; practice of law, Great Falls, from 1913; mem. Wuerthner & Wuerthner, from 1946; chief dep. atty., Cascade Co., 1921-23; mem. Mont. Ho. Reps., 1925-27, Senate, 1927-31; mayor Gt. Falls, Mont., 1932-41. Pres. Mont. Municipal League, 1939-40. Served as bandmaster, U.S. Army, World War I. Mem. Am. (state del., mem. ho. dels.), Mo. State (past pres.), Cascade Co. (past pres.) bar assns., American Judicature Soc., Sunshine Internat. Air Route Council (past pres.), Gt. Falls C. of C. Republican (dir. speakers bur. State Central Com.). Lutheran. Mason (33 degree, K.T., Shriner), Elk, Moose, Eagle. Clubs: Lions (1st dist. gov., dir. 1930-31), Lawyers (U. Mich.), Meadowlark Country. Composer mus. score The Awakened Rameses (Mich. Union opera), 1911. Home: Great Falls, Mont. †

WURF, JERRY, labor union official; b. N.Y.C., May 18, 1919; s. Sigmund and Lena (Tannenbaum) W.; A.B., N.Y.U., 1940; m. Mildred Kiefer, Nov. 26, 1960; children—Susan, Nicholas and Abigail. Worked in cafeteria, N.Y., 1940-43; an organizer local 448 Hotel and Restaurant Employees, 1943, organizer, adminstr. union's Welfare Fund, 1947; organizer in N.Y. for Am. Fedn. of State, County and Municipal Employees, 1947-58, exec. dir. dist. council 37, 1959-64, internat. pres., 1964-81; v.p. exec. council AFL-CIO. Mem. exec. com. Com. for Nat. Health Ins., Leadership Conf. on Civil Rights; trustee 20th Century Fund; mem. vis. com. Brookings Instn.; Mem. Am. Arbitration Assn. (dir.), Council on Fgn. Relations. Clubs: Nat. Democratic, Federal City. Home: Washington, D.C. Dec. Dec. 10, 1981.

WURM, JOHN NICHOLAS, bishop Roman Catholic Church; b. Overland, Mo., Dec. 6, 1927; s. Anthony Ernest and Estelle Rose (Leonard) W. B.A., Kenrick Sem., 1950; M.A., St. Louis U., 1958, Ph.D., 1969. Ordained priest, 1954; prin. Corpus Christi High Sch., 1960-63, Rosati-Kain High Sch., St. Louis, 1963-72; assoc. supt. schs. Archdiocese St. Louis, from 1972; vis. prof. ch. history Kenrick Theol. Sem., St. Louis, 1974-76, consecrated bishop, 1976, aux. bishop of, St. Louis, 1976-84; pastor Basilica of St. Louis, from 1976; dep. dir. Notre Dame Study Cath. Edn., St. Louis, 1969-70; mem. state com. North Central Assn., from 1972. Home: Saint Louis, Mo. Dec. Apr. 27, 1984.

WYATT, EDWARD AVERY, IV, newspaper editor; b. Petersburg, Va., Mar. 10, 1910; s. Edward Avery and Bessie Sutherland (Spain) W.; m. Martha V. Seabury, Aug. 31, 1940 (dec. Feb. 1963); children—Edward A., V. Elizabeth. A.B., Randolph-Macon Coll., 1931; student (Nieman fellow), Harvard, 1939-40. Reporter News Leader, Richmond, Va., 1930-31; asso. editor Progress-Index, Petersburg, Va., 1931-39, editor, from 1940; dir. Petersburg Newspaper Corp. Author: Along Petersburg Streets, 1943; Co-author: Petersburg's Story, A History, 1960; Contbr. articles on hist. subjects to mags.; Editor: Petersburg Imprints, 1786-1876, 1949. Past chmn. Va. State Library Bd.; Trustee Petersburg Mus., Mchts. Hope Ch. Restoration Found., Va. State Coll. Found., Tabb St. Ch. Found. Mem. Am. Soc. Newspaper Editors, Soc. of Cincinnati, Phi Beta Kappa, Omicron Delta Kappa, Phi Delta Theta. Episcopalian. Club: Rotarian. Home: Petersburg, VA.

WYCHE, IRA THOMAS, army officer; b. Ocracoke, N.C., Oct. 16, 1887; s. Lawrence Olin and Lorena (Howard) W.; B.S., U.S. Mil. Acad., 1911; grad. Mounted Service Sch., 1916, Field Arty. Sch., 1924, Command and Gen. Staff Sch., 1925, Army War Coll., 1934; m. Mary Louise Dunn, Dec. 15, 1917; 1 dau., Elizabeth. Commd. 2d lt., 1911; promoted through grades to maj. gen., 1942; comdr. 79th Inf. Div., Western Front, 1944; apptd. inspector general, A.U.S., Jan. 1947, 1948. Decorated Distinguished Service Medal, Legion of Merit, Silver Star Medal, Bronze Star (with 2 clusters), Army Commendation Ribbon (U.S.); Officer Legion of Honor (France); Croix de Guerre with palm (France). Mem. Master of Foxhounds Assn., Army and Navy Club. Home: Pinehurst, N.C. †

WYCKOFF, DONALD DARYL, business educator; b. Santa Monica, Calif., Apr. 28, 1936; s. Donald K. and Mary Gladys (Hammer) W.; m. Valerie M. Abdou, Aug. 30, 1958; children: Michele, Abigail. B.S., M.I.T., 1958; M.B.A., U. So. Calif., 1968; D.B.A., Harvard U., 1972. Vice pres. Cosmodyne Corp., Torrance, Calif., 1959-68; dir. Logistics Systems, Inc., Cambridge, Mass., 1968-72; prof. Bus. Sch., Harvard U., Boston, 1972-80, James J. Hill prof. transp., 1980-85; pres. D. Daryl Wyckoff Assocs., Inc., Marblehead, Mass., 1973-85; dir. Charles River Assos., Midway Airlines, Rusty Pelican. Author: Organizational Formality and Performance in the Motor Carrier Industry, 1974, Railroad Management, 1976, Truck Drivers in America, 1979, (with others) The Owner Operator: Independent Trucker, 1975, Operations Management: Text and Cases, 1975, The Motor Carrier Industry, 1977, The Domestic Airline Industry, 1977, The Chain Restaurant Industry, 1978, Management of Service Operations, 1978, The U.S. Lodging Industry, 1981; contbr. (with others) articles to profl. jours. Mem. transp. com. New Eng. Council, 1976—; bd. dirs. North Shore Vocat. Sch., 1979-80; trustee Winsor Sch., Boston, 1980-85. Mem. Transp. Research Forum (nat. v.p. 1974-75, pres. New Eng. chpt. 1975-76), Beta Gamma Sigma, Phi Sigma Kappa. Republican. Episcopalian. Club: Corinthian Yacht. Home: Marblehead, Mass. Died May 1985.

WYCKOFF, PETER HINES, physicist; b. Bklyn., June 1, 1913; s. Peter C. and Martha (Schofer) W.; B.S. in Elec. Engring., Carnegie Inst. Tech., 1936; M.S., Cal. Inst. Tech., 1937; m. Evelyn C. Jauquet, Nov. 17, 1942; 1 child, Peter S. Research engr. Westinghouse Research Labs., East Pittsburgh, Pa., 1937-41; physicist USAF, 1946-48, chief Atmospheric Physics Labs., 1948-58, chief Aerophysics Lab., 1958-61; mem. Upper Atmospheric Rocket Research Panel, 1953-61, Tech. Panel on Rocketry U.S. Nat. Com. for IGY, 1954-61; asst. dir. physics research IIT Research Inst. (formerly Armour Research Found.), Chgo. 1961-64; program mgr. weather modification NSF, 1964-73. Served from 1st lt. to lt. col. USAAF, 1941-46. Fellow AAAS, Am. Inst. Aeros. and Astronautics (asso.); mem. IEEE, Optical Soc. Am., Am. Phys. Soc., Am. Meteorol. Soc., Am. Geophys. Union, Sci. Research Soc. Am., Sigma Xi, Eta Kappa Nu, Phi Kappa Phi, Tau Beta Pi, Sigma Pi Sigma. Home: Falls Church, Va. Dec. Dec. 17, 1981.

WYLAND, RAY ORION, educator; b. Jewell County, Kan., Apr. 15, 1890; s. Warren William and Ellen (Howard) W.; A.B., U. of Ill., 1915; B.D., Garrett Bibl. Inst., 1918; student U. of Chicago, 1918-19; A.M., Columbia U., 1929, Ph.D., 1934; m. Ruby Arnold, Oct. 12, 1915; 1 son, Ray Orion. Ordained to ministry M.E. Ch., 1910; pastor chs. in Ill. conf., 1910-15, in Rock River Conf., 1915-18; with Y.M.C.A., Chicago, 1918-19, United Americans, 1920-22; asst. dir. edn. Boy Scouts of America, N.Y. City, 1922-24, dir. relationships, 1924-29, nat. director edn., 1930 to 1944, dir. Division of Relationships, 1944-52; mgr. Mountain States Nat. Sch. and Library Divs., The Grolier Soc., Inc. from 1952. Chairman Co-ordinating Council of Nature Activities. Member advisory board and chairman committee on visual edn. Inst. of Oral and Visual Edn. Cons. Econ. and Social Council, U.N. Mem. N.E.A., Religious Edn. Assn., Phi Delta Kappa, Alpha Phi Omega (co-founder, mem. exec. bd., 1926-48). Rep. Meth. Rotarian (dir. N.Y. Rotary, 1938-40, v.p. 1940-41, pres. 1942-43), Pres. Strathmore Assn. of Scarsdale, 1941-42; chmn. Labor Relationships Com. Nat. Republican Club, 1945-46. Editor: Principles of Scoutmastership, 1929. Author publs. relating to Boy Scouts field; contbr. to ednl. and religious publs. Home: Tujunga, Calif.

WYLER, WILLIAM, motion picture director, producer; b. Mulhouse, France, July 1, 1902; s. Leopold and Melanie (Auerbach) W.; educated in schools at Mulhouse to 1918;

student Ecole Superieure de Commerce, Lausanne, Switzerland, 1919, Conservatory of Music, Paris, 1920; m. Margaret Sullavan, 1934 (div. 1936); m. Margaret Tallichet, Oct. 23, 1938; children—Catherine Leonie, Judith Margaret, Melanie, David. Commd. maj. U.S. Army Air Forces, June 17, 1942. Awarded Air Medal, in European Theatre of Operations, June 7, 1943, Legion of Merit, 1945. Recipient Acad. of Motion Picture Arts and Sciences award for direction Mrs. Miniver, 1943, for direction The Years of Our Lives, 1947, Acad. award for direction of Ben Hur, 1959; D.W. Griffith award Dirs. Guild; Irving Thalberg award; others. Mem. Am. Vets. Com., Air Force Assn., Screen Directors Guild, Acad. of Motion Picture Arts and Sciences. Democrat. Jewish religion. Clubs: Hillcrest; Sun Valley Ski. Dir. notable motion pictures, including: The Little Foxes; Mrs. Miniver; The Best Years of Our Lives; The Heiress, 1948; Dead End, Jezebel, Wuthering Heights, Detective Story, 1951; Roman Holiday; The Desperate Hours, 1955; Friendly Persuasion, 1956; The Big Country, 1957; Ben Hur, 1958; The Children's Hour, 1962; The Collector, 1964; How to Steal a Million, 1965; Funny Girl 1968; The Liberation of L.B. Jones, 1970. Decorated Chevalier de la Legion d'Honneur; Star Solidarity; Order Merit (Italy); honored Directors Retrospective, U.S. Film Festival, 1972. Author: (with Axel Madsen) William Wyler, 1973. Home: Beverly Hills, Calif. Died July 29, 1981.*

WYLIE, TURRELL VERL, educator; b. Durango, Colo., Aug. 20, 1927; s. Vernon Glenn and Myrtle Lucy (Davis) W.; m. Sharrie Louise Stevenson, July 31, 1969. B.A., U. Wash., 1952, Ph.D., 1958. Mem. faculty U. Wash., Seattle, 1958-84; prof. Tibetan studies, 1968-84, chmn. dept., 1969-72. Author: The Geography of Tibet, 1962; Contbr. articles to profl. jours. Served with AUS, 1946-47. Ford Found. fellow, 1955-57; Rockefeller Found. grantee, 1960-63; Am. Council Learned Socs. fellow, 1973-74. Mem. Assn. Asian Studies, Am. Oriental Soc., Tibet Soc. Home: Seattle, Wash. Died Aug. 25, 1984.

WYMAN, PHILIP, piano mfr.; b. Fitchburg, Mass., June 2, 1889; s. Alfred A. and Flora (Wright) W.; B.A., Harvard, 1910, H.H.D., Cincinnati Coll. Conservatory Music, 1960; m. Frances Smith, Sept. 1914 (div.); m. 2d, Frances Perin, August, 1935. Vice pres. Baldwin Piano Co., Cin., 1954-62, vice chmn. bd., 1962-64, hon. chmn., from 1964; v.p. Coll. Conservatory of Music of Cin., 1955-57, trustee emeritus, 1957-62, past chairman board; v.p. Cincinnati Music Festival Assn., 1948-60; mem. exec. com. Cin. Summer Opera, from 1956, chmn. exec. com., 1961-66. Dir. Brand Names Found., 1956-57. Served from lt. to capt., Signal Corps, U.S. Army, 1917-19. Clubs: Commonwealth, Garret, Queen City, Camargo, Cincinnati Country, Harvard (Cin.); Mill Reef (Antigua, B.W.I.): Bath (Miami Beach, Fla.). Home: Cincinnati, OH. †

YADIN, RAV-ALOOF YIGAEL, archeologist; b. 1917; M.A., Ph.D., Hebrew U., Jerusalem. Chief. gen. staff br. Hagana Hdqrs., 1947; chief operations, gen. staff, Israel Defense Forces, 1948; chief gen. staff br., 1949, chief staff, 1949-52; archeol. research fellow Hebrew U., 1953-54, lectr. archeology, 1955-59, asso. prof., 1959-63, prof., 1963-84. Author: The Scroll of the War of the Sons of Light against the Sons of Darkness, 1955; The Message of the Scrolls, 1957; (with N. Avigad) A Genesis Apocryphon, 1958; Hazor I: The First Season of Excavations; Hazor II: Second Season; Hazor III, 1961; The Art of Warfare in Biblical Lands, Finds in the Bar-Kochba Caves, 1963; The Ben Siran Scroll from Masada, 1965; Masada, Herod's Fortress and Zealots Last Stand, 1966. Address: Jerusalem, Israel. Died June 28, 1984.

YAMAOKA, GEORGE, lawyer; b. Seattle, Jan. 26, 1903; s. Ototaka and Jhoko (Watanabe) Y.; student U. Wash., 1921-24; J.D., Georgetown U., 1928; m. Henriette d'Auriac, Mar. 18, 1933; 1 dau., Colette Miyoko (Mrs. Henry Sonderegger). With Japanese Govt. Commn., Phila. Sesquicentennial Expn., 1926; adviser Japanese Consulate Gen., 1928-29, Japanese del. London Naval Conf., 1929-30; admitted to N.Y. bar, 1931, Japanese bar, 1949; practice in N.Y.C., from 1931, Tokyo from 1949; assoc. firm. Hunt, Hill & Betts, 1930-40, partner, 1940-56; sr. partner Hill Betts & Nash, 1956 60, sr. partner Hill, Betts, Yamaoka & Logan, Tokyo, 1956-60, Hill, Betts, Yamaoka, Freehill & Longcope, 1960-70, Hill, Betts & Nash, from 1970. Chmn. bd. Yasuda Fire & Marine Ins. Co.; dir. Ehrenreich Photo Optical Industries, Inc.; sec., dir. Bank Tokyo Trust Co., N.Y.C. Okura & Co. (Am.), Inc., Jiji Press (N.Y.) Ltd., 24 Gramercy Park, Inc. Chmn. Am. Def. Supreme Comdr. Allied Powers Internat. Mil. Tribunal Far East, 1946-49; mem. adv. panel internat. law U.S. State Dept., 1972-74. Decorated 3d Order Sacred Treasure Japanese Govt., 1968. Mem. Am., Fed., N.Y., 1st (Tokyo) bar assns., Assn. Bar City N.Y., N.Y. County Lawyers Assn., Consular Law Soc. (pres.-elect), Am. Fgn. Law Assn., Internat. Law Assn., Maritime Law Assn. U.S., Japanese C. of C. (dir.), Japan Soc. N.Y. (hon. dir.), Japanese Am. Assn. N.Y. (hon. pres.). Clubs: Paris Am. (sec.); Marco Polo, Downtown Athletic, World Trade Center (adv. bd.), Nippon (N.Y.C.); American (Tokyo); Hodogaya (Japan) Country; Kasumigaseki (Japan) Country. Home: New York, N.Y. Died Nov. 19, 1981.

YARDUMIAN, RICHARD, composer; b. Phila., Apr. 5, 1917; s. Haig Y. and Lucia (Atamian) Y.; m. Ruth Elsie Seckelmann, Jan. 9, 1937; children—Vahaan, Vartan (dec.), Miryam, Aram (dec.), Sarah (dec.), Nishan, Rebekah, Rachel, Esther Marie, Dara, Anahid, Mira-Estelle, Vera Renata. Student piano with George F. Boyle, student conducting with Pierre Monteaux, student harmony and counterpoint with William F. Happich, student harmony and counterpoint with H. Alexander Matthews; D. Sacred Music, Maryville Coll. ((hon.)), 1972; Mus.D. (hon.), Widener Coll., 1978. Tchr. advanced piano; pres. bd. dirs. The Lord's New Ch., Bryn Athyn, Pa., 1957-79, v.p., 1979-85, music dir., 1939-85; Bd. dirs. Phila. Chamber Orch.; co-founder, bd. dirs. Chamber Symphony of Phila., 1965; trustee Philharmonia Orch.; trustee, v.p. Grand Teton Music Festival. Composer: Three Preludes for Piano, 1936, 39, 44, Armenian Suite, 1937, Symphonic Suite, 1939, Three Pictographs for Orch., 1941, Danse for Piano, 1942, Desolate City, 1944, Prelude and Chorale for Piano, 1944, Chromatic Sonata for Piano, 1946, Psalm 130, 1947, Monologue for Solo Violin, 1947, Violin Concerto, 1949, middle movement, 1960; Epigram: William M. Kincaid for flute and strings, commd. by William Kincaid, 1951, String Quartet No. 1, commd. by Phila. String Quartet, 1955, Cantus Animae et Cordis for string orch., 1955, Passacaglia, Recitatives & Fugue for piano and orch., commd. by Rudolf Firkusny, 1957, Chorale-Prelude on Veni Sancte Spiritus (chamber orchestra), 1958, Symphony No. 1, commd. Eugene Ormandy, 1961, Create in Me, anthem commd. Princeton Theol. Sem. for Sesquicentennial, 1962, Symphony No. 2, Psalms for contralto and orch., 1964, Magnificat for Women's Voices, commd. by Hollins Coll., 1965; for chamber orchestra Come, Creator Spirit (mass in English), commd. Fordham U. for 125th anniversary, 1966; oratorio Abraham, commd. by Maryville Coll. for Sesquicentennial, 1971; Chorales, composed for The Lord's New Ch., 1980-85, Four Chorale-Preludes for Organ, 1976, Two Chorale-Preludes for Orchestra: Jesu, meine Freude, Nun komm der Heiden Heiland, 1978, To Mary in Heaven; poem by Robert Burns Voice and Piano, 1952, Voice and Orch., 1978; Ee Kerezman (Resurrection), Chorale-Prelude for Orch.; recs. for, Columbia, RCA, EMI, HNH, CRI, Varese-Sarabande; Contbr. to: Music Jour. Served with inf. U.S. Army, World War II. Recipient Edward B. Benjamin restful music award, 1958; Eugene Ormandy Commn. award, 1961; Composer award Lancaster Symphony, 1975; Gold medal award for excellence Armenian Bicentennial Commemoration Com., 1976. Mem. ASCAP, Phila. Mus. Soc., Mus. Fund Soc. Home: Bryn Athyn, Pa. Died Aug. 15, 1985.

YARGER, ORVAL FRANCIS, government official; b. Paris, Ill., Oct. 12, 1908; s. Boyd Lee and Mary (Lanigan) Y.; B.Ed., Ill. State U., 1932; postgrad. U. Ill., 1933-34; M.B.A., Northwestern U., 1935; m. Rosie Jepsen Rasmussen, Aug. 13, 1936; children—Orval Jens, Williams Carl. Partner, finance mgr. The Co-Op Bookstore, Normal, Ill., 1933-80; instr. bus. adminstrn. Central Y Coll., Chgo., 1936-39; spl. agt. FBI, Washington, 1941-49; intelligence officer CIA, various fgn. locations, 1950-54; dir. inspections, insp. in charge AID, Dept. State, various U.S., fgn. locations, from 1954, also dir. comml. fishing and transport Europe, Africa, Cobrecaf Corp., Concarneau, France, 1961-80; partner with Andre Auger & Consorts, LaRochelle, France, 1960-80. Mem. Ex-FBI Agts. Soc. Home: Normal IL

YATES, OTIS WEBSTER, clergyman, educator; b. Morrisville, N.C., May 23, 1888; s. Joseph and Ardelaine Frances (Scott) Y.; grad. high sch., Cary, N.C., 1910; A.B., Wake Forest (N.C.) Coll., 1914; Th. M., Southern Bapt. Theol. Sem., 1917; m. Margaret Elizabeth Culley, Oct. 1, 1917; children—Otis Webster, Anne Culley, Margaret Elizabeth. Head of dept. of Bible and Greek, Bethel Coll., Russellville, Ky., from 1918, also engaged in pastoral work in surrounding villages and country, dean of coll., 1920-31, acting pres. 1927-29, pres., 1930-31. Democrat. Baptist. Rotarian. Home: Russellville, Ky. Deceased.

YATMAN, ELLIS LAURIE, lawyer; b. Dedham, Mass., June 17, 1888; s. James Octavius and Martha Ellen (Laurie) Y.; A.B., Brown U., 1911; LL.B., Harvard, 1915; m. Marion Fay, Oct. 4, 1919; 1 son, Thomas Laurie. Admitted to R.I. bar, 1916, Mass. bar, 1947, also fed. cts.; asst. city solicitor, Providence, 1919-28; judge probate ct., Providence, 1928-35; mem. firm Chace and Yatman, Providence, 1936-71; chmn. bd. Case & Risley Press Paper, Inc., from 1962. Trustee Providence YWCA, 1932-40; bd. dirs. Home for the Aged, Providence. Mem. Am., R.I. (pres. 1959-60, editor-in-chief jour. 1955-57, asso. editor 1957-63) bar assns., Am. Law Inst., Am. Judicature Soc., Phi Beta Kappa, Delta Upsilon. Conglist. Mason (32). Home: Providence, R.I. †

YENTER, RAYMOND A., army officer; b. Iowa, Aug. 17, 1887; commd. capt. Cav., Nat. Guard of Iowa, 1915 and inducted into Fed. service for Mexican border crisis, 1916-17; commd. maj. Cav. Organized Res., 1920; capt. Cav. Iowa Nat. Guard, 1921, and advanced to brig. gen. of the line, Mar. 1936; entered Fed. service, Feb. 1941, as comdr. 75th Field Arty. Brigade, Camp Forest, Tenn. Deceased.

YINGLING, HAL CHARLES, coll. prof.; born Tiffin, O., Sept. 20, 1890; s. Louis Wright and Ella (Brenneman) Y.; B.S., Heidelberg Coll., Tiffin, 1910; M.S., Ohio State U., 1916, grad. student summers 1933-38; Ph.D., 1942; m. Delia Hoppes, Sept. 12, 1917; children—Mavis Aileen, Hal Charles, Neville Maxine. Instr. high sch., Old Fort, O., 1911-12, Massillon, 1912-14; asst. prof. entomology, Tex. Agrl. and Mech. Coll., 1916-19; prof. of biology, Augustana Coll., from 1919. Mem. Genetics of America, Am. Assn. Univ. Profs., A.A.A.S., Sigma Xi. Republican. Presbyterian. †

YOAKAM, GERALD ALAN, educator, author; b. Eagle Grove, Ia., Nov. 18, 1887; s. Eugene George and Olive Louisa (Mason) Y.; A.B., U. of Iowa, 1910, A.M., 1919, Ph.D., 1922; m. Helen Marie Swain, Aug. 2, 1911; children—Barbara Jeane, Richard David. Prin. supt. and county supt. schs. in Iowa, 1910-18; prin. U. of Ia. Elementary Sch., 1919-20; dir. teacher training State Teachers Coll., Kearney, Neb., 1920-23; prof. edn. and head dept. elementary edn., U. of Pittsburgh, 1923-32, prof. edn. and dir. of courses from 1932. President International Council for the Improvement of Reading Instruction, 1950-52; dir. reading conferences U. Pitts. from 1940. Member N.E.A., National Society for Study of Edn., Am. Assn. U. Profs., Nat. Council on Research in English (pres. 1948), Am. Assn. Sch. Adminstrs., A.A.A.S., Pa. Edn. Assn., Phi Kappa Phi, Phi Delta Kappa. Meth. Clubs: Edgewood Country, Authors, Faculty. Author or co-author books relating to field. Asso. editor Journal Educational Research; cons. editor American Education Press; mem. Yearbook Com. Nat. Soc. of Edn., 36th Yearbook, Part I, 1936; National Council on Research in Elementary School English, 1940. Home: Pittsburgh, Pa. †

YOCHELSON, LEON, physician; b. Buffalo, July 23, 1917; m. Ruth E. Jolley, Sept. 6, 1942; children—David, Roger, Deborah. B.A. in Psychology magna cum laude, U. Buffalo, 1938, M.D., 1942. Diplomate Am. Med. Bd. Examiners, Am. Bd. Psychiatry and Neurology (psychiatry). Med. officer St. Elizabeth's Hosp., Washington, 1942-43, 46-48; clin. prof. psychiatry George Washington U. Sch. Medicine, 1949-59, prof., 1959-82, chmn. dept., 1959-70; tng. analyst Washington Psychoanalytic Inst., 1958-82; chmn. Psychiat. Inst. of Washington, Psychiat. Inst. Found., Psychiat. Insts. Am.; pres. med. staff Springwood-At-Leesberg Hosp.; guest lectr. Cath. U. Am., St. Johns U. (Minn.); cons. to VA, HEW, NIMH; chmn. com. on psychiat. hosps. Am. Fedn. Hosps., 1974-82, v.p., 1976-82; dir. Nat. Commn. on Confidentiality Health Records, 1976-82. Contbr. articles to profl. jours. Served to maj. M.C. AUS, 1943-46. Fellow Am. Psychiat. Assn., Am. Coll. Psychiatrists, Am. Coll. Psychoanalysts (founding); mem. Am. Psychoanalytical Assn., Washington Psychiat. Soc. (sec., pres.), Washington Psychoanalytic Soc., Med. Soc. D.C. (chmn. mental health com., mem. ethics com.), Profl. Assos. of Psychiat. Inst. (chmn.), Nat. Assn. Pvt. Psychiat. Hosps. (chmn. com. on allied orgns.), Med. Soc. St. Elizabeth's Hosp. (past pres.), Alpha Omega Alpha. Home: Washington, D.C. Dec. June 22, 1982.

YOCOM, HARRY BARCLAY, prof. zoology; b. Pennsville, Ohio, July 12, 1888; s. Franklin R. and Elizabeth S. (Penrose) Y.; A.B., Oberlin Coll., 1912; A.M., U. of Calif., 1916, Ph.D., 1918; m. Florence Torrey, Aug. 18, 1917 (died Feb. 1920); 1 dau., Elizabeth Madeline (Mrs. Dean R. Barlow); m. 2d, Catherine W. Beckley, Sept. 19, 1921. Instr. in zoology, Wabash Coll., 1912-13, Kan. State Agrl. Coll., 1913-15; grad. asst., U. of Calif., 1915-17; prof. zoology, Washburn Coll., 1917-18; asst. prof. zoology, Coll. City of N.Y., 1919-20; asst. prof. zoology, U. Oreg., 1920-25; asso. prof., 1925-26, prof., 1926-47, head of department, 1943-45, professor emeritus, from January 1, 1947; associate director Institute Marine Biology, 1942-47. Served as 1st lt., Sanitary Corps, U.S. Army, during World War I. Fellow A.A.A.S.; mem. Western Soc. Naturalists, Oreg. Acad. Science, Am. Assn. Univ. Profs., Sigma XI, Phi Sigma. Clubs: U. of Oreg. Faculty, Eugene Round Table. Home: Eugene, Oreg. Deceased.

YODER, FRED ROY, ret. educator; b. nr. Hickory, N.C., Dec. 12, 1888; s. Colin M. and Emma C. Yoder; A.B., Lenoir Rhyne Coll., Hickory, N.C., 1910, LL.D., 1941; A.M., U. N.C., 1915; student U. Mo., 1915-17, U. London, 1919; Ph.D., U. Wis., 1923; m. Wilma Porter, June 22, 1923; children—Hubert, Thomas, Elaine. Prin. high sch. N.C., 1910-14; instr. econs. and sociology La. State U., 1917; instr. sociology U. Mo., 1919-20; asst. prof. agrl. econs. and rural sociology State U. of Wash., 1920-21; asso. prof. agrl. econs. N.C. State U., 1921-22; with State U. Wash., 1923-54, prof. sociology and chmn. dept., 1923-47; prof. sociology Lewis and Clark Coll., 1955-57; prof. sociology and econs. Western Ky. State U., 1957-58; prof., chmn. dept. social scis. Campbellsville (Ky.) Coll., 1958-68, chmn. dept. bus. and econs., 1969-71. Served with U.S. Army, 1918-19; overseas, France, Germany; 1st lt. AAC, 1943-44. Mem. Am. So., Rural sociol. socs., Am. Country Life Assn., Am. Farm Econ. Assn., Am. Econ. Assn., Am. Polit. Sci. Assn., Am. Hist. Soc., Nat. Council Social Studies, So. Hist. Soc., So. Econ. Assn., So. Polit. Sci. Assn. Nat. Grange, Loyal Order of Moose, Democrat. Conglist. Rotarian. Author: Introduction to Agricultural Economics, 1929, rev. edit., 1938; Introductory Sociology, 1944; History of the Yoder Family in North Carolina, 1970; numerous monographs and articles. Home: Pullman, WA. †

YOHE, CURTIS MILLER, railway official; b. Connellsville, Pa., Sept. 22, 1887; s. James Buchanan and Mary Margaret (Sykes) Y.; LL.B., Cornell U., 1910; m. Elsie May Close, Dec. 15, 1914; children—Curtis Miller (dec.), Barbara Close, Mary Ann, Elsie May, Curtis Miller, III.

Purchasing agt. Pittsburgh & Lake Erie R.R., 1921-28, v.p., 1929-52, pres. since 1952; asst. to pres. N.Y.C. Lines, 1928-29; officer and dir. various railroads and subsidiary properties; Pitts. Forgings. Co., Flannery Mfg. Co., dir. Mellon Nat. Bank & Trust Co. Trustee Dollar Savs. Bank. Mem. Carnegie Hero Fund Commn. Mem. Zeta Psi. Presbyterian. Clubs: Duquesne, Rolling Rock Country, Fox Chapel Golf. Home: Pittsburgh, Pa. Deceased.†

YOLLES, TAMARATH KNIGIN, (MRS. STANLEY FAUSST YOLLES) physician; b. Bklyn., Feb. 27, 1919; d. Max H. and Bessie (Krokoff) Knigin; m. Stanley Fausst Yolles, Oct. 10, 1942; children—Melanie A., Jennifer C. A.B., Bklyn. Coll., 1939; M.D., N.Y. U., 1951. Research asst. U. Minn., St. Paul, 1939-40; asst. parasitologist Army Med. Sch., Walter Reed Army Med. Ctr., Washington, 1941; parasitologist C.E. U.S. Army, Brit. Guiana, 1941-43; asso. dir. Area Lab. Trinidad Sector and Base Command, 1943-45; parasitologist NRC Schistosomiasis Project, N.Y. U. Coll. Medicine, 1946-47; intern USPHS Hosp., S.I., N.Y., 1951-52; commd. surgeon USPHS, 1954, advanced through grades to asst. surgeon gen. (rear adm.), 1970; dep. chief medicine Public Health Service Outpatient Clinic, Washington, 1959-61, health maintenance officer Office Surgeon Gen., 1961-64; dir. div. commd. personnel ops. Office Sec. HEW, Rockville, Md., 1968-71; asst. adminstr. for orgn. devel. Health Services and Mental Health Adminstrn., Rockville, 1971-72, cons. to adminstr., 1972-73; prof. clin. community medicine Sch. Medicine, SUNY, Stony Brook, 1972-73, prof. community medicine, 1973-85, asso. dean continuing med. edn., 1977-85; mem. Nat. Acad. Sci.-NRC Commn. Emergency Med. Services, 1976-85; chmn. Regional Emergency Med. Service Council, 1976-85. Decorated medal of Freedom, 1947. Mem. AMA (commn. emergency med. services, governing council sect. on med. schs.), Am. Soc. Parasitologists, Am. Trauma Soc., Am. Public Health Assn., Suffolk Heart Assn. (dir.), Am. Coll. Emergency Physicians, Am. Assn. Emergency Physicians, Suffolk County Acad. Medicine (trustee), Suffolk County Med. Soc. (dir.), Traffic Safety Bd. (Chmn.), Am. Soc. Tropical Medicine, Alpha Omega Alpha. Home: Stony Brook, N.Y. Died July 29, 1985.

YORK, JOHN Y., JR., air force officer; b. Yorkville, Wayne County, W.Va., Apr. 10, 1890; s. James Franklin and Dora (Billups) Y.; B.S., W.Va. Univ., 1913; J.D., U. of Mich., 1916; grad. Army Indsl. Coll., 1927; M.B.A., Harvard Grad. Sch. Bus. Adminstrn., 1929; grad. Army War Coll., 1938; m. Ida Lee Harris, Dec. 6, 1917; children—Elizabeth Anne, Ida Louise, Isla Jean. Began legal practice, 1916; entered army, 1917 as 2d lt. Air Corps; commd. regular army, 1920; promoted through grades to major gen., 1944. Mem. Beta Theta Pi. Club: Army and Navy Country (Washington). Home: Arlington, Va. †

YOST, CHARLES WOODRUFF, diplomat; b. Watertown, N.Y., Nov. 6, 1907; s. Nicholas Doxtater and Gertrude (Cooper) Y.; m. Irena Oldakowska, Sept. 8, 1934; children—Nicholas, Casimir, Felicity. Grad., Hotchkiss Sch., 1924; A.B., Princeton, 1928; student, U. Paris, 1928-29; LL.D., St. Lawrence U., Princeton, Hamilton Coll.; Dr. Social Sci., U. Louisville. Entered fgn. service, 1930, served as vice consul, Alexandria, 1931-32, Warsaw, 1932-33, free-lance journalist, 1933-35; with Dept. State, 1935-45; asst. to chmn. U.S. delegation San Francisco Conf., 1945; sec. gen. U.S. delegation Potsdam Conf., 1945; charge d'affaires U.S. Legation, Bangkok, 1945-46; polit. adviser U.S. delegation UN Gen. Assembly, 1946; 1st sec. Am. embassy, Prague, 1947; counselor Am. legation, Vienna, 1947-49; spl. asst. ambassador-at-large Council Fgn. Ministers and UN Gen. Assembly, 1949; dir. Office Eastern European Affairs, Dept. State, 1949-50; minister-counselor Am. embassy, Athens, Greece, 1950-53, dep. high commr. to, Austria, 1953-54, U.S. minister to, Kingdom of Laos, 1954-55, rank of ambassador, 1955-56; minister Am. embassy, Paris, 1956-58, U.S. ambassador to, Syria, 1958, Morocco 1958-61; U.S. dep. rep. to UN, 1961-66; sr. fellow Council Fgn. Relations, N.Y.C., 1966-69; chief U.S. rep. to UN, 1969-71; distinguished lectr. Sch. Internat. Affairs Columbia; also counselor UN Assn., 1971-73; pres. Nat. Com. on U.S.-China Relations, 1973-75; sr. fellow Brookings Instn., 1975; spl. advisor Aspen Inst., 1976-81. Author: The Age of Triumph and Frustration: Modern Dialogues, 1964, The Insecurity of Nations; International Relations in the Twentieth Century, 1968, The Conduct and Misconduct of Foreign Affairs, 1972, History and Memory, 1980. Recipient Rockefeller Pub. Service award, 1964. Mem. Council Fgn. Relations, AAAS. Died May 22, 1981.

YOST, HENRY THOMAS, JR., educator; b. Balt., Jan. 22, 1925; s. Henry Thomas and Martha (Minsker) Y.; B.A., John Hopkins, 1947, Ph.D., 1951; M.A. (hon.), Amherst Coll., 1965; m. Martha Jean Thomas, June 12, 1948; 1 dau., Brenna Duncan. Mem. faculty Amherst Coll., 1951-81, prof. biology, 1965-81, Rufus Tyler Lincoln prof., 1976-81, chmn. com. ednl. policy, 1961-62. Mem. exec. com. Mass. PAX, 1960-81; sci. adv. bd. Consumers Union, 1959-81. Pres., Western Mass. Health Planning Council, Valley Health Plan. Served with AUS, 1943-46. Adam T. Bruce fellow Johns Hopkins, 1950-51; fellow Chester Beatty Research Inst., London, Eng., 1962-63, 69-70. Fellow A.A.A.S.; mem. N.Y. Acad. Scis., Radiation Research Soc., AAUP, (nat. council 1965-66, 68-71, mem. com. profl. ethics, 1965-68, mem. com. teaching, research and publ. 1968-73, chmn. com. on relations with fed. and state govts. 1973-81), Genetic Soc. Am., Soc. Devel. Biol. Bot. Soc. Am. Author: Cellular Physiology, 1972; (with W.M. Hexter) The Science of Genetics, 1976; also articles in field. Home: Amherst, Mass. Died Nov. 15, 1981.

YOUNG, ARIBERT LEE, lawyer; b. Terre Haute, Ind., Sept. 8, 1923; s. John D. and Birdie J. (Peak) Y.; student Okla. A. and M. U., 1942-43, Purdue U., 1946-47; LL.B., Ind. U., 1950; m. Mabel A. Cook, Sept. 7, 1946; children—Richard Alan, Deborah Jean, Douglas Edward. Admitted to Ind. bar, 1950, Supreme Ct. U.S., 7th Circuit Ct. of Appeals, Supreme Ct. Ind.; practiced in Indpls., 1950-80; sr. partner Kightlinger, Young, Gray & DeTrude; pres. Meridian Parking, Inc. Served with AC, USNR, 1942-46. Mem. Am., Ind., Indpls. bar assns., Fedn. Ins. Counsel (sec.-treas., dir.), Lawyers-Pilots Bar Assn., Phi Delta Phi. Methodist. Club: Columbia (Indpls.). Contbr. articles to profl. jours. Home: Indianapolis, Ind. Died June 5, 1980.

YOUNG, CHARLES J(ACOB), electronic research; b. Cambridge, Mass., Dec. 17, 1899; s. Owen D. and Josephine (Edmonds) Y.; A.B., Harvard, 1921; m. Eleanor L. Whitman, 1923; children—John Peter, David Whitman; m. 2d. Esther M. Christensen, 1929; children—Neils Owen, Esther Van Horne. Radio engr. Gen. Electric Co., Schenectady, N.Y., 1923-29; electronic development engr. RCA Mfg. Co., Camden, N.J., 1929-42; asso. lab. dir. RCA Labs., Princeton, 1942-1984. Recipient Modern Pioneer award N.A.M., 1946. Fellow Inst. Radio Engrs., Sigma Xi. Home: Princeton, N.J. Died Oct. 2, 1984.

YOUNG, DEFORREST EUGENE, utilities company executive; b. Joplin, Mo., Mar. 29, 1920; s. Oral S. and Blanche M. (Trent) Y.; m. Virginia Lee Carter, June 1, 1942; children—Stephen K., Bradley E. Student, Mo. So. Coll., 1938-40. Bookkeeper The Gas Service Co., Joplin, Mo., 1940-42, asst. chief clk., 1947-50, office mgr., 1950-59, mgr. date processing, 1959-67, asst. treas., 1967-70, asst. sec., 1969-70, treas., 1970-82, v.p., 1978-82; acct. United Zinc Smelting Corp., Joplin, 1942-47. Mem. Fin. Execs. Inst. Home: Kansas City, Mo. Dec. Feb. 16, 1982.

YOUNG, ELIZABETH (MARY HAWORTH), columnist; b. (Mary Elizabeth Reardon) Riverside, Clinton County, O.; d. John Francis and Anne (Brennan) Reardon; ed. grade and high schs.; special student, Wilmington (O.) Coll., 1924-26; m. William Howard Young, Mar. 13, 1930 (died Nov. 23, 1948); children—Mary Elizabeth, Amelia Ann. Office girl, Wilmington (O.) Daily News-Journal, 1923-24, news reporter, 1924-26; editor, The Community News, weekly paper, Columbus, Ohio, 1926-28; advertising solicitor, Ohio State Journal, 1925-29; advertising solicitor, The Lima (Ohio) Daily News, 1929-30; feature writer, The Washington (D.C.) Post, 1933-34, assistant woman's editor, columnist, 1934-44; now syndicated writer on human relations for The Washington Post and King Features. Received Annual Americanism award, 1943, for contribution to community edn. in better citizenship, by Am. Legion Post No. 46 (Washington). Mem. Women's Nat. Press Club, Am. Newspaper Womens Club, Theta Sigma Phi (hon.), Arts Club of Washington. Home: Washington, D.C. Died Nov. 1, 1981.

YOUNG, FERDINAND HENRY, business exec.; born Brooklyn, June 2, 1889; s. Henry Young and Caroline (Stein) Y.; m. Ann Wolff, Apr. 30, 1919; children—Bernice, Elvira, Marion, Virginia. Vice pres. and dir. in charge prodn., Abbott Labs., North Chicago; chmn. bd. Abbott Labs. Export Co., Chicago, Abbott Labs. Internat. Co.; dir. Abbott Labs., Ltd., Canada. Home: Lake Bluff, Ill. †

YOUNG, GEORGE HOOPER, univ. dean; b. Elkhorn, Wis., Dec. 3, 1915; s. J. Howard and Winifred (Hooper) Y.; m. Lillian Latham, June 16, 1941. B.A., U. Wis., 1938, LL.B., 1941. Bar: Wis. bar 1941. Practiced with firm Stroud, Stebbins, Wingert & Young, Madison, 1941-50; asso. prof. law U. Wis., 1950, prof., from 1953, dean Law Sch., 1957-68. Contbr. articles to legal publs. Mem. Am. Law Inst., Am., Wis., Dane County bar assns., Am. Judicature Soc., Order of Coif, Phi Eta Sigma, Phi Delta Phi. Home: Madison, Wis.

YOUNG, H. ALBERT, lawyer; b. Kiev, Russia, May 30, 1904; came to U.S., 1905, naturalized, 1926; s. Harry and Rose (Morsoff) Y.; m. Ann Blank, Mar. 22, 1931; children—Ronell (Mrs. William Douglass), Stuart B., H. Alan. B.A., U. Del., 1926; J.D., U. Pa., 1929. Bar: Del. bar 1929, U.S. Dist. Ct 1933, 3d Cirucit Ct. U.S 1933, Supreme Ct. U.S 1944. Sr. ptnr. firm Young, Conaway, Stargatt & Taylor, Wilmington, Del., 1959-82; atty. gen., Del., 1951-55; atty. for Del. Legislature, 1935-37, Del. State Republican Com., 1965-70; chmn. Com. Adoption Uniform Comml. Code, 1964-70; participant arguments before U.S. Supreme Ct. in segregation cases, 1954; chmn. adv. com. on implementation ABA standards for criminal justice U.S. Supreme Ct., 1973-82; vice chmn. Del. Bd. Bar Examiners. Bd. dirs. Jewish Fedn. Del., Kutz Home for Aged, Jewish Community Center.; Fellow Brandeis U., Hebrew U. Fellow Am. Coll. Trial Lawyers, Internat. Acad. Trial Lawyers (dir. 1965-71), Am. Bar Found.; mem. Am. Law Inst., Del. Bar Assn. (pres. 1961-63), Ill. Bar Assn., ABA (ho. of dels.), Am. Judicature Soc. Jewish. Home: Wilmington, Del. Dec. May 29, 1982.

YOUNG, J. NELSON, lawyer, educator; b. Rossville, Ill., Nov. 13, 1916; s. Jesse Bowman and Lula (Nelson) Y.; m. Zerla Gingerich, Nov. 20, 1940; 1 dau., Marynel. B.S., U. Ill., 1938, J.D., 1942. Bar: Ill. bar 1942, U.S. Supreme Ct. bar 1955; C.P.A., Ill. Assoc. firm McDermott, Will & Emery, Chgo., 1946; asst. prof. law U. Ill., 1946-51, assoc. prof., 1951-53, prof., 1953-81; prof. law U. N.C., Chapel Hill, 1981-85; vis. prof. Harvard U., 1958-59; research staff Ill. Commn. on Revenue, 1963; cons. bank tax study Adv. Commn. Intergovtl. Relations, 1974. Author: (with Nowak and Rotunda) Constitutional Law, 1978, 2d edit., 1983, (with others) CCH Study of Federal Tax Law—Individual Income Tax, 1983, Taxation Business Enterprises, 1983. Served with USNR, 1942-46. Mem. Am. Bar Assn., Ill. Bar Assn., Am. Law Inst., Am. Inst. C.P.A.'s, Am. Acctg. Assn., Internat. Fiscal Assn., Ill. C.P.A. Soc. Home: Chapel Hill, N.C. Died June 17, 1985.

YOUNG, MILTON R., former U.S. senator; b. Berlin, N.D., Dec. 6, 1897; s. John Young and Rachel (Zimmerman) Y.; m. Patricia M. Byrne, Dec. 27, 1969. Student, N.D. State U., Graceland Coll. Mem. N.D. Ho. of Reps., 1933-34; mem. N.D. Senate, 1935-45, U.S. Senate from N.D., 1945-81. Republican. Home: La Moure, N.D. Dec. May 31, 1983.

YOUNG, RALPH AUBREY, economist; b. Cheyenne, Wyo., June 12, 1901; s. Benjamin and Virginia (Crawford) Y.; A.B., Ohio Wesleyan U., 1923, LL.D., 1969; M.B.A., Northwestern U., 1925; Ph.D., U. Pa., 1930; m. Louise Merwin, Sept. 5, 1925; children—Merwin Crawford, Anne Alexandra, Ralph Aubrey. Instr. U. Pa., 1925-28; research staff Nat. Indsl. Conf. Bd., 1928-29, 32-34; spl. bus. analyst Dept. of Commerce, 1929-30; Social Sci. Research Council fellow, 1930-31; asst. prof. U. Pa., 1931-37, assoc. prof., 1937-40, prof., 1940-45; research staff and dir. financial research program, Nat. Bur. Econ. Research, 1938-45; asst. dir. div. research and statistics Bd. Govs. Fed. Res. System, 1946-47, asso. dir., 1947-48, dir., 1948-59, adviser to bd., 1960-65, chmn. com. to review regulatory activities, 1975-76, sec. fed. open market com., 1960-65, dir. bd.'s div. internat. finance, 1961-65; cons. div. central banking services IMF, 1966-76; dir. Independence Sq. Income Securities Fund, Temporary Investment Fund; trustee Trust for Short-Term Fed. Securities; dir. Westchester Corp.; lectr. Geo. Washington U., 1948-62. Mem. research adv. bd. Com. for Econ. Devel., 1944-56, asso. mem., 1956-66; com. on research in finance Nat. Bur. Econ. Research, 1938-58; mem. bd. Nat. Acad. Econs. and Polit. Sci., 1954-60; mem. Conf. Bus. Economists; trustee Joint Council Econ. Edn., 1962-65. Fellow Center for Advanced Study, Wesleyan U., 1968. Fellow Am. Statis. Assn.; mem. Beta Gamma Sigma, Phi Gamma Delta. Meth. Club: Cosmos (Washington). Author numerous books on banking and finance, latest being: Monetary Instruments in the United States: Role of the Federal Reserve System. Home: Washington, D.C. Died Apr. 20, 1980.

YOUNG, RALPH CHILLINGWORTH, chemist; b. Phoenix, N.Y., Oct. 20, 1889; A.B., Syracuse U., 1912, A.M., 1913; Ph.D., Mass. Inst. Tech., 1929. Chemist, U.S. Dept. Agr., 1917-18; instr. chemistry, Syracuse U., 1919-21; with Mass. Inst. Tech. from 1922, as instr., research associate and associate prof. inorganic chemistry. Fellow Am. Acad. Arts and Sciences; mem. Am. Chem. Soc. Address: Arlington, Mass. †

YOUNG, ROY NORTON, cement cons.; born Beloit, Kan., Sept. 15, 1887; s. William Henry and Fannie (Web) Y.; B.S., Kan. State College, 1914; m. Jessie McKinnie, Jan. 21, 1919; children—Estelle, Janet, Barbara. Assistant chemist, draftsman Western States Portland Cement Co., Independence, Kan., 1915-16; chief chemist Sandusky Portland Cement Co., York, Pa., 1917; fellowship, asst. chem. engr., later asso. chem. engr. Nat. Bur. Standards, Washington, 1918-23; asst. chem. engr. Lehigh Portland Cement Co., Allentown, Pa., 1924-31, chem. engr. in charge process, 1931-44, asst. v.p., operating mgr., 1944-46, v.p., operating mgr., 1946-54, cement mfg. cons. Mem. Sigma Tau, Sigma Alpha Epsilon. Republican. Presbyn. Contbr. tech., trade jours. Home: Asheville, N.C. †

YOUNG, SAMUEL ROLLO, ret. railroad exec.; b. Coatesville, Pa., Mar. 3, 1887; s. Samuel Scott and Sallie Pusey (Hammond) Y.; graduate State Normal Sch. (West Chester, Pa.), 1904; grad. Lehigh U. (Bethlehem, Pa.), 1909; m. Cidney Alta Young, Oct. 17, 1912; children—Samuel Richard, Robert George. Civil engr. Consolidation Coal Co., Van Leer, Ky., 1909-10; rodman Sunbury div. Pa. R.R., 1910-12; farmer, Coatesville, Pa., 1912-15; civil engr. Midvale Steel & Ordnance Co., 1915-16; asst. engr. Atlanta & West Point R.R.-The Western Ry. Ala.-Ga. R.R., 1916-17, div. engr., 1918, dist. engr., 1918-20, asst. chief engr., 1920-31, chief engr., 1931-44, asst. gen. mgr., 1944-47, pres. and gen. mgr., 1947-53, pres., chief exec. ofcr., 1953-56; past pres., dir. Augusta Union Sta. Co., Augusta & Summerville R.R., Savannah River Terminal Co.; past chmn. bd. control Atlanta Joint Terminals, ret.; dir Trust Co. of Georgia Assos. Pres. College Park Bd. Edn., 1927-29; mem. Atlanta-Fulton County Joint Planning Bd., 1948-72. Mem. Am. Soc. C.E., Soc. Am. Mil. Engrs., Georgia Engring. Soc., Newcomen Soc., Atlanta Hist. Soc., Pa.-Scotch Irish Soc.,

Alpha Tau Omega. Presbyn. Mason. Clubs: Kiwanis, Capital City (Atlanta). Home: College Park, GA. †

YOUNG, STEPHEN M., lawyer, former U.S. senator; b. May 4, 1889; s. Judge Stephen M. and Belle (Wagner) Y.; LL.B., Western Res U., 1912; M. Civil Law (hon.), Kenyon Coll.; LL.D. (hon.), Central State Coll.; Chubb fellow Yale; Dr. Pub. Service, Rio Grande Coll.; m. Ruby L. Dewley, 1911 (dec. 1952); 2 children; m. Rachel Bell, 1957 (dec. 1982); Admitted to Ohio bar, 1911; asst. pros. atty. Cuyahoga Country, 1917-18, chief criminal pros. atty. Cuyahoga County, 1919-21; mem. Ohio Gen. Assembly, 1913-17; mem. 73d, 74th, 77th, 81st Congresses, Ohio at large; mem. U.S. Senate from Ohio, 1959-71. Mem. Ohio Commn. Unemployment Ins., 1931-32. Served with AUS, World War II; allied mil. gov. Province Reggio Emilia, Italy, 1945; lt. col. Res. Decorated Bronze Star, Purple Heart, Army Commendation ribbon; Order of Crown (Italy). Mem. Cuyahoga County Bar Assn. (past pres.), War Vets. Bar Assn. Cleve. (past pres.). Democrat. Home: Washington, D.C. Dec. Dec. 1, 1984.

YOUNG, WARREN HOWARD, federal judge; b. Chgo., Sept. 9, 1916; s. Elmer Leonard and Clarice Agnes (Anderson) Y.; B.A. in Econs. with honors, Northwestern U., 1938; J.D., Harvard, U., 1941; m. Ruth Ann Haskell, Dec. 16, 1957; children—Rodney, Lauren (Mrs. Ron Speas), Jonathan, Deborah, Gar, Timothy. Admitted to Ill. bar, 1941, V.I. bar, 1950; asso. firm Carney, Crowel & Leibman, Chgo.; sr. partner Young, Isherwood, Carney & Marsh, St. Croix and St. Thomas; U.S. dist. ct. judge Dist. V.I., St. Croix, 1971-80. Pres. V.I. Title & Trust Co., 1950-71, Young-Clark Ins., Ltd., 1952-71, Pentheny Ltd., 1963-71. Chmn. com. fund raising Boy Scouts Am., chmn. bd. trustees; v.p., dir. Coast Guard Alumni Found., 1969-71. Served with USCGR; PTO. Mem. Am., Fed., V.I. bar assns., Am. Judicature Soc., World Peace Through Law Center, Lawyers-Pilots Assn. (charter), Nat. Lawyers Club, Navy League, Internat. Platform Assn. Clubs: St. Croix Tennis, St. Croix Yacht, V.I. Ski Divers, V.I. Soaring, Naui Scuba Diver Home: Christiansted, St Croix. Dec. June 6, 1980.

YOUNG, WILLIAM TANDY, JR., advt. exec.; b. Pine Bluff, Ark., Mar. 11, 1897; s. William Tandy and Eddine (Hudson) Y.; m. Margaret Wilson, 1937 (dec. 1949); m. Francigene Sheridan, Nov.15, 1952; children—William Tandy III, Collier Young Genet, Sheridan. Student, U. Ind. Ret. pres. Leo Burnett Co., Inc., Chgo.; former dir. and part owner Wilson Milk Co., Indpls., pvt. real estate investments, 1963-81; Pres. Arlington Park Jockey Club, Arlington Heights, Ill. Trustee Palm Beach Day Sch. Served with U.S. Army, World War I; brig. gen. USAAF, World War II. Decorated Legion of Merit, Silver Star U.S.; Croix de Guerre France). Clubs: Racquet (Chgo.); Brook (N.Y.C.); Everglades (Palm Beach), Bath and Tennis (Palm Beach). Home: Palm Beach, Fla. Died Sept. 1, 1981.

YUNKERS, ADJA, artist; b. Riga, Latvia, July 15, 1900; s. Karland Adeline (Stahl) Y.; student Leningrad Art Sch., 1914-15, Hamburger Kunstgewerbe Schule, 1920-22; m. Kerstin Bergstrom, Feb. 24, 1946 (div.); m. 2d, Dore Ashton, July 8, 1952; children—Alexandra Louise, Marina. Came to U.S., 1947, naturalized, 1953. One-man shows Gallery Maria Kunde, Hamburg, Germany, 1920, Dresden, Germany, 1924, Copenhagen, Denmark, 1946, Oslo, Norway, 1946, Stockholm, Sweden, 1945-47, New Sch. Social Research, N.Y., 1946, Whitney Mus. Am. Art, 1972, Mass. Inst. Tech., 1973, other large museums U.S.; tchr. cutting and printing wood blocks in color New Sch. Social Research, from 1947, also Parsons Sch. Design; instr. Barnard Coll., N.Y.C.; represented in collections in Germany, Sweden, Norway, Belgium, Holland, France, Switzerland, Italy, N.Y. Pub. Library, Mus. Modern Art. Met. Mus., Bklyn. Mus., Boston Mus. Fine Arts, Fogg Mus., Balt. Mus. Art, others; former teaching staff Cooper Union, N.Y.C.; tchr., guest critic in painting Columbia U., from 1967; mural commn. Syracuse U., 1967; tapestry commn. Stony Brook U., L.I., N.Y. Guggenheim fellow, 1949-50, 54-55; Ford Found. grantee, 1959-60. Recipient Bronze medal Chgo. Art Inst., 1961; Gold medal 2d Norwegian Internat. Print Biennale, Fredrikstad, 1974. Editor, pub. art mag. Creation (Stockholm), 1942-43, Ars, 1942-44, Ars Konstserie, 1944-46, Blanco, 1974. Address: New York, N.Y. Died Dec. 24, 1983.

ZABLOCKI, CLEMENT JOHN, congressman; b. Milw., Nov. 18, 1912; s. Mathew and Mary (Jankowski) Z.; m. Blanche Janic, May 26, 1937 (dec. July 1977); children: Joseph, Jane. Ph.B., Marquette U., 1936, LL.D. (hon.), 1966; LL.D. (hon.), Alverno Coll., 1969, Sogang U., Seoul, Korea, 1974, Jagiellonian U., Cracow, Poland, 1975, U. Notre Dame, 1979. High sch. tchr., 1938-39, organist, choir dir., 1932-48, state senator 3d dist., Wis., 1942-48; mem. 81st-98th Congresses from 4th Wis. Dist., chmn. fgn. affairs com., chmn. subcom. on internat. security and sci. affairs; mem. spl. congl. study mission to West Europe, 1951, South Asia and Far East 1953, Near, Middle and Far East, Southeast Asia and Pacific 1955, chmn. spl. study mission to, Poland, 1963, Southeast Asia and Pacific 1963, Far East, Southeast Asia, India, Pakistan 1965, chmn. Congl. delegation to Poland, 1965, Congl. mem. mission to People's Republic of China, 1974; Congl. adviser UN World Food Conf., Rome, 1974; U.S. del. UN 14th Gen. Assembly, 1959; Congl. adviser U.S. delegation Commn. on Disarmament, 1971-74; mem. Commn. on Orgn. Govt. for Conduct Fgn. Policy; del. Mutual Balance Force Reduction Conf., Vienna, Austria, 1974; mem. Japan-Am. Friendship Commn. Mem. adv. bd. Georgetown U. Center Strategic Studies. Named Alumnus of Yr. Marquette U., 1979. Mem. Cath. Order of Foresters, St. Vincent Conf., Polish Nat. Alliance, Polish Am. Fedn., Polish Assn. Am., Polish Roman Cath. Union, Milw. Musicians Assn., Holy Name Soc. Democrat. Roman Catholic. Clubs: KC, Eagles. Home: Milwaukee, Wis. Dec. Dec. 3, 1983.

ZACK, ALBERT JOSEPH, labor union official; b. Holyoke, Mass., Nov. 22, 1917; s. Charles Sumner and Mary (Crean) Z.; ed. pub. schs., N.J.; m. Jane Lillian Nesworthy, May 27, 1939; children—Linda Jane (Mrs. Keith Tarr-Whelan), Allen Young. News editor Springfield (Mass.) Daily News, 1942-46, radio sta. WSPR, Springfield, 1946-47; pub. relations dir. Ohio CIO Council, Columbus, 1947-52; asst. pub. relations dir. CIO, Washington, 1952-55; asst. pub. relations, dir. AFL-CIO, 1955-57, dir. pub. relations, 1957-80. Democrat. Club: Nat Press (Washington). Home: Washington, D.C. Dec. Oct. 28, 1981.

ZANE, HARRY S., freight traffic mgr.; b. Kansas City, Kan., July 7, 1888; s. Joseph and Carrie Zane; m. Ona Robinson, July 28, 1906; 1 son, Harry S. Entered career in railroad work with C., M., St. Paul & Pacific R.R., advancing through positions of responsibility to be freight traffic mgr. sales and service, Chgo., from 1918. Address: Chicago, Ill. Deceased.

ZARTMAN, LEONARD STORY, lawyer, bus. exec.; b. Rochester, N.Y., Sept. 18, 1926; s. Leonard S. and Eva (Cushman) Z.; A.B., Yale, 1948; LL.B., Columbia, 1953; m. Barbara Jean Flower, Aug. 2, 1969; children—Eve C.; (by previous marriage) Lydia, Sarah G., Nathaniel S., Dana S., Mary W. Admitted to N.Y. bar, 1953; practiced in Rochester, 1953-68; mem. firm. Nixon, Hargrave, Devans & Doyle, 1953-64; atty. Eastman Kodak Co., 1964-68, asst. to gen. counsel, 1970, asst. sec., 1971-73, sec., 1973-82; spl. asst. to Pres. Nixon, 1969; gen. counsel Small Bus. Adminstrn., Washington, 1969-70. Served with USNR, 1944-46; as capt. USMCR, 1950-52. Mem. Am., Monroe County (N.Y.) bar assns. Home: Rochester, N.Y. Died Oct. 9, 1982.

ZATURENSKA, MARYA (MRS. HORACE V. GREGORY), poet, biographer; b. Kiev, Russia, Sept. 12, 1902; d. Abram and Johanna (Lubovska) Zaturensky; brought to U.S., 1910, naturalized, 1914; student (scholar) Valparaiso U., 1921-23, U. Wis. Library Sch., 1925; D.Litt. (hon.), U. Wis., 1977; m. Horace V. Gregory, Aug. 21, 1925; children—Joanna (Mrs. S.H. Zeigler), Patrick Bolton. Recipient Shelley award Poetry Soc. New Eng., 1935; Pulitzer prize in poetry, 1938; Guarantors award Poetry mag., 1941; also others. Author: (poetry) Threshold and Hearth, 1934, Cold Morning Sky, 1937, The Listening Landscape, 1941, The Golden Mirror, 1944, Selected Poems, 1954, Terraces of Light, 1960, Collected Poems, 1966; The Hidden Waterfall, 1974; (with husband) History of American Poetry Since 1900, 1946, The Mentor Books of Religious Poems, 1957, The Crystal Cabinet, 1962, The Silver Swan, 1966; (biography) Christina Rosetti: A Portrait with Background, 1949, rev., 1970; also introduction to poetry vols. Editor: Selected Poems of Christina Rossetti, 1969; Collected Poems of Sara Address: Palisades, N.Y. Teasdale, 1966. Jan. 19, 1982.

ZATZ, SIDNEY ROSS, lawyer; b. Chgo., Mar. 28, 1913; s. Max and Goldie (Rosovich) Z.; Ph.B., U. Chgo., 1933, J.D. cum laude, 1935; m. Shirley R. Meyerovitz, Apr. 19, 1975. Admitted to Ill. bar, 1935, since practiced in Chgo.; ptnr. firm Arvey, Hodes, Costello & Burman, and predecessors, from 1980; dir. Peerless Weighing and Vending Machine Corp. Bd. dirs. Palos Community Hosp. Served as officer USNR, World War II. Mem. Ill., Chgo. bar assns., Am. Assn. Hosp. Attys., U. Chgo. Law Sch. Alumni Assn. (dir.), Phi Beta Kappa, Order of Coif. Club: Standard (Chgo.). Home: Chicago, Ill. Dec. 1980.

ZECH, ROBERT FRANCIS, accountant; b. Chgo., July 29, 1911; s. Nicholas P. and Minnie (Boll) Z.; m. Betty Ruth Smith, Jan. 28, 1943; children—Adrienne (Mrs. Carlos Urrutia), Robert S., Lisa. B.A., Williams Coll., 1933; student, Northwestern U., 1933-34. C.P.A., numerous states. With Arthur Andersen & Co. (C.P.A.'s), 1934-74, partner charge Dallas office, 1951-68. Mem. adv. com., past chmn. financial mgmt. conf. Tex. A. and M. U.; Chmn. Civil Service Bd., Dallas, 1959-68; treas., v.p. Jr. Achievement Dallas, 1954-62, pres., 1962-68, dir., 1954-72, bd. govs., 1972-81; mem. adv. council Dallas Community Chest Trust Fund, 1965-67; mem. Dallas Assembly, 1962-64; Bd. dirs. Dallas Council World Affairs, 1969-71, Dallas Child Guidance Clinic, 1976-81; bd. dirs., exec. com. Dallas Grand Opera Assn., 1972-81. Served to lt. comdr. USNR, 1942-45. Mem. Am. Inst. C.P.A.'s, Tex. Soc. C.P.A.'s, Dallas C. of C. (bd. dirs. 1968-70), Garoyle, Zeta Psi, Beta Alpha Psi. Club: City (Dallas). Home: Dallas, Tex. Died Feb. 14, 1981.

ZECHMEISTER, LÁSZLÓ KÁROLY ERNÖ, prof. organic chemistry; b. Györ, Hungary, May 14, 1889; s. Charles and Irene (Mocsáry) Z.; student Polytech. Inst., Zurich, Switzerland, 1907-11 (diploma in chemistry, 1911; Dr. Engring., 1913); married. Began as asst., Kaiser Wilhelm-Inst. für Chemie, Berlin, 1912; instr. Danish Royal Vet. Acad., Copenhagen, 1921-23; prof. of chemistry and dir. chem. lab., Med. Sch., U. of Pécs, Hungary, 1923-40; prof. organic chemistry, Calif. Inst. Tech., Pasadena, Calif., from 1940; Guggenheim fellow, 1949; Sigma Xi lecturer, 1948. Awarded Pasteur medal, Paris, 1935; Claude Bernard medal, Paris, 1947. Member Hungarian Acad. Science (received the great prize of this Acad. 1937), Roy Danish Acad. Sci. (foreign mem.), Jr. Am. Chem. Soc. Author: Textbook of Organic Chemistry, 1930, 1932; Carotinoide, 1934; Principles and Practice of Chromatography (by. L. Z. and L. Cholnoky), 1941, 43; and about 200 research papers. Editor: Progress in the Chemistry of Organic Natural Products, 1938. Address: Pasadena, Cal. †

ZEIGLER, EARL FREDERICK, clergyman, educator; b. Barnard, Kan., Jan. 13, 1889; s. Frank and Marietta (Finney) Z.; A.B., Ohio Northern U., 1913, D.D., 1933; B.D., Presbyterian Theol. Sem. of Chicago, 1918; A.M., University of Chicago, 1926; m. Mabel E. Faulkner, June 28, 1911; children—Mary Margaret (Mrs. R. G. Stoll), Ruth (Mrs. Howard P. Hartman), Earl Frederick, James Faulkner. Teacher and superintendent of various schools in Ohio, 1907-15; ordained to ministry Presbyterian Church, 1918; pastor Pullman (Ill.) Church, 1916-18, First Ch., Rochelle, Ill., 1918-22, Union Ch. and Berea Coll., Berea, Ky., 1922-29; dean Presbyn. Coll. of Christian Education, 1929-37; Editor Bd. of Christian Edn., Presbyn. Ch. U.S.A., 1937-57. Awarded Blackstone Fellowship in New Testament, Presbyn. Theol. Sem., Chicago, 1918; also preaching prize same inst., 1918. Republican. Author: Toward Understanding Adults, 1931; The Way of Adult Education, 1938; Why Give?1940; Clothed With Power, 1950; Interpreting Ordination Vows, 1951; Understanding My Trusteeship, 1952; Older Persons in the Church Program, 1957; Christian Education of Adults, 1958. Contbr. to religious jours. Home: Philadelphia, Pa. Deceased.

ZELLE, M(AX) R(OMAINE), lab. research adminstr.; b. Polk County, Iowa, Oct. 11, 1915; s. Guy C. and Clara (Ringgenberg) Z.; B.S., Iowa State U., 1937, Ph.D., 1940; m. Evelyn Hansen, Dec. 24, 1937; children—Claire Christine, Phillip Wayne. Asst. county agt., Audubon, Ia., 1935-36; asst. prof. genetics Purdue U., 1941-44; biologist NIH, Bethesda, Md., 1946-48; prof. bacteriology Cornell U., 1948-58; geneticist, div. biology and medicine AEC, 1950-51, 57-58, chief biology br., 1958-60, asst. dir. biol. scis., 1960-61; prof. genetics and dir. Center Radiol. Scis., U. Wash., 1961-62; dir. div. biol. and med. research Argonne Nat. Lab., 1962-69; prof., chmn. dept. radiology and radiation biology Colo. State U., Ft. Collins, 1969-80; cons. biology div. Oak Ridge Nat. Lab., 1947-49, 52-57, summer guest investigator, 1952, 54, 56. Mem. bd. advisers Phoenix project U. Mich., 1966. Adviser to U.S. delegation UN Sci. Com. on Effects Atomic Radiation, 1958-62; cons. Bur. Radiol. Health FDA, Dept. Health, Edn. and Welfare, 1969-73, Plowshare Programs Office AEC, 1972. Served to lt. (j.g.) USNR, 1944-46. Fellow A.A.A.S.; mem. Am. Inst. Biol. Scis., Genetics Soc. Am., Soc. Am. Microbiols., Am. Soc. Naturalists, Radiation Research Soc. (councilor 1960-63, sec.-treas. 1972-75), Health Physics Soc. (pres. Central Rocky Mountain chpt. 1975-76), Scabbard and Blade, Sigma Xi, Phi Kappa Phi, Alpha Zeta. Club: Cosmos (Washington). Home: Fort Collins, Colo.

ZEUSLER, FREDERICK A., coast guard officer; b. Baltimore, Md., May 20, 1890; s. Ernst Carl and Anna (Schaefer) Z.; grad., pub. schs. and Polytechnic Inst. (Baltimore), U.S. Coast Guard Acad., 1911; m. Clarice Louise Palmer, Aug. 15, 1916; children—Clarice Louise (Mrs. David Shawe), Jean Ann (Mrs. Leslie Olson). Graduate Coast Guard Acad., 1911, and advanced through grades to rear adm., 1945; sea duty, 26 yrs.; oceanographer in Bering Sea, Arctic and on ice patrols; lecturer and instr. U. of Wash., 3 yrs.; exec. officer, ballistics and seamanship instr., Coast Guard Acad., 3 yrs.; ordnance officer and twice communications officer at C.G. Hdqrs.; navigator and exec. U.S.S. McCulloch, 1917, U.S.S. Chattanooga, 1918-19; comdr. Ketchican Dist. and subsector comdr., 1940-44; D.C.G.O. 13th Naval Dist., 1944-46; for physical disability Nov. 1946; exec. asst. to pres. Alaska Steamship Co. from 1947. Tech. advisor Pan American Com. Conf., 1934. Mem. Naval Inst., Nat. Geog. Soc., Assn. Maritime Law, Sigma Xi. Clubs: Explorers, Sojourners, Propeller, Mason (Shriner.) Author numerous papers and handbooks pertaining to Alaska and oceanography. Home: Seattle, Wash. †

ZIEGLER, CHARLES M., state ofcl., civil engr.; b. Noble Co., Ind., May 23, 1888; s. Christ M. and Barbara (Popp) Z.; B.S., U. Mich., 1913; m. Bertha Ory, Jan. 10, 1925; children—Elizabeth Lou (Mrs. Herman Quimrbach), Rosemary Eames (Mrs. Roy Warren), Phyllis Marie (Mrs. Bruce Harlan), Barbara Ann. With engring. dept. Ann Arbor (Mich.) R.R. Co., 1913-14, Dept. Pub. Works, City of Saginaw, Mich., 1914-17; asst. city engr., Saginaw, 1917-18; with U.S. Govt., McCook Field, Dayton, O., 1918-19; gen. engring. work, including Mich. State Coll. bldgs., 1933-39; city assessor, Lansing, Mich., 1939-43; successively asst. dist. engr., dist. engr., constrn. engr., dept. state highway commr., Mich. State Highway Dept., 1919-33, state highway commr. from 1943 (elected, 1943, to fill unexpired term, re-elected, 1945, 49, 53). Mem. Mich. Engring. Soc. (past pres.), Am. Assn. State Highway Ofcls. (past pres.), Am. Rd. Builders Assn., Tau Beta Pi. Club: Lansing (Mich.) Engrs. (past pres.). Home: Lansing, Mich. †

ZIEMER, GREGOR, author; b. Columbia, Mich., May 24, 1899; s. Robert and Adell Von Rohr (Grabau) Z.; m. Edna E. Wilson, May 29, 1926; 1 dau., Patsy. B.A., U. Ill., 1922; M.A., U. Minn., 1923; Ph.D., U. Berlin, 1934. Mem. Staff Park Region Jr. Coll., head journalism dept.; supr. of schs, Philippine Islands, 1926-28; founder Am. Colony Sch., Berlin, 1928; Berlin corr. N.Y. Herald, London Daily Mail, Chgo. Tribune; lectr., radio newscaster WLW, Cin. in, U.S., WLW (since Berlin sch. closed by war); joined spl. war agy., 1944; overseas with SHAEF; v.p. Internat. Enterprises, Inc., 1948; pub. edn. Am. Found. for Blind, 1952-64; dir. Inst. Lifetime Learning, Long Beach, Calif., 1966-71, freelance writer, from 1971; producer, dir. numerous radio programs, from 1966. Author: (with dau. Patsy) Education for Death, new edit, 1972, The Making of the Nazi, 1941, Should Hitler's Children Live, 1946, Whirlaway Hopper, 1962, Too Old for What? , 1968, Witness on Water Skis, 1975, Let'm Eat Grass, 1975, Brigand of Montserrat, 1979; motion picture Let's Listen to Lifetime Learning; radio Giant Step Forward; TV One Empty Rocking Chair,; Contbr.: (with dau. Patsy) to mags. Lectures of Americanism. Served as lt. col. 4th Armored Div. 3d Army, 1945; mil. govt. work in Bavaria with SHAEF to help organize newspapers in Germany. Recipient Westinghouse citation, 1958, award Freedoms Found. for series Am. Heritage, 1969; named Man of Year for work with blind, 1960. Mem. Am. Pub. Relations Assn. (pres. 1960, Silver Anvil award 1956, 58, 60, Paul Revere citation 1958), Am. Legion, Lake City (Minn.) C. of C. (Bicentennial com.), Council of Nat. Orgns., Overseas Press Club, Assn. Radio News Analysts, Cuvier Press Club, Tau Kappa Alpha, Kappa Delta Pi, Beta Sigma Psi. Address: Rancho Palos Verdes, Calif.

ZIMBALIST, EFREM, violinist; b. Rostow on Don, Russia, Apr. 9, 1889; s. Aaron and Maria Z.; early mus. tng. under father; studied in Imperial Sch., St. Petersburg, Russia, with Leopold Auer; m. Alma Gluck, June 15, 1914; children—Maria Virginia (Mrs. Henry F. Bennett, Jr.), Efrem; m. Mary Louise Curtis Bok, July 6, 1943 (dec. 1970). Debut in Berlin at 17; toured through Germany and England; came to U.S., 1911, and has appeared in all the leading cities; has made two world tours, also six tours of the Orient. Composer of (works for orchestra) American Rhapsody, Concerto for Violin and Orchestra; Landara (an opera; concerts for piano and orchestra); also string quartet; violin sonata and many songs and minor pieces for violin and piano. Dir. Curtis Inst. of Music, Phila., 1941-68. Home: Reno, Nev. Dec. Feb. 22, 1985.

ZIMINSKY, VICTOR D., business executive; b. Boston, Mar. 2, 1899; s. Andrew and Honora (O'Leary) Z.; m. Mary Evelyn Monahan, Oct. 24, 1927 (dec. 1961); children: Victor D., Mary Patricia. Student, Boston U.; LL.D., Providence Coll., Suffolk U.; D.C.S., Holy Cross Coll. Buyer E. T. Slattery Co., Boston, 1918-28; v.p. Franklin Simon & Co., 1928-36, Gimbel Bros., N.Y.C., 1939-47; pres., dir. The Union News Co., N.Y.C., 1947-56; pres., chmn. bd. Victor D. Ziminsky Co., Inc., 1956-84; hon. dir. Crown Cork & Seal Co., Inc.; dir. Overseas Service Corp.; hon. trustee N.Y. Bank for Savs. Mem. adv. council Lavelle Sch. Blind.; Trustee Cath. Charities N.Y., St. Patrick's Cathedral, N.Y.; hon. chmn. bd. regents Oblate Coll.; mem. adv. council St. Vincent's Hosp., Westchester; trustee Al Smith Meml. Fedn.; bd. dirs. Holy Name Center for Homeless Men. Knight Sovereign Order of Malta; Knight Assn. Knights and Ladies Equestrian Order Holy Sepulchre Jerusalem. Mem. Am.-Irish History Soc., Friendly Sons St. Patrick. Roman Catholic. Clubs: Union League (N.Y.C.); Westchester Country (Rye, N.Y.). Home: Scarsdale, N.Y. Dec. May 12, 1984.

ZIMMERMAN, WILLARD PAUL, glass manufacturer; b. Washington Court House, Ohio, June 18, 1894; s. Samuel W. and Florence (Cockerill) Z.; A.B., Miami U., Oxford, Ohio, 1917, LL.D., 1973; LL.D., Toledo U., 1964; m. Ruth McCoy, Mar. 27, 1918; children—Doris Jean, Willard Paul. Sales mgr. Am. Seeding Machine Co., 1920-27; sec.-treas. Hemingray Glass Co., 1927-33; plant mgr. Owens-Ill. Glass Co., 1933-36, gen. mgr. indsl. and structural div., Toledo 1936-38; exec. v.p. Owens-Corning Fiberglass Corp., 1946-56, cons., after 1956; dir. Ohio Citizens Trust Co. Trustee, Toledo Hosp., Inst. Med. Research, Miami U. Served as regt. adj., U.S. Army, World War I. Recipient Distinguished Service award Nat. Found. and Hall of Fame, 1963. Mem. AIM, U. S., Ohio chambers commerce, Res. Officers Assn., Am. Legion, 40 and 8, Ind. Soc. Chgo., Delta Kappa Epsilon, Sigma Delta Psi. Republican. Presbyn. Clubs: DKE (N.Y.C.); Toledo, Iverness (Toledo); Boca Raton, Royal Palm Yacht and Country (Boca Raton, Fla.). Mason (hon. 33 deg.). Home: Toledo, Ohio. Dec. Oct. 3, 1979

ZIMMERMANN, BERNARD, surgeon, educator; b. St. Paul, June 26, 1921; s. Harry Bernard and Mary Robertson (Prince) Z.; m. Elizabeth Caldwell, June 18, 1949; children—Bernard III, Andrew Caldwell. Student, Harvard U., 1939-42, M.D., 1945; Ph.D., U. Minn., 1953. Intern Boston City Hosp., 1945-46; mem. faculty U. Minn., 1953-60, prof. surgery, 1959-60, W.Va. U. Med. Sch., from 1960, chmn. dept., 1960-73; Head exptl. surg. facility Naval Med. Research Inst., Bethesda, Md., 1946-48; mem. cancer chemotherapy study sect. HEW, from 1959; mem. surgery tng. com. Nat. Inst. Gen. Med. Scis. Author: Endocrine Functions of the Pancreas, 1952; Contbr. articles to med. jours.; Editorial bd.: Jour. Surg. Research, 1960-73. Bd. dirs. St. Paul Inst. and Sci. Museum, 1956-60; pres., dir. W.Va. div. Am. Cancer Soc. Fellow dept. surgery U. Minn., 1948-53; clin. fellow Am. Cancer Soc., 1950-53; Am. scholar cancer research, 1953-58; Damon Runyon fellow cancer research, 1952-53. Mem. A.C.S. (com. pre-and postoperative care), Am., Central surg. assns., Soc. Univ. Surgeons, Halsted Soc. (pres.), Nat. Soc. Med. Research (sec.-treas.), Am. Soc. Exptl. Pathology, Soc. Head and Neck Surgeons, Soc. Exptl. Biology and Medicine, Minn. Acad. Medicine (sec.-treas. 1959-60), Minn. Territorial Pioneers. Unitarian (past trustee). Home: Morgantown, WV.

ZINK, CHARLES GEORGE, JR., coal co. exec.; b. Fitchburg, Mass., Feb. 11, 1923; s. Charles G. and Elizabeth (Schott) Z.; B.S. in Mineral Engring. and Mineral Econs., Pa. State U., 1947; postgrad. air pollution, Mass. Inst. Tech., 1958; m. Mary Elizabeth Bosley, Apr. 11, 1953; 1 son, David C. Mgr. indsl. sales Hudson Coal Co., Scranton, Pa., 1954-60; v.p. Glen Alden Fuel Sales Co., Wilkes Barre, Pa., 1960-67; exec. v.p. Glen Alden Coal Co., 1965-67; v.p. Glen Alden Export Co., 1963-67; v.p. Blue Coal Co., also Blue Coal Export Co., 1967-75; v.p. Lehigh Valley Coal Sales Co., Lehigh Valley Coal Export Co., Jeddo-Highland Coal Co., 1975-82. Mem. Anthracite Producers Adv. Com.; fuels engring. cons. mem. export expansion council Dept. Commerce, from 1964, mem. Pa. Coal Research Bd., 1962-70; chmn. Elm Park Inst., 1967; asst. adminstr. (anthracite) Nat. Def. Exec. Res.; chmn. adv. com. U.S. Dept. Interior, 1971, mem. R.R. Task Force NE Pa., 1973. Bd. dirs. Anthracite Inst., Pa. Sci. and Engring. Found., Moses Taylor Hosp. vice chmn. Anthracite Export Assn. Served with USAAF, World War II. Decorated Air medal with oak leaf cluster. Mem. Am. Inst. Mining Engrs. (sec. 1968), Soc. Mining Engrs., Internat. Briquetting Assn., Am. Water Works Assn., Am. Mining Congress (land, air water use com. 1968), Theta Chi (sec. 1971). Methodist. Mason (Shriner, Jester). Co-developer trade marking process for coal; devel. chem. treatment for coal. Home: Scranton, Pa. Died Feb. 4, 1982.

ZINNEMAN, HORACE HELMUT, physician, educator; b. Frankfurt/Main, Germany, Oct. 10, 1910; s. Lazar Ludwig and Lea (Margulies) Z.; came to U.S., 1938, naturalized, 1942; M.D., U. Vienna, 1937; m. Ruth May York, Oct. 10, 1941. Intern, Lincoln (Nebr.) Gen. Hosp., 1939-40; practice medicine specializing in internal medicine, Lincoln, 1940-50; resident in internal medicine Med. Sch., U. Minn., 1951-52, mem. faculty, 1952-80, prof. medicine, 1968-80; mem. staff Mpls. VA Hosp., 1952-79. Served with U.S. Army, 1943-46. Decorated Bronze Star medal. Diplomate Am. Bd. Internal Medicine. Fellow A.C.P.; mem. Am. Assn. Immunologists, Central Soc. Clin. Research, Soc. Exptl. Biology and Medicine, Minn. Med. Assn. Asso. editor Minn. Medicine, 1970-80; contbr. to publs. in field. Home: Saint Paul, Minn. Died Aug. 17, 1980.

ZIOLKOWSKI, KORCZAK, sculptor; b. Boston, Sept. 6, 1908; married; 10 children. Works represented in permanent collections, including, San Francisco Art Museum, Judge Baker Guidance Center, Boston, Symphony Hall, Boston, Vassar Coll., Poughkeepsie, N.Y.; sculptor: marble portraits of Paderewski (First Sculptural prize for World's Fair 1939), Georges Enesco, Artur Schnable, Wilbur L. Cross, John F. Kennedy; commd. works include Noah Webster Statue (marble) on Town Hall lawn, West Hartford, Conn., Wild Bill Hickok; granite portrait, Deadwood, S.D., Chief Sitting Bull, Mobridge, S.D., Robert Driscoll, Sr; marble, First Nat. Bank Black Hills, Rapid City, S.D.; study of Walt Disney, Ray Kroc, both at Crazy Horse, Chief Henry Standing Bear, Kennedy Meml. Library, Boston; carving mountain into equestrian figure of Sioux Chief Crazy Horse at request of Indians as meml. to Indians of N.Am, Custer, S.D., 1948—; asst. to: (Gutzon Borglum) carving mountain into equestrian figure of Mt. Rushmore Nat. Meml, S.D. Chmn. bd. dirs. Crazy Horse Found. Mem. Nat. Sculpture Soc. Home: Sturgis, N.D. Dec. Oct. 20, 1982.

ZOOK, RALPH TAYLOR, petroleum producer; b. Newville, Pa., Dec. 5, 1889; s. Eli J. and Rebecca Jane (Huey) Z.; ed. mech. elec. engring., Williamson Sch., Delaware County, Pa., 1906-09; m. Imogen Leuffer, Mar. 6, 1918 (died Oct. 19, 1922); 1 son, Edward Leuffer (dec.); m. 2d Martha Bannon Jones Feb. 16, 1937; two daughters, Sally, Polly. Original mem. Planning and Coordination Com. for Petroleum Industry under N.R.A.; trustee Pa. State Coll., 1932-34; past pres., hon. life mem. Pa. Grade Crude Oil Assn.; dir. and hon. life mem. Bradford Dist. Oil Producers Assn.; dir., past pres. Ind. Petroleum Assn. of America; member production committee for Dist. No. 1, Prodn. Com., Nat. Oil Policy Com. and Petroleum Industry War Council under Petroleum Adminstrn. for War; industry adviser to Sec. Ickes in negotiations of Anglo-Am. Oil Agreement; mem. exec. com. Am. Petroleum Inst., 1945-49; vice chmn. Bradford Aviation Commn., 1944-51; mem. Nat. Petroleum Council. Republican. Presbyterian. Mason (32 deg., Shriner). Clubs: Bradford Valley Hunt, Penn Hills. Home: Bradford, Pa. †

ZORNOW, GERALD BERNARD, photographic mfr.; b. Pittsford, N.Y., Mar. 3, 1916; s. Theodore A. and Dora Eleanor (Sweeney) Z.; B.A., U. Rochester, 1937; m. Gaylord Baker, July 9, 1940 (dec.); 1 dau., Marian Gaylord. With Eastman Kodak Co., 1937-82, beginning as sales trainee, successively mgr. Kodak exhibit World's Fair, tech. rep. med. div., salesman Chgo. area, asst. mgr. Northeastern sales div., then sales mgr. div., mgr. Pacific No. sales div., San Francisco, asst. gen. sales mgr., Rochester, N.Y., 1937-56, dir. sales, apparatus and optical div., 1956-58, v.p., 1958-63; v.p. marketing Eastman Kodak Co., 1963-69, exec. v.p., 1969-70, chmn. exec. com., from 1970, also dir.; chmn., exec. com., pres. Eastman Kodak Co., 1970-72, chmn. bd., 1972-76; dir. Dreyfus-Marine Midland Inc., Marine Midland Bank-Rochester, Marine Midland Banks, Inc.; chmn. Marketing Sci. Inst. Bd. dirs. Rochester Community Baseball, Inc.; trustee U. Rochester, United Community Chest Greater Rochester. Served to capt. USMCR, World War II. Mem. Rochester C. of C. (trustee). Home: Rochester, N.Y. Died Aug. 29, 1984.

ZUCKER, ADOLF EDWARD, coll. prof.; b. Ft. Wayne, Ind., Oct. 26, 1890; s. Friedrich and Marie (Kremmer) Z.; prep. edn., Concordia Coll., Ft. Wayne; A.B., U. of Ill., 1912, A.M., 1913; Ph.D., U. of Pa., 1917; studied Sorbonne, Paris and Universities of Munich and Berlin; m. Lois Miles, Sept. 6, 1916; 1 son, John Miles. Instr. German, U. of Pa., 1916-17; instr. modern langs., Tsing Hua Coll., Peking, China, 1917-18; asst. prof. English, Peking Union Med. Coll., 1918-22; prof. modern langs. and comparative lit., U. of Md., 1923-35; prof. German lit., U. of N.C., 1935-37; prof. of German lit., and head dept. Ind. U., 1937-38; chmn. div. of humanities U. Md., 1938, emeritus; research dir. Carl Schurz Memorial Found., 1941-43; Fulbright fellow, Vienna, 1952. Director of University of Maryland. European Program, Heidelberg, 1950-51; Am. del. to Goethe Bi-centennial, Frankfurt, 1949. Textbook censor, Allied Control Council, Headquarters. Frankfurt, Germany, 1945-46; lecturer for Office Mil. Govt. at German univ., 1947. Mem. Modern Lang. Association of America, Modern Humanities Research Association, Society for Advancement Scandinavian Studies, Am. Assn. Univ. Profs., Soc. for History of Germans in Md. Author: Amerika und Deutschland, 1953. Author, editor or co-translator of books relating to field; editor: The Forty-Eighters, 1950. †

ZUDANS, ZENONS, research center exec.; b. Latvia, Aug. 10, 1918; came to U.S., 1959, naturalized, 1964; m. Irene Pilaps, Apr. 22, 1943; children—Inta, John, Andrew. B.S., U. Latvia, 1943; Ph.D., U. Pa., 1966. Technician Latvian Dept. Industry, Riga, 1940-41; engr. Inst. Indsl. Methods Prodn., Riga, 1942-45; mech. engr. Oberbayerische Forschungsanstalt, Oberammergau, W. Ger., 1944-45; transp. officer UNRRA, W. Ger., 1945-47; mech. engr. COBAST, Sao Paulo, Brazil, 1947-58, Budd Co., Phila., 1959; sr. v.p. Franklin Research Center, Phila., from 1959. Author: Thermal Stress Techniques in the Nuclear Industry, 1965; mem. editorial bd.: Nuclear Engring. and Design, from 1981, Jour. of Computers and Structures, from 1971. Fellow ASME; mem. Am. Nuclear Soc., Am. Concrete Inst. Home: West Chester, PA.

ZURN, EVERETT FREDERICK, business executive; b. Erie, Pa., Mar. 31, 1908; s. John Arthur and Clara (Ackerman) Z.; m. Elizabeth Jane Henderson, Oct. 29, 1932; children: Eleanor Jane (Mrs. Peter B. Hutt), Susan Catherine (Mrs. James M. Smith, Jr.), James Arthur. Student, Denison U., 1927-29; A.B., U. Pitts., 1931; Litt.D. (hon.), Mercyhurst Coll., Erie, 1966; LL.D. (hon.), Grove City (Pa.) Coll., 1977. With J.A. Zurn Mfg. Co., Erie, 1931-56, pres., 1952-56, Zurn Industries, Inc., Erie, 1956-65, chmn. bd., 1965-73, chmn. exec. com., 1973-85; dir. First Nat. Bank Pa., 1966-77, Times Pub. Co., Erie.; Mem. President's Water Pollution Control Adv. Bd., 1965-68; past vice chmn. environmental com. B.I.A.C., Paris, 1972-73; mem. regional export expansion council Dept. Commerce, 1962—, chmn., 1967-69; mem. Nat. Expansion Council, 1967-69; mem. U.S. trade missions to, Burma, 1962, Japan, 1962, Greece, 1964. Mem. lay adv. com. Pa. Med. Soc.; mem. adv. council Coll. of Engring. Found. of U. Tex.; Alternate del. at large Democratic Nat. Conv., 1952, 56, del. at large, 1960-68; mem. Electoral Coll., 1944; Bd. dirs. Hess Found., 1962-65; trustee emeritus St. Vincent Health Center, pres. bd. trustees, 1962-65; bd. corporators Hamot Med. Center; adv. bd. Pa. State U. Behrend Coll.; trustee Mercyhurst Coll., 1969-73. Recipient Behrend Coll. Medallion Pa. State U., 1983. Mem. ASME, Am. Soc. Naval Engrs., Navy League, Newcomen Soc., NAM (dir. 1970-73), Pa. C. of C. (past dir.), Phi Delta Theta. Presbyn. Clubs: Erie (Erie), Kahkwa (Erie), Aviation (Erie). Home: Fairview, Pa. Died Mar. 1985.

ZWEMER, RAYMUND LULL, biologist; b. Bahrain; Mar. 30, 1902; s. Samuel Marinus and Amy Elizabeth (Wilkes) Z.; student English Sch., Cairo, Egypt, 1916-18; A.B., Hope Coll., Mich., 1923; Ph.D., Yale, 1926; Nat. Research fellow Harvard, 1926-28; Guggenheim fellow U. Buenos Aires, 1941; m. Dorothy Ingeborg Bornn, Sept. 13, 1929; children—Raymund Wilkes, Suzanne (Mrs. R.A. Visser), Theodore, Jane (Mrs. R.L. Koeser). Instr., Columbia, 1928-31, asst. prof., 1931-44; worked with minister of pub. health, Uruguay, 1942; chmn. Interdeptl. Com. on Cooperation with Am. Republics, 1944; asso. chief Div. Cultural Cooperation, U.S. Dept. of State, 1944-47; exec. dir. Interdeptl. Com. on Sci. and Cultural Cooperation, 1945-47; exec. sec. Nat. Acad. Scis. and NRC, 1947-50; chief, sci. div. Library of Congress, 1950-55; chief div. internat. cooperation for sci. research UNESCO, Paris, 1956-57, dir. Bur. Personnel and Mgmt., UNESCO, 1958; asst. sci. adviser Dept. of State, 1958-61, mem. U.S. delegations NATO Sci. Com. meetings, Paris, also CENTO Sci. Council meetings, London, Ankara, Tehran, 1958-61; asso. editor Am. Physiol. Soc. publs. Am. Jour. Physiology and Jour. Applied Physiology, 1961-65; dir. Biol. Info. User Survey, 1961-62; dir. trans. project Fedn. Am. Socs. for Exptl. Biology, 1962-66, exec. editor Fedn. Procs., 1966-67, project dir., exec. editor Neurosci, Transl., from 1967. Ofcl. U.S. del. to 2d PanAm. Congress on Endocrinology, 1941; various offices U.S. Book Exchange, Inc., Washington, 1948-56, chmn. bd., 1950-51; asso. editor Anat. Record, 1950-55; cons. in physiology Naval Med. Research Inst., 1949-55; convenor finance com. Internat. Anat. Nomenclature Com., 1965, mem. main com., 1975; del. to Com. on Data for Sci. and Tech., Internat. Union Biol. Scis., 1970; mem. adv. com. Sci. News, 1971-81; trustee Biol. Abstracts, 1949-56, 62-67, v.p., 1953, pres., 1954-55, treas., 1963-64. Recipient A. Cressy Morrison prize N.Y. Acad. Sci., 1937. Fellow A.A.A.S.; mem. Council Biol. Editors, Am. Assn. Anatomists (chmn. com. anat. nomenclature), Council on Biol. Scis. Information (dir. from 1967, sec. 1967-68), Spl. Libraries Assn. (pres. Washington chpt. 1955), Am. Inst. Biol. Scis. (mem. steering com. biol. scis. communication project 1961-63, mem. pension fund com.), Fedn. Am.

Socs. for Exptl. Biology (chmn. com. on biol. handbooks 1959-72), Am. Physiol. Soc., Am. Assn. Phys. Anthropologists, Washington Acad. Sci., Sigma Xi, Gamma Alpha; also hon. mem. Soc. Medicine Montevideo Uruguay, Biol. Soc. Argentine Med. Assn. Republican. Rotarian. Club: Cosmos (Washington). Home: Silver Spring, Md. Died Oct. 5, 1981.

ZWORYKIN, VLADIMIR KOSMA, business executive; b. Mourom, Russia, July 30, 1889; s. Kosma and Elaine (Zworykin); E.E. Petrograd Inst. Tech., 1912; student Coll. de France, Paris, 1912-14; Ph.D., U. Pitts., 1926; D.Sc., Bklyn. Poly. Inst., 1938, Rutgers U., 1972; m. Tatiana Vasilieff, Apr. 17, 1916; children—Nina (dec.), Elaine; m. Dr. Katherine Polavitsky, Nov. 1951. Came to U.S., 1919, naturalized, 1924. Research with Westinghouse Elec. and Mfg. Co., 1920-29; dir. electronic research RCA Mfg. Co., 1929-42; assoc., research dir. RCA Labs., 1942-45; dir. electronic research, 1946-54, v.p., tech. cons., 1947-54, hon. v.p., cons., from 1954. Recipient Morris Liebmann Meml. prize 1934; Modern Pioneer award Am. Mfrs. Assn., 1940; Rumford medal Am. Acad. Arts and Scis., 1941. Howard N. Potts medal Franklin Inst., 1947;

Presdl. Certificate of Merit, 1948; Chevalier Cross of French Legion of Honor, 1948; Lamme Award, 1949, Edison Medal, 1952, AIEE; medal of honor IRE, 1951; Gustave Trasenster award, 1959; Cristoforo Columbo award, 1959; Faraday medal Brit. Inst. Elec. Engrs., 1965; Nat. Medal of Sci., 1966; Golden Plate award Am. Acad. Achievement, 1967. Served with Signal Corps. Russian Army, World War I. Named to Nat. Inventors Hall of Fame, 1977. Fellow IEEE, TV Soc. (Eng.) (hon.), Instituto Internazionale della Communicazoni (Italy) (hon.), Am. Phys. Society, AAAS; hon. mem. Soc. Motion Picture and TV Engrs., Brit. Instn. Radio Engrs.; mem. Am. Philos. Soc., N.Y. Acad. Scis., Electron Microscope Soc. Am., Nat. Acad. Engring. (Founders medal 1968), Société Française des Electroniciens et des Radioelectriciens (hon.), Am. Acad. Arts and Scis., Nat. Acad. Scis. U.S.A., French Acad. Sci., Sigma Xi. Co-author: Photcells and Their Applications, 1932; Television, 1940, rev. 1954; Electron Optics and the Electron Microscope, 1946; Photoelectricity and Its Application, 1949; Television in Science and Industry, 1958. Developer iconoscope, electron microscope, other advances in radio, TV and electronics. Home: Princeton, N.J. Died July 29, 1982.